# THE OXFORD
# CLASSICAL DICTIONARY

# THE OXFORD CLASSICAL DICTIONARY

EDITED BY

N. G. L. HAMMOND

AND

H. H. SCULLARD

SECOND EDITION

**OXFORD**
**AT THE CLARENDON PRESS**

*Oxford University Press, Walton Street, Oxford* OX2 6DP

*Oxford New York Toronto*
*Delhi Bombay Calcutta Madras Karachi*
*Petaling Jaya Singapore Hong Kong Tokyo*
*Nairobi Dar es Salaam Cape Town*
*Melbourne Auckland*

*and associated companies in*
*Berlin Ibadan*

*Oxford is a trade mark of Oxford University Press*

*Published in the United States*
*by Oxford University Press, USA*

*ISBN 0–19–869117–3*

*Printed in Great Britain by*
*William Clowes Ltd.*
*Beccles, Suffolk*

# PREFACE

THE preparation of this edition was undertaken by the present editors in 1964 on the understanding that the material would be assembled rapidly and that the Clarendon Press would give some priority to the printing. Almost all the material was collected in the years 1964–6, and the galley-proofs were corrected and returned by the contributors in the course of 1967–8. The preparation of the original edition extended over some fifteen years, in consequence of many unforeseen factors and especially the intervention of war. This time the shorter period of gestation has made the task of co-ordination less difficult for the editors and has probably given the Dictionary a more even tone.

In planning the new edition the editors were of the opinion that very many articles of the original edition would have to be replaced or altered in the light of new discoveries and new outlooks, and after detailed consideration it was decided that every article of the original edition should be submitted to revision or replaced. In fact a considerable proportion of them have been replaced by new articles, which appear above the initials of the contributors. The other articles have all been scrutinized, and some have been altered or added to either by the original contributor or by another contributor. In the latter case the article appears over the initials of the original contributor, to which the initials of the second contributor are usually but not always appended. Thus all articles and in particular the bibliographies have been brought up to date, that is up to within the years 1967–8, when the contributors returned their corrected proofs. In a few cases the editors have added references to important works which were published after that time.

The original edition, of which the entire planning was *ab initio*, was produced by a team of six editors and three editorial assistants. On this occasion, the model being to hand, it seemed that two editors might be sufficient, especially as one of them, H. H. Scullard, had been an editor of the first edition. Any faults in the present edition should be laid at their joint door. They have worked in close harmony and at a similar pace, with Hammond primarily responsible for Greek affairs and Scullard for Roman affairs. They owe a special debt to a few scholars who read through articles on certain topics and gave advice: Professor H. W. Parke for religion and mythology, Professor G. E. L. Owen and at a later stage Professor D. Furley for philosophy, Professor Gordon Williams for Latin literature and language, Mr. B. Nicholas for Roman law, and Professor the Revd. Dr. H. Chadwick for some Christian writers. They are grateful also to the contributors for their co-operation, which has made it possible to work to the above timetable.

The editors have introduced only a few changes. They have allowed a little more space for the archaeological background, without departing from the principle that this is a classical and not an archaeological dictionary. They have included more places, peoples, and persons (for example, lesser rulers, whom a reader may wish to identify) than there were in the first edition. They have paid more attention to the later Roman Empire, including in particular more emperors and leading Christian writers. In order to make space for these additions and keep the length of the dictionary within bounds, the editors have withdrawn a few of the long articles and all the briefest entries, which were merely cross-references for the most part (for example 'ABRAXAS, *see* Amulets'). They have added an 'Index of names etc. which are not the titles of entries in the Dictionary', and they are confident that this Index will greatly increase the usefulness of the dictionary as a worl of reference.

The spelling of names in the latinized form has been taken over from the original edition, bu it has not been rigorously applied, where a contributor has preferred a different but current form Romans are listed, as before, under their familiar names (a few more having been transferred t their *cognomina*). It is probably preferable for the reader to look, for instance, for the two con spirators under the headings BRUTUS and CASSIUS rather than under either IUNIUS an CASSIUS, or BRUTUS and LONGINUS, which a rigid classification under either *nomina* o *cognomina* would require. Where it seemed that it might be useful to the reader, the serial numbe in Pauly–Wissowa has been added to Roman *nomina*. Except in this respect, and in respect of som Supplementbände, reference has not been made in general to Pauly–Wissowa, *Real-Encyclopädie* nor to *The Cambridge Ancient History* nor to the *Prosopographia Imperii Romani*. Readers ar asked to bear these standard works of reference constantly in mind.

The editors are very grateful to Mrs. S. Argyle for her unfailing help and meticulous attentior to detail. She has played the major part in seeing the material through the press, adding cross-references, standardizing details of presentation where advisable, checking points of bibliography and bringing many matters to the attention of the editors. They are grateful too to the staff of the Clarendon Press, and in particular to the Printer's reader, for their courtesy and consideration.

N. G. L. H.
H. H. S.

*October 1969*

# FROM THE PREFACE TO THE FIRST EDITION

THE idea of the present work, the publication of which has been inevitably delayed by the war, was first conceived in 1933. It is designed to cover the same ground, though on a different scale, as the well-known dictionaries by Sir William Smith on Greek and Roman antiquities and on Greek and Roman biography, mythology, and geography. The eighth edition (1914) of Lübker's *Reallexikon* was taken as a general model, but with certain modifications in principle and with certain differences in emphasis. The present work is intended to be less purely factual than Lübker. It devotes more space to biography and literature, less to geography and to bibliographical information, aiming in this latter respect at no more than referring the reader to the best work, in English and foreign languages, on the various subjects. A special feature is the inclusion of longer articles designed to give a comprehensive survey of the main subjects and to place minor characters, places, and events, the choice of which has been necessarily selective, against their appropriate literary or historical background. The *terminus ad quem* is, generally speaking, the death of Constantine (337), and proportionately less space has been allotted to persons who lived later than the second century A.D.; but a few prominent figures of later ages, such as Augustine, Eustathius, Photius, Psellus, Thomas Magister, Triclinius, and Tzetzes, who are important for the student of classical antiquity, have been included. Christian writers, as such, have been excluded.

The editors of the dictionary at its inception were Mr. J. D. Denniston, for Greek literature; Professor J. Wight Duff, for Latin literature; Professor H. M. Last, for Greek and Roman history and geography; Professor A. D. Nock, for Greek and Roman religion; Sir David Ross, for Greek and Roman philosophy, mathematics, and science. Professor R. G. Collingwood advised on matters concerned with art and archaeology until his death in 1943. In 1937 Professor Last found himself unable to continue his editorship, and his place was taken by Professor M. Cary and Dr. H. H. Scullard, who are alone responsible for the selection and form of articles on history, geography, law, archaeology, and art. In 1944 Professor Wight Duff died, and Professor A. Souter agreed to see the articles on Latin literature through the press; and in 1945 Professor H. J. Rose took over from Professor Nock the final stages of the editorship of articles connected with religion. In the autumn of 1939 Sir Paul Harvey undertook the complicated and laborious task of securing uniformity in such matters as spelling, transliteration, and abbreviations, and of adding the requisite cross-references. He had all but completed this work when in June 1948 illness compelled him to relinquish it. Professor Paul Maas has placed his many-sided learning at the Delegates' disposal in the final stages, and contributed the short bibliographical articles at the end of the book. Valuable help and advice have also been received from Mr. R. Syme and Professor A. Momigliano.

Every effort has been made by the editors to incorporate the results of recent scholarship and to bring the work as much up to date as possible, but a task which involved communication with so many widely scattered contributors has been made much harder by the interruptions of war and the difficulties of present production. For any omissions therefore, particularly in the bibliographies, the reader's indulgence is sought.

*June 1948*

|  |  |
|---|---|
| M. C. | A. D. N. |
| J. D. D. | W. D. R. |
| J. W. D. | H. H. S. |

# SIGNS

\* before Greek or Latin words denotes words not actually extant.
[—], names of authors or works in square brackets indicate false or doubtful attributions.
A small number above the line indicates the number of an edition.

# ABBREVIATIONS USED IN THE PRESENT WORK

## A. GENERAL

| | | | |
|---|---|---|---|
| ad fin. | ad finem | l.c. or loc. cit. | loco citato |
| ad loc. | ad locum | lit. | literally |
| ad init. | ad initium | n. | note |
| al. | alias, aliter, etc. | n.d. | no date |
| ap. | apud | no. | number |
| arg. | argument | n. plur. | neuter plural |
| art. | article | N.S. | New Series |
| b. | born | N.T. | New Testament |
| c., cc. | century, centuries | OE | Old English |
| c. | *circa* | OIr | Old Irish |
| comm. | commentary | ON | Old Norse |
| d. | died | OP | Old Persian |
| E.T. | see Engl. Transl. | O.T. | Old Testament |
| ed. | editor, edition, edidit, or edited by | op. cit. | opus citatum |
| Engl. Transl. or E.T. | English Translation | pl., pls. | plate, plates |
| esp. | especially | Ps.- | Pseudo- |
| f., ff. | and following | qu. | query |
| fl. | floruit | q.v., qq.v. | quod vide, quae vide |
| Fr. | French | repr. | reprint |
| fr., frs. | fragment, fragments | str. | strophe |
| Hebr. | Hebrew | s.v. | sub voce |
| ib., ibid. | ibidem | Suppl. | Supplement |
| id. | idem | temp. | tempore, in the time of |
| inf. | infra | tr. or transl. | translation or translated by |
| l., ll. | line, lines | v., vv. | verse, verses |

## B. AUTHORS AND BOOKS

| | | | |
|---|---|---|---|
| AE | L'*Année Épigraphique*, published in *Revue Archéologique* and separately, 1888– | Acad. index Herc. | *Academicorum philosophorum index Herculanensis editus a F. Buechelero*, 1869 |
| AJArch. | *American Journal of Archaeology*, 1897– | Ael. | Aelianus |
| | | NA | *De natura animalium* |
| AJPhil. | *American Journal of Philology*, 1880– | VH | *Varia Historia* |
| ARW | *Archiv für Religionswissenschaft*, 1898– | Aen. | *Aeneid* |
| | | Aesch. | Aeschylus |
| ATL | B. D. Meritt, H. T. Wade-Gery, and M. F. McGregor, *The Athenian Tribute Lists*, i–iv, U.S.A. 1939–53 | Ag. | *Agamemnon* |
| | | Cho. | *Choephori* |
| | | Eum. | *Eumenides* |
| | | Pers. | *Persae* |
| Abh. followed by name of Academy or Society | *Abhandlungen* | PV | *Prometheus Vinctus* |
| | | Sept. | *Septem contra Thebas* |
| | | Supp. | *Supplices* |
| Abh. sächs. Ges. Wiss. | *Abhandlungen der sächsischen Gesellschaft der Wissenschaften* | Aeschin. | Aeschines |
| | | In Ctes. | *Against Ctesiphon* |
| Abh. zu Gesch. d. Math. | *Abhandlungen zur Geschichte der mathematischen Wissenschaften*, 1877– | In Tim. | *Against Timarchus* |
| | | Aët. | Aëtius |
| | | Alc. | Alcaeus |
| Abh. zu Gesch. d. Med. | *Abhandlungen zur Geschichte der Naturwissenschaften und d. Medizin*, 1922– | Alcidamas, *Soph.* | Alcidamas, Περὶ σοφιστῶν |
| | | Alcm. | Alcman |
| | | Alex. Polyh. | Alexander Polyhistor |

| | |
|---|---|
| Altheim, *Hist. Rom.* | F. Altheim, *Römische Religions-* |
| *Rel.* | *geschichte*, tr. H. Mattingly, 1938 |
| *Amer. Acad. Rome* | *Memoirs of the American Academy* |
| | *at Rome*, 1915– |
| *Amer. Hist. Rev.* | *American Historical Review*, 1895– |
| Amm. Marc. | Ammianus Marcellinus |
| Ammon. | Ammonius grammaticus |
| *Diff.* | Περὶ ὁμοίων καὶ διαφόρων λέξεων |
| Anac. | Anacreon |
| Andoc. | Andocides |
| *Anecd. Bach.* | *Anecdota Graeca*, ed. L. Bachmann, |
| | 1828–9 |
| „ *Bekk.* | *Anecdota Graeca*, ed. I. Bekker, 3 |
| | vols., 1814–21 |
| „ *Ox.* | *Anecdota Graeca* e codd. MSS. |
| | Bibl. Oxon., ed. J. A. Cramer, |
| | 4 vols., 1835–7 |
| „ *Par.* | *Anecdota Graeca* e codd. MSS. |
| | Bibl. Reg. Parisiensis, ed. J. A. |
| | Cramer, 4 vols., 1839–41 |
| *Ann. Ist.* | *Annali del Istituto di Corrispon-* |
| | *denza Archaeologica*, 1829– |
| Anon. *De Com.* or | Anonymus *De Comoedia* |
| Περὶ κωμ. | |
| *Ant. Class.* | *L'Antiquité classique*, 1932– |
| *Ant. Journ.* | *Antiquaries Journal*, 1921– |
| Ant. Lib. | Antoninus Liberalis |
| *Met.* | *Metamorphoses* |
| *Anth. Lat.* | *Anthologia Latina*, ed. A. Riese, |
| | F. Buecheler, and E. Lom- |
| | matzsch, 1869–1926 |
| *Anth. Lyr. Graec.* | see Diehl |
| *Anth. Pal.* | *Anthologia Palatina* |
| *Anth. Plan.* | *Anthologia Planudea* |
| Antig. Car. | Antigonus Carystius |
| Antip. Sid. | Antipater Sidonius |
| *Anz.* followed by | *Anzeiger* or *Anzeigen* |
| name of Academy | |
| or Society | |
| Ap. Rhod. | Apollonius Rhodius |
| *Argon.* | *Argonautica* |
| Apollod. | Apollodorus mythographus |
| *Bibl.* | *Bibliotheca* |
| *Epit.* | *Epitome* |
| Apollonius | Apollonius paradoxographus |
| *Mir.* | *Mirabilia* |
| Apollonius Dyscolus | |
| *Pron.* | *De pronominibus* |
| App. | Appian |
| *BCiv.* | *Bella Civilia* |
| *Hann.* | Ἀννιβαϊκή |
| *Hisp.* | Ἰβηρική |
| *Ill.* | Ἰλλυρική |
| *Mac.* | Μακεδονική |
| *Mith.* | Μιθριδάτειος |
| *Pun.* | Λιβυκή |
| *Sam.* | Σαυνιτική |
| *Syr.* | Συριακή |
| *App. Verg.* | *Appendix Vergiliana* |
| Apsines, *Rhet.* | Apsines, *Ars Rhetorica* |
| Apul. | Apuleius |
| *Apol.* | *Apologia* |
| *Asclep.* | *Asclepius* |
| *De deo Soc.* | *De deo Socratico* |
| *De dog. Plat.* | *De dogmate Platonis* |
| *Flor.* | *Florida* |
| *Met.* | *Metamorphoses* |
| Ar. | Aristophanes |
| *Ach.* | *Acharnenses* |
| *Av.* | *Aves* |
| *Eccl.* | *Ecclesiazusae* |
| *Eq.* | *Equites* |

| | |
|---|---|
| *Lys.* | *Lysistrata* |
| *Nub.* | *Nubes* |
| *Plut.* | *Plutus* |
| *Ran.* | *Ranae* |
| *Thesm.* | *Thesmophoriazusae* |
| *Vesp.* | *Vespae* |
| Ar. Byz. | Aristophanes Byzantinus |
| Aratus *Phaen.* | Aratus, *Phaenomena* |
| *Progn.* | *Prognostica* |
| *Arch. Ael.* | *Archaeologia Aeliana* (Newcastle- |
| | upon-Tyne), 1815– |
| *Arch. Anz.* | *Archäologischer Anzeiger* in *Jahr-* |
| | *buch des [kaiserlichen] deutschen* |
| | *archäologischen Instituts* (*JDAI*) |
| *Arch. Class.* | *Archeologia Classica*, 1949– |
| Ἀρχ. Ἐφ. | Ἀρχαιολογικὴ Ἐφημερίς, 1910– |
| *Arch. Journ.* | *Archaeological Journal*, 1845– |
| *Arch. Pap.* | *Archiv für Papyrusforschung*, 1900– |
| *Arch. Rep.* | *Archaeological Reports* published by |
| | the Hellenic Society, 1955– |
| Archil. | Archilochus |
| Arist. | Aristotle |
| *An. Post.* | *Analytica Posteriora* |
| *An. Pr.* | *Analytica Priora* |
| *Ath. Pol.* | Ἀθηναίων Πολιτεία |
| *Cael.* | *De Caelo* |
| *Cat.* | *Categoriae* |
| [*Col.*] | *De Coloribus* |
| *De An.* | *De Anima* |
| *Div. Somn.* | *De Divinatione per Somnia* |
| *Eth. Eud.* | *Ethica Eudemia* |
| *Eth. Nic.* | *Ethica Nicomachea* |
| *Fr.* | *Fragmenta* |
| *Gen. An.* | *De Generatione Animalium* |
| *Gen. Corr.* | *De Generatione et Corruptione* |
| *HA* or *Hist. An.* | *Historia Animalium* |
| *Int.* | *De Interpretatione* |
| [*Lin. Ins.*] | *De Lineis Insecabilibus* |
| [*Mag. Mor.*] | *Magna Moralia* |
| [*Mech.*] | *Mechanica* |
| *Mem.* | *De Memoria* |
| *Metaph.* | *Metaphysica* |
| *Mete.* | *Meteorologica* |
| [*Mir. Ausc.*] | see *Mir. Ausc.* under M |
| [*Mund.*] | *De Mundo* |
| [*Oec.*] | *Oeconomica* |
| *Part. An.* | *De Partibus Animalium* |
| *Ph.* | *Physica* |
| [*Phgn.*] | *Physiognomonica* |
| *Poet.* | *Poetica* |
| *Pol.* | *Politica* |
| [*Pr.*] | *Problemata* |
| *Resp.* | *De Respiratione* |
| *Rh.* | *Rhetorica* |
| [*Rh. Al.*] | *Rhetorica ad Alexandrum* |
| *Sens.* | *De Sensu* |
| *Soph. El.* | *Sophistici Elenchi* |
| *Top.* | *Topica* |
| [*Xen.*] | *De Xenophane* |
| Aristid. Quint. | Aristides Quintilianus |
| Aristox. *Fr. Hist.* | Aristoxenus, *Fragmenta Historica* |
| *Harm.* | *Harmonica* |
| *Rhythm.* | *Rhythmica* |
| Arn. | Arnobius |
| *Adv. Nat.* or *Adv.* | *Adversus Nationes* |
| *Gent.* | |
| Arnim (von) | see *SVF* |
| Arr. | Arrian |
| *Anab.* | *Anabasis* |
| *Epict. Diss.* | *Epicteti Dissertationes* |
| *Peripl. M. Eux.* | *Periplus Maris Euxini* |
| *Tact.* | *Tactica* |

| | |
|---|---|
| Artem. | Artemidorus Daldianus |
| Asc. | Asconius |
|   *Corn.* | Commentary on Cicero, *Pro Corneleo de maiestate* |
|   *Mil.* | Commentary on Cicero, *Pro Milone* |
|   *Pis.* | Commentary on Cicero, *In Pisonem* |
|   *Verr.* | Commentary on Cicero, *In Verrem* |
| Ath. | Athenaeus |
| *Athenaeum* | *Athenaeum* (Pavia), Nuova Serie, 1923– |
| Athenagoras, *Leg. pro Christ.* | Athenagoras, *Legatio pro Christianis* = Πρεσβεία περὶ Χριστιανῶν |
| *Auct. ad Her.* | *Auctor ad Herennium* |
| August. | Augustine |
|   *Ad Rom.* | *Expositio* of *Epist. ad Romanos* |
|   *De civ. D.* | *De civitate Dei* |
|   *In Evang. Iohan.* | *Tractatus in Evangelium Iohannis* |
|   *Ep.* | *Epistulae* |
|   *Retract.* | *Retractationes* |
| Aul. Gell. | see Gell. |
| Aur. Vict., *Caes.* | Aurelius Victor, *Caesares* |
| [Aur. Vict.], *De Vir. Ill.* | [Aurelius Victor], *De Viris Illustribus* |
| Auson. | Ausonius |
|   *Cent. Nupt.* | *Cento Nuptialis* |
|   *Grat. Act.* | *Gratiarum Actio* |
|   *Mos.* | *Mosella* |
|   *Ordo Nob. Urb.* | *Ordo Nobilium Urbium* |
|   *Prof. Burd.* | *Commemoratio Professorum Burdigalensium* |
|   *Technop.* | *Technopaegnion* |
| *BAct.* | *Bellum Actiacum*: see *BAegypt.* |
| *BAegypt.* | *Carmen de Bello Aegyptiaco sive Actiaco* (papyrus fragment) |
| *BAfr.* | *Bellum Africum* |
| *BAlex.* | *Bellum Alexandrinum* |
| *BCH* | *Bulletin de Correspondance Hellénique, 1877–* |
| *BGU* | *Berliner Griechische Urkunden* (*Ägyptische Urkunden aus den Kgl. Museen zu Berlin*), 1895– |
| *BICS* | *Bulletin of the Institute of Classical Studies*, London, 1954– |
| *BIFAO* | *Bulletin de l'Institut français d'Archéologie Orientale*, Cairo, 1901– |
| *BKT* | *Berliner Klassikertexte, herausgegeben von der Generalverwaltung der Kgl. Museen zu Berlin*, 1904– |
| B.M. | British Museum |
| B.M. *Coins, Rom. Emp.* | *British Museum Catalogue of Coins of the Roman Empire*, 1923– |
| *BN* | *Beiträge zur Namenforschung*, Heidelberg, 1949– |
| *B. phil. Woch.* | *Berliner philologische Wochenschrift*, 1881–1920 |
| *BSA* | *Annual of the British School at Athens*, 1895– |
| Bacchyl. | Bacchylides |
| Badian, *Stud. Gr. Rom. Hist.* | E. Badian, *Studies in Greek and Roman History*, 1964 |
| Baehr. | E. Baehrens |
|   *FPR* | *Fragmenta Poetarum Romanorum*, 1886 |
|   *PLM* | see *PLM* |
| Basil. *De Virg.* | Basilius, *De Virginitate* |
| Beazley, *ABV* | J. D. Beazley, *Attic Black-figure Vase Painters*, 1956 |
|   *ARV²* | *Attic Red-figure Vase Painters²*, 1963 |

| | |
|---|---|
| *Beitr.* | *Beitrag, Beiträge* |
| Beloch | K. J. Beloch |
|   *Gr. Gesch.* | *Griechische Geschichte²*, 1912–27 |
|   *Röm. Gesch.* | *Römische Geschichte bis zum Beginn der punischen Kriege*, 1926 |
| Bengtson, *Strategie* | H. Bengtson, *Die Strategie in der hellenistischen Zeit* (Munchener Beiträge zur Papyrusforschung und Rechtsgeschichte 26 (1937), 32 (1944), 36 (1952)) |
|   *Röm. Gesch.* | *Grundriss der römischen Geschichte* (1967) |
| Bérard, *Bibl. topogr.* | J. Bérard, *Bibliographie topographique des principales cités grecques de l'Italie méridionale et de la Sicile dans l'antiquité*, 1941 |
| *Ber. Sächs. Ges. Wiss.* | *Berichte über die Verhandlungen der [Kgl.] sächsischen Gesellschaft der Wissenschaften zu Leipzig*, 1848 |
| *Berl. Abh.* | *Abhandlungen der preuß. Akademie d. Wissenschaften zu Berlin*, 1786–1907; 1908– |
| Berve, *Alexanderreich* | H. Berve, *Das Alexanderreich aus prosopographischer Grundlage*, 1927 |
| *Bibl. Éc. Franc.* | *Bibliothèque des Écoles françaises d'Athènes et de Rome*, 1877– |
| Bidez–Cumont | J. Bidez and F. Cumont, *Les Mages hellénisés*, 2 vols., 1938 |
| Bieber, *Sculpt. Hellenist. Age* | M. Bieber, *Sculpture of the Hellenistic Age²*, 1961 |
| Blass, *Att. Ber.* | F. Blass, *Die Attische Beredsamkeit*, 2nd ed. 1887–98 |
| *Boll. Fil. Class.* | *Bollettino di filologia classica*, 1894–1929; N.S. 1930– |
| *Bonner Jahrb.* | *Bonner Jahrbücher*, 1895– |
| *Bresl. phil. Abh.* | *Breslauer philologische Abhandlungen* |
| Brommer, *Vasenlisten²* | F. Brommer, *Vasenlisten zur griechischen Heldensage²*, 1960 |
| Broughton, *MRR* | T. R. S. Broughton, *The Magistrates of the Roman Republic*, 1951–60 |
| Bruns, *Font.* | C. G. Bruns, *Fontes iuris Romani antiqui⁷*, 1919 |
| Budé | Collection des Univ. de France, publiée sous le patronage de l'Assoc. Guillaume Budé |
| Buecheler, *Carm. Epigr.* | F. Buecheler, *Carmina Latina Epigraphica*, 2 vols. with Supplem. by E. Lommatzsch, 1895–1926 |
| *Bull. Com. Arch.* | *Bullettino della Commissione archeologica comunale in Roma*, 1872– |
| *Bull. Ist. Dir. Rom.* | *Bullettino del Istituto di diritto romano*, 1888– |
| *Bull. Rylands Libr.* | *Bulletin of John Rylands Library*, 1903– |
| Burnet, *EGP* | J. Burnet, *Early Greek Philosophy⁴*, 1930 |
| Bursian | C. Bursian, *Geographie von Griechenland*, vol. ii, 1872 |
| *Jahresb.* | Bursian's *Jahresberichte über die Fortschritte der Altertumswissenschaft*, 1873– |
| *Byz. und Neugr. Jahrb.* | *Byzantinisch-neugriechische Jahrbücher*, 1920– |
| *Byz. Zeitschr.* | *Byzantinische Zeitschrift*, 1892– |
| *CAF* | T. Kock, *Comicorum Atticorum Fragmenta*, 1880–8 |
| *CAH* | *The Cambridge Ancient History*, 1923–39 |
| *CAH²* | 2nd edition, 1961– |

| | |
|---|---|
| CCAG | Catalogus Codicum Astrologorum Graecorum, 9 vols., Brussels, 1898–1953, ed. F. Cumont et al. |
| CGF | G. Kaibel, Comicorum Graecorum Fragmenta, 1899 |
| CHJ | Cambridge Historical Journal, 1924– |
| CIA | Corpus Inscriptionum Atticarum, 1825– |
| CIE | Corpus Inscriptionum Etruscarum, 1893– |
| CIL | Corpus Inscriptionum Latinarum, 1863– |
| CISem. | Corpus Inscriptionum Semiticarum, 1881– |
| CJ | Classical Journal, 1905– |
| CMG | Corpus Medicorum Graecorum, 1908– |
| CML | Corpus Medicorum Latinorum, 1915– |
| CPhil. | Classical Philology, 1906– |
| CPL | Corpus Poetarum Latinorum, 1894–1920 |
| CQ | Classical Quarterly, 1907– |
| CR | Classical Review, 1887– |
| CRAcad. Inscr. | Comptes rendus de l' Académie des Inscriptions et Belles-lettres, 1857– |
| CRF | see Ribbeck |
| CSEL | Corpus Scriptorum Ecclesiasticorum Latinorum, 1866 ff. |
| CVA | Corpus Vasorum Antiquorum, 1925– |
| Caes. | Caesar |
|   BCiv. | Bellum Civile |
|   BGall. | Bellum Gallicum |
| Callim. | Callimachus |
|   Aet. | Aetia |
|   Ap. | Hymnus in Apollinem |
|   Cer. |     ,,   ,, Cererem |
|   Del. |     ,,   ,, Delum |
|   Dian. |     ,,   ,, Dianam |
|   Epigr. | Epigrammata |
|   Jov. | Hymnus in Jovem |
|   Lav. Pall. | Lavacrum Palladis |
| Calp. | Calpurnius Siculus |
| Carm. Arv. | Carmen Arvale |
| Carm. Epigr. | Carmina Epigraphica ('pars posterior' of Anthologia Latina) |
| Carm. Pop. | Carmina Popularia in Diehl's Anth. Lyr. Graec. ii, pp. 192–208 |
| Carm. Sal. | Carmen Saliare |
| Cary–Warmington, Explorers | M. Cary and E. H. Warmington, The Ancient Explorers, 1929 |
| Cass. Dio | Cassius Dio |
| Cassiod. | Cassiodorus |
|   Var. | Variae |
| Castagnoli, Stud. urb. | F. Castagnoli (ed.), Studi di urbanistica antica, 1966 |
| Cat. Lit. Pap. | H. J. M. Milne, Catalogue of the Literary Papyri in the British Museum, 1927 |
| Cato, Agr. or Rust. | Cato, De Agricultura or De Re Rustica |
|   Orig. | Origines |
| Catull. | Catullus |
| Celsus, Med. | Celsus, De Medicina |
| Censorinus, D.N. | Censorinus, De die natali |
| Chalcid. in Tim. | Chalcidius, in Platonis Timaeum |
| Charisius, Gramm. | Charisius, Ars Grammatica |
| Christ–Schmid–Stählin | W. von Christ, Geschichte d. griechischen Literatur, revised by W. Schmid and O. Stählin, ii. i⁶ 1920, ii. ii⁶ 1924. See also Schmid–Stählin |
| Chron. Marcell. | Marcellinus, Chronicon |

| | |
|---|---|
| Chron. Min. | Chronica Minora |
| Chron. Pasch. | Chronicon Paschale |
| Cic. | Cicero (Marcus Tullius) |
|   Acad. | Academicae Quaestiones |
|   Acad. Post. | Academica Posteriora (= Plasberg, Bk. IV) |
|   Acad. Pr. | Academica Priora (= Plasberg, Bk. I) |
|   ad Brut. | Epistulae ad Brutum |
|   Amic. | De Amicitia |
|   Arch. | Pro Archia |
|   Att. | Epistulae ad Atticum |
|   Balb. | Pro Balbo |
|   Brut. | Brutus or De Claris Oratoribus |
|   Caecin. | Pro Caecina |
|   Cael. | Pro Caelio |
|   Cat. | In Catilinam |
|   Clu. | Pro Cluentio |
|   Corn. | Pro Cornelio de maiestate (fragmentary) |
|   Deiot. | Pro rege Deiotaro |
|   De Imp. Cn. Pomp. | see Leg. Man. |
|   De Or. | De Oratore |
|   Div. | De Divinatione |
|   Div. Caec. | Divinatio in Caecilium |
|   Dom. | De Domo sua |
|   Fam. | Epistulae ad Familiares |
|   Fat. | De Fato |
|   Fin. | De Finibus |
|   Flac. | Pro Flacco |
|   Font. | Pro Fonteio |
|   Har. Resp. | De Haruspicum Responso |
|   Inv. Rhet. | De Inventione Rhetorica |
|   Leg. Agr. | De Lege Agraria |
|   Leg. | De Legibus |
|   Leg. Man. | Pro Lege Manilia or De Imperio Cn. Pompeii |
|   Lig. | Pro Ligario |
|   Luc. | Lucullus or Academica Posteriora |
|   Marcell. | Pro Marcello |
|   Mil. | Pro Milone |
|   Mur. | Pro Murena |
|   Nat. D. | De Natura Deorum |
|   Off. | De Officiis |
|   Orat. | Orator ad M. Brutum |
|   Part. Or. | Partitiones Oratoriae |
|   Phil. | Orationes Philippicae |
|   Pis. | In Pisonem |
|   Planc. | Pro Plancio |
|   Prov. Cons. | De Provinciis Consularibus |
|   QFr. | Epistulae ad Quintum Fratrem |
|   Quinct. | Pro Quinctio |
|   Q Rosc. | Pro Roscio Comoedo |
|   Rab. Post. | Pro Rabirio Postumo |
|   Red. Pop. | Post reditum ad Populum |
|   Red. Sen. | Post reditum in Senatu |
|   Rep. | De Republica |
|   Rosc. Am. | Pro Sexto Roscio Amerino |
|   Scaur. | Pro Scauro |
|   Sen. | De Senectute |
|   Sest. | Pro Sestio |
|   Sull. | Pro Sulla |
|   Tog. Cand. | Oratio in Senatu in toga candida (fragmentary) |
|   Top. | Topica |
|   Tusc. | Tusculanae Disputationes |
|   Verr. | In Verrem |
| Cicero, Comment. Pet. | Cicero (Quintus), Commentariolum Petitionis |
| Cichorius, Röm. Stud. | C. Cichorius, Römische Studien, 1922, repr. 1961 (cited by chapter and section) |

Claud., *Cons. Hon.*　Claudianus, *De consulatu Honorii*
　*Cons. Stil.*　　*De consulatu Stilichonis*
Clem. Al.　Clemens Alexandrinus
　*Protr.*　　*Protrepticus*
　*Strom.*　　*Stromateis*
Cod.　Codex
*Cod. Iust.*　*Codex Iustinianus*
*Cod. Theod.*　*Codex Theodosianus*
*Codd. Lat. Ant.*　E. A. Lowe, *Codices Latini Anti-*
　(Lowe)　　*quiores*, 1934–
*Coll. Alex.*　see Powell
Collingwood–Myres,　R. G. Collingwood and J. N. L.
　*Roman Britain*　　Myres, *Roman Britain and the*
　　*English Settlements*[2], 1937
Collingwood–Wright,　R. G. Collingwood and R. P.
　*RIB*　　Wright, *The Roman Inscriptions*
　　*of Britain*, i, 1965
Columella, *Rust.*　Columella, *De re rustica*
*Comm. in Arist.*　*Commentaria in Aristotelem Graeca*
　*Graeca*
Conon, *Narr.*　Conon Mythographus, *Διηγήσεις*
*Const.*　*Constitutio*
Conway, *Ital. Dial.*　R. S. Conway, *Italic Dialects*, 1897
Cook, *Zeus*　A. B. Cook, *Zeus: a Study in*
　　*Ancient Religion*, vol. i, 1914;
　　vol. ii, 1925; vol. iii, 1940
Cornutus, *Theol.*　Cornutus (L. Annaeus), *Ἐπιδρομὴ*
　*Graec.*　　*τῶν κατὰ τὴν Ἑλληνικὴν Θεολογίαν*
　　*παραδεδομένων*
*Corp. poes. ep. Graec.*　*Corpusculum poesis epicae Graecae*
　*lud.*　　*ludibundae*, vol. 1, *Parodia et*
　　*Archestratus*, P. Brandt, 1888;
　　vol. 2, *Syllographi Graeci*,
　　C. Wachsmuth, 1885
*cos., cos. suff.*　*consul, consul suffectus*
Cramer, *Anecd. Par.*　see *Anecd. Par.*
*Cul.*　*Culex*
Cumont, *Rel. or.*　F. Cumont, *Les Religions orientales*
　　*dans le paganisme romain*[4], 1929
Cyril, *Adv. Iul.*　Cyrillus, *Adversus Iulianum*

*DCB*　*Dictionary of Christian Biography*
　　*and Literature*, ed. H. Wace and
　　W. C. Piercy, 1911
D.L.　see Diog. Laert.
*DTC*　*Dictionnaire de Théologie Catho-*
　　*lique*, ed. A. Vacant, E. Mangenot
　　and E. Amann, 15 vols.,
　　1903–50
Dam. *Isid.*　Damascius, *Vita Isidori*
Dar.–Sag.　Ch. Daremberg and E. Saglio, *Dic-*
　　*tionnaire des antiquités grecques*
　　*et romaines d'après les textes et*
　　*les monuments*, 1877–1919
*De Com.*　see Anon. *De Com.*
De Sanctis, *Stor.*　G. De Sanctis, *Storia dei Romani*,
　*Rom.*　　1907–1966
*De Vir. Ill.*　*De Viris Illustribus* (auctor ignotus)
Déchelette, *Manuel*　J. Déchelette, *Manuel d'archéologie*
　　*préhistorique, celtique et gallo-*
　　*romaine*, 1908–14
Degrassi, *ILLRP*　A. Degrassi, *Inscriptiones Latinae*
　　*Liberae Rei Publicae*, i, 1957; ii,
　　1963
*Délos*　*Explorations archéologiques de*
　　*Délos*, Paris, 1909–
Dem.　Demosthenes
　*De Cor.*　　*De Corona*
　*Lept.*　　*Against Leptines*
　*Meid.*　　*Against Meidias*
Demetr. *Eloc.*　Demetrius [Phalereus], *De Elocu-*
　　*tione* = *Περὶ ἑρμηνείας*

Demiańczuk, *Supp.*　J. Demiańczuk, *Supplementum*
　*Com.*　　*Comicum*, 1912
Democr.　Democritus
Dessau, *ILS*　H. Dessau, *Inscriptiones Latinae*
　　*Selectae*, 1892–1916
Did. Iul.　Didius Julianus, see S.H.A.
Diehl, *Anth. Lyr.*　E. Diehl, *Anthologia Lyrica Graeca*,
　*Graec.*　　1925; 2nd ed. 1942; 3rd ed.
　　1949–52
　*Poet. Rom. vet.*　　*Poetarum Romanorum veterum*
　　*reliquiae*, 1911
Diels, *Dox. Graec.*　H. Diels, *Doxographi Graeci*, 1879
　*Vorsokr.*　　*Fragmente der Vorsokratiker*[5], 1934
*Dig.*　*Digesta*
Dio Cass.　Dio Cassius
Dio Chrys.　Dio Chrysostomus
　*Or.*　　*Orationes*
Diocl. Magn.　Diocles of Magnesia
Diod. or Diod. Sic.　Diodorus Siculus
Diog. Laert. or D.L.　Diogenes Laertius
Diogenian.　Diogenianus Paroemiographus
Diom.　Diomedes Grammaticus
Dion. Calliphon.　Dionysius Calliphontis filius
Dion. Hal.　Dionysius Halicarnassensis
　*Ant. Rom.*　　*Antiquitates Romanae*
　*Comp.*　　*De Compositione Verborum*
　*De Imit.*　　*De Imitatione*
　*Dem.*　　*De Demosthene*
　*Isoc.*　　*De Isocrate*
　*Lys.*　　*De Lysia*
　*Pomp.*　　*Epistula ad Pompeium*
　*Rhet.*　　*Ars Rhetorica*
　*Thuc.*　　*De Thucydide*
　*Vett. Cens.*　　*De Veterum Censura*
Dion. Thrax　Dionysius Thrax
Dionys. Per.　Dionysius Periegeta
Diss.　Dissertatio
*Diss. Pan.*　*Dissertationes Pannonicae*, 1932–
Dittenberg. *SIG*　W. Dittenberger, *Sylloge Inscriptio-*
　　*num Graecarum*[3], 1915–24
*Diz. Epigr.*　see Ruggiero
Donat.　Aelius Donatus
*Dox. Graec.*　see Diels
Duff, *Minor Lat.*　J. W. and A. M. Duff, *Minor*
　*Poets*　　*Latin Poets*, Loeb, 1935
Dunbabin, *Western*　T. J. Dunbabin, *The Western*
　*Greeks*　　*Greeks*, 1948

*EGF*　G. Kinkel, *Epicorum Graecorum*
　　*Fragmenta*, 1877
*ERE*　see Hastings
Edmonds, *FAC*　J. M. Edmonds, *Fragments of Attic*
　　*Comedy*, i, 1957
*Enc. Brit.*　*Encyclopaedia Britannica*
Ennius, *Ann.*　Ennius, *Annales*
*Entretiens Hardt*　Fondation Hardt. *Essaies sur*
　　*l'antiquité classique*, 1952–
*Eph. Epigr.*　*Ephemeris Epigraphica, Corporis*
　　*Inscriptionum Latinarum*
　　*Supplementum*, Berlin, 1872–
Epicurus, *Ep.*　Epicurus, *Epistulae*
*Epigr. Gr.*　G. Kaibel, *Epigrammata Graeca ex*
　　*lapidibus conlecta*, 1878
Epiph. *Adv. Haeres.*　Epiphanius, *Adversus Haereses*
*Epit.*　*Epitome*
*Epit. Oxyrh.*　*Epitome Oxyrhynchica* of Livy
Eratosth.　Eratosthenes
　[*Cat.*]　　[*Καταστερισμοί*]
*Ἔργον*　Τὸ *Ἔργον τῆς Ἀρχαιολογικῆς*
　　*Ἑταιρείας*, Athens, 1956–
*Etym. Magn.*　*Etymologicum Magnum*
Euc.　Euclid

| | |
|---|---|
| Eudem. | Eudemus |
| Eunap. | Eunapius |
| *VS* | *Vitae Sophistarum* |
| Eup. | Eupolis |
| Eur. | Euripides |
| *Alc.* | *Alcestis* |
| *Andr.* | *Andromache* |
| *Bacch.* | *Bacchae* |
| *Beller.* | *Bellerophon* |
| *Cyc.* | *Cyclops* |
| *El.* | *Electra* |
| *HF* | *Hercules Furens* |
| *Hec.* | *Hecuba* |
| *Hel.* | *Helena* |
| *Heracl.* | *Heraclidae* |
| *Hipp.* | *Hippolytus* |
| *Hyps.* | *Hypsipyle* |
| *IA* | *Iphigenia Aulidensis* |
| *IT* | *Iphigenia Taurica* |
| *Med.* | *Medea* |
| *Or.* | *Orestes* |
| *Phoen.* | *Phoenissae* |
| *Rhes.* | *Rhesus* |
| *Sthen.* | *Stheneboea* |
| *Supp.* | *Supplices* |
| *Tro.* | *Troades* |
| Eus. or Euseb. | Eusebius |
| *Chron.* | *Chronica* |
| *Hist. Eccl.* | *Historia Ecclesiastica* |
| *Praep. Evang.* | *Praeparatio Evangelica* |
| Eust., *Il.* | Eustathius, *ad Iliadem* |
| Eutocius, *In Arch.* | Eutocius, *In Archimedis circuli* |
| *circ. dim.* | *dimensionem* |
| | |
| *FAC* | See Edmonds |
| *FCG* | see Meineke |
| *FCGM* | see Olivieri |
| *FGrH* | F. Jacoby, *Fragmente der griechischen Historiker*, 1923– |
| *FHG* | C. Müller, *Fragmenta Historicorum Graecorum*, 1841–70 |
| *FIRA* | see Riccobono |
| *FOR* | *Forma Orbis Romanae. Carte archéologique de la Gaule romaine*, ed. A. Blanchet (1931– ) |
| *FPG* | F. W. A. Mullach, *Fragmenta Philosophorum Graecorum*, 1860–81 |
| *FPL* | see Morel |
| *FPR* | see Baehr. (Baehrens) |
| *FUR* | *Forma Urbis Romae*, Rome, 1960, ed. G. Corettoni et al. |
| Farnell, *Cults* | L. R. Farnell, *The Cults of the Greek States*, 1896–1909 |
| *Hero-Cults* | L. R. Farnell, *Greek Hero-Cults and Ideas of Immortality*, 1921 |
| Festus, *Gloss. Lat.* | W. M. Lindsay's second ed. of Festus in his *Glossaria Latina*, vol. iv |
| Firm. Mat. | Firmicus Maternus |
| *Err. prof. rel.* | *De errore profanarum religionum* |
| Fleck. *J. Suppl.* | *Fleckeisens Jahrbücher für klassische Philologie*, Suppl. xxiv, 1898 = *Neue Jahrbücher f. d. klassische Altertum* |
| Forbes, *Stud. Anc. Technol.* | R. J. Forbes, *Studies in Ancient Technology*, 9 vols., 1957–64 |
| Frank, *Econ. Survey* | *An Economic Survey of Ancient Rome*, Ed. T. Frank, 5 vols., U.S.A. 1933–40 |
| Frazer, *GB* | J. G. Frazer, *The Golden Bough: a Study in Magic and Religion*[3], 13 vols., 1911–15 |
| Frere, *Britannia* | S. S. Frere, *Britannia*, 1967 |
| Friedländer, *Rom. Life* | L. Friedländer, *Darstellung aus der Sittengeschichte Roms*[9-10], 1921–3, revised by G. Wissowa[6]; *Roman Life and Manners under the Early Empire*, Engl. Transl. from ed. 7, 1908–13 |
| Frontin. | Frontinus |
| *Aq.* | *De Aquae Ductu Urbis Romae* |
| *Str.* | *Strategemata* |
| Fronto, *Ep.* | Fronto, *Epistulae* |
| Fulg. | Fulgentius |
| *Myth.* | *Mitologiae tres libri* |
| Funaioli, *Gramm. Rom. Frag.* | H. Funaioli, *Grammaticae Romanae fragmenta*, 1907, vol. i alone published |
| *GB* | see Frazer |
| *GDI* | H. Collitz et alii, *Sammlung der griechischen Dialektinschriften*, 1884–1915 |
| *GGM* | C. Müller, *Geographici Graeci Minores*, 1855–61 |
| *GLP* | see Page |
| *GRBS* | *Greek, Roman and Byzantine Studies*, U.S.A. 1958– |
| Gai. *Inst.* | Gaius, *Institutiones* |
| Gal. | Galen |
| *Libr. Propr.* | Περὶ τῶν ἰδίων βιβλίων |
| *Nat. Fac.* | Περὶ φυσικῶν δυνάμεων |
| Gell. | Aulus Gellius |
| *NA* | *Noctes Atticae* |
| German. | Germanicus |
| *Arat.* | *Aratea* |
| *Gesch.* | *Geschichte* |
| *Gloss. Lat.* | see Lindsay |
| Glotz, *Hist. grecque* | G. Glotz, R. Cohen, and P. Roussel, *Histoire grecque*, i–iv. 1, 1925–38 |
| *Gnomon* | *Gnomon, Kritische Zeitschrift für d. gesamte klassische Altertumswiss.*, 1925– |
| Gomperz | T. Gomperz, *Griechische Denker*, 1896. Engl. Transl. ('Greek Thinkers'), vol. i, 1901; vol. ii, 1902; vol. iii, 1905; vol. iv, 1912 |
| Gorg. | Gorgias |
| *Hel.* | *Helena* |
| *Pal.* | *Palamedes* |
| *Gött. Anz.* | *Göttingischer gelehrte Anzeigen*, 1739– |
| *Gött. Nachr.* | *Nachrichten von der Gesellschaft der Wissenschaften zu Göttingen*, 1845– |
| Gow and Page | A. S. F. Gow and D. L. Page, *Greek Anthology: Hellenistic Epigrams*, 2 vols., 1965 |
| *Gramm. Lat.* | see Keil |
| *Gramm. Rom. Frag.* | see Funaioli |
| Greenidge, Clay, Gray, *Sources* | A. H. J. Greenidge, A. M. Clay, and E. W. Gray, *Sources for Roman History 133–70 B.C.*, 1960 |
| Grenier, *Manuel* | A. Grenier, *Manuel d'archéologie gallo-romaine*, 1931–4; = vol. v of Déchelette's *Manuel d'archéologie préhistorique* |
| Guthrie, *Hist. Gk. Phil.* | W. K. C. Guthrie, *History of Greek Philosophy*, 1965– |
| *HR Rel.* | see under Peter |
| Halm, *Rhet. Lat. Min.* | K. Halm, *Rhetores Latini Minores*, 1863 |
| Hammond, *Epirus* | N. G. L. Hammond, *Epirus*, 1967 |
| Hammond, *Hist. G.* | N. G. L. Hammond, *History of Greece*[2], 1967 |

Hansen, *Attalids* — C. V. Hansen, *The Attalids of Pergamum*, 1947
Harp. — Harpocration
Harv. Stud. — *Harvard Studies in Classical Philology*, 1890–
Harv. Theol. Rev. — *Harvard Theological Review*, 1908–
Hastings, *ERE* — J. Hastings, *Encyclopaedia of Religion and Ethics*, 12 vols., 1908–21; Index vol. 1926
Heath, *Hist. of Greek Maths.* — T. L. Heath, *History of Greek Mathematics*, 2 vols., 1921
Hercher, *Epistolog. Graec.* — R. Hercher, *Epistolographi Graeci*, 1873
Hdn. — Herodianus
Hdt. — Herodotus
Head, *Hist. Num.* — B. V. Head, *Historia Numorum*², ed. 2, 1911
Hell. Oxy. — *Hellenica Oxyrhynchia*
Heph. — Hephaestion
Heraclid. Pont. — Heraclides Ponticus
*Hermes* — *Hermes, Zeitschrift für klassische Philologie*, 1866–
Hermog. — Hermogenes
Id. — Περὶ ἰδεῶν
Inv. — Περὶ εὑρέσεως
Prog. — Προγυμνάσματα
Herod. — Herodas
Hes. — Hesiod
Op. — *Opera et Dies*
Sc. or Scut. — *Scutum*
Th. or Theog. — *Theogonia*
Hesp. — *Hesperia: Journal of the American School of Classical Studies at Athens*, 1932–
Hieron. — Hieronymus (Jerome)
ab Abr. — *ab Abraham*, the chronological reckoning from the first year of Abraham followed in Jerome's translation and enlargement of Eusebius' Chronicle
Adv. Iovinian. — *Adversus Iovinianum*
Chron. — *Chronica* = ab Abr.
De script. eccles. proleg. — *De scriptoribus ecclesiasticis (prolegomena*
De Vir. Ill. — *De Viris Illustribus*
Ep. — *Epistulae*
Hignett, *Hist. Athen. Const.* — C. Hignett, *A History of the Athenian Constitution*, 1952
Himer. *Ex. Nap.* — Himerius, *Excerpta Napolitana*
Hippoc. — Hippocrates
[Ep.] — *Epistulae*
Hippol. — Hippolytus
Haer. — *Refutatio omnium Haeresium*
Hist. — *Historia*, Baden-Baden, 1950–
Hist. Aug. — *Historia Augusta* (see S.H.A.)
Hom. — Homer
Il. — *Iliad*
Od. — *Odyssey*
Homil. Clement. — *Clementine Homilies*
Hor. — Horace
Ars P. — *Ars Poetica*
Carm. — *Carmina* or *Odes*
Carm. Saec. — *Carmen Saeculare*
Epist. — *Epistulae*
Epod. — *Epodi*
Sat. — *Satirae* or *Sermones*
Hsch. — Hesychius
Hyde, *Greek Mariners* — W. Hyde, *Ancient Greek Mariners*, 1947
Hyg. — Hyginus
Fab. — *Fabulae*
Poet. Astr. — *Poetica Astronomica*

Hymn. Hom. Ap. — *Hymnus Homericus ad Apollinem*
Bacch. — „ „ „ *Bacchum*
Cer. — „ „ „ *Cererem*
Mart. — „ „ „ *Martem*
Merc. — „ „ „ *Mercurium*
Pan. — „ „ „ *Panem*
Ven. — „ „ „ *Venerem*
Hymn. Mag. — *Hymni Magici*
Hymn. Orph. — *Hymni Orphici*
hyp. — hypothesis
IG — *Inscriptiones Graecae*, 1873–
IG Rom. — *Inscriptiones Graecae ad res Romanas pertinentes*, 1906–
ILN — *Illustrated London News*
ILS — see Dessau
IPE — *Inscriptiones orae septentrionalis Ponti Euxini*, 1885
I. l. de Gaule — *Inscriptions latines des trois Gaules*, ed. P. Wuilleumier, 1963
Iambl. — Iamblichus
Myst. — *De Mysteriis*
Ibyc. — Ibycus
Il. — *Iliad*
Indo-Germ. Forsch. — *Indogermanische Forschungen*, 1891–
Inst. Iust. — *Institutiones Iustiniani*
Iron Age in S. Britain — Ed. S. S. Frere, *The Iron Age in Southern Britain*, 1958
Isae. — Isaeus
Isid. — Isidorus
Etym. or Orig. — *Etymologiae* or *Origines*
Isoc. — Isocrates
Bus. — *Busiris*
Paneg. — *Panegyricus*
It. Alex. — *Itinerarium Alexandri*
It. Ant. — *Itineraria Antonini Augusti*
JDAI — *Jahrbuch des [kaiserlich] deutschen archäologischen Instituts*, 1886– (contains *Archäologischer Anzeiger*)
JEg. Arch. — *Journal of Egyptian Archaeology*, 1914–
JHS — *Journal of Hellenic Studies*, 1880–
JNES — *Journal of Near Eastern Studies*, Chicago, 1942–
JÖAI — *Jahreshefte des Österreichischen Archäolog. Instituts in Wien*, 1898–
JRS — *Journal of Roman Studies*, 1911–
JTS — *Journal of Theological Studies*, 1899–
JWI — *Journal of the Warburg and Courtauld Institute*, 1937–
Jahrb. — see [Neue] Jahrb.
Jahrb. f. cl. Phil. Suppl. — *Jahrbücher für classische Philologie, Supplementband*
Jahresb. — see Bursian
Jerome — see Hieron.
Jones, *Cities E. Rom. Prov.* — A. H. M. Jones, *The Cities of the Eastern Roman Provinces*, 1937
Later Rom. Emp. — *The Later Roman Empire 284–602*, 1964
Joseph. — Josephus
AJ — *Antiquitates Judaicae*
Ap. — *Contra Apionem*
BJ — *Bellum Judaicum*
Vit. — *Vita*
Journ. Bib. Lit. — *Journal of Biblical Literature*, 1890–
Journ. Phil. — *Journal of Philology*, 1868–1920; Index, 1923
Journ. Sav. — *Journal des savants*, N.S. 1903–

| | |
|---|---|
| Julian. | Julianus Imperator |
| *Apophth.* | *Apophthegmata* |
| *Ep.* | *Epistulae* |
| *Mis.* | *Misopogon* |
| *Or.* | *Orationes* |
| Just. *Epit.* | Justinus, *Epitome* (of Trogus) |
| Juv. | Juvenal |
| κ. | κατά |
| Kaibel | see *CGF* and *Epigr. Gr.* |
| Keil, *Gramm. Lat.* | H. Keil, *Grammatici Latini*, 8 vols., 1855–1923 |
| Kern | O. Kern |
| *Orph. frag.* | *Orphica Fragmenta*, 1922 |
| *Rel. d. Griech.* | *Die Religion der Griechen*, 1926 |
| Kirk-Raven, *Presocratic Philosophers* | G. S. Kirk and J. E. Raven, *The Presocratic Philosophers*, 1957 |
| *Kl. Pauly* | *Der Kleine Pauly* 1964– |
| *Kl. Schr.* | *Kleine Schriften* (of various authors) |
| *Klass. Phil. Stud.* | *Klassische Philologische Studien* herausg. von E. Bickel u. C. Jensen |
| *Klio* | *Klio, Beiträge zur alten Geschichte*, 1901– |
| Klotz, *Scaen. Rom. Frag.* | Ed. A. Klotz, *Scaenicorum Romanorum Fragmenta*, 1953 |
| Körte, *Men. Rel.* | A. Körte, *Menandri Reliquiae* |
| Kroll, *Rhet.* | W. Kroll, *Rhetorik*, 1937; written as article for *PW*, but published separately |
| Kühn | K. G. Kühn, *Medicorum Graecorum Opera* |
| *LEC* | *Les Études Classiques*, 1932– |
| LSJ | Liddell and Scott, *Greek-English Lexicon*, 9th ed., revised by H. Stuart Jones, 1925–40 |
| LXX | Septuagint |
| Lactant. | Lactantius |
| *Div. Inst.* | *Divinae Institutiones* |
| Lambrechts, *Sénat* | P. Lambrechts, *La Composition du Sénat romain 117–192*, 1936 |
| Latte, *RR* | K. Latte, *Römische Religionsgeschichte*, 1960 |
| Laur. | Laurentian Library |
| *Leipz. Stud.* | *Leipziger Studien zur klassischen Philosophie*, 1878–95 |
| *Lex.* | *Lexicon* |
| *Lex. Mess.* | *Lexicon Messanense* |
| *Lib. Colon.* | *Libri coloniarum* |
| *Lind. Temp. Chron.* | Chr. Blinkenberg, *Die Lindische Tempelchronik*, 1915 |
| Lindsay, *Gloss. Lat.* | W. M. Lindsay, *Glossaria Latina*, Paris, 1930 |
| Lippold, *Griech. Plastik* | G. Lippold, *Die Griechische Plastik (Handbuch der Archäologie)*, 1950) |
| Livy, *Epit.* | Livy, *Epitomae* |
| *Per.* | *Periochae* |
| Lobeck, *Aglaoph.* | C. A. Lobeck, *Aglaophamus*, 1829 |
| Loeb | Loeb Classical Library |
| [Longinus], *Subl.* | [Longinus], Περὶ ὕψους |
| Luc. | Lucan |
| Lucian | |
| *Alex.* | *Alexander* |
| *Anach.* | *Anacharsis* |
| *Catapl.* | *Cataplus* |
| *Demon.* | *Demonax* |
| *Dial. D.* | *Dialogi Deorum* |
| *Dial. Meret.* | *Dialogi Meretricii* |
| *Dial. Mort.* | *Dialogi Mortuorum* |
| *Hermot.* | *Hermotimus* |
| *Hist. conscr.* | *Quomodo Historia conscribenda sit* |

| | |
|---|---|
| *Ind.* | *Adversus Indoctum* |
| *Iupp. Trag.* | *Iuppiter Tragoedus* |
| *Macr.* | *Macrobii* |
| *Nigr.* | *Nigrinus* |
| *Salt.* | *De Saltatione* |
| *Symp.* | *Symposium* |
| *Syr. D.* | *De Syria Dea* |
| *Trag.* | *Tragoedopodagra* |
| *Ver. Hist.* | *Verae Historiae*, 1, 2 |
| *Vit. Auct.* | *Vitarum Auctio* |
| Lucil. | Lucilius |
| Lucr. | Lucretius |
| Lugli, *Fontes* | G. Lugli, *Fontes ad Topographiam Veteris Urbis Romanae Pertinentes*, vols. i–iv, viii, 1953–62 |
| Lycoph. | Lycophron |
| *Alex.* | *Alexandra* |
| Lycurg. | Lycurgus |
| *Leoc.* | *Against Leocrates* |
| Lydus, *Mens.* | Lydus, *De Mensibus* |
| *Mag.* | *De Magistratibus* |
| Lys. | Lysias |
| *MAMA* | *Monumenta Asiae Minoris Antiquae*, ed. Sir William M. Calder and J. M. R. Cormack, vols. i–viii, 1928–62 |
| *MDAI* | *Mitteilungen des deutschen archäologischen Instituts, Athenische Abteilung* (A) 1876– *Römische Abteilung* (R) 1886– |
| *MGH* | *Monumenta Germaniae Historica*, 15 vols., 1877–1919, repr. 1961 |
| *AA* | *Auctores Antiquissimi* |
| *MH* | *Museum Helveticum*, 1944– |
| Macrob. | Macrobius |
| *Sat.* | *Saturnalia* |
| Magie, *Rom. Rule Asia Min.* | D. Magie, *Roman Rule in Asia Minor*, U.S.A. 1950 |
| Malcovati, *ORF* | H. Malcovati, *Oratorum Romanorum Fragmenta*², Turin, 1955 |
| Manitius | M. Manitius, *Gesch. der lat. Lit. des Mittelalters*, 1911–12 |
| Marcellin. | Marcellinus |
| *Marm. Par.* | *Marmor Parium (IG 12(5), 444)* |
| Marquardt | J. Marquardt |
| *Privatleben* | *Privatleben der Römer*², besorgt von A. Mau. 2 vols., 1886. These together make up vol. vii of *Handbuch der römischen Altertümer*, von Joachim Marquardt und Theodor Mommsen |
| *Staatsverw.* | *Römische Staatsverwaltung*², 1881–5 |
| Mart. | Martial |
| *Spect.* | *Spectacula* |
| Marx | F. Marx, *C. Lucilii Carminum Reliquiae*, 1904–5 |
| Mattingly–Sydenham, *RIC* | H. Mattingly and E. A. Sydenham, *Roman Imperial Coinage*, 1923– |
| Meineke, *FCG* | A. Meineke, *Fragmenta Comicorum Graecorum*, 1839–57 |
| *Mélanges d'arch.* | *Mélanges d'archéologie et d'histoire de l'École française de Rome*, 1881– |
| *Mél. Masp.* | *Mélanges Maspéro*, 1934–7 |
| Men. | Menander |
| *Epit.* | Ἐπιτρέποντες |
| *Her.* | Ἥρως |
| *Pk.* | Περικειρομένη |
| *Sam.* | Σαμία |
| Meyer, *Forschungen* | Ed. Meyer, *Forschungen zur alten Geschichte*, 1892–9 |

Michell, *Econom.* H. Michell, *The Economics of*
*Anc. Gr.* *Ancient Greece*², 1957
Migne, *PG* Migne, *Patrologiae Cursus, series*
*Graeca*
*PL* *Patrologiae Cursus, series Latina*
Min. Fel. Minucius Felix
*Oct.* *Octavius*
Mir. Ausc. *De Mirabilibus Auscultationibus*
(auctor ignotus)
*Mnemos.* *Mnemosyne*, 1852–
Mommsen Th. Mommsen
*Ges. Schr.* *Gesammelte Schriften*, 8 vols.,
1905–13
*Röm. Forsch.* *Römische Forschungen*, 2 vols. (1 in
2nd ed.), 1864–79
*Röm. Staatsr.* *Römisches Staatsrecht*, i, ii, ed.
3, 1887, iii, 1888
*Röm. Strafr.* *Römisches Strafrecht*, 1899
Mommsen–Mar- *Manuel des antiquités romaines*,
quardt, *Manuel* 1887–1907, a French transl. of
Mommsen's *Römisches Staatsrecht*
*Mon. Anc.* *Monumentum Ancyranum*
*Mon. Ant.* *Monumenti Antichi pubblicati per*
*cura della Reale Accademia dei*
*Lincei*, 1890–
*Mon. Piot* *Monuments Piot*, 1894–
Morel, *FPL* *Fragmenta Poetarum Latinorum*
*epicorum et lyricorum . . . post*
E. Baehrens, ed. W. Morel, 1927
Münzer, *Röm. Adels-* F. Münzer, *Römische Adels-*
*parteien* *parteien und Adelsfamilien*,
1920
*Mus. Belge* *Musée Belge*, 1897–
*Myth. Vat.* *Mythographi Vaticani*, ed. Bode,
1834

*Nachr. Ges. d. Wiss.* see *Gött. Nachr.*
*Gött.*
Nash, *Pict. Dict.* E. Nash, *Pictorial Dictionary of*
*Rome* *Ancient Rome*, 1961–2
Naevius, *fr. com.* Naevius, *fragmenta comoediarum*
Nauck see *TGF*
Nemes. Nemesianus
*Cyn.* *Cynegetica*
*Ecl.* *Eclogae*
Nep. Nepos
*Att.* *Atticus*
*Epam.* *Epaminondas*
⎧ (1) [*Neue*] *Jahrbücher für Philologie*
⎪ *und Pädagogik*, 1826–97
⎪ (2) *Neue Jahrbücher für d. klas-*
⎪ *sische Altertum*, 1898–1925
[*Neue*] *Jahrb.* ⎨ (3) *Neue Jahrbücher für Wissen-*
⎪ *schaft und Jugendbildung*,
⎪ 1925–36
⎪ ((1), (2), and (3) form a continuous
⎩ series)
Nic. Nicander
*Alex.* *Alexipharmaca*
*Ther.* *Theriaca*
Nic. Dam. Nicolaus Damascenus
Nilsson, *Feste* M. P. Nilsson, *Griechische Feste v.*
*religiöser Bedeutung m. Ausschluss*
*d. attischen*, 1906
*GGR* *Geschichte der Griechischen Religion*
i², 1955, ii², 1961
Non. Nonius
Nonnus, *Dion.* Nonnus, *Dionysiaca*
Norden, *Ant.* E. Norden, *Die Antike Kunstprosa,*
*Kunstpr.* *vom 6. Jahrh. v. Chr. bis in d.*
*Zeit d. Renaissance*, 1898, rp.
with supplements 1909

*Not. Dign.* [*occ.*] [*or.*] *Notitia dignitatum in partibus*
*occidentis orientis*
*Not. Scav.* *Notizie degl iscavi di antichità*, 1876–
*Nov.* *Novellae*
*Num. Chron.* *Numismatic Chronicle*, 1861–
*Numen.* Numenius

O.C.T. Oxford Classical Texts
*ODCC* *Oxford Dictionary of the Christian*
*Church*, ed. F. L. Cross, 1958
*OGI* *Orientis Graeci Inscriptiones Selectae*,
1903–5
*ORF* see Malcovati
*Od.* *Odyssey*
Ogilvie, *Comm.* R. M. Ogilvie, *Commentary on*
*Livy 1–5* *Livy, Books 1–5*, 1965
Olivieri, *FCGM* A. Olivieri, *Frammenti della Comme-*
*dia Greca e del Mimo nella Sicilia*
*e nella Magna Grecia*, 1930
*Op. Arch.* *Opuscula Archaeologica*, Lund,
*Or.* *Oratio*
1935–
Origen, *c. Cels.* Origen, *Contra Celsum*
Oros. Orosius
*Orph. Lith.* *Orphica, Lithica*
Ov. Ovid
*Am.* *Amores*
*Ars Am.* *Ars Amatoria*
*Fast.* *Fasti*
*Hal.* *Halieuticon Liber*
*Her.* *Heroides*
*Ib.* *Ibis*
*Medic.* *Medicamina faciei*
*Met.* *Metamorphoses*
*Pont.* *Epistulae ex Ponto*
*Rem. Am.* *Remedia Amoris*
*Tr.* *Tristia*
Overbeck J. Overbeck, *Die antiken Schrift-*
*quellen zur Geschichte d. bilden-*
*den Künste bei den Griechen*, 1868

π. περί
*PACA* *Proceedings of the African Classical*
*Associations*, 1958–
*PBSR* *Papers of the British School at*
*Rome*, 1902–
*PCPS* *Proceedings of the Cambridge*
*Philological Society*, 1882–
*PG* see Migne
*PGM* *Papyri Graecae Magicae*, ed. by
Karl Preisendanz, 2 vols., 1928–31
*PIR* *Prosopographia Imperii Romani*
*Saeculi I, II, III*, 1st ed. by
E. Klebs and H. Dessau, 1897–8;
2nd ed. by E. Groag and A.
Stein, 1933–
*P–K, GL* A. Philippson and E. Kirsten, *Die*
*Griechischen Landschaften* i–iv,
1950–9
*PL* see Migne
*PLG* T. Bergk, *Poetae Lyrici Graeci*,
1882, rp. 1914–15
*PLM* *Poetae Latini Minores*, ed. E.
Baehrens, 5 vols., 1879–83; rev.
by F. Vollmer, only vols. i, ii,
and v completed 1911–35
*PP* *La Parola del Passato*, Napoli, 1946–
*PPF* H. Diels, *Poetarum Philosophorum*
*Graecorum Fragmenta*, 1901
*PSAS* *Proceedings of the Society of Anti-*
*quaries, Scotland*, 1866

| | | | |
|---|---|---|---|
| *PSI* | *Papiri Greci e Latini, Pubblicazioni della Società italiana per la ricerca dei papiri greci e latini in Egitto,* 1912– | *Philol.* | *Philologus,* 1846– |
| | | *Philol. Suppl.* | *Philologus,* Supplement, 1860– |
| | | Philostr. | Philostratus |
| *PW* | A. Pauly, G. Wissowa, and W. Kroll, *Real-Encyclopädie d. klassischen Altertumswissenschaft,* 1893– | *Imag.* | *Imagines* |
| | | *VA* | *Vita Apollonii* |
| | | *VS* | *Vitae Sophistarum* |
| Page, *GLP* | D. L. Page, *Greek Literary Papyri,* 1942– | Phld. | Philodemus |
| | | Phlegon, *Mir.* | Phlegon, *Miracula* |
| | | Phot. | Photius |
| *Poet. Mel. Gr.* | *Poetae Melici Graeci,* 1962 | *Bibl.* | *Bibliotheca* |
| *PAmh.* | *Amherst Papyri,* 1900– | Pickard-Cambridge– | A. W. Pickard-Cambridge, *Dithy-* |
| *PAntin.* | The *Antinoe Papyrus* of Theocritus | Webster, *Dithy-* | *ramb, Tragedy and Comedy,* 2nd ed. |
| *P Antinoop.* | *Antinoopolis Papyri* | ramb² | revised by T. B. L. Webster, 1962 |
| *PBerol.* | *Berlin Papyri* | Pind. | Pindar (ed. C. M. Bowra, 1947) |
| P. Cairo Zeno | C. C. Edgar, *Zenon Papyri,* 4 vols., 1925–31 | *Isthm.* | *Isthmian Odes* |
| | | *Nem.* | *Nemean* „ |
| *PEleph.* | *Elephantine Papyri,* 1907 | *Ol.* | *Olympian* „ |
| *PFouad* | P. Jouguet and others, *Les Papyrus Fouad I,* 1939 | *Pyth.* | *Pythian* „ |
| | | Pl. | Plato |
| *PGiess.* | *Griechische Papyri im Museum des oberhessischen Geschichtsvereins zu Giessen* | *Alc.* | *Alcibiades* |
| | | *Ap.* | *Apologia* |
| | | *Chrm.* | *Charmides* |
| *PGhôran* | P. Jouguet, *BCH* 1906, 103 ff. | *Cra.* | *Cratylus* |
| *PHib.* | *Hibeh Papyri,* 1906 | *Cri.* | *Crito* |
| *PIand.* | *Papyri Iandanae,* 1912– | *Criti.* | *Critias* |
| *PLips.* | *Griechische Urkunden der Papyrussammlung zu Leipzig* | *Epin.* | *Epinomis* |
| | | *Euthphr.* | *Euthyphro* |
| *PLondon* | *Greek Papyri in the British Museum,* ed. F. G. Kenyon and H. I. Bell | *Grg.* | *Gorgias* |
| | | *Hipparch.* | *Hipparchus* |
| *PLund* | *Papyri Lundenses* | *Hp. Mi.* | *Hippias Minor* |
| *PMilan.* | *Papiri Milanesi* | *La.* or *Lach.* | *Laches* |
| *POsl.* | *Papyri Osloenses* | *Leg.* | *Leges* |
| *POxy.* | *Oxyrhynchus Papyri,* ed. B. P. Grenfell and A. S. Hunt, 1898– | *Menex.* | *Menexenus* |
| | | *Phd.* | *Phaedo* |
| *PRyl.* | *Catalogue of the Greek papyri in the John Rylands Library at Manchester,* 1911– | *Phdr.* | *Phaedrus* |
| | | *Phlb.* | *Philebus* |
| | | *Prm.* | *Parmenides* |
| *PTeb.* | *Tebtunis Papyri,* 1902–38 | *Prt.* | *Protagoras* |
| *PVat. II* | *Il Papiro Vaticano Greco II,* ed. M. Norsa and G. Vitelli, 1931 | *Resp.* | *Respublica* |
| | | *Symp.* | *Symposium* |
| Parker, *Roman Legions* | H. M. D. Parker, *The Roman Legions*², 1958 | *Soph.* | *Sophista* |
| | | *Tht.* | *Theaetetus* |
| *Parod. Epic. Gr. Rel.* | *Parodorum Epicorum Graecorum reliquiae,* vol. i of *Corpusculum Poesis Epicae Graecae Ludibundae,* P. Brandt and C. Wachsmuth, 1888 | *Ti.* | *Timaeus* |
| | | Platner–Ashby | S. B. Platner and T. Ashby, *A Topographical Dictionary of Ancient Rome,* 1929 |
| | | Plato Com. | Plato Comicus |
| Parth. | Parthenius | Platon. | Platonius |
| *Amat. Narr.* | *Narrationum Amatoriarum libellus* (Ἐρωτικὰ παθήματα) | *Diff. Com.* | *De Differentia Comoediarum* |
| | | Plaut. | Plautus |
| Paulus, *Sent.* | Julius Paulus, *Sententiae* | *Amph.* | *Amphitruo* |
| Paus. | Pausanias | *Asin.* | *Asinaria* |
| Pearson, *Lost Histories of Alexander* | L. Pearson, *The Lost Histories of Alexander the Great,* 1960 | *Bacch.* | *Bacchides* |
| | | *Capt.* | *Captivi* |
| *Peripl. M. Rubr.* | *Periplus Maris Rubri* | *Cas.* | *Casina* |
| Pers. | Persius | *Cist.* | *Cistellaria* |
| Peter, *HR Rel.* | H. Peter, *Historicorum Romanorum Reliquiae,* vol. i², 1914, ii, 1906 | *Curc.* | *Curculio* |
| | | *Men.* | *Menaechmi* |
| Petron. | Petronius | *Merc.* | *Mercator* |
| *Sat.* | *Satura* | *Mostell.* | *Mostellaria* |
| Pf. | R. Pfeiffer | *Stich.* | *Stichus* |
| Pfuhl | E. Pfuhl, *Malerei u. Zeichnung d. Griechen,* 3 vols., 1923 | Pliny | Pliny (the Elder) |
| | | *HN* | *Naturalis Historia* |
| Pherec. or Pherecyd. | Pherecydes | Pliny | Pliny (the Younger) |
| *Phil. Unters.* | *Philologische Untersuchungen,* 1880– | *Ep.* | *Epistulae* |
| *Phil. Wochenschr.* | *Philologische Wochenschrift,* 1921– | *Pan.* | *Panegyricus* |
| Philo | Philo Judaeus | *Tra.* | *Epistulae ad Traianum* |
| *CW* | Edition of Philo Judaeus by L. Cohn and P. Wendland, Berlin, 1896–1916 | Plotinus, *Enn.* | Plotinus, *Enneades* |
| | | Plut. | Plutarch |
| | | *Mor.* | *Moralia* |
| *In Flacc.* | *In Flaccum* | *Amat.* | *Amatorius* |
| *Leg.* | *Legatio ad Gaium* | *An seni* | *An seni respublica gerenda sit* |

| | | | |
|---|---|---|---|
| *Comp. Ar. et Men.* | *Comparatio Aristophanis et Menandri* | *Onom.* | *Onomasticon* |
| *Conv. sept. sap.* | *Convivium septem sapientium* | Polyaenus, *Strat.* | Polyaenus, *Strategemata* |
| *De Alex. fort.* | *De fortuna Alexandri* | Polyb. | Polybius |
| *De def. or.* | *De defectu oraculorum* | Pompon. | Pomponius |
| *De exil.* | *De exilio* | Porph. | Porphyry |
| *De fac.* | *De facie in orbe lunae* | *Abst.* | *De Abstinentia* |
| *De fort. Rom.* | *De fortuna Romanorum* | *De Antr. Nymph.* | *De Antro Nympharum* |
| *De frat. amor.* | *De fraterno amore* | *Plot.* | *Vita Plotini* |
| *De garr.* | *De garrulitate* | Powell, *Coll. Alex.* | J. U. Powell, *Collectanea Alexandrina*, 1925 |
| *De gen.* | *De genio Socratis* | | |
| *De glor. Ath.* | *De gloria Atheniensium* | Powell and Barber, *New Chapters* | J. U. Powell and E. A. Barber, *New Chapters in the History of Greek Literature*, 1921; Second Series, 1929; Third Series, J. U. Powell alone, 1933 |
| *De Is. et Os.* | *De Iside et Osiride* | | |
| *De lat. viv.* | *De latenter vivendo* | | |
| *De mul. vir.* | *De mulierum virtutibus* | | |
| *De mus.* | *De musica* | *praef.* | *praefatio* |
| *De prof. virt.* | *De profectu in virtute* | Preisendanz | see *PGM* |
| *De Pyth. or.* | *De Pythiae oraculis* | Preller–Robert | L. Preller, *Griechische Mythologie*[4], bearbeitet von C. Robert, 1894 |
| *De sera* | *De sera numinis vindicta* | | |
| *De soll. an.* | *De sollertia animalium* | *Prisc. Inst.* | Priscian, *Institutio de arte grammatica* |
| *De superst.* | *De superstitione* | | |
| *De tranq. anim.* | *De tranquillitate animi* | *Proc. Brit. Acad.* | *Proceedings of the British Academy*, 1903– |
| *Quaest. conv.* | *Quaestiones convivales* | | |
| *Quaest. Graec.* | „ *Graecae* | *Procl.* | *Proclus* |
| *Quaest. Plat.* | „ *Platonicae* | *In Ti.* | *In Platonis Timaeum commentarii* |
| *Quaest. Rom.* | „ *Romanae* | Procop. | Procopius |
| *Quomodo adul.* | *Quomodo adulescens poetas audire debeat* | *Aed.* | *De Aedificiis* |
| | | *Goth.* | *De Bello Gothico* |
| *Vit.* | *Vitae Parallelae* | *Vand.* | *De Bello Vandalico* |
| *Aem.* | *Aemilius Paulus* | *Progr.* | *Programm* |
| *Ages.* | *Agesilaus* | Prop. | Propertius |
| *Alc.* | *Alcibiades* | *Prosop. Att.* | J. Kirchner, *Prosopographia Attica*, 1901–3 |
| *Alex.* | *Alexander* | | |
| *Ant.* | *Antonius* | *Prosop. Rom.* | = *PIR* |
| *Arat.* | *Aratus* | Prudent. | Prudentius |
| *Brut.* | *Brutus* | *c. Symm.* | *contra Symmachum* |
| *C. Gracch.* | *Gaius Gracchus* | *Perist.* | *Peristephanon* |
| *Caes.* | *Caesar* | Ptol. | Ptolemaeus mathematicus |
| *Cam.* | *Camillus* | *Alm.* | *Almagest* |
| *Cat. Mai., Min.* | *Cato Maior, Minor* | *Geog.* | *Geographia* |
| *Cic.* | *Cicero* | *Harm.* | *Harmonica* |
| *Cim.* | *Cimon* | | |
| *Cleom.* | *Cleomenes* | Quint. | Quintilian |
| *Crass.* | *Crassus* | *Ep. ad Tryph.* | *Epistula ad Tryphonem* (introductory to the following) |
| *Dem.* | *Demosthenes* | | |
| *Demetr.* | *Demetrius* | *Inst.* | *Institutio oratoria* |
| *Flam.* | *Flamininus* | Quint. Smyrn. | Quintus Smyrnaeus |
| *Luc.* | *Lucullus* | | |
| *Lyc.* | *Lycurgus* | *RAC* | *Reallexikon für Antike und Christentum*, Stuttgart, 1941– |
| *Lys.* | *Lysander* | | |
| *Mar.* | *Marius* | *RGVV* | *Religionsgeschichtliche Versuche und Vorarbeiten*, ed. A. Dieterich, R. Wünsch, L. Malten, O. Weinreich, L. Deubner, 1903– |
| *Marc.* | *Marcellus* | | |
| *Num.* | *Numa* | | |
| *Pel.* | *Pelopidas* | | |
| *Per.* | *Pericles* | *RIB* | see Collingwood–Wright |
| *Phil.* | *Philopoemen* | *RIDA* | *Revue Internationale des Droits de l'Antiquité* |
| *Pomp.* | *Pompeius* | | |
| *Pyrrh.* | *Pyrrhus* | *RK* | see Wissowa |
| *Rom.* | *Romulus* | *RLÖ* | *Der römische Limes in Österreich*, 1900– |
| *Sert.* | *Sertorius* | | |
| *Sol.* | *Solon* | *Rav. Cosm.* | *Cosmographia Anonymi Ravennatis* |
| *Sull.* | *Sulla* | *Rend. Ist. Lomb.* | *Rendiconti d. R. Istituto Lombardo di scienze e lettere*, 1864– |
| *Them.* | *Themistocles* | | |
| *Thes.* | *Theseus* | *Rend. Linc.* | *Rendiconti della reale accademia dei Lincei*, 6th Ser. 1892–1924; 7th Ser. 1925– |
| *Ti. Gracch.* | *Tiberius Gracchus* | | |
| *Tim.* | *Timoleon* | | |
| [Plut.], *Cons. ad Apoll.* | [Plutarch], *Consolatio ad Apollonium* | *Rend. Pont.* | *Rendiconti della pontificia accademia romana di archeologia*, 1921– |
| *Vit. Hom.* | *Vita Homeri* | *Rer. nat. scr. Graec. min.* | O. Keller, *Rerum naturalium scriptores Graeci minores*, 1877 |
| *X orat.* | *Vitae decem oratorum* | | |
| *Poet. Rom. Vet.* | see Diehl | *Rev. Arch.* | *Revue archéologique*, 1844– |
| Poll. | Pollux | *Rev. Bibl.* | *Revue biblique*, 1892– |

| | | | |
|---|---|---|---|
| *Rev. Ét. Anc.* | *Revue des études anciennes*, 1899– | SPCK | Society for Promoting Christian Knowledge |
| *Rev. Ét. Grec.* | *Revue des études grecques*, 1888– | *SVF* | H. von Arnim, *Stoicorum Veterum Fragmenta*, 1903– |
| *Rev. Ét. Lat.* | *Revue des études latines*, 1923– | Sall. | Sallust |
| *Rev. Hist.* | *Revue historique*, 1876– | *Cat.* | *Bellum Catilinae* or *De Catilinae coniuratione* |
| *Rev. Hist. Rel.* | *Revue de l'histoire des religions*, 1880– | *H.* | *Historiae* |
| *Rev. Phil.* | *Revue de philologie*, Nouv. Sér. 1877– | *Iug.* | *Bellum Iugurthinum* |
| *Rh. Mus.* | *Rheinisches Museum für Philologie*, 1827–, Neue Folge, 1842– | Satyr. | Satyrus Historicus |
| | | *Vit. Eur.* | *Vita Euripidis* |
| *Rhet.* | see Spengel | *Sav. Zeitschr.* | *Zeitschrift der Savigny-Stiftung für Rechtsgeschichte, romanistische Abteilung*, 1862– |
| *Rhet. Her.* | *Rhetorica ad Herennium* | | |
| *Rhet. Lat. Min.* | see Halm | | |
| Ribbeck, *CRF* | O. Ribbeck, *Comicorum Romanorum Fragmenta* | Schanz–Hosius | M. Schanz, *Geschichte d. römischen Literatur*, revised I⁴ 1927 and II⁴ 1935 by C. Hosius; III³ 1922, Hosius and Krüger; IV. i² 1914 and IV. ii. 1920, Schanz, Hosius, and Krüger |
| *TRF* | O. Ribbeck, *Tragicorum Romanorum Fragmenta* [both in *Scaenicae Romanorum Poesis Fragmenta³*, 1897–8]², 1962 | | |
| Riccobono, *FIRA* | S. Riccobono, *Fontes Iuris Romani AnteIustiniani*, 1941 | | |
| | | Schmid–Stählin | W. Schmid and O. Stählin, *Geschichte d. griechischen Literatur* I. i 1929, ii 1934. iii (1940), iv (1946), v (1948), See also Christ–Schmid–Stählin |
| *Riv. d. Arch. Crist.* | *Rivista di archeologia cristiana*, 1924– | | |
| *Riv. Fil.* | *Rivista di filologia*, 1873– | | |
| *Riv. ital. per le sc. giur.* | *Rivista italiana per le scienze giuridiche*, 1886– | | |
| Robin | L. Robin, *La Pensée grecque et l'origine de l'esprit scientifique²* 1932; Engl. Transl. *Greek Thought* | schol. | scholiast or scholia |
| | | *Schol. Bern.* | *Scholia Bernensia ad Vergilii bucolica et georgica*, ed. Hagen, 1867 |
| Rohde, *Griech. Roman* | E. Rohde, *Der griechische Roman u. s. Vorläufer³*, 1914 | *Schol. Bob.* | *Scholia Bobiensia* |
| | | *Schol. Cruq.* | *Scholia Cruquiana* |
| *Röm.* | Römisch | *Schol. Dan. Aen.* | *Scholia Danielis* (Pierre Daniel, first publisher in 1600 of Supplements to Servius' Commentary on Virgil) |
| *Röm. Forsch.* | see Mommsen | | |
| *Röm. Gesch.* | see Beloch | | |
| *Röm. Mitt.* | see *MDAI* | | |
| Roscher, *Lex.* | W. H. Roscher, *Ausführliches Lexikon d. griechischen u. römischen Mythologie*, 1884– | *Schol. Flor. Callim.* | *Scholia Florentina in Callimachum* |
| | | Schroeder, *Nov. Com. Fragm.* | O. Schroeder, *Novae Comoediae fragmenta in papyris reperta exceptis Menandreis*, 1915 |
| Rose, *Handb. Gk. Myth.* | H. J. Rose, *Handbook of Greek Mythology⁶*, 1958 | | |
| Rostovtzeff | M. Rostovtzeff | *Scol. Anon.* | *Scolia Anonyma* in Diehl's *Anth. Lyr. Graec.* II, pp. 181–92 |
| *Roman Empire²* | *The Social and Economic History of the Roman Empire²*, 1957 | *Scol. Att.* | *Scolia Attica* in Diehl's *Anth. Lyr. Graec.* II, pp. 181–9 |
| *Hellenistic World* | *The Social and Economic History of the Hellenistic World*, 3 vols., 1941 | Scullard, *Rom. Pol.* | H. H. Scullard, *Roman Politics 220–150 B.C.*, 1951 |
| | | *Etr. Cities* | *The Etruscan Cities and Rome* (1967) |
| Ruggiero, *Diz. Epigr.* | E. de Ruggiero, *Dizionario epigrafico di antichità romana*, 1886– | Scymn. | Scymnus |
| | | sel. | selected |
| Rumpf, *Malerei u. Zeichn.* | A. Rumpf, *Malerei und Zeichnung*, 1953 | Semon. | Semonides |
| | | Sen. | Seneca (The Elder) |
| Rut. Namat. | Rutilius Namatianus, *De Reditu* | *Con. Ex.* | *Controversiarum Excerpta* |
| | | *Controv.* | *Controversiae* |
| *SC* | *Senatus consultum* | *Suas.* | *Suasoriae* |
| *SEG* | *Supplementum epigraphicum Graecum*, 1923– | Sen. | Seneca (The Younger) |
| | | *Apocol.* | *Apocolocyntosis* |
| S.H.A. | Scriptores Historiae Augustae | *Ben.* | *De beneficiis* |
| *Alex. Sev.* | *Alexander Severus* | *Clem.* | *De clementia* |
| *Aurel.* | *Aurelian* | *Constant.* | *De constantia sapientis* |
| *Clod.* | *Clodius* | *Dial.* | *Dialogi* |
| *Comm.* | *Commodus* | *Ep.* | *Epistulae* |
| *Did. Iul.* | *Didius Iulianus* | *Epigr.* | *Epigrammata super exilio* |
| *Hadr.* | *Hadrian* | *Helv.* | *Ad Helviam* |
| *Heliogab.* | *Heliogabalus* | *Prov.* | *De Providentia* |
| *M. Ant.* | *Marcus Antoninus* | *QNat.* | *Quaestiones Naturales* |
| *Marc.* | *Marcus* | *Tranq.* | *De tranquillitate animi* |
| *Max.* | *Maximinus* | Serv. | Servius |
| *Sev.* | *Severus* | *Praef.* | *Praefatio* |
| *Tyr. Trig.* | *Tyranni Triginta* | *Serv. Dan.* | see *Schol. Dan. Aen.* |
| *SIG* | see Dittenberg, *SIG* | Sext. Emp. | Sextus Empiricus |
| *SMSR* | *Studi e materiali di storia delle religioni*, 1925– | *Math.* | *adversus Mathematicos* |
| | | *Pyr.* | Πυρρώνειοι ὑποτυπώσεις |

| | |
|---|---|
| id. Apoll. | Sidonius Apollinaris |
| *Carm.* | *Carmina* |
| *Epist.* | *Epistulae* |
| Sil. | Silius Italicus |
| *Pun.* | *Punica* |
| Simon. | Simonides |
| Simpl. | Simplicius |
| *in Cael.* | *in Aristotelis de Caelo Commentarii* |
| *in Phys.* | *in Aristotelis de Physica Commentarii* |
| Sitz. followed by name | *Sitzungsberichte* |
| of Academy or Society | |
| Sitz. Wien | *Sitzungsberichte der Akad. der* |
| | *Wissenschaften in Wien, 1848–* |
| Socrates, *Hist. Eccl.* | Socrates, *Historia Ecclesiastica* |
| Solin. | Solinus |
| Soph. | Sophocles |
| *Aj.* | *Ajax* |
| *Ant.* | *Antigone* |
| *El.* | *Electra* |
| *Fr.* | Fragments, *TGF* or A. C. Pearson, |
| | 1917 |
| *OC* | *Oedipus Coloneus* |
| *OT* | *Oedipus Tyrannus* |
| *Phil.* | *Philoctetes* |
| *Trach.* | *Trachiniae* |
| Sozom. | Sozomen |
| *Hist. Eccl.* | *Historia Ecclesiastica* |
| Spengel, *Rhet.* | L. Spengel, *Rhetores Graeci*, 1853–6, |
| | vol. I pars ii. iterum ed. |
| | C. Hammer, 1894 |
| *Stadiasmus* | *Stadiasmus Maris Magni* (in *GGM* |
| *=Periplus* | I. 427) |
| Stat. | Statius |
| *Achil.* | *Achilleis* |
| *Silv.* | *Silvae* |
| *Theb.* | *Thebais* |
| Steph. Byz. | Stephanus Byzantius or Byzantinus |
| Stith Thompson | Stith Thompson, *Motif-Index of* |
| | *Folk-Literature*, 6 vols. in Indiana |
| | University Studies, 96–7, 100–1, |
| | 105–6, 108, 110–12; also published |
| | as FF Communication 106–9, |
| | 116–17, 1932–6 |
| Stob. | Stobaeus |
| *Ecl.* | Ἐκλογαί |
| *Flor.* | Ἀνθολόγιον |
| Strab. | Strabo |
| Strack, *Reichsprägung* | P. L. Strack, *Untersuchungen zur* |
| | *römischen Reichsprägung des* |
| | *zweiten Jahrhunderts*, 1931 |
| *Stud. Doc. Hist. Iur.* | *Studia et Documenta Historiae et* |
| | *Iuris*, Rome, 1935– |
| *Stud. Etr.* | *Studi Etruschi*, Firenze, 1927– |
| *Stud. Gesch. Kult.* | *Studien zur Geschichte und Kultur* |
| *Alt.* | *des Altertums*, 1907– |
| *Stud. Ital.* | *Studi italiani di filologia classica*, |
| | 1893– |
| *Studi stor.* | *Studi storici per l'antichità classica*, |
| | 1908–15 |
| *Suda* | Greek Lexicon formerly known as |
| | Suidas |
| Suet. | Suetonius |
| *Aug.* | *Divus Augustus* |
| *Calig.* | *Gaius Caligula* |
| *Claud.* | *Divus Claudius* |
| *Dom.* | *Domitianus* |
| *Gram.* | *De Grammaticis* |
| *Iul.* | *Divus Iulius* |
| *Ner.* | *Nero* |
| *Poet.* | *De Poetis* |
| *Rel.* Reiff. | *Reliquiae*, ed. Reifferscheid |
| *Rhet.* | *De Rhetoribus* |

| | |
|---|---|
| *Tib.* | *Tiberius* |
| *Tit.* | *Divus Titus* |
| *Vit.* | *Vitellius* |
| *Vita Luc.* | *Vita Lucani* |
| *Supp. Aesch.* | H. J. Mette, *Supplementum Aeschy-* |
| | *leum*, 1939 |
| *Supp. Com.* | see Demiańczuk |
| *Supp. Epigr.* | see *SEG* |
| Susemihl, *Gesch. gr.* | F. Susemihl, *Geschichte d. griechi-* |
| *Lit. Alex.* | *schen Literatur in d. Alexandriner-* |
| | *Zeit*, 1891–2 |
| Sydenham, *CRR* | E. A. Sydenham, *The Coinage of* |
| | *the Roman Republic*, 1952 |
| *Syll. Graec.* | see *Corp. poes. ep. Graec. lud.* |
| *Symb.* | *Symbolum* |
| *Symb. Osl.* | *Symbolae Osloenses*, Oslo, 1922– |
| *Symb. Philol. Daniels-* | *Symbolae Philologicae O. A.* |
| *son* | *Danielsson octogenario dicatae*, |
| | Uppsala, 1932 |
| Syme, *Rom. Rev.* | R. Syme, *The Roman Revolution*, |
| | 1939 |
| *Tacitus* | *Tacitus*, 2 vols., 1958 |
| Symmachus, *Relat.* | Symmachus, *Relationes* |
| *TAM* | E. Kalinka and R. Herberdey, *Tituli* |
| | *Asiae Minoris*, Vienna, 1901– |
| *TAPA* | *Transactions of the American Philo-* |
| | *logical Association*, 1870– |
| *TGF* | A. Nauck, *Tragicorum Graecorum* |
| | *Fragmenta²*, 1889 |
| *TRF* | see Ribbeck |
| *Tab. Agn.* | *Tabula Agnoniensis* |
| Tac. | Tacitus |
| *Agr.* | *Agricola* |
| *Ann.* | *Annales* |
| *Dial.* | *Dialogus de Oratoribus* |
| *Germ.* | *Germania* |
| *Hist.* | *Historiae* |
| Tarn, *Alexander* | W. W. Tarn, *Alexander the Great*, |
| | 1948 |
| Tatianus, *Ad Gr.* | Tatianus, *Oratio ad Graecos* |
| Taylor, *Voting* | L. R. Taylor, *The Voting Districts* |
| *Districts* | *of the Roman Republic*, 1960 |
| Ter. | Terence |
| *Ad.* | *Adelphoe* |
| *An.* | *Andria* |
| *Eun.* | *Eunuchus* |
| *Haut.* | *H(e)autontimorumenos* |
| *Phorm.* | *Phormio* |
| Tert. | Tertullian |
| *Ad Nat.* | *Ad Nationes* |
| *Adv. Valent.* | *Adversus Valentinianos* |
| *Apol.* | *Apologeticus* |
| *De Anim.* | *De Testimonio Animae* |
| *De Bapt.* | *De Baptismo* |
| *De Monog.* | *De Monogamia* |
| *De praescr. haeret.* | *De praescriptione haereticorum* |
| *De Spect.* | *De Spectaculis* |
| Teubner | Bibliotheca Scriptorum Graecorum |
| | et Romanorum Teubneriana, |
| | 1849– |
| Theoc. | Theocritus |
| *Epigr.* | *Epigrammata* |
| *Id.* | *Idylls* |
| Theog. | Theognis |
| Theoph. *ad Autol.* | Theophilus, *ad Autolycum* |
| Theophr. | Theophrastus |
| *Caus. Pl.* | *De Causis Plantarum* |
| *Char.* | *Characteres* |
| *Hist. Pl.* | *Historia Plantarum* |
| Theopomp. | Theopompus Historicus |

Thomson, *Hist. Anc. Geog.*   J O. Thomson, *A History of Ancient Geography*, 1948

Thuc.   Thucydides

Tib.   Tibullus

Timoth.   Timotheus

  *Pers.*   *Persae*

Tod.   M. N. Tod, *Greek Historical Inscriptions*, i², 1946, ii, 1948

*Trag. Adesp.*   *Tragica Adespota* in Nauck's *Tragicorum Graecorum Fragmenta*, pp. 837–958

trib.   *tribunus*

trib. pot.   *tribunicia potestas*

Tzetz.   Tzetzes

  *Chil.*   *Historiarum variarum Chiliades*

Ueberweg–Praechter, *Grundriss*   F. Ueberweg, *Grundriss d. Geschichte d. Philosophie*, Pt. i, *Das Altertum*; 12th ed. by K. Praechter, 1926

*VCH*   *Victoria County History*

Val. Max.   Valerius Maximus

Varro, *Ling.*   Varro, *De Lingua Latina*

  *Rust.*   *De Re Rustica*

  *Sat. Men.*   *Saturae Menippeae*

Vatin.   Vatinius

Vell. Pat.   Velleius Paterculus

Verg.   Virgil

  *Aen.*   *Aeneid*

  *Catal.*   *Catalepton*

  *Ecl.*   *Eclogues*

  *G.*   *Georgics*

*Vit. Aesch.*   *Vita Aeschyli* (O.C.T. of Aeschylus)

*Vit. Eurip.*   *Vita Euripidis* (O.C.T. of Euripides)

Vitr.   Vitruvius

  *De Arch.*   *De Architectura*

Vopiscus, *Cyn.*   Vopiscus, *Cynegetica*

*Vorsokr.*   see Diels

Walbank, *Polybius*   F. W. Walbank, *A Historical Commentary on Polybius*, 1957–

Walz   C. Walz, *Rhetores Graeci*, 9 vols., 1832–6

Warde Fowler, *Rel. Exper.*   W. Warde Fowler, *The Religious Experience of the Roman People*, 1911

Warmington, *Indian Commerce*   E. H. Warmington, *The Commerce between the Roman Empire and India*, 1928

Webster, *Later Greek Comedy*   T. B. L. Webster, *Studies in Later Greek Comedy*, 1953

Wegner, *Herrscherbild.* (1939)   M. Wegner, *Die Herrscherbildnisse in antoninischer Zeit*, 1939

  *Herrscherbild* (1956)   *Das römische Herrscherbild*, 1956

*Westd. Zeit.*   *Westdeutsche Zeitschrift für Geschichte und Kunst*, 1882–1909

*Wien. Stud.*   *Wiener Studien*, 1879–

Wilamowitz   U. von Wilamowitz-Moellendorff

  *Hell. Dicht.*   *Hellenistische Dichtung in der Zeit des Kallimachos*, 1924

Wilhelm, *Urkunden*   A. Wilhelm, *Urkunden dramatischer Aufführungen in Athen*, 1905

Winter, *KB*   F. Winter, *Kunstgeschichte in Bildern*, 1935 ff.

Wissowa, *RK*   G. Wissowa, *Religion und Kultus d. Römer*², 1912

  *Ges. Abh.*   *Gesammelte Abhandlungen zur römischen Religions- und Stadtgeschichte*

Xen.   Xenophon

  *Ages.*   *Agesilaus*

  *An.*   *Anabasis*

  *Ap.*   *Apologia Socratis*

  *Cyn.*   *Cynegeticus*

  *Cyr.*   *Cyropaedia*

  *Hell.*   *Hellenica*

  *Mem.*   *Memorabilia*

  *Oec.*   *Oeconomicus*

  *Symp.*   *Symposium*

  *Vect.*   *De Vectigalibus*

*YClS*   *Yale Classical Studies*, 1920–

*Z. für die öst. Gym.*   *Zeitschrift für die österreichischen Gymnasien*, 1850–

Zeller, *Phil. d. Gr. Gesch. d. gr. Phil.*   E. Zeller, *Die Philosophie d. Griechen Grundriss d. Geschichte d. Griechischen Philosophie*¹³, 1928

  *Plato*, etc.   *Plato and the Older Academy*, Engl. Transl. 1888

Zonar.   Zonaras

**ABACUS,** a counting-board, the usual aid to reckoning in antiquity. The Egyptians, Greeks, and Romans alike used a board with vertical columns, on which (working from right to left) units, tens, hundreds, or (where money was in question) e.g. $\frac{1}{8}$ obols, $\frac{1}{4}$ obols, $\frac{1}{2}$ obols, obols, *drachmae*, sums of 10, 100, 1,000 *drachmae*, and talents were inscribed. When an addition sum was done, the totals of the columns were carried to the left, as in our ordinary addition. The numbers might be marked in writing or by pebbles, counters, or pegs.     W. D. R.

**ABARIS,** a legendary servant of Apollo, similar to Aristeas (q.v. 1), and believed to be a Hyperborean (q.v.). He lived without food, and travelled everywhere bearing the golden arrow, the symbol of the god (Hdt. 4. 36). Pindar assigned him to the time of Croesus (fr. 283 Bowra). Later authorities tell of his presence in Athens (*Suda*, s.v.) and of his helping the Spartans by directing the performance of sacrifices which prevented all plagues thereafter (Apollonius, *Mir.* 4).     W. K. C. G.

**ABDERA,** a flourishing Greek city lying on the coast of Thrace (q.v.), to the east of the mouth of the Nestus (Diod. 13. 72. 2; Strab. 7. fr. 46; Hdt. 7. 126). Originally a Clazomenian colony, founded in the seventh century B.C., it was reoccupied by colonists from Teos (among them Anacreon, q.v.) in the second half of the sixth century (Hdt. 1. 168; Pind. *Paean* 2); its site was near Bulustra, a corruption of the name it bore in the Middle Ages, Polystylon. Like Aenus (q.v.), Abdera owed its wealth (it was the third richest city in the Delian League, with a contribution of fifteen talents) to its corn production (see the coins), and to the fact that it was a port for the trade of Upper Thrace, and also a centre for commerce with the Odrysian rulers (*see* THRACE). Abdera was one of the resting-places chosen by Xerxes (q.v.) in his journey along the northern shores of the Aegean in 480 B.C. (Hdt. 7. 120). In 431 B.C. Abdera, under Nymphodorus, an Athenian *proxenos* (Thuc. 2. 29. 1), was the protagonist in the attempt to unite Thrace and Macedon with Athens. Nymphodorus arranged an alliance between Athens and his brother-in-law, the Odrysian ruler, Sitalces (q.v.). Abdera was incorporated in the kingdom of Macedonia by Philip II (q.v.), and after the death of Alexander the Great (q.v.) it was in the hands of the successive masters of Macedonia. Abdera was a 'free city' under the Romans (Pliny, *HN* 4. 42). The coin types of Abdera reached perfection in the third quarter of the fifth century B.C. Though 'Abderites' was a by-word for stupidity (Cic. *Att.* 4. 17. 3; 7. 7. 4), Abdera boasted among its citizens Democritus (q.v.) and Protagoras (q.v.).

S. Casson, *Macedonia, Thrace and Illyria* (1926); W. Regel, *Ath. Mitt.* 1887, 161 ff.; Avezou–Picard, *BCH* 1913, 117 ff.; M. Feyel, *BCH* 1942–3, 176 ff. (bibliography); D. I. Lazarides, *Prakt. Arch. Et.* 1952 (1955), 260 ff.; 1954 (1957), 160 ff.; 1955 (1960), 160 ff.; 1956 (1961), 139 ff.; Head, *Hist. Num.*², 253 ff., 891; M. L. Strack and H. von Fritze, *Die Ant. Münzen Nordgriechenlands* (1912), ii. *Thrakien*, 1. 1; J. M. F. May, *The Coinage of Abdera* (1966).     J. M. R. C.

**ABYDOS,** Milesian colony on the Asiatic side of the Hellespont, at its narrowest point, opposite Sestos (*see*

HERO AND LEANDER). Xerxes crossed here to Europe early in 480 B.C. From 477 to 412 Abydos was a member of the Athenian Empire. In 411 B.C. the Spartan fleet was defeated by the Athenians near Abydos. In 200 the town, until then a free city, fought heroically against Philip V of Macedon, but was forced to surrender. Three years later Antiochus III made Abydos one of his chief bases of support. Later it probably belonged to Pergamum, but as an autonomous State.

Magie, *Rom. Rule Asia Min.*, 752 ff, 1012 ff,     V. E.

**ACADEMY,** (1) a park and gymnasium in the outskirts of Athens sacred to the hero Academus (or Hecademus), now under excavation; (2) the school or college established there by Plato, possibly as early as 385 B.C. This was organized as a corporate body with a continuous life of its own and survived down to its final dissolution by Justinian in A.D. 529.

There can be little doubt that Plato's chief object in the foundation was to train men for the service of the State, and there is evidence that a number of his pupils played a considerable part in the political life of their cities. But his method of training consisted of a thorough education in science and philosophy, and the school is better known for its contributions to these subjects. Under Plato and his immediate successors a great deal of important work was done in mathematics and astronomy. But later more purely philosophical interests became paramount. In the third and second centuries B.C., under Arcesilaus and Carneades, the Academy became known as the chief sceptical school, though there is some doubt as to the exact length to which their scepticism went. In the following century this tendency was abandoned. After that we know practically nothing of the institution for several centuries, though occasional indications justify us in believing in its continued existence. It does not emerge into the light again until the fifth century A.D., when it appears as a centre of Neoplatonism, particularly under the leadership of Proclus (q.v.). It was also active in the production of commentaries on Plato and Aristotle, some of which still survive and preserve information of great value.

Histories of Ancient Philosophy: Zeller; Gomperz; Robin. J. Burnet, *From Thales to Plato* (1914), ch. 12; G. C. Field, *Plato and His Contemporaries* (1930), ch. 3; W. Jaeger, *Aristotle*, ch. 1 (Engl. Transl. 1934); H. Cherniss, *The Riddle of the Early Academy* (1942); R. E. Witt, *Albinus and the History of Middle Platonism* (1937); T. Whittaker, *The Neo-Platonists* (1918), ch. 9.     G. C. F.

**ACAMAS,** in mythology, son of Theseus, brother of Demophon (qq.v.); eponym of the tribe Acamantis. When Diomedes went to Troy to ask for the return of Helen, Acamas accompanied him; Laodice, daughter of Priam, fell in love with him and had by him a son, Munitus (Parth., *Amat. Narr.* 16). After the Trojan War, according to one account, it was he, not Demophon, who came to Thrace and met and deserted Phyllis. While in Cyprus he opened a mysterious box she had given him, and, frightened by what he saw in it, galloped wildly away, fell, and was killed by his own sword (schol. Lycophron 495).

Acamas and Demophon appear in art chiefly in late

archaic and early classical representations of the Sack of Troy, rescuing their grandmother Aethra. Both were shown in Polygnotus' Troy at Delphi (Brommer, *Vasenlisten*², 164, 198). H. J. R.; C. M. R.

**ACARNAN,** eponym of Acarnania; in mythology, son, with Amphoterus, of Alcmaeon (q.v. 1) and Callirhoë. When Alcmaeon was murdered, Callirhoë prayed Zeus, who was her lover, to make her sons grow up immediately; he granted her prayer, and they avenged his death on Phegeus and his sons (Apollod. 3. 91–93). H. J. R.

**ACARNANIA,** a district of north-west Greece, bounded by the Ionian Sea, the Gulf of Ambracia, and the river Acheloüs. It contained a fertile plain along the lower Acheloüs, but was ringed off on other sides by mountains. Neolithic pottery has been found in a cave on the Krithote peninsula, and there are traces of Early and Middle Helladic occupation. Mycenaean remains are scanty: house foundations near Astacus, and a tholos tomb reported from Chrysovitsa. A part of the shadowy 'mainland' in the *Odyssey*, its inhabitants long remained semi-barbarous. In Thucydides' day they still went about carrying arms (1. 5). In the seventh century the best sites on the seaboard were occupied by settlers from Corinth. The Acarnanians formed a confederacy in the fifth century, if not earlier, fortified their cities, and invoked Athenian help against the Corinthian colonists (Thuc. 2. 68), and later against the Ambraciotes and the Peloponnesians in 429–426 B.C.; but they were subdued by Agesilaus in 390 and remained under Spartan rule until 375, when they joined Athens' Second League. They supported Boeotia in its triumph over Sparta but reverted to Athens in resisting Philip of Macedon. Subsequently they became dependants of Macedonia. In 314, at the instance of Cassander, they replaced their early cantonal league by a federation of newly founded cities (their largest town being Stratus). Frequent frontier disputes with the Aetolians led to the partition of Acarnania between Aetolia and Epirus *c.* 255; but after the fall of the Epirote monarchy *c.* 230 the Acarnanians recovered their independence and acquired from Epirus the island of Leucas. Though they sided with Philip V of Macedon against the Romans (200), they were allowed by the latter to retain their confederacy until 30 B.C.

BSA 1931–2, 1947; P.–K. *GL* 2. 2. 368 ff.; J. A. O. Larsen, *Greek Federal States* (1968), 89 ff. M. C.; N. G. L. H.

**ACASTUS,** in mythology, son of Pelias (*see* NELEUS); he took part in the Argonautic expedition and the Calydonian boar-hunt. When Peleus (q.v.) took refuge with him, Acastus' wife (variously named) loved him, and being repulsed, accused him to her husband of improper advances. Acastus, therefore, contrived to steal Peleus' wonderful sword and leave him alone on Mt. Pelion, where he was rescued by Chiron (*see* CENTAURS). Afterwards Peleus took Iolcus, putting to death Acastus' wife and, by some accounts, Acastus himself (Apollod. 3. 164–7, 173; schol. Ap. Rhod. 1. 224; cf. Paus. 3. 18. 16). H. J. R.

**ACCA LĀRENTIA** (less correctly **Larentina**), an obscure Roman goddess, whose festival (Larentalia or Larentinalia) was on 23 Dec. A story current in Sulla's time (Valerius Antias ap. Gell. 7. 7. 5–7) makes her a prostitute, contemporary with Romulus (or Ancus Martius, Macrob. *Sat.* 1. 10. 12), who became rich by the favour of Hercules and left her property to the Roman people; another, perhaps invented by Licinius Macer, says she was wife of Faustulus (q.v.), mother of the original Fratres Arvales (q.v.) and adopted mother of

Romulus (Macrob. ibid. 17). The name looks as if there should be some connexion with Larunda (q.v.). That she had another festival in April (Plut. *Quaest. Rom.* 35) is probably a mis-statement, but see E. Tabeling, *Mater Larum* (1932), 57 and Latte, *RR* 92.

Mommsen, *Röm. Forsch.* ii. 1 ff. H. J. R.

**ACCIUS,** LUCIUS, born in 170 B.C. at Pisaurum in Umbria where his family had an estate. He was a friend of Pacuvius (q.v.) and at the same games both produced plays, Accius aged 30 and Pacuvius 80. He lived at least to 90 B.C. (Cicero knew him—*Brut.* 107). He did not belong to the circle of Scipio: his friend and patron was Brutus (q.v. 2) Callaicus (*cos.* 138 B.C.), and Accius composed a dedication in Saturnians for the temple built to celebrate his Spanish victories. He made an educational tour to Athens and the Greek cities of Asia Minor.

WORKS: (1) *Didascalica*: a work in nine books which dealt with the history of literature, particularly drama, from Homer and Hesiod to Accius himself. Twenty-two lines remain, some of which are sotadic, some trochaic and iambic, some seem to be prose; it may be that the work was in mixed verse and prose (like Varro's Menippean satires)—though allowance must be made for the inaccuracy of ancient quotation and for the possibility that some of the verses were quoted by Accius from other authors. The work may have been in dialogue-form, with a Greek expounding Greek literary history; if so, it belonged to the popularizing Peripatetic genre to which Cicero's *Brutus* belongs. His chronology of Roman drama was in error by forty-three years since he assumed that Livius Salinator (*cos.* 219, 207 B.C.) had been the owner of Livius Andronicus. The mistake was corrected by Varro. (2) *Pragmatica*: another work on drama, in trochaic metre. (3) *Parerga*: of unknown content, also poetical. (4) *Annales*: books of hexameter poetry not on history, but on months and festivals (like Ovid's *Fasti*). (5) *Sotadica*: apparently a collection of mixed erotic verse (Pliny, *Ep.* 5. 3. 6, Gellius 6. 9. 16.). Accius interested himself in the question of spelling-reform, and engaged in heated controversy with Lucilius (q.v. 1)—cf. Varro *de ling. Lat.* 10. 70. (6) *Tragedies*: it was as a tragedian that Accius' fame grew throughout antiquity, acclaimed the greatest Roman tragedian in the first century A.D. (cf. Vell. Pat. 1. 17; Columella *praef.* 30). Fragments of some forty-six named plays are extant. Most of the recognizable plays were translated from Euripides, some from Sophocles, a few from Aeschylus; a number of his plays seem to have had post-Euripidean originals. Sufficient fragments of *Bacchae* and *Phoenissae* are extant to allow some comparative judgement: Accius clearly was at least as free with his originals as Ennius (q.v.). In the case of the *Armorum Iudicium* it has been suspected that Accius used a play of Aeschylus but added to it from the *Ajax* of Sophocles. He continued the writing of *fabulae praetextae* (q.v.) with a *Brutus* (on the founding of the Republic) and *Aeneadae vel Decius* (on the self-immolation of the young Decius Mus at Sentinum in 295 B.C.). Accius created for the expression of tragic sentiment a style that was vigorous, elevated, solemn, and sonorous, which excited the interest and admiration of later rhetoricians—characteristic features are frequent alliteration, paronomasia, word-play, antithesis, careful parallelism of cola, and neologisms (but Grecisms are very few indeed). He was much quoted by Cicero (with whom his *Atreus* was a favourite) and imitated by Virgil (Macrob. *Sat.* 6). Even in the fragments there is a strong impression of a turbulent, almost wayward, personality, a man of influence in his own time and of great importance for the development of Latin literature: he was a scholar who devoted himself to collecting and criticizing the work of his predecessors and considering questions of authenticity (like a

Hellenistic Greek scholar) and he was the last real tragedian in Rome, an original poet in his own right who
stamped his Greek material with a powerful style of his
own.

FRAGMENTS. E. H. Warmington, *Remains of Old Latin* ii (Loeb,
1936), 326 ff. (with trans.). Dramatic fragments only: Ribbeck, *TRF*[1];
Klotz, *Scaen. Rom. Frag.* i, 190 ff. Non-dramatic: Morel, *FPL*, 34 ff.
*Didascalica*: Funaioli, *Gramm. Rom. Frag.*, 25 ff. GENERAL: F. Leo,
*Gesch. d. röm. Lit.* (1913), 384 ff. For an attempt to discern contem-
porary politics: B. Biliński, *Accio ed i Gracchi* (Accad. Polac. di
Science e Lett. fasc. 3; Rome, 1958). G. W. W.

**ACCLAMATIO** at Rome was public applause or disapproval (often combined with action), especially on
important occasions such as triumphs or games. In the
Republic *principes viri* could gauge public opinion in this
way; though the shouts might be contrived (as by Clodius
(q.v. 1) against Pompey: Cic. *Q. Fr.* 2. 3). Under the
Empire claques spread even at recitations and declamations. The imperial family was greeted in public by
words soon ritually fixed. In the Senate, as discussion
disappeared, *acclamatio* provided the only expression of
opinion. By the second century A.D. it became a recognized procedure, recorded in the minutes. It thus came
under official control, losing its dangerous spontaneity.
The mob, protected by numbers and anonymity, always
retained a certain freedom of protest. The vestigial
popular assemblies, municipal councils, and ultimately
the Church, also used *acclamatio* as a procedure.

Dar.–Sag. 1. 18; Mommsen, *Röm. Staatsr.* iii. 349, 951. E. B.

**ACESTES** (Αἰγέστης, Αἰγεστος), in mythology, son of
a Trojan woman of noble rank, exiled for some reason by
Laomedon (various accounts in Dion. Hal. *Ant. Rom.*
1. 52. 1 ff.; Serv. on *Aen.* 1. 550; schol. Lycophron
953 ff.), and a non-Trojan father, usually said to be the
Sicilian river-god Cri(m)nisus. He founded Egesta
(Segesta) in Sicily, and hospitably received Aeneas (*Aen.*
1. 550 and 5. 36 ff.). H. J. R.

**ACHAEA** (Ἀχαία) is a name derived from Ἀχαιοί, which
in Homer refers particularly to Achilles' men and
Agamemnon's followers. Ἀχαιοί may also appear in the
forms Aḫḫijava and Ekwesh in Hittite and Egyptian texts
cf 1400–1200 B.C. Considerable Mycenaean remains have
been found, e.g. in the regions of Aegium, Dyme, Pharae,
and Patrae (see E. T. Vermeule, 'The Mycenaeans in
Achaea', *AJArch.* 1960, 1 ff.) It is held that Achaea was
not spared by the upheavals of the beginning of the Iron
Age, and there may be good justification for the part
played by Achaea in 'migration' saga. In historical times
the name was restricted to south-east Thessaly (Ἀχαία
Φθιῶτις) and the north coast of the Peloponnese between
Elis and Sicyon. Here a narrow territory, with good soil in
the plains and on hill terraces, extends between the almost
harbourless Corinthian Gulf and a steep range of mountains with some passes of importance into Arcadia.
Twelve small towns, forming a federal State, divided
this territory; they met at the sanctuary of Poseidon
Heliconius until Helice fell into the sea (after an earthquake in 373 B.C.), later generally at Aegium. For the
topography, history, and remains of Achaea, see J. K.
Anderson, 'A Topographical and Historical Survey of
Achaea', *BSA*, 1954, 72 ff. Some remains of the classical
period have been found at Aegium and Leontium (destroyed by Philip V?). Patrae (modern *Patras*) has considerable remains of the Roman Odeum.

The Achaeans sent colonists to Sybaris, Croton,
Metapontum, Caulonia in south Italy; otherwise they
had an unimportant early history, remaining neutral in
the Persian Wars and most of the wars between Greeks.
In the third and second centuries the Achaean Confederacy (q.v.) became the chief power in Greece, eventually
including nearly all the Peloponnesus and part of central
Greece. T. J. D.; R. J. H.

From 146 B.C. this area was attached to the Roman
province of Macedonia, but in 27 B.C. it became the centre
of the senatorial province of Achaea, which included
Aetolia, Acarnania, part of Epirus, Thessaly, and the
Cyclades, with the governor (a proconsul of praetorian
rank) residing at Corinth. Temporarily, from A.D. 15 to
44, Achaea was again joined to Macedonia as an imperial
province governed by the imperial legate of Moesia.
Nero's proclamation of freedom for Greece (67) was
withdrawn by Vespasian (70 or 74). At latest from the
time of Antoninus Pius, Epirus became a separate province and Thessaly was added to Macedonia. Rome
allowed some regional and fluctuating confederacies to
revive, while a Panachaean League, under a Helladarch
and high priest, became responsible for the imperial cult.
A wider Panhellenic League (Panhellenion) was created
by Hadrian, whose favour Greece, and especially Athens,
enjoyed. Cities like Athens, Sparta, Patrae, Corinth, and
Elis flourished, but in some parts much land apparently
fell into the hands of wealthy men whose great estates
overshadowed the poorer cities; yet in more remote
districts moderate and small landowners may have continued to make a moderate living. H. H. S.

P.-K., *GL* iii. 1, *Der Peloponnes*, pt. 1, 164 ff.; S. Accame, *Il
dominio romano in Grecia dalla guerra acaica ad Augusto* (1946);
J. A. O. Larsen in Frank, *Econ. Survey*, 259 ff. (437 ff. for the bound-
aries of the province), *Representative Government in Greek and Roman
History* (1955), and *Greek Federal States* (1968), 80 ff. for the Leagues;
E. Groag, *Die römischen Reichsbeamten von Achaia bis auf Diokletian*
(1938) and *Die röm. Reichs. von Achaia in spätrömischer Zeit* (1946);
U. Kahrstedt, *Das Wirtschaftliche Gesicht Griechenlands in der
Kaiserzeit* (1954).

**ACHAEAN CONFEDERACY.** An early Achaean Confederacy, organized at an unknown date, lasted through
the fourth century. It was notable for the admission of
non-Achaeans (Calydon). As an ally of Sparta it escaped
dissolution after the King's Peace. The later Achaean
Confederacy, apparently regarded as a continuation of
the old, was founded in 280 B.C. by the union of four
cities, to which the remaining Achaean cities soon were
added. It acquired importance through the incorporation
of non-Achaeans, who were admitted on terms of equality,
so that Dorians and Arcadians could become Achaean
statesmen. When Sicyon was admitted after the expulsion
of its tyrant in 251, Aratus (q.v. 2) of Sicyon soon became
the leading Achaean statesman and adopted a definitely
anti-Macedonian policy. The later admission of Megalopolis and other Arcadian cities led to hostility with Sparta
and paved the way for reconciliation with Macedonia.
During the Cleomenic War (see CLEOMENES III) Aratus
himself asked for Macedonian help and permitted the
Achaeans to join the Hellenic League of Antigonus Doson
(224). This alignment lasted till Achaea went over to
Rome in 198. The new alliance led to the incorporation
of almost the entire Peloponnesus, but also led to frequent
clashes with the Roman authorities. After the Achaean
War of 146 the Confederacy was dissolved, but a smaller
Achaean Confederacy soon was organized and continued
under the Empire (see ACHAEA).

At the head of the Confederacy were two generals until
a single general was substituted in 255. Immediate re-
election was forbidden, and prominent leaders commonly
served every second year. Alongside of the general stood a
board of ten *demiourgoi*, who shared in the administration
and presided over the assemblies. The federal deliberative
bodies were a *boule* and an *ekklesia* in which all male
citizens over 30 could take part. For a regular meeting of
either or both bodies the term *synodos* was used; for an
extraordinary meeting, *synkletos*. There were apparently
four regular meetings a year, at first attended by both the
*ekklesia* and the *boule*. Then, shortly before 200 B.C., a

law was passed to the effect that the *ekklesia* could not be summoned except to extraordinary meetings to deal with a question of alliance or war. The subject was announced in advance, and only this one subject could be acted on. The vote was taken by cities, the votes apparently being weighted in proportion to the size of the cities. Other business, even elections, was handled by the *boule*. See *also* FEDERAL STATES.

Polybius; Livy, bks. 31–45; *SEG* xiv. 375 (federal *boule*). G. Niccolini, *La confederazione achea* (1914); F. W. Walbank, *Aratos of Sicyon* (1933); A. Aymard, *Les Assemblées de la confédération achaienne* (1938) and *Les Premiers rapports de Rome et de la confédération achaienne* (1938); J. A. O. Larsen, *Representative Government in Greek and Roman History* (U.S.A., 1955), index and *Greek Federal States* (1968), 80 ff. Early Achaea: *Robinson Studies* ii (U.S.A., 1954), 797 ff. *See also under* FEDERAL STATES. J. A. O. L.

**ACHAEMENIDS,** descendants of Achaemenes (Hakhamanish), the eponymous founder of the Persian royal house. According to Herodotus (7. 11) and the Behistun inscription, he was the father of Teispes, ancestor of Cyrus and Darius. At first kings only of Parsumash, a vassal State of the Median Empire, the Achaemenids extended their sovereignty over Anshan and Parsa; Cyrus II (q.v.) or III challenged and conquered Astyages, and the Median Empire passed to the Persians (550 B.C.). Campaigns in the north and east, the conquest of Lydia and the defeat of Nabonidus of Babylonia, brought the whole of western Asia into one vast empire, to which Cambyses added Egypt. A collateral branch of the family assumed the succession with Darius (q.v.), the greatest of the Achaemenids. His reign marks the climax of Persian rule. Subsequent reverses, e.g. the failure of Xerxes' Greek expedition, and harem intrigues weakened the dynasty, until with the defeat of Darius III Codomannus by Alexander in 330 B.C. the line perished.

Achaemenes; Teispes; [? a Cyrus and a Teispes]; Cyrus I, *c.* 645–602; Cambyses I, *c.* 602–559; Cyrus II, 559–530; Cambyses II, 530–522; Darius I, 522–486; Xerxes I, 486–465; Artaxerxes I Longimanus, 465–424; Xerxes II, 424–423; Darius II Nothus, 423–404; Artaxerxes II Mnemon, 404–359; Artaxerxes III Ochus, 359–338; Arses, 338–336; Darius Codomannus, 336–330.

CLASSICAL SOURCES for Achaemenid Persia. Herodotus; Ctesias, *Persica*; Xenophon, *Cyropaedia, Anabasis*, etc.; Strabo, bks. 11–17. CUNEIFORM. F. H. Weissbach, *Keilinschriften der Achämeniden* (1911); R. Kent, *Old Persian* (U.S.A. 1953). Archaeological: L. van den Berghe, *Archéologie de l'Iran ancien* (Leiden, 1959); Dandamayev, *Iran pri pervykh Akhemenidov* (1963). MODERN WORKS. G. C. Cameron, *History of Early Iran* (U.S.A. 1936); A. Christensen, 'Die Iranier', *Handbuch der Altertumswissenschaft* iii. 1, 3; A. Godard, *L'Art de la Perse ancienne* (1930); E. Meyer, *Geschichte des Altertums* iii (1937); R. N. Frye, *The Heritage of Persia* (1962), ch. 3. M. S. D.; R. N. F.

**ACHAEUS** (1), eponym of the Achaeans; in mythology, son of Poseidon (Dion. Hal. *Ant. Rom.* 1. 17. 3), Zeus (Serv. on *Aen.* 1. 242), Xuthus (Apollod. 1. 50), or Haemon (schol. *Il.* 2. 681).

**ACHAEUS** (2) of Eretria (b. 484–481 B.C.), Athenian tragic poet, to be distinguished from the Achaeus (? of Syracuse) who won a Lenaean victory *c.* 330. He wrote 44 (or 30 or 24) plays, the first produced about 447 B.C., and won one victory. He was probably dead when the *Frogs* was produced in 405 (*Suda*, s.v.). Of nineteen known titles more than half are probably satyric; the philosopher Menedemus thought his satyric plays second only to those of Aeschylus (Diog. Laert. 2. 133). The Alexandrians placed him in the *Canon* (*see* ARISTOPHANES 2) and Didymus wrote a commentary on him. Euripides is said to have adapted one line from him (Ath. 6. 270b) and he is twice quoted by Aristophanes (*Vesp.* 1081, *Ran.* 184). Athenaeus (10. 451c) describes him as lucid in style, but liable to become obscure and enigmatical.

*TGF* 746–59. A. W. P.-C.; D. W. L.

**ACHAEUS** (3) (d. 213 B.C.), general of Antiochus III (q.v.) and his kinsman (whether cousin or maternal uncl is uncertain). In 223–2 he recovered most of Seleuci Asia Minor from Pergamum; but he was encouraged b Antiochus' difficulties in the East to proclaim himsel independent (220). His soldiers refused to follow hir against Antiochus, but he maintained himself in Asi Minor until the king was at liberty to deal with him After a two years' siege in Sardes he was betrayed t Antiochus and barbarously executed.

Polyb. bks. 4–8; H. H. Schmitt, *Untersuchungen zur Geschicht Antiochos' des Grossen und seiner Zeit* (1964), 30 f., 158 ff., 181 ff P. Meloni, *Rend. Linc.* 1949, 535 ff., 1950, 161 ff. G. T. C

**ACHARNAE,** the largest Attic deme (the figure 3,00 hoplites in Thuc. 2. 20. 4 is too high; 1,200 is mor likely), lay around Menidi in the north-west corner o the Attic plain, near the pass from the Thriasian plai along which Archidamus and the Spartans marched i 431 B.C. Although made famous as charcoal-burners b Aristophanes, the Acharnians gained a livelihoo primarily from the growing of corn and the cultivatio of vines and olives. They were also noted for their braver (Pind. *Nem.* 2. 16) and had, appropriately, a sanctuary t Ares.

Thuc. 2. 19–23; Ar. *Ach.* A. Milchhöfer, *Kartenvon Attika* (188 ii. 42 ff.; S. Dow, 'Thucydides and the number of Acharnia Hoplitai', *TAPA* 1961, 66 ff. C. W. J. I

**ACHATES,** in mythology, faithful companion of Aenea (*Aen.* 1. 312 and often); he killed Protesilaus (schol *Il.* 2. 701).

**ACHELOÜS,** the longest of Greek rivers, rising i central Epirus and debouching after a course of 150 mile (mostly through mountain gorges) at the entrance to th Corinthian Gulf. Its lower reaches constituted the frontie between Acarnania and Aetolia. It had no value as a lin of communications.

**ACHERON,** a river of Thesprotia in southern Epirus which breaks through an impenetrable gorge into th Acherusian plain where a lake lay in ancient times. Th entrance to Hades was reputed to be there at the con fluence of the Cocytus and Pyriphlegethon streams whic joined the Acheron river below the lake. The setting o Odysseus' evocation of the dead in the *Odyssey* draws o the scenery of the Acherusian plain, and the Oracle o the Dead by the confluence of the rivers (Hdt. 5. 92. 7 has been excavated.

S. I. Dakaris, *Tò "Εργον* 1958, 95 ff. et seq.; *Prakt. Arch. Et.* 196 (1963), 114 ff. et seq.; *Antike Kunst* 1963, Beiheft i. 51 ff. N. G. L. H

**ACHILLES** (*Ἀχιλλεύς*), in mythology, son of Peleus anc Thetis (qq.v.); usually said to be their only child, but cf Lycophron 178 and schol. there. The etymology of hi name is unknown, though there could be a connexior with the river-name Acheloüs, and a possible form of th name occurs for persons in Linear B. All the evidence goes to show that he was a man, real or imaginary, anc not a 'faded' god, and that his widespread cult (Leuke ir the Black Sea, Olbia, and elsewhere in that region sporadically in Asia Minor; Epirus; doubtfully ir Thessaly; Elis; Croton in Italy) is the result chiefly o solely of the *Iliad* (see Farnell, *Hero-Cults*, 285 ff.). Hi portrait was drawn once for all by Homer, and late writers merely added details from their own imagination or possibly from obscure local legends of which we know nothing.

In the *Iliad* he appears as a magnificent barbarian somewhat outside the circle of Achaean civilization though highly respected for his prowess. He, alone among

Homeric figures, keeps up the old practice of making elaborate and costly offerings, including human victims, at a funeral (*Il.* 23. 171 ff., condemned as 'evil deeds', 176); contrast the sceptical attitude of Andromache (22. 512–14). His treatment of the body of Hector is of a piece with this (22. 395, again stigmatized as 'unseemly deeds', and 24. 15 ff.). So also is his furious and ungovernable anger, on which the whole plot of the *Iliad* turns; in 24. 560 ff. he is himself conscious of this weakness and afraid that it may overcome his chivalrous pity for Priam. When not roused by anger or grief, he is often merciful (21. 100 ff.), but in his fury he spares no one and has no respect even for a visible god (22. 15–20). Apart from his valour in battle, he is a pathetic figure, being conscious of the fated shortness of his life (9. 410 ff., cf. 19. 408 ff.). He is capable of the most generous sentiments, witness his devoted friendship for Patroclus throughout the poem and his strong detestation of lying (9. 312), an unusual thing in a Homeric Greek.

He comes to Troy, apparently, of his own free will, not as in any sense a subject of Agamemnon, at the head of a contingent of fifty ships (*Il.* 2. 685), and there distinguishes himself in a series of engagements during which he takes twelve towns along the coast and eleven inland (9. 328–9), including Lyrnessos, where he captures Briseïs (2. 690). Agamemnon, on being compelled to return his own captive, Chryseïs, to her father (1. 134 ff.), takes Briseïs from Achilles by way of compensating himself (ibid. 320 ff.). At this insult, Achilles refuses further service and begs his mother Thetis to move Zeus on his behalf (352 ff.). She succeeds in inducing the god to punish Agamemnon and his army; a false dream encourages the king to go out against the Trojans, who, hearing that Achilles is no longer fighting, profit by their strategic superiority (their reinforcements are close at hand, Agamemnon can get none from nearer than Greece) to offer battle, instead of merely standing on the defensive (9. 352 ff.). The result is a series of engagements in which Agamemnon loses far more men than he can afford (*Il.* 2–8). Now Agamemnon offers a full and handsome honour-price to Achilles, who puts himself in the wrong by refusing it (9 *passim*), but is later induced to let Patroclus go at the head of his followers, the Myrmidones (16. 1 ff.), to keep the Trojans from actually burning the Greek camp. Patroclus, however, is killed fighting (16. 786 ff.), and Achilles, on hearing the news, is frenzied with grief (18. 15 ff.), hastily reconciles himself to Agamemnon, goes out the next day, routs the Trojans, and kills Hector (19–22). He is wearing armour specially made for him by Hephaestus (18. 468 ff.), as his own had been worn by Patroclus and fallen into the hands of Hector. He then gives Patroclus a magnificent funeral (23) and, warned by his mother (24. 137), lets old Priam ransom Hector's body.

His death is foretold in the *Iliad* (22. 359–60); he is to be slain by Paris and Apollo. The *Odyssey* (24. 35 ff., a doubtfully authentic passage) describes the fight over his body, his funeral, and the mourning of Thetis and the other sea-nymphs over him. Later authors add the following details, among others.

He had his education from Chiron (see e.g. Pind. *Nem.* 3. 43 ff., developing *Il.* 11. 832). When the contingents were gathering for the Trojan War, Peleus, or Thetis, knowing that he would die at Troy, hid him in Scyros, dressed as a girl. Here he met Deïdameia, daughter of Lycomedes, king of the island, who bore him Neoptolemus (q.v. 1). Calchas having told the Greeks that Troy could not be taken without him, Odysseus with envoys found him and discovered his sex; after which he went willingly with them (so unnamed and rather doubtful cyclic poets in schol. *Il.* 19. 326, and many later writers). On the way to Troy, the Greeks landed in

Mysia, and there Achilles wounded Telephus (q.v. 1) in battle, afterwards healing him (so the *Cypria*, which also makes Achilles marry Deïdameia after the affair in Mysia). Still according to the same poem, the army then reassembled in Aulis, where the affair of Iphigenia (q.v.) occurred, went on to Tenedos, where Achilles and Agamemnon had a quarrel, and finally reached Troy, where a number of exploits of Achilles are recorded (killing of Cycnus and Troïlus, checking of a plan to abandon the enterprise, etc.). After the events in the *Iliad*, Troy was reinforced successively by the Amazon Penthesilea and by Memnon (qq.v.), who were both slain by Achilles. Immediately afterwards he was killed by Apollo (or Paris, or Apollo in the shape of Paris). So far the *Aethiopis*.

Further details are mostly erotic. Achilles and Patroclus were lovers (e.g. Aesch. fr. 135 Nauck); other loves were Troïlus (Serv. on *Aen.* 1. 474), Polyxena daughter of Priam (Hyg. *Fab.* 110), Helen (Lycophron 171 f., where he merely dreams of her; Paus. 3. 19. 13, where he is united to her in Leuce), and, oddest and earliest, Medea (Ibycus and Simonides ap. schol. Ap. Rhod. 4. 814; Lycoph. 174; in the Elysian Fields). The story that he was made invulnerable by Thetis (save for the heel in which he traditionally got his death-wound, originally no doubt from a poisoned arrow) by being plunged into Styx is not found earlier than Statius (*Achil.* 1. 134, whereon see schol. 269). It is a common folk-tale.

Achilles is very popular in art, especially Attic vase-painting, from the sixth century; early he is often bearded, from the late archaic period regularly beardless. Favourite scenes are: the ambush, death, and battle over the body of Troïlus; Achilles' armour brought by Thetis; the fight with Hector and the ransom of his body; the funeral games of Patroclus; fights with Penthesilea and Memnon; dicing with Ajax; the battle over, and rescue of, Achilles' body; later, among the daughters of Lycomedes (Roman paintings and sarcophagi, perhaps inspired by the fourth-century picture by Athenion). He is also shown as a baby brought by Peleus to Chiron.

'Achilleus', in Roscher's *Lexikon*; for Achilles as historic, D. L. Page, *History and the Homeric Iliad* (1959), 197 ff. In art, Brommer, *Vasenlisten*[2], 249 ff.; D. von Bothmer, *Amazons in Greek Art* (1957), (Penthesilea); Schauenburg, *Bonner Jahrb.* 1961, 215 ff.
H. J. R.; C M. R.

## ACHILLES TATIUS

**ACHILLES TATIUS** (1), Greek romancer from Alexandria, author of 'The Adventures of Leucippe and Cleitophon' (Τὰ κατὰ Λευκίππην καὶ Κλειτοφῶντα), flourished in the second century A.D., as recent papyrus discoveries demonstrate (thus confirming Altheim's acute hypothesis), and not in the fourth–sixth century A.D., as was previously believed. Of his life nothing certain is known: the *Suda* ascribes other works to him (two lost, an *Etymology* and a *Miscellaneous History of Many Great and Illustrious Men*, and one partly preserved, *On the Sphere*, the authorship of which is, however, debated) and says that the writer was later in life converted to Christianity and even became a bishop, which is doubted by most scholars. The novel, in eight books, follows the usual patterns of the genre (a much hindered love—between the two protagonists—triumphs in the end over numberless difficulties, terrifying dangers, and complicated adventures—voyages, shipwrecks, tortures, guiles, abductions, attacks by pirates and robbers, etc.); the story is told—this is unusual in the genre—in the first person by Cleitophon himself, whom Achilles pretends to have met in Sidon. The author's style is typically Atticistic in that it is characterized by an extreme Attic purity of diction (occasionally marred by vulgarisms), *apheleia* (short, asyndetic sentences), *isokola* and sound-effects, detailed descriptiveness (sophistic *ekphraseis*: Achilles relishes describing objects, animals, places, natural phenomena in their minutiae), propensity to declamations and disquisitions (e.g. on the effect of tears; often of the antithetic type, e.g. on love for women and paederasty, on fame and calumny). Achilles Tatius shows an uncommon ingenuity in inventing *coups de théâtre* (e.g. 'apparent deaths': Leucippe is made by him to die three times and is each time unexpectedly resuscitated; unforeseen letters and arrivals are also exploited for effect). The numerous and irrelevant interruptions relegate the plot into the background; the characterization of the personages—which, as Rohde has noted, shows a propensity towards realism, as a reaction against the idealism prevailing in the genre—is poor. Achilles Tatius was much admired by Byzantine critics for his diction and style, whereas his licentiousness scandalized them (cf. e.g. Phot. *Bibl.*, *Cod.* 87 and *Anth. Pal.* 9. 203).

EDITIO PRINCEPS. Heidelberg 1601; preceded by Latin translations (Della Croce; 1544 [partial], 1554 [complete]).
STANDARD EDITION. E. Vilborg (Stockholm, 1955).
COMMENTARIES. F. Jacobs (Leipzig, 1821); E. Vilborg (Stockholm, 1962).
CRITICISM. Rohde, *Griech. Roman*, 498 ff; W. Schmid, *PW*, s.v. Achilleus Tatios; Christ–Schmid–Stählin II 2⁶, 1046 ff; A. Lesky, *Gesch. d. griech. Litt.* (1963²), 921 ff. (especially for new papyrus evidence); H. Rommel, *Die naturwissenschaftlich-paradoxographischen Exkurse bei Philostratos, Heliodoros und Achilleus Tatios* (1923); H. Sexauer, *Der Sprachgebrauch des . . . A. Tatius* (Diss. Heidelberg, 1899); A. Stavroskiades, *Ach. Tat., ein Nachahmer des Platon, Aristoteles, Plutarch, Aelian* (Diss. Erlangen, 1889); H. Dörrie, *De Longi Achillis Tatii Heliodori memoria* (Göttingen, 1935).
Latest English Translation by S. Gaselee (Loeb, 1917, repr. 1947); numerous translations into modern languages (English, French, German, Italian) since 1546 (a list in Gaselee, Introd., xvi).
G. G.

**ACHILLES TATIUS** (2) (probably 3rd c. A.D.), author of a Greek commentary on Aratus, the only surviving part of his work Περὶ σφαίρας.

Ed. E. Maass, *Commentariorum in Aratum Reliquiae* (1898), 25.

**ACHILLEUS,** rebel in Egypt, A.D. 296–7, not the Domitius Domitianus of the coins, but his chief assistant. Domitianus revolted in summer 296 and was conquered by Diocletian in person early in 297. His revolt was probably due to economic distress connected with Diocletian's reform of the coinage.

W. Seston, *Dioclétien et la tétrarchie* (1946), 137 ff. | H. M.

**ACILIUS** (*PW* 4), GAIUS, Roman senator and historian, who interpreted for Carneades, Diogenes, and Critolaus in the Senate in 155 B.C., wrote a history of Rome, in Greek, from early Italian times to his own age, certainly to 184 B.C. (Dion. Hal. 3. 67. 5); it appeared *c.* 142 (Livy, *Per.* 53: reading *C. Acilius*). His senatorial tradition is seen in the anecdote of Scipio and Hannibal (Livy 35. 14. 5). His work was reproduced in Latin by a Claudius, probably Claudius (q.v. 11) Quadrigarius, who would then have incorporated it in his annalistic form.

Peter, *HRRel.* i² (1914), cxxi, 49; *FGrH* iii. c 881 ff.; Scullard, *Rom. Pol.*, 224 n. 1., 249. A. H. McD.

**ACRAE** (modern *Palazzolo Acreide*), founded by Syracuse in 663 B.C., stands on a hill protected by steep declivities, commanding the westward route from the Syracusan plain. It enjoyed local self-government, but its fortunes were throughout its history linked with those of its metropolis. Remains of a theatre and council-house attest its prosperity under Hieron II (q.v.). Extensive catacombs reveal it as still flourishing in the fifth century A.D.

Bérard, *Bibl. topogr.*, 39 f.; L. Bernabò Brea, *Akrai* (1956).
A. G. W.

**ACRAGAS** (Lat. *Agrigentum*, modern *Agrigento*—until 1927 *Girgenti*) was founded *c.* 580 B.C. by the Geloans in Sican territory in south-west Sicily. One of the most substantial Hellenic cities in size and affluence, it occupied a large bowl of land, rising to a lofty acropolis on the north and protected on other sides by a ridge. Its early access of power was owed to the tyrant Phalaris (q.v.). In 480 Theron (q.v.) was the ally of Gelon (q.v.) in his victory at Himera. After expelling Thrasydaeus, Theron's son, Acragas had a limited democratic government, in which Empedocles (q.v.), its most famous citizen, took part in his generation. Acragantine sixth- and fifth-century prosperity is attested by a remarkable series of temples, the remains of which are among the most impressive any Greek city can offer.

Sacked by the Carthaginians in 406, Acragas revived to some extent in the time of Timoleon (q.v.) and Phintias (286–280 B.C.), but suffered much in the Punic Wars. By Verres' time it was again wealthy, and with the rest of Sicily received full Roman citizenship after Julius Caesar's death. In the post-Roman period its inhabited area contracted to the old acropolis, but it has always been one of the principal cities of Sicily; even so, the modern city by no means covers the area of its ancient counterpart.

Ancient descriptions: Pindar, *Pyth.* 12 init.; Polyb. 9. 27; Strab. 6. 2. 5. Modern works: Bérard, *Bibl. topogr.*, 40 ff.; Dunbabin, *Western Greeks*; P. Griffo, *Agrigento—a guide²* (1956); P. Marconi, *Agrigento* (1929). Good plan of the ancient city in *Fasti Archaeologici* 1957 (1959), plan A. A. G. W.

**ACRISIUS,** in mythology, son of Abas, king of Argos, and his wife Aglaïa, father of Danaë and brother of Proetus (q.v.). After Abas' death the two brothers quarrelled; in their warfare they invented the shield. Proetus, defeated, left the country, returned with troops furnished by his father-in-law Iobates, and agreed to leave Argos to Acrisius, himself taking Tiryns; both were fortified by the Cyclopes. See schol. Eur. *Or.* 965. Cf. PERSEUS (1). H. J. R.

**ACRON,** HELENIUS (2nd c. A.D.), wrote commentaries (now lost) on Terence (*Adelphi* and *Eunuchus* at least) and Horace; but evidence for a commentary by him on Persius is slender. The extant pseudo-Acron scholia on Horace (ed. O. Keller, 2 vols., 1902–4) appear in three recensions of which the earliest dates from the fifth century. Alongside of excerpts from Porphyrion (q.v.), these scholia may contain genuine Acron material; but their attribution to him (not made in any MS. before the 15th c.) is probably due to a humanist. *See* SCHOLARSHIP, LATIN.

Schanz–Hosius, § 601. J. F. M.

**ACROSTIC.** Acrostics were perhaps composed in Latin earlier than in Greek. They were used by Ennius and the composers of Sibylline oracles (Cic. *Div.* 2. 110–12). Phlegon (q.v.) cites two examples from oracles (*Mir.* 10: Keller, 76 ff.). Cf. also *Anth. Pal.* 14. 148 (to Julian the Apostate), *GGM* 1. 238–9 (where the acrostic determines the authorship of a work), Dionysius Periegeta (*GGM* 2. 102 ff., 109 ff., 513 ff.), the acrostic prologues (of uncertain date) to Plautus' plays, and the beginning and end of the *Homerus Latinus*, giving (Silius) -Italicus as the author. A comedy-prologue of the third century B.C. has a series of lines beginning with α, β, etc. (Page *GLP* 324).

H. Diels, *Sibyllinische Blätter* (1890). J. D. D

**ACTA.** Under the Roman Republic magistrates took an oath, on entering office, to respect the laws of the State. With the fall of the Republic and the increasing scope and importance of the Emperor's enactments (loosely called *Acta*), it was desirable that these should acquire a permanence comparable with that of the laws. Magistrates therefore, emperors included (Dio Cass. 60. 10), took the oath to observe the *Acta* of previous emperors, except those whose *Acta*, directly after their death, were explicitly rescinded (*rescissio actorum*) or at least excluded from the oath. Thus no oath was taken to observe the *Acta* of Tiberius, Gaius, Galba, Otho, Vitellius, Domitian, or Caracalla; though it is clear from the evidence of Gaius, *Inst.* 1. 33 (citing an edict of Nero) and *Digest* 48. 3. 2 (citing an edict of Domitian), that the wise enactments of even bad emperors might survive their death. The exact definition of *Acta* was not easy. The term was eventually held to cover the 'Constitutiones Principum' (i.e. *edicta*, *decreta*, and *rescripta*); but the difficulties arising from a loose definition of it were apparent when Julius Caesar's *Acta* were ratified by the Senate after his murder (Cic. *Phil.* 1. 16 ff.). A second difficulty concerned the relation of the *Acta* of the living emperor to those of his predecessors. The first recorded case of an oath to observe such *Acta* was that taken by all the magistrates to observe the *Acta* of Julius Caesar in 45 B.C. (Appian, *BCiv.* 2. 106). Similar oaths were taken to observe the *Acta* of Augustus in 29 and in 24 B.C. (Dio Cass. 51. 20; 53. 28). At first moderate emperors, as Tiberius and Claudius, sought to restrict the oath to the *Acta* of Divus Augustus, excluding their own *Acta* (Suet. *Tib.* 67; Tac. *Ann.* 1. 72; Dio Cass. 60. 10), but, with the increase of autocracy, the oath came to include the *Acta* of reigning emperors.

The *Acta Senatus* (or *Commentarii Senatus*) constituted the official record of proceedings in the Senate under the Roman Empire, the senator responsible for the record being, since the reign of Tiberius, selected by the Emperor (Tac. *Ann.* 5. 4). The *Acta Diurna* were a gazette, whose daily publication dates from 59 B.C. (Suet. *Iul.* 20); it recorded important social and political news, and was read not only at Rome but also in the provinces (Tac. *Ann.* 16. 22). The *Acta Senatus* were preserved and could be consulted by senators. Tacitus used, or depended on authorities who used, both these (e.g. *Ann.* 15. 74) and the *Acta Diurna* (*Ann.* 3. 3). J. P. B.

**ACTAEON,** in mythology, son of Aristaeus (q.v. 1) and Autonoë, daughter of Cadmus (q.v.). A keen hunter, he one day came upon Artemis bathing; offended at being thus seen naked by a man, she turned him into a stag and he was chased and killed by his own hounds; so first in Stesichorus ap. Paus. 9. 2. 3 (fr. 59 Page, *Poet. Mel. Gr.*); most famously in Ovid, *Met.* 3. 138 ff. Other versions of his offence were that he was Zeus' rival with Semele (Acusilaus, fr. 33 Jacoby = Apollod. 3. 30) or that he boasted that he was a better hunter than Artemis (Eur. *Bacch.* 339–40), and that he wished to marry Artemis (Diod. Sic. 4. 81. 4). But to see any deity uninvited brings destruction (Callim. *Lav. Pall.* 101–2).

Actaeon torn by hounds under Artemis' eyes is found in many works of art from the early fifth century. In early pictures he sometimes wears a deerskin, and was shown sitting on one in Polygnotus' Underworld, but the first in which he sprouts antlers are after the middle of the century. Artemis surprised bathing appears first in Pompeian painting.

Brommer, *Vasenlisten²*, 336 f. See also P. Jacobsthal, *Marburger Jhrb. f. Kunstwissenschaft*, 5 (1900); Caskey–Beazley *Attic Vase Paintings in the Museum of Fine Arts, Boston* ii (1954), 46 ff., 83 ff. H. J. R.; C. M. R.

**ACTE,** CLAUDIA (*PW* 399), freedwoman of Nero (or possibly Claudius), came from Asia Minor: hence her alleged descent from the Attalidae. In A.D. 55, encouraged by Seneca in Agrippina's despite, Nero made her his mistress, but from 58 onwards she was gradually supplanted by Poppaea (q.v.). Her wealth is attested by records of her household and estates in Italy and Sardinia. She deposited Nero's remains in the tomb of the Domitii.

Tac. *Ann.* 13. 12; Suet. *Nero* 28, 50; Dio Cass. 61. 7. G. E. F. C.

**ACTIUM,** a flat sandy promontory on the coast of Acarnania (q.v.), at the entrance to the Ambracian Gulf, forming part of the territory of Anactorium. There was a temple of Apollo there at least as early as the fifth century B.C. Actium was the site of Antony's camp in 31 B.C., and gave its name to the naval battle fought just outside the gulf, in which he was defeated by Octavian (2 Sept.). Octavian commemorated his victory by founding Nicopolis (q.v. 3) on the other (northern) side of the strait.

Augustus developed the local Actian Games in honour of Apollo into a quinquennial festival, modelled on the Olympian; these *Actia* were later adopted by several other Greek States. An Actian 'era' was established, with probably a double initial date of 32/1 or 31/30.

P-K, *GL* ii. 380 f.; W. W. Tarn, *JRS* 1931, 173 ff., 1938, 165 ff.; G. W. Richardson, *JRS* 1937, 153 ff.; H. Volkmann, *Cleopatra* (1958), 176 ff., 230 f. G. W. R.

**ACTS OF THE PAGAN** (or **HEATHEN**) **MARTYRS** is the name given by modern scholars to about a dozen fragments of Alexandrian nationalist literature, preserved on papyri mostly written in the second or early third century A.D. The majority of the fragments give, in dramatic form, reports of the hearing of Alexandrian embassies and of the trials of Alexandrian nationalist leaders before various Roman emperors. The episodes related, of which the dramatic dates range from the time of Augustus to that of Commodus, are probably basically historical and the accounts appear to be derived to some extent from official records. But they have been coloured up, more in some cases than in others, for propaganda purposes, to caricature the emperors, to stress the fearless outspokenness of the Alexandrians, who are sometimes surprisingly rude to the emperors, and to represent their punishment, usually execution, as martyrdom in the nationalist cause. This literature is in general bitterly hostile to Rome, reflecting the tensions between Alexandria and her overlord during the first two centuries of Roman rule. These included antagonism between the Greeks and Rome's protégés, the Jews, and three episodes concern their quarrels. But despite the violent hatred expressed by the Greeks for the Jews, anti-Semitism is only a subsidiary feature in these primarily anti-Roman compositions.

H. Musurillo, *The Acts of the Pagan Martyrs, Acta Alexandrinorum* (1954; with commentary); also Teubner text (1961). E. M. S.

**ACUSILAUS,** of Argos, lived 'before the Persian Wars' (Joseph. *Ap.* 1–13) and compiled Γενεαλογίαι, translating and correcting Hesiod, with ingenious conjectures but no literary merit.

*FGrH* i. 2.

**ADAERATIO,** the term used during the later Roman period for the commutation into money of levies or issues in kind. The transaction was sometimes unofficial, sometimes official, and might be made at the initiative of the government, the tax-collector, or the taxpayer in the case of levies, or of the distributor or recipient of issues. The rate of commutation might be settled by bargaining, or fixed by the government at the market price or at some arbitrary sum. Nearly all *adaeratio* was into gold from the mid fourth century. Levies of expensive objects, such as horses, oxen, or uniforms, were commuted from an early date in order to distribute their incidence over a number of taxpayers. The regular land-tax, payable in grain, wine, oil, and meat, was still normally levied in kind in the East in the mid fifth century, being commuted as a special privilege, on the basis of five years' average of prices. Anastasius commuted most of the land-tax to gold. In the West the land-tax was already all paid in gold in the mid fifth century. The rations (*annonae*), fodder (*capitus*), and uniforms of the troops were mostly commuted by the early fifth century; those of the civil servants were first officially commuted in 423, those of the higher officers of State in 439.

S. Mazzarino, *Aspetti sociali del quarto secolo* (1951), ch. 4.
A. H. M. J.

**ADAMKLISSI,** the site of two Roman monuments in the plain of the Dobrudja (S. Roumania): (1) a military funeral altar inscribed with the names of at least 3,000 Roman casualties, commemorating either the defeat of Cornelius Fuscus (A.D. 86), or that of Oppius Sabinus the year before, in the Dacian War of Domitian (cf. Em. Doruţiu, *Dacia* 1961, 345 ff.), (2) a *tropaeum* dedicated to Mars Ultor by Trajan in 109 to commemorate his victories over the Dacians. In the near-by valley Trajan founded a small city, Tropaeum Traiani.

Florea Bobu Florescu, *Monumentul de la Adamklissi²* (1961), German transl. *Das Siegesdenkmal von Adamklissi* (1965); I. A. Richmond, *PBSR* 1967, 29 ff. J. J. W.

**ADEIA,** permission given by the Athenian *ekklesia* to make proposals or give information under special circumstances: e.g. proposals (1) to revoke sentences of *atimia* (q.v.), or to remit State debts; (2) to rescind a special clause forbidding the alteration of certain laws or decrees (Thuc. 2. 24. 1; 8. 15. 1); (3) to impose an *eisphora* (q.v.), or to borrow from the treasury of Athena. For a grant of *adeia*, at least in case (1) above, a quorum of 6,000 votes was necessary. *Adeia* was also necessary, for noncitizens, to make supplication to the assembly or lay information about crimes of which it took cognizance (*see* EKKLESIA). A similar procedure was observed in many other Greek States. A. W. G.

**ADIABENE** (*Hadiab*), district of the two Zâb rivers in north Mesopotamia. A Seleucid eparchy, it became a vassal kingdom, later a satrapy, of Parthia, and was constantly involved in her internal disputes and in her wars with Rome. One of the dynasties of Adiabene embraced Judaism (Joseph. *AJ* 20. 17–37). Trajan's army overran Adiabene in A.D. 116 and Caracalla's in 216, but neither campaign had more than a momentary effect on the status or allegiance of the country. It was absorbed into the Sassanid Empire at the time of the final collapse of Parthia. M. S. D.; E. W. G.

**ADLECTIO.** A man could enter the Roman Senate (*see* SENATUS) either by holding a magistracy or by having his name placed on the senatorial roll (in the Republic, by the censors). Admission by this second means (which Sulla temporarily suppressed) was known technically as *adlectio* under the Principate, when *adlectio* was also employed to accelerate the magisterial careers of senators; an ex-quaestor, for instance, who was *adlectus inter praetorios*, like Germanicus in A.D. 9 (Dio Cass. 56. 17), could proceed directly to the consulship. Princes of the imperial house might be adlected by the Senate—e.g. Germanicus and Drusus, son of Tiberius, in A.D. 9 (Dio Cass. 56. 17), following the precedent set for Octavian in 43 B.C. (Augustus, *Res Gest.* 1). Though the right of adlection had been largely employed by Julius Caesar, it was exercised cautiously by the first emperors, and only in connexion with the holding of an official *lectio senatus* or the tenure of the censorship: by Augustus probably, and certainly by Claudius (*ILS* 968) and by Vespasian

and Titus (*ILS* 1024). After Domitian the right of *adlecti* was exercised as a normal power of the Emperor. Me were adlected *inter quaestorios* (i.e. to the rank of ex quaestors in the *cursus honorum*), *inter aedilicios, inte tribunicios, inter praetorios*. *Adlectio inter consulares* wa an innovation of Macrinus and met with opposition (Di Cass. 78. 13); under the constitution of Diocletian an Constantine it became common. J. P. E

**ADONIS** (Ἄδωνις), in mythology, the son of Cinyra (q.v.), king of Cyprus, by an incestuous union with hi daughter Myrrha or Smyrna, according to the usual myth (Ov. *Met.* 10. 298–559, 708–39). The beautiful youth wa beloved by Aphrodite. While hunting he was killed b a boar, or, in some accounts, by the jealous Hephaestus or by Ares disguised as a boar. Panyasis (in Apollod *Bibl.* 3. 14. 4) calls Adonis the son of Theias and Smyrna Aphrodite concealed the infant in a box and entruste it to Persephone, who was unwilling to restore him ti Zeus decreed that Adonis should spend part of each yea on earth with Aphrodite, part in the underworld wit Persephone. Adonis was a divinity of vegetation an fertility, whose disappearance marks the harvesting of th crops (cf. Euseb. *Praep. Evang.* 3. 11. 12). He is akin t the Babylonian Tammuz; the name Adonis may b simply the Semitic title 'Adon', 'Lord', by which he wa known in Phoenicia. Byblos was especially sacred t Adonis, and his death, which annually stained the rive Adonis with his blood, was localized at the near-b Aphaca (Lucian *Syr. D.* 6–9). He was worshipped a Amathus in Cyprus, and it was probably from Cypru that his cult was carried, by the fifth century, to Athens where he was, at least partially, identified with Eros. Hi cult existed only in conjunction with that of Aphrodit (q.v., § 3), to whom swine seem to have been sacrifice only where she was associated with Adonis.

THE ADONIA. At Byblos there was a period of mourn ing for the dead Adonis, but his resurrection (Lucian loc. cit.) is borrowed from the Osiris cult, not origina At Alexandria the rites consisted of a magnifice pageant of the wedding of Adonis and Aphrodite; th next day women carried his image to the sea-shore ami lamentations (Theoc. *Id.* 15). The mourning of th women and the setting out of the ephemeral 'Gardens o Adonis' on the house-tops marked the festival at Athens There was perhaps considerable variation in the conten as in the date of the festival, and much of the origina intent of the rites appears to have been forgotten. I fifth-century Athens they were held in April, in Ptolemai Egypt perhaps in September, while under the Empir the accepted date was 19 July. The cult was especiall popular with women.

W. W. Baudissin, *Adonis und Esmun* (1911); J. G. Frazer, *Adon Attis Osiris* i. Separate studies on the *Adonia*: Nilsson, *Feste*, 384 ff. F. Cumont, *Syria* 1927 and 1935; A. S. F. Gow, *JHS* 1938 (detaile commentary on Theoc. 15); F. R. Walton, *Harv. Theol. Rev.* 1938 P. Lambrechts in *Mélanges Is. Lévy* (1955); W. Atallah, *Adonis dan la littérature et l'art grecs* (1966). F. R. W

**ADOPTIO,** a legal act by which a Roman citizen— whether he is in the *patria potestas* (q.v.) of another or i *sui iuris*, i.e. himself a *paterfamilias*—enters anothe family and comes under the *patria potestas* of its chief When the adopted person is *sui iuris* the act is called *adrogatio*. Both entail the consequences of a *deminutio capitis* (q.v.) *minima*.

2. *Adrogatio* effects the fusion of two families, fo together with the *adrogatus* all the persons under hi power (*potestas, manus*) and all his property pass into th family of the *adrogator*. In early times a public act wa necessary for the validity of *adrogatio*: the vote of th *comitia curiata*, preceded (since it involved the extinctio of a family and its *sacra*) by an investigation by th

pontiffs; by the time of Cicero the *comitia* were replaced by thirty lictors, who gave their assent as the representatives of the *curiae*. Since the *comitia* met only in Rome, *adrogatio* could take place only there until, certainly under Diocletian and probably before, a new method of *adrogatio*, by imperial rescript, was introduced. The old form thereafter disappears.

3. *Adoptio* of a *filius familias* had a more private character. Its form was the same as that of *emancipatio* (q.v.) save that after the third sale the final stage was not a manumission but a collusive claim by the adopter that the son was in his *potestas*. These formalities were finally abolished by Justinian and replaced by a simple declaration before a magistrate.

4. The effect of both *adoptio* and *adrogatio* was to place the adopted person for all legal purposes in the same position as if he had been a natural child in the *potestas* of the adopter. The adopted son took his adoptive father's name and rank. He acquired rights of succession on death in his new family and lost all such rights as he had in his old family. Moreover, *adoptio imitatur naturam*, and therefore an adoptive relationship was, for example, as much a bar to marriage as a natural one. (Another result was the rule that the adopter must be older than the person adopted—according to Justinian at least eighteen years older.)

5. Adoption (of both kinds), since it was a method of acquiring *patria potestas* and continuing the agnatic family, could originally be by men only. Adoption by women *ad solatium liberorum amissorum*, perhaps first allowed by Diocletian, shows a new conception. *Adrogatio*, since it involved the extinction of one family in order to preserve another, was subject to other restrictions— in particular that the adopter must have no children and must either be over the age of sixty or for some reason have no prospect of begetting children.

6. Since *adoptio* destroyed the adopted person's rights of succession in his old family, and a subsequent *emancipatio* by the adoptive father would likewise destroy his rights in his new family, Justinian, in order to remove this possibility of injustice, made a drastic change in the character of *adoptio*. In the ordinary case it was to do no more than create rights of succession in the new family (so-called *adoptio minus plena*). For all other purposes, including the retention of existing rights of succession, the person adopted was to remain in his natural family. *Adoptio* was to have its full effect (so-called *adoptio plena*) only when the adopter was a natural ascendant (e.g. maternal grandfather) and therefore less likely to indulge in capricious emancipation.

7. The testamentary adoptions recorded in non-legal sources in the late Republic and Principate, and which may have been influenced by Greek practice, would seem to have created only an obligation (from which the praetor could give dispensation) to take the testator's name. In the case of Caesar's adoption of Octavian legal effect was given to the adoption by a posthumous *adrogatio*.

G. Desserteaux, *Effets de l'adrogation* (1892); F. Wieacker, *Eos* 956; G. Lavaggi, *Stud. et doc. hist. et iuris* xii (1946); W. Schmitt-enner, *Oktavian u. das Testament Cäsars* (1952). And see textbooks under LAW AND PROCEDURE, ROMAN, I. A. B.; B. N.

**ADOPTION, GREEK.** The Code of Gortyn includes the earliest detailed reference to adoption in Greece. There it takes place *inter vivos*; the adoptive father must not himself be an adopted son, but otherwise he was free to adopt, whether or not he already had children of his own. The adoptive son was allowed some rights of inheritance, but these were not as great as those of a son by birth.

From Athens we have abundant but not altogether reliable evidence in the speeches of fourth-century orators, particularly Isaeus. In Attic law the original purpose of formal adoption was to enable a citizen who had no son to choose an heir, usually if not always from among his relatives. (It is likely enough that in all periods more informal adoptions took place which did not give the same legal and financial privileges.) By the time of Isaeus we hear of three types of adoption: (i) *inter vivos*; (ii) testamentary; (iii) posthumous, in which case a man who had neither left a son nor adopted a son in his will was after his death assigned a son by adoption to carry on his family. The principle that adoption imitates nature (*see* ADOPTIO) is not accepted in Greece, and the adoption of a daughter's husband was a regular practice. Isaeus reiterates the view that religious considerations were important: a son must be adopted so that the family rites may be kept up and the continued existence of the family assured. In earlier times this may well have been so, but the circumstances in which adoption, particularly testamentary and posthumous, was employed suggest that by the fourth century financial factors weighed more heavily. This view is supported by the evidence that a man sentenced to suffer hereditary disabilities might normally give his sons away in adoption, thus saving them from the financial penalties of his sentence at the cost of extinguishing his branch of the family (cf. Plut. *Mor.* 834 b).

Elsewhere inscriptions are almost our only source of evidence. Many adoptive formulae are used, either of the type Διονύσιος Εὐρήμονος φύσει δὲ Λαμπρίου or Πασιφῶν Ἐπιλύκου καθ' ὑοθεσίαν δὲ Δαμοκλεῦς (or κατὰ θυγατροποίαν when a woman is adopted). These formulae are not a safe guide to the relative frequency of adoption in different parts of Greece. Very few Attic inscriptions have the local formula γόνῳ δέ. Yet the number of occurrences in Rhodes, greater there than in all the rest of Greece, surely reflects some special situation. It seems clear, for instance, that in Rhodes by the second century B.C. adoption was used as a means of manipulating priesthoods normally confined to particular families, so that in some cases an old man had to arrange for his adoption into the right family. There are signs elsewhere that adoption could amount to what we should rather call fosterage (see Cameron's article, cited below), and again that it might be used as a kind of apprenticeship. (Note the mention of adoption with reference to medical practice in the Hippocratic Oath.)

At least by the early years of the Roman Empire a person might be adopted by a city or a group within it as υἱὸς (θυγατὴρ) τῆς πόλεως or υἱὸς τοῦ δήμου. This might be traced back to some privilege granted to war-orphans such as is mentioned in Pericles' Funeral Speech (Thuc. 2. 46), but the earliest explicit reference to adoption by a community belongs to the second century B.C. (a Rhodian adopted by the Delians: cf. Hiller, *J. Oest. Inst.* 1901, 164 ff.)

Dar.–Sag. s.v. adoption; PW, s.v. adoptio (1). A. Wentzel, 'Studien über die Adoption in Griechenland', *Hermes* 1930, 167 ff. contains useful material despite the mistaken argument that Rhodian adoption is a sign of Roman influence; A.!Cameron, 'θρεπτός and related terms', in *Anatolian Studies presented to Buckler* (1939), 27 ff.; M. S. Smith, 'Greek Adoptive Formulae', *CQ* 1967, 302 ff. M. S. S.

**ADRASTUS,** the name of several mythological persons, the only one of importance being the son of Talaus, king of Argos. His name, if it means 'the unescapable', is very appropriate to a warrior-prince and gives no grounds for supposing he was originally a god. In historical times he had a cult at Sicyon and Megara (see Farnell, *Hero-Cults*, 334 ff.). Probably much of the tradition concerning him is derived from the lost cyclic epic *Thebais*; whether it has any historical content is doubtful.

When a young man he was driven out of Argos by dynastic rivalries and took refuge in Sicyon with his mother's father Polybus (q.v.). He married Polybus' daughter and succeeded him as king (*Il.* 2. 572 and scholiast there; Pind. *Nem.* 9. 9 ff., with schol.); afterwards he returned to Argos, making terms with Amphiaraus (q.v.). While reigning there he received in his house Tydeus and Polynices (qq.v.), both exiles, and recognized in them the lion and boar to whom he had been bidden marry his daughters, Argeia (to Polynices) and Deipyle (to Tydeus) (see, e.g., Apollod. 3. 58–59). He then undertook to restore them, and began by attempting to set Polynices on the throne of Thebes. The army was led by himself, his two sons-in-law, and Parthenopaeus (originally Adrastus' brother, in later accounts son of Atalanta, q.v.), Amphiaraus, Capaneus, and Hippomedon—the famous Seven against Thebes; in some lists the exiles are omitted and Mecisteus and Eteoclus substituted (see Wilamowitz-Moellendorff, *Aischylos Interpretationen* (1914), 97 ff.). On the march to Thebes the army halted at Nemea, and there were shown the way to water by Hypsipyle (q.v.). While she was thus engaged her charge, the baby Archemorus, was killed by a serpent; Amphiaraus secured her pardon and the Nemean Games were founded in memory of the infant (see especially Eur. *Hypsipyle*, ed. G. W. Bond 1963). The attack on Thebes was a complete failure, only Adrastus escaping home, thanks to his marvellous horse, Arion. Our chief authorities here are Aeschylus, *Septem* and some odes of Pindar, notably *Ol.* 6. 12 and *Pyth.* 8. Ten years later Adrastus led the sons of the Seven, the Epigoni, against Thebes with better success; the city fell, but Adrastus' son Aegialeus was killed in the fighting. According to the earlier story (Paus. 1. 43. 1) the aged Adrastus died of grief on the way home; a sensational and late account (Hyg. *Fab.* 242. 5) makes father and son burn themselves alive *ex responso Apollinis.* H. J. R.

**ADRIA,** modern *Atria*, a coastal city in the north of the Po delta, now 12 miles from the sea. Perhaps Venetic in origin, it was probably one of the twelve Etruscan cities north of the Apennines. It had a large Greek population, and from the late sixth century onwards was an important entrepôt for Greek and Etruscan trade with the Po valley and Northern Europe. Varro (*Ling.* 5. 161) derives *atrium* from Atria.

*Mostra dell' Etruria Padana e della città di Spina* (Bologna, 1960), *passim.* D. W. R. R.

**ADRIANUS** of Tyre (*c.* A.D. 113–93), sophist, pupil and successor of Atticus Herodes at Athens. He subsequently taught rhetoric at Rome and his works included μελέται, epideictic speeches, and treatises on ἰδέαι and στάσεις.

**ADRIATIC SEA** (ὁ Ἀδρίας; *mare Adriaticum* or *superum*). This term was used indifferently with that of 'Ionian Sea' (q.v.) to denote the gulf between Italy and the Balkan Peninsula. Its southward limit was extended by some authors to include the sea east of Sicily. In neolithic times seafarers from the south settled round the Gulf of Valona at the entry to the Adriatic, and in the Bronze Age there is evidence of trade in Baltic amber (q.v.), perhaps in Bohemian tin (q.v.), and in weapons from the north to Italy and Greece with ports of call in Albania, for instance in the Mati valley. Seafarers from the Adriatic occupied the Nidhri plain in Leucas, where they practised burial under a tumulus such as occurred in Albania in the Middle Helladic period. Greek exploration of the Adriatic was said to be the work of the Phocaeans, who penetrated to its upper end by 600 B.C. (Hdt. 1. 163); but Greek colonization was settled from Corinth and Corcyra in the late seventh and the sixth centuries, their chief foundations being Apollonia and Epidamnus (qq.v.). Emigrants from Cnidos occupied Black Corcyra (*Cur-*

zola), and Syracusans (probably refugees from Dionysi◦ I) took possession of Issa (*Lissa*). But the north Dalm◦ tian coast was not colonized. Temporary settlemen◦ were made by Rhodes in south Apulia (Strabo 14. 654 probably in the sixth century). In central Italy Ancor (q.v.) was a solitary Greek foundation. Adria and Spi◦ (qq.v.) at the Po estuary throve on trade with the Etru◦ cans from the early fifth century, and finds of coins in th◦ Po valley indicate Tarentine trade up the Adriatic in th◦ fourth century.

Adriatic commerce and colonization were impeded b◦ the brigandage of the Illyrians on the South Dalmatia◦ coast, where deep recesses and off-shore islands provide◦ ideal pirate bases. This nuisance was eventually su◦ pressed by the Romans, who swept the Adriatic with◦ war-fleet after the First Punic War (229 and 219 B.C.◦ and from the time of Augustus patrolled it with a regul◦ police flotilla. But Greek trade in the Adriatic fell aw◦ after 300 B.C., and the Romans made little use of this s◦ except on the crossings from Brundisium and Ancor◦ (qq.v.)

R. L. Beaumont, *JHS* 1936, 159 ff.; Hammond, *Epirus*, 326 ff.
M.

**ADULIS** or **ADULE,** on the west coast of the Red S◦ (at Zulla in Annesley Bay near Massawa), was used b◦ Ptolemy II and III for elephant-hunts, and became a◦ important export-mart for African and re-exporte◦ Indian wares, a caravan-route leading thence inlan◦ Greeks and Indians frequented it. When the Axumi◦ kingdom rose (1st c. A.D.; *see* AXUMIS) Adulis becam◦ their main port and base (for voyages to E. Africa an◦ India), surpassing all others in the third century A.◦ Two famous inscriptions (combined in *OGI* 54) a◦ among its monuments.

*Periplus M. Rubr.* 4; Pliny 6. 172; Ptol. *Geog.* 4. 7. 8; 8. 16. ◦ Cosmas, ed. Winstedt, 101B ff. E. H. ◦

**ADULTERY.** I. In GREEK STATES the punishment ◦ adultery (μοιχεία) ordinarily took the form of priva◦ self-help. A law of Draco allowed a man to kill anyo◦ caught in the act with his wife, mother, sister, or daughte◦ according to a law of Solon the offended husband cou◦ deal with the adulterer as he liked. The adulterer coul◦ however, buy himself off by paying a money penalty. ◦ was also open, alike to interested persons and to others ◦ the first instance, to enter a legal prosecution against hi◦ Penalties were very severe and differed in the individu◦ States. The husband of a woman convicted of adulte◦ was compelled to repudiate her, otherwise he becam◦ liable to *atimia* (q.v.) by a law of Solon. In the Graec◦ Egyptian papyri some marriage contracts (so the olde◦ one, *PEleph.* 1) prescribe a pecuniary penalty for adu◦ tery.

II. ROMAN LAW (except as indicated below) took co◦ nizance only of adultery by the wife. Until the legislati◦ of Augustus (below) its punishment was left either to t◦ outraged husband (cf. Gell. 10. 23; Val. Max. 6. 1. 13)◦ to the judgement of a family council. It is probably ◦ this practice that is attributable the legend of a law ◦ Romulus (Dion. Hal. 2. 25) punishing the adulteress wi◦ death. In the late Republic it would entitle the father ◦ the husband to sue for *iniuria* (q.v.), but this was tr◦ also of the seduction of an unmarried woman. Adulte◦ would also be a ground for the husband's retaining pa◦ of the dowry on divorce (*see* MARRIAGE, LAW OF), but ◦ was not brought within the criminal law until the *L◦ Iulia de adulteriis coercendis* (18 B.C.). The right of se◦ redress was regulated: the father might kill his adultero◦ daughter and her adulterer if caught in the act in his ◦ her husband's house; a husband might not kill his wi◦

and only in certain circumstances the adulterer. A special court (*quaestio*), presided over by a praetor, was created to try cases of adultery. The normal penalty was *relegatio* (q.v.) of both wife and adulterer (but *in diversas insulas*), confiscation of parts of their property, and for the woman loss of half her dowry. The husband with clear evidence must divorce immediately, or be punished as a *leno* (procurer). The accusation must be made by husband or father within sixty days after the divorce; thereafter it could be made within four months by anyone (both periods counting only *dies utiles*, i.e. days on which the court sat).

The penalties of the *Lex Iulia*, to which a special title is dedicated in Justinian's *Digest* (48. 5), were made more severe by the Christian emperors. Constantine introduced the death-penalty (which Justinian confirmed) but restricted the right of making a charge against the guilty person to the husband and the relatives of the wife.

Adultery by the husband was never as such a crime, but his illicit intercourse with a respectable woman constituted the crime of *stuprum* under the *Lex Iulia*, and in the fifth century (*Cod. Iust.* 5. 17. 8) his adultery in the matrimonial home or his adultery with a married woman anywhere entitled his wife to divorce him without incurring the penalties by then imposed for unjustified divorce (*see* MARRIAGE, LAW OF).

GREEK LAW. J. H. Lipsius, *Das attische Recht* i (1905), 429 ff.; A. Berger, *Strafklauseln in d. Papyrusurkunden* (1911), 218 ff.
ROMAN LAW. Mommsen, *Röm. Strafr.* (1899), 627 ff, 688 ff.; Ph. Lotmar, *Mélanges Girard* ii (1912), 143 ff.; E. Volterra, *Studi econ.-giur. dell'Univ. Cagliari*, 1928; *Studi Bonfante* ii (1930); *Rend. Ist. Lomb.* 1930; B. Biondi, *Studi Sassaresi* xvi (1938).
A. B.; B. N.

**ADVOCATUS.** The parties to a Roman civil trial might entrust the presentation of their case to advocates (*advocati, patroni, causidici*). These men, who appear as a class in the late Republic under the influence of Greek rhetoric, and of whom Cicero (q.v. 1) and the Younger Pliny (q.v.) are prominent representatives, were orators rather than lawyers. They would necessarily have or acquire some knowledge of law, but their reputations were founded on their skill in forensic rhetoric. They and the jurists (*see* JURISPRUDENCE) regarded each other as distinct classes, with different (and in the eyes of the other class inferior) functions, though occasionally an advocate might become a jurist. Advocates were supposed to give their services gratuitously: the *Lex Cincia* (q.v.) forbade the acceptance of any reward, and the ban was repeated by Augustus and more than once in the first century A.D., but evidently to no purpose, and by the end of the second century it was accepted (*Dig.* 50. 13. 1. 9 ff.) that advocates might claim an *honorarium* (or *palmarium*, if payment was conditional on the case being won.). In the later Empire, with the disappearance of the professional jurist, the advocates, at least in the East, are no longer merely orators, but are qualified lawyers who have studied at a law school and form a privileged corporation. Their number is limited, their fees are regulated, and they are attached to a particular court. The majority of the compilers of the *Digesta* (q.v.) were advocates.

Advocates must be distinguished from legal representatives. In the earliest procedure, *per legis actiones* (*see* LAW AND PROCEDURE, ROMAN), the parties must in general be present in person; under the formulary procedure they might appoint representatives (*cognitores, procuratores*: Gai. *Inst.* 4. 82 ff.) who would take their place in the proceedings. But in either case they might also employ the services of an advocate.

F. Schulz, *Roman Legal Science* (1946), 43 ff., 108 f., 268 ff.
A. B.; B. N.

**AEACUS,** in mythology, son of Zeus and Aegina (daughter of the river-god Asopus), ancestor of the Aeacidae, the (post-Homeric) genealogy being:

Aeacus ⚭ Endeis (daughter of Sciron of Megara)

Thetis ⚭ Peleus     Hesione ⚭ Telamon ⚭ Eriboea
Achilles ⚭ Deidameia     Teucer     Aias ⚭ Tecmessa
Neoptolemus     Eurysaces

Some accounts give Aeacus a third, illegitimate son, Phocus, who was killed by his brothers; they consequently left the island of Aegina (so named from their grandmother). Aeacus was celebrated for his piety. In response to his prayers to Zeus Hellenios a drought came to an end (Isoc. 9. 14–15 and later authors). Because the population of the island was scanty, or had died of a plague sent by Hera, he besought Zeus to help him, and the god turned a swarm of ants into men, who were, therefore, called Myrmidones (Hes. fr. 76 Rzach; Ov. *Met.* 7. 517 ff.). He judged between the gods (Pind. *Isthm.* 8. 25); built part of the walls of Troy (Pind. *Ol.* 8. 31; no other authority). After his death he became a judge of the dead (Isoc. loc. cit; Plato, *Ap.* 41 a, *Grg.* 523 e). H. J. R.

**AECAE,** a Roman town (modern *Troia*) 14 miles southwest of Foggia in northern Apulia. It sided with Hannibal (q.v.) and later became a stage on the Via Traiana. The largest of all the Apulian centuriation (q.v.) systems covered over a hundred square miles east of the town.

*CIL* ix, 85. T. Ashby and R. Gardner, *PBSR* 1916, 141 ff.
G. D. B. J.

**AEDESIUS** (d. *c.* A.D. 355) of Cappadocia, Neoplatonist, pupil of Iamblichus and teacher of Maximus, Chrysanthius, Priscus, and Eusebius Myndius. He set up a school of philosophy in Pergamum. No writings remain; biography by Eunapius.

**AEDILES.** The aediles originated as two subordinate officials of the *plebs*, created to assist the tribunes, whose sacrosanctity they partly shared, either for the maintenance of the prison, or, as is more likely, to superintend the common temple (*aedes*) and cult of the *plebs*, that of Ceres (q.v.). Soon their functions began to extend to the administration of public buildings in general, particularly to the oversight of the archives, both *plebiscita* and *senatus consulta*. With the addition in 367 B.C. of two *aediles curules*, elected from the patricians, the aedileship became a magistracy of the whole people. After the admission of plebeians the curule magistracy was held alternately by either order, but in the Empire was omitted by patricians. The office was elective—either in the *concilium plebis*, or, for the *curules*, in the *comitia tributa*—and annual, being held after 367 for the consular, not the tribunician, year (*see* CALENDARS, §8). *Curules* ranked below praetors, *plebeii* at first below tribunes but eventually with the *curules*. The office was non-essential in the *cursus honorum*, but its connexion with the games rendered it useful to men with political ambitions, and it was the first office to confer full senatorial dignity and the *ius imaginis* (*see* IMAGINES). The competence of either branch was the same. Their duties were the *cura urbis*, *cura annonae*, and *cura ludorum sollemnium*. *Cura urbis* meant care for the streets of Rome, traffic regulations, public order in religious matters and cult practices, care for the water-supply and the market, especially the supervision of weights and measures. Consequently they had powers of minor jurisdiction. Fines exacted went to separate chests for *plebeii* and *curules*. Out of the *cura urbis* developed the *cura annonae*, the maintenance and distribution of the corn-supply (see ANNONA), a heavy charge until Julius Caesar created special *aediles Ceriales* for this duty, which passed under Augustus to the *praefectus annonae* and other officials. Care for the public games, which grew out of their urban administration, increased in importance with the growth of wealth and political rivalry in the later Republic, till the greater part of the expense was borne by the aediles as a means of gaining popularity and votes. Augustus, however, transferred the games to the praetors. The *ludi Romani* and the *Megalesia* fell to the *curules*, the *ludi Ceriales* and *plebeii* to the plebeians. Aediles are also found as the normal minor administrative officials of all Roman municipalities (see MUNICIPIUM), and in corporate bodies such as *vici* (see VICUS) or *collegia* (see CLUBS, ROMAN). *See also* AERARIUM.

Livy; Dion. Hal.; Cicero, *Verrines*, 2 and 5. 14. G. De Sanctis on origins, *Riv. Fil.* 1932, 433 ff. Mommsen, *Röm. Staatsr.* ii³. 470 f. H. Siber, *Römisches Verfassungsrecht* (1952), 200 ff.; Broughton, *MRR*. A. N. S.-W.

**AEDITUUS** (older **Aeditumus**), properly the keeper or sacristan of a consecrated building, *aedes sacra*. In practice two kinds of official were so named, (*a*) a man of rank and standing, who was responsible for the upkeep of the building, (*b*) a servant, often a slave, who did the actual work of cleaning, etc.

Marquardt–Wissowa, *Röm. Staatsverw.* (1881–5), iii². 214 ff.; Latte, *RR* 410. H. J. R.

**AËDON** (Ἀηδών), in mythology, daughter of Pandareos, the son of Hermes and Merope. She married Zethus and had two children, Itylus and Neïs. Envying Niobe (q.v.), Amphion's wife, for her many children, she planned to kill them, or one of them, at night; but Itylus was sleeping in the same room as they and she mistook the bed and so killed him. In her grief she prayed to be changed from human form, and became a nightingale (ἀηδών).

Schol. *Od.* 19. 518. Rose, *Handb. Gk. Myth.* 282 and 340B. H. J. R.

**AEDUI**, a Gallic tribe which occupied most of modern Burgundy. They appealed to Rome against the Arverni and Allobroges (121 B.C.) and received the title of *fratres consanguineique*. During the Gallic War they gave valuable though not whole-hearted support to Caesar, and when they finally joined Vercingetorix in 52 their support was lukewarm. Under the Empire they became a *civitas foederata*, and were the first tribe to furnish Roman senators. *Duoviri* replaced the *Vergobretus* as magistrates, and the hill-fort Bibracte was abandoned for Augustodunum (c. 12 B.C.). They took part unsuccessfully in the rebellions of Sacrovir (A.D. 21) and Vindex (68). In the third century the region suffered heavily from civil war and barbarian invasion; the panegyrist Eumenius celebrates the relief measures of Constantius and Constantine.

*CIL* xiii. 400. O. Hirschfeld, *Kl. Schr.* (1913), 186 ff.; C. Jullian, *Hist. de la Gaule* (1907–26), iii. 535 ff.; vi. 423 ff. C. E. S.

**AEGAE** (*Vodena*, now *Edessa*), early capital of Macedon, commanding the route from the Macedonian plain to upper western Macedonia. Formerly called Edessa, it formed a base for the Macedonian conquest of the coastal plain c. 640 B.C., was renamed Aegae, and remained the cult-centre of the royal house even after Archelaus moved the court to Pella (q.v.). Its strong position is illustrated in S. Casson, *Macedonia, Thrace, and Illyria* (1926), fig. 69. N. G. L. H.

**AEGEAN SEA**, between Greece and Asia Minor. To it the modern name Archipelago was originally applied, but the ancient Greeks derived the name Aegean variously from Theseus' father Aegeus (q.v.), who drowned himself in it; from Aegea, Amazonian queen, who was drowned in it; from Aegae city. They subdivided it into *Thracian*, along Thrace and Macedonia to the north coast of Euboea; *Myrtoan*, south of Euboea, Attica, Argolis, west of the Cyclades; *Icarian*, along (Asiatic) coasts of Caria and Ionia; *Cretic*, north of Crete. Some, like Strabo, treated the last three as separate, ending the Aegean at Sunium in Attica. The whole Aegean contains many islands in three groups: along the Asiatic coast, including Lesbos, Chios, Samos, Rhodes; a small group off Thessaly; Euboea and the Cyclades, a continuation or reappearance of the mountains of the Greek mainland.

Cary, *Geographic Background*, chs. 1. and 2. E. H. W.

**AEGEUS** (Αἰγεύς), almost certainly a humanization of Poseidon of Aegae; hence Theseus (q.v.) is sometimes called his son, sometimes Poseidon's. In legend, however, he is a king of Athens, son (usually) of Pandion and Pylia, daughter of Pylas, king of Megara. Born in Megara, he afterwards conquered Attica. Probably Athenian claims to the Megarid in historical times have much to do with this and similar legends. Having no children, he consulted Delphi, and was told in riddling phraseology to be continent till he reached home (Eur. *Med.* 679, and schol.), but did not understand, and begat Theseus on Aethra, daughter of Pittheus, king of Troezen, who understood the oracle and purposely brought it to pass that the divinely ordained child should be his grandson. Later, he gave Medea a refuge on her flight from Corinth (see MEDEA), and married her; their son was Medus (Hyg. *Fab.* 26. 1, from some Alexandrian source). On her trying to poison Theseus when he arrived in Athens, Aegeus drove her out (different account in Hyginus, ibid. 2). Theseus freed him from the attacks of Pallas and his fifty sons, who were trying to overthrow him, and afterwards left for Crete to meet the Minotaur (see MINOS). On returning, however, he forgot to change the black sails of his ship, and Aegeus, seeing them and thinking his son dead, killed himself by leaping off the Acropolis or into the sea, hence, in this account (but see preceding article), called the Aegean (Αἰγαῖον πέλαγος) after him. See, for connected accounts, Plutarch, *Theseus*, and Apollod. 3. 206 ff.

H. J. R.

**AEGIMIUS**, a legendary king, son (or father, schol. Pind. *Pyth.* 1. 121) of Dorus, eponym of the Dorians. Being attacked by the Centaurs, he asked Heracles to help him, and in gratitude for his aid adopted Hyllus (q.v.) and made him joint heir with his own sons.

**AEGINA**, an island in the Saronic Gulf, inhabited from late neolithic times and in contact with Minoan Crete and Mycenae. It was conquered c. 1100 B.C. by the Dorians under Deiphontes (q.v.), son-in-law of Temenus of Argos. Early in the seventh century (probably) it fell to the Argive tyrant Pheidon (q.v.) and struck the first coins of Greece proper, the long-lived silver 'tortoises'. Throughout the archaic period it was a naval power, often in rivalry with Samos (war with King Amphicrates; voyages of Sostratus of Aegina and Colaeus of Samos; establishments at Naucratis (q.v.); attack c. 520 on Samians settled in Crete).

In 506 began the long struggle with Athens. The Athenian fleet that won Salamis was raised ostensibly against the Aeginetans who had 'medized' in 491; but at Artemisium, Salamis, and Plataea they fought on the Greek side, winning the prize for valour and much besides. To this period belongs the temple of Aphaea (q.v.) with its splendid sculptures now in Munich.

When Athens founded the Delian League (q.v.), Aegina may have become a member, but war broke out between Athens and Aegina in 459. A decisive naval defeat in 459 led to the capture of the 'eyesore of the Piraeus' and its forced inclusion in the Delian League (458), to which it paid 30 talents yearly. The Aeginetans helped to foment the Peloponnesian War, and on its outbreak were expelled from their island, which was occupied by Athenian cleruchs, among them the families of Aristophanes and Plato. Restored by Lysander in 405 they received a Spartan harmost, and till its bequest to Rome by Attalus of Pergamum the island played a minor, mainly passive, role. Its supreme glory is to have inspired some of Pindar's greatest poetry, including the eighth Pythian.

IG i². 191 f.; POxy v. 842, cols. 1, 2, 3. A. Furtwängler and others, Heiligtum der Aphaia (1906); G. Welter, Aegina (1938, with good bibliography). A. Andrewes, 'Athens and Aegina, 510–480 B.C.', BSA 1936–7, 1 f.; N. G. L. Hammond, 'The War between Athens and Aegina c. 505–481 B.C., Hist. 1955, 406 f.; D. M. MacDowell, 'Aegina and the Delian League', JHS 1960, 118 f.    P. N. U.; N. G. L. H.

**AEGIS,** attribute of Zeus and Athena, usually represented as a goatskin. When Zeus shakes the aegis (Il. 17. 593 ff.) a thunder-storm ensues and he puts fear into the hearts of Achaeans. Athena and Apollo use the aegis to disperse enemies and to protect friends (Il. 15. 229, 307; 21. 400).

The aegis made by Hephaestus (Il. 15. 307 ff.) for Zeus is indestructible, resisting even lightning (Il. 21. 400). That of Athena (Il. 5. 738) is surrounded by Fear, Fight, Force, and Pursuit, and has a Gorgon-head in the centre. In art the aegis appears as an attribute of Athena from mid sixth century on (A. Rumpf, Chalkidische Vasen (1927), 143). It is shown as a short cloak worn over the shoulders or, like a shield, over the left arm; it is bordered with snakes and has often the head of Gorgo in the centre. It is assumed that originally the aegis was conceived as a storm-cloud (Aesch. Cho. 585) and came to be regarded as a goatskin because of the similarity of words αἴξ goat and καταιγίς hurricane.

Dar.-Sag. s.v.; N. Prins, De Oorspronkelijke Beteekenis van de Aegis (1931); Cook, Zeus iii. 837.    G. M. A. H.

**AEGISTHUS,** in mythology, surviving son of Thyestes (see ATREUS; so Aesch. Ag. 1605); but a version apparently Sophoclean (see Dio Chrys. 66. 6; cf. Apollod. Epit. 2. 14; Hyg. Fab. 87 and 88. 3–4) makes him the incestuous offspring of Thyestes and his daughter Pelopia after the murder of the elder sons. His name suggesting the word αἴξ, a story is told, in connexion with that mentioned above, that he was exposed and fed by a she-goat (Hyg. ibid. and 252). When adult, he returned to Argos to avenge his father. All this is post-Homeric; the Odyssey (3. 517 ff.) evidently thinks of him as a baron having an estate near the domains of Agamemnon, and gives no reason for the quarrel except Aegisthus' intrigue with Clytemnestra (q.v.; cf. 1. 35 ff.). For his murder of Agamemnon and the revenge taken by Orestes, see the appropriate articles.

The death of Aegisthus is a favourite subject in archaic and classical art (Brommer, Vasenlisten², 321 f.; and see under CLYTEMNESTRA, ORESTES).    H. J. R.; C. M. R.

**AEGRITUDO PERDICAE,** an anonymous Latin epyllion narrating the calamitous love of Perdicas for his mother, Castalia. Its ascription to Dracontius (q.v.) is unwarrantable, though it almost certainly belongs to his period, and probably to Africa.

TEXTS: Riese, Anth. Lat. ii² (1906), no. 808; PLM v². 238.    A. H.-W.

**AELIANUS (1),** CLAUDIUS (c. A.D. 170–235), generally known as 'Aelian', of Praeneste, where he was pontifex. He taught rhetoric in Rome, but later confined himself to writing. Extant works: Π. ζῴων ἰδιότητος (De Natura Animalium), a collection of excerpts and anecdotes of a

paradoxical or moralizing character, concerned chiefly with the animal world; Ποικίλη ἱστορία (Varia Historia), a similar collection dealing with human life and history; Ἐπιστολαὶ ἀγροικικαί, short stylistic exercises in letter form. Fragments exist, chiefly in the Suda, of Π. προνοίας and Π. θείων ἐναργειῶν, collections designed to illustrate the workings of providence and divine justice.

Aelian's philosophical ideas, notably that of universal reason as manifested in the animal creation, derive from Stoicism; he is especially bitter against the Epicureans. His excerpts, largely derived from intermediate sources (Sostratus, Alexander of Myndos, Pamphilus, etc.), often supplement our knowledge of earlier writers. He enjoyed a reputation for Attic purity of diction (Suda, Philostratus); he affects Herodotean simplicity (ἀφέλεια) and lack of arrangement. His works enjoyed great subsequent popularity, and were much drawn upon by Christian writers. He is probably to be distinguished from the author of a Tactica (see article below).

Suda; Philostr. VS 2. 31. Editions: R. Hercher 1858 (preface); id. (Teubner) 1864; De Nat. An.: A. F. Scholfield (Loeb, 1958–9). Criticism: W. Schmid, Atticismus (1889) iii. 1 f. (language); M. Wellmann, Hermes 1891, 1892, 1896, 1916 (sources of Π. ζ. ἰ.); F. Rudolph, Leipz. Stud. 1884 (sources of Π. l.).    W. M. E.

**AELIANUS (2),** author of a Tactica (in Greek), probably in Trajan's reign, on the long-dead Macedonian phalanx, mostly taken from Asclepiodotus (q.v.). Its value is slight.

TEXT: H. Köchly and W. Rustow, Griechische Kriegsschriftsteller (1855).

**AELIUS (1,** PW 105**) PAETUS CATUS,** SEXTUS (cos. 198 B.C.), a Roman jurist, and author of the Tripertita, so called because it contained first the law of the XII Tables, then an account of its development by legal interpretation, and finally the legis actiones. Pomponius (q.v. 6) says of it: 'ueluti cunabula iuris continet'. He also mentions a collection of legis actiones (Ius Aelianum) which, he says, superseded the Ius Flavianum (see FLAVIUS 1). This may be identical with the third part of the Tripertita. No fragment of either work survives.    A. B.; B. N.

**AELIUS (2),** LUCIUS, born probably c. A.D. 100, had the same name, L. Ceionius (PW 7) Commodus, as his father. He became praetor in 130, cos. I in 136, and was adopted (as 'L. Aelius Caesar') later in 136 (CIL vi, 10242) by Hadrian as his successor. Aelius received the tribunicia potestas in Dec. 136 and was cos. II in 137. Elegant, luxurious, and consumptive, he nevertheless governed the two Pannonias well (136–7). He died on 1 Jan. 138, honoured but not deified.

S.H.A. Hadr. and Ael.; Dio Cassius bk. 69; Diz. Epigr. iii. 638 ff.; Lambrechts, Sénat, no. 36; Strack, Reichsprägung, ii. 166 ff.; B.M. Coins, Rom. Emp. iii. J. Carcopino, Rev. Ét. Anc. 1940, 284 ff.; Grénade, Rev. Ét. Anc. 1950, 258 ff.; R. Syme, Athenaeum 1952, 306 ff.; Tacitus ii. 601. See also under HADRIAN and VERUS, LUCIUS.    C. H. V. S.; M. H.

**AELIUS (3,** PW 117**) PROMOTUS,** physician from Alexandria, probably belonging to the period between Hadrian and Pertinax (A.D. 138–93). He wrote a book on curative methods called Δυναμερόν, sections of which remain.

**AEMILIANUS,** MARCUS AEMILIUS (PW 24), Emperor A.D. 253. His patria was Djerba. While governor of Moesia he repelled a Gothic invasion and was saluted Emperor by his troops in opposition to Trebonianus Gallus (253). His reign lasted only three months. When news reached Rome that Valerian had been proclaimed Emperor, Aemilianus was assassinated by his own soldiers.

G. M. Bersanetti, Riv. Fil. 1948, 257 ff.    H. M. D. P.; B. H. W

**AENEAS (1)** (Αἰνείας or Αἰνέας), son of Anchises and the goddess Aphrodite, a famous Trojan leader in Homer's

*Iliad* and the hero of Virgil's *Aeneid*. In the *Iliad* he is said to have been respected equally with Hector (5. 467), and honoured like a god (11. 58). He fought against Diomede (bk. 5), Idomeneus (bk. 13), and Achilles himself (bk. 20). His actions are not strikingly heroic, and more than once he is protected or rescued by one of the gods, to whom he exhibits marked piety (20. 298, 347). Aeneas was descended from the younger branch of the Trojan royal house (20. 230 ff.), and had a grudge against Priam, who came of the elder branch, for not giving him his due (13. 460). But he himself hoped to succeed to the kingship (20. 180), and Poseidon prophesies that he and his descendants will rule over the Trojans (20. 307). Aeneas is thus the one Trojan hero who has a definite future before him.

From this hint tradition developed the legend of his flight from Troy with his father Anchises (q.v.), his son Ascanius (q.v.), and his ancestral gods (*see* PENATES) (Xen. *Cyn.* 1. 15), and the legend of his subsequent wanderings. Arctinus represents him as retiring to Mt. Ida, and afterwards he was thought to have visited or founded many places on the mainland of Greece and elsewhere, which either had names resembling his own, like Ainos in Thrace and Aineia in Chalcidice, or possessed temples of Aphrodite, often with the cult title Αἰνείας, such as those in Leucas, at Actium, and at Elymus in Sicily. This story of his wanderings was developed with the addition of other places, such as Delos and Crete, by later writers, especially by Hellanicus, Timaeus, and Dionysius of Halicarnassus. The association with Sicily acted as a stepping-stone both to Rome and to Carthage. Stesichorus may have asserted that Aeneas reached 'Hesperia', but the story that he came to Latium appears first in Hellanicus. It became popular after the wars with Greece, when patriotism urged the Romans to seek a founder within the cycle of Greek legend, but among the enemies of Greece. Among Roman writers this development is found in Naevius and Ennius, in Q. Fabius Pictor and later historians, including Livy. Considerations of chronology later made Aeneas the founder, not of Rome itself, but of Lavinium (q.v.), the head of the Latin League. The connexion of Aeneas with Carthage was known to Varro, and there is a possible earlier reference to the meeting of Aeneas and Dido in a fragment of Naevius (q.v.). Archaeological evidence shows that the legend of Aeneas was known in Etruria from the end of the sixth century B.C.

Virgil thus inherited a flat and disconnected story of Aeneas' wanderings, a legend of his association with the foundation of Rome, and a hero with no definite characteristics, except a scrupulous piety. Out of this material he constructed the epic of the *Aeneid*. The legends of the wanderings he wisely telescoped into the third book, while the association with Rome is developed into the great national theme of the poem. Virgil's portrait of Aeneas is based on the piety ascribed to him by Homer, but this is amplified in the full sense of the Roman *pietas* into a devotion to his father, to his mother and the gods in general, and to the great destiny of Rome.

The *Aeneid* ends with the slaying of Turnus by Aeneas, but other writers tell of his meeting with Dido's sister, Anna, on the banks of the Numicius (Ov. *Fasti* 3. 601 ff.) and of his purification in the river and his assumption to heaven with the title of Indiges (Ov. *Met.* 14. 581 ff.).

Aeneas' flight from Troy, with Anchises on his back and Ascanius at his side, is shown in late archaic and early classical vase-paintings of the sack of Troy; also on a late sixth-century coin of Aeneia (Macedonia); also on scarabs and as terracottas of *c.* 500 B.C. in Etruria. Combats with Aias and Diomedes are also found (Brommer, *Vasenlisten*[2], 273 f., 278, 287).

J. Perret, *Les Origines de la légende troyenne de Rome* (1942); F. Bömer, *Rom und Troia* (1951); E. D. Phillips, *JHS* 1953, 66 f.;

R. D. Williams, *Vergili Aeneidos liber tertius* (1962), 3 ff; Ogilvie, *Comm. Livy. 1–5*, 33 (Aeneas in Etruria), 39 f. (Lavinium). Cf. also S. Weinstock, *JRS* 1960, 114 ff. and A. Alföldi, *Early Rome and the Latins*, 250 ff., tor Lavinium; K. Schauenburg *Gymnasium* 1960 176 ff., for Aeneas and Rome.                          C. B.; C. M. R

**AENEAS** (2), commonly called *Tacticus*, probably the Aeneas of Stymphalus who was general of the Arcadian Confederacy in 367 B.C., wrote several military treatises (epitomized later for Pyrrhus), of which the one on the defence of fortified positions, probably written soon after 357, has survived. As advice to the defenders of a besieged town it is rather elementary, though it contains interesting details; but its real value is the light it throws on social and political conditions in early fourth-century Greece, for it is assumed throughout that the chief danger to the defence is not so much the enemy without the wall as the opposing faction within, who will betray the city if they can. Philologically, the work, as an early non-Attic document, has some interest for the study of the growth of the Hellenistic *Koine*.

Illinois Greek Club, *Aeneas Tacticus* (Loeb, 1923); L. W. Hunter, *Aineiou Poliorketika* (1927); D. Barends, *Lexicon Aineium* (1955), with Bibliography.                                    W. W. T.

**AENESIDEMUS** of Cnossos, Sceptic, probably of the Ciceronian period. Philo seems to have borrowed from him an account of the τρόποι τῆς ἐποχῆς (grounds of suspense of judgement). Works: Πυρρώνειοι λόγοι, Ὑποτύπωσις εἰς τὰ Πυρρώνεια, Κατὰ σοφίας, Περὶ ζητήσεως, Πρώτη εἰσαγωγή. His aim was to restore the sceptical character which the teaching of the Academy had under Antiochus' influence lost. Diogenes Laertius (in the life of Pyrrhon) and Sextus Empiricus give many details of his teaching, which was substantially followed by Sextus himself. The τρόποι τῆς ἐποχῆς were directed against the reliability of the senses.                    W. D. R.

**AENIANES,** situated east of Dodona in the Homeric Catalogue (*Il.* 2. 749), moved probably through Cassopaea into the upper Spercheus valley, where their tribal state became a member of the ancient Amphictiony centred on Anthela (*see* AMPHICTIONIES). This state survived into Roman times.

P.-K. *GL* 1. 1. 242 f.; Hammond, *Epirus*, 375 f.          N. G. L. H.

**AENUS,** a flourishing Greek city, originally an Aeolic foundation (Hdt. 7. 58. 3), on the coast of Thrace (q.v.), 11 miles from Doriscus, on the east side of the mouth of the Hebrus (Alcaeus, fr. 29 Lobel); the modern *Enez* is on the site of the ancient city. Like Abdera (q.v.), Aenus owed its wealth to its geographical situation. Not only did it command the trade that descended the Hebrus valley, but also it provided an alternative route to the Bosporus and the Dardanelles for trade that wished to reach the Aegean from the Black Sea; merchandise could be disembarked at Odessus, sent overland to the Hebrus valley, and then down to Aenus. Aenus thus lay at the entrance to the natural route to the rich cornlands, ranches, forests, and fruit-producing regions of eastern and central Thrace. It also derived considerable revenue from its fisheries. Aenus was an Athenian tributary state contributing 12 talents to the Delian League in 454 B.C. The subsequent lowering of the tribute of Aenus was due partly to the rise of the Odrysian power (*see* THRACE), and partly to the Athenian development of the sea-route from the Black Sea, which diverted commerce from the land-route by the Hebrus valley. Possibly, after the rise of the Odrysian power, Aenus passed out of Athenian control, but this was later re-established; Aenus supplied peltasts at Pylos (q.v.) in 425 B.C., and was an ally of Athens in Sicily in 415 B.C. (Thuc. 4. 28. 4; 7. 57. 5). Between 341 and 185 B.C. Aenus passed through th nds of the Macedonian, Egyptian, and Pergamene ngs, until in 185 B.C. it was declared a 'free city' by e Romans (Pliny, *HN* 4. 43). The coin types of Aenus ached perfection in the third quarter of the fifth cenry B.C.

S. Casson, *Macedonia, Thrace and Illyria* (1926), esp. 255 ff.; Head, *st. Num.* 246 ff.; M. L. Strack and H. von Fritze, *Die Ant. inzen Nordgriechenlands* ii (1912), *Thrakien*, 1, 1; J. M. F. May, *nos, its History and Coinage*, 474–341 B.C. (1950). J. M. R. C.

**EOLIAE INSULAE,** the volcanic Aeolian Islands, miles north-east of Sicily, had a flourishing Neolithic lture based on the obsidian industry and well repented in the Diana plain and Castello (Lipari), a natural rtress with a succession of Neolithic, Bronze Age, reek, and Roman settlements. The islands took full mmercial advantage of their position between east and est in the Early Bronze Age (Capo Graziano culture): ported pottery (MH, LH I–II, Mycenaean IIIA 1 and has established the first absolute dates in the prestory of western Europe. Aegean (LH IIIA) contact ntinued in the Middle Bronze Age (Milazzese culture): ntact with the peninsular Apennine Culture agrees th the Liparus legend (Diod. Sic. 5. 7) and gave rise to e Late Bronze Age–Early Iron Age Ausonian culture, v.) with its parallels at Milazzo for the proto-Villanovan nfields of the mainland. The Cnidian-Rhodian colony Lipara was founded in 580–576 B.C., and conquered 252 by Rome; under the Empire it had the status of a hall provincial town with Roman citizenship. The ands produced obsidian, sulphur, alum, pumice, and ral.

*PW* s.v. Basileia, Didyme, Erikussa, Euonymos, Hiera (now lcano), Lipara, Meligunis, Phoenikussa, Strongyle (now Stromboli), termessa; L. Bernabò Brea, *Boll. d'Arte* 1951, 31 ff.; id. *Minos* 52, 5 ff.; id. *Sicily before the Greeks*[2] (1966); M. Cavalier, *Antiquity* 57, 9 ff.; Lord W. Taylour, *Mycenaean Pottery in Italy* (1958); Bernabò Brea and M. Cavalier, *Bull. Paletn. It.* 1956, 7 ff.; id. *eligunis–Lipara*, 2 vols. (1960, 1965); Dunbabin, *Western Greeks*, ex, s.v. Lipara. D. W. R. R.

**EOLIS,** the territory of the northernmost group of reek immigrants to the western coast of Asia Minor, tending from the entrance of the Hellespont to the outh of the Hermus—a linguistic and ethnological, not geographical, unit. Near the end of the second millenum B.C. the Aeolians, deriving from Boeotia and hessaly, planted their first settlements in Lesbos, and ence expanded northwards to Tenedos, and along the ainland coast to the east and south. The Troad was cupied much later (perhaps in the seventh century B.C.) ' secondary colonization, principally from Lesbos. here must have been considerable racial fusion with the cal barbarian inhabitants. Most of the Aeolian cities rived such prosperity as they enjoyed primarily from riculture, commerce being of minor importance in esbos. The Aeolian settlements in the south were ouped together in a league, whose origin was probably ligious. Its members were Aegae, Aegirusa, Cilla, Cyme, ryneum (where the temple of Apollo was perhaps the ntral sanctuary of the league), Larissa, Myrina, Neonchos, Pitane, Smyrna (later resettled by Ionians), and emnos. The most important cities in the north were: tandros, Assos, Cebren, Gargara, Ilium, Neandria, and epsis.

J. M. Cook, *The Greeks in Ionia and the East* (1962). D. E. W. W.

**EOLUS,** (1) the ruler of the winds (perhaps by derivan 'the changeable'); in *Od.* 10. 2 ff. a mortal, son of ppotes; he lives in Aeolia, a floating island, with his sons and six daughters, who have married one another; can tie up the winds in a sack to prevent them blowing. *Aen.* 1. 51 ff. he is a minor god and keeps the winds in

a cave on Aeolia. Sometimes confused with (2) a son of Hellen (q.v.), eponym of the Aeolians and the Aeolidae:

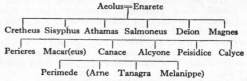

Canace killed herself, or was killed by her father, because of incest with Macareus (Ov. *Her.* 11). Arne, or Melanippe, became by Poseidon mother of (3), another ancestor of the Aeolians; see Hyg. *Fab.* 186 and Rose ad loc.; Euripides, frags. of Μελανίππη ἡ δεσμῶτις and *M.* ἡ σοφή. H. J. R.

**AEPYTUS,** in mythology, son of Cresphontes, king of Messenia, also called Cresphontes (see *TGF* 497) and Telephontes (Hyg. *Fab.* 137. 3). Fleeing, as a child, when his father was killed by Polyphontes, he returned with false news of his own murder and, after narrowly escaping death from his mother Merope, killed Polyphontes, thus becoming king. H. J. R.

**AEQUI,** primitive Italic tribe inhabiting the valleys of the Himella, Tolenus, and upper Anio (q.v.); their dialect probably resembled Oscan (q.v.). Expanding from the highlands towards Latium, by 500 B.C. they held the mountains behind Tibur and Praeneste (qq.v.), and for seventy years, despite their small numbers (Livy 6. 12), they proved even tougher enemies to the Hernici, Latins, and Romans (qq.v.) than their Volscian allies. They established themselves on the Alban Hills and were not expelled until 431 (*see* ALGIDUS). Thereafter, however, Aequi are only casually mentioned until 304, when they apparently occupied their original central Italian area. Rome now almost exterminated them; she established Latin colonies at Carsioli and Alba Fucens (qq.v.), gave the surviving Aequi *civitas sine suffragio* and rapidly romanized them (Livy 9. 45; 10. 1. 9). The Aequian nation thus disappeared, although a *municipium Aequiculorum sive Aequiculanorum* is still recorded after 90 B.C. (Pliny, *HN* 3. 106); its name survives in the district Cicolano north of the Fucine Lake. Their name (*aequi*) gave rise to the tale that the Aequi invented the *ius fetiale* (Livy 1. 32).

G. Devoto, *Gli antichi Italici* (1951), 127 ff. E. T. S.

**AERARII,** a class of Roman citizens who had incurred the censors' reproof and condemnation for some moral or other misbehaviour. They were condemned to pay *tributum* at a higher rate than other citizens (*aerarii* is obviously connected with *aes*). Such an individual, *aerarius factus*, might receive additional punishment, e.g. be *tribu motus* (after 304 B.C. this involved relegation to one of the four urban tribes), but it has been clearly demonstrated by Fraccaro that *aerarium facere* is not identical with *tribu movere*.

The origin of the custom is obscure. Mommsen's theory, though now discredited, has enjoyed wide acceptance. He argued that an *aerarius* originally had no landed property and therefore was not registered in any Servian tribe; he was exempted from voting and military service, but had to pay a poll-tax in proportion to his means. Fraccaro, however, has clearly demonstrated that an *aerarius* should not be opposed to a *tribulus* and that *all* citizens were members of tribes from the beginning.

Mommsen, *Röm. Staatsr.* ii[2], 392 ff. A. H. J. Greenidge, *Infamia* (1894), applied *aerarius* to the centuries instead of the tribes. P. Fraccaro, *Athenaeum* 1933, 150 ff. (= *Opuscula* ii. 149 ff.). Cf. Taylor, *Voting Districts*, 10 f. H. H. S.

**AERARIUM,** derived from *aes*, denotes 'treasury'. The main *aerarium* of Rome was the *aerarium Saturni*, so called from the temple below the Capitol, in which it was placed. Here were kept state documents, both financial and non-financial (including *leges* and *senatus consulta* which were not valid until lodged there), and the state treasure, originally mainly of bronze, *aes* (hence the name), but including also ingots of gold and silver and other valuables. The *tabularium* (q.v.) was built near it in 78 B.C.

The *aerarium* was controlled by the quaestors under the general supervision of the Senate, with a subordinate staff of *scribae*, *viatores*, etc. The *tribuni aerarii* (q.v.), men of a property-class a little below the knights, were probably concerned with making payments from the tribes into the treasury. The *aerarium sanctius* was a special reserve, fed by the 5 per cent tax on emancipations. Treasure was withdrawn from it in 209 B.C. and on other occasions. Caesar in 49 B.C. insisted on seizing the reserve for his own uses.

Caesar placed two aediles in charge of the *aerarium*, Augustus two *praefecti* (28 B.C.) and then two praetors (23). Claudius (A.D. 44) placed it again under the quaestors, Nero, finally, in A.D. 56 under two *praefecti*. These officials are last attested in the mid fourth century. In the earlier Empire at least the *aerarium* remained the official repository for state documents and cash; payments from it could be ordered by the Senate and, in practice, by the Emperor. *Bona caduca*, *bona damnatorum*, and other revenues were increasingly diverted to the *fiscus* (q.v.). The details of this process, especially as regards the provincial *tributum* (q.v.), remain obscure.

The *aerarium militare* was founded by Augustus in A.D. 6 to provide for the pensioning of discharged soldiers. Augustus provided for it a capital sum of 170,000,000 sesterces from his own funds and an income from the *centesima rerum venalium* and the *vicesima hereditatum* (*see* VECTIGAL). It was administered by three ex-praetors (*praefecti aerarii militaris*), at first chosen by lot, later by the Emperor.

O. Hirschfeld, *Die kaiserlichen Verwaltungsbeamten* (1905), 13 f.; A. H. M. Jones, *JRS* 1950, 22 ff.; F. Millar, *JRS* 1964, 33 ff.
H. M.; F. G. B. M.

**AES,** bronze, i.e. copper, as generally used with alloy of tin, etc.

*Aes*, by itself, can denote (1) a document recorded in bronze, e.g. the ground-plan of a colony, (2) 'stipendium', 'military pay', and from that 'military service', (3) the bronze list of recipients of free corn (*aere incisi*). *Aes*, with explanatory adjectives, has a wide range of uses: thus *aes alienum* (or *circumforaneum*) = 'debt', *aes multaticium* = 'money raised by fines', *aes equestre* = the grant to the knight to buy his horses, *aes hordearium* = the allowance for the keep of the horses. *Aes et libra* represented the old method of purchase, by touching the scales with a piece of bronze.

All these uses depend on the fact that bronze was the first metal employed by the Romans to measure values (*see* COINAGE, ROMAN). Most important is the reckoning with cardinal numbers and the genitive *aeris*, representing originally pounds of bronze, but, subsequently, perhaps, smaller amounts, as the *aes* fell from the full pound to two ounces, one ounce, a half, and even a quarter. The characteristic meaning, however, seems to be the original, 'pounds', so that, even in later days, when the silver *sestertius* was the unit of reckoning, it was equated to the old pound of bronze. When Gaius gives the limit fixed by the *Lex Voconia* as 100,000 *aeris*, he does not mean anything different from the 100,000 *sestertii* recorded by Dio Cassius.

H. Mattingly, 'Aes and Pecunia', *Num. Chron.* 1943, 21 ff.
H. M.

**AESCHINES** (1) (*c.* 397–*c.* 322 B.C.). Athenian ora whose exchanges with Demosthenes (q.v. 2) in the cou in 343 and 330 provide a large part of the evidence for relations of Athens and Macedon in the 340s and 330s. His origins were sufficiently obscure to all Demosthenes' invention full play. He probably did receive the usual formal training in rhetoric, but a hoplite service of some distinction in the 360s and ea 350s, and a period as an actor, he embarked on a pul career as a supporter first briefly of Aristophon (q and then of Eubulus (q.v. 1), during whose supervisior the city's finances Aeschines' brother, Aphobetus, wa Theoric Commissioner (*see* THEORIKA). In 347/6 b Aeschines and Demosthenes were members of the bo (q.v.) and their disagreements led to sixteen years enmity. Early in 346 (though many have dated the af to 348/7) when alarming news reached Athens of the tension of Macedonian influence to Arcadia, Eubu supported by Aeschines took the lead in urging Athen protest to Arcadia and to seek to organize a Comm Peace, which would provide for common action agai aggressors and so make it unnecessary for any state seek Macedonian help. Aeschines was sent on an emba to Megalopolis (q.v.) where he sought to dissuade assembly of the Arcadians from dealings with Phi Whether through the indifference of the Greek states through the new threat to Greece caused by the refusa the Phocian tyrant, Phalaecus, to permit access to Therm pylae (q.v.), the key-point for the defence of Greece, initiative of Eubulus and Aeschines proved abortive. embassy of ten, including Aeschines and Demosther was hastily sent to negotiate peace terms with Phi Their return to the city was closely followed by a Ma donian embassy, and on the 18th and 19th Elapheboli when the peace was debated and voted, Aeschines pla a notable if ineffectual part. Demosthenes, realizing t peace was essential and that the only form of peace wh Philip would accept was a plain alliance with Ath and her allies of the Second Athenian League (q. made himself responsible for getting the decree of Phi crates (q.v.) passed: Aeschines strove without success a Common Peace open to all the Greeks. The ten amba adors then set off again to secure Philip's oath to treaty which he did not render until his forces were position to attack Phocis. When the ambassadors returr with this alarming news, it was decided in the *boule* recommend an expedition to save Phocis, but by r Skirophorion, when the people met, it was known t Philip had occupied Thermopylae; Demosthenes' p posal was not even read out and he was himself shou down. Aeschines then made a speech, which Dem thenes chose to regard as proof that Aeschines had b won over by Macedonian bribery. The truth was proba far different; since Phocis could not be saved, Aeschi sought to reconcile the Athenians to the fact by report vague suggestions of Macedonian proposals for cent Greece which were very much what Athens was seeki

From that day Demosthenes was implacably oppo to Aeschines as well as determined to destroy the Pea while Aeschines was gradually won over to support it a seek its extension into a Common Peace. In 346/5 Dem thenes with the support of Timarchus began a prose tion of Aeschines for his part in the peace negotiatio Aeschines replied by charging Timarchus with breach the law forbidding those whose misconduct was not ious from addressing the assembly; the *Against Timarc* was successful and Demosthenes was forced to recogn that the time was not ripe to attack Aeschines. By mid the mood of Athens had clearly begun to change; early the year Philocrates had been successfully prosecuted Hyperides (q.v.) and in the *de Falsa Legatione* Den sthenes attacked Aeschines, the advocate of mer amending a discredited peace, as if he had been the orator really responsible in 346 for Athens' accepting the Peace. Aeschines replied in a speech of the same title and, supported by Eubulus and Phocion (q.v.), was narrowly acquitted. Aeschines continued to have some influence in the assembly, and in 340/39 was sent as one of Athens' representatives to the Amphictionic Council (*see* AMPHICTIONIES), on which occasion he appears to have displayed a serious lack of judgement in relation to the affairs of central Greece: at a time when the war against Philip had recommenced and there was a clear need to avoid exacerbating the divisions of Greece, Aeschines replied to Locrian charges against Athens with such a vigorous attack on the conduct of the Amphissans that hostilities began and Philip was the more easily able to intervene.

Aeschines was a member of the embassy sent to negotiate with Philip after Chaeronea, but from then on he withdrew from politics only to re-emerge on two occasions when circumstances seemed favourable for an attack on Demosthenes. The first was in early 336 when Ctesiphon proposed that Demosthenes should be crowned in the theatre at the Dionysia (q.v.) for the excellence of his services to the city: earlier Demosthenes had been similarly honoured without protest but, at a time when Demosthenes' gloomy predictions after Chaeronea seemed mocked by the opening of the Macedonian invasion of Persia, Aeschines indicted the decree under the Graphe Paranomon (q.v.). However, the murder of Philip made the future too uncertain for Aeschines to be confident of success, and he decided not to proceed with the indictment for the moment. In 330 after the defeat of Persia at Gaugamela and the failure of Agis' revolt, which Demosthenes had chosen not to support, Athens was in almost complete isolation with no prospect of liberation from Macedon, and Aeschines thought the moment suitable for him to proceed with his prosecution of Ctesiphon. In the *Against Ctesiphon*, after adducing minor, if perhaps valid, legalistic considerations concerning the details of the original decree, he reviewed the career of Demosthenes, somewhat selectively, and sought to show that Demosthenes was unworthy of the crown. In the *de Corona* Demosthenes replied with all the devastating effect that his great rhetorical gifts could command, and Aeschines failed to secure the necessary fifth of the jury's votes to save him from a fine and the limitation of the right to prosecute. He chose to retire from Athens to Rhodes, where he taught rhetoric.

The supremacy of Demosthenes as an orator has to a large extent beguiled posterity into the opinion that he alone fully appreciated the menace of Macedon and correctly diagnosed the causes of Philip's success, and Aeschines has been represented as an opportunist with little judgement and less principle. In fact, there was no obvious way of saving Athens and Greece, and it is probable that Aeschines no less than Demosthenes sought to maintain his city's power and independence.

SPEECHES. The only genuine speeches of Aeschines known to the critics of the Roman period were the three that we have: a fourth, concerning Delos, was rejected by Caecilius (q.v.4). Aeschines was a man of dignified presence and fine voice, who deprecated the use of extravagant gestures by an orator, preferring a statuesque pose. Proud of his education, he displays it by frequent quotation of poetry. In the use of historical argument he cannot compare with Demosthenes, but in a battle of wits he more than holds his own. His vocabulary is simple but effective, though occasional obscurities may be found in his sentences. Ancient critics ranked him lower than he deserves; the fact is that he was not aiming at literary perfection; his object was to produce a powerful effect on his audiences, and he was justified by the result.

For general bibliography, *see* ATTIC ORATORS and DEMOSTHENES (2).

Text: Blass (Teubner, 1908). Text and translation: Adams (Loeb); Martin and Budé (Budé). Index: S. Preuss (1896). For complete Scholia see 1865 Teubner edition of Aeschines (ed. F. Schultz).

G. L. C.

**AESCHINES (2) SOCRATICUS** (4th c. B.C.), of the Athenian deme Sphettus, one of Socrates' most devoted adherents, was present at his master's condemnation and death. He founded no school of philosophy, but is said to have had Xenocrates as a pupil. He also wrote speeches for the lawcourts, and taught oratory. He fell into great poverty, but found a refuge at the court of Syracuse; whether in the time of Dionysius I or in that of Dionysius II (i.e. after 368) is not known; he returned to Athens after the expulsion of Dionysius II in 356. He is best known as the author of Socratic dialogues which were highly esteemed for their style and their faithfulness to Socrates' character and way of speaking. Those which were pretty certainly genuine are Μιλτιάδης, Καλλίας, Ἀξίοχος, Ἀσπασία, Ἀλκιβιάδης, Τηλαύγης, Ῥίνων; seven others passed under his name, but were judged by antiquity not to have the genuine Socratic character.

Ed. H. Dittmar (1912). More fragments of the Ἀλκιβιάδης in POxy. xiii. 88–94. W. D. R.

**AESCHYLUS.** (*See also* TRAGEDY.)

I. LIFE (525/4–456 B.C.)

Aeschylus, son of Euphorion of Eleusis, a member of a Eupatrid family, was born 525/4 B.C. (*Marm. Par.*) and witnessed the end of tyranny at Athens in his youth, and the growth of democracy throughout his life; he fought at Marathon (*Marm. Par.*), where his brother Cynegirus met a noble death, and probably at Salamis (schol. Aesch. *Pers.* 429; Pausanias (1 14. 5) adds Artemisium, and the *Life* Plataea, but these reports are much less certain). On the strength of Ar. *Ran.* 885–7 many have believed that he was initiated into the Mysteries. It is not clear what inference should be drawn from Aristotle's statement (*Eth. Nic.* 3. 1) that when accused of revealing the Mysteries, he replied that he did not know that what he said was something which might not be uttered. (Clement of Alexandria (*Strom.* 2. 461) says that he obtained acquittal by proving that he was not initiated; there is no agreement as to the plays in which the supposed revelation was made.) But his temperament was profoundly religious and intensely patriotic, and the effect upon it of the great events of his youth and manhood was seen in his assertion of the supremacy of Justice and his conception of Divine Government.

His first appearance in tragedy seems to have been very early in the fifth century (*Suda*, s.v. 'Pratinas'); his first victory was in 484 (*Marm. Par.*). Of his extant plays, the *Persae* was produced in 472, the *Septem contra Thebas* in 467, and the *Oresteia* (*Agamemnon*, *Choephoroe*, and *Eumenides* with the lost satyric *Proteus*) in 458. The *Supplices*, in view of certain archaic features, used commonly to be regarded as the earliest extant play, but in 1952 a fragmentary Hypothesis was published (*POxy.* 2256,3) from which it appears that the Danaid trilogy (see below, II) was produced in competition with Sophocles; there is an indication that 463 may be the date. The *Prometheus* was probably one of the latest plays (see below, II). Aeschylus seems to have paid two visits to Sicily, the first not many years after the foundation by Hieron in 476 of the new city of Aetna, the second after the production of the *Oresteia*. On the first visit he wrote a play (*Aetnae* or *Aetnaeae*) in honour of the new city, and gave a performance of the *Persae* at Hieron's request; the second ended with his death at Gela in 456. No better reason for these visits need be sought than the attraction of such a centre of literary men as Hieron's court; the causes imagined by old writers—his defeat by Sophocles in 468, or by Simonides in the composition of an epitaph on the heroes of Marathon, or the collapse of the wooden theatre during one of his plays, or the unpopularity caused by the terrifying effect of the *Eumenides*—may be dismissed. The epitaph on his monument at Gela, in which his fighting at Marathon is mentioned, but not his poetry, may (as Paus. 1. 14. 5 asserts) or may not have been composed by himself. After his death the Athenians decreed that anyone desiring to produce the works of Aeschylus should be granted a chorus by the archon (*Vit. Aesch.*). In view of this, not too much must be made of Aristophanes' allusion (*Ran.* 807) to disagreements between Aeschylus and the Athenians. The figures in the *Life* and in the *Suda* giving the number of his plays and victories are uncertain or corrupt. The catalogue of his plays in the Medicean MS. includes 72 titles, but omits 10 plays ascribed to him elsewhere, most of them probably correctly. The statement in the *Life* that his plays gained many victories after his death may well be true.

## II. Works

The trilogies or tetralogies of plays connected in subject which are recorded with complete or virtual certainty are (1) *Laius, Oedipus, Septem contra Thebas*, and the satyric *Sphinx*; (2) *Supplices, Aegyptii, Danaides*, and the satyric *Amymone* (*POxy.* 2256, 3); (3) *Oresteia* (see above); (4) *Λυκούργεια*, including *Edoni, Bassarides* or *Bassarai, Νεανίσκοι*, and the satyric *Lycurgus*. The *Prometheus Δεσμώτης* was followed by the *Prometheus Λυόμενος*; it is a matter of debate whether the *Prometheus Πυρφόρος* (if not satyric and identical with the *Prometheus Πυρκαεύς*) came first or third in the trilogy, if such a trilogy was ever completed. Certain peculiarities in the extant play have led a few scholars to doubt its Aeschylean authorship; others suppose that it was written for production in Sicily and perhaps not given its final form by Aeschylus. No connexion of subject can be traced between the plays produced in 472—*Phineus, Persae, Glaucus Potnieus*, and the satyric *Prometheus* (? *Πυρκαεύς*), but a number of titles have been grouped together with greater or less likelihood:

*Myrmidones, Nereides, Phryges*, or *Ἕκτορος Λύτρα*, with choruses attendant upon Achilles, Thetis, and Priam (*see* B. Snell, *Scenes from Greek Drama*, 1964).

*Ὅπλων Κρίσις, Threissae, Salaminiae*, the first turning upon the contest for the arms of Achilles, the second on the death of Ajax, the third perhaps on the misfortunes of Teucer.

*Argivi, Eleusinii* (which corresponded in subject to Euripides' *Supplices*), perhaps preceded by *Nemea*.

On the Argonautic story: *Argo, Lemnians, Hypsipyle, Cabiri*. (The statement in Ath. 10. 428 f. that Aeschylus brought drunkards on the stage for the first time in the *Cabiri* suggests a satyric play.)

*Semele* or *Ὑδροφόροι, Xantriae, Bacchae, Pentheus* (order and some titles uncertain), with the satyric *Διονύσου Τροφοί*. (See E. R. Dodds, *Euripides, Bacchae*[2] (1960), xxviii ff.; H. Lloyd-Jones, *Aeschylus* (Loeb) ii. 566 ff.)

The satyric *Δικτυουλκοί*, about the infant Perseus (for important papyrus fragments see Lloyd-Jones, op. cit. 531 ff.), may have followed *Polydectes* and perhaps *Phorcides*, though this too could be satyric.

Besides these, *Telephus* and *Mysi* probably belong to one group, *Memnon* and *Ψυχοστασία* to another, *Ixion* and *Perrhaebides* to a third. *Ψυχαγωγοί* (cf. Hom. *Od.* xi), *Penelope, Ὀστολόγοι*, may possibly have formed a tetralogy with the satyric *Circe* (Wilamowitz *Aeschylos Interpretationen*, 246, n. 1), but *Ὀστολόγοι* and *Ψυχαγωγοί* could themselves have been satyric.

The titles not enumerated above include: *Athamas*,

*Aetnae* or *Aetnaeae* (see Lloyd-Jones, op. cit. 593 ff.), *Alcmene, Atalante, Heliades, Heraclidae, Thalamopoioi, Ἱερεῖαι, Callisto, Cares* or *Europa* (for a papyrus fragment see Lloyd-Jones, op. cit. 599 ff.), *Cressae, Niobe* (for a papyrus fragment see Lloyd-Jones, op. cit. 556 ff.), *Palamedes, Propompoi, Toxotides* (on the death of Actaeon), *Philoctetes* (see Dio Chrys. 52), *Orithyia*; and the satyric plays *Θεωροὶ ἢ Ἰσθμιασταί* (for important papyrus fragments see Lloyd-Jones, op. cit. 541 ff.), *Cercyon, Κήρυκες, Leon, Sisyphus* (possibly two plays, *Σ. δραπέτης* and *Σ. πετροκυλιστής*).

## III. Character of his Work

It was Aeschylus who in all probability organized the external presentation of the drama on the lines which were to become traditional—the rich costumes, the decorative (though probably not in his time thick-soled) cothurni, the solemn dances. He seems to have had a special liking for gorgeous or impressive spectacular effects, such as were presented in the *Supplices* and *Eumenides* and, indeed, in nearly all his plays, though in a certain fondness for the barbaric (cf. Ar. *Ran.* 928 ff., 962 f.) and in some experiments in mechanical devices which may have bordered on the grotesque his successors did not follow him. The Egyptian and oriental dresses in the *Supplices* and *Persae* are of a piece with his enjoyment of the geography of strange lands. The Persian Wars affected him as they affected Herodotus. His love of long and magnificent descriptions—the battle of Salamis in the *Persae*, the armour of the heroes in the *Septem*, the fall of Troy in the *Agamemnon*—is characteristic, and in a trilogy there was room for it. In other respects, too, he was a master of impressiveness—the long silences of some of his characters, the recurrent refrains (*ἐφύμνια*) of many choral odes, the solemn grandeur of Darius in the *Persae*, the litany of invocation in the *Choephoroe*, are sufficient illustrations. It must also have been he who created the tragic dialogue in the forms which became regular, though in him they sometimes show (especially in stichomythia, as compared e.g. with Sophocles) a certain stiffness, and there is not much adaptation of style to speaker. His characters are 'typical', in the sense that in most there is not much minute drawing of the details of character—Danaus is the cautious father, Pelasgus the constitutionally-minded king, Atossa the royal mother, Eteocles the champion and defender of his city, Prometheus the victim and the unyielding opponent of tyranny, and so on—and that most are the embodiment each of some great passion or principle which determines all their words and acts.

The characters share the greatness of the issues which are worked out in their destiny. A man's destiny depends on the interaction of two factors, his own will and the higher powers that rule the world; each of the great personages of Aeschylus possesses a will that can rise to the conflict; but the Clytemnestra of the *Agamemnon* stands above them all as one in whom the imagination of a poet is added to a commanding and relentless personality. Not that Aeschylus is incapable of pathos; but even in Cassandra there is no lack of strength.

His choruses are all very distinctly characterized, though still 'typical'; the foreboding solemnity of the old men of the *Agamemnon*, tremulous, not what they were, but not prepared to endure an Aegisthus, contrasts sharply with the fussy, noisy terror of the women in the *Septem*; and the tender sympathy of the Oceanids with the savage joy of the Erinyes in their horrible office. The chorus in most plays serves as a foil to set off in relief the character of the leading personage. Now and then, as in the Watchman in the *Agamemnon* and the Nurse in the

*hoephoroe*, there is a thoroughly homely character with
ttle human touches.

In the *Frogs* of Aristophanes Aeschylus is made to
efend the 'high-flown' language with which he is taunted
n the ground that great thoughts and minds need great
ords for their expression, in other words, that the
randeur of his style is of a piece with that of his charac-
rs and conceptions. The defence was a just one in a
oet who had fought at Marathon; the critics belonged
· an age when grandeur did not come naturally and was
ot taken seriously. He is not afraid of compound words
f which each embodies a whole picture; of epithets
rung together in a mass, passing rapidly from one
etaphor to another, rather than giving for comparison
s Sophocles does) a single picture clearly and beautifully
rawn; of phrases suggesting the outline of some great
naginative idea, not so minutely analysed as to be
xpressible in simple language. He lives in a world of
etaphor, and his metaphors are drawn from a wide
nge of sources in human life and the natural world, and
sometimes strange, often give pictures of incomparable
eauty. An image or related images are repeated or
eveloped throughout a play or trilogy (e.g. birds of prey
· the *Supplices*, the net in the *Oresteia*).

The plot of an Aeschylean play is usually of the
nd which Aristotle calls simple or straightforward
πλῆ), i.e. uncomplicated by περιπέτεια or by recognition
:enes of the kind which often compose the crisis in his
ıccessors' plays; events move relentlessly forward, as
ıe divine plan works itself out. The connected trilogy
as a form specially fitted for the presentation of the
ivine operation in its slow but certain working, and the
·rms of surprise, which were very telling and almost
ecessary when the action was confined to a single play
ıd a single day, were less natural to Aeschylus. For
hat Aeschylus taught was the lesson of the ultimate
ıstice of Providence, in whose designs the rival claims,
hether of men or of supernatural powers, were at last
·conciled and contending wills brought to work to-
:ether within the universal scheme of ordered government
ıd goodwill towards men, which is what the name of
eus signifies to him, and in which there is room for both
pollo and the Eumenides. That at least was the moral
· the *Oresteia* and the Prometheus trilogy, and probably
· the Danaid trilogy also, as is strongly suggested in the
ıoruses of the extant play. Everything that is of the
ature of ὕβρις, unless it has become incurable, must be
runed of its selfishness and its excess—the Danaids' re-
·ction of Aphrodite, the irreconcilability of Prometheus,
ıe savagery of the age of the Titans and the Furies.
eus himself (this is perhaps the boldest of Aeschylus'
naginations) has had to grow in wisdom and learn the
·irit of good government. The current ideas of inherited
/il, of the curse upon a house and the fatality of great
rosperity, Aeschylus takes over but purifies. The curse
ill not fall on a man unless he calls it out by his own
rongdoing and so gives the demon in the house his
ıance, nor will wealth, perilous though it be, harm its
ossessor if he keeps himself free from ὕβρις; the stroke
· Justice, however long delayed, will never fail to fall
here it is deserved, but there may be at last, by the
·ace of God, an escape from the fatal chain of evil, and
ıe cruellest suffering, like that of Io, may be seen in the
ıd to have been only a step in a great and beneficent
esign of the Divine Will.

In the history of his own time, no less than in
gend as he interpreted or refashioned it, Aeschylus read
ıe same lessons. The antithesis of tyranny and freedom
as in the air the poet breathed, and it is not far below
ıe surface in any play. The failure of Persia was unmis-
kably the downfall of ὕβρις, and as for Athens, the
ılvation of the State lay in freedom and righteousness

and in the reconciliation, through moderation on either
side, of rival claims—that is the moral of Athena's
speeches in the *Eumenides*, a play which ends in a great
festival of reconciliation, recalling at every point the
Panathenaea, the festival of united Athens (see W. Headlam, *JHS* 1906).

LIFE AND WORKS. H. W. Smyth, *Aeschylean Tragedy* (1924); B.
Snell, *Aischylos und das Handeln im Drama* (1928); G. Méautis,
*Eschyle et la trilogie* (1936); G. Murray, *Aeschylus* (1940); G. Thom-
son, *Aeschylus and Athens²* (1946); F. R. Earp, *The Style of Aeschylus*
(1948); F. Solmsen, *Hesiod and Aeschylus* (1949); K. Reinhardt,
*Aischylos als Regisseur und Theologe* (1949); E. T. Owen, *The
Harmony of Aeschylus* (1952); J. de Romilly, *La Crainte et l'angoisse
dans le théâtre d'Eschyle* (1958). *See also* TRAGEDY, GREEK: works by
Kitto, Lesky, D. W. Lucas, Pohlenz. On the MSS., A. Turyn, *The
Manuscript Tradition of the Tragedies of Aeschylus* (1943); R. D.
Dawe, *The Collation and Investigation of Manuscripts of Aeschylus*
(1964); *Repertory of Conjectures on Aeschylus* (1965).
   TEXT. U. von Wilamowitz (1914); G. Murray (O.C.T., 2nd ed.
1955); P. Mazon (Budé, 6th ed. 1953); H. W. Smyth (Loeb, 1926;
vol. ii reprinted 1957, with appendix by H. Lloyd-Jones containing
the principal papyrus fragments); H. J. Mette, *Die Fragmente der
Tragödien des Aischylos* (1959).
   COMMENTARIES. A. Sidgwick (each play separately); P. Groeneboom (ditto, but not *Supplices*); H. J. Rose, *A Commentary on the
surviving plays of Aeschylus*, 2 vols. (1958); *Persae*, H. D. Broadhead
(1960); *Septem*, T. G. Tucker (1908); *Supplices*, T. G. Tucker (1889);
J. Vürtheim (1928); *Prometheus*, G. Thomson (1932); *Oresteia*, G.
Thomson, incorporating the work of W. Headlam (1938); *Agamemnon*,
E. Fraenkel (1950); J. D. Denniston and D. Page (1957); *Choephori*,
U. von Wilamowitz, *Aischylos Oresteia* II (1896); T. G. Tucker
(1901); *Eumenides*, A. W. Verrall (1908). Also U. von Wilamowitz,
*Aischylos Interpretationen* (1914); G. Italie, *Index Aeschylus* (1955).
   TRANSLATIONS. Prose: W. and C. E. S. Headlam (1909). Verse:
G. Murray (collected, 1952); R. Lattimore and others, 2 vols. (1954,
1956, in *The Complete Greek Tragedies*); P. Vellacott (Penguin Books,
1956, 1961).                               A. W. P.-C.; R. P. W.-I.

**AESCULAPIUS,** latinized form of *Asclepius* (q.v.),
was brought to Rome from Epidaurus at the instance of
the Sibylline Books, perhaps seconded by Delphi, after
a plague in 293 B.C. Legend told how the sacred snake,
incarnating the god, itself chose the Insula Tiberina for
its abode, and there on 1 January 291 a temple was dedicated to Aesculapius (Livy 10. 47; *epit.* 11; Ov. *Met.* 15.
622–745; *Fasti* 1. 289–94). The cult was patterned directly
on that of Epidaurus, but of the minor deities worshipped
there only Hygieia was received, to whom, from about
180 B.C. (Livy 40. 37), the name of the Italic goddess
Salus was sometimes applied. They received a joint cult
from the military in various parts of the Empire, but the
relative strength of Aesculapius in Dacia and Spain may
be due to Greek or Oriental elements there. The Aesculapius worshipped with Caelestis in and about Carthage
is a Semitic god of the Eshmun type.

W. A. Jayne, *The Healing Gods of Ancient Civilizations* (U.S.A.
1925), ch. 7; J. Toutain, *Les Cultes païens dans l'Empire romain* i
(1907), 330 ff.; E. J. and L. Edelstein, *Asclepius* (1945).   F. R. W.

**AESEPUS,** god of the Mysian river of that name,
Hesiod, *Theog.* 342.

**AESERNIA,** modern *Isernia*, with interesting ancient
remains, strong site near the upper Volturnus River controlling north-west Samnium (q.v.). A Latin colony,
established here after the Samnite Wars (263 B.C.), was
staunchly pro-Roman until Social War insurgents captured it (90 B.C.) and made it their capital. Strabo (5. 250)
exaggerates its unimportance; it became a flourishing
*municipium*.

Castagnoli, *Stud. urb.* 79 ff.                          E. T. S.

**AESERNINUS,** grandson of Asinius Pollio (q.v.), an
orator under Tiberius.

**AESOP,** famed as a teller of fables used metaphorically
to illustrate a point, lived as a slave on the island of Samos
in the early sixth century B.C. Ancient chronological
reckoning put his death in the year 564, four years before
Croesus became king of Lydia. The name Aesop as that

of a sculptor appears in a contemporary inscription from Sigeum in the Troad. Aesop the fabulist came originally not from Phrygia (this was a later literary invention), but from Thrace, according to the testimony of the local chronicler Eugeon of Samos who wrote before 431 B.C. What Eugeon said about Aesop's origin is implied by Herodotus in speaking of Rhodopis of Thrace as Aesop's fellow slave, and his other statements are not in conflict with Herodotus' account of Aesop (ii. 134–5). As Herodotus lived on the island of Samos before the year 456 B.C., he was well acquainted with its historical traditions. The belief of the Delphians in Herodotus' time, that Aesop was unjustly killed as a scapegoat by their ancestors, was a mistaken belief and is easily explained, with its cause, as a myth. It is very improbable that Aesop ever went to Delphi. Likewise purely mythical is the much later story that he acted as diplomatic courier for King Croesus.

The ancient testimonies about Aesop are assembled in B. E. Perry's *Aesopica* i. 211–41; and the total meaning of them, as outlined above, is analysed in detail by the same author in his *Babrius and Phaedrus* (Loeb, 1965), xxx–xlvi.                                   B. E. P.

**AESOPUS** (1st c. B.C.), tragic actor, 'gravis' (Hor. *Epist.* 2. 1. 82), contemporary of Roscius (Quint. *Inst.* 11. 3. 111 'Roscius citatior, Aesopus gravior'). He gave Cicero lessons in elocution (*Auct. ad Her.* (3. 21. 34) suggests that he was greatly his senior) and supported Cicero's recall from exile (*Sest.* 120–3); he returned to the stage for Pompey's *ludi*, 55 B.C., without much success (*Fam.* 7. 1. 2). See *Div.* 1. 80; *Tusc.* 4. 55; *QFr.* 1. 2. 14. His son, M. Clodius Aesopus, was rich enough to be a wastrel (Hor. *Sat.* 2. 3. 239; Pliny, *HN* 9. 122).                     G. C. R.

**AETHRA,** in mythology, daughter of Pittheus, king of Troezen, and mother of Theseus by Aegeus (qq.v.). Since Theseus was often called son of Poseidon, various explanations grew up. Aethra was sent by Athena (hence called Apaturia, the Deceitful) to the island of Hiera or Sphairia, where Poseidon met her (Paus. 2. 33. 1); Poseidon visited her the same night as Aegeus (Apollod. 3. 208, Hyg. *Fab.* 37. 1); it was a tale invented by Pittheus to save her credit (Plut. *Thes.* 6.) Her appearance as waiting-maid to Helen (*Il.* 3. 144) also needed explanation; a story apparently as old as the Cycle (*Iliu Persis*, fr. 3 Allen, cf. Apollod. 3. 128) says the Dioscuri carried her off while Theseus was in Hades, as reprisal for his kidnapping of Helen, and her grandsons, Demophon and Acamas (qq.v.), fetched her home when Troy fell.

Aethra is shown in late archaic and early classical vase-paintings as Helen's old slave rescued by her grandchildren at the sack of Troy. In Polygnotus' Troy at Delphi she was still in attendance on Helen. There are also pictures of a story unknown to surviving literature, where Theseus draws his sword on her. (Brommer, *Vasenlisten*[2], 163).                         H. J. R.; C. M. R.

**AËTION,** painter (and sculptor?), dated by Pliny 352 B.C. In his most famous picture, the 'Marriage of Alexander and Roxane' (not before 327), Roxane was seated in the marriage chamber, Alexander standing before her, Hephaestion leaning on Hymen; Erotes fluttered round the chief actors and played with Alexander's arms in the background. Aëtion was probably not the sculptor mentioned by Theocritus (*Epigr.* 8) and Callimachus (*Epigr.* 24).                       T. B. L. W.

**AËTIUS,** eclectic of the first or second century A.D., summarized in his Συναγωγὴ περὶ ἀρεσκόντων the opinions of the Greek philosophers on natural philosophy. These *Placita* are reproduced in the ps.-Plutarchean *Epitome* and in Stobaeus' *Eclogae*, and have been edited by H.

Diels in *Doxographi Graeci* (1879), 273–444. They fo one of our most important sources for the opinions of t philosophers whose works have for the most part perishe but must be used with caution: the tradition they repr sent derives in part from the περὶ φυσικῶν δοξῶν of The phrastus (q.v.), but augmented and modified by Sto Epicurean, and later Peripatetic theories.          W. D.

**AETIUS,** FLAVIUS, d. A.D. 454, a Roman patrician, w born at Durostorum (near Silistra in Bulgaria), the son Gaudentius, a high-ranking military officer. He w profound influence with Valentinian III (q.v.) and t came the effective ruler of the Western Empire, bei consul three times (432, 437, 446), an unprecedented d tinction for one who was not a member of the imper house. Appointed *patricius* in 433 he fought successfu thereafter against barbarians and rebels in Gaul, his ma achievement being the destruction of the kingdom of t Burgundians (q.v.) centred on the city of Worms. In 4 the Britons appealed to him in vain for help against t barbarian invaders of their island. In 451 he joined for with the Visigoths and defeated Attila and the Huns the battle of the Catalaunian Plains; but he could little to oppose Attila when the Huns invaded Italy 452. He was assassinated at the instigation of Petroni Maximus, the later Emperor.                         E. A.

**AETNA,** (1) Europe's highest active volcano (10,705 in 1950), lying between Tauromenium and Catana Sicily. The lower slopes are remarkably fertile, prin pally in vines, olives, lemons, and oranges, and are thic populated; woods and scrub cover the middle slopes; upper are desolate. Eruptions were attributed to a gi (Typhon or Enceladus) beneath the mountain. T Sicani traditionally removed westwards because of the They have been more frequent, apparently, in mode times. The ancients recorded comparatively few, though those of 475, 396, and 122 B.C. were notable.

C. S. du Riche Preller, *Italian Mountain Geology*, iii (1923).
                                                      A. G.

**AETNA,** (2) the name given to Catana when Hiero (q.v.) settled a colony there. In 461 these colonists we expelled, and transferred themselves and the name Sicel *Inessa* (perhaps *Poira*, between Paternò and Ce turipae). Ducetius (q.v.) captured Inessa–Aetna in 4 but it subsequently became a Syracusan strongho Dionysius I (q.v.) garrisoned it with Campanians wh Timoleon (q.v.) had trouble in dislodging. It suffered Verres' hands, but its later fortunes are unknown.

Dunbabin, *Western Greeks*, 131 f.; D. Adamesteanu, Κώκαλος 1 169 ff., where, however, a Hieronic foundation at Civita, west Paternò, rather than at Catana is postulated. *See also* EMPEDOCLE
                                                      A. G.

*AETNA,* Latin didactic poem of unknown authorsh It attempts to explain the volcanic activity of Mt. Et

The poem is ascribed to Virgil in our earliest MSS. a included amongst his *juvenilia* by the *vita Donati*, whe however, doubt is expressed about its authenticity. F if any, would now maintain the ascription. There is consensus of opinion about date, but the style and lan age seem to point to the Silver Age. Since the poem d not mention Vesuvius, it can hardly be later than eruption of A.D. 79. There has been much speculati about authorship.

Rejecting mythological explanations, the author arg that the controlling force behind eruptions is w operating at high pressure in narrow subterranean ch nels, and that the volcanic fire, produced by friction, g a nutritive material especially in the lava-stone (*la molaris*). The poem is embellished by digressions. C assage (222–81) extols physical science; another (603–45) arrates the devotion of two brothers who rescued their arents during an eruption. *Aetna* makes hard reading, artly because of its corrupt text, partly because of the ifficulty of the subject-matter and the author's style. He rains after brevity, overloads words and phrases, inulges freely in metaphor and personification; in his erse mythological allusions details are taken for granted s well known. Nevertheless, the work does not lack olish or animation. It also shows an earnest enthusiasm or the study of nature. The scientific sources of *Aetna* re uncertain, though Posidonius may well have been one. imilarities of thought and expression in Seneca's *Naturales Quaestiones* seem to indicate, not a debt to eneca, but a common source. Amongst poets Lucretius the author's principal model, but he also seems much fluenced by Virgil.

TEXTS. Teubner (*PLM* i, Vollmer–Morel, 1930), O.C.T. (Goodar, 1966). With comm.: H. A. J. Munro (1867). With comm. and ansl.: R. Ellis (1901). With comm. and ind. verb.: F. R. D. Goodar (1966). With transl.: Duff, *Minor Latin Poets*.
A. M. D.; F. R. D. G.

**ETOLIA**, a country bordered on the west by the wer and middle valley of the river Acheloüs, and on the st by Mt. Oxya, the watershed between Aetolia and Ialis. It contains the southern continuation of the Pindus ountain range. While the mountains of north Aetolia n north and south, the main range of southern Aetolia ns east and west, cutting off the rich plains of central etolia by Lake Conope and Lake Trichonis from the ast of the Corinthian Gulf. The coast between the ouths of the Acheloüs and the Euenus contains shallow goons but no good harbour. While five coastal towns, pecially Pleuron and Calydon, were known to Homer, e religious centre of classical Aetolia lay inland at hermum near Lake Trichonis, and its history was enrely that of a land power. Seclusion from the sea left etolia undeveloped in the fifth century B.C. (Thuc. 1. 5), tle urbanized, and organized in tribes who formed a mmon front against Demosthenes' invasion (426 B.C.). grew in power after 370 B.C. when the Aetolian Conderacy was formed as a close-knit federal State (Tod no. 7). The natural avenues of expansion lay in Acarnia and northwards to Amphilochia and Malis; but etolia did not develop successfully along these lines til the third century B.C. *See* AETOLIAN CONFEDERACY.

W. J. Woodhouse, *Aetolia* (1897).; K. D. Stergiopoulos, *'H ἀρχαία τωλία* (1939); P.–K. *GL* 2. 2. 299 ff.
N. G. L. H.

**ETOLIAN CULTS AND MYTHS.** The chief vinities of Aetolia were Artemis, Apollo, and Athena edication of statues of all three by Aetolians at Delphi, us. 10. 15. 2; of Artemis and Apollo only, id. 10. 16. 6). he cult centre of Artemis Laphria was Calydon (later trae, id. 7. 18. 8–13); Apollo was worshipped at alydon, but principally at Thermum; Athena is associad with Pleuron (Stat. *Theb.* 2. 726–31; Dion. Calliphon. 9 = *GGM* i. 240). At Phistyon the Syrian Aphrodite e ATARGATIS), to whom the epithet Phistyis was here plied, shared a temple, from at least 213/12 B.C., with e Mother of the Gods and the Virgin (Parthenos), posbly local deities in origin; the cult is known only from scriptions. The cults of Dionysus (cf. Paus. 7. 21. 1–5), eracles, Zeus Soter, and some others are also known. Prominent in myth are Aetolus, the reputed founder, d the family of Oeneus, Althaea, Meleager, and eianira (qq.v.). For the Calydonian boar-hunt *see* ELEAGER (1).

J. de Keitz, *De Aetolorum et Acarnanum sacris* (Diss. Halle, 1911); . J. Woodhouse, *Aetolia* (1897); E. Kirsten, *PW* xx, 1304 ff., s.v. chträge (Phistyon); for the inscriptions see *IG³* ix. 1 and G. affenbach, *Sitz. Berl.* 1936; for the myths, C. Robert in L. Preller, iechische Mythologie ii. 1 (1920), 85 ff.
F. R. W.

**AETOLIAN CONFEDERACY.** The looser tribal organization of the Aetolians gave way during the fourth century B.C. to a federal State (*sympoliteia*, q.v.), which acquired considerable power already in the latter part of that century and retained it even during the first period of the Roman intervention. In the third century the Aetolians exercised a protectorate over Delphi and through their expansion secured a controlling interest in the Amphictionic League (*see* AMPHICTIONIES). Since they normally were hostile to Macedonia, they naturally became Rome's first active allies within Greece proper. Their later hostility to Rome and co-operation with Antiochus III proved their downfall. Their conquests and outside influence were lost, and in 189 B.C. the Aetolians were forced to accept a treaty as subject allies of Rome. The Confederacy was not dissolved, but all its importance and influence were gone.

At the head of the Confederacy was a general elected annually. The primary assembly had two regular meetings a year and could be summoned for special sessions. In this body the votes seem to have been counted by heads and not, as in some federal States, by cities. The *boule* or *synedrion*, in which the cities were represented in proportion to population, contained some thousand members. Hence, particularly in time of war, much of the leadership fell to a smaller body, the *apokletoi*, itself containing over thirty members, probably a committee of the *boule*. The cities contributed to the federal treasury in proportion to the number of their representatives in the *synedrion*. At no time did the leadership of the Confederacy pass out of the hands of the Aetolians proper. This was in part because the more distant States were not made regular members, but merely bound to the Confederacy by *isopoliteia* (q.v.), which involved civil rights, protection, and potential citizenship but no participation in federal affairs unless residence was established in a community possessing active citizenship. Grants of *asylia* (q.v.) by the Aetolians were not infrequent and were highly prized on account of their extensive use of piracy and the right of reprisal. *See also* FEDERAL STATES.

G. Klaffenbach, introduction to *IG³* ix. 1 with references to the widely scattered sources; R. Flacelière, *Les Aitoliens à Delphes* (1937); J. A. O. Larsen, *TAPA* 1952, 1 ff.; *Greek Federal States* (1968), 78 ff.
J. A. O. L.

**AETOLUS** (*Αἰτωλός*), eponym of the Aetolians. His legend seems to be founded on traditions of the relation between certain Greek peoples. Endymion, king of Elis, had three sons, Paeon, Epeios, and Aetolus; he set them to race at Olympia, promising the kingship to the winner. Epeios won, hence the ancient name *Ἔπειοί* for the people of the district; Paeon left the country and gave his name to the district of Paeonia; Aetolus had later to leave because of a blood-feud, and went to Aetolia, which is called after him (Paus. 5. 1. 3–8).
H. J. R.

**AFER,** GNAEUS DOMITIUS (*PW* 14) (d. A.D. 59), of Nemausus (*Nîmes*), considered by Quintilian the best orator of his age. After his successful prosecution of Claudia Pulchra, cousin of the elder Agrippina, in A.D. 26, he enjoyed a distinguished, but sinister, reputation. Prosecuted by the Emperor Gaius in 39, he saved himself by flattery and was made consul (Sept. 39).
J. P. B.

**AFRANIUS** (1), LUCIUS (b. *c.* 150 B.C.), Latin poet; Cicero's report of him (*Brut.* 167) suggests that he was an orator and therefore a Roman citizen. He was the most prolific composer of *comoediae togatae*, whose representation of domestic life in Italian towns he made more artistic and involved, with wider and coarser appeal. His plays were performed even in imperial times, the most renowned being *Divortium, Epistula, Fratria* *rivignus,*

*Vopiscus.* He admired Terence, from whom he confessedly borrowed, and was compared by Horace (*Epist.* 2. 1. 57) with Menander. He portrayed chiefly family life and the 'middle classes'. *See* TOGATA.

FRAGMENTS. O. Ribbeck, *CRF*² 164 (Teubner,³ 1897); F. Leo, *Gesch. d. röm. Lit.* (1913), 375 ff.; W. Beare, *The Roman Stage*² (1964), 128 ff. E. H. W.

**AFRANIUS** (2) (*PW* 6), Lucius, of Picene birth (*ILS* 878), served under Pompey (q.v.) in Spain and against Mithridates. His triumph (Cic. *Pis.* 58) was probably won in a praetorian province between these two legateships, possibly in 69 B.C. As consul in 60 he was overshadowed by his colleague Metellus (q.v. 9) Celer, and was therefore ineffective on Pompey's behalf. His consular province was one of the Gauls, probably Cisalpina, but there is no evidence that he ever proceeded to it. From *c.* 53 he governed Hispania Citerior as Pompey's legate with three legions, and in 49 commanded at Ilerda. Pardoned by Caesar, he returned to Pompey, though charged with treachery by other Pompeians. He escaped from Pharsalus, but was captured and executed after Thapsus. G. E. F. C.

**AFRICA, ROMAN.** The Punic Wars (q.v.) made Rome heir to the Carthaginian Empire. In 146 B.C. she left most of the continental territory in the hands of Masinissa's descendants, but formed a new province in the most fertile part. This covered about 5,000 square miles of the northern part of Tunisia, north-east of a frontier line (the *fossa regia*) from Thabraca to Hadrumetum; it was governed by a praetor from Utica. Except for this community and six others of Phoenician origin who had deserted Carthage, most of the land became *ager publicus.* Though the attempt by Gaius Gracchus to found a *colonia* at Carthage failed, Roman and Italian traders and farmers settled in the province in large numbers, and many of Marius' veterans settled west of the *fossa regia*. After the battle of Thapsus (46 B.C.) Caesar added to the province (Africa Vetus) the Numidian territory of Juba I (Africa Nova); his colonial foundations in Africa included Clupea, Curubis, and Neapolis, and his plan to colonize Carthage was carried through by Octavian. A substantial territory in Numidia centred on Cirta was given to his supporter P. Sittius (q.v.) and a numerous following.

2. Under Augustus, after various changes of boundary, the united province (Africa Proconsularis) extended from Cyrenaica to the river Amsagas. At least eleven colonies were founded in it, and the flow of Italian immigrants was substantial. Thirteen colonies were founded on the coast of Mauretania, which, however, was ruled by the client prince Juba II. The enlarged province was governed by a proconsul from Carthage, who also commanded the Legio III Augusta. Under Gaius the command of the legion was handed over to an imperial *legatus* who became responsible for the government of Numidia and the frontier districts. The provincialization of North Africa was completed by Claudius with the creation of two provinces in Mauretania. Resistance to Roman rule on the fringes of the Sahara and in the mountainous regions such as the Kabylie and Aurès was no more than sporadic and for over three centuries the whole area from Cyrenaica to the Atlantic was protected by only one legion and auxiliaries. The frontier ran from Arae Philaenorum through Cydamus (*Gadhamès*), Nefta, Vescera (*Biskra*), and Auzia (*Aumâle*) to the Atlantic south of Volubilis.

3. Urban life in North Africa was of pre-Roman origin. In spite of the destruction of Carthage, a number of towns of Phoenician or Carthaginian origin survived on the coast, notably Hadrumetum and Lepcis Magna and places between; on the north and west coast, Icosium,

Tingi, and Lixus appear to have been Carthaginian settlements of some size. In a few places Carthaginian language and institutions survived into the second century A.D. Over large areas of the interior, the influence of Carthaginian civilization on the primitive Berber tribes was profound especially in central Tunisia and in the region of Cirta where Numidian dynasties had encouraged it. However, under Roman imperial rule, urbanization was on a vastly increased scale. Over 500 communities ranked as separate *civitates*, of which a large number obtained the rank of *municipium* or *colonia*. The area of densest urbanization was in the vicinity of Carthage and in the Bagradas valley, where some of the towns were only a dozen miles apart; among these may be mentioned Thuburbo Maius, Thibiuca, Membressa, Vaga, Bulla Regia, and Simitthus. In the centre of Tunisia, Macta, Sufes, Sufetula, and Ammaedara were notable. The last named, like the Numidian towns of Theveste, Thamugadi, Lambaesis, and Diana Veteranorum, owed its origin to the Third Legion. *Equites Romani* of African origin are known from the mid first century A.D., soon followed by senators. During the second century African senators, the best known being the orator Fronto, formed the largest western provincial group. The influence of Africans reached its height under Septimius Severus, born at Lepcis Magna.

4. The wealth of Africa was proverbial throughout the Roman period, and consisted largely of agricultural products. Of these corn was the chief, and the amount annually exported, largely through Carthage which became the largest city in the west after Rome, amounted to perhaps over half a million tons. The most productive districts for cereals were the Bagradas valley and the region round Cirta and Sitifis. From the second century olive-growing was equally prosperous in the drier regions of central Tunisia, and in Numidia and Mauretania. Productivity depended largely on the maintenance of irrigation systems of various kinds which Roman settlers introduced. Africa was notable for the vast estates in the hands of a few men, the largest landowner being the emperor. These were to some extent balanced by the estates of more modest size owned by members of the municipal upper class. Epigraphy reveals complicated systems of tenure which applied to the *coloni* on the large estates. Other exports from Africa were marble, wood, precious stones, dyes, gold-dust, and wild animals for show in Rome and elsewhere. There is evidence that the inhabitants of Carthage and other ports gained considerable profits from trade. The arts and crafts of Africa lacked the refinement of those of Italy and the northern shores of the Mediterranean; there were, however, vigorous and effective local schools of sculptors and mosaic makers.

5. During the third century, Africa suffered less than most provinces in the west from imperial usurpations, although the consequences of the failure of Gordian I were serious. Christianity spread more rapidly than in any other western province, first in the urbanized areas but making rapid strides in Numidia after *c.* 200. The work of Tertullian and Cyprian (qq.v.) were of considerable importance in the development of Latin Christianity.

6. In Diocletian's administrative changes, the provinces of Numidia, Byzacena, Tripolitana, Mauretania Sitifensis, and Mauretania Caesariensis formed the diocese of Africa, the proconsular province being strictly outside the diocesan system, and Mauretania Tingitana being part of the diocese of Spain. The military forces of the area were put under a *comes Africae*, and the frontier was divided into districts each under a *praepositus limitis*, a system unique in the Empire. Throughout the fourth century, North Africa was affected by a serious division among the Christians; the Donatists, condemned

schismatics by imperial legislation from Constantine onwards, were particularly strong in the rural areas of Numidia and Mauretania where social discontents were growing and where the government's authority was declining. Augustine of Hippo was active in stimulating the orthodox against the schismatics. In spite of these troubles, the area remained relatively prosperous in comparison with the devastated provinces of northern Europe, and it was a decisive stage in the collapse of the Roman Empire when it was conquered by the Vandals in 429. The invaders found Africa an easy prey, since the defensive system was suited for no more than policing and the suppression of sporadic tribal revolts.

Atlas archéologique de la Tunisie (1st series by E. Babelon, etc, 1892–1913; 2nd series by R. Cagnat and A. Merlin, 1914–32); A. Piganiol, Atlas des centuriations romaines de Tunisie³ (1959); S. Gsell, Atlas archéologique de l' Algerie (1911).
Inscriptions: CIL viii and Supplements; R. Cagnat, etc., Inscriptions latines de l'Afrique (1923); A. Merlin, Inscriptions latines de la Tunisie (1944); Inscriptions latines de l'Algerie i by S. Gsell (1923), ii, pt. i by H. G. Pflaum (1957).
S. Gsell, Histoire ancienne de l'Afrique du Nord i–viii (1914–29); P. Romanelli, Storia delle province romane dell'Africa (1959); R. M. Haywood in Frank, Econ. Survey iv; L. Teutsch, Stadtewesen in Nordafrika (1962); T. R. S. Broughton, The Romanization of Africa Proconsularis (U.S.A. 1929); G. C. Picard, La civilization de l'Afrique romain (1959); B. E. Thomasson, Die Statthalter der röm. Provinzen Nordafrikas, 2 vols. (1960). J. Baradez, Fossatum Africae (Paris 1949); B. H. Warmington, The North African Provinces from Diocletian to the Vandal Conquest (1954). R. Cagnat, L'Armée romaine d'Afrique² (1912); A. Berthier, Les Vestiges du christianisme dans la Numidie antique (1943); P. Monceaux, Histoire littéraire de l'Afrique chrétienne (1901–22); W. H. C. Frend, The Donatist Church (1952); J. I. Miller, The Spice Trade of the Roman Empire (1969), see index.
W. N. W.; B. H. W.

**AFRICANUS** (1), JULIUS (*PW* 45), a speaker of the first century A.D. from Gaul, ranked by Quintilian, who knew him, alongside of Domitius Afer and admired for his force (*Inst.* 10. 1. 118; 12. 10. 11). He delivered a loyal address to Nero after Agrippina's death (*Inst.* 8. 5. 15).

**AFRICANUS** (2), SEXTUS CAECILIUS (*PW* 29) (*c.* A.D. 150), a Roman jurist, almost certainly a pupil of Salvius Julianus (q.v. 2). His *Quaestiones* (9 books) record for the most part the views of his master, edited without any systematic arrangement, and usually introduced by a simple '*ait*', '*inquit*', or '*respondit*', without mention of Julian's name. He is not a fluent writer, indeed his texts are sometimes hardly intelligible. A reconstruction of this work has been edited by O. Lenel, *Sav. Zeitschr.* 1931. His *Epistulae* are known from one citation, and there are indications that he also wrote a commentary on the *Lex Julia de adulteriis*.                    A. B.; B. N.

**AFRICANUS** (3), JULIUS (*PW* 47), a Christian philosopher of Aelia Capitolina, went *c.* A.D. 220 on an embassy to Elagabalus which secured city rank and the title of Nicopolis for Emmaus, and established a library in the Pantheon for Severus Alexander. His principal works were the *Chronographies* (Χρονογραφίαι) in five books, a synchronization of sacred and profane history from the Creation to A.D. 221, which was the basis of Eusebius' *Chronicle*, and Οἱ Κέστοι in twenty-four books, a miscellany of information, chiefly relating to magic, on various topics ranging from medicine to tactics. He also wrote a letter to Origen, in which he questioned the authenticity of the story of Susannah, and a letter to a certain Aristides, in which he harmonized the two genealogies of Christ.

H. Gelzer, Sextus Julius Africanus (1880–98); W. Reichardt, Die Briefe des Sextus Julius Africanus an Aristides und Origenes (1909).
A. H. M. J.

**AFTER-LIFE.** In Greek and Roman thought, bound by no generally received dogma or revelation, numerous and often contradictory concepts of the after-life existed side by side. These peoples were concerned primarily with this life, but, certain philosophers apart, a belief in some sort of survival after death was almost universal. That the dead live on in the tomb was perhaps the most primitive, and most enduring, concept of all. There they still feel human wants, which are satisfied both by the household objects buried or burned with the body and by the continued tendance regularly paid to the dead by their families. Already in Mycenaean times this tendance seems to have given rise, in the case of individuals especially powerful both in life and death, to the continuing cult of heroes by persons not related to them and eventually by the whole community. By a different line of development arose festivals such as the Attic Anthesteria in which the dead in general received attention.

**2.** The belief that the dead dwell together in a common, subterranean abode, the realm of Hades and Persephone, dark and gloomy like the grave, found its classic expression in Homer (especially *Od.* 11), and so became fixed as the popular eschatology of all antiquity. Thither all mortals must repair, there good and evil alike lead a shadowy and cheerless existence. The dead need nothing and are not to be feared, for Homer's aristocratic society, separated from the ancestral tombs, has forgotten or ignores the older ideas (which, however, reappear in the post-Homeric age), and the elaborate funeral rites are in the main but meaningless survivals.

**3.** A totally different conception, that of Elysium or the Isles of the Blest, situated at the ends of the earth, appears in Homer (*Od.* 4. 561–9) and Hesiod (*Op.* 167–73) as the place to which certain favoured heroes, exempted from death, are translated by the gods. Elysium appears to be a survival from Minoan religion; when a later age concerned itself with the fate of the blessed *dead*, Elysium was transferred to the nether regions, in conformity with Greek ideas and the Homeric picture.

**4.** By the sixth century the Eleusinian Mysteries, an old, probably pre-Greek, agrarian cult, through an association of its chthonic divinities and the powers of the underworld, had begun to promise to its initiates a happier lot in the after-life (*Hymn. Hom. Cer.* 480–2; Ar. *Ran.* 154–8, 455–9); apparently, there as in this world they will continue to celebrate the Mysteries. A more clearly ethical note was struck in some mystic speculation, notably that reflected in Pind. *Ol.* 2 and frs. 131 and 133 Bergk. The divine origin of the soul was affirmed; popular ideas of punishment after death were combined with a doctrine of metempsychosis, and assurances of blessedness were held out to those who, throughout a series of existences in this and the other world, should lead pure lives. These or similar ideas were entertained by Pythagoreans and by Orphics, and had wide currency, but it is doubtful that there was any consistent doctrine of 'Orphism'.

**5.** Hitherto the hope of immortality had been at most based on intuition or religious teaching. Plato, whose eschatology was profoundly influenced by 'Orphism', however much he scorned its baser manifestations, first supplied this hope with a philosophic foundation, by arguments based on anamnesis, the Theory of Ideas, and ethical considerations. The precise nature of immortality he never defines, but his intense conviction that to the good man nothing but good can come and that the highest part of man's nature is allied to God has had far-reaching consequences.

**6.** Aristotle denied the power of survival to all but the intellectual part of man's tripartite soul, and even this is deprived of all sensibility. The Hellenistic age was, in general, little inclined to speculate on the after-life. The Academy adopted a thoroughly sceptical attitude. Epicurus and his followers attacked the fear of death with the claim that the soul, like the body, was composed of material atoms, and was dissipated at death. While some Stoics admitted a limited survival, at least of the souls of the wise, until the next cosmic conflagration, Panaetius denied even this. Posidonius, however, reverted to Platonic language and imagery, and the first century B.C. witnessed a considerable revival of interest in the after-life.

7. The Thraco-Phrygian cults of Dionysus and Sabazius and the hellenized mysteries of Attis and of Isis offered to many adepts the assurance of a blessed after-life—whether the dead was thought of as inhabiting the old underworld, or whether his continued existence was transferred to the celestial spheres. This belief in a celestial immortality, which was in no sense limited to the mystery religions, derived its popularity from the new concept of the universe as a series of concentric spheres around the earth and from philosophic speculations on the soul, whether in the Platonic sense of something from the world of Being which had descended into the world of Becoming, or the Stoic sense of something essentially Fire. Such ideas found easy acceptance in the cult of Mithras (q.v.), who was identified with the Sun, and in that more general solar piety which played so large a part in the later religious life of antiquity.

8. A final word on the specifically Italic concepts of the after-life: the ghosts of the dead join the undifferentiated mass of *Manes* or *Lemures* in the underworld (*Inferi*), and can return only at certain specified times, as at the feast of the Lemuria in May; no idea of divine retribution is discernible. On this primitive core of belief was superimposed the whole range of Hellenic conceptions, at first through Magna Graecia and through Etruria, which had combined Greek ideas with an elaborate demonology, and later by direct contact with Greece and the East. From the latter years of the Republic on, the Graeco-Roman world was essentially one in its development of religious and philosophic ideas of the after-life.

A. Brelich, *Aspetti della morte nelle iscrizioni sepolcrali dell'impero romano* (Diss. Pannonicae 1, 7, 1937); F. Cumont, *After Life in Roman Paganism* (U.S.A. 1922); *Recherches sur le symbolisme funéraire des Romains* (1942); A. Dieterich, *Nekyia²* (1913); Farnell, *Hero-Cults*; W. K. C. Guthrie, *Orpheus and Greek Religion* (1935), ch. 5; I. M. Linforth, *The Arts of Orpheus* (U.S.A. 1941). C. H. Moore, *Ancient Beliefs in the Immortality of the Soul* (1931); G. E. Mylonas, 'The Cult of the Dead in Helladic Times', *Robinson Studies* i (U.S.A. 1952); M. P. Nilsson, *Minoan-Mycenaean Religion²* (Lund, 1950); 'Early Orphism', *Harv. Theol. Rev.* 1935; A. D. Nock, *Harv. Theol. Rev.* 1932, 1940; E. Rohde, *Psyche* (Engl. Transl. of 8th ed., 1925); Mrs. A. Strong, *Apotheosis and After Life* (1915). *See* PSYCHE, SOUL, TRANSMIGRATION.          F. R. W.

**AGAMEMNON,** in mythology, son of Atreus and brother of Menelaus (qq.v.); king of Mycenae, or Argos; probably an historical person, who, if not overlord of some or all of the princes of the Mycenaean era, was the most important of them.

In Homer, Agamemnon is commander-in-chief of the Greek expedition against Troy. In the *Iliad* he is a man of personal valour, but lacking resolution and easily discouraged. His quarrel with Achilles (q.v.) supplies the mainspring of the poem's action. The *Odyssey* (1. 35 ff.; 4. 512 ff.; 11. 405 ff.; 24. 96–97) tells how, on his return, he was carried by the wind outside his own territory to the barony of Aegisthus (q.v.), the lover of his wife Clytemnestra, sister of Helen, who treacherously set upon him and his men at a banquet and killed them all, Clytemnestra also killing Cassandra, daughter of Priam, whom Agamemnon had brought back with him. This story later authors retell with elaborations and small changes, e.g. the scene is generally (as in Aesch. *Ag.*) transferred to Argos.

The *Cypria* is the earliest evidence for the sacrifice of Agamemnon's daughter Iphigenia (q.v.). The cause of it was the offence given to Artemis by Agamemnon, who after a successful hunt boasted that he was a better hunter than she. Calchas, when the fleet was wind-bound at Aulis, explained that the goddess was the cause and the

sacrifice must be made to appease her. Iphigenio was therefore sent for to Aulis on the pretext that she was to be married to Achilles. For sundry variants, see Rose, *Handbook of Greek Mythology*, 119 and notes.

In other stories Agamemnon appears as a subsidiary figure, or is handled with more or less disregard of tradition, as in the fantastic perversion of the legend in Hyginus, *Fab.* 88.

In historical times Agamemnon had cults at several places (see Farnell, *Hero-Cults*, 321 and note 55). The remarkable statement (Lycophron 335 and 1369, with schol.) that he was called Zeus at Sparta has never been satisfactorily explained. In any case, there is no earlier evidence for it, and it seems to be a development of the Hellenistic period.

Agamemnon's children in all accounts include Orestes (q.v.). A quite unsupported story (Hyg. *Fab.* 121) gives him an illegitimate son, Chryses, by his slave-concubine Chryseis (*Il.* 1. 111, etc.). His daughters are Chrysothemis, Laodice, and Iphianassa in *Il.* 9. 145; Iphigenia, whom Homer does not mention, seems to be a later substitution for Iphianassa.

In archaic and early classical vase-painting Agamemnon appears in occasional Trojan scenes, separating Ajax and Odysseus when they quarrel or supervising the voting on their claims. In Polygnotus' Troy he was judging the lesser Ajax; in his Underworld leaning on a sceptre and holding the speaker's staff. His death is very rarely illustrated (*see under* CLYTEMNESTRA). The Chryses story is now found on a silver cup of the first century B.C. (see Corbett and Strong, *BMQ* 23 (1961) 68 ff.)

Brommer, *Vasenlisten²* 334 f.          H. J. R.; C. M. R.

**AGANIPPE,** in mythology, daughter of the river-god Permessus (Paus. 9. 29. 5: spelling 'Ter-'), nymph of the spring of that name on Helicon (Callim. *fr.* 696 Pf.), sacred to the Muses.

**AGAPENOR** (*Ἀγαπήνωρ*), in mythology, leader of the Arcadian contingent against Troy (*Il.* 2. 609); son of Ancaeus (q.v.). On the way back from Troy he arrived at Cyprus (Lycoph. 479 ff.), where he founded Paphos and a temple of Aphrodite and settled (Paus. 8. 5. 2).

**AGASIAS,** (1) sculptor, son of Dositheus, of Ephesus. He signed the Borghese warrior in the Louvre (Winter, *KB*, 382. 3), a nude figure striding forward to parry an attack from above, showing remarkable knowledge of anatomy and probably deriving from an earlier group. The signature and another from Thessaly are dated late second to early first century B.C.

Lippold, *Griech. Plastik*, 382; G. M. A. Richter, *Three Critical Periods* (1951), 48; Bieber, *Sculpt. Hellenist. Age*, 162 ff.
T. B. L. W

**AGASIAS,** (2) sculptor, son of Menophilus, of Ephesus, known from signatures in Delos, of about 100 B.C. One base may belong to the wounded warrior of Delos, part of a group (Winter, *KB*, 350. 1; C. Picard, *BCH* 1932, 491).
T. B. L. W

**AGATHARCHIDES,** Greek grammarian and Peripatetic of Cnidos, became guardian to a young Ptolemy (? Soter II) of Egypt, c. 116 B.C.

WORKS: (i) Τὰ κατὰ τὴν Ἀσίαν, on the Diadochi; (ii) Τ.κ.τ. Εὐρώπην, on history ? 323 B.C. to fall of Macedon (iii) Περὶ τῆς Ἐρυθρᾶς θαλάσσης; [(iv, epitome of (iii) not Agatharchides'? (v) on Trogodytes—same as (iii)?]; (vi) epitome of writers on (?) wonders; (vii) historical Ἐκλογαὶ ἱστοριῶν; (viii) Intercourse of Friends.

Extracts survive from (iii), in Photius and Diodoru bk. 3, dealing with elephant-hunts; name of 'Red' Sea tc.; Ethiopians; gold-mining on Egypto-Ethiopian frontier; races and animals west of Red Sea; cause of flooding of the Nile in summer; Arabians, especially Sabaeans.

FGrH n. 86; GGM i. liv-lxxiii, 111-95 (Red Sea); E. H. Bunbury, Hist. of Anc. Geog. (1879) ii. 50 ff.; A Berthelot, L'Afrique sahar. et soudanaise (1927) 215 ff.; Thomson, Hist. of Anc. Geog. 136, 175, 182, 210; Hyde, Greek Mariners, 196 ff. E. H. W.

**AGATHARCHUS** (5th c. B.C.), painter, of Samos. He made a 'scene' for Aeschylus (probably for a revival at the time of the Peloponnesian War), and was compelled by Alcibiades (c. 430 B.C. ?) to paint his house (with perspective scenes?). He wrote a book on 'scene-painting', which inspired Anaxagoras and Democritus to write on perspective. He was the first painter to use perspective on a large scale (isolated instances occur on vases from the late sixth century B.C.).

Overbeck, 1118-25; Pfuhl, 723; A. Rumpf, JHS 1947, 13; Malerei und Zeichn. 121; J. White, Perspective in Ancient Drawing and Painting (1956); T. B. L. Webster, Bull. Rylands Libr. 1962, 243. T. B. L. W.

**AGATHIAS** (c. A.D. 531-c. 580), surnamed Scholasticus, 'the Advocate', was born in Aeolis, studied in Alexandria and Constantinople, and practised law in the latter city. A good scholar with fine taste, he is best known as compiler of a seven-book Circle of recently written poetic epigrams, many of which entered the Greek Anthology (q.v.). Anth. Pal. 4. 3. is his preface to it, including a table of contents (113-33). The Anthology contains about a hundred of his epigrams: some are little more than conceits in the Alexandrian manner, but the love poems are warm and effective. In metre, vocabulary, and style he is deeply indebted to Nonnus.

Later (Hist., pref., p. 11. 5 Bonn), Agathias embarked upon a History designed to bring up to date the narrative of Procopius' Wars. Only the years 553-9, however, are covered in the five books completed at the author's death. Agathias' poetic interests can be seen in the elaborate vocabulary and in his expressed determination to make the work pleasing as well as informative (iii. 1). He accordingly treats his material (mainly military—the campaigns of Narses in Italy and the end if the war in Lazica) in a rhetorical and moralizing way. But we owe to his industry and curiosity three important excursuses, one on the Franks and the others on the history and customs respectively of Sassanid Persia; the last of these makes use of the Persian Royal Annals. Though himself a Christian, Agathias tried to exclude from his secular history specific references to Christianity. The motivation, however, is recognizably Christian; unlike his model, Procopius, Agathias makes no use of the concept of τύχη as a force in history. The work appears to have been well received, and was at once imitated and continued by Menander Protector.

History, ed. R. Keydell (Berlin, 1967); forthcoming monograph by A. Cameron. W. S. Teuffel, Studien und Charakteristiken (1889²) 296 ff.; G. Franke, Quaeestiones Agathianae (Breslau, 1914); A. Mattsson, Untersuchungen zur Epigrammsammlung des A. (1942; A. and A. Cameron, 'The Cycle of Agathias', JHS 1966, 6 ff. (dating publication to A.D. 567/8); A. Cameron, 'Herodotus and Thucydides in A.', Byz. Zeitschr. 1964, 33 ff. O. Veh, 'Der Geschichtsschreiber A. von Myrina', Wissenschaftliche Beilage zum Jahresbericht 1952/53 des Gymnasiums Christian-Ernestinum Bayreuth 18 ff., 35 ff. G. H.; A. M. C.

**AGATHINUS**, CLAUDIUS (c. A.D. 50-100), pupil of the Stoic L. Annaeus Cornutus and of Athenaeus (q.v. 3) of Attaleia, the founder of the pneumatic school of medicine. He was the teacher of Archigenes (q.v.). Adopting some of the tenets of the empirical and methodical schools of medicine, he founded an eclectic school. Works: Περὶ ἐλλεβόρου; Περὶ ἡμιτριταίων (on semi-tertian fevers); Περὶ σφυγμῶν (on the pulse). W. D. R.

**AGATHOCLES**, tyrant and king of Syracuse, was born at Thermae Himeraeae in 361 B.C., migrating to Syracuse in Timoleon's time. He distinguished himself in wars against Acragas and the Bruttii (c. 325) but, intriguing against the ruling oligarchy, was exiled, restored, and exiled again. In 317 he overthrew the oligarchs, and ruled as tyrant with the support of the lower classes. Suppressing attempts to raise a coalition against him, he captured most of eastern Sicily. Carthage intervened when he attacked Acragas, and he was blockaded in Syracuse after a heavy defeat at Licata (311).

With the resource of desperation Agathocles slipped out of Syracuse and landed in Africa, where, obtaining help from Ophellas (q.v.) of Cyrene, he nearly succeeded in capturing Carthage; meanwhile, Carthaginian attacks on Syracuse failed. He returned to Sicily to defeat an alliance organized by Acragas, but, going back to Africa, he found that things had deteriorated in his absence; whereupon he abandoned his army and made good his own escape (307). His ruthless campaigns in Sicily ensured that thereafter he ruled the major part of a pacified island. He assumed the title of king in 304. Subsequently he intervened in Italy, and even captured Corcyra (c. 300). Family animosities frustrated his attempts to found a dynasty, and before his death (289) he 'restored Syracusan freedom'. But his own career had made the gesture illusory, and his real legacy was a continuing anarchy. However, history may give him less than his deserts, for the bulk of the information about him is ultimately derived from his bitter enemy Timaeus (q.v. 2).

H. J. W. Tillyard, Agathocles (1908); H. Berve, Die Herrschaft des Agathokles (Sb. Akad. München 1952, Heft 5). A. G. W.

**AGATHON**, after the three great masters the most distinguished tragic poet, son of Tisamenus of Athens, and remarkable for his personal beauty, won his first victory at the Lenaea in 416 B.C., when he was probably under thirty years of age (Pl. Symp. 198 a). The Symposium of Plato represents a feast in honour of his victory. In 411 he heard and approved of Antiphon's speech in his own defence (Arist. Eth. Eud. 3. 5)—this may mean that his sentiments were not on the democratic side—and in the same year he was caricatured in Aristophanes' Thesmophoriazusae, but about 407 he went to the court of Archelaus in Macedonia (Ar. Ran. 83-85; Ael. VH 13. 4; Anecd. Ox. iv. 269; Pl. Symp. 172 c), and died there, probably about 401. He came under the influence of the sophists, Gorgias and Prodicus (Pl. Prt. 305 d). His speech in Plato's Symposium is in the manner of Gorgias, and some quotations from his tragedies are in a pointed, epigrammatic style, probably due to sophistic influence. His originality was shown by the composition of a tragedy (Antheus, not Ἄνθος) in which characters and plot were his own invention, not taken from legend (Arist. Poet. 9); traces of the plot may perhaps be found in Alexander Aetolus (Powell, Coll. Alex. 122) and Parth. Amat. Narr. 14; by making choral odes, for the first time, mere interludes (ἐμβόλιμα) without reference to the plot (Poet. 13), and by the free use in tragedy of the chromatic scale and various florid musical figures (Plut. Quaest. conv. 3. 1. 1). Aristophanes (Thesm. 101 ff.) parodies his lyrics and hints that they are voluptuous and effeminate. Aristotle also criticizes him (Poet. 18) for including too lengthy a story, such as the whole sack of Troy, within a single plot. He was evidently a 'modernizer' in tragedy, who sat loose to tradition but was not without genius, though less than forty lines of his work survive. (TGF 763-9). A. W. P.-C.; D. W. L.

**AGDISTIS**, a form of the Phrygian mother-goddess; at Pessinus Cybele (q.v.) was called Agdistis (Strabo 469,

567). According to the myth (*see* ATTIS), she was originally androgynous. Her cult spread to various parts of Anatolia, to Egypt (by 250 B.C.), to Attica (with that of Attis in Piraeus 4th–3rd, cc., *IG* ii². 4671; at Rhamnus, 83/2 B.C.), Lesbos, and Panticapeum. At Lydian Philadelphia her private shrine (1st c. B.C.) enforced a strict moral code (*SIG* 985; O. Weinreich, *Sitz. Heid.* 1919). There and elsewhere Agdistis appears with *theoi soteres*. *See* ANATOLIAN DEITIES.

H. Hepding, *Attis* (1903); Hiller v. Gaertringen, *ARW* 1926. Rhamnus inscription: K. A. Rhomaios, Ἑλληνικά 1928; P. Roussel, *Rev. Ét. Anc.* 1930. F. R. W.

**AGELADAS (Hageladas),** Greek sculptor of Argos, reputed teacher of Myron, Polyclitus (2), and Phidias (qq.v.). It is uncertain whether our records regarding Hageladas refer to two sculptors of that name or to only one. In the latter case his activity must have extended from the last two decades of the sixth century B.C., when he made statues of athletes at Olympia in 520, 516, and 507 B.C. (cf. Pausanias 6. 14. 11; 10. 6; 8. 6), to much later; for he made a Heracles Alexikakos, 'Averter of Evil', of which the name is thought to have been derived from the plague of 430 B.C. His most famous work was a bronze statue for the sanctuary of Zeus at Ithome, commissioned by the Messenians who had settled at Naupactus (Paus. 4. 33. 2). It is perhaps reproduced on coins of Messene, on which appears a striding Zeus, hurling a thunderbolt with one hand, an eagle perched on the other. For the people of Aegium he made another statue of Zeus 'as a boy', also in a striding attitude (Paus. 7. 24. 4), which is apparently reproduced on Roman coins of that city. A contemporary extant bronze statue by an unknown sculptor, the striding 'Poseidon' from the Artemisium, now in Athens, may give us some visualization of these statues.

G. M. A. R.

**AGENOR** (Ἀγήνωρ), name of several mythological persons, the most important being the king of Tyre (or Sidon), father of Europa (q.v.). On the disappearance of his daughter, he sent out his sons to look for her, bidding them not come back without her; hence Phoenix, Cilix, and Cadmus founded respectively the Phoenician and Cilician peoples and Thebes in Boeotia. His genealogy, which varies somewhat (see Stoll in Roscher's *Lexikon*, s.v. 'Agenor'), links various Eastern peoples together. H. J. R.

**AGENTES IN REBUS (or RERUM).** The detested *frumentarii* (*see* POLICE) were abolished by Diocletian, and he or his successors replaced them with the vaguely named *agentes in rebus*, to take charge of the Postal Service (q.v.), but in fact (at least before long) also to take over the police duties of the *frumentarii* (cf. Aur. Vict. *Caes.* 39. 44). Soon equally detested, they were practically abolished by Julian, but under his successors reached an establishment of several thousand. By the middle of the fourth century A.D. they were attached to the Magister Officiorum (q.v.), forming a *schola* under a *princeps*, with promotion based fairly strictly on seniority. Senior ranks were popularly called *curiosi* (at least implying 'spies'), and this term later became official. One or two of them were regularly sent to inspect each province. Their secret service functions and their abuse of their wide powers are amply attested in the *Codes* and the literary sources. There were many applicants for the career, and they were carefully selected. By the time of the *Theodosian Code* (and probably earlier), freedmen, Jews, and heretics were excluded; relatives of *agentes* had preference for entry, and various dignitaries had limited rights of

nomination. From the highest grade of their service, these trusted agents usually went as *principes* to various *officia* and sometimes then went on to govern provinces. They ultimately retired to high rank and numerous privileges

E. J. Holmberg, *Zur Gesch. d. cursus publicus* (1933), 104; Jones *Later Rom. Emp.* ii. 578 (with notes); W. G. Sinnigen, *Byz. Zeitschr.* 1964, 78 ff. E. E

**AGER PUBLICUS.** I. IN ITALY. During her conquest of Italy Rome penalized such communities as offered stubborn resistance or subsequently rebelled, by confiscating a part (usually a third) of their territories. The use to which the public land should be put was from an early date—according to tradition as far back as 486 B.C.—disputed between the patricians, who preferred to maintain public ownership, under which they could occupy it as *possessores* (*see* POSSESSIO), and the plebs, who wished it to be distributed among themselves. As the *ager publicus* grew by conquest, the patricians became more liberal. Some land was distributed to individuals (*viritim assignatus*); part of the territory taken from Veii was so treated in 393. More was allocated to colonies of Roman citizens; this practice, according to tradition, dates back to the early fifth century. Larger areas were devoted to the Latin colonies which Rome planted after the dissolution of the Latin League in 338. By the Licinio-Sextian law of 367 (*see* STOLO) no citizen might occupy more than 500 *iugera* of this land.

The defections of the allied communities during the Second Punic War were punished by extensive confiscation of land, and the conquest of Cisalpine Gaul added large areas to the *ager publicus*. Most of the Gallic land was devoted to colonies, and the remainder was distributed in small holdings (173 B.C.). Elsewhere few colonies were planted, and vast tracts, especially in the south, remained in the hands of the State. The best of this land was leased by the censors and brought in a good rent to the State, but large tracts were occupied by *possessores*, being mostly used for ranching. The *possessores* were supposed to pay dues, and the size of their tenures was legally limited by the Licinio-Sextian laws. But the laws were regularly evaded or ignored, and the collection of dues was lax.

Under the agrarian law of Ti. Gracchus (133) a commission was set up to resume for the State public land occupied in excess of the Licinio-Sextian limit (increased in favour of *possessores* who had sons) and to distribute them in small holdings, which were to remain public and pay a *vectigal*. Much land was distributed under this scheme, which was revived by C. Gracchus in 123–122 B.C., until in 119 the land commission was suppressed. C. Gracchus also planned several colonies, one of which at least was planted. By the agrarian law of 111 the Gracchan small holdings, whose *vectigal* had been abolished in 122, and the holdings of *possessores* within the Gracchan limit were declared private land, the *vectigal* which had been reimposed in 119 on the latter being abolished. After this law the following categories of land remained public: (*a*) open spaces at Rome; (*b*) roads; (*c*) lands leased by the censors, notably the *ager Campanus*; (*d*) lands assigned to Roman and Latin colonies and *municipia* corporately; (*e*) holdings allotted on condition of maintaining the roads; (*f*) lands granted to state creditors (*in trientabulis*); (*g*) pastures on which contiguous owners had exclusive rights (*compascua*); (*h*) all other public lands, which were henceforth to be common pasture. Sulla confiscated the territories of many cities which opposed him for the benefit of his veterans. Caesar in 59 distributed the *ager Campanus* to Pompey's veterans. Octavian in 30 expropriated cities which had favoured Antony to find land for his veterans, but compensated the owners in money or provincial land.

II. IN THE PROVINCES. According to Gaius the *dominium* in all provincial soil was vested in the Roman people or the Emperor; but this theory, which probably did not arise till the first century A.D., had no practical import. The public land acquired under the Republic comprised (*a*) the estates of prominent opponents, in so far as these were not immediately sold or given away; (*b*) the territories of cities which were, like Carthage and Corinth, destroyed or were merely, as were a few Sicilian and Pamphylian communities, punished by the loss of their lands; (*c*) the royal lands of kings who were deposed or bequeathed their kingdoms to Rome. These comprised some Macedonian estates, Attalid lands in the Chersonese, and an extensive tract of desert in Cyrenaica; the Bithynian and Pontic royal lands seem to have been assigned by Pompey to the cities of the new province. Most of the provincial public lands (except in Cyrenaica) seem to have alienated by the beginning of the Principate, some, such as Carthage and Corinth, being devoted to Roman colonies. Under the early Principate more royal lands were added to the *ager publicus*, notably the γῆ βασιλική of Egypt and extensive domains in Cappadocia.

The *ager publicus*, both in Italy and the provinces, was swelled by *bona vacantia, caduca*, and *damnatorum*. These sources, negligible under the Republic, became important under the Principate owing to the severe *leges caducariae* passed by Augustus and to the frequent condemnations of wealthy men. All public lands gradually passed under the administration of the Emperor, and most seem eventually to have been assimilated to the imperial estates; *see* DOMAINS (*b, Imperial*).

M. Weber, *Römische Agrargeschichte* (1891); E. G. Hardy, *Six Roman Laws* (1901), 35 ff.; A. H. M. Jones, *JRS* 1941, 26 ff.; Tenney Frank, *JRS* 1927, 141 ff.; L. Zancan, *Ager publicus* (1935); G. Tibiletti, *Athenaeum* 1948, 173 ff., 1949, 3 ff., 1950, 245 ff.; A. Burdese, *Studi sull'ager publicus* (1952); E. Badian, *Hist.* 1962, 209 ff.
A. H. M. J.

**AGESILAUS** (444–360 B.C.), Spartan king, son of Archidamus and half-brother of Agis II, secured the succession in 399, largely through Lysander's influence, in preference to Leotychidas, whose legitimacy was suspect. Lysander had hoped to use Agesilaus for his own ends, but was quickly brought to heel. As commander in Asia Minor from 396, Agesilaus overran Phrygia and routed Tissaphernes, but failed to check the growing Persian naval menace. Recalled with his army in 394, he took the overland route and reached Coronea almost unopposed. The ensuing battle with the Boeotian and allied forces was a Pyrrhic victory, and Agesilaus had to evacuate the country. He won minor successes, however, in the vicinity of Corinth and in Acarnania (391–388). He condoned, on grounds of expediency, Spartan intervention against Mantinea, Phlius, and Olynthus (in violation of the principle of autonomy enjoined by the peace of Antalcidas), and the still more flagrant occupation of the Cadmea by Phoebidas (382), and attempt on the Piraeus by Sphodrias (378). The alliance between Thebes and Athens resultant on this policy was unshaken by Agesilaus' invasions of Boeotia in 378 and 377. His refusal in 371 to admit Epaminondas' claim to represent all Boeotia at the peace congress in Sparta precipitated the Battle of Leuctra. In the years of Sparta's humiliation he organized the defence of the city (370 and 362) and sought to augment the State revenues by foreign service (in Asia Minor with Ariobarzanes 364, and in Egypt with Nectanebo 361). He died on the homeward voyage from Egypt (360).

Despite his poor physique and a strain of romanticism, Agesilaus was typically Spartan in his qualities and limitations. He was an efficient soldier, but a better tactician than stategist, and he failed to understand the importance of sea-power. The narrowness of his loyalties

dissipated those moral assets by virtue of which alone Sparta could maintain her hegemony.

Xenophon, *Agesilaus* (the encomiastic tribute of a personal friend), *Hellenica*; *Hellenica Oxyrhynchia*; Nepos, *Agesilaus*; Plutarch, *Agesilaus*. H. Lins, *Kritische Betrachtung der Feldzüge des Agesilaos in Kleinasien* (1914).
D. E. W. W.

**AG(G)ENIUS URBICUS** (perhaps 5th c. A.D.), *gromaticus*, author of a commentary on Frontinus' treatise *De controversis agrorum*.

**AGIADS** (Ἀγιάδαι) was the name of the senior royal house at Sparta. The Agiad dynasty enjoyed a ceremonial precedence over the other (Eurypontid) house, but possessed no constitutional privileges. The most notable Agiad kings were Cleomenes I and III, Leonidas, and Pausanias (qq.v.).

**AGIS II,** son of Archidamus, king of Sparta c. 427–c. 399. Though active in the Archidamian War, he first gained distinction in the campaign of 418 against the Argives and other enemies of Sparta. After failing to utilize what appeared to be a strategic advantage, he subsequently won a decisive victory near Mantinea, which restored Spartan authority in the Peloponnese and Spartan prestige throughout Greece. In 413 he was sent to occupy Decelea as a permanent base for plundering Attica. Remaining here, he attempted to exert an autocratic control over Spartan policy, but his influence waned when the centre of war moved to Asia. He collaborated with Lysander in the blockade of Athens in 405–404, and in his last years reduced Elis by a successful invasion. As a military leader he was at least competent and energetic, but, like so many Spartan kings, he seems to have lacked constructive statesmanship.

Thucydides, bks. 5 and 8.
H. D. W.

**AGIS III,** king of Sparta (338–331 or 330 B.C.), Eurypontid, organized the resistance of the Greeks against Macedonia during Alexander's Asiatic campaign. Assisted by the Persian admirals' gifts of ships and money, he assembled an army, consisting mostly of 8,000 Greek mercenaries, fugitives after Issus. He was successful in Crete and then in Peloponnesus, where some States revolted from Macedonia (331). Athens, however, stood aloof (in spite of Ps.-Dem. 17), and so did Megalopolis, Messene, and Argos. While besieging Megalopolis, Agis was forced to meet Antipater and an army almost twice as numerous as his own. After a hard struggle, he was beaten and died heroically. His death put an end to all Greek revolts against Alexander.

Arrian, Diodorus, Curtius. Berve, ii. no. 15; Glotz, *Hist. grecque* iv. 194 f.; E. Badian, *Hermes* 1967, 170 ff.
V. E.

**AGIS IV** (c. 262–241 B.C.), son of Eudamidas, ascended the Eurypontid throne at Sparta in 244. Heavy mortgages, large estates in single hands, and a depleted citizenbody were evils he resolved to cure by a return to 'Lycurgus' constitution'. In 243, as ephor, his supporter Lysander introduced relevant bills; in 242 Agis deposed new, reactionary ephors, and Leonidas, the Agiad king whom he had already impeached, fled to Tegea. Supported by his rich uncle Agesilaus, Agis now burnt the mortgages; this done, Agesilaus turned against him and while Agis was absent assisting his Achaean allies against Aetolia, Leonidas returned and seized power. Arriving back, Agis took sanctuary; but the ephors decoyed him out and executed him.

High-minded but unrealistic, he fell before cleverer men: his death became the legend around which a new generation rallied.

Plut. *Agis*. Beloch, *Gr. Gesch.* iv; W. H. Porter, *Hermathena* 1935; P. Cloché, *Rev. Ét. Grec.* 1943; E. Gabba, *Athenaeum* 1957; A. Fuks, ibid. 1962; *CQ* 1962; *CPhil.* 1962.
F. W. W.

**AGONES,** public festivals at which competitors contended for a prize, were a distinctive feature of Greek life. Most of these festivals were under the patronage of a god or hero, the smaller gatherings depending on local support, the larger drawing spectators from all parts of the Greek world. The best-known were the Olympic, Pythian, Nemean, and Isthmian games, together with the Dionysia and Panathenaea at Athens (qq.v.). In most cases chariot-races, foot-races, and field events were the chief attractions, but at Athens the first place was given to the dramatic competitions in honour of Dionysus. *See also* ATHLETICS. Introduced at Rome in 186 B.C., contests in the Greek manner became fairly common towards the close of the Republic. A regular quinquennial festival (Neronia) was established by Nero, a quadrennial *Agon Capitolinus* by Domitian in A.D. 86, and an *Agon Solis* by Aurelian in 274.

Friedländer, ii. 117 ff. F. A. W.

**AGONIUM,** name given to 9 Jan., 17 March, 21 May, and 11 Dec. in the Roman calendar. It does not denote a festival of any particular god, and the ancients were in doubt of its meaning, witness the etymologies (Festus, 9 Lindsay, and note in his larger ed. *Gloss. Lat.* iv. 104). Possibly it is a latinization of ἀγών, in its old sense of 'assembly'. The January entry may have displaced the name of the festival of Janus, presumably *\*Ianuar.*

H. J. R.

**AGORA,** the forum or civic centre of a Greek city. For the Agora of Athens *see* ATHENS, TOPOGRAPHY.

R. Martin, *Recherches sur l' Agora grecque* (1951); R. E. Wycherley, *How the Greeks built Cities*² (1962). H. A. T.

**AGORACRITUS,** Greek sculptor, a native of Paros and pupil of Phidias. Pliny (*HN* 36. 17) records that he was defeated in a competition for a statue of Aphrodite and then sold his statue to the people of Rhamnus, where it served as a statue of Nemesis. Pausanias (1. 33. 3), who attributes the statue to Phidias, gives a detailed description of it and of its base. It represented the goddess standing, holding an apple-branch in one hand and a phiale in the other, and wearing a crown decorated with deer and images of Victory. Excavations at Rhamnus have brought to light a colossal female head, now in the British Museum, corresponding to Pausanias' description, as well as fragments of the base, now in Athens. A Roman relief at Stockholm preserves versions of four of the figures on the base. Furthermore, a standing figure on a coin of Cyprus represented holding a branch in one hand and a phiale in the other has by some been thought to reproduce the statue; but not enough of the head is preserved to make the interpretation convincing. In addition Agoracritus is known to have made a colossal marble statue of the Mother of the Gods for the Metroon of the Athenian Agora, and bronze statues of Athena Itonia with Zeus-Hades in Coronea (Paus. 9. 34; Strab. 9. 411). Of the Mother of the Gods a number of reproductions, large and small, have been identified, and recently the head of the Zeus-Hades has been recognized in heads in the Barberini Collection, Naples, and Sweden (cf. Andren, *Rend. Acc. Pont.* xxxv (1962–3), 27 ff.). G. M. A. R.

**AGORANOMOI** (ἀγορανόμοι), overseers of the market, an office known in more than 120 Greek states. In classical times they were usually elected by lot. In Athens there were ten, five for the city and five for the Piraeus. They kept order in the market, saw to the quality and correct weight of goods, and collected market dues. They had power to punish small infractions of their rules with fines, from the proceeds of which they maintained and extended the market buildings; for graver offences they initiated prosecutions before the dicasteries and presided at the trials. *See also* METRONOMOI, SITOPHYLAKES, ASTYNOMOI. A. W. G.

**AGRICOLA.** (1), GNAEUS JULIUS (*PW* 49) (A.D. 40–93), of Forum Julii (*Fréjus*), was son of Julius Graecinus, senator, and Julia Procilla; he married Domitia Decidiana, and had one son (died an infant) and one daughter. He was educated at the University of Massilia. He was *tribunus militum* to Suetonius Paulinus in Britain (A.D. 61); quaestor of Asia (64); *tribunus plebis* (66); praetor (68); commissioner for the recovery of temple property (68); recruiting officer for Mucianus (69); legate of the Twentieth Legion, in Britain (71–73); legate of Aquitania (74–77); consul (77); legate of Britain (from 78).

His career, in particular the British governorship, is described in his *Life* by Tacitus, his son-in-law. Previous experience in Britain, shrewd intelligence, provincial sympathies, and an exceptional eye for country, enabled Agricola both to pacify civilians and to advance far into Scotland, where his permanent outposts at Inchtuthil (*JRS* 1919 and 1953–65), Fendoch (*PSAS* lxxiii. 110 ff.), Stracathro (*JRS* 1961, 123), and others yet to be confirmed by excavation, blockaded the Highlands. The advance was by stages. North Wales was reconquered and Anglesey occupied (Tac. *Agr.* 18); the west coast ('silvas ac aestuaria', *Agr.* 20) was annexed. Then came a preliminary advance to the Tay (*Agr.* 22), gripping the Tweed crossing at Newstead and followed by a consolidation between Forth and Clyde (*Agr.* 23) with forts at Camelon and near Mumrills and Cadder and perhaps signal-posts at Bar Hill and Croy Hill (G. Macdonald, *Roman Wall in Scotland*,² 1934). This marked the limit of conquest permitted by Titus. The fifth campaign was probably in south-west Scotland, where Agricolan forts are now known at Dalswinton, Glenlochar, Gatehouse of Fleet, and Loudon Hill. The sixth (A.D. 83) marked a fresh advance northwards beyond the Forth (made possible by a change of emperor) and the foundation of a fortress for Legio XX at Inchtuthil. Marching camps extend to Auchinhove. In the seventh the Highlands were spurred to defeat at 'mons Graupius' perhaps not far short of Inverness. Agricola was then recalled after a rather specialized experience which did not fit him for service elsewhere. Roman historians were most struck by his circumnavigation of Britain (*Agr.* 38; Dio Cass. 39. 50. 4; 66. 20. 1–2); kindred explorations were also made (Plut. *De def. or.* 18; cf. Dessau, *Hermes* 1911, 156).

His civil policy involved the encouragement of urbanization and the foundation of self-ruling *civitates* in southern Britain to fill the administrative gap caused by moving the garrison north. The Verulamium forum inscription (*JRS* 1956, 146 f.), too, illustrates *Agr.* 21. 1. The great extension of the governor's military duties caused the appointment of a *legatus iuridicus* in A.D. 79 (*ILS* 1011).

Tacitus, *Agricola*, ed. R. M. Ogilvie and I. A. Richmond (1967). I. A. Richmond, *JRS* 1944, 34.ff.; Frere, *Britannia*, ch. 6. I. A. R.; S. S. F.

**AGRICOLA** (2), SEXTUS CALPURNIUS, waged war as governor of Britain for Marcus and Verus (A.D. 163); was legate in the German phase of the Marcomannic War and governor of *Tres Daciae* in 167–8. British inscriptions attest his military building at Corbridge and Chesterholm in Tynedale and at Ribchester on the Ribble; also a change of garrison at Carvoran on Hadrian's Wall. I. A. R.

**AGRICULTURAL IMPLEMENTS.** Manual implements for cultivating the soil were the essential tools of the farmer throughout classical antiquity. Persistent tillage of the fallow between crops was necessary to the successful growing of cereals, and hoe cultivation was never superseded by the plough, since flat arable land was scarce both in Greece and Italy. Greek farmers seem to have made few improvements in the design of their implements. In ancient Italy, however, the great variety of soils encountered in the various regions produced much variety in the basic implements of tillage, the spade and the hoe. The foot-rest spade (*bipalium*) afforded greater penetration, and multiple-tined hoes (*bidentes*, *rastra*) helped to produce a fine, even tilth for the seed-bed. The advance of viticulture and the extension of orchards stimulated the development of specialized implements for the skilled operations of lopping and pruning, ranging from the simple bill-hook (*falx putatoria*) to the perfected form of the vine-dresser's knife (*falx vinitoria*), with which six different operations could be performed (Colum. *RR* 4. 25). Similar advances in design may be noticed in harvesting implements; the balanced sickle (*falx messoria*), though not invented by Roman farmers, was much improved by them; many other specialized harvesting implements are mentioned by the Roman authorities, including a 'spitted' sickle (*falx veruculata*), which probably improved the process of gathering in the stalks before cutting. Cato's handbook (2nd c. B.C.) and that of Palladius (4th c. A.D.) contain valuable inventories of farm equipment, including lists of iron implements. Machines are somewhat rare. The threshing-sledge (*tribulum*) was borrowed from Greece, and an improved version (*plostellum poenicum*) was one of many agricultural legacies from Carthage. Separation of the grain from the chaff was a laborious process in antiquity, whether effected by the back-breaking method of flailing with a hingeless stick, or by treading out with animals; the *tribulum*, a heavy board with flints embedded in the under-side, was an advance on earlier methods, and the process was still further improved by the substitution of sets of small wheels for the flint teeth as in the *plostellum poenicum*. But the most significant mechanical invention was the *vallus*, a reaping machine equipped with a row of sharp knives, which was driven through the standing corn by an animal harnessed at the rear, tearing off the heads of grain and depositing them in a container. This 'heading' machine is reported by Pliny the Elder and by Palladius as used on the open fields of northern Gaul, where it saved both time and manpower. A sculptured slab depicting a *vallus* was discovered in 1958 on a late Gallo-Roman site on the borders of Belgium and Luxemburg. *See* PLOUGHING.

Dar.-Sag., s.v. rustica res; *PW*, s.v. bidens, bipalium, crates, dolabra, Ernte, ligo, pala, pecten, plostellum punicum, rastrum, runco, sarculum, Sichel, traha, tribulum, vallus; Sir W. M. F. Petrie, *Tools and Weapons* (1917); F. Angelini, *Indagine sugli attrezzi a mano in agricoltura* i (1939), 3 ff.; E. M. Jope, in *A History of Technology*, ed. C. Singer, vol. ii (1956), 94 ff.; J. Le Gall, 'Les "falces" et la "faux" ', *Annales de l'Est*, Mem. 22 (1959), iv, 55 ff.; J. Kolendo, 'Techniques rurales: la moissonneuse antique en Gaule romaine', *Annales* (ESC), 15 (1960), 1099 ff.; K. D. White, *Agricultural Implements of the Roman World* (1967). K. D. W.

**AGRICULTURE** (Greek and Roman). The general technique of Greek and Roman agriculture, its utilization of most of the plants, animals, and tools employed until modern times, may have originated in the mesolithic and neolithic periods; but the beginning of the Iron Age, i.e. the dawn of history in Greece and Italy, witnessed a revolutionary change. The iron plough and other tools, now made of the new metal, increased agricultural production as never before. Most of the villagers of the Minoan and Mycenaean regions seem to have been serfs of their kings, but the periods of Homer, Hesiod, and Solon preferred small and economically independent agricultural units, and revolted successfully against the rule of big landlords. Small estates of knights and pea-

sants were now the rule. A few slaves, together with their owner's family, did all normal work. Free labourers were employed during harvest and for tasks for which the farmers and their servants lacked sufficient time. Small irrigation works and canals were necessary almost everywhere. After a year of cultivation the land was left fallow for one, and in some regions, for two years and was ploughed in autumn, in spring, and in summer (in some regions only twice in the year). The production of grain, flax, and vegetables was supplemented by arboriculture, olive-culture, viticulture, and especially pasturage, which were the most lucrative forms of land work.

**2.** The period of classical Greece witnessed a rational differentiation of the various agricultural plants and their habits, of the different kinds of soil, and of the appropriate manures, and production was stimulated by the growing demand for grain, meat, and vegetables in towns. The time had come for threefold rotation of crops (*IG* ii². 2493 and Xen. *Oec.* 16. 12–15). The agricultural production of Greece must have increased very greatly when the soil could be continuously cultivated without being exhausted. No wonder that the first capitalistic slave estates were established at this time, and that capitalists investing in land began to lease to tenants tracts which were too large for their own or their stewards' management. Small estates remained nevertheless the rule in the Greek motherland, and were common also in Sicily and on the Black Sea coast.

**3.** From Alexander to Augustus Mediterranean agriculture was improved by many inventions (especially machines for hoisting water). Suitable varieties of plants and animals were transferred from one part of the civilized world to another, and new crops developed in many countries. Attica seems to have produced 1,100,000–1,250,000 bushels of grain in Alexander's time, of which amount only *c.* 15–20 per cent. appears to have been wheat. The production of the Hellenistic East increased considerably. The two-crop system originating in the ancient East was improved under Greek management, and independent Greek cultivators were settled throughout the Seleucid Empire.

**4.** The Ptolemies refined and expanded the New Kingdom economy of Egypt in their state-controlled agriculture (cf. Wilbour Papyrus). Oil-seeds, grain, and textile plants had to be cultivated in each region of the Nile country according to an official schedule, which was revised each year. The seed, iron tools, and cattle for agriculture were commonly lent to the cultivators by the government. Almost the whole of the crop had to be paid (for taxes in kind, rent) or sold to the government, which built up a granary system for wheat export throughout the Nile country. Only a few large estates of distinguished owners were partly exempted. Handbooks on agriculture (the sources of Cato, Columella, the *Geoponica*, Mago, Varro) were used in this new cultivation system as well as by the more educated owners of large slave estates, which now superseded many of the peasant homesteads in all Mediterranean countries. Another characteristic of the same period was the surprising extent of division of labour and specialization in Greek and Roman agriculture, and the very common, almost capitalistic calculation of expenses, revenues, and profits.

**5.** The highest standard of ancient cultivation was reached in the Italian agriculture of the later Republic and early Principate. Big slave estates prevailed here, so long as prisoners of war were cheap. The varieties of plants, the rotation of crops, and the other methods of cultivation, amelioration, irrigation, and manuring, bookkeeping, the organization and division of labour, the buildings, tools, old and new machines were carefully selected from the technical as well as from the economic point of view, and similar methods spread to the provinces.

6. The Roman *villa* (q.v.) of this period underwent decisive changes, as soon as slave economy ceased to pay. Estate management of the highest type had to be confined to comparatively small tracts, so far as cheap labour for it was available. Most of the land had to be given to small tenants who were gradually bound to the soil (*see* COLONUS). This development did not mean the collapse of Graeco-Roman agriculture, but its final preservation. The agricultural methods of small peasants had not been much improved during the prevalence of slave estates; but the landlords of necessity now saw to it that their tenants should learn as much of the results of scientific agriculture as was suitable for their small economic units.

7. The unification of Mediterranean agriculture as seen to-day was completed from the second century A.D. onwards by the popularizing of plants, animals, tools, machines, and methods of estate agriculture under the peasantry of the Empire. Germanic and Oriental prisoners of war, who were settled throughout the Empire, were similarly taught, and transferred such knowledge to their home countries. Agriculture did not break down in Europe after the conquest of the Western Roman Empire. On the contrary, the agriculture of middle and northern Europe was modelled on Late Roman lines; it was a fundamental heritage of the Ancient World. *See also* AGRICULTURAL IMPLEMENTS, ARBORICULTURE, BEE-KEEPING, HORSES, LATIFUNDIA, OLIVE CULTURE, PASTURAGE, VILLA, VITICULTURE.

PW, s.v. 'Ackerbau' (Olck), 'Bauernstand' (Suppl. IV, Kornemann), 'Domaenen' (Suppl. IV, id.), 'Iunius' (104, Kappelmacher), 'Landwirtschaft' (Orth), 'Mago' (15, Klotz) 'Pontos Euxeinos' (Suppl. IX, Danoff), 'Porcius' (9, Helm), 'Terentius' (Suppl. VI Dahlmann); H. Bolkestein, *Economic Life in Greece's Golden Age*[2] (1958); E. Bréhaut, *Cato the Censor on Farming* (1933); V. Ehrenberg, *The People of Aristophanes*[2] (1962), ch. 3. 7; M. I. Finley, *Land and Credit in Ancient Athens, 500–200 B.C.* (1951); T. Frank, *Econ. Surv. I–V; An Economic History of Rome*[2] (1927); G. Glotz, *Le Travail dans la Grèce ancienne* (1920); H. Gummerus, *Der römische Gutsbetrieb als wirtschaftlicher Organismus* (Klio Suppl. 5, 1905); J. Hasebroek, *Griechische Wirtschafts- und Gesellschaftsgeschichte bis zur Perserzeit* (1931); V. Hehn, *Kulturpflanzen und Haustiere*[8] (1911); F. M. Heichelheim, *Wirtschaftsgeschichte des Altertums* (1938), Index s.v. Dreifelderwirtschaft, 'Gutsbetrieb als Wirtschaftsorganismus', 'Landwirtschaft', Zweierntenwirtschaft'; 'The Wilbour Papyrus', *Hist.* 1953, 129 ff.; 'Man's Role in Changing the Face of the Earth in Classical Antiquity', *Kyklos* 1956, 318 ff.; 'Römische Sozial- und Wirtschaftsgeschichte', *Historia Mundi* 1956, 397 ff.; *An Ancient Economic History*, i (1958), 332 ff., 340 ff., 371 ff., 451 ff., 515 ff. ii (1964), 112 ff., 219 ff.; art. 'Wirtschaftsgeschichte II, 2, A', *Handwoerterbuch der Sozialwissenschaften* (1962), 44, 144 ff.; *A History of the Roman People* (1962, with C. A. Yeo); *Kl. Pauly*, s.v. 'Bauernstand, Leges Agrariae'; W. E. Heitland, *Agricola* (1921); A. Jardé, *Les Céréales dans l'antiquité grecque* (1925); Jones *Later Rom. Emp.*, ch. 13, 20; J. Karayannopulos, *Das Finanzwesen des frühbyzantinischen Staates* (1958); Magie, *Rom. Rule Asia Min.*; Michell, *Econom. Anc. Gr.*, ch. 2; G. Mickwitz, *Engl. Hist. Rev.* 1937, 577 ff.; Cl. Préaux, *L'Économie royale des Lagides* (1939); Rostovtzeff, *Roman Empire; Hellenistic World*; L. Ruggini, *Economia e societa nell'Italia Annonaria* (1961); M. Schnebel, *Die Lamdwirtschaft im hellenistischen Aegypten* (1924); V. A. Sirago, *L'Italia agraria sotto Trajano* (1958); W. L. Westermann, *The Slave Systems of Greek and Roman Antiquity* (1955); C. A. Yeo, *Finanzarchiv* 1952, 321 ff., 445 ff. F. M. H.

**AGRI DECUMATES,** a territory including the Black Forest, the basin of the Neckar, and the Swabian Alb, annexed by the Flavian emperors between A.D. 74 and 98 to shorten communications between the Rhine and Danube armies, and lost to Rome c. A.D. 263. It had been occupied by the Helvetii and later by Suebi, but after the migration led by Maroboduus (c. 6 B.C.) there was no compact tribal community left, and a number of homeless Gauls settled there. The meaning of *Decumates* has been much disputed; it has been widely held that the term was derived from the Celtic word for ten, the *Agri Decumates* thus consisting of ten units, possibly cantons (cf. the *Decempagi* of the Mediomatrici).

The only classical reference to the *Agri Decumates* is Tac. *Germ.* 29. E. Hesselmeyer, *Klio* 1931, 1 ff.; E. Norden, *Alt-Germanien* (1934), 137 ff.; Tacitus, *Germania*, ed. Anderson (1938), 148 f. O. B.

**AGRIPPA** (1) **I,** MARCUS JULIUS (10 B.C.–A.D. 44), erroneously called 'Herod' in Acts of the Apostles xii, a grandson of Herod the Great (q.v.), lived at the imperial court from childhood until the death of his friend Drusus, Tiberius' son (A.D. 23). He then returned to Palestine, where he pursued a varied and impecunious career. He came back to Italy in 36 on borrowed money, but was imprisoned by Tiberius for treason. He had, however, cultivated the friendship of Gaius, who released him and appointed him king of the tetrarchy of his uncle Philip (q.v. 4) in 37 and of that of Herod (q.v. 2) Antipas also in 39. On a visit to Rome in 40 he courageously dissuaded Gaius from his proposal to desecrate the Temple. In 41 Claudius, whose accession he had assisted, added the province of Judaea (*see* ARCHELAUS 4) to his kingdom, and his rule was popular despite his generosity to Greek cities, especially Berytus. But his plan to fortify the northern suburb of Jerusalem and his ambitious foreign policy disquieted Claudius, who on his death annexed his whole kingdom.

Josephus, *BJ* 2. 178–83, 206–20; *AJ* 18. 143–301; 19. 236–363; Philo, *Leg.* 261–330. M. P. Charlesworth, *Five Men* (1936), 3 ff.; A. H. M. Jones, *The Herods of Judaea* (1938), 184 ff. E. M. S.

**AGRIPPA** (2) **II,** MARCUS JULIUS (b. A.D. 27/28), did not succeed his father Agrippa I in 44, but lived at Claudius' court until 49/50, when he was appointed king of Chalcis, (*see* ITURAEA). This principality had been granted to his uncle Herod (a brother of Agrippa I) by Claudius in 41 and ruled by Herod till his death in 48. In 53 Agrippa was transferred to the former tetrarchy of Philip (q.v. 4) together with Abilene and Arcene. Nero added four toparchies of Galilee and Peraea. Though his subjects were mostly gentiles, Agrippa maintained close relations with the Jews. He inherited his uncle's right to appoint the High Priests and to control the Temple treasury, and frequently visited Jerusalem (cf. Acts xxv–xxvi). But he supported the Roman government, and after unsuccessful attempts, first by argument and then by military action, to prevent the Jewish revolt in 66, he gave military help to the Roman commanders throughout the war and was present at the siege of Jerusalem; he was rewarded with an accession of territory. Indications in Josephus (q.v.) that he was dead before the publication of the *AJ* (93/94) and *Vita* are confirmed by epigraphic evidence against Photius' statement (*Bibl.* 33) that he died in 100.

Josephus, *BJ* 2. 335–526, *etc.*; *AJ* 20. 1–223. A. H. M. Jones, *The Herods of Judaea* (1938), 217 ff. E. M. S.

**AGRIPPA** (3), MARCUS VIPSANIUS (*PW* 2), the lifelong friend and supporter of Augustus, was born in 64 or 63 B.C. of obscure but probably well-to-do family. He accompanied Octavius to Rome from Apollonia after the murder of Caesar, helped him to raise a private army, prosecuted Cassius in the court set up by Pedius (q.v.1) in 43 (possibly as tribune), was prominent in the war against L. Antonius (q.v. 6), and became *praetor urbanus* in 40. Subsequently as governor of Gaul he suppressed a rebellion in Aquitania (q.v.), led a punitive expedition across the Rhine, and, either now or in 20, helped the Ubii to settle on the left bank. As consul (37) he fitted out and trained a new fleet for Octavian's war against Sextus Pompeius, converting the Lacus Avernus near Cumae into a harbour (Portus Julius) for the purpose, and in 36 won the two decisive naval engagements at Mylae and Naulochus, where his improved grapnel was highly effective. In 35 and 34 he took part in the Illyrian War. In 33 his munificent aedileship must have contributed greatly to the popularity of Octavian's cause. In 31 his vigorous naval operations were the primary cause of Antony's defeat; at Actium (q.v.) he commanded the left wing. He next (31–29), with Maecenas, managed affairs in Italy in

Octavian's absence. On Octavian's return he helped him to carry out a drastic *lectio senatus* and a census (29–28); he held a second and third consulship (28 and 27). When Augustus, seriously ill (23), handed him his signet-ring, he probably meant to indicate him as his most suitable successor. He was entrusted with the control of the eastern half of the Empire and probably granted the proconsular *imperium* for the purpose (23). Friction with M. Marcellus (q.v. 7) possibly may have been a secondary cause of this mission, which he performed from headquarters at Mytilene. He was recalled in 21 to represent Augustus in Rome; in 20 he proceeded to Gaul and in 19 to Spain where he put an end to trouble with the Cantabri (q.v.). In 18 he was associated even more closely with Augustus by the conferment of the *tribunicia potestas* for five years, and his *imperium* was apparently renewed for the same period. In 13 his tribunician power was renewed for five more years and his *imperium* made *maius* like that of Augustus. As one of the *quindecimviri sacris faciundis* (q.v.) he assisted in the celebration of the *ludi saeculares* in 17. His second mission to the East (17/16–13) is notable for the establishment of Polemon (q.v.) of Pontus in the Bosporan kingdom, the settlement of veteran colonies at Berytus and Heliopolis (qq.v.), and his friendship with Herod (q.v. 1) and benevolent treatment of the Jews. Early in 12 he went to Pannonia where there was a danger of revolt, but fell ill on his return and died about the end of March. After a public funeral he was buried in the mausoleum of Augustus.

Agrippa's immense wealth, due no doubt to his first marriage (see below) and his position as right-hand man of Augustus, was spent freely in the service of Rome and the Empire. For Rome he built the Pantheon (q.v.), the first great public baths (q.v.), a granary, a new bridge over the Tiber, two new aqueducts (Julia and Virgo), and a network of installations for the distribution of the water; he also cleaned out and repaired the sewers, and managed the entire water-system of the city till his death. His constructions in the provinces included buildings at Nemausus (q.v.) and a system of main roads radiating from Lugdunum (q.v.). By his will Augustus received the greater part of his property, including the whole of the Thracian Chersonese (q.v.); he also made generous bequests to the people of Rome.

He wrote an autobiography (now lost) and a geographical commentary (also lost, but used by Strabo and Pliny) from which a map of the Empire, displayed on the Porticus Vipsania built after his death, was constructed.

Agrippa was married three times: (1) *c.* 37, to Attica (q.v.), who bore him a daughter Agrippina (q.v. 1); (2) *c.* 28, to Augustus' niece Marcella, whom he divorced; and (3) in 21, to Julia (q.v. 2), by whom he had three sons, Gaius Caesar (q.v. 7), Lucius Caesar (q.v. 8), and Agrippa (q.v. 4) Postumus, and two daughters, Julia (q.v. 3) and Agrippina (q.v. 2). Through this Agrippina the Emperors Gaius and Nero were descended from him.

Upright, simple in his tastes, and avoiding undue distinction (he refused three triumphs), Agrippa was above all a man of action, equally successful both in war and peace. He was not without ambition, but consistently subordinated it to the interests of Augustus.

Vell. Pat. 2; Joseph. *AJ* 12. 3, 15. 10, 16. 2–6; Suet. *Aug.*; App. *BCiv.* 5; Cass. Dio 48–55. M. Reinhold, *Marcus Agrippa* (1933); R. Daniel, *M. Vipsanius Agrippa* (1933); Syme, *Rom. Rev.*, see Index; F. W. Shipley, *Agrippa's Building Activities in Rome* (U.S.A. 1933); Schanz–Hosius, ii. 329 ff.; for his geographical commentary, A. Klotz, *Klio* 1931, 35 ff., 386 ff. (fragments); for the map, J. J. Tierney, *Proc. Royal Irish Acad.* 1963, 151 ff. Iconography: F. Poulsen, *Röm. Privatporträts und Prinzenbildnisse* (1939) 11 ff. G. W. R.; T. J. C.

**AGRIPPA** (4) **POSTUMUS**, Marcus Vipsanius (*PW* Iulii 128), third son of Agrippa (3) and Julia, born after his father's death in 12 B.C., was adopted by Augustus along with Tiberius in A.D. 4 and hence renamed Agrippa Julius Caesar. He was a youth of fine physique but his depraved and contumacious character ultimately exasperated Augustus into disinheriting him. He was first sent to Surrentum, then condemned by the Senate to perpetual exile on Planasia (A.D. 7). Later a conspiracy to rescue him and place him at the head of a military insurrection was uncovered and suppressed. He was put to death immediately after the death of Augustus, it is not clear on whose instructions. The story of a visit by Augustus to Planasia some months earlier (Tac. *Ann.* 1. 5) is generally rejected. After Agrippa's death a slave of his called Clemens impersonated him with a view to overthrowing Tiberius, but was taken and killed (A.D. 16).

M. P. Charlesworth, *AJPhil.* 1923, 145 ff.; E. Hohl, *Hermes* 1935, 350 ff.; M. L. Paladini, *Acme* 1954, 313 ff. G. W. R.; T. J. C.

**AGRIPPA** (5), Sceptic, later than Aenesidemus (q.v.; date otherwise unknown). Diog. Laert. 9. 88 ff. ascribes to him five τρόποι τῆς ἐποχῆς (grounds of doubt), which are distinguished by Sext. Emp. *Pyr.* 1. 164 from those previously recognized by the Sceptics. W. D. R.

**AGRIPPINA.** (1) Vipsania Agrippina (d. A.D. 20) was daughter of M. Agrippa and granddaughter of Pomponius Atticus. Married to Tiberius, she bore him a son, Drusus, but he was forced by Augustus, against his will, to divorce her and marry Julia in 12 B.C. She then married Asinius Gallus (q.v. 5) and bore him at least five sons.

(2) Agrippina Major (*c.* 14 B.C.–A.D. 33), Vipsania Agrippina, the daughter of M. Agrippa and of Julia (daughter of Augustus). She married Germanicus (probably in A.D. 5), to whom she bore nine children. She was with Germanicus on the Rhine from 14 to 16 and in the East from 18 until his death in the following year. From 19 to 29 she lived in Rome, the rallying point of a party of senators who opposed the growing power of Sejanus. With Tiberius, whom she suspected (without evidence) of causing her husband's death, her relations were consistently bad, and he refused her request in 26 for leave to marry again. She was arrested in 29 on the instruction of Tiberius and banished by the Senate to Pandateria, where she starved to death in 33. She was survived by one son, Gaius (q.v. 1), and three daughters, Agrippina II, Drusilla, and Livilla.

(3) Agrippina Minor (A.D. 15–59), Julia (*PW* 556) Agrippina, the eldest daughter of Germanicus and Agrippina, was born on 6 Nov. A.D. 15 at Ara Ubiorum. In 28 she was betrothed to Cn. Domitius Ahenobarbus, to whom she bore one son, the later Emperor Nero, in 37. During the principate of her brother Gaius (37–41) her name, like those of her sisters, was coupled with the emperor's in vows and oaths; but when she was discovered at Moguntiacum late in 39 to be involved in the conspiracy of Gaetulicus, she was sent into banishment. She was recalled by her uncle Claudius, who married her in 49. Aided by Pallas, Seneca, and Burrus, she quickly achieved her ambitious purpose. Receiving for herself the title Augusta, she persuaded Claudius to adopt Nero as guardian of his own son Britannicus. She was generally believed to have poisoned Claudius, to make room for Nero (54). In the first years of Nero's rule she was almost co-regent with him but, after Pallas had fallen in 55 and Burrus and Seneca turned against her, she lost her power. In March 59 she was murdered at Baiae by a freedman, Anicetus, acting on Nero's instructions. She wrote an autobiography.

J. P. V. D. Balsdon, *Roman Women* (1962). J. P. B.

**AGROECIUS**, fifth-century bishop of Sens, wrote a treatise *De Orthographia* (ed. Keil, *Gramm. Lat.* vii. 113–25) as a supplement to Flavius Caper (q.v.).

Schanz–Hosius, § 1100.

**AGYRRHIUS** (*c.* 400 B.C.), Athenian democratic politician, restored the 'Theorika' (q.v.), and introduced payment for attendance at the Assembly, first one, later three obols.

**AHALA,** GAIUS SERVĪLIUS (*PW* 32). The legend that Servilius saved his country in 439 B.C. by killing Sp. Maelius (q.v.) with a dagger concealed under his armpit was probably invented as an aetiological myth to explain the *cognomen* (perhaps Etruscan) Ahala or Axilla (i.e. armpit) borne by the *gens Servilia*. When it was discovered that Servilii Ahalae occurred in the Fasti before 439, a different version was elaborated, according to which Servilius acted neither as a private citizen nor illegally, but as Master of Horse in Cincinnatus' second (fictitious) dictatorship. Later embellishments, due to political propaganda of Gracchan and Sullan times, include Servilius' exile from his ungrateful country. The legend of the tyrannicide and saviour of republican liberty decisively influenced a descendant of the *gens Servilia*, M. Brutus (q.v. 5).

Mommsen, *Röm. Forsch.* ii. 199 ff.; Ogilvie, *Comm. Livy, 1–5*, 550 ff.
P. T.

**AIAS** (*Aἴas*, Lat. *Ajax*). (1) Son of Telamon, king of Salamis, hence A. Telamonius (*see* AEACUS, TELAMON 1), but nowhere called an Aeacid till after Homer. In the *Iliad* he is of enormous (πελώριος) size, head and shoulders above the rest (3. 226–9). Only in a brief reference in the Catalogue (2. 557) is he connected with Salamis. He is a blunt, stolid man, slow of speech, of unshakable courage, who repeatedly leads the Greek attack or covers the retreat. His stock epithet is 'bulwark (ἕρκος)of the Achaeans' and his characteristic weapon a huge shield, evidently of Mycenaean pattern. Fighting Hector in a duel, he has rather the better of it (7. 206 ff.); he draws a wrestling-match with Odysseus, strength against cunning (23. 708 ff.). He is one of the three ambassadors who treat with Achilles (q.v.; 9. 169 ff.). In the *Odyssey* (11. 543 ff.) mention is made of his death in consequence of the arms of Achilles having been adjudged to Odysseus and not to him after the death of their owner. The story is probably that found in later authors, e.g. Sophocles (*Ajax*), that he went mad with anger and disappointment and finally killed himself; it was told in the *Little Iliad*.

In the *Great Ehoiai* (Hesiod, fr. 140 Rzach) and thence in Pindar (*Isthm.* 6. 34 ff.), Heracles visits Telamon and, standing on his lion-skin, prays that his new-born child shall be as stout (ἄρρηκτος) as the skin; Zeus, in answer, sends an eagle, αἰετός, and hence the baby is named Aias. From this develops (Lycophron 455 ff.) the tale that Aias was invulnerable save at one point, where the skin had not touched him when (in this version) he was wrapped in it. In the *Aethiopis* Aias carries off the body of Achilles, while Odysseus keeps off the Trojans (cf. *Od.* 5. 309). Of his death various stories were told; he died of an arrow-wound received from Paris, or, being invulnerable, was buried alive by the Trojans throwing clay on him (argument to Soph. *Aj.* ad fin.). When he killed himself his blood flowed on the ground and there sprang up the iris (ὑάκινθος), which also commemorates the death of Hyacinthus (q.v.); hence the markings on its petals recall the hero's name (Aἴas—αἰαῖ, see Ov. *Met.* 13. 394 ff.).

Aias had a cult in Salamis, Attica, Megara (?), the Troad, and Byzantium (Farnell, *Hero-Cults*, 307 ff. and note 58). That he was not originally a man at all, but a gigantic and supernatural being, is an ingenious theory (see, for instance, P. von der Mühll, *Der grosse Aias*, 1930) but based on slight evidence. Page more convincingly argues that he was a traditional figure of Mycenaean epic as the bearer of a man-covering shield and was drawn

into the story of the *Iliad* later (*History and the Homeric Iliad* (U.S.A. 1959), 232 ff.) Certainly from Homer on he was conceived as a very tall and powerful man, nothing more.

The suicide of Aias is a favourite theme in art in many media from the seventh century. Other subjects popular from the sixth are: combats with Hector and others, dicing with Achilles; lifting Achilles' body; and various phases of his quarrel with Odysseus over Achilles' arms (Brommer, *Vasenlisten²*, 275 ff.).

(2) Son of Oïleus or Ileus, the Locrian chieftain. In Homer Aias is leader of the Locrian contingent (*Il.* 2 527 ff.); he is 'much lesser' than the son of Telamon (hence often called Aias the Lesser), quick-footed, and often paired with his greater namesake as a brave fighter. He is, however, of hateful character and on occasion grossly rude (as 23. 473 ff.). Athena hates him (ibid. 774 *Od.* 4. 502); in the latter passage he is drowned by Poseidon for blasphemy against the gods while scrambling ashore after shipwreck. In the *Iliu Persis* Aias drags Cassandra away from the altar of Athena, pulling the Palladium with her. For his historical existence there is some argument in the Locrian custom of sending every year two virgins of their noblest families to serve in the temple of Athena of Ilium, if they were not killed on the way by the townspeople. From early in the third century B.C. the Aianteioi, the hero's own clan, undertook to furnish these girls (inscription published by A. Wilhelm *JÖAI* 1911, 168 f.; for the custom in general, see Lycophron 1141 ff. and schol. there; Polybius 12, fr. 5, Büttner–Wobst; Plutarch, *De sera* 557 d). It ended in the second century B.C. The Locrians had maintained that it was imposed for 1,000 years. It has seemed inconceivable to some scholars that this should be the result of an imaginary person's fabulous crime, and therefore the classical explanation, that it is a penance for Aias carrying off the Palladium or raping Cassandra at the altar of Athena, during the sack of Troy, has been accepted, but it seems to owe its imposition in historic time to the Delphic oracle. See further Farnell, op. cit. 294 ff and ibid. 293–4, for Aias' cult; A. Momigliano, *CQ* 1947, 49; Parke and Wormell, *Delphic Oracle* (1956), 326 ff.

The dragging of Cassandra from the image of Athena is frequently found in vase-painting and other arts from the beginning of the sixth century. In Polygnotus' Troy Aias was shown taking an oath about the assault before the Greek kings (Brommer, *Vasenlisten²* 282 ff.).

That two heroes so unlike should have the same name is curious, and at the same time an argument against supposing that they were originally one.
H. J. R.; H. W. P.; C. M. R

**AION** (*Aἰών*), a personification of (1) period of time, (2 passage of time, indefinitely long time (hardly eternity except in thought deriving from Plato, *Tim.* 37 d). In cult, (1) is represented by the festival at Alexandria (late and Greek but not unconnected with Egyptian ideas, see E. Norden, *Geburt des Kindes*, 28, and refs. there), at which an image was brought out of the inner sanctuary of the Κορεῖον, with the announcement that 'the Maiden (Κόρη) has brought forth Aion.' This is apparently the year; cf., for an allegedly Phoenician mythological figure of the same kind, Philon of Byblus ap. Euseb. *Praep. Evang.* 1. 10. 7. (2) perhaps in Eur. *Heracl.* 900, but cf. Wilamowitz-Moellendorff on *Hl* 660; cf. Heraclitus, fr. 79 Bywater. In cult he is late probably Orphic (Kern, *Relig. der Griechen* iii. 243) possibly Mithraic also (Cumont, *Textes et Monument* (1895–9), i. 76; *Rel. or.* (4. 140 and note 46), cf. the Iranian Zervan Akarana). Mythologically, Aion is a important character in Nonnus, *Dionysiaca*. His connexion with a number of figures showing a lion-headed deity is problematical, cf. Cumont, *Textes*, loc. cit., Nilsson, *GGR* ii. 478 ff. An inscription to him, of the Augustan period, comes from Eleusis, *SIG*, 1125. Cf. A. D. Nock, *Harv. Theol. Rev.* 1934, 53 ff. on the complexity of ideas attaching to this term (and on the publicist and patriotic sense of *Aeternitas* at Rome); C. Bonner, *Hesp.* 1944, 30 ff.                                    H. J. R.

**AISYMNETES**, according to Aristotle (*Pol.* 1285ª), a supreme ruler appointed by some early city-states in times of internal crisis, for life, for a prescribed period, or till the completion of his task, e.g. Pittacus (q.v.). Aristotle defines the office as an elective tyranny; Dionysius (5. 73) compares the Roman dictator. These *aisymnetai* have affinities with the early lawgivers (Solon, Zaleucus, Demonax, etc.), the difference being one of local nomenclature. Inscriptions (*SIG* 38, 57, 272, 642, 955) show regular magistrates so called in Teos, Miletus, Naxos, Megara, Selinus, and Chalcedon. The word first occurs in *Od.* 8. 258, meaning a referee.          P. N. U.

**AITHER** (*Αἰθήρ*), personification of the purer upper stratum of air (approximately the stratosphere), next to or identical with the sky; son of Erebus and Night (Hesiod, *Theog.* 124–5); of Chaos and Darkness (Hyginus, *Fab. praef.* 1); husband of Day and of Earth (ibid. 2–3).
                                                              H. J. R.

**AIUS LOCUTIUS**, the unknown divine 'sayer and speaker' who, a little before the battle of the Allia (q.v.) in 390 B.C., bade one M. Caedicius tell the magistrates that the Gauls were coming. After their departure a precinct (*templum*) and shrine (*sacellum*) were dedicated near Vesta's shrine, on the Nova Via, where the voice was heard.

Livy 5. 32. 6; 50. 5. Platner–Ashby, 3 f.          H. J. R.

**ALABANDA**, a city in northern Caria, on the Marsyas, a tributary of the Maeander, at the point where the road from Tralles branches westward to Halicarnassus and south to the coast opposite Rhodes. Its site (now *Arabhisar*) between two hills is likened by Strabo to a packsaddle. In the province Asia it was a *civitas libera* and the centre of a *conventus*. It was proverbial for opulence and comfort.                                              W. M. C.

**ALAE**, a term originally denoting the two contingents of *socii* normally posted on the legion's flanks; after the Social War (90–89 B.C.) it bore the more restricted sense of cavalry. In his Gallic campaigns Caesar employed contingents of tribal cavalry, mainly under native *praefecti equitum*, and many of these, no doubt, were embodied for service in the Civil Wars and placed under veteran officers. When Augustus organized the *auxilia* the cavalry contingents were called *alae* and commanded by equestrian *praefecti equitum* (the title *praefectus alae* becomes common later), and numbered either 1,000 men (*ala miliaria*), or 500 (*ala quingenaria*), subdivided into 24 and 16 *turmae* respectively. They commonly bore titles indicating the country from which they had been recruited (e.g. *Hispanorum*), or the emperor or general who had raised them (*Aelia, Siliana*), or as a mark of honour (*Augusta, pia, fidelis*), or to distinguish their armament (*sagittariorum*). In this way many units acquired a multiplicity of titles (e.g. *ala III Augusta Thracum sagittariorum civium Romanorum*).

By the middle of the first century A.D. the regular career of equestrian officers comprised the *tres militiae*— *praefectus cohortis, tribunus militum, praefectus alae*. Thus the command of an *ala* was held to be more important than the legionary tribunate. The pay of members of *alae*, though lower than that of legionaries, was above that of other auxiliary units: the basic rate was two-thirds that of the legionary.

In the Late Empire *alae* survived as cavalry units of the frontier armies.

*See* ARMIES (ROMAN), AUXILIA, LIMITANEI, MERCENARIES (ROMAN), PRAEFECTUS, SIGNA MILITARIA, STIPENDIUM.

G. L. Cheesman, *The Auxilia of the Roman Army* (1914); K. Kraft, *Alen und Kohorten an Rhein und Donau* (1951); Jones, *Later Rom. Emp.*                                  H. M. D. P.; G. R. W.

**ALAMANNI (ALEMANNI),** a Germanic people, who formed a loose confederation of tribes in western Germany in the third and later centuries A.D. Whether they were immigrants from eastern Germany or a regrouping of peoples who had been known to Tacitus, is obscure. At any rate, they were unknown to Tacitus under this name. They finally broke through the Roman *limes* (c. 260) and thenceforward lived south of the river Main in the old *Agri Decumates* (q.v.). Their raids on the Roman provinces had become serious in the thirties of the third century, and their warriors more than once penetrated into Italy itself. Their defeat by Julian in 357 at the battle of Strasbourg scarcely checked their raids, and they never ceased to devastate eastern Gaul. In the fifth century they settled permanently in Alsace and in northern Switzerland, which they converted into German-speaking countries. They were finally conquered by the Franks.                                        E. A. T.

**ALANS**, a people of nomadic pastoralists who lived in south-eastern Russia in the first two centuries A.D. After the arrival of the Goths (q.v.) in the Ukraine, they lived between the Volga and the Don. They often tried to cross the Caucasus; but the Roman emperors from Nero and Vespasian onward fortified the western exits of the Caucasus against them; and Arrian, when governor of Cappadocia, beat off an attack by them. In the fourth century they were driven westwards by the Huns, crossed into Gaul in 406, and in 409 reached Spain, where they were absorbed by the Vandals (q.v.).
                                                              E. A. T.

**ALARIC**, Visigothic leader (died A.D. 410), led his people from Lower Moesia in 395, devastated Greece, and in 401 entered Italy. Defeated by Stilicho (q.v.) at Pollentia (*Pollenzo*) in 402 and at Verona in 403, he besieged Rome itself three times in the years 408–10. He finally entered the city on 24 Aug. 410 and plundered it for three days. There is little reason to attribute any extensive damage of the city's buildings to his men. Intending to occupy Africa he marched to Rhegium, but his ships were wrecked in a storm, and the enterprise was abandoned. He died at Consentia (*Cosenza*) in that same year and was buried in the bed of the river Busentus.
                                                              E. A. T.

**ALASTOR**, in mythology, son of Neleus and brother of Nestor, (q.v.). Like all his brothers save Nestor himself, he was killed by Heracles (*Il.* 11. 693; Apollod. 1. 93). He married Harpalyce, daughter of Clymenus of Argos, but on the way home he was overtaken by Clymenus and robbed of his bride, for whom her father had an incestuous passion. To revenge herself, she killed her younger brother, cooked his flesh, and served it to her father at a feast. She then prayed to be taken from the world of men, and became a χαλκίς, here a night-bird of some kind (Parthenius 13, from Euphorion).

ἀλάστωρ, subst. or adj., in the latter case often with δαίμων added: an avenging power, as Aesch. *Ag.* 1501, where it is the supernatural agent who, according to Clytemnestra, exacts vengeance on Atreus' descendants for his crime (*see* ATREUS, AGAMEMNON). Hence the criminal himself, presumably as giving occasion for such punishment, e.g. Aesch. *Eum.* 236, where Orestes uses it of himself; hence occasionally a mere vague term of abuse, 'wretch', 'scoundrel', as Dem. 19. 305. H. J. R.

**ALBA FUCENS,** an ancient town just north of the Fucine Lake (q.v.) in central Italy, first mentioned as a Latin colony planted *in Aequis*, but near the Marsi, 303 B.C. (Livy 10. 1); perhaps the Via Tiburtina was now extended thus far east (*see* VIA VALERIA). Alba usually supported the Roman government, e.g. against Hannibal, the *socii* (90 B.C.), Caesar, and Antony; its recusant attitude in 209 was exceptional (App. *Hann.* 39; Livy 27. 9; 29. 15; *Epit.* 72; Caes. *BCiv.* 1. 15; Cic. *Phil.* 3. 6). Roman State prisoners were often kept here (Livy 30. 17; 45. 42; *Epit.* 61). Excavations at *Albe* (reports in *Ant. Class.* 1951, etc.) have revealed its extent and importance. Macro (q.v.) was a prominent native son.

P. L. MacKendrick, *The Mute Stones Speak* (1962), 95 ff.
E. T. S.

**ALBA LONGA,** on the Albanus Mons (q.v.), near modern *Castel Gandolfo,* a very ancient city traditionally founded *c.* 1152 B.C. by Ascanius (q.v.) (*Aen.* 3. 390 f.). Its necropolis contains tombs of *c.* 1100. Alba founded some, certainly not all, Latin cities (reject Livy 1. 52, *Aen.* 6. 773; and see A. Alföldi, *Early Rome and the Latins* (U.S.A. 1965), 236 f.). Apparently it once headed a league (of Prisci Latini? see Festus, 253 L.), the nature and members of which cannot be exactly determined: lists in Diodorus (7. 5), Dionysius (4. 92; 5. 61), and Pliny (*HN* 3. 69), like surviving lists of Alban kings, are untrustworthy. Alba lost its primacy in Latium perhaps in the seventh century B.C., allegedly through its destruction by Rome: some families are said to have migrated to Rome (Julii, Tullii, etc.: Livy 1. 29 f., Tac. *Ann.* 11. 24), while others joined neighbouring Bovillae and preserved Alban cults and memorials until late times (*Albani Longani Bovillenses: ILS* 6188 f.). Alba was never rebuilt, but modern *Albano* preserves its name (from *Albanum* = Domitian's Alban villa, which became a legionary camp under Septimius Severus and subsequently the nucleus of today's town). Alban wine and building stone (peperino) were famous.

M. Pallottino, *Arch. Class.* 1960, 27 ff.; F. Dionisi, *La scoperta topografica di Alba Longa* (1961); P. G. Gierow, *The Iron Age Culture of Latium,* 1 (Lund, 1966), 11, i (1964). E. T. S.

**ALBANIA** (Caucasian), the land (modern *Shirvan*) adjacent to the eastern Caucasus and the western Caspian, separated from Armenia by the river Cyrus (*Kur*). Its Caspian flat-lands were fertile, but the Albanian people remained a rude and warlike folk of herdsmen, hunters, and fishers, who traded by barter. Under a common king they had twelve local chiefs and spoke twenty-six different dialects; their chief worship was an orgiastic cult of the moon-goddess. Albania was explored by Pompey in 65 B.C. and was occasionally attached to the Roman Empire as a client State.

Strabo 11. 491 ff.; Pliny, *HN* 6. 15, 29, 39; Ptol. *Geog.* 5. 12. Cary, *Geographic Background,* 177. E. H. W.

**ALBANUS LACUS** (modern *Lago Albano*), a crater lake in the Albanus Mons (q.v.) near Rome. Its wooded banks in imperial times were studded with villas, e.g. Domitian's. Lacking natural outlets, its waters reach the Rivus Albanus, and thence the Tiber, via a tunnel through the crater rim built *c.* 397 B.C. The Romans reputedly excavated this *emissarium* to ensure the fall of Veii which, an oracle prophesied, awaited the overflow-

ing of the lake (Livy 5. 15–19). Actually their motive was to carry off the waters rapidly for irrigation purposes (Cic. *Div.* 2. 69); otherwise seepage through the porous subsoil would waterlog the districts below.

Ogilvie, *Comm. Livy 1–5,* 658 ff. E. T. S.

**ALBANUS MONS,** the Alban Hills and more specifically their dominating peak (*Monte Cavo,* 3,115 feet), 13 miles south-east of Rome. Until *c.* 1150 B.C. the Albanus Mons was an active volcano, discouraging dense population in Latium; the volcano, however, has been inactive in historical times. On the summit stood the Latin federal sanctuary of Jupiter Latiaris where Roman consuls celebrated the *Feriae Latinae* (Dion. Hal. 4. 49; the antiquity of the festival probably is underestimated). Remains exist, not indeed of the temple, but of the Via Triumphalis leading to it; here at least five Roman generals celebrated ovations after being refused regular triumphs in Rome (e.g. Marcellus in 211 B.C.: Livy 26. 21).

For early settlements, see P. G. Gierow, *The Iron Age Culture of Latium* i (Lund, 1966), ii (1964). E. T. S.

**ALBINOVANUS PĒDO,** a poet-friend addressed by Ovid in *Pont.* 4. 10, author of a *Theseid,* is mentioned by Martial (1 *praef.*; cf. 5. 5. 6) as one of his models in epigram. Under Tiberius he wrote a poem on Germanicus' North Sea expedition from which Seneca (*Suas.* 1. 15; cf. Baehr. *FPR,* p. 351) quotes over twenty hexameters as a typical Latin description of the ocean. Its rather turgid rhetoric does not exhibit the qualities in him which appealed to Martial; but the younger Seneca (*Ep.* 122. 15–16) calls him a 'fabulator elegantissimus' and gives his vividly amusing story about a noisy neighbour who turned night into day.

H. Bardon, *La Littérature latine inconnue,* ii (1956), 69 ff.
J. W. D.

**ALBINUS** (1), Platonist philosopher, pupil of Gaius. Taught at Smyrna, where Galen heard him lecture in A.D. 151–2. Extant writings are (i) a brief preface to Plato's dialogues (Πρόλογος or Εἰσαγωγή), concerned with their classification and the order in which they should be studied; (ii) a summary of Plato's doctrines ('Ἐπιτομή or Διδασκαλικός), designed as a handbook for the general public. (By a misreading the latter work is ascribed in the MSS. and earlier editions to an otherwise unknown 'Alcinous'.) Albinus' version of Platonism reveals the eclectic tendencies of his time, especially in its bold incorporation of Aristotelian elements. He attributes Aristotle's categories to Plato; he equates Plato's Demiurge with Aristotle's Unmoved Mover; he interprets Plato's transcendent 'Forms' as the thoughts of this Aristotelian God. Much of the raw material of Neoplatonism is present in Albinus, but he has no doctrine of the One and shows no tendency to mysticism.

TEXT AND FRENCH TRANSLATION. P. Louis (1945). Text also in C. F. Hermann's Teubner edition of Plato (1853), vi. 147 ff.
DISCUSSION. R. E. Witt, *Albinus and the History of Middle Platonism* (1937); J. H. Loenen, *Mnemos.* 1956, 296 ff., and 1957, 35 ff.
E. R. D.

**ALBINUS** (2) (4th c. A.D.), writer on metre and music. His works are lost.

Teuffel, § 405, 2 and § 407, 5; Schanz–Hosius, § 825.

**ALBION,** ancient (Celtic or pre-Celtic) name of Great Britain (but not Ireland), first recorded *c.* 525 B.C. by a Massiliote seaman (quoted by Avienius, q.v.) who spoke of Ireland, two days' sail from Brittany, 'alongside the island of the Albiones'. The name 'Albion' was used by the author of *De Mundo* (who said that it and Ireland were bigger than the Mediterranean islands, but smaller han Ceylon), but it was soon ousted by the Celtic Britannia'. A number of Latin geographic names begin alb- (cf. *also* 'Alpes'). The Romans, connecting 'Albion' vith *albus*, 'white', referred the name to the cliffs of Dover, perhaps rightly—W. J. Watson, *History of Celtic Place-names of Scotland* (1926), 10; the name Albion may be pre-Celtic—S. Casson, *Greece and Britain* (1943), 16; Ilyde, *Greek Mariners*, 122.

Avienius (ed. A. Holden, 1965), 90 ff.; Ps.-Arist. *de Mundo* 3; Pliny 4. 102; Ptol. 2. 31 and 7. 5. 11. E. H. W.

**ALBUCIUS** (1), TITUS (praetor *c.* 105 B.C.), orator: Lucilius satirized the absurdities of his Graecomania (88–93 Marx) and Cicero called him 'doctus Graecis vel potius plane Graecus' (*Brut.* 131). He was an Epicurean and after his condemnation in 103 B.C. for extortion in Sardinia he spent his exile in philosophical study at Athens (Cic. *Pro Scauro* 40, *Tusc.* 5. 108). C. J. F.

**ALBUCIUS** (2) **SILUS**, GAIUS, Augustan orator and teacher of rhetoric, from Novaria in Cisalpine Gaul. Though over-conscientious and distrustful of himself, he could command a grand simplicity, and Seneca classes him as one of the four outstanding practitioners of his time (*Cont.* 7 *pr.* 1–9; Suet. *Rhet.* 6).

A. Asserato, *Gaio Albucio Silo* (1967). C. J. F.

**ALBUM**, a whitened *tabula*, was used for publishing, in black writing, priestly notices, *fasti*, notices of *comitia* and Senate, *proscriptiones* and edicts (e.g. *album praetoris* with *formulae actionum*), also member rolls (e.g. *album senatorum*, *decurionum*, *iudicum*, *collegii*), and lists of recipients of corn. A. H. McD.

**ALBUNEA**, nymph of the *albulae aquae*, a sulphurous spring and brook rising at Tibur, where it forms the well-known waterfall, and flowing into the Anio. Near the fall was a dream-oracle (*Aen.* 7. 81 ff., needlessly doubted by Heinze and Wissowa, *RK* 211 n. 4). Albunea herself was called a Sibyl (Varro ap. Lactant. *Div. Inst.* 1. 6. 12); Servius on *Aen.* 7. 84 equates her with Leucothea (q.v.) and says the god [*sic*] Mefitis is her subordinate.

B. Tilly, *Vergil's Latium* (1947), ch. vi (= *JRS* 1934, 25 ff.). H. J. R.

**ALCAEUS** (1) (b. *c.* 620 B.C.), lyric poet, of Mytilene in Lesbos (Strabo 617), was still a boy when his brothers, Antimenidas and Cicis, overthrew the tyrant Melanchros (frs. 53, 75, Diog. Laert. 1. 74). Melanchros was succeeded by Myrsilus, who was helped by Deinomenes and Pittacus. Alcaeus' early years seem to have been spent in combating all three. At first he lost and went into exile at Pyrrha (schol. ad fr. 114), where he wrote fr. 42, and possibly fr. 130, in which political conditions are described in seafaring language. A fight followed, and to Alcaeus' delight Myrsilus was killed (fr. 332). He was succeeded by Pittacus, with whom Alcaeus seems at first to have been friendly, since both fought against Athens at Sigeum (Diog. Laert. 1. 74) *c.* 600 B.C. Here Alcaeus lost his shield and celebrated the fact (fr. 428). On the conclusion of peace Pittacus became all-powerful, and was attacked by Alcaeus, who regarded his election to power as an act of madness (fr. 348) ,and reviled him for his physical defects (Diog. Laert. 1. 81), his ambitious marriage (fr. 69), his riotous behaviour (fr. 70), and his craftiness (fr. 72). The result of the struggle was that soon after 600 B.C. Alcaeus went to Egypt (Strabo 37) and his brother Antimenidas became a mercenary of the king of Babylon (fr. 48). Alcaeus seems also to have been in Thrace (fr. 45) and to have had negotiations with the Lydians (fr. 69). Before Pittacus resigned his powers in

580 B.C. he forgave Alcaeus (Diog. Laert. 1. 75), who must have returned home. The rest of his life and the date of his death are unknown.

His works survive only in fragments. Edited by Aristophanes and Aristarchus in at least ten books (Heph. p. 74, 12 ff.), they seem to have been arranged according to subject, since Ὕμνοι (schol. Heph. p. 169, 28 ff.) and Στασιωτικά (Strabo 617) are mentioned, but the papyrus fragments give no indication of systematic arrangement. The remains indicate that Alcaeus wrote lyrical songs, usually monodies; many dealt with contemporary politics, while others are drinking-songs (frs. 335, 338, 346, 347, 366), sometimes with a meditative tinge (fr. 38), love-songs (fr. 71; cf. Theoc. 29–30, Hor. *Carm.* 1. 32. 11), hymns to Apollo (fr. 307), Hermes (fr. 308), and the Dioscuri (fr. 34). Sometimes he seems to write variations on themes of folk-song (fr. 10) or describes a festive scene (fr. 115). He writes in vernacular Aeolic, with occasional Homerisms. He uses two- or four-lined stanzas with a wide variety of metres, including the Greater and Lesser Asclepiads, the Sapphic and Alcaic stanzas, and other stanzas of his own invention. He occasionally employs an elaborate allegory (frs. 119, 326), but normally he writes directly and easily, and is at his best in describing simple sights or emotions.

TEXT. E. Lobel and D. L. Page, *Poetarum Lesbiorum Fragmenta* (1955).
CRITICISM. D. L. Page, *Sappho and Alcaeus* (1955), 147 ff.; C. M. Bowra, *Greek Lyric Poetry*², 130 ff. PW Suppl. xi, 8 ff. C. M. B.

**ALCAEUS** (2) is called by the *Suda* κωμικὸς τῆς ἀρχαίας κωμῳδίας and author of ten plays. His Πασιφάη took the fifth (last) prize in 388 B.C. (hyp. 4 Ar. *Plut.*). Fragments of seven other plays survive; the titles suggest that he specialized in mythological burlesques.

FCG i. 244–9; CAF i. 756 ff.; FAC i. 886 ff. K. J. D.

**ALCAEUS** (3) of Messene (fl. 200 B.C.) has some fifteen epigrams in the Greek Anthology, including several biting lampoons on Philip V of Macedon. Plutarch (*Flam.* 9) says that one of them was repeated all over Greece, and gives the king's bitter parodic reply. These are the earliest extant epigrams containing political invective. In technique, perhaps also in outlook, Alcaeus owes something to Cercidas (q.v.). His iambics, which must have been pasquinades too, are lost.

C. Edson, *CPhil.* 1948; F. W. Walbank, *CQ* 1942, 135 ff., 1943, 1 ff.; T. B. L. Webster, *Hellenistic Poetry and Art* (1964), ch. 1c. G. H.

**ALCAMENES**, Greek sculptor, probably of Athens, active during the whole of the second half of the fifth century B.C. He was called both a pupil and a rival of Phidias (cf. Pliny *HN* 36. 16; 34. 49 and 72). Like Phidias he worked in bronze, marble, and gold and ivory. A few of his works have been more or less tentatively identified in reproductions of Roman date. For instance, the seated statue that he made for the sanctuary of Dionysus 'near the theatre' (Paus. 1. 20. 3) appears on Roman coins of Athens. The Aphrodite of the Gardens, one of his most famous works (cf. Lucian *Eikones*, 6; Pliny 36. 16), has been recognized by some in the so-called Venus Genetrix type. The group of Procne and Itys in the Acropolis Museum has been thought to be the group dedicated by one Alcamenes (Paus. 1. 24. 3)—possibly but not necessarily identical with the sculptor. The most reliable attribution appears to be that of 'a Hermes of the Gateway', seen by Pausanias at the entrance of the Acropolis (1. 22. 8), and identified in two inscribed herms with a bearded head, one found at Pergamum, the other at Ephesus. The fame of the original is borne out by the large number of extant copies. The statement by Pausanias (5. 10. 8) that Alcamenes made the sculptures of the western pediment of the temple of Zeus at Olympia does not fit either the chronology or what is known of the style of Alcamenes, and must be due to a mistake.

G. M. A. R.

**ALCATHOUS** (Ἀλκάθοος or Ἀλκάθους), in mythology, son of Pelops and Hippodameia, to whom games (Alkathoia) were celebrated at Megara (Pind. *Isthm.* 8. 74 and schol. on *Nem.* 5. 46). A folk-tale (theme H 105, Stith Thompson) told by Dieuchidas (ap. schol. Ap. Rhod. 1. 517) says that, exiled for his share in the murder of his brother Chrysippus, he killed a lion (it haunted Cithaeron and had killed Euhippus, son of Megareus, king of Megara, who promised his daughter's hand and the succession to his throne to whoever slew it, Paus. 1. 41. 3), cut out its tongue, and when false claimants arose, used it to refute them. He then built temples to Apollo Agraios and Artemis Agrotera (Paus. ibid.) and walls for Megara; Apollo helped him, and rested his lyre on a stone still shown in Pausanias' time (ibid. 42. 2). His eldest son, Ischepolis, was killed on the Calydonian boar-hunt; one Callipolis brought the news and scattered the wood of a fire on which Alcathous was offering, whereat Alcathous killed him with one of the billets (ibid. 42. 6). H. J. R.

**ALCESTIS** (Ἄλκηστις), in mythology, a daughter of Pelias (*see* NELEUS) and wife of Admetus, king of Pherae in Thessaly. For some unknown reason she is the central figure of two interesting legends, one of them also moving and famous in literature, but both characteristic folk-tales. (1) When she was of age to marry, many suitors appeared, but her father would not give her to any who could not fulfil the prescribed condition of driving wild beasts yoked to a chariot. This is of course one of the innumerable stories told of extraordinary tasks set wooers (see Stith Thompson, H 335). In this instance it does not appear that Pelias apprehended any danger from Alcestis' marriage, or had any special reason for wanting her at home. Admetus succeeded, thanks to a divine helper. Apollo had shortly before killed the Cyclopes who made Zeus' thunderbolts (cf. Eur. *Alc.* 1 ff.), because he did not dare to avenge the death of his son Asclepius (q.v.) on Zeus himself. In consequence, he was banished from heaven for a time (the common punishment of a human manslayer is here transferred to a god), and made to serve a mortal. Admetus was renowned for his piety and treated his divine serf with every consideration, employing him (appropriately, as he is a god of flocks and herds, *see* APOLLO) to tend his horses or cattle. The god, in return for this, in a later form of the legend, because Admetus was very handsome and he loved him (first in Callimachus, *Ap.* 49, who does not mention the affair of the banishment) brought him a lion and a boar yoked, and he drove away with Alcestis behind this team (Hyg. *Fab.* 50. 51; source unknown; 50. 1 suggests another form of the story in which the successful candidate was allowed to choose whichever of Pelias' daughters he preferred). (2) At the bridal feast, Admetus forgot to sacrifice to Artemis (Apollod. 1. 105, who also had the story of the lion and boar), and on opening the bridal chamber found it full of serpents. The snake being a chthonian creature for the most part, this was an omen of imminent death, and Apollo again intervened. By the primitive method of making the Fates drunk (Aesch. *Eum.* 728) he persuaded them to promise that if anyone else would die on Admetus' behalf, he might continue to live. But no one would consent to die, except Alcestis (Eur., ibid. 15 ff. who makes no mention of the portent). That there was any baseness in accepting her offer did not occur to tellers of the legend before Euripides; elsewhere Admetus is a wholly admirable character. So far, the tale embodies popular moralizing (a man's truest friend a good wife). On the appointed day Alcestis according died, i.e. the rest of her life was transferred to her husband. Now comes a form of the widespread tale (Tammuz and Ishtar is the oldest known form) of the recovery from the lower world of one of a pair of lovers. It i sometimes said (Apollod., ibid. 106) that Persephon sent Alcestis back of her own accord; but the usual version is that Heracles (q.v.) intervened. Admetus, wit his usual piety, had received him hospitably in the mids of his own grief; by way of return for this, he set out t harrow Hell, and fought successfully either with Hade himself (Apollod., ibid.) or with the death-spirit, Thana tos, compelling him to give Alcestis back.

A. Lesky 'Alkestis der Mythus und das Drama', *Sitz Wien* 1925, gives the best analysis of the legend and dis poses of the view that Admetus is a faded god.

Apart from these tales, neither of the pair has much mythology. Admetus took part in the Argonautic ad venture, (Hyg. *Fab.* 14. 2 and elsewhere); the Calydonia boar-hunt (Apollod. 1. 67); the funeral games over Pelia (Chest of Cypselus in Paus. 5. 17. 9, where he drives chariot); perhaps in imitation of this, Statius (*Theb* 6. 310 ff.) makes him compete at the first Nemean game with a team of mares.

One account (Phanodemus ap. schol. Ar. *Vesp.* 1239 says that in his old age Admetus was driven into exil with Alcestis and their youngest child, Hippasus (th elder son, Eumelus took part in the Trojan War, *Il.* 2 713–14; he was a skilled charioteer, 23. 288–9, but ha ill success in the chariot-race at Patroclus' funeral, ibid 391 ff.; the daughter, Perimele, married Argos, son o Phrixus, Ant. Liberalis 23). The cause of the exile i not known, and the story is plainly connected with th famous skolion (quoted by Ar. *Vesp.* 1238), Ἀδμήτο λόγον ὦταῖρε μαθὼν τοὺς ἀγαθοὺς φίλει, said by Phano demus to refer to Admetus' kind reception by Theseus

There appears to have been no hero-cult of eithe Alcestis or her husband. H. J. R

**ALCHEMY** in antiquity was a mixture of chemical metallurgical, and glass technology, Greek philosophy mystical and syncretist religion, and astrology; it wa probably not yet concerned with the 'philosopher's stone nor with the transmutation of base metals into gold.

2. The word 'alchemy' is from the medieval Latin from the Arabic al-kīmiyā'; the etymology of this i dubious, but it is commonly derived from the Greek *chēmia*, which according to Plutarch meant Egypt (th black land), from the Egyptian km, 'black'. This is sup ported by the fact that Plutarch also quotes 'the pupil o the eye' as another meaning, which is true of km; and by the Coptic *chēme*, 'the black ⟨land⟩', Egypt, found in th place-name Pelchēm (which incidentally gave the Arabi form Bilkīm). But there was early confusion of *chēmi* with *chumeia* (iotacism), from the root of *cheō*, 'pour' *chumeia* being a metallurgical term; and, according to Pro fessor Dubs, alchemy is derived via the Arabic from th article *al* plus the Chinese *kiəm-iŏk*, 'sperm of gold' presumably through Jundishapur in the eighth century In any case ancient alchemy was never called by such name, being always referred to in such terms as 'th Work', 'the Sacred Art'.

3. The art is distinguished from the pure science o chemistry by its mixture of mystical and magical element with the technology. Its origins are obscure. Later dis tinctions, such as that between esoteric and exoteri alchemy, or theoretical and practical, are irrelevant, prob ably being developed between the eighth and twelft centuries. Alchemy in late antiquity was born of the con fluence of three streams: (1) *technology*, especially the art of glass colouring and metal-working, including makin

her metals *look like* gold and silver—the appearance as always very important; (2) *theory*, derived from reek philosophy: two doctrines are of special import-ace, that of the four elements (which held the field from mpedocles to Boyle), and that of the essential unity of l things, the *hypokeimenon* common to philosophers om the Presocratics to Aristotle and on, and found so in Orphics and Neoplatonists and others; which ads us to (3) *occult religion*, and the mystical and syn-etist magical beliefs of late Hellenistic times. The mbol of unity, the *ouroboros*, the snake eating its own il, is common in astrological, Gnostic, and apocryphal xts, as well as in alchemical ones. All of this points fairly efinitely to Egypt, to Alexandria, in about the second nd third centuries A.D.

**4.** The inventor was said to be Hermes, and alchemy linked with other occult sciences in the Hermetic terature of the first three centuries A.D., along with eo-Pythagorean, Neoplatonic, and Gnostic ideas. That lexandria was the early home of the art is most prob-ole, as the cradle of the Hermetic literature, of syn-etist philosophical movements, and of the ancient and ell-developed arts of the glassworker, potter, gold-nith, and jeweller: one man often combined several of nese skills, and Jewish craftsmen in these arts are men-oned in the Talmud. The earliest works are attributed Democritus or his teacher Ostanes; there might be me technological connexion with Democritus (cf. Sen. *p.* 90. 32–33). At this stage the art was concerned with olour-changes in glass and metals, especially with the roduction of alloys and the imitation of gold and silver. hen philosophy was added to technology: the funda-ental identity of the stuff of the universe; the permuta-ons of the four elements and four qualities (Aristotle); e lack of any clear distinction between animate and animate, which led to the idea of 'generation' not being mited to the animate; and the ideas of the 'pneuma' or irit that could flow through the universe, and its xhalations (Aristotle and the Stoics); all this widened e scope of the art and opened the way to (1) the idea of e transmutation of metals and (2) the introduction of ligion and astrology, which shared the belief in the sential unity of all things. It may have led to the search r a substance to achieve transmutation, and possibly so long life—much later known as the Philosopher's tone, or Elixir (probably derived by the Arabs (al-iksīr) om *xērion*, a desiccative powder for wounds, though ubs derives this also from the Chinese). Zosimus (fl. A.D. 300), much of whose work remains, seems to stand the beginning of this tradition. There must certainly e some doubt whether alchemy in classical times, or : least before the fourth century A.D., ever went much eyond the arts of the jeweller and goldsmith, concerned ith the alloying and imitation of gold and silver.

**5.** Their apparatus included furnaces, with bellows to roduce high temperatures; crucibles and retorts of vari-us kinds, of metal, pottery, and glass; the *bain-Marie*, ill used by chemists, going back to Mary the Jewess, ho is said also to have invented the *tribikos*, or three-out still, and the *kerotakis*, originally a warmed plate n which wax-mixed colours were kept soft for working, nd then used to subject molten metals to the action of apours to produce alterations in colour. The substances sed by these early alchemist-craftsmen can very often e identified, but when alchemy and astrology were fused ae language became more esoteric and difficult to inter-ret. The arts had always been kept secret in the families nvolved, and the admixture of magic, etc., made things orse. The 'seven stars in the sky' were identified with even metals—sun/gold, moon/silver, Mars/iron, Mer-ary/mercury, Venus/copper, Jupiter/tin, Saturn/lead—nd the symbols used for either or both.

**6.** There are no early Latin alchemical texts, but the general connexion between technology, secret arts, and astrology is evident in the fourth-century Firmicus Maternus' work: those born when Mercury is in the fourth station in the evening will be 'goldsmiths or goldminers or masters of certain hidden arts'; those born when the moon is between Mars and Venus will practise the 'arts of pigments or scents or stones and gems, and will often be colourers of metals'; and those 'who are polishers of precious stones or who give gems another colour with various pigments' are linked with 'those who know the secrets of the heavens or who easily learn secret and hidden matters'.

M. Berthelot, *Collection des anciens alchimistes grecs* (4 vols., 1887–8); E. O. von Lippmann, *Entstehung und Ausbreitung der Alchemie* (3 vols., 1919, 1931, 1954); Lynn Thorndike, *History of Magic and Experimental Science* (vol. 2, 1923); A. J. Hopkins, *Alchemy, Child of Greek Philosophy* (1934); A.-J. Festugière, *La Révélation d'Hermès Trismégiste* i (1944); F. Sherwood Taylor, *The Alchemists* (1951); E. J. Holmyard, *Alchemy* (1957); J. Read, *Through Alchemy to Chemistry* (2nd ed., 1961); *PW* i. 1338; *Ambix* (1937 on), esp. H. H. Dubs, 'The Origin of Alchemy', *Ambix* 1961, 23. S. J. T.

**ALCIBIADES** (*c.* 450–404 B.C.), son of Cleinias, Athenian general and statesman. Brought up in the house-hold of his guardian Pericles, he became the pupil and intimate friend of Socrates. His brilliance enabled him in 420 to assume the leadership of the extreme demo-crats, and his ambitious imperialism drew Athens into a coalition with Argos and other enemies of Sparta. This policy, half-heartedly supported by the Athenians, was largely discredited by the Spartan victory at Mantinea (418). Though Alcibiades temporarily allied with Nicias to avoid ostracism, the two were normally adversaries and rivals, and when the former sponsored the plan for a Sicilian expedition, Nicias vainly opposed it. Both were appointed, together with Lamachus, to command this armament, and received extraordinary powers (415). Alcibiades was suspected of complicity in the mutilation of the Hermae (*see* ANDOCIDES 1) and other profanations at Athens, and soon after the fleet reached Sicily he was recalled for trial. He escaped, however, to Sparta, where he gave the valuable advice that a Spartan general should be sent to Syracuse and that a permanent Spartan post should be established at Decelea in Attica.

In 412 his mission to Ionia caused many allies of Athens to revolt, but he soon lost the confidence of the Spartans and fled to Tissaphernes. He tried to secure reinstatement at Athens by winning the support of Persia and fomenting an oligarchic revolution, but he could not induce Tissaphernes to desert the Spartan cause. The Athenian fleet at Samos appointed him general, and for several years he skilfully directed operations in Ionia and the Hellespont, winning a brilliant victory at Cyzicus in 410. He returned to Athens in 407 and was entrusted with an extraordinary command. Against the powerful combination of Lysander and Cyrus he could effect little, and when in his absence a subordinate suffered defeat at Notium (406), his enemies roused popular suspicion against him. He then withdrew, and in 404 through the influence of the Thirty Tyrants (q.v.1) and Lysander he was murdered in Phrygia, where he sought refuge with Pharnabazus.

Alcibiades showed himself to be outstandingly able as a politician and later as a military leader, but his personal ambition and the excesses of his private life aroused the distrust of the Athenians, who twice discarded him when his leadership might have been a decisive factor (cf. Thuc. 6. 15. 3–4).

Thuc., bks. 5–8; Xen. *Hell.* bk. 1; Plato, *Alc.* 1 and *Symp.*; Plut. *Alc.* J. Hatzfeld, *Alcibiade*² (1951). H. D. W.

**ALCIDAMAS** (4th c. B.C.), rhetorician and sophist, was born at Elaea in Aeolis. He studied under Gorgias, and led the orthodox branch of Gorgias' followers, while Isocrates led the innovators; the difference consisted largely in the fact that Alcidamas emphasized the importance of a power of improvisation resting on wide knowledge, while Isocrates excelled in dialectical skill and delicacy of language. The works extant under Alcidamas' name are (1) Περὶ τοὺς γραπτοὺς λόγους γραφόντων ἢ περὶ σοφιστῶν, (2) (spurious) Ὀδυσσεὺς κατὰ Παλαμήδους προδοσίας. The most important of the lost works seems to have been that called Μουσεῖον.

Ed. F. Blass, in his *Antipho* (1892), 183. W. D. R.

**ALCINOUS** (Ἀλκίνοος), in mythology, son of Nausithous (*Od.* 7. 63), husband of Arēte, his first cousin (ibid. 66), king of the Phaeacians in Scheria (ibid. 6. 12, etc.), father of Nausicaa (q.v.). He received Odysseus hospitably (*see* ODYSSEUS) and sent him to Ithaca on one of the magic ships of his people (13. 70 ff.), though he had had warning of the danger of such services to all and sundry (13. 172 ff.). In the Argonautic legend (see especially Ap. Rhod. 4. 993 ff.) the Argonauts visit Scheria (here called Drepane) on their return from Colchis; the Colchians pursue them there and demand Medea. Alcinous decides that if she is virgin she must return, but if not, her husband Jason shall keep her. Warned by Arēte, she and Jason consummate their marriage. H. J. R.

**ALCIPHRON** (2nd or 3rd c. A.D.), sophist, whose *Letters*, supposedly written by Athenians of the fourth century B.C. (fishermen, farmers, 'parasites', hetairai) attest his wide reading in classical literature and preserve many reminiscences of New Comedy, especially of Menander. *See* LETTERS (GREEK), § 6.

Loeb text and translation, A. R. Benner–F. H. Fobes (1949, with letters of Aelian and Philostratus). Rohde, *Griech. Roman*, 343 ff. D. A. R.

**ALCM(A)EON** (1) (Ἀλκμέων, Ἀλκμαίων), in mythology, son of Amphiaraus (q.v.). After the expedition of the Seven against Thebes, he avenged his father's death on his mother Eriphyle, and afterwards became, by command of Apollo, leader of the expedition of the Epigoni, which took Thebes (or the expedition came first, the matricide afterwards, contrast Asclepiades in schol. *Od.* 11. 326, with Apollod. 3. 86). Being maddened by the Erinyes, he left Argos and went to Psophis where King Phegeus purified him and gave him his daughter Arsinoë or Alphesiboea, but as a famine visited the land he left, settled in the new land formed by the Acheloüs at its mouth, and therefore not seen by the sun when Eriphyle was killed, and married Acheloüs' daughter Callirhoë (*see* ACARNAN). But the brothers of Arsinoë waylaid and killed him, afterwards shutting their sister up in a chest and selling her as a slave. In Euripides' *Alcmeon at Corinth* he met Manto on his wanderings and had two children by her.

Alcmeon is present at the departure of Amphiaraus in sixth-century vase-paintings, especially a Corinthian krater in Berlin, and on the Chest of Cypselus (on connexion see H. G. G. Payne, *Necrocorinthia* (1931), 139 ff. with refs.).

M. Delcourt, *Oreste et Alcméon* (1959). In art, Brommer, *Vasenlisten²*, 337 f. H. J. R.; C. M. R.

**ALCMAEON** (2) of Croton, probably a younger contemporary of Pythagoras (q.v. 1) and certainly in contact with his school, wrote a book on natural science known to Aristotle and Theophrastus. As a physician he explained bodily conditions and human affairs in general by the interplay of opposites (health being an *isonomy* of hot and cold, wet and dry, etc., disease a *monarchy*).

He operated on the eye and discovered 'passages' linking the sense-organs to the brain, which he recognized as the seat of thought and feeling (followed by Plato but not Aristotle); and he compared the immortality of the soul to the endless circling of the heavenly bodies.

*Testimonia* and fragments in Diels, *Vorsokr.*¹¹ i. 210–16; Cardini, *Pitagorici* i (1958). J. Wachtler, *De Alcmaeone Crotoniata* (1896); Guthrie, *Hist. Gr. Phil.* i. G. E. L.

**ALCMAEONIDAE,** a noble Athenian family prominent in politics. Its first noteworthy member was Megacles who as archon, perhaps in 632/1 B.C., involved it in hereditary taint (*see* CYLON) first used against it about a generation later, when party-strife between the descendants of Cylon's followers and the Alcmaeonidae was resolved by the condemnation and expulsion of the whole family, living and dead. Within a few years, however they were back: Alcmaeon, son of Megacles, commanded the Athenian contingent in the first Sacred War (q.v.); the rich reward he received for his services to the Lydian king's emissaries at Delphi helped him to a victory in the chariot-race at Olympia (592?). His son Megacles (q.v.) increased the family's renown still further when he married the daughter of Cleisthenes (q.v. 2), the tyrant of Sicyon. His own daughter's marriage to Pisistratus (q.v.), however, broke down, in part because of the family curse. When Pisistratus was finally established as tyrant (c. 546), the Alcmaeonidae had to go into exile again but must have been allowed to return before the archonship of Megacles' son Cleisthenes (q.v. 1) in 525/4. Later, perhaps after the murder of Hipparchus (q.v. 1) in 514 Hippias (q.v. 1) expelled them yet again. After several unsuccessful attempts to return, and the loss of the fortified post which they set up at Leipsydrium inside Attica, they eventually succeeded, with the co-operation of Delphi, in effecting the overthrow of Hippias and their own restoration (511/10). The ancestral curse was invoked again by Cleomenes (q.v. 1) in the year of Cleisthenes' reforms (508/7) and caused another temporary withdrawal of the family. In 490 they were suspected of collusion with the Persian invasion-force, and the early victims of ostracism (q.v.) included another Megacles, nephew of Cleisthenes (486), and Xanthippus (q.v.), husband of Megacles' sister Agariste (484). During the remainder of the century individual members of the family flourished: what part it played collectively, if any, is not easy to show: the development of the democracy would tend to reduce both its influence and its vulnerability. Pericles, son of Xanthippus and Agariste, was able to ignore the Spartan appeal to the curse in 432/1, and Alcibiades, who also had an Alcmaeonid mother, does not appear to have been attacked on this score.

G. W. Williams, *Hermathena* 1951, 32 ff., 1952, 3 ff., 1953, 58 ff.; W. G. Forrest, *CQ* 1961, 232 ff.; T. L. Shear, *Phoenix* 1963, 99 ff. T. J. C.

**ALCMAN** (fl. 654–611 B.C., Jerome–Eusebius; 631–62 B.C., *Suda*), lyric poet, who lived in Sparta in the second half of the seventh century B.C. While some (ap. *Suda* s.v. Ἀλκμάν) said that he was a Laconian from Messoa, others (Crates ap. *Suda*) said that he came from Sardes in Lydia, and support for this has been found in fr. 16 where the poet may be addressing himself. In the latter case he would be an Asiatic Greek. He is also said to have been a slave who was granted his liberty because of his skill (Heraclid. Pont. fr. 2). His fragments show no direct reference to contemporary history, though fr. 41 may refer to the end of a war, and fr. 64 may be a tribute to Spartan methods of government. His work seems to belong to the period of peace which followed the Second Messenian War, and is mainly concerned with Spartan feasts and festivals. He wrote lyrical poems which were later collected in six books (*Suda*. loc. cit.). These seem to have been mainly choral and to have often been sung by choirs of maidens. From one more than half survives (fr. 1). Beginning with a myth which illustrates the punishment of pride, it goes on to give personal remarks about the girls who sing and is very hard to interpret. It has been variously ascribed to festivals of Artemis, the Dioscuri, Dionysus, and Helen; it seems to have been sung at night in some kind of competition against another choir. He wrote on cosmological notions, giving an important part to Thetis (fr. 5). Other fragments come from hymns to the Dioscuri (fr. 2), Hera (frs. 3, 60), Athena (frs. 43, 87, 120), Apollo (frs. 45–50), and Aphrodite (fr. 55), while one seems to describe a nocturnal festival of Dionysus (fr. 56). He also wrote in hexameters what may have been Preludes to recitations of Homer. In these he sometimes varies a Homeric theme (fr. 77) or speaks about himself (fr. 26). He uses a literary language which includes Dorian and Aeolic elements and shows echoes from Homer. References to the Issedones, the Rhipean mountains, and King Kolaxais of Scythia may perhaps be taken from the work of Aristeas of Proconnesus. He writes with unaffected charm about simple matters such as birds (frs. 26, 39, 40), horses (fr. 1, ll. 45–49, 58–59), food (frs. 17, 19, 20), and with magic about night and sleep (fr. 89). The *Suda* says that he was the inventor of love-poems, but his fragments give no evidence on this beyond the tender emotions which he describes between the different members of a choir. His metres are varied and usually simple, though in fr. 89 he shows an advanced technique. It is not clear that he used a triadic structure in his verse.

TEXT. Page, *Poet. Mel. Gr.*, 2–91.
CRITICISM. D. L. Page, *Alcman, the Partheneion*, (1951); A. Garzya, *Alcmane: i Frammenti* (1954); C. M. Bowra, *Greek Lyric Poetry²*, (1962), 16 ff.; *PW* Suppl. xi, 19 ff. C. M. B.

**ALCMENE,** in mythology, daughter of Electryon. When her husband Amphitryon (q.v.) killed her father by mischance, she left Argos for Thebes with him, but refused to allow him conjugal rights till he had avenged the death of her brothers on the Taphians and Teleboans. He gathered an army and set out; but during his absence his wife was visited by Zeus (*see* HERACLES). She thus bore Heracles to Zeus and Iphicles to Amphitryon ([Hesiod], *Shield* 1 ff.). The birth was delayed by Hera (*Il.* 19. 114 ff., much elaborated in Ov. *Met.* 9. 290 ff., Ant. Lib. 29 from Nicander). After the death of Heracles, she and her children were persecuted by Eurystheus; according to Euripides (*Heracl.*) they took refuge in Attica. Eurystheus attacked but was defeated and captured, the victory being bought by the sacrifice of Heracles' daughter Macaria to Persephone, in accordance with an oracle; Alcmene insisted on the death of Eurystheus. At her own death Alcmene was taken to the Islands of the Blessed and a stone substituted in her coffin (Pherecydes ap. Ant. Lib. 33. 3). She had a cult at Thebes and elsewhere (Farnell, *Hero-Cults*, 409).
H. J. R.

**ALESIA,** a town of the Mandubii, a client-state of the Aedui, modern *Alise-Ste Reine*, a hill-fort built by La Tène Celts. Excavation has revealed a Gallic town with *murus Gallicus*. In 52 B.C. Caesar besieged Vercingetorix here, and after beating off a large relieving army received his surrender. Siege-works corresponding to Caesar's minute description were discovered in 1860–5. A Gallo-Roman town on the hill, with some important buildings, has been excavated. It suffered damage in A D. 69 and *c.* 166, and in the third century, eventually falling into decay.

Caesar, *BGall.* 7. 68–89 (siege). J. Le Gall, *Alésie* (1963); J. Harmand, *Une Campaigne césarienne, Alesia* (1967). C. E. S.

**ALETES** (Ἀλήτης), in mythology, (1) son of Hippotas. Asking at Dodona how he might become king of Corinth, he was told he would be 'when one gave him a clod of earth on a day of many garlands'. He went there on a festival as a beggar, and was given earth by one of whom he asked bread; subsequently he became king through an intrigue on the occasion of a festival (schol. Pind. *Nem.* 7. 155). (2) Son of Aegisthus, *see* ERIGONE (2).
H. J. R.

**ALETRIUM** (modern *Alatri*), town of the Hernici (q.v.) 45 miles south-east of Rome. Always loyal to Rome after 358 B.C., Aletrium became a prosperous *municipium* (Cic. *Clu.* 46) and remained such (reject *Liber Colon.* 230). Its massive polygonal walls have survived almost intact, those surrounding the citadel being particularly remarkable.

L. Gasperini, *Aletrium*, i, *I documenti epigrafici* (1965); G. Lugli, *La tecnica edilizia romana* (1957), 131 ff. E. T. S.

**ALEUADAE,** the leading aristocratic family of Thessaly, who dominated the neighbourhood of Larissa. The military and political organization of the Thessalian national State was ascribed to Aleuas the Red. The earliest *tagus* (q.v.) who was certainly an Aleuad was Thorax; his intrigues with Persia caused a temporary eclipse of Aleuad influence after the invasion of Xerxes. The Aleuadae vigorously opposed the tyrants of Pherae and several times invited Macedonian intervention. Simus, at first a creature of Philip, later defied him, and the suppression of this movement against Macedonian domination finally broke the power of the Aleuadae.

H. D. Westlake, *Thessaly in the Fourth Century B.C.* (1935); *JHS* 1936, 12 ff. H. D. W.

**ALEXANDER** (1) **I,** king of Macedon *c.* 495–450 B.C. He submitted to Persia (492) and served with the Persian forces under Xerxes. Nevertheless he succeeded in helping the Greeks without arousing Persian suspicion; he advised the Greeks to abandon Tempe and is s iid to have given information to the Athenians before Plataea. For his services he was admitted as a Hellene to the games at Olympia, where he won a victory, and became proxenus at Athens. He endeavoured to hellenize his court, to which he invited Pindar. After the Persian retreat he annexed territory as far as the Strymon valley, capturing silver-mines in the Krusha Balkan, whence he issued the first Macedonian coinage on the standard used by Abdera. His further expansion was checked by the Delian League and Athens' reduction of Thasos. He was the first king of Macedon to enter Greek politics, to establish claim to Greek descent, and to introduce Greek ways into Macedonia.

F. Geyer, *Historische Zeitschrift*, Beiheft 19 (1930); J. Papastavrou, Μακεδονικὴ πολιτικὴ κατὰ τὸν 5ον π. X. αἰῶνα. Ἀλέξανδρος I (1936). N. G. L. H.

**ALEXANDER** (2) **II,** eldest son of Amyntas and king of Macedon 369–368 B.C. Invoked by the Aleuadae (q.v.) against Alexander of Pherae, he garrisoned Larissa and Crannon before a rebellion in Macedonia compelled him to return. Pelopidas ejected the Macedonian garrisons, arbitrated in Macedonia, and made alliance with Alexander. Shortly afterwards Alexander was murdered. He probably instituted the *pezetaeri* (*see* HETAIROI *and* ARMIES, GREEK AND HELLENISTIC, § 4). N. G. L. H.

**ALEXANDER** (3) **III** of Macedonia ('the Great'), 356–323 B.C., son of Philip II and Olympias of Epirus. Aristotle became his tutor, and he early showed his powers of intellect and command. Despite serious quarrels with Philip, occasioned by palace intrigues and uncertainty as to the succession, Alexander did succeed without difficulty (336), and immediately devoted himself to the plan of invading Asia which was part of his inheritance. To invade the Persian Empire with limited objectives was not difficult, experience having shown that a Greek army could penetrate to Mesopotamia and, with good cavalry, might defeat any Persian army. Distances were great and communications sometimes difficult; but an army could usually live on the land, and had nothing to fear, west of Iran, from a national resistance of hostile populations.

2. Having secured Macedonia, Greece, and his northern frontiers, Alexander crossed the Hellespont (334) with an army of about 40,000 men, of whom fewer than half were Macedonians, and fewer than a quarter were Greek contingents from city-members of the Corinthian League. His immediate object was certainly to liberate the Greek cities in Asia. This was quickly achieved, after the battle of the Granicus (near the Hellespont) had reduced the Persian advance forces to defending a few strong places. He now disbanded his fleet and proceeded to 'defeat the Persian fleet on land', by conquering its remaining bases in Phoenicia and Egypt. Having completed the conquest of western and southern Asia Minor, he was brought to action by the Persian 'Grand Army'. The battle of Issus (near Alexandretta) was fought on ground unfavourable to the Persian cavalry; it was won by the steadiness of the Macedonian infantry and Alexander's brilliant cavalry leadership. Shortly after, he refused peace on favourable terms—the first certain sign that, exceeding the more restricted aims of the Greeks and probably of Philip, he intended to conquer the whole Persian Empire. But though the way to Babylon and the East lay open, he adhered to his original plan and spent the next year in occupying Phoenicia, Palestine, and Egypt. The capture of Tyre represents his greatest military achievement, and with it Persia ceased to be a Mediterranean Power.

3. In 331 Alexander left Egypt for Babylonia, where Darius had collected another 'Grand Army'. At the battle of Gaugamela (in the plain of Mesopotamia), he outmanœuvred and defeated the Persians on their own terrain; Darius escaped, but now became a mere fugitive. Alexander proceeded to occupy the Persian capitals (Babylon, Susa, Persepolis, Ecbatana), where the vast treasures of the Empire were stored. The sack of Persepolis was probably unpremeditated, since it seems at variance with his policy towards the Persians in general (see 5a below). The death of Darius left Alexander free to assume the title of *Basileus* (Great King) and to treat further resistance as rebellion (330). In a great sweep from the Caspian to the south-east slopes of Hindu Kush he found little opposition (330–329), but the conquest of Bactria and Sogdiana (Russian Turkestan) cost him nearly three years of hard fighting. Here was a national resistance broken only by time, a strategy adapted to new conditions, and a final gesture of reconciliation, Alexander's marriage with the Sogdian Roxane.

4. The Indian Expedition (327–325) extended the eastern frontiers of the Empire to the Hyphasis (Beas) and lower Indus. The nations of north-western India, unable to combine, presented to Alexander an opportunity like that which the disunion of Greece had given to Philip. The only formidable opponent was Porus (king of the Paurava), and the only great battle (the 'Hydaspes battle') was another triumph for Alexander's versatility. Having overrun the Punjab, he turned back because the army refused to follow him further. The return journey to Persia became a voyage of discovery. With half of the army, part marching and part in ships newly built, he reached the Indus delta, whence the fleet was to make the unknown voyage to the Persian Gulf, while he took an equally dangerous land route to prepare its bases. This return march through Gedrosia has been called Alexander's 1812; exaggerated though its horrors may have been, it was certainly the nearest that he ever came to a great disaster. The fleet suffered too, but arrived safe (325–324).

5. The last year of Alexander's life reveals how great would have been his difficulties had he survived. Misgovernment and disloyalty among his subordinates, a mutiny of his Macedonians, a rising of Greek soldier settlers in Bactria, imminent war in Greece—these were the fruits of his policy, which may conveniently be summarized under two heads, (a) Alexander's conception of conquest; (b) his conception of himself.

(a) In the government of the Empire he made only one important innovation, some separation of fiscal from military authority in the western provinces, with a more centralized financial administration. To peoples used to being ruled, the change of rulers meant little; with the former rulers themselves, the Iranian nobility, the case was different. With striking originality, Alexander adopted the style and ceremonial of a Persian king; he drafted Iranian cavalry into his army, and had 30,000 boys trained to fight in the Macedonian style. He married into the Iranian nobility and eventually made his highest officers do likewise, and encouraged mixed marriages by the soldiers. This bold policy was not wholly successful *vis-à-vis* the Iranians themselves: most of his Asiatic governors turned out badly. To many of his Macedonian officers it was odious from the first, and gave rise to those unsavoury affairs of Philotas and Parmenion (qq.v.), of Cleitus (q.v.), and of Callisthenes (q.v.) and the Royal Pages, which show Alexander at his most tyrannical, besides suggesting an essential insecurity at the foundations of his power. Finally his plans for a new 'mixed' army occasioned the great mutiny of 324, when even the Macedonian soldiers, devoted hitherto, stated their grievances. To the Macedonians the situation was simple: they were the conquerors, the barbarians were the conquered. To Alexander it appeared that some at least of the barbarians should be partners in the Empire: the combined aristocracies of Macedonia and Iran were to be the ruling class.

(b) It is likely though not certain that in 324 Alexander officially requested the Greek cities to treat him as a god (Aelian, *VH* 2. 19; Hyperides 5, col. 31; Arrian, *Anab.* 7. 23. 2): this act perhaps contains a clue to his inner personality and aims. It is usually interpreted as a political manœuvre, a means of evading his obligations to the Greek city-members of the Corinthian League; but, if so, it was a very inept manœuvre, and failed of its purpose. Greek religion certainly allowed for the possibility of a man, a great benefactor, becoming a god; but there was no religious consciousness in Greece which could override the highly developed political consciousness, and there was no question of Alexander's deification appearing to any Greek as a 'revelation', or as compensating for the loss of his political birthright, complete autonomy. Alexander himself, however, may have believed in his own divinity: if Greeks in general could hail a benefactor as a god, who more likely to believe in his divinity than the benefactor himself? In 332–331 Alexander had gratuitously undertaken a long and dangerous march to the desert oracle of Ammon (oasis of Siwah), and his own propaganda later announced that he had been recognized as son of Ammon (Zeus) (Callisthenes ap. Strabo 17. 1. 43, and *see* AMMON). This may well have been a customary local formula addressed to a new pharaoh; but, equally, its effect can have been incalculable on one whose whole career reveals his extraordinary preoccupation with the gods of all nations and, rhaps, his emulation of the Greek gods, Heracles and onysus in particular.

**6.** It remains a debated question whether Alexander med at a universal monarchy. The chief evidence pporting this view is probably not authentic (Diodorus , 4. 3 ff.); in fact, there is no sign that he intended in e immediate future anything more than exploration, d perhaps conquest, on his southern and northern ntiers (Arabia and the Caspian). His desire in India conquer still further had been natural if, as is likely, he ought the eastern Ocean comparatively near. If he lieved in his own divinity, that does not make him cent on conquering the West as well as the East, since Greek god (except perhaps Zeus) was ever supposed hold a universal rule. What is certain is that he would ver have settled down.

**7.** Alexander was undoubtedly the greatest general his race and probably of antiquity. He profited by the lendid army of Philip, and by technical improvements siegecraft; but this does not explain his achievement, nich was due to a profound, if unconsidered, insight to the essentials of strategy, and a wonderful versatility. temperament an inspired leader of cavalry and a monster of celerity', he could nevertheless be patient ege of Tyre), and could fight a defensive battle until e moment came to strike (Gaugamela). No doubt he posed himself too readily, and in leading a charge he st control of the battle; yet to this personal courage d his powers of endurance he partly owed his continued cendancy over officers and men, despite their accumu-ing grievances. As a ruler, he must be judged by his ans for the Empire (above), which were grand and iginal, but perhaps impossible of execution, even by mself. His foundations of new cities show a superb preciation of strategic needs and economic possibilities. e was always eager to find some new thing, whether new land or a new piece of knowledge. His favourite ok was the *Iliad*, his favourite sport hunting, and his ly relaxation the symposium. His character was eroic' rather than amiable: extravagantly brave and nerous by nature, he was extravagantly passionate and vengeful when thwarted, vices which led him to great d spectacular crimes. In him the soul wore out the east, and he died, in his thirty-third year, of a fever hich might well have spared him had he ever known w to spare himself.

ANCIENT SOURCES. *Alexander-historians* (see under the separate mes). There are three main lines of tradition. (1) The 'good' dition includes perhaps Alexander's official *Journal* (see EPHE-RIDES) written by Eumenes of Cardia, and such letters of Alexander are genuine; the geographical work of his bematists Baeton and ognetus; the histories of Ptolemy I and Aristobulus, Nearchus' ok, and some valuable information in Eratosthenes. (2) An anti-exander tradition of the Greek opposition, which came to include heoretical element, of Alexander as a tyrant, corrupted by power d owing his success to Fortune. (3) The so-called vulgate tradition a name used to embrace Cleitarchus and some lesser writers, as esicritus and Chares; it is popular history, making the most of any terial that is in any way sensational. Callisthenes comes under no el, but as the earliest of all the writers was probably used by most the rest. Many writers are known, from the fourth century B.C. to e fourth A.D., of whom nothing survives but the name or a few gments; among them may be mentioned Anaximenes the rhetori-n, Ephippus the gossip-monger, Androsthenes and Polycleitus the ographers, Nymphis and Marsyas of Pella, historians, Anticleides e antiquarian, Hegesias, rhetorician and untrustworthy historio-apher. (For lists see Müller and Jacoby, below.)

Of extant writers the most important, Arrian, is noticed under his me. Plutarch's *Life* of Alexander is compiled from every kind of irce, good and bad; the first part of his *De Alexandri fortuna* is a ung man's passionate protest against slanders. Diodorus 17 is gely based on Cleitarchus. Curtius gives some invaluable informa-n mixed with much rubbish; he uses Cleitarchus extensively, but lemy and a hostile source from time to time, and so presents a angely inconsistent picture. Justin is almost worthless, except as owing the hostile tradition more consistently than elsewhere. veral extant works—the *Meltz Epitome, Itinerarium Alexandri, Oxyrhynchus* 1798, *Codex Sabbaiticus* 29—illustrate the transition the Romance. The problem of the modern historian is how far to e Diodorus and Curtius. C. Müller, *Scriptores rerum Alexandri*

*Magni* (1846); F. Jacoby, *FGrH* ii. nos. 117–53, and the notes; Berve, *Alexanderreich* ii, under the separate names (contemporaries only). For Ptolemy: H. Strasburger, *Ptolemaios und Alexander* (1934); E. Kornemann, *Die Alexandergeschichte des Königs Ptolemaios I* (1935). For others, L. Pearson, *The Lost Histories of Alexander the Great*, (1960). Full bibliographies in *CAH* vi. 529 ff. and in Glotz, *Hist. grecque* iv. i. 33 ff.; see also W. W. Tarn, *Alexander the Great* ii (1948).

MODERN LITERATURE. (*a*) *General histories*. Beloch, *Gr. Gesch.* iii, pt. i, ch. 16; J. G. Droysen, *Gesch. Alexanders des Grossen* (re-print, 1917); Glotz, *Hist. grecque* iv, pt. i, bk. i; W. W. Tarn, *Alexander the Great*, 2 vols. (1948); G. Radet, *Alexandre le Grand* (1931); U. Wilcken, *Alexander der Grosse* (Engl. Transl. 1932); F. Schachermeyr, *Alexander der Grosse* (1949).

(*b*) *Alexander's army*. Berve, *Alexanderreich* pt. i, 103; J. Kromayer and G. Veith, *Antike Schlachtfelder* iv, pt. 3 (1924); Tarn, op. cit. ii. 135 ff.; P. A. Brunt, 'Alexander's Macedonian Cavalry', *JHS* 1963, 27 ff.; E. W. Marsden, *The Campaign of Gaugamela* (1964).

(*c*) *Administration and political ideals*. Berve, op. cit. 221; Ed. Meyer, *Kl. Schr.*[1] i (1920); U. Wilcken, 'Alexanders Zug in der Oase Siwa' (*Sitz. Berl.* 1928, 576); Wilcken, 'Alexander der Grosse und die hellenistische Wirtschaft' (*Schmollers Jahrbuch* 1921, 349); G. T. Griffith (ed.), *Alexander the Great: the Main Problems* (1965); A. R. Bellinger, *Essays on the Coinage of Alexander the Great* (1963).

(*d*) *Prosopography*. Berve, op. cit. ii.

(*e*) *Review of recent Literature*. G. Walser 'Zur neueren Forschung über Alexander den Grossen' (1956) in Griffith, op. cit. 345 ff. See also *Greece aud Rome* xii (1965). W. W. T.; G. T. G.

**ALEXANDER** (4) **IV** of Macedonia (323–?310 B.C.), posthumous son of Alexander the Great and Roxane, succeeded to the Empire jointly with Philip Arrhidaeus, but never lived to rule, though the possession of his person was important to the 'legitimist' generals in the wars of the *Diadochi* (q.v.), and later (316) to Cassander (q.v.), the greatest enemy of Alexander's house. Prisoner though he then became, his name and cause were still useful to Antigonus in his efforts to re-unite the Empire under his own rule; and correspondingly his continued existence embarrassed Cassander, who finally put him to death. G. T. G.

**ALEXANDER** (5) **OF PHERAE,** tyrant 369–358 B.C., nephew of Jason (q.v. 2). Throughout his tyranny he was opposed by Larissa and other cities, which refused to recognize him as *tagus* (q.v.). His enemies received occasional support from Thebes and became increasingly formidable, especially after Pelopidas had organized a Thessalian Confederacy modelled upon that of Boeotia. Pelopidas, who three times visited Thessaly, defeated him at Cynoscephalae in 364, and Pherae was subsequently compelled to join the Boeotian alliance. Alexander was at first an ally but later an enemy of Athens. In 358 he was murdered by the sons of Jason.

The cruelties attributed to Alexander by a tradition which glorified Pelopidas may well be exaggerated. He possessed great energy but little judgement, and, unlike Jason, attempted to crush the Thessalian cities rather than win them by diplomacy.

Diodorus, bk. 15; Plutarch, *Pelopidas*, 26–35. M. Sordi, *La lega tessala* (1958), ch. 8; H. D. Westlake, *Thessaly in the Fourth Century B.C.* (1935), ch. 7. H. D. W.

**ALEXANDER** (6) **I**, king of Molossia in Epirus, 342–330 B.C. Philip II of Macedon, his brother-in-law, placed him on the throne, expelling Arybbas and subjugating Cassopaea; as king of the Molossi he united Epirus in the form of a symmachy with himself as *hegemon*. In-voked by Tarentum *c*. 333, he conquered most of south Italy, allied with Rome, and was defeated and killed at Pandosia; he had made Epirus an important power, coining gold and silver, and united to Macedon by his marriage with Cleopatra, sister of Alexander the Great.

P. R. Franke, *Alt-Epirus und das Königtum der Molosser* (1955); Hammond, *Epirus*, 534 ff. N. G. L. H.

**ALEXANDER** (7) **II**, king of Molossia 272–*c*. 240 B.C. During the Chremonidean War (see CHREMONIDES) he invaded Macedonia, was routed and deposed by the generals of Antigonus, who set up a republic (*c.* 263 B.C.). Restored with Aetolian help, he conquered Acarnania and divided it with Aetolia. He died shortly afterwards.

Hammond, *Epirus*, 588 ff. N. G. L. H.

**ALEXANDER** (8) (b. *c.* 315 B.C.), of Pleuron in Aetolia (hence called *Aetolus*), made his name as a tragic poet and was included in the *Pleiad* at Alexandria. *Circa* 285–283, he was entrusted by Ptolemy Philadelphus with the *diorthosis* (preliminary sorting-out) of the tragedies collected for the Library. Later, *c.* 276, he appears at the court of Antigonus Gonatas in Macedonia.

WORKS. The only trace of Alexander's tragedies is one title, *Αστραγαλισταί* (*Dice-players*), *TGF*² 817. Two elegies are known, the *Apollo* and the *Muses*. The first was a collection of love-stories with unhappy endings, framed as a series of prophecies uttered by Apollo himself. Thirty-four lines (fr. 3) survive from the story of Antheus and Cleoboea; the language is learned and the style extremely dry. The *Muses* contained literary history. A striking appreciation of Euripides in anapaestic tetrameters (fr. 7) must come from a similar work. From two epyllia, *Halieus* (*Fisherman*) and *Circa* or *Crica*, only a fragment apiece survives. Other works mentioned are *Phaenomena* (Alexander met Aratus in Macedonia), *Epigrams*, and *Ionic Poems* (without music; cf. Strabo 14. 648; Ath. 620 e) in imitation of Sotades.

TEXTS. Powell, *Coll. Alex.* 121 ff.; Diehl, *Anth. Lyr. Graec.* vi.² 74 ff. MODERN LITERATURE: G. Knaack, 'Alexandros (84)' in *PW* i. 1447 f.; W. von Christ, *Gesch. griech. Lit.* ii. 1⁶ (1920), 173 f.; Susemihl, *Gesch. gr. Lit. Alex.* i.187; L. N. Mascialino, *Lycophron* (Leipzig, 1964). E. A. B.

**ALEXANDER** (9) (*c.* 290–*c.* 245 B.C.), son of Craterus (q.v. 2), and his successor as viceroy of Corinth and Euboea, declared himself independent in 250–249 (not 252, as commonly held) at Ptolemy's instigation, and allied himself with the Achaean Confederacy. A short war with Athens and Argos ended in 249, Gonatas acquiescing in his usurpation. The Aetolian victory of Chaeronea (245) split his realm in two, and about this time he died (poisoned, an unlikely rumour claimed, by Gonatas), leaving his throne to Nicaea, his widow.

W. H. Porter, ed. Plutarch's *Aratus*, Introd. (1937). F. W. W.

**ALEXANDER** (10) **BALAS** (d. 145 B.C.), pretended son of Antiochus IV, became king of Syria after the defeat and death of Demetrius I (q.v. 4). He was a pawn of Pergamum and Egypt and had support from the Roman Senate, which feared (unnecessarily) a revival of Seleucid power; as a king, he was incompetent. His reign (150–145) was ended by his expulsion and death; it is important mainly as marking the beginning of a period of civil wars which hastened the disintegration of the Seleucid Empire.

H. Volkmann, *Klio* 1925, 373 ff. G. T. G.

**ALEXANDER** (11) 'Polyhistor', born *c.* 105 B.C. at Miletus, came as prisoner of war to Rome; freed by Sulla (*c.* 80 B.C.), he took the name L. Cornelius Alexander; he was pedagogue to a Cornelius Lentulus, and later taught C. Julius Hyginus. He was accidentally burnt to death at Laurentum. His vast literary output (*FGrH* 273), probably after 49 B.C., included compilations of material on various lands, Delphi, Rome, the Jews, wonder-stories, and literary criticism. Alexander followed Crates' school; industrious and honest, he lacked taste and originality.

F. W. W.

**ALEXANDER** (12) (2nd c. A.D.), son of Numenius, wrote a *τέχνη* in which the rival theories of Apollodorus and Theodorus were discussed; also *Π. σχημάτων* (based

on Caecilius), which influenced later writers. *See al* ANONYMUS SEGUERIANUS.

Spengel, *Rhet.* i. 427–60, iii. 1–6, 9–40. T. Schwab, *Alexan Numeniu, Rhetorische Studien*, 5. J. W. H.

**ALEXANDER** (13) **OF ABONUTEICHOS** (*Ἀβών τεῖχος*) in Paphlagonia, a contemporary of Lucian (q.v whose bitterly hostile account of him, *Ἀλέξανδρος ψευδόμαντις* (see M. Caster, *Études sur Alexandre ou faux prophète*, 1938) is our chief source of informatio He claimed to have a new manifestation of Asclepi (q.v.) in the form of a serpent called Glycon. With th divine aid, he gave oracles and conducted mysterie from which he carefully excluded all unbelievers, espec ally Epicureans, and all Christians. He got a considerab following, a prominent member being a Roman of son standing, named Rutilianus. He was personally han some and apparently popular with women especial to what extent, if any, he believed his own doctrine ca hardly be determined in the absence of any descripti of him other than Lucian's, which represents him as thorough impostor, applying to him all the stock abu of rhetorical controversial writings. The cult surviv its author.

Nilsson, *GGR* ii. 452 ff. H. J.

**ALEXANDER** (14) **OF APHRODISIAS** (fl. ear 3rd c. A.D.), Peripatetic philosopher. He began lectu ing at Athens in A.D. 198 or soon after, and dedicat his book *Περὶ εἱμαρμένης* to Septimius Severus an Caracalla. His teachers had been Aristocles of Messan Herminus, and Sosigenes. He was the ablest of th Greek commentators on Aristotle, and is treated wi great respect by his successors among these, who pr serve many fragments of his lost works. He is singula free from the mystical tendencies of his time. He assum the indissoluble unity of the mental faculties and deni the immortality of the soul and the reality of time, b apart from a few such individual doctrines confin himself to the attempt to explain Aristotle's views witho innovation or criticism, treating them, as no dou Andronicus (q.v.) had before him, as forming one c herent system. The extant commentaries are on *A Pr.* 1 (ed. M. Wallies, 1883), *Top.* (ed. M. Walli 1891), *Mete.* (ed. M. Hayduck, 1899), *Sens.* (ed. P. Wen land, 1901), *Metaph.* (ed. M. Hayduck, 1891; only bl 1–5 are by Alexander); the most serious loss is his cor mentary on the *Physics*. There are also extant under h name a work of his own *Περὶ ψυχῆς* (ed. I. Bruns, 188 *Ἀπορίαι καὶ λύσεις*, *Ἠθικὰ προβλήματα*, *Περὶ εἱμαρμέν Περὶ κράσεως καὶ αὐξήσεως* (all ed. by I. Bruns, 189 Of these *Περὶ ψυχῆς* 1, *Περὶ εἱμαρμένης* (tr. A. Fitzgera 1931), and *Περὶ κράσεως καὶ αὐξήσεως* are probab genuine. *Ἰατρικὰ ἀπορήματα καὶ φυσικὰ προβλήματα* a *Περὶ πυρετῶν* (ed. J. L. Ideler, *Physici et Medici Grae Minores* (1841), 3, 81), and *Προβλήματα ἀνέκδοτα* (ed. C. Bussemaker, *Aristotelis Opera* (1857) iv. 291), a spurious.

*Alexandre d'Aphrodise*, G. Théry (1926), P. Moraux (194 P. Merlon, *Monopsychism* (1963). W. D.

**ALEXANDRIA** (1) was founded by Alexander the Gre immediately after his conquest of Egypt; communicati with Europe by sea was important, and none of t existing harbours on the Delta coast could accommoda a large fleet. Whether he designed to make it the capi of the country is unknown; it was not till after Ptolen had established himself in possession of Egypt that t seat of government was transferred from Memphis Alexandria. But it grew rapidly, and was made a cent of learning as well as of commerce and industry by t second and third Ptolemies. Under the Romans it w e one city that counted in the province; and, despite sasters in the third century, it did not begin to decline l the Arab conquest shifted the connexions of Egypt om Europe to Asia.

The plan of ancient Alexandria is difficult to reconruct, as nearly all buildings have been destroyed and bris has covered the old levels. It lay on a neck tween the sea and Lake Mareotis, and the island of aros was linked with the mainland by a mole, seven ades (c. ¾ mile) long, so as to provide a double harbour. he chief edifices were by the eastern harbour—the mporium fronting the sea, the Palace on the east, the aesareum and Theatre, probably also the Museum and ibrary, behind; a wide street intersected the city from st to west, by which was the Gymnasium. The only e of these of which the site is certain is the Caesareum. he Temple of Sarapis stood in the western quarter. nder the early Ptolemies the city in all probability ssessed the normal organs of democratic government, it these may have lapsed, or been abolished before e end of the dynasty. Augustus definitely refused to ant any self-government, though the Alexandrian tizenship was allowed to continue and carried with it rtain privileges—e.g. it was the avenue to Roman tizenship for an Egyptian. In 200 Alexandria was given Senate by Severus, simultaneously with other Egyptian wns. Probably the control of the city was kept strictly the hands of the Prefect: the only special local official entioned is the head of the police. The Jews, who were merous and inhabited a special quarter, had their own hnarch and council under the Ptolemies, and Augustus nfirmed these privileges. **J. G. M.**

For archaeological material, excavations, etc, see the *Bulletin de la cité royale archéologique d'Alexandrie*, (1898– ), and the publican of the Musée gréco-romain (written first by E. Breccia and en by A. Adriani) *Le Musée gréco-romain* (1922–32) and *Annuaire Musée gréco-romain* (1933 (with title in Italian)—3, 1952). For litical history, constitution, etc., see especially P. F. A. Jouguet, *ull. Soc. arch. Alex.* 1948, 71 ff. (Ptolemaic period); H. A. Musurillo, *rts of the Pagan Martyrs* (1954), *passim*, esp. 83 ff., 106 ff. (particuly for Roman period). Cults: E. Visser, *Götter und Kulte im olemäischen Alexandrien* (Amsterdam, 1938); H. I. Bell, *Cults and reeds in Graeco-Roman Egypt* (1953). A detailed general survey lacking, but the historical guide to the Museum by Breccia, *exandria. ad Aegyptum²* (1922), is a good introduction; *see also* riani, *Repertorio d' Arte dell' Egitto greco-romano*, Ser. A i–ii culpture), Ser. C i–ii (archaeology and topography) (1961, 1963).

**LEXANDRIA** (2) 'ad Issum', near Iskenderun *lexandretta*) on the Gulf of Issus, was probably Myrian- us refounded by Alexander (333 B.C.). It lay six miles uth-west of the Cilician Gates (hence the alternative me 'Alexandria of Cilicia'), and was also the key of e Syrian Gates (*Beilan Pass*).

**LEXANDRIA** (3) 'Arachosion' (of the Arachosii) or lexandropolis, at or near Kandahar in Afghanistan, was unded or refounded by Alexander, 329 B.C. It lay on important trade-route between Merv (or else Meshed) d India through the Bolan and Mula Passes, Kabul, d Las Bela. It soon ceased to be a Greek town.

**LEXANDRIA** (4) 'Areion' (of the Arii), Herat in horassan, founded or refounded by Alexander, was the ief town in Ariana. It lay on an important trade-route om Merv (or else Meshed) through Kandahar to India.

**LEXANDRIA** (5) 'Eschate', or 'the Farthest' (*Khod-nd?*), hurriedly founded by Alexander on the Jaxartes a fortress held by Macedonians, Greek mercenaries, d local Asiatics, against savage peoples beyond. It as refounded by Antiochus I as an 'Antiocheia'.

Arrian, *Anab.* 4. 1. 3; Curtius 7. 6.

**ALEXANDRIA** (6) 'among the Paropamisadae' was a short-lived colony of Alexander, north of Kabul, at the junction of routes from Aria, Bactria, and India.

Arrian, *Anab.* 3. 28. 4 ff.; 4. 22. 5; Strabo 12. 514. **E. H. W.**

**ALEXANDRIAN POETRY.** This term commonly denotes the Greek poetry, other than the New Comedy of Athens, composed between *c.* 300 and *c.* 30 B.C., and is justified by the fact that till 145 (expulsion of the scholars by Ptolemy Physcon) Alexandria, thanks to its library and museum, was the literary capital of the Greek world. The distribution of this poetry over the period indicated is very uneven. Two decades of fairly intense activity form a prelude to Alexandria's Golden Age, which itself only lasts from *c.* 280 to *c.* 240. The writers who follow are all Epigoni, and the second century B.C. is the least productive in the history of Greek poetry. But the beginning of the first century witnesses a St. Martin's Summer of Alexandrian poetry thanks to Meleager and his contemporaries. Meleager's *Garland* becomes known at Rome, and soon Parthenius and others introduce their pupils to Alexandrian poetry as a whole, which is thus enabled to play an important part in shaping the course of Roman poetry.

2. The struggles of the *Diadochi* discouraged the production of any poetry except Comedy and the Epigram, but *c.* 300 a revival becomes visible in the southeastern corner of the Aegean, both on the mainland (Zenodotus and Menecrates of Ephesus, Hermesianax and Phoenix of Colophon) and in the neighbouring islands, where the chief representatives were Philetas of Cos, Simias of Rhodes, and Asclepiades of Samos. The last-named, together with his associates Posidippus and Hedylus, was mainly important as an epigrammatist, but the other two exerted a wider influence. Both were scholars as well as poets and reviving the tradition of another scholar-poet, Antimachus of Colophon, set an example of a learned poetry, appreciable only by the cultivated few, which their successors followed almost as a matter of course. Though very little of their work survives, it seems that Philetas, Simias, and their contemporaries experimented in most of the poetical forms which the next generation commonly favoured, i.e. Narrative Elegy, Epyllion or Short Epic, Cataloguepoem, Hymn, Iambus, Didactic Poem, Epigram, and Paignion. After 280 the leading figures are Aratus of Soli, chiefly but by no means solely a didactic poet; Theocritus of Syracuse, best known for his pastorals but active in many other fields; Callimachus of Cyrene, the most representative Alexandrian poet, thanks to the clarity with which he formulated his poetic creed and the consistency with which he practised it; and finally Callimachus' opponent, Apollonius of Rhodes, who dared to question his former master's ruling and to compose an Epic in the grand manner. Contemporary with these poets was, it seems, Herodas of Cos, whose *Mimiambi* reflect the spirit of the age no less by the archaism of their form than by the modernity of their content. Of Alexandrian tragedy (though its seven most famous writers were known as the Tragic Pleiad) and Satyr-play little can now be established. The *Alexandra*, attributed to Lycophron, one of the Pleiad, probably belongs to the early second century.

3. In the quarrel between Callimachus and Apollonius the victory went to the former, but the question remained unsettled. Thus after the Golden Age, while Euphorion and Eratosthenes cultivate the Epyllion, Rhianus and others revert to the longer Epic. Moschus and Bion continue the Pastoral down to *c.* 100, and the didactic poems of Nicander of Colophon are best dated about the middle of the second century. But at Alexandria the

savant had displaced the scholar-poet. For the poets referred to above see under their names.   E. A. B.

4. *General character of Alexandrian poetry.* In Alexandrian times the new material from the conquered East, the great scientific institutions like the Alexandrian Museum or the vast Hellenistic libraries, the prevailing Aristotelian spirit, and even the patronage of the kings, tended to foster science rather than poetry. The third and second centuries B.C. are the great age of Greek natural science, mathematics, and scholarship, but not of creative literature. All Alexandrian poets were hampered by the weight and the splendour of classical Greek literature. Unable to create original poetic forms, they mixed and mingled elements from the old and clearly defined types of poetry. Scholarly and highly polished verse became the main criterion of great art. This often led to an artificial and fastidious style, delighting in archaic words, scholarly allusions, and a number of intricate and varied metres. Moreover, as real religious feeling had on the whole declined in the Hellenistic world the gods and the heroes were humanized, and the Panhellenic versions of the myths were avoided; *delectare* takes the place of *prodesse*. Realism and individualism, which came to play such a prominent part in that period, gave love—both ideal and sensual—a central position in poetry. At the same time, big city life, which developed in the large Hellenistic cities, excited a longing for the tranquillity and the beauty of country life, such as we find in the Bucolic poets, the true precursors of the Roman *ruris amatores*. This turn to the simple and the rustic brought animals, children, slaves, and landscape into Alexandrian verse, subjects on the whole beyond the scope of classical poetry. It is fair, however, to stress that by conscious art many Alexandrians did all they could to rise above the limitations of their age.

G. Knaack, 'Alexandrinische Litteratur' in *PW* i. 1399–1407; W. von Christ, *Gesch. griech. Lit.* ii. 1⁶ (1920); Susemihl, *Gesch. gr. Lit. Alex.*; F. A. Wright, *A History of Later Greek Literature* (1932); E. A. Barber, *CAH* vii, ch. 8; A. Couat, *La Poésie alexandrine* (1882, Engl. Transl. by J. Loeb, 1931); Ph.-E. Legrand, *La Poésie alexandrine* (1924); Wilamowitz, *Hellenist. Dichtung*; Rohde, *Griech. Roman*; E. A. Barber, 'Hellenistic Poetry', ch. 8 and Appendix by G. Giangrande in *Fifty Years and Twelve of Classical Scholarship* (1968); A. Körte–P. Händel, *Die Hellenistische Dichtung* (1960); T. B. L. Webster, *Hellenistic Poetry and Art* (1964); A. Rostagni, *Poeti alessandrini* (1963).   C. A. T.

## ALEXANDRIANISM, LATIN.

The work of the 'Alexandrian' poets of the first century B.C. is distinguished from the earlier hellenizing movement, represented in epic and drama, by a difference of models and a corresponding difference of purpose. Their main interest was turned from the classical Greek writers to the poets of the third and second centuries, and their aim was not now to bring into Latin what was best in Greek literature but to promote the ideals of technical perfection presented by the Alexandrians. Alexandrianism was a movement of scholarship, and it found a natural home in Italy when the period of creative activity which had come with the Punic Wars and the first contacts of Rome with Hellenism had been succeeded by an age of criticism of which the beginnings are seen in Lucilius and Accius; and the social and political unrest in Italy which set in with the Gracchi may well have encouraged an attitude which turned men of letters upon themselves and on the pursuit of art for art's sake.

The movement begins with the work of poets writing near the beginning of the first century B.C. and bridging the gap between the old style and the new—the epigrams of Porcius Licinus, Valerius Aedituus, and Lutatius Catulus, and the bizarre erotic poems of Laevius. These pioneers were succeeded by a school of poets (associated with Cisalpine Gaul), of which Catullus is the only surviving representative, but which also included Valerius Cato, Cinna, Calvus, Cornelius Nepos, Ticida, and probably Furius Bibaculus. These poets and their followers, who turned away from the traditional idiom of Latin poetry and found new patterns in Alexandria are sometimes called *neoterici*, the 'Moderns'. The nam was sarcastically given to them by Cicero (οἱ νεώτερ *Att.* 7. 2. 1., 50 B.C.; 'poetae novi', *Orat.* 161, 46 B.C. who was impatient of their mannerisms and their sel conscious pretensions. In *Tusc.* 3. 45 (45 B.C.) he pu the worst face on their devotion to Alexandrian models calling them 'cantores Euphorionis'; the description wou utterly misrepresent the width of Catullus' own interest but Catullus and Calvus were dead when the words we written, and Cicero may be thinking (as Horace is *Sat.* 2. 5. 41) of lesser men who aped the fashion.

Four of the outstanding characteristics of the Gre Alexandrians reappear in their Latin successors: (1) t development of new genres, especially 'epyllion', eleg and epigram, all miniature forms replacing the larg scale epic and drama; (2) a regard for form, for concinni and symmetry in language and metre, which left a lasti impression on Latin literature; (3) the cult of erudit seen in the vogue of didactic verse, in wealth of myth logical allusion, and in the search for novelty in stor telling; (4) the emergence of a subjective and person way of writing—in elegiac and lyric a new individualis in narrative a sentimental treatment and a psychologic interest. Two differences probably tempered the excess of Alexandrian mannerism in transplanting: while Greece Alexandrian literature was a literature of e haustion, in Italy it was one of revolt and experimen and the first Italian Alexandrians, for all their *ars a doctrina*, were not confined, as were their masters, the sheltered life of the study.

Thus established, Alexandrianism exercised its i fluence throughout the century. The mock heroic *Cul* and the romantic *Ciris* of the *Appendix Vergiliana* a Alexandrian in technique, as were the lost elegies Gallus. In Virgil's *Eclogues* and *Georgics* the influen of Alexandrian models is strong; in his maturer wo Virgil learned to turn their lessons to his own purpos and to reconcile Alexandrian ideals with the tradition Latin epic. The combination of learning with inten individualism in Propertius reflects his avowed allegian to the masters of Alexandrian elegy; Ovid's elegies ov much to the same sources, while the *Metamorphoses* a the *Fasti* are akin to the narrative verse of Callimach but in Ovid the influence of Alexandrianism is fus with that of the rhetoric of the schools.   C. J.

## ALEXIS

(c. 375–c. 275), Middle and New Comedy po born at Thurii (*Suda*), but apparently living most his long life at Athens. Wrote 245 plays (*Suda*); the fi of his Lenaean victories came probably in the 350s (six after Eubulus, fourth after Antiphanes in the victor list, *IG* ii². 2325. 150), and he won a victory at t Dionysia in 347 (*IG* ii². 2318. 278). The good anonymo tractate on Comedy (§ 17, p. 9 Kaibel) makes Menand a pupil of Alexis—a relationship more plausible th that of blood alleged by the *Suda*.

About 140 titles and 340 fragments survive, but it difficult to assess from them the part played by Ale in the transition from the older to the newer forms Comedy. Three facts, however, are notable: Alexis us both the older form of the chorus which was address by the actors (fr. 237) and the newer form known b from Menander (fr. 107); the παράσιτος seems to ha received his common name from Alexis (fr. 178); a Alexis' Ἀγωνίς ἤ Ἱππίσκος, dating probably from t 330s, was an early example of the type of plot especia associated with New Comedy, involving both a love aff and a confidence trick. The fragments show sometin l reflection and beauty of language; fr. 70, carnal love crime against real Love; fr. 219, life as a carnival (influencing the profounder Menander, fr. 416 Koerte?); 228, old age as life's evening. Pleasant wit is revealed frs. 102, 163 (see Arnott, *Hermes*, 1965, 298 ff.). Of terest also are fr. 45, a verbally clever comparison man and wine; fr. 98, beauty-culture; fr. 108, part of postponed prologue (of the New Comedy type); fr. 4, a cook's cure for burnt pork; fr. 135 (from the * vos*, one of about a dozen mythological burlesques in *exis*), Heracles' teacher has a library of classical Greek thors; fr. 245, a man philosophizes about the nature Eros.

Alexis' fame continued down to Roman times. Gellius *A* 2. 23. 1) notes that Alexis' plays were adapted by *man comedians; Turpilius used his Δημήτριος as a odel; and Plautus' *Poenulus* may at least in part derive *m his Καρχηδόνιος.

FRAGMENTS. *FCG* iii. 382 ff.; *CAF* ii. 297 ff., iii. 744; Demiańczuk, *pp. Com.* 211; *POxy.* 1801. (*PBerol.* 11771 [text in Page, *GLP* no. J is sometimes attributed to Alexis, but only on the slenderest dence.) Interpretation: A. Olivieri, *Dioniso*, 1939, 279 ff. (un- iable).　　　　　　　　　　　　　　　　　　　　W. G. A.

**LFENUS** (*PW* 8) **VARUS, PUBLIUS**? (*consul suffectus* B.C.; *praenomen* inferred from designation of P. Ifenus Varus, *cos.* A.D. 2, presumably his son, as P. f.) as a pupil of the jurist Servius Sulpicius (q.v. 2) Rufus, any of whose *responsa* were published by Alfenus in his *igesta*, a work in forty books; two epitomes of this *rk* were used in Justinian's *Digest* (q.v.), one under e name of Paul. Alfenus is identified by Porphyrio .v.) with *Alfenus vafer* mentioned by Horace (*Sat* 1. 3. .o), who was a shoemaker of Cremona: this identifica- on, which has been widely accepted, is rejected by some .g. E. Fraenkel, *Horace* (1957), 89 f.). If from Cremona, s *novus homo* and his son were apparently the only isalpines to reach the consulship under Augustus. In Alfenus served with Asinius Pollio and Cornelius allus on a commission to confiscate land in Transpadane aul and divide it among war veterans; he acted prob- ly as a legate or prefect, or possibly was a pro- agistrate (cf. Broughton, *MRR* ii. 377 f. He was not ollio's successor as governor of Cisalpine Gaul, as is roneously stated by Servius on *Ecl.* 9. 10). He acted rshly towards Mantua (Servius, loc. cit.); Virgil's land the district was confiscated but was later returned (or e poet was compensated). Alfenus may be the Varus med in Verg. *Ecl.* 9; it is less certain whether *Ecl.* 6 as dedicated to him or to Quinctilius Varus.

L. De Sarlo, *Alfeno Varo e i suoi Digesta* (1940).　　　H. H. S.

**LFIUS (ALPHIUS) AVITUS**, a 'neoteric' (cf. .EXANDRIANISM) of Hadrian's time, used iambic di- .eters in poems on historical events.

Baehr. *FPR*; Morel, *FPL*; Schanz–Hosius, § 513, 3.

**LGIDUS**, the easternmost section of the outer edge the Albanus Mons (q.v.), famous for its temples of iana and Fortune and its fashionable villas (Hor. *Carm. aec.* 69; Livy 21. 62; Sil. 12. 536). The rim of the lbanus Mons is here pierced by a narrow pass which the equi (q.v.) seized in the fifth century B.C. (Diod. 11. 40 nplies the date 484). This pass, which the Via Latina .v.) later used, dominated the route to the Hernici .v.); consequently Cincinnatus and other Roman nerals strenuously tried to dislodge the Aequi, Postu- ius Tubertus finally succeeding in 431.　　　E. T. S.

**LIMENTA.** The purpose of the *alimenta* in the Roman mpire was to give an allowance for sustenance to poor ildren, and this was achieved by the investment of

capital in mortgage on land, the mortgage interest being paid to, and administered by, municipalities or State officials. The system originated in private philanthropy, the earliest known benefactor in this field being T. Helvius Basila in the late Julio-Claudian period (*ILS* 977). A later philanthropist, the Younger Pliny, who made a similar gift to Comum, has recorded his reasons for his endowment (*Ep.* 7. 18). Inscriptions record similar private benefactions both in Italy and in the provinces. Gifts from the imperial *fiscus* to Italian towns for this purpose were first made by Nerva and Trajan. According to two Trajanic inscriptions (*ILS* 6675; 6509) from Veleia, near Parma, and from the Ligures Baebiani, near Beneven- tum, landowners who received money from the Emperor's gift gave security in land, to the value of roughly 12½ times the sum received; on this they paid annual interest at the rate of 5 per cent. The total received annually in interest at Veleia was 55,800 sesterces, which was dis- tributed among 263 boys, 35 girls, and 2 illegitimate children. The boys received 16 sesterces a month, the girls 12, and the illegitimate children 12 and 10 respec- tively. The system was widely advertised by Trajan, on one of the bas-reliefs of the arch at Beneventum (illus- trated, Rostovtzeff, *Roman Empire*[2], 356, 361) and on coins with the legend ALIM[ENTA] ITAL[IAE] (Mattingly– Sydenham, *RIC* ii. 240). Its primary object was to increase the birth-rate among the poorer classes, partly, as Pliny suggests (*Panegyricus* 26), with a view to the recruiting of the Roman legions. There is no reason to think that the landowners needed or even welcomed the loans (which laid a perpetual charge on their property). As the system continued during the second century (there is inscriptional evidence from forty-six Italian towns), a civil service was created for its administration, with a senatorial *praefectus alimentorum* and subordinate equestrian *procuratores ad alimenta*. The *curatores* of the great roads of Italy also took part in this work.

*CAH* xi. 887 (bibliography). F. C. Bourne, *TAPA* 1960, 47 ff.; R. Duncan-Jones, *PBSR* 1964, 123 ff.; P. Garnsey, *Hist.* 1968, 367 ff.; A. R. Hands, *Charities and Social Aid in Greece and Rome* (1968), 108 ff.　　　　　　　　　　　　　　　　　　　　J. P. B.

**ALISO,** a fort on or near the Lippe established during the wars of Drusus, possibly the one mentioned by Dio (54. 33. 4) as set up in 11 B.C. 'at the point where the Lupia and the Elison unite'. The garrison resisted the advancing Germans after the defeat of Varus (q.v. 2) in A.D. 9 and regained the Rhine (Vell. Pat. 2. 120). Ger- manicus, in 15, refortified all the posts between Aliso and the Rhine and restored the road (Tac. *Ann.* 2. 7). Its site is uncertain; its identification with an important Roman fort excavated at Haltern, on the Lippe, 30 miles from the Rhine, is not widely accepted.　　　　　　　　O. B.

**ALLECTUS,** probably *rationalis* (finance minister) of Carausius in Britain. Allectus assassinated him in A.D. 293/4, but after three years' rule he was overthrown by Constantius I, whose praetorian prefect, Asclepiodotus, de- feated and slew him, probably somewhere in Hampshire.

P. H. Webb, *Num. Chron.* 1906, 127 ff., and in Mattingly– Sydenham, *RIC* v, ii, 427 ff., 558 ff.; E. Stein, *Hist. du Bas-Empire*, (1959), i. 78 ff., 446 ff.; R. A. G. Carson, *Journ. Brit. Arch. Assoc.* 1959, 33 ff.; D. E. Eichholz, *JRS* 1953, 41 ff.　　　C. E. S.

**ALLEGORY, GREEK.** As philosophy developed, many who valued its various doctrines were led by their admiration for the wisdom and inspiration of Homer and Hesiod to find similar views symbolically expressed in the early poetry. (The tendency survives, as in a modern scholar who depicts Homer as a pacifist because Zeus dislikes Ares in the *Iliad*.) Even the early philo- sophic critics of Homer's world-view accepted this stand- point, and competed with the poet by expressing their theories in 'poetic' style, whether by remoulding the myths to suit newer cosmogonies, or at least by using puns, personifications, and 'enigmas', either in verse (Parmenides, Empedocles) or in prose (Anaximander, Heraclitus). Hence the belief that Homer too 'philosophized in verse', and that allegorical treatment could make his teaching fully explicit. This belief was not altogether baseless, for Homer and Hesiod contain some traces of speculative thought and some genuinely allegorical passages. Allegorical interpretation could not develop fully until philosophy had more or less attained an independent life and an abstract (non-mythical) language of its own. Its most flourishing period was the late fifth century B.C., when Metrodorus of Lampsacus, the most thoroughgoing of all allegorists, studied Homer's 'physical' doctrines, and other adherents of Anaxagoras as well as Heracliteans and Sophists specialized (as Plato shows) in the 'hidden meanings' (ὑπόνοιαι: ἀλληγορία is a later word) of the poets. Once this method had been initiated by the philosophers for its *positive* results, it began to be exploited by 'grammarians' (first, apparently by Theagenes (q.v. 2) of Rhegium, who explained some allegories in Homer's Theomachy) for the *negative* purpose of defending morally offensive passages of Homer. But the leading allegorists were philosophers, who applied their treatment to offensive and inoffensive passages alike. The handmaid of this pseudo-science (never, be it noted, popular among the Greeks) was 'etymology' (q.v.), which dealt in the 'true' meanings, as revealed by assonances, of mythical words and names.

**2.** Plato attacked *positive* (philosophical) allegorism, chiefly on the ground that the authority of the poets (even if their teaching were ascertainable) cannot do duty for reasoned argument. *Negative* or defensive ('grammatical') allegorism he regarded as unimportant.

**3.** After Plato, among philosophers allegorism (mainly etymological) was practised by the Stoics (especially Chrysippus) for the illustration and corroboration of their own doctrines. This school, however, from Zeno (following Antisthenes, who was not an allegorist) onwards, admitted the presence of irrational 'opinion' (δόξα) in the poets, from which deeper meanings cannot be extracted. The Middle Stoics laid still more stress on this element; hence Cicero's Balbus (unlike the grammarians) refuses to interpret the Theomachy; and the Platonizing Stoic, Ariston of Chios, rejected allegorism entirely. In the first century A.D. the Stoic Seneca regarded it as an aberration of the grammarians; but his contemporary, the Stoic Cornutus (in his *De Natura Deorum* = *Theologiae Graecae Compendium*, Teubner), tried to recall Stoicism to something like the position of Chrysippus. Plutarch was Platonic enough to reject allegorism, but the Neoplatonists (except Plotinus) revived it in a distorted and exaggerated form (see e.g. Porphyry, *De Antr. Nymph.*).

**4.** As for the grammarians, Alexandrian scholarship (Aristarchus, etc.) rejected the allegorical interpretations of Homer. But Crates and his school, under Stoic influence, adopted the practice for the defence of Homer's good fame. It is ultimately from these grammarians that the bulk of the allegories found in the Homeric scholiasts and in the collection (first century A.D.) known as Heraclitus' *Quaestiones Homericae* (a veritable curiosity of literature) is derived. Their view is that Homer either erred or allegorized (cf. [Longinus] Π. ὕψους 9. 7), but (unlike Longinus) they are sure that he did not err: if Zeus binds Hera (for example), this means that aether is the boundary of air, and the two 'anvils' are the other two elements. Such is the standpoint also of Strabo (a Stoic of sorts, who regarded myth as the treacle disguising the pill of historical and philosophical truth), [Plutarch] (*Vit. Hom.*), Maximus of Tyre (for whom

poetry is elementary philosophy), Dio Chrysostom, and others. Some, but not all, of these used allegorical interpretation to vindicate Homer's omniscience against Plato.

**5.** Deliberately written allegories are rare in Greek and never extensive. Examples are Prodicus' *Choice of Heracles* (Xen. *Mem.* 2. 21) and Plato's parable of the Cave (*Resp.* 514 a).

J. Tate, *CR* 1927, 214; *CQ* 1929, 41, 142; 1930, 1; 1934, 105 and literature there cited; L. Radermacher, *Mythos und Sage bei den Griechen* (1938), esp. 293, n. 10.                              J.

**ALLEGORY, LATIN.** The main line of succession in allegorism leads from Stoicism not to Rome but to Alexandria; Origen, for example, had read Cornutus. Some Romans (Ennius, Varro), however, adopted Greek methods with the Roman gods, and the Stoic in Cicero's *De Natura Deorum* (2. 62–9) supplies examples of 'etymological' allegorism on these lines, deriving e.g. 'Neptunus' from 'nare'. But Horace, who knew Stoicism well, is more typically Roman in ignoring 'physical' and 'etymological' speculations, and merely contending for the moral meanings of the *Odyssey* (*Epist.* 1. 2) and of the tales of Orpheus and Amphion (*Ars P.* 391 ff.). Although the word ἀλληγορία first appears in a Roman author (Cicero), it has only a very restricted use, as a term of rhetoric.

Unlike medieval allegorism, which led both before and after the Renaissance to the creation of allegories on a large scale (Dante, Spenser), these theories did not result in any such sustained parallelism as marks *The Pilgrim's Progress* or *The Tale of a Tub*. They merely encouraged certain poetic conceits (like calling the sea 'Neptune') and numerous personifications, which range from Lucretius' Venus to the Philologia of Martianus Capella. These personifications are sometimes developed in poetry in a way which, as Propertius (2. 12) on the figure of Amor suggests, may indicate the influence of symbolic painting; this manner is most clearly seen in Ovid's picturesque Palace of the Sun, Home of Sleep, etc. (*Met.* 2. 1 ff.; 11. 592 ff.).

A few allegories come directly from Greek: Horace takes over Alcaeus' ship of State; Silius adapts the Choice of Heracles. Some rare examples are original and un- sophisticated like Tarquin's message to his son or Menenius Agrippa on the belly and the other members (Livy 1. 54; 2. 32). The most novel tendency was the allegorical representation of contemporary persons and events: the shepherds of Virgil (and of his imitators) correspond (to a degree still disputed) with real persons. To some modern scholars Aeneas has seemed a similar disguise for Augustus. Actual allusions in the *Aeneid* to contemporary events may excuse such a view; just as Virgil's profundity and deliberate ambiguities may excuse the older interpretation of the *Aeneid* which, from the time of Donatus onwards, found there an allegory of ideas rather than of facts (see D. Comparetti, *Vergil in the Middle Ages* (tr. of 1st ed., 1895), i, ch. 8; D. L. Drew, *The Allegory of the Aeneid*, 1927).           J.

**ALLIA,** a stream flowing into the Tiber 11 miles north of Rome (modern *Fosso Maestro*?), where the Gauls overwhelmed the Romans (18 July, 390 or 387 B.C.? Despite Diodorus (5. 114) the battle probably occurred east of the Tiber (Livy 5. 37; Plut. *Cam.* 18). See also AIUS LOCUTIUS.

M. Sordi, *I rapporti romano-ceriti* (1960), 1 ff.           E. T.

**ALLIFAE,** mountain town overlooking the Volturno (q.v.), the gateway between Samnium and Campania (qq.v.): modern *Castello d'Alife* (with interesting museum in nearby *Piedimonte d'Alife*). Strategic Allifae changed hands repeatedly in the Samnite Wars. Under ome it descended to lower ground and became a ourishing town (modern *Alife*, with well-preserved oman walls, etc.). E. T. S.

**LLOBROGES,** a tribe of Gallia Narbonensis, occupy- g modern Dauphiné and Savoy. The name seems to ean 'foreigners'. They were annexed to Rome in 121 c. by Cn. Domitius (q.v. 2) Ahenobarbus and Q. Fabius .v. 8) Maximus Allobrogicus. An attempted revolt was rushed by C. Pomptinus (61). On the other hand, they :sisted the invitations of Catiline (63) and Vercingetorix 2). Under the Empire the name gives place to Vien- enses (from the capital Vienna), surviving only as the rotecting god, Allobrox.

C. Jullian, *Hist. de la Gaule* (1908), ii. 515; vi. 330 ff. C. E. S

**L MINA.** A port at the mouth of the River Orontes in yria (now part of Turkey), excavated by Sir Leonard Voolley. It was established as a trading post by 800 B.C. nd visited by Cypriots and Greeks, mainly Euboeans nd islanders. The Greek interest became dominant, rith East Greeks and carriers of Corinthian pottery replac- g the islanders in the seventh century. It was probably major source of goods for Greece in the 'orientalizing' eriod. After a break during the period of Babylonian omination the port revived under the Persians and ourished until it was eclipsed by the foundation of eleucia in 301 B.C. It may be the Greek Posideion, said y Herodotus to have been founded by Amphilochus fter the Trojan War.

L. Woolley, *A Forgotten Kingdom* (1953); id., *JHS* 1938; J. oardman, *Greeks Overseas* (1964), 61 ff., 125. J. B.

**LOADAE,** in mythology, Otus and Ephialtes, sons of phimedeia, wife of Alōeus, and Poseidon. They grew ll they were 9 fathoms tall and 9 cubits broad when years old (*Od.* 11. 310–11). They imprisoned Ares a a bronze vessel for thirteen months (*Il.* 5. 385 ff.); ey meant to climb to heaven by piling mountains on ach other, but were killed by Apollo before they grew p (*Od.* 11. 315 ff.). A later variant (Hyg. *Fab.* 28) says ey tried to violate Artemis; Apollo sent a hind between em, and in shooting at it they killed each other. They ere punished in Tartarus (Hyg. ibid. and Rose ad loc.). n their cult (see Schultz in Roscher's *Lexikon* i. 254) ey have no such unholy characteristics. H. J. R.

**LPHABET, GREEK.** The various forms of local lphabet current in early Greece were all ultimately de- ived from a Phoenician (Semitic) source, which must ave reached the Aegean in the course of trade certainly y the second half of the eighth century (the date of the arliest Greek examples found as yet). The alphabet, as aken letter by letter from the Semitic model, runs: ΑΒΓ ΔΕϜΙΗΘΟΙΚΛΜΝΞΟΠΜϘΡΣΤ, but not all the Ϝreek states found a use for all the letters, though prob- bly all continued for some time to be repeated mechanic- lly in their order. Certain states found no use for Ϝ ('*vau*'), others for Ξ (properly, perhaps, a more complicated bilant than is implied by our *x*), or Ϙ ('*qoppa*', the *k* efore *o* and *u*); and for *s* some used Σ, but others pre- erred Μ ('*san*', perhaps corresponding to the English ronunciation of *z*). The most striking feature in the Ϝreek adaptation of the Phoenician model is that by ltering (consciously or unconsciously) the original signi- cance of ΑΕΙΟ and adding Υ Greek, unlike Phoenician, chieved an independent representation of vowel-sounds. ϘΧΨΩ are all Greek additions. Υ, from its sound nd shape, appears to be a variant of Ϝ, a vowel *u* derived rom the semivowel *u̯*; evidently it belongs to the very arly stage of adaptation, for no local alphabet lacks . Ω, an Ionic invention (see below), may also be a oublet, formed by breaking the Ο. The exact origins

of the three double-consonant letters ϘΧΨ are disputed, though it is generally agreed that they originated among the eastern Greeks. Another non-Phoenician letter Τ ('*sampi*'? *see* NUMBERS I (2) for the letter signifying 900) was used by many cities in the same eastern Ionic area for the sibilant rendered elsewhere by ΣΣ or ΤΤ; but it did not become widespread. Other Greek states also produced occasionally their own local symbol for some sound not covered by the common alphabet; but these too remained isolated experiments, except for Ϝ (see below).

An early form of the Greek alphabet is preserved by the archaic inscriptions from the Doric-speaking group of islands headed by Melos, Thera, and Crete. In it, as in many other 'epichoric' or local scripts, we find Ϝ, Ϙ, Μ, and Η = *h* (except for Crete, where Η stood, as in Ionic, for *eta*; see below); but it lacks the non-Phoeni- cian additions Ϙ, Χ, and Ψ, using Π (or ΠΗ), Κ (or ΚΗ), and ΠΣ. Ω is also absent. At a more developed stage the alphabets fall roughly into two main groups, 'blue' and 'red' in Kirchhoff's original colour-chart. The split lay in their usage of the signs Χ and Ψ. (1) The 'blue' alphabets used Χ for *kh* and Ψ for *ps* (if they used it at all; otherwise, ΦΣ); also (most of them) Ξ for *x*. The 'red' used Ψ for *kh* and Χ (occasionally ΧΣ) for *x*. Kirchhoff further identified the 'blue' as Eastern and the 'red' as Western, and this is still basically true; most of the central and western mainland and the western colonies are 'red', and most of the eastern mainland, the Aegean islands, and the Greek states in Asia Minor are 'blue'. But 'red'-users exist in the eastern sector (e.g. Euboea, the E. Argolid, Rhodes) and 'blue'-users in the western (e.g. Corinth's north-western colonies, and Selinus). Most colonies used the script of the metropolis (e.g. the colonies of Euboea and Achaea); but some, apparently, did not (e.g. Megara's northern and western colonies, and Syracuse).

One variety of the eastern alphabets, namely the East Ionic, eventually became predominant. In the Ionic dialect (as in many others) short *e* possibly had a close quality [e] (*see* PRONUNCIATION, GREEK), but there were two forms of long *e*, one open and the other close: [e:] and [ɛ:]. Through the absence of the h-sound in Ionic pronun- ciation, the aspirate-letter Η in this script stood not for an emphatic *h* with its (apparent) following vowel-sound *e*, but only for a lengthened vowel-sound [ɛ:]; again, it is uncertain whether this was originally a conscious or un- conscious alteration. The East Ionic alphabet appears also to have originated the new symbol Ω (see above) to represent [ɔ:]. [e:] and [o:] continued for a time to be denoted by Ε and Ο like the short vowels, but before 400 B.C. the development of the original diphthongs *ei* and *ou* into simple long vowels of close quality made it possible to use ΕΙ and ΟΥ not only for the original diphthongs but also for the [e:] and [o:] that had never been diphthongal (e.g. εἰμὶ κοῦρος, older ΕΜΙ ΚΟΡΟΣ).

The East Ionic alphabet was officially accepted at Athens in the archonship of Eucleides (403–402 B.C.) and thereafter gradually extended. Non-Ionic elements like Ϝ lingered locally for some time, and local differences, especially in vowel-pronunciation, still produced varia- tions in spelling. As Η could no longer express the rough breathing, a modification of it (Ͱ) was used for this pur- pose in some areas and has given rise to the sign '; another modification (˧) has produced the sign for the smooth breathing.

A. Kirchhoff, *Studien zur Geschichte des griech. Alphabets* (1887); E. S. Roberts, *Introduction to Greek Epigraphy* i (1887); C. D. Buck, *Comparative Grammar of Greek and Latin* (U.S.A. 1932), 68 ff., and *The Greek Dialects* (U.S.A. 1955), 17 ff.; A. Rehm in Otto's *Hand- buch d. Archäologie* i (1939), 191 ff.; G. Klaffenbach, *Griechische Epigraphik* (1957); A. G. Woodhead, *The Study of Greek Inscriptions* (1959); L. H. Jeffery, *The Local Scripts of Archaic Greece* (1961); M. Guarducci, *Epigrafia graeca* i (1967). J. W. P.; L. H. J.

**ALPHABET, LATIN.** It has generally been held that the original Latin alphabet of twenty letters (A B C D E F H I K L M N O P Q R S T V X) was borrowed directly from the Greek alphabet of Cumae in Campania. This city, a colony of Chalcis in Euboea, was regarded as the most likely source, because the ancient forms of certain Latin letters strongly resemble the Cumaean equivalents. Modern opinion, however, favours the view that Latin, like Oscan and Umbrian, owes its alphabet only indirectly to the Greeks, but directly to the Etruscans. For Latin the immediate source is said to be an early form of Etruscan script, derived itself most probably from Campania, but the possibility of a different origin cannot be definitely excluded. Be this as it may, the ultimate source is a western alphabet which contained the signs X = *ks* and H = *h*.

In the Latin adaptation of this alphabet the following points are noteworthy:

(1) C (<), i.e. Γ (Gamma), was at first used for *k* as well as for *g*. This peculiarity is usually ascribed to the influence of Etruscan, which made no distinction between voiceless and voiced stops (*see* PRONUNCIATION, GREEK, B. 1). Of the three signs thus available for the voiceless guttural, K was used originally before *a*, C before *e* and *i*, Ϙ (Greek Koppa) before *o* and *u* (as in Greek) and also before *u̯*. Eventually C was generalized for all positions except before *u̯*, where Ϙ continued. Relics of the old spelling are *Kalendae* and *Kaeso*. In the third century B.C. the introduction of G, a modification of C, gave the voiced guttural a separate symbol. C., Cn. = Gaius, Gnaeus are survivals.

(2) It has been held that Z originally occupied the seventh place in the alphabet and represented the voiced *s* (*z*), but was dropped when this sound became *r* in the fourth century B.C. There is, however, no certain occurrence of Z in any republican inscription. Afterwards it was reintroduced to express ζ in words borrowed from Greek, and found its place then at the end of the alphabet, its original position having been occupied by G.

(3) For Latin *f* the nearest equivalent in Greek was the voiceless Digamma (FH) which occurred in some dialects, and which must have approximated in pronunciation to Scottish *wh*, i.e. *hw*. F is a simplified form of FH. This use of F (in Greek = *u̯*) made it necessary to express *u̯* as well as *u* by V. Y (another form of V) was added late in the republican period to denote *v* (by then = *ü*) in words borrowed from Greek. I had to do duty for both *i* and *i̯*. The use of *u* and *i* for the vowels and *v* and *j* for the semivowels is a device of medieval times and not of the Latin period.

(4) An attempt to distinguish long vowels from short by writing the former double is attributed to the poet Accius (q.v.). Later the 'Apex' (a mark like an acute accent) was sometimes employed for the same purpose. *ei* for *ī* is common from about 150 B.C. after the diphthong *ei* had become *ī* in pronunciation. The occasional use of 'I longa' (e.g. FELIcI) starts in Sulla's time.

(5) For double consonants a single letter originally sufficed. The reform in this respect belongs to the second century B.C. and is ascribed to Ennius.

W. M. Lindsay, *The Latin Language* (1894), 1 ff.; F. Sommer, *Handbuch der lateinischen Laut- und Formenlehre* (1914), 23 ff.; Leumann–Hofmann–Szantyr, *Lateinische Grammatik* (repr., 1963), i. 44 ff.; M. Lejeune, *Rev. Ét. Lat.* 1957, 88 ff. J. W. P.; I. M. C.

**ALPHESIBOEA,** in mythology, daughter of Phegeus of Psophis and wife of Alcmaeon (q.v.). According to Propertius 1. 15. 15, she and not Callirhoë's children avenged him; perhaps a mere blunder, perhaps an unknown variant. H. J. R.

**ALPHEUS** (Ἀλφειός), the largest river of Peloponnesus, rises in south Arcadia near Asea and flows past Olympia to the Ionian Sea. Its main tributaries are t[he] Arcadian Ladon and Erymanthus. The Cladeus jo[ined] it at one corner of the ancient site at Olympia. [Its] waters were fabled to pass unmixed through the s[ea] and to rise in the fountain of Arethusa at Syracuse (Pin[dar] *Nem.* 1. 1; Ibycus, fr. 23 Bergk).

P-K, *GL* iii. 1. 285 ff. T. J. D; R. J. [

**ALPS.** Although the passes of the Alps were used f[or] trans-European commerce since prehistoric times, t[he] early Greeks had no knowledge of these mountain[s] though a vague notion of them may lurk in their specul[a]tions about the Hercynia Silva and the Rhipaean Mt[s] (qq.v); in Herodotus (4. 49) 'Alpis' is a tributary of t[he] Danube. By the fourth century Greek travellers in nor[th] Italy and Provence brought information about a 'pilla[r]' or 'buttress' of the north (Ephorus ap. Scymn. 188 but Apollonius Rhodius (4. 627 f.) could still believe th[at] the Rhone and Po were interconnected. The Roma[n] conquest of Cisalpine Gaul and Hannibal's invasion [of] Italy (Polyb. 3. 50–6; Livy 21. 32–7; the pass remai[ns] unidentified) brought more detailed knowledge, an[d] Polybius gave a good description of the western Alp[s] though he thought that they extended uniformly in [a] west-east direction. The campaigns of Caesar in Gau[l] and of Tiberius in Switzerland and Austria, opened u[p] the Alps thoroughly, and in the first two centuries A.[D.] at least five paved roads (Little and Great St. Bernar[d], Splügen, Maloja, and Brenner passes) were built acro[ss] them. Strabo defined the curve of the Alps with su[b]stantial correctness, and graphically described the vegetation and the predatory habits of the valley popul[a]tions.

The Romans distinguished the following chains: Alp[es] Maritimae, Cottiae (from Mte. Viso), Graiae (the S[t]. Bernard section), Poeninae (Mt. Blanc–Mte. Rosa[)], Raeticae (Grisons), Noricae (Tyrol), Carnicae, an[d] Venetae. They also gave the name of 'Alps' to the Au[s]trian and Dalmatian mountains. E. H. [

ROMAN PROVINCES. Augustus reduced the area north [of] Nice on both sides of the Var and constituted it as t[he] province of Alpes Maritimae in 14 B.C.; it was govern[ed] by a *praefectus*, later by a *procurator*. The district furth[er] north, after pacification, was left under the rule [of] Cottius (q.v.); later it was annexed by Nero and know[n] as Alpes Cottiae. These two little provinces forme[d] buffers between Italy and Gaul. After Diocletian Alp[es] Cottiae was restricted to an area east of the Alps, e[x]tended eastwards, and included in the diocese of Ita[ly] under a *praeses*. Alpes Maritimae was limited to west [of] the Alps and extended; it was united to the Gallic di[o]cese. In the second century a third Alpine province h[ad] been created, Alpes Atrectianae et Poeninae, comprisi[ng] part of Raetia; it included the Vallis Poenina (upp[er] Rhone valley, today *Valais*) with centre at Octodur[us] (Martigny) and was under a *procurator*. Diocletian r[e]named it Alpes Graiae et Poeninae. H. H.

Cary–Warmington *Explorers* 120 ff.; (Pelican) 146 ff.; Cary, *Ge[o]graphic Background* 7, 105, 108 ff., 247 ff., 276 ff. *et al.*; R. Heuberge[r], 'Die Anfänge des Wissens v. d. Alpen', *Zeitschrift für Schweizerisc[he] Geschichte* 1950, 337 ff.

**ALTAR.** The ancients distinguished between βωμό[ς], *altare*, the altar of a supreme god, ἐσχάρα, *ara*, that [of] a hero or demi-god, and ἑστία, *focus*, a domestic alt[ar], though these distinctions were not always observed. A[n] altar for the indispensable sacrifice was a necessary a[d]junct of a cult (save in the case of infernal deities, [to] whom offerings were made in pits, βόθροι, *scrobes*). Offe[r]ing tables or benches seem to have served in place [of] altars in prehistoric Greece. In Archaic Greece cru[de] block altars were the focus for worship before regul[ar] temples, *oikoi* for the cult images, were built. Later altars are either block-like or, in Ionia, have a broad flight of steps up to the sacrificial platform. Some of these are immense. The great altar of Pergamum was 40 feet high, while others at Syracuse and Parium are credited with a length of one stadium. Within the temples smaller altars served for incense or bloodless offerings. In Hellenistic times circular altars are common, while the Romans preferred the quadrangular form, and their cinerary urns were frequently in the form of altars. Altars were places of refuge, the suppliants being under the protection of the deity to whom the altar belonged.

E. Pernice, *Die Hellenistische Kunst in Pompeji*, vol. v (1932); W. Altmann, *Römische Grabaltäre der Kaiserzeit* (1905); F. Robert, *Thymélé* (1939); C. G. Yavis, *Greek Altars* (U.S.A. 1949).
F. N. P.; J. B.

**ALTHAEMENES,** in mythology, son of Catreus, king of Crete. Warned by an oracle that he would kill his father, he left Crete for Rhodes. Long after, his father came to seek him; Althaemenes took him for a pirate and killed him (Diod. Sic. 5. 59; Apollod. 3. 12–16).
H. J. R.

**ALTINUM,** modern *Altino* on mainland Italy near Venice, an important highway junction, where the Viae Postumia, Popillia, Annia (1), and transalpine Claudia Augusta met. In antiquity a fashionable resort town, which rivalled Baiae (q.v.), Altinum is today only a hamlet. Barbarian invasions in the Late Empire ruined it.
E. T. S.

**ALYATTES,** fourth Lydian king (c. 610–560 B.C.), of the house of Gyges, finally drove out the Cimmerians, extended his dominion to the Halys, and made a war on Cyaxares the Mede (585), during which occurred an eclipse (perhaps the one foretold by Thales). After the conclusion of peace through Labynetus (Nebuchadrezzar) of Babylon he continued the Lydian campaigns against Ionia, conquered Smyrna, but was foiled by Clazomenae and Miletus. He built temples to Athene near Miletus and made offerings to Delphi. The founder of the Lydian Empire, he was buried in a vast round-barrow tomb, described by Herodotus and Strabo and still visible.
Herodotus bk. 1; Strabo 13. 627. G. Radet, *La Lydie* (1893), 193–206.
P. N. U.

**ALYPIUS** (3rd or 4th c. A.D.), the author of an extant Εἰσαγωγὴ μουσική, the fullest source of our knowledge of Greek musical scales.
Ed. C. Jan, *Musici Scriptores Graeci* (1895), 357–406.

**AMADOCUS,** dynastic name in the royal house of the Odrysians, who controlled the Thracian hinterland: (1) courted by Alcibiades in 406 B.C. and an ally of Athens in 390 B.C.; and (2) one of the three Thracian kings who made alliance with Athens in 357 B.C. (Tod ii, no. 151), held central Thrace against the king of eastern Thrace, Cersobleptes, and invoked the help first of Athens and then of Philip II of Macedon in 352 B.C. who soon absorbed the kingdom into his own sphere of influence. See THRACE.
N. G. L. H.

**AMAFINIUS,** GAIUS, older contemporary of Cicero, popularized the philosophy of Epicurus in Latin. Cicero refers to him disparagingly (*Fam.* 15. 19. 2; *Acad. Post.* 1. 5. Cf. *Tusc.* 1. 6; 2. 7; 6, 7).
Schanz–Hosius, § 157 b.

**AMALTHEA** (Ἀμάλθεια), in mythology, a nurse of Zeus, variously described as a nymph or a she-goat (details in Stoll, in Roscher's *Lexikon* i. 262). Possibly

she was originally a theriomorphic goddess (cf. M. P. Nilsson, *Minoan-Mycenaean Religion* (1950), 466). Two principal legends, neither early, concern her. She was transformed into the star Capella (Aratus, *Phaen.* 162–4 and many later authors). Her horns were wonderful, flowing with nectar and ambrosia (schol. Callim. *Jov.* 1. 49). One of them broke off, and was filled with fruits and given to Zeus (Ov. *Fasti* 5. 121 ff.). This was the origin (the story is variously told) of the proverbial Ἀμαλθείας κέρας, *cornu Copiae*, first mentioned by Antiphanes ap. Ath. 503 b. It is very likely to be older than its connexion with Amalthea, for it is a widespread folk-motif, the magical object whose possessor can get anything he likes (or all he wants of some specific thing) out of it (see Stith Thompson, D 1470. 2. 3). Ovid has another version: when Achelous' horn was broken off in wrestling with Heracles (q.v.), the Naiads picked it up, filled it with flowers and fruit, and gave it to Bona Copia (*Met.* 9. 88–89); this is Latin, for there is no Greek goddess corresponding to Copia.
H. J. R.

**AMANUS,** the name applied to the mountain horseshoe of Elma Dagh above Alexandretta, together with Giaour Dagh which trends north-eastwards. It is separated from Taurus by the deep gorge of the Jihun. It is crossed by great passes, the Amanid Gates (*Baghche Pass* from the Cilician plain to Zeugma), and the Syrian Gates (*Beilan Pass*) carrying a Roman road from Tarsus into Syria. The part of Mt. Amanus which Cicero reduced to order (*Att.* 5. 20. 3) must be the heights that end in Ras-el-Khanzir.
E. H. W.

**AMARANTUS** of Alexandria (1st–2nd c. A.D.), an older contemporary of Galen (Gal. 14. 208, Ath. 8. 343 f.), was the author of a commentary on Theocritus (*Etym. Magn.* 156. 30, 273. 41), perhaps based on Theon's notes, and of a work Περὶ σκηνῆς, which probably gave historical and biographical accounts of stage performances and performers (Ath. loc. cit. and 10. 414 e).
J. F. L.

**AMASEIA,** capital of the kings of Pontus until soon after 183 B.C., and home of Strabo the geographer, was situated in a defile between massive heights, with a magnificent fortress commanding the middle valley of the Iris and the chief Pontic roads. Pompey gave it municipal status and made it the administrative centre of a large territory, but it later came under royal rule. Augustus attached it to Galatia in 3/2 B.C., and Trajan to his new Cappadocian province between A.D. 107 and 113. In the second century it received the titles metropolis, *neocorus*, and first city. It increased in importance with the development of the roads leading to the eastern frontier.
Strabo 12. 561. F. Cumont, *Studia Pontica* ii (1906), 138 ff.; iii (1910), 109 ff.; Magie, *Rom. Rule Asia Min.*, 180 and Index.
T. R. S. B.

**AMASIS** (1) became pharaoh c. 569 B.C. as champion of the native Egyptians against Apries (q.v.), but later 'becoming philhellene' granted the Greeks Naucratis (q.v.), maintained a Greek bodyguard, allied himself with Lydia, Samos, Cyrene, and perhaps Sparta, and made gifts to Greek shrines. These foreign alliances were dictated by the Persian peril, which overthrew Egypt in 525, shortly after Amasis' death. His long reign was remembered as a time of peace and prosperity attested by numerous great buildings, and Amasis himself as a great but unconventional and sometimes deliberately undignified figure.
Herodotus 1. 77 and bks. 2 and 3. G. Maspéro, *Popular Stories of Egypt*, 281 ff.; F. K. Kienitz, *Die politische Geschichte Ägyptens vom 7 bis zum 4 Jahrhundert vor der Zeitwende* (1953), 30 ff.
P. N. U.

**AMASIS** (2) (6th c. B.C.), potter, in Athens; probably father of the potter Cleophrades; known from eight signatures. The Amasis painter, who worked for him 555–525 B.C., painted black-figure *amphorae, oenochoae, lecythi*, cups. A formal but individual artist; note particularly his Apollo and Heracles (Boston), Dionysus and Maenads (Paris), wedding scene (New York).

Beazley, *ABV*, 150; S. Karouzou, *The Amasis Painter* (1956); D. von Bothmer, *Antike Kunst* 3 (1960), 71.

T. B. L. W.

**AMAZONS** (Ἀμαζόνες), in mythology, a people of female warriors, always situated on the borders of the known world (Themiscyra on the Thermodon, Aesch. *PV* 723–5, but they have been driven from there, Strabo, 11. 5. 4; on the Tanais, Pliny, *HN* 6. 19; the Caspian Gates, Strabo, ibid., citing Cleitarchus), and in all probability nothing more than the common travellers' tale of the distant foreigners who do everything the wrong way about, cf. Hdt. 2. 35. 2 (Egyptians). Attempts to find a sociological significance in the legend (Bachofen, *Mutterrecht*,[2] 1897, 88 and elsewhere) or other explanation postulating a foundation of fact are mistaken. Why this particular tale caught Greek fancy and was elaborated we do not know.

*Amazon customs.* Generally it is stated that they provide for offspring by meeting at certain seasons with men of another race, afterwards keeping their female children but getting rid of or disabling the boys (Justin 2. 4. 9–10, Diod. Sic. 2. 45. 3); they destroy the girls' right breasts to prevent them getting in the way in battle, ibid.; hence their name, fancifully derived from ἀ + μαζός. Their deities are Ares (e.g. Ap. Rhod. 2. 385 ff.) and Artemis (see below). Their occupations are hunting and fighting, their weapons being especially the bow and the 'Amazonian' crescent-shaped shield, but also axe and spear, all used on horseback.

*Amazon legends.* In the *Iliad* they are warred upon by Bellerophon (q.v.; *Il.* 6. 186) and by Priam (3. 189). After Homer Arctinus (*Amazonis*) and others represent them as coming to the help of Priam after Hector's death under their queen Penthesilea (q.v.), daughter of Ares. Achilles kills her, but is accused of being in love with her by Thersites, whom he kills in anger (cf. Quint. Smyrn. 1. 538–810). With these stories are connected the numerous legends that this or that place in Ionia was founded by Amazons (especially Ephesus, Strabo 12. 3. 21 and 1, 4; Pind. fr. 157 Bowra; Tac. *Ann.* 3. 61. 2; cf. schol. *Il.* 6. 186). They are often connected also with the following legends.

Heracles (q.v.) and his campaign against the Amazons to get their queen's girdle produced an echo in the legend of Theseus (q.v.), modelled as usual on that of the greater hero. Either because he had been with Heracles or on account of an expedition he undertook on his own behalf (Plut. *Thes.* 26 gives several versions), the Amazons attacked him in force, reached Attica, and besieged him in Athens itself. A great battle took place on the date of the later festival Boedromia (Boedromion, unknown day), and a chthonian ceremony in Pyanopsion (?) was interpreted as a sacrifice to the dead Amazons. In general, there was a strong tendency, perhaps especially among antiquarians, to explain nameless monuments and festivals whose original meaning had been forgotten by relating them to this event (examples in Plut. ibid. 27). The result was that the Amazons were defeated, or at all events so stoutly resisted that they agreed to retire from Attica. For the further history of the Amazon Hippolyta (or Antiope), who had become Theseus' prisoner, *see* HIPPOLYTUS (1).

Of Hellenistic date, on the other hand, is the legend, or rather cycle, which represents Dionysus (q.v.) as

meeting the Amazons and conquering them. It is par of his conquest of the East; references to it are found e.g., in Tacitus, loc. cit. and Plut. *Quaest. Graec.* 56 A Euhemerizing story in Diod. Sic. 3. 71. 4 represent them as his allies, and presumably goes back to som legend to that effect.

A favourite legend, originating in the writings o Alexander's contemporaries, represented him as meetin the Amazon queen beyond the Jaxartes. See Tarn *Alexander* ii, appendix 19.

Amazons are very popular in art from at least th end of the seventh century. They wear short tunics often from the fifth century showing one breast, some times 'Scythian' trousers, and are light-armed. Th statues of wounded Amazons at Ephesus in the mi fifth century (Pliny, *HN* 34, 53, confirmed by copies suggest that the story of their defeat there by Dionysu may be earlier than the literary evidence; see D. vo Bothmer, *Amazons in Greek Art* (1957).

Besides the articles 'Amazonen' in Roscher's *Lexikon* and *PW* see especially W. R. Halliday in *The Greek Questions of Plutarc* (1928), 209 ff. H. J. R.; C. M. R

**AMBARVALIA** (*Ambarvale sacrum, Lustratio agri*) (1) a private rite, described by Cato, *Agr.* 141; Verg. *G* 1. 338 ff., cf. *Ecl.* 3. 77; 5. 75 and Servius ad locc. Tib. 2. 1; *see* LUSTRATION *and* AMBURBIUM. (2) A Stat rite, in which, since even the earliest *ager Romanus* ha too large a circumference to be easily got about in on day, sacrifice was offered at particular points (Strab 5. 3. 2). That this was identical with the sacrifice to th Dea Dia performed by the Arval Brothers has bee repeatedly suggested (Wissowa, *RK* 562), but is denie by A. Kilgour, *Mnemos.* 1938, 225 ff. See also Latte *RR* 65; A. Momigliano, *JRS* 1963, 100 f. and *Mai* 1963, 47 f. H. J. R

**AMBER**, a fossil resin, has a wide natural distribution i northern Europe and is also found in Sicily: so far as i known, the amber from the classical Mediterranean wa Baltic. It has been found at Ras Shamra (Ugarit) an Atchana, and also appears in the *terremare* (*see* TERRA MARA) in northern Italy. The earliest amber from th classical world comes—probably via Wessex— from th Shaft-Graves at Mycenae (q.v.); amber is rare in Minoa Crete. J. M. Navarro deduced that during the Early an Middle Bronze Age amber travelled from west Jutlan across Germany along the rivers to the Po and the head o the Adriatic. The trade was probably conducted b central European middlemen who could exchange meta for amber for onward transmission both to the eas Mediterranean and westwards to Britain. Amber bead were common throughout Bronze Age Europe, an reached Brittany, central France, and the Iberian penin sula; a gold-bound amber disc from Isopata (LM III A and a crescentic necklace from Kakovatos in Elis (LI II A) have striking British affinities. In the Iron Age route starting from the East Baltic conveyed amber t Italy, particularly to the east coast, where Picenum reached its peak as a centre of an indigenous ambe industry in the sixth century B.C. Amber was common i Archaic Greece, but not after *c.* 550 B.C., and it is seldom mentioned by Greek authors; Thales was the first to not its power of attraction. The main centre of amber carvin under the Roman Empire was Aquileia: amber was b then a fashionable luxury and played an important par in imperial trade with the free Germans: see Pliny, *H* 37. 30–51 and Tac. *Germ.* 45, quoted by Cassiodorus i the sixth century A.D. in a letter of thanks for a large gi of Baltic amber sent to Theodoric.

J. M. de Navarro, *Geog. Journ.* 1925, 481 ff.; P. Marconi, *Mo Ant.* 1935, cols. 406 ff.; O. Brogan, *JRS* 1936, 220; A. Spekke, *Th Ancient Amber Routes* (1957); N. K. Sandars, *Bronze Age Cultures*

*France* (1957), 72 ff.; id., *BSA* 1958–9, 237 ff. (and A. E. Werner, ibid. 261 f.); id., *Antiquity*, 1959, 292 ff.; C. W. Beck et al., *Archaeometry* 1965, 96–109; id., *GRBS* 1966, 191–211; J. Jensen, *Act. Arch.* 1965, 43–86; D. E. Strong, *Catalogue of the Carved Amber* (British Museum) (1966). D. W. R. R.

**AMBIORIX,** chief of the Eburones, a Gallic tribe between the Meuse and Rhine who were freed by Caesar from dependence on the Atuatuci. However, in 54 B.C. Ambiorix revolted against Caesar: through treachery he destroyed the camp and forces of Titurius Sabinus at Atuatuca. He then induced the Nervii to besiege the winter-camp in their territory which Q. Cicero commanded. It was relieved only by Caesar's arrival. Ambiorix continued to resist (53–51) and though the land of the Eburones was devastated he evaded capture. H. H. S.

**AMBITUS,** a 'going round' (cf. *ambire*), or canvassing for public office. Personal contact with the electors in Rome was naturally allowed, but propaganda throughout Italy or among provincial citizens, although legal, was generally open to criticism. The State soon intervened against bribery and intrigue. The alleged law *de ambitu* of 432 B.C. is probably either a forgery or an anticipation of the *Lex Poetelia* (358), which forbade propaganda outside Rome but was soon disregarded, or of a law passed in 314 against the *coitiones*, i.e. societies of illegal canvassers. The scandalous increase of electoral corruption in the early second century required an elaborated legislation. From the *Lex Cornelia Baebia* (181) down to the laws enacted by Cicero (*L. Tullia*, 63), Pompey (*L. Pompeia*, 52), and Caesar (*L. Iulia*, 49) attempts were made to stop bribery by threatening heavy penalties (death, exile for ten years or life, etc.). Municipal authorities accordingly took steps to keep order in local elections. But the works of Cicero and the *Commentariolum petitionis consulatus* sometimes attributed to his brother Quintus expose the uselessness of such precautions. In the imperial age *ambitus* came to indicate an appointment illegally secured, and was punished with confiscation and deportation.

Mommsen, *Röm. Strafr.* 865 ff.; W. Kroll, *Die Kultur d. ciceronischen Zeit* (1933), i. 50 ff. P. T.

**AMBIVIUS TURPIO,** Lucius, actor and theatredirector in Terence's day. His experience as a player contributed much to the success of Caecilius Statius and Terence (q.v.). All Terence's plays were, the *didascaliae* record, produced by him.

**AMBRACIA** (modern *Arta*), situated north of the Bay of Actium, in the fertile valley of the lower Arachthus. It was founded as a Corinthian colony by Gorgos, son of the tyrant Cypselus. Its attempts to control the whole coastland of the Bay of Actium brought it into conflict with the Acarnanians and Amphilochians, who with Athenian aid inflicted a severe defeat upon the Ambracians in 426 B.C. Ambracia allied with Athens against Philip of Macedon, who subdued and garrisoned it. In 294 it was ceded by Cassander's son to Pyrrhus (q.v.) who made it his capital and spent lavishly on its adornment. After the fall of the Molossian monarchy it became a centre of conflict between Philip V of Macedon and the Aetolian Confederacy, from which it was wrested by the Romans after a siege (189). It then became a free city.

Hammond, *Epirus*, 140 ff. M. C.; N. G. L. H.

**AMBROSIA** and **NECTAR,** the food and drink respectively (but the reverse occasionally, see Ath. 39 a) of the gods. Their effect is to make those who take them immortal (Pind. *Ol.* 1. 60 ff., cf. *Il.* 5. 341–2). They will keep a corpse from decay (e.g. *Il.* 19. 38–39). The smell of ambrosia is extraordinarily sweet and will overpower bad odours (*Od.* 4. 445–6). Various things connected with the gods are 'ambrosial' (the fodder of Ares' horses, *Il.* 5. 369; the 'beauty', κάλλος, apparently a sort of magical wash, with which Athena treats Penelope, *Od.* 18. 192–3); mortals of high rank wear 'nectarean' garments (*Il.* 3. 385; 18. 25), perhaps 'sweet-smelling'. That nectar is originally some kind of honey-drink (mead?), ambrosia idealized honey, is probable (see Roscher in his *Lexikon* i. 282). H. J. R.

**AMBROSIUS,** c. A.D. 339–4 Apr. 397, bishop of Milan. Son of the praetorian prefect at Trier, he was educated at Rome, and began a legal career, quickly becoming consular of Aemilia with headquarters at Milan. On the death of the Arian Auxentius (probably 374, not 373 as in the Bodleian MS. of Jerome's chronicle) he was chosen bishop by popular acclamation, though only a catechumen. Over the emperors Gratian, Valentinian II, and Theodosius I (qq.v.), he exercised mounting influence, his objective being an orthodox empire from which error (Arianism, paganism, Judaism) would be excluded. He persuaded Valentinian II to withstand the plea of Symmachus (q.v. 2) and the Roman aristocracy for the restoration of the Altar of Victory (384). By mobilizing popular support he resisted the demand of Justina, Gratian's widow, that a church be given to the Arian Goths in the army at Milan (385–6). By 388 his influence could make it expedient for Theodosius (reluctantly and resentfully) to revoke an order commanding the church at Callinicum on the Euphrates to restore a synagogue burnt by intolerant zealots. More to his credit is his excommunication of Theodosius for ordering the massacre of 7,000 at Thessalonica (390), a decision to which Theodosius submitted in circumstances that are obscure: by 422, in the 'Life of Ambrose' by his secretary Paulinus, the story is already encrusted with legend. Though inclined to domineer, Ambrose had positive qualities, and was not merely the archetypal administrator-bishop. His letters (*ep.* 23 spurious), funerary panegyrics, and sermons are the principal western source for the period 374–97. He used his knowledge of Greek to study philosophy and theology: large borrowings from Philo, Origen, Plotinus, and Basil occur in his commentaries and sermons (which in 384–6 substantially moved Augustine towards conversion). His *de Officiis Ministrorum* is a Christian revision of Cicero. Though there is some narrowness and a too zealous fostering of the popular demand for relics of martyrs, yet there is breadth to Ambrose's vision of the responsibility of the church as being to society as a whole, not to its own private interests. His relations with Theodosius foreshadow the medieval conflicts between church and empire. His hymns, in iambic dimeters, enjoyed lasting popularity; they moved Augustine to tears (*Conf.* 9. 6).

WORKS: Migne, *PL.* xiii–xvii; *CSEL* 10 vols. J. R. Palanque, *Saint Ambroise et l'empire romain* (1933); F. Homes Dudden, *Life and Times of St. Ambrose* (1935); A. Paredi, *S. Ambrogio* (1960, E.T. 1964). H. C.

**AMBURBIUM,** a rite of lustration (q.v.) for the city, corresponding to the Ambarvalia (q.v.), for the fields. It is probable that it was annual, though if so it must have been one of the *feriae conceptivae*, or movable festivals, for it appears in no calendar. Beyond this we have no certain knowledge, for the conjecture of H. Usener (*Weihnachtsfest*², 310 ff.), that it was on 2 Feb. and ultimately christianized into Candlemas is too hazardous to accept even in the modified form proposed by Wissowa (*RK*, p. 142, n. 12), that it was held about then (see L. Delatte *Ant. Class.* 1937, 114 ff.). Lucan (1. 592 ff.) describes an *amburbium* of some kind, but it was clearly an extraordinary ceremony. H. J. R.

**AMEIPSIAS,** Athenian comic poet, contemporary with Aristophanes. His Κόννος (see PHRYNICHUS 2) was placed second to Cratinus' Πυτίνη and above Aristophanes' *Clouds* in 423 B.C. (hyp. 5 Ar. *Nub.*). Connus was Socrates' music-master, and the play may have had a similar character to *Clouds*. Socrates himself was a character (fr. 9 quoted by D.L. 2. 28, without naming the play) and the chorus consisted of φροντισταί, i.e. Sophists (cf. the φροντιστήριον in *Clouds*). Κωμασταί ('Revellers'; see PHRYNICHUS 2) won the first prize, defeating Aristophanes' *Birds*, at the City Dionysia in 414 (hyp. I Ar. *Av.*). We have seven titles.

*FCG* i. 199 f.; *CAF* i. 670 ff.; *FAC* i. 476 ff.            K. J. D.

**AMELESAGORAS,** author of a series of Greek miracle stories: cf. Ov. *Fasti* 6. 749 (see Frazer ad loc.), perhaps derived from Amelesagoras. Probably a priest of Eleusis. A fourth-century B.C. *Atthis* is doubtfully ascribed to him.

*FGrH* iii 330.

**AMELIUS** or **AMERIUS GENTILIANUS** (3rd c. A.D.), born in Etruria, was Plotinus' pupil A.D. 246–70. His literary work was devoted mainly to the exposition and defence of Plotinus' philosophy, of which, however, he had little true understanding.

**AMERIA,** modern *Amelia,* hill-town of southern Umbria. Although very ancient (Pliny, *HN* 3. 114), it is first mentioned by Cicero (*pro Rosc. Amer.* 15, 19, 20, 25), in whose day it was a prosperous *municipium.* It remained such in imperial times. Its massive polygonal walls are still well preserved.            E. T. S.

**AMICITIA** was a relationship of friendship between Rome and either another State (e.g. Egypt, established in 273 B.C.) or an individual (e.g. a king: see CLIENT KINGS); such *amici populi Romani* were recorded in a *tabula amicorum. Amicitia* involved only diplomatic recognition and not a formal treaty relationship or legal obligations. In private life, apart from purely personal friendships, *amicitia* might exist between individuals as a link formed for political ends, a political alliance based on common interest rather than on mutual affection. Where the status of one party (either Rome or an individual) was much greater than that of the other, the relationship tended to develop into patronage and *clientela.*

A. Heuss, *Die volkkerrechtl. Grundlagen der röm. Aussenpolitik* (1933); E. Badian, *Foreign Clientelae* (1958), 12 f., 44 f.; J. Hellegouar'ch, *Le Vocabulaire latin des relations et des partis politiques sous la République* (1963); P. A. Brunt, *PCPS* 1965, 1 ff.            H. H. S.

**AMICUS AUGUSTI,** a term used unofficially to indicate senators and equites who were admitted to the Roman imperial court. The *amici* were graded (by a practice which, in private families, dated from C. Gracchus and Livius Drusus: Sen. *Ben.* 6. 34) as *primae, secundae,* or *tertiae admissionis.* The term was also used in a narrower sense to indicate those who were chosen from this larger body as the Emperor's advisers (*consiliarii*) and travelling-companions (*comites*): cf. Suet. *Tit.* 7. 2; Pliny, *Pan.* 88.

J. A. Crook, *Consilium Principis* (1955).            J. P. B.

**AMISUS,** a sixth-century colony of Miletus or Phocaea, situated on the Euxine coast at the head of the one good commercial route into Pontus and Cappadocia. Athenians settled there in the mid fifth century and renamed it Piraeus. Declared free by Alexander the Great, it came under the kings of Pontus, probably by 250 B.C. After its capture in 71, Lucullus restored the city, and gave it freedom and additional territory—gifts confirmed by Pompey, when he shaped its municipal constitution, and by

Caesar. Antony gave it again to kings (40), but Augustus declared it a free and allied city (30), and it remained part of the province of Bithynia and Pontus until Diocletian. The territory included the fertile coastal plain of Themiscyra, and was extended westwards to the mouth of the Halys river. Its abundant coinage and the wide dispersal of its citizens attest a commercial importance which remains today.

Strabo 12. 547. F. Cumont, *Studia Pontica* ii (1906), 111 ff.; ii (1910), 1 ff.; Jones, *Cities E. Rom. Prov.,* see Index; Magie, *Rom Rule Asia Min.* 185 f., and Index; C. Roebuck, *Ionian Trade and Colonization* (1959), 123.            T. R. S. B

**AMMIANUS MARCELLINUS** (*c.* A.D. 330–95), the last great Roman historian, was a Greek who was born into a middle-class family at Antioch. He joined the army and in 353 was serving among the *protectores domestici* on the Eastern frontier under the command of Ursicinus, an officer whom he highly respected. With Ursicinus he also served in Gaul under the Caesar Julian (q.v.). He marched on Julian's fateful campaign in Persia in 363 and also visited Egypt and Greece. Finally, after 378 he settled in Rome, and it was in Rome and for Roman readers that he wrote his History. Accordingly, although his native language was Greek, he composed his great work in Latin. Originally in thirty-one books covering the years 96–378, the History was a continuation of the historical works of Tacitus. But books i–xiii have been lost; and the extant narrative begins with the events of 353. Thus, we possess Ammianus' account of the second half of the reign of Constantius II, and of the entire reigns of Julian, Jovian, Valentinian I, and Valens, together with the earlier part of the reign of Gratian. The narrative is written in extreme detail: it is never dull, and its general accuracy has never been called in question. Gibbon exaggerated when he said that Ammianus wrote 'without the prejudices and passions which usually affect the mind of a contemporary', for Ammianus makes no secret of his profound, though not uncritical, admiration of Julian. He was himself a pagan like Julian, though he writes tolerantly of Christianity. Discussion of Ammianus' historical sources has turned largely on the extremely detailed account of Julian's Persian campaign of 363. Another very long account of the same expedition is extant in Zosimus, who took it from Eunapius, who in turn drew on a memoir written by the physician Oribasius, another participant in the campaign. It appears that Ammianus drew heavily on Eunapius' narrative but supplemented it by what he had seen himself. His sources in other parts of his work are practically unknown. The work includes numerous digressions on a great variety of subjects, and some of these (e.g. those on social life in the city of Rome) are of great value.

Text by C. U. Clark (Berlin, 1910–15). A comprehensive study of Ammianus is a desideratum: there are partial studies by W. Ensslin 'Zur Geschichtsschreibung und Weltansschauung des Ammianus Marcellinus', *Klio,* Beiheft xvi (1923); E. A. Thompson, *The Historical Work of Ammianus Marcellinus* (1947); A. Cameron, *JRS* 1964, 15 ff.; id. *CQ* 1964, 316 ff.; A. Demandt, *Zeitkritik und Geschichtsbild im werk Ammians* (1965); R. Syme, *Ammianus and the Historia Augusta* (1968).            E. A. T

**AMMON** (or **AMO[U]N**), originally the god of the city of Thebes in Egypt. During the age of the Egyptian Empire Ammon became an imperial deity whose worship struck roots in Nubia, Syria, and Libya. Ammon appears in Greek literature chiefly by reason of his cult at the oasis of Siwa, which became known to Greeks after the colonization of Cyrene in the seventh century. In the temple at Siwa there was an oracle of Ammon whose fame in the Greek world came to rival that of Delphi and Dodona. In Greece Ammon was usually portrayed on coins and elsewhere with a head of Zeus to which the curling ram's horns of Ammon were added. Pindar and Herodotus testify to the authority of the oracle of Ammon, and we are

old that it was consulted by Cimon, Lysander, and
others. In the fourth century Athens had a theoric vessel
named the Ammonis, and public sacrifices to Ammon
were conducted by the magistrates. The oracle was probably at the height of its influence when it was visited by
Alexander the Great. Alexander's question and the
answer he received from the god are unknown to us, but
some modern writers have asserted that Alexander went
to the oracle to be deified. Actually the priests there did
but employ a conventional form in greeting Alexander
as the son of Zeus. The cult of Ammon seems to have
been popular with some members of the Ptolemaic
dynasty, but it certainly was not widespread in the
Mediterranean world during the Hellenistic and Roman
periods. We know of *thiasotai* of Ammon in Attica, and
Ammon was connected in some way with the cult of
Amphiaraus at Oropus (*IG* ii². 1282). Occasionally
Ammon is included among the Egyptian deities, though
here are only two such instances at Delos. Ammon is
represented in sculpture chiefly by busts, masks, and
relief medallions, most of which portray him in the conventional manner.

Cook, *Zeus* i 346 ff.; A. Erman, *Die Religion der Ägypter* (1934);
C. Meyer, art. 'Ammon' in Roscher's *Lexikon*; A. Wiedemann,
*Herodots Zweites Buch* (1890); U. Wilcken, *Alexander the Great*
(1932); C. J. Classen, *Hist.* 1959, 349 ff.; L. Vitali, *Fonti per la storia
della relig. Cyren.* (1932), 4 ff.; F. Chamoux, *Cyrène sous les Battiades*
(1953), 320 ff.; H. W. Parke, *The Oracles of Zeus* (1967), ch. ix.
T. A. B.

**AMMONIUS** (1) (2nd c. B.C.), pupil and successor of
Aristarchus (schol. *Il.* 10. 397; *Suda*, s.v.), wrote, besides
a commentary on Homer (*POxy.* ii. 121), other works
on the Homeric poems, e.g. a treatise on Plato's borrowings from Homer ([Longinus], *Subl.* 13. 3), and essays in
defence of Aristarchus' recension of the Homeric text
(schol. *Il.* 10. 397); these formed a valuable source for
Didymus. For his commentary on Pindar (schol. *Ol.*
1. 122 c) he used Aristarchus' work, but made independent additions (schol. *Nem.* 3. 16 b). The work on
Aristophanes (schol. *Vesp.* 947), sometimes entitled
Κωμῳδούμενοι (ibid. 1239), probably discussed the
individuals attacked in Old Attic Comedy.

H. Erbse, *Beitr. zur Überlieferung der Iliasscholien* (1960), 295 ff.
J. F. L.

**AMMONIUS** (2) **SACCAS,** of Alexandria, Platonist
philosopher, active in first half of third century A.D.,
famous as the teacher of Plotinus, who studied under him
232–42, as well as of Origen the Christian, Origen the
pagan, Longinus, and others. According to Porphyry
(*apud* Eus. *Hist. Eccl.* 6. 19) he was brought up as a
Christian but reverted to paganism as soon as he began
to think for himself. The epithet θεοδίδακτος and the
nickname Saccas (sack-carrier? wearer of sackcloth?)
would seem to imply a humble origin, though other interpretations have been proposed. He wrote nothing, and
no distinctive features of his teaching can be inferred
with any certainty from the few references to it in Nemesius, *nat. hom.* 2 and 3, and Hierocles *apud* Photium, cod.
251. Even the story of the vow of secrecy which his
pupils, like those of Pythagoras, took and subsequently
broke (Porph. *vit. Plot.* 3. 24) is not entirely free from
doubt. Nevertheless the teacher who evoked from
Plotinus the cry τοῦτον ἐζήτουν and retained him as a
disciple for eleven years has some claim to be considered
the Socrates of Neoplatonism.

Zeller, *Phil. d. Gr.* iii. 2⁵. 500 ff.; H. Dörrie, *Hermes* 1955, 439 ff.;
E. R. Dodds and others, *Les Sources de Plotin* (Entretiens Hardt V),
24 ff. E. R. D.

**AMNESTY.** There are few certain records of public
amnesties in Greek States, the earliest one being the law
of Solon (Plut. *Sol.* 19), who probably restored citizen
rights to every man who had lost them, unless he was dis-

franchised for murder or tyranny. Another act of general
reconciliation was the decree of the Athenian Assembly
after the restitution of democracy (403 B.C.), which excluded only the Thirty Tyrants (q.v. 1) and some of their
most important assistants. Aristotle (*Ath. Pol.* 39. 6)
quotes its chief regulation: μηδενὶ πρὸς μηδένα μνησικακεῖν.
The word ἀμνηστία is not used for this act before
Plutarch; its first known use is in a Milesian inscription
of the second century B.C. (*SIG* 633. l. 36). An amnesty
decree as part of a general proclamation of peace (φιλ-
άνθρωπα) was issued by Ptolemy VIII Euergetes II (118
B.C.) (*PTeb.* I. 5).

A. P. Dorjahn, *Political Forgiveness in Old Athens. The Amnesty of
403* (1946); Hignett, *Hist. Athen. Const.*; Rostovtzeff, *Hellenistic
World* 2, 874 ff.; 3, 1543. V. E.

**AMOEBEAN VERSE,** a device found mainly in
bucolic poetry, consists of couplets or 'stanzas' assigned
alternately to two characters (e.g. Theoc. 5 and 8; Verg.
*Ecl.* 3 and 7; cf. Hor. *Carm.* 3. 9). Such passages are
generally singing matches (sometimes preceded by mutual
abuse) in which each theme introduced by one character
is closely 'capped' by the other. J. F. M.

**AMPELIUS,** LUCIUS (2/3 c. A.D.), published a *liber
memorialis*, a handbook of knowledge, dedicated to a
Macrinus, not necessarily the emperor of A.D. 217–18.
It gives a summary of cosmography, geography with
*miracula mundi*, mythology (Euhemeristic in tendency),
and history (Oriental, Greek, and of the Roman Republic,
with constitutional interests); incidental references to
Trajan occur. Compendious in style, it was based, probably indirectly, on Nigidius Figulus and Varro, Alexandrian works, Euhemeristic genealogies of the gods, and,
in the historical part, Cornelius Nepos, Trogus, the
epitomized Livian tradition, and the tradition of the *De
Viris Illustribus.*

EDITIONS. E. Wölfflin (1854); E. Assmann (1935). Cf. E. Wölfflin,
*De L. Ampelii libro memoriali* (1854). A. H. McD.

**AMPHIARAUS** (Ἀμφιάραος, Ἀμφιάρεως), in mythology,
son of Oecles (or Apollo, Hyg. *Fab.* 70, a not unexampled
genealogy for diviners). On the return of Adrastus (q.v.)
from Sicyon, Amphiaraus made peace with him and
married his sister Eriphyle (Apollod. 1. 103). Foreknowing
the result of the expedition of the Seven against Thebes,
he would not take part in it till Eriphyle, bribed by
Polynices with the necklace of Harmonia, compelled him
(for the necklace, see Rose, *Handb. of Gr. Myth.*⁶, 185,
190, 194), it having been agreed between Amphiaraus
and Adrastus that in case of differences between them
she should decide. Before setting out, he commanded
his children to avenge his death on Eriphyle and to make
an expedition against Thebes (cf. ALCMAEON 1). He
attacked Thebes at the Homoloian Gate (Aesch. *Sept.*
570), was driven off, and, as he fled, was swallowed up in a
cleft in the ground made by Zeus' thunderbolt (rhetorical
description, Stat. *Theb.* 7. 771 ff.; for continuous account
see Apollod. 3. 60–77). Thus originated the very famous
oracular shrine of Amphiaraus (Farnell, *Hero-Cults*,
58 ff.; *see also under* OROPUS *and* AMMON).

Whether he was originally a man or a god is disputed;
his name ('very sacred') points to the former, as ἱερός is
not used of a god in classical Greek (though Hesiod,
*Theog.* 21, uses it of the 'race of immortals'). but if so,
the epic hero became identified with a local deity.

Polynices offering Eriphyle the necklace appears on
a number of fifth-century vases; and she is present
holding it in the scenes of Amphiaraus' departure popular in archaic art (*see* ALCMAEON 1). A mid-fifth-century
Attic vase shows the combats at Thebes and Amphiaraus'
chariot swallowed by the earth (Brommer, *Vasenlisten*²,
337 f., 344 f.). H. J. R.; C. M. R.

**AMPHICTIONIES** (from ἀμφικτίονες, 'dwellers round about') is the name for leagues connected with temples and the maintenance of their cults. Most important was the Amphictionic League organized around the temple of Demeter at Anthela near Thermopylae and later associated also with that of Apollo at Delphi (*see* DELPHIC ORACLE, § 6). In the earliest form known the League consisted of the following twelve tribes: Thessalians, Boeotians, Dorians, Ionians, Perrhaebians, Dolopians, Magnetes, Locrians, Aenianes, Phthiotic Achaeans, Malians, and Phocians. Thus it was possible to control the League by reducing the small tribes of central and northern Greece, as was done by Thessaly in the sixth and Aetolia in the third century B.C. The League, in co-operation with Delphi, administered the temple of Apollo and its property and conducted the Pythian Games. In the *synedrion*, which met twice a year, each tribe had two votes cast by two *hieromnemones* (q.v.), alongside of whom stood a number of *pylagorai*, later replaced by *agoratroi*. The *ekklesia* was less important and is seldom mentioned. During the fourth century B.C. a board of *naopoioi* and later of *tamiai* supervised the rebuilding of the temple and the administration of its funds. The latter even issued Amphictionic coins.

The League was not without political importance. An old Amphictionic oath forbade destroying cities within the League or cutting off their water-supply. Later efforts at Panhellenic legislation included decrees concerning Dionysiac guilds and currency. Violators of Amphictionic laws were tried by the *hieromnemones*, who could even proclaim sacred war against offenders. Strong States, however, disregarded Amphictionic judgements, and the League was important politically chiefly as a tool of powerful States. Votes frequently were transferred from one State to another: Delphi acquired two, those of Phocis were transferred to Philip II, and the Aetolians assigned votes to their friends. They themselves probably were not admitted to the League, but by their conquests acquired direct control of the votes of others, the maximum recorded being fifteen. Under Augustus six votes were added for Nicopolis and the total for the first time increased (from 24 to 30). Under Hadrian there was a readjustment to secure a more just representation, but the details are unknown.

A selection of documents in *SIG*³. G. Busolt, *Griechische Staatskunde* ii (1926), 1280 ff.; U. Kahrstedt, *Griechisches Staatsrecht* (1922), 383 ff.; R. Flacelière, *Les Aitoliens à Delphes* (1937); G. Daux, *Delphes au II et au I*ᵉʳ *siècle* (1936); V. Ehrenberg, *The Greek State* (1960), 108 ff.　　J. A. O. L.

**AMPHILOCHI**, a tribe of north-western Greece, occupying the wooded hill-country east of the Gulf of Ambracia and controlling the narrow passage above the coast from Acarnania and Aetolia to Ambracia. The only town, Amphilochian Argos, claimed as its founders Amphilochus, Alcmaeon, or Diomede. Amphilochia was the scene of many campaigns.

Hammond, *Epirus*, 246 ff.　　N. G. L. H.

**AMPHILOCHUS**, in mythology, brother of Alcmaeon (q.v. 1), and, in some accounts (as Apollod. 3. 82 and 86), his comrade in the expedition of the Epigoni and helper in slaying Eriphyle. After Homer he takes part in the Trojan War (e.g. Quint. Smyrn. 14. 366), and is celebrated as a diviner. He and Calchas left Troy together by land and came to Claros (Strabo 14. 1. 27). A number of local tales (or constructions of Greek historians) connect Amphilochus with the origins of places and peoples in Asia Minor, as Poseideion on the borders of Syria and Cilicia (Hdt. 3. 91. 1), the Pamphylian nation (ibid. 7. 91. 3), but above all the famous mantic shrine in Mallus (Strabo 14. 5. 16). Apollo killed him in Soli (Hesiod quoted ibid. 17).　　H. J. R.

**AMPHION** (Ἀμφίων) and **ZETHUS** (Ζῆθος), in mythology, the sons of Antiope (q.v.) and Zeus. Left behind by their mother at birth, they were found and reared by a shepherd. Amphion was given a lyre by Hermes and became a wonderful musician; Zethus was a herdsman. When, after long captivity, their mother escaped, they were full-grown, and recognizing her, they took her under their protection, killing or at least dethroning Lycus and putting to death his wife Dirce by tying her to the horn of a bull, as she had intended to do to Antiope. Dirce was turned into, or her bones were burned and thrown into the spring which bore her name. Amphion and Zethu now proceeded to wall the city later known as Thebe (from Zethus' wife Thebe, Apollod. 3. 45; Thebe is local nymph or minor goddess), Amphion drawing the stones after him by the magical music of his lyre. Amphion married Niobe (q.v.). See Euripides, fr. 179–22 Nauck, and later finds, Pickard-Cambridge in Powell *New Chapters* iii. 105 ff.; Apollod. 3. 43 ff.; Hyg. *Fab.* 7–

The brothers (called also τὼ λευκοπώλω, the Whit Horses, or Horsemen) were evidently alternative founder of Thebes to Cadmus (q.v.). For their cult in historic times: Farnell, *Hero-Cults*, 212 ff.　　H. J. I

**AMPHIPOLIS**, on the east bank of the Strymon which surrounds the city on three sides (hence its name 25 stades from its port, Eion; it was originally the site of a Thracian town, Ennea Hodoi (Hdt. 7. 114; Thuc. 100; 4. 102). After two unsuccessful attempts in 497 and 465 B.C., it was colonized by the Athenians, with other Greeks, under Hagnon, son of Nicias, in 437–436 B.C. It owed its importance partly to its strategic position commanding the bridge over the Strymon and the rout from northern Greece and the Hellespont, with all th lateral communications along the Thracian coast, and partly to its commercial wealth as the depot for the gol and silver mines of the Pangaean district (*see* GOLD SILVER, PANGAEUS), and as a centre for ship-timbe (Thuc. 4. 108). In Roman times the Via Egnatia (q.v. passed through Amphipolis and Eion on its way to th plain of Philippi (q.v.). In 424 B.C. Amphipolis sur rendered to the Spartan Brasidas (q.v.) without resist ance; the Athenians blamed Thucydides (q.v. 2), th historian, who was with his fleet at Thasos (q.v.) at th time. In 422 B.C. an unsuccessful attempt to recover was made by Cleon (q.v.), and in the battle both Cleo and Brasidas were killed. Amphipolis was to have bee restored to Athens by the Peace of Nicias (421 B.C.), bu it remained practically independent till its occupation b Philip II (q.v.) of Macedon in 357 B.C., after which it wa a Macedonian city, until the defeat of the Macedonian at Pydna in 168 B.C. Amphipolis was one of the principa mints of the kings of Macedon. Under the Romans became a 'free city', and the capital of Macedonia prim (Pliny, *HN* 4. 38).

Thucydides, 4. 102–8; 5. 6–11. J. Papastavru, 'Amphipoli Geschichte und Prosopographie', *Klio*, Beiheft 37 (1936) (biblic graphy); S. Casson, *Macedonia, Thrace and Illyria* (1926), 214 ff. W. M. Leake, *Travels in N. Greece*, 3, 183 ff.; P. Perdrizet, *BC* 1922, 36 ff.; Head, *Hist. Num.*² 214 ff.; H. Gaebler, *Die Ant. Münze Nordgriechenlands*, iii 2 (1935), 30 ff.; W. K. Pritchett, *Studies Ancient Greek Topography* (1965), 30 ff.　　J. M. R. C

**AMPHIS**, Middle Comedy poet, not anterior to Plat (fr. 6, which refers to τὸ Πλάτωνος ἀγαθόν). His twenty eight titles come chiefly from mythology and daily life but Γυναικοκρατία, *Government by Women*, sounds like a Aristophanic theme, and Διθύραμβος may have deal with musical innovations of the time (cf. fr. 14).

*FCG* iii. 301 ff.; *CAF* ii. 236 ff; *FAC* ii. 313 ff.　　W. G. V

**AMPHISSA**, in western (Ozolian) Locris, command the route leading west of Mt. Parnassus from Doris the Gulf of Crisa. Its traditional policy being enmity with Phocis and alliance with Thebes, Amphissa played a leading part in the Third Sacred War (q.v.), and was reduced to dependence by Onomarchus in 353 B.C. Independent again after the collapse of Phocis, it proposed, probably in the interest of Thebes, that Athens be fined by the Delphic Amphictiony, but Aeschines countered by accusing Amphissa of sacrilege in cultivating the Sacred Plain of Crisa (340); from this sprang the Amphissaean War, in which Philip II of Macedon captured Amphissa and destroyed its walls (338).

L. Lerat, *Les Locriens de l' Ouest* (1952); P.-K., *GL* 2. 2. 580.
N. G. L. H.

**AMPHITHEATRES.** The earliest known Roman amphitheatre is that of the Sullan colony (*c.* 80 B.C.) at Pompeii, called by its builders *spectacula* (*CIL* x. 852). Pliny (*HN* 36. 117–20) ascribes the introduction of amphitheatres at Rome to Curio (q.v. 2), the first permanent building being erected by Statilius Taurus in 29 B.C., at a time when such buildings were being constructed far and wide throughout the Empire. Architecturally, such examples as those of Emerita (8 B.C.; *Arch. Journ.* 1930, 113, pl. viii) with segmental arches, and of Nemausus (*Nîmes*), with heavy lintel construction, exhibit affinity to wooden prototypes, which continued to exist (Tac. *Ann.* 4. 62). In the Pompeian amphitheatre, the arena is sunk below ground level and the seats are supported on a mass of earth held by retaining walls; the façade has external staircases. Natural arenas on artificially constructed earth mounds were common in the provinces. Imperial architects, however, rapidly evolved very large self-contained buildings, in which problems of access and circulation were solved by remarkably ingenious use of balanced vaulting systems. The most famous is the Colosseum (q.v.). The arena was honeycombed with underground passages for stage effects, comparable with those of Julius Caesar's *Forum Romanum* (*JRS* 1922, 8 f.) The amphitheatre should be distinguished from the *ludus*, or gladiators' training-school, which has much less seating and a proportionately larger arena (Lundström, *Undersökningar i Roms topografi*, 22 ff.).

Ashby–Anderson–Spiers, *Architecture of Ancient Rome* (1927). See also bibliography s.v. COLOSSEUM. Methods of laying out the non-elliptical arena are discussed by J. A. Wright, *Archaeologia* 1928, 215. I. A. R.

**AMPHITRYON,** in mythology, son of Alcaeus.

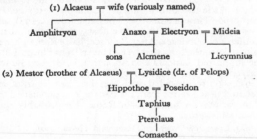

Taphius and the sons of Pterelaus quarrelled with Electryon and reaved his cattle. In recovering them, Amphitryon accidentally killed Electryon, and so had to leave his native Mycenae (or Argos), taking Alcmene and Licymnius with him. At her urging (*see* ALCMENE) he got together an army, partly by help of Creon I, king of Thebes, who made it a condition that Amphitryon should rid him of the uncatchable Cadmeian vixen, which was ravaging the country. Amphitryon obtained the help of Cephalus (q.v.) and his hound Laelaps, which never lost its quarry, and the impasse between the beast

which could not be caught and the beast which must catch was settled by Zeus turning both to stone. Amphitryon proceeded against Pterelaus and his people the Teleboans, but could not take their city while Pterelaus lived, nor could the latter die till a golden hair which Poseidon had planted in his head was removed. Comaetho, being in love with Amphitryon, finally betrayed Pterelaus, and their city, Taphos, was taken. *See further* ALCMENE, HERACLES.

Apollodorus 2. 50 ff.; a somewhat different account in Arguments 4 and 5 to [Hesiod], *Shield*. H. J. R.

**AMPHORA STAMPS** (GREEK). Stamps impressed on plain pottery amphoras, usually on their handles, before firing in the kiln. These amphoras were two-handled commercial containers having at the bottom not a base for standing but a knob or tip to facilitate shifting; when filled, such jars were corked or otherwise firmly closed. Not all were stamped. Most were probably made for the transport and storage of wine. The stamps were evidently control stamps, which seem to have endorsed the jars as of standard capacity, each according to its geographical class and particular size. Amphoras produced by different local centres are distinguishable by special features of shape, and the stamped ones most specifically by their stamps.

Typical Greek amphora stamps contain a name in the genitive, apparently that of the endorsing potter or pottery manufacturer; plus a name, sometimes with a title, introduced by the preposition *epi*, presumably a dating authority (in the most numerous class of stamps, the name of the month made the date more precise); plus sometimes an ethnic adjective ('Thasian, 'Knidian', etc.); and/or an identifying device, which may be the arms of the issuing state, as the 'rose' characteristic of the coins of Rhodes is common also in stamps on Rhodian amphoras. Some amphoras were stamped with a single name or device only; a few on the other hand named in their stamps other magistrates in addition to the presumed dating authority.

Stamped containers were issued by a limited number of Greek States, which were important as producers of wine (a few, probably, of oil), or as large-scale commercial handlers. For instance, the elaborately stamped early Thasian amphoras were made at a time of close state-control of the production and sale of the famous wine of Thasos, both wine and control being well attested in ancient literature and in epigraphical texts of the late fifth and early fourth centuries B.C. In contrast, Rhodian wine is very little mentioned by the ancients; and yet Rhodian amphora stamps are by far the most numerous class known to modern study. Presumably the standard Rhodian container facilitated the collection of port taxes which were the main source of revenue of the State of Rhodes. The wine contained was of ordinary grade consumed in bulk, for instance by the troops of Hellenstic times. Perhaps not all of it was made in Rhodes.

Although the original purpose of dating amphoras was no doubt to fix more closely the responsibility for their being standard containers, one effect must have been to date the contents, identifying the age or special vintage of the finer kinds of wine, and the freshness of the cheaper which was not worth drinking after a year. An incidental benefit is that to modern archaeological studies: as the chronology of these objects becomes better established, their very commonly found fragments quite often provide the best evidence available for dating an excavated deposit of the fourth to the first centuries B.C.

Excavations of the Athenian Agora, Picture Book No. 6, *Amphoras and the Ancient Wine Trade* (U.S.A., 1961). Short illustrated account of the history and uses of the commercial amphora, without bibliography.
V. R. Grace and M. S. Petropoulakou, Chapter 14, on the Greek

amphora stamps, in Ph. Bruneau ed., *Exploration Archéologique de Délos*, vol. 27, *L'Ilot de la Maison des Comédiens* (in press 1968), with a general review of the field, and a discussion of earlier publications.

New publications in this field are noticed currently by L. and J. Robert under 'inscriptions cérmiques' in their regular epigraphical bulletins published in the *Rev. Ét. Grec.* V. R. G.

**AMPLIATIO** means adjournment and was a peculiarity of Roman criminal procedure in the time of the Republic, exceptionally admitted by some laws on criminal matters. When a certain proportion of the jury regarded the evidence of guilt of the accused as insufficient for condemnation or discharge, they settled by the vote *non liquet* that the case was not quite cleared up and demanded by pronouncing the word *amplius* the reiteration of the evidence. The effect was not a simple adjournment, but a repetition of all proofs with the object of elucidating the case more thoroughly. Although normally *ampliatio* might take place only once, the system lent itself to abuse before an unscrupulous jury: thus in 138 B.C. when L. Aurelius Cotta (*cos.* 144) was prosecuted by Scipio Aemilianus, probably *de repetundis*, proceedings are said to have been repeated seven times. A restriction of *ampliatio* (to once or twice) was imposed in the *quaestio de repetundis* by the lex Acilia (*see* GLABRIO 2) and later Glaucia (q.v.) introduced the system of *comperendinatio* (the division of a trial into two parts), though evidence is lacking to show whether *comperendinatio* was applied to any other *quaestio*. The institution apparently fell into disuse in the early Principate. *See* LAW AND PROCEDURE, ROMAN, III.

J. P. Balsdon, *PBSR* 1938, 109 ff. A. B.; B. N.

**AMULETS** (Lat. *amuletum*), charms, objects worn for magical use, to protect the wearer against witchcraft, the evil eye, sickness, accidents, etc. (cf. modern mascots). Houses, walls, towns, etc., were protected in the same way. Any kind of material might be used, stones and metals as well as animals and plants, because every sort of material was supposed eventually to possess supernatural or magical virtue. Even parts of the body (hand, *fascinum, vulva*) had peculiar efficacy; thus the snout of a wolf, fixed upon the door, guarded against evil influences (Pliny, *HN* 28. 157), etc. The efficacy of the amulet might be enhanced by engraved figures, e.g. deities or symbols, especially on stones and metals (cf. the so-called 'Abraxas gems' and the Solomon gems in Byzantine times). Inscriptions (magical formulas, unknown magic words, the 'great name', alphabets, anagrams) are here often added, but such inscriptions were also thought effective by themselves, just as the inscriptions mentioning Herakles Alexikakos on houses (W. K. C. Guthrie, *The Greeks and their Gods* (1950), 240). A number of apotropaic charms written on papyrus have been found in Egypt (cf. also the illustrations in *POsl.* 1). The magical potency was secured and strengthened by a consecration of the amulet (cf. Orph. *Lith.* 366 ff.). The forms of amulets are innumerable (270 kinds in Flinders Petrie, *Amulets*); notable are rings, nails, keys, knots, etc. Special importance derives from the place at which or the circumstances (fitting times, stellar influences) in which the amulet was found or made. A crossway and a burial-place are considered to endue anything there found (plants, bones, skulls) with magic powers. Remains of men whose death had been a violent one (shipwrecked men etc.) were eagerly sought. 'Individual amulets' depend only on chance observation and vague ideas of connexion.

Belief in amulets remained active in Greece, as in Italy, in all classes of the populations through the whole of antiquity and still survives to-day.

Words for amulets: φυλακτήριον, περίαμμα, περίαπτον;

*amuletum* (for etymology see Walde–Hofmann, *La etym. Wörterbuch²* (1938), i. 42), *bulla, crepundia, fasci num, alligatura* (later), etc.

Kropatscheck, *De amuletorum apud antiquos usu* (1907); Freire Marreco, etc., art. 'Charms' in Hastings, *ERE*; cf. Flinders Petri *Amulets* (1914); C. Bonner, *Studies in magical amulets* (1950). S. F

**AMYCLAE,** an 'Achaean' town on the right bank of th Eurotas *c.* 3 miles south of Sparta, mentioned in the Homeric *Catalogue* as in the domain of Menelaus Accounts vary of its resistance to the Dorians (q.v.) bu not later than *c.* 750 B.C. it, and consequently the rest o S. Laconia (q.v.), fell. It was incorporated in Sparta territory as an *oba* (*see* SPARTA). But it reappears with it own magistrates in the Roman period (three ἔφοροι—*I* v. 1. 26, 2nd or 1st c. B.C.). Remains of the famou sanctuary and throne of Apollo Amyclaeus (*see* HYACIN THUS) have been excavated on the hill of H. Kyriak (probably north of the ancient town).

Paus, 3. 18. 7–19. 6. F. Kiechle, *Lakonien und Sparta* (1963). Fo the sanctuary and throne: Frazer, *Paus.*, ad loc.; E. Fiechter, *JDA* 1918; E. Buschor and W. von Massow, *Ath. Mitt.* 1927. A. M. W.; W. G. F

**AMYCUS,** in mythology, king of the Bebryces, a savage people of Bithynia. He was of gigantic strength and compelled all comers to the land to box with him, the loser to be at the absolute disposal of the winner. Wher the Argonauts arrived in his country, Polydeuces accepted his challenge, and being a skilled boxer overcame Amycus' brute force. In the fight Amycus was killed (Apollonius), or knocked out (Theocritus), and made to swear to wrong no more strangers, or, having lost the fight, was bound by Polydeuces (Epicharmus and Pisandrus ap. schol. Ap. Rhod. 2. 98).

Ap. Rhod. 2. 1 ff.; Theoc. 22. 27 ff. H. J. R

**AMYMONE** (Ἀμυμώνη), in mythology, daughter of Danaus. While at Argos (*see* DANAUS) she went for water, was rescued from a satyr and seduced by Poseidon, who created the spring Amymone in commemoration (Apollod. 2. 14; Hyg. *Fab.* 169, 169 a). H. J. R

**AMYNANDER,** king of Athamania which lay between Macedon and Aetolia, in 209 B.C. tried to mediate on behalf of the Aetolians with Philip V (q.v.) of Macedon. In the Second Macedonian War he supported the Romans and had the task of bringing in Aetolia on their side. He captured Gomphi and other Thessalian towns (198), and was sent by Flamininus on an embassy to Rome after the conference of Nicaea. After Cynoscephalae Rome allowed him to keep the forts that he had taken from Philip. Later he supported Antiochus on his arrival in Greece: he was driven from his kingdom by Philip, now Rome's ally (191), but recovered it with Aetolian help in 189. He secured peace-terms from the Senate, and persuaded the Ambraciotes to surrender to Rome. He probably died soon afterwards.

S. J. Oost, *CPhil.* 1957, 1 ff.; Hammond, *Epirus*, 614 ff. H. H. S

**AMYNTAS** (1), dynastic name in the royal house of the Macedonians. The most famous bearer of the name, Amyntas III, king of Macedon *c.* 393–370 B.C., increased the power of his kingdom by withstanding the pressure of the Illyrians and the Dardanian king, Bardylis, and by astute diplomacy. He managed to ally himself with whatever Greek state became his most powerful neighbour: the Chalcidian Confederacy (Tod, ii, no. 111), the Spartans who destroyed the Chalcidian Confederacy, the Athenians when they replaced Sparta (Tod, ii, no. 129) and then Jason of Pherae. His consolidation of Macedonia and is example in diplomacy were important factors in the success of his son Philip II. *See* MACEDONIA. N. G. L. H.

**MYNTAS** (2), a client-king of the Romans in Asia Minor. Originally secretary of Deiotarus (q.v.), he commanded the Galatian auxiliaries of Brutus and Cassius in 42 B.C. He deserted after the first battle of Philippi, and after Deiotarus' death received from Antony a kingdom which eventually comprised Galatia, Lycaonia, and parts of Phrygia, Pamphylia, and Pisidia. In 35 he received the surrender of Sextus Pompeius (q.v. 6). He accompanied Antony to Actium, but by a second timely desertion, before the battle, he won Octavian's favour and his kingdom was still further enlarged by the addition of Isauria and Cilicia Tracheia. In 25 he was killed during a campaign against the Homonades, an unruly mountain tribe on the southern borders of his realm. Though he left sons, the greater part of his kingdom was annexed by Augustus and made into the Roman province of Galatia (q.v.).

M. C.; T. J. C.

**ANABOLE,** strictly used of the striking-up of a musical instrument, especially of a lyre, by a bard when he began to sing (*Od.* 1. 155, 8. 266: ἀνεβάλλετο, Pind. *Pyth.* 1. 14.), but used in a special sense of a lyric solo introduced into a dithyramb (Ar. *Av.* 1385; Arist. *Rh.* 3. 9. 1) by Melanippides, Cinesias, and Timotheus. C. M. B.

**ANACHARSIS,** a Scythian prince of the royal blood who in the sixth century B.C. travelled extensively in Greece and elsewhere and gained a high reputation for wisdom. On his return to Scythia he was put to death for attempting to introduce the cult of Magna Mater which he had observed at Cyzicus. So much we learn from Herodotus (4. 76 f.). Diogenes Laertius (1. 10 ff.) and other late writers claim to know more; they give him a Greek mother, and bring him in 592 B.C. to Athens where he is Solon's guest and figures among the 'Seven Sages'; they credit him with many pithy sayings and even with (apocryphal) didactic poems. About his attitude to Greek culture there were apparently two traditions from an early date. Herodotus sees him as an ardent philhellene but mentions the claim that he thought poorly of all Greeks save the Spartans. It was the latter view which eventually prevailed. From Ephorus (fr. 42 Jacoby) onwards he appears as a type of the 'noble savage' who outstrips the Greeks in wisdom and virtue; in the *Letters of Anacharsis*, a Hellenistic composition (third century B.C.?), he becomes a mouthpiece for Cynic diatribes against a corrupt civilization. These letters were much relished: Cicero translated one of them (*Tusc.* 5. 90), and they furnished a model for Montesquieu's *Lettres Persanes* and Goldsmith's *Citizen of the World*.

R. Heinze, *Philol.* 1891; P. von der Mühll, *Festschrift für H. Blümner* (1914). Letters: text in R. Hercher, *Epistologr. Graeci* (1873), 102 ff.; text and comm., F. H. Reuters, *de A. epistulis* (Diss. Bonn, 1957). Sayings: *FPG* i. 232 ff. E. R. D.

**ANACREON** (b. *c.* 570 B.C.), lyric poet, son of Scythinus, born at Teos (*Suda* s.v. Ἀνακρέων), but left home *c.* 545 B.C. when it was threatened by the Persians (Strabo 644); to this he may refer in frs. 46 P. and 74 P. With other Teans he founded the colony of Abdera in Thrace (*Suda*, Strabo, l.c.). References to fighting here against Thracians may be seen in fr. 191 G. a commemorative epigram for a dead fighter, and in fr. 192 G. Here too he may have written fr. 72 P. to a Thracian girl. He was summoned to Samos by Polycrates, who wished him to instruct his son in music (Himer. *Ex. Nap.* in *Hermes* 1911. 422), and he was with the tyrant when the fatal messenger came summoning the latter to his death (Hdt. 3. 121). He is said to have made many references

to Polycrates in his poems (Strabo 14. 638), but none survives. To his Samian period must belong fr. 25 with its reference to civil strife, fr. 1 for the Magnesians on the Maeander, and many of his love-poems, which seem to have been to the taste of Polycrates. After the fall of Polycrates Hipparchus fetched him to Athens ([Pl.] *Hipparch.* 228 b); thence *c.* 514 B.C. he went to Thessaly, where two epigrams, fr. 198 G., a dedication by King Echecratidas, and fr. 199 G., a dedication by Queen Dyseris, show him consorting with royalty. He returned to Athens, where his memory was honoured later by Critias (fr. 8) and by a statue on the Acropolis (Paus. 1. 25. 1). His death, at an advanced age, was said to be due to a grape-pip sticking in his throat (Val. Max. 9. 8). His works were edited by Aristarchus in six books of μέλη, ἴαμβοι, and ἐλεγεῖα (Heph. p. 68. 22; 74. 11 ff.). The first class contains his lyric poems, mostly monodic, such as hymns to Artemis (fr. 3 P.), Eros (fr. 13 P.), and Dionysus (fr. 357/12 P.), love-songs to Cleobulus (frs. 14–15 P.) and other convivial or sympotic poems (frs. 11, 13, 18, 57 c, 65 P.). Of his iambic poems the most complete example is his cruel poem on Artemon (fr. 43 P.). His elegiacs contain commemorative poems, dedications, and epitaphs. He writes in an Ionic vernacular with very few traces of Homeric or Aeolic language. His metres are usually simple. He favoured a stanza made of Glyconics with Pherecrateans for *clausulae*, and often used a minor Ionic verse with anaclasis, called Anacreontic after him. He is remarkable for his combination of fancy and wit, which prevents him from taking himself or others too seriously. His poetry is concerned mostly with pleasure, but this may well be due to the circumstances of its performance, and it is unwise to deduce too much about his character from it. *See also* IAMBIC POETRY, GREEK, *and* LYRIC POETRY, GREEK.

TEXT: Page, *Poet. Mel. Gr.* 172–235; B. Gentile, *Anacreon* (1948). CRITICISM: U. von Wilamowitz-Moellendorff, *Sappho und Simonides* (1913), 102 ff.; L. Weber, *Anacreontea* (1895); C. M. Bowra, *Greek Lyric Poetry*² (1961), 269 ff.; *PW* Suppl. xi, 30 ff.
C. M. B.

**ANACTORIUM,** a joint colony of Corinthians and Acarnanians, was founded *c.* 620 B.C. on the south coast of the Gulf of Ambracia. It sent troops to fight at Plataea against the Persians. In 425 Anactorium was absorbed into Acarnania.

Hammond, *Epirus*, 62 and 425 f. N. G. L. H.

**ANAGNIA,** chief town of the Hernici (q.v.), in a fertile area of Italy (*Aen.* 7. 684); modern *Anagni* with well-preserved walls. In 306 B.C. Anagnia became a *civitas sine suffragio* (*see* MUNICIPIUM) which Pyrrhus and Hannibal later ravaged (Livy 9. 42 f.; 26. 9; App. *Sam.* 10). In the second century it acquired full citizenship (Festus 155 L.) and remained a *municipium* under the Empire (reject *Lib. Colon.* p. 230). Vitellius' general Valens and Commodus' concubine Marcia were born here (Tac. *Hist.* 3. 62; *ILS* 406). The numerous temples near Anagnia were still celebrated in Marcus Aurelius' time (Fronto, *Ep.* 4. 4).

S. Sibilia, *La Città dei Papi* (1939); Castagnoli, *Stud. urb.* 49 ff.
E. T. S.

**ANAGNOSTES,** a reader, often an educated slave, whose duty in Roman houses was to entertain his master and guests at table by an *acroama* in Greek and Latin. Cicero (*Att.* 1. 12. 4) mentions his distress at the death of his young reader Sosthenes. He had one, however, who ran away (Vatin. ap. Cic. *Fam.* 5. 9. 2). Atticus kept very good readers whom he thought indispensable at dinner parties (Nep. *Att.* 13. 3 and 14. 1). Gellius (3. 19) records similar entertainment at dinner with the philosopher Favorinus. The word is used of a scholar giving a *recitatio* in a theatre (Gell. 18. 5. 2 and 5). The *anagnostes* also took part in grammatical instruction. J. W. D.

**ANAHITA** (*Anaitis*, Ἀναῖτις), Persian goddess of the fertilizing waters (*Zend-Avesta*, Yašt 5). Artaxerxes II (404–358 B.C.) introduced the use of cult-images (Berossus ap. Clem. Alex. *Protr.* 5. 65. 3), and the cult spread to Armenia, Cappadocia, Pontus, and especially to Lydia. In Armenia sacred prostitution (q.v.) was practised (Strabo 532–3), and in Pontus Anahita possessed many *hierodouloi* (q.v.). In Lydia she was assimilated to Cybele and to Artemis Ephesia, and hence called Mater Anahita or Artemis Anahita, but Iranian traditions, notably the fire-cult, also persisted (Paus. 5. 27. 5–6). She was often called the Persian Artemis. *See* ANATOLIAN DEITIES.

Nilsson. *GGR* ii,² 672 ff. (with references to the earlier literature); S. Wikander, *Feuerpriester in Kleinasien und Iran* (1946). F. R. W.

**ANAKES** (Ἄνακες), old by-form of ἄνακτες, hence 'kings', 'lords'. A title especially of the Dioscuri (q.v., and see LSJ, s.v.), but also of the Tritopatores (?, q.v.), (Cic. *Nat.* D. 3. 53), and perhaps certain deities at Amphissa (Paus. 10. 38. 7, where MSS. have Ἄνακτες). H. J. R.

**ANALOGIA, DE,** Caesar's lost treatise inspired by the teaching of Antonius Gnipho (q.v.), written on a journey across the Alps (55 or 54 B.C.) and dedicated to Cicero. It defended the principle of Analogy (q.v.) and a reformed *elegantia* founded on the *sermo cotidianus*. Gellius (1. 10. 4) quotes from its first book the famous advice 'ut tamquam scopulum sic fugias inauditum atque insolens uerbum' (see H. Dahlmann, *Rh. Mus.* 1935, 258 ff.) J. W. D.

**ANALOGY** and **ANOMALY** were the watchwords of two opposing schools of thought about linguistic phenomena. In particular, the analogists held that nouns and verbs were capable of classification into orderly declensions and conjugations on the basis of similarity of form (ἀναλογία), whereas the anomalists were impressed by the many manifestations of irregularity (ἀνωμαλία) which actual usage sanctioned. Neither party viewed language in a true perspective or effected any appreciable change in living speech; but the discussion was not entirely barren in so far as it stimulated grammatical studies. The analogist at least had a standard he could apply in cases of genuine doubt; the strength of the anomalist's position lay in his readiness to accept language as he found it. Underlying the controversy was the question (already discussed in Plato's *Cratylus*; cf. Lucr. 5. 1028–90) whether language was a natural growth or an arbitrary convention; and though matters of style did not at first enter into the argument, the analogists tended to be allied with purists in their condemnation of barbarisms and solecisms, and anomalists with those who claimed a place for new coinages and modes of expression. Amongst the Greeks, the quarrel was most keenly pursued on the side of analogy by the grammarians of Alexandria (e.g. Aristophanes of Byzantium, Aristarchus, Dionysius Thrax), and on the side of anomaly by the Stoics (e.g. Chrysippus, who wrote four books Περὶ ἀνωμαλίας) and the scholars of Pergamum (e.g. Crates of Mallos). At Rome the Scipionic circle in their pursuit of *Latinitas* and *purus sermo* inclined to favour the analogical view (cf. Lucil. 964). Varro (*Ling.* bks. 8–10) gives both sides of the controversy but leans towards the analogists, as did Caesar (*See* ANALOGIA, DE) and 'Atticists' like Calvus. Cicero (e.g. *Orat.* 155–62), Horace

(*Ars P.* 70–72), and Quintilian (1. 6) give greater weig to the claims of *consuetudo*.

Norden, *Ant. Kunst.* i. 184 ff.; J. E. Sandys, *Hist. of Cla Scholarship* i (1921) (*passim*); G. L. Hendrickson, *CPhil.* 1906, 9 F. H. Colson, *CQ* 1919, 24. J. F. N

**ANATOLIAN DEITIES.** The outstanding characte istic of Anatolian religion is the worship of a moth goddess and her youthful male consort, embodiments the fertility principle, who reappear constantly under diversity of local, differentiating names, epithets, an forms. There is some evidence (J. Keil, *JÖAI.* xvi 1915) for a divine triad of mother, father, son, but th is a less constant feature. The apparent diversity whic masks the basic similarity of the great pair is due in pa to the strength of localism and to local differentiatio and development, in part to the complex racial bac ground of Asia Minor, and in part to identification wi various Hellenic divinities, each of whom might fitly l thought to represent one facet of the native god's co plex personality. Thus the male god, as supreme, mig be called Zeus; as giver of oracles, Apollo; and as heale Asclepius. Generally the goddess predominated i Asiatic cities, while in Hellenic foundations the god w accorded higher rank. The native names, such as Cybe (q.v.), Attis (q.v.), Ma, Wanax, seldom or never appe in Asia Minor on Greek inscriptions (though local ep thets do), and are known chiefly from Neo-Phrygian doc ments or from outside Anatolia. According to Cald (*CR* 1927, 161–3) this shows that while speakers the native languages used the old names, speakers Greek did not, except in the Mysteries (cf. the myst formula in Dem. *De Cor.* 260). Of the Mysteri themselves we know little, and that chiefly from no Asiatic sources. *See* AGDISTIS; ANAHITA; ATTIS; CYBEL EUNUCHS, RELIGIOUS; HIERODOULOI; METRAGYRTES; PR STITUTION, SACRED; SABAZIUS.

The inscriptions are our chief source of material: see especia the series *Monumenta Asiae Minoris Antiqua* (1928– ), and numero articles in *Anatolian Studies presented to Sir Wm. Ramsay* (192 *Anatolian Studies presented to W. H. Buckler* (1939), and L. Robe *Études anatoliennes* (1937). A valuable synthesis in Cumont, *Rel. o* ch. 3. F. R. V

**ANATOMY AND PHYSIOLOGY.** The earliest r cords of true anatomical observations are in fragmen of Alcmaeon (q.v. 2; *c.* 500 B.C.) of Croton. There ca be no doubt that he actually dissected animals, discerr ing the optic nerves and the tubes between the nose an ear cavities now known as 'Eustachian'. He even extende his researches to embryology, describing the head of th foetus as the first part to develop—a justifiable inte pretation of the appearances. His followers investigate especially the blood-vessels.

2. The theory of Empedocles (q.v.; *c.* 492–432 B.C.) Acragas of four elements was to control medical thoug for two millennia, but more immediately influential w his view taken from folk-belief that the blood is the se of the innate heat (θερμὸν ἔμφυτον)—'the blood is th life'. This led to the consideration of the heart as cent of the vascular system and chief organ of the *pneum* which was distributed by the blood-vessels. *Pneuma* w identified, in accord with certain philosophical tendencie with both air and breath. These views of Empedocl were rejected by the important Coan Medical Schoo then becoming prominent, but were widely accepted els where. Notably Diogenes of Apollonia, a contempora of Hippocrates of Cos, was led to investigate the bloo vessels, and his account of the vascular system is th earliest that is intelligible.

3. Early members of the so-called 'Hippocratic Co lection' (*see* HIPPOCRATES 2) are the treatises *On the sacr disease* of about 400 B.C. and *On the nature of man* whic

s but little later. The author of the former opened the skulls of goats and found the brain to resemble that of men in being cleft into symmetrical halves by a vertical membrane. The large veins of the neck are intelligibly described. The arteries are said to contain air, an idea gained from their emptiness in dead animals. *On the nature of man*, ascribed by Aristotle to Polybus, son-in-law of Hippocrates, contains the doctrine of the four humours. These—Blood, Phlegm (*pituita*), Black Bile (*melancholia*), and Yellow Bile (*cholē*)—make up the living body as the four elements make up non-living matter. This doctrine persisted till quite modern times and has left definite traces in the anatomical and, indeed, psychological nomenclature of our own day.

**4.** An interesting Athenian practitioner of the middle and late fourth century B.C. was Diocles (q.v.3) of Carystus. He drew his opinions from many sources, adopting the humours of Polybus and the innate heat of Empedocles, regarding with Aristotle the heart as seat of the intelligence but accepting also Sicilian pneumatism. His observations on the early human foetus are the first recorded. His work *On anatomy*, based to some extent on human material, has disappeared and we have no general early treatise on the subject. Our best representative of the anatomy of the fourth century is the tract in the Hippocratic Collection *On the heart*, of about 340 B.C. We cannot be sure that it is based on human dissection, but it discusses the anatomical similarities of man to animals. It places the innate heat in the heart. Air enters direct into the left ventricle, where takes place some subtle change of blood into spirit, and where too the intellect resides. The heart valves are described and experiments are suggested for testing their competence. The startlingly false statement that in drinking some of the fluid passes into the lungs may indeed, as the author of the tract claims, have been 'verified' by experiment: a coloured fluid was found to have stained the inside of the windpipe of a pig whose throat was cut while it was drinking the fluid. This experiment may well have been performed; and the fluid may have entered the windpipe as the animal was squealing. The view that drink passes into the lungs is also found in Plato's *Timaeus* and in other writings; it was opposed by, amongst others, Aristotle.

**5.** The direct contributions of Aristotle to human anatomy and physiology are unimportant and he did not dissect the human body (though he may have dissected a human embryo). The text of his account of the heart is corrupt and incomprehensible, but it was in any event very inadequate, nor did he make any proper distinction between arteries and veins, though he gave fair descriptions of several of these vessels. On the other hand, he gave excellent accounts of certain organs from the standpoint of comparative anatomy. Some were illustrated by drawings, the first anatomical figures recorded. We can confidently restore certain of them, for example, that of the organs of generation. His nomenclature of the uterine organs is still partially retained.

**6.** Among the noteworthy errors of Aristotle is his refusal to attach importance to the brain. Intelligence he placed in the heart. This was contrary to the views of some of his medical contemporaries, contrary to the popular view, and contrary to the doctrine of the *Timaeus*. Aristotle must have known all these, and it is conjectured that, having found the brain to be devoid of sensation, he concluded that it could not be associated with it. The function of the brain was to prevent the heart from overheating the blood. This was effected by the cold Phlegm (*pituita*) secreted in the nose, supposedly by the brain, an idea preserved in our anatomical term 'pituitary body'.

**7.** After Aristotle's time Alexandria became the chief medical centre. Herophilus (q.v.; *c.* 300 B.C.) of Chalcedon, of the earliest Alexandrian scientific generation, adhered to the humoral theory. He was the first to dissect the body publicly and investigated the anatomy of the eye, the brain, the nervous system, the vascular system, and the organs of reproduction. He recognized the brain as the central organ of the nervous system and the seat of intelligence; distinguished the cerebrum from the cerebellum; described the fourth ventricle of the brain and even its 'calamus scriptorius', which he named (ἀνάγλυφος κάλαμος); and described the meninges and the 'wine-press' (torcular, ληνός), a confluence of veins which modern anatomists, following Galen, still name after him. He was the first to grasp the nature of nerves other than those of the special senses, and he distinguished motor from sensory nerves. The modern anatomical terms 'prostate' (ἀδενοειδεῖς προστάται) and 'duodenum' (δωδεκαδάκτυλον) are derived, through Galen, from him. We owe to him also the first description of the lacteals and the first clear differentiation of arteries from veins. Pulsation was for him an active arterial process. He wrote an anatomy for midwives and is the first medical teacher recorded—perhaps apocryphally—to have had a woman pupil.

**8.** Erasistratus (q.v.) of Chios, a younger Alexandrian contemporary of Herophilus, abandoned the humoral doctrine and was the first to set forth a complete physiological scheme. Accepting the atomism of Democritus and its consequent 'materialism' he described the body as a mechanism, combining this with a pneumatic theory. Observing that every organ is equipped with a threefold system of branching vessels—veins, arteries, and nerves—he concluded that the minute divisions of these, plaited together, compose the tissues. Blood and two kinds of pneuma are the sources of nourishment and movement. Blood is carried by the veins, which take it to the heart. Air is taken in by the lungs and passing thence to the heart becomes changed into the first pneuma, the *vital spirit* (πνεῦμα ζωτικόν) which is sent to the parts of the body by the arteries. Carried by these to the brain it is there changed to the second pneuma, the *animal spirit* (πνεῦμα ψυχικόν), and distributed to the parts through the nerves, which are hollow. The so-called Anonymus Londinensis ascribes to Erasistratus an experiment designed to demonstrate *quantitative* changes associated with animal metabolism.

**9.** The view of Erasistratus that the heart is the centre and source not only of the arterial system but also of the venous system was ahead of all opinion until Harvey (1628). Perceiving that arteries though empty in dead bodies, yet when incised in the living contain blood, he sought to explain the presence of the blood in them as due to the escape of pneuma through the wound leading to a vacuum by which blood was sucked into the arteries from the veins through fine intercommunications between artery and vein. The view that arteries contain air was experimentally disproved by Galen 450 years later, but Erasistratus, having realized that the two systems communicate at their periphery, was not very far from the conception of a circulation.

**10.** Erasistratus advanced on Herophilus' knowledge of the nervous system, giving detailed descriptions of the cerebral ventricles, which he regarded as filled with animal spirit. He observed the cerebral convolutions, noting their greater elaboration in man than in animals, associated, as he thought, with man's higher intelligence. He made experiments on the brain and meninges, traced the cranial nerves into the brain itself, and distinguished cranial sensory from cranial motor nerves. He also attained a clear view of the action of muscles in producing movement, regarding their shortening as due to distension by animal spirit.

**11.** After Erasistratus anatomy and physiology declined at Alexandria. The schools that arose at Pergamum, Smyrna, Corinth, and elsewhere were poor substitutes. The human body ceased to be dissected and when Galen began his studies about A.D. 145 it was difficult to find even a skeleton in these schools. Nevertheless, two Ephesians of the first Christian century produced noteworthy anatomical works. Of these Rufus gave to many parts of the eye the names by which they are still known, and in his book on the pulse claimed that the heart strikes the chest-wall during contraction. Had this critical observation been known to Galen it should have led him to modify his physiological scheme, perhaps in the direction of a circulation. Soranus of Ephesus wrote a book on pregnancy with figures of the uterus. Indirect medieval copies of these are the first surviving anatomical drawings exhibiting details ascertainable only by human dissection.

**12.** Anatomical and physiological science in antiquity reached both its climax and its end with Galen (q.v.; A.D. 129–99), who spent his early years gleaning in many schools the traditions of his predecessors. Though he was an eclecticist and a dogmatist (thus he taught the humoral theory which had been abandoned by Erasistratus and others) he engaged in dissection and vivisection (of animals) and in carefully planned experiments, such as his famous experiment designed to demonstrate the irreversibility of the flow from the kidney to the bladder. His active professional life was passed at Rome, where he gave public demonstrations. He never dissected a human body, but made numerous accurate anatomical and physiological studies on a variety of animals, among them the Barbary ape, the structure of which is not very different from that of man. He also experimented on dogs, bears, cattle, and pigs, being struck with the resemblance of the latter to human beings.

**13.** Galen elaborated a complete physiological scheme which was generally accepted until modern times. It involves three kinds of pneuma or spirit in addition to air. The basic principle of life was drawn from the world-pneuma of air by breathing. Entering the body through the windpipe it passes to the lung and thence to the left ventricle, where it encounters the blood. His view as to the changes that then take place in the blood was most ingenious, and the errors that it involved remained current till the seventeenth century.

**14.** Galen believed that chyle, brought from the digestive system by the portal vessel, reaches the liver, and that that organ has the power of enduing it with a pneuma, innate in all living substance, which came to be called the *natural spirit* ($\pi\nu\epsilon\hat{\upsilon}\mu\alpha\ \phi\upsilon\sigma\iota\kappa\acute{o}\nu$). It then became venous blood. This is distributed by the liver through the venous system, ebbing and flowing in the veins.

**15.** One great branch of the venous system, a mere extension of a great trunk direct from the liver, was the cavity that we now call the right ventricle. The venous blood that entered this had two possible fates. Most of it, remaining awhile in the ventricle, left it to ebb back into the liver, having parted with its fumes or impurities, which were carried off to the lung and thence exhaled—hence the poisonous character of re-breathed air. A small fraction of the blood in the right ventricle, however, trickling through minute channels in the heart-substance, dripped slowly into the left ventricle. There, encountering the air brought through the lung, these drops of dark blood, charged with natural spirit, are elaborated into the higher *vital spirit*, which is the active principle of the bright arterial blood.

**16.** The arterial blood charged with vital spirits is distributed through the arteries to all parts of the body. Some passes to the so-called 'rete mirabile' ($\pi\lambda\acute{e}\gamma\mu\alpha$ $\mu\acute{e}\gamma\iota\sigma\tau\upsilon\nu\ \theta\alpha\hat{\upsilon}\mu\alpha$) at the base of the brain, and becomes

charged with yet a third pneuma, the *animal spirit* derive from the brain. This is distributed by the nerves. T 'rete mirabile', absent in man, is well developed in catt It was from experiments and observations on them th this remarkable system was derived.

**17.** Of Galen's positive anatomical knowledge the be presentation is his great work *On anatomical procedu* in sixteen books, of which nine survive in Greek whi the remainder have been recovered in modern times i Arabic translation. His treatise *On the uses of the par of the body of man* was the most popular of his gener anatomical works. *On anatomical operations* is a super experimental study. *On the anatomy of muscles* is a accurate and remarkable pioneer survey. *On bones, f beginners* is his only work based on human material an has influenced modern nomenclature. Among his term current in modern anatomy are apophysis, epiphysi trochanter, diarthrosis, and synarthrosis.

**18.** In pure anatomy Galen's best work was on th muscles, and his writings contain frequent referenc to the form and function of muscles of various animal Thus the dissection of the muscles of the orbit and laryn was performed on the ox, while those of the tongue a described from the ape. Occasionally he indicates th he is aware of the difference between the muscles he describing and those of man. His famous and intense teleological description of the structure and functior of the hand was derived from that of the Barbary ap There is perhaps in all literature no passage that is mo confident as to the exact details of the divine intention

**19.** Galen's anatomical and physiological writings a both voluminous and detailed. They are, however, i arranged, and, since he has no adequate technical nomer clature and is very argumentative, his meaning is ofte obscure. Though his account of the brain and of i related nerves is difficult, yet his classification and de scription of the cranial nerves remained in vogue unt quite modern times, and part of his nomenclature them survives even in current anatomy.

**20.** Perhaps Galen's most remarkable achievemen was his experimental investigation of the spinal cor the continuity of which at different levels was, he showe necessary for the maintenance of certain function Injury between the first and second vertebrae cause instantaneous death. Section between the third an fourth produced arrest of respiration. Below the sixt it gave rise to paralysis of thoracic muscles, respiratio being carried on only by the diaphragm. If the lesio were yet lower the paralysis was confined to the lowe limbs, bladder, and intestines. Galen's knowledge of th functions of the spinal cord was not developed an indeed was not adequately appreciated until well int the nineteenth century.

**21.** Galen's scientific works are among the most in fluential of all time. Nevertheless he established n school and he had neither disciples nor followers. On h death in 199 the prosecution of original anatomical an physiological inquiry ceased abruptly. Medical write after Galen, on the whole, restrict themselves to sun marizing and commenting upon the views of their pre decessors. Galen's influence and reputation in the Middl Ages are, at least in large part, to be accounted for by th fact that his strongly teleological views were, like those Aristotle, congenial to medieval thinkers.

Remains of fifth-century anatomists in Diels, *Vorsokr.*[10] (196( E. Krause, *Diogenes von Apollonia* (1908–9). M. Wellmann, *L Fragmente der Sikelischen Aerzte, Akron, Philistion und des Diok von Karystos* (1901). W. Jaeger, *Diokles v. Karystos* (1938). Aristotle anatomy mostly in *Historia animalium*, trans. by D'Arcy W. Thom son (1910). The fragments of Herophilus and Erasistratus collecte and translated by J. F. Dobson, *Proc. of Roy. Soc. of Med., Historic Section,* 1924 and 1927. J. Ilberg, *Die Ueberlieferung der Gynäkolog des Soranos von Ephesos* (1910). Soranus, *Gynecology,* transl. ( Temkin (1956). Ch. Daremberg, *Œuvres anatomiques physiologiqu et médicales de Galien* (2 vols. 1854). Max Simon, *Sieben Bücher Anatomie des Galen* (2 vols. 1906). J. S. Prendergast on Galen in *Proc. of Roy. Soc. of Med., Historical Section* 1926 and 1928. Very little of Galen is translated into English; there is, however, A. J. Brock, *Galen on the Natural Faculties* (Loeb, 1916); Galen, *On Anatomical Procedures*, transl. by C. Singer (1956); and a very good rendering of the famous passage *On the hand* by T. Bellott (1840). G. Senn, *Die Entwicklung der biologischen Forschungsmethode in der Antike* (1933). Survey by Charles Singer and C. Rabin, *A Prelude to Science* (1946); M. R. Cohen and I. E. Drabkin, *A Source Book in Greek Science*[2] (1958); Miriam Drabkin, 'A Select Bibliography of Greek and Roman Medicine', *Bull. of the Hist. of Medicine* 1942, 399 ff.; H. E. Sigerist, *A History of Medicine*, ii (1961). C. S.; A. W.

**ANAXAGORAS** (*c.* 500–*c.* 428 B.C.; Apollodorus ap. Diog. Laert. 2. 7), son of Hegesibulus, a native of Clazomenae, the first philosopher to reside in Athens. He came in 480, probably with Xerxes' army, and 'began to philosophize at Athens in the archonship of Callias (Calliades) at the age of 20, where he is said to have remained 30 years' (Demetrius of Phalerum ap. D.L. ibid.). The teacher and friend of Pericles, he was indicted by the latter's enemies on charges of impiety and medism; but with Pericles' aid he escaped to Lampsacus, where he founded a school and died in general honour and esteem. Accounts of the trial vary: the probable date is 450, not 432 (as Ephorus ap. Diod. 12. 38 f. and Plut. *Vit. Per.* 32 state). Anaxagoras' astronomical views, the main ground of the charge, were influenced by the fall of the meteorite at Aegospotami in 468–467. Only one work is ascribed to him: from bk. 1 a score of fragments is preserved by Simplicius.

Conflicting testimonies make modern reconstructions of Anaxagoras' system problematic. He accepts, like Empedocles, the Eleatic denial of 'becoming' and void, but unlike Empedocles presses this denial to the point of holding that in the beginning the world was a 'mixture' containing 'seeds' (σπέρματα) of every qualitatively distinct natural substance, organic and inorganic: these (flesh, blood, bone, gold, etc.) are infinitely divisible into parts like each other and the whole—hence Aristotle's name for them, 'homoeomeries' (ὁμοιομερῆ)—and are Anaxagoras' 'elements'. His theory thus conflicts both with atomism and with Empedocles' less drastic pluralism. Seeds take their quality from their prevailing component (fr. 12); but actually, at every stage of division, imperceptible portions of *every* other 'qualitied' thing remain, for (fr. 11) 'in everything there is a portion of everything except mind (νοῦς)'. This last Anaxagoras introduces as initiator of cosmic motion and animating principle of plants and animals. Mind, because itself separate and unmixed, can move other things.

Anaxagoras thus explains growth and nutrition without assuming qualitative change (cf. fr. 10): the characters which 'emerge' must have been present, imperceptibly, in the germ of food, and rendered apparent by regrouping. But much is obscure, e.g. the place of the 'opposites' (such as hot and cold, wet and dry) in Anaxagoras' scheme. Tannery, followed by Burnet and others, took these to be the basic ingredients of the 'seeds'. Cornford, identifying them with the things of which Anaxagoras says that there is a portion in everything (frs. 4, 6, 11, 12), used this dictum to explain only the qualitative differences in the seeds and not, as did Aristotle and the ancient commentators, all natural change. But this view, as well as discounting the ancient tradition, imported a gross ambiguity into Anaxagoras' words 'a portion of everything in everything'; and later writers have tried to save the literal sense of the dictum and at the same time save Anaxagoras from the vicious regress that seems to come from combining it with his other thesis that the characters which anything exhibits are those which predominate among its ingredients, e.g. that gold is the stuff in which gold predominates.

Anaxagoras' cosmology is a closely knit part of the

theory. *Nous* starts a rotatory motion (περιχώρησις) which gradually spreads. Thus seeds are separated out, the dense, moist, cold, and dark (ἀήρ) going to the centre, their opposites (αἰθήρ) to the circumference. The heavenly bodies are stones, torn from the earth, which motion renders red-hot (cf. ASTRONOMY). Anaxagoras follows the Ionian tradition of a flat earth, but knows the cause of eclipses. Whether he assumes only *one* world (cf. Cornford against Burnet, *CQ* 1934) remains controversial. Sense-perception depends on the contrast of unlikes.

Anaxagoras' great reputation in antiquity is endorsed on the whole by Aristotle. He solves the problem raised by Parmenides more subtly, if less simply, than the Atomists. His failure to use mind as a teleological principle, which Plato and Aristotle deplore, was fortunate for science.

Diels[11], ch. 59. A useful survey of modern literature in D. E. Gershenson and D. A. Greenberg, *Anaxagoras and the Birth of Physics* (1964), to which should be added C. Strang, *Archiv für Gesch. der Philosophie* 1963. On A.'s use of physiological ideas: G. Vlastos, *Philosophical Review* 1950. A. J. D. P.

**ANAXANDRIDES** (4th c. B.C.), Middle Comedy poet, possibly of Rhodian birth (Ath. 374 b), won the first prize ten times (*Suda* s.v.), three times at the Lenaea (*IG* ii[2]. 2325. 142). His first victory was in 376 (*Marm. Par.* 70), and he was active at least as late as 349 (*IG* xiv. 1098. 8). Forty-one titles have survived, and eighty citations; some of the titles look back to Old Comedy (e.g. *Cities, Huntsmen*), some forward to New Comedy (e.g. *Madman, Samia*), and many are mythological (e.g. *Anchises, Protesilaus*). The longer fragments reveal an elegant style and a moralizing strain which earned him a place in anthologies.

*FCG* iii. 161 ff.; *CAF* ii. 135 ff.; *FAC* ii. 42 ff. K. J. D.

**ANAXARCHUS** (4th c. B.C.) of Abdera, a follower of Democritus, with Sceptical tendencies, was the teacher of Pyrrhon the Sceptic. His nickname Εὐδαιμονικός implies that he treated happiness as the *summum bonum*. He accompanied Alexander the Great on his Asiatic campaigns and was much esteemed by him. He is usually represented in antiquity as a flatterer of Alexander, but this may be due to Peripatetic prejudice. He was cruelly put to death by the Cypriot prince Nicocreon.

Testimonia and fragments in Diels, *Vorsokr.*[11] ii. 235 ff. W. D. R.

**ANAXILAS** (1), tyrant of Rhegium, 494–476 B.C. By collusion with Samian refugees he tried to seize Zancle, then part of the dominions of Hippocrates (q.v. 1), but the Samians made a compact with Hippocrates and were expelled by Anaxilas in 490/489, who settled there other Greek colonists, chiefly Messenians (*see* MESSANA). Anaxilas fortified the straits against the Etruscans but, antagonistic to Gelon (q.v.), supported Carthage in 480. Afterwards he made his peace with Syracuse, and married his daughter to Hieron I (q.v.). In 477 he threatened Locri, but Hieron intervened; he died the next year.

E. S. G. Robinson, *JHS* 1946, 13 ff.; Dunbabin, *Western Greeks*, chs. 13–14; G. Vallet, *Rhégion et Zancle* (1958), 335 ff. A. G. W.

**ANAXILAS** (2) (4th c. B.C.), Middle Comedy poet, can be dated to the middle of the fourth century B.C. by the fact that in three of his plays (Diog. Laert. iii. 28) he ridiculed Plato. We have nineteen titles and some forty citations, the longest of which (fr. 22, from Νεοττίς) characterizes well-known hetairai.

*FCG* iii. 341 ff.; *CAF* ii. 264 ff.; *FAC* ii. 332 ff. K. J. D.

**ANAXIMANDER** (Ἀναξίμανδρος) (*c.* 610–540 B.C.) of Miletus wrote the first philosophic prose treatise *c.* 546 B.C. He held that the origin (ἀρχή) of all things was the

Infinite (τὸ ἄπειρον), which he regarded as the Divine (τὸ θεῖον), describing it as 'eternal and ageless' and as 'surrounding' and 'governing' the innumerable worlds. Each world he envisaged as the product of a number of pairs of conflicting opposites which are separated from one another out of the Infinite and 'pay due compensation to each other according to the assessment of Time for their injustice'. He thereby first conceived the universe as a cosmos subject to the rule of law. Anaximander revolutionized astronomy by treating the paths of the sun and moon as great circles passing beneath the earth and composed of fire wrapped in vapour. The visible sun is an aperture in the vapour equal in diameter to the earth. The earth remains freely in the centre and cannot fall, because there is no reason why what is situated in the middle and is equidistant from the extremities should move in one direction rather than another and it is impossible that it should move in opposite directions at once. He introduced into Greece the gnomon, which he used for astronomical observation, and drew the first map of the earth. He held an evolutionary theory of the origin of animals and men. *See also* ASTRONOMY.

Diels, *Vorsokr.*<sup>11</sup> i. 81 ff; Burnet, *EGP* 50 ff; W. Jaeger, *Theology of the Early Greek Philosophers* (1947), 17 ff.; Kirk–Raven, *Presocratic Philosophers*, ch. iii; C. H.Kahn, *Anaximander and the Origins of Greek Cosmology* (U.S.A., 1960); Guthrie, *Hist. Gk. Phil.* i. 72 ff.   A. H. C.

**ANAXIMENES** (1) of Miletus (fl. *c.* 546 B.C.), junior and perhaps pupil to Anaximander (q.v.), maintained in simple Ionic prose that the one cosmos, which comes into existence and perishes in a perpetual cycle, is encompassed and sustained by the infinite and eternally moving divine air or vapour (ἀήρ), which it breathes. The cosmos further consists of 'air', which, when rarefied, becomes fire, when condensed, progressively wind, cloud, water, earth, stone; from these lesser divinities all other things are formed. The earth is thin and flat, floating on air. Sun, moon, and stars are leaves of fire. They are exhaled from the earth and carried by air around it; they are invisible at night, behind high ground in the distant north. Anaximenes' astronomy is retrograde from Anaximander's; but his theory of condensation and rarefaction is the first strictly physical account of the relation of things to their primary constituent and had a lasting influence.

Diels, *Vorsokr.*<sup>11</sup> i. 90 ff.; Burnet, *EGP*, 72 ff.; Zeller–Mondolfo, *La filosofia dei Greci* I. ii (1938), 206 ff.; Kirk–Raven, *Presocratic Philosophers*, ch. iv; Guthrie, *Hist. Gk. Phil.* i. 115 ff.   A. H. C.

**ANAXIMENES** (2) of Lampsacus (*c.* 380–320 B.C.), historian and rhetorician, a pupil of Zoïlus. His historical work (*FGrH* 72) comprised *Hellenica*, *Philippica*, and a work on Alexander; [Demosthenes] xi was thought in antiquity to be his; xii is perhaps his also. He also wrote on Homer. The *Rhetorica ad Alexandrum*, first attributed to him by Victorius, on the ground of Quint. 3. 4. 9, is the sole surviving pre-Aristotelian manual of rhetoric.

Text of *Rhetorica*: M. Fuhrmann (1966); H. Rackham (Loeb). Translation, E. S. Forster, in *Works of Aristotle* xi (1924). See L. Radermacher, *Artium Scriptores* (1951), 200 ff.; V. Buchheit, *Das Genos Epideiktikon* (1960), 189 ff., argues against A.'s authorship of *Rhetorica ad Alexandrum*.   D. A. R.

**ANAXIPPUS**, New Comedy poet, 'in the time of Antigonus and Demetrius Poliorcetes' (*Suda*). Four comedies are plainly attributed to Anaxippus; and one fragment (49 vv.) of another is assigned to '(X)anthippus' —possibly a mistake for Anaxippus—the verbose but humorous speech of a cook who elevates the gastronomic art (see H. Dohm, *Mageiros* (1964), 156 ff.).

*FCG* i. 469 f., iv. 459 ff.; *CAF* iii. 296 ff.   W. G. W.

**ANCAEUS** (Ἀγκαῖος), in mythology, (1) son or grandson of Lycurgus of Arcadia (Hyg. *Fab.* 14. 14), an Argonaut (Ap. Rhod. 1. 164), the strongest next to Heracles, with

whom he is paired (ibid. 426, 531, etc.), killed in the Calydonian boar-hunt (Ov. *Met.* 8. 315, 391 ff.). (2) son of Poseidon (Ap. Rhod. 1. 187) and king of the Leleges of Samos; often confused with (1) (as Apollod. 1. 112 and 126). A skilled navigator, he steered the *Argo* after Tiphys died (Ap. Rhod. 2. 894). He planted a vineyard and was told by his servant that he should not live to drink its wine. On the grapes ripening, he pressed some of the juice into a cup, but the man remarked πολλὰ μεταξὺ πέλει κύλικος καὶ χείλεος ἄκρου and Ancaeus was killed by a boar before he could drink (schol. Ap. Rhod. 1. 188).   H. J. R.

**ANCHISES,** in mythology, son of Capys and grandson of Assaracus, belonged to the younger branch of the Trojan royal house. Spoken of with respect in the *Iliad*, he is chiefly famed for his marriage with Aphrodite while pasturing herds on the slopes of Ida, from which union Aeneas was born. Forbidden to reveal the name of his son's mother, he is said to have boasted of it among his friends, and for this was blinded or lamed by lightning. At the fall of Troy he was rescued by Aeneas, who carried him on his shoulders from the city, and subsequently shared his son's wanderings. Tradition gives many accounts of his death; Virgil places it at Drepanum in Sicily, and later describes him in the Elysian fields.

R. D. Williams, *Virgil, Aeneid* iii (1962), 3 ff.; R. G. Austin on *Aeneid* ii (1964), 247 ff.   R. A. B. M.

**ANCHISTEIS** (ἀγχιστεῖς), the kinship-group, extending to second cousins, which was the basis of family law at Athens; also called συγγενεῖς. In cases of homicide, the nearest male relative within this limit had to prosecute; in cases of intestacy, the nearest male relative within this limit could claim the property. Relatives on the father's side had precedence, but the mother's relatives were included.

W. K. Lacey, *The Family in Classical Greece* (1967).   A. W. G.

**ANCONA** (Ἀγκών, so called from the shape of its harbour, which resembles an elbow-joint), a town of Italy in the territory of the Piceni, with the only good natural harbour on the central east coast, but with a poorly developed hinterland. It is first mentioned as a colony of refugees from Dionysius I of Syracuse. It was used by Cinna (q.v. 1) as the mustering point of his expeditionary force against Sulla (84 B.C.), and it subsequently served as a port of embarkation to Dalmatia. Trajan rebuilt the harbour and erected a commemorative arch on a mound above it.

G. Annibaldi, *Il Museo naz. delle Marche* (1961), especially for Picene culture.   M. C.

**ANCYRA** (Ἄγκυρα, modern *Ankara*), a city in that part of Phrygia settled by the Galatians, one of whose three tribes, the Tectosages, made it their capital. It lies in a strong position, around the steep fortified crag which formed its acropolis, at an important road junction, and rose to prominence as the capital of the province Galatia, as again to-day as the capital of Turkey. On the walls of the temple of Rome and Augustus, the ruins of which still stand, was inscribed the bilingual record of the reign of Augustus known as the *Monumentum Ancyranum* (q.v.)   W. M. C

**ANDOCIDES** (1) (*c.* 440–*c.* 390 B.C.), a member of a distinguished aristocratic family, whose grandfather had been one of the ten Athenian envoys who negotiated the Thirty Years Peace of 446. In 415, shortly before the great expedition to Sicily was due to depart, the Athenians were greatly dismayed one morning to discover that in the night the statues of Hermes around the city had been mutilated: Hermes being the god of travellers, this act was presumably intended to affect the progress of the expedition, but it was also taken, curiously, as a sign that the democracy itself was in danger. In the subsequent accusations the young Andocides and his associates in a club, which was probably suspected of oligarchic tendencies, were named as having shared both in the mutilations and in profane parodies of the Eleusinian Mysteries, and were arrested. Andocides, to secure immunity and, as he claimed, to save his father, confessed to a share in the mutilations and gave an account of the whole affair which, though it may have been far from the truth, was readily accepted by the Athenians. This secured his release, but shortly afterwards, when the decree of Isotimides, aimed at him especially, forbade those who had confessed to an act of impiety to enter temples or the Agora, Andocides preferred to leave the city and began to trade as a merchant, in which role he developed connexions all over the Aegean and in Sicily and Italy. In 411, seeking to restore himself to favour at Athens, he provided oars at cost price to the fleet in Samos, and shortly afterwards returned to Athens to plead for the removal of the limitation on his rights. Unfortunately for him, the revolution of the Four Hundred had just installed in power the very class of citizens whom his confession had affected, and he was put into prison and maltreated. Released, perhaps at the fall of the Four Hundred, he returned to his trading, in the course of which he was for a while imprisoned by Evagoras (q.v.), the king of Cyprus. At some time after the re-establishment of the democracy in 410, he returned to the city to renew his plea (the speech *de Reditu* belongs to this occasion) but he was again unsuccessful. Returning finally under the amnesty of 403, he resumed full participation in public life, and in 400 (or 399) successfully defended himself in the *de Mysteriis* against an attempt to have him treated as still subject to the decree of Isotimides: the sixth speech of the Lysian corpus, *Against Andocides*, was delivered by one of his accusers. In 392/391 he was one of the Athenian envoys sent to Sparta to discuss the making of peace, and on his return in the debate in the assembly he delivered the *de Pace* urging acceptance of the proffered terms, which were in fact very similar to those of the King's Peace of 387/386. The Athenians, however, rejected the peace, and Andocides and the other envoys were prosecuted by the young Callistratus (q.v. 2). Andocides anticipated condemnation by retiring into exile, and we hear no more of him.

SPEECHES. In addition to the three speeches mentioned above, there is a fourth speech, *Against Alcibiades*, preserved under his name, which purports to be concerned with an ostracism in 415; most scholars regard this as a forgery of late date. Fragments of four other speeches are preserved.

Greek and Roman critics discovered in Andocides faults which, according to their canons, were serious; and admittedly the faults are there. He sometimes carries the use of parenthesis to absurd extremes; he cannot keep to one point at a time; his style is so loose that the argument is hard to follow. On the other hand, this inconsequential method of expression is at times effective, giving the impression of an eagerness which outruns premeditated art. He possessed a natural gift of expression, a fine flow of words, and a good narrative style. He was not a professional rhetorician, and if he neglected scholastic rules, it can at least be claimed for him that he was successful on his own unconventional lines.

For general bibliography *see* ATTIC ORATORS.
TEXT. Blass–Fuhr (Teubner, 1913).
TEXT AND TRANSLATION. Dalmeyda (Budé, 1930), Maidment Loeb, *Attic Minor Orators* i, 1941).
COMMENTARIES. *De Mysteriis* and *De Reditu*, E. C. Marchant

(1889); *De Mysteriis*, D. Macdowell (1962); *De Reditu*, U. Albini (1961); *De Pace*, U. Albini (1964).
INDEX (to A., Lycurgus, and Dinarchus). L. L. Forman (1897).
G. L. C.

**ANDOCIDES** (2) (fl. last quarter of 6th c. B.C.), a potter in Athens, known from nine signatures. Two important artists worked for him: 1. Andocides painter. Painted amphorae and cups in black- and red-figure (the black-figure parts perhaps by another), red-figure, and white-figure technique. Successor of Execias (q.v.). 2. Menon painter (probably called Psiax; worked also for the potter Menon, etc.). Painted amphorae, hydriae, and small vases in black-figure, black- and red-figure, and red-figure technique.

*ABV* 253; *ARV*² 1. T. B. L. W.

**ANDREAS** (d. 217 B.C.), physician of Ptolemy IV (Philopator). Works: Νάρθηξ (a pharmacopoeia, with descriptions of plants and roots); Περὶ δακέτων (on snake-bites); Περὶ τῶν ψευδῶς πεπιστευμένων (against superstitious beliefs); Περὶ στεφάνων (all lost except for fragments).

**ANDRISCUS,** an Adramyttian adventurer, claiming to be Philip, the son of Perseus (q.v. 2) and Laodice, appeared as pretender to the Macedonian throne. On approaching Demetrius I of Syria, Laodice's brother, he was handed over to Rome, but escaped and with Thracian help invaded Macedonia, where by two victories and repressive measures he established control in 149 B.C. Rejecting negotiations with Scipio Nasica, he defeated Juventius Thalna, but was crushed in 148 by Q. Caecilius Metellus (q.v. 3).

Livy, *Per.* 48–50; Polyb. 36. 9–10 and 17; Zonar. 9. 28. G. Colin, *Rome et la Grèce* (1905), 608. A. H. McD.

**ANDROGEUS** (Ἀνδρόγεως), in mythology, (1) son of Minos (q.v.) and Pasiphaë, was treacherously killed by his defeated rivals after a victory in the Panathenaic games, or (in another version) was sent by Aegeus king of Athens against the Marathonian bull and destroyed by it. To avenge him Minos besieged Athens, and was only appeased by an annual tribute of seven youths and seven maidens to be thrown to the Minotaur. Later he was honoured in Phalerum as κατὰ πρύμναν ἥρως. (2) Greek leader killed at Troy (Verg. *Aen.* 2. 370–3).

R. A. B. M.

**ANDROMACHE,** in mythology, daughter of Eëtion king of Thebe and wife of Hector (q.v.; *Il.* 6. 395 ff.). Her father and brothers were killed by Achilles, her mother taken prisoner but ransomed (ibid. 414 ff.). After the fall of Troy her son Astyanax was put to death by the Greeks (*Little Iliad*, fr. 19 Allen; *Iliu Persis*) and she herself became Neoptolemus' slave (ibid.). She bore him a son, Molossus, eponym of the Molossians. According to Euripides (*Andromache*) she narrowly escaped death at the hands of Neoptolemus' wife Hermione (q.v.) during the visit to Delphi in which he was killed (*see* NEOPTOLEMUS 1). After his death (Euripides) or before his marriage (*Aen.* 3. 327–9) she was handed over to Helenus, with whom she lived the rest of her life in Epirus. H. J. R.

**ANDROMEDA,** in mythology, daughter of Cepheus king of the Ethiopians and his wife Cassiepeia or Cassiope (Κασσιέπεια, Κασσιόπη). A principal source of our information about her is apparently the *Andromeda* of Euripides (Nauck², 392 ff.). Cassiepeia boasted that she was more beautiful than the Nereids; they complained to Poseidon, who flooded the land and sent a sea-monster to ravage it. On consulting Ammon, Cepheus learned that the only cure was to expose Andromeda to the monster, and she was accordingly fastened to a rock on the sea-shore. At this point Perseus (q.v. 1) came by on his way from taking the head of Medusa. He fell in love with Andromeda at sight, and got her and her father's consent to marry her if he could kill the sea-beast. This he did; but Andromeda's uncle Phineus, who had been betrothed to her, attacked him by open force (Ov. *Met.* 5. 1 ff.) or otherwise (ἐπιβουλεύοντος, Apollod. 2. 44). Perseus showed him and his followers the head of Medusa, turning them all into stone. He and Andromeda stayed for a time with Cepheus, and left their eldest son, Perses, with him; from Perses the Persian kings were descended. They then went on to Seriphus and thence to Argos and Tiryns (*see* PERSEUS 1). Their other children were Alcaeus, Sthenelus, Heleius, Mestor, Electryon, and a daughter Gorgophone (Apollod. 2. 43–9; other authorities in Nauck, loc. cit). The story is of a type widely distributed (Stith Thompson R111. 1. 3) and may well have had a share in forming the legend of St. George and the dragon (Politis in Λαογραφία 1913, 220 f.). (The traditional site in later time was Joppa.)

That Andromeda, Perseus, Cepheus, Cassiepeia, and the monster were all turned into the constellations bearing their names (the monster is Cetus) was asserted by Euripides, according to [Eratosthenes], *Catast.* 17, by the natural interpretation of his words; he may, however, merely mean that Euripides tells the story of her rescue. If the first interpretation is right, it is one of the very few Greek star-myths which can be traced back to an earlier date than the Alexandrian period.

Manilius 5. 22 ff., 540 ff.; [Eratosthenes] 15–17; Hyginus, *Poet. Astr.* 2. 9–12; schol. German. *Arat.* 77 ff., 137 ff., Breysig.

H. J. R.

**ANDRON** of Halicarnassus, author concerned with the genealogies of Greek cities and families (Συγγενικά or Συγγένειαι,) a popular subject in the fourth century B.C. The ascription of an *Atthis* to him is improbable.

*FGrH* i. 10.

**ANDRONICUS RHODIUS** (1st c. B.C.), Peripatetic philosopher, who recalled the attention of the school to the works of Aristotle and Theophrastus, which had sunk into neglect. He arranged the works of both in the order in which those of Aristotle and in part those of Theophrastus have survived; on his arrangement of Aristotle's works is based the list preserved by Ptolemy. He wrote a treatise in at least five books on the order of Aristotle's works, with discussion of their contents and authenticity, an account of his life, and a transcript of his will. In his work he had the assistance of the grammarian Tyrannio. Andronicus' editorial work is probably to be dated about 40 B.C., and his assumption of the headship of the Peripatetic school at Athens, if it can be accepted as historical, shortly thereafter. The work *De Passionibus* which passes under his name (bk. 1, ed. X. Kreuttner, 1885; bk. 2, ed. K. Schuchardt, 1883) is spurious.

M. Plezia, *De Andronici Rhodii studiis aristotelicis* (1946); I. Düring, *Aristotle in the Ancient Biographical Tradition* (1957), 413 ff.

W. D. R.

**ANDROS**, the most northerly of the Cyclades (q.v.). In the eighth century B.C. the island was dependent on Eretria. It submitted to Persia in 490, thus angering Athens. Pericles planted Athenian colonists there, halving its tribute to the League in 449. About 410 it revolted from Athens; as a free State it entered the second Athenian League (378–377). After the battle of Chaeronea the island came under Macedonian control, which remained more or less continuous until the occu-

pation by Pergamene and Roman forces in 200. After 1 Andros was associated with the Roman province of As

*IG* xii. 5; P-K, *GL* iv. 89 ff.; T. Sauciuc, *Andros* (1914); D. Paschalis, *Andros* (1925). W. A.

**ANDROSTHENES,** of Thasos, sailed with Nearch (q.v. 2) and wrote an account of the voyage and of l subsequent exploration of the inner Persian Gulf a Bahrein.

*See* ALEXANDER (3), Bibliography, Ancient Sources.

**ANDROTION** (c. 410–340 B.C.), of a distinguished a wealthy family, entered Athenian public life c. 386. I was the only atthidographer who was an active politici and was engaged in military and diplomatic matters for t next forty years. A pupil of Isocrates and member of t Council before 378, he opposed Demosthenes a Eubulus on the question of a Persian alliance again Macedon, and aimed to recover Athens' prestige by con bining a moderate conservative policy at home with energetic foreign policy against Persia. He was accus by Demosthenes (*Or.* 22) in 354–353 of making an illeg proposal (παράνομα), and was in exile in Megara betwee 350 and 340 where the eight books of his *Atthis* we written. This shows a deliberate shift of interest fro pre-history to contemporary events. Books 1–3 de with the early history to the end of the Peloponnesi War and books 4–8 the following sixty years to 34 It was the main source of Philochorus' *Atthis* for t historical period, and was one of Aristotle's sources f the *Athenian Constitution*.

*FGrH* iiiB. 324 *and see under* ATTHIS. G. L.

**ANGELS** (ἄγγελοι), 'messengers'. Hermes was co sidered the messenger of the Olympians, and nam Angelos (once Euangelos). The same function was atti buted to Iris (in the *Iliad* and *Homeric Hymns*), and Plato (*Cra.* 407 e, 408 b) the two are the divine angel Ossa ('fame') is called *angelos* (*Il.* 2. 93–94), likewi Hecate-Artemis (Sophron in schol. Theoc. 2. 12), whi signifies her intercourse with the nether world and tl dead. Hermes is once (*Epigr. Gr.* 575,1 (1st–2nd c. A.D. named the 'messenger of Persephone'. Thera has yield interesting sepulchral inscriptions (Christian), in whi the 'angelos' of the defunct is mentioned, *IG* xii. 3. 933 (Index, 257; in no. 1238 the protective genius of tl grave, cf. Hermes in Thessaly). The angels became ir portant in Gnostic and Neoplatonic systems (in the fo lowing order: gods, archangels, angels, demons, heroes they were connected with the planets (under Jewisl Chaldaean influence), dominated metals and plants, a their names had magic virtues (see *PGM*, Index). The cult flourished in Egypt and Asia Minor especially in tl second and third centuries A.D. and gained new life wi the Christians (Michael replacing Hermes, but al Apollo, etc.).

Th. Hopfner, *Griechisch-ägyptischer Offenbarungszauber* (vol. and xxiii of Wessely's *Studien zur Palläographie und Papyruskur* 1922, 1924) i, §§ 135 ff.; H. Leclercq, art. 'Anges' in Cabrol–Leclerc *Dictionnaire d'archéologie chrétienne* i. 2, col. 2080 ff.

S.

**ANGERONA,** DIVA, a Roman goddess, worshipped 21 Dec. (Divalia or Angeronalia), in the Curia Accule (Varro, *Ling.* 6. 23), or the *sacellum Volupiae*, whe there stood on the altar a statue of Angerona with h mouth bound up and sealed (Macrob. *Sat.* 1. 10. *CIL* i², p. 337). The ancients connected her name wi *angina* (Festus, 16, 12 Lindsay) or *angor* (Masurius a Macrob. ibid.); Mommsen with *angerere*, 'to raise u sc. the sun after the solstice, on the basis of the *Fa Praenestini* (*see* Latte, *RR* 134).

Wissowa, *RK* 241. H. J.

**ANGITIA,** or the **ANGITIAE,** Marsian goddess(es), principally worshipped on the Lacus Fucinus at Lucus Angitiae (now *Luco*), also at Sulmo, where the plural of the name is found (see, for the former, *Aen.* 7. 759). Her native name was Anagtia and she seems to have been a goddess of healing and very popular.

R. S. Conway, *Italic Dialects* (1897), 182, 289 f.; Wissowa, *RK* 49; Schirmer in Roscher's *Lexikon*, s.v. H. J. R.

**ANICETUS** (*PW*, s.v. Aniketos, 5), prefect of the fleet at Misenum, was freedman and tutor of Nero, who used him to murder Agrippina. Subsequently induced to confess himself Octavia's paramour, he was exiled to Sardinia (A.D. 62). A. M.

**ANIMALS, SACRED.** Neither Greece nor Italy regarded any beast as an incarnate god in classical times (unlike Egypt, with the practices of which land they became familiar), but various animals were sacred in one sense or another. (1) A number of beasts and birds are connected with individual gods; thus, the eagle is associated with Zeus, the cow and the peacock with Hera, the owl with Athena, the bull with Dionysus, and so forth; in Italy, the wolf and the woodpecker are creatures of Mars (e.g. Plut. *Rom.* 4). It is a tenable theory that some at least of these deities were originally theriomorphic. (2) Besides the consecrating of victims to gods and the dedication of a live creature to some deity (as the horses dedicated by Julius Caesar, Suet. *Divus Iulius* 81; such animals were unworked and called ἄφετοι in Greek, e.g. Pl. *Critias* 119 d) we occasionally hear of an animal living in a shrine, as serpents (q.v.) very commonly in chthonian cults (Erechtheus, on the Acropolis, Hdt. 8. 41. 2; Asclepius, Ar. *Plut.* 733); geese sacred to Juno (Moneta) (Livy 5. 47. 4). (3) Sporadically, we hear of some creature locally sacred and inviolable; e.g. tortoises on Mt. Parthenion (Paus. 8. 54. 7); these were regarded as sacred to Pan. Such phenomena have often been explained as survivals of totemism, but there is no evidence that this ever existed in Greece, see Rose, *Primitive Culture in Greece* (1925), 47 ff. Perhaps no one explanation can fit them all. For a full discussion see Nilsson, *GGR* i². 212 ff. *See also* BIRDS (SACRED). H. J. R.

**ANIO** (modern *Aniene*), a river of Italy rising in the Sabine country and separating it from Latium (Pliny, *HN* 3. 54). After flowing seventy-five miles west-south-west it joins the Tiber at the site of Antemnae just north of Rome. Landslides in A.D. 105 and later have changed but not destroyed its spectacular cascades at Tibur (Hor. *Carm.* 1. 7. 13; Pliny, *Ep.* 8. 17). It supplied two aqueducts, Anio Vetus (272 B.C.) and Anio Novus (A.D. 52), and below Tibur was navigable (Strabo 5. 238). Skeletal remains of Neanderthal man indicate very ancient habitation of its valley.

G. Colasanti, *L'Aniene* (1906); T. Ashby, *Aqueducts of Ancient Rome* (1935), 54, 252. E. T. S.

**ANIUS,** in mythology, king of Delos and priest of Apollo. His mother Rhoeo being with child by Apollo, her father Staphylus son of Dionysus set her afloat in a chest, which stranded on Delos. Anius, when he grew up, married Dorippa and had three daughters, the Oenotropoi, Oeno, Spermo, and Elais, who could produce wine, seeds, and oil, by grace of Dionysus. They thus supplied Agamemnon's army before Troy. Anius received Aeneas (*Aen.* 3. 80). See Lycophron 170, and scholiast there. H. J. R.

**ANNA PERENNA,** a Roman goddess, whose festival was on 15 March, i.e. the first full moon of the year by the old reckoning (1 March being New Year's Day). It was popular and merry (see Ov. *Fasti* 3. 523 ff., with Frazer's commentary). She is usually explained as being a year-goddess, and her name thought of as created from the prayer 'ut annare perennareque commode liceat', 'for leave to live in and through the year to our liking' (Macrob. *Sat.* 1. 12. 6). See, however, Altheim, *Terra Mater* (1931), 91 ff., who makes her 'Mother Perna', a form of Ceres with Etruscan connexions. She has no mythology, but Ovid (ibid.) tells two stories (? of his own invention), one identifying her with Anna the sister of Dido (546–656), the other with an old woman of Bovillae named Anna ('Granny'), who fed the plebeians during the secession to the Mons Sacer (663–74). On what follows, 675 ff., cf. Rose, *Handb. Gr. Myth.*, 324 and Latte, *RR* 138, who would connect it with a mime of Laberius.

H. J. R.

**ANNALS, ANNALISTS.** From the beginning of Roman history to 400 B.C. only scanty records were preserved, but the main lines of tradition are authentic in the fourth century, and from *c.* 300 B.C. the *tabulae pontificum* (q.v.) gave regular records of magistrates and events of cult importance. These tables were the first annals, from which Ennius took the title of his historical epic; but their character was still mainly sacral in Cato's day (*Origines*, bk. 4, fr. 77 Peter), and the variance in the foundation-dates of Rome indicates that the pontifical records were not in full chronicle form in the middle of the second century.

The senatorial historians, Fabius Pictor, Cincius Alimentus, Postumius Albinus, and C. Acilius (qq.v.), appear to have been more than annalistic writers, and rather discursive historians, following the Hellenistic κτίσεις and episodic histories; Cato's *Origines* continued their work in Latin. The evidence of both pontifical records and historiography sets the first regular annalistic history in the latter part of the second century B.C.

Under Cato's influence the 'old' annalists, Cassius (q.v. 2) Hemina and Calpurnius Piso (q.v. 1), began the systematic reconstruction of Roman history. Then the publication of the *annales maximi* in eighty books, *ab initio rerum Romanarum usque ad P. Mucium pontificem maximum*, presumably by P. Mucius Scaevola himself (Pontifex Maximus from 130 to *c.* 115 B.C.), set out in formal arrangement year by year the official events of the State, viz. elections and commands, civic, provincial, and cult business. The composition involved for the regal period legendary and antiquarian speculation, for the early Republic systematic reconstruction from the surviving records, and probably added to the framework of the *tabulae pontificum* from fuller records in the archives.

The publication was definitive, and the new material and its formal arrangement determined the character of 'late' annalistic history from Cn. Gellius to the Sullan annalists and Livy. The influence of rhetorical theory allowed, probably Gellius, certainly Valerius Antias and Claudius Quadrigarius (qq.v.) to elaborate the ceremonial form and expand the records in the light of senat rial constitutionalism, legalistic antiquarianism, and family interests, with conventional rhetorical composition; this led, particularly with Antias, to inaccuracy, invention, and tendentious falsification.

The annalistic form was thus established as a historiographical γένος. Licinius Macer (q.v. 1) and Aelius Tubero (q.v. 2) in following it appear to have checked their material, but Livy accepted both material and arrangement in its Sullan form, and his work enshrines the annalistic tradition. The form was adapted to the narration of contemporary history, and was used by the imperial annalists, imposing its conventions even on Tacitus.

Peter, *HRRel.* i², ii (repr. 1962–3); K. W. Nitzsch, *Die röm.*

*Annalistik* (1873); E. Kornemann, *Die Priestercodex in der Regia* (1912); F. Leo, *Gesch. röm. Lit.* i (1913), 259 ff.; De Sanctis, *Stor. Rom.* i. 16 ff.; Beloch, *Röm. Gesch.* 86 ff.; M. Gelzer, *Kl. Schr.* iii. 93, 104, 220 ff.; J. P. Balsdon, *CQ* 1953, 158 ff.; J. E. A. Crake, *CPhil.* 1940, 375 ff.; P. Fraccaro, *JRS* 1957, 59 ff. *See also* TABULA PONTIFICUM. A. H. McD.

**ANNIANUS,** a 'neoteric' (cf. ALEXANDRIANISM) of Hadrian's time, composed *carmina Falisca* on country themes.

Baehr. *FPR*; Morel, *FPL*. Schanz–Hosius, § 513.

**ANNICERIS,** of Cyrene, philosopher of the Cyrenaic school, probably lived under Ptolemy I, who died 283 B.C. He, Hegesias, and Theodorus 'the godless' became leaders of three divergent branches of the school, his own originality consisting, so far as we know, in stressing the importance of sympathetic pleasure.

Bibliography, s.v. CYRENAICS. W. D. R.

**ANNONA,** the Roman corn supply. Under the Republic, although there was a free market, the Senate maintained a general supervision, forbidding speculation and in a famine authorizing subsidized distribution. At least from 299 B.C., the aediles (q.v.) were in general charge of this. The quaestor (q.v.) at Ostia organized imports to the capital and the Senate watched his efficiency (*see* SATURNINUS 1). In emergencies other magistrates (e.g. praetors: Asc., *Corn.* 59) might have to act and special *curatores* (e.g. M. Scaurus (q.v. 1) about 104 B.C.) could be appointed. Nevertheless shortages were frequent. Most of the imports came from Sicily and Sardinia.

Gaius Gracchus (q.v. 4) first passed a *lex frumentaria*, offering fixed quantities of grain to each citizen at a subsidized price. Other Populares lowered the price, until Clodius (q.v. 1) made distributions free. A shortage in 57 led to Pompey's *cura annonae* with unprecedented powers. Caesar (q.v. 1) created two new aediles (*Ceriales*) to manage the whole organization and limited recipients of free grain to 150,000.

Augustus, after a famine, accepted a *cura annonae* in 22 B.C., raised the figure of recipients to 200,000 and put distributions under a board of prefects. Later he appointed an equestrian *praefectus annonae*—who became one of the highest equestrian officers—to organize supplies. By the time of Trajan there was a *fiscus frumentarius*. Claudius strengthened and expanded the *Annona* office, put an official in charge of Ostia, and offered encouragement to importers of grain. Large numbers of inscriptions to numerous grades of officials attest the size and elaborate organization of the office. Most of the grain was imported from Egypt and Africa, and imports were recognized as the Emperor's responsibility. The cities of Italy and the provinces looked after their own supplies, usually through special officials; but government help was often given in times of famine, and numerous local dignitaries are honoured for similar services.

Armies, under the Republic, were supplied by requisition and (chiefly) by compulsory purchases in the provinces. Under the Empire, similar methods were commonly used, but the organization of supplies was the Emperor's responsibility. Legionaries (but, after Nero, not the Praetorian Guard) had part of their wages withheld to pay for their provisions. Under Septimius Severus (q.v. 1) continued inflation (and the Emperor's dependence on the army) led to the legions' receiving their food free. The consequence of this was the *annona militaris*— an additional tax (in kind) imposed on Italy and the provinces at first exceptionally, but before long regularly (*see* INDICTIO), and the word 'annona' henceforth chiefly means this tax. The *mansiones* of the Postal Service (q.v.) were extended to store the produce received, which was generally collected by the soldiers in charge of the service

and managed by an *actuarius*. The chief effect, apart from the heavy burden on the provincials, was to increase the army's independence and the autonomy of provincial forces.

Annona often appears as a goddess on imperial coins with attributes connected with coins and ships.

*PW*, s.v. 'Annona', 'Frumentum'. D. van Berchem, *L'Annona militaire dans l'Empire romain au III* siècle (1937), *Les Distribution de blé et d'argent* (1939). E. B

**ANONYMUS** Ἀντατπικιστής, a contemporary opponent of Phrynichus (q.v. 3) the Atticist, who cites from good, but not always Attic, writers many words condemned by Phrynichus. *See* LEXICA SEGUERIANA.

**ANONYMUS SEGUERIANUS** (3rd c. A.D.) wrote a τέχνη τοῦ πολιτικοῦ λόγου, including references to the work of Alexander (q.v. 12), son of Numenius, which throw light on first-century rhetorical teaching.

Spengel, *Rhet.* i. 427–60; D. Matthes, *Lustrum* 1959, 76 ff.

**ANSER** (1st c. B.C.), a salacious erotic poet. Nothing remains of his poems. The only unequivocal reference to him is in Ovid (*Tr.* 2. 435).

R. Unger, *De Ansere Poeta* (1858); Schanz–Hosius, § 246.

**ANTAEUS** (Ἀνταῖος), in mythology, a giant, son of Poseidon and Earth, living in Libya; he compelled all comers to wrestle with him and killed them when overcome (Pind. *Isthm.* 4. 56 ff. and schol. Plato, *Tht.* 169 b). He was defeated and killed by Heracles (q.v.). That he was made stronger when thrown, by contact with his mother the Earth (Apollod. 2. 115), seems a later addition to the story. H. J. R.

**ANTAGORAS OF RHODES** (3rd c. B.C.), author of a *Thebais*, epigrams, and a *Hymn to Love*.

**ANTALCIDAS** (more correctly *Antialcidas*) (fl. 4th c. B.C.), Spartan agent and general, converted first Tiribazus (392 B.C.) and later Artaxerxes II (388) to the view that Persia had greater identity of interest with Sparta than with Athens. Having negotiated a Sparto-Persian alliance, he blockaded the Hellespont and forced Athens, and her allies, to agree to the peace which bears his name (386). Its terms abandoned the Greek cities of Asia Minor to Persia (Xen. *Hell.* 5. 1. 32–6). He undertook further diplomatic missions to Persia in 372 and 367, the second of which was a disastrous failure and may have occasioned his death by suicide. D. E. W. W.

T. T. B. Ryder, *Koine Eirene* (1965), 28 ff.

**ANTENOR** (1), in mythology, an elderly and upright counsellor in Troy during the siege, who advised the return of Helen to the Greeks, and in return for this (or, according to much later accounts, for betraying the city) was spared by the victors. Pindar says his descendants held Cyrene; but in the story current in Roman times he took with him the Eneti from Paphlagonia (who had lost their king at Troy) and, settling in Venetia at the head of the Adriatic, founded Patavium. R. A. B. M.

**ANTENOR** (2), Athenian sculptor, active *c.* 540–500 B.C. He made the first group of the tyrannicides Harmodius and Aristogiton (*see* CRITIUS). It was taken to Persia in 480, but restored to Athens by Seleucus I, or Antiochus I Soter, or Alexander the Great, and then stood, together with the group by Critius, in the Agora. Two signed bases by Antenor have been found on the Acropolis of Athens. One of them was dedicated by the potter Nearchus and supported the most imposing of the Maidens of the Acropolis (no. 681). A certain similarity to the Maidens on the east pediment of the temple of Apollo at Delphi has suggested to some the attribution of that pediment to Antenor.  S. C.; G. M. A. R.

**ANTHEMIUS,** Western Roman Emperor (A.D. 467–72), was the son-in-law of the Eastern Emperor Marcian and was elevated in order to combat the Vandals of Africa. A Greek and a philosopher, he was unpopular in Italy. In 472 Ricimer (q.v.) besieged him in Rome, where his forces were defeated and he himself beheaded. Sidonius Apollinaris addressed a Panegyric to him.  E. A. T.

**ANTHESTERIA,** the festival of the flowers, celebrated in the spring, in Athens on the 12th Anthesterion (Feb.–Mar.) and (as the frequent occurrence of the month name Anthesterion shows) in many other Ionian towns. The day before had its name, Pithoegia, from the opening of the wine-jars. The festival had two aspects, on the one hand that of merriment and rejoicing and, on the other, that of gloom. On the chief day, the 12th, the new wine was ceremonially blessed before Dionysus; everyone carried in wine and drank of his own jug, cf. Eur., *IT* 949–60; hence this day was called Χόες, the Jugs. A drinking contest was held. Small children were admitted to the festival and given little jugs; it was a school holiday. On the same day Dionysus was brought in on a ship set on wheels and married the wife of the (Archon-) Basileus, and in the evening, which according to religious reckoning belonged to the 13th, called the Χύτροι, pots with cooked fruits were brought to the dead and Hermes Chthonios. At the close of the All-Souls-festival the spirits were expelled with the cry: Θύραζε, κῆρες, οὐκέτ' Ἀνθεστήρια (cf. J. ter Vrugt-Lentz, *Mnemos.* 1962, 238 ff.).

Nilsson, *GGR* i², 594 ff.; L. Deubner, *Att. Feste* (1932), 93 ff.; G. van Hoorn, *Choes and Anthesteria* (1951); A. W. Pickard-Cambridge, *Dramatic Festivals of Athens*² (1967), 1 ff.  M. P. N.; J. H. C.

**ANTHIMUS** was a Greek doctor attached to the court of the Emperor Zeno (A.D. 474–91) who was involved in treasonable relations with the Ostrogothic king Theoderic Strabo in 481. He fled Roman territory and took refuge in Italy at the court of Theoderic the Great, who later sent him on a diplomatic mission to the Franks. He wrote some time after 511 a short Latin handbook of dietetics—*De observatione ciborum ad Theodoricum regem Francorum epistula*. The interest of this curious text, half medical textbook, half cookery book, is twofold: first, it provides a detailed and vivid picture of the eating and drinking habits of a Germanic people of the Völkerwanderung: beer and mead are drunk for pleasure, wine as a medicine; second, since Anthimus learnt his Latin from the lips of the common people and had no contact with the literary and grammatical tradition, the *De observatione ciborum* is a specimen of the popular Latin of late antiquity, deviating from classical norms in vocabulary, morphology, and syntax, and of great value to the Romance philologist.

Ed. E. Liechtenhan, *CML* 8 i; N. Groen, *Lexicon Anthimeum* (1926).  R. B.

**ANTHOLOGIA LATINA,** the title conventionally applied to a collection of poems made in Africa during the early sixth century A.D. It is composed partly of poems written by African poets during the Vandal occupation, partly of miscellaneous earlier pieces. The collection offers enormous variations of interest and literary quality: among much inferior work or outright rubbish are transmitted, for example, the *Pervigilium Veneris* (q.v.) and a number of shorter poems which in modern times have achieved the status of anthology pieces, such as the *De concubitu Martis et Veneris* of Reposianus (q.v.). It played an influential part in the development of

medieval Latin poetry. Much of the attention which has been devoted by modern scholars to the problems of the Anthology is due to the extremely interesting character of the chief MS., the seventh-century Codex Salmasianus (Parisinus lat. 10318), once the property of Claude de Saumaise (1588–1653).

The standard edition is that by A. Riese and F. Bücheler (2 vols., 1894, 1906); it contains much material having only an adventitious connexion with *A.L.* Some poems will be found in Duff, *Minor Lat. Poets.* Cf. also the useful introduction and bibliography in M. Rosenblum, *Luxorius* (1961).  E. J. K.

**ANTHOLOGY,** ἀνθολογία, 'bouquet', means a collection of poems, but was not so used until the Byzantine period. The greatest anthology of classical literature is the Palatine Anthology of Greek poetic epigrams (quoted as *Anth. Pal.*), so called because the only MS. was found in the Count Palatine's library at Heidelberg. From the fourth century B.C. onwards, many collections of poetic epigrams by individual poets or on special subjects were made, but these have been almost wholly lost. (For a fragment of one, arranged by subjects, see Page, *GLP,* 454–9; for a collection of one man's epigrams see Powell, *New Chapters III,* 187.) The first large critical anthology of which we know was the *Garland* collected about 80 B.C. by Meleager (q.v. 2). It contained Greek poems attributed to some fifty poets past and present, from Archilochus to Meleager himself. Most were in elegiac couplets; all were short, averaging eight lines. A scholiast asserts that Meleager arranged them alphabetically by the first letter of each poem, but modern critics believe he grouped them by authors and by subjects. About A.D. 40 Philippus (q.v. 7) of Thessalonica gathered a less abundant *Garland* of Greek epigrams written since Meleager. The poems are duller and more trivial: the Muses were now speaking Latin. During the reign of Hadrian, Straton (q.v. 3) of Sardis made a collection of epigrams on homosexuality, and the scholar Diogenianus produced an anthology perhaps devoted chiefly to convivial and satiric epigrams. About A.D. 568 the Byzantine poet and scholar Agathias (q.v.) compiled a seven-book *Circle* of new epigrams by his contemporaries and himself, which he arranged by subject. His metrical table of contents survives to show the scheme he followed (*Anth. Pal.* 4. 3. 113–33).

Not long before A.D. 900 Cephalas (q.v.) created a large, important, new anthology covering the whole history of the epigram. He used the collections of Meleager, Philippus, Straton, Diogenianus, Agathias, and others; and tried to arrange his material by subject, although he failed to carry out the plan consistently.

The anthology of Cephalas, and all those which preceded it, have been lost as wholes. However, many hundreds of the poems they contained have survived in two extant compilations.

About A.D. 980 an unknown Byzantine scholar (perhaps a group of scholars) made a large volume, which has come down to us in a unique MS., the Palatine Anthology. He based it on Cephalas' work, but he omitted some poems and added a great number of others. It contains some 3,700 epigrams, in fifteen books arranged thus: (1) pious epigrams by Christian poets; (2) a description (*see* EKPHRASIS) of the statues in one of the baths of Constantinople; (3) poems describing the sculptures in a Cyzican temple; (4) the poetic prefaces written by Meleager, Philippus, and Agathias for their anthologies; 5) love poems; (6) dedicatory poems for real or imaginary votive offerings; (7) epitaphs; (8) epitaphs and other poems by St. Gregory Nazianzen; (9) epideictic epigrams—displays of wit and imagination on curious facts, famous people, interesting works of art; (10) comments on life and morality; (11) convivial and satirical epigrams; (12) poems on homosexual love; (13) epigrams in unusual metres; (14) riddles and puzzles; (15) miscellaneous epigrams, including poems shaped like an axe and an egg.

Finally, the monk Planudes produced his own anthology of Greek epigrams, neatly arranged in seven books with complex subdivisions. It is not known what sources he used: certainly the collection of Cephalas; probably two others closely resembling the Palatine Anthology. He cut out many fine poems and bowdlerized some which he thought impure, but he included nearly 400 epigrams which are not in the Palatine MS.; in modern editions these are printed as 'Book 16' of the Greek Anthology. The result, called the Planudean Anthology, has survived in Planudes' own autograph (now in Venice, dated 1301, perhaps a mistake for 1299): it was the first collection of Greek epigrams to be printed (1494) and the only one known until the Palatine Anthology emerged from obscurity (1606), to supersede it.

The Greek Anthology is a mine of jewels choked with masses of lumber. Books 1, 2, 3, 8, 14 have little but historical interest; Books 4, 12, 13, 15 are curious, often fascinating; the remaining books contain some trivialities and some of the finest short poems in the world. (*See* EPIGRAM.)

TEXTS. F. Jacobs (1794–1814: still contains useful information); F. Dübner (1871–88: uncritical); H. Stadtmüller, 1–6 (1894), 7 (1899), 9. 1–563 (1906) (hypercritical); W. R. Paton (with English translations, 5 vols, 1916–18); P. Waltz and others (with introductions, French translations, notes, and indexes) 1–4 (1928); 5 (1928); 6 (1931); 7. 1–363 (1938); 9. 1–358 (1957); H. Beckby (with introductions, German verse translations, notes, bibliography, copious indexes, 4 vols, 1957–8).
STUDIES. R. Weisshäupl, *Die Grabgedichte der griechischen Anthologie* (1889); P. Sakolowski, *De Anth. Pal. quaestiones* (Leipzig, 1893); W. Rasche, *De Anth. Graecae epigrammatis quae colloqui formam habent* (Münster,1910); P. Kägi, *Nachwirkungen der älteren griech. Elegie in den Epigrammen der Anth.* (1917); Cichorius, *Röm. Stud.*, ch. 8; B. Stumpo, 'L'epigramma d'amore a Costantinopoli nel secolo VI d.C.', *Rend. Ist. Lomb.* 1924, 241 ff.; A. Wifstrand, *Studien zur griech. Anth.* (1926); P. Waltz, 'L'Anthologie grecque', *Bull. de l'Assoc. Guillaume Budé*, July 1928, 3 ff.; L. A. Stella, *Cinque poeti dell'Antologia Palatina* (1949); G. Luck, 'Die Dichterinnen der griech. Anthologie', *MH* 1954, 170 ff.; A. S. F. Gow, *The Greek Anthology: Sources and Ascriptions* (1958); A. S. F. Gow and D. L. Page, *Hellenistic Epigrams*, 2 vols. (1965) and *The Greek Anthology: The Garden of Philip*, 2 vols. (1968).                    G. H.

**ANTICĂTO or ANTICĂTONES** (Schanz–Hosius[4] i. 334 ff.), two (?) lost books by Caesar (A. Dyroff, *Rh. Mus.* 1895, 481 ff., thinks one by Hirtius) answering eulogies on Cato, whose death at Utica occasioned laudatory discourses on republican heroes by Cicero, Brutus, and Fadius Gallus.                    J. W. D.

**ANTICLEA** (Ἀντίκλεια), in mythology, daughter of Autolycus (q.v. 1), wife of Laertes, and mother of Odysseus (*Od.* 11.84–5). Later (as Sophocles, *Phil.* 417 and schol.) Odysseus' real father is Sisyphus (q.v.).    H. J. R.

**ANTICLEIDES** of Athens (fl. early 3rd c. B.C.) wrote a history of Alexander (containing a long digression on Egyptian antiquities), a substantial mythological work, *Nostoi*, reaching into historical times, perhaps as far as Pisistratus, and an account of Delian antiquities. He favoured unusual versions and rationalizations of legends (like the Atthidographers and Palaephatus) and invented romantic details of the Trojan War; some fragments show Peripatetic influence.

FGrH 140; Pearson, *Lost Histories of Alexander* 251 ff.
                    F. W. W.

**ANTICYRA,** Phocian town at the head of the gulf east of Cirrha. An excellent port and outlet for Phocian export, it shared the history of Phocis, being destroyed in 346 B.C. and captured by Roman generals. It gained a reputation from the medicinal plant hellebore (supposed to cure madness), which grew in its neighbourhood.

Le Lerat *Rev. Phil.* 1945, 12 ff.                    N. G. L. H.

**ANTIDORUS** (*c.* 300 B.C.) of Cyme was the first to abandon the name κριτικός and to call himself γραμματικό (Clem. Al. *Strom.* 1. 16. 79). He wrote a work on Home and Hesiod, of which the form and content are unknown and a treatise on λέξις, which was either a lexical study perhaps of Homeric expressions, or a work on styl (schol. Dion. Thrax, 3, 7, 448 H.; schol. *Il.* 23. 638–9)
                    J. F. L.

**ANTIDOSIS.** An Athenian who had been put to liturgy (q.v.) had a right to refuse it, by asking, at an officially fixed date, another wealthy citizen either to perform it in his stead or to agree to an exchange of properties (ἀντίδοσις). If the other citizen rejected this offer, a court decided which of them should perform the liturgy. Both parties had to divulge their whole estate on oath, three days after they had formally laid claim to their opponent's possessions before the magistrates. Only shares in the mines of Laurium had not to be declared because they were free from liturgy obligations.

A. M. Andreades, *History of Greek Public Finance* (1933), 283 ff. G. Busolt–H. Swoboda, *Griechische Staatskunde* i, ii (1920–6) M. I. Finley, *Land and Credit in Ancient Athens* (1951); H. Francotte *L'Antidosis en droit athénien* (1895); LSJ s.v.; Michell, *Econom. Anc Gr.* Index.                    F. M. H

**ANTIGENES** (5th c. B.C.), Attic dithyrambic poet, who wrote a dedicatory poem for tripods won at the Dionysia competition by the Acamantis tribe. The poem, preserved at *Anth. Pal.* 13. 28, is written in couplets, the first line of which is a dactylic tetrameter followed by a trochaic dipody, the second an iambic tripody followed by an alcaic decasyllable. Nothing else is known of him or his work.

TEXT. Diehl, *Anth. Lyr. Graec.* ii. 119.
CRITICISM. U. von Wilamowitz-Moellendorff, *Sappho und Simonides* (1913), 218 ff.                    C. M. B

**ANTIGONE** (1). In the versions of the legend of Oedipus (q.v.) best known to us, he and Iocasta have four children, Eteocles, Polynices, Antigone, and Ismene though Homer (*Od.* 11. 271 ff.) and the Cyclic epic *Oedipodia* (see Paus. 9. 5. 11) know nothing of offspring of the incest and the latter makes Euryganeia daughter of Hyperphas the mother of his children. Of these four the two sons are part of the story from the cyclic *Thebai* onwards; the daughters seem to be a later addition, or at least are unimportant until the fifth century B.C. The earliest certain mention of either appears to be Mimnermus fr. 21 Bergk, from which, combined with Phocylides ap. schol. Eur. *Phoen.* 53, it appears that Ismene was 'in converse with Theoclymenus' (unknown in such a context, perhaps a mistake for Periclymenus, one of the Theban heroes) and was killed by Tydeus (q.v.) at the instance of Athena by the spring which bears her name, i.e. the source of the river Ismenus. Ion of Chios (fr. 12 Bergk; both this and the passage of Mimnermus are from Sallustius' argument to the *Antigone*) said that both sisters were burned in the temple of Hera by Laodamas son of Eteocles, an otherwise unknown tale. Also, in the older stories neither the affair of the burial of Polynices nor the banishment of Oedipus is told. We have then a legend apparently of fifth-century Attic growth, whether pure invention or founded on some local tradition.

Omitting the spurious termination of the *Septem* of Aeschylus (see discussion by P. Groeneboom, *Aeschylus' Zeven tegen Thebe* (1938), 245 ff.), our materials are the *OT*, *OC*, and *Antigone* of Sophocles and the fragments of Euripides, *Antigone*, with their derivatives. Taking the Sophoclean plays in the order of events in the story, not of their composition, in *OT* 1480 ff. Oedipus takes farewell of his children and commends them to the fatherly care of Creon; they are mute figures. In *OC* he s a wandering beggar, faithfully tended by Antigone. Ismene, here as elsewhere the less resolute character, remains at Thebes, but comes to Colonus (324 ff.) to bring them news of happenings there. Creon, whose character has deteriorated in this play, kidnaps both sisters in an attempt to force Oedipus to return, but is himself taken by Theseus and the girls rescued (818–1096). Antigone advises Oedipus to grant Polynices an interview (1181 ff.), and vainly begs her brother to abandon the attempt on Thebes (1414 ff.); they address each other in terms of deep affection. In the *Antigone* Creon has forbidden Polynices to be buried after his and Eteocles' death at each other's hands (23 ff.); Antigone resolves to bury him despite this. Ismene is horrified, and will not do more than keep her secret (85). Antigone contemptuously casts her off and later (536 ff.) will have none of her attempts to confess herself a confederate. The attempt to give Polynices at least the formal minimum of burial succeeds (245 ff.), but later (407 ff.) Antigone is arrested while coming to pour libation and replace the dust which had been swept from the body. Creon now sentences her to be placed alive in a vault, despite the protestations of his son Haemon who is betrothed to her (635 ff.). In this he is doubly wrong, for it is impious to put a living person into the underground realm of Hades, and it is Antigone's betrothed husband who should deal with her (P. Roussel in *Rev. Ét. Grec.* 1922, 63 ff.; Rose in *CQ* 1925, 147 ff.). Tiresias warns him (988 ff.) that he is offending the gods by leaving dead bodies unburied; he sets out (1095 ff.) to bury Polynices and rescue Antigone, but finds her already dead by her own hand; Haemon kills himself over her body and Creon's queen Eurydice stabs herself from grief (1183 ff.).

Euripides, possibly using some tradition of the existence of descendants of Antigone, modified Sophocles' story; his play being lost, we have to reconstruct the plot chiefly from Hyginus (*Fab.* 72, which is not an accurate synopsis, see C. Robert, *Oidipus* (1915), 381 ff.; Rose, *Modern Methods in Class. mythology* (1930), 40 ff.; J. Mesk in *Wien. Stud.* 1933, 1 ff.). Creon, acting more correctly than in Sophocles, handed over Antigone, when taken, to Haemon to be put to death. He, instead of doing so, hid her among shepherds, and had a son by her. The child lived, grew, and came to Thebes on the occasion of certain games. Since he naturally competed naked, Greek fashion, Creon recognized him as one of his own race, the Sparti, because he had on his body the peculiar birthmark like a spear-head which all that family bore Hyg. *Fab.* 72. 3; Arist. *Poet.* 1454ᵇ22, very likely from this play). He denounced the young man as a bastard (fr. 168 Nauck) and ordered the deaths, apparently, of Haemon and Antigone. Hereupon, according to Hyginus 72. 3) Heracles vainly interceded; fr. 177 is an apostrophe to Dionysus, and Aristophanes' argument to Sophocles' *Antigone* says that Antigone was 'given in marriage' to Haemon, from which, together with general probability, it seems likely that Dionysus was the intercessor (if indeed the quotation is not from the *Antiope*) and the play ended with a reconciliation and formal union of the lovers.

The story in Hyginus is itself evidence that some development took place in the legend after Euripides, possibly at the hands of the fourth-century tragedians (so Mesk). One additional detail, of unknown date of origin, is the appearance of Argia, wife of Polynices, to help Antigone bury him (Hyginus 72. 1; Statius, *Theb.* 12. 177 ff.); she meets Antigone by moonlight; they put Polynices' body on Eteocles' still burning pyre, the flames of which divide (cf. ETEOCLES 2); they are taken and sentenced to death by Creon, but rescued by the arrival of the Attic army under Theseus.

Although the above stories are not of Theban origin, they had been adopted in Thebes by imperial times.

Pausanias was shown (9. 25. 2) a place outside the walls called σύρμα Ἀντιγόνης, 'Antigone's drag', said to be the spot where she dragged the body of Polynices, as it was too heavy for her to lift, to lay it on the pyre of Eteocles (see above; this suggests that the legend was popularized there in a rather late form). It was one of several alleged monuments of the mythical past of the city, doubtless rather a by-product of the tourist trade than the result of a real tradition.

See material collected briefly in Jebb's introduction to his edition of Sophocles, *Antigone*; more in Stoll's arts. 'Antigone' and 'Ismene' in Roscher's *Lexikon*.                    H. J. R.

**ANTIGONE** (2), in mythology, daughter of Eurytion son of Actor, king of Phthia. Peleus (q.v.) was purified by her father after the murder of Phocus (*see* AEACUS) and married her, with a third of the country for her dowry. Later he accidentally killed Eurytion at the Calydonian boar-hunt and fled to Iolcus (Apollod. 3. 163).    H. J. R.

**ANTIGONE** (3), in mythology, daughter of Laomedon, king of Troy. Because she vied in beauty with Hera, the latter turned her hair into snakes; afterwards she, or the other gods, turned her into a stork, which therefore preys on snakes (Ovid, *Met.* 6. 93–95; Servius on *Aen.* 1. 27; *Myth. Vat.* 1. 179).    H. J. R.

**ANTIGONUS** (1) **I** (probably 382–301 B.C.), 'Monophthalmus' son of Philip, a Macedonian noble, first appears holding a command in Alexander's army (334). He was left as satrap of Phrygia (333). In Alexander's lifetime he did useful work in Asia Minor, but he gave no indication of his future greatness. His opportunity came when his friend Antipater (q.v. 1) gave him command over the royal army in Asia (321). His successful campaigns against the 'rebels' Alcetas (320) and Eumenes (320 and 318–316), and the death of Antipater (319), gave Antigonus, alone of the generals, a prospect of reuniting all Alexander's Empire under himself, and this became his unceasing aim. The result was a coalition of the 'separatist' generals against him (Cassander in Macedonia, Ptolemy in Egypt, and Lysimachus in Thrace), but the war (315–311) left him as strong as before, though the occupation of Babylon and the eastern satrapies by Seleucus (312) greatly reduced the area he controlled. The peace of 311 lasted only a year, and his separate attempts to crush Seleucus (310–309), Ptolemy (306–305), and Cassander (304–302) finally convinced them all (with Lysimachus) that Antigonus himself (he had assumed the royal title in 306) must be crushed. In the decisive battle of Ipsus (in Phrygia) he was defeated and killed. Of his kingdom little is known. He is said to have governed well, and he certainly showed statesmanship in his policy towards the Greeks. His reputation rests on his greatness as a general, but in an age of peace he would probably have been a great ruler, and certainly could never have been a bad one.

Diodorus bks. 18–20; Plutarch, *Eumenes and Demetrius*; Berve *Alexanderreich* ii. no. 87; Bengtson, *Strategie* i (1937), 96 ff.
                    G. T. G.

**ANTIGONUS** (2) **II** (c. 320–239 B.C.), surnamed *Gonatas* (Euseb. 1. 238; meaning unknown), son of Demetrius I and Phila, was in charge of Demetrius' Greek possessions after 287. In 285, having lost much of Thessaly to Pyrrhus, he made peace; on Demetrius' death (284/3) he took the title of king. In 280 he marched on Macedon, but was repelled; Sparta meanwhile stirred up revolts in Greece. After a naval campaign he made a lasting peace with Syria (278); and having defeated 20,000 Gauls near Lysimacheia, he seized Macedonia. For ten months Cassandreia resisted, but by 276, when he married Antiochus' sister, Phila, he was acknowledged king of

Macedon. When in 274 Pyrrhus, back from Italy, attacked Macedon, many Macedonians deserted; Antigonus suffered defeats (274/3) and lost Thessaly and upper Macedonia. In 272, however, Pyrrhus invaded Peloponnesus, and Antigonus joined with Sparta to destroy him. He now re-established his power as far as Corinth. Shortly afterwards, subsidized by Egypt, Athens and Sparta began the Chremonidean War against him (probably 267–263/2), which ended with the fall of Athens. After a short-lived truce (261), in alliance with Antiochus II he resumed the war against Ptolemy, but made a separate peace in 255. Whether his naval victory off Cos, which secured him the Aegean, belongs to this or the Chremonidean War is uncertain. In 250/49, instigated by Egypt, Alexander, his governor of Corinth, revolted, and held Corinth with Chalcis until his death. But after defeating Ptolemy at sea off Andros (246), Antigonus tricked Alexander's widow, Nicaea, out of Acrocorinth (245). This fortress, however, Aratus seized in 243, and Antigonus' subsequent Aetolian alliance proved fruitless; to this period belongs his patronage of Peloponnesian tyrants. In 241/40 he made peace with Achaea, and died in spring 239.

Blunt, honest, and tenacious, Antigonus won not only Macedon, but also its people. Himself a philosopher, he gathered about him poets, philosophers, and historians; and his long reign, despite vicissitudes, re-established Macedon as a nation.

ANCIENT SOURCES. Plut. *Demetr.*, *Pyrrh.*, *Arat.*; Justin bks. 16 ff. For the early years the tradition echoes Hieronymus of Cardia, for the later the pro-Spartan Phylarchus. Inscriptions important. MODERN LITERATURE. W. W. Tarn, *Antigonos Gonatas* (1913); W. Fellmann, *Antigonos Gonatas . . . und die griechischen Staaten* (1930); C. F. Edson, *CPhil.* 1934. F. W. W.

**ANTIGONUS** (3) **III** (*c.* 263–221 B.C.), surnamed *Doson*, son of Demetrius the Fair (who was half-brother of Antigonus II), became guardian to Philip V on Demetrius II's death (229) and married Philip's mother Phthia (Chryseis). After expelling a Dardanian inroad he recovered most of Thessaly from invading Aetolians, but made an agreement leaving them Phthiotic Achaea, and renounced the re-establishment of Macedonian influence beyond Thermopylae. Early in 227, as sequel to a threatened mutiny by the army assembly, he took the title of king. An expedition to Caria in 227 was probably directed against Ptolemy: it brought acquisitions in the Aegean, alliances in Crete, and gains in Caria; but the islands generally remained independent, and Macedonian sea-power now rapidly decayed. Meanwhile the Achaean Confederacy was crumbling before Cleomenes; in 227/26 Antigonus received Achaean envoys favourably, and in 224, on Aratus' promise of Acrocorinth, he led his troops to the Isthmus. In two campaigns he recovered Arcadia, and in winter 224 set up a league of the allies, with himself as president. In 222 he crushed Cleomenes at Sellasia and occupied Sparta. But immediately he was summoned to expel the Illyrians from Macedon; having burst a blood-vessel in battle, he died in summer 221, after providing for Philip's succession.

The Achaean alliance and the Hellenic League stamp Antigonus as a statesman of generous vision. His policy mainly followed traditional lines; but his rehabilitation of Macedon gave it new life and a strong material background for Philip's wilder policies.

ANCIENT SOURCES. Polyb. 2; Plut. *Cleom.*, *Arat.* Justin bk. 28. MODERN LITERATURE. W. W. Tarn, 'Phthia-Chryseis', *Athenian Studies presented to W. S. Ferguson* (U.S.A. 1940), 483 ff.; P. Treves, *Athenaeum*, 1934–5; S. Dow and C. F. Edson, *Harv. Stud.* 1937; J. V. A. Fine, *AJPhil.* 1940; Maria T. Piraino, *Antigono Dosone re di Macedonia* (1954). F. W. W.

**ANTIGONUS** (4) of Carystus (fl. 240 B.C.), bronze-worker and writer, lived at Athens in touch with the Academy; worked under Attalus I at Pergamum.

WORKS. An inferior anecdotal collection survives: (1 Ἱστοριῶν παραδόξων συναγωγή (*Rer. Nat. scr. Graec. Min* i. 8 f.); Diog. Laert. and Athenaeus contain fragment from (2) *Lives of Philosophers*, personal character-sketche of contemporaries; (3) various works of art-history (4) Περὶ λέξεως (Ath. 3. 88 a; 7. 297 a; probably thi Antigonus).

A reliable biographer with a flowing, periodic style Antigonus achieved considerable popularity. He helpe to make the statues which celebrated Attalus' Galli victory.

U. von Wilamowitz-Moellendorff, *A. v. Karystos* (1881); Hansen *Attalids*, 360 ff. F. W. W.

**ANTILOCHUS**, in mythology, son of Nestor (q.v. 1) mentioned several times in the *Iliad* as a brave warrio and a fine runner (e.g. 15. 569–70). He brings Achille the news of Patroclus' death (18. 2 ff.), drives cleverly i the chariot-race (23. 402 ff.), and courteously cedes th second prize to Menelaus (596). His death is mentione (*Od.* 3. 111); it took place (*Aethiopis*, whence Pindar *Pyth.* 6. 28 ff.) while he was defending his father agains Memnon, when Paris had killed one of Nestor's horse and he called Antilochus to his help. H. J. R

**ANTIMACHUS** (probably b. *c.* 444), of Colophon poet and scholar. It is possible that he competed in poetic contest at the Lysandreia in Samos before Lysan der (died 395), cf. Plut. *Lys.* 18. 8. Further, the evidenc of Hermesianax, fr. 7, 41–46 and [Plutarch], *Cons. a Apoll.* 9. 106 b may be accepted that he loved one Lyd (probably his mistress, not his wife), and wrote hi narrative elegy with that title, a collection of 'heroi misfortunes', to console himself for her loss. Finally Heraclides Ponticus (fr. 91 Voss) records that Plato sen Heraclides to Colophon to collect Antimachus' poems. I is, therefore, probable that Antimachus died fairly earl in the fourth century B.C.

WORKS. Our sources mention five poems: *Thebai Lyde*, *Deltoi*, *Artemis*, *Iachine* (?). The *Thebais* was ar epic narrating the first expedition against Thebes. Fo his material Antimachus probably drew not only on th Epic Cycle but also on lyric and tragic versions of th story of Thebes. The *Lyde* comprised at least two book probably considerably more in view of Antimachus reputation for prolixity, which the fragments detailin the voyage of the *Argo* seem to justify. Other legend mentioned included those of Demeter's wanderings Bellerophon, and Oedipus. It is clear that except for th metre there was very little that was elegiac about th *Lyde*. Though it is possible that the poem contained preface in which Antimachus explained the circumstance that had produced it, there is no evidence that once em barked he turned aside from his narration of 'heroic mis fortunes' to bewail his own. The laments which accordin to Hermesianax filled the poem must have been those o the heroes and heroines. Though others, e.g. Mimnermus had inserted references to myth into their elegies, Anti machus was the real founder of Narrative Elegy an found many imitators. The *Deltoi* (? *Tablets*) was perhap a collection of short poems (? in elegiacs). The *Artemis* if the first part of *PMilan.* 17 contains excerpts from thi poem, was written in hexameters and its careful re cording of the goddess's titles and cults recalls the *Hym to Artemis* of Callimachus.

Later writers praised Antimachus for his sobriety an virility (cf. Asclepiades, *Anth. Pal.* 9. 63 and Poseidippus *Anth. Pal.* 12. 168), qualities which perhaps explai Plato's liking for his verse. But Callimachus (fr. 589 ff. found him stodgy and involved. What little survive seems to justify the more unfavourable verdict. Bu Antimachus' real importance is that as a scholar (h dited Homer) no less than poet he anticipated by some oo years the scholar-poets of Alexandria. Unlike his ost-Cyclic predecessors, Pisander and Panyassis, he not nly borrowed without change from early Epic, but also ractised all the arts of 'interpretation', variation, and ontamination which were to become so popular with the Iellenistic poets, and not least with Callimachus. In anguage, too, Antimachus anticipates the Alexandrians. The scanty fragments contain many 'glosses', neologisms, nd obscure periphrases.

TEXT. B. Wyss, *Antimachi Colophonii Reliquiae* (1936); Diehl, *Anth. Lyr. Graec.* i³, 100 f.; for *PMilan.* 17 see also A. Vogliano, *Papiri della R. Università di Milano* i (1937) 41 ff.; Del Corno, *Acme* 962; G. Wentzel, 'Antimachos (24)' in *PW* i. 2433–6; J. Trüb, *Kataloge in der griech Dichtung* (1952) 74 f.; on Callimachus' polemic gainst A. see M. Puelma, *Philol.* 1957, 90 f. E. A. B.

**ANTINOÖPOLIS** (*Sheikh Abâdeh*), in Middle Egypt, ounded in A.D. 130 by Hadrian in memory of Antinous q.v. 2), stood east of the Nile at the head of a new road o the Red Sea. Its constitution was Greek, modelled on hat of Naucratis, with special privileges; hellenized nhabitants were brought, e.g., from Ptolemais; it was also he metropolis of an Egyptian nome. After Diocletian it was the administrative centre of the Thebaid. Considerable remains of public buildings existed in 1800, but have been destroyed. The cemeteries were excavated by Gayet, the mounds explored for papyri by Johnson.

E. Jomard, *Description de l'Égypte, Antiquités*, ch. 15, pls. 53–61; E. Kühn, *Antinoöpolis* (1913); J. Johnson, 'Antinoë and its papyri' *JEg. Arch.* 1914); H. I. Bell, *JRS* 1940, 133 ff.; P. V. Pistorius, *Indices Antinoopolitani* (1939). J. G. M.

**ANTINOUS** (1), in mythology, chief of Penelope's suitors, son of Eupeithes (*Od.* 1. 383); killed by Odysseus 22. 8 ff.).

**ANTINOUS** (2, *PW* 5) was born probably between A.D. 110–12 at Bithynium ( = Claudiopolis) in Bithynia. His beauty and grace made him Hadrian's (q.v.) favourite. While accompanying the Emperor up the Nile in 130, he was drowned and contemporary gossip surrounded his death with romantic legend; some even said that he had given his life for his master. At Hadrian's instance, he was deified by many communities, and in Egypt Hadrian commemorated him by founding a new city called Antinoöpolis (q.v.); elsewhere he was honoured by cult, festivals, and statues.

B. W. Henderson, *Hadrian etc.* (1923), 130 ff.; C. W. Clairmont, *Die Bildnisse des Antinous* (1967); M. Yourcenar, *Hadrian's Memoirs* (rev. ed., 1963), 301 ff. C. H. V. S.; M. H.

**ANTIOCH** (Ἀντιόχεια) (1), capital of Seleucid Syria, on the left bank of the Orontes, some 15 miles from the sea, was founded in 300 B.C. by Seleucus I, in a favourable position between his Anatolian and Eastern possessions, on the edge of a large and fertile plain. Seleucia, at the mouth of the Orontes, became its harbour. The king transferred thither the 5,300 Athenian and Macedonian settlers whom Antigonus had planted at Antigoneia nearby in 307, and his successors enlarged the city and adorned it with splendid buildings. Antioch also contained a large Jewish community, whose privileges were said to go back to Seleucus I. Since it was the royal capital, its people played a large part in the dynastic revolutions of the later Seleucid era. After an interlude of Armenian rule (83–66) it was annexed by Pompey (64) and became the capital of the province of Syria; it was made an autonomous city by Caesar (47). Having sided with Pescennius Niger it was in A.D. 194 degraded by Septimius Severus, but was in 201 restored to its former rank, to which Caracalla added the title of colony. Antioch ruled an extensive territory. It was the third city of the East, after Alexandria and Seleucia on the Tigris. Its

wealth was derived from its position on the great commercial road from Asia to the Mediterranean, and from the exploitation of natural resources like wine and olive-oil, extensively produced by its immediate hinterland. The city was ruined when the Persian and Arab invasions put an end to its agricultural activities and to free navigation in the Eastern Mediterranean. Under the late empire, it had enjoyed an intense intellectual life, and also became a centre of Eastern monasticism. Excavation has brought to light a wealth of late antique art.

K. O. Müller, *Antiquitates Antiochenae* (1839); G. W. Elderkin and R. Stillwell (eds.), *Antioch on the Orontes* i–iv (U.S.A., 1934–58); G. Downey, *History of Antioch* (1961); A. J. Festugière, *Antioche paîenne et chrétienne* (1959); G. Tchalenko, *Villages antiques de la Syrie du Nord* (1953–8). A. H. M. J.; H. S.

**ANTIOCH** (2) (Pisidian: Ἀντιόχεια Πισιδίας or more correctly πρὸς Πισιδίαν 'towards Pisidia'), a city in Phrygia (so Strabo, confirmed by inscriptions), lying near the Pisidian border, called 'the Pisidian' to distinguish it from the other Phrygian Antioch on the Maeander, and hence wrongly assigned to Pisidia by Pliny and others. It was a Seleucid foundation, settled by colonists from Magnesia-on-the-Maeander, occupying a plateau above the river Anthios (mentioned on its coins) close to the modern *Yalvaç*. It was declared free by the Romans after the defeat of Antiochus the Great, but passed under Roman control as part of the kingdom of Amyntas (see GALATIA) in 25 B.C., and about the same time was made a Roman colony with the name Caesarea Antiochia. The colony was linked by military roads with the other colonies subsequently founded by Augustus to control Pisidia. Near it was a wealthy *hieron* of Mên Askaênos with wide estates and numerous temple-serfs (*hierodouloi*, q. v.), the site of which has been excavated. In Diocletian's provincial reorganization Antioch was assigned to Pisidia.

Jones, *Cities E. Rom. Prov.* (see Index); B. Levick, *Roman Colonies in S. Asia Minor* (1967); *PW* Suppl. xi, 49 ff. W. M. C.

**ANTIOCH** (3) (*Margiana*, modern *Merv*) was founded apparently by Alexander, destroyed by Asiatics, and refounded by Antiochus I. Here in a mountain-girt fertile plain a land-route from Seleuceia branched, forming silk-routes, (i) through Samarkand, (ii) through Balkh, to central Asia; a third went south through Herat and the Bolan Pass to India.

Strabo 516; Pliny *HN* 6. 46–47. E. H. W.

**ANTIOCH-IN-PERSIS** (4), the *Ionaca polis* ('Greek-town') of Ptolemy 6. 4. 2, probably stood on the Gulf of Bushire, whence a road must have run up to Persepolis, as now to Shiraz. It was founded by Seleucus I and re-colonized and enlarged by Magnesia-on-the-Maeander for Antiochus I (*OGI* 233). It was a Greek city, with Council, Assembly, and Prytanies, i.e. division into tribes; it worshipped the gods of Magnesia, and was the local centre for the official cult of the Seleucid dynasty.
W. W. T.

**ANTIOCHUS** (1) I (SOTER) (324–261 B.C.), son of Seleucus I (q.v.) and the Bactrian Apama. He ruled the eastern Seleucid territories from 293/2, and took over Seleucus' young wife Stratonice (whether for romantic or political reasons). On his accession (281) he renounced his father's ambitions in the West, and his treaty (278) with Antigonus (q.v. 2) Gonatas formed the basis of peace and friendship with Macedonia throughout the century. Northern Asia Minor, and later much of its southern and western coast, slipped from his grasp, the latter being lost mainly to Egypt ('First Syrian War', 274–271, and war of 263–261). His chief exploit was his defeat of the Gallic invaders of Asia Minor (273?—'the Elephant Victory'), which earned him his cult-name

'Soter'. Of his personal character and internal policy little is known, except that he was the greatest founder of cities after Alexander (*see* COLONIZATION, HELLENISTIC). His elder son Seleucus became co-regent in the East (280), but proved a failure, and may even have been executed for treason.

W. W. Tarn, *CAH*. vii. 701 ff.                    G. T. G.

**ANTIOCHUS** (2) **II** (THEOS) (*c.* 287–246 B.C.), second son of Antiochus I and Stratonice. His reign (commencing 261) comprises the most obscure period of Seleucid history. Most of the known facts bear on his relations with Egypt, and show that, by the 'Second Syrian War' (260–253), in alliance with Macedonia, he recovered most of what Antiochus I had lost, namely the coast of Asia Minor (except Pergamum, Caria, and Lycia) and places in Coele Syria. His Egyptian marriage, however, (to Berenice, daughter of Ptolemy II, 252) and repudiation of Laodice (q.v. 2) with her children, created a 'succession question' which became acute on his death.

W. W. Tarn. *CAH* vii, 710 ff.                    G. T. G.

**ANTIOCHUS** (3) **III** ('the Great') (*c.* 242–187 B.C.), second son of Seleucus II (q.v.), succeeded (223) to a kingdom already reduced by separatist movements (Bactria and Parthia), which threatened to spread to Media, Persis, and Babylonia and to Asia Minor (*see* ACHAEUS 3). His aim from the first was to restore and expand. His first attempt to conquer Ptolemaic Syria and Palestine was foiled by a Ptolemaic victory at Raphia ('Fourth Syrian War' 219–216). But by his 'Anabasis' in the East (212–206) he acquired Armenia, and regained Parthia and Bactria, as vassal kingdoms; and his demonstrations in 'India' (Cabul valley) and 'Arabia' (across the Persian Gulf) earned him, like Alexander, the title of 'Great'.

But Antiochus' expansion policy was ruined by his failure to recognize the advent of a new Power in the eastern Mediterranean, Rome. His notorious secret treaty with Philip V of Macedonia to partition the overseas possessions of Egypt (202) was not directed against Rome; but the Senate, already suspicious of Philip, took alarm when Antiochus, after conquering Ptolemaic Syria and Palestine (202–198), invaded Europe to recover Thrace (196). In the protracted diplomatic exchange of 196–193 he and the Senate were at cross-purposes, and finally he lost patience and invaded Greece. He was defeated by the Romans in two land battles, at Thermopylae and Magnesia (ad Sipylum), and also lost a naval campaign to them. By the peace of Apamea (188), despite its seaboard the Seleucid Empire ceased to be a Mediterranean Power, though it remained a great continental Power in Asia. Despite these errors of judgement in dealing with Rome, the triumphs of his youth, his unfailing energy, and his high conception of the Seleucid task in Asia suggest that Antiochus really was a great man.

ANCIENT SOURCES. The most important is Polybius, directly in bks. 2–21, and indirectly in Livy bks. 30–8.
MODERN LITERATURE. M. Holleaux, *Rome, la Grèce, et les monarchies hellénistiques* (1921), and in *CAH* viii, chs. 6, 7; W. W. Tarn, ibid. vii. 723 ff.; H. H. Schmitt, *Untersuchungen zur Geschichte Antiochos' des Grossen und seiner Zeit* (1964).                    G. T. G.

**ANTIOCHUS** (4) **IV** (EPIPHANES) (*c.* 215–163 B.C.), third son of Antiochus III, became king in 175. The tradition about him is unfavourable, mainly because of his policy towards the Jews. He controlled Judaea firmly (if tactlessly), because it was strategically important as a frontier province; and he wished to hellenize the Jews, probably because he believed in hellenization as an instrument of rule. But the result, apparent only after his death, was to stimulate and revive Jewish nationalism. Despite his reputation for eccentricity, Antiochus was probably not a mere tyrant or trifler: his policy of urbanization,

especially in the East, represents a notable achievemen at this date. His Egyptian war (169/8), 'preventive' i motive, could certainly have achieved the annexation o Egypt, had Rome not intervened. Finally, the easter expedition, on which he met his death, shows that he wa alive to the nascent danger from Parthia.

E. R. Bevan, *CAH* viii, ch. 16; S. K. Eddy, *The King is Dead* (196 chs. 8 and 9.                    G. T. C

**ANTIOCHUS** (5) **V** (EUPATOR) (*c.* 173–162 B.C.), son o Antiochus IV, reigned less than two years through th regent Lysias, and was put to death in Antioch whe Demetrius I (q.v. 10) arrived from Rome to claim hi throne.                    G. T. G

**ANTIOCHUS** (6) **VI** (EPIPHANES DIONYSUS) (*c.* 148 138 B.C.), son of Alexander (q.v. 10) Balas and Cleopatr Thea (daughter of Ptolemy VI). In the revolt at Antioc against Demetrius II (q.v. 11) he was put forward by th general Diodotus (later called Tryphon) as heir to th throne formerly usurped by his father. Tryphon soo deposed (142) and later killed him (138).                    G. T. C

**ANTIOCHUS** (7) **VII** (SIDETES) (*c.* 159–129 B.C.), secon son of Demetrius I (q.v. 10) of Syria, succeeded hi brother Demetrius II, who had become a prisoner i Parthia (139). Able and energetic, he quickly defeate and killed the pretender Tryphon in Antioch (138) reconquered Palestine (135–134), and temporarily re covered Babylonia from Parthia (130). But his eventua defeat and death in battle against the Parthians brough about the final loss of the Seleucid provinces in the East

E. R. Bevan, *CAH* viii. 529 ff.                    G. T. C

**ANTIOCHUS** (8) (HIERAX) (*c.* 263–226 B.C.), second so of Antiochus II (q.v.) and Laodice, became independen ruler of Seleucid Asia Minor when his brother Seleucu II (q.v.) was occupied with the 'Third Syrian War' (246 241). He defeated Seleucus' attempt to recover Asi Minor ('War of the Brothers', *c.* 239–236), allying him self with traditional enemies of the Seleucid House Pontus, Bithynia, and Galatians, and marrying a Bithynia princess, daughter of Ziaelas and sister of Prusias I. Th Galatian alliance, however, embroiled him with the risin power of Attalus I of Pergamum, who drove him from Asia Minor (230–228). After an unsuccessful attempt t raise Syria and the East against Seleucus, he became a exile (227), and died by violence in Thrace.

W. W. Tarn, *CAH* vii. 720 ff.                    G. T. C

**ANTIOCHUS** (9), the name of some kings of COM MAGENE (q.v.):

**ANTIOCHUS I,** son of Mithridates and Laodic (daughter of Antiochus VIII Grypus of Syria), submitte to Pompey in 64 B.C. and received a strip of Mesopotami In the Civil War he sent troops to Pompey. Later h helped the Parthians; in 38 was besieged in Samosata b Ventidius and then by Antony who probably remove him and made his brother Mithridates king. Antiochu built a royal mausoleum for his father at Arsameia (q.v. 2 and a monumental tomb for himself on Mt. Taurus a Nimrud Dagh where stood a statue of the deified king o a terrace among seated gods of colossal size. The monu ment shows a blend of Iranian and Greek elements i both art and religious ideas.

For the monument see R. Ghirshman, *Iran* (1962), 57 ff. H. Dörri *Der Königskult des Antiochus von Kommagene* (1964).

**ANTIOCHUS II,** son of I, was perhaps installed a king by Octavian, but in 29 B.C. he was summoned t Rome and executed for having murdered an ambassado.

**ANTIOCHUS IV,** who enjoyed the friendship of the Emperor Gaius in Rome, was installed by him in Commagene in A.D. 38, but was deposed soon afterwards. Claudius restored his kingdom in 41 and he reigned until 72; the portrait of his wife (and sister ?) Iotape appears on some of his coinage. His son was betrothed to Drusilla, daughter of King Agrippa I (q.v. She later married Felix, q.v.). Antiochus protected Cilicia against the Cietae (52) and for services under Corbulo against the Parthians he received part of Armenia (60). In the Jewish revolt he helped Vespasian and Titus (69–70), but in 72 he was accused by Paetus of intriguing with Parthia and was deposed. He lived in internment in Sparta and Rome.

For the numismatic evidence of the extent of his kingdom see Magie, *Rom. Rule Asia Min.* 1367 f.  H. H. S.

**ANTIOCHUS** (10) of Syracuse, Greek logographer of the fifth century B.C., wrote a history of Sicily from the mythical Cocalus to 424 B.C., and a history of Italy. He wrote the latter certainly, and the former probably, in Ionic. *See* HISTORIOGRAPHY, GREEK, § 2.

*FGrH* iiiB. 555.  K. J. D.

**ANTIOCHUS** (11) of Ascalon (b. *c.* 130–120 B.C.), founder of the 'fifth Academy', became the pupil, at Athens, of Philon (q.v. 3) of Larissa and of the Stoic Mnesarchus. In 88 he accompanied Philon to Rome, and made the acquaintance of L. Lucullus. He had probably already reacted against the teaching of Philon, and he soon abandoned the Scepticism of the Middle and New Academy and reverted to the teaching of the Old Academy. He was head of the Academy at Athens in 79–78, when Cicero attended his lectures. He joined Lucullus again at the time of the Second Mithridatic War (73), and died about 68. His doctrine was an eclectic one in which he maintained the essential agreement of the Academic, Peripatetic, and Stoic philosophies; in spite of lack of originality he had much influence. Cicero quotes him frequently.

H. M. Strache, *D. Eklektizismus v. Antiochos v. Askalon* (1921); G. Luck, *Der Akademiker Antiochos* (1953).  W. D. R.

**ANTIOCHUS** (12) of Athens (not later than A.D. 300), author of a popular compilation of astrological lore.

Ed. A. Olivieri, *Cat. Cod. Astr.* i. 108, and F. Boll, ib. vii 128. *PW* i. 2494 and Suppl. 4. 32.

**ANTIOPE** (Ἀντιόπη), in mythology, daughter of the river Asopus (*Od.* 11. 260) or Nycteus, king of Boeotia (tragedians, especially Euripides, see schol. ad loc.). Her story has come down chiefly through Euripides' tragedy *Antiope*, now lost (*see* AMPHION). Zeus loved her and approached her in the form of a satyr (Ov. *Met.* 6. 110; Nonnus, *Dion.* 16. 243). She then fled from her father to Sicyon, where she married Epopeus; Nycteus, dying by his own hand, bade his brother Lycus punish her. He attacked Sicyon, killed Epopeus, and carried Antiope off. Either then (Apollod. 3. 43), at Eleutherae, or before meeting Epopeus (Hyg. *Fab.* 8. 2) she bore her twin sons. Lycus and his wife Dirce put her in a dungeon and tormented her till at length she escaped.  H. J. R.

**ANTIPATER** (1) (Ἀντίπατρος) (397–319 B.C.), Macedonian general. He was one of Philip II's right-hand men in war and in diplomacy; in 347–346 he helped to negotiate the peace between Philip and Athens. After Philip's death he aided Alexander in the struggle for the succession, and during Alexander's absence in the East he was governor of Macedonia and 'general of Europe' (334–323). He made himself disliked in Greece by giving support to oligarchs and to tyrants, but he obtained the assistance of the Greek League founded by Philip, when

Agis III (q.v.) of Sparta organized rebellion against Macedon, and he defeated Agis decisively at Megalopolis (331).

After the death of Alexander, Antipater was caught by surprise when the Athenians, Aetolians, and Thessalians rose in revolt, and had to sustain a siege in Lamia; but after the arrival of Macedonian reinforcements and a victory at Crannon he broke up the rebel league (323–322). He now imposed a more oligarchic form of government upon Athens and drove Demosthenes, whose surrender he demanded, to commit suicide. In 321 he joined a coalition of Macedonian generals against the regent Perdiccas, and after Perdiccas' death he obtained the regency from a conference of generals at Triparadisus in Syria. He remained a loyal servant of the Macedonian dynasty, and his death in 319 precipitated the break-up of Alexander's Empire.

Diodorus, bks. 17–18, *passim.* Berve, *Alexanderreich* ii, no. 94. M. C.

**ANTIPATER** (2) of Tarsus (2nd c. B.C.), Stoic, successor of Diogenes (q.v. 3) of Babylon as head of the school at Athens and teacher of Panaetius. He defended himself in many writings against the criticisms of Carneades, and committed suicide at a great age. His views differed little from those of Chrysippus. Named works: Περὶ θεῶν, Περὶ μαντικῆς. His definition of the end of life (Stob. *Ecl.* 2, p. 76, 11, ed. Wachsmuth) has some importance in the history of ethics.

Testimonia and fragments in H. von Arnim, *SVF* iii. 244 ff. M. Pohlenz, *Die Stoa²* (1955).  W. D. R.

**ANTIPATER** (3) of Sidon (fl. *c.* 120 B.C.) has about seventy-five epigrams in the Greek Anthology (q.v.) and one more has turned up on papyrus (Page, *GLP*, 454 ff.). Most of them are artificial epitaphs and descriptive pieces, not infrequently adapted from earlier Hellenistic epigrams; but they contain some fine phrases, and the poems on the Roman destruction of Corinth (*Anth. Pal.* 7. 493 and 9. 151) are truly touching. Q. Lutatius Catulus (q.v. 2) knew him as a fluent improviser (Cic. *De Or.* 3. 194); Meleager imitated him in an amusing address to his tombstone (*Anth. Pal.* 7. 428, cf. 427).

T. B. L. Webster, *Hellenistic Poetry and Art* (1964), ch. 9.  G. H.

**ANTIPATER** (4) of Tyre (1st c. B.C.), who introduced Cato of Utica to the Stoic philosophy, died shortly before 44 B.C. Works: Περὶ καθήκοντος, Περὶ κόσμου, Περὶ οὐσίας, Περὶ ψυχῆς, Περὶ γάμου, Περὶ γυναικὸς συμβιώσεως.

**ANTIPATER** (5) of Thessalonica, Greek epigrammatist, became in about 11 B.C. a client of L. Calpurnius Piso Frugi, the cultured statesman for whose sons Horace may have written the *Ars Poetica*. His latest datable poem belongs to the years A.D. 12–15. In the Greek Anthology there are about eighty of his epigrams—graceful, witty, and unimportant; his attitude to life and art closely resembles Ovid's.

Cichorius, *Röm. Stud.* viii. 6 and 7.  G. H.

**ANTIPATER** (6), father of Herod (q.v. 1) the Great, was the son of the governor of Idumaea appointed by Alexander Jannaeus. As an Idumaean he was hated by many true Jews, but dominated the Jewish scene for a generation. He gained power with the support of the Pharisees and his friend Aretas III (q.v.) of Nabataea (he had married a Nabataean), and above all by supporting Hyrcanus, the legitimate heir to the Jewish kingdom, against his brother Aristobulus (*see* JEWS, A 2). Antipater advocated Hyrcanus' case to Pompey, though himself not pleased with Pompey's settlement. He realized, unlike many contemporaries, that Roman superiority in the

East would be permanent, and he channelled his ambitions into winning Rome's confidence. He helped Scaurus (q.v. 2) to reach terms with Aretas (62 B.C.), and Gabinius to reinstate Ptolemy Auletes in Egypt (55); above all, although he had supported Pompey until Pharsalus, he secured Caesar's favour by raising and leading troops to help him at Alexandria (48). He received as reward Roman citizenship and the administration of Judaea; his sons Phasael and Herod acted as governors of Jerusalem and Galilee. In 43 he raised funds for Cassius, but was murdered. Thus Rome's client, though an Idumaean, rendered Rome useful service by maintaining stability in a troubled area. H. H. S.

**ANTIPATER** (7), Aelius, of Phrygian Hierapolis (d. *c.* A.D. 212), a pupil of the rehtorician Claudius Hadrianus of Tyre. Under Septimius Severus he was *ab epistulis Graecis*, legate of Bithynia, and a consular. Teacher and friend of Caracalla and Geta, he lost imperial favour after Geta's death. He wrote a history of Severus (*F Gr H* 211). H. H. S.

**ANTIPHANES,** poet of Middle Comedy, exhibited his first play in 385 B.C. (Anon. *De Com.* 13) and won thirteen victories (*Suda*, s.v.), eight of them at the Lenaea (*IG* ii² 2325. 146). The number of plays attributed to him in antiquity ranged between 260 and 365; we have 134 titles and over 330 citations, many of them extensive. Several titles suggest mythological burlesque (including Ἀνθρωπο-γονία); others are evidently drawn from the plot of the play (e.g. Ἀκοντιζομένη, Ἀλιευομένη); others, again, refer to types or professions (e.g. Ἄγροικος, Ἀκέστρια, Φιλοθήβαιος —this last, one would suppose, political in character, but not necessarily to be dated in or even near the time at which Demosthenes was arguing for an alliance with Thebes). Like all poets of Middle Comedy, Antiphanes is often cited by Athenaeus for his references to victuals, but he is also the source of many gnomic passages in Stobaeus' anthology (e.g. frs. 41, 53, 86, 123). Among other citations of exceptional interest are frs. 122 (on metaphysics), 191 (on the difference between the tragedian's art and the comic poet's), and 209 (on music).

*FCG* iii. 3 ff.; *CAF* ii. 12 ff.; *FAC* ii. 162 ff. K. J. D.

**ANTIPHATES,** in mythology, king of the gigantic Laestrygonians in the *Odyssey* (10. 106). On Odysseus sending three of his crew to inquire who the people are, he kills one for his dinner, the others escaping. His people then destroy all Odysseus' fleet save his own ship.

H. J. R.

**ANTIPHILUS** of Byzantium has about fifty epigrams in the Greek Anthology (q.v.). Many are ingenious paradoxes or descriptions of freak accidents (*Anth. Pal.* 9. 86). Some (e.g. 9. 546) show a genuine love of ships and seafaring. He has an abjectly flattering address to 'Nero' (9. 178): if this is Tiberius, he wrote it about 5 B.C., if Nero, about A.D. 54.

Cichorius, *Röm. Stud.* 334 f.; K. Müller, *Die Epig. des A. von Byzanz* (1935). G. H.

**ANTIPHON** (1) (*c.* 480–411 B.C.), the Attic orator. A man of strong aristocratic prejudices, he never, or very seldom, appeared in court or spoke in public, but gained a great reputation by speeches composed for others. He suddenly came to the front in 411 B.C. as the brain of the oligarchic conspiracy, and was the leader of the extremists against the moderate counsels of Theramenes (q.v.). He went with Phrynichus and eight others to negotiate peace with Sparta in the hope of obtaining support for the oligarchs. The mission failed, and the murder of Phrynichus was followed shortly by the fall of the Four Hundred

and the flight of the leaders to Decelea. Antiphon a Archeptolemus remained, and were tried, condemne and executed. Antiphon delivered, in his own defenc the finest speech of the kind which had ever been hea (Thuc. 8. 68). When congratulated by Agathon (q.v.) its brilliance, he replied that he would rather have sati fied one man of good taste than any number of comm people (Arist. *Eth. Eud.* 1232ᵇ7).

WORKS. The *tetralogies* are oratorical exercises d signed to show in outline how speeches should be cor posed both for attack and defence. Each set contai (*a*) the prosecutor's opening speech, (*b*) the first spee for the defence, (*c*) the prosecutor's reply, and (*d*) t defendant's conclusion. *First Tetralogy*: a murder ca tried before the Areopagus. *Second Tetralogy*: a b has been accidently killed by a javelin in the gymnasiu and the boy who killed him is charged with murd *Third Tetralogy*: an old man, assaulted by a young ma has died of his wounds. *The Murder of Herodes* deals wi a real case. Herodes and the accused were on a voya together; one night Herodes went ashore and disappeare later, his companion was accused of murder. It is possi that the charge was trumped up to injure the defe dant's father, who was unpopular in Mytilene on politi grounds (§§ 74–80). *On the Choreutes* (*c.* 412 B.C.), d fence of a *choregos* who has accidently caused the dea of a boy singer by giving him a drug to improve his voi *Against a Stepmother*: a young man accuses his ste mother of having employed a slave-woman to pois his father. This may be a rhetorical exercise. A f fragments of other speeches survive; some of these m be the work of Antiphon (2), the sophist.

When Antiphon began to write there was no tra tion of prose style in the Attic dialect. His contempora Gorgias wrote in Attic, but his influence cannot ha been much felt before 427 B.C., when he first visit Athens. Antiphon then, was free to make experimen The result was a style which, though crude at times, always vigorous and precise. He was the first of exta writers to pay careful attention to 'periodic' expression, opposed to the 'running' style, which is more suita to narrative than to argument. He indulges freely antithesis both of word and of thought, and is able to jo together clauses so neatly balanced that they correspo even in the number of syllables. In vocabulary, he avoi colloquialisms, and has some partiality for poetical wor Some of the peculiarities of Thucydides may be trac to his influence.

He established a standard form of structure—introduction, describing the circumstances of the ca a narration of the facts; arguments and proofs, sometin interspersed with evidence; lastly, a peroration.

His manner is as dignified as his style; he frequen appeals to divine law, which punishes the guilty ev though he may escape human justice; he avoids perso lities, though in the *Herodes* the speaker exhibits righteous indignation against his persecutors. He rel on *a priori* probabilities (arguments from character, et at least as much as on the evidence of witnesses.

For general bibliography see ATTIC ORATORS.
TEXT. Blass–Thalheim (Teubner, 1914).
TEXT AND TRANSLATION. Gernet (Budé), Maidment (Loeb, *Minor Orators* i, 1941).
INDEX. F. L. van Cleef (U.S.A. 1895).
See also K. J. Dover, *CQ* 1950, 44 f. J. F.

**ANTIPHON** (2) of Athens (5th c. B.C.), contempor with Antiphon the orator and often confused with h sophist and interpreter of dreams, mentioned by Xe phon and Aristotle as an opponent of Socrates. Wor Ἀλήθεια, Περὶ ὁμονοίας, Πολιτικός, Περὶ κρίσεως ὀνείρ

Testimonia and fragments in Diels, *Vorsokr.*¹¹ ii. 334 ff.; M. Un steiner, *I Sofisti* iv (1962). W. D.

**ANTIPHON** (3), tragic poet at the court of the Elder Dionysius of Syracuse, by whom he was put to death Plut. *Quomodo adul.* 27; Philostr. *VS* 1. 15. 3).

*TGF* 792.

**ANTISTHENES** (1) (*c.* 445–*c.* 360 B.C. (Diod. 15. 76)), son of Antisthenes of Athens and of a Thracian woman Diog. Laert. 6. 1; Seneca, *Constant.* 18. 5), one of the most devoted followers of Socrates (Xen. *Symp.* 8. 4; *Mem.* 3. 11. 17). He was considered founder of the Cynic sect (Diog. Laert. 1. 15; 6. 13) and probably influenced the philosophy of Diogenes of Sinope, from whose nickname ὁ κύων the name of that sect is derived. He also influenced the doctrine of the Stoics.

The main principles of his philosophy were the following. Happiness (εὐδαιμονία) is based on virtue (ἀρετή). Virtue is based on knowledge and therefore can be taught. This is done through investigation into the meaning of words (ὀνομάτων ἐπίσκεψις). For he who knows the meaning of a word knows also the thing which it denotes. Whoever knows what virtue is cannot but act virtuously. Whoever has attained this knowledge can never lose it. Most pleasures (ἡδοναί) are treacherous and do not contribute to happiness. Only the pleasure which is the result of exertion (πόνος) is lasting and unobjectionable. The best government is that of the wise man.

He revered Heracles because he led a life of virtue and exertion, and considered Cyrus the model of a wise monarch. He preferred Odysseus to Ajax because he considered wisdom superior to brutal strength. He wrote dialogues (*Heracles, Aspasia, Cyrus, Protrepticus,* and others), interpretations of Homer, and fictitious orations *Ajax, Odysseus*).

Antisthenes' theory of language is taken by Aristotle to deny the possibility of contradiction (*Top.* 104ᵇ20–1) and of definition (*Metaph.* 1043ᵇ23–6).

*Antisthenis fragmenta* coll. A. W. Winckelmann (1842); Diogenes Laertius 6. 1–19; F. Dümmler, *Antisthenica* (1882); K. v. Fritz, *Hermes* 1927, 453 ff.; *Rh. Mus.* 1935, 19 ff.; R. Dudley, *A History of Cynicism* (1937), 1 ff.; F. Sayre, *The Greek Cynics* (1948); R. Höistad, *Cynic Hero and Cynic King* (1948). K. VON F.

**ANTISTHENES** (2) of Rhodes (fl. early 2nd c. B.C.), wrote Διαδοχαὶ φιλοσόφων; also a history, perhaps of Rhodes, down to his own time (used by Polybius via Zeno).

*FGrH* iii. 508.

**ANTISTIUS** (1, *PW* 47) **VETUS,** GAIUS, under whose father Caesar had served in Spain as quaestor, himself became Caesar's quaestor (date uncertain). He opposed Caecilius Bassus (q.v. 1; *see* CORNIFICIUS 1) in Syria in 45 B.C. (probably as *legatus*), but in 44 joined the Liberators. He was legate of Octavian in Illyricum (35–34?), *cos. suff.* 30), and, perhaps as governor of Hispania Citerior, fought against the Cantabri (26–24). His descendants held several consulships in the early Principate; Antistius 2) was his great-grandson.

Syme, *Rom. Rev.,* see index. T. J. C.

**ANTISTIUS** (2, *PW* 53) **VETUS,** LUCIUS, consul with Nero in A.D. 55, was legate of Germania Superior (55–6) and planned to connect the Rhine with the Rhône. In 62 he vainly urged his son-in-law Rubellius Plautus to take up arms against Nero. Proconsul of Asia (*c.* 64), he anticipated condemnation by suicide (65). He is perhaps the writer who was a source for Pliny, *HN* 3–6.

Ritterling, *Fasti des röm. Deutschland,* 16; Schanz–Hosius, ii, 653. A. M.

**ANTIUM** (modern *Anzio*), roadstead of Latium. Legends envelop its origin, but apparently it was Latin in the sixth century B.C. (Dion. Hal. 1. 72; Polyb. 3. 22). Shortly thereafter Volsci captured it, and for 200 years Antium was apparently the principal Volscian city. Most fifth-century records concerning it, including the record of the Latin colony in 467, are untrustworthy: the notorious annalist Valerius Antias hailed from here. But in the fourth century it was the centre of Volscian resistance to Rome, that ended only when Maenius (q.v.) captured the Antiate fleet and made possible the establishment of a citizen colony, 338 (Livy bks. 2–8; Dion. Hal. bks. 4–10). Antiate pirates, however, continued active even after 338 (Strabo 5. 232). After being sacked by Marius, Antium became a fashionable resort with celebrated temples (App. *BCiv.* 1. 69; 5. 26; Hor. *Carm.* 1. 35). Caligula and Nero were born here and, like later emperors, patronized the town (Suet. *Calig.* 8; *Ner.* 6). Antium nevertheless gradually declined. A pre-Julian calendar, ruined villas, and famous *objets d'art* like the Apollo Belvedere have been found here.

Pre-Volscian Antium: M. L. Scevola, *Rend. Ist. Lomb.* 1959, 417 ff.; 1960, 221 ff.; 1964, 89 ff. E. T. S.

**ANTONIA** (1, *PW* 112), daughter of the triumvir M. Antonius and his cousin Antonia, born between 54 and 49 B.C. She was promised in 44 to a son of the triumvir Lepidus, but married, *c.* 34, the rich Pythodorus of Tralles. She seems to have died before her father. Her daughter Pythodoris married Polemon (q.v. 1), king of Pontus (cf. *OGI* 377) and (later) Archelaus, king of Cappadocia (q.v.).

Cf. *PW,* s.v. Pythodoris, 1 and Pythodoros, 13. A. M.; T. J. C.

**ANTONIA** (2, *PW* 113), elder daughter ('maior' Suet. *Nero* 5. 1; wrongly 'minor' Tac. *Ann.* 4. 44, 12. 64) of M. Antonius and Octavia (q.v. 2), born in 39 B.C., was the wife of L. Domitius (q.v. 6) Ahenobarbus. Their children were Gnaeus, consul A.D. 32 (the father of Nero), Domitia (wife of C. Passienus Crispus), and Domitia Lepida (mother of Messalina (q.v. 1)). T. J. C.

**ANTONIA** (3, *PW* 114), younger daughter ('minor' Suet. *Calig.* 1. 1, *Claud.* 1. 6) of M. Antonius and Octavia, (q.v. 2), born 31 Jan. 36 B.C., married Drusus (q.v. 3); their children were Germanicus, Livilla, and Claudius (later Emperor) (qq.v. Cf. *IGRom.* iv. 206). After Drusus' death in 9 B.C. she refused to marry again. In A.D. 31 she gave information to Tiberius leading to the discovery of the conspiracy of Sejanus (q.v.). Her grandson, Gaius, on his accession conferred numerous honours upon her, including the name Augusta, but soon found her criticisms irksome, and, it was said, drove her to commit suicide (1 May 37). G. W. R.; T. J. C.

**ANTONIA** (4, *PW* 115), daughter of Claudius and Aelia Paetina, married in A.D. 41 Cn. Pompeius Magnus and afterwards Faustus Cornelius Sulla. Her first husband was put to death by Claudius, the second by Nero. She was killed some months after the Pisonian conspiracy, in which her complicity is possible: less likely is Suetonius' story (*Nero* 35) that her condemnation was caused by her refusal to marry Nero after Poppaea's death. A. M.

**ANTONINUS** (1) **PIUS,** Roman Emperor A.D. 138–61, was born in 86 at Lanuvium, near Rome, and was named *Titus Aurelius* (*PW* 138) *Fulvus Boionius Antoninus*. He was son of Aurelius Fulvus, of a consular family originally from Nîmes, and Arria Fadilla, also of provincial and consular descent. Antoninus became quaestor, praetor, and in 120 *cos. I ord.* By then he had married Faustina (q.v. 1). Appointed *IVvir consularis* (*see* HADRIAN), he administered this legal office in Etruria and Umbria, where he owned much property. Proconsul of

Asia between 133 and 136, he gained fame for his integrity and afterwards joined Hadrian's *consilium* (q.v.). Scrupulous, loyal, and gentle, he earned the respect of Hadrian, who, on the death of L. Aelius (q.v. 2) in 138, adopted him as successor, and made him in turn adopt both M. Annius Verus ( = M. Aurelius, q.v. 1), Faustina's nephew, and L. Ceionius Commodus ( = L. Verus, q.v.), son of Aelius. During Hadrian's last months, Antoninus, now holder of proconsular and tribunician power, was virtual ruler. At Hadrian's death, Antoninus' accession, on 10 July 138, was smooth. He persuaded a hesitant Senate to consecrate the late ruler. The Senate conferred on him himself the title *Pius* (devout) and on Faustina that of *Augusta*. Whether *Pius* commemorated his loyalty to the memory of his adoptive father or his general devotion to his own responsibilities and the gods is uncertain. The title *Pater Patriae*, refused at first, he accepted in 139, with a second consulship; he was *cos. III* in 140 and *IV* in 145.

His policy was unsensational, but beneficent and mildly progressive. Accession gifts (*aurum coronarium*; q.v.) were remitted entirely for Italy, and as to one-half for the provinces. Rome and Italy were the focus of an attention which reflected his *pietas*. His medallions of 140–4 advertise the coming (in 147) 900th anniversary of Rome's founding, and show his belief in her mission. He was fond of the life of a country gentleman in his villa at Lanuvium and perhaps never left Italy during his reign. By suppressing the four imperial supervisors (*IVviri consulares*) whom Hadrian (q.v.) had appointed, he returned Italy fully to senatorial control (S.H.A. *Ant.* 11. 6). Completely deferential to the Senate, of which no member was put to death, he nevertheless conceded to it no new powers, and used his advisory *consilium* on all matters. General administration was increasingly centralized. Rotation of office became slower and good officials at home and abroad remained unchanged for years. Permanent officials of the bureaucracy were made members of the *consilium* (*consiliarii*). Imperial control of jurisdiction continued, with experts to assist.

Antoninus dispensed nine 'liberalities' to a total of 800 *denarii* a head; established an alimentary fund (*see* ALIMENTA) to support *Puellae Faustinianae*, named in memory of Faustina (d. 140–1); lightened the provincial burden of the imperial post; helped many communities financially; and carried out much public building. But he cut down unnecessary public expenditure, and at his death left 675 million *denarii* in the Treasury (Dio 74. 8. 3). Modest and plain-living himself, he disciplined both freedmen and imperial procurators. Confiscation was rare, judicial clemency frequent.

Foreign affairs, though Antoninus' influence encouraged peaceful settlement, were uneasy. About 140–1 the British frontier was advanced (*see* WALL OF ANTONINUS); but the Brigantes were later to revolt. A restive Germany was further insulated by settling Britons in the Neckar lands. Revolt in Numidia and Mauretania (*c.* 145–50) was followed by Jewish and Egyptian risings. Dacian trouble (*c.* 158) caused the partition of that province into three under procurators (159). Kings were assigned to the Colchian Lazi, to the Quadi, and to the Armenians, whom Parthia was warned to leave untouched, though hostilities occurred later (*ILS* 1076); and Abgar of Edessa was admonished for aggressive conduct.

With the succession assured, and himself—another Numa—high in respect, Antoninus quietly furthered the centralization of government, relying chiefly on a friendly Senate. The general tone of harmony and well-being under Antoninus is well expressed by Aristides (q.v. 5), whose oration 'To Rome' pictures the Empire as a congery of happy, peaceful, and prosperous city-states under the aegis of Rome's beneficent hegemony and pro-

tection. Antoninus died at Lorium on 7 Mar. 161, entrusting the State to M. Aurelius. Deified by universal accord, he received all the usual honours, including commemorative column in the Campus Martius, whose base is now in the Vatican, and a temple in the Forum himself and Faustina.

I. ANCIENT SOURCES. *Literary*: The account of Antoninus *Historia Augusta* is uncritical. For Aristides' *To Rome*, J. H. Olive 'The Ruling Power &c.', *Trans. Am. Philosophical Soc.* 1953, 871 Minor references in Aurelius Victor and Eutropius; and fragments Dio Cassius bk. 70. The *Meditations* of M. Aurelius and Fronto *Letters* contain frequent allusions to Antoninus.
*Inscriptions*: W. Hüttl, *Antoninus Pius II* (1933).
*Coins*: B.M. *Coins, Rom. Emp.* iii (1936), iv (1940); Strac *Reichsprägung* iii; J. M. C. Toynbee, *CR* 1925, 170 ff.
II. MODERN LITERATURE. *Diz. Epigr.* s.v. 'Antoninus'; E. Bryant, *The Reign of Antoninus Pius* (1895); G. Lacour-Gaye *Antonin le Pieux et son temps* (1888); W. Hüttl, op. cit. i (1936 Wegner, *Herrscherbild* ii. 4 (1939); *Lex. der alt. Welt.* (1965), 335 s.v.; M. Hammond, *The Antonine Monarchy* (1959). For his temp and column at Rome, Nash, *Pict. Dict. Rome* i; for *Pius* C. H. Dod *Num. Chron.* 1911, 5 ff. Bibliography: A. Garzetti, *L'impero* Tiberio agli Antonini (1960), 690 ff.; A. Piganiol, *Hist. de Rom* (1962), 306 f., 581; Bengtson, *Röm. Gesch.* 348 ff.
C. H. V. S.; M.

**ANTONINUS** (2), ARRIUS (*PW* 9), maternal grand father of the Emperor Antoninus (q.v. 1) Pius, was co *suff.* in A.D. 69, proconsul of Asia under Vespasian, and consul again in 97 under his friend Nerva (q.v.). He addressed in three letters by the Younger Pliny, who say that his Greek verses recalled Callimachus and Heroda Probably, like his son-in-law Aurelius Fulvus, he cam from Nemausus: his wife Boionia Procilla was certain Narbonese.

Syme, *Tacitus*, App. 32, 87. G. E. F.

**ANTONINUS** (3) **LIBERALIS,** mythographer, prob ably of Antonine times, published a Μεταμορφώσεων συ αγωγή, based on Hellenistic sources, e.g. Nicander.

TEXT. E. Martini, *Mythographi graeci* ii. 1, 61: E. Oder, *Antonino Liberali* (1886).

**ANTONIUS** (1, *PW* 28), MARCUS, praetor (perhaps *p consule*) in 102 B.C., fought against the Cilician pirate He triumphed late in 100, was consul in 99, and cense (with L. Flaccus (q.v. 5) ) in 97. A friend of Mari (q.v. 1) with Arpinate connexions, he opposed the a herents of Saturninus, refused to support the recall Metellus (q.v. 6) Numidicus, in his censorship enrolle Italians as citizens (thus making the *Lex Licinia Muc* necessary), and defended Aquillius and Norbanus (q v.). He later turned against Marius, was prosecuted und the law of Varius (q.v. 1), but acquitted, and was kille after Marius' return to Rome (87). He and L. Crassus we the leading orators of their age, heard and admired b Cicero, who later drew idealized portraits of then particularly in the *Brutus* and the *De Oratore*. His orato was simple, depending mainly on *actio* for its effect, an (perhaps for that reason) he never published his speeche He left a rhetorical treatise (only the second in Lati after that of Cato (q.v. 1)), apparently incomplete.

Malcovati, *ORF*¹ 221 ff.; Badian, *Stud. Gr. Rom. Hist.* see Inde E. S. Gruen, *JRS* 1965, 67; U. W. Scholz, *Der Redner M. Anton* (1963). E.

**ANTONIUS** (2, *PW* 29) 'CRETICUS', MARCUS, s of (1), a weak and easy-going man, dominated by h noble wife Julia (*see* CAESAR 2). As praetor (74 B.C.) was given a special *imperium* (described as *infinitum*) deal with the pirates, perhaps in part to provide a for counterbalancing Pompey's (q.v.). Unsuccessful in h campaigns off Liguria and Spain and oppressive in h requisitioning (see Cic. 2 *Verr.* 3. 213), he was disastrous defeated by the Cretans in a naval battle, made a trea with them, and died soon after (*c.* 72). E.

NTONIUS (3, *PW* 19) 'HYBRIDA', GAIUS, son of
). An officer under Sulla, rewarded in the proscriptions,
e escaped prosecution *repetundarum* by appealing to the
ibunes on a technicality. As tribune (72 B.C. ?) he helped
▸ pass the *Lex Antonia de Termessibus* (q.v.). Expelled
om the Senate by the censors (70), he was helped to a
raetorship by Cicero (66), made an election compact with
is old comrade Catiline (q.v.) in 64 (see Asconius 82 ff.)
ıd was elected consul with Cicero. Given the province of
Iacedonia by Cicero, he agreed to march against Cati-
ne, but left the fighting to his legate Petreius (q.v.).
ppressive and unsuccessful in Macedonia, he was
rosecuted and, though defended by Cicero, convicted.
ecalled from exile by Caesar, he was censor in 42.

E. B.

NTONIUS (4, *PW* 30), MARCUS, 'Mark Antony' the
iumvir, eldest son of Antonius (2) Creticus, was born
83 B.C. After a dissipated youth he distinguished him-
elf as a cavalry commander under Gabinius (q.v. 2) in
alestine and Egypt (57–54), and then joined Caesar's
aff in Gaul, where, apart from an interval in Rome
3–52), he remained till the end of 50; in 51 he was
uaestor. As tribune in 49 he defended Caesar's interests
ı the Senate, fled to his camp when 'the last decree' was
assed, took part in the fighting in Italy, passed measures
estoring the sons of the proscribed and some of those
ondemned *de ambitu* under Pompey's law of 52, and was
eft in charge of Italy during Caesar's Spanish campaign.
ı 48 he served under Caesar in Greece and commanded
is left wing at Pharsalus. Caesar then sent him to Italy
ı his representative and *magister equitum* (till late in 47),
ut apparently was not wholly satisfied with his conduct,
ı he held no further post till 44 when he was Caesar's
onsular colleague. After the Ides of March he was at
rst conciliatory towards the Liberators, but he made an
nscrupulous use of Caesar's papers, and his recruiting
f armed supporters, followed by the irregular enactment
f a law which gave him Cisalpine Gaul and Gallia
omata for five years (June), strengthened the opinion
ıat he was preparing to step into Caesar's shoes. Further,
ıe activities of Octavian threatened his position as leader
f the Caesarian party. By early 43 he faced an armed
>alition consisting of Decimus Brutus (q.v. 6), whom he
as blockading in Mutina (q.v.), the new consuls Hirtius
ıd Pansa (qq.v.), both moderate Caesarians, and Octav-
n, backed by the Senate's authority and Cicero's
loquence; in April he was compelled by reverses at
orum Gallorum and Mutina to retreat to Gallia Nar-
onensis. He was joined there, however, by the governors
f the western provinces, Lepidus (q.v. 3), Pollio (q.v.),
ıd Plancus (q.v. 1), and subsequently reconciled with
▸ctavian.

By the *Lex Titia* (November 43) Antony, Lepidus,
ıd Octavian were appointed *tresviri rei publicae con-
ıituendae* (see TRIUMVIRI) for five years. The proscription
f their political and personal enemies was followed in
2 by the defeat of Brutus and Cassius at Philippi (q.v.),
vhere Antony established his reputation as a general. By
greement with Octavian he now undertook the re-
rganization of the eastern half of the Empire. In the
ourse of this task he met Cleopatra at Tarsus (q.v.) in
ı and spent the following winter with her in Egypt. The
efeat of his brother L. Antonius (q.v. 6) in the Perusine
Var compelled him early in 40, despite the distraction of
Parthian invasion of Syria (*see* LABIENUS 2), to return
▸ Italy, but a new agreement was reached at Brundisium
y which Antony surrendered his province of Gaul,
rhich Octavian had already occupied, and married his
ister Octavia (q.v. 2). In 39 they made the treaty of
Misenum (q.v.) with Sextus Pompeius, after which
ıntony left with Octavia to continue his task in the
̱ast. By 38 his lieutenant Ventidius (q.v.) had ex-

pelled the Parthians from Syria. In 37 new differences
between Antony and Octavian were settled at Tarentum,
and the Triumvirate was prolonged for another five
years; but this time he left Octavia behind when he departed for the East, and renewed his association with
Cleopatra on a permanent basis. This step was probably
not without its political motives. The support of the rich
kingdom of Egypt, to which he now restored some of its
old territories, was a valuable asset. For similar reasons he
saw to it that the able Herod (q.v. 1) was installed in his
kingdom of Judaea. The allegiance of Egypt and the
Hellenistic East was courted by religious propaganda:
Antony had already assumed the role of Dionysus, i.e. of
Osiris, and he and Cleopatra could now be represented
as a divine pair with Cleopatra as Aphrodite or Isis,
united for the benefit of Asia, as had been predicted at
Tarsus (Plut. *Ant.* 26). In 36, however, Antony's Parthian
expedition ended in a disastrous retreat, and the defeat
of Sextus Pompeius and the elimination of Lepidus from
the Triumvirate brought the rivalry between Antony and
Octavian into sharper focus. In 35 there was fresh cause
of offence when Octavia came to the East bringing
Antony Roman troops amounting in number only to one
tenth of what Octavian had promised and Antony refused to receive her. In 34 he annexed Armenia on the
pretext of the desertion in 36 of its king Artavasdes
(q.v. 1) and celebrated in Alexandria a triumph, followed
by a ceremony in which Cleopatra and her children—
including Caesarion (q.v.), whom Antony declared to be
Caesar's acknowledged son—were proclaimed as monarchs of the expanded Egypt and other territories inside
and outside the Roman Empire. An open breach with
Octavian followed; the year 33 saw an acrimonious exchange of accusations. Early in 32 Octavian frightened
many of Antony's supporters into leaving Rome (*see*
SOSIUS 1); Antony divorced Octavia; and Octavian
forcibly seized and published Antony's will, in which he
allegedly left bequests to his children by Cleopatra (an
impossibility in Roman law) and requested burial in
Alexandria. It was now easy for Octavian to procure the
annulment of Antony's remaining powers and a declaration of war against Cleopatra. Antony's legions were
supplemented by the Egyptian fleet and the forces of his
numerous client-kings, but the presence of Cleopatra in
his camp alienated a number of his Roman supporters
including Plancus (q.v. 1), Titius (q.v. 2), and Domitius
(q.v. 5) Ahenobarbus. Decisively defeated at Actium
(q.v.) in September 31, Antony attempted to defend
Egypt, but the general defection of his governors and
vassals made his cause hopeless. He committed suicide
before Octavian's entry into Alexandria (Aug. 30).

Of fine physique, and with a constitution which
excesses and hardships alike failed to ruin, Antony was a
natural soldier, and his courage, affability, and generosity
made him a great soldiers' leader. As a politician, though
by no means unskilful, he was sometimes led into serious
errors by his irascible temper and self-will. It was his
misfortune to face in Octavian a cooler, more single-
minded, and less scrupulous opponent. As an administrator he was not without ability: his arrangements in
the East, except where they concerned Cleopatra and her
family, were largely retained by Augustus. In oratory he
inclined to the florid Asian school; his only literary publication was an apologia of 31 *De sua ebrietate*; specimens
of his epistolary style can be seen in Cicero's correspondence, the thirteenth *Philippic* and Suetonius'
*Augustus.*

Antony was married (1) to Fadia; (2) to his cousin
Antonia, daughter of C. Antonius (3), whom he divorced
in 47; (3) in 47 or 46, to Fulvia (q.v.); (4) in 40, to Octavia.
By Antonia he had a daughter Antonia (q.v. 1); by Fulvia
two sons, Marcus and Iullus Antonius (qq.v. 7 and 8); by

Octavia two daughters Antonia (2) and (3), through whom he was the ancestor of the three emperors Gaius, Claudius, and Nero. His marriage to Cleopatra (37?) was not valid in Roman law. For their children see CLEOPATRA VII.

Cicero, *Letters* and *Philippics*; Caes. *BGall.* 7. 81, 8, *BCiv.* 1, 3; Vell. Pat. 2; Joseph. *AJ* 14–15, *BJ* 1; Suet. *Jul.*, *Aug.*; Plut. *Ant.*; App. *BCiv.* 2–5; Cass. Dio 41–51. J. Kromayer, *Hermes* 1894, 556 ff.; 1896, 70 ff.; Syme, *Rom. Rev.*, see index; A. Zwaenepoel, *LEC* 1950, 3 ff.; 1951, 47 ff.; J. Crook, *JRS* 1957, 36 ff.; F. Dumont, *Mélanges Levy–Brühl* (1959), 85 ff.; R. F. Rossi, *Marco Antonio* (1959); H. Buchheim, *Die Orientpolitik des Triumvirn M. Antonius* (1960); S. E. Smethurst, *Thought from the Learned Societies of Canada* (1960), 155 ff.; I. Becher, *Das Altertum* 1965, 40 ff.; Schanz–Hosius i. 388 f.; *ORF²* 468 ff. Iconography: O. J. Brendel, *Hommages à A. Grenier* (1962), 359 ff. *See also* ACTIUM, AUGUSTUS, CLEOPATRA VII. G. W. R.; T. J. C.

**ANTONIUS** (5, *PW* 20), GAIUS, second son of Antonius (2). As Caesar's *legatus* in 49 B.C. he was blockaded by a Pompeian fleet on the island of Curicta in the Adriatic and forced to surrender. After his praetorship in 44 he set out for Macedonia, but was besieged and captured in Apollonia by M. Brutus (March 43). He tried to incite the troops of Brutus to mutiny and was executed by his order, probably early in 42. G. W. R.

**ANTONIUS** (6, *PW* 23), LUCIUS, third son of Antonius (2). He was quaestor in Asia in 50 B.C. and stayed on in 49 in charge of the province 'pro quaestore pro praetore'; in 44, as tribune, he carried a law giving Caesar special powers in the appointment of magistrates, and after Caesar's death was made chairman of an agrarian commission. In the war of Mutina he served under his brother Marcus. As consul in 41, with the encouragement of Fulvia (q.v.) and in the supposed interests of Marcus (hence his assumed surname 'Pietas'), he asserted the rights of his office against Octavian, and championed the Italians dispossessed by the latter's settlements of veterans. The ensuing civil war ended in the surrender of Lucius at Perusia (q.v.), early in 40. Octavian pardoned him and sent him to a command in Spain, where he appears to have died soon afterwards. G. W. R.; T. J. C.

**ANTONIUS** (7, *PW* 32), MARCUS, called 'Antyllus' by the Greeks, elder son of the triumvir and Fulvia (q.v.). In 37 B.C. (at Tarentum) he was betrothed to Julia (q.v. 2). He assumed the *toga virilis* after Actium and was put to death by Octavian after the capture of Alexandria.
G. W. R.

**ANTONIUS** (8, *PW* 22), IULLUS, second son of the triumvir and Fulvia, was brought up in Rome by Octavia (q.v. 2) and married in 21 B.C. to Marcella, her daughter by Marcellus. Praetor (13), consul (10), and proconsul of Asia (7/6?), he was condemned to death (2 B.C.) for adultery with Julia (q.v. 2) and designs on the supreme power, and committed suicide. He wrote verse, including an epic *Diomedeia* in 12 books; Horace addressed *Carm.* 4. 2. to him. He had sons called Iullus and Lucius.

K. M. T. Atkinson, *Hist.* 1958, 327; Schanz–Hosius ii. 273.
T. J. C.

**ANTONIUS** (9) **CASTOR**, perhaps a freedman of M. Antonius (q.v. 4), was one of the Elder Pliny's sources for botany (*HN* 25. 9). Pliny mentions that he possessed his own botanical garden.

Schanz–Hosius § 495, 3.

**ANTONIUS** (10) **MUSA**, physician of Augustus, whom in 23 B.C. he cured of a serious illness. Apparently he was the first to introduce hydropathy at Rome. He wrote a work in several books on the properties of drugs. The extant works that pass under his name—*De herba*

*botanica* and *De tuenda valetudine ad Maecenatem*—ar spurious and later.

Ed. E. Howald and H. E. Sigerist, *CML* iv. W. D. I

**ANTONIUS** (11) **DIOGENES** (c. A.D. 100), author a tale of travels and adventures in twenty-four book entitled 'The wonderful things beyond Thule' (Τὰ ὑπ Θούλην ἄπιστα). The story, of which only Photius' abstra is extant (*Bibl.*, *cod.* 166), was of a fantastic character (th protagonist, amongst other things, reaches the Moon the erotic element is very much confined to the back ground, and the work, as Rohde has shown, belong rather to the genre 'Reisefabulistik' than to the gen: 'love-romance' proper.

TEXT. R. Hercher, *Erotici Scriptores Graeci* i. 233 ff. (Teubner). CRITICISM. Rohde, *Griech. Roman*, 269 ff.; Christ–Schmic Stählin II. ii⁶. 819 ff. *See also* NOVEL, GREEK. G. (

**ANTYLLUS** (2nd c. A.D.), physician, belonged to th pneumatic school; his chief contributions to medicin were in the sphere of dietetics, general therapeutics, an especially surgery. Works: Περὶ βοηθημάτων (on med: cine); Χειρουργούμενα (on surgery); Περὶ ὑδροκεφάλων: a lost except for frs. *See* SURGERY, § 6. W. D. F

**ANUBIS,** originally one of several local gods of the dea in Egypt, is represented on the monuments as a jacka In Hellenistic times his cult is both celestial and inferna and he is sometimes identified with Hermes under th name Hermanubis. He is an important member of th cult of the Egyptian deities only at Delos, though w know of a *thiasos* which worshipped him at Smyrna. I the Roman period he is represented at times as a soldie in armour. T. A. I

**ANYTE** of Tegea (fl. early 3rd c. B.C.) was an Arcadia poetess, much admired in her time and thereafter. Abou eighteen of her charming Doric epigrams, mostl sepulcral, are in the Greek Anthology (q.v.) and one cited by Pollux 5. 48. Her lyrics are lost, but she trans lated some of Sappho's spirit into her sensitive elegia quatrains. She was the first to make epitaphs for animals and one of the first to write pastoral descriptions of wil nature (e.g. *Anth. Pal.* 16. 228).

M. J. Baale, *Studia in Anytes vitam* (Haarlem, 1903); S. Colangel Stud. *Ital.* 1915, 280 ff.; F. Herrlinger, *Totenklage um Tiere in d antiken Dichtung* (1930); G. Luck, *MH* 1954, 174 ff.; Wilamowit: Hellenist. *Dichtung* i. 136 f. G. H

**ANYTOS** (5th–4th c. B.C.), a wealthy Athenian and democratic leader. General in 409 B.C., he failed t prevent the loss of Pylos, and is said to have escaped con demnation only by bribery. After the war, he was on of the restorers of democracy with Thrasybulus, provin himself an honest and moderate politician. Plato (*Men* 90 f.) introduces him as a well-bred man, but a passionat enemy of the sophists. He probably did not belong to th circle of Socrates, as some sources hint. He became on of the three accusers of Socrates, less for private reason than from an honest belief that he was doing the best fo Athens. Accounts about his banishment and murde may be later inventions.

*Prosop. Att.* 1324. V. I

**AORNOS,** the mountain stronghold between the Swa and Indus rivers captured by Alexander (327–326 B.C. has been identified by Sir Aurel Stein with Pir-sar, nortl of Buner. Two great ridges, Pir-sar and Una-sar, con verge at right angles; the 'rock' is Bar-sar on Pir-sar, cu off from the Una ridge (along which Alexander attacked by the Būrimār ravine (across which he constructed hi ramp). The operations can be understood only from map, which shows what a great feat of arms it was. 'Aornos' may represent Una (Unra).

Sir A. Stein, *On Alexander's Track to the Indus* (1929), chs. 17–22, with maps.
W. W. T.

**APAMEA,** a city on the Orontes which replaced the Macedonian military colony of Pella. It was founded by Seleucus I, or perhaps Antiochus I. It was the capital of a satrapy and the military headquarters of the Seleucid kingdom. A natural fortress, it was seized by Caecilius Bassus in 46 B.C. and endured a long siege. During the Principate it made only one issue of coins (under Claudius), but ruled a large territory; its citizen population numbered 117,000 under Augustus. Its ruins are being excavated (reports in *Ant. Class.* 1932, 1935–6). Apamea is by no means to be confused with its namesake in Phrygia, where the Romans concluded a peace with Antiochus III (q.v.) in 188 B.C.
A. H. M. J.

**APARCHE,** votive gift to a god. The custom which is expressed by the Latin word *votum* (q.v.), that a gift is promised and given if a certain condition is fulfilled by the god, was common in Greece too (cf. *Il.* 6. 305 ff.); it is expressed by the word εὐχή. The words ἀπαρχή, ἀκροθίνια express the idea that a part of something gained is given to the god. Generally these gifts were understood as a χαριστήριον, thank-offering. Cf. *IG* i². 625 εὐχωλὴν τελέσας σοι χάριν ἀντιδιδούς.

H. Beer, *Ἀπαρχή und verwandte Ausdrücke in griechischen Weihinschriften* (Diss. München, 1914); J. Rudhardt, *Notions fondamentales de la pensée religieuse, etc.* (1958), 219 ff.
M. P. N.

**APATURIA,** a festival characteristic of the Ionians (among the Dorians the Apellai (q.v. 2) corresponds to it). It is chiefly known from Athens, where it was celebrated by the phratries in the month of Pyanopsion (Oct.–Nov.). Its three days were called (1) δορπία (from a late meal), (2) ἀνάρρυσις (from the sacrifice of an animal), (3) κουρεῶτις. On this last day the children and young adult men and newly married wives were enrolled in the phratry. Three sacrifices are mentioned in connexion with this enrolling: the μεῖον (the lesser one) was probably brought on behalf of a child introduced into the phratry; the κούρειον (cf. κουρεῶτις) has its name from the shearing of the hair of the ephebes; the γαμηλία from the introduction of the newly married young women. *See also under* AETHRA.

L. Deubner, *Attische Feste* (1932), 232 ff. Note above all the inscription of the phratry of the Demotionidae, *IG* ii². 1237 = *SIG*³ 921.
M. P. N.

**APELLAI** (1) (Ἀπέλλαι), a festival of Apollo at Sparta and elsewhere, at Sparta the occasion for a citizen assembly which modern scholars often therefore call the Apella. Its procedure was defined by the *Rhetra* of Lycurgus; all Spartiatae could attend its (perhaps monthly) meetings which were presided over by the kings and Gerousia (q.v.), later (in the 5th c.) by the ephors (q.v.). It could only accept or reject proposals put before it, any right, formal or assumed, of initiating legislation or of amendment having been withdrawn by an addition to the *Rhetra*, ascribed to Kings Theopompus and Polydorus (see SPARTA). It expressed its opinion by acclamation, and if this seemed indecisive, by formal division.

The extent of its competence is uncertain but it had the right to decide disputed royal successions; to appoint military commanders; to elect ephors and other magistrates and members of the Gerousia; to decide on peace or war and the conclusion of treaties; and to approve the emancipation of helots. Any proposed change in the laws required its approval.

We hear also of a μικρὰ ἐκκλησία (Xen. *Hell.* 3. 3. 8)

apparently convoked on urgent occasions, but its composition is uncertain.

Arist. *Pol.* 1273 a; Thuc. 1. 79–87; Plut. *Lyc.* 6; *Agis* 8–11; Diod. Sic. 11. 50. (*and see* SPARTA).
W. G. F.

**APELLAI** (2). Ἀπέλλα is a Dorian word signifying assembly-place, assembly (*see preceding article*). In the plural it signifies a festival corresponding to the Athenian Apaturia (q.v.) at which the new members of the *gens* were introduced. The name of the month Apellaios proves that it was widely spread among the Dorians; otherwise it is known only through the inscription of the Labyadai at Delphi (*SIG*² 438).

Nilsson, *GGR* i.² 556.
M. P. N.

**APELLES** (4th c. B.C.), painter, of Colophon, later of Ephesus (sometimes called Coan because of the Coan Aphrodite). Pliny dates him 332 B.C. (because of the portrait of Alexander). He was taught first by Ephorus of Ephesus, then by Pamphilus (q.v. 1) of Sicyon. When in the Sicyonian school, he helped Melanthius to paint the victorious chariot of the tyrant Aristratus. He painted portraits of Philip, Alexander, and their circle, and a selfportrait. Anecdotes connect him with Alexander, Ptolemy, and Protogenes. He died in Cos while copying his Aphrodite, probably early in the third century.

SELECTED WORKS: 1. Aphrodite Anadyomene, in Cos, later in Rome. Aphrodite rising from the sea, wringing out her hair. 2. Alexander with the thunderbolt, in Ephesus. Alexander darker than nature so that the thunderbolt stood out. 3. Calumny, preceded by Envy, Intrigue, and Deception, and followed by Repentance and Truth, dragging her victim before a man with large ears, attended by Ignorance and Superstition. 4. Sacrifice, in Cos. Described by Herodas (4. 59). Copies of his works have been seen in the Herculaneum tragic actor (Gorgosthenes) (Pfuhl, fig. 653; Rumpf, pl. 51/1) and the Alexander mosaic (Pfuhl, fig. 648; Rumpf, pl. 48). The tone of his pictures was due to a secret varnish. He wrote a book on painting; he claimed to know when to take his hand from a picture (contrast Protogenes), and that his works had charm, χάρις (contrast Melanthius).

Overbeck, 591, 1067, 1073, 1090, 1446–8, 1481, 1687, 1726, 1745, 1748–9, 1751, 1759, 1766, 1772, 1774, 1827–1906, 1921; Pfuhl, 801; Rumpf, *Malerei u. Zeichn.* 147; *Ath. mitt.* 1962, 229.
T. B. L. W.

**APENNINE CULTURE** is the term used to describe the material aspects (almost exclusively ceramic) of the semi-nomadic pastoral economy diffused along the Apennine chain from the Bolognese in the north to the south-east tip of peninsular Italy throughout the Middle and Late Bronze Age. There are particularly significant concentrations in south-east Emilia (Toscanella Imolese), the Marche (Filottrano), Tuscany (Belverde), Latium (Pian Sultano), Campania (Ischia, q.v., has produced Apennine material associated with Late Mycenaean IIIA sherds), Puglia (Coppa Nevigata, Grotta Manaccora, and the Tarentino), and in Lipari (*see* AEOLIAE INSULAE). A division between two sequences, northern and southern, may be expressed typologically in terms of pottery traits and topographically by an east-west line between Termoli and Formia; the material from Lipari, however, has affinities with the northern rather than with the southern sites. In the Late Bronze Age the story of the Apennine Culture is closely linked with that of the *terremare* (*see* TERRAMARA).

S. M. Puglisi *Mon. Ant.* 1951, cols. 1 ff.; id. *La Civiltà Appenninica* (1959); R. Peroni *Arch. Class.* 1958, 243 ff.; id. *Mem. Linc.* 1960, 1 ff.; D. H. Trump *Proc. Prehist. Soc.* 1958, 165 ff.; id. *PBSR* 1963, 1 ff.; id. *Central and Southern Italy before Rome* (1966), 109 ff.; C. E. Östenberg, *Luni sul Mignone e problemi della preistoria d'Italia* (1967).
D. W. R. R.

**APENNINES,** Italy's mountain backbone, branch off from the Alps near Genoa. At first they are of moderate height (3,000–4,000 ft.) and run eastwards forming the southern boundary of Cisalpine Gaul (Northern Apennines); then, near Ariminum, they turn south-east, follow the line of the Adriatic coast and attain great altitudes—9,560 feet at the Gran Sasso (Central Apennines); approaching Lucania they become lower again, swing south and occupy virtually all south-west Italy (Southern Apennines: the granite Sila mountains of the Bruttian Peninsula, although geologically distinct, are generally reckoned a prolongation of the limestone Apennines. Italy's volcanic mountains, however—Albanus, Vesuvius, Vultur—are independent of the Apennine system). The 800-mile Apennine chain is not continuous and unbroken, but consists of tangled mountain masses of varying width, interspersed with numerous upland passes and fertile valleys suitable for agriculture or summer pasturage. Offshoots are numerous, e.g. Apuan Alps (Liguria), Volscian Mountains (Latium); some are completely separated from the main range, e.g. Mons Garganus (Apulia). The Apennines feed most Italian rivers except the Po and some of its tributaries, but, not being perennially snow-capped, supply inadequate amounts of water in summer, when consequently the rivers become mere rills or torrent-beds. The Apennines contain numerous mineral springs but little mineral wealth. In antiquity their cheeses, wolves, bears, goats, extensive forests, and brigands were famous.

Polyb. 2. 16; 3. 110 includes Maritime Alps in the Apennines; Strabo 2. 128; 5. 211; Lucan 2. 396–438; Varro, *Rust.* 2. 1. 5, 16; Pliny, *HN* 11. 240; 16. 197. C. S. du Riche Preller, *Italian Mountain Geology* (1923). E. T. S.

**APER,** MARCUS, an advocate of Gallic origin who attained the praetorship. He apparently visited Britain, perhaps as *tribunus laticlavius*. Tacitus studied his rhetorical methods, and in the *Dialogus* introduces him as a utilitarian vehemently defending lucrative court-oratory in the modern style as against poetry and the older fashions.

Tac. *Dial.* 2; 5–10; 16–23. Syme, *Tacitus*, App. 91. G. C. W.

**APEX,** a sort of mitre derived from the Etruscans, worn by Roman *flamines* and some other priests, or more properly the top of it (Suetonius ap. Servius on *Aen.* 2. 683, 'apex proprie dicitur in summo flaminis pilleo uirga lanata, hoc est in cuius extremitate modica lana est'. The *virga* was a twig or spike of olive-wood (Festus p. 9. 30 Lindsay); the *lana* was a woollen thread, *apiculum*, with which apparently the spike was tied on (ibid. 21. 10). The lower part of the head-dress was the *galerus*; that of the *flamen Dialis* was called *albogalerus*, being made of the skins of white victims sacrificed to Jupiter (ibid. 9. 29; Varro ap. Gel. 10. 15. 32). This was a close-fitting conical cap (Varro, *Ling.* 7. 44).

K. A. Esdaile, *JRS* 1911, 213 ff.; Wissowa, *RK* 499; Latte, *RR* 157, 404, and (for illustration) pl. 23. H. J. R.

**APHAEA** (Ἀφαία), a goddess worshipped in Aegina, where the ruins of her temple (famous for its pedimental sculptures, now in Munich) are still extant. She was identified with Britomartis (q.v.; Paus. 2. 30. 3); i.e. she was of similar character to Artemis (q.v.). H. J. R.

**APHRODISIUS,** SCRIBONIUS, slave and pupil of Horace's teacher, Orbilius, took up the subject of Latin orthography and strongly criticized the work of Verrius Flaccus (q.v. 8). Scribonia, Augustus' first wife, freed him (Suet. *Gram.* 19).

**APHRODITE,** Greek goddess of love, beauty, a fertility. The meaning of the name is uncertain, thou the Greeks, from Hesiod on (*Theog.* 188–206), deriv it from ἀφρός, 'foam', and told of the birth of Aphrod from the sea. She was worshipped throughout almost of the Greek world; the sanctuaries at Paphos (q.v.) a Amathus in Cyprus, at Cythera, and at Corinth we especially renowned. To Homer she is 'the Cyprian', a it was probably from Cyprus, in the Mycenaean age, th Aphrodite first entered Greece, though the Hellenic go dess doubtless owes something to earlier Aegean divi ties, such as Ariadne, whose cults she had absorbed. Gre tradition consistently pointed to an eastern origin f Aphrodite (cf. Hdt. 1. 105; Paus. 1. 14. 7), and it was fro Cyprus that Adonis, the consort of Astarte-Aphrodi was later to come to Athens. But the process of helleniz tion has already gone far in Homer, who makes Aphrod the daughter of Zeus and Dione, and the wife of Hephae tus; Ares, in later myth her husband, appears in t lay of Demodocus (*Od.* 8. 266–366) as her paramou Aeneas is her son by the Trojan Anchises (*Il.* passi *Hymn. Hom. Ven.* 5), and she is ever the partisan of t Trojans (another hint of her non-Hellenic origin) but i warrior, and when she is wounded by Diomedes, Ze reminds her that her sphere is not war but love (*Il.* 428–9).

Primarily, she is a goddess of generation and fertilit and in poetry often seems little more than a persor fication of the sexual instinct and the power of lov Occasionally she presides over marriage, and the beard Aphrodite of Cyprus seems to be an androgynous ty arising from the marriage ritual (*see* HERMAPHRODITU but marriage was a domain largely pre-empted by He Prostitutes, however, considered Aphrodite their patr (cf. Aphrodite Πόρνη, Ἑταίρα, Ath. 13. 572 e–573 a), a there was sacred prostitution (q.v.) in her cult at Corint but in general the public cult, at least, was staid and eve austere.

The evidence for Aphrodite as a goddess of veget tion is slight, but not to be dismissed out of hand. She closely associated with Adonis (q.v.), a divinity of veget tion; here too belong the cult names A. ἐν Κήπο A. Ἄνθεια, and her associations with the Charites, t Horae, and Eros (qq.v.) (cf. the sanctuary of Eros a A. ἐν Κήποις on the north slope of the Acropolis, Broneer, *Hesp.* 1932, 1935). The powers of fertility a generally chthonian (A. Μελαινίς, Paus. 2. 2. 4; 8. 6. 9. 27. 5; A. Ἐπιτυμβία at Delphi, Plut. *Quaest. Ro* 269 b), and to this trait may be due her frequent associ tion in cult with Hermes (q.v.).

Aphrodite was widely worshipped as a goddess the sea and seafaring (A. Ποντία, Εὔπλοια). The arme Aphrodite (ὡπλισμένη) or goddess of war (A. Ἄρε Στρατεία) was worshipped in Sparta, Cyprus, Cyther and elsewhere; this warlike character is probably a dire survival from her Oriental prototypes, and may al explain her associations, chiefly in myth, with Ares (q.v.

Two very common titles are Οὐρανία and Πάνδημ (see *PW*, s.vv.), but the philosophical interpretation these as representing intellectual and common love (I *Symp.* 180 d–181; Xen. *Symp.* 8. 9–10) is unjustifie The title Urania, in fact, seems frequently a mark of t Oriental goddess, and was a cult name at Cypru Cythera, and Corinth. It was also applied to vario foreign goddesses (e.g. the Scythian Argimpasa, Hdt. 59; the Arabian Allat, Hdt. 3. 8; Venus Caelestis Astarte at Carthage). Pandemus, on the other hand, t 'goddess of the whole people', represents the highe political idea to which Aphrodite attained, notably Athens, but also at Erythrae, Thebes, Cos, and Megal polis.

Apart from Hermes, Aphrodite has no strong ass

ciations in cult with the major Hellenic gods. Nor are her festivals, except in Cyprus, of great importance, though that at Delos, where Aphrodite has replaced Ariadne, was very ancient (Plut. *Thes.* 21; Callim. *Del.* 306–13), and several states had a month named for her. The myrtle and the dove are sacred to Aphrodite (cf. dove used for lustration of temple of Pandemus, *IG* ii². 659); the sacrifice of swine seems to mark the fertility cult and the presence of Adonis.

In the Hellenistic period the name 'Syrian A.', (on Delos A. *Ἀγνή*) designates Atargatis (q.v.).

The poets, as in the fragment of Aeschylus' *Danaides* and the magnificent exordium of Lucretius, exalt Aphrodite as the cosmic generative force pervading all nature.

Farnell, *Cults* ii, chs. 21–23; Nilsson, *Feste* (1906), 362 ff.; *GGR* i. 519 ff.; L. Preller–C. Robert, *Griechische Mythologie*⁴ (1894) i, 345 ff.; R. Dussaud, *Rev. Hist. Rel.* 1916, 1. See VENUS. F. R. W.

**APHRODITE IN ART.** Greek art took several hundred years to achieve a truly individual vision of Aphrodite. Archaic art represents her either in the Oriental type of a nude goddess or as a standing or seated figure distinguished only by attributes from other goddesses. (E. Suhr, *AJArch*, 1961, 389).

Classical art of the fifth century endows Aphrodite with majestic beauty and grave charm (G. M. A. Hanfmann, *AJArch*. 1962, 281). The famous images by Phidias, Alcamenes, and Agoracritus (A. W. Lawrence, *Class. Sculpt.* 1929) are lost, but we can admire in originals the poetic charm of Aphrodite rising from the sea (Ludovisi Throne: W. Hahland, *JÖAI* 1953, 27; E. Simon, *Die Geburt der A.*, 1959), the quiet dignity of Aphrodite on the swan (painted cup, London), the harmony of Aphrodite and Eros in the Parthenon frieze. An Aphrodite on a tortoise and one leaning on a pillar reflect monumental images of Periclean times (Schrader, *Phidias*, 1924).

'The finest statue not only of Praxiteles but in the whole world is the Aphrodite for the sight of which many have sailed to Cnidos', says Pliny (*HN* 36. 4. 20). Carved about the middle of the fourth century and known through Roman copies, this statue shows the goddess laying her garment on a hydria before taking a bath. The first convincing representation of the beautiful female nude, distinguished by an evasive charm, the Cnidian Aphrodite became a model for the numerous Aphrodites of Hellenistic and Roman times (T. Kraus, *Die A. von Knidos*, 1957). Of these the best known are Aphrodite of Cyrene, the popular Venus de Milo (J. Charbonneaux, *La Vénus de Milo*, 1958), the crouching Aphrodite by the Bithynian Doidalsas (R. Lullies, *Die Kauernde Aphrodite*, 1954), the armed Aphrodite of Acrocorinthus, and the various types described as 'Venus Genetrix'.

C. Blinkenberg, *Knidia* (1933);'A. W. Lawrence, *Later Greek Sculpture* (1927); O. Broneer, *The Armed Aphrodite* (1930); M. Bieber, *Röm. Mitt.* 1933. G. M. A. H.; J. R. T. P.

**APHTHONIUS,** AELIUS FESTUS (3rd c. A.D.), wrote four books *De Metris*, which now form the bulk of the *Ars Grammatica* of Marius Victorinus (ed. Keil, *Gramm. Lat.* 6. 31–173). This incorporation (not due to Victorinus himself) was effected before A.D. 400.

Schanz-Hosius, § 829. J. F. M.

**APICIUS,** proverbial cognomen of several Roman gourmets, especially M. Gavius (*PIR*² G 91), who lived under Augustus and Tiberius, made a science of his culinary expertise, and left some writings (Pliny, *HN* 10. 33; Sen. *Helv.* 10. 8–9; schol. Juv. 4. 23; etc.). The *De Re Coquinaria* ascribed to (Caelius) Apicius by the MSS.

was, however, compiled later and probably took its present form in the fourth century.

TEXT. Giarratano–Vollmer (1922); A. Marsili, (1957).
TRANSLATION (with text). B. Flower–E. Rosenbaum (1958); J. André (1965), French.
F. Vollmer, *Sitz. München* (1920), 6. L. A. M.

**APION,** son of Posidonius, a Greek (or Graeco-Egyptian) of Alexandria, pupil of Didymus, and successor to Theon as head of the Alexandrian school. He was later at Rome, under Tiberius and Claudius. He was nicknamed *Πλειστονίκης* (by himself), *cymbalum mundi*, and *propriae famae tympanum* (by Tiberius and Pliny, Pliny *HN* Pref. 25), and, for his industry, *Μόχθος*. He wrote on Egypt (cf. Josephus, *Ap.* 2. 143; and Gell. 5. 14. 10–30); he called up (so he said) Homer's spirit to ascertain the poet's parentage and birthplace, but published no account of the proceedings, and compiled, *inter alia*, an alphabetically arranged Homeric glossary, based, as was usual, on Aristarchus, and preserved only in fragments and in the derivative work of Apollonius Sophistes.

FRAGMENTS. *FGrH*. 616. A. Ludwich, *Philol.* 1917, 205; 1919, 90; K. Alpers, 'Theognostos, *Περὶ ὀρθογραφίας*' (Diss. Hamburg 1964), 54 ff. P. R. B. F.

**APIS,** the sacred bull worshipped in Memphis. His cult attained national prominence and under Ptolemaic and Roman rulers official recognition was given to it and to the feast-days connected with it. When the sacred animal died, a successor was chosen and the dead beast was mummified and entombed during a period of sorrow and fasting which lasted for seventy days. Apis is mentioned a few times in Greek inscriptions as one of the gods included among the Egyptian deities, but his chief importance for Graeco-Roman religion lies in the fact that the cult of Sarapis (q.v.) originated in the worship of the Osirified (*see* OSIRIS) Apis-bulls entombed in the temple at Memphis. T. A. B.

**APODEKTAI,** a board of ten officials at Athens, who received all the moneys from the revenue-collecting departments and paid them over to the spending departments, under the supervision of the *boule*. They were instituted by Cleisthenes; from the time of Pericles they were appointed by lot.

**APOLLINARIUS** (*c.* A.D. 310–*c.* 390) was a brilliant, original Christian thinker whose treatment of the incarnation ranks as one of the classic heresies (Apollinarianism). A champion of Nicene orthodoxy against Arius' teaching, he became bishop of Laodicea *c.* 360. As a counter to Julian's anti-Christian educational policy he rewrote parts of the Bible in classical forms. He was the author of numerous commentaries and treatises which (apart from works pseudonymously attributed to orthodox writers) survive only in fragments. His distinctive teaching was that the Logos took the place of the human rational soul in Christ. Only so, he argued, could his unity and moral integrity be secured; but this solution was soon rejected as mutilating Christ's humanity.

Texts in H. Lietzmann, *Apollinaris von Laodicea* i (1904).
J. N. D. K.

**APOLLO** (*Ἀπόλλων*, Epic also *Ἀππόλλων* or *Ἄπόλλων*, as *Il.* 1. 14), the most Greek of all gods, in art the ideal type of young, but not immature manly beauty. His functions are especially music, archery, prophecy, medicine, and the care of flocks and herds; with agriculture he has much less to do. He is often associated with the higher developments of civilization, approving codes of law (as Hdt. 1. 65. 6), inculcating high moral and religious principles (as id. 6. 86. 15; Aelian, *VH* 3. 44), and favouring philosophy (e.g. he was said to be the real father of Plato). In matters of ritual, especially of purification, his oracles are commonly regarded as the supreme authority. Politically, he is especially prominent in suggesting or approving schemes of colonization (Apollo Archegetes, q.v.). His cult was panhellenic and he is regularly spoken of with profound respect, some of the war-time plays of Euripides being an exception.

His name is not found on Linear B tablets and is of uncertain etymology, perhaps not Greek. Of his origin there are two principal theories. (1) He comes from somewhere north of Greece. In support of this it is urged that his seats of worship are numerous and ancient in the north; the legendary Apolline people, the Hyperboreans (q.v.), are always thought of as northerners and are real enough to send yearly offerings to Delos which follow a route from the north (Hdt. 4. 33; cf. Farnell, op. cit. *infra*, 99 f.); and the ritual of the Stepteria points north also. (2) He is Asianic, for his title Λύκειος and the name of his mother Leto suggest Lycia and the Lycian *Lada*; he has numerous connexions with that country and with the Oriental sacred number seven (e.g. his birthday is the seventh of the month, Hesiod, *Op.* 771); he is especially worshipped at Troy and warmly supports the Trojans in Homer. The question is yet undecided. (Short bibliography in Rose, *Handb. of Gk. Myth.*, 158 n. 2; add Bethe, 'Apollon der Hellene', in Ἀντίδωρον, Göttingen, 1924.)

It was conjectured as early as the fifth century B.C. (Euripides, fr. 781, 11–13 Nauck; Aesch. ap. [Eratosth.], *Catast.* 24 is uncertain) that Apollo was the Sun, and this theory prevailed in Hellenistic and imperial times and was for a while revived by modern scholars. It lacks, however, any real evidence (see Farnell, 136 ff.). It is more likely that the god's origins are to be sought in his titles of Nomios and Lykeios. If he was a god of herdsmen in wild country, it is highly probable that his interests would include archery, music, and medicine, and that he should be somehow connected with their worst enemy, the wolf, is equally reasonable; he can both send and stay that and other plagues. How and where he became a prophetic god is not known, but he is so from our earliest records.

Of his oracular shrines, Delphi was the chief, though others were important, notably Branchidae and Claros in Ionia, whereof the latter was particularly prominent in Hellenistic times. The method of divination was by possession, the medium being filled with the god, or his inspiration (see further Farnell, 179 ff. and DELPHIC ORACLE). Of his ritual perhaps the most remarkable was the Delphic Stepteria, held every eight years. In this, a boy, apparently personating the god, was led to a hut near the temple, called the palace of Python (see below); this was set on fire; the boy went away into supposed banishment; and finally all concerned were purified at Tempe and came back by the traditional sacred route known as the Pythian Way (see Farnell, 293). The ancients regarded the ritual as a sort of play commemorating the killing of Python (see below). Delphi, through the enterprise of its clergy, became the nearest approach to a Vatican which Greece possessed, though it had no formal authority to enforce its advice. Delphic propaganda may be traced in the tendency to introduce Apollo as adviser, inspirer, etc., into any and every myth which contains a prophet or a prediction. Delphi claimed to be the centre of the world, the famous stone called the *omphalos* (navel) marking the very spot. In art, Apollo is often represented as sitting on this, but the actual seat of his medium, the Pythia, was a tripod, hence continually associated with Apollo and his oracles.

Apollo's earliest adventure (for his birth at Delos, *see* LETO) was the killing of Python, a formidable dragon which guarded Delphi (in the earliest version, the

Homeric Hymn to the Pythian Apollo, 300 [122], it is a female and unnamed). He also killed Tityos, a giant who offered violence to Leto, *Od.* 11. 580. For other divine vengeances, *see* ALOADAE, NIOBE.

Of his many loves, the most famous was that for Coronis, mother of Asclepius (q.v.). For the adventures to which Asclepius' death led, *see* ALCESTIS. Very interesting is the tale of his unsuccessful rivalry with Idas (q.v.) for Marpessa. Another object of his affections was Cassandra (Alexandra), daughter of Priam. To win her he gave her the gift of prophecy, but having received it she would not grant him her love. He could not recall his gift but made it futile by causing her always to be disbelieved (Aesch. *Ag.* 1202 ff.). Somewhat similar, probably modelled upon this, is the story of the Cumaean Sibyl, as told by Ovid (*Met.* 14. 132 ff.). He bade her choose whatever she wished, and she asked to live as many years as she held grains of sand. But she forgot to ask for permanent youth, and, having denied him, received no more favours from him; hence she grew so old that she finally hung in a vessel, saying, when asked what she wanted, that she wished to die (Petronius. *Sat.* 48. 8; see Campbell Bonner in *Quantulacunque, Studies presented to Kirsopp Lake* . . . (U.S.A. 1937), 1 ff.). By Cyrene, granddaughter of the river Peneus, he became father of Aristaeus (q.v. 1); he was first attracted to her by observing her courage and prowess in hunting on Mt. Pelion, where she was fighting a lion bare-handed, and carried her off to that part of Africa which was afterwards named after her (Pind. *Pyth.* 9. 17 ff.; it was a foundation legend of the colony of Cyrene: see L. Vitali, *Religione Cyrenaica* (1932), 107 ff.).

Apollo was usually impartial in politics, though he shows Troy great favour in the *Iliad*. His principal departures from this attitude were during the Persian Wars, when the Delphic oracle began by being partial to the Persians, and the Peloponnesian War, when it was whole-heartedly of the Spartan faction; hence Euripides' attitude (see above).

In Italy, Apollo was introduced early, partly through Etruria (cf. the famous statue of him from Veii), partly direct from Greek settlements. Although now and then equated with native gods (as the deity of Soracte, *Aen.* 11. 785), he never had a generally accepted identification. At Rome his Republican cult seems to have been primarily that of a god of healing (the Vestals addressed him as *Apollo medice, Apollo Paean*, Macrob. *Sat.* 1. 17. 15) and of prophecy (cf. SIBYLLA, QUINDECIMVIRI). He had a shrine, *Apollinar*, outside the Porta Carmentalis, and a temple was erected in consequence of the plague of 433 B.C. Augustus, who had a special devotion to him partly owing to the nearness of the battle of Actium to one of his temples, erected a magnificent temple on the Palatine (thus receiving him *intra pomerium*). It was vowed in 36 and dedicated in 28; to it a celebrated library was attached. Thenceforward, under the Empire, Apollo Palatinus was in some sort the equal of Jupiter Optimus Maximus.

Apollo is very popular in art from the seventh century, as a youth, naked or robed, with bow or lyre, alone or with Artemis and sometimes Leto, the Muses or other deities, or in action-scenes (Niobids, Tityos, etc.).

*See also* ARISTEAS (1), DELOS, DELPHIC ORACLE, OMPHALOS, STONES SACRED, THEBES (1).

Farnell, *Cults* iv. 98 ff.; W. K. C. Guthrie, *The Greeks and their Gods* (1950), 73 ff., 183 ff.; Wissowa, *RK* 293 ff.; Latte, *RR* 221 f.; J. Gagé, *Apollon romain* (1955), J. Fontenrose, *Python* (U.S.A. 1959), K. Kerényi. *Apollo*² (forthcoming); for temples in Rome, Nash, *Pict. Dict. Rome* i. 28 ff.                                                    H. J. R.; C. M.

**APOLLODORUS** (1) (5th c. B.C.), painter, of Athens. Pliny dates him 408 B.C., but he must have been painting by 430, if Zeuxis (q.v.) 'entered the door opened b

Apollodorus'. He was the first to represent appearance (*species*) and was known as σκιαγράφος. Σκιαγραφία, common in Plato for illusionistic painting, means primarily plastic shading by a gradation of colour; on vases shading is not used for human figures until 425–400. Although only two of his pictures are mentioned, his importance was fully recognized in antiquity.

Overbeck, 1641–7; Pfuhl, 734; R. G. Steven, *CQ* 1933, 150; A. Rumpf, *JDAI* 1934, 10; *Malerei u. Zeichn.* 121.     T. B. L. W.

**APOLLODORUS** (2) of Gela. New Comedy poet, contemporary of Menander according to *Suda*. He has been identified with Apollodorus (q.v. 3) of Carystus, but Pollux 10. 138 and inscriptional evidence (see E. Capps, *AJPhil.* 1900, 45 ff.) prove his separate existence.

*FCG* i. 459 ff., iv. 438 ff.; *CAF* iii. 278 ff.     W. G. W.

**APOLLODORUS** (3) of Carystus, New Comedy poet, more famous than Apollodorus (q.v. 2) of Gela, and sometimes referred to as Apollodorus 'the Athenian' (which suggests the grant of Athenian citizenship). He composed forty-seven dramas and won five victories (*Suda*). A contemporary of Posidippus, he produced his first play *c.* 285 B.C. Ἑκύρα was the original of Terence's *Hecyra*: Ἐπιδικαζόμενος of Terence's *Phormio*. These Latin adaptations seem to indicate that Apollodorus was greatly influenced by Menander (q.v. 1), and that one of his characteristics was an obsessive attention to detail in the organization of his plots. Fr. 5, the folly of Greek fighting Greek.

*FCG* iv. 440 ff.; *CAF* iii. 280 ff.; Demiańczuk, *Supp. Com.* 8 f.; Page, *GLP*, no. 58. See E. F. Krause, *De Apollodoris Comicis* (1903); M. Schuster, *De Apollodoris Poetis Comicis* (1907); W. E. J. Kuiper, *Two Comedies by Apollodorus of Carystus: Terence's Hecyra and Phormio* (1938; too speculative); M. R. Posani, *Atene e Roma* 1942, 141 ff.; K. Mras, *Anz. Österreich. Akad.* 1948, 184 ff.; Webster, *Later Greek Comedy*, 205 ff.     W. G. A.

**APOLLODORUS** (4) of Alexandria, physician and scientist of the beginning of the third century B.C. His chief work, Περὶ θηρίων or Λόγος θηριακός (on poisonous creatures), was the primary source for all the later pharmacologists of antiquity (e.g. Numenius, Nicander, Heraclides of Tarentum, Sostratus, Aelian, Sextius Niger, Pliny, Dioscorides, Archigenes, Aemilius Macer). He seems also to have written a work Περὶ θανασίμων (or δηλητηρίων) φαρμάκων.

Fragments in O. Schneider, *Nicandrea*, 181 ff.     W. D. R.

**APOLLODORUS** (5) of Pergamum (*c.* 104–22 B.C.), rhetor who taught Octavianus (Suet. *Aug.* 89; Tac. *Dial.* 19) and others at Rome. His Τέχνη, dedicated to C. Matius, was translated into Latin by C. Valgius Rufus; but his real influence was due to his oral teaching, which was challenged by Theodorus (q.v. 3) of Gadara. His theories and those of his followers are known from Quintilian (2. 11; 3. 1). He insisted that all legal speeches should be composed of the four regular 'parts'—proem, narration, argumentation, peroration—in the regular order. This contrasts with the less rigid precepts of Theodorus.

M. Schanz, 'Die Apollodoreer und die Theodoreer', *Hermes* 1890.     D. A. R.

**APOLLODORUS** (6) of Athens (b. *c.* 180 B.C.), pupil of Aristarchus, left Alexandria (*c.* 146 B.C.), perhaps for Pergamum, and later moved to Athens, where he remained until his death. He was a scholar of great learning and varied interests.

WORKS. **1.** Chronological: Χρονικά or Χρονικὴ σύνταξις, dedicated to Attalus II of Pergamum and based on the chronological researches of Eratosthenes (q.v.), was written in comic trimeters and dealt in considerable

detail with successive periods of history, important incidents, philosophical schools, the life and work of individuals from the fall of Troy (1184 B.C.) to 144 B.C.; later it was continued, not certainly by Apollodorus himself, down to 119 B.C. **2.** Mythological: *Bibliotheca* (Βιβλιοθήκη), a study of Greek heroic mythology. The extant work of this name, which presents an uncritical summary of the traditional Greek mythology, belongs to the first or second century A.D. **3.** Theological: Περὶ θεῶν, a rationalistic account of Greek religion, much used by later writers. **4.** Geographical: a commentary on the Homeric Catalogue of Ships, an important work of scholarship based on Eratosthenes and Demetrius of Scepsis, and containing many quotations from poets and historians and many criticisms of earlier writes; Strabo found it a valuable source for books 8 to 10 of his *Geography*. The Γῆς περίοδος or Περὶ γῆς, a geographical guide-book in comic trimeters, was probably a later forgery. **5.** Critical and exegetical: commentaries on Epicharmus and Sophron; these probably included a critical recension of the text. **6.** Etymological: Ἐτυμολογίαι or Ἐτυμολογούμενα or Γλῶσσαι.

F. Jacoby, *FGrH* iiB. 244 and *Apollodors Chronik* (1902); [*Bibliotheca*], R. Wagner in *Mythographi Graeci*, i (1894), J. G. Frazer, with translation (Loeb, 1921); C. Robert, *De Apollodori bibliotheca* (1873); A. Diller, *TAPA* 1935, 296 ff.; M. van der Valk, *Rev. Ét. grec.* 1958, 100 ff. (*Bibliotheca*); R. Münzel, *De Apollodori περὶ θεῶν libris* (1883).     J. F. L.

**APOLLODORUS** (7) of Damascus, a Greek townplanner and architect who worked at Rome in the first century A.D. He planned the Forum of Trajan and designed, or supervised, the Basilica and Column of Trajan, and other adjacent architecture; and he built a bridge over the Danube. Trajan treated him with deference; but Hadrian, offended by Apollodorus' criticism of his architectural plans, found a pretext for banishing him in A.D. 129, and ultimately had him executed (Dio Cass. *Epit.* 69. 4). Apollodorus wrote works on military and civil engineering. For his surviving work on *Engines of War* see C. Wescher, *La Poliorcétique des Grecs* (1867), 137 ff.     H. W. R.; R. E. W.

**APOLLODORUS** (8) of Seleuceia on the Tigris, Stoic philosopher, the author of an *Ethics* and a *Physics* cited by Diog. Laert. 7. 102, 129; 125, 135. He also wrote logical works. Testimonia in H. von Arnim, *SVF* iii. 259–61.

**APOLLONIA** was the name of several Greek cities. The chief of these was in Illyria, founded *c.* 600 B.C. where the river Aous enters the coastal plain, with relatively easy communications across the Balkan range. It was founded as a Corinthian colony by 200 settlers (Steph. Byz. s.v.) and grew rapidly in size and prosperity, until it was able to destroy one of its neighbours, Thronium, by the middle of the fifth century. In the Hellenistic period its strategic position and its wealth attracted the Macedonian, Molossian, and Illyrian kings and also Corcyra. It joined Rome in 229 B.C., was treated as a free city and prospered greatly as the main base of Roman armies in the wars against Macedon. After 146 it was one of the terminal points of the Via Egnatia (q.v.), and it was Caesar's headquarters in the campaign of Dyrrhachium (48). In 45–44 Caesar gathered an army at Apollonia for his eastern campaigns, and at his death his grandnephew Octavius was stationed there as a cadet.

Recent excavations reported in *Buletin i universitetit Shtetëror të Tiranës, Seria shkencat shqërore* 1960, 1. 51 ff.; 1963, 3, 117 ff.     M. C.; N. G. L. H.

**APOLLONIUS** (1) **RHODIUS** (3rd c. B.C.) of Alexandria or less probably Naucratis, but generally called the

Rhodian owing to his retirement to Rhodes. Born c. 295 B.C., Apollonius was a pupil of Callimachus (*Vitae*, the *Suda*). According to *Vita* i (Mooney, 1) he turned late to writing poetry. This conflicts with the statement of the same authority that Apollonius gave a recitation of the *Argonautica* while still a stripling (ἔτι ἔφηβον ὄντα), was badly received, and retired to Rhodes, where he revised his poem, which then became famous. (At several places in bk. 1 the scholia cite the version of the *proekdosis* ( = the first edition), but the differences from the present text are not important.) *POxy* 1241, a list of Alexandrian librarians, establishes that Apollonius held the post of *Prostates* (director) of the Alexandrian library after Zenodotus and before Eratosthenes. *Vita* ii represents Apollonius as being appointed librarian after his return from Rhodes, but this dating and the *Suda*'s statement that he succeeded Eratosthenes as librarian probably originate in a confusion with Apollonius the Eidograph, who is known (from *POxy* 1241) to have followed Eratosthenes in this office. On the whole it is likely that Apollonius succeeded Zenodotus as librarian c. 260 and held the post till the accession of Euergetes in 247. The quarrel between Apollonius and his teacher Callimachus seems to have been one of the important episodes in the bitter literary controversy between the writers of long traditional epics and those of short and highly finished poems. The freedom with which Apollonius refashioned in his own style whole passages of Callimachean poetry suggests the turning of a purely literary discussion into a personal feud (cf. Pf. Call. ii, xli and vol. i *passim*). This may well have been enhanced by friction at the library, where Callimachus, who was never librarian, was presumably Apollonius' subordinate. Though Callimachus is said to have been victorious, and Apollonius to have retired to Rhodes, it appears that finally the long traditional epic won the day (cf. K. Ziegler, *Das hellenistische Epos* 1934). Tradition records a reconciliation between Apollonius and Callimachus, and that they were buried close to one another (Vit. Apollon. Rhod. A, in Schol., Wendel, 2. 5).

WORKS. *Verse*. In the fashion of the day Apollonius wrote poems, from which a few hexameters survive, on the Foundation (κτίσις) of Alexandria, Naucratis, Caunus, Cnidus, Rhodes, possibly Lesbos. A poem called *Canobus* was in choliambics. Of his *Epigrams* only *Anth. Pal.* 11. 275, an attack on Callimachus, is extant. Apollonius' *magnum opus* was the *Argonautica*, narrating in four books—he was the first epic poet to divide his own work into books—Argo's voyage to Colchis by the Propontis and Black Sea (bks. 1-2), the winning with Medea's aid of the Golden Fleece (bk. 3), and the return by the Danube, Po, Rhône, Mediterranean, and northern Africa (bk. 4). It is the great epic of the Alexandrian period, the only one before Virgil that in subject and extent (5834 hexameter lines) could aspire to a comparison with Homer. In real Alexandrian style Apollonius, who was both poet and scholar, delights in displaying his erudition and explaining the *aetia* (causes) of names, cults, relics, habits, etc., when recasting the celebrated myth. It is evident that he consulted a great number of authorities, and the excellent scholia record many of his sources. Apollonius was the first poet to place love—Medea's love for Jason—in the foreground of the action in an epic poem. The enormous effect this exercised upon subsequent writing has secured for the *Argonautica* a significant place in the history of the world's literature. Except for Sappho, no other Greek poet has so vividly portrayed the first awakening of love in a young woman's heart, nor followed so closely its psychological development. In this lies the perennial charm of book 3. Apollonius is also capable of delightful descriptions. Amazingly rich is, for instance, the shading, when portraying the appearance of morning and night,

and there are brilliant 'baroque' scenes of great plasti charm—e.g. that of Thetis and her sisters assisting Arg through the Wandering Rocks (4. 933 f.)—as well ǎ delightful 'genre' scenes, from which a delicate iron is not absent (e.g. 3. 43 f.). Moreover, he introduces number of striking new similes. But as an epic the woi is unsuccessful. Its main defect is a want of structur unity. The poet did not succeed in moulding into a whol the abundant erudite material he had collected; too ofte the narrative falls into long, disjointed, soulless passage At the same time Apollonius is weak in characterizatior Jason, his central hero, is highly uninspiring and blood less, completely lacking the energy of a heroic leade. Even Medea has no unity of character—Medea of book stands in sharp contrast with Medea of book 3—and ha little real epic grandeur. How short she falls in tha respect of Virgil's Dido! Apollonius' relation to the heroi past is in a sense almost 'modern'. There is no whole hearted, credulous admiration of the great past, bu rather an attitude of coolly critical superiority, and thi does not help in the writing of an epic. Apollonius vocabulary is mainly taken from Homer, but in Alexan drian manner he is continually varying and 'interpretin the Homeric words and phrases. Not a single line of th *Argonautica* could stand unaltered in Homer. Indeed, hi greatest achievement as a stylist lies in the subtle adapta tion of Homer's language to describe a new world c romantic sentiment. Metrically Apollonius' hexamete follows Homer rather than Callimachus. Apollonius wa much read and admired in late antiquity. The papyi show that he was highly esteemed in the imperial perioc and he is one of the few Alexandrian poets whose wor survived in medieval MSS.

*Prose*. Apollonius had some repute as a scholar. ⲁ tract of his *Against Zenodotus* is mentioned, also works o Archilochus, Antimachus, and Hesiod.

TEXT. H. Fränkel (1961); R. C. Seaton (1929); R. Merkel (1854 Powell, *Coll. Alex.*, 4 f. (fragments); C. Wendel, *Scholia Vetera* (193! republ. 1958); (with transl.) R. C. Seaton (Loeb, 1912).
COMMENTARIES. G. W. Mooney (1912); M. M. Gillies (bk. 3, 1928, F. Vian (bk. 3, 1961); A. Ardizzoni (bk. 3, 1958).
GENERAL. G. Knaack, 'Apollonios (71)', in *PW* ii. 126 ff.; Christ Schmid–Stählin ii. i⁶. 140 ff.; E. Delage, *La Géographie dans le Argonautiques d' A. de Rhodes* (1930); F. Mehmel, 'Virgil und Apol Rhodios, Untersuchungen über die Zeitvorstellung in der antike epischen Erzählungen', *Hamburger Arbeiten z. Altertumswissenschaft* (1940); P. Händel, *Beobachtungen z. epischen Technik des A. Rhodios* (1954); H. Fränkel, 'Das Argonautenepos des A.', *MH* 195' id., *Abh. Akad. Wiss. Gött. Phil.-hist. Kl.* III⁰ Folge, 55 (1964 H. Herter, 'Hellenistische Dichtung seit 1921, II Teil: Apolloniᴄ Rhodios', *Bursians Jahresbericht*, 285 (1944–55); H. Erbse, *Rh. Mu* 1963, 229 f. E. A. B.; C. A. ⸋

## APOLLONIUS (2, *PW* 112) of Perge mathematiciᶏ

(fl. 2nd half of 3rd. c. B.C.). Born at Perge in Pamphyliᶏ he studied at Alexandria with the pupils of Euclid. Ther he composed the first version, in eight books, of hi *Conics* for a geometer, Naucrates, 'somewhat too hurried ly' (*Conics* 1 praef.). He visited Ephesus and Pergamun where he stayed with one Eudemus, to whom he sub sequently sent the first three books of the revised versio of the *Conics*. After Eudemus' death the remaining book were sent to Attalus, perhaps King Attalus I of Perga mum (q.v.).

Of the *Conics* (κωνικά) the first four books survive i Greek and the next three in Arabic translation; the eight is lost. Apollonius states (*Conics* 1 praef.) that the fir four books form an elementary introduction, while th remainder are particular extensions (περιουσιαστικώτερο He claims no originality for the *content* of *Conics* 1-4, bᵘ says that he expounds the fundamental properties 'moi fully and generally' than his predecessors. This is ful justified: earlier writers on conics (*see* MATHEMATICS including Archimedes, had described them as sectior of a right circular cone by a plane at right angles to generator, and hence the parabola, ellipse, and hyperbola were known as 'section of a right-angled cone', 'of an acute-angled cone', and 'of an obtuse-angled cone' respectively. Apollonius generates all three from the most general type of circular cone, the double oblique. He then defines the fundamental properties in terms of the 'application of areas' familiar from Euclid, using the terms παραβολή, ἔλλειψις and ὑπερβολή, according as the applied figure exactly fits, falls short of, or exceeds that to which it is applied.

Apollonius did for conics what Euclid had done for elementary geometry: both his terminology and his methods became canonical and eliminated the work of his predecessors. Like Euclid, too, his exposition follows the logical rather than the original sequence of working. Investigation of the latter has revealed how 'algebraic' his methods are. His silence on some features of conics (e.g. the focus of the parabola) is not due to ignorance, but to the elementary nature of the treatise; the specialized investigations of books 5–7 cover only a selection of possible topics, but are enough to reveal Apollonius as an original mathematical genius second only to Archimedes in antiquity.

Commentaries to the *Conics* were written by Serenus (3) and Hypatia (q.v.). That by Eutocius on books 1–4 is extant. Pappus provides lemmata, including some to the lost book 8.

Of other works by Apollonius there survives only the λόγου ἀποτομή (*Cutting-off of a Ratio*), in two books, in Arabic translation. Pappus (bk. 7) describes briefly the contents of five more lost works: (1) χωρίου ἀποτομή (*Cutting-off of an Area*); (2) διωρισμένη τομή (*Determinate Section*); (3) ἐπαφαί (*Tangencies*); (4) νεύσεις (*Inclinations*); (5) τόποι ἐπίπεδοι (*Plane Loci*). Apollonius also wrote works on the *Cylindrical Helix* (Proclus in Eucl. 105), the *Comparison of the Dodecahedron and Eicosahedron* (Hypsicles, Euclid bk. 14, 2), and on unordered irrationals (Pappus in Eucl. 10, 219 Junge–Thomson). In his ὠκυτόκιον (*Quick Delivery*) he calculated limits for the value of π closer than those of Archimedes (q.v.) (Eutocius in Arch. 258). His καθόλου πραγματεία (*General Treatise*) dealt with the foundations of geometry (Marinus in Data Eucl. 234). Pappus (bk. 2) gives excerpts from a work in which Apollonius sets out a system of expressing large numbers by, in effect, using 10,000 instead of ten as a base (cf. ARCHIMEDES, *Sand-reckoner*).

In optics Apollonius wrote a work Περὶ πυρείου (*On the Burning-mirror*) (*Frag. Math. Bobiense*, ed. Heiberg, *Mathematici Graeci Minores* 88). In theoretical astronomy his work was of fundamental importance. From passages in Ptolemy's *Almagest* (4. 6 and 12. 1) it seems probable that it was he who first established the equivalence of eccentric and epicyclic models of planetary motion, and applied this to the determination of the moon's eccentricity and the stationary points of the planets. This was an essential foundation for the systems of Hipparchus and Ptolemy (qq.v.)

DATE. Evidence in *PW* ii. 151, further G. Huxley in *GRBS* 1963, 100 ff.

EDITIONS. Critical text of *Conics* 1–4, with Latin translation, Eutocius' commentary and fragments of lost works by J. L. Heiberg (Teubner, 1891, 1893). Of the Arabic version only part of book 5 has been published, with German translation, by L. Nix (1889). For the rest of books. 5–7 the basis is still Edmund Halley's Latin translation in the *editio princeps* of the Greek text (1710). λόγου ἀποτομή: no edition of the Arabic, Latin translation by Halley (1706). For the history of the text and editions see Heiberg's edition vol. ii, lvii ff.

TRANSLATIONS OF THE CONICS. T. L. Heath, *Apollonius of Perga* (1896, repr. 1961: much adapted, but with useful introduction). French, P. ver Eecke, *Les Coniques d'Apollonius de Perge* (1963: all seven books; the most useful translation). German, A. Czwalina, *Die Kegelschnitte des Apollonius* (bks. 1–4 only: 1926).

COMMENT. H. G. Zeuthen, *Die Lehre von den Kegelschnitten im Altertum* (1886, repr. 1966). Heath, *Hist. of Gr. Maths.* ii, 126 ff. very full summary, includes references to attempts to restore the lost works). O. Neugebauer, *Apolloniusstudien, Quellen und Studien z.*

*Gesch. d. Math.* (1929– ) B 2. 215 ff. (for Apollonius' 'algebra'). On Apollonius' astronomical contributions see O. Neugebauer in *Scripta Mathematica* 1959, 5 ff. G. J. T.

**APOLLONIUS** (3) (3rd c. B.C.), the finance minister of Egypt for about twenty years from 262 B.C., held an estate of some three square miles at Philadelphia in the Fayûm; it was reclaimed land, tenable at the king's will. His development of the estate can be traced from the correspondence of Zenon, his right-hand man; he was specially interested in the improvement of livestock, horticulture, and viticulture. He had extensive business interests in Egypt and the Levant and owned a merchant fleet, as is shown by the same correspondence; there is also mention in it of properties in Alexandria and at Memphis which he seems to have possessed. Zenon, a Carian from Caunus, entered his service soon after his appointment to office, and settled at Philadelphia probably in 256; thereafter he managed Apollonius' estates, and acquired businesses of his own, which he carried on for some years after Apollonius disappears as a landholder at Philadelphia (c. 242). Of his associates the most important was Cleon, an engineer employed in the reclamation of the Fayûm, whose works are recorded in other papyri besides those of Zenon.

M. Rostovtzeff, *A Large Estate in Egypt* (1922); Cl. Préaux, *Les Grecs en Égypte* (1947). Apollonius' development of the estate, and Zenon's management of it, are known particularly from the following collections of papyri: Cairo (*Cat. général des antiq. égypt. du Musée du Caire, Zenon Papyri*, ed. C. C. Edgar, 5 vols. 1925–40); Michigan, *Zenon Papyri*, ed. C. C. Edgar (U.S.A. 1931); Columbia, *Columbia Pap., Zenon Papyri*, ed W. L. Westermann and E. S. Hasenoehrl (2 vols, U.S.A. 1934–40). J. G. M.

**APOLLONIUS** (4) (2nd c. B.C.) of Alabanda, ὁ μαλακός, a pupil of Menecles of Alabanda. He founded a school of rhetoric at Rhodes, visited by Scaevola (121 B.C.) and M. Antonius (98 B.C.).

**APOLLONIUS** (5) perhaps of the 2nd c. B.C., author of Ἱστορίαι θαυμάσιαι, a compilation from Aristotle, Theophrastus, Aristoxenus, etc.

Ed. O. Keller, *Rerum Naturalium Scriptores* i. (1877), 43 ff. *PW* Suppl. iv. 45.

**APOLLONIUS** (6) (1st c. B.C.), sculptor, son of Archias, of Athens. Known from signature in Athens and on bronze herm of Polyclitus' Doryphorus (Winter, *KB* 393. 3); three other herms from the same villa in Herculaneum are also probably his.

**APOLLONIUS** (7), sculptor, son of Nestor, of Athens, signed the Belvedere torso in the Vatican (Winter, *KB* 394. 2). The supposed signature on the bronze boxer in the Terme is apparently an illusion (M. Guarducci, *Ann. della Scuola archeol. di Atene* 1959–60, 361). Apollonius may also have made the cult statue of Jupiter Capitolinus, dedicated 69 B.C., which is reflected in small bronzes.

T. B. L. W.

**APOLLONIUS** (8) of Citium, an Alexandrian physician of about 50 B.C. Works: (extant) commentary on Hippocrates Περὶ ἄρθρων; (lost) Πρὸς τὰ τοῦ Ταραντίνου (against Heraclides); Πρὸς Βακχεῖον; *Curationes*.

Ed. H. Schöne, 1896.

**APOLLONIUS** (9) **MOLON** (1st c. B.C.), rhetor, a native of Alabanda and pupil of Menecles. He lectured at Rhodes, visited Rome (87 and 81 B.C.), taught Cicero and other Romans, and won success as a pleader.

Cicero, *Brut.* 307, 312, 316: Diog. Laert. 3. 34. G. A. Kennedy, *The Art of Persuasion in Greece* (1963), 326 f.

J. W. H. A.

**APOLLONIUS** (10) **MYS,** member of the Herophilean school of medicine, worked for many years in Alexandria, towards the end of the first century B.C. He wrote Περὶ τῆς Ἡροφίλου αἱρέσεως, Περὶ εὐποςίστων φαρμάκων, and Περὶ μύρων.

**APOLLONIUS** (11) **SOPHISTA** (c. A.D. 100) compiled a *Lexicon Homericum* which is extant in an abridged form (ed. I. Bekker, 1833). A fragment of the unabridged work survives in a Bodleian papyrus. He used especially the commentaries of Aristarchus, on whose critical method he throws valuable light, and the glossary of Apion.

F. Martinazzoli, *Hapax legomenon* i. 2 (1957); H. Erbse, *Beitr. zur Überlieferung d. Iliasscholien* (1960), 206 ff.; H. Schenk, *Die Quellen des Homer-Lex. des A. Soph.* (1961). J. F. L.; R. B.

**APOLLONIUS** (12) of Tyana (Ἀπολλώνιος ὁ Τυανεύς), a Neopythagorean sage. According to our only full account, Philostratus' Τὰ ἐς τὸν Τυανέα Ἀπολλώνιον (time of Septimius Severus, see Rose, *Handb. of Gk. Lit.* 403, W. Nestle, *Griechische Religiosität* (1930–3), iii. 123 ff.), he was born at Tyana in Cappadocia, apparently about the beginning of the Christian era, and survived into the Principate of Nerva (for other datings, and the few known facts about him, see J. Miller in *PW* ii. 146 ff.). He led the life of an ascetic wandering teacher, possessed miraculous powers, visited distant lands, including India, was in danger of his life under Nero and again under Domitian, and saw by clairvoyance the latter's death (Philostr. 8. 25–6, cf. Cassius Dio 67. 18). Philostratus is highly untrustworthy (*PW* xx. 139 ff., F. Solmsen), and references elsewhere scanty; but Apollonius' existence and Pythagoreanism need not be doubted. An anti-Christian writer, Hierocles of Nicomedia, paralleled Apollonius with Christ, which provoked a reply (extant) from Eusebius. Of his writings (see *Suda*, s.v., 623 Bernhardy) there survive some doubtfully authentic letters and a fragment of his treatise *On Sacrifices* (Τελεταὶ ἢ περὶ θυσιῶν). H. J. R.

**APOLLONIUS** (13), son of Mnesitheus, named *Dyscolus*, of Alexandria (2nd c. A.D.). Of his life little is known; apart from a short visit to Rome, he did not leave Alexandria. His works are distinguished, even among grammarians, for obscurity of style and asperity of manner; but his method is genuinely critical, and his zeal for correcting errors extends to his own (cf. *Syntax*, p. 231. 15 Bekk.). For the history of grammar from Dionysius Thrax to his own day he is our chief source of information.

Of some twenty works, mostly on syntax, named in the *Suda*, four survive—on the *Pronoun, Conjunction, Adverb*, and *Syntax*. A conspectus of his doctrines is given in the *Syntax*, which deals mainly with Article, Pronoun, Verb, Preposition, and Adverb, successively. He approaches syntax from the parts of speech, not the sentence, beginning with the establishment of the 'correct' order of these, assuming that there must be a proper order for them as there is, in his view, for the alphabet; and he has much argument disproving such current opinions as that the function of the article is to distinguish genders, and that ὦ is its vocative. As a result, although he correctly settles many details, acutely arguing from function, not form, he nevertheless achieves no comprehensive, organic, system of syntax. His work is marked by a constant quest for principle. 'We must investigate what *produces* solecisms, and not merely adduce examples.' '*Why* do some verbs take the genitive, not the accusative?' In discussing forms and constructions he makes much use of alleged ἀναλογία (*see* CRATES (3) OF MALLOS), e.g. insisting on ἵμι, not εἷμι, by 'analogy' from the plural and dual; also τεθείκωμαι (pf. pass. subj.). He also makes use of what he recognizes to be false

analogy (συνεκδρομή), as when he explains that the usag γράφει τὰ παιδία (nominative) is permitted because i sounds the same as when παιδία is accusative, in which case the syntax is normal.

He himself writes Hellenistic κοινή, as befitted a technical writer; Atticism was confined to belles-lettres So we find such typical turns of syntax as ἐάν c. indic. εἰ c. subjunct., ἐπεὶ μή, etc. Apollonius takes no though for style, and his work is marked by frequent pleonasm anacoluthon, etc. He had a wide knowledge of literature and was familiar with Latin. Inevitably perhaps, he fall short of the comparative and historical methods available if not always adopted, to-day. But it would be hard to overestimate his influence on later Greek and Latin grammarians, notably Priscian, or to quarrel with Priscian's tribute, 'maximus auctor artis grammaticae'.

Edition, by Uhlig and Schneider in Teubner's *Grammatici Graeci* P. Maas, *De pronomine, pars generalis* (1911); E. Egger, *Apolloniu Dyscole: Essai sur l'hist. d. théories gramm. dans l'antiquité* (1854) A. Thierfelder, *Abhdl. d. Sächs. Akad. d. Wiss.* 43. 2 (1935); E. A Hahn, *TAPA* 1951, 29 ff.; H. Erbse, *Beitr. zur Überlieferung de Iliasscholien* (1960), 311 ff. P. B. R. F.; R. B

**APOLLONIUS** (14) of Tyre, the hero of an anony mous novel widely known in the Middle Ages. The oldest extant version (5th–6th c. A.D.) is in Latin, *Historia Apollonii Regis Tyrii*, but subject-matter (the usual story of a couple who become separated and are at last reunited after innumerable adventures involving pirates, enslave ment, apparent deaths, etc.) as well as an analysis of the 'Realien' suggest that there was a Greek original of the second or third century A.D.; an analysis of the diction on the other hand, has so far led scholars to opposit conclusions (some maintain the existence of such a Gree original, others affirm that the work was written directl in Latin). Certain critics distinguish two strata in the work, one pagan and one Christian.

TEXT. Riese (Teubner, 1871, 1893²); M. Ring (Posen–Leipzig 1888). Both important, neither definitive.
CRITICISM. Rohde, *Griech. Roman*, 435 ff.; Schanz–Hosius iv. 2 548 ff. (fundamental); Teuffel–Schwabe, *Hist. Rom. Lit.* (trans G. C. W. Warr) ii⁵ (1892), 548 ff;. R. Helm, *Der antike Roman* (1956), 47 ff. (good survey of problems). G. G

**APOLLOPHANES,** according to the *Suda* an Athenia comic writer. Once victorious, c. 400 B.C. (*IG* ii². 2325) In the Κρῆτες a character is introduced apparently speak ing Doric.

*FCG* i. 266–7; *CAF* i. 797 ff.; Demiańczuk, *Supp. Com.* 9.

**APOPHRADES,** unlucky, forbidden days, charac terized by gloomy rites (Plato, *Leg.* 800 d), e.g. th Plynteria (Plut. *Alc.* 34), on which no assembly or cour was held. Such were also the last two days of the Anthes teria, on which the dead visited their old houses an people chewed buckthorn and smeared the doors wit pitch to protect themselves. They were properly calle μιαραὶ ἡμέραι as opposed to καθαραί.

E. Rohde, *Psyche* i (1925), 237, n. 3. M. P. N

**APPARITORES,** public servants who attended Roma magistrates (cf. *apparere*). The most important classe were *scribae, lictores, viatores* (qq.v.), *accensi*, and *prae cones*. They were generally freedmen or sons of freed men. They received an annual salary from the State Although their appointment was technically annual, the were soon permitted to retain their posts indefinitely Organized into panels (*decuriae*), they formed corpora tions which were legally recognized by the State. It i uncertain whether the *apparitores* wore any characteristi uniform.

Mommsen, *Röm. Staatsr.* i³. 332 ff.; A. H. M. Jones, *Studies* Roman Government and Law (1960), 153 ff. P. 7

**APPELLATIO.** Until the end of the Republic th judgement of the private *iudex* (q.v.) in the formular system of civil procedure (*see* LAW AND PROCEDURE, ROMAN II) was not subject to appeal. Thereafter appeals were probably admitted. Certainly in the *cognitio extraordinaria* they became normal. Appeal was usually made in the first place to the magistrate who appointed the trial judge, but there might be further appeals, ending with one to the Emperor. *Appellatio* in its developed form had to be made orally or in writing (*libelli appellatorii*) to the judge whose decision was impugned, and he then transmitted all the documents in the case to the competent higher magistrate with a written report (*litterae dimissoriae*, *apostoli*). The hearing on appeal was a new trial, and fresh evidence was admissible. A frivolous appellant had to pay the other party four times his costs; Constantine punished him with *relegatio* (q.v.) *in insulam* and confiscation of half his property, but Justinian reverted to pecuniary penalties, at the court's discretion. Justinian made an extensive reform of the system of appeal, and the influence of his legislation can still be seen in modern continental law. His *Nov.* 82 settled the rule that all judgements except those of the *praefectus praetorio* were appealable.

In the widest sense *appellatio* is any recourse to a higher magistrate for the alteration or quashing of a decree of a lower one. In this sense the term is used with respect to ordinary administrative decisions of magistrates and judgments delivered in criminal cases. In the language of the later classical jurisprudence the term *appellatio* is used indiscriminately with *provocatio* (cf. *Dig.* 49. 1 and *Cod. Just.* 7. 62), the proper field of which in former times was criminal jurisdiction. Thus imperial constitutions speak of *appellatio* or *provocatio* against a nomination as *decurio* or *scriba* (*Cod. Just.* 7. 62. 4, 7).

E. Perrot, *L'Appel dans la procédure de l'ordo iudiciorum privatorum* (1907); R. Orestano, *L'appello civile in diritto romano*² (1953); R. Villers, *Studi de Francisci* i (1956); J. M. Kelly, *Princeps iudex* (1957). For criminal procedure *see also under* LAW AND PROCEDURE, ROMAN III, *and* PROVOCATIO.      A. B.; B. N.

**APPENDIX VERGILIANA,** a collection of Latin poems of various provenance, genre, and quality, ascribed to Virgil by ancient authorities and most MSS. which transmit them. Ascription to Virgil was early (Lucan knew the *Culex* as Virgilian), partly through deliberate forgery, partly association of anonymous pieces with a famous name. Internal evidence against Virgilian authorship is very strong. It now seems untenable for most of the collection and questionable for any part of it. The poems are mainly late Augustan or of the first century A.D., when they satisfied a demand for Virgilian *iuvenilia*, and they provide a fascinating sample of the second- and third-rate verse produced in abundance during this period.

The *vita Donati* of Virgil lists as his juvenile writings *Catalepton*, *Priapea*, *Epigrammata*, *Dirae*, *Ciris*, *Culex*, and *Aetna* (the last as doubtful). The *vita Servii* adds *Copa*. *Moretum* and *Elegiae in Maecenatem* had joined the collection by the ninth century (Murbach catalogue), probably earlier. Our MS. tradition is gravely corrupt and it is often hard to decide which faults are the authors', which the scribes'.

The CATALEPTON (κατὰ λεπτόν) contains fourteen poems, miscellaneous in subject and metre. Their quality ranges from the clumsiness of 9 to the brilliance of 10 (a parody of Catullus 4). The contemporary reference of several of the poems renders them enigmatic. It is possible (no more) that some are by Virgil.

CIRIS, an epyllion of Alexandrian inspiration, relates the story of Scylla, daughter of Nisus. The narrative, wilfully unbalanced, with elaboration of a few scenes, is often obscure in thought and affected in expression. Virgilian verses and phrases are ineptly adapted and by their inappropriateness betray the imitator. The *Ciris* is

also strongly influenced by Catullus 64. Though without much literary merit, the poem is an interesting specimen of its genre.

COPA, a pastiche of commonplaces and phrases from Virgil and Propertius, yet with a lively vigour which invests its trivial Epicureanism with considerable charm.

CULEX. A shepherd kills a gnat which has befriended him. The gnat's ghost later appears, reproaches the shepherd for ingratitude and describes the underworld. Though Lucan, Statius, and Martial believed the poem was Virgil's, the language, phraseology, and above all the fumbling adaptation of Virgilian phrases clearly show it is post-Virgilian. The author simulates the young Virgil writing to the young Augustus and thus places his ψευδεπίγραφον in an interesting historical context. The *Culex* also represents for the Roman Homer a counterpart to the *Batrachomyomachia*.

DIRAE (LYDIA). Transmitted as one poem in the MSS. but usually edited as two: *Dirae*, in which a dispossessed farmer curses the farm he has lost, and *Lydia*, in which the writer laments his separation from Lydia. Both poems have some originality and force.

ELEG. IN MAEC. (q. v.), two uninspired elegies on Maecenas' death.

MORETUM describes a humble farmer's preparation of his breakfast. It is an accomplished piece of work, realistic and mildly mock-heroic in tone. Its moral implications about country life link it in spirit with the *Georgics*.

PRIAPEA (3 poems). Pliny (*Epist.* v. 3. 6) mentions Virgil amongst those who wrote *versiculos severos parum*. He may mean the *Priapea*.

AETNA. *See* Art. AETNA.

TEXTS. Teubner (*PLM* i, Vollmer–Morel, 1930), O.C.T. (Clausen, Goodyear, Kenney, Richmond, 1965).
COMMENTARIES. *Catalepton*, R. E. H. Westendorp Boerma (1949–63); *Ciris*, R. Helm (1937); *Culex*, F. Leo (1891); *Dirae* (*Lydia*), A. F. Naeke (1847).
TRANSLATION. H. R. Fairclough, Loeb *Vergil* ii (not reliable).
STUDIES. *Ciris*, F. Leo, *Ausg. kl. Schr.* ii. 29 ff. (1902–7); *Copa*, Wilamowitz, *Hell. Dicht.* ii. 311 ff. (1924); *Culex*, E. Fraenkel, *JRS* 1952 1 ff.; *Dirae* (*Lydia*), E. Fraenkel, *JRS* 1966, 142 ff.    F. R. D. G.

**APPIAN** (*Appianos*) of Alexandria, born probably under Domitian, experienced the Jewish rising of A.D. 116, held office in Alexandria, and after gaining Roman citizenship moved to Rome to become an advocate and, through the influence of Fronto, *procurator Augusti*; under Antoninus Pius he wrote his 'Ρωμαϊκά. Ethnographic in arrangement, this work treated in turn the Roman conquests: Book i Βασιλική, ii 'Ιταλική, iii Σαυνιτική, iv Κελτική, v Σικελικὴ καὶ Νησιωτική, vi 'Ιβηρική, vii Άννιβαϊκή, viii Λιβυκή, (Καρχηδονική, Νομαδική), ix Μακεδονικὴ καὶ 'Ιλλυρική, x 'Ελληνικὴ καὶ Ἀσιανή, xi Συριακὴ καὶ Παρθική, xii Μιθριδάτειος; xiii–xvii 'Εμφυλίων (the Civil Wars, books 1–5); xviii–xxi Αἰγυπτιακῶν (the conquest of Egypt); xxii 'Εκατονταετία, xxiii Δακική, xxiv Ἀράβιος (the Empire to Trajan and the Dacian and Arabian campaigns). Books vi–ix, xi–xvii are complete, except for Νομαδική (viii) and Μακεδονική (ix), which with i–v are fragmentary; x, xviii–xxiv are lost.

The extant tradition goes back ultimately, in its successive parts, to an early annalist, Polybius, Posidonius, Sallust, Asinius Pollio in particular, then Livy, the memoirs of Augustus, and possibly Nicolaus of Damascus; but it probably came immediately from the composition of an early imperial annalist, whom Appian adapted to his ethnographic form. Loyal and honest, an admirer of Roman imperialism, he wrote in the plain κοινή, and though interested mainly in wars and unreliable about Republican institutions and conditions, preserves much valuable material, most notably in bk. 1 of the *Civil Wars*.

TEXTS. L. Mendelssohn (1879–81); P. Viereck, *Bell. Civ.* (1905); H. E. White (1912–13, Loeb). P. Meloni, *Libro Macedonico di Appiano* (1955); E. Gabba, *Appianno e la storia delle guerre civili* (1956); id., *Bell. Civ.* i (1958).    A. H. McD.

**APRIES** (*Hophra*), fourth pharaoh (589–570 B.C.) of the Saite XXVIth dynasty, relied like his predecessors on Ionian and Carian mercenaries. He made unsuccessful attempts to conquer Phoenicia and Cyrene, and was overthrown by a rising against his mercenaries which set Amasis on the throne.

Herodotus 2. 161 f., 4. 159; F. K. Kienitz, *Die politische Geschichte Ägyptens vom 7 bis zum 4 Jahrhundert* (1953), 27 ff., 161 ff.
P. N. U.

**APRONIUS**, LUCIUS, *cos. suff.* A.D. 8, served in Germany as legate of Germanicus (15) and received *triumphalia insignia* from Tiberius. Proconsul of Africa (18–21), he was again so honoured. He was in Rome 22–4; in 28 as propraetorian legate of Germania Inferior he fought against the Frisii.
H. H. S.

**APSINES** of Gadara (3rd c. A.D.), Athenian rhetor and rival of a certain Fronto of Emesa, author of Π. σχημάτων, Ζητήματα, and Μελέται. His Τέχνη (Spengel, *Rhet.* i. 329–414), which has come down with many interpolations, owed much to Hermogenes and is the latest complete τέχνη to survive.
J. W. H. A.

**APULEIUS**, born *c.* A.D. 123 of wealthy parents at Madaurus in Africa (August. *De Civ. D.* 8. 14), was educated first at Carthage (*Flor.* 18), then at Athens (*Apol.* 72), and at Rome (*Flor.* 17). After much travel (*Apol.* 23) he returned to Africa. Later setting forth on a journey to Egypt he fell sick at Oea (*Tripoli*) *c.* A.D. 155, where he was visited by an old friend, Sicinius Pontianus; the latter was anxious about his widowed mother Pudentilla, now betrothed to her brother-in-law, Sicinius Clarus. Pontianus, being on bad terms with his uncle, proposed to Apuleius that he should marry Pudentilla; after some hesitation, Apuleius, finding the widow wealthy and attractive, took her to wife. Sicinius Aemilianus (brother of Sicinius Clarus) accused Apuleius of having won her love by magic. The case was tried at Sabrata before the proconsul, Claudius Maximus. Apuleius defended himself with vigour (*Apologia*) and was acquitted, but left Oea for more congenial surroundings. He is next heard of at Carthage, enjoying renown as poet, philosopher, and rhetorician (*c.* A.D. 161). He was appointed chief priest of the province (*Flor.* 16), and delivered many florid declamations after the manner of the rhetoricians of the 'second Sophistic'. Statues were erected in his honour at Carthage and at Madaurus (the base of the latter has been discovered). He may have had a son named Faustinus. The date of his death is uncertain.

WORKS. (1) *Apologia* (or *Pro se de Magia*) is one of the most interesting and certainly the oddest of all Latin speeches. Apuleius' aim was not merely to rebut the charges against him but to make his opponents look ridiculous and to advertise his own powers of rhetoric. For its theme see above.

(2) The *Metamorphoses* (better known as 'The Golden Ass') is the sole Latin novel that survives entire. A delightful work, imaginative, humorous, and exciting, it tells the adventures of one Lucius who, being too curious concerning the black art, is accidentally turned into an ass, and thus disguised, endures, sees, and hears many strange things. He is at last restored to human shape by the goddess Isis. At the outset a Greek (1. 1), at the close he is referred to as 'a poor man from Madaura' (11. 27), and the story of his initiations into the mysteries of Isis and Osiris is probably to some extent autobiographical (cf. *Apol.* 55). Many stories are embedded in the novel, the most famous being the exquisite tale of Cupid and Psyche (4. 28–6. 24). Another version of the novel, briefer but in some details remarkably close, is given in the MSS. of Lucian (Λούκιος ἢ ὄνος). Both works probably

derive from the same original, the lost *Metamorphoses* of which the unknown Lucius of Patras was either the author or the narrator (Photius 96 b, 12 Bekker). The story of Cupid and Psyche (which, like the conversion of the hero in book xi, has no parallel in Λούκιος ἢ ὄνος) may be an adaptation of the Greek of 'Aristofontes Atheneus' (Fulg. *Myth.* 3. 6). The date is uncertain (an early work according to Purser, late (*c.* A.D. 180) according to Helm).

(3) The *Florida* are excerpts from declamations on varied themes, mainly trivial and showing an extravagance typical of the author. They contain much that is curious and amusing, while the description of the death of the comic poet Philemon has real beauty. They were largely composed between A.D. 160 and 170.

(4) The *De Deo Socratis* is a flamboyant declamation on the δαιμόνιον of Socrates, probably based on a Greek original.

(5) A Latin translation of a passage from Menander's Ἀνεχόμενος: Baehrens *PLM* iv. 104.

(6) *Lost works*: Poems (*Apol.* 6, 9; *Flor.* 9. 17, 18, 20); Speeches (*Apol.* 24, 55; *Flor.* 16; August. *Ep.* 138. 19); *Quaestiones Naturales*, *De Piscibus* (*Apol.* 36, 38, 40), *De Re Rustica*, *De Arboribus*, *Astronomica*, *Arithmetica*; *De Republica*, *De Proverbiis*; *Epitome Historiarum*; *Eroticus*; *Quaestiones Conviviales*; a translation of Plato's *Phaedo*; a novel entitled *Hermagoras* (Priscian, *Gramm. Lat.* 2. p. 85).

(7) *Doubtful Works*: opinion is now sharply divided on the authenticity of two works (i) the *De Dogmate Platonis*, an exposition of the philosophy of Plato, showing neither knowledge nor understanding. Book 1 deals with Plato's life and physical doctrine; book 2 (dedicated to 'my son Faustinus') sets forth his ethics. Book 3, in which he promised to deal with his dialectic, is missing; some have held that the Περὶ ἑρμηνείας, a treatise on formal logic, is the third book, but it is regarded by others as spurious. (ii) the *De Mundo* is a translation of the Περὶ κόσμου falsely attributed to Aristotle; it too is dedicated to Faustinus.

(8) *Spuria*: *Asclepius*, *Herbarius*, *De Remediis Salutaribus*, *Physiognomonia*.

The style of Apuleius is a development of Asianism (*see* RHETORIC, GREEK § 3), which finds its nearest parallel in Pliny (*HN* 9. 102; 10. 3; 10. 81). There is no justification for calling it *African Latin*. It is florid and extravagant, richly coloured with poetry, full of strange words, Graecisms, archaisms (*see* ARCHAISM), and idioms drawn from colloquial Latin; its fullest and most perfect development is seen in the *Metamorphoses*, where it finds appropriate scope and at times rises to great heights of beauty (e.g. *Met.* 11. 1). The works of Apuleius are tinged throughout by his personality—a rhetorician posing as philosopher, peacock-proud and full of an immense store of undigested and superficial learning. But his novel won him deserved renown. Indeed St. Augustine was not certain that he had not actually been turned into an ass, and warns the faithful against those who extol him as a thaumaturge whose powers surpassed those of Christ himself (*Ep.* 136. 1; 138).

TEXTS. *Met.*, R. Helm (1907, 1912, 1931); *Apol.*, R. Helm (1905); *Flor.* R. Helm (1910), *De Deo Soc.*, *Ascl.*, *De Dog. Plat.*, *De Mundo*, Περὶ Ἑρμηνείας, P. Thomas (1908), *Herbarius*, E. Howald and H. E. Sigerist, *CML* iv (1927).
COMMENTARIES. Complete, F. Oudendorp (1764 (1823)), G. F. Hildebrand (1842). *Apol.*, H. E. Butler and A. S. Owen (1914); C. Marchesi (1914). *Cupid and Psyche*, L. C. Purser (1910). Commentary on *Met.* bk. i by M. Molt, on bk. ii by B. J. De Jonge, on bk. v by J. M. H. Fernhout.
TRANSLATIONS. *Apol.* and *Flor.*, H. E. Butler (1909); P. Vallette (1924). *Met.*, W. Adlington (1566 and (revised by S. Gaselee) 1915); H. E. Butler (1910).
STYLE. Norden, *Ant. Kunstpr.*; M. Bernhard, *Der Stil des A.* (1927); W. Oldfather, etc., *Index Apuleianus* (U.S.A. 1934); J. Redfors, *Echtheitskritische Untersuchung der apuleischen Schriften De Platone und De Mundo* (1960).
*Bursian* 171 (1915) 147 ff.; 175 (1919) 1 ff. H. E. B.; M. S. S.

**APULIA,** a rather unhealthy region of south-eastern Italy (cf. Varro, *Rust.* 1. 6), extending from Mons Garganus to Calabria; modern *Puglia*. Its arid soil is fertile, especially in the coastal and northern plains; southern Apulia contains numerous hills, including Mons Vultur. Apulian wool was famous, summer migration of flocks having been practised there continuously since early times (Varro. *Rust.* 2. 1; Pliny, *HN* 8. 190). Its inhabitants were indiscriminately called Apuli; they included Messapic-speaking Peucetii and Daunii as well as Apuli proper who dwelt about Mons Garganus and spoke Oscan (Strabo 6. 283 f.). Although lacking Greek colonies, Apulia was much hellenized by 300 B.C. Between 326 and 317 it became subject to Rome, largely voluntarily, and remained loyal against Pyrrhus (Livy 8. 25, 37; 9. 12. 9 f., 20; Zonar. 8. 5). In the Hannibalic and Social Wars, however, many Apulians revolted (Livy 22. 61; Appian, *BCiv.* 1. 39); the consequent devastation ruined Apulia. Chief towns: Teanum, Sipontum, Luceria, Arpi, Herdonia, Venusia, Canusium, Barium.

P. E. Arias (ed.), *Ricerca archeologica nell'Italia meridionale* 1960), 95 ff. E. T. S.

**AQUAE MATTIACAE,** modern *Wiesbaden*. The thermal springs at Wiesbaden are mentioned by Pliny the Elder, who describes their action (*HN* 31. 20), and the site of the Roman baths has long been known. It had military importance because it commanded a stretch of the *limes* and several periods of military occupation have been detected, including a stone cohort fort.

*Der obergermanisch-raetische Limes*, B, Bd. ii, no. 31 (ed. E. Fabricius, 1909). P. S.

**AQUAE SEXTIAE,** modern *Aix-en-Provence*, the first Roman foundation in Transalpine Gaul, was established as a fort by C. Sextius Calvinus in 123 B.C. after his defeat of the Salluvii (q.v.) and in 102 B.C. was the scene of Marius' great victory over the Teutones. Under Augustus it was refounded as *Colonia Julia Augusta Aquis Sextiis*, initially with Latin rights (Pliny *HN* 3. 36). In A.D. 381 it became the capital of the province of Narbonensis Secunda. No major monuments survive, but a gate and the courses of four aqueducts are known.

M. Clerc, *Aquae Sextiae* (1916); F. Benoit, *FOR* v (1936), 65 ff.; Grenier, *Manuel* iii. 115 ff., iv. 68 ff. Battle: A. Donnadieu, *Rev. Ét. Anc.* 1954, 281 ff. A. L. F. R.

**AQUAE SULIS,** modern *Bath*, attributed by Ptolemy to the *civitas* of the Belgae. The hot springs were developed from the Flavian period and later attained great elaboration, outrivalling the largest Gaulish establishments. The water was led to a partly underground building containing a great lead-lined bath (73 × 29 feet), later vaulted, and two other swimming baths. Hypocaust systems and further plunge baths were later added at either end. To the north lay the tetrastyle temple of Sulis Minerva, of which the steps, pilasters in the Composite style, and fragments of altar and of the famous Gorgon pediment (30 feet wide) survive. Solinus records that coal was burnt on the altar. Facing the porticoed temple court to the east was a further building (a theatre?). Many inscriptions record visitors from Britain and abroad (Collingwood and Wright, *RIB* 138–78). A town-wall enclosing 22 acres was provided in the third century. The site was deserted in Saxon times, the ruins being described in an eighth-century poem.

F. J. Haverfield, *VCH* (Somerset) i. 219 ff.; W. H. Knowles, *Archaeologia* 1926. 1 ff.; I. A. Richmond and J. M. C. Toynbee, *JRS* 1955, 97 ff.; B. Cunliffe, *Antiquity* 1966, 199 ff. S. S. F.

**AQUEDUCTS** are justly regarded as one of Rome's most distinctive contributions to architecture and hygiene.

Rome's first aqueducts, Aquae Appia (312 B.C.) and Anio Vetus (272 B.C.), were tunnelled, no doubt owing much to inherited experience drawn from making the far older drainage-channels (*cuniculi*) and emissaries cut in the soft tufaceous Latian valley-floor (*PBSR* 1963, 74 ff.). Possibly this experience weighed with the builders even more than military considerations, which favoured the hidden underground channel. Such tunnels, like early railway tunnels, were cut in short lengths reached by vertical shafts, which later served for inspection and cleaning. To cross ravines and narrow valleys or to reach elevated points a conduit carried on arches was required, short bridges occurring sparingly on the Anio Vetus, as at Ponte Taulella, long arched sectors for the first time on the Aqua Marcia (144 B.C.). An alternative method of conveyance, employed for the Anio Vetus at Ponte Lupo, was the inverted siphon (Vitr. 8. 7; *ILS* 5348). All these principles were strikingly developed in the wide imperial world, the Pont du Gard near Nemausus (*Nîmes*) and the aqueduct of Segovia furnishing the most famous examples of storied bridges, the Aquae Marcia (144 B.C.), Claudia, and Anio Novus (A.D. 38–52) of Rome itself offering the most remarkable series of arched substructions, the four aqueducts of Lyons the finest series of inverted siphons, made of lead pipes in series bedded upon concrete. The cost and upkeep of these works was high. Aqua Marcia cost 180,000,000 sesterces, and Pliny (*Ep.* 10. 37) quotes 3,329,000 sesterces for the aqueduct of Nicomedia in Bithynia. The quality of water varied very much also (cf. Frontin. *Aq.* 120–2; *ILS* 5795). Smaller towns thus contented themselves with simpler underground systems, which were also much in vogue in military forts and fortresses, where wooden pipe-lines were often used. The channels and their course remained public property, often demarcated by *cippi*, and the water, on arrival, was distributed from *castella*, as at Nîmes and Thuburbo Maius, to public fountains, baths, and private consumers, the latter relying much upon overflow (*aqua caduca*). Supplies were regulated by gauge-pipes of standard bore (*calices*) or by time-limits (*CIL* vi. 1261, viii. 448). Development of water-power, as on the Aqua Traiana (A.D. 109; *see* JANICULUM), was rare. Rents were not designed to cover running costs or capital charges, and the works were usually a liability to the community rather than a source of income.

Under the Republic the aqueducts were maintained by censorial *locatio*; in the absence of censors, other magistrates, especially the aediles by virtue of their general *cura urbis*, were responsible for the water supply. Agrippa, as aedile in 33 B.C., assumed a general responsibility for the aqueducts which he kept till his death in 12 B.C. In the following year Augustus established a permanent board of *curatores aquarum* originally three in number, one being of consular rank. The functions of the *curatores* under the Empire are described by Frontinus who held office in the time of Trajan.

The principal aqueducts of Rome were the following: Appia, 312 B.C.; Anio Vetus, 272 B.C.; Marcia, 144 B.C.; Tepula, 125 B.C.; Julia, 33 B.C.; Virgo, 19 B.C.; Alsietina, 2 B.C.; Claudia, A.D. 47; Anio Novus, A.D. 52; Traiana, A.D. 109; Alexandriana, A.D. 226.

Frontinus, *De Aquis Urbis Romae*. T. Ashby, *Aqueducts of Ancient Rome* (1935); E. B. van Deman, *The Building of the Roman Aqueducts* (U.S.A. 1934); G. de Montauzan, *Les Aqueducs antiques de Lyon* (1909); E. Samesreuther, *Bericht der Röm.-Germ. Kommission* 1936, 24 ff.; J. B. Ward-Perkins, *PBSR* 1955, 115 ff.; for aqueducts at Rome, Nash, *Pict. Dict. Rome* i. 35 ff. I. A. R.; D. E. S.

**AQUILA** (1), PONTIUS (*PW* 17), of undistinguished family, probably from Sutrium, tribune in 45 B.C., annoyed Caesar by not standing up as he passed in triumph after Munda. He was one of Caesar's murderers, and in 43 served under D. Brutus in the war of Mutina. After defeating T. Plancus (q.v. 2) he was killed in the battle of 21 Apr., and shared the honour of a public funeral with Hirtius and Pansa (qq.v.).

E. Pais, *Dalle guerre puniche a Cesare Augusto* (1918), 313 ff.
T. J. C.

**AQUILA** (2) **ROMANUS** (3rd c. A.D.), rhetorician, whose treatise *De figuris sententiarum et elocutionis* (ed. Halm, *Rhet. Lat. Min.* 22–37) was partly based on the Greek of Alexander Numenius, but contains illustrations from Cicero's works (often misquoted from memory).

Schanz–Hosius, § 837. J. F. M.

**AQUILEIA**, a city 7 miles from the head of the Adriatic. In 186 P.C. Transalpine Gauls occupied this fertile site, which controls roads across the Julian Alps. Rome ejected them and founded a Latin colony (181 B.C.) to forestall similar intrusions and to exploit neighbouring gold-mines (Livy 39. 22, 54; 40. 34; H. Mattingly–E. S. G. Robinson, *Date of Roman Denarius* (1933), 22). Aquileia became a great military, commercial, and industrial stronghold; its amber trade was especially important (Strabo 4. 207 f.; 5. 214). In imperial times it was a *colonia*, sometimes dubbed *Roma secunda*, the capital of *Venetia et Istria*, one of the world's largest cities, until razed by Attila in 452 (Auson. *Ordo Nob. Urb.* 65 f.; Amm. Marc. 21. 11 f.; Procop. *Vand.* 1. 330). Its inhabitants fled to the neighbouring lagoons of Venice. Aquileia became a malaria-stricken village, but was still an important patriarchate in the fifteenth century. Ancient remains are numerous.

A. Calderini, *Aquileia Romana* (1930); S. Panciera, *Vita Economica di Aquileia* (1957). E. T. S.

**AQUILLIUS** (1) (fl. *c.* 174–154 B.C.), supposed Latin author of *Boeotia* (*Boeotis?*), a *comoedia palliata* which Varro attributed to Plautus.

O. Ribbeck, *CRF*² 33 (3rd ed. Teubner, 1897). E. H. W.

**AQUILLIUS** (2, *PW* 10), MANIUS, consul in 129 B.C., succeeded Perperna (q.v. 1) in Asia and completed the war against the allies of Aristonicus. With the help of a senatorial commission, he delimited and organized the province of Asia and built roads in it (Degrassi, *ILLRP* n. 456). He triumphed (126), was accused *repetundarum* and, though clearly guilty, acquitted.
E. B.

**AQUILLIUS** (3, *PW* 11), MANIUS, son of (2), chief legate of Marius (q.v. 1) against the Cimbri and his colleague as consul in 101 B.C., when he crushed the slave revolt in Sicily, personally killing the rebel leader, Athenion. He celebrated an *ovatio* (99?), was later accused *repetundarum* and, though guilty, acquitted through the efforts of his friends Marius and Antonius (q.v. 1). As head of a mission to Asia (89), he restored Ariobarzanes of Cappadocia and Nicomedes (q.v. 4) of Bithynia to their thrones, and then forced Nicomedes to attack Mithridates, thus starting the First Mithridatic War. Defeated by Mithridates, he was captured and killed amid public humiliation and ridicule. E. B.

**AQUILLIUS** (4, *PW* 23) **GALLUS**, GAIUS, a Roman jurist of the last century of the Republic, pupil of Q. Mucius Scaevola (q.v. 4). He was praetor (probably of the *Quaestio* (q.v.) *de ambitu*) in 66, contemporarily with Cicero, but thereafter devoted himself to the law; he died between 55 and 44 B.C. He is famous as the creator of the *formulae de dolo* (Cic. *Off.* 3. 14. 60; *Nat. D.* 3. 30. 74) which enabled the bad faith of either party to be pleaded in a lawsuit, and thereby added greatly to the flexibility of

the law; he also drafted the *stipulatio Aquil(l)iana* by which all kinds of debts could be converted into one *stipulati* (q.v.) so that they could be discharged by a singl *acceptilatio* (*Dig.* 46. 4. 18. 1). B. N

**AQUINCUM**, on the Danube at Budapest, was th centre of the Illyrian-Celtic Eravisci, later the provincia capital of Pannonia Inferior. Throughout the Roma period it was a key military base against the Quadi an the Sarmatian Iazyges. From Tiberius it was an auxiliar station and under Domitian was occupied by Legio I Adiutrix. Under Trajan this unit was detached fo service in Dacia and the East (*c.* A.D. 101–14/17), and it place was taken by Legio X Gemina, but it returned t become the permanent garrison of Aquincum, except fo two further periods of detachment, 161–7 and unde Septimius Severus, when its place was taken by I Flavia Felix. Around the camp a *canabae* (q.v.) develope its own administration, while the city of Aquincum, municipium (*Aelium*) under Hadrian and *colonia* (*Septimia* under Severus, developed quite separately on a site miles north of the legionary fortress. Aquincum wa abandoned with the rest of Pannonia (*c.* 400), its las mention being Sid. Apoll. 5. 107.

János Szilagyi, *PW* Suppl. xi, 61 ff. On legionary movements se A. Mócsy, *PW* Suppl. ix, s.v. 'Pannonia'.
F. A. W. S.; J. J. W

**AQUITANIA**, a name originally applied strictly to th area bounded by the Garonne, the Pyrenees, and the Bay of Biscay (modern *Gascony*). The Aquitani are describe as differing from the other Gauls in speech, customs, an physique, and archaeologically their culture is distin guished by several primitive Hallstatt survivals. The were divided into many small tribes which were defeate in 56 B.C. by P. Crassus (q.v. 5) and finally subdued afte campaigns in 38 and 27 B.C. Augustus made Aquitani an imperial province, governed from Burdigala (q.v. but extended it to include the Celtic tribes to the Loir which, as Strabo complains (4. 177), made ethnographica nonsense of the name. By the third century, howeve the original Aquitanian tribes, which had coalesced t nine, were granted administrative independence a Novempopulana, centred on Elusa (*Eauze*), so that th later provinces of Aquitanica Prima and Secund (capitals at Bourges and Bordeaux) in fact excluded them as did medieval Guyenne, while Gascony took its nam from the Vascones, a Pyrenean tribe. *See also* BURDIGALA LUGDUNUM (2).

G. Fabre, *Les Civilisations protohistoriques de l' Aquitaine* (1952 C. Jullian, *Hist. de la Gaule* ii (1908), 449 ff.; O. Hirschfeld, *K Schr.* (1913), 209. A. L. F. R

**ARA PACIS**, a monument dedicated on 30 Jan. 9 B.C by the Senate, as Augustus records in his Testament, t commemorate his safe return from Gaul and Spain. I was erected in the Campus Martius, where the Palazz Fiano now stands. The altar proper was surrounded by a walled precinct (11·6 × 10·6 m.) with doors on east and west. The walls of this precinct were sculptured with reliefs in two tiers: internally there were festoons slung from ox-heads above and fluting below; externally, the lower frieze was filled with a spreading floral pattern, the upper contained on east and west mythological scenes, on north and south a rendering of the procession on the consecration day (4 July 13 B.C.) with portraits of the imperial family and figures of lictors, priests, magistrates, and representatives of the Roman people. These reliefs rank among the most important products of Augustan art. The smaller reliefs on the inner altar showing Vestals, priests, sacrificial animals (a sheep and two steers or two heifers), etc., continue the procession on the outer walls.

Several sculptured slabs were brought to light about 1568; others were found in 1859 and 1903. They were identified (rightly, despite a recent attempt to prove the contrary) as parts of the Ara Pacis by F. von Duhn in 1879. In 1937–8 the site was thoroughly explored and the monument reconstructed, with most of its surviving sculptures, a short distance to the north of the Palazzo Fiano.

G. Moretti, *L' Ara Pacis Augustae* (1938); J. M. C. Toynbee, 'The Ara Pacis Reconsidered', *Proc. Brit. Acad.*, 1953. See also *JRS* 1960, 44 ff.; 1961, 153 ff.                F. N. P.; J. M. C. T.

**ARABIA.** Greeks of the Classical period were familiar with the coast of Arabia and with Arabia Petraea. They knew less about the other divisions into which by Ptolemy's time they had divided the peninsula—Arabia Felix in the south and Arabia Deserta. The Romans of the Empire took account, as their organization of the southern sector of their eastern *limes* reveals, of the historical role of the Arabs, their steady pressure on the settled lands in the north, their infiltration into the Syrian end of the Arabian peninsula, their seasonal movements of transhumation between the Desert and the Sown.

In the north confrontation with, and partial subjection to, the great powers of Mesopotamia and Babylonia are attested on the monuments of the Assyrian kings from Shalmaneser III (853) to Tiglath Pileser III (745–727), and Esarhaddon (680–669) and Babylonian Nabonidus visited Taima in person (552). The Persian King Darius I recorded the tributary status of Arabaya (cf. Hdt. 7. 69; 3. 97).

For the Greeks knowledge really began with Alexander. In preparation for his intended circumnavigation his admiral Hieron sailed down the Persian Gulf to Ras Mussendam, and Anaxicrates down the Red Sea through Bab-el-Mandeb to the south coast; the south-east (Oman) long remained unknown. The Seleucids planted some settlements along the coast between the Euphrates and Gerrha, and had a trade arrangement with Gerrha, which supplied Seleucia with spices. Ariston explored down to Bab-el-Mandeb for Ptolemy II, and that king, to chastise the hostile Nabataeans of Petra, tapped the 'incense route' south of them by a trade arrangement with the Lihyanites of Dedan (Al-'Ula); Miletus settled for him a colony, Ampelone, as a sea-port for Dedan. The fourth–third-century kingdoms in the south were Minaea on the Red Sea, Katabania at the Straits, and Sabaea, the Hadramaut, and Mahra along the south coast; by the second century Minaea had vanished, and a Sabaean-Homerite confederacy (Himyarites) dominated Yemen. Both terrain and climate had permitted an early flowering of Arabian civilization in southern Arabia.

In the north much had been achieved by the Nabataean Arabs; their territories as far as the Negev and Transjordan were developed with the aid of skilful water conservation. In the first century Petra grew great, and the Nabataeans finally extended from Damascus to Dedan. The interior was always unknown. Arabia exported frankincense and myrrh, gold and gems, and re-exported Indian spices and other products. The principal routes were the 'incense route' from Sabaea through Medina, Dedan, and Petra to Syria, and routes from Dhofar to Gerrha, from Gerrha across to Petra, and from Egypt to Babylonia via Jauf. Till Augustus' time the southern Arabs were jealous intermediaries of the sea-trade between India and Egypt; Roman Egypt, with direct voyages to south Arabia and India, broke their monpoly, and also diminished the importance of the 'incense route'.

Augustus sent a military expedition under Gallus (q.v. 4) to Arabia Felix (Sabaea), which failed; but Roman naval predominance in the Red Sea was secured and the reduction of Aden (Arabia Eudaemon) early in the

Principate facilitated the movement of Greek merchant convoys on their passage from Egypt to India and back (Anon. *Peripl. Mar. Erythr.* 26). Friendly diplomatic relations with the rulers of the Yemen and Hadramaut coasts replaced attempts at military control in Arabia. But in the north the construction of a military *limes* from Black Sea to Red Sea involved the absorption of the client kingdom of Nabataean Arabia into the Roman provincial system. Trajan sent Cornelius Palma (q.v.) to annex the land of the Nabataeans (q.v.) as a Roman province, and constructed a great road through it from Aela on the Red Sea to Damascus (this city being assigned to Syria). The provincial era started on 22 March 106. Of the two chief cities, Bostra and Petra (qq.v.), the former became the provincial capital, where during the second century Legio III Cyrenaica was stationed. The governors were at first senatorial legates, later equestrian *praesides*. Slightly enlarged to the north under Septimius Severus, the province under Diocletian was divided into two: the part around Bostra retained the name Arabia, the other part was later incorporated in Palaestina but (by *c.* 358) appears as Palaestina Salutaris.

Anon., *Peripl. Mar. Erythr.* in Muller, *Geogr. Gr. Min.* i.; Cary-Warmington, *Explorers*, ch. 4; F. Altheim and R. Stiehl, *Die Araber in der alten Welt*, I–II (1964–5); R. Dussaud, *La Pénétration des Arabes en Syrie avant l'Islam*; R. E. Brunnow and A. Domaszewski, *Die Provincia Arabia* i–iii (1904–9); Jones, *Cities E. Rom. Prov.* 292 ff.; H. C. Pflaum, *Syria* 1957, 136 ff. (for governors). See also J. I. Miller, *The Spice Trade of the Roman Empire* (1969).
                                       W. W. T.; E. W. G.

**ARACHNE** (i.e. 'Spider'), in Ovid, *Met.* 6. 5 ff., a Lydian woman, daughter of Idmon of Colophon, so skilled in weaving as to rival Athena, whom she challenged to a competition when the goddess visited her to warn her. On Athena's destroying her web, she hanged herself and Athena changed her to a spider. This seems to be originally a folk-tale (Stith Thompson A 2091. 1, 2231. 5).                                       H. J. R.

**ARADUS,** the main city of North Phoenicia, on an island off the coast, whose kings ruled a large area on the mainland. Captured by Alexander the Great, it regained its freedom under Antiochus II in 259 B.C. Federated with its former dominions (Gabala, Carne, Marathus, Simyra), it remained a vassal to the Seleucids. In the second and first century B.C., the federation was gradually dissolved. Captured after resisting Antony (38 B.C.), its prosperity continued as an important harbour for eastern trade. In the mountains opposite the island are the remarkable ruins of the main Aradian high-place, the temple of Zeus Baitokaikes.

H. Seyrig, *Revue numismatique*, 1964.                H. S.

**ARAE FLAVIAE,** *Rottweil* on the Neckar. In A.D. 74 the Roman Rhine–Danube frontier was shortened by carrying a road south-eastwards from Strasbourg to the Danube. A fort was built at the point where another road coming up from Vindonissa joined it and the settlement Arae Flaviae developed there. Domitian advanced the frontier further and removed the garrison. Arae Flaviae was thought to have lost its importance after A.D. 100 and no public administrative buildings have been found, but the description as a *municipium* in a recently discovered official order of A.D. 186 poses new problems.

W. Schleiermacher, in (*Gymnasium*) *Germania Romana: I. Römerstädte in Deutschland* (1960), 59 ff.                O. B.; P. S.

**ARAROS** (Ἀραρώς), son of Aristophanes, produced (after 388 B.C.) two of his father's plays, *Kokalos* and *Aiolosikon* (hyp. 4 Ar. *Plut.*). The first play of his own was produced in 375; we have fragments of five plays, and six titles.

*FCG* i. 343–6; *CAF* ii. 215–19; *FAC* ii. 12 ff.                K. J. D.

**ARATEA,** Latin poems translated from the Φαινόμενα and Προγνώσεις of Aratus (q.v. 1) (1) by Cicero, partly extant, a portion being in about 480 hexameters besides detached fragments of *Phaenomena* and *Prognostica*, sometimes inaccurate and monotonous; (2) by Germanicus, *Phaen.*, 725 hexameters, and fragments amounting to over 200 verses of *Progn.*, a more poetic and more independent adaptation than Cicero's, in which Germanicus corrects some astronomical errors in the original; (3) by Avienius (q.v.) in the fourth century, *Phaen.* in 1325, *Progn.* in 553 hexameters, considerably expanded from the Greek.

G. Sieg, *De Cic., German., Avieno Arati interpretibus* (1886). (1) Baehr. *PLM* i. 1–28; Cicero, ed. C. F. W. Müller, 4, v. 3, 360–94; W. W. Ewbank, *The Poems of Cicero*, 1933; V. Buescu, *Cicéron, Les 'Aratea'* (Bucharest, 1941); A. Traglia, *Ciceronis Poetica Fragmenta* ii (Rome, 1952). (2) *PLM* i. 142 ff.; A. Breysig, (Teubner,¹ 1899). (3) Ed. Breysig, 1889. J. W. D.

**ARATUS** (1), of Soli in Cilicia (*c.* 315–240/239 B.C.), was first taught by Menecrates of Ephesus, perhaps in that town. Later he went to Athens, where he imbibed Stoicism from Zeno and was introduced to Antigonus (q.v. 2) Gonatas. Antigonus *c.* 277 invited Aratus to the Macedonian court, where he celebrated the king's marriage to Phila, half-sister of Antiochus I. He also celebrated Antigonus' victory over the Celts (277) in a *Hymn to Pan*. Later Aratus went to Syria and joined Antiochus' court. There he completed his edition of the *Odyssey*, but eventually returned to Macedonia, where his death preceded that of Antigonus in 240/239.

Works. Aratus' best-known work, still extant, is an astronomical poem, entitled *Phaenomena*. This, undertaken at the request of Antigonus, versifies a prose treatise or treatises of Eudoxus of Cnidos (*c.* 390–337). After a proem to Zeus (1–18), and a brief reference to the poles, Aratus describes the northern and southern fixed stars (26–453), the circles of the celestial sphere (462–558), and the risings and settings of stars (559–732). The remainder of the poem (733–1154) deals with weather signs, in spite of a separate title (Προγνώσεις διὰ σημείων) an integral part of the poem. The *Phaenomena* achieved immediate fame (cf. *Anth. Pal.* 9. 25 (Leonidas of Tarentum); Callimachus, *Epigr.* 27) and found many commentators (the names of 27 are known); but the astronomical mistakes, which some commentators tried to remove by altering the text, were widely criticized, especially by Hipparchus (*c.* 190–120 B.C.), whose commentary survives. Nevertheless the poem enjoyed a great reputation among both Greeks and Romans (cf. Cic. *De Or.* 1. 69) till the end of antiquity. Latin translations of it were made by Varro of Atax, Cicero, Germanicus, Avienius (*see* ARATEA). Aratus' style is sober, being modelled on Hesiod, and the language, drawn mostly from Homer, is relatively simple (there are few 'glosses'), but the poem is not easy reading owing to the nature of the subject-matter. There are some bad errors in the formation of Epic words, and some neologisms. The metre is fairly correct, but the refinements introduced by Callimachus are lacking. The Stoic creed pervades the whole poem, while poetic colour is provided by digressions, the longest being the descriptions of the Golden Age (98–136) and of storms at sea (408–35).

Aratus wrote many other poems, now lost, e.g. *Epikedeia*, *Epigrams* (cf. *Anth. Pal.* 12. 129), *Elegies* (Macrob. 5. 20. 8), *Hymns*, *Paegnia*, and a collection of short poems with the title Τὰ κατὰ λεπτόν (the meaning is uncertain), from which the *Catalepton* attributed to Virgil takes its name. Other lost works had astronomical or medical titles.

Texts. E. Maass, *Arati Phaenomena* (1893); *Commentariorum in Aratum reliquiae* (1898, republ. Berlin 1958); J. Martin (text, commentary and trans., Florence, 1954); id., *Histoire du texte des Phénomènes d'Aratos* (1956).

General Literature. G. Knaack, 'Aratos (6)' in *PW* ii. 391–9; E. Maass, *Aratea* (1892); G. R. Mair, *Callimachus, Lycophron, Aratus* (Loeb, 1921), 359 ff.; W. W. Tarn, *Antigonos Gonatas* (1913), 223 ff.; Christ–Schmid–Stählin ii. 1⁶, 163 ff.; R. Böker, 'Die Entstehung der Sternsphäre A.'s', *Sb. Leipzig, Math.-nat. Klasse* 1952; W. Shadewaldt, *Griechische Sternsage*, Fischer Bücherei 129 (1956). Further bibliography in G. Sarton, *Hist. Science* I (1957), 207.
E. A. B.

**ARATUS** (2) (271–213 B.C.), a Sicyonian statesman educated at Argos, his refuge after his father's murder (264). He recovered Sicyon in 251, united it to the Achaean Confederacy for defence against Macedon, and solved its economic difficulties by subsidies from Ptolemy Philadelphus, whom he visited personally. As General of the Confederacy, normally each alternate year from 245, he seized Acrocorinth in 243 and defeated Gonatas' Aetolian allies at Pellene (241). In alliance with Aetolia (239–229) he frequently attacked Athens and Argos; additions to the Confederacy included Megalopolis (235) and Argos (229), and on Demetrius II's death (229) Aratus helped to liberate Athens. However, Spartan aggression cancelled these advances. Defeated at Mt. Lycaeus and Ladoceia (227) by Cleomenes III, he realistically opened negotiations with Macedon, and Doson's arrival in 224 preserved the Confederacy from disruption. In the crisis he held special powers, judicial and administrative. On Philip V's accession he called in Doson's Hellenic League against Aetolian aggression (220); in the subsequent war he successfully exposed the treachery of the court cabal under Apelles, and after the peace of Naupactus (217) vigorously resisted Philip's anti-Roman policy and proposed seizure of Ithome. His death (213), probably from consumption, was attributed popularly to Philip.

His *Memoirs* (Ὑπομνηματισμοί: Polyb. 2. 40) were pro-Achaean and apologetic in tone, and less reliable than Polybius claims (2. 40. 4).

Though not without personal rancour (e.g. against Lydiades or Aristomachus of Argos), Aratus' actions usually revealed a sound statesmanlike basis. His failure to organize a strong army was serious; but his major decisions were almost invariably correct, and both as a diplomatist and guerrilla leader he carried adaptability to the height of greatness.

Pclyb. 2. 37–71; bks. 4–5; Plut. *Agis, Cleomenes, Aratus*; *FGrH* 231. F. W. Walbank, *Aratos of Sicyon* (1933); W. H. Porter, ed. Plutarch's *Aratus*, introd. (1937). F. W. W.

**ARAUSIO,** a town in Gallia Narbonensis, modern *Orange*. Near here the Cimbri defeated Cn. Mallius and Q. Caepio (q.v. 1) with huge losses (105 B.C.). Under Augustus a colony for veterans of Legio II Gallica (*Colonia Firma Julia Secundanorum Arausio*) was established on land taken from the Tricastini; details of the centuriation are preserved on marble tablets, of which many fragments have been recovered. Important monuments survive, including the theatre, with an enigmatic semicircular structure adjoining, two temples, and the triumphal arch (with Tiberian inscription) which stands outside the north gate.

J. Sautel, *FOR* vii (1939), 104 ff.; Grenier, *Manuel* iii. 172 ff. (general), 398 ff. (temples), 754 ff. (theatre); I. A. Richmond, *JRS* 1933, 151 ff. (arch and walls); A. Piganiol, *Les Documents cadastraux de la colonie romaine d'Orange* (1962, Suppl. to *Gallia*); R. Amy et al., *L'Arc d'Orange* (1962, Suppl. to *Gallia*); G. C. Picard, *Le Trophées romains* (1959), 319 ff. Battle: C. Jullian, *Hist. de la Gaule* iii (1909), 65 ff. A. L. F. R.

**ARAXES,** properly the Armenian river now called Aras, Ras, or Yerash, rising in Bin Geul Dagh, then flowing eastwards across Erzerum and the Mogan Steppe. Until A.D. 1897 it joined the Kur (ancient Cyrus), but now flows separately into the Caspian. Swift and turbulent now, in Graeco-Roman times it marked a trade-route from the Caspian and the Cyrus to Artaxata and Asia Minor. Herodotus confuses the Aras with the Iaxartes or the Oxus. Xenophon calls it Phasis, his Araxes being probably the Khabur. The 'Araxes in Persis' is probably the Bendamir or Kum Firuz. E. H. W.

**ARBITRATION, GREEK.** The submission of a dispute to a neutral person or body, whose verdict the disputants engage themselves in advance to accept, was recognized among the Greeks from a very early period, and legend and history alike attest its frequent application. There is evidence for the existence of public arbitrators in numerous States, e.g. Sparta, Gortyn, Ephesus, and Lampsacus, but we have detailed knowledge only about Athens. There private διαιτηταί, not necessarily citizens, were frequently employed to settle claims on an equitable rather than on a legal basis (Arist. *Rhet.* 1. 13), while public arbitrators, appointed from citizens in their sixtieth year, were used, especially in the fourth century, for the settlement, under the auspices of the 'Forty', of private claims exceeding 10 drachmas in value, so as to lighten the work of the public courts (Arist. *Ath. Pol.* 53). Once accepted by both parties, the arbitral award became legally binding, but inasmuch as either party had the right of appeal to the lawcourt, these public διαιτηταί must be regarded as mediators rather than as arbitrators in the strict sense. Another important application of the same principle was the practice, especially frequent in the Hellenistic age, whereby a State invited a friendly neighbour-State to send a tribunal (δικασταὶ μετάπεμπτοι, ξενικὸν δικαστήριον) to deal with civil, and sometimes also with criminal, cases affecting its citizens; the visiting judges sought first to settle disputes 'out of court', but where the method of conciliation (σύλλυσις) failed, they had the right to pronounce legal judgements.

But it was in the field of inter-State relations that arbitration attained its greatest influence. Whether the Greeks originated this device for substituting equity for force is uncertain, but it was assuredly they who made it a recognized and frequent means of averting wars. The earliest recorded cases, such as the Spartan arbitration between Athens and Megara regarding the possession of Salamis, are known only from semi-legendary traditions; but the original text survives of an award of about 450 B.C. (*SIG* 56 = Tod 33), by which Argos sought to compose existing differences between her two Cretan colonies Cnossos and Tylissus and to prevent their future recurrence. After 450 peace-treaties normally contained a clause binding the contracting parties to submit to arbitration all eventual disputes (e.g. Thuc. 1. 78. 4, 140. 2, 144. 2, 145; 4. 118. 8; 5. 18. 4, 79. 4), and we may assume that this course was frequently followed, though circumstances sometimes arose in which the exacerbation of public feeling and the difficulty of finding a suitable arbitrator led to the neglect of this provision. Athens seems to have claimed the right to act as arbitrator in disputes among the members of her Empire (Plut. *Per.* 25), and later the Greek leagues sought by similar means to secure internal harmony.

It is upon inscriptions that we depend for our detailed knowledge of the operation of the arbitral machinery, the size, composition, and appointment of the tribunals, their procedure, the nature of the evidence laid before them, the formulation and publication of their awards, the penalties attaching to their infraction, and the character of the boundary-delimitations carried out by frontier commissions. Among the fullest and most interesting accounts of this kind are those relating to the arbitrations of King Lysimachus and, later, the Rhodians between Samos and Priene (*OGI* 13, *SIG* 599, 688), of the Megarians between Corinth and Epidaurus (*SIG* 471), of the Aetolians between Perea and Melitea in

Thessaly (ibid. 546 B), of the Senate between Melite and Narthacium (ibid. 674), of the Mylasians between Magnesia and Priene (ibid. 679), of the Milesians between Sparta and Messene (ibid. 683), of the Magnesians between Itanus and Hierapytna (ibid. 685), and of the Cnossians between Lato and Olus (ibid. 712; *Inscriptions de Délos*, 1513).

For the Athenian διαιτηταί see M. H. E. Meier, *Die Privatschiedsrichter u. d. öffentlichen Diäteten Athens* (1846); B. Hubert, *De arbitris atticis et privatis et publicis* (1885); A. Pischinger, *De arbitris Atheniensium publicis* (1893); T. Thalheim in *PW* v. 313 ff.; G. Busolt, *Griech. Staatskunde* (1920–6), 485 ff., 1111 ff.; R. J. Bonner, *CPhil.* 1907, 407 ff., 1916, 191 ff.; J. H. Lipsius, *Das attische Recht u. Rechtsverfahren* (1905), i. 220 ff.; H. C. Harrell, *Public Arbitration in Athenian Law* (1936). For the ξενικὰ δικαστήρια see E. Sonne, *De arbitris externis quos Graeci adhibuerunt* (1888); Thalheim in *PW* v. 573 f.; Busolt, op. cit. 557 f. For inter-State arbitration see Sonne, op. cit. H. F. Hitzig, 'Altgriech. Staatsverträge über Rechtshilfe', in *Festschrift F. Regelsberger* (1907); C. Phillipson, *International Law and Custom of Ancient Greece and Rome* (1911), ii. 127 ff.; A. Raeder, *L'Arbitrage international chez les Hellènes* (1912); M. N. Tod, *International Arbitration amongst the Greeks* (1913), *Sidelights on Greek History* (1932), 37 ff.; Busolt, op. cit. 1257 ff. M. N. T.

**ARBITRATION, ROMAN.** The history of Roman arbitration begins with the intervention of Rome as a great power in the politics of the Hellenistic world. Rome took the place of the kings who had often acted as international arbitrators between the free cities and leagues of the Greeks. Such disputes were referred to the Senate, which decided the general issue, but sometimes left particular points to a third party with local knowledge for settlement. Rome did not, in the earliest period, enforce the acceptance of her arbitral awards. While not abusing her influence, Rome tended to accept the state of affairs at the time when the appellants first came under her influence as the standard of reference. This practice tended, as her authority increased, to merge into the defence of the privileges of her allies. With the formation of provinces and the consolidation of the Empire, arbitration lost its international character, since, except by special permission, which was sometimes allowed, notably in Sicily, the subject peoples could not turn elsewhere. But senatorial adjudication of disputes between provincial communities of all categories continued to be frequent till the third century of the Empire. Such arbitration tended to merge with the general provincial administration, and was gradually replaced by the activity of special commissioners such as the *curatores* and *correctores* (q.v.) *civitatum*. Its existence illustrates the lively political self-consciousness of the cities of the Roman Empire.

ANCIENT SOURCES. Polybius, Livy bks. 30–45. Documents in Abbott and Johnson, *Municipal Administration in the Roman Empire* (1927).
MODERN LITERATURE. Ibid. ch. 11; E. de Ruggiero, *L'arbitrato pubblico presso i Romani* (1893); E. Badian, *Foreign Clientelae* (1957), chs. 4, 7. A. N. S.-W.

**ARBORICULTURE.** Neolithic Europe knew apple, and perhaps pear, cherry, and plum-trees; the ancient oriental regions also knew fig-trees and date-palms, pistachio, carob, walnut, peach, lemon, pomegranate, and almond-trees. Greece after the Persian Wars and especially in the Hellenistic age, as well as Italy after 200 B.C., imported and cultivated all these fruit-trees, so far as climate permitted. Under the Roman emperors many of them reached the Rhine, the Danube, and the Atlantic coast, and spread into Germanic and Slavic Europe, and from Iran even to China. Fig and date-trees had great economic importance for the Asiatic and African parts of the Mediterranean world and for southern Greece from Minoan times. The scientific experience of Greece and Rome was used for arboriculture with remarkable results. Orchards flourished everywhere, the methods of their cultivation being well known to us from papyri and contemporary authors. Cultivation of trees useful for their wood is found in Attica, and in the Ptolemaic and Roman Empires. State plantations of them were established, private plantations encouraged and even commandeered to lessen the scarcity of wood in Egypt and elsewhere. *See* AGRICULTURE.

Frank, *Econ. Survey* i–v, Index s.v. 'deforestation', 'forests', 'fruit', 'timber'; F. M. Heichelheim, *An Ancient Economic History* ii² (1964), 218 f.; Rostovtzeff, *Hellenistic World. Roman Empire* Indexes s.v. 'arboriculture', 'deforestation', 'forestry', 'forests', 'fruit-trees', 'timber', 'wood'. Michell, *Econom. Anc. Gr.³*, Index s.v. 'deforestation', 'timber'. F. M. H.

**ARCADIA,** a mountainous area in central Peloponnesus approaching the sea only in the south-west, near Phigalia. Its small valleys have a hard climate but are not infertile. Most of it is drained by the Alpheus and its tributaries, but large parts have no overground outlet for their waters, which disappear through swallow-holes; hence the north and east valleys either held lakes (Pheneus, Stymphalus) or became flooded. The most prosperous parts were the eastern plains, with Orchomenus, Mantinea, Tegea, lying at about 2,000 feet, and the Alpheus valley, where lay Heraea, the first Arcadian place to coin and one of the religious centres of Arcadia (C. Seltman, *Greek Coins²* (1955), 97). Arcadia offers few traces of Bronze Age civilization (except for infrequent fringe-sites such as Analipsis on the border between Tegeate territory and Laconia), and this is strikingly true of the late Mycenaean period (cf. F. Kiechle in *Kadmos* i (1962), 112 ff.). It is possible that refugees from the destruction of Messenian Pylos took refuge in Arcadia to form a heterogeneous population there in the southwest. Later Arcadia, particularly the mountain valleys, was a land of villages. It therefore carried little direct weight in the politics of Greece, but through Mantinea and Tegea it exercised considerable influence on the preoccupations of Sparta especially in the fifth century (cf. W. G. Forrest, 'Themistokles and Argos', *CQ* 1960, 221 ff.; A. Andrewes, 'Sparta and Arcadia in the early fifth century', *Phoenix*. 1952, 1 ff.). Recent archaeological discoveries have been made at Gortys (especially a curious bath-building) and Pheneus. Some later fortified sites remain to be identified: cf. *BCH* 1956, 522 ff. The chief strength of Arcadia was manpower, and from the early fifth century we hear of Arcadian mercenaries. From the mid sixth century it came under Spartan hegemony, but disaffection appeared from time to time related (though not necessarily simultaneously) to democratic developments and synoecism (cf. Strabo 7. 337) (*and see* MANTINEA). Under Epaminondas' direction an Arcadian Confederacy was formed as a counterweight to Sparta, but was weakened by particularism. For Arcadian participation in the Achaean Confederacy see MEGALOPOLIS.

Arcadia's dialect appears (resembling Cypriote) to preserve elements of Old Achaean (Mycenaean). The sequestered character of a good deal of Arcadian life preserved odd myths and cults: cf. the horse-headed Demeter of Lycosoura. The pastoral pursuits are reflected in the small Arcadian shepherd bronzes.

Paus. bk. 8 and Frazer's Commentary; W. Lamb, *BSA* 27 (1925), 133 ff.; C. Callmer, *Studien zur Geschichte Arkadiens* (1943); P-K, *GL* iii. 1, *Der Peloponnes*, pt. 1, 200 ff. T. J. D.; R. J. H.

**ARCADIAN CULTS AND MYTHS.** All the usual gods were worshipped in Arcadia; the most remarkable features of the cult were (1) Zeus on Mt. Lycaeon had a holy place, to enter which was death (by stoning, if it was deliberate; mysteriously within a year, if otherwise). It was reported as early as the time of Plato that human sacrifice was practised there, and that he who tasted the flesh of the human victim became a wolf. (2) Poseidon's

shrine at Mantinea stood open but might not be entered one Aepytus who disregarded this was blinded by mysterious wave. (3) Hermes by most reports was bor on Mt. Cyllene; there is little doubt that his cult origi nated in that region. (4) Demeter at Lycosura wa associated with a goddess Despoina, said to be he daughter by Poseidon; at Phigalia she was shown horse headed and bore the surname of Black (*see* ARCADIA); a Thelpusa, that of Erinys. In other words, she was a loca goddess identified with the normal Demeter, but of mor formidable character. (5) Pan is universally said to be a Arcadian god, as was natural enough, considering tha the country was largely pastoral. (6) Before a festival a Aliphera sacrifice was made to a godling called Myiagros 'fly-catcher', and it was believed that after this flie would not trouble the worshippers. Of myths, the mos important was the claim of the Arcadians that Zeus wa born in their country, and the source of the river Ned had sprung up for Rhea to wash herself and her infant. I was a kind of proverb or standing joke that the Arcadian had lived there since before the moon was created. *Se also* ARES.

W. Immerwahr, *Die Kulte und Mythen Arkadiens* (1891). H. J. R

**ARCADIUS** (1) of Antiocheia, a grammarian, of th later Empire, who wrote a (lost) Ὀνοματικόν (table of nou inflexions). To him is falsely ascribed an extant epitom from Herodian, probably made by Theodosius (end o 4th c. A.D.), to which a spurious conclusion was added i the sixteenth century.

Edition (Hdn. Epitome): M. Schmidt (1860). P. B. R. F

**ARCADIUS** (2), FLAVIUS, Eastern Roman Emperor (A.D 383–408), was the elder son of Theodosius I. Weak an irritable, he had little influence on the course of event in his time, and throughout his reign the governmen was effectively in the hands of his ministers, Rufinus (1 and Eutropius (2) (qq.v.), against whom the poet Claudia wrote vigorously, and Anthemius, of whom little is known E. A. T

**ARCAS,** eponym of Arcadia, son of Zeus and Callist (q.v.). Being left without a mother, he was reared b Maia. His grandfather Lycaeon, to test the omniscienc of Zeus, killed him and served up his flesh. The god over threw the table, destroyed the house with a thunderbolt turned Lycaon into a wolf, and restored Arcas to life Later, meeting Callisto in bear-shape, Arcas pursue her into the precinct of Zeus on Mt. Lycaeon. Both thu incurred the death-penalty (cf. ARCADIAN CULTS; Ovid *Met.* 2. 496, says nothing of the shrine but only that h did know her and was about to kill her), when Zeu turned them respectively into the Great Bear an Arctophylax.

Hyginus, *Poet. Astr.* 2. 1 and 4. H. J. R

**ARCESILAS I, II, III, IV,** second, fourth, sixth, an eighth kings of the Battiads, who ruled Cyrene (q.v. from its foundation (*c.* 630) for some 200 years. Informa tion on their reigns comes almost entirely from Herodotu and from Pindar and his scholiasts. In detail the chrono logy is uncertain. Arcesilas I (*c.* 591?–*c.* 575?) seems t have followed closely in the founder's footsteps. Arcesi las II, the Cruel (after 570), quarrelled with his brothers who seceded and founded Barca. They stirred up th Libyans against him, and he was defeated by them, an then murdered by his brother Learchus. He is th Arcesilas depicted supervising the loading of merchan dise on the famous cup in Paris (*CAH*, pls. i. 378) Arcesilas III (before 525–after 522) succeeded to monarchy stripped of its powers by the reform of Demonax of Mantinea. He seems to have tried to establish a demagogic tyranny, was forced into exile, collected mercenaries on Samos with the help of Polycrates, and regained power in Cyrene, only to be murdered later at Barca. In the meantime he had submitted to Cambyses when the latter conquered Egypt. Arcesilas IV (before 462–c. 440?) employed Pindar to celebrate his victory in the chariot-race at Delphi (462), but a democratic revolution led to his fall and the end of the dynasty.

Hdt. 4. 159–67, 200–5; Pind. *Pyth.* iv, v and scholia. F. Chamoux, *Cyrène sous la monarchie des Battiades* (1953). A. J. G.

**ARCESILAUS** (1), or **ARCESILAS** (both forms given in the sources), 316/5–242/1 B.C., son of Seuthes, or Scythes, of Pitane in Aeolia. Head of the Academy in the middle of the third century B.C., who gave the school its sceptical turn which it followed, with minor variations, until the age of Antiochus of Ascalon. (The term 'New Academy' is late, and was first applied by Antiochus. The term 'Middle Academy' may also derive from Antiochus. 'Second Academy' is a much later term.) Arcesilaus first studied in his home-town with the mathematician Autolycus, whom he followed to Sardis. On his father's death, his brother wanted him to study rhetoric, but Arcesilaus went to Athens and studied philosophy under Theophrastus. An intimate friendship with Crantor won him over to the Academy, where he came to know Polemo and Crates. On the death of Crates, a certain Socratides, elected scholarch on account of his age, resigned and gave his place to Arcesilaus, who headed the school until his death. He was a man of wide interests, many friends and acquaintances, famous for his wit, and an interesting, though harsh, teacher. He wrote some poetry—two epigrams by him are preserved in Diog. Laert.

Arcesilaus probably (but see D.L. iv. 24 = *Ind. Herc.* xvi. 14 ff.) published nothing, perhaps (D.L. iv. 32) to avoid any suspicion of dogmatism. What we know of his teachings derives from later sources. The present fashion to ascribe to members of the Academy under his guidance the composition of some of the spurious and dubious dialogues of the Platonic corpus (*Eryxias, Clitopho, De Justo*) should be treated with Academic doubt. A devoted reader of Plato, Arcesilaus believed that neither he nor Socrates had any doctrines of a 'dogmatic', positive nature, and based his teaching activities on the Socratic practice of arguing for and against any given point of view without reaching any conclusions, the result of which leads the student to the sceptical ἐποχή (withholding of judgement). How much this attitude may have been influenced by Pyrrhonian scepticism is debatable, but it is clear that the story of an esoteric teaching of Platonic doctrines of a more positive nature, revealed by him and his successors in the Academy only to their oldest pupils, is an aetological myth, used by late sceptics to find a distinction between the Academy and themselves, and by late Platonists to maintain an unbroken continuity of Platonism in Athens. It is now thought that, unlike Pyrrho, Arcesilaus did not consider ἐποχή as a mere attitude of mind whose function is mainly to make the sceptic imperturbable, but rather as a genuine philosophical position, which he believed was the original Platonic one, and which he used in his polemic, especially against the Stoics. The latter based their theory of truth on the concept of καταληπτικὴ φαντασία (clear and certain perception), followed and corroborated by συγκατάθεσις ('adsensio', certainty). Arcesilaus taught that, by using Platonic arguments against the reliability of our senses and by emphasizing contradictions within Stoic theory, one arrives at the principle of ἀκαταληψία (lack of certain perception). In his ethical teaching he maintained that the main moral principle is to follow what is reasonable (τὸ εὔλογον). This concept is nowhere sufficiently defined, but it probably means a common-sense attitude to moral issues rather than a complicated system of ethics.

SOURCES: Acad. index Herc. xv–xx. Diogenes Laertius iv. 28–45. Cicero, *Acad. Pr.* and *Lucullus, passim.* Sextus Empiricus, *Pyr.* i. 232–4; *Math.* vii. 150–8. Numenius ap. Euseb. *Praep. Ev.* xiv. 6. Wilamowitz, *Antigonos von Karystos* (1881), 57 ff.

MODERN DISCUSSIONS: V. Brochard, *Les Sceptiques grecs* (1887), 94 ff. Zeller, *Philos. d. Gr.⁵*, iii. i. 507 ff. Überweg–Praechter, *Grundriss*, 464 f.; 467–8; 141*. von Arnim in *PW* ii. 1164 ff. (Arkesilaos 19). P. Couissin, *Rev. Ét. Grec.* 1929, 373 ff; G. Gartmann, *Der Pseudoplatonische Dialog Eryxias* (Diss. Bonn 1949); H. Schmeken, *Philos. Jahrb.* (Fulda) 1950, 20 ff; A. Carlini, *Ann. Sc. Norm. Sup. di Pisa* 1962, 33 ff. J. G.

**ARCESILAUS** (2) (1st c. B.C.), sculptor, friend of L. Lucullus, working in Rome. Works: 1. Statue of Venus Genetrix for temple dedicated by Julius Caesar in 46 B.C. 2. Statue of Felicitas for Lucullus. 3. Centaurs carrying nymphs, for Asinius Pollio. 4. Lioness with Cupids for Varro. 5. Plaster model for crater with reliefs. His models, *proplasmata*, were sold at a high price. Probably a versatile adapter rather than an original artist.

Overbeck 2268–70; Lippold, *Griech. Plastik*, 386; Bieber, *Sculpt. Hellenist. Age*, 181, 184. T. B. L. W.

**ARCHAEOLOGY, CLASSICAL,** is the study of the ancient Greek and Roman world from sources other than transmitted texts; its primary concern is with material remains and tangible objects. Its upper chronological limit is not tied to the arrival of Greek-speaking and Italic peoples in the Mediterranean lands; in fact the prehistoric as far back as the neolithic commonly falls within the sphere of the classical archaeologist's activity. The lower limit is the breakdown of the pagan civilization of antiquity.

The traditional role of classical archaeology is the presentation and study of the different classes of artistic products, and its principal fields have consequently been the fine arts and architecture. From the sixteenth century in Italy, and the seventeenth and eighteenth centuries in France and England, studies were prosecuted with the aim of providing the best and most correct models for the training of practising architects and artists. To this end, for instance, the Society of Dilettanti (founded in London in 1733) financed a remarkable series of expeditions to study and publish the relics of antiquity; and at the beginning of the nineteenth century it was the view of Goethe and other critics that the arrival of the Elgin marbles sufficed to make London the centre of artistic study. With the reaction against classical taste in more recent times, the study of the antique has gradually lost its bearing on architectural practice and become an end in itself. Scholars have begun to pay more attention to the origins and evolution of architectural forms, the different kinds of secular buildings, and ensembles and city planning as revealed by modern excavations; and this has resulted in a greatly increased understanding of the development of ancient cities and living conditions.

In the realm of art, sculpture has been pre-eminent. The collecting of ancient statuary has a long history, and not least in England where King Stephen's brother, Henry of Blois, was concerned in transporting statues from Rome to Winchester, and in the first half of the seventeenth century Lord Arundel formed a notable collection and statues were collected on Delos for King Charles I. Puritanism perhaps partly accounts for the evident decline in interest after this time in England; and certainly it seems to have been the academies in Latin countries that fostered the study of the antique until the mid eighteenth century. But subsequently the acquisition of much of the Parthenon sculptures by Lord Elgin and the formation of national collections in European capitals gave rise to intense scholarly research in classical sculpture in the nineteenth century (especially in Germany, where art-history became an important subject in the universities and close contact was maintained with Rome through the Institute founded there in 1829). In the present century the study of classical sculpture has begun to suffer from a lack of fresh material and currently, perhaps, from a certain loss of interest in artistic values among classical archaeologists; but further advance may come from new technical approaches or from more serious study of comparative material such as terracotta figurines.

Classical painting (to leave aside Etruscan tombs) cannot be very effectively studied because of the loss of the Greek masterpieces, which are too distantly and uncertainly reflected in the Pompeian murals. Mosaics and Roman painting are only now being adequately studied. Greek painted vases, on the other hand, have been eagerly studied in the 200 years since they began to be recovered in large numbers from Italian cemeteries. In the present century interest has tended to shift from the interpretation of their figured scenes to accurate classification (which is likely in future to benefit from laboratory work on the chemical composition of the clays), analysis of forms and decoration, the recognition of individual artists and their interrelationship, and close dating. This work, in which Beazley has played a dominant part, has lent a new precision to archaeological field-work, because pottery, which had no scrap value and has proved relatively indestructible, provides the most abundant evidence for the dating of most archaeological contexts. An interesting old-established branch of Classical Archaeology is numismatics, which is mainly studied by specialists in contact with coin-collections but enters increasingly within the orbit of historians and archaeologists. Likewise common to history and archaeology, and tending to breed its own specialists, is the study of inscriptions (epigraphy). The discovery of the inscriptions themselves is largely due to the journeys of exploration which, over several centuries, have been directed to the recording of ancient remains and the discovery and identification of sites.

Having a great range of works of art in its repertory, Classical Archaeology has developed a bias in the direction of museum studies; and the museums have been supplied by excavation and illicit traffic in antiquities. From the mid eighteenth century, when the ransacking of Pompeii and Herculaneum commenced, excavation (both licit and illicit) was increasingly adopted as a means of procuring valuable works of art. In the 1870s, however, Schliemann demonstrated that it could be used as an instrument of historical inquiry; and from his labours, and those of successors like Evans, there emerged the image of a hitherto unsuspected civilization—that of Bronze Age Crete and Mycenae. The attraction of this Aegean civilization consisted not only in its revelation of an advanced economy and cultural life, but in the demonstration that the Greek legends of the Heroic Age had a historical foundation whose validity could be tested on the ground. Archaeology thus found itself engaged in making history out of pre-history; and British and American scholars, whose research in classical antiquities had been handicapped by lack of teaching in their home-countries, were quick to turn to this new field of pre-classical research. The significance of context in archaeology was recognized. New methods were developed; and in due course the instrument of stratigraphical excavation came also to be applied to elucidating the successive historical phases of classical civilization.

At the present time, thanks both to the organizing activity of foreign archaeological schools in Mediterranean lands and to the growing interest in archaeology in other countries, a high proportion of classical archaeologists gain experience of field-work, whether in excavation or in surface (and now also underwater) exploration. The most modern field exploration, such as that being conducted in Messenia by the University of Minnesota, favours a team-approach embracing the physical, biological, and social sciences; there is unlimited scope for work of this sort, which could profitably be supplemented by soundings to resolve particular problems. Excavation has already progressed far, especially in Italy, Western Asia Minor, and, above all, in Greece where the government has encouraged participation on the part of the foreign schools. Accessible sites of obvious appeal (such as Olympia, Delphi, Corinth, Delos, Pergamum, central Athens and Rome, Ostia, Carthage) have been extensively cleared; scores of others have been more or less methodically excavated, and interest is coming to centre increasingly on the fringes of the Greek and Roman worlds where native cultures were encountered. In this context, with the light that it is shedding on military activity and romanization, the Romano-British has become an important sector of Classical Archaeology.

Despite the increased emphasis now being laid on Archaeology as an autonomous discipline and a subject of specialized study, it remains true that research in Classical Archaeology is undertaken mainly by scholars who have specialized in classical studies. Certainly, much can be gained—especially in the less fully documented eras and sectors—from archaeological techniques that are coming to be applied to the study of other cultures. But at the same time there are many aspects of classical civilization in which even the most laborious use of these techniques and methods would not materially alter the conclusions that have been drawn from the various written sources; in general, a thorough grounding in ancient civilization and history is essential to the interpretation of the findings of archaeology, and there is an ever-increasing body of modern (not to mention ancient) literature in different languages which must be digested by those who pursue research in the classical field. It seems therefore natural that, while taking advantage of the skills developed in other fields of study, Classical Archaeology should continue to rank as a branch of the Classics.　　J. M. C.

**ARCHAISM** in Latin. The efforts of Ennius to hellenize Latin literature diverted the literary language of Rome away from the popular dialect, and literary Latin became in a sense a dead language. Writers wishing to invigorate their style would introduce from everyday speech words which came in time to appear archaic. We still find in Ennius the original quantity of terminations (e.g. *ponebāt*), nominatives in -*ōr* and -*ā* and elision of -*s* before consonants. The first declension genitive is always in -*āī* or -*ās*, the old genitive plural, e.g. *deum*, is common, and obsolete pronouns e.g. *mis*, *olli*, *sas*, and verbs like *morīmur*, *fūimus*. Many of these forms were metrically convenient for later writers, but, apart from such considerations, the success and prestige of the *Annals* stamped such archaisms firmly upon the literary language. Forms thus reintroduced are frequently of popular origin, and it is difficult to disentangle the archaic and the popular elements. Modernizing scribes have removed much of the archaic from Cato, but he still shows archaisms such as *praefamino* (imperative) and *prohibessis*. In Caesar and Cicero Latin prose reached its zenith of classical purity, but in Sallust we come to one who deliberately imitates the ancients. He is full of old words e.g. *prosapia*, *obsequela*, *dextumus*, and recalls early comedy in his fondness for frequentatives. In inflexion he uses e.g. *fide* (dat.), *vis* (acc. pl.), *nave* (adv.), *senati*, *nequitur*. Lucretius too is given to archaism, chiefly to show his admiration for Ennius. He uses forms like *in-*

*ndo, alid, rabies* (genit.), *vapōs* (nomin.), *scatit, confluxet, recesse*, infinitives in *-ier, escit, siet, fuat* and elision of preconsonantal *-s*. Archaisms are naturally not frequent in the impassioned poetry of Catullus, but some of the above are convenient and he shows *alis, alid, deposivit, componer, tetulit, recepso*. Horace's *Epistles* and *Satires* have many colloquialisms and a few archaisms, e.g. *erepsemus, surrexe*. Virgil, though a keen antiquarian, keeps archaism within bounds, retaining just enough to give to his work a grateful flavour of antiquity, e.g. *aulāī, olli, usso, admittier*. The Latinity of Propertius is quite peculiar. He shows many archaisms both in vocabulary and inflexion, e.g. *tergit, lenibunt, nullo, toto, uno* ( = *nulli*, etc.). The not infrequent archaisms in Livy occur mostly in legal formulae and hardly affect the general tone of his work, for by his time the struggle between the graecizing and archaizing schools had ended in victory for the former. Persius (1. 76–8) mocks Neronian archaizers, and this recurrent phenomenon reappears in Hadrian's time, when it became fashionable to prefer Ennius to Virgil. In Fronto and Apuleius we see a deliberate return to the obsolete diction of Ennius and Cato; and even Gellius, whose language is much purer, is full of archaisms like *edulcare, recentari, aeruscator*. In Christian writers, who wrote for the people at large, archaic words which had never died out of the spoken language again came into their own.

A. Ernout, *Recueil de textes latins archaïques* (1957), and texts of authors mentioned in the article. P. S. N.

**ARCHEDEMUS** of Tarsus, Stoic philosopher, probably a pupil of Diogenes (q.v. 3) of Babylon.

Testimonia in von Arnim, *SVF* iii. 262–4.

**ARCHEDICUS,** New Comedy poet, who foully slandered Demochares, nephew of Demosthenes (Polyb. 12. 13), in order to gain favour with Antipater.

*FCG* iv. 435 ff.; *CAF* iii. 276 ff.

**ARCHEGETES** (Ἀρχηγέτης), i.e. 'leader', 'guide', a title of Apollo (q.v.) in several places, e.g. Naxos in Sicily (Thuc. 6. 3. 1), where he had an altar; of Heracles at Sparta (Xen. *Hell.* 6. 3. 6); of Asclepius near Tithorea (Paus. 10. 32. 12). It signified that the god either personally shared in, or had shown approval of, the foundation of the colony or other institution in question and would protect it. *Archegetis* (ἀρχηγέτις) is used in like manner of goddesses. H. J. R.

**ARCHELAUS** (1), philosopher (fl. 5th c. B.C.), probably of Athenian birth, was a pupil of Anaxagoras (q.v.) and followed him in the main, but in some details adhered to the views of the Ionians and Empedocles. The tradition is consequently confused: he is credited both with accepting Anaxagoras' original 'mixture' of elements, from which the hot and the cold are first separated out, and also (improbably) with generating everything, as Anaximenes had, by condensation and rarefaction from air. He is said to have taught Socrates, but it is improbable that he anticipated Socrates by engaging in ethical speculation.

Testimonia and frs. in Diels, *Vorsokr.*[11] ii. 44 ff. W. D. R.

**ARCHELAUS** (2), king of Macedon *c.* 413–399 B.C. He organized the military strength of Macedonia by training infantry and building forts and roads (Thuc. 2. 100), and sought to foster hellenization by bringing Greek artists, especially Euripides, to his court, and by celebrating games at Dium. Moving his court from Aegae to Pella near the coast and adopting the Persian coin standard, he developed Macedonian trade. He maintained friendly relations with Athens, averted the revolt of Elimiotis by a marriage alliance, and captured Pydna (410); *c.* 400 he put the philo-Macedonian party into power at Larissa, probably annexing Perrhaebia.

F. Geyer, *Historische Zeitschrift*, Beiheft 19 (1930). N. G. L. H.

**ARCHELAUS** (3) (fl. 1st c. B.C.), Greek general of Mithridates VI, perhaps from Sinope or Amisus. After overrunning Bithynia and most of central Greece ('First Mithridatic War', 88–85 B.C.), he was twice defeated by Sulla, and commissioned by Mithridates to negotiate a peace. Falling under suspicion of treasonable dealings with Sulla, on the renewal of war (83) he deserted to Rome, and he assisted Lucullus early in the third war (74). His only defeats were by Rome's best general with an army better, and not much smaller, than his own.

Appian, *Mithridatica* 18 ff.; Plutarch, *Sulla* 11 ff. For army figures, see esp. Memnon (fr. 22, *FGrH* iii B, no. 434). G. T. G.

**ARCHELAUS** (4), on the death of his father Herod (q.v. 1) the Great, became ethnarch of the southern part of his kingdom—Judaea, Samaria, and Idumaea. His rule was so unpopular that in A.D. 6 Augustus deposed him at his subjects' request and annexed his territory as the province of Judaea. E. M. S.

**ARCHERMUS,** sculptor (6th c.) of Chios. According to Pliny, son of Micciades and grandson of Melas, father of Bupalus (q.v.) and Athenis. Inscribed plinth in Delos names Micciades and Archermus, probably as both dedicators and sculptors, and Melas, as a Chiote hero. It probably belonged to the Nike of Delos (Athens, N.M. 21). A signature of Archermus found on the Acropolis of Athens has been connected with the Nike (Acropolis Museum 693). Archermus is said to have been the first to represent Nike winged.

Overbeck 314 f.; A. E. Raubitschek, *Dedications from the Athenian Akropolis* (U.S.A. 1949), 484 ff.; G. M. A. Richter, *Archaic Greek Art* (U.S.A. 1949), 116. T. B. L. W.

**ARCHERS** (Greek and Hellenistic). In Homer the chieftains, except Teucer, Pandareus, and Paris, did not use the bow in war, but the rank and file did. In classical times the Persians were dreaded for their attacks with arrows, but Greek citizens were not organized into regular bodies of archers. Archery, which had gone out of normal use, was kept up only in Crete and the backward parts of Greece, such as Acarnania. Cretan archers, who were specially renowned, were frequently employed at all periods to supplement the ordinary citizen-soldier. Athens also in the fifth century imported Scythian mercenaries who acted both as police and as soldiers, and were reinforced by additional recruits from the poorer citizens up to a total of 1,600 (Thuc. 2. 13. 8). Mounted archers were few in the classical period. In the Hellenistic armies under Oriental influence the use of archers, whether mounted or on foot, was somewhat more frequent, but only the Parthians made them the main arm of their offensive.

H. Hommel, *PW* s.v. τοξόται; R. Cagnat, Dar.–Sag. s.v. 'Sagittarii'; W. W. Tarn, *Hellenistic Military and Naval Development* (1930), 87 ff.; F. E. Adcock, *The Greek and Macedonian art of war* (1957), 14 ff.; A. M. Snodgrass, *Arms and Armour of the Greeks* (1967). H. W. P.

**ARCHESTRATUS** of Gela, a contemporary of Aristotle, styled ὁ τῶν ὀψοφάγων Ἡσίοδος ἢ Θέογνις (Ath. 6. 310 a). Wrote a Ἡδυπάθεια, a sort of gastronomical Baedeker, the source of Ennius' *Hedyphagetica*.

Brandt, *Corpusc. poes. ep. graec. ludibundae* i. 114–93. J. D. D.

**ARCHIAS,** AULUS LICINIUS, a Greek poet of Antioch, arrived in Rome before 100 B.C. He celebrated Marius' Cimbric victory, and the Mithridatic victories of Lucullus (q.v. 2), who obtained for him the citizenship of Heraclea in Lucania (93 B.C.). Under the Lex Plautia Papiria he acquired Roman citizenship. This was contested by Gratius (62), and defended successfully by Cicero (*Pro Archia*). Cicero hoped for a laudatory poem from him, but (*Att.* 1. 16. 15) in vain, as he was engaged by the Metelli. He improvised in verse (Quint. *Inst.* 10. 7. 19). His epigram on the infant Roscius discovered asleep with a serpent coiled round him is mentioned by Cicero (*Div.* 1. 79): it may be inferred he was alive in 45. Forty-one epigrams in the Greek Anthology are headed 'Archias', but identification is not possible (he might be the elder Archias, cf. *Anth. Pal.* 9. 91).

Susemihl, *Gesch. gr. Lit. Alex.* i. 900. G. C. R.

**ARCHIDAMUS,** the name of several Eurypontid kings of Sparta. The most notable were:

ARCHIDAMUS II, who reigned from 469(?) B.C. (476, Diodorus) to 427–426; grandson of Leotychidas (q.v.). He distinguished himself on the occasion of the great earthquake in 465/4 (or 469/8; *see* SPARTA) and the subsequent Messenian War, after which we hear nothing of him for thirty years. Having failed to dissuade Sparta from going to war with Athens, he led the Peloponnesian forces to invade Attica in 431, 430, and 428; and to attack Plataea in 429. He left two sons, Agis II and Agesilaus II (qq.v.).

Thuc. bks. 1 and 2, *passim*; Diod. 11. 63–64.

ARCHIDAMUS III, who reigned from 361–360 to 338, son of Agesilaus II. He brought back the Spartan army after Leuctra (371), in which Diodorus wrongly states that he took part, and fought against the Arcadians (367, 364). He distinguished himself in the defence of Sparta against Epaminondas (362), and supported the Phocians in the Sacred War, but returned in disgust at the duplicity of their commander Phalaecus (346). Invited to help Tarentum against the Lucanians (*c.* 342), he landed with a force in Italy but soon fell in battle at Manduria (338). Isocrates' *Archidamus* purports to be the appeal of the king to a congress at Sparta (366–365) to refuse the Theban demand for the recognition of the independence of Messene. Pausanias mentions a statue of him at Olympia.

Xen. *Hell.* bks. 5–7; Theopompus *FGrH* 115 F 232; Diod. bks. 15 and 16; Plut. *Ages.* 19, 33–34, 40; Paus. 3. 10. 3–5; 6. 4. 9. E. Meyer, *Forschungen* (1892–9) ii. 505 f. A. M. W.

**ARCHIGENES** of Apamea in Syria, pupil of Agathinus (q.v.); well-known physician at Rome in the time of Trajan (A.D. 98–117). He belonged to the Eclectic school, but was chiefly influenced by the doctrines of the Pneumatic school. The leading principle of his therapeutics was to combat the eight δυσκρασίαι (bad temperaments). Galen's theory of the pulse was borrowed from that of Archigenes, while at other points Galen reacts against his teaching. Works: Περὶ τῶν κατὰ γένος φαρμάκων; Περὶ τόπων πεπονθότων; Περὶ καστορίου χρήσεως; eleven bks. of letters of medical advice; and many others: all lost except for frs. W. D. R.

**ARCHILOCHUS,** iambic and elegiac poet, of Paros, son of Telesicles (Ael. fr. 80) and a slave-woman. His date is disputed. The ancient authorities vary from the time of Romulus, 753–716 B.C. (Cic. *Tusc.* 1. 1. 3), to that of Gyges, who died *c.* 652 B.C. (Hdt. i. 12). The eclipse of the sun mentioned in fr. 74 is usually taken to be that of 6 Apr., 648 B.C., which is more likely than that of 14 Mar., 711 B.C. Though Archilochus took part in the colonization of Thasos (Euseb. *Praep. Evang.* 6. 8), which is dated *c.* 708 B.C. (Clem. Al. *Strom.* 1. 333 b), it was probably in the later stages. Archilochus mentions

contemporary events in a war in Euboea (fr. 3). Little is known of his life except of warfare in Thasos, and his quarrels with Lycambes in his attempts to marry Neobule (Hor. *Epist.* 1. 19. 23 ff.). Fr. 18 proves that he went to the Thracian mainland. He was killed in battle (Plut. *De sera* 7). Considerable remains of his work survive: (1) elegiac epigrams, probably songs sung to the flute over the wine, often about himself, sometimes influenced by epic language, but remarkable for their strongly personal note, whether about war (frs. 3, 6, 7) or wine (fr. 4); (2) iambic trimeters, also about himself, though in fr. 22 another character is represented as speaking. In them he seems to have assailed Lycambes (fr. 24), and fr. 25 has been referred to Neobule; (3) trochaic tetrameters catalectic, including lines on the colonization of Thasos (frs. 52–4), the approach of war (fr. 56), his own misfortunes (frs. 58, 67), the eclipse of the sun (fr. 74), and his own skill in poetry (frs. 76–7); (4) epodes, or stanzas of mixed metres, of which there are different types: (*a*) frs. 81–7 iambic trimeter followed by hemiepes, (*b*) frs. 88–97 iambic trimeters followed by iambic dimeters, and (*c*) fr. 104 dactylic hexameters followed by iambic dimeters. In this class he composed αἶνοι, fables of traditional character about the fox and the monkey, the fox and the eagle, the fox and the hedgehog, probably with personal references to himself and his circumstances; (5) tetrameters of mixed rhythms, (*a*) frs. 107–11, paroemiacs and ithyphallics, (*b*) frs. 112–17, dactylic tetrameters and ithyphallics; (6) Pindar (*Ol.* 9. 1) attributes to him the song of victory used by victors at Olympia. He was regarded as a great innovator (Plut. *De mus.* 28) in metre, language, and subjects, and the fragments support this reputation. They are less violent and abusive than we might expect (cf. Pind. *Pyth.* 2. 99). His language is mostly colloquial Ionic, though in his elegiacs he admits epic forms. *See also* IAMBIC POETRY, GREEK.

TEXT. Diehl, *Anth. Lyr. Graec.* i. 3. 3–49; F. Lasserre and A. Bonnard, *Archiloque: fragments* (1958).
CRITICISM. A. Hauvette, *Archiloque, sa vie et ses œuvres* (1905); F. Lasserre, *Les Epodes d'Archiloque* (1950); A. A. Blakeway, 'The Date of Archilochus' in *Greek Poetry and Life* (1936), 34 ff.; F. Jacoby, 'The Date of Archilochus', *CQ* 1941, 97 ff. PW Suppl. xi, 136 ff. C. M. B.

**ARCHIMEDES,** mathematician and inventor (*c.* 287–212 B.C.). Born at Syracuse, son of an astronomer Phidias, and killed at the sack of the city by the Romans under Marcellus, he was on intimate terms with its king Hieron II. He probably visited Egypt: he corresponded with the Alexandrian scholars Conon of Samos and Eratosthenes (qq.v.). Popular history (see especially Plut. *Marc.* 14–19) knew him as the inventor of marvellous machines used against the Romans at the siege of Syracuse and of other devices such as the screw for raising water (κοχλίας); for his boast 'give me a place to stand on and I will move the earth' (Simpl. *in Phys.* 1110. 5); for his determination of the proportions of gold and silver in a wreath made for Hieron (εὕρηκα, εὕρηκα, Vitr. 9. 9–12); for his construction of two 'sphaerae' (a planetarium and a star globe) which were taken to Rome (Cic. *Rep.* i. 21–2); and for his tomb, which by his wish depicted a cylinder circumscribing a sphere, with the ratio $\frac{3}{2}$ which he discovered between them (Plut. *Marc.* 17, Cic. *Tusc.* 5. 64–6).

His extant works, with the most important features of each are:

In Greek: (1) *On the Sphere and Cylinder*, bks. 1 and 2: the formulas for the surface-area and volume of a sphere and any segment of it. (2) *Measurement of the Circle*: by inscribing and circumscribing regular polygons of ninety-six sides upper and lower limits of $3\frac{1}{7}$ and $3\frac{10}{71}$ are found to the value of $\pi$; and Archimedes incidentally gives a rational approximation to $\sqrt{3}$ and to the square roots of several large numbers. (3) *On Conoids and Spheroids*:

determination of the volumes of segments of various solids formed by the revolution of a conic about its axis. (4) *On Spirals*: properties of tangents to the 'Archimedean' spiral, and determination of its area. (5) *The Equilibriums of Planes* or *Centres of Gravity of Planes*, bks. 1 and 2: the theory of the lever is propounded and the centres of gravity of various rectilinear plane figures (bk. 1) and of segments of conics (bk. 2) are established. (6) *Quadrature of the Parabola*: the area of a parabola is determined first by 'mechanical' (see below) and then by geometrical means. (7) *The Sand-reckoner*: description of system for expressing enormously large numbers in words (in effect a notation in which 100,000,000 is used as a base as we use 10). Archimedes employs it to express the number of grains of sand which, on certain assumptions, the universe is calculated to contain. It is the only surviving work of Archimedes touching on astronomy (see below), and is our best source for the heliocentric system of Aristarchus (q.v. 1). (8) *Method of Mechanical Theorems*: description of the method invented by Archimedes for finding by 'mechanical' means the areas and volumes of various figures (e.g. the parabola and the sphere). (9) *On Floating Bodies*: deals with the positions which segments of a solid of revolution can assume when floating in a fluid; for this Archimedes had to invent a science of hydrostatics *ab ovo*. The Greek text of the latter two works was discovered only in 1906, though *On Floating Bodies* was already known in Latin translation.

In Arabic: (1) *Book of Lemmas* (available only in Latin translation): a miscellany of fifteen problems in plane geometry. (2) *On the Heptagon in a Circle* (available in German translation): geometrical construction of a regular heptagon. Both these works have undergone alteration in the Arabic tradition.

The most notable characteristic of Archimedes' mathematical work is its freedom from the trammels of traditional Greek mathematics. It is true that in the *proofs* of those theorems for which the integral calculus would now be used (e.g. those determining the surface-area and volume of a sphere, the area of a parabola, and the volume of conoids) he uses the traditional Greek method of bypassing infinitesimals (invented by Eudoxus, q.v., and deployed in Euclid, bk. 10; it has been misnamed 'method of exhaustion' in modern works). But the *Method* reveals that for the *discovery* of these theorems he used a technique which consists essentially of dividing two figures into infinitely thin strips, weighing these strips against each other, and then summing them to get the ratio of the two whole figures. This is analogous to the procedure of the first practitioners of the integral calculus in the seventeenth century, but unlike them Archimedes recognized its lack of logical rigour, and used it only as a heuristic method. The same freedom of thought appears in the arithmetical field in the *Sand-reckoner*, which shows an understanding of the nature of a numerical system immeasurably superior to anything else from antiquity. It is this breadth and freedom of vision, rather than the amazing ingenuity which Archimedes everywhere displays in the solution of particular problems, which justifies his title not only as the greatest mathematician of antiquity, but as one of the greatest ever. His work in hydrostatics (see no. (9) above) was epoch-making (though the effect in antiquity was negligible). The same is true of statics, though here he probably had predecessors (*see* PHYSICS).

All his work in astronomy is lost except for an ingenious method of finding the sun's apparent diameter described in the *Sand-reckoner*, and a passage giving the distances of the heavenly bodies preserved in Hippolytus (*Haer.* 41, 18 ff. Wendland). This (highly corrupt) passage suggests that he had no mathematical theory of astronomy. However, his construction of a planetarium suggests the reverse. On this he wrote a work (περὶ σφαιροποιίας,

Pappus 8. 3), now lost. Other lost works include treatises on semi-regular polyhedra (Pappus 5. 34), on elementary mechanics (περὶ ζυγῶν or περὶ ἰσορροπιῶν, Pappus 8. 24 and 8) and on reflection in mirrors (κατοπτρικά, Theon *in Syntax. I*, 347 f. Rome). An epigram preserves a 'cattle-problem' attributed to Archimedes; this poses a problem in indeterminate analysis with eight unknowns. There is no evidence that Archimedes found the solution, which is in immense numbers. Fragments of a work entitled στομάχιον, dealing with a square divided into fourteen pieces for a game or puzzle, are preserved in Greek and Arabic.

Commentaries by Eutocius to *Sphere and Cylinder*, *Measurement of the Circle*, and *Equilibriums of Planes* survive.

EDITIONS. Critical text of Greek works (with Latin translation), fragments, some Arabic works in Latin translation, and of Eutocius' commentaries by J. L. Heiberg, 2nd ed. Leipzig (Teubner), 1910–15, 3 vols. German translation of texts concerning the *Heptagon in a Circle* in Carl Schoy, *Die Trigonometrischen Lehren des . . . al-Bīrûnî*, (1927), 74 ff. For the history of the text see Heiberg iii Prolegomena. For earlier editions see Heath's translation, xxix ff. For the texts of Archimedes that were available to Islam and the Latin West see M. Clagett, *Archimedes in the Middle Ages*, i (U.S.A. 1964).

TRANSLATIONS. T. L. Heath, *The Works of Archimedes* (1897), and *The Method of Archimedes* (1912), repr. in one vol., (U.S.A. 1957); French, P. ver Eecke, *Les Œuvres complètes d'Archimède*, (1921) (includes commentaries of Eutocius).

COMMENT. Heath, *Hist. of Greek Maths.* ii. 16 ff.; E. J. Dijksterhuis, *Archimedes* (Copenhagen, 1956; best detailed account, in English, of life and works). On the Heptagon see Tropfke, *Osiris* 1936, 636 ff. For the mechanical inventions see A. G. Drachmann, *The Mechanical Technology of Greek and Roman Antiquity* (Copenhagen, 1961).

G. J. T.

**ARCHIPPUS**, Athenian comic poet, won first prize (at the City Dionysia?) in 415 B.C. We have six titles, and four other plays were variously attributed to Archippus or Aristophanes. In his best-known play, *Fishes* (after 403, as the reference to the archon Euclides in fr. 27 shows), he exploited an idea similar to that of Aristophanes' *Birds*; fr. 27 concerns a treaty between Athens and the fishes. *Rhinon* no doubt satirized the man of that name who came into prominence in 404/403 (Arist. *Ath. Pol.* 38. 3 f.).

*FCG* i. 205 ff.; *CAF* i. 679 ff.; *FAC* i. 794 ff. K. J. D.

**ARCHITECTURE. I.** GREEK. With the decline of Mycenaean civilization (*see* MYCENAE) architecture in Greece was reduced to very simple materials and forms. Remains from the early centuries of the first millennium are slight (cf. H. Drerup, *Arch. Anz.* 1964, 2, 180 ff.). Most interesting are a number of clay models of houses or temples, some of which may have some affinity with the Mycenaean megaron or hall (*see* TEMPLE). Monumental architecture developed in the seventh century, and reached great heights in the sixth.

The architects concentrated their efforts mainly on the temple. To the simple rectangular *cella* which formed its nucleus they added an outer colonnade, or *pteron*, which served for both protection and decoration; and it was in the treatment of this that the great Orders of architecture were evolved.

The independent stoa too (q.v. 2) was tentatively developed in the archaic period. Some building types remained rudimentary until a comparatively late date. The Greeks were not very successful in designing council-houses and other covered halls, relying for the support of the roof on the multiplication of columns. The unroofed theatre (q.v.) remained simple in form in the fifth century and attained perfection in the fourth. Buildings such as the stadium and gymnasium (qq.v.) were open and informal in design until the late fourth century. Throughout the same period houses too (q.v.) were mostly unpretentious in plan and construction. Next to its temples, the most impressive architectural creation of the archaic and classical city was its fortification wall (*see* TOWNS).

The commonest Greek mode of construction was in unbaked brick on a stone foundation and socle (cf. HOUSES). This remained usual in the more modest buildings, throughout the classical period. Construction in solid stone, with some influence from Egypt, developed in important temples in the seventh and sixth centuries. Fine marbles were increasingly used where available—the western Greeks lacked ready supplies—with knife-edge joints and contintinuous highly polished surfaces. Fine masonry dispensed with bonding material, but used clamps and dowels. City-walls continued to be built in unbaked brick in their upper portions; but in the fifth and still more in the fourth century the best were of massive stone throughout, in styles which combine beauty with rugged strength. Fortification and terrace walls were sometimes built of carefully designed polygonal masonry; in the variety known as Lesbian the lines of the joints run in swinging curves (see R. Scranton, *Greek Walls*, U.S.A. 1941).

The great architectural Orders show traces of an origin in early wooden construction; but how the forms ultimately standardized for decorative purposes are related to the original constructional elements is not always clear. The Doric order may owe something to surviving Mycenaean capitals. The Ionic capital has oriental affinities; where the peculiar type known as Aeolic, found in Lesbos and the neighbouring mainland, stands in the line of development is uncertain. Both orders attained full stature in the sixth century, Ionic somewhat later than Doric; Doric in Greece proper, and the West, where there were interesting experiments and variations, Ionic in East Greece and the neighbouring islands, most notably in the vast temples of Hera at Samos and Artemis at Ephesus (q.v.). In the fifth century the Orders reached their highest point of refinement, both in general proportions and in perfection of detail, including their elegant mouldings (see L. Shoe, *Profiles of Greek Mouldings*, 1936, and *Profiles of Western Greek Mouldings*, 1952). At Athens Doric and Ionic were most subtly related and combined, even in the same building (*see* PARTHENON, PROPYLAEA).

The main elements of a Doric structure are, in elevation, the foundation; the euthynteria (levelling course); the three steps, forming a platform the top of which is the stylobate; the massive column shafts, rising from the stylobate without a base (after some variation, in its classic fifth-century form, the Doric column was in height, with capital, about $5\frac{1}{2}$ times its lower diameter, and had 20 shallow flutes); the capital, consisting of the echinus, a simple convex moulding swelling out from the top of the shaft, surmounted by the abacus, a flat rectangular slab; the architrave, constructed of plain blocks spanning the columns; the frieze, consisting of triglyphs (so called because they were divided vertically by grooves into three bars), normally placed over each column and the centre of each intercolumnation, alternating with metopes, square slabs set back from the face of the triglyphs; and, finally, the cornice (*geison*) surmounted by the gutter (*sima*). At the ends of the temple the horizontal and sloping cornices together formed the pediment.

The Ionic Order was lighter in proportions and more ornate in detail, with more elaborate mouldings. The column had a base, of which there were several local variations, and 24 flutes, more deeply cut than in Doric and separated by plain strips. The Ionic capital too had a convex moulding, carved with 'egg-and-tongue', but this was surmounted and partially masked by the characteristic volute member. The architrave consisted of three bands each projecting a little above the one below. Above it, over an 'egg-and-tongue' moulding, and in place of the Doric triglyph frieze, was a row of small projecting blocks, the dentils. Sometimes a continuous sculptured frieze was inserted at this point, instead of or occasionally in addition to the dentils.

In both orders the architects faced awkward problems at the corner of the building, in Doric with the triglyph frieze, in Ionic with the capital. The Corinthian capital invented in the later part of the fifth century, according to tradition by the sculptor Callimachus (q.v. 2), had the advantage that all four faces were the same, with volutes rising vertically from luxuriant bands of acanthus leaves. Corinthian was not a complete new order but a variant on Ionic. First found in a single capital (or possibly three) in the temple of Apollo at Bassae (q.v.), it was used for some time tentatively and experimentally, mainly in interiors. In the Olympieum (q.v.) at Athens, in the second century B.C., it assumed its classic form and was used on a vast scale. Imported to Rome (Sulla actually transported some columns from the Olympieum) it became the great imperial order.

In the finest temples, and sometimes in other buildings, certain subtle 'refinements' were introduced. The horizontal lines, from the foundations upwards, were given a slight but accurately planned upward curve. The columns had entasis, i.e. besides tapering upwards they had a slight outward curve or bulge, pronounced in some archaic temples, more delicate in the time of the Parthenon. They tilted slightly inwards, the corner columns diagonally. Besides their subtle optical and aesthetic effect, some of these features had a practical purpose giving the building greater stability and ensuring drainage for the stylobate.

Architects and sculptors worked in close collaboration; some artists were both, e.g. Scopas (q.v.). Most sculpture was meant to be seen in an architectural setting. The interior of the temple was designed to show off the great cult statue. Sculpture was applied to the structure of the building in the pediments and metopes of Doric temples; the continuous sculptured frieze, characteristic of Ionic, was incorporated in some Doric buildings too (Bassae, the Parthenon, temple of Hephaestus at Athens). Statues called acroteria stood on the summit and corners of the pediments. The essential structural members, such as the columns and architrave, were very rarely sculptured (*see*, however, CARYATIDES). Bright paint was freely applied to architectural details, as well as to sculpture. A few temples and stoas had paintings on their walls, in the form of frescoes or on wooden panels (*see* PAINTING, PROPYLAEA, STOA). Thus not only sculpture but painting served the master art.

*See* TERRACOTTAS for decoration in this material.

For architects *see* CALLICRATES (1), HERMOGENES (1), HIPPODAMUS, ICTINUS, PHILON (1), PYTHIUS, SCOPAS.

R. E. W.

II. ROMAN architecture represents a fusion of traditional Greek elements, notably the trabeated orders, with new structural principles based on the development of the arch and of a new building material, concrete. The element inherited from Greece catches the attention to-day, as it did that of the architects of the Renaissance, but it was in fact increasingly restricted to a few traditional building forms, such as the temple and the basilica (qq.v.), and to such secondary features as colonnades and porticoes, or else relegated to a superficial, decorative role. Already in the late Republic (e.g. in the façade of the Tabularium (q.v.); cf. the Colosseum) we find the three Orders (to which the Romans added a fourth, the 'Composite') used simply as a decorous adjunct to an arcuated façade; and the development of applied marble veneer, wall-mosaic, and moulded stucco facilitated a steady divergence between the traditional classical elements of the visible decorative surfaces and the functional realities

f the underlying structures. The process was not carried
 its logical conclusion before Byzantine times, but it
as already a significant factor in the first and second
enturies A.D.

The decisive developments in Roman concrete
rchitecture took place between c. A.D. 50 and 130 and
re embodied in such buildings as Nero's Golden House
ee DOMUS AUREA), Domitian's palace on the Palatine,
Iadrian's Villa, and the Pantheon (q.v.), as well as in the
partment-houses and warehouses of Ostia and, later,
he great 'imperial' baths (q.v.) or the Basilica of
Maxentius (see BASILICA). The revolutionary structural
roperties of the new material were used to create, for
he first time in history, an architecture in which the
ominant factor was not the solid masonry but the space
hich it enclosed. Instead of the rationality and structural
icidity of Greek architecture, this was an architecture of
lusion and suggestion, of subtly curvilinear forms and
bove all of inner light and colour and of soaring, vaulted
pace. The exterior architecture by contrast moved
teadily towards a functional severity comparable to that
f the aqueducts, bridges, and other monuments of
Roman engineering.

The great contribution of Greek architecture to
osterity was its perfecting of the Orders, that of the
Romans the first realization of the architectural signifi-
ance of interior space. Both proved to be achievements of
erennial significance, the former as an ever-fresh source
f rediscovered inspiration, the latter as one of the funda-
nental concepts of all subsequent architectural thinking.

J. B. W.-P.

A. Marquand, A Handbook of Greek Architecture (1909); T. Fyfe,
Hellenistic Architecture (1936); D. S. Robertson, Greek and Roman
Architecture² (1943); W. B. Dinsmoor, The Architecture of Ancient
Greece (1950; full bibliographies, 341 ff.); H. Plommer, Ancient and
Classical Architecture (Simpson's History of Architectural Develop-
ment, vol. i, revised, 1956); A. W. Lawrence, Greek Architecture²
Pelican History of Art, 1967); L. Crema, L'Architettura romana
.959); R. Martin, Manuel d'Architecture grecque (1965); A. Boethius
nd J. B. Ward-Perkins, Etruscan and Roman Architecture (Pelican
History of Art, 1969).

**RCHIVES.** I. GREEK (ἀρχεῖον, originally = 'magis-
rate's office', acquired a specialized sense in the Hellen-
tic period). Temple officials kept records of dedications
nd property from the archaic period onwards. Secular
ublic documentation, from beginnings in the sixth
entury B.C., gathered momentum in the fifth and reached
ts maximum efficiency in the Hellenistic age. Athens
ffers the most easily surveyed evidence. In the early
eriod each magistracy kept its own records, on pinakes
writing tablets—sometimes leukomata or whitened
oards) or papyri. These were co-ordinated into a record-
ffice, housed in the Metroon, at the end of the fifth
entury. Material thereafter readily available for research
nd quotation went back to the time of Solon and in-
luded historical documents such as the Themistocles-
ecree (SEG xviii. 153). These were αὐτόγραφα, recopied
rom time to time; many of the ἀντίγραφα of selected
tems usually of sacral or international importance,
n stone or bronze, have survived as the inscriptions
vhich, though the principal source for modern study,
hould not be mistaken for the archives themselves. It
ecame possible for citizens to deposit documents such
s wills in the ἀρχεῖον, and in some cases this was a legal
equirement. The registration of land-property and the
reservation of records were particularly elaborate in
Ptolemaic and Roman Egypt.

G. Busolt–H. Swoboda, Griechisches Staatskunde² (1926), i. 488 ff.,
. 1036 ff.; Hignett, Hist. Athen. Const. 12 ff., does not believe that
arly documents survived to the fourth century; G. Klaffenbach,
Bemerkungen zum griechischen Urkundenwesen (Sb. Akad. Berlin
960–6), with refs. to earlier literature. A. G. W.

II. ROMAN (tabularia, from tabulae as 'records'). From
he early Republic, as tradition shows, Rome had public
records, variously kept, though they were not systematically organized until the late fourth century B.C. We
know, for instance, of lists of magistrates (see FASTI),
copies of legislative acts and treaties, census details, and
priestly records that also referred to public affairs (see
TABULA PONTIFICUM and ANNALS), later edited for historical use. Some documents, e.g. copies of treaties in bronze,
were stored on the Capitol (see EPIGRAPHY); other records
were held in the magistrates' offices and the priestly colleges. The chief archives were the aerarium in the temple
of Saturn, after 78 B.C. moving to the Tabularium, which
still stands on the Capitol slope facing the Forum. It contained originally financial documents and later almost all
official records, including laws, plebiscita, senatus consulta,
as well as imperial 'constitutions' and decrees; the urban
quaestors were in charge. The temple of Ceres also held
first senatus consulta and then copies of plebiscita. Under
the Empire the tabularium Caesaris preserved all documents relating to landed property, and we may add the
archives of the imperial court departments along with
those of the municipia and provinces; Marcus Aurelius
established a register of Roman births in the provinces.

Mommsen, Röm. Staatsr. ii, i, 545 ff. A. H. McD.

**ARCHONTES,** the general term for all holders of office
in a State. But the word was frequently used of a particular
office, originally at least the highest office of the State.
Archontes are found in most States of central Greece,
including Athens, and in States dependent on or influenced by Athens.

In Athens there were at first three archons, the
basileus, the polemarch, and the archon eponymos, this
being probably the order in which they were first instituted. The royal house of Medontidae (see CODRUS)
continued to hold a hereditary life-office (probably as
basileis, not as archontes eponymoi, as Aristotle says) after
the institution of polemarch and archon, the two latter
being presumably elective. Later (c. 750 B.C.?) the three
archons were made ten-yearly, and in 683 yearly magistrates; all rights of the Medontidae had disappeared.
Shortly after this the number of archons was increased
to nine by the addition of six thesmothetai (q.v.). They
were elected by the people and were the chief magistrates
of the State. The archon eponymos was the most important because he had the widest range of duties. Political
struggles in the seventh and sixth centuries centred
upon the elections to this office till the tyranny of the
Pisistratids, who arranged that one of themselves or
their adherents should hold it. In 487 the lot (first from
an elected body of perhaps 500, later from a body of 100
chosen by sortition) was introduced as the mode of their
appointment, and therewith their political importance
ended. No influential politician held the office afterwards; before 487 Solon, Hippias, Themistocles, and
Aristides had been archons.

The nine archons and the secretary to the thesmothetai were each chosen from one of the ten phylai.
Solon's arrangement was preserved, by which the
archonship was open only to men of the highest or two
highest census-classes (see SOLON); it was opened to the
zeugitai in 457, never formally to the thetes, though
questions were not asked if one of the latter was chosen.

All ex-archons after their euthyna (q.v.) entered the
Areopagus, and remained life-members of that council.
This added considerable importance to their office in
early times; when the introduction of the lot as the
method of election affected a majority of the Areopagites,
the Areopagus too lost its political importance.

Like most public offices in Greece, the archonship
involved wide judicial as well as executive duties. In early
times the nine archons tried cases entirely themselves
(except those involving life or citizen rights, where there

was trial by the Areopagus or appeal to the citizen-body). The relationship between the archons and the Heliaia (q.v.) in the sixth century is obscure. In the developed democracy the archons (and other magistrates) were only required to examine a case to decide if it could be brought at all, and if so in what court, to collect the evidence, and to preside at the trial (*see* DIKASTERION).

The *ar chon eponymos* was so called because he gave his name to the year: the list of eponymous archons was kept continuously from 683 B.C., but the term *eponymos* was not officially used before Roman imperial times. He was chief magistrate until 487 and always remained the nominal head of the State. His archonship was a civil office, and was concerned especially with the protection of property; on entry into office he took an oath that at the end of his year everyone should hold what he held at the beginning: that is, he guaranteed the citizens against disorder and arbitrary executive action. Since property involved inheritance, the archon had to protect the family (and in particular orphans and heiresses), and in his judicial capacity had charge of all cases involving family and inheritance rights. He regulated certain religious festivals, particularly the City Dionysia, and had the charge of lawsuits arising from them.

7. The *Basileus* had certain religious duties and presided over the Areopagus. He had charge of the Lenaea and the Mysteries(qq.v.), and in general of all the religious duties of the former kings. He introduced lawsuits arising from these, and also those between claimants for a priesthood. His jurisdiction included all charges of impiety, and all homicide cases (because a man guilty of shedding blood must be kept away from sacred places till purified). *See also* POLEMARCHOS, THESMOTHETAI.

Aristotle, *Ath. Pol.* chs. 3, 8, 13, 55–9. T. J. Cadoux, *JHS* 1948, 70 f.; Hignett, *Hist. Athen. Const.* A. W. G.

**ARCHYTAS** of Tarentum flourished in the first half of the fourth century B.C. He was visited by Plato, and had a great reputation in antiquity. He is said to have been the founder of mechanics; he distinguished harmonic progressions from arithmetical and geometrical; he solved the problem of doubling the cube, by means of two half-cylinders. He worked out the ratios which underlie the relations of successive notes in the enharmonic, the chromatic, and the diatonic scales. In philosophy he belonged to the Pythagorean school. Frs. of his mathematical works remain, but the other frs. cited as from him are late fabrications.

Testimonia and fragments in Diels, *Vorsokr.*[11] i. 421–39. W. D. R.

**ARCISIUS** (Ἀρκείσιος), in mythology, father of Laertes and grandfather of Odysseus (q.v.); his own parentage is variously given. In one story, his mother was a she-bear (Ἀρκείσιος—ἄρκτος), Aristotle in *Etym. Magn.* 144. 25.

**ARCTINUS** of Miletus (? 8th c. B.C.), epic poet; author of the *Aethiopis* and *Iliu Persis*, and probably of the *Titanomachia*. *See* EPIC CYCLE.

*EGF*, 3, 6 ff., 33 ff., 49 ff.

**ARDEA**, a city of the Rutuli, a Latin people. Although three miles distant from the sea it served as a port for Latium. Archaeological remains (ditch and wall defences, acropolis, and temples that long served as federal sanctuaries for the Latin League) confirm the tradition that Ardea was once an important city, worthy of signing a separate treaty with Rome (444 B.C.). In 442 a Latin colony strengthened Ardea against the Volsci and in 390 Camillus, it was said, set out from here to repel the Gauls. Apparently, too, Ardea remained loyal in the Latin War (Livy 8. 12). A Samnite raid *c.* 315 B.C. and subsequently malaria caused Ardea to decline. However, the erection of

numerous villas and possibly the dispatch of a Hadrian colony prevented the village from entirely disappearin In republican times Ardea served as a State prison; late its fields supported the imperial elephants.

Verg. *Aen.* bks. 7–12; Dion. Hal. 1. 72; Livy 4. 7; 5. 43 f.; 39. 1 Cato fr. 58 P.; Strabo 5. 232; Diod. 12. 34; *Lib. Colon.* 23 B. Tilly, *Vergil's Latium* (1947), 31 ff.; A. Alfŏldi, *Early Rome a the Latins* (U.S.A. 1965); A. Andren, *Opuscula Romana* I (1954 1 ff. (acropolis excavations), iii (1961), 1 ff. E. T.

**AREITHOUS** (Ἀρηίθοος), a mythological characte surnamed Κορυνήτης, i.e. Club-man, because he foug with a club of iron; his armour had been given him b Ares. Lycurgus the Arcadian caught him in a narro road where he had no room to swing his club, ran hi through with a spear, and took his armour (*Il.* 7. 138 ff. H. J.

**ARELATE**, a town in Gallia Narbonensis, moder *Arles-sur-Rhône*. The *periplus* of Avienius (679) mention a Greek town Theline which preceded 'Arelatus', an the 'Rhodanusia' of Ps.-Scymnus (206) was presumabl in the vicinity; but archaeological vestiges are slight (c Jacobsthal–Neuffer, *Préhistoire* 1933, 51). Arelate cam into importance in connexion with the construction of the 'Fossa Marianae', and was used as a naval base by Caesar agains Massilia (49 B.C.). A colony of veterans of the sixt legion was founded here in 46 ('colonia Iulia Patern Arelate sextanorum'), but the town was much enlarge as appears, by Augustus, to whom the earliest survivin town-wall, and probably the still visible east gate, ar due. The *territorium* was created mainly at the expens of Massilia. Early buildings still partially surviving ar the forum, amphitheatre (136 m. × 107 m. externally and the theatre. The principal importance of Arelate wa due to its position as a port of trans-shipment for sea going vessels which were under the control of the fiv corporations of *navicularii Arelatenses*. In the Late Empire it acquired importance as the occasional residenc of emperors, in the fourth century a mint was set up, an in the fifth it became the seat of the praetorian prefectur Extensive baths (*La Trouille*) date from this period, an though the area within the walls was reduced, Ausoniu (19. 73–80) and the Emperor Honorius (Haenel, *Corp legum*, 238) attest its prosperity. After various vicissitude it was annexed by the Visigoths in A.D. 476.

L. A. Constans, *Arles antique* (1921); Grenier, *Manuel* i. 289 ff ii. 493 ff; iii. 157 ff. C. E.

**ARELLIUS FUSCUS**, Augustan rhetor, perhaps Greek. His style was brilliant but affected and undisc plined (Sen. *Controv.* 2 *praef.* 1). Ovid was one of h many pupils (ibid. 2. 2. 8–9). He had a son of the sam name.

Schanz–Hosius, § 336, 6.

**AREOPAGUS**, the 'Hill of Ares' (Ἄρειος πάγος) a Athens, north-west of the Acropolis (*see* ATHENS (TOPO GRAPHY)), and the ancient Council associated with i This Council was probably first called simply ἡ βουλή later, after the creation of a second Council (*see* BOULE it was known as ἡ ἐξ Ἀρείου πάγου βουλή or the like an its members as Ἀρεοπαγῖται.

2. During the monarchy and much of the aristocrat period the Council consisted exclusively of Eupatrid (q.v.), how chosen in early times we can only gues Under an arrangement introduced at latest by Solon came to comprise all the ex-archons, who entered it o the expiry of their term of office—and, at least in th fourth century, after passing the Council's own *dokimas* (q.v.)—and remained in it normally till death. The annu entry of nine new members in middle life maintained strength of 200–300. With this system of recruitment, th

reopagus gradually ceased to be exclusively aristocratic; or a time it represented the wealthy element and ventually came to include citizens of all classes (*see* RCHONTES, THETES); some more specifically political ffects of the system are suggested below (under 5). In te Roman times the Areopagus consisted of thirty-one nembers chosen by the proconsul.

**3.** ·Under the monarchy, the king summoned and pre-ided over the Council; of the annual magistrates, al-hough all nine archons apparently attended, only the Basileus is indicated as president. The original meeting-lace may have been the king's palace on the Acropolis; ter, and for a time exclusively (as the name indicates), it vas the Hill of Ares, and murder-trials before this Council lways took place there; meetings were also (at least in he fourth century) held in the Stoa Basileios. Some neetings were held in private, but the murder-trials were ublic and something is known of their procedure.

**4.** The original function of the Areopagus must have een to advise the king in his capacity as leader, priest, nd judge. As the monarchy declined, the influence of he Council increased; the tradition that in the seventh entury it was virtually in charge of the government (cf. Arist. *Ath. Pol.* 3. 6) is probably sound; it would be natural or the yearly magistrates to defer to the collective wis-lom of their ex-colleagues, serving for life. The general cope of the Council's activity probably remained un-hanged till the reform of Ephialtes, though the codifica-ion of the law rendered its jurisdiction less arbitrary, and o perhaps to some extent limited them. That before Solon it actually chose the archons (Arist. *Ath. Pol.* 8. 1 f.) s doubtful (cf. Arist. *Pol.* 1273$^b$35–1274$^a$2); nor would the reation of a second Council deprive it of probouleutic unctions, since these were hardly necessary in the pre-Solonian State (*see* BOULE, EKKLESIA); on the other hand, ts function of giving general advice must have continued s long as the archons remained the principal magistrates. Iowever, the functions for which we have specific vidence are wholly judicial. The Council judged in cases of deliberate homicide, wounding, and arson, and in a ariety of other matters, mainly of a religious character; t also exercised a 'guardianship of the laws' (νομοφυλακία), lealing, by means of the procedure called *eisangelia* q.v.), with attempts to subvert the constitution and with he improper use of their powers by magistrates. The enalties it could inflict included fines, exile with loss of property, and death; and its judgements were final.

**5.** Under the tyrants, the Areopagus came to be omposed entirely of their partisans (cf. Thuc. 6. 54. 6), nd must therefore have been discredited by their fall, hough it may have re-aligned itself behind Cleisthenes q.v. 1; *see also* BOULE). From 507/6 to 488/7 it was re-cruited from archons freely elected by the people for nerit, including such persons as Themistocles and Aristides, and this and the crises of 490 and 480/79 may explain the revival of influence which, according to Aris-otle (*Pol.* 1304$^a$17–24, *Ath. Pol.* 23. 1, 25. 1) it enjoyed or some years after 480. But with the rapid advance of he naval class and of democratic institutions the great owers of the Areopagus seemed out of place, and the gradual disappearance of its elected members after 487/6 weakened its resistance. In 462/1 Ephialtes (q.v. 4) de-prived the Areopagus of its 'guardianship of the laws' and apparently circumscribed its jurisdiction in other respects. It remained the court for deliberate homicide, wounding, and arson; and for some other matters, on which, how-ever, its judgements seem to have been no longer always final. It lost all political influence and became a minor, if venerated, part of the judicial system. A proposal to restore the νομοφυλακία in 403/2 (And. 1. 84) does not seem to have been put into effect. In the later fourth century we

find the Areopagus, both on its own initiative and on the instructions of the *ekklesia*, holding criminal investiga-tions (ζητήσεις)—particularly into allegations of treason-able conduct, e.g. desertion of the city after Chaeronea (q.v.) in 338 and acceptance of bribes from Harpalus (q.v.) in 323. Such investigations ended in reports (ἀποφάσεις) which could lead to trials in the dicasteries. In 337/6 a law against tyranny provided the penalty of outlawry for Areopagites who recognized an overthrow of the democracy: whether there was any real likelihood of such behaviour is not clear.

In the more oligarchical constitution favoured by the Romans the judicial functions of the Areopagus seem to have been extended, and it was associated with the *boule* in the administration. It was still in existence in the fourth century A.D.

G. Gilbert, *Const. Antiquities of Sparta and Athens* (1895), see Table of Contents; Busolt–Swoboda, *Griech. Staatskunde³* (i, 1920; ii, 1926), see Index; R. J. Bonner and G. Smith, *Adm. of Justice from Homer to Aristotle* (i, 1930; ii, 1938), see Indexes; H. T. Wade-Gery, *CQ* 1931, 1 ff. (*Essays in Greek History* (1958), 86 ff.) Hignett, *Hist. Athen. Const.* see Index; B. D. Meritt, *Hesp.* 1952, 355 f.; R. Sealey, *AJPhil.* 1958, 71 ff. T. J. C.

**ARES** (Ἄρης, Aeolic Ἄρευς; etymology unknown, but good Greek formation; it is uncertain whether the name appears on Linear B tablets), the Greek war-god, not in the sense of a warlike deity who leades his people into battle, but rather a deification of warlike spirit F. Schwenn, *ARW* 1923–4, 224 ff., finds difficulty in supposing this possible for early times and suggests that Ares was originally a deity of vegetation, who became a war-god secondarily by some unknown process. There is, however, no reason to assume that Ares was worshipped by the earliest Greeks. He is unpopular, is an important god only in Thebes and perhaps Athens (contrast Mars, q.v.), belongs especially to the northern and western communities (Aetolia, Thessaly, etc.), and has been con-sidered by some to be of Thracian origin (Farnell, op. cit. *infra*, 399 ff.). It is conceivable that he was 'projected' from some widespread rite of war-magic, earlier than civilization in any Greek people. He never develops into a god with any moral functions, like Zeus or Apollo, and in mythology he appears either as instigator to violence or as a tempestuous lover, a divine *miles gloriosus*. He frequently has Aphrodite (q.v. § 4) as his partner (e.g. at Thebes they are the parents of Harmonia, *see* CADMUS); he is associated with her, Athena, and Enyo in his temple at Athens (Paus. 1. 8. 4). It must be noted that Aphrodite (q.v.), like many mother-goddesses, has warlike qualities. Hence, as she is also thought of as wife of Hephaestus, the story that Ares is her paramour (*Od.* 8. 266 ff. and often later). In his ritual perhaps the most remarkable feature is that at Tegea he was worshipped by women under the title of Γυναικοθοίνας (Paus. 8. 48. 4); it should be remembered that women are often active in war-magic. Dogs were sacrificed to him (under his common title of Enyalios) at Sparta (Plut. *Quaest. Rom.* 290 d; Paus. 3. 14. 9), a procedure associated with purifica-tions and deities of an uncanny sort, such as Hecate. The name Enyalios as that of a god occurs on a tablet at Cnossos, and this deity may have been identified later with Ares.

In mythology, although son of Zeus and Hera, he is commonly the helper of foreign peoples, such as the Trojans, or unusually warlike ones, as the Amazons (q.v.). He is father, by various mothers, of numerous children, mostly sons and commonly of warlike, often violent and outrageous character, as Ascalaphus (*Il.* 13. 518; 15. 113 for Ares' fury at his death); Diomedes the Thracian (*see* HERACLES); Cycnus the brigand (*see* ibid.); Meleager in some versions of the story (Hyg. *Fab.* 14. 16); Phlegyas, eponym of a whole people of impious raiders and ferocious fighters (Paus. 9. 36. 2). Such genealogies seem to waver between the complimentary (a brave warrior is a 'shoot from Ares' stock', ὄζος Ἄρηος, in Homer) and the uncomplimentary, the god's own character being ferocious and unlovely. That he is the father of Eros (Simonides, fr. 24 Diehl) is a by-product of the original lack of any association between Eros and Aphrodite. Of his daughters, Harmonia has already been mentioned; by Agraulus daughter of Cecrops (see ATTIC CULTS AND MYTHS) he became the father of Alcippe, who was violated by Halirrhothius son of Poseidon. Killing him, he was tried by the Areopagus and acquitted (Apollod. 3. 180) or sent into a year's serfdom (Panyassis ap. Clem. Alex. *Protr.* 26, 22 Stählin). As early as Hesiod (*Th.* 934) Aphrodite bears him his Homeric attendants Deimos and Phobos (Fear and Rout). Cicero (*Nat. D.* 3. 60) adds Anteros to the family from some late author.

In Rome he was identified with Mars (q.v.).

In early art Ares is seldom shown by himself but often in assemblies of gods: in the Gigantomachy; the Birth of Athena; the wedding of Peleus and Thetis; the return of Hephaestus to Olympus; the introduction of Heracles; and on the Parthenon frieze. There is also an archaic tradition showing Ares and Aphrodite as a wedded couple in a chariot (see C. Karusos, *JDAI* 1937, 172 ff.). Early a bearded warrior, he is later shown naked and young (already on the Parthenon); and often as Aphrodite's lover.

Much material collected in Roscher's *Lexikon*, s.v. 'Ares' (Stoll-Furtwängler). Brief account in Rose, *Handbook of Gk. Myth.*[6], 157 f. For his cult, see especially Nilsson, *GGR* I[2]. 517 ff.
H. J. R.; C. M. R.

**ARETAEUS** of Cappadocia, medical author, a contemporary of Galen (*c.* 150–200), wrote in Ionic in imitation of Hippocrates. Works (extant but incomplete): Περὶ αἰτιῶν καὶ σημείων ὀξέων καὶ χρονίων παθῶν; Περὶ θεραπείας ὀξέων καὶ χρονίων παθῶν; (lost) Περὶ πυρετῶν; Περὶ γυναικείων; Περὶ φυλακτικῶν; Χειρουργίαι. His main merit is that he builds on the solid foundations of Archigenes (q.v.).

Ed. K. Hude, *CMG* ii (1923); F. Kudlien, *Unters. zu A. von Kapp.* (1964).
W. D. R.

**ARETAS,** the name of several kings of the Nabataeans (q.v.).

ARETAS II (*c.* 110–96 B.C.) in 96 tried to help Gaza (a gateway to the Mediterranean) against Alexander Jannaeus, who was defeated by his successor, Obodas I (*c.* 96–87) probably *c.* 94.

ARETAS III (*c.* 87–62) defeated Jannaeus and occupied Damascus, but yielded it to Tigranes before 70. He supported Hyrcanus (see JEWS, A. 2) and in 66 besieged Jerusalem, until he was compelled to leave by Scaurus (q.v. 2), who in 62 advanced to Petra but in return for 300 talents recognized Aretas as king of the Nabataeans.

ARETAS IV (9 B.C.–A.D. 39). On the death of Obodas III (30–9 B.C.) a certain Aeneas seized the throne and took the royal name. He was recognized by Augustus only after some delay caused by the intrigues of Syllaeus, the vizier of Obodas III, who had given bad advice to Aelius Gallus (q.v. 4) about the Roman attack on Arabia Felix: Syllaeus' later quarrels with Herod had provoked the latter to invade Nabataea (12 B.C.) and thus incur Augustus' displeasure. After recognizing Aretas, Augustus had Syllaeus executed for further intrigues. Aretas sent help to Varus (q.v. 2) against Judaea after Herod's death (4 B.C.). His daughter married Herod (q.v. 2) Antipas, who later divorced her: in due season Aretas, without consulting Rome, invaded Peraea and defeated Antipas. Aretas was saved from a Roman punitive attack because L. Vitellius (q.v. 2) withdrew when he heard of the death of Tiberius. Gaius granted Aretas control of

Damascus, which at the time of St. Paul's escape from the city (*c.* A.D. 40) was under an ethnarch of Aretas (2. Cor. xi. 32).
H. H. S

**AREUS** (*c.* 312–265 B.C.), son of Acrotatus, succeeded his grandfather, Cleomenes II, on the Spartan throne (309–308). In 280 he invaded Aetolia, after organizing a Peloponnesian coalition against Macedon; on his repulse this collapsed. In 272 he returned hurriedly from helping Gortyn in Crete, to drive Pyrrhus back from Sparta and assisted in his destruction at Argos. During the Chremonidean War he failed to force Craterus' Isthmus lines to relieve Athens; in 265 he fell outside Corinth. He was the first Spartan king to hold an elaborate court and to issue silver coins.

Beloch, *Griech. Gesch.* iv.
F. W. W

**ARGAS,** citharode and poet of the first half of the fourth century B.C., renowned for his badness (Plut. *Dem.* 4, schol. Aeschin. 2. 99). Hence his name was used as a term of abuse of Demosthenes by Aeschines (2. 99).

**ARGEI.** On 16 and 17 March a procession went to Argeos (Ov. *Fasti* 3. 791–2), i.e. to the twenty-seven *Argeorum sacraria* (Varro, *Ling.* 5. 45) situated at various points in the four Servian regions of Rome; Varro locates twelve (see Platner–Ashby, *Topog. Dict.* 51 ff.). The festival has been thought by some to date from the pre-urban period of independent village communities but more probably it reflects the stage (6th c.) when Rome was united in four regions which did not yet include the Capitoline and Aventine hills (cf. A. Momigliano, *JRS* 1963, 99 f.). On 14 May (15, Dion. Hal. *Ant. Rom.* 1. 38. 3), the Vestals, pontiffs, and others threw from the Pons Sublicius into the Tiber twenty-seven effigies of men in old-fashioned clothing (Ov. op. cit. 5. 621 ff.; Dion. Hal. loc. cit.; Varro, op. cit. 7. 44 and Ennius quoted there; see further Frazer on Ovid, loc. cit.). The ancients commonly explained this as a surrogate for human sacrifice (Ov. ibid., and other passages). Of moderns, Wissowa holds a similar view (art. 'Argei' in *PW*, = *Gesammelte Abhandlungen*, 211 ff.), and dates it from the third century B.C., the age of the document quoted in Varro, *Ling.* 5. 47 ff. This is generally rejected. That it is a vegetation rite, with the well-known drowning or bathing of a sort of Jack-in-the-Green, is unlikely, if only from the number of the figures (why more than one?) (L. Deubner, *ARW* 1925, 299 f.). Frazer suggests (*Fasti of Ovid*, iv. 91 and references there), that the puppets are 'offerings to the river-god to pacify him and induce him to spare the real persons using the bridge or otherwise approaching the stream. Latte (*RR* 412 ff.) proposes to interpret it as a more general ceremony of purification, linking it with the use of *oscilla* in the Compitalia (see LARES).
H. J. R.; H. W. P

**ARGENTARIUS** (1), MARCUS (fl. early 1st c. A.D.), is the gayest of the Greek epigrammatists whose work, collected in the *Garland* of Philippus (q.v. 7), has partly survived in the Greek Anthology. He carries on the tradition of Leonidas (q.v. 2) of Tarentum, writing about poverty and drink (*Anth. Pal.* 9. 229); as a humorist and punster he precedes Lucillius and Martial. He may be the eccentric Latin-speaking Greek rhetor mentioned by the elder Seneca (*Controv.* 9. 3 (26). 12–13).

R. del Re, *Maia* 1955, 184 ff.; S. G. P. Small (text, commentary, analysis), *YClS* 1951, 65 ff.
G. H

**ARGENTARIUS** (2), Augustan rhetor, a Greek; slavish follower of Cestius (Sen. *Controv.* 9. 3. 12–13)

e may be identical with the epigrammatist of the Greek
nthology.

**RGENTORATE**, modern *Strasbourg*. The Celtic
ıme (silver fort) hints at a pre-Roman settlement, of
hich traces have been found. Perhaps first occupied as
ιe of Drusus' *castella* by 'Ala Petriana Treverorum'.
was garrisoned *c*. A.D. 12–43 by Legio II Augusta, then
ʏ legionary detachments including one of XXI Rapax,
ho constructed the first basalt wall. *C.* A.D. 80 Legio
III was transferred here. Its fortress (606 × 300 m.)
as defended by an earth bank with 90 cm. thick re-
tment wall of small blocks and brick borders. From
ιe third century Argentorate was exposed to barbarian
tacks (an incident of which was Julian's victory, A.D.
57), and for increased protection the wall was fronted
ʏ another, 2 m. 50 cm. thick, of re-used masonry with
ıstions *c*. 25 m. apart. In this period the *canabae* (q.v.),
ʳeviously important, were given up and the civil popu-
tion crowded into the fortress.

R. Forrer, *Strasbourg-Argentorate* (1927); J. J. Hatt, *Hist.* ii,
)53/4, 234 ff.                                                    C. E. S.

**RGONAUTS** (Ἀργοναῦται), one of the oldest Greek
ıgas, based originally on a perhaps real exploit of the
ımi-historical Minyae, known as early as Homer (*Od.*
ᵵ. 70). It is attached by its origins to Thessaly but may
ıve been developed into its earliest extant version
ırough the influence of Milesian exploration in the
lack Sea. The chief surviving accounts are Pindar,
yth. 4; Apollonius Rhodius, *Argonautica* (both of these,
ʳpecially the latter, have very helpful scholia); Valerius
laccus, *Argonautica* and the 'Orphic' *Argonautica*;
ʳpollodorus, 1. 107 ff.; Hyginus, *Fab.* 12 ff. The later
ıthors all draw more or less on Apollonius, but not
xclusively.

2. Aeson son of Cretheus (*see* AEOLUS 2) was deprived of
ιe kingship of Iolcus in Thessaly by his half-brother
ᵉlias. His young son Jason (q.v.), on reaching manhood,
ıme to reclaim the throne. Pelias was afraid to refuse
ʷenly, so induced him (how, accounts vary) first to go
ıd fetch the Golden Fleece (*see* ATHAMAS) from Colchis.
ᵛith the help of Hera, who favoured him and had been
ısulted by Pelias, he got together a band of the noblest
ɛroes in Greece (lists differ widely, owing no doubt to
ınbitious families, many not Minyan, claiming an
ıncestor in the *Argo*; but all include Argos (q.v. 1*b*),
iphys the helmsman, Lynceus, whose sight was preter-
ıaturally keen, and a few more, among them Heracles
ıd Orpheus, both manifest intruders; cf. also Rose,
*landb. of Gk. Myth.*⁶, 295). Argos built him a ship, the
*lrgo*, by help of Athena; she was the first longship ever
ıade. They set sail for Colchis and had several adven-
ıres by the way. At Lemnos (*see* HYPSIPYLE) they stayed
ı year with the women of the island; at Cyzicus they
ɛre hospitably received by the eponym of the island
ınd Heracles rid him of the Gegeneis who infested the
ills. Driven back by a storm, they killed Cyzicus in a
ʳuffle at night, and mourned for him. At Cios, Heracles'
age Hylas was carried off by water-nymphs and he,
ʳaying to look for him, was left behind. After visiting
ıe Bebryces (*see* AMYCUS) they touched at Salmydessus
ınd learned from Phineus (q.v.) that to get to the Euxine
ıey must pass the Clashing Rocks (Symplegades), which
ɛ advised them to test by seeing if a dove could fly
ɛtween them before they met. The dove did so, and the
*lrgo* likewise passed; in some accounts the rocks became
tationary (at the present Bosphorus). Arrived finally at
̔olchis, they were confronted with a task set by King
ɛeetes; they must yoke a pair of fire-breathing bulls,
lough a field, sow it with teeth from Cadmus' dragon
ʳee CADMUS), and overcome the warriors who should

spring up. This Jason succeeded in doing with the help
of Medea (q.v.), and, still by her advice, he took the
Fleece that same night and fled, accompanied by her.

3. The story now divides into several main variants,
conditioned partly by the geographical ideas of different
periods, partly by the desire to bring the Argonauts into
connexion with places traditionally Minyan. (1) They
returned the way they came. (2) Because they did not
want to face the Symplegades again or for some other
reason, they ascended the river Phasis, got to the stream
of Ocean, and so sailed around till they reached the
Mediterranean again. (3) They went up the Ister
(Danube), thence got into the Eridanus (fabulous, but in
part the Po), down it to some part of the Mediterranean,
and so home. (4) From the Ister they got (via the Rhine?)
into the North Sea, and so down to the Straits of Gibraltar and through them. The subsidiary adventures vary accordingly; some of the commonest are, that they reached
Africa and there met a Triton who showed them the
way through the shallows near Cyrene and foretold the
founding of the colony by one of their descendants (Pind.
ibid. 19 ff.); they passed the Sirens (*see* ODYSSEUS) and
were protected against their song by Orpheus' still more
lovely playing (Ap. Rhod. 4. 891 ff.); they came to
Crete, and there encountered Talos (q.v.), who guarded
the island. Medea charmed him into a magic sleep, and
he was killed by destroying the fastening that closed his
one vein, thus letting out his blood, or whatever corresponded to it in him (Ap. Rhod. 4. 1638 ff., Apollod.
140–1; details vary, however). For their meeting with
Alcinous, *see* s.v.

4. Not only is the story diversified with details which
are pure *Märchen* (a feature of many sagas, since one good
story attracts another; cf. Rose in *Folklore* (1935), 16 f.)
but the motive of the voyage is of the same sort, together
with two principal episodes at least. To send a hero on a
dangerous journey to get rid of him, to confront a
dangerous visitor with tasks, to be helped in those tasks
by the daughter of a tyrant, wizard, or other formidable
person, are all well-known themes (Stith Thompson,
nos. H 1211, H 900, G 530, 2), and the Golden Fleece
itself seems a sort of magical treasure, the kind of thing
which fairy heroes go to look for. If a real voyage underlies the tale, it is deeply buried.

5. The Argo is shown on a Sicyonian metope at
Delphi before the mid sixth century; otherwise only the
funeral games of Pelias and the pursuit of the Harpies
occur often in archaic art (see H. G. G. Payne, *Necrocorinthia* (1931), 141 f.; E. Kunze *Archäische Schildbander*
(1950), 177 f.). Micon painted the Argonauts in the
Anaceum at Athens towards the mid fifth. The punishment of Amycus with all the Argonauts present is shown
on the Ficoroni cista and other fourth-century Italian
works, evidently reflecting a wall-painting (*see* J. D.
Beazley, *Etruscan Vase-painting* (1947), 58).

Roscher's *Lexikon*, arts. 'Argo', 'Argonautai' (Seeliger). J. R.
Bacon, *Voyage of the Argonauts* (1925); R. Roux, *Le Problème des
Argonautes* (1949). In art, Brommer, *Vasenlisten*², 346 ff.
                                                        H. J. R.; C. M. R.

**ARGOS** (1), in mythology, (*a*) a monster, of variously
stated parentage, who had a third eye in the back of his
neck, or four eyes, two before and two behind (Pherecydes
and the anonymous epic *Aegimius* ap. schol. Eur. *Phoen.*
1116), or many eyes (Aesch. *PV* 678 and most authors).
He was of huge strength and size, and killed a bull and a
satyr which were troubling Arcadia; he also took vengeance on the killers of Apis the son of Phoroneus (Apollod.
2. 4). When Io (q.v.) was turned into a heifer, Hera set
Argos to watch her (Aesch. loc. cit.), but by command
of Zeus, Hermes killed him (Apollod. ibid. 7 and many
authors). He turned into a peacock (Moschus, 2. 58 ff.,
schol. Ar. *Av.* 102), or Hera took his eyes to deck its

tail (Ov. *Met.* 1. 722–3). (*b*) An Argonaut, builder of the *Argo*, see ARGONAUTS. His parentage and nationality are variously given. (*c*) Eponym of the city Argos, Apollod. 2. 2–3.
H. J. R.

**ARGOS** (2), a city in the southern part of the Argive plain, 3 miles from the sea, at the foot of the Larissa hill which was occupied from prehistoric, through classical and Hellenistic, to Frankish and Turkish times. A low hill, the Aspis, which has remains of earlier Bronze Age occupation, formed part of the city. Middle Bronze Age (Helladic) remains have been found over a wide area (the Deiras ridge, and the South Quarter), and a Mycenaean cemetery with chamber tombs on the Deiras. Mycenaean Argos appears to have been at its height in Mycenaean III A–B (roughly later 14th–13th c.). Occupation (as opposed to burials) of the Geometric period has been found recently for the first time near the chapel of Panaghia tou Vrachou. Extensive remains of the classical and Roman city (which lay for the most part in the plain) have been found in following up earlier excavations: in the region of the classical Agora: bouleuterion (?) of the first half of the fifth century, stoa, tholos, a large building (heroon?) of Roman date, and late Roman baths; the theatre (restored under Hadrian) and the Odeion have also been investigated. Elsewhere Roman houses and interesting late mosaics have been found. Among interesting earlier remains are a hoplite panoply, spits, Argive Geometric, and seventh-century figured ware. A late Geometric krater recalls those from the Fusco cemetery at Syracuse, and the problem of the possible promotion of western colonization by Argos (cf. N. G. L. Hammond, *BSA* 1954, 99 ff.).

In the *Iliad* Argos was the kingdom of Diomedes, who owned Agamemnon's leadership; also, in a wider sense, Agamemnon's empire. In the Dorian invasion Argos fell to Temenus, the eldest of the Heraclids. It probably was the base from which the Dorians occupied northeast Peloponnesus, and retained the overlordship until the eighth or seventh century, when its ascendancy was challenged by Sparta. Early in the seventh century a strong king, Pheidon (q.v.), defeated the Spartans, presided in person over the Olympic Games, and made Argos the first power in Greece. It is doubtful if he was concerned with the issue of silver coinage in Aegina (see *Num. Chron.* 1950, 177 ff.). But his power died with him, checked perhaps by the rise of Corinth. Henceforth Argos maintained a suspicious neutrality, fighting once a generation with Sparta. Her heaviest defeat was *c.* 494 B.C., when Cleomenes was barely repelled from the walls by the women of Argos, rallied by the poetess Telesilla. In 480–479 the Argives observed a benevolent neutrality towards Persia. Shortly afterwards they set up a form of democracy. They were repeatedly allied with Athens against Sparta (461, 420, 395), but remained an ineffective power. Argos sided with Philip II of Macedon and was one of the last cities to join the Achaean League, after a period of rule by tyrants. The territory of Argos in classical times included Mycenae, Tiryns, Nauplia, Asine, and other strongholds in the Argive plain, but not the cities of the Acte east of Argos, nor Phlius and Cleonae in the northern hills. The great Argive goddess was Hera, worshipped at the Heraeum six miles north of Argos. The minor arts were important in the earliest period, but from the seventh century they shared in the general decline. Argive sculptors of the early classical period were pre-eminent; the greatest was Polyclitus (q.v. 2).

P-K, *GL* iii. 1. 93 ff.; C. W. Blegen, *Prosymna* (1937); *BCH* since 1950 for recent excavations; W. Vollgraff, *Le Sanctuaire d'Apollon pythéen à Argos* (1956); 'Le Théâtre d'Argos', *Mnemos.* 1951, 193 ff.;

P. Courbin, 'Une rue d'Argos', *BCH* 1956, 183 ff. History: G. Huxley, *Early Sparta* (1962), 26 ff.; W. G. Forrest, 'Themistokl and Argos', *CQ* 1960, 221 ff.; F. Kiechle, 'Argos und Tiryns nach d Schlacht bei Sepeia', *Philol.* 1960, 181 ff.; on the Athenian allian and the battle of Oinoe, L. H. Jeffrey, *BSA* 1966. Argive sculptur Beyen and Vollgraff, *Argos and Sicyon*; C. Picard in *Manuel d'arché logie grecque* iii (1948). The Argive Heraeum: C. Waldstein ar others, *The Argive Heraeum* (1902–5); P. Amandry, *Hesp.* 195 222 ff., for dating of the building remains.
T. J. D.; R. J. H

**ARGOS, CULTS AND MYTHS OF.** The mo famous cult of the Argolid was that of Hera, whose grea temple, however, was not in Argos itself but some dis tance away (*see* HERA). In the city itself, on the lowe acropolis (the Aspis), stood a very ancient temple ( Athena (*see* Vollgraff, *Mnemos.* 1928, 319). Of grea importance in historical times was Apollo Lykeios, whos temple stood in the Agora (Soph. *El.* 6 f.; Paus. 2. 19. 3 its foundation was ascribed to Danaus (q.v.). Also Apoll had a sanctuary on the acropolis with an oracle under th title Pythaeus (for excavation see W. Vollgraff, *L Sanctuaire d'Apollon pythéen à Argos* 1956). Myths con nected with the city and district are innumerable, near every important legend touching them at some point more local are the lists of Argive kings, of which th oldest is in a βουστροφηδόν inscription from the Aspi (Vollgraff, *Mnemos.* 1931–2, 369 ff.): Potamos (?Inachus Sthenelas son of Echedamidas, Hippomedon, Charo (otherwise unknown as a hero), Adrastus (q.v.), Orth agoras, Cteatus, Aristomachus, and Ichonidas. See, fo later lists, Apollod. 2. 1 ff., Hyg. *Fab.* 124.
H. J. R

See bibliography s.v. ARGOS (2).

**ARGOS** (3) **AMPHILOCHICUM,** traditionally found ed by Amphilochus after the Trojan War, on the easter shore of the Ambraciote Gulf. In its struggles agains Ambracia (Thuc. 2. 68) it was helped by Athens an Acarnania, and played its part in Athenian operations i north-west Greece in the early years of the Peloponnesia War. It maintained its independence, was the capital o the Amphilochi, and issued coins of Pegasus type *c.* 350 250 B.C.

P-K, *GL* 2. 1. 194 ff.; Hammond, *Epirus.*
N. G. L. H

**ARGUMENTUM,** an explanation of the circumstance in which the action of a play is supposed to open, ad dressed direct to the audience by the speaker of th prologue (which may be deferred, cf. Plaut. *Cist.* 155 *Mil.* 79). The *argumentum* forms part of all the prologue of Plautus except in the *Asinaria* and *Trinummus* (wher we are informed that it is unnecessary); no doubt it wa often translated from the Greek original (cf. the exposi tion uttered by Agnoia in Menander's *Perikeiromene*); i may vary from a brief statement (as in the *Truculentus* to a detailed account (e.g. *Amph.* 97–150). Frequently i anticipates the plot to some extent. Terence abandone the *argumentum* altogether. Cf. HYPOTHESIS.

G. Michaut, *Plaute* (1920), i. 101 ff.; G. Duckworth, *The Nature* Roman Comedy (1952), index s.v. 'argument' and 'prologue'. W. I

**ARIADNE,** in mythology, daughter of Minos (q.v.) an Pasiphaë. When Theseus (q.v.) came to Crete, she fe in love with him and gave him a clue of thread by whic he found his way out of the Labyrinth after killing th Minotaur. He then fled, taking her with him, bu (magically?) forgot and left her on Naxos (Dia). It i generally said that Dionysus found her there and marrie her; but Plutarch (*Thes.* 20, from Paeon of Amathus preserves a curious local legend and custom. Theseu left her there pregnant, and she died in childbed. I commemoration of this, every year at Amathus a youn man imitated a woman in childbed in honour of Ariadn Aphrodite (*see* APHRODITE, § 1). It is probable tha Ariadne was originally a goddess, Minoan in origin, bu with a Greek name meaning 'very holy'.

A figure shown with Dionysus in sixth-century vase-paintings, distinct from the nymphs who accompany the satyrs, has sometimes two children and is probably Ariadne. She appears in some early representations helping Theseus in the adventure of the Minotaur. Her desertion by Theseus on Naxos is found from the early fifth century, and remains popular later when it is joined by the sequel, Dionysus discovering Ariadne.

Nilsson, *GGR* i². 314 ff. In art, Brommer, *Vasenlisten²*, 166 f.; R. Hampe, *Frühe griechische Sagenbilder in Böotien* (1936), 78 f.; E. Kunze, *Archaische Schildbander* (1950), 127 ff., 170 f.
H. J. R.; C. M. R.

**ARIARAMNES** (280?–230?), eldest son of Ariarathes II (q.v.) of Cappadocia, and the leader who probably secured recognition of the independence of Cappadocia from the Seleucid kings perhaps before 250 B.C. He made his son Ariarathes III (q.v.) his co-ruler. T. R. S. B.

**ARIARATHES,** the name of several kings of CAPPADOCIA:

(1) **ARIARATHES I** (b. *c.* 404 B.C.) claimed descent from the house of Cyrus the Great. Satrap of Cappadocia, which then included Pontus, he resisted Alexander's appointee, and after Alexander's death was captured and killed by Perdiccas and Eumenes in 322, aged 82.

(2) **ARIARATHES II** (*c.* 301–*c.* 280 B.C.), escaped to Armenia in 322, and after 301 recovered Cappadocia, now separated from Pontus, perhaps with Armenian help, but remained nominally subject to the Seleucid kings.

(3) **ARIARATHES III** (*c.* 250–220 B.C.), co-ruler with his father Ariaramnes (q.v.), perhaps from before 250 B.C., married Stratonice, daughter of Antiochus II Theos, and added Cataonia to his realm. He was the first to issue coins with the royal title.

(4) **ARIARATHES IV EUSEBES** (220–163 B.C.), son of Ariarathes III, married (*c.* 192) Antiochis, a daughter of Antiochus III the Great, but after the battle of Magnesia (190) allied himself with Eumenes II of Pergamum, to whom he gave his daughter Stratonice in marriage, and the Romans. He remained a faithful ally of Rome against Pharnaces I of Pontus and the Gauls. Passing over two older princes whom Antiochis introduced and later admitted to be supposititious, he gave the succession to her late-born son Mithridates, as Ariarathes V.

(5) **ARIARATHES V EUSEBES PHILOPATOR** (163–130 B.C.), son of Ariarathes IV, rejected on advice from Rome a marriage alliance with Demetrius I of Syria, who then aided Orophernes, one of the supposititious children mentioned above, in expelling him from his kingdom. On appeal Rome divided the kingdom between them, but with the aid of Attalus II of Pergamum he recovered the whole (*c.* 157). Failing to obtain Orophernes' treasure from Priene, he sacked the city. He died while aiding Rome against Aristonicus (q.v. 1), but Lycaonia was added as a reward to the kingdom of his son. A lover of Hellenic culture, he became a citizen of Athens, and promoted Hellenism in his kingdom.

(6) **ARIARATHES VI EPIPHANES PHILOPATOR** (130–*c.* 116 B.C.), son of Ariarathes V. During his minority the ruthless regime of his mother Nysa stirred up strife, which Mithridates V of Pontus used to interfere in the kingdom and to arrange the marriage of Ariarathes with his daughter Laodice. On his coinage regnal years are numbered up to fifteen. He was assassinated by Gordius, a Cappadocian noble, perhaps at the instigation of Mithridates VI of Pontus.

(7) **ARIARATHES VII PHILOMETOR** (*c.* 116–*c.* 101 B.C.), son of Ariarathes VI. During the regency of his mother Laodice invasion by Nicomedes III of Bithynia led Mithridates also to invade Cappadocia, ostensibly to protect his sister, but when she married Nicomedes he changed his plea to protection of her son, whom he put upon the throne. Ariarathes' objections to the return of Gordius, his father's assassin, led to hostilities. During a conference in the presence of both armies Mithridates murdered the young king with his own hands, occupied the country, and placed his own son upon the throne. The coinage of Ariarathes VII numbers up to sixteen regnal years. *See* ARIARATHES IX.

(8) **ARIARATHES VIII,** second son of Ariarathes VI and brother of Ariarathes VII, was placed on the throne by the Cappadocian nobles in revolt against Ariarathes IX (q.v.), the son of Mithridates. Mithridates promptly expelled him and he died soon afterwards, the last of his dynasty.

(9) **ARIARATHES IX EUSEBES PHILOPATOR** (*c.* 101–87/86), son of Mithridates VI of Pontus, who placed him at the age of 8 on the throne of Cappadocia with Gordius as regent. Expelled by the Cappadocians in favour of Ariarathes VIII (q.v.) and restored by Mithridates, both he and a rival claimant sponsored by Nicomedes III of Bithynia and Laodice were disallowed by the Roman Senate, which offered the Cappadocians their freedom. They, however, requested a king and chose a noble, Ariobarzanes, who was probably installed by Sulla as proconsul *c.* 95 B.C. When Ariobarzanes was expelled by Mithridates' ally, Tigranes of Armenia, Ariarathes was restored, but was again removed by the Roman commission under Aquillius (89 B.C.). With the outbreak of the First Mithridatic War he returned to his claim, and should probably be identified with the Ariarathes (Arcathias), Mithridates' general in Macedonia, who died at Tisaeum in Thessaly before March of 86. Regnal years on his coinage number up to fifteen.

(10) **ARIARATHES X EUSEBES PHILADELPHOS** (42–36 B.C.) succeeded his brother Ariobarzanes III (q.v.), after being one of his vassals. At least six regnal years are numbered on his coinage, so it was in 36 B.C. that Antony executed him and replaced him with Sisines, one of the rival priestly family of Comana, who took the name Archelaus (*see also* CAPPADOCIA).

Diodorus Siculus 31. 19–22, 28, 32; Strabo 12. 533–540. Th. Reinach, *Trois Royaumes*; Magie, *Rom. Rule Asia Min.* see Index; B. Simonetta, 'Notes on the Coinage of the Cappadocian Kings', *Num. Chron.* 1961, 9 ff.; 1964, 83 ff.; O. Mørkholm, ibid. 1962, 407 ff.; 1964, 21 ff.; E. Badian, 'Sulla's Cilician Command', *Stud. Gr. Rom. Hist.* 157 ff. T. R. S. B.

**ARICIA,** modern *Ariccia*, at the foot of the Albanus Mons (q.v.), 16 miles south-east of Rome, on the edge of a remarkably fertile volcanic depression (*vallis Aricina*; the impressive, beggar-infested viaduct, which carried the Via Appia across this (Juv. 4. 117), survives). Founded in mythical times, Aricia was temporarily the leading city of Latium (*c.* 500 B.C.): under Turnus Herdonius it organized resistance to Tarquinius Superbus, helped Aristodemus (q.v. 2) of Cumae to crush the Etruscans (*c.* 505 B.C.), supplied the Latin League with a meeting-place (*caput aquae Ferentinae*), and had a prominent role in the Lake Regillus (q.v.) battle and ensuing *foedus Cassianum* (499–493). In 446 Aricia quarrelled with Ardea over boundaries. After participating in the Latin War it received Roman citizenship (Festus 155, L. represents this, probably inaccurately, as partial citizenship), and became a prosperous *municipium* (Cic. *Phil.* 3. 15). Such it remained, despite its sack by Marius (Livy, *Epit.* 80;

*Lib. Colon.* 230), until barbarian invasions ruined it. Aricia was the birthplace of Augustus' mother Atia, and is celebrated for its wealthy Temple of Diana Nemorensis, whose ruins still exist nearby in the woods surrounding Lake Nemi; its presiding priest was a runaway slave who had murdered his predecessor (*see* REX NEMORENSIS).

Strabo 5. 239; Verg. *Aen.* 7. 761 f.; Livy i. 50 f. etc.; G. Florescu, *Ephemeris Daco-romana* iii (1925) (documented); A. E. Gordon, *Cults of Aricia* (U.S.A. 1934); A. Alföldi, *Early Rome and the Latins* (U.S.A. 1965), 47 ff. E. T. S.

**ARIMASPEANS.** A legendary people of the far North, between the Issedones and the Hyperboreans. They were one-eyed, and fought with griffins who guarded a hoard of gold. Aristeas (q.v. 1) was said to have written an epic about them (Hdt. 3. 116, 4. 13 and 27; Aesch. *PV* 803 ff.). W. K. C. G.

**ARIMINUM,** modern *Rimini* with imposing Augustan monuments, an Umbrian and later Gallic town on the Adriatic which became a Latin colony, 268 B.C. (Vell. Pat. 1. 14; Beloch, *Röm. Gesch.*, 490, for magistrates; A. Sambon, *Monnaies ant. de l'Italie* (1903), 88, for coins; A. Bernardi, *Studi Ghisleriani* 1948, for the *Ius Arimini*). An important harbour and road-centre, Ariminum was the key to Cisalpine Gaul, controlling the bottle-neck between Apennines and Adriatic (Polyb. 3. 61, etc.; Livy 24. 44, etc.; Strabo 5. 217). It remained loyal to Rome against Hannibal (Livy 27. 10) and obtained Roman citizenship *c.* 89 B.C. (Pliny, *HN* 3. 115). Surviving sack by Sulla, occupation by Caesar, confiscation and colonization by the Triumvirs, attacks by Flavians (A.D. 69) and Goths (538), it became one of five towns composing the *pentapolis maritima* under the Ravenna exarchs (App. *BCiv.* 1. 67; 4. 3; Plut. *Caes.* 32; Tac. *Hist.* 3. 41; Procop. 2. 10).

G. A. Mansuelli, *Ariminum* (1941). E. T. S.

**ARIOBARZANES,** the name of some kings of CAPPADOCIA (q.v.):

(1) **ARIOBARZANES I PHILOROMAIOS** (*c.* 95–63/62), a Cappadocian noble whom the Cappadocians chose in preference to Ariarathes IX (q.v.) when the previous dynasty came to an end. His career consists almost entirely of a series of expulsions and restorations. Installed by Sulla (*c.* 95), driven out by Tigranes of Armenia, and restored by Aquillius (90/89 B.C.), driven out again the following year, and restored by Curio at Sulla's command in 85/84, he had to retire before Tigranes again in 78, suffered the ravages of the Third Mithridatic War, and the renewed attacks of Tigranes in 67. Pompey increased his kingdom to include, in the east, Sophene and Gordyene, and, in the west, Cybistra, restored his capital Mazaca, and gave him large loans. Yet in 63 or 62 (his coins have the numbers of at least thirty-two regnal years) he abdicated in Pompey's presence in favour of his son.

(2) **ARIOBARZANES II PHILOPATOR** (63/62–*c.* 52), son of Ariobarzanes I and Athenais, and married to Athenais, a daughter of Mithridates VI, had an uneasy reign, requiring the help of Gabinius in 57 to crush his enemies, and was assassinated shortly before Cicero became governor of Cilicia in 51, probably by members of a pro-Parthian faction. Years 7 and 8 are numbered on his coins.

(3) **ARIOBARZANES III EUSEBES PHILOROMAIOS** (52–42 B.C.), son of Ariobarzanes II, recognized by the Senate as king and commended to Cicero, who found him in 51 beset by enemies in his kingdom, including his mother, and by heavy debts to Pompey and other Roman nobles, remained loyal to Rome and aided Pompey in the war with Caesar. Caesar, however, confirmed him and added Armenia Minor to his kingdom. Cassius had him killed in 42 for refusing aid. Years 9 and 11 are numbered on his coins.

See bibliography s.v. ARIARATHES. T. R. S. B.

**ARION** (1) (*Ἀρείων*), in mythology, the wonderful horse of Adrastus (q.v.); at Thelpusa in Arcadia (Paus. 8. 25. 5) he was said to be the offspring of Poseidon and Demeter in horse-shape. He could speak (Propertius 2. 34. 37). He belonged successively to Poseidon himself, Copreus, Heracles (*see* CYCNUS 1), and Adrastus (schol. *Il.* 23. 346). H. J. R.

**ARION** (2) (*Ἀρίων*) (fl. 628–625 B.C.), son of Cycleus, of Methymna in Lesbos (*Suda*, s.v.), spent most of his life at the court of Periander, paid a profitable visit to Italy and Sicily, returned to Corinth after being thrown overboard and carried to land, it was said, by a dolphin (Hdt. 1. 23). He was an important figure in the history of the dithyramb, which he composed himself and taught Corinthian choirs to perform. He seems to have made it formal and stationary and to have given his poems names, i.e. definite subjects. The *Suda* connects him with the birth of tragedy, but this probably means no more than that his type of dithyramb helped eventually to produce tragedy. Nothing survives of his work, and a piece attributed to him by Aelian (*NA* 12. 45) is certainly spurious, being probably work of the fifth or fourth century B.C.

TEXT. Page, *Poet. Mel. Gr.* 506–7. See also Pickard-Cambridge-Webster, *Dithyramb²*, 97 ff.; C. M. Bowra, *MH* 1963, 121 ff. C. M. B.

**ARIOVISTUS,** king of the Suebi, invaded Gaul *c.* 71 B.C. at the invitation of the Sequani, and defeated the Aedui, then the pre-eminent Gallic tribe. He invited more Germans and defeated at Magetobriga (site unknown) a combined Gallic attempt to eject him. The Senate ratified his conquests by the title of 'friend'. In 58, however, Caesar, influenced by the petitions of Gallic chiefs, picked a quarrel with him, and after a difficult campaign routed him in the plain of Alsace. His death is mentioned incidentally in *BGall.* 5. 29.

Caesar, *BGall.* 1. 31–53; Cicero, *Att.* 1. 19. 2. Rice Holmes, *Ancient Gaul*, 37 ff., 553 ff., 636 ff.; C. E. Stevens, *Latomus*, 1952, 166 ff. C. E. S.

**ARISBE,** name of two cities: (1) in the Troad, from Arisbe daughter of Merops, wife of Priam, or Paris, afterwards of Hyrtacus, or daughter of Teucer of Crete and wife of Dardanus; (2) in Lesbos, from Arisbe, daughter of Macar (Steph. Byz., s.v.).

**ARISTAEUS** (1), son of Apollo and Cyrene (daughter of Hypseus, king of the Lapithae), a god or hero, protector of cattle and fruit-trees, whose cult originated in Thessaly, but is found also in Cyrene, Ceos, Boeotia, and elsewhere. Pindar in *Pyth.* 9 tells how Apollo, enamoured of Cyrene in Thessaly, carried her off to Libya, where Aristaeus was born. Virgil in *G.* 4. 315–558 narrates an otherwise unknown story of Aristaeus, which he is said by Servius on doubtful authority to have substituted for a eulogy of Gallus after his disgrace. Aristaeus had offended the nymphs by pursuing Eurydice, wife of Orpheus, who in her flight was bitten by a serpent and died. The nymphs in revenge destroyed his bees. On his mother's advice he takes counsel of Proteus, who explains the cause of his misfortune. Cyrene urges him to sacrifice cattle to the nymphs. Returning after nine days Aristaeus finds bees swarming in the carcasses. C. B

**ARISTAEUS** (2), of Croton, son-in-law and first successor of Pythagoras, is said to have written works or mathematics. In an extant fr. of a work Περὶ ἁρμονίας ascribed to him, the eternity of the world is inferred from that of God.

**ARISTAGORAS** (1) (fl. *c.* 500 B.C.), son-in-law of Histiaeus (q.v.), in whose absence he ruled Miletus. In 499 B.C. he is reported to have persuaded the Persians to undertake an expedition against Naxos. On the failure of this enterprise he profited by the widespread discontent of the Ionians to raise them in revolt. He restored freedom to Miletus, and combated the other tyrants, who all had Persian support. In winter 499/8 he went to Greece to obtain help. Refused by Cleomenes of Sparta, he was successful in Athens and Eretria: Athens sent twenty ships, quite a large section of her fleet, Eretria only five. Their help was ineffective. Before the final failure of the revolt Aristagoras emigrated to Myrcinus in Thrace, to perish there with his companions in a fight against the Thracians. It is difficult to believe that he was a great man.

Hdt. bk. 5. De Sanctis, *Riv. Fil.* 1931; A. R. Burn, *Persia and the Greeks* (1962). V. E.

**ARISTAGORAS** (2), comic writer of uncertain date. His Μαμμάκυθος ('The Simpleton') was possibly a *réchauffé* of Metagenes' Αὖραι (Ath. 13. 571 b).

FCG i. 218; CAF i. 710.

**ARISTARCHUS** (1) of Samos (*PW* 25), astronomer (fl. first half of 3rd c. B.C.), was a pupil of the Peripatetic Straton (q.v. 1) of Lampsacus. He is famous as the author of the heliocentric hypothesis in astronomy, that 'the fixed stars and the sun remain unmoved, and that the earth revolves about the sun on the circumference of a circle, the sun lying in the middle of the orbit' (Archimedes, *Sand-reckoner* 4–5); he combined with this the rotation of the earth about its own axis (Plutarch, *De fac. in orbe lunae*, 6). His only extant treatise, *On the sizes and distances of the sun and moon*, is, however, on the geocentric basis. Starting with six 'hypotheses', the treatise has eighteen propositions combining clever geometry with facility in arithmetical calculation. The ratios of sizes and distances which have to be calculated are really equivalent to trigonometrical ratios, and Aristarchus finds upper and lower limits to their values on the basis of assumptions equivalent to well-known theorems in trigonometry. The gross discrepancy of the results from reality (see Heath's edition, 330) is due partly to errors in the 'hypotheses', but mainly to the choice of method, which, though mathematically correct, is ill-suited for its purpose (*see* HIPPARCHUS 3). Aristarchus is said to have invented the hollow spherical sun-dial (σκάφη) (Vitruv. 9. 8), and to have added $\frac{1}{1623}$ of a day to Callippus' estimate of $365\frac{1}{4}$ days as the length of the year (Censorinus *de die natali* 19. 2, emended), and to have observed the solstice in 280 (Ptolemy, *Alm.* 3. 1).

Text, translation, and full commentary in T. L. Heath, *Aristarchus of Samos* (1913, repr. 1959). See 317 ff. of the latter for history of the text and editions. See also Pappus 6. 69–73. Aristarchus' life and works are discussed in Heath, 299 ff. T. H.; G. J. T.

**ARISTARCHUS** (2) of Samothrace (*c.* 217 to 145 B.C.) belonged to the school of Aristophanes of Byzantium at Alexandria and was tutor of Ptolemy VII Eupator, son of Ptolemy Philometor. He succeeded Apollonius ὁ εἰδογράφος as head of the Alexandrian Library (*c.* 153 B.C.). On the accession of Ptolemy VIII Physcon (145 B.C.) he left Alexandria for Cyprus, where he died. With him scientific scholarship really began, and his work covered the wide range of grammatical, etymological, orthographical, literary, and textual criticism. He was styled ὁ γραμματικώτατος (Ath. 15. 671 f.), and for his gift of critical divination was nicknamed μάντις by Panaetius (Ath. 14. 634 c). His name has often been used to typify

the complete critic (e.g. Cic. *Att.* 1. 14. 3. Hor. *Ars P.* 450). In matters of language he was an Analogist and an opponent of Crates (q.v. 3) of Mallos. The school which he founded at Alexandria and which lasted into the Roman imperial period had many distinguished pupils, e.g. Apollodorus and Dionysius Thrax. His writings fall into three main groups:

1. Critical recensions (διορθώσεις) of the text of Homer, Hesiod, Archilochus, Alcaeus, Anacreon, Pindar. For these, particularly for his double recension of the *Iliad* and *Odyssey*, he used symbols to indicate his suspicions of the genuineness of verses, wrongful repetition, confused orders of verses, etc. (*see* SCHOLARSHIP, GREEK). The *disiecta membra* of his commentaries surviving in medieval scholia often enable us to reconstruct his apparatus of critical signs; indeed they were so reconstructed for Homer by Byzantine scholars of the tenth century. In his treatment of textual problems in Homer he was more cautious than his Alexandrine predecessors and sought to remove corruption, conjecture, and interpolation by scrupulous regard for the best manuscript tradition, by careful study of the Homeric language and metre, by his fine literary sense, by emphasis on the requirements of consistency and appropriateness of ethos, and by his practice of interpreting a poet by the poet's own usage. He avoided allegorical interpretation, as practised by the Stoics. But his work seems to have had comparatively little influence on the traditional text of Homer.

2. Commentaries (ὑπομνήματα) on Homer, Hesiod, Archilochus, Pindar, Aeschylus, Sophocles, Ion, Aristophanes, Herodotus.

3. Critical treatises (συγγράμματα) on particular matters relating to the *Iliad* and *Odyssey*, e.g. the naval camp of the Greeks; and polemics against other writers and scholars, e.g. against Philetas and the *Chorizontes* (*see* HOMER, § 6), especially Xenon.

K. Lehrs, *de Aristarchi studiis Homericis*[3] (1882); A. Ludwich, *Aristarchs homerische Textkritik* (1884–5); D. B. Monro, *Homer's Odyssey*, Appendix (1901); A Römer, *Die Homerexegese Aristarchs* (ed. E. Belzner 1924); H. Erbse, *Hermes* 1959, 275 ff.; M. van der Valk, *Researches on the Text and Scholia of the Iliad* ii (1964), 84 ff. J. F. L.; R. B.

**ARISTARCHUS** (3) of Tegea, a contemporary of Euripides, dated by Eusebius (*Chron.* 2. 105) 455–454 B.C.; said by the *Suda* (s.v.) to have written seventy tragedies and won two victories. His plays included *Tantalus*, *Achilles* (adapted by Ennius), *Asclepius* (a thank-offering for recovery from illness, *Suda*, s.v.). No precise meaning can be attached to the *Suda*'s statement that Aristarchus πρῶτος εἰς τὸ νῦν μῆκος τὰ δράματα κατέστησεν.

TGF 728. 9. A. W. P.-C.

**ARISTEAS.** (1) of Proconnesus, a legendary servant of Apollo (cf. ABARIS), and reputed author of a poem on the Arimaspeans (q.v.). His story has three features of especial interest for Apolline religion (Hdt. 4. 13): (*a*) Ecstasis, literal separation of soul from body. Aristeas produces the semblance of death and appears at the same time elsewhere. (*b*) The taking of non-human shape. Aristeas accompanies Apollo in the form of a raven. (*c*) Missionary spirit. The object of Aristeas' miraculous disappearance from Cyzicus and reappearance at Metapontum is to spread the cult of the god.

E. D. Phillips, *The Legend of Aristeas: fact and fancy in early Greek notions of East Russia, Siberia and Inner Asia, Artibus Asiae* (1955), 161 ff.; J. P. D. Bolton, *Aristeas of Proconnesus* (1962).

(2) For the 'letter of Aristeas', *see* SEPTUAGINT.

W. K. C. G.

**ARISTIAS** (5th c. B.C.), son of Pratinas (q.v.) of Phlius, contended against Aeschylus in 467, when Aeschylus produced his Theban tetralogy and Aristias his father's *Perseus*, *Tantalus*, *Antaeus* (?), and Παλαισταὶ Σάτυροι (Arg. Aesch. *Sept.*, *POxy* 2256 fr. 2.). He achieved some fame as a composer of satyric plays (Paus. 2. 13. 5). His name is doubtfully restored, two places below that of Sophocles, in the list of Dionysiac victors in *IG* ii². 977 a.

*TGF* 726–8.                                              A. W. P.-C.

**ARISTIDES** (Ἀριστείδης) (1), Athenian statesman and soldier. His family is not named, but he was a cousin of Callias (q.v. 1). Although he is stated to have been an associate of Cleisthenes (q.v. 1), nothing certain is known of him until, as *strategos* in 490/89 B.C., he supported the plans of Miltiades (q.v.) at Marathon. In 489/8 he was archon. In 482 he was ostracized, apparently as a result of rivalry with Themistocles (q.v.). Two years later, on the approach of Xerxes, he was recalled in the general amnesty, and held the *strategia* at least for the next three years (480/79–478/7). He led the Athenian hoplites who landed on the islet of Psyttaleia in the battle of Salamis, commanded the Athenian army at Plataea, and helped Themistocles to secure the rebuilding of the walls of Athens against the wishes of Sparta. In 478 he commanded the Athenian contingent of the Greek naval forces, and was chiefly responsible for the secession of the Asiatic and island Greeks from the Spartan Pausanias (q.v. 1). When the Delian League (q.v.) was formed (spring 477), Aristides fixed the quota of each contributory State. Aristotle (*Ath. Pol.* 24) says that he also initiated the policy of democratic state-socialism; but this is doubtful. He was, apparently, still alive in 467.

He died a poor man, if it is true that the State had to support his children; earlier, he had been rich enough to stand for the archonship (*see* ARCHONTES). His reputation for honesty went back to his contemporaries, and dominated the later tradition about him. He was contrasted with the deceitful Themistocles, and this may have led to the conclusion that ideologically they were on opposite sides. But it is doubtful whether their rivalry was anything but personal, or persisted after Aristides' ostracism. They co-operated closely in the repulse of the Persians and the foundation of the Athenian Empire; and some at least classed Aristides equally with Themistocles as a party-leader on the popular side.

Plutarch, *Aristides*. On the tradition of his 'justice', I. Calabi Limentani, *Rend. Ist. Lomb.* 1960, 43 ff.        A. W. G.; T. J. C.

**ARISTIDES** (2), painter, of Thebes, pupil of Euxinidas (late 5th c. B.C.), and teacher of Euphranor (q.v.). His use of encaustic was further developed by Praxiteles (q.v.). Probably father and teacher of Nicomachus, whose son and pupil (see below) has been confused with the elder Aristides by Pliny. The statement that he was the *first* to represent the soul, the affections, and the emotions, though his colour was rather hard, is more credible of early than late fourth-century painting. He probably painted the Baby creeping to its dying mother's breast (before 335) and the Suppliant whose prayers could almost be heard.                                    T. B. L. W.

**ARISTIDES** (3), painter, son of Nicomachus. Of Pliny's list the 'Battle of Greeks and Persians' (for Mnason of Elatea) probably, and the portrait of Leontion, pupil of Epicurus (after 306), certainly, were by the younger Aristides.

Overbeck, 1762, 1772, 1778–85; Pfuhl, 789, 814; H. Fuhrmann, *Philoxenes von Eretria* (1931), 72.               T. B. L. W.

**ARISTIDES** (4) of Miletus (*c.* 100 B.C.), author (or arranger into 'Rahmenerzählungen') of the lost Μιλησιακά. Ancient references indicate that the Μιλησιακά were

erotic, often obscene, short stories (Ov. *Tr.* 2. 413–14; Plut. *Crass.* 32; ps. Luc. *Amores* 1). The genre, about whose exact nature there is no general agreement amongst scholars, seems to have had no direct connexion with the Greek novel (so Rohde, followed by Schmid and Lesky, against Bürger) but to have exerted, on the other hand, considerable influence upon the later, realistic novel: stories like Lucian's *Asinus*, the *Widow of Ephesus* in Petronius (*Sat.* 111 f.) and those contained in Apuleius' *Metamorphoses* (cf. *Metam.* 1. 1 ego tibi *sermone* isto *Milesio varias fabulas* conseram) seem to be specimens of the 'Milesian genre'.

Aristides' Μιλησιακά were translated into Latin by Cornelius Sisenna (cf. Ov. *Tr.* 2. 443–4; fragments in Buecheler–Heraeus, *Petronii Saturae*³, 237 ff.), and *Milesiae fabulae* became in Rome a generic title for erotic short stories. *See also* NOVEL, GREEK.

Christ–Schmid–Stählin, ii. 1², 481 ff.; W. Stählin, in Rohde, *Griech. Roman*, 605 ff.; W. Aly, *PW*, s.vv. Milesia, Novelle; A. Calderini, *Le Avventure di Cherea e Calliroe* (1913), Prolegomeni, 29 ff. (short but accurate discussion).                G. G.

**ARISTIDES** (5), AELIUS (A.D. 117 or 129–81 or later), public speaker and man of letters. Born of a land-owning family in Mysia, he studied Greek literature under Alexander of Cotiaeon, the tutor of Marcus Aurelius, and rhetoric at Athens, probably under Herodes Atticus. At the age of 26, when on a visit to Rome, he was struck down by the first of a long series of maladies, apparently psychosomatic in origin, which put an end to his hopes of a great public career and drove him to spend much of his time as a patient at the Asclepieum of Pergamum. The remainder of his life was passed mainly in Asia Minor, where he made his home in Smyrna and in the intervals of illness occupied himself in writing and lecturing. His writings were admired by his contemporaries for the purity of their Attic diction; today, with the exception of the *Sacred Teachings*, they are read chiefly for the incidental light which they throw on the social history of Asia Minor in the second century. They include addresses delivered on public and private occasions, model 'declamations' on historical themes, polemical essays, prose hymns to various gods, and six books (the last unfinished) of *Sacred Teachings* (Ἱεροὶ Λόγοι). (The two τέχναι of rhetoric transmitted under Aristides' name and edited by W. Schmid in the Teubner series are not from his hand.) Among the public addresses, Εἰς Ῥώμην paints an impressive picture of the Roman achievement as seen by an admiring provincial, while the Παναθηναϊκός provides a potted history of classical Athens, which was much used as a schoolbook in Byzantine times. Of the polemical works the most interesting are Π. ῥητορικῆς and Ὑπὲρ τῶν τεττάρων, designed as replies to Plato's charges in the *Gorgias*. The *Sacred Teachings*, a record of revelations made to Aristides in dream by Asclepius, are in a class apart: they are of major importance both as evidence for the practices associated with temple medicine (*see* MEDICINE. 1.) and as the fullest first-hand report of personal religious experiences which has come down to us from any pagan writer.

TEXT. W. Dindorf (1829, repr. 1964: includes scholia); B. Keil (1898: incomplete, only vol. ii published).
TRANSLATIONS WITH COMMENTARY. Εἰς Ῥώμην, J. H. Oliver, *The Ruling Power* (1953); Εἰς Δία, J. Amann (1931, German); Εἰς τὸν Σάραπιν, A. Höfler (1935, German).
DISCUSSION. A. Boulanger, *Aelius Aristide et la sophistique dans la province d'Asie* (1923); U. von Wilamowitz, 'Der Rhetor Aristeides', *Sitz. Berl.* 1925; C. A. de Leeuw, *Aelius Aristeides als Bron voor de Kennis van sijn Tijd* (1939); G. W. Bowersock, *The Sophists in the Roman Empire* (1969), ch. 3.
RELIGIOUS EXPERIENCES. G. Misch, *History of Autobiography in Antiquity* (Eng. trans. 1950) ii. 495 ff.; J. A. Festugière, *Personal Religion among the Greeks* (1954), 85 ff.
LANGUAGE AND STYLE. W. Schmid, *Der Atticismus* ii (1889).
SCHOLIA AND TRANSMISSION OF TEXT. F. W. Lenz, *Aristeidesstudien* (1964).                                   E. R. D.

**ARISTIDES** (6) **QUINTILIANUS** (probably 3rd or 4th c. A.D.), author of a work in three books Περὶ μουσικῆς which contains interesting material not found elsewhere, some of which may possibly go back to the school of Damon in the fifth century B.C. Book 1, dealing with ἁρμονική, ῥυθμική and μετρική, is a compilation based partly on Aristoxenus but containing some unique rhythmic and harmonic doctrines. Book 2, stylistically elaborate, deals with the value of music in education and psychotherapy, book 3 with the numerical relations thought to exist between music and the natural world. The metaphysical background has connexions with the teaching of Porphyry and Iamblichus, but Aristides should perhaps be reckoned a Neopythagorean rather than a Neoplatonist.

Ed. R. P. Winnington-Ingram (1963); German translation and commentary, R. Schäfke (1937). R. P. W.-I.

**ARISTIPPUS,** (1) a citizen of Cyrene and a companion of Socrates. His date is uncertain, but he was probably somewhat older than Plato. He appears, from the earliest evidence, to have been a professional teacher of rhetoric, a man of luxurious habits and, for a time, a courtier of Dionysius I. But his close friendship with Socrates, which is undoubted, suggests that there must have been something more in him than appears from this. He has sometimes been described as the founder of the so-called Cyrenaic school (*see* CYRENAICS), but this is almost certainly a mistake for

(2) a grandson of above through his daughter Arete. He appears to have been the first to teach the characteristic doctrine of this school, that immediate pleasure was the only end of action. This was combined with a sensationalist theory of knowledge and the belief that the present moment is the only reality. But it is uncertain how much of these developments should be ascribed to Aristippus himself.

Ed. E. Mannebach, *Aristippi et Cyrenaicorum Fragmenta* (1961), G. Giannantoni, *I Cirenaici* (1958). Zeller, ii. 1⁴. 336 ff., 361 ff.; T. Gomperz, *Greek Thinkers* (E.T. 1905) ii. 209 ff. L. Robin, *La pensée grecque* (1932, E.T.), 169 ff.; G. B. L. Colosio, *Aristippo di Cirene* (1925); C. J. Classen, *Hermes* 1958. G. C. F.

**ARISTOBULUS** (1) of Cassandreia, historian of Alexander, was one of the Greek technicians with the army. He wrote before Ptolemy I; his history was used by Arrian to supplement Ptolemy and was Strabo's basis for Alexander in India. He was better on geography and natural history than on military matters; but he knew much that was really important about Alexander himself, and must have had his confidence.

*See* ALEXANDER (3), Bibliography, Ancient Sources; Pearson, *Lost Histories of Alexander*, ch. 6. W. W. T.

**ARISTOBULUS** (2), an Alexandrian Jew, probably of the second half of the second century B.C., author of a commentary on the Pentateuch which is known only through quotations by Clement, Anatolius, and Eusebius. This has been thought by some scholars to be a much later work (of the 3rd c. A.D.) falsely ascribed to Aristobulus; but the character of the quotations does not necessitate this conclusion. If the earlier date be accepted, the book is the earliest evidence of contact between Alexandrian Jewry and Greek philosophy. Its object was twofold, to interpret the Pentateuch in an allegorical fashion and to show that Homer and Hesiod, the Orphic writings, Pythagoras, Plato, and Aristotle had borrowed freely from a supposed early translation of the O.T. into Greek. Though Aristobulus toned down the anthropomorphism of the O.T., his thought remained Jewish and theistic; it did not accept the pantheism of the Stoics or anticipate the Logos-doctrine of Philo.

Zeller, *Phil. d. Gr.* iii. 2⁴. 277 ff. W. D. R.

**ARISTOCLES** (1) of Pergamum (2nd c. A.D.), Peripatetic, studied under Herodes Atticus at Rome (c. A.D. 130–40) and practised as a sophist and teacher of rhetoric at Pergamum, and as a travelling lecturer in Ionia and Italy, and became suffect consul. Works: Τέχνη ῥητορική; letters; Μελέται; an address to the emperor Ἐπὶ τῇ διανεμήσει τοῦ χρυσίου. W. D. R.

**ARISTOCLES** (2) of Messana in Sicily (2nd c. A.D.), Peripatetic, teacher of Alexander (q.v. 14) of Aphrodisias. Works: Περὶ φιλοσοφίας; Πότερον σπουδαιότερος Ὅμηρος ἢ Πλάτων; Τέχναι ῥητορικαί; Περὶ Σαράπιδος; Ἠθικὰ βιβλία. His history of philosophy was probably superior to that of Diogenes Laertius in insight, his chief interest being in tracing the development of doctrine and in philosophical criticism.

Testimonia and fragments in Mullach, *FPG* iii. 206–21. H. Heiland, *Aristoclis Messanii Reliquiae* (1925). F. Trabucco, *Acme* 1958. W. D. R.

**ARISTOCRACY,** the 'rule of the best', was originally the rule of the nobility. How far the court aristocracy survived the dark ages is uncertain. Homer shows the king's authority and, in an equal measure, the importance of the assembly of the people, restricted by the chiefs of the noble families. Pretending to share descent from the gods with the king, the nobles were the ruling class of the city-state (*see* POLIS). They were the landowners, and owners of livestock, mostly living in town, prominent by birth, wealth, and personal prowess. They formed a class of knights (ἱππεῖς), connected by their unwritten laws of nobility, and by the old social and religious communities of tribe, brotherhood, and family (*see* PHYLAI, PHRATRIAI, GENOS). The nobles governed the State by means of the council, whose authority long remained unquestioned. After the eighth century B.C., however, military tactics changed, and rows of heavy-armed foot-soldiers (hoplites) displaced knights fighting in single combat. By subsequent economic evolution, new sources of wealth (mines, trade, industry) arose, and were utilized by nobles as well as by other people. In these circumstances aristocracy gradually changed its character, and non-aristocrats rose to the same political level as the nobles. Either the smaller communities, especially the phratries, were opened to the non-nobles, or else new ones with analogous rights were founded. Aristocracy became oligarchy (q.v.), but the moral standards and the political leadership of the nobility guided Polis society for a long time. Some noblemen like Theognis (q.v. 1) fought the upstarts, others like Pindar (q.v.) praised and consolidated their own ideals. Later on, aristocracy became the political and moral ideal of philosophy, the rule of the best and wisest men.

V. Ehrenberg, *The Greek State* (1960); W. G. Forrest, *The Emergence of Greek Democracy* (1966). V. E.

**ARISTODEMUS** (1), the traditional hero of the First Messenian War (c. 735–715 B.C.; *see* SPARTA). When the Messenians had withdrawn to their stronghold of Ithome in the fifth year of the war, he offered his daughter for sacrifice to the gods below, in response to a Delphic oracle. Eight years later he was elected king, and after carrying on guerrilla warfare for five years, signally defeated the Spartans. But in the following year he slew himself in despair on his daughter's grave.

Paus. 4. 9–13. For the value of his traditions, *see* ARISTOMENES (1) *and* MESSENIA. A. M. W.

**ARISTODEMUS** (2), nicknamed the Effeminate, repulsed Etruscan and other attackers of Cumae and exploited his constant popularity to support the people against the nobles (524 B.C.). Aristodemus again defeated the Etruscans twenty years later at Aricia (q.v.) and helped break their power in Latium (q.v.); seizing power, he became tyrant of Cumae. Later he harboured Tarquinius Superbus after the Battle of Lake Regillus (q.v.) and died c. 492. Despite his legendary features Aristodemus is the earliest truly historical figure at Cumae (q.v.).

A. Alföldi, *Early Rome and the Latins* (U.S.A. 1965), 50 ff.
E. T. S.

**ARISTODEMUS** (3), of unknown date (? 4th c. A.D.), compiled a history of Greece which included at least the period 480–431 B.C., perhaps as a handbook for students of rhetoric. Aristodemus drew on a pro-Athenian tradition and included Ephorus among a variety of sources; but the work is inaccurate, lacking in chronology, and makes no significant addition to the historical evidence. The fragments suggest that its value was negligible.

*FGrH* ii A 104; G. F. Hill, *Sources for Greek History*, (1951).
G. L. B.

**ARISTOGITON** (Ἀριστογείτων), Athenian tyrannicide. He and Harmodius, both members of the ancient family of the Gephyraei, provoked by private differences, plotted with others to kill the tyrant Hippias (q.v. 1) and his younger brother Hipparchus (q.v. 1) at the festival of the Panathenaea in 514 B.C. The plot miscarried: only Hipparchus was killed. Harmodius was at once cut down by Hippias' guards, Aristogiton arrested and executed after torture.

After the expulsion of Hippias in 511/10 the deed of Aristogiton and Harmodius received ample recognition, public and private. Bronze statues of them by Antenor (q.v. 2) were set up, and, these having been carried off by Xerxes in 480, were replaced in 477/6 by a second group designed by Critius (q.v.) and Nesiotes; the quatrain inscribed on the base (which may go back to the first group) was composed by Simonides (F 76 Diehl; *SEG* x. 320). Their tomb (or cenotaph) was placed in the Ceramicus; the polemarch sacrificed annually to them; and their descendants received free meals in the Prytaneum. Privately, scolia (q.v.) were sung claiming them as the men who gave Athens ἰσονομία (Ath. 695). All this fostered the popular belief that Hipparchus, not Hippias, was the tyrant and that Aristogiton and Harmodius, rather than the Alcmaeonidae (q.v.) and Spartans, had ended the tyranny; and despite the deliberate refutations of this view by Herodotus and Thucydides, it continued to influence the tradition.

F. Jacoby, *Atthis* (1949) 158 ff. M. Lang, *Hist.* 1954/5, 395 ff.; V. Ehrenberg, *Wien. Stud.* 1956, 57 ff.; T. R. Fitzgerald, *Hist.* 1957, 275 ff.; A. J. Podlecki, *Hist.* 1966, 129 ff.; G. M. A. Richter, *Sculpture and Sculptors of the Greeks* (1950), 199 ff. and figs. 565 ff.
A. W. G.; T. J. C.

**ARISTOMENES** (1), a traditional hero of Messenian resistance to Sparta (q.v.), usually assigned to the Second War of c. 650 B.C. With support from Argos and Arcadia, the story runs, he won a striking victory, at Stenyclarus. Defeated in the battle of 'The Great Trench' by the treachery of Aristocrates the Arcadian, he held out for eleven years, twice escaping after capture. After the fall of his stronghold, Eira, he lived in exile at Rhodes.

Paus. 4. 14–24, probably following Callisthenes and Rhianus, a Cretan poet of the third century B.C., whose works are lost. The story of Aristomenes and of Aristodemus (q.v. 1) was much embellished, if not virtually created, after the founding of Messene in 369.
MODERN DISCUSSIONS. E. Schwartz, *Philol.* 1937, 19 ff.; J. Kroymann, *Neue Philologische Untersuchungen* xi (1937); F. Jacoby, *FGrH* 265 F 38–46 Komm.; F. Kiechle, *Messenische Studien* (1959), 72 ff., 86 ff.; G. L. Huxley, *Early Sparta* (1962), 89 ff.
A. M. W.; W. G. F.

**ARISTOMENES** (2) Athenian comic poet, competed as early as 439 B.C. (*IG* xiv. 1097. 13) and as late as 388 B.C. (with *Admetus*, hyp. 4 Ar. *Plut.*). He produced Κολεοφόροι

(hyp. 1 Ar. *Eq.*, emended [from 'Υλο- or 'Ολο-] to conform with *IG* xiv. 1097) in 424 B.C.; he won the first prize at the City Dionysia (with Διόνυσος ἀσκητής) in 394 B.C. but the first of his two victories at the Lenaea cannot have been much after 440 (*IG*. ii². 2325. 120). We have fiv titles in all.

*FCG* i. 210 ff.; *CAF* i. 690 ff.; *FAC* i. 198 ff.     K. J. I

**ARISTON** (1) of Chios, pupil of Zeno of Citium founded an independent branch of the Stoic school an was, about 250 B.C., the most influential philosopher at Athens, with the exception of Arcesilaus. He apparently left behind him no writings except letters. He represente a return towards the views of the Cynics, taking n interest in logic or physics, and rejecting Zeno's recog nition of a distinction between the προηγμένα and th ἀποπροηγμένα (preferable and non-preferable) amon things indifferent, and holding that the end of life ἀδιαφορία, complete indifference to them all.

Testimonia in H. von Arnim, *SVF* i. 75–90. M. Pohlenz, *D Stoa²* (1955).     W. D. I

**ARISTON** (2) of Ceos, Peripatetic, probably succeede Lycon (q.v.) as head of the Lyceum c. 225 B.C. He was n an original philosopher but became an important sourc for the earlier history of his school: Diog. Laert. seems t have derived from him the wills of Aristotle and his suc cessors, Theophrastus, Straton, and Lycon, togeth with some biographical details and a bibliography o Straton and perhaps of Aristotle. Works: Lives (main anecdotal) of philosophers; Περὶ τοῦ κουφίζειν ὑπερηφανίας Τιθωνὸς ἢ περὶ γήρως; Λύκων; Ἐρωτικὰ ὅμοια; a sup plement to Theophrastus' Περὶ ὑδάτων. He continue the Theophrastean tradition of writing Χαρακτῆρες an was influenced in his writing of them by the lively sty of Bion (q.v. 1) of Borysthenes.

Ed. F. Wehrli (1952). P. Moraux, *Listes anciennes des ouvrag d'Aristote* (1951), 237 ff. (*contra*, I. Düring, *Class. et Med.* 1956).
W. D. I

**ARISTON** (3) of Alexandria, a Peripatetic associate with Antiochus of Ascalon at Alexandria in 87 B.C. H is quoted by Simplicius as an authority on Aristotle' *Categories*.

**ARISTONICUS** (1) (d. 128 B.C.), perhaps an illegiti mate son of Eumenes II of Pergamum. He led a formid able popular rising after the death of Attalus III and th bequest of his kingdom to Rome (133–130). His motive may have been mainly nationalistic and anti-Roman, bu his appeal was to the depressed classes, especially slave and non-Greeks. The name *Heliopolis* ('City of the Sun in connexion with his projected State, and the presence o Blossius (formerly tutor of the Gracchi), suggest 'Utopian' programme of social revolution. But if he wa really claiming the throne of Pergamum as Eumenes II as a recent and attractive attribution of a rare coin serie suggests, his aims may well have been more down-t earth. After some early successes in the field he wa captured by Roman forces and put to death.

G. Cardinali, 'La morte di Attalo e la rivolta di Aristonico' (*Sag . . . K. J. Beloch*, 1910, 269 ff.; Hansen, *Attalids* 134 ff.; E. S. Robinson, 'Cistophori in the name of King Eumenes', *Num. Chro* 1954, 1 ff.; L. Robert, *Villes d'Asie Mineure²* (1962), 252 ff.
G. T. C

**ARISTONICUS** (2), son of Ptolemaeus, an Alexar drian grammarian of the Augustan age (Strabo. 1. 2. 31 Much of his chief work—on the Aristarchan recension of Homer—is preserved in our scholia (cf. Nicanor). H also wrote Περὶ ἀσυντάκτων ὀνομάτων, commentaries o Hesiod and Pindar, and Περὶ τοῦ ἐν Ἀλεξανδρείᾳ Μουσείο

FRAGMENTS. L. Friedlander (1953); O. Carnuth (1869). CRITICISM. M. van der Valk, *Researches on the Text and Scholia the Iliad* 1 (1963), 553 ff.     P. B. R. F.; R. I

**RISTONOUS** (3rd c. B.C.), son of Nicosthenes, a Corinthian citharode. On a *stele* found at Delphi (*BCH* 894, 563 ff.) the Delphians give to him and his descendants certain privileges because of his hymns to the gods. The date has been fixed at 222 B.C. by Pomtow (*Klio* 1914, 305). Then follows a Paean to Apollo of forty-eight lines written in regular eight-lined stanzas of glyconics and pherecrateans.

Diehl, *Anth. Lyr. Graec.* ii. 297–300; Powell, *Coll. Alex.* 162 ff.; Powell and Barber, *New Chapters* 1. 45.  C. M. B.

**ARISTONYMUS**, comic writer, contemporary of Aristophanes (schol. Pl. *Ap.* 19 c), whom he attacks in his ῞Ηλιος ῥιγῶν.

*FGG* i. 196–7; *CAF* i. 668–9.

**ARISTOPHANES** (1), the greatest poet of the Old Attic Comedy, was the son of Philippus and the father of Araros (q.v.). It has been inferred (wrongly, perhaps) from *Ach.* 652 ff. that he lived, or owned property, on Aegina. Since he considered himself too young in 427 (*Ar. Nub.* 530 f. c. Schol.) to produce a play himself, he is unlikely to have been born earlier than 457, and may have been born as late as 445. He died in or shortly before 385. Eleven of his plays survive; we have in addition thirty-two titles (some of them alternative titles, and some certainly attributed to other authors) and nearly a thousand fragments. The surviving plays, and the datable lost plays*, are:

427: *Banqueters*\*, produced by Callistratus. It contained (frs. 198 and 222 and *Nub.* 529 c. Schol.) an argument between a profligate son and his father and also between the profligate and a virtuous young man.

426 (City Dionysia): *Babylonians*\*, produced by Callistratus. Dionysus was a character in the play (fr. 70), and by its 'attacks on the magistrates' it provoked a prosecution—apparently unsuccessful—by Cleon (Schol. Ar. *Ach.* 378).

425 (Lenaea, first prize): *Acharnians* ('*Ach.*'), produced by Callistratus; the 'hero' makes, and enjoys to the full, a private peace-treaty.

424 (Lenaea, first prize): *Knights* ('*Eq.*'), produced by Aristophanes himself; Cleon is savagely handled and worsted in the guise of a favourite slave of Demos, and a sausage-seller replaces him as favourite.

423 (City Dionysia, third and last prize): *Clouds* ('*Nub.*'), ridiculing Socrates as a corrupt teacher of rhetoric. We have only the revised version of the play, dating from the period 418–416; the revision was not completed and was never performed (Schol. *Nub.* 552).

422 (Lenaea, second prize): *Wasps* ('*Vesp.*'), produced by Philonides (q.v.), ridiculing the enthusiasm of old men for jury-service.

421 (City Dionysia, second prize): *Peace* ('*Pax*'), celebrating the conclusion of peace with Sparta.

414 (Lenaea): *Amphiaraus*\*, produced by Philonides (hyp. 2 Ar. *Av.*).

414 (City Dionysia, second prize): *Birds* ('*Av.*'), produced by Callistratus, a fantasy in which an ingenious Athenian persuades the birds to build a city in the clouds and compels the gods to accept humiliating terms.

411: *Lysistrata* ('*Lys.*'), produced by Callistratus, in which the women of all the Greek states compel their menfolk, by a 'sex strike', to make peace; and *Thesmophoriazusae* ('*Thesm.*')—datable in relation to Euripides' *Helena* and *Andromeda*, and by political references—in which the women at the Thesmophoria plan to obliterate Euripides, and an elderly kinsman of his takes part in the debate, disguised as a woman.

408: the first *Plutus*\* (Schol. Ar. *Plu.* 173).

405 (Lenaea, first prize): *Frogs* ('*Ran.*'), in which Dionysus goes to Hades to bring back Euripides, finds that he has to be the judge in a contest between Aeschylus and Euripides, for the throne of poetry in Hades, and ends by bringing back Aeschylus.

392: *Ecclesiazusae* ('*Eccl.*'); the date depends on a partially corrupt scholium (on *Eccl.* 193) and on historical references, and a case can be made for 391. In this play the women take over the running of the city and introduce community of property.

388: the second *Plutus* ('*Plu.*'), in which the god of wealth is cured of his blindness, and the remarkable social consequences of his new discrimination are exemplified.

After 388: *Aiolosikon*\* and *Cocalus*\*, both produced by Aristophanes' son Araros (hyp. 4 Ar. *Plu.*). *Cocalus* anticipated many of the characteristics of Menander (q.v. 1), according to *Vit. Ar.* = *Proleg.* (Dübner) XI.

In the first period, down to 421, Aristophanes followed a constant procedure in the structure of his plays, particularly in the relation of the parodos (entry of the chorus) and the parabasis (address by the chorus to the audience) to the rest of the play. From *Av.* onwards we see significant changes in this procedure, culminating, in *Eccl.* and *Plu.*, in the introduction of choral songs irrelevant to the action of the play (indicated in our texts by the word χοροῦ), and in *Plu.* the chorus seems, for the first time, something of an impediment to the unfolding of the plot (see COMEDY, MIDDLE). At the same time *Eccl.* and *Plu.* show a great reduction (though not a disappearance) of strictly topical reference. All the evidence suggests that Aristophanes was a leader, not a follower, in the changes undergone by comedy in the early fourth century B.C. Aristophanes' language is colourful and imaginative, and he is a master of lyric poetry in every vein, humorous, solemn, or delicate. He has a keen eye and ear for the absurd and the pompous; his favoured media are parody, satire, and exaggeration to the point of fantasy, and his favourite targets are men prominent in politics, contemporary poets, musicians, scientists, and philosophers, and—as is virtually inevitable in a comedian writing for a wide public—manifestations of cultural change in general. His sympathetic characters commonly express the feelings of men who want to be left alone to enjoy traditional pleasures in traditional ways, but they are also ingenious, violent, and ruthlessly self-seeking in getting what they want. Having been born into a radical democracy which had been created and strengthened by his father's and grandfather's generations, Aristophanes nowhere betrays sympathy with oligarchic reaction, least of all in 411, when this reaction was an imminent reality. His venomous attack on Cleon in *Eq.* is adequately explained by Cleon's earlier attack on him (see above), and his treatment of other politicians does not differ significantly from the way in which 'we' satirize 'them' nowadays. No class, age-group, or profession is exempted from Aristophanes' satire, and if we interpret his plays as moral or social lessons we never find the lesson free of qualifications and complications. In *Eq.* Cleon is worsted not by an upright and dignified man but by an illiterate and brazen cynic who beats him at his own game. In *Nub.* Socrates' 'victim' is foolish and dishonest, and in the contest between Right and Wrong, Right, who is characterized by bad temper, sexual obsession, and vacuous nostalgia, ends by 'deserting' to the side of Wrong. In *Thesm.* Euripides, sharply parodied in much of the play, triumphs in the end. In *Ran.* the end of the contest between Aeschylus and Euripides finds Dionysus in a state of complete irresolution. Modern sentiment admires the heroine of *Lys.*, but possibly Aristophanes and his audience found preposterous much in her which seems to us moving and sensible. Aristophanes' didactic influence (as distinct from his influence in raising the intellectual and artistic standards of comedy) does not seem to have been significant. Plato (*Ap.* 18 b c, 19 d) blames him for helping to create mistrust of Socrates. On the other hand, *Ach.* and *Lys.* do not seem to have disposed the Athenians to make peace (*Pax* did not mould public opinion, but fell into line with it), and Cleon was elected to a generalship shortly after the first prize had been awarded to *Eq.* The fact that Aristophanes survived not only Cleon's attacks but also (with his fellow comic poets) two oligarchic revolutions and two democratic restorations should not be forgotten.

Aristophanes was intensively studied throughout antiquity, and the plays which are now lost, as well as those which have survived, were the subject of commentaries (cf. Schol. Ar. *Plu.* 210).

*See also* COMEDY, OLD; COMEDY, MIDDLE; LITERARY CRITICISM, §§ 2, 3.

TEXT. Coulon (Budé).
COMMENTARY ON ALL PLAYS. Van Leeuwen (1892– ); Rogers (1902– ). Commentaries on Individual Plays. *Ach.*, Starkie (1909); *Eq.*, Neil (1901); *Nub.*, Starkie (1911); *Vesp.*, Starkie (1897); *Pax*, Platnauer (1964); *Av.*, Schroeder (1927); *Lys.*, Wilamowitz (1927); *Ran.*, Radermacher (1921, ed. 2 1954); *Plu.*, Holzinger (1940). Scholia. Dübner (1842); Koster (1960–[in progress]. Index. Todd (1932). Concordance. Dunbar (1883).
GENERAL. P. Boudreaux, *Le texte d' Aristophane et ses commentateurs* (1919); V. Ehrenberg, *The People of Aristophanes*² (1951); A. W. Gomme, 'Aristophanes and Politics', *CR* 1938; H.-J. Newiger, *Metapher und Allegorie: Studien zu Aristophanes* (1957); C. F. Russo, *Aristofane autore di teatro* (1962); W. Süss, 'Scheinbare und wirkliche Inkongruenzen in den Dramen des Aristophanes', *Rh. Mus.* 1954; J. Taillardat, *Les Images d'Aristophane* (1962).
K. J. D.

**ARISTOPHANES** (2) of Byzantium (*c.* 257–180 B.C.) succeeded Eratosthenes as head of the Alexandrian Library (*c.* 194 B.C.). He was a scholar of wide learning, famous for his linguistic, literary, textual, and scientific researches, and for his systematic study of punctuation and accentuation.

His edition of the *Iliad* and *Odyssey* made a distinct advance on the work of Zenodotus and Rhianus. Despite some capriciousness and boldness of treatment, due to a subjective method of criticism, his work showed much critical acumen; e.g. he was the first to put the end of the *Odyssey* at 23. 296. In his textual criticism he used symbols to show his doubts of the genuineness or satisfactoriness of verses (*see* SCHOLARSHIP, GREEK).

Besides editions of Hesiod's *Theogony*, Alcaeus, and Alcman, he produced the first collected edition of Pindar, whose works he arranged in seventeen books; in his texts of the lyric poets Aristophanes used signs to mark the ends of metrical *cola*. He probably compiled a complete and standard edition of Euripides, each volume of which perhaps contained eight plays (*CIA* ii. 992), and also the first critical edition of the comedies of Aristophanes; but to a later date belong the metrical ὑποθέσεις, traditionally ascribed to him, on seven of these comedies (*see* HYPOTHESIS). He was probably responsible for the somewhat unsatisfactory grouping of fifteen dialogues of Plato in trilogies.

His select lists of the best classical poets seem, along with those of Aristarchus, to have provided the basis for the classification of writers in the Alexandrian canon. He corrected and supplemented the biographical and literary information contained in the *Pinakes* of Callimachus. Introductions to some plays of Aeschylus, Sophocles, and Euripides, based on the *Didascaliae* of Aristotle and on Peripatetic research, are extant in an abbreviated form (*see* HYPOTHESIS). In the Π. προσώπων he treated the character-types in Greek Comedy. His interest in Menander led him to compile the treatise Παράλληλοι Μενάνδρου τε καὶ ἀφ᾽ ὧν ἔκλεψεν ἐκλογαί.

Of his lexicographical works the most important was the Λέξεις (or Γλῶσσαι), which perhaps consisted of a series of special studies classified according to dialect

or to subject. He produced two books of proverbs in verse (schol. Soph. *Aj.* 746) and four in prose (schol. Ar. *Av.* 1292). *See* PAROEMIOGRAPHERS.

The grammatical treatise Περὶ ἀναλογίας, in which he attempted to define the rules of Greek declension, was probably directed against Chrysippus' Περὶ ἀνωμαλίας and began the long controversy between Analogists and Anomalists (*see* ANALOGY).

The work Περὶ ζῴων appears to have been based on the studies of Aristotle, Theophrastus, and the Paradoxographers (q.v.). Excerpts survive in Byzantine miscellanies.

A. Nauck, *Aristophanis Byzantini grammatici Alexandrini fragmenta* (1848); K. Lehrs, *de Aristarchi studiis Homericis*³ (1882); U. von Wilamowitz-Moellendorff, *Textgeschichte der griechischen Lyriker* (1900); I. Wagner, *Die metrische Hypotheseis zu Aristophanes* (1908); T. O. H. Achelis, *Philol.* 1913, 414 ff., 518 ff., 1914, 122 ff.
J. F. L.

**ARISTOPHON** (*c.* 435–*c.* 335), Athenian politician, whose activities, extending from 403/2 to the late 340s, brought him into opposition first to the party of Callistratus (q.v. 2) over relations with Thebes, and later to Eubulus (q.v. 1) over finance and, perhaps, foreign policy. He successfully prosecuted Timotheus (q.v. 2) for his part in the Social War (357–355). In 346 he opposed the abandonment of Athens' claim to Amphipolis (q.v.) in the Peace of Philocrates (*FGrH* 115 F 166). He was attacked seventy-five times (never successfully) under the γραφὴ παρανόμων (q.v.), and, although the evidence for his life mainly concerns the period 363–350, the chance references to him in the orators show that he was a figure of the first importance.
G. L. C.

**ARISTOTLE** (Ἀριστοτέλης) (384–322 B.C.), son of Nicomachus, of the medical guild of the Asclepiadae, was born at Stagirus (later Stagira) in Chalcidice. Nicomachus was the physician and friend of Amyntas II of Macedon and Aristotle may have spent part of his boyhood at the court of Pella; he probably acquired in his father's surgery his interest in physical science. At the age of 17 he entered Plato's school at Athens, and here he remained to the death of Plato in 348–347, first as a pupil, later as a 'research student' working in comparative independence. It seems likely that in the study of zoology, even at this early date, he struck out a fresh line of research. When Plato was succeeded by Speusippus, who represented a tendency of Platonism repugnant to Aristotle, its tendency to 'turn philosophy into mathematics', he left the Academy, along with Xenocrates. They accepted an invitation from a former fellow student in the Academy, Hermias, the ruler of Atarneus and Assos in Mysia, who had gathered round him a small Platonic circle; at Assos they stayed till the fall and death of Hermias in 345, and Aristotle married Hermias' niece Pythias. From Assos he went to Mytilene, in the neighbouring island of Lesbos; his choice of a residence may have been due to Theophrastus, a native of the island. To his stay at Assos, and especially at Mytilene, belong many of his zoological inquiries; the island lagoon of Pyrrha is often mentioned in the *Historia Animalium*. In 343–342 Philip of Macedon invited him to come to Pella to act as tutor to Alexander. His teaching of Alexander was probably mainly in Homer and the dramatists, but he also composed for him a work on *Colonists* and one on *Monarchy*, and his instruction of Alexander in politics may have sown the seeds of his own interest in the subject. Any close intimacy with Alexander seems to have ended with the latter's appointment as regent for his father in 340; Aristotle probably then settled in Stagira.

2. In 335, soon after the death of Philip, Aristotle returned to Athens. Outside the city to the north-east

obably between Mt. Lycabettus and the Ilissus, lay a ove sacred to Apollo Lyceius and the Muses; here ristotle rented some buildings and founded a school; e buildings included a covered court (περίπατος) from hich the school took its name. Here he collected manu- ripts—the prototype of all the great libraries of tiquity—maps, and probably a museum of objects to ustrate his lectures, especially those on zoology. Alex- der is said to have given him 800 talents to form the llection, and to have ordered the hunters, fowlers, and hermen of the Empire to report to Aristotle any matters scientific interest; and the story probably has some undation in fact. Aristotle laid down rules for his mmunity, and established common meals, and a sym- sium once a month. Above all he organized research on grand scale, of which the account of the constitutions 158 Greek States was a good example. Under his adership Theophrastus carried on studies in botany d Aristoxenus in music, and fundamental histories earlier Greek thought were compiled by Theophrastus n physics, including cosmology· and psychology), udemus (mathematics, astronomy, and theology) and eno (medicine).

**3.** At some time during his second residence in Athens ythias died, and Aristotle lived afterwards with Herpyl- s, by whom he had a son Nicomachus. On the death of lexander in 323, Athens became the scene of an out- reak of anti-Macedonian feeling. A charge of impiety as brought against Aristotle, and rather than let the thenians 'sin twice against philosophy' he left the school Theophrastus' hands and retired to Chalcis, where he ed in 322 of a disease of the digestive organs. Diogenes aertius has preserved his will, in which he makes careful rovision for his relations, secures his slaves from being ld, and arranges for the freeing of some of them; his ill affords clear evidence of a grateful and affectionate ature.

**4.** An ancient tradition describes him as bald, thin- gged, with small eyes and a lisp in his speech, and as eing noticeably well dressed. We are told further that e had a mocking disposition which showed itself in his xpression. A number of extant statues, e.g. one in the ienna Museum, probably represent him.

**5.** The works connected with his name may be divided to three classes: (A) early popular works published by imself, mostly in dialogue form, and now lost; (B) memo- nda and collections of materials for scientific treatises, so now lost; (C) philosophical and scientific works, still xtant. Apart from the *Athenaion Politeia*, the whole xtant Aristotelian corpus, so far as it is authentic, be- ngs to the third class; of the other two our knowledge ests on frs., and on three lists which have come down om antiquity. (A) The dialogue *On Rhetoric*, or *Grylus*, odelled on the *Gorgias*, was probably written not long ter the death of Grylus in 362–361. Somewhat later, robably, was the *Eudemus*, or *On the Soul*, named after udemus of Cyprus, who died in 354–353. This was odelled on the *Phaedo* and accepted the doctrines of re-existence, transmigration, and recollection. To the me period belongs the *Protrepticus* (probably not a dia- gue), an exhortation to the philosophic life which was ry popular in antiquity and furnished Iamblichus with aterials for his *Protrepticus*, and Cicero with a model for s *Hortensius*. The dialogue *On Philosophy*, which gave account of the progress of mankind largely Platonic in aracter but asserting the eternal pre-existence of the orld and opposing the doctrine of Ideas and of Idea- umbers, belongs to about, or just after, the date of the rliest parts of the *Metaphysics*, i.e. to Aristotle's Assos eriod. To the period of his tutorship of Alexander be- ng *Alexander*, or *About Colonists*, and *On Monarchy*. ess is known of the other dialogues—*Politicus*, *Sophistes*,

*Menexenus*, *Symposium* (all probably modelled on Platonic dialogues of the same names), *On Justice*, *On the Poets*, *Nerinthus*, *Eroticus*, *On Wealth*, *On Prayer*, *On Good Birth*, *On Pleasure*, *On Education*.

(B) We know, from ancient accounts, of very large collections of historical and scientific facts which were made by Aristotle, sometimes in co-operation with others. The majority of these have been lost, and exist only in fragments. They must be dated during his headship of the Lyceum. *Pythionicai*, a list of the victors at the Pythian games, was compiled c. 335–334; *Nomima*, a collection of barbaric customs, and *Dicaiomata Poleon*, Pleas of the Cities, after 330. Of the *Politeiai*, accounts of the con- stitutions of Greek States, the *Athenaion Politeia* (written c. 329–328) was recovered from the sands of Egypt in 1890. Other collections of materials now lost were *Didascaliai* (records of the dramatic performances at Athens), *Aporemata Homerica* (Homeric problems), *Olympionicai* (records of victories at Olympia). Aristotle also made great collections of materials on physical prob- lems which were added to by successors, and worked up into the extant *Problems*.

(C) The works in the extant corpus may be classified as follows:

(*a*) Genuine: *Prior Analytics*, *Posterior Analytics*, *Topics*, *Sophistici Elenchi* (= *Top.* 9); *Physics*, *De Caelo*, *De Generatione et Corruptione*, *Meteorologica* (bk. 4 per- haps by Straton); *De Anima* and the following works known collectively as *Parva Naturalia*: *De Sensu et Sensibilibus*, *De Memoria et Reminiscentia*, *De Somno*, *De Somniis*, *De Divinatione per Somnum*, *De Longitudine et Brevitate Vitae*, *De Iuventute et Senectute*, *De Vita et Morte*, *De Respiratione*; *Historia Animalium* (bk. 10 and perhaps bk. 7, 8, 21–30, 9 are spurious, ? 3rd B.C.), *De Partibus Animalium*, *De Incessu Animalium*, *De Genera- tione Animalium*; *Metaphysics* (the earliest parts, bks. *A*, *Δ*, *K* (first part), *Λ*, *N* belong to the Assos period); *Nico- machean Ethics*; *Politics*; *Rhetoric*; *Poetics* (a fragment).

(*b*) Probably genuine: *De Interpretatione*, *De Motu Animalium*, *Eudemian Ethics* (probably earlier than *Eth. Nic.*).

(*c*) Of doubtful genuineness: *Categories*, *Magna Moralia*.

(*d*) Spurious: *De Mundo* (probably written between 50 B.C. and A.D. 100), *De Spiritu* (? c. 250 B.C.), *De Coloribus* (? by Theophrastus or Straton), *De audibilibus* (? by Straton), *Physiognomonica* (? 3rd c. B.C.), *De Plantis* (the original perhaps by Nicolaus of Damascus), *De Mirabilibus Auscultationibus* (compiled at dates ranging perhaps from the 2nd to the 6th c.), *Mechanica* (? by Straton), *Problems* (compiled perhaps as late as the 5th or 6th c.), *De Lineis Insecabilibus* (? by Theophrastus or Straton), *Ventorum Situs* (perhaps an extract from a work by Theophrastus), *De Xenophane, Zenone, Gorgia* (more properly *De Melisso, Xenophane, Gorgia*) (1st c. A.D.), *De Virtutibus et Vitiis* (c. 100 B.C.–A.D. 100), *Oeconomica* (of different periods, from 300 B.C. to A.D. 400), *Rhetorica ad Alexandrum* (? beginning of 3rd c. B.C.).

**6.** Strabo tells us (13. 54; cf. Plutarch, *Sull.* 26. 1) that Theophrastus left Aristotle's MSS. to Neleus of Scepsis in the Troad, whose successors kept them in a cellar to protect them from the book-collecting kings of Pergamum. They were sold (c. 100 B.C.) to Apellicon, who edited them badly. In 84 B.C. Sulla took them to Rome, where they were edited first by Tyrannion and then by Andronicus of Rhodes, towards the end of the first century B.C. Andronicus' edition is the basis of our present corpus. Until these editions were produced, the now extant works of Aristotle were unknown to the world, and he was known only through the works which are now lost. But when once the existing works came to be known, they were commented on by a series of commentators, mostly Neoplatonists, beginning with Aspasius (fl. *c.* A.D. 110) and ending with Sophonias (*c.* 1300).

**7.** The extant works were not prepared for publication, but they are for the most part too full and elaborate to be mere notes for lecture purposes. They rather suggest memoranda meant to be shown to students who had missed the lectures, and to preserve a more accurate record than memory or the notes of students could provide. The indications of date are slight; there are references which indicate that some of the works were begun early, and several which show that they were finished late in Aristotle's life. Many references imply an Athenian audience. The writings would probably reflect a progressive withdrawal from Plato's influence. Using this and other indications of date, we may say that Aristotle began by writing dialogues on the Platonic model, but that in the latest of these his protest against Plato's 'separation' of the Forms began to be felt. To the period of his stay in the Troad, in Lesbos, and in Macedonia belongs the earliest form of the extant works largely Platonic in character—the *Organon*, *Physics*, *De Caelo*, *De Generatione et Corruptione*, *De Anima* 3, *Eudemian Ethics*, the oldest parts of the *Metaphysics* and the *Politics*, and the earliest parts of the *Historia Animalium*. To the second Athenian period belong the rest of his works of research—*Meteorologica*, the works on psychology and biology, the *Constitutions*, and the other historical researches, the *Nicomachean Ethics*, the *Poetics*, the *Rhetoric*, and the completion of the works begun in the middle period.

**8.** It is impossible in a few pages to offer any useful summary of Aristotle's philosophy; for a philosopher's conclusions are worth little without his reasons for them, and Aristotle's reasons cannot be stated briefly. It may be more useful to offer a more general characterization. The main lines of his thought were to a large extent determined by his association with Plato and the Academy; and if we may distinguish his philosophical from his scientific works (though the distinction is only one of degree), it may be said that there is hardly a page of them which does not betray Plato's influence. The dialogues written before Plato's death seem to have shown little originality, and even in *Metaph. A*, written in the Assos period, Aristotle thinks of himself as still a member of the Platonic school. But by that time important differences begin to be apparent. Aristotle was an Ionian, with all the Ionian interest in observation and in the world of change. He felt unable to follow Plato in asserting the 'separate' existence of the Ideas, and unable to accept unchanging Ideas (as he mistakenly assumes that Plato did) as sufficient explanation of the facts of change and motion. The later development of Plato's thought, in which numbers took the place of Ideas as the explanation of the universe, he thought at least equally unsatisfactory. He is sometimes described as 'no mathematician', but this is an exaggeration. He was probably abreast of the mathematics of his time; he was interested in the astronomical theories of Eudoxus and Callippus (*Metaph. Λ.* 8) and his discussion of the problems of infinity and continuity is masterly. But he did not realize to anything like the same extent as Plato the importance of mathematics as the foundation of physical science. It is true that 'God always geometrizes'; in physical science mathematical precision is all-important, and from his failure to realize this he was led, in his physical works, to adopt and reason from assumptions which to common sense, in the absence of exact measurement, were highly plausible, but were mistaken; so that his influence on dynamics and on astronomy was a retarding one. The science in which he was most at home was biology, in which, in its early stages, exact measurement is less important. Here his combination of close observation with acute

reasoning made him *facile princeps* among the ancien 'Linnaeus and Cuvier have been my two gods,' Darw wrote, 'but they were mere schoolboys to old Aristot It is possible that Plato stimulated him to this study; at least one other member of the school, Speusipp tried his hand at biology. But in the main Aristotle w here reverting to the Ionian, pre-Socratic tradition curiosity about all sorts of natural phenomena.

**9.** The same passion for research was shown in h vast collections of materials about the constitutions Greek States, the history of the drama, the history the Pythian games; apparently nothing was too great too small to rouse his curiosity. One may even say th his political thought was to some extent modelled on h biological researches. He took over his original clas fication of constitutions from Plato's *Politicus*, with difference. But in one passage (*Pol.* 1290$^b$21–1291$^b$1 he envisages a classification which takes account of t various forms assumed in various States by the orga of the body politic, as biological classification takes a count of the forms assumed by the bodily organs; and can see in *Pol.* 4 and 6 an attempt to achieve for Stat such a precise description of their types as he gives f animals in the *Historia Animalium*.

**10.** His mind has two well-marked characteristic One is a sort of inspired common sense which mak him avoid extremes in any direction. In theory of kno ledge he is neither a rationalist nor an empiricist; recognizes the parts played both by the senses and by t intellect. In metaphysics he is neither a spiritualist n a materialist; he admits the claims both of mind and body, and regards the two as inseparable elements in t living being. In ethics he is neither a hedonist nor ascetic; he recognizes in pleasure an element, though secondary and consequential one, in the good life. politics he is neither an aristocrat nor a democrat; advocates the rule of the middle class, which he regar as the steadiest element in the State. He often writ what will not bear very close scrutiny; for many distin tions have become clear through later philosophical di cussion that were not clear in his day. But by virtue his strong common sense he rarely writes what anyo would regard as obviously untrue.

**11.** The other leading characteristic of his mind is tidiness and love of order; and by this philosophy h greatly benefited. For one thing, we owe to him, in t main, the classification of the sciences with which w habitually work. He divides them into the theoretica which aim simply at knowledge, the practical, which ai at improving conduct, and the productive, which ai at the production of things useful or beautiful; ar among the theoretical he distinguishes mathematic which studies things that are eternal and unchangeab but not substantial, physics, which studies things su stantial but subject to change, and 'first philosophy' theology, which studies what is both eternal and su stantial (*Metaph. E.* 1). And what is more importan he practises what he preaches. In a dialogue of Pla we are apt to find metaphysics and ethics, psychology an politics, all present together; the variety is part of t charm, but sometimes leaves the reader perplexed as what Plato is mainly driving at. To logic, to physic science, to zoology, to psychology, to metaphysics, ethics, to politics, to rhetoric—to each Aristotle devot one or more works in which, though with many fal starts, he sticks to one great subject with a wonderf feeling for relevance; the continuity he achieves is t more remarkable because none of the extant works w revised for publication, and several if not all of them co sisted originally of separate essays which he never broug formally into a whole. So it is that, while there ha always been philosophers who derived more inspiratio

om Plato, the working programme of the philosophical
iences has owed more to Aristotle.

**12.** His orderliness of mind shows itself also in the
evelopment of a terminology which has been of great
rvice to philosophy. When we talk or write philosophy,
e use a vocabulary which derives more from him than
om anyone else; and much of it has entered into the
eech of all educated men. Universal and particular,
emise and conclusion, subject and attribute, form and
atter, potentiality and actuality—these are a few of the
any antitheses which he first introduced by name. They
ave their danger, and much harm has been done by the
ib repetition of them when the danger has not been
cognized; but they have provided philosophy with a
amework that has been of great service.

**13.** His love of classification is another result of his
rderliness of mind. The leading categories—substance,
uality, and relation—received their names from Plato;
ut the idea of a complete classification of the *summa
nera* of nameable entities seems to be Aristotle's own;
r Plato never attempts a classification of categories in
is sense, and the 'greatest kinds' of the *Sophistes* cor-
spond rather to the *transcendentalia* which characterize
l existing things. Again Aristotle has a much more elabo-
te classification of the faculties of the soul than Plato.
ut it may be noted that he is singularly free from the
angers of faculty psychology. He thinks it important to
ark off mental activities into their kinds, but he does not
ink he has explained activities by referring to the
culties of which they are the manifestation; and his
istinction of the faculties is accompanied by an aware-
ess of the links between them. Sensation, for him, is
f particulars, and knowledge of universals; but sensa-
on is of particulars as characterized by universals, and
nowledge is of universals as exemplified in particulars.
gain, he has a most elaborate classification of animal
nds; but these form a *scala naturae* in which the transi-
on from one kind to another is never very wide, and the
wer kinds present analogues of what is found in the
gher.

**14.** Aristotle's work has till recently been treated as a
osed system of doctrine all held by him simultaneously,
d much ink has been wasted in the attempt to reconcile
e irreconcilable. This tendency requires correction in
vo ways. First, while some of his works (most notably
e account of the syllogism in the *Prior Analytics*) pro-
ed with assured mastery from point to point, others
.g. *De An.* 3, the *Metaphysics*, and the *Politics*) are little
ore than a series of ἀπορίαι to which only tentative
nswers are given. Secondly, Thomas Case and, on a
uch larger scale, Werner Jaeger have shown that there
 a great deal more development in his doctrine than has
itherto been recognized. As Jaeger has shown, the
neral tendency is from Platonic otherworldliness to a
rowing interest in the phenomena of the world around
. Yet Aristotle, while he became more of a scientist,
robably did not become less of a philosopher. The last
ook of the *Physics* and Λ of the *Metaphysics*, which
nnot be dated early (since they presuppose the highly
riginal treatment of the infinite and the continuous, to
hich apparently nothing in the Academy showed the
ay), show him still seeking for a super-sensuous ex-
lanation of change in the sensible world. W. D. R.

**15.** The foregoing account of Aristotle was written by
ir David Ross for the first edition of this Dictionary, and
ummarizes conclusions drawn from the most substantial
ad authoritative work done on Aristotle in this century.
or this edition it will be enough to notice some points
hich recent scholarship has left controversial. (A) The
esis of Case and Jaeger, that Aristotle for many years
dorsed and then progressively freed himself from
lato's metaphysics, may be said to have lost ground.

Partly this is due to fresh study of the crucial 'fragments'
(not only of their content but of their claim to authenticity), partly to a growing agreement that some of the
works which stress Aristotle's opposition to Plato (e.g. the
logical works) can plausibly be assigned in whole or part
to his years in the Academy. Many scholars no doubt remain broadly satisfied with the thesis; a few have reverted
to the treatment of Aristotle's work as a 'closed system'
which Ross rightly condemns; others argue that Aristotle's
later work shows a positive increase in sympathy with
Plato's aims, e.g. if one contrasts the analysis of substance in *Met. Z H*, or the enlargement of the idea of a
science in *Met. Γ*, with the apparently earlier treatment
of these topics in the *Organon*. (B) The belief that Aristotle's major treatises remained generally unknown until
their recovery and publication in the first century B.C. has
been weakened, partly by reconsideration of the debts of
Epicurus and the Stoics to Aristotle, partly by discussion
of the lists of Aristotle's works preserved in Diog. Laert.
and the *Vita Menagiana* and dating from the third/second
century B.C. (C) The picture of Aristotle as a serious and
honest researcher has been attacked at one point: his
accounts of the views of other thinkers, which serve as a
starting-point for many of his own theories and as a
foundation for later histories of philosophy, have been
argued to be systematically prejudiced. The thesis as a
whole has not won general assent, but it has been valuable
in stimulating discussion of the texts.

For Aristotle's views on ANATOMY AND PHYSIOLOGY,
ASTRONOMY, AFTER-LIFE, see under those titles. *See also*
DIALOGUE, GREEK; LITERARY CRITICISM, § 4; METEOROLOGY;
MUSIC, § 2; PAROEMIOGRAPHERS; PHYSICS, § 2.

LIFE. Texts in I. Düring, *Aristotle in the Ancient Biographical
Tradition* (1957). *Vita Aristotelis Marciana*, O. Gigon (1962).
WORKS AND DOCTRINE. R. Eucken, *Die Methode d. Aristotelischen
Forschung* (1854). V. Rose, *De A. Librorum Ordine et Auctoritate*
(1854); *A. Pseudepigraphus* (1863). T. Case, in *Enc. Brit.*[11] (1910).
Zeller, *Ph. d. Gr.* ii. 2⁴. W. Jaeger, *Aristoteles²* (Eng. transl. 1948).
W. D. Ross, *Aristotle⁶* (1955). D. J. Allan, *The Philosophy of A.*
(1952). I. Düring, *Aristotle* (1966).
TEXTS. I. Bekker, 1831 (with invaluable *Index Aristotelicus* by H.
Bonitz, 1870). Teubner texts of all works except *Cat.*, *Int.*, *An. Pr.*
and *Post.*, *Mete.*, *Mund.*, *Gen. An.*; *Rhet. Al.* in Spengel–Hammer,
*Rhet. Gr.* i, Fr. ed. V. Rose. O.C.T., *Cat.* and *Int.* (L. Minio-
Paluello), *An. Pr.* and *Post.* (W. D. Ross), *Top.* and *Soph. El.* (Ross),
*Phys.* (Ross), *Cael.* (D. J. Allan), *De An.* (Ross), *Gen. An.* (J. H.
Waszink), *Metaph.* (W. Jaeger), *Eth. Nic.* (I. Bywater), *Pol.* (Ross),
*Rhet.* (Ross), *Poet.* (R. Kassel), *Ath. Pol.* (F. G. Kenyon), *Fr. Sel.*
(Ross). *Mete.*, F. H. Fobes, 1919. *Mund.*, W. L. Lorimer, 1933. *Fr.
Dial. Sel.*, R. Walzer, 1934. With transl. in Loeb series (all except
*Hist. An.* and *Fr.*) and Collection Budé.
COMMENTARIES. *Comm. in A. Graeca* (Berlin, 1882–1909), with
*Supplementum Aristotelicum*, 1882–1903. S. Thomas Aquinas, comm.
on *Int.*, *An. Post.*, *Phys.*, *De Caelo*, *Gen. Corr.*, *Mete.* (Rome, 1882–6);
on *De An.*, *Metaph.* (Turin, 1924–6). *Organon*, J. Pacius (1597);
T. Waitz (1844–6). *Cat.* and *Int.*, J. L. Ackrill (1963). *An. Pr.* and
*Post.*, W. D. Ross (1949). *An. Post.*, J. Zabarella (1578). *Soph. El.*,
E. Poste (1866). *Phys.*, J. Pacius (1596); J. Zabarella (1600); W. D.
Ross (1936); bk. 2, O. Hamelin (1907). *Cael.*, *Gen. Corr.*, *Mund.*,
*Parva Naturalia*, J. Pacius (1601). *Gen. Corr.*, *Mete.*, J. Zabarella
(1600). *Gen. Corr.*, H. H. Joachim (1922); W. Verdenius and J. H.
Waszink (1946). *Mete.*, J. L. Ideler (1834–6); bk. 4, I. Düring (1944).
*De An.*, J. Pacius (1596); J. Zabarella (1605); A. Torstrik (1862);
F. A. Trendelenburg² (1877); G. Rodier (1900); R. D. Hicks (1907);
W. D. Ross (1961). *Parva Naturalia*, W. D. Ross (1955). *Sens.* and
*Mem.*, G. R. T. Ross (1906). *Somn. Vig.*, H. J. Drossaart Lulofs
(1943). *Insomn.* and *Div. Somn.*, id., 1947. *Juv.*, *Vit.*, *Resp.*, W. Ogle
(1897). *Hist. An.*, H. Aubert and F. Wimmer (1868). *Gen. An.*, id.,
1860. *Part. An.*, W. Ogle (1882); I. Düring (1943); bk. 1, J.–M. Le
Blond (1945). *Metaph.*, H. Bonitz (1848–9); W. D. Ross², (1953).
*Eth. Nic.*, J. A. Stewart (1892); J. Burnet (1900); R.-A. Gauthier and
J.-Y. Jolif, (1958); bk. 5, H. Jackson (1879); bk. 6, L. H. G. Green-
wood (1909); bk. 10, G. Rodier (1897). *Eth. Eud.*, A. T. H. Fritzsche
(1851). *Pol.*, F. Susemihl (1879); W. L. Newman (1887–1902);
bks. 1, 2, 3, 7, 8, F. Susemihl and R. D. Hicks (1894). *Rh.*, L. Spengel
(1867); E. M. Cope and J. E. Sandys (1877). *Poet.*, S. H. Butcher³
(1902); I. Bywater (1909); A. Gudemann (1934); G. Else (1957).
*Ath. Pol.*, J. E. Sandys², (1912); E. Kapp and K. von Fritz (1950).
*Fragm.*: *Protrepticus*, W. G. Rabinowitz (1957); I. Düring, (1961). *De
Iust.*, P. Moraux, (1957). *Spuria*: *Col.*, C. Prantl (1849). *Mech.*, J. P.
van Cappelle (1812). *Mus. Probl.*, F. A. Gevaert and J. C. Vollgraff
(1899–1902). *Lin. Ins.*, O. Apelt, *Beitr. z. Gesch. d. Gr. Phil.* (1891).
*Oec.* bk 1, B. A. van Groningen (1933).
TRANSLATIONS. Oxford Tr., ed. J. A. Smith and W. D. Ross
(1908–52, sometimes with important notes, esp. *An. Post.*, *De Caelo*,

*Parva Naturalia*, Lin. *Ins.*, biological works). *A. Werke in deutscher Übers.*, ed. E. Grumach, with comm.: *Eth. Nic.*, *Eth. Eud.*, *Magna Moralia* (F. Dirlmeier), *De An.* (W. Theiler) (1956–). French, with notes, J. Tricot (1934–). Loeb and Budé collections.

STYLE AND DICTION. H. Bonitz, *Arist. Studien* (1862) (syntax). R. Eucken, *De A. Dicendi Ratione* (1866) (particles); *Ueber d. Sprachgebrauch d. A.* (1868) (prepositions).

STUDIES OF PARTICULAR WORKS OR TOPICS. Logic: H. Bonitz, *Ueber die Categorien d. A.* (1853). G. Calogero, *I Fondamenti della Logica arist.* (1927). F. Solmsen, *Entwicklung d. arist. Logik und Rhetorik* (1929). J. Łukasiewicz, *Aristotle's Syllogistic*[2] (1957). W. and M. Kneale, *The Development of Logic* (1962). G. Patzig, *Die arist. Syllogistik*[4] (1963), *Aristotle on Dialectic* (Symposium Aristotelicum 1968). Physics: J. Zabarella, *De Rebus Naturalibus* (1590). P. Duhem, *Système du Monde* i (1913). A Mansion, *Introd. à la Physique Arist.*[4] (1946). F. Solmsen, *A.'s System of the Physical World* (1960). H. Carteron, *La Nition de Force dans le Système d'A.* (1924). G. Sorof, *De A. Geographia* (1886). O. Gilbert in *Die Meteorologischen Theorien d. gr. Altertums* (1907). Psychology: A. E. Chaignet, *Essai sur la Psych. d'A.* (1883). F. Brentano, *A. Lehre vom Ursprung d. menschlichen Geistes* (1911). F. Nuyens, *L'Évolution de la Psychologie d'A.* (1948). W. W. Jaeger, *Das Pneuma im Lykeion, Hermes,* 1913. Biology: J. B. Meyer, *A. Thierkunde* (1855). Metaphysics: W. W. Jaeger, *Studien zur Entstehungsgesch. d. Met. d. A.* (1912). F. Ravaisson, *Essai sur la Métaph. d'A.*[2] (1913). H. v. Arnim, *Die Entstehung d. Gotteslehre d. A.* (1931). J. Owens, *The Doctrine of Being in Aristotelian Metaph.*[2] (1963). Ethics: H. v. Arnim, *Die drei arist. Ethiken* (1924); *Das Ethische in A. Topik* (1927); *Eudemische Ethik und Metaphysik* (1929); *Nochmals die arist. Ethiken* (1929). R. Walzer, *Magna Moralia u. arist. Ethik* (1929). A. Mansion, *Autour des Éthiques attribuées à A.* (1931). K. O. Brink, *Stil und Form d. pseudarist. Magna Moralia* (1933). M. E. Hamburger, *Morals and Law: The Growth of A.'s Legal Theory* (1951). Politics: E. Barker, *Political Thought of Plato and A.* (1906). H. v. Arnim, *Zur Entstehungsgesch. d. arist. Politik* (1924). W. D. Ross, *The Development of A.'s Thought* (1957). Entretiens Hardt, *La 'Politique' d'A.* (1965). Rhetoric and Poetics: E. M. Cope, *Introd. to A.'s Rhet.* (1867). O. Kraus, *Neue Studien zur arist. Rhet.* (1907). L. Cooper, *The Poetics of A.* (1924); *Aristotelian Papers,* (1939). Mathematics: T. L. Heath, *Math. in A.* (1949). Method: J.-M. Le Blond, *Logique et Méthode chez A.* (1939). *A. et les Problèmes de Méthode* (Symposium Aristotelicum, Louvain 1961). A. and the Academy: L. Robin, *Théorie platonicienne des Idées et des Nombres d'après A.* (1908). H. Cherniss, *A.'s Criticism of Plato and the Academy* i (1944). P. Wilpert, *Zwei arist. Frühschr. über d. Ideenlehre* (1949). *Aristotle and Plato in the Mid-fourth Century* (Symposium Aristolicum. 1960).                    G. E. L. O.

**ARISTOXENUS**, born at Tarentum between 375 and 360 B.C., philosopher and musical theorist. He received a musical training from his father Spintharus and from Lamprus of Erythrae (not the Lamprus mentioned by Plato, *Menex.* 236 a). For some time he lived at Mantinea; and during a sojourn at Corinth (after 343) he became familiar with the exiled Dionysius the Younger (fr. 9). At Athens he became the pupil of the Pythagorean Xenophilus and finally of Aristotle. His reputation amongst his fellow-pupils at the Lyceum was such that he expected to succeed to the headship of the school; but the master passed him over in favour of Theophrastus. Aristoxenus is said by the *Suda* to have assailed Aristotle's memory; but though he retailed scandalous stories about Socrates (fr. 25–30) and alleged that most of Plato's *Republic* was plagiarized from Protagoras (fr. 33), the one extant reference he makes to Aristotle by name (*Harm.*, p. 31) is laudatory. Whether he ever returned to Italy is unknown; nor is there any evidence about the date of his death. The *Suda* gives the number of his books as 453.

WORKS. (*a*) *Principles and Elements of Harmonics*, of which three books are in part preserved. The first deals with the scope of the subject, movements of the voice, pitch, notes, intervals, and scales; ii covers the chief topics of i, but includes keys (τόνοι), modulation, and the construction of melody (μελοποιία) also, and is more polemical in tone; iii contains twenty-seven theorems on the legitimate combinations of intervals and tetrachords in scales. These three books do not give a complete theory of music; nor are they from a single work. The most probable view is that we have the remains of two treatises, the *Principles* (Ἀρχαί = i) and the *Elements* (Στοιχεῖα = ii and iii), both of which have suffered partly by curtailment and partly by the insertion of passages from other treatises. Further details of Aristoxenus' musical theory are found in later writers such as Plutarch

(*De mus.*), Cleonides, Aristides Quintilianus; and a sho fragment on Harmonics printed in *POxy.* iv. 667 is prol ably from some work of Aristoxenus.

(*b*) *Elements of Rhythm* (Ῥυθμικὰ Στοιχεῖα), of whi part of the second book is extant. It deals with the natu of rhythm (defined as a τάξις ἀφωρισμένη χρόνων), th primary unit of rhythm (ὁ πρῶτος χρόνος), feet, their di tribution between arsis and thesis, and their difference Since Aristoxenus refers to his earlier writings on music theory (282), this work is possibly later than the *Harmo ics*. Porphyry on Ptol. *Harm.* (78 Düring) quotes from work entitled Περὶ τοῦ πρώτου χρόνου; and passages base on Aristoxenus' theory of rhythm are found in lat authors, especially the Byzantine Michael Psellus (11 c.). An important fragment (*POxy.* i. 9), on the rhythm ization of cretic sequences, is attributed to a treatise Aristoxenus on rhythmical composition (see Powell an Barber, *New Chapters* ii. 178).

(*c*) Other musical works were: *On Music* (Περὶ μο σικῆς, at least four books; cf. Ath. 14. 619 d), *On Meloc* (Π. μελοποιίας, at least four books; cf. Porph., 125), C *Listening to Music* (Π. μουσικῆς ἀκροάσεως), *On Ke* (Π. τόνων), *On Auloi and Musical Instruments* (Π. αὐλ καὶ ὀργάνων), *On the Boring of Auloi* (Π. αὐλῶν τρήσεως *On Aulos-Players* (Π. αὐλητῶν), *On Tragic Poets* (Ι τραγῳδοποιῶν), *On Dancing in Tragedy* (Π. τραγικ ὀρχήσεως); and the obscurely entitled Πραξιδαμάντε seems to have contained musical material.

(*d*) Works of a biographical, historical, and miscell neous character were: the *Lives* (Βίοι ἀνδρῶν, includin biographies of Pythagoras, Archytas, Socrates, an Plato), *Pythagorean Maxims* (Πυθαγορικαὶ ἀποφάσεις *Comparisons* (Συγκρίσεις), *Educational Laws* (Νόμ παιδευτικοί), *Political Laws* (Νόμοι πολιτικοί, at lea eight books; cf. Ath. 14. 648 d), *Historical Notes* (Ἱστο ρικὰ ὑπομνήματα), *Short Notes* (Τὰ κατὰ βραχὺ ὑπομν *Miscellaneous Notes* (Σύμμικτα ὑπομν., at least sixtee books; cf. Photius *Bibl.* 176), *Scattered Notes* (Τ σποράδην), and *Table Talk* (Σύμμικτα συμποτικά).

Aristoxenus' presentation of the science of Ha monics differed in many important particulars from th of his predecessors and exercised a potent influence f many centuries (*see* MUSIC). His pride in his own achieve ments, his combativeness, his tedious proofs of the ob vious, and his parade of logic are sometimes irritatin but he shows himself a worthy pupil of Aristotle in h method of expounding by definition and subdivision int categories, and his system of musical theory is distinctl superior to the empirical and half-mystical investigatio of the Pythagoreans. He also had a deep interest in th ethical and educational value of music and showed strong preference for the older styles of composition. Th fundamental importance of his work on rhythm has als long been recognized. Like other Peripatetics, Aristoxenu did not restrict his inquiries to a single subject; but most what has been preserved from his other works is quote for its value as gossip. For his philosophical views we ha only the evidence of Cicero (*Tusc.* 1. 19) that Aristoxenu regarded the soul as a 'tuning' (*intentio*, ἁρμονία) of th body. This opinion, which would be attractive to musician, may have been taken from the later Pythago eans; for a somewhat similar view is expounded by Si mias the Theban, disciple of Philolaus, in *Phaedo* 86 but it is quite inconsistent with the earlier Pythagore doctrine of transmigration and could not have bee countenanced by Aristotle.

TEXTS. Harm.: Meursius (Leyden, 1616), Meibomius (Amsterdam 1652), P. Marquard (1868), R. Westphal (in *Aristoxenos* ii, 189 H. Macran (1902), R. da Rios (1954); and add *POxy.* iv. 66 Rhythm: Morelli (with *Aristidis oratio*, etc., Venice, 1785), R. Wes phal (in *Lehrsätze der gr. Rhythmiker,* 1861 and in *Aristox.* ii 189 P. Marquard (1868); and add *POxy.* i. 9. Fragments: F. Wehr *Aristoxenos* (1945).

COMMENTARIES. R. Westphal, *Lehrsätze* (1861), *System der ar hythmik* (1865), *Theorie der mus. Künste der Hellenen* (1885–89), *Aristoxenos* (1883–93); H. Macran, *Aristoxenus* (1902); L. Laloy, *Aristoxène de Tarente* (1904, with a useful lexicon); C. A. Williams, *Aristoxenian Theory of Musical Rhythm* (1911); R. da Rios, *Aristoxeni Elementa Harmonica* (1954).

TRANSLATIONS (of *Harm.*). Latin: Gogavinus (Venice, 1542: reprinted in Westphal, *Aristox.* ii); Meibomius (1652). German: . Marquard (1868). French: C. E. Ruelle (1871). English: H. Macran (1902). Müller (*FHG* ii) gives a Latin version of the fragments. J. F. M

**ARIUS** (1) **DIDYMUS** (1st c. B.C.) of Alexandria, philosophical teacher of Augustus. Works: a *Consolatio* addressed to Livia on the death of Drusus: a doxographical work of which Stobaeus preserves two long rs. on the Stoic and Peripatetic ethics. He is described as a Stoic, but seems to have shown an eclecticism imilar to that of Antiochus of Ascalon, by whom he was influenced.

Ed. Diels in *Doxographi Graeci*, 447–72. W. D. R.

**ARIUS** (2)(*c*. A.D. 260–336) was the most important of arly Christian heretics. Probably a Libyan by birth and pupil of Lucian presbyter of Antioch, he became a eading presbyter at Alexandria. About 319 (some argue 23) he began propagating subordinationist views about Christ's person (i.e. that the Son was subordinate to the Father). Controversy flared up, and he was condemned at the council of Nicaea (325). Though rehabilitated . 335 through the influence of Eusebius bishop of Nicomedia with the imperial family, he died shortly after. Three important letters and some fragments of his *Thalia* verse and prose popularizations of his doctrines) survive. His characteristic teaching was that the Son was a creature, created before time and superior to other creatures, but like them changeable and distinct in essence from the Father. J. N. D. K.

**ARMENIA,** a mountainous country of Asia. Strabo 11. 520 ff.) describes it as bounded on the east by Media Atropatene, on the north by Iberia, Albania, and Colchis, and on the west and south by the Euphrates, Cappadocia, and Commagene. The country was variously divided at different periods; some districts (e.g. Sophene, Gordyne) were often independent principalities. The Romans distinguished between Armenia Maior, the whole plateau ast of the Euphrates, and Armenia Minor, a small kingdom to the west of it.

Once the seat of the independent kingdom of Urartu, Armenia was incorporated into the Persian Empire, in which it formed a satrapy. Xenophon (*An.* 4. 2 and 3) describes the country as he saw it. Under Seleucid rule the Armenian cantons were administered by local governors, but when Magnesia (189 B.C.) the natives declared their independence, and one king, Artaxias, became sovereign over all Armenia Maior. The imperialistic ambitions of Tigranes (q.v. 1) the Great and his alliance with Mithridates VI, king of Pontus, brought him into conflict with Rome; after the campaigns of Lucullus and Pompey Armenia became a Roman protectorate. To restore and maintain this protectorate was the avowed aim of Augustus and the emperors who succeeded him. Armenia became the subject of a continual tug-of-war between the two world-powers, Rome and Parthia (and its successor, Sassanid Persia), each seeking to maintain control. A dynasty of Arsacid princes founded by Tiridates (q.v. 3) generally managed to maintain a balance, remaining Parthian in sympathy while professing friendship to Rome. Trajan temporarily reversed Roman policy y annexing the country.

Meanwhile Armenia Minor had suffered a bewildering succession of rulers between the time of Pompey and Nero: it was granted by Rome to various neighbouring ings. Under Deiotarus of Galatia in Pompey's day, it was ater seized by Pharnaces (q.v. 2), but after Zela it was given by Caesar to Ariobarzanes of Cappadocia (47). Antony gave it to Polemo of Pontus (37?) but after Actium Octavian installed Artavasdes, a former king of Media; later, however, in 20 B.C. it went to Archelaus of Cappadocia. Perhaps annexed by Tiberius, it was granted by Gaius in A.D. 38 to Cotys (grandson of Polemo I of Pontus). On the latter's death it was held by a son of Herod of Chalcis (54–72), and then was incorporated by Vespasian in the Roman province of Cappadocia.

Armenia was the first kingdom officially to adopt Christianity, and the new religion and its persecution by the Sassanids fostered a nationalistic spirit. In A.D. 387 the country was divided between Persia and Byzantium. The Arabs conquered it *c*. A.D. 653.

*See also* ARTAVASDES (1), TIGRANES (1–4), TIRIDATES (3).

*Rulers of Armenia* (to early 4th c. A.D.).

*Native Dynasty.* Artaxias I, 190 B.C.–161+; Artavasdes I, ruling before 138; Tigranes I? (App. *Syr.* 48); Tigranes II ("The Great'), 95–56/55; Artavasdes II, 56/55–34 (+30); Artaxias II, 33–20; Tigranes III, Tigranes IV, and Erato, 20–*c*. 6 B.C.; Artavasdes III, Tigranes IV, and Erato, *c*. 6 B.C.–A.D. 1.

*Rulers of miscellaneous origin.* Ariobarzanes (Mede), Artavasdes IV (Mede), Erato (restored), Tigranes V, A.D. 2–*c*. 12; Vonones (Parthian), *c*. 12–15/16; Orodes (Parthian), *c*. 15/16; Zeno (Artaxias III) (of Pontus), 18–*c*. 34; Arsaces I (Parthian), *c*. 34–36; Mithridates (Iberian), 36–*c*. 51; Radamistus (Iberian), *c*. 51–52.

*Arsacid Kings.* Tiridates I, 52 (crowned by Nero 66)–75+ [Tigranes VI, 60–61]; Sanatruces betw. 75+ and *c*. 110; Axidares, *c*. 110; Parthamasiris, *c*. 110–14 [Roman province 114–16]; Vologeses, 116–40/3; Sohaemus (of Emesa), 140/3–60, 164–85+; Pacorus, 160–63 [a king, father of Tiridates II]; Tiridates II, *c*. 217–*c*. 222; Chosroes I, *c*. 222–*c*. 250 [Time of troubles and Persian influence]; Tiridates III, *c*. 287–336/7.

SOURCES. (1) Classical: for the relations between Rome and Armenia see especially Strabo, bk. 11; Plutarch (*Lucullus, Pompey, Antony*); Tacitus (*Ann.* 12–15); Dio Cassius, bk. 68; Ammianus Marcellinus. (2) Oriental (unreliable): V. Langlois, *Collection des historiens de l'Arménie* (1877). (3) Numismatic: E. Babelon, *Les Rois de Syrie, d'Arménie et de la Commagène* (1890). No coins were minted in the Arsacid period.

MODERN WORKS. P. Asdourian, *Die politischen Beziehungen zwischen Rom und Armenien* (1911); A. Christensen, *L'Iran sous les Sassanides*[2] (1944); K. Güterbock, *Römisch-Armenien und die römischen Satrapien* (1900); C. F. Lehmann-Haupt, *Armenien einst und jetzt* (1910–31); J. Sandalgian, *Histoire documentaire de l'Arménie* (1917); E. Stein, *Gesch. des spätrömischen Reiches* (1929); id., *Histoire du Bas-Empire* I (rev. 1959), II (1949); F. Tournebize, *Histoire politique et religieuse de l'Arménie* (1900). M. S. D.; E. W. G.

**ARMIES, GREEK AND HELLENISTIC.** The composition of the Homeric army is never clearly stated in the epic, and was no doubt never exactly defined. Generally there is a distinction drawn between the champions (πρόμαχοι) and the general mass of soldiers (πληθύς). Probably only the chieftains were fully armed and armoured; the common soldiers equipped themselves as best they could.

2. There is no direct continuity between the Homeric army and the classical. In the latter (for which the Athenian can be taken as typical) the organization was based on the tribal system and property-qualification. The citizen of any age between eighteen and sixty, if not disabled, might be required at need to serve the State in a military capacity, as horseman, hoplite, or light-armed soldier, according to his assessment. In practice the hoplite was the chief unit. Cavalry were scarce in Greece, apart from Thessaly and Macedon, neither of which was a great military power between 550 and 375 B.C. The usual proportion of hoplites to cavalry in an army was ten to one. Light-armed citizen troops had no fixed equipment: they were only called out *en masse*, when an army marched πανδημεί into a neighbouring State or to resist such an invasion. Their numbers might be large,

but their military efficiency was slight. The Athenian hoplites were organized into ten tribal regiments; the cavalry were grouped into two divisions of five tribes each and were led by two hipparchs. Total numbers on the Athenian army-list (κατάλογος) are never clearly stated; the most important summary is in Thuc. 2. 13. 6 ff., which admits of various interpretations. Ordinarily young men from eighteen to twenty and older men from fifty upwards were retained for garrison duty only. The age-classes required were called up by reference to their year-archons (ἐπώνυμοι) or in the fourth century soldiers were alternatively summoned by the detachment (ἐν τοῖς μέρεσιν). The only standing army in fifth-century Athens were the τοξόται, archers mostly employed for police duties. They numbered 1,600 and were mainly hired from abroad.

3. Every Greek army had its local peculiarities, but the State with the most individual system was Sparta, where all the full citizens were equals, and therefore none was less than hoplite in status. Their cavalry were few and unsatisfactory. In the Persian wars the Spartans sent to Plataea a force of 5,000 citizens as hoplites, supported by 5,000 perioikoi. At that period they were divided into five territorial regiments, but at the battle of Mantinea (418 B.C.) the regiments were seven in number, subdivided into πεντηκοστύες and ἐνωμοτίαι, and in addition there was an eighth, separate, Scirite λόχος of 600. Thucydides reckoned the main hoplite force at Mantinea as 4,298 men, excluding the Scirites, and described them as five-sixths of the Spartan army. The cavalry force may have been 400, as in 424 B.C. (Thuc. 4. 55. 2). The early fourth century saw a further reorganization into five morai, subdivided into λόχοι, πεντηκοστύες, and ἐνωμοτίαι. The extent to which the army at Mantinea or later was composed of a blend of Spartans and perioikoi is uncertain, but the best theory is that Spartans and perioikoi were incorporated in the same organization, and that the changes of system correspond to increasing proportions of perioikoi and declining numbers of Spartiates. During the Peloponnesian War the Spartans were also compelled more and more to use Helots for foreign expeditions and garrison duty abroad. They were sent out under the command of one Spartiate with perhaps another Spartan or two as his lieutenants. In the fourth century Sparta like other Greek states was forced to employ mercenaries (q.v.).

4. The Macedonian army is best known as it was organized under Alexander the Great, but no doubt his system was taken over directly from Philip II, and its general lines may be much older. At that time the infantry consisted of the πεζέταιροι, about 3,000 strong, who formed the phalanx (q.v.), and the ὑπασπισταί, probably about twice as many, who were more lightly armed. The corps d'élite of the Macedonian cavalry were the ἑταῖροι, grouped in eight ἴλαι; but Alexander also had at his command large forces of Thessalian cavalry as well as Thracians, and special light-armed levies, such as the Agrianes. In addition he led into Asia the forces of his Greek allies and a certain number of mercenaries.

5. The armies of the Diadochi were in practice little else than mercenary bands, but with the founding of the Hellenistic kingdoms new national armies were established. (1) The army of the Ptolemies is best known from Polybius' account (5. 65) of the battle of Raphia (217 B.C.,) and from many casual references in inscriptions and papyri. The main divisions were (a) native Egyptians, (b) Macedonians, and (c) mercenaries. Of these the Macedonians were the most important, drawn from settlers with an obligation to provide military service, but the standing army mostly consisted of mercenaries who supplied the palace guard. (2) The army of the Seleucids was remarkable for the great variety of nationalities from which it drew its soldiers. Its phalanx was armed in the Macedonian style, but was no doubt of very mixed blood, and was raised from the military settlers (κάτοικοι). (3) The Macedonian army was still in theory based on its former system of citizen levies, but actually the manpower of Macedon had been seriously exhausted, and in later periods barbarian mercenaries from the north had to be hired in large numbers. (4) In the Hellenistic period the Achaean and Aetolian Confederacies were the chief military powers among the Greek States. Their forces were composed in varying proportions of citizens and mercenaries. They copied the royal armies in having more varied types of troops, and tended more and more to depend on professional soldiers.

See also ARCHERS, ARMS AND ARMOUR, ARTILLERY, HOPLITES, MERCENARIES (GREEK), WAR (GREEK ART OF).

J. Kromayer and G. Veith, Heerwesen und Kriegführung der Griechen und Römer (1928); P. Monceaux, Dar.–Sag., s.v. 'Exercitus'; On the Spartan army, H. T. Wade-Gery, Essays in Greek History (1958), 71 ff.; on Alexander's army, Tarn, Alexander ii. 135 ff., and on Hellenistic armies, G. T. Griffith, The Mercenaries of the Hellenistic World (1935). H. W. P.

**ARMIES, ROMAN.** Traditional accounts of the early Roman army are tendentious and may often reflect later conditions. It seems, however, probable that from the first military service was regarded as an essential feature of citizenship, but as the poor could not provide suits of armour, in practice service devolved upon the rich. This inequality was lessened by two reforms. (a) Citizens were grouped for service in accordance with their means (traditionally since Servius Tullius). Thus the richest provided the cavalry and the poorest the light-armed troops. (b) As the need for longer campaigns grew, pay was introduced (traditionally c. 400 B.C.). Thus gradually the State assumed responsibility for the maintenance of its soldiers.

2. By the time of the Punic Wars the Roman army consisted of a citizen militia levied according to seasonal requirements from citizens possessing a certain property qualification (although in a crisis even slaves might be enrolled), and organized in legions under consuls and military tribunes. The Socii were obliged by treaty to provide contingents, of equal numbers (theoretically) with those of Rome. They were commanded by praefecti, half of whom were Roman officials under the supreme control of the consuls.

3. This system of military service was radically altered by the Marian army reforms and the enfranchisement of Italy. By the former service in the legions was opened to all Roman citizens, and a professional army voluntarily enlisted replaced the conscript militia. By the latter Italians became eligible for military service. Consequently the separate contingents of Socii disappeared, and the Roman army now consisted of legions and of auxilia raised outside Italy. During the last century of the Republic the army became divided into de facto standing armies permanently stationed in certain of the provinces, and emergency armies raised to meet specific crises by generals with long-term commands. The men of the emergency armies, who were often induced to volunteer because of the general's personality and reputation, increasingly felt their allegiance owed to him rather than to the State: the generals in their turn recognized their need for the soldiers' political support. Thus the republican army disintegrated into a series of professional armies owing loyalty each to its own general.

4. Out of the armies of the triumvirs Augustus established a permanent standing army, composed of legions recruited from Roman citizens and auxilia from peregrini who were enfranchised after their service. The normal term of service in the legions was at first sixteen years—the maximum liability during the Republic—with an additional four years' liability as a veteran, serving in a

parate corps, 'sub vexillo'. In A.D. 6 service was extend-
d to twenty years 'sub aquila' and five years 'sub vexillo'.
y the second century service had become entirely 'sub
quila' and for twenty-five years. In addition Augustus
stituted the Praetorian Guard (*see* PRAETORIANI).

**5.** For the remainder of the Principate no substantial
terations were made, apart from the gradual elimina-
on of differences between legions and *auxilia*, a process
hich was the inevitable consequence of the extension of
oman citizenship. The policy of concentrating the
rmed forces along or near the frontiers, and the absence
f an adequate strategic reserve, led to the adoption of
mporary expedients and the increasing use of vexilla-
ons, and were partly responsible for the crises of the
ird century.

**6.** To some extent this problem was solved in the re-
rganization consummated by Constantine. The imperial
rces were divided into a mobile field army and station-
ry frontier garrisons. The praetorians were disbanded,
nd in place of their prefects *magistri militum* assumed
e highest command under the emperors.

*See further* ALAE, ARMS AND ARMOUR, ARTILLERY,
UXILIA, CANABAE, CENTURIO, COHORS, COMITATENSES,
OMITES, DIPLOMA, DONATIVUM, EQUITES SINGULARES,
ABRI, LEGATI, LEGION, LIMITANEI, MAGISTER MILITUM,
ANIPULUS, MERCENARIES (ROMAN), NUMERI, PALATINI,
RAEFECTUS, PRAETORIANS, PRIMIPILUS, SACRAMENTUM,
EGECRAFT (ROMAN), SIGNA MILITARIA, STIPENDIUM,
RIBUNI MILITUM, VELITES, VEXILLUM, WAR (ROMAN ART
F).

Kromayer–Veith, *Heerwesen und Kriegführung der Griechen und
Römer* (1928); Liebenam, *PW*, s.v. 'Exercitus' (1909); Parker, *Roman
egions²*; M. Marin y Pena, *Instituciones militares romanas* (1956);
. E. Smith, *Service in the Post-Marian Roman Army* (1958); Jones,
ater *Rom. Emp.*; A. Neumann, 'Disciplina militaris', *PW*, Suppl. x
965) 142 ff., E. Sander, 'Militarrecht', ibid. 394 ff.; G. R. Watson,
he *Roman Soldier* (1969); G. Webster, *The Roman Imperial Army*
969). H. M. D. P.; G. R. W.

**ARMINIUS,** a chieftain of the Cherusci (q.v.), born
18 B.C. He had the Roman citizenship, and served in
e Roman auxiliary forces, attaining equestrian rank. In
.D. 9 he lured P. Quinctilius Varus (q.v. 2) with three
gions into difficult country near the Saltus Teuto-
urgiensis (in the general neighbourhood of Detmold)
nd destroyed the whole force. In 15 he fought against
egestes, leader of the pro-Roman faction, whose daugh-
er Thusnelda he had married. Segestes was helped by
ermanicus (q.v.) and Thusnelda fell into the hands of
e Romans. In 16, though beaten by Germanicus and
ounded, Arminius again thwarted the Roman conquest
f Germany. In 17, helped by the Semnones and Lango-
ardi, he seriously weakened the power of Maroboduus
.v.); but presently, aspiring to kingship himself, he
ced armed rebellion. An offer by a Chattic chief to
oison him was rejected by Tiberius in 19, but he was
oon treacherously killed by his own kinsfolk. He was a
rudent tactician and a master of surprise attack; his
reatness was recognized by Tacitus: 'liberator haud
ubie Germaniae' (*Ann.* 2. 88). Much has been written,
ut little positive established, about his name, the period
f his service in the Roman forces, and the exact site of
is defeat of Varus: for the improbable suggestion that it
ave rise to the legend of Siegfried no solid grounds have
een discovered.

Strabo 201 f.; Vell. Pat. 2. 118 f.; Tac. *Ann.* 1–2; Cass. Dio 56.
9–22. L. Schmidt, *Gesch. d. deutschen Stämme* i² (1938), 100 ff.;
. Weerth, *Über neue Arminius- und Varusforschungen* (1951);
. Glaesener, *LEC* 1954, 31 ff.; E. Sander, *Gymnasium* 1955, 82 ff.;
. Bickel, *Rh. Mus.* 1955, 223 ff.; O. Höfler, *Siegfried, Arminius u.
Symbolik* (1961). A. M.; T. J. C.

**ARMS AND ARMOUR, GREEK.** Homeric equip-
ent is a special subject. No single description applies
o all the passages, but a large number are best inter-

preted in connexion with Minoan and Mycenaean arma-
ments, which are known from such representations as
those on the Shaft-grave daggers. Their characteristic
armour is a figure-of-eight-shaped shield made of one
ox-hide and swung from the neck by a strap. The only
protection used with it was a helmet. The chief weapon
was a long rapier-like sword. Towards the end of the
Bronze Age this style was displaced by the use of a much
smaller round shield carried on the arm. This change
involved the addition of a breastplate and greaves, while
the sword became shorter and was used for cut as well
as thrust. In the Homeric poems the champions begin by
throwing spears at each other, and when these are gone
they proceed to close combat with swords.

The standing type of the archaic and classical soldier is
the hoplite (q.v.). This was ultimately derived from the
soldier of the transition to the Iron Age. The trend was
towards heavier armour and fighting based on weight of
man-power. Shields were made of bronze, and spears
and swords of iron. In addition hoplites wore breast-
plates, greaves, and helmets as defensive armour. The
spear as used by hoplites and cavalry had become a pike
for thrusting, not throwing, and was usually some seven
feet in length. Only light-armed troops and some light
cavalry used instead the throwing spear (ἀκόντιον). Along
with the use of the spear as a pike, the sword (at least of
the Athenian hoplite) had developed a short, straight-
edged blade; it could only be used for very close fighting.

The fourth century saw the evolution of a more flexible
type of equipment than the hoplite's. Experiments were
first made with the peltast (q.v.), but the final change was
the establishment of the Macedonian type as employed in
the phalanx (q.v.). The spear (σάρισα) was increased still
more in length to a maximum of 17 feet, and the shield
reduced to a small target carried on the arm. The different ranks of the phalanx used different lengths of spear.
The equipment for light-armed infantry and light- and
heavy-armed cavalry was also specialized at this period.

J. Kromayer und G. Veith, *Heerwesen und Kriegführung der
Griechen und Römer* (1928); A. M. Snodgrass, *Arms and Armour of
the Greeks* (1967); id., *Early Greek Armour and Weapons* (1964); id.,
*JHS* 1965, 110 ff. (hoplite); W. W. Tarn, *Hellenistic Military and
Naval Developments* (1930). H. W. P.

**ARMS AND ARMOUR, ROMAN.** In the regal and
early republican period the Roman infantry was equipped
on the Greek model (possibly under Etruscan influence).
The *hasta* or thrusting spear was the chief offensive
weapon, and the defensive armour varied with the individual's means. The richest soldiers had corselets
(*loricae*) and light round shields (*clipei*), greaves (*ocreae*),
and helmets of leather (*galeae*) or of bronze (*cassides*).

**2.** By the time of Polybius, however, the *pilum* or
throwing spear had replaced the *hasta* as the Roman
national weapon, and was carried by the first two lines
(*hastati* and *principes*). For close fighting the two-edged
cut-and-thrust Spanish sword (*gladius*) had been introduced. The *clipeus* was superseded by the *scutum*, a long
shield of Samnite origin in two forms; the earlier oval,
the later rectangular with a slight cylindrical curve,
measuring four feet by two and a half feet, and metal-
bound at top and bottom. Both forms survived into the
Empire. A bronze plate (*pectorale*) was worn, probably
over a leather jerkin, by the poorer soldiers, and a coat
of mail (*lorica hamata*) by the richest. By contrast with
the heavy-armed legionary the *velites* were equipped with
only a small round buckler (*parma*) and a light spear
(*hasta velitaris*), sword, and a helmet without a crest
(*galea*). The legionary cavalry wore a helmet (*cassis*) and
cuirass, and carried a *clipeus* and two-pointed spear
(*hasta, tragula*), but no sword. The *Socii* were probably
armed like their corresponding Roman contingents.

**3.** During the last century of the Republic the *pilum*

became universal in the legion, and its construction was improved so as to increase its penetrative powers. The change from *clipeus* to *scutum* had made greaves unnecessary and they dropped out of use. The *auxilia* in general were armed with their national weapons.

4. The change to a permanent standing army brought with it the introduction of a special parade uniform, which for centurions included greaves, already obsolete in service dress. Otherwise for the legionaries there were few important changes, apart from modifications in the cuirass. Of special interest is the *lorica segmentata* (the name is modern) represented on Trajan's column, which consisted of breast and back plates strengthened by iron hoops round the body and arms. On the column of Marcus Aurelius the legionaries wear the *segmentata*, others the *hamata* and the *squamata*, or scale-armour. By contrast with the legionary *pilum* and *gladius*, the auxiliary infantry and cavalry carried a *lancea* and a *spatha* or long sword, probably of German origin; the infantry had oblong and the cavalry oval-shaped shields instead of the *scutum*. In addition there was a number of specialist contingents, whose names indicate their equipment (*funditores, sagittarii*).

5. The Roman army eventually lost its national character. The *gladius* was replaced by the *spatha*, and the *pilum* by the *spiculum* and *vericulum*, lighter versions of the weapon. In the late Empire there was considerable variation in equipment, of which some indication is given by the titles of units listed in the *Notitia Dignitatum*, e.g. *clibanarii* ('cuirassiers'), *cataphractarii*, the iron-clad horsemen of Persian pattern (J. W. Eadie, *JRS* 1967, 161 ff.), *scutarii*, named from their heavy shields.

P. Couissin, *Les armes romaines* (1926); Kromayer–Veith, *Heerwesen und Kriegführung der Griechen und Römer* (1928); Parker, *Roman Legions*; M. Marin y Pena, *Instituciones militares romanas* (1956). H. M. D. P.; G. R. W.

**ARNOBIUS,** a teacher of rhetoric at Sicca Veneria in Proconsular Numidia, was suddenly converted to Christianity (*c.* A.D. 295) and a year or two later, at the instance of his bishop, wrote seven books, *Adversus Nationes*, against the pagans. His work throws light on the Christian–pagan debate immediately before the Great Persecution, while the venom of his attack on traditional Roman paganism shows that this was by no means dead. His conversion seems to have been due, however, to profound disillusion with the old religion. The *Adversus Nationes* is directed against opponents who argued that, 'ever since the Christians have been on earth, the world has gone to ruin' (*Adv. Nat.* 1. 1), and that Christ was mortal, a magician no more important than Apollonius of Tyana or Zoroaster (ibid. 1. 52–53). In his answer Arnobius makes little use of the New Testament and none of the Old. His view of God is Platonic and of the soul derived from Stoicism. Christ is represented as a secondary deity. Indeed, apart from hope of his soul's salvation through Christ and his hostility to paganism Arnobius shows little trace of Christian theology. He reveals curious pagan beliefs current in Africa, while his remorseless critique of polytheism from material drawn from Varro and Lucretius anticipates St. Augustine's apologetic in the *De Civitate Dei*. His style is easy-flowing. He is the first Latin writer to use the word *deitas*, and the term *atheus* as applied to Christianity.

Ed. A. Reifferscheid, *CSEL* iv, and C. Marchesi, *Adversus Nationes* (Turin, 1934). P. Monceaux, *Histoire littéraire de l'Afrique chrétienne*, iii (1906), 241 ff.; F. Gabarrou, *Le Latin d'Arnobe* (1921); H. Hagendahl, *Le Prose métrique d'Arnobe* (Gothenburg, 1937); G. Bardy art. 'Arnobius', *RAC* i. 709 ff.; P. Courcelle, *The Conflict between Paganism and Christianity in the Fourth Century*, ch. 7 (ed. A. Momigliano, 1963); A. J. Festugière, 'Arnobiana', *Vigil. Christ.* vi (1952). W. H. C. F.

**ARPI,** the largest of the Daunian cities, lies some 3 miles north-east of Foggia, which in the Middle Ages inherited

its role as the main population centre of the Tavoliere ( Puglia. Thanks to its sheer size Arpi long escape detailed identification on the ground. Air photograph have now shown that the city was demarcated by massive earth rampart over 8 miles long and con taining eleven gateways. The site appears to hav grown from a central prehistoric nucleus and, like mos Daunian cities which suffered from the Hannibalic war and the spread of malarial conditions, was in decline b the late Republican period.

C. Drago, *Archivio Storico Pugliese* iii (1950), 161 ff.; J. S. I Bradford, *Antiquity* 1957, 167 ff. G. D. B.

**ARPINUM,** a Volscian hill-town in the Liris (q.v. valley; modern *Arpino*, with interesting polygonal walls Rome captured Arpinum from its Samnite conqueror and gave it *civitas sine suffragio*, 305–303 B.C. (Diod. 2( 90; Livy 9. 44; 10. 1). After 188 it enjoyed full citizenship being administered as a *praefectura* and, after 90, as *municipium* (Livy 38. 36; Festus 262 L.; Cic. *Planc.* 20) Subsequently Arpinum is seldom mentioned. Marius an Cicero (qq.v.) were both born on its territory (Juv. 8 237 f.); remains, possibly of Cicero's villa, still exis nearby.

L. Ippoliti, *Il luogo di nascita di Marco Tullio Cicerone* (1936 with bibliography; Castagnoli, *Stud. urb.* 21 ff. E. T. S

**ARRETIUM,** modern *Arezzo*, north-easternmost of th cities of Etruria and one of the latest founded. It is no certain when it passed under Roman rule, but in th third century B.C. it was an important base for Roma operations in North Italy, and it acquired additiona importance in the mid second century from the con struction of the Via Cassia (q.v.), of which it was the firs terminal. It became a *municipium* in the second century B.C. and a colony under Sulla, and again under Caesar From it comes a fine series of archaic bronzes, notably th Chimaera (cf. also Livy 28. 45, where Arretium supplie large quantities of bronze weapons for Scipio's Africa expedition); and for nearly a century after *c.* 30 B.C. it red-gloss table wares, both plain and relief-moulded (se TERRA SIGILLATA), dominated the markets of the Roma world.

Scullard, *Etr. Cities*, 165 ff. J. B. W.-P

**ARRIA** (1, *PW* 39) **MAJOR,** the wife of Caecina Paetus professed Stoicism. When her husband was condemne by Claudius for his part in the conspiracy of Camillu Scribonianus (A.D. 42), she stabbed herself and gav Paetus the dagger saying, 'Paete, non dolet' (Pliny, *Ep.* 3 16; Martial 1. 13). A. M

**ARRIA** (2, *PW* 40) **MINOR,** daughter of Arria (1), wa wife of P. Clodius Thrasea (q.v.) Paetus, mother o Fannia (who became wife of Helvidius Priscus), an relative of Persius. She wished to die beside her con demned husband (A.D. 66), but was forbidden. Banishe by Domitian, she returned to Rome under Nerva, an was a friend of Pliny the Younger. A. M

**ARRIAN** (FLAVIUS ARRIANUS, 2nd c. A.D.) of Bithyni governed Cappadocia under Hadrian and defeated th great Alan invasion of 134. He was a pupil of Epictetus whose teaching reinforced his natural sense and honesty if he claimed to imitate Xenophon, it was his onl affectation. He preserved the valuable *Discourses* o Epictetus; and beside military treatises and his los *History of Parthia* he wrote a history of Alexander' successors, based on Hieronymus of Cardia (large frag ments alone survive); the *Indike*, an account of Indi from Megasthenes and Nearchus, with a reproductio of Nearchus' account of his voyage; and his chief book the *Anabasis*, his history of Alexander. He calls Ptolemy and Aristobulus his sources, but his main source was Ptolemy, Aristobulus being used to supplement him; the vulgate and stories he quotes as λεγόμενα, 'so they say'. His sober narrative is the basis of Alexander's history, a welcome contrast to the romanticism, the slander, the absurd stories, so often met elsewhere, provided that it be remembered that Arrian is relying on writers who had been 'Alexander's men'. Purists condemn Arrian's style; it is more important that he wrote plainly and eschewed rhetoric. He is not a compiler, but a real historian who tried to go to the best sources; he illustrates Polybius' dictum that only men of action could write history, and but for this practical soldier we should know little enough about Alexander.

See ALEXANDER (3), Bibliography, Ancient Sources; A. B. Breebart, *Enige historiografische Aspecten van Arrianus' Anabasis Alexandri* (1960: English Summary, 160 ff.). W. W. T.

**AR(R)UNS,** an Etruscan *praenomen* (arnθ, arunθ, aranθ) borne by (1) a legendary Arruns in Tarchon's army allied with Aeneas (Verg. *Aen.* 11. 759 ff.), (2) a brother of Tarquinius Priscus, (3–4) a brother and son of Tarquinius Superbus, (5) a son of Porsenna, (6) a man of Clusium (Livy, 5. 33). H. H. S.

**ARRUNTIUS** (1, *PW* 7), Lucius, probably of non-senatorial family, was proscribed in 43 B.C., but escaped to Sextus Pompeius. He returned to Italy in 39 after the treaty of Misenum and commanded a division of Octavian's fleet at Actium. He was consul in 22, and as *XVvir sacris faciundis* took part in the *Ludi Saeculares* in 17. In spite of his wealth Arruntius was noted for the simplicity and severity of his life. He wrote a history of the (First?) Punic War.

Peter, *HRRel.* i. lviii f., 41 f.; Schanz–Hosius ii. 327 ff. G. W. R.

**ARRUNTIUS** (2, *PW* 8), L., consul in A.D. 6 and son of Arruntius (1). His wealth, connexions, energy, accomplishments, and integrity made him one of the most influential senators of his time. Augustus was believed, on his deathbed, to have said that he was both worthy of the supreme power and capable, if the chance came, of seizing it. Such a man naturally aroused the enmity of Tiberius' ministers, and perhaps the apprehension of Tiberius himself: though appointed by him governor of Nearer Spain, he was obliged to remain in Rome and administer the province by deputies for ten or more years (from 23 ?). In 31 a charge, probably of *maiestas*, brought against him by creatures of Sejanus (q.v.), was quashed by Tiberius; in 37, accused of *maiestas* and adultery through the contrivance of Macro (q.v.), he committed suicide, shortly before Tiberius' own death. Scribonianus (1) was his son by adoption.

R. S. Rogers, *CPhil.* 1931, 37 ff.; Syme, *Tacitus* 380 f., 442 f. T. J. C.

**ARRUNTIUS** (3) **STELLA,** Lucius (*cos. suff.* A.D. 101 or 102), poet-patron of Martial and Statius, gave games to celebrate Domitian's Sarmatian victory (93); wrote love-poems on Violentilla, whom he afterwards married (Mart. 1. 7; 4. 6; 5. 11. 2; 7. 14. 5; Stat. *Silv.* 1. 2).

Schanz–Hosius, § 416 a.

**ARRUNTIUS** (4) **CELSUS** (2nd c. A. D.), miscellanist, whose (lost) works included a grammar and (possibly) commentaries on Terence and Virgil.

Schanz–Hosius, § 606, 5.

**ARS,** a treatise. This meaning of the word, based on the opposition (common in literary criticism) between *ars* (τέχνη) and *natura* (*ingenium*, φύσις), is first found in the ps.-Ciceronian *Rhetorica ad Herennium*. The term is used mainly for technical works (*ars grammatica, ars arithmetica*); but *Ars Amatoria* was certainly Ovid's own title (cf. 2. 162). Horace's *Ars Poetica* is first so named by Quintilian (8. 3. 60). J. F. M.

**ARSACIDS,** the royal dynasty of Parthia (q.v.) *c.* 250 B.C.–*c.* A.D. 230. Arsaces, rebelling against the Bactrian satrap of Antiochus II Theos, became the first king of Parthia, and his descendants and successors (some 37 in number) bore his name as an official title. The Arsacids rapidly made Parthia a world-power second only to Rome: on the west they drove the Seleucids from Mesopotamia and more than once invaded Syria; in the east they reached India and extended their influence over the Indo-Scythian kingdoms. Their relations with Rome were generally hostile, yet they performed a great service to the western world in halting the constant menace of nomadic invasion from the north-east. Politically, the Arsacids were the heirs of the Achaemenids, from whom they claimed descent. They too made Media the centre of their empire and Ecbatana their capital; Ctesiphon (q.v.) was their winter residence. Although not themselves Persians, they adopted Persian religion and customs, and organization into satrapies. But Persia, never reconciled to the Parthian intruders, under the leadership of a new dynasty, the Sassanids (q.v.), shook off Parthian suzerainty and brought an end to Arsacid rule both in the Parthian Empire (*c.* 227 ?) and in Armenia (*c.* 253).

List of Parthian kings (N. C. Debevoise, *A Political History of Parthia* (1938), 270; J. Wolski, *Hist.* 1959, 222 ff., 1962, 138 ff.; id. *Berytus* xi (1956/7) 35 ff.; B. Simonetta, *Num. Chron.* 1956).

Arsaces I, *c.* 247–210/09; Arsaces II, 210/09–*c.* 191; Priapitius, *c.* 191–176; Phraates I, *c.*176–1; Mithradates I, *c.* 171–138/7; Phraates II, 138/7–*c.* 128; Artabanus I (II), *c.* 128–124/3; Mithradates II, *c.* 123–88/87; Gotarzes I, 91–81/80; Orodes I, 80–76/75; Sinatruces, 76/75–70 or 69; Phraates III, 70 or 69–58/57; Mithradates III, 58/57–55; Orodes II (q.v.), *c.* 57–*c.* 38/37; [Pacorus I, died 38]; Phraates IV (q.v.), *c.* 38–32; [Tiridates I (II), *c.* 30–25]; Phraates V (Phraataces), (q.v.), 2 B.C.–A.D. 4; Orodes III, 4–*c.* 6/7; Vonones I, 7/8–12; Artabanus II (III), 12–*c.* 38; [Tiridates II (III) (q.v. 2), *c.* 36]; [Cinnamus, *c.* 37]; Gotarzes II, *c.* 38–51; Vardanes, *c.* 39–47/48; Vonones II, *c.* 51; Vologeses I (q.v.), 51/52–79/80; Pacorus II, 78–115/16; Artabanus III (IV), 80–81; Osroes, *c.* 109–28/9; Parthamaspates, *c.* 117; Vologeses II, 105/6–47; Mithradates IV, 128/9?–47?; Vologeses III, 148–92; Vologeses IV, 191–208/9; Vologeses V, 208/9–28/9?; Artabanus IV (V), 213/14–26/27?; Artavasdes, 226/7–?

Tiridates I, brother and successor to Arsaces I, is legendary. An Artabanus I, successor to this Tiridates, was postulated by certain scholars in an attempt to improve the text of Trogus, *Prol.* 42.

SOURCES. Classical: Plutarch (esp. *Crassus* and *Antony*); Josephus (E. Täubler, *Die Parthernachrichten bei Josephus*, 1904); Tacitus (*Ann.* 13–15); Dio Cassius (*passim*).
Babylonian cuneiform texts (valuable for chronology): A. T. Olmstead, *CPhil.* 1937; J. N. Strassmaier, *Zeitschr. f. Assyriologie* iii (1888).
Chinese texts: F. Hirth, *China and the Roman Orient* (1885); J. J. M. de Groot, *Chinesische Urkunden zur Geschichte Asiens* (1921–6).
Coins (important): W. Wroth, *Parthia* (*B.M. Cat.*, 1903); R. H. Macdowell, *Coins from Seleucia* (1936).
GENERAL HISTORIES. G. Rawlinson, *The Sixth Oriental Monarchy* (1873); A. von Gutschmid, *Geschichte Irans* (1888); N. C. Debevoise, *Political History of Parthia* (1938). *PW*, arts. on individual kings.
Rome and Parthia: A. Günther, *Beiträge zur Geschichte der Kriege zwischen Römer und Parthern* (1922); F. A. Lepper, *Trajan's Parthian War* (1945); K. H. Ziegler, *Die Beziehungen zwischen Rom und dem Partherreich* (1964). M. S. D.; E. W. G.

**ARSAMEIA.** Name of two cities in Commagene: (i) Arsameia by the Euphrates (modern *Gerger*); (ii) Arsameia by the Nymphaeus (modern *Eski Kahta*) identified by remarkable inscriptions recording the sepulchral sanctuaries (*hierothesia*) set up, one at each site, by order of Antiochus (q.v. 9) I of Commagene.

K. Humann and O. Puchstein, *Reisen in Nordsyrien u. Kleinasien* (1890) 353 ff.; F. K. Dörner, *Forschungen in Kommagene* (1939); F. K. Dörner, etc., *Arsameia am Nymphaios* (1963).        E. W. G.

**ARSINOË I** (b. *c.* 300 B.C.), daughter of Lysimachus (q.v.) and of his first wife Nicaea. She married Ptolemy II when he was crown prince (*c.* 289–288), and had by him at least three children, Ptolemy III, Berenice, who married the Seleucid king, Antiochus II, and a Lysimachus. She was accused of plotting to kill her husband and was banished to Coptus (279–274). Her motive was perhaps jealousy, as Arsinoë II had returned to Egypt a short time before.        F. M. H.

**ARSINOË II** (*Philadelphus*) (*c.* 316–270 B.C.), daughter of Ptolemy I and Berenice I. She married (*c.* 299–298) Lysimachus (q.v.), who was strongly under her influence and gave her the towns of Heraclea, Tius, Amastris, and Cassandreia as special domains. After Lysimachus' defeat and death and a short marriage to her step-brother Ptolemy Ceraunus, Arsinoë fled to Egypt. She married her brother Ptolemy II in 276–275 or perhaps a year earlier. Arsinoë was queen of Egypt only for a few years (she died in 270), but they were years of the greatest expansion of Ptolemaic power overseas, and of the greatest brilliance of the Alexandrian court. Her influence on events seems to have been as great as, or greater than that of her husband, and the impact she left on posterity is comparable to that of Cleopatra VII. She and Ptolemy Philadelphus were deified as the Theoi Adelphoi already by 272 B.C., and her death was lamented in an elegy of Callimachus (fr. 228 Pf.). The Fayûm, colonized at this time, was called Arsinoïtes after her.        F. M. H.

**ARSINOË III** (*Philopator*) (b. *c.* 235 B.C.), daughter of Ptolemy III and Berenice II. She married her brother Ptolemy IV in 217, but fell into disfavour during his last years and was murdered in obscure circumstances in 206–205 or 204–203, shortly before or after her husband's death. A fragment of the autobiography of the great scholar Eratosthenes (Ath. 276 b) shows her as a fastidious and polished woman, disgusted by her husband's excesses.        F. M. H.

**ARSINOË** (1) (*Crocodilopolis*) was developed by Ptolemy Philadelphus as the metropolis of the district which he reclaimed in the Fayûm; its Egyptian predecessor was unimportant. The ruins are extensive, but have not been systematically excavated; they were the first source of papyri exploited in the Fayûm, and have produced large numbers of Roman and Byzantine documents, terracottas, etc.        J. G. M.

**ARSINOË** (2) (*Cleopatris*), now *Ardscherud* near Suez, at the northern end of the gulf, founded by Ptolemy II, was the capital of the Heroöpolite nome, and the terminal point of a canal from the Pelusiac arm of the Nile. It became one of the chief Egyptian ports, despite shoals and south winds, carrying Red Sea trade, but much less than Myos Hormos and Berenice (qq.v.). Near it Trajan established a garrison at Clysma, at the end of a new canal (from *Baboul*), cleared periodically through several centuries.

Warmington, *Indian Commerce*, 8 and index.        E. H. W.

**ART, GREEK RELIGIOUS.** A large proportion of Greek art served a religious purpose, at least in the earlier periods. The temple as a cardinal part of Greek life was known to Homer (cf. *Il.* i. 39); foundations of such temples dating from the late geometric period and terracotta models of such shrines have come to light in Samos, Perachora, Eleusis, Sparta, and Argos. And from the succeeding centuries, of course, many actual edifices are known. These buildings were regularly decorated with friezes and pedimental groups, and inside them were placed the cult statues of the respective deities. In addition, votive statues and reliefs were erected in the sacred precincts surrounding the shrines; for it was customary in Greece to dedicate a piece of sculpture to a deity, either in recognition of a favour received or in the hope of a favour to be granted. Accordingly, the earlier Greek sculptures that have survived to our time mostly come from sanctuaries.

The small cult figures current during the geometric age of the ninth and eighth centuries were mostly of wood and have all disappeared; but many geometric bronze and terracotta statuettes have been found in the sanctuaries of Olympia, Delphi, and elsewhere. Then, from the archaic period of *c.* 650–480 B.C. there exists a wealth of fine marble and limestone statues, as well as statuettes in various materials, discovered in sanctuaries all over the Greek world. Some still bear their dedicatory inscriptions. Thus, one of the life-size statues signed by Geneleos at Samos is inscribed: 'I am ... oche who has dedicated it to Hera' (*c.* 560 B.C.). Two female statues, also from Samos, one in the Louvre, the other in Berlin, were dedicated to Hera by Cheramyes (*c.* 575–550 B.C.). The famous Calf-bearer from the Athenian Acropolis is inscribed on its base with a dedication by '(Rh)onbos, son of Olos' (*c.* 560 B.C.). The Sacred Way to the temple of Apollo at Didyma in Asia Minor was lined with seated statues, some inscribed with their names (*c.* 560 B.C. and later). The intimate relationship felt by the Greeks towards their gods is shown by some of the inscriptions. For instance, an early archaic bronze statuette from Boeotia in Boston has the ingenious dedication: 'Mantiklos dedicated me to the far-shooting (god) of the silver bow, out of the tithe. Do thou, Phoebus, give something nice in exchange.'

There have also been preserved some outstanding examples of archaic architectural sculptures; for instance, the stupendous central Gorgon from a temple at Corfu (*c.* 600 B.C.), the three-headed Typhon from the Acropolis of Athens (*c.* 560–550 B.C.), and a number of metopes from mid sixth-century temples at Selinus and Foce del Sele. The 'Treasuries' belonging to various Greek city states were also erected in sanctuaries, and they too were decorated with sculptures, some of which have been found in fairly good preservation; e.g. the fine pediment and friezes of the Siphnian Treasury at Delphi (*c.* 530–525 B.C.), the metopes of the Athenian Treasury at Delphi (*c.* 510–500 B.C.), and some metopes of the late archaic temple of Foce del Sele, near Paestum in Italy.

The subjects represented in these early sculptures were mostly mythological—the legends about the gods and goddesses of Greece, which made Greek religion so colourful and human. And when other subjects were chosen, such as the battle of Greeks and Trojans on the pediments of the temple of Aphaea in Aegina (*c.* 500–480 B.C.), one finds a deity presiding in the centre of the contest. The same applies to the paintings of this period which, though they have practically all disappeared, are known from descriptions of ancient authors and by their 'reflections' on many vase-paintings. There too the majority represent the gods and heroes of Greek mythology that were worshipped by the Greeks; so they can also be considered as part of religious art, though the objects themselves mostly served a practical purpose.

In addition, single statues and reliefs were placed in sanctuaries as votive offerings to the deity—a custom that is responsible for the survival of the famous Maidens which had remained in place on the Acropolis of Athens during the whole of the archaic period and then been buried in trenches after the sack of Athens by the Persians in 480 B.C.

**2.** Our knowledge of fifth-century sculpture and architecture is largely derived from a few comparatively well-preserved sacred buildings—the temple of Apollo at Olympia, the Parthenon and the Erechtheum on the Athenian Acropolis, the temple of Apollo at Phigalia in Arcadia, and the temple of Hera at Argos. Their sculptural decoration ranges in date from *c.* 465 B.C. to the end of the century, and they bring before us the greatest artistic achievements attained during that unparalleled period. All reveal a religious spirit by the serenity that pervades them, bringing to mind Quintilian's statement that the gold and ivory statue of Zeus at Olympia by Phidias 'seems to have added something to the established religion'.

In addition, as in the archaic period, a few surviving single statues exemplify the prevalent Greek custom of erecting figures of victorious athletes in the sanctuaries of Greece, since the periodic athletic contests were held in these sacred precincts. Thus, the famous bronze Charioteer from Delphi (*c.* 470 B.C.) was part of such a votive offering, made after a victorious race. Much instructive information has also been derived from a series of votive reliefs erected in various sanctuaries showing deities enthroned or reclining, and human votaries approaching with gifts. It is furthermore noteworthy that portraits of prominent individuals—those of Pericles, Xanthippus, and Anacreon, for instance—were set up not in public places but in the sacred precinct of the Acropolis of Athens.

**3.** In the fourth century B.C., with the growing interest in individuality, the outlook changed. More and more civic buildings arose, and commemorative statues were often placed no longer in sanctuaries but in public market-places. A change in style reflects the new mentality. The single statues made by the prominent artists of the time, by Praxiteles and Lysippus for instance, show the new attitude. The Hermes and various Aphrodites by Praxiteles (some preserved in Roman copies) and the Apoxyomenos by Lysippus indicate a more human approach than Phidias' creations. In addition to the major deities, the secondary ones—satyrs, nymphs, Pan, and particularly Eros—now become prominent. And scenes from daily life, which already had made a frequent appearance on the later fifth-century vases, pervade the representations on vases and reliefs. Religious art was losing its former pre-eminent place—though the old tradition persisted for a considerable time. Thus, the portraits of Aeschylus, Sophocles, and Euripides which were set up by Lycurgus in 340–330 B.C. were placed in the theatre, that is, in a place sacred to Dionysus; and votive reliefs still crowded the sanctuaries of Asclepius and other beneficent deities.

**4.** In the Hellenistic age (*c.* 330–100 B.C.) Hellenic civilization spread throughout the Eastern Empire created by Alexander the Great and his successors. Art now became realistic in form and content. Artists became engrossed in depicting the life around them and the emotions of human beings. Pain and suffering, joy and exaltation, sleep and death were now for the first time convincingly rendered. Portraiture became an absorbing subject. Naturally side by side with these human subjects the Olympian gods retained a prominent place. But their character changed. Instead of the Apollo of

Olympia we have the Belvedere Apollo; instead of the Poseidon from Artemision we have the somewhat theatrical Poseidon from Melos; instead of Myron's Volneratus deficiens there comes the Laocoön; instead of the battles on the Phigalia and Mausoleum friezes we have the battle of Gods and Giants on the Pergamene altar. All are splendid creations in which the creative force of the new age found powerful expression. But the religious character has waned. Furthermore, new conceptions are added to the old. The Tyche of Antioch by Eutychides had many successors in the personifications of various cities. Oriental deities—Serapis, Isis, Harpocrates—were adopted in both Greece and Italy. Finally, the deification of the Hellenistic rulers and their families, represented on coins and in statues all over the Hellenistic world, had profound repercussions. The gods had descended from Olympus to earth. Greek art had extended its boundaries but had lost its sublimity. *See also* SCULPTURE, GREEK.

G. M. A. R.

**ARTABANUS III,** king of Parthia A.D. 12–*c.* 38, an Arsacid on his mother's side, gained the throne in a struggle against Vonones who fled to Armenia (11/12). When Germanicus (q.v.) installed Artaxias (Zeno) in Armenia (18), Artabanus acquiesced and renewed friendship with Rome. After strengthening his rule and his kingdom (a letter of his to Susa survives: see C. B. Welles, *Royal Correspond. in Hellen. Period,* U.S.A. 1934, 299 ff.) Artabanus challenged Rome by installing his son Arsaces on the Armenian throne (*c.* 34). Tiberius replied by encouraging rivals to the thrones of both Armenia and Parthia. Artabanus also faced an Iberian invasion of Armenia which he failed to stem, and fled to Hyrcania (36). Later he won his way back to Seleucia, and, somewhat chastened, he now met L. Vitellius on the Euphrates and accepted Rome's settlement in Armenia in return for recognition of his sovereignty in Parthia. Pressure from Parthian nobles forced him to flee again, but he was restored with the help of Izates, king of Adiabene. He died soon after.

N. C. Debevoise, *A Political History of Parthia* (1938), 152 ff.; U. Kahrstedt, *Artabanos und sein Erben* (1950). H. H. S.

**ARTABAZUS** (*c.* 387–*c.* 325 B.C), son of Pharnabazus (q.v.) and Apame. His consistent loyalty to Artaxerxes II (q.v.) was rewarded by his appointment as satrap of Dascylium, a position which was hereditary in his family. Under Artaxerxes III he revolted, and, aided successively by Chares and Pammenes, held out until 352, when he was forced to seek refuge in Macedonia. His return to Persia was arranged by Mentor, his brother-in-law, in 345. After Gaugamela he fled with Darius III, but deserted from Bessus to Alexander, who made him satrap of Bactria, a command which he resigned in 328.

D. E. W. W.

**ARTAPHERNES** (the earlier Greek form appears to have been Artaphrenes): (1) the half-brother of Darius and satrap in Sardes. After co-operating with Aristagoras (q.v. 1) in 499 B.C., he took a leading part in suppressing the Ionian Revolt. (2) His son, together with Datis, commanded the Persian expedition which was smashed at Marathon (q.v.). H. H. S.

**ARTAVASDES** (1) **I** of Armenia succeeded his father Tigranes before 52 B.C., and was Rome's ally when Crassus invaded Mesopotamia; but Orodes' simultaneous invasion of Armenia brought him over to Parthia's side, and he married his sister to Orodes' son Pacorus. The story of the performance of the *Bacchae* at the wedding feast in the Armenian capital has led to a suggestion that Artavasdes, who is said to have written Greek 'histories', was the unknown historian whom Plutarch followed in the Parthian part of his *Life* of Crassus; but the unknown was certainly an eastern Greek. Artavasdes remained Parthia's ally till Antony's invasion in 36, when Canidius defeated him and he became (in name) an ally of Antony; he deserted in the critical battle, and in 34 Antony in revenge entered Armenia with an army, seized the king by a trick and led him in captivity to Alexandria. He appeared in Antony's triumph there and was later put to death by Cleopatra, on the eve of the Actium campaign.

W. W. Tarn, *The Greeks in Bactria and India²* (1951), 51 ff.; H. Buchheim, *Die Orientpolitik des Triumvirn M. Antonius* (1960).
W. W. T.

**ARTAVASDES** (2), king of Media Atropatene, whose land and capital, Phraaspa, was attacked by M. Antonius (q.v. 4) in 36 B.C. Enmity with the Armenian Artavasdes (q.v. 1) and a quarrel with Parthia soon swung him to Antony's side. In 34 after defeating Armenia Antony gave part of Armenia to Artavasdes and betrothed his own son Alexander Helios to Artavasdes' young daughter Iotape. Later Artavasdes made an alliance with Tiridates (q.v. 2), and in 30, after they had been overcome by the Parthian Phraates, he fled to Octavian who granted him Armenia Minor. He died, in Rome, before 20 B.C.
H. H. S.

**ARTAXATA**, the capital city of Armenia, on the river Araxes, in the district of Ararat, *c.* 20 miles south-west of Erivan. It was founded by Artaxias I, traditionally with the advice and assistance of Hannibal (Strabo 11. 528; Plut. *Luc.* 31). It was several times captured by the Romans during their invasions of Armenia; Corbulo burnt it in A.D. 58 (Tac. *Ann.* 13. 41); it was rebuilt by Tiridates (3) brother of Vologeses (qq.v.) and renamed Neronia (Dio Cass. 63. 7), but reverted to its old name. It was seized by Statius Priscus (A.D. 163) when he invaded Armenia. He did not destroy it, but founded a new city, Caenepolis (later, Valarshapat) not far away, and this soon replaced Artaxata as capital.
M. S. D.; E. W. G.

**ARTAXERXES** (1) I (*Macrocheir*), king of Persia, son of Xerxes and Amestris, began his forty years' reign on his father's assassination in 464 B.C. He overcame disaffection in the court, in Bactria, and in Egypt, which, through Athenian support, resisted until 454. The peace of Callias (449) regulating relations with Athens was, on balance, a Persian diplomatic success. He was dominated by his mother; but his generous treatment of Themistocles, and of the Jewish and Egyptian minorities, suggests political sense rather than weakness.
D. E. W. W.

**ARTAXERXES** (2) II (*Mnemon*) (*c.* 436–358 B.C.), son of Darius II and Parysatis, ascended the Persian throne in 404. After crushing Cyrus' rebellion and repelling Spartan intervention in Asia Minor (peace of Antalcidas 386), he twice failed in the attempt to recover Egypt (385–383 and 374). He succeeded in suppressing the Satraps' Revolt (366–358), largely through mutual distrust among his enemies. His incapacity and subservience to the will of his mother and of his wife, Statira, caused a progressive decline and disintegration of the Empire.
D. E. W. W.

**ARTAXERXES** (3) III (*Ochus*) succeeded his father, Artaxerxes II, in 358 B.C. He secured his position by the wholesale execution of his brothers, and by crushing Orontes and Artabazus. In 343 (after a previous failure in 351) he reconquered Egypt with the aid of Mentor, who later recovered western Asia Minor. He was poisoned by his minister Bagoas in 338. Though he misjudged the strength of Macedonia, his achievement

in restoring the power and prestige of the central government indicates high qualities of statecraft and leadership.
D. E. W. W.

**ARTAXERXES** (4) (*Ardashir*), the name of several Sassanid kings, the greatest being Artaxerxes I (A.D. 211–12 to 241), son of Papak, founder of the New Persian Empire of the Sassanids. Taking advantage of the confusion in the eastern part of the Roman Empire to assume the kingship of Istakhr (Persepolis), and then to conquer the neighbouring principalities one by one, he finally defeated Artabanus V of Parthia in battle and entered Ctesiphon in 224. After further campaigns his empire included Iran, Afghanistan, and Baluchistan to the Oxus, Babylonia, Mesopotamia, and Armenia. He was responsible for the political and religious organization of the Sassanian Empire, and he founded many cities. He fought an indecisive campaign against Severus Alexander (230–2), but in a second invasion of Roman Mesopotamia (238) captured Carrhae and Nisibis. Towards the end of his reign his son Sapor (q.v.) became co-regent.
M. S. D.; E. W. G.

**ARTEMIDORUS** (1) of Tarsus (2nd and 1st cc. B.C.), grammarian. For his edition of the Bucolic Poets he wrote *Anth. Pal.* 9. 205. *See also* GLOSSA (Greek).

**ARTEMIDORUS** (2) (fl. 104–101 B.C.), a Greek of Ephesus, voyaged along Mediterranean shores, outer Spain (and Gaul?), and in Alexandria wrote eleven geographical books (Περίπλους, Τὰ γεωγραφούμενα, Γεωγραφίας βιβλία), often quoted. His records, especially of distances in western regions, including (misapplied) use of Roman measurements, were fair, with errors and confusions (K. Miller, *Mappaemundi* (1898), vi. 127 ff.). For eastern waters and Ethiopia Artemidorus relied on Agatharchides (q.v.), adding distances and details as far as C. Guardafui; for India, on Alexander's writers and Megasthenes (q.v.). He made two calculations of the inhabited world's length and two of its breadth, without determining positions by latitude and longitude.

GGM 1. 74 ff. Berger, *Gesch. d. wiss. Erdkunde d. Gr.* iv, 38 ff. E. H. Bunbury, *Hist. of Anc. Geog.* ii (1879), 61 ff.
E. H. W.

**ARTEMIDORUS** (3) (late 2nd c. A.D.), of Ephesus (but usually known as 'Daldianus', after his mother's native city, Daldis in Lydia), travelled extensively to collect dreams, and wrote an extant treatise ('Ονειροκριτικά) on their interpretation, a topic which had attracted the attention of serious men, as well as anecdote-mongers, since the Alexandrian age; also Οἰωνοσκοπικά and Χειροσκοπικά (palmistry). Artemidorus is important for the study of ancient folklore.

TEXT. R. Hercher (1964); R. A. Pack (1963). W. Reichardt, *De Artemidoro Daldiano* (1894); R. Dietrich, *Beitrage zu A.* (1910).
J. D. D.

**ARTEMIS** (Ἄρτεμις, occasionally Ἄρταμις), a goddess universally worshipped in historical Greece, but in all likelihood pre-Hellenic. The name yields no Greek etymology, Ἄρταμις being probably a popular assimilation of it to ἄρταμος (slaughterer, butcher; see O. Kern, *Relig. der Griechen* i (1926) 102). For features indicating a specifically Minoan origin, see M. P. Nilsson, *Minoan-Mycenaean Religion²* (1950), 432 ff.; the name occurs on a Linear B tablet as owner of a slave. She is often confused with Hecate and Selene (qq.v.), with the former owing to resemblance of character and functions, with the latter through learned speculation. Her proper sphere is the earth, and specifically the uncultivated parts, forests and hills, where wild beasts are plentiful; it is true that she is often a city-goddess, but this is a secondary development of her importance, especially among women; cf. Wilamowitz-Moellendorff, *Glaube der Hellenen* 1931–2) ii. 148, for a good sketch of her. Her place among he deities was not won immediately, for she plays a feeble and even ridiculous part in the *Iliad* (21. 470 ff.); but she is already a daughter of Zeus, 'lady of wild things' πότνια θηρῶν), sister of Apollo, a huntress and a 'lion unto women' (483), because their sudden and painless deaths re ascribed to her. Her functions as a birth-goddess and a bringer of fertility to man and beast, together with health to their offspring when born (she is often ουροτρόφος), are still obscure, at all events in the aristo-ratic circles for which Homer wrote; we may believe hat even then she was made more of among the common eople. She also was associated, in the Peloponnese particularly, with the fruitfulness of trees. Of mythology she as not much; for the story of her birth as Apollo's twin, ee LETO, DELOS; it is certain that she had originally nothing to do with him. The principal adventure which he never shares with her brother is the slaying of Orion q.v.). But it is highly probable that many of the stories of women or nymphs who bear children were originally nyths of Artemis (or some similar goddess), for being a giver of fertility she can hardly have been other than a mother-deity herself (see Farnell, op. cit. *infra*, 442 ff.); he strongest instance is perhaps Callisto, whose name is suspiciously like Artemis' title καλλίστη. However, for historical Greeks she was a virgin goddess, though a friend and helper of women in childbirth.

Concerning her cult, it is characteristic that she seldom as the larger cattle sacrificed to her. Goats are a common offering, and at Patrae Artemis Laphria was annually given a holocaust of wild beasts and birds, presided over by a priestess in a chariot drawn by stags like Artemis' own (Callimachus, *Dian.* 98 ff.; see Paus. 7. 18. 12, . Herbillon, *Cultes de Patras* (1929), 55 ff.). It is not, however, certain that this was as primitive a rite as it seems. Elsewhere her votaries simulate beast-shape, suggesting a theriomorphic form of Artemis herself. At Brauron in Attica, little girls in saffron dresses (to imitate he tawny hide of the bear?) danced before her; they were said ἀρκτεύειν, to play the bear, and were themselves called ἄρκτοι (Ar. *Lys.* 645 and schol.; Deubner, *Attische ?este* (1932), 207). The existence of the word νεβεύειν, to play the fawn, suggests a similar rite in Larissa and Demetrias (LSJ *Supplement* (1968); P. Clement, *Ant. Class.* 1934, 401 ff.). At Halae a pretence of human sacrifice was made, a few drops of blood being drawn from a man's throat with a sword (Eur. *IT* 1450 ff.); actual human sacrifice at Phocaea is alleged (Pythocles ap. Clem. Alex. *Protr.* 32, 7 Stählin; doubtfully authentic). These are some of her most characteristic and unusual rites; in many places there probably was little to distinguish her cult from that of any other important deity. That she develops into a city-goddess has already been said; occasionally she shows a connexion with agriculture (Farnell, 455 ff.).

Artemis is very often identified with foreign goddesses of a more or less similar kind. Mythologically, the most important of these identifications is with the goddess of a barbarous people in the Tauric Chersonese (*Crimea*), whose cult was said to have been imported by Orestes to Halae (see above). Historically, that having the widest-reaching results was probably with the great goddess of Ephesus, which was in many ways essentially right, hough the two cults had quite independent origins. From Ephesus the worship of this 'Artemis' was carried to Massilia by the Phocaeans, and thence again it made its way to Rome, where the Aventine temple of Diana (q.v.) had a statue modelled on the Ephesian type (Strabo 4. 1. 5). Identifications with other goddesses in Greece itself, besides Hecate and Selene, were not uncommon. A clear example is the so-called Artemis Orthia of Sparta (q.v., bibliography), where it is archaeologically certain that Orthia came thither with the Dorians, and therefore cannot have been originally the same as a pre-Hellenic deity; see *Artemis Orthia* (*JHS* Suppl. 5, 1929), 399 ff. There she was associated with the famous ordeal by scourging and with offerings of cheeses. No doubt many identifications were so complete that they now escape our notice.

From the seventh into the sixth century Artemis is commonly shown as Potnia Theron, often winged, as she sometimes is still in the fifth century. Early she normally wears a long dress, often with animal-skin, later a short tunic. She appears alone, with Apollo and sometimes Leto, or with other deities in conclave or Gigantomachy.

Farnell, *Cults* ii. 425 ff.; Nilsson, *GGR* i⁴ 481 ff.; W. K. C. Guthrie, *CAH* ii². 40. 27 ff. (1961, with bibliography).
H. J. R.; C. M. R.

**ARTEMISIA I,** princess of Caria, ruled under Persian suzerainty over Halicarnassus, Cos, Nisyrus, and Calyndus. She accompanied Xerxes' expedition with five ships. According to Herodotus, whose account (probably based on a Halicarnassian source) is strongly biased in her favour, she vainly urged Xerxes not to attack at Salamis (probably a prophecy *ex eventu*); she fought prominently in the battle and escaped pursuit by sinking an intervening Calyndian vessel. Afterwards she urged Xerxes to immediate retreat and transported part of his family to Ephesus.
P. T.

**ARTEMISIA II** succeeded her brother and husband Mausolus (q.v.) of Caria in 353–352 B.C. In his memory she started the building of the Mausoleum (q.v.), though she probably did not live to see its completion, and promoted a literary competition attended by the most famous rhetoricians (Isocrates, Theodectes, etc.); Theopompus won the prize. In 350 an attack on Rhodes by democratic exiles, relying on the support of Athens which Demosthenes (*Or.* 15) vainly tried to secure, gave Artemisia a pretext to subdue Rhodes and the adjacent islands. She died soon afterwards.

U. Kahrstedt, *Forschungen* (1910), 22 f., 114 f.; A. Momigliano, *Riv. Fil.* 1936, 54 ff.; Beloch, *Gr. Gesch.²* iii. pt. 2, 142 ff. P. T.

**ARTEMISIUM,** a promontory on the north-west coast of Euboea, so called from a temple of Artemis Proseoa on this site. The place is perhaps to be identified with the village of *Potaki* near the Bay of Penki. For the battle of Artemisium, *see* PERSIAN WARS.

G. B. Grundy, *The Great Persian War* (1901), 321 ff. P. T.

**ARTEMON** (1) (probably not later than 2nd c. B.C.), sometimes identified with Artemon (2) of Cassandreia or Artemon (3) of Pergamum, edited the letters of Aristotle with notes on the art of letter-writing.

Demetr. *Eloc.* 223, David on Arist. *Cat.* 24ᵃ28 Brandis.

**ARTEMON** (2) of Cassandreia (perhaps 2nd or 1st c. B.C.) wrote two bibliographical treatises, sometimes regarded as parts of a single work: (1) On the Collection of Books, (2) On the Use of Books, in the second book of which he discussed the three types of scolion.

*FHG* iv. 342 f.

**ARTEMON** (3) Ὁ ἀπὸ Περγάμου, also styled ὁ ἱστορικός, perhaps identical with Artemon (2) of Cassandreia, Cassandreia being his birthplace, Pergamum the scene of his literary activity (similar discrepancies in appellation often occur). He is several times mentioned in the scholia to Pindar for explanations of historical, geographical, and mythological problems.

*FGrH* 569. J. D. D.; K. J. D.

**ARTEMON** (4) of Miletus wrote, during Nero's reign, a book on dreams which come true, with special reference to cures by Sarapis, cited by Artemidorus.

*FHG* iv. 340.

**ARTEMON** (5) of Magnesia, date uncertain. Author of *Famous Exploits of Women* (Τῶν κατ᾽ ἀρετὴν γυναιξὶ πεπραγματευμένων διηγήματα), from which Sopater made excerpts.

**ARTILLERY.** In 399 B.C., at Syracuse, Dionysius I's artificers invented the first artillery (Diod. Sic. 14. 42. 1), the *gastraphetes*, shooting arrows only and somewhat resembling an early medieval cross-bow. Propellent force was supplied by a composite bow which, being too strong for a man to draw by hand, was bent by means of a mechanical stock. Later *gastraphetai*, some of which were stone-throwers, had winches (for drawing their bows) and bases.

*C.* 340 B.C., torsion catapults appear, possibly invented by Philip II's engineers (Polyidus?). Stock, winch, and base remain much the same, but two springs (τόνοι), i.e. bundles of rope made from animal sinew, horse-hair, or women's hair and held at high tension in a wooden metal-plated frame (πλινθίον), now provide propulsive power for each catapult. It took about seventy years of experimentation to develop torsion machines to full efficiency and reliability, a condition achieved *c.* 270 when calibrating formulae and lists of standard dimensions were introduced. Torsion catapults may not have ousted their non-torsion predecessors completely before the latter part of the third century.

The torsion καταπέλτης ὀξυβελής shot bolts only (main calibres from one-cubit bolt to four-cubit bolt), the λιθοβόλος hurled stone-shot (calibres ranging from ten minae to three talents). Both types had a maximum effective range certainly in excess of 300 yards. Schramm reached 387 metres with a full-size reproduction of a two-cubit ὀξυβελής employing horse-hair springs. Detailed modifications, devised between 200 B.C. and 25 B.C. and reflected in Vitruvius (10. 10–11), increased the power of standard catapults, perhaps by as much as 25 per cent.

Artillery figured most prominently in sieges (*see* SIEGE-CRAFT), in both attack and defence (e.g. Demetrius' siege of Rhodes, Diod. Sic. 20. 85 ff.). Onomarchus (Polyaenus, *Strat.* 2. 38. 2) and Alexander used it successfully in field operations, but lack of mobility severely restricted its usefulness here. It was probably quite important in Hellenistic naval warfare, *pace* Tarn, to judge by Demetrius' battle off Salamis (Diod. Sic. 20. 49–51) and Agrippa's performance at Naulochus (App. *BCiv.* 5. 118 f.) based on Hellenistic practice.

The static and mobile engines, illustrated on Trajan's Column and described by Heron Alexandrinus (*Cheiroballistra*), with all-metal πλινθία, were the most technically advanced and powerful arrow-shooting artillery ever produced and were probably designed by Greeks in Roman pay. From the fourth century B.C. onwards, Greek states large and small regarded artillery as a valuable subordinate arm and considered the production of catapults and the training of *catapeltaphetai* essential.

E. Schramm, in *Heerwesen und Kriegführung der Griechen und Römer* (J. Kromayer and G. Veith, 1928), 209 ff., with bibliography and illustrations; W. W. Tarn, *Hellenistic Military and Naval Developments* (1930), 101 ff.; E. W. Marsden, *Greek and Roman Artillery* (1969). E. W. M.

**ARULENUS RUSTICUS**, Q. JUNIUS (*PW* 149), *tr. pl.* A.D. 66, praetor 69, *cos. suff.* 92, Stoic philosopher and friend of Thrasea (q.v.) Paetus, like whom he was probably born at Patavium (see Pliny, *Epp.* i. 14. 3, on his brother Mauricus). Thrasea prevented him from vetoing the *senatus consultum* by which he was condemned to death.

He fought for Vitellius against Vespasian and was put death by Domitian because of a panegyric upon Thras and Helvidius Priscus (about 93). A. I

**ARUSIANUS MESSIUS** (late 4th c. A.D.), gramm rian, compiled an alphabetical list (*exempla elocutionu* of nouns, adjectives, verbs, and prepositions which ha more than one construction (ed. Keil, *Gramm. Lat.* 449–514). His citations from Sallust's *Historiae* a particularly valuable.

Schanz–Hosius, § 839. J. F. I

**ARVERNI,** a Gallic tribe, occupying modern *Auvergn* Craniometry and archaeology agree in assuming a co siderable pre-Celtic survival among the population. Th Arverni are reported as having long contested the prima of Gaul with the Aedui (Caesar, *BGall.* 1. 31. 3). In 2( B.C. they treated with Hasdrubal (Livy 27. 39. 6), and the next century, under Luernius and his son Bituitu their empire, according to Strabo (4. 2. 3), stretched far as the Pyrenees, the Ocean, and the Rhône. Bituitu was, however, defeated near the Rhône by Cn. Domiti Ahenobarbus and Q. Fabius Maximus (121), and sul sequently arrested at the peace conference, the Arverni empire being reduced to suzerainty over some neigl bouring tribes. In 52 Vercingetorix (q.v.), son of a form Arvernian king, led the Gallic revolt against Caesar, an defeated an attempt upon the hill-fort capital, Gergovi Under Augustus the capital was moved to Auguston metum (*Clermont-Ferrand*), and the tribe lost its powe of suzerainty; but it seemingly obtained the position *civitas libera.* Its principal temple—of Mercury Dumi —on the Puy-de-Dôme was famous for a statue erecte by the Greek Zenodorus at the cost of forty millic sesterces (Pliny, *HN* 34. 45). The region was devastate in the third century by the Alamanni, and after a hero struggle was ceded to the Visigoths in A.D. 475.

C. Jullian, *Hist. de la Gaule* ii. 546 ff., iii. 1 ff.; O. Hirschfeld, *Schr.* (1913), 200 f. C. É.

**ASCALABUS**, in mythology, son of Misme, an Att woman. His mother gave Demeter (q.v.), who was lookir for Persephone, a vessel of water, meal, and penny royal; he laughed at her for drinking it greedily, and sl threw what was left of it over him, whereat he became spotted lizard.

Anton. Lib. 24, citing Nicander; Ov. *Met.* 5. 446 ff. H. J. I

**ASCALAPHUS**, in mythology, (1) son of Ares (q.v. (2) son of Orphne (Ov. *Met.* 5. 539), a nymph of th river Acheron, or Gorgyra (Apollod. 1. 33), and Achero When Persephone was carried off by Pluto (*see* HADES Demeter obtained from Zeus a promise that she shoul return if she had eaten nothing in the lower worl Ascalaphus had seen her eat a few pomegranate-seed and betrayed her; Persephone turned him into an o (Ovid) or Demeter put him under a great stone (Apollod. H. J. I

**ASCANIUS**, the son of Aeneas (q.v. 1). According Virgil, his mother was the Trojan Creusa, and he accom panied his father to Italy after the fall of Troy (*Aen.* 2 Livy (1. 3) mentions an alternative version, that he w born from Aeneas' marriage to Lavinia after the found tion of Lavinium; and tells how he became king c Aeneas' death, but later left Lavinium and founded All Longa on the Alban Mount. Latin authors also call hi Iulus, and the *gens Iulia* claimed descent from him.

R. G. Austin on Verg. *Aen.* ii. 563, 598 (1964); Ogilvie, *Comm Livy 1–5*, 42 f. (on the political use which the Julii from 125 B. onwards made of the alleged descent). W. S. V

**ASCLEPIADES** (1) of Tragilus (4th c. B.C.), pupil of Socrates, wrote a work, Τραγῳδούμενα, on the myths of Greek tragedy and their treatment (*FGrH* i. 12), which probably became an important source for Mythographi.

**ASCLEPIADES** (2) of Samos, also called Sicelidas fl. 290 B.C.), was the chief epigrammatic poet of the Alexandrian period. In particular, he developed the love epigram, filling it with lyrical emotion and introducing some deathless symbols such as Love the archer and the child Eros. His friends Hedylus and Posidippus (2) followed and sometimes imitated him: the three published a collection of literary epigrams, the Σωρός. With Posidippus, he was attacked by Callimachus for praising the poetry of Antimachus (*Anth. Pal.* 9. 63). The 'Asclepiad' metres used by Alcaeus and Sappho bear his name because he revived them.

O. Knauer, *Die Epigramme des A. von Samos* (1935); A. Rostagni, *Poeti alessandrini* (1916) ch. 4; L. A. Stella, *Cinque poeti dell' Antologia Palatina* (1949); W. and M. Wallace, *TAPA* 1939, 191 ff. and *A. of Samos* (1941); Wilamowitz, *Hell. Dicht.* i. 146 ff. G. H.

**ASCLEPIADES** (3) of Prusa in Bithynia practised medicine in Rome, where he died at an advanced age (1st c. B.C.). A sensualist and materialist, influenced by Epicurus and Heraclides Ponticus, he accepted the atomic theory, rejecting all teleology and stressing the importance of phenomenal appearances. Opposed to the theory of humours and of the healing power of nature, he explained health as the unhindered movement of the bodily corpuscles, disease as their inhibited movement. His therapy, consisting in diet rather than in drugs, was based on the principle *tuto, celeriter, iucunde*, and made him equally well liked by high and low. His system influenced contemporary and later philosophers owing to its consistency and originality, and also as representative of a medical doctrine based on the theory of atoms in contrast to the Hippocratic and Galenic theories.

TEXT. Fragmenta, Ch. G. Gumpert (1749), not complete. List of writings: Susemihl, *Gesch. gr. Lit. Alex.* ii. 439.
LITERATURE. Summary, F. Überweg–K. Praechter, *Die Philosophie d. Altertums* (1926), 138 f., besides W. A. Heidel, *Harv. Stud.* 1911; T. C. Allbutt, *Greek Medicine in Rome* (1921); M. Wellmann, *PW* ii. 1632, still important, though antiquated in general characterization. For A.'s influence on the 17th c. see Cocchi, *Life of Asclepiades* (1762), i, and W. Dilthey, *Gesammelte Schriften* i (1922), 247. L. E.

**ASCLEPIADES** (4) of Myrleia in Bithynia (1st. c. B.C.) worked in Spain, and wrote on the history of Bithynia, and of scholarship; on Homer and Theocritus; and, as Atticist analogist, Περὶ ὀρθογραφίας. He insisted that grammar was a τέχνη: cf. Sext. Emp. *Math.* 1. 60–72.

*FGrH* iii C 697. P. B. R. F.

**ASCLEPIODOTUS** (1st c. B.C.), probably Posidonius' pupil, wrote on Greek and Macedonian military tactics. His book, the earliest extant specimen of a school treatise on a virtually dead branch of the military art, is a pedantic drill-book, in which the phalanx too often becomes a mathematical scheme. Probably it largely reproduces a lost work of Posidonius; but some things may go back through Posidonius to Polybius, and occasionally it gives an item of real value, as, e.g., that the famous Thessalian cavalry fought in a rhomboid formation.

K. K. Müller, 'Asklepiodotos' in *PW*; Illinois Greek Club, *Asclepiodotus* (Loeb, 1923). W. W. T.

**ASCLEPIUS** (Ἀσκληπιός, basic non-Ionic form Ἀσκλαπιός), hero and god of healing. In the *Iliad* he is a mortal, the 'blameless physician', taught his art by Chiron. To Hesiod and Pindar (*Pyth.* 3) he was the son of Apollo and Coronis, daughter of Phlegyas. Coronis proved faithless and with her lover Ischys was slain by Artemis, but Apollo (or Hermes, Paus. 2. 26. 6) snatched the unborn Asclepius from the pyre, and entrusted him to Chiron. For daring to restore Hippolytus to life, he was slain by a thunderbolt of Zeus. There were conflicting versions (cf. Paus. 2. 26. 3–7): Epidaurus (supported by Delphi) claimed to be his birthplace, and told how he was exposed by Coronis-Aigle and nurtured by a goat; in Messenia, Apollo and the Leucippid Arsinoë were considered his parents, in southern Arcadia, Arsippus and Arsinoë. His wife is generally called Epione, and his children include Machaon and Podalirius, the physicians of the *Iliad*, and the personifications Hygieia, Panaceia, Iaso, and (an Athenian addition) Aceso.

2. While many writers have classed Asclepius with the chthonian deities, Farnell has adduced strong evidence to show that he was in origin a hero, later elevated to full divinity; as a god, despite a few chthonian traits (e.g. the snake and possibly the rite of incubation), his associations are with the celestial divinities. His primary function, healing, is no criterion of his nature, for that art might be practised by gods, whether celestial or chthonian, or by heroes (cf. ἥρως ἰατρός at Athens). Unlike Trophonius, with whom he has been erroneously identified, he was not, except in a limited sphere, a giver of oracles, and even though, as Σωτήρ, he was on rare occasions invoked to protect from shipwreck and other ills, healing remained his chief concern.

3. The cult possibly originated at Tricca in Thessaly (Strabo 437; home of Machaon, *Il.* 4. 202), though the birth story is localized in eastern Thessaly. Thence he was carried, perhaps by the 'Phlegyans', into Phocis, where he was called Ἀ. Ἀρχαγέτας (Paus. 10. 32. 12), and Boeotia, and now probably originated his fateful alliance with Apollo. In the Peloponnesus, the cult at Titane contained certain archaic features (Paus. 2. 11. 6–8), and Hygieia may be native here. The cult at Gerenia in Messenia derived from Tricca, and even Epidaurus, despite its pretensions, never entirely forgot the Thessalian origin of Asclepius. At Epidaurus the hero, through his association with Apollo Maleatas, first attained real prominence, and Epidaurus became the metropolis from which many of the later shrines were founded: at Athens in 420 B.C. (with some non-Epidaurian influence), Pergamum (apparently 4th c.), Rome in 293–291 B.C. (see AESCULAPIUS), Balagrae of Cyrene (Paus. 2. 26. 9), and, in some degree at least, Lebene in Crete. At Cos local tradition (Herod. 2. 97) insisted on a Triccan origin. In instituting new shrines, a sacred snake, representing the god, was fetched from the mother temple; the famous story (Lucian, *Alex.*) of the charlatan Alexander's quackery at Abonuteichos is illuminating. Of the Hellenistic temples the greatest were at Epidaurus and Cos (cf. Herodas 4); under the Empire Pergamum ranked highest, and thence in Pausanias' time the cult was carried to Smyrna (Paus. 2. 26. 9).

4. The cult appealed strongly to the rising individualism of the fourth and ensuing centuries, since it provided a close personal relationship with the divine and could evoke a fervid personal devotion (as with Aelius Aristides) seldom found in the formal State religion. The number and magnificence of the temples and the quantities of ex-votos attest its popularity. The central feature of the cures was the ritual of incubation, amply described by Aristophanes (*Plut.* 653–747). Many of the recorded cures are sheer miracles, and while much was accomplished by auto-suggestion and the workings of faith, use was also made of pragmatic therapeutic methods: dietetic regimens, baths (at Pergamum in radio-active springs), and exercise. In a sense the great sanctuaries were sanatoria, equipped with theatres, gymnasia, and baths, but how far the secular physicians, sometimes designated as Asclepiadae, derived their science from the priestly craft remains an open question, though the

foundation of the temple at Cos (mid 4th c.) was perhaps due largely to disciples of Hippocrates. The chronic invalid Aelius Aristides is a valuable witness for the methods employed in his time in the cult. *See* MEDICINE, II. 9.

5. Usually associated with Asclepius were his children, especially Hygieia, personified Health; Telesphorus is a late Pergamene addition to the cult. The sacred snake regularly assists in the cures, sometimes also dogs, to which, at Piraeus, sacrifices were even ordained (*IG* ii². 4962). The organization of the cult followed normal lines; likewise the festivals for Asclepius, the Asclepieia, consisted of the usual hymns, processions, and sacrifices. Of the various paeans to Asclepius one, especially famous, continued in use at Athens for 500 years and more, and copies have been found also at Erythrae, in Macedonia, and in Egypt; late antiquity ascribed it to Sophocles, probably because of his famed 'reception' of Asclepius at Athens and consequent heroization as Δεξίων. Of epithets of Asclepius may be mentioned Σωτήρ, common on inscriptions, and Παιάν; Zeus Asclepius is late, as is σωτὴρ τῶν ὅλων and the title μύστης.

6. In art Asclepius generally appears as a mature, bearded man, similar to Zeus, but with a kindlier, milder expression; Calamis and Scopas portrayed him as beardless, and Boethus as a child. His most constant attributes are the staff (cf. rite of τῆς ῥάβδου ἀνάληψις at Cos, Hippocr. *Ep.* 11, 778 Kühn), and the snake, often coiled about the staff. Generally the god is standing, as in the fifth-century original from Emporion in Spain (R. Carpenter, *The Greeks in Spain* (U.S.A. 1925), 104 ff.); in the famous chryselephantine statue by Thrasymedes at Epidaurus, described by Pausanias (2. 27. 2) and figured on coins, Asclepius is seated, the staff in his left hand, his right extended above the head of a serpent, and beside the throne lies a dog. The scroll or tablet which he sometimes bears probably represents medical learning.

Farnell, *Hero Cults*, ch. 10; E. J. and L. Edelstein, *Asclepius* (2 vols., U.S.A. 1945); W. H. D. Rouse, *Greek Votive Offerings* (1902), ch. 5; A. Walton, *The Cult of Asklepios* (U.S.A. 1894); U. v. Wilamowitz-Moellendorff, *Isyllos von Epidauros* (1886); C. Kerényi, *Der göttliche Arzt* (1947. 1956²; Eng. trans., *Asklepios*, U.S.A. 1961). Special topics: R. Herzog, *Wunderheilungen von Epidauros* (1931); on paeans, J. H. Oliver, *Hesp.* 1936; F. Kutsch, *Attische Heilgötter und Heilheroen* (1913); on A. and Sophocles, F. R. Walton, *Harv. Stud.* 1935; W. S. Ferguson, *Harv. Theol. Rev.* 1944, 86; on A. and Aristides, A. J. Festugière, *Personal Religion among the Greeks* (1954), ch. vi; P. Schazmann and R. Herzog, *Kos*, vol. i, *Asklepieion* (1932); O. Deubner, *Das Asklepieion von Pergamon* (1938); C. Roebuck, *Corinth: Asklepieion and Lerna* (U.S.A. 1951); G. W. Bowersock, *The Sophists in the Roman Empire* (1969), ch. 5.                    F. R. W.

**ASCONIUS PEDIANUS,** QUINTUS (9 B.C.–A.D. 76; Hieron. *Chron.* on 76, the year he became blind being 64; see Clark), of Padua ('Livius noster', Asc. 68 [on Cic. *Corn.*]; Sil. *Pun.* 12. 212), a 'historicus clarus'. Quintilian (1. 7. 24) makes probable an early relationship with Livy. Servius on *Ecl.* 4. 11 implies that he knew Asinius Gallus (d. A.D. 33); *Suda* s.v. Ἀπίκιος connects him with Iunius Blaesus, *cos.* A.D. 10, not the consul of 28 (E. Klebs, *PW*). Lost writings are (1) *Vita Sallustii*, [Acron] on Hor. *Sat.* 1. 2. 41 (if the attribution is correct). (2) *Symposion*, imitating Plato, on physical exercises as promoting health and longevity (*Suda* and Pliny, *HN.* 7. 159). (3) *Contra obtrectatores Vergilii* (Donat. ap. Suet.). We possess only a fragment of his historical commentary on Cicero's orations(*Pis., Scaur., Mil., Corn., Tog. Cand.*), written between A.D. 54 and 57, and based on Cicero's published (and unpublished) works, except the letters to Atticus. Poggio found a ninth-century MS. at St. Gall: his copy is in Madrid (P. Matritensis). It was also copied by Sozomenus of Pistoja (S. Pistoriensis), and by Bartolomeo di Montepulciano (Laur. 54. 15). Included in *Sangallensis* was a fifth-century commentary on *Div.*

*Caec., Verr.* 1 and 2 to § 35. This is of grammatical character, and is quoted as pseudo-Asconius.

LIFE AND WORKS. J. N. Madvig (1828); Teuffel–Schwabe, *Gesch. d. röm. Lit.* (1900), § 295; Schanz–Hosius, § 476.
TEXTS. Kiessling–Schöll (1875): A. C. Clark (O.C.T. 1907); Th. Stangl, *Scholiastae Ciceronis Orationum* ii (1912); C. Giarretano (repr. 1965).                    G. C. R.

**ASCULUM PICENUM,** the capital of Picenum strongly placed amid imposing mountains near the Adriatic on the R. Truentus (Strabo 5. 241); modern *Ascoli Piceno*, with numerous ancient remains. Rome captured Asculum in 268 B.C. and continued the Via Salaria (q.v.) to it (Florus 1. 14). The Social War broke out here, but the Romans recovered the town after a two-year siege and grimly punished it (App. *BCiv.* 1. 38, 47, 48). In imperial times it was a *colonia* (Pliny, *HN* 3. 111). *See also* A(U)SCULUM.                    E. T. S.

**ASELLIO,** SEMPRONIUS (*PW* 16), historian, military tribune at Numantia in 134–133 B.C., wrote a history (*rerum gestae*) of his own times, not in annalistic form (*annales*) but, presumably under the influence of Polybius, with pragmatic treatment. Perhaps beginning at the destruction of Carthage, it included the year 137 B.C. in book 4, Ti. Gracchus' death in book 5, and Livius Drusus' death (91 B.C.) in book 14. In a celebrated fragment on the function of history (Gellius 5. 18. 8), he distinguishes between pragmatic *historia* and formal *annales*.

Peter, *HRRel* i², ccxlii and 179; M. Gelzer, *Kl. Schr.* iii. (1964), 93 ff., 104 ff.                    A. H. McD.

**ASIA** (continent). The name was probably derived from 'Assiuva', the Hittite designation of north-west Asia Minor; in Homer (*Il.* 2. 461) it denoted the hinterland of Ionia. Between 800 and 500 B.C. Greek explorers realized the existence of great land-masses beyond Europe and included all of these under 'Asia'. After 500 they separated Africa from Asia and fixed the boundaries of Asia at Suez and (usually) at the R. Don. Herodotus knew that a route led up the Don and into the Asian steppe; he had a fairly accurate conception of the Persian Empire as far as Babylonia, and sporadic information about Arabia, Iran, and north-west India; like most Greeks before Alexander, he gave Asia Minor a narrow neck at its eastern base. Greek knowledge of Asia progressed little until Alexander opened up the continent as far as the Syr Daria, the Himalayas, and the Jhelum, and the sea route between India and the Persian Gulf. The Hellenistic Greeks obtained some knowledge of the Ganges valley (*see* MEGASTHENES), and met Chinese travellers advancing across the Tarim basin (*see* SERES). But inner Arabia remained a secret to them, and their knowledge of the Caspian basin was inferior to that of Herodotus (*see* CASPIAN SEA, PATROCLES). The irruptions of the Parthians (250 B.C.) and of the Tochari and Sacae (150) into Iran virtually cut off the Greeks from central Asia.

In the second century A.D. the Roman emperors secured greater freedom of travel through the Parthian dominions, and Greek traders, advancing to Darau Kurghan, renewed contact with Chinese merchants and gained knowledge of the Pamirs, Tianshan, and Altai. In the first two centuries A.D. Greek traders also opened up the Indian coast as far as C. Comorin, and occasionally visited the Bay of Bengal and the Gulf of Tongking.

Cary–Warmington, *Explorers* (1929), 56 ff., 130 ff. (1963, Pelican), 73 ff., 157 ff.; Cary, *Geographic Background*, 151 ff. *See also* ARABIA, BACTRIA, HIPPALUS, INDIA, SERES, TAPROBANE.                    E. H. W.

**ASIA** (Roman province). Attalus III of Pergamum bequeathed his kingdom to the Romans. Annexed at his death in 133 B.C., it was constituted as *provincia Asia* by

Aquillius (*see* AQUILLIUS 2). Originally the province ⟨con⟩sisted of Mysia, the Troad, Aeolis, Lydia, Ionia, the ⟨isla⟩nds along the coast, and almost certainly Caria; part ⟨P⟩hrygia was given to Mithridates Euergetes of Pontus, ⟨and⟩ was not incorporated in the province till 116. Be⟨twe⟩en 56 and 50 the *conventus* of Laodicea, Apamea, and ⟨Sy⟩nnada, which lay along the route by which the governor ⟨of C⟩ilicia travelled to his province, were for convenience ⟨ass⟩igned to Cilicia. From 49 B.C. till *c.* A.D. 297 Asia ⟨inc⟩luded all the territory from Tyriaion to the sea, with ⟨its⟩ adjacent islands; it was bounded on the north by ⟨Bit⟩hynia, on the south by Lycia, and on the east (after 25 ⟨B.C.⟩) by Galatia.

⟨T⟩he province Asia was rich in natural resources and ⟨in⟩ the products of agriculture and industry (its dyed ⟨wo⟩ol fabrics were famous), and its harbours were entre⟨pot⟩s for the trade which crossed it by the Hermus and ⟨M⟩eander valley routes from the interior of Asia Minor ⟨an⟩d countries farther east. On this wealthy land the ⟨Ro⟩man republican governors and capitalists descended ⟨lik⟩e vultures, and its hatred of Rome had grown to white ⟨he⟩at when it joined Mithridates in 88–84 B.C. and partici⟨pat⟩ed in his massacre of 80,000 Italian residents in one ⟨da⟩y. In 84 Sulla reorganized Asia and (temporarily, at ⟨lea⟩st) revised its system of taxation; this year was used as ⟨th⟩e beginning of the provincial era in the eastern part of ⟨the⟩ province till the end of the imperial period. Asia con⟨tin⟩ued to suffer from arbitrary exactions during the civil ⟨wa⟩rs; order and prosperity returned to it with the founda⟨tio⟩n of the Principate. At the partition of provinces ⟨bet⟩ween Augustus and the Senate Asia became senatorial, ⟨wi⟩th a governor of consular rank who governed as pro⟨con⟩sul. He was assisted by three legates and a quaestor. ⟨Th⟩e governor landed at Ephesus, which the republican ⟨pub⟩*licani*, and later, also, the imperial procurators, made ⟨th⟩eir headquarters. Hence Ephesus rivalled Pergamum ⟨in⟩ importance, although Pergamum presumably con⟨tin⟩ued to be the seat of government of the proconsul. ⟨⟩Asia was a conglomeration of city territories; several ⟨of⟩ these cities had been autonomous in the Attalid ⟨pe⟩riod, and a few of those retained a titular freedom ⟨un⟩der the Romans. The cities, under the authority of ⟨th⟩e governor, continued to be administered by their own ⟨cou⟩ncils (membership of which was now for life) and magi⟨str⟩ates, often with the assistance of a *logistes* appointed by ⟨th⟩e Emperor, who controlled finance and expenditure. For ⟨pu⟩rposes of jurisdiction the province was divided into ⟨con⟩*ventus*. Pliny (*HN.* 5. 105 f.) listed nine of these, but ⟨hi⟩s list is perhaps incomplete; later (and earlier) there ⟨we⟩re more than nine. The number varied during both ⟨th⟩e Republic and the Principate. Provincial unity was ⟨ex⟩pressed in the *commune Asiae* (κοινὸν Ἀσίας), a General ⟨As⟩sembly of all the cities in the province, which met ⟨ann⟩ually in this or that city and provided for the official ⟨wo⟩rship of Rome and Augustus (*see* CONCILIUM). The ⟨hi⟩gh Priests of Asia (ἀρχιερεῖς τῆς Ἀσίας), who presided ⟨ov⟩er meetings of the κοινόν, should perhaps be distin⟨gu⟩ished from the Asiarchs (Ἀσιάρχαι), men of substance ⟨an⟩d benefactors of their own cities, the exact nature of ⟨wh⟩ose connexion with the κοινόν or its festival (κοινὰ ⟨Ἀσ⟩ίας) is still uncertain. City rivalries prevented the de⟨ve⟩lopment of any sense of provincial unity. In the first ⟨tw⟩o centuries of the Empire Asia enjoyed great pros⟨pe⟩rity, of which memorials survive in splendid ruins and ⟨ha⟩ndsome monuments all over the country, as well as in ⟨th⟩e works of Dio Chrysostom and Aelius Aristides. The ⟨cit⟩ies had changed from autonomous city-states into ad⟨mi⟩nistrative centres, but countless inscriptions attest the ⟨ea⟩gerness of members of the city aristocracies for public ⟨ser⟩vice, their generosity in providing civic amenities (at ⟨th⟩e expense of the rural populations they exploited) and ⟨th⟩e acquisition (by some families) of entry into the

imperial administrative aristocracy. Hellenism (and its vehicle, urbanization), completed its slow conquest of the inland regions, but the basic Anatolian element in the population of the interior was of enduring importance and stamped its own character on the religious movements that found a home there. The glittering, superficial society of the metropolitan cities of the coast, with its film-star heroes, the wealthy rhetors and sophists, was less receptive of these movements, and of Christianity in its earliest phase of expansion. The province shared in the universal sufferings of the third century, and in the fourth century, when the Anatolian roads led no longer westwards to Greece and Rome, but northwards to Constantinople, it lost its age-long position as an entrepôt of inter-continental trade. Meantime Diocletian (*c.* A.D. 297) had divided Asia into seven provinces: *see* e.g., LYDIA, PHRYGIA.

V. Chapot, *La Province romaine d'Asie* (1904); T. R. S. Broughton, in Frank, *Econ. Surv.* iv, pt. 4; Jones, *Cities E. Rom. Prov.* ch. 2; Magie, *Rom. Rule Asia Min.*; J. I. Miller, *The Spice Trade of the Roman Empire.* W. M. C.; E. W. G.

**ASISIUM**, modern *Assisi*, birthplace of Saint Francis and probably of Propertius, *municipium* of Umbria on the western slopes of the Apennines. It played little part in history until captured by Totila *c.* A.D. 545 (Procop. 7. 12). Its early imperial temple of 'Minerva' serves today as a church.

E. Zocca, *Assisi and its Environs* (Rome, 1950). E. T. S.

**ASIUS** of Samos (? 7th or 6th c. B.C.), poet (Ath. 3. 125 b ποιητὴν παλαιόν); author of genealogies, satirical poetry in hexameters (on the luxury of the Samians), and elegiacs.

*EGF* 202–5.

**ASKOLIASMOS** (ἀσκωλιασμός), a country sport in Attica. The players tried to keep their balance while jumping on an inflated and greasy wineskin (ἀσκός). The occasion seems to have been the Rural Dionysia (*see* DIONYSIA; Cornutus, *Theol. Graec.*, 60, 23 Lang; *Suda*, s.v.; Verg. *G.* 2. 384). That it was a religious or magical ceremony and that it belonged to any other festival seem to be mis-statements; see L. Deubner, *Attische Feste* (1932), 117, 135. H. J. R.

**ASMONIUS** (5th c. A.D.), author of works on grammar and metre (now lost) which Priscian used.

Schanz–Hosius, § 825.

**ASPASIA**, of Milesian family, lived with Pericles as his mistress from *c.* 445 B.C. after he had divorced his wife, till his death. She was a woman of considerable intellectual stature who conversed with Socrates and taught rhetoric. She was naturally enough the subject of politically inspired attacks, particularly in comedy. In addition to charges of immorality, she was supposed to have influenced Pericles unduly and to have induced him to start the Samian and Peloponnesian Wars. Aristophanes parodies these imputations in the *Acharnians* (515–539). She was prosecuted (the date is uncertain) for impiety and procuring by the comedian Hermippus (q.v. 1); but Pericles, the real object of this and the associated attacks, defended her passionately and successfully. Their son, excluded from citizenship under Pericles' own law of 451/0, was legitimated by decree after the death in the Plague of his two sons by his wife, and took his father's name; he was one of the generals executed after Arginusae (*see* PELOPONNESIAN WAR § 6). After Pericles' death in 429 Aspasia associated with Lysicles, a popular leader killed in 428. Her friendship with Socrates caused her to be remembered and written about by his followers, including Antisthenes (q.v. 1), Aeschines (q.v. 2), and Plato (*Menex.* 235 e–236 d, 249 d, e).

G. Busolt, *Gr. Gesch.* (1893–1904), iii. 505 ff. T. J. C.

**ASPASIUS** (*c.* A.D. 100–150), Peripatetic. His commentaries on Aristotle's *Cat.*, *Int.*, *Metaph.*, *Ph.*, and *Cael.*, and his *Libellus de naturalibus passionibus* are lost; his commentary on the *Eth. Nic.* survives in part (ed. G. Heylbut, 1889).

**ASPENDUS**, a Greek colony in Pamphylia, claiming descent from Argos. Its name (Estvediys on the early coins) is perhaps connected with the Asitawandas lately known from the inscriptions of Karatepe. Though assessed as a member of the Delian League (*IG*[2] i. 64), it preferred Persian rule, even resisting Alexander. Occupied by Ptolemy I, it was later subject to the Seleucids till 189 B.C., when C. Manlius admitted it to the alliance of the Roman people. Situated 8 miles from the mouth of the Eurymedon, which was navigable as far as the city, it was an important harbour. The ruins at *Belkis*, especially the theatre and the aqueduct, are unusually well preserved.

K. Lanckoroński, *Städte Pamphyliens* (1890) i. 85 ff.
A. H. M. J.; G. E. B.

**ASPER**, AEMILIUS (late 2nd c. A.D.), wrote commentaries (now lost) on Terence, Sallust (*Historiae* and *Cat.*), and Virgil, which dealt with subject-matter and diction and included parallels from Greek and Latin authors. Aelius Donatus (q.v. 1) probably borrowed freely from him. The *ars* extant under his name (ed. Keil, *Gramm. Lat.* 5. 547–54) is apocryphal.

A. Tomsin, *Étude sur le Commentaire Virgilien d' Aemilius Asper* (1952); Schanz–Hosius, § 598. J. F. M.

**ASPRENAS**, NONIUS, the name of two Augustan rhetoricians, Lucius and Publius, whose declamations are mentioned in Seneca's *Controversiae* and *Suasoriae*.

Schanz–Hosius § 336, 9 n. 11.

**ASSONANCE, GREEK.** Assonance is the recurrence of a sound in words which strikes the ear. The definition is, of necessity, subjective; and the Greek ear seems not to have noticed recurrences which strike our ear harshly; e.g. Eur. *Alc.* 160 ἐλούσατ', ἐκ δ' ἐλοῦσα; *IT* 1339, *Phoen.* 1174, *Or.* 238, Soph. *Phil.* 372. The Greeks tolerated such homoeoteleuta as Thuc. 2. 43. 6 ὁ μετὰ ῥώμης καὶ κοινῆς ἐλπίδος ἅμα γιγνόμενος ἀναίσθητος θάνατος (cf. [Andoc.] 4. 39, Pl. *Leg.* 949 c, Dem. 18. 238). Euripides, however, was taunted, perhaps unfairly, with putting in too many sigmas (Plato Com. fr. 30, Eubulus fr. 26–7).

(1) ALLITERATION. There are a few apparently intentional examples in Homer (e.g. Φ 181 χύντο χαμαὶ χολάδες, more in Aeschylus, not so many in Sophocles and Euripides. Alliterations in π are the most numerous. (The commonness of π as an initial letter does not wholly account for this.) Next come α and κ. The most famous example is Soph. *OT* 371 τυφλὸς τά τ' ὦτα τόν τε νοῦν τά τ' ὄμματ' εἶ. Cf. also Aesch. *Ag.* 819–20, *Cho.* 89, 566, Soph. *El.* 210, Eur. *Hipp.* 1201–2, *Phoen.* 488–9. In the prose of the pre-Socratics alliteration undoubtedly plays a part (cf. Heraclit. fr. 25, Democr. frs. 164, 193, 215, 258, Gorg. fr. 11. 4, 8), also perhaps in Thucydides (1. 69. 1, 81. 5–6; 6. 9. 1; 7. 68. 1), and Plato (*Ap.* 39 a, *Resp.* 609 a, *Leg.* 634 e, 666 e, 688 e, 730 c, 923 a), while it is virtually absent from Herodotus, Xenophon, and the orators. Plato's use of assonance is perhaps a legacy from earlier philosophers. At Pl. *Symp.* 197 d (Agathon) ἐν πόνῳ, ἐν φόβῳ, ἐν πόθῳ, ἐν λόγῳ κυβερνήτης the medial assonance is no doubt intentional.

(2) RHYME. Theognis (in marked contrast to Tyrtae has 'leonine' rhyme in one pentameter out of seven 173–83, 390–6), which can hardly be accidental. Ther little evidence for intentional rhyme in epic, or in trage but we can perhaps, as Herrmanowski suggests, dete tendency to employ it in proverbs (e.g. Soph. *OT* 110– and in *loci communes* at the end of a scene (e.g. Eur. *M* 408–9). There are more examples in comedy (e.g. *Ach.* 30–4, 1087–92, *Pax* 341–4; Alexis fr. 141. 9– Rhyme is clearly present in some of the late *Anacreon* (e.g. 38). In prose, Demosthenes does not seek rhym clauses, perhaps actually avoids them, while in Gorg Isocrates, and writers of the Isocratean school they are important part of the stock-in-trade, and double rhym often employed (e.g. Isoc. 4. 18 καινῶς διελθεῖν . ἀρχαίως εἰπεῖν).

(3) PUNNING ASSONANCE, extending over the grea part of the two words, including Cicero's 'immutati litterae quasi quaesitae venustates' (*Orat.* 84). With the pun is usually humorous; with the Greeks it often serious (Aesch. *PV* 693 ψύχειν ψυχάν), sometim the means for enforcing a philosophical lesson. T Aesch. *Ag.* 177 πάθει μάθος, Heraclit. fr. 114, Demo fr. 57, Pl. *Grg.* 493 a (σῶμα–σῆμα, πίθος–πιθανός). But Plato the pun, including puns on proper names, is of humorous or semi-humorous (*Leg.* 803 a τροπιδεία–τρόπ 834 d Κρῆς οὐκ ἄχρηστος, 956 e κληρώσεις–πληρώσ *Epin.* 982 e πορείαν–χορείαν), sometimes with a hit at sophists (*Symp.* 185 c Παυσανίου παυσαμένου, *Grg.* 49 λόγον καὶ ψόγον, in Callicles' mouth, *Prt.* 345 b χρόν πόνου, a backhanded compliment to Protagoras). Gorg λαβοῦσα–λαθοῦσα (fr. 11. 4) is a typical sophistic instan and φήμη–μνήμη, ῥώμη–γνώμη are common form in t style. Xenophon sometimes indulges in naïve puns (ε *An.* 2. 2. 1 Μένων–ἔμενε). For punning on proper nam see ETYMOLOGY, § 1.

O. Dingeldein, *Der Reim b. d. Griechen und Römern* (189 C. Riedel, *Alliteration b. d. griech. Tragikern* (1900); P. Herrman ski, *De homoeoteleutis quibusdam tragicorum* (1881); K. Polheim, *lateinische Reimprosa* (1925), 133 ff. (rhyme in Greek prose); Nord *Ant. Kunstpr.* 810 ff.; J. D. Denniston, *Greek Prose Style* (195 124 ff. J. D.

**ASSONANCE, LATIN.** Assonance in varying ma festations is native to Latin, aided by the structure of t language and abetted by stylistic developments.

(1) ALLITERATION. This appears in proverbs (Ot *Sprichwörter*, xxxii), prayers, legal formulae, etc.: 'flamma fumo est proxuma' (Plaut. *Curc.* 53); 'mer malae Maio nubunt' (see Ovid, *Fast.* 5. 490); 'ni utilius sale et sole' (Pliny, *HN* 31. 102); 'salua res e saltat senex' (Servius on *Aen.* 8. 110); (*b*) 'utique fruges frumenta uineta uirgultaque grandire bene euenire siris, pastores pecuaque salua seruassis' (Ca *Agr.* 141); (*c*) 'donum datum donatum dedicatumqu (*CIL* I[2]. 756); 'manu mancipio' (Thes. L. L. 8. 254. 7 'per lancem liciumque' (Gell. 11. 18. 9).

In early literature it is marked in Saturnians: 'quo uita defecit, non honos, honore | is hic situs quei nu quam uictus est uirtutei' (*CIL* I[2]. 1), 'inmortales morta si foret fas flere' (Naevius' epitaph, Gell. 1. 24. Plautus revels in it: 'sator sartorque scelerum et mess maxume' (*Capt.* 661), 'ex malis multis malum qu minimum est id minume est malum' (*Stich.* 120). Ennius its use ranges from the embarrassing ('nec cu capta capi nec cum combusta cremari', *Ann.* 359; Tite tute Tati tibi tanta tyranne tulisti', ibid. 109) to t noble ('lumine sic tremulo terra et caua caerula canden *Sc.* 292; 'o magna templa caelitum commixta ste splendidis', *Sc.* 196). Pacuvius has a fine example (246 'lassitudinemque minuam manuum mollitudine'.

In time, alliteration becomes increasingly integra with poetic art. Lucretius, though not entirely remov from the earlier manner, uses it with striking power in many memorable passages. The Augustans all make it do their bidding, Virgil especially (e.g. *Aen.* 2. 692 ff., 4. 651 ff.): it is now no longer an external ornament applied more or less selfconsciously, but an inner secret of sound, subtly deployed to serve emotion.

Prose employs alliteration constantly, often to point a rhetorical antithesis: contrast the naïveté of 'patrem primum, postea patronum proximum nomen habuere' (Cato, *Or. fr.* 200 M) with 'portum potius paratum nobis et perfugium putemus, quo utinam uelis passis peruehi liceat' (Cic. *Tusc.* 1. 119), or 'te non custodem ad continendas sed portitorem ad partiendas mercis missum putares' (Cic. *Vat.* 12). Tacitus especially likes alliterative pairs of words, sometimes on the archaic pattern: 'fortuna famaque' (*Hist.* 3. 32), 'largitio et luxus' (*Ann.* 4. 1), 'spes in uirtute, salus ex uictoria' (*Ann.* 2. 20), 'socordia ducum, seditione legionum' (*Hist.* 3. 46). Obtrusiveness returns with the second-century archaizers (Fronto, Apuleius).

(2) HOMOEOTELEUTON, often combined with alliteration, is another aspect of assonance. The Roman ear could take such thunder as this: 'coactus lacrimis omnium ciuium Romanorum qui in Sicilia negotiantur, adductus Valentinorum, hominum honestissimorum, omniumque Reginorum testimoniis multorumque equitum Romanorum' (Cic. *Verr.* 5. 158); it could be excited by this: 'tandem aliquando, Quirites, L. Catilinam furentem audacia, scelus anhelantem, pestem patriae nefarie molientem, uobis atque huic urbi ferro flammaque minitantem ex urbe uel eiecimus uel emisimus uel ipsum egredientem uerbis prosecuti sumus' (Cic. *Cat.* 2. 1). Poetry produces such effects as 'dulce ridentem Lalagen amabo, | dulce loquentem' (Hor. *Carm.* 1. 22. 23 f.), 'bello armantur equi, bellum haec armenta minantur' (Verg. *Aen.* 3. 540), flebant et cineri ingrato suprema ferebant' (id. ib. 6. 213), 'tendebantque manus ripae ulterioris amore' (id. ib. 6. 314).

(3) Such assonances tend inevitably towards a species of RHYME, as in the early magic formula 'terra pestem teneto, salus hic maneto in pedibus meis' (Varro, *Rust.* 1. 2. 27) or the sophisticated Virgilian 'limus ut hic durescit et haec ut cera liquescit' (*Ecl.* 8. 80). Rhetorical prose structure easily produces such turns as ' "in balneis desiluerunt." testis egregios! "dein temere prosiluerunt." homines temperantis!' (Cic. *Cael.* 63); they become exaggerated in Apuleius (e.g. *Met.* 11. 25 'tuo nutu spirant lamina, nutriunt nubila, germinant semina, crescunt germina'), Tertullian, and St. Augustine. Grammatical 'rhyme' is frequent in poetry: 'haec omnia uidi inflammari, | Priamo ui uitam euitari, | Iouis aram sanguine turpari' (Ennius, *Sc.* 97 ff.); 'terribilem cristis galeam flammasque uomentem, | fatiferumque ensem, loricam ex aere rigentem, | sanguineam, ingentem' (Verg. *Aen.* 8. 620 ff.); 'uile solum Sparte est, altae cecidere Mycenae; Oedipodioniae quid sunt nisi nomina Thebae? | quid Pandioniae restant nisi nomen Athenae?' (Ovid, *Met.* 15. 428 ff.).

The '*leonine*' *hexameter* with disyllabic rhyme occurs sometimes in Virgil (e.g. *Aen.* 3. 36, 10. 756) and other classical poets (e.g. Lucretius 1. 318; Ovid, *Ars Am.*, 1. 59, *Met.* 6. 247). Its special vogue in the eleventh century A.D. coincided with the full development of deliberate rhyming in the accentual hymn-form (first seen extensively in Sedulius and Venantius Fortunatus, 5th and 6th c.) and in secular medieval lyric: the potential of assonance is now 'modernized', and Latin poetry gains new beauty in a late blossoming.

J. Cousin, *Bibliographie de la langue latine* (1951), 215 ff. (valuable); A. Cordier, *L'Alliteration latine* (1939)—primarily concerning the *Aeneid*, but with important bibliographical treatment.—E. Wölfflin, *zur Alliteration* (1881, repr. in *Ausgewählte Schriften* [Leipzig, 1933], 225 ff., with detailed lists of 'allitierende Verbindungen'); id. in

*Archiv f. lat. Lex.* 1 (1884), 310 ff., 3 (1886), 443 ff.; C. Boetticher, *De alliterationis apud Romanos ui et usu* (diss. Berlin, 1884); O. Dingeldein, *Der Reim bei den Griechen und Römern* (1892); L. Mueller, *De re metrica²* (Leipzig, 1894), 560 ff.; Norden, *Ant. Kunstpr.*; W. J. Evans, *Alliteratio Latina* (1921); K. Polheim, *Die lateinische Reimprosa* (St. Petersburg–Berlin, 1925); F. J. E. Raby, *Christian Latin Poetry²* (1953), 20 ff. (useful bibliography); J. Marouzeau, *Traité de stylistique appliquée au latin* (1935), 42 ff.; L. R. Palmer, *The Latin Language* (1954); W. Beare, *Latin Verse and European Song* (1957); N. I. Herescu, *La Poésie latine* (1960), chs. 4–6; L. P. Wilkinson, *Golden Latin Artistry* (1963), 25 ff. R. G. A.

**ASSOS,** an impregnable site on the Gulf of Adramyttium, facing south towards Lesbos (it was originally colonized from Methymna) and controlling the coast road. The harbour is artificial. The public buildings rose in terraces on the steep hillside in a unified architectural scheme; impressive fortifications are still extant. Except in the fourth century B.C. the history of Assos is inseparable from the general history of the Troad. Ariobarzanes was besieged here in 365. Subsequently Hermias (q.v. 1) made Assos the centre for a school of Platonists, amongst whom Aristotle was numbered. It was the birthplace of the Stoic philosopher Cleanthes.

J. T. Clarke, F. H. Bacon, R. Koldewey, *Investigations at Assos 1881–1883* (1921). D. E. W. W.

**ASSYRIA** (Greek and Roman), the name applied by Herodotus (1. 178, 185, etc.), Xenophon (*Cyr.* 2. 5), and later writers (e.g. Pliny) to the whole country between the Armenian and Iranian mountains and the Syro-Arabian desert. More properly, Assyria denoted the ancient kingdom on the Upper Tigris, bounded on the north and east by the Masius range and the Kurdish hills—the centre of the great Assyrian Empire (c. 1000–612 B.C.). In the Parthian period the kingdom of Adiabene (q.v.) comprised most of the old territory of Assyria. Part of the Parthian city of Asshur, the ancient capital, can be reconstructed from excavations on the site.

The province of Assyria formed by Trajan in A.D. 116 and abandoned by Hadrian (Eutrop 8. 2; Ruf. Fest. 14 and 20) corresponds to the later Sassanid 'Asorestan', i.e. Lower Mesopotamia or Babylonia, including Ctesiphon (q.v.).

W. Andrae, *Das wiedererstandene Assur* (1938); A. Maricq, *Syria* 1959, 254 ff. M. S. D.; E. W. G.

**ASTERIA,** in mythology, sister of Leto (q.v.), mother, by Perses, of Hecate (q.v.). Being pursued by Zeus (Callimachus, *Del.* 38; Hyginus, *Fab.* 53, and several other authors; Nonnus, *Dion.* 2. 125, says it was Poseidon), who was in love with her, she turned into a quail, leaped into the sea (or was thrown into it), and then became Ortygia, i.e. Quail Island, afterwards Delos; the time and occasion of her turning into a quail are variously told. As her name means Starry, it appears as if the story were put together from disparate elements, perhaps an idea that the island was originally a falling star, i.e. meteorite, and also a desire to explain its alleged old name. See for more material Schirmer in Roscher's *Lexikon,* s.v. H. J. R.

**ASTRAGALUS.** Knucklebones (ἀστράγαλοι) were used especially by Greek women, in various simple games such as children now play with stones, and were also employed as dice. The four long faces of the knucklebones were of different shapes, one flat, one irregular, one concave, and one convex, and in dicing these had the value respectively of 1, 6, 3, 4. F. A. W.

**ASTROLOGY.** Ancient astronomy sought to reduce to mathematical order the apparent motions of the heavenly bodies. Astrology was concerned with the supposed effects of these heavenly bodies on human destinies. Its fundamental faith was that a universal 'sympathy' binds heaven to earth. And, as astronomy by prolonged observation had learned to predict the recurrence of heavenly phenomena, astrology professed to be a science which could forecast the earthly happenings which depend on the heavenly. This view of things, with its blend of religious and scientific elements, was first elaborated in the temples of Mesopotamia, and spread thence to Egypt. It had no great influence on Greek life until after the death of Alexander, when Greeks and Orientals mingled in the kingdoms of the Seleucids and Ptolemies. From this time on it became an increasingly important factor in the civilization of Greece and Rome, reaching its apogee in imperial times, and affecting every level of society. It is only the underworld of astrology that is represented by the casters of horoscopes, the *Chaldaei* and *mathematici*, assailed by Roman magistrates and satirists. At its highest it commanded the ardent allegiance of the best minds of the ancient world. Hardly a branch of ancient culture remained unaffected by it. The Stoic philosophers, trained in Greek thought, partially secularized this ancient temple wisdom, but gave it fresh currency. The astronomers Hipparchus and Ptolemy believed in it. It affected medicine profoundly. It found poetical expression in the *Astronomica* of Manilius and architectural embodiment in the Pantheon. It supplemented the *Ius Civile* by the concept of Natural Law. *See also* FATE.

TEXTS. *CCAG.* A. Bouché Leclercq, *L'Astrologie grecque* (1889); O. Neugebauer and H. B. van Hoesen, *Greek Horoscopes* (U.S.A. 1959); Cumont, *Rel. or.*, ch. 7 (a brilliant short account, with bibliography): Cumont, *L'Égypte des astrologues* (1937) which demonstrates the fresh light thrown on the ancient world by the progress of this branch of study. W. and H. G. Gundel, *Die astrologische Literatur in der Antike* (1967). B. F.

*Astrology and the Roman government.* Astrological studies and research were not hampered at Rome (witness the work and interest of Varro (2) and Nigidius Figulus, qq.v.), but on certain occasions (generally of some internal tension) measures were taken against professional astrologers who were practising their craft. These took the form of expulsion from Rome and Italy, though the rest of the Empire was unaffected. At least nine such expulsion orders are known between 139 B.C. and A.D. 93, based on magisterial order (in 139 and 33 B.C.), senatusconsultum (in A.D. 16 and 52), or imperial edict (as in 69). The measures, which sometimes included sorcerers, philosophers, and other diviners, branded such activities as temporarily undesirable, but they did not aim at establishing any permanent ban. Augustus, however, in A.D. 11 issued an edict which, besides publishing his own horoscope, forbade the prophesying of the date of the death of anyone and enacted that no diviner should prophesy secretly to any one person alone. The political implications are obvious: private consultations *de principis salute* might seem—or be—treasonable. These restrictions, though difficult to enforce, apparently remained 'on the statute book' until the fourth century. But Ulpian (early third century A.D.) clearly asserts that the theoretical study of astrology was legal during the Principate. Thus there is no contradiction with the reliance that so many emperors, as Tiberius, placed upon the art and its practitioners (*see* THRASYLLUS, BALBILLUS). Diocletian took the step of banning all divination throughout the Empire: 'ars autem mathematica damnabilis interdicta est' (*Cod. Iust.* 9. 18. 2). This again may have had only temporary effects, but with the Christian emperors of the fourth and fifth centuries political reasons were reinforced by religious motives, and the ban was made permanent. Thus Constantius in 357 made divination a capital offence, and the ban was repeated in 373 and 409 (*Cod. Theod.* 9. 16. 4, 8, 12).

F. H. Cramer, *Astrology in Roman Law and Politics* (U.S.A. 1954); R. MacMullen, *Enemies of the Roman Order* (U.S.A. 1967), ch. iv. H. H. S.

**ASTRONOMY.** From the earliest times the Greeks had used the rising and setting of certain stars as calendaric markers (e.g. Hes. *Op.* 619 ff.); but they had nothing that could be called astronomy in the scientific sense until comparatively late. The cosmological theories of the pre-Socratic philosophers, though containing occasional glimpses of the truth, were purely speculative. Most of the 'scientific discoveries' and feats attributed by later writers to the sixth-century philosophers, such as Thales' (q.v.) eclipse prediction, are unworthy of belief. During the fifth century, however, some of the concepts which are a necessary prerequisite for a science of astronomy were propounded. The sphericity of the earth was mentioned in Parmenides (q.v.) (A 44 D–K), who also stated that the moon receives its light from the sun (B 15). Empedocles (q.v.) not only said this but inferred the cause of solar eclipses (B 42). Anaxagoras said the same (A 77). Yet how unfamiliar all this was even in the late fifth century is shown by the remark of Thucydides (whose education was extraordinary for his time) that solar eclipses *seem* only to occur at new moon (2. 28). See also Plato *Crat.* 409 a–b. Whatever 'astronomical' activity there was in the fifth century centred on (*a*) the risings and settings of stars and perhaps description of the constellations (the zodiac was imported from Babylon as early as Cleostratus of Tenedos (2nd half of 6th c.), if the lines quoted from him are genuine); (*b*) observations of solstice and equinox, and establishment of luni-solar cycles. In the latter connexion the most famous name is Meton (q.v.). Both these activities were directed mainly towards practical, i.e. calendaric, purposes. There seems to have been general ignorance about the planets. Democritus, according to Seneca (*QNat.* 7. 3. 2) said that he *suspected* that there were several (*plures*) planets, but gave neither number nor names. In the same place Seneca attributes the introduction of knowledge of the planetary motions to Eudoxus (q.v. 1), and this is not unlikely: he is the first Greek who is *known* to have recognized the five planets (for it is impossible to sort out the genuinely early material from among what is attributed to Pythagoras and his school, and the passages in Plato, *Resp.* 616 d– 617 b and *Ti.* 38 c ff., where the five planets are hinted at, may well be later than Eudoxus' publication). But Eudoxus is also the first to have constructed a system of mathematical astronomy in his 'theory of homocentric spheres'. The observational data incorporated into this, namely crude synodic and sidereal periods of the heavenly bodies, were probably derived from a Babylonian source (Seneca, l.c., says Eudoxus imported 'the motions' from Egypt, but what is known of Egyptian 'astronomy' makes this highly unlikely). But the idea of constructing a geometrical model to account for the phenomena was peculiarly Greek. Eudoxus' system was of great mathematical elegance, and succeeded in reproducing the motions qualitatively, but it would take little observation to establish its disagreement with the facts. In particular no homocentric system could account for the obvious variations in size and brightness of, e.g., the moon and Venus. Nevertheless Callippus (q.v.) modified Eudoxus' system to eliminate some of the grosser discrepancies with the truth, and Aristotle provisionally accepted this modified system (*Cael.*, *Metaph.* Λ 8), and made what had probably been for Eudoxus a purely geometrical scheme into a physical mechanism with contiguous solid spheres. Other astronomical activity in the fourth century was concerned with the traditional subjects, the calendar (Eudoxus' *Octaeteris* and Callippus' 76-year cycle) and star risings, etc. (Eudoxus' *Phaenomena*). The earliest extant astronomical works, those of Autolycus (2) and Euclid (qq.v.), are nothing but a treatment of the latter in terms of elementary geometry. At this period Heraclides (q.v. 1) of Pontus put forward a new planetary system parently suggesting, among other things, that the earth evolves on its axis. The same idea was incorporated in the heliocentric hypothesis of Aristarchus (q.v. 1) of amos. Both of these, however, were purely descriptive nd non-mathematical. But there was also serious observation going on in the early third century: Aristyllus and 'imocharis in Alexandria attempted to fix the position of ars, and recorded details of occultations. Aristarchus o was an observer, but his only extant work, *On the izes and Distances of the Sun and Moon*, is more of a athematical exercise than a piece of serious astronomy. he third century probably saw a good deal of astronomical activity, including the production of mathematical heories, but our knowledge of it, even of the astronomical works of Archimedes (q.v.), is very slight. Important rogress was made by Apollonius (q.v. 2), who proved he equivalence of the (already existing)? epicyclic and eccentric theories for planetary motion, and applied them o the motion of the moon and the problem of planetary etrogradation. The ground was thus laid for the work of Hipparchus (q.v. 3), who used Apollonius' theoretical structure, extensive Babylonian eclipse records, and his wn systematic observations and practical skill to produce he first satisfactory theory for the motion of sun and oon (*c.* 150 B.C.). This was his greatest success, though e also made advances in every field of astronomy then tudied, in particular discovering the precession of the quinoxes. The only work of importance between him nd Ptolemy was done by Menelaus (q.v. 3), whose pherical trigonometry was probably the first. Ptolemy . A.D. 140) brought Greek astronomy to its acme. His *lmagest* ($\mu\alpha\theta\eta\mu\alpha\tau\iota\kappa\dot\eta$ $\sigma\dot\upsilon\nu\tau\alpha\xi\iota\varsigma$) is a systematic exposition of the whole field from first principles. He took over Hipparchus' solar and lunar theory, introducing a major orrection into the latter. He compiled a catalogue of tars, giving ecliptic co-ordinates and magnitudes, mostly rom his own observations. He constructed a theory of notion for the five planets (Hipparchus had refrained rom this because of the insufficiency of his data); for his he used the traditional epicycle and eccentric, but lso introduced an innovation of his own, the equant. It as thus possible to predict the position of all the known eavenly bodies at a given moment, all the details of clipses, the retrogradations of the planets (both times and rc-lengths), and the appearances and disappearances $\phi\dot\alpha\sigma\epsilon\iota\varsigma$) of the planets and fixed stars, all with accuracy y the standards of observation of the time (Ptolemy eckoned agreement within 10′ of arc as satisfactory). fter Ptolemy no significant advances were made in ntiquity: his system became canonical, and even the orrections that were applied to it by Islamic astronomers ere on points of detail, made possible by the longer eriod over which observations could be compared.

The astronomy of the Greeks covered only a part of hat is now comprised in the term. It was essentially a ystem for *predicting* the positions of the sun, moon, and lanets and the resulting phenomena rather than an xplanation thereof. Its basis, in the classical form, was in eometrical schemes of motion. There were also purely rithmetical schemes derived from Babylonian astronomy. It is not surprising to find these, in view of the eavy dependence of Hipparchus and Ptolemy on Babylonian records of astronomical observations. Yet they are igidly excluded from the *Almagest*: our knowledge of hem comes mostly from papyri and astrological works, e. the 'vulgar' astronomical literature. An early example s found in the $\dot\alpha\nu\alpha\phi\omega\rho\iota\kappa\dot\varsigma$ of Hypsicles (q.v.) of the econd century B.C. Physical astronomy, however, remained at a very low level (as did physics in general). It mostly ignored altogether in astronomical works. In ook 2 of Ptolemy's *Planetary Hypotheses* we do indeed nd an attempt to fit the kinematical models of the

*Almagest* into an explanatory physical system, but the theory of motion involved is as primitive as Aristotle's. Similarly such discussion as there was of the composition and evolution of the heavenly bodies remained at the level of speculation, and was carried on by philosophers rather than astronomers. Even the relative and absolute distances of the planets could not be determined scientifically (the *Almagest* gives only the distances of sun and moon). In such a situation the heliocentric hypothesis, with no physical or mechanical theory to support it, held no advantage over the geocentric, and suffered the severe disadvantage that for purposes of prediction all calculations must ultimately be geocentric. It is neither surprising nor reprehensible that Aristarchus' suggestion had no success in antiquity. Within its limits, Greek astronomy in its final development was highly successful, astonishingly so when we consider the crudity of observational instruments and the fewness of observations (Hipparchus and Ptolemy seem to have been the only astronomers who made *systematic* observations). The long life of the Ptolemaic system was not undeserved. For the effect which astronomical studies, in particular the theory of sundials, had on developments in mathematics, *see also* MATHEMATICS.

Best general account in J. L. E. Dreyer, *A History of the Planetary Systems from Thales to Kepler*, (1905), repr. as *A History of Astronomy from Thales to Kepler* (U.S.A. 1953). Particularly useful on the earlier period is P. Tannery, *Histoire de l'astronomie ancienne* (1893). For information on 'astronomy' in the pre-Socratics see T. L. Heath, *Aristarchus of Samos* (1913, repr. 1959). For a detailed account of the content of ancient works, J. B. J. Delambre, *Histoire de l'astronomie ancienne*, 2 vols. (1817), is still indispensable. See also D. R. Dicks, *Early Greek Astronomy to Aristotle* (1970). On Babylonian astronomy and traces of its methods in Greek texts see O. Neugebauer, *The Exact Sciences in Antiquity*[2] (U.S.A. 1957), chs. 5 and 6.
G. J. T.

**ASTURES,** an ethnographical group of north-western Spain, holding the northern coastline between the Callaeci and the Cantabri, and reaching south across the mountains. Before their conquest by Augustus they were known as rude and predatory highlanders. The census of Pliny, *HN* 3. 28 estimated 240,000 free men divided between the Transmontani of the north and the Augustani of the south. Pacified by Roman legions (26–19 B.C.), the Astures furnished gold, chrysocolla, minium, horses, and auxiliary troops. They formed an imperial *conventus*, whose capital Asturica Augusta (*Astorga*) was described by Pliny as 'urbs magnifica'. The quarters of the *Legio VII Gemina* (*León*) developed into a large place. Remains of Roman walls survive in both towns. An intricate road system, to aid transport of minerals, was constructed by the emperors from Augustus to Gratian.

A. Schulten, *Los Cantabros y Astures* (1943); M. Gómez Moreno, *Catálogo Monumental de España: Provincia de León* (1925); R. Syme, *AJPhil.* 1934, 293 ff.; I. A. Richmond, *JRS* 1931, 86 ff.
J. J. V. N.; M. I. H.

**ASTYANAX** or *Scamandrius* (*Il.* 6. 402), in mythology, young son of Hector and Andromache (qq.v.). At the capture of Troy he was flung from the walls by Neoptolemus (q.v. 1; *Little Iliad*, fr. 19 Allen) or killed by Odysseus (*Iliu Persis*). Astyanax' death is often shown in connexion with that of Priam in archaic and classical pictures of the Sack of Troy. Polygnotus in his Troy at Delphi showed Priam dead but Astyanax still alive, a baby at his mother's breast in the Greek camp (Brommer, *Vasenlisten*[2], 286).
H. J. R.; C. M. R.

**ASTYDAMAS,** the name of two poets of the fourth century B.C., father and son. The father was the son of Morsimus the son of Philocles (nephew of Aeschylus) (*Suda*, s.v.). It is uncertain to which some of the records about 'Astydamas' refer. One of the two was a pupil of Isocrates (436–338 B.C.) in rhetoric before he became a poet. The elder produced his first play in 398 B.C., and one of the two (probably the son) won his first victory in 372 (*Marm. Par.* 71). The elder is said to have lived to the age of 60 (Diod. Sic. 14. 43. 5), and if this is true the inscriptional records (*IG* ii.² 2320) which note Dionysiac victories in 341 with the *Achilles*, *Athamas*, and *Antigone*, and in 340 with the *Parthenopaeus* and *Lycaon* must refer to the son, and the ascription by the *Suda* and Photius of the *Parthenopaeus* to the father must be a mistake. The Athenians were so delighted with this play that they erected a statue to the poet in the theatre (Diog. Laert. 2. 43), and a fragment of the base of this survives, but he was not allowed to inscribe on it the conceited verses which made his name a byword for vanity (*Suda*, s.v. σαυτὴν ἐπαινεῖς). The son was evidently famous in his day. Aristotle notes (*Poet.* 14) that in his *Alcmaeon* he made the hero kill his mother unwittingly instead of deliberately as in the original legend, and Plutarch (*De Glor. Ath.* 7) speaks with very high praise of the *Hector*. Of the two poets less than twenty lines in all are preserved.

TGF 777–80. Wilamowitz, *Aischylos Interpretationen* (1914), 238 f.
A. W. P.-C.

**ASTYNOMOI,** an office found mostly in the Ionian States. In Athens there were five for the city and five for the Piraeus, elected by lot for one year. Their principal duties were to keep the streets clean and free of obstruction. They also had duties in relation to festivals; and in particular (at least *c.* 326) they enforced certain sumptuary laws. They could inflict small fines and introduce to the lawcourts more important cases within their jurisdiction. They had slaves as assistants. In many States they also had harbour and market duties (*see* AGORANOMOI). A law governing the duties of the *astynomoi* at Pergamum, passed probably in the second century B.C., is preserved in an inscription of the early second century A.D. (*SEG* xiii. 521). A. W. G.

**ASTYOCHE,** in mythology, sister of Priam and daughter of Laomedon (qq.v.; Apollod. 3. 146). She married Telephus (q.v. 1; Quint. Smyrn. 6. 135) and bore Eurypylus, who came to the Trojan War and was killed by Neoptolemus with many of his people, γυναίων εἵνεκα δώρων (*Od.* 11. 521). This the commentators explained either of the gift of a wife (Hermione) by Menelaus to Neoptolemus, or of the gift by Priam to Astyoche of the golden vine which was given Tros by Zeus as compensation for the loss of Ganymedes (*Little Iliad*, fr. 6 Allen), etc. See Eustathius *in Odyss.*, 1697, 30 ff. H. J. R.

**ASYLIA** means a guarantee against seizure of property by citizens of another State exercising the right of reprisal. Whenever there were no arrangements for the settlement of disputes between States the party wronged claimed the right to use self-help and to seize the property (e.g. a ship or its cargo), not only of the offending party, but of other citizens and metics of his State. Such seizure was designated by the verb συλᾶν and related words. Rights of reprisal were often proclaimed by one state against another. When *asylia* was granted to individuals it meant that whatever claims there were against his State his personal property was safe from seizure at the hands of citizens and residents of the State bestowing *asylia*. This form of *asylia* could be given to entire states. Another form, connected with a locality and not applying to the property of its citizens abroad, was the recognition by other States of the inviolability of a sanctuary or a sanctuary and the city in which it was located. Such sanctuaries were used as places of refuge; hence the later meaning of 'asylum'.

E. Schlesinger, *Die griechische Asylie* (1933), assembles the evidence and cites earlier literature. J. A. O. L.

**ATALANTA** (Ἀταλάντη), in mythology, daughter of Iasus, son of Lycurgus of Arcadia, and Clymene,

daughter of Minyas (Apollod. 3. 105), or of Schoeneus son of Athamas (Hesiod, fr. 20 Rzach). Boeotian and Arcadian legends often show connexion, but there is no need to suppose two heroines of the same name here for she is in all probability a by-form of Artemis (q.v.). She was a huntress, averse to marriage, loved by (1 Meleager (q.v. 1); Parthenopaeus was her son by him (Hyg. *Fab.* 99. 1, a late story, see Rose ad loc.); (2) Melanion (Milanion, i.e. Μειλανίων, Prop. 1. 1. 9), her firs cousin (Apollod., ibid.), or Hippomenes. She would marry no one who could not beat her in a foot-race (in Hyg. *Fab.* 185. 2, she follows the suitor and spears him if she can catch him; perhaps a reminiscence of a religious rite, see Rose ad loc.). Melanion, or Hippomenes got three golden apples from Aphrodite and delayed her by throwing them, thus winning. Their son was Parthenopaeus in most accounts. But (by the anger of Aphrodite, to whom he forgot to pay his vow, Ov. *Met* 10. 681 ff.) he lay with her in a holy place (Apollod. 108 Hyg., ibid. 6, Ov., ibid. 686); for this impiety they were turned into lions. In some versions (as Prop. 1. 1. 9 there is no race, but Melanion wins Atalanta's affection when hunting with her.

Atalanta wrestling with Peleus at the funeral games of Pelias is a very popular subject in archaic art, still sometimes found in classical. She is also regularly shown among the hunters of the Calydonian boar, a popular subject at all periods. Generally as a huntress, and in archaic art as an athlete, she wears a short tunic; as an athlete in classical art, briefs and a brassière (Brommer *Vasenlisten*², 235 ff., 240, 347). H. J. R.; C. M. R

**ATARGATIS** (Aramaic 'Atar-'Ata, according to Ronzevalle 'the divine 'Atā': cf. the epithet ἀγνή applied to her at Delos) or *Derceto*, the goddess of Hierapolis Bambyce in Syria. Her temple, rebuilt *c.* 300 B.C. by Stratonice, wife of Seleucus I, was plundered by Antiochus IV and by Crassus, but was still in Lucian's day one of the greatest and holiest in Syria. Her consort was Hadad; his throne was flanked by bulls, that of Atargatis by lions. At Ascalon, Atargatis was represented as half woman, half fish. Fish and doves were sacred to her; the myth records that, having fallen into a lake Atargatis was saved by the fish ([Eratosth.] *Cat.* 38), or in another version, that Atargatis was changed into a fish and her daughter Semiramis into a dove (Diod. Sic. 4. 2–6; 2. 20. 1–2; Ov. *Met.* 4. 44–8). Late in the third century B.C. her cult appears in Egypt, Macedon, and with civic status, at Phistyon in Aetolia and (early 2nd century at Thuria in Messenia. Natives of Hierapolis founded a shrine on Delos in 128–127, of which Athens soon took control. Atargatis was worshipped also in a number of other Hellenic cities, whereas in the west (apart from Rome, where Nero favoured her for a while) only a few dedications, from Italy, the Danubian provinces, and England, have been found. Since Atargatis was primarily a fertility goddess, the Greeks often recognized in her form of Aphrodite, but generally she was simply the 'Syrian goddess'. Astrologers identified her with the constellation Virgo, and a third-century 'creed' found in England (*RIB* 1791) accepts the *dea Syria* as one of several names or manifestations of the universal goddess At Thuria her cult included mysteries. Lucian, *De d Syria*, describes the cult in Syria; Apuleius, *Met.* 8– the life of her wandering Galli. *See* EUNUCHS, RELIGIOUS FISH, SACRED; METRAGYRTES.

C. Clemen, *Lukians Schrift über die syrische Göttin* (1938); Cumont, *Rel. or.*, ch. 5.; P. Lambrechts and P. Noyen, *La Nouve Clio*, 1954; S. Ronzevalle, *Mélanges de l'Université Saint Joseph* (Beyrouth), 1940; P. Roussel, *Délos colonie athénienne* (1916), 252 f H. Seyrig, 'Antiquités syriennes 78', *Syria*, 1960, 233 ff.; F. R. Walto *RAC* s.v. 'Atargatis'; E. Will, *Annales archéologiques de Syrie*, 19
F. R.

**ATE,** the personification of infatuation or moral blindness, in which right and wrong, advantageous and ruinous conduct cannot be distinguished. She is the subject of an elaborate allegory in *Il.* 19. 90 ff., the earliest in Greek, where she is daughter of Zeus (an early instance of the problem of the moral responsibility of Deity). She is daughter of Strife and sister of Lawlessness (Hes. *Theog.* 230). H. J. R.

**ATEIUS PRAETEXTATUS PHILOLOGUS,** LUCIUS, one of the chief scholars of the Ciceronian age. Born at Athens, he became a captive of war in 86 B.C., was brought to Rome and manumitted. He claimed to have written 800 books on all kinds of subjects (*miscellanea*, ὕλη) and took the name Philologus as an indication of his interests. According to Suetonius (*Gram.* 10) he helped Sallust by compiling a *Breviarium Rerum Romanarum* and Asinius Pollio by advising about the style of his history. Festus mentions his *Liber Glossematorum* and Charisius a work entitled *An amaverit Didun Aeneas.*

G. Funaioli, *Gramm. Rom. Frag.*, 137–41. Schanz–Hosius, § 195, 6.
J. F. M.

**ATELLA** between Capua and Naples in Campania (q.v.) (ruins near modern *Aversa*). Atella joined Hannibal (216 B.C.), but Rome soon recovered and grimly punished it (211 B.C.). It recovered, however, and became a prosperous *municipium*. The Atellana (q.v.), the vulgar farce staged in Oscan, which enjoyed popularity in Rome, possibly originated here. E. T. S.

**ATELLANA** (sc. *fabula*): in origin a native Italian farce, named after Atella in Campania but doubtless common in Oscan towns, and probably early known in Rome. It had stock characters: *Bucco*, 'the fool' (cf. Plaut. *Bacch.* 1088); *Dossennus*, perhaps wrongly connected with *dorsum* (and so 'Hunch-back') since it seems to reflect an Etruscan proper name and it was identified by Roman scholars with Manducus (Varro *Ling. Lat.* 7. 96); *Maccus*, also 'the fool' (cf. μακκοᾶν), the most frequently occurring name in titles of *Atellanae*; *Manducus*, originally a comic effigy carried in procession (Paulus Festi 115, Linds.; Plaut. *Rud.* 535 ff.), perhaps 'Glutton' (connected with *mandere*, Varro *Ling. Lat.* 7. 95); *Pappus*, 'the Gaffer' (cf. πάππος). It became a literary form (no doubt, because the inspiration provided by Greek New Comedy to produce *palliatae* had worn thin: *see* TOGATA) for a short time in the period of Sulla: its principal exponents were L. Pomponius (q.v. 1) of Bononia and Novius (q.v.). The action was set in a small Italian town that gave the dramatist opportunity to portray the humour and coarseness of provincial life. It seems to have been primarily low-life comedy, in coarse and obscene language; but the dramatic motifs were still drawn from Greek New Comedy. Surprisingly there are among the titles of Pomponius and Novius some which can only be interpreted as parodies of tragedies (e.g. Pomponius, *Agamemno Suppositus, Armorum Iudicium*; Novius, *Andromacha, Phoenissae*). The *Atellana* was sometimes used as an *exodium* (a 'follower') to a tragedy, like satyric drama in Athens, and these parodies may have been inspired by such occasions.

*Fabularum Atellanarum Fragmenta,* rec. P. Frassinetti (1955). Schanz–Hosius i. 245 ff.; W. Beare, *The Roman Stage³* (1964), 137 ff. P. Frassinetti, *Fabula Atellana* (1953). G. W. W.

**ATESTE,** the modern *Este*, has given its name to one of the principal Iron Age cultures of northern Italy, lasting from the ninth century B.C. until its peaceful annexation by Rome in 184 B.C. Until A.D. 589 it stood on the Adige, now some miles south, and throughout its history thus combined natural advantages for sea-trade, presumably coming through Adria (q.v.), with easy access to the land routes round the gulf. Already by the late seventh–early sixth centuries its products were not only reaching Felsina (q.v.) and the head of the Adriatic, but were also crossing the Alps to Carniola and the Tyrol. Noted for its production of sheet-bronze, particularly of *situlae*, Ateste was for 800 years the most important commercial and artistic centre of Venetia: its commercial position led to the incorporation of foreign (e.g. Oriental) elements, via Greek and Etruscan intermediaries, into a distinctive indigenous art-style.

G. Fogolari, *Il Museo Nazionale Atestino in Este* (1957); H. Müller-Karpe, *Beiträge zur Chronologie der Urnenfelderzeit nördlich und südlich der Alpen* (1959); *Mostra dell'arte delle situle* (Florence, 1961); G. Fogolari and O-H. Frey, *Stud. Etr.* 1965, 237 ff.; O-H. Frey, *Germania* 1966, 48 ff. D. W. R. R.

**ATHAMANES,** a tribal group related to the 'Hellenes', occupied the upper Acheloüs valley and the hill-country east of its watershed towards Thessaly. They formed a tribal state under a monarchy which was powerful in the Hellenistic period.

P.-K., *GL* 2. 1. 218 f.; Hammond, *Epirus*, 682 f. N. G. L. H.

**ATHAMAS,** in mythology, son of Aeolus (q.v. 2) and a character in a variously told story of a stepmother's cruelty (Stith Thompson, S31). He married first Nephele (a cloud-goddess), then Ino daughter of Cadmus; the order is reversed in Philostephanus ap. schol. *Il.* 7. 86; Hyg. *Fab.* 4, professedly from Euripides, introduces a third wife, Themisto, but omits Nephele. Nephele bore him Phrixus and Helle, and Ino in her turn Learchus and Melicertes. Ino was jealous of her stepchildren, and therefore caused the seed-corn to be roasted; when it consequently failed to grow, and Delphi was consulted, she induced the messengers on their return to say that the sacrifice of Phrixus and Helle, or Phrixus alone, was demanded. Nephele saved them, or him, by means of a golden-fleeced ram given by Hermes; the ram brought Phrixus to Colchis, where he married Chalciope, daughter of Aeëtes. Helle fell into the strait thenceforth named Hellespont (q.v.) after her. *See further* ARGONAUTS. In Hyginus, loc. cit., Themisto tries to murder the stepchildren and fails in the same manner as Aëdon (q.v.); cf. Stith Thompson, K1611. See Hyg. *Fab.* 1–5; Apollod. 1. 80 ff.; Ov. *Fasti* 3. 851 ff.; [Eratosthenes] 19; Hyg. *Poet. Astr.* 2. 20; schol. German. *Arat.*, 79, 142 Breysig. Several of these say that the ram became the constellation Aries. Cf. Pickard-Cambridge in Powell, *New Chapters* iii. 97. The rest of Athamas' story is less folk-tale and more myth. Because Ino had nursed Dionysus, Hera drove Athamas and her mad; Athamas killed Learchus, Ino ran from him carrying Melicertes, leaped into the sea, and she and her son were transformed into deities, Leucothea and Palaemon (Apollodorus and Hyginus, supra; Ov. *Met.* 4. 416 ff.; Rose, *Handbk. Gk. Myth.* 150 and authorities there cited).

At Halos in the Thessalian Achaea, the senior member of the clan claiming descent from Athamas was sacrificed to Zeus Laphystios if he entered the city hall. This was explained as retribution for Athamas' joining Ino in plotting against Phrixus (Hdt. 7. 197. 1). H. J. R.

**ATHANASIUS** (*c.* A.D. 295–373) was an outstanding theologian and church leader, and as a deacon played an influential part at the council of Nicaea (325). Appointed bishop of Alexandria in 328, he vigorously championed the Nicene doctrine of the consubstantiality (ὁμοούσιον) of Father and Son against Arianism, being five times deposed and exiled. Two of his exiles he spent in the West, to which he introduced monasticism. In the last decades of his life he developed the doctrine of the deity and personality of the Holy Spirit, and did much to promote understanding between the different anti-Arian groups in the church. His surviving writings include apologetic, dogmatic, and ascetic treatises, historical essays, and letters.

Migne, *PG* xxv–xxvii. Text ed. H. G. Opitz (Berlin Academy, 1934– ). J. N. D. K.

**ATHEISM.** 'Denial of the gods' (τὸ μὴ νομίζειν θεοὺς [εἶναι], J. Tate in *CR* 1936, 3, and 1937, 3) might mean atheism in the modern sense or a distaste for pagan mythology compatible with deep religious faith. The earliest motive for it was the moral inadequacy of the gods as depicted by Homer and Hesiod. Thus Xenophanes (q.v.) adduced the crimes imputed to them, and added that men everywhere created gods in their own image. Yet he upheld the existence of the divine, and taught a kind of pantheism. However, in the fifth century Ionian speculation and the Sophistic movement did make possible the doubt or denial of any form of deity. ἄθεος later became the term for this philosophical atheism (but see below). Of famous thinkers prosecuted for ἀσέβεια in this century, though political motives usually played a part in such prosecutions, Anaxagoras (q.v.) was a rationalist who sought to explain everything by natural causes and doubtless (though positive evidence is lacking) an atheist in the modern sense. Protagoras' (q.v.) position was strictly agnostic. Socrates (q.v. 1) is a more complex case. Perhaps the gods of his personal belief were not those of the State, but he conformed to official cults and was a man of deep religious feelings, sure of divine guidance. A certain Diagoras (q.v.) of Melos had always known in antiquity as 'the atheist' and was convicted of impiety at Athens *c.* 414 B.C. Often quoted for positive atheism is the fragment of the *Sisyphus* of Critias (q.v., fr. 23 Diels), which describes the gods as human inventions in the interests of law. Among the poets, Pindar defends the tradition by gently purging the myths of their crudities. Euripides exclaims against the folly of believing in such gods. Atheism was attributed to other contemporary philosophers, and Plato's attack in *Laws* 10 suggests that it was widespread in the next century. Aristotle's intellectual conception of divinity left no room for the traditional personal gods (*Metaph. Λ* 8 *fin.*), and the theological argument started in the Socratic schools led naturally to scepticism, and in once case at least— Theodorus the Cyrenaic—to actual atheism.

Besides 'unbelieving', ἄθεος meant 'abandoned by the gods', wicked, godless. (See lexica and K. Latte in *ARW* xx. 264.) The question of belief had not in general the importance which it has to-day (cf. A. D. Nock, *Conversion* (1933), 10 f.), and the word tended to be a term of abuse rather than a reasoned description, e.g. as applied to the Christians (Nock, *Sallustius* (1926), lxxxviii). Yet cf. also Theophrastus in Porph. *Abst.* 2. 7 and Plutarch *De Superst.*, where ἀθεότης is discussed and defined as a 'lack of sensitiveness to the divine'; also evidence in F. Cumont, *L'Égypte des astrologues* (1937), 135.

In general, see A. B. Drachmann, *Atheism in Pagan Antiquity* (London and Copenhagen, 1922.) W. K. C. G.

**ATHENA** (Ἀθάνα, Ἀθήνη, Ἀθηναίη(-α), Ἀθηνᾶ). The patron goddess of Athens in Attica and Athens in Boeotia, also extensively worshipped in many other places in Greece proper and the colonies and islands. There is no reasonable doubt that she is originally pre-Hellenic. Her name shows the non-Greek suffix -*na* found also, e.g., in Μυκῆναι; her most famous cult, that at Athens on the Acropolis, is on the site of a Mycenaean palace, the 'house of Erechtheus' of *Odyssey* 7. 81, cf. *Iliad* 2. 549; and her name appears in the form *a-ta-na po-ti-ni-ja* on a Linear B tablet at Cnossos. In Minoan fashion, she takes on occasion the form of a bird, as *Od.* 3. 371–2 (the owl, though regularly associated with her in classical times, is not the only bird with which she is connected

in cult). Her peculiar cult-statues, female yet fully armed, resemble the Mycenaean shielded goddess (*Ath. Mitt.* 1912, 129 ff. and pl. viii, often reproduced elsewhere). The conclusion is hardly avoidable (Nilsson, *Die Anfänge der Göttin Athene* (1921); *Minoan-Mycenaean Religion*[2] (1950), 417 ff.) that she is the tutelary goddess of Cretan and Mycenaean princes, especially the latter, retained in popular cult when the ancient citadels came to be reserved for the gods and not for rulers. Presumably she had been fervently worshipped by the subjects of those princes; at all events, she continued to hold a very high rank and to develop in several directions.

**2.** Besides her connexion with citadels, and consequently with cities (e.g. Verg. *Ecl.* 2. 61–2; *see* ZEUS), she has a rather decided association with water, hence her epithet *Tritogeneia*, whereof the first two syllables have something to do with water, though their exact meaning is unknown (cf. Farnell, op. cit. infra, 265 ff.). This, however, did not result in her becoming a deity of the sea, even by way of Athens' naval power; the hold of Poseidon was probably too strong.

**3.** She is regularly regarded as virgin. Her Elean title of Μήτηρ need mean no more than that mothers worshipped her (cf. the strange titles 'Maid', 'Wife', and 'Widow' applied to Hera (q.v.), and see Farnell, 302 ff., yet cf. E. Fehrle, *Kultische Keuschheit* (1910), 183 ff. That she is interested in fertility, both animal and vegetable, is not remarkable; she is a goddess of the State and on such increase its continued existence depends.

**4.** Her most conspicuous functions are perhaps those connected with war. She has a certain tendency to become a war-goddess in general, a kind of female Ares, as in *Iliad* 17. 398, where she is coupled with him as an expert in battles and liable to violent wrath; neither of them could have 'found fault with' the fury of the contest over the body of Patroclus. Normally, however, she is warlike in the sense that she fights for, or leads to battle, her chosen people, or hero (as Diomedes, *Il.* 5. 856, where she guides his spear into Ares' flank; Eur. *Heracl.* 349–50, where, though Hera leads the Argives, Athena leads Athens to fight against them). Or she protects them, as a strong warrior might a weaker one (Solon, fr. 3. 3–4 Diehl), though this does not refer only to war but to shielding Athens against all dangers. Hence also she is the inventor of sundry warlike implements, as the war-chariot (*Hymn. Hom. Ven.* 13) and the trumpet (she was called Σάλπιγξ in Argos, Paus. 2. 21. 3).

**5.** But, being female and goddess of that city which was perhaps nearer than any other in Greece to being industrialized, she is also a patroness of arts and crafts. Among these, spinning and weaving take a prominent place, as might be expected, and in general she is the goddess of women's work (*Hymn. Hom. Ven.* 14–15). But her influence extends much further than this, for all manner of handicraftsmen worship her, or regard her as their teacher, as potters (ps.-Hdt. *Vit. Hom.* 32; the scene is Samos, indicating that such worship of Athena is in no way purely Attic), goldsmiths (*Od.* 6. 233, again wholly unconnected with Athens). In Athens the Chalceia (literally the festival of smiths, χαλκῆς) was held in her honour, though Hephaestus seems to have had some share in it (Deubner, 35 f.). It is in such connexions as this that her title Ergane, 'the work-woman', is especially appropriate, and here also that her functions overlap to some extent those of Hephaestus, thus explaining their mythical connexion; see below. She is on occasion goddess of medicine also, since that is a highly skilled occupation, but this seems to be a development rather of Minerva (q.v.; see Ov. *Fasti* 3. 827).

**6.** Identifications between Athena and foreign goddesses are fairly numerous, e.g. Neith in Egypt (Plato *Tim.* 21 e), a Libyan goddess whose name is unknown

(Hdt. 4. 180. 2), and, most familiar, the Italian Minerva. It is not always possible to tell what caused the identification. Of Greek goddesses subordinate to her, the best known is Nike, whose temple on the Acropolis is one of the best preserved; she also had some connexion with Hygieia, whose name she bore as a title (Paus. 1. 23. 4).

**7.** That she became ultimately allegorized into a personification of wisdom is a not unnatural development of her patronage of skill; she passes from one sense of σοφία to another. The process has already begun in Hesiod (*Theog.* 886 ff.), where Metis, i.e. Good Counsel, is her mother (cf. Rose, *Folklore* (1935), 27 f.).

**8.** The principal myth concerning her is her birth, without mother (but cf. Hesiod, above), from the head of Zeus. It was fully developed by the time of Pindar (*Ol.* 7. 35; cf. scholiast there); Zeus' head was split with an axe by Hephaestus (or some other deity, the details varying in different accounts), and the goddess sprang out, fully armed and uttering her war-cry. Helios, adds Pindar, let his sons in Rhodes know of this, so that they might be the first to sacrifice to the new power. They did so, but in such haste that they forgot to take fire with them, and so offered the victims unburned, whence, as Athena was pleased with their devotion, the custom continued at her shrine among them. This is the goddess of Lindus, probably not originally Athena at all, who is not worshipped in this fashion, not being a chthonian goddess.

**9.** The above is no doubt a Rhodian myth; the following is Athenian. Hephaestus desired to marry her, and Zeus consented, but gave her leave to repulse his attentions. They struggled together, and his seed fell on the earth, which thus became fertile and in due season produced a boy. Athena took charge of the infant (possibly she was originally his actual mother, see above), hid him in a chest guarded by serpents and gave it to the daughters of Cecrops to keep, with instructions not to open it. They disobeyed, and at the sight of the serpents (or whatever the chest contained; chests are very common receptacles of sacred objects which must not be viewed at all, or only after some rite of initiation) they were so terrified that they leaped off the Acropolis and so perished. The child was called Erichthonius and remained a favourite of Athena (Rose, *Handb. Gk. Myth.*[6] 110 and references). In Attica also she strove with Poseidon for ownership of the land; she produced the olive-tree, thus outdoing the miracles which he performed, and won the contest; *see* POSEIDON.

**10.** That she was originally thought of as theriomorphic is not proved but suggested by her stock epithet γλαυκῶπις ('bright-eyed' or 'owl-faced'?).

**11.** Athena is constant in all forms of archaic and classical art from the seventh century, alone or with other deities or in scenes: her birth; the Gigantomachy; as patroness of heroes. She is generally armed (with helmet, aegis, shield, spear), and often has an owl, especially in fifth-century Athens.

Farnell, *Cults*, i. 258 ff., and the larger classical dictionaries. Attic cults, L. Deubner, *Attische Feste* (1932), 9 ff. Her place in Athens, C. J. Herington, *Athena Parthenos and Athena Polias* (1955); G. T. W. Hooker (ed.), *Parthenos and Parthenon* (1963); W. K. C. Guthrie, *CAH* ii². 40. 27 f. (1961, with bibliography). General discussion, Nilsson *GGR* i². 433 ff. In art, G. Beckel, *Götterbeistand in der Bildüberlieferung griechischer Heldensagen* (1961). H. J. R.; C. M. R.

**ATHENAEUM,** Hadrian's famous institute for lectures and recitations by rhetors and other literary men. Aurelius Victor (*Caes.* 14) calls it 'ludum ingenuarum artium'.

**ATHENAEUS** (1) (fl. *c.* A.D. 200), of Naucratis in Egypt. His only extant work, Δειπνοσοφισταί ('The Learned Banquet'), was probably completed after the death of Commodus in A.D. 192 (ib. 537 f.); other chrono-

logical inferences are uncertain. It belongs to the polyhistoric variety of the symposium form (*see* SYMPOSIUM LITERATURE), practised earlier by Aristoxenus and Didymus. It is now in fifteen books (originally perhaps 30); there is also an Epitome, which covers existing gaps. At the 'banquet', which extends over several days, philosophy, literature, law, medicine, and other interests are represented by a large number of guests, who in some cases bear historical names (e.g. Galen and Ulpian of Tyre); a Cynic philosopher is introduced as a foil; the Roman host, Larensis, probably the author's patron, is attested epigraphically (*CIL* vi. 212). The symposiac framework, if not devoid of occasional humour, is subordinate in interest to the collections of excerpts which are introduced into it. These relate to all the materials and accompaniments of convivial occasions; they are drawn from a vast number of authors, especially of the Middle and New Comedy, whose works are now lost; they are valuable both as literature and as illustrating earlier Greek manners. The order of these extracts sometimes suggests the use of lexica (Didymus, Pamphilus) or of διδασκαλίαι (*see* DIDASCALIA), as well as of lists of κωμῳδούμενοι; but Athenaeus has collected much independently from the great writers; he cites some 1,250 authors, gives the titles of more than 1,000 plays, and quotes more than 10,000 lines of verse.

ANCIENT SOURCE. *Suda.*
TEXT. G. Kaibel (Teubner, 1887–90).
TEXT AND TRANSLATION. C. B. Gulick (Loeb, 1927–41), 7 vols. Epitome: S. P. Peppink (1937–9).
COMMENTARY. J. Schweighäuser (1801–7).
CRITICISM. R. Hirzel, *Dialog* (1895) ii. 352. F. Rudolph, *Philol. Suppl.* vi (1891) (sources); K. Mengis, *Stud. Gesch. Kult. Alt.* 1920 (composition); C. A. Bapp, *Leipz. Stud.* 1885 (music and lyric); K. Zepernick, *Philol.* 1921 (trustworthiness); L. Nyikos, *Athenaeus quo consilio quibusque usus subsidiis Deipnosophistarum libros composuerit* (Diss. Basel, 1941). W. M. E.; R. B.

**ATHENAEUS** (2), author of an extant work on siege-engines (Περὶ μηχανημάτων) may probably be dated in the first century B.C.

Ed. R. Schneider, *Abh. d. Gesellsch. d. Wissensch. zu Göttingen* (Ph.-hist. Kl.) N.F. 12 (1912). E. W. M.

**ATHENAEUS** (3) of Attaleia practised medicine in Rome under Claudius (A.D. 41–54). Like many other physicians of that time he founded a new school, that of the Pneumatists. Imbued with Stoic ideas, but well trained in philosophy in general, Athenaeus assumed as basic elements the four qualities, together with the *pneuma* as the fifth. Health and disease he explained through their *eukrasia* (good temperament) and *dyskrasia* (bad temperament). His physiology was dependent on Aristotle. Details of his pathology are unknown. His system apparently was important in its speculative formulation rather than in its practical consequences. Athenaeus, who considered medical knowledge as part of general education, devised most elaborate dietetic rules, in which he included pedagogical as well as medical precepts, differentiated according to the different stages of life. The ideas of Athenaeus were highly estimated by Galen.

F. Kudlien, *Hermes*, 1962, 419 ff., dates Athenaeus at the end of the first century B.C. on account of Galen in *De causis contentivis*, who says that Athenaeus was a pupil of Poseidonius. But if this were true it would be strange that Celsus should not mention him. Perhaps Diels's date (beginning of the first century A.D.) is preferable (*Hermes*, 1918, 74, n. 1). Still further back one can hardly go unless a new investigation of the Pneumatic School, which is being prepared by Kudlien for *PW*, adds new data.

TEXT. Fragments from Oribasius in *Veterum et Clarorum Medicorum Graecorum Opuscula*, Ch. F. Matthaei (1808), not complete.
LITERATURE. M. Wellmann, 'Die pneumatische Schule', *Phil. Unters.* 1895, *PW* ii. 2034; no clear distinction between Athenaeus

and the teaching of his followers, whose importance seems exaggerated; cf. also T. C. Allbutt, *Greek Medicine in Rome* (1921); for the early history of Pneumatic theories, E. Neustadt, *Hermes* 1909; W. Jaeger, *Hermes* 1913; Allbutt, loc. cit. 224.      L. E.

**ATHENAGORAS,** Christian Apologist from Athens, addressed in A.D. 177 to Marcus Aurelius and Commodus a letter in which he refuted charges of atheism, Thyestian banquets, and Oedipean incest which were often brought against Christians. A powerful and lucid writer, he also wrote 'On the Resurrection of the Dead'.

E. Schwartz, *Texte und Untersuch. z. Gesch. d. altchrist. Lit.* iv. 2 (1891); J. Quasten, *Patrology* i (1950), 229 ff.      H. H. S.

**ATHENODORUS** of Tarsus, son of Sandon, was a Stoic, a friend of Cicero and Strabo, and a teacher of Augustus. He is to be distinguished from Athenodorus Cordylion of Tarsus, head of the Pergamene library whom Cato Uticensis brought to his home in Rome. He probably came to Rome with Octavian in 44 B.C. In his old age he was sent by Augustus to expel Boethus, Antony's ruler in Tarsus, where he then became the chief citizen. He probably represented the views of the Middle Stoa. He sent a summary of some views of Posidonius to Cicero who wanted them for his *De Officiis*. He wrote a work against the Categories of Aristotle, an account of Tarsus, a work addressed to Octavia (q.v. 2), and, like Posidonius, *On the Ocean*. Seneca used his ethical writings.

*FGrH* 746. Philippson, *PW*, Suppl. V, 47 ff.      H. H. S.

**ATHENS** (*'Aθῆναι*) (HISTORICAL OUTLINE). Archaeological remains are consistent with the Athenian tradition that in early times there were several kingdoms in Attica, and the thirteenth-century fortification of the Acropolis of Athens may be connected with the formation of the Athenian state by an act of union, which was attributed to Theseus (q.v.) and was celebrated annually (Thuc. 2. 15). Some such union enabled the Athenians to resist the Boeotians and the Dorians, remain a centre of Mycenaean traditions, and launch the Ionian migration from *c.* 1050 B.C. onwards. As elsewhere in Greece, the monarchy was succeeded by an aristocracy, when the archonship became the principal magistracy (*see* ARCHONTES). Though the archonship became an annual office in 683–682, and the Thesmothetai (q.v.) were instituted, the aristocracy retained and increased their power; for they not only monopolized political office, but controlled most of the land. An attempt by Cylon (*c.* 632) to overthrow them failed; and Draco's code (*c.* 624–621) left their powers untouched. In the ninth and eighth centuries Athens produced magnificent 'geometric' pottery, in the seventh the crude but vigorous 'early Attic'. Sculpture was comparatively little developed. Writing was in use from at least 700.

2. The authority of the aristocracy was challenged by Solon in 594 B.C. He liberated debt-slaves whether held on the land or sold abroad. He laid the foundations of democracy by establishing economic freedom, by making the *ekklesia* independent of the archons, by instituting the Heliaea and making the magistracies responsible to the people. He did not, however, secure internal peace; and after many years of struggle the popular leader Pisistratus made himself tyrant (first in 561–560 and finally *c.* 545). The tyranny lasted till 510, when his son Hippias was driven out. The sixth century saw a remarkable development of Athens. Her pottery, by its technical and artistic excellence, practically drove its rivals from all foreign fields; sculpture flourished; Solon was himself the earliest Attic poet, and the tyrants attracted poets from elsewhere—Athens was becoming a cultural centre. Material prosperity greatly increased, in agriculture,

manufacture, and trade; many foreigners settled in Athens, and by 500 the population was already large.

3. The attempt of the aristocrats to gain control after the expulsion of Hippias failed, and the reforms of Cleisthenes established a true democracy (*see* EKKLESIA, BOULE, AREOPAGUS). An active foreign policy was at first checked by an unsuccessful intervention in 498 in the Ionian Revolt; but the immense military and moral effort of Athens in two Persian wars (490 and 480–479) established her position as the most energetic and enterprising State in Greece; a fact, however, which soon drew her into rivalry with Sparta, the accepted leader. Sparta's refusal to champion the mainland Ionian States which revolted from Persia in 479 gave Athens her chance; in 477 the Delian League was founded, comprising most of the Aegean islands and the Greek cities of the Asiatic and Thracian coasts. The war with Persia was successfully continued till Cimon's victory at the Eurymedon (*c.* 467). Athens had a severe check when she supported an Egyptian revolt (459–454); but by the peace of 448 Persia practically recognized the Athenian Empire, agreeing not to sent her fleet west of Phaselis and of the Bosporus, nor her army nearer than three days' march of the Ionian cities. Before this, war had broken out with the Peloponnesians, in which Athens lost the battle of Tanagra (457), but won the campaign, conquering Boeotia and winning over Phocis, and gaining victories over Corinth and Aegina. Meanwhile she had reduced to submission a few seceding States in the League; she now strengthened her position by improving her fleet, by cleruchies (q.v.) and garrisons, by a better organization of the tribute, and by supporting democracies against oligarchies, by encouraging the States to look upon herself as their capital, and later by introducing her own coinage in the subject cities. The League had become an Athenian Empire. In 447 Boeotia and Phocis recovered their independence; but by the Thirty Years' Peace (445) the Peloponnesians recognized the Empire.

4. By the development of tragedy and later of comedy, history, and oratory, Athens had become indisputably the literary centre of Greece. During the ascendancy of Pericles, painting and sculpture flourished there as never before; between 447 and 431 the Parthenon, the Propylaea, and many other buildings were completed. Most Greeks eminent in art, letters, and science visited Athens, and many settled there. Socrates, himself an Athenian, laid the foundations of mental and moral science in an enduring manner, and assured to Athens the primacy in philosophical studies. Trade prospered, for Athens preserved the peace of the seas. Her power and her ambitions alarmed Sparta, and the rest of Greece was nervous; in 431 the Peloponnesian League and the Boeotians went to war, 'to free Greece from the tyrant city'. The war lasted, with an interval of uneasy peace, for twenty-seven years. By 404 the whole political structure of Cimon's and Pericles' generations was in ruins: Athens was a dependant of Sparta under the heel of the Thirty Tyrants (q.v. 1), her Long Walls (q.v.) destroyed, her fleet reduced to a dozen ships, her population barely half its former total.

5. Yet Athens made an astonishingly quick recovery. By 403 she had regained her democracy and her autonomy; ten years later she had a fleet, had rebuilt the Long Walls, and had successfully revolted with other cities against Spartan imperialism. In 377 a new maritime league was formed; in 376 Chabrias won back for Athens supremacy at sea. Athens supported Thebes in her struggle against Sparta till after Leuctra (371), and later assisted Sparta against Thebes, striving for a balance of power. But when Philip of Macedon began his policy of expansion (359), Athens could not decide definitely between war and peace, and became involved in half-

hearted wars. The maritime league lost its most powerful members in the Social War (357–355); but Athens was still strong at sea and controlled the Hellespont, indispensable for her food supplies. Inspired by Demosthenes, Athens resisted Philip successfully in the Bosporus region in 340; but after the defeat at Chaeronea (338) she was glad to secure peace with Philip with the loss of the Hellespont. Overawed by Alexander in 335, Athens reorganized her forces during his absence in the East; but in the Lamian War of 323–322 she was defeated on land and sea. She now had to admit a Macedonian garrison in Munychia, and to modify her constitution. It was the end of Athens as a considerable military power.

**6.** The fourth century was a time of material prosperity, and trade and manufacture had quickly revived; the arts and letters (especially oratory, at its greatest in Demosthenes) were as vigorous as before. Though an Athenian dicastery had condemned Socrates to death in 399 (on grounds that were largely political—*see* SOCRATES 1), philosophy and science still flourished and under the leadership of Plato and Aristotle were at their height. But after 322, though comedy, philosophy, and physical and historical science continued active in Athens, the decline in creative thought began; after 300 Zeno and Epicurus were her greatest figures, and, recognized by all as the cultural centre of the Greek world, she began to live on her past. Politically the story of the century after Alexander was one of frequent struggles to rid herself of Macedonian domination, often temporarily successful, but always with the help of one or other of the *Diadochi*, who, if successful, abused his power; they all wanted her as an ally and a military station; she was finally crushed between them in the war against Antigonus (q.v. 2) Gonatas (266–262), and her independence forfeited. She was free again in 228; and as a small State had comparative peace, while Rome was establishing her power in Greece. Her last independent action was when she sided with Mithridates against Rome. Reduced by Sulla after a siege (87–86), she pleaded her glorious past; but he retorted that he was there to punish rebels, not to learn ancient history. Thereafter Athens was a cultured university town to which men came from all parts of the Roman Empire, but with no history, and no creative thought.

*See also* ATTICA, PERSIAN WARS, PELOPONNESIAN WAR, and the articles on individual Athenians and particular political institutions.

ANCIENT SOURCES. The Ἀτθίδες (q.v.) or special histories of Athens written in the fourth and third centuries) have all been lost except Aristotle's *Constitution of Athens*. Frags. in *FGrH* 323–75.

MODERN WORKS. Besides the general histories of Greece, see G. De Sanctis, *Storia della repubblica ateniese*[2] (1612); P. Cloché, *La Démocratie athénienne* (1951); W. S. Ferguson, *Hellenistic Athens* (1911); P. Graindor, *Athènes de Tibère à Trajan* (1931), *Athènes sous Hadrien* (1934); J. Day, *An Economic History of Athens under Roman Domination* (U.S.A. 1942); Hignett, *Hist. Athen. Const.*; P-K, *GL* i. 753 ff.; A. H. M. Jones, *Athenian Democracy* (1959); C. Mossé, *La fin de la démocratie athénienne* (1962); J. Papastavrou, *PW*, Suppl. x (1965), 48 ff.; J. K. Davies, *Athenian Propertied Families* (1969); P. Mackendrick, *The Athenian Aristocracy 339–31 B.C.* (1969).

A. W. G.; N. G. L. H.

**ATHENS.** TOPOGRAPHY:

ACROPOLIS, the central fortress and principal sanctuary of the city throughout antiquity. Already in the thirteenth century B.C. the hilltop was enclosed by a massive wall; slight traces of a contemporary palace also survive: 'the strong house of Erechtheus' (*Od.* 7. 81). Much building activity occurred under Pisistratus and his sons. Fragments of architecture and sculpture exist from two large limestone temples and from a half-dozen smaller temples or treasuries. Of all these only one can be located with certainty, a peripteral Doric temple (c. 525 B.C.) of which the foundations are still visible on the north half of the hilltop. In 480 B.C. a new temple, of marble, was rising on the higher, southern part of the hill,

and an ornamental gateway was under construction at its west end. All these buildings were destroyed by the Persians together with scores of votive statues. The debris was used in levelling behind the new fortification walls now carried around the hilltop. In the 450s a colossal bronze statue of Athena Promachus by Phidias was erected in triumph over the final defeat of the Persians. The city's defences and the Agora having been put in order, Pericles set about the rehabilitation of the Acropolis; Phidias served as general superintendent. First came the Parthenon (447–432 B.C.) for which Ictinus and Callicrates were named as architects. Erected on the site of the unfinished temple, its size and elevation assured its easy dominance. There followed a new gateway, the Propylaea, designed by Mnesicles (437–432 B.C.). Although truncated in plan and never completed, this noble portal, perfectly scaled and fitted to its setting, became justly famous. On a bastion overlooking the approach to the Propylaea an old shrine of Athena Nike was replaced by a graceful marble temple. In the last quarter of the fifth century the old Pisistratid peripteral temple was succeeded by the Erechtheum, an Ionic building ingeniously contrived to shelter a number of cults including those of Athena, Poseidon, and the heroized king Erechtheus. Among many lesser sanctuaries on the hilltop may be noted that of Brauronian Artemis just inside the Propylaea. Of various service buildings the most conspicuous was the Chalkothēkē, a repository for bronze offerings, to the west of the Parthenon. Later ages respected the creation of Pericles and added few buildings. In the second century B.C., however, a tall pedestal was erected, probably by the Pergamene royal family, to carry a bronze quadriga as a pendant to the Nike temple; this was later rededicated to Agrippa. At some time after 27 B.C. the cult of Rome and Augustus was housed in a round temple to the east of the Parthenon. Pagan worship persisted on the Acropolis into the fifth century A.D.; the Parthenon and Erechtheum were eventually converted to Christian use, but scarcely before the sixth century.

ENVIRONS OF THE ACROPOLIS. The steep and sheltered south slope of the hill was developed as a 'theatre district' comprising the open-air Theatre of Dionysus (from *c.* 500 B.C.), the roofed Odeum of Pericles (*c.* 443 B.C.), and the unroofed Odeum of Herodes Atticus (*c.* A.D. 160). A two-storeyed colonnade, a gift of Eumenes II of Pergamum (197–159 B.C.), joined the two unroofed theatres and served as a sheltered promenade for the audiences of both. The south exposure and the presence of springs also made this area a natural choice for the Sanctuary of Asclepius (420 B.C.). Recent excavations have brought to light a sanctuary of 'the nymph' on the hillslope below the Odeum of Herodes. A broad road led from the Theatre of Dionysus around the east end of the Acropolis. It was bordered by tripods won as prizes in dramatic contests; the well-preserved monument of Lysicrates (334 B.C.) supported one such tripod. The Acropolis was approached from the Agora over the Panathenaic Way, named from its use by the procession in the national festival. Bordering this road on the slopes of the Acropolis was the Eleusinium, the principal sanctuary of Demeter and Persephone in the city. Higher on the north slope were various lesser sanctuaries, among them one of Eros and Aphrodite. The Areopagus, a low hill to the west of the Acropolis, was the seat of the council and court of the same name. Neither the meeting-place of this body, nor the Sanctuary of the Eumenides which is also attested by the authors, has yet been recognized. Prominent on a steep hill to the south-west of the Acropolis is the marble tomb of Antiochus Philopappus, an eastern prince and benefactor of Athens (A.D. 114–16).

AGORA, the civic centre, was conveniently situated midway between the Acropolis and the principal city gate

(Dipylon). It was bisected diagonally by the Panathenaic Way. Development can be traced from the early sixth century B.C. to the final destruction by the Heruli in A.D. 267. The area was sacked by the Persians in 480/79 B.C. and seriously damaged by the Romans in 86 B.C. The principal building periods are the Pisistratid era (older Temple of Apollo Patroüs, Enneakrounos, Altar of the twelve Gods), the time of Cimon (Old Bouleuterion, Tholos, Theseum, Stoa Poikilē), the post-Periclean years (New Bouleuterion, Stoa of Zeus, South Stoa, Mint, Southwest Fountain House), the second century B.C. (Gymnasium of Ptolemy, Stoa of Attalus II, Metroon), and the early Empire (Odeum of Agrippa, transplanting of the Temple of Ares, Market of Caesar and Augustus, Library of Pantaenus, Library of Hadrian). The architectural development proceeded from west to east. By the end of the second century B.C. the main square had taken shape. It was bounded on the west by the administrative buildings (Tholos, Bouleuterion, Metroön, Temple of Apollo Patroüs, Stoa of Zeus = Stoa Basileios), on the east by the Stoa of Attalus, on the north (not yet excavated) by the Stoa Poikilē and the Stoa of the Herms. On the south the Gymnasium of Ptolemy was installed in an old sanctuary of Theseus. The Temple of Hephaestus (450–400 B.C.) overlooked the Agora from the west. As the old square was given over to cultural purposes, new commercial facilities were provided further to the east in the market of Caesar and Augustus. Innumerable references in the ancient authors attest the intensity of the community life that was centred on the Agora.

PNYX, the meeting-place of the Athenian *ekklesia*, is a low hill west of the Acropolis. Three periods may be distinguished. (1) About 500 B.C. A section of the hillside sloping toward the middle of the city was smoothed as a seating floor, and a low terrace was erected for the speaker's platform. (2) 404/3 B.C. The auditorium was reversed and supported on an artificial embankment probably to gain protection against the wind; this change was attributed by Plutarch (*Them.* 19) to the Thirty Tyrants. (3) About 330 B.C. The auditorium was much enlarged, a great altar was erected above the speaker's platform, and two large colonnades were begun on the hilltop. Work on the colonnades was interrupted by the military situation and was never resumed. To the third period belong most of the visible remains, notably the rock-cut bema and the semicircular retaining wall. In the Hellenistic period the Pnyx was abandoned in favour of the Theatre of Dionysus.

SOUTH-EAST ATHENS. The principal monument in this area is the Temple of Olympian Zeus, begun by the Pisistratids and completed by Hadrian. Recent excavations between the Olympieum and the Ilissus have revealed a number of other temples and civic buildings, among them probably the Temple of Apollo Delphinius. A well-preserved arch marks the line of division between the old 'city of Theseus' and the new suburb, 'the city of Hadrian'. The only other visible remains of this suburb are a gymnasium and a number of bathing establishments with mosaic floors. Across the Ilissus lies the Panathenaic Stadium, first constructed by Lycurgus (338–326 B.C.), rebuilt in marble by Herodes Atticus (2nd c. A.D.), and restored by George Averof in 1896.

FORTIFICATIONS. The earliest enceinte of which remains exist was erected by Themistocles soon after the expulsion of the Persians (479 B.C.). In its length of 6½ kilometres the wall was pierced by a dozen gates of which the principal was the Dipylon in the north-west quadrant. To meet Macedonian threats in the late fourth century the system was strengthened by the addition of an outwork and moat on the low-lying north, east, and south sides, and by the walling off of a protrusion toward the south-west. The development of a new eastern suburb in

the time of Hadrian required an extension in that direction. After the disastrous Herulian raid of A.D. 267 a new and much smaller inner enclosure was hastily thrown up to the north of the Acropolis, but by A.D. 400 the old outer circuit was again functioning. Communication between Athens and her harbours were protected by a series of three long walls, the Northern and the Phaleric erected under Cimon, the Middle under Pericles. Demolished after 404 B.C. these walls were rebuilt in the fourth century B.C.

GENERAL. Paus. bk. i, and Frazer's commentary; W. Judeich, *Topographie von Athen²* (1931); I. T. Hill, *The Ancient City of Athens* (1953); J. Travlos, *The Development of the City Plan of Athens* (in Modern Greek) (1960).
ACROPOLIS AND ENVIRONS. M. L. D'Ooge, *The Acropolis of Athens* (1908); G. P. Stevens, 'The Periclean Entrance Court of the Acropolis of Athens', *Hesp.* 1936, 443 ff.; 'The Setting of the Periclean Parthenon', *Hesp.* Suppl. III (1940); 'The North-east Corner of the Parthenon', *Hesp.* 1946, 1 ff.; 'Architectural Studies concerning the Acropolis of Athens', ibid. 73 ff.; A. W. Pickard-Cambridge, *The Theatre of Dionysus in Athens* (1946); W. B. Dinsmoor, *The Architecture of Ancient Greece* (1950).
AGORA. Paus. bk. i, 2–17 with Frazer's commentary; R. E. Wycherley, *Literary and Epigraphical Testimonia* (1957); American School of Classical Studies, *The Athenian Agora, a Guide to the Excavation and Museum²* (1962), with detailed bibliography.
PNYX. K. Kourouniotes and H. A. Thompson, 'The Pnyx in Athens', *Hesp.* 1932, 90 ff.; H. A. Thompson and R. L. Scranton, 'Stoas and City Walls on the Pnyx', *Hesp.* 1943, 269 ff.
SOUTH-EAST ATHENS. J. Travlos, *The Development of the City Plan of Athens* (in Modern Greek) (1960); Annual reports in *Ergon* since 1960 (in Modern Greek).
FORTIFICATIONS. W. Judeich, *Topographie von Athen²* (1931); J. Travlos, *The Development of the City Plan of Athens* (in Modern Greek) (1960); S. E. Jakovidis, *The Acropolis in the Mycenaean Period* (in Modern Greek) (1962).                    H. A. T.

## ATHLETICS.

The Greeks were more interested in athletic contests between individuals than in team games, and athletic competitions were popular and numerous. At the major athletic festivals the athletic events were running, long-jumping, throwing the discus, throwing the javelin, wrestling, boxing, and the *pancratium*. The races were the stade-race (about 200 m.), the *diaulos* (two lengths of the stadium, about 400 m.), the long-distance race (up to 24 lengths of the stadium), and the race in armour. Jumping, throwing the discus, throwing the javelin, and wrestling were generally confined to the pentathlon (q.v.). There were also at many festivals horse-races and chariot-races.

There is no evidence of the standard of performance in any of the events. Phayllus (q.v. 1) is said to have jumped 55 feet, but this is impossible if the foot by which it was measured was of the usual length (viz. 12 inches or thereabouts). Probably a smaller foot (e.g. a child's) was used on this occasion (cf. Ar. *Nub.* 144 ff.). The Greeks always used weights, *halteres* (q.v.), for jumping; so the event cannot have been a triple jump (hop, step, and jump), in which the use of weights would have been impossible. The discus was a 'heavy' event and the δίσκουρα (discus-throw) was an indeterminate but comparatively short measure of distance (Hom. *Il.* 23. 523). The Greeks, however, were more concerned with the winning of the contest than with times and distances.

The habit of stripping naked for athletic contests is said by Thucydides (1. 6) to have been recently introduced, but he seems to be referring particularly to wrestling and boxing. It seems unlikly that the Greeks would ever have stripped completely naked for events involving running, though it was an artistic convention, even in early times, generally though not always, to portray athletes naked.

Athletic competitions were originally held at the funerals of chieftains (Hom. *Il.* 22. 162 ff. and 23, 630) and funeral games were not unknown in later times (Isoc. *Evagoras* § 1), but in general they were held at fixed times (*see* AGONES) and assumed a religious character which was not inherent in their origin. The Olympic

Games, which took place at four-yearly intervals without break from 776 B.C. to A.D. 393, were finally suppressed by the Christian Emperor, Theodosius, as being a pagan religious festival.

E. N. Gardiner, *Athletics of the Ancient World* (1930); H. A. Harris, *Greek Athletes and Athletics* (1964); J. Jüthner (F. Brein), *Die athletischen Leibesübungen der Griechen* (1965). R. L. H.

**ATHOS,** a headland on the easternmost of the Chalcidian promontories, with a conspicuous pyramid-shaped peak rising sheer from the sea to 6,350 feet. In 492 B.C. a Persian fleet was destroyed near it by a storm. To avoid the passage round Mt. Athos, Xerxes dug a canal through the neck of the promontory (483–481). This had a length of 1½ miles, a breadth of 65–100 feet, and a depth of 8–10 feet (Hdt. 7. 22–24; Strabo 7. 331). Despite the doubts expressed by ancient and modern writers, the canal was completed; the cutting is visible in places. The mountain was sacred to Zeus (Aesch. *Ag.* 289) and cast its shadow on Lemnos at sunset (Soph. *Fr.* 709). M. C.; N. G. L. H.

**ATIA** (1, *PW* Attii 34), daughter of M. Atius Balbus (q.v. 1) and of Julia, Caesar's sister, was the wife of C. Octavius (q.v. 4) and the mother of C. Octavius (the future Augustus) and of Octavia (2). After her husband's death in 58 B.C. she married L. Marcius Philippus (q.v. 5). She died in 43 in her son's consulship and received a public funeral. The legend that she had given birth to Augustus by Apollo had some circulation. A. M.; T. J. C.

**ATIA** (2, *PW* Attii 35), sister (presumably younger) of Atia (1). She married her sister's stepson, L. Marcius Philippus (q.v. 6), and had a daughter Marcia. T. J. C.

**ATILIUS** (1, *PW* 36) **CAIATINUS** (or **CALATINUS**), AULUS (*cos.* I, 258 B.C.), fought successfully in Sicily, and as praetor (probably; rather than proconsul) in 257 celebrated a triumph. As consul II (254) he stormed Panormus. He was the first dictator to lead an army outside Italy—to Sicily in 249. He was censor (247). He dedicated a temple to Spes in the Forum Holitorium (probably one of the three now under S. Nicola in Carcere). He was buried near the Porta Capena (epitaph, Cic. *Sen.* 61), and was reckoned by Cicero among the most famous men of old. H. H. S.

**ATILIUS** (2, *PW* 60) **SERRANUS**, AULUS, praetor in 192 B.C., commanded the Roman fleet against Nabis and Antiochus (192–191). Praetor again (173), he renewed the treaty relations with Syria on Antiochus Epiphanes' accession. Envoy to Perseus in 172 with Q. Marcius Philippus, he was consul in 170, in Liguria.

Scullard, *Rom. Pol.* 123, 199 ff., 259. A. H. McD.

**ATILIUS** (3), MARCUS, contemporary with Caecilius, composed *comoediae palliatae* of which very few fragments remain. He had a reputation for harshness, and could stir the emotions deeply. Licinius, in Cic. *Fin.* 1. 5, applies the term 'ferreus scriptor' to an Atilius who translated Sophocles' *Electra*.

FRAGMENTS. Ribbeck, *CRF²*, 32 (3rd ed. Teubner, 1897).
E. H. W.

**ATILIUS** (4, *PW* 39) **FORTUNATIANUS** (4th c. A.D.), metrician. The first part of his *Ars* (*metrica*) deals with general principles, the second with Horatian metres ed. Keil, *Gramm. Lat.* 6. 278–304). The work depends largely on earlier writers, especially Caesius Bassus (q.v. 2).

Schanz–Hosius, § 827. J. F. M.

**ATIMIA,** the loss of all or some civic rights in a Greek city. It originally implied outlawry, but later, especially in Athens, involved the loss of active rights only (or of some only of these). Deprivation might be temporary: a State-debtor's *atimia* ended automatically when the debt was paid. Permanent deprivation of all rights was the punishment for treason, bribery (of a magistrate), cowardice in face of the enemy, perjury in a lawcourt (after three convictions), and some offences against the citizenship laws. Permanent deprivation of some rights only was applied (1) if a man brought a *graphe* (q.v.) and (*a*) dropped it, or (*b*) failed to get one-fifth of the votes at the trial; (2) if a man had been convicted three times in a γραφὴ παρανόμων; (3) for certain moral offences.

A. W. G.

**ATLANTIS,** i.e. '(the island) of Atlas', 'the island lying in the Atlantic'. A very large island off the Straits of Gibraltar, which, according to myth, once ruled southwest Europe and north-west Africa, till, in an expedition to conquer the rest, its kings were defeated by the prehistoric Athenians (Plato, *Tim.* 24 e ff.). Its constitution is the chief subject of the unfinished *Critias*. Memories of Atlantic islands or of the great volcanic eruption of Thera may be behind the myth. It is interesting as the oldest surviving philosophical wonderland in Greek, a predecessor of Euhemerus' Panchaia (see EUHEMERUS), and of Iambulus (Diod. Sic. 2. 55–60).

Cf. W. A. Heidel, *Proc. American Acad. of Arts and Sciences* 1933, 189 ff.; J. Bidez, *Bull. acad. roy. Belgique* 1934, 101 ff. H. J. R.

**ATLAS** (Ἄτλας), probably 'very enduring', ἀ intensive +root of τλᾶν; in mythology a Titan, son of Iapetus and Clymene (Hesiod, *Theog.* 509). He is guardian of the pillars of heaven (*Od.* 1. 53); but later (as Hesiod, ibid. 517, Aesch. *PV* 347 ff.), he himself holds the sky up. Both are well-known popular explanations of why the sky does not fall (see Stith Thompson, A665. 2, A842). Atlas became identified with the Atlas range in north-west Africa, or a peak of it (first in Herodotus 4. 184. 5–6); sky-supporting mountains are also popular (Stith Thompson A665. 3), and found elsewhere in Greek (Ap. Rhod. 3. 161, on which see Gillies ad loc.); a later tale explaining that Perseus had turned him into stone with the Gorgon's head is in Ovid, *Met.* 4. 655 ff. He was variously rationalized into a king (Plato, *Critias* 113 a), a shepherd (Polyidus ap. schol. Lycophron, 879), and an astronomer (Diod. Sic. 3. 60. 2). From his position in the far west, he is naturally brought into conjunction with the Hesperides, as in Ovid, loc. cit.; he is their father in Diod. Sic. 4. 27. 2. In Homer (*Od.* loc. cit.), he is father of Calypso, but usually his daughters are the Pleiades (favourite subjects of popular speculation, Stith Thompson A773), Alcyone, Celaeno, Electra, Maia, Merope, Sterope, and Taygete, whose names and local connexions (Maia with Arcadia, Electra with Troy, etc.) show that the African localization of their father is no part of their story. Besides his connexion with Perseus (see above) and Heracles (q.v.), when the latter was seeking the apples of the Hesperides. Atlas offered to fetch them if Heracles would uphold the sky meanwhile; he then refused to take back the burden, until forced or cheated into doing so by the hero (e.g. Pherecydes ap. schol. Ap. Rhod. 4. 1396). Atlas upholding the sky was represented in art from early times, is a favourite subject in Hellenistic art, and develops into an ornamental support. H. J. R.

**ATLAS MOUNTAINS,** the great range which formed the backbone of Roman Africa. Its highest peaks are in the Great Atlas to the west, and Greek legend converted them into the bowed shoulders of the god who held up the heavens (*see* ATLAS). The chain slopes eastward through Middle and Little Atlas to the Aurès. On the north the Atlas buttresses the Tell or fertile coastal plain. Southward the mountains slope down to the Saharan desert, which runs eastward to touch Lesser Syrtis (q.v.). Between Tell and Sahara are the High Plateaux with much good grazing land; in the centre and the east lie the shotts or salt lakes. Suetonius Paulinus crossed Mt. Atlas in A.D. 42 (Pliny, *HN* 5. 14–15).

A. N. Sherwin-White, *JRS* 1944, 1 ff. W. N. W.

**ATREBATES** (1), a tribe of Gallia Belgica. Conquered by Caesar in 57 B.C., they contributed 4,000 men to the Gallic forces at Alesia in 52, under Commius (q.v.), and revolted again in 51. Under the Empire they were noted for their woollens. Their centre was at Nemetacum (*Arras*), an important road junction; the 'Arras hoard', which included the medallion depicting London's submission to Constantius in 296, was found at Beaurains, 2 miles to the south, in 1922.

Hoard: J. Babelon and A. Duquesnoy, *Arethuse* i (1924), 45 ff.; A. Evans, *Num. Chron.* 1930, 221 ff. A. L. F. R.

**ATREBATES** (2), an offshoot of a Gaulish tribe which had entered Britain before 54 B.C. and occupied a region between the Thames, the Test, and West Sussex. Successive rulers recorded by coins were Commius, Tincommius (qq.v.), Eppillus, and Verica; the last three appear to have had treaties with Rome. After A.D. 43 part at least of the area was ruled by Cogidubnus (q.v.) but eventually three *civitates* were created: (i) of the Atrebates with *caput* at Calleva (Silchester), (ii) of the Belgae with *caput* at Venta (Winchester), (iii) of the Regnenses with *caput* at Noviomagus (Chichester). An imperial tile-works of the reign of Nero existed at Pamber. Sub-Roman earthworks near Silchester suggest the survival of the town well into the Dark Age, a conclusion confirmed by the tombstone of Ebicatos inscribed in Ogham characters (perhaps sixth century).

C. E. Stevens in W. F. Grimes (ed.), *Aspects of Archaeology in Britain* (1951), 332 ff.; A. L. F. Rivet, *Town and Country in Rom. Brit.*[2] (1964), 139 ff.; Frere, *Britannia*, ch. iv and v; B. H. St. J. O'Neil, *Antiquity* 1944, 113 ff. S. S. F.

**ATREUS**, in mythology, son of Pelops (*see* TANTALUS) and husband of Aërope. From late epic on (*Alcmaeonis* ap. schol. Eur. *Or.* 995) he and his brother Thyestes are at variance. Hermes was wroth with the whole house for the death of his son Myrtilus (*see* PELOPS) and gave them a golden ram, the possession of which carried the kingship with it; Thyestes got this from Aërope, whose paramour he was; Atreus banished him, but later pretended a reconciliation. At the banquet held to consummate this, Atreus served up to Thyestes the flesh of the latter's own children, at which the sun turned back on its course in horror. *See further* AEGISTHUS. In another version (Apollod. *Epit.* 2. 12) Atreus by advice of Hermes offers to let Thyestes, who has seized the throne, keep it till the sun turns back; Thyestes agrees, and Zeus immediately turns the sun backwards, the rest of the story following much as above. There are numerous other variants; the story was much elaborated by the tragedians, see for instance Eur. *El.* 699 ff.; *Or.* 995 ff.; Seneca, *Thyestes*, passim. Continuous narratives, Apollod., loc. cit.; Hyg., *Fab.* 86–8; more in Roscher's *Lexikon*, art. 'Atreus' (Furtwängler). H. J. R.

**ATRIUM VESTAE**, an ancient precinct, east of the *Forum Romanum*, comprising the *aedes* and *lucus Vestae*, *Regia*, *domus publica*, and *domus Vestalium*. Republican remains of the last two underlie the existing *domus Vestalium*, built after Nero's fire of A.D. 64. The western ritual-kitchen is Flavian, while the eastern *exedra*, once

fronting a closed garden behind Nero's small peristyle, is Hadrianic. The Antonines, uniting the rooms groupe about the Neronian courtyard, added second and third stories. The enlarged peristyle now visible is Severan Later additions are of minor significance.

E. B. van Deman, *Atrium Vestae* (U.S.A. 1909); *Bull. Com.*, 1930 207 ff.; G. Lugli, *Roma antica* (1946), 202 ff.; Nash, *Pict. Dic Rome* 1, 154 ff. I. A. R

**ATTA**, TITUS QUINCTIUS (*PW* 21, d. 77 B.C.), Latin poet composed *comoediae togatae*, elegiac epigrams, and per haps *satura*. Fragments, and titles of eleven plays survive He excelled in character-drawing, especially feminine

FRAGMENTS. Ribbeck, *CRF*[2], 160 (3rd ed. Teubner, 1897).

**ATTALEIA**, now *Antalya*, a city of Pamphylia, founde by Attalus II, perhaps with Athenian settlers; on it imperial coins the city boasts kinship with Athens. In 7 B.C. it was mulcted of its territory by Servilius Isauricu for its complicity with the pirate king Zenicetes. Thes lands were probably utilized by Augustus for settling veterans, but Attaleia was not made a colony, a statu which it achieved only in the late third century. Apar from the city-walls the ruins are scanty.

K. Lanckoroński, *Städte Pamphyliens* (1890), i. 7 ff. A. H. M. J

**ATTALUS I** (SOTER) of Pergamum, 269–197 B.C., so of Attalus a cousin of Eumenes I, whom he succeede (241). He was the first to refuse 'tribute' to the Galatians and his great victory over them (before 230) was com memorated by his cult-name *Soter*, by the triumpha monument at Pergamum famous for its 'dying Gaul and probably by the title of King (which Eumenes ha never taken). His counter-attack on Antiochus (q.v. 8 Hierax who had co-operated with the Galatians, gaine him all Seleucid Asia Minor except Cilicia (229–228 but Achaeus (q.v. 3) (223–220), cousin and general of Antiochus III, deprived him of most of his conquests.

Attalus now inaugurated a 'western' policy which wa to give a new turn to the history of Pergamum. Th dangerous ambitions of Philip V of Macedonia prompte him to support Philip's enemies the Aetolians, first wit subsidies (220–217), and later with troops and a flee (210–207). After the peace of Phoenice (205), Attalu replied to Philip's acts of aggression near the Hellespon by renewing the war in alliance with Rhodes (201), an securing Roman intervention against Macedon in com mon with the Rhodians. During the 'Second Mace donian War' he co-operated with the Romans by sea. H died shortly before the final victory.

An excellent general and diplomatist, Attalus raise Pergamum almost to the rank of a Great Power. Betwee Philip and Antiochus, he chose to live dangerously, an his approach to Rome, though brilliantly successful i its immediate rewards (*see also* EUMENES II), ultimatel made Pergamum a pawn of Roman policy, beside precipitating the collapse of the Hellenistic political sys tem. Apart from politics, Attalus was a notable patron o literature, philosophy, and the arts, and enjoyed a con spicuous domestic happiness with his wife Apollonis o Cyzicus and their four sons.

Hansen, *Attalids*, esp. ch. 3; *and see under* PERGAMUM. G. T. C

**ATTALUS II** (PHILADELPHUS), 220–138 B.C., secon son of Attalus I, and brother of Eumenes II, whom h succeeded (160–159). Before 160 he showed himself skilful soldier and diplomatist, and was conspicuousl loyal to Eumenes, whom he could probably have sup planted, with Roman support, at any time after 168 (*se* EUMENES II). As king, he fulfilled the (by now) tradition Pergamene part of watch-dog for Rome in the East. H equipped and supported the pretender Alexander Bala to win the Seleucid throne from Demetrius I (153–150); likewise Rome supported Attalus in his two wars with Bithynia. Like all the Attalids, he was genuinely interested in letters and the arts.

Hansen, *Attalids*, esp. 123 ff.        G. T. G.

**ATTALUS III** (PHILOMETOR EUERGETES), *c.* 170–133 B.C., son of Eumenes II and successor of Attalus II (138). His short reign was famous only for its dénouement, the 'Testament of Attalus' bequeathing the kingdom of Pergamum to Rome (*OGI* 338). Its motive has never been perfectly explained, especially as Attalus was comparatively young and presumably did not expect a premature death. But the revolution after his death (*see* ARISTONICUS 1) suggests that he may have made and published this testament partly as an insurance against social revolution while he survived.

Hansen, *Attalids*, 134 ff.        G. T. G.

**ATTHIS** (Ἀτθίς), a type of literature dealing specifically with the history of Attica which became popular *c.* 350–250 B.C. under the influence of the Sophists and Peripatetics and the general conception fostered by Isocrates and the Orators of a return to the past glory of Athens. Hellanicus' history of Attica (Thuc. i. 97), published soon after 404 B.C., was not strictly an *Atthis*, but may have set the pattern for the longer works written after 350 B.C.

Cleidemus was recognized by Pausanias 10. 15. 5 as the first atthidographer, followed by Androtion, Phanodemus, Demon, Melanthius, and Philochorus whose *Atthis* ended shortly after the Chremonidean War. The later work of Ister (q.v.), of Cyrene described as Συναγωγὴ τῶν Ἀτθίδων, seems to have been an epitome of previous *Atthides*. Most atthidographers held priestly or political offices and produced other works on religious antiquities. Characteristics of the *Atthides* are their chronological arrangement, emphasis on mythology, and origins of cults and descriptions of political institutions. Scholia to Aristophanes and the *Marmor Parium* show their accepted value for dates. Their contents were traditional including the history of Athens from primeval times to contemporary events, and their length steadily increased. Although the authors adopted different interpretations of events (the *Atthides* perhaps reflected current political rivalries) they did not seek new sources of information and generally agreed on the main facts of history. The *Atthides* were often used by later commentators for constitutional and topographical details.

F. Jacoby, *Atthis, the local chronicles of Ancient Athens* (1949), who rejects the view of Wilamowitz, *Aristoteles und Athen* i (1893), that he first *Atthis* was compiled by an anonymous writer *c.* 380 B.C. from the records of the Exegetae; K. von Fritz, *Atthidographers and Exegetae* and L. Pearson, *The Local Historians of Attica, TAPA* 1940 and 1942. *See also* HISTORIOGRAPHY, GREEK, § 5.      G. L. B.

**ATTIANUS**, PUBLIUS ACILIUS (*PW*, s.v. Caelius 17, but inscriptions do not support the name *Caelius*, found only in S.H.A. *Hadr.* 1. 4), an equestrian of Italica, became guardian and adviser of the young Hadrian (q.v.). He was almost certainly *praefectus praetorio* when Trajan died in A.D. 117 and helped Plotina to secure Hadrian's succession. Probably in 119, Hadrian enrolled Attianus in the Senate with consular rank, ostensibly to honour him, but perhaps in fact to remove him from office because of his part in securing the execution of four 'consular' generals for a presumed plot (*see* HADRIAN). He was succeeded as prefect by Turbo (q.v.).

S. H. A. *Hadr.*; Dio Cassius bk. 69; R. H. Lacey, *The Equestrian Officials of Trajan and Hadrian, etc.* (Diss. Princeton, 1917), 16, p. 37; Lambrechts, *Sénat*, no. 2; Syme, *Tacitus*, see index.      C. H. V. S.; M. H.

**ATTIC CULTS AND MYTHS.** The chief goddess was of course Athena, her festivals being Arrhetophoria

(Pyanopsion and Scirophorion; for the month-names, *see* CALENDARS), Procharisteria (early spring; both the above are agricultural), Callynteria and Plynteria (Thargelion; ceremonial cleansing of temple and statue), Panathenaea (q.v., Hecatombaeon 28, Great Panathenaea every four years), and Chalceia (last day of Pyanopsion). Other gods and goddesses were celebrated at the following festivals: Demeter and Core—Scira (*see* SCIROPHORIA, Scirophorion 12), Thesmophoria (q.v., Pyanopsion 10 at Halimus, 11–13 at Athens), Haloa (Poseideon), Chloia (early spring, to Demeter Chloë and Core, at Eleusis), Lesser Mysteries at Agrae (Anthesterion), Greater Mysteries beginning at Athens and ending at Eleusis (Boedromion 15–22: *see* MYSTERIES). Dionysus—Anthesteria (q.v., Anthesterion 11–13; apparently a blend of his worship with an All Souls feast), Lenaea (q.v., Gamelion ? 12), Rural Dionysia (*see* DIONYSIA, Poseideon), Great or City Dionysia (Elaphebolion 9–13 or 14, see J. T. Allen in *Univ. of Calif. Publns.* xii, 35 ff.; this and the Lenaea were the great dramatic festivals), Oschophoria (Pyanopsion ? 8). Kronos—Kronia (Hecatombaeon 12). Zeus—Diasia (Anthesterion 23, to Zeus Meilichios, *see* ZEUS), Dipolieia (Scirophorion 14), Diisoteria (Scirophorion, at Piraeus), and some minor feasts. Apollo—Thargelia (q.v., Thargelion 7), Pyanopsia (Pyanopsion 7). Artemis—Munichia (Munichion 16); Brauronia (at Brauron, unknown date, *see* ARTEMIS), Tauropolia (Halae, unknown date), Elaphebolia (unknown, gave its name to the month Elaphebolion). There were also festivals, of which not much is known, to Poseidon, Hephaestus, Prometheus, the Eumenides, and some minor deities.

The best-known myths have to do with Athena and Poseidon (qq.v.). Heroic and aetiological tales centre on the vague and contradictory line of kings, dealing mainly with Cecrops (*see* CULTURE-BRINGERS), Erichthonius, Erechtheus (q.v.), and above all Theseus (q.v.). There is besides the story of Cephalus (q.v.) and Procris, and a few others little known. *See also* BENDIS, ERIGONE, NEMESIS (1).

S. Solders, *Die ausserstädtischen Kulte und die Einigung Attikas* (1931). L. Deubner, *Attische Feste* (1932).      H. J. R.

**ATTIC ORATORS.** Caecilius of Calacte in the Augustan age wrote 'On the style of the ten orators', namely Antiphon, Andocides, Lysias, Isocrates, Isaeus, Lycurgus, Aeschines, Demosthenes, Hyperides, Dinarchus. This 'canon', though ignored by Dionysius, was recognized by the ps.-Plutarch, Quintilian, and later writers. Its origin is unknown, but the arbitrary inclusion of a definite number of names in such a class is characteristic of Alexandrian scholarship.

ANCIENT SOURCES. Pseudo-Plutarch, *Lives of the Ten Orators*; Dionysius of Halicarnassus, *De Verborum Compositione* and *Letters to Ammaeus*; Demetrius, *De Elocutione*; Hermogenes Περὶ ἰδεῶν; [Longinus], *On the Sublime*.
MODERN WORKS. F. Blass, *Die attische Beredsamkeit²* (1887–98); R. C. Jebb, *The Attic Orators from Antiphon to Isaeus²* (1893); J. F. Dobson, *The Greek Orators* (1919); Grote, *History of Greece*; *CAH* vii; Croiset, *Histoire de la litt. grecque* v. G. Kennedy, *The Art of Persuasion in Greece* (1963).
TEXTS. *Oratores Attici*, I. Bekker (1828); do. G. S. Dobson (1828); Text and Translation of *Minor Attic Orators*, K. J. Maidment and J. O. Burtt (2 vols. Loeb). *Selections from the Attic Orators* (text and commentary), R. C. Jebb (2nd ed. 1888).
See also under the names of the various orators.      J. F. D.

**ATTICA**, a triangular promontory constituting the easternmost part of central Greece, separated from Boeotia by Mts. Parnes and Cithaeron and from Megara by Mt. Cerata. This area of about 1,000 sq. m. is dominated by four mountain systems, Aegaleos, Hymettus, Pentelicus, and Laurium, which divide the landscape into three interconnected plains, to the west the Thriasian plain with its chief town at Eleusis where Demeter gave corn to man, in the centre the larger but stonier Attic plain, and to the east the Mesogeia suitable for the vine, olive, and fig, as well as two smaller parcels of arable land to the north-east around Marathon and Aphidna. Attica's wealth, however, lay not so much in the light, sparsely watered soil, as in natural resources: excellent potter's clay, white and blue marble from Pentelicus and Hymettus, and silver and lead from Laurium (q.v.).

From Neolithic times so large a district encouraged the growth of many separate communities that were at first independent. The tradition of twelve townships in the time of Cecrops appears justified in the light of the copious Mycenaean remains from Eleusis, Marathon, Thoricus, and elsewhere. But then occurred the *synoekismos* (q.v.), a fusing of these disparate entities into a single Athenian state, an act attributed to Theseus though in fact a gradual process lasting probably until the seventh century (*see* ELEUSIS). The choice of Athens as capital was natural; not only was the city located within the largest plain, but it was also the centre of communications. That it had ready access to the sea at Phalerum and Piraeus was later to prove a consideration of the highest significance.

This ascendancy of Athens, religious as well as political (for the major rural cults were duplicated in the city), did not at first unduly weaken the importance and vigour of the Attic countryside. Power and wealth continued to be locally based as were men's loyalties, and the rich finds of archaic sculpture and pottery show that in the sixth century aristocratic families lived throughout Attica in a style (and with a following) akin to feudal barons. However, the tyranny of Pisistratus and the reforms of Cleisthenes broke the strength of these local associations by making everyone dependent upon the organized, central government at Athens, a dependency further intensified in the fifth century by the adoption of an aggressive foreign policy based on sea-power and sea-borne trade. Attica had now become an appendage to Athens and in an emergency such as the Peloponnesian War could be disregarded.

GENERAL LITERATURE. Cary, *Geographic Background*, 75 ff.; P-K, *GL* 1, pt. 3.; R. J. Hopper, *BSA* 1961, 189 ff.
TOPOGRAPHY. E. Curtius and A. Milchhöfer, text to *Karten von Attika* (1881–1900).
CULTS AND HISTORY. S. Solders, *Die ausserstädtischen Kulte und die Einigung Attikas* (1931).
MAPS. British Staff, 1 : 100,000; Curtius–Kaupert, *Karten von Attika* 1 : 25,000; Ἐλευθερουδάκης, 1 : 100,000; Greek Staff, 1 : 20,000.
C. W. J. E.

**ATTICA,** CAECILIA (*PW* Pomponii 78), daughter of Atticus, born 51 B.C. As a child she is frequently mentioned in Cicero's correspondence. Married to Agrippa through the good offices of Antony (*c.* 37), she was the mother of Agrippina (1). Suspected of misconduct with her tutor, Caecilius (q.v. 3) Epirota, she may have been divorced; or else she died young; at all events Agrippa married again *c.* 28.
T. J. C.

**ATTICUS** (1), TITUS POMPONIUS (*PW* 102, Suppl. 8), born in 110 B.C. as the son of a rich and cultured knight, was later adopted by an even richer uncle, whose wealth he inherited. He was a boyhood friend of Cicero, whose brother Quintus married Atticus' sister, and whose *Letters to Atticus* (which Atticus himself perhaps edited some time after Cicero's death) are the best source for his life and character. (There is also a useful, but uncritical, biographical sketch by his friend Nepos.) In 85 Atticus left Rome after realizing his assets in Italy, in order to escape the civil disturbances that he foresaw, and settled in Athens until the middle sixties (hence his *cognomen*). He there studied and adopted the Epicurean philosophy and henceforth combined a life of cultured ease and literary activity with immense success in business (where his methods were no better or worse than what we know of his contemporaries') and an infallible

instinct for survival. While urging Cicero privately t determined action on behalf of the Optimates (with who he sympathized), especially in 49, he himself refused t engage in politics and helped all prominent politician in need, from Marius to Octavian, without becomin embroiled in their differences. He was Cicero's literar adviser and publisher and himself wrote a *Liber Annal* (a chronological table of world, and especially of Roman history), which became a standard work, and othe historical books (all now lost). He lived to become friend of Agrippa, who married his daughter, and i 32 he committed suicide when suffering from an incurabl illness.

Cicero and Nepos (see above). Shackleton Bailey, *Cicero's Letter to Atticus*, i (1965), 3 ff.
E. F

**ATTICUS** (2), JULIUS, like Graecinus (q.v.), a Latin writer on vines in Tiberius' time, who was a source fo Columella (3. 17. 4) and Pliny (*HN* 17. 90.)

Schanz–Hosius § 497. 1.

**ATTICUS** (3) (*c.* A.D. 150–200), Platonist, opposed th infiltration of Peripatetic elements into Platonism, bu himself introduced into it certain doctrines proper t Stoicism.

**ATTILA,** king of the Huns (q.v.) (A.D. 434–53), at firs ruled jointly with his brother Bleda, whom he murdere in 445. The empire which he inherited from his predeces sors stretched from the Alps to the Caspian Sea. Hi major military campaigns were those of 441–3 and 44 against the Eastern Empire, where he ravaged th Balkan provinces and Greece; that of 451, when he in vaded Gaul but was defeated at the Catalaunian Plain by the Romans, led by Aetius, and the Visigoths; and that of 452, when he invaded Italy and sacked some of the most famous cities there. He intended to invade the Eastern Empire again in 453, but died during the nigh after his marriage to a girl called Ildico. He was of a blustering, arrogant character, a persistent negotiator but not pitiless. No detailed description has survived of any of his battles.

E. A. Thompson, *A History of Attila and the Huns* (1948). E. A. T

**ATTIS,** in mythology, the youthful consort of Cybele (q.v.) and prototype of her eunuch devotees. The myth exists in two main forms, with many variants. According to the Phrygian tale (Paus. 7. 17. 10–12; cf. Arn. *Adv. Nat* 5. 5–7), the gods castrated the androgynous Agdistis (q.v.); from the severed male parts an almond tree sprang and by its fruit Nana conceived Attis. Later Agdistis fell in love with him, and to prevent his marriage to another caused him to castrate himself. Agdistis is clearly a doublet of Cybele, though Arnobius brings them both into his account. Ovid (*Fasti* 4. 221–44) and others change many details, but keep the essential aetiological feature, the self-castration. In a probably Lydian version Attis, like Adonis, is killed by a boar. The story of Atys, son of Croesus, who was killed by the Phrygian Adrastus in a boar-hunt (Hdt. 1. 34–35) is an adaptation of this, and attests its antiquity, though the Phrygian is probably the older version.

In Asia Minor Attis bears his native name only in the Neo-Phrygian inscriptions, though the high priest and, under the Empire, all members of the priestly college at Pessinus had the title Attis. Attis is sometimes called Papas or Zeus Papas.

Whatever his original character, vegetation god or mortal lover of Cybele, in the early cult he remains a subsidiary figure, whose death is mourned but who is not, apparently, worshipped. He appears only rarely in Greece, but at Rome attained official status under laudius, and after *c.* A.D. 150 becomes an equal partner the cult. Under the later Empire he was invested with lestial attributes, and became a solar deity, supreme, l-powerful, and sometimes it seems a surety of im-ortality to his initiates. In art he is generally repre-nted as an effeminate youth, with the distinctive arygian cap and trousers. *See* ANATOLIAN DEITIES; BELE; EUNUCHS, RELIGIOUS.

J. Carcopino, *Mél. d' Arch. et d'Hist.*, 1923, 135 ff., 237 ff.; Cumont, *l. or.*; H. Hepding, *Attis* (1903); H. Graillot, *Le Culte de Cybèle* 12); H. Strathmann, *RAC*, s.v.; M. P. Nilsson, *GGR*², ii, 640 ff.; Lambrechts, *Attis: van herdersknaap tot god* (1962), with French umé; M. J. Vermaseren, *The Legend of Attis,in Greek and Roman* *t* (Leiden, 1966). F. R. W.

**UDAX** (probably 6th c. A.D.), grammarian, whose *De :auri et Palladii Libris excerpta* is extant (ed. Keil, *ramm. Lat.* 7. 320–62).

Schanz–Hosius § 1105.

**UFIDIUS** (1, *PW* 15) **BASSUS** (fl. mid 1st c. A.D.), e imperial historian, an Epicurean and subject to ill alth, which prevented a public career, wrote on the erman Wars (*Bellum Germanicum*), probably under iberius and glorifying his achievements of A.D. 4–16. e also wrote a history of his times, probably under laudius, which may have begun with Caesar's death, cluded Cicero's death (Sen. *Suas.* 6. 18; 23), and was ntinued by the Elder Pliny under the title *a fine ufidii Bassi*. This indicates an inconspicuous closing int, which may fall in A.D. 31, but is, on the evidence Tacitus' use of Pliny, better set *c.* A.D. 50. In authority e ranks among the great historians of the early Empire Quint. 10. 1. 103).

Peter, *HRRel* ii. cxxxv, 96; Ph. Fabia, *Les Sources de Tacite* (1893), 5, 355; cf. F. Münzer, *Rh. Mus.* 1907, 161 ff.; Syme, *Tacitus*, 4, 288, 697 ff. A. H. McD.

**UFIDIUS** (2, *PW* 6), GNAEUS, praetor in 107 B.C., rote a 'Graeca historia', probably of Rome (*Tusc.* 5. 2).

*FGrH* 814.

**UFIDIUS** (3), MODESTUS, commentator on Virgil and orace, in the first century A.D.

Schanz–Hosius § 264.

**UFIDUS** (modern *Ofanto*), the most important river southern Italy. A powerful stream in winter and uggish creek in summer, it rises near the Tyrrhenian a but flows into the Adriatic, through the territories of irpini and Apuli, past Canusium and Cannae. Horace, native of nearby Venusia, often mentions it. E. T. S.

**UGURES**, official Roman diviners, forming a *col-ium* which consisted originally of three but was adually increased to sixteen members (Livy 10. 6. 7–8 d *periocha* 89; Dio Cassius 42. 51. 4), one of the attuor amplissima collegia. Etymology uncertain; the aditional derivation from *aui+ger*(o) would give *\*auger*, t *augur*; that from the root *aug*(*eo*) (see E. Flinck *nn. Acad. Scient. Fennicae* 1921, 3 ff.), suggests rites fertility rather than divination, but the transition is t impossible, cf. AUGURIUM CANARIUM. Their business as not to foretell the future, but to discover by observa-n of signs (*auguria*), either casually met with (*oblativa*) watched for (*impetrativa*), whether the gods did or d not approve a proposed action. The most charac-ristic signs were given by birds (hence the traditional ymology). These might be chickens, which were carried y armies in the field for the purpose; food was given to em, and if they ate it so as to drop some from their aks, that was an excellent sign ('tripudium solistimum',

Cicero, *Div.* 2. 72, where see Pease). If wild birds were observed, the augur marked out a *templum* (cf. DIVINA-TION), i.e. he designated boundaries by word of mouth (see e.g. Varro, *Ling.* 7. 7–8, which gives the formula) within which he would look for signs, and divided this space into *sinistra*, *dextra*, *antica*, and *postica* (*pars*); the significance of the flight or cry of the bird varied according to the part in which it was heard or seen. The officiant faced south or east (H. J. Rose, *JRS* 1923, 82 ff). Such observations prefaced every important action public or (at least in early times) private, but to accept or reject augural advice was the responsibility of the magistrate or other person performing the action. For *augurium salutis*, *see* SALUS, and for augury in general *see* DIVINATION; RELIGION, ETRUSCAN. For the Auguratorium on the Palatine where Romulus is said to have taken the auspices for his new city, see Nash, *Pict. Dict. Rome* 1, 163.

Bouché-Leclercq, *Histoire de la Divination* iv. 209 ff.; Wissowa, *RK* 523 ff.; Latte, *RR* 67, 397; P. Catalano, *Contributi allo studio del diritto augurale* (1960). H. J. R.

**AUGURINUS**, SENTIUS, a young friend praised by Pliny (*Ep.* 4. 27; 9. 8) for writing 'Poems in Little' (*poematia*) marked by charm and tenderness, but some-times by satire. Pliny quotes eight hendecasyllabics by him in the manner of Catullus and Calvus. Possibly he is identical with Q. Gellius Sentius Augurinus, proconsul under Hadrian (*CIL* 3. 586).

Baehr. *FPR*; Morel *FPL*. J. W. D.; G. B. A. F.

**AUGURIUM CANARIUM.** Ateius Capito (in Festus, 358, 27 Lindsay) says that reddish (*rutilae*) bitches were sacrificed *canario sacrificio pro frugibus*, to 'deprecate' the fierceness of the Dog-star. Cf. Fest. (Paulus), 39, 13, from which it would appear that the place was near the Porta Catularia and the time fairly late summer, since the crops were yellowing (*flauescentes*). This seems to be the *sacrum canarium* of Daniel's Servius on *G.* 4. 424. The ritual name, however, was *augurium canarium*, as is shown by Pliny (*HN* 18. 14) who quotes from the *com-mentarii pontificum* (q.v.) the direction that the days (*dies*; it is not clear whether the rite lasted more than one day or the various days for different years are meant) for it should be fixed 'priusquam frumenta uaginis exeant nec (et *codd.*, corr. Ulrichs) antequam in uaginas perueniant', that is to say some time in spring (see L. Delatte, *Ant. Class.* 1937, 93 ff.). The name probably means 'augurium of the dog-days'. It is most unlikely that it was a sacrifice to the Dog-star; it may have been an augury in the sense that omens for the result of the harvest were taken from the victims, but if the second etymology given under 'AUGURES' is right, it is tempting to make it mean 'cere-mony of increase for the dog-days'. There is no evidence, though some probability, that the augurs took part and no reason to suppose it performed in honour of any god.

Latte, *RR* 68. H. J. R.

**AUGUSTA** (1) **PRAETORIA** (now *Aosta*), a colony founded with 3,000 Praetorians on the Duria Maior in Cisalpine Gaul by Augustus (24 B.C.); it was here that Terentius Varro had encamped the previous year when subjugating the Salassi (q.v. Strabo 4. 206; Cass. Dio 53. 25). Standing at the Italian end of the Great and Little St. Bernard Passes over Pennine and Graian Alps respectively, Augusta became and still remains the capital of this whole region (*Val d'Aosta*).

For inscriptions see P. Barocelli, *Inscriptiones Italiae* i, fasc. 1 (1932); for Roman monuments, F. Haverfield, *Ancient Town Planning* (1913). F. Eyssenhardt, *Aosta und seine Alterthümer* (1896); P. Toesca, *Aosta* (1911). E. T. S.

**AUGUSTA** (2) **RAURICA** (now *Augst*, near Basle), a colony founded by Munatius Plancus (q.v. 1) in 44 B.C. in the territory of the Raurici. Strengthened by Augustus, it formed with Aug. Praetoria and Aug. Vindelicorum a linked communication system and was a frontier post in the Upper Rhine valley. Though attacked by the Alamanni in A.D. 259/60, it flourished in the second and third centuries, as witnessed by the surviving remains: forum, temples, theatre, amphitheatre, basilica, baths, curia, dwellings; the city wall, begun in the third century, was uncompleted. Under Diocletian it was succeeded by a garrison nearer the Rhine in Castrum Rauracense (Kaiseraugst).

F. Stähelin, *Die Schweiz in röm. Zeit*[3] (1948), 95 ff., 597 ff.; R. Laur, *Führer durch Augusta Raurica*[3] (1959); for find of mid-fourth-century silver, R. Laur, *Der Silberschatz von Kaiseraugst* (1963).
H. H. S.

**AUGUSTA** (3) **TAURINORUM** (now *Torino, Turin*), an important Augustan *colonia* in Cisalpine Gaul, situated at the foot of the Mont Genèvre Pass over the Cottian Alps and at the confluence of the Duria Minor and the Padus (q.v.), which here became navigable (Pliny, *HN* 3. 123). Originally the capital of the Taurini, who were probably celticized Ligurians, it is apparently identical with the Taurasia captured by Hannibal, 218 B.C. (App. *Hann.* 5). Tacitus (*Hist.* 2. 66) records its burning in A.D. 69. Ancient authors seldom mention it. The modern city preserves the ancient street plan.

F. Haverfield, *Ancient Town Planning* (1913), 87; G. Bendinelli, *Torino Romana* (1928).
E. T. S.

**AUGUSTA** (4) **TREVERORUM**, modern *Trier* or *Trèves*, was founded by Augustus. It rapidly became the chief city of north-east Gaul, and an important trade centre between Gaul and the Rhineland; its colonial status, if not already conferred by Augustus, probably dates from Claudius. It was the seat of the *procurator provinciae Belgicae et duarum Germaniarum*; Postumus made it his capital, a precedent followed by Maximian and Constantius Chlorus (though it had been badly damaged by the Franks and Alamanni in 275/6), and it remained the capital of the Prefecture of Gaul from 297 until early in the fifth century, when it was abandoned to the Franks. Its bishop enjoyed a corresponding importance.

Trier grew far beyond the original settlement, to cover 700 acres. Notable ruins, mostly of the period when the city was frequently the imperial residence, survived into modern times—e.g. the 'Porta Nigra' (a late Roman gateway), remains of public halls, including an imperial audience hall, baths, and the first-century amphitheatre (restored by Constantius Chlorus). Excavation has revealed an extensive temple quarter (already used in pre-Roman times) outside the town, comprising about seventy shrines, a theatre, and priests' dwellings. Pottery (including samian ware) and cloth manufactured in Trier were widely exported; the city had an imperial mint from at least 296 and was also a centre of the Moselle wine trade.

K. Schumacher, *Siedelungs- und Kulturgeschichte der Rheinlande*, Bd. ii (1923).
O. B.; P. S.

**AUGUSTA** (5) **VINDELIC(OR)UM** (now *Augsburg*) probably dates from *c.* A.D. 6–9, when the legion stationed at Oberhausen nearby was sent away. It lay at the centre of a network of important roads and was from the first the administrative and trading centre of Raetia (cf. Tac. *Germ.* 41). Hadrian raised it to municipal status (122–3), and after the reorganization under Diocletian it remained the civil capital of Raetia Secunda. It became the seat of a bishop. Nothing of Roman Augsburg remains above

ground, but numerous sculptures and smaller obje have been found.

W. Hübener, *Jahrbuch d. Röm.-Germ. Zentral-museums, M*[a] 1958, 154 ff.
O.

**AUGUSTINUS**, AURELIUS (St. Augustine, A.D. 35 430), was born at Thagaste (*Souk Ahras*, Algeria), s of Patricius and a dominant Catholic mother, Moni He taught rhetoric at Carthage, Rome, and (384 to 3 at Milan. Patronized by Symmachus (q.v. 2), the pag orator, he hoped, by an advantageous marriage (to wh he sacrificed his concubine, the mother of a son, Ad datus—d. *c.* 390) to join the 'aristocracy of letters' typi of his age (*see* AUSONIUS). At 19, however, he had read *Hortensius* of Cicero. This early 'conversion to phi sophy' was the prototype of successive conversions: Manichaeism (q.v.), a Gnostic sect promising Wisdo and, in 386, to a Christianized Neo-Platonism (q.v patronized by Ambrose (q.v.), bishop of Mila Catholicism, for Augustine, was the 'Divine Philosoph a Wisdom guaranteed by authority but explored reason: *Seek and ye shall find*, the only Scriptural citati in his first work, characterizes his life as a thinker.

Though the only Latin philosopher to fail to mas Greek, Augustine transformed Latin Christianity by Neo-Platonism: his last recorded words echo Plotin (q.v.). Stimulated by abrupt changes—he was forcil ordained priest at Hippo (*Bône*, Algeria) in 391, beco ing bishop in 395—and by frequent controversies ( DONATISTS, PELAGIUS), Augustine developed his id with an independence that disquieted even his admire He has left his distinctive mark on most aspects western Christianity.

Augustine's major works are landmarks in the aba donment of classical ideals. His early optimism was so overshadowed by a radical doctrine of grace. This chan was canonized in an autobiographical masterpiece, t *Confessions* (*c.* 397–400), a vivid if highly selective sou for his life to 388 and, equally, a mirror of his chang outlook. *De Doctrina Christiana* (begun 396/7) sketch a literary culture subordinated to the Bible. *De Trinit* (399 to 419) provided a more radically philosophi statement of the doctrine of the Trinity than any Gre Father. *De Civitate Dei* (413 to 426) presented a d finitive juxtaposition of Christianity with litera paganism and Neo-Platonism, notably with Porphy (q.v.). After 412, he combatted in Pelagianism vie which, 'like the philosophers of the pagans', h promised men fulfilment by their unaided efforts. In *Retractationes* (427) Augustine criticized his supe abundant output of 93 works in the light of a Catho orthodoxy to which he believed he had progressively co formed—less consistently, perhaps, than he realized.

Letters and verbatim sermons richly docume Augustine's complex life as a bishop: the centre of a gro of sophisticated ascetics (notably Paulinus of Nola), t 'slave' of a simple congregation, he was, above all, man dedicated to the authority of the Catholic Chur This authority had enabled his restless intellect to wo creatively: he would uphold it, in Africa, by every mea from writing a popular song to elaborating the o explicit justification in the Early Church of a policy religious persecution (*see* DONATISTS).

WORKS. Migne, *PL* xxxii–xlvii; see C. Andresen, *Bibliograp Augustiniana* (1962). Consult especially: H.-I. Marrou, *St. Augu et la fin de la culture antique*[4] (1958); P. Courcelle, *Recherches sur Confessions* (1950), *Les Confessions de St. Augustin dans la tradi littéraire* (1963); R. Holte, *Béatitude et Sagesse* (1962); F. van Meer, *St. Augustine the Bishop* (Engl. trans. 1961); P. Bro Augustine of Hippo* (1967).
P. R. L.

**AUGUSTODUNUM** (modern *Autun*), a town Gallia Belgica, founded *c.* 12 B.C. in the plain of t Arroux to replace the hill-town Bibracte. It was l

t on a large scale (area *c.* 490 acres), and important
ildings (including two town gates) survive. It was
lebrated as a centre of learning both in the first and in
e fourth centuries A.D. It suffered for its fidelity to
audius II (A.D. 269), and was ruined after a seven-
onth siege. Its restoration under Constantius I is
lebrated by Eugenius, master of the local 'Scholae
aenianae'. But the reduced perimeter of the town wall
ows its depopulation.

H. de Fontenay, *Autun et ses Monuments* (1889); F. J. Haverfield,
*cient Town Planning* (1913), 121 ff.; Grenier, *Manuel* iii. (1956),
ff.; É. Thevenot, *Autun* (1932); id., *Les Voies rom. de la cité des*
*uens* (1969).                                                    C. E. S.

**UGUSTUS** (63 B.C.–A.D. 14). C. Octavius, born on
Sept. 63 B.C., was brought up by his mother Atia
v. 1), Caesar's niece, as his father C. Octavius (q.v. 4)
ed in 59. His teachers gave him a taste for literature
d philosophy, but Caesar himself introduced him to
oman life. Aged 12, he pronounced the *laudatio* of
s grandmother Julia; he was appointed pontifex; in
B.C. he accompanied his great-uncle in his triumph.
espite delicate health, he joined Caesar in Spain in 45.
Apollonia, where he had been sent with his friends,
Agrippa and Salvidienus Rufus, to complete his
idies, he learnt of Caesar's sudden death. The opening
Caesar's will revealed that Octavius had been adopted
d made his chief heir by the dictator. He decided to
turn to Italy and to avenge Caesar. The unexpected
uation imposed new duties and stimulated new ambi-
ns. Caesar had lived long enough to afford an inspiring
ample, but had died soon enough not to destroy the
oman traditionalism of his heir. Octavius was cautious
d superstitious, but exceptionally mature, clever, and
cided. In Italy he gained Cicero's sympathy and
ntony's distrust. He celebrated the *ludi Victoriae*
aesaris* and, while linking himself with the moderate
publicans, did not overlook Caesar's veterans. During
e conflict between Antony and Dec. Brutus (q.v. 6)
obtained from the Senate the rank of senator and
opraetor, and emerged victorious from the war of
utina (43 B.C.). But when the Senate refused their
ampion due honours, his legionaries forced his appoint-
ent as consul. He was recognized as Caesar's adopted
n under the name of Gaius Julius Caesar Octavianus.
e soon reached a compromise with Antony and M. Lepi-
is (q.v. 3). By the *Lex Titia* (27 Nov. 43) they secured
ficial acknowledgement of themselves as triumvirs *rei*
blicae constituendae* for five years. Octavian obtained
frica, Sicily, and Sardinia as his provinces. When on
Jan. 42 Caesar was recognized as a god, Octavian
came *divi filius*. In the triumviral proscriptions (q.v.)
was as ruthless as his colleagues: ambition and a touch
puritanical fanaticism made him cruel. During the
mpaign of Philippi he suffered from ill health. Under
ew settlement he held Spain, Sardinia, and for a short
ne Africa, and supervised the distribution of land to
e veterans. This task and the suppression of the
bellion of L. Antonius (q.v. 6), in which Salvidienus
ufus, M. Agrippa, and C. Maecenas became his close
llaborators, strengthened his hold on Italy and Gaul
o B.C.). In a transitory attempt to conciliate Sextus Pom-
ius, who had occupied Sicily and Sardinia, Octavian
arried his relative Scribonia (q.v.). In Oct. 40 the pact
Brundisium sealed a new reconciliation with Antony,
no married Octavian's sister, Octavia; Virgil's fourth
clogue records the contemporary enthusiasm. Octavian
vorced Scribonia and married Livia (q.v.), who shared
s traditionalism and simplicity and thus became a
rmanent force in his life. Salvidienus Rufus was now
ndemned to death, since he was suspected of meditat-
g revolt. In 38, when war with Pompeius broke out,
ctavian probably assumed the *praenomen* of *imperator*

(q.v.), which was ratified in 29 by the Senate. In 37 at
Tarentum Antony and Octavian confirmed their agreement and had their triumviral powers extended for
another five years (until Dec. 33?). With the defeat of
Pompeius and the downfall of Lepidus (36) the West was
in the hands of the *divi filius*.

**2.** Octavian was already winning over public opinion
in Italy. He put himself under the protection of Apollo.
He was perhaps granted *sacrosanctitas* or some other
form of tribunician privilege. He disbanded legions and
founded colonies. He saw definitely that his task was to
establish peace and restore Italy. The opposition to
Antony and Cleopatra reinforced his position at a
moment in which the consciousness of a united Italy
was just formed. Between 35 and 33 B.C. his campaigns
in Illyricum and Dalmatia, although not entirely successful, strengthened the eastern borders of Italy. Great
attention was given to the adornment of Rome, especially
under the aedileship of Agrippa (33 B.C.). Octavian's
party had originally won more support from the Italian
municipalities, but now a considerable part of the Roman
aristocracy joined. Antony's callousness towards Octavia
added a family justification to the rivalry. The triumvirate
was not renewed, but Octavian, like Antony, did not
abandon power and prepared for war against his partner.
In Oct. 32 Italy and the western provinces swore
allegiance to Octavian. They became his clients—an
important step towards the Principate and a substitute
for his triumviral powers. War was declared only against
Cleopatra. In 31 Octavian's position became more regular
when he assumed the consulship, which he held every
year until 23 B.C.

**3.** Octavian overthrew Antony in the campaign of
Actium (Sept. 31), founded Nicopolis (q.v. 3), and ascribed
his success to Apollo. In August 30 he became master
of Egypt and its treasure. His arrangements in the East
mainly preserved the dispositions of Antony. In 30
libations for his *genius* were granted by the Senate; his
tribunician competence was perhaps extended; he was
authorized to create patricians. In 29 he celebrated his
triumph and the temple of Janus was closed. Many
legions were disbanded; new distributions of land were
granted. In 28 Octavian held the census with Agrippa, reduced the Senate to some 800 members (later to 600), was
appointed *princeps senatus*, revived ancient religious ceremonies, and dedicated a temple of Apollo on the Palatine.
His policy was increasingly founded upon his prestige as
victor, peace-bringer, and defender of Roman tradition.
He was teaching the Italian people that Roman traditions
were their traditions and old Roman virtue the eternal
foundation of the Roman State. Poets, historians, and
artists were at his side. The Republic had to be solemnly
restored, because the Republic was deeply rooted in
tradition. Yet the restoration had to be reconciled with
the obvious fact that Octavian never seriously thought
of laying down his power. He effectively controlled the
State through his money and his soldiers (*see* ARMIES,
ROMAN, § 4).

**4.** On 13 Jan. 27 B.C., Octavian transferred the State
to the free disposal of the Senate and people, but he
received Spain, Gaul, and Syria (in addition to Egypt)
for ten years as his province with the greater part of
the army, while preserving his consulate (*see* IMPERIUM).
On 16 Jan. he received among many honours the title
Augustus (see following article), which proclaimed his
superior position in the State. The month Sextilis was
called Augustus. A golden shield was set up in the
Senate-house with an inscription commemorating his
valour, clemency, justice, and piety; a replica found at
Arles is dated 26 B.C. Possibly he was granted other
powers. The Republic was restored, because his powers
depended on the Senate and were formally to last only

for ten years. Yet the forces in his hands were over-whelming and supported a moral authority even greater. Half the Empire had already sworn allegiance to him. The oath was extended to the other provinces, and probably the soldiers took a special oath of allegiance to him. In the East the cult of Augustus was associated with the existing cult of Roma. In the West many forms of worship, especially of his *genius*, were widespread. Horace described him as Mercury in *Carm.* 1. 2.

5. Expansion of the frontiers and reinforcement of the Roman penetration in semi-conquered territories were equally considered. The frontiers between Egypt and Ethiopia were secured by the campaigns of Cornelius Gallus (29 B.C.) and C. Petronius (25). Augustus himself directed the main phase of the final submission of Spain and the urbanization and organization of Spain and Gaul (27–25). In 25 Terentius Varro (q.v. 4) Murena crushed the Salassi in Val d'Aosta, but Aelius Gallus failed to conquer Arabia Felix (25–24). Galatia was annexed (25) and Juba appointed king of Mauretania. These were difficult years: Augustus was critically ill in 25 and 23 B.C. In 26 Cornelius Gallus (q.v. 3) was condemned. In 23 or 22 the conspiracy of Varro Murena was discovered. In 23 young Marcellus (q.v. 7), who had married Augustus' daughter Julia in 25, died. As Augustus had no son, the problem of a successor was urgent. Constitutional reforms seemed necessary. In 24 Augustus had been granted dispensation from certain laws. In July 23 he resigned the consulship, but obtained an *imperium proconsulare maius* in the senatorial provinces and the *tribunicia potestas* for life; this included the absolute right of veto and involved complete control of the State—the very end of the Roman Republic. Agrippa was honoured with an eastern command (23) and the hand of Julia (21); their sons Gaius and Lucius were eventually regarded as the future heirs. In 22 Augustus refused the dictatorship, but accepted the *cura annonae*; Gallia Narbonensis (in 22) and Hispania Baetica were transferred to senatorial administration. Augustus' travels in Sicily, Greece, and Asia (22–19) were probably of great importance for the civil organization; the most apparent result was the reconciliation with Parthia, which recognized the Roman protectorate in Armenia. An expedition against the Garamantes in Africa was successful (19). Possibly some consular privileges were granted to Augustus by the Senate in 19. Moral and religious reforms marked the years 18 and 17 B.C. The *lex Iulia de adulteriis* made adultery a public crime; the *lex Iulia de maritandis ordinibus* made marriage nearly compulsory and offered privileges to married people. A *lex sumptuaria* tried to reduce luxury. Members of senatorial families were forbidden to marry into families of freedmen. In 17 the *ludi saeculares* were celebrated. In 18 the powers of Augustus were extended for five years, while a co-regency was conferred upon Agrippa, and a new *lectio senatus* was held. In 17 Augustus adopted Gaius and Lucius, and in 14 he gave the Bosporan kingdom to Polemo of Pontus—an unsuccessful settlement. Three years of residence by Augustus in Gaul (15–13) marked the importance of the organization of Gaul and its frontiers. T. Statilius Taurus was left in Rome as *praefectus urbi*. In 16–15 Raetia and Noricum were annexed as imperial provinces. About 15–14 the imperial mint of Lugdunum was founded, which meant a direct control of gold and silver coinage. At latest from *c.* 11 B.C. (when a new *lectio senatus* was made), the organization of the senatorial and equestrian orders and the *iuvenes* (qq.v.) was complete. A *consilium* of magistrates and other senators helped Augustus to prepare business for the full Senate. In 13 the powers of Augustus and Agrippa were extended for five years. Agrippa's death in 12 was a blow. The death of Lepidus left the post of

Pontifex Maximus open: Augustus, the head of th Roman Empire, became also the head of the Roma religion (12). An altar to Roma and Augustus was bui at Lugdunum (*Lyon*): later a similar altar was built Oppidum Ubiorum (*Cologne*). In both cases the alta was meant to be the focus of provincial loyalism.

6. The substitution of Tiberius' and Drusus' influen for that of Agrippa was marked by new military activit In several campaigns the frontier of Illyricum was a vanced to the Danube (13–9 B.C.) and later Moesia w made a province. Meanwhile Drusus attempted to a vance the Rhine frontier to the Albis (*Elbe*); he died 9 B.C. In 9 the Ara Pacis (q.v.) was dedicated and (in 7 the *collegia* (*see* CLUBS, ROMAN) were revised. In 8 t powers of Augustus were extended for ten years. Son time between 12 B.C. and A.D. 1 the Homonadeis southern Galatia were defeated and in 6 Paphlagonia w added to Galatia. In 6 Tiberius received *tribunic potestas*, but shortly afterwards retired to Rhod through jealousy of Gaius Caesar, who in 5 was pr claimed *princeps iuventutis*.

7. The great creative period of the life of August was over. His best collaborators were dead, includin the poets, Virgil and Horace. Livy was left to witness h decline, Ovid to experience the severity of his mor code. Augustus politically favoured the upper classe but he was careful to appeal in some measure to eve class. The division of Rome into fourteen *regiones* 7 B.C. gave the opportunity for associating the cult the *genius* of the Emperor with the popular cult of t Lares Compitales. By the *leges Fufia Caninia* (2 B.C.) a *Aelia Sentia* (A.D. 4) manumission was limited and ce tain classes of slaves were excluded from the possibili of Roman citizenship. Augustus was also conservati in bestowing citizenship on provincials. In 2 B.C. was saluted as *pater patriae*; he also banished Ju (q.v. 2). The deaths of Lucius Caesar (A.D. 2) and Gai Caesar (A.D. 4) thwarted Augustus' plans for the succe sion, and he was compelled to adopt Tiberius, wl again received *tribunicia potestas* for ten years. In A.D. Augustus' own powers were extended for ten yea Probably in A.D. 5 (as the Tabula Hebana (q.v.) fou in Etruria in 1947 has revealed) the elections of t magistrates were reformed: consuls and praetors we to be 'designated' by ten special centuries composed senators and judiciary *equites* taken from thirty-three the thirty-five tribes. This procedure (*destinatio*) reduce the power of the *comitia centuriata*. In A.D. 6 a ne system was introduced to pay discharged soldiers fro an *aerarium militare* (*see* AERARIUM); this superseded t necessity of founding military colonies, the last volutionary survival. The privileged position of Ita in taxation was reduced by the imposition of two n taxes on legacies and sales. Seven *cohortes* of *vigi* (q.v.) and three *cohortes urbanae* (q.v.) were establishe In foreign affairs the year A.D. 6 was marked by the a nexation of Judaea as a province and by the Pannoni rebellion which suddenly revealed the weakness of t Roman army, which had been reduced to twenty-eig legions (apart from the *auxilia*) and had been posted the borders without a central reserve. Tiberius took th years to crush the rebellion (6–9), while the loss of thr legions under Varus (q.v. 2) in Germany in 9 confirm the insufficiency of the military organization. August was shocked and decided to abandon Germany and retain only twenty-five legions: conquest would invo increasing the army. The year A.D. 9 saw the last soc law (*lex Papia Poppaea*), which mitigated the *lex Iulia maritandis ordinibus* and offered further inducements having children. In A.D. 13 Tiberius received *tribuni potestas* and *imperium proconsulare* for another ten yea Augustus himself was granted ten more years of pow

The decisions of his *consilium* were given the force of *senatus consulta*. In April A.D. 13 he deposited his will in the house of the Vestals. It included a *breviarium totius imperii* (a summary of the military and financial resources) and the so-called *Monumentum Ancyranum* (q.v.). His mausoleum had been ready for many years. He died on 19 Aug. A.D. 14 at Nola, and on 17 Sept. the Senate decreed that he should be accepted among the gods of the State.

8. He had preserved the calm beauty of his person until his old age. He had never forgotten his studies, but no philosophic influence is demonstrable in his government. He wrote a pamphlet against Brutus about Cato Uticensis, an exhortation to philosophy, an auto-biography dealing with the period before about 25 B.C., a biography of Drusus, a short poem about Sicily, a book of epigrams—all lost works—and planned a tragedy on Ajax. His style was clear and simple, but, if required, as majestic as his mind. When he entered political life, republican liberty was already dead. He tried to establish a government in which an accurate balance of classes and of countries gave the predominance to Roman tradition and Italian men without offending the provinces and without diminishing the Greek culture. He gave peace, as long as it was consistent with the interests of the empire and with the myth of his glory. But he intended especially that the peace was to be the internal peace of the State. He assured freedom of trade and wealth to the upper classes. He did his enormous work in a simple way, living a simple life, faithful to his faithful friends. His superstition did not affect the strength of his will. Yet, as he never thought of real liberty, so he never attained to the profound humanity of the men who promote free life.

Sources. *Monumentum Ancyranum* (q.v.); Suetonius, *Life* (ed. Adams, 1939; Levi, 1958); Appian, *BCiv.* (only until 35 B.C.); Dio Cassius 45 ff.; Velleius Paterculus, etc. The contemporary poets and monuments are invaluable. For the coins see *British Museum Catalogue* i (1923). The minor fragments of Augustus' works are collected in H. Malcovati, *Caesaris Augusti . . . fragmenta* (1962). Inscriptions in V. Ehrenberg and A. H. M. Jones, *Documents illustrating the reigns of Augustus and Tiberius*[1] (1955).
General Literature: *CAH* x is the best reference-work, but cf. Mommsen, *Röm. Staatsr.*, especially vol. ii[2] and M. Hammond, *The Augustan Principate*[2] (U.S.A. 1968). Later works: A. v. Premerstein, *Vom Werden und Wesen des Prinzipats* (1937; V. Arangio-Ruiz et al., *Augustus, Studi in occasione del bimillenario augusteo* (1938); Syme, *Rom. Rev.*; J. Buchan, *Augustus* (1937); H. Andersen, *Cassius Dio und die Begründung des Principates* (1938). G. Rodenwaldt, *Kunst um Augustus* (1942); M. Hammond, 'Hellenistic influences on the structure of the Augustan principate', *Am. Ac. Rome* 1940, I. M. Grant, *From Imperium to Auctoritas* (1946); G. E. F. Chilver, *Hist.* 1950, 408 ff.; E. T. Salmon, ibid., 1956, 456 ff.; M. A. Levi, *Il Tempo di Augusto* (1951); A. H. M. Jones, *Studies in Roman Government and Law* (1960); P. Sattler, *Augustus und der Senat* (1960); H. D. Meyer, *Die Aussenpolitik des Augustus und die Augusteische Dichtung* (1961); H. H. Scullard, *From the Gracchi to Nero*[2] (1963); G. W. Bowersock, *Augustus and the Greek World* (1965). For the portraits see O. Brendel, *Ikonographie des Kaisers Augustus* (1931) and *Augustus*, p. 374. See also K. Hönn, *Augustus im Wandel zweier Jahrtausende* (1938); P. Grenade, *Essai sur les origines du principat* (1961); A. la Penna, *Orazio e l'ideologia del principato* (1963).   A.M.

**AUGUSTUS, AUGUSTA** (Gk. Σεβαστός, Σεβαστή). On 16 Jan. 27 B.C. Octavian received the title 'Augustus' from the Senate, wisely preferring this to the alternative offer of 'Romulus'. The word *augustus* had been used in republican times at Rome only in a religious context— 'sancta uocant augusta patres', Ovid wrote (*Fast.* 1. 609) —and was readily contrasted with *humanus*. Though Augustus apparently intended that the title should be carried by his successor (Suet. *Tib.* 26), Tiberius at first hesitated to accept it (Dio Cass. 57. 2. 1; 8. 1. Compare the similar conduct of Vitellius in A.D. 69, Tac. *Hist.* 2. 52; 80). It was held by all Roman Emperors except Vitellius, and never by any other member of the imperial family. The title 'Augusta' was bequeathed by Augustus to his wife Livia, granted by Gaius to his grandmother Antonia, by Claudius to his wife Agrippina, and by Nero

to Poppaea. From Domitian's time it was normally conferred, on the initiative of the Senate, upon the wife of the reigning Emperor.   J. P. B.

**AULIS,** where the Greek fleet collected before sailing to Troy, is a small hill on the Euripus with a little land-locked harbour north and a deep bay south. The emigrants to Aeolis also claimed to have sailed thence (Strabo 9. 401), and Hesiod names it as a port (*Op.* 651); but it had no important later history. Recent excavations have revealed the temple of Artemis Aulideia (5th c. B.C., later modified and finally covered by a late Roman bath), remains of an enclosure possibly surrounding the ancient plane tree (Paus. 9. 19. 7) and of two fountains. Under the porch of this temple a circular structure may represent an earlier temple. The Mycenaean cemetery of Aulis has also been found and Mycenaean (?) walls on the hill above.   T. J. D.; R. J. H.

**AURELIA** (*PW* 'Aurelius' 248), of the family of the Cottae, was the mother of Caesar (q.v. 1). She watched over the conduct of his wife Pompeia (q.v.) and detected Clodius (q.v. 1) at the Bona Dea ceremony. She died in 54 B.C.   E. B.

**AURELIANUS,** Lucius Domitius (*PW* 36) (*c.* A.D. 215–75), a man of humble origin from Dacia Ripensis, played a prominent part in the military plot that destroyed Gallienus (q.v., early A.D. 268). Appointed by Claudius II to the chief command of the cavalry, he served with distinction against the Goths, and, after the death of Claudius, was raised to the throne by the army in place of Quintillus (*c.* May 270).

Barbarian invasions claimed his first attention. He defeated the Vandals in Pannonia and then repulsed a dangerous attack on Italy by the Juthungi, pursuing them over the Danube. He then visited Rome, and surrounded the city with walls, to prevent a surprise attack by the barbarians (see WALL OF AURELIAN). He also disposed of three rivals in the provinces—Septimus, Urbanus, and Domitianus.

Zenobia (q.v.), ruling Palmyra for her young son, Vaballathus, had occupied Egypt and Asia Minor up to Bithynia. Coins were struck for Vaballathus as colleague of Aurelian, but he was determined to restore the unity of the Empire. He marched eastward, stopping on the way to repulse the Goths and Carpi on the Danube. Judging that the old province of Dacia was now a liability he withdrew the Roman troops and much of the population and formed a new province of Dacia, south of the Danube. The main Palmyrene army under Zabdas met him north of Antioch on the Orontes. Aurelian won victories here and at Emesa. The provincials were won over by his leniency, and Zenobia withdrew to Palmyra. Aurelian followed and soon broke down resistance. Zenobia was captured on her way to seek aid from Persia, and Palmyra surrendered.

Marching back westward, Aurelian defeated the Carpi on the Danube, but was recalled by the revolt of Palmyra (273). Striking without delay, Aurelian deposed the new king, Antiochus, and reduced Palmyra to a village. A wealthy merchant of Alexandria, Firmus, who tried to save Zenobia's cause, was soon crushed.

Aurelian now turned west and ended the Gallic Empire at Châlons, assisted by the desertion of the Emperor Tetricus (q.v.) himself (early 274). Tetricus and Zenobia headed the captives from all Aurelian's victories in a magnificent triumph.

Early in 275 Aurelian set out against Persia, but was murdered at Caenophrurium, near Byzantium, in a military plot, fostered by his secretary Eros. Some time passed before Tacitus was appointed to succeed him—

the army offering the choice to the Senate, the Senate shirking the dangerous responsibility.

Aurelian's tireless energy and brilliant military talents restored the unity of the Empire after forty years of disaster; he was rightly hailed as *restitutor orbis*. He was a ruthless disciplinarian to the soldiers and civilian officials. He attempted a reform of the now worthless coinage, issuing new money for the old. In 274 he instituted a State cult of *Sol invictus* and seems to have had the aim of making it the universal religion of the empire. At the time of his death, he was planning to renew the persecution of the Christians.

L. Homo, *Essai sur le règne de l'empereur Aurélian* (1904); K· Gross, *RAC* i. 1004 ff. H. M.; B. H. W.

**AURELIUS**(1), MARCUS, Roman Emperor A.D. 161-80, was born in 121 and named *M. Annius* (*PW* 94) *Verus*. He was son of Annius Verus, a brother of Faustina the Elder (q.v.), and from a consular family of Spanish origin. Marcus' mother was Domitia Lucilla, whose family owned a large tile industry outside Rome, which, inherited by Marcus, passed into the *patrimonium Caesaris* (q.v.). He early gained the favour of Hadrian who justly nicknamed him *Verissimus*, made him a Salian priest when only 8, betrothed him in 136 to the daughter of L. Aelius (q.v. 2), and supervised his education; the best teachers of rhetoric, grammar, philosophy, and law were employed to form his frank, serene, and sensitive character. With Aelius' son Lucius ( = L. Verus, q.v.), he was adopted (as 'M. Aelius Aurelius Verus Caesar') by Antoninus Pius (q.v.) in 138. Quaestor in 139, and *cos. I ord.* with Pius 140, he was betrothed to Pius' daughter and his own cousin, Faustina the Younger (q.v.), whom he married in 145, as *cos. II*; a daughter's birth in 146 brought him also the *tribunicia potestas* and a proconsular *imperium*. Now aged 25, a son-in-law of Pius, himself a father, and enjoying subordinate collegiality with Pius, Marcus held a position clearly excelling that of Lucius, who did not even become *cos. I* until 154. This student, frail and yet austerely athletic, continued to live with Pius in close friendship and trust, ever loyal and deferential. About 146-7 he deserted rhetoric, taught by his faithful Fronto (q.v.), for Stoic philosophy, which inspired all his future life.

**2.** Succeeding, as M. Aurelius Antoninus, on 7 Mar. 161, Marcus immediately petitioned the Senate that L. Verus, his fellow-consul in that year (they were respectively *cos. III* and *cos. II*), should receive (as 'L. Aurelius Verus') the *tribunicia potestas*, the full proconsular *imperium*, and the title *Augustus*, i.e. joint authority with himself. For the first time the Principate became collegiate (except for the office of *pontifex maximus*), and the tie was emphasized by Verus' betrothal to Marcus' daughter Lucilla (q.v.), commemorated by a fresh alimentary institution (*see* ALIMENTA). Revolt in Britain and Chattan aggression were settled; but in the East the Parthians, seizing Armenia, defeated two Roman armies and, in Mar. 162, Marcus sent Verus thither with a strong force. Indulgent and dilatory, Verus did not arrive until 163; but Statius Priscus soon recovered Armenia (163-4), and Avidius (q.v. 3) Cassius invaded Mesopotamia and made it a Roman protectorate (165-6). Returning, Verus' troops brought a pestilence which swept the world. About 166 German tribes poured across the upper and lower Danube and even invaded north Italy. Two new legions were hastily recruited; able generals and Marcus' insistence on a strong Dacia, now made a 'consular' province with two legions, saved a critical situation. Marcus and Verus reached Aquileia in 168; the invaders sought terms, and Italy was freed. After they returned to Rome in early

169, Verus' death of apoplexy relieved Marcus of an embarrassing partner.

**3.** Marcus now contemplated the permanent subjection of central and south-eastern Europe north of the Danube. In 169, after auctioning imperial treasures to replenish the treasury, and marrying the widowed Lucilla to Ti. Claudius (q.v. 15) Pompeianus, Marcus left Rome. From 170 to 174 he fought the Marcomanni and Quadi; and in 175 he successfully attacked the Sarmatian Iazyges. 'Marcomannia' and 'Sarmatia' came near provincialization. But plans were shelved when Avidius Cassius revolted in 175; Marcus merely defined a neutral zone north of the Danube, and settled, in depopulated areas south of the river, semi-romanized tribesmen under obligation to defend the frontiers—the first step in the de-romanization of the frontier provinces. Though Cassius, proclaimed Emperor in Syria and Egypt, was soon murdered, Marcus set out in alarm for Syria. In 176 he visited Egypt (uneasy since a Delta revolt in 172), and returned, via Syria, to Rome, to celebrate a great triumph. When, in 177, German tribes again vexed Pannonia, Marcus raised his son Commodus (q.v.) to full collegiality as *Augustus*, consul, and holder of the *tribunicia potestas* and full proconsular *imperium*. He left Commodus, married to the highly born Bruttia Crispina, as his representative in Rome while he himself went north to defeat the Marcomanni in 178. He was in a position to possess their territory with that of the Quadi and Iazyges; but he died, swiftly and peacefully, on 17 Mar. 180, and Commodus soon abandoned the campaign. Marcus, sincerely mourned, was commemorated by a famous sculptured column still standing in Rome; equally well known is an equestrian statue in bronze, erected presumably during his lifetime and now on the Capitoline Hill.

**4.** Ironically, war thus dominated the philosopher's reign. To this is due much of the intensity of his *Meditations* (see below), compiled in solitude during his campaigns, and breathing high Stoic principles. But Stoicism endangered empire; 'self-sufficiency' did not encourage wide administrative experience based on personal contact. Marcus' faulty judgement in choosing Commodus as successor probably reflects fear lest the succession of another than his son might create dissension. Under Marcus the imperial bureaucracy increased because defence, administration, and economics were becoming more complex. Circuit judges (*iuridici*) were revived for Italy (*see* HADRIAN); *alimenta, fiscus, annona* (qq.v.), and even the care of minors, were controlled by permanent officials; registration of free-born children was compulsory; the various grades of officialdom received distinguishing titles. Marcus' obvious duties were faithfully discharged; jurisdiction claimed his full care; and Senate and Knights were honourably treated. But generally he was an improver rather than an innovator; foresight and imagination were lacking. Long wars and many largesses (seven, for a total of 850 *denarii* per head) emptied a treasury which auctions could not relieve; even the silver coin in circulation dropped sharply in volume. The plague of 166-7 meant a loss of population which perhaps was not fully recovered. As had Trajan and Hadrian, he felt it necessary to appoint commissioners (*curatores*; q.v.) for communities threatened with bankruptcy. The natural consequence was a loss of municipal initiative. Thus behind the façade of Antonine prosperity and meticulous but not foresighted government, economic stagnation and bureaucratic centralization prepared the way for the Severan monarchy and the crisis of the third century. C. H. V. S.; M. H

**5.** Marcus is one of the few rulers of empire whose writings have outlasted their practical achievements. The letters which as a young man he wrote (chiefly in Latin) to his tutor Fronto (q.v.) are somewhat self-conscious and only occasionally revealing; it is on the twelve books of *Meditations* (τὰ εἰς ἑαυτόν) that his fame rests. With the exception of the first book, in which he records his gratitude to his family, to his teachers, and to the gods, these aphorisms and reflections are arranged in no systematic order, and are often concise to the point of obscurity; they appear to have been transcribed—probably after his death, and with little or no editing—from the notebooks in which Marcus originally jotted them down for his private guidance. To this circumstance they owe their peculiar value as a personal document. Marcus had little to say to himself that had not been said before: a conservative thinker, he was resistant to the new ideas of his time and content for the most part to follow the Stoic tradition as it had been reshaped by Posidonius (q.v. 2). But he restated the old doctrines with a new intensity of religious and moral feeling, and in a lapidary style which is all his own; this has made his *Meditations* a breviary for contemplatives throughout the centuries.　　　　　　　　　　　　　　　　　　　E. R. D.

WRITINGS. *Letters*, ed. L. Pepe, with Ital. commentary (1957); *see also under* FRONTO. *Meditations*, ed. A. S. L. Farquharson, with Eng. trans. and commentary (2 vols., 2nd ed. 1952); ed. W. Theiler, with Germ. trans. and notes (1951). Discussion: E. V. Arnold, *Roman Stoicism* (1911); Wilamowitz, '*Kaiser Marcus*' (Vortrag, 1931); G. Misch, *A History of Autobiography in Antiquity* (Eng. trans., 1950); M. Pohlenz, *Die Stoa* (1948). ANCIENT SOURCES. *Literary*: Copious excerpts from Dio Cassius bks. 71–72 furnish useful material. Though the life of Marcus in the *Historia Augusta* is uncritical and confused by interpolation, it affords substantive information which can be supplemented from the related lives of L. Verus, Avidius Cassius, and Commodus. Aurelius Victor and Eutropius add further minor items. *Coins*: for coins as *Caesar*, Strack, *Reichsprägung* iii 12 ff.; in general, *B.M. Coins, Rom. Emp.* iv (1940). *Marcus' column*: G. Becatti, *Colonna di Marco Aurelio* (1957); Nash, *Pict. Dict. Rome* i. 276 ff. MODERN LITERATURE. *Diz. Epigr.*, s.v. 'Aurelius'; E. Renan, *Marc-Aurèle, etc.* (1882); H. D. Sedgwick, *Marcus Aurelius, a Biography*, etc. (1921); A. von Premerstein, *Klio* 1911, 1912, 1913; F. Carrata Thomes, *Il Regno di M.A.* (1953); C. Parain, *Marc-Aurèle* (1957); W. Görlitz, *Marc Aurel* (1954), with bibl. and summary of inscriptions on 284 ff.; C. H. Dodd (Eastern and Danubian campaigns in the light of the coinage) *Num. Chron.* 1911, 209 ff., 1913, 162 ff.; Wegner, *Herrscherbild* (1939), ii. 4; M. Hammond, *Journ. of Econ. Hist.* Suppl. VI (1964), 63 ff.; *The Antonine Monarchy* (1959); A. Birley, *Marcus Aurelius* (1966); Bengtson, *Röm. Gesch.* 348 ff. Bibliography: A. Garzetti, *L'impero da Tiberio agli Antonini* (1960), 696 ff.; A. Piganiol, *Hist. de Rome*⁵ (1962), 307 f., 581 f.

**AURELIUS** (2) (*PW* 46) **ANTONINUS**, MARCUS (A.D. 188–217), nicknamed CARACALLA (more correctly Caracallus). The elder son of Septimius Severus, he was created Caesar in A.D. 196 and Augustus in 198. His relations with his younger brother Geta, created Augustus in 209, always bad, worsened after the death of Septimius in 211. Their mother Julia Domna prevented a partition of the Empire, but in 212 Caracalla, the stronger character, procured the murder of Geta and became sole ruler.

In 213 he set out for Germany where the Alamanni are named for the first time as enemies of Rome. They were defeated, but the Cenni (? Chatti) were bought off with a subsidy. A strengthening of the wall along the *limes* of Upper Germany and Raetia may probably be attributed to Caracalla.

Caracalla's next objective was the East, where in his assumed role of a second Alexander he hoped for vast conquests. The year 214 was spent on the Danube fighting the Carpi and mobilizing an army, which included a phalanx of 16,000 equipped on the Macedonian model. In 215 the province of Osroene was enlarged to include Edessa, but an attack on Armenia failed. In 216 he invaded Media and spent the winter at Edessa preparing for a more intensive campaign, but was assassinated near Carrhae in April 217 (*see* MACRINUS).

Caracalla's chief claim to fame was his edict of 212 granting Roman citizenship to all communities inside the Empire (*see* CITIZENSHIP, ROMAN); his motive in fact was to obtain increased revenue from the inheritance tax. His financial difficulties also brought about inflation through the issue of a new coin, the so-called *Antoninianus*. Caracalla's crude but vigorous personality was attractive to the army.

Herodian 4. 1–13; Dio Cassius 77–8; S. H. A.; W. Reusch, *Der Historische Wert der Caracalla-vita*; Ch. Sasse, *Die Constitutio Antoniniana* (1958). H. M. D. P.; B. H. W.

**AURELIUS** (3) **VICTOR**, SEXTUS, an African, governor of Pannonia Secunda, A.D. 361, and *praefectus urbi*, 389, published *Caesares*, probably after 360, from Augustus to Constantius (360). Based on Suetonius, this imperial history treated biographical material after a moralizing fashion, in the tradition of Sallust and Tacitus; the writer is heathen, interested in prodigies. The *Origo Gentis Romanae* and *De Viris Illustribus* (republican biography) associated with the *Caesares* in a *historia tripertita* are not by his hand.

Ed. F. Pichlmayr (1911); G. Puccioni, *Origo Gentis Romanae* (1958); C. G. Starr, *Am. Hist. Rev.* 1956, 574; A. Momigliano, *Secondo Contributo alla storia degli stud. class.* (1960), 145 ff. (*JRS*, 1958, 56 ff.); id. *Conflict between Paganism and Christianity in the Fourth Century* (1963), 81, 96 ff. A. H. McD.

**AUREOLUS**, a soldier of humble origin from Dacia, became commander of the new cavalry corps based on Milan, helped Gallienus (q.v.) to overthrow Ingenuus in Pannonia (A.D. 258–9) and then, in 261, the Macriani, on the borders of Thrace. He also had a limited success in Gaul in 263 against Postumus. In 268, while Gallienus was fighting the Goths, Aureolus revolted at Milan. He was besieged there by Gallienus, and when the latter was assassinated, surrendered to Claudius, but his own soldiers killed him. H. M.; B. H. W.

**AURUM CORONARIUM.** Gold crowns were offered to rulers and conquerors in the ancient Orient and in the Hellenistic world. Similar offerings were made from the early second century to Roman generals (e.g. Plut. *Aem. Paul.* 34, 5) and rapidly came to be exacted by them. A law of Caesar (59 B.C.) enacted that it should not be demanded until a triumph had been formally decreed. Under the Empire, *aurum coronarium* went to the Emperor alone and was exacted with increasing frequency, not only for triumphs (see *Res Gestae* 21; Pliny *HN* 33. 54) but on imperial accessions, anniversaries, adoptions, and so forth, and then became an irregular form of taxation on communities.

Th. Klauser, *Röm. Mitt.* 1944, 129; *RAC*, s.v. F. G. B. M.

**AURUNCI**, neighbours of the Sidicini (q.v.) in the Latium–Campania (qq.v.) border region. Servius (*ad Aen.* 7. 727) identifies them with the Ausones (= Oscans, q.v.), the prehistoric inhabitants of much of southern Italy (called *Ausonia* after them). *C.* 313 B.C. Rome conquered and quickly assimilated the Aurunci. Principal towns: Aurunca (= the later Suessa), Minturnae, Sinuessa, and probably Cales. E. T. S.

**A(U)SCULUM SATRIANUM** (modern *Ascoli Satriano*) was a town 18 miles south of Foggia in Apulia; little survives. Here Pyrrhus defeated the Romans in 279 B.C. Like Salapia (q.v.) it suffered for its revolt in the Social War. Opposite the town on the western bank of the Carapelle there are traces of two superimposed centuriation systems mentioned by an entry in the *Liber Coloniarum*.

*CIL* ix. 62 ff. G. D. B. J.

**AUSONIAN CULTURE**, the name introduced in 1956 by L. B. Brea for the culture of the Late Bronze Age in the Aeoliae Insulae (q.v.), is closely related to the later Apennine Culture (q.v.) of the peninsula, with which the Islands had previously traded. The archaeological evidence coincides with the legend (Diod. Sic. 5. 7) that Liparus, son of the king of the Ausonians (*see* AURUNCI) in central Italy, founded a city on the island named after him. 'Ausonian I' is virtually confined to the Lipari acropolis. 'Ausonian II' is represented by villages and cremation cemeteries at Lipari and Milazzo (Mylae in north-east Sicily); the cemetery at Milazzo has much in common with Protovillanovan cemeteries on the mainland.

L. Bernabò Brea and M. Cavalier, *Bull. Paletn. It.* 1956, 7 ff.; L. Bernabò Brea, *Sicily before the Greeks*² (1966); R. Peroni, *Mem. Linc.* 1960, 1 ff.                                    D. W. R. R.

**AUSŎNIUS,** DECIMUS MAGNUS (d. *c.* A.D. 395), was born at Bordeaux about the beginning of the fourth century. His studies were pursued at Bordeaux and Toulouse. For thirty years he taught in his native town, first as *grammaticus*, then as *rhetor*. Distinguished enough to attract the attention of the court, he was called by Valentinian to Trèves to be tutor to Gratian. He was on the staff of father and son in the campaigns against the Alamanni (368–9). After holding minor positions he became governor of Gaul, and later of other provinces. Finally, in 379, he was made consul. After the murder of Gratian (383) he returned to his early home, and added to the number of his poems, enjoying epistolary intercourse with various eminent men.

His numerous poems, written in various metres (hexameter, elegiac, hendecasyllabic, etc.), are of considerable interest, in both subject-matter and style. There are over a hundred epigrams, some of which are in Greek and others translated from Greek. There are twenty-five letters. His correspondence with Paulinus (q.v.) of Nola is the most notable part of these. The *Ephemeris* includes many poems in various metres, dealing with daily life. The *Parentalia* is a collection of short poems in memory of deceased relatives of the poet. The *Commemoratio Professorum Burdigalensium* is of interest for the history of education. The *Ordo Nobilium Urbium* describes twenty notable cities of the Roman world. This account by no means exhausts the list of the minor poems, throughout which the author's minute knowledge of Virgil is apparent and his Christian faith is not obtruded. *See also* CENTO (LATIN).

His most important poem is the *Mosella* which still attracts readers. It is a rhetorically fashioned *laudatio* in 483 hexameters, and describes in considerable detail the various fish to be found in the river as well as some of the fine buildings on the banks and other features, the whole constituting a series of episodes, composed, like the rest of Ausonius' verse, according to rule.

Ed. R. Peiper (Teubner, 1886); H. G. Evelyn White, 2 vols. (Loeb, 1919–21); *Mosella*, C. Hosius (3rd ed., 1926). S. Dill, *Roman Society in the last century of the Western Empire* (1905); T. R. Glover, *Life and Letters in the Fourth Century* (1901); E. K. Rand, 'Decimus Magnus Ausonius', *Proc. Class. Ass.*, 1927; M. J. Byrne, *Prolegomena to an edition of the works of Ausonius* (U.S.A. 1916); S. Prete, *Ricerche sulla storia del testo di Ausonio, Temi e testi, 7* (1960); M. K. Hopkins, *CQ* 1961, 239 ff.                                    A. S.

**AUSPICIUM,** a term used by the Romans for certain types of divination, particularly from birds (*avis, specio*), designed to ascertain the pleasure or displeasure of the gods towards matters in hand. Despite ancient and modern attempts at definition, *auspicia* are hardly to be differentiated from *auguria*, and are not limited to signs derived from the number, position, flight, cries, and feeding of birds—particularly the sacred chickens, for which *see* AUGURES—but extend to other animals (Paul. ex Fest. 244 M. s.v. *pedestria auspicia*) or to inanimate phenomena. Festus and Paulus (261–262 M.), record five types: *ex caelo, ex avibus, ex tripudiis, ex quadripedibus,*

*ex diris*. Private auspices were early largely abandoned, save for weddings (Cic. *Div.* 1. 28 and other references, Latte, *RR* 264), but public ones, taken by magistrates possessing the *ius auspiciorum* (or *spectio*) were important in civil and military life, and were retained by Cicero in *Leg.* 3. 10. They appear at elections, inauguration into office, entrance into a province, etc., and in the conduct of wars the phrase *ductu auspicioque* frequently recurs (*Thes. Ling. Lat.* v. 2171, 8–27). Since ex-officials, however, and later, imperial legates lacked the *ius auspiciorum* (Cic. *Nat. D.* 2. 9, *Div.* 2. 76–7), even public auspices eventually fell into neglect, and at times pains were taken to avoid observing signs divinely vouchsafed (Cic. *Div.* 2. 77–8).

Observation was usually made from a *tabernaculum*, by a professional attendant of the magistrate (Cic. *Div.* 2. 71–2 preserves the ritual in the case of the sacred chickens), and *auspicia minora* (of the lesser magistrates) were sometimes superseded by *auspicia maiora* of consuls, praetors, or censors (Gell. 13. 15. 4). *Vitium*, a ritual defect or oversight, often nullified auspices, but *peremnia*, or rites at the crossing of streams (Cic. *Div.* 2. 77, Serv. *Aen.* 9. 24) provided against one type of *vitium*. Recrossing the *pomerium* (the bound between the civil and military spheres) required the taking of new auspices in order to avoid *vitium*, a famous instance being narrated by Cic. *Div.* 1. 33. For the military *auspicia ex acuminibus* see especially Cic. *Div.* 2. 77 and Pease ad loc.

P. Catalano, *Contributi allo studio del diritto augurale* (1960). For the subject in general and for bibliography, *see* DIVINATION, LEX, LEGES, AELIA ET FUFIA.                                    A. S. P.

**AUTOCRATES,** Athenian comic poet, ἀρχαῖος, according to the *Suda*, which adds 'he wrote also many tragedies'. Τυμπανισταί (or Τυμπανίστριαι, Hsch.) is the only title we have.

*FCG* i. 270; *CAF* i. 806; *FAC* i. 942 ff.                                    K. J. D.

**AUTOLYCUS** (1), in mythology, maternal grandfather of Odysseus. He 'surpassed all men in thievery and (ambiguous) swearing', by favour of Hermes (whose son he is in later accounts), *Od.* 19. 394 ff.; one of his thefts, *Il.* 10. 267; later stories in von Sybel in Roscher's *Lexikon*, s.v.                                    H. J. R.

**AUTOLYCUS** (2) of Pitane, astronomer (fl. 2nd half of 4th c. B.C.), author of two works on elementary spherical astronomy, the earliest Greek mathematical treatises that have come down to us entire: (1) *On the Moving Sphere* (περὶ κινουμένης σφαίρας) treats of the poles and principal circles of the sphere. Many of its propositions are used in the *Phaenomena* of Euclid (q.v.). (2) *On Risings and Settings* (περὶ ἀνατολῶν καὶ δύσεων), dealing with risings, settings, and visibility periods of stars, is in two books, which are in fact two versions of the same work. In a lost work (Simplicius *de Caelo*, 504 f.) Autolycus criticized the system of concentric spheres of Eudoxus (q.v.) on the ground that it did not account for the differences in the apparent sizes of some heavenly bodies at different times, and attempted to remedy this.

Critical text by J. Mogenet (Louvain, 1950). See 22 ff. of this for history of the text and editions, and 5 ff. for Autolycus' life and works. See also Pappus 6. 33 ff.
GERMAN TRANSLATION. A. Czwalina, Ostwalds Klassiker nr. 232 (1931).
COMMENT. P. Tannery, *Mém. Scient.* ii. 225 ff. On the two versions of *Risings and Settings* see Olaf Schmidt in transactions of *Den 11te skandinaviske Matematikerkongress i Trondheim 22–25 August 1949* (1952), 202 ff.                                    G. J. T.

**AUTOMEDON,** in mythology, Achilles' charioteer, son of Diores (*Il.* 17. 429 and often); hence by metonymy, any charioteer, as Juvenal 1. 61.

**AUTONOMY,** one of the leading ideas of the Greek *polis* (q.v.), meant not merely the right of self-government, but the right and the possibility of using its own laws and constitution. Therefore in the Peloponnesian War Sparta pretended to be fighting for the autonomy of the Greek States, which in the Athenian Empire had been forced to establish democratic governments. Autonomy was mostly connected with, but not clearly distinguished from, the idea of freedom (*eleutheria*). Ideally, it also demanded a large degree of economic self-sufficiency (*autarkeia*). Though mainly concerning the interior life of the *polis*, and responsible for the intensive cultural life of every single *polis*, autonomy was an instrument of inter-Hellenic policy, and the chief reason for the failure of all attempts to create political unity among the Greeks. As Persian and Macedonian supremacy over Greek towns was mainly based on local tyrants or oligarchies, autonomy thereafter implied a free democratic constitution. Under the Hellenistic kings, however, the autonomy of the Greek States was often very precarious, and sometimes it did not exclude even a royal garrison, compulsory taxation, or actual supervision by a king's official.

V. Ehrenberg, *The Greek State* (1960) (extended German edition 1965); A. Heuss, *Stadt und Herrscher des Hellenismus* (1937); A. H. M. Jones, *The Greek City* (1940); E. J. Bickerman, *RIDA* 1958, 13 f.
V. E.

**AUTRONIUS** (*PW* 7) **PAETUS,** PUBLIUS, was elected consul with P. Sulla (q.v. 2) for 65 B.C. Both were convicted of *ambitus* and the consulships went to their competitors. Involved in the 'First Catilinarian Conspiracy' (*see* CATILINE) of 66/65, then in that of 63, he is said to have plotted Cicero's death, was convicted *de vi* in 62 and went into exile in Epirus. E. B.

**AUXESIA** and **DAMIA,** obscure goddesses of fertility (Hdt. 5. 82. 2 ff.), worshipped at Epidaurus and Aegina, with ritual abuse (ibid. 83. 4); at Troezen, with ritual stone-throwing (Λιθοβολία, Paus. 2. 32. 2), where the local legend made them Cretan virgins stoned in a disturbance. *See* BONA DEA. H. J. R.

**AUXILIA.** During the last two centuries of the Republic Rome made good her deficiency in cavalry and light-armed troops with contingents raised outside Italy. These *auxilia* greatly increased in number during the civil wars and formed the nucleus of the permanent auxiliary army established by Augustus (*see* MERCENARIES). This force was recruited from provincials who had not yet received the franchise. Thus in the Julio-Claudian period Gallia Comata and Hispania Tarraconensis provided a large proportion of *auxilia*, while Narbonensis and Baetica, two more romanized provinces, were areas for legionary recruiting. Service was sometimes, as with the Batavi, accepted in lieu of tribute. As their numbers came to be kept up by local recruiting, the *auxilia* gradually lost their native character, and the titles borne by the units ceased to indicate the origin of their soldiers. Exception must be made of the Oriental cohorts of archers, which were maintained at strength by drafts from their home countries.

The auxiliary units generally bore titles which indicated the tribe or district from which they were raised (*Alpinorum, Alpina, Lusitanorum*): a few early units are named after their founders (*ala Siliana* after C. Silius). In addition they frequently bore honorific titles (e.g. *pia, fidelis, Augusta*), and descriptive ones (*miliaria, equitata, sagittariorum*, etc.). They were numbered, but not consecutively, a fresh series starting when new regiments were raised some time after the original levy. This inconvenient system renders difficult any assessment of the total strength of the *auxilia*. Probably

it ranged from 130,000 under Augustus to approximately 225,000 in the second century.

The *auxilia* comprised both cavalry and infantry, the former organized in *alae*, the latter in *cohortes*, either 1,000 or 500 strong, while there were some mixed units (*cohortes equitatae*). They were commanded generally by *praefecti*, in some cases by *tribuni*, who were of equestrian rank and mostly in their thirties when first appointed. Under them were centurions and decurions.

The pay of the auxiliary soldier was considerably lower than that of the legionary, ranging from as little as one-third of legionary pay for the *pedites* to two-thirds for the *alares* (*see* STIPENDIUM). After twenty-five years' service the auxiliary soldier received the franchise for himself and his descendants (*see* DIPLOMA).

During the second century the *auxilia* gradually became assimilated to the legions and after Caracalla's edict their distinctive character was largely lost. In the barbarian invasions of the third century many units were destroyed, and in the Constantinian reorganization *alae* and *cohortes* are regiments of the *limitanei*. The term *auxilia* remained as the designation of certain infantry units of the mobile field army and of the *limitanei*. *See* ALAE, COHORS, LIMITANEI, PALATINI, PRAEFECTUS.

G. L. Cheesman, *The Auxilia of the Imperial Roman Army* (1914); W. Wagner, *Die Dislokation der römischen Auxiliarformationen in den Provinzen Noricum, Pannonien, Moesien und Dakien von Augustus bis Gallienus* (1938); K. Kraft, *Alen und Kohorten an Rhein und Donau* (1951); Jones, *Later Rom. Emp.* H. M. D. P.; G. R. W.

**AUXIMUM,** modern *Osimo* with well-preserved ancient walls, hill-town of Picenum, 12 miles from the Adriatic. Becoming a Roman colony (128 B.C. ?), it developed into a flourishing place, which supported Caesar against Pompey. Much later it and four other cities constituted the Pentapolis under the Ravenna Exarchate.

E. T. Salmon, *Athenaeum* 1963, 3 ff. E. T. S.

**AVENTICUM,** chief city of the Helvetii (q.v.), modern *Avenches*. Under Vespasian (c. A.D. 73/4) a colony of veterans was founded there (Colonia Pia Flavia Constans Emerita Helvetiorum Foederata); the relationship of *coloni* and *incolae* is not very clear. It was sacked by the Alamanni (259/60). Walls (of the Flavian colony), east gate, theatre, forum, amphitheatre, baths, and private houses survive.

F. Stahelin, *Die Schweiz in röm. Zeit¹* (1948); G. T. Schwartz, *Die Kaiserstadt Aventicum* (1964). H. H. S.

**AVENTINE,** an abrupt plateau overlooking the Tiber and separated from the other hills of Rome by the Murcia valley. It formed *regio* XIII of Rome, while an eastward lobe (*regio* XII, *Piscina publica*) was known as *Aventinus* to Dionysius, Varro, and Festus, and later as *Aventinus minor*, though perhaps not originally so called (Cic. *Div.* 1. 107, quoting Ennius). The hill was *ager publicus* given to the *plebs* for settlement in 456 B.C. It already held two pre-republican temples, to Diana, patroness of a Latin league, and to Luna; also the Loretum, reputed a regal tomb, and the *armilustrium* (where arms were ritually purified). These connexions are with Latium rather than Rome, and the hill lay until A.D. 49 outside the *pomerium* (q.v.). Other early temples were those of Juno Regina (396–392 B.C.) and Jupiter Libertas (238 B.C.), the latter housing Varro's library presented by Asinius Pollio. Here also dwelt Ennius (q.v.), in the plebeian quarter whose early and thriving prosperity is represented by the *clivus Publicius*, a street development of 238 B.C. I. A. R.

**AVERNUS,** a deep lake near Puteoli. Its unusual name (fancifully derived from ἀ-ὄρνις), its reputed immense depth, and its situation amid gloomy-looking woods and mephitic exhalations inspired the belief that it led to the underworld (Strabo 5. 244; Verg. *Aen.* 6. 237 f.; Lucr. 6. 740 f.; Livy 24. 12). Agrippa temporarily remedied its lack of a natural outlet. E. T. S.

**AVIANUS** or **AVIENUS** (fl. *c.* A.D. 400), Roman fabulist; he dedicated his forty-two fables in elegiac metre to Macrobius (q.v.) Theodosius, who probably used him as a speaker in his *Saturnalia*. Nothing more is known of his life. His chief source is the Greek fabulist, Babrius (q.v.). With few exceptions, his fables are expanded paraphrases of their Babrian prototypes; and the exceptions are probably based on lost fables of Babrius. Avianus' style is picturesque; he expands his models by elaborating the descriptive element; but his effort to introduce Virgilian and Ovidian phrases produces a strained and sometimes mock-heroic effect. Mingled with classical echoes, there are frequent instances of a degenerate Latin (R. Ellis ed. xxxvi ff.). The metre is correctly Ovidian except for a few lapses showing the decline of metrical strictness in Avianus' age. Paraphrases, scholia, and quotations show that Avianus was popular in medieval schools. Stronger evidence is afforded by the *promythia* and *epimythia* attached to some of the fables to point a moral. Most of these were composed in medieval times; but some *epimythia* may come from Avianus himself.

TEXTS. E. Baehrens *PLM* v; A. Guaglianone (*Paravia* 1958), id. Ital. trans. in separate work (1958). Text with commentary. R. Ellis (1887). Text with translation. Duff, *Minor Lat. Poets*; (French) P. Constant (Garnier 1938) with Phaedrus, Publilius Syrus, and *Disticha Catonis*). Schanz–Hosius § 1019. Alan Cameron, 'Macrobius, Avienus, and Avianus', *CQ* 1967, 385 ff. A. M. D.

**AVIDIUS** (1, *PW* 8) **QUIETUS**, TITUS, from Faventia in Cisalpina, legionary legate not later than A.D. 82, proconsul of Achaea under Domitian, *cos. suff.* in 93, and governor of Britain in 98. He was a friend of Thrasea Paetus, Pliny the Younger, and of Plutarch who dedicated a book to him. His son was *cos. suff.* in 111. H. H. S.

**AVIDIUS** (2, *PW* 6) **NIGRINUS**, GAIUS, was probably son of an Avidius Nigrinus, proconsul of Achaea under Domitian and brother of (1) above. Avidius himself was tribune *c.* A.D. 105 and *cos. suff.* in 110. He then became governor of Dacia (rather than Upper Moesia; *ILS* 2417). He served in Achaea as imperial legate towards the end of Trajan's reign (*SIG*³ 827), either as actual governor, if Achaea (like Bithynia; *see* PLINY 2) had temporarily been transferred from the Senate to the Emperor, or as a special arbitrator between cities (*see* MAXIMUS 1). Rich, influential, and well connected (he was father-in-law of L. Aelius, q.v. 2), he was thought to be Hadrian's selected successor; but he became involved in the conspiracy of the four 'consulars' against Hadrian (q.v.) in 118, and was executed by senatorial order.

S.H.A. *Hadr.*; Dio Cassius, bk. 69. Lambrechts, *Sénat* no. 22; R. Syme, *Athenaeum* 1957, 310 ff.; id., *Tacitus*, see index. C. H. V. S.; M. H.

**AVIDIUS** (3, *PW* 1) **CASSIUS**, GAIUS (d. A.D. 175), was son of the equestrian C. Avidius Heliodorus, a rhetorician of Cyrrhus in Syria and an official under Hadrian and Antoninus Pius. Avidius became *cos. suff.* under Marcus Aurelius, between 161 and 168 (*CIL* xvi, 127) and afterwards governor of Syria. He drilled the Syrian legions into efficiency, thrust east against Parthia, subdued Mesopotamia, and captured Seleuceia and Ctesiphon (165–6). He was subsequently given supreme command over all the East, including Egypt, where he quelled a revolt in 172. In 175, apparently because Marcus was falsely reported to have died on the Danube, and reputedly with the encouragement of Faustina the

Younger (q.v.), Avidius had himself saluted as Emperor and for three months controlled Egypt and all the eastern provinces except Cappadocia and Bithynia. But Marcus' return to Rome meant the collapse of the revolt. Avidius himself was murdered by a centurion. Unrecognized by the Senate, he had issued no coinage. Marcus, visiting the East to restore its loyalty, displayed clemency to Avidius' family and supporters.

S.H.A. *Avidius Cassius*; Dio Cassius, bk. 72. Lambrechts, *Sénat* no. 694; R. Remondon, *Chronique d'Égypte* 1951, 364 ff. *See also under* AURELIUS (1). C. H. V. S.; M. H.

**AVIEN(I)US** (an inscription from Bulla Regia reveals his name as *Postumius Rufius Festus qui et Avienius*: see Alan Cameron, *CQ* 1967, 392 ff.) (4th c. A.D.), Latin writer to whom are ascribed: (i) *Descriptio Orbis Terrae* (title varies), 1,394 extant hexameters (material based, sometimes closely, but with omissions, additions, and amplifications, on Dionysius (q.v. 9) Periegetes) describing noteworthy things in physical and political geography, and reproducing in vigorous style much ancient ignorance which learned contemporaries could have corrected; (ii) *Ora Maritima*, 703 extant iambics (from a much larger work?) mostly about the coast from Massilia to Gades, with little order and much irrelevance, full of ancient nomenclature and ignorance, but giving interesting material from early records of Greek and Carthaginian voyages in the Atlantic *c.* 500 B.C.; (iii) *Aratea Phaenomena* (1,325 extant hexameters) and *Aratea Prognostica* (552 hexameters) based on Aratus, sometimes closely, often expanding, attractive in style; (iv) three short works (two personal, one on the Sirens and Ulysses). Avienius, born of a distinguished old family the Rufii Festi of Volsinii, held high office.

Ed. A. Holder, *Rufi Festi Avieni Carmina*, (1965).
*Descriptio Orbis Terrae*: P. van de Woestijne, *Ant. Class.* 1954, 29 ff.; 1955, 127 ff.; 1958, 375 ff.; and *Rev. Belge de Philologie* 1955, 74 ff.; 1957, 48 ff.; 1958, 51 ff.; 1959, 52 ff.; *Class. et Med.* 1956, 173 ff.; *id. De vroegste uitgaven van Avienus' Descr. Orb. Terr.* (1959) and in *Hommages à L. Herrmann* (1960), 757; and critical edition 1961.
*Ora Maritima*: A. Schulten (1922, 2nd ed. 1955); A. Berthelot (1934); S. Lambrino, *Bull. des Études portugaises* 1956; N. Lambroglia, *Riv. di Studi Liguri* 1949. Cf. also L. F. Vidal, *Estudios geographicos* 1949; and (on the *Aratea*) A. Vigevani, *Annali della Scuola Norm. Superiore di Pisa* 1947, 49 ff. E. H. W.

**AVĪTUS**, ALCIMUS ECDICIUS, bishop of Vienne (*c.* A.D. 490–518), a vigorous opponent of Arianism, author of sermons, letters, a biblical epic in five books, and a short poem on chastity.

EDITION. Peiper, *MGH* (1883).

**AXIONICUS**, Middle Comedy poet, perhaps late in the period (fr. 2 mentions Gryllis, a parasite of one of Alexander's generals). In Φιλευριπίδης, 'Lover of Euripides', fr. 4 is modelled on a tragic monody.

*FCG* iii. 530 ff.; *CAF* ii. 411 ff.

**AXONES**, the tablets of laws, in the Prytaneum at Athens, revolving on a vertical axis. Draco's and Solon's laws were written on them, and they were quoted by the number of the *axon*; the highest known number is sixteen (Plut. *Sol.* 23. 4). The axones were originally of wood, but copies were published on similar pillars of stone. Whether the stone slabs were called κύρβεις seems doubtful; it seems impossible clearly to distinguish between the two names, even to decide which is the earlier one. A fragment found at Chios shows that similar revolving slabs were used elsewhere too.

Cratinus, fr. 276. K. Holland, *AJArch.* 1941, 346 f.; Harrison, *CQ* 1961, 5 f.; E. Ruschenbusch, *Historia Einzelschriften* 9 (1966), 23 ff. V. E.

**AXUMIS** or **AUXUME** (modern *Axum*), a city in the Tigré province of Abyssinia. In the first century A.D. it became the royal seat of the Habashat or Axumites, who, through their port Adulis, traded busily with Arabians, Greeks, Romans, and Indians, eclipsing Meroë. In the second century A.D. the Axumites were powerful in Somaliland and possibly in Arabia also, controlling much of the traffic to India from that time until far in the Byzantine era. Fragments of their history are known from inscriptions and classical references. Some of the kings were Christians, and important relations were maintained with the West. The summit of Axumite influence was reached in the fourth and fifth centuries A.D.

See A. Wylde, *Modern Abyssinia* (1901) (for antiquities); A. H. M. Jones and E. Monroe, *Hist. of Abyssinia* (1935); E. A. Budge, *Hist. of Ethiopia* (1928), i; Warmington, *Indian Commerce*, index, 'Axumites' (for commerce); J. Bent, *The Sacred City of the Ethiopians* (1893), appendix by D. Müller (inscriptions); J. I. Miller, *The Spice Trade of the Roman Empire* (1969). E. H. W.

# B

**BABRIUS,** VALERIUS (?), probably a hellenized Roman, who composed not later than the second century A.D. (*POxy.* 10, n. 1249) μυθίαμβοι Αἰσώπειοι, being versions in choliambic metre of existing fables, together with some original additions. The work may have been originally in ten books (*Suda*); in the existing MS. tradition, and in that known to Avianus at the end of the fourth century, it consists of two, of which the second is incomplete. The metre, in which the stress accent begins to play a part, and the language, which is that of everyday life, are well adapted to the subject-matter. The collection enjoyed great popularity, and was paraphrased in prose and verse in the Middle Ages.

SOURCES. *Suda*; Avianus (*prooem.*).
EDITIONS. W. G. Rutherford (comment., 1883); O. Crusius (Teubner, pref., 1897); B. E. Perry (Loeb 1964).
CRITICISM. O. Crusius, 'De B. aetate', *Leipz. Stud.* ii (1879); E. M. Husselman, *TAPA* 1935, 104 ff. W. M. E.; R. B.

**BABYLON** (1) (modern *Bâbil*), principal city of the southern part of Mesopotamia (q.v.). Situated at a natural centre of trade-routes, it was one of the greatest cities of the ancient world. Contact with the Greek world of the LH IIIB period, as shown by cylinder seals discovered at Thebes, was probably made indirectly through Syria or Egypt. The city attained its highest prosperity under the Chaldaean kings of the New Babylonian Empire (626–539 B.C.). The history thereafter is one of gradual decline. The Persians, who conquered it in 539 B.C., made it the chief city of the Babylonian satrapy; it was the winter residence of the Great King. As a result of rebellions the walls and public buildings were at least partially demolished; but enough was left to impress Herodotus when he visited it about 450 B.C. His description (1. 178 ff.) is fairly accurate for what he saw, but what he was told is much exaggerated. Alexander entered Babylon without resistance in 331 B.C. His project of rebuilding it and making it the capital of his Empire was frustrated by his death there in 323 B.C.

In Hellenistic times Babylon was still a prosperous city with a considerable Greek population. A frequent bone of contention among Alexander's successors, it was more than once sacked. It suffered still more from the foundation of Seleuceia (q.v. 1) as the new commercial centre of Babylonia (Pliny, *HN* 6. 122). In the Parthian period Babylon was still sufficiently important to have its own city-governor, but it declined rapidly; Trajan in A.D. 116 found little but ruins. Many of the public buildings, temples, palaces, etc., and the city walls have been excavated.

R. Koldewey, *Das wiedererstehende Babylon* (Engl. Transl. 1915); E. Unger, *Babylon* (1931); O. E. Ravn, *Herodotus' Description of Babylon* (1942); S. A. Pallis, *The History of Babylon 538–93 B.C.* (1953); J. G. Macqueen, *Babylon* (1964).

(2) Fortified town at the head of the Delta of Egypt; the headquarters of a Roman legion under the early Empire. M. S. D.; J. G. McQ.

**BABYLONIA,** the more southerly of the two ancient kingdoms of Mesopotamia. Its geographical limits were not clearly defined. Ptolemy (5. 20) says that it was bounded by Mesopotamia, Arabian desert, the Persian Gulf, and the river Tigris. It was sometimes included in the wider designation Assyria (q.v.).

In 538 B.C. the New Babylonian Empire fell before the Persians, and the country became an Achaemenid satrapy. Conquered by Alexander and intended as the centre of his empire, it was disputed among the *Diadochi*; Seleucus I Nicator founded Seleuceia (q.v. 1) to replace Babylon as the capital city. When the eastern portion of the Seleucid empire passed to the Parthians, Babylonia became an important commercial and administrative centre; Ctesiphon, the Parthian residence, became the capital of the Sassanids.

Through all vicissitudes, until the Sassanian epoch, Babylonia retained its ancient civilization, the religion, cuneiform writing, and economic organization which it had inherited from Sumer. An attempt of Antiochus Epiphanes to hellenize it failed. In the Greek cities the native element was at first segregated, but most of the numerous Greek residents became orientalized, as the numerous business documents from Babylon and Orchoi (*Uruk*) testify. Babylonia had a considerable influence on Greece in the fields of astrology, astronomy, mensuration, and even perhaps literature (e.g. the *Epic of Gilgamesh* on the descriptions of Heracles). It also played an important part, politically and commercially, as the bridge between East and West. It was far more extensively cultivated than today, and was proverbially fertile (Hdt. 1. 193; Strabo 16. 742).

K. Holzhey, *Assur und Babel in der Kenntnis der griechisch-römischen Welt* (1921); J. Jordan, *Uruk-Warka* (1928); P. Schnabel, *Berossos und die babylonisch-hellenistische Literatur* (1923). *See also* SELEUCEIA I. Rostovtzeff, *Hellenistic World*; W. W. Tarn and G. T. Griffith, *Hellenistic Civilisation* (1952); O. Neugebauer, *The Exact Sciences in Antiquity* (1957). M. S. D.; J. G. McQ.

**BACAUDAE,** less correctly *Bagaudae*, a name of Celtic origin, but uncertain meaning, applied to insurgent peasants in Gaul and northern Spain. Its first known application was to the followers of Aelius and Amandus, suppressed in Gaul by Maximian in A.D. 285. In the early and middle fifth century prolonged revolts of this type occurred in Armorica and there were frequent outbreaks in north-east Spain. The revolts were perhaps connected with attempts to tie the peasants to the land, thus increasing their subjection to the landlords.

B. Czúth, *Die Quellen der Geschichte der Bagauden* (1965); PW Suppl. XI, 346 ff. B. H. W.

**BACCHANALIA,** the Latin name of the Dionysiac *orgia*. They are especially known because of the measures taken by the Roman Senate to repress them and an accompanying crime-wave in 186 B.C.: the senatorial decree is preserved (*CIL* i. 196; *ILS* 18), and Livy (39. 8–18) gives a long account of the episode. They were widespread in southern Italy. The first trace is an inscription of the fifth century B.C. from Cumae forbidding those who were not initiated into the Bacchic mysteries to be buried in a certain place (figured in Cumont, *Rel. or.* 197). Evidently they came from Campania to Rome, bringing much disorder under the cover of religion. A connexion may exist between the decree mentioned and a regulation of the Bacchic mysteries in Egypt by Ptolemy IV at the end of the third century B.C. (Cichorius, *Röm. Stud.* 21). In the first centuries A.D. the Dionysiac mysteries were very popular, as is proved e.g. by the many sarcophagi with Dionysiac motifs and the paintings in the Villa Item at Pompeii (their interpretation is highly controversial). Very important is the inscription of Agrippinilla (early second century A.D.), enumerating the officials of a Bacchic *thiasus*. Cumont believes that oriental elements were dominant, but it seems that these mysteries were fundamentally Greek.

Cumont, *Rel. or.* 195 ff.; O. Kern, *PW*, s.v. Mysterien (xvi. 1310); M. P. Nilsson, *The Dionysiac Mysteries of the Hellenistic and Roman Age* (Lund, 1957). The Cult in 186 B.C.: A. H. McDonald, *JRS* 1944, 26 ff.; A. Bruhl, *Liber Pater* (Paris, 1953), 82 ff.; D. W. L. van Son, *Livius' behandeling van de Bacchanalia* (1960, with English summary). The Agrippinilla inscription: A. Vogliano and F. Cumont, *AJArch.* 1933, 215 ff. The Villa Item paintings: A. Maiuri, *La villa dei misteri²* (1947); R. Herbig, *Neue Beobachtungen am Fries der Mysterienvilla in Pompeii* (1958); G. Zuntz, *Proc. Brit. Acad.* 1963, 177 ff.; Houtzager, *De grote wandschildering in de Villa dei misteri* (1963, with extensive English summary). M. P. N.

**BACCHEIUS** (Βακχεῖος) **GERON,** author of an *Εἰσαγωγὴ τέχνης μουσικῆς*, lived in the time of Constantine (A.D. 274–337). The work is in the form of question and answer; while following in the main the tenets of Aristoxenus, it borrows freely from other schools of musical theory.

Ed. C. Jan, *Musici Scriptores Graeci* (1895), 283–316. W. D. R.

**BACCHIADAE,** a clan of Heraclid descent so named after Bacchis, a king of Corinth, held a monopoly of political power at Corinth for a century or so before the rise of Cypselus (q.v.) *c.* 657 B.C. They laid the foundations of Corinth's ascendancy in naval warfare, maritime commerce, literature (*see* EUMELUS), and art, especially in pottery. The clan, consisting of some two hundred families, practised endogamy and retained its identity long after its expulsion by the tyrants. Members of the clan went to Illyria, whence they founded the Lyncestian royal family, and to Tarquinii, where they influenced Etruscan art.

E. Will, *Korinthiaka* 1955, 295 ff. N. G. L. H.

**BACCHYLIDES** (fl. 5th c. B.C.), lyric poet, of Iulis in Ceos, son of Midylus (*EM* 582, 20) and nephew of Simonides (Strabo 486, *Suda* s.v. Βακχυλίδης). He may have been born about 524–521 (*Chron. Pasch.* 304. 6), though Eusebius–Jerome gives his *floruit* both in 467 B.C. and in 431 B.C. Remains of fifteen epinician odes and six dithyrambs found in 1896 at Al-Kussiyah and supplemented by later finds may be arranged tentatively in a chronological order. He seems to have followed the fortunes of his uncle Simonides and to have been employed by the same patrons, a fact which sometimes brought him into competition with Pindar, who was almost his contemporary. His first activities may have been in Thessaly (fr. 15, Ode 14) and Macedonia, where he wrote his Encomium for Alexander son of Amyntas (fr. 20 B). About 485 B.C. he wrote Ode 13 for Pytheas of Aegina, and Ode 12 may belong to the same period. Again like his uncle, he wrote dithyrambs for the competitions at Athens, notably Ode 19, and Ode 18, which is unique in being a dialogue between the leader of the chorus, who takes the part of Aegeus, and the remainder,

who represent his followers. It is not clear whether this is a survival of an older form of dithyramb or has been influenced by the technique of Attic drama. Ode 17, which may belong to the early years of the Delian League, is really a paean sung by a Cean choir at Delos. The date of Ode 10, written for an Athenian victor in the Isthmian Games, is not known. About 476 B.C. Bacchylides accompanied Simonides to Sicily as the guest of Hieron (Ael. *VH* 4. 15) after writing Ode 5 for Hieron's victory in the horse-race at Olympia, an event celebrated by Pindar in *Ol.* 1. In Sicily he seems to have incurred the dislike of Pindar, who is thought to make disparaging references to him in *Ol.* 2. 86–8, *Pyth.* 2. 72–3, *Nem.* 3. 80–2. It is not known how long he stayed in Sicily, but his connexion with it was maintained with Ode 4 for Hieron's victory in the Pythian horse-race of 470 B.C., for which Pindar wrote *Pyth.* 1, and Ode 3 for the Olympian chariot-victory of 468 B.C., when Pindar may have written *Pyth.* 2. To his later years belong Odes 6 and 7 for Lachon of Ceos in 452. He is said to have been exiled to the Peloponnese (Plut. *De exil.* 14), and in this period he may have written Ode 9 for Automedes of Phlius, and the dithyramb *Idas* for the Lacedaemonians (20). The date of his death is not known.

Bacchylides also wrote hymns (frs. 1–2), paeans, of which fr. 4 contains a fine eulogy of peace, processional songs (frs. 11–13), maiden-songs (Plut. *De mus.* 17), hyporchemata (frs. 14–16), encomia, like that to Alexander (fr. 20 B) and to Hieron (fr. 20 C). His reputation has suffered by the comparisons with Pindar, which are at least as old as 'Longinus' (*De Subl.* 33). His gifts are of a different kind: a brilliant clarity and sense of narrative, a real love for the games which he describes, an absence of didactic fervour, a choice command of epithets, and occasional moments of magical beauty.

TEXT. B. Snell, 8th ed. (Teubner, 1961). COMMENTARIES. R. C. Jebb (1905); H. Jurenka (1898); A. Taccone (1907). CRITICISM. A. Severyns, *Bacchylide* (1933); W. K. Prentice, *De Bacchylide Pindari artis socio et imitatore* (Diss. Halle, 1900); W. S. Barrett, 'Bacchylides, Asine and Apollo Pythaieus', *Hermes* 1954, 421 ff. C. M. B.

**BACIS.** Although used by Herodotus (8. 20) as if a proper name, later references make it clear that Bacis was the generic title of a class of inspired prophets, characteristic of the growth of ecstatic religion in the seventh and sixth centuries B.C.

E. Rohde, *Psyche* (Engl. Transl. 1925), 292 ff.

**BACTRIA** (old Iranian name, Zariaspa; roughly part of northern Afghanistan, southern Uzbekistan, and Tadjikistan) received its name from the Bactrus, an affluent of the Oxus. This country in the middle Oxus Valley, with its chief city Bactra, was known to Greeks as the Jewel of Iran on account of its fertility. Traditionally the home of Zoroaster and the Zend Avesta, it formed an Iranian satrapy under the Achaemenids and fought heroically against Alexander. Seleucus exercised his authority over it only by force of arms; and yet not long after his death, it revolted under the leadership of Diodotus I, a Bactrian Greek. The newly founded kingdom of the Bactrian Greeks (Indo-Greeks, Yavanas), which withstood the challenge of Antiochus III, grew into a strong power, the more important kings, out of about forty, being Euthydemus I (235–200 B.C.), Demetrius I (200–185 B.C.) and II (180–165 B.C.), Eucratides I (171–155 B.C.), and Menander (155–130 B.C.). At the height of their power they ruled over almost all Afghanistan, parts of Soviet Central Asia, and a considerable area of what is now known as Western Pakistan. They also led an expedition into the Ganges valley but failed to annex any part of it. Among the later kings Heliocles I and Hermaeus are better known and their coin types were imitated by the Scythian and other successors. The Bactrian kingdom was known to the Chinese as Ta-hsia and Chang Ch'ien visited its northern part in 129–128 B.C., when it was under the possession of the Yueh-Chih, who crossed the Oxus and occupied the southern parts of Bactria in c. 100 B.C. and divided in among five *hsi-hou*, one of which was Kuei-shuang (Kushanas). About the beginning of the Christian era Ch'iu-ch'ueh (Kujula Kadphises), *hsi-hou* of Kuei-shuang became the master of the whole of Ta-hsia. His son Yen-kao-chen (Wima Kadphises) and the successor Kushan kings, most important among whom were Kanishka, Huvishka, and Vasudeva, ruled over a major part of northern India. Under the Kushanas the country became a centre of Buddhism. Bactria was the meeting-place not only for the overland trade between the western world on the one hand and India and China on the other but also for the cross-currents of religious and artistic ideas during several centuries.

W. W. Tarn, *The Greeks in Bactria and India²* (1951); A. K. Narain, *The Indo-Greeks* (1957) with a list of kings on p, 181.
A. K. N.

**BAEBIUS** (*PW* 44) **TAMPHILUS**, MARCUS, praetor in 192 B.C., with an advance guard covered the Roman landing in Greece against Antiochus. Consul in 181, he transported 40,000 mountain Ligurians to Samnium (*Ligures Corneliani et Baebiani*, *ILS* 6509). To him are attributed the Baebian measure on the number of praetorships (Livy 40. 44. 2) and the *Lex Baebia de ambitu* (Livy 40. 19. 11).

Scullard, *Rom. Pol.* 123, 171 ff.
A. H. McD.

**BAETICA**, the heart of the province originally (197 B.C.) called Hispania Ulterior. As the territory occupied by the Romans increased, an administrative division between Hither and Further Spain was formed beginning at the Mediterranean south of Carthago Nova (*Cartagena*) and running west-north-west to the Anas (*Guadiana*) at Lacimurga (*Villavieja*); thence northward to the Tagus (*Tajo*), beyond which the west was unconquered or unorganized. In 27 B.C. the old settled province east and south of the Anas was assigned to the Senate with the name Hispania Ulterior Baetica, or simply Baetica; Augustus took the rest of Spain (*see* LUSITANIA). Baetica was divided for judicial purposes into four *conventus* centred at Gades, Corduba, Astigi, Hispalis (Pliny *HN* 3. 7), comprising more than 175 town communities. By the time of Augustus' death, many of these towns had the *ius Latii* (q.v.), and spoke Latin, not Iberian (Strabo 3. 151). This Latinized culture developed chiefly in the rich Baetis (*Guadalquivir*) valley from which wine, oil, wheat, honey, sheep, fish, copper, lead, cinnabar, and silver were exported to Rome. The wealth of the country attracted pirate-bandits from Africa (A.D. 178), while the Vandals tarried there long enough to attach their name to the country (*Andalusia*).

R. Thouvenot, *Essai sur la province romaine de Bétique* (1940).
J. J. VAN N.; M. I. H.

**BAIAE**, reputedly named after Baios, Odysseus' companion, was a dependency, originally perhaps the port, of Cumae (q.v.) on an inlet of the Bay of Naples. Although never a *municipium*, Baiae became a fashionable resort because of its mild climate and beautiful surroundings. Great thermal buildings, impressive remains of which still survive, served its sulphur-springs (*aquae Cumanae*); and Julius Caesar, Caligula, Nero, Alexander Severus, and others built opulent villas nearby. Ulti-

mately, however, malaria, already present in republican times (Cic. *Fam.* 9. 12), and earthquakes ruined Baiae.

A. Maiuri, *The Phlegrean Fields³* (1958); R. F. Paget, 'The Great Antrum at Baiae', *PBSR* 1967, 102 ff.
E. T. S.

**BALBILLUS**, TIBERIUS CLAUDIUS, the astrologer, was probably a son of Thrasyllus (q.v.) and shared his father's lore. He won the friendship of the young Claudius (the future Emperor), but on Tiberius' death he retired to Alexandria. On Claudius' accession he returned to Rome and became an *amicus* of the Emperor. He accompanied Claudius to Britain as *comes*, *tribunus militum* of Legio XX, and *praefectus fabrum*; and he at some time followed an equestrian career, becoming procurator in Asia. He gained the goodwill of Agrippina and of Nero at least until A.D. 64/65, and was Prefect of Egypt (55–59). He lived until after A.D. 75 and enjoyed Vespasian's favour. He was at one time head of the Museum at Alexandria. Fragments from the *Astrologumena* of this learned man have been preserved (*Catalogus Codicum Astrologorum Graec.* VIII. iii. 103, iv. 233). Despite the objections of A. Stein (*PIR²* C 813), the identification, here assumed, of the astrologer with the prefect is generally accepted (cf. Syme, *Tacitus*, 508, n. 9: Magie, *Rom. Rule Asia Min.* ii, 1398 ff.: H. G. Pflaum, *Les Carrières procuratoriennes* (1960), 34 ff.).

F. H. Cramer, *Astrology in Roman Law and Politics* (U.S.A. 1954), 112 ff.
H. H. S.

**BALBINUS**, DECIUS CAELIUS (*PW* 20) CALVINUS and **PUPIENUS MAXIMUS**, MARCUS CLODIUS (*PW* 50), members of a board of twenty *consulares* appointed for the defence of Italy against Maximinus, were after the deaths of Gordian I and II in Africa chosen joint emperors by the Senate (A.D. 238). Both had had long senatorial careers. Constitutionally, on the model of the consulate, they had equal powers, each being Pontifex Maximus; but Balbinus was entrusted with the civil administration and Pupienus with the command of the army. To placate the people, Gordian III was given the status of Caesar.

At the news of Maximinus' murder Pupienus proceeded to Aquileia and sent back the former's legions to their provinces, and with his German bodyguard returned to Rome to share a triumph with Balbinus and Gordian. For a few days the joint government worked smoothly, but the praetorians, who resented the Senate's action, mutinied. The two Emperors were dragged from their palace and murdered after ruling for three months.

P. W. Townsend, *YClS* 1955, 49 ff.
H. M. D. P.

**BALBUS** (1), MARCUS ATIUS (*PW* 11), of a good senatorial family of Aricia, and related to Pompey, was the husband of Julia, sister of Caesar, and father of Atia, Augustus' mother. Praetor before 59 B.C., he was a commissioner under the *Lex Iulia Agraria* (q.v.).
E. B.

**BALBUS** (2), T. AMPIUS, called 'tuba belli civilis' (Cic. *Fam.* 6, 12. 3, a letter addressed to him), was tribune (63 B.C.), pro-Pompeian, and proconsul in Asia in 58 (Broughton, *MRR Suppl.* 4 f.; cistophori in his name were minted at Ephesus, etc.). After raising troops for Pompey at Capua (49), he served as *legatus pro praetore* in Asia. Exiled by Caesar, he was recalled (47/6) through Cicero's influence. He wrote history (Suet. *Iul.* 77).
H. H. S.

**BALBUS** (3), LUCIUS CORNELIUS (*PW* 69) (*Maior*), born in the *civitas foederata* of Gades, acquired Roman citizenship at Pompey's instance in 72 B.C. and took his name from the Cornelii Lentuli (for possible explanation see Syme, *Rom. Rev.* 44). He removed to Rome, where his political sense and the wealth derived from his adoption (*c.* 59) by Theophanes of Mytilene gave him enormous influence. Part architect of the coalition of 60 B.C., he gradually shifted his allegiance from Pompey to Caesar, serving the latter as *praefectus fabrum* in 62 and 59, and later managing his interests in Rome. In 56 he was prosecuted for illegal usurpation of the *civitas*, and successfully defended by Cicero in the extant speech. In the Civil War he was outwardly neutral, and persistently tried to persuade Cicero and Lentulus (q.v. 7) Crus to join him. Actually he favoured Caesar, and after Pharsalus became, with Oppius, Caesar's chief agent in public affairs. In 44 he supported Octavian, though cautiously, and in 40 became Rome's first foreignborn consul. Author of a published diary (now lost), and recipient and editor of Hirtius' commentaries, he had wide literary interests over which he constantly corresponded with Cicero. He bequeathed 25 *denarii* to every citizen of Rome.

On the difficult constitutional questions connected with Balbus' case in 56 see F. Münzer, *PW* cit.

G. E. F. C.

**BALBUS** (4), LUCIUS CORNELIUS (*PW* 70), nephew of Balbus (3), and distinguished as 'Balbus minor' in Cicero's letters, received the Roman citizenship with his uncle. In 49 and 48 B.C. he undertook diplomatic missions for Caesar; in 43 he was proquaestor in Further Spain under Pollio (q.v.), who complained of his tyrannical conduct at Gades and of his absconding with the paychest. He was honoured by Augustus with a pontificate and consular rank. Proconsul of Africa (21–20?), he defeated the Garamantes and other peoples and triumphed (27 Mar. 19), a unique distinction for one not born a Roman. He built a new town and docks at Gades and a theatre in Rome, which he dedicated in 13. He wrote a *fabula* (q.v.) *praetexta* on his mission of 49, and lengthy Ἐξηγητικά of uncertain scope.

Syme, *Rom. Rev.*, see index; P. Romanelli, *Storia delle province romane dell'Africa* (1959), 176 ff., 668 f.; Funaioli, *Gramm. Rom. Frag.* 540 f.; Schanz–Hosius i, see index; F. della Corte and E. Paratore, *Riv. cult. class. e med.* 1960, 347 ff. G. W. R.; T. J. C.

**BALBUS** (5), a writer on surveying (*see* GROMATICI). He was in charge of military surveying during the Dacian campaigns of Domitian or more probably of Trajan.

O. A. W. D.

**BALEARES INSULAE.** The name *Gymnesiae* (Γυμνήσιαι), used by early Greek voyagers, was replaced by *Baliares* or *Baliarides* from an Iberian original. The spelling was changed to *Baleares* in the Augustan period. Roman names of each island were *Maiorca* (formerly *Columba*), *Minorca* (formerly *Nura*), *Capraria, Menaria, Tiquadra,* and *Cunicularia* (formerly *Hannibalis*). Urban units included Iberian *Tuci*, Phoenician *Bocchori* and *Guiuntum*, and Roman *Palma* and *Pollentia* on Maiorca. Minorca had Iberian *Sanisera* as well as Phoenician *Mago* and *Iamo*. The characteristics of the natives most frequently mentioned by classical writers were their cavehomes, the absence of gold and silver, inhumation, polyandry, and their exceptional skill in the use of the sling. Although Roman title to the islands was recognized by the treaty of 202 B.C., they were not pacified till 121 by Q. Caecilius Metellus (Balearicus). Copper coins were minted under Tiberius by some of the towns, all of which received the Latin Right (*see* IUS LATII) from Vespasian. For administrative purposes the islands were attached to the *conventus Carthaginiensis* of Hither Spain. Diocletian made them an independent province. Escape from the severity of barbarian invasions may be inferred from the late reference (*Not. Dign.* 11. 71, ed. Seeck) to the Balearic dye-works, *bafii.* J. J. VAN N.

**BALL GAMES.** We know from Homer that ball games were played in early Greece, for it was a lost ball that roused Odysseus from his sleep in the bush and led to his discovery by Nausicaa. At Athens in the fifth century they were overshadowed by gymnastic exercises, but they were popular with youths, as archaeological evidence shows. A sculptured relief built into the Themistoclean ring-wall at Athens, and rediscovered in 1922, shows the details of a 'hockey match'. The ball is on the ground in the middle; two youths with sticks are engaged in a 'bully' for it; on either side of them stand two other pairs of youths with sticks.

Another relief represents a throw-in from the touchline: one youth is preparing to throw, the rest are waiting either to seize the ball in the air or to tackle the next possessor. This game, *Phaeninda*, was played with a small, hard ball and bore some resemblance to our Rugby, except that the ball was thrown and never kicked. Another game, more akin to handball or basketball, was played with a lighter ball, the Greek *sphaira*, Latin *follis*. Here tackling was not allowed, and the ball was thrown from hand to hand while the players were running at full speed. In a third type of game (*trigon*), the players were three in number and stood at the corners of a triangle, throwing balls quickly one to the other; both hands were used and caddies supplied the players with missiles.

Galen, *On the small ball* (*Scripta Minora* i. 93). F. A. W.

**BALLISTA (or CALLISTUS)**, praetorian prefect of Valerian, rallied the Romans at Samosata after his capture and dealt severe blows to the Persians on the Cilician coast. In A.D. 260, he joined Macrianus in setting up the younger Macrianus and Quietus as rivals to Gallienus. When the Macriani marched west, Ballista stayed with Quietus in Emesa, but fell a victim with him to Odaenathus. H. M.

**BANKS.** Loans and deposits were known to the Indo-European and Semito-Hamitic tribes, as their languages prove. The ancient oriental cultures had even an encashment business and exchange bills. But banking as a trade could not develop until the invention of coins allowed specialized bankers sufficient opportunities for a living. Institutions which may be called private banks are found in Mesopotamia from the seventh century B.C.; but banking business was here not separated from the administration of large estates. In early Greece the temples (e.g. the Artemisium at Ephesus) had almost regional monopolies of banking. But in the classical period the τραπεζῖται, who originated before 500 B.C. as money-changers and set up their 'tables' at festivals and markets, took over the business of the temples. By the fourth century they provided most of the loans and held most of the deposits, and individual bankers of note appeared (*see* PASION). Whether endorsements could be performed in classical Greece and contemporaneously in Mesopotamia is not certain; various new types of loan appear in our sources at this time (*see* BOTTOMRY LOANS, USURY). On the other hand, banking remained a risky trade. A banker's death meant loss of valuable customers and connexions, if not bankruptcy. The firms were small and banking terminology and book-keeping remained simple. Many bankers combined banking with commerce or manufacture.

In the city-states of the Hellenistic age the more important temples, private firms, and the cities themselves carried on the banking business without much change. But the Ptolemaic Empire created a public banking system which represents for us the most highly developed banking organization of antiquity. A network of royal banks was spread over the whole of Egypt with a central bank in Alexandria, provincial banks in all district capitals, branch establishment in smaller localities, and institutes of minor importance, which were let out to private bankers under the State bank's control. Thousands of employees found occupation in this vast institution, which had a monopoly for the banking business of Egypt, collected revenues, and paid out the charges of the monarchy. Endorsements (*PTeb.* 890) and even primitive exchange bills occur here. Lending was not monopolized by this State bank; the owners of large estates and the temples lent large sums to peasants and business people.

The Roman banks of the second and first centuries B.C. were comparatively small firms. The main business was done by *equites* and other men of wealth and not by specialized bankers. Their methods, however, were progressive and included primitive exchange bills. The so-called *permutatio*, a method of clearing between banks in and outside Rome, allowed payments to provincial residents and vice versa without actual transfer of money.

Augustus divided the Egyptian State bank into small and independent local institutions. The banking structure of republican Rome (with local variations) spread over the whole Empire. Gradually the banks of the Principate lost most of their paying business (money-exchange and lending) to local owners of large estates, a primitive state of affairs which became common throughout the rural districts of the Byzantine Empire. The banks which survived the breakdown of Roman coinage during the third century A.D. were indispensable for financial State transactions, and were therefore compulsorily enrolled in the *corpus collectariorum*, which was controlled by the government. Most of the earlier banking procedure was codified by Justinian I and preserved by Europeans and Arabs throughout the Middle Ages.

See also ATTICUS (1), CAECILIUS (5), NUMMULARII. A. Berger, *Encyclopedic Dictionary of Roman Law* (1953), art. 'argentarii', 'mensa', 'nummularius', 'permutatio', 'tessera nummularia'; H. Bolkestein, *Economic Life in Greece's Golden Age*² (1958), 124 ff.; J. C. A. M. Bongenaar, *Isocrates' Trapeziticus* (1933); A. Calderini, *Aegyptus* 1938. 244 ff.; J. Corver, *De Terminologie van het Crediet-Wezen in het Grieksch* (1934); V. Ehrenberg, *The People of Aristophanes*³ (1962), ch. ix; M. I. Finley, *Land and Credit in Ancient Athens, 500–200 B.C.* (1951), index; Frank, *Econ. Survey* i–v (index); A. Fruechtl, *Das Geldgeschaeft bei Cicero* (1912); G. Glotz, *Le Travail dans la Grèce ancienne* (1920), index; J. Hasebroek, *Hermes* 1920, 113 f.; F. M. Heichelheim, *An Ancient Economic History* ii (1964), 193 ff.; *Historia Mundi* 4 (1956), 411, 418 f., 442, 458, 468 f.; *Historia* 1962/3), art. 'Geld- und Muenzgeschichte (I)', 'Wirtschaftsgeschichte (II, 2, A)'; *Kl. Pauly*, s.v. 'Bankwesen'; R. Herzog, *Tesserae Nummulariae* (1919); E. Kiessling, s.v. 'Giroverkehr', in *PW* Suppl. IV; B. Laum, s.v. 'Banken', in *PW* Suppl. IV; Michell, *Econom. Anc. Gr.*, index; F. Oertel, in R. von Poehlmann, *Geschichte der sozialen Frage und des Sozialismus in der antiken Welt* ii⁴ (1925), 529 ff.; Cl. Préaux, *L'Économie royale des Lagides* (1939), index; Rostovtzeff, *Roman Empire*²; *Hellenistic World*; W. L. Westermann, *Journ. Econom. and Business History* 1931, 30 ff.; E. Ziebarth, *Beiträge zur Geschichte des Seeraubs und Seehandels im alten Griechenland* (1929), index. F. M. H.

**BANTIA,** near Venusia (q.v.) on the borders of Lucania (q.v.) (Pliny, *HN* 3. 98; Hor. *Odes* 3. 4. 15): modern *Banzi.* The great Marcellus fell near here in 208 B.C. Its surviving municipal regulations (*see* TABULA BANTINA) prove that it spoke Oscan *c.* 100 B.C. Under the Empire Bantia was a *municipium* (q.v.).

E. Vetter, *Handbuch der italischen Dialekte* (1953) 1. 13 ff. E. T. S.

**BARCINO** (modern *Barcelona*), *Colonia Faventia Iulia Augusta Pia,* a native foundation with dubious traditions of origin both Greek and Phoenician. Granted colonial immunity by Caesar, Barcino received full colonial status from Augustus. It was far less important to the earlier Roman Empire than Tarraco, but took the lead in the third century, when its restored and modernized town walls show its recovery from the Frankish invasion which ruined Tarraco. From this time, inscriptions record the gifts of wealthy citizens and the service of many imperial-cult officials. These, like the literary references, are chiefly of late date.

M. Almagro, *Carta Arqueologica de España, Barcelona* (1945); I. A. Richmond, *JRS* 1931, 86 ff.; A. Balil, *Colonia Iulia . . . Faventia Barcino* (Madrid, 1964). J. J. VAN N.; M. I. H.

**BAR COCHBA,** 'son of a star', is the name used by Christian writers to denote the leader of the second Jewish revolt in Palestine (A.D. 132–5), to whom Rabbi Akiba applied the prophecy in Num. xxiv. 17. The precise form of his real name, Shim'on (Simon) Ben or Bar (son of) Cosiba, which often appears in a distorted form in Jewish writers, has been given by the discovery of letters written by him and documents dated by the era of the 'liberation of Israel by Shim'on Ben Cosiba, Nasi (Prince of) Israel' in the Dead Sea caves. This era, apparently calculated from 1st Tishri (October) 131, is used also on the coins struck by the Jews during the revolt. Little is known of the course of the revolt (*see* JEWS, A), but there is epigraphic evidence that a large legionary force was needed to defeat the rebels, who held Jerusalem early in the revolt but later relied mainly on guerrilla tactics, and Bar Cochba's letters show that he had an important base at Engeddi and suggest disaffection among his troops towards the end of the war. Some of the rebels finally took refuge in the Dead Sea caves, while others made a last stand at Bethar, in the sack of which Bar Cochba was killed.

Dio Cassius 69. 12–14; Eusebius, *Hist. Eccl.* 4. 6. P. Benoit, J. T. Milik, and R. de Vaux, *Les Grottes de Murabba'at* (*Discoveries in the Judaean Desert,* ii) (1961), nos. 24, 43–4; *Israel Explorat. Journ.* 1961, 40 ff.; 1962, 248 ff. E. M. S.

**BARDYLIS I** founded a powerful kingdom early in the fourth century B.C. which threatened to destroy the Molossian and Macedonian kingdoms. The former was saved by Sparta and the latter by Philip II of Macedon. The centre of Bardylis' kingdom lay north of Lake Lychnitis, and his immediate subjects were probably Dardanians; but he controlled many Illyrian tribes and disposed of large and warlike forces.

F. Papazoglu, *Hist.* 1965, 143 ff.; N. G. L. Hammond, *BSA* 1966, 243 f. N. G. L. H.

**BAREA** (*PW* 2) **SORANUS,** Q. MARCIUS, *cos. suff.* A.D. 52, incurred Nero's anger for his just proconsulate in Asia (before 63). In 66 he was accused by a knight, Ostorius Sabinus, because of friendship with Rubellius Plautius and alleged plotting in Asia. He was condemned, on false evidence given by his former Stoic teacher Egnatius Celer (Juv. 3. 116), who, under Vespasian, was accused by Musonius and condemned. H. H. S.

**BARYGAZA** (*Broach*), near the mouth of the Nerbudda, on the Gulf of Cambay. After discovery by Hippalus (q.v.) of the use of monsoon winds, Greek ships sailed thither direct from Aden; conducted by royal pilots from the Kathiawar coast and towed to the town, they bought merchandise, presents, and Roman coins. To Barygaza were brought Indian and Chinese products from the north through Modura (*Muttra*) and Ozene (*Ujjain*), and from eastern and central India chiefly through Tagara (*Thair*?) and Paethana (*Paithan*). Barygaza sent Indian ships to the Persian Gulf, Somaliland, and Arabia. It was the chief port for Greek and Persian trade in north India.

*Periplus Maris Rubri,* passim; Ptol. *Geog.* 7. 1 ff. Warmington, *Indian Commerce,* index (for commerce). E. H. W.

**BASIL** of Caesarea (Cappadocia), *c.* A.D. 330–79. Born of wealthy Christian parents, he studied at Constantinople and Athens with Himerius and Prohaeresius, and met Libanius (qq.v.). After baptism (356) he began to organize monastic communities in Asia Minor for which he composed Rules. Solitary asceticism he discouraged. In 370 he became bishop of Caesarea, where he died after nine years of stormy controversies. A profound acceptance of classical culture appears in his writings. The ascetic Rules have many analogies with Musonius (q.v.) and Porphyry (q.v.). He wrote letters and sermons typical of the best epistolography and rhetoric of his time. His theology owes something to Plotinus (q.v.) whom he gratefully quotes. It is chiefly in the tract 'To the young' on reading pagan literature that a prickly, defensive tone appears. His Trinitarian terminology ('one *ousia*, three *hypostases*') he did not originate, but did much to interpret with the help of his friend Gregory (q.v. 2) of Nazianzus and his younger brother Gregory (q.v. 3) of Nyssa.

WORKS. Migne *PG* xxix–xxxii; Letters, ed. Y. Courtonne (1957– ), ed. R. J. Deferrari (Loeb 1926–34); *Ad adulescentes*, ed. F. Boulenger (1952). W. Jaeger, *Early Christianity and Greek Paideia* (1962); J. Quasten, *Patrology* iii (1960), 204 ff.　H. C.

**BASILICA,** the name applied to a wide range of Roman building-forms, most commonly and characteristically to the large, multi-purpose public halls which regularly accompanied the fora of the western half of the Roman world, corresponding roughly in function to the Greek and Hellenistic stoa. The earliest known was built in Rome by Cato in 184 B.C. The early basilicas of central Italy (Alba Fucens, Ardea, Cosa) were of the type represented later by Vitruvius' basilica at Fano (5. 1. 6–10) and by the Augustan Basilica Aemilia and Basilica Iulia in the Forum Romanum: timber-roofed, columnar halls, often with galleries, exedrae, and clerestory lighting, and with one long side facing the open area. An alternative, longitudinal (S. Italian?) form, with the entrance in one short side and a tribunal at the far end, is represented at Pompeii (early 1st c. B.C.; another early example at Corinth). The name came later, by extension, to be used of any large covered hall in domestic (Vitr. 5. 5. 2; Sid. Apoll. *Epist.* 2. 2. 8), commercial (*basilica vestiaria, basilica argentaria*), military (Veget. *De re militari* ii. 23), or religious (*Basilica Hilariana, CIL* vi 30973) use. The outstanding example of such development is the Basilica Nova of Maxentius, finished by Constantine. This was a huge vaulted structure, inspired by the central halls of the great 'imperial' bath-buildings (*see* BATHS), with a triple-bayed central nave (clear span 76 feet; 114 feet from floor to vault) buttressed on either side by three enormous, intercommunicating, barrel-vaulted exedrae. Trajan's more conservative, timber-roofed Basilica Ulpia, with internal colonnades and apses at the ends of the central nave, was widely imitated in Italy and the western provinces (outstandingly in the Basilica Severiana at Lepcis Magna, dedicated A.D. 217), and exercised an important influence on the Christian church-architecture of the fourth century.

J. B. Ward-Perkins, *PBSR* 1954, 69 ff.　J. B. W.-P.

**BASSAE,** in south-west Arcadia, near Phigaleia, the site of one of the best-preserved Greek temples. This was dedicated to Apollo, and built by Ictinus, the architect of the Parthenon, though the suggestion has been made that it is the work of two architects, Ictinus and a younger man to whom was due the engaged side walls and the Corinthian column. The orientation, determined seemingly by that of an earlier building, was towards the north instead of the east, and the early sunlight, instead of entering through the main doorway, was admitted to the *adytum* through an opening of unique kind in the eastern side-wall. Unique too were the ten engaged Ionic columns which decorated the side-walls of the *cella* internally, and the single central Corinthian column— one of the earliest of its kind, and one of the most

beautiful—between the *cella* and the *adytum*. The sculptured frieze (now in the British Museum) shows that it belonged to the late fifth century. Traces have been found of earlier occupation of the site, and the remains of archaic revetments would point to an earlier building, of which no other evidence has yet been found, though foundations of other archaic and classical buildings show that the temple was not isolated. *See* ICTINUS.

Paus. 8. 41. 7 ff.; C. R. Cockerell, *The Temples . . . at Aegina and . . . Bassae* (1860); W. B. Dinsmoor, 'The Temple of Apollo at Bassae', *Metr. Mus. Studies* iv. 204 ff.; *AJ Arch.* 1939, 27 f.; and 'The sculptured frieze from Bassae', *AJ Arch.* 1956, 401 ff.
T. J. D. and H. W. R.; R. J. H.

**BASSUS** (1), QUINTUS CAECILIUS (*PW* 36), an equestrian officer under Pompey in the Civil War. After Pharsalus he fled to Syria, where after a mutiny, in which Sextus Caesar (q.v. 5) was killed (46 B.C.), he won over two legions, seized Apamea (where he was besieged by Caesarian commanders), and negotiated with Deiotarus (q.v.) and the Parthians. After Caesar's death, both his troops and his besiegers soon joined C. Cassius (q.v. 6), who dismissed him unharmed.　E. B.

**BASSUS** (2), CAESIUS (1st c. A.D.), a friend of the satirist Persius and editor of his work. He himself was a lyric poet, and Quintilian (10. 1. 96) mentions him as the only one whose name might appear with that of Horace in a canon of Roman lyric poets. He is possibly the author of a metrical work to which later writers refer and part of which is preserved in a corrupted form under the name of Atilius Fortunatianus: ed. Keil, *Gramm. Lat.* vi. 255–72). The treatise *De Metris* printed in Keil, *Gramm. Lat.* vi. 305–12, is apocryphal.

Schanz–Hosius, § 385.　J. F. M.

**BASSUS** (3), SALEIUS, a well-esteemed epic writer who died young (Quint. *Inst.* 10. 1. 90, Juv. 7. 80). Vespasian assisted him financially (Tac. *Dial.* 5. 2; 9. 8).

Schanz–Hosius, § 411. 1.

**BASTARNAE,** a roving tribe which first appeared on the lower Danube *c.* 200 B.C. They were enlisted by Philip V and Perseus of Macedon against their enemies in the northern Balkans, and by Mithridates against the Romans. They defeated C. Antonius (*c.* 62 B.C.), but were subdued by M. Crassus (29–28 B.C.; cf. Cass. Dio 51. 23. 2–27. 3), and henceforth they generally appear as subject allies of Rome. One hundred thousand Bastarnae were transferred by Probus across the Danube into Thrace (*S.H.A. Prob.* 18. 1), and Diocletian settled others in Pannonia. Despite uncertainty in earlier writers the German nationality of the Bastarnae may be deduced from Strabo (7. 3. 17), Pliny, (*HN* 4. 100), and Tacitus (*Germ.* 46. 1). They appear to have been the first of the race to travel the migration route from the Baltic to the Black Sea, and their movement is recalled on the Peutinger Table, where the Carpathians are called Alpes Bastarnicae.　M. C.; J. J. W.

**BATAVI,** a Germanic people, living between the Old Rhine and the Waal, where their name is preserved in the Dutch district of Betuwe. They were an offshoot of the Chatti (q.v.), but helped Drusus in the conquest of western Germany in 12 B.C. and frequently thereafter were of much military value to the Romans. Remaining incorporated in the Empire after the Roman withdrawal to the Rhine in A.D. 9, they paid no taxes and helped Germanicus in his attacks on their fellow Germans in A.D. 16. Their warriors formed auxiliary regiments serving under their own chiefs in the Roman army by the middle of the first century A.D.; and they are also found until A.D. 68 in the personal bodyguard of the Emperors

was they, under the leadership of Civilis (q.v.), who
-aded the great revolt of A.D. 69–70. Thereafter they
ere not prominent in Roman history; and their re-
tionship to the Franks, who later occupied their terri-
ry, is obscure. E. A. T.

**ATHS,** one of the most characteristic and widely dis-
ibuted types of Roman building, found in all provinces
the empire and enjoyed by all classes of society. A
oman bath functioned on the lines of a modern Turkish
ath, the essential features being a changing-room
*podyterium*); a sweating-room (*caldarium*) heated by
e passage of hot air through hypocausts beneath the
oor and through ducts imbedded in the walls, and
quipped with a plunge bath; and an unheated *frigidarium*
ith a cold plunge. A fully equipped public bath might
addition include rooms for dry heat (*laconica*); rooms
an intermediate temperature (*tepidaria*); latrines; a
wimming pool (*natatio*); exercise grounds (*palaestrae*);
olonnades and gardens; cisterns; service-rooms and
oke-holes (*praefurnia*); and suites of lecture-halls,
braries, museums, and club-rooms. These buildings
ccupied a central position in the social life of the day;
ny community of any substance had at least one *thermae*
r public use, and private bath-suites are a common-
lace of domestic architecture in both city and country.
he Roman bath was first developed in Campania, the
arliest-known examples being found at Pompeii (q.v.),
tabian Baths, baths in Regio VIII, insula 5, early 1st c.
.c.). The first public baths in Rome were built by
grippa, *c.* 20 B.C. The high temperature and humidity
ade these buildings an important medium for the
evelopment of the new concrete-vaulted architecture.
he Baths of Titus and of Trajan in Rome already
lustrate the emergence of the great symmetrically
lanned 'imperial' type of bath-building, later repre-
ented in the capital by the Baths of Caracalla and Dio-
letian and in the provinces by such buildings as the
Iadrianic Baths at Lepcis Magna, the Antonine Baths
t Carthage, and the 'imperial' Baths at Trier. On a
maller scale, too, the influence of the capital (e.g. of
he baths of Hadrian's Villa) is visible in the elaborately
urvilinear vaulted forms of such buildings as the baths
t Thenae in Tunisia and the Hunting Baths at Lepcis
Magna. It was one of the few types of western Roman
uilding to be widely adopted in the eastern provinces,
here (as one sees at Ephesus and Miletus) it was
apidly assimilated to and finally replaced the Hellenistic
ymnasium.

W. J. Anderson, R. P. Spiers and J. Ashby, *The Architecture of
ncient Rome* (1927), ch. 6; Krencker and Kruger, *Die Trierer
aiserthermen* (1929). J. B. W.-P.

**ATO** (1), the Dalmatian, chieftain of the Daesitiates,
aised rebellion in Illyricum in A.D. 6, raided the Dalmatian coast, fought against the Romans in the valley
f the Save, and, after the capitulation of his Pannonian
llies in A.D. 8, retreated southwards. After vainly
efending several forts against the Romans, he surren-
ered and was interned at Ravenna (A.D. 9).

E. Koestermann, *Hermes* 1957, 345 ff. R. S.

**ATO** (2), the Pannonian, like his Dalmatian namesake,
evolted, tried to capture Sirmium (A.D. 6), and shared
n the subsequent fighting, but surrendered in A.D. 8
t the river Bathinus. Soon after, however, the Dalma-
ian chieftain captured and killed him. R. S.

**ATON** (Βάτων), New Comedy poet in the middle of the
hird century B.C.; an anecdote links him (if Βάτωνι is
ightly conjectured at Plut. *Mor.* 55 c) with Cleanthes

(d. *c.* 231) and Arcesilaus (d. 241). Frs. 3 and 5 travesty
Epicurus' teaching about 'the good' and pleasure.

*FCG* 1. 480 f., iv. 499 ff.; *CAF* iii. 326 ff. W. G. A.

**BAUBO** (*Babo*), a female daemon of primitive and
obscene character, doubtless originally a personification
of the *cunnus*. She appears in the Orphic version of the
Rape of Kore (Kern, *Orph. Frs.* 49 ff.), and on inscriptions from Paros and Asia Minor, and is mentioned by
Asclepiades of Tragilus (Harpocration, s.v. Δυσαύλης)
as mother of the Anatolian Mise. She has been thought
to have a part in the Eleusinian Mysteries (Ch. Picard,
*Rev. Hist. Rel.* 1927), but see L. Deubner, *Attische
Feste* (1932), 83 n. 3 and G. Méautis, *Les Dieux de la
Grèce* (1959), 68 ff. She survives in modern folklore
(R. M. Dawkins, *JHS* 1906). Other references in Picard,
loc. cit. and W. K. C. Guthrie, *Orpheus and Gk. Rel.*[2]
(1952), 136. W. K. C. G.

**BAVIUS** (1st c. B.C.), a poetaster, rescued from oblivion
by Virgil's contempt (*Ecl.* 3. 90).

Schanz–Hosius § 246.

**BEDRIACUM** (or **BETRIACUM**), near modern *Cal-
vatone* midway between Verona and Cremona in Cisalpine Gaul, gave its name to two decisive battles in A.D. 69.
Vitellius' troops defeated Otho's in the first, but were
themselves defeated by Vespasian's in the second some
months later. Both battles were apparently fought nearer
Cremona than Bedriacum. E. T. S.

**BEE-KEEPING** had the same importance for non-
tropical antiquity from palaeolithic times onwards as
sugar production has now. The culture of bees seems
to have begun as early as the Mesolithic period. Solon
introduced a law which regulated bee-keeping. Greek
towns (Teos, Theangela) and the Ptolemaic empire
introduced special taxes on bee-keeping and carefully
organized enterprises for honey-production. Different
methods of bee-keeping and breeds of bees were developed, the most important progress being made during
the centuries between Alexander and Augustus. One
bee-hive would produce 1–2½ and occasionally 3 *chous*
(*c.* 6–18 pints) of honey at one harvesting. The best
honey came from Attica (Hymettic region), Theangela,
Chalybon, Cos, Calymna, Rhodes, Lycia, Coracesium,
Thasos, Cyprus, several districts of Syria, Sicily (especially the Hyblaean region near Syracuse), Liguria, Noricum, and the south of Spain, the main honey-exporting
countries of the ancient world. The practical experience
of many generations of Greek and Roman bee-masters
was finally codified by a number of Greek and Latin
authors, the most distinguished being Aristotle, Virgil,
Varro, and Columella.

*See also* ARISTOTLE, COLUMELLA, HONEY, VARRO (2), VIRGIL. J. Klek,
*PW*, s.v. 'Bienenzucht' (Suppl. IV), Olck, ibid., s.v. 'Biene', 'Bienen-
zucht'; P. d'Héronville, *Mus. Belge* 1926, 161 f.; Frank, *Econ. Sur-
vey* i–v (index); T. J. Haarhoff, *Greece and Rome* 1960, 155 f.; F. M.
Heichelheim, *An Ancient Economic History* i[2] (1958), 348, 349, 531;
J. Klek–L. Armbruster, *Archiv für Bienenkunde* i. 6; ii. 17; iii. 8;
vii (1919–26); xvii (1936), 177 f.; xxi (1940), 37 f.; L. Koep,
*Reallex. für Antike und Christentum*, art. 'Biene'; M. Launey, *Rev.
Ét. Anc.* 1942, 25 ff.; Michell, *Econom. Anc. Gr.* 73 ff.; Cl. Préaux,
*L'Économie royale des Lagides* (1939), 233 ff.; L. Robert, *Ant. Class.*
1935, 170 f.; Rostovtzeff, *Roman Empire*[2]; *Hellenistic World* (indexes).
F. M. H.

**BELGAE.** According to Caesar, a population-group of
this name occupied lands to north of Seine and Marne.
They were the fiercest inhabitants of Gaul and boasted of
their German blood (cf. Strabo 4. 196). Certain tribes,
he says, had settled in Britain, and Belgae are actually
located there by later geographers. The Gallic Belgae

were subdued by Caesar in 57 B.C., but continued to give trouble for thirty years more.

Among the Gallic Belgae, archaeology distinguishes two cultural provinces separated by the Ardennes. The northern part is a backward region with Hallstatt characteristics; to the south, traditions of the Marne culture, notably the pedestal-urn, persist. Both experienced German penetration, cremation (a German practice) being normal. The northern group was reinforced under the empire by new settlers and rose suddenly to great prosperity under the stimulus of the Rhine market.

An exodus from the southern (pedestal-urn) group into Britain occurred c. 100 B.C., which developed into the kingdom of Cassivellaunus (q.v.), whose descendants extended their rule over all the south-east. About the time of Caesar's conquest, or perhaps after, a further exodus settled in Hampshire and Berkshire, spread over west (but not east) Sussex, and influenced the culture of the neighbouring Durotriges. Their rulers were the house of Commius (q.v.) and their culture was characterized by Bead-rim pottery.

Characteristics of the Belgae were their preference for woodland sites both for towns and for agricultural development, and their fondness for things Roman, which, however, made them no less hostile to Roman invasion; it appears, indeed, that it was Belgic areas which led opposition to the Roman conquerors.

C. F. C. Hawkes and G. C. Dunning, *Arch. Journ.* 1930, 150 ff.; Hawkes in *Problems of the Iron Age in Southern Britain* (ed. S. S. Frere, 1958), 14 f.; id., *Antiquity* 1968, 6 ff.                    C. E. S.

**BELISARIUS,** the famous general of Justinian, began his military career on the eastern frontier, but won his first great victory in A.D. 533–4, when he sailed to Africa and at the battle of Tricamarum overthrew the Vandal kingdom, which had plagued the Romans for a century. He also captured the last Vandal king Gelimer (q.v.). In 535 he began the conquest of the Ostrogothic kingdom of Italy by occupying Sicily. In 536 he took Naples and Rome, where he withstood a siege for over a year. In 540 he entered Ravenna, thus almost completing the conquest of the peninsula; and in the same year returned to Constantinople, taking with him King Witigis, many eminent Goths, and the royal treasure. After the Gothic reconquest of Italy Belisarius returned as commander-in-chief in 546, and after some successes was again recalled (549), leaving the completion of the war to Narses (q.v.), with whom he was on bad terms. He died in 565. Our extremely detailed knowledge of his campaigns is due to the historical works of his secretary, Procopius (q.v.).

J. B. Bury, *History of the Later Roman Empire* (1923), ii; E. Stein, *Histoire du Bas-empire* (1949), ii.                    E. A. T.

**BELLEROPHON** (Βελλεροφῶν, Βελλεροφόντης). In *Il.* 6. 155 ff., Glaucus the Lycian gives the following account of his ancestor Bellerophontes; the genealogy is Sisyphus—Glaucus I—Bellerophontes—Isandros, Hippolochus and Laodameia, Sarpedon being the son of Laodameia, and Glaucus II of Hippolochus. He was a man of remarkable beauty and valour, a native of Ephyre (generally identified with Corinth). Proetus, king of the Argives,* had a wife Anteia (Stheneboea in later accounts) who tried to tempt Bellerophon, and when he refused, told Proetus that he had tried to seduce her (cf. ACASTUS; Stith Thompson, K 2111). Proetus then sent Bellerophon to Lycia (in later accounts the king of Lycia, Iobates, was Proetus' father-in-law) with a letter to the king asking for his execution (cf. Stith Thompson, K 978).

* In Homer there is no hint that Ephyre was not in his domains; later, e.g. schol. *Il.* 6. 155, the geography is modernized, and Bellerophon has to leave Corinth because of a blood-feud and take refuge at Argos.

On reading this, the king set him first to fight the Chimaera (q.v.), then the Solymi, then the Amazons, and finally laid an ambush for him. Bellerophon survived all these trials, and the king made peace with him and married him to his own daughter. Afterwards, Bellerophon became 'hated of all the gods' and wandered along on the πεδίον Ἀλήϊον (to Homer at least the 'plain of wandering'). Later, he accomplishes his tasks with the help of the winged horse Pegasus, which Athena helped him to catch (Pind. *Ol.* 13. 63 ff.); he used him to take vengeance on Stheneboea (Euripides, *Sthen.*) and offended by trying to fly on him to heaven (Eur. *Beller.*). See further Rose, *Handb. Gk. Myth.*[6] 270 f.

Bellerophon on Pegasus attacking the Chimaera is found in Corinthian vase-painting before the mid seventh century, and in Athenian before the end, and continues to be found in various arts in later centuries (Brommer, *Vasenlisten*[2], 220 ff.).        H. J. R.; C. M. R.

**BELLONA,** the Roman war-goddess, older *Duellona*, rarely *Bellola*. Whether independent in origin or an offshoot of Mars, she is early, her name occurring in the formula of *devotio* (Livy 8. 9. 6). She had, however, no *flamen* and no festival, and her temple was vowed in 296 B.C. and built somewhat later (Livy 10. 19. 17). It was in the Campus Martius, near the altar of Mars, and often used for meetings of the Senate when held *extra pomerium*. Before it stood the *columna bellica*, used in formal declarations of war, cf. FETIALES. She was occasionally identified with Nerio, the ancient cult-partner of Mars (Augustine, *De civ. D.* 6. 10), commonly with the Greek war-goddess Enyo, and in imperial times at latest with the Cappadocian goddess Mâ.

Wissowa, *RK* 151, 348; Latte, *RR* 235. Temple: Platner–Ashby 82; Nash, *Pict. Dict. Rome* i. 202.                    H. J. R

**BELLUM AFRICUM,** a record of Caesar's war in Africa (winter 47–46 B.C.). Its ninety-eight chapters are monotonous to the layman, but as military history it is painstaking and straightforward. Both style and matter suggest that the author was a trained soldier, tribune or centurion, who took part in the campaign, though not a man in Caesar's confidence; Hirtius (q.v.) was certainly not the author (*see* BELLUM ALEXANDRINUM), but his claims to editorship are still upheld.        G. E. F. C

**BELLUM ALEXANDRINUM,** a work continuing Caesar's commentary on the Civil War. Thirty-three chapters describe the war at Alexandria from the point at which Caesar left off; then follow the campaign of Calvinus (q.v. 2) against Pharnaces (chs. 34–41), the war in Illyricum (chs. 42–7), and the disturbances during C. Cassius' tenure of Spain (chs. 48–64), both in the winter 48–47; and finally Caesar's campaign against Pharnaces (chs. 65–78) ending in the victory of Zela (2 Aug. 47). On one view held in antiquity (Suet. *Iul.* 56) Hirtius (q.v.) wrote this work and the *Bella Africum* and *Hispaniense* (qq.v.) besides: for the *Bellum Alexandrinum* stylistic comparison with *Bell. Gall.* viii makes his authorship quite probable, even though (contrast *Bell. Alex.* 19. 6) he took no part in the Alexandrian War.

K. Barwick, 'Caesars Commentarii und das Corpus Caesarianum', *Philol.* Suppl. xxxi (1938).                    G. E. F. C

**BELLUM CIVILE.** (1) Caesar's books on the war begun in 49 B.C. are *Commentarii Belli Ciuilis*. (2) The title of Lucan's poem, often miscalled *Pharsalia*, is *Bellum Ciuile*. (3) *Bellum Ciuile* is given as the title of the poem of 295 hexameters introduced into Petronius' *Satyricon* (119–24) to illustrate Eumolpus' implied criticism of the management of the same subject by Lucan, who is not named.        J. W. D.; G. B. A.

**ELLUM HISPANIENSE,** an account of the campaign which ended at Munda (45 B.C.), written by an eyewitness, certainly not Hirtius (see BELLUM ALEXANDRINUM), but probably from Caesar's army. The text is deplorable; but many meaningless passages are caused by the author's illiteracy and his incapacity to understand anything difficult. The work is interesting mainly as a study in half-educated Latin, which combines colloquialism with quotations from Ennius and schoolboy rhetoric. G. E. F. C.

**ELUS** (Βῆλος), hellenization of Ba'al, Bel, sometimes recognized as a divine title (Zeus Belus, Hdt. 1. 181. 2; Marduk?), oftener taken as the name of an ancient oriental king (of Assyria, Serv. on Aen. 1. 642); father of Ninivo (ibid.); ancestor of the founder of the dynasty of the Heraclidae in Lydia (Hdt. 1. 7. 3); father of Danaus (v.); founder of the rulers of Persia (Ov. Met. 4. 213). It thus forms a stopgap name for foreign genealogies, as Ixion for Greek. H. J. R.

**ENDIS** (Βένδις, Βενδῖς), a Thracian goddess, worshipped with orgiastic rites in Thrace (Strabo, 10. 3. 16, p. 470); at the Piraeus, where her cult was accepted officially in 430/29 B.C. for the benefit of resident Thracians, she had processions, a torch-race on horseback, and a vigil. It is made by Plato the opening scene of the Republic (327 a, 354 a). The date was Thargelion (Deubner, Att. Feste (1932), 219). She was apparently represented as carrying two (hunting?) spears (Hesych., s.v. δίλογχον).

Ferguson, Harv. Theol. Rev. 1944 and Hesp. Suppl. vol. 8 (1949), 131 ff.; M. P. Nilsson, Opuscula Selecta iii (1960), 55 ff. H. J. R.

**ENEFICIARII** were in the Roman army non-commissioned officers (principales) with administrative duties, who took precedence according to the rank of the officer under whom they served (beneficiarii consularis, procuratoris, legati legionis, praefecti, tribuni, etc.). They were so called, according to Vegetius (2. 7), because they owed their promotion to the beneficium of their commander: the title is at least as old as the time of Caesar (BC 1. 75; 3. 88). During the Empire, as soldiers were increasingly employed in administration, the number and variety of beneficiarii rose, and higher grades (cornicularii, commentarienses) were created. Especially from the time of Septimius Severus onwards we find them performing a wide range of non-military activities, which could all be described as police and civil-service functions. Appointment as beneficiarius usually presupposed some experience in one or more of the ranks of signifer, optio, and tesserarius, the non-commissioned grades employed on general duties. The pay of beneficiarii was probably twice the basic legionary rate. See POLICE, STIPENDIUM.

A. von Domaszewski, Die Rangordnung des römischen Heeres (1908); A. H. M. Jones, JRS 1949, 44 f. = Studies in Roman Government and Law (1960), 161 f.; R. MacMullen, Soldier and Civilian in the Later Roman Empire (1963). G. R. W.

**ENEVENTUM,** on the river Calor in southern Italy. Originally a stronghold of the Hirpini Samnites (see SAMNIUM) named Malventum, it fell some time after 300 B.C. to the Romans, who made it a Latin colony, changing its ill-sounding name to Beneventum, 268 B.C. (Vell. Pat. i. 14; Festus 25 L.). Thereafter its territorium expanded and Beneventum flourished. Under the republic it was a military base, later an opulent municipium; under the Empire a colonia and important road-centre (viae Appia, Traiana, qq.v.); under the Lombards a duchy. The ancient remains include Trajan's arch. (Polyb. 3. 90; Livy 27. 10, etc.; Strabo 5. 250).

Beloch, Röm. Gesch. 489, for magistrates; A. Sambon, Monnaies antiques de l'Italie i (1903), 114, for coins. E. T. S.

**BERENICE.** (1) BERENICE I, daughter of Lagus (father of Ptolemy I) and Antigone, was born c. 340 B.C., and died between 281 and 271. She married a Macedonian Philippus. The issue of this marriage were Magas, king of Cyrene, Antigone (m. Pyrrhus of Epirus), and other daughters. Berenice, already a widow, came to Egypt with her aunt Eurydice, who married Ptolemy I. The step-sister of the king, she presently (c. 317) became his mistress and succeeded Eurydice as his wife. Their children were Arsinoë II and Ptolemy II Philadelphus.

(2) BERENICE SYRA, daughter of Ptolemy II and Arsinoë I, was born c. 280 B.C. She married the Seleucid king Antiochus II after the Second Syrian War (252). Laodice, the king's divorced first wife, murdered Berenice and her son by Antiochus after his death in 246, before Ptolemy III could bring help.

(3) BERENICE II, daughter of King Magas of Cyrene and of Apama, daughter of Antiochus I, was born c. 273 B.C. She was betrothed to Ptolemy III, but after Magas' death Demetrius, a Macedonian prince, was called in by her mother to marry her. Berenice led a rebellion against them both, and Demetrius was killed by her orders. She married Ptolemy III in 247, who called a star 'The Lock of Berenice' after her, as Callimachus and Catullus tell us. After her husband's death she became joint ruler with her eldest son Ptolemy IV, but was murdered by him in 221. He nevertheless appointed a special Alexandrian priestess in his mother's honour in 211–210, the ἀθλοφόρος Βερενίκης Εὐεργετίδος. See PTOLEMY (1). F. M. H.

**BERENICE** (4) (b. A.D. 28), daughter of Agrippa I (q.v.), was married to Marcus, brother of Tiberius (q.v. 3) Julius Alexander in 41, and then in 46 to her uncle Herod, king of Chalcis (see ITURAEA). From his death (48) she lived with her brother, Agrippa II (q.v.). To quieten rumours of incest, she persuaded Polemon, priest-king of Olba in Cilicia, to marry her (53/54), but the marriage did not last long. She played some part in public affairs: in 66 she tried, at first single-handed and then with Agrippa, to prevent the Jewish revolt, and in 69, in Agrippa's absence, she supported the Flavian cause. Titus fell in love with her while he was in Judaea (67–70), and when she visited Rome with Agrippa (75) he openly lived with her, perhaps for some years. He deferred, however, to public opinion and did not marry her, and on her second visit (79) he dismissed her invitus invitam (Suet. Div. Tit. 7).

J. A. Crook, AJPhil. 1951, 162 ff. E. M. S.

**BERENICE,** the name of several Hellenistic towns. Chief among them were: (i) a foundation of Ptolemy II on the Egyptian coast of the Red Sea below Ras Benas, connected with Coptus on the Nile by a desert camel-track supplied with cisterns and stations. It became the chief Egyptian port for Arabia, east Africa, and India in the first and second centuries A.D. (Warmington, Indian Commerce, 6 ff., 51 ff., 73 ff.); (ii) Berenice Panchrysos, on the African coast of the Red Sea near the gold-mines of Jebel Allaki; (iii) Berenice Epideiris on the same coast at the Straits of Bab-el-Mandeb. E. H. W.

**BEROSUS** or **BEROSSUS** (Βηρωσός) (fl. c. 290 B.C.), priest of Bel, author of history of Babylon (Βαβυλωνιακά) in three books dedicated to Antiochus I. Book 1 dealt with origins to the Flood, book 2 reached Nabonassar (747 B.C.), and book 3 the death of Alexander. Its value lay in transmission of Babylonian history and astronomy to the Greek world.

FGrH 680. E. A. B.

**BERYTUS** (modern *Beirut*), a Phoenician city. It issued a municipal coinage, inscribed both in Greek and in Phoenician, from the reign of Antiochus IV, at first as Laodicea in Phoenice, later under its old name. Its merchants formed a wealthy colony in Hellenistic Delos. In 81 B.C., Tigranes made it a free city, and in *c.* 16 B.C. it became a Roman colony, with *ius Italicum*, veterans of two legions being settled in it by Agrippa. It received at this time a large accession of territory, perhaps at first including Heliopolis. A great trading town, it was also famed for its wine and linen, and from the third century for its school of Roman law.

R. Mouterde and J. Lauffray, *Beyrouth ville romaine* (1952).
A. H. M. J.; H. S.

**BESTIA,** LUCIUS CALPURNIUS (*PW* 23), as a Gracchan land commissioner, distributed land in Africa (*ILLRP* 475). As tribune in 120 B.C., he secured the recall of P. Popillius (q.v. 2) from exile. As consul (111) he was sent to Numidia, with Scaurus (q.v. 1) as one of his legates, to fight Jugurtha (q.v.). He made a peace, which was disavowed in Rome, and was later condemned by the commission set up by the law of Mamilius (q.v. 3). He returned at some time, but went into exile again in 90, to escape prosecution under the law of Varius (q.v. 1).
E. B.

**BETROTHAL, GREEK,** Ἐγγύησις, a contract to marry between a young man and the girl's father, formed an essential element in a marriage and was often in retrospect the best evidence that a legitimate marriage had been contracted. As a contract it was bilaterally actionable within the normal forms of Greek contract. By the second century B.C. the practice of formal ἐγγύησις had largely been superseded by a dowry-contract between husband and wife's father. (This is a brief statement of Athenian practice in high strata of society: regional and social variations were complex and must be taken into account.)

J. H. Lipsius, *Attische Recht u. Rechtsverfahren* ii. 2 (1912), 468 ff.; J. W. Jones, *Law and Legal Theory of the Greeks* (1956), 174 ff.; W. Erdmann, *Die Ehe im alten Griechenland* (1934), Index, s.v. Engyesis, and esp. 225 ff.; H. J. Wolff, *Written and Unwritten Marriages in Hellenistic and Post-classical Roman Law* (1939); W. K. Lacey, *The Family in Classical Greece* (1967).
G. W. W.

**BETROTHAL, ROMAN.** *Sponsalia* in republican times consisted of reciprocal *sponsiones*, and breach-of-promise actions (in the form of actions for damages) existed. The movement of classical Roman law was in the direction of removing constraint, and the term *sponsalia* came near to an informal agreement to marry, voidable at will (except that the intending husband was required to return such *dos* as had been given to him and the intending bride was expected to return the much more usual gift from her intending husband, the *donatio ante nuptias*, for gifts after marriage were excluded). The betrothal was solemnized with a kiss and the intending husband put an iron ring (*anulus pronubus*) on the third finger of the girl's left hand; it was the occasion for a party (also called *sponsalia*).

P. E. Corbett, *Roman Law of Marriage* (1930), 1 ff.; F. Schulz, *Classical Roman Law* (1951), 109 f.; H. F. Jolowicz, *Hist. Intro. to the Study of Roman Law*² (1954), 242; Marquardt, *Privatleben*, 38 ff.
G. W. W.

**BIBACULUS,** MARCUS FURIUS (*PW* 37), is said by Jerome to have been born at Cremona in 103 B.C. Suetonius makes him a pupil of Valerius (q.v. 7) Cato, another Cisalpine, and quotes two hendecasyllabic epigrams on Cato by him (*Gramm.* 11); Tacitus mentions him and Catullus together (*Ann.* 4. 34. 8: cf. Quint. 10. 1. 26) as the authors of lampoons on 'the Caesars' which Julius and Octavian ignored. These data seem to connect him with the circle of the *novi poetae* (and he may be the Furius of Catullus 11, 16, 23, and 26); but in that case Jerome's date must be some twenty years too early. A contemporary poet whom Horace accuses of bombast (*Sat.* 2. 5. 40) is identified by the scholia with Furius Bibaculus, author of a poem on 'the Gallic War', which may be the hexameter *Annales* (in at least eleven books) of one Furius from which Macrobius (6. 1) quotes some lines. The difficulty of ascribing a historical poem to the Bibaculus of Suetonius and Tacitus has suggested that there were two poets of the same name and that Jerome's date belongs to the epic poet—a precarious suggestion in view of the incompleteness of our knowledge of the literary currents of the time.

Fragments in Morel, *FPL*.
C. J. F.

**BIBRACTE** (modern *Mont-Beuvray*), a hill-fort, the original capital of the Aedui. Here in 52 B.C. the supreme command was conferred by a pan-Gallic council upon Vercingetorix. Its inhabitants were transferred *c.* 12 B.C. to a new town in the plain, Augustodunum (q.v.) (*Autun*), but inscriptions—*deae Bibracti*—at Autun kept the old name alive, and a cult survived on the site itself. Excavations have revealed numerous houses of the Gallic town, all rectangular and of dry stone, some with *atria* and even hypocausts. An important metal-workers' and enamellers' quarter was also revealed.

Bulliot, *Fouilles du Mont Beuvray* (1899); Déchelette, *Fouilles du Mont Beuvray de 1897 à 1901* (1904); id. *Manuel* ii. 946 ff. C. E. S.

**BIBULUS** (1), MARCUS CALPURNIUS (*PW* 28), Caesar's colleague in aedileship and praetorship, and finally in the consulate of 59 B.C., when after being forcibly prevented from vetoing the agrarian law he attempted from his house to invalidate legislation by 'watching the heavens'. His only departure from strict republicanism was to propose Pompey's consulate in 52. In 51 he governed Syria, and resisted the Parthians tenaciously. In the winter 49–48 he wore himself to death, trying to prevent Caesar's crossing to Epirus. He married Porcia, daughter of Cato and future wife of Brutus. G. E. F. C.

**BIBULUS** (2), LUCIUS CALPURNIUS (*PW* 27), son of (1) and Porcia (q.v.), joined his stepfather Brutus and was proscribed; but after Philippi he came to an understanding with Antony and recovered his rights. He served Antony both as a mediator, on several occasions, between him and Octavian and as a naval commander, and governed Syria for him from *c.* 34 B.C. till his death *c.* 32. His brief memoir of Brutus was used by Plutarch (*Brutus* 13, 23).

Peter, *HRRel.* ii. lxvii. Syme, *Rom. Rev.*, see index. A. M.

**BIDENTAL.** By Etruscan use, when lightning had struck any place, the supposed fragments of the bolt were collected, buried while a formula was pronounced (Lucan 1. 606–7), and the place walled in (ibid. 8. 864, and inscribed *fulgur conditum* or the like; it was tabu (ibid. 1. 608, 'dat . . . numen'), and anyone touching was *incestus* (Hor. *Ars P.* 471). This was called a *bidental*.

C. O. Thulin, *Etruskische Disciplin* (1909), i. 92 ff.; Latte, *RR* 81.
H. J. R.

**BILINGUALISM IN THE CLASSICAL WORLD**
The Greeks were conscious monoglots. Because they were intellectually pre-eminent and usually made a distinction (often misunderstood) between Greeks and Barbarians, they never gave foreign languages a place in their educational system. The Romans developed a bilingual culture (Marrou, op. cit. *infra*, ch. 3).
The early Romans were pioneers in a world where

you had to be either the hammer or the anvil. There was little opportunity for intellectual or artistic development. But in the third century B.C. came the impact of Greek culture on a nation of soldier-farmers. Their first conservative reaction was fear lest their established native tradition should be swamped by the intellectually brilliant Greeks, who had been established in Italy for some centuries but had kept aloof as they did in Massilia and elsewhere. Although in 240 B.C. Livius Andronicus produced a translation of the *Odyssey* which was eagerly received, and Philhellenism was strongly aided by Ennius, who said he had three hearts, Roman, Italian, and Greek, Cato the Censor supported the Nationalists and there were several expulsions of Greek teachers. But nothing could stop the enthusiasm for Greek art and letters as we may see, for example, from Cicero's speech on behalf of the Greek-speaking Archias. The earliest Roman historians, like Fabius (q.v. 6) Pictor, wrote in Greek. Where the population was mainly Greek, laws were promulgated in both languages; Roman officials could speak Greek. The Roman came to be at home in both languages, *vir utriusque linguae*, and to realize that he was thus enriching his own culture. The conversion of the Roman to Greek was of enormous importance for the Western Tradition; for it meant the preservation of the Greek cultural heritage and its spread throughout the civilized world particularly during the two centuries of peace established by Augustus. The Letters of Cicero and of Pliny the Younger, and the artistic achievement of Virgil (the first real friend of his national hero in Italy is a Greek) reveal the perfect harmonization of the two languages.

This co-operation extended to the fourth century A.D. Juvenal's outburst against the *Graeculus esuriens* is not typical. But when Constantinople became the centre of Greek influence and the Byzantine Empire began, it was difficult to find bilingual teachers in the West (*Codex Theodos.*xiii. 3. 11). St. Augustine complained about his Greek lessons. Greek was declining in his time; the teaching methods were barbarous; Latin-speaking children, as Quintilian tells us, were made to start with Greek, which was felt to be a *lingua peregrina*. Bilingual manuals were produced in the fourth and fifth centuries; they were practical books of words and phrases addressed to 'all who wish to speak Greek and Latin', and we have an example in the *Hermeneumata Pseudodositheana*. The bilingual tradition lasted for a considerable time at Constantinople; the speech of society and literature was Greek, but Latin remained the language of the Law. The loss of Greek in the West (after the two cultures had helped each other for some six centuries) is reflected in the declining standard of literature and civilization.

Roman education, beginning with diversity and hostility, produced a bilingual tradition the content of which became the basis of Western civilization.

G. Colin, *Rome et la Grèce de 200 à 146* (1905); H. I. Marrou, *History of Education in Antiquity* (1956); T. J. Haarhoff, *Schools of Gaul* (1920); *Vergil the Universal* (1937); *The Stranger at the Gate* (1938).
T. J. H.

**BIOGRAPHY, GREEK.** The impulse to celebrate the individual finds early expression in the dirge and funeral oration; but not until the fifth century, with its conscious recognition of the individual in various arts, do the first traces of biographical literature appear in Greece. Many of Thucydides' sketches approximate to this genre; and Ion of Chios and Stesimbrotus described important contemporary figures. In the fourth century appeared Isocrates' *Evagoras* and Xenophon's *Memorabilia* and *Agesilaus*, all forerunners of biography proper; though Isocrates' claim that the *Evagoras* was the first prose encomium of a living person is exaggerated.

Meanwhile the Platonic corpus was developing the figure of Socrates.

**2.** Aristotle gave biography a new impetus. Under his influence interest in ethical and cultural problems encouraged the writing of βίοι, 'ways of life' of peoples and individual types (e.g. Clearchus; Dicaearchus); simultaneously the history of rhetoric and the chronology of refinements in that art were recorded in compilations, and Aristotle himself gave such researches a literary form. Directly associated with Theophrastus was Aristoxenus, who stamped the so-called peripatetic biography with its most typical characteristics—combinations of legendary material, scandal, polemics, an interest in literary innovations, and a popular literary form in which character was revealed through a man's actions. Duris was more directly interested in personality, a trend carried further by Phaeneas, Idomeneus, and Neanthes, who treated not only literary figures but also, occasionally, men of action. Chamaeleon set a popular fashion by deducing wild stories from the works of those for whom reliable biographical data were scanty, a precedent followed by Hermippus of Smyrna, Satyrus, who ignored the distinction between men of letters and men of action, and Sotion, who instituted the διαδοχή—a semi-biographical account of successive teachers and pupils in various fields.

**3.** About 240 B.C. Antigonus of Carystus displayed a new accuracy in describing contemporaries from personal knowledge; and in the scholarly atmosphere of Alexandria there grew up a biographical form, which revalued the findings of the Peripatetics and re-established their chronological data. Commentaries and epitomes called for biographical introductions, which generally shed their narrative character: between the particulars of a writer's birth and death short notes gave specific details of his mode of life, friends, students, works, etc. Typical of this school is Posidonius' pupil, Jason; and Heraclides Lembus took still further a literary form which led ultimately to Suetonius.

**4.** Meanwhile, historians too, after Alexander, stressed the individual personality; Polybius, in his *Histories* (e.g. 10. 2) and *Life of Philopoemen*, and after him Panaetius, are associated with a development to which such memoir-writers as Aratus had contributed. There is, however, no proof that Peripatetic biography continued, treating political and military figures (as Leo claims). Two hundred years later Plutarch's *Lives* mark a new achievement, without continuous links with either previous biographers or Hellenistic historians. Like the Peripatetics Plutarch is discursive, and in contrast to the Alexandrians normally lets his hero's character be deduced from his actions; though his scheme is flexible, each *Life* forms a whole, generally with a strong moral bias. The *Comparisons* reveal his keen interest in psychology.

**5.** Later Philostratus rhetoricized and Eunapius broke up the Alexandrian form; Alexandrian too in origin, though more learned, were the Neoplatonist biographies of Porphyry and Marinus. Of the abridging and synthesizing of the materials of the literary biography an example survives in Diogenes Laertius. Much of Greek biography has perished. It seems clear, however, that the Peripatetic form, for all its weaknesses, constituted an artistic unity, though it failed to portray the development of character; whereas the Alexandrian studies, which had most influence at Rome, remained an accumulation of material lacking internal cohesion.

F. Leo, *Die griech.-röm. Biographie nach ihrer litt. Form* (1901); G. Misch, *Geschichte der Autobiographie* i² (1931; E.T. 1949); W. Uxkull-Gyllenband, *Plutarch u. die griech. Biographie* (1927); D. R. Stuart, *Epochs of Gk. and Roman Biography* (U.S.A. 1928); N. I. Barbu, *Les Procédés de la peinture des caractères ... dans les biographies de Plutarque* (1934).
F. W. W.

**BIOGRAPHY, ROMAN.** In the writing of biography, the Romans were not wholly dependent on the Greeks. The attitudes and customs of their own political and family life led them to put a special value on recording the achievements of their great men. We hear of songs at banquets praising the famous (Cic. *Tusc.* 4. 3), of dirges (*neniae*) at funerals, and of a native tradition of *laudationes funebres* (Dion. Hal. *Ant. Rom.* 5. 17). *Laudationes* (q.v.) were preserved (Cic. *sen.* 12) and kept among the family records, with the *imagines* (q.v.) of distinguished ancestors. Sepulchral inscriptions were important too, and became very elaborate, often giving details of private as well as public matters (cf. *laudatio Murdiae*, *CIL* vi. 2. 10230; *laudatio Turiae*, ibid. 1527, 31670). F. Leo denied the importance of the *laudationes* for the development of Roman biography, but Stuart (op. cit. *infra*, chs. 7 and 8) puts a more positive view, and with good reason.

**2.** A great deal of writing which can be called biographical owes its origin to the need to compose justifications for political or military action. The bulletins sent home by generals in the field, on which the claim for ·a triumph would rest, are autobiographical in the sense that events recorded centre on the commander's achievements; such writing naturally goes back to an early period. Various autobiographical works of the late republic were also in one sense or another justificatory; *perhaps* C. Gracchus' *ad Pomponium* (Cic. *Div.* 2, 62; cf. Plut. *Ti. Gracch.* 8); more certainly the three books of M. Aurelius Scaurus (Cic. *Brut.* 112), the five or more of P. Rutilius Rufus (Charisius, *GL* 1. 139. 18 Keil) and Q. Lutatius Catulus' book 'de consulatu et de rebus gestis suis' (Cic. *Brut.* 132). Sulla's memoirs (twenty-two books in all) owed something to the Greek precedent of Aratus; he became an important source to later historians. Cicero (many of whose speeches contain descriptions of the *vita* of client or opponent) wrote about his own career and achievement both in Latin and in Greek. Under the Principate, it was especially members of the imperial family and others closely connected with the regime who wrote political memoirs: Augustus, Tiberius, the younger Agrippina (Tac. *Ann.* 4. 54), Hadrian, Severus. Similar in tendency to these autobiographical works were the memoirs sometimes written by clients or freedmen of the great: Plotus (or Pitholaus?) on the Pompeii (Suet. *rhet.* 3), Tiro on Cicero (Asconius *in Milonianam* 43).

**3.** A somewhat different impression is given by writings designed to praise or defend not only political actions but private character or philosophy. The career of the younger Cato (q.v. 5) inspired works by Brutus (Cic. *Att.* 12. 41), Cicero (*Att.* 12. 40. 1), and Munatius Rufus (Plut. *Cat. Min.* 37)—this last an answer to Caesar's counterblast to Cicero, the *Anticato*. L. Calpurnius Bibulus (q.v. 2) wrote on the other philosopher-statesman, Brutus (Plut. *Brutus* 23). These were the beginnings of a considerable literature, with more than a touch of hagiography about it, which clustered around Stoic opponents of the Principate in the first century: the lives of Thrasea Paetus by Arulenus Rusticus and of Helvidius Priscus by Herennius Senecio are mentioned by Tacitus in the preface to his *Agricola*—a work which itself must have been influenced by this type of encomiastic biography, though it contains many other elements as well.

**4.** Apart from Tacitus, the principal extant 'biographers' are Nepos and Suetonius, with his continuators and imitators, the *Scriptores Historiae Augustae*. Nepos' collection of short lives of famous men owes much to Greek writing περὶ ἐνδόξων ἀνδρῶν; his *Atticus*, on the other hand, is more Roman, and at the same time more encomiastic in tone and content.

Suetonius' *Caesares* deals with the Emperors primaril as private individuals and does not profess to give history of their reigns; in terms of genre, the book not very different from his lives of poets, grammarian etc. Jerome (Suet. *Reliquiae*, 3 Reifferscheid) mention Varro, Santra, Nepos, and Hyginus as Suetoniu Roman predecessors. It looks as if Varro is meant to b the founder of the genre; but nothing of his work su vives to substantiate this. Of Santra we know littl Suetonius (*de gramm.* 14, *de poet.* 4) twice quotes h literary opinions. Hyginus (q.v. 1) seems to have com piled more than one collection of *viri illustres* (Gellius 14. 1 with Asconius *in Pisonianam* 12). *See* HISTOR AUGUSTA.

**5.** Revelation of intellectual or spiritual life is rare i Roman autobiography or biography. Cicero (*Bru* 313 ff.) tells us something of his education and develop ment; but the confessions in Marcus Aurelius' Εἰς 'Εαυτο are unique in pagan times; they may be compared wit the *Confessions* of St. Augustine.

F. Leo, *Die griechisch-römische Biographie* (1901); D. R. Stuar *Epochs of Greek and Roman Biography* (1928); G. Misch, *Geschich der Autobiographie* i² (1931; E. T. 1949); W. Steidle, *Sueton und d Antike Biographie* (1951).                    J. C. R.; D. A. ℞

**BION** (1) (*c.* 325–*c.* 255 B.C.), frequently referred to a *Bion the Borysthenite*, son of a freedman and of a forme hetaera of Borysthenes (= Olbia). Because of a frau committed by his father the family was sold into slavery But as slave of a rhetorician Bion received a good educa tion, was later set free, and inherited the fortune of h master. He went to Athens and studied in the Peripato (under Theophrastus) and the Academy (probably unde Xenocrates). But he was more strongly influenced b Crates the Cynic and by Theodorus the atheist an hedonist. Diogenes Laertius includes him among th adherents of the Academy. But he did not follow an particular philosophical creed. He imitated the causti humour, the criticism of conventions, and the shameless ness of the Cynics, and preached the Cyrenaic doctrin that happiness is achieved by adapting oneself to circum stances. He wandered from town to town lecturing fo money. In his writings, which later influenced Roma satire, he used a highly eclectic style.

*Sillographi Graeci*, ed. C. Wachsmuth, 73–7; Diogenes Laertiu 4. 46–58. R. Heinze, *De Horatio Bionis imitatore* (1889); *and see und* CYNICS.                                              K. VON ℞

**BION** (2) (fl. probably *c.* 100 B.C.), of Phlossa nea Smyrna. Seventeen fragments have been preserved fron his *Bucolica*. Some pieces seem complete, others to b excerpted from longer poems (? a *Hyacinthus*, a *Galatea* The bucolic element is very slight. The theme of severa pieces is playfully erotic, but in others Bion is sententiou and in one fragment, where he dwells on the vanity o human effort, seems to strike a more personal note. Bion' style is easy and the language simple. Since the Renais sance he has also been credited with the *Lament fo Adonis*, a highly coloured composition in ninety-eigh hexameters, which some MSS. wrongly assign to Theo critus. While this has the same theme as Theocritus 15 100–44 and in certain features (e.g. the refrain) recal Theocritus 1, the lyrical treatment is more akin to tha found in certain hymns of Callimachus, though Bion goe far beyond the latter in emotionalism. The chief argu ment for Bion's authorship of the *Lament for Adonis* drawn from the references to the poem in the *Lament fo Bion*, a work of some disciple of his, not, as some MSS assert, of Theocritus or Moschus. According to th *Lament for Bion* he spent most of his life in Sicily. Th fragmentary *Epithalamius of Achilles and Deidameia*, a epyllion introduced by two bucolic interlocutors, ha so been assigned by some to Bion, but without real justification.

TEXTS. A. S. F. Gow, *Bucolici Graeci* (1952), 153 ff.; U. von Wilamowitz-Moellendorff, *Bucolici Graeci*[2] (1910), 122, 130, 140; H. Legrand, *Bucoliques grecs* ii (1927), 185 ff.
GENERAL LITERATURE. G. Knaack, 'Bion (6)', in *PW* iii. 481; Wilamowitz-Moellendorff, *Reden und Vorträge*[4], i (1925), 292 f.; Ballarotti, *Theocritus* (1946). E. A. B.

**BIOTTUS** (2nd c. B.C.), Greek comic poet, mentioned only in didascalic lists. His Ποιητής was produced in 168–167 B.C., followed later by his Ἀγνοῶν (*IG* ii[2]. 2323, 212 and 238). No fragments remain.

*CAF* iii. 366.

**BIRDS, SACRED,** *see* ANIMALS, SACRED; some further particulars are given here. One of the most noteworthy associations of a bird with a deity is that of the swan with Apollo (for material, see Sir D'A. W. Thompson, *Glossary of Greek Birds*[2] (1936), 180 ff., q.v. in general for legends concerning birds). It was a fixed ancient belief that it could sing, at least when dying, an idea perhaps founded on the cry of the Whooper Swan; certainly no other species makes any but a harsh noise. It was also the form taken by Zeus to approach Leda (refs. ibid. 183), and there are several stories of metamorphoses into swan-form; when Horace hopes to become one, *Carm.* 2. 20. 9 ff., he means that he is to be recognized as a true poet, Apollo's singer. The connexion of the sparrow (στρουθός) with Aphrodite, as Sappho, fr. 1. 10, is not unreasonably to be explained by its fertility and lustfulness; the dove (περιστερά) is associated with her most probably because of her oriental connexions, it being the sacred bird of more than one Asianic mother-goddess (Atargatis, Lucian, *Syr. D.* 14; Ishtar and others). In the case of deities with pre-Hellenic connexions, the occasional bird-form which they assume (cf. ATHENA, § 1) may plausibly be associated with the epiphanies of Minoan divinities in that shape (see M. P. Nilsson, *Minoan-Mycenaean Religion*[2] (1950), 285 ff.); but some birds, e.g. Hermes' cock and Hera's peacock, are much later than their owners, being comparatively recent introductions into Greece. H. J. R.

**BIRTHDAY** (γενέθλιος ἡμέρα, *natalis*, sc. *dies*). The classical Greeks seem to have paid but little attention to the anniversary of their births. A child's birth was the occasion of congratulatory visits from friends and relations, and presents might be given to the child (Aesch. *Eum.* 7–8); but this was not confined to the actual day of the birth, but was carried out when the child was first seen by the giver, hence the name ὀπτήρια for such presents (Callim. *Dian.* 74, there given to an infant three years old); the word also means a sacrifice made by the father on first seeing the child (Eur. *Ion* 1127). Another word was γενέθλια, also used both of the sacrifice (ibid. 53, 805) and of the gift (Hesych., s.v.). But there is no definite proof of the yearly recurrence of this or of the family festival which accompanied it (Plato, *Symp.* 203 b) earlier than the date (conjecturally late 4th c.) of the Greek original of Plautus, *Pseudolus*, in which much stress is laid on its being Ballio's birthday (165 ff.). The nearest approach is the fact that the days of the month associated with gods are interpreted as being their birthdays as early as Hesiod, *Op.* 771 (a passage doubtfully part of the original poem) and *Hymn. Hom. Merc.* 19; it may therefore have been the custom to have some kind of remembrance, monthly rather than yearly, of the birthdays of human beings.

In Hellenistic times birthdays were more observed, particularly in the case of kings and other great persons. One of the most familiar instances of this is found on the Rosetta stone (*OGI* 90. 46), where the Egyptian clergy

decree solemnities for 'the day on which the birthday feast of the King is held'. This may of course have been connected in other cases, as it certainly was in this one, with the divine or quasi-divine honours given them; we may compare the celebration after their deaths of the birthdays of distinguished men in and just before that period, as Aratus at Sicyon (Plut. *Arat.* 53) and the founders of various philosophical schools. These had in some cases been regularly heroized and in others received from their followers and successors in the schools something like heroic honours, analogous to those paid to the founder of a city or colony. But some royal personages themselves kept their own birthdays as feasts, analogous to but more splendid than those of ordinary individuals in Rome or a modern country; Cleopatra VII is an example, Plut. *Ant.* 73, where it is expressly noted that on a special occasion she refrained from making any display on her birthday. It is quite possible that the growing belief in the personal *daimon* has something to do with the increased importance of the birthday in the case of private individuals (e.g. *Anth. Pal.* 6. 227; the epigrammatist Crinagoras sends a friend a piece of plate for a birthday present); to celebrate the birthday was to celebrate the anniversary of the deity's first manifestation of his care. See, for the belief, Th. Hopfner, *Griechisch-ägyptischer Offenbarungszauber* i, § 117 ff.

In Rome certainly a like belief had a direct connexion with birthday ceremonies, which are testified to from Plautus onwards (supposing that not all his references are taken over from Greek models) and even for quite humble persons, as Verg. *Ecl.* 3. 76, where a slave is speaking. This was the universal cult of the Genius (q.v.), attested for birthdays by Tibullus (2. 2. 5); at a birthday sacrifice 'ipse suos Genius adsit uisurus honores'. It was to him, then, that the ceremonial of the day was directed. Since in classical times he was precisely equivalent to the Greek personal *daimon*, it may be that Greek influence played a part; but certainly the Romans celebrated not only private birthdays and those of Emperors but also the *natales* of cities and all manner of institutions, since every one of them had its genius. The *natalis* of a temple, however, is presumably an annual honour paid to its god.

W. Schmidt, *Geburtstag im Altertum* (1908), and in *PW* vii. 1135 ff. H. J. R.

**BITHYNIA,** a territory in north-west Asia Minor, originally confined to the peninsula of Chalcedon, but gradually extended eastward to Heraclea and Paphlagonia, southward to the Mysian Olympus, and westward to Mysia and the Propontis. Although much of the land is mountainous, the Sangarius river with its tributaries and the valleys that run back from the Propontis form fertile plains and provide relatively easy communications. It was a well-watered region producing good timber, excellent pasturage, and all manner of fruits and grains, possessing fine quarries of marble, and good harbours, and crossed by the chief roads to the Anatolian plateau and to Pontus.

The Bithynians were of Thracian origin, and long kept their tribal identity among the peoples about them. They warred constantly with the Greek colonies on the coast, preserved a measure of autonomy under local dynasts during the Persian regime, and in 298/7 B.C. founded a dynasty of Thracian stock, beginning with King Zipoetes. By a combination of aggressive policies and judicious alliances (especially with the Galatians, whom they invited into Asia in 278/7), the Bithynian kings protected themselves against the Seleucids and their rival Heraclea (q.v. 3) and extended their power to Inner Paphlagonia, to the valleys of Nicaea and Prusa, and finally to the cities of the coast. They were active founders of cities, especially Nicomedes I and II and Prusias I, fostered commerce, to which the tribesmen had previously been inhospitable, and showed an interest in Greek culture. Wars with Pergamum in the second century lost Prusias I and II some territory, but otherwise changes were slight until in 75/74 Nicomedes IV bequeathed his kingdom to Rome (*see* NICOMEDES I–IV; PRUSIAS I–II).

In organizing the province of Bithynia-and-Pontus Pompey apparently divided all the land among the cities for convenience in maintaining order and collecting taxes. Nicaea, for instance, apparently had a common boundary with Dorylaeum. In the early Empire Bithynia-and-Pontus was at first a senatorial province, but the importance of the great highway to the eastern frontier and of maritime connexions with the Euxine coasts led imperial procurators to assume more than their regular authority. Special legates were sent under Trajan and Hadrian (Pliny and Julius Severus), and finally Marcus Aurelius made it imperial. In the time of Pliny and Dio Chrysostom peculation by magistrates, unwise and extravagant building, bitter rivalries between cities, and social discontent within individual cities created a bad situation, which they did their best to remedy.

Strabo 12. 563–6. Th. Reinach, *Trois royaumes de l' Asie mineure* (1888); M. I. Rostovtzeff, *BSA* 1918, 1 ff.; Jones, *Cities E. Rom. Prov.* 148 ff.; Magie, *Rom. Rule Asia Min.*, 302 ff. and index; G. Vitucci, *Il regno di Bitinia* (1953). T. R. S. B.

**BITON** (Βίτων) (3rd or 2nd c. B.C.), the author of a small extant work on siege-engines (Κατασκευαὶ πολεμικῶν ὀργάνων καὶ καταπαλτικῶν) and of a lost work on optics.

Ed. A. Rehm and E. Schramm, *Abh. d. Bayer. Akad. d. Wissensch.*, Ph.-hist. Abt., N.F. ii, 1929.

**BLAESUS** (1) of Capreae (? 2nd or 1st c. B.C.), author of σπουδογέλοια (perhaps akin to Menippus' satires).

Kaibel, *CGF* 191.

**BLAESUS** (2), QUINTUS JUNIUS (*PW* 41), probably a *novus homo* of municipal origin, was *consul suffectus* in A.D. 10. As legate of Pannonia he failed to break the mutiny which Tiberius' son Drusus finally reduced (14). When proconsul of Africa in 21, his command was prorogued and he defeated Tacfarinas (q.v.). Tiberius allowed his troops to hail him *imperator*, the last time a private citizen received this honour. He was uncle of Sejanus (q.v.), whose fall involved his own fate. H. H. S.

**BLOSSIUS** (*PW* 1), GAIUS, of Cumae, descendant of a prominent anti-Roman family of Hannibalic Capua and a student of Stoic philosophy, was a friend of Tiberius Gracchus (q.v. 3), after whose death he joined Aristonicus (q.v. 1). After Aristonicus' defeat he killed himself. His philosophical influence on both these men is difficult to gauge.

D. R. Dudley, *JRS* 1941, 94 ff. E. B.

**BOCCHUS**, king of Mauretania and father-in-law of Jugurtha (q.v.). His offer of alliance at the beginning of the Jugurthine War was rejected by Rome. In the later stages of the war he joined Jugurtha, at the price of the cession of western Numidia. With Jugurtha, he twice nearly defeated Marius; but, impressed by Roman strength, he was finally induced by Sulla to surrender Jugurtha and became a 'friend of the Roman People', even retaining part of Numidia. The surrender of Jugurtha to Sulla (with whom Bocchus maintained his connexion) was depicted on Sulla's signet ring and is shown on a coin of his son Faustus Sulla (Sydenham, *CRR*, no. 879). A second Bocchus, together with a Bogud (q.v.), held the throne of Mauretania at the time

of the Civil War between Caesar and Pompey. For the coinage, see J. Mazard, *Corpus Nummorum Numidic Mauretaniaeque* (1955), 61 ff. E. 

**BOEOTIA**, a district of central Greece, bordering o Attica, and of similar extent. Its heart consisted of th plains of Orchomenus and Thebes, which were goo wheat-land and bred horses (for the flooding of th northern plain, *see* ORCHOMENUS, COPAÏS). The south rough and mountainous, with good harbours on th Corinthian Gulf, but not easy of access; the north is hi country with a narrow seaboard; the east rolling countr watered by the Asopus. The south-east frontier is forme by Cithaeron and Parnes, the north-west, with Phoc and Locris, is not clearly marked.

The earliest prehistory from the Neolithic culture on wards is illustrated by the renewed excavations at Eutres (Neolithic, Early Helladic). Bronze Age (Helladic Boeotia was very important, as is clear from saga an from archaeological remains; *see* s.v. COPAÏS, ORCHO MENUS, THEBES 1. The region was earlier called th 'Cadmean' land, which was changed when the Boeotian arrived from Thessaly, some before and some after th Trojan War (Thuc. i. 12). The term 'Cadmean' seems t be the equivalent of Mycenaean or pre-Dorian. Thi substratum appears to have left its mark on the Boeotian dialect which is most closely related to Thessalian an Aeolic, but has west Greek (Dorian?) elements, and, i the south-east, traces akin to Arcadian. These non Dorian elements may well be explained as survivals o Mycenaean (Old Achaean) Greek. Orchomenus and th Oropus district were relatively late additions to th Boeotian territory. Twenty-nine small Boeotian town are named in the Homeric Catalogue. Some disappeared others were absorbed by more powerful neighbours; i classical times the independent cities numbered abou a dozen. The importance of Boeotia in Greek histor varied with the degree of Theban control (*see* THEBES 1 though some of her rivals, Thespiae and Plataea, ha more attractive histories. The Boeotians were, on th whole, a self-contained agricultural people who did no share in the overseas expansion of Greece. The prover Βοιωτίαν ὖν referred to their riches, and the slownes with which the Athenians taunted them. It is preserve by Pindar, the greatest of a number of Boeotian poet from Hesiod downwards who give it the lie. Th Boeotian contribution to ancient music was also im portant. Artistically Boeotia was always backward.

For the Boeotian Confederacy *see* FEDERAL STATES an THEBES (1).

Paus. bk. 9 and Frazer's commentary; Strabo 9. 400 ff. P-K, *GI* I. ii. 430 ff.; A. W. Gomme, 'The Topography of Boeotia', *BSA* xvi (1911–12), 189 ff.; W. A. Heurtley, 'Notes on the Harbours of S Boeotia, ib. xxvi (1923–5), 38 ff.; W. R. Roberts, *The Ancient Boeotian* (1895); M. Feyel, *Polybe et l'histoire de Béotie* (1942).
T. J. D.; R. J. H

**BOEOTIA, CULTS AND LEGENDS.** Stories of th earliest population are scanty and poor (see Paus. 9. 1. and 2; cf. Cauer in *PW* iii. 640–2). We may instance th shadowy figure of Aon, eponym of the Aones (Steph Byz., s.v.; schol. Stat. *Theb.* 1. 33), son of Poseidon Most of the tradition concerning Orchomenus is los (cf. MINYAS) and the bulk of the surviving tales ar Theban (*see* ADRASTUS, AMPHIARAUS, AMPHION, ANTIGONE CADMUS, ETEOCLES, OEDIPUS). Much of what we know is owing to Pausanias. Cf. HERACLES.

Of cults, several are remarkable. Plataea had th Daedala, apparently a sacred marriage (*see* MARRIAGE SACRED), combined with a remarkable fire-ceremon (Paus. 9. 3. 3 ff., cf. Plutarch, vol. vii, pp. 43–50 Bernar dakis). At Orchomenus existed the ancient cult of th Charites (Pind. *Ol.* 14. 4; Paus. 9. 38. 1, cf. Farnell *Cults* v. 428). On Helicon was the shrine of the Muses said to have been founded by Otus and Ephialtes (Paus. 29. 1 ff., Farnell, ibid. 435). Thespiae had the cult of Eros (Paus. 27. 1), and a virgin priestess of Heracles (ibid. 6); Lebadea the oracle of Trophonius (q.v.). At Chaeronea a stick said to be the sceptre of Agamemnon was the chief deity (Paus. 40. 11, see de Visser, *Die nicht menschengestaltigen Götter* (1903), 112). At Thebes(q.v. 1) itself may be mentioned the cult of Apollo Σπόδιος, the very ancient worship of Aphrodite, the so-called tomb of Amphion and Zethus (qq.v.) and the fertility-magic attaching, Athena's title of Onca and the imported cult of Hector (Paus. 11. 1 and 2; 16. 3; 17. 4; 18. 5), also the remarkable sanctuary of the Cabiri (q.v.) (ibid. 25. 5; see Kern in *PW* x. 1437 ff.). For a list of Boeotian cults, see Nilsson, *Feste*, topographical index under 'Böotien'.

For contacts with Arcadian myths and cults, see V. Bérard, *Les Cultes arcadiens* (1894), index under 'Béotie'. H. J. R.

**BOETHIUS**, ANICIUS MANLIUS SEVERINUS (c. A.D. 480–524), of high birth, son of a consul, himself became consul in 510. Theodoric, the Ostrogoth, who took an interest in learning, made him *magister officiorum*, and showed him great favour until he fell under the suspicion of treason, was imprisoned and finally put to death. In prison he wrote his famous work *De Consolatione Philosophiae*, conceived as a dialogue between himself and Philosophy, a mixture of prose and verse, largely Neoplatonic in content, using Greek sources, but showing the influence of Macrobius' commentary on the *Somnium Scipionis*, and, as regards the dialogue form, of Fulgentius (q.v.). Boethius was an accomplished Hellenist. His ambition was to provide a Latin translation of Aristotle, and then of Plato, with reconciling commentaries. He drew, for his commentaries, upon Alexandrian sources, and, of the task he had set before him, he left a translation of the *Organon*; commentaries, one on the *Categories*, two on the *De Interpretatione*; a translation and two commentaries on Porphyry's *Isagoge*; a commentary on Cicero's *Topica*, besides logical works of his own. He wrote also on music, geometry, and arithmetic. It is now agreed that Boethius is the author of five theological treatises that have come down under his name.

WORKS. Migne, *PL*, lxiii and lxiv; *De Consolatione*, ed. L. Bieler 1957: with bibliography); *Theological Tractates and the Consolation of Philosophy*, ed. H. F. Stewart and E. K. Rand (Loeb), also R. Peiper (1871); *De Arithmetica* and *De Musica*, G. Friedlein (1867).
COMMENTARIES. On *De Interpretatione*, ed. C. Meiser (1877–80); on *Isagoge*, ed. S. Brandt, *CSEL* xxxviii; on *Prior Analytics* (probably by Boethius), L. Minio-Paluello, *JHS* 1957.
H. M. Barrett, *Boethius* (1940); H. R. Patch, *The Tradition of Boethius* (1935); L. Minio-Paluello in *Mediaeval and Renaissance Studies* i. 2; J. Shiel, ibid. iv; P. Courcelle, *La Consolation de philosophie dans la tradition littéraire: antécédents et postérité de Boèce* 1967); recent bibliography in *Clavis Patrum Latinorum*, ed. E. Dekker (1961). F. J. E. R.

**BOETHUS** (1) (2nd c. B.C.), sculptor and metal-worker, son of Athenaion, of Chalcedon. Works (dated): (*a*) signature of dedication made by Boethus to Athena of Lindus about 180 B.C. in gratitude for the office of proxenus; (*b*) signature of statue of Antiochus IV (175–164 B.C.) in Delos (undated); (*c*) signed bronze archaizing term, found in the sea near Mahdia, probably support for winged boy also found there (Winter, *KB* 310. 1). No other work can be certainly associated with this Boethus.

A. Rumpf, *JÖAI* 1952, 86; Lippold, *Griech. Plastik*, 352. T. B. L. W.

**BOETHUS** (2) (2nd c. B.C.), sculptor, son of Apollodorus, of Carthage. Known from signature in Ephesus and Pausanias' description of gilded boy in Heraeum at Olympia (Overbeck, 1596).

**BOETHUS** (3) of Sidon (fl. 2nd c. B.C.), pupil of Diogenes (q.v. 3) of Babylon, was an unorthodox member of the Stoic school. In distinction from Chrysippus' monistic psychology he propounded a dualistic one, in which the rational faculties νοῦς and ἐπιστήμη were opposed to the irrational, ὄρεξις and αἴσθησις. A similar dualism appears in his derivation of soul from air and fire, of which the latter was probably regarded as the basis of reason. Similarly he rejected Pantheism and divided the universe into a part which was divine—the sphere of the fixed stars—and a part which was not. His divergences from orthodox Stoicism seem to be due to Aristotelian influence. He devoted himself specially to the study of astronomy and meteorology. Works: a commentary on Aratus' *Phaenomena*, Περὶ φύσεως, Περὶ εἰμαρμένης.

Testimonia in von Arnim, *SVF* iii. 265–7; M. Pohlenz, *Die Stoa* (1955). W. D. R.

**BOETHUS** (4) of Sidon, Peripatetic philosopher of the time of Augustus, a pupil of Andronicus of Rhodes and probably also of Xenarchus. After Andronicus' death he seems to have been head of the school at Athens. His commentaries on Aristotle, now lost, are referred to by later Greek commentators; Simplicius quotes him on the logic of the early Academy, while challenging his account of Aristotle's logic. W. D. R.

**BOGUD** (*Bogud, Bogus, Βόγος, Βογούας*), perhaps son of Bocchus I and brother of Bocchus II (qq.v.), with whom he shared the kingdom of Mauretania, taking the western half (the later Tingitana). He became Caesar's ally in 49 B.C.; in 48 he helped Q. Cassius (q.v. 5) in Spain; in 46 he was attacked by Cn. Pompeius (q.v. 5); in 45 he gave decisive assistance to Caesar at Munda. Later, perhaps in 41, at the suggestion of L. Antonius (q.v. 6), he attacked Octavian's lieutenant in Spain, but was forced to return by a revolt of his subjects and presently (38?) lost his kingdom to Bocchus, who aided the rebels. Bogud now took service with Antony. He fell at Methone in the Peloponnese fighting against Agrippa (31). His wife Eunoe was said to have had a love-affair with Caesar.

T. J. C.

**BOII**, Gauls who entered Italy *c.* 400 B.C. (reputedly via the Great St. Bernard) and established themselves between the Po and the Apennines, ousting Etruscans and Umbrians. Their chief city was Bononia. Their Iron Age civilization was not altogether primitive. Defeated by Rome *c.* 282 B.C., they signed a 45-year truce. They were conquered again at Telamon (q.v. 2) (225) and submitted until Hannibal's arrival encouraged them anew; with Ligurian and other allies they continued fighting Rome until they were subjugated, massacred, and mulcted of half their territory in 191. Military roads and colonies (Bononia, Parma, Mutina, qq.v.) consolidated the Roman victory and the Boii disappeared from Italy through either expulsion or assimilation (Livy 5. 35; 21–35; Polyb. 2. 17 f.; 3). Boii are also recorded in Gaul, where they supported the Helvetii, were defeated at Bibracte (58 B.C.), and settled on Aeduan territory (Caes. *BGall.* 1. 5. 28; 7. 9). Bohemia, which preserves their name, likewise contained Boii from early times until their extermination by Burebistas the Dacian *c.* 50 B.C.

The relationship of these various Boii is commonly but somewhat unconvincingly explained as follows (Strabo 5. 213): large numbers left the parent Gallic stock, entered Italy, were expelled thence after 191 and settled in Bohemia.

For bibliography see CISALPINE GAUL. E. T. S.

**BOIO**, an ancient Delphic priestess, to whom was attributed an Ὀρνιθογονία (description of transformations into birds) of unknown date.

Powell, *Coll. Alex.* 23–4.

**BOLA** (or **BOLAE**), town in Latium, which often changed hands between Romans and Aequi (q.v.) in the fifth century B.C. It disappears from history after 389 B.C. (Livy 6. 2. 14; Diod. 14. 117. 4). Its site is unknown, but was evidently somewhere near Algidus (q.v.).  E. T. S.

**BOLANUS**, VETTIUS (*PW* 25) commanded a legion under Corbulo in Armenia (A.D. 62), was *cos. suff.* about 66, and was sent by Vitellius as legate of Britain in 69. In that year, with his army depleted by the Civil Wars, he was necessarily inactive; but before his recall in 71 he had probably conducted important operations in Brigantia, perhaps penetrating into Scotland. He was proconsul of Asia, and raised to the patriciate perhaps by Vespasian.

Statius, *Silv.* 5. 2. E. Birley, *Roman Britain and the Roman Army* (1953), 10 ff., 46.  G. E. F. C.

**BOLUS** of Mendes (Egypt), contemporary of Callimachus (3rd c. B.C.), a writer on magic or pharmacology (*Suda*, s.v.). A work of his called *On Sympathy and Antipathy* was somehow attached to Democritus' name. The same work or another is a *materia medica* divided into artificial and natural (Χειρόκμητα and Φυσικὰ δυναμερά). He also wrote *Marvels* (Θαυμάσια). Bolus was one of the first in a considerable tradition of Paradoxographers (q.v.). Only fragments of his works survive.

FRAGMENTS. Diels-Kranz, *Vorsokr.* 68 B 300; *FGrH*, 263.
K. Ziegler, *PW*, s.v. Paradoxographoi; Max Wellmann, *Abh. d. Berl. Ak.* 1921, 4, 7 ff., 1928, 7, 9 ff.; J. A. Festugière, *La Révelation d'Hermès Trismégiste* i (1944), 197 ff., 222 ff., 432; J. H. Waszink, *RAC* ii. 502 ff.; W. Burkert, 'Hellen. Pseudopythagorica,' *Philol.* 1961, 232 ff.  D. J. F.

**BOMILCAR** (*PW* 5) in 111 B.C., while Jugurtha (q.v.) was in Rome under safe-conduct, murdered Massiva, a Numidian pretender, for him. He fought at the battle of the Muthul, but then tried to assassinate Jugurtha or surrender him to Metellus (q.v. 6). He was apprehended and killed.  E. B.

**BONA DEA**, a Roman goddess worshipped exclusively by women. It has been conjectured that her name is simply a literal translation of Agathe Theos, a Greek goddess related to Hygieia (q.v.) and that her worship was introduced in the third century B.C. (Latte, *RR* 228 ff.). Her proper name was allegedly Fauna, daughter (Varro ap. Macrob. *Sat.* i. 12. 27) or wife (Sex. Clodius ap. Arn. *Adv. Nat.* 5, 190, 2 Reifferscheid, cf. Plut. *Quaest. Rom.* 20) of Faunus (q.v.). Her official nocturnal ceremonial was held yearly at the house of the chief magistrate, under the leadership of his wife and with the assistance of the Vestals (Cic. *Har. Resp.* 37; Plut. *Caes.* 9). The room was decorated with vine-branches and other plants and flowers; myrtle, however, was excluded. Wine was brought in, but called milk and the covered jar containing it a honey-pot (Macrob. ibid. 25, and the other passages cited). It is not known how much of this was native and how much due to the superimposed ritual of Damia (cf. AUXESIA; Festus, 60, 1 ff. Lindsay). The sacrifice to Bona Dea was a sow (Macrob. ibid. 23), and in imperial times her temple stood on the Aventine below the *saxum*, hence her title Subsaxana (Platner–Ashby, 85).  H. J. R.; H. W. P.

**BONIFACIUS**, Roman general (d. A.D. 432), served in Africa, but when recalled to Italy refused to go and was widely believed to have invited the Vandals to cross from Spain in 429 to assist him against the central government. Unable to rid the country of his allies, he was reconciled to the government and died of a wound received when trying to suppress Aetius.  E. A. T.

**BONNA**, modern *Bonn*. Auxiliary troops were first stationed at Bonna *c.* 20/10 B.C. and remained in garrison there into the third century. The legionary fortress dates from the second quarter of the first century A.D. and was rebuilt several times. It was in use in the fourth century, very probably still by a military garrison. As well as the *canabae* there was also a separate civil settlement.

H. v. Petrikovits, *Das römische Rheinland* (1960), 43 ff., 60, etc.  P. S.

**BONONIA** (1) (modern *Bologna*), in Cisalpine Gaul, has always been a place of consequence. Villanovan settlements occupied the site from *c.* 1050 until 500 B.C. when Etruscans founded Felsina there. Felsina (q.v.) became the chief Etruscan city north of the Apennines (Pliny, *HN* 3. 115), but fell first to the Boii (q.v.), then to Rome (196 B.C.), and acquired the name Bononia (Livy 33. 37). Subsequently as Latin colony, *municipium*, imperial *colonia*, or part of the Ravenna exarchate, Bononia was always important (Livy 37. 57; Festus, 155 L.; Tac. *Ann.* 12. 58; Procop. *Goth.* 3. 11). Antony, Octavian, and Lepidus met near here to establish the Second Triumvirate (*CAH* x. 19). As a centre of the north Italian road system (Strabo 5. 216 f.), Bononia flourished and was able to survive a conflagration in A.D. 53 and Alaric's attack in 410 (Tac. loc. cit.; Zosim. 6. 10).

(2), see GESORIACUM.

For BONONIA (1) see the bibliography under CISALPINE GAUL, and A. Grenier, *Bologne, Villanovienne et Étrusque* (1912); A. Ducati, *Storia di Bologna* (1928).  E. T. S.

**BONOSUS** (3rd c. A.D.), son of a Gallic mother, but of British descent, was commander of the Roman fleet on the Rhine. Losing a squadron through carelessness to the Germans and fearing punishment, Bonosus revolted. He was crushed by Probus after a bitter struggle (A.D. 280).  H. M.

**BONUS EVENTUS**, personified 'good result', originally good harvest (Varro, *Rust.* 1. 1. 6), then success in general. He had a temple on the Campus Martius (Amm. Marc. 29. 6. 19), and was a popular deity, to judge by the many inscriptional dedications to him.

Wissowa, *RK* 267.  H. J. R.

**BOOKS, GREEK AND LATIN.** There is ample evidence not only of the use of writing in the Near East long before the earliest Greek literature, but also of the use of Greek in Crete and on the mainland for writing on clay tablets in the Bronze Age. But there is as yet no evidence that writing at this time was used for literary purposes in Greek, nor do we know what material was used later when the Homeric and Hesiodic works were written down. We may assume that it was some form of skin; its use was widespread throughout antiquity and Herodotus (5. 58) records that the Ionians, at a time when papyrus was unavailable, had long used skins. The antiquity of this practice is implied by the use among the Ionians of διφθέρα for a papyrus roll, just as βίβλος suggests that papyrus was first imported into Greece from the Phoenician town of Byblos. Thus while the *Iliad* may first have been recorded on skin, for Herodotus papyrus was and had been for long the normal writing-material and we may safely assume that it was available at least from the seventh century onwards. It was the dominant writing-material throughout antiquity, although the wooden tablet (which is of comparable antiquity, cf. Hom. *Il.* 6. 169) and skins or parchment were always in use.

Papyrus, as a writing-material, was made from the pith of a water-plant (*Cyperus papyrus*) which in antiquity grew plentifully in the Nile (Pliny, *HN* 13. 68 ff.). The

ith was cut into thin strips, which were laid down
a two layers, in one of which the fibres were laid.
orizontally, and in the other vertically. The two layers
ere fastened together by water and pressure, and the
urface polished. The size of the sheets was governed by
ae length to which the strips could be cut without weak-
ess, the widest being the best. Specimens are known as
road as 15 inches, but normal measurements from
Jreek times range from about 9 inches downwards. In
eight a roll might be as much as 12 or 13 inches (one
·gyptian papyrus reaches 19 inches); but 8 or 9 inches
s a more normal size for literary rolls, ranging down
o 5 inches for a book of poetry, or even 2 inches for
booklet of epigrams. In the Roman market names were
iven to various qualities according to their size; but
aese categories cannot be identified in the extant speci-
aens.

The sheets thus formed were glued together (κολλή-
aτα) to form a roll; the join between the sheets is all
ut invisible in rolls of good quality and did not obstruct
ae pen. The commercial unit was the roll (χάρτης)
ather than the sheet; Pliny states that a roll never con-
isted of more than twenty sheets, i.e. was not more than
bout 15 feet in length, but we know from documents
f rolls of fifty sheets, and no doubt rolls were made of
ifferent length for different purposes. On this as on
ther topics concerned with books Pliny's statements
eed to be treated with reserve. For practical use the
oll could be shortened (and may also have been sold
a sections), or lengthened by attaching additional sheets,
hough this would hardly have been done with expensive
olls designed for literary MSS. At least from the Alexan-
rian age onwards a roll of about 30–35 feet was the
orm for Greek and Latin literature, though some longer
aes are known. With writing of average size this would
uffice for a book of Thucydides. A single roll would
ften comprise two or more shorter works, e.g. some of
ae Homeric books. This approximate standardization
f the length of the roll is probably to be credited to the
lexandrian Library; it is noticeable that in later
Iellenistic and Roman times the average length of the
oll supplied the writer, e.g. Diodorus, with the natural
ivisions for his work.

The alternative material to papyrus throughout anti-
uity, if generally regarded as inferior, was vellum or (as
. was later known) parchment. This was made from the
kins of cattle, sheep, and goats, the skins being washed,
craped to remove the hair, smoothed with pumice, and
ressed with chalk. There is a slight difference between
ae hair- and the flesh-sides, the former tending to be
arker and retaining the ink better. Pliny's statement
HN 13. 17) that vellum was invented at Pergamum
hen Ptolemy Epiphanes (205–182 B.C.) placed an em-
argo on the export of papyrus in order to hamper the
rowth of the library of his rival bibliophile Eumenes II
f Pergamum (197–159 B.C.) can only mean, since skins
ad been used for writing for many centuries, that some
pecial refinement in their manufacture was introduced
here; to this the later Greek use of περγαμηνή gives some
upport. The extent to which vellum or parchment (there
s no regularly observed distinction between the terms)
vas used in the ancient world is probably disguised by
ae fact that almost all our material evidence for ancient
ooks comes from Egypt, where until the fourth century
..D. it would have been perverse to use anything but
apyrus. Documents on vellum have been found at Dura
n the Euphrates dating from the early second century
.C.; parchment rolls with texts of the Greek translation
f the O.T. have been found at Qumran and Murabba'at,
vhile a parchment roll of Xenophon's *Symposium* was
xcavated at Antinoöpolis in Egypt (perhaps an import).

Long after poems and other literary works were

written down as a matter of course, the normal method of
publication was oral. Books were essentially *aides-
mémoire* for the author or performer, not a primary means
of communication to an audience. This view of the book
as a *hypomnema* or substitute for recital persists until
Plato, if not later. Only in the fifth century B.C. and at
Athens do we find allusions to the circulation and collection of books and to the beginnings of a book-trade:
Eupolis (fr. 304, Kock) mentions the place 'where books
are for sale' and Plato (*Apol.* 26 d) makes Socrates say
that a copy of Anaxagoras could be bought from the
orchestra (presumably in the agora) for a drachma or
less. But though Thucydides clearly writes for the serious
student, Aristophanes can suggest that an interest in
books was something eccentric (see J. D. Denniston,
*CQ* 1927, 117), and in Xenophon it is an indication of
the size of a private library that it included a complete
Homer (*Mem.* 4. 2. 10). None the less, we learn from
him that by the end of the century books were an article
of export from Athens to the Black Sea (*Anab.* 7. 5. 14).

In the creation of the book in the modern sense it
may be surmised that the principal factors were the
Sophists, the development of prose, particularly forensic
prose, and the popularity of tragedy with the demand
for repeat performances and reading texts that it created.

There is little doubt that books and the book-trade
developed fast in the fourth century. Isocrates was the
first author whom we know to have written to be read
rather than recited; we may note, however, that throughout antiquity reading always meant reading aloud. From
a technical point of view the development was haphazard; it is likely that rolls might be either very short
or very long, though hardly as large as Egyptian ceremonial rolls exceeding 100 feet. Little help was given
to the reader and probably little attention was paid to
calligraphy (the earliest allusion is in Plato: *Laws* 810 b).
This at any rate is what the Timotheus papyrus, the
earliest literary papyrus to be found in Egypt dating
to the second half of the fourth century B.C., would
suggest, and on the first point its evidence is supported
by that of the nearly contemporary Derveni papyrus
recently found near Salonika. With the late fourth
century B.C. the evidence of the papyri first becomes
available, and continues without a break to the eighth
century A.D. (*see* PAPYROLOGY, GREEK).

No doubt the Alexandrian Library should also be
credited with certain other improvements in the technique of the book besides that of standardizing the length
of the roll that sharply separate the earlier and clumsy
literary papyri from those of the middle third century
B.C. onwards. In the earliest texts verse, except for
iambics and hexameters, is not written metrically; the
minimum of help is given the reader in dramatic texts;
lines from one column almost run into those in the next;
punctuation and spacing is even more occasional and
erratic than it is later. After the Alexandrian reform,
a standard literary text would have a column width of
not less than 2 and not more than 4 inches, including
the margin; for poetry the width was of course dictated
by the metre and in a sumptuous Homer might reach
nearly 10 inches, although 5 inches would be normal.
The writing was arranged in columns (σελίδες or
*paginae*) which do not correspond with the κολλήματα.
The number of lines varies with the height of the column
and the size of the writing; but numbers less than 25 or
more than 45 are exceptional. Neither in the roll nor
later in the codex, where reference was easy, as it could
never have been with the 'roll, was the ancient scribe
concerned to keep the same number of lines to a column.
The number of letters to a line similarly varied. There
were fixed rules governing the division of words at the
end of a line and to meet these the outer (right-hand)

edge of the column was usually uneven, though later the size of letters was adjusted to give a regular edge. About 18 to 25 letters to a line is normal; less than 16 is very exceptional. Conjectures based on the number of lines to a column or of letters in a line are therefore precarious.

It should perhaps be emphasized that the papyri have presented specimens of very different types of book; the school text, the amateur copy, the scholar's private text, the ordinary trade book, the *édition de luxe*. The quality of the text, as distinct from that of the script, is often inferior in the last-named category and Strabo's preference (13. 1. 54) on grounds of accuracy for the private copy is thus confirmed.

The writing on papyrus was normally on the side on which the fibres lay horizontally (*recto*), i.e. on the interior of the roll when folded, the side that was usually more highly polished; but frequently the other side (*verso*) of a document or literary text was subsequently utilized. Such copies were, however, for private use or, possibly, represent a form of cheap production for the market. Very occasionally the text on the recto is continued on the verso; such rolls are known as opisthograph, and references to them occur in ancient authors, as marks either of the poverty of the writer or the excess of his matter (Lucian, *Vit. Auct.* 9; Ezek. ii. 10; Pliny, *Ep.* 3. 5. 17; Juv. 1. 6). They were for private use, not for sale. Since the writing on the recto almost invariably precedes that on the verso (there are a few exceptions in the documents of the third century B.C. and in the late Byzantine Age), valuable evidence for dating may sometimes be obtained, especially when the verso of a literary roll has been used for a dated document.

The margins between columns are generally small, but those on the top and bottom of the roll may extend to 1½ or 2 inches, or even more. Here lines or words accidentally omitted are sometimes written, generally with an arrow to indicate the place in which they should be inserted. Deletions are made by a stroke of the pen or by placing dots above the words in question. An occasional note will be added in the margin but this is rarely, if ever, part of the original text; the commentaries that are found surrounding a text in Byzantine MSS. were invariably in classical times published as separate works (ὑπομνήματα). Occasionally, e.g. in MSS. of Homer, critical signs against the text refer to such commentaries.

Helps to the reader are strikingly rare in general, though they tend to increase in the Roman period as early Greek poetry became less readily intelligible. Words are not separated; enlarged initials are not used. Accents are found only in poetic texts, with negligible exceptions, and even here they are not systematically used. A rough breathing is sometimes inserted where misunderstanding might arise, and an apostrophe is sometimes placed between double consonants or after a final consonant in foreign, e.g. Semitic, words. Punctuation is uncertain and arbitrary: it takes the form either of a single point, generally about level with the top of the letter (there is no systematic use of high, medial, and low points), or of leaving a short space at the end of a clause. A short stroke (παράγραφος) was placed, from the fourth century B.C. on, below the beginning of a line in which a break occurs (often also indicated by spacing); the same symbol is used in drama to indicate a change of speaker. In the Roman period it is usual for the names of the characters to be written in the margin. Books were often illustrated; the few illustrations that survive are mostly of scientific or mathematical works, but there is one to a poem on the labours of Hercules and a few (two in colour) to works of prose literature. Titles were placed at the end of the roll, regarded as the part least liable to danger. Little informa-

tion about the author and title of the work was give though occasionally the number of lines, reckoned a conventional system, was added. In the Herodas M titles of individual poems were prefixed by the origin scribe. The normal means of identifying the conten of a roll was a label (σίλλυβος, *titulus*) of papyrus vellum, which projected from it as it lay on a shelf in a box; one that has survived has the words Πίνδαρ ὅλος, but there was no MS. attached. When not in us rolls were stored in boxes or buckets (τεῦχος, *caps capsilla, scrinium*) or laid on shelves in or pigeon-hol (*nidi*). Catullus (22. 4 ff.) gives a detailed descriptic of an elaborate roll. It was furnished with rollers ( which no specimen has been found in Egypt), the pr jecting knobs of which might be made ornamental colour or material. The roll itself might be enclose in a vellum cover (διφθέρα, *paenula*) which could t coloured and fastened with coloured strings, the papyr soaked in cedar-oil (Horace, *Ars P.* 332), and the lab coloured.

Just as Latin literature depends very largely on Gree so Latin books in the classical period in all essentia closely resembled their Greek models. The word *lib* looks back to a time when writings were inscribed o bark (as they were in other parts of the world); for th archives written on linen (*libri lintei*) in the time of th kings Livy quotes no authority earlier than the secon century B.C. Thus the main vehicle of Latin literatu was the papyrus roll (*charta, volumen*). One divergen from Greek practice seems to have been that in Lati MSS. words were divided, usually by points, a syste we find in one of the oldest surviving Latin litera texts, the *Carmen de Bello Actiaco* from Herculaneu and this was only given up under Greek influence the second century A.D. Very few fragments of wor of Latin literature have survived compared with Gree if only because our principal source is Egypt whe there was little reason for studying Latin (*see* PAPYROLOG LATIN); but by way of compensation Latin literature much richer than Greek in information about books an the book-trade. From the first century B.C. on we hear professional booksellers (*librarii*: the word also mea copyist; later *bibliopolae*) with their staffs of copyist many of Cicero's own works were published by Atticu who kept a large number of slaves trained in all th operations of book-production—including that of makir last-minute corrections at the author's request. In in perial times references in literature are frequent; boo shops were mainly to be found in the Argiletum wit advertisements of their wares suspended on the colum of the porticos (Mart. 1. 117. 9 f.). There are occasion indications of the price of books; Book 13 of Martial w sold by the bookseller Tryphon for four sesterc (13. 3. 2) while a handsome copy of another of his book was sold by Atrectus for twenty sesterces (1. 117. 17 There was no copyright in antiquity and the auth never gained directly from the sale of his books; equall the publisher or bookseller was in no position to prote his trade against anyone who cared to make a copy. W hear in Aulus Gellius (18. i. 11) of second-hand boo stalls at Brundisium, and we know from other authors th there was a considerable trade in old and rare book sometimes as much as 200 or 300 years old, sometim alleged by the seller to be much older (Pliny, *HN* 1. 83, 86; Quint. 9. 4. 39; Lucian, *Adv. Indoct.* 102).

An important innovation that was probably Roman origin was the development of the tablet. The tabl itself is as old as Homer; made normally of wood, eith whitened to take ink or covered with wax on whic writing was inscribed with a stilus, it consists usually two or more folds fastened together with thongs and necessary secured with a seal. One specimen from Egy as no less than nine leaves or eighteen sides. They were very generally used for private correspondence, legal documents, business purposes, and by authors for their rough notes or first drafts. It seems to have been in Rome first that parchment was substituted for wood; *membranae* is a technical term for the vellum notebook (Hor. *Sat.* 2. 3. 2, cf. 2 Tim. iv. 13), for which there is no Greek equivalent. Quintilian (10. 3. 31) refers to them as used by students for their lecture-notes, and there is no doubt that they were the prototype of the codex, though used at first for what may be called sub-literary texts or purposes. We first hear of their use for classical literature in Martial, who in his descriptions of gifts at the Saturnalia includes a number of books (14. 183–95), some of them specifically said to be *in membranis*. They were pocket-editions, and unless they were extracts or epitomes must have been cheap omnibus editions. But pretty clearly this experiment by an enterprising publisher was a failure; what gave rise to the modern form of book was the adoption of the notebook by the Christian Church for the Scriptures, it would seem from the first century onwards. It originated most probably in the Church of Rome; certainly from the early second century onwards almost all the biblical texts and all the N.T. texts with no significant exceptions found in Egypt are in codex-form, the papyrus codex being probably an adaptation of the parchment notebook. For non-biblical texts as for pagan literature the roll continued to be more commonly used than the codex down to the fourth century. Both the greater capacity and the ease of reference it afforded must have commended the codex to the Church. Outside Egypt the vellum notebook may have encouraged the use of vellum rather than papyrus for the codex, for which it offered certain advantages; but either material could be and was used in either form, and we find papyrus codices still being manufactured occasionally in the sixth century.

The papyrus codex was formed by taking a sheet twice the width of the page desired and folding it once vertically, thus producing a quire of two leaves. By similarly treating a number of sheets simultaneously, a quire could be made of any desired size. Specimens exist from quires of two leaves to quires of eighteen leaves, but these seem to have been early experiments and eventually it was found convenient to form quires of ten or twelve leaves. All the later codices are of this type. Care was taken in the arrangement of the leaves, to see that on facing pages recto faced recto and verso verso. When complete the codex, whether papyrus or parchment, was often bound in leather and secured with strings; examples are known from the late third century onwards. Most extant papyrus codices have only one column to a page, but there are some examples with two; here perhaps the arrangement of columns in the roll from which the codex is copied is deliberately preserved. Most papyrus codices vary in measurement between 12 inches by 8 inches and 8 inches by 7 inches, but there is considerable variety in format which has no significance for dating.

By the fourth century A.D. the victory of the codex over the roll was unmistakable; that of parchment over papyrus hardly less so. The reason for the first, apart from the enormous prestige that its use for the Scriptures gave it, may be found in the greater capacity and solidity of the codex at a time when books were increasingly used for reference; that for the latter may probably be found quite as much in the economic decay of Egypt and in the decline of international trade as in any inherent merits in the material. Constantine ordered fifty copies of the Scriptures for the churches in Constantinople, all to be written on vellum; and at about the same time St. Jerome records that the papyrus MSS. in the library of Caesarea, having become worn by use, were replaced by vellum copies. From this and the subsequent century come the earliest MSS. of classical authors (the finds of excavation apart) that have survived down to the present day. They are closer perhaps to the book-production of the Middle Ages than to that of classical antiquity. The classical book was severely anonymous, as perhaps fitted a tool rather than an object in its own right; we cannot find the name of a single scribe on any literary papyrus. The importance of preserving the exact text of the Scriptures leads to notes often of great interest on the history of the text, e.g. those in the Codex Sinaiticus at the end of Esdras and Esther recording the correction of the text from a MS. by Pamphilus. Similarly some of the earliest Latin MSS. which originated in the circle of the Symmachi in the late fourth century and the early years of the fifth record sometimes the copyist, the corrector, and the place of writing, and convey, as they were intended to do, both a challenge to the new religion and their owner's devotion to the old.

W. Schubart, *Das Buch bei den Griechen und Römern*[2] (1921: preferable to the posthumous and unannotated edition of 1961); T. Birt, *Kritik und Hermeneutik nebst Abriss des antiken Buchwesens* (1913); N. Lewis, *L'Industrie du Papyrus* (1935); E. G. Turner, *Athenian Books of the 5th and 4th Century* (1951); C. H. Roberts, 'The Codex', *Proc. Brit. Acad.* 1954; O. Jahn in *Sitz. Sächs. Gesellsch. d. Wissenschaften* 1851, 327 (on subscriptions in Latin MSS.); C. Wendel, *Die griechische-römische Buchbeschreibung verglichen mit der des vorderen Orients* (1949). F. G. K.; C. H. R.

**BOREAS,** the North wind. Cults of, or magic practices directed towards, winds are fairly common in Greece (*see* WIND-GODS and Farnell, *Cults* v. 448 f.; more in Fiedler, *Antiker Wetterzauber* (1931)). The most famous worship of Boreas was in Attica (Hdt. 7. 189, for his help against the Persians at Artemisium). Mythologically, he was 'son-in-law' of the Athenians, having carried off his bride, Oreithyia, daughter of King Erechtheus, from the Areios Pagos or the banks of the Ilissus (Plato, *Phdr.* 229 c–d). By her he had two sons, Zetes and Calais (*see* CALAIS AND ZETES).

Apart from this, hardly anything is told of him which does not arise from his physical characteristics. He is, for instance, son of Eos and Astraeus (Hes. *Theog.* 378–80), along with Zephyrus and Notus; in other words, winds come down out of the sky, where the stars and dawn are—an idea which competes with the conception of them as underground beings (as a kind of ghosts, cf. HARPYIAE, or because they come from below the horizon?), to whom black victims are sacrificed (e.g. Ar. *Ran.* 847). Even his begetting of horses (as *Il.* 20. 223) is a simple mythologizing of the speed of wind, or perhaps of some such belief as that in Verg. *G.* 3. 275, that mares can be impregnated by wind.

He is shown carrying off Oreithyia on Attic vases from the early classical period on, and on an akroterion of the Athenian temple at Delos of the later fifth century. He is shown as winged, with rough hair and beard.

H. J. R.; C. M. R.

**BORYSTHENES,** a river of Scythia (modern *Dnieper*). According to Herodotus (4. 53) it was the largest river after the Nile and the Ister (*Danube*), being navigable for forty days from the sea. This statement, and his failure to mention the falls at Dnieprostroi, show that Herodotus was unacquainted with the upper course of the Borysthenes. But the glowing terms in which he described its fisheries and meadows were not ill founded. The Borysthenes was the chief Greek trade route into Scythia, but this trade (as the record of finds shows) did not extend beyond the region of Kiev. M. C.

**BOSCOREALE,** a township between Vesuvius and Pompeii (2 k.), former hunting reserve of the Angevin kings. It would have remained in obscurity, but for the discovery nearby of several *villae rusticae*, buried in the eruption of Vesuvius in A.D. 79. Two, found on the farm of V. de Prisco, are specially noteworthy. The first, excavated 1893–4 (no longer visible: model in Pompeii Museum), contained ninety-four pieces of silver plate of Alexandrine and Roman workmanship, now in the Louvre. This treasure seems out of place in a large agricultural factory (presses and store for wine and oil, threshing-floor, with only modest residential wing) and may have been deposited there from elsewhere at the time of the catastrophe. The second, discovered four years later, belied its symmetrical farm-house plan by possessing the appurtenances of a finely decorated country mansion, with wall-paintings of the first century B.C. (now in the Museo Nazionale, Naples).

R. C. Carrington, *JRS* 1931, 110 ff.                    R. C. C.

**BOSPORUS** (1), THE THRACIAN, was a narrow strait joining the Black Sea with the Sea of Marmora and the Mediterranean and dividing Asia and Europe. Its direction is NE.–SW. and it is 17 miles long, and from 600 yards at the narrowest to 3,300 at the broadest in width. The current runs swiftly from the Black Sea into the Mediterranean, breaking against Serai Point, the shores of ancient Byzantium. The strait has been worn away in a fairly recent geological past as the exit for the water of the Black Sea, which was originally a lake. The Bosporus is noted for its wealth of fish, and many ancient Greek coastal towns bore fish as the device on their coins. The name records the legend of the crossing of Io (q.v.).                    S. C.; D. E. W. W.

**BOSPORUS** (2), THE CIMMERIAN, the *Straits of Kertch*, connected the Black Sea with the Sea of Azov (Maeotis, q.v.). The chief Greek settlements were Panticapaeum (q.v.) and Nymphaeum on its western shores in the Crimea, and Phanagoreia on its eastern in the Taman peninsula. A group of Greek cities, in close connexion with Scythians and Sindians, developed into a Bosporan group which extended its influence further into the Crimea (*see* CHERSONESUS 2, TAURIC). The lead was taken by Panticapaeum, first under its Archaeanactid rulers and then from 438 B.C. under the Spartocids (q.v.). This Bosporan kingdom, which Greeks might regard as a military tyranny, did not pass away rapidly as many Greek tyrannies, but developed into a Hellenistic monarchy and flourished for over 200 years. Its economic life began to suffer after c. 250 B.C., and pressure of Scythian and Sarmatian attacks increased until it was impelled to appeal for help to Mithridates VI of Pontus, whose general Diophantus in two campaigns drove back the Scythians. Thus, when Paerisades V (*see* SPARTOCIDS) was killed, all the Greek cities of the Bosporus, Crimea, and the northern shore of the Black Sea were added to Mithridates' realm, with the local capital at Panticapaeum.

After Mithridates' defeat by Rome, Pompey allowed the king's treacherous son, Pharnaces (q.v. 2), to hold his father's Russian dominions. After Pharnaces' defeat by Caesar at Zela, the kingdom was granted to Mithridates of Pergamum but in trying to get control of it he was killed by Asander who had married Pharnaces' daughter Dynamis. Asander, who won recognition from Antony and Octavian, ruled until 17 B.C. Strategic aspects of imperial defence, together with the economic importance of the kingdom, required Rome to establish strong government there. Rome promised the throne and marriage with Dynamis to Polemon (q.v. 1) of Pontus; in 14 B.C. Agrippa forced the Bosporans to accept this arrangement. He settled the kingdom, placing the autonomous city of Chersonesus (q.v. 3) under its protection.

Thus, as under Mithridates, the two shores of the Black Sea were under unified native rule. But Polemon and Dynamis soon quarrelled. When Polemon married Pythodoris, Dynamis sought help from a (Sarmatian) ruler Aspurgus whom she married: they finally overthrew Polemon (8 B.C.). Augustus accepted the situation and Dynamis was recognized as a vassal queen until her death in A.D. 7/8. Her husband Aspurgus gained control in 10/11 and received the royal title and Roman citizenship from Tiberius in 14/15. On his death (37/38) he left two sons, Mithridates (probably Dynamis' son) and Cotys, the son of a second wife, a Thracian princess named Gepaepyris. Though Gaius formally granted the kingdom to Polemon II of Pontus in 38, it was held by Gepaepyris and her stepson Mithridates, who was later recognized by Claudius (41). When Mithridates' half-brother Cotys soon afterwards revealed to Claudius that Mithridates was plotting revolt, Cotys was given the kingdom (44/45); Mithridates, defeated in battle, was taken prisoner to Rome, but was set free. Nero, to secure a base for his projected Sarmatian campaign, appears to have annexed the kingdom c. 62/63 (Cotys I being either dead or deposed). However, Cotys' son Rhescuporis was granted the kingdom in 68/69 and reigned until c. 90. Under later rulers (several named Rhescuporis, Cotys, and Sauromates) the kingdom, which was recognized as an important link in the defensive system of the Roman Empire, was allowed by Rome to issue gold and silver coins, and on occasion received military support. It enjoyed renewed economic prosperity in the second and third centuries, trading with Asia Minor and Scythian tribes and supplying corn for Roman armies on the Danube and in the east. Relations with the Alans (q.v.) appear to have been friendly, but the Greek cities were increasingly subjected to peaceful penetration by Sarmatians (q.v.), so that they gradually became 'Sarmatized' during the second century. But during the third the Alans joined the Goths in attacking the Empire, and Panticapaeum became a Gotho-Sarmatian city.

E. H. Minns, *Scythians and Greeks* (1913); M. Rostovtzeff, *Iranians and Greeks in South Russia* (1922), *Skythien und der Bosporus* (1931: literary and archaeological sources); M. Danoff, *PW*, Suppl. ix s.v. Pontos Euxeinos', 1118 ff. (with bibliography of recent Russian work); J. Boardman, *Arch. Rep.* 1962–3, 44 ff.; E. B. de Ballu, *L'Histoire des colonies grecques du littoral nord de la Mer noire*[2] (1962: a bibliography of Russian works, 1940–62).                    H. H.

**BOSTRA,** a commercial town in the north of the Nabataean kingdom (q.v.). In A.D. 106 it was refounded by Trajan as the capital of the province of Arabia. In the second century it became the camp of Legio III Cyrenaica and was made a colony by Severus Alexander. It was sacked by Zenobia (q.v.). The ruins are considerable and include the best-preserved theatre of the Roman world, recently restored.

R. E. Brünnow and A. von Domaszewski, *Die Provincia Arabia* iii (1909), 1 ff.                    A. H. M. J.; H.

**BOTANY.** Among the Greeks, as among other peoples, knowledge of herbs was linked not only with agriculture but also with medicine. It was somewhat esoteric and from an early date, certain drugs were imported from overseas, notably from Egypt, Mesopotamia, and even India. Plant-lore was the special preserve of the rhizotomists (ῥιζοτόμοι), who were differentiated from the physicians and doubtless represent an earlier cultural stratum. They were sometimes of evil reputation; thus Sophocles wrote a play (now lost), dealing with the magical practices of Medea, in which ῥιζοτόμοι appeared as the Chorus, probably employed on nefarious tasks: see also Lucian *Dial. D.* 13. 1. In gathering plants they practised complex rituals of which fragments are preserved by Theophrastus and Pliny.

**2.** The Hippocratic Collection mentions some three ndred herbal drugs but tells almost nothing of the ants themselves. Nevertheless, in the first half of the urth century botany was emerging as a separate disci-ne and attention was paid to it at the Academy even fore it was taken up at the Lyceum. Perhaps under e influence of the former, but chiefly inspired by cilian pneumatic views (*see* ANATOMY AND PHYSIOLOGY), the Hippocratic work *On the nature of the embryo* of out 360 B.C. It discusses germination of seeds and owth of plants and contains the first attempt at a getable physiology.

**3.** Aristotle treated plants as an order of beings lower an animals, linked with them through the 'zoophytes', ntinued downward into non-living matter, and possess-g only the lowest of the three faculties of soul i.e. trition, growth, and reproduction, but not locomotion perception. The pseudo-Aristotelian treatise *On ants* is probably later but may well contain, though in corrupt form, some genuinely Aristotelian material. e have, however, in addition to a considerable number botanical passages in other works of Aristotle, several eatises on plants by his pupil Theophrastus (*c.* 372–7 B.C.).

**4.** Theophrastus felt the need of a technical termino-gy and began to develop it. Like his master he was eply interested in generation and, having examined the rmination of seeds, with extraordinary acuteness made e distinction between monocotyledons and dicotyle-ns. In this and in many other matters he showed mself fully capable of following morphological homo-gies. Though ignorant of the nature of sex in flowers e had an approximately correct notion of the relation flower and fruit, distinguished hypogynous, peri-ynous, and epigynous types, and regarded the relation flowers to fruit as the essential floral element. He had clear view of plant distribution as dependent on soil d climate and, benefiting by the knowledge available om Alexander's expeditions, came near to a statement geographical plant regions. He has numerous good escriptions of the forms, habits, habitats, fructification, ltivation, and uses of plants, of which he discusses ore than 400 kinds.

**5.** The Alexandrian school produced no botanical orks of significance. Important, however, was the work the rhizotomist Crateuas (q.v., *c.* 100 B.C.), who served lithridates VI of Pontus. He wrote a herbal in which ach plant was represented by a figure. Of this there urvives a substantial fragment, copied from a very ncient and perhaps almost contemporary original. Since rateuas plant representation has been an important de-artment of botany.

**6.** The *Natural History* of Pliny (A.D. 23–79) records any current views on the nature, origin, and uses of ants. Being quite uncritical it is more interesting for lklore than for botany. On a higher plane is the *Materia 1edica* of Dioscorides (*c.* A.D. 60), which consists of a ries of short accounts of plants accompanied by terse escriptions which sometimes include habits and habi-ts. It is the most widely read botanical work ever enned. Early MSS. of versions and translations of it re to be numbered by the hundred. Many of its plant-ames have passed into modern terminology. After ioscorides there was no systematic extension of botanical nowledge in antiquity.

**7.** Difficulties in identifying the plants of Dioscorides d very early, perhaps during his lifetime, to the pre-aration of copies of his herbals provided with pictures the plants. A magnificent representative of this prac-ce in uncial letters is the Juliana Anicia MS. of 515 at ienna, the earliest surviving complete Greek herbal. llustrated Latin versions, abridgements, and modifica-

tions of Dioscorides were prepared in the time of Cassiodorus (*c.* A.D. 490–585), and a Latin work based on one of these versions but bearing the name of Apuleius is the commonest early medical text. A splendid half-uncial MS. of this *Herbarius Apuleii* at Leyden is almost contemporary with Cassiodorus himself and is our earliest complete Latin document of this type.

**8.** The question of the identification of plants men-tioned by classical writers frequently arises and can be answered for certain distinctive or economically impor-tant species. The question, however, ignores the seman-tics of plant-names. A modern plant-name—even a 'popular' one—presupposes a conception of species and of their constancy and limitations and an idea of classi-fication that was absent in antiquity. Greek and Latin writers, like modern unlettered peasants, constantly called the same plant by different names and different plants by the same name. The question as to what a par-ticular writer meant by a particular plant-name is there-fore, with the exceptions mentioned above, normally unanswerable.

H. O. Lenz, *Botanik d. alten Griechen u. Römer* (1859); J. Berendes, *Des Pedanios Dioskurides aus Anazarbos Arzneimittellehre* (1902); H. Bretzl, *Botanische Forschungen des Alexanderzuges* (1903); A. de Premerstein, *De codicis Dioskuridei Aniciae Julianae historia etc.* (1906); E. L. Greene, *Landmarks of Botanical History* (U.S.A. 1909); E. Howald and H. E. Sigerist, *Antonii Musae De herba vettonica Liber, Pseudo-Apulei Herbarius*, etc. (1927); Charles Singer, 'The Herbal in Antiquity', *JHS* 1927; G. Senn, *Die Pflanzenkunde des Theophrast von Eresos* (1933); R. Strömberg, *Theophrastea, Studien zur botanischen Begriffsbildung* (1937); R. M. Dawkins, 'Semantics of Greek Plant Names', *JHS* 1936; M. R. Cohen and I. E. Drabkin, *A Source Book in Greek Science*[2] (1958); *PW* s.v. Dioskurides; *PW* s.v. Theophrastus (in Suppl.-Bd. vii); J. I. Miller, *The Spice Trade of the Roman Empire* (1969). C. S.

**BOTTOMRY LOANS** (ναυτικόν, ναυτικὸς τόκος; *fenus nauticum* or *pecunia traiecticia*) are known from the fourth century B.C. They took the place of modern shipping-insurance, because they were repayable only if the ship or the cargo which had been pledged for them (especially in Greek law), safely reached its destination (ἑτερόπλουν) or returned to the original port (ἀμφοτερό-πλουν), according to the terms of a written contract. The debt was not forfeited if ship or cargo was lost by the debtor's fault. Creditors and debtors could be groups of persons in partnership.

The biggest loan we know of amounts to 70 *minae*. During the fourth century the rate charged for a voyage from Athens to the Pontus and back was 30 per cent. on the amount of the loan, from Sestus to Athens 12½ per cent., and from Byzantium to Athens 10–12 per cent. Roman law from Justinian I onwards allowed a rate (*usurae maritimae*) up to 12½ per cent. on *fenus nauticum.* The creditor had the right to send a supercargo (ἐπί-πλους), often a freedman or slave, with the ship to control loading, unloading, and repayment. Attic as well as Roman law made elaborate regulations for this institu-tion, which represented an important form of capital investment.

Klingmueller, *PW*, s.v. 'fenus'; Berger, ibid. s.v. 'iactus'; Schwahn, ibid. s.v. 'ναυτικὸς τόκος'; A. Berger, *Encyclopedic Dictionary of Roman Law* (1953), art. 'fenus nauticum', 'iactus mercium', 'lex Rhodia de iactu'; H. Bolkestein, *Economic Life in Greece's Golden Age*[2] (1958), 112 ff.; M. I. Finley, *Land and Credit in Ancient Athens, 500–200 B.C.* (1951), index; Frank, *Econ. Survey* i–v (index, s.v. 'loans, mercantile'); F. M. Heichelheim, *Ancient Economic History* ii (1964), 168, 194 ff.; Michell, *Econom. Anc. Gr.* index; U. E. Paoli, *Studi di diritto attico* (1930), pt. i; Rostovtzeff, *Roman Empire*[2]. F. M. H.

**BOUDICCA** (name uncertain, but 'Boadicea' has neither authority nor meaning), wife of Prasutagus, who was established as client-king of the Iceni (East Anglia) by the Romans. On his death (A.D. 60) he had left the Emperor coheir with his daughters, but imperial agents maltreated his family. Under Boudicca the Iceni, assisted by the Trinovantes, rose in rebellion while the governor, Suetonius Paulinus, was occupied in the west. Colchester, London, and Verulamium were successively sacked. Venturing a battle, however, with Paulinus' main force, Boudicca's troops were easily routed, and she herself took poison.

Tacitus, *Ann.* 14. 31–7; *Agr.* 16. 1–2; Dio 62. 1–12. Collingwood-Myres, *Roman Britain*, 99 ff.; D. R. Dudley and G. Webster, *Rebellion of Boudicca* (1962). C. E. S.

**BOULE** in Greek States, originally the council of nobles which the king summoned to advise him; later a specially appointed council to undertake, on behalf of the citizenbody, the day-to-day affairs of State. Its range of competence was equal to that of the citizen Assembly. In an oligarchy it might be in some respects independent of the Assembly—e.g. it might have the right of summoning the Assembly only when it wished; in a democracy it was its servant, acting as a general-purposes committee. In the former, members might be elected by vote (perhaps from a restricted number of citizens) or sit by hereditary right, for a term of years, or for life; in a democracy, members were generally chosen by lot, and served for a year only. Every 'constitutional' State (hereditary monarchy, oligarchy, or democracy) had a *boule* of one kind or another.

**2.** In Athens, the original Council was that of the Areopagus (q.v.). Solon, according to a tradition which can be traced back to *c.* 400 B.C., created a second Council of 400, 100 from each *phyle* (q.v.), with probouleutic functions. Some modern critics believe that this Council, like the certainly fictitious one ascribed to Draco (q.v.), was a fabrication of the oligarchs of the late fifth century. However, the Chians had a second Council, with fifty members from each of their *phylai*, by *c.* 550 B.C. (Tod 1); and what little we know of the Athenian *ekklesia* (q.v.) in the sixth century suggests that there was room for *probouleusis* in Solon's constitution. That we hear nothing of the activities of his Council—unless it, rather than the Areopagus, is the Council which resisted the efforts of Cleomenes (q.v. 1) to dissolve it in 508/7 (Hdt. 5. 72)—is not a strong argument against its existence. It has been suggested, but cannot be proved, that Solon himself alluded to its institution in words which Plutarch adapts (*Sol.* 19. 2).

**3.** Solon's Council, if historical, was replaced by that of Cleisthenes (q.v. 1), which, with modifications, was retained till late Roman times. It had 500 members, fifty from each of the ten new *phylai*. It was known simply as ἡ βουλή, or occasionally, to distinguish it from the Areopagus, as ἡ βουλή οἱ πεντακόσιοι. After 307/6 the number varied, partly owing to the creation and abolition of additional *phylai*; in the fourth century A.D. it was 300. Members served for one (Attic) year: a second term was possible after an interval. Membership was open to all citizens over thirty, including, at least from the late fifth century, the Thetes (q.v.); the method of appointment was by lot from πρόκριτοι selected by the demes (*see* DEMOI), each deme being allotted places in proportion to its size. Those on whom the lot fell had to pass a *dokimasia* (q.v.) before the outgoing Council. Councillors were paid from the time of Pericles; in the late fourth century the pay was five obols a day.

**4.** The Council met daily except on festive and unlucky days. Its business was prepared by a changing committee of fifty of its own members, the *prytaneis* (q.v.); its chairman, who served for a day and also acted as chairman of the Assembly if that met on his day, was in the fifth century chosen from the *prytaneis* and thereafter from the *proedroi* (q.v.), who were also Councilmembers. The Council had its own secretary, later secretaries (*see* GRAMMATEIS). Ordinary citizens and most

magistrates could communicate with the Council on through the *prytaneis*. Thus the Council was carefull protected from undue influence, internal or external. A exception to this tendency was its relation to the *strateg* (q.v.), who appear to have acquired the right both t attend the meetings and to make propositions. Th Council met usually in the βουλευτήριον (see ATHEN (TOPOGRAPHY)), on occasion elsewhere. Meetings wer normally public but could be held in secret if the Counc so decided. It was assisted in some of its tasks by com mittees of ten of its own members, viz. the τριηροποιο ἐπιμεληταὶ τοῦ νεωρίου, εὔθυνοι, λογισταί, and ἱεροποιο (see below).

**5.** The competence of the *boule* had three overlappin aspects—probouleutic, administrative, and judicial. A debates in the *ekklesia* (q.v.) were based on προβουλευ ματα formulated by it, and it often had to take action i accordance with the resultant ψηφίσματα. In general, i supervised and co-ordinated the work of the variou boards of magistrates and so gave unity to the whol administration. It was specifically entrusted with a wid variety of matters. It received foreign envoys befor they proceeded to the *ekklesia*, and made drafts o treaties. It saw to the building of new triremes and th maintenance of the whole fleet and of the docks. It financial duties were far-reaching. Through the πωλητα and *apodektai* (q.v.) it supervised the letting out o State contracts for the collection of taxes and rents fror State property, and the receipt of the revenue from th contractors and, in the fifth century, of the imperia tribute, in the reassessments of which it assisted; it als supervised the borrowing and repayment of loans fron the temple treasuries, the handing over of funds fron each annual group of treasurers to their successors, an the accounts kept by magistrates of the public money entrusted to them (*see* EUTHYNA, LOGISTAI). It had th care of public buildings, and of certain State cults an sacrifices. It was responsible for the preservation of al State archives (*see* GRAMMATEIS). In its judicial capacit it held various kinds of *dokimasia* (q.v.), and tried crimina cases arising out of *eisangeliai* (q.v.) and some othe types of criminal procedure. It took over from the Areo pagus the right of investigating illegal conduct on th part of magistrates. In certain circumstances it coul arrest accused persons pending trial, and could itsel impose fines up to a limit of 500 drachmas; for a severe penalty it had to refer the case to the *ekklesia* or a dicas tery (q.v.).

**6.** The *boule* was the keystone of the democrati constitution; without its assistance in the formation an execution of policy the *ekklesia* could never have exer cised its sovereignty wisely and effectively. That, in spit of its wide powers, the *boule* did not dominate the Stat was due to the annual change of its entire membership and to the *ekklesia*'s right of amendment and rejection o προβουλεύματα. It may be doubted whether the Coun cillors' pay was sufficient to induce the poorest bread winners to abandon work for a whole year, and there i evidence that in the fourth century the well-to-do were indeed, somewhat over-represented on the Council; ye the rule that membership could be repeated once onl meant that a large proportion of the population passe through its ranks, and it was therefore likely, in norma circumstances (for an alleged exception cf. Lys. 13. 20) to reflect adequately all points of view.

**7.** During the revolution of 411, the Cleistheni Council was temporarily replaced by a Council of 40 (see FOUR HUNDRED, THE); and the Thirty Tyrant (q.v. 1) likewise appointed a Council of their own, wit 500 members, which acted as a revolutionary tribuna The *boule* of the restored democracy played an im portant part in the revision of the laws. Its place in th constitution was not substantially changed by the vicissitudes of the Hellenistic period; under the Romans it shared its work of policy-making and administration with the Areopagus.

8. For the Council at Sparta, *see* GEROUSIA; for federal Councils *see* ACHAEAN CONFEDERACY, AETOLIAN CONFEDERACY, FEDERAL STATES.

G. Gilbert, *Const. Antiquities of Sparta and Athens* (1895), see Table of Contents; Busolt–Swoboda, *Griech. Staatskunde³* (i, 1920; , 1926), see indexes; R. J. Bonner and G. Smith, *Adm. of Justice from Homer to Aristotle* (i, 1930; ii, 1938), see indexes; Hignett, *Hist. Athen. Const.*, see index; A. H. M. Jones *Athenian Democracy* (1957) see index; V. Ehrenberg, *The Greek State* (1960), see index; A. G. Woodhead, *Hist.* 1967, 129 ff. For the Second Council at Chios, L. H. Jeffery, *BSA* 1956, 157 ff.; J. H. Oliver, *AJPhil.* 1959, 96 ff.                                                    A. W. G.; T. J. C.

**BOVIANUM VETUS,** a *colonia* in Samnium (q.v.) mentioned by Pliny (*HN* 3. 107). Mommsen sought it at a site near modern *Pietrabbondante*, with well-preserved remains of a theatre and temples, but the identification seems erroneous. Its role in the Samnite Wars in uncertain.

Mommsen, *CIL* ix. 257; E. T. Salmon, *Samnium and the Samnites* (1967), 13.                                                    E. T. S.

**BOVIANUM UNDECIMANORUM,** capital of the Pentri Samnites: modern *Boiano*. Prominent against Rome in the Samnite Wars, it remained loyal during the Hannibalic War. In the Social War, after temporarily serving as a capital for the Italians, it was reduced to a village by Sulla. Under Vespasian veterans from Legio Undecima Claudia colonized it: hence its name. *See* SAMNIUM.

Strabo 5. 250; Livy 9. 28. 31; 25. 13; App. *BCiv.* 1. 51; Pliny, *HN* 3. 107.                                                    E. T. S.

**BOVILLAE,** ancient town on the Via Appia (q.v.), 12 miles from Rome. Here survivors from destroyed Alba Longa (q.v.) allegedly found refuge: they included the Gens Julia which thereafter always maintained close associations with Bovillae. Here Milo killed Clodius (qq.v.), 52 B.C. By then Bovillae had greatly dwindled, but it remained a *municipium*, whose inhabitants in imperial times were styled Albani Longani Bovillenses.
                                                    E. T. S.

**BOXING.** In Greek and Roman boxing there was no classification of competitors by weight and so the advantage was generally with the heavier man. A contest lasted until one of the contestants was unable or unwilling to continue.

The Greeks bound leather thongs (ἱμάντες) round their wrists and knuckles, to protect them rather than to increase the severity of the blow. Sometimes the fingers, or some of them, were left free, though this may have been the practice in the pancratium (q.v.) rather than in actual boxing. For training they used softer padded gloves (σφαῖραι). Body-blows were not used to any extent and the face was always the principal target.

The Romans used the *caestus*, a glove weighted with pieces of iron and having metal spikes placed round the knuckles, and boxing became a gladiatorial show rather than an athletic sport.                                                    R. L. H.

**BRASIDAS** (d. 422 B.C.), Spartan general. Though prominent from 431, he held only subordinate commands until 424, when he was sent with a small force of Helots and Peloponnesians to damage Athenian interests in the Thraceward region. After saving Megara from an Athenian attack, he hurried northwards and rapidly won several important cities, including Amphipolis and Torone. He continued his operations after the conclusion of the armistice between Athens and Sparta in 423, by

supporting the revolts of Scione and Mende, though he was unable to protect them adequately. In 422 he surprised and defeated an Athenian army under Cleon at Amphipolis, but was himself mortally wounded.

Brasidas' resourcefulness and his talent for winning confidence gained the admiration of Thucydides, who contrasts him with other Spartan leaders. His success permanently injured the Athenian cause in a vital area.

Thucydides, bks. 4–5.                                                    H. D. W.

**BRAURON** (modern *Vraona*), on the east coast of Attica, was one of twelve independent townships united traditionally under Theseus (q.v.). Its early prominence is attested by remains from Neolithic to Mycenaean times. It was then deserted, and the classical settlement Philaidai had its centre further inland. Brauron regained its importance in the archaic period as a place sacred to Artemis (q.v.), whose cult was associated with Iphigenia (q.v.) whom some believed to be buried there. The cult was chiefly for women, and young girls, *arktoi*, performed a bear-dance at the annual Brauronia. Excavation of the site since 1945 has revealed many of the buildings and dedications of the classical sanctuary, which became inundated and abandoned apparently about the end of the third century B.C.

Eur. *IT* 1462 ff.; Paus. 1. 33. 1 and Frazer's commentary; L. Deubner, *Attische Feste* (1932), 207 f.; Πρακτικά and Ἔργον (excavation reports); J. Papadimitriou, 'The Sanctuary of Artemis at Brauron', *Scientific American* 1963, 110 ff.                    C. W. J. E.

**BRENNUS** (1), the Gallic king who traditionally captured Rome (in 390 B.C. or, according to Polybius' chronology, 387), and made the famous utterance: 'Vae victis.' Since neither Polybius nor Diodorus mentions him, it has been irresponsibly suggested that Brennus is a title which was mistaken for a name, or that historians transferred to him the name of the Gallic chieftain who invaded Greece in 280/79 B.C. But the former hypothesis is disproved on philological grounds, and the Greek accounts of Brennus, which can be traced back to fourth- or early third-century authors, are in any case anterior to the coming of the Celts.

J. Gagé, *Rev. arch.* 1954.                                                    P. T.

**BRENNUS** (2), leader of the Galatian invasion in 279 B.C. Following on the heels of another body of Gauls under Bolgius, Brennus overran Macedonia and invaded Greece in autumn. Checked by a Greek coalition at Thermopylae, he sent a detachment to Aetolia whereupon the Aetolian force withdrew from Thermopylae; he then turned the Greek position at Thermopylae, as the Persians had done in 480 B.C. (*see* PERSIAN WARS); and when the Greek forces scattered, he attacked Delphi. The detachment in Aetolia and the main column under Acichorius were harassed by guerrilla tactics, while Brennus was wounded at Delphi. During the general retreat northwards the Gauls were attacked by the Thessalians; Brennus committed suicide, and few escaped.                                                    N. G. L. H.

**BREVIS BREVIANS,** Latin phonetic tendency between fourth and first centuries B.C., a 'short' syllable 'shortening' a following long one which is preceded or followed by an accent. Hence *caléfacio* (from *cálēfácio*), but *feruéfacio*. A comprehensive study setting out the conditions under which shortening becomes permanent (*benĕ* and *malĕ*, but cf. e.g. *probĕ*) is wanted. Poetry in general accepts the shortened forms only when they have become stabilized, but early drama shows *breuis breuians* in active operation in scansions—such as *bonîs, quid ĕst, pessim(e) ŏrnatus*.                                                    O. S.

**BRICKSTAMPS, ROMAN.** Brickstamps bearing the names of kings occur already in ancient Egypt. Used in many places up to the present day (most frequently as trade marks), they are rarely of more than limited interest. Except for the brickstamps of military units throughout the Roman Empire, these inscriptions became historically and archaeologically important documents only after the fire of Rome in A.D. 64, when there was an unprecedented demand for burned bricks. For more than a century the building activity in the city made large-scale production of bricks profitable. With the raw materials at hand in the Tiber valley on estates largely owned by members of the upper class (often well known to us), the brick industry, which had started modestly in the last century of the Republic, thrived. The stamps indicate the *praedia* where the brick-yards were located and/or frequently the names of foremen or workers employed there.

Probably because of the preference for seasoned bricks, the owner of the *figlinae Brutianae*, M. Rutilius Lupus (*praefectus Aegypti* A.D. 113–17), introduced in A.D. 110 the consular date into his brickstamp. Dated stamps are erratically used, mainly by the big producers, from A.D. 110 to 164, except in A.D. 123 when every brickstamp had to bear a date, presumably at the behest of the government.

Stamps make it possible to trace the ownership of brick-yards for generations; e.g. those of Cn. Domitius Afer (q.v.; *cos.* A.D. 39) passed through inheritance and marriage to his descendant by law, the emperor Marcus Aurelius. By the early third century brick-production in Rome had become virtually an imperial monopoly. During the chaotic decades between Caracalla and Diocletian, brickstamps almost disappear, to be once more resurrected in Diocletian's reorganization of the brick industry, now part of the imperial bureaucracy (*c.* A.D. 300). Two centuries later, Theodoric's brickstamps, a fitting expression of the cultural aspirations of Ostrogoth rule, bring to a close the history of the ancient brick industry.

EDITIONS. H. Dressel, *CIL* xv. 1 (1891, incomplete); H. Bloch, *Supplement to CIL xv. 1 Including Complete Indices to the Roman Brick-Stamps* (1948), repr. from *Harv. Stud.* 1947 and 1948.
STUDIES. H. Bloch, 'I bolli laterizi e la storia edilizia romana', *Bull. Com. Arch.* 1936, 141 ff.; 1937, 83 ff.; 1938, 51 ff.; republished with indexes as vol. 4 of *Studi e Materiali del Museo dell'Impero Romano* (1947); id., *Scavi di Ostia* i (1953), 215–27 (list of all brickstamps of Ostia found *in situ*); id., 'The Serapeum of Ostia and the Brick-Stamps of 123 A.D.', *AJArch.* 1959, 225 ff.; id. 'Ein datierter Ziegelstempel Theoderichs des Grossen', *Röm. Mitt.* 1959, 196 ff.; R. Meiggs, *Roman Ostia* (1960).          H. B.

**BRIDGES.** Remains of causeway bridges are associated with Bronze Age road systems in the Argolid. Some of the bridges had water-passages with 'arches' composed of horizontal overlapping stones, and the type survived into the classical period. Timber bridges must have been built from an early period, and stone bridges constructed on the pillar-and-lintel principle are known from the fifth century B.C. The bridge over the sacred stream at Brauron has five parallel rows of orthostats spanned by lintels (*BCH* 1962, 681). In the Hellenistic period bridges up to 300 m. long were built, for instance, in northern Greece and in Asia Minor. Piers of masonry, carefully built on the rocky bed, were so shaped as to create an efficient slipstream, and they carried a removable roadway of planking. It is uncertain whether any surviving example of a stone bridge with true arches dates from before the Roman period. The Etruscan 'bridges', as at Veii and Vulci, are tunnelled spurs of natural rock, the built structures in stone being in fact Roman. For, while the wooden bridge (*pons sublicius*) is associated with the very existence of Rome, the stone bridge is a relatively late development, the earliest dated example

being *pons Aemilius* (Livy 40. 51. 4) of 179 B.C., given an arched superstructure in 142 B.C., and followed by *pon Mulvius* (q.v.) in 109 B.C. and *pons Fabricius* in 62 B.C Typical of the state of affairs outside Rome is Strabo' description (4. 1. 12) of the Narbonese *via Domitia* o the statement of Augustus (*Mon. Anc.* 4. 19): 'refeci uiar Flaminiam ... [.. et pontes in ea] omnes praete Muluium et Minucium.' Nearly all monumental bridge thus belong to the imperial age. In Italy the most com plete are those of Augustus at Ariminum and of Hadria at Rome, the most imposing those of Augustus at Narni and at Asculum, the most curious the bold foot-bridg of Val de Cogne (*JRS* 1939, 149). But they are far out classed in length by the Augustan bridge at Emerit and in height by the famous bridge which several Spanisl communities combined to erect over the Tagus gorg at Alcántara (A.D. 106). The tradition of wooden bridge building, however, continued in the hands of militar engineers (*PBSR* 1935, 34). Caesar's description of hi temporary wooden bridge on the Rhine (*BGall.* 4. 17) i famous (cf. *CR* 1908, 144). Vegetius (1. 10) describe pontoon bridges of boats, while many bridges of timbe more durably constructed than these must have carrie even the most important trunk roads. Bridges spannin powerful rivers, however, were usually built with ston piers and wooden superstructure, as the Flavian Rhin bridge at Moguntiacum or Trajan's Danube bridge, th latter some 1,120 metres long, with stone piers and seg mental arches of timber. British examples are th Thames bridge at London, the Tyne bridges at Corbridg and Newcastle upon Tyne (*pons Aelius*), where ston piers of the same kind are known to have been used. A Arelate (*Arles*) there was a famous permanent bridg of boats (Auson. *Ordo Nob. Urb.* 77), figured in a mosai at Ostia (G. Becatti, *Scavi di Ostia* (1961), iv, pl. clxxxiv)

S. Parnicki-Pudelko, *Archaeologia* xi (1959/60), 128 ff.; Hammond *Epirus* 235 f.; R. Delbrück *Hellenistische Bauten in Latium* i (1907) Ashby–Anderson–Spiers *Architecture of Ancient Rome* (1927); M. H Ballance, *PBSR* 1951, 78 ff.; P. Gazzola, *Ponti romani*, 2 vols (1963); for bridges at Rome, Nash *Pict. Dict. Rome* ii. 178 ff.
I. A. R.; D. E. S

**BRIGANTES,** the most populous tribe in Britain (Tac *Agr.* 17), whose territory, spanning the island (Ptol *Geog.* 2. 3. 16), included the legionary fortress of Ebura cum (*York*), a capital at Isurium (*Aldborough*), forts a Olicana (*Ilkley*), Cataractonium (*Catterick*), and Vino vium (*Binchester*), and native *oppida* at Camulodunun (*Almondbury*), Stanwick, and Rigodunum (perhap Ingleborough). Under Queen Cartimandua (q.v.) earl relations with Rome were friendly; later strife in th royal household compelled annexation by Cerialis an Agricola in A.D. 71–9 (Tac. *Agr.* 17, 20). The Pennin and forests of Lancashire and Durham were intersecte by garrisoned roads (Tac. *Agr.* 20) and lead-minin began by A.D. 81 (*CIL* vii. 1207). In the Ouse basi civil life gave rise to a town at Isurium and widesprea villas, as at Well, Castledykes, Gargrave, or Dalto Parlours. Systematic pacification of the uplands wa a commonplace under Hadrian (Juv. 14. 196), but unde Pius the tribe apparently lost much territory followin unlawful raiding (Paus. 8. 43). The eponymous goddes. *Brigantia* won local fame (Collingwood and Wright *RIB* 627, 628, 630, 1131, 2066, 2091, cf. 623; N. C Jolliffe, *Arch. Journ.* 1941, 36 ff.

I. A. Richmond, *JRS* 1954, 43 ff.; id. in R. E. M. Wheeler, *Th Stanwick Fortifications* (1954), 61 f.; Frere, *Britannia*, chs. 4, 6–8 I. A. R

**BRIGANTIUM,** also called Brigantia (modern *L Coruña?*), one of the mystery sites of Roman Spain. Th name, obviously Celtic, is found in Dio, Orosius, an two itineraries (*Bricantia* in Rav. Cosm.). The evidenc from the itineraries and Ptolemy would place it in or near modern Betanzos. But the lighthouse ascribed to it by Dio and Orosius is apparently that of La Coruña (*CIL* ii. 2559, 5639). Ptolemy's name, *Flavium Brigantium*, marks it as a recipient of Vespasian's grant of the Latin Right (*see* IUS LATII). J. J. VAN N.

**BRIGETIO,** *Ó-Szöny* on the Danube, was a legionary fortress and city in Pannonia. In the early second century A.D. it was occupied in turn by Legio XI Claudia and XXX Ulpia Victrix until the end of Trajan's reign when I Adiutrix became its permanent garrison. The civil settlement became a *municipium* (*Antoninianum*) by the early third century (*CIL* iii. 11007) and later a *colonia* (*CIL* iii. 4335).

L. Barkóczi, *Brigetio* (Diss. Pann. ii. 22 (1951) Budapest). J. J. W.

**BRIMO,** name or title of a goddess, often identified with Persephone (q.v.; as *Etym. Magn.* 213, 49), Hecate (q.v.; as ibid.; Ap. Rhod. 3. 861), or Demeter (q.v.; as Clem. Alex. *Protr.* p. 13, 4 Stählin). At Eleusis it was proclaimed that she had borne 'a holy child Brimos' (Hippolytus, *Haer.* 5. 8. 40, 96 Wendland, where both names are said to mean 'strong'). H. J. R.

**BRISEIS,** in mythology, daughter of Briseus of Lyrnessus and widow of Mynes; Achilles' slave-concubine, taken from him by Agamemnon and afterwards restored (*Il.* 1. 392; 19. 60, 296, and contexts). H. J. R.

**BRITANNIA** (the form Πρεταννικαὶ νῆσοι, used apparently by the earliest Hellenic visitor, Pytheas (*c.* 300 B.C.) should be cognate with Irish (q-Celt) *cruithin* (= Picts)). At the beginning of the Christian era the culture of Britain was divided fairly sharply by a line from Tyne to Exe, corresponding to a geological contrast of the Palaeozoic 'Highland' and the Caenozoic 'Lowland' zone. In the 'Highland zone', Bronze Age conditions prevailed among peoples of neolithic ancestry; in the 'Lowland' waves of Celts had imposed Iron Age cultures, the latest of whom, the Belgae (q.v.), overran the south-east (first arrival *c.* 100 B.C.). Caesar's invasions (55 and 54 B.C.), at least, retarded the formation of a Belgic *imperium*, which was, however, realized by Cunobelinus (d. *c.* A.D. 41); but disturbances in his old age invited intervention. A grotesque demonstration by Caligula (A.D. 40) indicated the trend of Roman policy, which was resumed by Claudius, who invaded Britain after Cunobelinus' death (A.D. 43). The army (four legions with accompanying *auxilia*) quickly overran the 'Lowland Zone' (A.D. 43–8), and a revolt under Boudicca (q.v.; A.D. 60) was crushed; but where Celtic civilization was combined with 'Highland Zone' conditions, as in east Wales (Silures) and Yorkshire (Brigantes), little was effected until the campaigns of an able succession of Flavian governors. The last of these, Agricola (probably A.D. 78–85), advanced far into Scotland, but after his recall the army was reduced to a garrison footing of three legions (making with the *auxilia* a strength of *c.* 50,000). Further withdrawal of troops compelled a retreat (*c.* 110) to the Tyne–Solway line, and *c.* 120 a definite frontier-line was drawn there (Hadrian's Wall). About this time the Ninth Legion disappeared. Rome had lost the initiative in Britain, a fact which anticipates the high water mark of progress soon reached in the Empire itself. Britain, indeed, is, in every respect of romanization, last in advance, first in retreat. This is its historical significance.

**2.** Britain was a typical imperial province, and its local government imitated the Gallic cantonal system. A late author (Gildas, 3) mentions twenty-eight *civitates*, which included, eventually, four *coloniae* (Colchester, Lincoln, Gloucester, York). New towns were created in Roman style, where even artisans wrote Latin. The negative aspect of romanization, however, was the virtual extinction of an attractive native art, based on the La Tène style. Towns were compelled to surround themselves with walls during the late second and early third centuries, possibly through nervousness at peasant discontent. Though their subsequent decay has been exaggerated, it certainly seems that less money was spent on them.

**3.** Rural life follows closely the lines of pre-history. Areas of easy settlement, populated since the Bronze Age, continue so, and the normal unit of habitation, the settlement of rude well-huts, persists, as it does in the little romanized 'Highland zone'. Elsewhere either the farm or imposing residences (like Washington's Mount Vernon) are the norm. Less romanized (and far less literate) than the towns, the villas and even the villages show increased prosperity. Moreover, the mineral wealth (mainly in argentiferous lead-mines worked as early as A.D. 49) increased the value of the province to Rome. The class distinction, however, manifest in the contrast between the Celtic spoken by the common man and the stilted Latin of his superiors, had the seeds of trouble.

**4.** After Hadrian, political history was fairly uneventful. The northern tribes continued troublesome, and *c.* A.D. 142 Antoninus Pius decided to push the frontier up to the Forth–Clyde isthmus (Antonine Wall). But the new line was never very satisfactory, and by the end of the century (exact date still controversial) was abandoned.

**5.** The usurpation of Albinus (A.D. 193–6) illustrates an evil from which the province was later to suffer, the removal of its garrison for overseas adventures; an incursion from the north ensued. The campaigns of Severus, however (A.D. 208–11), re-established the *status quo* behind Hadrian's Wall, which he had restored. Though garrisons in the 'Highland zone' would not be seriously reduced, Britain seems fairly peaceful in the third century. But the growing strength of Saxon piracy made necessary the erection of signal-stations and forts along the eastern and southern coasts (begun *c.* A.D. 280).

**6.** Britain, however, held firm, and the attempt of a Menapian seaman, Carausius, to blackmail Diocletian, by seizing it, into recognizing him as colleague caused little internal disturbance. Carausius, in fact, was assassinated in A.D. 294, and in A.D. 297 the imperial authority was re-established by Constantius Chlorus. From now Britain, already divided into two by Severus, was administered as four provinces. Christianity began to reach it, but old ways were still strong, and pagan temples were actually built *de novo*.

**7.** Continuous attacks, however, were undermining its powers of resistance and recovery; and a general assault in A.D. 367 was accompanied by a revolt of the frontier garrison. Order was restored with difficulty, but a vast capital destruction had been suffered. Adventurers, Maximus (A.D. 385) and Constantine (A.D. 407), withdrew the garrison, and it is doubtful whether after A.D. 410 there was ever a Roman army there again. Left to itself, Roman Britain, with buildings enlarged and new villages created, is likely to have become the prey of its peasantry, and it was a natural resource to enrol Saxons from overseas as *foederati*; they soon revolted and invited their Teutonic fellows. In the struggle of Celt and Teuton, Roman Britain disappeared almost completely (the precise extent of survival is very controversial), even Christianity vanishing from the Lowland zone. But, in truth, the Roman element was already in retreat, and in the Highland zone, though men spoke of 'Romania' and wrote Latin on the tombstones, the spirit was Celtic and the old Celtic art broke forth, though hesitatingly, once more.

Chief sources: Caesar, *BGall.* 4. 20–36; 5. 8–23. Tacitus, *Ann.* 12. 31–40; 14. 29–39; *Agricola.* Dio Cassius 60. 19–23; 76. 11–13. Collingwood and Wright, *RIB* i. R. G. Collingwood and J. N. L. Myres, *Roman Britain²* (1937: very full bibliography but out of date on some points); I. A. Richmond *Roman Britain²* (1963); Frere, *Britannia*; J. Liversidge *Britain in the Roman Empire* (1968); A. L. F. Rivet, *Town and Country in Roman Britain²* (1964); G. Simpson, *Britons and the Roman Army* (1964). On language, K. Jackson, *Language and History in Early Britain* (1953). On art, J. M. C. Toynbee, *Art in Roman Britain* (1962) and *Art in Britain under the Romans* (1964). Bibliography, W. Bonser, *A Romano-British Bibliography* (55 B.C.–A.D. 449) (1964).                    C. E. S.

**BRITANNICUS,** Tiberius Claudius (*PW* 92) Caesar, son of Claudius and Messalina, born 12 Feb. A.D. 41. His first surname was Germanicus; 'Britannicus' was added after Claudius' invasion of Britain. His stepmother Agrippina (q.v. 3) induced Claudius in 50 to adopt her son L. Domitius (Nero), who was three years older than Britannicus and so now took precedence over him; and she contrived to remove the tutors and officers of the guard who were loyal to Britannicus, thus ensuring Nero's accession on Claudius' death (54). Early in 55 Agrippina seems to have considered using Britannicus to prop up her failing influence, but he very soon died, almost certainly poisoned by Nero's order.

F. Giancotti, *Rend. Linc.* 1953, 254 ff., 1954, 587 ff. Iconography, V. H. Poulsen, *Act. Arch.* 1951, 129 ff.                    G. W. R.; T. J. C.

**BRITOMARTIS** (the name means 'sweet maid' in Cretan, Solinus 11. 8), a Cretan goddess, identified with Artemis (Solinus loc. cit. and Hesychius s.v.). She had a temple near Cydonia (Strabo 10. 4. 13). Minos loved her; she avoided him for nine months and finally, to escape him, leaped over a cliff into the sea, was caught in fishermen's nets (hence called Dictynna from δίκτυον), got away to Aegina, escaped from him again into a grove of Artemis, and was thenceforth worshipped there as Aphaea (q.v.).

See Callimachus, *Dian.* 189 ff.; Pausanias 2. 30. 3; Antoninus Liberalis 40 (no author quoted); [Verg.] *Ciris* 286 ff.; Rose, *Handb. of Gk. Myth.* 117 f.                    H. J. R.

**BRIZO,** a goddess worshipped by women at Delos, especially as protectress of sailing (Semus of Delos ap. Athen. 8. 335 a–b = *FHG* iv. 493). Her name is derived from βρίζειν 'to sleep', and she was credited with sending prophetic dreams. Bowls of all sorts of food, except fish (cf. FISH, SACRED), were offered to her in sacrifice.                    F. R. W.

**BRONZE.** The ancients used the words χαλκός, *aes*, indiscriminately for copper and for the harder and more fusible bronze, the compound of copper and tin. Implements of bronze are found in Egypt and Mesopotamia before 3000 B.C. During the third millennium (the Early Minoan period of Crete) the general use of bronze and the normal composition of the mixture (one part of tin to nine of copper) were established. Until the introduction of iron bronze remained the sole metal for utilitarian purposes, and afterwards it continued in general use to the end of antiquity for sculpture, many domestic objects, and, after the fifth century B.C., for small-denomination coins. Brass (ὀρείχαλκος, *orichalcum*, a mixture of copper and zinc) is not found before Roman imperial times, when a white metal formed by the addition of lead to bronze is also in use.

Copper is widely found in classical lands, where the principal sources of supply are, for Greece, Chalcis in Euboea and Cyprus, and, for Italy, Bruttium, Etruria, and Elba, while under Roman rule Spain produced largely. Tin (q.v.) is much rarer, though a little is still worked in Asia Minor; but Herodotus speaks of the metal as coming from the extremities of Europe (3. 115), and Spain, Brittany, and Cornwall seem to have been the main sources.

Several varieties of bronze were distinguished in antiquity—Corinthian, Delian, Aeginetan, Syracusan, Campanian—but these cannot be identified. The technical processes employed were: hammering into plates which were riveted together (σφυρήλατον), used in the making of utensils and, during the archaic period, of statues; and casting with wax, either solid (usually in the case of small statuettes) or hollow over a core of clay or plaster (πρόπλασμα, *argilla*) to produce large-scale sculpture. Relief decoration was produced in repoussé work (ἐμπαιστική); incised ornament is also common, especially on mirrors. Tin and copper solders were used in addition to riveting for joins. The dull patina of bronzes in museums is the result of time; ancient bronzes were kept bright, and the surface was often coated with gold or silver, or variegated with damascening and inlay, while enamelling on bronze was a Celtic practice.

Pliny, *HN* bk. 34. H. Blümner, *Technologie und Terminologie der Gewerbe und Künste bei Griechen und Römern* (1874–87) iv; Kluge and Lehmann-Hartleben, *Die Antiken Grossbronzen* (1927); W. Lamb, *Greek and Roman Bronzes* (1929); J. Charbonneaux, *Greek Bronzes* (1958); Forbes, *Stud. Anc. Technol.* ix; see also the introductions to the *Catalogues of Bronzes* of the British Museum (by H. B. Walters, 1893) and of the Metropolitan Museum, New York (by G. M. A. Richter, 1915).                    F. N. P.

**BRUCTERI,** a Germanic people, living north of the Lippe in the neighbourhood of the modern Münster. A powerful people, they were allies of the Cherusci, whom they assisted in resisting the invasions of Germany by Germanicus (q.v.). They also played a prominent part in the revolt of Civilis (q.v.) in A.D. 69–70, in which their priestess Veleda had much influence. They were heavily defeated (c. 98) by the Chamavi and Angrivarii, who occupied their land; but the Roman belief that some 60,000 Bructeri were killed is doubtless exaggerated: they retained their identity until much later times.                    E. A. T.

**BRUNDISIUM** (Βρεντέσιον, modern *Brindisi*), the best harbour on the Italian east coast, consisting of two arms of the sea which penetrate deeply into the land, and the nearest Italian town to the east Adriatic coast. A Messapian settlement, it was not colonized by Greeks, despite traditions of early Cretan and later Tarentine colonists. About 440 B.C. it entered into treaty relations with Thurii (*SEG* xvi. 582), but is little attested until 244 B.C., when the Romans constituted it a Latin colony. It became the terminal point of the extended Via Appia (q.v.) and the regular port of embarkation for Roman armies crossing to Greece or Epirus. Hence in 49 Caesar attempted to cut off Pompey's retreat from Italy by capturing it, and in 40 Antony besieged it when Octavian sought to prevent his returning to Italy. By the 'treaty of Brundisium' the triumvirs settled their differences. Virgil died there in 19 B.C. For so important a port— and it was a vital link in the communications system of the Roman Empire—its ancient remains are disappointingly meagre.

C. Picard, *Rev. Ét. Lat.* 1957, 285 ff.                    A. G. W.

**BRUTTEDIUS (BRUTTIDIUS) NIGER,** aedile A.D. 22; prosecuted Silanus (q.v. 9) for *maiestas* (Tac. *Ann.* 3. 66). He was a pupil of Apollodorus (Sen. *Controv.* 2. 1. 35–6). He was tempted to woo imperial favour by delation, and is probably the Bruttidius of Juv. 10. 83. His account of Cicero's death (Sen. *Suas.* 6. 20 f.) comes from an historical work by him.

Peter, *HRRel.* 2. 90–1.                    J. W. D.

**BRUTTII** inhabited the rugged south-west peninsula of Italy (modern *Calabria*; the name Bruttium lacks ancient authority). Earlier inhabitants were Morgetes and Oenotri (= Sicels?) and Chones (= Illyrians). Sabellian Lucani appeared near Laus *c.* 390 B.C., defeated Thurii (q.v.) (Polyaenus 2. 10), and imposed their Oscan language on the peninsula. In 356 the Oscanized inhabitants, asserting their independence from the Lucani, became known as Bruttii—probably a pre-Sabellian name which the Lucani adopted as their word for 'runaways' (Diod. 16. 15; Strabo 6. 253 f.; Justin 23. 1). The Bruttii conquered several Greek colonies on the fertile coastlands, became themselves partly hellenized (Festus, 31 L.), and reached their apogee in the third century. Rome, however, subjugated them for supporting Pyrrhus and seized half the Sila Forest (q.v.) (Zonar. 8. 6; Dion. Hal. 20. 15). When they revolted to Hannibal, Rome confiscated additional territory, ringed them round with colonies (Buxentum, Tempsa, Vibo, Croton, Thurii), and practically enslaved them (App. *Hann.* 61). Consequently the separate nation of Bruttii disappeared. In 71 B.C. Spartacus, following Hannibal's example, based his operations on Bruttian territory. Once famous for its ships' timber and pitch, Hannibalic depredations started its decline (but see Cassiod. *Var.* 8. 31). Chief towns: Consentia, Clampetia, and Greek coastal colonies.

J. Whatmough, *Foundations of Roman Italy* (1937), 335; G. Slaughter, *Calabria, the First Italy* (U.S.A. 1939); E. Vetter, *Handbuch der ital. Dialekten* i (1953), 119 ff.; A. de Franciscis, O. Parlangeli, *Gli italici del Bruzio* (1960). E. T. S.

**BRUTUS** (1), LUCIUS IUNIUS (*PW* Suppl. v, 356 ff.), the traditional founder of the Roman Republic, is probably an historical figure. There is no reason to suppose he was a god, or that his exploits were retrojections of achievements by later members of the *gens Iunia*, the more so since the name Brutus is likely to be a derogatory term or nickname which the annalists were at pains to explain rationalistically by assuming that Brutus feigned to be 'stupid' in order to escape suspicion from or vengeance at the hands of the Tarquins. His consulship in 509 B.C., and his alleged attempt to humanize some primitive cults, are probably fictitious or later embellishments to connect the origins of the republican institutions with the exploits of its alleged founder. On the other hand, the story of the capital punishment which he inflicted on his sons, and of his victory over the Etruscans at Silva Arsia, where he was killed, are best explained as part of an early popular legend or epic poetry.

Walbank, *Polybius* 339; Ogilvie, *Comm. Livy 1–5*, 216 f. P. T.

**BRUTUS** (2) **CALLAICUS,** DECIMUS IUNIUS (*PW* 57), as consul in 138 B.C. and proconsul, fought successfully in Iberia, triumphing over the Lusitani and Callaici. He accompanied Tuditanus (q.v. 2) to Illyricum and later opposed Gaius Gracchus. He was an orator, philhellene, and a patron of Accius (q.v.).

A. E. Astin, *Scipio Aemilianus* (1967), see index. E. B.

**BRUTUS** (3) **DAMASIPPUS,** LUCIUS IUNIUS (*PW* 58), fought for the government in the *bellum Sullanum*. Defeated by Pompey (83 B.C.), he was *praetor urbanus* in 82 and had four unreliable senators (including Scaevola (q.v. 4)) killed. He tried to relieve Marius (q.v. 2) at Praeneste, but was defeated by Sulla at the Colline Gate, captured, and executed. E. B.

**BRUTUS** (4), MARCUS IUNIUS (*PW* 52), as tribune in 83 B.C. established a colony at Capua. In 77, as a legate of Lepidus (q.v. 2), he commanded in Cisalpina, surrendered to Pompey at Mutina, and, after a promise of safe conduct, was executed. E. B.

**BRUTUS** (5), MARCUS IUNIUS (*PW* 53), the tyrannicide, son of Brutus (4) and Servilia (q.v.), was born probably in 85 B.C., and adopted (not later than 59) by his uncle (?) Q. Servilius Caepio; after this his legal name was Q. Caepio Brutus. In 58 he accompanied Cato (q.v. 5) to Cyprus, and in 53 was quaestor to Appius Claudius (q.v. 12) in Cilicia. He joined Pompey in the Civil War, but was pardoned by Caesar after Pharsalus. In 46 he was governor of Cisalpine Gaul, and in 44 *praetor urbanus*. He entered into the conspiracy against Caesar for patriotic reasons and with Cassius (q.v. 6) played a leading part in it. Soon after the deed he found it impossible to remain in Rome, and was assigned by the Senate in June the task of importing corn from Asia and later the unimportant province of Crete; in August, after a quarrel with Antony, he sailed instead to Greece. With money handed over to him by the retiring quaestors of Asia and Syria, and with the support of Q. Hortensius, governor of Macedonia, he raised an army, won over the troops of Vatinius (q.v.), and captured C. Antonius (q.v. 5) in Apollonia (Mar. 43). The Senate had already (in Feb.) voted him the command of all the troops in Illyricum, Macedonia, and Achaea, and later probably made his *imperium* formally *maius* and valid in Asia as well. Ignoring appeals to come to the aid of the republicans in Italy, and, later, his own condemnation under the law of Pedius (q.v. 1), he continued to collect men and materials in the East, campaigned against the Bessi in Thrace and by the successful siege of Xanthus forced the Lycians to give him financial aid. In the summer of 42 he and Cassius moved into Europe to meet Antony and Octavian; Brutus committed suicide after his defeat in the second battle of Philippi (23 Oct.).

Brutus impressed his contemporaries by his moral earnestness and independence of spirit. The affair of Scaptius and the Salaminians (Cic. *Att.* 5. 21, 6. 1) reveals him in a bad light, but alongside it should be placed his humane governorship of Cisalpine Gaul (Plut. *Brut.* 6). As a man of action he was not ineffective, but his temperament inclined him to study and contemplation; and this constituted the principal bond between him and Cicero, who dedicated several of his treatises to him. Their surviving correspondence is only a small part of what was published. Separate collections of Brutus' letters have also been lost; a group of Greek letters survives, most of which are certainly spurious. Brutus wrote books on virtue, duty, and patience, epitomes of histories, including that of Polybius, and poems. In philosophy his preference was for the Academics; in oratory he favoured the Attic school.

He married (by 51) a daughter of Ap. Claudius (q.v. 12) and after divorcing her in 45, Porcia (q.v.), daughter of Cato.

Cicero, *Letters* and *Philippics*; Vell. Pat. 2. 56–72; Plutarch, *Brutus*; App. *BCiv.* 2–4; Cass. Dio 44–7. G. Boissier, *Cicéron et ses amis* (1865), 405 ff.; Tyrrell and Purser, *The Correspondence of Cicero* (1904–33), vi², cix ff.; M. Radin, *Marcus Brutus* (1939); Syme, *Rom. Rev.*, see index; R. F. Rossi, *PP* 1953, 26 ff.; A. E. Raubitschek, *Phoenix* 1957, 1 ff.; Schanz–Hosius i. 394 ff.; *ORF*² 460 ff.; F. Portalupi, *Bruto e i neo-atticisti* (1955); L. Torraca, *Marco Giunio Bruto, Epistole greche* (1959). Iconography: H. Möbius, *Ἀρχ. Ἐφ.* 1953–4, 3, 207 ff. G. W. R.; T. J. C.

**BRUTUS** (6), DECIMUS IUNIUS (*PW* 55a in Suppl. v), probably son of Decimus Brutus (consul 77 B.C.) and Sempronia, the associate of Catiline: from the name Albinus given to him by Greek writers and on coins it is usually assumed he was adopted by a Postumius Albinus. As a young man he served under Caesar in Gaul and distinguished himself by a naval victory over the Veneti (q.v. 1) in 56. He successfully commanded a Caesarian fleet at Massilia in 49, and was appointed governor of Transalpine Gaul, where he suppressed a rebellion of the Bellovaci (46). He took part in the conspiracy against

Caesar, in spite of the marked favour shown him by the dictator, who gave him another provincial command in Cisalpine Gaul and designated him consul for 42. In Apr. 44 he went to his province, and in December refused to surrender it to Antony, who claimed it in virtue of the law he had passed in June. Besieged by him in Mutina (q.v.), he was released by the victory of Hirtius (q.v.) and Octavian in Apr. 43. With Hirtius dead and the other consul Pansa (q.v.) dying, the Senate placed Brutus in command of their troops, but their two veteran legions preferred to resume service under Octavian, who, moreover, failed to help Brutus with the pursuit of Antony. Brutus followed Antony into Transalpine Gaul and joined Plancus (q.v. 1) in June, but was presently deserted by him. He now planned to join Marcus Brutus in Macedonia, but was abandoned by his army, captured by a Gallic chief, and put to death by Antony's order.

Cicero, *Letters* and *Philippics*; Caes. *BGall.* 3, 7, *BCiv.* 1–2; Vell. Pat. 2. 56–64; App. *BCiv.* 2–3; Cass. Dio 44–6. Tyrrell and Purser, *The Correspondence of Cicero* (1904–33), vi². lxxxiv ff.; Syme, *Rom. Rev.*, see index. G. W. R.; T. J. C.

**BRYGUS,** potter, in Athens, late sixth to early fifth century B.C. Known from nine signatures. His best artist, the Brygus painter, decorated red-figure cups, plastic vases, etc. Note particularly Komos (Würzburg), Sack of Troy (Paris).

**BRYSON** of Heraclea on the Pontus, sophist, was probably a pupil of Eucleides of Megara and a teacher of Pyrrhon (qq.v.). He is best known as the author of an inconclusive attempt to square the circle (Arist. *An. Post.* 75ᵇ4; *Soph. El.* 171ᵇ16, 172ᵃ3 and Alexander, *Comm.* ad loc.).

**BUBASTIS,** a local cat-headed goddess of the city of Bubastis. Early identified with Isis, she was also identified by the Greeks with Artemis. A temple of Bubastis existed at Memphis, one of the many temples in the great complex of sacred structures there. The festival of the goddess is described in Hdt. 2. 60. Bubastis appears with the Egyptian deities, or with some of them, at Delos, Ostia, Nemi, and Rome. T. A. B.

**BUCEPHALUS (**or **BUCEPHALAS),** favourite horse of Alexander the Great, died after the battle on the Hydaspes (326 B.C.). In its memory, Alexander founded the town of Bucephala on the site. *See also* HORSES.

**BUILDING MATERIALS.** GREEK. In its developed stages Greek architecture was based on the use of finely dressed stone masonry, above all the white marbles available in many parts of the Aegean, including that of Mt. Pentelicus, used on the Parthenon (q.v.); but it contains many formal reminiscences of an earlier phase, when the principal materials were timber (together with tiles at all times the standard material for roofs and ceilings) and walls of puddled rubble or mud brick, often upon a socle of more massive stone masonry (e.g. the Temple of Hera at Olympia—q.v.). The dressed blocks were regularly fastened with cramps and dowels of wood or metal, but without mortar; and although exceptionally almost entire buildings might be of marble, including ceilings of quite large span (e.g. the Erechtheum—q.v.), considerations of cost frequently meant that the less conspicuous parts were built in local limestone (*poros*). Inferior materials were regularly surfaced with fine marble stucco to resemble masonry, but the use of marble veneer was a Hellenistic innovation, as was the introduction of coloured marbles (other than grey). Painted terracotta facings are characteristic of districts, such as much of Sicily and south Italy, where suitable fine

building-stones were not available. Bronze was used for many decorative purposes.

2. ROMAN. Roman building practice was everywhere based on the materials (stone, timber, crude brick and fired brick) locally available, supplemented where necessary by the importation of fine marbles and granites, roofing timbers, etc. In Rome itself the plentiful local supplies of soft, easily dressed, volcanic tufa were used from the sixth century B.C. onwards and remained in use at all periods as a general-purpose building material. Travertine, quarried near Tivoli, was discovered in the second century B.C. and was the fine building-stone *par excellence* of the later republic. Under Augustus its place was taken in monumental use by white marble, at first from Luni (Carrara), later from Greece and especially from Attica and Proconnesos (Marmara). Many of the earlier Italic temples were built largely of timber, with painted terracotta details; and timber-framed crude brick was widespread in Rome before the fire of A.D. 64.

It was the perfection and exploitation of concrete which constituted the chief contribution of the Romans to architecture (*see* ARCHITECTURE). This was a hydraulic cement which derived its unique strength from the use of the local volcanic ash (*pozzolana*, Latin *pulvis puteolanus*, from its first exploitation at Puteoli, in Campania). In Rome from the second century B.C. onwards it came to supersede the puddled clay rubble and timber ceilings of previous practice, replacing the simple traditional forms by vaulted chambers that were as strong as fine ashlar and far cheaper and more flexible to build. The aggregate was often skilfully graded by weight, the supreme example of this being the dome of the Pantheon, and the vaulting load might be further lightened by the incorporation of large jars. It was regularly used with a facing of stone or fired brick; but this was purely superficial, the strength of the structure being that of the concrete core. Outside Italy its place was taken by a tough mortared rubble, often strengthened with courses of brick, and in the eastern provinces much of the vaulting was carried out in brick, anticipating Byzantine practice. Roman masonry was regularly faced with other materials, including marble veneer, painted plaster, moulded stucco, and mosaic. Translucent window-glass was common. Gilt bronze was used occasionally for doors and roof-tiles, waterproof cement and lead and terracotta piping regularly for hydraulic installations.

3. GENERAL. Locally and for domestic building simple, practical materials persisted at all periods: crude brick or puddled rubble, often on a damp-resistant stone footing; drystone masonry; timber-framing; tiles, thatch, or puddled terrace roofs. These simpler materials are frequently reflected in the conventions of monumental architecture, and they were themselves regularly faced, usually with fine stucco, to imitate monumental masonry.

M. E. Blake, *(Ancient) Roman Construction in Italy*, vols. 1 (1947) and 2 (1959); G. Lugli, *La tecnica edilizia romana* (1957). J. B. W.-P.

**BULLA REGIA,** a town in the Bagradas valley in North Africa, now *Hammon Daradji*. Burials bear witness to the Punic and Numidian periods of its history. Later it came within Africa Proconsularis; an *oppidum liberum* under Augustus, it became a colony under Hadrian. Deities worshipped there include Apollo, Jupiter, Caelestis, Saturnus, and Diana. Extensive Roman ruins survive.

P. Quoniam, *CR Acad. Inscr.* 1952, 460 ff. H. H. S.

**BUPALUS.** Sculptor (6th c.) of Chios. Son of Archermus (q.v.) and brother of Athenis. Made statues of Tyche and the Graces in Smyrna and a caricature of Hipponax (q.v.), in return for which Hipponax satirized him; this was probably a grotesque labelled Hipponax. A Chiot signature on the Acropolis of Athens has been connected with Acropolis kore no. 675, and this may be an indication of the style of Bupalus.

Overbeck 315 ff.; A. Rumpf, *Arch. Anz.* 1936, 53; A. E. Raubit-schek, *Dedications from the Athenian Akropolis* (U.S.A. 1949), 486; G. M. A. Richter, *Archaic Greek Art* (U.S.A. 1949), 110, 138.
T. B. L. W.

**BURDIGALA,** a town in Gallia Aquitanica, modern *Bordeaux*. An important port, trading even with Britain, it had many strangers in the population. A praetor is mentioned as executive magistrate. Of remains, the amphitheatre (Palais-Gallien, perhaps as early as second century) and the important temple of Tutela (destroyed by Louis XIV) are notable. In the late Empire a reduced enceinte, *c.* 700×450 m., rectangular with bastions, was built. It was the birthplace (*c.* A.D. 320) of Ausonius, who celebrated its university. It fell under Visigothic rule from *c.* A.D. 413.

C. Jullian, *Inscriptions romaines de Bordeaux* (1887–90); Grenier, *Manuel* i. 410; R. Étienne, *Bordeaux antique* (1962). C. E. S.

**BUREBISTAS,** king of the Dacians, built up an extensive but impermanent empire in the Danubian lands (*c.* 60–44 B.C.). With the aid of a priest called Decaeneos he carried out a religious and moral reform in Dacia, pulling up all the vines (Strabo, 303 f.). In Pannonia he defeated and annihilated the Boii and other Celts; he harried the Greek cities on the coast of the Pontus; and he spread his power southwards over the Danube into Thrace. Pompey negotiated with him for assistance in 48 B.C. (cf. *SIG*[3] 762: decree in honour of the ambassador Acornion of Dionysopolis). Caesar was intending to march against him in 44. But Burebistas himself was assassinated about this time and his empire broke up into four or five separate kingdoms. R. S.

**BURGUNDIANS (BURGUNDIONES),** a Germanic people unknown to Tacitus, who appear on the upper and middle Main, though not on the Rhine, soon after A.D. 250. They had little contact with the Romans until *c.* 406, when they crossed the Rhine and established a kingdom in the province of Germania Prima with their capital at Worms. When they tried to occupy Belgica Prima they suffered an appalling defeat at the hands of Aetius and an army of Huns, losing (it is said) their king and 20,000 men. This event is commemorated in the *Nibelungenlied*. But their kingdom survived until it was overrun by the Franks in 534. They were converted to Arian Christianity (mid 5th c.) and to Catholicism in 516. E. A. T.

**BURRUS,** SEXTUS AFRANIUS (*PW* 8), equestrian procurator of Livia, Tiberius, and Claudius, came from Gallia Narbonensis (Dessau, *ILS* 1321). As Agrippina's favourite, he was appointed sole *praefectus praetorio* by Claudius in A.D. 51 and retained his post under Nero (q.v. 1). He was Nero's tutor and adviser for many years, and with Seneca was responsible for the first period of Nero's government. Unaffected in 55 by an unfounded accusation of conspiracy, he played an uncertain part in Agrippina's murder, but opposed Nero's designs against Octavia. That his death in 62 was due to poison is asserted by Suetonius and Dio, but regarded by Tacitus (*Ann.* 14. 51) as non-proven. A. M.

**BUSIRIS,** according to Greek mythology, an Egyptian king, son of Poseidon, who slaughtered on the altar of Zeus all foreigners who entered Egypt. Heracles is said to have come to Egypt and killed the wicked king with all his followers. Among classical writers, Herodotus,

Euripides, Isocrates, Diodorus, Virgil, Arrian, and others, it was a popular myth.

For vase representations of the Heracles–Busiris legend see Brommer, *Vasenlisten*[2], 19 f. For literary sources see Hiller von Gaertringen, *PW* s.v. Busiris (5), 1074 ff. T. A. B.

**BUTES,** name of several figures of Attic legend: (1) son of Teleon, an Argonaut who, charmed by the Sirens' song, plunged into the sea, but was rescued and taken to Lilybaeum by Aphrodite, by whom he became the father of Eryx. (2) Son of Poseidon Erechtheus (or of King Pandion), legendary ancestor of the family of the Eteobutadae, hereditary priests of that god in the Erechtheum. (3) Son of Boreas, driven mad by Dionysus for the rape of the nymph Coronis. R. A. B. M.

**BUTHROTUM** (now *Butrinto*, uninhabited), founded traditionally by the Trojan Helenus (q.v.) on a low hill at the seaward end of a narrow channel leading from a lake, possessed fine harbours and fisheries and was a port of call on the coasting route along Epirus. It has prehistoric remains, a fine theatre, and strong Hellenistic fortifications. The centre of a tribal union, it later became a Roman colony.

L. M. Ugolini, *Albania antica* iii (1942); Hammond, *Epirus,* see index; *Studime Historike* ii (Tiranë, 1966), 143 ff. N. G. L. H.

**BYBLOS** (modern *Gebeil*, Lebanon). A major port of Phoenicia, 26 miles north of Berytus (modern *Beirut*), which derived much of its prosperity from the export of timber. It was occupied already in the fourth millennium B.C. and had the reputation of being the oldest city in the world, according to Philo (q.v. 5) of Byblos. Egypt took an interest in Byblos from an early date and there are traces of relations with Bronze Age Crete and Greece. Excavations have yielded little of its later history, but for one of the earliest examples of alphabetic writing, the sarcophagus of King Ahiram (10th c. B.C.). It developed as a Phoenician port and capital, and was an independent kingdom with its own coinage under the Persians. It became a centre for the cult of Adonis. The Greeks took from its name their word for papyrus.

M. Dunand, *Fouilles de Byblos* (1939, 1951). J. B.

**BYSSUS** (βύσσος, prob. = Hebr. and Aram. *būṣ*) was the fibre from which a fine and often expensive material for garments, etc. (e.g. Aesch. *Sept.* 1039), was woven. It was long thought of as cotton, but analysis of Egyptian mummy wrappings (cf. Hdt. 2. 86) makes a fine linen more probable, although usage was perhaps not always consistent and the byssus grown and manufactured in Elis (Pliny *HN* 19. 20; Paus. 6. 26. 6) may have been cotton. There is no ancient evidence for the use of the silky byssus filaments produced by some molluscs (esp. pinna nobilis).

*PW* iii. 1108; Hehn–Schrader, *Kulturpflanzen und Haustiere*[2] (1911), 172, 189, 409. L. A. M.

**BYZACIUM.** The name, of uncertain Libyan or Phoenician origin, applied in Roman times to part of the province of Africa from the Gulf of Hammamet to the Gulf of Gabes, with the hinterland; it was probably the Βυσσάτις χώρα of Polybius (3. 23. 2). The chief town was Hadrumetum, which, like a number of others, was of Phoenician or Carthaginian origin. The area was extremely fertile in parts, and the olive was intensively cultivated; a procuratorial region was based on Hadrumetum. Under Diocletian it became a province with the name *Valeria Byzacena*. B. H. W.

**BYZANTIUM,** famous city on the European side of the south end of the Bosporus, bounded by the Golden Horn on the north, the Propontis on the south. The Greek city occupied only the eastern tip of the promontory, approximately the area now covered by the Old Serai. Of the various founders named in the sources the Megarians have the best claim, as cults and institutions show, but groups from the Peloponnese and central Greece probably also participated. The Eusebian foundation date is 659, but calculation from that of Chalcedon (q.v.) gives 668 (Hdt. 4. 144). No material earlier than the end of the seventh century has emerged from the (to date) slight excavations. Except during the Ionian Revolt, Byzantium was under Persian control from the time of Darius' Scythian Expedition to 478. In the Athenian Empire it paid 15 talents tribute, or more, which shows its wealth,—derived throughout the Greek period from fishing and levying tolls on passing ships. It revolted from Athens in 440–439 and in 411–408. Under Spartan control after Aegospotami (405), it joined the anti-Spartan sea league formed after the battle of Cnidos (394), which is attested by alliance coins. It came under Athenian influence again from c. 390, and it became a formal ally of Athens from c. 378

to 357 and then again when resisting Philip of Macedon in the famous siege of 340–339. Hecate traditionally helped the besieged on this occasion, and her symbol, the Crescent and Star, appeared on the coins of the city; this symbol later passed from Greece to Islam. It suffered from attacks and exactions by the Celts in the third century, and was on the winning side in Rome's Greek wars in the second century. Byzantium's strategic position helped it to enjoy a privileged status in the Roman Empire, briefly and terribly lost when it supported Pescennius Niger against Septimius Severus. Then it was besieged for over two years (summer 193 to winter 195 (?); Cassius Dio, 75. 12. 1, exaggerates in his detailed and brilliant account) and was brutally punished by loss of privileges and acts of destruction. The city was soon rebuilt and reinstated. Constantine refounded Byzantium as New Rome on 11 May 330, extending the bounds of the city and adorning it with magnificent buildings. It was known thereafter as Constantinopolis (q.v.). A. J. G

# C

**CABIRI,** non-Hellenic deities, probably Phrygian (earlier theories of Phoenician origin are not borne out by recent researches, Kern, *Rel. d. Griech.* (1926), i. 235 ff.), who promoted fertility and (at least from the fifth century) protected sailors. Their numbers varied, but one tradition gave four names, Axierus, Axiocersa, Axiocersus, Cadmilus (schol. Ap. Rhod. 1. 917). The Greeks also gave them the common title of Μεγάλοι Θεοί, and connected their worship in different places with more familiar cults, those of Demeter (material in Farnell, *Cults* iii. 367, n. 256), Hermes (ibid. v. 11 and 16), and Dionysus. With the first and last they had certainly an initial kinship, if the assumption of Phrygian origin is correct. (This would also facilitate the identification with the Corybantes and Curetes which took place in the Hellenistic period.) Their chthonian nature is confirmed by phallic rites and the presence of sacrificial pits at Samothrace (q.v.) and Thebes (Kern, loc. cit.). The historic centre of their worship was Samothrace, where mysteries were celebrated (Hdt. 2. 51; Ar. *Pax* 276), but it existed on other islands, notably Lemnos, and in Asia Minor (*see* MYSTERIES). On the mainland, the cult is found from the sixth century at Anthedon on the Boeotian coast and near Thebes. Pausanias' statement (4. 1. 7) that the Theban cult was founded from Athens was denied by Wilamowitz, but may be true. Probably under Orphic influence (W. K. C. Guthrie, *Orpheus and Gk. Rel.*[2] (1952), 123 ff.), it acknowledged an elder Cabirus and a child, and identified the former with Dionysus. The ἄνακτες παῖδες worshipped at Amphissa were thought by some to be the Cabiri (Paus. 10. 38. 7: cf. s.v. ANAKES). After Alexander the cult spread rapidly over the Greek world. At Samothrace it was patronized by the Ptolemies, and later by the Romans (*BCH* 1925, 245 ff., 258; Kern, op. cit. iii. 118; K. Lehmann-Hartleben, *AJArch.* 1939, xliv; J. H. Oliver, ibid. 464 ff.). In this period the Cabiri were often confused with the Dioscuri (q.v.), who shared their character as seamen's gods. In art we have representations of a pair of Cabiri, a younger and an older, the older, bearded figure usually reclining while the younger stands (best exemplified by the Κάβιρος and Παῖς at Thebes, but there are traces of the same pair at Samothrace), and later they became a pair of youths indistin-

guishable from the Dioscuri; so on coins, where also a hammer-wielding Cabirus appears.

See in general B. Hemberg, *Die Kabiren* (Uppsala, 1950), and for a summary of the Cabiri in art, O. Kern in *PW* x. 1477 ff.
W. K. C. G

**CACUS** and **CACA** (etymology uncertain; connexion with Caeculus founder of Praeneste, of whom a miracle involving fire is related, Servius on *Aen.* 7. 678, has often been suggested but remains unproved). The former is represented in *Aen.* 8. 190 ff. (cf. Dion. Hal. *Ant. Rom.* 1. 39. 2 ff., Prop. 4. 9) as a savage fire-breathing monster, son of Volcanus (q.v.), who lived on the Palatine (Aventine according to Virgil, but the Scalae Caci on the Palatine go far to prove him wrong: see Platner–Ashby, 465; Nash, *Pict. Dict. Rome* ii. 299). He terrified the countryside with his brigandage till he stole some of the cattle of Geryon from Heracles (q.v.), and was overcome and killed by the latter. Servius (on *Aen.* 8. 190) says that he was betrayed by his sister Caca, and by way of reward she was given a shrine 'in quo ei pervigili igne sicut Vestae sacrificabatur' (so the best MS., F; 'in quo ei per virgines Vestae sacrificabatur' the rest). This makes it tolerably plain that originally Cacus and Caca were a divine pair, the fire-god and fire-goddess of the Palatine settlement: cf. Latte, *RR* 60, who is doubtful about the deductions to be drawn from the legend.
H. J. R

**CADMUS,** in mythology, son of Agenor, king of Tyre. When his sister Europa (q.v.) disappeared, Agenor sent Cadmus with his brothers Cilix and Phoenix (the eponyms of Cilicia and Phoenicia), to seek her, with instructions not to return without her. Cadmus arrived at Delphi and was advised to settle where a cow, which he should find on leaving the temple, lay down. She led him to the site of Thebes, where he built the Cadmea, the citadel of the later town. To get water he killed a dragon, the offspring of Ares, and had to undergo a term of servitude. By advice of Athena, he sowed the dragon's teeth, and there came up a harvest of armed men, whom he killed by setting them to fight one another. Five survived and became the ancestors of the nobility of Thebes, the Spartoi (traditionally 'sown men'). He married Harmonia, daughter of Ares and Aphrodite, to whom he gave a robe and a necklace made by Hephaestus; the latter especially played a part in later events, *see* AMPHIARAUS. Their children were Ino, Semele, Autonoë, and Agave (*see* ACTAEON, ATHAMAS, DIONYSUS, PENTHEUS). Cadmus introduced writing into Greece (i.e., the 'Phoenician', or North Semitic alphabet). The discovery (1964) of a cache of inscribed Mesopotamian cylinder-seals in a Mycenaean site on the Cadmea raises the question whether there is any historic basis to the legend. In their old age he and Harmonia went away to Illyria and finally were turned into serpents. *See* ALPHABET.

A few late archaic vases show the wedding of Cadmus and Harmonia, in the chariot yoked with a lion and a boar; several fifth- and fourth-century ones show the fight with the dragon (Brommer, *Vasenlisten²* 339 f).

O. Crusius in Roscher's *Lexikon*, s.v. F. Vian, *Les Origines de Thèbes, Cadmos et les Spartes* (1963). H. J. R.; H. W. P.; C. M. R.

**CAECILIUS** (1) **STATIUS**, an Insubrian Gaul, probably from Mediolanum (*Milan*), taken prisoner (in 223 or 222 B.C.) and brought as slave to Rome (the *praenomen* Statius was common in north Italy and was regarded as a slave's name since its bearers normally came to Rome as prisoners of war); on manumission he took the name Caecilius and Statius became his *cognomen*. His *floruit* (Jerome, from Suetonius) is given as 179 B.C. and he died in 168 B.C. Best evidence for his early career is Terence *Hec.* 9–27: Ambivius (q.v.) Turpio encouraged him, produced his plays, and helped him from early failure to the position of the most highly regarded of comic poets in plots and emotional power (Varro, *Sat. Men.* 399) and in *gravitas* (Hor. *Epist.* ii. 1. 59), while Volcacius ranked him greatest of all. Some forty-two titles are known, of which sixteen seem clearly based on Menander. The most important fragments are preserved by Gellius 2. 23, three passages of his *Plocium* side by side with Menander's Greek. One passage shows a trimeter monologue turned into a polymetric *canticum*, close in style and metrical technique to Plautus. The passages are the best direct evidence for the procedure of *vortere*, the relationship of Roman plays to their Greek originals. Caecilius was the first of a distinguished series of writers from north Italy that includes Catullus and the Younger Pliny.

FRAGMENTS. E. H. Warmington, *Remains of Early Latin* i (1935), 468 ff. (with trans.), Ribbeck *CRF*. F. Leo, *Gesch. d. röm. Lit.* (1913), 217 ff. G. W. W.

**CAECILIUS** (2) of Novum Comum, one of Catullus' friends, composed a poem on Cybele (Catull. 35).

**CAECILIUS** (3) **EPIROTA**, QUINTUS, a man of letters of the Augustan age. He was the freedman of Atticus and the friend of Cornelius Gallus, after whose death (26 B.C.) he opened a school where he taught small groups of pupils. According to Suetonius (*Gram.* 16), he was the first to give public lectures on Virgil and other contemporary poets.

Schanz–Hosius, § 352. J. F. M.

**CAECILIUS** (4, *PW* 2) of Calacte in Sicily, first century B.C.; rhetorician, possibly to be identified with the Jewish *libertus* mentioned by Plutarch, *Cic.* 7. His range of interests (he wrote a history of the Sicilian slave-war as well as rhetorical works) and his literary outlook resemble those of Dionysius (q.v. 7) of Halicarnassus. His most important work, περὶ τοῦ χαρακτῆρος τῶν δέκα ῥητόρων, dealt with questions of authenticity in the orators. The titles κατὰ Φρυγῶν and τίνι διαφέρει ὁ Ἀττικὸς ζῆλος .τοῦ Ἀσιανοῦ; indicate his position as an exponent of Attic standards against 'Asianist' rhetoric (*see* RHETORIC, GREEK, § 3). He is much quoted by later writers as an authority

on figures (σχήματα); and his περὶ ὕψους gave 'Longinus' (q.v.) the incentive to attempt his own treatment of the subject.

FRAGMENTS: E. Ofenloch (1907). D. A. R.

**CAECILIUS** (5) **JUCUNDUS**, LUCIUS (1st c. A.D.), a Pompeian auctioneer, whose coarse features are known from a pair of priapic herms placed in his atrium by his freedman, Felix, which bore realistic heads of the master —wart and all! His trade was revealed by 127 waxed tablets, mostly receipts recording the proceeds of auction sales that Jucundus conducted, and dating with two exceptions from A.D. 52 to 62.

*CIL* iv. 3340. R. C. C.

**CAECINA** (1), **AULUS**, a friend of Cicero and a member of an old Etruscan family of Volaterrae (*Ceicna*; cf. the river Caecina, modern *Cecina* there). Cicero had defended his father in an inheritance case in 69 B.C. (cf. Cic. *Caecin.*). Caecina supported Pompey in 49 and wrote a pamphlet against Caesar; consequently he was exiled after Pharsalus (48); Cicero commended him to the governors of Sicily and Asia. He surrendered to Caesar in 46. Trained by his father, he was an expert in the *Etrusca disciplina*, on which he wrote; his work was used by Pliny (*HN* 2) and by Seneca (*Quaest. Nat.* 2. 3. 9). He has some repute as an orator.

Cic. *Fam.* 6. 5–9; 13. 66. H. H. S.

**CAECINA** (2, *PW* 24) **SEVERUS**, AULUS (*cos. suff.* 1. B.C.), a *novus homo* and an experienced soldier, from Volaterrae (*Not. Scav.* 1955, 145). Attested as legate of Moesia in A.D. 6, when he rescued Sirmium from the Pannonian insurgents, but had to protect his province from Dacian and Sarmatian raiders. In 7, commanding with M. Plautius Silvanus an army of five Roman legions, he won a great battle north-west of Sirmium and marched to join Tiberius at Siscia. In 14 he was legate of Germania Inferior and had trouble with a mutiny. In 15 he nearly suffered a serious disaster when crossing the 'pontes longi' on his return from the Ems to the Rhine. In 21 he proposed without success that wives should not be permitted to accompany their husbands on provincial commands. His own wife had given him six children (Tac. *Ann.* 3. 33). R. S.

**CAECINA** (3, *PW* 10) **ALIENUS**, AULUS (*cos. suff.* A.D. 69), born at Vicetia, was quaestor of Baetica in 68 and active for Galba. He is described as 'decorus iuventa, corpore ingens, animi immodicus, scito sermone' (Tac. *Hist.* 1. 53). Legate of a legion in Germania Superior, he was largely instrumental in the elevation of Vitellius, one of whose army-columns he led across the Great St. Bernard to Italy and to victory at Bedriacum. Honoured and enriched by Vitellius, and dispatched northwards to arrest the Flavian invasion, he negotiated with the enemy and was deposed from command by his own troops. Rescued after the fall of Cremona, Caecina acquired the favour of Vespasian, but conspiring, so it is alleged, with Eprius (q.v.) Marcellus in 79, he was summarily executed. R. S.

**CAELESTIS**, the epithet which the Romans applied to the Carthaginian goddess Tanit whom they often identified with Juno. That the goddess was brought to Rome in 146 B.C. by *evocatio* after the sack of Carthage is improbable, since the cult apparently did not spread outside Africa before the time of Septimius Severus (q.v.) whose coinage depicts Dea Caelestis seated on a lion. Her statue was brought to Rome by Elagabalus, and before A.D. 259 a shrine had been built on the Capitol at Rome near the temple of Juno Moneta. In Roman Carthage Juno Caelestis had an oracle and was the chief deity in the city. The epithet Caelestis was occasionally applied to Aphrodite and Diana, and also, probably under astrological influence, to the constellation Virgo.

G. Ch.-Picard, *Les Religions de l'Afrique antique* (1954), 100 ff.; Latte, *RR* 346 f.; on Virgo, see *PW* s.v. Virgo 8.                H. H. S.

**CAELIUS MONS,** the most south-easterly of the seven hills of Rome, lay south of the Esquiline: part of its northern side was apparently called Sucusa. Originally named Querquetulanus, its name Caelius was derived by antiquarians from Caelius Vibenna (q.v.). Archaeological evidence for early settlement is lacking, though it was included in the Septimontium. Crossed by the Servian Wall, it was densely populated in the Republic; after a devastating fire in A.D. 27 it was occupied by the houses and gardens of the wealthy.

The chief buildings on it were the following. The temple of Divus Claudius, begun by his widow Agrippina, mainly destroyed by Nero, and restored by Vespasian (only buttress walls and porticos survive). The Macellum Magnum, built by Nero (cf. *JRS* 1919, 179 ff.), perhaps on the site of S. Stefano Rotondo. Castra Peregrina, barracks for *peregrini* (q.v.) and *frumentarii* (*JRS* 1923, 152 ff.). In the eastern part lay the Castra Nova Equitum Singularium, barracks of the mounted bodyguard of the Emperor, built by Septimius Severus and used until Constantine disbanded the Equites Singulares in A.D. 312: they are now under St. John Lateran. The Sessorium, the residence of the Empress Helena, where Elagabalus had had a vast villa which included a small amphitheatre (Amphitheatrum Castrense), the great Circus Varianus (565 m. × 125 m.) and Thermae, which after a fire were restored by Helena, the Thermae Helenae. An atrium of the palace was made by Constantine into the Church of S. Croce in Gerusalemme. The grounds of the villa were cut by the Wall of Aurelian (270–2). For this last group of buildings, where excavation started in 1958, see Nash, *Pict. Dict. Rome*, s.vv. and plan i. 241.

A. M. Colini, *Storia e topografia del Celio* (*Mem. Pont. Acc.* 1944).                H. H. S.

**CAELIUS** (*PW* 35) **RUFUS,** MARCUS, b. 82 B.C. at Interamnia (*Teramo*), came under Cicero's tutelage in 66, but in 63 associated with Catiline (q.v.). In 59 he successfully prosecuted C. Antonius (q.v. 3) for *repetundae*; but in early 56 his prosecution of L. Bestia for *ambitus* failed, and Bestia's son L. Sempronius Atratinus charged Caelius with *vis*. According to Cicero, who with Crassus secured Caelius' acquittal, the attack was inspired by Caelius' ex-mistress Clodia (q.v.). Tribune and opponent of Pompey in 52, in Aug. 50 Caelius, now aedile, declared for Caesar; but in 48 Caesar's reluctance to cancel debts shook his enthusiasm, and as *praetor peregrinus* he opposed the official policy of Trebonius, *praetor urbanus*. The *senatus consultum ultimum* (q.v.) being passed, Caelius fled, joining Milo to start insurrection in Italy. He was captured and executed at Thurii (48).

Seventeen letters to Cicero (*Fam.* 8) show brilliant political insight, with agreeable attacks on the more pompous personalities; fourteen are written to Cicero in Cilicia on Roman affairs. His wit made him a master of invective (cf. Quintilian, 4. 2. 123). Catullus, whom Caelius supplanted as Clodia's lover, addresses him in poem 77, and surely also in 58.

Cic. *pro Caelio*, ed. R. G. Austin³ (1960); T. A. Dorey, *Greece and Rome* 1958; C. J. Fordyce, *Catullus* (1961).                G. E. F. C.

**CAENEUS** (Καινεύς), a Lapith (*see* CENTAURS), of whom three principal stories are told. (1) He was invulnerable, and therefore the Centaurs disposed of him by hammering him into the ground (Pind. fr. 150 Bowra, cf. Hyg. *Fab.* 14. 4 and Rose ad loc.). (2) He set up his spear to

be worshipped (schol. in Ap. Rhod. 1. 57, in *Il.* 1. 264) (3) He was originally a girl, Caenis, loved by Poseidon who gave her (invulnerability and) a change of sex (*Aen* 6. 448 and Servius there, and scholiasts as above). He was son of Elatus of Gyrtone (*Il.* 2. 746 and schol. 1. 264 Ap. Rhod. 1. 57).                H. J. R

**CAEPIO** (1), QUINTUS SERVILIUS (*PW* 49), praetor in 109 B.C., triumphed over Iberian rebels in 107. Made consul for 106, during a temporary reaction in favour of the Optimates due to the failure of Marius to finish the Jugurthine War, he passed a law giving senators a share (perhaps a majority) of seats on criminal juries (*see* QUAESTIONES, REPETUNDAE) and probably restricting rewards for successful prosecution. Sent to fight against the Tectosages, he took Tolosa and captured the sacred (but accursed) treasure there, said to be that taken by the Gauls from Delphi. The gold disappeared *en route*, not (it was thought) without his knowledge. In 105 his refusal to co-operate with the *novus homo* Cn. Mallius Maximus, his successor, against the Cimbri led to the disaster of Arausio and indirectly to Marius' series of consulships. Caepio had his *imperium* abrogated and on his return faced several trials on various charges; he was finally convicted by Norbanus (q.v. 1) in 103 and ended his days in exile at Smyrna.                E. B.

**CAEPIO** (2), QUINTUS SERVILIUS (*PW* 50), son of (1), brother-in-law and friend of Drusus (q.v. 2), unsuccessfully opposed Saturninus (q.v. 1) as quaestor in 100 B.C., but (with a L. Piso) coined money needed for the execution of his corn law (see Sydenham, *CRR*, no. 603: probably misdated). In 95 he was accused of *maiestas* in one of a series of political trials (*see* NORBANUS 1), was defended (half-heartedly) by L. Crassus (q.v. 3) and acquitted. Quarrelling with Drusus, originally for private reasons, he drew closer to his enemies and in 92 attacked (and was attacked by) Scaurus (q.v. 1), who had helped to defend his father, in a duel of inconclusive prosecutions. In 91 he was a leading opponent of Drusus. He was killed by Poppaedius (q.v.) in the Social War (90).

Badian, *Stud. Gr. Rom. Hist.* 34 ff.; E. S. Gruen, *JRS* 1965, 59 ff.                E. B.

**CAEPIO** (3), FANNIUS (*PW* 16), headed a conspiracy against Augustus, probably in 23 B.C. (*see* VARRO (4) MURENA). When prosecuted by Tiberius before the *quaestio maiestatis* he attempted to escape but was betrayed and executed.

**CAERE** (Etr. χaire; modern *Cerveteri* = *Caere vetus*), 30 miles north of Rome on the Tyrrhenian coast, was one of the wealthiest of the twelve cities of Etruria. The earliest finds date from Villanovan times, and its most brilliant period fell between the seventh and fifth centuries, during which its close contact with the East Mediterranean (via, for example, its port of Pyrgi, q.v.) is attested *inter alia* by a considerable quantity of imported Greek pottery and by the 'Caeretan hydriae', presumably the work of an *émigré* East Greek craftsman active from *c.* 530 to shortly after 510 B.C. Excavation has been mainly confined to tombs, which from the seventh century onwards take the form of elaborate chambered *tumuli*, laid out in streets. One of the most important is the Regolini-Galassi tomb: together with the contemporary tombs at Praeneste and Vetulonia (qq.v.) it affords our best evidence for the artistic repertoire of the Orientalizing period in Etruria. For its relations with Rome, *see* CAERITES.

L. Pareti, *La Tomba Regolini-Galassi* (1947); B. Pace et alii, *Mon. Ant.* 1955; J. M. Hemelrijk, *De Caeretaanse Hydriae* (Rotterdam, 1956); M. Pallottino, *La necropoli di Caere*⁵ (1960); Scullard, *Etr. Cities*, 97 ff.; M. Cristofani, *La tomba delle iscrizioni a Cerveteri* (1965); F. Roncalli, *Le lastre dipinte da Cerveteri* (1965).                D. W. R. R.

**CAERITES.** The ancient accounts of the so-called Caerite franchise are contradictory. They confuse together the earliest and the final stages of development of *civitas sine suffragio*. Caere received this status (*see* MUNICIPIUM) either as a reward for protecting the Vestal Virgins during the Gallic invasion of 390 B.C. (Gellius' and Strabo's view), or as a punishment for an otherwise unspecified revolt during the third century, which was possibly Livy's view. The latter is more probable, because the connexion with the Gallic invasion is unknown to Livy, and the common belief that the status of Caere was *ignominiosum* fits only the later date. The notion that Caere was the first *municipium* is a deduction from the improbable connexion of its franchise with the events of 390 B.C.

A. N. Sherwin-White, *The Roman Citizenship* (1939), 50 ff.; M. Sordi, *I rapporti Romano-ceriti* (1960). A. N. S.-W.

**CAESAR** (1), GAIUS JULIUS (*PW* 131), b. 100 B.C., son of C. Caesar (who died *c.* 85 without becoming consul) and Aurelia of the Cottae. His father's sister had married Marius; he himself in 84 married Cornelia daughter of Cinna (q.v. 1). Whether his early career shows political consistency is uncertain. Service in Asia (81); unsuccessful prosecution of Dolabella (*cos.* 81) and C. Antonius (q.v. 3) in 77, followed by retirement for study in Rhodes; service against the pirates (75–74); return to Rome when elected *pontifex* (73); support of Pompey (q.v.) in restoring tribunician rights (71–70); intrigue with the Transpadani in the year after his quaestorship (69); and at least one speech in favour of Pompey's commands (67–66). His 'Marianism' at least was sustained. He had supported the Lex Plotia (? 70) recalling the partisans of Lepidus (q.v. 2); and even after Cornelia's death in 68 and his remarriage to Sulla's grand-daughter Pompeia, he restored Marius' trophies during his aedileship in 65.

**2.** As aedile Caesar spent heavily, probably financed by Crassus (q.v. 4), whom he supported in designs on Egypt; Suetonius also implicates him in the alleged plot to murder the consuls (*see* CATILINE). In 63 he engineered the trial of Rabirius (q.v. 1), a demonstration against misuse of the *senatus consultum ultimum*; and he may have backed the bill of Rullus (q.v.). But his great achievement in 63 was to be elected *pontifex maximus*, defeating Catulus (q.v. 3) and other consulars. When he was accused of complicity with Catiline, Cicero abruptly dismissed the charge, and treated Caesar with great deference (e.g. *Cat.* iv. 9) when he opposed execution of the Catilinarians. His praetorship in 62 was suspended after he had supported Pompey's man Metellus (q.v. 10) Nepos; but he was quickly reinstated, and obtained Further Spain as his province, though his creditors apparently prevented his departure till June 61; meanwhile as witness at the Bona Dea trial in May he refused to depose against Clodius (q.v. 1), though he had divorced Pompeia because 'his family must be above suspicion'. In Spain he made a grandiose expedition through Lusitania to Callaecia, and on his return, greatly enriched, he claimed a triumph. This he had to forgo because the Senate refused him permission to stand for the consulate outside Rome, but forming a close compact with Pompey and Crassus (called in modern times 'the First Triumvirate') he secured election for 59.

**3.** Though showing respect to the Senate at the outset, Caesar ruthlessly overrode opposition and disregarded the vetoes of his colleague Bibulus (q.v. 1). Land for Pompey's veterans was quickly provided by a *Lex agraria*, extended by a hotly contested *Lex Campana* in June; and Pompey's eastern *acta* were confirmed. The *publicani* secured rebate on the Asiatic tax contracts of 61; Caesar also colonized Novum Comum, passed an important *Lex de repetundis*, compelled publication of the Senate's transactions, and (as *pontifex maximus*) transferred Clodius to the plebeians. Meanwhile a *Lex Vatinia* (? May) revoked the grant to Caesar of an insignificant province, and conferred on him Cisalpine Gaul and Illyricum for five years, legalizing his immediate possession of an army. The Senate added Transalpine Gaul, and Caesar left early in 58, to be engaged for the next nine years on the Gallic Wars (q.v.). In the early years there is no evidence of any discord with Pompey, now his son-in-law (*see* JULIA 1); but by Apr. 56 the attacks of Domitius (q.v. 4) looked dangerous, and Caesar met Pompey and Crassus at Luca. Pompey and Crassus became consuls for 55, and renewed Caesar's command for five years more, themselves receiving equivalent terms of *imperium* under a *Lex Trebonia*. Caesar was temporarily safe; thereafter he received from the Senate *supplicationes* of unprecedented length for his Gallic successes, and bribed nobles in Rome, and cities and kings abroad, to foster his designs. But in 54 Julia died, and in 53 Crassus was killed. Caesar approved of Pompey's measures in 52 (*BGall.* 7. 6), and gained on balance from Pompey's *Lex de Iure Magistratuum*, for his tribunes could now veto attempts to recall him before he could stand for the consulate, which a law of this year enabled him to do *in absentia*. Yet the crux was whether Pompey, who now had a fresh *imperium*, would support these attempts at recall. Although he opposed in 51 the motion of M. Marcellus (q.v. 4), after much hesitation he threw in his lot with Caesar's opponents. The final compromise of Caesar's tribune Curio (q.v. 2) failed, and on 1 Jan. 49 (pre-Julian) the Senate voted that Caesar lay down his command. On 10 Jan. Caesar crossed the Rubicon.

**4.** Caesar rapidly overran Italy, capturing Domitius (q.v. 4) at Corfinium on his way, but he failed to prevent Pompey's crossing to Greece. He therefore turned to Spain, where he forced Pompey's lieutenants Afranius and Petreius to surrender after some brilliant manœuvring near the town of Ilerda (2 Aug.). On his way home he received the capitulation of Massilia. In 48 he effected a crossing to Epirus, Antony later bringing the bulk of his army. Shortage of troops frustrated his blockade of Pompey at Dyrrhachium, and a sortie by Pompey inflicted considerable loss. But reinforced by Domitius Calvinus in Thessaly, Caesar fought a set battle against Pompey's force (still far superior numerically) at Pharsalus, where the courage of his veterans in withstanding cavalry brought complete victory (9 Aug. 48). He pursued Pompey to Egypt, and was involved through the winter in a difficult war against Ptolemy XIII and the Alexandrians, which ended in the establishment of Cleopatra, now his mistress, as queen. He proceeded to Asia Minor and defeated Pharnaces (q.v. 2) of Bosporus at Zela, the battle which occasioned his famous boast, 'Veni, vidi, vici'. He returned to Rome, but in Dec. 47 landed in Africa, where after four months he overcame the Pompeian forces under Scipio at Thapsus. The wars seemed over, and he celebrated four triumphs, Gallic, Alexandrian, Pontic, and African; but in 45 he was called to Spain to fight Pompey's sons and Labienus, and his victory at Munda—17 Mar., now Julian—was his hardest battle.

**5.** On his return from Ilerda Caesar was made dictator to hold elections, in Oct. 48 he was again appointed, in 46 he became dictator for ten years, and in 44 for life. He secured his consulate for 48, in 46 and 45 held nine months' consulates (the last without a colleague), and in 44 was consul again. In 44 he received tribunician *sacrosanctitas*, in 46 a *praefectura morum*. Other powers and honours, including a full *tribunicia potestas*, he refused, but received extraordinary emblems of royalty, statues, a purple robe, a temple to his Clementia, and a *flamen* (M. Antonius); and his head appeared on coins of 45–44. But full deification was given only after his death. The reforms of his period of power were necessarily sporadic and incomplete: he reduced the number of recipients of corn dole and abolished *collegia* (q.v.), but settled veterans in Italy and outside, founding numerous colonies, many for commercial reasons, especially Corinth and Carthage; he curtailed indiscriminate emigration and ordained that at least one-third of Italian herdsmen be freemen; he carried out public works in Italy, prepared standard regulations for Italian municipal constitutions, carried sumptuary laws, introduced the Julian calendar (beginning 1 Jan. 45 = 709 A.U.C. *see* CALENDARS, § 7), and abolished tax farming in Asia and perhaps in other provinces. His revision of debts was moderate, and offended extremists like Caelius (q.v.). He was lavish in granting citizenship (Cisalpine Gaul received it from a *Lex Roscia* in 49), and went outside Italy in recruiting the Senate, which he enlarged to 900. At the time of his death he was preparing wars against Parthia and Dacia. His famous 'clemency', which reached its climax with the recall of M. Marcellus (q.v. 4), attempted to conciliate the aristocracy. But his powers and honours, and especially perhaps his control of offices, even though he refused the title *Rex* in 44, were intolerable even to men who had been of his party, and on the Ides of Mar. 44 he fell to a conspiracy led by M. Brutus and C. Cassius, and died at the foot of Pompey's statue. By will dated 13 Sept. 45 he had 'adopted' his great-nephew C. Octavius (*see* AUGUSTUS, § 1), in the event that he had no son of his body; and to every citizen he left 300 sesterces, repeating a previous gift. His largesse to his soldiers had also been considerable, though their loyalty to him, the chief factor in his power, was in the main spontaneous. In 59 he had married Calpurnia (q.v. 1) as his third wife; among his numerous mistresses the most famous after Cleopatra was Servilia, half-sister of Cato and mother of Brutus.

**6.** WRITINGS: seven books *De Bello Gallico*, each covering a year from 58 to 52 (completed to 50 by Hirtius, q.v.) and three *De Bello Civili*. Both works show Caesar as the simple, efficient patriot, fighting necessary wars; but the propaganda (cf. *BCiv.* 1. 1–11; 3. 31–3, 82–3) never breaks unduly the masterly descriptions of warfare, studied in all later ages. The Commentaries were a new literary genre; their style (cf. Cicero, *Brutus*, 262; Hirtius' preface to book 8) is lucid and compressed, entirely free from rhetoric, and the diction is simple but brilliantly chosen. As the author of a (lost) work on 'Analogy' (q.v.) Caesar eschewed the 'inauditum atque insolens verbum' (Gellius, i. 10. 4), and he wrote a verse epigram to Terence, the 'puri sermonis amator' (*FPL* 91). As an orator he was second only to Cicero, but his (lost) *Anticato* in reply to Cicero (see CATO 5) was not a success.

**7.** Caesar's style mirrors the clear vision which was his outstanding quality. His generalship, unsurpassed in antiquity, rested chiefly on his sense of the moment to strike. As a statesman he had abandoned the palliatives of earlier reformers, and the urban populace was no longer first in his mind: the inchoate programme of his dictatorship finds coherence in the promotion of good government, economic development, and greater social equality in Italy and in the empire as a whole. Yet his radicalism, however far-seeing, went too far for the Italy of his day; and though the stories of trousered Gauls in the Senate or of an intended transference of the capital to the East are fabrications, they may point the direction in which Caesar was moving. But he legislated almost in spite of himself. The man who by 46 could say 'satis diu uel naturae uixi uel gloriae' (Cic. *Pro Marcello* 25) was ambitious for personal position rather than reform, and the Civil War (see Caes. *BCiv.* 1. 9. 2) was fought to save his *dignitas*. He was not, like Augustus, economical in the powers he held, nor did he understand the indirect exercise of *auctoritas*; again, the exaggerations of our sources about his honours, royal and divine, reveal something which even contemporaries thought about him. But his impatience was characteristic of his zest for life; his continued accessibility moved the reluctant Cicero; and his culture is another proof of his astonishing versatility which makes him one of the most impressive characters of antiquity.

ANCIENT SOURCES. After Caesar's own writings (above), with the *Bella* (*Alexandrinum*, *Africum*, *Hispaniense*, qq.v.) and the many references in Cicero (q.v. 1), the most important contemporary author is Sallust (q.v.): see R. Syme, *Sallust* (1964) against the view that the *Bellum Catilinae* was written to exculpate Caesar from revolutionary aims, and against the authenticity of the *Epistulae ad Caesarem senem*. Among later writers (*see* APPIAN, DIO (2) CASSIUS, LIVY, LUCAN, PLUTARCH, SUETONIUS (2), VELLEIUS) Suetonius, though his collation of contemporary material is sometimes perverse, provides invaluable evidence about Caesar's personality; but in Caesar's earlier career it is often difficult to evaluate the significance of incidents which less successful politicians of his generation would not have been recorded. For documentary (including numismatic) evidence see the particularly full entries in Broughton, *MRR*, especially on the years 49–44; note also Bruns, *Font.* 15–18, 28.

MODERN LITERATURE. (*a*) General: Mommsen, *History of Rome* iv–v, Engl. Transl. W. P. Dickson (1895); E. Meyer, *Caesars Monarchie und das Principat des Pompejus*³ (1922); T. Rice Holmes, *The Roman Republic* (1923); J. Carcopino, *César* (*Histoire générale*, ed. G. Glotz, *Histoire romaine* ii (1936)—for strong contrast see F. E. Adcock in *CAH* ix. 691 ff.); M. Gelzer, *Caesar der Politiker und Staatsman*⁶ (1960, E.T. 1968)—see discussion by R. Syme, *JRS* 1944, 92 ff.; J. P. V. D. Balsdon, *Julius Caesar* (1967). (*b*) Year of birth: for 100 B.C. (Mommsen supported 102, Carcopino 101) E. Badian, *JRS* 1959, 81 ff. seems decisive. (*c*) Early life: H. Strasburger, *Caesars Eintritt in die Geschichte* (1938); L. R. Taylor, *CP* 1941, 113 ff. (*d*) The year 59: F. B. Marsh, *History of the R. World 146–3 B.C.* (1935) 387 ff.; L. R. Taylor, *AJPhil.* 1951, 254 ff. (*e*) The legal issues preceding the Civil War ('Die Rechtsfrage', Mommsen, *Ges. Schr.* iv. 92): J. P. V. D. Balsdon, *JRS* 1939, 57 ff., 167 ff.; G. R. Elton, *JRS* 1946, 18 ff.; P. J. Cuff, *Hist.* 1958, 445 ff. (*f*) The dictatorship years: Syme, *Rom. Rev.* (1939), chs. iv–vi; J. H. Collins, *Hist.* 1955, 445 ff. (*g*) The conspiracy: A. Momigliano, *JRS* 1941, 149 ff. J. P. V. D. Balsdon, *Hist.* 1958, 80 ff.; V. Ehrenberg, *Harv. Stud.* 1964, 149 ff. (*h*) Writings: K. Barwick, 'Caesars Commentarii und das Corpus Caesarianum', *Philol.* Suppl. xxxi (1938); id., *Caesars Bellum Civile: Tendenz, Abfassungzeit und Stil* (1951); M. Rambaud, *L'Art de la déformation historique dans les commentaires de César* (1953); F. E. Adcock, *Caesar as Man of Letters* (1956). (*j*) See various papers published for the 2,000th anniversary of the Ides of March in *Greece and Rome* 1957 and *Cesare nel Bimillenario della Morte* (Edizioni Radio Italiana, 1956). For a survey of literature since 1935 see H. Collins, *Classical World* Dec. 1963. G. E. F. C

**CAESAR** (2) LUCIUS JULIUS (*PW* 142), brother of (3) and of Catulus (q.v. 2), was governor of Macedonia c. 94 B.C. Consul in 90, he commanded on the southern front in the Social War, winning a battle against Papius (q.v.) after several disastrous defeats. He passed the basic law offering the citizenship to the Italian allies (see Cic. *Balb.* 21) and, as censor in 89 with P. Crassus (q.v. 2) helped to enrol the first of them. With his brother (3) he opposed Marius, whom he had previously supported, and was killed in 87 after Marius' return. His daughter married Antonius (q.v. 2) and became the mother of Antonius (q.v. 4).

E. B.

**CAESAR** (3) STRABO (VOPISCUS), GAIUS JULIUS (*PW* 135), brother of (2) and of Catulus (q.v. 2), a distinguished orator and wit, is the chief speaker on wit and humour in Cicero's *De oratore*. He supported Marius and was land commissioner under a law of Saturninus (q.v. 1 and aedile (90 B.C.). Though he had not been praetor he tried to gain the consulship of 88, clashing violently with Marius and Sulpicius (q.v. 1), whom he thus brought together. He was killed after Marius' return in 87.

E. Bickel, *Rh. Mus.* 1957, 1 ff.; cf. Malcovati, *ORF*³ 272, no. 73.
E. B.

**CAESAR** (4), LUCIUS JULIUS (*PW* 143), was the son of (2), and father of (6); uncle of Antony. Quaestor in Asia in 77 B.C., he was consul in 64. In 63 he and Caesar were appointed to the antiquated office of *duumviri perduellionis* for the trial of Rabirius (q.v. 1). He was legate of Caesar in Gaul (52–49) but took no part in the Civil War; in 47 as *praefectus urbi* (q.v.) he was unable to check the disturbances caused by Dolabella (q.v. 3).

After Caesar's death he opposed Antony and was proscribed, but was saved by the intercession of his sister Iulia, Antony's mother. He wrote *Libri Auspiciorum* or *Augurales*.

Syme, *Rom. Rev.*, see index; Schanz–Hosius i. 600.    T. J. C.

**CAESAR** (5), SEXTUS JULIUS (*PW* 153), from the dictator's branch of the family, took his side in the Civil War. He served under him in Spain in 49 B.C., was quaestor in 48, and governor of Syria, probably 'pro quaestore pro praetore', from 47 to 46, when he was murdered by some of his own troops at the instigation of Caecilius Bassus (q.v. 1).    T. J. C.

**CAESAR** (6), LUCIUS JULIUS (*PW* 144), grandson of (2), played an important part in negotiations between Caesar and Pompey (49 B.C.). After failing to prevent the crossing of Curio (q.v. 2) to Africa, he joined the Pompeian forces there, was pardoned after the death of Cato (q.v. 5), but was mysteriously killed soon after.    E. B.

**CAESAR** (7), GAIUS (*PW*, Julius 134), eldest son of Agrippa and Julia, was born in 20 B.C. and adopted by Augustus in 17. Augustus evidently hoped that he or his brother Lucius would succeed him, and the favour he showed them probably caused Tiberius' retirement in 6. In 5, when he assumed the *toga virilis*, he was designated consul for A.D. 1, admitted to the Senate, and saluted by the *equites* as *princeps iuventutis*. From now on he was virtually heir apparent. In 1 B.C. he married Livilla (q.v.) and was sent with proconsular authority to the East. In A.D. 2 he had a conference with the Parthian king on the Euphrates and appointed a Roman nominee king of Armenia. This led to a revolt, which Gaius proceeded to suppress. Seriously wounded at the siege of Artagira, he died eighteen months later in Lycia on his way back to Italy (21 Feb. A.D. 4), greatly to Augustus' sorrow and dismay. He and Lucius were honoured in the following year by the naming after them of ten electoral centuries (*see* TABULA HEBANA).

Syme, *Rom. Rev.*, see index; M. L. Paladini, *Nuova Rivista storica* 1957, 1 ff.; P. Sattler, *Studien aus dem Gebiet der alten Gesch.* (1962), 1 ff. Iconography: L. Curtius, *MDAI* 1948, 53 ff.; F. Chamoux, *BCH* 1950, 250 ff., *Rev. Arch.* xxxvii, 1951, 218 ff.; *Bull. Soc. Nat. Ant. France* 1963, 205 f.; L. Fabbrini, *Rend. Linc.* 1955, 469 ff.
G. W. R.; T. J. C.

**CAESAR** (8), LUCIUS (*PW*, Julius 145), second son of Agrippa and Julia, was born in 17 B.C. and at once adopted by Augustus with his elder brother Gaius. In 2 B.C., when he assumed the *toga virilis*, he received the honours previously conferred on Gaius. He died at Massilia, on his way to Spain, on 20 Aug. A.D. 2.

Syme, *Rom. Rev.*, see index. Iconography: see no. 7.    G. W. R.

**CAESARAUGUSTA** (modern *Zaragoza*), in northeasterly central Spain. On the site of the Iberian Salduba Augustus built a colony which Strabo compares with Emerita (q.v.) for its civilizing effect on outlandish parts. Workmen imported from Italy took part in building its walls, which had a perimeter of about 2,900 metres. Literary and monumental records are scanty.

I. A. Richmond, *JRS* 1931, 86 ff.    M. I. H.

**CAESAREA** (1) **OF CAPPADOCIA** (formerly Mazaca), was created by the Cappadocian kings to be their capital. Ariarathes V gave it a Greek constitution (the laws of Charondas, q.v.) under the name of *Eusebeia under Argaeus*, which was changed to *Caesarea* by Archelaus in 12–9 B.C. From A.D. 17 it was the capital of the province of Cappadocia and an imperial mint. The name survives as *Kayseri*, but virtually nothing remains of the ancient city.    A. H. M. J.; G. E. B.

**CAESAREA** (2) **PALAESTINAE** occupied the site of the coastal city of Strato's Tower, so named presumably after one of the fourth-century kings of Sidon. It was captured by the Hasmonaean king Alexander Jannaeus soon after his accession (103 B.C.), removed from Jewish control by Pompey in 63 and attached to Syria, and restored to Herod the Great (q.v.) by Octavian in 30. Between 22 and 10 B.C. (or 12 B.C.; see *JTS* 1935, 22 ff.) Herod rebuilt the city on a lavish scale, renaming it Caesarea and providing it with a huge artificial harbour, *portus Augusti*. It rapidly developed into an important commercial centre, with a purple-dyeing industry. Herod intended it as a Greco-Syrian city, but many Jews also settled there, and tension over the claim of this large minority to citizenship led to riots (c. A.D. 60); the matter was referred to Nero, who decided against the Jews. Further disturbances (66), culminating in a massacre of the Jews, sparked off the revolt against Rome. Vespasian made Caesarea a colony with immunity from *tributum* (q.v.) *capitis*; Titus added immunity from *tributum soli*. It was the administrative capital of the province of Judaea under both the procurators (A.D. 6–66) and the legates (from 70).

L. Haefeli, *Cäsarea am Meer* (1923); M. Weippert, *Zeitschr. des Deut. Palestina Vereins* 1963, 172; G. Dell'Amore (ed.), *Caesarea* (1965); L. Kadman. *Corpus Nummorum Palaestinensium* ii (1956).
E. M. S.

**CAESAREA** (3) (modern *Cherchel*), a seaport in Mauretania. The old Carthaginian trading-station of *Iol* became Caesarea when Juba II (q.v.) and Cleopatra Selene made it the capital of their Mauretanian kingdom and a centre of Greek art. Under Claudius it received a colony of veterans and became the residence of the procurator of Mauretania Caesariensis. With a population of 100,000 Caesarea became the third most important African port; it traded with the Mediterranean and Atlantic, and was a naval base. Its best-known citizen was Macrinus (q.v.). Sacked by Moors and Vandals, it was refortified by Belisarius.

P. M. Duval, *Cherchel et Tipasa* (1946); S. Gsell, *Cherchel, antique Iol*[2] (1952, revised by M. Leglay). Excavation reports in *Libyca*, 1953 and subsequent years.    W. N. W.

**CAESARION** was the nickname conferred by the Alexandrians on Ptolemy XV Caesar (*PW*, Ptolemaios 37), eldest son of Cleopatra VII (q.v.). He was born in 47, probably on 23 June (Julian calendar), and Cleopatra claimed that Caesar (who had been with her in Alexandria from the preceding summer) was the father. In 44 he was associated with his mother as joint-king; in 34, at the 'Donations', he was named 'King of Kings'. A king claiming Caesar as his father might well seem a rival to Octavian, Caesar's adopted son and heir; and it was probably at his instigation that Oppius (q.v. 2) wrote his pamphlet denying the claim. Antony declared that Caesar had himself acknowledged the boy as his son. In 30 Cleopatra declared him to be of age, to stimulate the loyalty of the Alexandrians, then sent him away for safety, but he was tricked into returning and executed on Octavian's order. Caesar's paternity is still disputed.

H. Volkmann, *Cleopatra* (1958); J. P. V. D. Balsdon, *CR* 1960, 68 ff.; H. Heinen. *Hist.* 1969, 181 ff.    T. J. C.

**CAESELLIUS VINDEX,** LUCIUS (early 2nd c. A.D.), wrote a miscellany (now lost) entitled *Stromateus* or *Lectiones antiquae* (Aul. Gell. 6, 2. 1).

Schanz–Hosius, § 593.

**CAKES.** The ancients, especially the Greeks, had an enormous variety of cakes and bread (lists in Pollux 6. 72 ff., Athenaeus 643 e ff., cf. the lexicographers under the names of the different kinds). Of these, many were used in sacrifices (material collected in Lobeck, *Aglaophamus*, 1060 ff.; see also Eitrem, *Opferritus*, index under 'Kuchen'). Examples are the ἀμφιφῶν, stuck with lights and sacrificed to Artemis Munichia (Ath. 645 a); the βασυνίας, of wheat-flour and honey, sacrificed to Iris (ibid. 645 b); many kinds were in shapes of animals, etc. (ibid. 646 e, 647 a; schol. Thuc. 1. 126. 6, and often). Cakes are the poor man's offering (Porphyry, *Abst.* 2. 16), and often prelude a greater sacrifice (as Ar. *Plut.* 660 and schol.). The usual Latin name for a sacrificial cake is *libum* (as Ov. *Fasti* 1. 127–8). H. J. R.

**CALABRIA,** in antiquity the flat and arid but fertile south-eastern promontory or 'heel' of Italy, inhabited by Messapii (q.v.). Its prehistoric monuments resemble those of Sardinia. The Lombards seized Calabria *c.* A.D. 700, whereupon the Byzantines transferred its name to the south-western promontory or 'toe' of Italy—the Calabria of today.

O. Haas, *Messapische Studien* (1962). E. T. S.

**CALAIS** and **ZETES,** in mythology, sons of Boreas (q.v.), hence often called together the Boreadae. They took part in the expedition of the Argonauts (q.v.), and, being winged, freed Phineus from the Harpies (q.v.). They persuaded the others to leave Heracles behind at Cios (*see* HYLAS), for which he afterwards killed them, setting over their grave two stones, of which one moves when the north wind blows (Ap. Rhod. 1. 211, 1298; 2. 240 ff.).

Winged men common on vases from before the middle of the seventh century in no narrative context may sometimes be meant for Boreads. The type is used from the sixth for Calais and Zetes chasing the Harpies from Phineus' feast (Brommer, *Vasenlisten*[2], 351).

H. J. R.; C. M. R.

**CALAMIS,** Greek sculptor, active during the first half of the fifth century B.C. Perhaps from Boeotia. He worked in marble, bronze, and gold and ivory. His style was distinguished for its grace and refinement, and he was famous for his statues of horses. Pausanias (9. 16. 1) states that he made a statue of Zeus Ammon for Pindar, and a Hermes Criophorus for Tanagra (9. 22. 1); the latter is reproduced on Roman coins of that city. His most ambitious work was a colossal bronze statue of Apollo, 30 cubits high, which he made for Apollonia Pontica (Pliny 34. 39; Strabo 7. 319). It is perhaps reproduced on silver coins of that city. The Sosandra, praised by Lucian (*Eikones* 6) for the simple and orderly arrangement of its drapery, may have been the original of the so-called Aspasia, preserved in a number of Roman copies. His Apollo Alexikakos, which stood in the Ceramicus of Athens (Paus. i. 3. 4), has been thought to be reproduced in the Apollo of the Omphalos.

It is possible that this Calamis is identical with the artist by that name mentioned as a caelator, 'a chaser of silver cups' (Pliny 33. 156); but the Calamis, teacher of Praxias, belongs to the fourth century B.C. G. M. A. R.

**CALCHAS,** in mythology, son of Thestor; a diviner who accompanied the Greek army to Troy (*Il.* 1. 69 ff.). He reveals the reason for the plague on the camp (ibid.) and foretells the length of the war (2. 300 ff.). After Homer he is introduced into several episodes, as the sacrifice of Iphigenia (q.v.; Aesch. *Ag.* 201 ff., from the *Cypria* directly or otherwise); the building of the Wooden Horse (Verg. *Aen.* 2. 185, cf. Quint. Smyrn. 12. 3 ff.), and generally the actions fated to capture Troy. After the war he went to Claros, and there met Mopsus (q.v.). It had been foretold that Calchas would die when he met a better diviner than himself; Mopsus answered a question which he could not answer (the number of figs on a tree), and Calchas died of mortification (Strabo 14. 1. 27).

Another story of his death is that he died laughing at prophecy that he would not live to drink the wine of his vineyard (Servius on Verg. *Ecl.* 6. 72); cf. ANCAEUS. A oracle in Apulia was identified with his name (Strab 6. 3. 9). He is depicted on an Etruscan mirror from Vulci see, e.g. O. W. von Vacano, *The Etruscans* (1960), pl.

H. J. R.; H. W. I

**CALEDONIA,** the name used by Tacitus and Di Cassius for the Scottish Highlands, beyond the *ciuitate trans Bodotriam sitas* (*Agr.* 25). Others use the adjective sometimes of inland Britain (Florus 1. 45. 18; Stat. *Silv* 5. 2. 142), mostly of north Britain, referring to its sea (Lucan 6. 37), its north cape and monument with Gree letters (Solinus 22; Mommsen, *Addit.* 234), its frost (Claudian *IV Cons. Hon.* 26), fauna (id. *I Cons. Stil.* 2 247), pearls (Auson. *Mos.* 68), and people (Mart. 10. 44. 1 Claudian, *Laus Serenae* 45; Sid. Apoll. *Carm.* 7. 89). I wooded hills (*saltus*) were early famous (Florus 1. 17. 3 1. 45. 18; Pliny *HN* 4. 102) but vaguely located (op. cit. until Ptolemy (*Geog.* 2. 3. 8) placed δρυμὸς Καληδόνιο south-west of Beauly Firth. The name survives (Watson *Celtic Place-names of Scotland* (1926), 21) in Dunkeld Rohallion, and Schiehallion. It occurs as a personal (*Eph Epigr.* vi. 1077) and tribal (*ILS* 4576) name.

Agricola (q.v. 1) defeated the *Caledonii* without con quering them. In A.D. 197 they broke a treaty with Rom (Dio Cass. 75. 5), were reduced by Severus in 209, bu broke faith again in 210–11 (id. 76. 15). Dio (76. 12 divides non-Roman Britain into *Caledonii* and *Maeatae* Ammianus (27. 8. 5) distinguishes *Dicalydones* (cf. Ptol *Geog.* 2. 3. 1, ὠκεανὸς Δουηκαληδόνιος) and *Verturiones*, th latter of Fortrenn (Watson, op. cit. 68 f.). I. A. R

**CALENDARS.** Almost every ancient community had calendar of its own, differing from others in names o months and date of New Year. All were, at least originally lunar (*see* TIME-RECKONING). The months were either simply numbered (Protos was the first month in Phocis September the original seventh month in Rome) o named after festivals held or deities specially worshippe in them (Dios and Apellaios, the first two Macedonian months, from Zeus and Apollo; Anthesterion at Athens from the Anthesteria; Martius in Rome and several othe Italian communities, from Mars). Some of the Gree month-names are found in Linear B; both they and the Italian names are usually adjectival, the word for 'month being expressed or understood.

**2.** Of Greek calendars, the least imperfectly known is the Athenian. The names of the months were Hekatombaion Metageitnion, Boedromion, Pyanopsion, Maimakter ion, Poseideon, Gamelion, Anthesterion, Elaphebolion Mounichion, Thargelion, and Skirophorion. All are named after festivals, some very obscure to us and prob ably to fifth- and fourth-century Athenians, which occu in them. Each month was in length 29 or 30 days; a leap year, 384 ± 1, an ordinary year, 354 ± 1 days. A leap-yea was obtained by inserting a second (δεύτερος) or late (ὕστερος) month; of nine attested examples of the terms five are applied to a second Poseideon, four to a miscel lany of months.

**3.** The first day of the Athenian month was the 'new moon' (νουμηνία), determined presumably by observation of the first visibility of the new moon after conjunction The next nine days were the 'rising' month, μὴν ἱστάμενος and numbered forward, as with us: Βοηδρομιῶνος πέμπτη ἱσταμένου for Boedromion 5. The eleventh and twelfth were simply ἑνδεκάτη and δωδεκάτη. The thirteenth to the nineteenth were numbered forward in the style Βοηδρομιῶνος τρίτη ἐπὶ δέκα, Boedromion 13. The twentieth was called δεκάτη προτέρα and the twenty-first δεκάτη ὑστέρα. The next eight days, the 'waning' (φθίνων, month, were numbered backward in the style Βοηδρομιῶ-ος ἐνάτῃ φθίνοντος, Boedromion 22. In the late fourth century B.C. the phrase μετ᾽ εἰκάδας replaced φθίνοντος. The last day of the month was commonly called through-out the Greek world τριακάς, or thirtieth, but at Athens νη καὶ νέα, 'old and new'. The omitted day in a hollow month was the twenty-ninth, προτριακάς (IG 12. 1. 4), or Athens) δευτέρα φθίνοντος (Proclus' scholium on Hesiod's Works and Days 765). An examination of the attested distribution of leap-years at Athens fails to reveal any purposely devised scheme, as was the case, for example, in Babylon, where the so-called Metonic cycle was current. In Italy, at all events in Rome, days were num-bered backwards from the three fixed points, the kalendae (new moon), idus (full moon), and nonae (the ninth day, counting inclusively, before the Ides). Thus ante diem octavum kalendas Apriles is 25 Mar.; pridie nonas Iunias is 4 June.

4. The Athenians designated dates in their lunar calendar as κατὰ θεόν ('according to the moon'; see, recently, J. Pouilloux, Rev. Ét. Anc. 1964, 211). Dates in their festival calendar, on the other hand, were at times termed κατ᾽ ἄρχοντα ('archon's time'). Such dates were arbitrary modifications of the lunar calendar made by the chief magistrate in the form of intercalated or suppressed days. An example is Ἐλαφηβολιῶνος ἐνάτει ἱσταμένου τετάρτει ἐμβολίμωι, 'fourth intercalary Elaphebolion 9' (Hesp. 1954, 299). The vast majority of dates preserved to us are in terms of the festival calendar—an unfortunate fact for modern scholarship, because one can rarely be sure when a given date is a true lunar date or a modified one. The politicians, not the astronomers, ruled the calendar.

5. Athenian assemblies were convened in accordance with a third calendar, the 'prytany' calendar, which re-flects the division of the year according to the prytanies of the boule. The prytany comprises the length of time the bouleutai of any given tribe presided over the council. In inscriptions, the number and the day of the prytany are given by ordinary numerals: ἐπὶ τῆς Ἐρεχθηίδος ἐνάτης, τριακοστῇ τῆς πρυτανείας = thirtieth day of the ninth prytany, in which the tribe Erechtheis presided. Aristotle (Ath. Pol. 43. 2) records a schematic arrange-ment for this calendar in which the prytanies are of uniform length. All explicit evidence proving the lengths of prytanies at Athens confirms the Aristotelian fixed pattern. Until the end of the fifth century, the only calendar dates found in inscriptional sources are by pry-tanies. In the fourth and following centuries, the prytany and festival calendars began on the same day, the first new moon of the month Hekatombaion. Before 407 B.C., the prytany year totalled 366 days, a fraction of a day longer than a solar year.

6. The original Roman calendar consisted of ten months only, the later March–December, and must therefore have had an uncounted gap in the winter, between years (see especially Ov. Fasti 1. 27 ff., with Frazer's note; cf. Nilsson, Time-Reckoning, 223). The republican calendar, represented for us by the frag-mentary Fasti Antiates (see Mancini in Not. Scav. 1921, 140 for first publication) and literary descriptions (notably Censorinus 20. 4 ff., Macrob. Sat. 1. 13. 1 ff.; their chief ultimate sources are no doubt Varro and Verrius Flaccus), was introduced from Etruria by Tarquinius Priscus (so Junius Gracchus ap. Censorinum, ibid.), as is shown among other things by the month-name Iunius, pure Latin Iunonius, clearly connected with the Etruscan form of Juno's name, Uni. It is earlier, however, than the Capito-line temple (traditionally not dedicated till after the ex-pulsion of the kings), for of the feast-days which it marks in large capitals none is connected with that cult. Janu-ary, as containing the festival (*Ianuar, presumably the

Agonium of later calendars, 9 Jan.) of the god of gates who was on his way to be a god of all beginnings, must have been intended to be the first month, but the revolu-tion which expelled the Etruscan dynasty put a stop to this and March remained the first of the year till 601/153. March, May, Quintilis (July), and October had 31 days each (Ides on 15th, Nones on 7th), Feb. 28 and the rest 29 (Ides on 13th); total, 355.

7. To intercalate, a 'month' of 22 or 23 days, called Mercedonius or Intercalaris, was placed between the 23rd and 24th of Feb. This intercalating was so clumsily done that by the time of Julius Caesar the civic year was about three months ahead of the solar. In his capacity of Pontifex Maximus, he intercalated sufficient days to bring the year 708/46 to a total of 445 days (Censorinus, ibid. 8), which was thus the 'last year of the muddled reckoning', 'ultimus annus confusionis' (Macrob. ibid. 14. 3). From the next year onwards the Egyptian solar calendar (see TIME-RECKONING) was adapted to Roman use, by inserting enough days in the shorter months to bring the total up to 365 and arranging for the insertion of a day, not a month, between 23 and 24 Feb. in leap-year (hence called bissextile year, since the date a. d. vi. kal. Mart. occurs twice in it; the non-existent date '29 Feb.' is a modern absurdity). No substantial change was made thereafter till the reforms of Gregory XIII (promulgated by Bull, 24 Feb. 1582), whose calendar is now in general use.

8. The official year of the consuls (and of most other Roman magistrates) was appointed in 153 B.C. to begin on 1 Jan. That of the tribuni plebis began on 10 Dec.

E. Bickerman (see TIME-RECKONING); M. P. Nilsson, Primitive Time-Reckoning (Lund, 1920); 'Entstehung und religiöse Bedeutung des griechischen Kalenders', in Lunds Universitets Arsskrift, N.F., Avd. 1, Bd. 14, Nr. 21; 'Zur Frage von dem Alter des vorcäsarischen Kalenders', in Strena philologica Upsaliensis (1922); W. K. Pritchett, Ancient Athenian Calendars on Stone (U.S.A. 1963); F. Altheim, History of Roman Religion (1938), 104 ff.; A. K. Michels, The Calen-dar of the Roman Republic (U.S.A. 1967). H. J. R.; W. K. P.

**CALES,** town, probably Auruncan, on the borders of Campania (q.v.): excavations at modern Calvi have yielded seventh-century bucchero ware. In 334 B.C. a Latin colony was sent to Cales, presumably to counter-balance Samnite-controlled Teanum (see SIDICINI) and Cales became a centre of Roman authority in Cam-pania (Livy 8. 16; 10. 20). A quaestor navalis was stationed there (Tac. Ann. 4. 27; text uncertain). Cales was an important base in the Hannibalic War, but, sus-taining heavy losses, refused Rome further aid in 209 (Livy 27. 9). Rome reinforced it in 184 B.C. (Dessau, ILS 45). In Ciceronian and imperial times Cales was a municipium (q.v.), and the birthplace of Vinicius, Velleius Paterculus' patron (Cic. Leg. Agr. 2. 86; Tac. Ann. 6. 15). The fertile Ager Calenus was famous for its pottery. Numerous monuments survive.

A. Sambon, Monnaies antiques de l'Italie i (1903), 353; C. L. Woolley, JRS 1911, 199; L. Pareti, Storia di Roma i, ii (1952/3). E. T. S.

**CALIDIUS,** MARCUS, as praetor (57 B.C.) he helped to effect Cicero's return from exile; in 52 he supported Milo (Asc. Mil.). A leading Atticist pupil of Apollodorus in oratory (cf. RHETORIC, LATIN), he was praised by Cicero (Brut. 274 ff.).

Schanz–Hosius, § 139; Malcovati, ORF² no. 140.

**CALLEVA ATREBATUM,** modern Silchester, on the Hampshire–Berkshire border. The Roman town was enclosed by a polygonal earthwork (230 acres), and c. 100 was laid out in insulae. A flint wall erected c. 200 behind a slightly earlier bank reduced the enclosed area to c. 100 acres. The land within it was completely excavated 1890–1909. Shops, a dyeing industry, and some sixty houses were exposed, and of public buildings a *forum* with *basilica*, baths, a presumed *hospitium*, five small temples, and a small Christian church. The population was perhaps *c.* 2,000. The town was eventually deserted in circumstances still obscure.

Coins of Epillus (fl. A.D. 10), son of Commius, REX CALLE or CALLEV are known, but nothing earlier than a polygonal enclosure just before or just after 43 has appeared. *See also* ATREBATES (2).

Excavation Reports of public buildings and houses in *Archaeologia*, xl, xlvi, l, lii–lxii (1866–1910). Dating of defences and street-grid, *Archaeologia* xcii (1946), 121 ff. G. C. Boon, *Roman Silchester* (1957) is a complete study of the town and its remains.                         C. E. S.

**CALLIAS** (1), son of Hipponicus, of one of the richest families in Athens. He was cousin to Aristides (q.v.1), and married Elpinice, sister to Cimon (q.v.). He is said to have distinguished himself at the battle of Marathon; he won the chariot-race at Olympia three times. He was noteworthy for his diplomatic services to the State. He supposedly negotiated (*c.* 450 B.C.) the 'Peace of Callias' ending hostilities between Athens and Persia and recognizing each party's sphere of influence (*see* ATHENS: HISTORICAL OUTLINE § 3). The reality of this treaty was impugned by Theopompus (q.v. 3), and has been doubted by some modern scholars. The negotiations, according to the most circumstantial account (Diod. 12. 4), took place in Cyprus: if so, Callias' mission to the court of Artaxerxes (q.v. 1) at Susa, recorded by Herodotus (7. 151), may have been on another occasion. Callias was probably one of the negotiators of the Thirty Years' Peace with Sparta (446/5), and may also have been author of the alliances with Rhegium and Leontini made about the same time (*ATL* iii. 276). He was father of Hipponicus, a general in the Archidamian War who died at Delium, and grandfather of Callias (3).

The ancient evidence for the 'Peace of Callas' is listed in Hill-Meiggs-Andrewes, *Sources for Greek History* (1951), index i. 615; the numerous modern discussions extend from Grote (*History of Greece* (1888) iv. 422 ff.) to K. Kraft, *Hermes* 1964, 148 ff. and H. B. Mattingly, *Hist.* 1965, 273 ff.                         T. J. C.

**CALLIAS** (2), Athenian comic poet, won first prize at the City Dionysia in 446 B.C. (*IG* ii². 2318, col. 3), and was active at least until 430 (*IG* xiv. 1097. 5 f.). We have eight titles (including Ἀταλάνται), and thirty-five fragments; fr. 12 mentions Socrates. 'Callias the Athenian, a little earlier than Strattis' (Ath. 453 c) who composed a γραμματικὴ τραγῳδία (cf. 448 b, 276 a) might be the same person.

*FCG* i. 213 f.; *CAF* i. 693 ff.; *FAC* i. 170.                         K. J. D.

**CALLIAS** (3) (*c.* 450–370 B.C.), an Athenian nobleman, notorious for his wealth and his extravagance. He was ridiculed by comic poets, and attacked by Andocides whom he accused of sacrilege. More sympathetic pictures of his house and life are given by Xenophon (*Symposium*) and Plato (*Protagoras*). He was general in 391/0, and took part in the famous victory of Iphicrates (q.v.) over Spartan hoplites. As an old man, he was a member of the embassy sent to Sparta in 371/0.                         V. E.

**CALLIAS** (4) of Syracuse, lived at the court of Agathocles, tyrant of Syracuse (316–289 B.C.), and wrote a history of his reign in twenty-two books, variously described as Τὰ περὶ Ἀγαθοκλέα, Περὶ Ἀγαθοκλέα ἱστορίαι, etc. It so favoured Agathocles that Callias was suspected of accepting bribes; so Diod. Sic. (21. 17. 4) who, however, probably knew Callias only through the medium of Agathocles' enemy, Timaeus. The history had little influence on the tradition, which remained unfavourable to the tyrant, although, apart from the account written by

Agathocles' brother, Antandrus, it was the first important work on this subject. The fragments do not provide sufficient material to determine the contents of the work.

*FGrH* iii B. 564.                         G. L. B

**CALLICRATES** (1), a Greek architect of the fifth century B.C. He was associated with Ictinus and the sculptor Phidias in the building of the Parthenon (q.v.).

**CALLICRATES** (2) (d. 149–148 B.C.) of Leontium, the Achaean pro-Roman statesman, in opposition to Lycortas after the death of Philopoemen, announced in Rome in 181–180 B.C. his policy of subservience to Rome. General in 180–79, he repatriated Spartan and Messenian exiles and restored Spartan local rights. In 168 he prevented assistance to Egypt. After the Third Macedonian War with the detention of the leading independent Achaean politicians in Italy, he maintained his ascendancy with Roman support, despite his unpopularity with the masses until his death.

Polyb. 24. 8–10; 29. 23–5; 30. 13, 29, 32. G. Colin, *Rome et la Grèce* (1905), 233. De Sanctis, *Stor. Rom.* iv. 1. 247, 347.
                        A. H. McD

**CALLICRATIDAS**, Spartan admiral, who succeeded Lysander (q.v.) in 406 B.C. He resented Spartan dependence on Persian subsidies and refused to submit to humiliating treatment by Cyrus. He defeated a squadron under Conon at Mytilene and blockaded it there. Leaving 50 ships to maintain the blockade, he proceeded with 120 to attack an Athenian relief fleet of 150. In a battle off the Arginusae Islands he suffered a heavy defeat and was drowned. He displayed energy, spirit, and forthrightness, but his qualities are perhaps overrated by authorities hostile to Lysander.

Xenophon, *Hellenica* 1. 6. 1–33; Diodorus 13. 76–9, 97–9; Plutarch *Lysander* 5–7.                         H. D. W

**CALLIMACHUS** (1), Athenian polemarch and commander-in-chief in the campaign of Marathon (490 B.C.). He accepted Miltiades' plan to meet the Persians in the field. His part in the actual battle, in the last stage of which he was killed, has been obliterated by the personality and achievements of Miltiades, but his share in the victory was fully recognized in the wall-paintings on the Stoa Poikile (*c.* 460 B.C.), where he was portrayed among the Athenian gods and heroes, and in two surviving epigrams (Tod, 13).

H. Berve, *Miltiades* (1937), 78 ff.; C. Robert, *Die Marathonschlacht in der Poikile* (1895), 19 ff.; N. G. L. Hammond, *JHS* 1968, 41, 45 f.                         P. T.

**CALLIMACHUS** (2), Greek sculptor, active in the later fifth century B.C. Perhaps an Athenian. He is reputed to have been the inventor of the Corinthian capital (Vitr. 4. 1. 9–10) and to have made a golden lamp for the Erechtheum (Paus. 1. 26. 6–7); also a seated statue of Hera for a temple at Plataea (Paus. 9. 2. 7). He was noted for being the first artist to employ the running drill, and it is said of him that he spoiled his art by overelaboration (Pliny, *HN* 34. 92). His style has been recognized in a series of reliefs representing dancing Maenads. The signature 'Callimachus made it' on a relief in the Capitoline Museum representing Pan and the three Graces, in archaistic style, presumably is by a Roman copyist of that name. Still another Callimachus signed (together with Gorgias) a statue of Hellenistic style, found at Minturno.

                        G. M. A. R.

**CALLIMACHUS** (3) (*c.* 305–*c.* 240 B.C.) of Cyrene, son of Battus (hence Battiades in *epigr.* 21 Pf.; Catull. 65. 16; Ov. *Am.* 1. 15. 13, etc.). He is described as a pupil of Hermocrates of Iasos. Early in life Callimachus migrated o Alexandria and became a schoolmaster in its suburb Eleusis. Later he was given employment at the Alexandrian library and produced a *catalogue raisonné* in 120 volumes with the title Πίνακες τῶν ἐν πάσῃ παιδείᾳ διαλαμβάντων καὶ ὧν συνέγραψαν, the first scientific literary history. It is now clear that he never became *prostates* (director) of the library (cf. *POxy.* 1241, col. ii. 1). The quarrel between Callimachus and his pupil Apollonius—later known as Apollonius Rhodius—seems to have been one of the important episodes in the bitter literary controversy between the writers of long traditional epics and those of short and highly finished poems. The freedom with which Apollonius refashioned in his own style whole passages of Callimachean poetry suggests the turning of a purely literary discussion into a personal feud (cf. Pf. *Call.* ii, xli and vol. i *passim*). Callimachus was victorious and Apollonius retired to Rhodes, but it appears that finally the long traditional epic won the day (cf. K. Ziegler, *Das hellenistische Epos*, 1934). Tradition records a reconciliation between Callimachus and Apollonius and that they were buried close to one another (Vit. Apollon. Rhod. A, in Schol., Wendel, p. 2. 5). It was during this dispute that Callimachus wrote the *Ibis*, a wilfully obscure poem in mockery of Apollonius, which gave Ovid the idea for his poem of the same name. The literary critics of Callimachus were many and persistent, including such well-known names as Asclepiades and Poseidippus. These he vigorously counter-attacked till the end of his life. His fame and popularity in late antiquity must have exceeded that of every other Hellenistic poet, to judge by the great number of Callimachean papyri—even greater than those of Euripides—and the many quotations found in grammarians, metricians, lexicographers, and scholiasts; only Homer is more frequently quoted. One poem only of Callimachus can be definitely dated, the *Plokamos* (fr. 110 Pf.), which treats of events of the year 246/5; but a *terminus post quem* can also be found: (*a*) for the *Galatea* (fr. 378 Pf.), which speaks of the attack of the Gauls in 278 B.C.; (*b*) the *Ektheosis Arsinoes* (fr. 228 Pf.), which must have been composed after the death of the queen in 270 B.C.; and (*c*) Hymn IV *On Delos*, where Ptolemy II, who was deified in 270, is mentioned as θεὸς ἄλλος. If the *Sosibiou Nike* (fr. 384 Pf.) refers to Sosibius, who was later minister of Ptolemy IV and *pseudepitropos* of Ptolemy V, Callimachus must have still been composing remarkable poetry in the late forties of the third century.

## WORKS

*Verse.* Callimachus' longest and most famous poem was the *Aetia* (Αἴτια, Causes), a narrative elegy of roughly 7,000 lines in four books. It contained a series of aetiological legends connected with Greek history, customs, and rites; the length of the individual *aetia* varied. The poet imagined himself carried in a dream from Libya to Mount Helicon, where the Muses instructed him in all manner of legendary lore (cf. *Anth. Pal.* 7. 42). The extant fragments indicate that in the first two books Callimachus conversed with the Muses, but that in books iii–iv the various stories were not connected by a fictitious dialogue or otherwise. The number of *aetia* contained in the first three books is unknown; it is evident, however, that they received varied treatment, and that personal and realistic touches were introduced by the poet. The *Diegeseis* (expositions), which gave the arguments and other information on the poems of Callimachus (fragments of three separate *Diegeseis* have been found in papyri, all presumably going back to a common lost source, cf. Pf. *Call.* ii, xxviii and n. 1), contain the subjects of the last few *aetia* of book iii, and possibly all of book iv. The longest fragments of the *Aetia*, such as those from the stories of *Acontius and Cydippe* (fr. 75 Pf.), *Icus* (fr. 178 Pf.), or the *Sicilian Cities* (fr. 43 Pf.), come

from papyri. It appears that Callimachus published a second revised edition of the *Aetia* which was included in his collected works. As a general introduction to these, and perhaps as a more special introduction to the *Aetia*, he composed the *Answer to the Telchines* (the Retort to his Critics) (fr. 1 Pf.), in which he expounds his final and most polemic views on poetry. As last *aetion* to the revised edition we find the *Plokamos* (fr. 110 Pf.), also known from Catullus' adaptation (Catull. 66), which is followed by the Epilogue (fr. 112 Pf.), in which reference is made to the poetry of Hesiod, as at the beginning, in the *Somnium* (fr. 2 Pf.). In the final edition of Callimachus' works the *Aetia* were followed by a book of iambic poems of approximately 1,000 lines. The favourite metres are the scazon and iambic trimeter, but some pieces are in epodic form and there are other experiments. The thirteen poems included in this book are of miscellaneous content and character. In I–III and V Callimachus satirizes contemporary morals and literary attitudes. In IV and XIII he deals with his literary critics; VI describes Phidias' statue of Zeus at Olympia for an intending tourist; VII–XI are more on the line of the *Aetia*; XII celebrates the birth of a daughter to a friend Leon. A veritable *lanx satura*, the *Iambi* must have influenced Roman satire. Of Callimachus' lyrics very little survives, but enough to prove his skilful use of a variety of metres. His galliambics probably served as a model to Catullus and Varro. The most interesting fragment comes from the *Ektheosis Arsinoes* (fr. 228 Pf.). It is in archebuleans and shows Callimachus at his best as a court poet. Epic on the grand scale was avoided by him on principle. Instead, and as an answer to his critics, he composed the *Hecale*, the most famous epyllion (q.v.) in Greek literature The details of the narrative cannot be reconstructed, but we know that it described in about 1,000 lines the victory of Theseus over the bull of Marathon. In true Alexandrian manner the emphasis was laid not on the great heroic deed of Theseus, but on the noble poverty of Hecale, the old woman who had offered him hospitality on his way to Marathon. The scene of the rustic meal in particular was greatly admired and copied (cf. Ov. *Met.* 8. 620 f.; Ps.-Virgil, *Moretum*, etc.). The *Hecale*, which also contains a remarkable scene in which birds are the speakers, was yet one more *aetion*, explaining the name and cult of an Attic deme. As the *Argonautica* of Apollonius Rhodius depend in many points on the *Hecale* (cf. Pf. *Call.* i *passim*), the view that this was Callimachus' answer to the *Argonautica* is untenable. A small number of fragments from his minor epic and elegiac poems have survived. Of these fr. 384 Pf. from the *Sosibiou Nike* is the most interesting as it appears to be an endeavour to revive in elegiacs the Pindaric epinician ode. The only complete works of Callimachus which have been transmitted in medieval MSS. are his *Hymns* and his *Epigrams*. Of the *Hymns*, I–IV and VI are in hexameters, V in elegiacs. Up to a point Callimachus' model is the Homeric *Hymns*. His *Hymns*, however, were not intended to be recited at a public festival, still less to accompany religious ritual. They are literary pieces, meant for reading or recitation to a select audience. I, II, and IV contain political propaganda. The style varies. I (Zeus) reads at times like a humorous report of a learned controversy. III (Artemis) approximates to an epyllion. IV (Delos), which competes with the Homeric *Hymn* to the Delian Apollo, comes nearest to the traditional manner. II (Apollo), V (Baths of Pallas), and VI (Demeter) represent Callimachus' greatest originality in this department. By a combination of dramatic mime and lyric the poet brings to life the spectacle itself and the emotions of the spectators. In V and VI a 'Holy Story', pathetic in V, grotesquely gruesome in VI, contributes an epic element. I–IV are in the epic dialect, V–VI in Doric. Of

Callimachus' *Epigrams* some sixty survive. More interesting than the dedications and epitaphs, though some of the latter are excellent, are the occasional pieces, prompted by his own experiences and emotions, especially during early manhood. Of Callimachus' tragedies, comedies, and satirical plays mentioned by the *Suda* nothing survives.

*Prose.* Besides the *Pinakes* Callimachus wrote many other works in prose, e.g. a *Chronological Register of the Athenian Dramatic Poets*, a study on Democritus' writings and language, numerous encyclopaedias (*About Nymphs, Birds, Games, Winds, Rivers*, etc.), collections of Paradoxa and Glosses. His scholarly activities may also be judged from the distinguished men numbered among his pupils; they include not only Apollonius Rhodius, but Eratosthenes of Cyrene and Aristophanes of Byzantium.

It is clear that Callimachus was a poet of great originality and extraordinary refinement. His amazing productivity (the *Suda* credits him with more than 800 volumes) was accompanied by bold experimentation in his poetry and a great versatility of style. The scholarly element, it is true, often adds a frigidity to his verse, but the lively personal and realistic touches which appear never allow his writings to degenerate into arid selections of obscure myths.

Texts. R. Pfeiffer, *Callimachus* i–ii (1949–53); C. A. Trypanis, *Callimachus Aetia, Iambi, Hecale and other Fragments* (Loeb, 1958); for the hymns and epigrams also A. W. Mair, *Callimachus, Lycophron, Aratus* (Loeb, 1921). On the Callimachean papyri see R. A. Pact, *The Greek and Latin Literary Papyri*² (1965), 28 f.
General. Wilamowitz, *Hell. Dicht.*; H. Herter, 'Kallimachos(6)', *PW*, Suppl. v. 386 ff.; A. Körte–P. Händel, *Die Hellenistische Dichtung* (1960); T. B. L. Webster, *Hellenistic Poetry and Art* (1964); K. J. McKay, 'Poet at Play', *Mnemos.* Suppl. 6, 1962; id., 'Erysichthon', *Mnemos.* Suppl. 7, 1962.          C. A. T.

**CALLINUS**, elegiac poet, of Ephesus, lived in the first half of the seventh century B.C., when Cimmerians and Trerians were attacking Phrygia, Lydia, and Ionia (Strabo 627, 647). He refers to them in frs. 3 and 4. He also refers to the destruction of Magnesia by the Ephesians (Ath. 525 c). His one long fragment (fr. 1) summons men lying at a feast to take up arms and defend their country, and attributes the rank of demigod to the brave fighter. It is written in epic language, but with certain originalities of phrasing.

Text. Diehl, *Anth. Lyr. Graec.* i. 1, 3–5. commentary: T. Hudson-Williams, *Early Greek Elegy* (1926), 71 ff. criticism: C. M. Bowra, *Early Greek Elegists* (1938), 13 ff.          C. M. B.

**CALLIPHON**, philosopher of uncertain date (probably not before Ariston of Chios and Hieronymus of Rhodes, who flourished c. 250 B.C.). Cicero says he held that the supreme good consists in the union of pleasure and virtue.

**CALLIPPUS** of Cyzicus, astronomer (fl. 330 B.C.), went with Polemarchus to Athens, where he stayed with Aristotle. He corrected and added to Eudoxus' (q.v.) theory of concentric spheres designed to account for the movements of the sun, moon, and planets (Simpl. on *de Cael.* 493, 5–8 Heib.); Callippus added two more spheres in each case for the sun and moon, and one more for each of the planets (as to these changes see Arist. *Metaph.* 1073ᵇ32–8, Simpl. loc. cit. 497, 17–24). Callippus proposed a year-length of 365¼ days, and consequently introduced the 76-year cycle named after him, containing 27,759 days and consisting of 940 months—28 intercalary —as an improvement on Meton's cycle of 19 years (Geminus, *Isagoge* 8. 57–60); the first 76-year cycle began in 330–329 B.C.

On the concentric spheres see J. L. E. Dreyer, *History of the Planetary Systems* (1906), 103 ff. On the 'Calippic Cycle' see F. K. Ginzel, *Handbuch der Chronologie* ii (1911–14), 409 ff.          T. H.; G. J. T.

**CALLIRHOË** (1), in mythology, daughter of the river Achelous; for her story, *see* ACARNAN, ALCMAEON (1); (2) virgin of Calydon, vainly loved by Coresus, priest of Dionysus there, in a romantic and obviously late legend (Paus. 7. 21. 1–5).

**CALLISTHENES** of Olynthus, Aristotle's nephew, already known for works on Greek history, but not a wise man, accompanied Alexander's expedition as its historian. In his history he wrote up Alexander as champion of Panhellenism, partly propaganda against the Greek opposition; but he also made him son of Zeus, a far-reaching extravagance. He quarrelled with Alexander in 327 by opposing the introduction of *proskynesis* (his reasons remain doubtful), and was executed for alleged complicity in the Pages' conspiracy, which had its effect on the attitude of the Peripatetic school toward Alexander thereafter.

*See* ALEXANDER (3), Bibliography, Ancient Sources. T. S. Brown, *AJPhil.* 1949, 225 ff.; Pearson, *Lost Histories of Alexander* ch. 2; E. Mensching, *Hist.* 1963, 274 ff.          W. W. T.

**CALLISTO**, probably in origin a by-form of Artemis Καλλίστη; in mythology, daughter of Lycaon. She was loved by Zeus and bore him Arcas (q.v.). Either Artemis, angered at her unchastity, or Hera then turned her into a she-bear; or she was shot by Artemis. In her transformed shape, either Artemis mistook her for a real bear and killed her, or her own son pursued her (as a quarry or because she was trespassing on the precinct of Zeus Lycaeus), when Zeus took pity on them and transformed him into the constellation Arctophylax, her into the Great Bear.

See Apollodorus 3. 100–1; Ps.-Eratosthenes 1 and 8; Ov. *Met.* 2. 405 ff., *Fasti* 2. 155 ff.          H. J. R.

**CALLISTRATUS** (1), a διδάσκαλος of Old Comedy, possibly himself a comic poet, but better known as the man under whose name Aristophanes produced his three earliest plays.

**CALLISTRATUS** (2) of Aphidna, nephew of Agyrrhius (q.v.), was a talented orator and financier, who influenced Athenian policy from 377 to 361 B.C. Having prosecuted the ambassadors who proposed peace with Sparta in 391, he was elected strategus in 378 when the Second Athenian League was founded. He is known to have organized the finances of the league and is believed to have inspired its liberal constitution. With Iphicrates he prosecuted Timotheus for misconduct in 373 and acted as *strategos* in 372, when Spartan naval power was broken. Realizing that Thebes was becoming more dangerous than Sparta, he negotiated the peace of 371 with Sparta (Xen. *Hell.* 6. 3. 10 f.). Endeavouring to maintain the balance of power between Thebes and Sparta, he proposed the dispatch of Iphicrates to aid Sparta in 369. Since his policy failed to check Thebes, he was impeached and only saved by his oratory (366). When Timotheus' policy of imperialism failed, Callistratus perhaps regained popular favour by negotiating alliance with Arcadia, but in 361 he was impeached, and was condemned to death *in absentia*. After reorganizing the finances of Macedonia for Perdiccas II, he landed in Attica and was put to death. A realist and constructive statesman, he was thwarted by the rise of Thebes.

P. Cloché, *La Politique étrangère d'Athènes 404–338 B.C.* (1934).          N. G. L. H.

**CALLISTRATUS** (3), pupil of Aristophanes of Byzantium, edited Homer and other authors, and wrote Σύμμικτα, quoted by Athenaeus. He attacked his fellow-pupil Aristarchus for departing from his master's doctrines.

**ALLISTRATUS** (4), a Roman jurist of the first half of the 3rd c. A.D. He was evidently of Greek origin: his Latin is awkward, and his interest lay in the legal life of the Hellenistic provinces and the imperial rescripts directed to them. Works: *Quaestiones*, four books *De Iure Fisci*, *Institutiones*, an exposition of the edictal law (with title of which the meaning is not clear: *Ad Edictum Monitorium*), and of the procedure *extra ordinem* (*De Cognitionibus*).

R. Bonini, *I 'libri de cognitionibus' di Callistrato* (1964).
A. B.; B. N.

**ALLISTRATUS** (5) (3rd or 4th c. A.D.), a sophist who wrote Ἐκφράσεις (descriptions) of fourteen statues, in imitation of the Εἰκόνες of Philostratus of Lemnos.

TEXT. C. Schenkl and E. Reisch (Teubner, 1902).
TRANSLATION. A. Fairbanks (Loeb, with Philostratus, 1931).

**ALLISTUS**, GAIUS JULIUS (*PW* 306), an influential freedman of the Emperor Gaius, who took part in the conspiracy leading to Gaius' murder in A.D. 41. Under Claudius he increased his wealth and power in the post of *a libellis*, and was patron of the physician Scribonius (q.v. 3) Largus. He prudently refused help to Narcissus in accomplishing Messalina's downfall, but later was unsuccessful in championing the claims of Lollia Paulina to be Claudius' (fourth) wife. Agrippina, no doubt, secured his dismissal after Claudius' death, for nothing more is heard of him (*see* CLAUDIUS I). J. P. B.

**ALLIXENUS** (fl. c. 155 B.C.), a Rhodian Greek, wrote Περὶ Ἀλεξανδρείας. Athenaeus (5. 196 a; 203 e) quotes Callixenus on ships built by Ptolemy Philopator and on πομπή of Philadelphus.

*FGrH* iii. 627.

**CALPURNIA** (1, *PW* 126), daughter of Piso (q.v. 5) Caesoninus, married Caesar in 59 B.C. cementing an alliance between her husband and father. Though Caesar was prepared to divorce her to marry Pompey's daughter in 53, her affection for him was great, and she attempted to keep him from the Senate on the Ides of March (Plut. *Caes.* 63). After the murder she handed his papers and 4,000 talents to Antony. Her age is not known, but it is noteworthy that her brother Piso (q.v. 6) 'Frugi' lived until A.D. 32. G. E. F. C.

**CALPURNIA** (2, *PW* 130), third wife of Pliny the Younger, whom she accompanied to Bithynia. She was grand-daughter of L. Calpurnius Fabatus, a Roman knight of Comum (*ILS* 2721). See Pliny *Epp.* 6. 4. 7; 7. 5; 10. 120–1. G. E. F. C.

**CALPURNIUS** (1, *PW* 119) **SICULUS**, TITUS (fl. A.D. 50–60), was the author of seven pastorals associated until 1854 with four others which Haupt proved to be by Nemesianus (q.v.). Calpurnius' Neronian date is clear from allusions to the comet of A.D. 54 (1. 77–83), to the amphitheatre of 57 (7. 23–24), to Nero's speech for the people of Ilion (1. 45), and to the handsome young and divine ruler welcomed as the restorer of a Golden Age (cf. *Apocolocyntosis* 4: see SENECA 2, § 4) in 1, 4, and 7. These are his three courtly poems, placed at the beginning, middle, and end of the collection, while 2, 3, 5, and 6 are more strictly rural. In 2 Crocale's praises are sung alternately by a shepherd and a gardener (an innovation in pastoral); in 3 (possibly the earliest) Lycidas has thrashed his faithless sweetheart but swears repentance in a pretty love-song; 5 is an old herdsman's advice to his foster-son on managing goats and sheep, while 6 is a singing-match broken off by the ill temper of the competitors. Of the court-pieces, 1 represents two shepherds finding a poem by Faunus cut into the bark of a tree to prophesy a new Golden Age—they hope that their poetry will reach the emperor through their patron Meliboeus; and 4, the longest eclogue (169 lines), hints that they have had some success; 7 gives Corydon's impressions of the amphitheatre built by Nero at Rome.

The problems concerning Calpurnius have produced many theories. His name may imply that he was son of a freedman of C. Calpurnius Piso, who conspired against Nero in 65; the epithet 'Siculus' may mean literally 'Sicilian' or symbolize the poet's debt to Theocritus. 'Meliboeus' in 1 and 4, described as learned and a new Maecenas, has been questionably identified with Seneca, with Piso, and others. The contemporary Einsiedeln eclogues (q.v.) have unconvincingly been ascribed to Calpurnius. It has further been debated whether he could have written the *Laus Pisonis* (q.v.).

The situations, names, and phraseology in Calpurnius' poems are often reminiscent of Virgil, to whom (as Tityrus) he does notable homage in 4. 64–72. There are signs of the influence of Ovid, Propertius, and Tibullus. Calpurnius can take a cue from Theocritus and follow it up with some independence. He shows skill in coherent dialogue when he employs amoebean verse in eclogues 2, 4, and 6. *See also* PASTORAL POETRY, LATIN, § 5.

LIFE AND WORKS. Clementina Chiavola, *Della vita e dell'opera di Calpurnio Siculo* (1921).
TEXT. E. Baehrens, *PLM* iii; H. Schenkl, *Calp. et Nemes. bucolica* (1885) and in Postgate, *CPL*; C. Giarratano, *Calp. et Nemes. bucolica* (1924, with *Einsiedeln Ecl.*; repr. 1951); E. Raynaud, *Poetae Minores* (Classiques Garnier, 1931).
COMMENTARY. C. H. Keene, *Eclogues of Calp. and Nem.* (1887).
TRANSLATIONS. E. J. L. Scott (octosyllabic verse; 1890); J. W. and A. M. Duff (prose; Loeb, 1934).
SPECIAL STUDIES. M. Haupt, *De carminibus bucol. Calp. et Nemes.* (1854) ('Meliboeus' = Calp. Piso); F. Chytil, *Der Eclogendichter Calp. u. seine Vorbilder* (1894) ('Meliboeus' = Columella); J. Hubaux, *Les Thèmes bucoliques dans la poésie latine* (1930); E. Cesareo, *La poesia di Calpurnio Siculo* (1931). J. W. D.

**CALPURNIUS** (2, *PW* 40) **FLACCUS** (2nd c. A.D.), author of declamations (*see* DECLAMATIO) from fifty-three of which excerpts survive (Schanz–Hosius, 592).

G. Lehnert, *Calp. Flacc. Declamationes* (1903).

**CALVINUS** (1), GAIUS SEXTIUS (*PW* 20), as consul in 124 B.C. and proconsul fought successfully in Transalpine Gaul, triumphing over Ligurians, Vocontians, and Salluvians c. 122. He founded Aquae Sextiae (*Aix-en-Provence*), as a Roman garrison post. E. B.

**CALVINUS** (2), GNAEUS DOMITIUS (*PW* 43; cf. 11), served in Asia in 62 B.C., supported Bibulus (q.v. 1) when tribune in 59, and was praetor in 56. To secure election as consul he engaged in a scandalous compact with the consuls of 54 (Cic., *Att.* 4. 17. 2, etc.); disturbances followed revelation of the plot, but he was finally elected in July 53 for the rest of that year. He may have suffered exile in 51 (R. Syme, *Sallust* (1964), 217). In the Civil War he was Caesarian, fighting against Scipio in Thessaly, commanding the centre at Pharsalus, suffering defeat by Pharnaces (q.v. 2) at Nicopolis, and assisting Caesar in Africa. In 42, while bringing reinforcements to the triumvirs, he was trapped on the Adriatic by Ahenobarbus, and lost his whole force. Consul again in 40, he afterwards governed Spain, with notorious severity to the troops; in 36 he triumphed, and from his spoils decorated the Regia (q.v.). G. E. F. C.

**CALVISIUS** (*PW* 13) **SABINUS**, GAIUS, of obscure and probably non-Latin family, served under Caesar in Greece in 48 B.C. and became governor of Africa in 45. He tried to protect Caesar on the Ides of March (44). Antony's reappointment of him to Africa (Nov. 44) came to nothing (*see* CORNIFICIUS I). He was consul in 39. He commanded a fleet for Octavian against Sextus Pompeius (38), and was responsible for restoring order in Italy (36). Later he was governor in Spain and triumphed in May 28. His son was consul in 4 B.C. and his grandson in A.D. 26.

Syme, *Rom. Rev.*, see index. T. J. C.

**CALVUS,** GAIUS LICINIUS (*PW* 113) (82–?47 B.C.), orator and poet, son of the annalist C. Licinius Macer (q.v. 1). In oratory he practised a severe Atticism, but he was a vivacious speaker (Sen. *Controv.* 7. 4. 7). Cicero, who deplored his uncompromising Atticism and thought that over-fastidiousness of style impaired his effectiveness, pays tribute to his great abilities (*Brut.* 283–4, *Fam.* 15. 21. 4) and Quintilian's balanced judgement indicates that some critics placed him above Cicero (10. 1. 115). He left twenty-one speeches, of which those against Vatinius (one probably delivered in 54 B.C., when Cicero was defending) were still models for the student of oratory in Tacitus' time (*Dial.* 18, 21, 25). He was an intimate friend of Catullus and shared his attitudes and his tastes—the two are paired by Horace, Propertius, Ovid, and Pliny—and his writing was in the same genres—an 'epyllion' (on the story of Io), epithalamia (one in glyconics), elegiac verse, and epigrams (some attacking Caesar and Pompey): only a few lines survive.

FRAGMENTS in *ORF*², n. 165; Morel, *FPL.* C. J. F.

**CALYPSO** (Καλυψώ, 'she who conceals'), a nymph, daughter of Atlas (q.v.; *Od.* 1. 14 and 50 ff.). She lived on the island of Ogygie, 'where is the sea's navel', i.e. a great way from any known land, and there received Odysseus when shipwrecked on his way from Circe's island (cf. ODYSSEUS). Though she promised to make him immortal if he would stay and be her husband (5. 209), he desired to return home; therefore, at the command of Zeus, conveyed by Hermes (5. 105 ff.) she let him go in the eighth year (7. 259–61), providing him with materials and tools to construct a makeshift boat (σχεδίη, 5. 251; the description shows that it was not a 'raft'). After Homer, little is added to her story. In the *Odyssey* nothing is said of her having children by Odysseus; but in Hesiod, *Theog.* 1017–18 (an interpolation?) she has two sons, Nausithous and Nausinous. More commonly her son (by Odysseus or Atlas; in post-Homeric genealogies she is often daughter of Oceanus or Nereus) is Auson, eponym of Ausonia (S. Italy), also called son of Circe (see, e.g., schol. Ap. Rhod. 4. 553 and Eustathius on Dionysius Periegeta, 78). H. J. R.

**CAMARINA,** a Syracusan colony founded *c.* 599 B.C. at the mouth of the river Hipparis in southern Sicily, near modern *Scoglitti*. In constant dispute with the Syracusans, it was destroyed by them in 553 and again *c.* 484 after refoundation by Hippocrates of (q.v. 1). Gela Established once more in 461 by the Geloans, it supported the anti-Syracusan coalition in 427–4, but decided for Syracuse after 415 (cf. Thuc. 6. 75–88). Abandoned by Dionysius I (q.v.) in 405, it revived in the period of Timoleon. The supposition that it was finally destroyed and abandoned in 258 (Diod. Sic. 23. 9. 4–5) is invalidated by the discovery of buildings of Roman republican date. Strabo (6. 2. 5) records the site as deserted.

Bérard, *Bibl. topogr.* 44 f. for earlier literature. More recent researches: A. di Vita, Κώκαλος 1958, 83 ff., id., *Bollettino d'Arte* 1959, 347 ff., P. Pelagatti, ibid. 1962, 251 ff. A. G. W.

**CAMBYSES** (Kambūjiya), son of Cyrus the Great; king of Persia 530–522 B.C. The main achievement of his reign was the conquest of Egypt in 525 B.C. (Hdt. 3. 1–15). He planned further military expeditions against Carthage, Ethiopia, and Siwa Oasis, but the first proved impracticable, the second was a partial failure, and in the third the Persian force perished in the desert. The misfortunes may have changed him from a wise and tolerant ruler to the tyrannical madman of Herodotus' account. He died in Syria while returning to suppress the rebel Gaumata, the Pseudo-Smerdis.

J. V. Prašek, 'Kambyses', *Alte Orient* xiv. 2 (1913); *PW*, s.v. 'Kambyses' (C. F. Lehmann-Haupt). M. S. D.

**CAMELS.** The camel of the Graeco-Roman and Iranian worlds, including Bactria, was the one-humped Arabian species; the two-humped 'Bactrian' camel belonged to India, China, and central Asia; the 'Bactrian' camel sent to Xerxes with the Saca tribute is depicted at Persepolis as an Arabian with two humps. Camels were common draught-animals in Ptolemaic and Roman Egypt; Alexander and Ptolemy I utilized swift dromedaries for messages across the desert; Antiochus III had a camel corps, as had Romans (*dromedarii*) and Parthians later. But the real use of camels in war was shown by Surenas (q.v.), though seemingly he had no imitators.

O. Brogan, *PBSR* 1954, 126 ff.; E. H. Bull, *Antiquity* 1956, 117 f. W. W. T.

**CAMENAE,** Roman goddesses, identified since Livius Andronicus (*Odissia*, fr. 1) with the Muses. They seem, however, to be water-deities: they had a grove and spring outside the Porta Capena (Plut. *Numa* 13; Platner–Ashby 89) whence the Vestals drew water daily, and also a little shrine (*aedicula*, Servius on *Aen.* 1. 8, who says it was of bronze and dedicated by Numa; its dedication-day was 13 Aug., *fast. Antiates*). Libation was made to them with milk and water (Serv. Dan. on Verg. *Ecl.* 7. 21). Their shrine, being struck by lightning, was removed to the temple of Hercules Musarum (Servius, first citation above).

Wissowa, *RK* 219. H. J. R.

**CAMERINUM,** town of the Umbrians, (q.v.), modern *Camerino*, midway between Perusia (q.v.) and the Adriatic. Its inhabitants, known as Camertes, were sometimes mistaken for burghers of Etruscan Clusium (q.v.), whose earlier name was Camars. Camerinum signed a 'most equal' treaty with Rome before 300 B.C. and was favoured by her thereafter, even as late as imperial times. E. T. S.

**CAMILLA,** a legendary Volscian maiden, whose father, Metabus, in flight fastened her to a javelin, dedicated her to Diana, and threw her across the Amisenus river. After life as a huntress she joined the forces of Turnus, engaged in battle, and was killed by the Etruscan Arruns. Virgil alone (*Aen.* 7. 803; 11. 539–828) relates her story. See HARPALYCE (2). A. S. P.

**CAMILLUS** (1), MARCUS FURIUS (*PW* 44), the saviour and second founder of Rome after the Gallic invasion (387/6 B.C.). The splendour of his career is emphasized by the continuous embellishments which the account of it underwent from the fourth century B.C. onwards. He is said to have been military tribune with consular power in 401, 398, 394, 386, 384, and 381 B.C. Of five alleged dictatorships and four triumphs, those of 396 and 389 may be accepted. Political pamphleteers, especially from the time of Sulla, exploited the story of Camillus for propaganda purposes: so Livy (5. 51 ff.) puts into his mouth a programme foreshadowing the Roman traditionalism of Augustus' policy.

Camillus' earliest and greatest, and undoubtedly historical, victory was the capture of Etruscan Veii (*c.* 396 B.C.); soon afterwards he reduced Falerii. As a war memorial a golden basin was dedicated to Apollo in the treasury of the Massaliotes at Delphi. This fact need not be questioned, since contacts had long been established, through Etruria, between Rome and the Greek world, while Greek fourth-century historians (e.g. Aristotle) dealt with Camillus' career, or at any rate with the Camillus legend. Tradition alleged that Camillus, who had been exiled for appropriating some booty, retired to Ardea in exile, where he was appointed dictator when the Gauls attacked Rome: he levied an army, defeated the Gauls, and recovered the gold with which the Romans had bought off the invaders. Whether Camillus was ever actually exiled or not, the story was obviously invented to balance the defeat on the Allia and, despite traces of accounts drawn from the contemporary legends, the main elements in it were borrowed from the trial of the Scipios. If Camillus did nothing to prevent the catastrophe, nobody contributed more whole-heartedly to Rome's subsequent recovery. Although his home policy aimed at reasserting patrician influence, and he crushed the sedition of M. Manlius (q.v.) by force, his military reforms proved nevertheless favourable to the plebeians, since they gave recognition to individual merit and provided public pay, and he supported the plebeian claims to the supreme magistracies. In 367 during the struggle of the Licinian–Sextian rogations he vowed a temple to Concord; it was built at the foot of the Capitoline hill. Camillus' policy of appeasement at home enabled him successfully to lead the Romans against the Aequi and Volscians (389), although his subsequent victories were undoubtedly exaggerated by a tradition which in general regarded him as 'parens patriae conditorque alter urbis' (Livy 5. 49. 7).

Mommsen, Röm. Forsch. ii. 321 ff.; O. Hirschfeld, Kl. Schr. 1913), 273 ff.; E. Täubler, Klio 1912; E. Burck, Die Erzählungskunst des T. Livius (1934), 109 ff.; A. Momigliano, Secondo contributo alla storia degli studi classici (1960), 89 ff.; J. Hubaux, Rome et Véies 1958); Ogilvie, Comm. Livy 1–5, 669 ff. P. T.

**CAMILLUS** (2), LUCIUS FURIUS (*PW* 41), a son of Camillus (1). As consul in 349 B.C. he defeated the Gauls through the efforts of Valerius (q.v. 3) Corvus. Probably this success, and not an alleged Auruncan victory in 345, induced him to dedicate the temple of Juno Moneta Livy 7. 28). E. T. S.

**CAMILLUS** (3), LUCIUS FURIUS (*PW* 42), a grandson of 1). In 338 B.C. he and his fellow consul, C. Maenius, crushed the Latins and dissolved the Latin League—an exploit that earned them honorific statues in the Forum Livy 8. 13). Camillus' second consulship (325) was undistinguished owing to illness (Livy 8. 29). E. T. S.

**CAMILLUS,** an acolyte in Roman cult, fem. *camilla.* They might be the children of the officiant, but must have both parents alive (*pueri patrimi et matrimi*), be below the age of puberty, and of course free-born.

Latte, RR 407. H. J. R.

**CAMPANIA** lies between the Apennines and the Tyrrhenian Sea in Italy, extending from Latium to the Surrentine promontory. This fertile, volcanic plain annually produced three, sometimes four, cereal and vegetable crops. Its roses, fruits, olives (from Venafrum), and wines (from the isolated mountains Vesuvius, Gaurus, Massicus, Callicula) were also famous. In the Bay of Naples it possessed an excellent harbour, and Puteoli (q.v.) became Italy's chief port. The mild climate and beautiful luxuriousness of Campania constantly attracted invaders and reputedly sapped the martial energies of its inhabitants (Polyb. 3. 91). After 750 B.C. Greeks began colonizing the coast, drove back the indigenous population (known traditionally as *Ausones*, q.v.), and extended their influence even to Rome (*see* CUMAE). In the interior c. 600 an invading Etruscan minority established a league of twelve cities headed by Capua, but failed to capture Cumae (Polyb. 2. 17). The Greeks indeed badly defeated these Campanian Etruscans in 474. Invading Sabelli (q.v.), however, proved irresistible: they captured Cumae as well as Capua (c. 425), and imposed their language on, and merged with, the indigenous population (Diod. 12. 31. 76; Livy 4. 37). Thus, the nation of the Campanians was created. Their language was called, after the original inhabitants, Oscan (q.v.). The Campanians, although more civilized than their Samnite or Roman neighbours and although skilled mercenary soldiers, were no match for fresh Sabellian invaders and consequently sought Roman protection c. 343 B.C. Thereafter, although the Oscan and Greek languages long survived here, Campanian history is linked with Roman (*see* CAPUA). Campania witnessed heavy fighting in the wars of the Republic and suffered disasters like the eruption of Vesuvius. Nevertheless it remained a prosperous area with an excellent road-system and numerous villas. Augustus joined Campania to Latium to form his First Region; indeed the name was ultimately restricted to Latium, the *Campagna* of today.

K. J. Beloch, *Campanien*[2] (1890); A. Sambon, *Monnaies antiques de l'Italie* i (1903), 137; R. M. Peterson, *Local Cults of Campania* (Rome, 1919); J. Day, *YCIS* iii (1932), 167 (well documented); J. Whatmough, *Foundations of Roman Italy* (1937), 292; G. Spano, *La Campania felice nelle età più remote* (1941); E. Vetter, *Handbuch der ital. Dialekte* (1953), 1. 1 ff.; P. E. Arias (ed.), *Ricerca archeologica nell'Italia meridionale* (1960), 1 ff. E. T. S.

**CAMPS.** When the Roman camp (*castra*) was described by Polybius (6. 27–32) about 143 B.C., its stereotyped form was already taken for granted; indeed, no Roman historian troubles to describe it. It is associated with the earliest annals of Roman history (cf. Livy 10. 32. 9; 34. 46. 8; 40. 27. 1–7; 41. 2. 11), but its origins are doubtful. R. Lehmann-Hartleben assigns its introduction to the Etruscans and would connect it with Assyrian war-entrenchments (*Die Traianssäule* (1926), 10), while others would connect it with the *terramara* (q.v.) settlements of prehistoric Italy, too often assumed to be normally symmetrical (*Antiquity* 1939, 320). The augural principles associated with its planning certainly appear in the earliest Roman colonies of which we have archaeological knowledge, and its development is undoubtedly a Roman invention.

Polybius describes a camp for a consular army of two Roman legions with an equivalent number of Italian allies. It is square, and faces in the most convenient direction (contrast Veget. 1. 23). Its plan is based upon the general's tent (*praetorium*, q.v.) and the 100-foot street (*via principalis*), parallel therewith. The legions (each grouped as 1,200 *hastati*, 1,200 *principes*, 600 *triarii*, and 1,200 *velites*) and the bulk of the allies were encamped by *centuriae* (then of 60 men each) and *turmae* in parallel divisions along streets at right angles to the *via principalis*, and were divided at the position of the fifth cohort by a second large cross-street, hence called *via quintana*. The *praetorium* is flanked by six tribunes' tents disposed along the *via principalis*, with open spaces behind them serving respectively as *forum* and *quaestorium*. Then comes a third cross-street, behind which lay the *extraordinarii* (selected allied troops) with *auxilia* (foreign levies) on the flanks. The enclosing rampart (*vallum*) and ditch (*fossa*) were divided from the host by an *intervallum* 200 feet wide, serving for booty, and probably for the *velites*, about whose position there is ambiguity (Stolle, *Das Lager und Heer der Römer* (1912), 94–104). There are many points of resemblance between this Polybian plan and the camps of the second century B.C. excavated by A. Schulten at Numantia (q.v.), though the allotment of space differs considerably, maniples being grouped round a square rather than in long narrow *strigae*.

An imperial camp of the third century A.D. (*Rh. Mus.* 1893, 243) is described in the anonymous treatise *De Munitionibus Castrorum*. While Polybius had tried to describe common practice, this imperial camp is treated as a mere exercise in castrametation, using factors unlikely to be found in conjunction. The differences are striking. The proportion of the whole work is not square but *tertiata*, one-third being called *praetentura* and two-thirds *retentura*. Auxiliaries and irregulars take the place of *extraordinarii* and occupy the whole *praetentura*. The *via quintana* has moved to behind the *praetorium*. The legionaries are quartered around the whole encampment, lying between the *intervallum* and a street called *via sagularis*. The unit for all regulars is no longer the maniple, but the *centuria* of 80 men. The *quaestorium* has moved to behind the *praetorium* and such institutions as the hospital (*valetudinarium*), of which Polybius makes no mention, have appeared. Archaeology does not supply examples of imperial camps on so large and detailed a scale as the republican camps at Numantia. For defences and outlines, the British groups of Northumberland and Scotland are unrivalled. At Masada (q.v.), west of the Dead Sea, there is a remarkable series of small siege-camps, filled with temporary buildings in the manner of Numantia, while the manœuvre-camps of Cawthorn should also be noted.

H. Stuart Jones, *Companion to Roman History* (1912), 226 ff.; A. Schulten, *Numantia* i–iv (1914–31); Kromayer-Veith, *Heerwesen und Kriegsführung der Griechen und Römern* (1928); for Northumberland examples, I. A. Richmond, *Northumberland County History* xv. 116 ff. and id. *Proc. Brit. Acad.* 1955, 297 ff.; for Scottish examples, W. Roy, *Military Antiquities of the Romans in North Britain* (1793); for Masada, *see* s.v. MASADA; *De Munitionibus Castrorum*, ed. Lang (1848), von Domaszewski (1887). I. A. R.

**CAMPUS MARTIUS,** originally the Tiber flood-plain bounded by the Pincian, Quirinal, and Capitoline hills, though its precise limits, especially to the south, are still arguable. It was originally pasture, outside the *pomerium* (q.v.) and therefore used for army musters and exercises and for the *comitia centuriata*. In early times, the Campus contained the altar of Mars, from which it took its name, the *Villa Publica* (435 B.C.), and the temple of Apollo (431 B.C.); later came the famous altar to Dis and Proserpina, on which centred the Secular Games (q.v.). Republican public works, the *Forum Holitorium*, *Circus Flaminius* (221 B.C.), *Porticus Octavia* (168 B.C.) and *Minucia* (110 B.C.), and many unidentified temples, as in the *Forum Boarium* and Piazza Argentina, had, by the first century B.C., overrun its south end. The *Theatrum Pompei* (52 B.C.), with huge *porticus*, foreshadows the immense buildings of the Augustan *viri triumphales*: the temple of Neptune by Domitius Ahenobarbus (*c.* 32 B.C.), Statilius Taurus' amphitheatre (29 B.C.), Augustus' own *Mausoleum*, gardens, and crematorium (28 B.C.), *porticus Octaviae* (27 B.C.), and the *Saepta Iulia* (q.v., 26 B.C.), Agrippa's Baths, water-garden, aqueduct (q.v.), Pantheon (q.v.) and *porticus Argonautarum* (25 B.C.), the theatres of Marcellus and Balbus (the latter with *Crypta*) of 13 B.C., a monumental sun-dial (10 B.C.) of which the gnomon was an obelisk of Psammetichus II, and the *Ara Pacis* (q.v., 9 B.C.). Imperial buildings gradually filled the remaining space. Gaius projected an amphitheatre, and perhaps built the *Iseum et Serapeum* vowed by the triumvirs. Nero built *thermae* (A.D. 62–4) and Domitian the *Templum Divorum* (*Vespasiani et Titi*), a *stadium* (now Piazza Navona), and *odeum*. Hadrian added the *basilicae* of Matidia and Marciana, with a temple to the former. Pius honoured Hadrian with a temple (A.D. 145), and is himself commemorated by a crematorium and *columna Divi Pii*, with famous panels on its base, while the *templum divi Marci* is associated with the more famous

Column, with spiral reliefs of the Marcomannic war Eventually, the whole area was included within the Wall of Aurelian (q.v.).

F. Castagnoli, *Mem. Acc. Linc.* 1948, 103 ff.; for buildings, se Nash, *Pict. Dict. Rome*, s.vv. I. A. R.; J. P

**CAMULODUNUM,** modern *Colchester* (Essex). A site to the west of the Roman (and modern) town, was occupied *c.* A.D. 9 by the Belgic conquerors of the Trino vantes and was the capital and mint of Cunobelinu (q.v.), as well as the principal trading port of Britain (cf Fox, *Proc. Prehist. Soc. E. Anglia* vii. 159). Capture in Claudius' campaign of A.D. 43, it served as a base for the conquest of Britain, and in 49 a colony (*colonia Victricensis*) was founded close by, which was probably a first the provincial capital. This unwalled town wa sacked by Boudicca in 60 and was subsequently rebuil in regular *insulae* to cover an area of *c.* 108 acres. I defences were a clay bank, to which, as appears, a ston wall was added *c.* A.D. 180. Important remains are th substructures of a temple (probably that of Divus Clau ius), and the monumental west (Balkerne) gate. In th suburbs are temples and a large theatre. Samian potter was made here in the second century. Its subseque history is virtually unknown.

C. F. C. Hawkes and M. R. Hull, *Camulodunum* (1947); M. Hull, *Roman Colchester* (1957); *VCH Essex* iii. 7 ff. (I. A. Richmond 90 ff. (M. R. Hull). C. E.

**CANABAE,** the name given to the civil settlements tha grew up around the legionary fortresses, e.g. at Moguntia cum, Carnuntum, and Lambaesis. Many of their in habitants were veterans. *Canabae* were *vici* (q.v.) and ha magistrates with the titles of *magistri* or *curatores*, an probably a local council. During the second century A. some of them were given the status of *municipia* (q.v.), o *coloniae* (*see* COLONIZATION, ROMAN).

Soldiers who give *castris* as their birthplace were bor in the *canabae* of the camp where their fathers, who be fore A.D. 197 were unable to contract a legal marriage were stationed. During the second century A.D. a hig proportion of legionaries were recruited in this way.

R. MacMullen, *Soldier and Civilian in the Later Roman Empi* (1963), 119 ff. H. M. D. P.; G. R. W

**CANALS** (*fossae*, διώρυγες). Drainage and irrigatio canals were freely used throughout the ancient worlc Egypt and Mesopotamia depended entirely on a syster set up in prehistoric times and extended and main tained later. The water of Lake Copaïs (q.v.), from ver early times, was carried for many miles over the sur rounding plain in canals and under it in tunnels; in Italy the Etruscans built canals that laid the foundations of th prosperity of the Po valley (Pliny, *HN* 3. 20). These wer kept up even by the Gallic invaders and extended by th Romans. In southern Italy the Pomptine Marshes (q.v. posed a more difficult problem, never really solved. Th Via Appia (q.v.), however, was safeguarded against th water, and the canal built for this purpose by M Cethegus (*cos.* 160 B.C.) provided a popular transpor route (Hor. *Sat.* 5. 5). Latium and Etruria were, on th whole, kept well drained by means of canals and tunnel (*cuniculi*). Claudius converted the Fucine Lake int cultivable land by draining the water through tunnels which were repaired and improved in the second centur In Roman Africa, following up earlier Carthaginia efforts, the Romans built a system of canals that caugh all the available water and vastly extended the cultivabl area. Its remains are still an impressive sight.

Navigable canals were also known in Egypt (especiall in the Nile Delta) and Mesopotamia. Xerxes, for hi invasion of Greece, by-passed the stormy Athos (q.v eninsula by a canal nearly 20 feet wide across its neck. This was regarded as sacrilege ('Where Zeus wanted an land, he made one'), duly avenged by his defeat. Yet lere were one or two similar canals in Classical Greece, ld more were planned at various times and abandoned, otably—on different occasions from Periander to Nero, ho intended to set Jewish prisoners to work on it—one ross the Isthmus of Corinth. In Italy, the mouth of the o, and under the Empire that of the Tiber, frequently lled for canalization. So did river mouths in the pro-nces, e.g. the Rhône and the Rhine–Meuse, where nals were built, respectively, by Marius and Drusus .v. 3). Corbulo (q.v.), as legate of Lower Germany, con-ected the Meuse with the Rhine above the delta. In ritain, a system of canals linked Fenland with the Trent. Italy, Agrippa (q.v. 3) joined the Lucrine Lake to vernus and made them into one large land-locked rbour; and Nero envisaged, and actually started , a scheme to connect this with Rome, thus avoiding e difficulties posed by the Tiber mouth. Egypt remained e principal country of canals. Alexandria was con-ected with the Nile by the 'Canopus Canal'; and though gyptian schemes for digging through the Isthmus of ez had apparently failed, Ptolemy II, using some of eir workings, built a canal from the Nile (near Helio-olis) to the Bitter Lakes, which he connected with rsinoe (q.v. 2). This was kept up and improved, in part y new diggings, by various successors, last by Trajan d Hadrian. Alexandria thus became a centre for sea-orne trade between the East and the Mediterranean.

Dar.-Sag., 'Fossa'; S. Judson and A. Kahane, *PBSR* 1963, ff. (Etruscan *cuniculi*); Forbes, *Stud. Anc. Technol.* ii, ch. i. E. B.

**ANDIDATUS,** a candidate for a magistracy. Officially amed *petitor* (his rivals were therefore styled *competi-res*), he was called *candidatus* because he wore a white, r whitened, toga when greeting electors in the forum. le was then accompanied by a slave (*nomenclator*) who eminded him of the names of the electors, and by a rowd of partisans (*sectatores*), mostly freedmen, whose sk was to secure votes by bargaining and bribing, either irectly or through special agents. The *divisores* were harged with distributing money to the voting members f the tribes. To prevent or limit canvassing, legislation *de mbitu* (*see* AMBITUS) was enacted, but unsuccessfully. These ctivities frequently began a full year before the elections, ut candidature became official only with *professio* to, and onsequent *nominatio* by, the presiding magistrate or his olleague. Although this right of *nominatio* was shared in e imperial period by the Princeps, probably by virtue f his consular power, it is not to be confused with the ntirely unofficial recommendation of candidates by an fluential private citizen (*commendatio*), a practice repub-can in origin which was later widely employed by the mperors in order virtually to ensure the election of andidates of their own choosing.

Mommsen, *Röm. Staatsr.* i³. 477 ff.; ii². 921 ff. P. T.; E. S. S.

**ANIDIUS** (*PW* 2) **CRASSUS,** PUBLIUS, of obscure nd probably non-Latin family, served under Lepidus .v. 3) in Gallia Narbonensis and helped to bring about is *rapprochement* with Antony in May 43 B.C. He is robably the Crassus who led an army for Antony during e Perusine War. At the end of 40, after the peace of rundisium, he held a suffect consulship, and subse-uently served Antony in the East. Early in 36 he sub-ued the Iberians and Albanians in the region of the aucasus, and then joined Antony's Parthian expedition. robably left in command in Armenia, he brought his rmy to join Antony in 32, and took charge of all the land rces in the Actium campaign. After the battle he

deserted his troops and rejoined Antony in Egypt, where he was put to death by Octavian in 30.

Syme, *Rom. Rev.*, see index. T. J. C.

**CANINIUS** (1, *PW* 9) **REBILUS,** GAIUS, of praetorian family, served as Caesar's *legatus* in 52 B.C. against Vercingetorix. In 49 he was sent by Caesar to Pompey to arrange a compromise, and then fought under Curio (q.v. 2) in Africa. In 46 he was in Africa again with the status of proconsul, taking part in the campaign of Thap-sus; in 45 he served as a *legatus* in the campaign of Munda. On the last day of 45, on the sudden death of Q. Fabius Maximus, Caesar appointed him *consul suffectus* for the few hours of the year that remained. Apparently pro-scribed (43), he escaped to Sextus Pompeius in Sicily and there refounded Cephaloedium as a Roman *municipium*. His son and grandson also reached the consulship.

Syme, *Rom. Rev.*, see index; M. Grant, *From Imperium to Auctoritas* (1946), 192 f. T. J. C.

**CANINIUS** (2, *PW* 13) **RUFUS,** of Comum, a neigh-bour of the Younger Pliny, much occupied with his landed estates, but possessing an epic bent which Pliny encouraged, as he encouraged production of poetry in the case of Octavius and others. His literary interests are discernible from Pliny's letters to him (1. 3; 2. 8; 3. 7; 6. 21; 7. 18; 8. 4; 9. 33). J. W. D.

**CANIUS RUFUS,** from Gades, a poet and friend of Martial, who alludes to his versatility and merriment in epigram 3. 20 (cf. 1. 61. 9; 1. 69).

**CANNAE,** a village on the south bank of the Aufidus in Apulia, the site of Hannibal's great victory in 216 B.C. (Polyb. 3. 107–18; Livy 22. 43–9). L. Aemilius Paullus and C. Terentius Varro (qq.v.) with perhaps 48,000 infantry and 6,000 cavalry (rather than the 86,000 which Polybius implies) faced Hannibal's 35,000 infantry and 10,000 cavalry. Hannibal's convex crescent-shaped formation gradually became concave under pressure of the Roman centre which, being thus encircled and finally surrounded by Hannibal's cavalry in the rear, failed to break through and was cut to pieces. The long-debated question whether the battlefield lay north or south of the river has not been settled by recent archaeo-logical discoveries: the cemeteries, found in 1937 and after, are medieval, not ancient.

For a summary of the problems see Walbank, *Polybius* 1. 435 ff. For the burials and other excavations, F. Bertocchi, *Rend. Linc.* 1960, 337, *Studi annibalici* (1964) 93 ff., and N. Degrassi, ibid., 83 ff. H. H. S.

**CANTABRI,** a sea-coast and mountain tribe of Spain situated east of the Astures (q.v.). Their poverty and primitive characteristics are described by Strabo (3. 3. 7–8, pp. 155–6), who ascribes to them a sort of gynaeco-cracy (3. 4. 18, p. 165). They were finally reduced by the Romans in campaigns from 26 to 19 B.C. which were led by Augustus (26–25) and Agrippa (19). Those who survived this Cantabrian War were either deported from their mountain homes or remained under the super-vision of Roman troops. Juliobriga (modern *Reinosa*) was the only considerable town before Vespasian's colony of Flaviobriga. Pliny mentions *plumbum nigrum*, or lead, and magnetic iron, as natural resources.

On the wars see D. Magie, *CPhil.* 1920, and R. Syme, *AJPhil.* 1934. A. Schulten, *Los Cantabros y Astures* (1943). J. J. VAN N.

**CANTHARUS,** Athenian comic poet, victorious in 422 B.C. (*IG* ii². 2318). His Συμμαχία seems to have dealt with the ostracism of Hyperbolus in 417.

*FCG* i. 251; *CAF* i. 764–6; Demiańczuk, *Supp. Com.* 28.

**CANTIACI,** inhabitants of Kent who formed a *civitas* of Roman Britain, the only one to adopt not a tribal but a geographical title (Cantion, cf. Caesar, *BGall.* 5. 14) which perhaps goes back to Pytheas. Kent received numerous immigrations in the later pre-Roman period, and Caesar himself records four kings there (*BGall.* 5. 22). The Cantiaci, therefore, were probably an artificial grouping of these elements created by Rome (cf. the *Belgae* and *Regnenses*) for local-government purposes. The *caput civitatis* was Durovernum (*Canterbury*) (*Rav. Cosm.* 72), but Durobrivae (*Rochester*), where there had been a Belgic mint, was a secondary centre round which were many villas. *Richborough* (Rutupiae, q.v.), *Dover* (Portus Dubris), and *Lympne* (Portus Lemanis) were important ports and bases of the *Classis Britannica* and later became forts of the Saxon Shore, as did *Reculver* (Regulbium). A substantial pottery industry existed along the Thames estuary (Upchurch marshes) and iron was worked in the Weald.

*VCH Kent* iii; A. L. F. Rivet, *Town and Country in Rom. Brit.*[2] (1964), 144 f.; D. F. Allen in *Iron Age in S. Britain*, 97 ff.; *Archaeologia* 1944, 1 ff. S. S. F.

**CANTICA,** the lyric or musical portions of a Latin comedy (e.g. in Plautus, q.v. § 3) as contrasted with *diverbium*. Lyric *cantica* scarcely exist in Terence (q.v.). It seems clear that they represent an invention of Roman dramatists (*see* METRE, LATIN, 1 (B)).

**CANULEIUS** (*PW* 2), GAIUS, tribune of the plebs in 445 B.C., is reputed to have enacted a *rogatio* or *Lex Canuleia* that allowed intermarriage between patricians and plebeians, probably by recognizing the legitimacy of children of plebeian mothers, and by admitting them to the patrician *gentes*. Livy's lively but historically almost worthless account contains difficulties (e.g. the carrying of the law in the tribal assembly, and its connexion with the first plebeian attempts to win admission to the consulate), but the fact and approximate date of the law are indisputable.

De Sanctis, *Stor. Rom.* ii. 55 ff.; Ogilvie, *Comm. Livy 1–5*, 527 ff. On the question of intermarriage between patricians and plebeians see H. Last, *JRS* 1945, 31 ff. P. T.

**CANUSIUM,** city of Apulia (q.v.), on the river Aufidus (q.v.), of probable Daunian origin (cf. Pliny *HN* 3. 104): modern *Canosa*. Late Canosan pottery, necropolis finds, coins, and language indicate much hellenization by 300 B.C. (cf. Hor. *Sat.* 1. 10. 30). After submitting to Rome (318 B.C.), Canusium remained faithful until the Social War, which apparently caused it to decline somewhat (Strabo 6. 283; Livy 9. 20; App. *BCiv.* 1. 42, etc.). However, situated on the Via Traiana (q.v.), it soon recovered to become a *municipium*, an Antonine *colonia*, and the chief Apulian city in the sixth century (Procop. 3. 18). For a list of its decurions (A.D. 223) see Dessau, *ILS* 6121 (cf. 8703 *b*, 5188).

N. Jacobone, *Canusium* (1925). E. T. S.

**CAPANEUS** (Καπανεύς), in mythology, son of Hipponous and father of Sthenelus (*Il.* 4. 367; Hyg. *Fab.* 70. 1); one of the Seven against Thebes, cf. ADRASTUS. As he climbed on the walls, boasting that not even Zeus should stop him, he was destroyed by a thunderbolt (Aesch. *Sept.* 427; Eur. *Phoen.* 1172 ff. (from the cyclic *Thebais*?)). H. J. R.

**CAPENA,** the centre of a small independent territory on the west bank of the Tiber, south and east of Mt. Soracte. The original settlers were closely related to, if not identical with, the Faliscans (q.v.) and in classical times spoke a similar, near-Latin Indo-European dialect. Politically the city was closely associated with Etruscan Veii (q.v.),

and was annexed to Rome after the destruction of V in 396 B.C., but culturally the remains of its cemeteri reveal strong affinities also with the Faliscan cemeteri of Falerii and Narce (q.v.), as well as with the Sabi territories. Though a *municipium*, the city was of sm importance in Roman times and was eventually abandone It occupied the hill of Civitucola, 2 miles north of t modern Capena and is known chiefly from the co tents of its cemeteries. Near the south-east border of i territory, at Scorano, lay the important early river cross ing, market-town, and sanctuary of Lucus Feroniae (q.v.

*Not. Scav.* 1906, 1922, and 1953; G. D. B. Jones, *PBSR* 19 116 ff., 1963, 100 ff. J. B. W.

**CAPER,** FLAVIUS (late 2nd c. A.D.), grammarian, who lost treatises *De Latinitate* (containing citations from o Latin authors) and *De Dubiis Generibus* were freely use by later writers. The *Orthographia* and *De Verbis Dub* extant under his name (ed. Keil, *Gramm. Lat.* vii. 92–10 107–12) are apocryphal.

Schanz–Hosius, § 599. J. F. N

**CAPITO** (1), GAIUS ATEIUS (*PW* 7), of undistinguishe family, was tribune in 55 B.C. He opposed the consu Pompey and Crassus and stigmatized the latter's pr posed attack on Parthia as a war of unjust aggressio Unable to prevent Crassus' departure by announci adverse prodigies, he solemnly cursed him as he left t city (November). In 50 he received a *nota* from t censors on the ground that he had invented the sa prodigies: the punishment was, in Cicero's view, illogic (*Div.* 1. 29 f.). He is probably the Capito who distribut land to veterans by Caesar's appointment in 44.

J. Bayet, *Hommages à G. Dumézil* (1960), 31 ff. T. J.

**CAPITO** (2), GAIUS ATEIUS (*PW* 8), a Roman jurist the early Empire. He came of a modest family, b obtained the consulship (in A.D. 5), and was *curat aquarum* from A.D. 13 to 22, the year of his death. Wi his contemporaries 'maximae auctoritatis fuit' (Pompo *Dig.* 1. 2. 2. 47; cf. Tac. *Ann.* 3. 75), but his reputati did not last. His writings are referred to only once another jurist, though more plentifully by non-leg authors. This neglect is probably attributable at least part to his conservatism in legal matters, although politics he was a supporter of the new order. In bo these respects he contrasted sharply with his rival N Antistius Labeo (q.v. 1), whose subsequent reputatic was very different. It was indeed their rivalry that was t origin, if Pomponius' statement is true, of the schools jurists which came to be called Sabinians and Proculia (*see* SABINUS 2). Capito's later eclipse may also be attr butable to the fact that his writings (*De Iure Pontifici Coniectanea*, *De Iure Sacrificiorum*) seem to have bee principally concerned with sacral and constitutional la and were therefore probably soon considered obsolete

L. Strzlecki, *C. Atei Capitonis Fragmenta* (1960). Also Huschk Seckel–Kübler, *Iurisprudentia anteiustiniana* i[2] (1908), 62 ff. A. B.; B.

**CAPITOL, CAPITOLIUM, or MONS CAPITOL NUS,** one of the hills of Rome: an isolated mass left erosion, with two peaks, Capitolium proper and A It seems not to have been settled at all before the six century, but attained importance as the site of the gre temple started by King Tarquin and dedicated, in t first year of the Republic according to tradition, to Jupit Optimus Maximus, Juno, and Minerva; these deities h an earlier temple at the so-called Capitolium Vetus the Quirinal (Varro, *Ling.* 5. 158). At all periods, t hill was less an inhabited part of the city than a citadel a religious centre; here the consul took vows before goi his province and here he returned in triumph after a victory. The original platform of the temple (55 m. by 0 m. in area) still exists; but the original temple, often embellished, was burnt in 83 B.C. The new temple of Lutatius Catulus (69 B.C.), renovated and repaired by Augustus in 26 and 9 B.C., was burnt down in A.D. 69, while Vespasian's temple perished in the fire of A.D. 80. The last building was dedicated two years later by Domitian and cost 12,000 gold talents. It was plundered by Gaiseric (q.v.) in A.D. 455. The Tarpeian Rock (q.v.) lay close by, on the south-west shoulder of the hill. On the north summit of the hill, originally distinguished as the arx, lay the temple of Juno Moneta (344 B.C.), the auguraculum (an augur's observation post with primitive hut), and the temple of Concordia (216 B.C.). On the col between the hills, known as inter duos lucos, lay the aedes Veiovis (Vitr. 4. 8. 4) and the asylum associated with Romulus. The east face of the hill was occupied by the Tabularium (q.v.) and the approach-road from the Forum (clivus Capitolinus), paved in 174 B.C.

Both hill and the temple of Jupiter were reproduced in many cities of Italy and the Roman West, and either hill or temple or both in Roman Byzantium; Jerusalem, as refounded by Hadrian, was styled Aelia Capitolina. The right to erect such Capitolia was at first probably reserved for Roman coloniae.

E. Gjerstad, Early Rome, iii (1960), 168 ff.; for buildings, see Nash, Pict. Dict. Rome, s.vv.　　　　A. W. V. B.; I. A. R.; J. N.

**CAPPADOCIA** at one time designated the whole region between Lake Tatta and the Euphrates, and from the Euxine Sea to Cilicia; but the northern part became Cappadocian Pontus' or simply 'Pontus' (q.v. 2), and the central and southern part Greater Cappadocia. This latter consists of a rolling plateau, almost treeless in its western portion, some broken volcanic areas in the centre and west (the cone of Mt. Argaeus reaches 12,000 ft.), and the ranges, for the most part well watered and well timbered, of the Taurus and Antitaurus. A rigorous winter climate limits production to hardy cereals and fruits. Grazing was always important; the Persian kings levied a tribute of 1,500 horses, 50,000 sheep, and 2,000 mules, and Roman Emperors kept studs of race-horses here. Mines are mentioned of quartz, salt, Sinopic earth, and silver. Since the passes were frequently closed in winter the country was isolated, and consequently developed slowly.

In the second millennium B.C. this region of small principalities and temple states was penetrated by Assyrian trading colonies, and became subject to the Hittite rulers of Boghaz Köy. After their fall (c. 1200 B.C.) it lay open to Phrygian, and later to Cimmerian, invasion and devastation. The Medo-Persian conquest (585 B.C.) led to the formation of an Iranian nobility with feudal dominion over considerable districts. Besides these there existed large areas owned by temples and ruled by priests, such as the territories of Ma of Comana and Zeus of Venasa. Nobles and priests often rivalled the authority of the kings. The ordinary people lived in villages on the large estates or as serfs on the temple territories, supplying their masters with labour and revenues and the raw material for an active slave-trade.

The satrap Ariarathes (q.v. 1) refused to submit to Alexander and was killed by Perdiccas (322). His descendants, restored after 301, added Cataonia to their possessions, and were recognized as kings from c. 255 B.C. Ariarathes IV (q.v.) supported Antiochus III against Rome at Magnesia in 190, but he and his successors thereafter adopted a philo-Roman policy. Their efforts at Hellenization and urbanization made slow progress, as Mazaca and Tyana remained almost the only cities. Devastated by Tigranes (q.v. 1) of Armenia in the

Mithridatic Wars, Cappadocia was restored by Pompey, who gave the king large loans for reconstruction. Antony replaced this line, which had proved disloyal in the Parthian invasion, with the energetic Archelaus, who renamed Mazaca Caesarea and founded Archelais (Garsaura). He lost favour in Rome in his old age, and the military importance of Cappadocia led to its annexation in A.D. 17. A procuratorial province until Vespasian, it was joined (in A.D. 72) with the Galatian complex under a consular legate until Trajan, who, between 107 and 113, formed the new province of Cappadocia with Pontus which remained united to the time of Diocletian. The eleven royal strategiai remained the basis of the provincial administration. Development of commerce from the West, the transfer of legions to the upper Euphrates, and the system of military roads aided the belated advancement of native communities to city rank, but at most they hardly occupied a third of the territory. Imperial estates, beginning with the royal properties, steadily increased through confiscations.

See also ARIARAMNES, ARIARATHES, ARIOBARZANES.

Strabo 12. 533–40. Th. Reinach, Trois royaumes de l'Asie mineure (1888); Jones, Cities E. Rom. Prov. 175 ff.; W. E. Gwatkin, 'Cappadocia as a Roman Procuratorial Province', Univ. of Missouri Studies v (1930), no. 4; Magie, Rom. Rule Asia Min. 200 f. and index.
　　　　　　　　　　　　　　　　　　　　T. R. S. B.

**CAPREAE** (modern Capri), a beautiful, mountainous island near Naples (Strabo 5. 248). Neolithic people once dwelt here, and, in prehistoric times, legendary Teleboae (Mon. Ant. 1924, 305; Verg. Aen. 7. 735). In historical times Capreae was Neapolitan territory until Augustus, who often stayed here, gave Neapolis Aenaria in exchange (Suet. Aug. 92). Tiberius spent his last ten years on Capreae, amid wild debaucheries according to incredible ancient records. Ruined villas afford tangible memorials of his sojourn; he is said to have built twelve, named after various deities (Tac. Ann. 4. 67). After Tiberius the Caesars avoided Capreae except as a place of banishment, e.g. for Commodus' wife and sister (Dio Cass. 72. 4). Although arid, Capreae was fertile, but in antiquity never experienced municipal organization. The Romans knew its famous Blue Grotto.

H. E. Trower, Book of Capri (1924); A. Maiuri, Breviario di Capri (1938).　　　　　　　　　　　　　　　　E. T. S.

**CAPROTINA**, a title of Juno (q.v.), derived from the Nonae Caprotinae (7 July), i.e. Nones of the Wild Fig (caprificus), under which maidservants had a sham fight with stones, etc., and abused each other. It seems to be an old rite of fertility (fig-juice as equivalent to milk? cf. the Akikuyu rite in Man 1913, no. 3), grown unintelligible and relegated to slaves, though freeborn women also sacrificed on that day (Macrob. Sat. 1. 11. 36); see further Wissowa, RK 184, Latte, RR 106.　　H. J. R.

**CAPSA** (modern Gafsa), an oasis in southern Tunisia. The Libyan settlement there was destroyed by Marius in 106 B.C. (Sall. Iug. 89 ff.). It later revived, becoming a municipium under Hadrian and subsequently a colonia. Under the Byzantines, it was the centre of defence against the desert nomads.　　　　　　　　　　　　　B. H. W.

**CAPUA**, city in western Italy. Archaeological evidence indicates that Capua was founded before 600 B.C., probably by Etruscans; it was certainly Etruscan in the sixth century (Vell. Pat. 1. 7; Livy 4. 37). Capua gave its name to the entire surrounding plain, Ager Campanus (i.e. Capuanus), later called Campania (q.v.). But it specifically dominated the immediately neighbouring territory (Falernus Ager, Casilinum, Calatia, Suessula, Acerrae, Atella). Other Campanian cities (Suessa, Teanum, Nola, Nuceria, Neapolis, Cumae) pursued independent policies. After 474 B.C. Etruscan power in Campania declined and *c.* 440 Sabelli (q.v.) were becoming numerous in Capua; *c.* 425 they seized and soon oscanized it (Diod. 12. 31). Henceforth the Campani of Capua are frequently mentioned. Threatened by fresh Sabellian invaders *c.* 343, they sought Roman protection but immediately proved treacherous. Accordingly Rome confiscated the Falernus Ager, gave Roman citizenship to the *equites Campani* and *civitas sine suffragio* (see MUNICIPIUM) to the other Campani (Livy 7. 29–8. 14). Capua, however, retained its Oscan language and magistrates (*meddices*), the latter with somewhat curtailed powers after 318 when *praefecti Capuam Cumas* were appointed (Mommsen, *Röm. Staatsr.* ii³. 608). After 312 the Via Appia linked Capua still more closely to Rome. In the Samnite Wars Capua behaved equivocally and witnessed much fighting (Diod. 19. 76; Livy 9. 25); it continued, however, to prosper, becoming indeed proverbial for its luxuriousness and pride (Ath. 12. 36). By 218 it rivalled Carthage and Rome (Florus i. 16. 6). In 216 Capua revolted to Hannibal, but in 211 Rome recaptured and severely punished it, executing its prominent citizens, depriving the remainder of political rights and confiscating its territory, which as Roman public domain was partly used for colonies (194) but mostly rented out at a substantial profit until distributed to 20,000 colonists by Julius Caesar (59) (Livy 23. 2 f.; 26. 14 f.; Cic. *Leg. Agr.* 1. 7; Vell. Pat. 2. 44). Capua itself remained a populous town, but without municipal privileges until after 90 B.C. (Cic. *Sest.* 10). It suffered in the wars of the late Republic but under the Empire was a prosperous *colonia*, Augustus particularly favouring it (Dio Cass. 49. 14). It had declined somewhat, but was still a considerable city when Vandals sacked it (456). Saracens finally destroyed Capua (840), the church of Santa Maria alone escaping to give the town its modern name (*Santa Maria di Capua Vetere*). Its refugees settled at Casilinum, the Capua of to-day. Capuan perfumes and bronzes were famous (Cic. *Sest.* 19; Pliny *HN* 34. 95). Its large amphitheatre proves its fondness for gladiatorial shows; *see also* SPARTACUS.

J. Heurgon, *Capoue préromaine* (1942); A. Alföldi, *Early Rome and the Latins* (U.S.A. 1963), 183 f.; Scullard, *Etr. Cities*, 190 ff.; M. W. Frederiksen, 'Republican Capua', *PBSR* 1959, 80 ff.; A. Sambon, *Monnaies antiques de l'Italie* i (1903), 387; *Not. Scav.* 1924, 353 (for the magnificent Mithraeum); *Atti d. III conv. sulla Magna Grecia* (Villanovan settlement). *See also* s.v. CAMPANIA. E. T. S.

**CAPYS** (1), father of Anchises (*Il.* 20. 239); (2) companion of Aeneas (*Aen.* 10. 145) and founder of Capua; (3) king of Alba Longa (Livy 1. 3. 8).

**CARATĂCUS** (the form Caractacus is found only in an inferior manuscript), son of Cunobelinus. He took part in the resistance against the Roman invasion of A.D. 43 perhaps at Bagendon, near Cirencester, among his subjects the Dobunni (so emend Dio's Βοδούννων) rather than in Kent and Essex, as Dio states. He could easily escape over the Severn to the Silures of Monmouthshire, where he renewed hostilities against the governor Ostorius Scapula, by whom, however, he was defeated somewhere in the hills of the Welsh border. He fled to Cartimandua (q.v.), queen of the Yorkshire Brigantes, who surrendered him to the Romans (51). Tacitus puts into his mouth a rhetorical speech delivered at Rome to Claudius, who spared his life.

Dio 60. 20. 1–2; Tac. *Ann.* 12. 33–7. E. M. Clifford, *Bagendon, A Belgic Oppidum* (1961), 56 ff.; D. R. Dudley and G. Webster, *The Roman Conquest of Britain A.D. 43–57* (1965), see index. C. E. S.

**CARAUSIUS**, MARCUS AURELIUS MAUS(AEUS?) (cf. Dessau, *ILS* 8928), a Menapian of mean origin who was appointed *c.* A.D. 287 to a command in the English Channel. He aroused, however, the suspicions of Maxi-mian and fled to Britain, where he proclaimed himsel[f] emperor. An unsuccessful attempt to suppress him le[d] to a settlement whereby he could represent himself as [a] colleague of the Emperors (*c.* 290) and extend his rul[e] over north-eastern Gaul. His remarkable realm utilize[d] the support of Franks and possibly Picts; and he ma[y] have instituted the fortification of the Saxon shore. Th[e] Caesar Constantius, however, ejected him from Bou[-] logne (293), and he was assassinated by his *rationali*[s] Allectus.

P. H. Webb, *Reign and Coins of Carausius* (1907); C. H. V. Suther-land, *Coinage in Roman Britain* (1937), 62 ff.; Collingwood–Myres, *Roman Britain²*, 276 f.; W. Seston, *La Tetrarchie* (1946), 69 ff.; E. Stein, *Hist. du Bas-Empire* (1959), i. 67 ff., 433; R. A. G. Carson, *Journ. Brit. Arch. Assoc.³* 33 ff.; D. A. White, *Litus Saxonicum* (U.S.A. 1961), 19 ff.; Frere, *Britannia*, 335 ff. C. E. S.

**CARBO** (1), GAIUS PAPIRIUS (*PW* 33), supporter of T[i.] Gracchus (q.v. 3), on whose agrarian commission h[e] served from 130 B.C. As tribune in 131, he passed a la[w] extending secret ballot (see CASSIUS 4, GABINIUS 1) t[o] legislative comitia and unsuccessfully proposed a bi[ll] permitting iteration of the tribunate. Having turne[d] against Gaius Gracchus (q.v. 4), he won the consulshi[p] for 120 and—being an orator of some distinction—suc[-] cessfully defended Opimius against Decius (5) Subul[o] (qq.v.). Universally detested, he was prosecuted by youn[g] L. Crassus (q.v. 3) in 119 and committed suicide. He [is] among the alleged murderers of Scipio (q.v. 11) Aemi[-] lianus.

Malcovati, *ORF²*, 152 ff.; A. E. Astin, *Scipio Aemilianus* (1967[)] see index. E. [B.]

**CARBO** (2), GNAEUS PAPIRIUS (*PW* 38), seditious tri[-] bune in 92 B.C., fought in the Social War and in 8[7] supported Cinna (q.v. 1), who made him his colleagu[e] as consul in 85 and 84. As sole consul after Cinna'[s] death, he abandoned Cinna's Liburnian campaign an[d] continued his moderate policy, but gave equality i[n] citizenship to the Italians. After supporting a vote fo[r] disarmament, he gave up the consulship at the end o[f] the year. With Sulla advancing in Italy, he became consu[l] (82) with Marius (q.v. 2) and, with inexperienced levie[s] campaigned unsuccessfully in Picenum, Etruria, and Cis[-] alpine Gaul against Sulla, Metellus (q.v. 7), and Pompey. After failing to relieve Marius at Praeneste, he fled t[o] Africa. His name headed the proscription list and [on] captured by Pompey (whom he had once defended o[n] a criminal charge), he was ignominiously executed a[t] Lilybaeum. E. [B.]

**CARBO** (3), ARVINA, GAIUS PAPIRIUS (*PW* 40), so[n] of (1), was the only member of his family with Optima[te] sympathies, according to Cicero. He remained the enem[y] of L. Crassus (q.v. 3) who had accused his father. Durin[g] the Civil War he supported Cinna (q.v. 1) and, perhap[s] when on the point of going over to Sulla, he was execute[d] by Brutus Damasippus on orders from the Younge[r] Marius. He was probably tribune in 90 B.C. and is to b[e] distinguished from C. Papirius Cn. f. Carbo, brothe[r] of (2), who was tribune in 89 (or possibly 88, cf. [E.] Badian, *Stud. Gr. Rom. Hist.* 76 ff.), was joint author o[f] the *lex Plautia Papiria* (see Plautius 1), and died a[t] Volaterrae in 81.

Broughton, *MRR* ii. 30 f. H. H. [S.]

**CARCINUS** (1), son of Xenotimus of Thoricus, a trag[ic] poet mercilessly ridiculed, with his sons, by Aristophane[s] (*Pax* 781 ff., *Vesp.* 1497 ff.) and other comic poets. H[e] is probably identical with the general mentioned b[y] Thucydides (2. 23).

**CARCINUS** (2), son of Xenocles (1) and grandson o[f] Carcinus (1), a tragic poet who is said to have written 16[0] ays (*Suda*, s.v.) and won 11 victories (*IG* ii². 2325, according to a probable restoration) in the fourth century. He passed much time at the court of the younger Dionysus of Syracuse (Diod. Sic. 5. 5. 1). He is referred to by Aristotle, *Poet.* 16 (the recognition scene in the *Thyestes*) and 17 (a mistake in theatrical management in the *Amphiaraus*), *Eth. Nic.* 7. 7 (the endurance of Cercyon in the *Alope*), *Rh.* 2. 23 (an argument in the *Medea*—apparently she did not kill her children in this play) and 3. 16 (arguments of Iocasta in the *Oedipus*), and Plutarch (*De glor. Ath.* 7) praises his *Aërope* The phrase Καρκίνου ποιήματα is said to have been applied to obscure poems (*Suda*, s.v., etc.) but only on the strength of a single passage in the *Orestes*.

*TGF* 797–800. A. W. P.-C.

**ARCINUS** (3) **OF NAUPACTUS** (? 7th–6th c. B.C.), epic poet, probable author of the *Naupactia*, a Catalogue of Famous Women.

*EGF* 198–202.

**CARDIA**, a Greek city on the west side of the Thracian Chersonesus (q.v. 1), at the head of the Gulf of Melas, with a strategic position at the narrowest part of the isthmus. Founded jointly by Miletus and Clazomenae in the late seventh century B.C., it received an addition of Athenian colonists led by the elder Miltiades (q.v.), who strengthened its fortifications by constructing a wall across the isthmus, and was controlled by him and his successors, till it was abandoned to the Persians in 493. In the fifth century Cardia remained in the Athenian sphere of influence, and in the fourth it was the centre of a bitter struggle for possession between Athens and the kings of Thrace and then between Athens and Macedonia. In 352/1 Cardia joined Philip II and during the reign of Alexander was ruled by a tyrant Hecataeus. In the struggle between Alexander's successors, Lysimachus destroyed Cardia and removed its inhabitants to the new foundation of Lysimacheia nearby. Though Cardia was soon restored, Lysimacheia continued to serve as capital of the Chersonese, but by the time of the Elder Pliny, the latter had declined and Cardia had recovered something of its former importance.

U. Kahrstedt, *Beiträge zur Geschichte der thrakischen Chersones* (1954). E. I. McQ.

**CARIA**, the mountainous region inhabited by Carians in south-west Asia Minor south of the Maeander, with Greek cities (Cnidos and Halicarnassus) occupying the client peninsulas and mixed communities on the shores of the gulfs. Until the fourth century the pastoral Carians lived mainly in hill-top villages grouped under native dynasties and sanctuaries, the principal seat being Mylasa. The Carians themselves claimed to be indigenous; but in Greek tradition they came from the islands, and the interior of Caria is in fact lacking in prehistoric sites. They preserved their language until Hellenistic times, using a mainly alphabetic script; the relics that survive are not really intelligible, but it seems doubtful whether the language can have Indo-European affinities. The Carians were early associated with Ionians in mercenary service (especially under the Pharaohs). Subjected by Croesus and then by the Persians, they joined in the Ionian revolt (c. 499–494) and ambushed a Persian army. The coastal communities joined the Athenian League at the time of the Eurymedon campaign. Under the rule of the Hecatomnids (395–334), and especially of Mausolus, Caria was intensively hellenized and modern cities were planned to promote the Greek way of life, with the result that Caria was quickly absorbed in the later Greek world.

Strabo 14. 651 ff. J. and L. Robert, *La Carie* i (forthcoming). J. M. C.

**CARINUS**, Marcus Aurelius (*PW* 75), elder son of Carus (q.v.), left by him as Caesar in the West, when he marched against Persia (A.D. 282). Made Augustus before his father's death, Carinus succeeded him as colleague of Numerian and crushed the rebel 'corrector Venetiae', Julianus, in battle near Verona. Early in 285 Diocletian, appointed Emperor to succeed Numerian, ended a difficult campaign at the battle of the Margus in Moesia.

W. Ensslin, *PW*, s.v. VALERIUS (142), 2424 f. H. M.

**CARISTIA**, a Roman family feast, otherwise *cara cognatio*, celebrated on 22 Feb., immediately after the *dies parentales* (Feb. 13–21). Ovid (*Fasti* 2. 617 ff.) says it was a reunion of the surviving members of the family after the rites to the departed; Valerius Maximus (2. 1. 8) adds that no outsiders were admitted and any family quarrels were then settled. It is mentioned under the date in the calendar of Philocalus and under February in the *Menologia Rustica*.

Latte, *RR* 274, 339. H. J. R.

**CARMEN**: Cicero refers to the Twelve Tables (*Leg.* 2. 59) or an ancient sentence of execution (*Rab. Post.* 13, cf. Livy 1. 26. 6) as a *carmen*; the word is equally used of spells, prayers, oaths, oracles, epitaphs—in fact of any solemn saying or formula whose characteristic was not that it was in verse but that it was in rhythmical prose. It was not the fact that they were composed in verse that gave the *carmen Arvale* (q.v.) or the *carmen Saliare* (q.v.) this title, but the solemn formulaic rhythm which they shared with similar prayers that were not strictly in verse. An excellent example of the latter is the prayer on the occasion of the *lustratio agri* preserved by Cato (*Agr.* 141): it is composed in parallel clauses, in dicola and tricola, linked by anaphora or alliteration or placed in asyndeton, synonyms are linked, and the whole is characterized by measured movement and balance. That this was not just a Latin style but also Italic seems indicated by the fact that similar linguistic phenomena can be traced on the *tabulae Iguvinae* (q.v.).

Cicero *Brut.* 75 (cf. *Tusc.* 1. 2. 3, 4. 2. 3, Varro ap. Nonium 77, 2) refers to a report of Cato that in olden days *carmina* used to be sung at aristocratic dinners about the great deeds of ancestors. This report was built up into a most imaginative theory about the tradition of early republican history by Niebuhr (cf. Macaulay's preface to his *Lays of Ancient Rome*). Unfortunately it is clear that Cato did not know these *carmina* and their existence is open to considerable doubt (see A. D. Momigliano, *JRS* 1957, 104 ff.).

The word *carmen, carmina* came in the first century B.C. to be used as the 'poetic' word for poetry, and in this sense it was given full currency by the Augustans. (This development was very similar to the way in which the word *vates*—which originally meant 'soothsayer' or 'seer' and was used in no complimentary way by Ennius in reference to his predecessor, *Ann.* 7 prooem—came, through Varro's influence, to be used as the elevated word for 'poet', especially by the Augustans; see H. Dahlmann, *Philol.* 1948, 337 ff.)

C. Thulin, *Italische sakrale Poesie u. Prosa* (1906); G. Pasquali, *Preistoria della poesia romana* (1936); E. Norden, *Aus altröm. Priesterbüchern* (1939). G. W. W.

**CARMEN ARVALE** (see CARMEN). The Arval ritual-hymn would be invaluable if we possessed a correct copy. Unfortunately what we have (text: E. Diehl, *Altlateinische Inschriften*, 118) is most corrupt and its interpretation therefore doubtful. *Lases* equals *Lares*, *enos* may be *nos*, and *Marmar*, *Marmor* may be reduplicated forms of *Mars*. If *semunis*, *advocapit* represent *sēmōnes*, *advocabit* then they show dialectal changes, the former *ŏ* > *ū*, the latter (Faliscan? *b* > *p*. It was already obscure before the time of Aelius Stilo (see Schanz–Hosius i. 18). E. Norden, *Aus altrömischen Priesterbüchern* (1939), thinks the hymn not a pure relic of Italian ritual but influenced by Greek.

L. R. Palmer, *The Latin Language* (1954), 62 ff. P. S. N.

**CARMEN DE FIGURIS,** anonymous Latin poem (*c.* A.D. 400), describing figures of speech in 186 hexameters. Three lines are devoted to each figure, explaining its name and giving one or two examples. Material largely taken from Rutilius (q.v. 2) Lupus. Prosody late, aphaeresis of final *s* and ancient forms (*indupetravi, prosiet*) imitating pre-classical poetry.

Baehr. *PLM* iii. 272. O. S.

**CARMEN DE PONDERIBUS ET MENSURIS,** a Latin didactic piece of 208 hexameters, fourth to fifth century A.D., at one time erroneously ascribed to Priscian, but of uncertain authorship. It deals with weights and measures (giving Greek and Latin names), with the specific weight of different liquids, and with a test for an alloy of silver and gold.

Baehr. *PLM* v. 71; A. Riese, *Anth. Lat.*² 1. 2. 29. J. W. D.

**CARMEN NELEI.** Of this dim work five fragments (19 words) survive, embedded in Charisius and Festus. Charisius ranks it for age with the *Odissia* of Livius. The metre and content of three fragments suggest, if anything, a drama.

Morel, *FPR*.

**CARMEN SALIARE.** The fragments of the ritual-hymn of the Saliar priests (text: E. Diehl, *Poet. Rom. Vet.* 1) have come down in far too corrupt a state to allow us certainty of interpretation. It was already unintelligible in Republican times to the priests themselves. Interesting are the syncopated form *cante* (= *canite*), the termination of *tremonti* (cf. Dor. φέροντι), the diphthong, and -*s*- of *Leucesie* (= *Lucerie* 'god of light'), and the archaic superlative *dextumum*. The rest is quite uncertain and obscure.

Schanz–Hosius, i. 18. P. S. N.

**CARMENTIS or CARMENTA** (the latter form is found in Greek authors and very rarely in Latin, as Hyg. *Fab.* 277. 2), mythologically a prophetess, mother of Evander; she (Hyg. ibid.; Isid. *Etym.* 1. 4. 1 and 5. 39. 11) or more commonly Evander (as Tac. *Ann.* 11. 14. 4) taught the Aborigines to write. As Carmentis is also called a nymph (as *Aen.* 8. 336), she may have been a water-goddess; certainly she was a goddess of birth, worshipped by matrons (Plut. *Rom.* 21, *Quaest. Rom.* 56). Hence there are sometimes two Carmentes, Prorsa and Postverta in reference to the position of the child in the womb (Varro ap. Gell. 16. 16. 4). Her, or their, relation to the triad Parca Nona Decima, or Nona Decuma Morta (ibid. 3. 16. 11) is obscure, as is also the question whether Carmentis or the Carmentes are the older. A minor *flamen* was assigned to the goddess and a two-day festival (11 and 15 Jan.).

The shrine of Carmentis was at the foot of the Capitoline hill, near the Porta Carmentalis (a gate in the Servian Wall, so called from the shrine): see Platner–Ashby, 101, 405.

Wissowa, *RK* 220; Latte, *RR* 136. H. J. R.

**CARMINA TRIUMPHALIA,** songs sung, in accordance with ancient custom, by soldiers at a triumph (q.v.), either in praise of their victorious general or in a satiric ribaldry supposed to avert the evil eye from him.

Cf. Schanz–Hosius i⁴. 21 f.; Baehr. *FPR*, 330 f. J. W. D.

**CARMO** (modern *Carmona*), some 25 miles east of Hispalis (q.v.), was a stronghold of the Iberian chi Luxinius. It was prominent in the Second Punic War an in Galba's operations of 151 B.C.; in 49 B.C. it declare for Caesar, expelling its Pompeian garrison. Municip status is not attested before Gaius, but was probab earlier. Strength and prosperity, sustained into th Moslem period, are illustrated by the Roman walls wit towers and gates, still partly extant, and by a larg cemetery.

M. Fernández López and G. E. Bonsor, *Itinerario de la necropo romana de Carmona* (1889); G. E. Bonsor, *Archaeological Sketc book of the Necropolis at Carmona* (1931); J. de M. Carriazo–l Raddatz, *Madrider Mitteilungen* 1961, 71 ff. M. I. F

**CARNEA** (Κάρνεια), a Doric festival, whose freque occurrence is proved by the name of the month Karnei (Aug./Sept.) which is common to most Doric calendar this month was considered to be holy. Details are know from Sparta. A meal took place in bowers like tents in military fashion and there was a race of youths calle σταφυλοδρόμοι. A youth put *tainiai* on his head and ra away; if he was overtaken by the others, it was a goo omen; if not, a bad one. The festival belonged to Apoll but he has certainly ousted an old god Karnos or Ka neios. The fact that κάρνος signifies 'ram' has given ris to various hypotheses; the interpretation of the festiv is uncertain.

S. Wide, *Lakonische Kulte* (1893), 74 ff.; Nilsson, *Feste*, 118 ff GGR i². 531 ff. M. P. N

**CARNEADES** (214/3–129/8 B.C., Apollod. in Diog. I 4. 65), from Cyrene, son of Epicomus (or Philocomus studied in the Academy under Hegesinus, whom he su ceeded as its head at a date earlier than 155, when he wa sent by the Athenians on a political embassy to Rom along with the Peripatetic Critolaus and the Sto Diogenes of Babylon. He resigned his position as hea of the Academy in 137/6, owing to age and weakness, an was succeeded by a younger namesake. He published n writings, but his views and arguments were transmitte by his pupils, particularly Clitomachus (q.v.), and wer long influential.

Carneades was known as the founder of the New c Third Academy, which superseded the Middle Academ of Arcesilaus (q.v. 1). He argued, using terms taken fro the Stoics, that grasp of reality could come only throug 'presentations' (φαντασίαι, lit. 'seemings'), mental event of which we are directly aware. These presentations ma give true or false evidence, but there is no mark by whic one that is true can be known to be true. Since we ca therefore never be certain that any presentation, wheth arising from the senses or from the mind, is veracious, w must always reserve our judgement (ἐπέχειν) and nev assent. But a presentation may be persuasive (πιθανή i.e. seems true or probable, or not. Persuasive ones a usually true, the unpersuasive usually false. For the pu poses of life we have to assume, although we must n assert, the truth or falsity of many presentations. Th more important the decision, the more probable we wis the presentation to be on the acceptance of which we ac Probability is greater if associated presentations are als persuasive, greater still if each member of the grou retains its credibility after close examination (Sext Math. 7. 159–89, 403–25; *H.P.* 1. 227–9 gives an earli erroneous version).

Carneades also attacked the dogmatic philosophers i detail, exposing their inconsistencies and improbabilitie

Many of his arguments against a belief in gods, providence, prophecy, and fate are to be found in Cicero (particularly *Nat. D.* 3 and *Div.* 2). He frequently maintained the two sides of a question successively, with great force and rhetorical skill. His speeches delivered at Rome in 155 in favour of and, the next day, against just behaviour by men or states made a deep impression and were used by Cicero in *Rep.* 3.

By the so-called *Carneadea divisio* he maintained that there were only 9 possible ends of human action (Cic. *Fin.* 16 ff.). Which of them he himself thought the most probable Clitomachus could never determine; he argued both for pleasure *plus virtue* and for the *enjoyment* of the 'primary natural goods', but this may have been to show the inadequacy of the Epicurean and Stoic views. He believed that happiness was a broad term, and that something deserving the name was in the reach of most men.

The differences between the New Academy and the later so-called Pyrrhonian sceptics are set out by Sextus, *Pyr.* 1. 220–32; they all turn on Carneades' admission of probability.

H. von Arnim in *PW*, s.v. Karneades, and see the bibliography under SCEPTICS. F. H. S.

**CARNEISCUS**, Epicurean of the third or second century B.C., author of Φιλίστας, a discussion of friendship in which Praxiphanes (q.v.) was criticized.

Ed. W. Crönert, *Kolotes u. Menedemos* 60 (1906).

**CARNUNTUM**, on the Danube between Petronell and Deutsch-Altenburg, was an important Roman military base and the seat of government of Pannonia (Superior). At first part of Noricum, Carnuntum was probably added to Pannonia c. A.D. 14 when Legio XV Apollinaris was transferred there from Emona (q.v.). The legionary fortress was constructed at this date: the stone wall probably dates from Tiberius, while some rebuilding in stone appears to have taken place in A.D. 73 (*CIL* iii. 11194–6). The legion remained at Carnuntum, except for the years 62–71, until c. 114 when it was replaced by XIV Gemina Martia Victrix. The civil settlement became a *municipium* (*Aelium*) under Hadrian and a *colonia* (*Septimia*) under Severus, who was proclaimed Emperor there. It was often visited by emperors: thus M. Aurelius wrote there the second book of his *Meditations*; Diocletian, Galerius, and Maximian met there in 308; Valentinian stayed at Carnuntum in 375, and ordered the camp to be reconstructed. Carnuntum was flourishing in the second century before its destruction in the Marcomannic Wars, after which it was soon rebuilt. Under Septimius Severus the civilian town increased largely, but later diminished. About 400 Carnuntum was burnt down. Temples, private houses, baths, two amphitheatres, military and civil burial-places have been excavated.

E. Swoboda, *Carnuntum, seine Geschichte und seine Denkmäler* (1964). F. A. W. S.; J. J. W.

**CARRHAE** (modern *Harran*), city in north Mesopotamia, the Haran of Genesis xi. 31, Ezekiel xxvii. 23, etc., 25 miles south-west of Edessa. Haran and its temple of the moon-god Sin are first mentioned on a tablet from Mari about 2,000 B.C. It was an important provincial capital, trading city, and fortress in the Assyrian empire; the site yielded notable inscriptions of Nabonidus in 1956). A Macedonian military colony (probably without full city status) under the Seleucid dynasty, it preserved its native name in the Hellenized form 'Carrhae'. The disastrous defeat of the Roman general Crassus, who invaded Parthian Mesopotamia in 53 B.C., occurred near Carrhae (Plut. *Crass.* 19 ff.; Pliny *HN* 5. 85, etc.). Carrhae was included in the territory annexed as a re-

sult of the eastern war of M. Aurelius and issued coins as a Roman city from his reign until that of Gordian III. Severus gave it colonial status and additional titles attest further honours from Caracalla, who was visiting the temple of Sin in 217 when he was assassinated. It was a fortress city, changing hands more than once during the centuries of frontier warfare between Rome and Byzantium and Sassanid Persia. At the time of its final capture by the Arabs in 639 the city was inhabited jointly by Christians and pagan Sabians.

The town walls survive, with the principal gateways; but most of the visible remains, including the Great Mosque and the Castle, are Islamic.

Jones, *Cities E. Rom. Prov.* ch. 9; C. J. Gadd, *Anat. Stud.* 1958, 35 ff.; S. Lloyd and W. Brice, ibid. 1951, 77 ff. E. W. G.

**CARRIAGES.** In Greece, from the earliest times, the ἅμαξα (or ἀπήνη), a cart usually with two (but sometimes with four) wheels and drawn by mules or donkeys, was used to transport loads in peace and war. Made of light wood or wicker-work, it became the common means of transport for persons. (It is often simply called ζεῦγος, 'a yoke'.) It could be covered with canvas and used for sleeping *en route*. Men preferred to be seen on horseback; but the ἅμαξα had to be used on long journeys with heavy luggage.

In Rome, the *plaustrum* was a similar primitive vehicle, often drawn by oxen and used for all rustic purposes. (The pronunciation 'plostrum' was taken as marking a rustic.) Very early—probably via Etruria (cf. Livy 1. 34)—the Romans came across other (Celtic) vehicles and all other names of vehicles are Celtic. Some cannot have been very different from the *plaustrum*, and the old word continued to be used generically for all of them. Only the most important can be mentioned here. The first was the *carpentum*, a covered two-wheeled wagon for two or three passengers. In 395 B.C. (Livy 5. 25. 9), traditionally, matrons were allowed to use it freely in Rome, the *pilentum* (a four-wheeled luxury version) being approved for religious ceremonies, including weddings and funerals. The *carpentum* became the standard small vehicle (normally mule-drawn) of the Postal Service (q.v.), used even by emperors on their travels; though for them and other important people there may have been a four-wheeled version. For longer journeys with heavy baggage, the standard vehicle was the *raeda* (spelling varies), familiar by the late republic. It was a four-wheeler with bench seats and a removable canvas top, strongly built for heavy loads. (The *Theodosian Code* allows it a maximum of 1,000 lbs. in the public service, against 200 for any two-wheeler.) It was drawn by any number of mules up to twenty (eight or ten in the public service), giving varying speeds; but it was, of course, expensive to run. However, *raedae* could be hired for a journey. The *carruca* was an aristocratic form of *raeda*, highly ornate and used only by eminent personages. The *carrus* was a smaller vehicle, with two or four wheels, modelled on a Celtic war-chariot, but used (it seems) chiefly for freight. In the late *cursus publicus* heavy *angaria* ('post-wagons') appear, drawn by oxen and used for slow freight. No doubt they existed before and were more generally used—perhaps simply a version of the old *plaustrum*. For rapid transport for one or two persons, the *cisium* (an open *carrozza*), drawn by one or two animals, provided such speed that speed-limits had to be imposed; nevertheless, it remained liable to accidents. In Cicero's day (*Rosc. Am.* 19) one could cover 56 difficult miles in ten hours at night in relays of *cisia*. They could usually be hired at the town gates, and the corporations of *cisiarii* probably had interchange agreements. The *essedum*, originally the great Celtic war-chariot used (e.g.) by the Britons (cf. Caes. *BGall.* 4. 33), was very similar to the *cisium*. When used by nobles and emperors, it could be luxurious and very ornate.

The law of Oppius (q.v. 1) prohibited the use of carriages in Rome during daylight hours (other towns probably had similar regulations), and this seems to have been generally observed, with statutory exceptions (e.g. religious ceremonies), down to the Empire. It then gradually fell into disuse as far as important people were concerned.

Chiefly owing to such regulations, and to the fact that no shock-absorption was attempted in the case of any type of carriage, litters (φορεῖα, lecticae), of oriental origin and long frowned upon, except for the use of invalids and perhaps women, became increasingly popular in the Hellenistic age and the late Republic. Basically portable beds carried by slaves, they could be curtained and highly ornamented and were comfortable for short-distance travel. Cicero was in a litter when he met the soldiers who killed him. Caesar and various emperors imposed restrictions, but quite ineffectively, since later even spoilt children were used to them (Quint. 1. 2. 7). Roman litters became heavy and elaborate, requiring up to eight burly slaves, and the number of lecticarii in a wealthy household became a measure of opulence. The sedan chair (δίφρος, sella), at its simplest a chair carried by two porters, was freely on hire and common in the streets. When used by the rich, it could be a luxurious curtained box with a comfortable seat.

Dar.-Sag. 'Vehiculum' and individual Latin words; E. M. Jope in *History of Technology* (ed. C. Singer and others), vol. ii (1950), 537 ff.
E. B.

**CARRINAS** (*PW* 1), GAIUS, perhaps praetor in 83 B.C., commanded government troops against Sulla and was several times defeated in central and northern Italy. After the escape of Carbo (q.v. 2), he tried to join Marius (q.v. 2) at Praeneste, in fact marched on Rome with the Samnite Pontius (2) and shared his defeat at the Colline Gate. He was captured and executed. E. B.

**CARSIOLI,** 42 miles east of Rome on the Via Valeria (q.v.), town of the Aequi which Rome converted into a Latin colony (c. 298 B.C.). Always an important and flourishing stronghold in antiquity, it disappeared in medieval times. Meagre ruins between modern *Arsoli* and *Carsoli* mark its site.

A. Cederna, *Nat. Scav.* 1951, 169 ff. E. T. S.

**CARSULAE,** on the Via Flaminia (q.v.) in Umbria, 10 miles north of Narnia (q.v.). Although rarely mentioned in ancient literature, the town was an important one, to judge from its recently excavated site. Its remains include a gate and double temple (of Honos and Virtus? cf. Livy 27. 25. 7; Plut. *Marc.* 28. 1). E. T. S.

**CARTEIA,** a town near San Roque on the coast of S. Spain in Baetica, lay some 4 miles from Gibraltar. The recent discovery of Hispano-Carthaginian coins suggests a pre-Roman origin, Punic if not Phoenician (the derivation of the name from *Kart* = Phoenician 'City' is thus made more probable). It figures in the Second Punic War as a naval base, and in 171 B.C. it was made a 'colonia civium Latinorum et libertinorum', comprising over 4,000 sons of Roman soldiers and Spanish women, together with Carteians who enrolled—the first Latin colony outside Italy (Livy 43. 3). It was famous for its fisheries, which were advertised on the coinage.

Coinage: A. Vives, *La Moneda hispanica* iv (1924), 18 ff. H. H. S.

**CARTHAGE** (*Kart-Hadasht*; Καρχηδών; *Carthago*). This Phoenician colony on the Tunisian coast was traditionally founded from Tyre in 814 B.C., but in reality

somewhat later. It provided anchorage and supplies for ships trading in the west for gold, silver, and tin. It remained dependent on Tyre for about two centuries but outstripped other Phoenician colonies because of its position and better harbour.

2. Trade was more important for Carthage than for any other ancient state. Most of it was conducted by barter with backward tribes in Africa and Spain, where metals were obtained in exchange for wine, cloth, and cheap manufactures. Voyages of exploration were undertaken along the Atlantic coast of North Africa and Spain. Carthage maintained a monopoly of trade in the western Mediterranean, sinking ships of other states which entered. From the fourth century, Carthage also exported agricultural products and entered the Hellenistic economy. The city grew fast; it was surrounded by a massive wall 22 miles in length and an artificial harbour basin was built; the population may have reached 400,000.

3. The Constitution of Carthage was oligarchic, and its stability was admired by Aristotle. The chief magistrates were two shophets (Lat. *suffetes*) who were elected annually on a basis of birth and wealth. Military commands were held by separately elected generals. There was a powerful 'senate' of several hundred life-members. The powers of the citizens were limited. A body of 104 'judges' scrutinized the actions of generals and other officials. Largely through this body the ruling class was successful in preventing the rise of tyranny either through generals manipulating the mercenary armies or officials working on popular discontents. Military service was not obligatory on the Carthaginians, whose population was too small to control a large area by citizen armies: instead, mercenaries were raised from various western Mediterranean peoples.

4. In the fifth century, owing to set-backs in Sicily Carthage occupied much of the hinterland in Tunisia and in course of time developed a prosperous agriculture At the same time many small settlements were made along the coast, which Carthage controlled from the borders of Cyrenaica to the Atlantic. The native Berber population in areas near Carthage adopted some elements of settled life (e.g. at Thugga); in general they were harshly ruled by the Carthaginians and eager to revolt.

5. The chief external policy of Carthage was the control of sea-routes to the west. From c. 600 B.C. it was clear that rival claims must lead to war between Etruscans Carthaginians, and Greeks. The westward thrust o Phocaea and Massilia was crushed off Alalia in Corsica by the Etruscan and Carthaginian fleets (c. 535). Carthage established its control in southern Sardinia and consolidated its hold on Gades, Malaca, and other parts o southern Spain. Earlier Malchus had won successes in Sicily, and the western end of the island was held fo Carthage by Panormus, Lilybaeum, and Drepanum.

6. For three centuries Carthaginians and Greek fought intermittently for Sicilian territory and th allegiance of Sicans, Sicels, and Elymians. In 480 B.C. great Carthaginian army under the shophet Hamilca was defeated at Himera by the tyrants Gelon and Theron His grandson, Hannibal, avenged him by destroyin Himera (409); but the ensuing wars with Dionysius o Syracuse ended with Carthaginian power confined t the west of the island. Agathocles carried the war int Africa, but was defeated near Tunis (307).

7. With Rome Carthage had concluded treaties i 508 and 348, in which she guarded jealously her mono poly of maritime trade, while abstaining from any inter ference in Italy. When Pyrrhus attacked (280), her fle helped Rome to victory. But sixteen years later Sicilia politics brought the two Powers into conflict and pre cipitated the Punic Wars (q.v.), which ended with th destruction of the city (146).

**8.** Rome decreed that neither house nor crop should se again. But Carthaginian blood survived. The grim antheon, which had nerved the Phoenician warriors in attle and siege, still persisted, and Africa continued to orship Baal-Hammon, Tanit-pene-Baal, Eshmoun, nd Melkart. Proof of the practice of human sacrifice as come from the excavation of the so-called 'tophet' at 'arthage. Urban life and the rule of shophets continued in aany Berber towns. Carthage never developed an art of er own, and was content to copy Greece and Egypt. She nanufactured and exported carpets, rugs, purple dyes, wellery, pottery, lamps, tapestry, timber, and hides. Ier great carrying trade passed to Italians and Greeks. Ier agricultural skill, which had made excellent use of ae richly phosphated Tunisian plain, profited her Roman onquerors and her Berber subjects; Mago's thirty-wo books on scientific farming were translated into atin.

**9.** The site of Carthage was too attractive to remain noccupied for long. The attempt of C. Gracchus (q.v. 4) establish the colony of Junonia on the suburban land ailed, but the city site was colonized by Caesar and ugustus. It received colonial rank (*see* COLONIZATION, OMAN) and became the capital of proconsular Africa. Ireat buildings rose on Byrsa Hill, and by the second entury A.D. Carthage had become second only to Rome n the western Mediterranean. A few urban troops and cohort of the Third Augustan legion sufficed to keep rder. But through his control of the African corn-trade, ae proconsul was a potential danger to the Emperor, as as shown by the rebellions of Clodius (q.v. 2) Macer and ae Gordians (qq.v.).

**10.** Carthage became an outstanding educational ntre, especially famous for orators and lawyers. In the iird century the genius of Tertullian and the devotion of yprian made her a focus of Latin Christianity. Her ishop held himself the equal of the bishop of Rome, and ae played a great part in establishing western Christianity n lines very different from the speculations of the Greek iurches. As a great Catholic stronghold, she fought gainst the Donatist heresy. When the Vandals (q.v.) verran Africa, she became the capital of Gaiseric and is successors. After Belisarius' victory Catholicism was estored on stricter lines. Carthage remained loyal to ae East Roman Empire and beat off the earlier Moslem avasions, until captured in 697.

Carthaginian inscriptions in *CISem*. i; G. K. Jenkins and R. B. ewis, *Carthaginian Gold and Electrum Coins* (1963); P. Cintas, *ramique punique* (1950). S. Gsell, *Histoire ancienne de l' Afrique du ord* (1914–28); De Sanctis, *Stor. Rom.* iii (1); O. Meltzer, *Geschichte r Karthager*, i–ii (1879–96), iii (by U. Kahrstedt, 1913); V. Ehren-rg, *Karthago* (1927); G. Picard, *Le Monde de Carthage* (1956: T. Carthage 1964); G. and C. Charles-Picard, *La Vie quotidienne Carthage* (1958: E. T. 1961); B. H. Warmington, *Carthage* (1960); Audollent, *Carthage romaine* (1901); for Roman colonization, Teutsch, *Das Städtewesen in Nordafrika* (1962), 2 ff., 101 ff.
W. N. W.; B. H. W.

**ARTHAGE (Topography).** Carthage was situated on art of a peninsula which projected seawards (and east-ards) within the Gulf of Tunis; the isthmus, which nked it to the mainland in the west, was 2–3 miles wide the narrowest point. Topographical details are contro-ersial and the remains of Punic Carthage small. The arliest settlers (nothing earlier than *c.* 750 B.C. has yet een found) probably disembarked on the little bay of l Kram, which faces south and is protected by a small eadland from the east. Nearby were built the Sanctuary ophet) of Tanit (of which a dedicatory deposit contains reek vases of *c.* 725 B.C.) and the artificial harbours of arthage. The settlement gradually spread northwards to ae Byrsa hill, the citadel. Despite some modern doubts is should be identified with the Hill of St. Louis, and ae ancient harbours with the Salammbo lagoons. If the

walls of Punic Carthage were over 20 miles in circum-ference (Livy, *Epit.* 51), a large part of the enclosed area must have been sparsely populated; traces of a ditch out-side the wall which ran across the isthmus have been identified. The citadel (Byrsa) had its own walls (which perhaps also included the so-called Juno and Odeon Hills).

The fortifications were destroyed by Rome in 146 B.C.; Theodosius II (A.D. 425) and Belisarius (553) refortified the site. The main harbour (Cothon), which was small and artificial, comprised an inner circular naval port and an outer rectangular commercial basin: it is visible as two adjacent lagoons; traces of the paved bottom of the circular port and of a quay survive. Be-tween the harbour and citadel was the central meeting place (agora). Cemeteries spread over the slopes of the hills of St. Louis and of Juno, and Bordj el Djedid: graves of the seventh and sixth centuries show that this area was at this time outside the inhabited part. Traces of the residential quarter of the Hellenistic period have been found on the southern part of the St. Louis hill, and a new quarter developed in the district of Sidi Bou Said further north (*c.* 300 B.C.). No traces of Roman colonial delimitation of the land can with certainty be attributed to the Gracchan settlers of Junonia. Remains of cisterns, an aqueduct, amphitheatre, houses, and the proconsular palace survive from Roman Carthage. See especially Appian, *Pun.* 8. 95 ff., Strabo 17. 3. 4, Orosius 4. 22.

H. P. Hurd, *The Topography of Punic Carthage* (U.S.A. 1934); D. B. Harden, *Greece & Rome* 1939, 1 ff., *The Phoenicians* (1962), 30 ff.; C. Picard, *Carthage* (1951, with bibliography of excavation reports); G and C. Charles-Picard, *Daily Life in Carthage* (1961), 25 ff.; J. Feron and M. Pinard, *Cahiers de Byrsa* v (1955), 31 ff.; ix (1960–1), 77 ff. (on the Byrsa hill); J. Baradez, *Karthago*, 1958 [1960], 45 ff. (on the harbours); F. Reyniers, *Mélanges Piganiol* (1966), 1281 ff.; P. Gauckler, *Nécropoles puniques de Carthage* (2 vols. 1915); A. Audollent, op. cit. and L. Teutsch, op. cit. 101 ff. in biblio-graphy s.v. CARTHAGE.
H. H. S.

**CARTHAGO NOVA,** a town in Hispania Citerior, today *Cartagena*. It lay on a peninsula within one of the best harbours of the Mediterranean. Originally named Mastia, it was refounded as New Carthage by Hasdrubal in 228 B.C. as a base for the Carthaginian conquest of Spain. It was captured by Scipio Africanus in 209, visited by Polybius in 133 (described in 10. 10), and made a colony (*Col. Iulia Victrix N.C.*) by Julius Caesar or more probably by Octavian after a prior grant of Latin rights by Julius (cf. M. Grant, *From Imperium to Auctoritas* (1946), 215 ff.). During the Empire it was overshadowed by Tarraco, though remaining an impor-tant city until its destruction by the Vandals (A.D. 425). It was famous for the neighbouring silver-mines, which brought the Roman treasury a daily revenue of 25,000 *drachmae*, for a fish sauce called *garum*, for mackerel, and for esparto grass (*spartum*) used for ropes, baskets, and sandals.

For the topography see H. H. Scullard, *Scipio Africanus* (1930), Appendix I. Numerous articles by A. Beltrán are listed by J. M. Blázquez, *Emerita* 1962, 104 n. 3. Coinage: A. Vives, *La Moneda hispanica* (1924), i. 37 ff., iv. 28 ff.
H. H. S.

**CARTIMANDUA,** queen of the Brigantes (q.v.), whose treaty-relationship with Claudius protected the early northern borders of Roman Britain. In A.D. 51, true to her obligation, she handed over the fugitive Caratacus (q.v.), but was weakened by the resulting breach with her husband, the patriot Venutius, and twice required the help of Roman troops in the period 52–57. Later, plan-ning to deprive him of support, she divorced Venutius and married his squire Vellocatus; but with the Roman world otherwise engaged in 68–9 Venutius seized his chance and drove her out. The result was the conquest of

Brigantia under Vespasian and its incorporation in the province.

I. A. Richmond, *JRS* 1954, 43 ff.; Frere, *Britannia*, ch. v.
S. S. F.

**CARUS,** MARCUS AURELIUS (*PW* 77), born at Narbo, praetorian prefect of Probus, rebelled in Raetia in A.D. 282, and, after Probus had been murdered by his troops, announced to the Senate his accession as Emperor. Leaving Carinus as Caesar in the west, Carus marched east against Persia with his younger son and Caesar, Numerian. On the way he defeated the Quadi and Sarmatae on the Danube. Carus invaded Persia and captured Ctesiphon, but, venturing on a further advance, was killed, perhaps by treachery on the part of Aper, the praetorian prefect.

T. B. Jones, *CPhil.* 1942, 193 f.; P. Meloni, *Il regno di Caro* (1948).
H. M.

**CARVILIUS** (1, *PW* 9) **MAXIMUS,** SPURIUS, twice consul with Papirius Cursor: in 293 B.C. when he conquered the Samnites at Cominium and dedicated a statue of Jupiter Capitolinus made from their armour (Livy 10. 43; Pliny, *HN* 34. 43); and in 272, when he closed the series of triumphs over the Samnites (Zonar. 8. 6). His censorship (Vell. Pat. 2. 128) probably belongs to 289.
E. T. S.

**CARVILIUS** (2), freedman of Spurius Carvilius Maximus (*cos.* 235 B.C.). 'The Romans were late in beginning to teach for payment, and the first of them to open an elementary school was Spurius Carvilius' (Plut. *Quaest. Rom.* 59). It is unlikely that Carvilius' school was the first to be opened at Rome, where literacy is attested *c.* 450 B.C. (Livy 3. 44). Cicero's statement, that boys in the early Republic were required to learn the XII Tables by heart, points to the probability that schools existed before 250. Carvilius probably was the first to open a school for pay, earlier teachers having depended on voluntary gifts from pupils.

According to Plutarch, Carvilius was the first to differentiate between the letters C and G (*Quaest. Rom.* 54). Some scholars have attributed the distinction to Appius Claudius Caecus. *See also* EDUCATION, V 2.

A. Gwynn, *Roman Education* (1926), 29 ff.
T. J. H.

**CARYATIDES,** a Greek term for columns or pilasters the shafts of which were carved in the form of draped females. The most famous caryatides are those of the Athenian Erechtheum (q.v.), one of which is now in the British Museum. Others have been found at Delphi, notably in the porch of the Siphnian treasury.

The name seems to have come from Caryae in Laconia. Vitruvius (1. 1. 5) tells an unlikely tale to explain it; more likely is some connexion with the dancers who performed in honour of Artemis (Paus. 3. 10. 7). The simple term *Korai* is sometimes used; male equivalents were called Atlantes (*see* ATLAS).
H. W. R.; R. E. W.

**CASCA,** SERVILIUS (*PW* 52 f.). Two brothers so named joined the conspiracy against Caesar in 44 B.C. One, Publius Longus, took a leading part and was the first to strike on the Ides of March. In 43 he was tribune, but when Octavian marched on Rome he fled and joined Brutus. The brothers killed themselves after Philippi (*Anth. Lat.* 457).

A third Casca, with the *praenomen* Gaius, apparently from another *gens*, was tribune in 44; alarmed at the fate of Helvius Cinna (q.v. 3), he put out a statement asserting that he had nothing but the *cognomen* in common with the two conspirators.
T. J. C.

**CASILINUM,** town in Campania (q.v.), where the Via Appia and Latina (qq.v.) met and crossed the Volturnu (q.v.): modern *Capua* (a name it acquired in A.D. 85 when the inhabitants of nearby ancient Capua (q.v.) fleeing the Saracens, settled here). Casilinum resolutel resisted, but finally fell to Hannibal. It has always been strategic keypoint.
E. T. S

**CASINUM,** town on the Via Latina (q.v.), near th southern extremity of Latium (q.v.): modern *Cassino* with Saint Benedict's celebrated monastery on th mountain above it. Volsci and Samnites (qq.v.) succes sively held Casinum. Under Rome it was a flourishin *municipium*, where Mark Antony caroused in Varro' renowned villa.
E. T. S

**CASPIAN SEA** (also called 'Hyrcanian' from its SE coast). This large and brackish inland water was cor rectly described by Herodotus as a lake. In spite o partial exploration by Greeks, all subsequent writer thought that the Oxus and Iaxartes flowed into it; man believed that it was joined to the Black Sea (by the rive Phasis), or to the Sea of Azov; and the prevalent vie was that a channel linked it with a not far distant North ern Ocean. The first of these opinions may have ha apparent support from the remains of a prehistori channel between the Caspian and the Aral Sea, and th last may have been prompted by a vague knowledge o the Volga. About 285 B.C. Patrocles (q.v.) sailed u both sides, but failing to reach the north end, gav currency to the belief that one could sail from the Caspia to India by the Northern Ocean. Renewed exploratio after the reign of Tiberius led to the rediscovery of th Volga ('Rha' in Ptolemy), and Ptolemy restated the trut that the Caspian is a lake, though he got its shape wrong

Cary–Warmington, *Explorers* (1929), 136 ff., (1963, Pelican) 166 177, 185, 198; Thomson, *Hist. of Anc. Geog.*, index; Cary, *Geo graphic Background*, 177 f., 184, 189 ff., 198 f., 312. A. Herrmann *PW*, s.v. 'Kaspisches Meer'.
E. H. W

**CASSANDER** (*c.* 358–297 B.C.), son of Antipater (q.v. 1) joined Alexander in Asia (324). They seem to hav disliked one another intensely, but the tradition which makes him Alexander's murderer is false. When th Empire began to split up after the death of Antipate (319), Cassander drove the regent Polyperchon from Macedonia and most of Greece (319–316); hencefort his aim was to keep what he held, which involved resist ing the efforts of Antigonus to reunite the Empire unde himself. These efforts he finally joined in defeating (with Ptolemy, Lysimachus, and Seleucus) by the decisiv victory of Ipsus (301). His last four years were devote mainly to consolidating his position at home.

Ruthless and drastic though he was in politics, Cass ander was no barbarian. He founded two great cities Cassandreia and Thessalonica (*Salonika*), and he rebuil Thebes. As befitted the slayer of Alexander's mother son, and widow, he had friends among the Peripatetics the literary group which had least cause to cherish Alex ander's memory.

Diodorus, bks. 18–20. W. W. Tarn, *CAH* vi, ch. 15, and vii 75 ff.; Berve, *Alexanderreich* ii, no. 414; Bengtson, *Strategie* 134 ff.
G. T. G

**CASSANDRA** or **ALEXANDRA,** in mythology daughter of Priam (q.v.). In Homer, nothing is said o her being a prophetess; she is mentioned (*Il.* 13. 365 as being the most beautiful of Priam's daughters, an (in 24. 699 ff.) she is the first to see the body of Hecto being brought home. Nor is it clear that post-Homeri epic enlarged on the Homeric picture; its principal ne episode, assuming that Homer did not already know o it, is her mishandling by Aias (q.v. 2) the Locrian. Ho old the tradition of her prophetic gifts is we do not know, but in surviving literature it appears first in Pindar, *Pyth.* 11. 33 (474 or 454 B.C.; if the latter, then later than Aeschylus, *Agamemnon*, with which it has points of contact; perhaps both draw on the *Oresteia* of Stesichorus). In *Agam.* 1203 ff., Apollo has given her the power of prophecy, to win her love; as she cheats him, he turns the blessing into a curse by causing her always to be disbelieved. Later authors follow this form of the story, which indeed Aeschylus seems to imply was already well known when he wrote. There is, however, another (schol. *Il.* 7. 44 and Eustathius 663, 40) which says that she and Helenus, when children, had their ears licked by serpents while asleep and so got their prophetic gift. She commonly appears, in Tragedy and elsewhere, as foretelling vainly the evil results of successive events, such as the birth of Paris, and finally warning the Trojans against the Wooden Horse (as Verg. *Aen.* 2. 246). On the basis of this, Lycophron (*Alexandra*) takes occasion to put into her mouth a forecast of mythological and historical adventures of both Trojans and Greeks from the war to his own day. For her story *see* AGAMEMNON, AIAS (2).

In art she is chiefly represented at the moment when she clutches the image of Athena and Aias seizes her: a favourite scene in archaic and classical periods, by itself or as part of the Iliupersis. In archaic pictures she is naked. Polygnotus showed her in his Troy at Delphi, and apparently also that at Athens, sitting on the ground clasping the fallen image, while Aias at an altar took an oath about the assault.

Farnell, *Hero-Cults*, 329 ff.; J. Davreux, *La Légende de la prophétesse Cassandre* (1942); P. G. Mason, *JHS* 1959, 80 ff. In art, Brommer, *Vasenlisten²*, 282 ff. and Davreux, loc. cit.

H. J. R.; C. M. R.

**CASSIAN**, JOHN, *c.* A.D. 360–435, came from the East (Bethlehem, Egypt, Constantinople) to found monasteries at Marseilles, *c.* 415. He wrote *Instituta* or rules for his monastic communities, and then the more inward 'Conferences' (*Collationes*), using his recollections of famous Egyptian ascetics. He was the principal transmitter to the West of the best ascetic wisdom of the desert fathers. His good sense and moderation (exemplified in explicit refusal to pander to demands for miracles) and his psychological and spiritual penetration made him a determinative influence on western monasticism. His delicate critique of Augustine's doctrine of grace (*Coll.* 13) drew a charge of Semi-Pelagianism from Prosper (q.v.) of Aquitaine, and in the West he has never been a canonized saint.

WORKS. Ed. M. Petschenig, *CSEL* xiii, xvii. O. Chadwick, *John Cassian²* (1967).

H. C.

**CASSIODORUS** (FLAVIUS MAGNUS AURELIUS CASSIODORUS, SENATOR). Roman politician and writer (*c.* A.D. 490–*c.* 583). He was born in southern Italy of a senatorial family of distant Syrian origin. He had a large estate near Scylacium (q.v.). His father had been a prefect of the praetorium of Theodoric, king of the Goths, and he followed his father in the same career. Consul A.D. 514, *magister officiorum* between 523 and 527 in succession to Boethius, he became prefect of the praetorium of King Athalaricus in 533. In 535 he made an unsuccessful attempt (in collaboration with Pope Agapetus) to set up a Christian university in Rome. In 537 he retired and devoted himself increasingly to scholarship and religion. He may have been taken prisoner by the Byzantines and brought to Constantinople in 540. By 550 he was an influential man there. He must have gone back to Italy a few years later when Justinian pacified and reorganized the country. He established a religious community called Vivarium on his ancestral estate in Calabria. Its characteristic feature was the emphasis on the intellectual activities of the monks. Though the monastery of Vivarium did not survive beyond the seventh century, it had far-reaching importance for the preservation of ancient books and in creating a model of monastic life which was later to influence the Benedictine order.

Cassiodorus wrote among other works: (1) a brief summary of Roman history to A.D. 519 (within the context of a universal history) which is known as *Chronica*; (2) a great work on the history of the Goths in twelve books which are lost, but were summarized by Jordanes (q.v.) in the extant *Getica*; (3) a treatise on the soul; (4) a commentary on the Psalms; (5) *De Orthographia*; (6) the *Institutiones*, a very influential guide to the education of his monks in both secular and religious matters.

The history of the Goths which was written before 534 (but probably revised and brought up to date in different circumstances in 551) was meant to reconcile Goths and Romans. It brings together much important information not only on the Goths, but also on the Huns: truth, however, is sometimes distorted to please the Gothic masters. About 538 Cassiodorus edited under the title *Variae* the most important letters and edicts he had written on behalf of the Gothic kings. He also organized the Latin translation of Greek works (such as Flavius Josephus' *Jewish Antiquities* and the so-called *Historia Tripartita*, an ecclesiastical history from A.D. 306 to 439 compiled from Theodoretus, Socrates, and Sozomenus). He is one of the founders of western medieval civilization.

All the works in Migne, *PL* lxix–lxx. The *Variae* and the *Chronica*, ed. by Th. Mommsen in *MGH*. A condensed English translation of the *Variae* by T. Hodgkin (1886). *Institutiones*, ed. by R. A. B. Mynors (1937) and transl. into English with important introd. by L. W. Jones (1946). *De Anima*, ed. by J. W. Halporn, *Traditio*, 1960, 39; the commentary on the Psalms, ed. by M. Adriaen in *Corpus Christ.* (1958); *De Orthographia*, ed. H. Keil, *Gramm. Lat.* 7. 143. An excerpt from the Cassiodorus' lost history of his own family was first published by H. Usener, *Anecdoton Holderi* (1877). D. M. Cappuyns in A. Baudrillart, *Dict. hist. géogr. ecclés.* 11, 1949, 1349; J. J. van den Besselaar, *Cassiodorus Senator* (1945, in Dutch); W. Wattenbach-Levison, *Deutschlands Geschichtsquellen* i, 1952, 67; A. Momigliano, *Proc. Brit. Acad.* 1955, 207 ff.; id., *Entretiens Hardt* 4. 247 ff. (both repr. in *Secondo Contributo*, 1960); P. Riché, *Éducation et culture dans l'occident barbare* (1962), 200 ff.

A. M.

**CASSITERIDES** ('Tin Islands'), a name applied generically to all the north Atlantic tin lands, but especially to Cornwall and the Scillies (which may have served as depots for Cornish tin). They were probably first discovered by Phoenicians or Carthaginians from Gades; the latter eventually established an open-sea route from north-west Spain. A Greek named Midacritus (*c.* 600 B.C.?) is recorded to have imported tin from Cassiteris island (Pliny, *HN* 7. 197), but it is doubtful whether he actually reached the Cassiterides. The Carthaginians kept their tin-routes secret, hence Herodotus (3. 115) doubted the existence of the Cassiterides. Pytheas (q.v.) visited the miners of Belerium (*Land's End*) and their tin depot at Ictis (q.v., *St. Michael's Mt.*); but it was left to a Roman, P. Crassus (probably a governor in Spain *c.* 95 B.C.), to make the tin-routes generally known. Strabo, who enumerates ten Cassiterides (the Scillies group contains thirty islands), describes the Cornish tin and lead mines and the black cloaks and long tunics of the natives. The importance of the Cornish mines declined in the first century A.D., after the discovery of tin deposits in Spain. *See also* TIN.

Strabo 3. 175–6. T. R. Holmes, *Ancient Britain* (1907), 483 ff.; F. J. Haverfield, *PW*, s.v. 'Kassiterides'; Thomson, *Hist. of Anc. Geog.* 55, 195 f.

E. H. W.

**CASSIUS** (1, *PW* 91) **VECELLINUS**, SPURIUS, according to the Fasti, was consul in 502, 493, and 486 B.C., though bearing a plebeian name, and mediated the treaty made between Rome and the Latins in 493. This established peace throughout Latium, providing for mutual military assistance on equal terms, and held good till *c.* 380. Dubious legends attached to the name of Spurius (e.g. that in 486 he planned an agrarian law in the interest of the plebeians, aiming at royal power, and was condemned to death in 485) need cast no doubt upon the treaty. Its effect is discernible beneath the surface of Livy's narrative, which tends, through pride, to obscure the fact that Rome was only an equal partner.

For bibliography, *see under* LATINI. A. N. Sherwin-White, *The Roman Citizenship* (1939), 20 ff.; Ogilvie, *Comm. Livy 1–5,* 337 ff.
A. N. S.-W.

**CASSIUS** (2, *PW* 47) **HEMINA,** LUCIUS, the Latin annalist, treated Roman history from early Italian times (book 1) and the founding of Rome (book 2) to the Second Punic War (book 4), writing before the Third Punic War (cf. the title *Bellum Punicum posterior* of book 4); but fr. 39 (146 B.C.) indicates an extension. His interest in Italian origins, in etymological, religious, and social antiquities, and in synchronism (fr. 8), reflects the influence, especially, of Cato's *Origines.*

Peter, *HRRel.* i². clxv and 98. T. Frank, *Life and Literature in the Roman Republic* (1930), 172 ff. A. H. McD.

**CASSIUS** (3, *PW* 42) **DIONYSIUS** of Utica, wrote (1) (88 B.C.) a Greek translation (with additions) of the work of the Carthaginian Mago on agriculture, which became the standard work on the subject, used by all its successors in antiquity; (2) 'Ριζοτομικά, a compilation much used by Pliny the Elder. W. D. R.

**CASSIUS** (4, *PW* 72) **LONGINUS RAVILLA,** LUCIUS, as tribune in 137 B.C. passed a *lex tabellaria* introducing secret ballot in all trials before the People (except for treason). He was consul in 127, and as censor (125) he (with his colleague Cn. Servilius Caepio) brought the *Aqua Tepula* (an inferior aqueduct) to Rome. Renowned for severity as a *iudex* (called 'scopulus reorum'), he gained fame by formulating an important principle of investigation in the question '*Cui bono?* (= 'Who profited?'). In 113, when three Vestals had been accused of unchastity and two acquitted by the Pontifex Maximus Metellus (q.v. 5), he was appointed as special investigator and convicted them and other people involved. E. B.

**CASSIUS** (5, *PW* 70) **LONGINUS,** QUINTUS, probably cousin of the tyrannicide, was Pompey's rapacious quaestor in Further Spain *c.* 52 B.C. In 49, as one of the two tribunes who supported Caesar, he fled to his camp and in April summoned the Senate on his behalf. Caesar made him governor of Further Spain, where he surpassed his conduct as quaestor. While preparing an expedition against Juba (48) he was surprised by a rebellion of provincials and soldiers; peace was restored after the arrival of Bogud (q.v.) and Lepidus (q.v. 3), to whom he had sent for help. When his successor Trebonius (q.v.) also arrived (early 47), he left with his treasures, but his ship was wrecked. T. J. C.

**CASSIUS** (6, *PW* 59) **LONGINUS,** GAIUS, the tyrannicide, was quaestor to M. Crassus (q.v. 4) in 53 B.C., escaped from Carrhae (q.v.), collected the remnants of the army, and organized the defence of Syria, staying on as proquaestor till 51: in 52 he crushed an insurrection in Judaea and in 51 repelled a Parthian invasion. As tribune in 49 he supported Pompey and was appointed by him to a naval command; in 48 he operated in Sicilian waters but on the news of Pharsalus abandoned the war and presently (perhaps in spring 47) obtained Caesar's pardon and the post of *legatus. Praetor peregrinus* in 44, he played a leading part in the conspiracy against Caesar. Soon after the deed he was forced by popular hostility to leave Rome, and was assigned by the Senate

in June the task of importing corn from Sicily, and late the unimportant province of Cyrene. After quarrellin with Antony, he sailed instead for Asia (Sept. or Oct. and thence to Syria, where, early in 43, the governors o Bithynia and Syria, Marcius Crispus and Staius Murcu (q.v.), put their armies at his disposal. Caecilius Bassu (q.v. 1), whom they had been besieging, followed suit; force under A. Allienus on its way from Egypt to Dola bella (q.v. 3) was intercepted and made to join him; an after the capture of Laodicea he took over Dolabella' army too. After Mutina the Senate had given him, wit Brutus, command over all the eastern provinces and prob ably also *imperium maius*; but in the autumn they wer outlawed for the murder of Caesar under the law of Pediu (q.v. 1). After raising more troops and money and sub duing the Rhodians, who had refused their support Cassius crossed with Brutus to Thrace in the summer o 42 and encountered Antony and Octavian at Philippi(q.v.) In the first battle his camp was captured and, probabl under the impression that the day was altogether lost, h killed himself.

More keen-sighted and practical than Brutus, Cassiu seems nevertheless to have been less respected and les influential. He was a man of violent temper and sarcasti tongue, a strict disciplinarian, and ruthless in his exac tions. The charge of covetousness may have been we founded; but there is no convincing evidence that h was influenced by petty motives in the conspiracy agains Caesar. He married Brutus' half-sister Junia Terti (Tertulla), who survived till A.D. 22 (Tac. *Ann.* 3. 76).

Cicero, *Letters* and *Philippics*; Caes. *BCiv.* 3. 5, 101; Vell. Pat. 2 46–73; Joseph. *AJ* 14; Plut. *Crass., Caes., Brut., Ant.*; App. *BCiv* 2–4; Cass. Dio 40–7. Tyrrell and Purser, *Correspondence of Cicer* vi² (1933), cii ff.; Syme, *Rom. Rev.*, see index. G. W. R.; T. J. C

**CASSIUS** (7, *PW* 65) **LONGINUS,** LUCIUS, brothe of the tyrannicide, took Caesar's side in the Civil Wa and in 48 B.C. held a proconsular command in Greece Tribune in 44, he took no part in the conspiracy agains Caesar; he may have passed the *Lex Cassia* enabling Caesar to create patricians. He supported Octavia against Antony, and after their reconciliation in 43 flee to Asia, where Antony pardoned him in 41. Cassius (11 was probably his grandson. T. J. C

**CASSIUS** (8, *PW* 80) **PARMENSIS** (i.e. of Parma was, like Cassius (6) Longinus, among Caesar's murderers Horace (*Epist.* 1. 4. 3) thinks of Albius (Tibullus) a writing poetry to surpass that of this Cassius (confusec by the scholiasts with an inferior poet Cassius Etruscus Hor. *Sat.* 1. 10. 61). J. W. D

**CASSIUS** (9, *PW* 89) **SEVERUS,** Augustan orato whose speeches were brilliant but bitter (Sen. *Controv.* ; *praef.*; Quint. *Inst.* 10. 1. 116; 12. 10. 11; Tac. *Dial* 19 and 26). Like T. Labienus (q.v. 3), he had his works publicly burned (Tac. *Ann.* 1. 72; 4. 21; Suet. *Calig.* 16) He died in the 25th year of his exile about A.D. 34 (Euseb Chron.). J. W. D

**CASSIUS** (10, *PW* 37) **CHAEREA,** a centurion ir Lower Germany in A.D. 14. In 41, as a tribune in th Praetorian Guard, he was mocked by Gaius for hi supposed effeminacy. He played a leading part in th latter's murder (41). On Claudius' accession he wa executed. J. P. B

**CASSIUS** (11, *PW* 60) **LONGINUS,** GAIUS, a promi nent Roman jurist. After holding the urban praetorshij he was *cos. suff.* A.D. 30, proconsul of Asia 40–1, *legatu* of Syria 45–9. Exiled by Nero in 65 to Sardinia, he live to be recalled by Vespasian. His principal work was th *Libri iuris civilis,* known through a revised edition b

avolenus (q.v.) and citations in later jurists' works. He
njoyed high authority as a jurist, and his *responsa* are
ften cited. He was a pupil of Sabinus, after whose death
e became head of the Sabinian school; hence it is some-
mes called *schola Cassiana* (*Cassiani*). *See* SABINUS 2.

A. B.; B. N.

**CASSIUS** (12, *PW* 3), a Roman physician of the time of
Augustus and Tiberius (31 B.C.–A.D. 37). His specific
or the relief of colic was famous in antiquity.

**CASSIUS** (13, *PW* 8), Ἰατροσοφιστής, the author of
Ἰατρικαί ἀπορίαι καί προβλήματα φυσικά, not earlier than
he 3rd century A.D. The author must have been a rather
clectic member of the Pneumatic school of medicine.

Ed. J. L. Ideler, *Physici et Medici Graeci Minores* (1841) i. 144.

W. D. R.

**CASSIVELLAUNUS,** king presumably of the Catu-
ellauni (Herts.), appointed supreme commander of the
outh-eastern Britons on the occasion of Caesar's second
nvasion (54 B.C.). After an initial defeat in Kent, he
ndeavoured to avoid battle and hamper his enemies'
oragers—strategy which much embarrassed Caesar, who
vas able, however, to capture his capital (probably
Vheathampstead, cf. R. E. M. Wheeler, *Verulamium*
1936), 20). A peace was arranged through Caesar's agent
Commius, by which Cassivellaunus agreed to pay a
ribute and allow the independence of the Trinovantes
Essex). No coinage can be certainly attributed to him.

Caesar, *BGall.* 5. 11. 8; 18–22. Collingwood–Myres, *Roman
Britain*, 46 ff.; D. F. Allen, 'The Origins of Coinage in Britain',
*ron Age in S. Britain*, 97 ff.

C. E. S.

**CASTOR AND POLLUX.** The cult of the Dioscuri
q.v.) was introduced into Rome at an early date, tradi-
ionally (Livy 2. 20. 12; 42. 5) in 484 B.C., in consequence
f a vow made by A. Postumius at the battle of Lake
Regillus. In this connexion the famous legend (derived
rom Locri in Magna Graecia) arose, that they actually
ook part in the battle and brought word of it to Rome
Dion. Hal. *Ant. Rom.* 6. 13. 1–2). Their temple was in
he Forum (cf. Platner–Ashby, 102; Nash, *Pict. Dict.
Rome* i. 210 ff.); it was commonly called *aedes Castoris*,
he two brothers being not infrequently referred to as
*Castores*. Several indications point to the introduction of
he cult from Tusculum (Wissowa, *RK* 269 f.), but an
nscription from Lavinium, discovered in 1958, shows
hat their cult was known there about 500 B.C. with a
itle (*qurois*) directly derived from Greek (Degrassi,
*LLRP* ii. 1271; cf. S. Weinstock, *JRS* 1960, 112 ff.).
There is no evidence that the cult in Rome was under
he control of the *quindecimviri* (q.v.), like normal Greek
r other foreign worships. The most outstanding feature
f the ritual was the close connexion of the brethren with
he *equites*, whose ceremonial parade (*transvectio equitum*)
ook place on 15 July, the traditional date of the battle
Dion. Hal., ibid. 4; for the age of this, see S. Weinstock,
*MSR* 1937, 10 ff.). A controversial point is the con-
exion of the Castores with Juturna, whose *lacus* in the
orum is near their temple. F. Altheim (*RGVV* 1930,
ff.) argues that her name has an Etruscan suffix (*θur*),
neans 'daughter of Jupiter' or the like, and indicates close
ssociation between her and them. Other scholars hold
he nearness of the places of worship to be merely
ortuitous.

Wissowa, *RK* 268 ff.; Latte, *RR* 173 ff.     H. J. R.; H. W. P.

**CASTOR OF RHODES,** rhetorician, possibly to be
dentified with the son-in-law of Deiotarus, the Galatian
etrarch, published Χρονικά, synchronistic tables of
Oriental, Greek, and Roman history, from the Assyrian

Belus and Ninus and the Sicyonian Aegialeus to Pompey
(61–60 B.C.), adding the mythical period of Greek kings
to the tables of Eratosthenes and Apollodorus; the work
was used by Varro, Julius Africanus, and Eusebius.

*FGrH* ii B, 1130; BD, 814.     A. H. McD.

**CASTRA REGINA,** modern *Regensburg* (also known
by Celtic name Rataspona, hence modern *Ratisbon*), was
a Roman military station in Raetia on the Danube at the
mouth of the River Regen. From the Flavian period it
was garrisoned by an auxiliary cohort, replaced by Legio
III Italica under Marcus Aurelius when it became the
provincial capital.

J. J. W.

**CASTULO,** a city of the Oretani situated near the upper
Baetis (*Guadalquivir*) in the Saltus Castulonensis (*Sierra
de Segura*). Its importance, indicated by the description
*urbs valida ac nobilis*, derived from the lead and silver
mines nearby, and from its situation on an old route from
Valentia to Corduba. Hannibal chose a wife from Castulo. It was a key fortress which thrice changed hands in
the Hannibalic War. Pliny lists it among the *Latini
veteres* of early imperial Baetica.

M. Acedo, *Castulo* (1902); P. Spranger, *Hist.* 1958, 95 ff.

J. J. VAN N.; M. I. H.

**CATACOMBS,** a term derived from κατά κύμβας, a
locality close to the church of St. Sebastian on the Via
Appia, 3 miles south of Rome. The name may refer to
the natural hollows across which the road passes or to an
inn-sign, but was in use in the fourth and fifth centuries
A.D. for the Christian cemetery associated with St.
Sebastian's in the form *ad catacumbas* or *catacumbae*.
This famous cemetery was a series of narrow underground
galleries and tomb-chambers, cut in the rock. Their walls
are lined with tiers (up to seven are known) of coffin-like
recesses (*loculi*) for inhumation, holding from one to four
bodies apiece and sealed with a stone slab or with tiles.
The affinity to *columbaria* (q.v.) is evident, but the type
itself seems to have been immediately derived from
Jewish catacombs (H. W. Beyer and H. Lietzmann, *Die
Katakombe Torlonia*, 1930), where Jews, like Christians,
remained a household of the faithful, united in death as
in life. Catacombs were not confined to Rome: examples
are known at Albano, Alexandria, Hadrumetum, Kertsch,
Naples, Malta, and Syracuse. All are associated with soft
rocks, where tunnelling was easy.

The catacombs at Rome, however, are much the most
extensive, stretching for at least 350 miles. Their distribution, along the main roads outside the city, is explained
by their later growth out of, or side by side with, pagan
cemeteries lying beyond the city boundaries in conformity
with the law. That of St. Priscilla, on the Via Salaria,
grew out of the burial-ground of the Acilii Glabriones
(q.v. 4), possibly persecuted for their Christianity under
Domitian. The Domitilla catacomb, on the Via Ardeatina,
developed from the hypogeum of the Flavii. The official
organization by the Church of public catacombs, mainly
for the poor of the Roman Christian community, began
c. 200, when the then pope, St. Zephyrinus, directed
St. Callixtus to provide τό κοιμητήριον (see the third-
century Greek document known as the *Philosophumena*),
which is represented by the oldest part of the catacomb
beside the Via Appia that bears St. Callixtus' name today.
Another important catacomb near the same road is that
of Praetextatus.

In the tomb-chambers (*cubicula*) of the catacombs are
altar-tombs and arched recesses (*arcosolia*) for the bodies
of popes and martyrs. Walls and ceilings received paintings which represent the first development of Christian
art and are executed in the same technique and style as
contemporary pagan work. Their subjects are biblical

(scenes from the O.T. far outnumbering those from the N.T.) or symbolic (the Good Shepherd, Christus-Orpheus, Christ as Lawgiver, Eucharistic and celestial banquets, figures of Orantes, etc.). A few motifs are drawn from daily life and some are frankly pagan. A remarkable and probably private catacomb, dating from the fourth century and brought to light on the Via Latina in 1955, has paintings which include a medical class and six episodes from the Hercules cycle, as well as biblical scenes more elaborate and showing a much wider range of content than those in the official public catacombs. Furniture in the catacombs included carved sarcophagi, lamps, pottery vessels of various kinds, and painted glass medallions.

The presence of these large cemeteries is explained partly by the size of the Christian community in Rome and partly by the long periods of toleration. By about a century after the official recognition of the Church, the catacombs passed into desuetude and became centres of pilgrimage.

O. Marucchi, *Le catacombe romane* (1933); P. Styger, *Die römischen Katakomben* (1933); L. Hertling and E. Kirschbaum, *Le Catacombe romane e i loro martiri* (1949), E.T. 1960; E. Bick and R. Goebel, *Die Katakomben* (1961); J. Wilpert, *Die Malereien der Katakomben Roms* (1901); A. Ferrua, *Le pitture della nuova catacomba di Via Latina* (1960). On the Jewish catacombs of Rome, see G. B. Frey, *Rend. Pont.* 1937; H. J. Levi, 'The Jewish Catacombs and Inscriptions of Rome' (*Hebrew Union College Annual*, 1928, 299 ff.); E. R. Goodenough, *Jewish Symbols in the Graeco-Roman Period* ii, 1953, 3 ff.; iii, 1957, figs. 702–838. See also *Rivista di archeologia cristiana*, passim; *Jahrbuch für Antike und Christentum*, passim.          I. A. R.; J. M. C. T.

**CATANA** (Κατάνη, Latin *Catĭna*, modern *Catania*), founded from Naxos (q.v. 2) in 729 B.C., lies beside the sea at the southern extremity of the slopes of Mount Aetna; to the south stretches the fertile *Piana di Catania*, coveted by the Syracusans, whose superior power dominated Catana for much of its history. Its lawgiver Charondas was its most famous citizen in its early period. Hieron I (q.v.) removed the Catanaeans to Leontini and renamed the city Aetna, repeopling it with Dorian mercenaries. In 461 these were expelled (*see* AETNA) and the old name restored. The Athenians used Catana as a base in 415–413. Captured by Dionysius I (q.v.) in 403, it thenceforward formed part of the Syracusan Empire, with brief intervals of independence or subjection to Carthage. After 263, when the Romans captured it, it became a *civitas decumana*, and it flourished greatly under Roman rule (Cic. *Verr.* iii. 103) although it suffered in the first Servile War. Eruptions and earthquakes, especially those of 1169, 1669, and 1693, have left few ancient remains in the prosperous modern city.

Bérard, *Bibl. topogr.* 45 ff.; Dunbabin, *Western Greeks*, esp. 129 ff.
                                                                A. G. W.

**CATILINE** (LUCIUS SERGIUS [*PW* 23] CATILINA), of patrician (but not recently distinguished) family, served with Pompey and Cicero under Pompeius Strabo in the Social War. He then reappears as a lieutenant of Sulla both in the *bellum Sullanum* and in the proscriptions, when he killed his brother-in-law Marius (q.v. 3). There is no further record of him until his praetorship (68 B.C.), after which he governed Africa for two years. On his return he was prosecuted *repetundarum* and was prevented from standing for the consulates of 65 and 64, though finally acquitted with the co-operation of his prosecutor Clodius (q.v. 1). In 66/5 he was said to be involved in a conspiracy with Autronius and Sulla (q.v. 2); the details are obscured by gossip and propaganda. His frustrated ambition became his driving force: in the elections for 63 he made a compact with C. Antonius (q.v. 3) and gained the support of Caesar, Crassus (q.v. 4), and others, but was defeated by Cicero. He then began to champion the cause of the poor and discontented, especially dissolute

aristocrats, bankrupt Sullan veterans, and those whos land they had occupied. Again defeated for 62, he organ ized a widespread conspiracy, with ramifications through out Italy. Cicero, fully informed by his spies, could no take decisive action against him owing to lack of sufficien support; for Catiline, as a demagogue, a patrician, and a old Sullan, was both popular and well connected. I November Cicero succeeded in frightening Catiline int joining a force of destitute veterans that had assembled i Etruria; soon afterwards some Allobrogan envoys, care lessly approached by conspirators in Rome (*see* LENTULU 4), provided Cicero with the written evidence he needed and the leaders of the conspiracy in Rome were arreste and (after a vote in the Senate) executed. Antoniu marched out against Catiline, who was caught betwee him and Metellus (q.v. 9) Celer and defeated and kille by Petreius (q.v.) near Pistoria (early Jan. 62). Cicero wa hailed as saviour of Rome, but incurred much unpopu larity on account of the executions.

SOURCES. Chiefly Cicero, *In Catilinam* and Sallust, *Catilin* Modern discussions are numerous: the best perhaps still C. Joh Die *Entstehungsgeschichte der catilinarischen Verschwörung* (1876 G. Boissier, *La Conjuration de Catilina* (1905); E. G. Hardy, *Th Catilinarian Conspiracy* (1924); Z. Yavetz, *Hist.* 1963, 485; for rece bibliography, N. Criniti, *Aevum* 1967, 370 ff. On Sallust, see R. Sym *Sallust* (1964), 60 ff.                                    E. F

**CATIUS,** TITUS, an Insubrian, mentioned by Cicer (*Fam.* 15. 16) as a recently deceased writer on Epi cureanism.

Schanz–Hosius, § 157 b.

**CATO** (1) 'CENSORIUS', MARCUS PORCIUS (*PW* 9) (234 149 B.C.), was born of peasant stock in Tusculum. H fought as military tribune in the Second Punic War an was at Metaurus (207). His proof of legal ability an stern traditional morality impressed L. Valerius Flaccu with whom he began his political career. Quaestor in 204 he was in Sicily, and on his return via Sardinia brough Ennius to Rome (203–202). Plebeian aedile in 199, h became praetor in Sardinia in 198, expelling usurers *Leges Porciae de sumptu provinciali* and *de provocatione* ar probably to be dated here. Consul in 195 with I Valerius Flaccus, he opposed the repeal of the *Lex Oppi* and took the province of Spain; here, after extensiv operations, he settled the administration and initiated th development of Roman rule.

After distinguished service under Manius Aciliu Glabrio at Thermopylae (191), he prosecuted Q. Minu cius Thermus (190), and, himself a candidate, supporte charges of peculation against Glabrio in the censo elections for 189. He instigated and openly helped th attacks on L. Scipio, aiming to destroy the predominanc and Hellenistic influence of Scipio Africanus. His succes led to his censorship in 184 with L. Valerius Flaccus at a time when social deterioration among nobles an people gave his doctrines full scope. He taxed luxury strictly revised the senatorial and equestrian rolls, an checked the publicani; he also spent heavily on buildin e.g. 1,000 talents on the sewerage system. He represente a policy of reconstruction, moral, social, and economi The character of colonization at this time does no necessarily prove a predominantly agrarian policy on h part; he treated senators, *equites*, people, Latins, an provincials with equal regard to their traditional plac in the State. This conservatism was associated wit hatred of things Greek entering into Roman life, and h disguised his wide knowledge by a rustic pose in th cultivated senatorial society, which added ill manners t his natural robustness. He supported the *Lex Baebi* in 181, and opposed its modification and the repeal c the *Lex Orchia*; he attacked M. Fulvius Nobilior after th latter's censorship (179–178). In 171 he was patron in th

Spanish appeal against extortion, prosecuting P. Furius Philus. He supported the *Lex Voconia* (169), favoured the independence of Macedonia, and rejected war against Rhodes (167), and attacked Sulpicius Galba for his opposition to Aemilius Paullus' triumph. In 155 he spoke against the Athenian embassy of philosophers, and in 154 upheld the case of Ptolemy Philometor in the Egyptian question.

His embassy to Carthage (153), when he saw the new prosperity of the old enemy, brought into his policy the demand for the destruction of Carthage. The reason probably lies less in any commercial consideration than in distrust of Carthaginian resurgence and moral indignation at its character. In 151 he supported the return of the Achaean hostages, favoured Attalus II in a dispute with Prusias II, and approved of the prohibition of re-election to the consulship. In 150, despite the opposition of Scipio Nasica, he saw war declared on Carthage. In 149 he attacked Sulpicius Galba on behalf of the Lusitanians. He died in 149 aged 85 years, leaving two sons, Cato Licinianus by his first wife, Cato Salonianus by second marriage; the latter was grandfather of Cato Uticensis.

Cato's whole policy appears based on a conception of traditional government and life, with the single aim of establishing social solidarity again in Rome and Italy, administrative control in the West, but no more than security, with justice, in the East. His thought found expression also through his strong natural literary talent. He published his speeches: Cicero knew more than 150, and we have fragments of 80. He wrote an encyclopaedia for his first son, including agriculture, rhetoric, and medicine, and separate treatises on medicine, jurisprudence, and military science. We know of letters to his son, apophthegmata, and the *Carmen De Moribus*, a gnomic book of morality; the *Catonis Disticha* date from imperial times.

The *De Agri Cultura*, written *c.* 160 B.C., dealt with the development of vine, olive, and fruit-growing and grazing for profit in Latium and Campania; for all its lack of form, its details of old custom and superstition, and its archaic tone, it was an up-to-date work directed from his own knowledge and experience to the new capitalistic farming. The *Origines* in seven books, written from *c.* 168 to 149, following the Hellenistic κτίσεις histories and the senatorial historiography, included Aeneas, the founding of Rome (751 B.C.), the kings in book 1, the foundation traditions of the Italian cities in books 2 and 3, the Punic Wars to Cannae in book 4, the Rhodian debate of 167 B.C. in book 5, the prosecution of Sulpicius Galba (149) in book 7. He used Fabius Pictor, Hellenistic legends, local traditions, inscriptions, later inserting his own speeches; his treatment was discursive (*capitulatim*) and pragmatic, and, unlike the senatorial historiography, omitted the names of generals. The work, the first of its kind in Latin, inspired historical study and founded prose style; for to the principle of 'rem tene, uerba sequentur' he joined plain rhetorical device, including imitation from Greek, and a sense of effect in sentence structure and vocabulary. The style is the man, and if his talent moved narrowly in the expanding field of imperial politics, it touched greatness in his literary stimulus to the Roman tradition.

Livy 29. 25; 32. 27; bks. 34, 36, 38–9; 43. 2; 45. 25; Cicero, *De Senectute*; Nepos, *Cato*; Plutarch, *Cato Maior*; H. Malcovati, *ORF*² 2. P. Fraccaro, *Opusc.* i (1956), 115 ff.; W. Drumann–P. Groebe, *Geschichte Roms* v. 102 (1912); De Sanctis, *Stor. Rom.* iii. 2, 507, 517; iv. 1, 163, 438, 447, 579; B. Janzer, *Hist. Unters. zu den Redenfragmenten des M. Porcius Cato* (1937); F. della Corte, *Catone Censore* (1949); Scullard, *Rom. Pol.*; D. Kienast, *Cato der Zensor* (1954).

TEXTS. *De Agri Cultura*, H. Keil (1882–94); index by R. Krumbiegel (1897); G. Goetz (1922); E. Bréhaut, *Cato the Censor on Farming* (1933); W. D. Hooper–H. B. Ash (Loeb, 2nd imp. 1934); H. Jordan, *M. Catonis praeter librum de re rustica quae exstant* (1860);

Peter, *HRRel.* i, cxxvii, 55; Norden, *Ant. Kunstpr.*, 64; J. Hörle, *Catos Hausbücher* (1929); R. Till, 'Die Sprache Catos', *Philol.* Suppl. xxviii (1936).                                                 A. H. McD.

**CATO** (2), GAIUS PORCIUS (*PW* 5), grandson of (1) and of Paullus (q.v. 2), was in his youth a friend of Ti. Gracchus (q.v. 3). Consul in 114 B.C., he was disastrously defeated in Macedonia by the Scordisci and, on his return, convicted *repetundarum*. Probably a legate in the war with Jugurtha, he was condemned by the commission of Mamilius (q.v. 3) and went into exile, becoming a citizen of Tarraco.                                                 E. B.

**CATO** (3), LUCIUS PORCIUS (*PW* 7), grandson of (1), perhaps the tribune who in 100 B.C. opposed Saturninus (q.v. 1) and tried, with Pompeius (q.v. 2), to secure the recall of Metellus (q.v. 6) Numidicus. He fought successfully in the Social War until killed in his consulate (89).                                                 E. B.

**CATO** (4), GAIUS PORCIUS (*PW* 6), towards the end of 59 B.C. called Pompey 'privatus dictator' when prevented from prosecuting Gabinius (q.v. 2). In 56 as tribune he attacked Pompey again over the Egyptian business and proposed a bill to abrogate Lentulus (q.v. 5) Spinther's command. Milo (q.v.) made him ridiculous by buying his gladiators and auctioning the 'familia Catoniana'. After Luca he postponed the elections in the interests of Pompey and Crassus. In 54 he was prosecuted, and though apparently acquitted is not heard of again. Pompey in 56 was confident he was a tool of Crassus (Cic. *QFr.* 2. 3. 4.), and he may have been such throughout.                 G. E. F. C.

**CATO** (5) **UTICENSIS**, MARCUS PORCIUS (*PW* 20) (95–46 B.C.), great-grandson of Cato (1), nephew of Livius Drusus, and brought up in the Livian household with the children of his mother's marriage to Cn. Servilius Caepio. Quaestor probably in 64, in 63 he became tribune-designate in order to check Metellus (q.v. 10) Nepos, supported Murena's (q.v.) prosecution, and intervened powerfully in the Senate to secure the execution of the Catilinarians. As tribune he conciliated the mob by increasing the doles of cheap corn, but in all else remained uncompromising; Cicero (*Att.* 1. 18. 7; 2. 1. 8) deplores his lack of realism which prevented revision of the Asian tax-contracts (61 B.C.) and frustrated every overture of Pompey (q.v.) until the 'Triumvirate' was formed. In 59 he opposed Caesar obstinately and was temporarily imprisoned, but next year Clodius (q.v. 1) removed him by compelling him to undertake the annexation of Cyprus, over which, though King Ptolemy killed himself and Cato's accounts were lost on the voyage home, his reputation for fairness remained unimpaired. After Luca he persuaded his brother-in-law Domitius (q.v. 4) not to despair of the consulate, but the two were driven from the field; and Vatinius (q.v.) by bribery defeated Cato for the praetorship, which he subsequently obtained in 54. In 52, forsaking his principles, he supported Pompey's consulate: he himself stood for 51, but failed. In the war he strove to avert bloodshed of citizens but resolutely followed Pompey: he served in Sicily, whence Curio expelled him, then in Asia, and during the campaign of Pharsalus held Dyrrhachium. After Pompey's defeat he joined the Pompeians in Africa, composed their quarrels, and had Scipio made general. During the war he governed Utica with great moderation, and was honoured by the inhabitants when after Thapsus he compassed his famous death.

His character was not agreeable: his first wife Antistia proving unfaithful, he lent the second, Marcia, daughter of Philippus (*cos.* 56), to Hortensius. But his constitutionalism, a mixture of Stoicism and old Roman principles, was genuine. After death he was more dangerous than ever to Caesar, who in his *Anticato*, a reply to Cicero's pamphlet *Cato*, pitched the hostile case too high, and left the fame of Cato's life and death to give respectability to the losing side, and to inspire 'Republicans' a century later: 'uictrix causa deis placuit, sed uicta Catoni' (Lucan i. 128).

SOURCES. Plutarch's *Cato Minor* is wholly laudatory but rich in anecdote. See also the sources cited s.v. CAESAR (1). On Cato's portrait see *Acta Archaeologica* 1947, 117 ff.; on Cyprus, E. Badian, *JRS* 1965, 110 ff.                                                    G. E. F. C.

**CATREUS** (*Κατρεύς*), in mythology, son of Minos and Pasiphaë, father of Althaemenes, Aërope, Clymene, and Apemosyne. In consequence of the prophecy that one of them should kill him (*see* ALTHAEMENES) he sold Aërope and Clymene, who, however, married respectively Pleisthenes, who here replaces Atreus as father of Agamemnon and Menelaus, and Nauplius, her sons being Palamedes and Oeax. Apemosyne was killed by Althaemenes, who did not believe her when she told him that she had been violated by Hermes, and supposed her unchaste. See Apollod. 3. 12 ff.                              H. J. R.

**CATTIGARA** (*τὰ Καττίγαρα*), important city-port of the Sinae (Southern Chinese) near the mouth of river Cottiaris. *C.* A.D. 100, one Alexander discovered it by sea from India, on a gulf inhabited by fish-eaters. Cattigara may be *Hanoi* or *Kian-chi* in the Gulf of *Tongking*, or possibly *Canton*. After the Gulf of Siam Ptolemy makes the Chinese coast face west, so that by mere calculation with his figures Cattigara would fall in Borneo.

Ptol. *Geog.* 1. 14. 4–10, etc.; 7. 3. 3; 8. 27. 14. G. E. Gerini, *Journ. Royal Asiatic Soc.* 1897, 551 ff.; Warmington, *Indian Commerce,* 109, 125 f., 129, 177; A. Herrmann, *PW,* s.v. 'Kattigara'; Thomson, *Hist. of Anc. Geog.* 314 ff.                                    E. H. W.

**CATULLUS** (1), GAIUS VALERIUS (*PW* 123), was born at Verona in Cisalpine Gaul. St. Jerome gives the dates of his birth and death as 87 and 57 B.C. and adds that he died in his thirtieth year. The second date cannot be true: that Catullus was alive in 55 is proved by his references to Pompey's second consulship (113. 2), to the Porticus Pompei (55. 6), and to Caesar's invasion of Britain (11. 12, 29. 4), but he makes no reference to any event after 55. It is a reasonable hypothesis that he was born in 84 and died in 54. His family was of some standing in the province; his father was in a position to entertain Julius Caesar when he was governor (Suet. *Jul.* 73). He came to Rome young and for the rest of his life it was his home (68. 34–5), but he remained a northerner (39. 13) and did not lose touch with his province: he was back in Verona after the death of his brother in Asia (65. 68. 19 ff.), and it was to a villa at Sirmio on Lake Garda, presumably a family property, that he returned from foreign travel (31). At Rome he moved in fashionable society and there he fell under the spell of the woman whom he calls Lesbia. Her real name was Clodia (Apul. *Apol.* 10) and she was a married woman of some social position: if, as there are grounds for supposing (though the identification cannot be proved), she was the sister of P. Clodius Pulcher, Cicero's enemy, and the wife of Q. Metellus Celer, governor of Cisalpine Gaul from 64 to 62, she was some ten years Catullus' senior and the connexion must have begun by 59, when Metellus died. Catullus' last message to her (11) was probably written in 55 or 54. Between these years lay the story of happiness and disillusion which is contained in the twenty-five Lesbia poems: during that time he spent a year, 57–56, in Asia Minor, probably with his friend C. Helvius Cinna, in the entourage of the governor of Bithynia, C. Memmius (10, 46).

The poems fall into three groups. 1–60 are short occasional pieces, lyric, amatory, or satiric, mostly in phalaecian hendecasyllables or scazons (two are in sapphics

and there are examples of pure iambics, glyconics, asclepiadeans, and priapeans). 61–4 are longer poems: 61 a glyconic epithalamium for the marriage of Torquatus and Aurunculeia, 62 a fanciful wedding-poem in hexameters, 63 a galliambic poem suggested by the myth of Attis, 64, the longest, in 408 hexameters, a 'miniature epic' on the marriage of Peleus and Thetis, much of it occupied by a digression on the story of Ariadne. 65–116 are all in elegiacs: 66 (to which 65 is a preface) is a translation of a piece of Hellenistic court-poetry, Callimachus' poem on the Lock of Berenice; 67, 68, and 76 are of types which were to be developed in Augustan elegy; the rest are miscellaneous epigrams with a range of subjects like that of the first group. Catullus himself prefixed a dedication to Cornelius Nepos (q.v.) to a volume of his verses, but that cannot have included the whole collection as we have it, which must have been put together after his death: there is evidence that some poems have been lost in transmission.

The epithet *doctus* which is given to Catullus by his successors (Tib. 3. 6. 41; Ovid, *Am.* 3. 9. 62; Mart. 1. 61. 1) is itself a recognition of his acceptance of the literary ideals of Alexandrianism (q.v.). The scholarly concern for technical perfection which he learned from the Alexandrians lies behind all that he wrote and he does not leave his literary creed and standards in doubt: he admires the extreme Alexandrianism of his friend Cinna's *Zmyrna* (95) and he makes fun of the unadventurous representatives of the older tradition of poetry (14, 36). But though the influence of Alexandrian poetry on him is strong, it does not dominate his work. He translated Callimachus, but he also translated Sappho. The *Peleus and Thetis* is a deliberate essay in a characteristically Alexandrian genre: the romantic handling of the story and the disproportionate digression are Alexandrian and he indulges again and again in Alexandrian mannerisms—the learned allusion to gratify the scholarly reader, the devices of apostrophe and exclamation, tricks of style (anaphora and symmetry) and preciosities of rhythm (e.g. the 'spondaic' hexameter): but much of its technique is inherited from earlier Latin poetry and conventions of vocabulary and forms of phrase are derived from the tradition of Ennius and shared with Lucretius and Cicero. In the elegiac 68, in which verbal pattern is at its most intricate and allusion verges on pedantry, the native Latin ornament of alliteration is put to greatest use. While the conception of the *Attis* (63) must be drawn from a Hellenistic original, the power of its language and the skill with which Latin words are fitted to an exotic rhythm are Catullus' own. In the lyrics and epigrams too Catullus is *doctus*, but uses *doctrina* in his own way. The phalaecian metre was itself an Alexandrian invention, but Catullus makes it the vehicle for the brisk raciness or the pathetic simplicity of everyday Latin speech. The lament for the pet bird (3), the invitation to dinner (13), the lines on an old ship (4), all have their prototypes in selfconscious Hellenistic epigram, but Catullus' imagination has used these to produce something new, personal, and immediate.

In the short poems Catullus conveys his own feelings with simple and passionate sincerity. Some convey deep emotion, rapture or despair over Lesbia, sympathy for a friend, sorrow for his brother; others reflect the uninhibited vitality of a young privileged intelligentsia, its conventions, its enthusiasms, and its dislikes. His views of persons and events are the reactions of an individualist: his friends are those who share his sophisticated tastes and when he attacks Caesar and Pompey his attacks are not political but personal, inspired by fastidious indignation at the rise of upstarts under their patronage.

On the side of technique the importance of Catullus' work lies in the refinement of standards which reached its full development in his Augustan successors. His influence is to be seen in Horace's lyrics and much more in his fellow countryman Virgil, whose admiration for him shows itself in many verbal echoes: his elegiacs point the way to the art of Propertius. In the next century it was his epigrams that were remembered and Martial acknowledged him as his master.

ED.: E. Baehrens (Leipzig, 1885), Kroll (Leipzig³, 1959).
TEXT. R. A. B. Mynors (O.C.T. 1958). Comm.: R. Ellis (1889²), C. J. Fordyce (1961). Index: M. N. Wetmore (U.S.A. 1912).
GENERAL. Wilamowitz, *Hell. Dicht.* vol. ii, ch. 8; A. L. Wheeler, *Catullus and the Traditions of Ancient Poetry* (U.S.A. 1934); E. A. Havelock, *The Lyric Genius of Catullus* (1939).　　　　　C. J. F.

**CATULLUS** (2, *PW* 2), a mime-writer of the middle of the first century A.D. (Juv. 8. 185 ff., 13. 111; Mart. 5. 30. 3), whose lost works include a piece *Phasma* (The Ghost) called *clamosum* by Juvenal, and a realistic one, *Laureolus*, in which the crucifixion of a notorious bandit was staged (Mart. *Spect.* 7. 4; Suet. *Calig.* 57; Joseph. *AJ* 19. 94).
　　　　　　　　　　　　　　　　　　　　　　　J. W. D.

**CATULUS** (1), GAIUS LUTATIUS (*PW* 4), was consul in 242 B.C. when Rome determined to renew naval warfare against Carthage. His great service was his decision to attack when a Carthaginian fleet appeared off Aegates Insulae (W. Sicily); there he terminated the First Punic War by a naval victory, 10 Mar. 241. He negotiated peace terms with Hamilcar.　　　　　　　　　H. H. S.

**CATULUS** (2), QUINTUS LUTATIUS (*PW* 7), of noble (but not recently prominent) family, brother of two Caesares (qq.v. 2 and 3) and married first to a Domitia, then to a sister of Caepio (q.v. 1), was three times defeated for the consulship, until helped by Marius—then at the summit of popularity—to success for 102 B.C., probably through the mediation of the Caesares. Defeated by the Cimbri on the upper Adige, he had to retreat and give up the Po valley, but in 101, joined by Marius (who treated him with great courtesy) and assisted by Sulla (q.v. 1) as legate, he helped to win the victory of the Vercellae (perhaps near Rovigo, on the lower Po). Marius and Catulus triumphed jointly, and Catulus built a portico on the Palatine out of the spoils. Alienated from Marius, who received most of the credit for the victory, he became one of his chief opponents, drawing his friends away from him. He probably fought under L. Caesar in the Social War, opposed Marius and Cinna in 87, and after their return was prosecuted by Marius (q.v. 3) and committed suicide.

A cultured man, interested in philosophy, art, and literature, he was a link between the friends of Scipio (whom he knew in his youth) and the generation of Cicero, who greatly admired him and introduced him as a character in the *De Oratore*. He wrote light verse (two epigrams, one on young Roscius (q.v. 3), survive) and a monograph on his German campaign, and he was a competent—though not outstanding—orator. His funeral oration on his mother Popillia was the first example of a Roman woman being thus honoured. He was also a patron of literary men (e.g. Archias, q.v.); but he was not the centre of a literary circle.

Malcovati, *ORF³*, 218 ff. H. Bardon, *LEC* 1950, 145 ff. (on his alleged literary circle); id. *La Littérature latin inconnue* (1952), 115 ff.; Badian, *Stud. Gr. Rom. Hist.*, see index.　　　　　E. B.

**CATULUS** (3), QUINTUS LUTATIUS (*PW* 8), son of (2) and of a Domitia, perhaps escaped from Rome after the return of Cinna (q.v. 1) in 87 B.C., but seems to have come back. On Sulla's return he joined him and brought about the cruel death of Marius (q.v. 3) in revenge for his father's; but he opposed the lawlessness of the *Sullani*. Consul in 78 with Sulla's support, he opposed his colleague Lepidus (q.v. 2), carried a law against violence, and

secured Sulla a solemn funeral, at which the power of his veterans was displayed. When Lepidus rebelled, Catulus, as proconsul, was chiefly responsible for his defeat. Henceforth he was an acknowledged leader of the *Optimates*. He was entrusted with the rebuilding of the Capitoline temple, which he carried out lavishly, dedicating the temple in 69 (cf. *ILLRP* 367–8). During the seventies he defended the Sullan settlement, but finally acknowledged that it did not deserve to survive and accepted its modification (70). In 67 and 66 he opposed the laws of Gabinius and Manilius (qq.v.)—Pompey had offended him in 77—and in 65, as censor, the attempt of his colleague M. Crassus (q.v. 4) to enfranchise the Transpadanes. In 63 he was ignominiously defeated by Caesar in an election for the chief pontificate and tried to involve Caesar in suspicion as a Catilinarian. This was the end of his great *auctoritas*: in 61 he was asked his opinion in the Senate after two men much junior to him, and he died soon after. He was a mediocre orator and never equalled his father's interest in literature and philosophy.　　　　　　　　　　　　　　　E. B.

**CATUVELLAUNI**, the most powerful British Belgic tribe, occupying parts of Herts., Beds., Cambs., Bucks., and Northants. It is probable that Cassivellaunus (q.v.) ruled this tribe; later kings were Tasciovanus and his son Cunobelinus (qq.v.) who became the leading ruler in pre-Roman Britain. After A.D. 43 a *civitas* was created with *caput* at Verulamium (q.v.), though this town itself may have possessed municipal status. Building done by a *corvée* of this *civitas* is attested on Hadrian's Wall (Collingwood and Wright, *RIB* 1962). The region was mainly agricultural with important pottery industries near Radlett (Herts.) in the Nene valley and in Oxfordshire.

A. L. F. Rivet, *Town and Country in Rom. Brit.²* (1964), 145 ff.; Frere, *Britannia*, ch. iv.　　　　　　　　　S. S. F.

**CAUCASUS.** For long the Greeks knew only the name and great size of this range. Herodotus describes it as a vast high mountain with many primitive peoples, skirting the west side of the Caspian, and he knew of the Derbent pass. Others believed that it contained many lakes and large rivers. Alexander mistook the Hindu-Kush for part of the Caucasus, thus causing some confusion in Greek literature. Not much more was learnt until Pompey subdued the Iberi (*see* IBERIA). Strabo could give details of the Caucasus—a well-wooded barrier between the two seas and connected with the Armenian heights and Mt. Taurus; he described the customs of the natives and their use of snow-shoes and hides which served as toboggans. No accounts survive of subsequent discoveries.

Strabo 11, esp. pp. 499–506; Ptol. *Geog.* 5. 9. 14, 15. Thomson, *Hist. of Anc. Geog.* 170 f., 253 f., 363 f., etc.; Cary, *Geographic Background* 156, 177, 309 ff.　　　　　　　　E. H. W.

**CAUDINE FORKS**, the narrow defile where a Roman army was trapped by, and surrendered to, Gavius Pontius (q.v. 1), 321 B.C. (Livy 9. 2–6). It lay in the territory of the Caudini Samnites, somewhere between Capua and Beneventum, but cannot be certainly identified. The Arienzo–Arpaia valley, the traditional site, contains the significantly named hamlet Forchia, but seems too small; an objection that applies also to the valley between S. Agata de' Goti and Moiano. The plain between Arpaia and Montesarchio, although large enough, does not fit Livy's description.

P. Sommella, *Antichi campi di battaglia in Italia* (1967), 49 ff.
　　　　　　　　　　　　　　　　　　　　　　　E. T. S.

**CAULONIA**, Achaean colony on the 'sole' of the Italian 'boot', near *Punta di Stilo*, that shared the Pythagorean vicissitudes of Croton (q.v.), its probable metropolis. Dionysius (q.v. 1) of Syracuse captured Caulonia (389 B.C.) and transferred its inhabitants to Sicily. Sabellian assaults about a century later completed its ruin. E. T. S.

**CAVES, SACRED.** It would appear that Greek cave-sanctuaries mostly belong either to pre-Hellenic cults or to oriental importations: an exception is perhaps the cave-shrines of the Nymphs, common from Homer (*Od.* 13. 347 ff.) on. The most famous is that of Zeus on Mt. Dicte in Crete (cave of Psychro, M. P. Nilsson, *Minoan-Mycenaean Religion*² (1950), 393). This was vaguely remembered as his birthplace and belongs to the cult of the Cretan god identified with him. Hardly less celebrated was the cave of Trophonius at Lebadea (Farnell, *Hero-Cults*, 21; description, Paus. 9. 39. 5 ff.). Here the date of the cult is unknown. In Italy, one of the most celebrated holy caves was the Lupercal on the Palatine, where the Luperci met for their ritual (see Platner–Ashby, 321). This is undoubtedly old, but we have no reason to suppose the ceremony pre-Italic. Of imported cults in both countries, that most closely connected with caves, or artificial underground vaults, was Mithraism (*see* MITHRAS).

For Cybele and caves, cf. L. Robert, *Mélanges Bidez* (1934), 795 ff.; A. J. Festugière, *Rev. Bibl.* 1935, 382 f. H. J. R.

**CEBES** of Thebes, pupil of Philolaus the Pythagorean, and later of Socrates, plays an important part in the discussions in the *Phaedo*, and in the *Crito* is represented as one of those who were prepared to spend money in helping Socrates to escape from prison; the (suspect) 13th Platonic Letter represents him as still alive in 366. The extant dialogue (probably belonging to the 1st c. A.D.) called Κέβητος Θηβαίου Πίναξ makes no pretence to be by Socrates' friend, and has been ascribed to him by a mere error. It presents an eclectic doctrine which in spite of its Pythagorean setting owes more to Plato, Aristotle, and the Stoics than to the Pythagoreans.

Ed. K. Praechter (1893). W. D. R.

**CECROPS** (Κέκροψ), mythical first king of Athens (though Actaeus is sometimes called first king), was a child of the Attic soil, though some late writers said that he was of Egyptian or Cretan origin. Sometimes it is said that his father was Hephaestus. As an indication of his autochthonous origin Cecrops is often represented as of serpent shape below the waist. By Aglauros or Agraulos, daughter of Actaeus, he had three daughters, Pandrosos, Herse, and Aglauros II. He was succeeded upon the throne by Cranaus. According to some writers there were two Cecropes who had ruled in Athens, the second being a son of Erechtheus.

Among late writers Cecrops had the reputation of having been a great benefactor of mankind. The story that he had instituted monogamy among men had its origin in a rationalistic interpretation of his double nature. He was also credited with the institution of burial of the dead and with the invention of writing. During his reign the contest of Athena and Poseidon for possession of Athens took place, and in some accounts he was judge of the contest. In a small structure on the Acropolis at the south-west corner of the Erechtheum the Athenians saw the tomb of Cecrops.

ANCIENT SOURCES. Eur. *Ion* 1163 f.; Apollod. 3. 177 ff.; Paus. 1. 5. 3; schol. Ar. *Plut.* 773.
MODERN LITERATURE. Benjamin Powell, *Erichthonius and the Three Daughters of Cecrops* (1906); Cook, *Zeus* iii. 237 ff.; J. Harrison, *Themis* (1927), 261 ff. J. E. F.

**CELSUS** (1) **ALBINOVANUS**, a friend of Horace (*Epist.* 1. 3. 15–20; 8. 1), who rebukes him gently for writing poetry which is too slavishly imitative. M. S.

Schanz–Hosius, § 320, 279 n. 8.

**CELSUS** (2), AULUS CORNELIUS (*PW* 82), under Tiberius (A.D. 14–37), wrote an encyclopaedia comprising agriculture, medicine, military science, rhetoric, and probably philosophy and jurisprudence (*see* ENCYCLOPAEDIC LEARNING). Apart from a few fragments of the other sections only the medical books are preserved. The work, dealing with the whole of medicine, is most important for the reconstruction of Hellenistic doctrines. The introduction outlines briefly but admirably the history of medicine up to the author's time. Celsus, a layman, writing for his own instruction and that of other laymen, selected with sound judgement his material from different sources (*see* SURGERY, § 7). In philosophy he was a follower of the Sextii; in medicine he was influenced most strongly by Themison. The Latin of Celsus, the 'Cicero medicorum', became the model of Renaissance writing when his book, almost unnoticed in antiquity and in the Middle Ages, was rediscovered and printed at a very early date.

TEXT. F. Marx, *CML* i (1915); text criticism, H. Lyngby, *Textkritiska studier till Celsus' Medicina* (Göteborg, 1931).
TRANSLATION: with text, Loeb; James Greive (1756).
LITERATURE. Celsus' book not based on one Greek original, O. Temkin, *Bull. of the Inst. of the Hist. of Med.* 1935; opposite theories summarized, Marx, loc. cit. lxxiv; M. Wellmann, *Arch. f. Gesch. d. Med.* 1925; Celsus as philosopher, A. Dyroff, *Rh. Mus.* 1939. J. Ilberg, *Neue Jahrb.* 1907; G. Baader, *Forschungen und Fortschritte* 1960, 215 ff.; J. Scarborough, *Roman Medicine* (1969). L. E.

**CELSUS** (3), PUBLIUS JUVENTIUS (*PW* 13), a distinguished Roman jurist, praetor A.D. 106 or 107, *legatus* of Thrace, twice consul (the second time 129), proconsul of Asia, member of Hadrian's *consilium*. He was head of the Proculian School (*see* SABINUS 2), as his father, Juventius Celsus (whose pupil he probably was), had been before him. His reputation evidently greatly surpassed that of his father, of whom little is known. The son's principal work, and the only one of which extracts survive, was thirty-nine books of *Digesta*, but this incorporated material drawn from his earlier *Epistulae, Commentarii*, and *Quaestiones*. Celsus had a profound knowledge of the earlier literature, which he often cites, but he is a severe and caustic critic of other jurists' views. His constructions are original; his language is clear and as independent as his mind. *See also* JULIANUS (2).

F. Stella Maranca, *Intorno ai frammenti di Celso* (1915); F. Wieacker, *Iura* 1962; M. Bretone, *Labeo* 1963; *and see under* JURISPRUDENCE. A. B.; B. N.

**CELSUS** (4), author of the first comprehensive philosophical polemic against Christianity, the Ἀληθὴς λόγος, written *c.* A.D. 178–80, of which the greater part is quoted in Origen's *Contra Celsum*; and of a book of advice to converts from Christianity. Celsus wrote from the standpoint of a Greek and a Platonist, but put certain objections to Christianity in the mouth of Jews in Egypt familiar with the Logos-theory. The Ἀληθὴς λόγος is important evidence for the knowledge of, and attitude towards, the Christianity of the Greek world; it shows knowledge of Gnostic sects as well as of the 'Great Church'. Celsus' criticism became part of the material for the Neoplatonic polemic against Christianity.

R. Bader, Ἀληθὴς λόγος (1940). W. D. R.

**CELTIBERIANS**, a large ethnographical group in north central Spain, probably formed by a fusion of the Celtic invaders with the existing Iberians, whose traditions dominate the mixture. They were sheep-owners and fighters, living chiefly in hill-forts. From their native iron they developed the two-edged Spanish sword which was adopted by the Roman legions. After their first encounter with Cato (195 B.C.) a smouldering war against Rome flared up in 181 to 179 (peace of Tiberius Gracchus), 153 to 151, and finally 143 to 133 (the war of Numantia, q.v.).

The Romans brought down hill-forts, encouraged agriculture, and established a few towns. The region, incorporated in the imperial *conventus* of Clunia, became peaceful but not sophisticated (see Martial XII preface and 18, on his home Bilbilis, a Roman *municipium*).

A. Schulten, *Numantia*, 4 vols. (Munich 1914–31), esp. vol. i, introduction; P. Bosch-Gimpera, *Etnologia de la peninsula iberica* (1932), chs. 24 and 25.                                    M. I. H.

**CELTS,** a name applied by ancient writers (and extended by modern to the British Isles) to a population group occupying mainly lands north of the Mediterranean region from Galicia in the west to Galatia in the east. Their unity is recognizable by common speech and common artistic tradition. (1) Dialects of Celtic are still spoken (Ireland, Scotland, Wales, Brittany), or are attested by inscriptions, quotations, and place-names in this area. The language seems closely akin to the Italian group, showing like it a division between 'q' and 'p' renderings of the velar guttural. The significance of this division is still obscure. (2) The artistic unity is expressed in the La Tène style (called from the Swiss type-site), which appears *c.* 500 B.C. inspired by increasing trade contacts. It derived principally from living Italo-Greek styles, but archaic Hellenic motives which had survived in a Villanovan backwater are also noticeable, as well as eastern influences conveyed by way of Scythia. Out of these chronologically and regionally different borrowings the Celts evolved a very idiosyncratic art of swinging, swelling lines, at its best alive and yet reposeful.

The view is generally accepted that the primary elements of 'Celtic Culture' originate with the Bronze Age 'Urn-field people' of the Upper Danube (13th c. B.C.) on whom a warrior aristocracy from the east imposed itself *c.* 750. It is likely that the 'Urn-field people' spoke a 'proto-Celtic' language, though the 'Celtic race' is likely to be a product of the Hallstatt leaders. Induced probably by worsening climatic conditions of the Later Bronze Age and after, 'Urn-field' and subsequent 'Hallstatt' invaders brought peoples whom we may call Celts to Spain and to Great Britain as early as the eighth and seventh centuries. Southwards the Celts penetrated Italy, sacking Rome in 390. Typical Hallstatt graves are present in Bohemia in the seventh century, and Celts descended the Danube, entered the Balkans, and raided Delphi (279). Another band crossed the Hellespont (278) and founded a state called Galatia where Celtic was still spoken in the fifth century A.D.

Celtic culture is above all recognizable by common speech and common artistic tradition.

The ancients knew the Celts as fierce fighters and superb horsemen, and noticed the savagery of their religious rites conducted by the priesthood, the Druids, who derived their doctrine from Britain. But Celtic political sense was weak, and they were crushed between the migratory Germans and the power of Rome, to be ejected (e.g. from Bohemia and south Germany), or more or less assimilated (as Belgae, q.v.) by the former, and conquered outright by the latter.

GENERAL. T. G. E. Powell, *The Celts*[2] (1960) has all-round coverage and full bibliography; N. K. Chadwick, *Celtic Britain* (1963); A. Ross, *Pagan Celtic Britain* (1967).
SOURCES. J. Dinan, *Monumenta Historica Celtica* (1911); J. Zuriker, *Fontes Religionis Celticae* (1934–6).
LANGUAGE. G. Dottin, *Langue gauloise* (1920, with *corpus* of Celtic inscriptions); A. Holder, *Altkeltischer Sprachschatz* (1891–6); H. Pedersen and Henry Lewis, *Concise Comparative Celtic Grammar* (1937); R. Thurneysen, *Grammar of Old Irish* (1946); K. H. Jackson, *Language and History in Early Britain* (1953).
ART. P. Jacobsthal, *Early Celtic Art* (1944); C. Fox, *Pattern and Purpose* (1958); A. Varagnac and G. Fabre, *L'Art gaulois* (1964); F. Henry, *L'Art irlandais* (1963).                          C. E. S.

**CENOMANI,** Gauls, reputed to be Aulerci, who established themselves in Cisalpine Gaul *c.* 400 B.C. (Polyb. 2. 17; Strabo 5. 216). Their territory lay around Lake Garda. Chief towns: Brixia and probably Verona and Bergomum (Livy 5. 35). The Cenomani usually supported Rome, e.g. in 225 B.C. against Boii and Insubres and in 218 against Hannibal (Polyb. 2. 23, 24, 32; Livy 21. 55). In 200, however, they joined Hamilcar, but were quickly subjugated and romanized, disappearing from history (Livy 31. 10; 32. 30). In 49 B.C. Gallia Transpadana, including the Cenomani district, obtained Roman citizenship. For bibliography *see* CISALPINE GAUL.
                                                          E. T. S.

**CENSOR** (cf. *censere*, to estimate) was the title of a Roman magistrate who, although lacking *imperium* and the right to an escort of lictors, nevertheless possessed great authority, since he controlled public morals and supervised the leasing of public areas and buildings. The censorship was probably instituted *c.* 443 B.C. as a civil magistracy, in order to make up and maintain the official list of citizens, or *census* (q.v.)—a function previously fulfilled by the consuls. If a citizen was found guilty of suppressing or delaying information about his status and property, the censors (who always numbered two, in obedience to the principle of collegiality) were empowered to take judicial proceedings against him. The enrolment of the population, which generally took place in spring (probably in May), ended in a religious ceremony called *lustrum* ('cleansing', *see* LUSTRATION). Originally this ceremony was held *quinto quoque anno*, i.e. every four years, but from 209 B.C. onwards the formula was taken to mean every five years, and the interval between two celebrations was called a *lustrum*. The censors entered office in early spring and held it for eighteen months, the revised roll being issued twelve or fifteen months after their appointment. This registration took place in a special building in the Campus Martius. The *equitum census*, i.e. the making-up of the list of those liable to cavalry service, was held in the Forum. The censors had the right of striking off the names of those who had given false statements, or who no longer merited the privilege of fighting as knights, because of unbecoming behaviour at home or on military service, bad administration of provinces or public property, and the like.

A plebeian was elected to the censorship in 351 B.C., if not before, and one of the *Leges Publiliae* of 339 declared that at least one censor must be a plebeian, although two collegiate plebeian censors were not elected until 131. The power of the censors reached its zenith in the third and second centuries, and throughout the middle and later Republic the office stood at the head of the *cursus honorum*. Its prestige sprang largely from the power of the censors to revise the senatorial rolls and to strike off those who had not observed the *ordo magistratuum* or had acted against law and public morality. The authority of the censorship was greatly reduced by Sulla and, although down till the Augustan age several distinguished citizens filled the office, it soon became a dead letter. The Emperors tended increasingly either to assume responsibility for censorial functions themselves or to confer such responsibility upon lesser officials. This process reached its logical conclusion when Domitian appointed himself censor for life.

Mommsen, *Röm. Staatsr.* ii³. 1, 334 ff.; H. F. Jolowicz, *Hist. Introduction to the Study of Roman Law*[2] (1939), 36 f., 50 ff.; A. Klotz, *Rh. Mus.* 1939, 27 ff.; J. Suolahti, *The Roman Censors* (Helsinki, 1963), with full bibliography. For the censorial Fasti see also Broughton, *MRR*.                                    P. T.

**CENSORINUS** (3rd c. A.D.), a Roman grammarian (Prisc. 1. 4. 17), wrote *De accentibus* (lost), and a '*De die natali* uolumen illustre' (Sid. Apoll. *Carm.* 14 *praef.* 3), dedicated to Q. Caerellius on his birthday in A.D. 238, which is preserved. The first part deals with human life, particularly its origins, the second with time and its divisions. The work is derived from different sources, above all Varro, and also Suetonius (*De anno Rom.*), and is valuable for its mainly competent transmission of these. It is accompanied in the MSS. by an anonymous and noteworthy collection of articles on various topics, e.g. the universe, geometry, metre (our earliest source for Roman metre), and music, known (since L. Carrion's edition, Paris, 1583) as *fragmentum Censorini. See also* SCHOLARSHIP, LATIN.

TEXTS. O. Jahn (1845, rp. 1964); F. Hultsch (1867). Schanz–Hosius iii. 219 ff.                                                     A. H.-W.

**CENSUS,** a national register which was prepared at Rome from the time of the kings for taxation and military service. The holding of a census was at first the duty of the king, then of the consuls, and from 443 B.C. of the censors (q.v.). A census was normally held at intervals of five years. The citizens were registered in tribes and distributed into five classes according to their wealth: each class was subdivided into *seniores* and *iuniores*. They were required to state their full name and age and the amount of their property (*Tabula Heracleensis*, 145). The names of women and children were not included in the census, but parents gave information about their families (Dion. Hal. *Ant. Rom.* 4. 15). Under the later Republic the census was taken very irregularly, but it was revived by Augustus, who held it three times (*Res Gestae* 8). The last known census was held in Italy by Vespasian and Titus: it had come to be unnecessary here, as Italians had become exempt from direct taxation. The taking of a census was concluded with a religious purification (*see* LUSTRATION). In the *Tabula Heracleensis* the chief magistrates of Italian towns are ordered to take a census simultaneously with the holding of one in Rome, and this must have been done earlier in communities possessing Roman citizenship (see Livy 29. 15).

In some provinces, e.g. Sicily (Cic. *Verr.* 2. 131), a local census was held even in republican times, but it was not till the reign of Augustus that the census was organized by the imperial government. Information could be easily acquired in the municipalized senatorial provinces. Augustus was well informed by 7 B.C. about the wealth of the people of Cyrene (*SEG* ix. 1. 8). But new machinery had to be set up in the more backward provinces, where organized city life did not exist. A census was held in Gaul in 27 B.C., 12 B.C., A.D. 14 and 61, and, like the census held in Judaea in A.D. 6 after its annexation in the governorship of Quirinius, provoked popular resistance. Most of the inscriptions referring to officials of the census come from imperial provinces. The governor was normally responsible and records the fact in his inscriptions, but many other men of senatorial and later of equestrian rank were concerned with the matter (*ILS* iii, Index, p. 351); minor officials were entrusted with the duty in particular districts, e.g. Q. Aemilius Secundus, who when prefect of a cohort conducted the census of Apamea under Quirinius (*ILS* 2683). The census-return (*forma censualis*) included full details of the character and extent of cultivated land and the number of slaves owned (*Dig.* 50. 15. 4), and of other forms of property. This information was necessary to those responsible for levying the *tributum* (q.v.) *soli* and *tributum capitis*. It was probably the duty of governors to keep the register up to date, but no regular census-period seems to have been prescribed.

In Roman Egypt there was a census-period of fourteen years. Numerous papyri contain the census-returns made by householders, which gave full details of properties and occupants and had to be addressed separately to a number of different officials.

A. H. J. Greenidge, *Roman Public Life* (1901), 221 ff., 429 ff.; S. L. Wallace, *Taxation in Egypt* (1938), 96 ff.; G. Pieri, *L'Histoire du cens jusqu'à la fin de la rép. rom.* (1968).     G. H. S.; F. G. B. M.

**CENTAURS,** a tribe of wild, beast-like monsters usually thought of as having the upper part of a human being and the lower part of a horse. Centaurs live in woods or mountains of Elis, Arcadia, and Thessaly. In the *Iliad* they are described as 'beasts' (φῆρες; and cf. *Od.* 21. 303). Possibly the conception of horse-shaped centaurs originated with the horse-breeders of Thessaly. Myths of Centaurs must be very old, since they occur in Homer, in late Mycenaean, and in early orientalizing art. For the Greeks Centaurs are representative of wild life, animal desires, and barbarism. They are lustful and over-fond of wine. Their fight against the Lapiths, whose king Peirithous invited Centaurs to his marriage (*Il.* 1. 263; 2. 742; *Od.* 21. 295 ff.; [Hes.] *Sc.* 178 ff.) is famous. Either one (Eurytion) or several Centaurs attempted to rape the Lapith women. In the ensuing fray the Centaurs were routed, although they killed the invulnerable Caeneus. Heracles had a clash with them when he visited the Centaur Pholus. Attracted by the smell of wine, Centaurs assailed Heracles with rocks and stones, but were beaten back with fire-brands and arrows and fled to Cape Malea.

Individual Centaurs have myths of their own. Nessus offered to carry Deianira across the river Euenus and then attempted to rape her (Archilochus in Dio Chrys. 60). Heracles killed him with his sword or with arrows. This scene is a great favourite with archaic vase-painters. Before Nessus died he gave to Deianira the garment which later caused the death of Heracles (Soph. *Trach.*). Chiron is the wise and kind old medicine-man among the Centaurs. He is of divine origin, son of Kronos and Philyra (Pherecyd. in schol. Ap. Rhod. 1. 554; Apollod. 1. 9), well versed in medicine (*Il.* 4. 219) and other arts, and educates divine children and heroes, Achilles, Asclepius, and Jason. He also helps Peleus to woo Thetis (Apollod. 3. 13. 5). Chiron had a cult in Thessaly.

The Centaurs are sometimes children of Ixion (q.v.), but in Pindar the offspring of Centaurus, son of Ixion and Nephele, who mated with mares near Mt. Pelion (Pind. *Pyth.* 2. 44).

In art, the earliest Centaurs brandish boughs or hunt. The Nessus episode appears in the seventh century B.C. (J. M. Cook, *BSA* 1934–5, 191). The fight with the Lapiths occurs on the famous François vase (A. Minto, *Anthemon, Scritti in onore di Carlo Anti* (1955), 21 ff.) and in sculpture on the pediment of the temple of Zeus in Olympia. Later, Centaurs join the Dionysiac *thiasus* and are so shown on Roman funeral reliefs. (Cf. Nonnus, *Dion.* 14. 49, 149, 193.)

P. V. C. Baur, *Centaurs in Ancient Art* (1912); J. E. Harrison, *Prol. to the Study of Greek Religion* (1922), 380; P. Kretschmer, *Glotta* 1919; H. Payne, *Necrocorinthia* (1932); M. Ziemssen, *Kentaurendarstellungen auf griechischen Vasen* (1945); W. Havers, *Sprache* 1958; V. Karageorghis, 'Notes on some Centaurs from Cyprus' in Χαριστήριον εἰς 'Αναστάσιον κ. 'Ορλάνδον ii. 160 f. (1964).
G. M. A. H.; J. R. T. P.

**CENTO.** I. GREEK. A patchwork (*cento*, a patchwork cloak) of existing verses, sometimes humorous in intention, sometimes not. Trygaeus' improvisation at Ar. *Pax* 1090–4 is an early example, and in the *Frogs* (1264 ff., 1285 ff., and 1309 ff.) the cento is pressed into the service of literary criticism. Lucian (*Symp.* 17) mentions a 'very funny song', made of a medley of Hesiod, Anacreon, and Pindar. Cf. also *Anth. Pal.* 9. 381–2. 'Ομηροκέντρωνες were composed in Byzantine times, e.g. by the Empress Eudocia in the fifth century A.D. Many parodies, e.g. the one of Homer quoted by Dio Chrysostom in *Or.* 32 (see Brandt, *Corpusc. poes. ep. graec. ludib.* 100 ff.) are virtually centos.

G. Kaibel, *Epigrammata Graeca e lapidibus conlecta* (1878), 1009; E. Stemplinger, *Das Plagiat in der griech. Lit.* (1912), 193 ff.
J. D. D.

II. LATIN. The main victim of Latin cento-makers was Virgil: perhaps the sport began quite early (see Petronius 132. 11, and cf. the parodies in Donatus, *vit. Verg.* 43). The earliest extant specimen is the *Medea* of Hosidius Geta (late 2nd c.), in which the characters (even the Messenger) all speak Virgilian hexameters patchworked together, and the choral lyrics consist entirely of final *hemistichia*. An anonymous cento *de alea* (date uncertain) is an amusing squib, contrasting sharply with the vulgar and nasty *cento nuptialis* of Ausonius (q.v.), perpetrated *c.* 368 at Valentinian's request (and in the hope of going one better than the emperor). Ausonius describes his technique at some length in a prefatory letter.

Roughly contemporary with Ausonius' *facetiae*, Virgilian cento took a new turn. The Christian poetess Proba used it for rewriting parts of the Old and New Testaments ('cuius quidem non miramur studium sed laudamus ingenium', Isidore *de uir. ill.* 22); other Christian centos are the *de Verbi incarnatione* (once attributed to Sedulius), the *Tityrus* of Pomponius (an 'Eclogue' in which Meliboeus is instructed in the Faith), and the *de ecclesia* of Mavortius (?) which ends with an 'improvised' postscript after the poet had been hailed as *Maro iunior*. Proba's compilation may be the *centimetrum de Christo* declared apocryphal by Pope Gelasius in 494 (Migne 59. 162; cf. Isidore *de uir. ill.* loc. cit.), in a *decretum* whose authenticity is itself disputed (Schanz–Hosius, iv². i. 220, Teuffel–Schwabe, *Gesch. d. römisch. Lit.*⁶ (1913–20), iii. 449).

Apart from the formal genre, long passages that are largely centos occur in later poets, e.g. Columban (6th c.), Waldram (9th c.), and the author of the *Ecbasis Captiui* (10th c.), and now other writers besides Virgil are pillaged, Horace and Ovid among them.

Isidore, loc. cit. and *Orig.* i. 38. 25; Tertullian *de praescr. haeret.* 39.

TEXTS in *CSEL* xvi. i. 511 ff. (Schenkl, with important preface), Migne xix. 801 ff., Baehrens *PLM* iv. 191 ff.

Schanz–Hosius, loc. cit. and 31; Teuffel–Schwabe, loc. cit. and 278; Manitius, *Gesch. d. christlich-lat. Poesie* (1891), 11, 123 ff.; id., *Gesch. d. lat. Lit. des Mittelalters* (1910–11), i. 184, 597, 618; Bursian, *Jahresb.* 1929, 123. O. Delepierre, *Tableau de la littérature du centon* (London, 1874–5); L. Mueller, *de re metrica*² (1894), 585 ff.; T. R. Glover, *Life and Letters in the Fourth Century* (1901), 144 ff.; C. O. Zuretti, *Ausonii cento nuptialis* (*Stud. Ital.* 1904, 319); F. Ermini, *Il centone di Proba e la poesia centonaria latina* (1909); D. Comparetti, *Virgilio nel Medio Evo* (rev. G. Pasquali [1937]), i. 64 ff. (tr. E. F. M. Benecke, 53 ff.); F. J. E. Raby, *Christian Latin Poetry*² (1953), 16; id., *Secular Latin Poetry*² (1957), i. 44. R. G. A.

**CENTUMVIRI**, a special civil court at Rome, or, strictly, the panel, numbering in fact during the Republic 105 persons (three taken from each *tribus* (q.v.)) and in the Empire 180, from which a court (*consilium*) was chosen. The number forming a *consilium* is not known, but in the Empire there were usually four *consilia*, though the full court of 180 might sit for a particular case (Pliny, *Ep.* 4. 24; 6. 33). The presidents of the *consilia* were, in the late Republic at least, ex-quaestors, but Augustus assigned this duty to the *decemviri* (see VIGINTISEXVIRI). The president of the whole panel was apparently a *praetor hastarius* (Pliny, *Ep.* 5. 9. 5). The *centumviri* took only the second stage of the proceedings, in place of the more usual single *iudex* (q.v.). The first stage, before the *praetor urbanus* or *peregrinus* (Gai. *Inst.* 4. 31) was by *legis actio sacramento* (see SACRAMENTUM), even after *legis actiones* had otherwise been abolished by the *Lex Iulia de iudiciis* (see LAW AND PROCEDURE—ROMAN II). The extent of the court's competence is obscure. Recorded cases are mainly concerned with matters of inheritance, and the *querela inofficiosi testamenti* (see INHERITANCE § 5) was developed by the court (an apparently unique instance of court-made law in Rome), but its competence was evidently considerably wider (Cic. *De Or.* i. 38. 173). Its jurisdiction was alternative to that of the *unus iudex*.

What determined the bringing of a case before the *centumviri* is not known, but the court was evidently, at least at certain periods (Cic. *De Or.* 1. 57. 242 ff.; *Brut.* 39. 144 f.; Tac. *Dial.* 38; Pliny locc. citt.) a forum for *causes célèbres*. The court was presumably created after 241 B.C., when the number of *tribus* was increased to 35; its first recorded case was about a century later (Cic. *De Or.* 1. 40. 181, 1. 56. 238). B. N.

**CENTURIA** was the smallest unit of the Roman legion. Each legion contained 60 centuries (see LEGION, § 1; MANIPULUS).

According to tradition, Servius Tullius founded a new political assembly based on the centuries. The real date of this reform is doubtful, and many scholars prefer the middle or the end of the fifth century B.C. The assembly consisted of 18 centuries of horsemen, 6 of which were called *sex suffragia*, and 170 centuries of foot-soldiers. The foot-soldiers were divided into five *classes* (q.v.) according to their census. The first class fell into 40 centuries of *iuniores* (between 17 and 45 years) and 40 of *seniores* (between 46 and 60); the second, the third, and the fourth into 10 centuries of *seniores* and *iuniores* apiece, and the fifth into 15 of each category. Five centuries of non-combatants, including one of *capite censi* (*proletarii*), were attached; two of these centuries (of *fabri*) were apparently ranked with the first class. The age limit of sixty for the *seniores* disappeared in the centuries of the comitia.

Between 241 and 218 B.C. the distribution of the centuries underwent a reform about which Livy (1. 53. 12) and Cicero (*Rep.* 2. 22. 39) leave us uncertain, except to show that its object was to correlate the centuries and the local tribes, and that the first class was reduced to 70 centuries. Some scholars hold that each class was now equally divided into 35 centuries of seniors and 35 of juniors; but others with greater probability hold that the number of the centuries remained fixed at 193. The discovery of the Tabula Hebana (q.v.) has shown that Augustus created a system of voting for the *destinatio* of consuls and praetors in which senators and *equites* from thirty-three tribes voted in 10 (later 15) centuries.

The name *centuria* was also used for the block of 100 *heredia* (little allotments, theoretically each of 2 *iugera*), which was the unit for the delimitation of the *ager publicus* (see CENTURIATION).

*See* AUGUSTUS; COMITIA.

Chr. Meier, *PW*, Suppl. viii. 567. For the Servian classification, G. W. Botsford, *The Roman Assemblies* (1909), 66; A. Rosenberg, *Untersuchungen zur römischen Zenturienverfassung* (1911); P. Fraccaro, *Opusc.* ii (1957), 287 ff., 293 ff. (two fundamental papers of 1931 and 1934); G. De Sanctis, *Riv. Fil.* 1933, 289; H. H. Scullard, *A History of the Roman World*³ (1961), 423 ff.; A. Momigliano, *JRS* 1963, 119 (with bibliography). For the reform of the third century, De Sanctis, *Stor. Rom.* iii. 1, 376 ff.; P. Fraccaro, *Studi in onore di P. Bonfantet* (1930), 105 ff. U. Coli, *Studia Doc. Hist. Iur.* 1955, 181 ff.; L. R. Taylor, *AJPhil.* 1957, 337 ff.; E. Meyer, *Röm. Staat und Staatsgedanke* (1961), 492 (with bibliography). A. M.

**CENTURIATION.** Centuriation was a Roman agrimensorial technique designed for large-scale land partition. It is particularly associated with such important foundations as *coloniae* and many examples of *ager centuriatus* or *limitatus* are known in Italy and the Mediterranean provinces. The systems can be recognized by surviving stretches of the chequer-board grid of roads that normally divided the area into squares (*centuriae quadratae*) with sides of twenty *actus* (776 yds., 710 m.) and an area of 200 *iugera*. The *actus*, or 120 Roman feet, was the basic measurement involved. A *iugerum* was formed by 1 × 2 *actus* and two *iugera* formed a *heredium* in the form of an *ager quadratus*. In turn 100 *heredia* equalled the main land unit, the *centuria*. Its name was perhaps derived at first from its division among 100 settlers, each receiving a *heredium*. The lines of demarcation between *centuriae* were called *limites*, which were further termed *decumani* or *cardines*, the former theoretically running east–west, the latter north–south. In places like Lugo (near Ravenna), where the centuriation system had two main *limites* radiating from a central position, these were known as the *decumanus maximus* and the *cardo maximus*. The four subdivisions so created were called *dextra* and *sinistra* (north and south of the *decumanus*) and *ultrata* and *citrata* (west and east of the *cardo*). The evidence on the ground shows that the theoretical arrangements of the surveyors (*agrimensores, gromatici*) were considerably modified by topography and other local factors. Likewise there are *centuriae* of non-standard size and in early examples from Italy (Cosa, Cales, Lucera) the systems are based on parallel roads alone (*per decumanos solos*); otherwise most systems appear to be of early imperial date. Little is known of the internal arrangements within *centuriae*, but examples from Apulia and Tunisia show that intensive mixed farming was practised.

F. Blume, K. Lachman, A. Rudorff, *Die Schriften der römischer Feldmesser* (2 vols. 1848, 1852); E. Fabricius, *PW*, s.v. *limitatio*; P. Fraccaro, Enciclopedia italiana s.v. *agrimensura*; J. S. P. Bradford, *Ancient Landscapes* (1957), 145 ff. cf. *Antiquity* 1947, 197 ff.; A. Piganiol, *Atlas des centuriations romaines de Tunisie*[3] (1959).
G. D. B. J.

**CENTURIO.** The centurions were the principal professional officers in the Roman army. In the post-Marian army each of the ten cohorts had six centurions, whose titles, except in the case of the first cohort, were: (*secundus, tertius*, etc.) *pilus prior, pilus posterior, princeps prior, princeps posterior, hastatus prior*, and *hastatus posterior*. Between these centurions of the lower-ranking cohorts there was little difference in status apart from seniority. The first cohort had, probably from early in the Empire, only five centuries and was double the size of the others. Its centurions were *primus pilus, princeps, hastatus, princeps posterior*, and *hastatus posterior*. This group constituted the *primi ordines*, and within it a strict seniority was observed, with the post of *primus pilus* as the final honour.

During the Republic centurions were selected from the legionary soldiers; under the Principate, the majority of the centurions continued to be promoted legionaries, but some were *ex equite Romano*, i.e. men who had transferred from an equestrian career, or ex-praetorians (*evocati*). They were attracted by high pay (five times that of the praetorian soldier for the centurion, ten times for a member of the *primi ordines*), and good prospects on retirement. (*See also* PRIMIPILUS.)

Centurions are found also in the *Auxilia* and the Praetorians (qq.v.), but without the distinguishing titles of their legionary counterparts.

H. Wegeleben, *Die Rangordnung der römischen Centurionen* (1913); A. von Domaszewski, *Die Rangordnung des römischen Heeres* (1908); Parker, *Roman Legions*; E. Birley, *Carnuntina*, 1965.
H. M. D. P.; G. R. W.

**CEPHALAS,** CONSTANTINUS, held an official post in the palace at Constantinople in A.D. 917. Some time before this he compiled an anthology of Greek epigrams, on which the Greek Anthology (q.v.) was later based. Apparently he died or abandoned the task before completing it, since his collection is imperfectly edited and appears not to have been published in the normal way; but the material is invaluable.
G. H.

**CEPHALUS,** a hero, apparently Attic. He is eponym of the Attic *genos* Κεφαλίδαι (Hesych. s.v.), marries Procris (q.v.), and lives at Thoricus (Pherecydes, infra). He has, however, connexions outside Attica, for he takes part with his hound in the hunt for the Teumessian

vixen (*see* AMPHITRYON), in the Cyclic *Epigoni* (fr. 2 Allen); he marries Clymene daughter of Minyas (*Nostoi*, fr. 4 Allen). His principal adventures are: (1) his affair with Eos (q.v.), first in Hesiod (*Theog.* 986), where their son is Phaëthon the attendant of Aphrodite. Generally (e.g. Ov. *Met.* 7. 704, supported by much earlier evidence from art, see Roscher's *Lex.* s.v.), she carries him off. (2) His jealousy of Procris. To test her, he stayed away for eight years, came back in disguise, and succeeded in obtaining her favours (schol. V on *Od.* 11. 321, citing Pherecydes). (3) Her jealousy of him, because he spent so much time hunting (Pherecydes, ibid., cf. Ovid, ibid. 796 ff.). Learning that he was accustomed to call for a cloud, νεφέλη (Pherec.), or a breeze, *aura* (Ovid), to cool him, she supposed this the name of a mistress, followed him in hiding, and was killed by his throwing-spear, which he flung at her supposing her to be a beast (the spear never missed, Ov., ibid. 683; further fanciful details of the legend, Hyg. *Fab.* 189). That Cephalus was eponym of Cephallenia (Arist. in *Etym. Magn.* 144. 26) is hardly more than a pun. His father is regularly Deïon or Deïoneus.
H. J. R.

**CEPHEUS** (Κηφεύς), name of four or five mythological persons, the best known being the father of Andromeda (q.v.). Though generally called an Ethiopian from Euripides on, he and consequently the whole legend are very variously located; for particulars see Tümpel in Roscher's *Lexikon* ii. 1109–13.
H. J. R.

**CEPHISIA,** an Attic deme situated north-east of Athens at the modern *Kephisia*. A community of great antiquity to judge from both its name and its inclusion in the list of twelve townships traditionally brought together by Theseus (q.v.), it became widely known in the second century A.D. as the seat of one of Herodes (q.v. 2) Atticus' most luxurious villas, where amid groves, playing waters, and singing birds the great sophist held court.

Philochorus *FGrH* 328 F 94; Gell. *NA* 1. 2. 1–2 and 18. 10. 1; Philostr. *VS* 2. 1. 30; W. Peek, 'Attische Inschriften', *Ath. Mitt.* 1942, 136 ff.; A. Tschira, 'Eine römische Grabkammer in Kephissia', *Arch. Anz.* 1948/9, 83 ff.
C. W. J. E.

**CEPHISODORUS** (1) (fl. *c.* 400 B.C.), writer of Old Comedy (*IG* ii². 2325; Lys. 21. 4 Κηφισοδότῳ codd.). The Ἀντιλαΐς satirized the ἑταίρα Laïs.

*FCG* i. 267–9; *CAF* i. 800–2.

**CEPHISODORUS** (2) of Athens or Thebes, pupil of Isocrates, wrote a history of the Sacred War and a treatise directed against Aristotle.

*FGrH* ii. 112.

**CEPHISODOTUS** (1), sculptor, Athenian, probably father of Praxiteles (q.v.), and a brother-in-law of Phocion. Pliny dates 372, probably by his work at Megalopolis. No convincing attributions, since Rumpf has shown that the 'Irene' group goes back to an original of 350–320 B.C.

Overbeck, 878, 1137–43; Lippold, *Griech. Plastik* 223; A. Rumpf, *Archäologie* ii (1956), 80 ff.
T. B. L. W.

**CEPHISODOTUS** (2), sculptor, Athenian, son of Praxiteles. Pliny dates 296 B.C. (inscription of 344–343, published as signature of Cephisodotus, probably refers to dedicator). Selected works: 1 (with his brother Timarchus). Lycurgus and his sons, probably after Lycurgus' death 323. 2 (with Timarchus). Menander, in the theatre at Athens, probably after Menander's death, 291; copies of head at Boston, etc. (Winter, *KB* 320. 4). 3 (with Timarchus). Statues on the altar of the Asclepieum at Cos (Herod. 4. 1–26); fragments have been discovered.

4 (with Euthycrates, son of Lysippus). Anyte (fl. 284). 5. Symplegma (erotic group) in Pergamum. 6. Leto, later on the Palatine; reproduced on the Sorrento base. He continued the Praxitelean tradition into the third century.

Overbeck, 1331–41; Lippold, *Griech. Plastik* 299; Bieber, *Sculpt. Hellenist. Age* 20 f. T. B. L. W.

**CEPHISSUS** (*Κηφισός*), the name of several rivers, the best known being the Attic and the Boeotian Cephissus. The Attic Cephissus was the main river of the Plain of Athens, gathering all sources and streams of the mountains around, and emptying itself into the bay of Phalerum; its water, divided into many streams, irrigates the plain west of Athens (cf. Soph. *OC* 685); its clay-bed provided the material for Athenian pottery. The Boeotian Cephissus springs from the northern Parnassus, near Lilaea, and waters the plains of Phocis and northern Boeotia, debouching into the lake Copaïs.

Cary, *Geographical Background.* V. E.

**CERBERUS,** monstrous dog guarding the entrance to the lower world. According to Hesiod (*Theog.* 311) Cerberus is the son of Typhon and Echidna, has fifty heads and a voice like bronze. He is often referred to simply as 'the dog of Hades'. The canonical type of Cerberus, established in late archaic and classical literature and art (Eur. *HF* 611), shows him with three heads and mane or tail of snakes. Cerberus is most frequently mentioned in connexion with the descent of Heracles to Hades (*Il.* 8. 367; Apollod. 2. 5. 12). With the permission of Hades Heracles dragged Cerberus out of the lower world, showed him to Eurystheus, and then returned him to Hades. This episode is depicted with much gusto on the Caeretan *hydriae* in the Louvre (G. Roux, *Mélanges Picard* 1949, 896) and the Museo Villa Giulia (E. Pfuhl, *Malerei und Zeichnung der Griechen* (1923), pl. 36, fig. 154, and G. Q. Giglioli, *Arte etrusca* (1934), pl. 128, 3). The same scene appeared on the Amyclaean throne (Paus. 3. 18. 9, Frazer).

G. van Hoorn, *Studies pres. to D. M. Robinson II* (1953), 106; G. Hooker, *JHS* 1960, 112. G. M. A. H.

**CERCIDAS** (*c.* 290–*c.* 220 B.C.), of Megalopolis, was friendly with Aratus of Sicyon, who sent him *c.* 226 to Antigonus Doson to ask the latter's intervention on behalf of the Achaean Confederacy against Cleomenes (Polyb. 2. 48). In 222 before the battle of Sellasia Cercidas is mentioned as the leader of 1,000 men from Megalopolis (Polyb. 2. 65). Other authorities refer to his success as a lawgiver, alluding probably to the restoration of liberty at Megalopolis after the tyranny of Lydiadas (235). An alternative description of Cercidas as a Cretan (Diog. Laert. 6. 76) may indicate his residence in the island during that tyranny. Outside politics, he attained fame as a Cynic philosopher and poet.

WORKS. Literary sources have preserved only nine short fragments of Cercidas' verse. Of these one (fr. 14 Powell) is cited in the *Iambi*. It proves that the work was in the choliambic or scazon metre and may come from a diatribe against luxury. An attempt has been made (by A. D. Knox, *The First Greek Anthologist*, 1922) to claim Cercidas as the editor of an anthology of moralizing verse preserved in several papyri, and possibly the author of some of the pieces written in scazons. But his best-known work was his *Meliambi*, i.e. poems lyrical in form, but satiric in content. Substantial remains, preserved in *POxy.* 1082, show that Cercidas was a skilful and original metrist and a keen critic of social conditions in his day. Though a member of the property-owning class, he makes himself in these poems the mouthpiece of the poor and oppressed, and attacking the cult of

wealth and its attendant vices exhorts his fellows to mend their ways while there is yet time. In his use of verse to inculcate the Cynic view of life and in his mixture of the earnest and the jesting Cercidas was clearly influenced by Crates (2) of Thebes, whose example was followed about the same time by Menippus (1) of Gadara (qq.v.); but his opinions seem to have been formed chiefly by the example of the sect's founder, Diogenes, to whom he pays a glowing tribute (fr. 1), and by the teaching of Bion (q.v. 1) the Borysthenite. The so-called 'Diatribe Style', of which Bion is the reputed founder, finds frequent illustration in Cercidas' verse, but he combines with it other features, such as new and lengthy compounds, which derive rather from the dithyramb, Old Comedy, and Timon of Phlius. His skilful use of citations from Homer, of whose poetry he is said to be a warm admirer, and from Euripides is in the Cynic vein. The language of the *Meliambi* is a literary Doric which avoids local peculiarities and pedantic consistency. *See also* IAMBIC POETRY, GREEK.

TEXTS. Powell, *Coll. Alex.* 201 ff.; A. D. Knox, *Herodes, Cercidas, and the Greek Choliambic Poets* (Loeb, 1929), 190 ff.; Diehl, *Anth. Lyr.* iii³, 141–52.
GENERAL LITERATURE. G. A. Gerhard, 'Kerkidas (2)', in *PW* ix. 294 ff., also *Phoinix von Kolophon* (1909); Powell and Barber, *New Chapters*, 1 ff.; D. R. Dudley, *History of Cynicism* (1937), 74 ff.
E. A. B.

**CERCOPS OF MILETUS** (? 6th c. B.C.), epic poet, to whom (or to Hesiod) is ascribed the *Aegimius* (on the Dorian hero Aegimius who fought against the Lapithae).

*EGF* 82–5.

**CERES,** an ancient Italian corn-goddess, commonly identified in antiquity with Demeter (q.v.). Her name (Oscan *Kerrí*, see the 'Curse of Vibia', Conway 130, 1) suggests that of Cerus ('in carmine Saliari Cerus manus intellegitur creator bonus', Festus, 109, 7 Lindsay), but in cult she is found associated not with him but with Tellus (q.v.) Mater. This is shown by the juxtaposition of their festivals (Fordicidia, to Tellus, 15 Apr.; Cerialia, 19 Apr.) and the fact that the *feriae sementiuae* are celebrated in January in honour of both (Ov. *Fast.* 1. 657 ff., on which cf. Frazer). The occurrence of the Cerialia on the calendars and the existence of a *flamen Cerialis* testify to the antiquity of Ceres' cult at Rome, but her whole early history is extremely obscure, particularly her relations, if any, with non-Italian (Greek) deities; see, for some ingenious conjectures, Altheim, *Terra Mater* (1931), 108 ff. One of the many difficulties is to determine whether the rite of swinging attested by 'Probus' on Verg. *G.* 1. 385–9 as used at the *feriae sementiuae* is really, as he says, borrowed from the Attic *αἰώρα* (*see* ERIGONE) or an independent development. Another is the question whether the long list of minor deities invoked by the officiant on the same occasion (Servius on *G.* 1. 21) arises out of genuinely early ideas or is a relatively late priestly elaboration (see Rose, *JRS* 1913, 233 ff.).

There is, however, no doubt that Ceres' most famous cult, that on the Aventine (introduced 493 B.C.), is largely under Greek influence. She is there worshipped with Liber and Libera, the triad apparently representing the Eleusinian group of Demeter, Kore, and Iacchus (but see Altheim, op. cit. 15 ff.). The temple became a centre of plebeian activities, was supervised by the plebeian *aediles Cereris*, and was connected with the *ludi Ceriales* which became a prominent feature of the Cerialia. To this Greek cult belongs also, no doubt, the annual festival conducted by the women in August, called Greek and an initiation by Cicero (*Leg.* 2. 21); also probably Ceres' occasional association with the underworld (as in the 'Curse of Vibia', above), the purely Roman goddess in this connexion being Tellus (as Livy 8. 6. 10). *See also* MUNDUS.

Wissowa, *RK* 191 ff., 297 ff.; F. Altheim, *A History of Roman Religion*, passim; K. Latte, *RR* 71, 101, 161; H. Le Bonniec, *Le Culte de Cérès à Rome* (1958). Ceres' temple in Rome: Nash, *Pict. Dict. Rome* i. 227 ff. H. J. R.

**CERIALIS** CAESIUS RUFUS, QUINTUS PETILLIUS (*PW* 8) (*cos. suff.* A.D. 70, *cos. II suff.* 74), a relative of Vespasian, likewise perhaps Sabine by origin. Legate of Legio IX Hispana in Britain, he suffered a serious defeat in the revolt of Boudicca (61). With the Flavian forces at the capture of Rome, he was sent to restore order in Gaul and the Rhineland. He won a battle at Rigodulum, captured the city of the Treveri, and then proceeded to deal with Civilis and Classicus: after confused fighting the latter capitulated (towards the end of 70). Tacitus invents for him a notable oration in defence of the Roman rule in Gaul (*Hist.* 4. 73 f.). Cerialis was next appointed legate of Britain (71–4), in which command he shattered the power of the Brigantes and made extensive conquests in northern England (cf. Tac. *Agr.* 17). Nothing more is heard of him after his second consulship. The family ends with his son (*cos. II ord.* 83).

Syme, *Tacitus*, 175; 452 f. R. S.

**CERSOBLEPTES** (or **CERSEBLEPTES**, *IG*. ii. 65 b), the Odrysian king (*see* THRACE), son of Cotys I. Cersobleptes found himself, when he came to the throne in 360 B.C., engaged in a war, which he had inherited from his father, with Athens, and with two pretenders to the throne, Berisades and Amadocus. Charidemus (q.v.), the Athenian general, married Cersobleptes' sister, and continued to advise him, as he had done his father. In 359 B.C. the Athenian commander, Cephisodotus, was forced to make a treaty with Cersobleptes, which the Athenians repudiated. In the following year, Berisades and Amadocus joined forces, and, with Athenian help, forced Cersobleptes to sign a treaty dividing the kingdom of Cotys between the three princes, the Chersonese (q.v. 1) being ceded to Athens; Cersobleptes' share seems to have been the eastern part, Cypsela, Cardia, and the Propontis. Charidemus, however, persuaded Cersobleptes to renounce the treaty, and it was not till 357 that he was forced by the Athenian commander, Chares (q.v. 1), to surrender the Chersonese, and agree to the partition of Thrace. In the following years Philip II (q.v.) of Macedon proposed an alliance with Cersobleptes for the expulsion of the Athenians from the Chersonese, but nothing came of it. Meanwhile, through the agency of Charidemus, Athens secured Cersobleptes' goodwill, while his rival Amadocus (Berisades was now dead) turned to Philip. Philip invaded Thrace, and it was only his severe illness that prevented its subjection. In the peace of 346 B.C. between Athens and Philip, Cersobleptes was not included. 342 B.C. saw the last war between Philip and Cersobleptes, and in that year or the next the Odrysian kingdom passed into the control of Macedonia.

Demosthenes, 23; Head, *Hist. Num*². 257, 284; A. Hoeck, 'Das Odrysenreich in Thrakien', *Hermes* 1891, 76 ff. J. M. R. C.

**CERTAMEN HOMERI ET HESIODI,** ἀγὼν Ὁμήρου καὶ Ἡσιόδου, abbreviation of περὶ Ὁμήρου καὶ Ἡσιόδου καὶ τοῦ γένους καὶ ἀγῶνος αὐτῶν, title of an anonymous treatise preserved in a Florence MS. It is a joint life of Homer and Hesiod, written round an account of a contest between them supposed to have taken place at Chalcis (the circumstances inspired by Hes. *Op.* 650–60). Hesiod is adjudged victor, despite the crowd's acclamation of Homer, after each has recited 'the best' part of his poetry: the passages are chosen to show Homer as the poet of war, Hesiod as the poet of peace (cf. Ar. *Ran.* 1033–6). The

story is familiar to Varro and later writers, ignored in the Lives of Homer. The treatise as we have it dates from the Antonine period, but much of it was taken bodily from an earlier source (it agrees closely with a papyrus fragment of the third century B.C., P. Lit. Lond. 191), thought to be the Μουσεῖον of Alcidamas (q.v.), to which Stobaeus 4. 52. 22 ascribes two verses found in the *Certamen* (78–9), and which contained accounts of the deaths of Hesiod (cited in *Cert.* 240) and Homer (P. Michigan 2754, agreeing closely with the end of *Cert.*, but followed by what appears to be a transition to a new section). Some of the verses were current before this (78–9 = Theog. 425, 427; 107–8 = Ar. *Pax* 1282–3), and the contest of verses and riddles represents an early form (Rohde, *Kl. Schr.* (1901), i. 103 f.); but it is not known whether Homer and Hesiod were matched before Alcidamas.

A fragment ascribed to Hesiod (357 M.–W.) referring to an earlier contest with Homer in Delos is of uncertain origin and date.

TEXT. O.C.T. *Homeri opera* (1911–20), v. 218 ff. (Allen); U. von Wilamowitz-Moellendorff, *Vitae Homeri et Hesiodi* (1916), 34 ff.; A. Colonna, *Hesiodi Opera et Dies* (1959), 71 ff. CRITICISM. T. W. Allen, *Homer, the Origins and the Transmission* (1924), 20 ff.; E. Vogt, *Rh. Mus.* 1959, 193 ff.; K. Hess, *Der Agon zwischen Homer und Hesiod* (1960); M. L. West, *CQ* 1967, 433 ff. M. L. W.

**CESTIUS** (1, *PW* 7) **EPULO,** GAIUS, from a rich family which had recently entered public life, held the tribunate and praetorship, was *septemvir epulonum* (*see* EPULONES), died before 12 B.C., naming Agrippa as one of his heirs, and was buried in the large pyramidal tomb still to be seen in Rome by the Porta S. Paolo.

*ILS* 917 (his epitaph); Platner–Ashby, *Topog. Dict.* 478; Nash, *Pict. Dict. Rome* ii. 321 ff. T. J. C.

**CESTIUS** (2, *PW* 13) **PIUS,** LUCIUS, Augustan rhetor, a Greek from Smyrna; a popular teacher distinguished for his conceit, his outspoken wit, and his dislike of Cicero, to several of whose speeches he wrote answers.

Sen. *Controv.* 3 *praef.* 15–16; *Suas.* 7, 3. Schanz-Hosius, § 336, 8.

**CESTIUS** (3, *PW* 9) **GALLUS,** GAIUS, son of a consul and himself *cos. suff.* A.D. 42, was legate of Syria from 63 (or 65) to 67. In 66 he marched into Palestine to restore calm, but failed to occupy Jerusalem and on his withdrawal was defeated at Beth-horon. He died in 67. A. M.

**CETHEGUS,** PUBLIUS CORNELIUS (*PW* 97), of patrician (but not distinguished) family, fled with Marius in 88 B.C., returned with him in 87 and stayed in Rome. He then joined Sulla and took an active part in the proscriptions. During the next few years, though he held no high office, his knowledge of procedure and skill at intrigue gave him power equal to that of consulars. Antonius (q.v. 2) and the Luculli (qq.v. 2 and 3) obtained their commands by cultivating him and his mistress. E. B.

**CEYX,** in mythology, (1) king of Trachis, friend of Heracles, and father-in-law of Cycnus son of Ares ([Hesiod], *Sc.* 354 ff.). (2) Son of the Morning Star; husband of Alcyone daughter of Aeolus (1) or (2). He and his wife were turned into the birds which bear their names (see Sir D'A. W. Thompson, *Glossary of Greek Birds*² (1936), s.vv.) as punishment for calling themselves Zeus and Hera (Apollod. 1. 52); or, he was drowned and she, finding his body, leaped into the sea and both were changed by the pity of the gods (Ov. *Met.* 11. 410 ff.). H. J. R.

**CHABRIAS** (c. 420–357/6 B.C.) of Athens, a professional soldier who for over thirty years was frequently engaged in warfare for Athens (being a general at least thirteen times) and for the kings of Cyprus and Egypt in revolt from Persia. His greatest achievements were the defence of Boeotia in 378, during which he invented a useful method of defence against hoplites, the decisive naval victory over Sparta near Naxos in 376, and the extension of the Second Athenian League. After 370 he fought in the Peloponnese, and his fortunes seem to be linked to those of Callistratus (q.v. 2), with whom he was prosecuted by Leodamas, the βοιωτιάζων, in 366; like Callistratus he was restored to power shortly before the battle of Mantinea, and, when soon afterwards Callistratus was in exile, Chabrias was with Agesilaus (q.v.) in Egypt supporting King Tachos. After further campaigning as general for Athens in the Hellespont, he died, out of office, fighting gallantly for Athens at the battle of Chios in 357/6.

Nepos, *Chabrias*: Xen. *Hell.* 5. 1 ff.; Diod. 15. 29 ff.; Dem. 20. 75 ff. H. W. Parke, *Greek Mercenary Soldiers* (1933). G. L. C.

**CHAEREMON** (1), tragic poet of about the middle of the fourth century B.C., wrote a *Centaur* which Aristotle (*Poet.* 1) calls 'a rhapsody in which all metres were mixed'. ('Metres' probably do not include lyric metres.) The term 'rhapsody' may imply some affinity to epic poetry, but Athenaeus (608 e) called it a drama; his plays were better adapted for reading than for performance (Arist. *Rh.* 3. 12) and indulged in far-fetched and artificial metaphors, some of which might almost be parodies of the style of Aeschylus, though others are picturesque. Athenaeus' description of him (13, 608 d) as 'especially fond of flowers' is supported by several fragments in which they are mentioned, and a passage from the *Oeneus* shows some descriptive power and feeling for beauty of colour. A few epigrammatic and even cynical lines also survive.

*TGF* 781–92. A. W. P.-C.

**CHAEREMON** (2) of Alexandria, a Stoic, and Egyptian priest, teacher of the young Nero, wrote, *inter alia*, on Egyptian history and grammar (Σύνδεσμοι παραπληρωματικοί). Not extant.

*FGrH* 618.

**CHAEREPHON,** of Sphettus in Attica, an enthusiastic disciple of Socrates. He was banished by the Thirty Tyrants and returned with Thrasybulus in 403, but died before the trial of Socrates in 399. He is best known as having drawn from the Delphic oracle the saying that Socrates was the wisest of men; the story is related both by Plato and by Xenophon, and there is no reason to doubt its truth. The *Suda* refers to works of Chaerephon, but these were early lost. W. D. R.

**CHAERIS,** a pupil of Aristarchus, whose text of Homer he defended, wrote also a commentary on Pindar and Aristophanes, and a Τέχνη γραμματική, all lost.

**CHAERONEA** (Χαιρώνεια), in the Cephissus valley, was the northernmost town of Boeotia. It was subject to Orchomenus in the fifth century. It owes its fame to its position on the through-route from northern Greece, and to the defeat of the Athenians and Thebans by Philip in 338 B.C., which is commemorated by a colossal stone lion now restored and re-erected. In 86 Sulla won a decisive victory there over Mithridates' armies. Plutarch was born and lived at Chaeronea, and kept alive its customs.

N. G. L. Hammond, 'The two battles of Chaeronea', *Klio* 1938, 136 ff.; G. Soteriades, *Ath. Mitt.* 1903, 301 ff.; 1905, 113 ff.; P-K, *GL* I. ii. 430 ff. T. J. D.

**CHALCEDON,** Megarian colony on the Asiatic side of the Bosporus opposite Byzantium (modern *Kadiköy*). Cults and institutions confirm its Megarian origin. Traditionally founded (Eusebius) 685 B.C. Known archaeologically from inscriptions, coins, and chance finds, but no excavation to date. Called the 'city of the blind' (cf. Hdt. 4. 144) because its founders missed the then uncolonized site of Byzantium, with which city its history throughout antiquity was closely linked. A. J. G.

**CHALCIDICE,** the triple peninsula projecting from Macedonia, was inhabited originally by the Sithonians (Strabo 7, fr. 10), a branch of Edonian Thracians. Their name survived in 'Sithonia', the central promontory between the western 'Pallene' and the eastern 'Acte'. By the early seventh century the Bottiaei, displaced by the Argead Macedonians from the plain west of the Thermaic Gulf, 'Bottiaea' or 'Emathia', occupied the north-west portion of the peninsula, thereafter known as Bottice. The first Greek colonists from Chalcis in the eighth century dispossessed the Sithonians and founded around thirty settlements, giving the name 'Chalcidice' to the entire peninsula. Eretria founded colonies, e.g., at Dicaea and Neapolis; Andros at Sane, Acanthus, and Stagirus; and Corinth at Potidaea (q.v.) on the narrow isthmus of Pallene around 600 B.C.

Followers perforce of Xerxes, the cities joined the Delian League and became subjects of imperial Athens. Revolting in 432/1 they established a common capital at the former Bottic town Olynthus (q.v.), thus inaugurating οἱ Χαλκιδεῖς or the 'Chalcidic Confederacy', which became a most interesting specimen of ancient federalism. The member cities shared a common citizenship and common laws (Xen. *Hell.* 5. 2. 12); the confederacy struck a magnificent silver coinage, circulating especially in the Balkans and copied there by barbarian mints. In the 380s it extended its control to the north-west, depriving Macedonia of Anthemus and its capital Pella. But at the request of Acanthus and other States Sparta intervened in 382 and forced the confederacy to capitulate in 379 and become subordinate allies (Xen. *Hell.* 5. 3. 26). The Chalcidians soon joined the Second Athenian League (Tod, no. 123), but the creation of an Athenian cleruchy at Potidaea (c. 362) and other signs of Athenian ambition led to an unwise alliance in 356 with the Macedonian king Philip II (Tod, no. 158), who *more suo* cynically ceded to the Chalcidians Anthemus and Potidaea. The sequel was war in early 349. Aid from Athens was ineffective, and the capital Olynthus, taken by means of treachery, was destroyed in 348. Thus ended a remarkable experiment in federal government.

Ancient authors (e.g. Demosth. 9. 26) seem definitely to exaggerate the number of Chalcidic cities destroyed by Philip. Olynthus, resited or refounded, possibly by King Cassander (316–298), continued to exist as an important city throughout the Hellenistic period, as did Acanthus, Torone, Aphytis, and others. Land grants in Bottice were given by the kings to Macedonian nobles (Ditt. *Syll*[3]. 332), and new cities were founded by them, notably Cassandrea, created by Cassander in 316 on the site of the former Potidaea, which seems to have been the most important single city of Macedonia down to the Roman conquest. Antigonus II Gonatas founded Antigonea 'the Sandy' on the Bottic coast of the Thermaic Gulf and in all likelihood Stratonicea, probably the successor to Uranopolis, the curious creation of Cassander's eccentric brother Alexarchus. In 348–168 Chalcidice seems to have held a special place within the Macedonian realm, for the inscriptions reveal no instance of a citizen of any city in the peninsula being designated as a Macedonian.

Around 43 B.C. Q. Hortensius Hortalus, the proconsul

of Macedonia, founded a colony of Roman citizens at Cassandrea, which did not, however, displace the older Greek city. By the reign of Augustus a *conventus* of Roman citizens existed at Acanthus. In A.D. 268 Cassandrea successfully withstood a Gothic assault.

D. W. Bradeen, 'The Chalcidians in Thrace', *AJPhil.* 1952, 356 ff.; J. M. F. May, *The Coinage of Damastion* (1939); D. M. Robinson and P. A. Clement, *The Chalcidic Mint* (U.S.A. 1938); A. B. West, *The History of the Chalcidic League* (U.S.A. 1919); J. A. O. Larsen, *Greek Federal States* (1968), 58 ff.   C. F. E.

**C(H)ALCIDIUS** (Calcidius is more correct), 4th c. A.D., Christian translator and commentator on Plato's *Timaeus* (to 53 c only), using earlier Neoplatonic and Peripatetic exegetes, especially Adrastus, Gaius, Numenius, and Porphyry (q.v.). He dedicated his work to Hosius, according to MS. tradition the bishop of Corduba (d. 358), prominent under Constantine, but perhaps (since Macrobius and Isidore of Seville were ignorant of Calcidius) a high Milanese official of *c.* 395 whose epitaph survives. The *Timaeus* was read in Latin in his crabbed version throughout the Middle Ages.

Ed. J. H. Waszink (1962). Waszink, *Studien zum Timaioskommentar des Calcidius* (1964). Epitaph: E. Diehl, *Inscriptiones Latinae Christianae Veteres* (Berlin, 1925-31), 83.   H. C.

**CHALCIS,** the chief city of Euboea (q.v.), commanding the narrowest part of the Euripus channel. In the eighth century B.C. Chalcis, with its neighbour Eretria (q.v.), planted colonies in Italy and Sicily, and may already have led Greek settlement at the trading-post, Al Mina, in Syria. In the later eighth century she disputed with Eretria possession of the Lelantine plain, which lay between them. In the seventh century colonies were sent to the north Aegean shores. It was a great manufacturing and trading city, famous for its metal-work. In 506 it was compelled to cede part of its plain to Athenian cleruchs. The city made common cause, however, with Athens during the invasion of Xerxes. She led a revolt of Euboea against Athens (446), but was defeated and became a tributary ally until 411. A member of the Second Athenian League, from 350 she was a focus of Macedonian intrigues until 338, when, by imposing a Macedonian garrison, Philip II created here one of the three 'fetters' or 'keys' of Greece. The city was a great trade-centre of Hellenistic Greece, but was involved in the Macedonian and Syrian wars against Rome. For its participation in the Achaean Confederacy's struggle against Rome, Chalcis was partly destroyed (146); sixty years later it served as a base for the Pontic general Archelaus.

Strabo 10. 445-8; *IG* xii (9) 106 ff.   W. A. L.; J. B.

**CHALDAEAN ORACLES,** a poem in Greek hexameter verse, allegedly based on divine revelations, edited or composed by Julianus 'the Chaldaean', who lived under Marcus Aurelius. By the later Neoplatonists, from Porphyry to Psellus, it was regarded as a sacred book; upwards of 300 lines from it have been preserved by them. Its doctrine is an amalgam of Greek philosophical speculation (Platonist or Neopythagorean) with elements derived from several different oriental cults; it also taught the magico-religious practice of theurgy, which became, in Lewy's words, 'the last form of pagan religion'. Porphyry, Iamblichus, and Proclus are all said to have written commentaries on it.

FRAGMENTS. W. Kroll, *de oraculis Chaldaicis* (1894, repr. 1962), supplemented by J. Bidez, *Cat. des MSS alchimiques grecs* vi and *Mélanges Cumont* (1936), 95 ff.
DISCUSSION. H. Lewy, *Chaldaean Oracles and Theurgy* (Cairo, 1956; includes additional fragments, of disputable ascription); S. Eitrem, *Symb. Oslo.* 1942, 49 ff.; E. R. Dodds, *JRS* 1947, 55 ff. and *Harv. Theol. Rev.* 1961, 263 ff.   E. R. D.

**CHALYBES,** a people of the south-east coast of the Euxine, famed in Greek legend as the first workers of iron, which from early times they sent southward across Asia Minor and westward to the Aegean. Geographical sources locate them at various points from Paphlagonia to Colchis. Xenophon and Strabo appear to place them among the mountain tribes south of Trapezus, but both also mention other Chalybes near Cerasus who worked iron mines. The region is rich in iron and other minerals.

Magie, *Rom. Rule Asia Min.* 179.   T. R. S. B.

**CHAMAELEON** of Heraclea Pontica (*c.* 350–after 281), Peripatetic writer; almost no biographical details exist. Chamaeleon wrote works on satyric drama and comedy, and studies of a number of early poets, probably including Sophocles and Euripides, deducing biographical data from their works and references to them in comedy. These works, which were anecdotal and uncritical, are often cited by Athenaeus. His philosophical writings, Προτρεπτικός, Περὶ μέθης, Περὶ ἡδονῆς (this last attributed to Theophrastus Περὶ θεῶν), closely followed the Aristotelian tradition.

G. Scorza, *Riv. Indo-Greco-Italica* 1934; F. Wehrli, *Phainias von Eresos, Chamaileon, Praxiphanes* (1957).   F. W. W.

**CHAONES,** name of a tribal state (ἁ πόλις ἁ τῶν Χαόνων) in North Epirus which extended from the Dexari, probably near Berat (*FGrH* 1 F 103), to the river Kalamas (ancient Thyamis) in the sixth century but was eaten into later by the Illyrians and the Thesprotians. The royal house claimed descent from Helenus of Troy, and in 429 B.C. its representatives commanded the army under an annual *prostateia*; the capital was probably at Phoenice. As a part of the Epirote Alliance and then of the Epirote Confederacy the Chaonian State shared the history of Epirus until 170 B.C., when the Chaones and the Thesproti joined Rome and survived under the Roman settlement.

L. M. Ugolini, *Albania antica* 2 (1932); *Praktika* 1952, 279; Hammond, *Epirus*.   N. G. L. H.

**CHAOS.** 'The very first of all Chaos came into being', says Hesiod (*Theog.* 116); it is noteworthy that he implies by the verb (γένετο, not ἦν) that it did not exist from everlasting. What it was like he does not say; the name clearly means 'gaping void'. Later, presumably influenced by the ὁμοῦ πάντα of Anaxagoras (q.v.), it is described (Ov. *Met.* 1. 5 ff.) as a mixture of the 'seeds' (*semina*) or potentialities of all kinds of matter.   H. J. R.

**CHARAX** of Pergamum, living probably late in the period between Nero and the 6th c. A.D., published a World History in forty books, the Ἑλληνικά including at least ten books on Greek saga in Euhemeristic and allegorical fashion; Roman history began in book 12, with a second *syntaxis* for the Empire. He also wrote Χρονικά. *FGrH* ii. A, 482; C, 312.   A. H. McD.

**CHARES** (1) (*c.* 400–*c.* 325), famous Athenian soldier, probably more often general than any other Athenian of the fourth century save Phocion (q.v.), notorious for his treatment of the allies of the Second Athenian League: Isocrates' speech *de Pace* was directed at him especially (Ar. *Rhet.* 1418ᵃ32). He operated largely in the northern Aegean partly against Cersobleptes (q.v.) and the Chersonese (q.v. 1), in 352 winning back Sestos (q.v.), and partly against Philip (q.v. 1), notably at Olynthus and Byzantium (qq.v.). His troops were generally mercenaries, for whose payment he was largely left to provide himself. During the Social War (357–355) he was obliged to hire the services of his mercenaries to the rebellious satrap, Artabazus (q.v.) and won a great victory, 'sister to Marathon' as he claimed (Schol. ad Dem. 4. 19), but this precipitated the Persian ultimatum which abruptly ended the Social War. Chares fought in the campaign of

Chaeronea, and was one of those whose surrender was at first demanded by Alexander in 335. Shortly after, he retired to Sigeum and held command in Mytilene during the Persian offensive in the Aegean in 333 and 332. He was with the mercenaries at Taenarum in the mid 320s, but died before 324/3.

H. W. Parke, *Greek Mercenary Soldiers* (1933). G. L. C.

**CHARES** (2), of Mytilene, Alexander's chamberlain, wrote a history or memoir of him in at least ten books (*Historiai peri Alexandron*) such as a chamberlain would write, full of court ceremonial and personal gossip; but he probably witnessed the attempt to introduce *proskynesis* (prostration as a sign of obeisance), which he described.

See ALEXANDER (3), Bibliography, Ancient Sources, and Pearson, *Lost Histories of Alexander*, 50 ff. W. W. T.

**CHARES** (3), a writer of Γνῶμαι, from which over fifty lines are preserved, in a mutilated state, in a papyrus of the early third century B.C.

Powell and Barber, *New Chapters* i. 18.

**CHARIDEMUS** (4th c. B.C.), Euboean mercenary leader. He fought alternately for the Athenians, whose citizenship he gained, and for their enemy, the Thracian king Cotys (*c.* 360 B.C.). Having joined the satraps' revolt (362), he again went to Cotys, and after his murder he supported Cotys' young son Cersobleptes, whose sister he married. He was, however, highly honoured by Athens for helping to restore the Chersonesus to Chares. Thereafter as an Athenian general he fought against Philip of Macedon, and became bitterly anti-Macedonian. After the suppression of the Theban revolt in 335, Alexander pardoned the demagogues, but insisted on the surrender of Charidemus. He escaped and entered Persian service. He is said to have been executed by Darius for his outspokenness (333).

H. W. Parke, *Greek Mercenary Soldiers* (1933). V. E.

**CHARISIUS**, FLAVIUS SOSIPATER (late 4th c. A.D.), African grammarian. His *Ars grammatica* is a compilation and alongside of elementary material contains sections copied from learned sources which he names (e.g. Remmius Palaemon, Julius Romanus) and from which he took citations of Ennius, Lucilius, Cato, etc. It is to these borrowings that his work owes its value. Of the original five books, the first lacks its introduction, the fourth (dealing with style and metre) has gaps, and the fifth has to be pieced together from various sources. H. Keil's edition (*Gramm. Lat.* i. 1–296; 534–65) is superseded by that of K. Barwick (1925).

Schanz–Hosius, § 833. J. F. M.

**CHARITES**, goddesses personifying charm, grace, and beauty. Like the Nymphs and the Horae, the Charites are originally indefinite in number and stand for the joy and beauty produced by the blessings of fertile nature and by other things that evoke spontaneous emotion of pleasure. They make roses grow (Anacr. 44. 1. Bergk), they have myrtles and roses as attributes, and the flowers of spring belong to them (*Cypria* ap. Ath. 15. 682 e). Their varying names bespeak their qualities: *Thaleia*, the Flowering; *Auxo*, the Grower; *Kale*, the Beautiful; *Euphrosyne*, Joy; *Aglaia*, the Radiant, etc. In their further development they reflect the development of the truly Greek notion of *charis*. As representatives of beauty and grace they are naturally connected in mythology with Aphrodite (Paus. 6. 24. 7), but they are also present at all divine and human celebrations where Olympian joy prevails. They bestow their qualities of beauty and charm, on the one hand physical (*Anth. Pal.* 7. 600), on the other intellectual, artistic, and moral ('wisdom, beauty, and glory' Pind. *Ol.* 14. 6). In the Hellenistic poet

Hermesianax, Peitho (q.v.), Persuasion, becomes one of the Charites. Charites are fond of poetry, singing, and dance (Hes. *Th.* 64; Theog. 15) and perform at the wedding of Peleus and Thetis. χάρις is, however, not only grace but also favour and gratitude for favour. In Athens, statues of benefactors and decrees in their honour were placed in the precinct of Demos and Charites (W. S. Ferguson, *Hellenistic Athens*, 212, 238), and Aristotle says that 'the sanctuary of the Charites is placed in a prominent position' so that those seeing it may be reminded to requite one another's benefits (ἀνταπόδοσις, sc. χάριτος, *Eth. Nic.* 5. 1133ᵃ3).

Charites are always daughters of Zeus, but their mothers vary. From Hesiod on (*Th.* 907) their usual number is three. They play secondary parts in many myths and are connected with many divinities. Their most important cults were in Orchomenus, Paphos, Athens, and Sparta (Paus. 9. 35). Statues of Charites, shown as draped female figures, were seen in many archaic and classical sanctuaries. The type of three nude Charites, known throughout countless Roman copies, may go back to a famous Hellenistic painting. The Charities were Latinized as *Gratiae*.

S. Gsell, in Dar.–Sag., s.v. 'Gratiae'. G. Rodenwaldt, *JRS* 1938, 60. E. Paribeni, *Bolet. d'Arte*. 1951, 105; R. Pfeiffer, *JW* 1 1952, 20; K. Marót, *Musen, Sirenen und Charites* (1958); F. Rosado, *O tema das Graças na poesia clássica* (1962). G. M. A. H.

**CHARITON**, Greek romancer, author of a novel in eight books entitled *Chaereas and Callirhoe* (*Τὰ περὶ Χαιρέαν καὶ Καλλιρόην*), mentions his name and describes himself, at the beginning of his work, as a native of Aphrodisias and secretary to the orator Athenagoras. The name of the author and that of his birthplace have been suspected of being allegorical; the name of his employer has also come under suspicion, Athenagoras being the famous enemy of one of the novel's characters, Hermocrates. However, inscriptional evidence for the names Chariton and Athenagoras at Aphrodisias in Caria has been offered by Rohde. Papyrus fragments date Chariton not later than the second century A.D. (thus confirming Schmid's arguments): the presence in the novel of a genuine historical character (Hermocrates), the author's accuracy in avoiding hiatus, and the absence of *aphelia* apparent in his style, confirm Chariton's position as the earliest extant (instead of the latest, as was previously believed by most scholars) Greek romancer.

The story is that Chaereas and Callirhoe were married at Syracuse: soon after the marriage Chaereas, in a fit of jealousy, kicks his wife so severely that she is taken for dead. The desperate husband buries his wife, but tomb-robbers find her alive, take her to Miletus, and sell her as a slave. Chaereas is apprised of Callirhoe's abduction, and, in the course of his search for her, is himself captured and enslaved. After innumerable adventures, in which the exceedingly beautiful Callirhoe virtuously resisted the advances of numerous suitors, including no less a person than the king of Persia, the couple are at last reunited and return to Syracuse, where they lived happily ever after.

The traditional elements of the genre (apparent deaths, voyages, pirates, enslavements, shipwrecks, happy ending) are all present: the plot, in spite of its complicated nature, is narrated, without irrelevant digressions, with a great clarity (the novel has been described by Reitzenstein as a drama neatly divided in five acts) to which there corresponds a much less rhetorical style than that of the other romancers (Chariton strove to imitate, in particular, the Attic historians Thucydides and Xenophon).

EDITIO PRINCEPS. Villoison (Amsterdam, 1750).
STANDARD EDITION. W. E. Blake (1938).
ENGLISH TRANSLATION. W. E. Blake (1939).
COMMENTARY. D'Orville (Amsterdam, 1750; Leipzig, 1783², with notes by Reiske and others).

CRITICISM. W. Schmid, *PW*, s.v. Chariton (important for style); Rohde, *Griech. Roman* 517 ff.; Christ–Schmid–Stählin ii. 2⁶. 808 ff.; A. Lesky, *Gesch. d. griech. Litt.²* (1963), 918 ff.; J. Jakob, *Studien zu Chariton dem Erotiker* (Prgr. Aschaffenburg, 1903); W. E. Blake, 'Modal Usages in Chariton', *AJPhil.* 1936, 10 ff.; J. E. Rein, 'Zum schematischen Gebrauch des Imperfekts bei Chariton', *Ann. Acad. Sc. Fenn.* B 21, 2 (Helsinki, 1927); A. D. Papanikolaou, *Zur Sprache Charitons* (Diss. Köln, 1963); A. Calderini, *Le avventure di Cherea e Calliroe* (1913 with important *Prolegomeni*).                    G. G.

**CHARMADAS** (fl. *c.* 107 B.C.), member of the New Academy and pupil of Carneades. Sextus Empiricus describes him as having founded, with Philon of Larissa, the Fourth Academy. We learn from Cicero that he attacked the ordinary schools of rhetoric as Plato had done in the *Phaedrus*.                    W. D. R.

**CHARMIDES** (d. 403 B.C.), an Athenian of noble family, nephew and ward of Critias, uncle of Plato, and member of the Socratic circle. He is mentioned in Pl. *Symp.* 222 b, *Prt.* 315 a, Xen. *Mem.* 3. 6. 1, 7. 1–9, and plays a large part in the Platonic dialogue that bears his name. According to Xen. (*Mem.* 3. 7) he was encouraged by Socrates to take up political life. He assisted Critias in the oligarchic revolution of 404 and fell with him in battle in 403, when the democrats returned under Thrasybulus.                    W. D. R.

**CHARON** (1), in Greek mythology, the aged ferryman in Hades who for an obolus conveyed the shades of the dead across the rivers of the lower world. As a fee for Charon the Greeks used to put a coin into the mouth of the dead. He is first mentioned in the *Minyad* and by Aeschylus (*Sept.* 842) and introduced by Aristophanes in the *Ranae* (183). In art he is first seen on a terra-cotta of the sixth century B.C. He was painted by Polygnotus in Delphi (Paus. 10. 28. 1) and is often shown on white-ground *lecythi*. The Etruscans knew a demon *Charun* who is perhaps a hellenized native hammer-god. Virgil's famous description of Charon (*Aen.* 6. 298–315) embodies some Etruscan features.

F. de Ruyt, *Charun* (1934); F. Sullivan, *CJ* 1950, 11; G. van Hoorn, *Mél. Bijvanck* (1954), 141; H. Borza, *Orbis* 1955, 134; A. van Windekens, *BN* 1958, 161.                    G. M. A. H.

**CHARON** (2) of Lampsacus is called a predecessor of Herodotus (Plut. *De malign. H.* 859 b; Tert. *De Anima* 46; Dion. Hal. *Thuc.* 5; *Pomp.* 3. 7). He is listed in the *Suda* as 'born under Darius I' and as author of *Aethiopica, Persica, Hellenica, On Lampsacus, Chronicles* (*῏Ωροι) of the Lampsacenes, Πρυτάνεις ἢ ἄρχοντες τῶν Λακεδαιμονίων (ἔστι δὲ χρονικά), Κτίσεις πόλεων, Cretica,* and a *Periplus of the area outside the Pillars of Heracles.* This list, if correct, suggests a later date for Charon, since even Thucydides shows no knowledge of a chronological work based on Spartan magistrates; but there are no fragments from this work, nor from the *Hellenica* (cf. Thuc. 1. 97). Only ῏Ωροι and *Persica* can be cited by name, and the few surviving fragments can all be assigned to these works. The verbal quotations seem to indicate a less detailed treatment of historical incidents than in Herodotus, a similar interest in anecdote and romance, local legends and tradition, and a more archaic manner of writing. *See* LOGOGRAPHERS, HELLANICUS.

*FHG* i. 32–5; iv. 627–8; *FGrH* iii A, no. 262; F. Jacoby, *Abh. z. gr. Geschichtschreibung* (1956), 178 ff., repr. of *Stud. Ital.* 1938, 207 ff.; L. Pearson, *Early Ionian Historians* (1939), ch. 4; H. Fränkel, *Dicht. u. Philosophie d. frühen Griechentums* (1950), 450 f.                    L. P.

**CHARONDAS,** the lawgiver of his native town Catana, and other Chalcidic colonies, especially Rhegium. He is often associated with Zaleucus (q.v.), but he lived later, probably in the sixth century B.C. Aristotle emphasizes the precision of his laws, but he may have included later measures under the name of Charondas. His laws seem

to have embraced almost all departments of life. We do not know whether he established a new constitution, but he certainly was an aristocrat. The tradition in Diodorus is mostly legendary.

Arist. *Politics*, esp. 1274ᵃˑᵇ; Diodorus, 12. 11–19. Adcock, *CHJ* ii (1927); Mühl, *Klio*, Beiheft xxii, 1929; G. Vallet, *Rhégion et Zancle* (1958).                    V. E.

**CHAROPS,** a pro-Roman leader in Epirus, was educated at Rome; his grandfather, also Charops, had helped Flamininus against Philip V in 198 B.C. During Rome's war against Perseus (q.v.) he undermined Rome's trust in his political rivals. Polybius (30. 12) denounced his character in such terms as to suggest that he might have encouraged Rome's devastation of Epirus: thereafter until his death *c.* 159 B.C. he acted tyrannically in Epirus, but he was not overthrown although he had lost the favour of leading Romans.

H. H. Scullard, *JRS* 1945, 55 ff.; S. I. Oost, *Roman Policy in Epirus* (1954), 72 ff.; Hammond, *Epirus*, 626 ff.                    H. H. S.

**CHARYBDIS,** a sort of whirlpool or maelstrom in a narrow channel of the sea (later identified with the Straits of Messina, where there is nothing of the kind), opposite Scylla (q.v.; *Od.* 12. 101 ff.); it sucks in and casts out the water three times a day and no ship can possibly live in it. Odysseus, carried towards it by a current when shipwrecked, escapes by clinging to a tree which grows above it and dropping into the water when the wreckage is cast out (432 ff.).

Hence proverbially, a serious danger, as Horace, *Carm.* 1. 27. 19.                    H. J. R.

**CHATTI,** a Germanic people, who lived in the neighbourhood of the upper Weser and the Diemel. Although not mentioned by Caesar, they were the most powerful enemies of Rome in western Germany throughout the first century A.D. Overrun by Drusus in 12 B.C., they took part in the revolt of A.D. 9 and were later attacked by Germanicus, who in A.D. 15 burned their town of Mattium (exact site unknown), and by the generals of Claudius and Domitian. They fought a war in A.D. 58 against the Hermunduri for the possession of some salt-beds, took part in the revolt of Civilis (q.v.) in 69–70, and by their constant attacks sapped the strength of the Cherusci (q.v.). Their social and military organization was more highly developed than that of the other Germans: they were disciplined, they obeyed their officers' orders, and they had something like a commissariat. Their nobles took even less part in productive life than those of other Germanic peoples. They are occasionally mentioned later than the time of Tacitus as attacking the Roman Empire, but in the late Roman period we hear practically nothing of them. Their name appears to have survived in that of Hessen.

E. A. Thompson, *The Early Germans* (1965).                    E. A. T.

**CHAUCI,** a Germanic people, living on the North-Sea coast between the mouths of the Ems and the Elbe. Overrun in the Augustan conquest of western Germany, they apparently took no part in the revolt of Arminius (q.v.); but they more than once raided the Gallic coast from the sea during the first century A.D. Little is known of their history; but Tacitus comments on the great numbers of 'the noblest people among the Germans', and Pliny vividly describes the poverty-stricken lives of the coast-dwellers (*HN* 16. 2–4). Their relationship with the Saxons, who lived on that same coast at a later date, is unknown.                    E. A. T.

**CHERSONESUS** (1), Thracian, or *Gallipoli*, peninsula. This territory had a double importance in Greek history, as a wheat-growing district which produced a surplus for export, and more especially because it lay on a main passage between Europe and Asia. It was occupied in the eighth and seventh centuries by settlers from Miletus and other Ionian towns, the chief colonies being Cardia (near the Bulair isthmus) and Sestos (q.v.), at the principal crossing-point of the Dardanelles. It passed into the hands of the Elder Miltiades, probably by arrangement between Pisistratus and the native Thracian population, for whose protection he fortified the Bulair isthmus *c.* 560 B.C.). It remained in the possession of his family until 493, when the Younger Miltiades (q.v.), who had held the peninsula as a vassal of King Darius, abandoned it to the Persians. After the Persian Wars it was at once brought into the Delian League by the Athenians, who established colonies at Sestos, Callipolis, and elsewhere (*c.* 450). After a period of Spartan domination (404–386) the Athenians recovered control, but had some difficulty in keeping out the Thracian dynasts, and in 338 they ceded the peninsula to Philip of Macedon. After passing through the hands of various Hellenistic rulers, most of the Chersonese became a domain of the Pergamene kings (189). In 133 a large part of it was converted into Roman *ager publicus*, and under Augustus into an imperial estate.

S. Casson, *Macedonia, Thrace and Illyria* (1926), 210 ff.; U. Kahrstedt, *Beiträge zur Geschichte der thrakischen Chersones* (1954). M. C.

**CHERSONESUS** (2), Tauric, or *Crimea*. The main attractions of the Crimea to the Greeks were the fisheries of the Cimmerian Bosporus(q.v. 2: *Straits of Kerch*), the cornlands of the interior, and the partial protection which its peninsular situation gave against the mainland peoples of Russia. It was colonized by Milesians and other Ionians in the seventh century. The principal settlement was Panticapaeum (q.v.) on the Bosporus. In 438 most of the Chersonese came under the rule of a dynasty of Thracian stock but of Hellenic culture, under whom it attained great prosperity as a granary of Greece (*see* SPARTOCIDS).

*See* bibliography for BOSPORUS (2). M. C.

**CHERSONESUS** (3), city of, situated on the Crimean Riviera near *Sevastopol*, in a vine-growing district. This Milesian colony was refounded at some later date by Dorians from Heraclea Pontica. After a long period of independence it sought protection from Mithridates VI against Scythian inroads (*c.* 115 B.C.), and from his death in 63 B.C. until the third century it remained in the hands of his descendants, who held it as vassals of Rome. Nero provided it with a Roman garrison, and Hadrian gave it further protection by means of a wall across the Crimea. It remained an outpost of Greek civilization until the thirteenth century.

*See* bibliography for BOSPORUS (2) M. C.

**CHERUSCI,** a Germanic people, living around the middle Weser. They are the best known of the Germanic opponents of Rome in the first century A.D. Overrun in the Augustan conquest of western Germany, it was their chieftain Arminius (q.v.) who led the revolt of A.D. 9, which resulted in the destruction of Quinctilius Varus and his army. They successfully defended themselves against Germanicus' punitive expeditions in 15–16, inflicting heavy losses on the Romans. They expelled the tyrant Maroboduus from among the Marcomanni (A.D. 17), and defeated the attempt of Arminius himself to set up a tyranny over them. Thereafter they weakened themselves by their internal struggles which, together with the hostility of the Chatti (q.v.), reduced them to comparative impotence by the time of Tacitus. In later times they are rarely heard of.

E. A. Thompson, *The Early Germans* (1965), ch. iii. E. A. T.

**CHILDREN.** The role of children in the religious life

of antiquity was not inconsiderable, no doubt partly because of their sexual purity (see E. Fehrle, *Die kultische keuschheit* (1908–10), 112). Hence also in magic the prescription of child-mediums (*PGM* 5. 1; S.H.A. *Did. Iul.* 7. 10; in black magic, child victims, Hor. *Epod.* 5. 12 ff.; Lucan 6. 710). In family cult, an unmarried daughter would on occasion sing or lead off the hymn at the beginning of a symposium, when the third libation was poured (Aesch. *Ag.* 243 ff.). In like manner, after a Roman family dinner, one of the children would announce that the portion of food offered to the household gods was acceptable ('deos propitios', Servius on *Aen.* 1. 730; more in W. Warde Fowler in Hastings, *ERE* iii. 545). This was readily extended to public cult. Apart from the common occurrence of choirs of boys, girls, or both (Fehrle, loc. cit.), a striking instance is the ceremonial of the Arrhephoroi at Athens, wherein little girls, after long preparation, were entrusted with the carrying of very sacred objects from the Acropolis to the temple of Aphrodite in the Gardens (Paus. 1. 27. 3, cf. L. Deubner, *Attische Feste* (1932), 9 ff.). Cf. also the ritual at Brauron (*see* ARTEMIS). That the vestals (q.v.) develop out of the services of young daughters in domestic hearthcult is practically certain. Generally speaking, the presence of a παῖς ἀμφιθαλής, *puer patrimus et matrimus*, was necessary for all manner of rites, public and private, as diverse as a Roman marriage and the cutting of the olive-garlands at Olympia.

H. J. R.

**CHILDREN'S SONGS, GREEK.** Pollux (9. 123) gives a list of eighteen παιδιαί, children's songs often accompanied with some sort of action, and adds details about χαλκῆ μυῖα, a kind of Blind Man's Buff, χελιχελώνη, a kind of Prisoner's Base, and (9. 113) χυτρίνδα, a kind of Catch. Another such game was ἄνθεμα (Ath. 629 c).

J. M. Edmonds, *Lyra Graeca* (1952) iii. 536–43; Page, *Poet. Mel. Gr.* 463–7. C. M. B.

**CHILON** (*Χίλων*), Spartan ephor (556/5 B.C.), was the first 'to yoke the ephors (q.v.) alongside the kings' (Diog. Laert. 1. 68), i.e., presumably, to increase their powers in some unrecorded way. As ephor he may have helped to overthrow the tyranny at Sicyon (*PRyl.* 18). He is credited by modern scholars with a momentous change in Sparta's foreign policy which led to the development of the Peloponnesian League (q.v.). Universally accepted as one of the 'Seven Sages' (Plato, *Prt.* 343 a), he was worshipped as a hero at Sparta, but mainly for his political services (Paus. 3. 16. 4).

V. Ehrenberg, *Neugründer des Staates* (1925), 7–54; G. L. Huxley, *Early Sparta* (1962), 69 ff. and bibliography n. 486. W. G. F.

**CHIMAERA,** properly 'she-goat'; a triple-bodied monster, 'lion before, serpent behind, she-goat in the middle' (*Il.* 6. 181), of divine race (Hesiod, *Theog.* 319 ff., explains that it was the offspring of Typhon and Echidna) and fire-breathing, slain by Bellerophon (q.v.). In art, the goat is represented by the head and neck of one protruding from the creature's back, as in the famous bronze Chimaera at Florence (*CAH*, vol. i of plates, 336 f.). This is so oddly inorganic as to suggest an early misunderstanding of some kind, and there is much to be said for the theory of Anne Roes (*JHS* 1934, 21 ff.) that originally (in oriental art) it had wings ending in a goat-like head, a type known to exist (ibid. 23 and illustrations there). H. J. R.

**CHIONIDES** is treated by Aristotle (*Poet.* 1448ᵃ33) as one of the two earliest Attic comic poets, and it is probable that he was the first recorded comic victor at the City Dionysia, in 487 (*Suda* s.v.). Two plays ascribed to him, *Heroes* and *Beggars*, existed in Hellenistic times (Ath. [137 e and 638 d] doubts the authenticity of

*Beggars*) and the *Suda* mentions also the title '*Persians or Assyrians*'. *See* COMEDY, OLD, § 1.

FCG i. 27 ff.; CAF i. 4–7; FAC i. 6 ff.     K. J. D.

**CHIOS,** a large island lying off the Erythraean peninsula, roughly oblong in shape, but narrowing towards the centre through the broad indentation on the lengthy western side. The mountains of the north give way to fertile plains in the south. Chios was renowned in antiquity for its wine, corn, figs, and gum-mastic. The city of Chios, the focus of political, economic, and cultural life, was founded at the finest harbour of the eastern seaboard, and became highly prosperous. From the time of Homer (whose birthplace it claimed to be) Chios had a distinguished literary tradition, and schools of artists working in stone and metal flourished on the island.

After its occupation by Ionian settlers Chios was a consistent ally of Miletus against Phocaea, Erythrae, and Samos. Incorporated in the Persian Empire under Cyrus, it fought heroically in the Ionian Revolt, and was devastated after Lade. As a member of the Delian League, Chios remained loyal until 413; Athenian efforts to retake the city proved ineffective. It was pro-Athenian during the fourth century B.C. until the Social War (357–355), which resulted in a temporary Carian domination. Its relations with Rome were cordial; in 86 it was sacked by Zenobius, Mithridates' general, the inhabitants being transported to Pontus. Sulla restored them to their homes, and Chios enjoyed the privileges of a free city under the Empire, until these were suspended by Vespasian. *See also* BOULE.

J. M. Cook, *The Greeks in Ionia and the East* (1962); P. Argenti, *Bibliography of Chios from Classical Times to 1936* (1940); D. W. S. Hunt, *BSA* (1940–5), 29 ff.; J. Boardman, *Ant. Journ.* 1959, 170 ff. (on architecture).     D. E. W. W.

**CHLOË,** i.e. 'green', title of Demeter as goddess of the young green crops. She had a shrine near the Acropolis at Athens (Paus. 1. 22. 3) and a festival, the Chloia, perhaps on Thargelion 6 (Deubner, *Attische Feste*, 1932, 67).

**CHOERILUS** (1), an Athenian tragic poet, according to the *Suda* (s.v.) wrote plays from *c.* 523 B.C. onwards, winning thirteen victories, competed against Aeschylus and Pratinas, and, as some said, made innovations in the tragic mask and costume. Only one of his plays, the *Alope*, is known by name. One or two bold metaphors are quoted from him (*TGF* 719–20). He is probably not the Choerilus described in a line of an unknown writer (quoted by Plotius *de metris*) as 'King among the Satyrs'.

A. W. P.-C.

**CHOERILUS** (2) of Samos, epic poet of the late fifth century B.C., famed for his *Persica*. It was in more than one book, and contained a catalogue of the tribes that crossed the Hellespont with the Persians; it was still read in the third century A.D. (*POxy.* 1399). Fragments show skill and originality. Choerilus may also have written *Samiaca*. Lysander, when in Samos (*c.* 404), cultivated him in the hope of epic immortality, and Archelaus (q.v. 2) paid him to move to Macedon, where he died.

EGF 265–72; FGrH iii C. 545–7; Schmid–Stählin I. ii. 542 ff.
M. L. W.

**CHOERILUS** (3) of Iasus, epic poet; travelled with Alexander the Great; paid to celebrate him; a bad poet (Hor. *Epist.* 2. 1. 232–4; id. *Ars P.* 357–8; Porphyrion ad loc.).

EGF 308–11.

**CHOREGIA.** The main part of the expense of the production of dithyramb, tragedy, and comedy at the Dionysiac festivals at Athens was laid upon individual citizens of sufficient wealth. For dithyramb these *choregoi* were chosen by the ten tribes (Arg. ii to Dem. *Meid.*, cf. Ar.

*Av.* 1403–4); for tragedy and comedy at the Dionysia by the *Archon Eponymos*, at the Lenaea by the *Archon Basileus* (Arist. *Ath. Pol.* 56, 7); about the middle of the fourth century B.C. the appointment for comedy was transferred to the tribes (ibid.). No one could be obliged to serve as *choregos* until a year had elapsed after his last period of office (Dem. *Lept.* 8), but any citizen might volunteer to serve (Lys. 21. 1–6). No one under forty years of age might be *choregos* to a dithyrambic chorus of boys (Aeschin. *In Tim.* 11–12). The smaller expenses of dithyrambs performed at the Thargelia, Panathenaea, and Hephaestea were also laid upon individual *choregoi* (Antiphon 6. 11, Lys. 21. 2) and the same system was applied to some other entertainments, such as the exhibition of pyrrhic dancers (Isae. 5. 36). *Choregia* for the men's dithyramb, which involved a chorus of fifty members and the most highly skilled flute-players, was much more expensive than for tragedy; the boys' dithyramb and comedy might cost less than either (Lys. 19. 29, 42; 21. 1–5).

*Choregia* at the Great Dionysia probably began shortly before 500 B.C. for tragedy, and about 486 for comedy. The first dithyrambic victory is said to have been in 509. At the Lenaea comedy was introduced about 440, tragedy before 430. In 405, when there may have been a lack of rich men, *choregia* at the Great Dionysia was shared between two *choregoi* (Schol. Ar. *Ran.* 404); this arrangement probably lasted only a single year. (Such *synchoregia* at certain Rural Dionysia is attested by several inscriptions of later dates in the fourth century.) Under Demetrius of Phalerum, perhaps in 309, a State-appointed *agonothetes* was instituted to manage the festivals and share the expense with the State, which is frequently named in inscriptions as *choregos* (ὁ δῆμος ἐχορήγει), but *choregoi* reappear, with or without an *agonothetes*, in inscriptions of the first century A.D. (See Haigh, op. cit. *infra*, 54, 55.)

Dithyrambic poets were assigned to the several *choregi* by lot, and the *choregoi* then drew lots for the order of choice of a flute-player—a matter of great importance (Dem. *Meid.* 13–14; Antiphon 6. 11). It is probable that tragic and comic poets were also assigned by lot, but there is no record. *Choregoi* had nothing to do with the selection, payment, or dresses of actors, but if we can trust Plutarch, *Phocion* 19, they were responsible for the 'supers'. They chose the members of the chorus, provided a room for their practices, and paid the expense of their costumes and training (Arg. i to Dem. *Meid.*; pseudo-Xen. *Ath. Pol.* 1. 13, etc.). As it was a misfortune for a *choregos* to be assigned to a bad poet, so it was important for a poet to have a liberal *choregos*, since it depended upon him whether a play was well or badly presented in respect of costumes, mute characters (attendants, etc.) and other additions to the setting (παραχορηγήματα). An ambitious or public-spirited *choregos*, like Nicias, might provide a magnificent spectacle and so win the victory; a mean one, hiring cheap costumes, could ruin a play (Antiphanes fr. 204; Dem. *Meid.* 16, 61; Arist. *Eth. Nic.* 4. 2; Pollux 7. 78), though a negligent *choregos* might be brought to book by the archon (Xen. *Hieron* 9. 4).

The prize won by a successful *choregos* for dithyramb was a tripod, which he subsequently dedicated, often as a part of a more elaborate monument—the extant monuments of Lysicrates and Thrasyllus are instances—and the locality where most of the Dionysiac tripods were collected was named 'the Tripods'. Those gained at the Thargelia were erected in the precinct of Apollo Pythius (Isae. 5. 41; *Suda*, s.v. Πύθιον). The *choregoi* for comedy did not receive the tripod, nor, almost certainly, did the *choregoi* for tragedy; they erected tablets commemorating their victory, and some of these survive. There remain also some laudatory inscriptions erected by fellow tribesmen r citizens in honour of public-spirited *choregoi*. The choregic system was in use in many cities besides Athens, and a large number of inscriptions testify to its continuance in these to the end of the second century B.C., and in some much later. *See also* LITURGY.

A. Brunck, *Inscriptiones Graecae ad Choregiam pertinentes* (Diss. Philol. Halenses vii (1886)); E. Reisch, *De musicis Graecorum certaminibus* (1885) and art. Χορηγία in *PW* iii. 2 (1899); E. Capps, *Introduction of Comedy into the City Dionysia* (1903); A. Wilhelm, *Urkunden dramatischer Aufführungen in Athen* (1906); A. E. Haigh, *Attic Theatre*[3] (1907), Ch. 2 and App. B; K. J. Maidment, *CQ* 1935, 1 ff.; Pickard-Cambridge—Webster, *Dithyramb*[2]; Pickard-Cambridge—Lewis-Gould, *Dramatic Festivals of Athens*[2] (1968).
A. W. P.-C.; D. W. L.

**CHREIA,** a collection of witty or clever sayings, so called because designed for utility (χρησίμου τινὸς ἔνεκα, Hermog. *Prog.* c. 3); one of the varieties of *progymnasmata* (q.v.). Such collections were already being made in the fourth century B.C., e.g. by Theocritus of Chios and Demetrius of Phalerum, and some biographies of philosophers, e.g. that of Diogenes by Diogenes Laertius, consist largely of *Chreiai*; the ancestry of the genre may be seen in some parts of Xenophon's *Memorabilia*. The greatest extant collection is the *Gnomologium Vaticanum*, published in *Wien. Stud.* 1887–9. The *Chreia* of Machon (q.v.) is a collection of scurrilities.          J. D. D.; K. J. D.

**CHREMONIDES** (fl. 270–240 B.C.), Athenian nationalist statesman, pupil of Zeno. In the archonship of Peithidemus (probably 267/6) he carried a decree by which Athens joined the Peloponnesian anti-Macedonian coalition, supported by Ptolemy (*IG* ii[2]. 1. 686 and 687). The subsequent war, named after him (Ath. 5. 250 f.), ended with the surrender of Athens in 263–262. He found refuge with Ptolemy, and as Egyptian admiral was defeated off Ephesus by Agathostratus of Rhodes (*c.* 258); he was still admiral *c.* 240.

Beloch, *Griech. Gesch.* iv; W. W. Tarn, *JHS* 1934; F. Sartori, *Miscellanea di studi alessandrini . . . A. Rostagni* (1963), 117 ff.
F. W. W.

**CHRISTIANITY.** The life and teaching of Jesus Christ, the activities of St. Paul (Roman citizen though he was), the history and organization of the early Church, and even the importance of the New Testament as a source of knowledge of the Graeco-Roman world, these are topics too vast to be included in a classical dictionary (for some aspects, see, e.g., *The Oxford Dictionary of the Christian Church*, ed. F. L. Cross). This article, therefore, is confined primarily to the relations of Christianity with the Roman government.

The attitude of the Roman authorities towards primitive Christianity was influenced by two factors—first, their policy towards foreign cults in the city of Rome, and secondly, the repercussions of the long conflict between the Jews and the Seleucids to which Rome unwittingly found herself the heir.

The Roman Republic was famed for *religio*. Foreign observers, such as Polybius (6. 56), and citizens, such as Cicero (e.g. *Nat. D.* 2. 3. 8), testified to the reality of the Roman's devotion to his ancestral religion. This, however, was regarded in the nature of a contract rather than a creed or individual hope of salvation. The *pax deorum* implied that the gods protected the Roman people in return for receiving due worship and reverence from them. Acknowledgement (*recognitio*) of the ceremonies of the Roman people was to be one of the main demands made by the authorities on the Christians in the second and third centuries. The Senate as guardian of the common weal was responsible for the maintenance of traditional worship and, while not attempting to regulate the worship of the numerous alien population in Rome, suppressed as *prava religio* cults which appeared either horrific or subversive, and thus dangerous to the authority of the Roman gods. In 186 B.C. the *Bacchanalia* (q.v.) were suppressed in Rome on these grounds, and in the provinces the Druids suffered the same fate under Tiberius and Claudius.

Meantime, in the Jews Rome had encountered a people who had the strongest national sentiment, who had adherents and sympathizers in every part of the Mediterranean world, and who believed that their religion was to be the religion of mankind. Nevertheless, Rome and the Jews first met as allies against the Seleucids (1 Maccabees viii. 11). As the religion of an allied nation Judaism was tolerated and in the first century B.C. favoured against the clamant pressure of the Greek oligarchies in Asia Minor and the Greek islands.

The institution of the imperial cult (*see* RULER-CULT II), however, brought about a change in .Rome's relations with the Hellenistic world. Its peoples now found a centre of religious loyalty in a common Graeco-Roman culture, while Rome's relations with the Jews began to deteriorate. Fears of a world-wide Jewish rising led by some prophetic king of the Jews were rife by A.D. 33.

The Christian Church first became known to the authorities as a troublesome sect of Jews. At first, however, it benefited from the *de jure* acceptance that Judaism enjoyed. Acts, if written from an apologetic angle, shows Roman officials and the provincials, despite the Ephesus riot (Acts xix), as generally tolerant towards the new religion. The Jews, however, were determined to smother their rival, and attempted so far as possible to embroil the Christians with the authorities (cf. Acts xxiv. 2 ff.). Until 64 they were unsuccessful. Nero, however, found the Christians useful scapegoats for the Great Fire at Rome in that year. The Christians were punished, as the Bacchanals had been, for conspiracy and incendiarism inspired by *superstitio nova et malefica* (Suet. *Nero*, 16. 2). The popular reproach against the Christians recorded by Tacitus (*c.* 115: *Ann.* 15. 44) of 'odium humani generis' had been, however, one reserved for the Jews (cf. Tac. *Hist.* 5. 5. 1). A generation after the affair the writer of 1 Clement suggests that internecine rivalries within Judaism had their share in bringing about the deaths of Peter and Paul (1 Clement 4–5).

The Neronian persecution was neither followed up in Rome nor repeated elsewhere in the Empire. For the next century relations between the Christians and the remainder of the inhabitants of the Empire are shrouded in obscurity lit at rare intervals by well-commented incidents. Three factors dominate the period: first, the uninterrupted hostility between Jews and Christians, particularly in the province of Asia where both were numerous; secondly, the strongly apocalyptic tendency prevalent among the Christian communities and their expectation of the persecutions and disasters that would presage the Millennium of the Saints; and thirdly, despite increasing popular hostility, the comparative indifference of the authorities to them. Judaism, not Christianity, remained Rome's most intractable internal problem.

In 95 Domitian arrested his cousin Flavius Clemens, Domitilla, and Acilius Glabrio (4), consul in 91 (qq.v.). They were charged with 'atheism (ἔγκλημα ἀθεότητος) for which also many others who had drifted into the practices of the Jews were condemned' (Dio Cass. 67. 14). Clemens and Glabrio were killed; Domitilla was exiled. It is not easy to see an attack on Christianity in this. Suetonius, otherwise hostile to the Christians, does not connect these events with them, and Domitian's suspicions both of possible rivals to the throne and of *externa religio* in general, coupled with his merciless scrutiny of the Jews, may be sufficient explanation. The connexion of this incident with Judaism is further suggested by Nerva's recall of the victims of his predecessor's repression and the proclamation on his copper coinage FISCI IUDAICI CALUMNIA SUBLATA.

The real 'Domitianic persecution' was probably taking place in Asia. The 90s provide evidence for the alliance of Jewish and pagan adversaries of Christianity. This, combined with Christians' exaltation for martyrdom, produced the vivid picture of strife and persecution found in Revelation. The 'synagogue of Satan' (the Jews) of Rev. ii. 9 was henceforth associated with 'Satan's seat' (Rev. ii. 13), perhaps the altar of the imperial cult at Pergamum, where the martyr Antipas met his end.

The Asian provinces also provide the next information about the Christians. In 112 Pliny (q.v. 2) wrote to Trajan asking how to deal with the Christians in Bithynia. Like Tacitus and Suetonius, Pliny regarded them as an extravagant and noxious superstition (*superstitionem pravam, immodicam*) whose obstinacy rendered them worthy of punishment even if their practices did not. He had ordered the execution of Christians before writing to the Emperor about them. Trajan upheld Pliny's acts: Christians if denounced and proved to be such, were to be punished, but they were not actively to be sought out (*conquirendi non sunt*). If they recanted, they were to be freed. Anonymous accusations also were not to be accepted (*Ep.* 10. 96 and 97). Christians, so far as is known, took no part in the great Jewish rising of 115–17. They received a further measure of relief in 125, when Hadrian instructed the proconsul of Asia, Minucius Fundanus, in reply to a question by his predecessor, that Christians must be charged by regular accusation and proved to have acted contrary to the laws. The courts were open to hear accusations against them, but Christians were protected against vexatious attacks by the *calumnia* (malicious prosecution) procedure. In normal circumstances they could count on being left alone.

The legal position of Christianity in the first two centuries has caused difficulties to generations of scholars. Why were the early Christians persecuted at all? Christianity was certainly illegal. Pliny knew that there had been trials of Christians but he himself wanted to know whether punishment was attached to the Christian *nomen* or the *flagitia cohaerentia nomini*. The standard procedure against them was formal denunciation by a *delator* who had not merely to inform but conduct the prosecution in person with attendant risks for failure. Moreover, Trajan was not prepared to allow them to be treated as malefactors whom the authorities would be expected to destroy as a matter of course. Tertullian (*Apol.* 5) thought the procedure illogical. Others have done so too. *Maiestas* (treason), *flagitia* (crimes), atheism, and sheer *contumacia* all seem inadequate as explanations of the charges against them. Though it is true that we never hear of a Christian being prosecuted as a member of a *collegium illicitum*, it is probably in the assumption that Christians belonged to an illicit Judaistic organization suspected of criminal and antisocial proclivities that the answer must be sought. The opening words of Celsus' *Alethes Logos* (written *c.* 178), 'societies that are public are allowed by the laws, but secret societies are illegal' (Origen, *Contra Celsum* 1. 1), are significant. Even after the second fall of Jerusalem in 135, the Jewish religion was tolerated on grounds of antiquity (Origen, *Contra Celsum* 5. 41). The Christians, who in the eyes of the provincials were an off-shoot of Judaism, but had abandoned the Jewish law as well as that of their cities, had no *locus standi* in society. An illuminating statement of the Roman point of view is that of the proconsul of Africa, Galerius Maximus, at Cyprian's trial in 258. To Cyprian he said: 'You have long lived an irreligious life, and have drawn together a number of men bound by an unlawful association, and professed yourself an open enemy of the gods and religion of Rome' (*Acta Proconsularia* 3).

Under Hadrian and Antoninus Pius the Christians enjoyed a period of calm. The Church spread and its leaders travelled freely from place to place discussing increasingly varied opinions. Individuals such as Polycarp (q.v.), bishop of Smyrna, were well respected in the communities in which they dwelt and held their offices for decades. By the 150s, however, Christians had begun to replace the Jews in popular estimation as the enemies of the Empire and its civilization. Refusal to participate in the imperial cult and indeed in any form of activity connected with the pagan gods was regarded as deleterious to the rest of the community. Under Marcus Aurelius sporadic outbreaks of violence flared up into pogroms at Smyrna (*c.* 165) when Polycarp was seized and burnt and at Lyons in 177 when forty-eight members of the nascent Christian church were martyred. Personal denunciation by a rival philosopher led to the execution of Justin Martyr in Rome in 165. The Emperor himself, while not formally abandoning Trajan's rulings, is said by Melito, Bishop of Sardes, to have acquiesced in 'new instructions' (καινὰ δόγματα) that were circulated to the authorities in Asia facilitating the evil work of informers against the Christians (Euseb. *Hist. Eccl.* 4. 26. 5). In this reign, the Christians in the East touched the lowest point of unpopularity. They were the prey of popular rumour which attributed to them crimes such as incest, cannibalism, and child-murder as well as the more general and damning charge of atheism. Educated provincials, while less concerned with these accusations, regarded the Christians as disloyal citizens and their proselytizing as a disruptive force in the life of the Empire. Celsus' *Alethes Logos* and Lucian of Samosata's *De Morte Peregrini* (*c.* 165) provide important testimony for the views of thoughtful and observant pagans of the time. For their part, the Christian Apologists such as Justin, Melito of Sardes, Athenagoras, and Theophilus of Antioch attempted to refute the popular charges and claim toleration for themselves as loyal subjects while proclaiming the saving message for mankind.

Under Commodus and for most of the Severan period the Church enjoyed relative calm in Rome and the Greek-speaking east. There was now, however, a change in the character of the Christian communities. The Church's progress had originally been most strongly marked among the outer circle of semi-proselytes and inquirers in the Jewish synagogues to whom St. Paul had preached. The few documents that we have relating to the Church in the first half of the second century suggest an inward-looking body interested in perfecting itself before the Coming of the Lord. However, each decade brought new progress; merchants from the eastern Mediterranean carried the message into southern Gaul, and individuals such as Justin Martyr despairing of finding answers to their questionings from the current philosophies joined the Church's ranks. By 180 it was established in North Africa, and from now on the Church was to be Latin-speaking as well as Greek-speaking. Conflict with dissenting and non-orthodox movements, particularly Gnosticism, accelerated the establishment of common Rules of Faith, a recognized canon of Scripture and an organized hierarchy under the government of an urban episcopate. By 200 Christianity had ceased to be a Judaistic sect and was becoming one of the major religions of the Graeco-Roman world.

For reasons which are not clear Septimius Severus associated Jews and Christians in a ban which he imposed in 202 on conversion to either faith. This resulted in the first Empire-wide action against Christian converts. There were martyrs in Alexandria, Rome, Corinth, and Carthage, including Saints Perpetua and Felicitas at Carthage. In 212, however, Caracalla by granting Roman citizenship to nearly all free inhabitants of the Roman world rendered the Christians vulnerable to a general persecution: as Roman citizens the great majority of provincials could now be required to acknowledge the gods of Rome and participate in the imperial cult. So long as the Severan dynasty lasted, however, the Church suffered little molestation. Carthage is an exception, where outbreaks similar to those characteristic of the Hellenistic cities a generation previously took place. Elsewhere, persecutions arose out of local causes or even the personal embitterment of a provincial governor against the sect. It was in this period that the first buildings identifiable as churches were erected, in Dura Europos, Edessa, and in Cappadocia.

The removal of Alexander Severus in Mar. 235 ended the long period of quasi-toleration. Maximinus (235–8) associated the Christians with what he considered to be the weakness of the previous regime and acted against its leaders (Euseb. *Hist. Eccl.* 6. 28). In Rome Bishop Pontian and his rival Hippolytus were exiled to Sardinia, where they died. These measures did not last long and in the reigns of Gordian III and Philip (238–49) the Church again enjoyed a period of peace. Both Eusebius (*Hist. Eccl.* 6. 36) and Origen (*Contra Celsum* 1. 43) speak of large numbers of converts, and Origen, too, of Church office now becoming a desirable social asset. To Origen also the Church owed the beginnings of an intellectual ascendancy over paganism which it was never to lose.

The fall of Philip again brought a change of policy towards the Church. The danger to the Empire from the revived power of the Sassanids in the East and the combined pressure of Goths on the Danube and Franks and Alemanni on the Rhine frontier was increasing. The new Emperor, Decius (249–51), aimed at restoring traditional Roman virtue and discipline. He took the name of Trajan, revived the office of censor, and embarked on a skilful offensive-defensive campaign on the Danube frontier. At a time when the unity of the whole Empire behind its ruler was called for, the Christians were regarded as non-co-operators and their strength was feared. Decius' measures against them fell into two phases. In Jan. 250 he followed the precedent set by Maximinus and arrested senior members of the clergy; Pope Fabian was executed. Then in the late spring, orders were sent throughout the provinces for a general sacrifice to the gods of the Empire, perhaps a *dies Imperii* designed to inaugurate a new age of human happiness. Commissions were established to supervise the sacrifices, and those who performed were given a certificate (*libellus*) testifying to their act. Forty-three of these *libelli* have been recovered from various sites in Egypt. These measures took the Christians by surprise and had immense initial success. From Rome, Alexandria, Smyrna, and Carthage we hear of the flight or apostasy of clergy and droves of Christians thronging the temples to sacrifice (cf. Cyprian, *De Lapsis* 8, Euseb. *Hist. Eccl.* 6. 41, and the *Acta Pionii* (ed. Knopf and Krueger) 18). The government, however, had no means of following up their success and on the death of Decius (June 251) the danger passed. In a few years the Church had regained all the ground it had lost.

Once more, under Valerian (253–60), the Church faced the hostility of the Empire. The early part of Valerian's reign had been favourable to the Christians, but in the summer of 257 he attempted to suppress the Christian cult and enforce veneration of the gods of Rome on the Christian clergy. This was followed a year later by a much more severe edict including in its scope highly placed Christian laity and civil servants and aimed perhaps at diverting some of the wealth of the Church to the imperial fisc. In the West this was the most destructive and bloody of the persecutions, lasting through 258 and 259; the victims included Cyprian of Carthage.

Valerian's capture by Sapor in June 260 ended the persecution. His son Gallienus, perhaps in a bid for popular support against his rival the anti-Christian Macrianus, restored peace to the Church and ordered the return of its confiscated property. This peace, broken only by a threat of persecution by Aurelian in 275, lasted until Diocletian began to purge the civil service and army of Christians (*c.* 298). The last battle between Church and Empire had begun.

Why Diocletian started a full-scale attack on the Christians in 303 is not clear. The previous nineteen years of his rule had been characterized by conservative restoration under the aegis of the gods of Rome, Jupiter and Hercules. His rescript to the proconsul of Africa, Julianus (probably in July 297), shows that he hated foreign cults and religious innovation. It may be that he feared that the Christians were a powerful contrary influence on the fortunes of the Empire and must be made to conform. Pressed on by his avowedly anti-Christian Caesar, Galerius, Diocletian ordered on 23 Feb. 303 the destruction of church buildings, the surrender of the Scriptures, and the performance by clergy of an act of sacrifice. There was, however, to be no bloodshed. More stringent edicts followed, culminating in the spring of 304 when Diocletian was incapacitated by illness, with a command for a universal sacrifice.

In general these instructions were carried out without question in the provinces. But the Church was now immensely stronger than under Decius and Valerian. It had become the religion of the countryside as well as the cities of some of the great provinces bordering the Mediterranean. It had spread east into Armenia and Persia. Only the Celtic provinces of the Empire remained unassailable. Persecution was foredoomed to failure and Diocletian may have realized as much when he abdicated on 1 May 305.

While this ended the persecution in the West, the East suffered six more years of misery. By Apr. 311, however, Galerius admitted defeat and on his death-bed granted the Christians grudging toleration. For another year, however, Maximinus (q.v.), his successor as senior Augustus, maintained the repression and made a final but vain bid to rally the forces of tradition against the Christians. Meantime, whether convinced by a vision or not, Constantine having made himself master of the West called off the persecution. The Edict of Milan 313 marks the end of an era.

After a period of eleven years when Constantine combined veneration for the 'Unconquered Sun my companion' with that of Christ, the cause of Christianity triumphed at Chrysopolis in Sept. 324, and at the Council of Nicaea in 325 it became *de facto* the religion of the Empire. Thenceforth, paganism declined. Julian's attempted restoration (361–3) was shortlived. Under Theodosius the revolution was complete. Christianity had become the religion of the Mediterranean world.

Victory eventually went to the Church from a combination of circumstances. The turning-point would not seem to have come until after the failure of Valerian's persecution (260). The catastrophic events of the period 250–75 may have shaken the faith of many in the saving powers both of the immortal gods of Rome and in local territorial divinities. Where there is evidence, the rejection of the latter by Christian converts at this time was apparently complete. The bravery of martyrs and the Christian social message may also have had their effect in providing inspiration and refuge which the old gods failed to do. In the end, as Lactantius pointed out (*Div. Inst.* 5. 22. 18), God may have permitted the persecutions in order to bring the pagans within the community of the Church.

For works before 1938, see *CAH* xii. 775 ff., 794 ff., esp. E. G. Hardy, *Christianity and the Roman Government* (1906); L. H. Canfield, 'The Early Persecutions of the Christians', *Columbia*

*University Studies in History, Economics and Public Law*, 55, 1913; W. M. Ramsay, *The Church in the Roman Empire before 170* (1906); H. von Campenhausen, *Die Idee des Martyrismus in der alten Kirche* (1936); H. Last, *JRS* 1937, 80 ff.
Post 1939: G. E. M. de Ste Croix, *Past and Present* 1963, 6 ff.; W. H. C. Frend, *Martyrdom and Persecution in the Early Church* (1965); A. N. Sherwin-White, *Roman Society and Roman Law in the New Testament* (1963), and *JTS* 1952, 199 ff.; J. Vogt, 'Zur Religiosität der Christenverfolger im römischen Reich', *Sitzb. Akad. Heidelberg, Phil.-Hist. Kl.* 1962; 'Christenverfolgungen', i Historisch (J. Vogt) and ii Juristisch (H. Last), *RAC*, ii. 1159 ff.; *The Conflict between Paganism and Christianity in the fourth century* (1963), ed. A. Momigliano; J. D. Barnes, *JRS* 1968, 32 ff.
For documents in translation see J. Stevenson, *A New Eusebius* (1957); P. R. Coleman-Norton, *Roman State and Christian Church* (1966).                    W. H. C. F.

**CHRISTODORUS** (5th c. A.D.), prolific epic poet from Coptus in Egypt. Wrote an epic on the Isaurian victory of Anastasius in 497, versified histories (πάτρια) of Thessalonica, Nacle, Miletus, Tralles, Aphrodisias, and Constantinople (*Suda*, s.v.; cf. A. Cameron, *Hist.* 1965, 489) and a work on the pupils of Proclus (John Lyd, *De Magg.* iii. 26)—all now lost. Apart from two epigrams (*Anth. Pal.* 7. 697–8: cf. L. Robert, *Hellenica* 1948, 93), his only surviving work is an ἔκφρασις on the statues decorating the Baths of Zeuxippus in Constantinople (*Anth. Pal.* 2. 1–416). Both in diction and in metrical practice it shows clear traces of the influence of Nonnus, though not in all respects as strict as the master.

F. Baumgarten, 'De C. poeta Thebano' (Diss. Bonn 1881); A. Wifstrand, *Von Kallim. zu Nonnos* (1933), ch. i.        A. D. E. C.

**CHRISTUS PATIENS**, a play in 2,610 verses describing the Passion of Our Lord, bearing the name of Gregory the Nazianzene, but written by a Byzantine of the eleventh or twelfth century, possibly Constantine Manasses. It contains a very great number of lines from Euripides, and some from Aeschylus and Lycophron. It is of doubtful use for the textual criticism of Euripides, but portions of the lost end of the *Bacchae* have been recovered from it (See E. R. Dodds' edition of *Bacch.* (1960), 243 ff.).

TEXT. J. G. Brambs (Teubner, 1885); K. Horna, *Hermes* 1929, 429 ff.        J. D. D.; K. J. D.

**CHRYSEIS** (Χρυσηΐς), in mythology, daughter of Chryses, priest of Apollo at Chryse. She was taken prisoner and given to Agamemnon as his gift of honour (γέρας). On his refusal to let her father ransom her, Apollo, at Chryses' prayer, sent a plague on the Greek camp, which was not stayed till she was returned to him. Agamemnon compensated himself by taking Briseis (q.v.) from Achilles, thus starting the quarrel between them (*Il.* 1. 11 ff.). In a late legend (Hyg. *Fab.* 121) she has a son by Agamemnon.        H. J. R.

**CHRYSIPPUS** (c. 280–207 B.C.), son of Apollonius of Soli (Cilicia), successor of Cleanthes as head of the Stoa. He came to Athens about 260 and there first attended the lectures of Arcesilaus (q.v. 1), then head of the Academy. From him he got the training in logic and dialectic which he later used to great advantage in fighting the scepticism of Arcesilaus and the Middle Academy. He was converted to Stoicism by Cleanthes, whom he succeeded in 232. He devoted his life to elaborating the Stoic system in almost innumerable works and to defending it against the attacks of the Academy. He was so successful that his philosophy became identified with Stoic orthodoxy, and obscured that of his predecessors, from whom he differed in many points, especially in his logic and theory of knowledge. The catalogue of his works given by Diog. Laert. 7. 189–202 is not completely preserved.

FRAGMENTS. Von Arnim, *SVF* ii. 1–348; iii. 3–205; Diogenes Laertius 7. 179–202; E. Bréhier, *Chrysippe*² (1951); M. Pohlenz, 'Zenon und Chrysipp', *Nachricht. Götting. Gesellsch. Fachgruppe* i, N.F. ii, no. 9; *Die Stoa*² (1955); logic, B. Mates, *Stoic Logic*² (1961); physics, S. Samburský, *Physics of the Stoics* (1959).    K. VON F.

**CHRYSOGONUS**, LUCIUS CORNELIUS (*PW* 101), freedman of Sulla (q.v. 1), in collusion with two relatives of Sex. Roscius of Ameria (who had been murdered) placed the dead man's name on the proscription lists, to enable them jointly to buy his property at a nominal sum. He is the chief object of attack in Cicero's speech on behalf of Roscius (q.v. 1), whom he accused of his father's murder. When the case acquired political overtones, Sulla seems to have withdrawn his support.

Cicero, *pro Roscio Amerino.*                    E. B.

**CHRYSOSTOM**, JOHN (c. A.D. 354–407), bishop of Constantinople. Though educated at Antioch by Libanius, John turned to asceticism at home and later became a hermit. Ordained deacon at Antioch in 381 and priest (386), and pre-eminently a preacher, he reluctantly became bishop of Constantinople (398). Trouble with the Empress Eudoxia, Theophilus of Alexandria, and Asiatic bishops resenting his extension of Constantinople's quasi-patriarchal authority, caused his deposition by the Synod of the Oak (403). He was banished, recalled, banished again to Armenia (404), and died in exile (407).

Most eloquent of preachers (hence his name Chrysostom, 'the golden-mouthed') but not an outstanding theologian, he expounded Scripture in the Antiochene tradition according to its historical sense, practically and devotionally. Denunciation of luxury, care for the poor, interest in education are characteristic. The homilies *De Statuis*, occasioned by riots in 387, are notable; *De Sacerdotio* gives his conception of clerical duties. The *Liturgy of Chrysostom* is not his work.

EDITIONS. H. Savile (1612); B. de Montfaucon (Paris, 1718–38); Migne, *PG* xlvii–lxiv. Life by C. Baur, 2 vols. (Munich, 1929–39, E.T. 1959). See also J. A. de Aldama, *Repertorium Pseudochrysostomicum* (1965).        S. L. G.

**CICERO** (1), MARCUS TULLIUS (*PW* 29), the first of two sons of a rich and well-connected *eques* of Arpinum, was born on 3 Jan. 106 B.C., the year following the first consulship of C. Marius, with whose family (also from Arpinum) his grandmother Gratidia had marriage connexions. His intelligent and ambitious father (who was to die in the year of Cicero's canvass for the consulship), advised perhaps by L. Crassus (q.v. 3), gave his two sons an excellent education in rhetoric and rhetoric in Rome and later in Greece, with their two first-cousins as their fellow students. Cicero did military service in 90/89 under Pompey's father, Cn. Pompeius (q.v. 3) Strabo, and attended legal consultations of the two great Scaevolae (qq.v. 3 and 4). He conducted his first case in 81 (*Pro Quinctio*) and made an immediate reputation through his successful defence of Roscius of Ameria on a charge of parricide in 80, a case which reflected discreditably on the contemporary administration of the dictator Sulla. Cicero was then from 79 to 77 a student of philosophy and oratory both in Athens and in Rhodes, where he heard Posidonius (q.v. 2); he visited P. Rutilius (q.v. 1) Rufus at Smyrna.

**2.** He returned to Rome, his health greatly improved, to pursue a public career, and was elected quaestor for 75, when he served for a year in western Sicily, and praetor for 66, in each case at the earliest age at which he could legally become a candidate. By securing the condemnation of C. Verres (q.v.) for extortion in Sicily in 70 he scored a resounding success against Q. Hortensius, eight years his senior, whom he was to replace as the leading figure at the Roman Bar. In a cleverly disarming speech delivered during his praetorship (*De imperio Cn. Pompei*) he supported, against strong Optimate opposition, the tribune Manilius' proposal to transfer the command in the war against Mithridates to Pompey; this was the first public expression of his admiration for Pompey who was, with occasional short interruptions, henceforward to be the focus of his political allegiance. He was elected consul for 63—the first *novus homo* with no political background whatever since 94—because, in a poor field, Optimate voters were alarmed about the intentions of Catiline (q.v.), who might otherwise have been their candidate. Hampered by a weak and indeed suspect colleague, C. Antonius (q.v. 3), Cicero did very well to secure evidence which convinced the Senate of the seriousness of Catiline's conspiracy. After the last decree (*senatus consultum ultimum*) was passed, and Catiline left Rome for his army in Etruria, five conspirators prominent in Roman society and politics, including a praetor, P. Cornelius Lentulus Sura, were arrested and executed on 5 Dec. (the Nones). Although, after debate, the Senate, influenced by Cato (q.v. 5), had recommended their execution, the act itself, a violation of the citizen's right to a trial, could be justified only by the passing of the last decree and was Cicero's personal responsibility. Though approved in the first moment of panic by all classes of society in Rome, its legality was strictly questionable, and Cicero was unwise to boast as loudly of it as he did (even in a long and indiscreet letter to Pompey in the East, *Pro Sulla* 67, *Pro Planc.* 85, cf. *Fam.* 5. 7). He published his speeches of 63, including those against Catiline, in 60, wrote of his action in prose and verse, in Greek and Latin, and invited others, including Posidonius, to do the same; and to the end of his life he never wavered in his belief that he had acted rightly and had saved Rome from catastrophe.

**3.** Though it was unlikely that he would escape prosecution, Cicero refused overtures from Caesar, which might have saved him at the price of his political independence. In 58 P. Clodius (q.v. 1), whom he had antagonized in 61 when Clodius was charged with incest, moved a bill as tribune re-enacting the law that anyone who had executed a citizen without trial should be banished. Without awaiting prosecution Cicero fled the country, to Macedonia, and Clodius passed a second, certainly unconstitutional, bill, declaring him an exile. His house on the Palatine was destroyed by Clodius' gangsters, part of its site to be made a shrine of Liberty, and his villa at Tusculum was also badly damaged. With Pompey's belated support and with the support of the tribune Milo (q.v.), who employed violence as irresponsibly as Clodius had done in the previous year, Cicero was recalled by a law of the people on 4 Aug. 57 and was warmly welcomed on his return both in Italy and in Rome, which he reached on 4 Sept.

**4.** He returned to a busy winter, fighting to secure adequate public compensation for the damage to his property and, in the Senate and in the courts, supporting those chiefly responsible for his recall. Hopes of dissociating Pompey from his close political connexion with Caesar, attempts which Clodius was employed by Caesar to interrupt, were at an end when Caesar, Pompey, and Crassus revived their political union in Apr. 56, and Cicero was sharply brought to heel (*Att.* 4. 5, on his 'palinode'; cf. *Fam.* 1. 9 for his later account of his conversion). He at once spoke warmly in the Senate (e.g. in *De provinciis consularibus*) and on the public platform in favour of Caesar, as of a longstanding political friend. He claimed that it was the act of a realist, a *sapiens*, to accept the indisputable predominance of the Three ('temporibus adsentiendum', *Fam.* 1. 9. 21) and only revealed in conversation and in letters to such close friends as Atticus the deep wound which his pride—his *dignitas*—had suffered. He took no more part in the collapsing world of republican politics, devoting himself to writing, which he never regarded as anything but a poor substitute for active political life (the *De oratore* was published in 55, and the *De republica* finished in 51); and he was humiliated by briefs which, under pressure from Pompey and

Caesar, he was forced to accept. He defended Vatinius (q.v.) successfully and Gabinius (q.v. 2) unsuccessfully in 54. He was humiliated too by his failure, in a court packed with troops, to defend Milo adequately when, with the case already prejudiced, Milo was impeached for the murder of Clodius early in 52. The period brought him one consolation, when he was elected augur in 53 in the place of his earlier protégé, young P. Crassus (q.v. 5), who had been killed at Carrhae.

**5.** Cicero was out of Rome during the eighteen months preceding the outbreak of the Civil War, being selected under regulations following Pompey's *lex de provinciis* of 52 to govern Cilicia as proconsul from summer 51 to summer 50. He was a just, if not a strong, governor, but he regarded his appointment with horror as a second relegation from Rome. However, his dispatches recording the successful encounter of his troops with brigands on Mons Amanus earned a *supplicatio* at Rome and he returned, the *fasces* of his lictors wreathed in fading laurels, hoping that he might celebrate a triumph. Instead he was swept into the vortex of the Civil War.

**6.** Appointed District Commissioner at Capua by the government, he did not at first follow Pompey and the consuls overseas. Caesar saw him at Formiae on 28 Mar. 49, and invited him to join the rump of the Senate in Rome on terms which with great resolution Cicero refused to accept (*Att.* 9. 11 a, to Caesar; 9. 18). His long indecision up to this point which was anything but discreditable was now at an end, and he joined the Republicans in Greece, irritating their leaders by his caustic criticism, himself dismayed by the absence of any idealistic loyalty on their part to the cause of Republicanism. After Pharsalus, in which he took no part, he refused Cato's invitation to assume command of the surviving republican forces and, pardoned by Caesar, he returned to Italy. But political life was at an end, and he was utterly out of sympathy with Caesar's domination. All that he could do was to return to his writing, his only important speech being that delivered in the Senate in 46 (the year in which the *Brutus* was written) in praise of Caesar's pardon of M. Marcellus (*cos.* 51), who had done so much to precipitate the outbreak of the Civil War.

**7.** That Cicero was not invited to participate in the conspiracy to kill Caesar in 44 is not insignificant. He hailed the news of the murder on 15 Mar. with intemperate delight (e.g. *Fam.* 6. 15). Political life began again, and Cicero had all the prestige (*auctoritas*) of a senior consular. Within three months he was saying openly that Antony should have been killed too (*Att.* 15. 11. 2). He accepted the overtures of the young Caesar (Octavian), uncritical of the lawlessness of many of his acts, misled by his youth into a mistaken underassessment of his political acumen, and he closed his eyes to the fact that Octavian could never be reconciled to Brutus and Cassius. He struggled in speech after speech (the *Philippics*, the first delivered on 2 Sept. 44, the last on 21 Apr. 43) to induce the Senate to declare Antony a public enemy. After Antony's defeat in Cisalpine Gaul in Apr. 43, Octavian fooled Cicero for a time, perhaps with the suggestion that they might both be consuls together. But Octavian's intentions were different. After his march on Rome to secure the consulship for himself and his uncle Q. Pedius, and the formation of the Triumvirate, he did not oppose Antony's nomination of Cicero as a victim of the proscriptions which were the inauguration of the new regime. The soldiers caught Cicero in a not very resolute attempt to escape by sea. His slaves did not desert him, and he died with courage on 7 Dec. 43.

**8.** In politics he hated Clodius, with good reason, and he hated M. Crassus and, at the end of his life, Antony. For the character of Cato, eleven years his junior, he had unqualified respect, and he published a panegyric of

Cato in 45, after his death; but in politics, especially in the years following Pompey's return from the East in 62, he thought Cato's uncompromising rigidity (his *constantia*) impolitic, and Cato never concealed his distaste for Cicero's policy of temporizing expediency, both at this period and when he capitulated to the Three in 56. With Pompey Cicero never established the intimacy to which, particularly after Pompey's return in 62, he aspired, suggesting that he might play a second Laelius to Pompey's Scipio. Few of his contemporaries, perhaps, held him in higher esteem than did his constant opponent Caesar who, though often with an imperiousness which Cicero could not tolerate, was always friendly in his approach. Cicero was not a discriminating judge of the political intentions of others, being far too susceptible to, and uncritical of, flattery; and he was inevitably condemned to a certain political isolation. Loyally and not very critically devoted to the existing republican constitution, and fascinated by the mirage of a 'concordia ordinum', he was never a liberal reformer (*popularis*); yet he was never completely acceptable to the established *Optimates*, the worst of whom despised his social origin, while the rest mistrusted his personality as much as he mistrusted theirs. And, not having the *clientela* of the noble or of the successful general, he lacked *auctoritas*. It was this political isolation which (cf. *Att.* 1. 17; 1. 18. 1, of 61/60 B.C.) enhanced the importance for him of his close association with the knight T. Pomponius Atticus (q.v. 1), a man of the highest culture in both languages, his banker, financial adviser, publisher, and most generous and tolerant friend.

9. His marriage to Terentia had issue: Tullia, to whom he was devoted, whose death in 45 was the hardest of the blows which afflicted his private life, and M. Cicero (q.v. 4). His marriage survived the storms and stress of thirty years, until he grew irritated with Terentia and divorced her in winter 47/6, to marry the young Publilia, from whom in turn he was almost immediately divorced. Cicero was a good master to his slaves and, with the rest of his family, was devoted to Tiro, to whom twenty-one of his letters in *Fam.* 16 are addressed. He gave him his freedom in 53, 'to be our friend instead of our slave', as Quintus Cicero wrote (*Fam.* 16. 16. 1).

10. Cicero, who was never a really rich man, had eight country residences, in Campania, at Arpinum, at Formiae, and, his suburban villa, at Tusculum; in Rome he was extremely proud of his house on the Palatine, which he bought in 62 for 3½ million sesterces (*Fam.* 5. 6. 2).

11. Apart from the surviving histories of the late Republic and, in particular, Plutarch's *Lives* of Cicero and of his outstanding contemporaries, the bulk of our knowledge of him derives from his own writings, in particular from his letters, only a minority of which was written with any thought of publication. His reputation has therefore suffered from the fact that we have intimate knowledge of the most private part of his personal life; in this respect he has been his own worst enemy, and his critics have given undue prominence to his extremes of exaltation and depression and to the frequent expression of his evident vanity. (*See* J. P. V. D. Balsdon, 'Cicero the Man', in *Cicero*, ed. Dorey.)                    J. P. B.

WORKS

12. **Orations** (58, some incomplete, survive: about 48 are lost). *Pro Quinctio* (81). *Pro Sex. Roscio Amerino* (80). *Pro Roscio Comoedo* (77?). *In Caecilium Divinatio, In Verrem Act.* I, *Act.* II. i–v (70). *Pro Tullio, Pro Fonteio, Pro Caecina* (69). *Pro Lege Manilia, Pro Cluentio* (66). *Contra Rullum* I–III, *Pro C. Rabirio perduellionis reo, In Catilinam* I–IV, *Pro Murena* (63). *Pro Sulla, Pro*

*Archia* (62). *Pro Flacco* (59). *Post reditum ad Quirites, Post reditum in Senatu, De Domo sua* (57). *De Haruspicum responso, Pro Sestio, In Vatinium, Pro Caelio, De Prov. Cons., Pro Balbo* (56). *In Pisonem* (55). *Pro Plancio, Pro Rabirio Postumo* (54). *Pro Milone* (52). *Pro Marcello, Pro Ligario* (46). *Pro Rege Deiotaro* (45). *Philippicae* I–XIV (44–43). For historical context see §§ 1–11.

13. **Rhetorica.** The *De Inventione*, a largely technical treatment in two books of types of issue and appropriate arguments, was written in Cicero's youth (*De Or.* 1. 5), and probably intended as part of a larger work (cf. *De Inv.* 1. 9). After a gap of some thirty years Cicero returned, in his disillusionment after Luca, to writing about oratory, and by Nov. 55 (*Att.* 4. 13. 2) had finished the three books *De Oratore*. In this, probably the most carefully written of his literary works, and his most successful use of the dialogue (q.v.) form, Cicero advocates (through the mouth of the orator L. Crassus) a broadly based education for the orator, and deals with the general principles underlying the practice of oratory, though he still finds it hard to break away from the rules of the rhetoricians, e.g. in the classification of types of wit and humour in book 2. With the *De Oratore* Cicero himself coupled (*Div.* 2. 4) the *Brutus* and *Orator*, and in them we find the same call for a liberal education (*Brut.* 322, *Or.* 113 ff.). But his chief aim in writing them in 46 was to defend himself against criticism. The *Brutus* or *De Claris Oratoribus* gives a survey of Roman oratory and interesting details of Cicero's own training as an orator. An introductory section on Greek authors ends with a reference (51) to the Attic, Asiatic, and Rhodian schools of oratory, commending not only the *salubritas* of the *Attici*, but also the *celeritas* and *copia* of the *Asiatici*. Among the many orators discussed Calvus (q.v.) is criticized for his plain style (*exilitas*), and this introduces a polemic against the self-styled *Attici* among Cicero's contemporaries. Hortensius (q.v. 2), on the other hand, is quoted as an outstanding exponent of both types of Asianism, the one said to be balanced and epigrammatic, the other copious and ornate (325). The *Orator*, an attempt to sketch the perfect orator, continues to attack the *Attici*, while condemning the 'superfluous fat' of the *Asiatici*, from whom Cicero wishes to dissociate himself (25). A threefold classification of style—grandiose, plain, and intermediate—(20–2, 75–99) is coupled with the threefold task of the orator—*flectere, probare, delectare* (69). All three styles are necessary at different times, and the complete orator such as Demosthenes is able to use them all. Cicero claims merely to have tried. One of the features which distinguished the work of the *Asiatici* from that of the *Attici* was their excessive use of rhythm, and Cicero, having touched briefly in this subject in the *De Oratore* (III. 190–8), now treats it at length (168 ff.)—not without some inconsistencies—in defence of his own belief in the virtues of rhythmic prose. The same controversy enters into the brief *De Optimo Genere Oratorum*, written in 46 as an introduction to translations (not extant, possibly never completed) of the Greek orations *De Corona*. Demosthenes' all-round excellence, Cicero argues, should mean that 'Atticism' as a description of a severely plain style is a misnomer. The *Partitiones Oratoriae*, of uncertain date, but not before the late 50s, is a catechism in which Cicero answers his son's questions on the orator's craft. Almost equally technical is the *Topica*, written for Trebatius (q.v.) in 44, as an amplification of Aristotle's discourse on types of argument. Cicero thus returned in his final years to an exposition, for the benefit of student-orators, of the pedantic schoolroom instruction, from which he started in the *De Inventione*, and which he believed to be the groundwork of an orator's training, to be supplemented by a study of philosophy, law, and history.

**14. Philosophica.** These fall into two parts: (*a*) the political writings of the years immediately preceding Cicero's governorship of Cilicia, and (*b*) the works on epistemology, ethics, and theology which were produced in the incredibly short period between Feb. 45 and Nov. 44.

**15.** In the *De Republica*, a dialogue between Scipio, Laelius, and others, of which we have only parts of the six books (including the *Somnium Scipionis*, which thanks to Macrobius survived independently), Cicero discusses the best form of government, always with an eye on the history of the Roman State, and favours a constitution combining elements of all three main forms, monarchy, oligarchy, and democracy. His discussion reflects the troubled political conditions of the time and looks to a *rector* (for which part Cicero may at one time have cast Pompey) as a remedy for Rome's political sickness, but its chief value for subsequent ages lay in its assertion of human rights and the brotherhood of man, a notion which Stoic beliefs helped to foster. Cicero probably worked on the *De Legibus* immediately after doing most of the work on the *De Republica* (cf. *Leg.* 1. 15), but did not publish it. (It does not appear in the list he gives in *Div.* 2. 1 ff., and is not specifically mentioned in the *Letters*). In the three extant books (Macrobius quotes from a fifth book, and the reference to *iudicia* in 3. 47 has generally been taken to point to the subject of the fourth book) Cicero expounds the Stoic conception of a divinely sanctioned Law, based on reason, and discusses legal enactments connected with religion and magistracies.

**16.** Political inactivity under Caesar's dictatorship and the death of Tullia finally led Cicero to write on philosophical subjects which had always interested him, from the early days of his studies under the Epicureans Phaedrus (q.v. 3) and Zeno (q.v. 5), the Academics Philon (q.v. 3) of Larissa, Antiochus (q.v. 11) of Ascalon, and the Stoic Posidonius (q.v. 2), through the years of his association with Diodotus (q.v. 3) the Stoic, to the dark days immediately after the Civil War, when Matius urged him to write on philosophy (*Fam.* 11. 27. 5). What had formerly been for Cicero a useful exercise (cf. *Tusc.* 2. 9, and his claim (*Or.* 12) to be a product of the Academy rather than of the rhetoricians' workshops) and a source of oratorical material (cf. *De Or.* 1. 56 and *Or.* 113 ff.; the *Paradoxa Stoicorum*, published, it seems, as late as the beginning of 46, is an exercise in the preparation of such material) became now a haven of refuge (*Fam.* 7. 30. 2), a *doloris medicina* (*Acad. Post.* 1. 11). Cicero needed to reassure himself, and hoped as well to make a name for himself as a philosophical writer. (This is clear from *Off.* 1. 2 ff., where he admits his inferior philosophical knowledge, but against this balances his virtues as a stylist!) He had a profound admiration and respect for Plato ('*deus ille noster*': *Att.* 4. 16. 3) and Aristotle, and aimed at giving the Romans a philosophical literature, which would take the place of the Greek philosophers. The problem of how closely Cicero followed his Greek sources admits of no certain solution, since so much of the work of Hellenistic philosophers has been lost. Some scholars have taken Cicero's words: ἀπόγραφα sunt, minore labore fiunt; verba tantum adfero quibus abundo (*Att.* 12. 52. 3) too seriously. More trustworthy are his claims (*Off.* 1. 6) to follow the Stoics (in that work) not as a mere translator but drawing from Stoic sources as he thinks fit, and (*Fin.* 1. 6) to add his own criticism (*iudicium*) and arrangement (*scribendi ordo*) to the chosen authority.

**17.** Two lost works probably came first: the *Consolatio*, an attempt to console himself for the loss of Tullia, and the *Hortensius*, a plea for the study of philosophy, which profoundly affected St. Augustine (*Confess.* 3. 4. 7). In the list in *Div.* 2. 1, the *Hortensius* is followed by the *Academica*, a work originally in two books, entitled *Catulus* and *Lucullus*, of which only the second survives, but later recast in four books, of which we possess part of the first (*Academica Posteriora*). Here Cicero discussed the views of the New Academy, and in particular of Carneades (q.v.) on the impossibility of attaining certain knowledge. The recommendation (*Div.* 2. 150) to give unprejudiced consideration to different theories before approving *simillima veri* appealed to Cicero, who chose to regard himself as belonging to this philosophical school (*Tusc.* 2. 5, 4. 47).

**18.** But in moral questions Cicero was susceptible to the attractions of Stoic teaching, as is evident in the *De Finibus bonorum et malorum*, where he sets out and answers in turn the theories on the *summum bonum* propounded by the Epicureans and Stoics, before giving the views of Antiochus' so-called 'Old Academy' in book 5, and providing a somewhat unconvincing conclusion to the whole work. From the often difficult and sometimes tedious exposition of the schools' views on the principles of morality, Cicero turned in the *Tusculan Disputations* to the problems of death, grief, fear, passion, and other mental disorders, and of what is essential for happiness. Concerned largely to allay his own doubts, and impressed by Stoic teaching on these subjects, he writes here with a passionate intensity, and his language at times reaches heights of majesty and lyrical beauty never attained by any other Latin prose author.

**19.** Theological speculation next engrossed Cicero's attention. First came the *De Natura Deorum*—three books, each giving the view of a different school (Epicurean, Stoic, Academic) on the nature of the gods and the existence of a Divine Providence. Having allowed Cotta to present the sceptical Academic view in book 3, Cicero rounds off the debate with a typically Academic expression of his own opinion: that the Stoic's argument is more likely to be right (*ad veritatis similitudinem . . . propensior* 3. 95). Next, Stoic beliefs concerning Fate and the possibility of prediction are examined with a wealth of anecdote and quotation in the two books of the *De Divinatione*, published just after Caesar's murder (*Div.* 2. 4), and in this case Cicero displays no sympathy with Stoic views. He does, however, reaffirm (2. 148) his belief in the existence of a Divine Being, and maintains that it is prudent to keep up traditional rites and ceremonies. Finally, the fragmentary *De Fato* discusses the problem of Free Will and decides against Stoic fatalism.

**20.** The two genial and polished essays *Cato Maior de Senectute* (written probably just before Caesar's murder and included in *De Div.* list) and the *Laelius de Amicitia* show once again Cicero's anxiety to reassure himself in times of stress and danger, and his last work on moral philosophy *De Officiis* (finished Nov. 44) aims at giving advice, based on Stoic precepts and in particular (for books 1 and 2) on the teachings of Panaetius (q.v.), on a variety of problems of conduct (ostensibly to Cicero's son).

**21.** It was these three works, along with the *Tusc.* and the *Somnium Scipionis*, which continued to attract readers in the Middle Ages, when the work of Cicero the politician and orator was almost forgotten, to be rediscovered at the time of the Renaissance. Cicero's influence on European thought and literature as a philosopher who reproduced and commented on much that was interesting and important in Greek philosophy, as the creator of a philosophical vocabulary in Latin, and as an unusually sensitive writer of lucid and sonorous prose has been so pervasive as almost to defy assessment. Th. Zieliński's standard work, *Cicero im Wandel der Jahrhunderte* (1912), has been supplemented by M. L. Clarke and A. E. Douglas in *Cicero* (ed. Dorey, 1965).

**22. Poems.** Cicero's desire to win renown in as many fields as possible and his talent for manipulating words led almost inevitably to attempts at verse (cf. Plut. *Cic.* 40 for Cicero's facility as a versifier). After a boyhood epic, *Glaucus Pontius*, extant in Plutarch's time (*Cic.* 2) and some youthful poems mentioned by Julius Capitolinus (*Gord.* 3. 2), which are no more than names to us, Cicero early applied himself to a translation in hexameters of the *Phaenomena* of Aratus (q.v. 1). Of the first section (entitled *Aratus*) a large part has survived independently (469 lines), the only portion of Cicero's verse to do so. The second section, Cicero's *Prognostica*, is referred to by Cicero on occasion as a separate poem. The use by Virgil of some of the same material in *Georg.* 1 makes one regret that only fragments of this section survive. (The reference in *Att.* 2. 1. 11 and a comparison of lines quoted *Div.* 1. 14 and Isidore 12. 7. 37 have led some to suppose that Cicero revised the *Prognostica c.* 60; but the reference does not compel this interpretation and the quotation may be mistaken.) Other translations both of single lines and of extended passages from Homer and the tragedians which serve to embellish Cicero's philosophical writings are workmanlike rather than distinguished. After his consulship and again after his exile he thought to add to his reputation by composing the autobiographical poems *De Consulatu* and *De Temporibus Suis*, which were unlikely to appeal to contemporaries already satiated with Cicero's self-glorification. Of them little has survived except a passage of seventy-two lines from the *De Consulatu* (quoted *Div.* 1. 17) and the two notorious lines singled out, perhaps unfairly, for derision by contemporaries (cf. *Off.* 1. 77) and by Quintilian (11. 1. 24) and Juvenal (10. 122). More promising material was used by Cicero in his epic *Marius* which is of uncertain date: the subject suggests the 70s, whereas the style of the scanty fragments (for the main one see *Div.* 1. 106) suggests, but does not compel, a later date.

**23.** Cicero's verse lacks poetic imagination, vigour of movement, and variety of pauses: its chief interest lies in the possibility it affords of tracing the development of Latin hexameter verse from Ennius to Virgil. Conclusions are unsure owing to the fragmentary nature of Cicero's verse and the loss of other poets, but it seems likely that he made a significant contribution in lightening the movement of the hexameter, in obtaining a more frequent clash of ictus and accent in the first four feet and coincidence in the last two, and in refining the use of elision. For the latest assessment of Cicero's poems see G. B. Townend in *Cicero* (ed. Dorey). J. H. S.

**24. Letters** (931 in Tyrrell and Purser). Sixteen books *Ad Familiares* were published by Tiro, his literary executor. The sixteen books *Ad Atticum* cover the years 68 to 44; Cornelius Nepos saw them and acutely appreciated their value as a historical source (*Vita Attici* 16. 3). The previously accepted assumption that, because Asconius made no explicit reference to them, they were not published until the time of Nero, was challenged by J. Carcopino, but Carcopino's suggestion that they were published in 34/3 as part of Octavian's propaganda war against Antony is not convincing (but cf. A. Piganiol, *Rev. hist.* 1949, 224 ff., for a modification of this suggestion) and D. R. Shackleton Bailey, in his *Cicero's Letters to Atticus* i, ii (1965), 59 ff., has restated the case for a Neronian date. There are also twenty-seven letters written to his brother Quintus (*Ad Quintum fratrem*) during periods when the brothers were separated, chiefly when Quintus was in the provinces, from 59 to 54, and twenty-five letters of the correspondence of Brutus and Cicero (with one interesting letter of Brutus to Atticus, in criticism of Cicero, *Ad Brut.* 25 (1. 17), all from 43 B.C. There are, all told, ninety-nine different correspondents, writers, or recipients of letters, and the whole correspondence ranges over the years 68–43. Even so, a great many

important letters (for instance, Cicero's letter to Pompey in 63 about the execution of Catiline's supporters) have not survived. Cicero's own letters vary greatly in style. Some were careful and deliberate (e.g. *Fam.* 1. 9; 5. 7; 5. 12); others were written in haste, without thought of publication. As would be expected, more letters survived from the last years of his life (163 from 45, 122 from 44, and 101 from the first half of 43). When (for the first time, as far as we know) he thought of the publication of a volume of his letters in July 44, he wrote in terms of a quite small collection, seventy, which Tiro possessed, with the addition of others which Atticus would provide (*Att.* 16. 5. 5). J. P. B.

LIFE AND WORKS. G. Boissier, *C. and his Friends* (E.T., 1897); J. L. Strachan-Davidson, *C. and the Fall of the Roman Republic* (1894); E. G. Sihler, *C. of Arpinum* (U.S.A.–London, 1914); E. Ciaceri, *C. e i suoi tempi*[2] (1939–41); H. Strasburger, *Concordia Ordinum* (Leipzig, 1931); G. C. Richards, *C., a Study* (1935); H. J. Haskell, *This was Cicero* (1942); H. Willrich, *C. und Caesar* (1944); H. Frisch, *C.'s Fight for the Republic* (Copenhagen, 1946); F. R. Cowell, *C. and the Roman Republic* (1948); J. Carcopino, *C., the Secrets of his Correspondence* (E.T., 1951, reviewed, *JRS* 1950, 134; *CR* 1952, 178); F. Lossmann, *C. und Caesar im Jahre 54* (1962); K. Büchner, *Cicero* (Heidelberg, 1964); T. A. Dorey, ed., *Cicero* (1965); R. E. Smith, *C. the Statesman* (1966); M. Gelzer, *Cicero* (Wiesbaden, 1969).

TEXTS in Teubner, Loeb, and Budé series; also, in O.C.T.: *Speeches* (A. C. Clark and W. Peterson, 1908–16); *Rhetorica* (A. S. Wilkins, 1901–3); (*Ad Fam.*, L. C. Purser, 1901, repr. 1952 with corrections; *Ad Att.* i–viii, L. C. Purser, 1903, ix–xvi, D. R. Shackleton Bailey, 1961; *Ad Q. fr.*, *Ad M. Brut.*, Fragg., W. S. Watt, 1958). See also D. R. Shackleton Bailey, *Towards a Text of 'Ad Atticum'* (1960). *Scholia*, T. Stangl (1912); *Q. Asconii Pediani Commentarii*, A. C. Clark (O.C.T., 1907).

COMMENTARIES. (1) *Speeches*, C. Halm, rev. Laubmann–Sternkopf, Germ. (1886–93); *Pro Sex. Rosc. Am.*, G. Landgraf, Germ. (1914); *Div. in Caec.* and *In Verr.*, W. Peterson (1907); *In Verr.* iv, F. W. Hall (1907); v, R. G. C. Levens (1946). *De Imp. Cn. Pomp.* (*Pro Leg. Manil.*), J. C. Nicol (1899); J. R. King (1917); Pl. Fraccaro, A. Passerini, Ital. (1946). *Pro Cluent.*, W. Peterson (1899); *Pro C. Rab. perd.*, W. E. Heitland (1882). *In Cat.* i–iv, J. C. Nicol (1902); Pl. Fraccaro, A. Passerini, Ital. (1946). *Pro Archia*, J. S. Reid (1879); F. Richter, A. Eberhard, rev. H. Nohl, Germ. (1926); *Pro Flacco*, T. B. L. Webster (1931); *De dom.*, R. G. Nisbet (1939); *Pro Sest.*, H. A. Holden[9] (1933). *In Vatin.*, L. G. Pocock (1926). *Pro Cael.*, R. G. Austin[3] (1960); *De prov. cons.*, H. E. Butler, M. Cary (1924); *Pro Balbo*, J. S. Reid (1878); *In Pis.*, R. G. M. Nisbet (1961); *Pro Planc.*, H. A. Holden[3] (1891); H. W. Auden (1897); *Pro Milone*, A. B. Poynton[2] (1902); *Philippicae*, J. R. King (1868); i. ii, J. D. Denniston (1926); K. Halm, rev. G. Laubmann, Germ. (1905); ii, J. E. B. Mayor (1865); iii–vi, W. Sternkopf, Germ. (1912); vii–x, W. Sternkopf, Germ. (1913).

(2) *On Oratory*. *De Oratore*, A. S. Wilkins (1892); *Brut.*, A. E. Douglas (1966), O. Jahn, W. Kroll[6], Germ. (1962); J. Martha, Fr. (1892); *Orator*, J. E. Sandys (1885).

(3) *Philosophical Works*. *De Repub.*, H. Last, G. H. Poyser (1948); G. H. Sabine, S. B. Smith, *On the Commonwealth*, Introd. and Trans. (1929); C. Meissner, G. Landgraf, Germ. (1929); *Somnium Scipionis* (1915); *Academ.*, J. S. Reid (1885); *De Fin.*, J. S. Reid (1925); R. Rubrichi, Ital. (1938); *Tusc. Quaest.*, J. W. Dougan, R. M. Henry (1905–34); M. Pohlenz, Germ. (1957); *De Nat. Deor.*, A. S. Pease (1955); *De Divinat.*, A. S. Pease, i (1920); ii (1923); *Cato Mai.* (*De Senect.*), F. G. Moore (1903); *De Offic.* H. A. Holden[3] (1899); J. Higginbotham, *Cicero, on Moral Obligation*, Introd. and notes (1967).

(4) *Letters*. R. Y. Tyrrell, L. C. Purser (1885–1933); W. W. How, A. C. Clark, *Select Letters* (1925). D. R. Shackleton Bailey, *Cicero's Letters to Atticus* (1965–8).

TRANSLATIONS. Volumes of the Loeb Classical Library and, into French, volumes of the Association Guillaume Budé.

LEXICA. *Lexicon Ciceronianum Marii Nizolii* (1830); *Speeches*, H. Merguet (1873–4); *Letters*, W. A. Oldfather, W. V. Canter, K. M. Abbott (1938); *Rhetorica*, W. A. Oldfather, W. V. Canter, K. M. Abbott (1964); *De Inventione*, T. W. Fuchs (1937).

STYLE AND DICTION. J. Lebreton, *Études sur la langue et la grammaire de C.* (1901); Th. Zieliński, *Das Clauselgesetz in C.'s Reden* (1904); *Der constructive Rhythmus in C.'s Reden* (1920); H. D. Broadhead, *Latin Prose Rhythm* (1928); A. Traglia, *La lingua di C. poeta* (1950).

SPECIAL STUDIES. Orelli and Baiter, *Onomasticon Tullianum* (1838); O. E. Schmidt, *Der Briefwechsel des C.* (1893); *Ciceros Villen* (1899); A. H. J. Greenidge, *The Legal Procedure of C.'s Time* (1901); W. Warde Fowler, *Social Life at Rome in the Age of Cicero* (1922); W. Kroll, *Die Kultur der Cic. Zeit* (1933); J. Humbert, *Les plaidoyers écrits et les plaidoiries réelles de C.* (1925); K. Barwick, *Das rednerische Bildungsideal Ciceros* (1963); W. Rüegg, *C. und der Humanismus* (1946); P. Poncelet, *C. traducteur de Platon* (1957); M. van der Bruwaene, *La Théologie de C.* (1937), with bibliography on C.'s sources; B. Farrington, *Primum Graius Homo* (1927); H. Sjögren, *Commentationes Tullianae, de Ciceronis epistulis . . . . Quaestiones* (1910); E. Malcovati, *C. e la poesia* (1943); M. Rambaud, *C. et l'histoire romaine* (1953); Th. Zieliński, *C. im Wandel der Jahrhunderte* (1912).

**CICERO** (2), QUINTUS TULLIUS (*PW* 31) (102–43 B.C.), younger brother of Marcus Cicero (1) and similarly educated (they were both in Athens in 79 B.C.), had none of his brother's genius. He was impetuous and often tactlessly outspoken; yet he was an able administrator. Plebeian aedile in 65 and praetor in 62 (helped, no doubt, by the fact that Marcus was praetor and consul respectively when he was elected), he governed Asia from 61–59, receiving two long letters of advice and criticism from his brother in Rome (*QFr.* 1. 1 f.). He spent winter 57/6 in Sardinia as a legate of Pompey (q.v.), when Pompey received his corn commission, and was evidently a hostage for Marcus' good behaviour in politics. He was legate on Caesar's staff in Gaul from 54 to early 51, taking part in the invasion of Britain in 54 and winning deserved praise for his courage in holding out against the Nervii when the Gauls attacked the winter camps in 54 (*BGall.* 5. 40–52); though unwell, he drove himself so hard that his troops forced him to take some sleep at night (ibid. 40. 7). At Atuatuca a year later he took risks, probably with more excuse than Caesar allows, and was criticized (ibid. 6. 36–42). He was a valuable legate on Marcus' staff in Cilicia in 51/50, supplying (with C. Pomptinus) the military experience which Marcus lacked. He joined Pompey in the Civil War, was pardoned after Pharsalus and then, with his son, behaved badly in maligning his brother to Caesar (*Att.* 11. 9 f.). Victims of the proscription in 43, he and his son were betrayed by their slaves.

The twenty-seven surviving letters of Marcus to Quintus were written between 59 and 54, mostly when Quintus was serving abroad. Of the four short surviving letters of Quintus, one (*Fam.* 16. 16: 53 B.C.) congratulated Marcus on enfranchising Tiro and three (*Fam.* 16. 8: 49 B.C.; 16. 26 f.: 44 B.C.) were to Tiro. Quintus was a literary dilettante, writing four tragedies in sixteen days when in Gaul (*QFr.* 3. 5. 7). Though certainty is not possible (Balsdon, *CQ* 1963, 242 ff.), a strong case has been made out for believing that neither Quintus nor, indeed, a contemporary wrote the *Commentariolum Petitionis*, a long letter on Marcus' canvass for the consulship of 63 (M. I. Henderson, *JRS* 1950, 8 ff.; R. G. M. Nisbet, *JRS* 1961, 84 ff.; W. S. Watt, *M. Tulli Ciceronis Epistulae*, iii (O.C.T., 1958), 179).

Like his brother, Quintus owned property near Arpinum. His marriage to Pomponia, sister of Marcus' friend Atticus (q.v. 1) lasted from 69 to 44 and produced one son, but was never a happy one.

W. Wiemer, *Q. Tullius Cicero* (Diss. Jena, 1930). J. P. B.

**CICERO** (3), QUINTUS TULLIUS (*PW* 32) (66–43 B.C.), unstable son of (2), was harmed from childhood by the disputes of his parents, each of whom canvassed his sympathy against the other. His education was supervised during his father's absences on duty abroad by his mother's brother T. Pomponius Atticus (q.v. 1) to 54 and then by his uncle M. Cicero (1). With his cousin (4) he was taken out to Cilicia in 51–50, when his father was legate on his uncle's staff. The boys stayed for a time with King Deiotarus (q.v.) of Galatia (*Att.* 5. 17. 3). On the Republican side at Pharsalus and afterwards pardoned by Caesar, he then went to Asia with his father and sought to prejudice Caesar against his uncle (*Att.* 11. 10. 1). In 46 he was aedile at Arpinum (*Fam.* 13. 11. 3) and became Lupercus at Rome (*Att.* 12. 5. 1) and was perhaps active as such in the Lupercalia of 44, when Caesar was offered a crown. He was killed with his father in the proscriptions, in Dec. 43. J. P. B.

**CICERO** (4), MARCUS TULLIUS (*PW* 30), b. 65 B.C., spoilt son of the orator (1) and Terentia, was educated under his father's supervision and taken out to Cilicia by him in 51. He was a successful cavalry officer in the republican army in 49/8 (*Off.* 2. 45). Pardoned after Pharsalus, he would have liked to serve under Caesar in Spain (*Att.* 12. 7. 1), but instead was sent to Athens to study under the Peripatetic Cratippus. He served under Brutus, who praised him highly (*Brut.* 3 (2. 3). 6). After Philippi he joined Sextus Pompeius, but took advantage of the amnesty of 39. He was elected Pontifex and was colleague of Octavian (from 13 Sept. to 1 Nov.) as consul in 30; afterwards he governed Syria and was proconsul of Asia. There is no evidence to support the hypothesis (J. Carcopino, *Cicero, the Secrets of his Correspondence* (1951), 489 ff.) that his father's letters were published in 34/3 at the instigation of Octavian, partly to blacken his father's memory, and that he was an agent in the enterprise. Though he was, by his own admission, idle in his student days (*Fam.* 16. 21) and drank too much (Pliny, *HN* 14. 147) and though his distinguished public career may have been partly due to Octavian's repentance for his father's murder (cf. Sen. *Ben.* 4. 30), he cannot have been without considerable administrative ability.

J. P. B.

**CILICIA**, a district of southern Asia Minor. The name included various regions at various times, but came ultimately to designate the eastern half of the south coast. Of this the western portion (Cilicia Tracheia) is wild and mountainous, the eastern (Cilicia Pedias) is rich plainland. Here, after the Trojan War, came Greek settlers, bringing with them the name of the Cilices, who in Homer are located in the southern Troad (*Il.* 6. 397). Their leader, according to tradition, was Mopsus the seer, whose name survived in Mopsuestia and Mopsucrene and occurs as a personal name in later inscriptions. Identified wholly or partly with the Hilakku of the Assyrian records and with the Kelekesh of the Egyptian, the Cilicians were subject to the Assyrians in the eighth century; subsequently they were governed by a line of kings, at first independent, then under the Persians, bearing the name or title of Syennesis. After liberation by Alexander, possession of the country was disputed by the Ptolemies and the Seleucids; at the same time, at Olba in the eastern part of Tracheia, a sacerdotal dynasty maintained itself for several centuries, claiming heroic descent under the names of Teucer and Ajax. In the second century the pirates established themselves strongly on the coast of Tracheia; to deal with them the Romans c. 102 B.C. instituted a special command called the province of Cilicia. This, however, did not include either Pedias or even Tracheia; Cicero defines it as *Lyciam, Pamphyliam, Pisidiam Phrygiamque totam*, but this is probably exaggerated (*Verr.* 2. 1. 95). The pirates were not in fact suppressed until Pompey's campaign of 67 B.C. Pedias was included in the province c. 64 B.C., and in 56 a considerable area of the interior north of Taurus (while in the interior Pompey had also recognized the rule of a dynast, Tarcondimotus, who survived till he died fighting for Antony in 31 B.C., with his capital at Hierapolis-Castabala); but soon afterwards this province was dismembered and shared between Syria and Galatia, and under the early Empire it ceased to exist. Tracheia was at this time ruled by a succession of kings of Galatia, Cappadocia, and Commagene. In A.D. 72 Vespasian reconstituted the province of Cilicia to include Pedias and Tracheia only, under a praetorian legate.

Cilicia Pedias is among the most fertile parts of Asia Minor; it produced flax (now mostly replaced by cotton), vines, olives, and corn. It was also important strategically as affording the only route from Asia Minor to Syria. Tracheia had little to offer apart from ship-timber, which, however, was valuable to the Ptolemies (Egypt being lacking in timber), and later to the pirates.

Jones, *Cities E. Rom. Prov.* ch. 8; R. Syme in *Anatolian Studies Buckler* (1939), 299 ff.; Magie, *Rom. Rule Asia Min.* chs. 11, 12, 17.
G. E. B.

**CILO,** LUCIUS FABIUS (Septiminus Catinius Acilianus Lepidus Fulcinianus), *cos. suff.* A.D. 193, a Spaniard, was *comes* of Septimius Severus and Caracalla. After governing Narbonensis, Galatia, and Bithynia-Pontus, he accompanied Severus to the East against Pescennius Niger (193). He then governed Moesia Superior (195/6) and Pannonia Superior (197–202), was *praefectus urbi* (203/4–? 211) and *cos. II ord.* (204). He saved Macrinus' life after Plautianus' murder in 205, and later tried to reconcile Caracalla and Geta. After Geta's murder (212) his life was threatened by Caracalla but was saved by popular demonstrations.
H. H. S.

**CIMBRI,** a German tribe from north Jutland, where the district of Himmerland preserves their name. Towards the end of the second century B.C. over-population and encroachments by the sea drove them to migrate, in company with the Teutones (q.v.) and Ambrones. From the Elbe they arrived, by a roundabout route, in Noricum, where they defeated a Roman consular army (113 B.C.). They then turned west and entered the Helvetian territory between the Main and Switzerland, where a few of them settled; vestiges of a Cimbric element in the population are perhaps implied by inscriptions to Mercurius Cimbrianus at Miltenberg and Heidelberg (*ILS* 4595, 4596, cf. 9377). About 110 they entered the Rhône valley, defeating M. Iunius Silanus and then turning into the centre of Gaul. In 105 they were again in the south, where they won the great victory of Arausio (Orange), and then entered Spain, whence the Celtiberians drove them out. They now moved towards Italy. Marius defeated the Teutones and Ambrones, who took the western route, at Aquae Sextiae (*Aix-en-Provence*) in 102, and in 101 destroyed the Cimbri, who had travelled round the Alps and entered Italy by the north-east, near Vercellae, in the Po valley. A few of the Germans had remained in northern Gaul; the later Aduatuci claimed to be their descendants. A remnant of the Cimbri was found in Jutland by the naval expedition sent by Tiberius in A.D. 5 (*Mon. Anc.* 26).

L. Schmidt, *Geschichte der deutschen Stämme. Die Westgermanen²* (1938), i. 3 ff.; Tacitus, *Germania*, ed. Anderson (1938), 171 ff.
O. B.

**CIMINIUS MONS,** range of volcanic mountains rising to *c.* 3,000 feet, which separate southern from central Etruria. A crater lake (Lacus Ciminius: *Lago di Vico*) nestles amongst them. Fabius (q.v. 3) Rullianus won fame by penetrating their awe-inspiring, thickly wooded slopes in 310 B.C. (Livy 9. 36–9). Sutrium and Nepete (qq.v.) are keys to the region.
E. T. S.

**CIMMERIANS** (Κιμμέριοι, Assyrian Gimirri, the 'Gomer' of Ezek. xxxviii. 6, Genesis x. 2), a people driven from south Russia by the nomad Scyths (Hdt. 1. 16 f.). They overthrew Phrygia under the last King Midas (*c.* 676?), killed Gyges (q.v.), took the lower town of Sardis (*c.* 644), and terrorized Ionia (Strabo 647, citing Callinus and Archilochus), but were gradually destroyed by epidemics and in wars with Lydia and Assyria. Their name survived in the Cimmerian Bosporus (Straits of Kertch) and some place-names thereabout (though 'Crimea' itself is from Turkish *kirim*, a ditch, i.e. that across the isthmus of Perekop). In our *Odyssey* (11. 14 ff.) Cimmerians appear as a people on whom the sun never shines, near the land of the dead; but old variants Cheimerioi, Kerberioi (cf. Cerberus), rather suggest that the reading Kimmerioi has prevailed here only through the fame of the real Cimmerians.
A. R. B.

**CIMON,** Athenian statesman and soldier, son of Miltiades (q.v.) and Hegesipyle, daughter of the Thracian King Olorus. On his father's death in 489 he paid the fine of fifty talents which had been imposed upon him. He took part in an embassy to Sparta in 479 and from 479/8 or 478/7 held office frequently as *strategos*. In 478 he helped Aristides (q.v. 1) to win the allegiance of the maritime Greeks and from 476 to 463 commanded in all or nearly all the operations of the Delian League (q.v.). He drove Pausanias (q.v. 1) out of Byzantium and captured Eion on the Strymon from the Persian Boges (476/5). Soon after this he conquered Scyros; the Dolopian pirates who inhabited it were replaced by Athenian colonists and Cimon brought back 'the bones of Theseus' in triumph to Athens. These successes, coupled with his noble birth, his wealth, which he lavished on entertainments and public works, and his connexions—his (second?) wife Isodice was an Alcmaeonid and his sister Elpinice married Callias (q.v. 1)—made him very influential and he became the leader of the aristocratic party in opposition to Themistocles, and later to Ephialtes (q.v. 4) and Pericles. He is not said to have commanded in the operations against Carystus and Naxos (between 473 and 469), but this may simply be due to the brevity of our sources. His greatest military achievement soon followed (*c.* 468)—the Eurymedon campaign, in which the Persian fleet was totally destroyed, and several Greek cities, as far east as Phaselis (q.v.), joined the League. Next he subdued the Thracian Chersonese, driving out the remaining Persians, and, apparently in the same campaign, began the reduction of Thasos, which had seceded from the League, perhaps with the covert support of Alexander I of Macedon. This task Cimon completed after a two years' siege (465–463). On his return to Athens he was prosecuted on his *euthyna* (q.v.) by Pericles and other democrats, on a charge of having been bribed by Alexander not to attack Macedonian territory, but was acquitted. He now persuaded the Athenians, despite the opposition of Ephialtes, to assist Sparta against the insurgent helots, and himself led out a large force of hoplites (462). He was, however, soon sent home by the Spartans (who feared that the Athenians might intrigue with the helots), and with this ignominy Cimon's great influence at Athens ended. The democrats, led by Ephialtes and Pericles, stripped the Areopagus (q.v.) of most of its powers either during his absence or after his failure, and he was ostracized in 461. Four years later Cimon asked to be allowed to fight against the Spartans at Tanagra to prove his loyalty; this was refused, but he was recalled soon after. He took little part in politics, however, till *c.* 450, when he arranged a Five Years' Peace with Sparta and led a last expedition against Persia, to recapture Cyprus. On this campaign he died, and peace with Persia followed (*see* CALLIAS 1). Besides Isodice, Cimon married an Arcadian woman, apparently the mother of those three of his six sons who were called Lacedaemonius, Eleus and Thessalus after the three peoples whose *proxenos* (q.v.) he was. Lacedaemonius was *strategos* in 433/2 and commanded in the first expedition to Corcyra in 433.

In the later biographical tradition represented by Plutarch Cimon figured as a large-hearted, expansive, genial conservative; his foreign policy, in contrast with that of Pericles, one of goodwill towards the allies, friendship with Sparta, and war against the national enemy. There is some truth in this, but the Egyptian war took place during his exile, and he was as active as Pericles in opposing by force secession from the League. Attack were made on his character, some of them by Stesimbrotus, who came from Thasos.

Plutarch, *Cimon*. Meyer, *Forschungen* ii. 1 ff.; A. W. Gomme, *An Historical Commentary on Thucydides* i (1945), 326 f.; G. A. Papantoniou, *AJPhil.* 1951, 176 ff. J. Barns, *Hist.* 1953/4, 163 ff.; W. R. Connor *GRBS* 1963, 107 ff.          A. W. G.; T. J. C.

**CINAEDIC POETRY,** verses recited by κιναιδολόγοι, such as Sotades and Timon of Phlius. Originally accompanied by oriental instruments (Demetr. *Eloc.* 37; Polyb. 5. 37. 10), they were later recited (Pliny, *Ep.* 9. 17. 1; Strabo 648). They were of a satirical and scurrilous character (Petron. *Sat.* 23. 2) and said to be of Ionian origin (Ath. 620 e; cf. Plaut. *Stich.* 769).          C. M. B.

**CINAETHON OF LACEDAEMON,** epic poet, of uncertain date; supposed author of a *Telegonia* (? *Theogonia*), an *Oedipodea*, the *Ilias parva*, a *Heraclea*, and perhaps genealogies; to be distinguished from Cynaethus (q.v.). *See* EPIC CYCLE.

*EGF* 4, 8, 38, 196–8, 212.

**CINCINNATUS,** Lucius Quinctius (*PW* 27), an historical figure, although details of his career possibly were derived from popular poetry. In 458 B.C., according to tradition, when Minucius was besieged by the Aequi on Mt. Algidus, Cincinnatus was appointed dictator and dispatched to his rescue. He defeated the Aequi, freed Minucius, resigned his dictatorship after sixteen days, and returned to his farm beyond the Tiber. The story later underwent embellishments (e.g. the *Prata Quinctia* may have suggested the name of the hero, and various features may have been borrowed from the account of the rescue of C. Minucius in 217 B.C.), but undoubtedly it is based on more than the misinterpretation of some monument, a false etymology, or reduplication. But the story of Cincinnatus' second dictatorship in 439 has no foundation.

Ogilvie, *Comm. Livy 1–5*, 416 ff.          P. T.

**CINCIUS (*PW* 5) ALIMENTUS,** Lucius, Roman senator and historian, was praetor in Sicily in 210/9 B.C., and was captured by Hannibal (Livy 21. 38. 3). His history of Rome, written in Greek, set the foundation of the city in 729–728 B.C. and reached his own times. With the work of Fabius Pictor, it formed the basis of the senatorial historical tradition, especially of the Second Punic War. The constitutional antiquarian of the same name wrote towards Augustan times.

Peter, *HRRel.* i², ci, 40; *FGrH* iii c. 876 ff. Walbank, *Polybius* 29.          A. H. McD.

**CINEAS,** a skilful Thessalian diplomat, famous for his observations that Rome's Senate was an assembly of kings and war with Rome a battle with a hydra. King Pyrrhus (q.v.) sent him at least once and possibly twice to Rome to negotiate peace. His terms, however, proved unacceptable.

P. Lévêque, *Pyrrhos* (1957), 346 f.          E. T. S.

**CINESIAS** (*c.* 450–*c.* 390 B.C.), dithyrambic poet, of Athens, connected with the abolition of the Chorus from Attic comedy (Schol. Ar. *Ran.* 404), twice engaged in legal proceedings with Lysias, who disapproved of him (Lys. 21. 20; fr. 73). No fragments of interest survive from his work, but Aristophanes refers to him at *Av.* 1377; *Lys.* 860; *Eccl.* 330; *Ran.* 1437; fr. 198; and Plutarch (*De mus.* 30) regarded him as a corrupter of Attic music. *See* MUSIC § 10.          C. M. B.

**CINNA** (1), Lucius Cornelius (*PW* 106), of patrician birth, fought with distinction in the Social War and, against the opposition of Sulla, became consul in 87 B.C.

Trying to rescind the legislation that Sulla had carried by armed force, he was driven out of Rome by his colleague Octavius (q.v. 3) and was illegally deposed in favour of Merula. Collecting a force of legionaries and Italians, and supported by Carbo (q.v. 2), Sertorius, and Marius, he marched on Rome and captured it late in 87, after the death of Pompeius Strabo and the failure of Metellus (q.v. 7) Pius to relieve it. He punished those who had acted illegally, but tried (not altogether successfully) to stop Marius' indiscriminate massacre. Consul (86) with Marius, and, after Marius' death, with Valerius Flaccus, he managed to eliminate the use of force that had become accepted and to restore ordered government. He gained the co-operation of the *equites* and the People by financial reforms (*see* FLACCUS 6, *and* MARIUS 3), and that of the consulars (Perperna 3, Marcius Philippus 4, Scaevola 4, and Valerius Flaccus 6 (qq.v.)) and other responsible men by moderation and regard for *mos maiorum*. However, following Marius' precedent, he held the consulship again in 85 and 84 with Carbo, in view of the danger from Mithridates (whom he continued to fight) and of Sulla's ambiguous behaviour, though he tried to negotiate with Sulla. Embarking on a Liburnian campaign early in 84, perhaps to train an army for a possible conflict with Sulla's veterans, he was killed in a mutiny; after which Sulla rebelled and the government disintegrated. Our information on him is distorted by hostile sources.

H. Bennett, *Cinna and his Times* (1923); Badian, *Stud. Gr. Rom. Hist.* 206 ff.; C. M. Bulst. *Hist.* 1964, 307 ff.          E. B.

**CINNA** (2), Lucius Cornelius (*PW* 107), son of Cinna (1), took part in the revolt of Lepidus (q.v. 2), joined Sertorius (q.v.) in Spain, and was allowed to return, along with other Lepidani, by a *Lex Plautia* passed (in 70 B.C. ?) with the support of his brother-in-law Caesar; but was probably still debarred from a public career, as he reached the praetorship only in 44, after Caesar had reinstated the sons of the proscribed (49). As praetor he showed Republican sympathies: he expressed approval of the murder of Caesar, and was attacked on his way to the Senate (17 Mar.) and rescued by Lepidus. He procured the restoration of the deposed tribunes Flavus and Marullus, and on 28 Nov. refused the province assigned him by Antony. He married, perhaps at this time, Pompey's daughter, widow since 46 of Sulla (3). He may have been proscribed (cf. Sen. *clem.* 1. 9. 8).          T. J. C.

**CINNA** (3), Gaius Helvius (*PW* 12, cf. 11), a native of Cisalpine Gaul, a pupil of Valerius Cato, and a friend of Catullus, with whom he was probably in Bithynia in 57 B.C. (Catull. 10). He was a *doctus poeta* of the 'Alexandrian' school. His 'epyllion' *Zmyrna*, the work of nine years (Quint. 10. 4. 4), was a masterpiece of the 'new' Alexandrian manner and the admiration of his fellow poets (Catull. 95: cf. Verg. *Ecl.* 9. 35). Its subject, the Cyprian legend of the unnatural love of Zmyrna (or Myrrha) for her father Cinyras, gave opportunity for developing the Alexandrian interest in the psychology of passion and its allusive learning was such that within a generation or two it needed a commentary and the scholar L. Crassicius made his reputation by writing one (Suet. *Gramm.* 19). His *propempticon Pollionis*, a travel-poem in a Hellenistic genre, was prompted by a visit of the young Pollio (q.v.) to the East in 56 B.C.; he also wrote light verse in hendecasyllabics, scazons, and elegiacs.

He is usually identified with C. Helvius Cinna, tribune in 44, who carried a law deposing his colleagues Flavus and Marullus, who had offended Caesar, and was said to have drafted another permitting Caesar to marry additional wives and so get himself heirs. After Caesar's funeral he was torn to pieces by the mob, which mistook him for Cinna (2 above).

Morel, *FPL* 87 ff.; Schanz–Hosius i. 307 f. C. J. F.; T. J. C.

**CINNA** (4) **MAGNUS**, GNAEUS CORNELIUS (*PW* 108), son of Cinna (2) and grandson of Pompey, was consul in A.D. 5. According to a rhetoricized story (Sen. *clem.* 1. 9, Cass. Dio 55. 14–22) which some reject altogether, he plotted against Augustus during his absence in Gaul (possibly 16–13 B.C.), but was pardoned at the instance of Livia.

Syme, *Rom. Rev.*, see index; W. Speyer, *Rh. Mus.* 1956, 277 ff. T. J. C.

**CINYRAS,** mythical king of Cyprus and ancestor of the Cinyrades, the priests of Aphrodite at Paphos (Tac. *Hist.* 2. 3). Despite the legends which make Cinyras a king of Byblos (Strabo 755) or son of Sandocus, a Syrian immigrant to Cilicia (Apollod. *Bibl.* 3. 14. 3), he may represent the autochthonous culture in Cyprus (so Dussaud). Founder of the cult of Aphrodite in Cyprus, Cinyras introduced sacred prostitution (q.v.) there. He was the father of Adonis (q.v.) through unwitting incest with his daughter, Myrrha or Smyrna (Ov. *Met.* 10. 298 ff.); this story was sometimes told of Theias, who is also given as the father of Cinyras. As musician and seer, Cinyras is the son and favourite of Apollo. His name became proverbial for riches and beauty.

J. G. Frazer, *Adonis Attis Osiris* i, ch. 3; R. Dussaud, *Syria* 1950. F. R. W.

**CIRCE,** in Homer (*Od.* 10. 210 ff.) a goddess living on the fabulous island of Aeaea (ibid. 135), later identified, in Italy, with the promontory of Circeii in Latium. She is very powerful in magic; her house is surrounded by wild beasts who fawn on new arrivals (later, as *Aen.* 7. 19–20, they are men changed by her spells) and she turns Odysseus' men into swine. He is helped by Hermes to resist her spells by means of the herb moly, forces her to restore his men, and lives with her for a year, after which she gives him directions for his journey home, *see* ODYSSEUS. She is sister of Aeetes and daughter of Helios and Perse (*Od.* 10. 137–8). In Hesiod (*Theog.* 1011 ff., spurious?) she bears Odysseus two sons, Agrios and Latinus (*see further* ODYSSEUS). She touches the Argonautic legend, receiving Jason and Medea, and purifying both from the murder of Absyrtus (Ap. Rhod. 4. 557 ff.).

Odysseus and Circe, with the companions half-transformed, is a not very common subject in vase-painting from the mid sixth century on (Brommer, *Vasenlisten²*, 308 ff.). H. J. R.; C. M. R.

**CIRCEII,** town and isolated mountain on the Tyrrhenian coast south of Rome, originally the southern limit of Latium and, by popular etymology, the abode of Circe (q.v.). A Latin colony established here (393 B.C.) helped contain the Volsci (q.v.). Massive polygonal walls remain near modern *S. Felice Circeo*.

G. Lugli, *La tecnica edilizia romana* (1957), 148 ff. E. T. S.

**CIRCUS,** an enclosure for chariot-racing, planned with parallel sides and one semicircular end, all fitted with seats, and with an axial rib (*spina*) marked at each end by turning-posts (*metae*) dividing the area into two runs. The seating was arranged in storied groups. At the open end were the curved stables (*carceres*) for twelve teams of horses, who competed four, six, eight, or even twelve at a time under the colours of the different factions. These were red and white at first (Tert. *De Spect.* 5 and 9) and presently green (Suet. *Gaius* 55) and blue (Suet. *Vit.* 7), Domitian's purple and gold (Suet. *Dom.* 7) being temporary. There were seven laps to

each race, measured by movable eggs and dolphins, the emblems of the Heavenly Twins and Neptune, the horse gods (Dio Cass. 49. 43. 2).

The earliest example of a *circus* at Rome is the *Circus Maximus*, in the Murcia valley between the Palatine and Aventine hills, reputed to be of kingly origin, adorned during the Republic (Livy 8. 20. 1; 33. 27. 4; 39. 7. 8; 40. 2. 1; 41. 27. 6), and rebuilt by Caesar (Pliny, *HN* 36. 102). It measured 600 m. long by 150 m. wide; a lap was approximately 1,500 m. The second was the *Circus Flaminius* of 221 B.C., in the southern Campus Martius. The third was the *Circus Gai et Neronis* (Pliny, *HN* 36. 74) or *Vaticanus* (ibid. 16. 201), the site of Christian martyrdoms, close to the later St. Peter's basilica. Best preserved of all is the Circus of Maxentius on Via Appia, outside the city, dedicated in A.D. 309 (*ILS* 673).

In Italy, the *circus* is not infrequent, examples being known at Bovillae, Asisium (*CIL* xi. 5390), and Aquileia. The hippodromes of Constantinople, Alexandria, and Antioch were famous throughout the East. In the West, examples are known in Gaul at Lugdunum (*CIL* xiii. 1919), and Vienne; at Emerita, Toletum, Tarraco, Balsa, Zafra, and Urso in Spain, which was famous for its racing-stables (Pliny, *HN* 8. 166).

For circuses at Rome, see Nash, *Pict. Dict. Rome* i, 232 ff. I. A. R.

**CIRRHA,** a port to the east of Itea, owned tin-mines which were worked in prehistoric times. The site was occupied in the Early Helladic period and in the transitional period between the Middle Helladic and the Late Helladic periods. It flourished in the latter part of the Late Helladic period as the port of Mycenaean Crisa (q.v.) and it was especially prosperous in the seventh century. It was involved in the fate of Crisa, but it revived later as a port.

P-K, *GL* 1. 2. 686 ff. N. G. L. H.

**CIRTA** (modern *Constantine* in Algeria), a strong rock-fortress, commanding the gorges of the Ampsaga (*Rummel*), was the capital of Syphax and then of Masinissa, who encouraged the settlement of Italian merchants, and linked Cirta to the ports of Rusicade (*Philippeville*) and Chullu (*Collo*). Jugurtha captured it from Adherbal (112 B.C.) and massacred the Italian inhabitants. For help in overthrowing Juba I, Sittius (q.v.) and his followers were granted Cirta and the surrounding country by Caesar (46 B.C.). Under the Empire, the full name of Cirta was *Colonia Iulia Iuvenalis Honoris et Virtutis Cirta* and it was the centre of a unique confederation which included three other colonies, Rusicade, Chullu, and Milev. Cirta's great prosperity in the second and third centuries A.D. depended on its crops, marbles, and copper-mines. Its best-known citizen was Fronto (q.v.). Damaged in the civil wars of the early fourth century, it was restored by Constantine who renamed it *Constantina*, and became the capital of Numidia. There was a substantial community of Christians. Cirta retained some importance under Vandal and Byzantine rule.

L. Leschi, *Rev. Africaine* 1937; S. Gsell, *Inscr. Lat. Alg.* ii (1) (1957), 40 ff.; L. Teutsch, *Das Städtewesen in Nordafrika* (1962), 65 ff., 176 ff.; A. Berthier and R. Charlier, *Le Sanctuaire punique d'El Hofra à Constantine*, 2 vols. (1955). W. N. W.; B. H. W.

**CISALPINE GAUL,** the fertile, populous region between Apennines and Alps in north Italy. The migration of Gauls into Italy via the Brenner (*c.* 400 B.C.) was one phase of the great Celtic expansion (Livy 5. 33 f. mistakenly makes the Gauls arrive via the Western Alps *c.* 600). These Gauls, although successfully resisted by the Veneti, gradually ousted the Etruscans, pushed back the Umbrians and Ligurians, and made the Cisalpine area their own. Their gift for poetry, their art and material culture imply a certain degree of civilization; their iron implements, e.g. badly tempered swords, have been recovered from their inhumation burials. But in many ways they were savages: they practised head-hunting and human sacrifice and were addicted to drunken brawling. Occasionally they built excellent fortifications, but many Gallic settlements were mere collections of primitive huts. The Gauls were not very cohesive; they tended to form in groups around indivi-dual and often mutually hostile chieftains. Expert horsemen, they were savage fighters, ever ready to live either by plunder or by serving as mercenaries. In the fourth century B.C. their marauding bands, one of which captured Rome (390), terrorized Italy. After 330, how-ever, with an adaptability perhaps not surprising in so unstable a nation, these restless adventurers settled down about the Po and became skilful agriculturalists. How-ever, they retained their fighting qualities, as their an-nihilation of a Roman army at Arretium (284) proves. Subsequently they waged long and ultimately unsuccess-ful wars against Rome: *see* BOII, CENOMANI, INSUBRES, SENONES. Since any *tumultus Gallicus* threatened her national existence Rome pursued a policy of denationa-lization and even extermination; by 150 B.C. few Gauls remained in the Cisalpine plain (Polyb. 2. 35; Sall. *Iug.* 114; Cic. *Phil.* 8. 3). South Italians, including many Romans, replaced them and Cisalpine Gaul became known as Gallia Togata. Aerial photography has revealed the grid pattern, the so-called centuriation (q.v.) of the Roman settlements. Cimbri (q.v.) threatened in 101 and were repulsed by Marius. In 89 the Transpadane region received *Ius Latii*, the Cispadana apparently Roman citizenship. Probably it was Sulla who organized the Cis-alpine province with the Rubicon as its southern bound-ary (but see O. Cuntz, *Polybius u. s. Werk* (1902), 32). Roman citizenship was extended to the Transpadane region in 49, and in 42 the province was incorporated into Italy. Under Augustus the tribes inhabiting the Alpine foothills were conquered; thus the Alps became the frontier of Italy (Pliny, *HN* 3. 138). Its remarkable pro-ductivity and flourishing woollen trade enriched Cisalpine Gaul. 'Est enim ille flos Italiae, illud firmamentum imperi populi Romani, illud ornamentum dignitatis' (Cic. *Phil.* 3. 13). In Strabo's time (5. 217 f.), as in ours, it contained more large wealthy towns than any other part of Italy.

ANCIENT SOURCES. Strabo (5. 212 ff.) gives a valuable general account of Cisalpine Gaul, marred by anachronisms. Polybius' historical and geographical outline of Cisalpine Gaul down to the Hannibalic War, despite certain inaccuracies, is sober and scientific (books 2 and 3). For events after 202 the chief source is Livy 30–6, a confused account vitiated by rhetorical elaborations. Justin, Diodorus, Appian, and Dio Cassius are the principal subsidiary sources.
MODERN LITERATURE. G. A. Mansuelli and R. Scarani, *L'Emilia prima dei Romani* (1961); A. Bertrand and S. Reinach, *Les Celtes dans les vallées du Pô et du Danube* (1894); C. Jullian, *Histoire de la Gaule* i (1908); F. von Duhn in *Reallexikon der Vorgeschichte* (1924) s.v. 'Kelten'; T. G. E. Powell, *The Celts* (1958); J. Whatmough, *Prae-Italic Dialects* ii (1933), 166; *Foundations of Roman Italy* (1937); G. E. F. Chilver, *Cisalpine Gaul, Social and Economic History from 49 B.C. to the death of Trajan* (1941); C. B. Pascal, *The Cults of Cisalpine Gaul* (Brussels, 1964); for early Roman colonization, U. Ewins, *PBSR* 1952, 54 ff.; G. A. Mansuelli, *CR Acad. Inscr.* 1960, 65 f. E. T. S.

# CITIZENSHIP, GREEK (πολιτεία, a word which also denotes (i) the citizen body, (ii) the constitution). In Greek city-states citizenship expressed the fact that the *polis* was a community of free men, but it was originally not an individual right; it meant membership of a religious and social community (*see* POLIS). Descent from full citizen parents always conferred citizen status, and also membership of the smaller communities of family, *genos*, and *phratria* (qq.v.). The type of constitution depended on the number and quality of those who were full citizens, but in all constitutions the citizens tended to be exclusive.

In oligarchies it was more important to own landed property or to be wealthy than to be well born, and in democracies the rule of descent from citizen parents (ἐξ ἀμφοῖν ἀστοῖν) was not always strictly enforced. The share in citizens' rights varied among the sections of the people. Women might hold some rights, such as owning pro-perty, though not at Athens. Class differences were never fully removed, not even in radical democracy, though political rights could be equal. The *ethnikon*, used in the plural (οἱ Ἀθηναῖοι), indicated the State itself. Besides, the State could grant and withdraw citizenship. Such grants were seldom made in early times, except occasion-ally by tyrants or other leaders bent on increasing the number of their supporters; but they became frequent after the fourth century B.C. Inscriptions recording grants of citizenship are very numerous. Finally citizenship became an empty honour which might be obtainable by benefactions or even purchase, and in many cases people obtained two or more citizenships. Citizenship was lost either by *atimia* (q.v.) or banishment. The general duties of a citizen, e.g. submission to law, defence of the State and its constitution, worship of the State gods, were often confirmed by oath. In most cases citizenship granted to a stranger carried all the rights, though in later times not the duties, of a born citizen. In the Hellenistic Leagues every citizen of a member-state normally acquired a second citizenship, that of the League.

E. Szanto, *Griechisches Bürgerrecht* (1892); A. H. M. Jones, *The Greek City from Alexander to Justinian* (1940). V. Ehrenberg, *The Greek State* (1960; extended German ed. 1965). V. E.

# CITIZENSHIP, ROMAN. Roman citizenship de-pended either upon birth—descent from Roman parents on both sides, though one parent might be a *peregrinus* possessing *conubium*—or upon a grant made by the People, or, in the Empire, by the Princeps. It implied rights, privileges, and duties, *iura, honores, munera*. All citizens, after the union of the Orders, possessed *co-nubium*, etc., and, under the Republic, voting rights (*suf-fragium*) in the various assemblies, unless specifically disfranchised (*aerarii*; q.v.). The system of wealth classi-fication limited the value of the *suffragium* and deter-mined eligibility for magistracies (*honores*) and liability to *munera* (q.v.), especially military service. *Honores* were thus supplementary; there was no *ius honorum*. Rome gradually extended her citizenship to her allies and sub-jects, in whose incorporation *civitas sine suffragio* (*see* MUNICIPIUM) or *ius Latii* (q.v.; *also* LATINI) formed an intermediary stage. Citizenship brought the new Romans within the orbit of *iura, munera*, and *honores*, and entailed the surrender to Rome of the sovereignty of the com-munity concerned. Thus Roman citizenship was in-compatible with that of another independent state. But incorporated communities retained some rights of local self-government (*see* MUNICIPIUM). These principles, worked out in the incorporation between 380 and 250 B.C. of those places which formed the Roman territory down to 90 B.C., were revived by the incorporation of all Italy after the Social War (*see* SOCII, MUNICIPIUM, COMMERCIUM, LATINI). The consequent increase in the number of *municipia* inaugurated a change in the theory of Roman citizenship. Rome ceased to be a city-state and became the *communis patria* of all Italy. Municipal affairs began to supplant the Forum as the centre of interest for the mass of citizens, whose personal privileges, however, marked them as privileged élite when outside Italy. Next came the extension of the citizenship to provinces. From Caesar's dictatorship onwards Roman colonies and muni-cipalities were regularly established overseas and pro-vincial peoples were granted Latin rights and citizenship. Throughout the Principate these processes were accele-rated by the regular grant of citizenship to soldiers

recruited in the provinces and by wealthy provincial aristocrats entering the governing class of Rome, until the western provinces became Roman in both civilization and social rights (*see* COMMERCIUM). Finally, the *constitutio Antoniniana* conferred citizenship upon all free inhabitants of the empire (A.D. 212), without, however, affecting the status of their communities. (Cf. MUNICIPIUM, COLONIZATION, IUS ITALICUM.) The citizenship gradually lost its political importance: the abolition of *comitia* made the *ius suffragi* illusory; provincial Romans lost their former exemption from provincial taxation; senatorial *honores* fell only to the most distinguished of provincial citizens, though the municipal aristocracy commonly aspired to equestrian rank. But the social value remained unchanged, despite some assimilation of the rights of *peregrini* (q.v.) to those of citizens, and the *ius provocationis* remained a considerable judicial privilege guaranteed by the production of a birth-certificate or of a *diploma* of citizenship (*see* APPELLATIO). By the age of the Antonines, however, citizenship was mainly important as the symbol of imperial unity, the doctrine of the incompatibility of two citizenships had broken down with the frequent extension of the franchise to individual members of non-Roman communities (*see* PEREGRINI), and the political ambitions of ordinary men were satisfied in the service to their municipalities. So the spread of *civitas Romana* led to the elaboration of the theory that Rome was the *communis patria* of the whole civilized world.

For bibliography, *see* COLONIZATION, LATINI, MUNICIPIUM.
ANCIENT SOURCES. *CIL* xvi; *Digest* passim; *ILS* 212; *PGiess.* 40; Aelius Aristides, Eἰς 'Ρώμην; Tertullian, *Apol.*, etc.
A. N. Sherwin-White, *The Roman Citizenship* (1939); E. Gabba, 'Le origini della Guerra sociale', *Athenaeum* 1954; E. Badian, *Foreign Clientelae* (1958), chs. viii–x, on the unification of Italy; E. Kornemann, s.v. 'Conventus' in *PW*; Syme, *Tacitus*, chs. 34, 42–5, on provincial senators; A. N. Sherwin-White, *Roman Society and Roman Law in the New Testament* (1963), chs. 7–8, on provincial citizens; E. Condurachi, *Dacia* (1958). Also *see* CLAUDIUS (1).
A. N. S.-W.

## CITY-FOUNDERS (κτίσται, οἰκισταί, *conditores*)

played an important part in the city-state. In the Greek homelands, where the true origin of cities was no longer known, a god or legendary hero was looked upon as founder. But the founder is of greatest significance in the period of Greek colonization. No city sent out a band of colonists without appointing a founder, who had complete power over the colony until the new city's foundation was accomplished. If a band of exiles fo nded a city they selected one of their number to be founder. When a colony founded a colony in its turn, it always summoned a founder from the mother-city. The founders received heroic honours (*see* HERO-CULT) after death; there was probably no *polis* without a founder's cult. Sometimes a city changed its founder, thus symbolizing some important change in its constitution or fortunes, as when Amphipolis ousted Hagnon for Brasidas. Hadrian through his benefactions received the name of founder from many cities. J. E. F.

## CIVILIS, GAIUS JULIUS (*PW* 186) (1st c. A.D.),

a noble Batavian who had some grievances against the Roman government. When Antonius Primus wrote to him in A.D. 69, inciting him to create a diversion and so prevent Vitellian reinforcements from going to Italy, Civilis fomented a war of liberation under pretext of supporting Vespasian. With help from Germans beyond the Rhine he attacked the legionary camp of Vetera (q.v.), but was beaten off. The revolt, however, spread widely, finding support in the winter of A.D. 69–70 among Gallic tribes like the Treveri and Lingones. Roman troops at Novaesium took an oath of allegiance to the 'imperium Galliarum' and Vetera fell at last. But meanwhile the Flavian

generals were approaching. Cerialis (q.v.) won a battle near Trier and the Gallic movement collapsed. After mixed fighting along the Rhine towards the Batavian territory, Civilis finally capitulated. His fate is not known. R. S.

## CIVITAS.

For the abstract sense, *see* CITIZENSHIP, ROMAN. In the concrete sense, the word, like the Greek πόλις, from meaning originally any autonomous state, came to be applied under the Empire to any self-governing municipal unit, irrespective of its civic category. But technically it denoted the least privileged grade of provincial communities possessing local autonomy, however circumscribed (*see* PEREGRINI). Their form of government was republican, with magistrates, council, and a constitution fixed according to local custom. The development of *civitates* out of an unorganized village or tribal system was the first step in the municipal development of backward areas, notably in Spain and Africa. The *civitates*, which might later be given Roman municipal status (*see* MUNICIPIUM), were the basis of the provincial administration. The governors and procurators worked through them, leaving to the local authorities the actual performance of e.g. the census surveys and collection of taxes (*see* DECURIONES, MUNUS, MUNICIPIUM).

For bibliography *see* MUNICIPIUM, SOCII. A. N. S.-W.

## CLAROS,

oracle and grove of Apollo belonging to the Colophonians, who traced the cult back to Manto (daughter of Teiresias and mother of Mopsus) and Calchas. The sanctuary was discovered in 1907 by Makridi Bey in the valley a mile or so inland, and explored by him and Picard. Work was resumed by L. Robert in 1950, since when the main temple has been excavated with its altar and a smaller temple of Artemis. Of special interest is the rib-vaulted crypt under the temple cella, divided into an ante-room and adyton, and containing an omphalos and the well to which the (male) *prophetes* retired to drink the water of inspiration (according to Tacitus, he was told only the number and names of the consultants, and gave his responses in verse). The oracle evidently had a large clientele in Roman times; the earliest dedications reported are two statues of the sixth century B.C.

Strabo 14. 642; Tac. *Ann.* 2. 54; Paus. 7. 3. 1. K. Buresch, *Klaros* (1889); C. Picard, *Ephèse et Claros* (1922). For the recent excavations see *Arch. Rep.* 1959–60, 41 ff.; 1964–5, 46. J. M. C.

## CLASSICIANUS,

GAIUS JULIUS (*PW* 188) ALPINUS, perhaps originated from the Treveri. As procurator of Britain (A.D. 61) he favoured a policy of conciliation, and begged Nero to recall the harsher Suetonius (q.v.) Paulinus. His tombstone was found in London (*AE* 1936, 3; *RIB* 12).

Syme, *Tacitus*, 456; Frere, *Britannia*, 93. A. M.

## CLASSICUS,

JULIUS (*PW* 189), of royal stock among the Treveri (related presumably to C. Julius Classicianus, q.v.), and commanding as *praefectus* a cavalry regiment of his own tribe, joined Julius Civilis (q.v.) when his revolt spread into Gaul at the beginning of 70. Julius Tutor and the Lingonian Julius Sabinus were his close associates in the founding of the 'imperium Galliarum'. Classicus displayed great dash and vigour, shared in most of the fighting against the remnants of the Rhine legions and the generals of Vespasian, and remained loyal to Civilis, apparently to the end. His ultimate fate is unknown. R. S.

## CLASSIS

was at first the whole Roman army; later it was a division of the army in the reform attributed to Servius Tullius. Connected with the ancient meaning is also *classis* as 'navy'. In the Servian constitution the property owners were divided into five *classes* (apart from eighteen centuries of *equites* and four centuries of *fabri*, *cornicines*, and the like). The first three *classes* were infantry of the line, the last two light-armed troops.

The property ratings of the *classes* were perhaps at first expressed in terms of land or agrarian produce, and subsequently in terms of money. The monetary scales are variously given by ancient writers; probably they underwent several alterations (Livy 1. 43; Dion. Hal. 4. 16; Polyb. 6. 23. 15; 6. 19. 2; Gellius 6. 13; Gaius 2. 274; ps.-Asc. *Verr.* 2. 1. 41; Dio Cassius 56. 10; Cic. *Rep.* 2. 22). See CENTURIA.

G. De Sanctis, *Stor. Rom.* ii. 198, iii. 1, 353; A. Piganiol, *Annales d'histoire économique et sociale* 1933, 113 ff.; E. Cavaignac, *Rev. Phil.* 1934, 72 ff.; H. Mattingly, *JRS* 1937, 99 ff.; E. F. D'Arms, *AJPhil.* 1943, 424; H. Last, *JRS* 1945, 43 ff.; A. Momigliano, ibid. 1963, 120 ff. (with bibl.). A. M.

**CLASTIDIUM,** town near Placentia in Cisalpine Gaul (qq.v.). Here in 222 B.C. the Roman consul Marcellus (1) (q.v.) engaged in person and slew the Celtic enemy chieftain Viridomarus—the one certainly historical instance of *spolia opima* (q.v.). E. T. S.

**CLAUDIAN (CLAUDIUS CLAUDIANUS),** a Greek-speaking Alexandrian, came to Italy before A.D. 395 and, turning to Latin, scored an instant success by eulogizing his young patrons, Probinus and Olybrius, thereafter becoming court poet under the Emperor Honorius and official mouthpiece of his minister, Stilicho. His efforts won him an office with the style of *vir clarissimus*, a statue (*CIL* vi. 1710), and a rich bride selected by Stilicho's wife, Serena. His death (*c.* 404) may be inferred from his silence in the face of Stilicho's subsequent achievements. The poems have been transmitted in three groups: (1) *Panegyric on Probinus and Olybrius* (395); (2) *Claudianus maior*, a corpus of poems concerning Stilicho, made, therefore, probably before Stilicho's ignominious death (408). These include *Panegyrics* on consulships of Honorius (396, 398, 404), Mallius Theodorus (399), Stilicho (400); *Invectives* against Stilicho's rivals at the Eastern court of Arcadius, Honorius' brother, *In Rufinum* (396), *In Eutropium* (399); *Bellum Gildonicum* (398); *Epithalamium* and *Fescennina* on Honorius' marriage (398); *Bellum Pollentinum* (sive *Gothicum*) (402); minor poems of similar interest (e.g., *Laus Serenae*), but including epistles, idylls, and epigrams (e.g., *De sene Veronensi*) and a *Gigantomachia*; (3) *Claudianus minor*, i.e. the unfinished epic, *Raptus Proserpinae* (3 bks.), inspired possibly by the corn-shortage of 395–7 or the destruction of Eleusis (q.v.) by Alaric in 396.

Claudian is the last notable representative of the classical tradition in Latin poetry. Orosius (vii. 35) and Augustine (*De civ. D.* 5. 26), as well as his own clear predilection for the old religion, prove that he was not a Christian. In diction and technique he bears comparison with the best Silver Age work, but his considerable gifts of invective, description, and epigram are offset by a deplorable tendency to over-elaboration. His writings are a useful (and often highly distorted) historical source for his period, especially the political poems which were collected and republished separately by Stilicho after 404—a fact reflected in their separate manuscript tradition.

TEXTS. T. Birt, *MGH* x; J. Koch (Teubner, 1893). *Claud. min.* V. Paladini (with Ital. transl., 1952).
TRANSLATION. M. Platnauer (with text, Loeb, 1922).
COMMENTARIES. N. Heinsius (1665). J. M. Gesner (1759). *IV Cons. Hon.*, P. Fargues (1936). *VI Cons. Hon.*, K. A. Müller (1938). *In Ruf.*, H. L. Levy (1935). *In Eutr.*, A. C. Andrews (1931), P. Fargues (1933). LIFE AND WORKS. Birt, *Introd.* P. Fargues, *Claudien* (1933). Schanz-Hosius IV. ii. 3 ff. F. J. E. Raby, *Secular Latin Poetry*[2] (1957), 87 ff. W. Br.

**CLAUDIUS** (1) (TIBERIUS CLAUDIUS (*PW* 256) NERO GERMANICUS, 10 B.C.–A.D. 54), the Emperor, was born at Lyons on 1 Aug. 10 B.C. and was the youngest son of the Elder Drusus (q.v. 3) and of Antonia minor. Overshadowed by the strong personality of his elder brother Germanicus, and hampered by a weak constitution and continual illness (he suffered from some sort of paralysis: see T. de C. Ruth, *The Problem of Claudius*, U.S.A. 1924), he received no public distinction from Augustus beyond the augurate and held no magistracy under Tiberius, who considered his 'imminuta mens' an obstacle to high preferment (Tac. *Ann.* 6. 46). He first held office when on 1 July A.D. 37 he became suffect consul with his young nephew, the Emperor Gaius; for the rest, he received little from Gaius but insults. His proclamation as Emperor in 41 was largely accidental. After Gaius' murder he was discovered in the palace by a soldier, hiding behind a curtain in fear of murder; he was dragged to the Praetorian Camp and saluted by the Praetorian Guard while the Senate was still discussing the possibility of restoring the Republic. The Senate did not easily forgive him, and many senators supported the fruitless revolt of Scribonianus in Dalmatia in the following year. Chosen by the Guard, Claudius emphasized his interest in the army—a policy all the more necessary because of his own lack of military distinction. He took a personal part in the invasion of Britain (43) and was present at the capture of Camulodunum. By the end of his principate he had received twenty-seven imperial *salutationes*.

Though he was consul four times during his principate (in 42, 43, 47, and 51) and censor in 47/8, in policy he reverted from the pretentious absolutism of Gaius (who was, however, spared an official *damnatio memoriae*) to a less autocratic form of principate. He went further than his predecessors in extending the *civitas* (see e.g. the Volubilis inscriptions, *AE* 1916, 42; 1924, 66) and in the foundation of new colonies (e.g. Camulodunum in Britain). This liberal aspect of his policy is well revealed in his speech advocating that the chiefs of Gallia Comata should be granted the *ius honorum* (Dessau, *ILS* 212). With the Senate he was unpopular, not because he curtailed its powers, but from the circumstances of his accession and because of the insistence with which he urged its members to take their responsibilities seriously (see e.g. *BGU* 611). Other causes of his unpopularity were his intense interest in jurisdiction, especially the hearing of cases *intra cubiculum principis*, and the political power of his wives and freedmen. Claudius' principate is marked by the emergence of rich and powerful freedmen, especially Narcissus (q.v. 2), his *ab epistulis*, and Pallas (q.v. 3), his *a rationibus*. These private secretaries exercised ministerial functions and were, no doubt, heavily bribed by candidates for preferment. Claudius was incurably uxorious. His first wife bore him two children who died in infancy. Aelia Paetina, his second wife, bore him a daughter (Claudia Antonia, A.D. 27–66). He was married at the time of his accession to Valeria Messalina (q.v. 1), and had by her a daughter Octavia (born before 41, and later married to Nero) and a son, Britannicus (q.v.), born in 41 or 42. Messalina succumbed in 48 to the intrigues of Narcissus, and Claudius then married his niece Agrippina, who could count on the support of Pallas. She persuaded Claudius in 50 to adopt her son Nero as guardian of his own son Britannicus (four years Nero's junior). Four years later Claudius died: it was generally believed that Agrippina handed him a poisoned dish of mushrooms (13 Oct. A.D. 54). He was, nevertheless, consecrated and was the first Emperor after Augustus to receive this distinction. The *Apocolocyntosis*, probably by Seneca, is a satire on his consecration.

Claudius had in his youth acquired from Livy a

thorough knowledge of Roman history and great respect for Roman religion and tradition. He celebrated the *Ludi Saeculares* in A.D. 47, founded a College of Haruspices, expelled Jews from Rome (though in Judaea and in Alexandria he did his best to still the disturbances resulting from the anti-Semite policy of Gaius), and in Gaul he suppressed Druidism. He wrote books on Etruscan and Carthaginian history, on dicing, and on the history of Augustus' principate ('a pace ciuili'—i.e. from 27 B.C.). He also wrote an autobiography. None of these works has survived.

Claudius added a number of provinces to the Roman Empire: Britain (whose invasion had, perhaps, been contemplated by Gaius), the two provinces of Mauretania (whose last king, Ptolemy, had been deposed and executed by Gaius), and Thrace (in A.D. 46).

Ancient writers ascribed the responsibility for Claudius' administration, both on its good and its bad side, to his freedmen and wives. This view is now untenable for the early part of his principate, thanks to the survival of a large number of imperial enactments in inscriptions and on papyri covering a great variety of administrative problems. In these the approach to problems (generally from a historical point of view) is individual and the literary style is inimitably grotesque. They are clearly the expression of Claudius' own personality, and all of them reveal profound common sense. In the last four years of his principate, however, his powers were failing and Agrippina and Pallas exercised strong influence on his policy.

ANCIENT SOURCES. Tac. *Annals* bks. 11–12 cover the period A.D. 47–54, but we do not possess Tacitus' account of the first six—unquestionably the best and most important—years of Claudius' principate. For the rest, we depend chiefly on Dio Cassius bk. 60 and on Suet. *Divus Claudius*. For other sources, see *CAH* x. 973 f. The most important inscriptions and papyri (all of which are published by E. M. Smallwood, *Documents Illustrating the Principates of Gaius, Claudius and Nero* (1967)) are the letter to the Alexandrians (see H. I. Bell, *Jews and Christians in Egypt*), the Volubilis inscriptions (v.s.), the Anauni edict (*ILS* 206), the speech on the *ius honorum* of the Gauls (*ILS* 212; see on this Ph. Fabia, *La Table claudienne de Lyon*), and *BGU* 611.
MODERN LITERATURE. V. M. Scramuzza, *The Emperor Claudius* (U.S.A. 1940). A. Momigliano, *Claudius* (1934, repr. 1961 with exhaustive bibliography 1942–59). J. P. B.

**CLAUDIUS** (2) **II (GOTHICUS)**, MARCUS AURELIUS (*PW* 82) (VALERIUS), a soldier of Illyrian origin, one of the chief officers of Gallienus, chosen, after his assassination, to succeed him as emperor (early A.D. 268). Whether privy to the murder or not, he soon established friendly relations with the Senate, which had hated Gallienus.

An active soldier, he defeated the invading Alamanni near Lake Benacus, after his cavalry had suffered an initial set-back. Aurelian (q.v.) was appointed to command the horse.

In the West, the Gallic Empire, under Postumus and his successors, Marius and Victorinus, continued to hold aloof. When Augustodunum (*Autun*) revolted (269), however, Claudius sent no aid, and the city had to surrender to Victorinus.

The main achievement of Claudius was the decisive defeat of the Goths, who, even after Gallienus' successes, were plundering the Balkans. Claudius won two great battles, at Doberus and Naissus, and finally broke up their great host, absorbing many as soldiers or *coloni*. At the same time he took energetic steps against the pirate squadrons in the Aegean.

In the East, the Palmyrene government under Zenobia had begun by recognizing Claudius, but before the end of his reign had occupied Egypt and had pushed northward to Bithynia.

Claudius died of plague at Sirmium early in 270. His reputation, already solid as a victor over the Goths, was enhanced when Constantine later claimed (without any justification) to be his descendant.

P. Damarau, *Kaiser Claudius II Goticus* (1934). H. M.

**CLAUDIUS** (3, *PW* 123), APPIUS (decemvir, 451 B.C.), despite his patrician descent, supported the plebeian claims for a written code of laws and became the leader of the decemvirs. While his policy and high birth attracted the patricians, he pleased the plebeians by sharing power with their representatives at least in his second year of office. He thus hoped that the plebeians would compromise, and consent to abolish the tribunate in return for admission to the highest magistracies. His success as a lawgiver is attested by the survival of the decemviral code despite the violent opposition which his policy aroused. His ultimate failure (that he was murdered or escaped assassination by suicide is probable but not certain) together with the gloomy recollections of the civil struggle in which his dictatorship ended (*see* VERGINIA), gave rise to the legend of Appius' tyranny, which, embellished with details taken perhaps from the deeds of the later Claudii, and certainly from the stock-in-trade material supplied by Greek tyranny and its critics, overshadowed his work and memory.

Mommsen, *Röm. Forsch.* i. 295 ff.; Ogilvie, *Comm. Livy 1–5*, with bibliography, 476 ff., 503 ff. P. T.

**CLAUDIUS** (4, *PW* 91) **CAECUS**, APPIUS (censor in 312 B.C.) stands out as the first clear-cut personality in Roman history. He has rightly been compared with the aristocratic founders of Athenian democracy for, although a patrician, Appius used his censorship to increase the part taken by the lower classes in managing public affairs. He made citizens of low birth and even sons of freedmen senators. Their support, and also heavier taxation, enabled him to build during the eighteen months of his censorship the first aqueduct (*Aqua Appia*) and the Via Appia (q.v.) on which he founded a market (*Forum Appi*). It was meant as a first step towards Rome's expansion in southern Italy, which was indeed the cardinal principle of Appius' policy which he relentlessly pursued (and the major reason, eventually, for making him reject Pyrrhus' peace proposals). Whether he distributed the landless citizens of Rome throughout all the existing tribes, independently of their income, in order to establish a balance of power between the urban and the agrarian population, which alone had hitherto enjoyed full political rights, is a matter of dispute, although the step accords with his policy. He transferred the cult of Hercules from private to public superintendence, and perhaps helped Cn. Flavius (q.v. 1) to publish a book of forms of legal procedure. Despite his reforms Appius could still rely on senatorial support, as his subsequent career shows. As consul in 307 and 296 (when he dedicated a temple to Bellona) and praetor in 295, he took an active part in the wars against the Etruscans, Sabines, and Samnites. Despite old age and blindness, Appius was still one of the most authoritative statesmen when he persuaded the Senate to reject Pyrrhus' peace proposals (279/8), claiming that Rome had the right to consider as her property or at any rate her sphere of influence the whole of the southern mainland to the Straits of Messina. The speech he delivered on that occasion soon became famous, was poetically elaborated by Ennius, and still circulated in the age of Cicero. Appius was the first Roman prose-writer and author of moral apophthegms (e.g. 'faber est suae quisque fortunae'), which probably owed much to Graeco-Pythagorean sources.

Mommsen, *Röm. Forsch.* i. 301 ff.; P. Lejay, *Rev. Phil.* 1920, 105 ff.; Beloch, *Röm. Gesch.* 481 ff.; A. Garzetti, *Athenaeum*, 1947, 175 ff.; E. S. Staveley, *Hist.* 1959, 410 ff.; F. Cassola, *I gruppi politici romani* (1962), 128 ff. (with full bibliography). P. T.

**CLAUDIUS** (5, *PW* 102) **CAUDEX,** APPIUS (*cos.* 264 B.C.), formally commenced the First Punic War by crossing to Sicily with two legions. He relieved Messana by successive attacks on the camps of Hieron and Hanno (Polyb. 1. 11–12, 15). Philinus, however, described these Roman engagements as unsuccessful. H. H. S.

**CLAUDIUS** (6, *PW* 304) **PULCHER,** PUBLIUS, held the Sicilian command as consul in 249 B.C. To intensify the naval blockade of Lilybaeum he attacked the Carthaginian fleet at Drepana. The Carthaginian admiral, however, fell on the flank of the Roman line as its head entered Drepana harbour. Claudius lost 93 of his 123 ships in this the only serious Roman naval defeat in the First Punic War. The pious attributed his defeat to his disregard of religious form before the battle: when told that the sacred chickens would not eat, he drowned them: 'let them drink' (this anecdote is not found in Polybius). He was court-martialled and fined, and died soon afterwards.

Polybius, 1. 49–52. H. H. S.

**CLAUDIUS** (7, *PW* 29), QUINTUS, *tribunus plebis* in 218 B.C., was author of a law which forbade senators and their sons to own sea-going vessels capable of carrying over 300 *amphorae* (*c.* 225 bushels). Small vessels would suffice to transport their agricultural produce. He may be identified with the praetor of 208, unless the latter's *cognomen* was Flamen.

Livy 21. 63. For modern views of Claudius' motive see F. Cassola, *I gruppi politici romani* (1962), 216 ff. H. H. S.

**CLAUDIUS** (8, *PW* 300) **PULCHER,** GAIUS, augur (195 B.C.), praetor (180), was consul in 177, when, after repatriating Latins in Rome, he closed the Istrian War and crushed a Ligurian rising, recapturing Mutina in 176. He was military tribune in Greece in 171. Censor in 169 with Ti. Sempronius Gracchus, he intervened in the levies for Greece; his severity against the *equites* brought a prosecution in which he was nearly convicted. On the commission for settling Macedonia he died in 167. Strong-willed and conservative, he represented the traditional authority of the Senate in Roman and Italian affairs.

Scullard, *Rom. Pol.* 187, 203 ff. A. H. McD.

**CLAUDIUS** (9, *PW* 295) **PULCHER,** APPIUS, as consul in 143 B.C. won a victory over the Salassi in Cisalpine Gaul and, against the will of the Senate, celebrated a triumph, protected by a daughter who was a Vestal. Censor in 136, he became *princeps senatus* and one of the leading statesmen. An enemy of Scipio (q.v. 11), he married a daughter to Tiberius Gracchus (q.v. 3) when he too fell out with Scipio. He advised Tiberius during his tribunate, and then served on his agrarian commission until his own death (*c.* 130).

D. C. Earl, *Tiberius Gracchus* (1965); A. E. Astin, *Scipio Aemilianus* (1967), see index. E. B.

**CLAUDIUS** (10, *PW* 296) **PULCHER,** APPIUS, son of (9), as praetor in 89 or 88 B.C. enrolled some newly enfranchised allies. As an enemy of Cinna he left Rome in 87, was outlawed and struck off the Senate list by his own nephew Marcius Philippus (q.v. 4). As consul (79) he went to Macedonia (78), and, despite illness, won some victories, but died in 76. He was married to a daughter of Metellus (4) Baliaricus and was the father of P. Clodius (q.v. 1). E. B.

**CLAUDIUS** (11, *PW* 308) **QUADRIGARIUS,** QUINTUS, the Roman annalist of the immediate post-Sullan period, wrote a history of Rome in at least twenty-three books, from the Gallic sack to his own times. Book 3 included the Pyrrhic War, book 5 the battle of Cannae,

book 6 the year 213 B.C., book 9 (probably) Ti. Gracchus at Numantia, book 13 the year 99 B.C., book 19 the year 87 B.C.; the latest date preserved is 82 B.C., the latest book 23. If he is the Claudius who translated Acilius (Livy 25. 39. 12; 35. 14. 5), he presumably adapted the senatorial historian's material to his own annalistic form; the ἔλεγχος χρόνων of Κλαύδιος (Plut. *Numa* 1) is scarcely his. The choice of opening point shows his care in handling tradition, although in composition he may have used rhetorical methods of narrative elaboration. This, however, was probably not exaggerated, as by Valerius Antias. His style, as the fragments show, was simple, his vocabulary plain, with an archaic grace (Gellius 9. 13; 15. 1; 13. 29 (28)). He ranks with Valerius Antias as the leading annalist before Livy, and Livy followed him.

Peter, *HRRel.* i² (1914), cclxxxv, 205. W. Soltau, *Livius' Geschichtswerk* (1897); M. Gelzer, *Kl. Schr.* iii, 221 ff. (1964); M. Zimmerer, *Der Annalist Q. Claudius Quadrigarius* (1937). A. H. McD.

**CLAUDIUS** (12, *PW* 297) **PULCHER,** APPIUS, eldest son of (10), served in the East under his brother-in-law L. Lucullus (q.v. 2) in 72–70. As praetor in 57 he supported his brother P. Clodius (q.v. 1); from 56 to 55 he was governor of Sardinia. Consul in 54, he joined his colleague L. Domitius (q.v. 4) Ahenobarbus in a scandalous electoral compact with L. Memmius (q.v. 2) and Cn. Domitius Calvinus (q.v. 2), candidates for 53. After governing Cilicia (53–51), he was prosecuted by Dolabella (q.v. 3) *de maiestate*, for misconduct in Cilicia, and *de ambitu*, in connexion with his candidature for the censorship; but helped by Pompey, M. Brutus, and others he was acquitted on both counts and became censor (50), in which office he was surprisingly severe. In 49 he followed Pompey, and died in Greece early in 48. He wrote a work on augural discipline dedicated to Cicero, whose attitude towards this arrogant and unprincipled but influential aristocrat was understandably mixed (cf., e.g., *Fam.* 2. 13. 2). His wife was, it seems, a Servilia of the Caepio family and his daughters married Cn. Pompeius (q.v. 5) and M. Brutus.

Cic. *Fam.* 3. L. A. Constans, *Un Correspondant de Cicéron, Ap. Claudius Pulcher* (1921); Syme, *Rom. Rev.*, see index; Schanz–Hosius i. 598 f.; *ORF*² 419 f. T. J. C.

**CLAUDIUS** (13, *PW* 31), TIBERIUS (or perhaps TIBERIUS IULIUS), a freedman from Smyrna manumitted by Tiberius, served all the emperors from Tiberius to Domitian. Under Claudius he became a procurator, and at some later date (possibly on Vespasian's accession) was made *a rationibus*. Vespasian gave him equestrian rank. Banished by Domitian *c.* A.D. 82, he was recalled *c.* 89 on the intercession of his son Claudius (q.v. 14) Etruscus. He died in 92 aged nearly 90.

Statius, *Silv.* 3. 3, with the preface to the book; Martial, 7. 40. P. R. C. Weaver, *CQ* 1965, 145 ff. G. E. F. C.

**CLAUDIUS** (14, *PW* 143) **ETRUSCUS,** the wealthy son of (13) above and (Tettia?) Etrusca, patron of Statius and Martial, was probably knighted by Vespasian. He obtained from Domitian the recall of his exiled father. Statius' *Silvae* 3. 3 is dedicated to him. He was possibly nephew of Domitian's general Tettius Iulianus (*cos.* 83).

S. Gsell, *Essai sur le règne de l'empereur Domitien* (1894), 219 ff. A. M.

**CLAUDIUS** (15, *PW* 282) **POMPEIANUS,** TIBERIUS, son of an equestrian of Antioch, rose to senatorial rank and pursued a brilliant career; *c.* A.D. 167 he was governor of Lower Pannonia (*CIL* xvi. 123), where he stemmed the German invasions. He became *cos. I suff.* either before or soon after this governorship. In 169, he married Lucilla (q.v.), widow of L. Verus (q.v.), and in 173 was *cos. II ord.* He was now the trusted friend of M. Aurelius (q.v. 1), and his commander in all major campaigns. Under Commodus (q.v.) he retired into private life, thus escaping the repercussions of Lucilla's plot in 182. Though by 193 aged and infirm, he emerged again under Pertinax (q.v.), who, like Didius (q.v. 2) Julianus after him, vainly pressed him to assume a share of the imperial administration.

Lambrechts, *Sénat*, no. 705; H. G. Pflaum, *Journ. Sav.* 1961, 28 ff.; for representations on the column and reliefs of Marcus Aurelius, see bibliography in *Kl. Pauly* s.v. Claudius II 43.
C. H. V. S.; M. H.

**CLAUDIUS** (16) **MAMERTINUS** is the author of a speech delivered on 1 Jan. A.D. 362 in Constantinople, in which he thanked the Emperor Julian for the gift of the consulship. The kernel of the speech is an exaggerated eulogy of Julian. Involved in an embezzlement charge, he fell into disgrace in 368. *See* PANEGYRIC, LATIN.   A. S.

**CLAVUS ANGUSTUS, LATUS.** The *angustus clavus* was a narrow, the *latus clavus* a broad, purple upright stripe (possibly two stripes) stitched to or woven into the Roman *tunica*. The former indicated equestrian, the latter senatorial, rank. Under the Roman Empire the *latus clavus* was worn before admission to the Senate, on the assumption of the *toga virilis*, by sons of senators as a right (though, perhaps, the formal consent of the Emperor was required; cf. Suet. *Aug.* 38. 2); by others who aimed at a senatorial career (e.g. Ovid and his brother, *Trist.* 4. 10. 28 f.; Dio Cass. 59. 9. 5), with the Emperor's special permission. Military tribunes in the legions were distinguished as *tribuni angusticlavii* or *tribuni laticlavii* according as they were pursuing the equestrian or the senatorial *cursus honorum*.   J. P. B.

**CLAZOMENAE** (Κλαζομεναί), one of the twelve cities of the Ionian League, situated on the south shore of the Gulf of Smyrna on a small island joined to the mainland by a causeway. The original settlement was on the mainland, where large numbers of the terracotta sarcophagi peculiar to Clazomenae have been found. The move to the island came 'from fear of the Persians' (Paus. 7. 3. 9), apparently at the time of the Ionian Revolt (500–494 B.C.). About 600 B.C. Clazomenae successfully repulsed an attack by the Lydians under Alyattes, but later fell to Croesus. In the Delian League the city was at first assessed at one and a half talents, but during the Peloponnesian War this was raised to six and even to fifteen talents; the reason for this is not known. In the early fourth century the Clazomenians were engaged in hostilities with the men of Chytrion (or Chyton), a place on the mainland 'where the Clazomenians were formerly settled' (Strabo 645); it is not clear whether or not this is the original settlement. In 386 B.C. the island was claimed by the Persian King. Pliny and Pausanias say that the idea of constructing the causeway was due to Alexander; some scholars have rejected this evidence, but probably without justification. Distinguished Clazomenian philosophers were Anaxagoras in the fifth century B.C. and Scopelianus in the time of Domitian. The site is now called *Klazümen*, but the ruins are scanty.

J. M. Cook in Ἀρχ. Ἐφ. 1953–4; G. E. Bean, *Aegean Turkey* (1966), 128–36.   G. E. B.

**CLEANTHES** (331–232 B.C.), son of Phanias of Assos, disciple of Zeno of Citium and his successor as head of the Stoic School from 263 to 232. With him the sober philosophy of Zeno became pervaded by religious fervour. He considered the universe a living being, God as the soul of the universe, the sun as its heart. In ethics he stressed disinterestedness, saying that doing good to others with a view to one's own advantage was comparable to feeding cattle in order to eat them. He contended that evil thoughts were worse than evil deeds,

just as a tumour that breaks open is less dangerous than one which does not. Most famous among his works is his hymn to Zeus.

A. C. Pearson, *The Fragments of Zenon and Cleanthes* (1891); H. von Arnim, *SVF* i. 103–39; Poetical Fragments, Powell, *Coll. Alex.* (1955), 227–31; Diog. Laert. 7. 168–76, M. Pohlenz, *Die Stoa²*.
K. VON F.

**CLEARCHUS** (1) (*c.* 450–401 B.C.), a Spartan officer and a stern disciplinarian, held commands in the Hellespontine region from 409 onwards. He refused to withdraw from Byzantium in 403, was ejected by Spartan troops, and sought refuge with Cyrus II, who commissioned him to recruit, and later to command, the Greek mercenaries forming the core of his army. At Cunaxa his reluctance to expose his right flank made possible the decisive Persian cavalry charge. He held his troops together after the battle, but, with the other officers, was treacherously arrested at a conference with Tissaphernes and executed.   D. E. W. W.

**CLEARCHUS** (2), Middle Comedy poet, won at least one victory at the Lenaea *c.* 335–330 B.C. (*IG* ii². 2325. 154). We have three titles and five citations.

*FCG* iv. 562 ff.; *CAF* ii. 408 ff.; *FAC* ii. 542 ff.   K. J. D.

**CLEARCHUS** (3) of Soli, in Cyprus (*c.* 340–*c.* 250 B.C.), a polymath, wrote βίοι (ways of life, not biographies), paradoxes, erotica, an encomium on Plato, and zoological and mystical works. These are learned but sensational; attacks on luxury reveal a Peripatetic background.

O. Stein, *Philol.* 1931, 258–9. Fragments in F. Wehrli, *Klearchos* (1948).   F. W. W.

**CLEDONIUS** (5th c. A.D.), grammarian who taught in Constantinople and wrote an *Ars* (ed. Keil, *Gramm. Lat.* v. 9–79) which is explanatory of the *Ars* of Donatus. The treatise is preserved only in a sixth-century Berne codex which is our oldest MS. of a grammatical work.

Schanz–Hosius, § 1101.   J. F. M.

**CLEIDEMUS**, or **CLEITODEMUS** (fl. *c.* 350 B.C.), the oldest atthidographer, if we except Hellanicus, and an *exegetes* who is credited with a book on religious ritual. The *Atthis*, probably in not more than four books, was his chief work. The first two books which are most often cited dealt with the colonization of Attica, the monarchic period, and events to the time of Peisistratus, Cleidemus' main interest being apparently in the earlier history. The narrative extended at least to the Peloponnesian War and may have reached contemporary events. The work is also quoted as Πρωτογονία (the generic term *Atthis* for this type of literature derived from Hellenistic scholarship). The fragments show a tendency to rationalize myths and an interest in etymology. They contain references to matters of cult, constitutional points, and topographical details. The work was soon superseded by later *Atthides*.

*FGrH* iiiB. 323. *See under* ATTHIS.   G. L. B.

**CLEISTHENES** (1), Athenian statesman. He was of the family of the Alcmaeonidae (q.v.), a son of Megacles (q.v.) and Agariste, daughter of Cleisthenes (2) of Sicyon. He was archon under the tyrant Hippias (q.v. 1) in 525/4 B.C., but later in Hippias' reign, perhaps after 514, the Alcmaeonids along with other families were exiled again. It was said that it was Cleisthenes who persuaded the prophetess at Delphi (q.v.), in return for the family's services in the rebuilding of the temple, to recommend to all Spartans consulting the oracle the overthrow of the Athenian tyranny. When this had been accomplished by the Spartan king Cleomenes (q.v. 1) and the exiles had turned (511/10), Cleisthenes headed one of the two noble factions. His rival Isagoras, with the help of the aristocratic clubs (*see* HETAIRIAI), obtained the mastery and was elected archon for 508/7; Cleisthenes turned the tables on him by making an alliance with the people, and proceeded to pass far-reaching democratic reforms (*see* BOULE, DEMOI, EKKLESIA, OSTRACISM, PHYLAI, STRATEGOI, PRYTTYES). Isagoras now appealed to Cleomenes, who invoked the hereditary curse of the Alcmaeonidae, and Cleisthenes and his supporters judged it prudent to withdraw; but when Cleomenes arrived with a small force, expelled 700 more households, and attempted to set up a close oligarchy of Isagoras' friends, he met with strong popular resistance and was forced to retire in his turn, taking Isagoras with him; whereupon Cleisthenes and his partisans returned. The Athenians, fearing a war with Sparta, sought alliance with Persia: but the terms offered by the satrap of Sardis, though accepted by the Athenian envoys, were repudiated in Athens. It is reasonable to suppose that Cleisthenes had something to do with this attempt to get Persian help, and it has been conjectured that its abandonment involved his overthrow, since nothing further is recorded of him. However this may be, his democratic constitution was accepted and remained in force, and when he died he received a public tomb in the Ceramicus.

Cleisthenes was generally regarded as the creator of Athenian democracy, though the initial steps taken by Solon were not forgotten; on the other hand, Cleisthenes' constitution sometimes seemed aristocratic when contrasted with that of Ephialtes and Pericles.

V. Ehrenberg, *Neugründer des Staates* (1925), 55 ff.; id. *Hist.* 1950, 515 ff.; H. T. Wade-Gery, *CQ* 1933, 17 ff.= *Essays in Greek History* (1958), 135 ff.; T. J. Cadoux, *JHS* 1948, 109 f., 113 ff.; J. A. O. Larsen, *Essays . . . presented to G. H. Sabine* (1948), 1 ff.; E. Ruschenbusch, *Hist.* 1958, 398 ff.; C. W. J. Eliot and M. F. McGregor, *Phoenix* 1960, 27 ff.; P. Lévêque and P. Vidal-Naquet, *Clisthéne l'athénien* (1964); D. Kienast, *Historische Zeitschrift* 1965, 265 ff.                   T. J. C.

**CLEISTHENES** (2) of Sicyon, the greatest tyrant of the house of Orthagoras, which ruled for the record period of a century (*c.* 665–565 B.C.). His reign (*c.* 600–570) was marked by a strong movement against the Argive Dorian ascendancy: the three traditional Dorian tribes were renamed Piggites, Swinites, Assites, while the non-Dorian was called *Archelaoi* (Rulers), probably in relation to cult rather than politics; Argive rhapsodes were suppressed, the ancient Argive hero Adrastus was persuaded to find a tomb elsewhere and a new festival of Dionysus was established. His daughter Agariste (mother of the Athenian Cleisthenes) married the Alcmaeonid Megacles, after her suitors had spent a year in the tyrant's palace like successors of the suitors of Penelope. In the First Sacred War (q.v.) Cleisthenes took a leading part; he destroyed Crisa and for a while appears to have controlled the sea approach to Delphi.

P. N. Ure, *Origin of Tyranny* (1922), 258 ff., footnotes; A. Andrewes, *The Greek Tyrants* (1956); N. G. L. Hammond, 'The family of Orthagoras', *CQ* 1956, 45 ff.           P. N. U.

**CLEITARCHUS** of Alexandria, Alexander-historian, was most probably a secondary writer who was never in Asia and wrote under Ptolemy II, some time after 280 B.C. Little certainty can be obtained about his history, but if (as does seem certain) Diodorus book 17 substantially represents it in an abridged form, it contained much detailed straight narrative besides the patches of sensationalism which helped to make it popular. His sources can have included any of the more reputable historians who wrote before him (Callisthenes, Ptolemy, Aristobulus, Onesicritus, Nearchus), as well as popular beliefs and the poets who accompanied Alexander. He was used extensively by Curtius Rufus as well as by Diodorus (the

concurrences are frequent and striking). No critic of antiquity has a good word for him as a historian; but he was much read under the early Roman Empire and influenced the Romance.

*See* ALEXANDER (3), Bibliography, Ancient Sources; Pearson, *Lost Histories of Alexander*, ch. 8.         W. W. T.; G. T. G.

**CLEITUS** (1) ('the Black') (*c.* 380–328 or 327 B.C.), a Macedonian of noble birth and some distinction as a commander of cavalry. His fame, however, rests on two events: he saved Alexander's life at the battle of the Granicus; and he was himself killed by Alexander nearly seven years later, in a drunken quarrel, though the underlying grounds of difference were political questions of the first importance (Arrian, *Anab.* 4. 8. 1 ff.; Plutarch, *Alex.* 51, and—more hostile to Alexander—Curtius Rufus 8. 1. 19 ff.).

Berve, *Alexanderreich*, no. 427.           G. T. G.

**CLEITUS** (2) (d. 318 B.C.), a Macedonian noble, served under Alexander in Asia without special distinction. Sent home with Craterus and the 'veterans' (324), he played an important part in the Lamian War as admiral of the Macedonian fleet which closed the Dardanelles to the Greeks after two victories (322). For his continued loyalty to Antipater he was rewarded with the satrapy of Lydia (321), from which Antigonus expelled him (319). He became Polyperchon's admiral with the task of preventing Antigonus from invading Europe, but was defeated by Nicanor near the Bosporus and killed in Thrace soon afterwards.

Berve, *Alexanderreich* ii, no. 428.         G. T. G.

**CLEMENS**, FLAVIUS (*PW* 62) (*cos.* A.D. 95), grandson of Vespasian's brother Flavius Sabinus (the *praefectus urbi*) and husband of Flavia Domitilla (q.v.: the niece of Domitian), a person of inoffensive habits ('contemptissimae inertiae'), who was put to death, along with his wife, for *maiestas* soon after he laid down the consulate. They are said to have been guilty of ἀθεότης, or following Jewish practices (Dio 67. 14), and may have been Christians, as later tradition alleges. Domitian intended the succession to go to the two small sons of Clemens; they are not heard of after 96.         R. S.

**CLEMENT OF ALEXANDRIA** (TITUS FLAVIUS CLEMENS) was born *c.* A.D. 150, probably at Athens, of pagan parents. He was converted to Christianity and travelled extensively seeking instruction from Christian teachers and finally from Pantaenus, head of the Catechetical School of Alexandria, at that time an unofficial institution giving tuition to converts. Clement had a wide acquaintance with Greek literature; his writings abound in quotations from the Platonic and Stoic philosophers; also from Homer, Hesiod, and the dramatists (frequently drawn, it is thought, from anthologies and other secondary sources). His *Protrepticus* shows familiarity with the Greek Mysteries. After ordination he succeeded Pantaenus as head of the school, some time before 200, and held the office till *c.* 202, when, on the outbreak of the persecution under Septimius Severus, he left Alexandria and took refuge, perhaps with his former pupil Alexander, then bishop of Cappadocia and later of Jerusalem. Clement died between 211 and 216.

Much of his writings is lost, but the following important works survive nearly complete. These are: (1) The Προτρεπτικὸς πρὸς Ἕλληνας or 'Hortatory Address to the Greeks' (*c.* 190), designed to prove the superiority of Christianity to the pagan religions and philosophies. (2) The Παιδαγωγός or 'Tutor' (*c.* 190–5), an exposition of the moral teaching of Christ, not only in its general method, but also in detailed application to special points of conduct, such as eating and drinking, dress, and the use of wealth. (3) The Στρωματεῖς or 'Miscellanies' (probably c. 200–2), in eight books, the first seven dealing in the main with the subordination and inferiority of Greek to Christian philosophy. The eighth book is a fragment on Logic. In one of the MSS. two further pieces follow, generally known as *Excerpta ex Theodoto* and *Eclogae propheticae*.

The *Quis dives salvetur?* (Τίς ὁ σωζόμενος πλούσιος;) is an extant homily urging detachment from worldly goods. The Ὑποτυπώσεις or 'Sketches' (of which only fragments survive) was probably an exegetical work consisting of notes on passages of the Scriptures.

Clement's conception of Christianity has been criticized as tinged with Hellenism and humanism and as doctrinally imperfect. His name is often found in Christian calendars on 4 Dec., but in 1748 Benedict XIV expressly excluded him from the Roman martyrology. His writings, however, have much charm and are characterized by serenity and hopefulness.

TEXTS. O. Stählin (4 vols., 1905–36, in *Die griechischen christlichen Schriftsteller*); *Exc. ex Theod.* R. P. Casey (1934).
GENERAL LITERATURE. Eusebius, *Hist. Eccl.*; B. F. Westcott in *DCB*, s.v.; C. Bigg, *The Christian Platonists of Alexandria* (1886, revised 1913); O. Bardenhewer, *Geschichte der altkirchlichen Literatur* (ii², 1914), 40 ff.; H. Chadwick, *Early Christianity and the Classical Tradition* (1966). B. J. Kidd, *A History of the Church to A.D. 461* (1922), i, ch. 15.

**CLEMENT** of Rome, author of epistle (c. A.D. 96) from the Roman church rebuking the Corinthian church for arbitrarily deposing clergy. The plea for order sets many Hellenistic themes in a biblical framework, and expresses a positive attitude to the Empire.

Of the numerous works later attributed to Clement, the chief are (*a*) the second epistle, a mid second-century sermon of uncertain origin; (*b*) the Clementine Romance about Peter's travels and conflicts with Simon Magus, using themes from Hellenistic novels similar to Plautus' *Menaechmi* and the *Comedy of Errors*; the original, probably written c. 200, is buried in two widely divergent fourth-century recensions with a complex mutual relation, viz. *Homilies* (Greek) and *Recognitions* (Syriac and Rufinus' Latin); (*c*) *Apostolic Constitutions*, eight books of law and liturgy, c. 375; book 7 contains Hellenistic-Jewish prayers.

EPISTLES. Annotated ed. J. B. Lightfoot (1890). B. Altaner, *Patrology* (1960), 99 ff.; W. Jaeger, *Early Christianity and Greek Paideia* (1962), 12 ff. H. C.

**CLEOBIS** and **BITON**, the two Argive brothers mentioned by Solon to Croesus, in Herodotus' story (1. 31), as among the happiest of mortals. Their mother, presumably as Cicero says (*Tusc.* 1. 47) a priestess of Hera, found that her oxen were not brought in time for a festival, and they drew her car the 45 stades to the temple. She prayed to the goddess to grant them the greatest boon possible for mortals, and Hera caused them to die while they slept in the temple. The Argives honoured them with statues at Delphi, which have been discovered, their identity being ensured by an inscription.

*SIG* 5 *Supp. Epigr.* 3. 395. Cf. Ch. Picard, *Rev. Hist. Rel.* 1927, 365 ff. W. K. C. G.

**CLEOMEDES** (probably c. A.D. 150–200), astronomer, author of a popular work Κυκλικὴ θεωρία μετεώρων (*De Motu Circulari Corporum Caelestium*), largely founded on Posidonius, but with a certain number of optical discoveries which appear to be original.

Ed. H. Ziegler (1891). W. D. R.

**CLEOMENES** (1) **I** (reigned c. 519–490 B.C.), an Agiad king of Sparta, the son of Anaxandridas by his second wife. He pursued an adventurous and at times unscrupulous policy designed to extend and strengthen the Peloponnesian League (q.v.) and crush Argos (aims perhaps inherited from Chilon). He sought to embroil Athens with Thebes by referring the request of the Plataeans for help against Thebes to Athens (probably in 519, Thuc. 3. 68); later to attach her to the League by expelling the tyrant Hippias in 510, by interfering on behalf of Isagoras against Cleisthenes (q.v. 1) in 508, and by trying to organize two full-scale League expeditions (c. 506 and 504), the first to restore Isagoras, the second to restore Hippias. Both were frustrated by the obstruction of the Corinthians and of his colleague Demaratus (q.v.). The Argive army was ruthlessly crushed at Sepeia (near Tiryns, c. 494).

But he disliked distant commitments (he refused to interfere in the affairs of Samos (c. 515), or to support the Ionian Revolt (499)) and showed no certain awareness of the Persian danger before 491 when his attempt to punish Aegina for Medism was thwarted by Demaratus. He persuaded the Delphic Oracle to declare Demaratus illegitimate and had him deposed but the intrigue was exposed and he fled to stir up revolt among the Arcadians. Recalled to Sparta, he soon met a violent end. According to Herodotus he killed himself in a fit of insanity.

Herodotus (5. 39 ff.) may underrate Cleomenes; see J. Wells, *Studies in Herodotus* (1923), 74 ff.; G. L. Huxley, *Early Sparta* (1962), chs. 6 and 7. W. G. F

**CLEOMENES** (2) **III** (c. 260–219 B.C.), son of Leonidas, king of Sparta, imbibed ideals of social revolution from his wife Agiatis, Agis IV's widow. Becoming king in 235, he first moved in 229, when he annexed Tegea, Mantinea, Orchomenus, and Caphyae from Aetolia. Having provoked Achaea into war (228), he secured victories at Mt. Lycaeus and Ladoceia (227); he now seized despotic power at home (winter 227–226) and set up a 'Lycurgan' regime, cancelling debts, dividing up land, and restocking the citizen body from *perioeci* and metics. After his capture of Mantinea and victory at Hecatombaeum, a peace conference was called, but postponed owing to his illness; but meanwhile Aratus had opened negotiations with Antigonus III and war recommenced. By seizing Argos (225) and besieging Corinth (224) Cleomenes threatened to shatter the Achaean League; but Antigonus reached the Isthmus, Argos revolted, and Cleomenes was reduced to the defensive. In winter 223 he took Megalopolis; but after a decisive defeat at Sellasia (July 222) he fled to his patron Euergetes in Egypt. Imprisoned by Euergetes' successor, he broke out, tried in vain to stir up revolution in Alexandria, and committed suicide (winter 220–219).

An idealist and a nationalist, Cleomenes used social revolution as the tool of Spartan expansion. He was able to inspire allegiance, and his ideals lived on after him; but he devised no means of securing his gains.

Polyb. 2. 45–70; Plut. *Cleomenes, Aratus*. F. W. Walbank, *Aratos of Sicyon* (1933); E. Gabba, *Athenaeum* 1957; T. W. Africa, *Phylarchus and the Spartan Revolution* (U.S.A. 1961); B. Shimron, *Hist.* 1964. F. W. W.

**CLEOMENES** (3) of Naucratis was appointed financial manager of Egypt and administrative chief of the eastern Delta district by Alexander in 332–331 B.C., and was also entrusted with the completion of Alexandria. He made himself satrap of the whole of Egypt after a few years without the consent of Alexander, but was afterwards recognized and pardoned by him. Cleomenes became *hyparchos* of Egypt, with Ptolemy I as satrap, in 322–321; but the future king of Egypt brought serious charges against him, and executed him afterwards. The tricks with which Cleomenes exploited Egypt's wealth nd collected 8,000 talents are described in the second book of Ps.-Aristotle's *Oeconomica*.

A. M. Andreades, *BCH* 1929, 1 f.; F. M. Heichelheim, s.v. 'Sitos' in *PW*, Suppl. vi. 863 f.; G. Mickwitz, *Vierteljahrschrift für Soz.-und Wirtschaftsgesch.* 1939, 11 f.; F. Stähelin, s.v. 'Kleomenes' in *PW*. B. A. van Groningen, *Aristote, Le second livre de l'Économique* (Leyden, 1933), 183 ff. (commentary). F. M. H.

**CLEON**, Athenian politician, the son of a rich tanner. His first-known action in politics was to attack Pericles in 431 and 430; he succeeded him as 'leader of the people'. In 427 he proposed the decree (rescinded next day) to execute all the men of Mytilene after the suppression of its revolt. In 426 he attacked the *Babylonians* of Aristophanes as a libel on the State. In 425, after the Athenian victory at Pylos (q.v.), he frustrated the Spartan peace proposals, and later accused the generals in charge of the siege of Sphacteria of incompetence. Nicias (q.v. 1) offered to resign the command to him, and he was compelled to take it; with the help of Demosthenes (q.v. 1), the general on the spot, he was completely successful, forcing the Spartans to surrender. He doubtless approved, if he cannot be shown to have originated, the measure now passed greatly increasing the tribute paid by the allied states, and he was certainly responsible, in the same year, for an increase of the dicasts' pay from two to three obols. In 423 he proposed the decree for the destruction of Scione and the execution of all its citizens. In the late summer of 422, as *strategos*, he led an expedition to the Thraceward area, and recovered Torone and Galepsus, but failed in an attack on Stagira and was defeated by Brasidas before Amphipolis and killed.

We have a vivid picture of Cleon in Thucydides and Aristophanes. Both were clearly prejudiced against him; but in the absence of independent witnesses we cannot do much to correct the picture. Beyond doubt he was an effective, if vulgar and unscrupulous, speaker, and was vehement in his pursuit of power and glory for Athens; that he was corrupt is perhaps unlikely: but there is little to show that he was a far-sighted statesman or able administrator; as to his generalship, the undisputed facts include both successes and failures. By the fourth-century orators he was spoken of with respect; in the later history he is the conventional vulgar demagogue.

A. W. Gomme, 'Ελληνικά 1954, 1 ff. = *More Essays in Greek History and Literature* (1962), 112 ff.; M. L. Paladini, *Hist.* 1958, 48 ff.; A. G. Woodhead, *Mnemos.* 1960, 289 ff.; A. Andrewes, *Phoenix* 1962, 64 ff. A. W. G.; T. J. C.

**CLEONIDES** (beginning of 2nd c. A.D.), author of an Εἰσαγωγὴ ἁρμονική, one of the best sources for the harmonic theory of Aristoxenus (q.v.) of Tarentum.

Ed. C. Jan, *Musici Scriptores Graeci* (1895), 167–207, and H. Menge, *Euclidis Opera* 8 (1916), 186. W. D. R.

**CLEONYMUS** (fl. 305–270 B.C.), younger son of Cleomenes II, guardian to his nephew Areus, who ascended the Spartan throne in 309–308. In 303–302, answering a Tarentine appeal with 5,000 mercenaries, he forced the Lucanians to make peace, annexed Metapontum, and seized Corcyra. When Tarentum revolted he returned to Italy, but was defeated, and soon lost Corcyra. In 293 he helped Boeotia ineffectively against Demetrius; in 279 he seized Troezen, and attacked Messene and Megalopolis. Banished from Sparta c. 275 (Plut. *Pyrrh.* 26), he last appears accompanying Pyrrhus' Laconian invasion (272). Violent, and soured by missing the throne, he was a constant foe of the Antigonids.

Beloch, *Griech. Gesch.* iv; P. Meloni, *Giorn. ital. di fil.* 1950. F. W. W.

**CLEOPATRA I** (c. 215–176 B.C.), daughter of Antiochus III and Laodice. She married Ptolemy V in 193 and ruled after her husband's death in 180 as regent for her young son, Ptolemy VI, but died four years later.

W. Otto, *Zur Gesch. Zeit des 6 Ptol.* (Bayer. Abh. N.F. 11 (1934)), 23 f. F. M. H.

**CLEOPATRA II**, daughter of Ptolemy V and Cleopatra I, was born between 185 and 180 B.C. She married her brother, Ptolemy VI, c. 175–174. Later she was co-regent with him and his brother Ptolemy VIII from 170 until Ptolemy VI was restored as sole ruler. After his death in 146 Cleopatra's further life was a continuous struggle for power against her brother Ptolemy VIII by open war (short regency for Ptolemy VII in 146, rebellion 132–124) or diplomacy (marriage to Ptolemy VIII in 144, conciliation in 124). She survived her second husband, but died in 116 or 115. The details of the later stages of Cleopatra's career are very obscure: see especially W. Otto and H. Bengtson, *zur Geschichte des Niederganges des Ptolemäerreiches* (Bayer. Abh. N.F. 17, 1938), *passim*, which contains elaborate reconstructions of this period of Ptolemaic history, based to a considerable extent on the appearance and disappearance of Cleopatra II and III from the dating-prescripts of Greek and demotic papyri. F. M. H.

**CLEOPATRA III**, daughter of Ptolemy VI and Cleopatra II. Ptolemy VIII seduced and married her in 142 B.C., and made her co-regent, as a counterweight against her mother's influence. After his death in 116 her eldest son, Ptolemy IX, was made co-regent against her will. She incited unsuccessful rebellions in 110 and 108, but succeeded in 107 in giving her second son, Ptolemy X, his brother's throne. Her last years were filled with quarrels with this second son, who was accused by many of matricide. *See* CLEOPATRA II *and* PTOLEMY (1). F. M. H.

**CLEOPATRA VII** (*PW* 20), daughter of Ptolemy XII, born in 69 B.C., became joint-ruler of Egypt with Ptolemy XIII in 51. In 49 they supplied Cn. Pompeius (q.v. 5) with ships, men, and corn for his father's forces. Expelled in 48 by Ptolemy's party, she was reinstated by Caesar, who, after defeating her opponents, made Ptolemy XIV her new consort and departed early in 47 leaving three legions for her support. In the summer she bore a son whom she called Ptolemy Caesar, asserting that Caesar was his father. In 46, on his invitation, she came to Rome with her son and husband, returning to Egypt after his murder. Ptolemy XIV presently dying, supposedly poisoned by her order, she made her son co-ruler in his place.

In 42 her efforts to aid the Caesarians were thwarted by Cassius (q.v. 6) and by contrary winds. Summoned by Antony to Tarsus in 41 she vindicated her conduct and secured the death of her sister Arsinoe. Antony spent the winter in Alexandria, and after his departure she bore him twins: we cannot say if either yet contemplated a lasting association.

In 37 he summoned her to Antioch and they joined in a permanent political and personal alliance. Antony recognized the twins, and named them Alexander Helios and Cleopatra Selene; a third child born in 36 was called Ptolemy Philadelphus. In 48 Caesar had restored Cyprus to Egypt, and Antony now added further portions of the old Ptolemaic Empire including Cyrenaica. In return Cleopatra was to back him and his projects with the resources of Egypt. In 35 she gave money and stores to repair the losses of his Parthian expedition. Antony's rebuff of Octavia (q.v. 2) was probably due more to his resentment against Octavian and sense of the value of Cleopatra's support than to any special pressure exerted by her: his treatment of Herod (q.v. 1) shows there were limits to her influence.

In 34 they staged at Alexandria the so-called 'Donations', in which all the lands ruled by Alexander from the Hellespont to the Indus were nominally apportioned between Cleopatra and her children. She and Ptolemy Caesar were hailed not only as rulers of Egypt and Cyprus but as 'Queen of Kings' and 'King of Kings', i.e. overlords of this whole Empire; Alexander Helios became king east and Ptolemy Philadelphus west of the Euphrates, and Cleopatra Selene queen of Cyrenaica. Though much of this territory remained unconquered or governed by client-kings and Antony's lieutenants, the vision was attractive to the Greek-speaking world and was elaborated with the aid of religious and national symbolism.

The real extent of the threat to the integrity of the Roman Empire and to Octavian is hard to recover: at all events Cleopatra was a convenient focus for Octavian's propaganda and in 32 Rome declared war on her alone. She probably did not betray Antony at Actium and afterwards did her best to delay the inevitable end: but after his suicide she had to follow suit (10 Aug. 30) to avoid figuring in Octavian's triumph. She may have chosen death by the asp because it was a royal symbol.

Cleopatra was attractive rather than beautiful, with a lively temperament and great charm of speech. She was well-educated; and unlike her predecessors could speak Egyptian, besides numerous other tongues. She cared for her subjects' material welfare, entered into their religious beliefs, and was remembered by them with affection. Her image has been distorted by Roman propaganda and the subsequent tradition. She was, of course, not Egyptian, but Macedonian. She was admittedly ruthless towards her family, in the true Ptolemaic tradition. But she was not sexually lax, associating, to our knowledge, only with Caesar and Antony. Nor is it likely that she was concerned in this association merely to exploit sex for political ends. Ambitious for Egypt and for herself as Egypt's queen she certainly was—this was her crime in Roman eyes; and she sought to achieve her aims with their help; but this does not prove that she felt no affection or loyalty towards them; with men of their stamp, the contrary is probable, and is in some measure indicated by the evidence.

See also ACTIUM, ANTONIUS (4), AUGUSTUS, CAESAR (1), CAESARION, OCTAVIA (2), and PTOLEMY (XII–XV).

H. Volkmann, *Cleopatra* (1958), with an account of the sources and a full bibliography; J. G. Griffiths, *JEgArch.* 1961, 113 ff.; T. C. Skeat, ibid. 1962, 100 ff. Iconography: G. M. A. Richter, *The Portraits of the Greeks*, (1965), 269.          . T. J. C.

**CLEOPHON** (1), Athenian politician. He was a lyremaker, son of Cleippides, *strategos* in 429/8, apparently by a Thracian wife. He was already a public figure at the time of the ostracism of Hyperbolus (q.v.), and became 'leader of the people' after the restoration of democratic rule in 410 B.C. He introduced the διωβελία, a dole of two obols a day, the allotment of which is unknown. He apparently managed Athenian finances between 410 and 406; he was honest and died poor, and seems to have been efficient. But he was as violent in his manner as Cleon. He attacked both Critias and Alcibiades; and prevented the peace terms offered by Sparta after Cyzicus in 410 from being accepted, and again after Aegospotami in 405. He was prosecuted and condemned to death in 404.

E. Vanderpool, *Hesp.* 1952, 114 f.          A. W. G.; T. J. C.

**CLEOPHON** (2), Athenian tragic poet of whose plays some titles (*Suda*, s.v.) but no fragments survive. Aristotle mentions his unidealized characters (*Poet.* 2), his prosaic style (ibid. 22; *Rh.* 3. 7), and illustrates from him a method of evading a question (*Soph. El.* 15).

A. W. P.-C.

**CLERUCHY** (κληρουχία), a special sort of Greek colony in which the settlers kept their original citizenship and did not form an independent community. The term is confined to certain Athenian settlements founded on conquered territory (Greek and barbarian) from the end of the sixth century, especially during the Empire. It is often difficult to decide whether a settlement of the fifth century is a cleruchy, as ancient authors do not always distinguish cleruchies from other colonies. The chief certain or probable cleruchies down to the end of the fifth century are Chalcis (506, again *c.* 446), Naxos, Andros, the Chersonese Lemnos, and Imbros (*c.* 450), Hestiaea (*c.* 446), Aegina (431), Lesbos (427), Melos (416). (Definite evidence is lacking for an early cleruchy as such on Salamis, which seems to have had a unique position. The status of Scyros in the fifth century is uncertain.) These cleruchies did not survive Athens' defeat in 404. Later cleruchies are Lemnos, Imbros, and Scyros (from the early fourth century till the Roman period, with intervals), Samos (*c.* 361–322), Potidaea (361–356), Chersonese (353/2–338).

The numbers in a cleruchy varied from 4,000 (Chalcis) to 250 (Andros). Each settler (κληροῦχος) received an allotment (κλῆρος) which maintained him as a *zeugites* (q.v.). The theory, however, that the Athenians in this way swelled the numbers of hoplites at Athens conflicts with definite evidence that the cleruchs resided in the cleruchies, which may sometimes have served the purpose of garrisons in addition to providing land for the poor. As Athenian citizens cleruchs were liable for military service, paid war-tax (*eisphora*), and took part in religious activity at Athens. Distance, however, forced them to create organs for local self-government on the Athenian model, boule, ecclesia, and magistrates. In the fourth century at least cleruchies were supervised by officials sent out from Athens.

A. J. Graham, *Colony and Mother City in Ancient Greece* (1964), 166 ff.          A. J. G.

**CLIENS.** In early Rome a client was a free man who entrusted himself to another and received protection in return. In the late Republic and early Empire, clientship was essentially a social hereditary status consecrated by usage and reflected in the law. The rules of the law were far more binding for the special case of the freedman, who was *ipso facto* 'cliens' of his former owner (see FREEDMEN). The ordinary client might receive daily food, often converted into money (*sportula*) or assistance in the courts. In return he helped his patron in his political and private life, and showed him respect, especially by greeting him in the morning. Client and patron could not bear witness against one another, or at least the evidence could not be enforced. Dionysius (*Ant. Rom.* 2. 9–10) records other rules, many of which were out of use or are mere conjectures, for instance that the client must try to ransom his patron.

The Twelve Tables recognized the tie of clientship: 'patronus si clienti fraudem fecerit sacer esto' (8. 21).

In imperial times the client was practically confused with the parasite. Martial describes himself as a client. Clients were called *salutatores* because of their duty of daily salutation and *togati* because custom compelled them to wear the toga, by that time obsolescent.

In the provinces (especially in Gaul) the Roman clientship superimposed itself on pre-existing local forms of social ties. It is a controversial point whether the relations of certain vanquished states with Rome are to be described as clientship. But there is little doubt that Roman individuals and families built up large *clientelae* among foreigners: whole communities could become clients.

Mommsen, *Röm. Forsch.* i. 354 ff.; id., *Röm. Staatsr.* iii. 54 ff.; M. Gelzer, *Die Nobilität aus d. röm. Republik* (1912); L. Friedländer, *Darstellungen aus d. Sittengeschichte Roms* i⁹ (1919), 223 ff.; ii. 230 ff.; J. Carcopino, *Daily Life in Ancient Rome* (1941), 171 ff.; M. Lemosse, *RIDA* 1949, 37 ff.; E. Badian *Foreign Clientelae* (1958). See also PATRONUS.          A. M.

**CLIENT KINGS.** The first king to establish close and friendly contact with Rome was Hieron II (q.v.). By then Rome had developed the habit of expecting spontaneous subordination from her *socii* (q.v.) in return for protection: Roman nobles naturally saw a friendly relationship between strong and weak as one between patrons and clients (*see* CLIENS). Hieron preserved freedom in internal and (to some extent) in foreign affairs by adapting himself to this, supporting Rome in her wars and refusing to treat with her enemies (cf. Polyb. 1. 16. 10 f.). Demetrius (q.v. 7), as regent of Illyria, was less wise: taking his freedom too literally, he lapsed into 'ingratitude' and was attacked and deposed. These cases at once marked out the Roman attitude to client rulers, and they can be paralleled right down to, e.g., Deiotarus and Ariovistus (qq.v.) respectively. In return for the *beneficia* of freedom and protection (about which, however, she grew less conscientious), Rome expected 'free' allies (including kings) to remain *in officio*.

During the second century B.C. contact with rulers ranging from Hellenistic monarchs to Spanish chieftains demonstrated the essential weakness of monarchic states: however powerful in appearance, they were at the mercy of pretenders and succession troubles. This was freely exploited by the Senate where convenient, e.g. in the cases of Macedonia and Pergamum. To most kings, being recognized as king (*rex appellari*) and called 'friend and ally' by the Senate made the difference between security and anarchy. Once recognized, a king was normally as free as his *de facto* strength permitted; this would depend on his freedom from dynastic troubles, good relations with his neighbours, and distance from Rome. Though jealous of great royal power, the Senate (aware of its short duration) did not normally use more than diplomacy against suspect rulers: it took a long time to decide on war even against Jugurtha (q.v.). But open defiance was not tolerated. The result of this system was that the Republic knew no real frontiers: beyond the provinces (and within them) a penumbra of influence extended as far as distance and diplomacy would permit (*see*, e.g., ATTALUS II, MASINISSA, PHARNACES I). This inability to see kings otherwise than as clients embroiled Rome in trouble with Parthia (q.v.), which had no aggressive intentions, but was beyond the range of even effective diplomatic power: relations remained ambiguous, between equality and clientship, as long as the kingdom lasted.

In the final convulsions of the Republic, astute client kings acquired great power (*see* CLEOPATRA VII, JUBA I). But Augustus re-established them as *de facto* vassals, even making them liable to trial in Rome and deposition; he continued republican policy in using them to govern territory too difficult to administer directly; and he would annex their states when the time seemed ripe (*see* GALATIA, HEROD I), which the Republic (except in its final phase) had never claimed the right to do. Later Emperors differed in their policies; but the tendency was to absorb kingdoms within what came to be recognized as the frontiers of the Empire, while using the traditional techniques of diplomatic intervention whenever possible (e.g. in Parthia and Germany) beyond the frontiers. (See also names of individual kings and countries.)

P. C. Sands, *The Client Princes of the Roman Empire under the Republic* (1908); T. Yoshimura, *Hist.* 1961, 473 ff. (military contribution).  E. B.

**CLITOMACHUS** (187/6–110/09 B.C.), a Carthaginian, originally named Hasdrubal, migrated to Athens at the age of 24, and at 28 became the pupil of the sceptical Carneades (q.v.), founder of the 'New Academy'. From 140/139 he conducted his own school in the Palladium, but returned in 129/8 with many followers to the Academy, of which he became head two years later (*Acad. index Herc.* cols. 24, 30).

According to Diog. L. 4. 67 he wrote over 400 books; Sextus Empiricus *Math.* 9. 1 says that he was unnecessarily lengthy because he argued against the dogmatists from their own premisses. None of his work survives in its original form, but the arguments of Carneades, who left no writings, were preserved mainly by way of his efforts to record them. More than some other pupils he emphasized the refusal of Carneades to commit himself. His works included Περὶ ἐποχῆς (*On withholding assent*, Cic. *Luc.* 98), Περὶ αἱρεσέων (*On philosophical sects*, Diog. L. 2. 22), and a *Consolation*, addressed to the Carthaginians on their city's destruction (Cic. *Tusc.* 3. 54); he dedicated other books to the Romans L. Censorinus and Lucilius the poet.  F. H. S.

**CLITUMNUS,** a river near Trebiae in Umbria, famous for the white sacrificial kine on its banks (Verg. *G.* 2. 146). It flowed into the Tinia, and subsequently into the Tiber. Shrines of the personified Clitumnus and other deities adorned its source (called *Sacraria* in the Itineraries), attracting numerous tourists (Pliny, *Ep.* 8. 8; Suet. *Cal.* 43).  E. T. S.

**CLOACA MAXIMA,** originally an open water-course, later canalized, draining north-east Rome from the Argiletum to the Tiber by way of the Forum Romanum and Velabrum. Tradition ascribed its regulation to Tarquinius Superbus, and branch drains of the fifth century B.C. do exist. Much of the existing sewer, nowhere older than *c.* 200 B.C., is due to M. Vipsanius Agrippa in 33 B.C.

Nash, *Pict. Dict. Rome* i, 258 ff.  I. A. R.

**CLOATIUS VERUS,** Augustan lexicographer and grammarian, who wrote on the meanings of Greek words and on derivations of Latin words from Greek (cf. Gell. 16. 12, Macrob. *Sat.* 3. 19. 2). He may be the 'Cloatius' cited six times by Verrius Flaccus.  J. F. M.

**CLOCKS.** The hours (ὧραι, *horae*, not in the modern sense till Aristotle; δυώδεκα μέρεα τῆς ἡμέρης, Hdt. 2. 109. 3, but see J. Enoch Powell, *CR* 1940, 69 f.) were told in antiquity (1) by the sundial, ὡρολόγιον or -εῖον, *solarium*, consisting of a pointer, γνώμων, casting its shadow (hence the instrument is sometimes called σκιοθήρας) upon a convex surface, σκάφη (also πόλος, as being a sort of model of the sky) or (less commonly) a flat one. The inventor was Anaximander (Favorinus ap. Diog. Laert. 2. 1; Pliny, *HN* 2. 187 says Anaximenes), and the idea itself Babylonian (Hdt. loc. cit.). (2) By the water-clock, κλεψύδρα, *clepsydra*, ὑδροσκοπεῖον, consisting of (*a*) a vessel from which water flowed through a small orifice, (*b*) a graduated container into which the water flowed. But if the water-level in (*a*) was allowed to grow lower, the rate of flow would decrease; hence it was necessary either to keep the level in (*a*) constant or in some other way to compensate for the decrease. See Heron of Alexandria, vol. 1, 506. 23 Schmidt (Teubner, 1899), and the elaborate clock of Ctesibius (Vitruvius, *De arch.* 9. 8. 2 ff.). Ordinary clocks were, however, anything but accurate (Seneca, *Apocol.* 2. 2).

Convenient assemblage of facts in A. Rehm, *PW*, s.v. 'Horologium'. Cf. W. Kubitschek, *Grundriss der antiken Zeitrechnung* (1928), 188 ff.  H. J. R.

**CLODIA** (*PW* 66), second of the three sisters of P. Clodius (q.v. 1), born *c.* 95 B.C., had married her first cousin Metellus (q.v. 9) Celer by 62 (Cic. *Fam.* 5. 2. 6). Her bitter enemy Cicero (but gossip said she had once offered him marriage, Plut. *Cic.* 29) paints a vivid picture of her in his Letters from 60 B.C. onwards, and above all in his *Pro Caelio* of Apr. 56. Her affair with Catullus (q.v. 1—the identification with Lesbia is practically certain) began before the death of Metellus in 59, which Clodia was said to have caused by poison: by the end of that year Caelius (q.v.) was her lover. After the Caelius case her political importance ceases, but she may have been still alive in 45 (Cic. *Att.* 13. 38. 3, etc.). For bibliography *see* CAELIUS.                                         G. E. F. C.

**CLODIUS** (1, *PW* 48) **PULCHER,** PUBLIUS, youngest of six children of Ap. Claudius (10) Pulcher, was born *c.* 92 B.C. (since quaestor in 61). In 68 he corrupted the troops of his brother-in-law Lucullus (q.v. 2). During the next years he was apparently friendly with Cicero (Plut. *Cic.* 29), though accused of collusion in his prosecution of Catiline in 65. But in May 61 Cicero gave damaging evidence against him when he was on trial for appearing in women's clothes at the Bona Dea festival the previous December (*see* CAESAR 1): however, Clodius was narrowly acquitted by a jury bribed by Crassus. Next year, on returning from his quaestorian province of Sicily, he sought transference into a plebeian *gens*: this was at first resisted, but in Mar. 59 Caesar as *pontifex maximus* presided over *comitia curiata* at which the 'adoption' was ratified, and Clodius was elected tribune for 58. His measures included free corn for the *plebs*, restoration of *collegia*, repeal or modification of the *Leges Aelia et Fufia* (*see* LEX, LEGES), grant of new provinces to the consuls Gabinius (q.v. 2) and Piso (q.v. 5), bills ensuring the exile of Cicero (who departed in late March), the dispatch of Cato (q.v. 5) to Cyprus, and grant of title of king and control of Pessinus to Brogitarus ruler of the Galatian Trocmi. Clodius then turned against Pompey, allowing the escape of the Armenian prince Tigranes, threatening Pompey's life, and probably (Cic. *Dom.* 40, *Har. Resp.* 48) suggesting repeal of the *Lex Iulia Agraria* (*see* CAESAR 1). These attacks were continued in 57, when they were especially related to the question of Cicero's recall, and in the early part of Clodius' aedileship in 56; but after Luca his power to disrupt the 'Triumvirate' was weakened, though he continued to control large sections of the urban mob (*see also* MILO). He stood for the praetorship of 52, but owing to rioting the elections had not been held when he was murdered by Milo on 18 Jan. of that year. His clients among the *plebs* burned the Senate House as his pyre.

Clodius, who like two of his sisters used the 'popular' spelling of his name, probably saw the tribunate as a vital step in his political career: revenge on Cicero need not have been either his main aim in seeking *traductio in plebem*, nor (despite Cic. *Dom.* 41, *Sest.* 16) Caesar's aim in granting it. Moreover, the view that Caesar was at any time his patron seems misconceived. In 58–56 he may certainly have been allied with Crassus; but he was surely both opportunist and independent, for before as well as after Luca he was friendly with various *optimates* (Cic. *Fam.* 1. 9. 10, 19), and in 53 he was supporting the candidates of Pompey (Asconius, 26. 42). The one consistent motif is his courting of the *plebs urbana*.

The daughter of his marriage to Fulvia (q.v., later wife to Mark Antony) was momentarily married to Augustus (q.v.) in 42.

*See on* CAESAR (1), and add L. G. Pocock, 'Clodius and the Acts of Caesar', *CQ* 1924; E. Manni, 'L'Utopia di Clodio', *Riv. Fil.* 1940; E. S. Gruen *Phoenix* 1966, 120 ff.; R. G. M. Nisbet, ed. (1961) of Cic. *In Pisonem.* Cic. *De Domo* (ed. R. G. Nisbet, 1939), is an important but exceedingly complex source for the years 59–57.    G. E. F. C.

**CLODIUS** (2, *PW* 38) **MACER,** LUCIUS, *legatus* in Africa in A.D. 68, revolted from Nero and cut off the corn-supply of Rome. Though inspired by messages from

Galba (q.v. 1), he never recognized him; instead he called himself propraetor, and raised a new legion I Macriana liberatrix. Galba had him executed in October.

P. Romanelli, *Storia delle province romane dell'Africa* (1959), 279 ff.                                     A. M.; G. E. F. C.

**CLODIUS** (3, *PW* 52.) **QUIRINALIS,** PUBLIUS, from Arelate in Gaul, taught rhetoric in the Neronian age.

Schanz–Hosius, § 480.

**CLODIUS** (4, *PW* 17) **ALBINUS,** DECIMUS, belonged to a noble family. After distinguished military service in Dacia and Germany he was at the time of Commodus' death governor of Britain. As a potential candidate for the principate he was at first placated by Septimius Severus with the title of Caesar, but after Niger's death came into conflict with Septimius, who wished the imperial power to be confined to his own family. In reply Albinus was saluted Augustus by his army, and in A.D. 196 he crossed to Gaul in the vain hope of securing the support of the German legions before marching on Rome. He was killed in a battle near Lugdunum in 197.

Herodian 2. 15, 3. 7–8; Dio Cassius, bk. 73; *B.M. Coins, Rom. Emp.* v. lxxvii ff.; J. Balty, *Essai d'iconographie de l'empereur Clodius Albinus* (1966).                          H. M. D. P.; B. H. W.

**CLOELIA,** a Roman girl given as hostage to Porsenna (q.v.). She escaped across the Tiber to Rome, by swimming or on horseback, but was handed back to Porsenna who, admiring her bravery, freed her and other hostages. An equestrian statue on the Via Sacra later celebrated her exploit. Critics who dismiss the story as legend believe that the statue was dedicated to a goddess (Venus Equestris?) and that later Romans wrongly associated it with Cloelia.

Cf. Ogilvie, *Comm. Livy 1–5,* on Livy 2. 13.     H. H. S.

**CLUBS, GREEK.** The clubs here discussed may be defined as voluntary associations of persons more or less permanently organized for the pursuit of a common end, and so distinguishable both from the State and its component elements on the one hand, and on the other from temporary unions for transitory purposes. Despite the large number and great popularity of clubs in the Greek world, both in the Hellenistic and in the Greco-Roman period, literature makes surprisingly few references to them, and the available evidence consists almost entirely of inscriptions and, in the case of Egypt, papyri. These provide a picture which, if incomplete, is at least vivid and detailed.

2. Greek clubs, sacred and secular, are attested as early as the time of Solon, one of whose laws, quoted by Gaius (*Dig.* 47. 22. 4), gave legal validity to their regulations, unless they were contrary to the laws of the State; and we hear of political clubs (ἑταιρίαι) at Athens in the fifth century B.C. (Thuc. 3. 82; 8. 54; 65). In the classical period the societies known to us are mostly religious, carrying on the cult of some hero or god not yet recognized by the State, such as the votaries (ὀργεῶνες) of Amynus, Asclepius, and Dexion, the heroized Sophocles. With the close of Greek freedom, clubs become much more frequent and varied, and though many of them have religious names and exercise primarily religious functions, their social and economic aspects become increasingly prominent and some of them are purely secular. They are found throughout the Greco-Roman world, but are specially common in the cosmopolitan trade-centres such as Piraeus, Delos, and Rhodes, in Egypt, and in the flourishing cities of Asia Minor, and they appear to have played a valuable role in uniting in a common religious and social activity diverse elements of the population—men and women, slaves and free

tizens and aliens, Greeks and 'barbarians'. On the titles and aims of these guilds, their cults and festivals, their social and economic aspects, their membership and officials, their organization and finance, much light has been thrown by inscriptions, fully discussed by F. Poland (see below).

3. From the multifarious societies so revealed, incapable of a wholly satisfactory classification, three groups may be singled out for mention.

(a) Among the religious guilds a leading place is taken by those of the Dionysiac artistes (οἱ περὶ τὸν Διόνυσον τεχνῖται), which devoted themselves to the promotion of music and the drama. The earliest and most prominent of these was the Attic σύνοδος, founded probably in the early third century B.C. (though some scholars assign it to the late fifth) and traceable down to the close of the Roman Republic. Slightly later and less influential was the Isthmian and Nemean κοινόν, a federation of several local σύνοδοι with its centre at Thebes and branches at Argos, Chalcis, and elsewhere. To the third century belongs a similar κοινόν in Asia Minor, οἱ ἐπ' Ἰωνίας καὶ Ἑλλησπόντου, with Teos as its original centre, favoured by the Attalid kings, while in Egypt and Cyprus a guild of τεχνῖται flourished under the patronage of the Ptolemies. Under the Empire further titles and privileges were showered, especially by Hadrian, on the σύνοδος, a federal reorganization of the Dionysiac guilds, ἡ ἀπὸ τῆς οἰκουμένης περὶ τὸν Διόνυσον τεχνῖται, the existence of which is last attested in A.D. 291.

(b) In various cities wholesale merchants (ἔμποροι) formed associations of their own (Poland, 107 ff.), and in Athens they combined, for some purposes at least, with the shippers (ναύκληροι). In the second century B.C. two vigorous and wealthy societies, in which these two elements unite with the warehousemen (ἐγδοχεῖς), meet us on the island of Delos, the Heracleïstae of Tyre and the Poseidoniastae of Berytus (W. A. Laidlaw, History of Delos (1933), 212 ff.); the large and well-appointed clubhouse of the latter, which apparently served religious, social, and commercial ends, has been completely excavated (C. Picard, Explor. archéol. de Délos, vi, 1921).

(c) Numerous guilds, some of which probably date from the classical period, are composed of fellow workers in the same craft, industry, or trade, such as doctors, bankers, architects, producers of woollen or linen goods, dyers, fullers, launderers, tanners, cobblers, workers in metal, stone, and clay, builders, carpenters, farmers, gardeners, fishers, bakers, pastry-cooks, barbers, embalmers, transport workers. Their main function was religious and social rather than economic; and though we hear of troubles at Ephesus in which the guilds play a leading part (Acts xix. 24 ff.; Anatolian Studies presented to W. M. Ramsay (1923), 27 ff.), their chief object was not to modify conditions of labour or to champion the interests of the workers against their employers, but to offer their members opportunities of pleasurable intercourse in leisure hours.

4. Religious feeling and observance entered deeply into every department of Greek life, and among a people with so developed a social sense religion naturally tended to be an affair of the group rather than of the individual. Hence arose one of the main incentives to the formation of associations, and such glimpses as we gain of their activities suggest that religious rites played a prominent, though rarely (except at the earliest stage) the only role therein. Deities not recognized by the State were thus worshipped by their devotees, groups of compatriots settled in some foreign city, e.g. the Phoenicians and the Egyptians resident in Delos or Piraeus, maintained their native cults, most of the club-gatherings probably opened with some religious ceremony, and we have numerous references (e.g. IG ii². 1275 = F. Sokolowski, Lois

sacrées des cités grecques (1962), 126) to the participation of the guild in the funeral rites of its members, the provision or protection of their tombs, or the perpetuation of their cult as 'heroes'. Significant also is the large proportion of guild-names (Poland, Geschichte, 33 ff.; 57 ff.) which indicate religious activities (συνθύται, θεραπευταί, θρησκευταί, μύσται, etc.) or are derived from divinities (Ἀθηναϊσταί, Ἀφροδισιασταί, Ἡρακλεϊσταί, etc.), while their officials frequently bear titles of an unmistakably religious character. 'No point', remarks Poland, 'is more important for the historical evolution of the whole phenomenon than its relation to the deity. This is far more prominent than in the case of the Roman collegia; indeed, for many associations these religious aspects are the only thing which we learn about them.' A picture of unsurpassed vividness and detail is presented by an inscription (SIG 1109 = IG ii². 1368, translated in Tod, op. cit. infra. 86 ff.) of the second half of the second century A.D., which records the proceedings, punctuated by the interjections of enthusiastic members, of a general meeting of the Athenian society of Iobacchi, followed by a verbatim text of the new statutes of the society unanimously adopted thereat. These deal with the admission and subscriptions of members, the dates of periodical meetings, the maintenance of order and the penalties imposed for any disorderly behaviour, the religious ceremonies (including a sermon and a dramatic performance by officers and members of the society) which marked the principal meetings, the celebration of any auspicious event in the life of any member, the duties and privileges of the treasurer, and the attendance of members at the funeral of any of their number. There we see the portrayal of typical club-life, the social activities of which are founded upon and suffused by a common religious interest and loyalty.

E. Ziebarth, Das griech. Vereinswesen (1896); J. Oehler, Zum griech. Vereinswesen (1905); F. Poland, Geschichte d. griech. Vereinswesens (1909); M. N. Tod, Sidelights on Greek History (1932), 69 ff. For specific aspects or regions see M. San Nicolò, Aegyptisches Vereinswesen zur Zeit der Ptolemäer u. Römer (1913–15); P. Foucart, Des associations religieuses chez les Grecs (1873); F. Poland, s.v. 'Technitae' in PW; M. Radin, Legislation of the Greeks and Romans on Corporations (1910). The decrees and laws of the Attic societies are collected in IG ii². 1249–369; those of the Delian corporations in Inscriptions de Délos, 1519–23; for a selection of inscriptions relating to clubs see SIG³ 1095–120, Michel, 961–1018; for Egyptian religious associations A. D. Nock, etc., Harv. Theol. Rev. 1936, 39 ff. M. N. T.

**CLUBS, ROMAN.** The Latin words corresponding most closely to the English 'club' are collegium and sodalicium (sodalitas). The former was the official title of the four great priestly colleges, pontifices, VIIviri epulonum, XVviri sacris faciundis, and augures, and the word had religious associations even when the object of the club was not primarily worship. Few, if any, collegia were completely secular. Some took their name from a deity or deities, e.g. Diana et Antinous (ILS 7212), Aesculapius et Hygia (ibid. 7213), Hercules (ibid. 7315, etc.), Silvanus (ibid. 7317), and their members were styled cultores. Even when their name was not associated with a god collegia often held their meetings in temples, and their clubhouse (schola) might bear the name of a divinity (ILS 7218: Schola deae Minervae Aug.). The collegia illustrate the rule that all ancient societies from the family upwards had a religious basis.

Plutarch (Numa 17) attributes to Numa the foundation of certain collegia, but it is doubtful whether many existed before the Second Punic War. Complete freedom of association seems to have prevailed down to the last century of the Republic, though the action taken by the Senate against the Bacchanales in 186 B.C. shows that the government might intervene against an objectionable club. In the Ciceronian age the collegia became involved in political action; many were suppressed in 64 B.C. and again by Caesar, after a temporary revival by Clodius. By a *Lex Iulia* (probably A.D. 7, *ILS* 4966) Augustus enacted that every club must be sanctioned by the Senate or emperor. This sanction is sometimes recorded on club inscriptions, and it undoubtedly was freely given, though the policy of different emperors varied (Trajan absolutely forbade the formation of clubs in Bithynia: Pliny, *Tra*. 34). An extant *senatus consultum* (*ILS* 7212) shows that general permission was given for burial clubs (*collegia funeraticia* or *tenuiorum*), provided that the members met only once a month for the payment of contributions. In practice these clubs engaged in social activities and dined together on certain occasions, e.g. the birthdays of benefactors. After A.D. 100 the government seems to have viewed the clubs with little suspicion.

Many *collegia* were composed of men practising the same craft or trade, e.g. smiths, clothworkers, carpenters, sailors; but there is no evidence that their object was to maintain or improve their economic conditions. In most cases they were probably in name burial clubs, while their real purpose was to foster friendliness and social life among their members. Many clubs of *iuvenes* existed mainly for sport, and associations were formed among ex-service men (*veterani*). Several lists of members survive (e.g. *ILS* 6174–6; 7225–7). These are headed by the names of the *patroni* (*ILS* 7216 f.), wealthy men, sometimes of senatorial rank, who often had made gifts to the clubs. The members bore titles recalling those borne by municipal officials. The presidents were *magistri* or *curatores* or *quinquennales* (who kept the roll of members). Below these came the *decuriones*, and then the ordinary members (*plebs*). The funds were sometimes managed by *quaestores*. In these clubs the humbler population found some compensation for their exclusion from municipal honours. The fact that at the distributions of money or food a larger share was given to the officials or even to the *patroni* implies that the object of the clubs was not primarily philanthropic, though they no doubt fostered goodwill and generosity among their members. *See also* INDUSTRY, §§ 2, 5, and 7.

The evidence is almost entirely epigraphic, though Cicero often refers to the political activity of *collegia*. See *ILS* ii. 2, ch. 15 and iii. 2. 710 ff. Th. Mommsen, *De collegiis et sodaliciis* (Kiel, 1843); J. P. Waltzing, *Étude historique sur les corporations professionelles chez les Romains* (1895 ff.); E. Kornemann, s.v. 'Collegium' in *PW*; S. Dill, *Roman Society from Nero to Marcus Aurelius* (1905), 251 ff.; E. G. Hardy, *Studies in Roman History* i (1906), 129 ff. (Christianity and the Collegia); P. W. Duff, *Personality in Roman Private Law* (1938), chs. 4–5 (see also D. Daube, *JRS* 1943, 91 ff., 1944, 125 ff.). G. H. S.

**CLUENTIUS** (*PW* 4) **HABITUS**, AULUS, of a prominent family of Larinum, in 76 B.C. charged his stepfather Oppianicus and others with attempting to poison him; they were convicted after notorious bribery on both sides. In 66 the case was reopened by Oppianicus' son, who charged Cluentius with the murder of the Elder Oppianicus. Cicero conducted the defence and, by 'throwing dust in the eyes of the jury' (as he later boasted), won his case. The true facts cannot be disentangled.

Cicero, *Pro Cluentio*. G. S. Hoenigswald, *TAPA* 1962, 109 ff. E. B.

**CLUNIA**, a town in the territory of the Spanish Arevaci and later in Roman Tarraconensis, lay 25 miles northwest of Uxama (modern *Osma*). It may have been made a colony by Sulpicius Galba (q.v. 1): a long dedication to him (*CIL* ii. 2779) comes from here, and a coin (if genuine) names the city CLVNIA SVL(picia). Destroyed by Franks and Alemanni *c*. A.D. 300, the restored town was again destroyed by Germanic tribes in the fifth century. There are many remains: e.g. of a theatre, forum, temples.

A. Vives, *La Moneda Hispanica*, iv (1924), 111 ff.; P. de Palol, *Colonia Sulpicia* (1959). H. H. S.

**CLUSIUM** (Etr. *Clevsin*-, *Chamars*; modern *Chiusi*), i the province of Siena stands above the Via Cassia at th south end of the Val di Chiana. It was one of the twelv cities of Etruria, and one of the oldest in the north-eas The earliest finds are Villanovan, and the cremation ri continued uninterrupted, the ossuaries developing in th Orientalizing period into 'canopic urns', i.e. images of th dead. One of the earliest of the numerous chambe tombs produced the François vase, and a number ar painted. From the fifth century onwards, Clusium was centre of decorative bronze-working, specializing i braziers and candlesticks; throughout its history it wa also an important centre of stone-carving. The area ha produced an exceptionally large number of Etruscan in scriptions (*CIE* 475–3306). Clusium appears to hav passed into Roman hands at a comparatively late stage *See also* PORSEN(N)A.

R. Bianchi Baniinelli, *Mon. Ant.* 1925, cols. 209 ff.; Scullar *Etr. Cities*, 151 ff.; D. Levi, *Il Museo Civico di Chiusi* (1935). D. W. R.

**CLYMENE,** name of a dozen different heroines (for on *see* CATREUS), the best known being the mother of Phae thon (q.v.), wife of Merops, king of Ethiopia. Meanin simply 'famous', it is a stopgap name, like Creus Leucippus, etc., used where there was no genealogic or other tradition. H. J.

**CLYMENUS,** (1) euphemistic title of Hades, especiall at Hermione (Paus. 2. 35. 9, cf. Lasos ap. Athen. 624 e (2) The fabulous founder of the temple there, an Argiv (Paus. ibid.). (3) Name of several other mythologic persons, the best known being the father of Harpalyc (*see* ALASTOR). Variants to the story given there are th his daughter's transformation (to an owl, in this accoun took place while she was fleeing from him (*Paradoxc graphi*, 222 Westermann, where she is called Nyct mene, apparently by confusion with a like story c Epopeus, king of Lesbos (Hyg. *Fab.* 204)), and that h killed her (ibid. 206) and himself (ibid. 242. 4, Partheniu 13). H. J.

**CLYTEMNESTRA** (*Clytaem(n)estra*, Κλυταιμ(ν)ήστρα the shorter form is better attested; *Clutāemestra*, Liviu Andronicus, trag. 11, by iambic shortening), daughter c Tyndareos, sister of Helen and the Dioscuri and wife c Agamemnon (qq.v.). For the murder of her husband *see* AGAMEMNON.

Her legend was a favourite one among post-Homeri authors, and the central interest being her infidelity an murder, all manner of motives are discovered; for i Homer she is a weakly good woman (*Od*. 3. 266), over persuaded by the energetic scoundrel Aegisthus, an 'hateful' (ibid. 310) or 'accursed' (11. 410) only in retro spect. Her sole active cruelty is to kill Cassandra (11 422). Stesichorus (fr. 17 Diehl) blames Aphrodite, wh made Tyndareos' daughters unfaithful because h had neglected her. Aeschylus (*Ag*. passim) and othe after him (but the motive may be earlier, see Pinda *Pyth*. 11. 22 ff., cf. CASSANDRA) give her a double in centive, the sacrifice of Iphigenia (q.v.), and anger a Agamemnon's infidelities, the latter a non-Homeri reason. He also makes her a strong character, the leade in the whole affair, while Aegisthus is a blusterin weakling (cf. *Od*. 3. 310, ἀνάλκιδος Αἰγίσθοιο). Sopho cles and Euripides in their *Electras* still make her th more prominent figure, but tend to increase the re lative importance of Aegisthus again; Euripides (*E.* 1105–6) makes her somewhat sorry for all that ha happened. In Aeschylus, again, she tries to resist Oreste (*Cho*. 889 ff.) and threatens him with the Erinyes (924 whom her ghost afterwards stirs up against him (*Eun* 94 ff.); in the other tragedians she merely pleads for life

Her part in other legends is small; she brings Iphigenia to Aulis (Eur. *IA* 607 ff.), and Telephus (q.v.) gets a hearing from the Greeks by acting on her advice (Hyg. *Fab.* 101. 2; ? Euripidean). Her name occasionally occurs as a common noun meaning 'adulteress' (as Quintilian, *Inst.* 8. 6. 53), or 'murderess' (see Horace, *Sat.* 1. 1. 100, where 'fortissima Tyndaridarum' stands for Clytaemnestra). *See further* ELECTRA.

In archaic and early classical art Clytemnestra is regularly shown withheld by a nurse or Talthybios from rushing with a double axe to help Aegisthus stricken by Orestes. On one vase, which may not antedate Aeschylus, this scene is balanced by a death of Agamemnon, caught in the closed shirt and killed with a sword by Aegisthus, behind whom comes Clytemnestra with the axe. She is also once shown wielding an axe to kill Cassandra.

Höfer in Roscher's *Lexikon* ii. 1230 ff. In art, Brommer, *Vasen-listen*[2], 321. See also E. Vermeule in *AJArch.* 1966, 1 ff.
H. J. R.; C. M. R.

**CNIDOS**, a Greek city founded perhaps *c.* 900 B.C., and claiming descent from Sparta, situated on a long peninsula at the south-west corner of Asia Minor. Originally set on the south coast of the peninsula, it was transferred *c.* 330 to a magnificent strategic and commercial situation at the cape. Excavations were carried out there by Newton for the British Museum in 1857–9; and the fortifications and two protected harbours are still open to view. The Cnidians were a maritime people and colonized the Lipari Is. Failing in the attempt to convert their peninsula into an island they yielded to the Persians (after 546). After the Persian wars they joined the Athenian confederacy, but they warmly espoused the Spartan cause after 413. Subjected to Ptolemaic control in the third century and perhaps Rhodian in the early second, Cnidos was a *civitas libera* under Roman rule from 129 B.C. Notable citizens were Ctesias, Eudoxus the astronomer, Sostratus (architect of the Pharos of Alexandria), and Agatharchides. Cnidos was famous for its medical school, its wines, and the Aphrodite by Praxiteles.

C. T. Newton, *Halicarnassus, Cnidus and Branchidae* (1863); G. E. Bean and J. M. Cook, 'The Cnidia', *BSA* 1952. J. M. C.

**CODEX** (legal). The earliest-known collections of imperial *constitutiones* (q.v.) were the *Codex Gregorianus* (published *c.* A.D. 291) and *Hermogenianus*, a supplementary collection confined, apart from some later additions, to constitutions of the years 293–4, and published probably at about that time. Neither survives, but they can to some extent be reconstructed from other collections of legal texts. They were also used by Justinian (see below). They were unofficial collections by unknown authors (perhaps officials in the imperial chancery, Hermogenianus being possibly identical with the jurist of that name, q.v.). The next compilation, the *Codex Theodosianus* (438) was an official one, made on the orders of Theodosius II and containing in sixteen books general enactments from the time of Constantine.

In 528 (six months after his accession) Justinian ordered a commission including Tribonianus (q.v.) to make a new compilation to bring up to date and supersede the three previous ones. This was published in 529, but does not survive. For in 530 and in the three succeeding years, when the *Digesta* (q.v.) were being compiled, Justinian published many reforming constitutions, which made the first *Codex* obsolete. A new edition (*Codex repetitae praelectionis*) was therefore published in 534 by another commission, directed by Tribonianus. In twelve books it contains some 5,000 constitutions from the reign of Hadrian onwards. Unlike the *Codex Theodosianus*, it includes not only *leges generales*, but also

rescripts (*see* CONSTITUTIONES), but none later than Diocletian. The compilers were ordered to make interpolations in the same way as in the *Digesta* (q.v.).

Justinian's constitutions issued after the publication of the second Code (written mostly in Greek) are called *Novellae Constitutiones* (Novels). He never published a collection of them, though he had intended to do so. Three unofficial collections survive, the largest dating from not earlier than Tiberius II (578–82).

EDITIONS. The only complete modern edition of the *Codex Theodosianus* is *Theodosiani Libri XVI* by Mommsen and P. M. Meyer (1905) (translation with some notes by C. Pharr, 1952); the *Codex Iustinianus* and the *Novellae* are best found in the second and third volumes respectively of the stereotype edition of the *Corpus Iuris Civilis*, edited respectively by P. Krüger (1954[11]) and by R. Schöll and W. Kroll (1954[6]).
VOCABULARIES. O. Gradenwitz, *Heidelberger Index zum Theodosianus* (1925), *Ergänzungsband* (1929); R. v. Mayr, *Vocabularium Codicis Iustiniani* i (1920), ii (1923).
GENERAL WORKS. L. Wenger, *Quellen des röm. Rechts* (1953), 534 ff., 569 ff., 638 ff.; J. Gaudemet, *La Formation du droit séculier et du droit de l'église aux IVe et Ve siècles* (1957), 38 ff.; A. Cenderelli, *Ricerche sul Codex Hermogenianus* (1965). B. N.

**CODRUS**, supposedly king of Athens in the eleventh century B.C. According to the story current in the fifth century his father Melanthus, of the Neleid family, expelled from his Pylian kingdom by the Dorians (q.v.), came to Attica, and after killing the Boeotian king Xanthus in single combat during a frontier-war, was accepted as king of Athens in place of the reigning Theseid. During the reign of Codrus the Dorians invaded Attica, having heard from Delphi that they would be victorious if Codrus' life were spared; a friendly Delphian informed the Athenians of this oracle. Codrus thereupon went forth in woodcutter's garb, invited death by starting a quarrel with Dorian warriors, and so saved his country (see Lycurg. *Leoc.* 84–7). According to a simpler and probably older version, illustrated by a vase-painting of *c.* 450 (*ARV*[2] 1268, no. 1), the Dorians were defeated in a battle, in which Codrus was killed. Codrus was succeeded by his son Medon, and the kingship remained in the family until the eighth century; in a later version, Codrus was the last king and his descendants were archons (*see* ARCHONTES). Other sons of Codrus led the colonization of Ionia from Athens.

Codrus was worshipped as a hero, along with Neleus and the shadowy Basile (*IG* i[2]. 94 of 418/17); he was allegedly buried near the Acropolis (*IG* ii[2]. 4258); Pisistratus, and hence Solon and Plato, were believed to be descended from him. How much historical truth there is in his legend it is impossible to say. It has been argued that it was invented to support the claim of Athens to be the metropolis of Ionia.

A. Wilhelm, *Anz. Öst. Akad.* 1950, 366 ff.; *FGrH* 323a, F 23 comm. (in III b (Suppl.) (1954), i. 43 ff., ii. 49 ff.); R. E. Wycherley, *BSA* 1960, 60 ff.; G. T. W. Hooker, *JHS* 1960, 115. J. E. F. and A. W. G.; T. J. C.

**COELIUS** (1, *PW* 7) **ANTIPATER**, LUCIUS, jurist, rhetorician, and historian, the teacher of L. Crassus, writing after 121 B.C., introduced to Rome, from Hellenistic models, the form of the historical monograph. He wrote in seven books on the Second Punic War, Cannae appearing in book 1, Scipio's landing in Africa in book 6, the capture of Syphax in book 7; the work was dedicated to L. Aelius Stilo, the grammarian. Coelius used not only Roman sources, including family archives (Livy 27. 27. 13), but Silenus' Carthaginian account (Cic. *Div.* 1. 24. 49); his relation to Polybius is uncertain. Some antiquarian fragments indicate perhaps another work, certainly digressions. His style was Asianic, with rhythm, echoes of Ennius, striking word-order, and vivid presentation; he composed speeches within the narrative. The work was epoch-making, and its authority was recognized by Cicero, Brutus, Livy, who used him, and Hadrian.

Peter, *HRRel.* i² (1914), ccxi, 158; O. Meltzer, *De L. Coelio Ant.* (1867); Norden, *Ant. Kunstpr.* i, 176; De Sanctis, *Stor. Rom.* iii. 2. 176.
A. H. McD.

**COELIUS** (2, *PW* 12) **CALDUS**, Gaius, as tribune (107 B.C.) extended secret ballot to *perduellio* cases (*see* CASSIUS, 7). Praetor in 99 and consul in 94 (overcoming opposition due to his *novitas*), he perhaps governed Gaul during the Social War (see Broughton, *MRR Suppl.* 17). E. B.

**COERCITIO,** the right, held by every magistrate with *imperium*, of compelling reluctant citizens to obey his orders and enactments, by inflicting punishment. Against this compulsion, which magistrates exercised not as judges but as the holders of executive authority, no appeal was admitted. The law of *provocatio*, however, made it illegal to issue a capital sentence as a purely coercive measure. *Coercitio* was, therefore, applied in historical times in the case of minor offences only, and took the form of imprisonment, exactment of pledges, fine, relegation, and possibly flogging. But in military law magisterial compulsion always retained much of its primitive severity. *See also* LAW AND PROCEDURE, III. 10.

Mommsen, *Röm. Staatsr.* i³. 163 ff.; *Röm. Strafr.* (1899), 35 ff.; J. L. Strachan-Davidson, *Problems of the Roman Criminal Law* (1912), i. 97 ff. P. T.

**COGIDUBNUS,** client king of the British Atrebates (q.v.), *c.* A.D. 43–75. Tacitus (*Agric.* 14) notes his loyalty, rewarded by rule over additional *civitates*. An inscription from Chichester (Collingwood and Wright, *RIB* 91) records his title R(*ex et*) *legatus Aug*(*usti*) *in Brit*(*annia*). This, with its implication of senatorial and even praetorian status, was probably the gift of Claudius in 47. There are many evidences of his successful philo-Roman policy. The Fishbourne villa (*Antiquity* xxxix (1965), 177 ff.) may have been built for his old age. The *civitas Regnensium* derives its name from his kingdom.

Frere, *Britannia*, ch. 5. S. S. F.

**COHORS.** In the early Roman Republic the infantry provided by the *socii* was organized in separate *cohortes* of varying strength under Roman and native *praefecti*. In the legions the cohort was first used as a tactical unit by Scipio Africanus in Spain, but not for over a century (probably as part of the Marian reforms) did it permanently supersede the maniple. There were ten cohorts in a legion, and for administrative purposes each was divided into six centuries. (*See* CENTURIO; MANIPULUS.)

From the time of Scipio Aemilianus the general's personal bodyguard was known as the *cohors praetoria*, and the term continued to be used in this sense to the end of the Republic. An extension of meaning had developed by the middle of the first century B.C., when the term was used also to describe the entourage of personal friends and acquaintances which the provincial governor took with him. Both these usages led to developments in the Empire; the entourage of personal friends was the origin of the Emperor's *cohors amicorum*, the military *cohors praetoria* had its successor in the Praetorian Guard. (*See* PRAETORIANS.)

In the *Auxilia* the infantry units were called cohorts: these were 500 strong (*cohortes quingenariae*) or 1,000 strong (*cohortes milliariae*) and commanded generally by *praefecti*. There were also some mixed units (*cohortes equitatae*) of infantry and cavalry combined. (*See* AUXILIA.)

Besides the Praetorians, the urban troops and the *vigiles* were organized in cohorts under tribunes. (*See* COHORTES URBANAE, VIGILES.)

In the Late Empire certain units of the frontier armies still retained the title of cohort. They were commanded by tribunes.

Kromayer–Veith, *Heerwesen und Kriegführung der Griechen und Römer* (1928); Parker, *Roman Legions*; M. Marin y Pena, *Instituciones militares Romanas* (1956). H. M. D. P.; G. R. W.

**COHORTES URBANAE,** the police-force of Rome, created by Augustus and commanded by the *praefectus urbi* (q.v.). Regular police (q.v.) were contrary to republican notions, hence perhaps the resignation of the first prefect (*see* MESSALLA 3); when finally formed (in A.D. 13 ?) the force had to be used with tact. In dynastic crises the prefect and his cohorts might take an independent line, as in 41 and 69, but were normally as much at the Princeps' disposal as the praetorians. There were at first three, later three or four urban cohorts; their numbering was continuous (if not always strictly) with that of the praetorian cohorts. Each cohort was commanded by a tribune, and probably contained 1,000, later 1,500 men. The pay was apparently half that of the praetorians (*see* STIPENDIUM); for the tribunes and centurions, transfer to the praetorians was a common form of promotion. There were also single 'urban' cohorts at Lugdunum and Carthage, so called because originally withdrawn from Rome. The force was still in existence in the time of Constantine.

J. Marquardt, *Röm. Staatsverwaltung* (1881–5), ii². 481 ff.; O. Hirschfeld, *CIL* xiii, 250; M. Durry, *Les Cohortes prétoriennes* (1938), 12 ff.; A. Passerini, *Le coorti pretorie* (1939), 62 ff.; E. Echols, *CJ* 1961/2 25 ff.; H. Freis, *PW* Suppl. x (1965), 1125 ff. T. J. C.

**COINAGE, GREEK.** BEGINNINGS. A coin (νόμισμα) is a flattened piece of metal, of regulated weight, with a device stamped on one or both sides making it clear (though not always to us) what individual or community had put it out and would receive it again. It is therefore a special development of one of those objects (lumps of metal, tools, cattle, etc., *see* MONEY) used in primitive societies to measure value and store wealth; and it follows that for a long time coins circulated roughly at their bullion value (for electrum see below); there could be no question of imposing artificial rates, or of a wide difference between bullion and specie values, until communities were larger and more highly organized. The first coins were of electrum (λευκὸς χρυσός), originally held to be a metal of itself. Lydia was its main source and to Lydians Xenophanes (fl. 525), our best authority, attributed the first coinage. The foundation deposit of the Ephesian Artemisium (*c.* 600), in which the earliest-known coins, some already Greek (Miletus, Ephesus), lay side by side with typeless monetiform dumps of the same weight and metal, suggests a date say a generation earlier (*c.* 640–630) for their beginning. For a long time coin values were too high for regular domestic use; so presumably the first coins were meant to facilitate large payments by and to rulers, or civic authorities, who put them out, and merchants dealing in bulk. In fact they were little more than improved ingots bringing no immediate change in the daily way of life, which hardly began till 450–400 with the general increase in small change as we see in Aristophanes. Aegina, the only city west of the Aegean to join the Asiatic Greeks in founding Naucratis, was also the first (*c.* 625–600) outside Anatolia to adapt the invention to her own needs, with a silver coinage embodying the scale of values already established for the primitive iron currency of Greece: spit, handful of spits, two handfuls = ὀβολός, δραχμή, δίδραχμον (see § 4) 'Standards and Distribution'. Subsequently the invention of coinage as well as the change from artefact to silver bullion was some-mes associated through Aegina with Pheidon of Argos, g. by Ephorus; in the first, at least, chronology is ainst the tradition.

2. COIN TYPES. The type is a mark of origin and an nplicit guarantee, a badge or 'device' denoting a person r a community, in Asia, at first, often a person. Its gnificance was occasionally reinforced by an inscrip-on, like the koppa always added beneath Pegasus at orinth. The types of important cities like Corinth, egina, and later, Athens changed little. Their coins avelled widely, and uniformity was a valuable factor in eeping them familiar and acceptable. But the earliest ersonal badges on coins of Ionia—badges of rulers, ffice-holders, or merely of someone with large payments make or receive, reveal the essence of the coin type. he closest analogy is to a seal, as is clear from the pair f primitive coins, almost certainly from Ephesus, earing a stag; one is inscribed with an uncontracted enitive, Φανέος; the other reads Φανὸςἐμισῆμα: 'I am the adge of Phanes', a formula which occurs elsewhere on a eal-stone engraved with a different name and device. he type of these coins, the favourite beast of Artemis atroness of Ephesus, provides an obvious personal evice for a prominent citizen (or tyrant) whose name lready suggests the moon goddess; and shows, inci-entally, how a person's type may sometimes reveal his ity. Occasional types may be punning ('canting'), ke the φώκη at Phocaea, or the curious banker's table t fourth-century Trapezus; but the majority, whether ivic or personal, are concerned with deities. This is not, s has sometimes been thought, because of some special onnexion between religion and money, but because the ods were of the very texture of archaic Greek life. or a century it was quite exceptional for a coin to have nore than one type, and before the introduction of everse types (c. 530) direct representation of the god vas most unusual; the reference was oblique, through an nimal (e.g. the stag above), or an attribute (e.g. Apollo's yre at Delos); in the last analysis even so-called 'com-nercial' types (corn-ear at Metapontum, tunny fish at Cyzicus, silphium plant at Cyrene), or types sometimes hought to represent primitive currencies (double-axe at Tenedos), fall into the same category. After c. 530 the use of reverse types and the increase of inscriptions greatly widened the field. The old obverse type, usually retained and supplemented by an ethnic inscription on the reverse, left no doubt whence the coin came, and direct representation became general—at Corinth and Athens among the first. Once or twice outstanding oc-casions produced commemorative issues, usually on pieces of exceptional weight: the decadrachms struck simultaneously in Athens and Syracuse (479–478) cele-brating victory over the barbarians east and west; or Alexander's decadrachm struck at Babylon, one side showing him in mounted combat with King Porus on his elephant, the other standing in semi-oriental dress and holding, like Zeus, Nike and thunderbolt.

3. TECHNIQUE. Greek coins were always struck with dies, never cast like Roman Aes Grave by pouring molten metal into moulds, except for a few bronzes from the outlying west and north (Selinus, Olbia). In essence dies were prepared by engraving the device direct into an anvil (ἄκμων) or into a small block let into it (ἀκμονίσκος). A blank, globular or disk-like, of the required weight, probably heated, was then beaten into the sunken device by a short stout bar (χαρακτήρ, originally 'punch', later 'die', 'type'), its butt end resting on the blank while its top was struck by a hammer to force the blank into the die beneath. Thus the blank became a coin with a device in relief on one side (obverse), and a depression called an incuse on the other (reverse), reproducing a negative of the rough surface of the butt. In time (c. 530) the

practice arose of engraving the butt also with a device, and two-sided coins emerged. Dies were of toughened bronze till c. 400; later, rust marks show that they were sometimes of steel. Recent experiments suggest that one obverse should produce not less than 16,000 coins and that two to three reverse dies would be consumed in the process. At first the position of the axis of one die in relation to the other, when the coin is rotated, is arbitrary, but from the fifth century, with improved technique, in many places it became regular, sometimes providing valuable evidence for period and districts (e.g. at the Bactrian mint the position is regularly inverted until Euthydemus II; after him, parallel). Whether, before the Roman period, any dies were made by engraving a punch with a device (e.g. a head) in relief, and striking this into the still smooth surface of the die to produce a negative, which could then be finished off with a graver, is disputed.

4. STANDARDS AND DISTRIBUTION. Much has been written about the origins of Greek Weight Standards, but little established. It is certain that rough natural weights must have sprung up in the Aegean area with the use of unworked metals for currency, while others entered it from outside; and that by the seventh century indigenous and imported elements had been adjusted into a working relationship; for the first coinages embody hybrid standards, later called Euboic and Aeginetic, containing local elements arranged in a Mesopotamian framework of talent, manah (μνέα, μνᾶ), and shekel (στατήρ), whose weights and internal relations vary considerably from each other as well as from their model. These two standards roughly cover the major part of the Greek world down to Hellenistic times in a cruciform pattern: the Aeginetic makes the upright stretching from Crete and Caria over the mainland and up to the Macedonian border except for a strip covering the Isthmus, Attica, and Euboea; the cross-bar is the Euboic, centred on this strip, with extensions eastward over Samos to Lydia, and westward to Italy and Sicily, and colonial offshoots northwards from Corinth, into the Adriatic, from Chalcis, up the Aegean, to Chalcidice. The *Aeginetic standard* regulated the first silver coinage (see § 1) which replaced the old iron currency of mainland Greece. For the denominations see WEIGHTS, to which should be added the didrachm or stater (12·25–12·35 gm.), largest and commonest of all Aeginetan coins and theoretically important as revealing the eastern shekel-mina framework, though the pattern followed is western Semitic, with 50 shekels to the mina, not Mesopotamian, with 60. Mina and talent are necessarily only money of account. When in 450–425 bronze coinage was intro-duced 12 chalkoi were reckoned to the obol. Aeginetic drachms were early brought into the easy relationship of 70:1 with the light Euboic mina at Athens (Aristotle, *Ath. Pol.*); and some cities which, like Delphi, used the Aeginetic standard, long preferred to reckon their coinage in Euboic minas at this rate. The *Euboic standard* is more complex than the Aeginetic, and there is no sign of its having represented the silver equivalent of currency artefacts. It is used for electrum as well as silver, and exists in heavy and light form, one double the other; each form contains local versions, six in all, Lydo-Milesian, Samian, Chalcidian, Corinthian, Italo-Achaean, Attic, differing slightly in their weights and make-up. The relation of stater to mina is again western Semitic (50:1), with the single and significant exception of the Lydo-Milesian group, which retains the Meso-potamian relation of 60:1. The Euboic stater, however, is divided by 3, not 2 (except at Athens), to produce the lower denominations later called drachms. Here only the Lydo-Milesian and the Euboic-Attic versions can be dealt with. The *Lydo-Milesian* is the only surviving link

with the older unstamped currencies. It is used for the first electrum coins, and the typeless dumps preceding them (see § 1). The stater weighs 13·85–14·25 gm. with thirds and fractions according, giving a 60-stater mina of 825–855 gm., well within the limits of the heavy Euboic system; nor need it surprise us at this time and place to find the mina reckoned at 60 not 50 staters. Lydia had been in contact with Mesopotamia direct from Gyges onwards. In Ionia this stater continued in electrum (Miletus, Ephesus), sometimes losing weight, down to the Ionian Revolt, and in silver even later (Samos, Rhodes). *Euboic-Attic.* Though the weight system of Attica, as of Corinth, was a light Euboic, no coins were struck before the reform traditionally attributed to Solon, and the common Aeginetic stater-didrachms, with their rare drachms, filled the gap. These were reckoned at 35 staters (70 drachms) to the mina, because of their heavier weights, the normal reckoning, e.g. at Corinth, being 50 staters and 150 drachms. The reform gave the mina back its normal 50 staters, but these, following Aeginetic usage were thenceforth divided into 2, not 3 drachms. This left the old light Euboic mina for reckoning as before, with its normal weight and quota of 50 staters but with a new drachm, the half stater weighing 4·26–4·30 gm.; lighter than the intrusive Aeginetic, but heavier than the old Euboic third-stater drachm, as, struck e.g., at neighbouring Corinth. The first Athenian coins were not struck till after the reform; they are one-sided silver stater-didrachms and occasional fractions with changing heraldic-like types: the so-called *Wappenmünzen*. Few numismatists now would allow even the earliest to belong to Solon's archonship (594), and they are loosely dated in 575–525, along with their occasional electrum pieces which are fractions of the same standard. When reverse types were introduced (c. 530), the tetradrachm was added, perhaps under the influence of Chalcis and her northern colonies which used the heavy stater (tridrachm to them); the didrachm consequently ceased to be regularly struck, though still remaining nominally the stater, as the later gold coinages show. In the 20s Hippias inaugurated the familiar Athena owl series which continued with modifications till Roman times. In 350–325 bronze coins were introduced as at Aegina, the Attic obol being reckoned at 8 not 12 chalkoi owing to its lighter weight. By 525–500 the standard in its final form had reached Sicily, where it remained supreme till 300, and the Cyrenaica, where by 450–425 it had been transformed into another shape. With Alexander's adoption it became the most important in the ancient world and finally exercised a strong influence on the currency of Rome. *Other Standards.* Electrum first passed at ten times the value of silver (three-quarters of gold), but its true nature must soon have become apparent, for Croesus preferred to replace it, half-way through his reign, by a simultaneous issue of pure gold and silver pieces of identical weight (10·60–10·70 gm. with fractions, notably ⅓), leaving their exchange for adjustment at the current rate for the day (1 : 13⅓). The new gold stater has the value of the old electrum stater at 3 : 4; this was the first appearance of a double coinage (Hdt. 1. 94). His Persian successors at Sardis, taking over the idea and even types, developed an integrated system at different weights in which twenty silver pieces (5·35 gm.) passed for one gold (8·05 gm.). Darius I (c. 510) fractionally adjusted the weights, changed the types from the celestial lion and ox to the Great King at war, and gave his name to the gold piece. The resulting system lasted until Alexander. Meanwhile from 550–525 to 350–325 increasing supplies of gold coin and bullion within the Persian Empire and especially in the Thraco-Macedonian region, which briefly formed part of it, steadily depressed the commercial as against the official gold-rat and eroded the silver standards except in regions lik mainland Greece whose currencies were firmly base on silver. After the Peloponnesian War the *Rhodie* (tetradrachm 15·10–15·20 gm.) replaced the Euboic-Att and local standards in the currency of the Ionian coas while already in 425–400 Macedonian cities (e. Acanthus) began to issue staters of 14·00–14·50 gm instead of the old heavy Euboic stater. This implies th rough rate against gold of 12 : 1, which Philip II late adopted for the silver staters accompanying his issue of Euboic-Attic gold. Under Alexander the rate fell 10 : 1 and the position was stabilized by returning Croesus' plan of striking both metals on the sam standard. Unlike Croesus three Ionian cities, Cyzicu Phocaea, and Mytilene, with electrum coinages of grace ful style and wide circulation from 550–525 onward retained them till Alexander's conquest. All have type changing yearly (?), but only two have constant min marks in addition (tunny fish at Cyzicus, seal at Phocaea Mytilene has none, but we know that she and Phocae issued their coinages by treaty in alternate years (To ii. 112). These consist of sixths only (2·50–2·58 gm.), wit average gold content of 30–49 per cent; if staters wer struck none have survived save a unique emergenc piece of Mytilene. The stater, if not merely a unit o account, should weigh c. 15·00–15·60 gm. The standar named *Phocaic*, was used for silver too and was carrie westwards by Phocaeans to Massilia and its depen dencies, and also to Velia (c. 540), whence it sprea throughout Campania. Its historical importance lies i its adoption by the Romans for their earliest coinages *Cyzicene* staters weigh 16·05–16·15 gm., with sixths an twelfths according, and an average gold content o 37–47 per cent, not far below the daric with which the were roughly equated; whether they had a fixed rat either there or in the Athenian ἀρχή, within which the circulated in large numbers, is doubtful. In the fourt century they were in special demand in Black Sea ports With the rise of the Hellenistic kingdoms the face o Greek coinage altered. Apart from odd corners (e.g Crete) and a few privileged cities, autonomous issues ar rare except for bronze; and the bulk, east and west comes from larger units: kingdoms, states (Rome Carthage), leagues (Aetolian, Achaean, etc., and Brettian Only two major city-states, Athens and Rhodes coine continuously in the Aegean down to the first century B.C though there is much imitation of the tetradrachms o Alexander and Lysimachus in Anatolia. For Athen see above. The Rhodian standard fell steadily and it place abroad was largely taken in the second century by the *cistophoric* (staters 12·50–12·60 gm. falling): th pseudautonomous coinage of city-states under Perga mene and, later, Roman rule, named from its Dionysia type which is frequently mentioned in Roman records The larger kingdoms may have several mints but the are controlled from the centre and have little initiative types are prescribed and the coinages uniform; officials even dies, may pass from one to another. By Actiun Greek coinage is practically extinct. The considerable city coinages in bronze with Greek legends and loca types which appear, in the eastern provinces especially under the Empire, are Roman in appearance an conception, and are best considered under that head.

INTRODUCTORY. G. Macdonald, *Coin Types* (1905); *Evolution o Coinage* (1916); K. Regling, *Münzkunde* (Gercke–Norden, 3 (1931 ii, pt. 2); C. T. Seltman, *Greek Coins²* (1955); M. Hirmer–C. Kraay *Greek Coins* (1966), wide selection, with K.'s careful text to H.'s fin photographs. For general reference G. F. Hill, *Handbook of Greek and Roman Coins* (1899); F. von Schrötter, *Wörterbuch der Münzkunde* (1930).
ADVANCED. Head, *Hist. Num.²* (1911 and reprint) now unde revision but still indispensable though in parts out of date; in con junction with it should be studied the *British Museum Guide to the*

*Principal Coins of the Greeks*[3] (1959) with fifty-two dated plates; almost as valuable, but incomplete, is E. Babelon's *Traité des monnaies grecques* [*et romaines*] (1901–32), three parts in eight vols., I *Théorie et doctrine*, II *Description historique*, III *Planches*, which at B.'s death had reached Alexander except for Italy and Sicily (to 480 only); P. Gardner, *History of Ancient Coinage 700–300 B.C.* (1918), partly economic. Monographs on districts and cities are too many to list here, but see for modern methods of research: E. Boehringer, *Syrakus* (1929) to 435 only; G. K. Jenkins and R. B. Lewis, *Carthaginian Gold Coins* (1963); E. T. Newell, *Eastern and Western Seleucid Mints* (1938 and 1941); M. Thompson, *New Style Silver Coinage of Athens* (1963). Museum collections with discussion, *British Museum Catalogues* (*BMC*) *Italy–Cyrenaica* (1873–1927), since 1883 with increasingly valuable introductions; Bibliothèque nationale (Paris), E. Babelon, *Rois de Syrie* (1890); *Perses Achéménides* (1893). For further material, fully illustrated and described but not discussed, the British Academy's international series of public and private collections, *Sylloge Nummorum Graecorum* (*SNG* 1931– ) includes, among public collections, Aberdeen (Newnham Davis), American Num. Soc. (Berry), Ashmolean, B.M. (Lloyd), Copenhagen, Fitzwilliam; among private, Lockett, von Aulock. Among independently published collections: public, Bibl. Nat. Paris, J. Babelon, *Coll. Luynes* (1924); Bibl. nat. Brussels, P. Naster, *Coll. L. Hirsch* (1959); Boston, Mus. of Fine Arts, A. Baldwin-Brett, *Cat. of Gk. Coins* (1955); Fitzwilliam, S. W. Grose, *McClean Coll.*; private, R. Jameson, *Coll. Jameson* (1913–32); L. Forrer, *H. Weber Coll.* (1922).

ART. K. Regling, *Die Antike Münze als Kunstwerk* (1924); B. Ashmole, *Relation between Coins and Sculpture*; *Trans. of Internat. Num. Congress 1936* (1938); G. E. Rizzo, *Monete Greche della Sicilia*, 1946. G. F. Hill, *Select Greek Coins* (1927), excellent enlargements.

METROLOGY. In this highly controversial subject little is yet certain. F. Hultsch, *Gr. u. röm. Metrologie* (1882), still useful for the literary sources and discussions, as is E. Pernice, *Griechische Gewichte* (1894), for the archaeological; A. Segrè, *Metrologia e circolazione monetaria degli antichi* (1928); O. Viedebantt, *Antike Gewichtesnormen*, penetrating but limited in scope; J. Hamer, *Feingehalt der griechisch* [*und röm.*] *Münzen* (1906).

BIBLIOGRAPHY. Head's *Hist. Num.*[2] includes general bibliography to 1911; since then has appeared S. P. Noe's *Bibliography of Greek Coin-hoards*[2] (1937), American Numism. Soc. 'Num. Notes and Monographs', no. 78. Otherwise the only recourse is to regular indexes of numismatic periodicals, especially Amer. Numism. Society's *Numismatic Literature*, quarterly since 1947. E. S. G. R.

**COINAGE, ROMAN.** All mentions of coinage under the kings and the early Republic are unhistorical. Rome reckoned values in terms of oxen and sheep (hence *pecunia*, from *pecus*) down to *c.* 450 B.C., and later in uncoined bronze (*aes rude*), which was superseded in central Italy by cast bronze bars (*aes signatum*) bearing distinctive devices and related to the Roman pound (327·45 gm.) of 288 scruples.

2. By 290 B.C. Rome dominated central Italy, and tradition gives to *c.* 289 B.C. the establishment of triumvirs of the Roman mint, who continued the production of *aes signatum* and began that of *aes grave*, circular cast bronze *asses*, weighing 1 pound and marked I (= 1 *as*), together with subdivisions—true coins of which weight-variation was offset by defined face-value. Such currency was appropriate to an area familiar with bronze as a measure of value, and to a power now richer in bronze spoils and available copper mines. Each denomination bore its own characteristic types. There was no ethnic inscription.

3. The Pyrrhic War of 280 B.C. involved Rome in south Italy, with its long tradition of silver coinage; and he now produced, as extraordinary issues, struck silver didrachms. These 'Romano-Campanian' coins, of about 7·4 gm., were Greek in workmanship and style, and probably came from such mints as Naples and Tarentum: their Mars/Horse's head and Apollo/Horse types were accompanied by the legend ROMANO. Token bronze coins were also issued, similar to the earlier Neapolitan ΩΜΑΙΩΝ pieces. *Aes grave* continued at Rome under the mint-triumvirs, with stylistic improvement due perhaps to employment of Greek workers: the Janus or Mercury heads of the earlier *asses* were now replaced by Apollo. The *aes* weight-standard remained without obvious change, or even rose slightly. Corresponding *aes* issues were in production at other central Italian com-

munities. Bronze bars were by now being generally superseded.

4. Pliny, as correctly interpreted, assigns the first silver of Rome proper, under the *tresviri monetales*, to 269 B.C.; this consisted of didrachms, of about 7·1 gm., with types Hercules/Wolf and twins, obviously appropriate, and legend still ROMANO. The Pyrrhic war had taught Rome the importance of a regular south Italian currency, supervised by the *tresviri* but monetarily independent of her own value-marked *aes*. The First Punic War prompted a new silver didrachm issue of lighter weight (6 scruples, 6·8 gm.), with types Roma/Victory and legend ROMANO: these led to others of the same weight, whether during or after the war, on which ROMA replaced ROMANO; and *c.* 235 B.C. the Greek-style didrachms gave way to the more Roman-style *quadrigati* of the same weight, with types Young Janus/Victory in *quadriga*, and legend ROMA. There were concurrent changes in *aes* coinage: at first, in a series of issues with varying *as*-types, the weight began to drop, indicating the war-time necessity of over-valuation for bronze, and after *c.* 235 B.C., when the Janus/Prow *aes grave* appeared, with a full range of minor denominations, the *as* (originally weighing 1 pound) had sunk to semi-libral (half-pound) standard.

5. There is no certain evidence to show whether the mint of Rome worked in association with regional mints elsewhere from *c.* 269 until this time. But the Second Punic War undoubtedly found Rome as the only regular mint in operation, apart from special monetary emissions made by military leaders in the field. The strain of war was quickly reflected in the adoption of the triental standard for *aes*, followed closely by the quadrantal, itself unstable and waning. Hitherto the prime monetary unit had been the bronze fixed-value *as*, supplemented by silver traded at market value. About or just after 213 B.C. the silver *quadrigatus* gave way to the silver *victoriatus* (with *rev.* type Victory) of half its weight, i.e. *c.* 3·4 gm., still without defined face-value and struck also by Italian mints other than Rome: the stress of war had already resulted, *c.* 216, in the coining of the Janus/Oath-scene emergency gold. Finally, at a date which, not yet absolutely determined, archaeological evidence has suggested may be *c.* 211 B.C., Rome made the fundamental change, striking the silver *denarius* (of *victoriatus* weight) with types Roma/Dioscuri and legend ROMA. The obverse was marked X, = 10 *asses*: the coin was thus the silver equivalent of 10 reduced-weight bronze *asses*. Halves (*quinarii*, marked V and quarters (*sestertii*, marked IIS) were also coined. Henceforth the *as* was struck not cast. More gold, with types Mars/Eagle, marked as being of 60, 40, or 20 *asses*, was also produced, *c.* 209, drawing again on the state's extensive reserves of this metal. Internally the war had resulted in complete coinage-reform, with silver (aided by emergency gold) appearing as the major partner in a new system of bi-metallism. *Bigati* (*rev.* type Luna or Victory in *biga*) of denarial weight but without value-mark were probably produced for external purposes.

6. The pattern of Roman coinage was now set for many decades, upon the basis of silver *denarii* (with infrequently issued fractions) and a range of bronze, all struck, which tended to fall in weight, with the sextantal (2 ounce) *as* becoming uncial (1 ounce) in the later second century B.C.; the token nature of *aes* was now confirmed, although reckoning in *asses* or their multiples continued for a long time. In the rest of Italy the spread of the *denarius* resulted in the diminution of non-Roman silver coinages, though local *aes* in various categories was still frequent. Rome herself gained large bullion supplies in the century following the Second Punic War from war-indemnities and spoil: the gold 'Philippei' of

Macedon after 188 and 167 B.C. and the later *argentum Oscense* from Spain, on the denarial standard, were among major sources of coined metal. Gold, however, was not struck between *c.* 209 B.C. and the time of Sulla, who produced it during his eastern campaigns. The period of the Gracchi witnessed an internal monetary reform by which the *denarius* was valued at 16 *asses* (and marked XVI, and subsequently ✕) instead of 10. Soon after there was an increased production of plated *denarii*, some of which may have been issued alongside the normal pieces as a means of government profit, though many were perhaps the work of forgers, against whom later measures were directed.

7. The mint of Rome was in the temple of Juno Moneta, who thus gave her name to 'money'; and methods of production were those already elaborated for earlier coinages (*see* COINAGE, GREEK). In the course of time this mint was supplemented by others elsewhere, necessitated by the extension of colonies or the operation of armies in long-term campaigns: such 'military' issues were frequent from Sulla onwards. The mint of Rome continued under the supervision of the *tresviri*, progressively defined as *aere argento auro flando feriundo*, though certain issues of the first century B.C. were sometimes controlled by quaestors, aediles, or other magistrates through special authority (S.C. or EX S.C.). No coins of Rome bore magistrates' marks before the first *denarii*, of which some developed small pictorial symbols. These gave way to simple monograms, and these in turn to abbreviated names; after *c.* 150 B.C. these names might appear in fuller form, and ultimately excluded the legend ROMA.

8. The chronological arrangement of the republican denarial coinage and its associated *aes* is difficult, depending on the comparative analysis of hoards, the prosopographical identification of a long series of named *tresviri*, and the development of the coin-types. Normally an annual college of *tresviri*, of whom one seems to have acted as senior, struck in silver or bronze or both, producing a volume of coinage determined by higher authority; and the problem has been to accommodate the known or potential number of colleges within a given period of years. Prosopographical investigation is much assisted by study of type-development. Down to the Gracchan period *denarii* usually showed *obv.* head of Roma, *rev.* Dioscuri, or deity in *biga* or *quadriga*. Then the reverses changed, to show some incident illustrating the political or military services rendered by the moneyer's ancestors. After *c.* 100 B.C. such 'historical' types were increasingly invested with current political meaning, leading to type-sequences of party significance; and powerful *imperatores* like Sulla and Pompey did not hesitate, when coining on campaign, to use types of purely personal reference. Julius Caesar, as dictator, followed their example, and his final coinage (produced by *quattuorviri*) broke with all precedent and showed the portrait of a living man.

9. By now the coinage of Rome comprised abundant *denarii*, with some *aurei*: *aes* coinage had virtually ceased *c.* 80 B.C., when the *as* had sunk to ½ ounce standard, and earlier issues presumably continued as purely token money. During the second triumvirate coinage was struck in gold and silver by the triumvirs and their subordinates, who also coined in *aes*; and these coins were directed primarily to the political sympathies and the military necessities of Antony and Octavian in East and West respectively. The mint of Rome ceased coinage *c.* 40 B.C.

10. Augustus stabilized and modified the coinage-system of the Republic. He retained the *aureus* (at 42 to the Roman pound) and the *denarius* (at 84), in the relationship of 1:25, and struck a wide range of token coinage in *orichalcum* alloy (*sestertius, dupondius,* and *semis*) and copper (*as* and *quadrans*). Coinage in gold and silver tended to follow his own movements and military necessities in both East and West, but from *c.* 20 the mint of Rome was reopened, and from *c.* 15 B.C. another major mint, probably Lugdunum, was busy, though coinage at both could be periodic. Gold and silver (the latter substantially alloyed) generally stressed the Emperor's military powers, the *aes* his civil powers and the honours paid civically to him, whether at Rome by S(enatus) C(onsulto) or elsewhere in other ways. It is unlikely that there was any systematic difference in the control of the precious and non-precious coinages: the *tresviri a.a.a.f.f.* signed both at Rome down to *c.* 4 B.C., all names disappearing thereafter, when imperial slaves and freedmen operated the mint under imperial agency. In the provinces there was a large variety of civic and regional coinages, permitted by the *princeps*, and almost wholly of *aes*; those of the West were severely curtailed after Gaius' reign. The obverses, with few exceptions, showed the Emperor's portrait.

11. The major and 'official' mints of Augustus struck types which emphasized the imperial achievements, the imperial house, and the peace and prosperity of a new era secured by the Emperor through favour of the traditional gods. From this model all subsequent imperial coinage derived, and the *aes* continued to be marked SC though different Emperors varied the emphasis of their types at will until, in the third century A.D., the coinage (by proclaiming and promising everything) had come typologically to mean little or nothing. In the eastern provinces, however, there was another idiom. A very large number of Greek cities retained or gained the right to strike civic or regional *aes*, thus relieving the Emperor of a heavy economic obligation while adding to their own revenue. These coins, down to their disappearance *c.* A.D. 250, normally showed an imperial obverse portrait; the reverses were given up to representations of local gods and buildings or to themes of local history or mythology. Their inscriptions were normally in Greek. They were produced in quantity and form a rich commentary upon the continuing Hellenism of the flexibly organized eastern provinces of the Roman Empire.

12. Site-finds and hoards show that the imperial coinage proper was struck in large volume and circulated widely and over long periods. The *as* and its double, the *dupondius*, were for some time the commonest denominations, for civilians and soldiers alike. Silver and gold were probably restricted to the smaller number of the well-to-do, and also passed beyond the imperial frontiers in the service of luxury trades. This, together with growing imperial expenditure and other causes of economic maladjustment, soon resulted in monetary revision, in which Augustus' gold/silver bimetallism was, however, at first preserved.

13. Nero reduced the *aureus* from $\frac{1}{42}$ to $\frac{1}{45}$ of a pound, and the *denarius* from $\frac{1}{84}$ to $\frac{1}{96}$, increasing the amount of alloy in the silver. As the debasement of the silver, once begun, increased till it reached over 50 per cent under Septimius Severus, the coinage came to rest more and more on an essential gold basis. Caracalla, in A.D. 215, issued the so-called *antoninianus*, a coin of 2 (or possibly 1½) *denarii* substantially overvalued. Abandoned by Severus Alexander the coin was restored by Balbinus and Pupienus and, by the reign of Philip, had practically ousted the *denarius*. The *aureus*, reduced by Caracalla to $\frac{1}{50}$ of a pound, gradually fell in weight by the reign of Gallienus gold was struck on no single apparent standard. The debasement of the silver continued, and, in A.D. 259, the *antoninianus* became a mere copper piece, coated with silver. Under Trajan Decius it had fallen to the value of a *denarius*; now it

fluctuated at low and irregular values in the market. The *aes* coinage ran an even course down to Gallienus: Trajan Decius struck the *quadrans* after long intermission and introduced a double *sestertius*. But, when the silver piece collapsed, this coinage was suspended.

14. Aurelian called in the old money and issued new. He struck no regular *aureus*, and no good silver piece, but a slightly improved piece of silver-coated bronze marked XX.I. Whatever the value thus defined (the interpretation 'this 1 unit = 20 *sestertii* = 5 *denarii*' is not improbable), this reform carried the Empire over the immediate crisis, even though it was never fully effected in the West.

15. By the late third century the imperial mint-system had been greatly extended. Rome was still a major mint, but the urgency of frontier needs promoted the importance of Antioch, Siscia, and Milan: others in operation included Lugdunum, Ticinum, Serdica, and Cyzicus, apart from those temporarily established by provincial usurpers like the Gallic Emperors or Carausius in Britain. Alexandria, virtually continuous since Augustus, was still the official and imperial mint in Egypt, striking a debased Greek-style coinage with Greco-Egyptian types.

16. Diocletian began by standardizing his *aureus* at 70 to the pound and retaining the silver-washed unit of Aurelian. But in A.D. 294 he undertook a complete coinage-reform which provided (i) *aurei* marked Ƨ (60 to the Roman pound), (ii) good silver of Neronian weight marked XCVI (96 to the pound), (iii) large copper coins, with predominant *Genio Populi Romani* reverse, some of them marked XX I, (iv) small copper radiate-head coins, and (v) even smaller copper laureate-head coins. The XX I coins were probably worth 5 of the new *denarii communes* of his Price Edict; and 5 of the XX I coins may have been worth 1 silver piece: the value of the gold was probably not fixed in relation to that of the silver and copper. This monetary system was followed, with more or less completeness, by 15 mints extending from London to Alexandria.

17. About 309 Constantine introduced the lighter *aureus* of 72 to the pound, the famous *solidus*. Silver was hardly struck between A.D. 305 and 330. Then the $\frac{1}{96}$ of the pound reappears, succeeded, *c.* 350, by the *siliqua* ($\frac{1}{120}$ pound) and the *miliarense* ($\frac{1}{60}$). The subsidiary coinage of silvered bronze went through a series of changes and reductions, only partially intelligible to us. One reform fell under Constantius II (A.D. 348), another under Julian (363). *Pecunia maiorina* and *centenionalis* were names of coins not yet certainly identified. In the main, the *solidus* stood apart, in a privileged position, commanding a premium on its nominal value. Its issue was long regarded as the special prerogative of the Roman Emperor, and the barbarian successor-states were slow to usurp the right. It was, par excellence, the money in which tax payment was required.

18. The range of Diocletian's mints was in general continued later, though the weakness of the Western Empire in the fifth century saw ultimate contraction to Italy itself. Diocletian's change of types, modified by Constantine, also provided the basis for later usage. Late imperial coinage, more formal—even hieratic—in appearance, referred more and more to permanent aspects of the imperial rulers, and less to specific events; and each denomination tended to have its characteristic reverse type. Close uniformity in mint-control was exerted by *rationales*, dependent on the *comes sacrarum largitionum* who controlled the disbursement of bullion, itself protected by the Emperor's *comitatus*. The imperial name and features on the obverse were hallowed: but false coining was often rife, and was sternly repressed by edict.

19. The gradual development of independent money-systems among the barbarians of the West and the great reform of Anastasius in the East belong to another story.

(*a*) GENERAL. H. Mattingly, *Roman Coins*² (1962); G. F. Hill, *Historical Roman Coins* (1909); K. Regling in *PW*, s.v. 'Münzwesen' and in Gercke–Norden, *Einleitung in die Altertumswissenschaft*, 'Münzkunde'.

(*b*) EARLY ITALY AND THE ROMAN REPUBLIC. E. J. Haeberlin, *Aes Grave* (1910); H. A. Grueber, *British Museum Catalogue of Republican Coins*, 3 vols. (1910); M. von Bahrfeldt, *Die römische Goldmünzenprägung während der Republik und unter Augustus* (1923); E. A. Sydenham, *Aes Grave* (1926) and *The Coinage of the Roman Republic* (1952); H. Mattingly and E. S. G. Robinson, 'The Date of the Roman Denarius' (*Proc. Brit. Acad.* 1933); R. Thomsen, *Early Roman Coinage*, 3 vols. (1957–61).

(*c*) THE ROMAN EMPIRE. H. Mattingly and R. A. G. Carson, *British Museum Catalogue of Coins of the Roman Empire*, 6 vols., Augustus to Balbinus and Pupienus (1923–62); H. Mattingly, E. A. Sydenham, C. H. V. Sutherland, R. A. G. Carson (with P. H. Webb, J. W. E. Pearce and P. M. Bruun), *Roman Imperial Coinage*, vols. i–vii, Augustus to Constantine and vol. ix, Valentinian I to Theodosius I (1923–67); H. Cohen, *Description historique des monnaies frappées sous l'empire romain*², 8 vols. (1884–92); M. Bernhart, *Handbuch zur Münzkunde der römischen Kaiserzeit* (1926); M. Grant, *From Imperium to Auctoritas* (1946); P. L. Strack, *Untersuchungen zur römischen Reichsprägung des zweiten Jahrhunderts*, 3 vols. (1931–7). On coins as a source for imperial history see C. H. V. Sutherland, *Coinage in Roman Imperial Policy, 31 B.C.–A.D. 68* (1951) and H. Mattingly, *CAH* xii, 713 ff.      C. H. V. S.

**COLCHIS,** the region at the east end of the Euxine Sea, just south of the Caucasus mountains; the legendary home of Medea and the goal of Jason's expedition. The land was rich in timber, flax, hemp, wax, and pitch, and Phasis was the terminus of a northern trade route to central Asia. Its people consisted of many tribes; seventy languages, it is said, could be heard in the markets of Dioscurias. Greeks established trading posts on the coast. Colchis was conquered by Mithridates; it was assigned to Rome's client princes, and remained long under Polemon (q.v. 1) and Pythodoris. Under Hadrian there were Roman forts along the coast and the tribal chiefs were nominated by Rome.

Strabo, 11. 496–9; Arrian, *Peripl. M. Eux.* Magie, *Rom. Rule Asia Min.* (index).      T. R. S. B.

**COLLATIA,** in Latium (q.v.) about 10 miles east of Rome (modern *Lunghezza?*). Already under Roman control in regal times, it played a role in the Tarquin saga. Cicero (*de leg. agr.* 2. 96) records it as a village, Pliny (*HN* 3. 68) as non-existent. The Via Collatina, however, long continued in use.      E. T. S.

**COLLATIO LUSTRALIS.** The *collatio lustralis* (χρυσάργυρον) was a tax in gold and silver levied every five years (later four) on traders in the widest sense. It was instituted by Constantine (q.v.), and abolished in the East by Anastasius in 498; it continued to exist in the Ostrogothic and Visigothic kingdoms in the sixth century. From the late fourth century it was levied in gold only. Not only were merchants liable, but money-lenders, craftsmen who sold their own products, and apparently anyone who received fees. Prostitutes paid, and the fact that the government thus profited from sin made the tax unpopular with Christians. Doctors and teachers were expressly exempted. Landowners and peasants selling their own products were also immune, and rural craftsmen were declared exempt in 374. Painters were freed from the tax in 374, and clergy and veterans who practised crafts or trade were exempt if their assessment fell below a certain minimum. The tax was assessed on the capital assets of the tax-payer, including himself and his slaves and family. The rate of tax does not seem to have been heavy, but it caused grave hardship to poor craftsmen and shopkeepers. It was levied in each city by *mancipes* chosen by the merchants on the tax-register (*matricula*). The revenue went into the *largitiones*, but the collection was organized by the praetorian prefecture.      A. H. M. J.

## COLLEGIUM

(1) PRIVATE. Any private association of fixed membership and constitution: see CLUBS, ROMAN.

(2) MAGISTERIAL. A board of officials (or strictly speaking, of more than two officials). The principle of collegiality was so common a feature of all republican magistracies at Rome that its origins were embodied in the mythical figures of Remus and Titus Tatius (q.v.). To prevent the rise of a new monarchy disguised under the names of consulship or dictatorship, it was ordained that every magistracy should be filled by at least two officials, and in any case by an even number. They were to possess equal and co-ordinate authority, but subject to mutual control. Thus a decision taken by one consul was legal only if it did not incur the veto (*intercessio*) of the other. This principle led to alternation in the exercise of power, depending on age (*collega maior*), or, under the Empire, on domestic circumstances, the married being preferred to the single. Alternation gradually became a purely honorary distinction.

Mommsen, *Röm. Staatsr.* i³. 27 ff.; see, however, E. S. Staveley, *Hist.* 1956, 90 ff. P. T.

(3) PRIESTLY. The name *Collegium* was also applied to the two great priesthoods of the *Pontifices* (q.v.) and the *Augures* (q.v.) and to the *duoviri* (later *decemviri* (q.v.) and *quindecimviri*) *sacris faciundis*, who had charge of the Sibylline oracles and of the *Graecus ritus* in general. Minor religious 'Colleges' were the *Collegia Compitalicia*, concerned with the worship of the *Lares* (q.v.) at the *compita*, the *Collegium Capitolinorum*, responsible for the *Ludi Capitolini*, and the *Collegium Mercatorum*, who presided over the worship at the temple of Mercurius. The lesser priesthoods were known as *Sodalitates*: see SODALES.

Wissowa, *RK*, 404, 483 ff. C. B.

**COLLUTHUS** (5th c. A.D.), epic poet from Lycopolis in Egypt. Author of several panegyrics, an account of the Persian war of Anastasius (506), and a *Calydoniaka* (*Suda*, s.v.), now lost. His only surviving work is a *Rape of Helen* in uninspired hexameters clearly influenced by Nonnus, but not so strict in metrical practice, particularly in the regulating of accent at both caesura and word end (cf. A. Wifstrand, *Von Kallim. zu Nonnos* (1933), ch. i, esp. pp. 75–7).

Text: W. Weinberger, 1896, and a useful Loeb by A. W. Mair (1928, together with Oppian and Triphiodorus). Bibl.: R. Keydell, Bursian, *Jahresb.* 1931, 125 ff. A. D. E. C.

**COLONIA AGRIPPINENSIS** (*Colonia Claudia Ara Augusta Agrippinensium*), modern Cologne. In 38 B.C. Agrippa transferred the friendly tribe of the Ubii (q.v.) from the right to the left bank of the Rhine, and *c.* 9 B.C. an altar for the imperial cult (Tac. *Ann.* 1. 57) was consecrated at their tribal capital. About the same time two legions were stationed close by. These were transferred later and in 50 Claudius founded a colony in honour of Agrippina his wife (Tac. *Ann.* 12. 27) which was laid out in regular form. A fine naval base, the headquarters of the Rhine fleet, was built a little upstream and a large mercantile port developed between the colony and the river. The colonists and the Ubii merged rapidly, and the latter only adhered unwillingly to Civilis in 69–70. Cologne suffered in the wars of the third century, the naval base was abandoned by the middle of the century, but the city's fortifications were strengthened. Subsequently the bridge-head was massively fortified in the Constantinian period. The city was taken by the Franks in 355, but Julian drove them out the following year. They retook it in 463.

From the first century Cologne was the chief commercial city of the Rhineland and the capital of *Germania*

*Inferior*; it became a bishopric not later than the third century. Various manufactures are attested, and its glass was exported all over western and northern Europe.

K. Schumacher, *Siedelungs- und Kulturgeschichte der Rheinlande* ii (1923); A. Grenier, *Archéologie gallo-romaine* (1931), 345 ff.; H. v. Petrikovits, *Das römische Rheinland* (1960), 85 ff.

O. B.; P. S

**COLONIZATION, GREEK.** Colonization was always a natural activity for Greeks, living in a poor country. Mycenaean colonies of the Late Bronze Age have been revealed by archaeologists (e.g. at Miletus), the coast of Asia Minor and the islands off it were settled at the beginning of the Iron Age, and there was much colonizing in Asia under Alexander and in the Hellenistic period. Nevertheless, the greatest colonizing achievement, by which Greek cities were spread round the coasts of the Mediterranean and Pontus, is that of the archaic period *c.* 750–*c.* 550. The colonizing epoch precedes written history and the source material is inadequate. In the literature incidental accounts of colonies in Herodotus and, more notably, Thucydides (who was particularly interested in colonization) stand out as precious exceptions. Information on most of the colonies comes from brief notices in comparatively late writers, especially geographers like Strabo and the so-called Ps.-Scymnus. Archaeologists have striven to improve our knowledge, often most successfully. Interpretation of archaeological material, however, is often marred by the abuse of the dangerous argument from absence of finds, and the creation of bold theories of commercial, and even political, connexions on the sole basis of painted pottery. Archaeological evidence is most valuable for establishing the chronology, which otherwise depends largely on the foundation dates worked out by Greek chronographers and preserved by late compilers, notably Eusebius. These dates cannot be relied on as exact. However, where there has been thorough archaeological exploration in Sicily and southern Italy, the traditional dates have been in a general way confirmed, so they may be used (with reserve in detail) as a general chronological framework.

The regions colonized were determined by political and geographical factors. Greek settlers were excluded from politically advanced areas such as Egypt and the Syrian coast, though occasional trading settlements were established by invitation, as the unique Naucratis in the Delta (7th c.), and, probably, Posideum (modern Al Mina) at the mouth of the Orontes (8th c.). The colonists sought areas with a similar climate to Greece, suitable for the way of life they knew. Thus southern Italy (Magna Graecia) and Sicily were the first great areas of settlement. Here the Euboean cities Chalcis and Eretria were very active, especially the former, e.g. at Pithecusae (modern *Ischia*) and Cumae (*c.* 750), Naxos (734?), Zancle (*c.* 730?), and Rhegium (*c.* 720?). Corinth founded Syracuse (733) and Sparta Tarentum (706). Most of the colonies in southern Italy were Achaean, notably Sybaris (*c.* 720) and Croton (709). Seventh-century colonies include Gela (688) from Crete and Rhodes, Selinus (*c.* 628 from Megara Hyblaea, Himera (*c.* 648) from Zancle, Posidonia (*c.* 700?) from Sybaris; later still Acragas (580) from Gela.

Also in the eighth century colonies were established in the northern Aegean on the Thracian coast, though both chronological and other indications are exceptionally slight. Chalcis and Eretria, joined slightly later by Andros, colonized Chalcidice, founding, e.g., Torone (from Chalcis), Mende, and Methone (*c.* 710?) from Eretria; Acanthus (654) from Andros. Further east the Parians settled Thasos (first quarter of the seventh century), which in turn established many colonies on the coast opposite

The colonization of the Propontis, and especially the Pontus, was mostly later, probably partly because of the less attractive climate. Eighth-century dates for Sinope and its colony Trapezus (757) have not yet received archaeological confirmation. However, extensive archaeological investigation has so far been confined to the north and west coasts; here no material earlier than the second half of the seventh century has come to light. Miletus was the dominating mother-city in the whole region, founding in particular, Cyzicus (756?), Olbia (647). Beside Miletus Megara alone played an important role, founding Chalcedon (685), Byzantium (c. 667).

North-west Greece was a Corinthian preserve. Corcyra was settled c. 733 or c. 710, but the remaining colonies were not founded till the second half of the seventh century under the Cypselid tyranny, e.g. Epidamnus from Corcyra (c. 627), Leucas, Ambracia from Corinth.

In Africa Cyrene was settled from Thera c. 630. The Spanish and French coasts were a Phocaean area (Massilia c. 600). Here the Phocaeans met with determined resistance from the Phoenicians and Etruscans, who combined to force them to abandon Alalia in Corsica (c. 540).

The character of Greek colonization reflects that of the city-states from which it arose. Their economy was based on agriculture, and the overriding cause of the Greek colonizing movement was land hunger. Trade frequently followed the establishment of colonies and became very important for some, but colonies founded consciously for trade were exceptional, as, e.g., those of the northern Pontus, which Herodotus called *emporia*.

The process of founding a colony became regular. A founder (*oikistes*) was appointed, who first sought sanction from Delphi (hence Delphi's important role in colonization, though few, if any, of the oracles preserved are authentic), then led the expedition, chose the site, divided the land, and received heroic honours at death. Often a small preliminary party would be reinforced by later emigrants from the mother-city.

Normally a colony formed a new *polis*. However, the unity of colony and mother-city was symbolized by common participation in cults, by kindling the fire at the sacred hearth (Hestia) of the colony from that of the metropolis, and by summoning a founder from the metropolis when a colony itself colonized. The primacy of the metropolis in general terms was normally recognized, so that it was natural for a colony to turn to the mother-city for help in war or internal troubles. Thus, when circumstances were favourable, as when the distance was small or the mother city a sea-power, close associations of colonies and mother-cities and dependent colonies are found. The colonies of Corinth under the tyrants afford the most striking examples, or, later, those of Pisistratid and imperial Athens (*see* CLERUCHY). Bad relations could also occur; see the very revealing passages in Thucydides' account of Corinth's dispute with Corcyra about Epidamnus (1. 24 ff.).

The colonies generally formed enclaves of Hellenism on the edge of barbarian hinterlands, which were sometimes hostile; but friendly commercial relations were probably more usual. Mixed communities of Greeks and barbarians sometimes occurred, e.g. in Chalcidice, and the Pontus.

J. Bérard, *Expansion et colonisation grecques* (1960); J. Boardman, *The Greeks Overseas* (1964); A. J. Graham, *Colony and Mother City in Ancient Greece* (1964).                          A. J. G.

## COLONIZATION, HELLENISTIC.

The diffusion of Greek settlers through Asia and Egypt in the century after Alexander's conquests was as far-reaching in every sense as the earlier colonial movements. Macedonian settlers, as distinct from Greek, were an *élite*, and must have been relatively few. Greece in the fourth century had suffered cruelly from unemployment, but now the Macedonian rulers of the new lands needed Greek soldiers for their armies, and a Greek population attached to themselves (as their native subjects were not) to occupy places strategically or economically important. Alexander himself gave the lead. His greatest colony, Alexandria in Egypt, was one type of the new city, founded with an eye to trade and to creating a splendid Greek centre of administration. His military settlements in Sogdiana were likewise imitated by his successors wherever they had turbulent subjects to restrain or a dangerous frontier to hold.

In Egypt, apart from Alexandria itself (q.v. 1), the colonizing process was mainly for military purposes. Land (*kleros*) was assigned to soldiers individually, with a military obligation which passed to each occupant in successive generations. The 'cleruchs' did not form political communities, a lack which probably explains the failure, in time, of the Ptolemaic system to fulfil its original military object.

In Asia, the military *kleros* carried the same obligation; but the wide, open spaces allowed, and even demanded, communal groups of settlers. Most of the new Greek 'cities' began as military colonies. The possibilities of colonization on these lines were realized by Antigonus I and probably by the Ptolemies in their Asiatic provinces; but the greatest work was done by the first two Seleucids. Clusters of colonies in Bactria-Sogdiana to guard the northern frontier, and in Asia Minor and Syria to facilitate quick mobilizations in wartime, formed the backbone of the Seleucid military system, and ultimately of Greek civilization in Asia. Naturally they did not remain mere military centres. Greek civilians went to live there, and many foreigners; and in time they became self-governing cities (*poleis*) with the normal Greek institutions and the minimum of political interference from the king. Their citizen-body probably consisted always in the first place of Greeks (or Macedonians, Thracians, etc.) only, and Greek was always the official language, even in cities with large native populations. (Later foundations, e.g. of Antiochus IV, were often made by granting a city-charter and a Greek name to a native place containing few Greeks.) In northern India, in the 'Greek' Empire of the second century B.C., there are signs of a more liberal policy from the start towards the conquered, dictated mainly by the fewness of the Greek immigrants. In India the experiment did not survive to leave a permanent impression; but in the Near and Middle East the new cities, with all their limitations, remained for centuries the great representatives of civilization under Roman, and even under Parthian, rule.

V. S. Tscherikower, *Die hellenistischen Städtegründungen* (1927); A. H. M. Jones, *The Greek City from Alexander to Justinian* (1940); Rostovtzeff, *Hellenistic World*, esp. ii, 1053 ff.; M. Launey, *Recherches sur les armées hellénistiques*, esp. i (1949), 42 ff.; S. K. Eddy, *The King is Dead* (1961), 92 ff., 115 ff., 330 ff.; E. Bikerman, *Les Institutions des Séleucides* (1938), 74 ff. and 157 ff.; W. W. Tarn, *The Greeks in Bactria and India²* (1951), esp. ch. i, and 118 ff., 243 ff.; A. K. Narain, *The Indo-Greeks* (1957); G. Downey, *Ancient Antioch* (1963), chs. ii–iii; F. Cumont, *Les Fouilles de Doura-Europos 1922–3* (1926); A. R. Bellinger (ed.) and others, *Excavations at Dura-Europos* (1933–52); and *Final Report* I–VI (1943–59); L. Robert, *Villes d'Asie mineure²* (1962).                                                    G. T. G.

## COLONIZATION, ROMAN.

The earliest colonies of Roman citizens were small groups of 300 families sent to garrison the Roman coastline at Ostia (q.v.), Antium (338 B.C.), and Tarracina (329 B.C.). Others were added as the Roman territory expanded, through reluctance to maintain a permanent fleet. In 218 there were twelve such *coloniae maritimae*. After 200 B.C. citizen colonies were used to guard the coasts of Italy in general. *Coloni* retained their Roman citizenship because the early colonies were within Roman territory, and were too small to form an independent *res publica*; later colonies might be a mere enclave within an existing community. Thus citizen colonies are distinct from Latin colonies which, though largely manned by Romans, were autonomous states established outside Roman territory (*see* LATINI, IUS LATII). *Coloni maritimi* were normally exempt from legionary service, though the exemption was revocable, and were bound not to absent themselves by night from their colonies in time of war. About 177 B.C. the system of citizen colonies was reorganized. They were assimilated to Latin colonies, and the use of the latter abandoned. Henceforth citizen colonies were large—from two to five thousand men—and were employed for the same purposes as Latin colonies formerly. Generous allotments of land were given and their internal organization was changed also. They remained citizen colonies but received extensive powers of local government with annual magistrates—*duoviri, praetores,* or *duoviri praetores*—a council (*consilium*), and priestly officials. Not many of the new style were founded till the Gracchan age, when a further change took place in their employment. Henceforth colonies were founded not for strategic but for political reasons, either as an emigration scheme for the proletariat or to provide for veteran soldiers. But under the Principate strategic centres were usually chosen for such colonies.

The first foundation outside Italy was the Gracchan *Junonia* at Carthage. Its charter was revoked, but the *coloni* retained their allotments. In 118 B.C. Narbo Martius was successfully founded in Provence despite senatorial objections to overseas colonies. In 103–100 B.C. Saturninus and Marius proposed large-scale colonization in certain provinces, and effected a few settlements in Africa, Corsica, and Provence. But extensive colonization outside Italy became regular only under Caesar and Octavian. Some colonists were still drawn from the civilian population, notably at the refounding of Carthage and Corinth, also at Urso in Spain. Such colonies were known as *coloniae civicae*, being exceptional. Colonies sent to places where native communities already existed encouraged the romanization of the latter, which eventually received citizenship and municipal rights and coalesced with the colony. Augustus established numerous colonies not only in Narbonensis, the Spanish provinces, Africa, and Mauretania, but also in the East, notably the group in Asia Minor, surrounding the rebellious Homonadenses. Claudius began the regular colonization of the Balkan provinces and the northern frontier. These processes continued till Hadrian. Thenceforth no new colonies were founded. The increasing tendency to local recruitment of legionaries rendered veteran colonies unnecessary. Instead, the title of colony and *ius coloniae* became a privilege increasingly sought out by *municipia* as the highest grade of civic dignity. This process began when Claudius conferred the title upon the capital cities of certain Gallic communes, but only became considerable in the second century (*see* MUNICIPIUM, IUS ITALICUM). Colonies usually adopted the names of their founders and subsequent benefactors as titles of honour.

The arrangements for local government in Caesarean and imperial colonies were a more complex development of the earlier system. Colonial magistracies were always more uniform than municipal magistracies, and soon came to resemble a standardized, small-scale replica of the Roman constitution. Hence the later popularity of the *ius coloniae*. *Duoviri iure dicundo* replaced consuls and praetors; then came aediles and sometimes quaestors. *Pontifices* and augurs looked after cults and religion. The census was taken by *duoviri quinquennales*, replaced in some Italian colonies by *censores*. Ex-magistrates passed into the council of *decuriones* (q.v.), sometimes called *conscripti*.

Colonization was sometimes unofficial. In the later Republic casual immigrants established *pagi* and *conventus* (qq.v.) *civium Romanorum* in native communities, thus spreading Roman civilization and forming the basis of future *municipia*. See also AGER PUBLICUS.

ANCIENT SOURCES. (1) Republic: Scattered references in Livy, Cicero (esp. *Leg. Agr.* bk. 2), etc. Inscriptions, esp. Dessau, *ILS* 6087. (2) Empire: Strabo and Pliny, etc. Inscriptions, *CIL passim.* MODERN LITERATURE. E. T. Salmon, *Roman Colonization* (1969). (1) Republic: Beloch, *Röm. Gesch.*; E. Kornemann, 'Colonia' in *PW* (lists); H. Rudolph, *Stadt und Staat im römischen Italien* (1935); F. Wilson, *PBSR* 1937, 77 ff. (on Ostia); A. N. Sherwin-White, *The Roman Citizenship* (1939); E. T. Salmon, *Phoenix* 1955, 63 ff., *Athenaeum* 1963, 3 ff., *JRS* 1936, 47 ff.; (2) Empire. Above, and Abbott and Johnson, *Municipal Administration in the Roman Empire* (1926); T. R. S. Broughton, *The Romanization of Africa Proconsularis* (1929); E. Kornemann, 'Conventus' in *PW*; M. Grant, *From Imperium to Auctoritas* (1946); F. Vittinghoff, *Römische Kolonisation und Bürgerrechtspolitik* (1952); B. Levick, *Roman Colonies in S. Asia Minor* (1967). A. N. S.-W.

**COLONOS,** a small Attic deme whose territory included the hill Κολωνὸς ἵππιος (as distinguished from Κολωνὸς ἀγοραῖος, on which the Hephaesteum stands overlooking the Agora), was situated a mile and a half north of the Acropolis, near Plato's Academy. Here Oedipus found refuge and was buried; Theseus and Pirithous descended to Hades by the bronze threshold; and the assembly that set up the Four Hundred in 411 B.C. met in the sanctuary of Poseidon Hippios. The natural beauty of the place, now almost entirely lacking, was lovingly described by Colonos' most famous demesman, Sophocles.

Soph. *OC*, esp. 688 ff.; Paus. 1. 30. 4. E. Kirsten and W. Kraiker, *Griechenlandkunde*⁴ (1962), 150 ff. C. W. J. E.

**COLONUS.** (*a*) A member of a *colonia* (*see* COLONIZATION, ROMAN). (*b*) A tenant farmer. *Ager publicus* (q.v.) and municipal domains were normally let to *coloni*, as were the estates of private landlords when slave gangs were abandoned in the first century B.C., and also imperial estates. Private and imperial estates were usually managed by bailiffs (*vilici*), often slaves or freedmen of the owner, or farmers-general (*conductores, mancipes*), who cultivated a home farm and let the other farms to *coloni* and collected their rents. The rent was at first usually a fixed sum of money, later generally a share of the crops; on African estates the *coloni* also owed a few days' labour in the year on the home farm. On some municipal estates the tenure was perpetual, so long as a fixed rent charge (*vectigal*, q.v.) was paid. Nominally leases were for five years, but tenure tended to become hereditary. Perpetual tenure by emphyteutic leases (*see* EMPHYTEUSIS) was granted to *coloni* who reclaimed waste land. In order to simplify the collection of taxes Diocletian tied all the rural population to the places where they were registered. Landlords, finding this rule convenient, persuaded the government to enforce it against their tenants and to strengthen it. In 332 landlords were allowed to chain *coloni* suspected of planning to leave, and in 365 *coloni* were forbidden to alienate their property without their landlords' consent, and in 396 to sue their landlords except for increasing their rent. All these rules applied only to descendants of the tenants first registered (*originales, adscripticii*), and other tenants were free.

R. Clausing, *The Roman Colonate* (1925); M. Rostovtzeff, 'Studien zur Geschichte des römischen Kolonates' (*Arch. Pap.*, Beiheft i, 1910); Jones, *Later Rom. Emp.*, 795 ff. A. H. M. J.

**COLOR** in rhetoric was often applied to cast of style or embellishment of diction, but also specially to a type of argument, plea, or insinuation used to palliate (or occasionally exaggerate) an offence debated in a *controversia.* In this sense it is one of the main rubrics in the collection made by Seneca (q.v. 1). The danger was that a *color* might be too far-fetched (Sen. *contr.* 1. . 9 'longe arcessito colore') or supremely silly (9. 4. 22 colorem stultissimum induxit'). Seneca, on the Vestal who survived being thrown from the Tarpeian rock, cites Junius (q.v. 2) Otho's *color* 'Perhaps she prepared for her punishment and practised falling from the time when she began her offence'! (1. 3. 11). *Colores* might be published separately; Junius Otho was author of four books of them *contr.* 2. 1. 33).

Full discussion in S. F. Bonner, *Roman Declamation* (1949), 55 f.
J. W. D.; M. W.

COLOSSEUM, the medieval name of Amphitheatrum Flavium, near the Colossus Neronis, on the site of Nero's 'stagnum domus aureae'. It was begun by Vespasian and said to have been continued and completed by Titus and Domitian; the dedication took place under Titus in June A.D. 80. The axes measure 188 metres and 156 metres, the height 48·50 metres. Externally the building, which is of concrete faced with travertine, has three arcaded storeys with half-columns of the Doric, Ionic, and Corinthian orders, surmounted by a podium and a masonry with pilasters; there are windows in the podium and in the spaces between the pilasters. Above the windows were bronze *clipei* and next came mast-corbels for the awning, worked by sailors. The seating was in three tiers, with standing-room above it. The arena was cut off by a fence and high platform carrying marble chairs for guilds and officials, and, on the short axes, imperial or magisterial boxes. The arena was floored in timber, covering dens for beasts, mechanical elevators, and drains. Audiences, estimated at 50,000, were regulated outside the building in a plot bordered by bollards, and held tickets corresponding to the numbered arcades, whence an elaborate system of staircases commodiously served all parts of the auditorium.

The amphitheatre was restored by Nerva and Trajan CIL vi. 32254–5), Pius (S.H.A., *Pius* 8), between 217 and 238 (Dio Cass. 78. 25; S.H.A., *Elagabalus* 17, *Alex. Sev.* 24, *Max. et Balb.* 1. 14), in 250 (Hieron. *ab Abr.* 2268), after 442 (*CIL* vi. 32086–9) and 470 (*CIL* vi. 32091–2, 32188–9), about 508 (*CIL* vi. 32094), and in 523 Cassiod. *Var.* 5. 42).

G. L. Taylor and E. Cresy, *Architectural Antiquities of Rome* (1874), 114 ff.; C. Hülsen, *Röm. Mitt.* 1897; A. von Gerkan, *Röm. Mitt.* 1925, 11 ff.; G. Cozzo, *Architettura ed arti decorative* ii. (1922–3), 273 ff.; L. Crema, *L'architettura romana* (1959), 293 ff.; G. Lugli, *Roma antica* (1946), 319 ff.; Nash, *Pict. Dict. Rome* i. 17 ff.
I. A. R.; D. E. S.

COLOTES (1), Greek sculptor, native of Paros or Heraclea (in Elis?). Active in the second half of the fifth century B.C. He is said to have assisted Phidias in his work on the chryselephantine Zeus at Olympia Pliny 34. 87), and to have himself made several chryselephantine statues, as well as bronze figures of 'philosophers'. It has not been possible to recognize Roman copies of these statues. S. C.; G. M. A. R.

COLOTES (2) of Lampsacus (4th–3rd c. B.C.), pupil and fanatical admirer of Epicurus. Works: Against Plato's *Lysis*; Against the *Euthydemus* (both ed. by W. Crönert in *Kolotes u. Menedemus*, 1906); Against the *Gorgias*; Against the *Republic*; Ὅτι κατὰ τὰ τῶν ἄλλων φιλοσόφων δόγματα οὐδὲ ζῆν ἔστιν. From Plutarch *Adv. Coloten* we learn that the last-named work tried, in a superficial and ill-informed way, to show that any theory of knowledge other than the empiricism of Epicurus affords no secure basis for practical life.

R. Westman, *Plutarch gegen Kolotes* (1955). W. D. R.

COLOURS, SACRED. Three colours are especially important for sacral purposes in antiquity; they are white, black, and red, the last being understood in the widest possible sense, to include purple, crimson, even violet (cf. E. Wunderlich, 'Die Bedeutung der roten Farbe im Kultus der Griechen und Römer', 1925 (*RGVV* xx. 1), 1 ff.).

White is in general a festal colour, associated with things of good omen, such as sacrifices to the celestial gods (white victims are regular for this purpose in both Greece and Rome). See for instance *Il.* 3. 103, where a white lamb is brought for sacrifice to Helios (q.v.); the scholiast rightly says that as the Sun is bright and male, a white male lamb is brought for him, while Earth, being dark and female, gets a black ewe-lamb (cf. Verg. *G.* 2. 146 for the white bulls pastured along Clitumnus for sacrificial purposes). It is the colour of the clothing generally worn on joyous occasions (e.g. Eur. *Alc.* 923, Martial 4. 2, whereon see Friedlaender); of horses used on great festivals such as (probably) that of Demeter and Persephone at Syracuse (Pind. *Ol.* 6. 95, cf. J. Rumpel, *Lex. Pindaricum*, 1883, s.v. λεύκιππος, and cf. LEUCIPPUS). In Rome, white horses drew the chariot of a *triumphator* (J. Marquardt, *Röm. Staatsverw.* (1881–5), ii². 586).

Black on the contrary is associated with the chthonian gods and mourning (Homer and Euripides, locc. citt.), and with the dead (hence the Erinyes wear sombre clothing, φαιοχίτωνες, Aesch. *Cho.* 1049, as infernal powers). There are, however, exceptions. At Argos, white was the mourning-colour (Socrates of Argos in Plut. *Quaest. Rom.* 26); Plutarch's assertion that white was the colour of Roman mourning will hardly pass muster, see Rose, *Rom. Quest. of Plut.* (1924), 180. Hence to wear it at a festival was both ill-mannered and unlucky (Martial, loc. cit., cf. Ov. *Ib.* 102 and the scholiast there). The above facts easily explain why 'white' and 'black' respectively mean 'lucky' and 'unlucky' when used of a day, etc. The natural association of white with light and black with darkness is explanation enough, but it may be added that white garments are conspicuously clean (cf. *Od.* 4. 750 for clean clothes at prayer), black ones suggest the unwashed condition of a mourner; cf. DEAD, DISPOSAL OF. See further G. Radke, *Die Bedeutung der weissen und der schwarzen Farben* (Diss. Berlin, 1936).

Red has more complicated associations, for which see Wunderlich, op. cit. It would seem to suggest blood, and therefore death and the underworld (hence, e.g., the use of red flags in cursing, Lysias 6. 51), but also blood as the source or container of life, wherefore a red bandage or wrapping of some kind is common in ancient, especially popular medicine, and also the ruddy colour of healthy flesh and various organs of the body, wherefore it is associated with rites of fertility on occasion (e.g. statues of Priapus, Hor. *Sat.* 1. 8. 5). Perhaps because red, or purple, is the colour of light, red is on occasion protective, e.g. the *praetexta* of Roman magistrates and children. But it is also associated with the burning heat of summer, cf. AUGURIUM CANARIUM.

Other colours are of little or no sacral importance, but it may be noted that the veil (*flammeum*) of a Roman bride, often stated to be red, is distinctly called yellow (*luteum*) by Lucan (*Phars.* 2. 361) and Pliny (*HN* 21. 46).
H. J. R.

COLUMBARIUM. (1) A Roman dove-cot. These were sometimes small and fixed in gables (*columina*), sometimes very large tower-like structures (*turres*), fitted with nesting niches in rows, perches, and running water.

(2) *Columbarium* was also applied to the sepulchral chambers of large households or of *collegia* (Mommsen, *De collegiis*, 93), where ash-chests and urns were stored

in pigeon-holes (*loci*, *loculi*). These appear originally in Etruria (G. Dennis, *Cities and Cemeteries of Etruria* i². 10, 26) but are a feature of large Roman slave and freedmen groups attached to given households. The most striking are those of the Empress Livia, containing some 3,000 urns, the well-preserved *columbarium* of Pomponius Hylas, between Viae Appia and Latina, and the three *columbaria* of Vigna Codini (*CIL* vi. 4418–880, 4881–5178, 5179–538), all within the later city wall of Rome.

G. Lugli, *The Classical Monuments of Rome* i (1929), 400 ff.

I. A. R.

**COLUMELLA,** Lucius Iunius (*PW* 104) Moderatus, a Spaniard from Gades contemporary with Seneca. As a young man he served as a tribune with Legio VI (*CIL* ix. 235) about A.D. 36, probably in Syria. He came of a Spanish land-owning family and himself held estates in various parts of central Italy.

The *De Re Rustica*, which he was writing in A.D. 60–65, is a systematic treatise on agriculture in twelve books. Book 1 deals with general matters of buildings and labour, 2 with soils and crops, 3–5 with vines, olives, and fruit-trees, 6–7 with domestic animals, 8 with poultry and fishponds, 9 with game and bees, 10 (in verse) with gardening, 11 with the bailiff's duties and the farmer's calendar, 12 with the bailiff's wife's duties: the last two books were an addition to the original plan. The separate treatise *De Arboribus* seems to be part of an earlier and shorter treatment of the subject.

Columella writes as a successful practical farmer who is deeply concerned over the decline of Italian agriculture. He finds the causes of that decline in the growth of enclosures and the absenteeism of landlords and deplores its result in Rome's dependence on imported food: the essentials for recovery are knowledge, hard work, and personal interest on the part of the landowners. He draws mainly on his own experience but he also uses a series of authorities, from the Greeks to his own day, with whom he is prepared on occasion to disagree. His prose is direct and elegant, without affectation or extravagance: in book 10, in which he modestly accepts the invitation of *Georgic* 4. 147–8 and which he meant to be the climax of his work, his admiration for Virgil is not matched by his skill and his verses are dull and uninspired.

Text. W. Lundström–A. Josephson (Uppsala, 1897–1955: bks. 5 and 12 still lacking); H. B. Ash–E. S. Forster–E. H. Heffner (with transl.: Loeb, 1941–55).
Commentaries. J. M. Gesner² (Leipzig, 1773), J. G. Schneider (Leipzig, 1794), J. H. Ress (Flensburg, 1795); bk. 10, H. B. Ash (U.S.A. 1930).

C. J. F.

**COMEDY (GREEK), ORIGINS OF.** In many pre-literate cultures there are public occasions on which people pretend humorously to be somebody other than themselves, and it is a safe assumption that comedy, so defined, was of great antiquity among the Greeks (possibly of incomparably greater antiquity than tragedy). The word κωμῳδοί, 'κῶμος-singers', presupposes κῶμος, and a κῶμος is a company of men behaving and singing in a happy and festive manner. In the fourth century B.C. the City Dionysia included 'procession, boys' (i.e. boys' chorus), 'κῶμος, comedy and tragedy' (doc. ap. Dem. xxi. 10). The inscription which was erected in the fourth century to put on public view the records of victories at the City Dionysia from the beginning (*IG* ii². 2318) is headed ἀφ' οὗ (?) πρῶ]τον κῶμοι ἦσαν τῶ[ι Διονύσωι, and under each year the entries are in the order: boys' chorus, men's chorus, comedy, tragedy. It appears from these data that, so far as was known in the fourth century, a humorous adult male chorus was an archaic

feature of the City Dionysia, and it is probable that comedy was a specialized development from this. The question: 'when did the κῶμος first develop a dramatic character?' is not answerable. The practical question is: 'how far back, and to what parts of the Greek world can each ingredient of Old Attic Comedy be traced? There are three categories of evidence which help to answer this question, and five more which are of doubtful value.

A. 1. An Attic black-figure amphora of the mid sixth century B.C. depicts men disguised as horses, with riders on their backs, accompanied by a flute-player This shows that the animal-chorus so common in fifth century comedy far antedates known comedies. Another Attic vase showing men dressed as birds is contemporary with the earliest known comedies.

2. During the sixth century B.C. vase-painters (especially on the Greek mainland, including Attica commonly depict (i) dancers whose dress is exaggerated fore and aft for humorous effect—occasionally they wear a phallus of exaggerated size—and (ii) satyrs of various types, sometimes hairy, phallic, and in general grotesque. The distinction between (i) and (ii) is not absolute, for dancers may be found as participants in mythical scenes, and there is sometimes room for doubt whether the painter is depicting a satyr or a man dressed up. These facts suggest that in the archaic period men dressed as satyrs in order to enact scenes and incidents from mythology and (old or fresh) folklore. The most striking single item of evidence in this category is a Corinthian krater of the early sixth century, in which we see both a dancer wearing a mask and some naked beings of abnormal proportions, indicated by names which suggest demons rather than mortals, engaged in activity with large jars. Unfortunately, the interpretation of this vase is controversial, but if it really depicts a humorous dramatic performance it antedates all comparable evidence from Attica.

3. Archilochus in the seventh century and Hipponax at the end of the sixth composed many poems which contain unrestrained vilification and the grossest sexual humour These elements in Attic Comedy thus have a distinguished literary ancestry, and it is not necessary to account for them by reference to Dionysiac ritual of any kind.

B. 1. The earliest and best-known theory about the origin of comedy is Aristotle's (*Poet.* 1449ª10): that it began ἀπὸ τῶν ἐξαρχόντων τὰ φαλλικά. As it is hardly to be supposed that Aristotle had any information on the nature and content of phallic songs 200 years before his own day, it seems that having (reasonably) decided that the origins of both tragedy and comedy were to be sought in festivals of Dionysus, and having derived tragedy from the ἐξάρχων–chorus relationship in the serious and heroic dithyramb, he looked for a similar relationship in something gay and ribald, and found it in the phallic songs of his own day (he says: 'the phallic songs which are still customary in many cities'). Semus of Delos (ap. Ath. 622 c) speaks of φαλλοφόροι (at Sicyon?) who ridiculed members of their audience, and it is possible that the germ of the parabasis of Old Comedy lay in words or verses uttered in mockery of the public by men who accompanied the phallus in the procession in Dionysiac festivals at Athens. It must, however, be remembered that phallic songs as known to Aristotle and Semus may have been deeply influenced by literary comedy.

2. Equally, when Sosibius (*FGrH* 595 F 7) speaks of 'an old type of comic sport' at Sparta, he is not necessarily speaking of anything as old as the sixth century B.C. The clay models of grotesque masks found at the sanctuary of Artemis Orthia are as old as that, but we

do not know whether the masks were used for any dramatic purpose.

**3.** Although Aristotle (*Poet*. 1448ᵃ33) speaks of Epicharmus (q.v.) as 'much earlier' than the earliest poets of Old Attic Comedy, Chionides and Magnes, an alternative tradition (*Marm. Par.* 71, cf. Anon. *De Com.* 4) made Epicharmus a contemporary of Hieron, and references in frs. 98 and 214 support the latter tradition. Epicharmus may reasonably be ranked among the influences on Attic Comedy, but not among its ancestors.

**4.** The Megarians claimed to have originated comedy (Arist. *Poet*. 1448ᵃ31), and Ecphantides fr. 2, corrupt though it is, certainly says something about 'Megarian comedy'. This, however, only shows that some kind of comedy at Megara was contemporary with the earlier poets of Attic Comedy, and the Megarian claim recorded by Aristotle does not seem to rest on good grounds. The tradition that Susarion (q.v.) was Megarian is later than the tradition which made him Attic.

**5.** Extrapolation from extant comedies—a line of inquiry on which much time and ingenuity has been spent—is perilous. Our earliest complete play, *Acharnians*, was produced in 425 B.C. Very few of the citations from lost plays throw any light on the structure and composition of those plays, and, in any case, no citation can be dated with assurance earlier than 450 B.C. Since the fifth century was a period of rapid change in the arts generally, it is irrational to suppose that the form of comedy remained essentially unchanged until the time of Aristophanes. The most we can glean from extant comedies is the fact that they contain two disparate elements which may have entirely separate ancestries: (i) a disguised chorus which addresses itself directly to its audience, and (ii) dramatic scenes to which the chorus's disguise is irrelevant.

Pickard-Cambridge–Webster, *Dithyramb*²; L. Breitholtz, *Die dorische Farce im griechischen Mutterland* (1960). K. J. D.

**COMEDY (GREEK), OLD.** For practical purposes, 'Old Comedy' is best defined as the comedies produced at Athens during the fifth century B.C. An early form of comedy was composed in Sicily (cf. EPICHARMUS), the connexion of which with Attic comedy is hypothetical. At Athens itself no transition from Old to Middle Comedy occurred precisely in 400 B.C., but the two extant plays of Aristophanes which belong to the fourth century differ in character from his earlier work, above all in the role of the chorus (see § 2 below). The provision of comedies at the City Dionysia each year was made the responsibility of the relevant magistrate in 488/7 or 487/6 B.C. ('eight years before τὰ Περσικά', *Suda*, s.v. Χιωνίδης; cf. *IG* ii². 2325); Aristotle's statement (*Poet*. 1449ᵇ2) that before then comic performances were given by 'volunteers' (ἐθελονταί) is probably a guess, but a good one (cf. COMEDY (GREEK), ORIGINS OF). Comedies were first included in the Lenaea shortly before 440 B.C. (cf. *IG* ii². 2325). During the Peloponnesian War three comedies were performed annually at the City Dionysia and three at the Lenaea; before and after the war, five. In the fourth century they were performed also in the demes at the Rural Dionysia (cf. Aeschin. i. 157); we do not know how old this practice was. No complete plays of any poet of the Old Comedy except Aristophanes (q.v. 1) survive, and he belongs to the last stage of the genre, but we have a great many citations from the work of his elders (notably Cratinus, q.v.) and contemporaries (notably Eupolis, q.v.). Some of these support generalizations about Old Comedy based on Aristophanes, but where support is absent or doubtful it is important to remember Aristophanes' date and not to assume that the structural features common to his earliest plays constitute, as a whole, a formula of great antiquity.

**2.** The chorus, which had twenty-four members (cf. Ar. *Av.* 297 ff., with scholia ad loc. and *Ach.* 211), was of primary importance in Old Comedy, and very many plays (e.g. *Babylonians*, *Banqueters*, *Acharnians*) take their names from their choruses. In Aristophanes (the practice may have been different in Cratinus, q.v.) the chorus addresses the audience in the parabasis, which has a central position in the play, and again at a later stage. In parts of the parabasis the chorus maintains its dramatic role (as Acharnians, knights, clouds, jurymen, etc.), while in others it speaks directly for the poet; in the former case dramatic illusion is partly broken, in the latter case wholly. The entry of the chorus is sometimes a moment of violence and excitement; it may be (as in *Acharnians* and *Wasps*) hostile to the 'hero' of the play, and it has to be won over; thereafter it is on his side, applauding and reinforcing what he says and does. It is possible that the sequence hostility–contest–reconciliation between chorus and hero was a common formula.

**3.** The plots of Old Comedy are usually fantastic. In their indifference to the passage of time, the ease with which a change of scene may be assumed without any complete break in the action (places which in reality would be far apart can be treated as adjacent), and the frequency of their references to the audience, the theatre, and the occasion of performance, they resemble a complex of related charades or variety 'turns' rather than comedy as we generally understand the term. The context of the plot is the contemporary situation. In this situation, a character takes some action which may violate the laws of nature (e.g. in Aristophanes' *Peace* Trygaeus flies to the home of the gods on a giant beetle in order to release the goddess Peace from imprisonment and bring her back to earth) or may show a complete disregard for practical objections (e.g. in Aristophanes' *Acharnians* Dikaiopolis makes a private peace treaty with his country's enemies and enjoys the benefits of peace). Events in Old Comedy are sometimes a translation of metaphorical or symbolic language into dramatic terms, sometimes the realization of common fantasies; they involve supernatural beings of all kinds and the talking animals familiar in folklore. The comic possibilities of the hero's realization of his fantasy are often exploited by showing, in a succession of short episodes, the consequences of this realization for various professions and types. The end of the play is festive in character (Aristophanes' *Clouds* is a striking exception), a kind of formal recognition of the hero's triumph, but the logical relation between the ending and the preceding events may be (as in Aristophanes' *Wasps*) very loose, as if to drown the question 'But what happened *then*?' in the noise of song and dance and to remind us that we are gathered together in the theatre to amuse ourselves and Dionysus by a gay show.

**4.** Men prominent in contemporary society are vilified, ridiculed, and parodied in Old Comedy. Sometimes they are major characters, either under their own names (e.g. 'Socrates' in *Clouds* and 'Euripides' in *Thesmophoriazusae*) or under a very thin disguise (e.g. the 'Paphlagonian slave' in *Knights*, who is Cleon). Many plays, e.g. *Hyperbolus* and *Cleophon*, actually bore real men's names as their titles. The spirit in which this treatment was taken by its victims and by the audience raises (and is likely always to raise) the most difficult question in the study of Old Comedy. A man would hardly become a comic poet unless he had the sense of humour and the natural scepticism which combine to make a satirist, and prominent politicians are always fair game for satire. Equally, artistic or intellectual change is a more obvious and rewarding target for ridicule than traditional practices and beliefs. There is nothing in the comic poets' work to suggest that as a class they wished for an oligarchic revolution, and their own art was characterized by elaborate and continuous innovation. There is some evidence (schol. Ar. *Ach.* 67, cf. schol. Ar. *Av.* 1297) for attempts to restrict 'ridiculing by name' (ὀνομαστὶ κωμῳδεῖν) by legislation; their scope is not known, and their effect was obviously insignificant.

5. Mythology and theology are treated with extreme irreverence in Old Comedy; some plays were burlesque versions of myths, and gods (especially Dionysus) were made to appear (e.g. in Aristophanes' *Frogs* and Cratinus' *Dionysalexandros*) foolish, cowardly, and dishonest. Yet the reality of the gods' power and the validity of the community's worship of them are consistently assumed and on occasion affirmed, while words and actions of ill-omen for the community are avoided. It is probable that comic irreverence is the elevation to a high artistic level (Demodocus' tale of Ares and Aphrodite in *Od.* 8 may be compared) of a type of irreverence which permeates the folklore of polytheistic cultures. The essential spirit of Old Comedy is the ordinary man's protest—using his inalienable weapons, humour, and fantasy—against all who are in some way stronger or better than he: gods, politicians, generals, artists, and intellectuals.

6. The actors wore grotesque masks, and their costume included artificial exaggeration (e.g. of belly and phallus) for comic effect; the phallus may have been invariable for male roles until the fourth century. No limit seems to have been set, in speech or action, to the humorous exploitation of sex (normal or perverted) and excretion, and the vocabulary used in these types of humour eschews the euphemism characteristic of prose literature.

7. Most of the extant comedies of Aristophanes require for their performance four actors and, on occasion, supernumeraries, whose responsibilities can be precisely defined. Performance by three actors plus supernumeraries is possible only if we give the latter a degree of responsibility which blurs the distinction between actor and supernumerary.

A. Meineke, *Fragmenta Comicorum Graecorum* (1839–57), is a work of pre-eminent scholarship and judgement, and the first volume (*Historia Critica Comicorum Graecorum*) is fundamental. T. Kock, *Comicorum Atticorum Fragmenta* (1880–8); J. Demiańczuk, *Supplementum Comicum* (1912); the latest corpus of the fragments, J. M. Edmonds, *The Fragments of Attic Comedy*, vol. i (1957), is full of errors and absurdities, and should be used with great caution. T. Zieliński, *Die Gliederung der altattischen Komödie* (1885); P. Geissler, *Chronologie der altattischen Komödie* (1925); A. W. Pickard-Cambridge, *The Dramatic Festivals of Athens* (1953).
  *See also* : ARISTOPHANES (1); COMEDY (GREEK), ORIGINS OF; CRATINUS; EPICHARMUS.      K. J. D.

**COMEDY (GREEK), MIDDLE.** The term 'Middle Comedy', coined by Hellenistic scholarship, may be conveniently used to describe the period between Old and New Comedy (*c.* 404–*c.* 321 B.C.). It was a period of experiment and transition; different types of play seem to have predominated at different times; and probably no single type of play deserves to be labelled 'Middle Comedy' to the exclusion of all others.

2. The downfall of Athens, 404 B.C., vitally affected the comic stage; the loss of imperial power and political energy was gradually reflected in comedy by a choice of material less essentially Athenian and more cosmopolitan. In form at least the changes began early. Aristophanes' *Ecclesiazusae* and *Plutus*, now generally acknowledged to be early products of Middle Comedy, reveal the decline of the comic chorus. The parabasis has disappeared; instead of original lyrics composed for each choric song, interpolated pieces (ἐμβόλιμα) whose words are not preserved came to be used and their place was marked in the MSS. by the word *XOPOY*. By the

time of the *Plutus* (388), the part specially composed for the chorus is reduced to their opening song and a very few other verses addressed to the actors. Doubtless the decline of the chorus was gradual but not rectilinear throughout the period plays were written that took their titles from the chorus (a later example is Eubulus' *Stephanopolides*), and instances can be found of a chorus that still conversed with the actors (Aeschin. 1. 157: 345 B.C.) or sang specially composed lyrics (Eubulus, frs. 104 105); cf. also Alexis, fr. 237; Heniochus, fr. 5. Yet the typical chorus of New Comedy, completely without participation in the plot, must have become the norm by the end of the Middle Comedy period, together with the five-act structure that its four interludes make possible.

3. The obscene costume of Old Comedy, with grotesque padding and phallus, was probably given up during the period, but it is uncertain whether this change was gradual or promoted by appropriate legislation (Lycurgus' theatre reforms, *c.* 330 B.C., for instance?).

4. But the exact flavour of Middle Comedy is elusive. The pronouncements of ancient scholarship (e.g. Platonius, 11: emphasis on the lack of political criticism and the popularity of mythological burlesque; Arist. *Eth. Nic.* 4. 1128$^a$20: contemporary comedy (i.e. later Middle Comedy) had replaced the αἰσχρολογία of Old Comedy with ὑπόνοια) seem reasonably accurate, provided they are not interpreted too rigidly. In the absence of any complete play (after the *Plutus*) judgements must largely depend on the interpretation of the large number of fragments, often quoted with the titles of their plays; but it cannot be too strongly emphasized that the bias of the main preserver of these fragments, Athenaeus (q.v. 1), gives a distorted impression of the part that descriptions of food and drink played in Middle Comedy.

5. Yet titles and fragments, when carefully examined, can be very informative. The variety of subject, especially in contrast with New Comedy, is striking. Plays with political themes were produced mainly (but not exclusively) in the early part of the period (notable titles are Eubulus' *Dionysius*, Mnesimachus' *Philip*), and politicians such as Demosthenes and Callimedon were frequently ridiculed, if rarely criticized directly. As in Old Comedy philosophers were pilloried and their views comically misrepresented; Plato and the Pythagoreans seem to have been the commonest victims. In the earlier half of the period mythological burlesque played a dominant role, doubtless continuing the Old Comedy tradition. There may have been two types of such burlesque: straight travesty of the myth, with or without political innuendo, and parody of tragic (especially Euripidean) mythological treatments. The aim was often to reinterpret the story in contemporary terms: thus Heracles takes a book from Linus' library of classical authors (Alexis, fr. 135), and Pelops complains of the meagre meals of Greece when contrasted with the king of Persia's roast camel (Antiphanes, fr. 172). Among other popular themes were riddles, and the comedy of mistaken identity (modern scholars have posited Middle Comedy originals for Plautus' *Amphitruo* and *Menaechmi*).

6. Numerous fragments and titles show that a common characteristic of Middle Comedy was the observation of contemporary types, manners, and pursuits (e.g. κιθαρῳδός, μεμψίμοιρος, σκυτεύς, φιλοθήβαιος). This interest in the details of ordinary life clearly influenced the development of one particular type of comedy, dealing with a series of more or less plausible everyday incidents such as love affairs and confidence tricks, and based on a group of stock characters ultimately

(though often with caricature) drawn from life: the type of play mainly associated with New Comedy.

**7.** Virtually all the stock figures of New Comedy (e.g. cooks, courtesans, parasites, pimps, soldiers, angry old men, young men in love) can be identified in the fragments and titles of Middle Comedy. Although several of these characters go back at least to Old Comedy (thus the *miles gloriosus* has a prototype in Aristophanes' portrayal of Lamachus; titles bearing the names of courtesans are attributed to Pherecrates; Eupolis had a chorus of κόλακες), it is clear that the middle of the fourth century was the period which had the greatest influence on their typology —about then, for instance, the cook began to receive his typical attributes of braggadocio and garrulousness, and the term παράσιτος to be applied generally to the character hitherto called κόλαξ.

**8.** Plots of the New Comedy pattern already existed in Middle Comedy, e.g. Alexis' Ἀγωνὶς ἢ Ἱππίσκος (date *c.* 340–330) included a young man in love, a courtesan, and probably a confidence trick and a recognition. Some of the typical plot elements (e.g. the low trickery, the clever slave) go back to Old Comedy and probably beyond that to popular farce; and others (e.g. the recognition scenes) owe much to tragedy, especially Euripides. Though the question of origins is very complex, the part played by Middle Comedy must not be underestimated. Aristophanes is said to have originated the comic application of rape and recognition, but in a mythological burlesque: the Κώκαλος, a late play written in the Middle Comedy period; such burlesques may have represented an important stage in the development of certain typical New Comedy elements (significant titles here are Eubulus' *Auge* and *Ion* and Anaxandrides' *Helen*, all perhaps travesties of Euripidean plays famous for their rapes and/or recognitions). Consequently, when the *Suda* claims that Anaxandrides invented 'love affairs and rapes of maidens', this may mean that he was the first to use them as incidents of ordinary life in a non-mythical framework.

**9.** To fifty-seven poets Athenaeus assigns more than 800 plays: we know the names of about fifty poets (many of them non-Athenian), Antiphanes, Anaxandrides, Eubulus, Alexis, and Timocles (qq.v.) being the most prominent.

Meineke, Kock, Edmonds, vol. ii (1959: very unreliable, (as under OLD COMEDY). E. Fraenkel, *De media et nova comoedia quaestiones selectae* (1912). K. J. Maidment, 'The Later Comic Chorus', *CQ* 1935, 1 ff. F. Wehrli, *Motivstudien zur griechischen Komödie* (1936). Webster, *Later Greek Comedy*. K. Lever, 'Middle Comedy', *CJ* 1953–4, 167 ff. K. J. Dover, article on 'Greek Comedy' in *Fifty Years of Classical Scholarship* (ed. Platnauer, 1954), 96 ff.     W. G. A.

## COMEDY (GREEK), NEW

belongs to the last quarter of the fourth century and the succeeding, no longer exactly definable period during which creditable comedy continued to be written at Athens; an ancient tradition saw in the death of Philemon (264/3 B.C.) the end of the creative epoch.

**2.** Its significance is twofold. On the one hand, it is the final flowering of Athenian poetic genius: Menander (q.v.) is the last great poet of Athens, and New Comedy no less than Old Comedy, from which, with an infusion of tragic, principally Euripidean influence, it is ultimately descended, is Athenian national theatre, sustained by the resources of the state and the interest of the citizens. On the other hand, it is already of the Hellenistic era. Its creators hail from far and near and, though based on Athens, they must often have written for other cities. Its characters speak an Attic which foreshadows the international κοινή. Its servile names tell of economic expansion in the wake of Macedonian conquest: Getas, Daos, Libys, Syr(isc)os, Tibeios, etc. Set beside its mobile people, whom business, misfortune, or mer-

cenary service is constantly sending abroad, the folk of Old Comedy appear relatively stay-at-home. This restlessness is matched by an inner confusion: in place of the old, unselfconscious piety, fanaticism (e.g. *Priestess* and *Theophoroumene* of Menander) and experiment (e.g., for the first time, Sarapis in Menander's *Dagger*) enter in. Contemporary political conditions are noticed only where they impinge directly on the fate of individuals (e.g. the *tyrannis* of Dionysius of Heracleia in Menander's *Fisherman*). The people whom New Comedy so faithfully represents have more in common with the masses of the Graeco-Roman world than with the inhabitants of the classical *polis* who were not citizens unless 'politicians': because a great part of their political independence is gone, they live all the more intensely for self and family. Therefore, New Comedy remained 'modern'—νέα is less a chronological than a critical term—and popular down to the end of antiquity.

**3.** Discovery of long-lost children, love, intrigue of slaves are but some of the ever-recurring, inherited themes. Even where evidence is lacking it is not rash to suppose that the motifs encountered have had a complicated prehistory on the Attic stage. Originality is shown in another direction: in the accurate delineation of character and mood as well as in the artistic variation of traditional matter. In spite of the systematic repetition of fixed names and masks (consult T. B. L. Webster, *Greek Theatre Production*, 1956), the characters behind them, at any rate in the better plays, differ vividly and come alive with individual life. Antique burlesque has by no means disappeared; melodrama, under strong impulses from tragedy, gains ground. But the best work shuns both of these excesses.

**4.** The division into five acts separated by a non-dramatic chorus seems to have become general. In exposition, use is made, separately or in combination, of means developed by earlier drama, comic or tragic: prologue figure (e.g. Ἀήρ Philemon fr. 91; 'internally' too, e.g. Menander's Agnoia, not unprecedented, cf. *Knights* of Aristophanes), expository dialogue (e.g. Menander's *Heros*) and monologue (e.g. *PAntinoöp*. 15: Barns and Lloyd-Jones, *JHS* 1964, 25 ff.). The direct address to the 'gentlemen' (ἄνδρες) of the audience lingers, but the organic connexion with earlier comedy comes out still more strikingly in, e.g., the Taming of Cnemon (see MENANDER I). Iambic trimeter is the principal verse form, trochaic tetrameter coming next in importance; this metrical constraint does not impair colloquial vigour.

**5.** Being held inferior as a model of Attic speech, it did not find its way into the Byzantine schoolroom (minor exception: see Jäkel, *Menandri Sententiae*, 1964, Teubner). This proved fatal to the MS. tradition. Before the—thankfully unabating—papyrus discoveries, mostly of Menander, there were only the quotations preserved in various authors. Besides these two direct sources there are the adaptations of Plautus and Terence (qq.v.; consult also Ribbeck, *CRF*); far less important but not negligible are Alciphron, Aelian, Lucian, Libanius, Aristaenetus, and Theophylactus (qq.v.), where they are inspired by themes from New Comedy. Archaeology, finally, is an illustrative source of mounting value.

**6.** Philemon and Diphilus (qq.v.), along with the peerless Menander, formed the representative triad canonized by ancient critics; of the seventy or so remaining playwrights only a few, notably Posidippus and Apollodorus (3) of Carystus (qq.v.), are more than mere names for us.

Meineke, Kock, Demiańczuk, Edmonds (*as under* OLD COMEDY). Körte, Lloyd-Jones (*as under* MENANDER (1) where publication of other, more recent finds is cited too). P. A. E. F. Legrand, *Daos* (1910). O. Schroeder, *Novae com. fragm. in papyris reperta exceptis Menandreis* (Bonn, 1915) requires revision. D. L. Page, *Select Papyri*,

vol. iii, *Literary* (Loeb). T. B. L. Webster, *Monuments Illustrating New Comedy*, *BICS* Suppl. xi, 1961 (also *Lustrum* 1956, 111 ff.; 1961, 30), *Later Greek Comedy*.
     T. J. P. W.

**COMEDY (LATIN)**, see DRAMA, ROMAN.

**COMINIANUS** (early 4th c. A.D.), grammarian. His *Ars*, compiled for school use, is not extant, but is referred to respectfully by Charisius and was probably the basis of Dositheus (q.v. 2).

Schanz–Hosius, § 825.

**COMITATENSES**, i.e. units forming the Emperor's *comitatus*, were one of the two divisions in the Roman field army as reorganized by Constantine. They comprised both *vexillationes* (cavalry units of 500 men) and *legiones* (infantry units of 1,000 men) and were under the command of the *magistri militum*. See PALATINI.

D. van Berchem, *L'Armée de Dioclétien et la réforme constantinienne* (1952); Jones, *Later Rom. Emp.* 608 ff.      H. M. D. P.

**COMITES.** Under the Principate those who accompanied the *princeps* on his journeys abroad were semi-officially styled his *comites*. In the Constantinian reorganization the title was bestowed by official codicil upon the leading military and civil functionaries. The *comites* were classified in three grades (*ordinis primi, secundi*, and *tertii*).

*Comites* was also the title of certain mobile cavalry units which are first attested in the late third century.

Jones, *Later Rom. Emp.* 52 f. 104 ff.      H. M. D. P.; G. R. W.

**COMITIA.** In Rome *comitium* was the place of assembling; *comitia* meant an assembly of the Roman People summoned in groups by a magistrate with *ius agendi cum populo*. The convocation had to be on a proper day (*comitialis*), after the *auspicia* had been taken, on an inaugurated site. When only a part of the People was summoned, the assembly was strictly a *concilium* (Gell. 15. 27). When the whole People was summoned, but not by groups, the assembly was a *contio* (q.v.). In the *comitia* the majority in each group determined the vote of the group. The *comitia* voted only on business presented to them by magistrates, and they could not amend proposals. As the three main divisions of the Roman People were *curiae, centuriae, tribus* (qq.v.), the three types of *comitia* were *curiata, centuriata, tributa*. A special form of the *comitia curiata* and *centuriata* was the *comitia calata* (it is disputed whether they were summoned by the *pontifices* who played an important part in them). The resolutions of the *comitia* (and possibly of the *concilia plebis*) depended for their validity on a formal ratification by the patrician senators (*see* PATRUM AUCTORITAS).

**2.** (*a*) *Comitia curiata*. The most ancient *comitia* were the *curiata* (*see* CURIA 1), dating from the age of the kings. Their competence was progressively limited by the *comitia centuriata*. In historical times they formally confirmed the appointment of magistrates by a *lex curiata* (q.v.) *de imperio*, and witnessed the installation of priests, adoptions, and the making of wills, when the *pontifex maximus* perhaps presided at these ceremonies. The monthly announcement by the *pontifices* of the day on which the *nonae* would fall was probably made before the *curiae*. In Cicero's time the 30 *curiae* were represented in the *comitia* only by 30 lictors (Cic. *Leg. Agr.* 2. 12. 31).

(*b*) *Comitia centuriata*. The *comitia centuriata*, on a timocratic basis (*see* CENTURIA), were traditionally instituted by Servius Tullius. Many modern scholars prefer a later date (after 450 B.C.). The enacting of laws, the election of the magistrates *cum imperio* and of the censors, the declaration of war and peace, and the infliction of the death penalty—at least for political charges and offences —were concerns of *comitia centuriata*: the relation

between *provocatio* (q.v.) and trial by *comitia centuriata* is a matter of dispute (see for opposite views Mommsen's and Kunkel's works). An interval (*trinundinum*—probably of twenty-four days) was observed after the notification of a meeting, during which preliminary discussions (*contiones*) of the proposals (*rogationes*) were held. In the judicial *comitia* a preliminary investigation before a *contio* had to be held, lasting for three days; after a *trinundinum* and perhaps a further *contio* the vote was taken. The *comitia centuriata* met 'extra pomerium' (q.v.), usually in the Campus Martius, in military order. But in the last period of the Republic the voting centuries were no longer identical with the tactical field-units. The *Lex Caecilia Didia* (98 B.C.) forbade the presenting in the same bill of proposals dealing with unrelated subjects. The formula by which the magistrate proposed the law was: 'uelitis iubeatis Quirites rogo'. Approbation was expressed by the formula 'uti rogas'; rejection by 'antiquo'. The method of voting is described s.v. VOTING (2). The voting groups were unequal, and the wealthier citizens consequently exercised a preponderating influence. In the third century B.C. this disparity was lessened; but the *comitia centuriata* never became democratic.

(*c*) *Comitia plebis tributa*. The assemblies of the plebs were not strictly *comitia* but a *concilium*. But when *plebiscita* were given equal validity with the laws (287 B.C.), the *concilium plebis* was as a rule called *comitia*. It was divided in conformity with the territorial tribes (*see* TRIBUS). In them the tribunes of the plebs and the plebeian aediles were elected, trials were held for non-capital offences, and nearly every form of business was enacted. The procedure was quicker than in the *comitia centuriata*.

(*d*) The *comitia populi tributa* were founded in imitation of the *comitia plebis tributa*, at an uncertain date. They differed from the former in that they were convoked by consuls or praetors, and patricians were admitted. They elected quaestors, *aediles curules, tribuni militum a populo*, enacted laws, and held minor trials.

**3.** From *c.* 250 B.C. the Pontifex Maximus and from 104 B.C. (except during the period from Sulla to 63 B.C.) *pontifices, augures*, and *decemviri sacrorum* were elected by special *comitia* of seventeen tribes.

**4.** The *comitia* in Rome decayed with the extension of the Roman territory, which made it impossible for individuals to attend, and with the growing oligarchic spirit of the leading class, which avoided any reform of them. An attempt of Augustus to give to the *decuriones* of the colonies a chance to vote without coming to Rome was too late (Suet. *Aug.* 46). The election of magistrates was transferred to the Senate by Tiberius; only the declaration of the result (*renuntiatio*) was still performed before the People. The judicial functions also lapsed; and the last law known to us is an agrarian law of A.D. 98. The *comitia* continued a formal existence at least until the third century A.D.

**5.** The *municipia* and *coloniae* had *comitia*, at which (in republican times and at least in the first century of the Empire) magistrates were elected. In republican times they had also some legislative powers.

*See also* CURIA (1), CENTURIA, CLASSIS, LEX CURIATA, TRIBUS.

Mommsen, *Röm. Staatsr.* iii; G. W. Botsford, *The Roman Assemblies* (U.S.A. 1909); A. H. J. Greenidge, *Roman Public Life* (1901); G. Rotondi, *Leges publicae populi Romani* (1912); G. Nocera, *Il potere dei comizi e i suoi limiti* (1940); U. von Lübtow, *Das Römische Volk* (1955); E. Meyer, *Röm. Staat und Staatsgedanke*[3] (1964); L. R. Taylor, *Roman Voting Assemblies* (1966); H. Siber, *Sav. Zeitschr.* 1937, 233 ff.; G. Beseler, ibid. 356 ff.; C. H. Brecht, ibid. 1936, 261 ff.; U. Kahrstedt, *Rh. Mus.* 1917, 258 ff.; H. Last, *JRS* 1945, 30 ff.; F. Cornelius, *Unters. zur frühen röm. Geschichte* (1940); A. C. Roos, *Med. Nederl. Akad.* 1940, n. 3; H. Siber, *PW* xxiii, 128; E. S. Staveley, *AJPhil.* 1953, 1 ff.; J. Bleicken, *Hermes* 1957, 345 ff.

(*comitia calata*); P. Brunt, *JRS* 1961, 81 ff.; C. Nicolet, *Rev. Hist. Droit Franc. Étranger* 1961, 341 ff.; G. V. Sumner, *Athenaeum* 1962, 37 ff.; E. S. Staveley, *Hist.* 1962, 299 ff.; L. R. Taylor, *Athenaeum* 1963, 51 ff.; U. Hall, *Hist.* 1964, 267 ff. On trials W. Kunkel, *Untersuchungen zur Entwicklung des röm. Kriminalverfahrens* (1962); cf. P. Brunt, *Tijdschrift voor Rechtsgeschiedenis* 1964, 440 ff. On the possible relevance of the Brindisi elogium to the comitia centuriata, F. Cassola, *I gruppi politici romani nel III sec. a. C.* (1962), 289 (with bibl.) and A. Guarino, *Labeo* 1963, 89 ff. See also A. K. Michels, *The Calendar of the Roman Republic* (U.S.A. 1967).　　　　A. M.

**COMITIUM,** the chief place of political assembly in Republican Rome (Varro, *Ling.* 5. 155; Livy 5. 55) occupying an area north of the Forum between the Clivus Argentarius and the Argiletum. The topographical problems are difficult. It has been argued that the comitium was an open slope, perhaps stepped like a theatre descending to an open space in front of the *Rostra* and the *Graecostasis*. The Curia stood on the northern rim, the *carcer* and perhaps the *Basilica Porcia* on the west. The site was consecrated like a templum and the buildings apparently orientated by the cardinal points. The area was restricted by Caesar to a small space containing the successive republican *rostra* respectively associated with all but the first and last of five levels ranging from the sixth century B.C. to 52 B.C. The numerous monuments and statues which filled it have perished, excepting the ancient group consisting of a *sacellum*, a tufa cone, and an archaic *cippus* of ritual law (*ILS* 4913), all sealed in damaged condition below a black marble pavement (*lapis niger*) itself at least once altered in position.

E. B. van Deman, *JRS* 1922, 6 ff.; E. Gjerstad, *Opusc. Archeol.* ii (1941), 97 ff.; E. Sjöqvist, *Stud. Pres. D. M. Robinson* i (1951), 400 ff.; L. Richardson, *Archaeology* 1957, 49 ff.; Nash, *Pict. Dict. Rome* i, 287 ff.　　　　I. A. R.; D. E. S.

**COMMAGENE,** in north Syria, became an independent kingdom in 162 B.C. when its governor, Ptolemy, revolted against the Seleucids. His son Samos was succeeded as king by Mithridates Callinicus (*c.* 96–*c.* 70). The latter's son, Antiochus I (q.v.), submitted to Pompey in 64 B.C. and was rewarded with a piece of Mesopotamia; he was deposed by Antony in 38 B.C. for abetting the Parthian invasion. On the death of Antiochus III Tiberius annexed the kingdom in A.D. 17, but it was restored by Gaius in A.D. 38 to King Antiochus IV (q.v.), who, after being deposed by Gaius, was reinstated by Claudius in 41 and reigned till 72, when Vespasian, on account of his alleged Parthian sympathies, finally annexed the kingdom and incorporated it in Syria. The royal house claimed descent, through the satrapal dynasty of Armenia, from Darius, and, by a marriage alliance with the Seleucids, from Alexander; its genealogy and its religion, a superficially hellenized Zoroastrianism, are illustrated by the pretentious funeral monument of Antiochus I. On the annexation the country was divided into four city territories, Samosata (the royal capital, founded by King Samos *c.* 150 B.C.), Caesarea Germanicia (founded by Antiochus IV in A.D. 38), Perrhe, and Doliche. Commagene remained a separate κοινόν within the province of Syria.

E. Honigmann, *PW*, Suppl. iv, 978–90; K. Humann and O. Puchstein, *Reisen in Kleinasien* (1890); F. K. Doerner and T. Goell, *Arsameia am Nymphaios* (1963). For the monuments of Antiochus I at Nimrud Dagh see R. Ghirshman, *Iran* (1962), 57 ff.; H. Dörrie, *Der Königskult des Antiochus von Kommagene* (1964).　　A. H. M. J.

**COMMENDATIO.** Under the Roman Republic distinguished consulars influenced the elections of magistrates by open canvassing (*suffragatio*) on behalf of their friends. This practice, when employed by an emperor, was known as *commendatio*, and the recommended candidates (*candidati Caesaris*) were elected without opposition. Augustus at first canvassed in person (Suet. *Aug.* 56), but after A.D. 8 (Dio Cass. 55. 34) announced the names of his candidates in writing.

*Commendatio* was first employed for magistracies between the quaestorship and the praetorship (for which the Princeps recommended four candidates; Tac. *Ann.* 1. 15), but by the end of Nero's principate it was employed for the consulship also (Tac. *Hist.* 1. 77). The *Lex de imperio Vespasiani* (Dessau, *ILS* 244) granted to the Emperor the right of *commendatio*, apparently for all magistracies without limitation of number. Henceforth the consuls appear to have been the Emperor's nominees (cf. Pliny, *Pan.* 77, 'praestare consulibus ipsum qui consules facit').　　　　J. P. B.

**COMMENTARII** (ὑπομνήματα) were memoranda, originally of a private character, e.g. *tabulae accepti et expensi*, note-books for speeches, legal notes, etc. Their public use (excluding the false *commentarii regum*) developed in the priestly colleges (e.g. *commentarii pontificum, augurum*), and in the magistracies (e.g. *commentarii consulares, censorii, aedilium*), and with the provincial governors. Under the Empire, the *commentarii principis*, like the Hellenistic ἐφημερίδες, represented a court journal, and the system spread in the imperial administration, under the influence of the ὑπομνηματισμοί of the *praefectus Aegypti*. The Emperors' *commentarii* of campaigns and audiences, constitutions, rescripts, epistles, and edicts, had official authority.

From the business *commentarii* arose the literary form, autobiographical in character, written in plain style as a basis of full history, yet directed to the reading public, e.g. Sulla's ὑπομνήματα and, above all, Caesar's *commentarii*.

A. Rosenberg, *Einleitung und Quellenkunde zur röm. Geschichte* (1921), 2; cf. J. B. Bury, *Ancient Greek Historians* (1909), 232 ff.; F. Bömer, *Hermes* 1953, 210 ff.　　　　A. H. McD.

**COMMENTARII or LIBRI PONTIFICUM,** general name for the records kept by the *Collegium Pontificum* in Rome. They included *commentarii sacrorum*, of which an idea may be formed from the existing *acta Arvalium* (*see* FRATRES ARVALES) and *acta ludorum saecularium*, save that these are records of ritual actually performed, the pontifical *commentarii* being directions for the performance of ritual when necessary. They probably contained not only this, but also the text of prayers, sacred laws, and other relevant matter. The details are often extremely obscure, since neither the *commentarii* themselves nor any sufficient number of what may be safely regarded as verbatim quotations have come down to us. How old any kind of written liturgy, etc., was in Rome we do not know.

G. Rohde, *RGVV* 1936.　　　　H. J. R.

**COMMERCE, GREEK AND ROMAN.** A certain amount of trade with valuable raw materials and products of craftsmanship can be proved for Neolithic Greece and Italy from finds and excavations, and in an increasing degree for the same regions during the Bronze and Iron Ages. Many early traders seem to have been warriors, sailors, pirates, and craftsmen simultaneously. Those of the Minoan and Mycenaean town cultures were, perhaps, employees and serfs of their rulers after the model of the ancient oriental cultures. They had connexions with and brought their products to all Mediterranean coasts and even to middle Europe. We have, however, no evidence of barter in cheap products from published Linear B inscriptions, but its existence is self-evident.

2. The development of Greek trade after the migrations (*see* COINAGE, GREEK for later dates) is closely connected with the invention of coins *c.* 600 B.C., and especially those of small denominations *c.* 570 B.C. Sale of cheap goods like grain, oil, pottery, small hardware, etc., became easier and paid better than exchange by barter. The Phoenician traders in valuable products of foreign

countries lost their earlier importance for Greece and Italy, and gave way to native trade centres (e.g. Corinth, Athens, Aegina; the ports of Asia Minor, the Black Sea, and Magna Graecia). Three Greek commercial crafts developed during the later seventh and sixth centuries B.C., all free and independent, but without much working capital, those of the *naukleros* (a sea-merchant with his own ships), the *emporos* (a sea-merchant using the ships of others), and the *kapelos* (a petty trader in small districts).

**3.** The Classical Greek Age carried Hellenic trade patterns to neighbouring countries. Greek imports and exports of cheap goods, grain, oil, wine, cattle, Corinthian, Attic, and other pottery, metal products, etc., as well as inter-regional commerce, grew in such a degree that the markets (*agorai*) of Athens and of other towns became surprisingly efficient, and their *kapeloi* were able to specialize in single products and crafts like those of middlemen for imported products. The sea-merchants began to specialize as well, e.g. as foreign agents and as exclusive transport merchants. Some of the *emporoi* became land merchants. *Deigmata* (mercantile exchanges) were built in large ports. 'Corners' of merchant associations tried occasionally to increase prices. The foreign population of Athens grew enormously. Greek imports of valuable foreign products were also more intensive than in earlier centuries, Greece being wealthier than before the Persian Wars. Greek export trade with valuable merchandise reached the Atlantic coasts and India.

**4.** Rome became, during the same period, a modest river port and centre of communications for the middle Italian trade, and had a certain importance for the salt trade of its neighbours. It introduced market days and festivals (*nundinae, ludi Apollinares, ludi Romani, ludi plebeii*), and created the *Forum Boarium* for foreign merchants. The beginnings of the Roman law of sales were of future importance.

**5.** The campaigns of Alexander, the *Diadochi*, and the Roman generals from the Punic Wars to Augustus unified the immense region between the Atlantic Ocean and India, the Sahara, Rhine, Danube, and the Ukraine. The Greek economic structure was imitated everywhere, but not without being modified and adapted to new conditions. The towns of the Greek mother country, and many of the *poleis* and hellenized Phoenician towns in the East, preserved much of the economic structure of the pre-Alexander days. Main centres of such an economic type were Syracuse, Tarentum, Naples, Carthage, Massilia, and Cyrene in the West; Alexandria in Egypt, Corinth, Athens, Ephesus, Miletus, Apamea, Delos, and Rhodes in the old country; Olbia, Tanaïs, Byzantium, Thessalonica, and Sinope in the North, Antioch on the Orontes, Seleuceia in Pieria, Sidon, Tyre, Seleuceia on the Tigris, and Alexandria Charax in the East. The main trade was in cheap goods, the commercial crafts and their trading methods were not materially altered, but trade associations became more common and some of the *emporoi* were more specialized than during the classical period.

**6.** On the other hand, compulsory state planning was the most characteristic trade condition for the Egyptian countryside, for Hellenistic India, and to a lesser degree the more barbaric regions of the Seleucid, the Pergamenian, the southern Arabian, and the Parthian empires, which gradually developed a separate Semitic-Iranian Hellenism. In Ptolemaic Egypt, for example, the trade in oil, soda, salt, perfumes, beer, mining products, textile, leather, metal products, and (perhaps) papyrus was monopolized, so that the government was able to control the price and quality of such merchandise and to claim special fees for the right to buy and to sell, very few enterprises being privileged. Prices and trade conditions of grain, cattle, fish, game, wood, wine, slaves, and the

whole of the import and export trade were more or less government-controlled.

**7.** Roman civilization followed the Greek example, but modified it. Italy's essential imports of cheap products could not be paid for in full by her trading exports. Therefore the supply of Rome with raw materials for military purposes and grain was largely dependent on tribute. The exports of Italy, especially those in pottery, hardware, wine, and oil, spread over the whole of the Mediterranean during the last two centuries B.C., but by political as well as economic methods. The foreign trade in valuable products was much more important in the Latin than in the Greek part of the ancient world. Rome was the economic centre. Its main ports were Puteoli and later Ostia; its main provincial import and export harbours Aquileia in north Italy; Narbo and Arelate in Gaul; Utica and Cyrene in Africa; Athens, Delos, Pergamum, Ephesus, Apamea, Antioch, and Alexandria in the East. The Roman commercial crafts *navicularii* (= *naukleroi*), *mercatores* (= *emporoi*), *caupones* (= *kapeloi*) of the second century B.C. and their pattern of trade were similar to the Greek practice, albeit not so specialized; but from the first century onwards *caupo* (and later *kapelos* as well) meant an innkeeper, *mercator* a *kapelos* or a small *emporos*. The great capitalists, already known from Alexander's time in the East, became a special craft, that of the *negotiatores*, who were at the same time merchants, bankers, and owners of workshops and large estates. They almost superseded the Greek type of great *emporoi* and absorbed the main business in all Roman provinces up to the time of Caesar.

**8.** A large area of the Old World remained outside the Greek, Latin, and the not very different Semitic-Iranian regions of Hellenism, which were in close commercial exchange. Britain, Germany, southern Russia, western Siberia, and India were visited by Mediterranean merchants; but their trade habits had to be assimilated to alien conditions. Valuable products of the Hellenistic world even reached China and central Africa, as finds and Chinese reports prove.

**9.** The time of the Roman Principate began with an absolute commercial supremacy of Rome and Italy, and free Empire trade (wherever advisable). It ended with a far-reaching economic autarky of the Roman provinces and state control over commerce. Britain and Dacia only were added to the central zone of ancient commerce during that period. The foreign trade of the Roman Empire was considerable, as finds and many Latin and Greek words in Irish, German, Pahlavi, Semitic, Iranian, and even a few in Indian and Mongolian languages prove. A few Roman merchants reached China, and Chinese merchants seem to have come to Iran and the most eastern parts of the Empire either via ocean or caravan routes.

**10.** The internal changes were more revolutionary. The imports and exports of most of the earlier centres for cheap products gradually lost importance for private buyers, because such merchandise could be, and as a rule was, produced locally or in a consumer's own province. In such circumstances only the inter-provincial import and export of valuable goods remained lucrative from about the third century A.D. A considerable amount of local trade was done by large estates and state institutions which did not require real merchants for this purpose. During the first century A.D. the *negotiatores* had spread as *pragmateutai* to the Hellenistic East, and the merchants and traders had been able to specialize in the Hellenistic way throughout the Latin provinces of the Empire, and in regions and provinces like Egypt which had not known free trade during the Hellenistic period; but from about the time of Hadrian all important commercial crafts had to be saved from complete collapse by the Roman government. The *collegia* (*see* CLUBS) of merchants—originally private organizations—were bound, regulated, and privileged by the state, first those of the transport merchants, then those of the other crafts. The Hellenistic trade control had not been completely dissolved by the Roman government in many provincial regions. Now a new compulsory system with characteristic legal regulations arose wherever state necessities were concerned. The end of free trade for many centuries had come. Prices and trade conditions were controlled by magistrates whenever difficulties arose.

11. The commerce of the Late Roman Empire up to the Islamic conquest has often been underestimated. This was no period of 'house-economy'. The trade in valuable products was equal to that of earlier centuries. Jewels, perfumes, ivories, valuable textiles and glasses of the Mediterranean world were well known in northern Europe, Abyssinia, India, central and even eastern Asia. Trade in cheap products had suffered owing to Diocletian's system of taxation in kind, the decrease of the Roman and Greek town population during the third century A.D., and the autarky of many large feudal and church estates; but it was doubtless on the average superior to that of classical Greece (with the exception, perhaps, of Athens). The markets of Rome, Alexandria, Antioch, Constantinople, and many other towns were in normal years as full as ever of all that the population required. On the other hand, the strict and well-organized government control of the conditions of sale, and the codification of Roman commercial law, were novelties. Foreign trade was, if possible, restricted to certain frontier places, so that arms for prospective enemies as well as raw materials and victuals, as far as they happened to be scarce in the Empire, could not be exported. Profitable imports, e.g. Chinese silk, became state monopolies. Government officials controlled the quality and prices of all merchandise in their districts as well as the quantities allowed to a merchant. The variety of products is well known from Diocletian's Price Edict and the Church Fathers. On the other hand, the purchasing power of the Empire population had much decreased, and only in big towns and very wealthy country districts could the earlier specialization of commercial crafts be maintained to any extent. Not much difference existed, as a rule, between *negotiator* and *mercator*, between *emporos* and *kapelos*. Traders were very often craftsmen simultaneously, and comparatively few big merchant firms remained; but on the whole the standard of Late Roman commerce was sufficient for the needs of the period, and we may justly consider its controlled organization as indispensable for the future world-wide progress of commerce during the Islamic and the later European Middle Ages.

*See* AEGINA, AFRICA, ALEXANDRIA (1), AMBER, ANTIOCH (1), APAMEA, AQUILEIA, ARABIA, ARELATE, ATHENS, BANKS, BOTTOMRY LOANS, BRITANNIA, BYZANTIUM, CARTHAGE, CIRTA, COINAGE (GREEK, ROMAN), CONSTANTINOPLE, CORINTH, CYRENE, DELOS, EPHESUS, ERANOS, EUDOXUS (3), EUXINE SEA, FORUM BOARIUM, GLASS, HANNO (1), INDIA, INDUSTRY, INTEREST, ISTRIA (1), LAMPSACUS, LAODICEA, LIBYA, LIGHTHOUSES, LUDI, MALACA, MARBLE, MASSILIA, METICS, MILETUS, MONEY, MONOPOLIES, NABATAEANS, NARBO, NEAPOLIS, NUMIDIA, OLBIA, OSTIA, PALMYRA, PANTICAPAEUM, PERGAMUM, PHOENICIANS, PIRAEUS, POTTERY, PTOLEMY (1), PURPLE, PUTEOLI, PYTHEAS, RAVENNA, RED SEA, RHODES, SAMOS, SARDINIA, SCYTHIA, SELEUCIA (1,2), SERES, SHIPS, SICILY, SIDON, SINOPE, SLAVES, SOLON, SPAIN, SYRACUSE, SYRIA, TANAIS, TARENTUM, TARTESSUS, THASOS, THESSALONICA, THRACE, THULE, TIN, TYRE, USURY, UTICA, WINE.

J. L. Myres, in *CAH* iii, ch. 25; M. N. Tod, ibid. v, ch. i; T. Frank, ibid. viii, ch. xi; M. Rostovtzeff, ibid. viii, chs. 18, 20; xi, ch. 3; W. W. Tarn, ibid. ix, ch. 14; F. Oertel, ibid. x, ch. 13; xii, ch. 7. A. Berger, *Encyclopedic Dictionary of Roman Law* (1953), art. 'caupo', 'commercium', 'consistentes', 'ius commercii', 'lex Claudia', 'lex Rhodia', 'mercator', 'navicularii', 'negotiator', 'negotiatores', 'nundinae', 'receptum nautae', 'societas'; H. Bolkestein, *Economic Life in Greece's Golden Age²* (1958), chs. 5, 6; G. M. Calhoun, *The Business Life of Ancient Athens* (1926); M. P. Charlesworth,*Trade Routes and Commerce of the Roman Empire²* (1926); V. Ehrenberg, *The People of Aristophanes³* (1962), chs. 5, 6, 12; M. Finkelstein, *CPhil.* 1935, 320 ff.; M. I. Finley, *The Ancient Greeks* (1963), index; T. Frank, *An Economic History of Rome²* (1927); *Econ. Survey* i–v (indexes, s.v. 'commerce', 'trade'). G. Glotz, *Le Travail dans la Grèce ancienne* (1920), pt. i, chs. 1, 6. pt. ii, chs. 1, 3, 5. pt. iii, chs. 4, 10. pt. iv, ch. 6; J. Hasebroek,*Trade and Politics in Ancient Greece* (1933) id., *Griechische Wirtschafts- und Gesellschaftsgeschichte* (1931), F. M. Heichelheim, *Wirtschaftsgeschichte des Altertums* (1938), index, s.v. 'Fernhandel', 'Gueterumlauf','Kaufmannsberuf','Nahhandel'; *An Ancient Economic History* i (1958), 388 ff., 437 ff., 482 f., 490 ff., 494 ff., ii (1964), 171 ff. *Römische Social- und Wirtschaftsgeschichte*, in *Historia Mundi* iv (1956), 397 f. art. 'Wirtschaftsgeschichte ii, 2 A, in *Handwörterbuch der Sozialwissenschaften* (1962, 44), 144 f.; Jones, *Later Rom. Emp.* ch. 21; Michell, *Econom. Anc. Gr.*, index, s.v. 'commerce', 'trade'; G. Mickwitz, *Virteljahrsschrift für Sozial- und Wirtschaftsgesch.* (1939), 13 ff. *Geld und Wirtschaft im römischen Reiche des 4. Jahrh. n. Chr.* (1932); Cl. Préaux, *L'Économie royale des Lagides* (1939). Rostovtzeff, *Hellenistic World*; *Roman Empire²* (indexes, s.v. trade). L. Ruggini, *Economia e società nell'Italia Annonaria* (1961); Warmington, *Indian Commerce*; E. Ziebarth, *Seeraub und Seehandel im alten Griechenland* (1929); J. H. Miller, *The Spice Trade of the Roman Empire* (1969). F. M. H.

**COMMERCIUM** was the right of any *Latinus* (*see* LATINI) to enter into contracts with a Roman according to the forms of Roman law and enforceable in the Roman courts without recourse to the *ius gentium* (and vice versa). Without it a foreigner could only secure his rights by the help of the *praetor peregrinus*. *Conubium* similarly was the right to contract a legal marriage with a member of another state without either party forfeiting inheritance or paternity rights. Without *conubium* a Roman's children by a foreigner took the citizenship of the foreigner. These complementary rights formed an essential part of *ius Latii* (q.v.). Their development, unparalleled in the ancient world until the later stages of some Greek cities, belongs to the period before the growth of large states in Latium, and was encouraged by the continental environment of the numerous small *populi* of the plain-dwellers, *Latini* (q.v.). In 338 B.C. Rome temporarily suspended these rights between certain Latin peoples, and again between certain Hernici in 308. This was only a temporary expedient in punishment for their revolts. The Latin colonies, including the so-called 'Last Twelve' founded between 268 and 181 B.C., all shared these rights not only with Rome but with one another, for, being often contiguous and also adjacent to Roman colonies, they could not flourish without such connexions. These *iura* also formed the chief practical benefit of *civitas sine suffragio* (*see* MUNICIPIUM), and could be granted to other *socii Italici* by special dispensation. By the Social War they were perhaps common throughout Italy. Under the Empire *conubium* was sometimes withheld from *ius Latii*, but the spread of Roman citizenship inside Latin communities rendered this rare. The grant of either to *peregrini*, however, remained exceptional. *Conubium cum peregrinis mulieribus* was thus given as a reward upon discharge to the praetorian troops, when required, and also along with the citizenship to the auxiliary troops drawn from the provinces.

These conceptions could also be applied to the relations between any communities of *peregrini*. Thus in 168 B.C. Macedonia was split up into four districts which were forbidden *commercium* or *conubium*, as an exceptional expedient to avoid the creation of a new province.

For bibliography, *see* LATINI, IUS LATII. A. N. S.-W.

**COMMIUS**, appointed king of the Atrebates by Caesar 57 B.C., acted as cavalry leader and general diplomatic agent, especially in Britain. He joined the revolt of 52, however, and evaded attempts at capture and assassination. He finally retired to Britain, where he founded a dynasty (British Atrebates inscribed coins may be his).

C. Hawkes and G. C. Dunning, *Arch. Journ.* 1930, 291 ff.; R. P. Mack, *The Coinage of Ancient Britain* (1953), 31 ff.; Frere, *Britannia*, index. C. E. S.

**COMMODIANUS,** Christian Latin poet, variously assigned to the third, fourth, and fifth centuries A.D., and to Syria (Gaza), Gaul, and Africa, wrote the *Instructiones*, eighty short poems in acrostic form, and *Carmen apologeticum*, a metrical exposition of Christian doctrine. The language is noteworthy for its vulgar content, the versification for its rude hexameters, in which quantity plays little part.

TEXTS. B. Dombart, *CSEL* xv; J. Martin, *Corp. Christ., SL* cxxviii (1960). A. F. van Katwijk, *Lexicon Commodianeum* (1934). L. Krestan, *RAC*, s.v. *Commodianus*. A. H.-W.

**COMMODUS,** LUCIUS AELIUS AURELIUS (*PW* 89), sole Emperor A.D. 180–92, elder son of Marcus Aurelius, was born in A.D. 161. During his father's principate he was gradually advanced to the status of joint-ruler which he attained in 177 (Caesar in 166, *imperator* in 176, consul, *tribunicia potestas*, and Augustus in 177). In 177, after his marriage to Crispina, he accompanied his father to the second German-Sarmatian War.

On his accession in 180, he changed his name to M. Aurelius Commodus Antoninus. Peace was concluded on the German frontier, restrictions and controls being imposed on the tribes in return for subsidies and the evacuation of occupied territory. Commodus maintained a peaceful policy on all frontiers; the only serious trouble was in Britain where the Antonine Wall was overrun, the situation being restored by Ulpius Marcellus.

At first Commodus retained some of his father's ministers, e.g. Tarrutenius Paternus as praetorian prefect. But soon he resorted to government by means of favourites and displayed hostility to the Senate, which was exacerbated by an abortive conspiracy promoted by Lucilla and Ummidius Quadratus (182). For the next six years Rome was virtually governed by the praetorian prefects Perennis (182–5) and Cleander (186–9).

Commodus finally came under the influence of his concubine Marcia, his chamberlain Eclectus, and Laetus, who became praetorian prefect in 191. The intoxication of power seems to have deranged his mind. Senatorial persecutions were redoubled, Rome was rebaptized *Colonia Commodiana*, and the Emperor regarded himself as the incarnation of Hercules (title of *Hercules Romanus*). To perfect the impersonation he determined to appear in public on 1 Jan. 193 as both consul and gladiator, and this so outraged the feelings of his advisers that they suborned an athlete called Narcissus to strangle him.

Herodian, bk. 1; Dio Cassius, bk. 72; S.H.A. *Comm.*, J. M Heer, *Der historische Wert der Vita Commodi* (1901); F. Grosso, *La lotta politica al tempo di Commodo* (1964). H. M. D. P.; B. H. W.

**COMMON PEACE** (κοινὴ εἰρήνη), the phrase used by Diodorus Siculus, following Ephorus, and by some contemporaries (though not by Demosthenes, Isocrates, or Xenophon) to describe a series of peace-treaties in Greece in the fourth century B.C. applicable to all cities on the basis of autonomy. Such treaties were concluded in 387/6 (the King's Peace), 375, 371 twice, 365 (possibly), 362/1 and 338/7 (the League of Corinth), and proposed on other occasions; their principles strongly influenced the foreign policies of leading cities between 387 and 338 and were used as the basis of their relations with Greece by Philip II, Alexander, and Antigonus I.

T. T. B. Ryder, *Koine Eirene* (1965). T. T. B. R.

**COMMUNES LOCI,** 'commonplaces' (in Greek κοινοὶ τόποι, traced back as far as Gorgias and Protagoras by Cicero, *Brut.* 46–7), were 'arguments that could be transferred to many cases' (Cic. *Inv. Rhet.* 2. 48). They could be practised separately in schools (Quintilian 2. 4. 22), and published separately (id. 10. 5. 12). Some were directed against vices (id. 2. 1. 11); some discussed topics

of importance in court, such as the value of witnesses (Cic. *Cael.* 21 f.: *Part. Or.* 48 f.); others, like those listed in Cic. *De Or.* 1. 56 ('de dis immortalibus, de pietate, de concordia', etc.) were begrudged to oratory by philosophers. The variety was much increased by the declaimers of the first century A.D., because such passages could be easily learnt up and inserted more or less appropriately in declamations (see S. F. Bonner, *Roman Declamation* (1949), 60 f.); and by this route they appear in Silver Age literature. Thus the *locus de indulgentia* can be instructively traced from Lysias (24. 17) through Cicero (*Cael.* 39 f.: see Austin's note) and the Elder Seneca to Juvenal.

L. Arbusow, *Colores Rhetorici²* (Göttingen, 1963), 91 ff. (mainly medieval). M. W.

**COMMUNIO,** common ownership by two or more persons of a thing (including land) or of an undivided group of things (e.g. inheritance), originating in a contract by the parties (*societas, see* CONTRACT), or, independently of their intention, in a common inheritance or legacy. In early law (*consortium, societas ercto non cito*: Gai. *Inst.* 3. 154 a, b) a legal transaction in relation to the thing by one owner affected the rights of all (e.g. alienation transferred ownership of the whole), but in classical law such a transaction affected only the particular co-owner's notional share, or, if it did not admit of such divided effect, was void. (Thus a purported creation of a usufruct (*see* SERVITUTES) over the whole affected only the creator's share, and a creation of a praedial servitude was void. There were special rules as to manumission of a common slave.) In the material enjoyment of the property each co-owner could exercise the full rights of an owner, subject to the veto of any other co-owner (*ius prohibendi*). Disputes were adjusted by an action for division of the property (*actio communi dividundo*; *actio familiae erciscundae*, for division of inheritance). The judge divided the property among the co-owners in proportion to their shares, with equalizing payments where necessary. Profits, expenses, and damages, incurred by individual joint owners, were also apportioned by the judge.

A. Berger, *Zur Entwicklungsgeschichte der Teilungsklagen* (1912); S. Riccobono, *Essays in Legal History*, Intern. Congress of Historical Studies 1913; J. Gaudemet, *Régime juridique de l'indivision* (1934). On *consortium*: F. Wieacker, *Societas* (1936); F. de Zulueta, *JRS* 1935. A. B.; B. N.

**COMPRECATIONES.** Aulus Gellius (13. 23. 1–2) quotes from the *libri sacerdotum populi Romani*, that is to say the *commentarii pontificum* (q.v.), the following forms of address, which he calls *comprecationes deum immortalium* (since they are in the accusative, it would appear that some verb meaning 'to invoke' is to be supplied): *Luam Saturni, Salaciam Neptuni, Horam Quirini, Virites Quirini, Maiam Volcani, Heriem Iunonis, Moles Martis Nerienemque Martis*. It is clear that each pair consists of a well-known deity associated with an obscure one, or in two cases, a plurality of such. Since family relationships among Roman deities are unknown, and Gellius distinctly says that these prayers 'ritu Romano fiunt', no such word as *uxor* or *filia* can be supplied (contrast, e.g., *Terentia Ciceronis, Tullia Ciceronis*). It therefore remains to suppose that the genitives mean that the lesser deity is somehow active in the sphere presided over by the greater one, and are therefore used in a sense which could equally well be expressed by an adjective.

K. Kerényi, *SMSR* 1933, 17 ff.; Latte, *RR* 55. H. J. R.

**COMUM,** modern *Como*, birthplace of the Elder and the Younger Pliny, of whom the latter owned large properties there and was a notable benefactor. A flourishing centre of the South Alpine Iron Age Golaseccan culture, it came under Celtic rule in the fourth century B.C. and in

196 B.C. it passed within the Roman orbit. After 89 B.C. it received a first group of colonial settlers, and in 59 B.C., at the hands of Julius Caesar, a second group, under the name of *Novum Comum*. During the Empire it became a *municipium*, with territories bordering on those of Mediolanum and Bergomum. In late antiquity it was an important military base for the protection of north Italy. The principal surviving remains are those of the Ca' Morta Iron Age cemetery, in the Civic Museum, and the chequer-board street-plan of the Roman town, still faithfully reflected by that of the modern city.

D. Randall-MacIver, *The Iron Age in Italy* (1927); J. Whatmough, *The Foundations of Roman Italy* (1937), 136 ff.; G. E. F. Chilver, *Cisalpine Gaul* (1941). J. B. W.-P.

**CONCILIABULUM,** a type of large village which down to the Social War formed political centres for the Roman country-folk. They replaced the *tribus rusticae*, whose structure as civic units was shattered by the territorial expansion of Rome in the third century. Beginning 'beyond the tenth milestone' they covered the Roman territory except where other *oppida* existed. Official announcements were published in them, but as in other villages, their powers of self-government were slight, since they possessed neither municipal territory nor jurisdiction (*see* VICUS) until during the Ciceronian age they were assimilated to *municipia* (q.v.). A. N. S.-W.

**CONCILIUM** was a general name for any Assembly; it was often used to denote the Popular Assemblies at Rome, especially the Plebeian Assembly (*Concilium Plebis, see* COMITIA).

The provincial *concilia* (κοινά) were assemblies of delegates from the constituent cities or tribes of a province or of several associated provinces (e.g. Gallia Comata, *infra*) or of such parts of certain provinces as had, at an earlier stage, been (or formed part of) independent kingdoms or states (e.g. the separate κοινά of Bithynia, Pontus, or Lycia). The original basis of their organization was ethnic, not provincial. The *Commune Asiae*, properly τὸ κοινὸν τῶν Ἑλλήνων τῆς Ἀσίας, given by Octavian in 29 B.C. the task of carrying on what came to be the cult of Rome and Augustus, was the continuation of the κοινόν of representatives of the earlier Pergamene kingdom, which had likewise been concerned with questions of cult and honours to individual benefactors. In the less romanized western provinces such ethnic assemblies, tied to the imperial cult, were a useful instrument of romanization. Augustus' stepson, Drusus, inaugurated a *concilium* of the three provinces of Gallia Comata at Lugdunum (12 B.C.). With the Flavian emperors appear *concilia* organized on a provincial basis, e.g., in Baetica, Gallia Narbonensis, and Africa. Eventually the *concilia* received an official organization which covered the whole of the Roman Empire except Egypt.

The nature and functions of the *concilia* varied from province to province. The *concilia* ordinarily met once a year at a central point of their district (e.g. Carthage in Africa, Ephesus, Pergamum, Smyrna, or other important cities in Asia). Their primary function was the worship of 'Roma et Augustus', and their president was also chief priest of this cult. Games and festivals were often associated with the religious ceremonies. But the *concilia* also served as channels of communication between the provinces and the emperors, and in the first century A.D. they often rendered good service in reporting on bad governors and facilitating their condemnation in the Roman courts. But they never acquired powers of legislation or taxation; they lost all significance in the troubled times of the third century; and an attempt by Constantine to reanimate them (without emperor-worship) proved ineffectual.

E. G. Hardy, *Studies in Roman History* i (1906), ch. 13; P. Guiraud *Les Assemblées provinciales dans l'empire romain* (1887); E. Kornemann, *PW*, s.v. κοινόν (Suppl. iv) and 'Concilium'; Magie, *Rom. Rule Asia Min.*; J. A. O. Larsen, *Representative Government* (1955), 106 ff. M. C.; E. W. G.

**CONCORDIA,** personification of agreement between members of the Roman state or of some body or bodies within it (*Concordia provinciarum, militum* or *exercituum, imperi*, etc., on coins; occasionally inscriptions are dedicated to the *Concordia* of a town, guild, or the like). Her oldest and principal temple, near the Forum (Platner –Ashby, 138 ff.), was allegedly dedicated by Camillus in 367 B.C. (end of disturbances over the Licinian Rogations), restored by L. Opimius in 121 B.C. (death of C. Gracchus) and re-dedicated by Tiberius in A.D. 10 as Concordia Augusta, which from then on became a frequent title, apparently with reference to agreement between members of the imperial family. She had also a shrine near the above temple, dedicated in 304 B.C. (Livy 9. 46. 6), and another on the Arx in 216 B.C. (Livy 22. 33. 7; 23. 21. 7). The former was a political gesture, the latter commemorated the end of a mutiny. *See* HOMONOIA.

Wissowa, *RK* 328 f.; Latte, *RR* 237, 322; A. Momigliano, 'Camillus and Concord', *CQ* 1942, 111 ff. Temple: Nash, *Pict. Dict. Rome* i, 292 ff. H. J. R.

**CONDATE,** a common place-name in the Celtic provinces of the Roman Empire (as Condate Redonum, Rennes, etc.), meaning 'confluence'. *See also* LUGDUNUM (1).

A. Holder, *Alt-Celtischer Sprachschatz*, s.v. (thirty examples cited). A. L. F. R.

**CONDUCTOR** was a person who either contracted with a private person for the carrying out of some work, such as the construction of a building (Vitruv. 1. 1. 10), or who leased land, either cultivating it himself or subletting to *coloni* (*see* COLONUS 2). In the second century A.D. the term, while continuing to signify a private contractor or lessee (*Dig.* 19. 1. 52 *pr.*; 40. 7. 40. 5), is also widely used for persons contracting for the exploitation of imperial properties. In this period *conductores* leased, for instance, both the actual mineshafts and other concessions in the mining-area of Vipasca (*ILS* 6891) and contracted for imperial *horrea* (*Dig.* 20. 4. 21. 1; cf. *ILS* 5914), and imperial flocks in Italy (*CIL* ix. 2438). The inscriptions of the imperial estates in Africa (*CIL* viii. 25902; 25943; 26416) show that the *conductores* were men who both cultivated parts of the estates themselves and acted as middlemen between the *procuratores* (q.v.) and the *coloni*, from whom they were entitled to fixed proportions of the produce and fixed amounts of service. The inscription from the *Saltus Burunitanus* (*ILS* 6870) contains a *libellus* of the *coloni* to Commodus complaining of the connivance of the procurators and the *conductores* who exacted excessive services and had even sent troops against them. The function of *conductores* as middlemen continues in the imperial and private estates of the Late Empire.

From the beginning of the second century the word is also used for the individual collectors of the *portoria* (q.v.) who replaced the companies of *publicani* and were themselves replaced in the latter half of the century by imperial procurators (q.v.); *conductores* are not attested in connexion with any other tax.

In the second century, and possibly on occasion earlier (*AE* 1962, 288), *conductor* was also used for those who contracted for the *vectigalia* of local communities (Gaius 3. 145; *CIL* iii. 1209; 1363). F. G. B. M.

**CONFARREATIO,** the oldest and most solemn form of Roman marriage, confined to patricians and in classical times obligatory for the three *flamines maiores* and the *rex sacrorum*, who must also have been born of such marriages (Gaius 1. 112). The ceremony is imperfectly known, but outstanding features were that bride and bridegroom sat with veiled heads on joined seats, which were covered with the hide of a sheep (Servius on *Aen.* 4. 374); a cake of *far* (spelt) was used in some way (perhaps eaten by the parties), and the whole rite was in honour of Jupiter Farreus (Gaius, ibid.). The *flamen Dialis* and the Pontifex Maximus were present (Servius on Verg. *G.* 1. 31) and there must be ten witnesses (five, a sacred number, for each of the two *gentes* concerned?) (Gaius, ibid.). The marriage was indissoluble save by an elaborate ceremony, *diffarreatio* (Festus, 65. 17 Lindsay, cf. Plutarch, *Quaest. Rom.* 50; see Rose ad loc.; he speaks of 'horrible, extraordinary, and dismal rites'). See MARRIAGE CEREMONIES, § 2 *and* MANUS.

Rossbach, *Die römische Ehe* (1853), 95 ff.; P. E. Corbett, *The Roman Law of Marriage* (1930), 71.　　H. J. R.

**CONFLUENTES**, modern *Coblenz*, lay at the meeting of the Moselle with the Rhine (traces of a bridge over the former have been noted). From a Julio-Claudian (early Claudian?) fort it developed into an important road junction. Sacked by Germans in A.D. 259/60, its renewed walls were standing in 354. By the mid fifth century it was held by Franks. The name corresponds with the Celtic Condate (q.v.).　　H. H. S.

**CONGIARIUM.** Under the Republic this term designated gifts of wine or oil made by magistrates, candidates for office, or generals. Later these distributions consisted, at first mainly, and then exclusively, of money. From the time of Augustus *congiaria* were given by Emperors only or under their authority, and were associated with such events as the accession of a new Emperor, imperial birthdays, victories, or the erection of buildings. The recipients were identical with the *plebs frumentaria* who received doles of corn. Distributions of *congiaria* are frequently represented on imperial coinage.

D. van Berchem, *Les Distributions de blé et d'argent à la plèbe romaine sous l'Empire* (1939), 119 ff.　　G. H. S.

**CONON** (1) (c. 444–392 B.C.), an Athenian of noble birth. He was admiral of the squadron based on Naupactus in 414, and from 407 to 405 commanded the fleets operating in the Aegean and Hellespont. At Aegospotami he alone of the Athenian generals was on the alert, and slipped away to find refuge with Euagoras. He inspired the programme of reviving Persian sea-power, and his efforts were crowned with success when he annihilated the Spartan fleet at Cnidos (394). He crossed in triumph to Athens, completed the rebuilding of the Long Walls, and even dreamed of a new Athenian Empire. The visit of Antalcidas to Tiribazus in 392 converted the satrap to a pro-Spartan policy. Conon, who was in Sardis on a diplomatic mission, was arrested, and although he succeeded in escaping, died shortly afterwards.

D. E. W. W.

**CONON** (2) of Samos (3rd c. B.C.), astronomer and mathematician. After travelling in the western part of the Greek world in search of astronomical and meteorological observations, he settled in Alexandria. He is best known for his discovery (c. 245 B.C.) of the new constellation Βερενίκης Πλόκαμος between Leo, Virgo, and Boötes, recounted in Catullus' imitation (c.66 B.C.) of Callimachus' elegy on the Coma Berenices. He wrote an astronomical work *De Astrologia* of which nothing remains, and was well known for his researches into solar eclipses. In mathematics, he wrote a work Πρὸς Θρασυδαῖον on the mutual sections and contacts of conic sections. He was a close friend of Archimedes, who always praises highly his mathematical work, and regrets his early death.

W. D. R.

**CONON** (3), mythographer, who dedicated his work to Archelaus Philopator (Philopatris) of Cappadocia (36 B.C.–A.D. 17), published διηγήσεις, fifty tales from Greek saga, Atticist in style, based on a Hellenistic handbook, and preserved in Photius.

*FGrH* i. 26; Photius (ed. R. Henry, vol. 3, 1962).

**CONSCRIPTI.** This obscure term may refer either to an official list or *album* of senators, the *patres* 'on the list'; or to an early union of two different kinds of senators—i.e. *patres ⟨et⟩ conscripti*—either patricians and plebeians, though the struggle of the Orders renders this unlikely, or the *patres* of different communities incorporated in Rome.　　A. N. S.-W.

**CONSECRATIO**, the process of making anything into a *res sacra*. We are best informed of the ceremonial in the case of a temple (*aedes sacra*) and the ground on which it stood. The latter must be the property of the Roman people; e.g. Trajan saw no objection to the moving from its place of an old temple at Nicomedia, because it could not have been dedicated in Roman form (Pliny, *Tra.* 49, 50; cf. Mommsen, *Staatsr.* iii. 734). Furthermore, dedication must be authorized by the state (Cic. *Dom.* 136). Usually the Senate, the People, or in later times the Emperor appointed some person, or persons (*duumviri*, Livy 23. 21. 7 and often), with a natural tendency, if the temple had been vowed by a magistrate in office, to appoint him or some relative. It remained for the gods to accept the gift through their earthly agents, the *pontifices* (e.g. Justinian, *Inst.* 2. 1. 8). It was proper for the whole college to be present (Cic., ibid. 117); the minimum requisite was for one of them to be there. He held one of the *postes* of the entrance door and pronounced the necessary formula (ibid. 119, 121). Like all ceremonies, this must be gone through without interruption, hesitation, or stumbling (e.g. ibid. 134, 141; Pliny, *HN* 11. 174). The dedicator also held a doorpost (Livy 2. 8. 7), and went through a form of prayer (ibid. 8), dictated to him by the pontiff (Cic., ibid. 138, 'quid praeiri ... ius fuerit' and Livy, *infra*), containing a clause to the effect that he gave the building (or other object) to the god (Servius on Verg. *G.* 3. 16). The ceremony was necessary also if a new building was put up on ground already consecrated (Livy 9. 46. 6).

Of the other consecrations less is known; the goods of a condemned man were on occasion consecrated by a magistrate, who covered his head, employed a flute-player to drown ill-omened sounds, and had by him a small portable altar (*foculus*) for incense (Cic., ibid. 123–4).

A title-deed (*lex dedicationis*) seems regularly to have been drawn up, at all events for important dedications. To judge by the provincial specimens which alone have been preserved (Bruns, *Fontes*, nos. 90, 92) it was recited by the dedicator under the direction of the pontiff and contained a precise statement of the size of the ground on which the object stood, the conditions under which it was to be used, etc. See DEDICATIO.

Convenient assemblage of material (requiring some revision) in J. Marquardt, *Röm. Staatsverwaltung* (1881–5), iii². 269 ff. For discussion of the ceremony of holding the *postis*, see Latte, *RR* 200.　　H. J. R.

**CONSENTES DI,** the Roman version of the Athenian Twelve Gods. Their gilt statues stood in the Forum (Varro, *Rust.* 1. 1. 4), later apparently in the Porticus Deorum Consentium (see Platner–Ashby, 421; Nash, *Pict. Dict. Rome* ii. 241 ff.). As there were six male and six female, they may well have been the twelve worshipped at the *lectisternium* (q.v.) of 217 B.C. (Livy 22. 10. 9), Jupiter and Juno, Neptune and Minerva, Mars and Venus,

Apollo and Diana, Volcanus and Vesta, Mercury and Ceres (Wissowa, *RK* 61).                    H. J. R.

**CONSENTIUS** (5th c. A.D.), grammarian. His extant treatises *De nomine et verbo* and *De barbarismis et metaplasmis* (ed. Keil, *Gramm. Lat.* v. 338–85, 386–404) are excerpts from a complete grammar. His illustrations drawn from the speech of his own times make him valuable for the study of vulgar Latin.

Schanz–Hosius, § 1103.                    J. F. M.

**CONSILIUM PRINCIPIS.** A Roman magistrate was always at liberty to summon advisers in deliberation or on the bench. Under the Roman Empire a body of advisers summoned by the Emperor acquired the character of a Privy Council. At first it was unofficial, and no more than an indeterminate collection of 'amici Caesaris' who had been summoned by the Princeps to act as assessors in a judicial inquiry (Tac. *Ann.* 3. 10; 14. 62) or as advisers in problems of administration. Hadrian went further and, in judicial inquiries, summoned 'amici', 'comites', and jurisconsults, 'quos tamen senatus omnes probasset' (*Vita* 18). Severus Alexander established a regular *consilium* of seventy members, who assisted him in the framing of *constitutiones*; twenty of them were jurisconsults, the rest the Emperor's nominees, chiefly, no doubt, senators (*Vita* 16). Its members were known as *consiliarii Augusti*, some of them—perhaps only the *equites*—receiving salaries. The body was reorganized under Diocletian, membership being made permanent, and its name was changed to *sacrum consistorium* (q.v.). This *consilium* is to be distinguished from the regular *consilium* established by Augustus, and known as the *consilium semestre*, consisting of the two consuls, one member of each of the other colleges of magistrates, and fifteen senators chosen by lot, who retained their membership for six months (Dio Cass. 53. 21. 4 ff.; Suet. *Aug.* 35. 3). This body prepared business for the Senate in collaboration with the Princeps (see, for example, the *senatus consultum* conveyed in the fifth of the Augustan edicts from Cyrene, *JRS* 1927, 36). Its character was altered slightly in A.D. 13 and again after Tiberius' accession, but the institution came to an end after Tiberius retired from Rome in A.D. 26.

J. A. Crook, *Consilium Principis* (1955).                    J. P. B.

**CONSISTORIUM.** The name given to the imperial *consilium* from the time of Diocletian (q.v.), since the members no longer sat but stood in the Emperor's presence. It functioned both as a general council of state and as a supreme court of law. Its membership depended upon the Emperor's choice but normally included the principal civil and military officers of the *comitatus*, former holders of these offices, and also *comites consistoriani* who held no office; these last included legal experts, mostly drawn from the Bar. The consistory was still an active council of state in the fourth century, but its time was increasingly filled by ceremonial business, and by the fifth century its proceedings appear to have become entirely formal. Its sessions were called *silentia*, and its ushers *silentiarii*. Its minutes were kept by the imperial *notarii*, who in the fifth century were replaced by *a secretis*, drawn from the *agentes in rebus* or *memoriales*.

Jones, *Later Rom. Emp.* 333 ff.                    A. H. M. J.

**CONSOLATIO** (λόγος παραμυθητικός). Topics of comfort and consolation are found in many places in Greek literature (e.g. *Il.* 5. 381 ff., Eur. *Alc.* 416 ff.). The sophist Antiphon, the Academic philosopher Crantor (q.v.), and the popular philosophy of the Cynics all contributed to the formation of a set repertoire of arguments which occur again and again in both Greek and Roman writing. The *consolationes* which have come down to us concern chiefly death, sometimes exile, rarely other misfortunes. Simple letters or philosophic treatises, they differ according to the author's style and personality, the circumstances which dictated them, and the character of the recipient. Yet they all wear a fundamental likeness.

Of the stock arguments (*solacia*), one group is applicable to the afflicted person, the other to the cause of the affliction. Among the former the commonest thoughts are: Fortune is all-powerful—one should foresee her strokes (*praemeditatio*); has a loved one died?—remember that all men are mortal; the essential thing is to have lived not long but virtuously; time heals all ills; yet a wise man would seek healing not from time but from reason, by himself putting an end to his grief; the lost one was only 'lent'—be grateful for having possessed him. As to death, the cause of the affliction, it is the end of all ills: the one who is lamented does not suffer; the gods have sheltered him from the trials of this world. To these *loci communes* consolers sometimes add eulogy of the dead, and almost always examples of men courageous in bearing misfortune.

The tone is usually one of extreme intellectualism: reason is the supreme consoler. Seneca, however, views family affections as precious sources of comfort, and Christian consolers (Ambrose, Jerome, Paulinus of Nola), while resorting to pagan arguments, were enabled to renew the genre by the stress laid upon feeling and by the character of their inspiration, which was at once biblical, ethical, and mystic.

A good idea of the Greek material can be obtained from Ps.-Plato, *Axiochus*, and Ps.-Plutarch, *Consolatio ad Apollonium* (an anthology of consolatory topics). Plutarch's own *Consolatio ad Uxorem* is a moving example of the effectiveness of the τόποι in a deeply-felt bereavement. For Latin, see especially: *Tusc.* 1 and 3; Sulpicius ap. Cic. *Fam.* 4. 5; Sen. *Dial.* 6 (*ad Marciam*), 11 (*ad Polybium*), 12 (*ad Helviam matrem*; exile); *Ep.* 63, 81 (ingratitude), 93, 99, 107 (runaway slaves).

A. Gercke, *De Consolationibus* (*Tirocinium philologum* Berl.) 1883; K. Buresch, 'Consolationum . . . historia critica' (*Leipz. Stud.* ix. 1), 1886; C. Martha, *Études morales sur l'antiquité³* (1896), 135 ff.; J. D. Duff, *Sen. Dial.* 10, 11, 12 (two last being *Consolationes*), 1915; Ch. Favez, Introductions to his edns. of Sen. *Ad Helviam* (1918) and *Ad Marciam* (1928); *La Consolation latine chrétienne* (1937); R. Kassel, *Untersuchungen zur griechischen und römischen Konsolationsliteratur* (1958); R. Lattimore, *Themes in Greek and Latin Epitaphs* (1962), 215 ff.                    C. F.

**CONSOLATIO AD LIVIAM,** an elegiac poem of condolence, of 474 lines, addressed to the Empress Livia on the death of her son Drusus, campaigning in Germany 9 B.C., whose body was brought to Rome for burial. Date and authorship have been much discussed. The traditional ascription to Ovid is obviously false, indeed the imitation of Ovid's manner is not very expert. The poem is almost certainly a fictitious exercise in a recognized genre, the *consolatio* (q.v.; *see also* EPICEDIUM).

TEXTS. PLM ii. 2; F. W. Lenz, *P. Ovidii Nasonis Halieutica²*, etc. (1956).
COMMENTARY. A. Witlox (1934).
TRANSLATION. J. A. Mozley, *Ovid: Art of Love*, etc. (Loeb, 1939). See also Bickel, *Rh. Mus.* 1950, 193 ff.; J. Esteve-Forriol, *Die Trauer- u. Trostgedichte in d. röm. Lit.* (Diss. Munich, 1962), 56 ff.                    E. J. K.

**CONSTANS,** Roman Emperor (*c.* A.D. 323–50), was the fourth or fifth son of Constantine the Great. On the death of his father in 337, he became Emperor of Italy, Africa, and Illyricum. In 340 he defeated and killed his brother Constantine II (q.v.), who had invaded northern Italy, and thus became Emperor of the entire West. In 343 he visited Britain, the last legitimate Roman Emperor to do so. He was overthrown and killed in Gaul by Magnentius (q.v.) in 350.                    E. A. T.

**CONSTANTINE,** known to history as 'the Great', FLAVIUS VALERIUS CONSTANTINUS (*PW* 2) (*c.* A.D. 285–337), was born at Naïssus, the son of Constantius Chlorus and his concubine, Helena. When Constantius (q.v. 1) was appointed Caesar (293) Constantine was kept by Diocletian at his court. He showed great promise as an officer, served with Galerius against Persia, and was at his court in 305, when the old Augustus abdicated. The new ruler, Galerius, with both Caesars—Severus and Maximin Daia—devoted to him, was superior in all but name to his fellow Augustus, Constantius, and Constantine was virtually a hostage for his father's good behaviour. In 306 Constantius requested Galerius to release Constantine for service in Britain; Galerius reluctantly consented. Constantine, fearing interruption by Severus, hastened to Britain and assisted his father in Scotland. When Constantius died at York (25 June), Constantine was proclaimed Augustus by the troops, urged on by the Alamannic king, Crocus; Galerius, smothering his resentment, granted Constantine the rank of Caesar; the rank of Augustus of the West was given to Severus.

**2.** The rise of Maxentius in Rome reacted on the fortunes of Constantine. The old Emperor Maximian, returning to power to help Maxentius, visited Constantine in Gaul, gave him in marriage his daughter Fausta (already betrothed to him in 293) and the title of Augustus. Constantine made no move, when first Severus and then Galerius unsuccessfully attacked Maxentius, but he sheltered Maximian when driven from Rome after a vain attempt to depose his son. At the Conference of Carnuntum in 308 Constantine was called on to resign the title of Augustus and become Caesar again, under Licinius as second Emperor. Both he and Maximin Daia refused to be satisfied with the makeshift title of 'Filii Augustorum' and retained the full rank of Augustus. In Gaul, meanwhile, Constantine had successfully defended the Rhine against Franks, Alamanni, and Bructeri. He was absent on one of these expeditions in 310 when Maximian, restless and discontented, seized Massilia. Constantine turned and forced the old man to surrender and commit suicide. As the connexion with the Herculian dynasty was now discredited, Constantine emphasized his hereditary claim to the throne by alleging descent from Claudius (q.v. 2) Gothicus.

**3.** In 311 Galerius died and a new grouping of powers began. Constantine and Maxentius sought support in Licinius and Maximin Daia respectively. Early in 312 Constantine invaded Italy, broke up a stubborn resistance in the north by great victories near Turin and Verona, and then marched on Rome. Maxentius gave battle and found defeat and death at the Mulvian Bridge. Welcomed as deliverer by the Senate, Constantine replaced Daia as senior Augustus. In 313 Licinius visited Milan, married Constantia, sister of Constantine, and with him issued certain regulations in favour of the Christians, known as the 'Edict of Milan'. Licinius then struck down his eastern rival, Maximin, and the two kinsmen Emperors were left to rule East and West in harmony. The concord was unstable. A first war, fought in 314 or 316 was decided in favour of Constantine by victories at Cibalae and in the Mardian plain. The result was the cession to Constantine of territory as far as Thrace. In 317 Crispus and Constantine II, sons of Constantine, and Licinius II, son of Licinius, were appointed Caesars. But trouble soon arose again. Licinius, jealous and suspicious, began to persecute the Eastern Christians. In 323 Constantine, in beating back a Gothic invasion, violated the territory of Licinius; war followed. Victorious in great battles by land and sea—Adrianople, Chrysopolis, and the Hellespont—Constantine forced the abdication of Licinius, who soon afterwards was executed (324).

**4.** Constantine now held the whole Empire, reunited under his own hand. He completed the administrative work of Diocletian and introduced innovations. A substantial field army was created under new commanders, *magister peditum* and *magister equitum*, responsible directly to the Emperor: its soldiers (*comitatenses*) had higher pay and privileges than the frontier troops (*limitanei*). The number of Germans seems to have increased, especially in the higher ranks. The separation of civil and military commands, begun by Diocletian, was completed. At the highest level, the praetorian prefects and the *vicarii* now had purely administrative and judicial functions; the former as well as the latter controlled fixed territorial circumscriptions. In a reorganization of the central government consequent on the change in the role of the praetorian prefects, the *magister officiorum* controlled the imperial bureaux (*scrinia*), a new corps of guards (*scholae*) which replaced the praetorians, and a corps of couriers and agents (*agentes in rebus*); the *quaestor sacri palatii* was the chief legal adviser; and the *comes sacrarum largitionum* and the *comes rei privatae* handled the revenues and expenditures in gold and silver. The Emperor's council (*consistorium*) had the above as permanent officials as well as *comites*. At first these were strictly those who served at court or as special commissioners, but the title was soon given freely as an honour. Constantine gave senatorial rank to many, and reopened a number of official posts to senators who began to recover some of the political power they had lost in the third century.

**5.** The founding of Constantinople (q.v.) on the site of Byzantium was of great consequence. The need for an imperial headquarters near the eastern and Danubian frontiers had been recognized by Diocletian, who preferred Nicomedia. The strategic importance of Byzantium was impressed on Constantine in his war with Licinius. Major works were begun in 326, the *consecratio* of the site took place in 328, and the *dedicatio* in 330 with both traditional pagan rites and Christian ceremonies. From the beginning it was to be 'New Rome', though formally slightly lower in rank. Many of the traditional features of Rome were reproduced (e.g. a Senate, and free corn for the populace), but the pagan temples and cults of the old capital were conspicuously absent. As an imperial city in a Greek environment, the foundation in the end emphasized the division of the Empire between Greek- and Latin-speaking *partes*.

**6.** The transformations in Constantine's religious outlook are disputed; he probably went through more than one change. Highly emotional, and superstitious like all his contemporaries, he became convinced of the superiority of the God of the Christians, and of the need to secure this divine support for himself and the Roman Empire, after his victory over Maxentius. He was perhaps impressed by the growth of Christianity in spite of the persecutions. While ruler of the West only, where paganism was deeply entrenched, he gave much material support to the Church and privileges to the clergy. After he had settled in the East where Christians were more numerous his assertion of the new religion became more emphatic. He openly rejected paganism, though without persecuting its adherents, favoured Christians as officials, and welcomed bishops at court. His actions in church matters were, however, his own, and designed solely to maintain the unity of the Christian Church as essential to the unity of the Empire. He failed entirely in the Donatist schism in North Africa in the years following 312; in the East he called the first general council of the Church to Nicaea in 325 to deal with the Arian controversy, but his apparent success was rapidly seen to be superficial.

**7.** Constantine had a yearning for popularity; he was open-handed to all, to the detriment of the economy, and was forced to increase taxation in spite of the confiscation of the vast temple treasures. He tried but could do little to stop corruption in the steadily growing bureaucracy. He successfully established a gold coinage of 72 *solidi* to the pound but the *denarius* continued to depreciate. The greater part of taxation was in kind and we have the first laws designed to prevent *coloni* and other productive workers, not to mention *curiales*, from leaving their homes and work.

**8.** The prestige of the Empire abroad seemed fully restored, and most of Constantine's last years were peaceful; in 332 the Goths were repulsed on the Danube and thousands of Sarmatians were admitted within the Empire as potential recruits. A Persian war threatened but did not break out till after his death. At court, however, in a mysterious scandal, he ordered the execution of his eldest son Crispus and his wife Fausta in 326. His other sons, Constantine II, Caesar in 317, Constantius II, Caesar in 323, and Constans, Caesar in 333, were groomed for the succession with two sons of his half-brother. With so many descendants and relatives, Constantine, the advocate of hereditary succession, could do little but hope they would rule together in amity after his death. He was baptized on his death-bed, such a postponement being common at the time, having brought Christianity from the status of a powerful, though persecuted, minority to effective supremacy in the religious life of the Empire, and having built a new capital on a site deliberately chosen for its strategic importance and well equipped to face the permanent dangers on the Danube frontier.

J. Burckhardt, *Die Zeit Constantins des Grossen*[3] (1898); N. H. Baynes, 'Constantine the Great and the Christian Church' (*Proc. Brit. Acad.* 1929); A. Piganiol, *L'Empereur Constantin* (1932); A. H. M. Jones, *Constantine and the Conversion of Europe* (1948); J. Vogt, *Constantin der Grosse und sein Jahrhundert*[2] (1960); Jones, *Later Rom. Emp.* 77 ff. H. M.; B. H. W.

## CONSTANTINE II, Roman Emperor (A.D. 317–40),
second son of Constantine the Great, was born in Arles in Feb. 317 and on 1 Mar. was proclaimed Caesar. He became ruler of Britain, Gaul, and Spain on his father's death in 337. In 340 he invaded northern Italy so as to overthrow his brother Constans, but was defeated and killed at Aquileia. E. A. T.

## CONSTANTINE III (Flavius Claudius Constantinus), Roman Emperor, at first a usurper but recognized by Honorius in A.D. 409. He was elevated by the army in Britain in 407 and immediately crossed to Gaul, taking with him some, but not all, of the British forces. He established himself at Arles, won over Spain to his cause, unsuccessfully invaded Italy, and in 411 capitulated at Arles to the generals of Honorius and was put to death there. E. A. T.

## CONSTANTINOPLE. Constantinople was founded by Constantine on the site of Byzantium in A.D. 324, shortly after his victory over Licinius near the city. Constantine states that he 'bestowed upon it an eternal name by the commandment of God', and the new foundation was probably intended as a memorial of the final victory which God had given him. The new city therefore, as Eusebius states, was probably never sullied by pagan worship. Some old temples of Byzantium were preserved, but apparently only as museums, and the city was amply adorned with churches, notable among which were those of the Holy Apostles, where Constantine and his successors were buried, SS. Sophia and Eirene. The building of the city was quickly pushed on, private persons being encouraged to build houses by the grant of imperial lands in Asia Minor or of bread rations in perpetuity, and it was formally inaugurated on 11 May 330. It was

adorned with numerous works of art taken from pagan temples.

The city was styled the New Rome from the beginning, and was the normal imperial residence in the Eastern parts. It lacked the constitutional prerogatives of Rome, however, until in 340 Constantius II created its Senate, with quaestors, tribunes of the plebs, and praetors; henceforth, one of the consuls was normally inaugurated at Constantinople. On 11 Dec. 359 the first prefect of the city took office. Its administration was modelled on that of Rome, with a *praefectus annonae, praefectus vigilum,* and *magister census*; Justinian renamed the *praefectus vigilum* the *praetor plebis* enhancing his rank and salary, and created a new police officer, the *quaesitor*, whose function it was to see that visitors to the city returned home after completing their business, and to provide work for the able-bodied unemployed and to give begging licences to those unable to work. Like Rome Constantinople was divided (after 413) into fourteen regions (one across the Golden Horn and one outside the walls), each under a *curator*. As at Rome, there was a free issue of bread, inaugurated 18 May 332 for 80,000 persons.

The bishop of Constantinople, as bishop of the capital, acquired great prestige. In 381 the Council of Constantinople declared that he 'should have the primacy of honour after the bishop of Rome, because it was the New Rome', and in 451 the Council of Chalcedon gave him patriarchal jurisdiction over the dioceses of Thrace, Asiana, and Pontica; in the late sixth century he assumed the title of ecumenical.

In 425 a university was established. Its professors, five for Greek rhetoric and ten for Greek grammar, three for Latin rhetoric and ten for Latin grammar, one for philosophy and two for law, had a monopoly of higher teaching and were appointed by the Senate.

Constantinople grew rapidly. The Constantinian walls were demolished in 413, and the present walls built about a mile further west; the area of the city was doubled. The imperial import of corn under Justinian amounted to 8,000,000 *artabae*, enough to feed about 600,000 persons. The prosperity of the city was largely due to the fact that it housed the imperial court, the Senate, the palatine ministries, the praetorian prefecture of the East, and the two *magistri militum praesentales*. It was also the seat of the supreme courts of appeal with all their lawyers, of a university with its students, and of the patriarchate with its numerous clergy. It was thronged with petitioners and litigants ecclesiastical, civil, and military.

The Notitia of the city, drawn up under Theodosius II, gives interesting statistical information. There were in the city 20 (or 21) public bakeries, 120 private bakeries, 9 public baths (*thermae*), 153 private baths, and 4,388 houses (*domus*) apart from blocks of flats.

Of the buildings of the early period there survive the 'Burnt Column' of Constantine, the Hippodrome with its two obelisks, the aqueduct of Valens, the Theodosian Walls, the basilica of S. John of Studion, a mosaic floor from the Great Palace, Justinian's churches of S. Sophia, S. Eirene, and SS. Sergius and Bacchus, the palace of Justinian on the sea of Marmora and several huge cisterns.

C. Diehl, *Constantinople* (1924); Jones, *Later Rom. Emp.* 83 f. 687 ff.; M. Maclagan, *The City of Constantinople* (1968). A. H. M. J.

## CONSTANTIUS (1, *PW* 1) (CHLORUS), Flavius Valerius (Fl. Iulius before he became Caesar; the nickname Chlorus occurs first in Byzantine sources), b. A.D. 250 of Illyrian stock, served with distinction as officer and governor, and was called by Diocletian in A.D. 293 to become Maximian's Caesar in the West. He had earlier married Theodora, stepdaughter of Maximian,

and put away Helena, his concubine, the mother of Constantine.

The first task allotted to Constantius was the recovery of Britain, held by the usurper Carausius. In 293 he stormed Boulogne; but Allectus, who murdered Carausius, was left in peace for three years. In 296 Maximian came up to guard the Rhine, and Constantius and his praetorian prefect, Asclepiodotus, put to sea. Asclepiodotus, landing in fog near Clausentum (*Bitterne*), routed and killed Allectus in Hampshire. Constantius, separated from him, came up the Thames and reached London in time to cut to pieces the marauding survivors of the beaten army. Constantius showed mercy to the island and restored its defences. In 298 he gained a spectacular victory over the Alamanni at Langres.

The abdication of Diocletian in A.D. 305 left Constantius in the West as senior Augustus, but hampered by his Caesar, Severus, a creature of Galerius. Constantine remained with Galerius, virtually as a hostage. In 306 Constantius asked that his son might be restored to him. Constantine, travelling with desperate speed, reached Britain just in time to help his father in a last victory, over the Picts, and to succeed him when he died at York.

Constantius was an able general and a generous and merciful ruler. Though not a Christian himself, he was as lenient to the Christians under persecution as his loyalty to Diocletian would allow, and stopped as soon as Diocletian abdicated. The stories of his descent from Claudius (q.v. 2) Gothicus are inventions of Constantine's propagandists.

J. Moreau, *Jahrbuch für Antike und Christentum*, ii (1959), 158 ff.
H. M.; B. H. W.

**CONSTANTIUS II** (FLAVIUS JULIUS CONSTANTIUS), Roman Emperor (A.D. 324 to 361), was the third son of Constantine the Great. On his father's death in 337 he became ruler of the East. His reign was largely spent in repelling Persian attacks and in suppressing usurpers. He appointed his cousin Gallus (q.v. 8) to rule as Caesar at Antioch, but put him to death in 354. In 355 he appointed Julian to act as Caesar in Gaul. Julian rebelled at Paris in 361, and Constantius died at Mopsucrenae on 3 Nov. while marching to suppress him. He was deeply interested in theology and was an opponent of Athanasius (q.v.), but despite many efforts he solved none of the religious questions which vexed the Empire in his day.
E. A. T.

**CONSTANTIUS III**, Roman Emperor in A.D. 421, married in 417 Honorius' sister Placidia (q.v.), who bore him the future Emperor Valentinian III. In 418 he settled the Visigoths in south-western Gaul. Appointed Augustus in Feb. 421, he died in Sept. in that year.
E. A. T.

**CONSTELLATIONS.** The first evidence of knowledge of the constellations possessed by the Greeks appears in the poems of Homer and Hesiod. Homer speaks of the Pleiades, the Hyades, Orion, the Great Bear ('also called by the name of the Wain, which turns round on the same spot and watches Orion; it alone is without lot in Oceanus' bath', *Od.* 5. 271 f.), Sirius ('called Orion's dog', 'rises in late summer', 'a baleful sign, for it brings to suffering mortals much fiery heat'), the 'late-setting' Boötes. Hesiod mentions the same stars, his name for Boötes being, however, Arcturus. The inference is that, at first, the observations of the sky were all directed to practical utility, the needs of persons following various callings, the navigator, the farmer, etc. The stars served as signs to guide the sailor, or as indications of the

weather, times, and seasons. Calypso tells Odysseus to sail in such a way as always to keep the Great Bear on his left. Hesiod marks the time for sowing at the beginning of winter by the setting of the Pleiades in the early twilight, or the early setting of the Hyades or Orion, the time for harvest by the early rising of the Pleiades, threshing-time by the early rising of Orion, vintage-time by the early rising of Arcturus and so on; for Hesiod, spring begins with the late rising of Arcturus. Then, later, legends came to be attached to the various constellations, often owing to supposed resemblances in shape, and poetic fancy played its part.

**2.** (1) *Orion*, Ὠρίων (Ὠαρίων, Hesiod), was perhaps the constellation to which a Greek legend was earliest attached. A Boeotian legend made him a mighty hunter, ultimately killed by Artemis, or, according to a later version, by a scorpion sent by her. In art he is represented with a club in his right hand, a sword dependent from his belt (ξιφήρης Ὠρίων, Eur. *Ion* 1153) and a lion's skin on his left arm. In Ps.-Eratosthenes *ad Arat.* an alternative name Ἀλεκτροπόδιον ('cock's foot') appears. The three stars of the belt were in Latin *Iugulae*, and in Greek astrological texts Χάριτες ('graces').

(2) *The Great Bear*, ἡ Ἄρκτος = the Wain, ἡ Ἄμαξα, which is no doubt the earlier name. To the former name attaches the story that Callisto, beloved of Zeus, was turned into a bear by Hera and thereon placed by Zeus in the heavens. Another story is that the two bears were placed in the heavens as constellations, and that they were two bears which had hidden and nourished Zeus, when a youth, in Crete for a year (Aratus 30–5). With the 'Wain' is connected the name of the star called Βοώτης ('oxen-driver') by Homer; when the Wain becomes the Bear, Boötes is naturally called Arcturus (Ἀρκτοῦρος, 'Bear-guard', Hesiod; Ἀρκτοφύλαξ, Eudoxus and Aratus 92). Another name for the Great Bear was Ἑλίκη (Aratus 3; Apoll. Rhod. 3. 1105) implying convolutions; one interpretation is 'snail's-house', from a supposed resemblance in shape; the other rests on the revolution of the Bear round the pole. The Romans called it *Septentriones*, 'seven threshing-oxen' (*trio* = 'threshing-ox' in Varro and Gellius) going round and round. Βοώτης would be the suitable attendant for such a team, and perhaps there was an earlier Greek name corresponding to *Septentriones* which dropped out of use.

(3) *The Little Bear*. The Greeks, we are told, sailed by the Great Bear, the Phoenicians by the Little Bear (Aratus 39). Thales advised the Greeks to follow the Phoenician lead, the reason being that the Little Bear is the better guide to the position of the north pole. The Little Bear was commonly called *Cynosura* (κυνόσουρα, 'dog's tail', Aratus 36); another name was 'Callisto's dog' (schol. in Arat. 27).

(4) *Boötes* (Βοώτης), *Arcturus* (Ἀρκτοῦρος, Ἀρκτοφύλαξ) see *Great Bear*.

(5) *Hyades*, Ὑάδες, a group of stars, the morning setting of which marked for Hesiod the time for ploughing. The name is derived from ὗς, 'swine', and it was regarded as representing a sow with four young; this is a more likely derivation than the alternative one from ὕειν, 'to rain', because it corresponds to the Latin *suculae* (Cic. *Nat. D.* 2. 111).

(6) *Pleiades*, a group of seven stars near the Hyades. Hesiod calls them the seven daughters of Atlas by Pleione; their names were Halcyone, Merope, Celaeno, Electra, Sterope, Taÿgete, Maia (Aratus 262 f.). The name Pleiades may be derived from πλεῖν, 'to sail', since their early rising in spring marks for Hesiod the beginning of the sailing season. The spelling of the word as Πελειάδες is, however, supposed to justify the early Greek view of them as a flight of doves. Another significant name for them is βότρυς, cluster or bunch of grapes

schol. on *Il.* 18. 486). The Latin name is *Vergiliae*
Plaut. *Amph.* 275), perhaps derived from *virga*, a twig.

**3. The Zodiac.** The Greeks obtained their knowledge
of the twelve signs of the zodiac and the constellations in
them from the Babylonians, to whom the Egyptians of
the Ptolemaic period were similarly indebted. It was
probably Cleostratus of Tenedos who imported this
knowledge into Greece in the second half of the sixth
century B.C. (see Pliny, *HN* 2. 3; Hyginus, *Poet. Astr.* 2.
13). The pictorial representations of the constellations,
or most of them, passed over to Greece, as has been
inferred from a number of boundary stones (see L. W.
King, *Babylonian Boundary Stones in the British Museum*,
(1912)).

(7) The *Ram* (Κριός). According to Pliny this name
was first used by Cleostratus. The story is that it was the
ram with the golden fleece which bore Phrixus and Helle
over the sea (whence 'Hellespont'). It was sacrificed to
Zeus, who placed it among the stars; the fleece was the
object of the Argonauts' quest.

(8) The *Bull*, Ταῦρος, is in the Greek legend the bull of
the Europa-story.

(9) The *Twins*, Δίδυμοι, *Gemini*. They were variously
identified as Castor and Pollux, Amphion and Zethus,
Theseus and Heracles, Apollo and Heracles, Triptolemus
and Iasion. The notion of them as Apollo and Heracles
seems to go back to the time when the Greeks first
became acquainted with the signs of the zodiac; they
appear, however, in Babylonian texts.

(10) The *Crab*, Κάρκινος, *Cancer*, the fourth sign of
the zodiac, was easy, from its appearance, to picture as
a crab. An earlier name for it was ὄνων φάτνη, 'Asses'
Crib' (see Aratus 898 f.), representing a crib and two
asses.

(11) The *Lion*, Λέων, *Leo*, the fifth sign, was associated
with the hot harvest-season. Greek legend made it the
Nemean lion killed by Heracles. Its main star is *Regulus*.

(12) The *Virgin*, Παρθένος, *Virgo*, the sixth sign, is
represented with wings and holding an ear of corn
(στάχυς, *spica*). Aratus tells the story that she was the
daughter of Zeus and Themis and dispensed justice on
the earth, but, when men became vicious, she was translated to heaven; hence the alternative name of the constellation, Δίκη, Justice. She became, later, associated
with the succeeding sign, the *Scales*, Ζυγός, *Libra*; hence
the treatment of *Spica* by Aratus as a separate constellation. Other names attached to the constellation from
time to time were: Demeter (because of her holding the
ear of corn), Athena, Isis, Atargatis, Tyche (= Τύχη,
Ps.-Eratosth. *Cat.* 9), and Erigone, daughter of Icarius
or Icarus (Manilius 5. 251).

(13) The *Scales*, Ζυγός, *Libra*. The original Greek
name was χηλαί, *Claws* (of the Scorpion). The name
*Balance* is of Babylonian origin. The *Scales* were at
first represented as held in the claws of the Scorpion;
later, separated from the Scorpion, they were pictured
either alone or as held by a female or male figure.

(14) The *Scorpion*, Σκορπίος, is of Babylonian origin.
The Greek story is that it was sent by Artemis to kill
Orion.

(15) The *Archer*, Τοξότης, *Sagittarius*, was represented sometimes as a Centaur, sometimes as a creature
with two feet, standing upright. Ps.-Eratosth. (*Cat.* 28)
says of him: 'Most men call him a Centaur. Others
dispute this, because he does not appear to have four
legs, but stands upright and shoots with his bow. But
none of the Centaurs used a bow.' The figure is of
Babylonian origin.

(16) The *Sea-Goat* or *Horned Goat*, Αἰγόκερως, *Capri-
cornus*, the tenth sign of the zodiac, is of Babylonian
origin. It is a Goat-Fish, with the head of a goat and a
fish-tail. Epimenides identified it with the Cretan goat

which brought up Zeus; others make it Pan under the
name *Aegipan*. Theogenes caused it to be adopted as
part of the Arms of Augustus, and it was put on the
banners of the Augustan legions (G. Thiele, *Antike
Himmelsbilder* (1898), 69).

(17) *Aquarius*, Ὑδροχόος, *water-pourer*. 'The man that
holds the watering-pot' of the rhyme is represented as
pouring out water from an urn variously described as
ὑδρία, κάλπις, or κάλπη, *urna*. Legends identify it
sometimes with Deucalion, sometimes with Ganymede.

(18) The *Fishes*, Ἰχθύες, *Pisces*, one north and one
south, tied together by δεσμά or συνδεσμός (Aratus 243,
245). The northern one was also called 'swallow-fish' by
the Chaldaeans = χελιδονία ἰχθῦς, the other ὁ νότειος (schol.
in Arat. 242, Boll 196). The idea of this constellation
came perhaps from the *Water* (ὕδωρ) of which Aratus
made a separate constellation (Thiele 13).

**4.** Beginning with the fifth century the constellations
(their observed positions, risings, and settings) were used
by Meton, Euctemon, and Democritus for the purposes
of the calendar (παραπήγματα) and weather-indications
(ἐπισημάσιαι). By the time of Eudoxus (first half of 4th
c.) the following constellations were known and described
in literature, with various legends attached. We take
first those in the northern hemisphere.

(19) *Lyra*, Λύρα, containing the bright star Vega, is
mentioned in connexion with the Twins. Apollo being
one of the Twins, the association is appropriate, as
legend has it that Apollo presented the lyre to Orpheus.
The Lyre was used by Democritus and Euctemon for
calendar-making (Diels, *Vorsokr.*[5] ii. 143); it was also of
significance in the calendar of Caesar (Plut. *Caesar*, 50).

(20) The *Swan* (Ὄρνις, 'Bird', *Olor*, *Cygnus*), belonging, like the *Eagle*, to the Milky Way, touches the northern
tropic circle. Aratus (279) says that its right wing
stretches out to the right hand of Cepheus. Legend
connects it with the story of Leda and the Swan.

(21) The *Eagle*, Ἀετός, *Aquila*, was used by Democritus (Diels, loc. cit.). According to the legend, Zeus
used the Eagle to carry Ganymede to Olympus.

(22) The *Dolphin*, Δελφίς, *Delphinus*, known to Democritus (Diels, *Vorsokr.*[5] ii. 144), and used for the calendar
by Euctemon and Eudoxus, was supposed to have been
placed in the heaven by Poseidon for having helped him
towards his marriage to Amphitrite.

(23) The *Horse*, Ἵππος, *Equus*, a constellation on the
equator with back southwards; according to Aratus
(283) his head is touched by the hand of the Ὑδροχόος,
'water-pourer', in the *Catasterismi* and later he became
Pegasus.

(24) The *Crown* (northern), Στέφανος, *Corona*, is
mentioned by Aratus (71), next after the *Kneeler* (Heracles), as placed in the heaven to commemorate Ariadne;
also used for the calendar by Euctemon.

(25) The *Charioteer*, Ἡνίοχος, *Auriga*, a constellation
between the Twins, the Bull and the north pole, was
first conceived as a man holding reins and driving a
horsed chariot (Thiele 4. 28; F. J. Boll, *Sphera* (1903),
111); he was then combined by astronomers with a still
older constellation, the goat, Αἴξ, *Capella*, with two kids
(Ἔριφοι), so that he carries the former on his shoulder
and the latter on his left hand. Legend associated him
with Bellerophon.

(26) The *Kneeler* (ὁ ἐν γόνασιν) is described by Aratus
as 'like to a toiling man resting' on one knee with both
arms raised, and the tip of his right foot on the head of
the Dragon. He is represented as Heracles, with a club
in his right hand and the lion's skin on his left arm, in his
fight with the Dragon which watched the Garden of the
Hesperides. Others identified him with Theseus, Ixion,
Prometheus, etc.

(27) The *Serpent-holder* (Ὀφιοῦχος, *serpentarius*) holds

a serpent in his hands. His head is near and opposite to the Kneeler; he is above the Scorpion. Identified by ps.-Eratosth. *Cat.* 20 with Asclepius, and so with Ὑγίεια.

(28) The *Dragon*, Δράκων, *Draco*, passes in and out enclosing the Bears in coils turned opposite ways. Its head is under the foot of the Kneeler (Heracles). It was variously identified with the dragon killed by Cadmus, the dragon which watched over the Garden of the Hesperides, or the Python killed by Apollo.

(29) *Cassiopeia* (earlier spelling *Cassiepeia*), a group of stars represented (*a*) by Aratus (192–3) as in the form of a key, (*b*) as a queen sitting on a throne with arms uplifted as if in agony about her daughter Andromeda. In another picture she is shown chained to two trees.

(30) *Andromeda* is represented by Aratus (203) as having her hands bound, agreeably to the story (cf. Eur. fr. 124 N.).

(31) *Perseus* is pictured running, unclothed save for a chlamys, with a sword in his right hand, wings on his feet, and Medusa's head in his left hand. Aratus (249–50) does not mention the Gorgon's head. The constellation includes Algol (Arabic: (*Head of*) *the Demon*).

(32) *Cepheus*, husband of Cassiopeia and father of Andromeda. His position in the heavens is described by Eudoxus (ap. Hipparch. *in Arat.* 1. 2. 11) and Aratus (179 f.). His upraised right hand touches the Swan's right wing; his feet are just below the tail of the Little Bear.

(33) The *Arrow* (Ὀϊστός, *Sagitta*) is under the Eagle. It is supposed to represent the arrow with which Heracles killed the Eagle gnawing the liver of Prometheus.

(34) The *Triangle* (called Δελτωτόν, Aratus 233) is below Andromeda, between her and the Ram (Eudoxus ap. Hipparch. *in Arat.* 1. 2. 13).

The southern constellations are the following:

(35) *Cetus* (Κῆτος, the *Sea-Monster* or *Whale*), represented as the Sea-Monster sent to kill Andromeda, is some distance south of her and Perseus. Its head is on the equator, near to the feet of the Ram (cf. Aratus 354). It is said to occupy more space in the heavens than any other constellation.

(36) The *Eridanus* (or Ποταμός, *River*), alternatively called Oceanus and by some identified with the Nile. Eudoxus described it as Ποταμός, starting from the left foot of Orion and lying below the Cetus (Hipparch. *in Arat.* 1. 8. 6). The legend connects it with Phaëthon who fell into it when struck by Zeus with a thunderbolt. Later combined with ὕδωρ from Aquarius (Boll 136–8).

(37) The *Hare* (Λαγωός, *Lepus*), a constellation described as under the feet of Orion and pursued by the Great Dog (Sirius) behind it (Aratus 338).

(38) The *Great Dog*, Κύων, *Canis Major*. Its feet lie, like the bend of the river Eridanus, on the southern tropic (Eudoxus ap. Hipparch. *in Arat.* 1. 10. 37). The bright star of the constellation, Sirius, was known to the Egyptians as *Sothis*; the early morning rising of Sirius more or less coincides with the beginning of the rising of the Nile.

(39) *Procyon*, Προκύων, *Antecanis*, the *Little Dog*, was called Procyon because its morning rising is just before that of Sirius, its position being a little more to the north (schol. in Arat. 450. It is just under the Twins. Cf. Hipparch. *in Arat.* 2. 2. 13, etc.).

(40) *Argo*, Ἀργώ, is described by Aratus (349–50) as being marked by stars only in the half of the ship from the mast to the stern. Hipparchus objects to this part of the description. Argo's position is near the hind legs and the tail of the Great Dog.

(41) The *Southern Fish* (Ἰχθῦς Νότιος, *Piscis Australis*) is described by Aratus (386–8) as being under the Sea-Goat (Αἰγόκερως) and turned towards the Cetus. It receives the water poured out by Aquarius. It is alternatively called the *Great Fish* (schol. in Arat.).

(42) The *Water-Snake* (Ὕδρα, Aratus 444, 519; Ὕδρας Hipparch. *in Arat.* 1. 11. 9). Its head reaches the middle of the Crab, its coils are below the Lion and its tail above the Centaur. On its coils respectively are the *Bowl* (Κρατήρ) and the *Raven* (Κόραξ), a representation which is of Babylonian origin. It was identified with the Hydra killed by Heracles (schol. in Arat. 443). The scholium also has the story that the Raven is a servant of Apollo who was sent to fetch a cup of pure water for a sacrifice; the servant found a fig-tree on the way and waited for the figs to ripen; ultimately he carried back to Apollo a snake and the cup, saying that the snake had prevented him from drawing the water from the spring.

(43) The *Centaur* (Κένταυρος). According to Eudoxus (ap. Hipparch. *in Arat.* 1. 2. 20) and Aratus (501–3) its back is along the winter tropic, like the Argo and the middle of the Scorpion; Aratus says (437–8) that the part like a man is under the Scorpion and the hinder (equine) part under the *Claws*. Hipparch. *in Arat.* 1. 8. 19–23, correcting this, says that it is almost wholly under Virgo except for the right shoulder, right hand, and forelegs, which are partly under the Claws. In his left hand he is supposed to hold a thyrsus, and a hare dependent; on his right lies an animal (Θηρίον) which has been differently understood as a dog or a wolf or a panther (Boll 143–8).

(44) The *Altar* (Θυτήριον, *Ara*) is in front of the fore-feet of the Archer (between them and the fore-feet of the Centaur). Aratus uses the name θυτήριον (403), Eudoxus and Hipparchus θυμιατήριον (Hipparch. *in Arat.* 1. 8. 14; 11. 9, etc.); so Ptolemy.

(45) The *Southern Crown*, Στέφανος Νότιος, is under the feet of the Archer. It is probably identical with the nameless stars δινωτοὶ κύκλῳ in Aratus (400). The name Στέφανος is later than Hipparchus but is used by Geminus and Ptolemy. Alternative names, according to schol. in Arat. are Οὐρανίσκος, Prometheus, wheel of Ixion (Ἰξίονος τροχός). Others again call it πλοῖον (Boll, 150).

5. We may assume that Eudoxus gives in his works, entitled *Phaenomena* and the *Mirror* (Ἔνοπτρον) respectively, a description of all the constellations known in his time. According to Hipparchus (*In Arati et Eudoxi phaenomena* 1. 2. 2) the books were separate works, though they agreed in all but a few particulars. Hipparchus quotes freely from both. The poem of Aratus, *Phaenomena*, was a popular version of Eudoxus so far at least as lines 19–732 are concerned. The commentary of Hipparchus gives three names which do not appear in Aratus: Πρόπους = η of the Twins; in a text from Teucros a variant Τρίπους occurs; as to this see Boll 126 f.); Προτρυγητήρ, *Vindemiatrix*, herald of the vintage = ε of Virgo; *Canopus*, omitted in Aratus, according to schol., because not visible in Greece: = α of Argo: on this see Hipparch. *in Arat.* 1. 11. 7. Called the 'pilot of Menelaus'.

6. Geminus (Εἰσαγωγὴ εἰς τὰ φαινόμενα, c. 3) gives a list of the constellations, which he divides into three classes, those in the zodiac and those to the north and south of it respectively. The list does not differ substantially from that given above, but Geminus mentions separately the following stars:

The *Crib* (Φάτνη); two *Asses* (Ὄνοι): as to these see under *Crab* (10) above: Καρδία λέοντος (the Heart of the Lion, *Cor Leonis*, which Hipparchus calls ὁ ἐν τῇ καρδίᾳ τοῦ λέοντος), with the alternative name Βασιλίσκος, *Regulus*; Λίνοι, *Bands*, between the two fishes in the constellation of that name, and Συνδεσμός, *Knot* (see *Fishes* (18) above); Ὄφις, the *Snake* held by Ophiuchus; Προτομὴ Ἵππου καθ' Ἵππαρχον = *Equuleus*, *Little Horse* (apparently Hipparchus has not the name, but Ptolemy has); Θυρσόλογχος, *Thyrsus-staff*, which according to Hipparchus 'the Centaur wields'; Ὕδωρ, the *water* from Aquarius (see *Eridanus* (36) above); Κηρύκιον καθ' Ἱππαρχον, 'Herald's staff, according to Hipparchus' (= Caduceus), mentioned by Valens as held in Orion's left hand (perhaps Egyptian in origin, Boll 167); Γοργόνιον, the Gorgon's Head, 'at the end of Perseus' right hand'; 'the small stars close together at the end of Perseus' right hand are made into the Ἅρπη (Sickle)'; Βερενίκης πλόκαμος, Coma Berenices, so called by the courtier-astronomer Conon in honour of Berenice and celebrated in the poem of Callimachus: Ptolemy (Alm. 2. 56) calls this last constellation Πλόκαμος simply.

7. The Milky Way, Γαλαξίας κύκλος, is described by Aratus (400) as 'that wheel with glaring eyes all round which they call Milk'. Democritus was the first to recognize that it consisted of stars packed very closely together. The name arose out of the legend of Hera's milk which was spilt when she refused the breast to the infant Heracles. Popularly and poetically it was variously regarded as the way to the Home of the Gods, the one-time orbit of the sun, Phaëthon's course, the souls' meeting-place, etc.

8. The positions of the various constellations and stars in the heavens were shown on globes or 'spheres'. Even Thales and Anaximander are credited by the Doxographi with the construction of such globes. Eudoxus is certain to have had one; so had Hipparchus; and Ptolemy gave detailed instructions for the construction of a globe which would even allow for the change in the position of the poles with precession (Alm. 8. 3). The globe on the shoulders of the Atlas Farnese in the Naples Museum represents such a globe, and is attributed to a date not later than A.D. 150. It shows the constellations with the principal great circles on the heavenly sphere, but not individual stars; the positions of the constellations show that the artist avoided the mistakes of Aratus pointed out by Hipparchus; he was aware, and made use, of Hipparchus' corrections. A fragment of a similar globe of blue marble is preserved in the Berlin Museum (No. 1050 A); this has separate stars shown in yellow colour within the contour of the figures representing the constellations.          T. H.

9. We know, through fragmentary preserved astrological literature, that in Egypt of the Hellenistic-Roman period many fanciful 'constellations' were invented which may reflect, at least in part, late Egyptian and Babylonian traditions. These new groupings were distinguished as the sphaera barbarica in contrast to the conventional sphaera graecanica. The first evidence for this distinction is found with Nigidius Figulus (1st c. B.C.), later on with Manilius (3) and Firmicus Maternus (qq.v.). The constellations of the sphaera barbarica had little influence on astronomy but greatly affected Islamic, Hindu, and finally western astrology and its artistic representations.

10. A 'catalogue of stars' has as its purpose the localization of individual stars in a precise fashion, enabling later astronomers to establish changes in stellar positions. The first catalogue of this type, listing probably between 800 and 900 stars, was compiled by Hipparchus in the second century B.C. The ways in which Hipparchus defined the positions of stars is known to us through his Commentary to Aratus and Eudoxus; the most important method of describing the location of a star consists in giving the distance of the star from the north-pole and the point of the ecliptic at which the great circle from the pole to the star meets the ecliptic. These mixed equatorial ecliptic coordinates appear again in Indian astronomy (so-called 'polar longitudes'). There is no evidence for the consistent use of ecliptic coordinates; in particular, latitudes (perpendicular to the ecliptic) are never attested.

The first catalogue of stars in the modern sense of the word is contained in Book 7 of the Almagest (for A.D. 137). There one finds for 1,022 stars, distributed among forty-eight constellations, their ecliptic co-ordinates and magnitude (ranging from 1 to 6). This catalogue of stars remained the prototype for practically all major oriental and western catalogues until modern times.

F. Boll–W. Gundel, 'Sternbilder' in Roscher, Lex. vi. 867 ff. F. Boll, Sphaera (Leipzig, 1903); W. Gundel, 'Dekane und Dekansternbilder', Studien der Bibl. Warburg 19 (1936); H. Vogt, 'Der Kalendar des Claudius Ptolemäus' (= Boll, Griechischer Kalender v), Sitz. Heidelberg. Akad. d. Wiss., Phil.-hist. Kl., 1920; A. Rehm, 'Parapegmastudien, mit einem Anhang: Euktemon und das Buch De signis', Abh. d. Bayer. Akad. d. Wiss., Phil.-hist. Abt., 1941; C. H. F. Peters–E. B. Knobel, 'Ptolemy's Catalogue of Stars', Carnegie Inst. of Washington, 1915; E. B. Knobel, 'Chronology of Star Catalogues', Mem. Royal Astron. Soc. 43 (1875–7), 1 ff.; A. Scherer, Gestirnnamen bei den indogermanischen Völkern (1953); F. Saxl, Verzeichnis astrologischer und mythologischer illustrierter Handschriften des Lateinischen Mittelalters in Römischen Bibliotheken (1915); F. Saxl, Verzeichnis astrologischer und mythologischer illustrierter Handschriften des Lateinischen Mittelalters II: Die Handschriften der National-Bibliothek in Wien (1927); F. Saxl–H. Meier, Catalogue of Astrological and Mythological Illuminated Manuscripts of the Latin Middle Ages III: Manuscripts in English Libraries, ed. H. Bober (1953); IV: Astrological Manuscripts in Italian Libraries, Patrick McGurk (1966); P. Kunitzsch, Arabische Sternnamen in Europa (1959); Untersuchungen zur Sternnomenklatur der Araber (1961); F. Gössmann, 'Planetarium Babylonicum oder die sumerisch-babylonischen Sternnamen', Scripta Pontificii Inst. Biblici 1950 (to be used with some caution).          O. N.

CONSTITUTIONES, the generic name for legislative enactments by Roman Emperors, which were made in different forms. In the first place the Emperors possessed the ius edicendi like all higher magistrates (see EDICTUM); imperial edicta were issued for enactments of a general character (cf. Caracalla's edict on citizenship, q.v.), to a less extent for law reforms. This purpose was better served by decreta (decisions in civil or criminal trials passed by the Emperor) and rescripta (imperial decisions upon special points of law, in answer both to petitions, libelli, addressed to him by a litigant, and to the inquiry of a judicial official in complicated cases, relationes). The rescripta were also called epistulae, when directed in the form of a letter to the inquiring official or subscriptiones when written on the libellus itself and signed by the Emperor. Such constitutiones, although in form they merely interpreted existing law, often in substance laid down new rules. The Romans had no theory of the binding force of precedent in general, but such rulings, coming from the Emperor, were regarded as authoritative for future cases, unless their context showed them to be 'personal'. In the later Empire attempts were made to limit the general effect of rescripta. Another type of constitutiones was the imperial instructions (mandata) given to officials, especially to provincial governors. These were more concerned with administrative matters, but exceptionally they touched civil law, e.g. in dealing with legal relations (marriage, wills) of military persons.

At the beginning of the Principate there was no clear basis for the Emperor's legislative power, apart from edicta as expressions of his magisterial imperium (proconsulare). The first Emperors used therefore to give effect to their legislative intentions by means of the Senate, before whom they pronounced personally (oratio) or by a quaestor their motion for approval by the senators. The resolution of the Senate became later a mere formality, so that an imperial oratio was simply a kind of publication of an imperial law. By the middle of the second century, however, constitutiones themselves were recognized as having the force of law (legis uicem [uigorem] optinent). The numerous quotations of imperial rescripts in the works of the classical jurists excerpted in the Digest show how productive was this activity of the Emperors in the times of the Antonines and their successors. From the time of Diocletian and Constantine, at the latest, the legislative power of the Emperors was formally and clearly unlimited: they issued directly general enactments (leges generales), laying down new legal rules with unrestricted validity. For collections of constitutions, *see* CODEX.

For bibliography see under LAW AND PROCEDURE, ROMAN, § 1 (books on History and Sources). A. B.; B. N.

**CONSUL,** the supreme civil and military magistrate of Rome under the Republic. The etymology of the word *consul* is uncertain: it has variously been derived from *cum-esse* (Niebuhr), from *cum-salire* (Mommsen), and from *consulere* (De Sanctis). In any case it was not the original designation of the chief magistrates: Livy (3. 15. 12) and the Greek translation of their title (στρατηγός or στρατηγὸς ὕπατος) show that they were in the first instance called 'praetores'. This name (from *prae-ire*, to march ahead) and its Greek equivalent emphasize the military character of the magistracy. The name of 'consul' may have come into use earlier, but it is unlikely to have become the official title of the eponymous praetors until some time after a third praetorship had been created in 366 B.C. (*see* PRAETOR).

According to the traditional account, which has the support of the *fasti* (q.v.), the dual magistracy dated from the first year of the Republic in 509. The two principles of annuality and equal collegiality constituted the answer of the Romans to the threat of a return of monarchical rule. This view has its adherents among moderns, but many alternative theories have also been propounded in recent years. A small minority see the transition from monarchy to Republic as a gradual evolution. Others who accept the traditional 'revolution' claim to find the antecedents of the consuls in two civil or military assistants of the kings. Others again believe that the dual consulship of equals was a comparatively late development from what in the early fifth century had been either a single magistracy or a college of two or more unequal partners.

Analysis of the *fasti* suggests that the tradition may have been wrong in regarding the consulship as an office from which plebeians were at one time excluded by law. In the fifth century, however, plebeian consuls were few, and it was not until 367 that the Licinian plebiscite provided for the compulsory election of at least one consul of plebeian status. Assisted perhaps by the creation of a third praetorship in 366, the *comitia* repeatedly violated this enactment in spirit, if not in letter, during the next twenty-five years, and it was only after what was probably a more precise formulation of the measure in 342 that the election of a plebeian became a regular annual occurrence. Even then the patricians continued to fill the other consulship until 172.

Throughout the Republic candidates for the consulship were elected by the people in the *comitia centuriata*, but, as they were proposed by the senators from their own ranks, liberty of choice was greatly restricted. It disappeared under the Empire when the *comitia centuriata* were suppressed and the Emperors either recommended the candidates or themselves assumed the consulship. Under the Republic the consuls entered office on 15 Mar. (after 153 B.C. on 1 Jan.) and retained it for a whole year; under the Empire they retained it from two to four months only. Consequently, while during the Republic consuls, except *suffecti* (that is, other men appointed in case of the death, illness, or resignation of a consul), both gave their names to the year, despite differences of rank arising from their age (*collega maior*) or the polling (*collega prior*), consuls during the Empire did so only if they entered office on 1 Jan. (*consules ordinarii*, to be distinguished from their successors *consules suffecti*). A further distinction during the Empire depended on whether consuls were single or married, and the number of their children. Moreover, the Emperors often appointed themselves or their relatives and protégés consuls, entirely

disregarding the legal age limits, which had been carefully fixed in 180 B.C. by the *Lex Villia Annalis* (*see* VILLIUS). In the age of Cicero no one under forty-two could be elected consul; under the Empire even children could be invested with the office, which was conferred upon Honorius at birth. But the consulship survived in the Western Roman Empire until A.D. 534.

Mommsen, *Röm. Staatsr.*, ii³. 1. 74 ff.; De Sanctis, *Stor. Rom* i. 403 ff. (cf. *Riv. Fil.* 1929, 1 ff.); M. Holleaux, Στρατηγὸς ὕπατος (1918); E. S. Staveley, *Hist.* 1956, 90 ff. (on origins); Ogilvie, *Comm. Livy 1–5*, 230 f.; F. Cassola, *I gruppi politici romani* (1962); A. E. Astin, *The Lex Annalis before Sulla* (1958); A. Lippold, *Consules* (Bonn, 1963) (dealing with 264–201 B.C.). For lists of consular Fasti, A. Degrassi, *Inscr. Ital.* xiii, i (1947), Republican, and *I Fasti consolari dell' impero romano* (1952); Broughton, *MRR*; E. J. Bickerman, *Chronology of the Ancient World* (1968), 170 ff. P. T.; E. S. S.

**CONSUS,** a Roman god whose festivals (Consualia) were on 19 Aug. and 15 Dec., possibly in connexion with the ending respectively of the harvest and the autumn sowing. He seems connected with Ops (q.v.), by the dates of his festivals. The most reasonable explanation of his name is that it is connected with *condere* and he is the god of the store-bin or other receptacle for the garnered grain. This, as corn was often stored underground, may account for his subterranean altar in the Circus Maximus, uncovered only on his festival days (Varro, *Ling.* 6. 20; Dion. Hal., *Ant. Rom.* 2. 31. 2); for its alleged inscription (Tert., *De Spect.* 5) see v. Blumenthal and Rose, *ARW* 1936, 384; 1937, 111. The ancients commonly supposed his name to have something to do with *consilium* (Dion. Hal., ibid. 3) or, because his altar lay in the Circus, identified him with Poseidon Hippios (Livy 1. 9. 6). He had also a temple on the Aventine, probably vowed or dedicated by L. Papirius Cursor about 272 B.C. (see Platner–Ashby, 141). His characteristic offering was firstfruits (Dion. Hal., ibid.). Horses and asses were garlanded and rested on his festival (Plut., *Quaest. Rom.* 48, whereon see Rose). Whether he was originally honoured with circus games is doubtful.

Latte, *RR* 72. H. J. R.

**CONTAMINATIO:** a word used by modern scholars to express the procedure of Plautus and Terence in incorporating material from another Greek play into the play which they were 'translating'. The precise sense in which Terence's critics intended *contaminare* (*Andr.* 16, *Heaut.* 17) is not clear, for the word was being used not descriptively but pejoratively; but the concern of the critics was with the Greek plays and their intention to preserve them from violence. The practice which it was intended to condemn is clear since Terence makes it explicit (*Andr.* 9 ff.) that it referred to his 'translating' Menander's *Andria* and incorporating some parts of the *Perinthia*. He goes on to claim the precedent of Naevius, Plautus, and Ennius, and prefers their *neglegentia* to the *obscura diligentia* of his critics (these words too are not being used descriptively, but in the interest of producing assonance and antithesis—as is common in the ambitious rhetoric of Terence's prologues). The fragments of Naevius and Ennius are too meagre to judge, but Plautus (q.v.) gives evidence of the procedure criticized in Terence.

G. E. Duckworth, *The Nature of Roman Comedy* (1952), 202 ff. G. W. W.

**CONTIO** (*conventio*) was a public gathering at Rome which even non-citizens, though illegally, used to attend. It was summoned by a magistrate or priest, either as a preliminary to legislation, in which case the measures to be passed were announced, or as a political assembly, called to discuss questions of public moment or the programmes of the political leaders. A magistrate could cancel a meeting summoned by an inferior (*contionem avocare*), and a tribune could veto or adjourn it (*intercessio* and *obnuntiatio*). The right of addressing the audience (*contionem dare*) depended on the will of the president who addressed the assembly from the platform (*ex superiore loco*), while the debaters spoke *ex inferiore loco*. The meetings generally took place near the rostra, in daytime, on *dies fasti*. As the kings had done, so the Emperors alone summoned the meetings to address the people in solemn circumstances.

Mommsen, *Röm. Staatsr.* i³. 191 ff.; G. W. Botsford, *The Roman Assemblies* (1909), 139 ff.; A. H. J. Greenidge, *Roman Public Life* (1911), 158 ff.          P. T.

**CONTRACT, ROMAN LAW OF.** For the earliest contractual forms, *see* NEXUM, STIPULATIO. The classical law had no single principle of contract but rather, on the one hand, a form (*stipulatio*) into which any agreement could be cast, and on the other, a list of contracts (i.e. of typical circumstances in which an agreement would be given legal effect). Unless an agreement were clothed in the form of a *stipulatio* or satisfied the requirements of one of the listed contracts, neither party could sue on it. According to Justinian's classification (*Inst.* 3. 13. 2), which was based on that of Gaius (3. 89), contracts arose in four ways (*a*) *re*, by the handing over of a thing; (*b*) *verbis*, by formal words (*stipulatio*, q.v.; *dotis dictio*, *see* MARRIAGE); (*c*) *litteris*, by written entries in the account book of the creditor; (*d*) *consensu*, by a simple agreement within defined limits. The contract *litteris* was obsolete or obsolescent in the time of Gaius, and its exact character is obscure. The 'list of contracts' mentioned above comprises in fact those arising *re* and *consensu* (and certain other specific agreements of minor importance—the so-called clothed pacts—which were made actionable in the course of time by the praetor (*see* EDICTUM) or by imperial *constitutiones* (q.v.)). The four 'real' contracts were: (1) *mutuum*, a loan for consumption, i.e. of things such as money and food which can ordinarily be used only by being consumed; the borrower was obliged to return an equivalent in quantity and quality; the payment of interest, with a maximum of 12 per cent., reduced by Justinian to 4 per cent., required a special agreement, normally a *stipulatio*; (2) *commodatum*, a gratuitous loan for use; (3) *depositum*, a handing over of a thing for gratuitous safe-keeping, the depositee having no right to use it; (4) *pignus*, a pledge (*see* SECURITY). The consensual contracts were: (1) *Emptio venditio*, sale. This contract is made when the parties agree on a thing to be sold and a price (in money). Thereafter, although the thing belongs to the seller until it is handed over, the buyer bears the risk of its being damaged or destroyed (unless by the fault of the seller), and is correspondingly entitled to any accruing benefit. The seller must guarantee to the buyer undisturbed possession of the thing and, in the law of Justinian, the absence of serious but latent defects of quality. (This liability for latent defects was the result of a development to which the edict of the *aediles* (q.v.) *curules* concerning the sale of slaves and beasts made a large contribution.) (2) *Locatio conductio* (hire) included not only the hiring or leasing of a movable or immovable, but also contracts of employment in the form either of the hire of services or of the placing out of a job of work to be done (distinguished in modern terminology as *locatio conductio operarum* and *operis* respectively). Here, as in sale, the reward must be fixed and in money. Where a reward was not intended or was inappropriate because of the social position of the person rendering the services, the contract would be: (3) *Mandatum*, an undertaking to perform a gratuitous service for another at his request. Even though the contract was in principle gratuitous it was common to pay an *honorarium*, and in the late classical law it was possible to claim it in a special proceeding

(cf. ADVOCATUS). (4) *Societas* (partnership), an agreement to co-operate for a common purpose, each party making some contribution, of either capital, skill, or labour, and each sharing equally, unless otherwise agreed, in profits and losses (*see also* COMMUNIO). These contracts were flexible not only because they rested on a formless agreement but even more because the parties were obliged to observe *bona fides* in the making and execution of them, and in the hands of the jurists *bona fides* was a fertile concept.

For agreements which did not fall within these types the praetor could grant a special action (*actio in factum*). These exceptions were eventually (but probably not in the classical law) generalized into the category of what are now, following a Byzantine terminology, called 'innominate contracts', enforced by *actio praescriptis verbis*. An innominate contract is any agreement which does not conform to any of the types listed above (e.g. a contract of exchange, which was not sale since it had no money price, or a contract of employment in which a reward was intended but was not fixed at the time of the agreement), but only if it has been performed on one side (e.g. the services have been rendered). The importance of this type of contract is that it provides a general principle which (subject to the requirement of performance on one side) fills the gaps left by the traditional typical contracts.

See the text-books mentioned under LAW AND PROCEDURE, ROMAN, § 1. P. De Francisci, *Synallagma* i (1913), ii (1916). P. Bonfante, *Scritti giuridici* ii. S. Riccobono, *Studi Bonfante* ii (1930). V. Arangio-Ruiz, *Responsabilità contrattuale*² (1933); *Il mandato in dir. rom.* (1949); *La società in dir. rom.* (1950); *La compravendita in dir. rom.* (1954). T. Mayer-Maly, *Locatio conductio* (1956); F. de Zulueta, *Roman Law of Sale* (1945); A. Watson, *Contract of Mandate* (1961); B. Nicholas, *An Introduction to Roman Law* (1962), 159 ff.          B. N.

**CONTUBERNIUM** (from *taberna*) meant a 'dwelling together', as of soldiers or animals, but especially cohabitation between slave and slave or slave and free. Since a slave lacked juristic personality, a *contubernium* was not a marriage but a factual situation, at the pleasure of the owner, creating no legal consequences despite the use of such words as *uxor*, *maritus* or *pater*, even in legal texts. Children were the property of the mother's master; no slave woman could be guilty of adultery; manumission of one or both parents need not extend to their issue. It is impossible to determine how widespread *de facto* slave 'families' were: there was little place for them in Cato's estate management or in the mines, much more among urban slaves, increasing under the Empire. Despite a certain 'humanitarian' trend in imperial law (e.g. *Dig.* 33. 7. 12. 7; but cf. 33. 7. 20. 4), there was never a significant diminution of an owner's legal right to separate them.

For bibliography, *see* FREEDMEN; SLAVERY.          M. I. F.

**CONVENTUS**, 'assembly', is technically used (1) for provincial assizes; (2) for associations of Italians abroad.

(1) In most provinces, by the late Republic, assizes were held in fixed centres, in each for a defined district (later called *conventus iuridicus*). The system was probably borrowed from Hellenistic practice, and in the East Cicero still used the Greek term διοίκησις. The *conventus*, under the Empire, sometimes (e.g. in Spain) had their own imperial cult.

(2) By the early second century B.C., Italians (especially in the East) united for religious and other purposes under elected' *magistri*. These associations called themselves 'Italici' [later 'cives Romani'—but the Greeks from the start called them 'Ρωμαῖοι] qui [e.g.] Argi negotiantur' (or similar informal titles). Owing to their race, and often to special concessions, they obtained a position of great local importance, and the governor would rely on them

for service on juries and on his *consilium* and for advice on local conditions. Under the Empire these *conventus civium Romanorum* (as they came to be called) even passed decrees together with Greek city authorities. In some provinces (e.g. the Gauls) local associations (each normally under a *curator*) united under a *summus curator* for the province. *Curatores* were often Romanized natives. With the spread of Romanization, especially in the West, the *conventus* naturally disappeared.

Ruggiero, *Diz. Epigr.*, s.v. E. B.

**CONVERSION,** abandonment, more or less sudden, of one way of living in favour of another, a genuine phenomenon and occasionally testified to in antiquity. The most famous case is that of the young rake Polemon, who strayed into Xenocrates' lecture-room and was so impressed by his discourse on temperance that he turned philosopher (Diog. Laert. 4. 16). Horace professes (*Carm.* 1. 34) to have been converted from materialism by thunder from a clear sky, which at least shows that such a thing was supposed to be possible. But religious conversion, i.e. the abandonment of one religion for another, did not take place under polytheism; a believer in certain gods would not cease to believe in them because he was attracted to and became a devotee of another. A mystery-cult might attract a man to a religious life as a monastic order does today, but that again is not abandonment of former beliefs. Only Judaism and Christianity produced conversions in this sense.

A. D. Nock, *Conversion* (1933), and in *Pisciculi Franz Joseph Dölger dargeboten* (1939), 165 ff., also art. 'Conversio' in *RAC*. H. J. R.

**COOKERY.** The surviving evidence is regrettably incomplete for ancient methods of cookery. The only extant cookery book is that ascribed to Apicius (q.v.); but remnants of what must once have been an extensive literature (especially in Greek) are preserved by Athenaeus, and there are numerous incidental references elsewhere, especially in the Roman agricultural writings and (for the *haute cuisine* of his day) the *Cena* of Petronius. The contents of some Roman kitchens have come to light *in situ* at Pompeii; but Greek culinary objects of various periods, found in the Athenian agora and elsewhere, had for the most part been broken and discarded. Further information comes from vase-paintings and terracotta figurines.

Bread, which for the greater part of the period formed the basis of the diet, was as early as the sixth century B.C. often produced in commercial bakeries, which became increasingly common later. But it could also be baked at home, from flour ground within the household on saddle-stones or, later, rotary querns (*see* MILLS). (The mortar proper (ὅλμος, *pila*) was used for dehusking grain and for pounding other foods (e.g. dried fish), while the smaller θυεία (*mortarium*) was probably similar to our mixing-bowl.) The dough was kneaded on a kneading table (κάρδοπος, μάκτρα) and baked either 'under the ashes'— under a tile or dome-shaped cover (πνιγεύς, *testu*) with burning charcoal heaped over it—or in a small oven (probably = κρίβανος, *clibanus*), heated from below and often portable, or else, in Roman times, in a large baking-oven (*furnus*), which was pre-heated from within, the fire being removed before cooking began. All these ovens could be used for other foods also. For the kneaded barley μᾶζα, which served the poorer classes in Greece, the dough was prepared in a large bowl after the grain had been parched on a φρύγετρον and perhaps roughly crushed.

Other foods could be prepared either by dry heat (grilling, frying, roasting) on a brazier (ἐσχάρα) or over an open fire, often with the help of spits or a grill (probably = τάγηνον); or else they could be boiled or stewed. For

the latter purpose pots (χύτραι) or covered 'casserole (λοπάδες) were used, which could be heated either in larg 'barrel cookers' or on small braziers or on tripods o gridirons over charcoal burning on the hearth. Sometime wood appears to have been burnt in the hearth an sausages, sucking pigs, etc., smoked above it, the smok escaping through the roof or a vent in the wall. From Roman sites water-heating contrivances, at times highl ornamented, are also known, some of which sugges cooking by the *bain-marie* process.

The ancient kitchen also contained ladles, spoons strainers, graters, meat-hooks, cleavers, knives, and th like, often very similar to their modern counterparts. I general its equipment was more portable and, at least i Greece, less tied to a purpose-built room than is usua nowadays; but many of its implements, like the cookin methods employed, show a remarkable degree of con tinuity, especially in Greece, from ancient to moder times. *See also* FOOD AND DRINK, MEALS.

B. A. Sparkes, 'The Greek Kitchen', *JHS* 1962, 121 ff.; 196 162 f. (with copious references); B. Flower and E. Rosenbaum *Apicius, The Roman Cookery Book* (1958), esp. 29 ff. by J. Liversidge *PW*, s.v. Kochbücher, Kochkunst. L. A. M

**COPAÏS,** a lake, now drained, which in early day covered most of the west plain of Boeotia. It took it name from Copae on its north side. The swallow-hole on its east side were cleared and enlarged, and canals dug north and south to lead the Cephissus and other stream to them round the edge of the plain. Shafts for uncom pleted tunnels were also bored on the low hills in th north-east corner and between Copaïs and Lake Helic on the east. The drainage works were usually ascribed to the Minyans of Orchomenus. The outlets were said to have been blocked by the Theban hero Heracles: perhaps the Thebans stopped them during their wars against Orchomenus. In classical times, in spite of attempts to drain it, the lake was always swampy, and famous for eels (Ar. *Ach.* 880 ff.). On what afterwards became an island in the lake is the Mycenaean fortress called Gla (formerly identified by some with Arne), the importance of which has been shown by renewed excavations there: a great citadel with elaborate double gates from which roads lead, especially to the site of Hagia Marina, an elaborate palace of two wings and two megara, and a great enclosed space, the so-called 'Agora', divided from the palace precinct and containing other buildings, but apparently an integral part of the whole establishment. The complex was built in Late Helladic III, and shows signs of violent destruction after no long period of use.

P-K, *GL* I, ii. 466 ff. E. J. A. Kenny, *Annals of Archaeology and Anthropology* 1935, 189 ff.; U. Kahrstedt, *Arch. Anz.* 1937, 1 ff. T. J. D.; R. J. H.

**COPTUS** (modern *Keft*), chief city of the 5th nome of Upper Egypt, on the west bank of the Nile, was the starting-place of several routes to the Red Sea, especially one eastwards to Kosseir. But Ptolemy II caused this route to be less important than that to Berenice (q.v. 2), on the Red Sea, which became a well-equipped camel-track and the principal link between the Mediterranean and eastern waters. It was developed by Augustus; in the third century it temporarily fell into the hands of the native Blemmyes and was almost destroyed by Diocletian (A.D. 292), but recovered and maintained itself in the Byzantine Age. Part of a customs tariff survives on a papyrus from Coptus.

Warmington, *Indian Commerce*, 6 ff., 14 ff., 50 f., 104 f.; Kees, *PW*, s.v. 'Koptos'. E. H. W.

**CORA,** modern *Cori*, strongly placed at the north-west angle of the Volscian mountains in Latium (q.v.). Latins and Volsci (q.v.) disputed its possession before 340 B.C.

After 338 B.C. it was an ally of Rome and later a *municipium*. Fine remains exist of polygonal walls and two temples.

G. Lugli, *La tecnica edilizia romana* (1957), 134 ff.; Castagnoli, *Stud. urb.* 13 ff.    E. T. S.

**CORAX** of Syracuse (5th c. B.C.) is said to have been the first teacher of rhetoric. He perhaps taught the division of a speech into προοίμιον, ἀγών, and ἐπίλογος. Tisias (q.v.) was his pupil. (*See* RHETORIC, GREEK § 1)

L. Radermacher, *Artium Scriptores* (1951), 28 ff.; G. A. Kennedy, *The Art of Persuasion in Greece* (1963), 58 ff.    D. A. R.

**CORBILO** (probably the equivalent of St. Nazaire or Nantes), a town of the Veneti on the Loire, to which British tin was shipped for conveyance across Gaul to Massilia (*Marseille*) and the Mediterranean coast. The transit across Gaul was made in thirty days. Scipio Aemilianus (*c.* 135 B.C.) met traders from Corbilo at Massilia or Narbo, but failed to extract information about Britain from them. The town declined when the Cornish tin trade languished.

Strabo 4. 190; Diod. 5. 22. Cary, *JHS* 1924, 172 ff.    E. H. W.

**CORBULO,** GNAEUS DOMITIUS (*PW* 50, Suppl. iii), through the six marriages of his mother Vistilia (Pliny, *HN* 7. 162) was connected with many prominent families: one of his stepsisters married the Emperor Gaius. Probably *cos. suff.* A.D. 39, in 47 he was legate of Germania Inferior when he successfully fought against the Chauci led by Gannascus, but was not allowed by Claudius to go further. A strict disciplinarian, he made his troops dig a canal between the Meuse and Rhine. Proconsul of Asia under Claudius, he was soon after Nero's accession made *legatus* of Cappadocia and Galatia with the command against Parthia in the war about the control of Armenia. This started in earnest only in 58, when Corbulo had reorganized the Roman army in the East. He captured Artaxata and Tigranocerta, installed Tigranes as king of Armenia, and received the governorship of Syria. But Tigranes was driven out of Armenia, the war was renewed in 62, and at Corbulo's request a separate general, Caesennius Paetus (q.v.) was sent to Armenia. After Paetus' defeat, Corbulo obtained in 63 a *maius imperium*, restored Roman prestige, and concluded a durable agreement with Parthia: Tiridates, the Parthian nominee to the throne of Armenia, admitted a Roman protectorate. Corbulo probably did not abuse his popularity, but his son-in-law Vinicianus (q.v.) conspired. In Oct. 66 Nero invited Corbulo to Greece and compelled him to commit suicide. His daughter Domitia Longina became wife of Domitian in 70. It was the homage of the new dynasty to the name and influence of the greatest general of his time. The account of his achievements in Tacitus (*Ann.* bks. 12–15) and Dio Cassius (bks. 60–63) derives ultimately to a great extent from Corbulo's own memoirs.

M. Hammond, *Harv. Stud.* 1934, 81 ff.; Syme, *Tacitus*, see index. Portrait: F. Poulsen, *Rev. Arch.* 1932, 48 ff.    A. M.; G. E. F. C.

**CORCYRA** (Κέρκυρα), popularly identified with the Phaeacia of the *Odyssey*. In comparison with the bare rocks and heathland of other Ionian islands, Corcyra has an almost tropical luxuriance, thanks to its heavier rainfall. Today it is the staging-post between Greece and Italy, but, rather surprisingly, it was not always so. Its prehistoric links are with the north, not with Greece, and there is no evidence of any contact between Greek lands and Corcyra until the arrival of colonists, perhaps Eretrians at first (a tradition supported by the Euboean cow and calf among its coin types) and then Corinthians, traditionally in 733 B.C. Recent excavations have revealed Geometric pottery of the latter part of the eighth century. While there are fine architectural fragments of early

temples, Corcyra's chief artistic treasure is the splendid but terrible Gorgon pediment, which seems to epitomize the bitterness of the struggle with the mother city, Corinth. The standard of Corcyrean behaviour in war was set by Periander, the ferocious tyrant of Corinth: kidnapping of firstborns, revenged by murder among the olives. It shared with Corinth the foundation of Epidamnus (q.v.), and perhaps of other colonies in Illyria; but it resented the dominion of the tyrant Periander, and after his death it became a competitor of Corinth in Adriatic waters. Pursuing a policy of isolation, it stood out of the Persian Wars; but in 435 it was drawn into open hostility against Corinth, in consequence of a scramble for the control of Epidamnus, and to escape defeat it sought an alliance with Athens (433), which it renewed several times. It received protection from the Athenian fleet in 433, and again in 427 and 425, when Corinthian fleets attempted to co-operate with disaffected elements on the island; in 427 and 425 the Corcyrean democracy disgraced its victory by wholesale massacre of the oligarchs. In 410 Corcyra shook off the Athenian connexion, but in 375 it joined the Second Athenian League, and so drew upon itself a Spartan expeditionary force, which it beat off after a prolonged siege (373). By 360 it had again detached itself, but *c.* 340 it rejoined Athens in a vain attempt to prevent the intrusion of Macedonia into Adriatic waters. After the death of Alexander it became an object of dispute between various mainland dynasts, Cassander, Demetrius, and Pyrrhus, and was occupied for a time by the Syracusan tyrant Agathocles. In 229 it was captured by the Illyrians, but was speedily delivered by a Roman fleet and remained a Roman naval station until at least 189. At this period it was governed by a prefect (presumably nominated by the consuls), but in 148 it was attached to the province of Macedonia.

J. Partsch, *Die Insel Korfu* (1887); P–K, *GL* 2. 2. 422 ff.; Έργον 1954, 64 ff.; Hammond, *Epirus*, 363 f.    M. C.; S. B.

**CORDUBA** (modern *Cordoba*), a city on the middle Baetis (*Guadalquivir*), founded by M. Claudius Marcellus in 152 B.C., and raised to colonial status, with the title Patricia, some time after 49 B.C. It was sacked by Caesar in 45 for its Pompeian allegiance, and later settled with veterans by Augustus. It was the chief centre of Roman life and letters in the republican Spains; under the Empire it had few rivals, and retained capital importance in the administration of Baetica. Its republican poets were succeeded by the Senecas and Lucan; its Bishop Hosius (Ossius) was the dominant figure of the Western Church throughout the earlier fourth century. Its wealth was sustained by oil, wool, precious metals nearby (*Mons Marianus*), a flourishing business interest, and a waterway navigable by small ships. Decline cannot be inferred from the scantiness of Roman remains, overlaid by its brilliant Moslem period.    M. I. H.

**CORFINIUM,** town of the Paeligni (q.v.) on a strong site on the Via Valeria (q.v.) controlling a strategic bridgehead across the R. Aternus near modern *Corfinio*: remains exist at the church of *San Pelino* (i.e. Paelignus). Corfinium is unrecorded until the Social War when the Italians made it their seat of government and renamed it Italia, intending it to become the permanent capital of Italy (90 B.C.). They were quickly obliged, however, to transfer their seat of government first to Bovianum and then to Aesernia (qq.v.). After the Social War Corfinium became a Roman *municipium*. In 49 B.C., garrisoned by Domitius Ahenobarbus, it offered temporary resistance to Julius Caesar (Caesar, *BCiv.* 1. 15 f.; App. *BCiv.* 2. 38; Suet. *Iul.* 33 f.; Lucan, 2. 478 f.). Subsequently Corfinium received colonists on several occasions, but apparently was never styled *colonia* (*Lib. Colon.* 228, 255). Inscriptions indicate that it remained a flourishing *municipium* in imperial times, but its later history is unknown. Presumably it was destroyed in medieval times.

Diod. 37. 2. 4; Strabo 5. 241; Vell. Pat. 2. 16. D. Ludovico, *Dove Italia nacque* (1961). E. T. S.

**CORINNA,** lyric poetess, of Tanagra (fr. 2; Paus. 9. 22. 3), thought in antiquity to be an elder contemporary of Pindar, with whom various legends, none very trustworthy, connect her (*Suda* s.v. Κόριννα; Plut. *de Glor. Ath.* 4; Ael. *VH* 13. 25; schol. Ar. *Ach.* 720). But her language may mean that she did not write before the third century B.C. She wrote narrative lyrical poems on Boeotian subjects for a circle of women (fr. 2), with titles such as *Boeotus, Seven against Thebes, Euonymie, Iolaus, Return of Orion*. A papyrus at Berlin contains substantial remains of two poems. In the first (fr. 4) she describes a contest in song between the mountain gods Cithaeron and Helicon. Since Helicon is defeated, the contest may stand for the competition between her own kind of art and that of the Hesiodic school. In the second the seer Acraephen foretells the high destiny of the daughters of Asopus, who are married to gods. The material used may go back to epic sources, and is based on legends of colonization. Both are written in regular stanzas of fixed length in which a metre is repeated and the stanza closed with a *clausula*. She uses simple verse-forms, such as minor ionics and choriambic dimeters. She also wrote lyric nomes, and fr. 5 B, called *Orestes*, seems to be a choral hymn for a spring festival. Her text is in the reformed Boeotian spelling of the third century and if she wrote earlier, must have been transliterated from what she wrote. She normally keeps to her own dialect, but sometimes admits Aeolic and Homeric forms.

TEXT. Page, *Poet. Mel. Gr.* 326 ff.; W. Cronert, *Rh. Mus.* 1908, 166 ff.
COMMENTARY, etc.: U. von Wilamowitz-Moellendorff, in *Berl. Klass. Text.* v (2), 19 ff.; Page, *Corinna* (1953); E. Lobel, *Hermes* 1930, 356 ff.; P. Maas, *PW* xi. 1395. C. M. B.

**CORINTH,** the isthmus city controlling communications between north Greece and Peloponnesus and the eastern and western seas. The city lay north of the citadel (Acrocorinth), 2 to 3 miles from the sea, with ports, Lechaeum and Cenchreae, on both gulfs. Finds of Mycenaean pottery make it likely that the 'wealthy Corinth' of the Achaean catalogue in the *Iliad* was there and not at the site of classical Corinth.

At the Dorian conquest Corinth probably fell to Temenus the conqueror of Argos. Later the kingship gave place to the Dorian oligarchy of the Bacchiadae, under whom Corinth founded Corcyra and Syracuse (both traditionally 733 B.C.), led the way in shipbuilding (Ameinocles of Corinth built ships for Samos in 704) and naval warfare (battle with Corcyra, 664), and developed a great pottery industry. In its latest phase the Bacchiad government may have fallen under the ascendancy of Pheidon of Argos. About 657 it was overthrown by the tyrant Cypselus, under whose house Corinth reached its greatest prosperity and power (commemorated by dedications at Olympia and Delphi), while the discontented Bacchiad Demaratus, according to tradition, emigrated to Tarquinii and became the father of Tarquinius Priscus, king of Rome (Blakeway, *JRS* 1935, 129 ff.).

The chronology of the Corinthian tyranny is disputed, but archaeological evidence supports the dating of fourth-century historians, according to which Periander died in 585, and his nephew and successor Psammetichus (Cypselus II) was overthrown soon after.

The tyranny was replaced by a constitutional government, based apparently on a board of eight executive

magistrates and a council of eighty (*FGrH* 90; Nic. Dam. F 60). Trade still flourished and craftsmen still enjoyed special consideration. The city fostered friendly relations with the rising powers of Athens and Sparta; mediated between Athens and Thebes over Plataea (519), between Athens and Cleomenes of Sparta (507), Gela and Syracuse (491); supported Sparta against the medizing Polycrates of Samos, and Athens against Aegina; and fought well against Persia at Salamis, Plataea, and Mycale.

With the growth of Athenian imperialism Corinth's relations to Athens deteriorated, though even at the revolt of Samos from Athens in 440 she opposed Peloponnesian intervention; but Athenian interference at Megara and in the Corinthian Gulf had already led to fighting between Athens and Corinth in 459, and disputes between Athens and Corinth over Corcyra and Potidaea led to the outbreak in 431 of the Peloponnesian War. Corinth suffered severely, losing ships, trade, and colonies, and after the temporary peace of 421 was for a while estranged from Sparta, but at Mantinea in 418 was again fighting on the Spartan side. The Sicilian expedition of 415 increased her hostility to Athens: Corinthians under Gylippus took a leading part in the struggle at Syracuse and till the fall of Athens in 404 continued among Athens' most implacable foes. But shortly afterwards Corinth combined with Athens, Argos, and Boeotia to make war against the tyrannical rule of Sparta. During this 'Corinthian War' (395–386) a democratic government was established *c.* 392 with Argive help, but after the war it was replaced by an oligarchy. In the troubled times of Epaminondas and Philip II Corinth aimed at a neutral policy in Greece proper, but when Sicilian Greeks sought help against local tyrants and Carthage she sent out Timoleon in 344 and helped to repeople Syracuse, whose coins now showed the Corinthian *pegasus*. After the battle of Chaeronea (338) Corinth was made the gathering place of the new Hellenic League; here Philip, its author, and Alexander proclaimed their crusade against Persia.

In the Hellenistic period Corinth became a centre of industry, commerce, and commercialized pleasure, and also a key fortress that frequently changed hands in the dynastic struggles of the period. In 243 it joined the Achaean Confederacy; in 224 it sided against Aratus and Macedon with Cleomenes III of Sparta, and on the latter's overthrow passed again under Macedon till Flamininus' victory over Macedon in 198–6, when it was declared free like all other Greek cities and became the chief city of the Achaean Confederacy. As such it suffered heavily when Rome sought to curtail the Confederacy's power, and in 146 it was completely destroyed by Mummius.

Refounded in 44 B.C. as a Roman colony, it became the capital of the province of Achaea and was visited by apostles, emperors (including Nero, who made a vain attempt to cut a canal through the Isthmus), philosophers, Gothic hordes, and earthquakes. Its destruction by one of these last in A.D. 521 is cited by Procopius as evidence that God was abandoning the Roman Empire.

American School of Classical Studies at Athens, *Corinth* (1929 *et seq.*); J. G. O'Neill, *Ancient Corinth* (1930); H. G. Payne, *Necrocorinthia* (1931); *Perachora* i (1940) ii (1962); T. J. Dunbabin *JHS* 1948, 59 ff.; N. G. L. Hammond, *BSA* 1954, 93 ff.; E. Will, *Korinthiaka*, with full bibliography (1955). P. N. U.; N. G. L. H.

**CORIOLANUS,** GNAEUS MARCIUS (*PW* 51, Suppl. v. 653 ff.), was probably the eponymous hero or god of the Volscian town Corioli, from the capture of which he was reputed to have won his *cognomen*. He is said to have withdrawn from Rome when charged with tyrannical conduct and opposing the distribution of corn to the starving plebs; he then led a Volscian army against Rome, from which he was turned back only by the entreaties of his mother Veturia and his wife Volumnia (491 B.C.); he was then put to death by the Volscians. The sources of Dionysius 8. 62 and other evidence show that the story did not arise from the misinterpretation of any monument (especially the temple of the *Fortuna Muliebris*, reputedly built where Coriolanus' womenfolk had met him). Nor was it a fiction invented either to glorify some patrician family, or in imitation of some incidents in Greek history (although some details may have been borrowed from the stories of Achilles or Themistocles), or, finally, to provide an example of some legal customs and institutions. Rather, the legend reflects the period when Rome suffered severely from famine and Volscian pressure.

Mommsen, *Röm. Forsch.* ii. 113 ff.; E. T. Salmon, *CQ* 1930, 96 ff.; D. A. Russell, *JRS* 1963, 21 ff.; Ogilvie, *Comm. Livy 1–5*, 314 ff.
P. T.

**CORITANI,** a British tribe occupying part of the eastern midlands (Leics., Notts., Lincs.); the coins (formerly attributed to the Brigantes) and other remains suggest a Belgic aristocracy ruling indigenous inhabitants. The tribe, having been under pressure from the Catuvellauni, probably welcomed the Roman advance. A *civitas Coritanorum* was created with *caput* at *Ratae* (Leicester) (*Rav. cosm.* 92, Ptolemy, *Geography* 2. 3. 20); part of its land was reserved for the fortress of Legio IX (later II Adiutrix) at Lindum (q.v.), and subsequently used for a *colonia*. A Coritanus, M. Ulpius Novantico, is recorded on a diploma of 106. Industries included horse-raising, and the production of iron and building-stone.

A. L. F. Rivet, *Town and Country in Rom. Brit.²* (1964), 148 f.; D. F. Allen, *The Coins of the Coritani* (1962).               S. S. F.

**CORN.** Among the cereals used for human or animal food, maize was unknown in antiquity, and rice (ὄρυζα, *oryza*) remained confined to medicinal use. Rye (βρίζα, *secale*) and oats (βρόμος, *avena*) were 'northern' grains, which, though known, made little impact in the Mediterranean world. Millet (especially 'common' millet; κέγχρος, *milium*) was grown, but mainly as a fodder and emergency crop. The main grains throughout were wheat and barley. In Italy, where barley (*hordeum*) was grown largely for fodder, the husked species of wheat, known as *far* and eaten as porridge (*puls*), were dominant in early times (especially the tetraploid emmer; the hexaploid spelt was primarily a 'Gallic' grain) and survived in ritual use (*mola salsa*). But as baked bread began to establish itself they gradually gave way to the 'naked' species (*triticum*), which alone are suitable for baking, since husked grain required parching before it could be freed from its husks. But even among the naked wheats the tetraploid species (especially *triticum durum*), which are still grown there but are now used mainly for 'pasta', were more common than the hexaploid *triticum vulgare*, the Roman *siligo*, which comprises all modern bread wheats. In Greece, on the other hand, the husked wheats (ζειά, ὄλυρα) appear to have been unimportant, and it was barley (κριθή), ground into groats (ἄλφιτα) and 'kneaded' into μᾶζα, that yielded some of its early dominance to naked wheat (πυρός), ground into flour (ἄλευρα) and eaten as bread; but barley (also used in ritual as οὐλαί) never wholly lost its importance. Throughout the ancient world naked wheat finally came to be known as 'corn' (σῖτος, *frumentum*) in the sense of 'staple grain'. *See also* ANNONA.

N. Jasny, *The Wheats of Classical Antiquity* (1944); L. A. Moritz, *CQ* 1955, 129 ff.; id. *Grain-mills and Flour in Classical Antiquity* (1958).               L. A. M.

**CORN SUPPLY, GREEK.** Cereals, especially wheat, were the staple in the Greek diet (*see* FOOD AND DRINK). Given the terrain and its limited technology, the growth of population (q.v.) created a supply problem already in the archaic period, which remained permanently acute and was intensified by war or natural disaster. On the mainland of Greece and in the islands a few regions, particularly Boeotia and Thessaly (q.v., were fully self-sufficient; even the Peloponnese imported some corn, at least in war-time (Thuc. 3. 86. 3). The main sources were southern Russia, Egypt, Cyrene (q.v.), and Sicily (q.v.). In the fourth century B.C. Athens imported annually more than a million bushels (or twice that on another interpretation of Dem. 20. 31–2).

Even Athens, for all her silver resources (*see* LAURIUM), had to employ her political influence and power to maintain her corn supply, openly so when her empire gave her full control of the Aegean Sea in the fifth century B.C. (e.g. Tod, no. 61). In the fourth century she managed by diplomacy, notably with the Bosporus (Crimea).

There were also substantial internal controls. In Athens (the only state for which there is any detailed information) corn supply was on the agenda of the main Assembly meeting in each prytany (Arist. *Ath. Pol.* 43. 4); there were special supervisory officials, *sitophylakes* (q.v.), and various regulations prohibiting corn exports and stimulating imports. In view of the evident tensions which the subject aroused (e.g. Lys. 22; Dem. 20; [56]), it is curious that the trade was left largely to foreigners and metics (q.v.). From the late fourth century B.C. on, special purchasing officials, *sitonai*, are attested in a number of states.

F. M. Heichelheim, 'Sitos', *PW*, Suppl. vi (1935); L. A. Moritz, *Grain-Mills and Flour in Classical Antiquity* (1958); A. Jardé, *Les Céréales dans l'antiquité grecque* (1925); J. Hasebroek, *Trade and Politics in Ancient Greece* (1933); K. Köster, *Die Lebensmittelversorgung der altgriechischen Polis* (1939); L. Gernet, *L'Approvisionnement d'Athènes en blé* (1909); C. Mossé, *La Fin de la démocratie athénienne* (1962), pt. i.               M. I. F.

**CORN SUPPLY, ROMAN,** *see* ANNONA.

**CORNELIA** (1, *PW* 407), the second daughter of Scipio Africanus, married Ti. Sempronius Gracchus (q.v. 2). Of her twelve children only three reached maturity: Sempronia, who married Scipio (q.v. 11) Aemilianus, and the two famous tribunes Tiberius and Gaius Gracchus (qq.v. 3 and 4). After her husband's death she did not remarry (she refused an offer by Ptolemy VII Physcon) and devoted herself to the management of her estate and the education of her children. Traditions vary about how far she encouraged or attempted to restrain the political activities of her sons, but she did check Gaius' attack on Octavius (q.v. 2). Some of her letters were known to Cicero, who admired their style, but the authenticity of two fragments preserved in MSS. of Nepos has been much disputed and must be regarded as uncertain, although many have taken them to be genuine. She was cultured, with pronounced philhellenic interests, and after her sons were killed she continued to entertain many guests at her home at Misenum.

Plut. *Tiberius* and *Gaius Gracchus.* J. Carcopino, *Autour des Gracques* (1928), 47, 107; B. Förtsch, *Die politische Rolle der Frau* (1935), 56; G. Corradi, *Cornelia e Sempronia* (1946); on the letters see also H. Last, *C.AH* ix. 56 n. 1 and bibliography there.   A. E. A.

**CORNELIA** (2, *PW* 417), the cultured daughter of Metellus (q.v. 11) Scipio, married P. Crassus (q.v. 5) in 55 B.C. and in 52 Pompey. After Pharsalus she accompanied him to Egypt, where she saw him murdered. She returned to Italy.               G. W. R.

**CORNELIUS** (1, *PW* 18), GAIUS, quaestor of Pompey and friend of Gabinius (2) (qq.v.), whom he supported as his colleague in the tribunate (67 B.C.). He tried to introduce various reforms, but met with stiff resistance from the Optimate interests that he threatened, and achieved little of importance except for a law requiring a praetor to abide by his edict (q.v.) in administering justice (which had hitherto not been compulsory). Attempts to accuse him of *maiestas* led to a trial in 65; but Cicero successfully defended him, no doubt in order to please Pompey.

Asconius, *In Cornelianam*. W. McDonald, *CQ* 1929, 196 ff.
E. B.

**CORNELIUS** (2, *PW* 369) **SEVERUS,** Augustan poet. Of his hexameter poem on the Sicilian War of 38–36 B.C., perhaps part of a longer *Res Romanae*, Quintilian says (10. 1. 89) that if he had maintained the level of the first book he would have been second only to Virgil; Seneca (*Suas.* 6. 26) quotes a passage of twenty-five hexameters on Cicero's death. The nature of the 'carmen regale' ascribed to him by his friend Ovid (*Pont.* 4. 16. 9; cf. 4. 2. 1) is unknown. *Cf. AETNA* (3). C. J. F.

**CORNELIUS** (3, *PW* 168) **LABEO** (? second half of 3rd c. A.D.) wrote a (lost) history of Romano-Etruscan religion.

**CORNIFICIUS** (1, *PW* 8), QUINTUS, of recent senatorial family, was an orator and poet and a friend of Catullus and Cicero (cf. Cat. 38. 1, Cic. *Fam.* 12. 17–30). He wrote a lost epyllion *Glaucus*. As *quaestor pro praetore* in 48 B.C. he recovered Illyricum for Caesar and helped to defend it against the Pompeian fleet. Praetor (47 or 45), in 46 he went to the East, perhaps as governor of Cilicia; presently, however, Caesar assigned him to Syria and the war against Bassus (q.v. 1); what he did in this regard is not known. In the summer of 44, probably by Caesar's appointment, he went as governor to Africa Vetus, and continued to hold it for the Senate in disregard of the pretensions of Calvisius (q.v.) Sabinus. In 43 the Triumvirs proscribed him and assigned the province to T. Sextius (q.v. 1), governor of Africa Nova, who eventually defeated and killed him near Utica (42).

F. L. Ganter, *Philol.* 1894, 132 ff.; Syme, *Rom. Rev.*, see index; Schanz–Hosius i. 308 ff.; *FPL* 90. T. J. C.

**CORNIFICIUS** (2, *PW* 5), LUCIUS, a friend of Octavian, in 43 B.C. prosecuted M. Brutus for the murder of Caesar. In 38 he was one of Octavian's naval commanders in the war against Sextus Pompeius. In 36 he was cut off with three legions at Tauromenium, but extricated them and after a perilous march joined Agrippa at Tyndaris. He was consul in 35, and later proconsul of Africa, triumphing on 3 Dec. 32. He rebuilt the temple of Diana on the Aventine, and used to commemorate his march of 36 by riding to his dinner engagements on an elephant.

Syme, *Rom. Rev.*, see index; Platner–Ashby, 149 f. T. J. C.

**CORNIFICIUS** (3), by some regarded as the author of *Rhetorica* (q.v.) *ad Herennium*, cannot be certainly identified among several Cornificii.

**CORNOVII,** a tribe of western Britain (Staffs., Cheshire, Shropshire), with *caput* at Viroconium (q.v.). Legionary fortresses existed in their territory at Viroconium and later at Deva, and auxiliary forts also were long maintained, whether because of tribal unrest or as a protection against the Welsh. Perhaps because of this rural insecurity few villas occur, the resources of the *civitas* being concentrated at Viroconium. Industries include salt, copper, and lead workings. The *Notitia* records a *cohors I Cornoviorum* at Newcastle.

A. L. F. Rivet, *Town and Country in Rom. Brit.*² (1964), 150 f.; I. A. Richmond in Foster and Alcock, *Culture and Environment* (1963), 251 ff. S. S. F.

**CORNUTUS** (1), LUCIUS ANNAEUS, born *c.* A.D. 20 at or near Leptis, as a freedman of Seneca, or of one of his relatives, assumed the name Annaeus, and became a teacher of philosophy and rhetoric at Rome, *c.* A.D. 50, including Lucan and Persius among his pupils. Persius dedicated to Cornutus his fifth satire, and in 62 bequeathed him a sum of money, which he refused to accept, and his library. In collaboration with Caesius Bassus, Cornutus edited the posthumous poems of his disciple, omitting any passage which might appear to contain allusions to Nero. He was exiled in 63, 64, or 65, the cause is a matter of dispute, as is the question whether he later returned to Rome and resumed his literary activity. Cornutus was equally versed in Greek and Latin literature and wrote on Aristotle's logic (in Greek), and on rhetoric, the poetry of Virgil, etc. (in Latin). His one extant work (unless he wrote *Octavia*—see V. Cioffi, *Riv. Fil.* 1937, 246 ff.) is the Ἐπιδρομὴ τῶν κατὰ τὴν Ἑλληνικὴν θεολογίαν παραδεδομένων, or Summary of the Traditions concerning Greek Mythology; in this, he expounds, mainly following Chrysippus, the principles of Stoic criticism of myths, which he explains allegorically. In the Middle Ages scholia on Persius and Juvenal were wrongly attributed to him: cf. Teuffel, § 299. 2; Schanz–Hosius, §451. Christ–Schmid–Stahlin ii⁶. § 518.

TEXTS. C. Lang (Teubner, 1881). The fragments of Cornutus' minor works collected by R. Reppe, *De L. Annaeo Cornuto* (1906). P. Decharme, *La Critique des traditions religieuses chez les grecs anciens* (1905); B. Schmidt, *De Cornuti Theologiae Graecae compendio* (Diss. Halle, 1912); J. Tate, *CQ* 1929, 41 ff.; G. Rorca Serra, *Bull. Assoc. G. Budé* 1963, 388 ff.; Nock in *PW* Suppl. v. 995 ff., s.v. Kornutos. P. T.

**CORNUTUS** (2) **TERTULLUS,** GAIUS IULIUS (*PW* 196), probably from Perge in Pamphylia, was a friend of the Younger Pliny. His career was: legate of Crete and Cyrene, proconsul of Gallia Narbonensis, a period of quiet under Domitian, *praefectus aerarii Saturni* (A.D. 98–100), *cos. suff.* 100 with imperial approval (Pliny was his colleague in these last two offices), curator of the Via Aemilia (*c.* 104), governor of Aquitania (111–12), of Pontus-Bithynia (*c.* 115) and proconsul of Asia (or possibly of Africa) in 117/18. His life illustrates the emergence of the more civilian senatorial careers.

*ILS* 1024. J. Reynolds, *PCPS* 1963, 1 ff.; S. Jameson, *JRS* 1965, 54 f. H. H. S.

**CORONIS,** in mythology, daughter of Phlegyas, and mother of Asclepius (qq.v.). While with child by Apollo, she had an intrigue with (or married) Ischys son of Elatus, an Arcadian. Apollo learned this from a crow which brought word to Delphi (Pindar emends the story; Apollo knew it by his omniscience), and sent Artemis to kill Coronis. But when she was on the funeral pyre, he took the unborn child from her womb and gave him to Chiron to bring up (so Hesiod, fr. 123 Rzach; Pindar, *Pyth.* 3. 24 ff.). The local legend of Epidaurus omits the affair of Ischys and the killing, and says Coronis was also called Aegla (Isyllus, 46 ff.). Apollo turned the crow black for bringing the bad news (Ov. *Met.* 2. 632). H. J. R.

**CORRECTOR.** Since 'free' cities were technically independent of the governor (*see* SOCII), they were, on the whole, left to run their own affairs by the early Roman emperors. Trajan first sent a praetorian to Achaea to regulate the state of the free cities, which was apparently unsatisfactory. (Pliny, *Ep.* 8. 24, gives him advice.) Pliny (q.v. 2) himself, though actually governor, had special powers to perform a similar task for the cities in Bithynia (see, e.g., *Ep.* 10. 18. 3), and Cornutus Tertullus (*ILS* 1024) succeeded him. Senior Roman senators with various titles (often *corrector* = διορθωτής) soon appear in various eastern provinces, all with a similar mission (e.g. *ILS* 1067; and cf. HERODES ATTICUS 1).

In Italy, Domitian seems to have begun serious interference in local government (*see* CURATOR REI PUBLICAE). Officials supervising various regions appear in the second century A.D. (e.g. *ILS* 1040; 2768–9); by the early third we find a consular *corrector Italiae* (*ILS* 1159), later several more, as well as *correctores* of Italian regions, where Diocletian established them as regular governors.

Ruggiero, *Diz. Epigr.*, s.v.

E. B.

CORSICA (Κύρνος), a rugged island in the Mediterranean off western Italy, consisting mostly of mountains that rise 9,000 feet and fall sheer into the sea on the west. The eastern coast, however, has good harbours. The tradition that Corsica's earliest inhabitants were Iberians mixed with Ligurians is credible but unprovable. About 535 B.C. Etruscans, helped by Carthaginians, expelled the colony which Phocaeans had established at Alalia thirty years earlier. The island, which apparently fell under Etruscan control for some time, later came under Carthaginian influence. By sending expeditions in 259 and 231, Rome ousted the Carthaginians and organized Corsica with Sardinia as one province (subsequently in imperial times, exactly when is unknown, Corsica became a separate province). Rome colonized Mariana and Aleria on the east coast but exercised only nominal authority over the wild interior. Corsica produced ship-building timber, bitter-tasting honey, granite, cattle; the Romans did not work its mines. Vandals, Goths, Ravenna Exarchs, and Saracens successively followed the Romans as masters of the island.

Strabo 5. 223 f.; Pliny, *HN* 3. 80 (number of Corsican towns exaggerated); Hdt. 1. 165 f.; Diodorus 5. 13 f.; Theophr. *Hist. Pl.* 5. 8. 1; Seneca's picture of Corsica as inhospitable and unhealthy (*Dial.* 12. 7 f.; *Epigr.* 1 f.) is untrustworthy: Corsica was his place of exile In general ancient authors seldom mention Corsica. E. Michon, *Mélanges de l'École française de Rome* 1891, 106; F. von Duhn, *Italische Gräberkunde* (1924) i. 112; E. Pais, *Storia della Sardegna e della Corsica* (1923).

E. T. S.

CORSTOPITUM, a Roman military post near Corbridge, Northumberland. The name, possibly corrupt, is of uncertain etymology (Corstopitum, *It. Ant.* 464. 3; Corielopocarium, *Rav. Cosm.* 432. 6). Here the road from York to Scotland bridged the Tyne, branching to Carlisle and Tweedmouth. The place began as a Flavian bridge-head fort, with timber buildings and turf rampart (*Arch. Ael.* ser. 4, xv (1900), 255) garrisoned by the *ala Petriana* (Collingwood and Wright, *RIB* 1172). It lay empty when Hadrian's Wall was built, but important buildings were erected in A.D. 139 (*RIB* 1147) and 140 (*RIB* 1148) under Lollius (q.v. 4) Urbicus and in 163 (*RIB* 1149) under Calpurnius Agricola (q.v. 2), presumably connected with the reoccupation of Scotland. Severus and his sons built granaries *c.* 205 (*RIB* 1151, 1143), a large unfinished courtyard-building (probably a storehouse), and also legionary work-compounds, all restored or altered under Constantius I (*c.* 297) and Valentinian I (369). Late fourth-century silver plate, gold rings (*CIL* vii. 1300), and a gold coin-hoard attest prolonged use as an administrative centre.

*Arch. Ael.* ser. 4, xxxvii, 1959, 10 ff. (bibliography to 1958); ibid. 59 ff. (defences), 85 ff. (baths); ibid. xxxix, 1961, 37 ff. (mausoleum).

I. A. R.

CORTONA (Etr. *Curtun-*), 18 miles south-east of Arretium, was an important Etruscan stronghold with a commanding view of the Val di Chiana. The archaeological evidence does not indicate that it is older than the late seventh century B.C. After the defeat of the Etruscans in 311 B.C. by Quintus Fabius, Cortona and the two other leading cities of the interior, Pisa and Arretium (q.v.), made treaties with Rome. Large stretches of the fifth-century city wall are still extant, as are two earlier tumuli (*meloni*) and a Hellenistic mausoleum (the so-called

'Tanella di Pitagora'). The most notable piece of local figured bronze-work in the Museo dell' Accademia Etrusca di Cortona (founded 1726) is a magnificent fifth-century lamp with sixteen lights, depicting a *gorgoneion*.

A. Neppi Modona, *Cortona etrusca e moderna* (1926); Scullard *Etr. Cities*, 156 ff.

D. W. R. R.

CORUNCANIUS (1), TIBERIUS, from Tusculum, consul in 280 B.C., triumphed over Etruscan Volsinii and Vulci and guarded Rome against Pyrrhus' advance. He was the first plebeian Pontifex Maximus (254/3) and an early jurist: 'primus profiteri coepit' (Pompon. *Dig.* 1. 2. 2. 38), i.e. admitted the public, or at any rate students, to his consultations. Thus jurisprudence became professional instead of a mystery.

H. H. S.

CORUNCANIUS (2, *PW* 1 and 2), GAIUS and LUCIUS, formed the Roman embassy to Teuta, the Illyrian queen, in 230 B.C., demanding satisfaction for the murder of Italian merchants by Illyrian pirates; this was refused, and they were themselves attacked, L. Coruncanius being killed. This outrage precipitated the First Illyrian War (Polyb. 2. 8).

Badian, *Stud. Gr. Rom. Hist.* 1 ff.

A. H. McD.

CORYTHUS, the name of several obscure mythological persons, including (1) son of Zeus and husband of Electra (q.v. 2) daughter of Atlas; his sons were Dardanus and Iasius (Iasion), *see* DARDANUS; Servius on *Aen.* 3. 167. (2) Son of Paris and Oenone (qq.v.). His story is variously told; the least unfamiliar account is in Parthenius, 34, from Hellanicus and Cephalon of Gergis. He came to Troy as an ally; Helen fell in love with him and Paris killed him. Nicander, quoted ibid., calls him son of Paris and Helen.

H. J. R.

CŌS, one of the Sporades islands, occupied in Myc. IIIC, then colonized by Dorians, perhaps from Epidaurus, as part of the Doric hexapolis. In the Peloponnesian War it suffered from both Spartans and Athenians. In 366, after internal strife, the townships (*demoi*) were merged in one capital city, on the north-east coast. The island revolted successfully from Athens in 354, but came under the control of Alexander of Macedon. It subsequently oscillated between Macedon, Syria, and Egypt, to find its greatest glory as a literary centre under the protection of the Ptolemies and as the home of Philetas and Theocritus. In the second century Cos was loyal to the Romans, even before it became a *libera civitas* in the province of Asia. The Emperor Claudius, influenced by his Coan physician Xenophon, conferred *immunitas* on the island. Here in the fifth century B.C. Hippocrates laid the foundations of medical science. The Asklepieion and part of the agora have been excavated.

Strabo 14. 657–8. P–K, *GL* iv. F. III; W. R. Paton–E. L. Hicks, *Inscriptions of Cos* (1891); A. Maiuri, *Nuova silloge epigrafica di Rodi e Cos* (1925); Herzog, etc., *Kos: I. Asklepieion* (1932); A. N. Modona, *L'isola di Coo nell'antichità classica* (1933); I. Kontes, *Ai ellenist. diamorph. tou Asklep.* (1956); J. M. Cook–G. Bean, *BSA* 1957, 119 ff.

W. A. L.

COSA, the modern *Ansedonia*, situated on a commanding rocky promontory on the coast of Etruria, 4 miles south-east of Orbetello. Excavation has revealed no trace of Etruscan *Cusi*, which may have occupied the site of Orbetello itself. The surviving remains are those of the Latin colony founded in 273 B.C. (Vell. Pat. 1. 14. 7), to which belong the irregular circuit of walls, of fine polygonal masonry, and the neatly rectangular street-plan. The majority of the individual buildings, including the arx and the forum, a basilica and several temples, date from the town's period of maximum prosperity, in the second century B.C. Thereafter it declined rapidly, and by the first century A.D. had been virtually abandoned in favour of Succosa, on the level ground to the east, beside the harbour and the Via Aurelia.

F. E. Brown, *Am. Ac. Rome* 1951, 7 ff., F. Castagnoli, ibid. 1956, 147 ff.; F. E. Brown, and E. H. and L. Richardson, ibid. 1960; E. T. Salmon, *Roman Colonization* (1969).                     J. B. W.-P.

**COSCONIUS**, QUINTUS (1st c. A.D.), a scholar who wrote on grammar and law. His works are lost.

Cf. Schanz–Hosius, § 196. 2.

**COSMAS INDICOPLEUSTES**, fl. A.D. 540–50, Alexandrian merchant. He travelled in Palestine, Sinai, Ethiopia, and throughout the Red Sea trading area, but, despite the title which he received about the eleventh century, there is no evidence that he visited India. His 'Christian Topography', full of astonishing and curious information, is a naïve attempt to base a description of the form of the cosmos on scripture as opposed to pagan science, but is more interested (and competent) in theology than in geography or astronomy. The unnamed target of Cosmas' polemic is John Philoponus (q.v.), his monophysite contemporary at Alexandria. His own doctrinal sympathies are with Theodore of Mopsuestia, the divine most valued by the Nestorians of Sassanid Persia with whom Cosmas had personal contact.

Ed. E. O. Winstedt (1909). W. Wolska, *La Topographie chrétienne de Cosmas* (1962).                     H. C.

**COSSUS**, AULUS CORNELIUS (*PW* 112), the hero of two alleged wars with Fidenae (437–435 and 428–425 B.C.) of which only the second is probably historical. He won the *spolia opima* (q.v.) by killing Lars Tolumnius of Veii, whose inscribed breastplate he dedicated to Jupiter Feretrius. This inscription was read by the Emperor Augustus, who stated that Cossus performed the feat as consul in 428 (Livy 4. 20). This fact need not (but can) be interpreted as an invention of Augustus designed to block the claim of M. Crassus (q.v. 6) to a triumph. According to other traditions Cossus was military tribune in 437 and *magister equitum* in 426.

Cf. Ogilvie, *Comm. Livy 1–5*, 563 f.                     H. H. S.

**COTTA** (1), GAIUS AURELIUS (*PW* 96), nephew of Rutilius (q.v. 1) Rufus, was a distinguished orator and, with Drusus (q.v. 2) and Sulpicius (q.v. 1) Rufus, a member of a circle of ambitious young nobles around L. Crassus (q.v. 3). He was exiled by the commission set up by Varius (q.v. 1), but returned with Sulla. Consul in 75 B.C., he had to meet popular discontent and passed a law (rescinding one of Sulla's) which allowed tribunes to stand for higher offices. He governed Cisalpine Gaul, but died before he could triumph. In Cicero's dialogue *De Natura Deorum* he champions the Academic philosophy.

*ORF³* 286. G. Perl, *Philol.* 1965, 75 ff.                     E. B.

**COTTA** (2), MARCUS AURELIUS (*PW* 107), brother of (1), as consul in 74 B.C. was sent to defend Bithynia against Mithridates (q.v. 6). Attacking the king, he was defeated by land and sea near Chalcedon and had to be relieved by Lucullus (q.v. 2). He continued the war in Bithynia, sacking Heraclea (q.v. 3) after a long siege (Memnon, *FGrH*, no. 434, chs. 27–39). Though he paid much of the booty into the Treasury, he was later prosecuted and convicted, perhaps of peculation.     E. B.

**COTTA** (3), LUCIUS AURELIUS (*PW* 102), brother of (1), as praetor (70 B.C.) helped in the modification of the Sullan constitution by passing a law under which criminal juries were to consist in equal parts of senators, *equites*, and *tribuni aerarii* (qq.v.). In 66 he successfully prosecuted the consuls designate, Autronius and P. Sulla (2; qq.v.),

for *ambitus*, and himself became consul in 65. Despite a reputation for bibulousness, he was elected censor in 64. He supported Cicero both against Catiline and during his exile, but (as a relative of Caesar) was neutral in the Civil War; in 44 he was expected (being a *quindecimvir*) to propose that Caesar should be called king outside Italy as the sacred books were said to require.     E. B.

**COTTIUS**, MARCUS JULIUS (*PW* 197), son of a native king named Donnus, offered no opposition to Augustus' pacification of the Alpine regions and was recognized as ruler over a number of native tribes with the title of *praefectus civitatium* (*ILS* 94, cf. Pliny, *HN* 3. 138). He erected an arch in honour of Augustus at Segusio (*Susa*) in 7–6 B.C. (*ILS* 94), and improved the road over the Mt. Genèvre (Ammianus 15. 10. 2). The territory, annexed by Nero after the death of his son, was commonly known as the *Alpes Cottiae*.     R. S.

**COTYS, COTYT(T)O** (Κότυς, Κοτυ(τ)τώ, a Thracian goddess worshipped with orgiastic rites (Aesch. fr. 57 Nauck). Her cult was known in Athens in Eupolis' time, and included some rite of washing or dipping, see the fragments of his *Baptae* in *CAF* i. 273 ff. These point to the rites as being practised at the time in Corinth: cf Nilsson, *GGR* i². 835.     H. J. R.; H. W. P.

**CRAGUS**, a Lycian god identified with Zeus (Lycophron 542 and schol.), humanized into a son of Tremiles (eponym of the Tremileis or Lycians), after whom Mt. Cragus was named (Steph. Byz. s.v.).

**CRANNŌN**, a city of Thessaly, commanding a small level area among the low hills which separate the eastern and western plains. The Scopadae, the leading local family, were rivals of the Aleuadae (q.v.), but *c*. 515 B.C. they were involved in a mysterious disaster and lost much of their influence. The smallness of its plain and the proximity of Larissa checked the development of Crannon. A Pheraean named Deinias became tyrant, probably in the fourth century, and with support from the tyrants of Pherae. In the Lamian War Antipater defeated the Greek confederates near Crannon (322).     H. D. W.

**CRANTOR** of Soli in Cilicia (*c*. 335–*c*. 275 B.C.), philosopher of the Old Academy. Having left his native town for Athens, he became a pupil of Xenocrates, and formed close friendships with Polemon, Crates, and especially Arcesilaus, to whom he left his property on his death. It was under his influence that Arcesilaus abandoned the Peripatos for the Academy (Diog. Laert. 4. 22; 24; 25; 29).

Crantor's commentary on Plato's *Timaeus* was the first of the long line of ancient commentaries on the Platonic dialogues. His work *On Grief* (Περὶ πένθους) was much admired by later writers, among them Cicero, who used it as a model for his own *Consolatio*, written on the death of his daughter Tullia; but from what we know of him, Crantor's claim to fame lay in his attention to style, rather than in any great originality of thought.

F. Kayser, *De C. Academico* (1841, the fragments); *FPG* iii. 131–52. E. Zeller, *Plato*, etc., Engl. Transl. (1888), 619 f.; K. Buresch, *Leipz. Stud.* 1887; Susemihl, *Gesch. Gr. Lit. Alex.* i. 118 f.     C. J. R.

**CRASSUS** (1) **DIVES MUCIANUS**, PUBLIUS LICINIUS (*PW* 72), brother of P. Scaevola (q.v. 2), son-in-law of Ap. Claudius (q.v. 9), and father-in-law of C. Gracchus (q.v. 4). Noble, wealthy, and an eminent lawyer and orator, he was a key figure in the faction that opposed Scipio (q.v. 11) Aemilianus and sponsored Ti. Gracchus (q.v. 3). He took Tiberius' place on the agrarian commission and, acquiring popularity as a Gracchan, was lected consul and Pontifex Maximus late in life. As consul (131 B.C.) and proconsul he fought against Aristonicus (q.v. 1) and was killed after a defeat (130). He was succeeded by Perperna (q.v. 1).　　　　　E. B.

A. E. Astin, *Scipio Aemilianus* (1967), see index.

CRASSUS (2), PUBLIUS LICINIUS (*PW* 61), as tribune *c.* 106 B.C.) passed a famous sumptuary law. In his consulate (97) the Senate prohibited human sacrifice. After commanding in Iberia for several years, he triumphed over the Lusitani (93). He fought in the Social War and, as censor (89) with L. Caesar (q.v. 2), enrolled the first of the Italians. In 87 he helped to defend Rome against Marius (whose friend he had probably been somewhat earlier) and Cinna, and killed himself after their victory. His son (4) escaped to Spain.　　　　　E. B.

CRASSUS (3), LUCIUS LICINIUS (*PW* 55), outstanding orator and—even more than his rival Antonius (q.v. 1)—master and model of Cicero, who idealizes him, particularly in the *De oratore*, where he is the chief speaker. Born 140 B.C., he was taught by Coelius (q.v. 1) and studied law in the house of the Scaevolae (q.v.), into whose family he married. In his political début he successfully prosecuted C. Carbo (q.v. 1); in the affair of the Vestals (*see* CASSIUS 4) he defended a relative; and at an uncertain (but apparently later) date he supported the *popularis causa* of the colony of Narbo, which, with Domitius (q.v. 3), he helped to establish (cf. Sydenham, *CRR*, nos. 520 ff.). Quaestor in Asia, he used part of his time there for study and on his return became a leading barrister. In 106 he supported the jury law of Caepio (q.v. 1) in a great speech—using Popular methods for Optimate policies—which became famous but attracted the censure of Rutilius (q.v. 1) on moral grounds. Not prominent in factional strife in the 90s, he became consul in 95 with Q. Scaevola (q.v. 4) Pontifex, and they passed a law against aliens who had been illegally enrolled as citizens (chiefly in the censorship of Antonius and Flaccus (q.v. 5) in 97-96). A little later (it seems) he became an *adfinis* of Marius, after defending Caepio (q.v. 2). He governed Gaul, but failed to gain a triumph. In 92, as censor, he quarrelled with his colleague Domitius (q.v. 3); but they agreed in prohibiting the teaching of rhetoric in Latin—a measure in part intended to prevent the path to social advancement and a political career from being widened. Crassus was the teacher of a new generation of ambitious aristocratic orators (Drusus 2, Sulpicius 1 Rufus, and Cotta 1 qq.v.), whom he imbued with his ideas; and he supported Drusus in his tribunate (91), which aimed at putting them into practice. Rallying the Senate behind the tribune, he attacked the consul Marcius Philippus (q.v. 4) in his famous 'swan song'. His death soon after was a disaster for Drusus' cause.

As an orator, he is praised by Cicero for his *gravitas* and dignity. His style was Asianic, but not to excess, combining rhythm and ornamentation with pure Latinity.

Malcovati, *ORF*² 237 ff. Cic. *Brut.* and *De Or.*, *passim.* U. W. Scholz, *Der Redner M. Antonius* (1963), 55 f., 94.　　E. B.

CRASSUS (4) (DIVES), MARCUS LICINIUS (*PW* 68), son of (2), escaped to Spain in 87 B.C., joined Sulla after the death of Cinna, played a prominent part in the *bellum Sullanum* and made a fortune in the proscriptions. After his praetorship, he defeated Spartacus (72-71); but Pompey, crucifying many fugitives, claimed the credit for the victory, thus making an enemy of Crassus. Reconciled for the moment, they were elected consuls, 70, and greatly modified the Sullan constitution. In the next few years Crassus further increased his fortune: relying on his connexions, financial power, and astuteness,

and helping any eminent or promising man in need, he tried to gain unchallenged *auctoritas*. After 67, disliked by many Optimates and overshadowed by Pompey's special commands, he resorted to unorthodox tactics to gain control of the state machinery and perhaps an *imperium* to match Pompey's. He shielded those involved in the 'first conspiracy' of Catiline (q.v.), assisted Catiline up to his defeat in the elections for 62 (but not in his plans for revolution), supported the ambitions of young Caesar (without detaching him from Pompey), tried to gain the support of the Transpadanes by enrolling them as citizens during his censorship (65—he was foiled in this by his colleague Catulus (q.v. 3)), perhaps sought a mandate to annex Egypt, and hoped to profit by the legislation of Rullus (q.v.). Failing in all his plans, he left Rome before Pompey's return.

He was soon back, opposing Pompey's demands, with Optimate support; but he did not succeed in securing a refund for the Asian *publicani*, in whose over-optimistic bid his interests were involved. When Caesar returned from Spain, Crassus helped him to secure the consulate (59), and Caesar persuaded both him and Pompey to give each other passive (and Caesar active) support. As consul Caesar secured what each of them wanted and received Gaul as his reward. After his departure, P. Clodius (q.v. 1), whom Crassus had aided earlier, exploited the continuing suspicion between Crassus and Pompey and, for his own purposes, drove a wedge between them, as also between Crassus and Cicero. Early in 56, when Pompey seemed ready for an Optimate alliance, Caesar intervened: meeting Crassus at Ravenna and Pompey (perhaps with Crassus) at the so-called Conference of Luca, he arranged for them to be consuls in 55 and have special commands in Syria and Spain respectively after, while he retained Gaul. This was carried out against all opposition; and late in 55 Crassus set out for Syria (despite the solemn curses pronounced by the tribune Capito (q.v. 1)), hoping to regain a military reputation equal to that of his allies by a victory over the Parthians. After some successes and further preparations in 54, he crossed the Euphrates in 53, though deserted by the Armenians; but he was defeated near Carrhae (q.v.) by the Surenas (q.v.) and killed while trying to extricate himself.

Crassus saw the key to success in wealth and a reputation for wealth. Neglecting his early military ability for too long, he finally found unarmed power insecure in the changed conditions of the late Republic and died before he could profit by the lesson. Had he been less unlucky in his war, he might well have played the decisive part in history which he had mapped out for himself.

A. Garzetti, *Athenaeum* 1941, 1; 1942, 12; 1944-5, 1; F. E. Adcock, *Marcus Crassus, Millionaire* (1966).　　　　　E. B.

CRASSUS (5), PUBLIUS LICINIUS (*PW* 63) (*c.* 85-53 B.C.), younger son of the triumvir. He accompanied Caesar to Gaul, first as *praefectus equitum* (58), then as *legatus* (57). In the victory over Ariovistus his resolute handling of the reserve was decisive. In 57 he subdued the coastal Gallic tribes and perhaps explored the Cassiterides (Strabo 3. 175-6). In 56 he defeated the Aquitanians and returned to Rome where he supported the consular candidature of his father and Pompey. His elder brother Marcus as quaestor (54) then served under Caesar in Gaul. Publius in 55 married Cornelia, daughter of Metellus Scipio. He commanded a body of Gallic horse under his father in the Parthian war of 53. His vigorous leadership involved them in heavy losses which he refused to survive.　　　　　C. E. S.

CRASSUS (6), MARCUS LICINIUS (*PW* 58) (*cos.* 30 B.C.), grandson of M. Crassus (4), was at first a partisan of Sex.

Pompeius, then an Antonian. The precise date of his desertion to Octavian has not been recorded; the consulate was probably his reward. Appointed proconsul of Macedonia, he conducted highly successful campaigns in 29 and 28 (Dio Cass. 51. 23 ff.). Having killed a king of the Bastarnae with his own hands, he claimed the *spolia opima*, to the annoyance of Octavian, himself jealously monopolizing military glory. The claim was rebutted on the grounds that Crassus had not been fighting under his own auspices; Octavian may have used as an argument the linen corslet in the temple of Jupiter Feretrius, which purported to show that Cornelius Cossus (q.v.) was consul (not merely military tribune) when he earned the *spolia opima*. The incident may have accelerated the regulation of Octavian's constitutional position (as E. Groag argues, *PW* xiii. 283 ff.). Crassus was permitted to hold a triumph (27), after which nothing more is heard of this ambitious (and perhaps dangerous) *nobilis*. His son by adoption is M. Licinius Crassus Frugi (*cos.* 14 B.C.).

Syme, *Rom. Rev.*, see index. R. S.

**CRASSUS (7) FRUGI LICINIANUS,** Gaius Calpurnius (*PW* 32), of a long and illustrious line, was suffect consul under Domitian, and is possibly to be identified with C. Calpurnius Piso Licinianus, *cos. suff.* early A.D. 87 (W. Henzen, *Acta Fr. Arv.* cxviii, line 67). For conspiring against Nerva, he was exiled to Tarentum. His later plotting against Trajan caused his removal to an island, where, becoming suspect in Hadrian's reign, he was killed by a procurator while trying to escape.

For his tomb inscription, *CIL* vi. 31724; S.H.A. *Hadr.*; Dio Cassius bk. 68. Stech, *Senatores* (1912), no. 872; Lambrechts, *Sénat*, no. 31. C. H. V. S.; M. H.

**CRATERUS (1)** (*c.* 370?–321 B.C.), Macedonian officer of Alexander the Great. Beginning as commander of a *taxis* (brigade) of Macedonian infantry (at the Granicus), he advanced to be senior *taxiarch* (at Issus and Gaugamela), and, after Parmenion's death, virtually Alexander's second-in-command. When the army was divided he frequently held separate commands, and distinguished himself particularly in Bactria and Sogdiana (329–328), and in India at the Hydaspes battle. In 324 he was delegated to lead home the discharged Macedonian veterans, and to replace Antipater as regent of Macedonia and overseer of Greece, a distinction which illustrates Alexander's confidence in him. He was generally recognized as the best soldier on Alexander's staff, and he would certainly have played a commanding part among the 'Successors', had he not been killed in the very first battle, against Eumenes of Cardia, near the Hellespont.

Berve, *Alexanderreich*, no. 446. G. T. G.

**CRATERUS (2)** (321–*c.* 255 B.C.), son of Craterus (1) and Phila, Antipater's daughter, was appointed governor of Corinth and Peloponnesus (*c.* 280), and later viceroy of Attica and Euboea, by his half-brother, Antigonus II, whom he served loyally. In 271 he tried to assist Aristotimus, the Elean tyrant (Plut. *Mor.* 253 a), and in 266 checked Areus of Sparta at the Isthmus (Paus. 3. 6. 4–6).

The ψηφισμάτων συναγωγή, a collection of Athenian decrees with a scholarly commentary (*FGrH* 342), was perhaps the work of this Craterus.

W. W. Tarn, *Antigonos Gonatas* (1913); *CAH* vii; Bengtson, *Strategie* ii. 347 ff. F. W. W.

**CRATES (1),** Athenian comic poet, won three victories at the City Dionysia, the first almost certainly in 450 (Hieron. *Chron.* Ol. 82. 2, *IG* ii². 2325. 52); he was an actor before he was a poet (Anon. *De Com.* 7). We have

six titles. *Animals* depicted a situation in which animal§ refuse to be eaten by men. It seems to have contained comic prophecy of an era in which all work will perform itself (*see* METAGENES *and* PHERECRATES). Aristophane§ (*Eq.* 537 ff.) speaks of him affectionately, and Aristotl⸱ (*Pol.* 1449ᵇ7) says that he was the first to discard ἰαμβικⁱ ἰδέα and create plots which were 'general' (καθόλου), i.e⸱ to advance beyond the ridiculing of real individuals.

*FCG* i. 58 ff.; *CAF* i. 130 ff.; *FAC* i. 152 ff. K. J. D

**CRATES (2)** (*c.* 365–285 B.C.), son of Ascondas oⁱ Thebes, Cynic philosopher. Having come to Athens a a young man he first attended the lectures of Bryson oⁱ the Megaric School, but was soon converted to Cynicism by Diogenes of Sinope and decided to live henceforth in Cynic poverty. He married Hipparchia, sister o Metrocles of Maronea, having converted both brothe⸱ and sister to Cynicism. In her company he led a wandering life, preaching the gospel of voluntary poverty an⸱ independence, consoling people in distress, and recon⸱ ciling enemies. He became so universally beloved tha⸱ people wrote on their doors 'welcome to Crates, the goo⸱ spirit' (Julian, *Or.* 6. 201 b). He wrote a great man⸱ poems, mostly by revising the poems of famous poets s⸱ as to give them a Cynic content. His letters were praise⸱ for their style, but those which have come down to u are spurious. He is said by Diogenes Laertius (6. 98) t⸱ have written tragedies of a very lofty character in whic⸱ his philosophy was displayed. One fragment expresse⸱ cosmopolitan sentiments.

H. Diels, *PPF* 216 ff.; *TGF* 809–10; Diogenes Laertius 6. 85–93 E. Schwartz, *Charakterköpfe* ii. 1 ff.; D. R. Dudley, *A History o Cynicism* (1938), 42 ff.; Höistad, *Cynic Hero and Cynic King* (1948⸱ 126 ff. K. VON F. and A. W. P.-C

**CRATES (3)** of Mallos, son of Timocrates, was a contemporary of Demetrius of Scepsis (Strabo 14. 676) an⸱ Aristarchus. He visited Rome as envoy of Attalus oⁱ Pergamum, probably in 168 B.C., when his lectures during his recovery after breaking his leg in the Cloac⸱ Maxima, greatly stimulated Roman interest in scholarship (Suet. *Gram.* 2). He was the first head of the librar⸱ at Pergamum, and wrote, *inter alia*, on Homer, Hesiod Euripides, Aristophanes, and Aratus, usually with ⸱ philosophic and antiquarian bias; on Attic; and o⸱ 'anomaly'. See also *Anth. Pal.* 11. 218.

The Pergamenes and the Alexandrians were divide⸱ on the rival principles of 'analogy' and 'anomaly' ir language. Aristophanes and Aristarchus, of Alexandria in editing Homer sought the correct form (or meaning⸱ of a word by collecting and comparing its occurrences ir the text, a procedure more novel in their age than in ours Further, they tried to classify words by their types o⸱ form (cf. our declensions), in order by reference to the type to decide what was correct in any doubtful o⸱ disputed instance. Thus in Homer Aristarchus accented Κάρησος after Κάνωβος, πέφνων after τέμνων, οἰῶν after αἰγῶν; and similarly as to inflexions (*see* APOLLONIU§ (13) DYSCOLUS). Crates, on the contrary, borrowed hi⸱ linguistic principles from the Stoics, and sought in literature a meaning which he already knew *a priori*. Not onl⸱ words (*see* ETYMOLOGY) but literature likewise they though⸱ a μίμησις θείων καὶ ἀνθρωπείων (Diog. Laert. 7. 60), a⸱ accurate reflection of truth, and on this basis they carrie⸱ to ludicrous extremes the allegorical method of interpretation, in order to secure the support of Homer fo⸱ Stoic doctrines. In such features as inflexion they sa⸱ only confusion wrought upon nature's original product⸱ by man's irregular innovations and perversion§ Cleanthes had named this unruly principle of languag⸱ ἀνωμαλία, illustrating it without much difficulty fro⸱ the Greek declensions. This term and doctrine, and th⸱

allegorical method, were adopted by Crates and his school, to whom, consequently, the Alexandrian classification of forms (Crates seems to have written chiefly on noun anomalies) seemed futile in practice and wrong in principle.

The Alexandrians did valuable work; yet they had inevitable difficulty in deducing their types and rules from the facts: in such discrepancies, and when they proceeded by 'analogy' to adapt the facts to their rules, as even Aristarchus sometimes did, Pergamene criticism was, so far, justified. But neither did the Stoics (and Pergamenes) themselves follow usage *simpliciter*, but only usage controlled by their theory: cf. Diog. Laert. 7. 59.

The controversy gained importance with the growth of purism (*see* GLOSSA), and its extension from Greek to Latin; it is reflected in Varro's *De lingua Latina*. Compromises attempted by both Greek and Roman scholars left the problem unsettled. 'Quare mihi non inuenuste dici uidetur, aliud esse Latine, aliud grammatice loqui' Quint. *Inst.* 1. 6. 27.

H. Steinthal, *Geschichte d. Sprachwissenschaft bei den Griechen u. Römern²* (1891), 121 ff.; H. J. Mette, *Parateresis: Untersuchungen zur Sprachtheorie des Krates von Pergamon* (1952); J. Collart, *Entretiens Hardt*, 9. 119 ff. P. B. R. F.; R. B.

**CRATEUAS,** botanist and physician to Mithridates the Great (111–64 B.C.) to whom he dedicated the plant *mithridatia*, probably the mall, liliaceous *Erythronium Dens-canis* L. (Pliny, *HN* 25, 26, 62). Crateuas was the author of at least two works, both of which are known today only by fragments. (i) A herbal, whose title has not been preserved, in which coloured drawings of plants were accompanied by descriptions and their medical uses (Pliny 25. 4, 8). Dioscorides' Περὶ ὕλης ἰατρικῆς was based, in part, on Crateuas' writings and often refers to him. Some of the drawings in the so-called Juliana Anicia manuscript of Dioscorides (Cod. Vindobon. med. gr. 1) may be based on Crateuas' original drawings. This MS. also contains fragments from Crateuas' herbal. (ii) Ῥιζοτομικόν (schol. Nic. *Ther.* 681), a pharmacological work which discussed the medical uses of plants with details regarding their 'varieties' (εἴδη) and names.

*Dioscorides* ed. M. Wellman (1906–14), iii. 139 sq. (fragments); M. Wellman, 'Krateuas'. *Abh. Gött. Ges.* ii/1 (1899); *PW* xi, 1644; J. Stannard, 'Dioscorides and Renaissance Materia Medica', *Analecta Medico-Historica* 1 (1966); E. Mioni, *Un ignoto Dioscoride miniato* (1959). J. S.

**CRATINUS** was regarded, with Aristophanes and Eupolis, as one of the greatest poets of Old Attic Comedy. He won the first prize six times at the City Dionysia and three times at the Lenaea (*IG* ii². 2325. 50, 121). We have twenty-seven titles and over 460 fragments. The precisely datable plays are: Χειμαζόμενοι at the Lenaea in 426 (hyp. 1 Ar. *Ach.*), *Satyrs* at the Lenaea in 424 (hyp. 1 Ar. *Eq.*), and Πυτίνη at the City Dionysia in 423 (hyp. 6 Ar. *Nub.*). Three more are approximately datable: Ἀρχίλοχοι treats (fr. 1) the death of Cimon as recent, and therefore comes not long after 450; Διονυσαλέξανδρος (see below) attacked Pericles for 'bringing the war upon Athens', and must belong to 430 or 429; and fr. 71 of Θρᾶτται suggests that Pericles has just escaped the danger of ostracism (444/3). We do not know when Cratinus died; Ar. *Pax* 700 ff. speaks of him (in 421) as dead, but the context is humorous and its interpretation controversial. One category of titles is especially characteristic of Cratinus: Ἀρχίλοχοι, Διόνυσοι, Κλεοβουλῖναι, Ὀδυσσῆς, Πλοῦτοι, and Χίρωνες (see also TELECLIDES). In Ὀδυσσῆς it appears from fr. 144 that the chorus represented Odysseus' crew; it is possible that the 'new toy' of fr. 145 was a model of his ship brought into the orchestra. The play is mentioned by Platonius (*Diff. Com.* 7 and 12) as an example of 'Middle

Comedy' ahead of its time, i.e. as containing no ridicule of contemporaries. There are papyrus fragments of Πλοῦτοι, one of which indicates that the chorus explained its identity and role to the audience in the parodos. The hypothesis of Διονυσαλέξανδρος is also largely preserved in a papyrus; in this play Dionysus—as the title suggests —was represented as judging the goddesses and carrying Helen off to Troy; there was a chorus of satyrs, which in the parabasis addressed the audience 'about the poets'. In Πυτίνη Cratinus made good comic use of his own notorious drunkenness (cf. Ath. 39 c), represented himself as married to Comedy, and adapted in self-praise the compliment paid to his torrential fluency and vigour by Ar. *Eq.* 526 ff.

Cratinus' language and style were inventive, concentrated, and allusive, and Aristophanes was obviously much influenced by him, but Platonius (*Diff. Com.* 14) describes his work as comparatively graceless and inconsequential. It is clear from Ath. 495 a, Hdn. ii. 945, and Galen *Libr. Suis* 17 that Cratinus was the subject of commentaries in Hellenistic times.

*FCG* i. 43 ff.; *CAF* i. 11 ff.; *FAC* i. 14 ff. K. J. D.

**CRATIPPUS OF ATHENS,** author of a continuation of Thucydides' history at least to Conon's restoration of Athenian naval power (394 B.C.), was a contemporary of Thucydides (Dion. Hal. *Thuc.* 16). We need not dismiss him as a late Hellenistic writer who claimed earlier authority, but rather keep him in the running for identification with the Oxyrhynchus historian (q.v.) whose *Hellenica* evidently continued Thucydides (q.v. 2).

*FGrH* ii A 13; C 2. A. H. McD.

**CRATYLUS,** a younger contemporary of Socrates. He pressed the doctrine of Heraclitus to an extreme point, denying to things even the slightest fixity of nature. According to Aristotle he was Plato's first master in philosophy, and Plato drew the conclusion that since fixity does not exist in the sensible world there must be a non-sensible world to account for the possibility of knowledge. Plato in his *Cratylus* makes Cratylus maintain that falsehood is impossible and that all words in all languages are naturally appropriate to the meanings in which they are used, and exhibits him as uncritically accepting Socrates' glib etymologies.

Testimonia in Diels, *Vorsokr.*¹¹ ii. 69–70; D. J. Allan, 'The Problem of Cratylus', *AJPhil.* 1952. W. D. R.

**CREMERA,** modern *Fossa di Formello* (variously called *Valca* or *Valchetta*), stream flowing past Veii (q.v.) to join the Tiber at Fidenae (q.v.). Three hundred members of the Fabian clan perished on its banks (477 B.C.), after establishing a blockhouse from which to raid Veientane territory. E. T. S.

**CREMONA,** a Latin colony, founded in 218 B.C. as a bulwark against Insubres and Boii (qq.v.) on the north bank of the Padus (q.v.) in north Italy (Polyb. 3. 40; Tac. *Hist.* 3. 34). Cremona staunchly supported Rome against Hannibal, although thereby it suffered so severely that in 190 it required additional colonists (Livy 21. 56; 27. 10; 37. 46). Its territory was confiscated for a colony of veterans c. 41 B.C. (Verg. *Ecl.* 9. 28). However, it continued prosperous until its destruction by Vespasian's troops in A.D. 69 (Tac. *Hist.* 3. 33 f.). Thereafter, although an important road centre, Cremona did not really revive until the ninth century. E. T. S.

**CREMUTIUS (*PW* 2) CORDUS,** AULUS, the historian, writing under Augustus (Suet. *Tib.* 61. 3) and Tiberius, treated the period from the Civil Wars to at least 18 B.C. (Suet. *Aug.* 35. 2). He refused to glorify Augustus, and celebrated Cicero, Brutus, and Cassius, 'the last Roman'. Prosecuted for treason at the instigation of Sejanus (Tac. *Ann.* 4. 34–5), he committed suicide (A.D. 25). His work was burnt, but copies, preserved by his daughter, were republished under Gaius (Dio 57. 24. 4). The Elder Pliny and Seneca used his work.

Peter, *HRRel.* ii (1906), cxiii and 87; Syme, *Tacitus*, 337.
A. H. McD.

**CREON** (*Κρέων*), a stopgap name ('prince', 'ruler') given to several subsidiary figures, as (1) a king of Corinth. Medea and Jason (qq.v.) visited him, and Medea killed him by magic and fled, leaving her children behind (Creophylus ap. schol. Eur. *Med.* 264); the children were killed by the Corinthians. Euripides himself makes her kill Creon's daughter, Jason's betrothed, with a poisoned costume which catches fire when worn, Creon being killed in trying to save her (*Med.* 1136 ff.), and murder her own children (ibid. 1273 ff.). (2) An early king of Thebes, sometimes confused with (3). He purified Amphitryon (q.v.) from blood-guilt on his arrival in Thebes, helped him in his campaign against the Teleboans, and afterwards married his daughter Megara to Heracles (Apollod. 2. 57. 70). (3) Brother of Iocasta, *see* OEDIPUS. He offered her hand and the kingdom to anyone who would rid Thebes of the Sphinx (Eur. *Phoen.* 45 ff.). After Oedipus' fall and again after the death of Eteocles he became king, or regent, of Thebes, *see* ANTIGONE (1). During the attack by the Seven he lost his son Menoeceus (q.v.). According to the Attic account, Theseus was persuaded to intervene and compel him to grant burial to the bodies of the Seven (Eur. *Supp.*, passim). In Statius (*Theb.* 12. 773 ff.) Theseus kills Creon in the resulting battle. (4) The oldest occurrence of the name is *Il.* 9. 84, where he is father of Lycomedes, commander of part of the Greek outpost; otherwise unknown.

H. J. R.

**CRESILAS**, Greek sculptor, fl. *c.* 450–430 B.C.; native of Cydonia, Crete, but active mostly in Athens. His signature appears on five bases of statues, three found on the Acropolis of Athens, one in the Argolid, and one in Delphi. Another inscribed base, found at Pergamum, evidently supported a copy, transported from elsewhere. Among his works mentioned by Pliny (34. 74) is a portrait statue of Pericles, of which the head survives in several Roman copies, two (in the Vatican and the British Museum) inscribed 'Pericles'. On a fragmentary base, found on the Acropolis, appear parts of the names of Pericles and Cresilas, and it probably served to support the original statue. Of his other works, the statue of an Amazon, which he made for Ephesus, in competition with Phidias, Polycletus, Phradmon, and Cydon (cf. Pliny 34. 53), is probably reproduced in a figure in the Capitoline Museum. Of his Volneratus deficiens, 'a man wounded and dying', the general design is perhaps preserved in a bronze statuette at Modena, in a warrior on a black-figured lecythus in Paris, and in a (considerably restored?) bronze statuette in St. Germain-en-Laye.

G. M. A. R.

**CRETE.** I. PREHISTORIC, *see* MINOAN CIVILIZATION.
II. GREEK AND ROMAN. In historical times Crete was predominantly Dorian, but the transition from the Bronze Age may not have been so abrupt; Cnossos remained an important centre, and the 'Eteocretans' may have retained something of the Minoan culture and tongue. Of Homer's 'Crete of the hundred cities' more than fifty are known, Cnossos, Gortyn, and Lyttos being at first the most important, and later Cydonia with them. The island's position on sea-routes to and from Cyprus, the Levant, and Egypt secured it an important place in

the history of the development of archaic Greek art and important innovations were attributed to a Cretan Daedalos. It had a reputation as the home of mercenary slingers and archers, and of lawgivers (*see* GORTYN for an early code). Aristocratic society persisted in the island and the constitutions (though without kings) resembled closely that of Sparta, which was said to have been derived from the Cretan. The chief magistrates were called *kosmoi*. In the classical period the island lay outside the main currents of Greek history; she refused to aid the defence against Persia in the fifth century. From the middle of the third century her foreign relations centred on the new and unstable league (κοινὸν τῶν Κρηταιέων) and the intrigues of Macedon. In 216 the cities accepted Philip V as protector, but strife soon returned both against Rhodes and still more between the cities, especially Cnossos and Gortyn. By this time Crete was reputed a home of pirates second only to Cilicia. These activities were encouraged by Philip, who realized his hope of thereby injuring Rhodes. The pirates supported Mithridates VI of Pontus against Rome, and when M. Antonius intervened to chastise them he was beaten off Cydonia (74); but Q. Metellus with three legions crushed the islanders and destroyed Cnossos (68/67). Crete became a Roman province, and was united with Cyrene (except when the latter was briefly held by Cleopatra Selene). The old league was adapted as a *concilium provinciae*. In the early Empire Roman traders were numerous at Gortyn, where an imperial mint was established. *See also* ARCHERS.

*Inscr. Creticae* (ed. M. Guarducci, 1935– ) i–iv; Strabo 10. 474–84; Arist. *Pol.* 2. 10; Polyb. 6. 45–7. Mijnsbrugge, *The Cretan Koinon* (U.S.A. 1931); E. van Effenterre, *La Crète et le monde grec de Platon à Polybe* (1948); E. Kirsten, *Die Insel Kreta im funften und vierten Jdt.* (1936); P. Demargne, *La Crète dédalique* (1947); F. R. Willetts, *Cretan Cults and Festivals* (1955); id., *Ancient Crete, A Social History* (1965).
W. A. L.

**CREUSA** (*Κρέουσα*), feminine of Creon (q.v.). The best-known 'princesses' who bear this quasi-name are: (1) daughter of Erechtheus king of Athens. She was violated by Apollo and bore a son whom she exposed; Hermes brought him to Delphi, and thence after growing to young manhood he was brought back to Athens by Creusa's husband Xuthus, who supposed him his own son and called him Ion (q.v. 1). He became the ancestor of the Ionians (Eur. *Ion*). (2) Wife of Aeneas and mother of Ascanius; she died in trying to escape from Troy and her ghost warned Aeneas of his future adventures (*Aen.* 2. 651 ff.).

H. J. R.

**CRINAGORAS** (b. *c.* 70 B.C.), elegiac poet, of Mytilene, son of Callippus, took part in embassy to Caesar at Rome in 45 B.C., and to Augustus in 26–25 B.C. In Rome he was the friend of Octavia, and there wrote his epigrams nos. 29, 11, and 41. No. 29 is concerned with the marriage of Octavia's stepdaughter to Juba, no. 19 with Tiberius, no. 31 with Drusus. Ep. 24 has been connected with the disaster of Varus. He is more interesting for his connexions with others than for his own sake, since his work is usually rhetorical and undistinguished.

TEXT. M. Rubensohn, *Crinagorae Mytilenaei Epigrammata* (1888). CRITICISM. J. S. Phillimore, *Dublin Review* 1906; E. Norden, 'Das Germanenepigramm des Krinagoras', in *Sitz. Berl. Akad.* 1917, 668 ff.; Cichorius, *Röm. Stud.* viii, 4 ff.
C. M. B.

**CRISA**, on a spur close to the modern *Chryso*, controls the roads from the coast of the Crisaean Gulf to Amphissa and to Delphi. It was a Mycenaean site of some importance, but its greatest prosperity was attained in the seventh century B.C. when it founded Metapontum. In the First Sacred War (*see* SACRED WARS) Crisa was destroyed and its fertile plain was dedicated to Pythian

Apollo. The name Crisa and the name Cirrha (q.v.) were often interchangeable as our sources show.

P-K, *GL* i. 2. 686 ff. and 715 n. 63. N. G. L. H.

**CRITIAS** (c. 460–403 B.C.), one of the Thirty Tyrants at Athens, of an aristocratic family, to which Plato's mother (his first-cousin) also belonged. He was an early associate of Socrates, and of the sophists, and was himself active as a writer (*see below*). He was implicated in the mutilation of the Hermae, but released on the evidence of Andocides (q.v.). He seems to have played but a small part in the Revolution of the Four Hundred (q.v.). After their overthrow, either in 411 or 407, he proposed the recall of Alcibiades to Athens. In his exile, perhaps a consequence of the second exile of Alcibiades in 406, he went to Thessaly and, according to one story, intrigued with the *penestae* against their masters. On the surrender of Athens in 404 he returned, as a violent pro-Spartan, and was made one of the Thirty (q.v. 1). In Xenophon's narrative he appears as the leader of the extremists, violent and unscrupulous, and the proposer of the execution of his colleague Theramenes; but Aristotle in the *Politics* (1305ᵇ26) makes Charicles the leader. He was killed fighting against Thrasybulus (q.v.), spring 403. His reputation did not recover after his death; but Plato, much as he disliked the excesses of the Thirty, honoured his memory in his Dialogues.

Critias wrote elegiac poems and tragedies. In later days it was uncertain whether certain plays were the work of Euripides or of Critias (*Vit. Eur.*). A long fragment of the *Sisyphus* gives a rationalistic account of the belief in the gods, and the *Pirithous*, which is described by Ioannes Diaconus *In Hermogenem*, and of which some fragments are known from papyri, is probably his work.

Xen. *Hell.* ii. 3–4; *Mem.* i. 2. For his works, see *TGF* 770–5; Diels, *Vorsokr.* 88. Powell and Barber, *New Chapters* iii. 148 ff.
A. W. G. and A. W. P.-C.; A. A.

**CRITIUS**, Greek sculptor, fl. c. 480–460 B.C., probably an Athenian. Six statue bases bearing the combined signatures of Critius and Nesiotes have been found on the Acropolis of Athens. One of these gives the name of Epicharinus and may be identical with that which supported the statue of Epicharinus, 'who practised the race in armour', seen by Pausanias (1. 23. 9). The general composition is perhaps preserved in a bronze statuette in Tübingen and on a coin of Cyzicus. The fame of Critius and Nesiotes today rests on the group of the Tyrannicides Harmodius and Aristogiton which they were commissioned to make in 477 B.C. (*Marm. Par.*, Ep. 1. 1. 70 f.), to replace those by Antenor (q.v. 2). Copies of these figures have been identified on coins, vases, reliefs, and in full-size statues. The most complete marble copies are in the Naples Museum; fragmentary ones are in the Conservatori, British, and Metropolitan Museums, the Boboli Gardens, etc. A piece of the marble base on which the original bronze group stood has been found in the Athenian agora. Based on a resemblance to this well-authenticated work a number of attributions of extant sculptures have been made to Critius, the best-known being the 'Critius Boy', found on the Acropolis and dating from c. 480 B.C. G. M. A. R.

**CRITO** (Κρίτων) (1), a contemporary and devoted friend of Socrates, referred to in Plato's *Apology*, *Phaedo*, and *Euthydemus*. In the *Crito* he plans for Socrates to escape from prison. Seventeen (lost) dialogues ascribed to him by Diogenes Laertius are of doubtful authenticity.

**CRITO** (Κρίτων) (2), one of the latest poets of the New Comedy; he won second prize with 'Εφέσιοι in 183 B.C. and with Αἰτωλός in 167. From Φιλοπράγμων, *The Busy-*

body, eight lines are preserved, in which Crito calls the Delians παράσιτοι τοῦ θεοῦ.

*FCG* iv. 537 ff.; *CAF* iii. 354 f.

**CRITO** (3) of Argos, a Neo-Pythagorean philosopher, of whose Περὶ φρονήσεως Stobaeus (2, 157–8) quotes 15 lines of Doric prose, about the mind as created by God so as to enable man to contemplate God.

H. Thesleff, *The Pythagorean Writings of the Hellenistic Period* (Acta Academiae Aboensis, humaniora 30, 1 (1965)), 109. D. J. F.

**CRITO** (Κρίτων) (4), physician at Trajan's court c. A.D. 100 (his full name was T. Statilius Crito). We have (in Galen) considerable fragments of his works Κοσμητικά and Περὶ τῆς τῶν φαρμάκων συνθέσεως.

**CRITOLAUS** (*PW* 3), of Phaselis, head of the Peripatetic school in the second century B.C. His dates are unknown, but he was probably an old man when he took part, with Carneades the Academic and Diogenes the Stoic, in the philosophers' delegation to Rome in 156/5 B.C. He was the successor—though probably not the immediate successor (Wehrli, frs. 1, 3, 4)—of Aristo of Ceos as head of the Peripatetic school, and his period of office marks a reaction against the worldly and rhetorical preoccupations of his predecessors since Lyco, and a renewal of the scientific and philosophical activities of the school. Only fragments, and no titles, of his writings have survived. They show some acquaintance with Aristotelian doctrines, though much of it may be second-hand. His teachings, as far as one can reconstruct them, are essentially Peripatetic, with some traces of Stoic influences. He defended the Aristotelian doctrine of the eternity of the world against the Stoic idea of ἐκπύρωσις, and in ethics he held the highest good, in true Aristotelian fashion, to be a composite of the three kinds of goods, those of the soul, those of the body, and external goods. In psychology he taught that the soul was made of the 'fifth essence'—probably a compromise between Aristotelian cosmology and Stoic materialism.

He was a severe critic of rhetoric, and, like Plato, refused to recognize it as a proper art (τέχνη). But he recognized the superiority of Demosthenes, and the story that the latter learnt his rhetoric from the *Rhetoric* of Aristotle may have been his invention.

F. Wehrli, *Die Schule des Aristoteles* (1944–59), x. 49 ff.; A.-H. Chroust, *Antiquitas Hungarica* 1965, 369 ff. J. G.

**CROESUS**, last king of Lydia (c. 560–546 B.C.), son of Alyattes. He secured the throne after a struggle with a half-Greek half-brother, and completed the subjugation of the Greek cities on the Asia Minor coast. His subsequent relations with the Greeks were not unfriendly; he contributed to the rebuilding of the Artemisium at Ephesus and made offerings to Greek shrines, especially Delphi; anecdotes attest his friendliness to Greek visitors and his wealth (Κροίσειοι στατῆρες, but *see* COINAGE, GREEK). The rise of Persia turned Croesus to seek support in Greece and Egypt, but Cyrus anticipated him: Sardis was captured and Croesus overthrown. His subsequent fate soon became the theme of legend: he is cast or casts himself on a pyre, but is miraculously saved by Apollo and translated to the land of the Hyperboreans or becomes the friend and counsellor of Cyrus.

Herodotus, bk. 1; *FGrH* 90 (Nic. Dam.) F 65, 68; Bacchylides 3. British Museum *Cat. Sculpture* (1928) 1. i. 38; *Louvre, Vases antiques gr.* 197; G. Radet, *La Lydie* (1893), 206 ff. P. N. U.

**CROTON** (Κρότων), modern *Crotone*. Originally a Messapic settlement (J. Whatmough, *Prae-Italic Dialects* (1933) ii. 258), Croton became an Achaean colony c. 710 B.C. Its situation, near the celebrated temple of Hera

Lacinia in the 'toe' of Italy on an indifferent but important harbour, was bracing (Strabo 6. 216 f.; Polyb. 10. 1). Croton became a flourishing city twelve miles in circumference; it founded some colonies (Terina, Caulonia) and dominated others (Lametium, Scylacium). Famous for its doctors, athletes (including Milon, q.v.), Heracles cult, and especially for its Pythagorean brotherhood (between c. 530 and 455), Croton reached its apogee after destroying Sybaris (510). It even sent a ship to the battle of Salamis (Hdt. 8. 47). Shortly thereafter, however, its defeat by Locri and Rhegium (qq.v.) presaged its decline. Although still populous when captured by Dionysius (379), internal, Lucanian, Bruttian, Pyrrhic, and Hannibalic wars ultimately ruined Croton. A Roman colony (194 B.C.) failed to revive it (Diod. 14. 103 f.; 19. 3, etc.; Livy 24. 3; 34. 45).

See the bibliography s.v. MAGNA GRAECIA and add D. Randall-MacIver, *Greek Cities of Italy and Sicily* (1931); P. Larizza, *Crotone nella Magna Grecia* (1934); Bérard, *Bibliogr. topogr.* 48.     E. T. S.

**CROWNS AND WREATHS** were awarded by the Romans as decorations for valour; of these the highest was a wreath of grass (*corona obsidionalis, c. graminea*) granted to the deliverer of a besieged army. Pliny (*HN* 22. 6 ff.) lists eight recipients, ending with Augustus. Next came the *c. triumphalis* (*c. laurea*), a wreath of bay worn by the *triumphator* (*see* TRIUMPH), and the *c. ovalis* (*c. myrtea*), a myrtle-wreath worn for an *ovatio* (q.v.). During the Empire, of the awards which were allowed outside the imperial house, one, the *c. civica*, was theoretically open to all ranks, though there is no certain instance of its conferment after the reign of Claudius. It was a crown of oak-leaves and awarded for saving the life of a fellow soldier. Later, it was revived by Septimius Severus as a crown of gold (*c. civica aurea*) and given to centurions. Other decorations were awarded on a fixed scale and some were confined to particular ranks. Men below the centurionate were eligible for the lesser decorations of *torques, armillae,* and *phalerae* (necklaces, bracelets, and embossed discs worn on the corselet). Centurions could have these and the *c. vallaris* or the *c. muralis*, crowns awarded to the first man over the enemy's rampart or over the wall of a besieged town. A *primipilus* (q.v.) might be awarded the *c. aurea*, a plain gold crown, besides the *hasta pura* or silver spear-head. Officers of higher rank could receive the *vexillum*, a small standard mounted on silver, the *hasta pura*, and *coronae* according to a sliding scale. A mere *tribunus militum* was eligible for the *c. aurea*, a *legatus* of quaestorian rank might have the *c. vallaris* or *c. muralis* as well, and a *legatus* of praetorian rank all three. *Legati* of consular rank alone seem to have been awarded the *c. classica* (*c. navalis, c. rostrata*), a wreath decorated with a ship's prow, which was given for a naval victory.

Parker, *Roman Legions* 228 ff.     G. R. W.

**CRUCIFIXION** appears to have been a form of punishment borrowed by the Romans from elsewhere, probably Carthage. As a Roman penalty it is first attested in the Punic Wars. It was normally confined to slaves (*servile supplicium*), and later in the Empire to *humiliores*; it was not applied to soldiers, except in cases of desertion. Constantine the Great abolished the penalty (not before 314). The method of execution admitted variations, but the general practice was to begin with flagellation of the condemned, who was then compelled to carry a cross-beam (*patibulum*) to the place of execution, where a stake had been firmly fixed in the ground. He was stripped and fastened to the cross-beam by nails or cords, and the beam was drawn up by ropes until the man's feet were clear of the ground. The beam was then fastened to the upright. Some support for the body was provided by a ledge

(*sedile*) which projected from the upright, but a foot rest (*suppedaneum*) is rarely attested, though the feet were sometimes tied or nailed. Death probably occurred through exhaustion: this could be hastened by breaking the legs (*crurifragium*). A military guard was normally posted at the place of execution. After removal of the body the cross was usually destroyed.     G. R. W

**CTESIAS** (late 5th c. B.C.) of Cnidos, Greek doctor at the Persian court who assisted Artaxerxes at the battle of Cunaxa, and was sent as envoy to Evagoras and Conon, 398 B.C. Author of a far from trustworthy history of Persia (Περσικά) in twenty-three books, written in Ionic, of a geographical treatise (Περίοδος) in three books and of the first separate work on India ('Ινδικά).

J. Gilmore, *Fragments of the Persika of Ctesias* (1888); *FGrH* iii C 688.     G. L. B

**CTESIBIUS,** inventor (fl. 270 B.C.), was the son of a barber in Alexandria, and employed by Ptolemy II. He was the first to make devices employing 'pneumatics', i.e. the action of air under pressure. His work on the subject is lost, but descriptions of some of his inventions are preserved by Philon (2), Vitruvius, and Heron (qq.v.). These include the pump with plunger and valve (Vitr. 10. 7, Heron, *Pneum.* 1. 28), the water-organ (Vitr. 10. 8), the first accurate water-clock (Vitr. 9. 8. 4 ff.) and a war-catapult (Philon, *Belop.* 43). No great theoretician, Ctesibius was a mechanical genius, some of whose inventions were of permanent value. It is probable that many of the basic ideas in the works of Philon and Heron on mechanical devices derive from him.

A. G. Drachmann, *Ktesibios Philon and Heron* (Copenhagen, 1948).     G. J. T

**CTESIPHON,** on the river Tigris, c. 60 miles above Babylon. Founded as a Parthian military camp opposite the Hellenistic Seleuceia (q.v. 1), it became the winter residence of the Arsacids. After the destruction of Seleuceia (A.D. 165) it was the chief city in Babylonia. Artaxerxes made it the capital of the new Sassanian Empire, and his successors built palaces and added new suburbs. In 636 the 'seven cities' of Ctesiphon were taken by the Arabs. Part of the fortifications still stand, and the impressive ruins of a Sassanid palace.

M. Streck, *Alte Orient* xvi. 3/4 (1917); Honigmann, *PW*, Suppl. iv 1102 ff.; O. Reuther, *Antiquity* 1929, 434 ff.; J. H. Schmidt, *Syria* 1934, 1 ff.     M. S. D.

**CUICUL** (modern *Djemila*), a mountain-town lying between Cirta and Sitifis on the main road linking Numidia and Mauretania. Originally a *castellum*, dependent on Cirta, it became a colony under Nerva. In the second century A.D. it received an influx of romanized Berbers; agricultural prosperity developed and many public buildings were erected; its best-known citizen was Claudius Proculus, governor of Numidia (A.D. 208–10). Its extensive ruins include a Christian basilica, baths, theatre, baptistery, Caracalla's arch, and a temple of the *gens Septimia*.

A. Ballu, *Rev. Africaine* 1921; Y. Allais, *Djemila* (Paris, 1938); L. Leschi, *Djemila²* (Algiers, 1953); P. Monceaux, *Cuicul chrétien* (1923). Excavation reports in *Libyca* 1953 and subsequent years.     W. N. W

**CULLEO,** QUINTUS TERENTIUS (*PW* 43), a senator, captured by the Carthaginians and released by Scipio in 201 B.C.; to show his gratitude he marched in Scipio's triumphal procession in a freedman's cap. As *tribunus plebis* in 189 (or 188) he carried a measure to enrol sons of freedmen in the rustic tribes. As praetor (187) he examined the evidence of unlawful registration by Latins on the citizen oll. The statement (Antias, apud Livy) that he was chairman of a special *quaestio* set up to try L. Scipio belongs to a false account of the procedure then adopted. He served on commissions to Africa in 195 and 171.

H. H. S.

**CULTURE-BRINGERS.** All folklore (see Stith Thompson, A 500 ff.) contains stories of persons, divine or human, who introduced mankind in primitive days to the arts, religious observances, etc. Greek tradition is no exception. Prometheus (q.v.) is the great culture-hero of Attic belief (Aesch. *PV* 442 ff.); Cadmus (q.v.) introduces letters; Triptolemus, by direction of Demeter (q.v.), teaches men to plant corn. Similar Latin stories are late and artificial; for examples, see JANUS, SATURNUS. Gods figure occasionally in this capacity (Athena invents horsemanship, Dionysus introduces the vine, etc.). Lists of such inventors are late, but common, see Kremmer, *De catalogis heurematum* (Diss. Leipzig, 1890). H. J. R.

**CUMAE,** Italy's earliest Greek colony, founded on the coast near Naples by Chalcis, traditionally in 1050, actually *c.* 750 B.C., in fertile territory inhabited in pre-Hellenic times but now deserted. After its foundation Greek civilization spread further in Italy (A. Blakeway, *JRS* 1935, 135). Cumae soon acquired wealth and power. From 700 to 500 it exercised wide dominion and colonized Neapolis, Dicaearchia (= Puteoli), Abella, distant Zancle (= Messana), and possibly Nola (qq.v.). Cumae is inseparably associated with the Sibyl whose oracular cavern still exists (*Aen.* 6); but its first real personality is Aristodemus (q.v. 2), who repulsed the Etruscans. In 474 Cumae with Syracusan aid crushed Etruscan power in Campania, but was itself conquered by Sabelli (q.v.) *c.* 421 and became an Oscan city (Diod. 11. 51; 12. 76). Subsequently coming under Roman control it obtained *civitas sine suffragio* in 338 and *praefecti Capuam Cumas* in 318. It staunchly supported Rome in the Hannibalic and Social Wars, discarded Oscan for Latin in 180, and ultimately obtained full citizenship. But, as Puteoli rose, Cumae, despite repeated colonizations and the erection of villas nearby, declined. However, its inaccessible citadel was still strategically important in Belisarius' time.

A. Sambon, *Monnaies antiques de l'Italie* i (1903), 139, 283; E. Gabrici, *Mon. Ant.* 1913–14; D. Randall-MacIver, *Greek Cities of Italy and Sicily* (1931), 1; Bérard, *Bibliogr. topogr.* 50; Dunbabin, *Western Greeks*; E. Vetter, *Handbuch der ital. Dialekte* (1953) i. 91 f.; A. Maiuri; *The Phlegraean Fields* (1957); on harbour, R. F. Paget, *JRS* 1968, 152 ff. See also s.v. MAGNA GRAECIA. E. T. S.

**CUNAXA,** northward from Babylon, was the scene of the battle between Cyrus (q.v. 2) the younger and Artaxerxes II (401 B.C.). Artaxerxes' scratch army—he had only two satraps with him besides Tissaphernes—consisted of perhaps 30,000 infantry (Xenophon's estimate of 900,000 is ridiculous), but at least 6,000 horse. Cyrus, who had brought only 2,600 horse, had failed before he started. Tissaphernes, with Artaxerxes, was in the centre with a strong cavalry force; Cyrus put his 10,400 Greek hoplites under Clearchus on his right instead of opposite Tissaphernes, and took the centre himself with only 600 horse; Ariaeus with Cyrus' Asiatic troops was on the left. Clearchus routed the infantry of Artaxerxes' left, but neglected to turn against his centre; while he uselessly pursued the beaten infantry, Tissaphernes threw in his cavalry, killed Cyrus, outflanked Ariaeus who fled, and gained a decisive victory.

W. W. Tarn, *CAH* vi. 7; A. Boucher, *L'Anabase de Xénophon* (1913) pt. i, ch. 8. W. W. T.

**CUNOBEL(L)INUS,** son of Tasciovanus, king of the Catuvellauni at Verulamium. Perhaps as a result of the *clades Variana* in A.D. 9, he moved (in defiance of Caesar's treaty) against the Trinovantes and made Camulodunum his capital, where he established his mint. Later he conquered Kent and could be regarded as 'rex Britanniarum' (Suetonius, *Calig.* 44.{2). Camulodunum (Lexden Heath, near the later colony) became a notable centre of Roman imports, and his coins bear Latin inscriptions and emblems of mythology. About A.D. 40 a quarrel with his son Amminius, who fled to Rome, prompted Caligula's abortive demonstration. He died before 43; and a mound at Lexden Heath may be his grave (*Archaeologia* 1926–7, 241 ff.). He was prominent in medieval fable, whence Shakespeare derived the material for 'Cymbeline'.

D. F. Allen, *Archaeologia* 1944, 1 ff.; C. E. Stevens in *Essays presented to O. G. S. Crawford* (ed. W. F. Grimes, 1951), 332 ff. C. E. S.

**CUPIDO AMANS,** a short anonymous Latin poem, third century A.D., in 16 hexameters.

*Anth. Lat.* (Riese) 240. Duff, *Minor Lat. Poets.*

**CURATOR.** A *cura* was originally not an office, but a duty forming part of an office; thus the *cura annonae* was (normally) the aediles' task, the *cura morum* the censors'. A *cura viarum* (or of individual *viae*) is mentioned in connexion with various magistracies and by the late Republic we find it occasionally entrusted to a *privatus* with some experience. The first major independent *cura*, however, was the *cura annonae* of Pompey (q.v.) in 57 B.C. This *cura* was later conferred on Augustus, and others (notably a *cura morum*) were offered to him, as perhaps to Caesar before him. But Augustus, in accordance with a general tendency to empty the regular magistracies of content, instituted boards of *curatores* (with previous experience as magistrates) to take charge of administrative tasks like the *annona*, the roads, and the Tiber (qq.v.). Such *curatores*, both in Rome and in municipalities, became common under the Empire. The title is also used for the presidents of organizations like Conventus and Clubs (qq.v.).

Ruggiero, *Diz. Epigr.*, s.v. E. B.

**CURATOR REI PUBLICAE** (or **CIVITATIS,** etc.). Officials of the central government supervising city affairs appear in the East under Trajan (perhaps even under Domitian): their office is not yet distinguished from that of *corrector* (q.v.) and terminology overlaps. In the second century A.D. they become more common, are normally called λογισταί and seem to be chiefly in charge of the finances of one city, or at most two or three. In Italy and the West, the early emperors sporadically interfered in local government of citizen communities: when 'elected' local magistrates, they would govern through a prefect. A praetorian *curator* of colonies and *municipia* is found under Domitian (*ILS* 1017), and from the time of Trajan we frequently find men supervising cities, sometimes several towns concurrently or in succession. In western provinces they appear more gradually in the second century. Appointed by the Emperor (often on local recommendation), they are usually of senatorial or equestrian standing. Municipal notables appear quite early and become common under the Severi. Their duties come to embrace most aspects of local government. After Diocletian the office became municipal (though important men could be chosen to honour a town) and lost much of its power to the regional governor.

Ruggiero, *Diz. Epigr.*, s.v., and (for Africa) C. Lucas, *JRS* 1940, 56 ff. E. B.

**CURETES,** (1) a people hostile to the Calydonians (*Il.* 9. 529). (2) Semi-divine beings (Hesiod, fr. 198 Rzach, calls them θεοί) inhabiting Crete, who protected the infant Zeus by dancing about him and clattering their weapons so that his cries were not heard (Callim. *Jov.* 52 ff., and many authors). The origin of the legend is plausibly derived from the Cretan rite (see J. Harrison, *Themis*² (1927), 1 ff.; Nilsson, *Minoan-Mycenaean Religion*² (1950), 475 ff.) of a ceremonial (not provably a dance) in honour of Zeus Kouros. They are often confused with the Corybantes attendant on Rhea (see Rose, *Handb. Gk. Myth.*, 171). See further H. Jeanmaire, *Couroi et Courètes* (1939), and for the religious confraternity bearing this name at Ephesus in and after the time of Strabo, Ch. Picard, *Éphèse et Claros* (1922), 279 ff., etc. H. J. R.

**CURIA** (1) was the most ancient division of the Roman People, already existing under the kings. The *curiae* were thirty in number (ten for each Romulean tribe). Some bore local names (Foriensis, Veliensis), others personal ones (Titia). They were probably composed of families, who were, originally at least, neighbours. Probably both patricians and plebeians were always included (Dionysius 4. 12. 20). The head of the *curia* was the *curio* who was at least 50 years of age and was elected for life; the head of the college of the *curiones* was a *curio maximus*, who until 210 B.C. was always a patrician: details of their election are uncertain. The *curiae* were probably the basis of the oldest military organization and certainly the elements of the oldest Roman assembly (see COMITIA). Each *curia* had its own meeting-place called after the *curia*. The *curiae* had a special devotion for Iuno Quiritis: the Fornacalia and the Fordicidia were their most famous festivals. A comparable subdivision of the tribe is to be found at Iguvium (Umbria).

*Curia* was also the name given to the assembly-places of many other corporations, and especially to the senate-house (see below). As a voting section of the citizens the *curia* is attested in Latium (Lanuvium) and in many Italian and provincial *municipia* and *coloniae*, both of Latin and Roman status. It was especially common in Africa. During the Empire *curia* was also the usual name for the municipal senates, to which the elections of the magistrates were transferred from the people. It was largely constituted from ex-magistrates chosen for life (at least in the West) and in the Late Empire turned into a hereditary caste, called the *curiales*, whose lives and property were under the control of the state as security for the collection of taxes. See also CURIALIS, DECURIONES.

G. Humbert, Dar.-Sag. i. 2. 1627; Mommsen, *Röm. Staatsr.* iii. 99; F. Altheim, *Epochen d. röm. Geschichte* i (1934), 70; C. W. Westrup, *Rev. Int. Droits Ant.* 1954, 462 ff.; P. de Francisci, *Primordia Civitatis* (1959), 572 ff.; A. Momigliano, *JRS* 1963, 108 (with bibliography). For the *curiae* in *municipia* W. Liebenam, *Städteverwaltung im römischen Kaiserreiche* (1900), 214 ff.; Mommsen, *Juristische Schriften* i. 303 ff.; Jones, *Later Rom. Emp.* II. 724. A. M.

**CURIA** (2), the Senate-house of Rome, situated on the north side of the Comitium (q.v.) in the Forum and ascribed to Hostilius. It was restored by Sulla in 80 B.C., burnt after the death of Clodius in 52, and rebuilt by Faustus Sulla. Julius Caesar began a new building on a slightly different site in 44, forsaking the old orientation by cardinal points, which was restored by Domitian in A.D. 94, and later by Diocletian after the fire under Carinus in 283. The Caesarian plan, always retained, was a sumptuous oblong hall (25·20 × 17·61 m.), with central door facing a magistrates' dais and with lateral marble benches. The hall was separated from the record-office (*secretarium senatus*) by an *atrium* or *chalcidicum*, dedicated by Domitian to Minerva. Diocletian's building, of tile-faced concrete coated with imitation stucco blockwork, was preserved to full height as part of a church and restored in 1935–7.

Nash, *Pict. Dict. Rome* i. 301 ff. I. A. R.

**CURIALIS,** member of a city council (*curia*), or son or descendant of one in the male line. City councillors, or decurions (q.v.), had tended during the Principate to become a hereditary class, since only the richest citizens could bear the financial burden involved and normally property descended from father to son. From the middle of the second century wealthy citizens became increasingly reluctant to serve on the council, but were compelled to do so if legally nominated. Many exploited various exemptions. Roman senators and members of the equestrian service were excused local office and so were farmers of state lands or taxes, shippers serving the *annona*, doctors, professors, and other categories. From the time of Diocletian the government made increasing efforts to prevent these exemptions from being misused, and in particular to forbid *curiales* to obtain honorary offices. The government's efforts, however, were not very effective, and the curial class was gradually drained of its wealthier members.

Jones, *Later Rom. Emp.* 737 ff. A. H. M. J

**CURIATIUS MATERNUS,** senator, poet, and dramatist, at whose house the scene of Tacitus' *Dialogus* is laid. He speaks there as champion of poetry. His (lost) *praetextae*, *Domitius* and *Cato*, belong to Vespasian's time. On his origin, see Syme, *Tacitus*, appendix 90.

**CURIO** (1), GAIUS SCRIBONIUS (*PW* 10), after early forensic activity and an unsuccessful tribunate (90 B.C.), served under Sulla in the East and later enriched himself in the proscriptions. Consul in 76 B.C., he opposed Sicinius (q.v.), then fought in Macedonia as proconsul and triumphed (73). He supported Verres (q.v.) and was active in the courts and in politics in the 60s and 50s, consistently opposing Caesar, but defending Clodius (q.v. 1) and hence often hostile to Cicero, who wrote a pamphlet attacking him and later (needing his help) wanted to deny authorship. He died in 53 (see Cic. *Fam.* 2. 2). E. B.

**CURIO** (2), GAIUS SCRIBONIUS (*PW* 11), son of (1), moved in the circle of Clodius (q.v. 1) and Antonius (q.v. 4), but in the 50s B.C. was on the Optimate side with his father, and was implicated in the affair of Vettius (q.v. 3). He was quaestor in 54, tribune in 50 (elected as an enemy of Caesar, who had offended him). Resentful at the Optimates' opposition to his own schemes, alarmed at the drift to civil war (which they encouraged), and bribed by Caesar with a vast sum, he carried a disarmament resolution in the Senate by a large majority and, when it was ignored, joined Caesar at the end of his tribunate. After negotiating on his behalf, he served under him in 49, hoping to win Cicero to his cause; after occupying Sicily he crossed to Africa, where, after initial successes, he was defeated and killed by Juba (q.v. 1).

W. K. Lacey, *Hist.* 1961, 318. E. B.

**CURSES.** A curse is in general a wish, expressed in words and with magical effect, that evil may befall a person or persons or, sometimes, the curser himself.

I. The Greek word ἀρά reflects a prehistoric stage of Greek religion, signifying the address to supernatural forces, prayer as well as curse (personified as Ἀρά, secondarily combined with Erinys, goddess of revenge; cf. ἀρητήρ in the *Iliad*). Originally the curse (just as its opposite, the blessing) worked by its own inherent quality (*mana*), the power of its magic formula (see MAGIC); this may be spoken or written or both; it may also be accompanied or symbolized by action (cf. the modern Greek φασκέλωμα and the Italian *il fico*, etc.), the gesture and the intonation intensifying the emotional character of the curse. The curse was always a powerful weapon in the hands of the weak and the poor, as also against unseen or unknown foes. So we often meet with such imprecations (*dirae*) in funeral inscriptions against those who violate graves (especially in Asia Minor). Numerous leaden tablets magic nails, amulets, etc., cf. the magic papyri, inscribed with imprecatory formulas or words or signs, testify to the popularity of cursing (ἀναθεματίζειν), resorted to in all centuries by all sorts of people on any provocation (in the 4th c. B.C. even by well-to-do Athenians). When the tablets are buried in tombs, not only the spirits of the dead are invoked, but also the infernal deities, Persephone, Hades, Erinyes (cf. *Il.* 9. 453 ff.); elsewhere Hermes, Gaia, Demeter (at Cnidos), Hecate, and all sorts of demons are favourites (cf. the Roman *devotio*: see s.v.). Especially to be noted are the 'hereditary curse', infectious through generations (cf. Aeschylus' *Oresteia*), and the curse, uttered in vain, that returns to the curser, destroying him and his family (cf. *SIG*³ 41. 14). The ἀραί, *dirae*, developed into a special literary genus (cf. Sophron, Ovid's *Ibis*, Horace *Epod.* 10; Tib. 1. 5. 49 ff.). Later Christians might use ancient curses in inscriptions, simply prefixing a cross.

II. In the development of human society and ethics the curse plays an important role, just as does the oath (the two being often combined, cf. *Il.* 3. 279). The curse, expressed by the community through its representatives (magistrates, priests), had an enormous effect (cf. the blessing or curse uttered by parents or dying people). The culprit ('infecting' his countrymen, as Plato puts it, *Leg.* 9. 881 e 5) was thus in the position of a man guilty of sacrilege, and so the legal powers could enforce their rights even in cases where only the gods could help. Enemies and traitors were cursed, just as those who removed landmarks or maltreated guests and suppliants. The curses of the Bouzygai at the Athenian Bouphonia (*see* SACRIFICE § 2) may illustrate how ethical principles might be enforced by cursing the offenders, and 'public curses' were as terrifying to the Greeks (cf. the *dirae Teiae*, *SIG* 37–8) as to the Romans (cf. Crassus on his departure for the Orient, Plut. *Crass.* 16). The weakening of the fear of the old gods already recognizable in official use in the third century B.C. reduced the importance of the curse, but we can still see its effect in ecclesiastical ritual.

K. Latte, *Heiliges Recht* (1920), 61 ff.; E. Ziebarth, *Hermes* 1895, 57 ff.; Cf. W. W. Fowler, *Roman Essays and Interpretations*, 15 ff.; W. K. C. Guthrie, *The Greeks and their Gods* (1950), 270 ff.; Nilsson, *GGR* i². 800 ff.; A. E. Crawley, Hastings, *ERE* iv. 367 ff.; *IG* iii. 3; A. Audollent, *Defixionum Tabellae* (1904); R. Wünsch, *Antike Fluchtafeln²* (1912); recently found tablets: Nilsson, op. cit. ii². 221.
S. E.

**CURSUS HONORUM.** As the Roman magistracies developed and the relative degrees of responsibility were established, it was natural that normally they should be held in ascending order of importance. This custom became increasingly inflexible. The basic pattern, after preliminary military service, was quaestorship–praetorship–consulship–censorship. If the tribunate of the *plebs* and the aedileship were held, the former usually and the latter always followed the quaestorship. For various reasons neither tribunate nor aedileship could be made obligatory, and the consulship was probably only a *de facto* prerequisite for the censorship; but in or soon after 197 B.C. tenure of the praetorship became a legally necessary qualification for the consulship. Omission of the quaestorship, already rare, was prohibited by Sulla. This *certus ordo magistratuum* acquired further rigidity from the *lex annalis* (see VILLIUS). In the early Principate the pattern was extended. The vigintivirate became a prerequisite for the quaestorship, and all except patricians were obliged to hold either the tribunate of the *plebs* or the aedileship. Between vigintivirate and quaestorship the military tribunate was usually held; this is often thought to have been an obligatory step in the *cursus* (cf. esp. Suet. *Aug.* 38. 2), but either it was not so or exemptions were frequent. Provincial governorships and the new nonmagisterial posts (*see* CURATOR *and* PRAEFECTUS) were normally held at fixed points within the framework, though variations in these facilitated flexibility in careers. A similar *cursus* developed for equestrian careers (*see* EQUITES), especially for the senior prefectures, but it was always subject to greater variations than the senatorial *cursus*. A *cursus* was observed also in municipal magistracies.

A. Astin, *The Lex Annalis Before Sulla* (1958); Mommsen, *Röm. Staatsr.* i³. 536; E. Birley, *Proc. Brit. Acad.* 1953, 197.    A. E. A.

**CURTIUS** (*PW* 7, 9), the hero of an aetiological myth invented to explain the name of *Lacus Curtius*, a pit or pond in the Roman Forum, which by the time of Augustus had already dried up. Three Curtii are mentioned in this connexion: (1) a Sabine Mettius Curtius who fell from his horse into a marsh while fighting against Romulus; (2) C. Curtius, consul of 445 B.C. who consecrated a site struck by lightning; (3) and most important, the brave young knight M. Curtius who, in obedience to an oracle, to save his country, leaped armed and on horse-back into the chasm which suddenly opened in the Forum.

Ogilvie, *Comm. Livy 1–5*, 75 ff. For the Lacus Curtius see Platner–Ashby 310 f., Nash, *Pict. Dict. Rome* i. 542 ff.    P. T.

**CURTIUS** (4) **MONTANUS** was prosecuted under Nero for his satiric poems, and excluded from holding any public office (Tac. *Ann.* 16. 28; 29; 33). In A.D. 70 he attacked M. Aquillius Regulus in a fierce speech in the Senate (Tac. *Hist.* 4. 42). He became one of Domitian's advisers (Juv. 4. 107).

**CYBELE** (Κυβέλη; Lydian form Κυβήβη, Hdt. 5. 102), the great mother-goddess of Anatolia, associated in myth, and later at least in cult, with her youthful lover Attis (q.v.). Pessinus in Phrygia was her chief sanctuary, and the cult appears at an early date in Lydia. The queen or mistress of her people, Cybele was responsible for their well-being in all respects; primarily she is a goddess of fertility, but also cures (and sends) disease, gives oracles, and, as her mural crown indicates, protects her people in war. The goddess of mountains (so Μήτηρ ὀρεία; Meter Dindymene), she is also mistress of wild nature, symbolized by her attendant lions. Ecstatic states inducing prophetic rapture and insensibility to pain were characteristic of her worship (cf. especially Catull. 63).

By the fifth century Cybele was known in Greece, was early associated with Demeter (H. Thompson, *Hesp.* 1937, 206) and perhaps with a native Μήτηρ θεῶν, but except possibly for such places as Dyme, Patrae (Paus. 7. 17. 9; 20. 3), and private cult associations at Piraeus, where Attis also was honoured, it is likely that the cult was thoroughly hellenized. Cybele was officially brought to Rome from Asia Minor in 205–204 (for the conflicting legends see Graillot, op. cit. *infra*, ch. 1), but under the Republic, save for the public games, the Megalesia, and processions (Lucr. 2. 624 f.), she was limited to her Palatine temple and served only by Oriental priests (Dion. Hal. *Ant. Rom.* 2. 19. 3–5). After Claudius admitted Attis to public status, the priesthood was opened to citizens, and was henceforth controlled by the *XVviri sacris faciundis* (see QUINDECIMVIRI). The cycle of the spring festival, while not fully attested till A.D. 354, began to take form then. The rites began on 15 Mar. with a procession of the Reed-bearers (*cannophori*), and a sacrifice for the crops. After a week of fastings and purifications, the festival proper opened on the 22nd with the bringing of the pine-tree, symbol of Attis, to the temple.

The 24th was the Day of Blood, commemorating the castration and probably the death of Attis. The 25th was a day of joy and banqueting, the Hilaria, and after a day's rest the festival closed with the ritual bath (*Lavatio*) of Cybele's image in the Almo. The rubric for the 28th (*Initium Caiani*) is apparently unrelated. The relation of this spring festival to the Hellenistic mysteries of Cybele is uncertain. Of the later mysteries, in which Attis figured prominently, we again know little. The formulae preserved (Firm. Mat. *Err. prof. rel.* 18; Clem. Al. *Protr.* 2. 15) mention a ritual meal; the carrying of the κέρνος, a vessel used in the *taurobolium* to receive the genitals of the bull; and a descent into the παστός, probably an underground chamber where certain rites were enacted.

The ritual of the *taurobolium* originated in Asia Minor, and first appears in the West in the cult of Venus Caelesta (i.e. -is) at Puteoli in A.D. 134 (*ILS* 4271, but cf. 4099 of A.D. 108). From the Antonine period, numerous dedications to Cybele and Attis record its performance in this cult 'ex vaticinatione archigalli' (i.e. with official sanction), on behalf of the Emperor and the Empire. From Rome the rite spread throughout the West, notably in Gaul. It was performed also on behalf of individuals, and was especially popular during the pagan revival, A.D. 370–90. In the rite, the recipient descended into a ditch and was bathed in the blood of a bull, or ram (*criobolium*), which was slain above him (Prudent. *Perist.* 10. 1011–50). It was sometimes repeated after twenty years; one late text (*ILS* 4152) has 'taurobolio criobolioq. in aeternum renatus' (a concept possibly borrowed from Christianity), but in general the act was considered rather a 'thing done' for its own value than as a source of individual benefits.

A belief in immortality was perhaps part of the cult from early times, and the after-life may at first have been thought of as a reunion with Mother Earth. Later, Attis became a solar god, and he and Cybele were regarded as astral and cosmic powers; there is some evidence that the soul was then thought to return after death to its celestial source.

Thanks to its official status and early naturalization at Rome, the cult spread rapidly through the provinces, especially in Gaul and Africa, and was readily accepted as a municipal cult. Its agrarian character made it more popular with the fixed populations than with the soldiery, and it was especially favoured by women.

Cybele is generally represented enthroned in a *naiskos*, wearing either the mural crown or the *calathos*, carrying a patera and tympanum, and either flanked by lions or bearing one in her lap.

*See also* AGDISTIS, ANAHITA, ANATOLIAN DEITIES, ATTIS, EUNUCHS, METRAGYRTES.

J. Carcopino, *Mél. d'Arch. et d'Hist.* 1923; Cumont, *Rel. or.*; Farnell, *Cults* iii; J. G. Frazer, *Adonis Attis Osiris*³ (1922); H. Graillot, *Le Culte de Cybèle* (1912); H. Hepding, *Attis* (1903); M.-J. Lagrange, *Rev. Bibl.* 1919; Oppermann, s.v. 'Taurobolia', in *PW*; in Roscher, *Lex.*, Drexler and Höfer, s.v. 'Meter'; R. Duthoy, *The Taurobolium* (Leyden, 1969). F. R. W.

**CYCLADES,** the islands regarded as circling round the sacred isle of Delos. They enjoyed a flourishing and individual culture in the Early and Middle Bronze Age, and from the seventeenth century several were settled from Minoan Crete. After 1400 they fell within the Mycenaean sphere and continued inhabited after the decline of the Mycenaean cities of the mainland. About 1000 B.C. Ionic-speaking settlers from continental Greece occupied these islands. In the eighth century Eretria exercised control over some of them, as did the tyrants Pisistratus (Athens), Polycrates (Samos), and Lygdamis (Naxos) in the sixth; but no power could protect the islanders from the invading Persian fleet in 490. After the Persian Wars the islanders entered an Athenian

League centred at Delos (478–477), and Athens soo became mistress of the Cyclades. They were also enrolle in the second Athenian League (378–377), but th triumph of Philip of Macedon ended Athenian hegemony Antigonus of Macedon founded a League of Islande with headquarters at Delos. In the prolonged struggl between Macedon and Egypt in the third century th Cyclades often changed masters; late in the century the suffered from Cretan piracy and the rivalries of Perga mum, Rhodes, and Syria. In the Mithridatic War th islands were reduced by Archelaus (88), nor was tran quillity restored until the triumph of Augustus.

*IG* xii (5); P-K, *GL* ivc; C. Zervos, *L'Art des Cyclades* (1957) K. Scholes, *BSA* 1956, 9 ff.; I. Ström, *Acta Arch.* 1962, 221 ff. W. A. L.; J. B.

**CYCLOPES** (Κύκλωπες), gigantic one-eyed beings o whom at least two separate traditions exist. In Home they are savage and pastoral; they live in a distant coun try, having no government or laws. Here Odysseu (q.v.) visits them in his wanderings and enters the cav of one of them, Polyphemus, who imprisons him and hi men and eats two of them morning and evening, unt they escape by blinding him, while in a drunken sleep and getting out among the sheep and goats when h opens the cave in the morning (*Od.* 9. 106 ff.). Poly phemus is son of Poseidon, and the god, in answer to hi prayer for vengeance, opposes the home-coming o Odysseus in every possible way, bringing literally to pas the curse that he may return alone and find trouble whe he arrives (ibid. 532–5). Out of this, or by conflation o it with some local legend, grows the story of the amorou Polyphemus (Theocr. 11 and elsewhere). He lives i Sicily (one of many identifications of Homeric with late known western places) and woos Galatea (q.v.).

But in Hesiod (*Theog.* 149) the Cyclopes are three Brontes, Steropes, and Arges (Thunderer, Lightener Bright), who make thunderbolts and in general ar excellent craftsmen; they are like the gods except tha they have but one eye each, and are sons of Earth an Heaven. They often appear (as Callim. *Dian.* 46 ff.) a Hephaestus' workmen, and are often again are credited wit making ancient fortifications, as those of Tiryns, an other cities of the Argolid (schol. Eur. *Or.* 965). Ther they are called ἐγχειρογάστορες, simply 'workmen (Willamowitz-Moellendorff, *Glaube der Hellenen* (1931-2), i. 277). Schol. Hesiod. *Theog.* 139, makes these build ers a third kind of Cyclopes.

See Roscher in his *Lexikon*, s.v. 'Kyklopen', and S. Eitrem in *PW* s.v. H. J. R

**CYCNUS,** (1) a son of Ares, a brigand, waylaying an robbing those who brought tithes to Delphi (Argument 2 and 3 to [Hesiod], *Sc.*). According to that poem Heracles and Iolaus met him in company with Are himself in the precinct of Apollo (58). Clad in his armou the gift of the gods, and drawn by Arion (q.v.; 120) Heracles asked Cycnus to let him pass, then, as he woul not, engaged with him, encouraged by Athena (325 ff.) killed him, and then, when Ares attacked him, wounde the god in the thigh. Pindar (*Ol.* 10. 15) says Heracle fled before Cycnus, which the scholiast explains, quotin Stesichorus, as meaning that he at first fled before Are He also says that Cycnus' object was to build a templ of skulls to Apollo. (2) Son of Poseidon. He was kille by Achilles before Troy, according to several author from the *Cypria* on. Ovid (*Met.* 12. 83 ff.) adds tha he was invulnerable and Achilles choked him to death Poseidon then turned him into a swan (κύκνος). (3) Kin of Liguria, kinsman of Phaethon (q.v.); mourning fo his death, he also became a swan (Hyg. *Fab.* 154. 5) (4) Son of Apollo, a handsome boy. Because a much-tried lover left him, he drowned himself in a lake, ever after frequented by swans, into which he and his mother, who also drowned herself, were turned (Antoninus Liberalis 12).                                   H. J. R.

**CYLON,** an Athenian nobleman; winner of the *diaulos* at Olympia, perhaps in 640 B.C. He married the daughter of Theagenes (q.v. 1), tyrant of Megara, and with his help and a few friends seized the Acropolis at Athens, with a view to a tyranny, in an Olympic year (632 ?). The masses, however, did not follow him, and he was besieged. He himself escaped; his friends surrendered and, though suppliants at an altar, were killed. Hence arose the ἄγος, or taint, which attached to those said to be responsible, especially to Megacles the archon and his family, the Alcmaeonidae (q.v.).                              A. W. G.

**CYME,** the most important and powerful of the Aeolian cities on the seaboard of Asia Minor, occupying a site of natural strength midway between the mouths of the Caicus and the Hermus, and facing north-west towards Lesbos. Its history is a record of external domination, by Persians (though Cyme participated in the Ionian Revolt, and belonged to the Delian League and the second Athenian League), Seleucids, Attalids, and Romans. A severe earthquake devastated the city in A.D. 17. Hesiod's father came from Cyme to Boeotia. Its most distinguished son was Ephorus (q.v.). The inhabitants were famous for their easy-going temperament.
                                                D. E. W. W.

**CYNAETHUS** of Chios, according to schol. Pind. *Nem.* 2. 1, was chief among the later, spurious Homeridae (q.v.), composed the Homeric Hymn to Apollo (cf. Ath. 22 b), and was the first to recite Homer at Syracuse (c. 504 B.C.). How much fact this report contains is debatable.

H. T. Wade-Gery, *Essays in Greek History* (1958), 17 ff.
                                                M. L. W.

**CYNEGEIRUS,** brother of Aeschylus, fought and fell at Marathon (490 B.C.) in a bold attempt to seize a Persian ship by the stern. This exploit was immortalized in the Painted Portico (c. 460), and was variously elaborated by historians (e.g. the source of Justin 2. 9. 16 ff.) and rhetoricians (e.g. Polemon).                          P. T.

**CYNICS** (κυνικοί), followers of the principles of Diogenes of Sinope, who had received the nickname of κύων (dog) because he rejected all conventions, tried to live on nothing, and advocated and practised shamelessness (ἀναίδεια). Since Antisthenes had probably influenced the philosophy of Diogenes, many considered and still consider him the real founder of the sect.

The Cynics were never organized in a school like the Stoics, Epicureans, Peripatetics, etc., and had no elaborate philosophical system. Since therefore everybody was at liberty to adopt those of Diogenes' principles which appealed to him and to neglect the rest, there has been and still is much argument as to who was a true Cynic and who was not. The variety was greatest during the century following the death of Diogenes. His most faithful disciple Crates of Thebes preached the gospel of simplicity and independence, and comforted many in those troubled times by demonstrating that he who needs next to nothing, renounces all possessions, and keeps aloof from social entanglements, can live happily in the midst of war and disorder. Onesicritus adapted Cynic philosophy to the life of a soldier or sailor, and compared Diogenes' principles with those of the Indian ascetics. Bion of Borysthenes and Menippus imitated

Diogenes' caustic wit in their satirical writings. They were the first to mingle Cynicism with Hedonism. Cercidas derived theories of social reform from Cynic doctrines. Crates and Teles originated the type of Cynic who wandered all over Greece with stick and knapsack, teaching and preaching.

After having flourished in the third century B.C., Cynicism gradually faded out in the second and first centuries B.C., retaining only some literary influence (Meleager of Gadara). It was revived in the first century after Christ. The beginnings of this revival are unknown; but under the reign of Vespasian and his successors the Orient and Rome swarmed with Cynic beggar philosophers (Dio Chrys. 32. 10). Educated men like Dio himself, however, also adhered to Cynic principles; and the contrast between the true Cynic and the depraved Cynicism of the beggar philosophers became a commonplace in the literature of the Empire (Dio, Lucian, Julian). While the aristocratic opposition to the emperors was connected with Stoicism, middle-class criticism was sometimes voiced by Cynics who contrasted their ideal of the philosopher king with the actual conduct of the emperors. They therefore were frequently banished from the capital.

Outstanding among the Cynics of the first and second century after Christ were Demetrius, Dio, Demonax, Peregrinus Proteus, Oenomaus of Gadara, Sostratus, and Theagenes. Only very few Cynics of the following centuries acquired any renown. The last one mentioned by name is Sallustius, who lived at the end of the fifth century (*Suda*, s.v.; Dam. *Isid.* 342ª 27 ff.). But the Cynic beggar philosophers are frequently alluded to in literature up to the sixth century.

D. R. Dudley, *A History of Cynicism* (1938); F. Sayre, *The Greek Cynics* (1948); R. Höistad, *Cynic Hero and Cynic King* (1948).
                                                K. VON F.

**CYPARISSUS** (Κυπάρισσος), i.e. Cypress, in mythology son of Telephus (q.v. 1), a Cean (Ov. *Met.* 10. 106 ff.), who grieved so much at accidentally killing a pet stag that the gods turned him into the mournful tree; or a Cretan, who was so metamorphosed while fleeing from the attentions of Apollo, or Zephyrus (Servius on *Aen.* 3. 680).                                             H. J. R.

**CYPRIAN** (THASCIUS CAECILIUS CYPRIANUS), c. A.D. 200–58. Son of rich parents possibly of senatorial rank, he became bishop of Carthage (248) soon after baptism and was quickly beset by Decius' persecution (250), for which his writings are a major source. His letters and tracts, from which much of the old Latin Bible can be reconstructed, deal mainly with difficulties within the Christian community resulting from the persecution, especially the terms and proper authority for restoration of apostates and the avoidance of a split between the rival advocates of laxity and rigour. In 256–7 his theology led to a split with Rome, whose Bishop Stephen recognized the baptism of Novatian's community (since 251 separated on rigorist grounds). In Valerian's persecution (257) he was exiled to Curubis, and on 14 Sept. 258 executed at Carthage, the authorities treating him with the respect due to his class. More an administrator than a thinker, he writes with the effortless superiority of a high Roman official, liking correct procedure and expecting his clergy and *plebs* (and in practice his episcopal colleagues) to accept his authority. He speaks of bishops as magistrates, *iudices vice Christi*, and his language finds many analogies in Roman law. His application of juridical categories to the conception of the church permanently influenced Western catholicism. His *Life* by his deacon Pontius, the earliest Christian biography, aims to show him as the equal of the glorious martyr Perpetua, pride of African Christianity.

Ed. W. von Hartel (*CSEL* 3); Letters, ed. L. Bayard (1945); *Passio*, ed. R. Reitzenstein, Sitz. Heidelberg 1913; *de Unitate*, ed. M. Bévenot, *The Tradition of MSS* (1961). E. W. Benson, *Cyprian* (1897); H. Koch, *Cyprianische Untersuchungen* (1926); A. Beck, *Römisches Recht bei Tertullian und Cyprian* (1930). H. C.

**CYPRIOT SYLLABARY,** the system of writing native to Cyprus between the beginning of the seventh and the end of the third century B.C. It is also known as the Classical Syllabary, to distinguish it from the undeciphered Cypro-Minoan scripts found in the island from 1550 to 1050 B.C. and themselves derived from the Cretan Linear A. Undoubtedly descended from these—from which, however, it is separated by a lacuna covering the whole of the Cypro-Geometric period—the Classical Syllabary is subdivided into Paphian, confined to Paphos and archaic Curium, and the Common Cypriot of the rest of the island. It is exclusively the vehicle both of the Cypro-Arcadian dialect and of the still unintelligible Eteo-Cypriot language. Of some 800 texts now known to us, quite the most celebrated is the Bronze Tablet of Idalium. The syllabary now consists of fifty-six signs, five vowels (without distinction between the long and the short) and fifty-one combinations of consonant and vowel. The Cypriot Syllabary was deciphered by G. Smith in 1871.

O. Masson, *Inscriptions Chypriotes Syllabiques* (1961). T. B. M.

**CYPRUS** is an island in the Levant some 50 miles south of Cilicia Tracheia. Its extreme measurement is 140 by 60 miles. It is shaped like the skin of an animal, with the neck pointing towards north Syria. Excavations have revealed a distinctive Neolithic culture of high quality, which began before the outset of the sixth millennium B.C. with a preceramic phase, closed about 2300 B.C. with the chalcolithic. In the Early Bronze Age intruders from western Anatolia arrived in such strength that the earlier culture was speedily submerged; prosperity increased, more particularly on the north coast, and the beginnings of urbanization can be detected. Contacts with Asia Minor and Syria were superseded in the Late Bronze Age by Aegean influences: the first Mycenaeans arrived towards the end of the fifteenth century, traders and colonists established themselves during the fourteenth, soon after the middle of the thirteenth massive immigration, extending throughout the island to both town and country, caused the native culture, hitherto distinct, to become fused with the Mycenaean. All the main elements of Mycenaean life have now been found, except Mycenaean architecture, tomb-types and road-systems. The mining and smelting of copper, attested for the Early Bronze Age, were extensively practised. Enkomi, predecessor of Salamis (q.v.), appears to have been the chief Mycenaean city, and its close connexions with Syria are illustrated by finds at Ras Shamra (Ugarit). Among Aegean imports were two modes of syllabic writing called Cypro-Minoan, of which the earlier has been ascribed to the sixteenth century. These scripts, which have not been deciphered, survived in the Cypriot Syllabary (q.v.) as a vehicle for Greek down to about 200 B.C. Inscriptions also prove the survival into the Hellenistic age of a non-Greek tongue. The native name of the island in Mycenaean times seems to have been Alashia, as in the Hittite and Egyptian texts; but *Kypros* is attested by the Pylos tablets of the thirteenth century. Egyptian connexions, constant in the Late Bronze Age, may indicate a temporary domination in the fifteenth century.

Cyprus was not directly affected by the Dorian invasion and no Dorian settlement was made in the island—although its neighbour Rhodes was completely dorianized;

nor is it likely that its population received any reinforcement in the Age of Migrations. The Greek stock, which took root in the Mycenaean period, should therefore be exclusively Achaean. That this was in fact the case is proved by the survival of Achaean dialect forms (mostly as Arcadian) in the Cypriot Greek of the Classical age. The survival of the Bronze Age scripts also testifies to the absence of any drastic change at the beginning of the Iron Age. But Cyprus had some share in the general changes of the time, and about 1000 B.C. Iron Age peoples from Syria appear to have immigrated: Cypriot art was again altered and deeply modified. Towards the close of the ninth century Phoenicians from Tyre colonized the ancient Greek city of Citium, the Kittim of the Bible; and their influence, although never profound, reached a climax in the fourth century, when much of central Cyprus came within their control. The island was known to Homer, but not intimately. By 709 Cyprus had passed under Assyrian overlordship. More than half a century of independence, however, preceded annexation by Amasis, it would seem, shortly after 570; and until 525 it was ruled by Euelthon of Salamis as governor for the Egyptians. Each Cypriot city retained, however, a semi-autonomous kingship; these kingdoms went back to the Bronze Age, and they continued down to Ptolemaic times.

In 525 Cyprus fell to the Persians under Cambyses. In 498 a Cypriot rising in sympathy with the Ionian Revolt was crushed. After the Persian Wars Cyprus was briefly liberated by Cimon; but the island did not again enjoy freedom from Persian overlordship and the Phoenicians whom this favoured until Evagoras of Salamis, one of the greatest of Cypriots, organized in 411 a wider movement of philhellenism. Persian control, re-established after the fall of Evagoras, was conceded by Greece in 387 at the Peace of Antalcidas. In 351 the nine kings of Cyprus engaged in a revolt which seems to have been short-lived. In 333 the island declared for Alexander, and in his capture of Tyre its fleet was a decisive factor. On Alexander's death Cyprus passed first to Antigonus and then to Ptolemy. By him the kingships which had survived from Mycenaean times were suppressed and the cities furnished with the democratic institutions of the Greek city-state—a form of government to which they did not take readily. The island remained under the Ptolemaic dynasty for nearly two and a half centuries. It was annexed by Rome in 58 B.C. and attached to the province of Cilicia. Presented by Caesar to Cleopatra in 47 but reclaimed by Augustus after Actium, Cyprus was ceded in 22 B.C. by him to the Senate, to become a minor senatorial province. Such it remained until the reforms of Diocletian.

J. L. Myres, *Handbook of the Cesnola Collection* (1914); S. Casson, *Ancient Cyprus* (1937); Sir G. Hill, *A History of Cyprus* (1940); C. F. A. Schaeffer, *Enkomi-Alasia* (1952); P. Dikaios, *A Guide to the Cyprus Museum* (1953); *The Swedish Cyprus Expedition*, iv. 1A, *The Stone Age and the Early Bronze Age*, P. Dikaios and J. Stewart (1962); iv. 2, *The Geometric, Archaic and Classical Periods*, E. Gjerstad (1948); iv. 3, *The Hellenistic and Roman Periods*, O. Vessberg and A. Westholm (1956); V. Karageorghis, *Arch. Anz.* 1963, 498 ff.; Jones, *Cities E. Rom. Prov.*, ch. xiii; H. W. Catling, *Cypriot Bronzework in the Mycenaean World* (1964). T. B. M.

**CYPSĔLUS,** tyrant of Corinth *c.* 657–625 B.C., son of Ëétion, who traced descent from the pre-Dorian Lapithi, and Labda, a lady of the Dorian clan of the Bacchiadae, overthrew the long-established oligarchical rule of the Bacchiadae at Corinth. He soon obtained the support of the Oracle at Delphi, which issued *vaticinia post eventum*; for instance, that his career was foretold and that he escaped destruction by the Bacchiads only through being hidden as a babe in a jar (*cypsele*). Herodotus calls him bloodthirsty, but later writers contrast his mild rule with that of his son Periander. He had no bodyguard; probably his severity was confined to rival aristocrats while the masses supported him. The fine local pottery (late Proto-corinthian and early Corinthian) was exported (especially to the West) in immense quantities throughout his reign. On the route to Italy and Sicily he founded the colonies of Leucas, Ambracia, and Anactorium. The earliest Corinthian coins may go back to him, as may also some of the dedications made by his house at Olympia and Delphi.

E. Will, *Korinthiaka* (1955); P. N. Ure, *Origin of Tyranny* (1922), ch. 7, footnotes; A. Andrewes, *The Greek Tyrants* (1956).
P. N. U.; N. G. L. H.

**CYPSELUS, CHEST OF,** a chest of cedar-wood decorated with figures in ivory, gold, and wood, exhibited at Olympia in the temple of Hera. It is said to have been the one in which the infant Cypselus (q.v.) was hidden, and afterwards to have been dedicated by either Cypselus or his son Periander. Nothing of this famous chest survives, but Pausanias' long description of the decorations (5. 17. 5) suggests that they were in the style of the vase-paintings of that time, i.e. of the seventh to sixth century B.C. The shape of the chest was doubtless that of the *kibotoi* that appear on Greek vases from the sixth century down. A contemporary dedication by the Cypselids is the inscribed gold bowl in the Boston Museum.
S. C.; G. M. A. R.

**CYRANIDES** (Βίβλοι κυρανίδες or κοιρανίδες), a Greek work, in four books, on the magical curative properties of stones, plants, and animals. The name is of uncertain origin. If κυρανίδες is its original form, this may mean 'inscribed on columns' (from a Coptic word)—that being the account the work itself gives of its history; if κοιρανίδες, it means 'queens among books'. The compilation may be ascribed to the first or second century A.D., though part of it may go back to the Hellenistic age. It describes itself as the work partly of Cyranus king of Persia and partly of Harpocration (the medical and astrological writer).

Ed. C. E. Ruelle in F. de Mély, *Les Lapidaires de l'antiquité et du moyen âge,* ii (1898–9). W. D. R.

**CYRENAICS,** the 'minor Socratic' school founded at Cyrene by Aristippus (q.v. 1 and 2), which became the pioneer of Epicureanism. The chief other members were Theodorus, Hegesias, and Anniceris. The main tenet of the school was the treatment of the pleasures of the senses as the end of life. The school seems to have come to an end c. 275 B.C.

G. Giannantoni, *I Cirenaici* (1958); E. Mannebach, *Aristippi et Cyrenaicorum Fragmenta* (1961). W. D. R.

**CYRENE,** the great North-African city, situated some miles inland in the fertile territory called after it Cyrenaica. This area lies roughly midway between the Egyptian Delta to the east and Tunisia to the west, but deserts and great distances cut it off from the other civilized regions of Africa, and its natural contacts are northward, with Crete and Greece. The ancient site has been extensively explored archaeologically, so that the city's material remains are well known from its earliest days down to the seventh century A.D.; they contribute richly to our knowledge of ancient art, architecture, and epigraphy.

Cyrene was founded from Thera in c. 630 B.C., under the leadership of Battus. Its foundation is perhaps better known than that of any other Greek colony of the archaic period, in spite of some legendary contamination, because we have not only an exceptionally full account in Herodotus (4. 150–8) but also, it seems, the substance of the actual decree of Thera arranging for the colonization, preserved in a fourth-century inscription of Cyrene (*SEG* ix. 3). These sources reveal the arrangements appropriate to a forced colonial expedition made necessary by food shortage.

The city prospered greatly and received further settlers from Greece more than once; it founded other cities itself in the neighbouring region, as Barca, Euhesperides. Cyrene's territory was rich in corn, wool, oil, and silphium (trade in this medicinal plant became a monopoly of the Battiad kings); the horses were famous. Battus and his successors (the Battiads) ruled as kings for about 200 years, though not without political strife; see Hdt. 4. 159–64. During this time they beat off an Egyptian attack (c. 570), but submitted to Cambyses in 525 and formed part of Darius' empire. Cyrene regained its independence, probably between 479 and 474, and sheltered the Athenian survivors from the Egyptian Expedition (c. 455). The Battiad monarchy ended, probably c. 440, when Arcesilaus IV was deposed and a democratic reform took place, with extension of citizenship and tribal reorganization on Cleisthenic lines.

Cyrene submitted to Alexander the Great, but a period of confusion and civil war followed his death (323), when a Spartan leader captured and lost the city. This enabled Ptolemy to send Ophellas (q.v.) to subdue the whole country. It was probably at this time that the 'Ptolemaic' constitution was introduced, known to us from an inscription (*SEG* ix. 1: cf. M. Cary, *JHS* 1928, 222 ff.: others would date it later, e.g. even c. 265 B.C.). It established a liberal oligarchy, with a privileged citizen body of 10,000, two councils, and a popular court of perhaps 2,101; Ptolemy was permanent *startegos*. After a brief revolt by Ophellas (312–309) and a popular rising (c. 306) Ptolemy reconquered Cyrene and installed as governor his stepson Magas who continued to act for him until 274 when Magas married Apama, daughter of Antiochus I of Syria and declared his independence. However, he was reconciled with Ptolemy II before his death in 253. At this time, it seems, the cities of Cyrenaica sent for two philosophers, Ecdelus and Demophanes(q.v.), who devised a federal constitution for all the cities: they probably also established the port of Cyrene as a separate city, named Apollonia. Cyrenaica still remained under Egyptian control until the Roman Senate assigned it as a separate kingdom to Euergetes, brother of Ptolemy VI Philometor (163): when the brother became king in Egypt as Ptolemy VII Euergetes (145), Cyrenaica was again united to Egypt. On his earlier inoperative will of 154, bequeathing Cyrene conditionally to Rome in the event of his early death, see *JHS* 1933, 263 ff. In fact he left it to his illegitimate son Ptolemy Apion, who in turn bequeathed it to Rome (96) which annexed the royal land but left the cities free. Disorders led Rome to establish it as a regular province in 74, to which Crete was added in 67. After Antony had temporarily granted it to his daughter Cleopatra Selene, Augustus re-established it, with Crete, as a regular senatorial province (cf. CYRENE, EDICTS OF).

Cyrene suffered much devastation from the Jewish revolt in the reign of Trajan, and Hadrian brought in fresh colonists. In the Later Empire, Cyrene and the other cities of the Pentapolis (q.v.) were hard pressed by nomadic tribes from the desert.

U. von Wilamowitz-Moellendorff, *Kyrene* (1928); L. Malten, *Kyrene* (1911); J. Boardman, *The Greeks Overseas* (1964), 169 ff.; G. Pesce, *Enc. dell'arte antica,* s.v. Cirene (1959); Ruggiero, *Diz. Epigr.,* s.v. 'Cyrenae' (Paribeni), supplemented by *SEG* ix; E. S. G. Robinson, *British Museum Catalogue of the Greek Coins of Cyrenaica* (1929); on the foundation and *SEG* ix. 3, L. H. Jeffery, *Hist.* 1961, 139 ff., A. J. Graham, *JHS* 1960, 94 ff., and *Colony and Mother City in Ancient Greece* (1964), ch. 4 and app. 2; F. Chamoux, *Cyrène sous la monarchie des Battiades* (1953); Jones, *Cities E. Rom. Prov.,* ch. 12; P. Romanelli, *La Cirenaica romana* (1943); *PBSR* 1958, 30 ff. and 137 ff.; 1964, 1 ff. A. J. G. and B. H. W.

**CYRENE, EDICTS OF,** five edicts of Augustus, discovered in an inscription of Cyrene, published in 1927. The first four belong to 7–6 B.C. and apply to the senatorial province of Cyrenaica and Crete alone; the fifth (which introduces a *senatus consultum*) belongs to 4 B.C. and applies to the whole Empire. The documents definitively prove that Augustus received an *imperium maius* over the senatorial provinces and demonstrate the emperor's ably balanced policy towards the provincials.

In the first edict Augustus establishes the procedure that criminal cases involving a capital charge against a Greek should be tried by mixed Graeco-Roman juries of a certain census, unless the accused prefers to have an entirely Roman jury. The system is modelled on the *quaestiones perpetuae* of Rome. Roman citizens except Greeks who had received Roman citizenship are not allowed to be accusers in cases involving murders of Greeks. The second edict approves the conduct of the governor towards some Roman citizens. The third establishes that the provincials who have obtained Roman citizenship should continue to share the burdens of their original Greek community unless they had special privileges. Under the fourth, all legal actions between Greeks, other than capital ones, were to have Greek judges, unless the defendant preferred Roman judges. The fifth edict communicates a *SC* which establishes that charges of extortion can be examined by five senatorial judges, after a preliminary examination by the whole Senate. This marks a beginning of the judicial function of the Senate.

TEXT in *SEG* ix. 1, 1944, v. 8. Short English Commentary: J. G. C. Anderson, *JRS* 1927, 33 ff.; 1929, 219 ff.
A. v. Premerstein, *Sav. Zeitschr.* 1928, 419 ff.; 1931, 431 ff.; J. Stroux–L. Wenger, *Abh. d. Bayer. Akad.* 1928, 2 Abh.; F. de Visscher, *Les Édits d'Auguste découverts à Cyrène* (1940). H. M. Last, *JRS* 1945, 93 ff.; A. N. Sherwin-White, *PBSR* 1949, 5 ff.; J. Bleicken, *Senatsgericht und Kaisergericht* (1962).     A. M.

**CYRIL OF ALEXANDRIA** (d. A.D. 444), bishop from 412 after his uncle Theophilus. He continued Theophilus' suppression in Egypt of all error (paganism, Judaism, heresy), though his monks probably had not his approval for their murder of Hypatia (q.v.) in 415. Polemic in his Old Testament commentaries presupposes the continuing vitality of pagan cult in Egypt. He replaced the Isis-cult at Menuthis by translating thither relics of SS. Cyrus and John. About 435–40 he wrote twenty books (only 1–10 extant in full) refuting Julian (q.v. 1) point by point, so that his refutation is the principal source for reconstructing Julian's work, besides containing many quotations from Porphyry, Hermes Trismegistus (qq.v.), and other pagan sources. In 430–1 his zeal for orthodoxy and the honour of Alexandria led him to attack Nestorius of Constantinople, who was deposed at the council of Ephesus (431). But the resulting schism between Antioch and Alexandria could be healed (433) only by cautious concessions on Cyril's part, and in the controversy between the 'monophysites' and the defenders of the 'two-nature' Christology of the council of Chalcedon (451) both sides were able to appeal to his statements, the interpretation of which became an issue in theological debate under Justinian.

Ed. Migne, *PG* lxviii–lxxvii; J. Quasten, *Patrology* 3 (1960), 116 ff.     H. C.

**CYRIL OF JERUSALEM,** bishop from c. A.D. 350, d. 386. His twenty-four catechetical lectures are a basic source for liturgical history and for the topography of fourth-century Jerusalem. He wrote with a strong sense that he presided over the mother of all churches whence the faith had spread to the West, and advanced the ecclesiastical status of his see despite fierce opposition from the provincial metropolis, Caesarea.

Ed. W. K. Reischl and J. Rupp (1848–60); J. Quasten, *Patrology* 3 (1960), 362 ff.     H. C.

**CYRUS** (1) (*Kurash*), son of Cambyses and descendant of Achaemenes, the founder of the Achaemenid Persian Empire (559–529 B.C.). According to a legend of his birth and upbringing (Hdt. 1. 107–30), he was related to Astyages, king of Media (denied by Ctesias, *Persica* exc 2). Heir only to the throne of Anshan, he soon challenged his Median overlord. Capturing Astyages, he entered Ecbatana in 549 B.C. Thenceforward the Persians became the ruling race, though their kinsmen the Medes still held privileged positions in the State. Cyrus' defeat of Croesus of Lydia (Hdt. 1. 71 ff.) gave him Asia Minor, that of Nabonidus Babylonia, Assyria, Syria, and Palestine. Campaigns in the north and east extended his boundaries over almost all the Iranian plateau. The extent of his conquests is known from the lists of peoples subject to Darius. This vast empire he administered with wisdom and tolerance. In the conquered territories he was welcomed as a liberator; he respected their customs and religion, honouring Marduk at Babylon and freeing the captive Jews to build their temple in Jerusalem. To the Greeks he became a model of the upright ruler.

There are conflicting legends of his death (Xen. *Cyr.* 8. 7. 2 ff.; Hdt. 1. 204 ff.); it is probable that he died in battle. His grave is at Pasargadae (Strabo 15. 730; Arrian, *Anab.* 6. 29. 8).

The best sources for Cyrus' reign are the official cuneiform records.
F. H. Weissbach, *Keilinschriften der Achämeniden* (1911).
CLASSICAL SOURCES. Hdt. bk. 1; Ctesias, *Persica* bks. 7–9; Xen. *Cyropaedia* (a fanciful biography).
MODERN WORKS. J. V. Prašek, 'Kyros der Grosse', *Alte Orient* xiii. 3 (1912); F. H. Weissbach, *PW* Suppl. iv (1924), s.v. 'Kyros (6)'; W. Eilers, 'Kyros', *BN* 1964. *See also under* ACHAEMENIDS.
M. S. D.; R. N. F.

**CYRUS** (2) II, younger son of Darius II and Parysatis, and his mother's favourite. He was given an overriding command in Asia Minor in 408 B.C. when he had barely come of age. In Sardes he met Lysander; their friendly co-operation meant victory for Sparta in the Peloponnesian War. Cyrus was summoned to the court in 405 on his father's fatal illness, but Arsaces, the elder brother, succeeded as Artaxerxes II, and only Parysatis' influence saved Cyrus when accused of treason by Tissaphernes. On his return to Asia Minor he began to gather mercenaries (amongst whom Xenophon enlisted), ostensibly for an expedition against Pisidia. In the spring of 401 he set out with some 20,000 men; his true destination was not revealed until the army struck the Euphrates at Thapsacus. At Cunaxa (q.v.), some 45 miles from Babylon, Artaxerxes made his stand. Cyrus' deficiency in cavalry proved fatal, and he lost his life in a desperate attack on his brother's bodyguard. He had youthful faults of impetuosity and superficiality, but his personal charm, his energy, and his gift of leadership, were the qualities of a potentially great ruler.

Xenophon, *Anabasis* and *Hellenica*; Ctesias, *Persica*. F. H. Weissbach, *PW* Suppl. iv (1924), s.v. 'Kyros (7)'.    D. E. W. W.

**CYTHERA,** an island off Cape Malea (Peloponnesus) with rich *murex* deposits, which attracted an early Minoan colony (MM II–LM I). Perhaps c. 550 B.C. Sparta seized it from Argos, installing a garrison and governor (Κυθηροδίκης); its inhabitants became *perioikoi* (q.v.). An obvious strategic threat to Sparta, 'better sunk beneath the sea' said Chilon (q.v.), it was captured by Nicias (q.v. 1) and held for Athens from 424 to 421 and again from 393 to 386. Lost to Sparta in 195 (*see* LACONIA) it was restored by Augustus in 21 B.C.

In myth it was the birth-place of Aphrodite (Hes. *Theog.* 192).

P-K, *GL* iii. 2. x (a); *Arch. Rep.* 1963–4, 25 f.; 1964–5, 27; 1965–6, 21 f.     W. G. F.

**CYZICUS,** a Milesian colony traditionally founded in 756 B.C. and refounded in 675 (a date corroborated by finds of early pottery), on the island of Arctonnesus, among a Myso-Phrygian population. The site rivalled Byzantium in defensibility and commercial importance. The island could be joined to or cut off from the mainland at will; it sheltered two harbours, and practically all the shipping of the Propontis came to Cyzicus to avoid the inhospitable northern shore. Its coinage of electrum staters, called Cyzicenes, became famous everywhere.

Cyzicus was a member of the Delian League, to which it gave the largest annual contribution from the Hellespontine region, 9 talents. It was the scene of Alcibiades' naval victory over the Spartans in 410. It preserved much of its commercial importance in the fourth century, and continued to do so in the Hellenistic age, when it cultivated especially good relations with the Attalid kings. Under Rome it remained a free city and was rewarded

with an increase of its already large territory for its courageous resistance in 74 to Mithridates. Loss of freedom for a time and some diminution of territory followed the killing of Roman citizens, probably trade rivals, in 20 B.C. Further outbreaks caused definitive loss of the privilege in A.D. 25. Hadrian built a huge temple at Cyzicus, probably giving the city at the same time the titles of *metropolis* and *neocorus*. Later emperors gave aid after earthquakes. An earthquake in the reign of Justinian (6 Sept. 543) gave him a chance to use the marbles of Cyzicus in Saint Sophia.

Strabo 12. 575–6. F. W. Hasluck, *Cyzicus* (1910); *Arch. Rep.* 1959–60, 34; Jones, *Cities E. Rom. Prov.*; C. Roebuck, *Ionian Trade and Colonization* (1959); Magie, *Rom. Rule Asia Min.* 81 and index.
T. R. S. B.

# D

**DACIA** was situated in the loop of the lower Danube, consisting mainly of the plateau of Transylvania, but extending in a wider sense eastward to the Sereth and north to the Vistula. The Dacians were an agricultural people, but under the influence of Celtic invaders in the fourth century B.C. they absorbed Celtic culture and developed the gold, silver, and iron mines of the Carpathians. From c. 300 B.C. they traded with the Greeks, who frequently confused them with the Getae (q.v.), by way of the Danube; from the second century they also had relations with the Greek cities of Illyria and with Italian traders. Their chief import was wine.

The separate Dacian tribes were united by Burebistas (q.v.) c. 60 B.C. and under him they conquered Celtic and Illyrian peoples to the south and west, threatening the Roman province of Macedonia. After his death the power of Dacia declined because of internal struggles. For a time the Dacians were regarded as a serious threat. Caesar was planning a campaign against them before his death (Suet. *Div. Iul.* 44. 3). Some years later Octavian (App. *Ill.* 23) also fearing a possible alliance between Antony and the Dacians, sought a marriage alliance with Cotiso, one of the rival Dacian kings (Suet. *Aug.* 63). Under Augustus the Dacians caused few problems, but their military power revived under Decebalus (q.v.) with victories over Oppius Sabinus (85) and Cornelius Fuscus (86). After a Roman victory at Tapae (south-west Transylvania) Domitian made peace, recognizing Decebalus as a client ruler. Conquest of Dacia was effected by Trajan in the First and Second Dacian Wars (101–2, 105, cf. Cass. Dio 58. 6–14). Decebalus' stronghold Sarmizegethusa (Gradistea Muncel south of Oraştie) was taken and destroyed. These campaigns are depicted on the spiral frieze of Trajan's Column (*see* FORUM TRAIANI).

Roman Dacia comprised most of Transylvania, but it did not reach to the Theiss in the west or extend, initially at any rate, beyond the Aluta (*Olt*) in the east. Under Hadrian the province was twice subdivided, into *Superior* and *Inferior* in 118–19, while part of *Superior* was detached to form *Porolissensis*, probably in 124 (cf. *JRS* 1961, 66 f.). A further reorganization occurred probably in 168 when the three provinces (*Tres Daciae*) were placed under one governor.

There was a great influx of people from other provinces into Dacia, especially from the Illyrian and the eastern provinces. Some came as skilled miners, e.g. the Dalmatians at Alburnus Maior (*Roşia Montana*: cf. *CIL* iii. 921 ff.). Cities developed; the most important were the

*coloniae* at Sarmizegethusa and Apulum. As a result of the Gothic invasions (mid third century) Dacia was abandoned under Aurelian (270). In the fourth century Dacia was the name of provinces along the south bank of the lower Danube (cf. *Not. Dign.*, index).

ON DACIAN CULTURE. V. Parvan, *Dacia* (1928).
DACIAN WARS. C. Patsch, *Sitz. Wien* 217, 1 (1937).
THE ROMAN PROVINCE. C. Daicoviciu, *La Transylvanie dans l'antiquité* (published in *La Transylvanie*, Bucureşti, 1938); A. Stein *Die Reichsbeamten von Dazien* (Budapest, 1944), supplemented by C. Daicoviciu and D. Protase, *JRS* 1961, 63 ff.
SARMIZEGETHUSA. C. and H. Daicoviciu, *Sarmizegethusa* (*Les Citadelles et les agglomérations daciques des Monts d'Oraştie*) (Bucarest, 1963). M. C.; J. J. W.

**DAEDALUS,** a legendary artist, craftsman, and inventor of archaic times. He has a significant name, for artful works were called δαίδαλα. His father (Paus. 9. 3. 2) Eupalamus or 'Skillhand' was descended from Erechtheus (Pherecydes, *FGrH* i. 146). Daedalus was born in Athens, but had to leave the city because he killed his nephew Perdix who surpassed him in skill (*Suda*, s.v. Πέρδικος ἱερόν). He went to Crete, where he made the cow for Pasiphaë, the labyrinth for the Minotaur, a dancing ground (χορός), a small wooden statue of Aphrodite, and the famous thread for Ariadne. Enraged by the aid that Daedalus had rendered to Pasiphaë, King Minos imprisoned him and his son Icarus, but Daedalus constructed two pairs of artificial wings and flew away. He crossed safely to Sicily; Icarus, however, approached the sun too closely so that the wax of his wings melted and he drowned in the Aegean Sea.

In Sicily Daedalus was protected by the Sicanian king, Cocalus; Minos, who arrived in pursuit of him, was suffocated in a steam bath (constructed by Daedalus?) by the daughters of Cocalus (A. C. Pearson, *Fragments of Sophocles* (1917) ii,3). Daedalus had constructed in Sicily a reservoir for the river Alabon, a steam-bath at Selinus, a fortress near Agrigentum, and a terrace for the temple of Aphrodite on Mt. Eryx (Diod. 4. 78 after Antiochus).

Daedalus was also considered the inventor of carpentry and of such things as the saw, the axe, the plumb-line, the auger, and glue. He also invented the mast and the yards of boats (Pliny, *HN* 7. 198). As tangible evidence of his skill a folding chair was shown in the temple of Athena Polias on the Acropolis (Paus. 1. 27. 1). His skill in metalwork was attested by the golden honeycomb in the temple of Aphrodite on Eryx. A multitude of archaic temples and archaic statues, especially wooden ones in

Greece and Italy, were believed to be by his hand (Overbeck, *Antike Schriftquellen* (1868), 119). He first made figures which had open eyes, walked, and moved their arms from their sides, whereas earlier works had their feet closed and their arms fixed to their sides (*Suda Δαιδάλου ποιήματα*). Several later archaic artists were considered pupils of Daedalus, and a demos of the *phyle* Cecropis in Attica was named the Daedalids.

The legend of Daedalus unites many heterogeneous elements. Certain features seem to go back to Cretan and Dorian tales, others betray an Attic origin. The propensity of the Greeks to recognize their own gods and legends in foreign countries enabled them to recognize works of Daedalus in architecture and sculpture of the natives in Sicily, Sardinia, and even in the pyramids of Egypt (Diod. 4. 30; 1. 97; Paus. 10. 17. 3). Since the name of Daedalus had come to stand for art of extremely archaic character, any very archaic statue was easily ascribed to Daedalus. The notion of uncanny superhuman skill inherent in the character of Daedalus accounts for such folkloristic traits as the legend of living statues (Pind. *OL.* 7. 52; Eur. *Hec.* 836; F. Brommer, *MDAI* 1950, 80). The chronology of the Daedalids being faulty (Robert, *Archäologische Märchen* (1886)), it is not possible to determine the lifetime of Daedalus from ancient authors. It is also controversial whether a historical artist Daedalus gave the impetus to the formation of the legends, or is a purely mythological figure representative of accomplished craftsmanship.

Daedalus is represented on vases, gems, and in sculpture in Greece (J. D. Beazley, *JHS* 1927, 222) and Etruria (G. M. A. Hanfmann, *AJArch.* 1935, 189 ff.), and in Roman wall-painting and sculpture usually with Icarus or Pasiphaë.

C. Picard, *Manuel arch. grecque* i (1935), 77; W. Miller, *Daedalus and Thespis* (1931), ii. 1; B. Schweitzer, *Xenokrates von Athen* (1932), 20. T. J. Dunbabin, *PBSR* 1948, 1; G. Becatti, *Röm. Mitt.* 1853–4, 22; V. Cronin, *The Golden Honeycomb* (1954); A. van Windekens, *BN* 1958, 161. G. M. A. H.

**DAIMACHUS** of Plataea (first half of 4th c. B.C.), perhaps the first of several Boeotian writers of Hellenica, is Ephorus' source for early Boeotian history, and is important if Jacoby rightly assigns to him the *Hellenica* from Oxyrhynchus (q.v.; *Gött. Nachr.* 1924, i), whose author shows a close knowledge of Boeotian affairs. A younger Daimachus wrote Ἰνδικά a century later.

*FGrH* ii A. 65 and 66. G. L. B.

**DAIMON** (δαίμων). In Homer this word, which means 'allotter' (of fate, cf. Dem. 18. 208), may be applied to one of the great gods, but its use has peculiar features. It has no feminine form and rarely a plural (this is frequent in later literature). It has been observed that, whilst the Homeric poet in his own narrative constantly refers to the anthropomorphic gods, in the words which he puts in the mouth of his personages the cause of events is ascribed not to these but to a *daimon*, or a general phrase, θεός τις, θεοί, Ζεύς, is used: these phrases, however, are never exactly equivalent to *daimon*. *Daimon* appears to correspond to the supernatural power, the mana, not as a general conception but in its special manifestations, and always with the overtones of a personal agent. δαιμόνιος is 'strange', 'incomprehensible', even 'uncanny'. As *daimon* refers to the lot of a man, the word comes sometimes near the significance of 'fate', σὺν δαίμονι, πάρος τοι δαίμονα δώσω. An expression occurring in tragedy, ὁ παρὼν δαίμων, proves that the old reference to a special manifestation was not forgotten, although a general sense is frequent in later writers, e.g. in the compounds ὀλβιοδαίμων, εὐδαίμων, κακοδαίμων. Heraclitus says: ἦθος ἀνθρώπῳ δαίμων 'a man's character is his fate', but 'fate' is not quite a correct translation. Finally people spoke of a good and

an evil *daimon* of a man, which follows him through his life. The application of the word to cult gods is extremely rare, but it was appropriate to less well-defined gods. Hesiod calls the deceased of the Golden Age 'wealth-giving' *daimones*, and Aeschylus in the same sentence calls the ghost of Darius δαίμων and θεός. Thus the word seemed to be appropriate to lesser gods. Since Plato *daimones* were conceived as beings intermediate between gods and men, and Xenocrates allowed that they were of a mixed nature, and that ἡμέραι ἀποφράδες (*see* APOPHRADES) and festivals involving mourning, fasting, or improper language belonged to beings of this nature— an idea developed by Plutarch (R. Heinze, *Xenocrates* (1892), 167 f.). Finally, Christianity which made the pagan gods evil beings impressed upon the word the significance which 'demon' now has in common language.

M. P. Nilsson, *ARW* 1924, 363 ff.; *GGR* i². 216 ff.; H. J. Rose, *Harv. Theol. Rev.* 1935, 243; E. Hedén, *Homerische Götterstudien* (1912); E. Brunius–Nilsson, *Δαιμόνιε* (Diss. Uppsala, 1955); H. Nowak, *Zur Entwicklungsgesch. des Begr. D.* (Diss. Bonn, 1960); H. J. Rose and others, *La Notion du divin* (*Entretiens sur l'ant. class.* i, 1952). M. P. N.

**DALMATIA,** a Roman province on the east coast of the Adriatic north of Epirus, took its name from the Delmatae, a warlike Illyrian tribe, partly celticized, who inhabited the region behind Salonae (q.v.). At one time they were subject to the Illyrian kingdom (*see* ILLYRICUM) but revolted from Gentius and maintained their independence after his defeat by the Romans (168 B.C.). Because of their attacks on Roman allies they were invaded by the Romans in 156–155 B.C. and their capital Delminium (Županac: cf. Patsch, *PW*, s.v. Delminium) was destroyed. More campaigns against them were made in 118–117 and 78–77; in 51 they defeated troops sent against them by Caesar and during the Civil War they sided with the Pompeians and defeated Caesar's legates Q. Cornificius and A. Gabinius (48–47 B.C.). In 46, however, they submitted through a threat of invasion by Caesar himself. After further fighting under P. Vatinius (45–44), Octavian conquered most of their territory (34–33). After more disturbances (16 B.C.), they were attacked by Tiberius (11–9 B.C.), and finally conquered in the great Illyrian rebellion of A.D. 6–9, led by the Daesitiates of Bosnia (*Bellum Delmaticum, ILS* 3320). Probably in A.D. 9 Illyricum was divided into two imperial provinces, *Illyricum superius* and *inferius*, known by the Flavian period as Dalmatia and Pannonia (q.v.). The Roman province of Dalmatia included Illyricum south of the Save and reached eastward almost to the Danube. It was governed by *legati Augusti pro praetore* of consular rank who resided at Salonae, of whom one Camillus Scribonianus (q.v. 1) revolted in A.D. 42. Following the reforms of Gallienus (mid third century), the senatorial legates were superseded by equestrian *praesides*. Under Diocletian Dalmatia was divided into *Dalmatia*, with capital at Salonae, and *Praevalitana* or *Praevalis*, capital Scodra; the former was in the *dioecesis Pannoniarum*, the latter in *dioecesis Moesiarum*.

C. Patsch, *Sitz. Wien* 1932, 1933; *Archaeologisch-epigraphische Untersuchungen zur Geschichte der röm. Provinz Dalmatien* i–viii (Wissenschaftl. Mitteilungen aus Bosnien und der Hercegovina iv (1896)–xii (1912)). On governors see A. Jagenteufel, *Die Statthalter der römischen Provinz Dalmatia von Augustus bis Diokletian* (Öst. Akad. der Wiss., Schriften der Balkankommission, Antiqu. Abteil. XII, Wien, 1958). A. Betz, *Untersuchungen zur Militärgeschichte der römischen Provinz Dalmatien* (1939); G. Alföldy, *Bevölkerung und Gesellschaft der römischen Provinz Dalmatien* (Budapest, 1965); J. J. Wilkes, *Dalmatia* (1969). F. A. W. S.; J. J. W.

**DAMASCUS** was the capital of Demetrius III and Antiochus XII, under whom it issued municipal coins (some under the name of Demetrias, which the city received during Demetrius' reign). Menaced by the Ituraeans, it invited Aretas III, (q.v.), king of Nabataea, to protect it in 85 B.C., but was independent in 69. Annexed by Pompey in 64, it was granted by Antony to Cleopatra, reannexed by Octavian, granted by Gaius to the Nabataean kingdom, and finally annexed c. 62. It was made a colony by the Emperor Philippus. It derived its wealth from the caravan trade, from its woollen industry, and from the multifarious products of its territory, which included not only its own fertile oasis but from 24 B.C. a large (formerly Ituraean) area up to Mt. Hermon. The main surviving monument is the *peribolos* wall of the temple of Zeus Damascenus, the Semitic god Hadad.

C. Watzinger and K. Wulzinger, *Damaskus* (1922). A. H. M. J.

**DAMASTES** of Sigeum, a contemporary of Herodotus and pupil of Hellanicus (q.v.), wrote on *Events in Greece* (he mentioned a Persian visit of Diotimus, a *strategos* of 433–432 B.C.); on *Poets and Sophists*; on *Peoples and Cities*; on the *Ancestors of those who fought at Troy*: his *Periplus* was based on Hecataeus (q.v. 1). Strabo (1. 3. 1) criticized Eratosthenes for trusting him. Only scanty fragments survive.

*FHG* ii. 64–67; *FGrH* i, no. 5. J. L. M.

**DAMNATIO MEMORIAE.** This formed part of the penalty of *maiestas* (see PERDUELLIO). It implied that the *praenomen* of the condemned man might not be perpetuated in his family, that images of him must be destroyed, and his name erased from inscriptions. Bad emperors were not exempt from such a fate. Nero (Suet. *Nero* 49) and Didius Julianus (Dio Cass. 73. 17) were declared *hostes* and condemned to death by the Senate in their lifetime. In other cases the Senate voted a posthumous *damnatio memoriae* (which included *rescissio actorum*). Claudius prevented the Senate from condemning the memory of Gaius (Dio Cass. 60. 4. 5); but formal decrees were passed after the deaths of Domitian (Suet. *Domit.* 23), Commodus (*Vita* 20), and Elagabalus (*Vita* 17).

F. Vittinghoff, *Der Staatsfeind in der röm. Kaiserzeit* (1936). J. P. B.

**DAMNUM INIURIA DATUM.** Some cases of unlawful damage to property were dealt with in the XII Tables, e.g. damage committed by quadrupeds or in violation of agricultural interests (illicit cutting of trees or crops, grazing on another's pasture, and the like). But these were only special provisions; general rules on this matter were first laid down by a statute of unknown date (probably of the 3rd c. B.C.), *Lex Aquilia*, which introduced civil liability for wilfully or negligently killing or injuring another man's slave or beast (belonging to a herd), and for damage done to other kinds of property by burning, breaking, or destroying. The interpretation of jurists and the praetorian edict considerably extended the narrow provisions of the law to other kinds of damage, enlarged the circle of persons qualified to sue—the *lex* admitted only the owner of the damaged thing—and reformed the manner of assessing damages. The title IX. 2 of the *Digest* demonstrates how fertile was the contribution of the classical jurisprudence in the evolution of these doctrines.

H. F. Jolowicz, *Law Quarterly Review* 1922; D. Daube, ibid. 1936; F. H. Lawson, *Negligence in the Civil Law* (1950). A. B.; B. N.

**DAMOCLES,** courtier of Dionysius I. When he excessively praised the tyrant's happiness, the latter symbolically feasted him with a sword hung by a hair over his head (Cic. *Tusc.* 5. 61, and passim).

**DAMON** (1), Pythagorean from Syracuse, famous for his friendship with Phintias (not Pythias). An oft-told story: Phintias, sentenced to death by Dionysius (I or II), and

reprieved, comes back at the last moment to save Damon who had gone bail for him.

**DAMON** (2), Athenian, one of the earliest and most important Greek writers on music, a pupil of Prodicus and tutor of Pericles, much esteemed by Socrates and Plato. Plato ascribes to him (*Resp.* 400 a–c) views about the ethical effects of various rhythms, and Plato's own views about the ethical effects of different scales can probably also be traced to Damon (*Resp.* 424 c). Much in Aristides Quintilianus is probably due to him. He is said to have invented the 'relaxed Lydian' mode (ἡ ἐπανειμένη Λυδιστί).

Testimonia and fragments in Diels, *Vorsokr.*[11] i. 381–4; F. Lasserre, *Plutarque de la Musique* (1954), 74 ff. W. D. R.

**DAMOPHILUS,** a celebrated painter and modeller. Pliny says that he and a certain Gorgasus 'united both arts in the decoration of the temple of Ceres at Rome near the Circus Maximus' (*HN* 35. 154). The temple was dedicated in 493 and this is early evidence of a Greek artist in Rome. He should probably not be identified with the painter Demophilus of Himera, who was said to have taught Zeuxis (q.v.) (ibid. 61) or with Demophilus the author of a treatise on proportion (Vitr., bk. 7 praef.).

O. Vessberg, *Kunstgeschichte der römischen Republik* (1941), 15 ff. T. B. L. W.

**DAMOPHON** (2nd c. B.C.), sculptor, of Messene, repaired Phidias' Zeus at Olympia. Made statues of gods and goddesses for Messene, Aigion in Achaea, and Megalopolis, and large groups for Messene, Megalopolis, and Lycosura in Arcadia. The last comprised Demeter and Despoina enthroned, Artemis, and a Titan Anytus. The heads of Demeter, Artemis, and Anytus and part of Despoina's veil have been discovered (Winter, *KB* 373. 1–4). The style is academic in its reminiscences of the fifth and fourth centuries. The veil accurately copies contemporary textiles. Other works have been attributed to Damophon on grounds of style.

Overbeck, 745; 1557–64; Lippold, *Griech. Plastik* 350; Bieber, *Sculpt. Hellenist. Age* 158; the veil, A. J. B. Wace, *AJ Arch.* 1934, 107; other works, A. W. Lawrence, *Later Greek Sculpture* (1927), 121. T. B. L. W.

**DAMOXENUS,** New Comedy poet, foreign to Athens, as his name signifies; he mentions Epicurus, and Adaeus of Macedon who perished at Cypsela, 353 B.C. Fr. 2, a cook philosophizes; fr. 3, a handsome youth plays ball.

*FCG* iv. 529 ff.; *CAF* iii. 348 ff.

**DANAUS.** The following genealogy, artificial but not very late (it is due to Pherecydes, fr. 21 Jacoby), shows the relationships of Danaus.

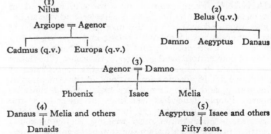

Since the names Aegyptus, Danaus, and Phoenix are simple eponyms of the Egyptians, Danai, and Phoenicians, the artificial nature of the whole is clear; but it may be taken as representing the historical theory of the day. Stubbings (*CAH* 2², 14. 11 ff.) argues for Danaus as a Hyksos refugee and founder of the Shaft grave dynasty at Mycenae. Danaus' direct ancestry is:

(6)
Zeus ⚯ Io

Epaphus

Libye ⚯ Poseidon

Belus          Agenor

This adds the eponym of North Africa to the complex; this detail is as old as Aeschylus, *Supp.* 313 ff.

Of Danaus' daughters, only two are named in any old source (the lists in Apollod. 2. 16–20 and Hyg. *Fab.* 170 are late and artificial). These are Amymone (q.v.), and Hypermestra. Of Aegyptus' sons, only Lynceus has a real name; the rest are given names in the above lists. The two fathers quarrelled; to settle the dispute Aegyptus was desirous that his sons should marry Danaus' daughters, while Danaus and his offspring were strongly opposed. (This has no sociological significance, see Rose in *Folk-Lore* xxvii. 226 ff.) As the weaker party, Danaus and his family fled to Argos, where they claimed help and shelter from their kin; the story, with numerous subsidiary details, is in Apollodorus (2. 12 ff.), Pausanias (2. 16. 1 ff.; 19. 3–7; 25. 4; 37. 1–2); Hyginus (*Fab.* 168 ff.). The oldest parts of it doubtless go back to the *Danais* (Rose, *Handbook of Greek Lit.* (1964), 69) and much is due to the Aeschylean trilogy of which the *Suppliants* is the surviving part. Aegyptus' sons pursued them, and Danaus consented to the marriage, secretly instructing his daughters to kill their husbands on the wedding night. Except Hypermestra, who spared her husband Lynceus and helped him to escape, they obeyed him. Danaus imprisoned Hypermestra, but finally, perhaps through the intervention of Aphrodite (Aeschylus, fr. 44 Nauck), released her.

So far the story is fairly consistent in its main outlines, though many details differ in different authors. It now divides into three main accounts. (*a*) Lynceus returned, killed Danaus and his daughters except Hypermestra, and became king and ancestor of the royal Argive line (schol. Eur. *Hec.* 886). (*b*) The daughters were purified by Athena and Hermes (Apollod. 22) after burying the heads of their husbands in Lerna, their bodies outside the city, a strange detail never satisfactorily explained. Danaus married them off by offering them as prizes in a foot-race (Pind. *Pyth.* 9. 112 ff.). (*c*) They were punished in Hades by being set to fill a leaky jar with water ([Plato], *Axiochus*, 371 e, and often later, as Hor. *Carm.* 1. 11. 22 ff.). Here again, no generally accepted explanation exists.

Campbell Bonner, *Harv. Stud.* 1902, 129 ff.          H. J. R.

**DANCING.** From earliest times, the dance played an important role in the lives of the Greeks, and was sometimes regarded by them as the invention of the gods. It was generally associated with music and song or poetry in the art called μουσική, and frequently made use of a body of conventionalized gestures, χειρονομία. The dance had a place in religious festivals, in the secret rites of mystery cults, in artistic competitions, in the education of the young, and even in military training, especially in Sparta. People danced at weddings, at funerals, at the 'naming-days' of infants, at harvests, at victory celebrations, in after-dinner merrymaking, in joyous κῶμοι or dance processions through the streets, in animal mummery, and even in incantations. However, there is no evidence for anything like the 'ballroom' or 'courting' dances of modern times. Performances by professional dancers were enjoyed, especially at dinner-parties, but such dancers were almost all slaves and courtesans.

Among particularly famous dances of the Greeks were the γέρανος (a nocturnal serpentine dance the name of which is probably derived from the root *ger-, 'to wind', and not from the word for 'crane'); the pyrrhic and related dances by men and boys in armour; the παρθένειον, a song-dance performance by maidens; the ὑπόρχημα, a lively combination of instrumental music, song, dance, and pantomime; the skilful 'ball-playing' dance; and the uproarious ἀσκωλιασμός, performed on greased wine skins. In the worship of Dionysus the wild ὀρειβασία, or 'mountain-dancing' of frenzied women, apparently borrowed from the East, had in early days produced something akin to dance mania; but by classical times it was toned down into a prepared performance by a θίασος, or group of trained devotees.

In the Athenian theatre, the τυρβασία of the cyclic choruses, the lewd κόρδαξ of comedy, the stately ἐμμέλεια of tragedy, and the rollicking σίκιννις of the satyr play were distinctive. The actors in the φλύακες plays of Magna Graecia apparently at times burlesqued the dignified dances of the religious festivals.

In the first century B.C. a new type of dance performance was introduced by the *pantomimi* Pylades and Bathyllus. It was a highly stylized portrayal, usually by one dancer, of a legend or mythological story, the performer changing his mask and costume to represent each character in turn. He was assisted by a chorus of singers and an orchestra. Still later, elaborate dance spectacles similar to that described by Apuleius (*Met.* 10. 29–34) were staged, sometimes in arenas.

The Romans were much more restrained than the Greeks in their use of the dance. Some of them, including Cicero (*Pro Mur.* 6. 13), openly expressed contempt for dancers. There are records of a few ancient dances used in religious ceremonies—e.g. the leaping and 'three-foot' dances (*tripudia*) of the armed Salii and the Arval Brethren, and the 'rope dance' of maidens in honour of Juno (Livy 27. 37. 12–15). Etruscan and Greek dancers, from the fourth century B.C. on, exerted some influence, and the introduction of various Oriental cults brought noisy and ecstatic dances to a disapproving Rome. Dancing by professionals, usually slaves, often furnished entertainment at dinner-parties. With the coming of the *pantomimi*, popular interest in the dance became almost incredibly great. As the Empire advanced, public dance performances were increasingly erotic and sensational, and they were finally suppressed under the influence of the Church.

Athenaeus 1. 25–27, 37–40; 14. 25–30. Lucian, Περὶ ὀρχήσεως. Plato, *Laws* 7. 814 e–817 e. Lillian B. Lawler, *The Dance in Ancient Greece* (1964); *The Dance of the Ancient Greek Theatre* (1964).
L. B. L.

**DANUVIUS,** the Roman name for the *Danube*. Originally it referred to the upper course of the Danube only, the part below the Iron Gates being known as Ister (q.v.). The upper course of the Danube remained unknown to the Greeks. Herodotus (2. 33) said that its source was in Pyrene (the Pyrenees?), Ephorus in the 'Pillar of the North' (the Alps?), Timaeus in the Hercynian Forest (q.v.), Timosthenes in a Celtic lake, Apollonius Rhodius in the Rhipaean Mts. (q.v.). The identity of the Danuvius and the Ister was first asserted by Sallust (fr. 3. 79 M.), probably as a result of Octavian's Illyrian expedition in 35 B.C. In 16 B.C. Tiberius discovered the real sources, and in 13–12 the bend of the middle course (Strabo 7. 289). Strabo described the Danube with considerable accuracy and Ptolemy knew its windings (*Geog.* 3. 8. 3; 8. 7. 2).

Cary, *Geographic Background* 273 ff.; 301 ff.          E. H. W.

**DAPHNE** ('laurel'), in mythology, daughter of a river-god (Ladon, generally; Peneus, Ov. *Met.* 1. 452; but

Phylarchus and Diodorus of Elaea made her daughter of Amyclas, eponym of the town Amyclae, Parth. 15). Apollo loved her, and, as she would have none of him, pursued her; fleeing from him, she prayed for help and was turned into the tree bearing her name.          H. J. R.

**DAPHNE,** a park near Antioch, dedicated by Seleucus I to the royal gods, especially Apollo. It contained their temples, which were served by priests appointed by the Crown, and a theatre, stadium, etc., where the kings celebrated games in their honour. Daphne was famed for its natural beauties and was a favourite and not very reputable pleasure resort of the Antiochenes. Pompey enlarged its area, and it appears under the Principate to have been the property of the emperors, who had a palace there in the fourth century and protected its famous cypresses. The Antiochenes, however, celebrated their Olympia in its precincts. A theatre and several villas and baths have been excavated.

*Antioch on the Orontes* ii (1938), ed. R. Stillwell.          A. H. M. J.

**DAPHNIS,** in mythology, a Sicilian shepherd. According to Stesichorus (ap. Aelian, *VH* 10. 18) and Timaeus (ap. Parth. 29) he was son or favourite of Hermes, and loved by a nymph, Echenaïs, who required of him that he should be faithful to her. This he was, till a princess made him drunk and so won him to lie with her. Thereupon the nymph blinded him; he consoled himself by making pastoral music, of which he was the inventor, or it was first invented by the other shepherds, who sang of his misfortunes; the language of our sources is ambiguous. But Theocritus 1. 66 ff. tells allusively a different story. In this, apparently, Daphnis will love no one, and Aphrodite to punish him inspires him with a desperate passion. Sooner than yield to it he dies of unsatisfied longing, taunting and defying her to the end, mourned by all the inhabitants of the country, mortal and immortal, and regretted by the goddess herself.
          H. J. R.

**DARDANI,** a warlike Illyrian tribe, which was in its eastern parts intermingled with Thracians, in the south-west of Moesia Superior. The Dardani first appear as a united nation under a king in 284 B.C. Their frequent raids harassed the kingdom of Macedonia as well as the later Roman province. They were fought by Sulla (85 B.C.), Appius Claudius Pulcher (78–76), C. Scribonius Curio (75–73); after unsuccessful campaigns under Antonius Hybrida (62) and L. Calpurnius Piso (57) the troops of M. Antonius engaged the Dardani (39); finally, they were subdued by M. Licinius Crassus (q.v. 6) apparently without fighting (29 or 28). Although the Dardani were recruited into the Roman army (for *alae* and *cohortes Dardanorum* cf. indexes of *CIL* xvi and Dessau *ILS*) they were never completely pacified and in the second century Marcus Aurelius is said to have made soldiers out of the 'bandits of Dardania' (*vita Marci* 21. 7).

C. Patsch, *Sitz. Wien* 214, 1 (1932), and (on the *latrones*) *Wiss. Mitt. Bos. Herceg.* 1902, 123 ff.; N. G. L. Hammond, *BSA* 1966, 239 ff.
          F. A. W. S.; J. J. W.

**DARDANUS.** In *Iliad* 20. 215 ff. we have the genealogy Zeus–Dardanus–Erichthonius–Tros, and thereafter

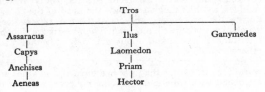

But as Priam is regularly called Δαρδανίδης, which by Homeric usage is either son or grandson of Dardanus, this passage is probably an interpolation. Later authors give two accounts of Dardanus. (*a*) He was a Samothracian, son of Zeus and Electra and brother of Iasion; either because he was driven out by Deucalion's flood (Lycophron 72–73 and schol.) or because Iasion was killed by the thunderbolt for assaulting Demeter (Apollod. 3. 138, a later form of the old ritual myth in *Od.* 5. 125 ff.), Dardanus left Samothrace and came to the mainland; for another account, see Diodorus Siculus 5. 48–49. (*b*) He and Iasius (Iasion) lived originally in Italy, their real or reputed father being Corythus (q.v. 1); either the brothers separate, Iasius going to Samothrace and Dardanus to the Troad, or Dardanus kills Iasius. Servius on *Aen.* 3. 167 mentions three other accounts, that he was an Arcadian, a Cretan, and a native of the Troad. The constants are that he was Electra's son and founded Dardania.          H. J. R.

**DARES OF PHRYGIA,** priest of Hephaestus at Troy (*Iliad* 5. 9) and reputed author of a lost pre-Homeric account of the Trojan War (Aelian, *VH* 11. 2). A supposed Latin prose translation survives, *Daretis Phrygii de Excidio Troiae Historia* (5th c. ?), with an alleged dedication by Sallust to Cornelius Nepos. It has little merit, but was widely used by medieval writers on the Trojan War. *See* DICTYS CRETENSIS.

TEXT. F. Meister (Teubner, 1873).          G. C. W.

**DARIUS I** (OP *Darayavaush*), Achaemenid king of Persia, 521–486 B.C. He came to the throne after overthrowing a usurper, Gaumata the Magian, who was impersonating Bardiya (Smerdis), the dead brother of Cambyses (Hdt. 3. 68 ff.). The first years of his reign were spent in quelling revolts in Persia, Babylonia, and the Eastern provinces. By 519 order was restored, and Darius could undertake the reconstruction necessitated by the recent anarchy. His division of the Empire into provinces governed by satraps (q.v.) was retained with little change throughout the Achaemenid period and even later. The true successor of Cyrus, his organization was framed to centralize authority while allowing to each province its own form of government and institutions. He was a worshipper of Ahura Mazda, but showed a wise tolerance towards the religions of his vassals. His financial reforms created a new national economy based on a yearly fixed tax. His campaigns were designed to consolidate the frontiers of the Empire; he developed commerce, building a network of roads, exploring the Indus valley and the Mediterranean, and connecting the Nile with the Red Sea by canal.

In 512 Darius penetrated into Europe on a punitive expedition against the Scythians. A revolt of the Greek cities in Ionia was suppressed (499–494); he then prepared to punish the Greeks for their interference. Storms off Mt. Athos checked this expedition (492), and a third, undertaken after further preparation, ended in a Greek victory at Marathon (490 B.C.). Darius died soon after.

G. B. Grundy, *The Great Persian War* (1901); R. Kent, *Old Persian* (U.S.A. 1953). P. J. Junge, *Dareios I* (Leipzig, 1944). J. V. Prašek, 'Dareios I', *Alte Orient* xiv. 4 (1914).          M. S. D.; R. N. F.

**DARIUS II,** son of Artaxerxes I, ruled over Persia 424–405 B.C. On his father's death he emerged triumphant from a dynastic struggle. His subsequent misgovernment, due in part to the influence of his consort and half-sister Parysatis, who proved much the stronger character, gave rise to a succession of abortive revolts in Syria, in Lydia (before 413), and in Media (410). More serious was the loss of Egypt in 410. These set-backs were partially balanced by the successful intervention of

Persian diplomacy, directed by Tissaphernes, Pharnabazus, and Cyrus, in the Peloponnesian War.

D. E. W. W.

**DARIUS III** (c. 380–330 B.C.), a collateral of the Achaemenid house, was raised to the throne in 336 by the vizier Bagoas, who met the same death at Darius' hands as he had himself inflicted on Artaxerxes III and Arses. In Alexander's invasion Darius was outgeneralled and outfought at Issus and Gaugamela, his defeats being aggravated by his personal cowardice. He attempted to rally the Eastern provinces, but was hunted down in 330, and his own followers, who had previously deposed him in favour of Bessus, stabbed him to death on Alexander's approach.

D. E. W. W.

**DASCYLIUM,** seat of the Persian satrap of Hellespontine Phrygia, close to Δασκυλῖτις λίμνη and famous for its hunting park (Xen. *Hell.* 4. 1. 15; *Hell. Oxy.* 17. 3; Strabo 575). The site has recently been identified by excavations at Hisartepe near Ergili, at the south-eastern corner of Lake Manyas, which therefore must be Δασκυλῖτις λίμνη. Hisartepe was the source of several Graeco-Persian relief sculptures now in Istanbul Museum, and its situation accords with Xenophon's description. The excavations produced Greek pottery of the early seventh century B.C. onwards, Greco-Persian reliefs and tomb-stelae, and Achaemenid clay seals of Xerxes' reign.

The site at Eşkel Limanı, on the Sea of Marmara east of the mouth of the River Rhyndacus, is not the satrap's seat, as was previously thought, but may be the Dascylium of the Athenian Tribute Lists.

J. A. R. Munro, *JHS* 1912, 57 ff.; K. Bittel, *Arch. Anz.* 1953, 1 ff.; E. Akurgal, *Anatolia* i (1956), 20 ff.; *ATL* i. 258 f., iii. 207, iv. 30 f.

D. J. B.

**DEA DIA,** a corn-goddess worshipped by the Fratres Arvales; chief festival in May.

Henzen, *Acta fratrum Arualium* (1874), 3 ff.

**DEAD, DISPOSAL OF.** Cremation and inhumation were the only native methods in the classical cultures, others being known (e.g. Hdt. 2. 86–8; Ap. Rhod. 3. 202–7 and Nymphodorus ap. scholiast, ibid.), but not normally practised. It does not appear that these two methods corresponded to different eschatological beliefs. In some cases they arose from racial difference (some Iron Age people in Italy cremated, others inhumed), but even this is not invariable (Homer's people always cremate, but seem to be descended from the inhuming Mycenaeans). In the Roman Empire considerations of economy or convenience had a good deal to do with the choice (see A. D. Nock, *Harv. Theol. Rev.* 1932, 357), and this may well have been true elsewhere. The essential thing was apparently to cover the body, burned or not, with earth (three handfuls will do for a ceremonial burial, Hor. *Carm.* 1. 28. 35, which is wholly Greek in tone; Antigone scatters a thin coating of dust over Polyneices, Soph. *Ant.* 255–6); the Roman definition of a buried body was one of which no bone showed above ground (Q. Mucius Scaevola ap. Cic. *Leg.* 2. 57, see the whole passage), or in a vault of some kind, such as a natural or artificial cave. Such constructions often held a number of bodies, e.g. *columbaria* (q.v.) used in imperial Rome and many earlier erections; pits in the earth, when used, varied considerably in size, pattern, and the number of corpses they contained.

**2.** This covering cut off the dead from the sight of the celestial gods, with whom they had no more to do (see Soph. *Aj.* 589, and its imitation in Verg. *Aen.* 11. 51), thus avoiding pollution or offence of them and their altars (cf. Soph. *Ant.* 1016 ff.). It was also a kindness to the departed, who were generally held to need burial in order to admit them to the lower world (e.g. *Il.* 23. 71 ff. *Aen.* 6. 325—*Od.* 24. 1 ff. is abnormal and such passages as *Aen.* 2. 646, Lucan 7. 819 are philosophical, no popular). Hence it was a universal act of piety to bury or at least allow the burial of, any dead person, friend or foe; to be left unburied was the lot of certain criminals after execution (at Athens, Plat. *Resp.* 4. 439 e, with Adam's note; traitors were so used, e.g. Soph. *Ant.* 26 ff. imitated by Aesch. *Sept.* 1013 ff. (a spurious passage) Soph. *Aj.* 1047 ff.; Roman law regularly allowed the burial of executed criminals, *Dig.* 48. 24, with occasional exceptions, Tac. *Ann.* 6. 29. 2). Suicides were sometimes given abnormal burial, or even none (Athens, see Aeschines 3. 244, hand of corpse buried separately; Rome, 'cautum fuerat in pontificalibus libris ut qui laqueo uitam finisset, insepultus abiceretur', Servius on *Aen* 12. 603; but this certainly was not regularly observed).

**3.** A regular funeral (ταφή, *funus*) was carried out as follows, omitting local, national, and chronological differences (see below). After the body had been bathed (e.g. *Il.* 7. 425; *Aen.* 6. 219), dressed (in clothes such as might have been worn in life, not in a shroud), and laid on a couch, it was lamented by the relatives and others present (excess in this respect was forbidden in classical times, e.g., by the XII Tables 10. 4 Bruns) and then carried to the place of burning or inhumation (ἐκφορά, *exsequiae*), attended by a more or less large crowd. The pyre, if the body was burned (πυρά, *rogus*), was often, in archaic Greece and under the Empire in Rome, an elaborate structure, and the amount of grave-gifts burned with the body or placed in the tomb might be very large, though customs varied enormously, the classical tendency being towards moderation in this respect also (see, e.g., Plutarch, *Solon* 21, XII Tables 10. 2 Bruns). The ashes, in a case of cremation, were placed in a vessel, the shape, material, and size of which varied in different times and places; for an unburned body a coffin (σωρός or λάρναξ, *capulus*) would normally be used, while later the stone sarcophagus, often elaborately carved, became very popular with those who could afford it. In either case, body and container would be put in one of the receptacles already described. If the body could not be found, a funeral would still be held, a dummy of one kind or another being sometimes used (example in *JHS* 1936, 140). The tomb, then and at intervals afterwards, became the centre of family ritual directed towards the dead.

**4.** Of the differences in funeral practice above referred to, the following are the most interesting and important. In the Heroic Age of Greece, as described by Homer (especially *Il.* 23, funeral of Patroclus), the whole ceremony was most elaborate. This may be due, as regards some details, to the fact that Achilles (q.v.) retains some of the manners of an earlier time. Achilles himself, as chief mourner, is fasting and unwashed (43 ff.) till the rites are completed. The body lies in state and is formally bewailed by the women (19. 282 ff.; cf. 24. 664 and 710 ff., the mourning for Hector). In a hot climate the ceremony probably did not last long; in the *Iliad* both Patroclus and Hector are miraculously kept from decay (19. 29 ff.; 23. 184 ff.), and the lying-in-state continues for several days. When the pyre is complete, the body is brought to it by a procession of warriors in full armour, and is covered with hair shorn from the mourners' heads; Achilles, as chief mourner, holds the head of the corpse during the procession, and he and some others keep watch over the pyre till morning. Then beasts are slaughtered and their fat laid about the body, together with other food-offerings and sacrifices of horses, dogs, and human beings, presumably to attend the dead in the next world (127 ff.). After the pyre has burned, the ashes are quenched with wine and the bones collected and put in an urn (237 ff.). A barrow of earth is then heaped above them (245 ff.), which was often marked by a post or other such object (331). Both the barrow and the post were called σῆμα, the former also τύμβος.

5. Of the funerals of the Minoan and Mycenaean ages we know nothing, but the tombs varied very much in size, elaboration, and number and value of offerings buried with the dead (see e.g. M. P. Nilsson, *Minoan-Mycenaean Religion*[2] (1950), 257; H. Schliemann, *Mycenae and Tiryns* (1878), 41 ff., 88 ff.). Nor is it known whether it was the custom then to have the elaborate games after the funeral proper which are described in Homer (*Il.* 23. 259 ff.). Every contestant receives a prize of some sort, and some of them were the property of the dead; this possibly represents a compromise between burying all his goods with him and allowing them to be inherited.

6. In the classical Greek period some remnant of the ancient magnificence was still to be seen in public funerals, especially those given at Athens to citizens killed in war (Diod. Sic. 11. 33. 3; Thuc. 2. 34), on which occasion a speech in their honour was made by one of the leading men (ἐπιτάφιος λόγος).

7. In Rome the funeral of a prominent man of good family, whose ancestors had held public office, was a remarkable ceremony. After the wailing (*conclamatio*) the corpse was laid out, fully dressed (in official robes, if he himself was or had been a magistrate), on a bed in the *atrium*, feet to the door. The household was *funesta*, i.e. in a state of taboo, not to be approached by, e.g., a pontiff, and to mark it as such, cypress or pitch-pine was hung outside the door. This condition lasted till a certain time after the funeral, when the heir formally swept out the pollution of death from the house with a special sort of broom (Festus, 68. 8 ff. Lindsay). The corpse was escorted to the place of inhumation or cremation, not only by living relatives and the general public, who were formally invited to attend, but by his dead kin, represented by actors or other suitable persons wearing their *imagines* (q.v.) and official robes. There were also professional mourning women, *praeficae*, who sang a dirge, *nenia* (q.v.), and musicians, often so noisy as to make the din almost proverbial (Hor. *Sat.* 1. 6. 43). The origin of all this was probably Etruscan; for details and references, see Marquardt, *Privatleben*[2] (1886), 2, 346 ff. In the case of a son, the funeral might be conducted at night with very little ritual, in which case the household did not become *funesta* (Rose in *CQ* 1923, 191 ff.). For Roman funerals, *see further* LAUDATIO FUNEBRIS, GLADIATORS.

8. Both Jews and Christians objected to cremation, which thus became ultimately extinct, and the latter in early times to elaborate sepulchres, hence the simple *loculi* or niches characteristic of the catacombs. Later they, when able to afford it, fell in with the common use of sarcophagi. See above, § 3.

Dar-Sag., s.v. 'funus'; D. S. Robinson, *Excavations at Olynthus*, xi (1942); G. Karo, *An Attic Cemetery* (1943). Forthcoming books on Greek and Roman burial customs by D. Kunz, J. Boardman, and J. M. C. Toynbee in the series 'Aspects of Greek and Roman Life'. H. J. R.

**DEAE MATRES,** deities known from Gallo-Roman monuments and inscriptions widely spread in the Celtic regions of the Roman Empire, but especially concentrated in the Rhineland and adjacent areas. *Matronae* is one certain alternative name, and there is a wide range of epithets, many incorporating tribal or local names, e.g. *Matres Treverae*. The most usual portrayal is of three seated women, in flowing robes with large hats, holding baskets of fruit or provisions of some kind. This is the triad presentation of the territorial nature and mother goddess; single figures with similar attributes are known under such names as Rosmerta, Maia, and Sirona (*see*

*also* EPONA). The cult of the Matres was brought by the army to Britain where, as in Ireland, local goddesses in triple form had long been established.

L. Hahl, *Bonner Jahrb.* 1960, 9 ff.; A. Ross, *Celtic Britain* (1967). *See* bibliography under RELIGION, CELTIC. T. G. E. P.

**DECAPROTI** (δεκάπρωτοι) first appear in A.D. 66 and become common throughout the Eastern provinces of the Roman Empire in the second and early third centuries; the office was abolished in Egypt and probably elsewhere in A.D. 307–8. *Decaproti* were probably in origin a finance committee of the city council, concerned with civic revenues and endowments. By the second century they were collecting imperial taxes and levies, and in the third this was their chief function; in Egypt they were responsible for the imperial land revenue. They were liable to make good deficits from their own property. Normally ten in number, the board had a varying membership, sometimes increasing to twenty. They were elected, and probably held office for five years.

E. G. Turner, *JEg.Arch.* 1936, 7–19. A. H. M. J.

**DECARCHIES,** (1) the committees, usually of ten oligarchic, pro-Spartan citizens, installed by Lysander (q.v.) after the Peloponnesian War in cities detached from the Athenian Empire. Possessing full executive powers, and sometimes supported by a garrison under a Spartan commander (*see* HARMOST), they collected their cities' share of the war-tax levied by Sparta (*Ath. Pol.* 39. 2). The Thirty Tyrants (q.v. 1) and the Ten at the Piraeus are the best-known examples. Many decarchies, especially in the Asiatic cities, were abolished in the reaction against Lysander (403–402 B.C.); the rest fell after the Spartan defeat at Cnidos (394) or by the King's Peace (386). (2) The same name was given to the governments instituted by Philip II of Macedon in the Thessalian cities in 344.

R. E. Smith, *CPhil.* 1948, 145 ff.; D. Lotze, *Abh. Sächs. Akad.* 1964, 68 f. A. M. W.: W. G. F.

**DECEBALUS,** king of the Dacians, acquired prominence through his war against Domitian (A.D. 85–9) and organized his realm. Though defeated by Roman armies, he was able to secure a favourable peace from Domitian when the revolt of the German and Sarmatian allies beyond the Danube imperilled the whole frontier, namely recognition, a subsidy, and the loan of skilled artisans. The growth of his power seemed dangerous to Trajan, who made war upon him and, after two campaigns (101–2), imposed fairly stringent terms of peace. Decebalus, it is said, did not abide by them: war began again in 105 with a serious Dacian incursion into Moesia. Trajan now resolved to make an end and convert Dacia into a Roman province. The land was invaded, Sarmizegethusa, the capital, was taken. Decebalus, hunted down, evaded capture by suicide (106). R. S.

**DECELEA,** a small Attic deme with its centre at Tatoi on the foothills of Mt. Parnes, had a view over the Attic plain as far as Piraeus. It was occupied by the Spartans from 413 to 404 B.C. as a permanent garrison on Attic soil. There are slight remains of a fortification, but they cannot be identified positively as the Spartan fort.

Thuc. 7. 19, 27–8; A. Milchhöfer, *Karten von Attika* (1883) vii–viii. 2 ff.; Θ. Ἀ. Ἀρβανιτοπούλου, Δεκέλεια (1958). C. W. J. E.

**DECEMPRIMI,** the ten senior members of the local council of a Latin or Roman municipality, formed with the yearly magistrates a group which in times of crisis represented the community in dealings with the central government. They are mentioned in the republican period only, but in the fully developed Empire a similar group of *decaproti* (q.v.) emerges as specially liable to Rome for the collection of the imperial taxes. The connexion between the two groups is obscure. *See* DECURIONES. A. N. S.-W.

**DECEMVIRI** was the name given to several Roman magistracies held by ten men:

(1) *Decemviri stlitibus iudicandis* judged suits to decide whether a man was free or a slave. It is doubtful whether they are to be identified with those *iudices* whose *sacrosanctitas* was declared together with that of the tribunes (Livy 3. 55). They are first definitely attested in a document *c*. 139 B.C. By Augustus they were probably made sectional presidents of the centumviral tribunal. *See* CENTUMVIRI, VIGINTISEXVIRI.

(2) *Decemviri sacris faciundis* kept the Sibylline books. Originally *duoviri*, they were increased to *decemviri* in 367 B.C. to include plebeians, and in Sulla's time to *quindecimviri*.

(3) *Decemviri legibus scribundis*. Tradition records that in 451 B.C. the Roman constitution was suspended and complete power was entrusted to ten patricians to prepare a code of laws. They prepared ten tables of law, and a new college of *decemviri* was appointed for 450 to complete the work. Although the new board included plebeians, it composed two additional tables which were unfavourable to the plebeians (e.g. codifying the prohibition of intermarriage between the Orders). It was dominated by Ap. Claudius (q.v. 3) and retained office until the murder of Verginia (q.v.) led to its resignation. The ancient constitution was restored and the consuls of 449 published the Twelve Tables. The substantial authenticity of the tradition (apart from the single episodes) depends on the reliability of the *Fasti*, which is difficult to deny. Further, since tradition pictures the second decemvirate as hostile to the plebeians, it would have hardly invented the plebeian *decemviri*. Thus both colleges may be accepted, though this is a very controversial conclusion. The Twelve Tables (q.v. for the content) represent a compromise between patricians and plebeians. It is doubtful whether the decemvirate was contemplated as a provisional magistracy or as one designed to replace permanently the consulate and tribunate. The majority of patricians and plebeians, however, were probably unfavourable to the second *decemviri*, fearing their tyrannical tendencies.

Diod. 12. 24–26; Livy 3. 32; Dionysius 10. 54; Cic. *Rep.* 2. 36. E. Täubler, *Untersuchungen zur Geschichte des Decemvirats* (1921); G. De Sanctis, *Riv. Fil.* 1924, 266 ff.; W. Soltau, *Sav. Zeitschr.* 1917, 1; J. Elmore, *CPhil.* 1922, 128 ff.; Beloch, *Röm. Geschichte* 236 ff.; U. von Lübtow, *Das Römische Volk* (1955), 286 ff.; Ogilvie, *Comm. Livy 1–5*, 451 ff.; R. Werner, *Der Beginn der röm. Republik* (1963), 280 ff. On *dec. stlitibus iud.* G. Franciosi, *Labeo* 1963, 163 ff. *See also* TWELVE TABLES. A. M.

**DECIDIUS SAXA**, LUCIUS, described by Cicero as 'ex ultima Celtiberia' but deriving from Italian and probably Samnite stock (compare the proscribed Cn. Decidius defended by Caesar), was admitted to the senatorial career by Caesar, becoming tribune of the plebs in 44 B.C. He had previously been a centurion or an equestrian officer. An Antonian partisan, Saxa commanded along with C. Norbanus the advance-guard of the Caesarians in the campaign of Philippi. Later governing Syria for Antony, he was defeated and killed in the Parthian invasion (40).

R. Syme, *JRS* 1937, 127 ff. R. S.

**DECIUS** (1), GAIUS MESSIUS (*PW* 9) QUINTUS, Emperor A.D. 249–51, a native cf Pannonia, but connected on his mother's side with an old Italian family, was city prefect before being appointed by Philip to restore discipline in the Danubian armies. His troops, however, forced him to assume the purple and Philip was subsequently

killed by his own men. In 250 the Carpi invaded Dacia, the Goths, under Kniva, Moesia. Decius was defeated near Beroea. The following year, in an attempt to intercept the Goths on their way home, he and his son Herennius were defeated and killed at Abrittus.

Decius was a staunch upholder of the old Roman traditions; his assumption of the additional surname of Trajan indicates an attitude favourable to the Senate. His persecution of the Christians resulted from his belief that the restoration of state cults was essential to the preservation of the Empire. There were many apostates and martyrs, but the death of Decius cut short the persecution (*see* CHRISTIANITY).

Zosimus 1. 22–23; Zonaras 12. 20. K. Gross, *RAC* 3, 611 ff. B. H. W.

**DECIUS** (2, *PW* 15) **MUS**, PUBLIUS, performed heroic but probably legendary feats as military tribune in the First Samnite War (343 B.C.; Livy 7. 34 f.). During his consulship (340) a battle with the Latins, somewhere in Campania (E. Pais, *Storia di Roma* (1926–7), iv. 196), made him famous. Actually Decius may not have been present (Beloch, *Röm. Gesch.* 374); he was popularly believed, however, to have ensured Rome's victory by solemnly 'devoting' himself and the enemy to the gods below and then charging into the enemy ranks to his death (Livy 8. 9)—an exploit more probably to be attributed to his son. For the possibility of his Capuan origin see J. Heurgon, *Capoue préromaine* (1942), 260 ff. E. T. S.

**DECIUS** (3, *PW* 16) **MUS**, PUBLIUS, son of (2) above, consul in 312, 308, 297, 295 B.C.; censor in 304. Duris, a contemporary, mentions his death at the battle of Sentinum (q.v.) in 295 (see Diod. 21. 6. 2). Later tradition (Livy 10. 28) insisted that this was another case of *devotio* (see preceding article); in fact, if any *devotio* is historical, it is probably his (but see Beloch, *Röm. Gesch.* 440). Even so, the real hero of Sentinum probably was his colleague, Fabius (q.v. 3) Rullianus. E. T. S.

**DECIUS** (4, *PW* 17) **MUS**, PUBLIUS, son of (3) above, consul 279 B.C. Pyrrhus defeated him at Ausculum. The story that he, like his father and grandfather, 'devoted' himself in the battle is unknown to most ancient authorities and should probably be rejected (Plut. *Pyrrh.* 21; Dion. Hal. 20. 1). E. T. S.

**DECIUS** (5, *PW* 9) **SUBULO**, PUBLIUS, a dissolute man, but a good orator, moved in Gracchan circles and, as tribune in 120 B.C., unsuccessfully prosecuted Opimius (q.v.). Accused *repetundarum* (119), he was acquitted, no doubt owing to his connexions among the *equites* (q.v.), who thus first demonstrated their new power. Praetor in 115, he was humiliated by the consul M. Scaurus (q.v. 1). He probably died soon after. His son (apparently) was adopted by a relative of Saturninus (q.v. 1), becoming C. Appuleius Decianus, and, remaining loyal to Saturninus after his death, had to go into exile in Asia (98 or 97).

E. Badian, *JRS* 1956, 91 ff. E. B.

**DECLAMATIO** as a technical term for the form of rhetorical training which consisted of exercises on invented themes came into use in the later part of Cicero's lifetime. Such exercises had been part of the stock-intrade of the Greek rhetorical schools of the third and second centuries B.C. (and had an ancestry in earlier rhetorical and philosophical training) and in Cicero's youth the use of them was already part of the recognized technique of the training of the orator in Rome: his own rhetorical handbook *De Inventione* and the anonymous treatise *Ad Herennium* give many examples. The Greek chools had distinguished between θέσεις, abstract general themes, and ὑποθέσεις, themes related to particular persons or situations; in Latin usage these terms were rendered respectively by *quaestiones* (e.g. 'an uxor ducenda?', 'an accedendum ad rem publicam?') and *causae* (e.g. the case, cited by Cic. *de Or.* 2. 100, of a man who contravenes a law forbidding a foreigner to climb the city wall and thereby repels an enemy attack and saves the city).

In the period following Cicero's death the practice of declamation acquired a new status and a new importance which may reasonably be connected with the changed conditions of the Principate. The courts still offered employment to the workaday advocate, but with the restriction of free political life the opportunity for the type of oratory by which the great advocates of the Republic, Cicero, Calvus, or Hortensius, had won their reputation had disappeared; the elevation of the declamation to be a genre in its own right, cultivated for its own sake, could provide an ambitious speaker with a new avenue to public attention. The declamation now had two recognized forms, one deliberative and the other forensic, denoted by two new technical terms. In the *suasoria*, an historical or mythological personage was given advice on his course of action in a particular situation: e.g. 'Should Sulla resign the dictatorship?' (Juv. 1. 16), 'Should Cato commit suicide after Utica?' (Pers. 3. 45), 'Should Alexander cross the Ocean?' (Sen. *Suas.* 1). In the *controversia* (this term, which in earlier usage had referred to the issue on which a case turned, was extended to denote the whole exercise) an invented legal case was argued on both sides before an imaginary jury. Though the ostensible purpose of the *controversia*, as of the *causa* in Cicero's day, had been practice in the handling of a case and the acquiring of resource and effectiveness in presenting it, the themes were drawn from an unreal romantic world of unlikely situations, of tyrants and tyrannicides, wicked stepmothers, erring Vestal virgins, pirate chiefs and their daughters, identical stepbrothers and sons disinherited twice over, and for the most part the points of law argued (though some may have been suggested by historical incidents or by Greek codes) were not those which a pleader could expect to encounter in the business of a Roman court. On these far-fetched and often complicated themes the professional declaimer and his pupils (the term *scholasticus* is applied to both) exercised a tortuous subtlety in the *divisio*, the analysis of the issues, and a fantastic ingenuity in the invention of *sententiae* (q.v.), neat and pointed observations, epigrams or paradoxes, in the contrivance of *colores*, the complexions or twists given to a case by way of extenuation or insinuation, in the use of rhetorical figures, and in the manipulation of the *locus communis* and the *descriptio*, the purple passage of moralizing or local colour on the vicissitudes of fortune or a storm at sea. We have a large number of examples of the genre in the collection of excerpts made (with comments) by the Elder Seneca under the title of *Oratorum et Rhetorum Sententiae Divisiones Colores*, which represents the rhetoricians of his own lifetime (he quotes from more than a hundred of them), and in the two collections of complete declamations spuriously attributed to Quintilian. The speaker's aim was not persuasion but the applause which was accorded to novelty, however extravagant, and ingenuity, however perverse; far from preparing the pupil for the realities of the courts, the technique tended rather to disable him. What had been in Cicero's time a practical exercise and a private activity, confined to the school or, at most, a circle of friends, became a public performance and a fashionable entertainment. The exhibitions given by the rhetoricians and their pupils were attended not only by students and their parents but by the literary society of

Rome: in Seneca's reminiscences we find such visitors to the schools as Pollio, Agrippa, Maecenas, and Augustus himself.

The declamation had its critics: the Elder Seneca deplores the bad taste, lack of discipline, and self-advertisement which it encourages, Tacitus its superficiality and unreality (*Dial.* 28 ff.); Petronius puts into the mouth of his hero Encolpius a lively exposure of its absurdities (*Sat.* 1–2); Quintilian pleads for the restoration of its proper function of 'iudiciorum consiliorumque imago' (2. 10. 1–12). But its influence was pervasive and its vogue lasted long. The schools of the developing provinces took it over from Rome; the declamations of Seneca's contemporary Gallio were being studied as classics in the time of St. Jerome, and the declamatory tradition left its mark on the Christian apologists. Its strangest legacy is in the medieval collection of tales known as the *Gesta Romanorum*, in which some of its romantic extravaganzas reappear as light reading for the monastery.

H. Bornecque, *Les Déclamations et les déclamateurs d'après Sénèque le Père* (1902); G. Boissier, *Tacitus and other Roman Studies* (E. T. 1906), 163 ff.; Norden, *Ant. Kunstpr.* i. 248 ff.; T. S. Simonds, *The Themes treated by the Elder Seneca* (U.S.A. 1896); E. P. Parks, *Roman Rhetorical Schools* (U.S.A. 1948); S. F. Bonner, *Roman Declamation in the Late Republic and Early Empire* (1949); A. D. Leeman, *Orationis Ratio* (Amsterdam, 1963), 224 ff.; A. Gwynn, *Roman Education* (1926), 155 ff. C. J. F.

**DECLAMATIONES PSEUDO-QUINTILIANEAE**, two sets of rhetorical pieces ascribed by the MSS. to Quintilian. (1) The so-called *declamationes maiores*, nineteen in number, were already by the fourth century A.D. circulating under the name of Quintilian, as quotations in Servius prove: and there is evidence that they were 'edited' by scholars of that period. It is generally supposed that these highly coloured declamations can hardly be from the hand of Quintilian (see *Inst.* 2. 10. 4 f. for his views on unreal declamations), but date and authorship remain quite uncertain. (2) The *declamationes minores* are the last 145 of a collection originally numbering 388. Each has a *thema* and short treatment of it; their derivation from some rhetorical school is ensured by the frequent presence of *sermones*, giving a master's hints on the treatment of the *controversia*. That the master was Quintilian is unprovable, though not impossible; the doctrine is not unlike that of the *Institutio* (Ritter in his edition, 512–14, lists parallels), though, here too, the themes may be too highly coloured to be Quintilianic.

TEXTS. *Quintiliani quae feruntur declamationes XIX maiores*, ed. G. Lehnert (1905). *M. Fabii Quintiliani declamationes quae supersunt CXLV*, ed. C. Ritter (1884).
COMMENTARY. P. Burman (Leyden, 1720). For attempts to date the declamations see Schanz–Hosius ii. 756 f. S. F. Bonner in *Fifty Years of Classical Scholarship* (ed. Platnauer, 1954), 373. M. W.

**DECUMA.** In Italy one-tenth of the grain harvest (one-fifth of the fruit harvest) on *ager publicus* (q.v.) was paid to the Roman Treasury; it was farmed out by the censors to *publicani* (q.v.). In Sicily, all land not made *ager publicus* (and then treated accordingly) or belonging to free cities (*see* SOCII) was *decumanus*: the tithes previously paid to Carthage and Syracuse were appropriated by Rome. Sardinia seems to have been under a similar system (we do not know for how long). In Sicily (where the *Verrines* give detailed information for the late Republic) the tithe was sold to contractors at Syracuse in accordance with the law of Hieron (q.v. 2), extended by the Romans to the whole province and adapted by the law of Rupilius (q.v.); the purchasers made individual contracts (*pactiones*) with the farmers, under the supervision of the governor. In 75 B.C. the sale of the tithe for fruits was transferred to Rome. A further *decuma* could be requisitioned against pay; the details are not clear, but it gave rise to chicanery and exploitation. The Asian tithe, under the law of C. Gracchus (q.v. 4), was sold in Rome by the censors. The immense amounts needed for this contract led to the growth of the powerful companies of *publicani* (q.v.). Collection seems to have been through *pactiones* with individual cities. Pompey probably extended this system to the provinces he organized. Caesar converted the Asian tithe into a fixed *tributum* (q.v.), payable directly and assessed at two-thirds the tithe. In Sicily a *tributum* had taken the place of the tithe by the time of Augustus and in other provinces the development was similar.

J. Carcopino, *La Loi d'Hiéron et les Romains* (1914).  E. B.

**DECURIONES,** the local councillors of the fully developed Roman municipal system, both in colonies and municipalities, whether Latin or Roman. They were recruited from the ex-magistrates and by censorial appointment at the quinquennial census, holding office for life. The qualifications were those required for the magistracies and included criteria of wealth, age, status, and reputation. The minimum age-limit of twenty-five was frequently neglected, minors of influential families being elected *honoris causa*. The *decuriones*, whose number varied with the size of the municipality, formed the *consilium* of the magistrates, and in practice controlled the public life of the community. Local administration and finance, the sending of deputations and petitions to Rome or to the provincial governors, the voting of honorary decrees and statues, fell to them, since the popular assemblies played little part except at the magisterial elections. The *decuriones* were also responsible for collecting the imperial taxes due by their municipality, and personally liable in case of default, a liability which became an intolerable burden in the later Empire and led to the breakdown of the municipal system. The decurionate became an hereditary inescapable *munus* of the wealthy, who degenerated from a ruling class to a tax-collecting caste, known as *curiales* (q.v.). For bibliography *see* MUNICIPIUM.  A. N. S.-W.

**DEDICATIO,** the other side of *consecratio* (q.v.). Strictly speaking, only one who is himself in touch with *res sacrae*, in other words a priest expert in the ways of the gods, can consecrate anything; hence we do not hear, for instance, that M. Horatius Pulvillus consecrated the Capitoline temple, but that he dedicated it. But the owner (State or individual) of a *res profana* can if he chooses give it to a god, as he might to another human being or another State. This giving to a god, or removing from the secular (*noa, profanus*) sphere into the sacred (*tabu, sacer*) being accomplished in due form, the object, which a moment before anyone might handle, because it was a common thing, now becomes charged with *numen*, and to have anything to do with it requires more or less precaution and observance of proper ritual. Thus, a block of carved stone is in itself unremarkable, but if it has been dedicated to a god for use as an altar, it is impiety to touch it save in the performance of an act of worship, usually sacrifice (Hor. *Carm.* 3. 23. 17).

Though only objects dedicated and consecrated by permission or direction of the State could in Roman law be really *res sacrae* (*see* CONSECRATIO), in practice anyone might privately dedicate, e.g., a chapel on his own property to such gods as he chose to worship, though occasionally a non-Roman cult was prohibited by decree of the Senate or other competent authority.  H. J. R.

**DEDICATIONS.** I. GREEK. In the early period of Greek literature dedication, in the modern sense, of literary works did not exist. When Hesiod, Theognis, and Empedocles addressed poems to Perses, Cyrnus, and Pausanias, their intention was not that of a modern dedicator, to gratify the dedicatee or obtain a *cachet* from his name. The person addressed was no more than a

target for the arrows of instruction or exhortation. Nor obviously, do the *Epinicians* of Pindar come into account here. The first Greek to dedicate a book seems to have been Dionysius Chalcus, who in the middle of the fifth century B.C. dedicated his poems to a friend (Ath. 15 669 d–e). In the fourth century Isocrates (*To Nicocles* and perhaps Theophrastus (Ath. 4. 144 e) adopted the practice, which became extremely common in the Hellenistic age. Thus Archimedes addressed his *Psammites* to Gelon, Apollonius of Perga the first three books of his *Conica* to Eudemus, the last five to Attalus I. Diogenes Laertius actually finds it 'arrogant' in Chrysippus to 'write so many books and dedicate none of them to a king' (7. 185), and mentions (4. 38) the only king to whom Arcesilaus did *not* dedicate anything. In the Roman period of Greek literature the practice remains frequent. Notable examples are the literary treatises of Dionysius of Halicarnassus (some in the form of letters) and the anthologies of Meleager and Philippus (*Anth. Pal.* 4. 1–2). J. D. D.

II. LATIN. There are various degrees of explicitness in Latin literary dedication, but no system. In general, epic and history avoided a dedicatory address—but there are exceptions. Motives vary from flattery of a monarch to a friendly gesture, from desire to honour a patron to need to instruct a pupil.

Catullus dedicated his poems to Cornelius Nepos (it is, however, uncertain how much of the extant collection was covered by that address) and Horace dedicated *Odes* 1–3 to Maecenas: both collections are prefaced by a poem written specially for the purpose (the same may be true of *Epistles* 1. 1). Virgil dedicated the *Georgics* to Maecenas. But, in *Epodes* and *Satires* 1, a poem which addresses Maecenas simply comes first in the collection, as the letter to Augustus begins *Epistles* 2. Propertius casually addresses Tullus in a way that scarcely suggests dedication. A programmatic poem, without address, opens Horace *Odes* 4, but other odes address individuals. The *Eclogues* have no dedication (nor does the first poem address anyone), though single *Eclogues* are addressed to Asinius Pollio, Alfenus Varus, and Cornelius Gallus. Lucretius, appropriately to a didactic work, addresses Memmius almost as a pupil, as Horace in the *Ars Poetica* addresses the sons of Piso. Dedications were not necessary (Persius prefaces his collection by an angry poem in scazons on inspiration; Juvenal by no address at all), especially in the case of epic: yet Lucan addresses Nero and Valerius Flaccus Vespasian. Statius (in his *Silvae*) and Martial used prose letters to introduce and dedicate some of their books.

The same lack of system can be seen in prose works: Cicero dedicated a number of his rhetorical and philosophical works to friends and contemporaries with an interest and reputation in those fields. Livy felt no obligation to address an individual, but Velleius Paterculus dedicated his work to M. Vinicius and Valerius Maximus to Tiberius. Sallust does not address any individual, nor Tacitus—except in his Ciceronian *dialogus de oratoribus*. The social status of the writer, the nature of the work, the writer's immediate circumstances, his random whim or fancy—any, or all, of these may explain a dedication, or the lack of it.

R. Graefenhain, *De more libros dedicandi ap. scr. Graec. et Rom. obvio* (1892); F. Stephan, *Quomodo poetae Graecorum Romanorumque carmina dedicaverint* (1910); J. Ruppert, *Quaestiones ad hist. dedicationis librorum pertinentes* (1911).  G. W. W.

**DEDITICII** were individuals, communities, or nations which made a formal, unconditional surrender of themselves, their property, territory, and towns to the Roman State. *Deditio* was usually performed by defeated enemies who preferred to throw themselves on Rome's mercy—

*deditio in fidem*—rather than suffer total sack and destruction—*expugnatio*. But any community which wished to place itself under the total protection of Rome could surrender by *deditio*. *Dediticii* were regarded as suppliants and usually treated with generosity. They had no political rights and were *cives nullius certae civitatis*, until Rome settled their future status, either by restoring to them the right of self-government, *leges et iura*, and recognizing them as ordinary *peregrini* (q.v.), or even by granting them the status of a *civitas libera* (*see* socii) or, on occasion, full treaty rights (*see* foedus). *Deditio* is not itself a form of treaty-alliance, nor is it normally a permanent status, although the *Lex Aelia Sentia* (A.D. 4) placed slaves of ill repute who were given their liberty in the category of *dediticii* instead of granting them Roman citizenship.

Livy, passim, esp. bks. 1–10; Caesar, *BGall.*, passim. A. Heuss, *Klio*, Beiheft xxxi (1933); E. Täubler, *Imperium Romanum* (1913); A. H. M. Jones, *Studies in Roman Government and Law* (1960), 129 ff. A. N. S.-W.

**DEIANIRA** (*Δηάνειρα*), in mythology, daughter of Oeneus and wife of Heracles. He first heard of her from Meleager's ghost in Hades, according to Bacchylides 5. 170. He won her in combat from Achelous (cf. amalthea), and on the way home he entrusted her to the centaur Nessus to carry across a river; Nessus tried to assault her and Heracles killed him with one of his poisoned arrows. Dying, he gave Deianira some of his blood, assuring her it was a potent love-charm. Years later, when she had borne Heracles several children, he brought Iole home from Oechalia; Deianira, to regain his affection, smeared the blood on a garment and sent it him. The poison caused his death, whereat she killed herself. See Sophocles, *Trachiniae*. H. J. R.

**DEIOTARUS**, tetrarch of western Galatia, attacked by Mithridates (q.v. 6), became a loyal Roman ally in all the wars in Asia from Sulla to Pompey, who, in his Asian settlement, greatly increased Deiotarus' territory. The Senate, perhaps adding more to it, gave him the royal title. Pompey also increased the territory of Deiotarus' son-in-law, Brogitarus, chief of the Trocmi in eastern Galatia. In 51 B.C. Deiotarus put his forces at the disposal of Cicero and Bibulus (qq.v.). In the Civil War, after following Pompey, he joined Caesar after Pharsalus and assisted Calvinus (q.v. 2) in his Pontic campaign, seizing the rest of Galatia. Caesar made him give up some of his gains, and on Caesar's final return to Rome (45) Deiotarus' enemies raised complaints about him, and his friend Cicero defended him in an extant speech. On Caesar's death, he reoccupied his lost territories, bought recognition from Antonius (q.v. 4), but then joined Brutus (q.v. 5). Before the final battle at Philippi he deserted to the Triumvirs and escaped punishment, dying peacefully in 40. He had organized two legions on the Roman model, one of which later became XXII Deiotariana.

F. E. Adcock, *JRS* 1937, 12 ff. E. B.

**DEIPHOBUS** (*Δηίφοβος*), in mythology, son of Priam; he plays a fairly prominent part in the fighting in the *Iliad*, and in the *Odyssey* is associated with Helen (5. 276), and the hardest fighting at the capture of Troy is about his house (8. 517–20). All later authors say he was married to Helen after Paris' death. H. J. R.

**DEIPHONTES** (*Δηϊφόντης*), in mythology, a descendant in the fifth generation of Heracles. He married Hyrnetho, daughter of Temenus king of Argos, and was favoured by him above his own sons, who therefore murdered their father and strove with Deiphontes, with

results variously described by different authors (collected by Stoll in Roscher's *Lexikon*, s.v.). H. J. R.

**DELIAN LEAGUE, THE,** is the modern name given to the great alliance formed in 478–477 B.C. against the Persians. In 478 the Greeks, led by Pausanias the Spartan regent, campaigned in Cyprus and secured Byzantium; but Pausanias abused his power and was recalled to Sparta. At the allies' request Athens accepted the leadership, the Peloponnesians were content to withdraw from overseas responsibilities, and a new alliance was formed. The sacred island of Delos, a traditional Ionian festival centre, was chosen as headquarters. Athens provided the commander of the allied forces and determined which cities were to provide ships and which money; the treasurers also, ten *hellenotamiai*, were Athenians, and the Athenian commander Aristides was responsible for the first assessment. But at the outset policy was determined at meetings on Delos at which every member had an equal vote. The nucleus of the alliance was formed by the Ionian cities of the west coast of Asia Minor, the Hellespont and the Propontis, and most of the islands in the Aegean. Chios, Samos, Lesbos, and some of the other states with a naval tradition provided ships; the remainder brought annual tribute to the treasury at Delos. Every member took an oath of loyalty which was permanently binding.

At first the original objectives were vigorously pursued. Persian garrisons were driven out of Thrace (except at Doriscus on the Hebrus) and the Chersonese, Greek control was extended along the west and south coast of Asia Minor, new members joined until there were nearly 200. A climax was reached when Cimon, commanding 200 Athenian and allied ships, destroyed the Persian land and sea forces at the mouth of the Eurymedon (c. 466). But meanwhile situations were developing which had not been anticipated. Carystus in Euboea was forced to join (c. 472), Naxos was not allowed to secede and had to accept a dictated settlement (c. 467), and in 465 the rich island of Thasos revolted because Athens was encroaching on her economic interests on the mainland. Thasos had to surrender in 462 and stiff terms were imposed, but a large colony of Athenians and allies, who had settled on the Strymon to exploit the riches of the area, was wiped out by the natives. There was clearly a danger that Athens would use the alliance increasingly in her own interest, but fighting against Persia was soon resumed. In 460 a strong force sailed to Cyprus and was soon diverted to Egypt to support Inaros, a Libyan prince who was leading a revolt against Persia. At first the joint forces were highly successful and the Persians were blockaded in Memphis, but strong Persian reinforcements reversed the situation and in 454 the Greeks had to capitulate. Meanwhile Athens had involved herself in war with the Peloponnesians. She now abandoned her offensive on the mainland and concentrated on maintaining control over her allies. The treasury was moved from Delos to Athens for greater security and disaffection among the allies was firmly suppressed. Cimon, who had been ostracized in 461 when his policy of good relations with Sparta was discredited, was specially recalled and, after negotiating a five years' truce with Sparta, he led another strong force to Cyprus. But after initial successes he died, the fleet returned, and war with Persia was not resumed.

The death of Cimon made it easier to reverse Athenian policy and, though the evidence is not satisfactory, it is highly probable that peace was negotiated by Callias at the head of an Athenian embassy. The main terms were that the Persian fleet was not to sail west of Phaselis, nor outside the Euxine; Persian satraps were not to attempt to force back Athenian allies into the Persian Empire; and the Greek cities of Asia were to be autonomous. The alliance of 478–477 had been primarily directed against Persia; the peace was followed by an unsettled period in the Aegean and political conflict in Athens. Pericles, now the recognized champion of the people, encouraged the Athenians to convert the alliance into an empire. He first invited the Greeks of the mainland and of the east to a congress at Athens to discuss common problems, particularly the rebuilding of temples destroyed by the Persians, and the policing of the seas. Sparta led a movement for abstention, the congress was not held, and Athens made the vital decisions herself. The alliance was not dissolved, tribute was to continue, and the reserve brought from Delos was used for the rebuilding of Athenian temples. Discontent among the allies was forcibly suppressed and the policy of imposing small Athenian garrisons and political residents which was begun in or even before the 50s was further developed. It was probably now that Athens enforced the use of her own coins, weights, and measures on the allies and required them all to bring standard offerings of cow and panoply to the Great Panathenaic festival which was held at four-year intervals. Cleruchies (q.v.) of Athenians were settled in allied territory, partly for the benefit of poorer Athenians, but also to add to Athenian security. The first known was at Andros in 450, together perhaps with Naxos and Euboea (? Carystus): the Chersonese was settled by Pericles in 447. By now only Chios, Samos, and Lesbos contributed ships, the rest paid tribute and had no effective means of resisting. The allies no longer took part in discussions of policy. In Athenian official language the 'allies' had now become 'the cities which the Athenians control'.

Athens was able to suppress her allies when they revolted; she had more serious trouble from the mainland cities over which she had gained control in the 50s. Boeotia, conquered in 457, revolted in 446 (or 447), and a small Athenian force, underestimating the danger, was overwhelmed at Coronea. This defeat was followed by the revolt of Megara, and also of Euboea, and, with the expiry of the truce, the Spartans brought a Peloponnesian army into Attica. Pericles who had taken the main Athenian army to Euboea returned and was able to negotiate a Spartan withdrawal as a preliminary to peace. In 446–445 the Thirty Years' Peace was agreed, in which Athens renounced her ambitions on land, but was free to consolidate her empire. Euboea was now crushed and bound more closely to Athens and in Athens Thucydides (q.v. 1), son of Melesias, who had opposed Pericles' policies, was ostracized. In 440, however, there came a severe shock when Samos challenged the right of Athens to interfere in a quarrel with Miletus. An attempted political settlement failed and a fierce war followed. Samos surrendered after a long siege and had to give up her fleet, pull down her walls, and pay a heavy indemnity. Athens had no more trouble from her allies until war with the Peloponnese seemed imminent. When war broke out she had a firm control, she was able to enforce regular tribute payment except in the less accessible areas of Caria, and she was able to demand that allied cases involving the major penalties of death, exile, loss of rights, and property confiscation should be heard at Athens. The people's courts played an increasing part in the control of empire.

Sparta, posing as the liberator of Greece, expected large-scale revolt from Athens; she was disappointed. Several of the smaller cities in Chalcidice had established their independence in 432 by settling inland at Olynthus, and in 428 Lesbos revolted and drew against herself a large Athenian force; but there was no general movement and Lesbos was crushed. Athens was able in 425 to increase the tribute assessment to a total of nearly 1,500

talents (the original assessment is said to have been 460 talents), and to use Milesians and other allies in her expeditions. In 415 when Melos refused to join her alliance, Athens reduced the island, put to death the men, and enslaved the women and children, an episode long remembered as the most ruthless act of Athenian imperialism. When the Athenian fleet and army were lost at Syracuse revolt spread more widely. Euboea was lost in 411, Thasos, Chios, and other Ionian cities broke away and appealed for help to Sparta, but even now some cities remained loyal and in most of those that revolted there was a pro-Athenian party. The reasons are complex. Most important was the Athenian championing of democracy. When revolts had been crushed Athens had usually imposed democracies; Sparta was the traditional champion of 'the better elements'. Liberation by Sparta might mean government by a narrow oligarchy. Athens also, in spite of the curtailment of liberties, had brought positive benefits to many of the poorer cities. Piracy had been suppressed to the great advantage of trade, and the Athenian navy offered well-paid service, particularly attractive to the islanders. The city of Athens, especially after the great building programme of Pericles, was a magnet to the leading men in the cities, and the poorer classes found more consideration and more opportunities for employment in Athens than in any other Greek city.

The allies did not in fact make a substantial contribution to the defeat of Athens, and when Sparta took Athens' place the cities soon had reason to regret the change. In less than thirty years they were again eager to unite under Athenian leadership, this time against Spartan aggression. But in 377 Athens repudiated cleruchies, garrisons, political domination, and other aspects of her rule that had been especially resented in the fifth century.

ANCIENT SOURCES. Hill–Meiggs–Andrewes, *Sources for Greek History* (1951). index, 354 ff.
MODERN LITERATURE. H. Nesselhauf, *Untersuchungen zur Geschichte der Delisch-Attischen Symmachie* (*Klio*, Beiheft xxx, 1933); *ATL*, vol. iii. More concisely in general Histories of Greece: N. G. L. Hammond² (1967); J. B. Bury³ (1951); *CAH* v.     R. M.

**DELLIUS** (*PW* 1), QUINTUS, joined first Dolabella (q.v. 3), then Cassius (q.v. 6), then Antonius (q.v. 4), who used him on many missions, and finally (just before Actium) Octavian—hence called *desultor bellorum civilium* by Valerius Messalla (q.v. 3), whose own record was rather similar. He wrote an account of Antony's Parthian War, which is a source of Plutarch's account in his *Antony*.
E. B.

**DELOS,** a small island (less than 2 square miles) regarded as the centre of the Cyclades. According to legend the birthplace of Apollo and Artemis, it was from earliest historical times sacred to Apollo, who was honoured by song, dance, and games in a festival (*panegyris*) to which came men and women from the islands and coasts of the Aegean as early as the eighth century (cf. *Homeric Hymn to Apollo*). The island had once been occupied, according to Thucydides, by Carian sea-rovers, who were driven out by Minos of Crete. The pre-Hellenic inhabitants, of whose occupation stone huts on Mt. Cynthus and in the plain afford evidence, were displaced by colonists from continental Greece before *c.* 1000 B.C., and the island was already famous in the *Odyssey*. Its history proper begins in the sixth century, when Pisistratus of Athens, to further his control of the Cyclades, purified Delos, and the Samian tyrant Polycrates extended his patronage to it. Delos was important as the centre of an Ionian amphictiony.

When the invading Persian fleet arrived in 490 Datis respected the sanctuary. In 478–477, when a maritime league was formed to ensure Greek independence,

Delos was naturally chosen as seat of the common treasury (*see* DELIAN LEAGUE). On the removal of the treasury to Athens (454) Delos came under more direct Athenian control, but did not pay tribute. In 426 Athens again purified the island, and Nicias inaugurated a quinquennial festival ('Delia') in a *theoria* of great pomp, possibly in 418/17 to inaugurate also the new temple of Apollo built by the Athenians. After the Peloponnesian War Athenian control of Delos was interrupted until the formation of Athens' second maritime league (378/7), when the administration of the Delian temples was re-organized under Athenian officials called Amphictions (cf. 'Sandwich Marble', *IG* ii². 1635, relevant to the financial period 377–373). When Athens lost her sea power, her administration of Delos stopped (314).

Henceforth for a century and a half the sanctuary was administered by local officials known as *hieropoioi*, while Egypt and Macedon contended for hegemony of the Aegean. During this period Delos enjoyed the usual institutions of a city-state. For the supervision of temple of Apollo, and all edifices within his *temenos*, the *ekklesia* entrusted its powers to the *hieropoioi*, who ranked next to the Archon, the head of the State. The first political relationship of the free Delians was with the League of Islanders (i.e. inhabitants of island-cities of the Aegean), the formation and protection of which are attributed by some to the Ptolemaic kings. The federal treasury—perhaps the seat of the League—was at Delos, where federal festivals were from time to time instituted in honour of the Hellenistic princes who happened to be paramount in the mid Aegean. The stoas of Antigonus Gonatas and Philip of Macedon were notable buildings of the third century. Delian monuments of this period reveal the pretensions not only of the Egyptian and Macedonian, but also of the Pergamene and Syrian kings. Early in the third century Delos was a centre of the corn trade of the Aegean; buyers came from Macedonia and other northern places. A foreign colony was growing up, foreign banking firms were flourishing; the occurrence of Italian names indicates commercial bonds with southern Italy. Delos enjoyed a kind of neutrality (see Laidlaw, *A History of Delos*, app. B); but at last she presumed to support Perseus of Macedon against Rome, and after his defeat at Pydna Rome handed over the island to her ally Athens, who removed the old inhabitants and sent her cleruchs to replace them (166), who in turn were later transformed into a cosmopolitan population. To damage Rhodian trade, Delos was made a free port.

In the third great period of Delian history the chief annual magistrate of the Athenian colony bore the title *Epimeletes*. After a servile outbreak (of unknown date), the cleruchy was, it is argued, dissolved; there was a wider organization of the Athenians and foreign traders. Already there existed guilds (κοινά) of Italian residents (*Hermaistai*, or *magistreis Mirquiri* sc. Mercurii, and others); the function of the Delian magistri has been much debated; it is improbable that there was a *conventus civium Romanorum*, as alleged by A. Schulten and E. Kornemann. There were also powerful Oriental guilds (e.g. the *Poseidoniastai* of Berytus), and trade guilds (e.g. the Oil-Sellers). Traders' vessels filled the Sacred Harbour and the Merchant Harbour to the south, and slaves constituted one of the chief commodities of exchange. Decline, however, set in after Archelaus, general of Mithridates of Pontus, sacked the island in 88; and in 69 the pirates, allies of Mithridates, attacked Delos, now a Roman naval centre, and enslaved the inhabitants. After Pompey suppressed the pirates some measure of prosperity returned to the island; a legatus of Lucullus, C. Valerius Triarius, repaired the town and built a wall to protect the inhabitants; and there is evidence of a Jewish colony. Before the end of the first century, however, the

trade-routes had altered, and Delos began to be abandoned both as entrepôt and as cult-centre. When Julius Caesar planted a colony of Romans on the old site of Corinth the fate of Delos was sealed, though a small group of inhabitants lingered on in the early Christian era.

The archaeological exploration of Delos, carried on by the French School (Athens) since 1873, first by A. Lebègue, then by Th. Homolle and many others, has been recorded contemporaneously in the *Bulletin de Correspondance Hellénique*, and since 1909 definitively in *Exploration archéologique de Délos*. It has revealed the remains of public buildings—temples, colonnades, theatre, gymnasium, etc., of agoras, and of warehouses and private dwellings of the second century B.C.; these, with a wealth of inscriptions, make a notable addition to the knowledge of Greek and Graeco-Roman civilization. The inhabited areas were on the sheltered western side, the sanctuary of Apollo (*Délos* xii) being close to the Sacred Harbour and south of the Sacred Lake and the celebrated Lion Terrace (*Délos* xxiv); further to the south were the theatre quarter (*Délos* viii) and the docks, quays, and warehouses (cf. *BCH* 1916, 5 ff.). North-west of the sanctuary was the Pillared Hall (Salle Hypostyle, *Délos* ii, ii *bis*), unique in Greek architecture and perhaps some sort of exchange. The most ancient worship may have centred on the sanctuary of Artemis, the site of which, identified in 1929, is nearer to the Sacred Harbour; here was found a very ancient treasure of gold, ivory, and bronze (cf. *BCH* 1947–8, 148 ff.). Some stress the importance of the temple of Leto in primitive times (e.g. Bethe, *Hermes* 1936, 351 ff., ibid. 1937, 190 ff.; *Die Antike* 1938, 81 ff.). The discoveries at the Artemision in 1946 gave rise to Gallet de Santerre's examination of Delos in pre-history and the problems of settlement on Mt. Cynthus and in the western plain respectively. The splendour of the *hieron* of Apollo eclipsed that of all others; to quote Homolle, among the temples of Greece there is none, not even the Parthenon, whose administration can be as minutely studied and as surely known as that of the temple of Apollo at Delos. Conditions regarding the letting of temple landed property, and the granting of temple loans, were defined as early as the fourth century in a document known as the Sacred Contract (cf. *Hermes* 1926, 86 ff.). Below Mt. Cynthus clustered on terraces the sanctuaries of the oriental gods (*Délos* xi, xvi). Delian records refer to a public gymnasium, and to palaestras, the identification of which is a matter of dispute (*Délos* xxv; *BCH* 1952, 562 ff.)

Evidence of the wealth and importance of foreign traders in the later second century B.C. is derived from the so-called Agora of the Italians (Schola Romanorum, Ἰταλικὴ Πάστας), the largest building of Delos and unique in the Greek world (*Délos* xix; cf. *BCH* 1881, 390 ff.; 1884, 113 ff.); also from the 'Establishment of the Poseidoniasts' of Berytus (*Délos* vi). The cosmopolitan character of the population at the end of the second century is indicated in an ephebe list of 119/18 (*BCH* 1931, 438 ff.). Thanks to the wealth of inscriptions it was possible to undertake prosopographical studies of the Romans and Italians on Delos (*BCH* 1884, 75 ff. (Homolle), ibid. 1912, 5 ff. (Hatzfeld); *Rev. Ét. Grec.* 1916, 188 ff. (Lacroix)). Also, the economic situation of the island with reference to commodities, prices, and wages in the period of independence has been the subject of particular investigation (e.g. G. Glotz, *J. des Savants* 1913, 16 ff., 206 ff., 251 ff.; *Rev. Ét. Grec.* 1916, 281 ff.). Valuable information was derived from the examination of stamped amphora handles (*BCH* 1952, 514 ff.).

In the course of the excavations a wealth of objects relating to daily life was found (*Délos* xviii), but few artistic bronzes among them. There is a fine collection

(Delos Museum) of lamps of black and red clay ranging in date from the fifth century to the early Christian era (*BCH* 1908, 133 ff.). There is a large collection of terra-cotta braziers (ibid. 1905, 372 ff.; ibid. 1934, 203 ff.; ibid. 1961, 474 ff.), and of terra-cotta figurines (*Délos* xxiii). Vases range from the earliest periods to the Attic red-figure period, the finest having been recovered from the older temple of Hera (*Délos* x); cf. *BCH* 1911, 350 ff. —archaic vases; ibid. 1913, 418 ff.—relief vases). Wall paintings and mosaics have survived, the former useful in assessing domestic cults (*Délos* ix). Some mosaics are very elegant, notably those in the House of the Masks (*Délos* xiv) and the House of Dionysus and House of the Dolphins (*Piot Mon. et Mém.* xiv).

Of the architectural adornment of the island, the theatre apart, little remains. Much marble sculpture was found, ranging in date from Naxian work of the seventh/sixth century to commonplace productions of the first century. Many portrait statues of the Graeco-Roman period are extant (*Délos* xiii), some of Hellenistic princes and some of official Romans (e.g. C. Billienus (*Délos* v. 41 ff., pl. 60)). There remain *in situ* the base and torso of the famous archaic and colossal statue of Apollo (Déonna, *Les Apollons archaïques*, 191 ff.), offering of the Naxians, as were the impressive lions (of Naxian marble) guarding the Processional Way leading to the Sacred Lake.

The detailed publications are those of the *Exploration archéologique de Délos* (in twenty-five volumes, 1909–61). The inscriptions are in *IG* xi and in *Inscriptions de Délos*, 1926–50. There is a selection in *Choix d'inscriptions de Délos* i (Textes historiques ed. F. Durrbach, 1921).
C. A. Lebègue, *Recherches sur Délos* (1876); T. Homolle, *Les Archives de l'intendance sacrée à Délos* (1887); V. de Schoeffer, *De Deli insulae rebus* (Berlin, 1889); id. s.v. Delos in *PW* iv. 2459 ff.; W. Koenig, *Der Bund der Nesioten* (1910); W. S. Ferguson, *Hellenistic Athens* (1911), ch. ix, 'Athens and Delos'. S. Molinier, *Les 'Maisons sacrées' de Délos au temps de l'indépendance de l'île, 315–166/5 av. J.C.* (1914); P. Roussel, *Délos colonie athénienne* (1916); id. *Les Cultes égyptiens à Délos* (1916); J. Hatzfeld, *Les Trafiquants italiens dans l'Orient hellénique* (1919); id. 'Les Italiens résidant à Délos,' *BCH* 1912, 5 ff.; A. E. R. Boak, 'The Magistri of Campania and Delos', *CPhil.* 1916, 25 ff.; M. Lacroix, 'Les Étrangers à Délos pendant la période de l'indépendance' in *Mélanges Glotz* (1932); M. Bulard, *La Religion domestique dans la colonie italienne de Délos* (1926); id. *Peintures murales et mosaïques de Délos, Piot Monuments et Mémoires* xiv (1908); Ch. Dugas, *Le Trésor de céramique de Délos* (1930); W. A. Laidlaw, *A History of Delos* (1933); R. Vallois, *L'Architecture hellénique et hellénistique à Délos jusqu'à l'éviction des Déliens*, I *Les Monuments* (1944); id. *Les Constructions antiques de Délos: Documents* (1953); W. Déonna, *La Vie privée des Déliens* (1948); M. Gallet de Santerre, *Délos primitive et archaïque* (1958); J. A. O. Larsen in Frank, *Econ. Survey* iv, 334 ff.; A. Plassart, 'La Synagogue juive de Délos' in *Mélanges Holleaux* (1913). On the contents of the Museum of Delos see N. M. Kontoleontos, Ὁδηγὸς τῆς Δήλου (1950), 138 ff.; for other publications see *CAH* viii, 792 f. W. A. L.

**DELPHI** is situated on the lower southern slopes of Parnassus, some 2,000 feet above the Gulf of Corinth. It attained importance at an early date and some have accepted the idea of a special connexion with Crete (cf. *The Delphic Hymn to Apollo*, 391–9, 514–23, for Apollo's Cretan priests, Κρῆτες ἀπὸ Κνωσοῦ Μινωΐου, and J. Defradas *Les Thèmes de la propagande delphique* (1954), 55 ff.), which is hardly supported by any volume of finds at Delphi, and may be due rather to memories of Cretan greatness as a centre of culture and ritual. Middle Helladic and later pottery has been found on the site, which also has the remains of Mycenaean houses. Subsequently Corinth seems to have played some part in the development of the oracle to judge from the pottery found, not unrelated to the activity of that city in western colonization and Apollo's function as Leader.

For the history of the oracle, see the following article. The sanctuary consisted of a *temenos* enclosed by a wall. Inside it were the monuments dedicated by the States of Greece to commemorate victories and public events, together with some twenty 'treasuries' a small theatre, and the main temple of Apollo (q.v., § 4) to which the Sacred Way wound up from the road below.

Tradition claimed (cf. *The Hymn to Apollo*, 295–6) Trophonius and Agamedes as the builders of the first temple of Apollo. There may have been others before the building which was destroyed by fire in 548 B.C. This destruction led to a reorganization, architectural rather than religious, of the *temenos*, involving the construction of the Polygonal Wall below the temple platform and the destruction of buildings and treasuries of which only architectural and sculptural elements now survive (cf. the Sicyonian *monopteros*). The great new temple was completed in the last decade of the sixth century with the aid if not the donations of the Athenian family of Alcmaeonidae then living at Delphi in exile. This new temple (partly described in the *Ion* of Euripides) was destroyed by an earthquake in 373. A new temple was built by subscription, its pedimental sculptures being made by two Athenians, Praxias and Androsthenes. This building survived until Roman times and was repaired by Domitian. The physical organization of the oracle, the cleft in the rock and the emanations from it, together with the position of the *adyton* or Holy of Holies where the Pythia gave her responses have been the subject of much controversy (cf. P. Amandry, *La Mantique apollinienne à Delphes* (1950), 201 ff.). The supposed *omphalos* (q.v.), the reputed centre of the earth, turns out to be the top of a pillar from the *iconostasis* of a church (*BCH* 1951, 210 ff.). A marble *omphalos* of Roman period has been found.

The sanctuary was attacked by the Persians in 480 and by the Gauls in 279, but suffered little damage. Nero despoiled it of 500 statues. Julian attempted a revival of the sanctuary, but the oracle announced to him its own decline, and in A.D. 390 it was finally closed by Theodosius in the name of Christianity. Excavations were begun by French archaeologists in 1880, when the village of Kastri was removed from the site to its present position.

Apart from the revelation of the main buildings of the enclosure and the remains of numerous memorials mentioned by Pausanias (such as the base of the Serpent Column commemorating Plataea and Lysander's memorial for Aegospotami), there have been notable finds of sculpture: the very archaic metopes of the Sicyonian *monopteros* and the metopes of the Athenian Treasury, the frieze of the Siphnian Treasury, pedimental sculptures of the 'Alcmaeonid' temple, important for sculptural chronology, the bronze Charioteer, and the remnants of the memorial set up by a Thessalian dynast the originals of which may be by Lysippus. Fragments of gold relief and ivory carving in the archaic style, including some heads of considerable size with inlaid eyes, which may have come from some work of art in these precious materials, were found buried under the Sacred Way.

Below the modern road and the Castalian Spring (the earlier form of which has recently been established) are public buildings (palaestra, etc.), the archaic temple of Athena Pronaia, and the fourth-century Tholos, in the area called the Marmariá, where lie also boulders which have fallen from the cliffs above (the Phaedriades).

F. Poulsen, *Delphi* (1920); E. Bourguet, *Les Ruines de Delphes* (1914); P. de la Coste-Messelière, *Au musée de Delphes* (1936); Pierre Birot, 'Geomorphologie de la région de Delphes', *BCH* 1959, 258 ff. S. C.; R. J. H.

**DELPHIC ORACLE**, in classical times the supreme oracle of Greece, presided over by Apollo. Its site was supposed to be the centre of the earth, marked by the sacred navel-stone (*omphalos*, q.v.). It had been a holy place from remote antiquity (remains of pre-Greek sacrifices have been found), and the presiding genius was originally an earth-spirit. Apollo was recognized by the Greeks themselves as a late-comer (Aesch. *Eum.* 1 ff., etc.). Aeschylus' account emphasizes the peaceful nature of the transfer to Apollo, but the legend of his killing a chthonian monster (*Hymn. Hom. Ap.*, Eur. *IT* 1244 ff.; see also J. E. Fontenrose, *Python: a Study of Delphic Myth and its Origins* (U.S.A. 1959)) suggests a different and more plausible tradition; the ecstasies and sex of the Pythia may be due to the original chthonian nature of the cult (but cf. K. Latte, *Harv. Theol. Rev.* 1940, 9 ff.).

**2.** Responses were given by the Pythia, who may have been originally appointed as a young virgin, but in later times at least was elderly (see Parke–Wormell, 35), in a state of frenzy induced by means not now ascertainable with certainty. Faith in the power of the god to take possession was complete, and the consequent emotional suggestion would doubtless add powerfully to the effect of such practices as chewing bay-leaves (Apollo's plant) or drinking holy water. Excavation has rendered improbable the post-classical theory of a chasm with mephitic vapours. The riddle of the prophecies is not entirely soluble. Efficient accumulation and use of information can account for much, but there remain exceptions, whose explanation will always be a mystery. After purification and sacrifice, inquirers approached the oracle in an order determined partly by lot. Right of precedence might be granted as a privilege (προμαντεία, Farnell, *Cults* iv. 214 n.). A male prophet put their question and interpreted the Pythia's answer, commonly in verse. Advice was sought both by private individuals (e.g. concerning marriage, childlessness, commercial enterprises) and States. Slaves were manumitted by dedication to the Delphic god.

**3.** In religion Delphi gave answers on all questions of cult, fostering the worship of Olympian and local deities impartially and adopting a generally conservative attitude on religious questions. The best way to worship was 'according to ancestral custom' or 'the City's custom' (Parke–Wormell, 321). It seems, however, to have welcomed Dionysus—with whose ecstatic worship Delphic prophecy has been thought to have much in common—and assisted in the propagation of his cult. At Delphi itself Dionysus was received into partnership, his grave was shown in the inner sanctuary, and for three winter months Apollo was believed to hand over the shrine to Dionysus and retire to the far north. The trieteric festivals of Dionysus at Delphi were orgiastic, and women were officially sent from the Greek States (including Athens) to take part in them. An authority on all cult-practices, Apollo was above all the god of *katharsis*, especially purification after homicide, from which the primitive conception of automatic *miasma* never entirely disappeared.

**4.** Politically, Delphi came to the fore in the great period of colonization, its advice being regularly sought on the choice of site and patron deity. Tradition assigned many laws of Greek cities also to the god, e.g. the constitution of Lycurgus at Sparta. Other political prophecies, with a few striking exceptions difficult to explain, suggest extensive knowledge of the situation and a leaning to conservatism which did not exclude attempts (not always successful) at a politic adaptation to changing conditions. Thus in spite of aristocratic sympathies, Delphi is said to have foretold the power of most of the tyrants (Pisistratus is an exception), it favoured Croesus until his fall, discouraged Greek resistance to Persia, was pro-Spartan in the Peloponnesian War, supported Philip of Macedon.

**5.** Questions of individual morality, which were left untouched by the city-states, deeply interested the oracle, and it seems to have shown great firmness on moral issues. It sponsored the notion that purity was a matter, not only of ritual, but also, and primarily, of the spirit, and that the intention might be more important than the deed. (Cf. esp. the story of Glaucus, Hdt. 6. 86, and

other examples in Parke–Wormell, ch. viii.) In this it reached the high-water mark of religious ethic in pagan antiquity. The famous exhortations carved on the temple, though not especially exalted in tone, were also moral precepts—'Know thyself' and 'Nothing too much'.

**6.** The importance of Delphi is above all that it provided a meeting-place for the otherwise isolated city-states of Greece. The unique position and universal prestige which it enjoyed, and which were necessary if it was to discharge this function, cannot now be completely accounted for, but besides the impressiveness of its prophetic method (as contrasted with 'sane' procedures like the inspection of victims or the flight of birds), one may mention the attraction of its famous Panhellenic Pythian games (founded after the First Sacred War about 590 B.C.) and its connexion with a powerful religious league of northern States, the Delphic Amphictiony (*see* AMPHICTIONIES). The early history of the Amphictiony is obscure, but it seems certain that its original centre was further north, and Delphi was probably not included until the middle of the seventh century. In the fifth century, with the recognition of Delphi as a common centre of worship, the Amphictionic Council became representative of the Greek states as a whole (Parke–Wormell, 177 f.). Macedon was admitted to membership after the assistance given by Philip against the Phocians in the Third Sacred War (355–346 B.C.).

**7.** In Hellenistic times the influence of Delphi and of the League rapidly declined, though the new kings thought it due to their royalty to flatter the oracle, which was still a centre of information for the Greek world. Delphi was seized by the Aetolian Confederacy about 300 B.C. and suffered later from barbarian invasions. Its treasure was unscrupulously used by Sulla. Under the Roman Empire it enjoyed a somewhat artificial revival in Hadrian's time, but astrology provided an alternative source of prophecy and there were rival oracles. The decline of Delphi was already almost complete when Christianity became the official religion under Constantine.

On the general subject of oracular prophecy, *see* ORACLES, DIVINATION.

For a full account of the Delphic oracle and bibliography, see H. W. Parke and D. E. W. Wormell, *The Delphic Oracle*² (2 vols., 1956), and its review by W. G. Forrest in *CR* 1958, 67 ff.
W. K. C. G.

**DEMADES** (fl. 350–319 B.C.), Athenian politician. A brilliant orator and diplomat, who recognized that Athens must come to terms with Macedon and did not scruple to stand in Macedonian pay, he rendered good service after the battle of Chaeronea, when he checked the intransigence of the Athenian people, rebuked Philip's insolence, and secured honourable terms of submission for Athens. After Philip's death he survived an impeachment by Hyperides, and when Alexander marched into Greece he again mediated between Athens and Macedon (335). During Alexander's absence in the East he remained in power, together with Phocion; he prevented Athens from supporting King Agis III (q.v.) against Macedon, and he procured the deification of Alexander. Accused of receiving a bribe from Harpalus (q.v.), he offered no defence and was fined; and after Alexander's death he was disfranchised. Reinstated in 322 to avert Antipater's attack on Athens, he used his influence to procure the deaths of Demosthenes and Hyperides. In 319 he was detected by Cassander in an intrigue with Antigonus, and was summarily executed by him while on an embassy to Macedonia. Nothing survives of his speeches (which were not committed to writing) except some picturesque phrases, e.g. 'Macedon without Alexander would be like the Cyclops without his eye'.

A fragment Ὑπὲρ τῆς δωδεκετείας, included in the oratorical Corpus, is certainly not by Demades.

P. Treves, *Athenaeum* 1933, 105 f.; *Rend. Ist. Lomb.* 1958, 327 f.
N. G. L. H.

**DEMARATUS**, a Eurypontid king of Sparta, *c.* 510–491 B.C. He obstructed his colleague Cleomenes I (q.v.) on the invasion of Attica (*c.* 506), and again when he prevented the arrest of the medizing party at Aegina (491). Dethroned on a false charge of illegitimacy by Cleomenes, he fled to King Darius. He accompanied Xerxes in 480, presumably in hopes of recovering his throne from the Persians, if victorious, and repeatedly warned him (according to Herodotus) that Sparta would undoubtedly resist him. Rewarded for his services with four cities in Asia Minor, he resided there until his death, many years later. A. M. W.

**DEMETER** (Δημήτηρ), the Greek corn-goddess, identified in Italy with Ceres (q.v.). It seems certain that the last two syllables of her name mean 'mother', but the first is more difficult. The ancient explanation, that δη- is a by-form of γη- and she is the 'earth-mother', breaks down owing to the absence of evidence of any such by-form of that or any other word beginning with γ. More likely, especially in view of Nilsson's demonstration (see below) that her most famous cult turns wholly on the processes connected with corn, is the suggestion of Mannhardt (see Farnell, op. cit. infra, 29 f.) that it is to be connected with ζειά, spelt, although this also is dubious, seeing that the form δηαί is attested (by Hesychius, s.v.) only as the Cretan for 'barley', and Demeter is not particularly connected with Crete, and the Dorian and other dialects call her Δαμάτηρ, indicating an *a*, not an *e* in the original form of her name.

Of her functions, however, there is no doubt. She is the goddess who governs the fruits of the earth, especially, though not quite exclusively, bread-corn. She would appear to have thrown off very early a younger double of herself, the 'Virgin' (Κόρη), who is regularly (not quite invariably) worshipped with her, and seems to be essentially the power which is in the corn itself and appears and disappears with it. Being thus connected with very important happenings at the surface of the earth, it is in accordance with a common tendency of Greek and other religions that she should become associated also with the depths of the earth; so Demeter becomes in mythology the mother-in-law, Kore (Persephone) the wife, of the death-god. It may reasonably be conjectured that originally the latter was the consort, not of Hades, but of Pluton, god of the wealth (especially the wealth of corn) which the earth produces. The story, first found in the Homeric Hymn to Demeter, is that Hades carried off Kore; Demeter, after vainly searching for her daughter, wandered to Eleusis and there was received, in disguise as an old woman, into the house of Celeus the king, to nurse his son. She put the child in the fire every night to burn his mortal nature away, but was interrupted by Metanira, Celeus' wife, and so hindered from making him immortal as she had planned. She then revealed herself to the Eleusinians, who built her a temple. Meanwhile Zeus, to persuade her to come back to Olympus and to let the earth bring forth, had Kore returned to her; but Kore, as she had eaten some pomegranate-seeds in the other world, could not return entirely, but spends some part of every year underground. As Nilsson (*ARW* xxxii. 79 ff.) points out, the myth agrees well with the historical celebration of the Eleusinian Mysteries (*see* ELEUSIS, MYSTERIES) and with Greek climatic conditions. The Great Mysteries are in Boedromion, 16–17 and 19–22, and connected with the return of Kore; the time is early autumn, when the fields are growing green again after the drought of summer. The Lesser Mysteries of Agrae are in Anthesterion; it is spring, and they lead up to the summer harvest and the following period of dryness, during which Kore, the young corn or seed-corn, is indeed under the earth, stored away in the great grain-jars. That the ritual of the Mysteries (which, at Eleusis, are even older than Demeter, being pre-Hellenic) had to do with the death and rebirth of the corn and that in time hopes of human immortality came to be read into this ritual is fairly clear, but the details remain extremely obscure (see bibliography below). Eleusis claimed to be the centre from which knowledge of agriculture sprung, Demeter having sent Triptolemus the Eleusinian to teach the rest of mankind (Callimachus, *Cer.* 20–2; Ov. *Met.* 5. 645; and many authors and representations in art).

Of other festivals of Demeter, one of the most famous and widely spread was the Thesmophoria (q.v., to Demeter Thesmophoros, 'bringer of treasures'; and *see* THEBES 1). In Athens it was held on Pyanopsion 11–13, and consisted of a series of rites, largely magical, performed by women for the fertility of the soil; connected with it was the ritual of the Scirophoria (q.v.), on Scirophorion 12.

In Arcadia Demeter appears as the consort of Poseidon (probably in his capacity of 'earth-holder' or husband of Earth, γαιήοχος, *see* POSEIDON). The Black Demeter of Phigalia and the Demeter Erinys of Thelpusa were both said to have been mated with by Poseidon in horse-shape, and the former was shown horse-headed (Paus. 8. 25. 4 ff., 42. 1 ff.), while it was doubtful if the child she bore was a foal or the local goddess Despoina. That a darker side of her nature was stressed here is clear from her titles. However, even the normal Demeter could be very formidable, since being a giver of plenty she could also bring famine. When Erysichthon (q.v.) offended her it was insatiable hunger that was his punishment. Another trace of her tendency to become a goddess of the depths of the earth and not simply of the corn is shown in the Athenian use of Δημήτρειοι, 'Demeter's people', as a euphemism for the dead (Plut. *De fac.* 943b).

Since she is a mother-goddess, the question who her husband was never consistently answered. In Arcadia (see above) he was Poseidon; according to Hesiod (*Theog.* 912–13) Zeus was Persephone's father; a story, probably a very old ritual myth, in the *Odyssey* (5. 125 ff.) says that she lay with Iasion (cf. DARDANUS) in a ploughed field, and that when Zeus heard of it he killed Iasion with the thunderbolt. To be the consort of a mother-goddess is very dangerous, cf. ANCHISES. Hesiod adds (ibid. 969 ff.) that their child was Plutus (q.v.). This is characteristic for all such goddesses; the important thing is that they should be fertile, not that they should be wives.

Demeter is shown in archaic and classical art with Triptolemus, Persephone, or both, or awaiting Persephone's return. She carries a sceptre, ears of corn, or torches, and is often difficult to distinguish from Persephone.

Farnell, *Cults* iii. 29 ff.; L. Deubner, *Attische Feste* (1932), 40 ff.; Nilsson, *Feste* 311 ff.; *GGR* i². 456 ff. J. Béquignon, 'Déméter déesse acropolitaine', *Rev. Arch.* 1958, 149 ff. H. J. R.

**DEMETRIAS**, a city of Magnesia on the Gulf of Pagasae. Formerly located below Mt. Pelion, it is now proved to have adjoined Pagasae on the western shore of the inner bay. Demetrius Poliorcetes founded it *c.* 293 B.C. by a 'synoecism' of many small Magnesian towns; he built massive fortifications and made the best use of an admirable site, so that it became important as a military and commercial centre. Though occupied by a Macedonian garrison as one of the 'fetters of Greece', it enjoyed some measure of self-government. Liberated from Philip V by Rome, Demetrias supported the Aetolians and Antiochus in 192–191. It was then regained by Philip and remained in Macedonian hands until the overthrow of Perseus. Its fortifications were partly demolished, and, although the principal city of the Magnesian League, it gradually declined.

The adjacent sites of Demetrias and Pagasae have been more thoroughly investigated by archaeologists than any in the interior of Thessaly.

F. Stählin and E. Meyer, *Pagasai und Demetrias* (1934); *PW* Suppl. ix.                                                      H. D. W.

**DEMETRIUS** (1), writer of Old Comedy (Diog. Laert. 5. 85). His Σικελία may be assigned to *c.* 400 B.C.

*CGF* i. 264–6; *CAF* i. 795–6.

**DEMETRIUS** (2) (5th/4th c. B.C.), sculptor, of Alopece. Made realistic portraits of Corinthian general Pellichus; Lysimache, priestess of Athena Polias in Athens; Simon, Athenian Hipparch. The realistic style can be seen on some contemporary Attic vases and on coins of Cyzicus.

Overbeck nos. 897–903; Lippold, *Griech. Plastik* 226; D. M. Lewis, *BSA* 1955, 4.                                      T. B. L. W.

**DEMETRIUS** (3) of Phalerum (b. *c.* 350 B.C.), son of Phanostratus, Athenian Peripatetic philosopher and statesman, began his political life in 325/4 and was probably elected *strategos* for many of the next few years. He escaped death as a pro-Macedonian in 318, and Cassander made him absolute governor at Athens, where he held power for ten years. As *nomothetes* he passed comprehensive legislation under Theophrastus' influence (317/16–316/15); military and other service was limited, various forms of extravagance were curbed, measures were taken to regularize contracts and titles to property and *nomophylakes* were set up. When Poliorcetes took Athens (307), Demetrius fled to Boeotia, and was later librarian at Alexandria (297). He died in disgrace under Philadelphus.

WORKS: moral treatises, popular tales, declamations, histories, literary criticism, rhetoric, and collections of letters, fables, and proverbs. Though an outstanding orator, Demetrius produced mainly a superficial amalgam of philosophy and rhetoric. He assisted his fellow Peripatetics, and under him Athens enjoyed peace.

*FGrH* ii B 228; F. Wehrli, *Demetrios von Phaleron* (1949). W. S. Ferguson, *Hellenistic Athens* (1911); E. Bayer, *Demetrios Phalereus der Athener* (1942); S. Dow and A. H. Travis, *Hesp.* 1943; *PW* Suppl. xi, 514 ff.                                      F. W. W.

**DEMETRIUS** (4) I of Macedonia, *Poliorcetes* (336–283 B.C.), son of Antigonus I (q.v.), married (321) Antipater's daughter Phila, and became a leading warrior in an age of war. His first important campaign (317–316) was against Eumenes (q.v. 3); his first independent command, against Ptolemy, ended in disaster at Gaza (312). Nevertheless he became henceforth the brilliant instrument of his father's policy of reuniting Alexander's Empire. His best performances were in Cyprus (306), which he won from Ptolemy by the naval victory of Salamis, and in Greece (307 and 304–302), where his harnessing of the Greek instinct for political freedom in his revived 'League of Corinth' achieved more than many victories. His famous siege of Rhodes (305) was a failure, and would have been unimportant politically had it succeeded; it repays study as a military *tour de force* and an apt expression of 'the Besieger's' personality.

The defeat of Ipsus and the death of Antigonus (301), for which Demetrius by his impetuosity was partly to blame, destroyed Antigonus' Empire in Asia, and reduced Demetrius' power to a precarious thalassocracy. But he kept a foothold in Greece, and after Cassander's death

(297) and the murder of two kings and the queen-mother, he had (through Phila) the best claim to the throne of Macedonia, and he was accepted as king by the army (294).

He was always a conqueror rather than a ruler, and age taught him no wisdom. While he established his control over Greece (293–289), he planned to regain his father's Empire in Asia. He possessed the finest man-power and the greatest fleet; but the Macedonians, who wanted peace not war, deserted to Lysimachus and Pyrrhus (qq.v.) when they simultaneously invaded Macedon; and Demetrius had lost his kingdom (288). He led into Asia no 'Grand Army', but a small force of mercenaries (287). He was trapped in Cilicia and surrendered to Seleucus (285), who hospitably encouraged him to drink himself to death (283). 'Bonis initiis malos euentus habuit.'

Diodorus, bks. 19, 20; Plutarch, *Demetrius*. W. W. Tarn, *CAH* vi, ch. 18; vii, ch. 3. G. Elkeles, *Demetrios der Städtebelagerer* (1941); P. Treves, *Riv. Fil.* 1931, 73 ff., 355 ff.                            G. T. G.

**DEMETRIUS** (5) 'the Fair' (ὁ καλός), son of Demetrius (4) Poliorcetes, and half-brother of Antigonus Gonatas. He was sent by Antigonus to take Cyrene from Ptolemy II (*c.* 255 B.C.). He gained Cyrene without opposition, but was murdered soon after at the instance of Berenice II (q.v.).                                                              M. C.

**DEMETRIUS** (6) II of Macedonia (*c.* 276–229 B.C.), son of Antigonus II and Phila, defeated Alexander of Epirus and dethroned him in 264 (Just. *Epit.*26. 2. 11). On succeeding Gonatas (*see* ANTIGONUS 2) in 239 he divorced Stratonice, Antiochus I's daughter, who had no male issue, and married an Epirote princess, Phthia, also called Chryseis. (His marriage to Nicaea, Alexander of Corinth's widow, was probably unconsummated: Plut. *Arat.* 17.) In 239–238 the Aetolian Confederacy, which sought to annex Epirote Acarnania, united with Achaea against Macedon ('Demetrian War'). Active at first in the west, Demetrius saved Acarnania, but lost Atintania; he assisted Argos against Achaea, and detached Boeotia, part of Phocis, and Opuntian Locris from Aetolia; and his general Bithys defeated Aratus, probably in 237–236. About this time, however, the Epirote monarchy was overthrown and the new republic joined the Confederacies; Demetrius allied himself with Agron of Illyria to protect Acarnania, but was called north by a Dardanian inroad. Defeated, he died in 229, leaving one son, Philip, by his wife Phthia.

A shadowy figure, Demetrius by his lack of vigour brought the Macedonian monarchy to a low ebb.

Plut. *Aratus*; Just. *Epit.* 28. V. Costanzi in *Saggi di storia antica offerti a G. Beloch* (1910); Beloch, *Griech. Gesch.* iv; P. Treves, *Rendiconti Accademia Lincei* 1932; M. Feyel, *Polybe et l'histoire de Béotie* (1942), 83 ff.                                                  F. W. W.

**DEMETRIUS** (7) of Pharos (d. 214 B.C.) betrayed Corcyra to Rome (229) and became a dynast in northwest Illyria. He helped Antigonus at Sellasia (222). In 220, breaking the treaty with Rome, he sailed past Lissus, to ravage the Aegean islands. Pursued by the Rhodians, he sold his assistance against Aetolia to Macedon. When expelled by the Romans (219), he fled to Philip V, whose anti-Roman policy he mainly inspired. In 215 he urged Philip to seize Ithome, and later perished in a rash expedition against Messene. Polybius (3. 19. 9) characterizes him as foolhardy, and wholly without judgement.

Polybius (the only reliable account). Cf. Walbank, *Polybius*; M. Holleaux, *Rome et la Grèce* (1921); Badian, *Stud. Gr. Rom. Hist.* 1 ff.                                                                F. W. W.

**DEMETRIUS** (8) I of Bactria (*c.* 200–185 B.C.), son and successor of Euthydemus I (q.v.), annexed Arachosia and Drangiana to his kingdom. According to some scholars he advanced as far east as Pataliputra (*Patna*) and 'consciously imitating Alexander' he 'intended, following his ideas, to make of his empire a kind of partnership of Greek and Indian, typified by his bilingual coinage'. But evidence for his far-reaching conquests and other achievements is lacking and the bilingual coins are now accepted to be the issues of a Demetrius contemporary which Eucratides I. Demetrias-in-Arachosia (somewhere between Seistan and Ghazni), mentioned in Isidore's *Parthian Stations*, perhaps owes its origin to Demetrius I. His silver coins bear his portrait wearing elephant scalp on the obverse and Heracles standing on the reverse.

W. W. Tarn, *The Greeks in Bactria and India*² (1951); A. K. Narain, *The Indo-Greeks* (1957). A. K. N.

**DEMETRIUS** (9) (*c.* 180–165 B.C.), probably related to Antimachus I, was an early contemporary of Eucratides I. He is the first among the Indo-Greeks to issue bilingual coins, with Greek and Kharosthi characters. A Demetrius known as king of 'India' in the classical sources must be identified with him.

A. K. Narain, *The Indo-Greeks* (1957). A. K. N.

**DEMETRIUS** (10) I Soter of Syria (187–150 B.C.), second son of Seleucus IV. As a hostage in Rome he saw the kingdom pass first to his uncle (Antiochus IV) and then to his cousin (Antiochus V). In 162 he escaped and won the throne for himself. He crushed the rebel general Timarchus in the east and reconquered the insurgent Jews in Palestine (161). His ability made him feared by neighbouring Powers and suspect to Rome (though the Senate had recognized his title in 160). He died in battle against a pretender, Alexander Balas, whom the kings of Pergamum and Egypt had suborned against him.

H. Volkmann, *Klio* 1925, 373 ff. G. T. G.

**DEMETRIUS** (11) II Nicator of Syria (*c.* 161–125 B.C.), eldest son of Demetrius I, reigned 145–139 and 129–125. In 141 he made war upon Parthia, but was captured, and did not obtain his release until 129. His reign well illustrates the difficulties of the later Seleucids. He won his kingdom from one pretender, lost part of it almost immediately to a second, and was finally murdered after losing the remainder to a third. G. T. G.

**DEMETRIUS** (12) of Scepsis in the Troad (b. *c.* 214 B.C.), grammarian, archaeologist, and polymath, wrote sixty books on the sixty-line Trojan catalogue (*Il.* 2).

**DEMETRIUS** (13) IXION (2nd c. B.C.), a grammarian, contemporary with Aristarchus, who seceded from Alexandria to Pergamum and disputed Aristarchan textual principles. He also compiled an Atticist Lexicon.

**DEMETRIUS** (14) LACON (2nd c. B.C.), Epicurean, pupil of Protarchus of Bargylia and younger contemporary of Zeno of Sidon. He criticized Carneades' attack on the possibility of proof, and expounded Epicurus' doctrine of time.

Ed. W. Crönert, in *Kolotes u. Menedemos* (1906), 100, and V. de Falco (1923). W. D. R.

**DEMETRIUS** (15) (probably 2nd or 1st c. B.C.) compiled in Greek a short guide to letter-writing which enumerates twenty-one types of letter, with one or two examples of each type (ed. V. Weichert, 1910).

**DEMETRIUS** (16) of Magnesia (fl. 50 B.C.), friend of Atticus, wrote in Greek on concord (Περὶ ὁμονοίας),

and on homonymous towns and writers; much of his biographical detail was transmitted to Diog. Laert.

*FHG* iv. 382.

**DEMETRIUS** (17). The treatise Περὶ ἑρμηνείας, 'On Style', is traditionally ascribed to Demetrius (3). This is most unlikely to be right. The author probably belongs to the late Hellenistic or early Roman period, though no indications are decisive. The distinctive feature of the book is that it treats of four types (χαρακτῆρες) of style, adding the δεινὸς χαρακτήρ to the traditional μεγαλοπρεπής, ἰσχνός, and γλαφυρός (*see* LITERARY CRITICISM IN ANTIQUITY § 6). Much of the material is Peripatetic; the examples come from poets and historians as well as orators, and among the orators Demosthenes has not the dominant position which later rhetoric usually assigns to him. Many minor fourth-century figures are quoted; this has been thought to indicate an early date, but the same is true of Rutilius Lupus' treatise on figures (C. Halm, *Rhetores Latini Minores* (Leipzig, 1863), 3 ff.), which is an abridgement of the younger Gorgias (q.v. 2, first century B.C.). Particularly noteworthy parts of Περὶ ἑρμηνείας are the sections on letter-writing (§§ 223–35) and on χάρις (in the chapter on τὸ γλαφυρόν, §§ 128–89).

EDITIONS. L. Radermacher (1901); W. Rhys Roberts (1902).—See also D. M. Schenkeveld, *Studies in Demetrius On Style* (Amsterdam, 1964).
TRANSLATIONS. W. Rhys Roberts (Loeb, 1927); T. A. Moxon (Everyman, 1934); G. M. A. Grube (1961; with extensive introduction and notes). D. A. R.

**DEMETRIUS** (18) of Tarsus (1st c. A.D.), a grammarian, one of the characters in Plutarch's *De defect. orac.*, where he is said (c. 2) to be on his way home from Britain to Tarsus. Perhaps identical with a Demetrius who dedicated two tablets with Greek inscriptions, now in the York Museum; and possibly also Demetrius (17). See W. Rhys Roberts, in Loeb *Demetrius*, 272 ff.

**DEMETRIUS** (19) the Cynic lived in Rome under Gaius, Nero, and Vespasian, and belonged to the strongly anti-monarchical branch of the Cynic school. He was exiled to Greece under Nero (A.D. 66) but returned in the time of Vespasian.

**DEMETRIUS** (20) of Troezen (probably 1st c. A.D.) wrote works on literary history (Ath. 1. 29a). The only known title is that of his work on philosophers, Κατὰ σοφιστῶν (Diog. Laert. 8. 74).

**DEMINUTIO CAPITIS.** Loss or change of status. The term is first found in Cicero (*Top.* 4. 18, 6. 29) but is no doubt older. '*Caput*' is a common legal word for the individual as such or as the member of a group, and hence for his status. Civil capacity in Roman law depends on three elements: freedom (*libertas*), Roman citizenship (*civitas*), and membership of a Roman family (*familia*). The loss of one of these three produces *capitis deminutio*: *see* PATRIA POTESTAS. Classical Roman law sometimes distinguishes three degrees of *deminutio capitis*. (*a*) *Maxima*, when the individual loses his freedom and therefore also his citizenship and family rights. This occurs by capture in war (*but see* POSTLIMINIUM) or, later, as a punishment. (*b*) *Media* (or *minor*), when he loses citizenship and family rights, usually as a punishment, as in the case of *aquae et ignis interdictio* (*see* EXSILIUM) or *deportatio* (*see* RELEGATIO). (*c*) *Minima*, when he loses family rights (*mutatio familiae*) by *adoptio* or *adrogatio* (*see* ADOPTIO), *emancipatio* (q.v.), entry into *manus* (q.v.). Terminology, however, varies. A given kind of *capitis deminutio* does not always entail all the same results, and the term sometimes refers to the event producing the effects and sometimes simply to the effects themselves.

The three-fold division is best regarded as a convenient but loose classification of the effects. The importance of a change of family lies in the breaking of agnatic ties and therefore the loss of rights of inheritance and guardianship (qq.v.); but the reforms of the Praetor and of Justinian, with their emphasis on cognatic relationship, progressively removed these effects (see INHERITANCE, LAW OF; ADOPTIO; GUARDIANSHIP). It may also result in extinction of debts, of personal servitudes (see SERVITUTES), failure of a will, etc. *Capitis deminutio* does not invariably result in a loss of status. A person adopted from one family to another remains in the same status; one who is emancipated achieves a higher status. But there is a loss of rights in the original family.

Gaius 1. 158–64; 2. 145; 3. 153; Ulp. *Epit.* 11. 9–13; *Inst. Iust.* 1. 16; *Dig.* 4. 5. F. Desserteaux, *Études sur la formation historique de la capitis deminutio* i (1909), ii (1919–26), iii (1928); W. W. Buckland, *A Text-Book of Roman Law*[3] (1963), 135 ff.; M. Kaser, *Iura* 1952, 48 ff. B. N.

**DEMIOURGOI** (δημιουργοί), 'public workers', are in Homer such independent craftsmen as metal-workers, potters, and masons, and also seers, doctors, bards, and heralds (though not beggars! *Od.* 17. 383). Plato and Xenophon use the word thus. But in pre-Solonian Athens they comprised all who gained their livelihood other than from the soil, perhaps including wage-earners. They enjoyed a short-lived right of supplying two of the archons (580 B.C.) (Arist. *Ath. Pol.* 13. 2); they do not subsequently appear as a separately organized class. As the highest, often eponymous officers, *demiourgoi* appear in several States; though perhaps of greatest antiquity in Elis and Achaea, they are most often mentioned in Dorian records. Their exact function varied from State to State. In the Achaean Confederacy they formed a council of ten, who assisted the general; the Arcadian Confederacy imitated this organization, based originally on local representation, as also in Elis, where the *demiourgoi* formed a special caste. *Demiourgoi* appear in the Argolid, Megarid, Messenia, Thessaly, Delphi, Locris, Phocis, Crete, and several Aegean islands; examples from Cilicia, Pamphylia, and Pisidia date from Roman times.

Evidence mainly epigraphical. V. v. Schoeffer, *PW*, s.v. 'Demiurgoi'; M. Guarducci, *Riv. Fil.* 1930; K. Musakawa, *Hist.* 1957, 385 ff. F. W. W.

**DEMOCEDES** of Croton (6th c. B.C.), one of the most famous physicians of his time, practised first in Aegina and Athens, then at the court of Polycrates of Samos. After the murder of Polycrates in 522 B.C. he won much favour at the court of Darius, but later returned to Croton; on the defeat of the aristocrats by the democrats under Theages he fled to Plataea. He married a daughter of the wrestler Milon.

Testimonia in Diels, *Vorsokr.*[11] i. 110–12. W. D. R.

**DEMOCHARES** (c. 360–275 B.C.), Athenian orator and democratic statesman, who rose to power after the expulsion of Cassander's agents in 307. During the 'Four Years' War' against Cassander (307–304) he fortified Athens and made an alliance with Boeotia. Exiled at a date which cannot be securely determined, he returned in Diocles' archonship (288–287?), and recovered Eleusis from Macedon. He secured financial aid from Lysimachus, Antipater, and Ptolemy; and in 280–279 (archon: Gorgias) had a decree passed honouring Demosthenes, his uncle. Sincere and patriotic, he was handicapped by doctrinaire political views.

His written works consisted of Speeches, and a History, mainly of Athens, in over twenty-one books, rhetorical and lacking in objectivity.

F. Jacoby, *FGrH* ii. 75; *Lives of X Orators*, 851 (decree passed by Demochares' son Laches, 271–270); W. S. Ferguson, *Hellenistic Athens* (1911); Beloch, *Griech. Gesch.* iv. 2, 445. F. W. W.

**DEMOCRACY** (δημοκρατία, the 'rule of the people'). This term becomes common with Thucydides and Aristophanes, but is known to Herodotus (6. 43), and is presumed by Aeschylus (*Supp.* 604). The germs of Greek democracy grew from the fact that the *polis* (q.v.) derived from the old assembly of the armed people, and always preserved some traces of that origin. Beginning with Thersites (*Il.* 2. 212), there were always movements against the rule of the noble and the rich, as the lower ranks of free people tried to win full citizenship. The development towards democracy may be first perceived in Hesiod and Solon. The suppressed and exhausted demos found leaders in tyrants or lawgivers, and during the sixth and fifth centuries B.C. many city-states achieved a more or less democratic constitution, especially under the influence of Athens where Cleisthenes (q.v. 1) had created the essential foundations of democracy. He used the expression for equality, *isonomia*, for democracy itself. Athens became the most perfect and by its power the most influential democracy. Its ideal form is proclaimed by the Periclean Funeral Speech (Thuc. 2. 35 ff.), its leading ideas were law, freedom, and equality.

The sovereign authority in democracy was the Assembly, which decided by majority. The principal task of the council (see BOULE) and the magistracies (q.v.) was to prepare measures and to carry them into effect. In the Assembly and popular courts almost the whole people participated, and as council and magistracies were continually changing their personnel, the people became the actual ruler. Every citizen had full liberty of speech (παρρησία), but even the most extreme democracy could not dispense with leadership. During most of the fifth century it was in the hands of aristocratic *strategoi* (q.v.), in the fourth century government was controlled by unofficial and irresponsible leaders ('demagogues'). That was one of the reasons for the decline of democracy. Other reasons were: the ease with which the Assembly could make and unmake laws, the strong individualism arising from the very ideals of freedom and equality, and the general mistrust of any person who grew powerful. Political philosophers always regarded democracy, and especially its 'deviation', ochlocracy, as a bad constitution.

Schoeffer, *PW*, Suppl. i. 346 ff.; T. R. Glover, *Democracy in the Ancient World* (1927); A. H. M. Jones, *Athenian Democracy* (1957); V. Ehrenberg, *The Greek State* (1960). V. E.

**DEMOCRITUS** of Abdera, b. 460–457 (Apollodorus ap. Diog. Laert. 9. 41); this date is more likely than the others mentioned (470–469 Thrasyllus, 500–497 Eusebius), because it agrees best with Democritus' own words, quoted from the *Mikros Diakosmos* by Diog. Laert. 9. 41, that he was forty years younger than Anaxagoras. According to the same source he wrote his *Mikros Diakosmos* 730 years after the fall of Troy; Ferguson argues that the only possible one of the traditional dates for this is Ephorus' 1135—giving 405 B.C. for Democritus' work. Tradition is unanimous that he lived to be very old (e.g. Lucian *Macrob.* 18 says he was 104). His father was a substantial citizen of Abdera in Thrace, called Hegesistratus, Athenocritus, or Damasippus. The story (Diog. Laert. 9. 34) that Xerxes left some magi behind, after he had been entertained by Democritus' father in Abdera, and that Democritus learnt 'theology and astrology' from them, must be a legend, since the magi would have had to stay about thirty years (moreover, the same story is told of Protagoras, Philostr. *VS* 1. 10. 1). Democritus is said to have travelled to Egypt to learn geometry, to Persia, the Red Sea, to India, and Ethiopia—and to Athens, 'but no one knew me' (fr. B. 116, quoted by Diog. Laert., who also says that Demetrius of Phalerum denied the story of this visit). In later antiquity he was known as 'the laughing philosopher' (γελασῖνος), probably because of his ethical ideal of 'cheerfulness' ($\epsilon \vartheta \theta \nu \mu i \eta$). There is a legend that he blinded himself—Tertullian (*Apol.* 46 d) typically says it was to prevent his desiring women—but Plutarch (*de curios.* 521 d) denies it.

As his teachers tradition mentions Leucippus (q.v. 3) and, less confidently, Anaxagoras (q.v.) and an unnamed Pythagorean (Diog. Laert. 9. 34 and 38). He referred to Protagoras (ibid. 42); probably Protagoras (q.v.) was much older than Democritus, and the story (Philostr. *VS* 10) that Democritus taught him must be wrong. Plato never mentions him by name, but almost certainly took account of his views in the later dialogues (see Hammer-Jensen, Wilpert, op. cit.). Aristotle refers to him frequently in many connexions and with great respect.

WORKS. Diog. Laert. 9. 46–9 mentions seventy titles, arranged in tetralogies (with some exceptions) by Thrasyllus and classified as follows: Ethics, Physics, Unclassified, Mathematics, Music (which includes philological and literary criticism), Technical, and Notes ($\dot{\upsilon} \pi o \mu \nu \dot{\eta} \mu a \tau a$). The later history of these books is unknown; only small fragments survive today; even Simplicius in the sixth century seems to have relied on summaries.

It seems impossible to separate the contributions of Leucippus and Democritus to the atomic theory; the most sustained of recent efforts to do so, by C. Bailey, is marred by mis-statements of the evidence. Aristotle and Theophrastus refer most doctrines to both or either of them indiscriminately. Aristotle's account of the origin of the theory (*Gen. Corr.* A 8) correctly relates it to the Eleatics. The Eleatics argued that what is real is one and motionless, since empty space is not a real existent; for motion is impossible without empty space, and plurality is impossible without something to separate the units. Division of what is real into units in contact, i.e. with no separating spaces, is ruled out because (*a*) infinite divisibility would mean there are no real units at all, and (*b*) finite divisibility is physically inexplicable. Against these arguments, says Aristotle, Leucippus proposed to rescue the sensible world of plurality and motion by asserting that empty space, 'the non-existent', may nevertheless serve to separate parts of what does exist from each other. So the world has two ingredients: being, which satisfies the Eleatic criteria by being 'full', unchanging, and homogeneous, and non-being or empty space. The pieces of real being, since it is their characteristic to be absolutely indivisible units, are called atoms. They are said to be solid, invisibly small, and undifferentiated in material; they differ from each other in shape and size only (perhaps also in weight), and the only change they undergo is in their relative and absolute position, through movement in space.

By their changes of position the atoms produce the compounds of the changing sensible world. Compounds differ in quality according to the shape and arrangement of the component atoms, their congruence or otherwise (i.e. their tendency to latch together because of their shape), and the amount of space between them. The motion of atoms is an original, unexplained property (Melissus had criticized Empedocles and Anaxagoras for their theories of the origin of motion); changes of motion occur through random collisions, though certain patterns are recognizable, such as the whirl or vortex, which has the effect of sorting out the atoms by size and shape. Our world is not unique but one of an indeterminate number. A world is produced by accident out of the infinitely numerous atoms moving through the infinite void; and the atomists produced an account of the evolution of progressively more complex stages of organization, including human cultures (traces in Diodorus 1. 7–8; and see Lucretius, book 5).

The soul, which is the cause of life and sensation, is made of fine round atoms, and is as perishable as the body. Perception takes place through the impact of $\epsilon \ddot{\iota} \delta \omega \lambda a$ (films shed from the surfaces of sensible objects) upon the soul-atoms through the sense-organs. Perceptible qualities are the product of the atoms of the sensible object and those of the perceiving soul. There is a distinction between 'dark knowledge' ($\gamma \nu \dot{\omega} \mu \eta \sigma \kappa o \tau i \eta$) of sensible properties which exist only 'by convention', and 'genuine knowledge' ($\gamma \nu \dot{\omega} \mu \eta \gamma \nu \eta \sigma i \eta$) of atoms and void. The senses provide clues, but they have to be interpreted to provide real knowledge.

Many fragments of Democritus deal with ethics, but they are mostly very short and hard to fit together to make a consistent and comprehensive doctrine. His ethical ideal seems to include the idea that the soul-atoms should be protected from violent upheavals; well-being ($\epsilon \dot{\upsilon} \epsilon \sigma \tau \dot{\omega}$) which leads to cheerfulness ($\epsilon \dot{\upsilon} \theta \upsilon \mu i \eta$) is a matter of moderation and wisdom (B 191). It is important not to let the fear of death spoil life, and to recognize the limits to which man is necessarily confined (B 199, 203). Pleasure is in some sense the criterion of right action, but there must be moderation in choosing pleasures (B 189, 207, 224, 231). In social ethics, Democritus was apparently prepared to link his view of contemporary society with his theory of the evolution of human communities; he saw that a system of law is by nature necessary for the preservation of society, and that citizens must make positive contributions to their society. Some fragments show that he was a democrat (B 251, cf. B 255).

Little is known (though much is written) about the mathematics of Democritus. A high reputation has been accorded to him on the strength of a tribute paid by Archimedes (*Method*, Introd.) though it is withdrawn elsewhere (*Sphere and Cylinder*, 1). He must have been a diligent biologist, for Aristotle quotes him often.

Democritus is a figure of great importance who has suffered through the triumph of his opponents, Plato, Aristotle, and the Stoics, in the following centuries. He defended the infinite and perishable universe, efficient or 'mechanical' causes, and the atomic theory of matter, as opposed to the finite and eternal cosmos of Aristotle, teleology, and the continuous theory of matter. The best brains preferred his opponents' arguments, and Epicurus and Lucretius were his only influential followers. Great honour was paid to him by post-Renaissance scientists but by then his books were lost.

1. ANCIENT SOURCES. Diels, *Vorsokr.*[11]

2. MODERN LITERATURE. (i) General: K. Lasswitz, *Geschichte der Atomistik* (1890); Heath, *Hist. of Greek Maths.*; H. Cherniss, *Aristotle's Criticism of Presocratic Philosophy* (1935); S. Sambursky, *The Physical World of the Greeks* (1956); Kirk-Raven, *Presocratic Philosophers*; E. A. Havelock, *The Liberal Temper in Greek Politics* (1957); J. Kerschensteiner, *Kosmos* (1962); Guthrie, *Hist. Gk. Phil. ii.* (ii) Special: P. Natorp, *Die Ethika des D.* (1893); A. Dyroff, *Demokritstudien* (1899); I. Hammer-Jensen, 'D. und Platon', *Arch. f. Gesch. d. Philosophie* 1910; C. Bailey, *The Greek Atomists and Epicurus* (1928), reviewed critically by R. Philippson, *Gnomon* 1930; R. Philippson, 'Democritea', *Hermes* 1929; S. Luria, 'Die Infinitesimallehre der antiken Atomisten', *Quellen und Studien zur Geschichte der Mathematik*, B 2 (1933); H. Langerbeck, $\Delta o \xi \iota s \ \dot{\epsilon} \pi \iota \rho \upsilon \sigma \mu i \eta$, *Studien zu D.'s Ethik und Erkenntnislehre* (*Neue philologische Untersuchungen* 1935), reviewed critically by E. Kapp, *Gnomon* 1936; H. Weiss, 'D.'s Theory of Cognition', *CQ* 1938; K. von Fritz, *Philosophie und sprachliche Ausdruck bei Demokrit, Platon und Aristoteles* (1938); G. Vlastos, 'Ethics and Physics in D.', *Phil. Rev.* 1945–6; id. 'On the Prehistory in Diodorus', *AJPhil.* 1946; W. Schmid, 'Die Atomistik', in Schmid–Stählin, *I.* v (1948), 224 ff.; P. Wilpert, 'Die Elementenlehre des Platon und D.', in *Natur, Geist, Geschichte*, Festschrift Wenzl (1950); V. E. Alfieri, *Atomos Idea* (1953); K. von Fritz, 'D.'s Theory of Vision' in *Science, Medicine and History* (Essays . . . Charles Singer) (1953); J. Davison, 'Protagoras, D. and Anaxagoras', *CQ* 1953; J. Mau, 'Studien zur erkenntnistheoretischen Grundlage der Atomlehre im Altertum', *Wissenschaftliche Zeitschrift der Humboldt-Universität zu Berlin*, 2. 1952/3; id. *Zum Problem des Infinitesimalen bei den antiken Atomisten* (1954); J. McDiarmid, 'Phantoms in Democritean Terminology' *Hermes* 1958; id. 'Theophrastus De Sensibus 66', *AJPhil.* 1959; id. 'Theophrastus De Sensibus 61–2', *CPhil.* 1960; J. Ferguson, 'On the Date of Democritus', *Symb. Oslo.* 1965; D. J. Furley, *Two Studies in the Greek Atomists* (1967); Thomas Cole, *Democritus and the Sources of Greek Anthropology* (1967). D. J. F.

**DEMODOCUS**, the minstrel of Alcinous (q.v.), blind but very gifted (*Od.* 8. 44–5; 62–4). He sings of the loves of Ares and Aphrodite (ibid. 266 ff., if genuine), is sent an honourable portion of meat by Odysseus at Alcinous' feast (474 ff.), and makes him weep with his songs of the Trojan War (521 ff.). H. J. R.

**DEMOI** (δῆμοι), generally villages like κῶμαι, but in Athens, where they are best documented, and in certain other states, e.g. Eretria, Cos, and Rhodes, they also acted as the smallest political divisions. This role they received at Athens from Cleisthenes (q.v. 1), who used them as the cornerstone of his fundamental arrangement of the citizenry into ten *phylai* (q.v.) or tribes, thirty *trittyes* (q.v.), and as many as 150 demes (later about 170). He divided the demes into three groups: those of the town, or approximately the extent of modern Athens, Piraeus, and the coast as far as the airport; those of the interior; and those of the coast. Each tribe included demes from these three regions, and within a tribe the demes from each region constituted a trittys.

Because the demes were originally natural townships and within Athens itself probably natural wards, they varied greatly in size. The differences were reflected in the Council of 500 where each deme was represented according to its population; the number of a deme's representatives was not vitally affected by movement since after the initial registration under Cleisthenes membership became hereditary and did not depend upon residence. Acharnae (q.v.), the largest, sent twenty-two members to the *boule* (in the fourth century) and may have provided 1,200 hoplites; Halimous had three representatives and scarcely a hundred members; many were still smaller.

The demes maintained lists of their own members, every Athenian being registered in his familial deme at the completion of his eighteenth year, and on these registers all citizens depended for recognition of their citizen rights, though a rejected applicant might appeal to a dicastery. They also kept records of all properties held within their territory and of the metics, who, unlike citizens, were enumerated strictly in their place of residence. They could thus furnish the State with the censual and cadastral information necessary for such institutions as *ephebeia*, *eisphora*, and *liturgies* (qq.v.).

The demes were also corporations with strong local associations; they performed certain police duties; they could hold land, had cults and officials; they held meetings, presided over by the *demarchos*, at which the demesmen passed measures ordering their own affairs. Being almost microcosms of the State, they provided an Athenian citizen with a basic experience and understanding of the meaning of responsible government and civic duty.

B. Haussoullier, *La Vie municipale en Attique* (1884); A. W. Gomme, *The Population of Athens in the Fifth and Fourth Centuries B.C.* (1933); E. Kirsten, 'Der gegenwärtige Stand der attischen Demenforschung', *Atti del terzo congresso internazionale di epigrafia greca e latina* (1959), 156 ff.; C. W. J. Eliot, *Coastal Demes of Attika* (1962). C. W. J. E.

**DEMON** (fl. *c.* 300 B.C.), author of an *Atthis* in at least four books. The fragments all belong to the period of the kings and suggest an antiquarian rather than historical interest, perhaps influenced by the Peripatetics and comparable with Ister. The work was criticized by Philochorus.

*FGrH* iii B. 327, and *see under* ATTHIS. G. L. B.

**DEMONAX** of Cyprus (2nd c. A.D.), Cynic philosopher, known only by the life of him ascribed to Lucian. He was of good family but elected to live in poverty; his teachers were Epictetus, Timocrates of Heraclea, Agathobulus, Demetrius. He avoided the grossest excesses of the Cynic school; he admired Socrates and Aristippus as well as Diogenes. He cannot be credited with any independent philosophical views. He starved himself to death when nearly 100 years old. W. D. R.

**DEMOPHANES** and **ECDELUS** (not Megalophanes and Ecdemus, as Plut. *Phil.* 1; cf. Ziegler, *Rh. Mus.* 1934, 228 f.) (3rd c. B.C.), two Megalopolitans, followers in exile of Arcesilaus of the Athenian Academy, and renowned for their services to the republican cause, in 251 B.C. helped Aratus to liberate Sicyon, and about the same time had the tyrant Aristodemus murdered, thus freeing their own city. They were also called in to establish a federal constitution in Cyrene, either by Demetrius the Fair (q.v. 5), or, less probably, after his assassination (*c.* 250). They were later famous as Philopoemen's teachers. F. W. W.

**DEMOPHON** (Δημοφῶν), in mythology, son of Theseus and brother of Acamas (q.v.). He and his brother, being shadowy figures, are often confused, both being lovers of Laodice and Phyllis. His part in the Trojan War is the doublet of his brother's. While returning he stayed in Thrace and there met Phyllis, a princess who fell in love with him. He left her, promising to return when he had settled affairs at Athens; but she, weary with waiting, hanged herself and was turned into an almond-tree, which put forth leaves when Demophon came at last and embraced it (Servius on Verg. *Ecl.* 5. 10; Hyg. *Fab.* 59; Ov. *Her.* 2). The Athenians claimed to possess the Palladium (q.v.), which came somehow into Demophon's hands (*Suda*, s.v. ἐπὶ Παλλαδίῳ; Clem. Al. *Protr.* 36, 15 ff. Stählin).

On representations of Demophon in art, *see under* ACAMAS.
H. J. R.

**DEMOSTHENES** (1) (d. 413 B.C.), son of Alcisthenes, Athenian general. After an unsuccessful invasion of Aetolia in 426 he won two brilliant victories against a Peloponnesian and Ambraciot army invading Amphilochia. In 425 his occupation of Pylos led to a most valuable success, the capture of a body of Spartan hoplites on the adjacent island of Sphacteria. He surprised Nisaea in 424, but failed to take Megara, and in a triple attack on Boeotia, for which he was perhaps responsible, he was unable to land troops at Siphae, since the enemy was forewarned. He was not again entrusted with a major command until 413 when he was sent to reinforce Nicias at Syracuse. After failing to regain Epipolae by a night attack, he urged withdrawal from Syracuse, which was delayed until the Athenians lost control of the sea and were driven to attempt escape by land. The rearguard, led by Demosthenes, surrendered on the sixth day, and he was subsequently executed.

Demosthenes apparently had no political ambitions and enjoyed no political influence. He showed inventiveness in trying to break the military stalemate produced by Periclean strategy, but his plans tended to be too elaborate. He was a skilful tactician and an inspiring leader.

Thucydides, bks. 3, 4, 7. M. Treu, *Hist.* 1956, 420 ff.
H. D. W.

**DEMOSTHENES** (2) (384–322), the greatest Athenian orator. When Demosthenes was 7 years old his father died, leaving the management of his estate to his brothers, Aphobus and Demophon, and a friend, Therippides. The trustees mismanaged the business, and Demosthenes at the age of 18 found himself almost without resources. He claimed his patrimony from his guardians, who spent three years in attempts to compromise. In the meantime, he was studying rhetoric and legal procedure under Isaeus (q.v. 1); at 21 he brought a successful action against his guardians; but two more years elapsed before he received the remnants of the property. By now he was engaged in the profession of *logographos* and the reputation gained in private cases led to his being employed as an assistant to prosecutors in public trials. From 355/4 onwards he came more and more to devote himself to public business. It is not clear how far Demosthenes' sympathies were engaged in his first public trials, the prosecutions of Androtion (q.v.) and Leptines in 355 and of Androtion's associate, Timocrates, in 353: *Against Androtion* and *Against Timocrates* he wrote for Diodorus, and in any case the political tendency of the trials is unsure; *Against Leptines* Demosthenes did deliver himself, and, since Leptines' law was defended by Aristophon (q.v.), it is possible that all three trials centred on his policy and that Demosthenes was one of his opponents. This would be consistent with the policy he supported in *On the Symmories* in 354/3: a rumour came that the Great King was preparing to attack Greece, as he had threatened to do in 356/5, and Demosthenes, arguing that the city was not properly prepared, opposed the advocates of war, certainly not the Eubulus (q.v. 1) group, possibly that of Aristophon. In 353/2 he turned on Eubulus: *On the Syntaxis* seems directed partly against the allocation of surpluses to the *theorika* (q.v.)—at § 30 he sneers about the public works of Eubulus—and partly against the policy of abstaining from all but essential military enterprises.

For the next few years Demosthenes was regularly on the losing side. Early in 352 in *For the Megalopolitans* he argued in favour of promising to support Arcadia, if Sparta carried out her plan of exploiting Thebes' preoccupation with the Sacred War: since Athens based her policy on concord with Phocis and Sparta, the decision to do no more than give a guarantee to Messenia was probably right. A few months later Demosthenes wrote *Against Aristocrates* for use in the attack on a proposal to honour Charidemus (q.v.) in gratitude for his offices in the cession of the Chersonesus (q.v. 1) by Cersobleptes (q.v.): the speech is notable both as a source of information about the law of homicide and also for the manner in which it regards Cersobleptes, not Philip, as the real enemy in the north. In late 352 Philip's attack on Cersobleptes carried him very near the Chersonesus, and Demosthenes' eyes were opened. In early 351 he delivered the *First Philippic* which pleaded for more vigorous prosecution of the war for Amphipolis: his proposals were not accepted; deeper involvement in the long fruitless struggle may have seemed to endanger the power to defend the vital areas of Thermopylae and Chersonesus. Late in 351 in *On the liberty of the Rhodians* he urged support of the Rhodian demos against the oligarchs supported by the Carian dynasty: but the Persian attack on Egypt prompted caution, and Demosthenes' arguments were far from strong. In mid 349 Olynthus (q.v.), which had by then lapsed from Philip's alliance, was attacked by Philip and appealed to Athens for help: in the three *Olynthiacs*, delivered in quick succession, Demosthenes demanded the fullest support and, in the last, an end to the law assigning surpluses to the Theorika; again he scathingly alluded to the works of Eubulus. There is, however, no reason to suppose that the three expeditions voted were not supported by Eubulus or indeed that they satisfied Demosthenes, and there are some reasons for thinking that the implementation of his proposals could have brought even greater disaster than the loss of Olynthus. Early in 348 the party of Eubulus involved the city in a costly and inconclusive intervention in Euboea to prevent the island falling into the control of those hostile to Athens: Demosthenes later claimed to have been alone in opposing the expedition; either he was not truthful or he had taken a curious view of Athens' interests. One consequence of his opposition to Eubulus

was that he became embroiled in an absurd wrangle with Midias, a prominent supporter of Eubulus, who had slapped his face at the Dionysia of 348: the case was settled out of court and the speech *Against Midias* was ·never delivered.

In mid 348 before the fall of Olynthus Demosthenes successfully defended Philocrates (q.v.) when he was indicted under the Graphe Paranomon (q.v.) for his proposal to open negotiations with Philip, and in 347/6, when Demosthenes like Aeschines (q.v. 1 for all the events of 346) was a member of the *boule* (q.v.), the partnership continued and Demosthenes played a leading part in securing acceptance of the Peace of Philocrates. On the two embassies to Macedon he cut a poor figure before Philip and got on badly with his fellow ambassadors, but the decisive moment came after the second embassy's return in the assembly on 16 Scirophorion, when it was known that Philip had occupied the Gates and that Phocis could not be saved. Demosthenes was shouted down and Aeschines made the speech to which Demosthenes constantly recurred. What Demosthenes wanted that day is not clear: if he did want the city to denounce the new peace, to march out to support Phocis attacked by the Macedonians and Thessalians from the north and the Thebans from the south, his judgement was seriously awry. From that day Demosthenes determined to undo the Peace, but shortly after in *On the Peace* he counselled caution, and for the moment contented himself with the attack on Aeschines from which he was forced to desist by the successful countercharge against his own associate, Timarchus.

The year 344 brought Demosthenes his opportunity to attack the Peace. Rumours reached Athens that Philip was preparing to intervene in the Peloponnese in support of Argos and Messene, and Demosthenes went on an embassy to those cities to warn them of the dangers of consorting with Philip: Philip protested, and shortly after Demosthenes' return the embassy of Python and all Philip's allies protested against his misrepresentations, and offered to turn the Peace into a Common Peace; first reactions were favourable, but in the assembly Hegesippus (q.v. 1) succeeded in having the status of Amphipolis referred to Philip—an oblique way of sabotaging the whole affair—while Demosthenes' contribution was the *Second Philippic* in which he denounced Philip as not worth an attempt at negotiation. (The alternative reconstruction would deny this conjunction and put Python's embassy in early 343.) In mid 343, after the success of Hyperides' (q.v.) prosecution of Philocrates, Demosthenes judged the moment suitable to resume his attack on Aeschines; *On the false embassy* sought to exploit the support of Eubulus' party for continuing the Peace and to suggest that Aeschines was really responsible for Philip's use of the peace negotiations to intervene in Phocis in 346. With the support of Eubulus and Phocion (q.v.) Aeschines was by a narrow margin acquitted. With the final collapse in early 342 of proposals to amend the Peace, Philip began to intervene directly in Greece, and amidst mounting hostility to Macedon Demosthenes went on an embassy to the Peloponnese to set about the organization of an Hellenic alliance for the war he was determined to have. For the moment his efforts came to little, but in 341 in *On the Chersonese* and shortly after in the *Third Philippic* he defended the aggressive actions of Diopeithes against Cardia by arguing that, since Philip's actions already amounted to war, it was absurd to heed the letter of the Peace. Not long after he delivered the *Fourth Philippic* (of which the authenticity was long doubted but is now widely accepted); in it Demosthenes appears so confident of his control that he dismissed the Theoric distributions in words inconceivable in 349, and he successfully demanded an appeal to Persia to join in attacking Philip. In 341/40 he also formed an alliance with Byzantium, and by autumn 340, when Philip finally declared war and seized the Athenian corn-fleet, Demosthenes was in full charge of the war he had sought, though he was unable to restrain Aeschines from his unwise intrusion at Delphi into the rivalries of Central Greece (*see* AESCHINES 1). In mid 339 he moved the suspension of the allocation of surpluses to the *theorika*, and with Thebes unlikely to side with Philip after having expelled the Macedonian garrison from the Gates, Demosthenes could expect not to have to face Philip in Greece. The sudden seizure of Elatea threw Athens into horrified perplexity, but Demosthenes proposed and effected alliance with Thebes, which he later pretended always to have wanted, and Athens and Thebes fought side by side at Chaeronea in autumn 338.

Demosthenes was present at the battle, and returned so quickly to organize the city's defences that Aeschines could accuse him of running away. He provided corn, repaired the walls, and was so much the man of the hour that he was chosen to deliver the Funeral Oration for 338 (which has not survived). With Philip in Greece, the people looked to Demosthenes and he successfully met the frequent attacks on him in the courts. In 337/6 he was Theoric Commissioner, and Ctesiphon proposed that he be crowned at the Dionysia (q.v.) for his constant service to the city's best interests: perhaps encouraged by the opening of the Macedonian attack on Persia, Aeschines indicted Ctesiphon, but with the changing events of the next few months he preferred for the moment to let the case lapse. Demosthenes, hoping that the death of Philip was the end of Macedonian domination in Greece, sought to foment troubles for his successor, but Alexander quickly marched south and Demosthenes had to accept the new monarch. In 335 Demosthenes actively aided the Thebans in their revolt and narrowly escaped being surrendered to Alexander. From then on he seems to have looked to Persia to accomplish the liberation of Greece: such at any rate seems to be the meaning of the many charges of receiving money from the Persians. Demosthenes gave no support to Agis at any stage and, when Persia was crushed at Gaugamela and the revolt of Agis collapsed, Athens was left in disastrous isolation. Aeschines seized the opportunity to renew his attack on Demosthenes through Ctesiphon. The case was heard in mid 330, and Demosthenes defended his acts in *On the Crown*, which is his masterpiece. He declined to fall into the trap of discussing recent events and with supreme art interspersed his discussion of events long past with lofty assertions of principle. Fewer than one-fifth of the jury voted for Aeschines, and he retired to Rhodes. Demosthenes was left in triumph, and the city settled down to acceptance of Macedonian rule, until in 324 word reached Greece that at the coming Olympia Nicanor (q.v. 1) was to make public a rescript ordering the restoration of exiles. Since this would affect the cleruchy on Samos, an agitation began which was to end in the Lamian War. Demosthenes led a deputation as *architheoros* to protest. Subsequently he engaged in the discussion at Athens about divine honours for Alexander, having also taken the lead in dealing with the sudden appearance of Harpalus (q.v.) by proposing first that Harpalus be kept prisoner and his money stored on the Acropolis, and later that the Areopagus investigate the losses. It is difficult to assess Demosthenes' policy in this year: he may have foreseen the new uprising under Leosthenes (q.v.) and planned to involve Athens, but, since the especial ally of Leosthenes was Hyperides, who led the attack on Demosthenes in the prosecution of early 323, Demosthenes appears to have been at odds with the war-party. Equally unsure is his guilt in the Harpalus trial: the Areopagus declared him guilty of appropriating 20 talents, and he was found

guilty and fined 50 talents, but, even if he did take the money, he may have intended to use it in service of the State; the whole affair is most obscure. He retired into exile, and lent his support to Hyperides in the creation of the alliance for the Lamian War. He was then recalled to Athens, but after the Macedonian victory at Crannon in 322 he left the city again, and was condemned to death by the decree of Demades (q.v.). Pursued by the agents of Antipater (q.v. 1), he committed suicide in Calauria (322).

Modern opinions of Demosthenes' political importance have varied greatly, often in discernible relation to contemporary events (cf. Knipfing, *Amer. Hist. Rev.* 1921, 657 ff.). He has been lauded as a solitary champion of liberty and censured as the absurd opponent of progress. With the latter view English scholars have, happily, had little sympathy, but the high esteem in which the works of Demosthenes have been rightly held as works of art has tended to obscure the possibility that, while his devotion to liberty is one of the supreme monuments of liberty, his methods and his policies were not the best suited to attain their end, and that those of his opponents, which we must largely infer from his attacks, were no less directed to maintaining the city's power and independence, and perhaps more apt.

Demosthenes has much to say about Philip's success being due to bribery and was convinced that his own opponents had been corrupted, but in his obsession with this dubitable view he seems blind to the real problem of his day, which was how Greece could be united to counter effectively the military power of the new national state so far greater than the power of any single city-state. There was much to be said against Demosthenes' determination to involve the full military resources of Athens in a war in the north, in particular that in such a war Athens stood to gain most and the other Greeks would not unite for that result. For the defence of Greece itself against invasion there was a real hope of uniting the cities in a Common Peace, and this appears to have been the policy of Demosthenes' opponents. There was perhaps more enthusiasm than judgement in his military assessments, and since the defeat of Chaeronea appears to have produced a Greece that could never wholeheartedly unite in a war of liberation, it is possible that, if such a decisive battle was inevitable, his opponents might have united Greece for it more effectively. But the situation of Greece was tragic, and Demosthenes was certainly of heroic stature.

*Private law-court speeches* (δίκαι). The series of private speeches begins with those against Aphobus and Onetor (363–362), in which Demosthenes claimed recovery of his property from his guardians, and continues throughout his life (*Against Dionysodorus*, 323–322). Several private speeches attributed (perhaps wrongly) to Demosthenes were delivered on behalf of the Apollodorus who was his opponent in the For Phormio. The speech *For Phormio* (350) and the first *Against Stephanus* (349; the second *Stephanus* is undoubtedly spurious) raise a question of professional morality. Pasion, the banker, appointed his chief clerk Phormio trustee for his sons; the elder son, Apollodorus, subsequently claimed a sum of money allegedly due to him, but Phormio proved that the claim had been settled some years previously. Apollodorus then prosecuted Stephanus, one of Phormio's witnesses, for perjury. If, as Plutarch states, Demosthenes wrote *Stephanus A* as well as *For Phormio*, he was guilty of a serious breach of faith, for while the earlier speech extols Phormio's character, the later one contains insinuations against him. The evidence for the authenticity of *Stephanus A* is, however, inconclusive (Paley and Sandys II, xxxix–l; Pickard-Cambridge, *Demosthenes*, 220–4). Aeschines asserts that Demosthenes showed to Apollodorus a speech composed for Phormio, but this may be a misrepresentation of some attempt by Demosthenes to act as mediator.

The subjects of the private speeches include guardianship, inheritance, claims for payment, bottomry-loans, mining rights, forgery, trespass, assault, etc. In the *Callicles* (which has flashes of humour, seldom found in Demosthenes) the plaintiff alleges that the defendant has flooded his land by blocking a watercourse; in the *Conon*, a brilliant piece of writing, combining Lysianic grace and Demosthenic force, some dissolute young rowdies and their father are summoned for assault.

Demosthenes had many rivals in his lifetime; but later critics considered him the greatest of the orators. His claim to greatness rests on his singleness of purpose, his sincerity, and his lucid and convincing exposition of his argument. In many instances he produces a great effect by the use of a few ordinary words. In his most solemn moments his style is at its plainest and his language most moderate. A master of metaphor, he uses it sparingly, and hardly at all in his most impressive passages. His style varies infinitely according to circumstances; sometimes as simple as Lysias, now polished like Isocrates, again almost as involved as Thucydides, he follows no scholastic rule; long and short periods follow each other, or are mingled with passages in the running style not prepared according to any regular system. Thus his carefully prepared utterances give an impression of spontaneity. Such was his control of language that he was generally able to avoid hiatus (q.v.) without any dislocation of the order of words. He had an instinctive aversion to a succession of short syllables, and even tribrachs are of comparatively rare occurrence.

TEXTS. Teubner, *ed. maior*, Fuhr–Sykutris, 3 vols. (1914–27), *ed. minor* Blass–Fuhr, vols. i–ii (1928–33); Blass, vol. iii (1923); O.C.T., Butcher–Rennie, 3 vols. Text with translation, Loeb, 7 vols. (J. H. Vince, A. T. Murray, and N. W. and N. J. de Witt); Budé, 10 vols.
COMMENTARIES. H. Weil, *Plaidoyers politiques de D.*, 2 vols. (1883–6); *Harangues de D.*, 1 vol. (2nd ed. by Dalmeyda); Paley and Sandys, *Select Private Orations*, 2 vols.; *Androtion* and *Timocrates*, W. Wayte; *Midias*, W. W. Goodwin; *Leptines*, J. E. Sandys; *On the Crown*, W. W. Goodwin; *Philippics, Olynthiacs, Peace, Chersonese*, 2 vols., J. E. Sandys. Index: B. Preuss, 1892.
TRANSLATIONS. *Orations*, C. R. Kennedy, 5 vols. (Bohn); A. W. Pickard-Cambridge, *Public Orations of D.*, 2 vols.; Lord Brougham, *On the Crown*.
For general bibliography, *see* ATTIC ORATORS. Especially useful for a general account, A. W. Pickard-Cambridge, *D. and the Last Days of Greek Freedom* (in Heroes of the Nations series, 1914), and G. Mathieu, *Démosthène, l'homme et l'œuvre* (1948). Further select bibliography: A. Schaefer, *D. und seine Zeit*[2] (1885–7); P. Treves, *Demostene e la libertà greca* (1933); A. Momigliano, *Filippo il Macedone* (1934); F. R. Wüst, *Philipp II von Makedonien und Griechenland* (1938); W. Jaeger, *D., der Staatsmann und sein Werden*[2] (1963); E. Badian, *JHS* 1961, 31 ff. (for modern discussion on Harpalus). There are many debatable questions of fact about the career of D.; the account given above is based on views developed in a series of articles: G. L. Cawkwell, *Rev. Ét Grec.* 1960, 1962, *CQ* 1962, 1963, *JHS* 1963.
G. L. C.

**DEMOSTHENES** (3) of Bithynia (? 2nd c. B.C.), epic poet, author of *Bithyniaca*.

*FGrH* iii. 699.

**DENTATUS** (1), LUCIUS SICCIUS (*PW* 3) or SICINIUS, called by ancient writers 'the Roman Achilles', was a legendary embodiment of the civic and military virtues of the plebeians in their struggles against both patricians and external enemies. Since the chronology of his largely fictitious career was unknown, Dentatus was later connected with the Decemvirs, by whose leader, Appius Claudius, he is said to have been treacherously murdered (449 B.C.).

Ogilvie, *Comm. Livy 1–5*, 475 f.
P. T.

**DENTATUS** (2), MANIUS CURIUS (*PW* 9), Roman plebeian hero, consul in 290, 284 (*suffectus*), 275, 274 B.C.; censor in 272. After ending the Samnite War (290),

he conquered Sabines (q.v.) (290), Senones (284), Pyrrhus (275), Lucani (274). He triumphed in 290 (the sources incredibly say twice) and 275. About 289 Dentatus partly drained Lake Velinus and in 272 commenced Rome's second aqueduct (*Anio Vetus*). He died in 270. The rhetorical accounts of his humble birth, incorruptibility, and frugality resemble the tales told of C. Fabricius (q.v.) Luscinus, and derive largely from Cato who idealized him.

G. Forni, *Athenaeum* 1953, 170 ff.
E. T. S.

**DENTISTRY** in antiquity was part of general medicine; diseases of the teeth were explained and treated in accordance with the theories on other diseases. The operative technique was excellent (the Hippocratic treatment of the fracture of the mandible is famous); extractions were performed at an early date. The methods of preserving the teeth, however, consisted mainly of medicinal and dietetic means; fillings for that purpose were unknown. Loose teeth were fastened with gold wire (Hippocrates, Π. ἄρθρων 32; *The XII Tables* 10. 8). Toothache being considered a chronic disease and one of the greatest torments (Celsus 6. 9), hygienic prescriptions were extensively advocated. Cleansing of the teeth with tooth-powder, the tooth-pick (*dentiscalpium*), chewing (σχινίζειν τοὺς ὀδόντας) were recommended in addition to innumerable remedies against bad breath, a favourite topic of Latin epigrammatists. False teeth were set, but only by technicians, the artificial teeth being carved from ivory or other animal teeth. Such protheses, used by the Etruscans and Romans, served primarily to hide physical defects and to correct deficiencies of speech, but had probably to be removed before meals. Physicians and dentists refrained from making protheses, either on account of their technical insufficiency, or because their importance for the process of digestion was not appreciated

V. Guerini, *A History of Dentistry* (U.S.A. 1909), surveys the Etruscan and other archaeological findings. K. Sudhoff, *Gesch. d. Zahnheilkunde*[2] (1926), dissertations on ancient authors enumerated, 75, 97, 102. W. Artelt, 'Gesch. d. Anatomie d. Kiefer u. d. Zähne', *Janus* 1929. Instruments, J. S. Milne, *Surgical Instruments in Greek and Roman Times* (1907).
L. E.

**DERCYLLIDAS**, a Spartan commander sent out in 411 B.C. to procure the revolt of Abydos and Lampsacus (qq.v.) from Athens. Dercyllidas achieved both goals, though Lampsacus was recovered almost immediately by Athens. Appointed harmost of Abydos, Dercyllidas was slandered by the Persian satrap Pharnabazus to Lysander (q.v.) in 407 and publicly disgraced. However, in 399 he was dispatched to Asia Minor in succession to Thibron to make war on Pharnabazus and Tissaphernes. Concluding an armistice with Tissaphernes, he campaigned against Pharnabazus and won over most of Aeolis, securing nine cities and a vast treasure in no less than eight days. During a truce which was concluded between the belligerents Dercyllidas crossed to the Thracian Chersonese, where he strengthened the Greek cities by building a wall across the isthmus to keep out the Thracians. In 397 he was ordered by the ephors to attack Tissaphernes, and obtained an offer of peace terms. But the Persians began to equip a fleet, and in 396 Agesilaus (q.v.) took over Dercyllidas' forces, though he employed him as one of three commissioners sent to Tissaphernes during a diplomatic exchange. After this Dercyllidas appears to have returned to Sparta, but in 394, he was sent to Amphipolis to inform Agesilaus of a Spartan victory at Corinth in the Corinthian War, and from there was sent on to the Hellespont to report the news to the allied Greek cities in the area. He was subsequently reappointed harmost of Abydos, and after the battle of Cnidos, succeeded in holding Abydos and Sestos loyal to the Spartan alliance despite the efforts of

Pharnabazus to win them over. An efficient general and a bachelor fond of adventures abroad, Dercyllidas showed a considerable amount of unscrupulousness and cunning, and for this reason was nicknamed Sisyphus, though the achievement of Agesilaus somewhat dimmed his own successes.

Thuc. 8. 61. 1, 62; Xen. *Hell.* 3. 1. 8–10, 16–27; 3. 2; 3. 4. 6; 4. 3. 1–2; 4. 8. 3–6; Diod. 14. 38. 2–3, 6–7; 39. 5–6; Ath. 11. 500c; Plut. *Lyc.* 15. 2. E. I. McQ.

**DE REBUS BELLICIS,** an anonymous treatise addressed to the Emperors Valentinian I and Valens (A.D. 364–75). The author explains plans for reforming the imperial financial policy, the currency, provincial administration, the army, and the law. He describes a number of machines with which he believes that the army should be equipped; and coloured illustrations of these machines survive in the MSS.

TEXT in E. A. Thompson, *A Roman Reformer and Inventor* (1952). E. A. T.

**DESTINATIO** (lit. 'marking out') became a technical term during the Principate of Augustus denoting a new stage in the election of consuls and praetors. As is now revealed by the Tabula (q.v.) Hebana, a Lex Valeria Cornelia of A.D. 5 assigned an important preliminary role in such elections to a select assembly comprising senators and all the *equites* enrolled in the judicial decuries. This body met on the Palatine, voted in ten units (increased to fifteen in A.D. 19 and to twenty in A.D. 23), and reached a corporate decision. The candidates whom it chose were known as *destinati*. Details of procedure given in the Tabula Hebana prove (1) that the number of *destinati* never exceeded the number of places to be filled, and (2) that the vote of the select assembly was succeeded by a vote of the full assembly on the Campus Martius. *Destinatio*, therefore, did not in theory guarantee election (cf. the non-technical use of the term in Livy 39. 32. 9), but, like the vote of the Republican *centuria praerogativa* (q.v.), it may frequently have done so in practice. In A.D. 15 freedom of choice was probably withdrawn from the full *comitia*, but the view that the *destinatio* procedure was also reduced at this time to a ceremonial formality is difficult to reconcile with the detailed modifications made to procedure in A.D. 19 and is not warranted by Tacitus' statement that elections were transferred to the Senate (*Ann.* 1. 15). It is probable that the *equites* soon voluntarily ceased to attend the select assembly through lack of interest. The hypothesis that they were deliberately included in the first instance in order to facilitate the election of *novi homines* does not stand up to analysis.

G. Tibiletti, *Principe e magistrati repubblicani* (1953)—with bibliography (283 ff.); A. H. M. Jones, *JRS* 1955, 9 ff.; Syme, *Tacitus* ii. 756 ff.; P. A. Brunt, *JRS* 1961, 71 ff.; W. K. Lacey, *Hist.* 1963, 167 ff. E. S. S.

**DETESTATIO SACRORUM.** A patrician, if *sui iuris*, had certain rites belonging to his *gens* (*sacra gentilicia*) to perform. If, therefore, he wished to become legally the son of a member of another *gens* (*arrogatio*) or cease to be a patrician (*transitio ad plebem*), he must, after investigation by the pontifices to make sure that the rites of his own *gens* did not become extinct, attest before them and the *comitia calata* that he renounced them. This was called *detestatio sacrorum*.

Gellius 5. 19. 5–10; 15. 27. 3, cf. 7. 12. 1; Cicero, *Dom.* 34 ff., *Orat.* 144; Servius on *Aen.* 2. 156. Mommsen, *Rom. Staatsr.* ii³. 37; ii. 38 f., 136 ff. H. J. R.

**DEUCALION** (Δευκαλίων), name of several mythological persons, the only important one being Prometheus' son, the Greek Noah. When Zeus flooded the

earth in wrath at the sins of the Bronze Age, or of Lycaon (q.v. 3), he and his wife Pyrrha, daughter of Epimetheus, by Prometheus' advice built an ark (λάρναξ, Apollod. 1. 47) and floated in it till the waters subsided. When their ark grounded, they were advised by a message from Zeus or an oracle from Themis to throw their mother's bones over their shoulders. Realizing that this meant the stones of the earth, they did so, and those thrown by Deucalion became men, those thrown by Pyrrha, women (Ov. *Met.* 1. 318 ff.; Apollod. 1. 46 ff.). They became the parents of Hellen (q.v.; ibid. 49). H. J. R.

**DEVA,** the river *Dee*, whence the name was applied to the legionary fortress at its mouth, modern Chester. Some early occupation c. A.D. 50 can be inferred, but the legionary fortress with earth bank and timber buildings dates from 74–8 and was used first by II Adiutrix and XX Valeria Victrix, subsequently by the latter alone. Timber was replaced by stone with stone wall c. 100. Chester was damaged c. 300 and was perhaps abandoned with the disappearance of Legio XX in 367. An extramural amphitheatre and civil settlement, possibly with colonial status, are known.

F. H. Thompson, *Roman Chester* (1959), summarizing much excavation, catalogued up to 1920 by P. H. Lawson, *Chester Arch. Journ.* xxvii. 163 ff. For inscriptions, R. P. Wright and I. A. Richmond, *Roman . . . Stones in the Grosvenor Museum, Chester* (1956); *RIB* 445 ff. C. E. S.

**DEVOTIO.** It was open to a Roman general, if the battle was going against him, to vow (*deuouere*) himself and the enemy's army with him to Tellus and the Manes (Livy 8. 9. 4 ff.). He wore his ceremonial costume (*toga praetexta*), with his head covered (*uelato capite*) and his feet on a weapon (*telum*, probably a spear or javelin; perhaps to bring himself into direct contact with Mars, cf. Mars Hasta). One hand touched his chin (? cf. the dedicator holding the door-post of the temple he dedicates, *see* CONSECRATIO). He then recited after a pontifex a formula of prayer asking for victory and the destruction of the enemy. At the end of this, he said: *legiones auxiliaeque hostium mecum deis manibus Tellurique deuoueo*. Then, girt with the *cinctus Gabinus* (*see* GABII), he sought death among the enemy. He might, however, substitute for himself any soldier from a legion (ibid. 10. 11), presumably with a corresponding change of formula. If he or his substitute was killed, the gods had clearly accepted the vow and must therefore accept the rest of it. If the substitute was not killed, but the victory won, an image at least 7 feet high must be buried in his place; if the general was not killed, he could never again offer sacrifice acceptably. The enemy must not get the weapon on which he had stood. Cf. s.v. DECIUS (2) MUS.

Latte, *RR* 125, 204. H. J. R.

**DEXIPPUS,** PUBLIUS HERENNIUS (fl. *c.* A.D. 253–76), Athenian sophist and statesman, published a Χρονικὴ ἱστορία to A.D. 269–70 in twelve books, a history of the *Diadochi* in four books, and Σκυθικά, a work on the Gothic Wars from A.D. 238 to Aurelian, preserved largely in Zosimus. In rhetorical composition and in style he follows Thucydides.

*FGrH* ii A, 452; C, 304. A. H. McD.

**DIADEM** (διάδημα), reputedly invented by Dionysus (Diod. 4. 4. 4), was originally any band wound about the head (esp. by priests, etc.). Later it denoted particularly the purple band with white decorations worn by Persian kings round the tiara. This was adopted, in the form of a white band with decorated edges, by Alexander and his successors as an emblem of royal power. As such it was refused by Julius Caesar in 44 B.C. and avoided by Roman Emperors until Constantine made it (as a purple band fitted with jewels and pearls) a regular part of the insignia of the reigning Augustus and Augusta.

A. Alföldi, *Röm. Mitt.* 1935, 1 ff.; H. W. Ritter, *Diadem und Königsherrschaft* (1965). L. A. M.

**DIADOCHI** (*Διάδοχοι*, 'Successors'). This term was applied in a special sense to the more important of Alexander the Great's officers who ultimately partitioned his Empire, viz. Antigonus I, Antipater, Cassander, Lysimachus, Ptolemy I, Seleucus I (qq.v.). The 'age of the *Diadochi*' represents a period extending from Alexander's death (323 B.C.) at least to the battle of Ipsus (301), which ended the efforts of Antigonus I (q.v.) to re-assemble the whole Empire under his own rule, and perhaps to the battle of Corupedium (281), which fixed the main political boundaries of the Hellenistic world for the next century. G. T. G.

**DIAGORAS**, lyric poet, of Melos. Though Eusebius–Jerome gives his *floruit* as 466 B.C., he seems to have been active in the last quarter of the fifth century (Ar. *Av.* 1071 ff., *Nub.* 828 ff.). Renowned for his atheism (Cic. *Nat. D.* 1. 2, 63), he disparaged the Mysteries (schol. Ar. *Av.* 1071; Lys. 6. 17), was condemned to death, and fled (Diod. Sic. 13. 6). Fragments, perhaps from *Encomia*, show no trace of atheism, and the story was that he lost his faith because the gods did not punish a man who broke his oath (Sext. Emp. *Pyr.* 9. 53).

TEXT. Page, *Poet. Mel. Gr.* 382–3.
CRITICISM. U. von Wilamowitz-Moellendorff, *Textg. d. griech. Lyr.* (1900), 80 ff.; F. Jacoby, *Diagoras ὁ ἄθεος* (Berlin, 1960); L. Woodbury, 'The date and atheism of D. of Melos', *Phoenix* 1965, 178 ff. C. M. B.

**DIALECTIC.** If Aristotle really said that Zeno discovered dialectic (Diog. Laert. 9. 25), he was inaccurate. Zeno set the example of exploring the consequences of an hypothesis, and Socrates set the example of seeking truth by question and answer alone; but the creator of the notion of dialectic was Plato (*Resp.* 531–9, and Adam's commentary, esp. ii. 168–79). He regards it as the highest of human arts, by which men attain the greatest insight into the best things. It deals solely with the unseen, not even using the visible as an aid. Its only medium is speech, the responsible use of question and answer in the pursuit of truth. He represents it sometimes as the synopsis of the one in the many and the many in the one, by which we define realities and discern which fall under which; sometimes as the exploration of the consequences of an hypothesis, by which we render our opinions more systematic. Once he suggests that dialectic can ultimately overcome its hypothetical character and reach the 'unhypothesized beginning' (*Resp.* 511 b). For Aristotle (see *Top.* 1. 1–2 and *Soph. El.* 34) its hypothetical character makes it inferior to deduction from premisses known to be true. Nevertheless, it has its uses: (1) ultimate premisses, which cannot themselves be deduced, can sometimes be made evident by exploring the consequences of their denial, and that is hypothetical thinking; (2) dialectic provides good training; (3) even winning the argument is worth something, and Aristotle's handbook of dialectic, the *Topics*, gives disproportionate attention thereto.

R. Robinson, *Plato's Earlier Dialectic*[2] (1953), 69 ff.; papers of the Third Symposium Aristotelicum, *Aristotle on Dialectic* (1968). R. R.

**DIALECTS, GREEK.** From the inscriptional evidence it appears that each of the Greek city-states possessed and used in its public documents its own individual dialect. This multitude of dialects falls into three distinct groups: (1) Attic-Ionic, spoken in Attica, the Ionic colonies on the southern seaboard of Asia Minor, and certain islands; (2) Aeolic in Lesbos and the neighbouring mainland and,

with an admixture of West Greek elements, in Thessaly and Boeotia; (3) Arcado-Cyprian, which is not employed in extant literature; (4) West Greek comprising (a) North West Greek in Phocis, Locris, Elis, and Aetolia, and (b) Doric in the Peloponnese and the Doric colonies in various islands and Magna Graecia.

(1), (2), and (3) have common characteristics which set them off as a group ('East Greek') from (4). (2) and (3) have much in common, and they may be classed together as 'Achaean'. To this group belongs the language of the Linear B texts from the Bronze Age palaces of Cnossos, Pylos, Mycenae, and Thebes, with a closer resemblance to (3). There are difficulties in the way of regarding 'Mycenaean' as the ancestral form of both (1) and (3).

The decipherment of Linear B brought support to the hypothesis that the isolation of Arcadian from Cypriot and the mixed character of Cretan Doric were due to the movement of Dorian tribes into the Peloponnese and Crete after the end of the Bronze Age. It was once believed that the distribution of the dialects reflects three successive invasions of Greek-speaking peoples into the Balkan peninsula, but modern dialect geography suggests that the comparatively slight differences between the dialects could easily have evolved in a relatively short time once the different Greek tribes had settled in their respective localities.

The dialects of the literary texts are not identical with those that appear in the inscriptions. This is not due merely to MS. corruption but to the strict literary formalism that forced a Greek writer to use the traditional language of the genre he was practising in preference to his native dialect. The dialect was, in fact, regarded as an integral part of the particular art form. Thus the epic dialect, arising from a fusion of Aeolic and Ionic elements, was utilized by all writers of Greek epic down to Byzantine times. The elegy was a creation of the Ionians. Yet because the hexameter was traditionally wedded to the epic dialect, it is this dialect (in an Ionicized form) that appears in elegy whether by Ionians like Archilochus and Callinus, the Laconian Tyrtaeus, the Athenian Solon, or the Megarian Theognis. Similarly the choric ode was developed among the Dorians; consequently Pindar, a Boeotian, Bacchylides, an Ionian, and the Attic dramatists must give their language at least a Doric flavour. It was because of this traditionalism in language that only few of the Greek local dialects achieved literary rank, and even these few discard much that would have seemed narrow and provincial. In this respect, too, Greek art idealized; the language itself represents a compromise between individual and local peculiarities.

EPIC POETRY dialect is basically Ionic, the most characteristic features of which are the change of *ā* to *η*, the *ν ephelkustikon*, the pronouns *ἡμεῖς, ἡμᾶς, ὑμεῖς, ὑμᾶς*, the particle *ἄν* and the infinitive in *-ναι*, and verbal forms in *-σαν* (*ἔδοσαν, ἔθεσαν*, etc.). It contains, further, numerous Aeolic elements such as *ἄμμε, ὕμμε*, etc., datives in *-εσσι*, genitives in *-οιο*, infinitives in *-μεν(αι)* and the particle *κε*. The dialect exhibits, further, features from different chronological stages of the language, and there can be little doubt that so composite and artificial a language is a product of a long poetical tradition which passed from an Aeolic to an Ionic sphere.

The language of Hesiod is practically identical with that of Homer. He has a few Aeolisms absent from Homer which may come from his native Boeotian—*αἴνημι, τριηκόντων*, etc. We find, further, Dorisms derived possibly from Locris, where he settled: *τέτορα, ἦν* 'they were', acc. plur. *-ᾱς* and participles like *δήσᾱς*. The epic dialect exercised a strong influence on all subsequent poetry, which constantly exhibits such features as *-οιο, -εσσι*, the omitted augment, and the inconsistent treatment of *ϝ*.

MELIC POETRY. The intensely personal character of this genre precluded any rigid formalism of language. The poems of Sappho and Alcaeus are written in their native Lesbian dialect. Characteristic are the o in στρότος, βροχέως, etc., the diphthongs in αὔως, ναύοις, χεύατο, etc., the diphthong which appears after the loss of ν before s (παῖσα, λίποισα, and the acc. plur. ἀπάλαις, στεφάνοις, etc.), the double consonants in ἔμμι, ὔμμε, σελάννα, φαεννός, etc., datives in -εσσι, infinitives in -μεναι, and the -μι conjugation of contracted verbs (κάλημι, etc.). It would be absurd to attribute hyper-Aeolisms to native speakers. It follows that φαῖμι, Κρονίδαις, and the like are later corruptions.

Anacreon of Teos used his native Ionic with but few Aeolisms or epicisms (πτερύγεσσι, ὀχάνοιο, δακρυόεσσα, etc.).

Corinna of Tanagra wrote in Boeotian. Characteristic are εο > ιο (ἐκόσμιον), preservation of ϝ (ϝάδομη), verbal forms in -νθι and -νθη, ἰώνγα for ἔγωγε, τύ, τίν, τεοῦς for σύ, etc. and βανά = γυνή. The text in our version appears with the later orthography (αι > η, η > ει, ει > ι, οι > υ). The usual epic features are present.

For the CHORIC ODE the traditional dialect was Doric, the chief characteristics of which are the retention of ᾱ and ϝ, the preservation of the group τι (δίδωτι, ϝίκατι, etc.), aorists in -ξ (ἐδίκαξα), the article τοί, ταί, 1st person plur. in -μες (φέρομες), futures in -σεω, and the particle κα. Alcman, though he writes in the language of Sparta, nevertheless avoids certain local peculiarities such as the change of the intervocalic -σ to h (Ποhοιδάν). In view of the influence of Lesbian Melic poetry on the choric ode it is not surprising that Apollonius (Pron. 107. 13) describes Alcman as συνεχῶς Αἰολίζων. Aeolic features are ἔμματα, κλεννά, ἔχοισα, etc. Epic influence is apparent in ἐδμεναι, παίδεσσι, the free augment, etc. As with Corinna, the orthography of our text has been modernized: σιός (θεός) embodies a change of θ > s first attested in the fourth century B.C.

The language of other poets of this genre (Stesichorus, Ibycus, Simonides, Bacchylides, Pindar) has no such close connexion with a local dialect. It is an artificial creation, a mixture, varying with the individual author, of Aeolic, Ionic, and epic elements with the basic Doric, which is progressively reduced to a few representative elements, such as ᾱ, genitives like Κρονίδᾱ, Μουσᾶν, and verbal forms like πτάσσοντι.

IAMBIC and TROCHAIC poetry were written in Ionic. Hipponax, in particular, and his imitator Herodas, used an especially popular variety containing many non-Hellenic words. Solon, however, apart from quotations and reminiscences of epic and Ionic poetry, used his native Attic dialect. This dialect appears, further, in the trimeters and tetrameters of Attic drama. It has been suggested that the few Doric elements present indicate a possible Doric origin of this particular art form.

COMEDY. Both Epicharmus and Sophron employed the popular dialect of Syracuse, where the common Doric was infused with local peculiarities such as ψίν (σφίν), κίκραμι (κεράννυμι), κάρρων (κρέσσων). Even so popular a genre, however, did not wholly escape the influence of epic and tragedy.

PASTORAL POETRY. The dialects affected by Theocritus (epic in Id. 12, 22, and 25, Lesbian in 28–30, and 'choral' Doric in 16–18 and 24) have that combination of the learned and the artificial that we expect from an Alexandrian poet. Even the fuller Doric, in which the majority of the idylls are written, has been designated as 'salon-Doric'. For while it contains the common Doric features enumerated above, its artificiality is revealed by hyper-Doric forms like φιλάσω. The dialect contains a few more locally restricted Dorisms such as the acc. plur. in -ος, ἐντί = εἰσί, infinitives in -εν, and the second person sing. in -ες (συρίσδες), which may derive from the Doric

of Sicily or Cos. The usual epic elements are present (see above). Aeolic colouring is given by the predominance of participial forms in -οισα, but γελάοισα is hyper-Aeolic for γέλαισα.

EPIGRAM. The earliest inscriptional epigrams were written in the local dialects, so that even the Ionian Simonides composed the epigrams he wrote for Doric cities in a conventional Doric. The local peculiarities of the epigrams have often been obscured in the tradition: thus the MS. version of the epitaph on the Corinthians who fell at Salamis contains the words ποτ' ἐναίομεν, whereas the stone itself presents the Doric ποκ' ἐναίομες. The poets of this genre drew largely on Homeric material in composing their hexameters, but the oldest epigrams exhibit fewest traces of this influence. It is noteworthy that even such borrowings assume a native guise: thus Ποσειδάωνι ἄνακτι appears in a Corinthian epigram as Ποτειδάϝωνι ϝάνακτι. The evidence of the Linear B texts shows that the internal digamma in the god's name is a 'hyper-form'.

PROSE. A prose literature was first developed in Ionia, and Ionic became the language of historical and scientific prose; representative names are Hecataeus of Miletus, Antiochus of Syracuse, Hellanicus of Mitylene, and Hippocrates of Cos; even the Athenian Thucydides gave his history an Ionic flavour by avoiding local Attic peculiarities such as ττ and ρρ. The early λογογράφοι wrote in a simple unadorned Ionic. Herodotus, however, was a more self-conscious artist and dignified his native Ionic with archaic speech forms—uncontracted verbs, iterative imperfects (ποιέεσκε), and the numerous epic expressions which earned him the epithet Ὁμηρικώτατος.

Our estimate of the Homeric elements in the dialect of Herodotus must be linked with an examination of the textual tradition, for our MSS. present a picture of his dialect which can hardly be authentic. We find hyper-Ionic forms like Κροισέω, and suspicion is cast on the genuineness of the uncontracted verb forms by impossibilities such as κέεται, which is a false resolution of κεῖται. Moreover, the fact that another hyper-form νοῦσος is identical with the Homeric form, where it is metrically conditioned, whereas the derived verb, which does not occur in Homer, has the normal form νοσέω, suggests that the text of Herodotus was corrupted at an early date by editors ignorant of the Ionic dialect, who 'ionicized' his language while regarding the Homeric epics as a source of early Ionic. Thus, they took the omission of the augment to be an Ionic trait. This led to curious misunderstandings. The augmented imperfect of ὁράω, for instance, was *ἠγοραον, which in Ionic would appear as ἑώρων. The editors ionicized this by omitting the first vowel, so that the MSS. present the impossible ὥρων, the true unaugmented form being ὅρων. Ionic, further, was distinguished from Attic by the crasis of o + a > ω: thus ἑωντῷ contrasts with the Attic ἑαυτῷ. It is perhaps to a false generalization of this equivalence of ων and αυ in the respective dialects that we owe the Herodotean θῶυμα. At any rate, this form never appears in the inscriptions, which present, on the contrary, examples of θαύμων, θαύμασις. Similarly the extension of the form αὐτέων to the masculine and neuter rests on a misunderstanding of the relationship of the true Ionic feminine form αὐτέων to the contracted Attic αὐτῶν. Both rest on an early αὐτάων, which in primitive Ionic would appear as αὐτήων.

THE Κοινή. The liquidation of the independent city-states and the political unification of Greece encompassed the destruction of the ancient dialects and their absorption into a new common language. Xenophon, who passed his life among Greeks of different origin and dialect, epitomizes this process and may be regarded as the first writer of the κοινή. It was in this common language that the Septuagint and the Greek New Testament were written. In the first century the archaist revival we know as Atticism strove to approximate the language of prose literature to that of classical Attic. In spite of numerous revolts this archaistic literary language has maintained itself against the increasingly divergent popular language, so that the modern Greek must learn the καθαρεύουσα which he writes in addition to the δημοτική which he speaks.

C. D. Buck, *The Greek Dialects* (Revised ed. U.S.A. 1955).
J. Chadwick, 'The Prehistory of the Greek Language', *CAH*[2], ch. xxxix; O. Hoffmann and A. Debrunner, *Geschichte der griechischen Sprache*, 2 vols. (1953–4); A. Meillet, *Aperçu d'une histoire de la langue grecque*[6] (1948); L. R. Palmer, 'The Mycenaean Language' in *The Interpretation of Mycenaean Greek Texts* (1963) 36 ff.; id. 'The Language of Homer', in A. J. B. Wace and F. H. Stubbings, *A Companion to Homer* (1962) 75 ff.; A. Thumb, *Handbuch der griechischen Dialekte*, vol. i (revised by E. Kieckers, 1932); vol. ii (revised by A. Scherer, 1959). L. R. P.

**DIALECTS, ITALIC.** Latin together with Oscan and Umbrian as well as the dialects of various mountain tribes of central Italy, Marsi, Marrucini, Hernici, Vestini, etc., forms the Italic branch of the Indo-European family of languages. This excludes, in the north, Celtic, Ligurian (now generally considered Indo-European, cf. Kretschmer, Kuhn's *Zeitschr. f. vgl. Sprachforschung*, 38. 108), and Venetic (of Illyrian origin); in central Italy, Etruscan (q.v.); and, in the south, Messapian (probably Illyrian in descent). But the term Italic Dialects is more commonly confined to Oscan and Umbrian, the two chief non-Latin dialects of the group. Oscan inscriptions have been found in Samnium, Campania, Apulia, Lucania, Bruttium, but Pompeii, and more recently Capua, have furnished most. The earliest are coin-legends of c. 450–350 B.C., while the latest are graffiti from the walls of Pompeii after the first earthquake in A.D. 63. Most are written in the Oscan alphabet, which is derived through Etruscan from Chalcidic Greek. But a few, including the longest, the Tabula (q.v.) Bantina, are in the Latin alphabet, while others from south Italy are in Greek. Oscan was more than a mere *patois*. While Latin was still confined to Rome and Latium, Oscan was the chief language of central Italy. Our knowledge of Umbrian is derived almost entirely from the Tabulae (q.v.) Iguvinae, a more extensive document than any representing any other dialect save Latin. Some of the tablets are written in the Umbrian alphabet, also derived through Etruscan from Greek, the rest in the Latin alphabet. The following are some of the main features which distinguish Osco-Umbrian from Latin.

(a) PHONOLOGY

(i) $qu$ $gu$ appear as $p$, $b$ (Latin *qu*, *u*): O. *pis*, U. *pisi* (= quis). O. *bivus* (= vivi).
(ii) Syncope of short medial vowels: O. *actud* (= agito).
(iii) *nd* > *nn*: O. *upsannam* (= operandam).
(iv) *s* retained before nasals: O. *fisnam* (= fanum), U. *sesna* (= cena).
(v) *bh*, *dh* > *f*: O. *tfei*, U. *tefe* (= tibi).
(vi) *kt* > *ht*, *pt* > *ft*: O. *Uhtavis* (= Octavius), O. *scriftas* (= scriptae), U. *screhto* (= scriptum).
(vii) *ks* > *ss*, *s*: O. *destrst* (= dextra est).

(b) MORPHOLOGY

(i) First decl. genit. sing. ends in -*ās* (cf. paterfamilias), also nomin. plur.
(ii) Second decl. genit. sing. ends in -*eis*; dat. sing. in *oi*; nomin. plur. both nouns and pronouns in -*ōs*; genit. plur. only in -*ōm*.
(iii) Third decl. genit. sing. in -*eis* (from *i* stems); accus. sing. of consonantal stems in -*om* (from *o* stems); in the nomin. plur. consonantal and vocalic stems are kept distinct, the former ending in -*ĕs* with syncope of

the *e*, the latter in -*ēs* as in Latin: O. *humuns* (= homine but *tris* (= tres).
(iv) In the verb, moods, tenses, voices are like Lati but
(a) Present infin. active ends in -*om*: O. *ezum*, U. *ero* (= esse).
(b) Future indic. has -*s*- (it is a short vowel *s*- aori subjunctive): O. *deiuast* (= iurabit), U. *fere* (= feret).
(c) Future perfect has -*us*-: O. *dicust* (= dixeri U. *benust* (= venerit).
(d) Characteristic of the perfect is an -*f*- type: ( *aikdafed* (= decrevit). Oscan has also a -*tt*- perfec and Umbrian an -*l*- and -*nki*- perfect, but the -*t* and -*s*- types of Latin are lacking.
(e) A peculiar third sing. subjunctive passive is e.g. ( *sakrafir*, U. *ferar* (= feratur).

(c) SYNTAX

The syntax is very similar to the Latin with son differences in case-usage. Thus
(i) The locative is quite common: O. *eisei terei* (= in ( territorio).
(ii) Genitive of time: O. *zicolom XXX nessimum* (= ( diebus XXX proximis).
(iii) The genitive of respect is much less restricte than in Latin.

(d) VOCABULARY

There is a considerable number of words in Osc Umbrian which do not appear at all or in the same for in Latin, though they can be paralleled in other Ind European languages:
e.g. *her*- (= velle): O. *herest*, U. *heri*. Cf. χαίρω.
*touta*- (= civitas): O. *toutad praesentid* (= popu praesente).
*medes*- (= ius): O. *meddiss*, U. *mersto* (= iustum. C *modus*.
*hontro*- (= inferus): O. *huntruis* (= inferis), U. *hond* (= infra).
*ner*- (= vir): O. *nerum* (genit. plur.), U. *nerf* (accu plur.). Cf. *Nero*.
*pur*- (= ignis): U. *pure-to* (= ab igne). Cf. πῦρ.
*ais*- (= sacer): O. *aisusis* (= sacrificiis). Cf. Etru *aisar* (= dei), L. *aestimo*.
Peculiar to Oscan are, e.g.:
*deiua*- (= iurare) connected with *deiuo (= deus).
*egmo*- (= res). O. *egmazum* (genit. plur.).
*eituam*- (= pecuniae). Also in Marrucinian.
*feihúss* (= muros). Cf. τεῖχος: same root as L. *fing figura*.
*puklum* (= filium). Also Paelignian *puclois* (= pueris.
*tanginom* (= sententiam). Cf. L. *tongere* and Eng 'think'.
Peculiar to Umbrian are, e.g.:
*anouihimu* (= induitor). Same root as L. *induo*, *exu*
*gomia* (= gravidas). Cf. L. *gemo* and γέμω.
*nertru* (= sinistro). Cf. νέρτερος.
*uend*- (= vertere): U. *ahauendu* (= avertito). Cf. Eng 'wind'.

Many words are used in a sense either unknown i Latin or passing out of use. Thus
O. *kasit* (= caret) means *decet*, *oportet*.
O. *castrous* (= castrum), U. *castruo* means *fundus*.
O. *carneis* (= caro), U. *karu* means 'portion', cf. κείρ But Umbrian also has the meaning 'piece of flesh
U. *emantur* (= accipiantur) shows the original meanin of Latin *emo*, 'take', found in compounds *adim demo*.

O. *urust* (oro) is used in the technical sense 'plead, argue': cf. Festus 'orare antiquos dixisse pro agere'.

E. Vetter, *Handbuch der italischen Dialekte* (1953); A. Ernout, *Le Dialecte ombrien* (1961); J. W. Poultney, *The Iguvine Tablets* (1959).
P. S. N.

**DIALOGUE, GREEK.** Diogenes Laertius (3. 48) defines a dialogue as 'a discourse consisting of question and answer on some philosophical or political subject, with due regard to the characters of the persons introduced and the choice of diction'. It is essentially a μίμησις, an artistic reproduction of 'good talk' or informal discussion in which, while a single theme is pursued, some digression and inconsequence is permissible and proper; the theme must be of more than topical interest, though it usually arises out of the experiences of particular persons at a particular time.

The most important source of dialogue was the actual conversation of Socrates with all and sundry; yet the Σωκρατικὸς λόγος is foreshadowed in the incorporation of quasi-philosophical conversations in the narrative of Herodotus and Thucydides, notably that between Solon and Croesus (Hdt. 1. 30–2) and the Melian Dialogue (Thuc. 5. 85–113). The influence of Attic Drama is also plain, and the affinity to dialogue of the Mimes of Sophron is recognized by Aristotle.

The earliest Socratic dialogues may have been simply notes taken by those who talked with or listened to Socrates (cf. Pl. *Tht.* 142–3); later these developed into freer μιμήσεις in the hands of Plato, Xenophon, Aeschines (of whom considerable fragments survive), and other disciples. Plato's dialogues differ widely in literary merit: some show supreme dramatic power and artistry; in others the dialogue form becomes almost a convention, the chief speaker (sometimes an unnamed 'stranger') a mouthpiece for Plato's own teaching, and the interlocutors otiose. Of the earlier works Jaeger's saying is true, that 'his desire was to show the philosopher in the dramatic instant of seeking and finding, and to make the doubt and conflict visible'; for such an aim dialogue was wholly suitable.

Aristotle's dialogues, extant only in fragments, won him high literary fame in antiquity. Most were written before the death of Plato. Although some fragments show Aristotle still retaining the Socratic technique of question and answer, his usual method was probably that of long expository speeches, like those in Cicero's dialogues, with the leader (sometimes Aristotle himself) summing up.

After a long and almost total eclipse, dialogue reappears with Plutarch and Lucian. Some fourteen genuine dialogues of Plutarch survive, philosophical or semi-philosophical in character. His best work lacks Plato's depth and dramatic power, yet has a quiet charm and illuminates for us the interests of contemporary cultured society. In Lucian the influences of Socratic dialogue, the New Comedy, and Menippus combined to stimulate a genius unique amongst ancient writers. Though he employed many other forms, his fame rests principally on his satiric dialogues, brilliant exposures of every sort of dogma, prejudice, and humbug. In the twilight of classical antiquity dialogue is still represented in the work of Julian and Synesius.

Aeschines Socraticus, ed. H. Krauss (Teubner, 1911); Aristotle, *Fragments*, ed. Valentin Rose (Teubner, 1886); A. and M. Croiset, *Histoire de la litt. grecque* (1910–14) iii (Plato, Xenophon, etc.), v (Plutarch and Lucian); M. Croiset, *Essai sur la vie et les œuvres de Lucien* (1882); H. W. and F. G. Fowler, *Lucian* (Engl. Transl. with introduction, 1905); R. Hirzel, *Der Dialog* (1895); id. 'Plutarch' (*Das Erbe der Alten* iv, 1912); W. Jaeger, *Aristoteles²* (1948: Engl. Transl. by R. Robinson); F. Wehrli in *Aristote et les problèmes de méthode* (Symposium Aristotelicum, Louvain, 1961). R. H.

**DIALOGUE, LATIN.** The art of dramatic dialogue

early attained a high proficiency in Rome, especially in the comedies of Plautus and Terence, the Roman public being quite keen to appraise the quick give and take of conversation, as is shown by the popularity of the *altercationes* in forensic rhetoric (Cic. *Brut.* 164). Dialogue played a considerable part in the *Satura* from the time of Ennius, one of whose *saturae* seems to have been a dialogue between *Mors* and *Vita*; and many satires of Lucilius, Horace, and Persius are largely dialogue, though it plays a smaller part in Juvenal. Prose dialogue at Rome began with M. Junius Brutus, who composed his three books *De Iure Civili* in the form of dialogues with his son (Cic. *De Or.* 2. 224). These, like Cicero's, and the Roman dialogue generally, followed the Aristotelian rather than the Platonic model: the principal part in each dialogue was played by one interlocutor (sometimes the author himself) who expounded his view dogmatically in long speeches, the part of the other characters being reduced to a minimum. Each dialogue was preceded by a *mise en scène* giving the place and the occasion of, with the names of the participants in, the conversation. Cicero's long series begins with the political dialogues, *De Republica* and *De Legibus*, proceeds to the rhetorical dialogues (namely *De Oratore* and *Brutus*), and ends with the philosophical and theological *Academica, De Finibus, Tusculanae Disputationes, De Divinatione, De Natura Deorum*, etc. While Cicero's dialogues reproduced the conversation and manners of high society, a less polished, though not more Roman, stratum was represented in Varro's dialogue *De Re Rustica*. Seneca's *dialogi* are dialogues only in name. Tacitus' *Dialogus* resumes the Ciceronian tradition in its discussion of the decline of oratory. Minucius Felix used the dialogue form in his *Octavius* in the interest of Christian polemic (a use which persisted till the time of St. Augustine); in form and setting he is to some extent indebted to the *Atticae Noctes* of Aulus Gellius (q.v.). Macrobius (q.v.) used the dialogue form in a work deeply indebted in material to Gellius, though in form he depends closely on Plato, as he says himself (*Sat.* 1. 1. 7). The *De Consolatione* of Boethius (q.v.) is a dialogue between the author and Philosophy.

R. Hirzel, *Der Dialog* (2 vols. 1895); R. E. Jones, *AJPhil.* 1939, 307 ff. R. M. H.; G. W. W.

**DIANA** (root DI, cf. Zeus, Iup-piter; probably 'bright one', which says nothing for or against ancient and modern theories of her identity with the moon), an Italian goddess anciently identified with Artemis (q.v.). Altheim (*Griechische Götter in alten Rom* (1930), 93 ff.) supposes her cult actually derived from that of Artemis Orthia, through Etruria, but see A. E. Gordon in *TAPA* 1932, 177 ff.; *California Publ. in Class. Arch.* ii, 1934, 4 ff. Her cult was widespread; see Birt in Roscher's *Lexikon* i. 1003–4 for details. One of her most famous shrines was on Mt. Tifata near Capua (Vell. 2. 25. 4 and elsewhere in literature, supported by much inscriptional evidence); the name Tifata means 'holm-oak grove' (Festus, 503. 14 Lindsay), which suits Diana's character as a wood-goddess (see below) excellently. Most famous of all was her ancient cult near Aricia (on the shore of the volcanic lake known as *Speculum Dianae*, below the modern Nemi, i.e. *nemus*). Her temple stood in a grove, which was recorded as dedicated to her by Egerius Baebius (?) of Tusculum, *dictator Latinus* (Cato, *Orig.* 2, fr. 21 Jordan). It was therefore an old religious centre of the Latin League and it is probable, though direct proof is lacking, that the foundation of her temple (probably preceded by an altar) on the Aventine, traditionally by Servius Tullius (Livy 1. 45. 2 ff.), was an attempt to transfer the headquarters of this cult to Rome, along with, what Livy mentions (ibid. 3), the headship of the

League. *See further* REX NEMORENSIS, and for the Massiliote and Ephesian connexions of the Aventine temple, *see* ARTEMIS.

That she was largely a goddess of women is shown by the processions of women in her honour at Aricia (Prop. 2. 32. 9–10; Ov. *Fasti* 3. 268–9), also by the character of many of the votive offerings there, which have clear reference to children and childbirth; see further Frazer on Ovid, ibid. 267, Wissowa, *RK* 248. That she is a moon-goddess (see Preller–Jordan, *Römische Mythologie*[3] (1881–3), i. 312) is an idea resting on no real evidence (cf. JANUS). Warde Fowler (*Rel. Exper.*, 235) plausibly calls her a 'wood-spirit', for certainly she is commonly worshipped in wooded places. The central idea of her functions would seem to have been fertility, especially human, though probably not confined to that; for the development of such a deity into one of political importance, cf. Juno and Hera.

At Aricia she was associated with Egeria (q.v.), and Virbius, an obscure male deity (Ov. *Met.* 15. 544; Servius on *Aen.* 7. 84 and 761; *see* HIPPOLYTUS 1). Identifications with foreign deities are common all over the West.

In general see Latte, *RR* 169 ff. Aventine temple: Platner–Ashby, 149 f., and for its date and political significance, A. Momigliano, *Rendiconti dei Lincei* 1962, and *JRS* 1963, 106. Temple at Mt. Tifata: J. Heurgon, *Capoue préromaine* (1942), 299 ff., A. de Franciscis, *Archivio storico di Terra di Lavoro* (1956), 301 ff.            H. J. R.

**DIATRIBE.** For examples of the διατριβή in Greek, characteristic of the Cynic and Stoic schools, *see* EPICTETUS 2, TELES. A large number of Roman writers, even when not professed philosophers, imitated the Greek διατριβή. Cato in his speeches resorts to the polemic methods of the popular moralists of Greece. In Lucilius the employment of diatribist writings is above all literary. On the other hand, Varro's satires are so much akin to Menippus' works that they can be in their general features reconstituted, thanks to comparison with the dialogues of Lucian, another successor of Bion's disciple. Even Cicero in the *Tusculans* and *Cato Maior* presents long passages inspired by the opponents of systematic philosophy—by Ariston of Chios in particular. From this epoch of soul-stirring moral crisis, the popular preachers in their harangues to Roman crowds had recourse to the arsenal of themes belonging to the diatribe. Horace mocks them, but he willingly admits that his own satires are *Bionei sermones*; and his independence of thought does not debar him from using the same weapons. Among his contemporaries one must segregate the disciples of Q. Sextius (q.v. 2), founder of a sect which was rather original in spite of the eclectic character of its doctrine. Its ascetic vegetarianism is based, not on Pythagorean metaphysical conceptions, but on reasons of empirical ethics and hygiene which rest diatribic themes on the exercise of the will. Fabianus, an important 'Sextian', had an enormous influence upon the schools of rhetoric.

The elegiac poets and the prose-writers (especially Livy) who urge a return to the simplicity of ancient times found, like the fabulist Phaedrus, in this tradition, rejuvenated in accordance with the Roman spirit, those moralizing *loci communes* which appeared suitable to the needs of their period.

Seneca's works mark the point of departure for a fresh evolution, a neo-Stoicism in which, thanks to him, the diatribe makes its formal re-entry into philosophy. Notwithstanding manifold inconsistencies, Seneca towards the end of his life becomes more and more faithful to the moral principles which he had borrowed from Bion and Ariston. If Lucan and Persius return to orthodox Stoicism, Juvenal, the last of the great Roman

satirists, is especially influenced by *rhetores* whose diatribist themes he develops at length.

Among Christian writers Tertullian shows what profi the advocates of the new religion could draw from thi pagan tradition.

R. Heinze, *De Horatio Bionis imitatore* (1889); H. Weber, *D Senecae genere dicendi Bioneo* (1895); R. Schütze, *Iuvenalis ethicu* (1905); P. Wendland, *Die hellenistisch-römische Kultur*[3] (1912); C Favez, *Senecae ad Helviam matrem de consolatione* (1918); A. Oltra mare, *Les Origines de la diatribe romaine* (1926); Th. Brandt *Tertullians Ethik* (1928). O. Weinreich, *Zeitschrift für Kirchen geschichte* 1942, 39 ff.; L. Radermacher, *Weinen und Lachen* (1949 115 ff.            A. O. (transl. J. W. D.

**DICAEARCHUS**, a Greek from Messana, who live most of his life in the Peloponnese, especially at Sparta pupil of Aristotle and contemporary of Theophrastus Fl. *c.* 326–296 B.C. Fragments only survive of his works

I. POLITICAL. (i) Βίος Ἑλλάδος, the first attempt a a universal history of culture, from the Golden Age t Dicaearchus' time. (ii) Πολιτεῖαι (*Constitutions*) of Pellene Corinth, Athens, and Sparta. (iii) Τριπολιτικός, per haps a delineation of a 'mixed' constitution, containin elements of monarchy, aristocracy, and democracy. Prob ably this and others of Dicaearchus' work were in dialogu form. (iv) Ὀλυμπικός and Παναθηναϊκός, both probably i form political orations. (v) Περὶ τῆς ἐν Ἰλίῳ θυσίας, o Alexander's sacrifice before the battle at the Granicus.

II. BIOGRAPHY AND LITERARY HISTORY. (i) Βίοι, o the lives and writings of Plato and other philosophers (ii) Π. Ἀλκαίου, probably a biography and an exegetica commentary. (iii) Works on Homer, titles unknown (iv) Ὑποθέσεις τῶν Σοφοκλέους καὶ Εὐριπίδου μύθων (se HYPOTHESIS). (v) Π. μουσικῶν ἀγώνων, on competition in music and poetry. The last three works were impor tant sources for later scholars, containing much in formation about Homer and the Dramatists.

III. PHILOSOPHICAL. (i) Π. ψυχῆς, a dialogue on th corporeal nature and mortality of the soul, apparently consisting of two parts, Λεσβιακός and Κορινθιακός (ii) Π. φθορᾶς ἀνθρώπων, maintaining that man is de stroyed more by man than by natural disasters. (iii) A work on future things, title unknown, but apparently no identical with (iv) Π. μαντικῆς. (v) Ἡ εἰς Τροφωνίο κατάβασις, 'Descent into the Trophonian Cave', includ ing immoralities of priests therein. (vi) Letter (? philo sophical) to Aristoxenus.

IV. GEOGRAPHICAL. Περίοδος γῆς, cartography (an description?) of the known world, establishing fo geographers a main parallel of latitude from the Straits o Gibraltar to the Himalayas and the assumed eastern Ocean it included perhaps 'Measurements of Mountains i Greece', whose heights Dicaearchus over-estimated.

Dicaearchus was a learned, fertile, and remarkabl versatile author, of an original and genuinely scientifi turn of mind. He influenced many subsequent writer including Eratosthenes, Cicero, Josephus, and Plutarch Cicero, who admired him greatly (*Att.* 2. 2. 6; 13. 31 *Tusc.* 1. 77), took him as the exemplar of the βίος πρακτικός, Theophrastus as that of the βίος θεωρητικός.

FHG ii. 225 ff.; GGM i. 97–110, 238–43. F. Wehrli, *Dikaiarcho* (1944); Thomson, *Hist. of Anc. Geog.* 134, 142, 153 ff.; *PW* Suppl. xi            E. H. W

**DICAEOGENES**, a tragic poet, probably of the latte half of the fifth century B.C., wrote a *Medea* and a *Cyprian* (Aristotle, *Poet.* 16, mentions the recognition scene).

*TGF* 775–6.

**DICING** with six-sided dice (κύβοι, *tesserae*) or four sided knucklebones (ἀστράγαλοι, *tali*; natural or manu factured from, e.g., ivory) was a popular amusement i both Greece and Rome, either by itself or in associatio with board games. In Rome, where even Emperors (esp

Claudius) were keen players, high sums were often staked; and dicing was officially illegal except at the Saturnalia. *Tesserae* may have been used in varying numbers, but *tali* were normally used in fours, the best (though statistically not the rarest) of the thirty-five possible throws being when each showed a different face (prob. = *Venus*). *Canis* was the worst throw with both *tali* and *tesserae*, but its precise nature is uncertain. Cheating, sometimes with loaded dice (μεμολυββωμένοι), was not unknown, and to help prevent it the dice-box or 'tower' was soon introduced. Finds of ancient dice, which include an Etruscan pair, are not uncommon.

*PW*, s.v. *lusoria tabula* (Lamer), xiii, 1900 ff., esp. 1933 ff.

L. A. M.

**DICTA CATONIS** ('Dionysius', sometimes added to Cato's name, remains a puzzle), the title given to a versified handbook of morality, partly pagan, partly Christian, which, dating in its original form probably from the third century A.D., was widely studied in the Middle Ages and translated into many European languages. The title 'Cato' was perhaps an unknown author's or compiler's recognition of Cato the Elder as the first moralist of Rome.

The collection consists of (*a*) its most important part, four books of hexameter *Disticha* (288 lines); (*b*) preceding them, 57 *breves sententiae* in prose; (*c*) four short *praefationes*, that to book 1 being in prose, the rest in hexameters; (*d*) 16 additional lines from the Zürich and Verona MSS. of 'Cato'; (*e*) 78 single lines (*Monosticha*), besides a considerable number of lines of Catonian origin (Baehrens thought 52) in a *carmen monostichon* constituting rules for life, *Praecepta Vivendi*, and two short poems, possibly Catonian, *De Musis* and *Epitaphium Vitalis Mimi*. Bahrens accepted the ascription of the *Praecepta* to Columbanus, but its affiliation is rather with a poem ascribed by Dümmler to Alcuin (205 lines published by Dümmler, *MGH, Poet. lat. aevi Carolini* i. 275, 1880). This ascription Boas supports with proofs in *Alcuin und Cato* (1937), reprinting Dümmler's text with marginal notes to indicate borrowings from *Disticha* and *Monosticha*. Alcuin, he believes, used, not the medieval vulgate of 'Cato', but a fragment of the same family as the Veronese fragment.

The collection has bequeathed many debatable questions, e.g. which are the oldest parts, the prose or the verse? whether or not there once existed a larger *Corpus Catonianum*? how much is pre-Christian? what alterations were made by a Carolingian recension?

The maxims, not without worldly cunning and selfishness, inculcate on the whole a homely morality: they represent, as proverbs do, the experience of the past, traceable sometimes to Greece, though occasionally the influence of Horace or Ovid appears. The final couplet of the *Disticha* (4. 49) emphasizes the terseness aimed at.

TEXT. Baehrens, *PLM* iii. 205 ff.; Duff, *Min. Lat. Poets* (with transl.). Editions of *Disticha* (with varying amounts of the rest): G. Némethy², 1895; J. Nève, 1926; P. Constant (with Fr. transl. and including Phaedrus, Publilius Syrus, and Avianus), 1938; M. Boas, 1952. Eng. transl. without text, W. J. Chase (U.S.A. 1922).

See also A. Hermann, *RAC* ii. 935 ff. with bibliog. 941; E. Stechert, *De Catonis quae dicuntur distichis* (Diss. Greifswald 1912); M. Boas, *Die Epistola Catonis* (Akad. Amsterd. 1934); *Alcuin und Cato* (1937). Articles on MSS and relevant questions by M. Boas listed in his ed. of *Disticha*, lxxx ff.; O. Arngart, 'The Distichs of Cato and the Proverbs of Alfred, *Bull. Soc. Lettres Lund* 1951/2, 95 ff.; R. Hazelton, 'Chaucer and Cato', *Speculum* 1960, 357 ff.

J. W. D.; A. M. D.

**DICTATOR.** The dictatorship, which is found as a permanent office in other Latin states, was added to the Roman constitution soon after the expulsion of the kings to provide a temporary, extraordinary magistracy in military—and later domestic—crises, *rei gerundae causa*. Any connexion with Etruscan or Oscan magistracies is obscure (*see* MEDDIX). Originally a major colleague of

the consuls, known as *praetor maximus*, the dictator soon became completely independent, holding undivided authority of military character, not subject to veto or appeal, both abroad and at Rome. Twenty-four lictors indicated his quasi-regal power, which, however, was rather a concentration of the consular authority than a limited revival of the kingship. The dictator was not elected by the people, but nominated by a consul on the Senate's proposal. A *lex curiata* confirmed the nomination. After 361 B.C. *consulares* were normally selected, earlier the 'best man' was chosen. The dictator (who was also known as *magister populi*, master of the infantry) immediately appointed a *magister equitum* (q.v.) as his subordinate. Other magistrates remained in office but were subject to the dictator, who held his post for six months at most, the length of a campaigning season, or else retired when his particular task was done. This time limit rendered the dictatorship comparatively useless outside Italy, and its importance declined in the third century. Dictators were increasingly employed for minor purposes—holding elections or celebrating festivals or fixing the 'sacred nail', etc.—and popular agitation, long unsuccessful, was able by 300 B.C. to subject the dictatorship to *provocatio* (q.v.). Despite a revival during the invasion of Hannibal it was never again employed for its original purpose after 216 B.C., perhaps because of senatorial jealousy of independent authorities. After 202 B.C. even the dictators with limited competence were no more appointed. Later dictatorships (*see* SULLA I, CAESAR I) differed widely from the original in scope and purpose.

Livy bks. 1–25 and Dion. Hal. *passim*; Polybius etc. Art. 'Dictator' in *PW* with 'Magister Equitum', ibid. Suppl. v (lists); Mommsen, *Röm. Staatsr.* ii. 141 ff.; Beloch, *Röm. Gesch.* 75 ff.; A. Rosenberg, *Staat der alten Italiker* (1913), 89 ff.; E. Meyer, *Kl. Schr.* (1924) ii. 272; H. Siber, *Römisches Verfassungsrecht* (1952), 103 ff.; E. S. Staveley, *Hist.* 1956, 101 ff. (discussion of modern literature, 1940–54); A. Alföldi, *Early Rome and the Latins* (1965). A. N. S.-W.

**DICTYS CRETENSIS,** a Cretan of Cnossos, companion of Idomeneus at Troy, and reputed author of a Trojan War diary, actually composed perhaps in the second or third century A.D. (*PTeb.* ii. 268). This work, supposedly discovered during Nero's reign, was translated into Latin prose by L. Septimius (4th c.?) and with Dares (q.v.) formed the chief source drawn upon by medieval writers on the Troy-saga.

TEXT. W. Eisenhut (Teubner, 1958). G. C. W.

**DIDACTIC POETRY** includes under one name many works which have little in common, except that their subject-matter is not love or war but science, philosophy, or some art or craft. The Greeks hardly regarded it as a separate genre, but classed it under the general head of ἔπη. For works of this nature *see* the articles on HESIOD, the Pre-Socratic philosophers, MENECRATES (2), ARATUS (1), NICANDER, MARCELLUS (9), MANETHO, DIONYSIUS (9) PERIEGETES, OPPIAN. For Latin works *see* LUCRETIUS, CICERO (1), (*Prognostica*), VARRO (3), MACER (2), VIRGIL (*Georgics*), OVID (*Halieutica*), GRATTIUS, MANILIUS (3), GERMANICUS (*Phaenomena*), COLUMELLA (book 10), NEMESIANUS, TERENTIANUS, SERENUS (2), CARMEN DE FIGURIS, CARMEN DE PONDERIBUS, AVIENIUS.

**DIDASCALIA.** The word means primarily the 'teaching' of a play or dithyramb to the chorus which was to perform it by a poet or the professional trainer employed, and then, more generally, the production of the play or dithyramb. (In Plutarch and other late writers the term may also be applied to the group of plays performed.) In the plural Διδασκαλίαι refers to the records of performances, including the names of victorious tribes, *choregoi*, poets, actors, and flute-players for each year, and of the plays performed at the Dionysiac festivals; it appears that the name of the true author was recorded when a play was produced in another name, but see Schol. Eur. *Andr*. 445. Aristotle's lost works included one book entitled Διδασκαλίαι and one book of Νῖκαι Διονυσιακαὶ ἀστικαὶ καὶ Ληναϊκαί. These must have been completed from the official records; it is not known whether these were engraved on stone from the first or not; but it is generally agreed that the inscriptions, of which large fragments remain (*IG* ii². 2318–25, with some other scraps), and which were probably engraved in the third century or late fourth century B.C., were based on the work of Aristotle so far as this went, and brought up to date afterwards; and that Aristotle was also the source from which the scholars of Alexandria and Pergamum (Athenaeus 306 e) (including the authors of the Hypotheses to the plays in our manuscripts) must have drawn; it is not known how far his researches went beyond the official records, nor in what year his record began. The inscription numbered *IG* ii². 2318 probably carried the record back to 502 B.C. or a few years earlier, and is generally thought to correspond to Aristotle's Νῖκαι; the other inscriptions are likely to have drawn upon his Διδασκαλίαι.

See E. Reisch in *PW* v. 1 (1903), s.v. 'Didaskaliai'; A. Wilhelm, *Urkunden dramatischen Aufführungen in Athen* (1906); E. Capps, *Introduction of Comedy into the City Dionysia* (1903), and arts. in *AJPhil*. 1899 and 1900, *AJArch*. 1900, and *Hesp*. 1943; Pickard-Cambridge, *Dramatic Festivals of Athens* (1953), ch. 2; G. Jachmann, *De Aristotelis didascaliis* (1909). A. W. P.-C.

**DIDASCALIAE** at Rome. Plautus' *Stichus* and *Pseudolus* (in A), Terence's plays and Donatus' commentary thereon are prefaced by brief remarks concerning first performance, games at which performed, presiding magistrates, producer, composer, and type of music, Greek original, order of play in author's works, consuls of the year, etc. They were often incomplete; varying in different manuscripts; source unknown; nevertheless of fundamental importance.

See Schanz–Hosius, 105. W. B.

**DIDIUS** (1, *PW* 5), TITUS, as colleague of Norbanus (q.v. 1. tribune 103 B.C.), vainly tried to intercede against his prosecution of Caepio (q.v. 1). Praetor in Macedonia, he triumphed in 100 or 99. Consul with Q. Metellus Nepos (98), he helped to pass the *lex Caecilia Didia*, which, after the troubles of 100–98, established procedure for valid legislation and gave the Senate power to decide on contested validity: among other provisions, an interval of three *nundinae* was imposed between promulgation of a law and voting on it, and 'tacking' unrelated measures in a single bill was forbidden. He then commanded in Spain against the Celtiberians and by treacherous massacres gained the rare honour of a second triumph (93). A legate in the Social War, he was killed in June 89. E. B.

**DIDIUS** (2, *PW* 8) JULIANUS, MARCUS, a rich senator, was chosen by the praetorians after a mock auction of the Empire to succeed Pertinax on 28 Mar. A.D. 193, in preference to the latter's father-in-law Flavius Sulpicianus. He promised to restore the memory of Commodus, whose disloyal prefect Laetus was executed. But his election was unpopular with the masses and above all with the provincial armies; within a few weeks Septimius Severus was proclaimed Emperor at Carnuntum and Pescennius Niger in the East. The praetorians went over to the former and upon their direction the Senate deposed Julianus, who was murdered in his deserted palace on 1 June A.D. 193.

Herodian 2. 6–13; Dio Cassius bk. 73; *B.M.Coins, Rom. Emp.* v, lxix. 11–18. H. M. D. P.; B. H. W.

**DIDO,** legendary daughter of a king of Tyre, known by Virgil as Belus; she is said to have had the name of Elissa at Tyre, and to have been called Dido (? 'The Wanderer') at Carthage. Her husband, called Sychaeu by Virgil, was murdered by her brother Pygmalion, no king of Tyre, and Dido, escaping with some followe to Libya, there founded Carthage. At this point legen diverge. The older story, narrated by Timaeus, was th in order to escape marriage with the king of Liby (Iarbas in Virgil) Dido built a pyre as though for a offering and leapt into the flames. The Roman form the story, which gained currency at the time of the Pun Wars and was probably followed by Naevius and Enniu brought Aeneas to Carthage, but Varro, who adopts i makes Dido's sister Anna, not Dido herself, perish fc love of Aeneas. The story contained in the first an fourth books of the *Aeneid* may have been invented b Virgil himself. Aeneas, shipwrecked on the coast c Libya, is brought by Venus to the palace and entertaine by Dido, who falls in love with him. After a while Aenea departs, warned by Mercurius to leave Carthage an pursue his destiny, and Dido throws herself on the pyr Ovid in *Heroides* 7 presents Dido's lamentation in rhetorical form. Modern sentiment has reviled Aenea treatment of Dido, but his desertion of her in obedienc to divine command is an essential element in his 'piety (*see* AENEAS 1).

For the sources see A. S. Pease, *Verg. Aen.* 4 (1935), 14 ff.
C.

**DIDYMA,** oracular sanctuary of Apollo 10 miles sout of Miletus. It was in the hands of the priestly clan c Branchidae, by which name it was commonly known, an was, with Delphi, the most cosmopolitan of Greek oracles it received gifts from Pharaoh Necho and Croesus. Th archaic temple, from which little survives, was destroye by the Persians, probably in 494 B.C.; and in 480 th Branchidae were removed by Xerxes to Sogdiana, wher their descendants were massacred by Alexander the Great The cult statue of Apollo Philesios by Canachus was als carried off, but it was restored by Seleucus I. Thereafte the cult was administered by the Milesian State, with a annually elected *prophetes* and other officials. The build ing of a new temple over 350 feet long was commence c. 300 B.C.; of unconventional design, with a raise stage-like chamber behind the *pronaos*, and a sunke hypaethral *sekos* which contained a dainty shrine, it i one of the most magnificent ruins of the ancient world The Didymeia ranked among the great games of Roma times.

Inscriptions and architecture (T. Wiegand) *Didyma* (1941–58) G. E. Bean, *Aegean Turkey* (1966), ch. xi. J. M. C

**DIDYMUS** (1) (*c.* 80–10 B.C.) belonged to the schoo founded at Alexandria by Aristarchus (q.v. 2) and himsel taught there. A scholar of immense learning and industr (cf. his nickname Χαλκέντερος and Βιβλιολάθας, th latter because of occasional self-contradictions due to hi having forgotten what he had said in earlier books), b is said to have written 3,500 or 4,000 works. His im portance for literary history consists primarily in hi careful compilation of the critical and exegetical wor of earlier scholars. He was not an original researche but rather a discriminating variorum editor and scrupulous transmitter of learning that might otherwis have been lost.

WORKS: 1. He sought to reconstitute lost recension by Aristarchus of the Homeric text by the comparison c copies and by the examination of Aristarchus' com mentaries and special treatises. His results were muc used by the scholiasts. 2. Commentaries, with abundan mythological, geographical, historical, and biographica information, on Homer, Hesiod, Pindar, Bacchylides Choerilus, Aeschylus, Sophocles, Ion, Euripides, Achaeus Cratinus, Aristophanes, Phrynichus, Eupolis, Menan der, Thucydides, Antiphon, Isaeus, Isocrates, Aeschines

Demosthenes, Hyperides, Dinarchus. Much of the oldest scholia to Pindar, Sophocles, Euripides, and Aristophanes is ultimately derived from Didymus. A papyrus fragment of his commentary on Demosthenes' *Philippics* illustrates well his compilatory method. 3. Lexicography: *Λέξεις τραγικαί* and *Λέξεις κωμικαί*. These collections formed a valuable source for scholiasts and lexicographers, e.g. Hesychius. *On Corrupt Expressions, On Expressions of Doubtful Meaning, Metaphorical Expressions, On Proverbs*, a chief source of the extant works of the *Paroemiographi* (q.v.). 4. Grammar: *On Orthography, On Analogy among the Romans, On Inflexions*. 5. Literature and antiquities: *On Lyric Poets, Ξένη ἱστορία* (on myths and legends), *Miscellany* (*Σύμμικτα συμποσιακά*), *On the Axones of Solon*, works on the death of Aeneas, the birthplace of Homer, etc., and a polemic against Cic. *Rep.*, which was answered by Suetonius; but this last may be by his namesake Claudius Didymus.

M. Schmidt, *Didymi Chalcenteri grammatici Alexandrini fragmenta* 1854); A. Ludwich, *Aristarchs homerische Textkritik* (1884–5); C. Lehrs, *Die Pindarscholien* (1863); H. Diels u. W. Schubart, *D. Kommentar zu Demosthenes* (1904); A. Körte, *Rh. Mus.* 1905; P. Foucart, *Mémoires de l'Institut National de France* 1909. M. van der Valk, *Researches on the Text and Scholia of the Iliad* i (1963), 536 ff.
J. F. L.; R. B.

**DIDYMUS** (2), CLAUDIUS, the Younger (1st c. A.D.), an Atticist lexicographer, wrote on the incorrect diction of Thucydides (*Περὶ τῶν ἡμαρτημένων παρὰ τὴν ἀναλογίαν Θουκυδίδῃ*), abridged the *Attic lexicon* of Heracleon of Ephesus, and wrote a monograph comparing Latin with Greek.
P. B. R. F.

**DIEKPLUS** (*διέκπλους*), a naval manœuvre which the Greeks apparently borrowed from the Phoenicians in the Persian Wars. The ships of one line, feinting to ram the galleys of the opposing line, swept between them (*διεκπλεύσαντες*), damaging their oars or rudder-oar, and circled about to strike the helpless craft in the rear. To prevent this, a fleet was drawn up in two lines, either in file, as at Artemisium (U. Wilcken, *Hermes* 1906, 103 ff.), or in staggered formation, as at Arginusae (Xen. *Hell.* 1. 6. 29). With the heavier ships of Hellenistic times, the insertion of *lembi* in the lines (Polyb. 16. 4. 8 ff.), and the Roman reliance on boarding (ibid. 1. 22–3, 51), the *diekplus* was less often used.

H. T. Wallinga, *The Boarding-Bridge of the Romans* (Groningen, 1956).
C. G. S.

**DIES FASTI, NEFASTI.** On the Roman calendar (*see* CALENDARS) certain days were marked *F*, meaning *fas* or *fastus*, literally 'days of speaking', when the formal words necessary to transact legal business might be spoken, i.e. the courts were open and the day was not a festival. Others were *N*(*efasti*), when for one reason or another legal business might not be done (properly speaking, it was not impossible, but to do it was a *vitium* and must be expiated by a sacrifice). See Varro, *Ling.* 6. 29 ff. for other classes of days: *C*(*omitialis*), when public assemblies might be held; *EN*(*dotercisus*) or *intercisus*, lawful during the pause in the middle of the sacrificial ritual; *Q*(*uando*) *ST*(*ercus*) *D*(*elatum*) *F*(*as*), 15 June, when the shrine of Vesta (q.v.) was cleansed; *Q*(*uando*) *R*(*ex*) *C*(*omitiauit*) *F*(*as*), 24 Mar., 24 May, when the *rex* (q.v.) *sacrorum* had certain formal duties. On existing calendars, the sign NP, probably *nefas, feriae publicae*, is used somewhat erratically for many of the *dies nefasti. Dies religiosi* are any days, whether *nefasti* or not, supposed to be unlucky, e.g. the anniversary of Cannae.
H. J. R.

**DIETETICS** was originally the regulation of life for those who were training for the games, and this type of dietetics was practised as long as games were held. In the fifth century Herodicus of Selymbria, Plato says (*Resp.* 406 a), tried to heal the sick by prescribing a certain regimen; from then on dietetics became an established means of treating patients, like surgery or pharmacology.

Still more important than dietetics for athletes and the sick was that for the healthy as advocated by Greek physicians. If diseases due to a disturbance of the bodily balance can be healed by diet, it must be likewise possible to prevent diseases by a diet which preserves this balance undisturbed. Such prevention is the more necessary since the bodily balance is constantly changed by whatever a person does, eats, or drinks, by exercises and the seasons; it must be constantly restored so as to avoid the danger of falling into disease at almost any moment. The healthy no less than the sick, it was therefore claimed, should fall under the permanent supervision of the physician.

For their dietetic rules the physicians determined with minute accuracy the quality of all factors influencing the body from without or within. They regulated with great care every detail of life according to the necessities of health alone, and without paying any attention to the demands of business activities, politics, or normal life. They admitted that the poor had to content themselves with what was possible for them, but wanted the rich, who alone had the means of living a healthy life, to do so, even if it meant giving up everything else. Strange as it seems, people accepted this medical philosophy, believing as they did that health is the greatest blessing in this life of uncertainty and change. Such ideas became the more plausible, at least for the upper classes who were not restrained by any considerations of occupation, especially since political independence was gradually destroyed in the city-states. Yet even among the poor dietetic measures in as far as they could be applied were very common.

There can be no doubt that the demand of physicians on the healthy was responsible for much nervousness. People became too conscious of their bodies; besides, they were unable to endure sudden and unforeseen changes, and in addition tended to remain aloof from all useful activity, a consequence deplored by philosophers and statesmen. Yet it was not until Greek medicine was transmitted to the Romans that a certain change took place. The Romans insisted that the healthy man could do whatever he pleased, for otherwise he could not fulfil his duties as a citizen; dietetics they thought only good for weaklings and scholars. In the Roman Empire, however, even this opposition was overcome. With the rise of autocratic government and the beginning of the archaistic movement the Greek conception won the day and its reign was uncontested until the heathen ideal of bodily health vanished before the new God.

ANCIENT SOURCES. Hippocrates, *Περὶ διαίτης ὑγιεινῆς*; *Περὶ διαίτης* bks. 1–4; Galen, *Ὑγιεινόν*, bks. 1–6; Philostratus, *Περὶ γυμναστικῆς*.
MODERN LITERATURE. General, L. Edelstein, *Die Antike* (1931). Relation to gymnastics, L. Englert, *Studien z. Gesch. d. Med.* (1929). Medical content, J. Marcuse, *Diätetik im Alterthum* (1899); W. W. Jaeger, *Paideia* (U.S.A. 1944), iii. 3 ff., 44 f., overemphasizes the educational value of dietetics as of medicine in general. For the strong opposition to the dietetics ideal and its reasons see L. Edelstein, 'The Relation of Ancient Philosophy to Medicine', *Bulletin of the History of Medicine* 1952, 307 ff. A compromise between Greek and Christian ideas was attempted by some early Church fathers (A. Decker, *Kenntniss und Pflege des Korpus bei Clemens von Alexandreia*, 1936). Greek dietetics, despite its general similarity with Hindu medical dietetics, lacks the emphasis which the latter puts on 'the knowledge of the long and perfect life' (H. A. Zimmer, *Hindu Medicine*, U.S.A. 1948, lxviii f.). The counterpart of the Hindu dietetics of the soul practised by the priest (Zimmer, op. cit., xliii) among the ancients is the ethical dietetics taught by philosophers.
L. E.

**DIEUCHIDAS** of Megara (4th c. B.C.) wrote annals of Megara (*Μεγαρικά*), and ascribed the recension of Homer to Solon.
FGrH iii. 485; J. A. Davison, *CQ* 1959, 216 ff.

**DIFFERENTIAE,** distinctions between words of similar form (*ora, hora*) or meaning (*metus, timor, pavor*) formulated by rhetoricians and grammarians as an aid to correct diction. The earliest Latin examples are in the ps.-Ciceronian *Rhetorica ad Herennium* and Varro's *De Ling. Lat.* Many *differentiae* were discussed by miscellanists (Suetonius in his *Prata*, Aulus Gellius), by lexicographers (Verrius Flaccus, Nonius especially in book 5), and by grammarians. Anonymous lists compiled from various sources were sometimes attributed to great names (*Diff. Catonis*, etc.) and many items were incorporated in glossaries. Many *differentiae*, however, do not correspond with the actual usage of Latin authors.

G. Brugnoli, *Studie sulle Differentiae Verborum* (1955). Schanz–Hosius, § 1121.                                        J. F. M.

**DIGESTA,** a title applied by the classical jurisprudence to treatises on the law as a whole (*see* JURISPRUDENCE), and by Justinian to the main part of his codification, published after the first Codex and *Institutiones*. An alternative name for this part of Justinian's work was *Pandectae*, a counterpart of Greek origin to the Latin name formed from *digerere*. By the constitution of 15 Dec. 530, beginning with the words 'Deo auctore', the Emperor initiated the work by giving instructions to his minister of justice Tribonianus (q.v.) for its composition by the collection of passages from the works of classical jurists. Precisely three years later the collection was published by the Constitution 'Tanta', which contains precious indications on the origin and formation of the work, but nothing on the method by which the editorial commission (five professors and eleven advocates under the presidency of Tribonian) accomplished their task. The *Digesta* came into force on 30 Dec. 533. They contain excerpts from works of jurists of more than three centuries; the earliest is Q. Mucius Scaevola (q.v. 5), and the latest are Modestinus, Hermogenianus (qq.v.), and Charisius, but 95 per cent of the work is taken from authors of the period between A.D. 100 and 250. Justinian records that two thousand books with three millions of lines were read by the compilers for this purpose, but only a twentieth, 150,000 lines, were selected. A not quite accurate list of authors and works excerpted (Index Florentinus) is annexed to the best MS. of the *Digest*, preserved at Florence. The collection is divided into fifty books, the books into titles with headings taken chiefly from, and arranged in the order of, the praetorian edict. The excerpts ('fragments') vary in length from a few words to several thousand, but each has an *inscriptio* indicating its author and the work from which it is taken.

It was certainly a strange idea of the Emperor or his counsellors to construct a code of existing law by compiling passages written three to five centuries before, and presenting them as his own opinion (const. 'Omnem' 6: 'omnia nostra facimus'). The compilers, moreover, did not restrict themselves to collecting legal rules and formulations of a general character: they copied passages with historical reminiscences, etymological observations, quotations taken from Homer, polemics and divergent opinions, precious of course from a historical point of view, but superfluous and embarrassing in a work which according to a strict order of Justinian should have been a codification, since the jurists' opinions were to be considered as current and valid law. The task of the compilers was very difficult; the mosaic compilation of more than 9,000 fragments could not produce a perfect result; repetitions and contradictions were unavoidable (though strictly forbidden by Justinian) in such an enormous work, completed in less than three years. Another reason for the insufficiency of the work was the order of the Emperor that the compilers might alter and improve any-

thing that seemed to them 'superuacuum uel imperfectun uel minus idoneum' (const. 'Tanta' 10). Such alterations i the classical texts, by omission, addition, or substitution are called 'interpolations' ('emblemata Triboniani') The simplest merely suppress references to institution which had been abolished or had become obsolete, suc as *mancipatio* (q.v.) and *res mancipi*, *in iure cessio* (se DOMINIUM), *dotis dictio* (*see* MARRIAGE), *fiducia* (se SECURITY), or else replace them by modern terms. Sometimes the need for compression leads to the conflation o several passages into one or to the omission or abbreviation of arguments so as to produce an unintelligible o chaotic text. On the other hand, superfluous additions were made in explanation of a word or a rule. But a grea number of interpolations were far from being merely formal alterations, as when the classical decision wa restricted to special matters of fact or changed into a opposite one in conformity with the new law of imperia constitutions of post-classical times, and with reforms o Justinian himself, or under the influence of new lega doctrines and ideas. It is clear that such a method sometimes brought confusion into the precise constructions o the classical jurists.

The detection of interpolations engaged the attentior of the humanist lawyers of the sixteenth century, but i was only in the sixty years beginning *c.* 1880 that the attempt to distinguish by this means the 'classical' from the 'Byzantine' law became the chief interest of scholars In the first four decades of this period a number of criteria for the identification of interpolations were propounded and much of undeniable validity was achieved. Thereafter, the uncritical application of increasingly subjective criteria, particularly in the field of language and style, led to exaggerated claims which left few texts unscathed. There was, moreover, a failure to distinguish between merely verbal interpolations and those which effected a substantial change in the law; and the concentration on the search for interpolations led to an excessively clear-cut distinction between the classical law and the law of Justinian to the exclusion of the possibility of the texts' having been altered and edited in the interval. These and other considerations have led in recent years to a diversion of interest in other directions, and in particular to the examination of the fate of the texts in the postclassical period and the related study of the 'vulgarization of the law in this period and the identification of a classica revival in Justinian's time and immediately before. And within the classical law there has been a greater readiness to recognize divergences and developments.

MODERN EDITIONS. Mommsen, *Digesta Iustiniani* (2 vols. 1866 1870); Mommsen, P. Krueger, *Corpus iuris civilis* i (16th stereo typed ed. 1954). A pocket-edition by Bontante, Fadda, Ferrini Riccobono, Scialoja contains some useful suggestions (vol. i, 1908 vol. ii, 1931). Important works of reference: A. Guarneri-Citati Indice delle parole e frasi ritenute interpolate² (1927); Supplem. i Studi Riccobono i and Festschrift für P. Koschaker i (1939). Index Interpolationum quae in Iustiniani Digestis inesse dicuntur (initiated by L. Mitteis and edited under the direction of E. Levy and E. Rabel 3 vols. and 1 Suppl., 1929–35). *Vocabularium iurisprudentiae Romanae* in 5 volumes (not yet finished). *See also* the bibliographies under LAW AND PROCEDURE, ROMAN, § 1, and JURISPRUDENCE.          A. B.; B. N

**DIKASTERION** (δικαστήριον) was the ordinary Greek term for 'lawcourt'. In Athens until the beginning of the sixth century B.C. all verdicts were given by magistrate (*see* ARCHONTES) or by the Areopagus (q.v.) or the *epheta* (q.v.). Solon (q.v.) seems to have instituted a system by which an assembly of citizens (*heliaia*, q.v.) heard appeal against magistrates' verdicts, or authorized the impositior of penalties above certain limits. The next stages o development are obscure, but presumably appeals be came so usual that magistrates practically ceased to giv verdicts and the assembly did not have time to hear al the cases referred to it. A system of juries was therefore set up, in which each jury consisted of a number of citizens who tried a case on behalf of all the citizens.

**2.** For the period after the middle of the fifth century we have fuller information. Volunteers for jury service (who had to be over 30 years old) were called for at the beginning of each year, and a list of 6,000 jurors for the year was drawn up. To encourage volunteers, each juror received a small fee for each day on which he sat to try a case. This payment was introduced by Pericles (q.v.), who probably fixed it at 2 obols; it was raised to 3 obols not later than 425. Since the payment was less than an able-bodied man would earn by an ordinary day's work, one of its effects was that many of the volunteers were men who were too old for work. This state of affairs is satirized by Aristophanes in the *Wasps*.

**3.** The number of jurors who formed a jury varied according to the type of case, but was usually several hundred. In one trial it is said to have been 6,000. In the fourth century odd numbers (e.g. 501) were used, to avoid a tie in the voting, but there is no evidence for odd numbers in the fifth century. It is not known what method was used in the fifth century for allocating jurors to courts. By the early fourth century a system of lot was used for this purpose, and later in the century a more complicated system of lot (described in detail in Arist. *Ath. Pol.* 63–6) was introduced. The aim was to prevent bribery by making it impossible to know beforehand which jurors would try which case.

**4.** Each trial was arranged and presided over by a magistrate or group of magistrates. Different magistrates had responsibility for different types of case. The (eponymous) *archon* (see ARCHONTES) had charge of cases concerning family and inheritance rights. The *basileus* had charge of most cases connected with religion. The *polemarchos* (q.v.) had charge of cases concerning non-Athenians. The *thesmothetai* (q.v.) had charge of a wide variety of cases; in general any type of public case which did not clearly fall within the province of another magistrate came to them. The *strategoi* (q.v.) had charge of cases concerning military and naval service. The *hendeka* (q.v.) had charge of cases of theft and similar offences. Many types of private case were the responsibility of the *eisagogeis* or of the Forty, and there were several lesser boards of magistrates with responsibility for particular types of case, such as the *apodektai* and the *nautodikai* (q.v.).

**5.** In the fifth century and the first half of the fourth each magistrate sat regularly in the same court. The *heliaia* (q.v.) was the court of the *thesmothetai*, the Inserted Court (τὸ Παράβυστον) was the court of the *hendeka*, and the Odeum (q.v.) was probably the court of the *eisagogeis*. Other courts were the New Court (τὸ Καινόν), the Court at Lykos (τὸ ἐπὶ Λύκῳ), the Kallion, the Triangular, Greater, and Middle Courts (τὸ Τρίγωνον, τὸ Μεῖζον, τὸ Μέσον), and the Painted Portico (ἡ στοὰ ἡ ποικίλη). In Aristotle's time magistrates no longer sat regularly in the same courts, but were allocated to courts by lot each day. Distinct from all these courts were the Areopagus (q.v.) and the other special homicide courts (see EPHETAI), in which a different procedure was followed.

**6.** When anyone wished to bring a prosecution, he gave his charge to the appropriate magistrate. It was the responsibility of the accuser to deliver the summons to the accused. The magistrate held an inquiry (ἀνάκρισις), at which he heard statements and evidence from both parties. Some trivial cases could be decided by the magistrate forthwith, but generally the purpose of the inquiry was simply to satisfy him that the case should be taken to court.

**7.** At the trial the magistrate presided, but he did not give directions or advice to the jury, and did not perform the functions of a modern judge. The accuser spoke first, and the accused afterwards. If either party was a minor, a woman, or a non-citizen, the speech was made by the nearest adult male relative or patron; but otherwise each party had to speak for himself, unless clearly incapable, though he might deliver a speech written for him by a professional speech-writer, and he might call on friends to speak too in his support. In the course of his speech he could request to have laws or other public documents read out to the court. He could also call witnesses. Until some date in the first half of the fourth century, witnesses gave their evidence orally, and might be questioned by the speaker who called them (but not cross-examined by his opponent). Later in the fourth century witnesses gave evidence beforehand in writing, and at the trial merely signified assent when their statements were read out. Women, children, and slaves could not appear in court as witnesses, but a written record of a slave's statement could be produced as evidence if the statement had been made under torture. A certain length of time (varying according to the type of case) was allowed for each party to make his speech, the time being measured by a water-clock.

**8.** When the speeches of the parties were over, the jury heard no impartial summing-up and had no opportunity for discussion, but voted at once. In the fifth century each juror voted by placing a pebble or shell in an urn; there was one urn for condemnation and one for acquittal. In the fourth century each juror was given two bronze votes, one with a hole pierced through it signifying condemnation and one unpierced signifying acquittal, and he placed one in a 'valid' (bronze) urn and the other in an 'invalid' (wooden) urn; this method helped to ensure that the voting was secret and that each juror cast only one vote. When all had voted, the votes were counted, and the majority decided the verdict. A tie meant acquittal. There was no appeal from the jury's verdict.

**9.** For some offences the penalty was laid down by law, but for others the penalty had to be decided by the jury. In such cases, when the verdict had been given against the accused, the accuser proposed a penalty and the accused proposed another (naturally more lenient). Each spoke in support of his proposal, and the jury voted again to decide between them. Penalties regularly imposed were fines or damages, confiscation of property, confinement in the stocks, partial or total disfranchisement (see ATIMIA), exile, or death. Long terms of imprisonment were not imposed.

**10.** The chief fault of the Athenian lawcourts was that a jury could too easily be swayed by a skilful speaker. Most jurors were men of no special intelligence or legal experience; yet, without expert advice or guidance, they had to distinguish true from false statements and valid from invalid arguments, and they had to interpret the law as well as decide the facts. It says much for the Athenians' alertness and critical sense that the system worked as well as it did. The advantages were that the large juries were hard to bribe or browbeat, and that the lawcourts and the people were as nearly as possible identical, so that an accused man felt that he was being judged by the Athenian people, not merely by some government official or according to an obscure written rule. Thus the institution of popular juries was one of the Athenians' greatest democratic achievements.

*See* DIKE, PARAGRAPHE, SYKOPHANTAI.

J. H. Lipsius, *Das attische Recht und Rechtsverfahren* (1905–15); H. Hommel, 'Heliaia', *Philol.* Suppl. xix (1927); R. J. Bonner and G. Smith, *The Administration of Justice from Homer to Aristotle* (1930–8); F. Lämmli, *Das attische Prozessverfahren in seiner Wirkung auf die Gerichtsrede* (1938); S. Dow, 'Aristotle, the Kleroteria, and the Courts', *Harv. Stud.* 1939, 1 ff.; Hignett, *Hist. Athen. Const.*; R. Turasiewicz, *De servis testibus in Atheniensium iudiciis* (1963); D. M. MacDowell, *Athenian Homicide Law* (1963); M. Lavency, *Aspects de la logographie judiciaire attique* (1964).          D. M. M.

**DIKE** (1) (*Δίκη*), personification, mostly literary, of Justice. One of the Horae (Hesiod, *Theog.* 902), she reports to Zeus the wrong-doings of men (*Op.* 256 ff.), and similar ideas occur in later authors. In Aratus (*Phaen.* 96 ff.), she is the constellation Virgo, who finally left the earth when the Bronze Age began; some (as Ov. *Met.* 1. 149–50) call her Astraea in this connexion. In art she is sometimes shown punishing Injustice (see Paus. 5. 18. 2; cf. von Sybel in Roscher's *Lexikon* i. 1019). She catches an evil-doer (Eur. *Heracl.* 941); will not suffer a murderer to live (Acts xxviii. 4), perhaps from popular (pagan) belief. Cf. Schrenk in G. Kittel, *Theologisches Wörterbuch zum Neuen Testament* ii. 180 ff.          H. J. R.

**DIKE** (2) (δίκη) in Athenian law was the general term for 'case'. The principal distinction was between public cases (δίκαι δημόσιαι) and private cases (δίκαι ἴδιαι). But often, confusingly, the term *dike* without qualification was used for private cases only, in contrast with *graphe* and other types of public case.

2. The following distinctions may in general be made between public and private cases. (*a*) A private case concerned a wrong or injury done to an individual. A public case was brought for an offence which was regarded as affecting the community as a whole. For some offences, which could be regarded as either public or private, both types of case were legally permitted. (*b*) A private case could be brought only by the person who claimed that he had suffered wrong or injury. A public case could be brought by any citizen, unless disqualified. (*c*) In a private case damages or compensation might be awarded to the accuser. In a public case any fine or penalty was paid to the State. However, to encourage public-spirited citizens to prosecute offenders on behalf of the State, financial rewards were given to successful accusers in certain kinds of public case (notably *phasis* and *apographe*; see 3 (*f*) and (*g*) below). This had the unintended effect of encouraging the rise of *sykophantai* (q.v.). (*d*) To deter *sykophantai* penalties were imposed, in most kinds of public case, on an accuser who dropped a case after starting it, or who failed to obtain at least one-fifth of the jury's votes: he had to pay a fine of 1,000 drachmas, and he suffered partial disfranchisement (see ATIMIA), so that he could not bring similar prosecutions in future. These penalties did not apply in private cases.

3. The commonest kind of public case was *graphe* (q.v.). Sometimes this term was loosely used of any kind of public case, but more often the following special types of public case were distinguished from it. (*a*) *Eisangelia* (q.v.). Prosecution was initiated by denunciation to the *boule* or *ekklesia*, which might either decide to try the case itself or refer it to a lawcourt. (*b*) *Probole*. The accuser made a denunciation to the *ekklesia*. The *ekklesia* voted on it, but this hearing did not constitute a trial; if the accuser proceeded with the case, a trial was held subsequently in a lawcourt. This procedure was used against men accused of being *sykophantai* or deceiving the people of Athens, and also against those accused of violating the sanctity of certain festivals. The speech of Demosthenes *Against Meidias* relates to a case of this type. (*c*) *Apagoge*. The accuser began proceedings by arresting the accused and handing him over to the appropriate magistrates, usually the Eleven (see HENDEKA). This procedure was used especially against thieves caught in the act and against persons caught exercising rights to which they were not entitled. The speeches of Antiphon *On the Murder of Herodes* and Lysias *Against Agoratus* concern cases of *apagoge*. (*d*) *Endeixis*. The accuser made a denunciation to the magistrates, who arrested the accused. This procedure too was used against persons accused of exercising rights to which they were not entitled. The case of Andocides *On the Mysteries* is the

best-known example. (*e*) *Ephegesis*. The accuser led the magistrates to the accused, and they arrested him—a procedure very similar to *endeixis*, and used for the same type of offence. (*f*) *Phasis*. This name was given to cases against men who broke regulations concerning trade or mines, guardians who mismanaged their wards' property, and some others. If the prosecutor won the case, he was rewarded with half of the fine exacted or property confiscated. (*g*) *Apographe*. The accuser listed property which he alleged was due to the State and was being withheld. If he won the case, he was rewarded with three-quarters of the property recovered. Several surviving speeches were written for this type of case, e.g. Lysias *On the Property of Aristophanes* and [Demosthenes] *Against Nicostratus*.

In addition, a case arising from an accusation made at a *dokimasia* (q.v.) or a *euthyna* (q.v.) was similar to a public case in some respects.

4. A special type of private case was *diadikasia*. This was used when a right (e.g. to claim an inheritance) or an obligation (e.g. to perform a trierarchy) was disputed between two or more persons. Its distinctive feature was that there was no accuser or accused: all the claimants were on equal terms. When there was only one claimant for an inheritance, so that no trial was necessary, the formal award to the claimant was called *epidikasia*.

5. Homicide cases (δίκαι φόνου) were treated differently from others. If a person was killed, his relatives (see ANCHISTEIS) were required by law to prosecute the killer. The prosecution followed a special procedure of proclamations, pre-trials, and oaths. The trial was not held in an ordinary law court, but at one of several special open-air courts, with the Areopagus (q.v.) or the *ephetai* (q.v.) as the jury.

*See* DIKASTERION, PARAGRAPHE, SYMBOLON.

J. H. Lipsius, *Das attische Recht und Rechtsverfahren* (1905–15); R. Maschke, *Die Willenslehre im griechischen Recht* (1926); G. M. Calhoun, *The Growth of Criminal Law in Ancient Greece* (1927); U. E. Paoli, *Studi di diritto attico* (1930); R. J. Bonner and G. Smith, *The Administration of Justice from Homer to Aristotle* (1930–8); F. Pringsheim, *The Greek Law of Sale* (1950); L. Gernet, *Droit et société dans la Grèce ancienne* (1955); J. W. Jones, *The Law and Legal Theory of the Greeks* (1956); A. Kränzlein, *Eigentum und Besitz im griechischen Recht* (1963); D. M. MacDowell, *Athenian Homicide Law* (1963); A. R. W. Harrison, *The Law of Athens: the family and property* (1968).          D. M. M.

**DINARCHUS** (*Δείναρχος*) (c. 360–c. 290), the last of the 'ten orators'. A Corinthian by birth, he lived at Athens, and studied under Theophrastus. Being a *metoikos*, and therefore debarred from public speaking, he composed a large number of speeches for others. The first of these was written c. 336, but he did not come into prominence till c. 324, when he wrote a speech against Demosthenes in the Harpalus affair (see DEMOSTHENES 2). He prospered particularly after the death of Alexander, when, as his biographer Dionysius of Halicarnassus remarks, the other orators having been executed or banished, there was nobody left worth mentioning. Under the oligarchy established by Cassander, 322–307 B.C., he was active and prosperous, but on the restoration of democracy in 307 he retired to Chalcis in Euboea, where he lived till 292. Returning to Athens, through the intercession of Theophrastus, he was robbed of a large sum of money by his host Proxenos, and brought the latter to justice. Nothing is known of his life after this, nor the date of his death.

WORKS. Of sixty speeches which Dionysius considered genuine we possess only three—*Against Demosthenes*, *Against Aristogiton*, and *Against Philocles*, which are all connected with the affair of Harpalus. The authenticity of the first of these was doubted by Demetrius, but it is very similar to the others in style and matter. Three other speeches, *Against Boeotus II*, *Against Theocrines*, and *Against Mantitheus*, which appear in the Demosthenic Corpus, have sometimes been ascribed to Dinarchus.

Dinarchus marks the beginning of the decline in Attic oratory. He had little originality, except some skill in the use of new metaphors; he imitated his predecessors, especially Demosthenes (Hermogenes, *Id.* 2. 11 calls him κριθινὸς Δημοσθένης, 'a small-beer Demosthenes'), but developed no characteristic style of his own. He knew the technique of prose composition and had command of all the tricks of the orator's trade. He was competent up to a point, but his work is careless and lacking in taste. Thus, the arrangement of his speeches is incoherent; his sentences are long and formless, certain figures of speech, e.g. epanalepsis and asyndeton, are ridden to death, and his invective is so exaggerated as to become meaningless. Numerous examples of minor plagiarisms are collected by Blass (*Att. Ber.*² iii. 2. 318–21); in particular, a passage about Thebes in *Demos.* 24 is based on Aeschines 1. 133, and *Aristog.* 24 is suggested by Demosthenes 9. 41.

For general bibliography, see ATTIC ORATORS.
TEXT. Blass (Teubner, 1888). Index, see ANDOCIDES.
TEXT AND TRANSLATION. J. O. Burtt, *Minor Attic Orators* ii (Loeb).
J. F. D.

**DINON** (Δίνων rather than Δείνων) of Colophon, father of Cleitarchus (q.v.), wrote a history of Persia in at least three *syntaxeis* (perhaps Assyria, Media, Persia), certainly down to Artaxerxes Ochus. Following Ctesias' Περσικά, it represents the trend towards the romantic Alexander-histories. Widely read, it is used in Plutarch's *Artaxerxes*.

*FGrH* iii C, 522.
A. H. McD.

**DIO** (1) **COCCEIANUS,** later called Chrysostomos (*c.* A.D. 40–after 112, Greek orator and popular philosopher. Born of wealthy family in Prusa in Bithynia, Dio began a career as a rhetorician at Rome, but soon fell under the spell of the Stoic philosopher Musonius. Involved in a political intrigue early in the reign of Domitian, he was banished (*relegatus*) both from Rome and from his native province, and spent many years travelling through Greece, the Balkans, and Asia Minor as a wandering preacher of Stoic-Cynic philosophy. Rehabilitated by Nerva, he became a friend of Trajan, but continued to travel widely as an epideictic orator. He later retired to his family estates in Bithynia, became a notable in the province, and was prosecuted before the proconsul Pliny in connexion with a public building contract.

Of the 80 speeches attributed to him, two are actually the work of his pupil Favorinus. Many are display-speeches, but others, e.g. those delivered before the Assembly and Council at Prusa, deal with real situations. His themes are varied: mythology, the Stoic-Cynic ideal monarch, literary criticism, popular morality, funeral orations, rhetorical descriptions, addresses to cities, etc. He sees himself as a teacher of his fellow men, and his stock ideas are the Stoic concepts of φύσις, ἀρετή, and φιλανθρωπία. His language and style are atticist, though he avoids the extreme archaism of some of his contemporaries of the Second Sophistic, and often aims at an easy, almost conversational style, suggestive of improvisation. Plato and Xenophon are his main models. Dio idealizes the Hellenic past, and feels himself the heir to a long classical tradition, which he seeks to revive and preserve. His Stoic-Cynic philosophy has lost its erstwhile revolutionary élan, and become essentially conservative, though he still insists on the philosopher's right to free speech and criticism. His Greek patriotism is in no way anti-Roman. Like his contemporary Plutarch, he reflects the attitudes and culture of the upper classes of the eastern half of the Empire, who were beginning to reach out to a share in political power. He gives a vivid and detailed picture of the life of his times.

TEXT: H. v. Arnim (1893–6); G. de Budé (1915–19).
TEXT AND TRANSL.: J. W. Cohoon, H. L. Crosby (Loeb, 5 vols., 1932–51).
STUDIES: H. v. Arnim, *Leben u. Werke des D. von Prusa* (1898); W. Schmid, *Der Attizismus in seinen Hauptvertretern,* i (1887), 72 ff.; M. Cytowska, *De Dionis rhythmo oratorio* (1952); J. Moling, *D. u. die klassischen Dichter* (1959); R. MacMullen, *Enemies of the Roman Order* (1967), 46 ff.
R. B.

**DIO** (2) **CASSIUS** (*Cassius Dio Cocceianus*) of Nicaea (Bithynia), son of Cassius Apronianus, governor of Cilicia and of Dalmatia, entering the Senate under Commodus, became praetor (A.D. 194), *consul suffectus* (about 205), and consul for the second time with Alexander Severus in 229. Besides a biography of Arrian and a work on the dreams and portents of Septimius Severus, he wrote a Roman history from the beginnings to A.D. 229, of which books 36–54 (68–10 B.C.) are fully preserved, 55–60 (9 B.C.–A.D. 46) in abbreviation, 17, 79–80 in part. Xiphilinus (11th c.) epitomized from book 36 (missing Antoninus Pius and M. Aurelius' first years); Zonaras (12th c.) gives the tradition of books 1–21, 44–80 in books 7–11 of his Ἐπιτομὴ Ἱστοριῶν, following Xiphilinus from Trajan.

The narrative, which took ten years to prepare and twelve years to write, appears to be based on republican annalistic tradition, Livy or Livy's sources (from 68 to 30 B.C.), imperial annalistic tradition, and for contemporary events his own high authority. Unreliable about republican institutions and conditions, from Caesar onwards he used his constitutional experience, at first colouring events with his ideas of imperial absolutism (cf. Maecenas' speech in 52. 14–40), but later handling his material with full knowledge. Annalistic in arrangement, although modified to meet requirements of subject-matter, his narration concentrated on political aspects, in the manner of Thucydides, giving a rhetorical narrative in Atticist style.

TEXTS. J. Melber (1890–1928, Teubner); U. P. Boissevain (1895–1931); E. W. Cary (1914–27, Loeb). Syme, *Tacitus,* 271, 365; F. Millar, *Cassius Dio* (1964).
A. H. McD.

**DIOCLES** (1) (d. after 408 B.C.), Syracusan democrat opposed to Hermocrates (q.v.). He remodelled the Syracusan constitution; because his legislation was later thought obscurely phrased, and as after his death he received hero-worship, some scholars envisage an archaic hero-lawgiver distinguishable from the demagogue.

Diodorus bk. 13. W. Hüttl, *Verfassungsgeschichte von Syrakus* (1929), 85 ff.
A. G. W.

**DIOCLES** (2), Athenian comic poet, 'contemporary of Sannyrion' (q.v.) 'and Philyllius' (q.v.) according to the *Suda,* i.e. *c.* 400 B.C. We have six titles and fourteen fragments. He was also credited with the invention of a percussion instrument.

*FCG* i. 251 ff.; *CAF* i. 766 ff.; *FAC* i. 896 ff.
K. J. D.

**DIOCLES** (3) of Carystus, according to Pliny the second physician after Hippocrates in time and fame, a contemporary of Aristotle (384–322 B.C.), lived at Athens. He was the first physician to write in Attic, avoiding hiatus. His books dealt with animal anatomy, physiology, aetiology, symptomatology, prognostics, dietetics, botany. The fragments show the influence of the Sicilian school of which his father, Archidamus, was also an adherent, and of Empedocles (four humours, importance of the heart, the pneuma), of Hippocrates (the body considered as organism), of Aristotle (methodological concepts and terminology). Diocles' originality, it seems, consists in uniting these different trends. That in the details of scientific research he was independent is certain.

TEXT. Fragments, M. Wellmann, *Die Fragmente d. sikelischen*

*Ärzte* (1901); M. Fränkel, *D. Carystii fr. quae supersunt*, Diss. Berl. (1840).

LITERATURE. General discussion, Wellmann, loc. cit., and *PW* v. 802; F. Heinimann, *MH* 1955, 158 ff.; F. Kudlien, *Sudhoffs Archiv* 1963, 456 ff. W. Jaeger, *D. v. Karystos* (1938), points to Aristotelian influence and argues for a later date of Diocles than had formerly been assigned; the date 340–260 B.C. (Jaeger, *Sitz. Berl.* 1938) seems too late; cf. review of Jaeger's book by L. Edelstein, *AJPhil.* 1940. Cf. also F. Heinimann, op. cit.; F. Kudlien again makes Diocles an older contemporary of Aristotle but has not refuted all the arguments that speak for influence of the latter upon Diocles. L. E.

**DIOCLES** (4), mathematician (*? c.* 200 B.C.), wrote a work, important in the history of conic sections, *On Burning-Mirrors* (περὶ πυρείων). It is preserved only in a defective Arabic translation and in two long extracts by Eutocius (*Comm. in Arch.* Heiberg², iii. 66 ff., 160 ff.). The first solves the problem of finding two mean proportionals ('doubling the cube'), the second a problem propounded by Archimedes which amounts to a cubic equation.

The unpublished Arabic text is in Chester Beatty MS. 5255. COMMENT. Heath, *Hist. of Greek Maths.* i. 264 ff.; ii. 47 ff. DATE. Hitherto it has been supposed that Diocles is later than Apollonius, since the quotations by Eutocius contain references to the *Conics*. But from the antiquated terminology reflected by the Arabic version it seems probable that he wrote between Archimedes and Apollonius. G. J. T.

**DIOCLES** (5) of Magnesia (it is not known which Magnesia), a younger friend of the Cynic Meleager of Gadara, therefore probably born *c.* 75 B.C. He must have lived part of his life in Cos. He is mentioned only by Diogenes Laertius, who describes him as the author of an Ἐπιδρομή (compendium) τῶν φιλοσόφων. Diogenes makes large use of this work, but Nietzsche went much too far in describing Diogenes' work as simply an epitome of that of Diocles. (*See* DOXOGRAPHERS.) W. D. R.

**DIOCLES** (6), Greek rhetor of the Augustan age, whose declamations betrayed moderate Asianist tendencies.

Sen. *Controv.* 7. 1. 26.

**DIOCLETIAN** (GAIUS AURELIUS VALERIUS (*PW* 142) DIOCLETIANUS), originally named Diocles, a Dalmatian of low birth, who rose to be commander of the Emperor Numerian's bodyguard. Chosen by the army near Nicomedia in November A.D. 284 to avenge his master's death, he struck down the praetorian prefect, Aper. He then marched westwards to defeat Numerian's brother, Carinus, at Margus (early 285). He at once chose Maximian, an old comrade, to be his Caesar and sent him to Gaul to suppress the Bacaudae (insurgent peasants). Quickly victorious, Maximian was raised to the rank of Augustus early in 286.

The frontier situation was serious; Diocletian fought the Alamanni (288/9), Sarmatians (289 and 292), Saracens (290, in which year also Tiridates III was established as Roman nominee on the throne of Armenia), and was engaged against a serious revolt in Egypt (292/3). In the West, Carausius, admiral of the Channel fleet, revolted in 287 to escape condemnation for neglect of duty, seized Britain and a part of northern Gaul, and frustrated all attempts to reduce him. The Emperors were forced to leave him in peace, but did not recognize him.

In view of the many difficulties of the government, Diocletian in 293 established his famous 'tetrarchy'. Himself Augustus in the East he took Galerius to be his Caesar, while to Maximian, Augustus in the West, was assigned Constantius Chlorus. The two Caesars were bound to their Augusti by marriage with their daughters. Constantius blockaded Bononia (*Boulogne*) and wrested it from Carausius, who was soon afterwards murdered by his assistant, Allectus. A great expedition in 296 under Constantius and his praetorian prefect, Asclepiodotus, destroyed Allectus and recovered Britain. In 298 Constantius gained a spectacular victory over the Alamanni at

Langres. Maximian in 297 crossed to Africa and defeated the troublesome confederacy of the Quinquegentanei. In Egypt a fresh revolt broke out under Domitius Domitianus and Achilleus in 296, but was suppressed by Diocletian in person at Alexandria in 297.

Taking advantage of the situation, the Persian King Narses expelled Tiridates from Armenia. Diocletian summoned Galerius from the Danube frontier where he had been engaged against the Carpi. Defeated in the first campaign in 297 near Carrhae, Galerius brought up reinforcements and in 298 won a complete victory. The peace treaty consolidated Roman Mesopotamia and added seven small satrapies north of the upper Tigris to the Empire; Armenia and Iberia again became dependent on Rome. All trade between the two empires was directed through Nisibis.

In 303 Diocletian visited Rome for the first time, to celebrate his *Vicennalia*. A collapse in health the following year almost cost him his life, and on 1 May 305 he abdicated with Maximian, leaving Constantius and Galerius Augusti in West and East respectively, with Severus and Maximin Daia as their Caesars. His years of retirement were spent at Salonae (where remains of his palace survive), broken only by a return to public life, in 308, to help Galerius to re-establish order in the government at the Conference of Carnuntum. Diocletian died in 316, saddened by the civil wars, the collapse of his system of imperial succession, and the persecution of his kindred by Maximin Daia and Licinius.

Diocletian's genius was as an organizer, and many of his administrative measures lasted for centuries. The tetrarchy was an attempt to provide each part of the Empire with a ruler and to establish an ordered, non-hereditary succession. It broke down when his dominating personality was removed, but for most of the fourth century more than one Emperor was the rule. To raise the dignity of the imperial office Diocletian assumed an oriental court ceremonial and seclusion; he took the name Jovius and called Maximian Herculius to emphasize their quasi-divine authority. Each member of the tetrarchy had his own staff (*comitatus*), and was often on the move in his territory, though Nicomedia, Treviri, and Sirmium often provided the imperial residence, while Rome was of lesser importance.

In order to ensure more detailed supervision of affairs, many provinces were divided, the number probably being doubled. All provinces except Asia and Africa and the divisions of Italy were governed by equestrian *praesides* who had judicial, financial, and executive powers. In the later part of his reign, Diocletian began an important reform, separating military from civil power in the frontier provinces; a number of provincial armies were put under the command of *duces*, thus leaving the *praesides* to concentrate on their civilian duties. To supervise the *praesides*, Diocletian grouped the provinces into twelve units called dioceses (*see* DIOECESIS), each under a *vicarius* (equestrian), who was technically a deputy of the praetorian prefects, of which each member of the tetrarchy had one. Senators were almost excluded from both military and civil commands.

Diocletian's conception of imperial defence was conservative; he made little or no effort to increase the size of the élite field army (*comitatus*), which had been formed in the late third century. Instead, a massive programme of building and reconstruction of defensive works was undertaken on all frontiers, and these defences were to be held by sheer force of numbers; the number of soldiers in the Roman army was perhaps nearly doubled.

The increase in the size of the army and the administration was a heavy burden on the resources of the Empire. Diocletian introduced a new system of taxation to take into account the depreciation of money values and to regularize arbitrary exactions in kind. It was based on the *iugum*, the unit of land and the *caput*, the human unit, and was revised every fifteen years (*indictio*). The greater part of the State's revenue and expenditure was now in kind. He attempted to create a unified currency but could not establish confidence in it. In 301 he tried to halt the rapid rise in prices by the *Edictum de pretiis* which fixed maximum prices and wages. In spite of savage penalties it soon became a dead letter as goods disappeared from the market.

**10.** Diocletian was an enthusiast for what he believed was the old Roman religion, tradition, and discipline, which he held could reinforce imperial unity. Many legal decisions show his insistence on the maintenance of Roman law in the provinces where no doubt it had been neglected in the preceding decades. This policy formed the background to the persecution of the Christians undertaken in 303, possibly on the insistence of Galerius, less prudent than his Augustus. Four edicts were issued before the abdication and enforced with varying degrees of severity, most harshly in Palestine and Egypt. Diocletian's administrative measures did much to preserve the unity of the Empire for another century; they were completed by Constantine, who was also able, however, to introduce a number of innovations.

C. Costa in *Diz. Epigr.* ii. 1793 ff.; K. Stade, *Der Politiker Diokletian und die letzte große Christenverfolgung* (1926); W. Ensslin, *Zur Ostpolitik des Kaisers Diokletian* (1942); W. Seston, *Dioclétien et la tétrarchie* i (1946); Jones, *Later Rom. Emp.* 37 ff.
H. M.; B. H. W.

**DIODORUS** (1) of Sinope, New Comedy poet, brother of Diphilus (q.v.); a family monument (*IG* ii². 10321) suggests that he became an Athenian citizen (see Webster, *Later Greek Comedy* 152). He seems to have had two plays produced at the Lenaea of 288 (*IG* ii². 2319. 61, 63), and to have been a comic actor at Delos in 284 and 280 (*IG* xi. 105. 21, 107. 20). Fr. 2, the parasite's divine rites.

*FCG* iii. 543 ff.; *CAF* ii. 420 ff.; G. M. Sifakis, *Studies in the History of Hellenistic Drama* (1967), 26.
W. G. A.

**DIODORUS** (2) **CRONUS** of Iasos (fl. *c.* 300 B.C.), one of the masters of Megarian dialectic. Among his pupils were Zeno of Citium and Arcesilaus, both of whom owed much to him. He repeated the arguments of Zeno of Elea against the possibility of motion; his most famous argument, the κυριεύων, was directed against the possibility of that which is not actual, and played a considerable part in controversies over freewill.

P.-M. Schuhl, *Le Dominateur et les possibles* (1960). W. D. R.

**DIODORUS** (3) **SICULUS** of Agyrium, flourished under Caesar and Augustus (to at least 21 B.C.), wrote (*c.* 60–30 B.C.) a World History, his Βιβλιοθήκη, in forty books from the earliest times to Caesar's Gallic War (54 B.C.). He began with an ἀρχαιολογία: book 1 Egypt, book 2 Mesopotamia, India, Scythia, Arabia, book 3 North Africa, books 4–6 Greece and Europe (1–5 fully preserved, 6 fragmentary); books 7–17 covered from the Trojan War to Alexander the Great, books 18–40 from the Diadochi to Caesar (7–10 fragmentary, 11–20 fully preserved, 21–40 fragmentary). The narrative reproduces in its successive parts the tradition of Hecateus, Ctesias, Ephorus, Theopompus, historians of Alexander (including Aristobulus and Cleitarchus), Hieronymus, Duris, Diyllus, Philinus, Timaeus, an early Roman annalist, Polybius, Posidonius. This material was added to the framework of a chronographical work, dependent on Apollodorus. Despite his universal conception of history and his aim of writing for the Graeco-Roman world, his work is undistinguished, with confusion arising from the

different traditions and chronologies, a compilation only as valuable as its authorities, but thus valuable to us.

TEXTS. I. Bekker (1853–4); L. Dindorf (1866–8); F. Vogel–C. T. Fischer (1888–1906); C. H. Oldfather *et al.* (1933–, Loeb). Tarn, *Alexander* 63 ff.; G. T. Griffith in *Fifty Years of Class. Scholarship* (ed. M. Platnauer, 1954), ch. 6.
A. H. McD.

**DIODORUS** (4) of Alexandria (*PW* 53), mathematician and astronomer (1st c. B.C.), wrote a work, *Analemma*, on the construction of plane sundials by methods of descriptive geometry. Only the section on the determination of the meridian from three shadow-lengths survives, in Latin and Arabic versions, but later treatments of the subject are found in Vitruvius, Heron, and Ptolemy's *Analemma* (*see* MATHEMATICS § 7). The work was important enough for Pappus (q.v.) to write a commentary on it (iv. 246 Hultsch).

ANALEMMA: Proclus, *Hypotyposis*, 112 Manitius; *Anth. Pal.* 14. 139. The method of determining the meridian is preserved and identified as Diodorus' by al-Bīrūnī (see E. S. Kennedy in *Scripta Mathematica* 1959, 251 ff.). The same method is given (without author) by Hyginus, *Gromatici Veteres* ed. Lachmann (Berlin, 1848), i. 189 ff. (see Mollweide in *Monatliche Correspondenz* 1813, 396 ff.). The 'analemma construction' is found in Vitruvius, 9. 8, 8–10 and Heron, *Dioptra* 35. Other works by Diodorus are referred to in *Comm. in Aratum* ed. Maass, 30 ff. (astronomical) and Marinus, *Comm. in Euclidis Data*, *Eucl. Opp. Omn.* vi. 234, 17 (mathematical).
G. J. T.

**DIODOTUS** (1) **I**, satrap of Bactria-Sogdiana under Antiochus I and II, rebelled in 256–255 B.C., the fifth regnal year of Antiochus II, and declared his independence. He used the coin-types of Antiochus II, but substituted sometimes his name and sometimes his portrait for those of Antiochus. He also issued, towards the end of his career, coins with his own name, type—'Zeus hurling thunderbolt'—and portrait. A unique coin with the title 'Soter' may also be attributed to him. He died *c.* 248 B.C. and was succeeded by his son Diodotus II (q.v.).

A. K. Narain, *The Indo-Greeks* (1957). A. K. N.

**DIODOTUS** (2) **II**, (*c.* 248–235 B.C.), son of Diodotus I. Some of his coins bear the name of Antiochus but mostly they have his name, portrait, and type. The Parthians entered into an alliance with him.

A. K. Narain, *The Indo-Greeks* (1957). A. K. N.

**DIODOTUS** (3), Stoic, teacher of Cicero *c.* 85 B.C., lived later in Cicero's house. He died *c.* 60 and made Cicero his heir.

**DIOECESIS.** To facilitate the control of the provincial governors by the central bureaucracy Diocletian divided the Empire (including Italy) into twelve dioceses, each administered by a *vicarius*. These *vicarii* were officially deputies of the praetorian prefects (*agens vices praefectorum praetorio*). After Constantine, the prefects ruled directly the dioceses in which their seats were located. The proconsuls of Asia, Africa, and Achaea, were not subject to vicarial authority. The Diocletianic dioceses were Britain, Gaul, Viennensis, Spain, Africa, Pannonia, Moesia, Thrace, Asiana, Pontica, and Oriens. Italy was in practice divided between the *vicarius Italiae* in the north and the *vicarius in urbe Roma* in the south. Few changes occurred till the decline of the diocesan organization in the fifth century. *See* VICARIUS.

Jones, *Later Rom. Emp.* 47 f., 373 ff. B. H. W.

**DIOGENES** (1) of Apollonia (prob. Phrygian, not Cretan Apollonia), son of Apollothemis and younger (?) contemporary of Anaxagoras (cf. Diog. Laert. 9. 57; fl. *c.* 440 or 430 B.C.), was an eclectic philosopher, carrying on the Ionian tradition with additions from Anaxagoras and Leucippus. Little is known of his life. He almost certainly visited Athens, where his views aroused prejudice and were parodied by Aristophanes in the *Clouds* (423 B.C.).

WORKS: *On Nature* (Περὶ φύσεως), from which Simplicius quotes extensive fragments. Others cited, *Against the Sophists* (i.e. Cosmologists), a *Meteorology*, and *The Nature of Man*, are mere titles.

Diogenes revived the teaching of Anaximenes, whom he could scarcely have 'heard' (D.L. ibid.), that the primary substance is Air, endowing it with mind or intelligence, divinity, and all-disposing power. Its infinite transformations are effected by rarefaction and condensation. Diogenes argued that if things in the world, including Empedocles' elements, are to be affected by one another, they must be differentiations of the same underlying substance (fr. 2). Air is also the principle of soul and intelligence in living creatures, and essentially alike in all; it differs, however, in degrees of warmth for different species and individuals. Diogenes' physiological theories of generation, respiration, and the blood are important in the history of medicine, and Aristotle has preserved his account of the veins (*Hist. An.* 511b30 f.). His cosmology follows traditional lines, with its flat round earth, but bears some resemblance to that of Anaxagoras. The heavenly bodies are pumice stones filled with fire. But he is no mere reactionary: like the Hippocratic writers he displays the scientific interest in details typical of his age. *See also* ANATOMY AND PHYSIOLOGY § 2.

ANCIENT SOURCES AND TEXT OF FRAGMENTS. Diels, *Vorsokr*[5]. ii. 516–9. A. Maddalena, *Ionici* (1963), 244 ff.

MODERN LITERATURE. Zeller–Nestle, *Philosophie der Griechen* i. 2[7] (1922); Zeller–Mondolfo ii (1938); Burnet, *EGP* (translates frs.); Guthrie, *Hist. Gk. Phil.* A. J. D. P.

**DIOGENES** (2) (*c.* 400–*c.* 325 B.C.), son of Hicesias of Sinope, ὁ κύων, founder of the Cynic sect. According to some authors (Diog. Laert. 6. 20–21) he came to Athens as an exile after he and his father, who had been in charge of the mint in Sinope after 362 (*Recueil général des monnaies grecques de l'Asie mineure*, 193), had been accused of παραχαράττειν τὸ νόμισμα. At Athens he lived in extreme poverty and continued παραχαράττων τὸ νόμισμα in a metaphorical sense, by rejecting all conventions. Whether he was a personal disciple of Antisthenes (D.L. 6. 21 and passim) is doubtful on chronological grounds. But he seems to have been influenced by his philosophy, since there are many similarities in outlook, and since the originality of Diogenes apparently consisted more in the way in which he applied his philosophy in everyday life than in his theories as such.

His main principles were the following: Happiness is attained by satisfying only one's natural needs and by satisfying them in the cheapest and easiest way. What is natural cannot be dishonourable or indecent and therefore can and should be done in public. Conventions which are contrary to these principles are unnatural and should not be observed.

From this there results in practical life self-sufficiency (αὐτάρκεια), supported by ἄσκησις (training of the body so as to have as few needs as possible), and shamelessness (ἀναίδεια). Mainly on account of the latter quality Diogenes was called κύων (dog), from which appellation the name of the Cynics is derived.

He illustrated his simple principles by pointed utterances and drastic actions. He probably wrote dialogues and tragedies, the latter in order to show that the tragic heroes could have avoided misfortune by following his principles. But many of the works attributed to him by later authors were spurious.

Although Theophrastus described his way of living and his disciple Metrocles collected anecdotes about him, the tradition about his life is obscured by the fact that soon after his death he became a legendary figure and the hero of pedagogic novels (Eubulus, Cleomenes) and satirical dialogues (Menippus, Bion). The tradition on his philosophy was obscured by the tendency of the Stoics to attribute their own theories to him because they wanted to derive their philosophy from Socrates through the succession Antisthenes, Diogenes, Crates, Zeno.

It is uncertain whether Diogenes lived in Corinth for many years (so D.L. 6. 74; Dio Chrys. 8. 4; Julian, *Or.* 7. 212), and how, when, and where he died, since the tradition is conflicting.

His disciple Crates spread his philosophy. Diogenes had great influence on later literature through his caustic wit. He is stated (D.L. 6. 73, 80) to have written tragedies in which his doctrines were expounded, but the plays named as his were also ascribed to others. They were probably never acted.

Diogenes Laertius 6. 20–81; tragic fr. in Nauck, *TGF* 807–9. E. Schwartz, *Charakterköpfe* (1943), ii. 1 ff.; K. von Fritz, *Philol.* Suppl.-Bd. xviii. 2; *Studi di Filologia Class.* N.S. v. 133 ff.; D. R. Dudley, *A History of Cynicism* (1937), 17 ff.; F. Sayre, *Diogenes of Sinope* (1938); R. Höistad, *Cynic Hero and Cynic King* (1948). K. VON F.

**DIOGENES** (3) of Seleuceia on the Tigris, commonly called Diogenes of Babylon (*c.* 240–152 B.C.), pupil of Chrysippus, succeeded Zeno of Tarsus as head of the Stoic school. He visited Rome in 156–155 and greatly stimulated interest there in the Stoic creed. His most famous pupil was Panaetius, and his main influence was on the grammatical doctrine developed by the school. Works: Περὶ φωνῆς τέχνη; Διαλεκτικὴ τέχνη; Περὶ τῆς Ἀθηνᾶς; Περὶ μαντικῆς; Περὶ τοῦ τῆς ψυχῆς ἡγεμονικοῦ; Περὶ εὐγενείας (all lost).

Testimonia and fragments in von Arnim, *SVF* iii. 210–43. M. Pohlenz, *Die Stoa*[2] (1948–55), i. 180 ff., ii. 91 ff. W. D. R.

**DIOGENES** (4) of Tarsus, Epicurean of uncertain date, but probably identical with the author of a book on ποιητικὰ ζητήματα (who fl. *c.* 150–100 B.C.).

**DIOGENES** (5) of Oenoanda (near modern *Incealiler* in Turkey), an Epicurean of the second century A.D., was unknown before the discovery, in 1884, of parts of an inscription set up at his expense to proclaim the philosophy of Epicurus.

Diogenes, who was dying of a heart disease, issued his manifesto 'out of compassion' for his fellow men. In the Epicurean tradition he wished them to be freed from superstitious fear and to discover the true source of ἀταραξία. Though much of the text remains still buried, the published fragments include sections on Epicurean Physics and Ethics, an attack on ψευδοδοξία and the doctrines of rival philosophies, thoughts on old age, some original sayings of Epicurus, and Diogenes' testament. Part of the *Physics* is in the form of a letter (Περὶ ἀπειρίας κόσμων) written from Rhodes, where Diogenes may have been connected with an Epicurean school. Another epistle, from a son to his mother, was attributed by Cousin to Epicurus himself (*BCH* 1892, 68 ff.; cf. R. E. Philippson, *PW* Suppl. v (1931)).

TEXT. J. William (Leipzig, 1907, with comm.); A. Grilli (Milan, 1960); C. W. Chilton (Leipzig, 1967).
STUDIES. Ueberweg–Praechter, *Grundriss* 578 f.; C. W. Chilton, *AJArch.* 1963, 285 f.

**DIOGENES** (6) **LAERTIUS**, also called Laërtius Diogenes, author of an extant compendium on the lives and doctrines of the ancient philosophers from Thales to Epicurus. Since he omits Neoplatonism and mentions no philosopher after Saturninus, he probably lived in the first half of the third century A.D. Nothing whatever is known of his life, not even where and with whom he studied philosophy.

After an introduction on some non-Greek 'thinkers', such as the Magi, and some of the early Greek sages, he divides the philosophers into two 'successions' (*see* PHILO-SOPHY, HISTORY OF), an Ionian or Eastern (I. 22–VII) and Italian or Western (VIII), and ends with the 'sporadics', important philosophers who did not found sucessions (IX–X). This arrangement disperses the Presocratics in books I, II, VIII, and IX.

In X. 138 Diogenes speaks of giving the finishing touch to his entire work; but the book is such a tissue of quotations industriously compiled, mostly from secondary sources, that it could have been expanded indefinitely. Diogenes usually drew his material on any one philosopher from more than one earlier compilation, depending by preference on such writers as Antigonus of Carystus, Hermippus, Sotion, Apollodorus of Athens, Sosicrates of Rhodes, Demetrius and Diocles of Magnesia, Pamphila, and Favorinus, all of whom were themselves industrious compilers. Thus Diogenes' material often comes to us at several removes from the original. Fortunately, he usually names his sources, mentioning over 200 authors and over 300 works by name. As a rule he changes sources continually. Hence his reliability and value also change from passage to passage. For example, his account of Stoic doctrine (VII. 39–160) is reliable and his long quotations from Epicurus are invaluable when separated from the inserted marginalia that sometimes interrupt the sense. But some lives, as Heraclitus', are mere caricatures, and some summaries of doctrine are vitiated by philosophic distortion: for instance, Aristotle's doctrines are viewed through Stoic, perhaps also Epicurean, eyes.

Diogenes also wrote some wretched poetry, which he quotes more than two score times and of which he published a separate edition, not extant (I. 39).

He *may* have been a Sceptic, for he shows Sextus Empiricus' impartiality towards all schools. He includes praise of Epicurus and the Cynics, addresses part of his work to a woman interested in Platonism (III. 47) and another part to a person interested in Epicurus (X. 29); and once he speaks of a Sceptic as '*our* Apollonides' (IX. 109). Any or all of these passages may, however, have come from Diogenes' sources.

TEXTS. H. Huebner (1828); C. G. Cobet (1850, with Latin trans., on app. crit.); O.C.T., H. S. Long (1964). Crit. edits. of parts: Presocratics: Diels–Kranz; bk. 3, Plato: Breitenbach, Buddenhagen *et al.* (1907); bk. 5, 1–35, see ARISTOTLE; bk. 7, Stoics: von Arnim; bk. 8, 1–50, Pythagoras: A. Delatte (1922); bk. 10, *see* EPICURUS.
STUDIES. E. Schwartz in *PW* v. 738 (1905); R. Hope, *The Book of Diogenes Laertius* (1930); A. Biedl in *Studi e Testi* 184 (1955)—all three with bibliog.                                                    H. S. L.

**DIOGENIANUS** (1), Epicurean. Eusebius quotes many passages from his polemic against Chrysippus' doctrine of fate. His date is unknown, but he probably belongs to the second century A.D., when the polemic of the New Academy against Chrysippus was at its height.

Ed. A. Gercke, *Jahrb. für klassische Philologie*, Suppl. 14. 748.
                                                                              W. D. R.

**DIOGENIANUS** (2), of Heraclea, of the age of Hadrian. Besides geographical indexes, a collection of proverbs, and other works, he compiled in five books an alphabetically arranged epitome of the Lexicon of Pamphilus as abridged by Vestinus. This epitome was used by Hesychius, who refers to it under the title of Περιεργο-πένητες, by Photius and other Byzantine lexicographers, and by the scholiasts on Plato, Callimachus, and Nicander.

Edition, E. L. von Leutsch and F. G. Schneidewin, *Paroemio-graphi* i. 177, ii. 1. Norden, *Hermes* 1892, 625. R. Reitzenstein,

*Geschichte d. griech. Etymologika* (1897), 417 ff.; K. Latte, *Hesychii Alexandrini lexicon* i (1953). x. ii ff.                    P. B. R. F.; R. B.

**DIOMEDES** (Διομήδης), in mythology (1) a Thracian, son of Ares and Cyrene, king of the Bistonians (Apollod. 2. 96). To capture his man-eating horses was the eighth labour of Heracles (q.v.).

(2) Son of Tydeus (q.v.), and Deipyle, daughter of Adrastus (q.v.; Hyg. *Fab.* 69. 5 and often). He took a prominent part in the Trojan War, wounding Aphrodite and Ares by help of Athena, and overcoming a number of the foremost Trojans (*Il.* 5. 1 ff.), but behaving chivalrously to his hereditary guest-friend Glaucus the Lycian (q.v.; ibid. 6. 119 ff.). He and Odysseus raid the Trojan camp, killing Rhesus (q.v.; 10. 219 ff.). Throughout the poem, and especially in the second half, he is the author of wise and bold counsels. His part in the expedition of the Epigoni against Thebes (cf. ADRASTUS) is mentioned in the *Iliad* (4. 406, cf. Apollod. 3. 82 ff.). In the post-Homeric Trojan cycle he is conspicuous. He shared with Odysseus in the murder of Palamedes (q.v.; Paus. 10. 31. 2, quoting the *Cypria*). He and Odysseus brought Philoctetes from Lemnos (Hyg. *Fab.* 102. 3; cf. PHILO-CTETES). The same pair stole the Palladium from Troy (Hesychius and the *Suda* s.v. Διομήδειος ἀνάγκη, from the *Little Iliad*). Two other cycles of his adventures are: (*a*) In Calydon; his grandfather Oeneus having been robbed in old age of his kingship by the sons of Agrius, Diomedes killed them all but two, gave the throne to Oeneus' son-in-law Andraemon, and brought Oeneus to the Peloponnesus (Apollod. 1. 78). (*b*) After the return from Troy he found his wife Aegialeia unfaithful, came to Italy, where his companions were turned into birds (Stith Thompson, *Index*² 88), and finally received heroic or divine honours after his death or disappearance (Farnell, *Hero-Cults*, 289 ff.). Diomedes is not a favourite figure in art, but is shown sometimes from the early fifth century, in combat with Aeneas or Hector, and in scenes from the Doloneia and the theft of the Palladium, generally in company with Odysseus (Brommer, *Vasenlisten*², 287 f., 305 f., 334).                                      H. J. R.; C. M. R.

**DIOMEDES** (3) (late 4th c. A.D.), grammarian, who wrote an *Ars grammatica* in three books (ed. Keil, *Gramm. Lat.* i. 299–529). His work is of value because, though he rarely mentions his sources, he clearly relied upon earlier grammarians who discussed and illustrated the usages of Republican authors. Parallels between his work and that of Charisius (q.v.) seem to indicate that he borrowed from his contemporary.

Schanz–Hosius, § 834.                                          J. F. M.

**DION** (*c.* 408–354 B.C.), brother-in-law and son-in-law of Dionysius I, was in an influential position at his court and that of his successor. Impressed by Plato's teaching when that philosopher visited Sicily in 389, he tried to make Dionysius II an example of the 'philosopher king'; but, suspected of aiming to supplant him, he was forced into exile. Residing in Athens, he was closely associated with the Academy. In 357, after Dionysius' hostility had intensified, he led a small expedition to Sicily and succeeded in liberating Syracuse. But, as a member of the tyrants' family and oligarchic by political disposition, he lost his hold on popular enthusiasm; the Syracusans preferred his lieutenant Heracleides, who had won a great victory over Dionysius' admiral Philistus. Dion withdrew to Leontini, but was recalled when Dionysius counter-attacked. Once the danger was over, his discord with Heracleides revived, and Dion finally had him assassinated. Dion's rule became increasingly authoritarian, despite his alleged attempts to govern on Platonic principles, and in 354 he was murdered at the instigation of his follower and fellow Academic Callippus.

Historical tradition, based chiefly on his Platonic connexions, has been generous to Dion. A capable soldier, he lacked resolution and foresight, and the political circumstances of post-liberation Syracuse proved too much for him.

*See also* DIONYSIUS I, DIONYSIUS II, PLATO (1).

H. Berve, *Dion* (1956); Renata von Scheliha, *Dion* (1934)—an especially laudatory treatment; H. D. Westlake, *Durham University Journal*, N.S. vii (1946), 37 ff. A. G. W.

**DIONE** (Διώνη), consort of Zeus at Dodona, Farnell, *Cults* i. 39, who conjectures that she is the local form of the Earth-Mother; but her name is simply a feminine of Zeus (cf. Cook, *Zeus*, ii. 350 and note 6), which suggests rather a sky-goddess. Nothing definite is known of her cult (which was practically confined to Dodona and Athens, where it was introduced in the late fifth century); if the original consort of Zeus, she was ousted by Hera (q.v.), and from Homer (*Il.* 5. 370) on she is one of his mistresses or secondary wives, mother of Aphrodite, or even Aphrodite herself. H. J. R.

**DIONYSIA.** Many festivals of Dionysus had special names, e.g. the Anthesteria (q.v.), the Lenaea (q.v.), etc.; the latter are, however, in inscriptions styled Διονύσια τὰ ἐπὶ Ληναίῳ or ἐπιλήναια Δ. (Arist. *Ath. Pol.* 57; *IG* ii². 1496 A, b 105, 1672, 182) and the term Dionysia was given to such festivals at which dramatic performances took place. With the great and ever increasing popularity of the drama, Dionysia were instituted almost everywhere; their origin is found in Athens. Athens had (a) τὰ κατ' ἀγρούς, (b) τὰ ἐν ἄστει or τὰ μεγάλα Δ. The rustic Dionysia were celebrated in Poseideon and the city Dionysia in Elaphebolion.

(a) Rustic Dionysia are known from many Attic demes (those at Piraeus and at Eleusis being apparently specially important) through inscriptions, but only because of the dramatic performances which took place at them, and these are obviously borrowed from the city Dionysia. Fortunately Aristophanes gives a vivid description of the procession at the merry rustic festival (*Ach.* 247 ff.). First comes the daughter of Dicaeopolis as *kanephoros*, then two slaves carrying the phallus, and last Dicaeopolis himself singing an obscene lay in honour of Phales. Plutarch, *Non posse suav. vivi sec. Epic.* 1098b, mentions the cries and the riot at the rustic Dionysia. A special feature was the ἀσκωλιασμός, youths balancing on a full goat-skin; *see* ASKOLIASMOS. There are remains of theatres at Thoricus, Rhamnus, and Icaria.

(b) The City Dionysia were celebrated in honour of Dionysus Eleuthereus. This god was introduced into Athens by Pisistratus from the village of Eleutherae in the borderland between Attica and Boeotia. A temple was built to him on the southern slope of the Acropolis, and a second temple was erected close at hand, probably in the last years of the fifth century B.C. The orchestra where the dramatic performances took place was adjacent; the stone theatre was built by Lycurgus about 330 B.C. The fact that tragedy has its origin in this cult does not necessarily contradict the commonly accepted opinion of Aristotle that tragedy arose from the dithyramb and the *satyrikon* (i.e. a primitive impersonation by satyrs). At Eleutherae Dionysus was called μελαναιγίς, 'he who is clad in a black goat-skin', and a myth tells of a duel between Xanthus and Melanthus in which Dionysus appeared.

The City Dionysia was a great festival to which people flocked from all parts. The statue of Dionysus was brought to a temple in the Academy and, coming hence, the god made his epiphany with much pomp; phalli were carried in the procession, which went to the temple on the southern slope of the Acropolis where sacrifices were performed. Inscriptions give the information that, after the sacrifice, the ephebes carried Dionysus into the theatre by torchlight in order that he might be present at the dramatic performances (M. P. Nilsson, *JDAI* 1916, 336 ff.; P. Stengel, ibid. 340 ff.). When the theatre was filled with people the surplus of the State revenues was carried through the orchestra and the sons of men who had fallen in war were given panoplies.

The performances at the City Dionysia comprised lyric choruses sung by men and boys as well as tragedies and comedies. The Marmor Parium, ep. 43, gives the information that Thespis performed the first drama ἐν ἄστει at a date which is mutilated, but must fall between 536 and 532 B.C.; the *Suda* says 535. Comedy was introduced later, a few years before the Persian Wars (*see* COMEDY, OLD). For the very important but badly mutilated inscriptions which enumerate the victories see A. Wilhelm, *Urkunden dramatischer Aufführungen (Sonderschriften des österreichischen archäologischen Instituts* vi) (1906).

L. Deubner, *Attische Feste* (1932), 134 ff.; A. E. Haigh, *The Attic Theatre*³, revised by Pickard-Cambridge (1907); A. W. Pickard-Cambridge, *The Theatre of Dionysus in Athens* (1946); id., *The Dramatic Festivals of Athens*² (1967). M. P. N.; J. H. C.

**DIONYSIUS** (1) **I** (*c.* 430–367 B.C.), tyrant of Syracuse, was originally an adherent of Hermocrates (q.v.). After the Syracusan failure to relieve Acragas in 406, he induced the assembly to elect new generals, himself among them. Later he supplanted his colleagues, obtained a bodyguard, and was regularly re-elected *strategos autokrator*. But he failed to halt the Carthaginian advance, and was faced with an aristocratic revolt. In this situation he negotiated an unfavourable peace with Carthage, overcame the domestic opposition, and converted Ortygia into a personal stronghold. With his power consolidated he prepared to meet the Carthaginians on better terms, and enlisted large forces of mercenaries and armaments-workers. Meanwhile he destroyed Naxos (q.v.), planted settlers of his own in Leontini and Catana, and extended his control over many of the native Sicels.

Reopening hostilities in 397 he captured Motya (q.v.) after a notable siege, but next year Himilco (q.v. 2) advanced to Syracuse, defeating Dionysius' fleet and besieging the city. Dionysius averted a Syracusan uprising and, helped by Peloponnesian intervention and plague among the Carthaginians, overcame the crisis. A further Carthaginian attack in 392 was repulsed, and he was able to make an advantageous peace. The war also strengthened his hold on the interior of Sicily, and by 390 the island was divided into Syracusan and Carthaginian 'empires', separated by the River Mazarus. The phrase 'archon of Sicily', appearing in Athenian documents concerning him, seems to be a *de facto* statement of his position, not an official title.

He next intervened in Italy. In alliance with Locri and the Lucanians he defeated a coalition of Italiot Greeks at the River Elleporus (388) and destroyed Rhegium (386). His victories, and good relations with Taras, gave him effective control over most of Magna Graecia, and by friendship with Alcetas of Molossia and by colonizing Issa he brought his influence to the Adriatic. Fortified by this increase of empire he again made war on Carthage (382), but was heavily defeated at Cronium (375?) and ceded territory beyond the Halycus. A third war, begun in 368, brought him to Lilybaeum and was in progress when he died.

In Greece his close relationship with Sparta was an important factor in the political situation. The Athenians tried vainly to counter it, and in 387 and 373 his intervention seriously affected them. In 368/7 an alliance between Dionysius and Athens was finally achieved, but the tyrant died as soon as it was made.

His rule brought prosperity to Syracuse, but was expensive. Magnificent silver coinage went to pay his mercenaries, and many subterfuges to keep his treasury filled are reported. Although his government is traditionally considered oppressive (a tradition partly due to Plato, whose visit to his court was not a success), there is nothing to show that he was unpopular with the bulk of the Syracusan people. He fancied himself a tragic poet; but though he won the Athenian Lenaea in 367 with his *Ransoming of Hector* (an award which perhaps had political overtones) his plays are generally regarded as poor. His possession of Aeschylus' desk and the pen, writing-tablets, and harp of Euripides did not apparently add to his inspiration.

He married (1) Hermocrates' daughter, who committed suicide in 405, (2) Aristomache of Syracuse and Doris of Locri simultaneously. His successor was the eldest son of the last-named. He was a tyrant in the grand manner. If his character had few attractive features, the success of his rule in its combination of vigour, skill, and panache was and remains impressive.

K. F. Stroheker, *Dionysios I* (1958); A. G. Woodhead, *The Greeks in the West* (1962), 89 ff.; for the tragedies see Nauck, *TGF²* 793 ff.
A. M.; A. G. W.

**DIONYSIUS** (2) **II**, eldest son of Dionysius I (q.v.), succeeded his father in 367/6 B.C., when about 30 years of age. He made immediate peace with Carthage, and the first decade of his reign passed undisturbed save within the court, where rival factions contended for influence over an inexperienced ruler. While maintaining his father's empire Dionysius lacked his military ambitions and political shrewdness. He welcomed philosophers to his court, and himself wrote poetry and philosophic studies. His chief minister was the historian Philistus (q.v.). The attempt of Plato to turn him into a philosopher-king miscarried, and resulted in the repudiation of both Plato and Dion (q.v.) (366/5 B.C.). A further visit by Plato in 361 only widened the breach.

During Dionysius' absence in Italy (357/6) in connexion with two newly founded colonies in Iapygia, Dion seized Syracuse, although Ortygia resisted until 355. Dionysius held Rhegium till *c.* 351 and Locri till 347/6, when he recovered Syracuse. But by 344 he was blockaded on Ortygia by Syracusan rebels under Hicetas of Leontini, assisted by a Carthaginian fleet. He surrendered to the recently arrived Timoleon (q.v.), whom he probably thought he could use against his enemies; but he was held for a time at Catana, and then shipped to Corinth where he lived many years, a famous object-lesson on the fate of tyrants.

H. Berve, *Dion* (1956); Renata von Scheliha, *Dion* (1934); Glenn R. Morrow, *Plato's Epistles* (1962).
A. G. W.

**DIONYSIUS** (3), AELIUS, an important Atticist lexicographer, of the age of Hadrian. He compiled ten books of Ἀττικαὶ λέξεις. See PAUSANIAS (4).

**DIONYSIUS** (4) **THE AREOPAGITE,** an Athenian mentioned in Acts xvii. 34 as converted at Athens by St. Paul's preaching. Of the works ascribed to him, (1) Περὶ τῆς οὐρανίας ἱεραρχίας, (2) Περὶ τῆς ἐκκλησιαστικῆς ἱεραρχίας, (3) Περὶ θείων ὀνομάτων, (4) Περὶ μυστικῆς θεολογίας, (5) 10 letters, (6) a Liturgy, the four first-named are a daring fusion of Christianity with Neoplatonism, and had an enormous influence throughout the Middle Ages. They are certainly not by St. Paul's Dionysius; they draw on Proclus (q.v.) and probably date from *c.* 500. It has been conjectured that the ascription of them to the Areopagite is due to confusion between him

and another Dionysius (? Dionysius of Rhinocolura, *c.* 370), but it is arguable that the author deliberately tried to pass them off as the work of a contemporary of St. Paul.

Ed. Migne, *PG*, vols. 3, 4.        W. D. R.

**DIONYSIUS** (5) of Byzantium (fl. *c.* A.D. 175), a Greek. Of his Ἀνάπλους τοῦ Βοσπόρου, 'Voyage up the (Thracian) Bosporus', part of a Latin translation survives (Pierre Gilles, *de Bosp. Thrac., Libri III*).

*GGM* 11. i ff.; Gk., C. Wescher, 1874.

**DIONYSIUS** (6) **CHALCUS** (5th c. B.C.), poet, so called after his introduction of bronze currency into Athens; he took part in the colonization of Thurii (Plut. *Nic.* 5), wrote sympotic elegies, some of which began with a pentameter (Ath. 602c), of a somewhat riddling character, with notable metaphors.

TEXT. Diehl, *Anth. Lyr. Graec.* i. 1, 88–90. Criticism. R. Reitzenstein, *Epigramm und Skolion* (1893), 51; Wilamowitz, *Hell. Dicht.* i. 97.        C. M. B.

**DIONYSIUS** (7) of Halicarnassus, rhetor and historian, who lived and taught at Rome for many years from 30 B.C. His enthusiasm for all things Roman finds its clearest expression in his *Roman Antiquities* (Ῥωμαϊκὴ Ἀρχαιολογία) which began to appear in 7 B.C. The first ten of the twenty books survive; in its complete form the work went down to the outbreak of the First Punic War. A moralizing history, a panegyric, and a vast exercise in μίμησις, it is also a work of careful research and a valuable supplement to Livy. Dionysius regarded it as his masterpiece, and it exemplifies the literary theories he taught. These are to be found in his *scripta rhetorica*, especially: (i) περὶ μιμήσεως, of which only fragments survive, in which the judgements on individual authors coincide largely with those in Quintilian 10. 1; (ii) a series of discussions of the orators (Lysias, Isocrates, Isaeus, Demosthenes); the preface to this collection (περὶ τῶν ἀρχαίων ῥητόρων) explains Dionysius' distaste for 'Asianic' rhetoric (Μυσὴ ἢ Φρυγία τις ἢ Καρικόν τι κακόν), his hopes for an Atticist revival, and his consciousness that this happy change is due to the sound taste of the Roman governing class; (iii) a group of occasional works: *On Dinarchus*, *On Thucydides*, two letters to Ammaeus (one on Demosthenes' alleged indebtedness to Aristotle, the other again on Thucydides), and a letter to Cn. Pompeius on Plato, of whose 'dithyrambic' style Dionysius (like Caecilius and unlike 'Longinus') was very critical; (iv) περὶ συνθέσεως ὀνομάτων, the only surviving ancient treatise on word-arrangement and euphony, perhaps the most interesting and most difficult of his works: the detailed critique on *Odyssey* 11. 593–6 in ch. 20 is a fascinating example of his technique.

Dionysius makes great use of traditional critical categories (χαρακτῆρες λέξεως, ἀρεταὶ λέξεως, see LITERARY CRITICISM, § 6) and, especially in the books on the orators, frequently gives the impression of 'awarding marks' on inflexible principles; he is none the less an acute and sensitive stylistic critic, and he understood the importance of linking historical study of the orators with the purely rhetorical and aesthetic.

*Antiquitates*, ed. C. Jacoby (1885–1925), E. Cary (Loeb, 1937–50); *Opuscula*, ed. H. Usener–L. Radermacher (1899–1929). W. Rhys Roberts, *Three Literary Letters* (1901); *On Literary Composition* (1910). S. F. Bonner, *The Literary Treatises of Dionysius: a study in the development of critical method* (1939).      D. A. R.

**DIONYSIUS** (8) of Heraclea on the Pontus (*c.* 328–248 B.C.) studied under Heraclides Ponticus, Menedemus, and Zeno, and became one of the most voluminous writers of the Stoic school. He also wrote poetry (including a tragedy, Παρθενοπαῖος) and was an admirer and imitator of Aratus. An attack of illness in old age led him to abandon the Stoic creed that pain is not an evil and to adopt the view that pleasure is the end of life (hence his nickname ὁ μεταθέμενος). He starved himself to death.

Testimonia in von Arnim, *SVF* i. 93–96. W. D. R.

**DIONYSIUS** (9) **'PERIEGETES'** ('The Guide'), Greek author, in Hadrian's time (?), of Περιήγησις τῆς οἰκουμένης in 1,185 hexameters (for schoolboys?), describing in pseudo-epic style the known world chiefly after Eratosthenes, taking little account of subsequent discoveries: land, elliptic (east–west), three continents; ocean, with inlets; Mediterranean; Libya; Europe; islands; Asia. Lost works attributed to Dionysius: Βασσαρικά = Διονυσιακά; Λιθικά (on gems); Ὀρνιθιακά; Γιγαντιάς.

*GGM* 11. xv ff., 103 ff.; A. Garzya, *Dionysii Ixeuticon* (Teubner, 1963; prose-paraphrase of the Ὀρνιθιακά); E. H. Bunbury, *Hist. Anc. Geog.* (1879) ii. 480 ff.; *PW* v. 915–25. Thomson, *Hist. Anc. Geog.* 228 f., 302, 304, 329 f. E. H. W.

**DIONYSIUS** (10) of Philadelphia, reputed author of an extant poem, Ὀρνιθιακά, which may, however, be by Dionysius Periegetes.

Ed. F. S. Lehrs, *Poetae Bucolici et Didactici* (1851).

**DIONYSIUS** (11) of Samos, Hellenistic 'cyclographer', published a κύκλος ἱστορικός in seven books, a mythographical romance or, perhaps more probably, a mythological handbook.

*FGrH* i. 15.

**DIONYSIUS** (12) **SCYTOBRACHION,** an Alexandrian grammarian of the second or first century B.C., who appears to be cited also as Dionysius of Mytilene (or Miletus), wrote a mythological romance, Euhemeristic in tone and claiming authority by false reference to old writers. He treated of the Argonauts, followed here by Diodorus (books 3–4), the Trojan War, Dionysus and Athena, and the Amazons, and wrote Μυθικὰ πρὸς Παρμένωντα.

*FGrH* i. 228, 509. A. H. McD.

**DIONYSIUS** (13) of Sinope, Middle (?) Comedy poet. The learned cook provides humour in one piece (fr. 2).

*FCG* iii. 547 ff.; *CAF* ii. 423 ff.

**DIONYSIUS** (14) of Thebes, poet, teacher of Epaminondas (Nep. *Epam.* 2), regarded by Aristoxenus (ap. Plut. *De mus.* 31) as a practiser of the old style of music.

**DIONYSIUS** (15) surnamed **THRAX** (c. 170–c. 90 B.C.), son of Teres, of Alexandria, was a pupil of Aristarchus and later a teacher of grammar and literature at Rhodes, where his pupils provided him with the silver for a model to illustrate his lectures on Nestor's cup (Athenaeus 489, 492, 501). His only surviving work is the Τέχνη γραμματική, an epitome of pure grammar as developed by the Stoics and Alexandrians (see GRAMMAR). The work is essentially Alexandrian, but there are traces of Stoic influence. It defines grammar as an ἐμπειρία, but includes ἀναλογία (see CRATES (3) OF MALLOS) among its parts; classifies accents, stops, letters, and syllables; defines the parts of speech, with lists of their qualifications (cases, moods, etc.), and subdivisions, if any, giving examples; and concludes with some paradigms of inflection. There is no treatment of syntax in the work. It had, however, an immediate vogue which lasted until the Renaissance, and its authority was continued in the catechisms derived from it which then took its place. Latin grammar early fell under its influence (see, e.g., Remmius Palaemon), and through Latin most of the modern grammars of Europe are indebted to it. Through

Syriac and Armenian adaptations its influence spread far beyond Europe. An immense corpus of commentary grew up in Hellenistic, Roman, and Byzantine times around Dionysius' brief text.

EDITION. Uhlig, in Teubner's *Grammat. Gr.* (1883).
SCHOLIA. Hilgard, same series (1901). R. H. Robins, *Ancient and Mediaeval Grammatical Theory in Europe* (1951), 36 ff.; V. di Benedetto, *Ann. della Scuola Normale Superiore di Pisa* 1958, 169 ff.; 1959, 87 ff. P. B. R. F.; R. B.

**DIONYSIUS** (16) (? 2nd c. A.D.), a Greek, son of Calliphron, author of Ἀναγραφὴ τῆς Ἑλλάδος (for schoolboys?); 150 feeble iambics survive: preface (acrostics); Ambracia–Peloponnesus; [gap]; Cretan cities; Cyclades and Sporades Islands.

*GGM* i. lxxx, 238–43.

**DIONYSUS,** the god much more of an emotional religion than of wine (q.v.). He is rarely mentioned in Homer, for, like Demeter, he was a popular god who did not appeal to the Homeric knights, but the myth that Lycurgus persecuted him and his nurses is told (*Il.* 6. 130 ff.). From Hesiod (*Theog.* 940 ff.) on, his parents are Zeus and Semele (q.v.).

The general opinion, shared by both ancient and modern authors, that he came from Thrace is well founded. His cult was widely spread in Thrace (see RELIGION, THRACIAN), and the Thracian and Macedonian women were especially devoted to his orgia. The myths of invasions of Boeotia and Attica by Thracians are not to be wholly disregarded. They may be ascribed to the very beginning of the last millennium B.C., and the Thracians may have brought the cult to Greece. However, there was a certain connexion between Dionysus and Minoan religion, and the occurrence of his name in isolation on Linear B tablets suggests that he was not unknown in Greece in primitive times. Our legends may describe a revival or reintroduction. Boeotia and Attica were its chief seats; in the Peloponnese it is less common. Myths, e.g. of Pentheus and the daughters of Minyas, prove that it swept over Greece like wildfire and that the cause was its ecstatic character which seized chiefly on the women. They abandoned their houses and work, roamed about in the mountains, whirling in the dance, swinging thyrsi and torches; at the pitch of their ecstasy (see ECSTASY) they seized upon an animal or even a child, according to the myths, tore it apart, and devoured the bleeding pieces (Farnell, op. cit. *infra*, 302 ff.). This so-called omophagy is a sacramental meal; in devouring the parts of the animal the maenads incorporated the god and his power within themselves. Dionysus was sometimes believed to appear in animal form; he is called 'bull', 'bull-horned', etc. He himself and his maenads are clad in fawn-skins. Sometimes it is told that the maenads wore masks. The mask was characteristic of his cult; his image sometimes consisted of a mask and a garment hung on a pole, but these masks are human. This feature reminds us of primitive customs and is important with regard to the fact that the drama has its origin in the cult of Dionysus. The descriptions of his orgia referred to, in which the votaries are depicted as capable of all kinds of miracles, possessed by the god, enjoying communion with wild life, vegetable and animal, and able to overcome any human resistance (e.g. Eur. *Bacch.* 680 ff.), are mythical and literary, but votaries did in fact bear the god's name, *bakchoi* (Pl. *Phaed.* 69 c). Orgia of a milder kind were celebrated in historical times on Mt. Parnassus by official cult associations of women, and there is a trace of the omophagy in a State cult. The frenzy of the orgia was tamed by Apollo, who admitted Dionysus at his side at Delphi and brought his cult into the gentler forms of State religion.

Ancient authors say, however, that Dionysus also

came from Phrygia. The Phrygians, who were a Thracian tribe, believed that Dionysus (cf. Phrygian Diounsis: W. M. Calder, *CR* 1927, 160 ff.) was bound or slept in the winter and was free or awake in the summer. They knew also of a child-god. This Dionysus is apparently a god of vegetation. His other name, Bacchus, is a Lydian word. It is remarkable that the Dionysiac festivals of the Lenaea (q.v.) and the Anthesteria (q.v.), the spring festival in which Dionysus made his epiphany coming from the sea, are common to all Ionians, whilst other festivals of Dionysus are isolated. At Delphi Dionysus was venerated as a child in a winnowing fan and awakened by certain rites. It seems that Dionysus in a somewhat changed form came from Asia Minor across the sea. This Dionysus was a god of the vegetation, not of the crops but of the fruit of the trees including the vine. The phallus which was carried in the Dionysiac processions belongs to him as a god of fertility; he is never represented as phallic himself, but the Sileni and Satyrs who surround him are; they are daemons of fertility. This Dionysus was the god of wine, but wine has no great place in his cult in the early age, especially not in the orgia. The festivals of viticulture are few and rarely attributed to him, and we find him connected with a variety of plants—corn (Diod. Sic. 4. 4. 2), trees (Farnell, 96, 118 ff.), figs (Ath. 3. 78c; Hesychius s.v. συκάτης), ivy (Eur. *Bacch.* 106 etc.). On Attic vases he is, however, constantly represented with a drinking-horn, or a cantharus, and vine-branches. As time went on, he was more and more thought of as the god of wine, and we hear of wine-miracles in certain festivals.

A point of view particularly emphasized by some scholars is that he was the Lord of souls. The opinion of Rohde that the belief in immortality was introduced into Greece by Dionysus is now abandoned. While others, e.g. Miss Harrison, refer to the fact that the Anthesteria was devoted to the dead, these rites have nothing to do with Dionysus; the connexion had no intrinsic reason. Other similar festivals are too little known. But among the mystics Dionysus was associated with the Nether World, an idea which perhaps originated among the Orphics, in whose doctrines Dionysus had a great place. Thus Dionysus was introduced into mysteries other than the old orgia, but no one of them can be proved to be of old origin. Such mysteries became very popular in the Hellenistic and even more in the Roman age. In spite of the opinion of Cumont, these late mysteries of Dionysus seem to owe more to Greek than to Oriental tradition. That the idea of a happier life in the other world prevailed in them is proved by the fact that sarcophagi are often decorated with Dionysiac myths (see below). Dionysus was an ever popular subject of myths and stories in classical literature. Not to speak of his early adventures in escaping from Hera's jealousy (*see* ATHAMAS), his campaigns in the East are known to Euripides: their extension to India is modelled after those of Alexander the Great; they were celebrated in a voluminous epic by Nonnus at the end of antiquity. See BACCHANALIA, MAENADS.

Dionysus first appears in art in the early sixth century, and is thereafter exceedingly popular, especially in vase-painting: alone; with satyrs and nymphs or maenads; escorting Hephaestus to Olympus; sailing his vine-ship; with Semele, Ariadne, or Oenopion; drinking with Heracles. On the monument of Lysicrates he turns the pirates to dolphins; on Roman sarcophagi his eastern triumph is popular. In archaic art he is always bearded and robed; later often naked and young. The birth from Zeus' thigh and the handing of the baby to the Nymphs are shown on some fifth- and fourth-century vases.

E. Rohde, *Psyche* (1925); Farnell, *Cults* v. 85 ff.; J. E. Harrison, *Proleg. to the Study of Greek Religion* (1922), 364 ff.; Nilsson, *GGR* i¹.

564 and, for the Minoan connexions, *Minoan-Mycenaean Religion*¹ (1950), 492 ff.; W. F. Otto, *Dionysos* (1933), is highly speculative. The festivals: Nilsson, *Studia de Dionysiis atticis* (Lund, 1900); *Feste* 258 ff.; L. Deubner, *Attische Feste* (1932), 93 ff. The late mysteries: Cumont, *Rel. or.* 195; *AJArch.* 1933, 232 ff.; Rose, *Handb. Gk. Myth*⁶. 149 ff.; W. K. C. Guthrie, *The Greeks and their Gods* (1950), ch. 6; H. Jeanmaire, *Dionysos* (1951, speculative). M. P. Nilsson, 'The Bacchic Mysteries of the Roman Age', *Harv. Theol. Rev.* 1953, 175 ff.                    M. P. N. and H. J. R.; C. M. R.

**DIOPHANTUS** of Alexandria (date uncertain, between 150 B.C. and A.D. 280) was the first Greek to make any approach to an algebraical notation. He wrote Ἀριθμητικά in thirteen books, six of which survive, and a tract on Polygonal Numbers. A third work, Πορίσματα, is lost, but some propositions in the theory of numbers are quoted from it in the *Arithmetica*. Diophantus works with numbers purely arithmetically and not geometrically as did classical Greek mathematics. His work is in a tradition going back ultimately to Babylonian mathematics (*see also* HERON), but probably contains much that is original. In the preface to the *Arithmetica* he defines 'species' of numbers, which are, besides units (denoted by *Mo* for μονάδες), the various powers up to the sixth of the unknown quantity, for which he appropriates the word ἀριθμός denoted by the symbol *s*. Its powers he denotes by Δ^Y (for δύναμις, square), K^Y (for κύβος, cube), etc. He has a symbol Λ for *minus*, denoting λεῖψις, a 'wanting', contrasted with ὕπαρξις, 'forthcoming' or *plus*. Minus, he explains, multiplied by a plus gives minus, minus by minus, a plus. Expressions containing more than one 'species' he arranges according to powers, first the positive terms, then the negative terms all together. He shows how to solve simple and quadratic equations; he does not recognize negative roots of equations or negative numbers standing by themselves. His problems are mostly indeterminate or semi-determinate equations (single or simultaneous) of the second degree, and his methods are extraordinarily varied and ingenious; his object is always to find a solution in positive numbers (not necessarily integral as generally required in modern indeterminate analysis). The typical sort of problem solved is this: to find three numbers such that the product of any two of them *plus* their sum, or *plus* any given number, is a square. It was Diophantus' work which led Fermat to take up the theory of numbers, in which he made his world-famous discoveries.

CRITICAL TEXT, with Latin translation and scholia, by P. Tannery, (Teubner, 1893, 1895).
TRANSLATIONS. T. L. Heath, *Diophantus of Alexandria*², (1910, adapted, good commentary). French, P. ver Eecke (1926); German, G. Wertheim (1890); A. Czwalina (1952).
On Diophantus' date see Jakob Klein in *Quellen und Studien zur Gesch. d. Math.* B3 (1936), 133 n. 23.
COMMENT. Heath, *Hist. of Greek Maths.* ii. 440 ff.
T. H.; G. J. T.

**DIOS** wrote a history of Phoenicia cited by Josephus (*AJ* 8. 147–9; *Ap.* 1. 113–15).

**DIOSCORIDES** (1) (fl. 230 B.C.) has about forty epigrams in the Greek Anthology (q.v.), some based on the work of his predecessors Asclepiades (2), Callimachus (3), and Leonidas (2) (qq.v.). Eight deal with famous poets; many are paradoxical anecdotes. The rest—save one hate poem (*Anth. Pal.* 11. 363)—are lively love poems in the sharpest epigrammatic style.

Gow and Page, 1463 ff.                    G. H.

**DIOSCORIDES** (2) **PEDANIUS** (1st c. A.D.) of Anazarbus, army physician, was well versed in pharmacological literature and had studied the subject of his interest from early youth in extensive travels before composing his book; he was ambitious as expert rather than as writer. All this he tells us himself. He lived under Claudius and Nero (41–68); Erotianus mentions him.

WORKS: 1. Π. ὕλης ἰατρικῆς, books 1–5, almost 600 plants, nearly 1,000 drugs. 2. Π. ἁπλῶν φαρμάκων, or Εὐπόριστα, books 1–2.

The *Materia medica* is a conscious attempt to give a system, not an alphabetical list of drugs. Remedies from the vegetable, animal, and mineral kingdoms are described in careful subdivisions. The observation is minute, the judgement sober and free from superstition. Dioscorides' book superseded all earlier literature and became the standard work of later centuries, in the East no less than in the West. *See* BOTANY § 6; MEDICINE, 1 (*j*).

TEXT. *Materia medica*, M. Wellmann, i–iii (1907–14), contains both works; Wellmann's proof of genuineness of the second work (*Die Schrift d. D. Π. ἁπλῶν φαρμάκων*, 1914) not wholly convincing. Certainly spurious, Π. δηλητηρίων φαρμάκων; Π. ἰοβόλων, K. Sprengel, in C. G. Kühn, *Medici Graeci* xxvi (1830); *De herbis femininis*, H. F. Kästner, *Hermes* 1896; list of plant synonyms, Wellmann, *Hermes* 1898.
TRANSLATIONS. Latin, H. Stadler, *Romanische Forschungen* (1896 seq.); H. Mihăescu, *Iaşi* (1938). English, R. T. Gunther, *The Greek Herbal of Dioscorides* (1934).
LITERATURE. Survey, M. Wellmann, *PW* v. 1131, here Π. ἁπλῶν φαρμάκων spurious. Ch. Singer, *Studies in the History and Method of Science* ii (1921), also for illustrations (Codex Julia Anicia). T. C. Allbutt, *Greek Medicine in Rome* (1921). Arabic tradition, M. Meyerhof, *Quellen u. Studien z. Gesch. d. Naturw. u. d. Med.* (1933), 103.                                                      L. E.

# DIOSCURI (Διόσκουροι, Attic -κοροι), the Sons of Zeus, a title (*Hymn. Hom.* 33. 1, of uncertain date; Hdt. 2. 43. 2; and often in Attic authors; not in any early passage) of the Tyndaridae (cf. TYNDAREUS), Castor and Polydeuces (latinized Pollux). They are the brothers of Helen, *Il.* 3. 237 ff., where it is apparently stated that they are dead, but cf. *Od.* 11. 300 ff., where they are 'alive' although 'the corn-bearing earth holds them', and the author explains that they are honoured by Zeus and live on alternate days, 'having honour equal to gods'. Here and in Hesiod they are sons of Tyndareus and Leda; later, as in Pindar (*Nem.* 10. 80), Polydeuces is son of Zeus, his twin Castor of Tyndareus, and at Polydeuces' request they share his immortality between them, living half their time below the earth, the other half in Olympus. The Homeric hymn (*supra*) makes them both sons of Zeus, and an account of which there is no certain mention earlier than Horace (*Sat.* 2. 1. 26) makes them both born from an egg, like their sister (*see* HELEN). They had a cult in Lacedaemon, where they were symbolized by the *dokana*, two upright pieces of wood connected by two cross-beams (Plut. *De frat. amor.* 478 a–b), and in many other States, chiefly but not exclusively Dorian (Argos, Athens, Dorian colonies in Sicily, etc.). *See* ANAKES.

The chief events in their mythology are three. When Theseus kidnapped Helen they made an expedition to Attica, recovered her, and carried off Aethra (q.v. for references). They took part in the Argonautic expedition, and on it Polydeuces distinguished himself in the fight against Amycus (q.v.). Their final exploit on earth was the carrying off of the two daughters of Leucippus, the Leucippides, Phoebe and Hilaeira. Thereupon the nephews of Leucippus, Idas and Lynceus, pursued them (Pind. op. cit. 60 ff., who makes it a cattle-raid; Theoc. 22. 137 ff.). In the resulting fight Castor and both the pursuers were killed; the sequel of the shared immortality has already been mentioned, but some ingenuity seems to have been spent in determining whether they have since been always together or always separate, one being in Hades while the other is in Olympus (Rose, *Handb. Gr. Myth.*[6] 248, note 4). They are often identified with the constellation Gemini (as Ps.-Eratosthenes 10), and are connected with stars as early as Euripides (*Hel.* 140). Of the miracles attending their cult, the most famous is that connected with the battle of the Sagra, which gave rise to the Roman story

of their appearance at Lake Regillus (Cic. *Nat. D.* 2. 6). The Locrians, being at war with the Crotonians, appealed for help to Sparta and were told that they might have the Dioscuri, whom they accepted. In the battle, which resulted in a complete victory for them, two gigantic youths in strange dress were seen fighting on their side (Justin 20. 3. 8; *Suda* s.v. ἀληθέστερα τῶν ἐπὶ Σάγρᾳ).

It is a still unsettled controversy whether they are in origin heroes of more than usual celebrity and popularity (they received divine honours here and there) or heroized ('faded') gods. In favour of the former view it may be urged that the earliest evidence (Homer, Hesiod fr. 94. 13, 27, and 31 Rzach) knows nothing of their being anything more than important human beings, honoured after death as several others of their kind were; that they do not become more than heroes till relatively late and even in late traditions and theologizings retain much of their human origin, becoming stock examples of the possibility of transcendent human virtue attaining superhuman rank (as Horace, *Carm.* 3. 3. 9). For such a career a close parallel can be found in that of Heracles (q.v.). On the other side, however, can be cited a not inconsiderable list of divine twins, the most celebrated being the Sanskrit Açvins. These are often connected with horses; the Dioscuri are on occasion λευκόπωλοι, 'riders on white steeds', and Castor especially is a notable horseman. They not uncommonly have astral connexions, such as we have seen the Dioscuri have, though not very early and possibly only through one of their most picturesque functions, that of saviours of those in peril from storms at sea. In this capacity they appear as twin lights of St. Elmo's fire, which it would not be a hard thing to confuse mythologically with stars; see, for instance, Pliny, *HN* 2. 101. Certainly they are not infrequently seen in art with stars over the curious round caps which they wear. Moreover, possible traces of other twin gods have been discovered elsewhere in Greece, as for instance the Theban pair, Amphion and Zethus (*see* AMPHION), who are also sons of Zeus. But it cannot be said that these arguments are cogent as against the earlier date of the Homeric and Hesiodic passages; the original divine nature of the twins is no more than a possibility.

There is but one important identification of the Dioscuri with other figures; they tend to be confused with the Cabiri (q.v.). See, for some very interesting monuments connected with this and similar cults, F. Chapouthier, *Les Dioscures au service d'une déesse* (1935); in these, they (or deities identified with them) are grouped on either side of Helen. The connecting link is the common function of rescuing mariners.

In art they appear before the middle of the sixth century on metopes of the Sicyonian building at Delphi, with the Argo, and rustling cattle with Idas. In Attic black-figure they are shown with Tyndareus and Leda. Later the most popular subjects are: the Rape of the daughters of Leucippus; as Argonauts; at the Theoxenia; at the delivery to Leda of Nemesis' egg containing Helen. *See also* CASTOR AND POLLUX.

Farnell, *Hero-Cults* 175 ff., and Nilsson, *GGR* i[2]. 406, for their cult and the controversy as to their origin. Roscher's *Lexikon*, s.v.; in art, Brommer, *Vasenlisten*[2], 360 ff.                         H. J. R.; C. M. R.

# DIOSCURIDES or DIOSCORIDES (1st c. B.C. or A.D.) is reputed to have written *On Customs in Homer*, in which he is said to have interpolated the Homeric text, *On the Life of Homer's Heroes, Recollections* of sayings of famous men, *The Spartan Constitution, On Institutions*. But these may not be the work of one Dioscurides. Lengthy fragments survive in Athenaeus, Plutarch, and others.

*FHG* ii. 192 ff. R. Weber, *Leipziger Studien* ii (1888).
                                                      J. F. L.; R. B.

**DIOTIMA,** legendary priestess at Mantinea and teacher of Socrates; Plato in *Symp.* 201 d puts in her mouth his metaphysic of love. It is impossible to say whether Plato's fiction had any basis in fact, since we have no independent testimony.

**DIOTIMUS** (fl. 3rd c. B.C.) has a few epideictic and sepulchral poetic inscriptions in the Greek Anthology: *Anth. Pal.* 7. 173 is a good specimen of his quiet pathos.
Gow and Page, 1719 ff. G. H.

**DIOTOGENES,** the nominal author of Pythagorean treatises on Holiness and on Kingship, is otherwise unknown. His Περὶ βασιλείας defines the king as god's lieutenant on earth and the embodiment of law; it draws on an eclectic tradition and has been variously dated between early Hellenistic times and the second century A.D.

Stobaeus, 1. 93, 4. 79–81 W–H (Περὶ ὁσιότητος); 4. 263–70 W–H (Περὶ βασιλείας). *See* ECPHANTUS. G. T. G.

**DIPHILUS** of Sinope, brother of Diodorus (q.v. 1), New Comedy poet, born *c.* 360–50 B.C., lived most of his life at Athens, but died at Smyrna probably at the beginning of the third century (the reference to him in Plaut. *Mostell.* 1149 is useless for establishing his death date: see M. Knorr, *Das griechische Vorbild der Mostell. des Plaut.* (1934), 7 f.). Wrote about 100 plays, winning three Lenaean victories (*IG* ii². 2325. 163). About sixty titles are known, mostly typical of New Comedy; the nine or so with a mythical connexion (e.g. *Danaides, Theseus*) need not all have been mythological burlesques: some could have taken their titles from a man aping a myth hero (cf. Ath. 10. 421 e on *Herakles*), others from a divine prologue (e.g. *Heros*). An unusual title is Αἱρησιτείχης, which was altered to Στρατιώτης when the play was rewritten, presumably for a second production (Ath. 11. 496 f: the two titles appear as separate entries in the Piraeus book catalogue, *IG* ii². 2363). Diphilus' reference to 'gilded Euripides' (fr. 60: cf. the parody in fr. 73) suggests gentle ridicule shot with admiration. Many interesting fragments: fr. 17, the nationality of one's guests is important to a cook (cf. fr. 43); fr. 38, unfilial conduct of Ctesippus, son of Chaereas; frs. 69, 70, Archilochus and Hipponax anachronistically become Sappho's lovers; fr. 91, a vivid description of an unattractive woman.

A play of Diphilus was the original of Plautus' *Rudens*; the Κληρούμενοι, of Plautus' *Casina*; the Συναποθνῄσκοντες of Plautus' lost *Commorientes* (Terence, *Ad.* 6, used a scene omitted by Plautus); and possibly Σχεδία, of Plautus' *Vidularia*. Although Diphilus' originals may have been completely remodelled in the Roman adaptations, certain characteristics common to all these latter can doubtless be attributed to the Greek poet: a delight in lively theatrical effects, with clearly contrasted scenes and characterization perhaps less sensitive than that of Menander.

FRAGMENTS. *FCG* iv. 375 ff.; *CAF* ii. 541 ff.
INTERPRETATION AND CRITICISM. A. Marigo, 'Difilo Comico', *Stud. Ital.* 1907, 375 ff.; G. Coppola, *Atene e Roma* 1924, 185 ff.; W. H. Friedrich, *Euripides und Diphilos* (1953); Webster, *Later Greek Comedy* 152 ff. W. G. A.

**DIPLOMA,** a pair of small bronze tablets recording the privileges granted to a soldier on discharge. These *diplomata militaria*—the term is modern—of which well over 200 are extant, were given to auxiliaries and *classiarii* from the time of Claudius, and to members of the praetorian and urban cohorts from the time of Vespasian. The latest known is of A.D. 306. Down to about A.D. 140 the auxiliary and marine received personal citizenship, the legalization of his past or future marriage, and civic rights for his descendants. After this date, no doubt because the citizenship was already held by many in the *auxilia*, the form for them was brought into line with that of the *diplomata* granted to the praetorians. Citizenship was still given to those requiring it, but this privilege was not extended to existing children; the grant of *conubium* remained, as it was necessary for the marriage of a citizen with a peregrine.

The legionary did not normally receive a diploma. The only exceptions to this rule are the two *Adiutrices* legions recruited from *classiarii* in A.D. 68–9, and some soldiers of *X Fretensis* who were non-citizens enlisted in the same crisis. Two *diplomata* are extant, both of the third century, which were issued to members of the *equites singulares* (q.v.).

*CIL* xvi (texts of *diplomata*; ed. H. Nesselhauf). Konrad Kraft, *Zur Rekrutierung der Alen und Kohorten an Rhein und Donau* (1951), 106 ff. H. M. D. P.; G. R. W.

**DIPYLON,** a double gateway in a city-wall, the most famous example being at Athens in the Potters' Quarter (Cerameicus). The gateway comprised a rectangular courtyard open on the land side, closed by two double doors on the city side; each corner was enlarged to form a tower; a fountain-house adjoined the gateway on the city side. The complex dates from the time of Themistocles, but was rebuilt in the third century B.C. Through the Dipylon passed a broad road leading from the Agora to the Academy. A similar though smaller gateway 75 metres to the south-west protected the passage of the Sacred Way leading to Eleusis. Between the two gates stood the Pompeium, the marshalling place for the Panathenaic Procession (early 4th c. B.C.). From the eleventh century B.C. onward the area was the principal burial-ground of Athens. Bordering the road outside the Dipylon proper were the tombs of those who fell in war; here Pericles delivered the Funeral Oration. Nearby lay Harmodios and Aristogeiton, Cleisthenes and Pericles. The Sacred Way also was bordered by tombs of leading Athenian families and by small sanctuaries relating to the dead.

W. Judeich, *Topographie von Athen*² (1931), 135 ff., 400 ff. G. Gruben, *Arch. Anz.* 1964, cols. 384 ff. H. A. T.

**DIRGE** in Greek literature. The ancient critics seem to have distinguished between two kinds of dirge, the ἐπικήδειον sung actually over the dead body (Procl. ap. Phot. *Bibl.* 321ᵃ30), and the θρῆνος, a song sung in memory of the dead (Ammon. *Diff.* 54). The difference does not seem to have been observed by the Alexandrine editors of the lyric poets, and the Dirges of Simonides (frs. 7–12) and of Pindar (frs. 114–23) may well have included both kinds. The earliest evidence for such dirges is in *Il.* 18. 50–1, 314–16, 24. 472–4. In these a company laments, but the leader has a special part as ἔξαρχος.

E. Reiner, *Die rituelle Totenklage der Griechen* (1938), and H. Färber, *Die Lyrik in der Kunsttheorie der Antike* (1936), i. 38 f., ii. 53 f.
For the dirge in Latin literature, *see* EPICEDIUM, NENIA. C. M. B.

**DISCUS** (δίσκος), a flat circular piece of stone or metal, somewhat thicker in the centre. Extant specimens vary in weight from 3 to 15 pounds and in diameter from 3 to 12 inches, but many of these were dedicatory offerings rather than athletic implements. In throwing the discus, the athlete first swung the discus back in his right hand with a straight arm and turned his body to the right so that the left shoulder pointed in the direction of the throw. He then threw the discus with an underarm pull. The style varied in detail with the weight of the discus used. Throwing the discus was always an event for heavy men and it would seem that at the Olympic Games a heavy discus was used. The *balbis*, from which the throw was made, was a space defined by lines in front and at the sides but not at the back. The method of throwing is illustrated in vase-paintings and by statues, notably the *diskobolos* of Myron. R. L. H.

**DISSOI LOGOI** (labelled by H. Stephanus Διαλέξεις), a short surviving sophistic work written in Doric about 400 B.C., perhaps in Cyprus, perhaps at Cyrene. The contents have no originality; they are reminiscent now of Protagoras, now of Hippias, now of Gorgias, and confirm Plato's account of the ethical relativism characteristic of the Sophists.

Ed. Diels, *Vorsokr.*[11] ii. 405–16. W. D. R.

**DITHYRAMB.** The origin of the word διθύραμβος is not known, though it is almost certainly not of Hellenic origin. It first appears in Archilochus (fr. 77), who calls it the song of Dionysus and says that he, under the influence of wine, leads others in singing it. It was, then, from the beginning a choral song to Dionysus, though it need not yet have had any very definite form. It was reduced to order by Arion at Corinth c. 600 B.C., when it was sung by a regular choir and made to treat a definite subject. From Corinth it was brought to Athens by Lasos of Hermione (*Suda* s.v. Λᾶσος), and it soon became a subject for competition at the festivals of Dionysus. The first victor is said to have been Hypodicus of Chalcis in 509–508 B.C. (*Marm. Par.* 46). Hence till about 470 B.C. it attracted poets of great eminence such as Simonides, who won fifty-six prizes (fr. 79), Lasos, Pindar (frs. 60–77, not all for Athens), and Bacchylides (Odes 15–21). At this period it was composed like other choral odes, with regular strophe and antistrophe. The surviving fragments do not suggest any close connexion of their subjects with Dionysus or any special Dionysiac spirit, though the large element of narrative in them may be due to Arion's example. But about 470 B.C. its character began to change. The change, associated with the names of Melanippides, Cinesias, Philoxenus, and Timotheus, was largely musical, and since no note of their music survives, it is hard to estimate what happened. In the main the music seems to have become more important than the words and to have led to a degeneration of the text. A protest against this movement is to be seen in some lines of Pratinas (fr. 1). Other elements in the change were the abolition of the correspondence of strophe and antistrophe, the introduction of solo-songs, and the development of a pompous, affected language. The movement continued into the fourth century in the hands of Polyidus and Telestes. After the fourth century the dithyramb seems to have lost its importance, even at Athens, though before 300 B.C. the State took charge of the expenses of production. Inscriptions from Delos, from 286 to 172 B.C., show that at the Delian Dionysia and Apollonia competitions were still held, as they were at Miletus in the third century and at Teos and Samos in the second. Polybius (4. 20) notes that the Arcadians commonly sang dithyrambs in his time. The habit lasted in Athens into the imperial age, though no fragments of importance survive.

Pickard-Cambridge–Webster, *Dithyramb*[2], 1 ff. C. M. B.

**DIVERBIUM,** dialogue in a comedy as distinct from *cantica* (q.v.).

**DIVINATION** (μαντική). Prediction by supernatural means of future events and interpretation of past occurrences is found throughout Greek and Roman civilization, showing contacts at various points, such as necromancy, prophecy, extispicy, or astrology, with Oriental cultures. The present account sketches Greek and Roman uses together, and for the sake of brevity neglects much of their chronological development.

**2.** Our most important ancient source, Cicero's *D[e] Divinatione*, in 1. 11 and 2. 26 (possibly after Posidonius) divides the art into natural (or intuitive) and artificial (o[r] inductive) types. This distinction is generally valid fo[r] Greek and Roman civilization, but originally all divina[-] tion arises from one root: it is based on a concept tha[t] the soul of the prophet is in open contact with the whol[e] world around him (*see* MAGIC).

**3.** Of Natural Divination no form seems more primi[-] tive than dreams, often mentioned from Homer onward[.] These might either be understood by the dreamer o[r] require professional interpreters, whose lore, base[d] partly on empiricism but chiefly on supposed resem[-] blances (Arist. *Div. Somn.* 2. 464[b]7), was preserved i[n] practical dream-books, such as the *Onirocritica* of Artemi[-] dorus and Astrampsychus, or discussed in theoretica[l] works, like Aristotle (op. cit.), Synesius, *De Insomniis*, an[d] Macrobius, *Comm. in Somnium Scipionis.* A specialize[d] form is incubation (q.v.; ἐγκοίμησις), practised at health[-] shrines, like those of Asclepius, by persons desirous o[f] cures, and hence called iatromancy. Necromancy, o[r] evocation of spirits of the dead, is already well develope[d] in *Od.* 11, but though long employed, especially at cer[-] tain localities (*psychomantia*), it was less respectable tha[n] most other methods. Related to it are varieties in which[h] forms of the dead or of gods or demons appear on the[e] surface of liquids or on mirrors.

**4.** Very important is prophecy (*vaticinatio*), in which[h] the *vates* acts as the medium or mouthpiece (προφήτης) of a divine or demonic power possessing him, the process being related to poetic inspiration (cf. Plato, *Phaedr.* 244 a–b), and known as ἐνθουσιασμός; cf. [Arist.] *Probl.* 30. 1. 954[a]34–8. μαντική is almost certainly related to μαίνομαι and, being ἔνθεος, implies ἔκστασις in the sense of 'not being yourself'. This ecstatic or 'frenzied' type of prophecy is greatly elucidated by the observations of modern abnormal psychology. Like telepathy and clair-voyance and like the ventriloquists (ἐγγαστρίμυθοι), the freer forms of prophecy, such as those of the shadowy Bacis (q.v.) and Musaeus (q.v. 1), seem hardly to have become institutionalized, but with the Sibyls (q.v.) and the oracles (q.v.), e.g. Delphi (q.v.), Dodona (q.v.), Lebadea, Oropus, and Ammon (q.v.), prophetic power became resident at fixed sites, where a succession of media regularly answered consultants. *See*, however, PROPHECIES.

**5.** Artificial divination may be roughly divided into prognostications from animate beings or from plants, and those from lifeless objects. Its oldest type is perhaps augury (*see* AUGURES) or the observation and interpretation of the number, species, flight, cries, eating, and other symbolic acts of birds. It was common in Greece from the time of Tiresias, Melampus (Porphyry, *Abst.* 3. 3), and Calchas (*Il.* 2. 308–32), and at Rome was entrusted to the college of augurs (*see* AUSPICIUM). Auguries might be deliberately sought (*inpetratiua*) or offered to men unsought (*oblatiua*; cf. Serv. *Aen.* 6. 190), a variety of the former type more convenient for military use being the Roman observation of the sacred chickens. Similar features might be noted in the case of other animals, especially from their chance appearances during a journey (ἐνόδια; cf. A. S. Pease on Cic. *Div.* 1. 26). Still more important were indications derived from human beings, e.g. from their involuntary motions or twitchings (παλμός, salisatio), from sneezing, and from the large class of omens, where man is merely the tool of a temporarily possessing, superhuman, power (e.g. *Od.* 18. 112–17). Most important, during a long period and over a wide geographic range, is extispicy (or haruspicy), based on observation of the entrails—especially the liver (hepato-scopy) of sacrificial animals, for which *see* HARUSPICES. Predictions were also derived from miraculous growths nd actions of plants, e.g. of 'birth-trees' (see Donat. *Vit. Verg.* p. 2 Brummer), the residence of an 'external soul'.

6. Divination from lifeless objects has varied forms. The classification by Varro (ap. schol. Dan. *Aen.* 3. 359; sid. *Etym.* 8. 9. 13) into four elemental groups (*geomantis, aëromantis, pyromantis, hydromantis*) is suggestive ut unduly formal. Numerous are above all the uses of ots (cleromancy), in which a divine power guides the fall f dice or knuckle-bones (astragalomancy) or the drawing often by the hand of an innocent child) of inscribed *ortes* from some receptacle. This practice was often ocalized at particular sites, such as Claros, Praeneste, Antium, the fountain of Clitumnus, and Patavium. The nscribed lot is naturally later in origin than the introduction of writing, and from it was perhaps derived ibliomancy, or the random consultation of books to liscover prophetic advice. The great poets were often o used (rhapsodomancy), perhaps as being themselves livinely inspired. Thus we find the *sortes Homericae*, the *ortes Vergilianae*—eight cases in the *Augustan History* alone—and, with the Christians, the *sortes Biblicae*.

7. The interpretation of weather-signs (as in Aratus 733) approaches more nearly to empirical science, yet nany unusual meteorological phenomena (storms, neteorites, aurora borealis, etc.) and many arising from he earth (earthquakes, faulting, etc.), as well as teratological births of men and beasts (see above), were called ostenta, portenta, monstra, prodigia (q.v.) (Cic. *Div.* 1. 93), nd considered precursors of social, political, or dynastic changes. Such were recorded in priestly records (especally at Rome) and used as sources by various historians e.g. Livy, from whom Julius Obsequens, by a reverse process, compiled his *Prodigiorum liber*). For the vast eld of astrology in its various forms, increasing with the Driental influences following the conquests of Alexander, ree ASTROLOGY.

8. Popular belief at most periods commonly accepted older, socially or politically established, forms of divination, though many looked askance upon others as charatanry; and we may remember the famous gibe of Cato hat a haruspex could not but laugh on meeting a colleague. Some philosophers also accepted the art with little question, but Xenophanes, the Epicureans, Carneades, and others rejected it, and Panaetius expressed doubts of its reality. Some Peripatetics admitted intuitive but disallowed inductive divination (Cic. *Div.* 1. 5, 113; 2. 100), but most Stoics (notably Posidonius) vigorously defended both types, basing their justification upon the powers of gods, fate, and nature (Cic. *Div.* 1. 125), or upon the loctrine of συμπάθεια. Mystics in the second century of our era, and later, attempted to revive interest in the Delphic oracle, which was in Cicero's time (*Div.* 1. 37–38; cf. Plut. *De Pyth. or.*; *De def. or.*) already in neglect, and various collections of oracles, with infiltration of Christian elements, date from this period. Yet after a fitful respite, during which apologists like Origen attacked pagan divination as the work of malign demons, Theodosius, in the fourth century, by a series of edicts forbade various mantic rites, and though these sometimes survived under Christianized guise the prestige of the pagan divination was at an end.

GENERAL. A. S. Pease, commentary on Cicero, *De Divinatione* (1920–3); A. Bouché-Leclercq, *Histoire de la divination dans l'antiquité* (4 vols. 1879–82).
GREEK. W. R. Halliday, *Greek Divination* (1913); Nilsson, *GGR* i², 164 ff.; ii², 229 ff.; 467 ff.
ROMAN. W. Warde Fowler, *The Religious Experience of the Roman people* (1911), ch. 13.
SPECIAL SUBJECTS. Dreams: E. R. Dodds, *The Greeks and the Irrational* (1951), ch. 4; ecstatic prophecy: ibid., ch. 3; oracles: see s.v.; oracular literature: Nilsson, op. cit. ii², 479 ff.; involuntary motions: H. Diels, *Beitr. zur Zuckungsliteratur des Okzidents u. Orients* (1907–8); oracles by dice, etc.: F. Heinevetter, *Würfel- u. Buchstabenorakel in Griechenl. u. Kl. Asien* (1912); views of philosophers: F. Jaeger, *De oraculis quid veteres philosophi iudicaverint*

(1910); for the Stoa cf. K. Reinhardt, *Kosmos u. Sympathie* (1926), 214 ff. A. S. P.; J. H. C.

**DIVISIO,** which had other rhetorical and logical connotations, was, in the vocabulary of the *controversia*, a skeleton plan of the argument. Students would have this dictated by their master (Quint. 2. 6. 1); a grown declaimer might sketch it before he declaimed (Sen., *Controv.* i. pr. 21). Seneca (q.v. 1) in his collection of *controversiae* regularly extracts the skeleton for us (e.g. *Controv.* i. 7. 11 'fere hac usi sunt divisione'); the full declamation would clothe the bones in flesh (Ps.-Quint. *Decl.* 270 *sermo*). Perhaps declaimers did not always insert a formal division in their declamation; when they did, it would naturally follow the *narratio*, as did the *partitio* in judicial oratory (Quint. 4. 5).

S. F. Bonner, *Roman Declamation* (1949), 56 f. M. W.

**DIVITIACUS** (1) (1st c. B.C.), an Aeduan Druid, leader of the philo-Roman party. After the defeat of his tribe by Ariovistus (*c.* 61 B.C.) he appealed unsuccessfully for help at Rome. He regained influence against his brother Dumnorix by supporting Caesar (58), whom he urged in the name of the Gallic tribes to expel Ariovistus. In 57 he assisted Caesar by attacking the Bellovaci and secured favourable terms for them.

Caesar, *BGall.* 1. 16–20; 31–2; 2. 5–15; Cic. *Div.* 1. 41. 90.

**DIVITIACUS** (2), king of the Suessiones *c.* 100 B.C. and overlord of other tribes in both Gaul and Britain.

Caesar, *BGall.* 2. 4. 7. C. E. S.

**DIYLLUS** of Athens, a son of the atthidographer Phanodemus, and author of a universal history (Ἱστορίαι) in twenty-six books including that of Sicily for the period 357–297 B.C. The first part began with the Sacred War and overlapped and enlarged Ephorus' narrative down to 341, and the second and third parts continued with increasing detail until the death of Cassander, 297. Diyllus was one of the major sources of Diodorus and was considered a satisfactory authority by Plutarch.

*FGrH* ii A. 73. G. L. B.

**DOBUNNI,** a British tribe with Belgic aristocracy ruling an indigenous population. The coins, at first uninscribed, show affinity with those of Commius (q.v.) of the Atrebates; later, inscribed coins record the following rulers: *Anted-rig, Eisu, Catti, Comux, Corio,* and *Boduocus*. By emending Dio's Βοδούννων, otherwise unknown (60. 20), to Δοβούννων it can be suggested that part of the tribe (under Boduocus) made its peace with Claudius. An auxiliary fort was placed at Cirencester and another at Gloucester (*see* GLEVUM) where later (49) a fortress for Legio XX was established. The *caput civitatis* was created at Cirencester (Corinium) on the evacuation of the military in early Flavian times and a very large forum-and-basilica was built (550 × 345 feet). Two inscriptions (*RIB* 114, (Cirencester) and 2250 (Kenchester)) attest local self-government.

Corinium became the second city in Britain in size (240 acres within its third-century walls), and in the fourth century was very probably promoted capital of *Britannia Prima* (*RIB* 103). The *civitas* included the iron-working district of the Forest of Dean; its wealthy villas, including some of the largest in Britain (Woodchester, Chedworth, etc.), attest the prosperity of its agriculture which was primarily engaged on beef and wool.

D. F. Allen in E. M. Clifford, *Bagendon, a Belgic Oppidum* (1961: coinage); A. L. F. Rivet, *Town and Country in Rom. Brit.*² (1964), 151 ff.; J. S. Wacher, *Antiquaries Journal* 1964, 9 ff. (forum); P. D. C. Brown and A. D. McWhirr, ibid. 1967, 185 ff. (amphitheatre); J. C. Mann, *Antiquity* 1961, 316 ff. (B. Prima). S. S. F.

**DODONA** (Δωδώνη), a sanctuary of Zeus (under the cult-title of Naïos) in Epirus, famous as the centre of an oracle. It is first mentioned in the *Iliad* (16. 233) where the prophets, the Selli (Σελλοί) are described as 'of unwashed feet and sleeping on the ground'. In the *Odyssey* and elsewhere in early mythology it appears that the responses of the oracle came from a sacred oak. Also a dove was associated with the tree and was described as having spoken originally to reveal its sanctity. When Herodotus visited Dodona in the mid fifth century B.C. the oracle was operated by three priestesses instead of the Selli. Strabo (probably wrongly) attributed the change to the introduction of the cult of Dione. In later times the priestesses were themselves called doves (πελειάδες). The new method of consultation was for the inquirer to write his question on a leaden strip which was folded and put in a jar before being extracted by the prophetess. Numerous specimens of questions have been found; a few from States, but mostly from private persons vividly revealing their domestic or professional problems. In the late fifth and fourth centuries the oracle was consulted occasionally by such states as Athens and Sparta which found it a convenient alternative to Delphi. In the reign of Pyrrhus, Dodona was made the religious centre of his kingdom and the festival of the *Naïa* was developed. The sack by the Aetolians in 219 B.C. was followed by a restoration, but the sanctuary never really recovered from the Roman ravaging of Epirus in 167 B.C. The festival of the *Naïa* was revived and lasted till the third century A.D. Late legends also explained the oracle as conveyed by the murmur of a sacred spring or the echoes of a brazen gong. The magnificent theatre beside the sanctuary has recently been restored.

ANCIENT SOURCES. (*a*) Inscriptions: the consultants' questions are published in Collitz, *Dialekt-Inschriften*, 1557–98, and in *SIG³*, 1160–6, and those recently found in Πρακτικά (1929 ff.), Ἠπειρωτικά Χρονικά (1935), and Ἔργον (1954 ff.). (*b*) Literature: Hom. *Il.* 16. 233–5, *Od.* 14. 327 f. = 19. 296 f.; Hdt. 2. 55–7; Strabo 327–9 and bk. 7, frs. 1–3 (Jones).
MODERN LITERATURE: Excavation reports in C. Carapanos, *Dodone et ses ruines* (1878), and in the periodicals listed in (*a*) by D. Evangelides and S. I. Dakaris; full summary of results by the latter in Ἀρχ.Ἐφ. 1959 (1964); Nilsson, *GGR* i². 423 ff.; Hammond, *Epirus*; H. W. Parke, *The Oracles of Zeus* (1967). H. W. P.

**DOGS.** From earliest times in Greece and Italy, the dog was domesticated for hunting, guarding the house and flocks, and as the companion of man. Odysseus' hound, Argos, who, at the age of 20, signified the approach of strangers by pricking his ears, but showed his recognition of his master by wagging his tail and dropping his ears in affection, was bred for hunting wild goats, deer, and hares (*Od.* 17. 291–327). Homer mentions shepherds' dogs also (*Il.* 10. 183; 12. 303) and Hesiod the sharp-toothed watchdog (*Op.* 604).

The ancients knew many types of dogs. In Greece, the mastiff-like Molossian from Epirus was used mainly as a sheepdog and a watchdog (Arist. *HA* 608ᵃ, Lucr. 5. 1063 ff., Hor. *Epod.* 6. 5). The best-known hunting dog was the Laconian, a type subdivided by Xenophon into Castorian and the smaller Vulpine, believed to have been originally a cross between dog and fox. Points and faults of physique and habit, breeding and training are described in detail (Xen. *Cyn.* 3–4; 7). It was also used as a sheepdog (Varro, *Rust.* 2. 9, Hor. loc. cit.). The Cretan hound, famous for its agility and powers of tracking, may have been the cross between the Molossian and the Laconian which Aristotle describes (loc. cit.).

All these types were introduced into Italy, where there were also native breeds, the Umbrian, a sheepdog and hunter, noted for its keen nose (*vividus Umber*—Verg. *Aen.* 12. 753), but lacking in courage, the Salentine, a sheepdog (Varro, loc. cit.) and the shaggy-coated Etruscan, lacking speed, but keen-nosed. In hounds,

monochrome coats were regarded as a sign of poor breeding, but Columella (*Rust.* 7. 12. 3) recommends an all-white dog for the shepherd, to avoid mistaking it for a wolf in the half-light, and an all-black guard dog for the farm, to terrify thieves in daylight and to be less visible to intruders at night.

From Gaul came the *vertragus*, a type of greyhound swift-footed and used for coursing (Mart. 14. 200. 1) and from Britain a small shaggy terrier of poor appearance but great courage (Grattius, *Cyn.* 174 ff.). In the late Empire, *Scottici canes*, Irish wolfhounds, were imported as a novelty for the *ludi* of A.D. 393 (Symmachus, *Epist.* 2. 77). For pet dogs *see* PETS.

J. M. C. Toynbee, 'Beasts and their names in the Roman Empire' *PBSR* 1948, 24 ff. S. W.

**DOKIMASIA,** the examination of candidates for office at Athens, before the *thesmothetai* (except candidates for the *boule*, who were examined by the outgoing *boule*). Men already chosen, whether by lot or by vote, but primarily the former, were formally interrogated to ascertain whether they were eligible: e.g. whether they were 30 years old; whether (in the case of certain offices at certain periods, e.g. the archonship: *see* ARCHONTES) they belonged to a particular census-class; and whether they were not precluded from one office, because they had held it before, or were holding another, or through being under some form of *atimia* (q.v.). A. W. G.

**DOLABELLA** (1), GNAEUS CORNELIUS (*PW* 134), after serving under Sulla, became consul in 81 B.C. and later governor of Macedonia, triumphing in 78. Caesar unsuccessfully prosecuted him *repetundarum*. E. B.

**DOLABELLA** (2), GNAEUS CORNELIUS (*PW* 135), praetor in 81 B.C. As proconsul (80–79), he plundered Cilicia with the help of his legate Verres (q.v.), who later helped to convict him *repetundarum*. He lost his possessions, went into exile, and is not heard of again.

On the Republican Dolabella, see E. Badian, *PBSR* 1965, 48; E. S. Gruen, *AJPhil.* 1966, 385. E. B.

**DOLABELLA** (3), PUBLIUS CORNELIUS (*PW* 141), born c. 80 B.C., prosecuted Appius Claudius (q.v. 12) in 50. He commanded a Caesarian fleet in the Adriatic (49), and fought at Pharsalus, Thapsus, and Munda. As tribune for 47 (after adoption by a plebeian) he provoked serious riots in attempting to carry a law for the cancellation of debts. In 44 Caesar, despite Antony's opposition, undertook that Dolabella should become consul in his own place when he left for Parthia: on his death Dolabella associated himself with the assassins and assumed the vacant consulship, Antony not now demurring. In April his drastic suppression of Caesar-worshippers delighted Republicans: but his appointment by the Assembly to the governorship of Syria for five years apparently made him a Caesarian again. Reaching Asia in Jan. 43, he took Smyrna by surprise and killed Trebonius (q.v.); on the news, the Senate declared him a public enemy. He proceeded to Syria to face Cassius, but was forced to take refuge in Laodicea; on its capture he committed suicide (July).

Dolabella was notorious for his dissipation and chronic insolvency; hence, it seems, much of his political conduct and his marriages to Fabia and Tullia (q.v. 2): Cicero found him an uncomfortable son-in-law. Augustus' friend Dolabella was probably his son by Fabia and father of no. 4; his two sons by Tullia, born in 49 and 45, probably both died in infancy.

T. Rice Holmes, *The Roman Republic* (1923) iii. 516; Syme, *Rom. Rev.*, see index; M. Polignano, *Rend. Linc.* 1946, 240 ff., 444 ff. G. W. R.; T. J. C.

**DOLABELLA** (4), Publius Cornelius (*PW* 143), probably grandson of no. 3, was consul in A.D. 10, and (14 to *c.* 20) *legatus pro praetore* in Dalmatia, where he kept the legions quiet in 14 and built or rebuilt a number of military roads from Salonae (q.v.) to the legionary camps and the mountainous country beyond. In 23/24, as proconsul of Africa, he ended the war against Tacfarinas (q.v.). His descendants held consulships in 86 and 113.

T. J. C.

**DOLICHENUS, JUPITER**, local god or Baal of Doliche, now Tell Duluk, in Commagene. Originally a Hittite-Hurrite god of thunder and fertility, he formed with a consort a divine pair which, romanized as Jupiter Dolichenus and Juno, was carried westwards by soldiers, slaves, and merchants. With their twin acolytes the Castores, they gained popularity during the second and third centuries A.D. in many western military centres and at Rome. Dolichenus, now a god of the Universe, embraced the heavens, safety, success, and military triumph. He is generally depicted wearing Roman military costume, standing on a bull, and holding a thunderbolt and double-axe. *See* SYRIAN DEITIES.

The evidence, entirely archaeological, is discussed by P. Merlat, *Jupiter Dolichenus* (1960). For his temple on the Aventine in Rome, see Nash, *Pict. Dict. Rome* i. 521 ff. M. A. R. C.

**DOMAINS.** (*a*) CIVIC. Most cities owned land corporately. Some was acquired by conquest, some by escheat, some by confiscation. When cities came under Roman rule, conquest was ruled out, and escheated and confiscated estates normally went to the Roman People. The cities, however, continued to acquire the land, chiefly by gifts and bequests; though cities could not inherit under Roman law, they probably could do so under peregrine law (till A.D. 212), and legacies were legalized by Nerva; moreover, *fideicommissa* were doubtless always valid. The domains owned by a city did not necessarily lie within its territory; Arpinum owned land in Cisalpine Gaul and Cos estates in Cyprus. The rent from domains was often an important part of the civic revenues.

(*b*) IMPERIAL. The nucleus of the imperial domains was formed by the estates of successive Emperors, which normally passed to their successors. They were enlarged by a vast flow of bequests not only from friends, dependents, and freedmen, but from strangers: some emperors refused to accept bequests from persons unknown to them, but others were so grasping as to quash wills under which they did not benefit. Furthermore, the estates of persons condemned for *maiestas* were sometimes bestowed on the emperor; by the second century this was probably the regular practice. In Egypt the imperial domains were, from the Flavian period, managed by a special department (λόγος οὐσιακός) separately from the public lands. In other imperial provinces, where there were only scattered public domains, they and the imperial estates were probably administered by the same staff. In the public provinces the Emperor's procurators, who at first managed only his estates, later, perhaps under the Flavians, assumed control of public lands; at this date the domains in Africa were grouped in *regiones* and *tractus*. Public and imperial domains were thus assimilated (except in Egypt) and were both included in the *patrimonium*.

(*c*) ROYAL. Alexander and the Successors claimed to own the land of their kingdoms, excluding the Greek cities. This theory was most vigorously exploited by the Ptolemies in Egypt. They granted lands, it is true, to the gods in perpetuity, to their friends for life, and to their soldiers at first on a life and later on a hereditary tenure, and they even granted private possession in perpetuity

of some land. But they seem to have maintained their title to the land which was granted (γῆ ἐν ἀφέσει), and the rest, the royal land (γῆ βασιλική), they exploited directly by rack-renting it to the peasants. In Cyrenaica also the Ptolemies seem to have claimed ownership of all the land save the territories of the Greek cities. The Seleucids also made grants of land to their friends and soldiers, but they did not generally disturb tenures, but merely levied the customary dues from the natives. They gradually alienated the χώρα βασιλική by gifts and sales to cities, or to individuals with permission to incorporate the land in cities; by founding new cities; and by recognizing native communities as cities. When the Attalids succeeded to Seleucid Asia Minor, they probably found little royal land. The Bithynian and Cappadocian kings owned extensive royal lands. The Macedonian and other European kings, on the other hand, possessed little—probably only family estates and the territories of communities which had been conquered and destroyed.

(*d*) SACRED. Many gods owned land; especially in Egypt and Asia Minor. These were probably acquired in the main by gifts and bequests; partly perhaps by the foreclosure of mortgages, for the gods, controlling large reserves of cash, engaged extensively in money-lending. In Egypt the sacred lands were administered by the Crown under the Ptolemies, and the Roman government maintained the system. In Asia Minor the sacred lands were often managed by the high priests of the god, some of whom were independent dynasts or subject only to the suzerainty of the Crown. In cities the sacred lands were generally administered by public magistrates, and with the spread of cities the independent temples of Asia Minor mostly passed under municipal control.

O. Hirschfeld, *Kl. Schr.* (1902), 516 ff. (for (*b*)). M. Rostovtzeff, *Studien zur Geschichte des römischen Kolonates* (*Arch. Pap.*, Beiheft i, 1910); id., *Hellenistic World* (for (*c*) and (*d*)). E. Kornemann, *PW*, Suppl. iv. 227 ff. A. H. M. J.

**DOMINIUM.** In early Roman law ownership of things was closely connected with the power over persons: the rights of a *pater familias* over wife and children were similar to those over slaves and cattle; they all derived from his sovereign position as head of the *familia* (*see* PATRIA POTESTAS). It may be that in the early law private ownership was confined to movables, title to land not being as clearly distinguished as it later was from possession (*see* POSSESSIO): in the early proceeding (*see* VINDICATIO, SACRAMENTUM) both parties asserted ownership, and the issue was therefore one only of relatively better title, whereas in the *vindicatio* of the classical law the plaintiff asserted, and had in some way to prove, ownership.

Proof of ownership was to some extent facilitated by the method of acquisition by prescription known as *usucapio*: a person who acquired a thing in good faith from a non-owner by a transaction (*iusta causa, iustus titulus*, e.g. sale) which would normally transfer ownership, became owner after one year (if the thing were a movable) or two years (if immovable), provided that the thing had at no time been stolen (*see* FURTUM). *Usucapio* had also another application. Ownership of *res mancipi* (*see* MANCIPATIO) could be transferred only by *mancipatio* or *in iure cessio* (a kind of collusive *vindicatio* (q.v.) preserved in its primitive form). If, however, the thing were simply delivered, the recipient could become owner by *usucapio* after one or two years. Until then the holder (who was only *in via usucapiendi*) was unprotected by the old *ius civile*, but the praetors later intervened to enable him to retain and if necessary to recover the thing (*see* VINDICATIO). In this way, a kind of praetorian ownership developed (Gai. *Inst.* 2. 40). The holder of a *res mancipi* acquired by delivery was said to have it *in bonis* (bonitary owner); he is put by the praetor for almost all purposes in the position of the full civil law ('quiritary') owner (*dominus ex iure quiritium*). The holder of a thing acquired from a non-owner in the conditions set out above (*bonae fidei possessor in via usucapiendi*) is protected against everyone except the *dominus ex iure quiritium* or the bonitary owner. The distinction between *res mancipi* and *res nec mancipi* was finally abolished by Justinian, and bonitary ownership disappeared with it.

*Dominium* was in principle unlimited, but was subjected from the earliest times to restrictions in the public interest by legislation and by the censors (q.v.), and in the private interest by *servitutes* (q.v.). Provincial land belonged to the State (Gai. *Inst.* 2. 7), and could not be owned by individuals (unless by special grant of *ius Italicum* it had been assimilated to land in Italy). The distinction was, however, technical rather than practical since the interest of individuals in such land was effectively protected. (*See also* EMPHYTEUSIS.)

Ch. Appleton, *Histoire de la propriété prétorienne*, i, ii (1889–90); V. Scialoja, *Teoria della proprietà*, i, ii (1928–31); P. Bonfante, *Corso di diritto romano* ii. 1 (1926). M. Kaser, *Eigentum u. Besitz im ält. röm. Recht²* (1956); *Sav. Zeitschr.* 1956; *and see* textbooks *under* LAW AND PROCEDURE, ROMAN, 1. B. N.

**DOMITIAN** (TITUS FLAVIUS (*PW* 77) DOMITIANUS), son of the Emperor Vespasian, was born 24 Oct. A.D. 51. At the time of his father's rebellion against Vitellius in 69 he was in Rome, and in December was besieged on the Capitol with his uncle Flavius Sabinus (q.v. 3). He escaped, and on Vitellius' death was saluted as Caesar and was temporarily at the head of affairs. This brief taste of power, which abruptly ended with Vespasian's arrival in 70, may have coloured Domitian's outlook. He had dreamed of heading a Germanic invasion and of rivalling his brother's exploits; instead, he found himself condemned to a position of inferiority. Vespasian intended him to succeed the childless Titus, and he held two ordinary consulships (73 and 80) and five suffect consulships; yet neither under Vespasian nor under Titus did he exercise any real power.

The effect on Domitian's character was probably unfortunate. When he succeeded Titus in 81 he seems to have been an embittered man, determined to exert his powers to the full. His reign falls into two halves. Down to the rebellion of L. Antonius Saturninus (q.v. 3) in 88 he avoided bloodshed and ruled firmly but equitably; afterwards he became more and more ruthless, until his reign culminated in a Terror (93 to 96).

Domitian accentuated the absolutist tendencies of Vespasian. He was consul ten times during his Principate (with seven successive consulates in 82–8). He wore the dress of a *triumphator* even in the Senate and was accompanied by twenty-four lictors. He habitually exercised the right of *adlectio*, using it to draft distinguished *equites* and provincials into the Senate, while in 84 or 85 he became *censor perpetuus*. This was a serious blow to the Senate, whose composition he now completely controlled. He only consulted it perfunctorily, relying for advice on the *consilium principis*, in which senators and *equites* served equally. In fact Domitian broke the spirit of the Senate, compelling it to vote as he willed, and, after 88, bringing back all the horrors of *maiestas* and *delatio*. This may have been partly caused by financial embarrassment, though, as his major expenses occurred before 93, it may be argued that revenge was at least as important a motive. The increase of legionary pay from 225 to 300 *denarii* annually, military campaigns, extensive public works and buildings, such as the temple to Jupiter on the Capitol, the temple to Jupiter Custos on the Quirinal, and his magnificent Alban villa, in addition

to *congiaria* amounting in all to 225 *denarii* a head, all helped to swell expenditure.

In foreign policy Domitian aimed at strengthening existing frontiers, and his much-maligned campaign against the Chatti in 83 was a successful attempt to annex Mt. Taunus and complete the line of defence from Main to Neckar. In 85 the Dacian king Decebalus defeated and killed Oppius Sabinus, legate of Moesia. Another defeat followed in 86 or 87 and the Roman general Fuscus (q.v.) was slain and an eagle captured. In 88 the Roman forces won a victory at Tapae; but under pressure from a defeat of the Pannonian army, which he was leading in person, at the hands of the Marcomanni and Quadi, Domitian made an honourable peace with Decebalus and returned to Rome to triumph in 89. The Sarmatians invaded again in 92, and Domitian, taking the field in person, won some success. The only other serious fighting was that of Agricola (q.v. 1) in Britain. Agricola was recalled in 84, possibly because Domitian was jealous of his success.

In administration of the Empire Domitian showed himself careful and efficient, choosing good governors and punishing bad ones. Procurators and freedmen were strictly controlled, and exaction of taxes was severe but fair. Domitian also made attempts to raise the general standard of morality, and, as censor, strictly enforced the laws against immorality, suppressed castration, and checked theatrical licence. In 83 he executed three Vestal Virgins for immorality. In 90 the Chief Vestal, Cornelia, was condemned to be buried alive.

Domitian's strictness on the question of public morality accorded ill with the sensuality of his private life, a point emphasized by his opponents among the aristocracy and 'philosophers'. Other causes of his unpopularity were his attempt to impose Greek refinement on the Romans, his virtual suppression of the Senate, and the Oriental flattery of himself which amounted, at least unofficially, to an assumption of divine honours. Earlier Domitian had treated this opposition with comparative indifference, but in his later years, feeling that he could trust nobody, he turned to persecution. The philosophers were twice banished from Italy (probably 89 and 95). Many plots were made, though our authorities give the most flimsy reasons for Domitian's executions. The fact that the Emperor was childless increased both his own suspicion and the hopes of the plotters; until he executed him in 95, Domitian had destined the two sons of Flavius Clemens (q.v.) as his heirs; what he intended to do afterwards we do not know.

A vicious circle was thus set up; every unsuccessful plot caused more executions, which in their turn led to another plot. Finally the Emperor's own wife, Domitia (*see* CORBULO), feeling herself insecure, joined with the two praetorian prefects and some of the court officials in a plot which succeeded, and Domitian was murdered on 18 Sept. 96. It is almost certain that his successor Nerva (q.v. 1), who was adopted by the Senate on the same day, was privy to the conspiracy. The army, or at least the praetorian guard, was resentful at the murder.

Suet., *Dom.* (ed. J. Janssen, 1919), is a fairer source than most; see also Tac., *Agr.* (esp. 39–43), Dio 67, Pliny, *Pan.*: and for flatter Martial's earlier books and Statius, *Silvae.* M. McCrumm and A. G. Woodhead, *Select Documents of the Principates of the Flavian Emperors* (1961). Among recent works (for which S. Gsell, *Essai su le règne de l'empereur Domitien* (1896), laid a foundation which is still invaluable) see K. von Fritz, 'Tacitus, Agricola, and the Problem of the Principate', *CPhil.* 1957. R. L. J.; G. E. F. C.

**DOMITIANUS**, TITUS FLAVIUS (*PW* 78), son of Flavius Clemens (q.v.) and Flavia Domitilla; he and his brother were adopted by Domitian and received respectively the names of Domitian and Vespasian. Their tutor was Quintilian. A. M.

**DOMITILLA**, FLAVIA (*PW* 227), Domitian's niece, was accused with her husband, the consul Flavius Clemens (q.v.), in A.D. 95 of atheism, probably because she favoured Christian (though others would say Jewish) rites. She was exiled. The early-Christian Coemeterium Domitillae on the Via Ardeatina is somehow connected with her. Eusebius 3. 18, which refers to Domitilla as a niece of Clemens, is probably a simple mistake, not evidence for another person.

H. Leclercq, *Dict. d'arch. chrétienne* iv. 1401; P. Styger, *Die röm. Katakomben* (1933), 63 ff. A. M.

**DOMITIUS** (1, *PW* 18) **AHENOBARBUS**, GNAEUS, plebeian aedile (196 B.C.), praetor (194), and consul (192) in Gaul. In the absence of Scipio Africanus he was in effective command at Magnesia. He may have been in Greece in 169–168 and 167, but this Domitius was more probably his son, consul in 162. A. H. McD.

**DOMITIUS** (2, *PW* 20) **AHENOBARBUS**, GNAEUS, as consul (122 B.C.) and proconsul in Transalpine Gaul defeated the Allobroges and Arverni (qq.v.) in two great battles in the Rhone valley, once with the help of Fabius (q.v. 8). He treacherously seized the Arvernian king Bituitus and later led him in his triumph (*c.* 120). He built stone trophies in Gaul to commemorate his victories and began the Via Domitia (q.v.), perhaps establishing a garrison at Narbo (q.v.) to guard it; and he probably made treaties with the defeated tribes. His censorship (115, with L. Metellus Diadematus) was marked by unusual severity. He died *c.* 104. E. B.

**DOMITIUS** (3, *PW* 21) **AHENOBARBUS**, GNAEUS, son of (2), concerned (with Crassus, q.v. 3) in founding the colony of Narbo (cf. Sydenham, *CRR*, nos. 520 ff.), kept up his inherited Gallic connexions. Tribune in 104 B.C., he was not co-opted to a priesthood in his father's place; he unsuccessfully prosecuted Scaurus (q.v. 1)—whom he blamed for this—and passed a law transferring the election of priests of the four major colleges from the colleges themselves to the *minor pars populi* (seventeen tribes drawn by lot). Elected Pontifex Maximus, soon after he became consul (96), and censor (92) with Crassus (q.v. 3), with whom he quarrelled violently, but agreed in forbidding rhetorical teaching in Latin. He died soon after. E. B.

**DOMITIUS** (4, *PW* 27) **AHENOBARBUS**, LUCIUS (*cos.* 54 B.C.), husband of Cato's sister Porcia, supported Verres (Cicero then calls him 'princeps iuuentutis'—*Verr.* 2. 1. 139) and resisted Manilius (q.v. 2) in 66 B.C. Relentlessly hostile to the 'Triumvirate', in 58 (as praetor) and in 56 he specifically threatened Caesar's position in Gaul, the scene of his grandfather's victories; he thus precipitated the conference of Luca, which postponed his consulate to 54. In 49 the Senate granted him Gaul, but his march northwards, unsupported by Pompey, ended in capitulation at Corfinium, though by Caesar's clemency he survived to defend Massilia and to fall at Pharsalus. Domitius mobilized clients from the Marsi and Paeligni, and tenants from the great estates which Sullan bounty had given him. But his pretensions could make him ridiculous (Cic. *Fam.* 8. 14. 1), and he shared the brutality of his *gens* (Suet. *Nero* 2). G. E. F. C.

**DOMITIUS** (5, *PW* 23) **AHENOBARBUS**, GNAEUS, was with his father, (4) above, at Corfinium in 49 B.C. and like him dismissed unhurt by Caesar. In 44 he accompanied M. Brutus to Macedonia, and in 43 was condemned (perhaps unjustly: Suet. *Nero* 3, App. *BCiv.* 5. 261) for participation in the murder of Caesar. From 44 to 42 he

commanded a fleet in the Adriatic against the Triumvirs, but he joined Antony before the treaty of Brundisium, was formally reinstated in his civic rights, and governed Bithynia from 40 to 35 or later. In 36 he took part in the Parthian expedition and in 35 supported C. Furnius, governor of Asia, against Sextus Pompeius. He was consul in 32; early in the year he and Sosius (q.v. 1) fled to Antony. He opposed the personal participation of Cleopatra in Antony's war with Octavian, and went over to the latter before Actium, already suffering from a fever which proved fatal. He left one son (Domitius 6).

Syme, *Rom. Rev.*, see index. G. W. R.; T. J. C.

**DOMITIUS** (6, *PW* 28) **AHENOBARBUS**, LUCIUS (*cos.* 16 B.C.), the husband of Antonia, the elder daughter of M. Antonius and Octavia, the Princeps' sister. Alleged to have been proud, bloodthirsty, and addicted to chariot-racing, he was aedile in 22, when he behaved arrogantly to the censor Plancus; proconsul of Africa (12); legate of Illyricum between 7 and 2, when he marched from the Danube to the Elbe, setting up an altar to Augustus on the farther bank of the latter river. The direction of his march is uncertain. Next, in command of the army of Germany, he constructed the causeway across the marshes between the Rhine and the Ems known as the *pontes longi*, after which nothing more is heard of him until his death in A.D. 25 (with obituary notice, Tac. *Ann.* 4. 44).

Syme, *Rom. Rev.*, see index. R. S.

**DOMITIUS** (7, *PW* 66) **MARSUS**, Augustan poet, acknowledged by Martial as one of his models (1 *praef.*; 2. 77; 5. 5. 6; 8. 56. 24). To light poetry he added an epic *Amazonis* (4. 29. 8). Quintilian 6. 3. 102 ff. gives some information about a work of his on *urbanitas*, on which see E. S. Ramage, *CPhil.* 1959, 250 ff.

Baehr. *FPR*; Morel, *FPL*; Schanz–Hosius ii⁴. 174 ff.; H. Bardon, *La Litt. lat. inconnue* ii (1956), 52 ff. J. W. D.; G. B. A. F.

**DOMUS AUREA** (Golden House) was the name given to the residence built by Nero after the great fire of A.D. 64. It linked the palace on the Palatine with imperial properties on the Esquiline and included new palatial buildings and landscaped gardens covering the valley between the Palatine, the Caelian, and the Oppian, about 125 acres in all. The main block of new buildings was on the southern slope of the Oppian, and there was a large ornamental lake where the Colosseum (q.v.) now stands. As befitted its situation in a royal park, the main wing of the palace (now covered by the courtyard and reservoirs of the baths of Trajan) followed Hellenistic landscape architecture, with frontal colonnade and angular planning, permitting different vistas to be enjoyed. The treatment, however, is domestic when compared with the Flavian palace on the Palatine. The main entrance was from the Roman Forum along the new Via Sacra (q.v.) reaching a vestibule which housed a colossal bronze statue of Nero, on the site of Hadrian's Temple of Venus and Roma.

G. Lugli, *Roma ˚antica* (1946), 348 ff.; E. B. van Deman, *Am. Ac. Rome* 1925, 115 ff. C. C. van Essen, *Meded. Kon. Nederl. Akad. Wetenschappen*, 1954, 371 ff.; A. Boethius, *The Golden House of Nero* (1960); Nash, *Pict. Dict. Rome* i, 339 ff. I. A. R.; D. E. S.

**DONATISTS.** The Donatists were members of a puritanical Church of the Martyrs in fourth- and early fifth-century Roman Africa. Their schism from the African Catholics derived from the events of the Great Persecution (303–5). Whereas in the East the authorities' primary demand was the performance of sacrifice by Christian clergy, in Africa it was the surrender of the Scriptures. Those who complied, however, were dubbed *traditores* or 'surrenderers'. The death of Mensurius, bishop of Carthage (311), accentuated divisions, since more moderate Christians accepted that the Church on earth must be a 'mixed body' containing both righteous and sinners. Behind the ecclesiastical dispute lay cultural and economic divisions between the more urbanized and latinized Proconsular Africa and the more rural and native Numidia and Mauretania. Thus, when the arch-deacon Caecilian was elected bishop in Mensurius' stead by the Carthaginian Christians, a strong party called in the Numidians in opposition. These dissidents first elected Majorinus, and on his death a Numidian cleric, Donatus of Casae Nigrae (on the borders of the Sahara) as rival bishop.

Meantime, Constantine had ordered the return to Caecilian of confiscated church property, and also ex-empted Caecilian's clergy from a number of fiscal burdens. The opposition therefore appealed to Constan-tine for arbitration by Gallic bishops as to who was right-ful bishop of Carthage, but he commissioned Miltiades, bishop of Rome, himself an African, to convoke an episcopal tribunal. This decided for Caecilian (Oct. 313), but the Donatists now asserted that one of Caecilian's consecrators, Felix of Apthunga, had been a *traditor* and therefore incapable of performing a valid consecration. While their complaints were again rejected at the Council of Arles (Aug. 314), it was not until Feb. 315 that Felix was cleared, and only in Nov. 316 that Constantine decided that Caecilian was lawful bishop. By then Donatus' church had won wide acceptance throughout Africa, but apart from a precarious foothold in Rome the movement did not spread outside Africa. Here, despite the exile of Donatus by Constans (q.v.) in 347, the Dona-tists remained the majority church until *c.* 400. Their theologians included Macrobius, Donatist bishop of Rome, and Tyconius. Their support of the revolt of Firmus (372–5) left them unscathed, but an internal schism (392–3), and the failure of Gildo's revolt (398), laid them open to counter-attack by St. Augustine and the African Catholics. A series of imperial rescripts banned the movement (405), and in 411 a great conference of over 500 bishops at Carthage, presided over by the imperial commissioner Marcellinus, went against them. Years of persecution followed, ended only by the arrival of the Vandals in 429. Donatism, however, survived and re-emerged in strength in Numidia at the end of the sixth century. It may have persisted into the Moslem period.

Theologically the Donatists were rigorists, following the tradition of Tertullian (q.v.) and Cyprian (q.v.), holding that the Church of the saints must remain holy, and that sacraments dispensed by a *traditor* were not only invalid but infected the recipients. They combined puritanism with zeal for martyrdom which in this epoch included an expression of protest against inequitable social and economic conditions. Extremists, drawn from *coloni* and seasonal workers in Numidia and Mauretania, became known as Circumcellions, perhaps through their association with the shrines of martyrs (*cellae*). They ex-tended the martyr's traditional *agon* against the Devil, represented by persecuting authorities, to the Devil exploiting the poor through the agency of landowners. The Donatist leaders also accepted a theory of Church–State relations which, despite their appeals to Constantine (313) and Julian (361), practically equated the Roman Empire with the apocalyptic image of Babylon.

Donatism produced its own art forms, but not, so far as is known, a Bible in a language other than Latin. With the Coptic and Syrian Churches, it represents the general tendency towards cultural and religious groupings by regions which characterized both halves of the Empire from the late third century onwards.

The chief sources are Optatus, *De Schismate Donatistarum* (ed. C. Ziwsa, *CSEL*, xxvi), written *c.* 365 and 385, Augustine, Anti-Donatist

works (*CSEL*, li, lii, and liii), and the *Gesta* of the Conference of Carthage in 411, Migne, *PL* xi, 1223–1438. Some Donatist *Acta Martyrum* are published in *PL* viii, and early documents by H. von Soden, *Urkunden zur Entstehungsgeschichte des Donatismus* (1913). D. Voelter, *Der Ursprung des Donatismus* (1883); L. Duchesne, *Mélanges d'arch.* 1890, 590 ff.; P. Monceaux, *Histoire littéraire de l'Afrique chrétienne* iv–vii (1912–23); A. Berthier, *et al.*, *Les Vestiges du Christianisme antique dans la Numidie centrale* (1942); G. G. Willis, *St. Augustine and the Donatist Controversy* (1950); W. H. C. Frend, *The Donatist Church* (1952), and art. s.v. in *RAC*; H. J. Diesner, *Kirche und Staat im spätrömischen Reich* (1963; articles on the Circumcellions); E. Tengström, *Donatisten und Katholiken* (1964).
W. H. C. F.

**DONATIVUM,** a supplement to the regular pay of a soldier in the legions and the praetorian and urban cohorts. Originally a share of booty, donatives were paid in money to commemorate a joyful event, or left by emperors in their wills. After Claudius each new accession was the occasion for a donative. The amount granted to each praetorian was at the death of Augustus 250 *denarii*, to the *urbanicianus* 125, and to the legionary 75. These amounts coincided with those of a *stipendium* (q.v.) at the time. Gradually, however, because of the political import-ance of the Guard, the differences became disproportion-ately greater. When Hadrian adopted L. Aelius Caesar, the praetorians got 5,000 *denarii* each, the urban troops 2,500, and the legionaries apparently only 225. (The annual pay at the time for these three branches of the army was, in *denarii*, 1,000; 500; 300.) A similar distri-bution of five times their annual pay was made to the praetorians by Marcus Aurelius on his accession.

A. von Domaszewski, 'Der Truppensold der Kaiserzeit', *Neue Heidelberger Jahrbücher* (1900); M. Durry, *Les Cohortes prétoriennes* (1938); A. Passerini, *Le coorti pretorie* (1939), 114 ff.
H. M. D. P.; G. R. W.

**DONATUS (1),** AELIUS, the most famous grammarian of the fourth century A.D., who numbered amongst his pupils the future St. Jerome. He wrote two *artes* and commentaries on Terence and Virgil. (i) The *Ars minor* (ed. Keil, *Gramm. Lat.* iv. 355–66), intended for begin-ners, deals, in the form of question and answer, with the eight parts of speech. (ii) The *Ars maior*, or *secunda* (ed. Keil, ibid. 367–402), is more comprehensive and includes the *vitia et virtutes orationis*. These works became favourite school-books in the Middle Ages. (iii) The extant Terence commentary (which omits the *Heauton-timorumenos*) is not in its original form but is apparently a (6th c.) compilation made from two copies found in the margins of Terence MSS. P. Wessner (ed. 2 vols., 1902–5) prints the commentary as found in our manuscripts; H. T. Karsten (ed. 2 vols., 1911–12) attempts to restore the original form. In this work Donatus owed much to Aemilius Asper (q.v.). (iv) Of the Virgil commentary only the preface (ed. Wölfflin, *Philol.* 1867, 154) and the 'Life' of Virgil with an introduction to the *Eclogues* (ed. J. Brummer, *Vit. Verg.* 1912; C. G. Hardie, O.C.T. 1954) are extant. But the commentary of Servius (q.v.) contains much material derived from it, and the so-called Servius Danielis is claimed to be virtually Donatus (cf. E. K. Rand, *CQ* 1916, 158 ff.). Some of the more learned notes in glossaries (e.g. the *Liber Glossarum*) may also come ultimately from Donatus' commentary. *See also* SCHOLAR-SHIP, LATIN, IN ANTIQUITY.

Schanz–Hosius, § 832.
J. F. M.

**DONATUS (2),** TIBERIUS CLAUDIUS (late 4th c. A.D.), wrote a continuous (but tedious) commentary (*Interpreta-tiones Vergilianae*) in twelve books on the *Aeneid* (ed. H. Georgii, 2 vols., 1905–6), in which he deals with the poet's thought, style, rhetoric, and learning. It has no clear affiliation with earlier or contemporary commenta-tors and is mentioned by no later writer.

Schanz–Hosius, § 248. 3.
J. F. M.

**DORIANS,** the last of the northern invaders into Greece (c. 1100–1000 B.C.), who settled especially in Elis, Laconia, Argos, Corinth, Sicyon, Epidaurus, Megara, and Aegina, and crossed the seas to occupy Crete, Melos, and Thera, and the south coast of Asia Minor. Greek tradition associated the invasion with the return of the Heraclidae and traced the route of invasion from Doris (q.v.) via Delphi (where the priesthood came of Dorian families) to Naupactus, whence the invaders crossed by sea into Peloponnesus. As they spoke a dialect of Greek, it is probable that they were of related stock to the earlier invaders and had previously inhabited the fringes of the Mycenaean world, being at that time already organized in the three tribes commonly found later in Dorian communities, the Hylleis, Dymanes, and Pamphyli. The area whence the invaders came was probably Epirus and south-west Macedonia.

Culturally the Dorian invaders were inferior to the Mycenaeans; bringing little with them except the iron slashing sword and long bronze clothing-pin, they ended Mycenaean civilization, plunging Greece into the Dark Age, out of which the Greek *polis* or city-state emerged. In the Orientalizing and Archaic periods the Dorian element contributed largely to the development of Greek art in architecture, pottery, sculpture, and choral lyric. They possessed a restraint and architectonic power which blended with Ionic grace in Athens to produce the acme of Greek art. Politically the Dorians split into two main channels; at Sicyon, Corinth, Argos, and Aegina the Dorian conquerors gradually lost their monopoly of franchise and became merged in the subject people; but Sparta and Crete retained a peculiar political form, in which the subject-peoples were serfs and dependents, while the franchised Dorians constituted a ruling military class, with a special organization of men's clubs.

V. R. d'A. Desborough and N. G. L. Hammond, 'The end of Mycenaean Civilization and the Dark Age', *CAH*² ii. xxxvi; Hammond, *Epirus*, 370 f. N. G. L. H.

**DORIEUS,** a younger half-brother of the Spartan king Cleomenes I (q.v.). Jealousy and discontent drove him to lead a colonizing expedition to Cinyps on the north African coast (near modern *Tripoli*), whence the Carthaginians expelled him after three years. Returning to Sparta he next founded a settlement in west Sicily near Heraclea Minoa, where, before long, he and most of his followers were killed by the joint forces of Segesta and the Phoenicians. He had previously taken part with Croton in the destruction of Sybaris (510 B.C.).

Dunbabin, *Western Greeks*, 348 ff.; A. Schenk Graf v. Stauffenberg, *Hist.* 1960, 181 ff. A. M. W.; W. G. F.

**DORIS,** a small area in central Greece enclosing the headwaters of the Cephissus. Its small plain, containing the Tetrapolis of Pindus, Erineus, Boeum, and Cytinium, is traversed by the route from Malis to Phocis which turns the defences of Thermopylae and was used by the Persians and Galatians. The Dorians of Peloponnesus, and the Spartans particularly, claimed Doris as their metropolis (Tyrtaeus, fr. 2); possibly during the invasion period a section of Dorian invaders halted there. Represented on the Amphictionic Council, Doris was championed by Sparta (Thuc. 1. 107). In the fourth century it fell into the power of Onomarchus and later of Philip. Fourth-century walls are extant at Cytinium.

P-K, *GL* 1. 2. 657 ff. N. G. L. H.

**DOROTHEUS** of Sidon (1st or beginning of 2nd c. A.D.), an astrological poet who had great vogue with the Arabian astrologers.

Ed. (along with Manetho) H. Koechly (1858); V. Stegemann, *Die Fragmente des D.* (1939–43).

**DOSIADAS,** author of a poem called Βωμός because of its shape, preserved in *Anth. Pal.* 15. 26 and manuscripts of Theocritus, written in mixed metres and purporting to be a dedication by Jason, in extremely obscure, allusive language. The poem is a παίγνιον like the *Syrinx* of Theocritus and seems to come from the same circle and age.

TEXT. Powell, *Coll. Alex.* 175–6 with notes; U. von Wilamowitz-Moellendorff, *Bucolici Graeci*, 152–3.
CRITICISM. Wilamowitz, *De Lycophronis Alexandra* (1884), 12 ff. C. M. B.

**DOSITHEUS** (1) of Pelusium (fl. *c.* 230 B.C.), pupil of the astronomer Conon. He continued a connexion between the Alexandrian astronomers and Archimedes which had begun with the latter's studies in Alexandria; Archimedes dedicated several of his books to Dositheus. Observations by him on the time of appearance of the fixed stars (some of them made at places further north than Alexandria) and on weather-signs are recorded in the *Parapegma* of Geminus and elsewhere. He wrote a work Πρὸς Διόδωρον in which he discussed Aratus' *Phaenomena* and Eudoxus' researches, and a work on the calendar, Περὶ τῆς Εὐδόξου ὀκταετηρίδος. W. D. R.

**DOSITHEUS** (2), surnamed *Magister* (possibly late 4th c. A.D.), grammarian, whose bilingual *Ars grammatica* (ed. Keil, *Gramm. Lat.* vii. 376–436; J. Tolkiehn, 1913) was intended for Greeks who wished to learn Latin. The Latin part was probably based on the *Ars* of Cominianus, and the Greek (now interspersed with the Latin) was originally interlinear. Under Dositheus' name there are also preserved in various forms the remains of a bilingual school-book now known as the *Pseudo-Dositheana Hermeneumata* (ed. G. Goetz, *Corp. Gloss. Lat.* iii). Originally it contained twelve sections: vocabularies, *Hadriani sententiae, fabulae Aesopiae, de manumissionibus, narratio de bello Troiano*, etc. The contents are of various dates (some possibly 3rd c. A.D.) and have value for the light they throw on social life.

Schanz–Hosius, § 836. J. F. M.

**DOSSEN(N)US** (Hor. *Epist.* 2. 1. 173) probably identical with Manducus, the guzzler in *Atellana* (q.v.).

**DOXOGRAPHERS,** designation of those ancient authors who wrote on the doctrines of philosophers.

This type of literature was inaugurated by Aristotle, who used to discuss the views of his predecessors in the introductory chapters of his systematic works. His disciple Theophrastus was the first to write a special work on the subject. He collected the doctrines of the Pre-Socratics in sixteen books (φυσικῶν δόξαι) and arranged them according to topics, the first book dealing with the first principles (περὶ ἀρχῶν), the last (most of which is preserved) with the theory of sense-perception. The works of the Hellenistic authors who wrote on the lives (περὶ βίων) and of those who wrote on the succession of the philosophers (περὶ διαδοχῶν) contained doxographic elements. This is especially true of the history of philosophy ('Επιδρομὴ τῶν φιλοσόφων) of Diocles (q.v. 5) of Magnesia. Some of this material has found its way into the work of Diogenes Laertius.

Arius Didymus, the teacher of Augustus, wrote a summary (ἐπιτομή) of the doctrines of the Stoics. A complete doxography of the philosophy of the pre-Christian era was composed by Aëtius (q.v.).

*Doxographi Graeci* ed. H. Diels (1879); Burnet, *EGP* 33 ff.; Kirk-Raven, *Presocratic Philosophers*², 1 ff. K. VON F.

**DRACO** (Δράκων), according to Athenian tradition, was a lawgiver who introduced new laws in the archonship of Aristaechmus (perhaps 621/20 B.C.). This was the first time that Athenian laws were put down in writing (Arist. *Ath. Pol.* 41. 2). According to one account (Arist. *Ath. Pol.* 4) he established a constitution based on the franchise of hoplites (q.v.), but elsewhere he is only said to have made laws against particular crimes. The penalties were very severe: when asked why he specified death as the penalty for most offences, he replied that small offences deserved death and he knew of no severer penalty for great ones; and the fourth-century orator Demades remarked that Draco wrote his laws in blood instead of ink (Plut. *Sol.* 17). Solon (q.v.) repealed all his laws except those dealing with homicide.

Such was the tradition current in Athens in the fifth and fourth centuries. At that period no one doubted that the homicide laws then in force were due to Draco; this is shown by references in Attic speeches, and also by an inscription of 409/8 which contains part of the current law and describes it as 'the law of Draco about homicide' (*IG* i². 115).

Modern scholars have treated the tradition with varying degrees of scepticism. Some have doubted whether Draco existed at all. The hoplite constitution is generally regarded as spurious (being perhaps an invention of fifth-century oligarchic propagandists), but many accept that Draco introduced laws about homicide and other offences. Details of his laws cannot now be known; it cannot be assumed that the homicide laws current in the fifth and fourth centuries had remained unaltered since his time.

Hignett, *Hist. Athen. Const.* 305 ff. D. M. M.

**DRACON** of Stratonicea, in Caria, predecessor or contemporary of Dionysius Thrax; author of a number of works on grammar, metric, and particular lyric poets (Sappho, Alcaeus, and Pindar), cited in the *Suda*. The extant Περὶ μέτρων ποιητικῶν ascribed to him (ed. G. Hermann, 1812) has been shown to be a sixteenth-century forgery.

J. D. D.

**DRACONTIUS**, BLOSSIUS AEMILIUS, a Christian, a lawyer and *vir clarissimus*, well trained in rhetoric, lived in Carthage towards the end of the fifth century A.D. For eulogizing in verse the Roman Emperor he was imprisoned by Gunthamund, the Vandal king, but subsequently released. His secular works, marked by unrestrained rhetoric, consist of a collection of short hexameter poems entitled *Romulea*, including rhetorical exercises, epithalamia, and mythological epyllia (*Hylas*, *De Raptu Helenae*, *Medea*); the anonymous *Orestis Tragoedia*, now proved Dracontian, probably belongs to this collection. The Christian poems, written in prison, comprise (a) a short elegiac poem of repentance addressed to the king (*Satisfactio*), (b) *De Laudibus Dei* in three books of hexameters; this, his chief work, shows some poetic imagination, appeals by its personal interest, but is marked by digressions, repetitions, and lack of unity. Dracontius displays a considerable knowledge both of Scripture and of classical Roman literature. Though he is well versed in the poetic diction, exhibiting numerous echoes of the classical poets, his language is often harsh and obscure, the syntax audacious, and the prosody faulty. That the anonymous *Aegritudo Perdicae* is Dracontian cannot be proved.

EDITIONS. F. Vollmer, *MGH* xiv (1905), *PLM* v⁴ (1914). Introd., text, trans., and commentary of (1) *Satisfactio*, by Sister M. St. Margaret (U.S.A. 1936); (2) *De Laudibus Dei*, by J. F. Irwin (U.S.A. 1942). Teuffel, *Gesch. d. römisch. Lit.* (1913–20) iii⁶. 466 ff.; Schanz–Hosius, iv. 2. 58 ff.; F. J. E. Raby, *Christian Latin Poetry* (1953), and *Secular Latin Poetry* (1957: with bibliography); D. Romano, *Studi Draconziani* (1959). A. H.-W.; F. J. E. R.

**DRAMA, ROMAN.** HISTORY: see the articles on LIVIUS ANDRONICUS, NAEVIUS, PLAUTUS, ENNIUS, PACUVIUS,

ACCIUS, CAECILIUS, TERENCE, TRABEA, ATILIUS, AQUIL(L)IUS (1), TURPILIUS, TOGATA FABULA, TITINIUS, AFRANIUS, ATTA, ATELLANA FABULA, MIMUS, VARIUS RUFUS, ASINIUS POLLIO, SENECA (2).

2. THEATRE AND STAGE: Rome's first stone-built theatre was constructed in 55 B.C. by Pompey, it seated perhaps 9,000 (though Pliny says 40,000). A previous attempt, actually started in 155 B.C., was frustrated by the consul P. Scipio Nasica, reportedly on moral grounds. Previously the stage had been wooden and the seating temporary—that there was seating is proved by the decree allocating the front rows to senators, in 195 B.C. (Livy 34. 54. 3). The stage had three doorways, and at either end an open passage led into the projecting wing. The doors never seem to have been used to reveal action within to the spectators; all action took place outside (hence the fixed convention of speaking back into the house to set the circumstances of the action, e.g. opening of *Miles*), and a complicated scene like *Most.* iii. 2 (690–857) will have taxed the producer's ingenuity considerably. By convention, entrance or exit right was to or from the centre of the town (the market-place), and left was to or from the harbour or country. The word *angiportus* seems to have been a relative term for a street leading from a longer street (so it could be side-street, lane, or alley-way). Occasionally characters take concealment in the *angiportus* or make their escape by it; in this sense it seems to have been a notional alley-way between the stage-houses, not actually represented on the stage, but again notionally reached through one or other of the doors or exits. Much of the action, like this, took place by agreed conventions, so that, e.g., a character in concealment and eavesdropping on a speech or dialogue did not need to be really in hiding but simply standing at the back of the stage. Actors wore costumes and masks so that gestures became very important, and were a series of conventional signs of their own.

This is a very brief summary of a highly complex and controversial subject: for details and for later developments the following works should be consulted: G. E. Duckworth, *The Nature of Roman Comedy* (1952), 79 ff.; M. Bieber, *The History of the Greek and Roman Theater*² (1961); W. Beare, *The Roman Stage*³ (1964), 159 ff. and appendices. G. W. W.

**DRESS.** There are three striking points of difference between ancient and modern dress. Firstly, in both Greece and Rome women's dress in outward appearance was very similar to men's, and a Greek wife could, and often did, wear her husband's cloak out of doors. Secondly, there was very little fashionable alteration in the garments worn by both sexes, and none of our present-day bewildering changes in the body contour. Thirdly, wearing apparel was usually home-made and the same piece of homespun cloth could serve as a garment, a blanket, or a shroud.

2. The two garments worn in Greece by men and women alike were the tunic (χιτών) and the cloak (ἱμάτιον). The tunic had two main varieties, the Ionic made of linen, the Doric usually made of wool. The Doric tunic of women, often called a peplos (πέπλος), was in Athens the earlier kind of women's dress. It was simply a rectangle of cloth, in length rather more than the wearer's height, in breadth about twice the span of her arms. It was sometimes decorated with elaborate figured patterns (*see also* WEAVING). Before wearing, it was first folded along the upper edge so that the overlap would reach to the waist. It was then placed around the body, and fastened on the shoulders—in earlier times, at least, with large pins. It was sleeveless. As the tunic hung from the shoulders, openings for arm-holes were left on each side; the lengthier opening along the one side could be sewn up, or pinned. The peplos might or might not be secured at the waist with a girdle. The Ionic tunic of women was of

much lighter stuff. It was a long and very wide cylinder, sewn up at the sides, and was usually worn with a girdle. The upper edges were often caught at short intervals along the arm with brooches, or by stitches, to form long, full sleeves. Under either type of tunic women might wear the στρόφιον, a soft band around the body, below the breasts. In early times men customarily wore the long Ionic χιτών. Later they adopted (except for ceremonial and religious occasions) a Doric χιτών, similar to that of the women, but of knee-length or even shorter. It was pinned on the shoulders; for active exercise or for hard work it took the form of the ἐξωμίς, fastened on the left shoulder only, with the right arm left free. The cloak ἱμάτιον) of both men and women, for outdoor wear, was essentially a rectangular piece of stuff, woollen or linen. It could be draped according to individual taste, sometimes in very elaborate folds, but it was usually drawn away from one shoulder. Young men often wore a short flowing cape-like cloak (χλαμύς) for riding (see also EPHEBOI).

3. Roman women customarily wore an under-tunic —tunica interior—a short shirt-like garment, with or without sleeves. With it could be worn a strophium or mamillare, a soft leather band beneath the breasts. Over the tunic the unmarried woman wore the girded tunica exterior, reaching to the floor. A married woman wore instead the stola, a long, full garment, half covering the feet when the stola was girded up into folds under the breast. There was a coloured border around the neck of the stola, and around the lower edge of the garment there was an instita, which may also have been a coloured border. Usually the stola, like the Greek Ionic χιτών, had sleeves formed by means of fastenings at intervals along the arms. Both matrons and unmarried women made use of the palla, a rectangular piece of stuff like the Greek ἱμάτιον, worn only out of doors, and draped as the wearer wished. The men of Rome wore a tunica resembling the Greek χιτών, and an outer garment, the toga (q.v.), which they probably adopted from the Etruscans, but which became the distinctive badge of Roman citizenship.

4. At first the toga was worn alone next to the skin, but later one or more tunics underneath became usual— Augustus in cold weather wore four—and at all times the tunic was the usual indoor dress. The tunic of a senator had a broad purple stripe, latus clavus (q.v.), running from each shoulder to the hem, front and rear; that of the knight had two narrow stripes, angustus clavus (q.v.). There were, however, other garments worn on special occasions. The synthesis was a light brightly coloured garment especially suited for banquets; the lacerna an open mantle, fastened by a brooch on the shoulder, used in cold weather; the paenula, a sleeveless cloak, with a hole for the neck and a hood attached, used especially by travellers.

5. The Greeks had a broad-brimmed hat (πέτασος) for men, and a flat-brimmed one with high peaked crown for women, but seldom wore them; the conical cap (πῖλος) of workmen, sailors, and travellers seems to have had a wider use. They had sandals, slippers, soft shoes, and boots; of the latter, one type (κρηπῖδες) was worn by soldiers. At home the Greeks often went barefoot. Roman coverings for both head and feet were much like those of the Greeks. They had two special kinds of boot, the caliga, a heavy marching boot for soldiers, laced on the instep and secured by thongs, and the calceus, made in the case of senators of red leather with an ivory crescent and with thongs wound round the legs and tied in front.

A. J. B. Wace and Lady Evans in Cambridge Comp. Gr. Stud.⁴ (1931); L. M. Wilson, The Clothing of the Ancient Romans (1938); Lady Evans and E. B. Abrahams, Ancient Greek Dress (1964).
F. A. W.; L. B. L.

**DRUSILLA,** JULIA (PW 567) (born probably in A.D. 16), the second daughter of Germanicus and Agrippina. She was married to L. Cassius Longinus (cos. A.D. 30) and afterwards to M. Aemilius Lepidus the son of either Paullus (q.v. 5) or Lepidus (q.v. 5). Her name, like her sisters', was compulsorily included in vows and oaths after the accession of her brother Gaius. She was his favourite sister, and it was rumoured that their relations were incestuous. She was named as Gaius' heir during his illness (late 37), but died in 38. Public mourning was enforced throughout the Empire and, though there was no precedent in Roman history for the consecration of a woman, she was consecrated as Panthea, probably on the anniversary of Augustus' birthday.                J. P. B.

**DRUSUS** (1), MARCUS LIVIUS (PW 17), probably a descendant of Paullus (q.v. 1) and Salinator, as tribune (122 B.C.) combined with the consul Fannius (q.v.) in exploiting the People's reluctance to extend the citizenship as a weapon against C. Gracchus (q.v. 4). He proposed the establishment—never carried out—of large citizen colonies and the exemption of Latins from corporal punishment, and brought about Gracchus' defeat in the tribunician elections. Consul (112) and proconsul, he fought in Macedonia, triumphing in 110. Elected censor (109) with Scaurus (q.v. 1), he died in office, whereupon Scaurus was forced to abdicate.

H. C. Boren, CJ 1956, 27.                E. B.

**DRUSUS** (2), MARCUS LIVIUS (PW 18), son of (1), grandfather of Livia (q.v.) and for a time brother-in-law and friend of Caepio (q.v. 2). Eldest of a circle of ambitious young nobles around L. Crassus (q.v. 3), to whom he owed his oratorical training and some of his ideas, he was brilliant, hard-working, and arrogant. Having been quaestor and aedile, he became tribune (91 B.C.) after the conviction of his uncle Rutilius (q.v. 1), and, with the help of Crassus and Scaurus (q.v. 1), proposed a solution for all the major political problems: 300 equites were to be raised to the Senate (where their influence would be minimal) and criminal juries chosen from the enlarged Senate; colonies and land distributions were to provide for the poor; and the Italians were to be enfranchised. The ruling oligarchy was intended to get the credit and reap the political benefit, and the equites (in particular) were to be eliminated as a political force. Extreme oligarchs and factional enemies (led by Marcius Philippus (q.v. 4)), equites led by Caepio (with whom he had quarrelled), Italians unwilling to give up ager publicus as the price of citizenship, and probably Marius, whose political future was threatened, combined against him. After Crassus' death Philippus gained the upper hand and had the laws already passed invalidated. Drusus himself was assassinated. The commission of Varius (q.v. 1) and the Social War were the immediate consequences.

E. Badian, Hist. 1962, 225 (with recent bibliography).        E. B.

**DRUSUS** (3), NERO CLAUDIUS (PW 139), second son of Ti. Claudius Nero (q.v. 3) and Livia (q.v.), was born in 38 B.C. about the time of her marriage to Octavian. His praenomen was originally Decimus. After Nero's death in 33 he was brought up by Octavian. In 19 he was permitted to stand for magistracies five years before the legal minimum ages, and in 18 he was quaestor. In 15 with Tiberius he subdued the Raeti and Vindelici (see RAETIA). In 13 he was left in charge of the Three Gauls by Augustus: he organized a census and on 1 Aug. 12 dedicated an altar to Rome and Augustus at Lugdunum (q.v. 1). Augustus apparently considered him his best general, since he entrusted the invasion of Germany to him. Drusus applied himself to the task in four successive campaigns (12–9). He used as his chief base first Vetera, then Mogontiacum (qq.vv.); he also built a number of auxiliary forts beyond the Rhine. In 12, after routing the Sugambri, he sailed from the Lower Rhine, along a canal dug for the purpose (*fossa Drusiana*), through the lakes of Holland into the North Sea, won over the Frisii (q.v.), took Borkum, defeated the Bructeri (q.v.) in a naval encounter on the Ems, and invaded the country of the Chauci (q.v.), where his ships were stranded by the ebb-tide; with Frisian help he got away safely. He began the year 11 in Rome as urban praetor, then subdued the Usipetes, and after bridging the Lippe marched through Sugambrian territory into that of the Cherusci (q.v.), as far as the Weser. After celebrating an *ovatio* (q.v.) in Rome he renewed the war in 10 with the title of proconsul, attacking the Chatti (q.v.); and returned to Rome with Augustus and Tiberius. In 9 as consul he fought the Chatti, Suebi, Marcomanni (qq.v.), and Cherusci, and reached the Elbe; but died in summer camp after illness brought on by a fall from his horse. Tiberius, hastening from Ticinum, reached him before his death.

Drusus' expeditions had been extremely audacious, and the Senate bestowed on him and his descendants the surname of Germanicus: but his military achievements were more apparent than real. He was popular, and considered to hold Republican sentiments. He was buried in the mausoleum of Augustus; a cenotaph was also built at Mogontiacum. An unknown poet wrote for his mother the *Consolatio ad Liviam* (q.v.). He married Antonia (q.v. 3); their children were Germanicus, Livilla, and Claudius.

L. Schmidt, *Gesch. d. deutschen Stämme* i² (1938), 93 ff.; K. Christ, *Drusus und Germanicus* (1956). On the circumstances of his birth, *PIR*² C 857. Iconography. L. Fabbrini, *Bolletino d'Arte* 1964, 304 ff.
A. M.; T. J. C.

**DRUSUS** (4) JULIUS (*PW* 136) CAESAR (*c.* 13 B.C.–A.D. 23), the son of Tiberius (later Emperor) and Vipsania. He married Claudia Livia (Livilla), sister of Germanicus. He was successful in suppressing the mutiny of the Pannonian legions after Augustus' death, was consul in A.D. 15, and commanded in Illyricum A.D. 17–20, celebrating a triumph on his return to Rome. He was consul again in 21, was given the *tribunicia potestas*—and therefore indicated as Tiberius' prospective successor—in 22, but died in the next year, poisoned—it was later suspected —by his wife, who had been seduced by Sejanus. He was popular, though dissolute and cruel, and his relations with Germanicus (q.v.) were friendly, in spite of mischief-makers. His son Tiberius Gemellus was put to death by the Emperor Gaius; his last-known male descendant (through his daughter Julia) was Rubellius Plautus, who was murdered by Nero's orders in 62. J. P. B.

**DRUSUS** (5) JULIUS (*PW* 137) CAESAR (A.D. 7–33), as second of the surviving sons of Germanicus and Agrippina, was regarded, after the deaths of his father in 19 and of Drusus, son of Tiberius, in 23, as a likely successor to Tiberius after his elder brother Nero. Sejanus secured his arrest in 30 (a year after Agrippina and Nero were arrested), and he died, imprisoned in the palace, in 33.
J. P. B.

**DRYOPE**, in mythology, daughter of Dryops (q.v.). Apollo possessed her by a trick and she had by him a son, Amphissus, who became king of the city so called. Her mortal husband was Andraemon, son of Oxylus. The nymphs, who had long been her playfellows, finally carried her off and made a spring and a poplar appear where she had been; she became the nymph of the spring, and her son built a sanctuary for the nymphs. So far Nicander in Ant. Lib. 32. Ovid, *Met.* 9. 330 ff., says that while suckling Amphissus she wanted flowers for him to play with and by mishap plucked lotus-flowers, which were the nymph Lotis transformed. The plant

trembled and bled, and when Dryope tried to run away she turned into a lotus-tree. H. J. R

**DRYOPS**, eponym of the Dryopes; his parentage is variously given, and the history of his people, allegedly Pelasgian, i.e. pre-Hellenic, obscure, but they are stated to have emigrated widely (from the Spercheius valley to Parnassus, the Argolid, Arcadia, etc.); hence perhaps the differing stories which make him the son of gods or men belonging to several of these regions. Cf. DRYOPE.

Weizsäcker in Roscher's *Lexikon*, s.v.; J. E. Fontenrose, *Python* (U.S.A. 1959). H. J. R

**DUCENARII.** Augustus, probably in A.D. 4 (Dio 55, 13), added to the three existing *decuriae*, or jury panels, all filled by members of the equestrian order, a fourth decury from the *ducenarii*, i.e. citizens resident in Italy who had a census rating of 200,000 HS or more, half the property qualification of the *equites*. To the new decury he entrusted cases of minor importance (Suet. *Aug.* 32). Caligula added a fifth decury (Suet. *Gai.* 16).

In the Principate the equestrian officials of the imperial service came to be graded in categories as *sexagenarii*, *centenarii*, *ducenarii*, and later *trecenarii*. These grades referred to their salaries of 60,000, 100,000, 200,000, and 300,000 sesterces respectively. *See* PROCURATOR.

In the Late Empire *ducenarius* remained a grade of the equestrian order, the ranks being now *egregii*, *centenarii*, *ducenarii*, *perfectissimi*, and finally *eminentissimi*, the praetorian prefects. Rank was not confined to holders of office: their ranks and privileges were retained by past holders, and honorary grants became increasingly common. The result was that with inflation of the numbers of rank-holders the prestige of the ranks diminished. The *egregiatus*, the lowest grade, was most affected, and it may be significant that it is last recorded in 324. The perfectissimate was divided into three grades.

While the former army ranks continued to be used in units whose traditions went back to the Principate, in the new formations of the field-army new ranks were adopted. The non-commissioned officers were, in ascending order, *circitor*, *biarchus*, *centenarius*, *ducenarius*, *senator*, *primicerius*. Payment was now mainly in units of rations (*annonae*), of which the *centenarius* received 2½ and the *ducenarius* 3½. The *centenarius* is stated by Vegetius (ii. 8) to have been named from the number of men under his command.

Military ranks were adopted by the civil service of the Late Empire, which prided itself on being a *militia*. The majority of the ranks employed were survivals from the army of the Principate, but the new series of grades in the field-army, including *ducenarius*, was used also, e.g. by the *agentes in rebus*, the imperial couriers.

H. G. Pflaum, *Les Procurateurs équestres sous le haut-empire romain* (1950); *Les Carrières procuratoriennes équestres sous le haut-empire romain* (1960–1); A. H. M. Jones, 'The Elections under Augustus', *JRS* 1955, 15 f. (*Studies in Roman Government and Law*, 40 ff.); *Later Rom. Emp.* 8; 525 f.; 530; 578; 583 f.; 599; 634. G. R. W

**DUCETIUS**, a Hellenized Sicel who for a brief period welded the native communities of eastern Sicily into a formidable union, aiming with a Sicel federation to conquer the Siceliot Greeks. He helped the Syracusans to overthrow their ex-tyrants' mercenaries (461 B.C.), and established a capital at Menaenum near Caltagirone (*c.* 454), later moving to Palice. He captured Inessa and Morgantina (q.v.), and later defeated a Syracusan-Acragantine force; a dedication at Olympia (*SEG* xv. 252) perhaps commemorates his victory. Next year the tables were decisively turned. Ducetius appeared alone at Syracuse as a suppliant, was spared and sent in exile to Corinth. In 446 he returned as founder of Cale Acte,

perhaps under Syracusan auspices. His intentions thereafter remain obscure, and were in any case frustrated by
his death *c.* 440. With him died all real hope of a permanently strong native power in Sicily.

Diod. Sic. bks. 11–12. A. G. Woodhead, *The Greeks in the West*
1962), 82 f.; D. Adamesteanu, Κώκαλος 1962, 167 ff.          A. G. W.

**DUILIUS** (*PW* 3), GAIUS, consul (260 B.C.), censor (258),
and dictator to hold elections (231). As commander of
Rome's newly created fleet Duilius liberated Segesta and
defeated the Carthaginian fleet off Mylae in Sicily,
thanks largely to the adoption of the *corvus* (260). He
celebrated the first naval triumph. In the Forum a column
(*columna rostrata*) was erected, ornamented with the
bronze beaks (*rostra*) of the captured vessels with a laudatory inscription, of which a copy (or restoration) of
imperial times exists (*ILS* i. 65. A. Degrassi, *Inscr. Ital.*
13. 3. 69, *ILLRP*, n. 319. Cf. a briefer elogium, *ILS* 55,
*Inscr. Ital.* 13. 3. 13). Duilius was escorted through Rome
by night with torches and music, a Greek rather than
Roman honour. From the booty of Mylae he built a
temple to Janus in the Forum Holitorium.          H. H. S.

**DUMNONII,** a tribe in south-west Britain (Devon,
Cornwall, part of Somerset), apparently formed from
diverse Iron Age groups. After an initial military occupation a self-governing *civitas* was created in Flavian
times with *caput* at Isca (q.v., *Exeter*) (*It. Ant.* 486, 8 and
17, *Rav. Cosm.* 16). Villas are few and Romanization
concentrated in Isca. The population was perhaps mainly
cattle-raising, but from the mid third century the tin of
Cornwall, famous in pre-Roman times, was re-exploited;
and milestones attest road construction from Gordian III
down to Constantine. Two inscriptions (Collingwood and
Wright, *RIB* 1843–4) attest work on Hadrian's Wall by
a *corvée* of the Dumnonii. In the post-Roman period
Celtic Christianity and independence were long maintained under the princes of Dumnonia.

H. O'N. Hencken, *Archaeology of Cornwall and Scilly* (1932),
chs. 4–7; A. Fox, *Roman Exeter* (1952); A. L. F. Rivet, *Town and
Country in Rom. Brit.²* (1964), 153 ff.; A. Fox, *South West England*
1964), chs. vii–ix.          S. S. F.

**DUMNORIX,** brother of Divitiacus (q.v. 1) and leader
of the anti-Roman party among the Aedui. He conspired
in 61 B.C. with Orgetorix, the Helvetian. He acted against
Caesar, who only spared him at Divitiacus' request.
Ordered in 54 to accompany Caesar to Britain, he refused
but was cut down in attempting to escape.

Caesar, *BGall.* 1. 3. 9; 18–20; 5. 6–7.          C. E. S.

**DUOVIRI NAVALES.** First chosen by the Roman
people in 311 B.C., after the annexation of Campania
Livy 9. 30. 4), the *duoviri navales* 'for repairing and
equipping the fleet' were thereafter elected or appointed,
apparently at irregular intervals as need arose, until *c.*
50 B.C. This post was created for the defence of the
Italian coasts; it played no part in Rome's great wars, for
the ordinary squadron of a *duovir navalis* comprised only
ten warships (Livy 40. 18. 7–8).

J. H. Thiel, *Roman Sea-power before the Second Punic War* (1954),
ff.          C. G. S.

**DURIS** (1), potter and vase painter in Athens, working
510–465 B.C. Known from two potter's and thirty-eight
painter's signatures. Painted red-figure cups, etc.,
including ὅπλων κρίσις (Vienna), Eos and Memnon
Paris). A fine but slightly mannered artist, who continues
into the early classical period.

Beazley, *ARV²* 425.          T. B. L. W.

**DURIS** (2) (*c.* 340–*c.* 260 B.C.), son of Scaeus (Paus. 6.
13. 5), tyrant of Samos, historian and critic, a pupil of
Theophrastus.

WORKS: (1) Various writings on literature, music, and
painting, anecdotal in character. (2) *Samian Chronicle*,
two books mentioned. (3) *Histories* ('Ιστορίαι or Μακεδονικά
(Ath.); Ἑλληνικά (Diog. Laert.)): at least twenty-three
books, becoming increasingly fuller, and covering from
370 to *c.* 280. (4) *History of Agathocles*: four books cited
(excerpts, Diod. Sic. books 19–21). Duris' historical influence was small: careless of style, he aimed at sensationalism and emotional impact.

*FGrH* ii A 76. K. von Fritz, *Entretiens Hardt* iv, 85 ff.; F. W.
Walbank, *Hist.* 1960, 216 ff.; L. Ferrero, *Miscellanea di studi alessandrini . . . . A. Rostagni* (1963), 68 ff.          F. W. W.

**DUROTRIGES,** a British tribe in Dorset and surrounding areas, whose pre-Roman coinage suggests a
Belgic aristocracy ruling an indigenous population with
close contacts with Armorica. The tribe offered heavy
resistance to the Roman advance by Legio II Augusta
commanded by Vespasian, and much of its territory may
have become an imperial estate. The *caput* of the *civitas*
was probably Durnovaria (*Dorchester*), but later the
area was divided, the *Durotriges Lindinienses* being
centred on *Ilchester* (Lindinis). *RIB* 1672–3 record work
by a *corvée* of the latter on Hadrian's Wall. The *civitas*
was largely agricultural but important stone quarries were
exploited at Ham Hill. Christian mosaics are known from
the villas at Frampton and Hinton St. Mary.

D. F. Allen in *Iron Age in S. Britain* 97 ff. (coins); R. E. M.
Wheeler, *Maiden Castle* (1943); I. A. Richmond and J. W. Brailsford,
*Hod Hill* (1968); C. F. C. Hawkes, *Arch. Journ.* 1947, 27 ff.; C. E.
Stevens, *Proc. Somerset Nat. Hist. and Arch. Soc.* 1952, 188; J. M. C.
Toynbee, *JRS* 1964, 1 ff. (Hinton).          S. S. F.

**DUX,** a title sometimes given during the third century
A.D. to an officer performing duties above his rank (e.g.
*primipili* as *duces legionum*). With the separation of civil
and military authority which was begun by Diocletian,
the military command of some frontier zones was given
to equestrian *duces*. This reform was probably completed
by Constantine: henceforth military and civil command
were only occasionally united. Under Valentinian I the
*duces* were regularly given senatorial status.

R. Grosse, *Römische Militärgeschichte*, 8 ff.; 152 ff.: Jones, *Later
Rom. Emp.* 44, 144, 608 ff.          H. M. D. P.; G. R. W.

**DYEING,** like fulling (q.v.), with which it was sometimes combined, was commercially practised throughout
antiquity. Dyestuffs (φάρμακα, *medicamina*), among which
purple (q.v.) always ranked highest, were derived either
from vegetable substances, such as madder-root, whortle-
berry, saffron, reseda, and gall-nuts, or from insects or
molluscs (e.g. cochineal and purple). Textiles were
usually dyed before spinning; and the main 'immersion'
in the vat (from which dyeing was called βάπτειν, *tinguere*)
was normally preceded by washing with detergents and
often also by steeping in a mordant solution (πρόστυμμα)
to produce bright, even, and fast colours. There were
guilds of dyers both in Ptolemaic Egypt and in Rome
(*infectores*), where in imperial times dyeing became a
luxury trade. Quotations from Hellenistic textbooks
(βαφικά) survive in Pliny, *HN* 9. 136–8, and in 'chemical'
papyri.

H. Blümner, *Technologie der Gewerbe und Künste* i² (1912), 225 ff.;
Forbes, *Stud. Anc. Technol.* iv. 99 ff. (with full bibliography); J. I.
Miller, *The Spice Trade of the Roman Empire* (1969).          L. A. M.

**DYRRHACHIUM** (modern *Durazzo*), originally the
name of the headland under which the city of Epidamnus
was situated, became the name of the town itself *c.* 300
B.C. (it first appears on coins of the 5th c.). The city

passed successively through the hands of Cassander and Pyrrhus. In 229 it was besieged by the Illyrians, but was delivered and occupied by a Roman force. It served, together with Apollonia (q.v.), as a base for the Roman armies in Greece and the Balkan lands, and in 148 became the terminal point of the northern fork of the Via Egnatia (q.v.). In 48 Pompey made Dyrrhachium into his main base on the Adriatic, and he beat off an attack by Caesar

on his entrenched camp nearby (Caesar, *BCiv.* 3. 41–72). After the battle of Actium Octavian drafted evicted partisans of Antony from Italy to Dyrrhachium. (*See also* EPIDAMNUS.)

R. L. Beaumont, *JHS* 1936, 166 ff.; articles in *Buletin për shkencat shoqërore* 1957. 1; *Buletin i Universitetit Shtetëror të Tiranès, Seria shkencat shoqërore* 1958, 4; 1959, 2; 1962, 2; and *Studia Albanica* 1966, 1.,                                                                                    M. C.

# E

**EBURACUM** ('Εβόρακον, Ptol. *Geogr.* 2. 3. 10; 8. 3. 7; Eboraci, *Cod. Iustinian.* 3. 32. 1; S.H.A. *Severus* 19, etc.; *JRS* 1921, 102; *CIL* vii. 248; Eburacum, *It. Ant.* 466. 1, etc.; *Eboracen(sis)*, Collingwood–Wright, *RIB* 674; *Ebur(acensis)*, *RIB* 648), modern *York* on the Ouse. Here, on the east river-bank, lay the fortress of Legio IX Hispana, founded during the campaigns of Cerialis in A.D. 71–4, and rebuilt by Agricola *c.* 79 and under Trajan in 108 (*RIB* 665). In 122 Legio VI Victrix replaced the Ninth. The fortress wall was partly rebuilt late in the second century and again more thoroughly after Pictish invasions a century later. It was the seat of the northern command and capital of Lower Britain (*CIL* xiii. 3162); Severus and Constantius I died there. The *canabae* lay east of the Ouse; the mercantile settlement west of the river became a *colonia* before 237, with trade connexions extending to Bordeaux (*RIB* 674, 678; *JRS* 1921, 102), and a bishopric before A.D. 314.

S. N. Miller, *JRS* 1925, 176 ff.; 1928, 61 ff.; S. Wellbeloved, *Eburacum* (1842); I. A. Richmond, *Arch. Journ.* 1946, 74 ff.; *R. Com. Hist. Mon.* York, vol. i, *Eboracum* (1962).                I. A. R.

**ECBATANA** (*Agbatana*, OP *Hangmatana*, modern *Hamadan*) in northern Media, on the Iranian plateau. Traditionally founded by Deioces (Hdt. 1. 98) as the capital city of the Median Empire, it became the summer capital of the Achaemenid Empire, and like Susa and Babylon a royal residence (Strabo 11. 522–4; Xen. *Cyr.* 8. 6. 22). Alexander captured Ecbatana in 330 B.C. and plundered a vast sum from the treasury (Strabo 15. 731). It remained a royal residence in Parthian times. The site has not yet been systematically excavated; the palace and fortifications are described by Herodotus (1. 98), by Polybius (10. 27. 6 ff.), and others.

*A Guide to Hamadan* (Tehran, 1954).                M. S. D.

**ECHECRATES** of Phlius (fl. *c.* 367 B.C.), pupil of Archytas and Eurytus, was one of the last members of the Pythagorean school, and survived to the time of Aristoxenus. In Plato's *Phaedo*, Phaedo recites to Echecrates, apparently in the Pythagorean συνέδριον at Phlius, the account of Socrates' last discourses and death. Plato is said to have visited Echecrates at Locri.

Testimonia in Diels, *Vorsokr.*¹¹ i. 443.                W. D. R.

**ECHIDNA**, i.e. 'Snake' in mythology, a monster, child either of Phorcys and Ceto or of Chrysaor and Callirhoë daughter of Oceanus (Hesiod, *Theog.* 295 ff., where it is not clear which parents are meant). She was half-woman, half-serpent, mated with Typhon (q.v.), and bore Orthus (Geryon's hound), Cerberus, and the Hydra (*see* HERACLES), the Chimaera (q.v.), and, by Orthus, the Sphinx and the Nemean lion.                H. J. R.

**ECHION** ('Εχίων, 'snake-man'), (1) one of the surviving Sparti, *see* CADMUS; he married Agave and begat

Pentheus (q.v.). (2) Son of Hermes and Antianeira, daughter of Menetus. He and his twin brother Erytus joined the Argonauts (q.v.; Ap. Rhod. 1. 51 ff.). Their home was Pangaeon (Pind. *Pyth.* 4. 180) or Alope (Apollonius). They joined the Calydonian boar-hunt (Ov. *Met.* 8. 311).                H. J. R.

**ECHO** ('Ηχώ). There are two mythological explanations of echoes, neither very early. (*a*) Echo was a nymph vainly loved by Pan, who finally sent the shepherds mad and they tore her in pieces; but Earth hid the fragments which still can sing and imitate other sounds (Longus 3. 23). (*b*) *See* NARCISSUS (1).                H. J. R.

**ECLECTICISM,** a type of approach to philosophy which consists in the selection and amalgamation of elements from different systems of thought. Eclecticism in the full sense first began in the second century B.C. coinciding with a general decline in the originality of Greek thought. The traditional opposition between the major schools of philosophy tended to give way to a recognition of the real similarities between them; the Academic Antiochus of Ascalon, for example, held that the doctrines of the Old Academy, the Peripatos, and the Stoa were in essence indistinguishable. Panaetius and Posidonius incorporate elements of both Platonism and Aristotelianism into Stoic teaching; and Cicero and Seneca follow a similar trend, in abstracting ideas from various different Greek philosophers and attempting to fit them to the Roman context. But the prime example of systematic eclecticism are the Neoplatonists, in whose works the doctrines of Platonism, Aristotelianism, and other earlier systems meet to form a new unity.

E. Zeller, *A History of Eclecticism in Greek Philosophy* (Engl. Transl. 1883).                C. J. R.

**ECLOGA** (ἐκλογή), originally a selection, and so sometimes a fine passage from a work (Varro ap. Charisius 120. 28 K.: cf. Cicero's *eclogarii*, *Att.* 16. 2. 6; equivalent to his ἄνθη, ibid. 11. 1). *Eclogae* is common in the wider sense of *brevia poemata* (schol. Cruq. Hor. *Sat.* 2. 1); Suetonius (*Vit. Hor.*) calls Hor. *Epist.* 2. 1 an *ecloga*, and grammarians gave the name to the *Epodes.* Pliny, *Ep.* 4. 14. 9, thinks it suitable for his own sportive hendecasyllabics; Statius (*Silv.* prefaces to books 3 and 4) calls some of his *Silvae* by the term, and Ausonius his poem *Cupido cruci adfixus.* Its most famous application is to Virgil's *Bucolics.* It may not be Virgil's own title, though it has some MS. authority, and Suetonius seems to know it when recording certain *Antibucolica* (*Vit. Verg.*). Applied to the pastorals of Calpurnius and Nemesianus (*see* PASTORAL POETRY, LATIN), it was perpetuated in Carolingian and Renaissance usage.                J. W. D.

**ECPHANTIDES,** Athenian comic poet and contemporary of Cratinus (q.v.), won four victories at the City

Dionysia (*IG* ii². 2325. 49), but we have only two titles and five fragments.

*FCG* i. 12 ff.; *CAF* i. 9 ff.; *FAC* i. 12 ff.   K. J. D.

**ECPHANTUS**, a Pythagorean from Syracuse (or Croton; Iamblichus, *VP* 267), taught that the world is spherical and consists of monads moved by ψυχή or νοῦς and directed by πρόνοια. A treatise *On Kingship* is falsely attributed to him; it regards the king mystically as a mirror of god and essential part of a divinely ordered society. This work has been variously dated between the early Hellenistic period and the second century A.D.; but neither content nor analysis of syntax and vocabulary furnishes a decisive criterion.

*Vorsokr.*⁶ i. 442 ff. Stobaeus, iv. 244–5, 271–9 W–H (περὶ βασιλείας); cd. L. Delatte, *Les Traités de la royauté d'Ecphante, Diotogène et Sthénidas* (1942); E. R. Goodenough, 'The political philosophy of Hellenistic kingship' *YClS* 1928, 55 ff.; Tarn, *Alexander* ii. 409 ff.
G. T. G.

**ECSTASY** (ἔκστασις). In classical and good Hellenistic Greek this word and the corresponding parts of ἐξίστημι describe either a pathological condition, madness or unconsciousness, or, colloquially, the state of being beside one's self' with anger, etc. (LSJ, s.vv.); Aristotle, *Mem.* 451ᵃ9, is a very dubious contrary instance. Later they signify a trance-state in which the soul, quitting the body, sees visions, as Acts x. 10; xxii. 17 (SS. Peter and Paul respectively have symbolic revelations). A state of this sort is clearly meant to be induced by the ritual of *PGM* iv. 475 ff.; cf. Dieterich, *Mithrasliturgie*², 2 ff. (the magician mounts up to heaven). The loftiest application of the word is to the Neoplatonic union with deity, Plotinus, *Enn.* 6. 9. 11. Contrast ἐνθουσιασμός, in which the subject's body is possessed by a god. See further Hopfner, *Offenbarungszauber* ii, pars. 79 ff.; 102, and Fr. Pfister, *Pisciculi Franz Joseph Dölger dargebracht* (1939), 178 ff.; the word is characteristic of transcendental sects and philosophies.   H. J. R.

**EDESSA** (modern *Urfa*, from the native *Urhai*, whence also Gk. Ὀρροηνή, Lat. *Orr(h)ei*), capital of Osroene (q.v.), favourably situated in a ring of hills open to the south and surrounded by a fertile plain. It was founded as a military settlement by Seleucus I and acquired the Macedonian name Edessa. Later its official title as a city was Antiochia beside Kallirhoe. When Osroene asserted its independence, traditionally in 132 B.C. during the break-up of the Seleucid Empire, Edessa became the royal residence. From the time of Pompey, who made a treaty with Abgar II and allowed him an enlarged Osroene to rule over, Edessa played an ambiguous role in the wars and tensions between Rome and Parthia. Its sympathies were often with the Arsacids when prudence dictated compliance with Rome. Captured and sacked in A.D. 116 and again by L. Verus, it eventually became a Roman colony (Cass. Dio 77. 12), and thereafter issued a copious coinage. Christianity reached Edessa early, and the town became the most important bishopric in Syria. At the court of Abgar IX was Bardesanes (Bar Daisān) who was converted to Christianity (*c.* 180) but later was regarded as a heretic; he was not a Gnostic but taught an astrological fatalism. Edessa was several times besieged and more than once captured by the Sassanid Persians; Heraclius recovered it, but in A.D. 638 it fell to the Arabs. It had long been a centre of literary productivity in the Syriac language, the local form of Aramaic. The population of Edessa was predominantly Semitic and had closer affinities with its Iranian than with its more Hellenized western neighbours. Mosaics in the tombs of its aristocratic families vividly reflect their social habits.

A. R. Bellinger and C. B. Welles, *YClS* 1935, 95 ff.; R. Duval, *Histoire politique, religieuse et littéraire d'Edesse* (1892); L. Hallier,

*Untersuchungen über die Edessa Chronik* (1892); Jones, *Cities E. Rom. Prov.*, ch. 9; J. Levy, *Syria* 1957 (mosaics), 1961 (new excavations).   E. W. G.

**EDICTUM.** The higher Roman magistrates (*praetores, aediles, quaestores, censores*; in the provinces the governors) had the right to proclaim by edicts the steps which they intended to take in the discharge of their office (*ius edicendi*). Such edicts were put up in the Forum on an *album* (q.v.). Legally they ceased to be binding when the magistrate left his post (normally after a year), but customarily they were confirmed by his successors, so that for the most part the rules laid down in the edict remained continuously valid (*edictum tralaticium*). Among the magisterial edicts that of the *praetor urbanus* was of special importance for the development of the private law. The province of the *praetor*, as of all jurisdictional magistrates, was in form merely to apply the existing *ius civile*, but in his edict he was able, apart from providing model *formulae*, to promise new actions and other remedies and thus in substance to create a mass of new rules (*ius praetorium, honorarium*). In the formulation of his edict, and in its administration during his year of office, the praetor would rely on the advice of jurists (*see* JURISPRUDENCE). It was no doubt this indirect professional control which enabled the edict to play its vital formative function in the private law (*see* LAW AND PROCEDURE, ROMAN II. 4). On the order of Hadrian, the jurist Salvius Julianus (q.v.) composed a revised edition of the praetorian edict (*c.* A.D. 130), which was confirmed by a *senatus consultum*. It thus acquired a permanent form and the praetors lost the right to alter it. The edict of the *aediles* (q.v.) *curules* (concerning principally market sales of slaves and animals) was perhaps annexed to it. The later classical jurists wrote extensive commentaries on Hadrian's edict, which were freely excerpted by the compilers of Justinian's *Digesta* (q.v.), and the edict has been largely reconstructed on the basis of these excerpts (O. Lenel, *Edictum perpetuum*³ (1927)).   A. B.; B. N.

**EDUCATION.** I. THE EARLY PERIOD. Little is known of the training of children in the pre-classical period, but the myths preserve the traditions of Chiron (q.v.) and of Phoenix (q.v. 1) as ideal educators, teaching their pupils all the then known skills. The educational ideal of Phoenix was the 'speaker of words and doer of deeds' (*Il.* 9. 443). But the Mycenaeans provided technical instruction for scribes and poets, the latter developing, for the purposes of improvised recitation, the techniques of the stock episode, the catalogue and the verbal formula for recording the details of religious ritual as well as geographical and historical fact. The study of history, as recorded in the poetry, was thus an early element in education. The art of writing *may* have perished in the collapse of Mycenaean civilization, but poetry survived as the major educational instrument, preserving the traditions of the people, while its techniques continued to be taught and transmitted to culminate in the epics of Homer (q.v.), and ultimately to be transformed by the sophists (q.v.) and their forerunners into the techniques of prose rhetoric, which formed the most typical stream of the whole of ancient education.

II. SPARTA. Certain Dorian states like Crete (q.v.) and classical Sparta (q.v.) practised a totalitarian and militaristic form of education. Sparta had been a leader of culture, but in classical times its educational system was entirely adapted to the purposes of maintaining military strength. From the age of 7 the child was entirely under the control of the State, living in barracks away from parents. The aim of education was to produce efficient soldiers, and though their training included music and how to read and write, physical education received first priority. Girls, too, were educated in the interests of the state, to be the future mothers of warriors. For them, too, gymnastics and sport were emphasized, though dancing, singing, and music were not neglected.

III. CLASSICAL ATHENS. 1. *Elementary Education*. The introduction of alphabetic writing (*see* ALPHABET) into Greece in the second half of the eighth century implies the development of schools for its instruction, but these could have been originally professional schools of poets, priests, and scribes. Evidence for common elementary schools is much later. The traditions relating to Tyrtaeus (q.v.) in about 650 B.C. and the school laws of Solon (q.v.) of 594 B.C. are not well authenticated, but the institution of ostracism (q.v.) presupposes widespread literacy by the time of Cleisthenes (q.v. 1). There is mention of schools among the allies of the Mytilenaeans in about 600 B.C. (Ael. *VH* 7. 15), at Astypalaea in 496 B.C. (Paus. 6. 9. 6), at Chios in 494 B.C. (Hdt. 6. 27), at Troezen in 480 B.C. (Plut. *Them.* 10), and at Mycalessus in 413 B.C. (Thuc. 7. 29), and the general picture presented by the literary record, though queried by some scholars, is confirmed by Attic vase-paintings of the period.

There were three branches of elementary education, normally but not necessarily taught in different establishments. The *grammatistes* taught reading, writing, and arithmetic as well as literature, which consisted of learning by heart the works of poets, selected because of their value for moral training (Homer being the chief author studied); the *kitharistes* taught music and the works of lyric poets; the *paidotribes* gymnastics, games, and deportment. The pupil would normally start with the gymnastic lesson, then proceed to the lyre-school and finish the day with letters, but this sequence was not rigid, and as education was private, fee-paying, and not compulsory, parents might choose not to educate their children in all three branches. A training in letters would be a minimum of schooling. Girls, too, as we see from the vase-scenes, might receive an education in all three branches as well as in dancing, though not normally in the same schools as the boys and possibly not to the same extent. Boys were always accompanied to school by a *paidagogos*. The head teacher was normally a freeman enjoying the same social status (and receiving similar remuneration) as a doctor or any other democratic worker. The assistant masters might be slaves or freemen. Discipline was firm both at home and at school. The symbol of the *paidotribes*' power to punish was his forked stick, that of the other teachers the *narthex*; but for actual formal punishment in the schoolroom during the classical period the sandal was used, though other methods are attested for later times. There is no evidence of formal, written examinations, but pupils were regularly tested by recitation and were expected to give public proof of knowledge or skill in the regular public literary, musical, or athletic competitions, all of which are illustrated in vase-scenes. Despite the popularity of sport and contrary to much modern opinion, there was little real harmony between the intellectual and cultural sides of education. Xenophanes, Euripides, and Epaminondas opposed the athletic ideal which Pindar, Aristophanes, and Xenophon supported, while Plato, Isocrates, and Aristotle did not exclude but subordinated the physical to the intellectual. The schools themselves competed for the pupils' time and fees.

2. *Higher Education*. After elementary school a boy might enter a professional school of law or medicine or enrol in one of the schools of rhetoric or philosophy, or in courses offered by itinerant sophists either for personal culture and civic efficiency or in order to become a tertiary teacher himself. Some of these higher schools prescribed propaideutic courses (as geometry for Plato's Academy) and thus was born *secondary* education. The most famous higher schools were Isocrates' school of rhetoric, founded about 390 B.C., Plato's Academy (q.v. with its scientific, mathematical, and philosophical curriculum founded soon after, and Aristotle's Lyceum (*see* ARISTOTLE § 2) founded in 335 B.C.

3. *The Great Educators*. The sophists were itinerant teachers, claiming, each in his own way, to train pupil for civic efficiency. They believed in the power of knowledge to form human character, they offered wide curricula, they belonged to the liberal, democratic tradition of Greek education, they were progressive and pragmatic in their views and methods and they sought to enhance and transmit the cultural heritage against which Socrates (q.v. 1) and Plato (q.v. 1) so violently reacted. Socrates is said to have been in his younger days the head of a scientific school, but his chief importance for education rests upon his equation of virtue with knowledge and on his 'Socratic' method of teaching. Plato sets forth in the *Republic* and in a less extreme form in the *Laws* an idea state of a totalitarian mould and a corresponding system of education in which everything, including most forms of literature and art, which does not serve the ends of the state, is rigidly excluded. The *Timaeus*, which was virtually the only Plato known to the Middle Ages, provided for them the rationale for the *Quadrivium*, which, however, derives ultimately from Hippias. In his early work he strongly opposed the teaching of rhetoric, but later allowed it to be taught in the Academy alongside the scientific and other studies. In his concept of a school in permanent buildings staffed by specialists sharing a unified and integrated curriculum was born the idea of the secondary school, while in founding the Academy he may be said to have invented the University. Xenophon (q.v. 1) too was anti-sophistic (as was the fashion of fourth century educational thought), but he advocated a purely practical non-intellectual type of curriculum, with specialist teachers for each age group and the training of character through toil, and through the imitation of great examples. Isocrates (q.v.) restored the old tradition which Socrates and Plato had tried to suppress, and he owes much to the sophists in curriculum and teaching method. His path to the teaching of civic efficiency and of morality was through rhetoric, to which the other subjects of his curriculum were subservient. Amongst these ancillary subjects, which included, significantly, the study of history, he distinguished between useful, or cultural, and purely disciplinary subjects (like eristic and mathematics). He sought to oust the poets from their pre-eminent position in the curriculum by developing equivalent forms of composition in *prose*. His standpoint on the place of physical education in the curriculum has already been noted. The other main controversy among educational thinkers concerned the relative importance for learning of nature and nurture, of heredity and environment. The old aristocratic view—of Pindar, for example —was that heredity was all-important. The sophists had reconciled the claims of the two factors and Socrates and Plato had made grudging concessions to their view. Isocrates, though he vacillated at times, yet on the whole presented a balanced view, with due recognition of the claims of teaching. Aristotle (q.v.) taught rhetoric in the Academy, became the tutor of Alexander and founded the Lyceum, the greatest research institute of antiquity.

4. *Teaching Methods*. The methods of private tuition at home, individual attention in a group situation, and group instruction are all attested in our sources, not only for letters and music but also for gymnastics (Plato *Polit.* 294 d e). Memoriter learning and testing by recitation were common techniques.

Pedagogic skill was most highly developed in rhetorical teaching. Pupils memorized commonplaces, stock situations, and stock phrases together with sample passages like Gorgias' *Funeral Oration* as material for future 'improvisation'. They were trained in the psychology and techniques of persuasion and in the art of arguing both sides of cases. Both the sophists and Isocrates supplemented this training by curricula furnishing a wide background of general knowledge (*see* RHETORIC, GREEK).

The sophists developed the 'long' and the 'short' forms of discourse. The former corresponds to the lecture method, which even Socrates and Plato, though preferring the dialectic (q.v.) method and the seminar, frequently employed. The 'short' form is a dialectic or question-and-answer method, in which, unlike the Socratic method, the respondent makes a real contribution to the argument. This method was developed by Isocrates into a seminar technique of group discussion and group criticism. The Socratic method, which seems to depend for its rationale on the Theory of Ideas (*see* PLATO I) and which proceeds, after reducing the pupil to a state of *aporia* (or puzzlement), to bring to light knowledge lying dormant in the pupil's soul, is well illustrated in the geometry lesson of Plato's *Meno*. The 'play-way' method was recommended by Plato in the teaching of elementary arithmetic, but in general Plato was hostile to any form of experimentation in scientific teaching. The 'activity' method is advocated by Xenophon (q.v. 1) in the *Cyropaedia* where pupils learn justice by practising it in real life group situations.

IV. HELLENISTIC EDUCATION. 1. The pattern of education somewhat incompletely established by classical Athens was brought in the early years of the Hellenistic era to a definitive form which endured with but slight changes to the end of the ancient world. The greater attention paid to the education of the common man is reflected in the many separate philosophical treatises on education by such thinkers as Aristippus, Theophrastus, Aristoxenus, Cleanthes, Zeno, Chrysippus, Clearchus, and Cleomenes. The Hellenistic school was well integrated with society, participating in community rites and ceremonies and welcoming parents and citizens to its functions.

2. *Organization.* The State exerted more legislative control over education. Though schools were normally still run as private enterprises, the trend towards public ownership is exemplified in Teos, Miletus, Delphi, and Rhodes, where private benefactors had established foundations for the payment of teachers' salaries. Most cities provided at least one gymnasium (q.v.) for the purposes of education. Such gymnasia were designed to accommodate not only physical training but also teachers of literature, philosophy, and music. A public library was usually close by to complete the academic complex. The *gymnasiarchos* (q.v.) was a state official elected for one year to control the gymnasium as a whole and to supervise all aspects of the education (whether public or private) of the *epheboi* (q.v.) and the *neoi*. He might be expected to subsidize the school's finances from his own pocket, to buy oil for the athletes, and even to pay the salaries of one or more of the teachers. The increasing financial burdens of the office led to its decay in imperial times to a mere liturgy with wealth the only qualification. The *paidonomos* had similar duties in respect of elementary education. An important duty of both officers was the organization of the regular public competitions for both public and private schools which were the ancient substitute for the public examination and which were designed to facilitate the task of pupil promotion, to test the efficiency of the teacher, and to serve as the basis of the award of prizes for both teacher and pupil. Class loads tended to be high, as the recorded complaints of teachers indicate. The two most significant administrative developments in this period were the concentration of all educational activity for each age level into *one* building, and the division of the pupils into clear-cut

educational age groups—*paides* (up to 14), *epheboi* (15–17), and *neoi* (18 and over). Girls, too, were educated at all age levels. In some cases they came under the control of the same officials as the boys and shared the same teachers, occasionally perhaps even the same classrooms. In other cases separate state officials were responsible for them. At Athens the term *epheboi* (q.v.) had a different meaning than elsewhere and *neoi* was not an educational term. Education remained private but the general pattern no doubt was similar. The ephebic institution for the 18-plus group was military in character until towards the end of the second century B.C. when its programme came to include humane studies.

3. *Elementary Education* continued the classical pattern with but little change.

4. *Secondary Education* had originated in Athens from the preparatory courses required for entry to the higher schools. While still retaining this function it also became now an extension of general education for all pupils. Physical education and music continued, but of greater significance is the extension of elementary literary education to the secondary level, combining, in many instances, with mathematics and science to form the ancient ideal of *enkyklios paideia* (*see* ENCYCLOPAEDIC LEARNING) or 'general education'. This, of course, looks back to the syllabi of Hippias and Isocrates and forward to the medieval *Seven Liberal Arts*. There was, however, a constant tendency for literary studies to push out all the others. Homer and the other classics were studied in minute detail according to a rigidly formalized lesson plan. In later times the study of grammar (in the modern sense) and composition, and preliminary rhetorical material became common.

5. *Higher Education.* From the secondary school of the *epheboi* a youth was promoted at the age of 18 to the school for the *neoi*, in which gymnastics and music combined with literary and philosophical studies. These tertiary schools may, as Nilsson says, have influenced the Athenian *ephebic institution* (*see* EPHEBOI). Their standards were not high and for really serious higher education a youth must go to one of the great centres of learning—to Athens, Pergamum, and Rhodes for philosophy and rhetoric, to Cos, Pergamum, or Ephesus for medicine, to Alexandria for the whole range of higher studies (*see* MUSEUM).

6. *The Teachers.* Teachers, in the municipal systems, were elected by the people for one year at a time and supervised by the *gymnasiarch* and *paidonomos*. There were three grades of literary teacher—*grammatist* (elementary), *grammaticus* (secondary), and *rhetor* or *sophist* (tertiary). To compensate for the shortage of efficient teachers the *paidonomos* might engage skilled itinerant teachers for short periods. Ordinary teachers received but little more pay than a skilled workman, salaried state teachers being better off than private ones. The music teacher received most, then the literary teacher, then the *paidotribes*. A good teacher might expect to receive gifts, prizes at the competitions, and in some cases exemptions from taxes. Highly qualified teachers as well as state educational officials were amply rewarded. Some contemptuous references to teachers are recorded, but generally they were well respected, as is clear from many funerary monuments.

V. ROME. 1. *The Old Education.* The pupil was trained *in gremio matris* until the age of 7. The father then personally assumed responsibility for the boy's education, teaching him his letters, manly exercises, and the use of weapons as well as moral and social conduct and a knowledge of the laws. The boy accompanied his father everywhere, to ceremonies, social occasions, even to the Senate. With the assumption of the *toga virilis* at about the age of 16 came the *tirocinium fori* during which he was attached to some notable citizen for political experience, to be followed by the *tirocinium militiae* for his military training. This old aristocratic system of parental training and political apprenticeship, so favoured by such reactionaries as Cato (q.v. 1), persisted right into imperial times.

2. *Schools*. The evidence is scant, but elementary Latin schools must have existed from earliest times under Greek and Etruscan influence. Writing was known and Etruscan teaching alphabets have survived. The references to Verginia's attendance at school in 449 B.C. (Livy 3. 44. 6; Dion. Hal. 11. 28) and to schools at Falerii and Tusculum (Livy 5. 27; 6. 25) at the time of Camillus, if doubtfully authentic, do at least imply a long tradition of schooling. Plutarch (*Quaest. Rom.* 59) cannot be correct in saying that Spurius Carvilius (q.v. 2) was the first 'to open a letter school'. With the aristocratic hellenizing tendencies of the third and second centuries B.C. a system of Greek primary and secondary schools developed. These in turn created a demand for Latin secondary schools which could not develop until there was a Latin literature to teach—a want soon satisfied by Livius (q.v. 1) Andronicus' translation of the *Odyssey* and later by the *Annales* of Ennius. The programme was enlarged in 26 B.C. when Q. Caecilius (q.v. 3) Epirota introduced the study of Virgil and 'other new poets'. Tertiary education ran a similar course. Greek rhetoric, already taught at Rome in the second century B.C. and stimulated by the lectures of Crates (q.v. 3) of Mallos in 168 B.C., later generated Latin rhetoric when in 95 B.C. Plotius Gallus founded a Latin rhetorical school. Despite the inhibiting legislation of 92 B.C. the *Rhetorica ad Herennium* (q.v.) appeared between 86 and 82 B.C. as the first Latin textbook of rhetoric. There thus arose two parallel systems of education, one Greek, one Latin, using similar material and methods and sharing the same students. To be 'learned in *both* tongues' was the badge of culture. Two noteworthy features of Roman education were the exclusion of physical education from the schools and the inclusion of girls in the benefits of education. Education was to become predominantly literary and rhetorical but these studies lent themselves readily to moral training, an ideal never absent from Greek or Roman education.

3. *Teachers*. (*a*) The *litterator* or *ludi magister*, like the Greek *grammatistes*, offered an elementary education in reading, writing, and arithmetic for boys and girls from about 7 to 11 years of age. (*b*) The Romans adopted the Greek custom of assigning *paedagogi* to their children. In some cases these helped with the teaching. (*c*) The *grammaticus* taught grammar and literature and general subjects to the 12 to 15 age group as a general education and as a preparation for rhetoric. Originally he taught rhetoric too and a demarcation dispute persisted until the first century A.D., but the two professions were properly distinct. The typical lesson plan consisted of *praelectio* or preliminary explanation by the master; *lectio* or reading aloud by the pupil of the passage previously prepared and perhaps memorized; *enarratio* by master or systematic word by word explanation (by question and answer method) of details of word-endings, grammar, mythology, history, science, or general knowledge; and *iudicium* or final aesthetic judgement. Though expert teachers of mathematics, science, and music existed, these were for potential specialists only and it was the *grammaticus* who taught all the subsidiary subjects in the school. Normally this was done incidentally in the literature lesson as the subject-matter arose in the course of the *enarratio*. (*d*) The *Rhetor*. With the decay of political oratory under the Empire the emphasis in rhetorical education shifted to the training of pupils, who entered these schools at about the age of 16, for the career of advocate. The Latin rhetorical schools followed the Greek methods based on the formula: *inventio, dispositio, elocutio, memoria*. The pupil was introduced to his subject by a preliminary set of exercises (*progymnasmata* (q.v.)), and then mastered the art of declamation (*see* DECLAMATIO) with its division into *suasoriae*—deliberative rhetoric—and *controversiae*—legal rhetoric. As with the *grammaticus* general knowledge and moral behaviour were taught incidentally. For more advanced instruction a scholar would go abroad, preferably to Athens. Rhetorical teaching has been criticized by both ancient and modern writers for the unreality of its themes and for its irrelevance to real life. But recent scholarship has shown that many of the actual themes and most of the principles involved were very relevant to the practice of law in the imperial courts. The training certainly fitted the student for participation in the practice of public declamation, which was a very real feature in the cultural life of the time. The difficulty of the themes he had to grapple with provided excellent mental training and the experience of sustaining the classroom themes was a good basis for the thrust and parry of advocacy in the courts. In addition rhetorical studies were regarded as good preparation for administration and thus led to a career in the public service. (*e*) *Law Schools*. At first law was taught by the *tirocinium fori*, but with the development of legal theory there arose a class of legal experts (*iurisprudentes* (*see* JURISPRUDENCE)), who might be consulted on points of law by advocates and others, and who accepted pupils. Under the Empire they were granted official recognition and by the second century regular law schools were conducted by them in conjunction with their consultative practices. Rome's most original contribution to education was her law schools.

4. *State Control*. Though Athens, not Sparta, set the pattern for subsequent education, yet some measure of State support and control was to prove necessary for the spread of educational opportunity. The Troezenian decree and so-called Solonic laws (which may properly belong to the beginning of the fourth century) are early examples of State interference. The trend was continued in the Hellenistic State officials and the municipal schools founded on private benefactions. In Rome early State interest is revealed by the decrees of 173, 161, 154, and again of 92 B.C. expelling tertiary teachers. Though the Roman State did not ever institute special educational magistrates on the Hellenistic model, the Emperors exercised the same control through their ordinary powers as well as by granting immunities and privileges to, and conferring honours on, teachers, and by acting as 'benefactors'. Caesar attracted Greek teachers to Rome by granting them citizenship, while Augustus exempted them from his expulsion decree (Suet. *Caes.* 42. 2; *Aug.* 42. 3). Vespasian instituted the first chairs of Greek and of Latin rhetoric at Rome, to the latter of which he appointed Quintilian. Trajan gave the *munus educationis* to 5,000 needy children. Hadrian extended this benefit and also was the founder of the Athenaeum (q.v.). Marcus Aurelius created a chair of rhetoric and four chairs of philosophy at Athens. Public municipal schools were endowed by benefactors (as in Hellenistic times) and direct intervention by the Emperor or his delegates in such matters as choice of teachers and salary scales became common in the late Empire. Julian (q.v.) forbade Christians to teach in A.D. 362 but the ban was lifted in 364. And in 529 Justinian closed the Neoplatonist schools in Athens (*see* NEOPLATONISM). A proper national system of education never did develop, but with increasing State control education became constantly more widespread.

VI. Education as we know the term began in Greece where the basic theoretical and practical issues were first clearly enunciated and debated, where after much experimentation effective teaching methods were developed and curricula established and where the main lines of future educational development were laid down. Mathematical and scientific studies found a place in the curricula but the main emphasis was always on humane studies based on the traditional literature. Some few thinkers sought an ideal harmony of mind and body which was never fully realized in practice even in Greece and much less in Rome. Rome perfected the Greek methods and appropriated and handed on the Greek culture, but her original contribution was the systematic study of legal theory and the foundation of legal schools. The *Quadrivium* of Hippias (and of Plato)—arithmetic, astronomy, geometry, and music, and the *Trivium* of grammar, rhetoric, and dialectic deriving ultimately from the sophists and Isocrates, were the curricula inherited by the Middle Ages and designated by Martianus Capella as the *Seven Liberal Arts*. From beginning to end the ideal of the 'speaker of words' was never lost and the whole educational structure culminating in the elaborate methods of advanced rhetoric was designed to produce effective public speakers. Of all the lessons which the modern, democratic school has learnt from Greece and Rome, this is the one it has learnt least effectively.

F. A. G. Beck, *Greek Education, 450–350 B.C.* (1964) (lists the ancient sources and archaeological evidence); A. A. Bryant, 'Boyhood and Youth in the days of Aristophanes', *Harv. Stud.* 1907; M. L. Clarke, *Rhetoric at Rome* (1953); C. A. Forbes, *Greek Physical Education* (1929); A. Gwynn, *Roman Education* (1926); W. Jaeger, *Paideia* (1944–5); F. Kühnert, *Allgemeinbildung und Fachbildung in der Antike* (1961); R. C. Lodge, *Plato's Theory of Education* (1947); H. I. Marrou, *A History of Education in Antiquity* (1956); E. Mikkola, *Isokrates* (1954); M. P. Nilsson, *Die hellenistische Schule* (1955); E. Ziebarth, *Aus dem griechischen Schulwesen²* (1914).
F. A. G. B.

**EETION** ('Ήετίων), name of eight different mythological persons (see Schultz in Roscher's *Lexikon*, s.v.). The only well-known one is the father of Andromache (q.v.), king of the Cilician city of Thebe. Achilles captured and plundered the city, killing Eetion and his sons, but giving him honourable burial (*Il.* 6. 414 ff.).                    H. J. R.

**EFFATUS (AGER, LOCUS).** An augur (*see* AUGURES) who marked out a *templum* on the ground was said *liberare effarique* that space (see Servius on *Aen.* 1. 446), that is to free it (from profane use, cf. Livy 5. 54. 7) by the use of the proper words. But *effari* was used of marking off land for other purposes; the ground on which Rome (and presumably other cities regularly founded) stood was *ager effatus* (Gellius 13. 14. 1).

Latte, *RR* 42.                    H. J. R.

**EGERIA** (etymology uncertain, whether from *egero*, cf. *infero* : *inferius*; or connected with the gentile name Egerius, and if the latter, whether the goddess or the *gens* is prior), a goddess, probably of water, worshipped in association with Diana (q.v.), at Aricia (Verg. *Aen.* 7. 762–3), and apparently with the Camenae (q.v.) outside the Porta Capena in Rome (Juvenal 3. 17 and Mayor ad loc.). Women with child sacrificed to Egeria for easy delivery (Festus, 67. 25 Lindsay; Wissowa, *RK* 100, 219, 248 f.; cf. Altheim, *Griechische Götter*, 127; A. E. Gordon, *Univ. of California Publ. Class. Arch.* ii, 1934, 13 f.). She was said to have been Numa's consort and adviser (Livy 1. 21. 3 and often); cf. NUMA.

Latte, *RR* 170.                    H. J. R.

**EGG** (*in ritual*). Eggs play no great part in ancient ritual. They occur in chthonian offerings (Nilsson in *ARW* xi. 530 ff.), as life-givers (?); an egg is one of the materials used for purifying the ship of Isis (Apuleius, *Met.* 11. 16; not Greek ritual); but they were used for Greek purifications also (Lucian, *Dial. Mort.* 1. 1; *Catapl.* 7), including the so-called Hecate's suppers (schol. Lucian, 125. 24 Rabe); probably in the Greek instances simply as articles of food, either for the impurities to pass into so that they might be thrown away,

as food otherwise tainted might be, or as bribes to the uncanny powers which they might eat instead of anything more valuable. At meals, eggshells were smashed or pierced to prevent sorcerers using them (Pliny, *HN* 28. 19). There was also a form of divination, ῳοσκοπία, by putting eggs on the fire and observing how they sweated or burst; Orpheus was supposed to have written on this (Kern, *Orph. frag.* 333).                    H. J. R.

**EGNATIUS** (1, *PW* 9), GELLIUS, Samnite general who organized the coalition of Samnites, Gauls, and Etruscans whose defeat at Sentinum (q.v.) made Rome mistress of central Italy, 295 B.C. (Polyb. 2. 19; Livy 10. 21. 29). Egnatius, like the Roman general Decius (q.v. 3) Mus, fell in the battle. The suggestion that Egnatius is only a fictitious composite of two other Samnite generals, *Gellius* Status (captured 305) and Marius *Egnatius* (Social War hero), is unconvincing.                    E. T. S.

**EGNATIUS** (2, *PW* 36) **RUFUS,** MARCUS, of senatorial family, won popularity as aedile (probably 21 B.C.) by organizing a private fire-brigade, and, without observing the legal interval, held the praetorship in the following year. In 19, no less illegally, he presented himself to the consul C. Sentius Saturninus (q.v. 2) as a candidate for the other consulship, which had been left vacant for Augustus and declined by him; Sentius refused to accept his candidature and rioting ensued. Egnatius then plotted to assassinate Augustus on his return from the East, but was detected and executed.

F. Millar, *A Study of Cassius Dio* (1964), 87 f.
G. W. R.; T. J. C.

**EGYPT UNDER THE GREEKS AND ROMANS.** Egypt had been little affected by Greece before Alexander's conquest. Trade with Greece had mainly consisted in bartering corn for silver at Naucratis, and foreign manufactured articles rarely went up country. Greek mercenaries were employed at times, but did not settle; and travellers like Herodotus and Plato collected information but imparted none. Whether Alexander formed any plans for hellenizing Egypt is unknown: his one foundation there, Alexandria, was primarily a seaport, and he does not seem even to have garrisoned Memphis, the strategic centre of the lower Nile valley, while the south was left to itself. He was formally recognized as king at Memphis, and then passed out of Egyptian history. If he had any scheme, it would doubtless be known to Ptolemy Soter, if to anyone; but how far Ptolemy's organization of Egypt was his own and how far inherited from Alexander can only be guessed.

2. The development of Alexandria as the home of a new Graeco-Egyptian culture was begun by Soter: a typical instance of the syncretism attempted is the conception of Sarapis built up by a committee of theologians. Ptolemais, founded to control Upper Egypt, was more purely Greek in its organization; also reclaimed lands in the Fayûm were given to veterans of the army, providing a reservoir of troops and a guard for the desert frontier. But Hellenism did not spread amongst the natives for many decades; stray references, e.g. to gymnasia in some provincial towns, are the only indications of Greek influence. Ptolemy Philadelphus, less occupied with external policy than his father, could pay more attention to the advancement of culture in Alexandria, and spent money freely in securing Greek writers and artists; but he had to make concessions to Egyptian ideas, e.g. by issuing a copper coinage on the local standard to circulate alongside of the Greek silver. Attempts to introduce Greek practices, e.g. that of Apollonius in farming, were short-lived; the recruiting of Egyptians to be trained in a phalanx in 218 was more

significant of their recovery of position than of the growth of Hellenism. The difference in tone between the decree formulated by the synod of priests at Canopus in 237 and that similarly passed at Memphis in 196 shows the revival of nationalism in religion.

3. The second century B.C. witnessed a gradual supersession of Greeks by Graeco-Egyptians in the Alexandrian official circles. By the reign of Epiphanes most of the Ptolemaic possessions outside Africa, except Cyprus, were lost, isolating Egypt from the Greek political world; and the Ethiopian rulers of Meroe had pushed their frontier down to Philae. The latter probably fostered risings in the Thebaid, and the constant dynastic quarrels of the royal house, which started with the sons of Epiphanes, disturbed the whole country. To these in part the numerous concessions granted to the natives may be ascribed, as bribes for their support; but the Egyptian element at court must also have counted for something in securing them. Polybius seemingly found no pure Greeks even at Alexandria: he described the population as Egyptians, mercenaries, and Alexandrians of mixed stock; and, as there was little to tempt fresh Greek settlers, the Graeco-Egyptians would tend to become more and more Egyptian.

4. Greek influence, in short, was never more than a veneer in the interior of Egypt under the Ptolemies. In Alexandria the Museum maintained a contact with Greek culture, particularly in philosophy, which absorbed some Egyptian elements, but it did not touch the natives; the Greek language was used officially, but the native language persisted, to revive as Coptic; the Greek gods were only known in the country as synonyms for local deities, and in the artificial triad of Sarapis, Isis, and Harpocrates the latter two, who were mainly Egyptian in their attributes, were more generally worshipped than Sarapis. The royal house itself became egyptianized, in sympathies if not in blood: the monuments relating to it, especially in temples, are predominantly Egyptian; and the whole policy of government was changed accordingly in its orientation.

5. The Roman conquest of Egypt had disastrous results. Augustus treated Egypt as a personal estate, which was exploited without any consideration for the welfare of the inhabitants. The wealth of the land had not been seriously depleted under the Ptolemies: there is little evidence of destitution, and, though the conditions of life outside the towns were primitive, they did not deteriorate. Roman rule was marked by decay for over three centuries: the revenues were spent abroad and capital was drained to Rome, land went out of cultivation, and many of the agriculturists were reduced to vagabondage. It was not till the imperial authority grew weaker in the fourth century that there was any revival of prosperity in Egypt: then large estates of a feudal type were formed in some districts, in others monastic bodies acquired considerable properties—for both of which analogies can be found in Ptolemaic times —and contemporary documents suggest a distinct amelioration in the life of the natives. The changes in the administration of Egypt under the Roman Emperors illustrate this point. Augustus probably intended to keep the existing scheme of organization in being when he conquered the country: certainly many of the Ptolemaic official titles were retained, and the functions of these officials were seemingly little altered; the chief novelty, the Prefect, might be described as a viceroy substituted for a king. But, as the machinery had to be gradually adapted to a new ideal of government, the Ptolemaic civil service lost such independence as it had possessed— for instance, the heads of the former finance department, the *dioecetes* and *idiologus*, became of executive instead of administrative rank, and the presence of an army of

occupation deprived the *epistrategus* of his military powers. In the lower grades of officials, whose main duties were in the collection of revenues for the Emperor, there was a steady trend towards compulsory service: many of the Ptolemaic taxes had been farmed freely, but under the Romans the posts became liturgies. The local magistrates, under various titles—gymnasiarch, *exegetes*, eutheniarch, *cosmetes*, *agoranomus*—had one common responsibility, that of making up the sum assessed upon their town, if they could not extract it from the collectors, or these from the taxpayers. Septimius Severus attempted to remedy matters by converting the bodies of magistrates into senates, presumably with the idea of increasing the local control; but as the burden on the community as a whole was not lightened, the measure did nothing to check the impoverishment of the country.

6. In Alexandria Roman rule completed the fusion of the Greek and Egyptian elements, which thereafter formed a nationalist opposition to the imperial officials; the gymnasiarchs were usually in the forefront of any popular movement. There was apparently some revival of Greek culture, as shown by the study of Greek literature, and Sarapis worship became more influential. Hadrian may have realized the possibility of improving the condition of the country, by encouraging this tendency, when he founded Antinoopolis on a Greek model; but though his foundation prospered, his experiment was not repeated, except by Septimius Severus in a summary and ill-considered fashion. Romanization was never attempted: veterans from the army settled sporadically in the country, but they were soon absorbed into the mass of the natives; Latin was hardly ever used, except in official or military documents, or studied; formal mention of the emperors was occasionally made in Egyptian style on temple walls, and Roman festivals were occasionally observed, but in neither case was there any real meaning. In Byzantine times a resident in Egypt might boast of Macedonian descent, or quote Homer; no one showed any knowledge of the existence of Rome. *See also* PTOLEMY (1).

ANCIENT SOURCES. There is no connected account of any period in the history of Egypt under Greek or Roman rule, and very little first-hand evidence of value, except for passages in Polybius, the later, fragmentary books of Diodorus, and the *De bello Alexandrino*. The scraps of information given by Roman writers are far from trustworthy. The important inscriptions can be found in *OGI* and *IGRom*. The papyri discovered and published during the last fifty years provide the chief material: their evidence is necessarily fragmentary, but they have revolutionized the old views on the social and economic conditions of the country.

MODERN LITERATURE. (*a*) General history: A. Bouché-Leclercq, *Histoire des Lagides* (1903–7); E. R. Bevan, *History of Egypt under the Ptolemaic Dynasty* (1927); J. G. Milne, *History of Egypt under Roman Rule*[3] (1924); W. Schubart, *Aegypten von Alexander dem Grossen bis auf Mohammed* (1922).

(*b*) Military: J. Lesquier, *Les Institutions militaires de l'Égypte sous les Lagides* (1911); id. *L'Armée romaine d'Égypte d'Auguste à Dioclétien* (1918); M. Launey, *Recherches sur les armées hellénistiques* (2 vols. 1949–50), *passim*.

(*c*) Organization: L. Mitteis und U. Wilcken, *Grundzüge und Chrestomathie der Papyruskunde* (1912); A. Stein, *Untersuchungen zur Geschichte und Verwaltung Aegyptens unter römischer Herrschaft* (1915); V. Martin, *Les Épistratèges* (1911); E. Biedermann, *Der Βασιλικὸς γραμματεύς* (1913); P. Jouguet, *La Vie municipale dans l'Égypte romaine* (1911); B. A. van Groningen, *Le Gymnasiarque des métropoles de l'Égypte romaine* (1924); F. Oertel, *Die Liturgie* (1917); A. Stein, *Die Präfekten von Ägypten in der römischen Kaiserzeit* (1950).

(*d*) Taxation: U. Wilcken, *Ostraka aus Aegypten und Nubien* (2 vols. 1899); V. Martin, *La Fiscalité romaine en Égypte aux trois premiers siècles de l'Empire* (1926); S. L. Wallace, *Taxation in Egypt from Augustus to Diocletian* (1938).

(*e*) Social and Economic: Claire Préaux, *L'Économie royale des Lagides* (1939); Rostovtzeff, *Hellenistic World*; *Roman Empire*[2]; A. C. Johnson, *Economic Survey of Ancient Rome—Roman Egypt* (1936); J. G. Winter, *Life and Letters in the Papyri* (1933); J. G. Milne, *Catalogue of Alexandrian Coins* (Ashmolean Museum) (1933).

(*f*) Religion: W. Otto, *Priester und Tempel im hellenistischen Aegypten* (1905–8); H. I. Bell, *Jews and Christians in Egypt* (1924); *Cults and Creeds in Graeco-Roman Egypt*[2] (1954).

(*g*) Law: R. Taubenschlag, *The Law of Greco-Roman Egypt in the light of the Papyri*[2] (1955).

(h) Literary texts from Egypt: R. A. Pack, *The Greek and Latin Literary Texts from Greco-Roman Egypt*[2] (1965).

References to numerous articles in periodicals will be found, classified, in the bibliographies in *CAH* vii, ch. 4; x, ch. 10; xi, ch. 16. The general bibliography of Graeco-Roman Egypt published annually in the *Journal of Egyptian Archaeology* came to an end in 1939. An annual survey of inscriptions from Graeco-Roman Egypt has continued to date. *Chronique d'Égypte* provides information regarding current publications.                    J. G. M.

**EGYPTIAN DEITIES.** The chief deities of Egyptian origin worshipped in the Graeco-Roman world were Sarapis, Isis (qq.v.), and Harpocrates (*see* HORUS). Anubis (q.v.) appears with the group in some places and Ammon, Bubastis, and Osiris (qq.v.) at others. Temples of these deities such as the one at Delos, for instance, might contain among the 'associated gods', in addition to those mentioned, a dozen or more Egyptian, Greek, or syncretized deities. A minor deity of the group was sometimes Bes, an old, crude, comic god much beloved by the common people. The popularity of Bes, Harpocrates, and other minor members of the cult was enhanced by the influence of the pottery industry which sent out from Alexandria many statuettes, jars, jugs, and vases with representations of these deities. In the Hellenistic age most of the foundations of the cult of the Egyptian deities in the Aegean area seem to have become public cults very quickly, and most of their ceremonies and properties came under the regulation and direction of the magistrates of the city-states. In connexion with many of these cults there were societies of *melanephoroi* and some system of periodic services was probably carried out. In the later period, especially in the West as, for instance, at Pompeii, the cult was probably served by a professional priesthood, and at many of the temples the old Egyptian mysteries of Osiris were celebrated. Something of the nature of these mysteries is disclosed to us by Apuleius in his *Metamorphoses* (book 11), and Plutarch (*Concerning Isis and Osiris*) shows how they could receive a philosophic interpretation. The cult of the Egyptian deities was one of the last great pagan worships to succumb to Christian pressure. The temple at Alexandria was destroyed about 291, but the cult lingered longer at Philae. The cult seems to have commanded strong interest among official classes in Rome during the fourth century.

A. Alföldi, *A Festival of Isis in Rome under the Christian Emperors of the Fourth Century* (Diss. Pann. ii. 7, Budapest, 1937); T. A. Brady, *The Reception of the Egyptian Cults by the Greeks* (Univ. of Missouri Studies x. 1935); Cumont, *Rel. or.*; S. Dow, 'The Egyptian Cults in Athens' (*Harv. Theol. Rev.* 1937); G. Lafaye, *Histoire du culte des divinités d'Alexandrie* (1884); J. G. Milne, 'Graeco-Egyptian Religion' (*ERE* vi, 374 ff.); A. D. Nock, *Conversion* (1933); P. Roussel, *Les Cultes égyptiens à Délos* (1916); J. Toutain, *Les Cultes païens dans l'empire romain* (1907–); P. M. Fraser, 'Two Studies in the Cult of Sarapis in the Hellenistic World' (*Opusc. Atheniensia* (4°), 3, 1960). id., 'Current problems concerning . . . the cult of Sarapis' (ibid. 7, 1967). *See also under* ISIS, SARAPIS.                    T. A. B.

**EILEITHYIA(E)** (*Εἰλείθυια(ι)*), the goddess(es) of birth identified by the Romans with Lucina (*see* JUNO). She was evidently in origin a local Minoan nursing or mother goddess. Her cavern sanctuary at Amnisus, mentioned in *Od.* 19. 188, has been excavated by Marinatos, showing a continuous cult from the neolithic to the classical periods (*Crete and Mycenae* (1960), 115, and pl. 2). Her name, in the form 'Eleuthia', occurs in a tablet from Cnossus. She has no myth properly speaking, appearing simply as a subordinate figure in various stories of birth, *see* HERACLES, LETO. She is often identified with, or her name used as a title of, Hera; she is identified also with Artemis (q.v.), owing to that goddess's functions in connexion with childbirth (see, for instance, Farnell, *Cults* i. 247, n. 28c; ii. 567–8, n. 41). She is also on occasion the daughter of Hera (as Pausanias 1. 18. 5 (Crete)), or the partner of Artemis (as Diod. Sic. 5. 72. 5, where

she and Artemis are both daughters of Zeus). At Olympia, she is associated in cult with Sosipolis (for whom see Farnell, *Cults* ii. 611; M. P. Nilsson, *Minoan-Mycenaean Religion*[2] (1950), 503, n. 2). Her cult is widespread and she occasionally develops into a city-goddess.

R. F. Willetts, *CQ*, 1958, 221.                    H. J. R.; H. W. P.

**EINSIEDELN ECLOGUES,** two incomplete Latin pastorals (87 hexameters in all) first published in 1869 by Hagen from a tenth-century MS., early products of Nero's reign. In the first a competing shepherd belauds the minstrelsy (Nero's) which eclipses that of Mantua (Virgil's); in the second the shepherd Mystes sings the return of the Golden Age. The authorship, sometimes credited to Calpurnius (q.v. 1) Siculus, remains uncertain. The name of Mystes may be derived from Horace, *Carm.* 2. 9. 10, as that of Glycera(nus), or be chosen to reinforce the irony at the expense of a purely material and political 'Golden Age'. The poem begins with the same words as Calpurnius' fourth in celebration of the Golden Age, but satiety ('satias mea gaudia vexat') makes the Golden Age a great bore, 'quod minime reris'. This is an ironical answer to Calpurnius rather than Calpurnius himself. *See* PASTORAL POETRY, LATIN, § 5.

TEXT. E. Baehrens, *PLM* iii; A. Riese, *Anthol. Lat.* nos. 725, 726; C. Giarratano (with Calp. and Nemes., 1924).
TRANSLATION (with text). Duff, *Minor Lat. Poets.*
SPECIAL STUDY. S. Loesch, *Die Einsiedler Gedichte* (with text, facsimile, 1909) [supports Lucan's authorship, whose works present Stoic parallels to Apollo's praises, Ecl. 1. E. Groag, *PW* iii. 1379, maintains Calpurnius Piso's authorship]; W. Schmid, *Bonner Jhrb.* 1953, 63 ff.; W. Theiler, *Stud. ital.* 1956.                    J. W. D.; C. G. H.

**EIRENAEUS** (Lat., Minucius Pacatus), a grammarian of the Augustan age, pupil of Heliodorus the metrist, and cited by Erotian. *See also* GLOSSA (GREEK).

**EIRENE,** peace personified. Apart from her appearance as one of the *Horae* (Hes. *Theog.* 902), and a number of mentions in poetry (serious, Bacchylides, fr. 3 Jebb; Euripides, fr. 453 Nauck; semi-serious, Aristophanes, *Pax* 221 ff.), she has no mythology and little cult. At Athens, however, we hear of actual worship of her at a public festival; at the Synoikia (schol. Ar. *Pax* 1019), on Hecatombaeon 16, a sacrifice was offered to her, which the scholiast says was bloodless (perhaps a mere conclusion from the text of Aristophanes there, see Deubner, *Attische Feste*, 37 f.). It dates from the peace with Sparta in 374 (Isoc. 15. 109–11). It was for this occasion that the famous statue of her by Cephisodorus (see Roscher, *Lex.* i. 1222, *CAH*, pls. ii, 80a) was produced: the goddess holds on one arm the infant, Plutus. Two or three times the name is found applied to a heroine or Bacchante (see Roscher, ibid.), but not for women till much later.

H. J. R.

**EISANGELIA** (*εἰσαγγελία*) in Athenian law was a type of prosecution for an offence against the State, often translated 'impeachment'. The accuser denounced the offender to the *boule* (q.v.) or the *ekklesia* (q.v.). Either body might decide either to try the case itself or to refer it to a *dikasterion* (q.v.), or the *boule* (which had no authority to impose any heavier penalty than a fine of 500 drachmas) might refer it to the *ekklesia*.

*Eisangelia* was used for accusations of treason or of other serious offences for which no different procedure was prescribed by law; it was fundamentally a procedure for dealing with unprecedented or extraordinary crimes. But towards the end of the fifth century B.C. a law (quoted in Hypereides 4. 7–8; cf. Dem. 49. 67) was passed listing certain offences for which *eisangelia* was the regular procedure; they included treason, subversion of the democracy, formation of conspiratorial clubs, taking bribes to make proposals contrary to the public interest, and breaking promises to the State. The procedure could still be used for other offences too, and in the fourth century some quite trivial charges were made in this way.

Well-known cases of *eisangelia* are those against Alcibiades (q.v.) for profaning the Mysteries in 415, and against the generals at the battle of Arginusae in 406 for failing to rescue the shipwrecked sailors. Surviving speeches written for this type of case are those of Lycurgus *Against Leocrates* and Hypereides *For Lycophron* and *For Euxenippus*.

In addition, the name *eisangelia* was given to two other quite distinct types of prosecution: for maltreatment of an heiress or orphan, and for improper conduct of an arbitration.

See DIKE (2).

R. J. Bonner and G. Smith, *The Administration of Justice from Homer to Aristotle* i (1930), 294 ff. D. M. M.

**EISPHORA,** the name of an extraordinary property tax in ancient Greece which is known from Aegina, Athens, Mende, Messene, Miletus, Mytilene, the Koinon of the Nesiotes, Orchomenus, Potidaea, Siphnus, Sparta, Syracuse, and the Ptolemaic Empire. It was a quantitative land tax in Mende and in Ptolemaic Egypt, a quantitative property tax in Messene, a distributable property tax in Potidaea and fourth-century Athens, and a property tax of some kind in fifth-century Athens and other states mentioned.

Pollux 8. 130—a much-disputed passage which might nevertheless be trustworthy, at least in its dating—recalls a progressive *eisphora* system attributed to Solon. Thuc. 3. 19 (for 428–427 B.C.) and the (perhaps) earlier inscription *IG* i². 92 are the first certain sources for an *eisphora* in Athens.

The much-discussed tax was remodelled at Athens in 378–377. The whole taxable capital in the state had to be valued (the amount of the first assessment being 5,750 talents). The taxpayers were divided into *symmoriai* (q.v.) which were financially nearly equal. A certain percentage of the whole assessment ($\frac{1}{100}$, $\frac{1}{50}$, $\frac{1}{12}$, etc.) had to be paid, as the necessity arose. Even fortunes exempt from liturgies (q.v.) had to be assessed for the *eisphora*. Some years after 378–377 the so-called *proeisphora* was introduced, according to which the 300 richest citizens had to pay the whole levy in advance and reimbursed themselves later on from the other taxpayers.

For bibliography *see* FINANCE (GREEK AND HELLENISTIC), LITURGY, SYMMORIA. R. Thomsen, *Eisphora. A Study of Direct Taxation in Ancient Athens* (1964); and of still useful earlier research A. M. Andreades, *A History of Greek Public Finance* (1933), index, s.v. 'eisphora', 'liturgies', 'symmories'; H. Bolkestein, *Economic Life in Greece's Golden Age* (1958), 144; M. I. Finley, *Studies in Land and Credit in Ancient Athens* (1951), 14, 90, 93, 106; A. W. Gomme, *A Historical Commentary on Thucydides* ii (1956), 278 ff.; B. A. van Groningen, *Mnemosyne* 1928, 395 ff.; A. Th. Guggenmos, *Die Geschichte des Nesiotenbundes* (Phil. Diss. Wuerzburg 1929), 33; F. M. Heichelheim, *An Ancient Economic History* ii² (1964), 135, 138; W. Huettl, *Verfassungsgeschichte von Syrakus* (1929), 103; Michell, *Econom. Anc. Gr.*, index; A. Momigliano, *Athenaeum* 1937, 422 ff.; Cl. Préaux, *L'Economie royale des Lagides* (1939), index; Rostovtzeff, *Hellenistic World*, index; W. Schwahn, *Rh. Mus.* 1933, 247 ff.; A. Segré, *Stud. Ital. Fil. Class.* N.S. 1947, 157 ff.; G. E. M. de Ste Croix, *Class. et Mediaevalia* 1953, 20 ff.; proeisphora, *PW* Suppl. ix, s.v.; for the texts cp. Dittenberg. *SIG*, index; LSJ. F. M. H.

**EKKLESIA** (ἐκκλησία, in some States ἁλία, ἁλιαία, ἀγορά, ἀπέλλα), the Assembly of adult male citizens summoned (ἔκκλητοι) as of right, the ultimate authority in most Greek cities, though varying in composition, procedure, and competence with the political complexion of each. In monarchies and oligarchies membership was often subject to qualifications of birth, wealth, and age; meetings tended to be few, summoned at discretion (σύγκλητοι) by the executive or Council, and permitted only to accept or reject proposals on a few issues of general interest such as war, peace, and alliance; to elect magistrates from the restricted circle of those qualified to stand; and perhaps to judge serious criminal cases on appeal. In a radical democracy all adult citizens could attend; there were frequent statutory meetings besides those specially summoned; free debate and the amendment and initiation of proposals were allowed; and the Assembly's competence was extended to cover the suspension of those magistrates whom it still elected (*see* SORTITION), the control of all the magistrates and of the Council, the decision on all important political and financial issues, and a share in the actual administration, including even the conduct of wars, and in legislation. Most Assemblies met in the Agora, the general 'gathering-place' also used for the market.

**2.** At Athens, as elsewhere, the character of the *ekklesia* developed with progress towards democracy. At first it probably decided only issues of peace and war, and formally elected the magistrates; as political tension increased, it may have shared in other important decisions, e.g. to appoint Dracon and Solon as lawgivers and to divide the archonship of 580/79 between the classes (*see* EUPATRIDAI). Solon may have granted, or formalized, a power of passing decrees or laws; and he supposedly entrusted the people with judicial responsibilities. The earliest attested decrees are those granting Peisistratus a bodyguard (561/60) and abolishing torture (510/09?); the earliest laws passed in the Assembly were perhaps those of Cleisthenes; we know of no judicial acts on its part before its possible condemnation of the exiled Peisistratids (510/09?) and the partisans of Isagoras (508/7). Significant additions to its judicial powers were made by Ephialtes (q.v. 4). Membership may originally have been confined to freeholders; the apparent participation of craftsmen in 580/79 supports the tradition that under Solon's constitution all citizens might attend. Regular statutory meetings, at first one each prytany (*see* PRYTANIS), almost certainly date from Cleisthenes.

**3.** The fully democratic Athenian *ekklesia* was open to all adult male citizens over 18. It met on the Pnyx or, from the late fourth century, in the theatre of Dionysus; occasionally in Piraeus; and in the Agora if a ballot was needed. Meetings were summoned by the *boule* (q.v.); there were four statutory meetings in each prytany; extra meetings were called if the *boule* thought fit or the *strategoi* (q.v.) demanded it. The chairman of the *boule* for the day presided (*see* PRYTANIS, PROEDROI). The *boule* prepared the agenda and drafted resolutions (προβουλεύματα) which the Assembly debated and could accept, reject, or amend. It could not debate a matter on which there was no προβούλευμα, but could require the *boule* to prepare one for the next meeting. To some extent the agenda was governed by law, certain matters coming up regularly once a prytany (continuation in office of magistrates, corn-supply, etc.), others annually (ostracism, review of the laws). Every citizen present had the right to speak (ἀγορεύειν); magistrates had no privileges. Ambassadors and heralds from foreign States might be permitted to address the Assembly. Voting was by simple majority and generally by show of hands (χειροτονία); secret balloting by tribes and a quorum of 6,000 were required in some cases affecting individuals (ἐπ' ἀνδρί), viz. some trials, ostracism (q.v.), and grants of citizenship or *adeia* (q.v.). The ballots, except for ostracism, were ψῆφοι, pebbles; hence, by extension, any decree was a ψήφισμα. Numerous ψηφίσματα are preserved in inscriptions. All have a regular prescript, specifying, in its fullest form, the archon of the year, prytanizing tribe, day and number of the prytany, secretary, chairman, and mover of the decree, which often reproduces the προβούλευμα with amendments if any at the end.

**4.** The scope of the *ekklesia*'s competence has already been indicated. To some extent its activity had been limited by sortition and the dicasteries (qq.v.). Thus it elected only the magistrates for war and a few others, and judged only in cases brought by *eisangelia* (q.v.). Its main work was the making of decrees, and here its competence was manifold and far-reaching. The only restraint it recognized was that of the laws (νόμοι); an illegal decree might provoke the *graphe paranomon* (q.v.). In the fifth century the Assembly passed not only laws but also some decrees of general or permanent application tantamount to laws; after 403/2 laws and decrees were kept distinct and the revision of the laws was entrusted to *nomothetai* (q.v.).

5. The *ekklesia* was the embodiment of Athenian democracy. It gave the whole people a direct share in government. In routine matters it relied greatly on the *boule*, but the most important decisions were fully debated. Sometimes a decision was emotional and foolish, but on the whole the Assembly behaved responsibly. It was fairly representative of the people at large: to judge from a hostile estimate (Thuc. 8. 72), the normal peace-time attendance in the fifth century, even if no quorum was needed, was still well over 5,000, a very fair proportion of the citizen-body (*see* POPULATION, GREEK), considering that many lived in the country. After the Peloponnesian War, when the masses were poorer, payment for attendance was introduced, one obol per meeting at first; by 327 it was six, and nine for the 'principal' meeting in each prytany. The social composition of the meetings varied with circumstances (e.g. the absence of hoplites or sailors on expeditions) and the agenda.

6. So long as the Athenians were free to choose, the *ekklesia* retained its fully democratic character; the timocratic constitutions imposed during the generation following Alexander's death, and after the Roman conquest, involved certain modifications, such as exclusion of the poorer citizens, the abolition of pay, and the extension of election to the archons.

7. For the Spartan Assembly, *see* APELLAI (1); for federal Assemblies, ACHAEAN CONFEDERACY, AETOLIAN CONFEDERACY, FEDERAL STATES.

G. Gilbert, *Const. Antiquities of Sparta and Athens* (1895), see table of contents; Busolt–Swoboda, *Griech. Staatskunde³* (i, 1920; ii, 1926), see indexes; R. J. Bonner and G. Smith, *Adm. of Justice from Homer to Aristotle* (i, 1930; ii, 1938), see indexes; H. T. Wade-Gery, *CQ* 1933, 22 ff.; *Essays in Greek History* (1958), 143 ff.; Hignett, *Hist. Athen. Const.*, see index; A. H. M. Jones, *Athenian Democracy* (1957), see index; V. Ehrenberg, *The Greek State* (1960), see index s.vv. 'assembly', 'Ecclesia'; G. T. Griffith in *Ancient Society and Institutions, Stud. V. Ehrenberg* (1966), 115 ff.
A. W. G.; T. J. C.

**EKPHRASIS**, the rhetorical description of a work of art, one of the types of *progymnasma* (rhetorical exercise, q.v.). Similar, but shorter, descriptions in verse are common in the *Anthology*. The efflorescence of the representational arts in the second century A.D. gave an impetus to this type of writing, of which Nicostratus of Macedonia (2nd c. A.D., author of an Εἰκόνες) is perhaps the first exponent. Lucian's *De Domo* (Περὶ τοῦ οἴκου) is on the same lines. In his *Imagines* (Εἰκόνες) the beautiful Pantheia is compared to famous works of art. The earliest extant collection is that of Philostratus (q.v. 3), perhaps not descriptions of actual pictures. *See also* CALLISTRATUS (5) *and* PAULUS (2).

On the description of works of art in Greek literature, in general, see P. Friedländer, *Johannes von Gaza und Paulus Silentiarius* (1912), 1 ff.
J. D. D.

**ELAGABALUS** (1), the Baal of Emesa in Syria. His young priest, on becoming Emperor in A.D. 218 (see the following art.), carried to Rome the sacred black stone, or baetyl, of Elagabalus, enshrined it on the Palatine with the Carthaginian Caelestis as its bride, and for a brief period made the 'deus invictus Sol Elagabalus' the chief deity of Rome.
F. R. W.

**ELAGABALUS** (2, *PW*, s.v. VARIUS (10) AVITUS) (Roman Emperor A.D. 218–22), born Varius Avitus Bassianus, was a son of Julia Soaemias and grandson of Julia Maesa (*see* JULIA 7 and 8), and took his name from the sun-god of Emesa, Elah-Gabal, of whom he was hereditary priest. In his fifteenth year he was saluted Augustus at Emesa under the title of M. Aurelius Antoninus, his mother alleging he was the son of Caracalla. After the defeat of Macrinus he spent the winter at Nicomedia and only reached Rome in 219. His chief interest was the advancement of his religion. Two magnificent temples were built for the Sun-god, whose midsummer festival was celebrated by his priest with a ceremonial no less ludicrous than obscene. His mother attended debates in the Senate, and also presided over a 'female senate' which formulated rules of etiquette. Meantime positions of responsibility were given to mere palace servants.

In alarm for her own position and the continuance of the Severan dynasty Maesa induced him to adopt his cousin Alexianus (Severus, q.v. 2, Alexander) as Caesar (221). Jealousy and intrigue ensued till an opportune bribe by Mamaea, Alexianus' mother, induced the Praetorians to murder Elagabalus and his mother (222).

Herodian 5. 5–8; Dio Cassius, bk.'79; S.H.A. K. Gross, *RAC* iv, 987 ff.; K. Hönn, *Quellenuntersuchungen zu den Viten des Heliogabalus und des Severus Alexander* (1911). Temple in Rome: Nash, *Pict. Dict. Rome* i. 537 ff.
H. M. D. P.; B. H. W.

**ELATEA** ('Ελάτεια), a Phocian town of strategic importance; commanding the routes from Phocis to Boeotia by the Cephissus valley, from Phocis to Opus on the Euboean Straits, and from Boeotia to Thermopylae over Mt. Callidromus. The most famous citizen of Elatea was Onomarchus (q.v.). Philip II of Macedon occupied it in Sept. 339 B.C., threatening Boeotia a few miles south and Athens which lay three days' march distant; by fortifying the town he blocked all routes from Boeotia northwards. In 305 Cassander, while occupying the same position, was defeated by the Athenians under Olympiodorus (q.v. 1).
N. G. L. H.

**ELATUS** ('Έλατος), 'Driver', the name of (1) a Trojan ally killed by Agamemnon (*Il.* 6. 33); (2) one of Penelope's wooers (*Od.* 22. 267); (3) the eponym of Elatea (Paus. 8. 4. 2–4); (4) a Centaur (Apollod. 2. 85); (5) a Lapith, father of Polyphemus the Argonaut (schol. Ap. Rhod. 1. 40); father of Taenarus eponym of Taenaron (ibid. 102).
H. J. R.

**ELEA** (or **ELIA** or **VELIA**), modern *Castellamare di Bruca* (under excavation since 1927), Phocaean colony on the Tyrrhenian coast of southern Italy south of Paestum (q.v.), founded *c.* 540 B.C. It repelled the Lucani, allied itself with Rome (3rd c. B.C.?), and thereafter enjoyed quiet prosperity. It is chiefly famed for its Eleatic school of philosophers.

*PW* viii A, 2399 ff.; A. G. Woodhead, *The Greeks in the West* (1962), 65 f.; P. Mingazzini, *Atti e Mem. d. Soc. Magna Grecia* 1954, 3 ff.
E. T. S.

**ELEATIC SCHOOL** ('Ελεατικὸν ἔθνος, Pl. *Soph.* 242 d), a philosophical school represented by Aristotle and the doxographic tradition as having been founded at Elea in Lucania by Xenophanes (q.v.), and by Plato (perhaps jokingly) as having begun earlier still, but now agreed to have started with Parmenides (q.v.) of Elea at the end of the sixth century. There is no close connexion between Xenophanes' monotheism, reached by a critique of Homeric theology, and Parmenides' closely argued proof that what exists is single and indivisible and unchanging. It is Parmenides whose theories are defended by the other major representatives of the 'school', Zeno (1) and

Melissus (1) (qq.v.); Zeno shows paradoxes in the ideas of plurality, divisibility, and change, and Melissus maintains a modified version of Parmenides' conclusions against the pluralism of Empedocles and the atomists. Unlike Zeno, Melissus was not from Elea nor apparently a pupil of Parmenides, and with him the 'school' ended, though Gorgias (q.v. 1) tried his hand at an essay in the Eleatic style.                                                    G. E. L. O.

**ELECTRA** ('Ηλέκτρα, Doric Ἀλέκτρα), in mythology, (1) daughter of Oceanus, wife of Thaumas, mother of Iris and the Harpyiae (q.v.; Hes. *Theog.* 265 ff.). (2) Daughter of Atlas, one of the Pleiads, born in Arcadia (Apollod. 3. 110), usually located on Samothrace (as Ap. Rhod. 1. 916 and schol. there); mother by Zeus of Dardanus (q.v.) and Iasion (Iasius) (schol., ibid.). (3) Daughter of Agamemnon and Clytemnestra (qq.v.). She does not appear in Epic, the first certain mention being in the *Oresteia* of Stesichorus (see Vürtheim, *Stesichoros' Fragmente und Biographie*, 1919, 46). Where Stesichorus, or his alleged predecessor Xanthus of Sicily (ibid.), found the name is quite unknown; one or the other made a bad pun on it in defiance of quantity, interpreting the Doric form as meaning 'unwedded', as from α privative + λέκτρον. In Tragedy she becomes one of the central figures of the story. Sophocles (*El.* 12) makes her rescue Orestes (q.v.), then a young child, from the murderers of his father. In the *Choephoroe* of Aeschylus she is unalterably hostile to her mother and Aegisthus (q.v.), welcoming her brother, joining with him in the invocation to Agamemnon's ghost, but not actively helping the killings. Her role in Sophocles is similar, but more developed. In Euripides (*El.*), she is almost a monomaniac from hate and brooding over her wrongs, helps to kill Clytemnestra, and at once goes half-mad with remorse. In his *Orestes* she appears as a desperately faithful nurse and helper to her mad brother, and shares his wild exploits throughout; ibid. 1658 and Hyg. *Fab.* 122. 4, she marries Pylades; in Hyginus (ibid. 1–3) she meets Orestes and Iphigenia at Delphi and nearly kills the latter, who she thinks has murdered him. The source of this story is unknown, see Rose ad loc. For her appearances in art, see Robert, *Bild und Lied* (1881), 150 ff. It is fairly clear that the development of her story is due to the poets mentioned and their fellows, not to tradition.                                                H. J. R.

**ELEGIAC POETRY, GREEK.** The Greek elegiac is a development of the epic hexameter in the direction of melic verse by adding to it a so-called 'pentameter', which consists of two 'hemiepes' verses combined into a single line in the form:

$$-\smile\smile-\smile\smile-\,|\,-\smile\smile-\smile\smile-$$

The pentameter is a single unity in so far as the final syllable of the first half must be long and hiatus is not allowed between it and the following syllable, but it reveals its construction from two separate parts by the break which is required at the end of the first half and does not allow a word to be carried from one half to the other. The word ἐλεγεῖον, first used by Critias (fr. 2. 3), is connected with ἔλεγος, and in antiquity there was a popular notion that the elegiac was in some sense a lament, the 'flebilis elegeia' of Ovid (*Am.* 3. 9. 3). This seems highly unlikely, since most early types of elegiac have no relation to laments. It is more likely that ἔλεγος is connected with some foreign word for 'flute', such as survives in Armenian *elegn-*, and that the elegiac was originally a flute-song. This is supported by the references to the flute in early elegists such as Archilochus (fr. 123 Bergk), Mimnermus (Strabo 14. 643), and Theognis (241, 533, 825, 943), and by the use of the flute for purposes for

which the elegiac was used, such as military life and convivial occasions. The inventor of the elegiac is not known, and the ancients who ascribed it variously to Archilochus, Callinus, and Mimnermus may have known no more than we do. It makes its first appearance at the end of the eighth century and may have found most of its characteristic uses at an early date. It seems to have started in Ionia, but to have found its way quickly to the mainland of Greece. Its main uses may be classified (1) Sympotic. Flute-songs were sung over the wine, and the elegiacs of Archilochus (frs. 1–13), though they belong mostly to camp-life, are of this kind. So, too, is Callinus fr. 1, as its opening words μέχρις τεῦ κατάκεισθε show, though it is full of martial spirit. This type may be seen in all the known fragments of Mimnermus, in the collection ascribed to Theognis, in some short pieces of Anacreon (frs. 96–112), and in poets of the fifth century like Ion of Chios and Critias. To this class belong certain short poems sung in memory of dead men, like the Attic couplet on Cedon (Scol. Att. 23 D), which are sometimes mistaken for epitaphs. (2) Military. Long elegiac poems of an exhortatory kind were addressed to soldiers by Tyrtaeus, and it seems to have been his example which emboldened Solon to use the elegiac as a means for political discussion and propaganda. (3) Historical. Mimnermus told the history of Smyrna in his elegiac *Smyrneis*, Semonides that of Samos, Panyassis that of the Ionian colonization. This type may well have been a development of the first type, since Mimnermus certainly included historical pieces in his *Nanno*. (4) Different from these types was the use of the elegiac for inscribed dedications. Examples are attributed, without certainty, to Archilochus (fr. 16) and Anacreon (frs. 107–8). It is not known why the elegiac was used for this purpose. (5) Epitaphs. The elegiac was also used in inscriptions to commemorate the dead, who were either made to speak in the first person or had something simple said about their name, home, etc. This seems to have become a popular use in the middle of the sixth century B.C., especially in Attica, and may perhaps have been derived from the commemorative elegiac. Both epitaphs and dedications were inscribed without the author's name, and though many are attributed to well-known poets, such as Simonides, the attributions are extremely uncertain. The elegiac epitaph survived for centuries and was still popular in the fourth century A.D. (6) Lament. This use seems to have existed and even to have been popular at an early date in the Peloponnese, since Echembrotus (*c.* 586 B.C.) was famous for his elegies sung to the flute and for their gloomy character (Paus. 10. 7. 4). No early examples of this kind survive, but perhaps traces of it may be seen in the epitaph on the Athenian dead of Coronea (*CQ* 1938, 80–8), in the elegiacs of Euripides (*Andr.* 103–16), and in Plato's lines on Dion of Syracuse (fr. 6). These main types survived until the end of the fifth century, and probably till the end of the fourth. After this the differences between them tended to be obliterated and the elegiac was put to new uses, largely because instead of being composed for a practical end it was often composed as a literary exercise. About 300 B.C. the changes were already apparent, and may perhaps be connected with the names of Anyte and Addaeus; in the next generation, that of Philetas and Asclepiades, there is no doubt about them. With these, and later, authors the elegiac is used in the following new ways: (1) Descriptive. Scenes are described, of country or town life, or even from mythology. This became more and more popular and lasted into the Byzantine age. (2) Love-poems. On the whole this type is very rare in the sixth and fifth centuries, though the second book of Theognis shows its existence. It was a department of the sympotic elegy. It was developed in intensity and intimacy by Plato, and became common at

Alexandria. (3) Imitations of earlier forms, especially of dedications and epitaphs, which were often written just as literary pieces and betray themselves by their lack of exactness in giving names and their occasional confusion of real epitaphs with commemorative elegies. Along with these new forms the old forms survived and were still popular. After comparative inactivity in the fourth century the elegiac developed a new strength in the third, and was one of the forms of poetry most popular with the Alexandrians, who made its rules stricter and polished its technique. In the Roman period it continued its life and had a considerable flowering in the Augustan age, to which Antipater of Thessalonica, Bianor, and Euenus belong. The tradition was carried on in the first century A.D. by Antiphilus and Julius Polyaenus, and in the second by the distinguished figure of Lucian. After a century of comparative barrenness there was a considerable revival in the fourth century, when the Emperor Julian used the form and Palladas was the last distinguished pagan to express his feelings in it. Even in the sixth century, when classical Greek was a dead language, it was still used for the composition of elegiacs by such notable poets as Agathias Scholasticus, Paul the Silentiary, and Macedonius. After this outburst in the reign of Justinian it seems to have passed into disuse, though lines attributed to Cometas (*Anth. Pal.* 9. 586) may have been written as late as the reign of Constantine VII (A.D. 911–59).

TEXTS. Diehl, *Anth. Lyr. Graec.*; J. M. Edmonds, *Elegy and Iambus* (Loeb, 1931); T. Hudson-Williams, *Early Greek Elegy* (1926); W. Peek, *Griechische Vers-Inschriften* i (1955). CRITICISM. C. M. Bowra, *Early Greek Elegists* (1928). C. M. B.

## ELEGIAC POETRY, LATIN.
Ennius (ed. Vahlen², 215 f.) and Lucilius (Books 22–5) used the elegiac couplet for short occasional poems. Its real literary history begins *c.* 100 B.C. with the epigrams of Valerius (4) Aedituus, Porcius (1) Licinus, and Q. Lutatius Catulus (2) (qq.v.). These pieces, clearly Greek in inspiration (Day, 103 f.), are all concerned with love, and it is predominantly as a medium for love poetry that the elegy was developed during the first century B.C. Catullus' work includes many short epigrams, but his most ambitious and rewarding elegies are the longer poems (65–68) in which Hellenistic structures and techniques are informed by a new, specifically Roman and contemporary approach to love and poetry. What might be called the 'classic' type of love-elegy, the cycle of short poems centred upon the poet's relationship with a single mistress, appears to have originated with Cornelius Gallus (q.v. 3; cf. Ov. *Tr.* 4. 10. 51 ff.): his 'Lycoris', rather than Catullus' Lesbia, was the prototype of Tibullus' Delia, Propertius' Cynthia, Ovid's Corinna, and Lygdamus' Neaera. Latin love-elegy is a good example of a literary form almost every feature of which is derived from Greek models but which as a whole has no analogue in Greek literature: as the ancients regarded originality it is an original Roman creation, though not explicitly claimed as such by, e.g., Quintilian, who merely observes (*Inst.* 10. 1. 93) *elegia quoque Graecos provocamus*. Its brief history is the record of an increasing domination of the poet's experience by conventional literary and rhetorical elements: Ovid's *Amores*, in fact, compared with the elegies of Catullus or even Propertius, constitute almost a new kind of love-poetry. Somewhat outside the genre stands the delightful cycle of poems associated with the name of Sulpicia (q.v. 1).

It was natural that the elegiac couplet should be treated in Latin as something of an all-purpose metre, as it was in Greek. Its most versatile practitioner was, of course, Ovid. In the *Heroides*, *Ars Amatoria*, and *Remedia Amoris*, though the genres were formally different, the dominating theme was still love. For the *Fasti* Callimachus and Propertius, for the *Ibis* Callimachus afforded

his models. The *Tristia* and the *Epistulae ex Ponto*, on the other hand, represent what is in effect a new genre, for all the formal allegiance which they owe to the traditional origins of the metre (cf. *Am.* 3. 9. 3 f.). The range of possible applications is also illustrated by the other surviving elegies of the Augustan or immediately post-Augustan period: the elegies of the *Catalepton* (one or two probably by Virgil himself), the *Copa* (see APPENDIX VERGILIANA), the *Elegiae in Maecenatem*, the *Consolatio ad Liviam* (qq.v.), and the pseudo-Ovidian *Nux* (see OVID).

After Ovid the metre was used chiefly for epigrams and short occasional poems. Among the many examples transmitted in the *Anthologia Latina* (q.v.) those attributed to Seneca have a limited historical interest, those attributed to Petronius some poetic merit. The fixed association of the elegiac couplet with the epigram in Latin is largely due to Martial, whose favourite metre it was and who rivals and occasionally even excels Ovid in technical virtuosity. The most remarkable individual elegy of the imperial age is the *De reditu suo* of Rutilius Namatianus (q.v.). Among other poets who made use of the metre Claudian and Ausonius should be mentioned.

*The Metre*. The elegiac hexameter differs little from the heroic. The special effects appropriate to epic were not often required in elegiac writing, and the general character of the line is smooth and fluent. Of five pentameters by Ennius which survive four end in disyllables, and it may be that this rhythm was the most satisfactory to the Roman ear: certainly, though the epigrammatists mentioned above (§ 1) and Catullus freely admitted words of from three to five syllables to the end of the line, following Greek practice, the disyllabic ending became the rule in Propertius' later poems and in Ovid (however, in *Her.* 16–21, the *Fasti*, and the poems of exile he reverts occasionally to the looser usage). After Catullus elision became both rarer and, when used, less harsh. These developments were undoubtedly dictated by artistic preferences, but Catullus' 'un-Augustan' usages must not be interpreted as evidence of technical incapacity: the occasionally harsh rhythms of, e.g., *Carm.* 76 are part of the designed effect of the poem (cf. Harrison, *CR* 1943, 97 ff.). From the very beginning the Latin couplet, unlike the Greek, tended to be self-contained: genuine enjambment between couplets is extremely rare. For modern Latin verse-writing, from the Renaissance onwards, the strict Ovidian form of the couplet has generally been the preferred model. It is above all ideally suited to pointed expression, conveyed through variation and antithesis: half-line responding to half-line, pentameter to hexameter, couplet to couplet.

ORIGINS AND HISTORY. *A. A. Day, *The Origins of Latin Love-Elegy* (1938); *G. Luck, *Die römische Liebeselegie* (1961). INDIVIDUAL POETS. A. L. Wheeler, *Catullus and the Traditions of Ancient Poetry* (1934); K. F. Quinn, *The Catullan Revolution* (1959); K. F. Smith, *The Elegies of Albius Tibullus* (1913); H. E. Butler and E. A. Barber, *The Elegies of Propertius* (1933); *Critical Essays on Roman Literature: Elegy and Lyric*, ed. J. P. Sullivan (1962). METRE. *M. Platnauer, *Latin Elegiac Verse* (1951). Cf. also *E. Lissberger, *Das Fortleben der Römischen Elegiker in den Carmina Epigraphica* (diss. Tübingen, 1934).

(* = with bibliography) E. J. K.

## ELEGIAE IN MAECENATEM.
Tradition ascribes to Virgil two such *Elegiae* (wrongly combined in the MSS. and divided by Scaliger). As they were written after Maecenas' death (8 B.C.), Virgil (d. 19) cannot be the author. In the former elegy the unknown poet tells us that Lollius (either consul 21 B.C., cf. Hor. *Carm.* 4. 9. 33, or another Lollius) made him write this poem. This elegy defends Maecenas against the charge of weakness and love of ease.

The second elegy contains the farewell words of the dying Maecenas, who expresses gratitude to his friend Augustus.

Their date is disputed. By some they are dated shortly after Maecenas' death; on the strength of *El.* 1. 1–2 many ascribe to the same poet the anonymous *Consolatio ad Liviam*. Others rightly reject this on account of metre and diction, though the Maecenas elegies follow the *Consolatio* in places. As both *Consolatio* and Maecenas elegies borrow from Ovid's *Metamorphoses, Tristia,* and *Ex Ponto* (I–III), it is probable that the Maecenas elegies were written after A.D. 13.

TEXTS. Teubner (*Poet. Lat. min.* i, Vollmer); O.C.T. *Appendix Vergiliana* (q.v.) (1965).
COMMENTARY. J. Middendorf (diss. Marburg, 1912).
TRANSLATION. Duff (with text), *Minor Lat. Poets.*
DATE. F. Skutsch, *PW* iv. 944 (8 B.C.); F. Lillge, *De Eleg. in Maec. quaest.* (1901, 8 B.C.); B. Axelson, *Eranos* (1930, 1, not before Statius); A. Witlox, *Consolatio ad Liviam,* xiv (1934, under Nero); E. Bickel, *Rh. Mus.* 1950, 97 ff.
STYLE AND METRE. Th. A. A. M. Copray (diss. Nijmegen, 1940, *Eleg. in M.* not by the poet of *Consol.*). P. J. E.

**ELEMENTS.** Hesiod conceived the Universe as a family of divine powers descended partly from the Void (Chaos) but mainly from the Earth. The early Ionian cosmologists saw it as consisting of (Thales, Anaximenes, Heraclitus) or evolved out of (Anaximander) a single divine substance, unbegotten as well as everlasting. Parmenides regarded Nature as the product of the mixture in different proportions of two self-identical 'forms' (μορφαί), Light and Night, existing (like all Nature) only 'in belief', and transferred by a Daemon the world-government exercised by the Ionian divine substance (ἀρχή). These 'forms' Empedocles converted into four real 'roots' (ῥιζώματα), viz. Earth, Air, Fire, Water, which are the ultimate, exclusive, and eternal constituents combined in different ratios to form the Universe. He thus originated the conception of physical elements.

The atomists illustrated the relation between atoms and objects from that of letters to words, and Antisthenes may have called the simple sensibles in his theory of knowledge στοιχεῖα (cf. Pl. *Tht.* 201 e), sc. the 'elements' or ABC of the world. Plato was the first to give the name στοιχεῖα to such elements as the Empedoclean 'roots' (Eudem. fr. 31 Wehrli, cf. Pl. *Soph.* 252 b), but he himself held that not these but the geometric figures constituting them are alone genuine physical elements (*Ti.* 48 b; 56 b), and that the One and the Dyad are the στοιχεῖα of the Forms. Aristotle (*Metaph. Δ* 3, etc.) defined and classified the usage of στοιχεῖον, embracing now, among other things, the elementary demonstrations inherent in all mathematical and logical proof (whence Euclid's '*Elements*'). The physical sense, however, prevailed, though the metaphor was forgotten; so that when St. Paul speaks of 'beggarly elements' (Galatians iv. 9) he refers to natural phenomena, including now heavenly bodies, worshipped as spirits or angels. In Latin Lucretius, continuing the old image of letters for atoms, first translated στοιχεῖα by *elementa*; which term Cicero presently adopted to denote the Empedoclean 'roots'.

H. Diels, *Elementum* (1899). A. H. C.

**ELEPHANTINE,** on an island below the first cataract of the Nile, had been a military and business frontier station and a religious centre in Pharaonic times; but under the Ptolemies its religious importance was gradually transferred to the island of Philae above the cataract, and the Roman camp and customs station were at Syene, on the east bank of the river. Of the buildings seen by Jomard on Elephantine, the only interesting monument that remains is the Nilometer mentioned by Strabo. Many ostraca, chiefly customs receipts, have been found; also Aramaic papyri containing the records of Jewish mercenaries.

E. Jomard, *Description de l'Égypte, Antiquités,* ch. 3, pls. 30–7; H. G. Lyons, *Report on the Temples of Philae* (1908); A. E. P. Weigall, *Guide to the Antiquities of Upper Egypt*[2] (1913), 414 ff.; B. Porten, *Archives from E.* (U.S.A. 1969). J. G. M.

**ELEPHANTS.** The ancient world knew the two surviving species of elephant, the Indian or Asiatic (*Elephas maximus*) and the African (*Loxodonta africana*). Subspecies of the former require no mention, but the latter comprises two groups: *Loxodonta africana* or Bush elephant and *Loxodonta africana cyclotis* or Forest. These African varieties differ in structure and habitat, the Forest being considerably the smaller. It is this latter smaller Forest elephant that was known to, and used by, the Ptolemies and Carthage. When during the last century the opening-up of the interior of Africa revealed the Bush elephant, which is larger than the Indian, the ancient writers, who said that the African was smaller than the Indian, were considered to be wrong. But now that the smaller African subspecies has been distinguished, it is clear that they were right: the African elephant known to the ancients was smaller than the Indian. It was found in Ethiopia and the hinterland of the Red Sea, whence the Ptolemies obtained their supply, and in the forests at the foot of the Atlas mountains, which supplied the Carthaginians. The appearance of these elephants is shown on the fine coins minted by the Barcid generals in Spain.

Ivory was known to the Greeks long before the elephant. The Greeks first met the beast as a weapon of war when Alexander in a desperate struggle defeated the 200 Indian elephants of Porus (q.v.) on the Hydaspes (326 B.C.); the Romans first encountered it when Pyrrhus used his Indian elephants ('Lucanian oxen') in his invasion of Italy. Alexander himself did not try to use elephants for battle, but war-elephants were exploited to the full by his successors, particularly the Seleucids and Ptolemies, in their mutual struggles. This was the great age of the war-elephant. When the Seleucids gained control of the sources from which Indian elephants came, the Ptolemies had to look elsewhere and sent large-scale hunting expeditions to Ethiopia, using Indian mahouts to break in these African elephants. When Indians and Africans met in the battle of Raphia (217), the latter were defeated, but they were heavily outnumbered. The Carthaginians (some time before 264) built up a force of war-elephants drawn from the Atlas region. These contributed to their victories over Regulus (q.v. 1) and the Mercenaries, but although in general elephants were effective when used for the first time, they were liable to get out of hand. The Romans gradually took their measure, both the Indians of Pyrrhus and the Africans of the Barcids; finally, Scipio Africanus checked Hannibal's at Zama (q.v.) by leaving lanes in his ranks, while the Indians of Antiochus the Great failed to win him the battle of Magnesia. Seleucids and Numidians continued to make some use of them, but the Romans themselves used them only sporadically for war (e.g. at Pydna, 168, Numantia, 153, Thapsus, 46). Their main use by the Romans was for the arena or ceremonial purposes. The supply during the Empire was kept up by an imperial herd in Latium. Though the Parthians apparently did not use war-elephants, the Sassanids revived their use.

S. Reinach, Dar.-Sag., s.v. 'Elephas'; Sir W. Gowers and H. H. Scullard, *Num. Chron.* 1950, 271 ff. H. H. S.

**ELEPHENOR,** in mythology, leader of the Abantes of Euboea (*Iliad* 2. 540), killed by Agenor (4. 463–70). He is son of Chalcodon in both passages; Hyginus (*Fab.* 97. 10) says his mother was Imenarete, a dubious name. Lycophron 1034 and the schol. there make him survive the Trojan war, previous to which he had gone into exile from Euboea for accidentally killing his grandfather Abas. H. J. R.

**ELEUSINIA,** a word signifying games celebrated at Eleusis, never the Eleusinian Mysteries. The games were celebrated every fourth year (the second of the Olympiad) and on a lesser scale every second year. The prize was a certain quantity of grain from the Rarian field. We know also of a procession and certain sacrifices.

A. Rutgers van der Loeff, *De ludis Eleusiniis* (1903); L. Deubner, *Attische Feste* (1932), 91 ff. M. P. N.

**ELEUSIS,** the most important town of Attica after Athens and Piraeus, on a land-locked bay with a rich plain, was a strong prehistoric settlement and remained independent of Athens, with its own kings, perhaps as late as the seventh century B.C. It had a naturally defended acropolis, held by the Thirty Tyrants in 403, and many walls and houses are preserved. Its fame depended chiefly on the mysteries celebrated in honour of Demeter and Persephone, which attracted visitors from all Greece. Work of all periods is visible in their sanctuary; the Mycenaean megaron, cogently identified as the first shrine of the goddesses, was replaced in geometric times by an apsidal (?) temple, then by an archaic temple, and, finally, under Pisistratus, by the magnificent *telesterion*, a square hall with rock-cut seats like a theatre, rebuilt and enlarged by Ictinus. There was much building in Roman times, including the splendid Propylaea finished by Marcus Aurelius. The sanctuary ceased to exist after A.D. 395, a victim of Alaric and Christianity.

K. Kourouniotes, *Eleusis* (E.T. 1936); J. N. Travlos, 'The Topography of Eleusis', *Hesp.* 1949, 138 ff.; G. E. Mylonas, *Eleusis and the Eleusinian Mysteries* (1961). C. W. J. E.

**ELIS,** the plain of north-west Peloponnesus, famed for horse-breeding. It was occupied by a people akin in race and language to the Aetolians, coming in from the north. There are fairly extensive remains of Mycenaean occupation, with a concentration on the lower Alpheus near Olympia and at Olympia itself. In the Catalogue of the Ships (*Il.* 2. 592) the boundaries of Nestor's kingdom extend to the Alpheus. For the problem thus presented and that of the cattle raid in *Il.* 11, *see* PYLOS in Triphylia *and* MESSENIA. Mycenaean tombs (of LH IIIB–C date) have been found at Dhiasela near the Alpheus (*BCH* 1957, 574 ff.). Sub-mycenaean and Protogeometric burials occur on the site of the later city of Elis, and what has been described as a 'vast' geometric cemetery near Killini (*BCH* 1957, 568). Of interest is the τεῖχος Δυμαίων on the Araxus promontory, for its Mycenaean cult and habitation, and the continuity of occupation to Byzantine times. There is also a curious burial mound of Mycenaean date at Samiko, not far from the well-known site of Kakovatos. The Eleans' small neighbours of Pisa, Lepreum, and Triphylia long kept an uneasy independence. Their boundaries with the Arcadians of Heraea were established by treaty (Tod 5; early 6th c. ?). The Eleans presided over the Olympic Games, traditionally set up in 776 B.C.; but they may not have had effective control until two centuries later (*see* PISA). They lived a country life and had little concern with politics; a council of 90 life-members formed a closed circle within the oligarchy (Arist. *Pol.* 1306ᵃ12 ff.). They were early and loyal allies of Sparta, until in 420 Sparta championed the independence of Lepreum, whereupon Elis joined Athens and Argos; she was punished in 399 with the loss of Triphylia, which after 369 was united with Arcadia. Elis was now for a brief period a moderate democracy. In the third century the Eleans were allies of Aetolia and fought frequent wars with the Arcadians.

The town of Elis on the Peneus was built *c.* 471, and replaced Olympia as a political centre. It was an open and extensive town, of which considerable remains have been excavated including the theatre (*BCH* 1964, 755).

P-K, *GL* iii. 2. 2. 323 ff. Excavations: *JÖAI* 1911, Beiblatt 97 ff.; 1913, Beibl. 145 ff.; 1915, Beibl. 61 ff. T. J. D.; R. J. H.

**ELIS, SCHOOL OF,** was founded by Phaedon (q.v.; Diog. Laert. 1. 19; 2. 105; 126). Little is known of the members of the school other than its founder.

**ELOCUTIO NOVELLA,** a phrase used by Fronto (q.v., ed. M. P. J. van den Hout, 146. 15) in writing to his pupil M. Aurelius expressing the modern style of Latin which he advocated. This fresh mode was a reaction against the outworn conventions of the Silver Age and an attempt to combine the virile elements of Early Latin authors with the vigorous current of contemporary speech. Gellius and Apuleius also represent the movement.

R. Marache, *La Critique littéraire de langue latine et le développement du goût archaïsant au IIᵉ siècle de notre ère* (1952); Norden, *Ant. Kunstpr.* 361 ff. J. W. D.

**ELOGIUS,** QUINTUS, Augustan writer of memoirs cited as a first-hand authority on the Vitellian family by Suetonius (*Vit.* 1).

**ELYMAIS** (Hebr. *Elām*), a region between Babylonia and Persis, to which the name Susiana (properly the name of the district around Susa (q.v.)) was often extended in Hellenistic times. Elymais is primarily the hill country, Susiana the fertile plain. After Cyrus conquered Elymais and made Susa a principal residence city, Iranian influences gradually prevailed throughout the region. Elymais remained for the most part an autonomous ally rather than a subject of the Seleucid successors of Alexander, unlike Susa itself. Similarly, after the initial conquest by the Parthian Mithridates the Great, kings of Elymais asserted their autonomy. They issued coins, at first with the native name Kamniskires, from the second century B.C. onwards. Autonomy ended with the conquest and annexation of the kingdom by the Sassanid Ardashir (*see* ARTAXERXES 4).

U. Kahrstedt, *Artabanos III* (1950), 39 ff.; G. F. Hill, *Brit. Mus. Cat. Arabia*, etc. (1922). E. W. G.

**EMANCIPATIO** is the release of a *filius* or *filia familias* from family ties and the *patria potestas* by a voluntary renunciation of the *pater familias*. The *emancipatus* became a person *sui iuris* and, if male, a *pater familias* even though he had not yet a family of his own. *Emancipatio* entailed the consequences of a *deminutio capitis* (q.v.) *minima*. It was first made possible by taking advantage of the rule of the Twelve Tables that a father who sold his son three times was deprived of his *potestas* (*see* PATRIA POTESTAS § 2). The sales (by *mancipatio*, q.v.) were made to a friend, who made two intervening manumissions (which restored the son to the father) and after the third sale either made a third manumission or mancipated the son back to the father for him to make the manumission, the advantage of the latter method being to vest in the father the rights of succession, etc., to the son. Since the Twelve Tables referred only to sons, it was held, illogically, that for daughters or grandchildren one *mancipatio* was sufficient. Justinian finally abolished these formalities and substituted a simple declaration before a magistrate. The Emperor Anastasius had earlier (502) introduced *emancipatio per rescriptum principis*, where the son was absent. Justinian preserved this as an alternative method, applicable to all cases.

Gaius, *Inst.* 1. 132; *Inst. Iust.* 1. 12; *Dig.* 1. 7; *Cod.* 8. 48 (49). P. Moriaud, *La Simple Famille paternelle* (1910); cf. the republication of the Latin documents by P. M. Meyer, *Juristische Papyri* (1920), no. 9; P. Bonfante, *Corso di diritto romano* i (1925), 60 ff. A. B.; B. N.

**EMBATERION.** The ἐμβατήριον was properly a marching-tune (Polyb. 4. 20. 12). Hence it was also a marching-song, such as the Spartans sang when under arms (Ath. 630 f.; schol. Dion. Thrax 450. 27), like the anapaests attributed to Tyrtaeus (*Carm. Pop.* 18–19; cf. Dio Chrys. 2. 59).

**EMERITA AUGUSTA** (modern *Mérida*), a colony on the Anas (*Guadiana*) founded by Augustus in 25 B.C. for veterans of legions V and X. Built rapidly on a grand scale, it was linked with Baetica by a 64-arch bridge and with the north by Augustus' great trunk road, which crossed the Tagus by the bridge of Alconétar. Its aqueducts were fed from a large reservoir constructed nearby; Agrippa presented it with a great theatre; its gateway was depicted on its coins. Many monuments partly survive. The colony was reinforced by Otho. It was the premier city of Spain to Ausonius, and to the Visigoths a wonder, both for its architecture and for its saint, Eulalia.

I. A. Richmond, *Arch. Journ.* 1931, 99 ff.; M. Almagro, *Guia de Merida* (1961). M. I. H.

**EMESA,** in Syria Apamene, on the Orontes, now *Homs*. It was for long the centre of an Arab sheikhdom. One of these rulers was Sampsigeramus whose friendship with Pompey caused Cicero to poke fun at Pompey as an eastern potentate. Under the Flavians Emesa became Roman, but the dethroned Sampsigerami are still mentioned in inscriptions. Emesa was the native city of Julia Domna, Mamaea, Elagabalus (2), and Severus (2) Alexander (qq.v.). When Elagabalus became Roman Emperor (A.D. 217), Emesa began to flourish; it became a metropolis and received *ius Italicum*, and it was famed for its temple of the Sungod Baal and the games. It was conquered by the Arabs in 636.

H. Seyrig, *Syria* 1952, 204 ff., 1953, 12 ff. H. H. S.

**EMONA,** modern *Ljubljana* in the upper Save valley, was a city in south-western Pannonia on the main route between north-east Italy and the Danube. Under Augustus it was a legionary base occupied probably by Legio XV Apollinaris: on the transfer of this legion to Carnuntum (q.v.) *c.* A.D. 15 it was settled with a *colonia* of legionary veterans (cf. *CQ* 1963, 268 ff.).

J. Šašel, *PW* Suppl. xi, 540 ff. J. J. W.

**EMPEDOCLES** (*c.* 493–*c.* 433 B.C.; 444–441, his *floruit* ap. Diog. Laert. 8. 74, is too late), son of Meton and grandson of the Empedocles who won the horse-race at Olympia in 496, belonged to the aristocracy of Acragas in Sicily. Combining the roles of philosopher, scientist, poet, orator, and statesman with those of mystagogue, miracle-worker, healer, and claimant to divine honours, he acquired legendary fame. Tradition associates him with Pythagoreans, and Theophrastus (ap. D. L. 8. 55) calls him a follower and imitator of Parmenides. He championed democracy at Acragas after 472, declined an offer of the kingship, was later exiled and fled to the Peloponnese, where he recited his *Purifications* at Olympia. He visited Thurii shortly after its foundation (Apollod. ap. D. L. 8. 52). The place and manner of his death, about which there are conflicting stories, are unknown. He died aged 60 (Arist. ap. D. L. 8. 52; 74).

WORKS: two hexameter poems of considerable poetic merit (totalling 5,000 verses), (1) *On Nature* (Περὶ φύσεως), (2) *Purifications* (Καθαρμοί). About 350 verses of (1) and 100 of (2) are extant. Other writings are probably wrongly ascribed.

Empedocles' philosophy is the first pluralistic answer to Parmenides. Accepting the Eleatic contention that real being is permanent, he denies its unity and immobility. The All is a spherical *plenum*: within it four ultimate kinds or 'roots' (ῥιζώματα), fire, air, water, and earth—to which Empedocles assigns divine names—mingle and separate under the contrary impulses of Love (Φιλία) and Strife (Νεῖκος), to cause the arising and perish-

ing of 'mortal things'. Generation and decay are nothing save the compounding (in fixed ratios) and dissolution of eternally unchanging 'elements'. Empedocles imagines a World-cycle in which Love, the unifier of unlikes, and Strife, which divides and so joins like to like, alternately predominate. The four stages are: (i) Love controlling the Sphere, with the elements wholly mingled and Strife enveloping it on the outside; (ii) Strife passing in and Love going out; (iii) Strife victorious and the elements completely separated; (iv) Love returning and Strife withdrawing. Our world (cf. Arist. *Gen. Corr.* 334ᵃ6; *Cael.* 301ᵃ14) falls in period (ii): sexual generation has succeeded a phase of 'whole-natured forms' (fr. 62). A corresponding world occurs in (iv), where union in haphazard wise of limbs and organs, originating separately, produces monsters (frs. 57–61). (This interpretation of the World-cycle is not universally accepted: see bibliography.)

Empedocles' cosmology, described by the doxographers, begins with the separating off of the elements, first of all air and fire. His obscure astronomy mingles penetration with *naïveté*. Two hemispheres, a bright and a dark, revolving round the spherical earth, produce day and night. The sun is the rays of the diurnal hemisphere focused back from the earth's surface. More significant are his biological theories of pores and 'effluences' and of vision, later adapted by Plato and Aristotle. He explains sense-perception on the principles of symmetry and 'like perceives like'. The blood round the heart is the organ of thought.

The *Purifications*, prima facie a complete contrast to the poem *On Nature*, shows Empedocles in close relationship with the Orphic tradition in Acragas (cf. Pind. *Ol.* 2) and raises the problem of reconciling its doctrine of transmigration with the physical teaching. But the theological and mystical flavour of the cosmological poem, and the remarkable parallels with religious (exhibited by Cornford and Kranz), point to a possible vindication of the unity and consistency of his thought.

Empedocles' theory of matter is a step on the road to Atomism; and Aristotle, after criticism, incorporates it in his own philosophy. Empedocles was, through his disciple Gorgias, the parent of Sicilian rhetoric, and Galen calls him the founder of the Sicilian medical school. His importance in Greek thought is far-reaching.

ANCIENT SOURCES AND TEXT OF FRAGMENTS. Diels, *Vorsokr.*¹¹ i. 276–375.
MODERN LITERATURE. (1) General: Zeller–Nestle, *Philosophie der Griechen* i. 2⁷ (1922) (E.T. 1881); Th. Gomperz, *Greek Thinkers* i (1901); Burnet, *EGP* and *Greek Philosophy* Part i: *Thales to Plato* (1914); L. Robin, *La Pensée grecque*² (1932); H. Cherniss, *Aristotle's Criticism of Pre-Socratic Philosophy* (U.S.A. 1935): Guthrie, *Hist. Gk. Phil.* ii. (2) Special: J. Bidez, *La Biographie d'Empédocle* (1894); C. Millerd, *On the Interpretation of E.* (U.S.A. 1908); F. M. Cornford, *From Religion to Philosophy* (1912); E. Bignone, *Empedocle, Studio critico* (1916); W. Kranz, *Hermes* 1935. For a dissentient view of the World-cycle see F. Solmsen's development of a thesis of H. von Arnim in *Phronesis* 1965. A. J. D. P.

**EMPHYTEUSIS,** in late Roman law a lease in perpetuity or for a long term. It was more akin to ownership than to an ordinary lease, and the Emperor Zeno (*c.* 480) resolved a controversy by ruling that it was *sui generis*. As regulated by Justinian (*Cod.* 4. 66. 2–4), it was alienable (but the owner could pre-empt or claim a fine) and inheritable; it was protected by a variant of the *vindicatio* (q.v.); and it was terminable only for non-payment of rent for three years. It derived from earlier institutions, developed (from Greek models) in the third and fourth century A.D., originally for grants of imperial lands, especially *ius perpetuum*, a perpetual lease of land belonging to the *fiscus* (q.v.), and *ius emphyteuticarium* (ἐμφύτευσις), a long-term lease applicable to lands of the *patrimonium* (q.v.) *Caesaris*. Justinian merged in it the similar instituion of the Principate by which State or municipal land was granted in perpetuity or for a long term at a small rent (*vectigal*—hence the land was called *ager vectigalis*). The tenant had *possessio* (q.v.), and at least in some circumstances a variant of the *vindicatio*, but to what extent it had the other characteristics of *emphyteusis* is disputed.

L. Mitteis, *Zur Gesch. der Erbpacht im Altertum* (1901); F. Lanfranchi, *Studi sull'ager vectigalis* i (1938); ii (= *Ann. Univ. Camerino, sez. giur.* 1939); iii (= *Ann. Triestini* 1940); M. Kaser, *Sav. Zeitschr.* 1942, 34 ff.; L. Bove, *Ricerche sugli agri vectigales* 1960); E. Levy, *West Roman Vulgar Law, The Law of Property* ,1951), 43 ff., 77 ff. B. N.

**EMPORION** (modern *Ampurias*), a colony of Massilia on the Spanish coast about 75 miles north-east of Barcelona. A double city, Emporia or Emporiae, was formed by a settlement of the native Indigetes, separated by a wall which the Greeks guarded at night. It was the landing port of Roman expeditions in 218, 211, and 195 B.C. In 45 B.C. Caesar added some legionary veterans, but it was not until Augustus that Emporiae was made a *municipium civium Romanorum*, comprising the Roman, Spanish, and Greek inhabitants. Its coinage represents all three elements. Excavations since 1909 have distinguished the original Massiliote port (Palaeopolis) from the expanded Greek Neapolis and the Roman city. Numerous finds, extending into the Christian period, are housed in the archaeological museum of Barcelona.

M. Almagro, *Ampurias* (English ed. 1956) and *Las Necropolis de Ampurias* i, ii (1953, 1955). M. I. H.

**EMPUSA,** a Greek bogy-woman, appearing in fantastic forms (see Ar. *Ran.* 288 ff., the scholiast there, and the lexicographers, s.v.). Later demonology took her more seriously: Philostratus (*VA* 2. 4) recommends abusing her if met, whereupon she will flee squeaking; she is an amorous fiend, like a Lamia, who will sooner or later eat her human lover (4. 25); Apollonius rescues a young man from her. H. J. R.

**ENA, SEXTILIUS,** a Spaniard from Corduba, who wrote narrative verse on events of the Augustan period (Sen. *Suas.* 6. 27).

See Baehrens, *FPR*; Morel, *FPL*.

**ENCAUSTIC,** the technique of painting on stone or wood with heated wax as a medium for applying colours (Pliny, *HN* 35. 149). Encaustic decoration of architecture and ships preceded its use for pictures. Statues were coloured encaustically, which explains the statement that the technique was perfected by Praxiteles (q.v.); Praxiteles particularly liked those of his statues which were painted by Nicias (q.v. 2). An early fourth-century Apulian vase in New York (G. M. A. Richter, *Handbook of Greek Art* (1959), 395) shows an encaustic painter colouring a marble Herakles. The chief encaustic painters in Pliny's list are Polygnotus, Pamphilus (1), Pausias (qq.v.), Aristides (q.v. 2), and Nicias. The majority of the preserved mummy portraits (first to fourth century A.D.) are painted in encaustic on wood and show the combined use of brush and spatula for applying colours.

Overbeck, 1072, 1751, 1817; Pfuhl, 660, 796, 816, 821, 921. T. B. L. W.

**ENKTESIS.** Ἔγκτησις, ἔμπασις, and related words, commonly further defined by the addition of γῆς καὶ οἰκίας, are used to describe the right to own real property within a state. Since this right normally belonged only to citizens, it became the practice to make special grants of *enktesis* to foreigners, generally together with other rights and honours such as *proxenia* and even *isopoliteia*.

Examples and formulas are given by W. Larfeld, *Handbuch der griechischen Epigraphik* (1898–1907), i. 520 ff.; ii. 794 f.; *SIG*, index; Tod ii, index. J. A. O. L.

**ENCYCLOPAEDIC LEARNING.** In Greece the Sophists were the first who claimed to impart to pupils all the knowledge they might want in daily life. We are especially told of Hippias of Elis (Pl. *Hp. Mi.* 368 b; Cic. *De Or.* 3. 127) that he mastered all the subjects of instruction (τέχναι), later on called by Aristotle (*Pol.* 1337ᵇ15) ἐλευθέριαι ἐπιστῆμαι, or the branches of knowledge requisite for a freeman. Among them were astronomy, geometry, arithmetic, music, and grammar. When Quintilian (*Inst.* 1. 10. 1) speaks of 'orbis ille doctrinae quem Graeci ἐγκύκλιον παιδείαν uocat', he means the ordinary course of instruction for a pupil before taking up his special subject of study. Notwithstanding the value the Greeks attached to encyclopaedic knowledge, they never got so far as to compose an encyclopaedia.

It was reserved for the practical-minded Romans to lay down in a compilation the results attained by the scientific researches of the Greeks. Shortly after 184 B.C. Cato (q.v. 1) wrote a work for the benefit of his son on medical science, agriculture, and rhetoric, perhaps also on military science and jurisprudence.

Much more important was Varro's encyclopaedia, the *Disciplinae* in nine books on (i) *grammatica*, (ii) *dialectica*, (ii) *rhetorica*, (i) *geometria*, (v) *arithmetica*, (vi) *astrologia*, (vii) *musica*, (viii) *medicina*, (ix) *architectura*. The first seven books formed the foundations for the so-called seven liberal arts, which as *trivium* (grammar, dialectic, rhetoric) and as *quadrivium* (geometry, arithmetic, astronomy, and music) were still practised in the Middle Ages.

During the reign of Tiberius, Celsus (q.v. 2) composed an encyclopaedia named *Artes* probably containing the subjects agriculture, medicine, military science, rhetoric. Of these only the *libri medicinae* have come down to us. Pliny's *Naturalis Historia* (A.D. 77) is an encyclopaedia of nature and art. The *Prata* of Suetonius (q.v. 2) was rather a collection of 'uaria et miscella et quasi confusanea doctrina' (Gellius, *Praef.* 5) than a real encyclopaedia.

In the fifth century the *artes liberales* were once more treated by Martianus (q.v.) Capella between 410 and 439 in his bizarre work, *De Nuptiis Philologiae et Mercurii*. This encyclopaedia comprises, however, only the first seven *artes* dealt with by Varro. Neither is the book a strictly scientific manual, as Martianus dishes up his only half-understood learning borrowed from various sources in the shape of a Menippean satire, i.e. in prose alternated with poetry. The wedding of Mercury with Philology is the background that serves as a setting to the whole.

Boethius (q.v., *c*. 480–524) was so far interested in encyclopaedic learning that he made arithmetic, music, geometry, and astronomy the foundation of his purely philosophical works laid down in four text-books.

In the sixth century it was Cassiodorus (q.v.) who wanted to give the monks of his monastery 'Vivarium' a summary of the worldly sciences in his *Institutiones*. Therefore he laid down in seven chapters the seven liberal arts.

Finally, mention must be made of the *Etymologiae* or *Origines* by Isidorus (q.v. 2) of Seville (*c*. 570–636), an encyclopaedia which, starting from etymology, treated everything briefly that seemed to him worth knowing.

M. Guggenheim, *Die Stellung der liberalen Künste oder encyklischen Wissenschaften im Alterthum* (1893); Norden, *Ant. Kunstpr.* 670; *PW* Suppl. vi. 1256. P. J. E.

**ENDELECHIUS,** Severus Sanctus, friend of Paulinus of Nola, and professor of rhetoric at Rome (A.D. 395). The only work preserved is a poem *De mortibus boum* (A. Riese, *Anthologia* (1894), no. 893), thirty-three Asclepiadic stanzas, naïve in content but elegant (though not Horatian: several unrelated rhymes) in form. A dialogue between cowherds, it recommends Christianity as a protection from cattle-plague. The plague mentioned may be that of A.D. 386, the date of composition around 400, and the dramatic setting, and thus the author's home, Gallia Lugdunensis or Aquitania.

W. Schmid, *RAC* 5. 1960. O. S.

**ENDOWMENTS** can be divided into two groups, those given to state institutions and public corporations, and the private ones. The first group was called *epidoseis* in Greece, if the givers were citizens. They emerged after the Peloponnesian War, were an important factor in town finances, and were given in money or in kind (especially in grain). There was a difference between 'gifts' and *epidoseis* in Athens; the purpose of the *epidoseis* (cancellation of debts, war expenses, use for public buildings, roads, or libraries, foundation of schools and offices, grain provision, public festivals, distribution of food, etc.) and the terms on which they were to be collected, had to be defined in a published decree.

The private endowments had very different purposes. We hear of donations to temples and synagogues, sacrifices, processions, the making of statues of gods, festivals for kings and Roman Emperors, sacrifices for a dead person or care for his grave, donations and legacies to gymnasia, sports festivals, and clubs. The gifts were often in real estate (land, houses, and even villages). If the donation was intended to last for a long period or for ever, an administrative body had to be appointed and rules laid down specifying how a given capital should be invested and how its interest should be applied.

Many precautionary measures against betrayal of trust were provided (oaths, witnesses, state control, fines and punishment, legal actions, curses, blessings, disavowal of the endowment or its transfer to another body, etc.). Several hundreds of such endowments are known to us, a symbol of the public generosity of the ancients. The economic crisis of the third century A.D. marked the approximate end of these general endowments.

In Roman law only juridical persons of public law were permitted to receive and administer endowments, mainly subdivisions of the *aerarium, fiscus, patrimonium, res privata*, or of municipal exchequers and a few *collegia*. Justinian I, if not one of his predecessors during the fifth century A.D., made endowments under ecclesiastical administration for *piae causae* legal also. The donor had, in all these cases, the right to stipulate for which lawful purposes his endowment was to be used.

*See* CLUBS (GREEK *and* ROMAN), COLLEGIUM, FINANCE (GREEK AND HELLENISTIC).

A. M. Andreades, *History of Greek Public Finance* (1931), index, s.v. 'Epidoseis'; A. Berger, *Encyclopaedic Dictionary of Roman Law* (1953), art. collegia, collegia funeraticia, confirmatio donationis, donatio, donatio sub modo, ecclesia, paenitentia, piae causae, revocare donationem, universitas, usucapio pro donato; O. Broneer, *Hesp.* 1939, 181 ff.; M. I. Finley, *Studies in Land and Credit in Ancient Athens* (1951), 90; Frank, *Econ. Survey* i–v, index, s.v. 'foundations'; F. M. Heichelheim, *PW* art. 'Sitos'; *RAC* art. 'Domaene'; Jones, *Later Rom. Emp.* ch. 22; A. Kuenzi, *Epidosis* (1923); R. Laqueur, *Epigraphische Untersuchungen zu griechischen Volksbeschluessen* (1927); B. Laum, *Stiftungen in der griechischen und römischen Antike* i, ii (1914); Magie, *Rom. Rule Asia Min.*, index; A. Manzmann, *Griechische Stiftungsurkunden* (1962); Michell, *Econom. Anc. Gr.* 270, 275, 385; Rostovtzeff, *Hellenistic World*; *Roman Empire*² (indexes); H. Volkmann, *Neue Jahrb. f. Antike* 1939, 3 ff.; E. Ziebarth, 'Stiftungen', *PW* Suppl. vii; For the texts cp. also Dittenberg. *SIG*; *LSJ*; Preisigke-Kiessling, *Papyruswörterbuch* (indexes, s.v. 'ἐπίδοσις'). F. M. H.

**ENDYMION** (᾿Ενδυμίων), in mythology, a remarkably beautiful young man, either king of Elis (Apollod. 1. 56 and others) or a Carian (Aristophanes ap. Hesych., s.v.

᾿Ενδυμίωνα); his grave was shown on Latmos (Hesych. ibid., Paus. 5. 1. 5), or at Elis (ibid.). Of several tales told of him (see v. Sybel in Roscher's *Lexikon*, s.v.) the most celebrated is that he was loved by the Moon. In the Elean version (Paus. ibid. 4) she bore him fifty daughters, evidently the fifty months of an Olympiad; usually (as Apollod., loc. cit.), he sleeps everlastingly, either because Zeus granted it to him as a boon or for some other reason. H. J. R

**ENIPEUS** (᾿Ενιπεύς), god of a river (in Thessaly, or Elis, schol. *Od.* 11. 238, cf. Strabo 8. 3. 32), loved by Tyro, daughter of Salmoneus (q.v.). As she wandered beside it, Poseidon took the form of the river-god and possessed her, making a wave curve over them to hide them. She bore Pelias and Neleus. H. J. R

**ENNIANISTA**, 'an enthusiast for Ennius', a title claimed by a reader (ἀναγνώστης) who gave a public *recitatio* clamorously applauded in the theatre at Puteoli from Ennius' *Annales*. The incident, recorded by Gellius (18. 5), illustrates archaizing taste in the second century A.D. J. W. D.

**ENNIUS**, QUINTUS, born in 239 B.C. in Rudiae in Calabria, a meeting-point of three civilizations: Greek (from Tarentum), Oscan, and Latin (from Brundisium)— so Ennius said he had three hearts (Gell. 17. 17). In 204 B.C. Cato brought him back with him to Rome from Sardinia (Nepos, *Cato* 1, 4) where Ennius was serving with the Roman army. There, like Livius Andronicus, he lectured on poetry (Suet. *de gramm.* 1), but anecdotes tell of his *paupertas* (Cic. *Sen.* 14). In 189 B.C. the consul M. Fulvius Nobilior took him, after the fashion of Hellenistic generals, on his Aetolian campaign (which Ennius celebrated in the *Annales* and in his *Ambracia*, which may have been a play). The son of his new patron, in 184 B.C., took advantage of his position as a *triumvir coloniae deducendae* and made Ennius a Roman citizen (*Ann.* 377 V. and Cic. *Brut.* 79). Anecdotes connect him with Scipio Nasica (Cic. *de orat.* ii. 276) and Servius Sulpicius Galba (Cic. *Luc.* 51). His influence was great: Caecilius (q.v. 1) was *Enni primum contubernalis* (Jerome on 179 B.C.) and Pacuvius (q.v.) was his nephew. He died in 169 B.C. aged 70 (Cic. *Brut.* 78) and there was a story (no more) that his statue was in the tomb of the Scipios (Cic. *pro Arch.* 22).

*Tragedies*: some twenty titles are known, of which twelve are Euripidean, perhaps three Aeschylean, none is certainly Sophoclean, and one original was by an obscure contemporary of Euripides (the *Achilles* of Aristarchus: Plaut. *Poen.* 1 ff.). Real possibilities exist in the fragments of Ennius for comparison with Greek originals (e.g. *Alexandros* and *Telephus* from papyri), especially in the case of *Medea*. Here the changes in Ennius' translation of the nurse's opening speech are interesting: mythology is simplified and explained, so that of the first 5½ lines only 3½ are translated, and are expanded to fill 7; the fine vivid style of Euripides is made solemn and bombastic with alliteration and assonance. The speech *Med.* 214 ff. has been turned by Ennius into a polymetric *canticum* (scen. 259 ff. V.) and, more important, the great monologue of Medea before she slays her children shows dactylic tetrameters in Ennius and has therefore undergone the same treatment (*see* LIVIUS (1) ANDRONICUS, NAEVIUS, PLAUTUS, *and* CAECILIUS (1) STATIUS). Here and in the translation, e.g., of *Eumenides* 905 ff. (scen. 151 ff. V.), artificiality, a desire for careful patterning of language, and a delight in highflown usages have all contributed to substitute a rather grand formality for the natural ease of the Greek. It is possible to see in the fragments, however, something of the grandeur of the composition and to understand Cicero's admiration. Apart from these Greek tragedies, Ennius wrote *praetextae*, of which *Sabinae* (the rape of the Sabine women; it contained a motif taken from Eur. *Phoen.* 571 ff. in scen. 370 ff. V.) is an example and perhaps *Ambracia* (the dactyls of scen. 367 V. could be part of a *canticum*).

*Comedies*: nothing worth while can be said of Ennius' comedies, of which antiquity saw fit to preserve four separate lines.

*Saturae*: four books of mixed verse, distinguished carefully by the ancient world (e.g. Diom. *Gramm. Lat.* i. 485, 30 ff.) from the literary form invented by Lucilius (q.v. 1). Some seventy lines are preserved together with a long prose paraphrase of the fable of the crested lark (Gell. 2. 29). The subject of another *satura* was a contest between Life and Death.

*Scipio*: a special poem celebrating the great Scipio Africanus, probably not a *praetexta*. Excellent group of four lines quoted by Macrob. *Sat.* 6. 2. 26 (= var. 9 ff. V.). The barbarous hexameter (*sparsis hastis longis campus splendet et horret*: parodied by Lucilius 1190 M.) is quoted from this poem.

*Epicharmus*: Ennius translated one of the poems falsely attributed to Epicharmus of Sicily. It was on the subject *rerum natura* and the opening was a dream by Ennius (quoted by Cicero, *Luc.* 51).

*Hedyphagetica*: a composition based on a gastronomic poem of Archestratus of Sicily (end of 4th c. B.C.).

*Euhemerus*: a prose work based on the ἱερὰ ἀναγραφή of Euhemerus (q.v.). The remarkable fact about this work is that the deity whose majesty was most seriously infringed was not just a figure of the Greek Pantheon but Jupiter Optimus Maximus, the national god of the Roman State. Extensive fragments are quoted polemically by Lactantius.

*Annales*: a work of decisive originality especially in its application of the dactylic hexameter to epic; it contained eighteen books and Ennius seems to have been writing it up to the time of his death. The title is based on the public records, the *annales pontificum* (cf. Servius on Verg. *Aen.* 1. 373); its arrangement was on the historical pattern of consular years. The epic opened with a dream in which Homer appeared to Ennius and told him that he was his own reincarnation (6 and 15 V. and schol. on Pers. *prol.* 2); this is symptomatic of the pride which characterized his attitude to his predecessors (book 7 prologue, 213 ff. V.). Book I contained the story of the flight from Troy and the founding of Rome down to the death of Romulus; it also contained a famous *concilium deorum* on the Homeric pattern, parodied by Lucilius (q.v. 1). Books 2–3 the story of the other kings; book 6 Pyrrhus; books 8–9 the Punic Wars (but omitting the first Punic War since Naevius had dealt with that); books 10–12 the Macedonian War; book 13 the war against Antiochus 192 B.C. Books 15–18 the Istrian campaign and later events, but the details of these books are irrecoverable (see Gell. 17. 21. 43). Little more than this general outline can now be known of the architecture of the work. Stylistically it followed the lead of Livius Andronicus: archaisms are a very strong element (some, like *endo* for *in* and *induperator*, were metrically conditioned) and in the formation of compounds (like *altivolans, altisonus, omnipotens*) Ennius followed Naevius rather than Livius; but in the main the work represents the reaction in Latin of a style suitable for epic, remote from prose on the one hand, and from the excessive use of archaic features on the other. Metrically the work legislated for the Latin hexameter and Virgil's metrical practice differs only in refinements of detail. The epic is perhaps the most remarkable achievement in Latin, and is the culmination of a literary activity so varied, both in prose and verse, that

it rivals the achievement of the most distinguished Hellenistic Greek writers. The meagre fragments that survive conceal a most serious loss for the understanding of Latin literature.

I. Vahlen, *Ennianae Poesis Reliquiae*[2] (1903); E. H. Warmington, *Remains of Old Latin* (1935), 2 ff. (with trans.). Commentary on *Annales* by E. M. Steuart (1925); H. D. Jocelyn, *The Tragedies of Ennius* (1967); O. Skutsch, *Studia Enniana* (1967). E. Norden *Ennius und Vergilius* (1915); B. Snell, 'Euripides' *Alexandros*', *Hermes*, Einzelschr. 5 (1937); E. W. Handley and J. Rea, *The Telephus of Euripides*, *BICS* 1957; S. Mariotti, *Lezioni su Ennio* (1951).
G. W. W.

**ENNODIUS**, MAGNUS FELIX (A.D. 473/4–521), of Gaul, bishop of Pavia, author of a biography of his predecessor Epiphanius, a panegyric of Theodoric, letters, model speeches, miscellaneous poems (sacred and secular), and other writings. His work is noteworthy for its combination of pagan and Christian elements; preoccupation with form is dominant.

TEXTS. W. Hartel, *CSEL* vi; F. Vogel, *MGH, AA* vii. J. Fontaine, *RAC*, s.v. *Ennodius.* A. H.-W.

**EOS** ('Ήώς, 'Έως, *Aurora*), the dawn-goddess, a figure of mythology rather than cult. She is daughter of Hyperion and Thea (Hesiod, *Theog.* 372); she drives over the sky in a chariot and pair (*Od.* 23. 246), the horses being Lampos and Phaethon, i.e. Shiner and Bright. In other words, she is an important luminary, but less so than the Sun with his four-horse car. Her stock epithets, especially in Homer, are ῥοδοδάκτυλος (rosy-fingered) and κροκόπεπλος (saffron-robed), with obvious reference to the colour of the sky at dawn.

For some unknown reason, she is imagined as very amorous; an aetiological myth (Apollod. 1. 27) attributes this to the jealousy of Aphrodite, because Eos had been Ares' mistress. Hence most of the stories about her consist of kidnappings of handsome men to live with her (? a euphemism for sudden and mysterious death, see E. Rohde, *Psyche*[4] (1907), index under 'Entrückung'). The oldest of these lovers, so far as our documents go, is Tithonus; she leaves his bed to shine (*Od.* 5. 1). In *Hymn. Hom. Ven.* 218 ff. she asks Zeus to make him immortal, but forgets to ask immortal youth for him; so at last he becomes helpless with old age although he talks perpetually, and she shuts him up in a bedchamber. An old, perhaps original form of the story (see J. Th. Kakridis, *Wien. Stud.* 1931, 25 ff.) is that in Hellanicus (fr. 140 Jacoby), that he became a cicada, which chirps ceaselessly. Memnon (q.v. 1) was their son. A quite obscure lover is Clitus, a cousin of Amphiaraus (q.v., *Od.* 15. 250). Cephalus (q.v.) is much better known; in Ovid, *Met.* 7. 711 ff., Hyginus, *Fab.* 189. 2–3, it is Eos who suggests to him that he should try Procris' constancy. In Hyginus also (ibid. 5 ff.) Artemis gives Procris the means to be revenged on Cephalus. This opposition between the amorous and the virginal goddess might be suggested by *Od.* 5. 121 ff.; there Eos makes Orion (q.v.) her lover, and the jealousy of the gods finds expression in Artemis killing him with her arrows, an unusual detail, for she regularly kills women, not men.

In art she is generally winged, and is popular from the later sixth century: balancing Thetis at the Psychostasia of Achilles and Memnon or at their fight; or carrying Memnon's body from the field (Brommer, *Vasenlisten*[2], 259 ff., 290). From the fifth century she is shown pursuing or carrying off Cephalus or Tithonus, not always clearly distinguished (see Caskey–Beazley, *Attic Vase Paintings in the Museum of Fine Arts, Boston* (1931–63), ii. 37 f.). She sometimes appears in a two-horse chariot, going about her business as the Dawn. H. J. R.; C. M. R.

**EPAMINONDAS** (d. 362 B.C.; date of birth uncertain) was a pupil of Lysis the Pythagorean, but his early career is otherwise in doubt. Though he co-operated actively in the restoration of Theban power (379-371 B.C.), his individual part is not distinguishable till 371, when he was Boeotarch for the first time. While representing Thebes at the peace negotiations he refused to allow the Boeotian cities to be separately sworn, and consequently Agesilaus with the concurrence of Athens excluded Thebes from the treaty. Epaminondas was one of the commanders who met the invading Spartan army at Leuctra. Here he introduced the variant of a slanting attack by the left wing, which had been strengthened to the depth of fifty men (λοξὴ φάλαγξ). The crushing defeat of the Spartan army which followed made Epaminondas famous. More than a year later he invaded the Peloponnese (winter 370/69) to help the Arcadians to throw off Spartan control. When this was achieved without fighting, Epaminondas made the first recorded invasion of the Eurotas valley. He pressed home the moral advantage of this operation by establishing Messenian independence. His later invasions of the Peloponnese (369 and 367) had less effect. In 364 he decided to challenge the Athenian supremacy at sea, and led a fleet as far as Byzantium. But when war broke out again in Arcadia he commanded the Boeotians, and after a daring attempt to seize Sparta by surprise, he won an inconclusive victory at Mantinea, where he died of wounds.

The nobility of Epaminondas' character greatly impressed tradition. His political creations, independent Messenia and Arcadia, survived with somewhat different consequences than he had intended. His new strategy ended the military supremacy of Sparta and led to the innovations of Philip II and Alexander.

Plutarch's *Life* (as excerpted by Paus. 9. 13 ff.). H. W. P.

**EPAPHRODITUS** (1,), Nero's freedman and secretary, helped him to unmask the Pisonian conspiracy and accompanied him in his final flight. He was again secretary (*a libellis*) of Domitian, by whom he was killed (A.D. 95), apparently because he had helped Nero to commit suicide. Epictetus (q.v. 2) was his slave. He is probably not the man to whom Flavius Josephus dedicated his *contra Apionem* and *Jewish Antiquities*.

R. Laqueur, *Der jüdische Historiker Flavius Josephus* (1920), 23 ff.; L. A. Constans, *Mélanges d'arch.* 1914, 383 ff. A. M.

**EPAPHRODITUS** (2) of Chaeronea (1st c. A.D.) in his youth was a slave of the Alexandrian scholar Archias, who became his teacher. After obtaining his freedom from the governor of Egypt, M. Mettius, he taught at Rome and acquired a large library. He died in the reign of Nerva at the age of 75.

WORKS: Commentaries on Homer's *Iliad* and *Odyssey* (Steph. Byz., s.v. Λαπίθη, etc.; *EM* 165. 3, etc.), which dealt with etymology, grammar, and interpretation. Commentaries on Hesiod's *Scutum* (*Etym. Gud.* 36. 13) and Callimachus' *Aetia* (schol. Aesch. *Eum.* 2). Λέξεις, probably an etymological work (schol. Ar. *Vesp.* 352). Περὶ στοιχείων (schol. Theoc. 1. 117). J. F. L.

**EPEIUS** ('Ἐπειός), in mythology, (1) son and successor (as king of Elis) of Endymion (q.v.; Paus. 5. 1. 4). (2) Maker, with the help of Athena, of the Wooden Horse (*Od.* 8. 493). He was son of Panopeus, a poor warrior but an excellent boxer (*Il.* 23. 664 ff.); casts the weight very badly (ibid. 839-40). In Stesichorus (*Iliu Persis*, fr. 1 Vürtheim; Athenaeus, 457a) he is water-carrier to Agamemnon and Menelaus, and Athena pities his hard toil and (presumably) inspires him. This may be local tradition or Stesichorus' invention. H. J. R.

**EPHEBOI** (ἔφηβοι) meant in normal usage boys who had reached the age of puberty and could refer to any age

from 15 to 20. But at Athens it was also used in a technical sense to denote members of the Ephebic College. This institution was founded *c.* 335 B.C. on the initiative of Epicrates for the more efficient compulsory military training of youths reaching their 18th year. This age-group had always been liable to be called upon for military service but there is no clear evidence of any organized training institution before *c.* 335 B.C. The people elected a *kosmetes* to take charge of the whole organization and ten (later twelve) *sophronistai* (one from each tribe) to assist him, under the general jurisdiction of the *strategoi* (q.v.). Six teachers were appointed comprising two *paidotribai* (for physical training) as well as four separate instructors in the use of heavy armour, the bow, the javelin, and the catapult. At the end of the first year, which was spent in exercises and on guard duty in Munychia and Acte in common barracks, a review was held and the ephebes were granted a shield and spear by the State. Perhaps it was at this stage that they took the ephebic oath. In the second year they undertook duties in the country serving as *peripoloi*. During the two-year period they were exempt from civic duties and excluded from civic rights such as suing and being sued in the courts (except in certain cases). Thereafter they became full-citizens. After 305 B.C. the training was no longer compulsory and by 282 B.C., if not before, it was reduced to one year. About the same time the number of *paidotribai* was reduced from two to one. The *sophronistai* are mentioned for the last time in 303 B.C., though they do reappear in the time of Hadrian. With the end of compulsion the State no longer paid the ephebes the daily allowance (of 4 obols) and from now on the *ephebia* became an institution for a wealthy élite and numbers declined, though they did increase again later. Teachers probably continued to be paid by the state, but the *kosmetes* had to assume more and more of the financial burden himself, as the office became more and more of a liturgy. From *c.* 118 B.C. the *paidotribes* became a permanent, not an annual officer. Inscriptional evidence is scanty from about the middle of the third to near the end of the second century B.C., by which time the *ephebia* emerges as an *educational* institution, still retaining some of its military character, but emphasizing not only civic and religious duties but also philosophy and literature. Indeed, an inscription of 123/2 B.C. (*IG*² 1006) shows that the ephebes attended philosophical lectures in the Ptolemaeum, Lyceum, and Academy. From 118 B.C. onwards foreigners were admitted. The *ephebia* was still flourishing in the second century A.D. but began to decay towards the end of the third.

In other parts of the Hellenistic world the school systems recognized the three age groups of *paides*, *epheboi*, and *neoi* and in this context the *epheboi* are the 15 to 17 age-group (*see* EDUCATION, § IV. 2). This is Nilsson's interpretation of the inscriptional evidence (which he refers to a younger age-group than other authorities), and on this view there are no ephebic colleges of the Athenian pattern outside Athens. The Hellenistic *neoi* belong to the same age-group as the Attic *epheboi* and Nilsson believes that the programme of the schools for the *neoi*, combining physical (as distinct from military) training with cultural studies was a potent influence on the Athenian *ephebia* of the first century B.C.

M. P. Nilsson, *Die hellenistische Schule* (1955); H. I. Marrou, *A History of Education in Antiquity* (1956); S. Dow, *TAPA* 1960; C. Pélékidis, *Histoire de l'éphébie attique* (1962); O. W. Reinmuth, 'The Foreigners in the Athenian ephebia', *Univ. of Nebraska Studies in Lang.* 9, 1929. F. A. G. B.

**EPHEMERIDES** (ἐφημερίδες), diaries, a term applied particularly to the Royal Journal of Alexander the Great, kept by Eumenes (q.v. 3) of Cardia. Its importance as providing official documentation for the early historians of Alexander may have been overrated by many modern writers. Only Callisthenes seems likely to have had direct access to it, and he may not have needed it much, since he could write using his own notes on events still fresh. That Ptolemy had access to it, writing many years later, is possible, but only just. Almost certainly it was never published in full. The surviving quotations from it, relating mainly to Alexander's drinking habits and to his last illness, tell us little about its scope, and even cast doubts on the authenticity of these excerpts themselves. Nevertheless, it is possible that the military and administrative detail in Arrian's history (and sometimes in that of Curtius Rufus) represent material from the Diary, by whatever channels it may have been transmitted.

Fragments in *FGrH* ii B i, No. 117 (1927). H. Endres, *Die offiziellen Grundlagen der Alexanderüberlieferung* (1913); C. A. Robinson, *The Ephemerides of Alexander's Expedition* (1932); L. Pearson, *Hist.* 1954, 429 ff.
G. T. G.

**EPHESIA GRAMMATA,** formulae used in learned magic, see Eust. *Od.* 1864, 15. Cf. MAGIC, § 6.

**EPHESUS,** a city at the mouth of the Caÿster on the west coast of Asia Minor, which rivalled and finally displaced Miletus, and owing to the silting up of both harbours has itself been displaced by Smyrna as the seaport and emporium of the trade of the Maeander valley. Ephesus was founded by Ionian colonists under the leadership of Androclus, son of the Athenian king Codrus. It had little maritime activity before Hellenistic times, was oligarchic in temper and open to native influences. Ephesus maintained itself against the Cimmerians and also against the Lydian kingdom until its capture by Croesus, who contributed to the construction of the great temple of Artemis and dedicated the columns fragments of which are preserved in the British Museum. Under the Persians Ephesus shared the fortunes of the other seaboard cities; it was a member of the Delian League, but revolted *c.* 412 B.C. and presently sided with Sparta. The temple was burned down on the night of the birth of Alexander the Great, under whose control the city passed in 334. The city was replanned by Lysimachus *c.* 294 and passed with the kingdom of Attalus III to the Romans in 133. It had meantime grown to a size and importance rivalled in the East only by Alexandria and the Seleucid capitals, and under the Roman Empire it was the real (though not the titular) capital of the province Asia, and the residence of the proconsul. At this time, as earlier, the Temple treasury acted as a bank, in which deposits were made by cities, kings, and private persons. Acts xix gives a vivid picture of conditions in Ephesus in the middle of the first century A.D. In the provincial reorganization of Diocletian, Ephesus became the metropolis of the reduced province of Asia. The temple and part of the city have been excavated; among the notable ruins uncovered are the Prytaneum (where copies of the cult statue of the Artemisium were found), arcaded streets, baths, gymnasia, temples and churches, and a library, almost all being of Roman imperial times. Among famous citizens were the scurrilous poet Hipponax, the philosopher Heraclitus, Zenodotus and Artemidorus, and the painter Parrhasius.

*Enc. Brit.* (1964), 'Ephesus', see bibliography; F. Miltner, *Ephesos* (Vienna, 1958); G. E. Bean, *Aegean Turkey* (1966), ch. 7.
W. M. C.; J. M. C.

**EPHETAI** (ἐφέται) were an Athenian jury, fifty-one in number. Their origin and early history are obscure, but by the fifth century B.C. they seem to have been selected by lot from citizens over 50 years of age, and to have been concerned with homicide cases only. Under the presidency of the *basileus* (see ARCHONTES) they sat at the Palladion to try persons accused of unintentional killing, of complicity (βούλευσις) in killing, or of the killing (whether intentional or not) of a slave, a metic, or a foreigner; at the Delphinion to try persons accused of killing who defended themselves by claiming that the act was committed lawfully; and at Phreatto to try persons accused of a second killing when already exiled for the first. Thus they tried almost all kinds of homicide not considered important enough for trial by the Areopagus (q.v.). A likely exception is the formal trial of unknown killers and of homicidal animals and inanimate objects; these cases were heard at the *prytaneion*, possibly by the *ephetai* but more probably without any jury. The *ephetai* also took part in the procedure for pardoning a man exiled for unintentional homicide if there were no surviving relatives of the killed man. Some scholars have suggested that by the end of the fifth century the fifty-one *ephetai* had been replaced by ordinary heliastic jurors under the same name, but this view has not been universally accepted.

*See* DIKE (2), § 5.

G. Smith, 'Dicasts in the Ephetic Courts', *CPhil.* 1924, 353 ff.; R. J. Bonner and G. Smith, *The Administration of Justice from Homer to Aristotle* i (1930), 97 ff.; Hignett, *Hist. Athen. Const.* 305 ff.; D. M. MacDowell, *Athenian Homicide Law* (1963), 48 ff., 118 ff.
D. M. M.

**EP(H)IALTES** (Ἐφιάλτης, Ἐπ-), in mythology, (1) a giant; (2) one of the Aloadae (q.v.); also (3) a demon of nightmare. See Rose, *Handb. Gk. Myth.*[6]

**EPHIALTES** (4), Athenian statesman. About 465 B.C. he led a naval expedition beyond Phaselis (q.v.). Poor, incorruptible, and determined, he replaced Themistocles as the leading politician on the popular side, his principal opponent being Cimon (q.v.). He successfully prosecuted a number of the Areopagites for their conduct in office. He resisted the sending of help to the Spartans in 462 during the helot revolt, on the ground that Sparta was Athens' rival for power. With the help of Pericles, now beginning his political career, he took advantage either of Cimon's absence or of the revulsion of feeling on his inglorious return to pass measures stripping the Aeropagus (q.v.) of its more important powers (462/1); but so great was the hatred that he had aroused that he was murdered later in the same year. He was buried in the Ceramicus.

E. Manni, *Rend. Linc.* 1947, 308 ff.; R. Sealey, *CPhil.* 1964, 11 ff.; E. Ruschenbusch, *Hist.* 1966, 369 ff.
A. W. G.; T. J. C.

**EPHIALTES** (5), of Trachis, is said to have shown to Xerxes the path by which the Persians outflanked Leonidas at Thermopylae. The Delphic Amphictions set a price on his head (479 or 478), and the Spartans honoured as a hero another Trachinian who assassinated Ephialtes from personal motives (some ten years later, on his return from Thessaly, where he had taken refuge).
P. T.

**EPHIPPUS** (1), Middle Comedy poet, named in the Victors' List immediately before Antiphanes with one victory (*IG* ii². 2325. 145). Of the twelve known titles, six may indicate myth burlesque; in Βούσιρις, Heracles fought drunk (fr. 2). Ridicule is frequent: fr. 14, a full-length portrait of an elegant 'hypoplatonic' youth (cf. Webster, *Later Greek Comedy*, 51 f.). Fr. 5 (how a fish larger than Crete is prepared for the table) has an early reference to Celts (Webster, ibid. 40 ff.).

*FCG* i. 351 ff., iii. 322 ff.; *CAF* ii. 250 ff.
W. G. A.

**EPHIPPUS** (2), an Olynthian hostile to Macedonia, contemporary with Alexander, wrote a pamphlet of malicious gossip which started the legend of Alexander's excessive drinking.

*FGrH* ii. 126.

**EPHORS** ('Έφοροι, probably from ἐφορᾶν, but conceivably connected with οὖρος, 'a guardian'), magistrates in several Dorian States (Sparta, Thera, Cyrene, Euesperides, Heraclea Lucaniae). At Sparta they were elected annually by the citizens, and the senior ephor gave his name to the year. Combining executive, judicial, and disciplinary powers, they profited by the scarcity of written laws, and by the fifth century B.C., when they were five in number, they dominated the State (subject only to their rendering account to their successors). Their relationship to the monarchy suggests an origin in some early dispute between kings and aristocracy. Each month they exchanged oaths with the kings, the king swearing to observe the laws, the ephors to support the king. They had a general control over the kings' conduct, could prosecute them before the Gerousia, settle disputes between them, and enforce their appearance before their own board at the third summons. Two ephors accompanied the king on campaign. In administration they negotiated with representatives of other States, convoked and presided over the Gerousia and Apella (qq.v.), gave orders for mobilization and dispatch of the army.

Besides possessing general powers of civil jurisdiction they could depose and prosecute other magistrates. In trials before the Gerousia they both presided and executed the sentences. In disciplinary matters they enforced the Lycurgan κόσμος for the citizens, including supervision of the State education; they dealt more arbitrarily with the *perioeci*, and even more so with helots, through the *Krypteia* (q.v.). Briefly abolished by Cleomenes III (227–222 B.C.), the office survived until at least A.D. 200.

Most ancient writers ascribed the creation of the office to Lycurgus (q.v. 2) or to King Theopompus (c. 700 B.C.). A list of ephors was cited by some going back to 754, but they wrongly believed that Theopompus was on the throne in 754, and the list is undoubtedly false. Whether its 'creator' invented the office or merely adapted some surviving primitive Dorian institution remains unclear.

W. den Boer, *Laconian Studies* (1954), 197 ff. (with bibliography).
A. M. W.; W. G. F.

**EPHORUS** of Cyme (c. 405–330 B.C.), contemporary of Theopompus and a pupil of Isocrates. His various works included a history of Cyme ('Επιχώριος λόγος), a treatise on style (Περὶ λέξεως), and two books (Περὶ εὑρημάτων) which aimed at satisfying the demand for popular information on diverse topics characteristic of the period. His importance rests on his universal history ('Ιστορίαι) in thirty books. Beginning with the Return of the Heracleidae on the theory that this was the first period of verifiable fact, it reached the siege of Perinthus, 341. Book 30 was added by his son Demophilus to complete the work with an account of the Sacred War. The arrangement was on a subject system (Diod. Sic. 5. 1. 4) merging later into an annalistic framework.

Our knowledge of Ephorus largely depends on the fact that he was the chief source of Diodorus books 11–16, whose abridgement follows him very closely (see fr. 191). He consulted numerous authorities, correcting Herodotus by Ctesias, using a strongly biased Athenian source for the Pentecontaetia, perhaps Hellanicus or Andromon, and colouring Thucydides' account of the Peloponnesian War under the influence of fourth-century pamphleteers. He wisely preferred the Oxyrhynchus historian (q.v.) to Xenophon, and consulted Callisthenes and political pamphlets like those of Lysander and Pausanias. Although he failed in criticism of sources and was no military expert, he was, except for Xenophon, the most important historian of the fourth century. His work was known to Polybius, was extensively used by Diodorus

and Strabo, and was one of the sources of Polyaenus, Pompeius Trogus, and Plutarch. His influence lasted well into the Roman Empire. *See also* HISTORIOGRAPHY, GREEK, § 4.

*FGrH* ii A. 70; G. L. Barber, *The Historian Ephorus* (1935, with bibliography).                                                          G. L. B.

**EPHRAEM SYRUS**, c. A.D. 306–73, was born at Nisibis, where he lived until Jovian's surrender to the Persians (363) forced him to move to Edessa. He wrote (mainly verse) in Syriac; he could read Greek and was influenced by Hellenistic rhetoric. His 'hymns' contain many historical references, e.g. to the situation at Nisibis, to the sufferings of the Church under Julian and the restoration of church life under the Persians, and to the Arian controversy. Greek adaptations of his verses were current during his lifetime, and the fame he enjoyed is attested by Jerome. A small proportion of his works has been critically edited.

D. Hemmerdinger-Iliadou and J. Kirchmeyer in *Dictionnaire de Spiritualité* iv (1959), 800 ff.; E. Beck, *RAC* v (1961), 520 ff.   H. C.

**EPIC CYCLE**, ἐπικὸς κύκλος, a collection of early Greek epics, artificially arranged in a series so as to make a narrative extending from the beginning of the world to the end of the heroic age. Apart from the *Iliad* and *Odyssey*, we possess only meagre fragments of the poems involved, and our knowledge of what poems were involved is itself incomplete. We are best informed about those that dealt with the Trojan War and related events: there were six besides the *Iliad* and *Odyssey*, and summaries of their contents are preserved in some Homer MSS. as an extract from the *Chrestomathia* of Proclus (*see* NEOPLATONISM; but some think an earlier Proclus). Apollodorus and Hyginus (*see* MYTHOGRAPHERS) draw on a related source for their accounts of the Trojan War. Among monumental sources, the 'Tabula Iliaca' (*IG* xiv. 1284) is of particular interest.

2. The poems were composed by various men, mainly or wholly in the seventh and sixth centuries B.C. (Earlier dates given by chroniclers are valueless.) The Cycle is not mentioned as a whole before the second century A.D. But a Trojan Cycle, at least, seems to have been drawn up not later than the fourth century B.C., since Aristoxenus (*Vitae Homeri*, p. 32 Wil.) knew an alternative beginning to the *Iliad* evidently meant to link it to a preceding poem. Indeed, some of the Trojan epics seem designed merely to cover an allotted span of events; Arist. *Poet.* 1459ᵃᵇ criticizes the *Cypria* and *Little Iliad* for their lack of a unifying theme.

3. The cyclic poems (this term by convention excludes the *Iliad* and *Odyssey*) were sometimes loosely attributed to Homer; but Herodotus rejects this for the *Cypria* (2. 117) and queries it for the *Epigoni* (4. 32), and later writers generally use the names of obscurer poets or the expression ὁ (τὰ Κύπρια, etc.) ποιήσας. The poems seem to have been well known in the fifth and fourth centuries, but little read later; no papyrus fragment of them has been identified. Proclus' knowledge of them is demonstrably indirect.

4. The poems known or presumed to have been included in the Cycle, and the poets to whom they were ascribed, were as follows.

(1) In first place stood a theogony (O.C.T. *Homeri Opera* v. 96–8). Comparison with Apollodorus and *Orphica* indicates that an Orphic theogony was chosen, but doctored.

(2) *Titanomachia*: Eumelus (q.v.) or Arctinus of Miletus.

(3) *Oedipodia* (6,600 lines): Cinaethon of Lacedaemon.

(4) *Thebais* (7,000 lines): Homer (but more often anonymous). Highly esteemed by Pausanias (9. 9. 5), who says

that even Callinus knew the poem as Homer's; but if the name is correct, Callinus may only have alluded to the legend and to 'earlier singers'. On the subject of this and the following poem, see ADRASTUS.

(5) *Epigoni* (7,000 lines): Homer. ('Antimachus' in schol. Ar. *Pax* 1270 might mean Antimachus of Teos, but may be a confusion with the *Thebais* of Antimachus (q.v.) of Colophon. Cited by Herodotus and parodied by Aristophanes. The first line survives, and implies another poem preceding.

(6) *Cypria* (11 books): Homer, Stasinus of Cyprus, or Hegesias of (Cyprian) Salamis. The poem dealt with the preliminaries of the Trojan War (wedding of Peleus and Thetis, judgement of Paris, rape of Helen) and all the earlier part of the war down to the point where the *Iliad* begins. Fr. 1 implies no poem preceding. It was familiar to Herodotus, Euripides, Plato, and Aristotle. The title, τὰ Κύπρια (ἔπη), seems to refer to the poem's place of origin: cf. τὰ Ναυπάκτια ἔπη, ἡ Φωκαΐς.

(7) *Iliad*. There were alternative versions of the beginning and end which linked it with the adjacent poems above, § 2; schol. T *Il.* 24. 804).

(8) *Aethiopis* (5 books): Homer or Arctinus. The main events were the deaths of Penthesilea, Thersites, Memnon (qq.v.), and Achilles. The title refers to Memnon's Ethiopians; there was an alternative title *Amazonia*.

(9) *Little Iliad* (4 books): Homer, Lesches of Mytilene or Pyrrha, Thestorides of Phocaea, Cinaethon, or Diodorus of Erythrae. The suicide of Ajax, the fetching of Philoctetes and Neoptolemus (qq.v.), the wooden horse, Sinon (q.v.), the entry into Troy. (The last part, which overlaps the *Iliu Persis*, is omitted by Proclus, and may have been omitted from the poem when it formed part of the Cycle.) The poem must have acquired the name 'Ιλιάς independently of the *Iliad*, and then been called 'little' (μικρά) to distinguish it.

(10) *Iliu Persis* ('Ιλίου πέρσις, gen. -ιδος) (2 books): Arctinus or Lesches. The Trojan debate about the horse, Laocoon (q.v.), the sack of Troy, and departure of the Greeks. Aeneas left the city before the sack, not as in Virgil. The same title was given to a poem of Stesichorus.

(11) *Nostoi* (5 books): Homer, Agias (or Hegias) of Troezen, or Eumelus (q.v.). The returns of various Greek heroes, ending with the murder of Agamemnon, Orestes' revenge, and Menelaus' homecoming. The *Odyssey* alludes to these events—so much that it cannot have been intended to accompany the *Nostoi*—and its poet knew Ἀχαιῶν νόστος as a theme of song (1. 326, cf. 10. 15). Stesichorus also wrote *Nostoi*.

(12) *Odyssey*. Aristophanes of Byzantium and Aristarchus put the end of the poem at 23. 296, and so perhaps counted what followed as part of the *Telegonia*.

(13) *Telegonia* (2 books): Eugammon of Cyrene. An element of romantic fiction was conspicuous here (see ODYSSEUS, § 3). The appearance in a Cyrenean poet of Arcesilaus as a son of Odysseus suggests a sixth-century date (Arcesilas, q.v.), and Eusebius dates Eugammon to 566.

5. Various other early epics were current in antiquity, and some of them may have been included in the Cycle. Their remains are collected by Kinkel in *EGF*.

TEXTS. T. W. Allen, *Homeri opera* (O.C.T. 1911–20) v. 93 ff.; E. Bethe, *Homer, Dichtung und Saga* ii (1922), 149 ff. (Proclus only: A. Severyns, *Recherches sur la Chrestomathie de Proclos* iv (1963).)
DISCUSSION. F. G. Welcker, *Der epische Cyclus²* (1865–82); U. von Wilamowitz-Moellendorff, *Homerische Untersuchungen* (1884), 328 ff.; D. B. Monro, *Homer's Odyssey, Books XIII–XXIV* (1901), 340 ff.; J. Wackernagel, *Sprachliche Untersuchungen zu Homer* (1916), 181 ff.; Bethe, op. cit., 200 ff., 371 f. ff.; A. Rzach, *PW* xi. 2347 ff.; W. Kullmann, *Die Quellen der Ilias* (1960). M. L. W.

**EPICEDIUM** (ἐπικήδειον sc. μέλος, see DIRGE), in Latin literature a poem in honour of a dead person. The term is not found in Latin before Statius; the thing itself is older, for the *nenia* and *laudatio funebris* (qq.v.) contained its essentials. Strictly speaking, the *epicedium* was a song of mourning chanted over a corpse (*cadauere nondum sepulto*, in contrast with ἐπιτάφιον, Serv. ad Verg. *Ecl.* 5. 14), but it came to mean more generally a poem honouring a deceased person, scarcely distinguishable from a θρῆνος (see DIRGE). Themes appropriate to the *Consolatio* (q.v.) were naturally also in place in the *epicedium*, despite the different purposes of the two types of poem. There is also a close relation with the metrical epitaphs, several of which (Buecheler, *Carm. Epigr.* 1109; 1111; 1189; 1237) are really *epicedia*.

The constituent elements in the *epicedium* are lamentation and eulogy. Accompanying these (notably in the *Consolatio ad Liviam* or *Epicedion Drusi*, and in Statius) are consolatory reflections—irrevocability of fate, necessity of submission, faith in survival. Other customary features are frequent employment of mythology, apostrophes and invocations, indignation against destiny or the gods, thoughts on the vanity of birth or youth or merit, justification of lament, hope or assurance that the dead will be received in the other world by the *Manes*, finally (in Statius) description of last hours and of obsequies.

The metres are principally the hexameter and the elegiac couplet. Length varies considerably: the shortest pieces are about ten lines long; the longest (*Consol. ad Liv.*) is 474. Their literary worth is also very variable: contrast a masterpiece by Propertius with the poverties of the *Elegiae in Maecenatem*.

See especially: Catullus 101; Verg. *Ecl.* 5. 20–44; *Aen.* 6. 860–86; Hor. *Carm.* 1. 24; Propert. 3. 7; 18; 4. 11; Ov. *Am.* 3. 9; *Pont.* 1. 9; *Consol. ad Liviam* and *Elegiae in Maecenatem* (authors unknown); Mart. 5. 37; 6. 85; Stat. *Silv.* 2. 1; 6; 3. 3; 5. 1; 3; and 5; Auson. *Epiced. in patrem*; *Parentalia*.

Some *Epicedia* semi-parodically concern animals: Catull. 3; Ov. *Am.* 2. 6; Stat. *Silv.* 2. 4 and 5. There are of course Greek models and parallels for this theme; see *Anth. Pal.* 7. 189–216.

O. Schantz, *De . . . consolatione ad Liviam deque carminum consol. . . . historia* (1889); A. Pais, 'Degli epicedii latini' (*Riv. di filol.* 1890); O. Crusius, *PW*, s.v.; E. Galletier, *Étude sur la poésie funéraire romaine d'apres les inscriptions* (1922), 200 ff., 267 f.; G. Herrlinger, *Totenklage um Tiere in der ant. Dichtung* (1930); R. Lattimore, *Themes in Greek and Latin Epitaphs²* (1962); commentaries on Statius' *Silvae* by F. Vollmer (1898), H. Frère–H. J. Izaac (1944). C. F.; D. A. R.

**EPICHARMUS,** a Sicilian writer of comedy, was active during the first quarter of the fifth century B.C., as is clear from his references to Anaxilaus of Rhegium (fr. 98) and to Aeschylus (fr. 214). He was probably a native of Syracuse (our earliest evidence for this is Theocr. *Epigr.* 18 and *Marm. Par.* 71), but other cities laid claim to him; Arist. *Poet.* 1448ª32 is ambiguous, but may mean that the Sicilian Megarians regarded him as their own. Aristotle also says that Epicharmus was 'much earlier than Chionides and Magnes' (q.v.), and if this is true he must have been an established poet during the last part of the sixth century.

The titles and fragments of his plays (now significantly augmented by papyri) indicate that he was particularly fond of mythological burlesque; Heracles and Odysseus were the 'heroes' of many of these burlesques. *Logos and Logina* is shown by fr. 87 to have been mythological in character, a fact which could hardly have been guessed from its title. Some titles, like those of Attic comedies, are plurals, e.g. *Islands, Persians, Sirens*. It is a pity that no fragment enables us to decide beyond doubt how many actors these plays required or whether they required a chorus. The abundance of plural titles constitutes a prima facie case for a chorus. Certain fragments (6, 34) suggest that there *may* have been three actors on stage simultaneously, but this evidence is far from decisive. The scale of his plays is also uncertain. His language is Sicilian Doric, and is as colourful and sophisticated as that of Old Attic Comedy; he uses a variety of metres κατὰ στίχον, but there are no lyrics among the extant fragments.

A considerable number of philosophical and quasi-scientific works were attributed to Epicharmus in antiquity. The hard core of these may have been a collection of maxims made from his plays (cf. Theocr. loc. cit.), but as early as the fourth century B.C. the *Pseudepicharmeia* were regarded as forged (Aristoxenus fr. 45 Wehrli), and continued to be so regarded by critical historians, though the less critical treated them without scruple as genuine works of Epicharmus. A certain Alcimus argued that Plato derived much of his doctrine from Epicharmus (Diog. Laert. iii. 9 ff.), but it is hardly credible that the passages cited in support of this allegation were composed early in the fifth century; one of them (fr. 171) appears to parody the technique (πάνυ μὲν οὖν) of Platonic dialogue. The tradition that Epicharmus was a Pythagorean first appears in Plutarch (*Numa* 8).

Kaibel, *CGF* i. 88 ff.; Olivieri, *FCGM* i; Pickard-Cambridge-Webster, *Dithyramb*² 230 ff.; L. Berk, *Epicharmus* (1964). K. J. D.

**EPICRATES**, Middle Comedy poet, of Ambracia. In fr. 11 (before 347 B.C.) Epicrates cleverly describes scientific research in botany by Plato and his disciples.

*FCG* ii. 365 ff.; *CAF* ii. 282 ff.

**EPICTETUS** (1) (fl. 520–500 B.C.), potter and vase-painter in Athens, known from one potter's and thirty-nine painter's signatures, chiefly on red-figure cups with dainty compositions. One vase signed by Epictetus is attributed to the Cleophrades painter, a successor of Euthymides (q.v.) and a forerunner of the strong style, who painted from 510 to 480; he should perhaps be known as Epictetus II.

Beazley, *ABV* 254, 404; *ARV*² 70, 181. T. B. L. W.

**EPICTETUS** (2) (c. A.D. 55 to c. 135), of Hierapolis (Phrygia), Stoic philosopher. He grew up as a slave of Epaphroditus (q.v. 1), who allowed him to attend the lectures of Musonius Rufus and later set him free. Epictetus then began to teach philosophy in Rome. When in 89 Domitian banished the philosophers from Rome, he went to Nicopolis (Epirus), where he continued teaching to the end of his life. He acquired a large audience and many distinguished followers, among them Flavius Arrianus (*see* ARRIAN; *cos. c.* A.D. 130), who collected his lectures (διατριβαί), probably in eight books, four of which have come down to us, and later published a summary of his philosophy in the famous Manual (ἐγχειρίδιον). Through these posthumous publications he had great influence on the Emperor M. Aurelius.

Though Epictetus considered logic useful because it prevents us from being deceived by faulty arguments (Arrian 1. 17), he was but little interested in the purely theoretical side of philosophy, except theology. He taught that the universe is the work of God, and that Divine Providence manifests itself in its unity and order.

Contrary to the early Stoics he did not teach for the few and for the self-reliant, but for the many and the humble. He used to say that only he who had become aware of his weakness and his misery could profit from the teaching of the philosophers. He taught the common brotherhood of man. Wrongdoers, he thought, should not be punished as criminals, but pitied, because they are more unhappy than their victims.

Like the early Stoics he wanted to make man free and independent of the vicissitudes of fortune. We must not,

he said, let our happiness depend on things which are not in our power. The only thing which is always in one's power is one's own self and one's will. This we must keep unblemished. We must be indifferent to death, pain, and illness, and even the loss of our dearest relatives must not touch us. For all this not only belongs to the external world, but also happens through Divine Providence, which is always good.

*Epicteti Dissertationes ab Arriano digestae*, ed. H. Schenkl² (1916) ed. Souilhé-Jagu (Budé, 1943–63); A. Bonhöffer, *Epiktet und die Stoa* (1890); *Die Ethik des Stoikers Epiktet* (1894); Th. Colardeau, *Étude sur Épictete* (1903); D. S. Sharp, *Epictetus and the New Testament* (1914); M. Pohlenz, *Die Stoa*² (1955–9). K. VON F.

**EPICURUS** (*b.* Samos, 341 B.C.; *d.* Athens, 270 B.C.), moral and natural philosopher. His father, Neocles, a schoolmaster, was an Athenian of the deme Gargettus, who emigrated to the Athenian colony in Samos; his mother's name was Chaerestrate. As a boy he was taught by the Platonist Pamphilus. At 18 he was required to go to Athens to serve as an ephebe; Xenocrates was then head of the Academy and Aristotle was in Chalcis, and Menander was in the same class as Epicurus. He rejoined his family, who had left Samos, in Colophon. At this time or earlier he studied under Nausiphanes, from whom he learnt about the atomist philosophy of Democritus. When he was 32 he moved to Mitylene in Lesbos, and then to Lampsacus on the Hellespont; in both places he set up a school and began to acquire pupils and loyal friends.

He returned to Athens about 307/6, and bought a house, with a garden which became the eponymous headquarters of his school of philosophy. Apart from occasional visits to Asia Minor, he remained in Athens until his death in 270, when he bequeathed his garden and school to Hermarchus of Mitylene.

(The main sources for his biography are those collected by Diogenes Laertius, 10. 1–21.)

**2.** THE EPICUREAN SCHOOL in Athens consisted of a group of people who lived together on Epicurus' property, secluding themselves from the affairs of the city and maintaining a modest and even austere standard of living, in accordance with the Master's teaching. The company included slaves and women. Contemporary Epicureans often mentioned in the literature were his most devoted companion, Metrodorus of Lampsacus, who died before Epicurus; Leonteus and his wife Themista, also of Lampsacus; Hermarchus of Mitylene, the second head of the school in Athens; and a slave called Mys.

The school was much libelled in antiquity, perhaps because of its determined privacy and also because of Epicurus' professed hedonism. The qualifications which brought this hedonism close to asceticism were ignored, and members of rival schools accused the Epicureans of many kinds of profligacy. In Christian times, Epicureanism was anathema because it taught that man is mortal, that the cosmos is the result of accident, that there is no providential god, and that the criterion of the good life is pleasure. Centuries of prejudice have produced such caricatures as Sir Epicure Mammon, in Ben Jonson's *Alchemist*, and the modern use of the word 'epicure'.

**3.** WRITINGS. Diogenes Laertius (10. 26) reports that Epicurus wrote more than anyone else—about 300 rolls. Most of these are lost, including his thirty-seven books *On Nature*—of which there are a few, much mutilated papyri extant from Herculaneum. Apart from fragmentary quotations, the following three letters and two collections of maxims have been preserved, the first four all in the 10th book of Diogenes Laertius:

(1) Letter to Herodotus: a summary of his philosophy of nature.

(2) Letter to Pythocles: a summary of meteorology (possibly not authentic Epicurus but the work of a pupil).

(3) Letter to Menoeceus: a clear, elementary summary of Epicurean morality.

(4) *Κύριαι Δόξαι (Ratae Sententiae, Principal Doctrines)*: forty moral maxims.

(5) *Gnomologium Vaticanum (Vatican Sayings)*: eighty-one similar short sayings, discovered in a Vatican MS. by C. Wotke in 1888.

Apart from the letter to Menoeceus, and a few of the maxims, Epicurus' surviving writings are needlessly difficult, clumsy, ambiguous, badly organized, and full of jargon. Present-day knowledge and appreciation of Epicurus' system depends very largely on the poem of Lucretius, *De rerum natura*. Although this was written more than 200 years after the time of Epicurus, it appears to contain very little philosophical doctrine which was not taught by Epicurus himself.

4. DOCTRINES. The purpose of philosophy is practical: to secure a happy life. Hence moral philosophy is the most important branch, and physics and epistemology are regarded as subsidiary. (For this tripartition, see Sextus Empiricus, *Math.* 11. 169, and for the comparative evaluation K. *Δ.* 11 and Diogenes Laertius 10. 30.)

(a) *Moral Philosophy*. 'We say that pleasure is the beginning and end of living happily' (Letter to Menoeceus 128). It is a datum of experience that pleasure is naturally and congenitally the object of man's pursuit. Since it is a fact, however, that some pleasures are temporary and partial, and involve pain as well, it is necessary to distinguish between pleasures, and to take only those which are not outweighed by concomitant or subsequent pains. Pain is caused by unsatisfied desire; so one must recognize that those desires which are natural and necessary are easily satisfied; others are unnecessary, and if one views them properly they do not cause distress. The limit of pleasure is the removal of pain; to seek always for more pleasure is simply to spoil one's present pleasure unnecessarily with the pain of unsatisfied desire. Pleasure is not so much the process of satisfying desires, but rather the state of having desires satisfied.

Pleasure of the soul, consisting mainly of contemplation or expectation of bodily pleasure, is more valuable than bodily pleasure. The ideal is *ἀταραξία*, freedom from disturbance. The study of philosophy is the best way to achieve the ideal: by teaching that the soul dies with the body, being made of atoms as the body is, it frees a man from fear of death and life after death; by teaching that the gods do not interfere and that the physical world is explained by natural causes, it frees him from fear of the supernatural; by teaching him to keep out of competitive life in politics and administration (the slogan was *λάθε βιώσας*), it frees him from the distress of jealousy and failure; by teaching him to avoid intense emotional commitments, it frees him from the pain of emotional turmoil.

Epicurean morality was less selfish than it seemed. Starting from the idea of pleasure, Epicurus found a place for most of the conventional virtues (though not for the Aristotelian *μεγαλοπρέπεια* or *μεγαλοψυχία*), and especially for those of temperance and loyalty. The Epicurean communities were famous even among their enemies for the friendship which bound members to each other and to the founder.

(b) *Canonic* was explained in a book (now lost) called *Κανών*, which means 'Straight edge' or 'Rule'. Its subject matter was how to distinguish true from false propositions. It taught that sense-perception, the mechanics of which are explained in the physics, is reliable, in the sense that the mental image formed by means of sensation always corresponds to the physical object which caused the sensation. This physical object is always an *εἴδωλον* (idol)—an extremely fine 'film' of atoms given off from the surface of compounds in the physical world.

In normal sense-perception, a stream of similar *εἴδωλα* proceeding from the surface of an object without intermission activate the soul-atoms of the perceiver in the sense-organs, and the soul-atoms by their motions somehow picture the characteristics of the external object. The picture is retained in the mind as a memory. Delusions occur when single or damaged *εἴδωλα* cause an image to form which looks like those formed by continuous streams of *εἴδωλα*; a man is deluded only by judging it to *be* one of the latter. Thus Epicurus hoped to answer those who doubted the validity of sense-perception: *judgements* can be wrong, but sense-perception itself always corresponds accurately with something in the external world; and judgement can be improved by philosophy. (Letter to Herodotus 46–52, Lucretius IV).

(c) *Physics*. Epicurus adopted the atomist theories of Democritus, with some changes which can often be seen as attempts to disarm Aristotle's criticisms of atomism.

Epicurus' metaphysical argument for the existence of unchanging and indestructible atoms and void comes from Leucippus and Democritus, who were themselves responding to the Eleatic school. Arguments about being and not-being show that there must be permanent elements; arguments about divisibility show that there must be indivisibles; the fact of motion shows that there must be void in which the elements move.

Change is explained as the rearrangement of unchangeable atoms. The cosmos itself is a combination of atoms which came together at some point of time by purely natural causes, and it will perish similarly by the dispersal of its component atoms. Our cosmos is one of an indefinite number, past, present, and future.

Gods exist, living a happy life sempiternally in the intercosmic spaces. They take no thought for our cosmos, or for any other; such concern would detract from their perfect Epicurean contentment. It is good for man to respect and admire them, but not to expect favours or punishments from them.

Atoms move naturally downwards, because of their weight, unless they collide with other atoms. All combinations are due to collisions. Since collisons would be inexplicable if only downward motion occurred, it must be that there are deviations from the straight downward path—not large enough to be observable, nor frequent enough to create an unpredictable, random universe. This theory of deviation (*clinamen* or swerve) also accounts for the fact that actions of animals, including men, are not determined wholly by their genetic constitution and their environment (Lucretius 2. 62–332).

Our cosmos developed out of a collection of atoms in space, in which first the sky, air, sea, and earth were separated from each other by natural motions, and later the earth grew vegetation and finally animal species. No gods intervened: natural motions are enough to account for the development of everything in the world. A theory of the survival of the fittest accounts for the apparently purposive features of living things.

Epicurus contradicted the Aristotelian cosmology on all these points: the infinite universe, the plurality of worlds, the perishability of our world, the existence of void, the finite divisibility of matter, the 'evolution' of natural kinds, the rejection of a divine first cause, the rejection of final causes. The Aristotelian world picture gained much wider allegiance, both in antiquity and in the Middle Ages, and it was not until the rise of the 'mechanical philosophy' in the 17th century that Epicureanism again became a serious rival to Aristotelianism.

For fuller bibliography, see Haussleiter in Bursian, *Jahresb.* 1943, 1 ff., and P. DeLacy, 'Some Recent Publications on Epicurus and Epicureanism', *Classical Weekly* 1955, 169 ff.

H. Usener, *Epicurea* (1887; standard work, containing the extant writings and fragments, except papyri).

EDITIONS, TRANSLATIONS, AND COMMENTARIES: E. Bignone (1922;

Ital. trans., sel. frs., and notes); P. von der Muehll (1922; text only); C. Bailey (1926; text, Eng. trans., sel. frs., comm.); R. D. Hicks (1925; Loeb Classical Library, Diogenes Laertius vol. 2; text and trans.); G. Arrighetti (1960; text, Italian trans., comm.; includes frr. of Περὶ Φύσεως); Russel M. Geer (1964) Eng. trans. only).

MODERN LITERATURE (selection): C. Giussani, *Studi Lucreziani* (Lucr. vol. i, 1896); W. Crönert, *Kolotes und Menedemos* (1906); R. D. Hicks, *Stoic and Epicurean* (1910); C. Bailey, *The Greek Atomists and Epicurus* (1928), reviewed critically by R. Philippson, *Gnomon* 1930, 46 ff.; E. Bignone, *L'Aristotele perduto e la formazione filosofica di E.* (1936); W. Schmid, *E., Kritik der platonischen Elementenlehre* (1936); B. Farrington, *Science and Politics in the Ancient World* (1939); C. Diano, 'La psicologia d'Epicuro e la teoria delle passioni', *Giornale critico della filosofia italiana* 1939, 105 ff.; 1940, 151 ff.; 1941, 5 ff.; 1942, 5 ff. and 121 ff.; W. Schmid, 'Götter und Menschen in der Theologie Epikurs', *Rh. Mus.* 1951, 97 ff.; G. Freymuth, *Zur Lehre von den Götterbilden in der epikureischen Philosophie* (Deutsche Akad., 1953); N. W. DeWitt, *Epicurus and his Philosophy* (1954; over-enthusiastic); P. Merlan, *Studies in Epicurus and Aristotle* (1960); W. Schmid, article 'Epikur' in *RAC*; Knut Kleve, *Gnosis Theon* (*Symb. Oslo*. Suppl. 1963); David J. Furley, *Two Studies in the Greek Atomists* (1967); B. Farrington, *The Faith of Epicurus* (1967); Marie Boas, 'The Establishment of the Mechanical Philosophy', *Osiris*, 1952, 412 ff.; R. H. Kargon, *Atomism in England from Heriot to Newton* (1966); *PW* Suppl. xi. D. J. F.

**EPIDAMNUS,** a joint colony of Corcyra and Corinth, founded *c.* 625 B.C. as a port of call on the Adriatic coast and a focus of trade from Illyria. This trade was at first constituted as a monopoly for the benefit of the ruling oligarchy, which further strengthened its ascendancy by restricting industrial pursuits to public slaves. By 435 the commons had nevertheless gained control and expelled the oligarchs; when put under siege by the latter, they invoked the aid of Corcyra, and when this was refused they applied to Corinth. The Corinthians reinforced the democracy with new settlers, but shortly afterwards the city was recaptured by the Corcyraeans. This scramble of Corinthians and Corcyraeans for Epidamnus was a contributory cause of the Peloponnesian War. For the later history of Epidamnus, *see* DYRRHACHIUM.

Recent excavations reported in *Buletin për Shkencat Shoqërore* 1957. I. 61 ff. M. C.

**EPIDAURUS,** one of the small States of the Argolic Acte, on a peninsula of the Saronic Gulf. It was originally Ionic, but dorized from Argos (Paus. 2. 26. 1); unlike Argos, it used a 'Western' alphabet. It owed religious dues to Argos (Thuc. 5. 53), but was politically independent, and at one time controlled Aegina (Hdt. 5. 82). Its fame lay in the sanctuary of Asclepius, situated in an inland valley. The great temple of Asclepius (early 4th c.) does not appear to have been preceded on its site by an earlier temple. On nearby Mt. Kynortion Asclepius to some degree replaced his father Apollo, who as Apollo Maleatas from the middle of the seventh century took over the cult of a local hero which appears to go back to Mycenaean and earlier times (Πρακτ. 1948 (1949), 90 ff.). Entered by a propylaeum, the sanctuary contained the great temple with the gold and ivory statue of the seated god by Thrasymedes of Paros, other small temples, porticoes, baths, a gymnasium and palaestra, inns and priests' houses. The chief extant buildings are the *tholos*, a round building of the mid fourth century by Polyclitus the younger, with beautiful Corinthian columns, and one of the most perfect of Greek theatres, which well preserves its fourth-century plan. The building accounts of temple and *tholos* are preserved. Though there are earlier dedications, the buildings and the chief fame of Asclepius belong to the fourth and later centuries. The cult, originally perhaps Thessalian, was transferred from Epidaurus to other towns, notably to Athens and Rome (Paus. 2. 26. 8). The inscriptions recording cures, wrought by sleeping in a dormitory attached to the temple and following the prescriptions of the priests, are important for the history of ancient medicine.

P. Kavvadias, *Τὸ ἱερὸν τοῦ Ἀσκληπίου ἐν Ἐπιδαύρῳ* (1900); *Fouilles d'Épidaure* (vol. i only, Athens, 1893); *Ἀρχ. Ἐφ.* 1918, 115 ff. A. Defrasse, *Épidaure* (1895; architectural restorations); R. Herzog, *Die Wunderheilungen von Epidauros* (1931). T. J. D.; R. J. H.

**EPIGENES** (1) of Sicyon is said (*Suda*, s.vv. Θέσπι and Οὐδὲν πρὸς τὸν Διόνυσον) to have been the 'firs tragic poet', after whom Thespis was either second o sixteenth in the line of succession. He may have compose 'tragic choruses' of the type which Herodotus (5. 67 speaks of as produced at Sicyon in the sixth centur B.C., having reference to the sufferings of heroes, bu transferred by the tyrant Cleisthenes to the worship o Dionysus. A. W. P.-C.; D. W. L

**EPIGENES** (2), Middle Comedy poet, dated befor 376 B.C. by his reference to Hecatomnus, king of Caria

*FCG* iii. 537 ff.; *CAF* ii. 416 ff.

**EPIGONI** ('Ἐπίγονοι), sons of the Seven against Thebe (*see* ADRASTUS). They were: Alcmaeon and Amphilochus sons of Amphiaraus; Aegialeus, of Adrastus; Diomedes of Tydeus; Promachus, of Parthenopaeus; Sthenelus, o Capaneus; Thersander, of Polynices; Euryalus, o Mecisteus. (Apollod. 3. 82; a different list, Hyg. *Fab*. 71. H. J. R

**EPIGRAM,** ἐπίγραμμα, means 'inscription'. Since vers inscriptions were more memorable than prose, the wor came to denote a poetic inscription. In and after th Alexandrian period, it also meant a brief poem (usually i elegiac couplets) suggested by a single event, whethe grand (the death of a hero) or trivial (the death of a pe grasshopper). The great treasury of Greek literary epi grams is the Anthology (q.v.). Many others have bee collected from other sources—classical writers, stones pottery, and papyrus. No comparable collections of Lati epigrams exist; and there is as yet (1969) no book on th history of the epigram in Greece and Rome.

GREEK EPIGRAMS. Poetic epigrams were written i classical Greek for over 2,000 years. In the history of thi small but interesting form of literature there are fiv stages.

(1) *Archaic*. The earliest extant inscriptions in vers come from the eighth century B.C.: two lines written o 'Nestor's goblet' from Ischia (*Gymn*. 1956, 36 f.), a imperfect sentence on a Dipylon jug (Friedländer an Hoffleit 53). Thenceforward brief poetic epigrams wer placed on graves (ibid. 1, late seventh century), offering (ibid. 10, 750–650 B.C.), and even road-signs (ibid. 149 citing Pseudo-Plato, *Hipparchus* 228 d–e). At first the were in dactylic hexameter, echoing epic rhythm and phrasing; later, because of its melancholy associations sententious tone, and compact shape, the elegiac couple came to predominate. Iambic and trochaic epigrams ar found, but are less common. Typically, the archaic epi gram was a brief address in which a tombstone or votiv tablet (or sometimes the dead man) spoke to the passer by, giving him the necessary facts with strongly re strained emotion. This control and purpose made th epigram into an art-form.

(2) *Classical*. Epigrams were attributed by Gree critics to famous poets from Homer onwards, althoug not many are authentic. As far as we know, the firs eminent poet to write verse inscriptions was Simonide (q.v.), whose few genuine epigrams have a grave intensit of feeling which is enhanced by their brevity and imper sonality. Euripides wrote a fine couplet on the Athenia troops lost in Sicily (Plut. *Nic*. 17). The epigrams at tributed to Plato may not all be his (W. Ludwig, *GRBS* 1963); but Aristotle himself composed the inscriptio for the statue he set up at Delphi to honour his friend Hermias (Diog. Laert. 5. 1. 6). Many verse inscription by unknown authors have been preserved from *c.* 450 B.C. onwards. Their style grew more elaborate and their ton

partly influenced by tragedy) more emotional; they conveyed more facts than earlier epigrams; but, like the Attic funerary sculptures, they were nobly serene and sincere.

(3) *Hellenistic*. In the new era after Alexander's conquests the epigram was transformed. Poets still wrote real inscriptions in verse; but now they also created and published poems which, though brief and direct, like inscriptions, were never meant to be carved in stone. Several motives encouraged this development. Some poets whose profession it was to compose verse-inscriptions found that field too limited and extended their range of subjects: such was Leonidas (q.v. 2) of Tarentum. Other took to competing with one another or with their 'classical' predecessors in writing epigrams on interesting themes: such were Asclepiades (q.v. 2) and his friends Hedylus (q.v.) and Posidippus (q.v. 2). Most Alexandrian authors liked experimenting with established patterns and infusing new material into them: so Callimachus' (q.v. 3) address to his dead friend Heraclitus (*Anth. Pal.* 7. 80) is a development of the epitaph. They loved brevity, too (Call. fr. 465 Pf.), and the epigram must be brief (*Anth. Pal.* 6. 327). And, as true lyrical poetry ceased to be created and sung, poets now voiced more of their personal emotions through the elegy and its shorter but more versatile derivative the epigram. The themes treated in books 5, 11, and 12 of the Anthology, love and wine, now grew so popular that they almost dominated epigrammatic poetry. But there were other new departures: fictitious votive and funerary inscriptions (e.g. *Anth. Pal.* 6. 45, 301; 7. 725, 740); short poems on famous men, works of art, natural beauties, or curiosities —called 'epideictic' because they displayed the poet's skill (*Anth. Pal.* 9. 24, 374, 507, 713 f.); a few hate-poems (*Anth. Pal.* 12. 43 + 11. 275) and some joke-poems (more would be written later); sympathetic sketches of the life of poor folk (*Anth. Pal.* 6. 4, 226); portraits of women (*Anth. Pal.* 6. 353-4); and epitaphs on pet animals, a fancy invented by Anyte (q.v.). Unassuming as their subjects are, the language and style of these small poems are sensitive and the structure of their verse is skilfully varied.

(4) *Graeco-Roman*. In 196 B.C. Alcaeus (q.v.3) of Messene extolled T. Quinctius Flamininus, the 'liberator' of Greece (*Anth. Pal.* 16. 5). Greek poets now began— in the epigram as in other media—to address Romans and to influence Roman poetry. Among them there was none to compare with Catullus; yet Antipater of Sidon, Erucius, and Zonas wrote graceful epigrammatic poetry, while Philodemus (qq.v.) expressed ardent sensuality in lively colloquial speech (*Anth. Pal.* 5. 46, 132). About 80 B.C. Meleager (q.v. 2) did a great service to literature by publishing a fine anthology of epigrams covering about six centuries, the *Garland*. His own poems often imitated earlier authors, especially Asclepiades, but they were sweetly eloquent. Another *Garland* issued *c.* A.D. 40 by Philippus (q.v. 7) of Thessalonica contained Greek epigrammatists who wrote after Meleager's time: the most interesting of a dull group is Marcus Argentarius (q.v.). With him the Greek epigram started a new trend, its last important phase of growth. Many of his epigrams are jokes, with an unexpected quip in the last few words— a paradox or a pun. The modern concept of epigram thus created, and strengthened by the drastic humour of the contemporary mime, was worked out by Lucillius, who, like his imitators Nicarchus and Martial (qq.v.), concentrated on wit, humour, and point.

(5) *Byzantine*. The epigrammatists who wrote in the Byzantine era reflected the conflicting spiritual attitudes of their time. Devout Christians, such as St. Gregory of Nazianzus (writing *c.* A.D. 385), composed poems of unimpeachable orthodoxy, staunch sincerity, and re-

grettable monotony. Others, although doubtless Christian by profession and high in imperial favour, wrote epigrams which were surprisingly pagan in feeling, full of the joy of life and the raptures of love, and closely imitative of pre-Christian models: such was the consul Macedonius of Thessalonica (*c.* A.D. 550), Paulus Silentiarius, and his friend Agathias (qq.v.), who assembled an important anthology of new epigrams. (For specimens of their light gay poems see *Anth. Pal.* 5. 216-41.) And one notable poet, Palladas (q.v.), although recognizing that the Olympian cults were dead, could not accept the Christian creed, and from his cynical despair produced the last powerful and original poetic epigrams in Greek literature.

LATIN EPIGRAMS. In epigrammatic poetry, as in other fields, the Romans began with a crude but robust tradition of their own, extended and refined it by imitating the Greeks, and then endeavoured, sometimes with success, to outdo their masters. The earliest-known Latin epigrams are funerary inscriptions. The Saturnian epitaphs of the Scipios (*CIL* i². 7, 9, 10, 11) are not elegant, yet their force and brevity command respect. Ennius, the first great transmitter of Greek thought and style to the Romans, composed a quasi-epitaph—the first extant Latin poem in elegiac verse—asserting his own immortality, and wrote two even more grandiose epigrams glorifying Scipio. Poetic epitaphs on three early poets are recorded by Gellius (1. 24): those on Naevius and Plautus were perhaps written by later admirers, but the naïve quatrain of Pacuvius may be his own. The little-known writer Pompilius' epigram on himself traced his ancestry back through Pacuvius and Ennius to the Muses. Such poems are in the style of the Roman *elogium*, terse and proud.

Erotic epigrams in Latin appeared in the second century B.C. Gellius (19. 9) admiringly cites amatory poems by Porcius (q.v. 1) Licinus, Valerius Aeditus, and Q. Lutatius Catulus—all adaptations of well-known Greek themes. Accius is known to have written similar poems, as well as poetic inscriptions in Saturnians for a new temple of Mars; and a cruel satiric epigram on lovers' baby-talk (Morel 42) is attributed to Papinius (= Pompilius?). With Catullus (q.v.) both the love-epigram and the invective epigram caught fire and blazed up. For centuries there had been nothing in Greek to match the passionate agony of his *Odi et amo* (Cat. 85) or the bitter contempt of his denunciations of Caesar (Cat. 29, 52, 57, 93). Although he is often called a lyricist, Catullus wrote relatively few lyrics: like the Alexandrians, he chose to pour his emotions into the epigram and the elegy. His friends Calvus and Cinna also composed amatory, and Calvus invective, epigrams: their work is lost, but two humorous poems by Furius Bibaculus survive (Morel 80-1).

Thenceforward the writing of epigrams became extremely popular. The Younger Pliny (q.v., *Ep.* 5. 3) justifies himself for composing such poems by naming over a score of his predecessors, beginning with Cicero (q.v. 1) and closing with Ennius. We hear of epigrams by Brutus, Varro, Maecenas, Julius Caesar, Augustus, Tiberius, and many others: few have survived. Virgil (q.v.) began his career by making epigrams, including a parody of Catullus (*Catalepton* 10 ~ Catullus 4). Ovid (q.v.) too composed epigrams, and introduced some into his longer poems (*Met.* 14. 443-4, *Trist.* 3. 3. 73-6). Martial (q.v.) later cited (1 praef.) as his own models, besides Catullus, three authors of the early Empire whose reputations were partly based on their epigrammatic poetry: Domitius (q.v. 7) Marsus (whose book, named *Hemlock*, must have been satiric), Albinovanus (q.v.) Pedo, and the soldier and statesman Cn. Cornelius Lentulus (q.v. 9) Gaetulicus. Little of their work remains; but from the same era we have an anonymous collection of Priapea, rather more dirty than witty. Criticism of the emperors was voiced in anonymous epigrammatic pasquinades (see Suet. *D. Aug.* 70, *Tib.* 59, *Nero* 39, *Dom.* 23, and Morel 153–4); and the *probrosa carmina* which brought disaster on their authors (Tac. *Ann.* 4. 31, 6. 39, 16. 28), if not satires, were epigrams.

The reign of Nero, so fertile in literature, produced original and interesting epigrams by Seneca (2) and Petronius (3) (qq.v.), which have in part survived. The young Emperor himself wrote amatory epigrams, and patronized Lucillius (q.v.), who was perfecting the witty surprise-ending epigram in Greek. Lucillius was followed in the Flavian epoch by Martial (q.v.), most prolific and versatile of all extant epigrammatic poets and the chief model for modern epigrammatists. After him no important innovations were made in form or (until the Christians) in subject. His patron the Younger Pliny prided himself on his own epigrams, which—perhaps through his wish to be true to literary convention—were rather improper; but they have practically vanished. We have the impression that most epigrammatic poetry of the Roman Empire was satirical, comical, or amorous. It is strange to see Γ man *gravitas* still asserting itself in the epitaph written for himself by L. Verginius (q.v. 2) Rufus, who was thrice offered the imperial throne but *imperium adseruit non sibi sed patriae* (Pliny, *Ep.* 6. 10. 4). The sophistication of a later epoch comes out in the light epitaph Hadrian (q.v.) wrote for his horse (*PLM* 4. 126), his bantering exchange with the poet Florus (q.v.; Morel 136), and his playful address (of doubtful authenticity) to his soul in contemplation of death, Morel 137).

The last great pagan Latin poet, Claudian (q.v.), produced some well-turned but conventional epigrams, while Ausonius, like the Byzantine Agathias (qq.v.), wrote some which betray none of their author's Christian faith, being pagan in subject, sensuous in mood. In a remarkable return to the initial function of the epigram, three more devout Christian writers composed poems to be inscribed on objects of religious veneration: Prudentius (q.v.) expounding pictures of biblical scenes (doubtless in a basilica), Paulinus (q.v.) of Nola describing ecclesiastical buildings, and Pope Damasus explaining the holy places of Rome. (On such poetical descriptions see Friedländer and Hoffleit 54.) Though aesthetically undistinguished, these poems are valuable historically. Many hundreds of epitaphs, pagan and Christian, which have survived on stone, use conventional, imitative, often painfully inexpert verse to convey naïve and touching sentiments. The history of classical Latin epigram closes with the poets of the *Anthologia Latina* (q.v.), a group of mediocre sixth-century versifiers writing in North Africa under the Vandals. The least unimportant among them is Luxorius (q.v.), who tried to be a North African Martial; but he and his readers cared only for paradoxes or crudities, and scarcely understood the true beauties of the epigram, concision, deftness, and taste.

GREEK EPIGRAMS. 1. *General*: H. Beckby, *Anthologia Graeca²*, 4 vols. (Munich, 1965–7, with German verse translations); J. Geffcken, *Griechische Epigramme* (1916) and *Neue Jahrb.* 1917, 88 ff.; F. Hiller von Gaertringen, *Historische griech. Epigramme* (1926); R. Keydell, s.v. Epigramma, *RAC* 5. 539 ff.; W. R. Paton, *The Greek Anthology*, 5 vols. (1916–18, with Engl. transl.); W. Peek, *Griechische Vers-Inschriften I*(1955); S. Pfohl, *Bibliog. d. Griech. Versinschriften*(1964); R. Reitzenstein, *Epigramm und Skolion* (1893); P. Waltz et al., *L'Anthologie palatine*, 5 vols.(1928–57, with Fr. transl., notes, indexes).

2. *Archaic*: P. Friedländer with H. B. Hoffleit, *Epigrammata* (U.S.A. 1948).

3. *Classical*: U. von Wilamowitz-Moellendorff, *Sappho und Simonides* (1913).

4. *Hellenistic*: E. Bignone, *L'epigramma greco* (1921); M. Gabathuler, *Hellenistische Epigramme auf Dichter* (1937); A. S. F. Gow and D. L. Page, *Hellenistic Epigrams*, 2 vols. (1965); Knaack in Susemih', *Gesch.gr. Lit. Alex.* ii, ch. 36; A. Rostagni, *Poeti alessandrini* (1916); T. B. L. Webster, *Hellenistic Poetry and Art* (1964), chs. 2, 9, and 10; Wilamowitz, *Hell. Dicht.* 1. 119 ff.

5. *Special studies*: F. J. Brecht, *Motiv- und Typengeschichte des griech. Spottepigramms*(*Philol.* Suppl. 22, 1930); Cichorius, *Röm. Stud.*, ch. 8; Gow and Page; G. Herrlinger, *Totenklage um Tiere in der Antike Dichtung* (1930); P. Kägi, *Nachwirkungen der älteren griech. Elegie in den Epigrammen der Anthologie* (1917); B. Kock, *De Epigrammatum graecorum dialectis* (Göttingen, 1910); R. Lattimore, *Themes in Greek and Latin Epitaphs* (U.S.A. 1942); G. Luck, 'Die Dichterinnen der griech. Anthologie', *MH* 1954, 170 ff.; W. Peek, *Griech. Grabgedichte* (1960); W. Rasche, *De Anthologiae Graecae epigrammatis quae colloquii formam habent* (Münster, 1910); B. Stumpo, 'L'epigramma d'amore a Costantinopoli nel secolo VI d.C.', *Rend. Ist. Lomb.* 1924, 241 ff.

LATIN EPIGRAMS: E. Baehrens, *PLM* 4; F. Bücheler, *Carmina Epigraphica* (Leipzig, 1895); supplements by E. Engström (1912). E. Lommatzsch (1926); E. Galletier, *Étude sur la poésie funéraire romaine d'après les inscriptions* (1922); R. Lattimore, *Themes in Greek and Latin epitaphs* (U.S.A. 1942); W. Morel, *FPR*; M. Rosenblum, *Luxorius* (U.S.A. 1961); W. Speyer, *Epigrammata Bobiensia* (1962).

See also ANTHOLOGY and the names of individual epigrammatists.

G. H.

**EPIGRAPHY, GREEK,** *[note]* is the study of inscriptions written on durable material, such as stone or metal, in Greek letters and expressed in the Greek language. Coin-legends are regarded as falling within the province of the numismatist, painted mummy-labels and ink-written texts on ostraca (fragments of coarse pottery), specially numerous in and characteristic of Egypt, are claimed by the papyrologist, and painted inscriptions forming part of the original decoration of vases are assigned primarily to ceramics, though texts subsequently incised or painted on pottery and the stamps on Rhodian and other amphorae are usually regarded as epigraphical materials. The study covers an area coextensive with the lands inhabited or visited by Greeks who left behind written memorials, and a period of well over a millennium, from the appearance of the earliest extant examples of Greek writing down to the close of the fourth century A.D. or even later, when Greek merges into Byzantine history. The materials are to a large extent scattered in the various places where they were found, though much has been done to collect and protect them in museums in Greece (especially the Epigraphical Museum at Athens and the local collections at Eleusis, Corinth (31), Sparta, Olympia (32), Thebes, Delphi (33), etc.), Asia Minor (30, 42), Egypt (notably at Alexandria (56) and Cairo(57)), and elsewhere; there are important collections, e.g., in Berlin, Paris (55), the British Museum (54), and the Ashmolean Museum at Oxford (127).

2. Epigraphical studies have a very long history (2, 10, 11). Herodotus discusses, in the light of archaic dedications copied by him at Thebes, the Phoenician origin of the Greek alphabet and its later modification under Ionian influence (Hdt. 5. 53–61), and he frequently appeals to inscriptions as historical sources, as do also Thucydides and most of the Greek historians and orators. Philochorus edited a collection of Ἐπιγράμματα Ἀττικά early in the third century B.C., and about the same time Craterus published a Ψηφισμάτων συναγωγή with historical commentary, while a century later Polemo of Ilium received the nickname στηλοκόπας for his tireless attention to the inscribed records. The study revived in the fifteenth century with the activity of Ciriaco de' Pizzicolli (Cyriac of Ancona) (126) in copying ancient inscriptions in the course of his travels, and the seventeenth and eighteenth centuries witnessed a dozen attempts to collect the available material in *corpora*. The modern period opens with the travels of Pouqueville, Leake, Gell, Osann, Letronne, and others, August Boeckh's acceptance in 1815, under the auspices of the Berlin Academy, of the task of preparing a new and comprehensive *corpus* on a geographical basis (28), and the issue by J. Franz in 1840 of the first adequate general work on Greek epigraphy (7). Thus were laid the foundations on which scholars have built during the past century, aided by the enhanced

* In this article figures in brackets refer to corresponding items in the appended Bibliography.

opportunities of travel which followed the liberation of Greece, the systematic excavations carried out by Greek and foreign archaeologists on many Hellenic sites—the Acropolis, Corinth (31), Olympia (32), Delphi (33), Delos (29, 38), Gortyn, Priene (44), Miletus, Pergamum (46), Magnesia (43), Sardis (47), and others, of which the most recent and prolific is the Athenian Agora—and the improved technique of decipherment, restoration, and publication, in which the 'squeeze' and the photograph play a valuable part. The most ambitious and fruitful enterprise of this period is that of the Berlin Academy, which, shortly before the completion of Boeckh's great work, embarked on the publication of a series of *corpora*, united in 1903 under the single title of *Inscriptiones Graecae* (29), which was to contain all the Greek inscriptions of Europe; the Vienna Academy undertook the preparation of a *corpus*, of which only the firstfruits have appeared (30), of Asia Minor; and Syrian (49), Bulgarian (36), and Roumanian *corpora* are planned or already begun.

**3.** Greek epigraphy comprises two main provinces, palaeographical and historical, though there is a certain overlap between them in so far as palaeographical criteria are used for the determination of the provenance and the date of an inscription, and so for its assignment to its historical context.

I. Inscriptions afford by far the earliest extant examples of Greek writing, and are thus invaluable for the study of the origin and development of the Greek alphabet and script (9–13, 24, 25). The persistent tradition which spoke of the Phoenicians and their semi-mythical King Cadmus as those who taught the Hellenes to write is confirmed by the use of the word φοινικήϊα (Hdt. 5. 58; *SIG* 38. 37) to denote letters, by the 'retrograde' direction of the earliest Greek inscriptions, by the Greek letter-names, by the identical order of the alphabets of Phoenicia (as inferred from the cognate Hebrew) and of Greece (as indicated by many early *abecedaria*, by the numerical values given to the letters, and by the unbroken tradition of the Greek language), and by the striking resemblances between the letter-forms used in the most archaic inscriptions of the Greeks and their Phoenician counterparts, as found, e.g., in the inscription of Ahiram from Byblus and on the 'Moabite Stone'. The Phoenician alphabet of twenty-two consonants the Greeks rapidly and skilfully transformed (71, 72) into an instrument suited for the representation of their own language, either discarding or giving new phonetic values to letters they did not require, and making further additions, as utility or consistency demanded, at the close of the alphabet, which, as they first learned it, ended with Τ. In this process of development and adaptation each community or group of communities made its own experiments, and thus a large number of local variations arose (71), but the resultant alphabets fall into four main classes: (1) those of Crete, Thera, and early Melos, in which ΞΦΧΨ are lacking, (2) those of Attica and certain islands, in which ΦΧ represent the sounds φχ, but ΞΨ are wanting, (3) the 'Eastern Group', including also Corinth, Argos, and Sicyon, in which ΞΦΧΨ represent ξφχψ respectively, and (4) the 'Western Group', in which Ξ is not used and ΦΧΨ represent φξχ respectively. The original 'retrograde' direction of the script gave place to the 'boustrophedon' style, in which the lines run alternately from right to left and from left to right, and this was succeeded by the exclusive use of the left-to-right direction (72). Greek aesthetic sense, notably that of the Athenians, demanded greater simplicity, symmetry, and uniformity in the letter-forms and insisted on their arrangement in straight horizontal lines. Indeed, in the sixth century B.C. the 'stoichedon' style appears, and enjoys, especially at Athens, a long vogue;

in this there is an exact alignment of letters not only horizontal but also vertical (73). Down to the close of the fifth century Athens used an alphabet of only twenty-one letters,

$$ \text{ABΛΔΕΞΗΘΙΚLΜΝΟΠΡΣΤΥΦΧ,} $$

in which E denotes ε, ει, η, O denotes ο, ου, ω, and H retains its original value as an aspirate; but in 403 B.C. the Milesian alphabet of twenty-four letters was officially adopted in its place, and soon all Greece followed the Athenian lead and used the alphabet

$$ \text{ΑΒΓΔΕΞΗΘΙΚΑΜΝΞΟΠΡΣΤΥΦΧΨΩ.} $$

Since that time the Greek alphabet has neither gained nor lost a letter, though various influences modified their forms. (1) The fourth century witnessed an excessive simplification, due perhaps in part to economic motives, leading to the frequent representation of A or Δ by Λ, of H or N by ΙΙ, etc.; but this hampered the reader and proved a passing phase, dying out in the third century. (2) Another temporary fashion was the substitution of rectilinear for curved forms, partly in the engraver's interest and partly because of the archaic appearance of some of the resultant forms. (3) Far more lasting and potent was the tendency towards elaboration of the script, due to a recoil from the old simplicity and a desire to display the designer's ingenuity; this led to the addition of serifs or of 'apices' to the letters, the substitution of Λ for A, and the invention of various ornamented forms, and flourished in the two centuries before and after Christ, but died down *c.* A.D. 200. (4) Ultimately the influence of the cursive style triumphed, and the epigraphical script became a mere copy on stone of the forms convenient to papyrus or parchment, with its tendency to make the letters taller and narrower, to substitute curved for straight lines, and to reduce or eliminate the necessity of removing pen from paper. We thus reach an alphabet of the type

$$ \text{ΑΒΓΔΕΖΗΘΙΚΛΜΝΞΟΠΡΣΤΥΦΧΨΩ.} $$

Numbers were either written out in words or indicated by numeral signs. The Greek numeral systems are of two classes, in the first of which there are many striking local divergences. (1) In the acrophonic system (74), illustrated by inscriptions from about 460 to 100 B.C. and used sporadically even later, the initial letters of πέντε, δέκα, ἑκατόν, etc., stand for the values indicated by those words; Ι represents the unit; and there are usually compound signs for 50, 500, 5,000, etc. Thus in Attica ΜΧΧΗꝒᴬΔΔΔΓΙ = 12186 and ΤΤꝒΗΡꝶΗΓΗΙΙC = 2 talents, 5607 drachmas, 2½ obols. (2) In the alphabetic system, traceable back to the fifth century, widespread in the Hellenistic period and completely dominant by 100 B.C., the letters in their alphabetical order (with the retention of F and Ϙ in their original places after ε and π and the addition of ϡ after ω) indicate the nine units, nine tens, and nine hundreds, so that ΤϘΗ = 398 and ΜΒΡΠϹ = 12186. Frequently these alphabetic numerals, which are used for ordinal as well as for cardinal numbers, are distinguished by a superposed horizontal line. Inscriptions also furnish abundant materials for the study of Greek punctuation, ligature, monogram, and abbreviation, which consists in the omission either of the end or of some part of the interior of a word; the latter method of contraction is especially frequent in, but by no means confined to, the *nomina sacra*, e.g. Θ(εό)s, Χ(ριστό)ν, Κ(ύρι)ε.

II. Even more important than the form of inscriptions is their content. They are historical documents as well as palaeographical specimens, and there is no aspect of Hellenic thought or speech, writing or action on which they do not throw valuable light. Apart from such outstanding documents as the Attic tribute quota-lists and assessments (110, 111), the law-code of Gortyn (63, 64), the chronological table known as the 'Parian Marble' (65), the poems of Isyllus and Maiistas, the Delphic paeans (87), the cure-records from the Epidaurian Asclepieum, the official autobiography of Augustus in the bilingual *Monumentum Ancyranum* (66, 67), Diocletian's Edict (68, 69), and the philosophical confession of Diogenes of Oenoanda (70), inscriptions with their authentic, first-hand, contemporary records, characterized by extraordinary detail and objectivity, immeasurably enrich our knowledge of the ancient world (4, 5). They offer materials, often the sole materials available, for the study of all the Greek dialects (75–7); they provide uniquely valuable evidence of grammatical and orthographical usage and of phonetic changes (78); they give to the student of Greek literature thousands of dedicatory poems, metrical epitaphs, and other verse compositions (79–87), as well as countless examples of prose and extensive records of dramatic contests and victories (122); they preserve several hymns accompanied by the musical notes to which they were chanted. To the archaeologist they supply hundreds of signatures of sculptors (88, 89), potters, and painters. In the sphere of religion we owe to them a wealth of detailed knowledge of cult titles and ritual laws (94–6), temple organization and finance, priestly appointment and tenure, religious festivals and societies, oracles, confessions and thanksgivings, prayers and curses (97), not to speak of the light they throw upon Jewish and Christian beliefs and practices (16–23). In the political realm they preserve the *ipsissima verba* of laws, decrees (very many of which record the bestowal of citizenship, προξενία (100), and other privileges) (99), edicts and rescripts (108), treaties (101, 102), arbitral awards (5, 103–4), legal judgements (105), economic and fiscal regulations, financial records (109–12), specifications and accounts relating to public buildings (90–93), boundaries of States or public domains, lists of eponymous or other magistrates, census-surveys, and other documents, confirming, correcting, or supplementing the data derived from literary sources. Finally, in the field of private and social life, where literature is least helpful, inscriptions aid us with their countless records of legal and commercial transactions—contracts, sales, leases, mortgages and guarantees, loans and deposits, wills and endowments (106–7), dowries and manumissions of various types, civil or religious—of clubs and societies (5, 115), schools and scholars, examinations and prizes (116), their thousands of stamped amphora-handles and mercantile inscriptions (112), and their myriads of epitaphs with varying formulae, often revealing interesting local peculiarities (119–21). Even where such inscriptions are of little or no value individually, they frequently serve, taken in large numbers, as the bases of inductions which are of real importance, linguistic or historical.

The fullest epigraphical bibliography is (1) J. J. E. Hondius, *Saxa loquuntur* (1938), 55 ff. Here only a brief selection can be given. On almost every aspect of the study light is thrown by the works of M. Holleaux (esp. *Études d'épigraphie et d'histoire grecques*, ed. by L. Robert, 1938– ), L. Robert (esp. *Hellenica* i–xii, 1940–60), U. von Wilamowitz-Moellendorff (esp. *Kl. Schr.* v. 1 (1937)), and A. Wilhelm (esp. *Beiträge zur griech. Inschriftenkunde* (1909)). Current discoveries and discussions are recorded annually in the *Supplementum Epigraphicum Graecum*, founded by J. J. E. Hondius in 1923 and now edited by A. G. Woodhead, and J. and L. Robert contribute to the *Revue des études grecques* an invaluable critical summary of the epigraphical publications of each year.

HISTORY OF THE STUDY. (2) S. Chabert, *Histoire sommaire des études d'épigraphie grecque* (1906).

INTRODUCTIONS. (3) C. T. Newton, *Essays on Art and Archaeology* (1880), 95 ff.; (4) M. Cary, *Documentary Sources of Greek History* (1927), 1 ff., 126 ff.; (5) M. N. Tod, *Sidelights on Gk. History* (1932), 11 ff.; (6) G. Pfohl, *Die inschriftliche Überlieferung der Griechen* (1964).

COMPREHENSIVE TREATMENTS. (7) J. Franz, *Elementa Epigraphices Graecae* (1840); (8) S. Reinach, *Traité d'épigraphie grecque* (1885); (9) E. S. Roberts and E. A. Gardner, *Introduction to Gk. Epigraphy*, i. *Archaic Inscriptions*, ii. *Attic Inscriptions* (1887–1905); (10) W.

Larfeld, *Handbuch d. griech. Epigraphik* (1902–7); (11) id. *Griech. Epigraphik*[1] (I. von Müller's *Handbuch* i. 5, 1914); (12) F. Hiller von Gaertringen, *Griech. Epigraphik* (Gercke–Norden's *Einleitung* i. 9, 1924); (13) A. Rehm, *Die Schrift und die Schriftzeugnisse* (W. Otto's *Handbuch d. Archäologie* i (1937), 182 ff.); (14) G. Klaffenbach, *Griech. Epigraphik*[2] (1966); (15) A. Woodhead, *The Study of Greek Inscriptions* (1959).

CHRISTIAN INSCRIPTIONS. (16) O. Marucchi, *Christian Epigraphy* (1912); (17) C. M. Kaufmann, *Handbuch d. altchristlichen Epigraphik* (1917); (18) L. Jalabert–R. Mouterde, *Inscriptions grecques chrét.* in *Dict. d'archéol. chrét.* vii (1926), 623 ff.; (19) H. Grégoire, *Recueil des inscr. grecques-chrétiennes d'Asie mineure* (1922); (20) G. Lefebvre, *Recueil des inscr. grecques-chrétiennes d'Égypte* (1907); (21) N. A. Bees, *Corpus d. griech.-chr. Inschriften von Hellas* i. 1 (1941); cf. also no. (98).

JEWISH INSCRIPTIONS. (22) J. B. Frey, *Corpus Inscriptionum Judaicarum* (1936–); (23) S. Klein, *Jüdisch-palästinisches Corpus Inscriptionum* (1920).

PHOTOGRAPHS AND FACSIMILES. (24) H. Roehl, *Inscriptiones Graecae antiquissimae* (1882); (25) *Imagines inscr. Graec. antiquiss.*[3] (1907); (26) O. Kern, *Inscriptiones Graecae* (1913); (27) J. Kirchner, *Imagines inscr. Atticarum*[2] (1948).

CORPORA, i.e. complete collections for given localities. (28) A. Boeckh, etc., *Corpus Inscriptionum Graecarum* (*CIG*; 1825–77); (29) *Inscriptiones Graecae* (*IG*; 1873– ) [includes Europe only: i[2], ii/iii[2] Attica; iv Argolis (iv[2]. 1 Epidaurus); v Laconia, Messenia, Arcadia; vi* Elis, Achaea; vii Megaris, Boeotia; viii* Delphi; ix Phocis, Locris, Aetolia, Acarnania, Ionian Islands, Thessaly (ix[2]. 1 Aetolia, Acarnania); x* Epirus, Macedonia, Thrace, Scythia; xi† Delos; xii† Aegean Islands except Delos; xiii* Crete; xiv Sicily, Italy, and W. Europe; xv* Cyprus]; (30) *Tituli Asiae Minoris*† (1901– ); (31) B. D. Meritt, *Corinth* viii. 1 (1931); (32) W. Dittenberger-K. Purgold, *Inschriften von Olympia* (1896); (33) E. Bourguet, etc., *Fouilles de Delphes* iii (1909– ); (34) M. G. Demitsas, ῾Η Μακεδονία (1896); (35) E. Kalinka, *Antike Denkmäler in Bulgarien* (1906); (36) G. Mihailov, *Inscriptiones Graecae in Bulgaria repertae* (1956– ); (37) B. Latyschev, *Inscriptiones antiquae orae septentrionalis Ponti Euxini Graecae et Latinae* i[2], ii, iv (1885–1916); (38) F. Durrbach, P. Roussel, etc., *Inscriptions de Délos* (1926– ); (39) W. R. Paton–E. L. Hicks, *The Inscriptions of Cos* (1891); (40) A. Maiuri, *Nuova silloge epigrafica di Rodi e Cos* (1925); (41) M. Guarducci, *Inscriptiones Creticae* i–iv (1935–50); (42) *Monumenta Asiae Minoris Antiqua* i–viii (1928–62); (43) O. Kern, *Inschriften von Magnesia am Maeander* (1900); (44) F. Hiller von Gaertringen, *Inschriften von Priene* (1906); (45) W. Judeich, *Altertümer von Hierapolis* (1898); (46) M. Fraenkel, *Inschriften von Pergamon* i, ii (1890–5); (47) W. H. Buckler–D. M. Robinson, *Sardis* vii. 1 (1932); (48) W. M. Ramsay, *Cities and Bishoprics of Phrygia* (1895–7); (49) L. Jalabert, R. Mouterde, etc., *Inscriptions grecques et latines de la Syrie*† (1929– ); (50) *Publications of the Princeton Univ. Archaeological Expeditions to Syria* iii (1907–22); (51) F. Preisigke-F. Bilabel. *Sammelbuch griech. Urkunden aus Ägypten* (1915– ); (52) G. Oliverio, *Documenti antichi dell' Africa Italiana* i, ii (1932–6); (53) G. Oliverio-G. Pugliese Carratelli-D. Morelli, 'Supplemento Epigrafico Cirenaico' in *Annuario della Scuola Archeologica di Atene*, N.S. xxiii/xxiv. 219 ff.

COLLECTIONS. (54) *The Collection of Ancient Greek Inscriptions in the British Museum* i–iv (1874–1916); (55) L. Robert, *Collection Froehner*, i. *Inscr. grecques* (1936); (56) E. Breccia, *Iscrizioni greche e latine* [Alexandria Museum] (1911); (57) J. G. Milne, *Gk. Inscriptions* [Cairo Museum] (1905).

SELECTIONS. (58) G. Dittenberger, *Sylloge Inscriptionum Graecarum*[3] (1915–24); (59) G. Dittenberger, *Orientis Graeci Inscriptiones Selectae* (1903–5); (60) C. Michel, *Recueil d'inscr. grecques* (1900–27); (61) M. N. Tod, *Selection of Gk. Historical Inscriptions* i[2] (1946), ii (1948); (62) J. Pouilloux, *Choix d'inscr. grecques* (1960).

SINGLE INSCRIPTIONS. (63) J. Kohler-E. Ziebarth, *Das Stadtrecht von Gortyn* (1912); (64) for the Gortyn Code see M. Guarducci, *Inscr. Cret.* iv, no. 72; (65) F. Jacoby, *Das Marmor Parium* (1904), and further references in this Dictionary, s.v. Marmor Parium; (66) E. G. Hardy, *The Monumentum Ancyranum* (1923); (67) J. Gagé, *Res gestae Divi Augusti*[2] (1950), and references in G. Pfohl, *Die inschriftliche Überlieferung der Griechen*, (1964) 42–4; (68) T. Mommsen–H. Blümner, *Der Maximaltarif des Diocletian* (1893); (69) E. R. Graser in Frank, *Economic Survey*, and references in G. Pfohl, op. cit. 45 f.; (70) *Diogenis Oenoandensis fragmenta* ed. J. William (1907), and ed. A. Grilli (1960), and ed. C. W. Chilton (1967).

SCRIPT. (71) A. Kirchhoff, *Studien zur Geschichte d. griech. Alphabets*[4] (1887); (72) L. H. Jeffery, *The Local Scripts of Archaic Greece* (1961); (73) R. P. Austin, *The Stoichedon Style in Gk. Inscriptions* (1938); (74) M. N. Tod, 'The Greek Numeral Notation' in *BSA* xviii. 98 ff., xxviii. 141 ff., xxxvii. 236 ff., xlv. 126 ff.

DIALECT AND GRAMMAR. (75) H. Collitz, F. Bechtel, etc., *Sammlung d. griech. Dialekt-Inschriften* (1884–1915); (76) E. Schwyzer, *Dialectorum Graecarum exempla epigraphica potiora* (1923); (77) C. D. Buck, *The Greek Dialects* (1955); (78) K. Meisterhans-E. Schwyzer, *Grammatik d. attischen Inschriften*[3] (1900).

METRICAL INSCRIPTIONS. (79) G. Pfohl, *Bibliographie der griech. Vers-Inschriften* (1964); (80) id. *Monument und Epigramm* (1964); (81) G. Kaibel, *Epigrammata Graeca ex lapidibus conlecta* (1878); (82) E. Hoffmann, *Sylloge epigrammatum Graecorum* (1893); (83) P. Friedländer-H. B. Hoffleit, *Epigrammata* (1948); (84) W. Peek, *Griechische Vers-Inschriften*: i. *Grab-Epigramme* (1955); (85) id. *Griechische Grabgedichte, griechisch u. deutsch* (1960); (86) F. Hiller

* Not published by 1967. † Partially published.

on Gaertringen, *Historische griech. Epigramme* (1926); (87) J. U. owell, *Collectanea Alexandrina* (1925).

ART AND ARCHITECTURE. (88) E. Loewy, *Inschriften griech. Bildhauer* (1885): (89) J. Marcadé, *Recueil des signatures de sculpteurs recs* (1953–); (90) A. Choisy, *Etudes épigr. sur l'architecture grecque* 884); (91) H. Lattermann, *Griech. Bauinschriften* (1908); (92) R. L. cranton, 'Greek architectural inscriptions as documents' in *Harvard Library Bulletin* xiv. 159 ff.; (93) F. G. Maier, *Griech. Mauerbau-Inschriften* (1959).

RELIGION AND MAGIC. (94) J. von Prott–L. Ziehen, *Leges Graecorum Sacrae* (1896–1906); (95) F. Sokolowski, *Lois sacrées de l' Asie Mineure* (1955); (96) id. *Lois sacrées des cités grecques: Supplément* (962); (97) A. Audollent, *Defixionum tabellae* (1904); (98) E. Gabba, *Iscrizioni greche e latine per lo studio della Bibbia* (1958).

POLITICS AND LAW. (99) H. Swoboda, *Die griech. Volksbeschlüsse* 890); (100) P. Monceaux, *Les Proxénies grecques* (1886); (101) R. on Scala, *Die Staatsverträge des Altertums* (1898); (102) H. Bengton, *Die Staatsverträge des Altertums* ii (1962); (103) A. Raeder, *L'Arbitrage international chez les Hellènes* (1912); (104) M. N. Tod, *International Arbitration amongst the Greeks* (1913); cf. s.v. ARBITRATION, GREEK; (105) R. Dareste–B. Haussoullier–T. Reinach, *Recueil es inscr. juridiques grecques* (1891–1904); (106) B. Laum, *Stiftungen d. griech. u. röm. Antike* (1914); (107) A. Mannzmann, *Griech. Stiftungsurkunden* (1962); (108) C. B. Welles, *Royal Correspondence the Hellenistic Period* (1934).

FINANCE AND COMMERCE. (109) B. D. Meritt, *Athenian Financial Documents of the fifth Century* (1932); (110) id.–A. B. West, *The Athenian Assessment of 425 B.C.* (1934); (111) B. D. Meritt–H. T. Wade-Gery–M. F. McGregor, *The Athenian Tribute Lists* (*ATL*) iv (1939–53); (112) R. Hackl, *Merkantile Inschriften auf attischen Vasen* (1909); (113) L. Robert, *Études de numismatique grecque* (1951); 14) M. N. Tod, 'Epigraphical Notes on Greek Coinage' in *Num. Chron.* 1945, 108 ff.; 1946, 47 ff.; 1947, 1 ff.; 1955, 125 ff.; 1960, 1 ff. SOCIAL AND PRIVATE LIFE. (115) F. Poland, *Geschichte d. griech. Vereinswesens* (1909); cf. s.v. CLUBS, GREEK; (116) E. Ziebarth, *Aus griech. Schulwesen*² (1914); (117) L. Moretti, *Iscrizioni agonistiche reche* (1953); (118) L. Cohn-Haft, *The Public Physicians of Ancient Greece* (1956); (119) K. Strausberg, *De titulis Graecis sepulcralibus* 937); (120) G. Pfohl, *Untersuchungen über die attischen Grabschriften* (1953); (121) R. Lattimore, *Themes in Greek and Latin Epitaphs* (1942); (122) A. Wilhelm, *Urkunden dramatischer Aufführungen in Athen* (1906); (123) B. D. Meritt, *The Athenian Year* 961); (124) W. K. Pritchett, *Ancient Athenian Calendars on Stone* 1963).

OTHER TOPICS. (125) R. Cagnat–G. Lafaye, *Inscriptiones Graecae d res Romanas pertinentes* i, iii, iv (1906–27); (126) E. W. Bodnar, *Cyriacus of Ancona and Athens* (1960); (127) M. N. Tod, 'Epigraphical Notes from the Ashmolean Museum', *JHS* 1951, 172 ff.
                        M. N. T.

**EPIGRAPHY, LATIN,** the study of Latin texts inscribed on durable objects, usually of stone or bronze. It is concerned both with the form of the inscriptions and with their content, and so impinges on many other fields, e.g. palaeography, philology, history, law, religion. It excludes, but cannot ignore, texts on coins and gems; it has a strong interest in Greek inscriptions of the Roman period; unlike Greek epigraphy, it includes some texts written with pen and ink, e.g. those on *amphorae*.

2. The first-known collection of Latin inscriptions was made c. A.D. 800 and preserved in MS. at Einsiedeln. On this, as on subsequent collections made by early antiquaries, and on the transcriptions of artists who drew ancient monuments, we rely for knowledge of many lost texts; but it must be remembered that these have sometimes been over-imaginatively restored, even forged. Serious study began in the eighteenth century, among its outstanding early exponents being Bartolommeo Borghesi; a great advance was made in the nineteenth, with the plan for a complete corpus of Latin inscriptions, undertaken in Germany, chiefly on the initiative of Th. Mommsen.

3. The oldest of all Latin inscriptions is a craftsman's label on a gold *fibula* from Praeneste, of the late seventh century B.C. (*ILS* 8561), the oldest on stone a religious regulation on a *cippus* from the Forum Romanum, probably of the late sixth (*ILS* 4913). Examples are rare before the third century, not common before the second; the majority are early imperial, but they continue to the end of the ancient world, and after. They come from all parts of the Roman Empire, and are particularly valuable in providing evidence from the provinces as well as from Rome and Italy; the yield from the eastern provinces is small, but from the west, especially Africa, it is large.

4. The texts may be formal documents such as laws, treaties, legal contracts, wills (*acta*), or records of individuals and their activities (*tituli*), whether inscribed in their honour, at their commission, or, quite casually, by themselves (*graffiti*); epitaphs form the largest single group. The earliest show the Latin language at a date well before any surviving literature, the later its development in everyday usage (*see* LATIN, LANGUAGE, SPOKEN, VULGAR). They give information on governmental policy and administration, on persons and events, and on many aspects of life and thought on which the literary sources are silent or inadequate. The cumulative evidence even of trivial examples may be enlightening; and any text may prove more informative than it appears, if it is considered in its archaeological context. Something of the range may be summarily indicated as follows.

(*a*) The public *acta* include a series of laws of the Republic and early Empire, e.g. a judiciary law which is probably that of C. Gracchus and the *Lex de imperio Vespasiani* (*FIRA* i. 84 f.; 154 f.); some *senatus consulta*, e.g. much of the *s.c. de Bacchanalibus* of 186 B.C. (*ILS* 18); and many magisterial documents, especially edicts, letters, rescripts, and public speeches of emperors (cf. *ILS* 206, 423, 705, 212). Also noteworthy are the Fasti of consuls, local magistrates, and triumphing generals (*Inscriptiones Italiae* xiii. 1) which clarify the chronological framework of Roman history, and the Calendars (*Inscriptiones Italiae* xiii. 2) essential to the study of official Roman religion. For the inscribed autobiography of Augustus, *see* MONUMENTUM ANCYRANUM.

(*b*) The *tituli* of men in public life (*ILS* 1 f., 862 f.) present the administrative personnel of Rome, provide lists of the offices and achievements of individuals, often otherwise unknown, tell something of the official in action, his social and personal background, even his ideals and ambitions (cf. the Scipionic epitaphs, *ILS* 1–7). Taken as a whole, they show developments in the administrative system, e.g. from the simple career of a republican senator to its complex imperial counterpart in which the magistracies may be a minor element in a string of appointments created by emperors; they illustrate the emergence of the equestrian civil service and that of the imperial slaves and freedmen; they contain details indicative, e.g., of changes in the sources of recruitment of officials, as from Italy to the provinces, or of significant connexions between families in public life. Laudatory inscriptions also indicate the honours and titles accorded to, the qualities admired in, public men at different periods. Imperial inscriptions provide evidence for the titles and powers of emperors and for their policies and propaganda.

(*c*) Local government is illustrated by inscriptions containing municipal charters, careers of municipal officials, decrees of local authorities, records of public works and services, with some details of their finances (often supplied by private generosity), occasionally, as at Pompeii, election notices (*ILS* 6044 f.).

(*d*) Military affairs appear in the inscriptions of units and individual soldiers (*ILS* 1986 f.) which throw light on the organization and deployment of all branches of the armed forces. They reflect in general on foreign policy, in detail on sources of recruitment, terms of service, lines of promotion, the religious and other interests of the men, relations with civilians, prospects on demobilization, especially the prospect of Roman citizenship for men in auxiliary units, for which virtually all our information derives from military *diplomata* (*CIL* xvi).

(*e*) Religious affairs are documented by a number of dedications and building inscriptions (*ILS* 2957 f.) which show the character and organization of particular cults, the interaction of Roman and provincial cults, the tendency to syncretism, the introduction and development of new cults, especially the imperial cult. There are also accounts of ceremonies, like that of the Augustan *Ludi Saeculares* with its reference to the *carmen saeculare* of Horace (*ILS* 5050). Some views on after-life can be found in epitaphs. For Christianity, see below.

(*f*) Social developments, such as the progress of urbanization and romanization in the provinces, may be traced, e.g., from building inscriptions, the records of local government, changing forms of nomenclature. The history of nomenclature itself, important for its ethnic, social, and political implications, is very largely dependent on epigraphic evidence. There is also information, especially in epitaphs, on family relationships, average age of marriage, expectation of life (calculated roughly from ages at death), social gradings, social mobility, conditions of living in each class. Other aspects of ordinary life are illustrated, e.g., by inscriptions concerning *collegia* (*ILS* 7212 f.) which refer to club rules and the activities of members, or *ludi* (*ILS* 5051 f.) which show the popular types of entertainment, the performers, and the attitudes of their fans.

(*g*) Economic life is illustrated in part by references to crafts and trades on tombstones, but most valuably by the makers' stamps and salesmen's labels on many objects. These may help to show the organization of industries and commerce, both private and under imperial control, and are very often precisely datable (*see*, e.g., BRICK-STAMPS, SAMIAN WARE). There is also some information on prices and costs, e.g. in building inscriptions, and for a wide range of goods at the end of the third century A.D. in Diocletian's Edict on Prices (*CIL* iii. 1926 f.).

(*h*) Christian inscriptions begin as a group barely differentiated from the pagan texts of their time, but develop formulae and other features of their own, especially after the Peace of the Church. The earlier texts are often very humble tombstones or pilgrims' *graffiti* (cf. Kaufmann, *Handbuch*, 303 f.). Later they include more ambitious items, as, e.g., building inscriptions for churches. The set of verse *elogia* on popes and martyrs, written by Pope Damasus (366–84) and finely cut by Philocalus in letters which may have been especially designed for the purpose, form a landmark in this development of a specifically Christian epigraphic tradition (Kaufmann, *Handbuch*, 327 f.). All told they illustrate the character of early Christian society, the organization of the Church, the survival of pagan features, and the emergence of new ideas, including heresies.

**5.** Most inscriptions were incised. The more important were cut with care, and, from the late Republic onwards, often with art; lines and letters were painted on to the surface (lines sometimes faintly chiselled), in the more formal cases with mechanical aids, otherwise free-hand; the width and depth of strokes, occasionally also the height, were varied with a view both to legibility and to aesthetics; there was careful attention to the layout and proportions of the text in relation to the context. Incised letters on stone might be picked out in red, on bronze in white. Other methods were, e.g., to fix metal letters to stone by pegs (such letters rarely survive, but see *ILS* 4921 b for a reference to them in a temple inventory; texts may be deducible from the positions of the pegholes), to insert letters formed of strips of metal, coloured marble, or mosaic tesserae, to paint them, even to write them with pen and ink.

**6.** The letters (*see* ALPHABET, LATIN) were originally very like those of the early Greek alphabet in Italy. By the Augustan period, cutters had developed (i) the formal Latin capital (*scriptura monumentalis, litterae lapidariae, litterae quadratae*), a carefully designed letter, beautifully adapted to a monumental context and well illustrated on the base of Trajan's Column; (ii) a small, neat capital (*scriptura actuaria*), derived from the brush-painted letters used for ephemeral public notices as illustrated on Pom-

peian walls, and suited for recording long documents, e.g. the laws. Later, a larger version of the brush-painted letter was used on stone for private and some minor public inscriptions (Rustic capitals). Rounded letters (*scriptura uncialis*), borrowed from the forms used in papyri and parchments, appear from the late third century A.D., and the cursive hand in common use is frequent at all dates in *graffiti*, in waxed tablets such as those found at Pompeii (*CIL* iv. 3340 f.), and also appears occasionally on stone-cut texts of a crude type.

**7.** In addition the cutters used signs: (i) stops between words and phrases (occasionally syllables), in the form of round dots, squares, triangles, and, later, more elaborate shapes like ivy-leaves (*hederae distinguentes*); (ii) from the Sullan age to mid third century A.D., the *apex*, recalling an acute accent, to mark vowels long by nature; (iii) from the end of the Republic, the superscript bar to mark abbreviations. There was no uniformity of practice in the use of such signs and cutters often misplaced them, being more interested in their decorative value than their significance. For figures, *see* NUMBERS, ROMAN.

**8.** Of the cutters we know little, but two workshop advertisements survive, from Palermo (*ILS* 7680) and Rome (*ILS* 7679). There are also a few signatures, like that of Aemilius Celer who painted notices at Pompeii (*ILS* 5145) or Philocalus who cut the inscriptions of Pope Damasus (*ILCV* 963), and some references to the craft on tombstones.

**9.** The drafts from which the cutters worked were no doubt often written in cursive letters and difficult to read, which may account for some nonsensical letter-groups in inscriptions. The existence of virtually identical, but quite elaborate funerary texts at widely distant places (cf. *ILS* 2082 from Rome and 2257 from Burnum) may suggest the existence of handbooks from which an unimaginative client might choose a text. In addition there was heavy use of conventional formulae in all inscriptions and this often makes it possible to restore damaged texts with confidence. Restored letters are conventionally printed within square brackets [ ].

**10.** Most texts were composed with great brevity, though a trend to verbosity is apparent in the fourth century A.D. Space was also saved by abbreviating words, often drastically, by ligaturing letters and, sometimes, by using *sigla* (e.g. 7 = centurion), all of which present difficulties to the modern reader (most handbooks list those in common use). The resolutions of abbreviations and *sigla* are conventionally printed within round brackets ( ).

**11.** Some inscriptions are precisely dated by the consular year or an emperor's tribunician year, and even by the day of the month; others can be assigned within more or less exact chronological termini on grounds of content, e.g. prosopography, the use of a particular title, formula, or spelling, and occasionally of the material on which they appear; thus, marble is rare in Rome before the end of the Republic. Letter-forms may be an approximate guide, but are inevitably a subjective one, and liable to mislead because of the idiosyncrasies or gaucheries of the cutters.

INTRODUCTORY. R. Bloch, *L'Épigraphie latine* (1952); H. P. V. Nunn, *Christian Inscriptions* (1952); G. Susini, *Il lapicida romano* (1966).
GENERAL ACCOUNTS. R. Cagnat, *Cours d'épigraphie latine*[4] (1914); J. E. Sandys, *Latin Epigraphy*[2] (revised S. G. Campbell, 1927); I. Calabi, *L'uso storiografico delle iscrizioni latine* (1953), with very full bibliography; O. Marucchi, *Christian Epigraphy* (1912); C. M. Kaufmann, *Handbuch d. altchristlichen Epigrafik* (1917); H. Leclercq, 'Inscriptions latines chrétiennes' in *Dict. d'archéol. chrét.* vii (1926).
REFERENCE. E. de Ruggiero et al., *Dizionario epigrafico di antichità romane* (1886– ); H. Thylander, *Étude d'épigraphie latine* (1952).
ILLUSTRATION. F. Ritschl, *Priscae latinitatis monumenta epigraphica ad archetyporum fidem . . . repraesentata* (1862); E. Hübner, *Exempla scripturae epigraphicae latinae e Caesaris morte ad aetatem Iustiniani* (1885); A. E. and J. S. Gordon, *Album of Dated Latin Inscriptions, Rome and the Neighbourhood*, i *Augustus to Nerva* (1958), ii *A.D.* 100–

:9 (1964), iii *A.D. 200–525* (1965); Degrassi, *ILLRP, Imagines* .965).

PALAEOGRAPHY. J. Mallon, *Paléographie romaine* (1952) and *'RAcad. Inscr.* 1955, 126 f.; L. Robert, ibid. 195 f.; J. S. and . E. Gordon, *Contributions to the Palaeography of Latin Inscriptions* .957).

CORPORA. *Corpus Inscriptionum Latinarum* (*CIL*) (1863– ); vol. i ontains all republican inscriptions, vol. xvi all military diplomata, .egardless of provenance, the rest are arranged geographically— Spain; iii Provinces of Asia and the Levant, Greek-speaking rovinces of Africa and Europe, Illyricum; iv Pompeii, Herculaneum, tabiae; v Cisalpine Gaul; vi City of Rome; vii Britain; viii Africa; : Calabria, Apulia, Samnium, Sabini, Picenum; x Bruttium, .ucania, Campania, Sicily, Sardinia; xi Aemilia, Etruria, Umbria; ii Narbonese Gaul; xiii The Three Gauls and Germany; xiv Latium; v City of Rome (*instrumentum domesticum*); volumes are brought up » date from time to time by supplements. There are also many naller corpora: (i) *regional*: e.g. Italy, *Inscriptiones Italiae* (in rogress); H. Pais, *Additamenta ad CIL vol. V* (1888); H. Bloch, *The oman brick-stamps not in CIL vol. XV* (1947); Britain, Collingwood- Vright, *RIB* (1965); *Africa*, R. Cagnat, A. Merlin, L. Chatelain, nscriptiones latines du Maroc* (1942); A. Merlin, *Inscriptiones latines : la Tunisie* (1944); St. Gsell, *Inscriptions latines de l'Algérie*, i 922), ii, ed. H. G. Pflaum (1957); J. M. Reynolds and J. B. Ward- erkins, *The Inscriptions of Roman Tripolitania* (1952); *Gaul*, E. sperandieu, *Inscriptions latines de Gaule* (*Narbonnaise*) (1929); P. Vuilleumier, *Inscriptions latines de Trois Gaules* (1963); *Germany*, . Vollmer, *Inscriptiones Bavariae* (1915); *Jugoslavia*, B. Hoffiller nd B. Saria, *Antike Inschriften aus Jugoslavien* (1938); A. and J. ašel, *Inscriptiones latinae quae in Iugoslavia inte annos MCMXL et 1CMLX repertae et editae sunt* (1963); Latin inscriptions found in ireek-speaking areas are usually included in regional corpora of ireek inscriptions: (ii) *by type*, e.g. G. B. de Rossi, A. Silvagni, and . Ferrua, *Inscriptiones Christianae urbis Romae saec. VII*, (and series eries (1922–56); H. Zilliacus, *Sylloge inscriptionum Christianarum eterum Musei Vaticani* (1963); J. B. Frey, *Corpus inscriptionum iudaicarum* (1936–56); M. J. Vermaseren, *Corpus inscriptionum et ionumentorum Mithraicorum* (1956–60); M. H. Callender, *Roman mphorae* (1965).

RUNNING RECORDS of newly-published inscriptions and epigraphic iork. *Eph. Epigr.* (1877–1913); *Ann. Epigr.* (appears separately and ι *Rev. Arch.*) (1880– ); *JRS* (Roman Britain only) (1921– ). Cf. also . M. Reynolds, 'Inscriptions and Roman Studies 1910–1960', *JRS* 960, 204 ff.

SELECTIONS. (i) *General*: H. Dessau, *Inscriptiones Latinae Selectae* (*LS*) (1892–1916); A. Degrassi, *Inscriptiones latinae liberae reipublicae* (*ILLRP*) (1957–63); E. Diehl, *Inscriptiones latinae Christianae eteres* (*ILCV*) (1925–31), supp. ed. J. Moreau (1961): (ii) *by type*: iistory, G. McN. Rushforth, *Latin historical inscriptions, illustrating* he history of the early Empire² (130); A. R. Burn, *The Romans in triain²* (1969); R. H. Barrow, *A Selection of Latin Inscriptions* (1934); . Ehrenberg and A. H. M. Jones, *Documents Illustrating the Reigns ' Augustus and Tiberius²* (1955); E. M. Smallwood, *Documents llustrating the Principates of Gaius, Claudius and Nero* (1967); M. 1cCrum and A. G. Woodhead, *Documents of the Principates of the 'lavian Emperors* (1961); E. M. Smallwood, *Documents Illustrating he Principates of Nerva, Trajan and Hadrian* (1966); *language* A. :rnout, *Recueil de textes latins archaïques* (1916); E. Diehl, *Atlantein- che Inschriften* (1930); E. Diehl, *Vulgärlateinische Inschriften* (1910); iw, S. Riccobono *et al.*, *Fontes iuris Romani anteiustiniani* (*FIRA*) 1941–3); *verse*, F. Buecheler, *Carmina latina epigraphica* (1895), .upp. ed. E. Lommatsch (1926). J. M. R.

**:PILYCUS,** cited by Athenaeus as a writer sometimes f Old (4. 140a) Comedy, sometimes of Middle (e.g. . 28e). The Κωραλίσκος has a Doric title, and was writ- en partially in Doric.

*FCG* ii. 887 f.; *CAF* i. 803 f.; Demiańczuk, *Supp. Com.* 40.

**:PIMELETES.** (*a*) In Greek cities this title was given ither to regular magistrates who managed special depart- nents, such as the water supply, the docks, or festivals, r to special commissioners elected for some temporary eed, such as the erection of a public building. (*b*) In 'tolemaic Egypt the *epimeletes* was in the third century he chief financial official of the *nomos* (q.v. 1). In the econd century he was subordinate to ὁ ἐπὶ τῶν προσόδων nd he was sometimes responsible for a part of a nome mly. (*c*) In the Roman period *epimeletes* is often the ranslation of the Latin *curator*. A. H. M. J.

**:PIMENIDES,** religious teacher and wonder-worker f Crete. According to Plato (*Leg.* 1. 642 d) he was at .thens, performing religious rites and prophesying, bout 500 B.C. Others said that he purified the city after he slaughter of Cylon's associates about 600 B.C. (Arist. 4*th. Pol.* 1, etc.; Diels, *Vorsokr.*⁵ i. 29 f.). With the

variations in date go the legends of his great age (157 or 299), and miraculous sleep of fifty-seven years (Diog. Laert.; Diels, ibid. 28). The stories of wanderings out of the body (cf. *Suda*; Diels, ibid. 29) rank him with Aristeas (q.v.), Hermotimus, etc., but his god was the Cretan Zeus, and Plutarch says that the men of the time called him Κούρης νέος (Diels, ibid. 30). Tradition assigned to him a *Theogony* and a *Cretica*, also *Katharmoi* and other mystical writings.

Sources and fragments in Diels–Kranz, *Vorsokr.*⁵ i. 27–37; *FGrH* 457. See also Kirk–Raven, *Presocratic Philosophers* 23, 44 f.
W. K. G. C.

**EPIPHANIUS,** *c.* A.D. 315–403, born in Eleutheropolis, Palestine. He became a monk and in 367 bishop of Salamis (Constantia), Cyprus. He hated Greek culture, attacked the use of images in churches, and violently opposed both Origen's followers and the Arians as heretics adulterating the faith with 'hellenism'. They are the principal villains in his highly informative *Panarion* or 'Medicine-chest' for curing eighty heresies (375). A tract on biblical weights and measures contains important matter on the Old Testament versions.

Ed. K. Holl (1915–33, 3 vols., incomplete); P. de Lagarde, *Sym- mikta* ii (1880), 150 ff.; R. P. Blake and H. de Vis, *Epiphanius de Gemmis* (1934). W. Schneemelcher in *RAC* 5 (1961), 909 ff. H. C.

**EPIPHANY.** In Homer the gods regularly appear visibly and have dealings with men—fighting, helping, loving (cf. RELIGION, MINOAN-MYCENEAN). Poetic or mythical epiphanies, regarded as belonging to the distant past, persist throughout Greek literature, and sometimes serve the ends of religion by giving the *aition* for a living cult, e.g. the Homeric Hymn to Demeter. Even the *märchenhaft* story of Baucis and Philemon suggests this by its ending. Dionysus especially appeared with mani- festations of power to compel unbelievers, as in Euri- pides' *Bacchae*. In historical epiphanies the cult-motive is always prominent. In the famous story of Philip- pides, Pan demands worship at Athens in return for his help (Hdt. 6. 105). Two common types are (i) epiphanies to help or terrify in battle, frequent in Herodotus (8. 64; 8. 36 ff., etc.), and cf. in Roman saga the Dioscuri at Lake Regillus (Dion. Hal. *Ant. Rom.* 6. 13); (ii) healing epiphanies. Asclepius in effecting cures always *appeared* to the sufferer, usually in a dream (incubation) but some- times waking, as in the Isyllus-inscription (for which *see* HYMNS) and *SIG* 803. Frequent Hellenistic inscriptions record epiphanies connected with the foundation of cults (e.g. the *Soteria* at Delphi; Dionysus 'in the tree' at Magnesia, Kern, *Inschr. von M.* 215 b). The genuineness of the belief cannot be doubted (cf. Acts xiv. 10–12), though cases of fraud were recognized (Pisistratus, Hdt. 1. 60). The term *epiphaneia* was used also to denote miracles in which the deity was not thought to be seen (Dion. Hal. *Ant. Rom.* 2. 68). Deified living rulers were hailed as θεοὶ ἐπιφανεῖς, because their power was felt. In general see F. Pfister in *PW*, Suppl. iv. 277 ff.; A. D. Nock, *JHS* 1928, 38 ff.; cf. also the remarks of Nock in 'A Vision of Mandulis Aion', *Harv. Theol. Rev.* 1934, 53 ff., esp. 67 ff. W. K. C. G.

**EPIRUS** ("Ηπειρος, 'Mainland'), north-west area of Greece, from Acroceraunian point to Nicopolis, with harbours at Buthrotum and Glycys Limen (at Acheron's mouth); bordered on south by Gulf of Ambracia, and on east by Pindus range with pass via Metsovo to Thessaly. Three limestone ranges parallel to the coast and the Pindus range enclose narrow valleys and plateaux with good pasture and extensive woods; alluvial plains were formed near Buthrotum, Glycys Limen, and Ambracia. Epirus had a humid climate and cold winters. In terrain and in history it resembled upper Macedonia. Known in the *Iliad* only for the oracle at Dodona, and to Herodotus for the oracle of the dead by Acheron, Epirus received Hellenic influence from the Elean colonies in Cassopaea and the Corinthian colonies at Ambracia and Corcyra, and the oracle at Dodona drew pilgrims from northern and central Greece especially. Theopompus knew fourteen Epirote tribes, probably of Dorian and Illyrian stocks, of which the Chaones held the plain of Buthrotum, the Thesproti the plain of Acheron, and the Molossi the plain near Dodona, which forms the highland centre of Epirus with an outlet southwards to Ambracia. A strong Molossian State, which included some Thesprotian tribes, existed in the reign of Neoptolemus *c.* 370–368 B.C. (Ἀρχ. Ἐφ. 1956, 1 ff.). The unification of Epirus in a symmachy led by the Molossian king was finally achieved by Alexander (q.v. 6), brother-in-law of Philip II of Macedon. His conquests in southern Italy and his alliance with Rome showed the potentialities of the Epirote Confederacy, but he was killed in 330 B.C. Dynastic troubles weakened the Molossian State, until Pyrrhus removed his fellow king and embarked on his adventurous career (q.v.). The most lasting of his achievements were the conquest of southern Illyria, the development of Ambracia as his capital, and the building of fortifications and theatres, especially the large one at Dodona (q.v.). His successors suffered from wars with Aetolia, Macedon, and Illyria, until in *c.* 232 B.C. the Molossian monarchy fell. An Epirote League with a federal citizenship was then created, and the meetings of its Council were held probably by rotation at Dodona or Passaron in Molossis, at Gitana in Thesprotis, and at Phoenice in Chaonia. It was soon involved in the wars between Rome and Macedon, and it split apart when the Molossian State alone supported Macedon and was sacked by the Romans in 167 B.C., when 150,000 captives were deported (*see* CHAROPS). Central Epirus never recovered; but northern Epirus prospered during the late republican period, and Augustus celebrated his victory at Actium by founding a Roman colony at Nicopolis. Under the Empire a coastal road and a road through the interior were built from north to south, and Buthrotum was a Roman colony. Ancient remains testify to the great prosperity of Epirus in Hellenistic times. *See* CHAONES, MOLOSSI, THESPROTI.

Carapanos, *Dodone et ses ruines* (1878); D. Evangelides in Ἠπειρωτικὰ Χρονικά, 1935; L. M. Ugolini, *Albania antica* i (1927), ii (1932), iii (1942); P–K, *GL* 2. 1. 11 ff.; P. R. Franke, *Alt-Epirus u. d. Königtum der Molosser* (1955); *Die Antiken Münzen von Epirus* (1961); E. Lepore, *Ricerche sull'antico Epiro* (1962); S. I. Dakaris, Οἱ γενεαλογικοὶ μῦθοι τῶν Μολοσσῶν (1964); Hammond, *Epirus*.                                          N. G. L. H.

**EPISTATES.** (*a*) At Athens the ἐπιστάτης τῶν πρυτάνεων, chosen daily by lot from the *prytaneis*, during his day of office held the State seal and keys, and in the fifth century B.C. presided in council and assembly. In the fourth century he selected the *proedroi* by lot, and from them, also by lot, the ἐπιστάτης τῶν προέδρων who presided. Similar ἐπιστάται are found in other Greek cities; but sometimes the title is equivalent to the Athenian *prytaneis*. (*b*) In Ptolemaic Egypt the *epistates* was a royal official who administered justice in each *nomos* and sub-district. These officials were distinct from the ἐπιστάται τῶν φυλακιτῶν (*see* POLICE, GREEK). (*c*) In Ptolemaic Egypt the ἐπιστάτης ἱεροῦ was the superintendent, probably appointed by the Crown, of a native temple. (*d*) In all Hellenistic kingdoms the ἐπιστάτης was a high commissioner appointed by the king to control a subject city. He sometimes, perhaps generally, had a royal garrison to maintain public order. He frequently exercised an informal and in theory probably voluntary jurisdiction, settling suits out of court, preferably by arbitration. At Thessalonica and

at Seleuceia in Pieria he is known to have possessed a constitutional power of veto over legislation.

On (*d*), M. Holleaux, *BCH* 1933, 25 ff.; A. Heuss, *Klio*, Beihef xxxix (1937), 23 ff.; 58 ff.                                          A. H. M. J

**EPITADEUS,** a Spartan ephor (q.v.), who (probably soon after 400 B.C.) introduced a law authorizing the transfer of property including land by gift or bequest, a method perhaps already much practised in secret. To this measure, and to the wealth accruing to Sparta after the Peloponnesian War, the concentration of the territory of Laconia and Messenia in a few hands (Arist. *Pol.* 2. 1270ᵃ) was mainly due.

D. Asheri, *Athenaeum* 1961, 45 ff.                                          A. M. W.

**EPITAPHIOS,** a funeral speech, delivered, according to Athenian custom, by a citizen chosen on the grounds of his high moral and mental qualities (Thuc. 2. 34), at a public funeral of those who had fallen in battle. This practice, unique to Athens (Dem. 20. 141), was continued into Roman times and was clearly a solemn and important occasion, but before Hyperides the only certain names of speakers chosen are those of Pericles in 440 and 431, Demosthenes after Chaeronea, and Archinus at some intervening date.

The conventional form comprised a tribute to the virtues of the dead, a summary of their country's glorious achievements in the past, a consolation to their relatives, and an exhortation to the survivors to imitate their virtues. Thucydides professes to record in full the speech thus delivered by Pericles at the end of the first year of the Peloponnesian War. The speaker follows the usual form, except that, instead of enlarging on past history, he tells of the glories of Athens in her maturity.

As a contrast to the impersonal austerity of Pericles we have the speech of Hyperides on Leosthenes and others who died in the Lamian War (322 B.C.). Hyperides, who was an intimate friend of the dead general, shows deep personal feeling, and a unique feature of this speech is his reference to the hope of personal immortality. A passage in Lycurgus (*Leoc.* §§ 39–40) is in effect a condensed *Epitaphios* on the dead at Chaeronea.

In addition to these genuine speeches we possess a florid fragment by Gorgias and a speech, composed under Gorgian influence, attributed to Lysias, which, though it cannot be referred with certainty to any definite occasion, may well be genuine (see J. Walz, 'Der Lysianische Epitaphios' (*Philol.* Suppl. 29. 4)). A similar composition attributed to Demosthenes is almost certainly spurious. Finally, Socrates in Plato's *Menexenus* recites a funeral speech which, he affirms, was composed by Aspasia to be delivered by Pericles.

G. Kennedy, *The Art of Persuasion in Greece* (1963), 154 ff.; F. Jacoby, *JHS* 1944, 37 ff.; M. Pohlenzi, *Symb. Oslo* 1947, 46 ff.                                          J. F. D.

**EPITHALAMIUM, GREEK.** The ἐπιθαλάμιον was strictly a song sung by young men and maidens before the bridal-chamber (Dion. Hal. *Rhet.* p. 247), like the contents of Sappho's Book 7, Theocritus 18, etc. It was distinguished from the γαμήλιος, which could be sung at any festival connected with a wedding (Eust. 1541. 49), and from the ὑμέναιος, the processional song which accompanied the newly wed couple to their home, and is described by Homer (*Il.* 18. 491–6) and Hesiod (*Sc.* 273–80).

H. Färber, *Die Lyrik in der Kunsttheorie der Antike* (1936), i. 37 f., ii. 49 ff.                                          C. M. B.

**EPITHALAMIUM, LATIN.** There are extant some seventeen Latin verse epithalamia. Epithalamia by Calvus, Ticidas, and Ovid are among those that have perished.

The earliest and finest extant examples are the sixty-first and sixty-second poems of Catullus, who also in his sixty-fourth poem recounts the love and marriage of Peleus and Thetis. The influence of Sappho is discernible in Catullus, and her influence, direct or indirect, is sometimes suggested in the later rhetorical epithalamia of epic character. There are single examples by Statius, Ausonius (a cento), Paulinus of Nola, Ennodius, Venantius Fortunatus, and Luxorius (a cento). *Anthologia Latina* (Riese) 742 is an anonymous epithalamium. Claudian, Sidonius, and Dracontius have each left two epithalamia. A few verses by Gallienus are described as an epithalamium (S.H.A. *Gallieni Duo* 11. 8, and *Anthologia Latina* 711). The *Medea* of Seneca contains an epithalamium (56–115) which may well have owed something to one in Ovid's lost play with that title. The *De nuptiis Philologiae et Mercurii* by Martianus Capella is in mixed prose and verse, and a thing apart.

R. Reitzenstein, 'Die Hochzeit des Peleus und der Thetis', *Hermes* 1900, 73 ff.; A. L. Wheeler, 'Tradition in the Epithalamium', *AJPhil.* 1930, 205 ff.; E. A. Mangelsdorff, *Das lyrische Hochzeitsgedicht bei den Griechen und Römern* (1913); J. Fries, *Ein Beitrag zur Ästhetik der römischen Hochzeitspoesie* (1910); C. Morelli, 'L'epitalamio nella tarda poesia latina', *Stud. Ital.* 1910, 319 ff.; E. F. Wilson, Pastoral and Epith. in Lat. Lit.', *Speculum* 1948, 35 ff.; R. Muth, Hymenaios und Epithalamion', *Wien. Stud.* 1954, 5 ff.; A. d'Errico, L'epitalamio nella lett. lat. dal fescennino nuziale al c. 62 di Catullo', *Ann. d. Facoltà di Lett. e Filosofia della Univ. di Napoli*, 1955, 73 ff; R. Keydell, *RAC* v (1961), 927 ff.　　　　　　　　　G. B. A. F.

**EPITHETS, DIVINE.** In considering the very numerous surnames or epithets of gods it is necessary first to distinguish between those appearing only as literary (especially epic) ornaments and those known to have been used in cult. Thus we have no proof that Athena was ever addressed in ritual as γλαυκῶπις; it is her stock epithet in Homer, Zeus' pet-name for her (*Il.* 5. 373). It seems unlikely that Ares was prayed to as βροτολοιγός; he is so addressed by Athena (*Il.* 5. 31), which is a very different thing, and it is his stock epithet as ibid. 846). In Latin such ornaments are abundant; thus in Virgil, Mars is *durus* (*Ecl.* 10. 44); *impius* (*G.* 1. 11); *indomitus* (*Aen.* 2. 440); *saeuus* (*Aen.* 11. 153). These are certainly not cult-epithets, and in some cases the name of the god hardly means more than 'war, strife'. The epithet is purely poetical in *Aen.* 9. 717, where he is called *armipotens*, and in 11. 8 where *bellipotens* is used instead of his name. But there are many border-line cases, hard to decide. We have no instance of Athena being called Pallas in cult, yet it is not easy to suppose that so familiar a name was never used for her by worshippers; Zeus' stock epithet, 'cloud-gatherer', appears in the voc., νεφεληγερέτα, in epic in many places where it is syntactically a nom., strongly suggesting that its form had become fixed by some ancient liturgical phrase, which, however, is quite lost to us. The immediate function of the epithet in epic is often to form with the proper name a convenient metrical unit. Now and then an epithet is used to avoid mentioning an ill-omened name; Hades in Sophocles, *OC* 1606, is Zeus χθόνιος, and in Aesch. *Supp.* 231 he is even Zeus ἄλλος.

2. But coming to those epithets which are guaranteed by their occurrence in liturgical formulae, dedications, and the official names of temples, we may distinguish the following classes. (1) Purely local, meaning that the deity in question is worshipped, or has a temple or altar, at such-and-such a place. Thus Apollo Δήλιος is simply Apollo who is worshipped in Delos, and differs from the Pythian, or any other similarly named Apollo, no otherwise than as Our Lady of Lourdes does from Our Lady of Loretto. Dionysus Κυδαθηναιεύς (Dittenberger, *SIG* 1109. 16 and elsewhere) is nothing but the Dionysus who has a cult in the Attic deme Κυδαθήναιον. The Bona Dea (q.v.) Subsaxana gives rather the address of her temple

than any characteristic of her own; cf. St. Mary's le Strand, St. Martin's in the Fields. Such titles are of no more than topographical interest. At most they may tell us something of the history of the cult, if the title does not fit the immediate locality; a Demeter Ἐλευσία worshipped at Pheneos in Arcadia (Paus. 8. 15. 1) manifestly has something to do with the famous cult at Eleusis, and the local legend said as much. In like manner, the vow of a temple to Venus Erucina, i.e. the Aphrodite of Eryx, in Rome (Livy 22. 9. 10) was made by advice of a Sibylline and therefore Greek oracle. (2) Titles indicating association with another god. These are often of some historical importance, and at times puzzling. Apollo Κάρνειος (*SIG* 736. 34 and 69) has behind him a history of identification, cf. CARNEA; Athena Ἡφαιστία (ibid. 227. 20) need surprise no one, in view of the resemblance of some functions of the two deities; but it is less easy to see why she had a temple at Megara under the title Αἰαντίς (Paus. 1. 42. 4). In Latin these most characteristically take the form, not of an adjective applied to the god's name but of a genitive following it, as in the much-quoted *comprecationes* (q.v.) in Gellius 13. 23 (22). 2, *Luam Saturni, Salaciam Neptuni, Horam Quirini*, etc. Here in all cases the first of the pair is the less important, and the phrases mean 'Lua (etc.) who is associated with or belongs to the sphere of activity of Saturnus (etc.)', as is now pretty generally agreed. Adjectives are, however, used in the *Tabulae Iguvinae*, as I A 3, *Iuve Krapuvi* (*Ioui Grabouio*), 8, *Trebe Iuvie* (*Trebo Iouio*), though the meaning of the first adjective is not certain. (3) Undoubtedly the largest and most important class of epithets, however, have reference to the functions of the god or goddess, either in general or with reference to some particular occasion on which his or her power was manifest. Thus, Zeus has a great number of titles denoting his control of the weather and all that depends on it; he is Βροντῶν, Thunderer, Κεραύνιος, God of the Thunderbolt, Ὄμβριος, Sender of Rainstorms, Ὑέτιος, Rainer, and as a natural consequence Γεωργός, Farmer; also Οὔριος, God of Favourable Winds, and so forth. Examples may be had from Farnell, *Cults* (index under 'Zeus'), and reference there; the corresponding entry in the index to A. B. Cook's treatise on Zeus would supply abundant instances of every kind of title mentioned in this article. Aphrodite has epithets denoting her power over the sexual life of mankind, as Ἀμβολογήρα, 'delayer of old age'; her connexion with love whether licit or illicit, for example Πάνδημος 'Goddess of the whole people', in her Athenian worship as a deity of marriage (Farnell, ii. 658), and on the other hand Ἑταίρα and even Πόρνη (ibid. 667). These last belong to an extremely curious sub-class in which the characteristics of the worshipper are transferred to the deity; both signify the goddess who is worshipped by harlots. Hera in like manner is called Παῖς, Τελεία, and Χήρα at her three shrines in Stymphalus, in other words Maid, Wife, and Widow (Paus. 8. 22. 2); she naturally received the worship of women of all ages and conditions. The local legend was somewhat at a loss to explain the third title, since Zeus cannot die, and invented a quarrel between the two leading to a separation; clearly the sense of such epithets was no longer remembered when Pausanias wrote.

3. Of epithets referring to a particular manifestation of a god's activity two Roman examples may be given. Mars Ultor (see Platner–Ashby, 220, 329) owed his title to his supposed intervention on Augustus' behalf at Philippi and apparently in the recovery of the standards taken by the Parthians. Jupiter's titles Custos and Conservator (Tacitus, *Hist.* 3. 74) refer *inter alia* to the thank-offerings made him by Domitian after his escape from the Vitellians when they took the Capitol.

**4.** Epithets having reference to the higher (moral or civic) qualities of a deity are not uncommon, though less so than those which are due to his natural functions. It is to be noted that there is a tendency in later ages to read such qualities into an old title; thus Athena Προναία at Delphi, so named from the fact that her shrine was in front of the temple of Apollo, had so decided an inclination to become Πρόνοια that some manuscripts of Herodotus 8. 37. 2 have been infected by it. As genuine examples may be instanced Apollo Ἀρχηγέτης (*see* APOLLO), Athena Βουλαία (of the Senate), Venus Verticordia.

**5.** Late hymns, for instance those of the Orphic collection, have a strong tendency to heap up epithets, including the most unheard-of and fanciful, e.g. no. 28 (Abel), to Hermes.

C. F. H. Bruchmann, *Epitheta deorum quae apud poetas Graecos leguntur* (Teubner, 1893); J. B. Carter, *De deorum Romanorum cognominibus* (Teubner, 1898) and *Epith. deor. q. a. p. Latinos leguntur* (Teubner, 1902) are useful, but there is room for a large and exhaustive work. H. J. R.

**EPITOME** (ἐπιτομή). I. GREEK. The production of summaries or abbreviated versions of longer works, especially scientific works, was much practised in the post-classical era. Thus Pamphilus' Glossary was reduced from 95 books to 30, and then to 5. Strabo was often epitomized (*GGM* 2. 529 ff.). Aristophanes of Byzantium epitomized Aristotle's *Historia animalium*, and the epitome was later epitomized by Sopatros. The first two books of Athenaeus and part of the third survive only in an epitome. But the most important of all Greek epitomes is Proclus' prose summary of the *Epic Cycle*, which has come down to us through Photius, and is a most important source for Greek mythology. J. D. D.

II. LATIN. In Rome the rhetorical education of imperial times produced both encyclopaedic scholarship (*see* QUINTILIANUS), which tempts abbreviation, and compendious works of factual or illustrative information, especially in history: we have Valerius (q.v. 8) Maximus, and Martial knew an epitome of Livy. Short histories, however derivative, might be stylish (*see* FLORUS); but the trend by the third century A.D. was towards schematic summary. We may note Livy's *Periochae* (q.v.) and the reduction of Pompeius Trogus (q.v.) to Justinus' epitome. While the original authors remained, on papyrus, there was no loss; but during the change to parchment, the taste for epitome limited their chances of survival. Trogus was lost, and only the senatorial traditionalism of the fourth century saved Livy's best books (1–10, 21–45). Concise writing set its fashion. Late historians used the epitome to introduce their accounts of contemporary events (*see* EUTROPIUS 1, FESTUS 3), and it gave Roman background to the Christian interpretation of history (*see* OROSIUS); likewise in the new biography (*see* AURELIUS (3) VICTOR, MARIUS (5) MAXIMUS, HISTORIA AUGUSTA.)

Meanwhile practical 'digests' continued, e.g. the grammatical work of Julius (q.v. 6) Romanus, preserved partly by Charisius and Diomedes. Festus (q.v. 2) epitomized Verrius Flaccus (q.v. 8) on Augustan scholarship. Cassiodorus (q.v.) proves the value of this modest transmission of knowledge that would have otherwise been lost.

M. Galdi, *L'epitome nella letteratura latina* (1922). A. H. McD.

**EPONA.** The name, meaning 'The Great Mare', is that of a Celtic goddess known from a large number of dedications in Roman Gaul, and widespread from Spain to the Balkans, and northern Britain to Italy. The dispersal is due to devotees in the army, but the original cult area was in north-eastern Gaul, and monuments are frequent between the Saône and Seine, around the Mosel and its tributaries, and east of the Rhine to the *limes*. Alesia was a centre of the cult. The goddess is generally depicted riding on a horse, sometimes with attendant mares and foals, or seated and flanked by horses. In some of the latter instances she holds a basket of provisions, and is thus to be identified with the nature goddesses (cf. DEAE MATRES). Epona is mentioned by Juvenal (8. 157), and minor authors. The mare-goddess is found in single and triple form in insular Celtic mythology.

R. Magnen and E. Thevenot, *Epona, déesse gauloise* (1953), for inventory and map. *See* bibliography s.v. RELIGION, CELTIC.
T. G. E. P.

**EPONYMOI** (ἐπώνυμοι) are those who give their name to anybody or anything. They were of three kinds in antiquity. (1) Gods were the *eponymoi* of cities, as Apollo of Apollonia and Athena of Athens. (2) Heroes were the *eponymoi* of tribes, demes, γένη or *gentes*, and some other divisions of the populace. When Cleisthenes divided the Athenians into ten tribes, the Delphic oracle chose ten Attic heroes to be their *eponymoi*; forty-two other heroes became the *eponymoi* of the successive years of military service from 18 to 59. (3) In many cities the presiding magistrate was the eponym of the year, as the archon in Athens, the *stephanephoros* in Miletus, the consuls in Rome. J. E. F.

**EPOPEUS** ('Επωπεύς; corrupted to Epaphus by Hyginus, *Fab.* 7. 1; 8. 2–3), the king of Sicyon who protected Antiope (q.v.). He is post-Homeric, first in the *Cypria*, where a version of his story was told in an episode (Proclus ap. Phot.). Eumelus (in Paus. 2. 1. 1) said that he was son of Alōeus the son of Helios, and father of Marathon, the eponym of the Attic region of that name.
H. J. R.

**EPOREDIA,** modern *Ivrea*, founded at the foot of the Alps in north-western Cisalpine Gaul (q.v.) as a Roman colony (100 B.C.) to watch over the Salassi. Controlling the approaches of the *Val d'Aosta* and the Alpine passes, Eporedia became and remained a town of consequence.

U. Ewins, *PBSR* 1952, 70 ff. E. T. S.

**EPRIUS** (*PW* s.v.) **MARCELLUS,** TITUS CLODIUS, born of humble parentage at Capua, was praetor A.D. 48, legate of Lycia and proconsul of Cyprus, and *cos. suff.* in 62. After his Lycian legateship in 57 he was prosecuted for extortion, but secured acquittal by bribery and had his accuser exiled. In 66 he was one of the accusers of Thrasea (q.v.) Paetus, and received 5 million sesterces after the condemnation. After the Flavian entry into Rome in 70 he became a champion of the new government, and engaged in fierce controversies with Helvidius (q.v.) Priscus (Tac. *Hist.* 4. 6–8, 43). He was rewarded with the proconsulate of Asia, perhaps with special powers, for three years (70–3), and obtained a second consulate (*suff.*) in May 74. He also held three priesthoods, and was regarded not only as one of the most powerful orators of the age but as an intimate counsellor of Vespasian (Tac. *Dial.* 8, *Hist.* 2. 95). But just before Vespasian's death he was accused by Titus (q.v.) of conspiracy with Caecina (q.v. 3) Alienus, was condemned by the Senate, and committed suicide.

*ILS* 992; *AE* 1956, 86. J. A. Crook, *AJPhil.* 1951, 162 ff.
G. E. F. C.

**EPULONES,** the latest in date of the *quattuor amplissima collegia* of Roman priests. They were first instituted in 196 B.C. (Livy 33. 42. 1), and were then three in number (*tresviri epulones*), the bill for their creation being brought in by C. Licinius Lucullus, then tribune of the *plebs*, who was himself one of the first members. Their business was to organize and supervise the *epulum Iovis* and the similar public banquet which had by that time become a prominent feature of several festivals, as the *Ludi Romani* (cf. Cicero, *De Or.* 3. 73). They were later increased to seven and continued to be called *septemviri epulones*, although under Caesar their number became ten (Dio Cassius 43. 51. 9).

Wissowa, *RK* 423; 518; J. Marquardt, *Römische Staatsverwaltung* (1881–5) iii². 347 ff.; Latte, *RR* 399.　　　H. J. R.

**EPYLLION** (ἐπύλλιον, diminutive of ἔπος), a literary type popular from Theocritus to Ovid, was a narrative poem of about 100 to 600 hexameters; the subject was usually taken from the life of a mythical hero or heroine, the love motif being prominent in later epyllia. *See* THEOCRITUS, CALLIMACHUS (3), EUPHORION (2), CATULLUS (1), VIRGIL, OVID.

M. M. Crump. *Epyllion from Theocritus to Ovid.* (1931)　A. M. D.

**EQUITES. 1.** *Origins and Republic.* The early history of the cavalry at Rome is overlaid with legend and speculation. The kings are said to have enrolled 300 *celeres* or *trossuli* (later doubled) for the legion (q.v.). They wore loin-cloths, tunics with the *clavus* (q.v.), *trabeae* (short embroidered cloaks), and *mullei* (strapped red shoes); they were armed with lances and their horses were adorned with *phalerae* (silver disks). Their insignia, in various adapted forms, later became the distinctive attire of patricians, magistrates, and senators. 1,200 *equites* were allegedly added by Servius (q.v. 1). These 1,800 had their horses supplied and maintained by the State (hence *equites equo publico*), drawing on the property of widows and orphans. They had to serve ten campaigns. In the centuriate assembly they formed eighteen *centuriae* (q.v.), later including (it seems) those too old for service. This voting privilege survived in essence as long as the assembly. In the classical Republic these *equites* were enrolled by the censors (q.v.), after financial, physical, and moral scrutiny (*recognitio*). After 304 B.C. (but not regularly in the late Republic) they paraded to the Capitol in the *transvectio* on 15 July. Men of aristocratic birth always had preference for enrolment.

About 400 B.C., men on their own horses (*equites equo privato*) were added to the cavalry. They did not share the voting privilege, but were given at least some of the status marks, of the others. In the third century Roman cavalry proved increasingly ineffective in war and by 200 was largely replaced by *auxilia* (q.v.). But *equites* retained their social eminence and became a corps from which officers and the staffs of governors and commanders were drawn. This new 'equestrian' service was within the reach of any wealthy and well-connected family and the old exclusiveness was undermined. In the 120s senators (but not their families) were excluded from the 18 centuries, and this marks the beginnings of the later *ordo equester* as a separate class in the State. C. Gracchus (q.v. 4), by his law on the Asian tax, gave the wealthiest of non-senators a chance of new enrichment; and his friend Acilius Glabrio (2) turned over the *repetundae* (q.v.) court to (essentially) the same class of men.

The result of all this was a transformation of the *ordo*. By the first century B.C. the wealthiest non-senatorial class (especially the powerful *publicani*, q.v.), from which Gracchan juries were taken and whose sons served on equal terms with those of senators, claimed and increasingly received the title and the privileges of the old *equites*, achieving final recognition in the law of Roscius (q.v. 2) Otho in 67. (In modern works it is they who are customarily designated as *equites*.) The ineffectiveness of the censorship after Sulla (with the sole exception of 70 B.C.) made membership of the *centuriae* difficult to control, and the *equus publicus* disappears from record. These new *equites*, like the post-Sullan Senate, were a disparate class, vastly increased by the enfranchisement of Italy: round a Roman aristocratic core were grouped leading men from colonies and *municipia*—akin in background—and *publicani* and *negotiatores* (chiefly financiers), many of similar background, but some self-made men. A landed interest (and, of course, free birth) was essential to all of them for social recognition (cf. Cic. *Off.* i. 151). Senators and *equites*, in the late Republic, thus formed a plutocracy sharing both landed and business interests, in a continuous range of proportions.

In social standing, *equites* were almost equal to senators, freely intermarrying even with patrician nobles and gaining entry to the Senate (though not the consulate—*see* NOBILITAS) if they wanted it (see Cic. *Sest.* 97). But as a class they preferred the pursuit of money and pleasure to political responsibility, and they thus formed the non-political section of the upper class rather than (as in the Empire) an intermediate class. Their history is an important part of that of the late Republic, particularly in view of their control of the *quaestiones* (q.v.) during most of that time. Various Populares (first perhaps C. Gracchus) tried to mould them into a political force opposed to the Senate and the *nobilitas*; but their social and economic interests, especially after the enfranchisement of Italy, were basically too similar to permit this. Sulla (q.v. 1), after decimating them in the proscriptions, followed the example of Drusus (q.v. 2) and deprived them of leadership by adlecting the most prominent survivors to the Senate, and of power by taking the courts from them. But strengthened by the influx of Italians and by increasing financial power, wooed by Pompey, and largely restored to the courts by the law of L. Cotta (q.v. 3), they rose to unprecedented influence in the 60s, when Cicero and the Senate—aware of the basic community of interests of the two classes—tried to unit them behind the *Principes* in a *concordia ordinum*. Yet, though often united on a single issue (e.g. against threats to financial stability by demagogues or threats to freedom of profiteering by statesmen), sometimes even for a lengthy period, they were too disparate in composition and too non-political to form a stable grouping. Preventing necessary reform (especially in the provinces), they remained a disruptive and irresponsible element with no programme or allegiance, until the Civil War substituted military for economic power. Caesar deprived them of the Asian tithe, but opened a new avenue for them by making prominent *equites* his political and financial agents (*see* BALBUS 2, OPPIUS 2). The support of these men, as well as the precedent, proved important to Augustus.

Pliny, *HN* 33. 8–36. A. Alföldi, *Der frühröm. Reiteradel u. seine Ehrenabzeichen* (1952: on this, see A. Momigliano, *JRS* 1966, 16 ff.); H. Hill, *The Roman Middle Class in the Rep. Period* (1952: reviewed by M. Gelzer, *Gnomon* 1953, 319 ff. = *Kl. Schr.* i (1962), 222 ff.); M. I. Henderson, *JRS* 1963, 61 ff.; P. A. Brunt, *Second Intern. Conference of Economic History*, 1962 (1965), 117 ff.; C. Nicolet, *L'Ordre équestre a l'époque républicaine*, i (1966).　　　E. B.

**2.** With the establishment of the Empire the *equester ordo* ceased to be a political force, though, especially under Augustus, individual *equites* played an important unofficial part as advisers of the emperor, and the holders of the major equestrian posts had a steadily increasing importance in the administration of the Empire. The *equites*, in the wider sense (see below) provided the holders both of military prefectures and tribunates and of a wide range of posts in the imperial civil administration (*see* PROCURATOR), as it developed from its slight beginnings under Augustus.

Augustus, in accordance with his policy of reviving traditional rituals, restored the long-disused *transvectio* of 15 July, while allowing men handicapped by age or ill health to parade on foot, and those over 35 to have the choice of retaining or giving up the (notional) *equus publicus*; the occasion was also combined with a *recognitio* by Augustus of the physical and moral fitness of the *equites*

(Suet. *Div. Aug.* 38–9). Those who took part in this ceremony (more than 5,000 on occasion under Augustus, Dion. Hal. *Ant. Rom.* 6. 13) formed the *turmae equitum Romanorum*, headed by *seviri equitum Romanorum*, usually young men of senatorial birth (who before holding the quaestorship were technically *equites*) and, when such existed, by scions of the imperial house with the title *Principes iuventutis* (q.v.). These *equites* formed a distinct corporation which might dedicate statues or play a role in the funeral of an Emperor. They were called *equites equo publico*; the *equus publicus* was granted, and could be removed, at the pleasure of the Emperor. It seems that Emperors also granted the title of *eques equo publico* to some persons, like a boy who died at the age of 9 (*ILS* 1316) or the Spartan C. Julius Spartiaticus (*AE* 1927, 2) who almost certainly did not attend the parade in Rome.

Augustus also established four *decuriae* of *iudices* or *selecti* (each of 1,000, but comprising 3,000 men in all, since the fourth was made up of members of the other three) who were of equestrian rank, but, according to Pliny, *HN* 33. 30–3, were not as such called *equites* until A.D. 23. In the *Tabula Hebana* (q.v.) of A.D. 19, however, and presumably in the *Lex Valeria Cornelia* of A.D. 5 which it cites, they are called *equites omnium decuriarum quae iudicior(um) publicor(um) caussa constitutae sunt*. The panels were filled by the Emperor—a duty Tiberius neglected while on Capri (Suet. *Tib.* 41)—who also dismissed *iudices* for misconduct (Suet. *Dom.* 83). In theory (Pliny, *HN* 33. 30) no one could be admitted to the *decuriae* who was not of citizen birth. But Livia browbeat Tiberius into appointing a new citizen (Suet. *Tib.* 51) and Claudius found that *peregrini* from some Alpine tribes had actually served on the *decuriae* (*ILS* 206). Owing to the pressure for places—since after a regulation of A.D. 23 membership seems to have conferred the gold ring and the right to sit in the 14 rows—Gaius added a fifth *decuria*. Inscriptions from Italy and the provinces in the first three centuries attest men chosen for the *decuriae* by the Emperor (a minority being also *equo publico*); the appointment was perhaps sometimes a sinecure.

These two groups were small sub-classes within the much wider class of Roman citizens of the requisite census of 400,000 sesterces (Pliny, *HN* 33. 32) and of, normally, free birth. Thus, Strabo records that recent censuses had disclosed 500 men of equestrian census at both Gades and Patavium (Strabo 169; 213) and Josephus mentions *equites* of Jewish origin in Judaea in A.D. 66. Pliny the Younger gave money to his friend Romatius Firmus, a *decurio* (q.v.) of Comum *ad implendas equestres facultates* (*Ep.* 1. 19). The census and free birth seem to have been sufficient conditions for a man to be called *eques Romanus*; but an authorization by the Emperor may have been required. Emperors could certainly remove a man's equestrian rank, or award it to persons not formally qualified, such as centurions or *liberti*. *Primipili* (q.v.) when promoted to military prefectures or tribunates thereby gained equestrian rank.

The possession of equestrian rank in this wider sense (which unlike senatorial status passed only *de facto*, not formally, from father to son) spread widely through the provinces, following the extension of the citizenship—from the very beginning of the Empire in Narbonensis and Baetica, and in the first century and after in Africa and the Greek East; the Danubian provinces, Germany, Gaul, and Britain were little represented, or not at all. It was the landed *bourgeoisie* of the municipalities and Greek cities among whom equestrian rank spread; they were thus qualified to take up equestrian military or civilian posts, but were not obliged to do so, and many remained content with local or provincial offices—which are frequently attested also for those who take up posts in the

Roman service. Prominent provincial families, in which a member has equestrian rank in one generation, often acquire senatorial status in the next generation (e.g. *IGRom.* iv. 910). Similarly, from the Flavian period on, it became increasingly common for equestrian office-holders to be adlected into the Senate by the Emperor.

From the latter part of the second century equestrian officials in the imperial service began to acquire regular appellations of rank—*vir eminentissimus* for the Praetorian Prefects, *vir perfectissimus* for the other Prefects and higher procurators, *vir egregius* for the rest. In the later third century, with a substantial replacement of senatorial governors by *equites*, and then more markedly with the reforms of Diocletian (q.v.), the higher military posts, and almost all administrative posts, passed into the hands of *equites*. During the first half of the fourth century repeated attempts, evidently not entirely successful, were made to confine equestrian rank to office-holders, and exclude *curiales* (q.v.). In the same period the equestrian title *perfectissimus* (*egregius* disappears in the reign of Constantine) was steadily extended to officials of minor rank, eventually being awarded in three grades. By the end of the century this process had been overtaken by a similar diffusion of senatorial honours among officials, and at this point the *equester ordo* ceases to be a recognizable element in the Roman State.

See bibliography above and A. Stein, *Der römische Ritterstand* (1927); H. Petersen, *JRS* 1955, 47 ff.; Jones, *Later Rom. Emp.* 525 ff.; R. Duncan-Jones, 'Equestrian Rank in the Cities of the African Provinces', *PBSR* 1967, 147 ff. F. G. B. M.

**EQUITES SINGULARES IMPERATORIS**, probably created by the Flavians, were a mounted bodyguard of the Emperor. Chiefly Germans and Pannonians, they numbered at first 500 and later 1,000. Their relationship to the Praetorian guard was similar to that of the *auxilia* to the legions. They had their own camp near the Lateran under the command of two Praetorian tribunes.

M. Durry, *Les Cohortes prétoriennes* (1938). H. M. D. P.

**ERANOS.** In Homer and later authors this word meant a meal to which each partner contributed his share; but from the fifth century B.C. it was mostly a loan, free of interest, given to an individual by a number of friends. Creditors could form a club under an ἀρχέρανος, ἐρανάρχης, or προστάτης ἐράνων, who paid out the loan and received it in repayment. Each partner's claim was transferable, and repayment of sums greater than the original loan could be agreed upon, so that an *eranos* could be profitable business. Papyri from Alexandria suggest that this type of loan was often used by Hellenistic Jews to evade the biblical prohibition of interest.

M. I. Finley, *Studies in Land and Credit in Ancient Athens* (1951), index; E. Leider, *Der Handel von Alexandria* (1933), 82 ff. LSJ; E. Ziebarth, *PW*, s.v.; *Seeraub und Seehandel im alten Griechenland* (1929), 58; *Kl. Pauly*, s.v. F. M. H.

**ERASISTRATUS** of Ceos, physician, lived in Alexandria together with and after Herophilus (first half of the 3rd c. B.C.). His school still flourished in Galen's time; his books were read as late as the fourth century A.D. A scholar and philosopher rather than a practitioner, Erasistratus became more and more interested in scientific research, which included even quantitative experiment; working incessantly, he tried to complete his knowledge and did not shrink from admitting earlier mistakes. On the basis of the Democritean atomism and in connexion with Straton's system he apparently developed original ideas (e.g. that of a discontinuous vacuum); although relying on mechanistic principles of explanation, such as the *horror vacui*, he also believed that nature does nothing in vain. His anatomical studies led to the clear distinction of sensory and motor nerves; in post-mortem dissections he recognized the changes of the body due to disease; he was interested in comparative anatomy. In physiology he studied the growth of the body and the process of digestion; he theorized on the flow of the blood through the veins and that of the pneuma through the arteries. All diseases he explained by one cause, viz. plethora, repletion of the body through undigested nutrition; yet he did not neglect the local differences of illness nor the constitution of the patient. In therapy he emphasized the dietetic method and violently opposed phlebotomy and purgation.

TEXT. R. Fuchs, *Erasistratea* (Diss. Berl. 1892); *Hermes* 1894, 171 ff. Erasistratus in the fourth century A.D., Themistius, *Or.* 20. List of writings, Susemihl, i. 810.
TRANSLATION AND COMMENTARY. J. F. Dobson, *Proc. Royal Society of Med.*, Section Hist. of Med. (1927), indispensable translation and interpretation of more important fragments.
MODERN LITERATURE. Survey, M. Wellmann, *PW* vi. 333. Quantitative experiment, H. Diels, *Sitz. Berl.* 1893, 101 ff. W. Jaeger, *Hermes* 1913, 58 ff.; Charles Singer, *Enc. Brit.*[14], s.v. 'Medicine, history of'. On Erasistratus' theory of the heart and the veins see I. M. Lonie, 'Erasistratus, the Erasistrateans and Aristotle', *Bulletin of the History of Medicine* 1964, 395 ff. His research into the nervous system is discussed in its historical context by F. Solmsen, *MH* 1961, 188 ff.
L. E.

**ERATOSTHENES** of Cyrene (*c.* 275–194 B.C.), pupil of Callimachus and Lysanias, after spending several years at Athens, where he came under the influence of Arcesilaus and Ariston, accepted the invitation of Ptolemy Euergetes to become royal tutor and to succeed Apollonius Rhodius as head of the Alexandrian Library. The most versatile scholar of his time, he was the first to call himself φιλόλογος. By the Alexandrian specialists he was styled βῆτα (which probably means, not 'second rate' but next after the best' specialist in each subject), and πένταθλος, 'all-rounder', his best work being in geography.
WORKS (known in fragments only). 1. Literary criticism. His most important work in this field was the treatise *On Ancient Comedy*, in at least twelve books; this dealt with literary, lexical, historical, and antiquarian matters, and problems of the authorship and production of plays. His Καταστερισμοί treated the constellations and their mythology; the extant work of this name is probably not genuine. 2. Chronology. Χρονογραφίαι represented the first scientific attempt to fix the dates of political and literary history. He also compiled a list of Olympian victors. 3. Mathematics, astronomy, geography. Besides investigating arithmetical and geometrical problems (cf. his 'sieve' method of finding prime numbers), he dealt in *Platonicus* with mathematical definitions and with the principles of music, and he wrote geometrical works *On Means* and *Duplication of the Cube*. In his *On the Measurement of the Earth* (probably part of the *Geographica*—see below) he treated mathematical geography, in which he was a pioneer, calculating with a high degree of accuracy the circumference of the earth and, with much less accuracy, the magnitude and distance of the sun and moon. He was the first systematic geographer, and his *Geographica* (Γεωγραφικά, three books), in which he sketched the history of the subject and dealt with physical, mathematical, and ethnographical geography, is often mentioned, sometimes disapprovingly, by later geographers, e.g. Strabo. But Archimedes had evidently regarded him as an equal. 4. Philosophy. His essays had perhaps a mainly ethical interest. He wrote also a history of philosophy. 5. Poetry. His short epic *Hermes* described the birth of the god, his youthful exploits, and his ascent to the planets. The short epic *Anterinys* or *Hesiod* dealt with the death of Hesiod and the punishment of his murderers. [Longinus] (*Subl.* 33. 5) praises the elegy *Erigone*, which told the myth of Erigonus and his daughter.

See MAPS, GEOGRAPHY.
*FGrH* ii B 241; G. Bernhardy, *Eratosthenica* (1822); C. Strecker, *De Lycophrone Euphronio Eratosthene comicorum interpretibus* (1884); Heath, *Hist. of Greek Maths.* ii. 104 ff.; E. Hiller, *E. carminum reliquiae* (1872); Powell, *Coll. Alex.*; [*Catasterismi*], A. Olivieri in *Mythographi Graeci* iii, 1 (1897); R. M. Bentham, 'The Fragments of Eratosthenes', an important unpublished thesis, University of London (1948); I. Thomas, *Greek Mathematics* (Loeb, 1939, 1941), i. 100, 290 ff.; ii. 260 ff.; A. Thalamas, *Géographie d'Eratosthene* (1921); E. H. Bunbury, *History of Ancient Geography* I. xvi (1879); E. H. Berger, *Geschichte der wissenschaftlichen Erdkunde der Griechen*[2], 406 ff.; 441 ff. (1903). Thomson *Hist. Anc. Geog.* 124, 134 ff., 158 ff.; D. R. Dicks, *The Geographical Fragments of Hipparchus* (1960), especially commentary on bk. ii of H., and index, s.v. Eratosthenes.
J. F. L.; E. H. W.

**ERECHTHEUM,** the third outstanding building on the Athenian Acropolis, begun in 421 B.C. and finished, after a lapse, in 407 B.C.; built of Pentelic marble, with friezes of black Eleusis stone to take applied white marble relief sculpture. Exact details of its construction are known from a contemporary inscription. It is tempting to accept W. Dörpfeld's restoration of the original design as a long rectangular building with projecting porches placed centrally on the sides, but there is no certain evidence of this. The main structure is divided into four compartments: the largest (east cella) has a prostyle-hexastyle Ionic portico; the west end is closed by a wall with engaged columns and corner piers. At this end is a unique and boldly projecting (though small) south feature—the 'porch of the maidens', with draped female figures (caryatids) serving as supports—and, nearly opposite on the north side, a still more boldly projecting porch with Ionic columns (partly reassembled in early twentieth century) standing on a lower level and having the tallest Order of the whole composition. The Erechtheum is remarkable no less for the elegance and elaboration of its decorative detail than for the complexity of its plan.
The temple replaced to some extent the large sixth-century temple of Athena whose foundations can be seen between it and the Parthenon, and both were on the site of the presumed Mycenaean palace. We know from Pausanias (1. 26. 5–27. 3) that the Erechtheum housed a number of ancient cults (this may partly account for its complicated form) and many sacred spots and objects—the venerable image of Athena Polias, a golden lamp made by Callimachus (*see* CALLIMACHUS 2), a salt well and the mark of Poseidon's trident, an altar of Poseidon and Erechtheus (q.v.), and altars of Butes and Hephaestus. Near the west end of the building were shrines of Cecrops and Pandrosos, and the original sacred olive of Athena.

See also ALCAMENES.
*IG*, i[2], 372 ff.; G. P. Stevens and J. M. Paton, *The Erechtheum* (U.S.A. 1927); W. Judeich, *Topographie von Athen* (1931), 259 ff.; W. B. Dinsmoor, *Architecture of Ancient Greece* (1950), 187 ff., 360 (bibliography); I. T. Hill, *The Ancient City of Athens* (1953), ch. 17, 179 ff.
T. F.; R. E. W.

**ERECHTHEUS** ('Ερεχθεύς), a fabulous king of Athens, often confused with Erichthonius (*see* ATHENA) and perhaps identical with him originally. Like him, Erechtheus was son of Earth and reared by Athena, *Iliad* 2. 547 ff., where his worship is mentioned (for which see Farnell, *Hero-Cults*, 11; *Cults* i. 393; iv. 47–52). Cf. *Od.* 7. 80 f., from a comparison of which with the other Homeric passage it would seem that Athena and Erechtheus were honoured together in a predecessor of the historical Erechtheum (the old royal palace?). The chief legend of Erechtheus concerns his daughters, of whom there were three (Eur. fr. 357 Nauck; *Ion* 10 adds a fourth, Creusa q.v. 1). They included Chthonia (Erechtheus' children vary greatly from one account to another, for obvious genealogical reasons); when Eumolpus (q.v.) the Thracian, son of Poseidon and Chione, invaded Attica, Erechtheus inquired of Delphi how he might win the victory. He was told that he should do so if he sacrificed one of his daughters. Chthonia, therefore, was sacrificed by consent of her mother Praxithea, probably by her own also, the story forming the plot of Euripides' *Erechtheus*, known by its frequent citations in later authors (to those quoted in Nauck, 464 ff. add Hyginus, *Fab.* 46 and 238. 2, and Rose ad locc.). The other daughters killed themselves; Erechtheus' own fate is variously told. H. R. J.

**ERETRIA**, a city of Euboea (q.v.). It joined its neighbour Chalcis (q.v.) in trade in Syria, and colonizing in Italy, Sicily, and the North Aegean. In the late eighth century they fought over the Lelantine plain. Aristagoras of Miletus sought its aid for the Ionic revolt against Persia and in the avenging expedition sent by Darius the city was besieged and burnt. About 445 B.C. Athens planted a colony, but in 411 Eretria revolted with the rest of Euboea. A member of the second Athenian League (378–377), it again revolted (349), and subsequently was the victim of Athenian and Macedonian intrigues. In the second Macedonian war Quinctius Flamininus sacked the city, which after the Roman victory was nominally free. Eretria took little part in the struggle of the Greek leagues against Rome, and in the time of Augustus still ranked as the second city of Euboea. Its walls, temple of Apollo, theatre, and some public buildings have been excavated.

*IG* xii (9), 11 ff.; 'Αρχ. Δελτ. 1961/2, 144 ff. for buildings.
W. A. L.

**ERETRIA, SCHOOL OF,** founded by Menedemus (q.v. 1) as a continuation of the school of Elis, is mentioned by Diog. Laert. 1. 17–19; 2. 105; 126; Strabo 9. 393; Cic. *Acad.* 2. 129. Menedemus had a large following, but only one follower, Ctesibius, is known by name. The last trace of the school is in the title of a work of the Stoic Sphaerus against it. W. D. R.

**ERGITIUM,** mentioned by the Ravenna Cosmography and the Peutinger Table, was a town in the northern Apulian plain between Teanum Apulum (q.v.) and Sipontum. Its site has now been identified at Il Casone, 4 miles south-east of San Severo. The Roman settlement possessed a centuriation system based on 16-*actus* squares in the area to the north. G. D. B. J.

**ERICHTHONIUS,** an Attic hero, usually son of Hephaestus; for the circumstances of his birth, *see* ATHENA. But Apollodorus (3. 187) says 'some' name Atthis daughter of Cranaus as his mother. Being born, he was taken care of by Athena, who put him into a chest and gave him into the charge of the daughters, or a daughter, of Cecrops (q.v.; Eur. *Ion* 21 ff.; 270 ff., and later authors, as Apollod. ibid. 189; Hyg. *Fab.* 166. 4–5); all agree that they opened the chest, which Athena had forbidden them to do, and then out of fright (because the child had wholly or partly serpent form or had a serpent with him) or driven mad by the anger of the goddess, leapt off the Acropolis and so were killed. Or the serpent killed them (Apollod. ibid.). This scene is not very common in art, but the birth is a fairly popular subject, see Furtwängler–Reichhold, *Gr. Vasenmalerei* iii. 95 and plate 137. Erichthonius became king of Athens, fostered the cult of Athena (Apollod. ibid.), received from Athena two drops of the blood of the Gorgon (q.v.), of which one poisoned and the other healed (Eur. *Ion* 999 ff.), and was the inventor or introducer of sundry things, as chariot-driving ([Eratosth.] *Catast.* 13; Hyg. *Poet. Astr.* 2. 13; hence he is sometimes identified with the constellation Auriga), silver (Hyg. *Fab.* 274. 4). He is often confused with Erechtheus (q.v.). H. J. R.

**ERIDANUS** ('Ηριδανός), mythical river, having Electrides (Amber-) Islands at its mouth. Named by Hesiod (*Theog.* 338) as a real river, the Eridanus was placed first in unknown northernmost Europe, or in western Europe, flowing into the Northern Ocean. Herodotus (3. 115) and Strabo (5. 215) doubted its existence. Aeschylus called it 'Spanish', meaning the Rhône (see Pliny, *HN* 37. 32).

Greek authors from the time of Pherecydes agreed to identify the Eridanus with the Po, and Roman writers followed suit (since there are no islands at the mouth of the Po, some authors sought these in the east Adriatic). The description of the Eridanus as an amber-river may embody the memory of an early amber-route from Jutland up the Elbe and Rhine (Rhenus) and down the Rhône (Rhodanus) or across the Alps to north Italy (*see* AMBER). E. H. W.

**ERIGONE** ('Ηριγόνη), in mythology, (1) daughter of Icarius (q.v.), loved by Dionysus, who approached her disguised as a grape-cluster (Ov. *Met.* 6. 125). When she found her father's body she hanged herself, and the Athenian virgins began to do the same till her ghost was appeased by the αἰώρα and other honours (Hyginus, *Fab.* 130 and *Poet. Astr.* 2. 4; cf. Rose, *Greek Myth*[6].). (2) Daughter of Aegisthus (q.v.) by Clytaemnestra (q.v.). She was rescued by Artemis from Orestes (q.v.), who had killed her brother Aletes and wanted to kill her, and made a priestess in Attica (Hyg. *Fab.* 122. 3). According, however, to Cinaethon ap. Paus. 2. 18. 6, Orestes had by her an illegitimate son Penthilus.

F. Solmsen, *TAPA* 1947, 242 ff. H. J. R.

**ERINNA,** poetess, of the Dorian island of Tēlos (*Suda*, s.v. "Ηριννα), who probably lived at the end of the fourth century B.C., not, as the *Suda* says, in the time of Sappho, since her art shows affinities to that of Theocritus, and Asclepiades seems to have edited her work (*Anth. Pal.* 7. 11). Writing in local Doric with a few Aeolisms, she was famous for her *Distaff* ('Ηλακάτη), a poem in 300 hexameters in memory of her friend Baucis. Remains of this on a papyrus have recently been added to the few lines known from quotations, and show that in it Erinna described experiences of girlhood shared with Baucis and lamented her death. The title may refer to the time of spinsterhood which it describes. She herself died at the age of nineteen (*Anth. Pal.* 7. 11. 2). There also survive three epigrams, one dedicatory (*Anth. Pal.* 6. 352) and two inscriptions for Baucis' tomb (*Anth. Pal.* 7. 710 and 712). A line from what seems to have been a Propempticon (fr. 2) is of doubtful authenticity (Ath. 283 d).

TEXT. Diehl, *Anth. Lyr. Graec.* i. 4, 207–13; P. Maas, *Hermes* 1934, 206 ff.
CRITICISM. C. M. Bowra, in *Greek Poetry and Life* (1936), 325 ff.
C. M. B.

**ERINYES,** spirits of punishment, avenging wrongs done to kindred, especially murder within the family or clan (cf. ORESTES, ALCMAEON 1), but also lesser offences (see *Il.* 9. 454, 571; 15. 204), even against those who are no kin but have a claim on our pity (beggars, *Od.* 17. 475, though there it is rather hoped than stated that there are such avengers for them if wronged). They once stop a violation of the course of nature (*Il.* 19. 418), where they silence the horse Xanthus, given human utterance temporarily by Hera (407). Hence the dictum of Heraclitus (fr. 29 Bywater = 94 Diels–Kranz), that if the sun left his course the Erinyes would find him. But these passages go much beyond popular ideas, more in keeping with which are their associations with oaths (*Il.* 19. 259; Hesiod, *Op.* 803–4).

This early connexion of the Erinyes with offences other than manslaying makes against Rohde's theory (*Psyche*⁴ i. 270), accepted also by Nilsson (*GGR* i². 100 ff.), that originally an Erinys is the ghost of the person slain, though this will fit the other facts (close connexion with blood guilt, greater importance of the Erinyes of an elder brother or a parent, doubtful potency of those of a beggar; see the Homeric passages above) very well. It is on the whole more reasonable to suppose that they were from the first curses, actual or conditional, personalized, as Farnell argues (*Cults* v. 438–9), since a curse (cf. CURSES) is not a mere form of words but the stirring up of mysterious powers which work automatically when once set going. They are early associated with Earth (Hesiod, *Theog.* 185; cf. *Il.* 19. 259), which helps to explain Demeter Erinys (cf. DEMETER), an earth-goddess, as repository of powers of vengeance. As they regularly work by disturbing the mind (*Od.* 15. 233–4), it is understandable that very similar deities are called *Maniai* (Paus. 8. 34. 1). Being of the earth, they are often confused with kindlier powers who send fertility, Eumenides, Σεμναί, etc.; their cult under their own name is extremely rare (see Farnell, ibid. 437 ff.). It is possible that the name Erinys occurs on a tablet from Cnossos.

E. Wüst, *PW* Suppl. viii. H. J. R.

**ERIPHUS**, Middle Comedy poet, as the two mythological titles, Αἴολος and Μελίβοια, suggest.

*FCG* iii. 556 ff.; *CAF* ii. 428 ff.

**ERIS**, personification of strife (discord, rivalry, competition; there are two kinds, one bad and one good, the latter being emulation between fellow workers, Hesiod, *Op.* 11 ff.). Generally, however, she is definitely Strife. Thus she accompanies Ares in Homeric battle-scenes, as *Il.* 4. 440–1, where she is his sister and companion; *Theog.* 225 ff., she is daughter of Night and mother of Battles, Slaughters, Disputes, Lawlessness, etc.

She emerges into fuller mythical personality in the *Cypria*. Zeus, having decided on the Trojan War, to relieve Earth of the burden of so many human beings (fr. 1 Allen), lets Eris be present at the marriage of Peleus and Thetis (qq.v.). There she stirs up a quarrel between the goddesses as to which is the most beautiful, this leading to the Judgement of Paris (*see* PARIS) and so to the war. But the details are uncertain; we have no written pre-Alexandrian authority for the 'apple of Discord'. In Hyginus, *Fab.* 92. 1, from a Greek source perhaps about contemporary with the Emperor Claudius (see Rose, *Hygini Fabulae*, p. viii), Eris (Discordia) comes to the door, throws in an apple, and says the most beautiful may pick it up; other authorities (listed by v. Sybel in Roscher's *Lex.* i. 1338. 50 ff.) make her inscribe the apple 'for the fairest'. This is obvious *Märchen* (*see* FOLK-TALES), but when it was added to this myth is unknown. H. J. R.

**EROS**, god of love in Greek mythology. Eros personified does not occur in Homer, but the Homeric passages in which the word *eros* is used give a clear idea of the original significance. It is the violent physical desire that drives Paris to Helen, Zeus to Hera, and shakes the limbs of the suitors of Penelope (*Il.* 3. 442; 14. 294; *Od.* 18. 212). A more refined conception of this Eros who affects mind and body appears in the lyric poets of the seventh and sixth centuries B.C. Because his power brings peril he is pictured as cunning, unmanageable, cruel (Alcman 36 Diehl; Ibycus 6 Diehl; Sappho 137 Diehl; Theog. 1231); in Anacreon and in vase-paintings he smites the lovestruck one with an axe or a whip (*Deltion* 1927–8, 106). He comes suddenly like a wind

and shakes his victims (Sappho, Ibycus); Furtwängler recognized a pictorial equivalent of this image in the Eros who carries off a girl on vases and gems. Eros is playful, but he plays with frenzies and confusion. On the other hand, he symbolizes all attractions which provoke love. He is young and beautiful, he walks over flowers, and the roses are 'a plant of Eros' of which he makes his crown (*Anacreontea* 53. 42). He is sweet and warms the heart (Alcman 101 Diehl). Sappho sums up his essence, calling him 'bitter-sweet'.

Already Hesiod connects Eros with Aphrodite (q.v. § 3 and see *Theog.* 201), but many authorities hold this connexion not to be original. With Himeros and Pothos he is a constant companion of Aphrodite, although he can appear with any god, whenever a love story is involved, e.g. as ἀμφιθαλής at the marriage of Zeus and Hera (A. D. Nock, *CR* 1924, 152).

Hesiod seems to have transformed the Homeric conception of Eros. Although he describes Eros in terms almost identical with Homer as the god who 'loosens the limbs and damages the mind', he also makes him together with Earth and Tartarus the oldest of gods, all-powerful over gods and men. Building on this idea of Eros as a cosmic principle Parmenides found a place for Eros (Diels, *Vorsokr.*⁷ i. 243, fr. 13), perhaps as the power which leads contrasts together? This philosophic conception contributed to the Euripidean picture of omnipotent Eros (Ath. 13. 561), took abstruse mythological shape in Orphic cosmogonies (Ar. *Av.* 693), and formed the background for the famous Platonic discussions of Eros in *Symposium* and *Phaedrus*. (J. Stannard, *Phronesis* 1959, 120.)

Hellenistic poets continue the more playful conception of Anacreon and sing the tricks which Eros plays on mortals, the tribulations of those who try to resist him, and the punishments which he receives for his misdeeds. His bow and arrows, first mentioned by Euripides (*IA* 548 f.), play a great part in these accounts. He becomes a humanized genre figure in Rococo style. Frequently a plurality of Erotes is introduced (Ath. 13. 562; *Anacreontea*; *Anth. Pal.*; Ap. Rh. 3. 114). The usage originated because the Greeks drew no sharp distinction between love passion and the god who symbolized it; both could multiply. For the relation of Eros to Psyche *see* PSYCHE. Eros had some old cults and enjoyed much individual worship. He was always the god of love directed towards male as well as female beauty. Hence his images in the gymnasia, his cult by the Sacred Band in Thebes (Ath. 13. 561; 602), and the altar in Athens erected by the lover of Hippias (Ath. 13. 602 d). As a god of fertility Eros is celebrated in the very old cult in Thespiae, and in the joint cult with Aphrodite on the north slope of the Athenian Acropolis. In Thespiae Eros was represented by an aniconic image; in Athens phallic symbols have been found in the sanctuary. In both cults festivals were celebrated; that in Thespiae was called Erotidia. The festival in Athens was celebrated in the spring month of Munichion (O. Broneer, *Hesp.* 1932, 31; 1935, 125). In Philadelphia the worshippers called themselves Erotes after the god. In Athens a procession of Erotes is represented on a relief performing the functions of worshippers. Another cult centre was Parion in Mysia.

In art Eros grows young. He begins as a fairly grown-up boy in the archaic period, is a young boy in classical art, and becomes a playful putto in the Hellenistic age.

Cook, *Zeus* ii. 2, 1039; C. T. Seltman, *BSA* 1923–4, 87; P. Friedländer, *Studi e testi* (1939), 53; W. Strobel, *Eros* (1952); H. Gollob, *Die Metamorphosen des Eros* (1958); H. Chalk, *JHS* 1960, 32; K. Schauenberg, *Antike und Abendland* 1961, 77.

G. M. A. H.; J. R. T. P.

**EROTIAN**, grammarian and doctor of the Neronian age, compiled an extant glossary to Hippocrates.

**ERUCIUS** (1) of Cyzicus (fl. *c.* 40 B.C.), a Greek with a Roman name, is the author of fourteen epigrams in the Greek Anthology. One touching poem about a Greek woman captured by Romans (*Anth. Pal.* 7. 368) may refer to his mother; another (7. 377) expresses bitter hatred for Parthenius (q.v.); a third (6. 96) cites or coincides with a line of Virgil (*Ecl.* 7. 4).

Cichorius, *Röm. Stud.* viii. 3.                                        G. H.

**ERUCIUS** (2) **CLARUS,** Sextus, a friend of the Younger Pliny whose recommendation (*Ep.* 2. 9) gained him the lower senatorial magistracies *c.* A.D. 97–101. After successful service in the Parthian War and the capture of Seleucia (116) he became suffect consul in 117. After the disgrace of his uncle C. Septicius Clarus, praetorian prefect, in 122, he held no further office until under Pius he became Praefectus Urbi and consul II in 146 when he died. He had literary tastes (Aul. Gell. *NA.* 7. 6. 12; 13. 18. 12).                              H. H. S.

**ERYSICHTHON,** in mythology, son of Triopas, of Dotion in Thessaly. Wanting timber, he was so misguided as to start cutting down a sacred grove of Demeter, though warned not to do so by the goddess herself in human form. He was thereupon plagued with insatiable hunger, to satisfy which he ruined himself and all his household. Thus far Callimachus (*Cer.* 23 ff.); the tale can be traced back no earlier than Hellanicus (Crusius in Roscher's *Lex.* i. 1373. 56). Lycophron (1393, where see schol.; cf. Ov. *Met.* 8. 847 ff.) says he had a daughter Mestra, granted by her lover Poseidon power to change shape. She was sold in various beast-forms, escaped and came back to be resold, and he lived on the proceeds.

Zieliński, *Philol.* 1891, 138 ff. = *Iresione* ii. 1 ff.; K. J. McKay, *Erysichthon: a Callimachean comedy* (Leiden, 1962).       H. J. R.

**ERYTHEIA,** 'the red, or blushing, one', i.e. sunset-coloured. Name of (1) one of the Hesperides (q.v.; Apollod. 2. 114); (2) the daughter of Geryon, and also his island (Steph. Byz., s.v.; Paus. 10. 17. 5).

**ERYTHRAE** (Ἐρυθραί), one of the twelve cities of the Ionian League, on the coast opposite the island of Chios. Founded according to tradition by a party from Crete, and later by Ionians under Cnopus son of Codrus, the city was prosperous from the start, but has little individual history. Falling in turn, with the rest of Ionia, under the Lydians and then under the Persians, Erythrae was later a member of the Delian League; her assessment of seven talents is among the highest in Ionia. In the fourth century the city had some dealings with Mausolus, satrap of Caria, but their nature is not known. Pliny observes that the river Aelon at Erythrae had the curious property of causing hair to grow on the body. For the legend of the blind fisherman and the statue of Heracles see Pausanias. 7. 5. 5–8. The ancient name has changed, through the forms *Ritri* and *Litri*, to the present *Ildir*; the ruins are not abundant, but the city-wall, over two miles long, is well preserved in part, and the theatre has recently been excavated.

G. E. Bean, *Aegean Turkey* (1966), 153–9.               G. E. B.

**ERYX,** an Elymian settlement and a mountain (*Monte San Giuliano:* 751 m. above sea-level) above Drepana in west Sicily. An attempt by Dorieus (q.v.) to establish a settlement in the 'neighbourhood failed. Dependent on Segesta in the fifth century B.C., Eryx was occupied later by the Carthaginians, though temporarily seized by Pyrrhus (278 or 277). Phoenician masons' marks are found on the walls, and Punic legends appear on the

coinage from the fourth century. The Elymian settlement, perhaps on a lower height than the famous temple of Astarte-Aphrodite-Venus (where is the modern town of S. Giuliano), was evacuated in 259 during the First Punic War, and the inhabitants were transferred to Drepana. L. Junius seized both heights and established a fort on the lower slopes to isolate Drepana (249). Hamilcar Barca captured the old town, but not the temple and lower fort (244); thus he failed to relieve Drepana, although maintaining his position until 241. The temple underlies a medieval castle: see *Not. Scav.* 1934, 264 ff.; *JHS* 1936, 218 ff.                                  H. H. S

**ESQUILINE.** The name, in the form \**Esquiliae* (from *ex-colo,* cf. *inquilinus*), denoted the eastern plateau formed in Rome by *montes Oppius* and *Cispius,* the *regio Esquilina* being the second of the republican Four Regions (Varro, *Ling.* 5. 49–50). In the Iron Age and much later it was used as a cemetery (von Duhn, *Italische Gräberkunde* (1924), i. 468), ultimately for paupers (Hor. *Sat.* i. 8. 8–13). It was included by the republican Wall and provided later sites for Nero's Golden House and Trajan's *Thermae.* Under Augustus the name was applied to Regio V, outside the republican Wall, containing various gardens and the Sessorium, an imperial residence. The Arch of Gallienus (*CIL* vi. 1106) recalls the *porta Esquilina* of the republican Wall.                          I. A. R

**ETEOCLES,** (1) an ancient king of Orchomenus, founder of the local cult of the Charites (Paus. 9. 34. 9 ff.). (2) In mythology, the elder son of Oedipus (q.v.) After the blinding and retirement of their father, he and his brother Polynices twice insulted him, once by setting before him certain vessels which had belonged to Laius, and once by giving him a portion of meat less honourable than a king should have (Cyclic *Thebais,* frs. 2 and 3, Allen). He therefore cursed them (for conjectural details, see Rose, *Handbook of Greek Myth.*[6], index), and the curse was fulfilled thus. He and Polynices agreed to reign in alternate years, Eteocles taking the first year; Polynices left Thebes and married Argeia (*see* ADRASTUS). At the end of the year Eteocles would not give up his throne; Polynices returned with the Seven, and the two brothers met and killed each other. See references in Rose, loc. cit.                              H. J. R

**ETEOCLUS,** son of Iphis, a somewhat obscure Argive hero. At a fairly early stage of the tradition he seems to have replaced Parthenopaeus (q.v.) as one of the Seven against Thebes, cf. ADRASTUS (see Paus. 10. 10. 3). Then Aeschylus (*Sept.* 458) or his authority included both him and Parthenopaeus, apparently so as to be able to leave Adrastus out of the actual assault; hence later writers (as Soph. *OC* 1316 and Eur. *Supp.* 872) use the same list.

See Wilamowitz-Moellendorff, *Aischylos Interpretationen* (1914) 100.                                             H. J. R

**ETHIOPIA,** the land of the Ethiopians or 'Burnt-Faced Men', was a name usually applied by the Greeks to any region in the far south (but north of the Equator). Under the influence perhaps of Homer (*Od.* 1. 22, etc.) who distinguished between Western and Eastern Ethiopians, Aeschylus (*Supp.* 284–6) made the Ethiopians extend to India, and Herodotus (esp. 3. 17–23; 7. 69–70) distinguished between the woolly-haired Ethiopians (negroes) and the straight-haired ones (primitive Indians) The tendency to confuse Ethiopians with Indians continued throughout ancient times (e.g. in Aesch. *Supp.* 284 ff.). But from Herodotus onward Ethiopia designated especially the lands south of Egypt—Nubia, Sennaar

Kordofan, and north Abyssinia. This country was visited since 665 B.C. by the Greeks, some of whom penetrated in the wake of Cambyses as far as Korosko, and various Ethiopian peoples became known in Greece by their tribal names. Under the Ptolemies the African coast was explored by sea as far as Somaliland and Cape Guardafui; the Blue and the White Nile and the Atbara were clearly distinguished (*see* NILE); and the Ethiopian city of Meroë (q.v.) received a veneer of Hellenic culture (Diod. 3. 38 ff.; Strabo 16. 773–4; 785–7). An Ethiopian raid into Egypt (25 B.C.) was repelled by the Romans, who established a frontier area from Assuan and Maharrakah. In the first century A.D. a powerful Ethiopian State arose in Abyssinia (*see* AXUMIS).

E. A. W. Budge, *The Egyptian Sudan* (1907); P. Paulitschke, *Geogr. Erforschung des afrikanischen Kontinents* (1884). E. H. W.

**ETRUSCAN LANGUAGE.** Etruscan is commonly believed to be an insoluble mystery. The ancients themselves considered that it did not resemble any other known language (Dion. Hal. 1. 30. 2). However, some texts which present an unquestionable affinity with it have been found in Lemnos. It is now sometimes admitted that it did not belong to the Indo-European group of languages, but was a remnant of the prehistoric Mediterranean linguistic substratum, which was broken up and transmuted under the pressure of protracted Indo-European infiltrations, and emerged only where this pressure had been less successful.

We possess some 10,000 inscriptions dating from the seventh century to the time of Augustus. They mostly consist of epitaphs, which generally are comparatively late (third to first centuries B.C.), very short, and stereotyped in phraseology. A few are outstanding for their length, their subject, and sometimes their early date: the liturgical text written on the wrappings of an Egyptian mummy now in Zagreb (1,190 words, second–first century); the tile from Capua (300 words, fifth–fourth century), dealing with funeral ceremonies; the *Cippus Perusinus* (130 words), a legal document, concerning a point of burial rights; the *elogium* on the sarcophagus of a magistrate of Tarquinii, relating his career (59 words); a lead plate from Magliano, with names of deities and funeral offerings (70 words). To these and some others must be added now the two inscriptions on sheets of gold leaf (16 and 9 lines), which were excavated in 1964 in Pyrgi (q.v.), the harbour of Caere (*Cerveteri*), together with a Punic inscription on a similar gold sheet and apparently of similar content (11 lines): this find raised great hopes that a bilingual group had been discovered, but the study of these fascinating texts is only at its beginning.

In order to interpret Etruscan inscriptions, three different methods have been used. For many years, Etruscologists presupposed that Etruscan was akin to other better-known languages, and therefore fancied that they could interpret it as connected with e.g., Greek, Latin, Finnish, or Albanian. This etymological method has proved a complete failure, though it can explain a few words, which the Etruscans had borrowed from their neighbours or from commercial contacts. It is generally agreed now that we must rely upon the internal evidence of the records themselves, and nearly all we know of Etruscan comes from the patient effort of linguists who have scrutinized those words and constructions which recur in various contexts. However, this empirical method has recently been supported by a third: since Etruscan civilization itself developed as a part of a common Italic culture, an Etruscan ritual inscription from Cortona may not be altogether dissimilar from, for instance, the Umbrian ritual inscription of Iguvium (q.v.); parallel formulas may have expressed, among contem-

porary priesthoods, a certain uniformity of prayer and approach. This comparative method, which naturally has to be carefully checked, has opened new perspectives, especially in the general survey of the inscription of Zagreb.

The Etruscan alphabet is known to us under two aspects: first, theoretical model alphabets of 26 letters inscribed on ivory tablets, terracotta vases, etc., which were perhaps introduced in Etruria by Phoenician merchants; secondly, the alphabets actually used in surviving inscriptions; the archaic ones (seventh–sixth centuries) have 23 letters, the later (fourth–first centuries) 20 letters as the theoretical alphabet contained characters which were not needed by Etruscan phonetics. The Etruscan alphabet in turn provided, with some modifications, the Latin, Oscan, Umbrian, and Venetic alphabets.

In the majority of the oldest inscriptions, words are separated by dots. However, around the middle of the fifth century, and within certain limited districts (south Etruria and Campania), a syllabic punctuation appears. This system, which propagated itself in Venetic and recurs in Lemnian, has been interpreted as an obscure inheritance of earlier contacts with the Aegean world.

Besides proper names, there are about 150 root-words the meaning of which is approximately established. Some were preserved by Greek and Latin authors, like *ais*, plur. *aisar*, 'god'. The funerary inscriptions have provided us with a fair knowledge of the vocabulary of relationship: *clan*, plur. *clenar*, 'son'; *seχ*, 'daughter', etc. The verb *lupu* means 'to die'; the nouns *avil*, 'year', and *tiv*, 'moon' and 'month'. From the number of the years that the dead had lived we can infer the value of the numerals, while the first six are also found written on dice. There is now an almost general agreement as to their order, *θu, zal, ci, śa, maχ, huθ*. Tens were formed by adding -*alχ*: thus *ci* (3), *cealχ* (30). Names of magistrates have also been identified, e.g. *zilaθ* = *praetor*; *purθne* (Greek πρύτανις?).

The adaptation of Greek mythological names found on mirrors, and the simpler constructions of the funerary inscriptions have laid the basis of our knowledge of Etruscan phonetics, morphology, and syntax. They seem to be dominated by a great variety of rules and anomalous possibilities. The genitive is generally marked, for masculine nouns, by -*s*, for feminine, by -(*a*)*l*; but masculine nouns ending in a dental or sibilant consonant take the -(*a*)*l* termination (*arnθ, arnθal*), and feminine nouns ending in -*l, -a, -uia, -u* take the -*s* (*ramθa, ramθas*). For some nouns a complete paradigm can be drawn: nom. *meθlum* ('nation'); gen. *meθlum-e-s*; loc. *meθlum-t/θ*; dat. *meθ lum-e-ri*. A peculiarity of Etruscan morphology is a tendency to the superimposition of suffixes, without changing the meaning: *laris-al-is-la* = *larisal*, 'of Laris'. For verbs also, the value of different endings has become clearer: the stems are often used as imperatives (*tur*, 'to give' and 'give'); the 3rd sing. perfect ends in -*ce* (*turce, turuce*, 'he gave'). There are a great number of particles and pronouns (-*c* and (*u*)*m* = Lat. *que; nac*, 'so').

The general impression is that of a language which has never been systematically fixed. Although considerable progress has been achieved in recent years, the insufficiency of our present state of knowledge is illustrated by the difficulty of achieving an accurate translation of the Pyrgi inscriptions, despite the help of a Punic bilingual.

The majority of Etruscan inscriptions have been published in *Corpus Inscriptionum Etruscarum*, which is still in progress: i (1893–1902): Fiesole, Volterra, Siena, Arezzo, Cortona, Chiusi, Perugia; ii. 1 (1907): Orvieto, Volsinii; ii. 2 (1923): Populonia, Vetulonia, Vulci; ii. 3 (1936): Tarquinia; iii. 1 (1912): Faliscan Territory; Suppl. i (1911): the inscription of Zagreb. *Testimonia Linguae Etruscae*[2] (1968) by M. Pallottino is a useful collection of 900 inscriptions, with a complete reference system and excellent indexes. New discoveries are published yearly in *Studi Etruschi*. For the new Pyrgi inscriptions see s.v. PYRGI; M. Pallottino, *Archeol. Class.* 1964, 49 ff. J. Heurgon, *JRS* 1966, 1 ff.

A. Trombetti, *La lingua etrusca* (1928); M. Pallottino, *Elementi di lingua etrusca* (1936) and *Etruscologia*[5] (1963), 341 ff.; G. Devoto, 'Etrusco e peri-indoeuropeo', *Stud. Etr.* 1944, 187 ff.; K. Olzscha, 'Confronti di parole etrusco-umbre', *Stud. Etr.* 1961, 485 ff.; on the alphabet, J. A. Bundgård, 'Why did the art of writing spread to the West?' *Anal. Rom. Instituti Danici*, 1965, 11 ff.; on syllabic punctuation, E. Vetter, 'Die Herkunft des venetischen Punktiersystems', *Glotta* 1935, 114 ff., F. Slotty, *Beiträge zur Etruscologie* i (1952); on names, W. Schultze, *Zur Geschichte Lateinischer Eigennamen* (1904), H. Rix, *Das etruskische Cognomen* (1963), E. Fiesel, 'Die Namen des griech. Mythos im Etruskischen', *Zeitschr. f. vergleich. Sprachforschung*, Erg. Heft, 1928.                                    J. H.

**ETRUSCANS** (Tyrsenoi, Tyrrheni), the earliest historical occupants of the territories between the Tiber and the Arno (approximately the modern Tuscany) and Rome's principal early rivals for the hegemony of central Italy. They formed a loose confederation of politically independent cities with a common religious centre at Volsinii, and at the height of their power (*c.* 500 B.C.) they controlled an empire extending from the Po to central Campania; but though a vigorous and cultured people, they lacked the political cohesion of the Romans, by whom they were one by one finally conquered and absorbed.

The oldest Etruscan cities (Caere, Populonia, Rusellae, Tarquinii, Veii, Vetulonia, Volaterrae, Vulci, qq.v.) lay on or within easy reach of the coast, whence Etruscan rule spread inland towards Umbria and the middle Tiber valley (Arretium, Clusium, Cortona, Perugia, qq.v.) and, shortly before 500 B.C., northwards across the Apennines. At its fullest extent northern Etruria was coterminous with the Umbrians and Picenes (qq.v.), with the Ligurians, with the Veneti of Ateste (q.v.), and the Golaseccan Iron Age peoples of the southern Alps (*see* COMUM). In this direction Etruscan power was broken in the late fifth century by the invading Celts (q.v.). The corresponding southward expansion, complete by the mid sixth century (Etruscan Capua was founded *c.* 600 B.C.), was shortlived. The expulsion of the Tarquins from Rome was followed by the campaign in which Aristodemus (q.v. 2) drove the Etruscans from Campania, and in 474 B.C. Etruscan naval expansion, which at one time achieved control of Corsica, was conclusively checked in a battle off Cumae by the Campanian Greeks and Hieron of Syracuse. During the fifth century the Samnites swept the Etruscans out of Campania; Veii was destroyed in 396 B.C., and by the end of the third century the whole of Etruria was in Roman hands.

Already by the time of Varro and of the Emperor Claudius the Etruscans were a matter for antiquarian speculation, and the broad lines of the modern dispute as to their origins had taken shape. Herodotus (1. 94) believed them to be immigrants from Lydia, whereas Dionysius of Halicarnassus (1. 30), writing under Augustus, maintained they were indigenous. In the past the evidence of Herodotus has been generally accepted, but recently the growing body of archaeological information, with its clear indications of a continuity of native development and absence of identifiably Asiatic features, has led a number of scholars to follow Dionysius in regarding them as indigenous. The discussion turns on three aspects of the subject—the language of the Etruscans, their culture, and their political identity. The conclusions, though related, are not necessarily the same in each case.

The Etruscan language (q.v.) is not a member of the Indo-European or any other identifiable group of languages, and it is still quite uncertain whether it was an autochthonous local survival or an exotic intruder from abroad, or again, if it was an intruder, by whom it was introduced. The evidence of archaeology is more explicit. It is firmly established that the material culture of the historical Etruscans was rooted in, and derived without any sharp break from, that of the Early Iron Age Villanovan (q.v.) inhabitants of Etruria. Although there were a great many derivative elements, at first from the eastern Mediterranean and later from Greece, there is nothing that could not have been due to purely commercial contacts. Much has sometimes been made of the shift in burial practice from cremation (the Villanovan rite) to inhumation; but it is now evident that this took place within the framework of a single developing culture and does not necessarily imply the arrival of fresh peoples. In its most characteristic material aspects the Etruscan civilization unquestionably took shape on Italian soil.

On the other hand, Etruscan religion and astrology include many elements that seem to derive from the ancient east (*see* RELIGION, ETRUSCAN); and the rich princely tombs that contain many of the finest oriental or orientalizing pieces (e.g. the Regolini Galassi tomb at Caere, the Barberini and Bernadini tombs at Praeneste) appear with a suddenness suggestive of a new historical situation. These and other similar phenomena have been taken by many to indicate the arrival of a small, alien aristocracy, analogous to the Normans in south Italy or the Turks in Anatolia, whose talents lay in the fields of warfare and political organization rather than of material culture and who have consequently left little direct mark on the archaeological record.

What is beyond question is that, whether the Tyrsenoi were in origin such a conquering minority, or whether they merely represent the sum of the Early Iron Age peoples of Etruria, they had by the end of the seventh century become a single people with a single common language and a single broadly uniform culture, that of the historical Etruscans. Pending the systematic excavation of one of the Etruscan cities, our knowledge of their civilization comes largely from the grave goods and the carved or painted decoration of its cemeteries. Etruscan metalwork was outstanding. Their jewellery displays an extraordinary technical virtuosity and their bronzework, especially their furniture and fine household goods, was widely exported both within the Mediterranean (cf. Ath. 1. 28; 15. 700) and to Celtic Europe, major centres of production being Vulci, Capua, and the cities of eastern Tuscany. Surviving masterpieces include the Chimaera of Arezzo and the Capitoline Wolf. Although sculpture in stone was practised wherever local materials were favourable, as in the bas-reliefs of Chiusi and the alabasters of Volaterrae, the principal sculptural medium was painted terracotta, which was widely used for decorating the timber superstructures of temples and even on occasion for life-sized figured groups. The workshops of Falerii, Caere, and Veii in particular were active over large areas of southern Etruria and Latium, including Rome. The magnificent series of tomb-paintings at Tarquinii (also at Chiusi, Orvieto, and Veii) affords a vivid glimpse of Etruscan life and aspirations: scenes of banqueting, music and dancing, hunting, racing and wrestling, side by side with the grim figures of the underworld in a striking contrast of gaiety and fatalism. In every medium the techniques and much of the vocabulary were borrowed initially (from Greece and from the Orient), but, despite continuous contact with and influence from the Greeks in south Italy, the development is individual and unmistakably Etruscan.

Most of the obscurities of Etruscan history derive from the fact that it reaches us through an alien and largely hostile tradition, recorded when Etruria was already a spent force. Etruria was in fact the civilized power with which Rome was in closest contact during the earliest, formative stages of her own development. Religion, civil institutions, warfare, architecture, art, and engineering, these are some only of the fields in which Rome's debt to Etruria was deep and lasting.

*Corpus Inscriptionum Etruscarum* (1893– ); G. Dennis, *Cities and Cemeteries of Etruria*[3] (1883); D. Randall MacIver, *Villanovans and Early Etruscans* (1924); G. Q. Giglioli, *L'arte Etrusca* (1935); M. Pallottino, *The Etruscans* (1955 = Engl. Transl. of *Etruscologia*, of which 5th ed. is 1963), *Art of the Etruscans* (1955); L. Banti, *Il Mondo degli Etruschi* (1960); J. Heurgon, *La Vie quotidienne chez les Étrusques* (1961, Engl. Transl. 1964); E. Richardson, *The Etruscans, their Art and Civilization* (1964) (with excellent bibliographies, covering individual sites and subjects); Scullard, *Etr. Cities*.

J. B. W.-P.

**ETYMOLOGICA** (Greek). The earliest etymological studies are known only from (usually nameless) reproduction in the philosophers. The first-known title is the Περὶ ἐτυμολογίας of Heraclides Ponticus, now lost, as also the Ἐτυμολογικά of Chrysippus. Under Atticist influence etymology flourished among the later Alexandrians and under the early Empire, e.g. in the lexica of Eirenaeus, Demetrius Ixion, and Caecilius of Calacte. These works were absorbed by Dionysius, Vestinus, Phrynichus, and others of the second century A.D. From them, and from later redactions and conflations, e.g. by Orus, Orion, and Helladius, the Byzantine *Etymologica* are mainly derived. *See* ETYMOLOGICUM MAGNUM.

R. Reitzenstein, *Geschichte d. gr. Etymologika* (1897). P. B. R. F.

**ETYMOLOGICUM MAGNUM,** an extant lexicon of uncertain date, but used by Eustathius, who became Archbishop of Thessalonica in A.D. 1175, and based mainly on the E. Gudianum (of *c*. A.D. 1100) and the E. Magnum Genuinum (late 9th c., as yet unpublished), the E. Gud. itself being a conflation of the E.M.G. and the E. Parvum, both of which were completed under the direction of Photius.

E. Magnum: T. Gaisford (1841); R. Reitzenstein, *Gesch. d. griech. Etymologika* (1897), 212 ff. P. B. R. F.

**ETYMOLOGY** (in Greek and Roman times). Men have always seemed prone to toy with derivations and to see lessons in mere words. Thus in *Od.* 19. 562–7 the gates of *ivory* and *horn* by their very names—in Greek—proclaim the *frustration* and *fulfilment*, respectively, of the dreams that pass through them. Proper names have always been especial objects of such interest. L. Lersch (*Sprachphilosophie d. Alten* (1838–41), 3. 3 ff.) quotes some seventy examples—a selection only—mainly from Homer, Hesiod, Pindar, and Tragedy. Thus Aias is related by Sophocles to αἰάζειν, by Pindar to αἰετός; Euripides connects Zethus with ζητέω. Such play upon personal names continues up to the present day in Greek, and was much practised in late antiquity. (*See* ALLEGORY, GREEK.)

2. Unfortunately, Greek etymology did not remain the sport of amateurs, but was involved in sophistic and philosophical speculations on the origin of everything, including, inevitably, language. Was 'horse', or, it might be, some other—perhaps unrevealed—name, as much a natural property of the animal as its shape and constitution, or was a name only an artificial label by convention attached to this or that? Many of the Greek thinkers adopted the former view, with its consequences. Cratylus, pupil of Heraclitus, said that knowledge of Nature's names was required for real speech; without that utterance was mere noise. Indeed, in his old age, despairing of ascertaining Nature's names, he gave up utterance and used only gestures. Such a theory is paralleled in primitive (and later) practices, when, for example, healing virtues in things are deduced from their names, and the prescription swallowed with as much faith as the medicine: cf. E. S. McCartney, *AJPhil.* 1927, 326; E. R. Huc, *Travels in Tartary* (1850), i. 75.

3. If, then, words are not mere tokens of sensation and belief, to trace them to their ultimate origins would elucidate not the history of human opinion but Nature's own ἔτυμος λόγος. From this theory, constantly active though repeatedly challenged, arose a systematic practice of etymology, not only among its adherents. Early examples, with parodies of his own, figure largely in Plato's *Cratylus*, sometimes hitting the truth, if only by accident. Aristotle, who rejected the theory, has derivations: δίκαιον, δικαστής, from δίχα (*Eth. Nic.* 1132[a]31), μακάριον from χαίρω (ibid. 1152[b]7), σωφροσύνη (after Pl. *Cra.* 411 e) from σῴζειν τὴν φρόνησιν, and (cf. Athenaeus 40 b) μεθύειν from drinking μετὰ τὸ θύειν.

4. The Stoics, accepting the naturalistic theory, sought to relate the apparent chaos of current language to the rule of law hypothetically pervading Nature's works, by four principles stated in the Augustinian *Principia Dialecticae*. Nature forms words (i) κατὰ μίμησιν, by imitating things, e.g. *stridor, clangor*, or their impressions on the senses, as *crux* and *voluptas* are, respectively, unpleasant and pleasant in name (sound) as in fact; (ii) καθ' ὁμοιότητα, e.g. *crura*, which are 'longitudine atque duritia inter membra cetera ligno crucis similiora'; (iii) not from the thing but from something associated with it in one of various relations, viz. (*a*) *per efficentiam*, as '*foedus* a foeditate porci'; (*b*) *per effecta*, as '*puteus* quod eius effectum potatio est'; (*c*) *per id quod continetur*, as *urbs* from *orbis*; (*d*) *per id quod continet*, as *horreum* from *hordeum*; (*e*) *by metonymy*, as *mucro* for *gladius*; (iv) κατ' ἀντίφρασιν, as '*lucus*, quod minime luceat', '*bellum*, quod res bella non sit'. The operation of natural law was obscured, so they said, by human irregularity, ἀνωμαλία (*see* CRATES (3) OF MALLOS).

5. The Atticist movement (*see* GLOSSA, GREEK) furnished a new impulse for etymologists, and a new aim, viz. to test the admissibility of a word to 'correct use' by relating it to its στοιχεῖον, which in the derivative had probably suffered loss, accretion, metathesis, crasis, or other mutation. In this connexion a terminology for many such πάθη was evolved; cf. Pseudo-Trypho, Περὶ παθῶν. Atticism regarded not the usage of good writers but what was right for them to use (see Phrynichus; *contra*, Sext. Emp. *Math.* 1. 98). Etymology appears with analogy as a touchstone of diction in the Atticist Eirenaeus (early 2nd c. A.D.), and remained one of the criteria of fully developed purism, Greek and Latin. 'Latinitas est incorrupte loquendi obseruatio secundum Romanam linguam; constat autem, ut adserit Varro, his quattuor: natura (meaning *etymologia*), analogia, consuetudine, auctoritate' (Diom. 439). This new etymology appears in Philoxenus (1st c. B.C.), one of Varro's main sources, and is fully developed in Seleucus (under Tiberius), whose results resemble those of the *Cratylus*, from which he borrows.

6. At Rome (as elsewhere) aetiological etymologies were early popular: 'nomina haec numinum in indigitamentis inueniuntur, i.e. in libris pontificalibus, qui et nomina deorum et rationes nominum continent' (Serv. on Verg. *G.* 1. 21). There are also examples in the early poets. Under Greek influences the etymological fashion took firm hold of Latin literature and scholarship, with like results as in Greek: Paullus, s.v. 'miles': 'militem Aelius (i.e. Stilo) a mollitia κατ' ἀντίφρασιν dictum putat: sic ludum ["school"] dicimus, in quo minime luditur' (cf. Quin. *Inst.* 1. 6); cf. Diom. and § 4, *supra*. The taste for etymology grew in late antiquity. Martianus Capella (*c*. A.D. 420) and Isidore of Seville (*c*. A.D. 570–636) are among its most enthusiastic practitioners.

7. It would be idle to analyse minutely a practice, popular and highly esteemed, often surprisingly correct and even acute (cf. Pl. *Cra.* 405 c–d), which constantly produced such results as, ἕσπερος, ἀπὸ τοῦ ἔσω περᾶν πάντα τὰ ζῷα, and, γραμματική, διὰ τὸ τήκειν καὶ καθαίρειν τὰ γράμματα, and, ἔντερον, παρὰ τὸ ἐντὸς ῥέειν: so we are told that the (Greek) vowels number seven because there

are seven planets. Neither Greeks nor Romans, early or late, came within reach of a scientific, historical method in etymology. Their rules are but statements of their arbitrary practices, with a multiplication of terminology that did nothing for the advancement of knowledge.

E. Schwyzer, *Griechische Grammatik* i (1939), 29 ff.; F. Müller, *De veterum imprimis Romanorum studiis etymologicis* (1910); K. Woldt, *De analogiae disciplina apud grammaticos Latinos* (1911); H. Steinthal, *Gesch. d. Sprachwissenschaft bei den Griechen u. Römern* (1891) i. 331 ff. *See also under* GRAMMAR, GLOSSA (GREEK).

P. B. R. F.

**EUANGELUS** appears to be a New Comedy poet. One fragment (10 trochaic tetrameters) is preserved of Ἀνακαλυπτομένη—a master discusses with a cook the preparations for a wedding-banquet.

FCG iv. 572; CAF iii. 376.

**EUANTHIUS** (4th c. A.D.), author of a commentary on Terence. The only parts remaining are certain sections of the treatise *De comoedia* which is now prefixed to the commentary of Aelius Donatus (q.v.).

Cf. Schanz–Hosius, § 836. 1.

**EUBOEA,** also called Long Island (*Makris*), since it stretched from the Gulf of Pagasae to Andros. It shared the culture of the Cyclades in the Bronze Age. The chief cities in antiquity were Chalcis and Eretria (qq.v.). Other cities were Histiaea, Geraestus, and Carystus, famous for its marble. In the eighth century Chalcis and Eretria were powerful mercantile cities, who led the islanders to found a trading post at Al Mina (q.v.) in Syria by about 800. They established colonies on the north-west shores of the Aegean and in Italy and Sicily and fought over the Lelantine plain, which lay between them, in the eighth century. Eretrian control of some of the Cyclades passed to Athens, who later compelled Chalcis to cede part of the plain (506). In 490 the Persian general Datis attacked Euboea and captured Eretria and Carystus. Euboean contingents fought the Persians at Salamis and Plataea. Owing to Boeotian intrigues, the whole island revolted from Athens in 446, but it was reconquered by Pericles, who planted cleruchies in it. The cities remained tributary allies of the first Athenian League but revolted in the Peloponnesian War (411). They were enrolled in the second Athenian League (378–377) and incorporated in a Euboean Confederacy (341). After much turmoil, while the Thebans and Philip II of Macedon intrigued against Athens, the whole island came under the control of the Macedonian monarchy, by whose fortunes it was affected for the rest of the third century. In 196 Flamininus, the liberator of Greece, revived the Euboean Confederacy. Euboea was temporarily occupied by Antiochus of Sytia (192–191); for aid given to the Achaean Confederacy against Rome the federation was dissolved (146). The island was attached to the province of Macedonia, and fell into decay in the Roman imperial period.

IG xii (9); P–K, *GL* i. 2. Geyer, *Topographie und Geschichte der Insel Euboea* (1903); J. Boardman, *BSA* 1952, 1 ff., 1957, 1 ff.; W. Wallace *The Euboean League and its Coinage* (1956); W. G. Forrest, *Hist.* 1957, 160 ff.
W. A. L.; J. B.

**EUBULEUS** (Εὐβουλεύς), properly a euphemistic title of Hades, 'the good counsellor' (schol. Nic. *Alex.* 1 and elsewhere); one of a group of Orphic chthonian deities (Kern, *Orph. frag.* 32 c–e). He is humanized into a swineherd (fr. 51), son of Dysaules and brother of Triptolemus, who gave Demeter news of the rape of Persephone; or his swine were swallowed up with Persephone, which is why swine are thrown into chasms at the Thesmophoria (fr. 50).

Nilsson, *GGR* i². 463.
H. J. R.

**EUBULIDES** of Miletus, dialectician of the Megarian school, taught at Athens. He wrote a lampoon against Aristotle. He is said to have taught Demosthenes dialectic and rhetoric. He is best known for his eristic arguments, of which the most famous are the ψευδόμενος and the σωρίτης; but some of those ascribed to him by Diogenes Laertius are of older date.

As LOGICIAN. W. and M. Kneale, *The Development of Logic* (1962), 113 ff.
As PAMPHLETEER. I. Düring, *Aristotle in the Ancient Biographical Tradition* (1957), 388.
W. D. R.

**EUBULUS** (1) (c. 405–c. 335 B.C.), probably the most important Athenian statesman of the period 355–342. In 355, after thirteen years' struggle to regain Amphipolis and the Chersonese and the brief but disastrous Social War, the imperialistic advocates of war were discredited and the State near bankruptcy. Rising under the aegis of Diophantus of Sphettus, Eubulus by means of his position as a Theoric Commissioner gradually assumed control of the whole of Athens' finances, and raised public and private prosperity to a level probably not attained since the fifth century. An extravagant version of the sort of methods he probably followed is to be found in Xenophon's *De Vectigalibus*, but the most important guarantee of economic recovery was a law which made it difficult for the assembly to draw on the routine revenues of the State for inessential military operations. Thus he was able to employ the annual surpluses on a programme of public works: the distribution of money to the people, τὸ θεωρικόν, probably instituted in this period, engaged only a small part of the moneys controlled by the Theoric Commission.

In the wider spheres of policy, to judge from the allusions of Demosthenes, he sought to concentrate Athens' military resources on the defence of the essential interests of Athens and of Greece, and to exclude Philip from Greek affairs by uniting the Greeks in a Common Peace, his chief associates being Midias, Aeschines, and Phocion. The expedition to Thermopylae in 352, the intervention in Euboea in 348, and the attempt to unite the Greeks against Philip in 347/6 (or 348/7) are the chief fruits of this policy. Like almost all Athenian statesmen, he felt himself forced to accept the peace negotiated in 346 by Philocrates and Demosthenes. After Philip used the peace to intervene in Phocis, Demosthenes determined to renew the war, but Eubulus and his supporters sought to maintain and extend the peace. By mid 344 the opposition of Demosthenes and Hegesippus was beginning to weaken Eubulus' influence; in 343 the parties were fairly evenly balanced; but in 342 Demosthenes and the war-party were in full control. No more is heard of Eubulus after Chaeronea, and he may, like Aeschines, have retired from active politics. By 330 he was dead.

*See* THEORIKA. A. M. Andreades, *A History of Greek Public Finance* (1933), index; G. L. Cawkwell, *JHS* 1963, 47 f.; G. Glotz, *Histoire grecque* iii (1941), index, s.v. 'Eubule'.
G. L. C.

**EUBULUS** (2), Middle Comedy poet, with six Lenaean victories (IG ii². 2325. 144: the victors' list puts him two places after Anaxandrides, two before Antiphanes (qq.v.). He composed 104 plays (*Suda*). Some fifty-eight titles are extant, about half indicating mythological burlesque or parody of tragedy (note eleven titles identical with Euripides, a further eight with other tragedians), and parody of 'tragic' language is not uncommon in the fragments (direct parody of Euripides at frs. 26 [his sigmatism], 27, 67). Other notable titles: Διονύσιος (fr. 25: a character sketch of the tyrant), Πορνοβοσκός, Σκυτεύς, Σφιγγοκαρίων (a cook or slave who posed Sphinx-like riddles—a selection in fr. 107), and several that have the name of courtesans: e.g. Κλεψύδρα.

There is some metrical variety in the fragments: lyrics in frs. 35, 104 (choric song of the Στεφανοπώλιδες of the title?), 112, 139; anapaests in frs. 63, 77, 138; dactylic hexameters (for oracles or riddles) in frs. 28, 107. Several interesting passages: fr. 12 (from the Ἀντιόπη), in Boeotian dialect; fr. 90, Procris' hound in the lap of luxury; frs. 116–17, the bad women of myth outnumber the good.

FCG i. 355 ff., iii. 203 ff.; CAF ii. 164 ff.; Demiańczuk, Supp. Com. 40 f. D. Fedele, Dioniso 1947, 137 ff. W. G. A.

**EUCLEIDES** (1) of Megara (c. 450–380 B.C.), associate of Socrates and founder of the Megarian school. He was present at the death of Socrates and thereafter housed Plato and other members of the circle. Among his pupils were the logicians Eubulides and Stilpon (or Stilpon's teacher) (qq.v.). Cicero puts him in the tradition of Eleatic monism, and this may be connected with the report that he held the good to be one thing, having no opposite but named in many ways—e.g. as God, wisdom (φρόνησις), intelligence (νοῦς). His positive doctrines are otherwise unknown, but his practice of attacking the conclusion and not the premisses of an opponent's argument is attested and puts him in the 'eristic' tradition which dates from late in the fifth century, rather than in that of the Eleatics or (at his best) Socrates. Hence his leadership of a school of logicians whose contribution to philosophy was minimal but whose interest in logical paradoxes was taken over by the Stoic logicians.

Diog. Laert. ii. 106–12. G. E. L. O.

**EUCLEIDES** (2), Athenian archon in 403/2 B.C., which, being the year of the re-establishment of democracy, is very often quoted. From that time Athenian official inscriptions used the Ionian instead of the Attic alphabet, an important fact for epigraphic research though Ionian letters had sometimes been used before at Athens. E. V.

**EUCLID** (Εὐκλείδης), mathematician (fl. c. 300 B.C.), lived under Ptolemy I (306–283) and taught at Alexandria; his fame rests on his great textbook the Elements, στοιχεῖα, in thirteen books (Books 1–6 on plane geometry, 7–9 on the theory of numbers, 10 on irrationals, 11–13 on solid geometry). This work at once superseded those of earlier writers of Elements (Hippocrates of Chios, Leon, Eudoxus (q.v. 1), Theudius). Euclid made full use of his predecessors' work but added much of his own, while altering the whole arrangement. Most of the MSS. contain the recension by Theon of Alexandria, but the Vatican MS. 190 containing an earlier edition was discovered and edited by F. Peyrard (1814–18), and forms the basis of the authoritative text by J. L. Heiberg. Commentaries were written by Heron of Alexandria, Pappus, Simplicius. Fragments of these have come down to us, mostly through the Arabic (an-Nairīzī); but most valuable of all is the extant commentary of Proclus on Book 1. The so-called 'Book 14' is by Hypsicles (q.v.): 'Book 15' is an inferior compilation by a pupil of Isidorus (7th c. A.D.).

Of other works by Euclid some belong to elementary geometry: (1) the extant Data; (2) the lost Pseudaria, Fallacies (see Proclus 70); (3) On Divisions (of figures), (Περὶ διαιρέσεων), extant only in Arabic translation; the proofs of all but four of the propositions are missing.

To higher geometry belong the following: (1) three books of Porisms (Πορίσματα), (2) Surface-loci (Τόποι πρὸς ἐπιφανείᾳ), (3) four books of Conics (Κωνικά). These works are lost, and all we know of them is contained in Pappus (7, on the 'Treasury of Analysis'). Other extant works are: the Phaenomena, an astronomical textbook containing 16 or 18 propositions in primitive spherical geometry, partly based on Autolycus' (q.v. 2) On the Moving Sphere; Optics; Catoptrica (not genuine in its present form). Euclid wrote also on 'The Elements of Music': two works are attributed to him, the Sectio canonis (Κατατομὴ κανόνος) and an Introduction to Harmony, the former only containing excerpts from the original work, the latter being by Cleonides, a pupil of Aristoxenus. See also MATHEMATICS and MUSIC, § 4.

EDITIONS. Euclidis Opera Omnia, ed. J. L. Heiberg and H. Menge (with Lat. trans.), 8 vols. (Teubner, 1883–1916), contains Elements (with scholia) (i–v), Data (with Marinus' commentary) (vi), optical works (vii), Phaenomena, musical works and fragments (viii). A supplement by M. Curtze (1899) contains Gerard of Cremona's Latin translation of an-Nairīzī (Anaritius). The Arabic text of On Divisions was published with French translation by F. Woepcke, Journal Asiatique 1851, 233 ff. R. C. Archibald published an English translation from Woepcke's French, with additions, in Euclid's Book on Division of Figures (1915). al-Hajjaj's Arabic translation of the Elements was published from Codex Leidensis 399. 1 as far as the beginning of bk. 7 by Besthorn, Heiberg, and others (Copenhagen, 1897–1932).
TRANSLATIONS. Elements, T. L. Heath, 3 vols. (1925², repr. New York 1956, with historical introduction and commentary). Bks. vii–ix (French), J. Itard, Les Livres arithmétiques d'Euclide, (1961, with commentary). Data, C. Thaer (German, 1962). Optics and Catoptrica, ver Eecke (French, 1938).
COMMENT. Proclus, Comm. on Elem. I, ed. Friedlein (Teubner, 1873). French translation by ver Eecke (1948). German by M. Steck (1945). For history of text and editions of the Elements see Heiberg, Litteraturgeschichtliche Studien über Euklid (1882), and Heath's translation i, introduction. General: Heath, Hist. of Greek Maths. i. 354 ff. E. J. Dijksterhuis, De Elementen van Euklides (1929, 1931). Optics: A. Lejeune, Euclide et Ptolemée (1948). Catoptrica: Lejeune, Recherches sur la Catoptrique grecque (1954), 112 ff. Attempts to restore the Porisms were made by Simson, Opera Quaedam Reliqua (1776), 315 ff., and Chasles, Les trois livres des Porismes d'Euclide rétablis (1860). For editions and discussions of various works on mechanics and statics in Arabic and Latin versions which are attributed to Euclid, and which derive in part from early Greek sources, see Moody and Clagett, The Medieval Science of Weights (U.S.A. 1952), and Clagett, Science of Mechanics in the Middle Ages (U.S.A. 1959). T. H.; G. J. T.

**EUDEMUS** of Rhodes (second half of the 4th c. B.C.), pupil and friend of Aristotle. No account of his life survives, though Simplicius mentions a biography by a certain Damas (in Arist. Phys. 924. 13 Diels). He is said to have had a strong claim to succeed Aristotle as head of the Peripatos; but, in the event, Theophrastus was preferred over him. Later, he may have returned to Rhodes to set up his own school; but he remained faithful to the letter of Aristotle's teaching, and evidently continued in close contact with Theophrastus, who shared his conservative tendencies. A fragment of a letter survives, in which he consults him about the interpretation of a passage in Aristotle's Physics (Simpl. Phys. 923.11).

Eudemus compiled histories of arithmetic and geometry, astronomy, and theology. He also wrote on logic and rhetoric, and possibly on zoology. But we have detailed knowledge only of his work on physics, from which numerous passages are preserved by Simplicius. For the most part it represents a simple paraphrase of Aristotle's Physics, though there are occasional points of difference, where Eudemus attempts to reduce Aristotle's treatment to a more rigid scheme.

In the nineteenth century, Eudemus was held to be the author of the Eudemian Ethics, a work which is now generally regarded as an authentic part of the Aristotelian corpus.

F. Wehrli, Eudemos von Rhodos (1955); L. Spengel, Eudemi Rhodii Perip. fragm. (1866 and 1870; not sufficient); U. Schoebe, Quaestiones Eudemeae (1931; frs. of and comm. on the first book of the Physics). C. J. R.

**EUDORUS** (1), in mythology, a Myrmidon captain, son of Hermes and Polymele (Il. 16. 179 ff.).

**EUDORUS** (2) of Alexandria (fl. c. 25 B.C.), eclectic philosopher. Chief works (lost): Διαίρεσις τοῦ κατὰ φιλοσοφίαν λόγου; commentaries on Timaeus, Categories, Metaphysics, Aratus' Phaenomena; Περὶ τοῦ Νείλου. He is reckoned as a Platonist but owed much to Stoicism.

Dörrie, Hermes 1944, 25 ff.

**EUDOXUS** (1) of Cnidos (c. 390–c. 340 B.C.) was an outstanding mathematician and did work of importance in astronomy and geography; he was versatile in 'philosophy' in general. According to the not entirely trustworthy ancient biographical tradition (see especially Diog. Laert. 8. 86 ff.), he was a pupil of Archytas (q.v.) in geometry and of Philistion (q.v.) in medicine; he came to Athens to hear the Socratics when about 23, later spent some time in Egypt studying astronomy with the priests, then lectured in Cyzicus and the Propontis, visited the court of Mausolus, and finally returned to teach at Athens where he was acquainted with Plato; he drew up laws for Cnidos, and died aged 52.

In geometry he invented the general theory of proportion, applicable to incommensurable as well as commensurable magnitudes, found in Euclid Book 5 (scholion in Heiberg, *Euclidis Opera Omnia* v, 280). This greatly helped to assure the primacy of geometry in Greek mathematics (see MATHEMATICS). He also developed the method of approach to the limit (misnamed 'method of exhaustion' in modern works) which became the standard way of avoiding infinitesimals in mathematics. (see MATHEMATICS, § 3). He was thus able to prove that cone and pyramid are one-third of cylinder and prism respectively with the same base and height (Archimedes, *Method* pref.). Of his solution to the problem of doubling the cube nothing concrete is known.

In astronomy he was the first to construct a mathematical system to explain the apparent movement of the heavenly bodies: that of the 'homocentric spheres'. The report on this contained in Simplicius *Comm. on de Caelo* 492. 31 ff. (from which the title of the work is known to have been Περὶ ταχῶν) reveals both the high level of mathematics and the low level of observational astronomy of the time: Eudoxus combined uniform motions of concentric spheres about different axes with great ingenuity to produce, e.g., a qualitatively correct representation of the retrogradations of some planets; but the incorporated observational data are both few and crude, and the discrepancies of the results with observable fact often gross (for later corrections *see* CALLIPPUS *and* ASTRONOMY). Its adoption in a modified form by Aristotle was responsible for its resurrection in later ages. More practical (and also very influential) was Eudoxus' description of the constellations, with calendaric notices of risings and settings, which appeared in two versions named ἔνοπτρον and φαινόμενα. The latter is the work of his about which we know most, as it was adapted by Aratus (q.v. 1) for his immensely popular poem of the same name, and the commentary of Hipparchus (q.v. 3) on both is extant (see Manitius' ed. (Leipzig, 1894) 376, for refs. to Eudoxus). Another calendaric work was the ὀκταετηρίς ('8-year Cycle'). The papyrus treatise named Εὐδόξου τέχνη, though composed much later, contains elementary calendaric and astronomical information probably taken mostly from Eudoxus.

The γῆς περίοδος, in several books, was a work of mathematical and descriptive geography.

FRAGMENTS. F. Lasserre, *Die Fragmente des Eudoxos von Knidos* (1966).
LIFE. G. Huxley, *GRBS* 1963, 83 ff.
MATHEMATICS. Heath, *Hist. of Greek Maths.* i. 320 ff.; O. Becker, *Eudoxosstudien* i–v in *Quellen u. Studien z. Gesch. d. Math.* B2 and B3 (1951).
HOMOCENTRIC SPHERES. G. Schiaparelli, *Le sfere omocentriche* (1875), German transl. in *Abh. zur Gesch. d. Math.* i (1877), 101 ff. Dreyer, *History of the Planetary Systems* (1906), 87 ff. O. Neugebauer, *Exact Sciences in Antiquity²* (1957), 153 ff.
CALENDAR. Geminus, ed. Manitius (1898), 108 ff., 210 ff. Böckh, *Ueber die vierjährigen Sonnenkreise der Alten* (1863).
Εὐδόξου τέχνη. Editio princeps, including the interesting illustrations, *Notices et extraits des manuscrits XVIII* 2 (1865), 25 ff. Fr. Blass, *Eudoxi Ars Astronomica* (Kiel Festschrift, 1887). Translated by P. Tannery, *Histoire de l'astronomie ancienne* (1893), 283 ff.
GEOGRAPHY. Fragments collected by Brandes, *N. Jahrb. f. Philol.* Suppl. xiii (1847), 221 ff., also in *4te Jahresb. d. Vereins v. Freunden d.*

*Erdkunde zu Leipzig.* (1865), 58 ff. See further Gisinger, *Die Erdbeschreibung des Eudoxos von Knidos* (1921). G. J. T.

**EUDOXUS** (2) of Rhodes (fl. 225–200 B.C. ?), historian, perhaps identical with the author of Περίπλοι (*GGM* i. 565), which may have formed a part of Eudoxus' histories.
*FGrH* ii. 79.

**EUDOXUS** (3) of Cyzicus (2nd c. B.C.), Greek navigator. After 146 B.C. he was sent by Ptolemy Euergetes II of Egypt with a stranded Indian guide to find the sea-route to India; sent again later, he was on his return blown some way down east Africa, consorted with natives, returned to Alexandria with some wreckage there said to be part of a ship of Gades (*Cadiz*), decided that Africa could be circumnavigated, and determined to go round it to India, avoiding Ptolemaic exactions. Having collected cargoes at various ports, he set out from Gades, with music-girls, doctors, and carpenters on board, but was driven aground south of Morocco. Returning, he saw perhaps Madeira, failed to persuade Bocchus of Morocco to help him, cut across land to the Mediterranean, and, with much greater equipment, sailed again down west Africa, and disappeared.

Strabo 2. 98–102. J. Thiel, *Eudoxus van Cyzicus* (1939, in Dutch); Cary–Warmington, *Explorers* 98 ff.; (Pelican) 123 ff.; J. Carcopino, *Le Maroc antique* (1943), 156; Thomson, *Hist. Anc. Geog.* 185; Hyde, *Greek Mariners* 200 ff., 245 ff. E. H. W.

**EUENUS** of Paros (5th c. B.C.), poet and Sophist, of whom some twenty elegiac verses and two hexameters have come down. He gave metrical form to the rules of rhetoric and added to current terminology (Pl. *Phdr.* 267 a).

**EUETES,** said by the *Suda* to have been an Athenian writer of comedy contemporaneous with Epicharmus, but it is likely that the *Suda* is really referring to the similarly named tragedian of about that date.

**EUGAMMON** of Cyrene (6th c. B.C.), epic poet, author of the cyclic *Telegonia* (see EPIC CYCLE).
*EGF* 57–9.

**EUGENIUS,** FLAVUS, usurper A.D. 392–4 in the West. He taught rhetoric at Rome and was a friend of Symmachus who commended him to Arbogast, the Frankish *magister militum*, by whose influence he became *magister scrinii*. When Arbogast secured the death of Valentinian II (392) he proclaimed Eugenius as Augustus, but Eugenius failed to secure recognition from Theodosius or help from Ambrose. Nominally a Christian, he sympathized with the pagan revival and restored the altar of Victory in the Senate-house. In 394 Theodosius defeated him and Argobast on the Frigidus and Eugenius was killed.

Coinage: Mattingly–Sydenham, *RIC* ix. H. H. S.

**EUGRAPHIUS** (early 6th c. A.D.), author of a commentary on Terence (ed. P. Wessner in *Donati Commentum*, iii. 1). His interest is chiefly in the rhetorical qualities and characterization of the plays and often he does little more than paraphrase the text of Terence. He probably knew the commentary of Donatus on Terence and that of Servius on Virgil. The work is found in two versions, one of which contains interpolations.

Schanz–Hosius, § 1117. J. F. M.

**EUHEMERUS** (Εὐήμερος,) of Messene, while in the service of Cassander (q.v.) 311–298 B.C., wrote a novel of travel which was influential in the Hellenistic world. The substance of the novel is known from fragments and from an epitome by Eusebius (q.v.). Euhemerus described an imaginary voyage to a group of islands in the uncharted waters of the Indian Ocean and the way of life on its chief island, Panchaea. The central monument of the island, a golden column on which the deeds of Uranus, Cronus, and Zeus were recorded, gave the novel its title Ἱερὰ ἀναγραφή, 'Sacred Scripture'. From this moment Euhemerus learnt that Uranus, Cronus, and Zeus had been great kings in their day and that they were worshipped as gods by the grateful people. Earlier authors had written of imaginary utopias but the utopia of Euhemerus was particularly relevant to the position of those Hellenistic rulers who claimed to serve their subjects and on that account to receive worship for their services. The novel could be interpreted according to taste as supporting the traditional belief of Greek epic and lyric poetry which drew no clear line between gods and great men; as advancing a justification for contemporary ruler-cults; or as a work of rationalizing atheism. At the same time Euhemerus was influenced by the beliefs of the wider world which had been opened up by the conquests of Alexander the Great, and his novel reflected the awareness of new ideas in an exciting situation.

The theory of god and man which was advanced by Euhemerus seems to have made little impression on the Greeks, but Diodorus (q.v. 3) Siculus, apparently taking the romance for fact, embodied it in his sixth book, which survives in fragments. In Latin it had more success after the publication of the *Euhemerus* of Ennius (q.v.), and euhemerizing accounts of such mythological figures as Faunus exist. The Christian writers, especially Lactantius, liked to use it as evidence of the real nature of the Greek gods. Euhemerus' name survives in the modern term 'euhemeristic', applied to mythological interpretation which supposes certain gods (e.g. Asclepius) to be originally heroes.

Fragments: edited by G. Némethy (1889), G. Vallauri (1956)' and Jacoby, *FGrH* 63; see also J. Vahlen, *Ennianae poes. reliquiae²* (1903), cxx f.; 223 f. Studies: R. von Pöhlmann, *Gesch. der sozialen Frage³* (1925), 293 ff.; P. van Gils, *Quaestiones Euemereae* (Thesis, Kerkrade–Heerlen 1902); Nilsson, *GGR* ii 272; H. F. van der Meer, *E. of Messene* (Diss., Amsterdam 1948); H. Dörrie, *Abh. Akad. Gött.* 1964, 218 f.　　　　　　　　　　　　　　　　H. J. R.

**EUMELUS** (fl. *c.* 730 B.C.), Corinthian poet, of the Bacchiad family (*see* CORINTH). The works ascribed to him are folios (only fragments survive; all except the first were epics):

1. A *Prosodion* written for the Messenians (*see* LYRIC POETRY, GREEK, § 2). 2. *Corinthiaca*: a history of the Corinthian kingship from Helios at least as far as Glaucus. A prose version was known to Aristobulus q.v. 2) and Pausanias. 3. *Βουγονία*. Subject uncertain. 4. *Europia*. Apparently various legends connected with Thebes. 5. The *Titanomachia* (*see* EPIC CYCLE) was ascribed to Eumelus or to Arctinus. 6. The *Nostoi* (*see* EPIC CYCLE) seems to be ascribed to Eumelus in schol. Pind. *Ol.* 13. 31.

The authenticity and antiquity of these works has been questioned, but can be defended for the *Prosodion* and *Corinthiaca*.

*EGF* 185 ff.; *FGrH* iii B. 378 ff. with comm. 297 ff.; É. Will, *Korinthiaka* (1955), 124 ff.; C. M. Bowra, *CQ* 1963, 145 ff.　　　　　　　　　　　　　　　　　　　　M. L. W.

**EUMENES** (1) **I** of Pergamum (d. 241 B.C.), the son of Eumenes the brother of Philetaerus (q.v. 2), succeeded Philetaerus as ruler (never king) of Pergamum in 263, when he threw off Seleucid suzerainty with Egyptian assistance. After defeating Antiochus I near Sardes (262), he greatly extended his frontiers, and though he probably lost most of his gains to Antiochus II (*c.* 258), he maintained his independence till his death. He regu-

larly bought immunity from the plundering bands of the Galatians.

Hansen, *Attalids* 22 ff.; and *see under* PERGAMUM.　　G. T. G.

**EUMENES** (2) **II** (d. 160 or 159 B.C.) was the eldest son of Attalus I of Pergamum, whom he succeeded (197). He continued Attalus' policy of co-operation with Rome, and was perhaps mainly responsible for embroiling Rome with Antiochus (196–192), as Attalus had done with Philip V. In the war against Antiochus Eumenes assisted Rome with his fleet, and later stood a short siege in Pergamum; at Magnesia (189) he commanded the right wing with distinction. The peace of Apamea (188) gave him the Thracian Chersonese and most of Seleucid Asia Minor; and he secured these gains by cultivating the goodwill of Rome, which was further shown by the Senate's intervention in his favour, so as to end his wars with Bithynia (186–183) and (though ineffectively) Pontus (183–179). He was naturally the champion of the *status quo* in the East, and hence unpopular with all dissatisfied parties. The 'Third Macedonian War' (171–168), long regarded as 'inevitable', was hastened by his visit to Rome to accuse Perseus (172). Rome's failure to win the war quickly is said to have induced him to negotiate secretly with Perseus; but he cannot have seriously considered reversing a successful policy of thirty years. Nevertheless, he certainly forfeited the Senate's confidence, though it was only transferred to his brother Attalus.

Eumenes was a worthy successor to Attalus I, and carried his policy to its logical conclusion, greatly to the advantage of Pergamum (taking the short view). His ability is unquestioned, and the unfavourable tradition is due partly to this very success, which made him many enemies. His best memorial was perhaps the city of Pergamum itself, which he adorned with a splendid sequence of buildings.

Hansen, *Attalids*, esp. ch. 4.　　　　　　　　　　　G. T. G.

**EUMENES** (3) of Cardia (*c.* 362–316 B.C.), secretary to Philip of Macedon and to Alexander. He became (330?) principal secretary (ἀρχιγραμματεύς), and kept the Royal Journal (*see* EPHEMERIDES). Some military experience, too, came his way, and on Alexander's death he was immediately appointed satrap of the hitherto unconquered Cappadocia. It was in the wars of the 'Successors' (*see* DIADOCHI) that he proved himself a born general. He remained steadfastly loyal to the legitimate heirs and to the idea of a united Empire, and co-operated with the regents against the separatist generals. Driven from Asia Minor by Antigonus, he escaped to the Eastern satrapies, where he organized a fresh 'loyalist' front. After the indecisive battle of Paraecene (317), Eumenes' fate was decided at Gabiene by the desertion of his picked Macedonian corps. He was executed by vote of the Macedonians of both armies. He was the Themistocles of the period, an able Greek among able Macedonians, their equal in warcraft, their superior in diplomacy, which included skilful management of his Macedonian colleagues by tact, and of his Macedonian soldiers with the aid of an Alexander-cult instituted by him.

Diodorus, bk. 18 *passim*; Plutarch, *Eumenes*. Berve, *Alexanderreich*, no. 317; A. Vezin, *Eumenes von Kardia* (1907).　　G. T. G.

**EUMENIUS**, born at Autun *c.* A.D. 264, of Greek origin, a teacher of rhetoric, became Constantius' *magister memoriae* (q.v.) and was subsequently appointed by him to the headship of the school at Autun, a less exalted but more lucrative post. Soon afterwards (298) he delivered a public oration, in which he propounded reasons for rebuilding the war-damaged school, promised to donate his salary to the project, solicited court approval, and lavished much praise on the emperors. This speech is above the general level of the *Panegyrici* (some unplausibly identified with Eumenius). *See* PANEGYRIC, LATIN.

É. Galletier, *Panég. Lat.* i (1949), 103 ff.; W. S. Maguinness, *Greece and Rome* 1952, 97 ff.                    A. H.-W.

**EUMOLPUS**, mythical ancestor of the Eleusinian clan of the Eumolpidae, as his son Ceryx was of the Κήρυκες. He appears first in the Homeric Hymn to Demeter (184 and 475) as one of the rulers of Eleusis instructed by the goddess in the Mysteries. According to Apollod. 3. 201 ff. he was son of Poseidon and Chione daughter of Boreas (q.v.). To conceal her shame, she threw him into the sea; Poseidon saved him, brought him to Ethiopia, and entrusted him to his daughter Benthesicyme. When adult, he married Benthesicyme's daughter, but also tried to rape her other daughter, for which he was banished. During his exile he visited Eleusis, where he founded the Mysteries (Lucian, *Demon.* 34), or at least became somehow connected with them (Plut. *De exil.* 607 b). Finally, he succeeded Tegyrius, a Thracian king, but was sent for again by the Eleusinians to help them against Erechtheus (q.v.), in which campaign he was killed. An alternative genealogy, which can be traced back to the late fifth century B.C., made him the son of Musaeus (q.v. 1). See Nilsson, *GGR* i². 688 n. 4.                    H. J. R.

**EUNAPIUS**, Greek sophist. He was born in Sardes *c.* A.D. 345 and studied there under Chrysanthius and later in Athens under Prohaeresius. When he returned to Sardes he entered the circle of local neo-Platonists, learned theurgy and medicine, and mainly taught rhetoric. An admirer of the Emperor Julian and a convinced opponent of Christianity, he wrote to defend his old faith. His history (now lost except for fragments) continued that of Dexippus (q.v.) and went in fourteen books from A.D. 270 to 404; it was concluded about 414. Owing to its very anti-Christian attitude, it was later republished in an expurgated edition. It is a disputed point whether the new edition was prepared by Eunapius himself. Photius (*Bibl.* 77) saw both editions. We know little about Eunapius' sources except that he used his friend Oribasius' (q.v.) memoir on Julian. His relation to Ammianus is uncertain. He complained about the lack of reliable information on contemporary events in the Western part of the Empire. He was an important source not only to the pagan Zosimus (q.v.), but to the Christians Philostorgius, Socrates, and Sozomenus. The *Lives of the Sophists* written about A.D. 396 are extant. They follow Philostratus' model and on the basis of first-hand information deal mainly with fourth-century Neoplatonists. Eunapius gives an idealized picture in order to compete with the biographies of Christian saints. He died *c.* A.D. 420.

Fragments of the Histories in *FHG* iv, 7; L. Dindorf, *Hist. Gr. Min.* i (1870), 205. The best critical edition of the lives of the sophists by C. Giangrande (1956) with important introd. Text by W. C. Wright (Loeb, 1922). E. A. Thompson, *Ammianus Marcellinus* (1947), 28 ff. and 134 ff.; id., *A History of Attila* (1948), 16 ff.; W. R. Chalmers, *CQ* 1953, 165 ff.; A. F. Norman, ibid. 1957, 129 ff.; A. D. E. Cameron, ibid. 1963, 232 ff.                    A. M.

**EUNEOS** (Εὔνεως), and **THOAS** (Θόας), sons of Jason and Hypsipyle (q.v.). They came to Nemea while their mother was in captivity there, and were admitted to the house by her; later, they recognized her and took her away (Eur. *Hyps.*, ed. G. W. Bond (1963), 25 and 41).

**EUNUCHS, RELIGIOUS**, generally self-castrated, were frequently associated with the cult of the Anatolian mother-goddess. The custom probably originated here, rather than with the Semites, among whom it is found as a religious institution chiefly at Hierapolis-Bambyce, where many of the cultural ties were with Anatolia.

Best known are the Galli of Cybele and Atargatis, who were temple attendants or wandering mendicants (cf. METRAGYRTES) rather than priests (Lucian, *Syr. D.* 43); they are seldom mentioned in inscriptions. Though the Archigalli in the West seem not to have been eunuchs, the heads of the cult at Pessinus, the Attis and Battakes, probably were, at least in earlier times. There were eunuchs in the service of Hecate at Lagina (*BCH* 1920, 79; 84), and Strabo (641) says that the Megabyzi, the chief priests of Artemis at Ephesus, were formerly eunuchs.

Many explanations of the practice have been offered, as that the act was intended to increase the fertility of the goddess or to assimilate the worshipper to her. These may have been contributory or secondary ideas, but the basic motive was probably the desire to make oneself permanently pure. Certain rites only the chaste could perform; the eunuch, at least in a negative sense, possesses the purity of a virgin or child (at Ephesus virgins were the colleagues of the Megabyzus). In other words, the importance lay not in the act but in its consequences.

The chief ancient sources are Lucian, *Syr. D.*, Catullus 63, *Anth. Pal.* 6. 217–20, and the texts collected in H. Hepding, *Attis* (1903), and F. Cumont, *L'Égypte des astrologues* (1937), 132 f. A *lex sacra* of Eresus forbidding Galli entrance to a sanctuary, *CR* 1902, 190; the Galli at Rome, J. Carcopino, *Mél. d'Arch. et d'Hist.* (1923). Origins of rite and comparative material: A. D. Nock, *ARW* 1925; L. H. Gray in *ERE*, s.v. 'Eunuch'.                    F. R. W.

**EUNUS**, a Syrian slave in Enna, led a slave revolt in Sicily. Calling himself Antiochus, he collected a large army, chiefly of slaves, gained control of much of Sicily and defeated several Roman commanders. He struck bronze coins (see *CAH*, Pls. iv. 2). Piso (q.v. 1), with a consular army, began to retrieve the situation (133 B.C.) and Rupilius defeated and captured Eunus, who died in prison.                    E. B.

**EUPATRIDAI** (εὐπατρίδαι), one of the terms (cf. εὐγενεῖς, γενναῖοι, γνώριμοι) for Greeks noble by birth, i.e. members of named γένη (*see* GENOS), tracing their descent from heroic times, and, in the aristocratic stage of a city's development, monopolizing the government. They were generally rich landowners. At Athens, in the early sixth century, the Eupatridai appear as one of four distinct classes in the citizen-body, the other three being the 'farmers' (ἄγροικοι, γεωργοί, γεωμόροι), the Demiourgoi (q.v.), and the Thetes (q.v.). Of these the farmers and Demiourgoi were now beginning to dispute with the Eupatridai the monopoly of office which these had previously enjoyed (*see* ARCHONTES, AREOPAGUS). In 580/79, by a temporary compromise, the chief archonship was replaced by a committee of ten, of whom only five were Eupatridai (Arist. *Ath. Pol.* 13. 2). Solon (q.v.) ended the controversy by making wealth, not birth or occupation, the criterion of eligibility for office, but the Eupatrid families continued to exercise great influence, to hold certain priesthoods, and to interpret religious law (*see* EXEGETES). An individual γένος called Eupatridai has been alleged, mainly on the strength of a passage of Isocrates (16. 25). Εὐπατρίδης was also used to translate *patricius* (q.v.).

Busolt–Swoboda, *Griech. Staatsk*³. (i, 1920; ii, 1926), see indexes; H. T. Wade-Gery, *CQ* 1931, 1 ff. (*Essays in Greek History* (1958), 86 ff.); Hignett, *Hist. Athen. Const.*, see index; F. R. Wüst, *Hist.* 1957, 176 ff., 1959, 1 ff.; R. Sealey, *Hist.* 1960, 178 ff., 1961, 512 ff.; N. G. L. Hammond, *JHS* 1961, 76 ff.                    A. W. G.; T. J. C.

**EUPHANTUS** of Olynthus, tutor of Antigonus Gonatas, to whom he dedicated a treatise Περὶ βασιλείας. He also wrote contemporary history ('Ἱστορίαι) and several tragedies.

*FGrH* ii. 74.

**EUPHEMUS,** a hero, son of Poseidon, connected with the foundation-legend of Cyrene. Sailing with the Argonauts, he was given a clod (symbol of sovranty) by Triton as they returned from Libya, and told (in Pindar's account) that if he dropped it into the sea near Taenarum his descendants in the fourth generation would rule in Libya. It fell, however, by Thera, whence, in the seventeenth generation after Euphemus, Battus colonized Cyrene. (Pind. *Pyth.* 4. *See* EURYPYLUS (3), also Hdt. 4. 150 and Ap. Rhod. 4. 1730.)

In Homer (*Il.* 2. 846) a Euphemus is mentioned as leader of the Cicones, and in Plato (*Phdr.* 244 a) one as father of the poet Stesichorus. According to Hesychius, Euphemus was an epithet of Zeus in Lesbos.      H. J. R.

**EUPHORBUS,** in mythology, a Dardanian, son of Panthoos, who wounded Patroclus (*Il.* 16. 806 ff.), and was afterwards killed by Menelaus (17. 45 ff.). Pythagoras claimed to have been Euphorbus in a former incarnation and to recognize his shield (Hor. *Carm.* 1. 28. 9 ff., and commentators there).      H. J. R.

**EUPHORION** (1), son of Aeschylus, is said (*Suda*, s.v.) to have exhibited plays written by his father but not produced in his lifetime, and to have won four victories with them. In 431 B.C. he defeated both Sophocles and Euripides (Arg. Eur. *Med.*).      A. W. P.-C.

**EUPHORION** (2) (b. *c.* 275 B.C.—but that date has been challenged as too early), of Chalcis in Euboea, studied philosophy at Athens. In poetry he was a pupil of Archebulus of Thera. After enriching himself by a liaison with the elderly widow of Alexander, ruler of Euboea and Corinth, he was appointed librarian at Antioch in Syria by Antiochus the Great (223–187) and was buried there or at Apamea (the *Suda*).

WORKS. (1) *Verse.* Apart from epigrams (*Anth. Pal.* 6. 279; 7. 651) Euphorion seems to have confined himself in the main to the composition of epyllia and composite epics, akin to catalogue-poems, on mythological subjects. The *Suda* mentions three works, *Hesiod*, *Mopsopia* or *Miscellanea* (Ἄτακτα), *Chiliades*. The second was a collection of Attic legends, Mopsopia being an old name for Attica. The third guaranteed the eventual punishment of persons who had defrauded Euphorion of money by a recital of oracles fulfilled after the lapse of 1,000 years. Of the further titles cited in the fragments several are proper names, perhaps those of the addressees. The content of these poems was apparently mythological, as was certainly that of seven others, among which the *Thrax* seems to have been a medley of myths. The *Curses* or *Goblet-thief* was directed against a man who had robbed Euphorion of such an article, if fr. 9 belongs to this poem, imprecated on the thief many unpleasant ends recorded in myth; cf. Ovid's *Ibis*. The *Replies* (Ἀντιγραφαί) *to Theodoridas* was also in verse, a poetic epistle. The attribution to Euphorion of love-elegies in the Roman manner is based on a misunderstanding. (2) *Prose.* The following works are cited, *About the Isthmian Games*, *About the Aleuadae*, *About the makers of songs*, a lexicon to Hippocrates.

The scantiness of Euphorion's surviving fragments makes an estimate of his work difficult. In subject-matter he seems to have preferred the Trojan Cycle, local legends of a gruesome character, and topics of aetiology and geography. His narrative technique consisted in undue amplification of detail and vain repetition, leading up to very summary treatment of the climax (frs. 44, 51; Lucian, *Hist. conscr.* 57). His sentiment was mawkish (fr. 92) and he indulged in childish etymologies (frs. 57, 136). His proverbial obscurity is due partly to the many and difficult mythological references, partly to

his language, of which 'glosses' (cf. *Anth. Pal.* 11. 218, an attack on Euphorion by Crates of Mallos) and neologisms, including truncated words, formed an important part. His basic vocabulary was drawn from Homer, whom he termed 'untouchable' (fr. 118), but he was also indebted for this and for many themes to Hesiod and others. The papyrus fragments reveal him as a barefaced plagiarist of his immediate predecessors, Callimachus and Apollonius Rhodius. But [Lycophron] in the *Alexandra* is probably Euphorion's debtor. *See also* EPYLLION.

Euphorion exercised considerable influence on later poets. Among the Greeks, Nicander, Parthenius, Nonnus imitate his language or borrow his themes. At Rome his epyllia (*see* EPYLLION) were well known to the generation of Catullus and Gallus (hence *cantores Euphorionis*, Cic. *Tusc.* 3. 45). Virgil's debt to him for subject-matter is illustrated by Servius. Of extant Latin poems the *Ciris* perhaps reproduces Euphorion's technique most closely.

TEXTS. Powell, *Coll. Alex.* 28 ff. For the latest papyri see K. Latte, *Philol.* 1935, 129 ff. V. Bartoletti, *Papiri greci e latini*, 14 (1957), no. 1390; Page, *GLP* 489 ff.; L. G. Westerink, *Mnemos.* 1960, 329; *POxy* 30 (1964), 2526.
GENERAL LITERATURE. F. Skutsch, 'Euphorion (4)', in *PW* vi. 1174 ff.; A. Meineke, *Analecta Alexandrina* (1943), 3 ff.; F. Scheidweiler, *Euphorionis fragmenta* (1908); L. Alfonsi, 'Euphorione e l'elegia', *Miscellanea di studi alessandrini* 1963, 455 f.; A. Barigazzi, 'Il Dionysos di Euforione', ibid. 416 f.; F. della Corte, P. Treves, A. Barigazzi, V. Bartoletti, L. Alfonsi, 'Euforione e i poeti latini', *Maia* 1965, 158 f.; P. Treves, *Euforione e la storia ellenistica* (1955).
      E. A. B.; C. A. T.

**EUPHRANOR,** sculptor and painter, of the Isthmus; later settled in Athens. Pliny dates him 364 B.C. (by battle of Mantinea). Pupil of the elder Aristides (q.v. 2). His sculptures, some of them colossal, included Paris, Alexander and Philip in chariots, and a Priestess of great beauty. His Apollo Patroos has been found in the Athenian Agora (H. A. Thompson, *Hesp.* 1937, 77). His paintings included Cavalry battle before Mantinea, Theseus with Democracy and Demos, the Twelve Gods. He wrote on symmetry and colours. Critics remarked on his large heads and slim bodies, but he seemed to portray the dignity of heroes and himself called his Theseus 'beef fed', in contrast to the 'rose fed' Theseus of Parrhasius (q.v.).

Overbeck 1785–1810; Lippold, *Griech. Plastik* 260; Rumpf, *Malerei u. Zeichn.* 132.      T. B. L. W.

**EUPHRATES,** the longest river of western Asia, and the more westerly of the Two Rivers of Mesopotamia. Rising in the Armenian mountains, it flows south-west to the Taurus, then south-east, receiving its three main tributaries the Murat Su, the Balikh, and the Khabur on the left bank. In the alluvial plain of Babylonia, which it inundates yearly, it was in antiquity connected with the Tigris (q.v.) by numerous navigation and irrigation canals. In classical times it was crossed by a number of bridges, e.g. at Zeugma (q.v.) and Babylon. It served as a political boundary between Armenia and Cappadocia, Sophene and Commagene, and Upper Mesopotamia and Syria (Strabo 16. 746–9; Pliny 5. 83; Ptol. 5. 12). The Parthian Empire reached the permanent limit of its expansion westwards at the Euphrates over against Syria in 53 B.C. After the Romans in A.D. 66 recognized the rule of a Parthian Arsacid king over Armenia they began the construction of a military *limes* along the upper and middle course of the river; forts along its right bank guarded for more than 500 years the imperial frontier against first the Parthian, later the Sassanid kings.

F. R. Chesney, *Expedition for the Survey of the Rivers Euphrates and Tigris* i, ii (1850); V. Chapot, *La Frontière de l'Euphrate* (1907); D. Oates, *Studies in the Anc. Hist. of Northern Iraq* (1968).
      M. S. D.; E. W. G.

**EUPHRON,** New Comedy poet, dated to the middle of the third century B.C. by his allusion to Nicomedes of

Bithynia (fr. 11. 2). Nine titles are known. Fr. 1, the great discoveries of cooks (see H. Dohm, *Mageiros* (1964), 131 ff.).

FCG i. 477 f., iv. 486 ff.; CAF iii. 317 ff.      W. G. A.

**EUPHRONIUS** (late 6th–early 5th c. B.C.), potter and vase-painter in Athens, known from seventeen signatures. He signed five red-figure vases as painter (510–500 B.C.), notably Calyx Crater with Heracles and Antaeus (Paris), and Psycter with Hetaerae (Leningrad). Experimented with new positions, character contrast, etc., within ripe archaic conventions. As potter he employed Onesimus and the Pistoxenus painter.

Beazley, *ABV* 403; *ARV*² 13, 313, 858.      T. B. L. W.

**EUPOLEMUS** (fl. *c.* 150 B.C.), a hellenized Jew, wrote Περὶ τῶν ἐν τῇ Ἰουδαίᾳ βασιλέων, a popular history of the Jews in a rhetorical style.

FGrH iii. 723/4.

**EUPOLIS** was regarded as one of the greatest poets of the Old Attic Comedy (e.g. Hor. *Sat.* 1. 4. 1). His first play was produced in 429 B.C. (Anon. *De Com.* 10); he won three victories at the Lenaea and at least one at the City Dionysia (*IG* ii². 2325. 59, 126). The datable plays are: Νουμηνίαι at the Lenaea in 425 (hyp. 1 Ar. *Ach.*), Μαρικᾶς at the Lenaea in 421 (schol. Ar. *Nub.* 551), *Flatterers* at the City Dionysia in 421 (hyp. 1 Ar. *Pax*), *Autolycus* in 420 (Ath. 216 d), and Βάπται after 424 (fr. 78 refers to Ar. *Eq.*) but before 415 (schol. Aristid. 3. 444 D relates a story which, though untrue, presupposes 415 as the last possible date for Βάπται). *Cities* is to be dated *c.* 420 B.C.; it has many personal references in common with Ar. *Nub.*, *Vesp.*, and *Pax*. Δῆμοι must be later than 418 (fr. 110 B [*FAC*] refers to the Mantinea campaign) and earlier than 406 (fr. 98 shows that the Younger Pericles is still alive); 412 is the most probable date (Körte, *Hermes* 1912, 276 ff.). Eupolis died 'in the Hellespont, during the Peloponnesian War' (*Suda*), some time after 415 (Eratosth. ap. Cic. *ad Att.* 6. 1. 18). We have nineteen titles and over 460 fragments, including substantial papyrus fragments of Δῆμοι and (if the identification is correct) Προσπάλτιοι.

*Flatterers* ridiculed Callias, son of Hipponicus, for cultivating the company of sophists, and may be regarded as a comic poet's view of the kind of scene described by Plato, *Prt.* 314 ff. Μαρικᾶς was an attack on Hyperbolus, comparable with Aristophanes' attack on Cleon in *Eq.* (cf. Ar. *Nub.* 553). In Δῆμοι great Athenians of the past were brought up from the underworld to give advice to the present. In Ταξίαρχοι the luckless Dionysus is subjected to hard military training under Phormio. Eupolis' style was 'bitter and indecent' to the author of *Vit. Ar.* 11 (cf. Anon. *De Com.* 10), 'inventive, powerful, and attractive' to Platonius (*Diff. Com.* 15). The longer fragments do not stand up well to comparison with Aristophanes.

FCG i. 104 ff.; ii. 426 ff.; CAF i. 258 ff.; FAC i. 310 ff. (unreliable on Δῆμοι).      K. J. D.

**EURIPIDES.**

I. LIFE (*c.* 485–*c.* 406 B.C.)

**1.** Euripides was born probably in 480 or 485 B.C. As both the ancient 'Life' and the related biography by Satyrus, of which papyrus fragments are extant, draw many of their 'facts' from Old Comedy, little reliable information can have survived; in particular stories of his domestic misfortunes are suspect. His home was at Phlya, east of Hymettus, and as his family had an ancestral priesthood of Apollo Zosterios it must have been respectable, and if he was challenged to an *antidosis* (q.v.) (Arist. *Rh.* 3. 15) he must have been rich. It is not known

why Aristophanes could raise a laugh by referring to greengrocery in connexion with his mother Cleito. The cave on Salamis in which he used to compose (Philochorus fr. 21) was probably a family property; the habit of solitude which this suggests may be behind the tradition that he was surly and unconvivial (Alexander Aetolus 7). Unlike Sophocles he was not politically prominent, but he went on an embassy to Syracuse (Arist. *Rh.* 2. 6. and schol.) and composed an elegy or epitaph on those who fell in the attack on that city (Plut. *Nic.* 17); he may also have written the epinician ode to celebrate Alcibiades' victory at Olympia in 416 or 420 B.C. (Plut. *Alc.* 11, *Dem.* 1; see Bowra, *Hist.* 1960, 68). He was clearly involved in the intellectual movement associated with the sophists, whether or not he was personally acquainted, as tradition asserts, with Anaxagoras, Socrates, and others. According to Diogenes Laertius (9. 54) it was at Euripides' house that Protagoras first read his sceptical work on the gods. He is said (Satyr. *Vit. Eur.*, col. 10) to have been prosecuted by Cleon for impiety, and his undoubted addiction to books (Ar. *Ran.* 943, etc., Ath. 3 a), when reading was still a highly intellectual pastime, fits the picture. Possibly, though there is no firm evidence, it was the unpopularity caused by his attitudes and associates that caused him to accept an invitation to the court of Archelaus in Macedonia, probably in 408 B.C. There he died not long before Feb./Mar. 406, when Sophocles dressed his chorus in mourning at the Proagon (q.v.) to the tragic performances. That he was torn to pieces by the royal hounds is unlikely in view of Aristophanes' silence.

II. WORKS

**2.** Euripides first competed at the Dionysia in 455 (*Vit. Eur.* 32) and won his first victory in 441 B.C. (*Marm. Par.* 60); he was victorious again with the *Hippolytus* in 428 and after his death (? 405) with the *Bacchae* and *Iphigeneia in Aulis*, but on only two other occasions; in the 'Life' it is said that he was indifferent to theatrical success. According to the *Suda* he produced tragedies on twenty-two occasions (eighty-eight plays if all were shown at the Dionysia) and wrote ninety-two plays. Not all his plays need have been produced at Athens and in some cases authorship was in doubt; in particular *Peirithous*, *Rhadamanthys*, and *Tennes* were attributed by some to Critias, and although Euripides undoubtedly wrote a *Rhesus* the extant play of this name is not certainly his. Probably seventy-eight plays, including the three claimed for Critias, were known to Hellenistic scholars; among the plays which did not survive the fourth century were several satyr-plays. Some eighty titles are known.

The plays which we possess are of two kinds: (1) a selection of ten plays made about A.D. 200 for use in schools; they may have been contained in a single codex, and they have been transmitted with scholia, though those belonging to the *Bacchae* are lost. They are *Alcestis*, *Medea*, *Hippolytus*, *Andromache*, *Hecuba*, *Troades*, *Phoenissae*, *Orestes*, (*Bacchae*), and *Rhesus*. (2) The Laurentian MS. (known as L) contains in addition to the select plays, except *Troades*, nine plays numbered in the following sequence: *Helen*, *Electra*, *Heracleidae*, *Heracles*, *Supplices*, *Iphigeneia in Aulis*, *Iphigeneia in Tauris*, *Ion*, *Cyclops*, that is to say, taking their Greek titles, one beginning with Ε, 3 with Η, 4 with Ι and one with Κ. Such a quasi-alphabetical grouping by first letters is found also in ancient lists of the plays, and it can be taken as certain that what we have here is a sequence of plays in the order of the Alexandrian edition (see Barrett, *Eur. Hipp.* (1964), 50 ff.). This is of great importance since the plays are not selected, but a fair sample of Euripides' work. Without them we should be wholly ignorant of at least one important type of play.

**3.** The dates of the following plays are known (lost plays in brackets). (*Peliades*) 455; *Alcestis* (with *Cressae*, *Alcmaeon in Psophis*, *Telephus*) 438, second prize; *Medea* (with *Philoctetes*, *Dictys*, *Theristae*) 431, third prize; *Hippolytus* 428, first prize; *Troades* (with *Alexander*, *Palamedes*, *Sisyphus*) 415, plays connected in subject, second prize; *Helena* (with *Andromeda*) 412; *Orestes* 408; *Bacchae* and *Iphigeneia in Aulis* (with *Alcmaeon in Corinth*) produced posthumously, probably 405; *Phoenissae* (with *Oenomaus*, *Chrysippus*) after 412 and before 408, so also (*Hypsipyle*, *Antiope*); *Rhesus*, if our play is Euripides' work, is earlier than any other extant play (Ritchie, *The Authenticity of the Rh. of Eur.* (1964)).

As the technique of Euripides shows a remarkably steady development, especially in the use of resolved feet in trimeters (Ceadel, *CQ* 1941, 66; Zieliński, *Tragodoumenon Libri Tres* iii (Cracow, 1925)), it is possible to arrange the remaining plays in an approximate order with some confidence. Certain lost plays are given a *terminus ante quem* by references in comedy. Most of the following dates should have an error of not more than four years: *Heracleidae* 430, *Andromache* 426, *Hecuba* 424, *Supplices* 422, *Heracles* 417, *Electra* 417 (this play is often dated to 413 because of a supposed reference to the fleet in Sicilian waters l. 1347, but this is less than certain), *Iphigeneia in Tauris* a little before *Helena* of 412, *Ion* a little later; *Cyclops* being a satyr-play is not comparable with the rest, but probably a late work. Earlier than Aristophanes' *Acharnians* of 425 are (*Oeneus*, *Phoenix*, *Bellerophon*, *Ino*, *Thyestes*), than the (*Georgoi*) of 424 (*Cresphontes*), than the *Clouds* ? 423 (*Aeolus*), than the *Wasps* 422 (*Theseus*, *Stheneboia*), than the *Thesmophoriazusae* 411 (*Erechtheus*, *Melanippe the Wise*).

**4.** New papyri continue to throw light on lost plays; for the older finds see D. L. Page, *Greek Literary Papyri* (Loeb, 1942); no. 21, doubtfully attributed to Sophocles, is now known to be from Eur. *Telephus*, see *POxy.* 27 (1962), 2460; a new frag. of *Cresphontes* 2458 in same volume, also new information especially on the *Aeolus* in the collection of hypotheses (q.v.) 2455, 2457. A fragment of the *Erechtheus* awaits publication.

### III. CHARACTER AND CONTENT OF HIS WORK

**5.** In Euripides' plays the attitude to the myths which are the basis of virtually all Greek tragedy seems to have changed. Here judgement must be more than usually subjective and not all are agreed, but there appears a loss of confidence in the innate significance of the old stories and a readiness to give them an unnatural twist in order that they may fulfil momentarily a new purpose. Jason and Medea, selfish male and passionate woman, belong only intermittently to the heroic world; in the *Hecuba* the demagogues of the fleet are closer at hand behind the scenes than in Sophocles' *Ajax*; in the *Electra* an invented character, Electra's peasant husband, takes a leading part, and Apollo's dubious oracle is flatly rejected; even in the *Bacchae* Dionysus is vindicated amid pious sophistries broadly marked with a fifth-century origin. As Aristophanes makes Euripides claim in the *Frogs* (959), he brings into tragedy the familiar, everyday things of life; and the emotions too are more poignant and less sublime. Instead of developing what is latent in the myth like Sophocles he seems often to impose an alien significance upon it, or to use it as a means of producing brilliant but irrelevant effects. In his later years Euripides used myth almost for pure entertainment in his numerous plays of intrigue. These were a natural development of the revenge play in which a hero, such as Orestes, returns home in secret, is recognized by his friends, and by some stratagem overthrows the usurper. When success includes the murder of a mother, dramatic excitement is subordinate to the moral problem. But Euripides extended the treatment to plots of pure adventure where no moral problem was involved, and diverted his audience with brilliant scenes of recognition, cunningly planned escapes, and salvation snatched from catastrophe. *Iphigeneia in Tauris*, *Helen*, and *Ion* belong to this class and so did many lost plays. They end in unalloyed happiness, and in the *Andromeda* this was accompanied by the wish-fulfilments of triumphant love. Such things must have seemed to many a profanation of myth; really they showed a new kind of sensibility. At the same time the energy of Euripides' lyric narrative and an antiquarian enthusiasm for detail in describing cult and genealogy suggest an anticipation of the Alexandrian spirit. It is not irrelevant that the great age of poetry in Greece ended with the fifth century, and thereafter prose was the medium of serious thought.

**6.** About Euripides' power of portraying character there is both disagreement and confusion. Obviously he had an interest in states of mind, particularly abnormal ones, and a real power of projecting himself into a situation. Stories of violent or depraved passion clearly attracted him. [Longinus] observed justly that he bestowed his attention especially on madness and love and that he wrote with such vividness that one felt he had been present at the scenes he represented (15. 4–5). Above all he was aware, as perhaps no one had been before him, of the conflict which can arise within men's minds, of the agony caused by conflicting purposes; these are revealed in their heat in Medea, in retrospect by Phaedra in the *Hippolytus*, and we know now in the (*Chrysippus*). This analysis of man's predicament has earned him the name of 'irrationalist' (E. R. Dodds, *CR* 1929, 102; *The Greeks and the Irrational* (1951), 186 f.). The same idea is present in the denial that passion is an urge inspired by an external force for which a man is not responsible; cf. *Troad.* 988 'It was your own mind that became Cypris when you saw him' (of Helen and Paris). This is a title not less deserved than Verrall's 'rationalist'. Yet insights of this kind are only one element in the creation of character, and in spite of unforgettable moments we do not find many whole men or women in Euripides' plays. This is partly because within the narrow limits of a Greek play it is difficult, when situations change rapidly, to indicate at all fully the accompanying changes in states of mind. It may not be incredible that the gentle and pathetic Creusa, as she appears in the first half of the *Ion*, should appear as a potential murderess in the second, but nothing is done to ease the transformation. And it is partly because Euripides was not so much concerned to present life-like characters as to exploit to the full the rhetorical possibilities of every situation. Especially in the set debates of which the plays are full each character makes the best of his case, and it need cause no surprise if in doing so they fail to reveal the inward process of the spirit.

**7.** It cannot be doubted that Euripides was fascinated by the rapidly developing art of rhetoric—not that Sophocles was indifferent to it, but, as Quintilian said (10. 1. 67), for anyone who wished to prepare himself for speaking Euripides would be far the more helpful. The question arises whether the challenging generalizations in which the plays abound, the persuasive urging of unconventional views, are a product of the born pleader's desire to argue every case, or whether we can detect a point of view which is Euripides' own. It has been generally believed that Euripides was the child of the sophists (in fact he was their contemporary), openly attacking and quietly sapping established religion if not ordinary morality. It is true that a dramatist is unable to speak except through the mouths of others and that his views can never with certainty be identified as those expressed by any of his characters, not even the chorus. Yet Hecuba's 'random thoughts' (*Hec.* 603, cf. 800) have little to do with Hecuba. The weight of a play can appear to be on one side rather than another. In the *Hercules Furens* the denial that the innocent can be contaminated and pass on the infection of shed blood is too emphatic to be misunderstood, and so is the repetition of Xenophanes' famous attack on Homer's adulterous gods (1233–4, 1340–6). Both *Hippolytus* and *Bacchae* seem to imply that natural forces, however divine, if conceived as persons, turn out morally inadequate. The tradition of 'the philosopher of the stage', pupil of the rationalist father-figure Anaxagoras, is in agreement with the picture presented by comedy of Euripides as Socrates' crony (Ar. *Ran.* 1491, fr. 37 B; Telecleides fr. 39, 40), intellectually pretentious and unconventional. And apart from the surviving plays the numerous fragments which refer to contemporary speculation in physics and cosmology, wholly unparalleled in the works of any other dramatist, must imply a strong interest in these activities.

Of late it has been denied both that we can hope to know anything about Euripides' opinions and that these opinions were as sceptical as has been supposed (see *Entretiens Hardt* vi). While some may have identified his position too confidently with that of the more nihilistic sophists, there is little doubt where in general his sympathies lay. Further we may suspect in particular that he was attracted by a vague pantheism resting on a belief in a divine, quintessential aether, as in the system of Diogenes (q.v. 1) of Apollonia. To regard as divine the aether, the material from which soul is fashioned, was by no means in conflict with conventional belief, and Euripides brings the notion into his plays for no apparent reason but that he is interested in it (*Supp.* 533, 1140, *Hel.* 1015, *Or.* 1086, fr. 839. 10, 935 (with *Troad.* 884), 971; cf. Ar. *Ran.* 892). In fact this idea is more emphasized than anything obviously derived from Anaxagoras, though there are traces of his physical doctrines in fr. 783, *Or.* 839, and in the passages cited by Satyrus from the (*Peirithous*), whose authenticity is doubted, probably wrongly (frs. 593, 912).

It is a difficult question how far Τύχη (Chance) appears as a force in her own right, independent of the gods or contrasted with them. Usually she represents what is incalculable for man without reference to the question whether she is subject to a divine plan or is a merely random force. In the group of plays sometimes known as the Τύχη dramas, especially the *Ion* (Solmsen, 'Gestaltung des Intriguenmotivs in den Trag. des Soph. und Eur.', *Philol.* 1932, 1), coincidences and narrow escapes necessarily give Chance an important part in the action; but at *Hec.* 488 the alternative is squarely put: Is Zeus or Chance supreme? And the *Hercules Furens*, though there is no agreed interpretation of the play, can be read as the blank negation of divine purpose.

**8.** The events of the last third of the fifth century have left a clear mark on the plays. The noble ode in praise of Athens (*Med.* 824–65) shows the patriotic exaltation with which Euripides entered the period of war; it is maintained in the *Heracleidae*, the celebration of an incident on which Athenian pride loved to dwell, and in the (*Erechtheus*); growing bitterness appears in the ugly denunciation of Spartans and their ways in the *Andromache* (445 ff.); the *Supplices* too was called by an ancient critic 'encomium of Athens', but the political arguments, at times quite Thucydidean in quality, are balanced with surprising evenness; there may even be a touch of satire in the funeral praises of the outrageous Capaneus. Athena's words at the end are connected with an Argive alliance, actual or prospective. (*Bellerophon*) fr. 286 reveals the naked immorality of power politics. There is wide agreement that the *Troades* was composed with reference, if not to the capture of Melos, to the coming attack on Sicily. Weariness of war shows itself also in the *Helen*

(1151–64). In the numerous intrigue plays written in the last decade of his life Euripides perhaps turned his back on the sad Athenian scene in favour of a more fanciful world, but Delphian Apollo continued to receive hard knocks, especially in the *Ion*, because as a Dorian partisan he could be assailed with comparative impunity. There is an undertone of continuous hostility to demagogues and to the shams and deceptions of politics from the *Hecuba* (254), through the *Supplices* (726), *Orestes* (885–952), to the *Iphigeneia in Aulis* (337). Like most men of property he doubtless had no love for extreme democracy, and Dionysus' comment on Euripides' claim to have been moved by democratic sentiment 'that is a subject you had best leave alone' (Ar. *Ran.* 952) suggests that his attitude was notorious.

The idea that Euripides was particularly hostile to women can have arisen quite naturally from his fondness for plots in which wicked and licentious women figured; but this fondness is likely to have been the result of his interest in the springs of passion or, as in the incestuous plot of the *Aeolus*, in a problem of ethics, rather than of a belief in the depravity of women; bad men and good women are no rarity in his works. Again his plays contain many highly quotable generalizations about female wickedness, but it was part of the rhetorical technique to put statements about particular cases in general form.

## IV. STRUCTURE AND TECHNIQUE

**9.** Few of Euripides' plays show the mastery of structure which was achieved by Sophocles; only *Hippolytus*, *Iphigeneia in Tauris*, and *Bacchae* approach the highest standard. The *Medea*, which can in fact be performed by two actors, achieves remarkable concentration, but the unmotivated entrance of Aegeus is a blemish. Many complicated plots are handled with dexterity, notably in the *Ion*, but they give no positive impression of grace and symmetry, while some plays, especially the *Andromache*, are conspicuously lacking in coherence. The disconnexion of the two halves of *Hercules Furens* seems to be purposely emphasized by the second prologue in the middle of the play, and may be meant to indicate that the incoherence of the drama extends to the universe. The *Troades* would certainly have been assigned by Aristotle to the category of episodic plays, but this was the natural form to produce the effect which Euripides here desired. The *Phoenissae*, a mere pageant of myth, is less successful.

He seems willingly to have sacrificed some continuity for the sake of the advantages secured by his special type of prologue and exodos, or final scene. The first speaker usually states the facts which the audience needs to know, and these in the case of unfamiliar myths may be numerous. Occasionally, as in the *Medea*, some attempt is made to give the character in question a motive for speaking, but usually there is no pretence of dramatic illusion, and as it is often convenient to allude to things which no human being could know the speaker is sometimes a god, in the *Hecuba* a ghost. In the *Troades* an opening dialogue between two offended deities casts a sinister shadow over the victorious Greeks who before long will be reduced to the level of their victims. Had printed programmes been available Euripides would doubtless have begun his plays at the beginning of the action.

No less than eleven of the plays end with the appearance of a deity generally, if not always, introduced aloft by means of the *mechane* or crane. But the purpose is not the proverbial one of cutting a knot which the dramatist is unable to untie, except in the single case of the *Orestes*. Indeed in the *Iphigeneia in Tauris* a tempest is invented purely to give an occasion for Athena to intervene. Usually the divinity does no more than tidy up by announcing the future destinies of the characters; this is sometimes combined with the establishment of some still-existing cult. In the three plays which end with the epiphany of Athena there is a local or patriotic interest. In addition we must suppose that the operation of the *mechane* supplied an element of spectacle. Only in the *Hippolytus* and the *Bacchae* is the deity an integral part of the play as representing a force which has been dominant in the action, and to some extent in the *Electra* where the Dioscuri condemn Apollo's oracle which commanded the matricide. In two plays, *Medea* and *Hecuba*, one of the characters is allowed suddenly to develop prophetic powers in order to perform the function usually allotted to the 'god from the machine', which suggests that these deities are to be regarded as a dramatic convenience providing in addition a little incidental spectacle and not, in general, as evidence for Euripides' religious beliefs. Iris in the second prologue of *Hercules Furens* (822–42) and Athena at the end of the *Ion* are a partial exception to this, since they speak for other deities, Hera and Apollo, who dominate from a distance their respective plays.

**10.** Euripides' usual style is less elevated and magnificent than Sophocles'. The discrepancy increases in the later plays as the rhythm of the iambics grows more irregular with the frequent use of resolved feet, particularly of two or more in a single line, and with the freer division of the line between speakers. Aristophanes was fond of describing it by the term λαλιά 'chatter' and by contemptuous diminutives (*Ran.* 91, 954; *Ach.* 398, 447). Aristotle put it more sympathetically (*Rhet.* 3. 2. 5), 'Art is cleverly concealed when a speaker puts together words chosen from the language of ordinary speech, as Euripides does, who was the first to show the way', cf. [Longinus] 40. 3. This is not universally true. Euripides uses at times highly ornamental language, and Aristotle (*Poet.* 22. 7) quotes a case where he adds distinction to a line of Aeschylus by substituting θοινᾶται for the more pedestrian ἐσθίει. It is difficult to find sure examples of colloquial usage, for the tone of tragic language could be varied only within narrow limits. In his Messengers' speeches especially he achieves extraordinary vividness. In the *Hercules Furens* and all plays probably subsequent, except the *Electra*, there is a growing tendency to use trochaic tetrameters in place of iambics for the more animate passages.

**11.** Aristotle stated (*Poet.* 18. 1456ᵃ25) that the Chorus ought to take an active part as in Sophocles, not as in Euripides. In fact the use of the Chorus in Euripides' earlier plays is not strikingly different from that of Sophocles, and even in two late plays (*IT* 1284 ff., *Ion* 747 ff.) they make a notable intervention in the action. But it is true that they tend to become detached spectators and even in the *Bacchae*, where their expression of the beauty and terror of Dionysiac worship is a vital part of the play, they are ignored by the actors whenever more than one is present on stage. But the most marked change in the character of the Chorus, which is manifest in the *Troades* and subsequent plays, is due to innovations in the music (*see* MUSIC, § 10; Pickard-Cambridge–Webster, *Dithyramb²* 38 ff.). The old principle of one syllable to one note was abandoned and, to a considerable extent, the strophic system; in consequence greater skill was required in performance and there was new scope for professional virtuosity, cf. Arist. *Pr.* 19. 15. A papyrus fragment of the *Orestes* with musical notation (Turner, *JHS* 1956, 95) shows ὡς sung to two notes, and εἰειειει-λίσσετε in Aristophanes' parody (*Ran.* 1314) refers to the same point. In many of Euripides' later odes we find a structureless cascade of words with much excited repetition; the music is clearly taking charge. It is easy to believe that Euripides encouraged the great innovator Timotheus and wrote for him the prelude to his *Persae* (Plut. *Mor.* 795 d, Satyr. *Vit. Eur.* 39). It is said also that Cephisophon helped Euripides with the composition of

his music (Ar. *Ran.* 944, fr. 580). This new emotional music was particularly suitable for monodies, solo performances which were sometimes ornamental, e.g. *Ion* 82–183, but sometimes replaced an iambic speech at a dramatic climax, e.g. Creusa's startling outburst (*Ion* 859–922). The extreme case is the use of a monody in place of a Messenger's speech (*Orest.* 1369–1502). In the absence of the music, whatever it might mean to us, these often diffuse and vacuous lyrics mark a change for the worse, but there is the occasional triumphant success when it seems that Euripides has widened the existing range of human sensibility as when Ion celebrates the glory of a summer morning at Delphi (*Ion* 82–111) or the Chorus of the (*Phaethon*) describes how the world goes about its business at the rising of the sun (*Supp. Eur.* 70).

**12.** After his death Euripides became the most admired of the tragic poets and his plays were often revived. Tragedy carried his rhetorical tendencies still further; but his influence was exerted mainly on comedy, perhaps on Middle Comedy in plays of intrigue like Aristophanes' *Cocalus*, certainly on New Comedy with its *bourgeois* loves: 'peripeteiai, violations of maidens, substitution of children, recognitions by means of rings and necklaces, these are the very stuff of New Comedy, and it was Euripides who developed them' (Satyr. *Vit. Eur.* col. 7).

LIFE AND WORKS. G. Murray, *Euripides and his Age²* (1946); G. M. A. Grube, *The Drama of Euripides* (1961); M. Pohlenz, *Die griechische Tragödie²* (1954); A. Lesky, *Die tragische Dichtung der Hellenen²* (1964) (with bibl. of recent work); P. Decharme, *Euripide et l'esprit de son théâtre* (1893, E.T. by J. Loeb, 1905); W. Nestle, *Euripides, der Dichter der griechischen Aufklärung* (1901); A. Rivier, *Essai sur le tragique d'Euripide* (1944); W. Zürcher, *Die Darstellung des Menschen im Drama des Euripides* (1947); G. Zuntz, *The Politica Plays of Euripides* (1963); L. Séchan, *Études sur la tragédie grecque dans ses rapports avec la céramique* (1926); H. D. F. Kitto, *Greek Tragedy³* (1961); D. W. Lucas, *The Greek Tragic Poets²* (1959). Entretiens Hardt vi (1958); T. B. L. Webster, *The Tragedies of Euripides* (1968).

TEXT. G. Murray, O.C.T. (1901–13); with French Tr., L. Méridier, H. Grégoire, L. Parmentier, and F. Chapoutier (Budé, 1923– , 6 vols. published); H. von Arnim, *Supplementum Euripideum* (1913, including Satyrus' *Bios*); most of the longer papyrus fragments in Page, *GLP* i. 54 ff.; *POxy.* 27 (1962); *TGF* 361–716.

COMMENTARIES. F. A. Paley (3 vols., 1872–80²); *Alcestis*, A. M. Dale (1954); *Bacchae*, E. R. Dodds (1960²); R. P. Winnington-Ingram, *Euripides and Dionysus* (1948); *Electra*, J. D. Denniston (1939); *Helena*, A. C. Pearson (1903), A. Y. Campbell (1950); A. M. Dale (1966); *Hercules Furens*, U. von Wilamowitz-Moellendorff (1895²); *Hippolytus*, W. S. Barrett (1964); *Ion*, U. von Wilamowitz-Moellendorff (1926), A. S. Owen (1939); *Iphigeneia in Aulis*, E. B. England (1891); *Iphigeneia in Tauris*, M. Platnauer (1938); *Medea*, D. L. Page (1938); *Orestes*, N. Wedd (1895); *Phoenissae*, A. C. Pearson (1909). Incomplete plays, *Hypsipyle*, G. W. Bond (1963); *Telephus*, E. W. Handley and J. Rea (1957); *Cretes*, R. Cantarella (1964); *Alexander*, Br. Snell, *Hermes Einzelschrift* v (1937). See also Pickard-Cambridge in Powell and Barber, *New Chapters* iii. 105 ff.. On text and transmission U. von Wilamowitz-Moellendorff, *Analecta Euripidea* (1875), A. Turyn, *The Byzantine Manuscript Tradition of the Trag. of Eur.* (1957); G. Zuntz, *An Inquiry into the Transmission of the Plays of Euripides* (1966).

TRANSLATIONS. R. Lattimore and D. Grene, *The Complete Greek Tragedies* (Euripides in 2 vols. 1959).

CONCORDANCE. Allen and Italie (1954).

SCHOLIA. Ed. E. Schwartz (1887–91). D. W. L.

**EUROPA** (Εὐρώπη), in mythology, daughter of Agenor king of Tyre (cf. CADMUS), or of Phoenix (Φοῖνιξ, 'the Phoenician', *Il.* 14. 321): i.e. her father, originally nameless, is later given an appropriate name 'the proud one', first in Herodotus (4. 147. 5). Zeus loved her, and so turned himself into, or sent, a beautiful bull, which swam to the sea-shore where she was playing and enticed her by its mildness to climb on its back. Once there, she was carried away to sea, and landed in Crete. There she bore Zeus two or three children, Minos, Rhadamanthys, and, in post-Homeric accounts, Sarpedon (in other words, the later forms of the legend reflect a belief, true or false, of a connexion between Crete and Lycia; Apollod. 3. 2 ff.). For their subsequent adventures, see under their names. She was then married to Asterius, king of Crete, who adopted her sons. Zeus gave her the bronze man Talōs (Ap. Rhod. 4. 1643; cf. ARGONAUTS, TALOS) to guard the island, a hound which never missed its quarry ([Eratosthenes] 33; cf. AMPHITRYON), and a javelin which never missed its mark (ibid., cf. Ov. *Met.* 7. 681 ff.). These passed afterwards to Minos, thence to Procris (q.v.) for curing a disease which afflicted him, and so to her husband Cephalus. After her death Europa was worshipped as a goddess, her festival being the Hellotia (Nilsson, *Griechische Feste*, 95), i.e. she was popularly identified with some Cretan goddess. For a Cretan myth resembling hers, see Nilsson, *Minoan-Mycenaean Religion*[2] (1950), 480 f. Also the fayence plaque from Dendra showing a woman seated on a bull has usually been accepted as evidence for some form of this myth in Mycenaean times (see Nilsson, *GGR* i[2]. 356). The bull became the constellation Taurus ([Eratosth.] 14).                                                          H. J. R.

**EUROPE.** The name Εὐρώπη originally stood for central Greece (*Hymn. Hom. Ap.* 250; 290). It was soon extended to the whole Greek mainland and by 500 B.C. to the entire land-mass behind it. The boundary between the European continent and Asia was usually fixed at the river Don. Homer vaguely knew dark regions of the west and north, but his range of information hardly extended north of Greece or west of Sicily.

The Mediterranean seaboard of Europe was chiefly opened up by the Greeks between 800 and 500 B.C. (*see* COLONIZATION, GREEK). The Atlantic coasts and 'Tin Islands' were discovered by the Phoenicians (*see* CASSITERIDES); Pytheas (q.v.) circumnavigated Britain and followed the mainland coast at least to Heligoland. The Baltic Sea was probably not entered by Greek or Roman ships; Scandinavia was almost wholly unknown until quite late during the Roman Empire after the invasions by the Goths; and Thule (q.v.) remained a land of mystery.

The prehistoric amber (q.v.) routes across Europe from Jutland and the Baltic were unknown to later explorers. The Greeks penetrated by way of the Russian rivers as far as Kieff or perhaps Smolensk; central and north Russia remained to them a land of mythical peoples and of the fabulous Rhipaean Mts. (q.v.); north of the Balkans they located the equally mythical Hyperboreans (q.v.). Greek pioneers ascended the Danube to the Iron Gates, and the Rhône perhaps to Lake Leman. But Herodotus had only a hazy notion of central Europe, and the Hellenistic Greeks knew little more (*see* ALPS, HERCYNIAN FOREST).

The land exploration of Europe was chiefly accomplished by the Roman armies. These completed the Carthaginian discovery of Spain; under Caesar they made Gaul known; under Augustus' generals, M. Crassus, Tiberius, and Drusus, they opened up the Balkan lands, the Alpine massif, and the Danube basin (*see* DANUVIUS). Roman traders rediscovered the amber route from Vienna to the Baltic, and Trajan revealed the Carpathian lands by conquest (*see* DACIA). Tiberius and Drusus also overran west Germany to the Elbe, but central Germany remained little known outside Europe.

Cary-Warmington, *Explorers* 12 ff.; 108 ff.; 229 ff.; (Pelican) 21 ff.; 132 ff. Cary, *Geographic Background* 231 ff.; M. Ninck, *Die Entdeckung von Europa durch die Griechen* (1945). A. Schoening, *Germanien in d. Geog. des Ptolemaeus* (1962); G. Schuette in *Classica et Mediaevalia* 1951, 236 ff.; O. Brogan, *JRS* 1935, 195 ff.; H. J. Eggers, 'Der römische Import im freien Germanien', *Atlas der Urgeschichte* i (1951); H. C. Broholm, *Danmark og Romerriget* (1952); R. E. M. Wheeler, *Rome beyond the Imperial Frontiers* (1955), 21 ff.
                                                                        E. H. W.

**EUROPUS** (*Dura*) on the middle Euphrates, founded as a Seleucid military colony *c.* 300 B.C. At first mainly Greek in character, it became gradually orientalized; the Arsacids refortified the city, and under Parthian rule it thrived by commerce and agriculture. Occupied by the Romans in A.D. 165, it became a strongly garrisoned fortress on the Euphrates *limes*, but its prosperity rapidly declined. It was besieged and destroyed by the Sassanids *c.* A.D. 257.

The importance of Europus is mainly archaeological. Excavation of the material remains has added considerably to our knowledge of life and culture in Mesopotamia under Hellenistic, Parthian, and Roman rule. The discoveries include well-preserved architectural remains, temples of Greek and Oriental gods, a Christian church and a synagogue, public and private secular buildings, and a Roman camp; frescoes and reliefs of great value for the history of art and religion; military equipment; inscriptions, parchments, and papyri including fragments of a Seleucid code, numerous Greek contracts, and important Roman military archives.

F. Cumont, *Les Fouilles de Doura-Europos 1922–3* (1926); J. Johnson, *Dura Studies* (U.S.A. 1932); M. Rostovtzeff and collaborators, *Excavations at Dura-Europos, Preliminary Reports* (from 1929) and *Final Reports* of which those already published include parts of vol. iv (Pottery, Textiles, Lamps, Bronzes, etc.), v. i (Parchments and Papyri ed. Welles, etc.), vi (Coins, ed. Bellinger) and viii. i (The Synagogue, ed. Kraeling, etc.); M. Rostovtzeff, *Dura-Europus and its Art* (1938); C. B. Welles, 'The Population of Roman Dura', *Studies . . . in honour of A. C. Johnson* (1951).
                                                                M. S. D.; E. W. G.

**EURYBIADES,** a Spartan nobleman, was the first recorded admiral of the Peloponnesian League (481–480 B.C.). Despite the smallness of Sparta's contingent (10 ships at Artemisium, 16 at Salamis), he held chief command over the allied Greek fleet against Xerxes. He gave general support to Themistocles (a ridiculous story alleges that he was bribed at Artemisium), but opposed his scheme to cut off Xerxes' retreat after Salamis by breaking the bridges over the Hellespont. A statue seems to have been erected in his honour at Sparta.

G. B. Grundy, *Great Persian War* (1901), 543 ff.; C. Guratzsch, *Klio* 1925, 62 ff.                                                      P. T.

**EURYCLEIA,** Odysseus' nurse, a woman of good family bought by Laertes (*Od.* 1. 429 ff.). She recognizes Odysseus (19. 392 ff.); keeps the maids in their quarters while the Wooers are killed (21. 380 ff.).

**EURYCLES,** GAIUS JULIUS, son of Lachares of Sparta, who was executed by Antony for piracy, fought at Actium on the side of Octavian, who rewarded him with the Roman citizenship and allowed him to become ruler of Sparta. He exercised a sort of tyranny, and his influence extended over the Eleutherolaconian towns (*see* LACONIA) and elsewhere. Cythera (q.v.), which Augustus handed over to Sparta in 21, became his personal possession. Towards 7 B.C. he visited the court of Herod (q.v. 1) and Archelaus (*see* CAPPADOCIA), making mischief at the former; on his return to Greece he was the cause of widespread disturbances which led to his being accused twice before Augustus and banished, perhaps before 2 B.C. He seems to have died soon after this. Under the more discreet rule of his son Laco his memory was rehabilitated and games called Eurycleia were established and long maintained at Sparta.

G. W. Bowersock, *JRS* 1961, 112 ff.                          A. M.; T. J. C.

**EURYDICE** (1) (Εὐρυδίκη, 'wide-judging', i.e. 'princess', a stopgap name like Creusa, q.v. 1), name of a dozen mythological characters, the best known being Orpheus' wife (cf. ORPHEUS). Pursued by Aristaeus (q.v. 1), she was fatally bitten by a snake. Orpheus then descended to Hades and so charmed the infernal powers by his playing that he was permitted to bring her to the upper world again if he did not look back at her on the way. Breaking this taboo, he lost her. See especially Verg. *G.* 4. 454 ff., and for the distribution of the story, Stith Thompson, F 81. 1.                                                          H. J. R.

EURYDICE (2), originally called *Adea* (*c.* 337–317 B.C.), daughter of Amyntas (nephew of Philip II of Macedon) and Cynane (daughter of Philip II and the Illyrian Audata), was betrothed to the feeble-minded Philip (q.v. 2) Arrhidaeus before 323 when he succeeded to Alexander's throne (jointly with Alexander's infant son). Her royal blood endeared her to the Macedonian soldiers, whose protection enabled her to marry Philip Arrhidaeus (322), make trouble for the regent Antipater (321), depose his successor Polyperchon from the regency, and try to rule Macedonia, using Cassander as her minister, and excluding Alexander's son from the succession (317). Her undoing was Olympias, against whom the Macedonians would not fight. Philip and Eurydice became her prisoners, and after Philip's murder Eurydice obeyed an order to commit suicide. In an age of violence her blood, brains, and courage were not enough.

G. H. Macurdy, *Hellenistic Queens* (1932), 40 ff., 48 ff.
G. T. G.

EURYMEDON (now *Köprüçayi* or *Pazarçayi*), one of the principal rivers of the south coast of Asia Minor. Rising in the Pisidian mountains it flows southwards for something over 100 miles into the Mare Lycium. Eight miles from its mouth is the city of Aspendus, and further up the ruins of Selge stand high above its right bank. It was reckoned navigable in antiquity at least as far as Aspendus. At the mouth of the Eurymedon in or about 467 B.C. the Athenian Cimon gained a double victory over the Persian forces by sea and then by land; a well-known epigram attributed to Simonides perhaps celebrates this victory (fr. 142 Bergk). G. E. B.

EURYPONTIDS (Εὐρυπωντίδαι) was the name of the junior royal house at Sparta. The most notable Eurypontid kings were Agesilaus, Agis II and IV, Archidamus II, and Leotychides (qq.v.). *See also* AGIADS.

EURYPYLUS, in mythology, (1) son of Euhaemon; leads a contingent to Troy (*Il.* 2. 736); takes part in several battle-scenes and is wounded; tended by Patroclus (11. 809 ff.). According to the local legend of Patrae (Paus. 7. 19. 6 ff.), after the war he looked into a chest which contained an image of Dionysus made by Hephaestus, and went mad. He was promised at Delphi a cure when he found a 'foreign sacrifice'. Coming to Patrae, he found human sacrifice practised there, which, according also to Delphi, was to stop when a foreign king brought a foreign god. Both oracles were thus fulfilled and the cult of Dionysus established there under the title of Aesymnetes (see J. Herbillon, *Les Cultes de Patras*, 1929) Some, however, made this Eurypylus son of Dexamenus. (2) Son of Telephus (q.v. 1) and Astyoche sister of Priam (q.v.). (3) Son of Poseidon, a Triton, who meets the Argonauts and gives one of them, Euphemus, a lump of earth as pledge of possession of part of Africa (Cyrene) (Pind. *Pyth.* 4. 20 ff., Ap. Rhod. 4. 1551 ff.). H. J. R.

EURYTION, in mythology, (1) Geryon's herdsman, *see* HERACLES. (2) A centaur (*Od.* 21. 295 ff.); getting drunk and misbehaving at Peirithous' wedding-feast, he began the quarrel between centaurs and men. (3) Brother of Pandarus (q.v.; Verg. *Aen.* 5. 495 ff.). (4) *See* PELEUS.

EUSEBIUS of Caesarea (*c.* A.D. 260–340). Born in Palestine, Eusebius was trained in the tradition of Alexandrian Christian scholarship by Pamphilius, who died as a martyr in 310 during the Diocletianic persecution. Eusebius himself escaped. He became bishop of Caesarea (*c.* 314) and was a moderate supporter of Arius (*c.* 320). At the Council of Nicaea he was exonerated from the charge of heresy, vainly tried mediation, and ultimately signed the Nicene creed. He attended the council of Tyre in 335 which condemned Athanasius. He was in close touch with Constantine in whose honour he delivered an oration in 335 for the *tricennalia*. After Constantine's death he wrote a life—or rather a panegyric —of the Emperor, the authenticity of which has been disputed by some modern scholars. Diocletian's persecution and the transformation of the Roman Empire into a Christian kingdom by Constantine were the main sources of inspiration for Eusebius' historical and theological thought. He repudiated chiliastic expectations and had little sympathy for asceticism. He tried to demonstrate the superiority of the Bible over pagan philosophy and history, but showed himself well acquainted with the ways of Greek thought (as one would expect from an admirer of Origen) and attributed importance to pagan achievements as a preparation for Christianity. The coincidence of the *Pax Augusta* with the emergence of Christianity was to him providential. He used Hellenistic theories to justify Christian monarchy but went beyond them in regarding Constantine as the inheritor of the promise to Abraham. His *Praeparatio Evangelica* (after 312?) and the later *Theophania* (extant in a Syriac translation and in Greek fragments) are attacks against Greek philosophy in which it is argued that at its best (especially Plato) Greek philosophy coincided with or derived from biblical doctrine. The *Demonstratio Evangelica* (of which little more than the first half is preserved) argues for the fulfilment of Hebrew prophecy in Christ. Commentaries on the Bible—of which those on Isaiah, the Psalms, Luke are partly extant in excerpts—buttressed the same interpretation.

In the line of the great Christian chronographers, Eusebius organized universal history in a brief chronicle accompanied by careful chronological tables from the time of Abraham's birth. The Greek original is lost, but an Armenian version, a Latin adaptation by St. Jerome (q.v.), and various Greek derivations have come down to us. Perhaps the most important work by Eusebius is the *Ecclesiastical History* from its origins. It has probably no precedent, though Eusebius was influenced by Flavius Josephus, the Acts of the martyrs, the biographies of Greek philosophers, and in general by the methods of Hellenistic erudition. The work in its present form ends with A.D. 324, but there were earlier editions. It is uncertain when it was published for the first time: 303 and 312 are possible dates. It was enlarged in successive editions to describe the reversal of the situation after the great Persecution and the triumph of the Church. Eusebius devoted a special pamphlet to the martyrs of Palestine (an enlarged version of which is preserved in the Syriac translation) and he wrote an attack *Against Hierocles* on the subject of the comparison between Christ and Apollonius of Tyana. His *Ecclesiastical History* was a model for all the later ecclesiastical histories, which imitated his characteristic method of quoting authorities and documents. Rufinus (q.v. 2) translated it into Latin and continued it up to A.D. 395.

All the works in Migne, *PG* xix–xxiv; most of them in better editions in the Berlin series of *Griechische Christliche Schriftsteller* (the ed. of the *Eccl. Hist.* by Ed. Schwartz, 1903–9, is one of the masterpieces of classical scholarship: it is accompanied by Th. Mommsen's ed. of Rufinus' translation). The *Eccl. Hist.* available in Greek and Engl. transl. in the Loeb series (K. Lake and J. E. L. Oulton, 1926–32). The commentary of the *Eccl. Hist.* by H. Valesius (1659) is still useful. The *Chronica* in the editions by A. Schoene (1866–75) and J. Karst (1911), who does not entirely replace Schoene. Text, Engl. transl., and comm. of *Praep. Evang.* by E. H. Gifford (1903). Engl. transl. of *Dem. Evang.* by W. J. Ferrar (1920). Engl. transl. of the life of Constantine and of the tricennalian speech by E. C. Richardson in *Library of Nicene and Post-Nicene Fathers* i (1895). Text and Engl. transl. of the *Contra Hieroclem* in the Loeb series (F. C. Conybeare, 1912). E. Schwartz, *PW* vi (1907), 1370; H. Berkhof, *Die Theologie des Eusebius von C.* (1939); id. *Kirche und Kaiser* (1947); D. S. Wallace-Hadrill, *Eusebius of C.* (1960), with bibl., to be supplemented by the most recent ed. of B. Altaner, *Patrologie*; J. Moreau, *Dict. Hist. Géogr. Eccles.* 15 (1963), 1437. For Eusebius as a historian R. Laqueur, *Eusebius als Historiker seiner Zeit* (1929); J. Sirinelli, *Les Vues historiques d'Eusèbe de Césarée durant la période prénicéenne* (1961); A. Momigliano, *The Conflict between Paganism and Christianity in the IV cent.* (1963), 89 ff.; cf. also H. Zimmermann, 'Ecclesia als Objekt der Historiographie', *Sitz. Oesterr. Ak.* 235, 4 (1960). Among the recent studies on the life of Constantine cf. F. Vittinghoff, *Rh. Mus.*1953, 330 ff.; F. Scheidweiler, *Byz. Zeitschrift* 1956, 1 ff.; J. Moreau, *Hist.* 1955, 234 ff.; F. Winkelmann, *Die Textbezeugung der Vita C.* (1962); id. *Byz. Beiträge*, 1964, 91 ff.                                                    A. M.

**EUSTATHIUS** (12th c. A.D.), born and educated at Constantinople, was deacon at St. Sophia and taught rhetoric in the Patriarchal School until in 1174/5 he became Metropolitan of Thessalonica, in which position he continued till his death (*c.* 1194). His works of classical scholarship were written before 1175. Henceforward he devoted himself to the practical duties of his spiritual office and to combating the prevailing corruption of monastic life.

WORKS. (1) Classical. *Commentary on Pindar*, of which only the introduction survives; this gives information about lyric poetry (especially Pindar's) and Pindar's life, and shorter notes on the Olympian games and the pentathlon. The *Paraphrase of Dionysius Periegetes* has discursive scholia, valuable for citations from earlier geographers, historians, the complete Stephanus Byz., and the lost works of Arrian. The *Commentaries on Homer's Iliad and Odyssey* (Παρεκβολαὶ εἰς τὴν Ὁμήρου Ἰλιάδα [Ὀδύσσειαν]) are a vast compilation, in which the *Iliad* commentary is twice as long as that on the *Odyssey*. They are evidently based on Eustathius' lectures. Prefaces deal with the differences between the poems and with the cultural importance of Homer. The notes discuss chiefly questions of language, mythology (interpreted allegorically), history, and geography. Their value consists particularly in the assemblage of material drawn from the old scholia and the lost writings of earlier scholars and lexicographers. His quotations from classical authors are taken mostly at second hand. He often illustrates a point by reference to the customs and observances of his own time.

(2) His other works include a history of the conquest of Thessalonica by the Normans; several polemics, e.g. the famous treatise *Inquiry into Monastic Life*; letters to the Emperor, church dignitaries, and others; speeches and addresses, homilies and tracts, some of which have historical value. Eustathius was the outstanding scholar and orator of his time, enthusiastic for the traditional learning, for the preservation of books, for sound principles of education, and for the moral reawakening of monasticism. He is regarded as a saint by the Orthodox Church, and portrayed in a fresco of *c.* 1320 in the church of the Virgin in Gračanica.

*Commentaria ad Iliadem et Odysseam*, G. Stallbaum (1825–30); T. L. F. Tafel, *Eustathii Metropolitae Thessalonicensis opuscula* (1832); Migne, *PG* cxxxv, cxxxvi; A. B. Drachmann, *Scholia Vetera in Pindari Carmina* iii (1927); C. Müller, *Geogr. graeci minores* ii (1861); S. Kyriakides, *Eustazio di Tessalonica. La espugnazione di Tessalonica* (1961); T. Hedberg, *E. als Attizist* (1935); Ph. Kukules, Θεσσαλονίκης Εὐσταθίου τὰ λαογραφικά, 2 vols. (1950). P. Wirth *Untersuch. zur byzantinischen Rhetorik mit bes. Berucksichtigung der Schriften des Eustathios* (Diss. Munich 1960).      J. F. L.; R. B.

**EUSTOCHIUS** of Alexandria, physician, became a pupil of Plotinus in Plotinus' old age (Porph. *Plot.* 7) (prob. *c.* A.D. 265), and is said to have edited his master's works.

**EUTHYCLES,** writer of (?) Old Comedy (Ath. 3. 124 b). We possess but two titles, Ἄσωτοι ἢ Ἐπιστολή and Ἀταλάντη, the first of which looks more like Middle than Old Comedy.

*FCG* ii. 890; *CAF* i. 805.

**EUTHYDEMUS** (1) of Chios, Sophist, an older contemporary of Socrates. In the *Euthydemus* Plato presents him as a ridiculous figure. He has sometimes been thought to be unhistorical and merely a mask for Plato's criticism of Antisthenes. His historicity is proved by independent references by Aristotle; but Plato may have used him quite freely for the purpose of pillorying eristic views and arguments.                                    W. D. R.

**EUTHYDEMUS** (2) I, originally from Magnesia ad Sipylum (*c.* 235–200 B.C.), probably a satrap of Diodotus II (q.v.), killed him and became king of Bactria-Sogdiana. He consolidated Bactria into a strong state. In 208 B.C. he was attacked by Antiochus III, who failed to subdue him. His kingdom included also Aria and Margiana. His coins are found in large numbers. On his gold and silver money his portrait occurs on the obverse and Heracles-seated-on-rock on the reverse. Some of his portraits are masterpieces of art.

A. K. Narain, *The Indo-Greeks* (1957).      A. K. N.

**EUTHYDEMUS** (3) II, (*c.* 200–190 B.C.), belonging to the family of Euthydemus I and Demetrius I, distinguished from his first namesake by his coins with Heracles-standing type, was probably a sub-king. He is one of the three Indo-Greeks who issued nickel coins.

A. K. Narain, *The Indo-Greeks* (1957).      A. K. N.

**EUTHYMIDES** (end of 6th c. B.C.), vase-painter in Athens, known from seven signatures on large red-figure vases, including Arming of Hector (Munich). He breaks with archaic conventions; his heavy figures show new studies of movement.

Beazley, *ARV*² 26.      T. B. L. W.

**EUTHYMUS.** Temesa in south Italy was haunted by the ghost of Polites (q.v.), a companion of Odysseus, whom the inhabitants had killed for raping a girl. It could be kept quiet only by giving it the prettiest girl in Temesa every year. One year, when the sacrifice was to be made, Euthymus, a notable boxer, said to be son of the river Caecinus, arrived, pitied and then loved the girl, encountered the ghost, and drove it off for ever (Paus. 6. 6. 4–11).

Nilsson, *GGR* i². 183.      H. J. R.

**EUTHYNA,** the examination of accounts which every officer of the State underwent on expiry of his office, at Athens and generally elsewhere. It was primarily an examination into the handling of public money, by ten *logistai* (q.v.) at Athens. If the *logistai* were not satisfied, or if some qualified citizen brought a charge against a magistrate, they must bring the matter before a dicastery and preside at the trial. Even after discharge the magistrate was not entirely free; for thirty days after, ten *euthynoi*, chosen by lot by the *boule* from its own number, were prepared to examine any complaint, on a public or private matter, against an outgoing magistrate, and, if it was sound, brought it before a dicastery.

In democratic states the *euthyna*, though in the vast majority of cases a formality, was the most effective means for the control of the executive; and it put a powerful weapon into the hands of the sycophants (*see* SYKOPHANTAI).

Arist. *Ath. Pol.* ch. 48.      A. W. G.

**EUTROPIUS** (1), the historian, who took part in Julian's Persian campaign (A.D. 363) and was *magister memoriae* of Valens, published a survey of Roman history (*Breviarium ab urbe condita*) in ten books. Beginning with Romulus, he reached the Sullan Civil War in book 5,

Caesar's death in book 6, and covered the Empire to Jovian's death (A.D. 364) in books 7-10. The subject-matter for the Republic is based upon the Epitome of Livy, for the Empire upon the end of the Epitome, an expanded adaptation of Suetonius, and an 'Imperial History', closing with personal knowledge of events. The work is short, but well balanced, showing good judgement and impartiality. It was translated into Greek by Paenius about 380, adapted into Greek by Capito of Lycia, and used by Hieronymus (Jerome), Orosius, Isidore, and Paulus Diaconus.

EDITIONS. H. Droysen (ed. minor 1878; ed. maior 1879); C. Wagener (1884); F. Rühl (1887). W. Pirogoff, *De Eutropii breviarii A.U.C. indole ac fontibus* (1873); M. Galdi, *L'epitome nella lett. latina* (1922); A. Momigliano, *Conflict between Paganism and Christianity in the fourth century* (1963), 86. A. H. McD.

**EUTROPIUS** (2), minister of the Emperor Arcadius (q.v. 2) and a eunuch, he was the most influential man in the East from A.D. 395 to 399, when he became consul, the first eunuch to hold the office. In that year his political rivals overthrew him and banished him to Cyprus. The poet Claudian wrote vigorously against him. E. A. T.

**EUTYCHES** (6th c. A.D.), author of an *Ars de verbo* in two books (ed. Keil, *Gramm. Lat.* v. 447-89) and of a treatise *De aspiratione* (now incorporated in the *De orthographia* of Cassiodorus; ed. Keil, *Gramm. Lat.* vii. 199-202).

Schanz–Hosius, § 1116.

**EUTYCHIDES** (early 3rd c. B.C.), sculptor and painter of Sicyon, pupil of Lysippus.
WORKS: (1) Statue of Timosthenes, a boy victor at Olympia. (2) Tyche of Antioch. Tyche seated, supported by the river god Orontes and crowned by Seleucus and Antiochus. Many copies of Tyche and Orontes have survived, the best probably the marble group in the Vatican (Winter, *KB* 340. 1). The bold composition is Lysippan; the drapery has a new realism. The original of a seated girl in the Conservatori (Winter, *KB* 371. 4) is ascribed to Eutychides because of its likeness in composition. (3) Eurotas. A copy has been recognized in a river-god in the Vatican (Winter, *KB* 340. 2). (4) Dionysus, belonging to Asinius Pollio.

Overbeck, 1516; 1530-6; Lippold, *Griech. Plastik* 296; Bieber, *Sculpt. Hellenist. Age* 40; T. Dohrn, *Die Tyche von Antiocheia* (1963). T. B. L. W.

**EUTYCHIUS PROCULUS** (2nd c. A.D.), from Sicca, a teacher of Marcus Aurelius and author of (lost) grammatical works.

Cf. Schanz–Hosius, § 606. 7.

**EUXENIDES,** mentioned by the *Suda* as an Athenian writer of comedy contemporaneous with Epicharmus.

**EUXINE SEA** was the Greek name for the Black Sea. The name is euphemistic, and some authors (Pindar, Euripides) call it Ἄξεινος. This sea apparently remained closed to traffic from the Aegean in prehistoric times, and the details of the Argonaut story may have been added at quite a late date. The Euxine was opened up in the seventh century by Milesians and other Ionian Greeks; by 600 it had become ringed with Greek settlements (*see* COLONIZATION, GREEK), and it remained a Greek lake until the Middle Ages. The earliest surviving description of the Euxine Sea is by Herodotus, who had personal knowledge of its northern coasts and gave a fairly accurate account of it, though he greatly overestimated its length. A more detailed description of the south coast is contained in the geographical work attributed to Scylax (*c*. 340 B.C.). An excellent survey of the whole coast was written by Arrian in the days of Hadrian; a later 'Periplus of the Euxine Sea' is an extract from this work and from other Greek geographies.

Herodotus, bk. 4, esp. chs. 85-86; Scylax, chs. 67-92; Arrian, *Periplus Maris Euxini*; Ps.-Arrian, with same title. The last three works in *GGM* i. M. C.

**EVADNE** (Εὐάδνη), in mythology, (1) a daughter of Poseidon, who became by Apollo mother of Iamus, ancestor of the prophetic clan of the Iamidae in Olympia (Pind. *Ol.* 6. 29 ff., see Wilamowitz, *Isyllos*, 178). (2) Daughter of Iphis and wife of Capaneus, one of the Seven against Thebes. She burned herself on his funeral pyre (Eur. *Supp.* 980 ff.). H. J. R.

**EVAGORAS** (Εὐαγόρας, *c*. 435-374/3 B.C.), a member of the Teucrid house, the traditional rulers of Cyprian Salamis. Exiled during his youth, which fell in a period of Phoenician domination, he gathered some fifty followers at Soli in Cilicia, and with their aid established himself as ruler of Salamis in 411. His subsequent policy aimed at strengthening Hellenism in Cyprus by co-operation with Athens, and his court became a centre for Athenian *émigrés*, of whom Conon was the most distinguished. A clash with Persia was ultimately inevitable, but he postponed the issue by assisting in the revival of Persian sea-power culminating in the triumph of Cnidos. War finally came in 390 and dragged on for ten years. In alliance with Akoris of Egypt, Evagoras at first more than held his own. He not only extended his rule over the central cities of Cilicia, but also captured Tyre and dominated Phoenicia. In 382 Persia mobilized an overwhelming armament. Evagoras lost control of the sea at Citium in 381, and was forced to sue for peace, obtaining not unfavourable terms through dissensions among the Persian commanders. In 374 he was assassinated in a palace intrigue.

K. Spyridakis, *Evagoras I von Salamis* (1935). D. E. W. W.

**EVAGRIUS SCHOLASTICUS,** *c*. A.D. 536-*c*. 600, wrote a Church History from 431 to 594, which is the only continuous narrative of the period. Credulous but honest, he used good sources, both ecclesiastical and secular.

Ed. J. Bidez and L. Parmentier (1898). H. C.

**EVANDER** (Εὔανδρος), in Greece a minor god or daemon, belonging to the circle of Pan and worshipped in Arcadia, especially at Palantion, where he had a temple; in Italy connected with the worship of Faunus (identified with Pan) and regarded as the first settler at Rome. According to tradition he was the son of Hermes and of a nymph, daughter of the river-god Ladon, known as Themis and identified in Italy with the prophetic goddess Carmenta (or Carmentis). Through Atlas, grandfather of Hermes, he was connected with the Trojan Dardanus (Verg. *Aen.* 8. 134-7). A more human genealogy made him the son of Echemos of Tegea, whose grandfather was Pallas (q.v. 2). As a boy he is said to have welcomed Priam and Anchises in Arcadia and conducted them to the city of Pheneos (*Aen.* 8. 165). He left Arcadia owing either to the hostility of Argos or to a famine, and reaching Italy landed on the left bank of the Tiber and made a settlement on the neighbouring hill, which he called after his native city (or his grandfather) Pallanteum (*Aen.* 8. 54), afterwards the Collis Palatinus. He instituted there the worship of Faunus (Pan Lycaeus) and established the Lupercalia (q.v.; Ov. *Fasti* 2. 279 ff.). According to Virgil, Hercules visited him and slew the monster Cacus, who had stolen his cattle; Evander in memory established the cult of Hercules at the Ara Maxima (*Aen.* 8. 185-275; Livy 1. 7). Aeneas, on the outbreak of war against the Latins, made his way up the Tiber and appealed to Evander for aid. Evander welcomed him as a kinsman, conducted him over the site of the future Rome, and sent back with him his own son Pallas, who was subsequently slain in battle by Turnus (*Aen.* 10). Evander was thus used by the Romans to supply a legendary connexion between Greece and Rome and an aetiological explanation of place-names and cults.　　　　　　　　　　　　C. B.

**EVOCATIO.** Gods, being in a sense the highest class of citizens, are sometimes thought of as conquered when their city is taken(Verg. *Aen.* 1. 68 = 8. 11, 'uictos penatis', sc. of Troy), but more commonly (as Aesch. *Sept.* 218, on which see Groeneboom; Verg. *Aen.* 2. 351 f.) as leaving it. It was therefore not unnatural to hasten the fall of a city by inducing its gods to leave it, especially that god which particularly protected it. This the Romans did by promising the deity a cult in Rome at least as good as the one given by the city in question (Pliny, *HN* 28. 18). The formula of evocation is given by Macrobius, *Sat.* 3. 9. 7–8. The only instance recorded is the evoking of Juno Regina from Veii (Livy, 5. 21 ff.), if that of Juno from Carthage in 146 B.C. (Servius, *Aen.* 12. 841) be rejected.

Wissowa, *RK* 383 and note 7; W. Warde Fowler, *Rel. Exper.* 206; Latte, *RR* 125; V. Basanoff, *Evocatio* (Paris, 1947).　　　H. J. R.

**EXECIAS** ('Εξηκίας) (third quarter of 6th c. B.C.), potter and vase-painter in Athens, known from eleven signatures (two vases are inscribed 'Execias painted and made'). Painted amphorae, calyx craters, cups, pinakes. Note particularly Achilles and Ajax dicing (Vatican), death of Ajax (Boulogne), both excellent compositions showing a psychological insight unique in black-figure.

Beazley, *ABV* 143.　　　　　　　　　　　　T. B. L. W.

**EXEGETES** (ἐξηγητής), an interpreter or expounder, usually of sacred lore. Herodotus (1. 78. 2) gives this title to the college of diviners at the Telmessian oracle in Lycia. The Athenians traditionally considered Apollo Pythius their *exegetes*. From c. 400 B.C., if not earlier, Athens had official *exegetai*, expounders of the *patria*, the sacred and ancestral laws. The evidence about their numbers and functions is unclear and disputed. There were (1) at least one *exegetes* elected by the Demos from the Eupatridae; (2) at least one *exegetes* chosen by the Pythia, called *exegetes Pythochrestos*; (3) at least two *exegetai* of the Eumolpidae, who expounded Eleusinian *sacra*. The Athenian *exegetai* were generally concerned with the unwritten sacred law, but they often pronounced on secular and domestic questions (e.g. duties and obligations) untouched by statutes and of possible religious implications. Other cities too had *exegetai*, official or unofficial.

ANCIENT SOURCES, both literary and epigraphic are conveniently collected in J. H. Oliver, *The Athenian Expounders of the Sacred and Ancestral Law* (1950), 122 ff.
MODERN LITERATURE. Oliver, op. cit.; Ph. Ehrmann, *De juris sacri interpretibus Atticis* (1908); A. Persson, *Die Exegeten und Delphi* (1918); K. von Fritz, *TAPA* 1940, 91 ff.; F. Jacoby, *Atthis* (1949), ch. i; H. Bloch, *AJPhil.* 1953, 407 ff.　　　　　J. E. F.

**EXSILIUM.** A Roman citizen or *peregrinus* being threatened by criminal proceedings on account of a capital crime could—even after their inception—leave Roman territory and escape to that of another State before a capital sentence was pronounced against him. This voluntary self-banishment, called *exsilium* (later the same term was used for indicating the banishment pronounced by a judgement in a criminal trial), was tolerated by the magistrates; in the last century of the Republic, however, it became a legal institution, when magistrates were strictly ordered to allow the condemned person time to escape before executing the capital sentence. Thus *exsilium* became a substitute for the death penalty. Its effect was to prohibit the return of the wrongdoer to Roman territory. After his escape a decree, more administrative than jurisdictional in character, pronounced by the *comitia* or a high magistrate, excluded him from all legal protection and threatened him with death in case of illicit return (*aquae et ignis interdictio*). In later times *exsilium* lost its strict technical meaning, being used not only by historians and orators, but even in some juridical texts (if they are not interpolated) indiscriminately for voluntary and involuntary emigration, for legally prescribed banishment, for escape before and after judgement, and generally for all categories of expulsion, from the mildest form of *relegatio* (q.v.) to the severest one of *deportatio*. Because of these different uses of the word we must consider in each case whether it refers to temporary or perpetual expulsion, whether or not it is followed by loss of citizenship, by confiscation (total or partial) of property, and so on. In its old technical sense *exsilium* was perpetual and general, without any gradation; it resulted in loss of citizenship and of all property. See RELEGATIO.

G. Crifo, *Ricerche sull' 'exilium' nel periodo repubblicano* i (1961); V. de Villa, *Studi Albertario* i (1953).　　　　　　　　　A. B.

**EXSUPERANTIUS** (*PW* 2), IULIUS, in his *opusculum*, preserved in a Sallust MS., describes the Civil War of Marius and Sulla to the death of Sertorius. The dependence upon Sallust (*Jugurtha* and *Histories*) in subject-matter, without understanding of republican institutions or personalities, and in style, without feeling for phraseology, points to the fourth to fifth century A.D., when Sallust was in fashion.

Edited by C. Bursian (1868); G. Landgraf–C. Weyman, *Archiv für lat. Lex.* 1902, 561.　　　　　　　　　　　A. H. McD.

# F

**FABIANUS PAPIRIUS,** a philosopher of the older school (Sen. *Dial.* 10. 10), pupil of the Elder Sextius and of Blandus, taught the Younger Seneca. His declamations are copiously illustrated in Sen. *Controv.* book 2: cf. *praef.* 4–5.

**FABIUS** (1, *PW* 48) **AMBUSTUS,** QUINTUS, was *tribunus militum consulari potestate* in 391 B.C. Another tradition assigned his office to 390 and made him responsible for the Gallic attack on Rome, because when sent as ambassador to Clusium he had treacherously murdered a Gallic chief. Thanks to the authority of his father or to his popularity among the plebeians, he had escaped an

attempted patrician prosecution. This story was no doubt invented as an honourable explanation of the Roman defeat at the Allia. It may, however, be inferred from Livy (6. 1. 6–7) that the Roman military chiefs were actually prosecuted after the Celts had retired, although sudden death or suicide seems to have saved Fabius.

O. Hirschfeld, *Kl. Schr.* (1913), 269 ff.; Ed. Meyer, *Kl. Schr.* ii (1924), 312 ff.　　　　　　　　　　　　　P. T.

**FABIUS** (2, *PW* 44) **AMBUSTUS,** MARCUS, consul 360, 356, and 354 B.C., *princeps senatus* and a patrician leader after the Gallic catastrophe, aimed at re-establishing patrician influence at home and at reasserting the power of Rome over her neighbours. Successful against the Hernici (356 B.C.) and in 354 against the Tiburtini, over whom he triumphed, he was defeated by Tarquinii. As dictator in 351, he failed to prevent the readmission of the plebs to the consulate. The attempts in the traditional account to conceal or ignore his defeat in 354 demonstrate his authority and that of his family.

Beloch, *Röm. Gesch.* 352, 361 ff. P. T.

**FABIUS (3, *PW* 114) MAXIMUS RULLIANUS,** QUINTUS, a hero of the Samnite Wars; consul 322, 310, 308, 297, 295 B.C., censor 304 (after 310 his colleague was always P. Decius Mus), dictator 315 (Diod. 19. 101 records a second, probably apocryphal, dictatorship in 313). He celebrated triumphs over Samnites, Etruscans, Gauls. Of the exploits attributed to Rullianus the following deserve mention: his Samnite victory (325), when the dictator Papirius Cursor apparently impeached him for fighting against orders; his defeat by Samnites at Lautulae (315); his Etruscan expedition, reputedly through the Ciminian Forest (310); his annihilation of the Samnite, Gallic, Etruscan coalition at Sentinum (295) (*see* EGNATIUS 1). The untrustworthy account of Rullianus in our principal source, Livy (books 8–11), whom details in Diodorus, Valerius Maximus, Frontinus, and others supplement, derives partly from Fabius Pictor but more from later annalists. It borrows incidents from the career of Rullianus' great-grandson, Fabius Cunctator; e.g. Rullianus–Papirius Cursor resemble Cunctator–Minucius; the censor Rullianus restricting the rabble to four city tribes suggests Cunctator confining freedmen to those tribes; Rullianus rescuing his son, the consul Fabius Gurges (292) (*see* PONTIUS 1), anticipates Cunctator serving under his own son (213 B.C.).

E. T. Salmon, *Samnium and the Samnites* (1967), 220 ff. E. T. S.

**FABIUS (4, *PW* 53) BUTEO,** MARCUS (*cos.* 245 B.C.), censor 241, and *princeps senatus* from 214 if not from 220. His naval victory off Aegimurus and subsequent shipwreck are improbable. Probably he, not Fabius Cunctator, delivered the Roman ultimatum at Carthage in 218. As dictator he filled up the Senate after Cannae (216).

H. H. S.

**FABIUS (5, *PW* 116) MAXIMUS VERRUCOSUS, CUNCTATOR,** QUINTUS, consul I (233 B.C.), triumphed over the Ligurians and dedicated a temple to Honos; censor (230), consul II (228), dictator I between 221 and 219 (probably 221). He probably did not deliver the Roman ultimatum to Carthage (*see* FABIUS 4). After the disaster at Trasimene he was elected dictator II, but quarrelled with his *magister equitum,* Minucius (q.v. 2) Rufus. By religious observances he restored the people's morale and stated his policy of dogging Hannibal's heels and avoiding further pitched battles. He allowed Hannibal to ravage Campania unchecked and later at Callicula to cross the Apennines to Apulia, being duped by the Carthaginian advance at night behind a herd of oxen with burning faggots tied to their horns. Fabius' strategy of exhaustion, which was opposed by many Romans, was only justified as a temporary expedient, since there was yet no real reason to distrust the Roman legions. But when these were defeated at Cannae (216) Fabius' policy had to be continued and the abusive title Cunctator, the Delayer, now became an honour: 'unus homo nobis cunctando restituit rem' (Ennius, Vahlen, 370). As suffect consul III (215) in Campania Fabius covered the road to Rome, while Marcellus and Gracchus parried Hannibal's attacks. Presiding over the elections, he was re-elected consul IV (214) and helped to recover Casilinum. In 213 he served as legate to his inexperienced son, now consul. In 209 he was consul V and *princeps senatus*;

he recovered Tarentum through internal treachery. He strenuously opposed Scipio's determination to invade Africa (205), and died in 203. He was pontifex for twelve years, augur for sixty-two and exploited the political advantages of these priesthoods. A patrician of the older type, courageous, cautious, and unimaginative, Fabius inspired admiration rather than affection. Rightly called the Shield of Rome, he at length wore down Hannibal's strength: 'subsequendo coercuit' (*Elogium*). It was Scipio's bolder strategy which humbled Carthage—yet it was Fabius that had made its application possible. *See also* PUNIC WARS.

For Fabius' political position see Scullard, *Rom. Pol.,* index; F. Cassola, *I gruppi politici romani nel III sec. a. C.* (1962), chs. 6, 7 (on which see E. S. Staveley, *JRS* 1963, 185 ff.); J. E. A. Crake, *Phoenix* 1963, 123 ff. The attribution of a fragment of an *elogium* from Brundisium to Fabius (e.g. by G. Vitucci, *Riv. Fil.* 1953, 43 ff.) may be wrong (see, e.g., Broughton, *MRR* Suppl. 2). H. H. S.

**FABIUS (6, *PW* 126) PICTOR,** QUINTUS, Roman senator and historian, who took part in the Second Punic War, consulting the Delphic oracle after Cannae, wrote a History of Rome in Greek, the first of the senatorial Histories interpreting Roman institutions and policy to the Greek world. It treated the Greek association of Roman origins in Aeneas, set the foundation of the city in 748/7 B.C., and passed, probably in discursive fashion, to the Gallic and Punic Wars and his own times; his use of Diocles of Peparethus (Plut. *Rom.* 3; 8) is now disputed. Polybius, though criticizing his Roman bias (Polyb. 1. 14; 58; 3. 8–9), follows his authority. Dionysius and Livy cite him; Diodorus' use is uncertain. The Latin annals, if not a later adaptation, may belong to Ser. Fabius, the work *de iure pontificio* to Fabius Servilianus. Fabius' History, political in purpose, probably owed more to Hellenistic historiography than to the pontifical tradition, and it set the standard for senatorial history.

Peter, *HRRel.* i² (1914), lxix, 5, 112; *FGrH* iii. C 845 ff. F. Leo, *Gesch. der röm. Lit.* i (1913), 85; Beloch, *Röm. Gesch.* 95; M. Gelzer, *Kl. Schr.* iii (1964), 51 ff.; Walbank, *Polybius* i. 27 ff.; A. Alföldi, *Early Rome and the Latins* (1965), esp. ch. 4. A. H. McD.

**FABIUS (7, *PW* 109) MAXIMUS AEMILIANUS,** QUINTUS (*c.* 186–130 B.C.), born of L. Aemilius Paullus and Papiria and adopted by the Fabii Maximi, accompanied Paullus to Greece in 168. Praetor in Sicily (149); consul (145), he consolidated the position against Viriathus in Spain (145–144). Legate at Numantia in 134/3, he died in 130. His career followed the rise of his brother, Scipio Aemilianus.

H. Simon, *Roms Kriege in Spanien 154–133 v. Chr.* (1962), see index. A. H. McD.

**FABIUS (8, *PW* 110) MAXIMUS (ALLOBROGICUS),** QUINTUS, son of (7) and nephew of Scipio (q.v. 11), under whom he perhaps served as quaestor in Spain. As praetor (*c.* 124 B.C.) and proconsul he commanded in Spain, as consul 121 and proconsul in Transalpine Gaul (with Domitius, q.v. 120) triumphing *c.* 120 and building the first triumphal arch (*Fornix Fabianus*) in Rome. He may have been censor 108. The Fabii remained the chief patrons of the Allobroges. E. B.

**FABIUS (9, *PW* 102) MAXIMUS,** PAULLUS, son of Q. Fabius Maximus (*cos. suff.* 45 B.C.), owed his *praenomen* to his ancestor Paullus (2). An intimate friend of Augustus, he was consul in 11 B.C., proconsul of Asia, and *legatus Augusti* in Nearer Spain (3/2 B.C.). Rumour said that he accompanied Augustus on a secret visit to Agrippa (q.v. 4) Postumus in A.D. 14, and that his death, which followed shortly, was suicide, occasioned by the betrayal of the secret to Livia by his wife Marcia, daughter of Philippus (6). Africanus Fabius Maximus (*cos.* 10 B.C.), named after Scipio (11), was his brother, and Paullus Fabius Persicus (*cos.* A.D. 34), probably his son.

Syme, *Rom. Rev.*, see index. For coin-portrait, M. Grant, *From Imperium to Auctoritas* (1946), 387.                              T. J. C.

**FABIUS** (10, *PW* 140) **RUSTICUS,** from Spain, was perhaps not a Roman senator. He wrote a History, whose prose style led Tacitus (*Agr.* 10. 3) to compare him to Livy. His work had won recognition before the end of Domitian's reign, but it is uncertain whether his unawareness that Britain was an island, which was demonstrated by Agricola's fleet in A.D. 84, indicates composition before 84. His work dealt with Nero's reign and possibly A.D. 69, but its limits are not known. He was hostile to Nero and praised his friend and patron Seneca. He is mentioned by Tacitus, but the extent to which his work was used directly or indirectly (via the Elder Pliny?) is controversial.

Peter, *HRR* ii, 112 f.                              H. H. S.

**FABIUS** (11, *PW* 90) **IUSTUS,** Lucius, born *c.* A.D. 65, probably of Spanish or Narbonese origin, was a friend of the Younger Pliny and one of Trajan's generals; Tacitus dedicated his *Dialogus* to him. In 97 he probably commanded a legion, was *cos. suff.* in 102, perhaps held a military command in 106/7 (governor of Moesia or on Trajan's staff?), and *c.* 109 was governor of Syria.

R. Syme, *JRS* 1957, 131 ff.                              H. H. S.

**FABLE** (αἶνος, μῦθος, λόγος, ἀπόλογος), a feature of the popular tradition of the Greek as of other races. It is typically an anecdote of animal life with a moralizing application; it may, however, be drawn from inanimate nature or directly from human experience, and it merges into the *chreia*, the aetiological myth, and the humorous anecdote. Theon, *Progymn.* 3, defined a fable as λόγος ψευδὴς εἰκονίζων ἀλήθειαν. It is questionable whether Greek Fable is substantially indebted to that of any other race. Foreign sources are occasionally mentioned; e.g. Libya (Aesch. fr. 139), Egypt (Pl. *Phdr.* 275 b), Lydia (Callim. *POxy.* 1011), Sybaris (Ar. *Vesp.* 1259). Instances of its employment occur throughout Greek literature; among the earliest are Hesiod *Op.* 202 and Archilochus frs. 86 and 89; it is not found in Homer. The earlier popular type upon which writers drew appears to have been in prose form. By the end of the fifth century B.C. the body of native Fable was in general ascribed to Aesop, said to have been a slave in Samos in the sixth century (Hdt. 2. 134); his name is already familiar to Aristophanes and Plato. The earliest collection of Greek fables was probably the Λόγων Αἰσωπείων συναγωγαί of Demetrius of Phalerum (Diog. Laert. 5. 80), presumably in prose. The earliest extant collection is that of Babrius (q.v.), in choliambic verse. In Hellenistic and later times the Fable was found useful in rhetorical training (Hermogenes Προγυμνάσματα ad init.), and further collections were made with this object, e.g. the δεκαμυθία of Nicostratus (*Suda*, Νικ.) in the second century A.D. The Fable so adapted reached its final form in the medieval collections associated with the name of Aesop, which survive in several recensions, the latest being edited by Maximus Planudes.

LATIN FABLE. As represented in Latin literature Fable is in general derivative from the Greek Aesopic form. It was well adapted for use in the *Satura*, especially in that of the Horatian type. Aulus Gellius (2. 29) cites part of an adaptation by Ennius of an Aesopic fable; Lucilius (988 Marx) uses another. Horace sometimes gives fables *in extenso* (*Sat.* 2. 6. 79 ff.; *Epist.* 1. 7. 29 ff.), sometimes merely alludes to them (*Sat.* 2. 3. 299; *Epist.*

1. 3. 19). The first extant Latin collection was in iambic verse, by Phaedrus (q.v. 4), a freedman of Augustus, who published his five books under Tiberius and Caligula. The MS. tradition is probably the result of selection; an Appendix of fables ascribed to Phaedrus is added. Phaedrus acknowledges his formal debt to Aesop, whilst seeking to improve upon him (4 *prol.* 11). The collection includes besides definitely Aesopic material much that is derived from the author's experience or imagination. He writes professedly (1 *prol.* 3) for entertainment and instruction; at the same time a desire for literary recognition is certainly a leading motive. He incurred the displeasure of Sejanus (3 *prol.* 41), no doubt on account of indiscreet allusions to contemporary events. He has been called a better story-teller than fabulist (Nisard); he is certainly at his best in anecdote, whilst his work lacks in general the peculiar genius of the best Greek Fable. His versification is adroit and finished; and in the terse and vigorous simplicity of his style he shows himself a pupil not unworthy of the preceding epoch. His diction is in general classical, but shows traces of contemporary tendencies. The Phaedrian collection was later paraphrased in prose under the title of *Romulus* (the 'Latin Aesop'). In the third century Titianus, of whose work nothing further is known, composed prose fables (Auson. *Ep.* 16 *praef.*); the extant collection of Avianus (4th or 5th c.), consisting of forty-two fables in elegiac verse, is of no particular literary merit. These later authors appear to have drawn principally on Babrius.

A. Hausrath, *PW* vi, xix (Phaedr.); W. G. Rutherford, ed. *Babrius* (introd.; 1883); E. Rohde, *Der gr. Roman³* (App.), 1914; W. Wienert, *Die Typen d. gr.-röm. Fabel* (1925); K. Meuli, *Herkunft u. Wesen der Fabel* (1954); B. E. Perry, *Studium Generale* xii (1959), 17 ff.; M. Moigaard, *La Fable antique* i (1964), ii (1967); D. Nisard, *Poetes lat. d. l. décad.* i (1877) (Phaedr.); L. Hervieux, *Les Fables latines* (1893); O. Crusius, *PW* ii (Avian.); Editions: (Gr. Aesop) K. Hausrath (Teubner, 1957–9); B. E. Perry, *Aesopica* (1952); (Babrius) W. G. Rutherford (1883); (Phaedr.) L. Müller (Teubner, 1903); J. P. Postgate (1919); (Babrius and Phaedr.) B. E. Perry (Loeb, 1965); (Avian.) A. Guaglianone (1958); (*Romulus*) G. Thiele (1910).
                                                            W. M. E.; R. B.

**FABRI.** In the early Roman army there were two separately organized centuries of *fabri*, or armourers. They were commanded by *praefecti*. By the time of Caesar, and probably much earlier, these separate centuries of *fabri* had ceased to exist, and this kind of technical work was done by skilled legionaries. The title of *praefectus fabrum* remained as a convenient designation for the A.D.C. to the general.

J. Suolahti, *The Junior Officers of the Roman Army in the Republican Period* (1955), 205 ff.                              G. R. W.

**FABRICIUS** (*PW* 9) **LUSCINUS,** GAIUS, hero of the war with Pyrrhus (q.v.), consul in 282, 278 B.C., censor in 275. He negotiated for Rome with Tarentum (284) and with Pyrrhus (280, 278). He rescued Thurii from Sabellian besiegers (282) and was twice awarded triumphs for his victories over Bruttii, Lucani, Samnites, and Tarentines. His personality lies concealed under the rhetorical stories of his poverty, austerity, and incorruptibility; he rejected alike bribes from Pyrrhus and the proffered aid of would-be poisoners of Pyrrhus. Similar tales are told of the other plebeian hero M'. Curius Dentatus (q.v. 2), whom Cicero (cf. *Paradoxa* 50) constantly cites with Fabricius as a typical specimen of Roman virtue.

A. Passerini, *Athenaeum* 1943, 92 ff.; P. Lévêque, *Pyrrhos* (Paris, 1957); E. T. Salmon *Samnium and the Samnites* (1967), 255 ff.
                                                            E. T. S.

**FABULA** (besides meaning 'story', 'talk', 'fable') was the general Latin term for 'play'; special types were *F. Atellana* (see ATELLANA); *crepidata*, possibly = *palliata* (*crepida* was a type of Greek shoe, worn with the *pallium*);

*palliata*, adaptation of Greek New Comedy; (*pallium* = Greek cloak); *praetexta(ta)*, serious drama on Roman historical subjects (*praetexta* was the magistrate's toga); *riciniata*, a mime (*see* MIMUS II; *ricinium*, properly a woman's mantle, which could be used to veil the head; possibly this made it useful in the mime); *saltica*, libretto for pantomime (*see* PANTOMIMUS); *stataria*, 'quiet' play, opposed to *motoria*, 'bustling' play (cf. Ter. *Haut.* 36–40); *tabernaria*, 'private-house comedy' (?), apparently identical with *togata*; *togata*, Roman comedy, nearly always concerned with lower life; *trabeata*, a form of *togata* dealing with upper middle-class life, invented by Maecenas' freedman Melissus (the *trabea* was worn by the *equites*). W. B.

**FADIUS GALLUS,** MARCUS, friend of Cicero, who addresses to him *Fam.* 7. 23–7. In 45 B.C. he was among those who wrote anti-Caesarian eulogies of Cato. See ANTICATONES.

**FAESULAE,** modern *Fiesole*, an Etruscan town in the hills above Florence, probably on the site of an Iron Age sanctuary. The Orientalizing period is represented nearby by the Montagnola tomb at Quinto Fiorentino, which is similar to the Pietrera tumulus at Vetulonia (q.v.). The parallels at Populonia, Volaterrae, and Felsina (qq.v.) for the carved stone funerary stelae (*c.* 520–470 B.C.) of Faesulae draw attention to the importance of its position as a point of contact with Etruria Padana. The best archaeological evidence for the town itself dates from the early third century B.C., the date of the town wall, the cemetery, and the temple. Extensive remains of the Roman baths are also visible. Faesulae favoured Rome in the Second Punic War but in the Social War was defeated by Cato (q.v. 3). It subsequently became a *colonia* for Sulla's veterans; this led to unrest among the expropriated landowners as demonstrated in the course of the Catilinarian conspiracy.

M. Lombardi, *Faesulae* (Rome, 1941); A. de Agostino, *Fiesole* (Rome, 1949); G. Maetzke, *Stud. Etr.* 1955–6, 227 ff.; id. and G. Caputo, ibid. 1959, 41 ff.; *Not. Scav.* 1961, 52 ff.; Scullard, *Etr. Cities*, 168 ff. D. W. R. R.

**FALERNUS AGER,** a section of Campania (q.v.), centring on modern *Carinola*, between the Mons Massicus and the Volturnus taken by Rome from Capua (338 B.C. or later) and distributed among Roman citizens (Livy 8. 11. 22; 9. 41). Its exact extent and the origin of its name are alike uncertain. Its celebrated wine was already deteriorating in Pliny's day (*HN* 14. 62). E. T. S.

**FALISCANS,** the Early Iron Age inhabitants of the territory between Monte Cimino and the Tiber, and northern neighbours of Veii and of the closely related peoples of Capena, south and east Mt. Soracte. Their principal city was Falerii Veteres (*Civita Castellana*). In 241 B.C. the Romans captured and destroyed Falerii, transplanting its inhabitants to a new site, Falerii Novi, 3 miles to the west, where they remained throughout the Roman period, migrating once more to their old homes in the early Middle Ages. Though culturally and politically under strong Etruscan influence, the original Faliscan settlers were an independent branch of the same Urnfield peoples as the Villanovans and the Latins. They spoke and wrote an Indo-European language closely akin to Latin. The contents of the Faliscan cemeteries are now in the Villa Giulia Museum in Rome, together with a fine series of architectural terracottas from the temples of Falerii Veteres. The latter included the famous shrine of

Juno Curitis, described by Ovid (*Am.* 3. 13. 1 ff.), one of whose wives was of Faliscan origin.

W. Deecke, *Die Falisker* (1888); *Mon. Ant.* 1894; M. W. Frederiksen and J. B. Ward-Perkins, *PBSR* 1957, 67 ff. J. B. W.-P.

**FANNIUS** (*PW* 7), GAIUS (*cos.* 122 B.C.), the Gracchan annalist, son-in-law of Laelius and pupil of Panaetius, served at Carthage (146 B.C.) and in Spain (141), and became tribune (142?), praetor (126?), and consul (122), opposing C. Gracchus' Italian legislation in a celebrated speech (Cic. *Brut.* 26. 99–100). He wrote a History, perhaps from the origins of Rome, but probably of his own times (this depends on the date of the *Drepana* reference of fr. 3). He included speeches verbatim in his narrative, like Cato, and portrayed contemporary personalities. His work was authoritative, recognized by Cicero, Sallust, who praised its *veritas*, and Brutus.

Peter, *HRRel.* i², cxciii, 139; P. Fraccaro, *Opusc.* ii (1957), 103, 119; Broughton, *MRR* i. 519, n. 2. A. H. McD.

**FANUM FORTUNAE,** modern *Fano*, near the mouth of the Metaurus (q.v.) in Umbria: important highway junction, where the Via Flaminia (q.v.) reached the Adriatic. Named after a Temple of Fortune, it also contained Vitruvius' celebrated basilica (Vitr. 5. 1. 6). Neither has survived, but the Arch of Augustus (who made Fanum a *colonia*) is intact. E. T. S.

**FASCES** were bundles of rods (*virgae*), customarily made of elm or birch and bound together by red thongs. Introduced to Rome from Etruria during the late monarchy, they symbolized the tenure of *imperium* and were carried by an equal number of lictors (q.v.) in the fore of all Roman officials who held an active power of command. Originally axes were attached to the *fasces*, but from the early Republic these were removed within the city boundary—no doubt as an act of deference to the body which was the source of magisterial authority (compare the custom of dipping the *fasces* before the people). Only the lictors of dictators continued to carry axes in Rome. The *fasces* of the Emperors and of victorious republican generals were decked with laurel. The basic number of *fasces*, to which were entitled the king, the consul, and the promagistrate of consular rank, was twelve. Other magistrates received such a number as corresponded with the relative strength of their authority—praetors six, dictators and perhaps those with provincial *imperium maius* twenty-four. *Fasces* fewer than six were given to those who had a delegated *imperium*—e.g. five to the legates responsible to the emperor for the management of the imperial provinces. The *insignia* carried by lictors were of several types—e.g. bundles of *bacilli* when they attended municipal magistrates, some form of dummy rods when they attended the Roman consul who did not have the turn of power—but the generic term *fasces* appears to have been reserved to denote the traditional bundles of *virgae*.

Mommsen, *Röm. Staatsr.* i³. 373 ff.; K. Heinz-Vogel, *Sav. Zeitschr.* 1950, 62 ff.; E. S. Staveley, *Hist.* 1963, 458 ff. E. S. S.

**FASTI,** the old calendar of *dies fasti* and *dies nefasti* for legal and public business, which received definite publication by Cn. Flavius in 304 B.C. (Livy 9. 46. 5), came to cover also lists of eponymous magistrates (*fasti consulares*), records of triumphs (*fasti triumphales*), and priestly lists (*fasti sacerdotales*). We know of the sacral calendars of Fulvius Nobilior (189 B.C.) and Verrius Flaccus (at Praeneste), and have fragments of the pre-Julian calendar of Antium (*c.* 70 B.C.) and twenty calendars from the close of the Republic to Claudius; also *fasti* of the Feriae Latinae and two rustic *menologia*, and in book-form the calendar of A.D. 354, the *fasti Idaciani*, and the *Chronicon*

*Paschale*. Of *fasti consulares* we have the exemplar of Antium (*c*. 70 B.C.) and the *fasti Capitolini*, which were set up on or near the new Regia (q.v.) of 36 B.C. and then continued to A.D. 13; the *ludi saeculares* were added, until A.D. 88. *Fasti triumphales* appear in the fragments of Tolentino and Urbisaglia, and also from the Regia, where a list from Romulus to 19 B.C. was added about 12 B.C., presumably by Augustus as Pontifex Maximus.

The authenticity of the *fasti* is now scarcely in doubt, but they were subject to systematic editing, even before the work of Verrius Flaccus and Atticus. On archaeological evidence it is argued that the consular names down to *c*. 450 B.C. simply represent eponymous magistrates still under the kings. The case is yet unproven, but the reconstruction for the fifth century B.C. was necessarily speculative, perhaps politically tendentious; it was sound in its main lines for the fourth century, and from *c*. 300 B.C. appears consistently accurate, presumably using full regular records. This suggests that the inclusion of magistrates' names and cult notices followed directly on the Flavian publication, and may be associated with the *tabula pontificum* (q.v.).

*Inscript. Italiae* xiii. 1 (1947), 2 (1963); De Sanctis, *Stor. Rom.* i. 1; G. Costa, *L'originale dei fasti consolari* (1910); *I fasti consolari* (1910); E. Pais, *Fasti triumphales pop. Rom.* (1920–3); *I fasti trionfali del popolo Romano* (1930); Beloch, *Röm. Geschichte*, 1 ff.; K. Hanell, *Das altröm. eponyme Amt* (1946); E. Gjerstad, *Opusc. Romana* iii (1960), 99 ff.; cf. P. Fraccaro, *JRS* 1957, 59 ff.; A. K. Michels, *The Calendar of the Roman Republic* (U.S.A. 1967). A. H. McD.

**FASTING** (νηστεία), in the sense of abstinence from all food for a stated time, such as a day, is very rare in classical religions, both Greek and Roman. There is, for instance, no evidence whatever that anyone, priest or layman, was expected to come fasting to a sacral meal such as normally followed the killing of a victim. For Greece, however, we may cite two well-known instances. At the Thesmophoria the second day was called Nesteia, at all events at Athens (cf. ATTIC CULTS AND MYTHS), because, as it would appear, the women conducting the rite took no food then; there was a day at Taras (Tarentum) having the same name (cf. Aelian, *VH* 5. 20, who gives an aetiological story not to be taken too seriously); it probably was part of some rite of Demeter or a similar deity. In like manner, the *ieiunium Cereris* at Rome (Livy 36. 37. 4–5) was instituted by advice of the Sibylline Books, and therefore belongs to the Greek, not the native cult of that goddess. The other outstanding example of a ritual fast in Greece is, like the former, connected with the cult of Demeter. The Eleusinian formula in Clem. Al. *Protr.* 2. 21. 2 (p. 16. 18 Stählin) specifies that the initiate had fasted before drinking the *kykeōn*. Details are, however, lacking. Various statements to the effect that some person would not eat (e.g. Achilles after the death of Patroclus, *Il.* 19. 303 ff.; the beasts after the death of Daphnis, when they show human grief, Verg. *Ecl.* 5. 25–26) should not, therefore, without further proof, be taken to imply ritual fasting. The general prescription of light diet, that the body might hinder the soul as little as possible, for those engaged in divination, especially by dreams, extended to actual fasting in some cases, to judge from Tert. *De Anim.* 48. The later mystery-cults, on the other hand, seem to have used ritual fasting quite commonly, e.g. that of Attis (Sallustius, *De dis et mundo* iv, p. 8. 22 Nock). It is to be remembered that they are not Greek but Oriental in origin. The many prescriptions of fasting in the use of magic (q.v.) are not all evidence for any prolonged abstinence; for example, the application of the remedy in Pliny, *HN* 26. 93 (the touch of a naked girl's hand). She should do it *ieiuna ieiuno*, but this condition is satisfied if the ceremony is carried out before operator or patient has breakfasted. However, some examples of real fasting, extending on occasion over more than one day, are to be found (see Ziehen, loc. cit. *infra*, 94. 43 ff.).

What might be called partial fasting, i.e. abstinence during a certain period or for the whole of life from some specified food or class of foods, is common enough. The best-known examples are the vegetarian diets of the Orphics (*see* ORPHISM) and Pythagoreans (*see* PYTHAGORAS 1; also J. Haussleiter, *Der Vegetarismus in der Antike*, 1935), but many others exist, as the food-taboos of the *flamen Dialis* at Rome (he might not, e.g., eat beans, Gellius 10. 15. 12) and the very curious restriction on the priestess of Athena Polias at Athens, who might not eat green cheese unless it was imported (Strabo 9. 1. 11).

L. Ziehen in *PW* xvii. 88 ff. P. R. Arbesmann, *Das Fasten bei den Griechen und Römern, Religionsgeschichtliche Versuche und Vorarbeiten*, ed. A. Dieterich *et al.*, xxi. 1 (1929). H. J. R.

**FATE.** The words for fate in Greek and Latin are all transparent metaphors: the earliest of them, *moira* and *aisa*, mean 'share', 'portion', and, as abstractions denoting, in the first instance, the distinctive events of a man's life, they belong to a very naïve outlook, which stops short of both logic and religion. One's share is above all else death; as such *moira* may be either a fact of nature, a special destiny, an outcome of divine anger or of divine decree, or all of these together, as in Achilles' angry and inconsequent reply to Thetis at *Il.* 18. 115–21. *Moira* consoles, it does not enlighten; and talk of *moira* is more congenial to the epic heroes than to their poet, who dispels the certainty of fate with the scales of Zeus, in which are weighed the 'dooms' (*keres*) of opposing parties. In the epic only a sudden reversal, not the sum of life, comes from fate; a hero does not regard his rank and privileges as *moira*. Of course, one's 'share' may also signify, not fate, but what one deserves, as when something threatens to happen 'beyond' *aisa*. In the sense of 'fated share' or 'lot', however, *moira* and *aisa*, though sometimes referring to a favourable turn, always interrupt the normal course of things. It follows that *moira* is not one man's portion of a great whole, from which all are served; the working of fate does not conform to a general plan or dispensation, any more than does the gods' intervention to an orderly system of divine government. Twice in the epic *moira* has the quite exceptional meaning 'good fortune' (*Il.* 3. 182, where Agamemnon, as the great king, is 'born to good fortune'; *Od.* 20. 76), which has intruded, incongruously, from the language of little people, for whom *moira*, as later *tyche*, was the single factor of existence. In epic accounts of violent death *moira* is very often personified as a form of external compulsion, and called 'deadly', 'unspeakable'. In these contexts *moira* is easily heard as 'doom', 'destruction', a malevolent power like *ker*, so that the Moirai are enrolled by Hesiod among the offspring of Night, beside 'the *Keres* of pitiless vengeance'—not as powers of fate, but as a vague plurality of 'Dooms' (*Theog.* 217, 220–3. The dispensers of fate are usually the gods, less often the Moirai (*Il.* 24. 49), at first the individual lots personified, later members of a group whose names and number vary.

**2.** In the epic the gods spin, with a thread, the great realities—death, trouble, riches, homecoming—around a man, as if he were a spindle. From this image come the 'harsh Spinners', *Clothes* (*Od.* 7. 197), and the spinning Moirai (Callinus 1. 9 f.). Hesiod made the Moirai, like the Horai, a group of three, daughters of Zeus and Themis, with the names Clotho, Lachesis ('Getting-by-lot'), and Atropos ('Irresistible') (*Theog.* 904–6), but these three goddesses do not reappear together before Plato, who first describes them as occupied with a common task and singing in harmony (*Rep.* 10. 617 b–621 a). The gods' spinning takes place usually at the moment of birth, once t marriage as well (*Od.* 4. 207), and so answers to the custom of bringing gifts to the newborn child and to the bridal pair. The 'gifts of the gods', an easy metaphor (*Il.* ₃. 65), can also be real: Peleus received them at birth (*Il.* ₂4. 534), and at his wedding. The Moirai, bringing good fortune, attend the marriage of Peleus and Thetis (first on the François Vase), and later that of Zeus and Themis, and of Zeus and Hera. On these occasions the Moirai did not spin, but rather sang, a motif originating with the Muses; later they both spin and sing for Peleus (Catullus ₂4. 320–83). The Moirai may either finish their spinning at birth, so as to determine the life ahead—this leads to the burlesque fantasy of Seneca, who has Clotho produce from a little box the spindles of Claudius and his likeated cronies (*Apoc.* 3)—or continue throughout a man's ife, until all the thread has been drawn off the distaff, bringing death. They also weave, and a birth-goddess Rhapso, the 'Stitcher', was worshipped at Athens. Many other images occur. The Chest of Cypselus showed, beside certain allegorical figures, two old women at work with mortar and pestle, no doubt brewing good and ill for mankind (Pausanias 5. 18. 2). 'We do not know the goal that ate (*potmos*) has marked for our running' (Pindar, *Nem.* ₉. 6–7). Later the Fates write their decrees; these are kept in a huge archives office, according to Ovid (*Met.* 15. ₅08–15). In Greek art two, three, or four Moirai are shown together, mostly as maidens of pleasing appearance. In mythical context the Moirai are generally propitious deities. They are present at great beginnings: together with Time, at the founding of the Olympian Games by Heracles, and at the birth of Aphrodite and of Athena. According to Pindar Tyche, 'Success', was one of the Moirai, stronger than her sisters (Pausanias 7. 26. ₈). Since their power is exerted especially at birth, they are sometimes viewed as deities of childbearing, and in this role they receive cult service. The Moirai and Eileithyia visit heroines giving birth, in order to assist or retard the labour; Lachesis 'the glorious midwife' delivers Asclepius (Isyllus 49 f.).

3. It is obvious that 'fate' itself cannot be worshipped. But as birth-goddesses—associated in a number of cults with powers like Artemis, the 'birthday nymphs', the Childrearer'—the Moirai can help in time of need, and votive records in this sense are fairly common: such, for example, is a parent's dedication to the 'Saviour Moirai', returning 'thanks for himself and his children'. Athenian brides offered cuttings from their hair to the Moirai, and women swore by them. The Moirai also promote the growth of crops, as their kinship with the Horai in Hesiod's *Theogony* may already intimate, and so receive sacrifice at seed-time, and a thank-offering after the harvest; in a cult legend of Arcadia they persuade Demeter to lay aside her grief and revive the crops (Pausanias ₈. 42. 3).

4. Misfortune is often attributed, not to the gods of cult, but to a *daimon*, an animate power that is not identifiable, a lesser god it may be, one of a multitude who hover around us (Hes. *Op.* 122–6). A man owes his lot to a personal *daimon*; more explicitly, a *daimon* 'gets-by-ot', and executes, the *moira* of each man ([Lysias] *Epit.* ₁8; Pl. *Phd.* 107 d; Aristotle *apud* Clement, *Strom.* 6. ₈. 53); in the myth of Er Plato repudiates this widespread idea (*Rep.* 10. 617 e; cf. 629 d). The *daimon* himself was good' or 'evil', according as a man's affairs prospered or miscarried (Theognis 161–4); or each man has both a good and an evil *daimon* who accompany him through ife. Against such fatalism speculative writers—Heraclitus, Epicharmus, Democritus, and Xenocrates—urged that a man's *daimon* was no more than his 'character', and Posidonius made the two *daimones* a parable of reason and emotion contending in the human soul. Although a man might worship his *daimon*, sometimes beside *tyche*, it

was more natural to view him as evil (Menander *apud* Clement, *Strom.* 5. 14. 130, an ethical protest) and to ascribe a hard fate to a cruel malevolence; the epic once says 'a hateful *daimon* attacked him', bringing sickness (*Od.* 5. 396), and the same feeling is vividly expressed in the stories of the menacing apparition that compelled Xerxes to attack Greece against better counsel (Herodotus 7. 12–18), and of Brutus' 'evil *daimon*' (Plut. *Brut.* 36 and 48).

5. At the outset fate and the gods exist side by side, without disturbing each other. The epic gods do not as a rule maintain order and justice among mankind, so why discriminate between their ways and fate? When the heroes give a determinist account of behaviour or suffering, they speak indifferently of *moira* and the gods. The gods taken collectively often assign *moira*, but the interference of Olympian gods acting from personal, and usually partisan, motives does not enter this kind of thinking. Of course, the poet can feign that a god's designs are crossed by a hero's fated share, and that the god gives way: thus Poseidon reluctantly sees that Odysseus' *aisa* is to escape death (*Od.* 5. 288 f.). Here fate is not a matter of conviction, but of poetic intent. It is, however, possible to believe that the Olympian gods are constrained, not indeed by Fate as a higher power, but by their own *moirai*. Even a god cannot escape his allotted portion, Croesus learned from the Delphic oracle (Herodotus 1. 91); the lesson is acknowledged, and exemplified, by the captive Prometheus (Aesch. *Prom.* 103–5). This is no more than a corollary of the traditional view that the Olympian gods, having arrived in a world already made, exercise dominion according to a scheme of 'shares' (*Il.* 15. 187–9) or of 'honours' (Hes. *Theog.* 112 f.). The gods of cult and folklore, on the other hand, are often superior to fate. Apollo, in consequence of his oracular function, was believed to have influence with the Moirai, persuading them to delay the fall of Sardis (Herodotus 1. 91), and also, with the help of wine, to prolong the life of Admetus (Aesch. *Eum.* 723–8). In later times various deities—Apollo, Asclepius, Isis, Serapis—had in the eyes of their worshippers the power of contravening fate.

6. Fate is a problem only for the supreme god, Zeus. In the epic the problem is never envisaged. When Zeus, as 'the steward of war for mankind' (*Il.* 19. 224), weighs two 'dooms' against each other, the image does not imply that he consults fate as a higher authority, or ratifies it as a lesser. The issue is momentarily in doubt, as the poet wishes, but Zeus remains master of the situation: a steward weighing goods does not inquire of fate, and neither does Zeus. Since Zeus is not presumed to will things for the best, it would be pointless to ask whether his will has free play. Here again the poet may imagine for dramatic purposes a conflict which did not exist in real belief: so Zeus proposes to defer the *moira* of a hero on the field (*Il.* 16. 431–43; 22. 167–81). Hesiod, Pindar, and Aeschylus, in their mythical expositions of divine power and goodness, ally the Moirai with the government of Zeus, and the doctrine led to worship of the Moirai linked with Zeus as *Moiragetes*, 'leader of the Moirai', which was introduced at Athens, along with other religious innovations of a moralizing bent, by the mid fifth century; similar cults were widely adopted thereafter.

7. After the fourth century fate was often viewed as a general scheme ruling the world at large, and circumscribing the whole life of the individual, an idea which reflects the influence of scientific determinism, working through astrology and popular philosophy, and which was expressed by the term *heimarmene*—properly meaning fate, but coloured by a false etymology, so that it was understood to signify the 'chain' of mechanical causation. In earlier usage a man received his 'appointed portion',

*moira* qualified as *heimarmene*, a cognate word, but detached from its literal sense and heard as 'fated'. The substantive *heimarmene*—first attested on a late fifth-century vase, which shows Heimarmene beside Helen and Paris—during the next century replaced *moira*, now felt to be old-fashioned and poetic, in living speech. The Stoics analysed *heimarmene*, which Zeno had made the active principle of matter, as 'the connexion and succession' of causes (Cic. *Div.* 1. 55). Thus it happened that irrational fate and rational determinism—which was otherwise called 'necessity', *ananke*—converged in *heimarmene* and became inseparable. A perfunctory synthesis of *heimarmene*, providence, and nature was the earliest and most popular form of Stoic doctrine, but Posidonius placed god, nature, and *heimarmene* at descending levels, appearing as mind, soul, and matter respectively; and as a vague dualism came to dominate speculative thinking, fate and matter were commonly identified, and opposed to god and spirit. Saviour religions, mystical and gnostic philosophy, and even astrology itself, promised to bring release from the oppressive power of fate.

8. The Latin Parcae were assimilated in all respects to the Moirai. But originally *\*parica*, from *parere*, was a common noun meaning 'childbearing': *Parca Maurtia*, inscribed at Lavinium about 300 B.C., is the 'childbearing given by Mars', the principal god of the community. Parca was differentiated as Nona, Decuma, Morta, bringing a nine-months' birth, a ten-months' birth, and a stillbirth (*mors*) respectively, so that the three Parcae belonged to native Roman belief; it was no doubt their number, as well as their nature, that caused them to be identified with the Moirai. Livius Andronicus used Morta to render the epic *moira* meaning 'death'. In Latin fate is *fatum*, 'what is said', a term probably deriving from a belief in spoken magic (cf. Pliny, *HN* 28. 2. 14–16) rather than from prophecy. In another dedication at Lavinium the goddess of birth receives the epithet *fata*: she 'says', and thus fixes, the lot of the newborn child. In funerary epigrams the Parcae determine a person's fate by saying, *dicere*, or chanting, *canere, carmen*. *Fatus* is a personal deity, who could be either gracious or malign (Petronius 42, 71, 77), much like *daimon*. Dedications are also addressed to the *Fatae*, always plural, and a tomb-painting depicts, under the title *Fata divina*, three hooded figures, two women and a taller bearded man between them.

Nilsson, *GGR* i². 361 ff., 'Das Schicksal'; W. C. Greene, *Moira: Fate, Good and Evil in Greek Thought* (1944); D. Amand, *Fatalisme et liberté dans l'antiquité grecque* (1945); W. Theiler, 'Tacitus und die antike Schicksalslehre', *Phyllobolia, Festschrift für P. v. der Mühll* (1945), 35 ff. N. R.

**FAUNUS** (from root of *favere*, 'kindly one', euphemistic), a *numen* anciently identified with Pan, whose festival (5 Dec., Hor. *Carm.* 3. 18. 10) was kept in the *pagi* with dancing and merry-making. He was primarily of the forests, and especially connected with the mysterious sounds heard in them, hence his titles (or identification with) Fatuus and Fatuclus (Servius on *Aen.* 6. 775), both meaning 'the speaker'. As a god of herdsmen he was further identified with Inuus, whose name the ancients connected with *inire* and interpreted as the fertilizer of cattle (ibid.). He had female counterparts, Fauna (cf. BONA DEA) and Fatua (Cornelius Labeo in Macrob. *Sat.* 1. 12. 21). A more formidable side is shown by his identification (Servius, ibid.) with Incubo, a *numen* either of nightmare or (Petron. *Sat.* 38. 8) of buried treasure. He was on occasion oracular (*Aen.* 7. 81 ff.; Dion. Hal. 5. 16. 2–3 and elsewhere). For his alleged connexion with the Lupercalia (q.v.), see H. J. Rose, *Mnemosyne* 1933, 386 ff.

Wissowa, *RK* 208 ff.; Latte, *RR* 83. H. J. R.

**FAUSTINA** (1, *PW* s.v. Annius 120), ANNIA GALERIA, called 'the Elder', was daughter of M. Annius Verus (*cos. III* in A.D. 126) and aunt of M. Aurelius. She married the future Emperor Antoninus (q.v. 1) Pius *c.* 110 or later, and bore him two sons and two daughters, one of whom was Faustina (q.v. 2) 'the Younger'. Faustina the Elder became *Augusta* on the accession of Antoninus in 138. Later tradition questioned her character, but the pair lived in harmony until her death in 140/1, when Antoninus consecrated her and named a new alimentary charity *Puellae Faustinianae* (*see* ALIMENTA) after her. She shared his commemoration in a temple in the Roman Forum.

*Diz. Epigr.* i. 944 ff.; Wegner, *Herrscherbild* ii. 4 (1939); Strack, *Reichsprägung* iii; *B.M. Coins, Rom. Emp.* iv; Nash, *Pict. Dict. Rome* i 26 ff. C. H. V. S.; M. H.

**FAUSTINA** (2, *PW* s.v. Annius 121), ANNIA GALERIA, called 'the Younger', was the younger daughter of Antoninus Pius and Faustina (1) the Elder (qq.v.); she was born *c.* A.D. 125–30. First betrothed by Hadrian's wish to L. Verus (q.v.), in 139 Antoninus betrothed her instead to her cousin M. Aurelius (q.v. 1), whom she married in 145. She became *Augusta* after her first child's birth in 146. Ancient authority groundlessly interpreted her lively temperament as a sign of faithless and disloyal character, not above collusion with Avidius (q.v. 3) Cassius. She accompanied Marcus during his northern campaign in 170–4 and—now *Mater Castrorum*—to the East in 175. There she died. Marcus, who apparently loved her genuinely, consecrated her and founded in her memory a second charity of *Puellae Faustinianae* (*see* ALIMENTA).

*Diz. Epigr.* i. 508. *See also under* FAUSTINA (1) *and* AURELIUS (1). C. H. V. S.; M. H

**FAUSTULUS**, probably a by-form of Faunus (q.v.; if a deity *favet*, he is *faustus*), but humanized into a herdsman, husband of Acca (q.v.) Larentia, who found Romulus (q.v.) and Remus being suckled by the she-wolf. In a further rationalization his wife was the she-wolf herself (*lupa*, loose woman, prostitute). He reared the twins, and when Remus was brought before Numitor for an act of brigandage, told Romulus the whole story, whereupon the twins and their grandfather killed Amulius.

Livy 1. 4. 6 ff. H. J. R.

**FAVENTINUS**, MARCUS CETIUS, made an abridgement of Vitruvius (q.v.) which Palladius and Isidorus used.

**FAVONIUS** (1 *PW* 1), MARCUS, of municipal birth, admirer and excessive imitator of Cato (q.v. 5), especially in rude forthrightness. He attacked Clodius (q.v. 1) in 61 B.C., and vehemently (but ineffectually) opposed Caesar, Pompey, and Crassus in the 50s. Aedile in 53, praetor (after a failure) in 49 and active on Pompey's side, he was pardoned after Pompey's death. Tired of civil war, he kept out of the plot against Caesar, but later joined the 'liberators', was captured at Philippi and executed.

E. B.

**FAVONIUS** (2) **EULOGIUS**, a rhetor from Carthage in Augustine's time, wrote a *Disputatio de somnio Scipionis*.

Ed. Holder (1901); R. E. van de Weddingen (Coll. Latomus, 1957). M. Sicherl, *Beitr. z. Kritik und Erklärung des F. E.* (1959).

**FAVORINUS** (Φαβωρῖνος), rhetor with philosophical interests of the period of the Second Sophistic. He was born at Arles (Arelate), a congenital eunuch, perhaps about the beginning of Domitian's reign, obtained his Greek education at Marseilles, and later may have heard Dio of Prusa at Rome. Two of the speeches attributed to Dio (Nos. 37 and 64) are almost certainly by Favorinus

His speaking tours took him to Athens, Corinth, and Ionia, where he became the bitter rival of the rhetorician Polemo. He knew Plutarch and was the teacher of Herodes Atticus, Gellius, and Fronto. At Rome he moved in the circle of the Emperor Hadrian, was advanced to the rank of an *eques*, and held the office of a provincial high priest. About A.D. 130 he fell into disfavour, being supplanted by Polemo, and was exiled to Chios. Antoninus Pius let him return to Rome, where he recovered his status and influence and lived the rest of his life, dying around the middle of the second century.

Of his speeches, Περὶ φυγῆς and Κορινθιακός were autobiographical; but most were on general topics, e.g. Περὶ τύχης ('On Fate'), some with strongly sceptical implications. He also published two miscellanies, the earliest known examples of the type later produced by Aelian and Athenaeus, embodying the fruits of his reading: Ἀπομνημονεύματα ('Memoirs') and Παντοδαπὴ ἱστορία ('Miscellaneous History'). Numbers of his *sententiae* are found in florilegia. The titles of nearly thirty of his works are known. So far as the evidence shows, he wrote and spoke Greek by preference.

J. L. Marres, *De F. Arel. vita studiis scriptis* (Utrecht, 1853) (includes fragments no longer satisfactory); W. Schmid in *PW* vi 2078 (best account of life); Zeller, *Phil. d. Gr.* III. 2⁴, 76 f.; *FHG* iii. 577 ff. (hist. fragments only); M. Norsa and G. Vitelli, *Il papiro vaticano greco II*: Φαβωρίνου Περὶ φυγῆς, 'Studi e Testi' 53 (1931); E. Mensching, *Favorin von Arelate I*, 'Texte und Kommentare' 3, Berlin, 1963 (fragments of the miscellanies with introd. and comm.; part II to follow); Brink in *OCD¹*, s.v.; A. Barigazzi, *Favorino, Opere* (1966).                                                                    H. S. L.

**FEBRIS,** the *numen* of fever (it is rash to assume that it was malaria, the early history of which is imperfectly known, see P. Fraccaro, *Studi Etruschi* 1928, 3 ff.). She had three temples in Rome alone (Valerius Maximus 2. 5. 6), in which *remedia* (amulets?) which had proved efficacious were placed. Dedications to her have been found in various parts of the Roman Empire (see Wissowa, *RK* 246), some of which call her Tertiana and Quartana, clearly referring to malaria.            H. J. R.

**FEDERAL STATES** first appear in Greece in the fifth century B.C., were most numerous and influential in the Hellenistic age, and continued under Rome as local governments in parts of Greece and Asia Minor. Though their influence on the course of events was considerable, they are particularly important as one of the two chief instruments used by the Greeks for creating unities larger than city-states, namely the *symmachia* (q.v.) and the federal State (*sympoliteia*, q.v.). Organizations of both types commonly are called leagues, but to differentiate, it may be well to call federal States confederacies. A distinguishing mark is that while the *symmachia* claimed to preserve the freedom of its members, the *sympoliteia* limited their freedom by the creation of a federal government. Hence the King's Peace led to the dissolution of the Boeotian and other federal States.

**2.** Federal States developed from tribal units (Boeotians, Arcadians, etc.), and so frequently, even in Roman imperial times, a federal State was called an *ethnos* instead of a *koinon*, and c. 300 B.C. the states of Greece were classified as *ethne* (federal States and tribal States) and *poleis* (*IG²* iv. 1. 68). *Koinon* and *ethnos* are not synonyms, *koinon* meaning 'commonwealth' and *ethnos* 'nation' as in the phrase, 'the *koinon* of the *ethnos* of the Phocians' (*IG* vii. 3426). In some tribes cities developed early, but did not cause the dissolution of the tribe, and such conditions in time led to the growth of federal States. In other tribes, e.g. the Aetolians, a looser ethnic organization was long retained and later transformed into a *sympoliteia*. In either case, if a powerful State was to be developed, it was necessary to overstep the ethnic boundary and incorporate units outside the tribe. This policy was not employed extensively before the third

century B.C., when it was used most successfully by the Achaeans. In most cases federal citizenship seems to have included civil rights in all cities of the confederacy but the rights to vote and hold office only in one.

**3.** From the very beginning oligarchic States seem to have been more ready than democratic States to adopt representative government, though it must be noted that information is so scanty as to make generalizations dangerous. There is extant a description of the oligarchic Boeotian Confederacy as it was in the early fourth century. The right to vote depended on a property qualification, apparently the hoplite census, and the local governments were uniform with one-fourth of the active citizens serving as the *boule* and the rest as the *ekklesia*. For federal purposes the country was divided into eleven parts. Thebes, with subject communities, controlled four; Orchomenus and Thespiae, together with smaller communities grouped with them, controlled two each; Tanagra, one; the other two districts each included three towns. Each of the eleven parts furnished one Boeotarch, sixty federal *bouleutai* and an unknown number of judges, supplied equal contributions to the federal treasury, and furnished 1,000 hoplites and 100 horsemen to the army. The other numbers are precise, those for the soldiers (obviously) approximate; undoubtedly all active citizens of military age could be called. The federal *boule* was the final authority and thus the federal government was representative. The Confederacy, founded about 447 B.C., was dissolved at the King's Peace. The later confederacy of the time of Epaminondas was democratic; it had Boeotarchs, and a primary assembly meeting at Thebes and dominated by the Thebans. The Arcadian Confederacy organized in 370 had a form of government that suggests democracy with a *boule*, a primary assembly called the Ten Thousand, and a single general as its chief executive. An inscription which mentions the *boule* also lists fifty *damiorgoi* by cities showing an inequality of representation, thus suggesting, whatever was their relation to the *boule*, a system of representation in proportion to population also for this body.

**4.** The functioning and duties of the central government varied from State to State. The frequency with which the head of a confederacy was named general indicates that the federal government was concerned largely with foreign affairs. Apparently as many details as possible were left to the cities. There were federal treasurers and a treasury, but seldom taxes collected directly by federal authorities. Instead cities contributed their quotas, commonly on the ratio of their representation in the federal council. The amount collected varied according to the need, so that, when much booty was taken, the cities could hope for a reduction of their contributions. The federal secretaries must have been busy handling the many communications to the federal government from foreign and domestic sources. The judicial system varied. In Aetolia the *synedrion* seems to have been the only federal court, while for early Boeotia, Acarnania both early and late, and Lycia, a federal judiciary is clearly attested.

**5.** Whatever the constitutional form, the government of a federal State, through relatively greater activity of magistrates and council and less full attendance at meetings of the primary assembly, in practice functioned more nearly like a representative government than that of a normal city-state. The Boeotian Confederacy and many of the later confederacies took the step outright and dispensed with the primary assembly, which, however, was retained by the Aetolians as long as their Confederacy flourished and by the Achaeans to about 200 B.C. The Thessalian Confederacy, organized in 194 B.C., had as its chief organ of government a *synedrion* of over 300 members; each of the four Macedonian republics organized in 167 B.C. had a *synedrion* consisting of elected representatives; and the Lycian Confederacy flourishing in the same period is said by Strabo to have had a *synedrion* in which the cities, depending on their size, each had one, two, or three votes. The Lycian inscriptions from imperial times at first surprise the reader by quoting decrees passed by an *ekklesia*, but closer study shows that this was itself a representative body.

6. Only a few of the better-known States have been mentioned. Notice also that, when dates have been given to a Confederacy, these apply only to the government described and do not exclude the existence of a confederacy with a different form of government at other times.

ANCIENT SOURCES. Boeotian constitution: *Hell. Oxy.* 16 (11). Arcadian *damiorgoi*: Tod 132 (date: M. Cary, *JHS* 1922, 188). Thessalian *synedrion*: *IG* ix. 2. 261. Lycian Confederacy: Strabo 14. 664; documents in *TAM* ii.
MODERN LITERATURE. General: E. A. Freeman, *History of Federal Government* (ed. Bury, 1893); G. Fougères in Dar.–Sag., s.v. 'Koinon'; G. Busolt, *Griechische Staatskunde* ii (1926), 1395–575; J. A. O. Larsen, *Representative Government in Greek and Roman History* (U.S.A. 1955); *Greek Federal States* (U.S.A. 1968); V. Ehrenberg, *The Greek State* (1960), pt. i, ch. iii. Special: Federal coinage, M. O. B. Caspari, *JHS* 1917. Lycia: Jones, *Cities E. Rom. Prov.* ch. iii. Federal ctizenship: Larsen, *Symb. Oslo.* 1957, 5 ff.
　　　　　　　　　　　　　　　　　　　　J. A. O. L.

**FELICITAS,** a goddess of good luck, not heard of till the middle of the second century B.C., when L. Licinius Lucullus dedicated her temple on the Velabrum (see Platner–Ashby, 207); another was planned by Julius Caesar and erected after his death by M. Aemilius Lepidus where the Curia Hostilia had stood (ibid.). She is associated with Venus Victrix, Honos, and Virtus at Pompey's theatre (*Fast. Amit.* on 12 Aug.); with the Genius Publicus and Venus Victrix on the Capitol (ibid., 9 Oct.); with the *numen Augusti* (*Fast. Praenest.* on 17 Jan.). Thereafter she is important in official cult under the emperors, appearing frequently on coins (*Felicitas saeculi* with figure of the goddess) and in addresses to the gods in dedications, etc., immediately after the Capitoline triad.

Wissowa, *RK* 266–7.　　　　　　　　　　　　　H. J. R.

**FELIX,** MARCUS ANTONIUS (*PW* 54), freedman of Antonia, Claudius' mother, was brother of Pallas (q.v. 3). Perhaps sent in A.D. 52 to Samaria with the rank of procurator during the trial of Ventidius Cumanus, he was soon appointed procurator of Judaea, where unrest increased during his administration. He was St. Paul's judge. Accused by the Jews of Caesarea, he was acquitted. He married (1) Drusilla, granddaughter of Antony and Cleopatra, and (2) Drusilla, daughter of Agrippa I. He was succeeded by Festus (q.v. 1) *c.* 60.

E. Schürer, *Geschichte des jüdischen Volkes* i⁴. 571 ff.; A. Momigliano, *Annali Scuola Normale Pisa* 1934, 388 ff.　　　A. M.

**FELSINA,** modern *Bologna*, the most important of the Etruscan cities north of the Apennines, was established in the mid sixth century B.C. on the site of the flourishing Iron Age settlement that has given its name to the Villanovan culture (*see* VILLANOVANS), and continued its function as an entrepôt for trade with northern Europe. The Certosa cemetery has produced the finest of a number of late-sixth-century bronze *situlae* decorated with *repoussé* figures, quantities of Greek pottery imported presumably via Spina and Adria (qq.v.), and a number of fifth-century funerary stelae, some of which bear the earliest representations of Gauls to be found in the Mediterranean world. The Roman colony of Bononia (q.v. 1) was founded in 189 B.C.

A. Grenier, *Bologne villanovienne et étrusque* (1912); P. Ducati, *Storia di Bologna* i (1928); G. Mansuelli, *Atti e Mem. Dep. St. Patria Romagne* 1943–5, 1 ff.; id. *Stud. Etr.* 1957, 13 ff.; id. and R. Scarani, *L'Emilia prima dei Romani* (1961); *Mostra dell'Etruria Padana e della città di Spina* (1960); *Preistoria dell'Emilia e Romagna*, 2 vols. (1962–3); Scullard, *Etr. Cities*, 198 ff.　　　D. W. R. R.

**FENESTELLA** (52 B.C.–A.D. 19 or, possibly, 35 B.C.–A.D. 36), the antiquarian annalist, wrote a Roman history in at least twenty-two books, perhaps from the origins, certainly to 57 B.C.; the citations of Asconius reflect his special authority for the Ciceronian period. The fragments, which, however, may come also from works on constitutional and social antiquities, show his wide antiquarian interests and critical ability, in the Varronian tradition. The Elder Pliny used him, and an epitome was made. *See* SCHOLARSHIP, LATIN, IN ANTIQUITY.

Peter, *HRRel.* ii. cix. 79; L. Mercklin, *De Fenestella* (1844); J. Poeth, *De Fenestella* (1849).　　　　　　　　　　　A. H. McD.

**FERENTINUM,** modern *Ferentino*, town of the Hernici (q.v.), whose loyalty to Rome in 306 B.C. secured a measure of independence for it until 90 B.C. Its well-preserved walls, with polygonal lower and squared upper courses, are singularly interesting: the two styles may be coeval (1st *c.* B.C. for the citadel fortifications).

G. Lugli, *La tecnica edilizia romana* (1957), 127 ff.　　E. T. S.

**FERALIA,** Roman All Souls' Day, 21 Feb., last of the *dies parentales* (beginning at noon on 13 Feb.), during which each household made offerings at the graves of its dead (Ov. *Fasti* 2. 533 ff.). It is marked NP in imperial calendars (cf. DIES FASTI), but F in the Fasti Antiates; what public ritual, if any, was performed and whether any change in this respect took place under Augustus is unknown.　　　　　　　　　　　　　　　　H. J. R.

**FERIAE,** the Latin term for a day of festival. The basic notion included not only the honouring of gods, but also the abstention from work. Hence, the phrase '*ferias observare*' used of treating work as taboo for ritual reasons. In late times there were recognized piacular ceremonies for work done on *feriae*. Festivals could be of various kinds: some fixed by the regular calendar of the *Fasti* (*stativae*); others such as the *Feriae sementivae* dedicated to Tellus and Ceres were announced annually (*indictivae*). Movable festivals, which were held annually on days appointed by priests or magistrates, were known as *conceptivae*. Besides public festivals the period assigned to private ceremonial might be classed as *feriae*—e.g. the *denicales* or ten days of mourning.

Latte, *RR passim*; A. K. Michels, *The Calendar of the Roman Republic* (U.S.A, 1967), 69 ff., 130 ff. For Feriae Latinae *see* JUPITER § 5.
　　　　　　　　　　　　　　　　　　　　H. W. P.

**FERONIA** (Fē-, Verg. *Aen.* 7. 800; Hor. *Sat.* 1. 5. 24; and elsewhere), an Italian goddess, officially received in Rome before 217 B.C. (Livy 22. 1. 18), and given a temple in the Campus Martius (*Fast. Arval.* on 13 Nov.). Her principal place of worship was the *lucus Capenatis*, later Lucus Feroniae (q.v.), near Mt. Soracte (Cato, *Orig.* 1, fr. 26 Jordan; Verg. *Aen.* 7. 697; Strabo 5. 2. 9; Pliny, *HN* 3. 51). Her cult, however, is shown by inscriptional and other evidence to have been widely spread in central Italy (see Wissowa, *RK* 285 f.; Latte, *RR* 189). Of her functions and the etymology of her name, which may be Etruscan, nothing is known, and the ancients seem to have been equally uncertain, to judge by the variety of guesses recorded (Wissowa, ibid. 286). Strabo (loc. cit.) says that a ceremony of fire-walking was performed in her precinct, but this seems to be a confusion with the so-called Apollo of Soracte (see Verg. *Aen.* 11. 785 ff. and commentators there). Near Tarracina slaves were set free in her shrine (Servius on *Aen.* 8. 564); perhaps on Greek analogies.

Latte, *RR* 189 f.　　　　　　　　　　　　　　H. J. R.

**FESCENNINI (VERSUS),** ribald wedding-songs (Catull. 61. 126–55); cf. the licentious verses sung by soldiers at triumphs. Ancient etymologies were: Fescennium, a town in Etruria, and *fascinum* (= witchcraft, which the songs were supposed to avert). Similar verses were said to be exchanged at harvest-festivals between masked entertainers; such performances were thought to have been the origin of drama (q.v.). For a possible parallel see Hor. *Sat.* 1. 5. 51–70; but see *PW* s.v. 'Fescennini'. On ancient explanations of the origin of Roman drama, see C. O. Brink in *Entretiens Hardt* ix, 175 ff.                                                    W. B.

**FESTIVALS** (Greek). A festival is a sacred rite repeated yearly or with regular intervals of a certain number of years (every eight, four, two years; in this case there is often a lesser celebration in the intervening years, and except for the Dionysiac orgia, the enlargement consists of games); it is celebrated by an assembly at a certain time and after the introduction of the calendar on a certain day or days, often at full moon. The Roman custom of *feriae conceptiuae*, the day of which was fixed by the magistrate within certain limits, is not known in Greece. A remarkable circumstance is that most of the old festivals took place at full moon, generally on the twelfth day of the lunar month, except for those of Apollo which fell on his holy day, the seventh, and those of his mythological sister Artemis which fell on the day before. It is apparent that many rites are predeistic, i.e. magical rites efficient without the interference of any personal god, and only subsequently attached to the cult of a god. Sometimes a great god took possession of a festival which belonged to a lesser god— as happened with Apollo and the Hyacinthia, in which a preliminary sacrifice was offered to the hero Hyacinthus, in fact a pre-Greek god.

Aristotle remarks that in early times festivals chiefly took place after the harvesting of crops and fruits, and in fact a survey of the Greek festivals of early origin proves that most of them were agrarian. This corresponds to the old mode of life in which the people subsisted on the products of their own land, and to the fact that agrarian customs are bound up with the seasons and in consequence easily conform to a calendrical regulation. There is, therefore, much evidence for such festivals in the more backward regions of Greece. The old rites contained in them are very important for the history of Greek religion. Even at an early date people flocked together to a sanctuary at a given time. Their original purpose was to perform worship, but to this were added games, merrymaking, and markets. Such festivals were called *panegyreis* and take place even in modern Greece in a manner very reminiscent of the old. The most famous of the ancient *panegyreis* are the great games, the Olympia, Pythia, etc. (qq.v.).

The state of things described above was already in an early time changed by town life. The cult was the concern of the State and its magistrates had charge of it. They performed the rites and arranged the festivals. Almost every god who was not too unimportant had his festival day on which the people went to his temple. Although old rites were carefully preserved, the procession and the sacrifice including the meal that followed became the most prominent parts of the festival, in which great pomp was displayed. The sixth century B.C., in which great temples were built, marked a great advance in this direction, especially due to the tyrants. The Athenian democracy developed this during its heyday; the lavish sacrifices were a means to humour the people. In early times the colonies sent embassies (θεωροί: see THEOROI) to the festivals of the mother town, and the cities to the national games. The Athenians enjoined on their colonies and allies to send sacrificial animals, etc., to the Panathenaea and the Great Dionysia, and on these occasions displayed their glory to them. In the Hellenistic age it became very common for the cities to send embassies to each others' festivals, especially to the games. New festivals were instituted, many in commemoration of political events, but these are uninteresting, comprising only processions, sacrifices, and games. These festivals were for a great part an expression of the political aspirations of the cities.

Nilsson, *Feste*; L. Deubner, *Attische Feste* (1932–59); P. Stengel, *Die griech. Kultusaltertümer*[3] (1920), 190 ff. (including the games); Nilsson, *GGR* i[2]. 826 ff. (the *panegyreis*).                         M. P. N.

**FESTIVALS** (Roman). *See* FERIAE.

**FESTUS** (1), PORCIUS (*PW* 36, a very full discussion (1953) of the chronological difficulties), succeeded Felix (q.v.) as a procurator of Judaea *c.* A.D. 60 (date very uncertain). He fought against the Sicarii and a pseudo-prophet and was involved in the controversy between the Jews and Agrippa II. He carried on the trial against St. Paul, whom he sent to Rome (Acts xxv–xxvi). He died in A.D. 62.                                              A. M.

**FESTUS** (2), SEXTUS POMPEIUS (late 2nd c. A.D.), scholar, epitomizer of the *De significatu verborum* of Verrius Flaccus (q.v. 8). Of his work (alphabetically arranged in twenty books) the first half is lost. Festus himself was epitomized in the eighth century by Paulus Diaconus. The standard edition (including Paulus) is that of W. M. Lindsay (1913) whose later edition in *Glossaria Latina* iv (93–467) incorporates Festus material gleaned from glossaries. *See* SCHOLARSHIP, LATIN.

Schanz–Hosius, § 341.                                            J. F. M.

**FESTUS** (3, *PW* 11), RUFIUS, *magister memoriae* under Valens, wrote a *Breviarium rerum gestarum populi Romani* from the origins to the accession of Valens. The first part described the conquest of the Roman provinces, the second the eastern wars from Sulla, especially the Parthian Wars. Dedicated to Valens, it appeared after the Gothic peace (A.D. 369), at the height of the Persian War. It represents ultimately the epitomized Livian tradition and a compendious imperial History.

Ed. W. Förster (1874); C. Wagener (1886); J. W. Eadie, *The Breviarium of Festus* (1967). A. Momigliano, *Conflict between Paganism and Christianity in Fourth Century* (1963), 95, 98.     A. H. McD.

**FETIALES,** Roman priestly officials who conducted international relationships, as treaties and declarations of war. They were twenty (Varro ap. Non. 529), forming a *collegium* (Livy 36. 3. 7), variously said to have been founded by one or another of the kings; who its head was is not known, but it deliberated on questions affecting the state of war or peace (Varro, ibid.), though only in an advisory capacity, like all priestly *collegia*; the commonwealth decided what action should be taken.

Our chief informant as to their ritual is Livy. He states (1. 24. 4 ff.) that to make a treaty two *fetiales* were sent. One of these was the *uerbenarius* or *uerbenatus* (see Pliny, *HN* 22. 5; Varro ap. Non. 528), who carried herbs (*uerbenae, sagmina*) from the Arx; the other was the *pater patratus* (of doubtful meaning, most probably a 'fully-created father', i.e. not merely one by nature, but also formally appointed by the state). He, after the terms of the treaty had been read aloud in the presence of the other state's *fetiales*, pronounced a conditional curse on Rome if she were the first to break it, confirming this by killing a pig with a *lapis silex*, probably a neolithic implement, cf. JUPITER; STONES, SACRED. On occasion several pairs of *fetiales* might be sent (Livy 30. 43. 9).

If an injury were received from another state, the *pater patratus* crossed the border, first announcing, with his head veiled in a woollen garment (*filum*), who he was and what he came for, calling on Jupiter, *fas*, and the boundaries themselves to hear him and swearing to Jupiter that his errand was just. This formula was several times repeated at various stages of the journey. If within thirty-three days satisfaction was not given, he formally denounced the offending nation to all the gods and returned to Rome. The Senate would then be consulted by the chief magistrate, and, if it voted for seeking satisfaction *iusto pioque bello*, the *fetialis* went once more to the boundary, and there, after formally declaring a state of war in the presence of at least three adults, cast across it either an ordinary spear or a cornel stake sharpened and hardened in the fire (*hastam praeustam sanguineam*; to translate the last word by 'bloody' is a many-times-refuted blunder) (Livy 1. 32. 5 ff.). In case of war with a distant nation, the spear was cast upon a piece of land near the *columna bellica* in Rome (*see* BELLONA), which by a legal fiction was considered hostile territory. This was first done in the war with Pyrrhus (Servius on *Aen.* 9. 53 (52)), and was still in use under Marcus Aurelius (Dio Cassius 71. 33. 3; see Frazer on Ov. *Fast.* 6. 206). Other functions of the *fetiales*, however, as the formal claim (*clarigatio*) for satisfaction, described above, seem to have gone comparatively early out of use. Generally the office appears to have lapsed in the last century of the Republic and been revived by Augustus. (For changes by the end of the third century B.C. see F. W. Walbank, *CPhil.* 1949, 15 ff.) By a kind of pun, the origin of the *ius fetiale* was credited to the Aequicoli ('Plain-dwellers', misunderstood as 'cultivators of equity').

Wissowa, *RK* 550 ff.; T. Frank, *Roman Imperialism*, ch. 1; *CPhil.* 1912; Mommsen–Marquardt, *Manuel* i. 280 ff., vii. 377; Latte, *RR* 121 ff.; Ogilvie, *Comm. Livy 1–5*, 127 ff. H. J. R.

**FIBULA** (περόνη, πόρπη). The primitive brooch or fibula, of violin-bow form resembling the modern safety-pin, is found in late-Bronze-Age times in Greece, northern Italy, and central Europe. A single centre of diffusion is highly probable, and it is now widely accepted that the fibula is an Aegean invention, developed in the thirteenth century out of a Minoan type of pin which had the end bent to prevent slipping. By further bending until the end, flattened into a catch, could engage the point, the fibula was produced, and the addition of a spiral coil at the angle to increase the tension is also of early date. Later improvements enlarge the bow so as to grip more cloth. Large fibulae from mainland Greece, of late-Geometric times, have broad catchplates with incised figure decoration; the Cypriote type has a double-arched bow, the Asiatic a stilted one. The 'spectacle' type, in which the bow is replaced by spiral coils of wire, is considered of Danubian origin by some authorities. It was current in Greece, and imitated in bone and ivory in the seventh century. After 600 B.C. the fibula falls into comparative disuse in Greece, and no new types appear until Roman times. In Italy the development is unbroken and the types more varied: the bow looped, bent, threaded with disks, or thickened into the 'leech' or 'boat' form; the catchplate set transversely or fantastically prolonged. In the fifth century the simpler 'Certosa' type becomes universal and gives rise to the La Tène forms, in which the spiral spring is bilateral, and ultimately to the Roman in which, under the early Empire, a hinge replaces the spiral.

C. Blinkenberg, *Fibules grecques et orientales* (1926); R. Hampe, *Frühe griechische Sagenbilder* (1936); J. Sundwall, *Die älteren italischen Fibeln* (1943). F. N. P.

**FIDEICOMMISSUM.** A testator could make bequests out of his inheritance by legacy (*legatum*) or *fideicommissum*. The principal forms of *legatum* were: (1) *per vindicationem*, which enabled the legatee to claim his legacy directly by *vindicatio* (q.v.) from anyone in possession of it, and which was therefore confined to specific things of which the testator had *dominium* (q.v.) *ex iure Quiritium*; (2) *per damnationem*, which confined the legatee to a claim

against the heir, but which had a much wider scope (e.g. legacy of an annuity, or of a debt owed to the testator, or of an act to be performed by the heir). Whereas a *legatum* had to be left in a prescribed form and was chargeable only on an heir appointed by will, a *fideicommissum* was an informal request by the testator to any person who benefited from the inheritance (by will or on intestacy, by legacy or even by another *fideicommissum*). Such requests were originally not legally enforceable, but were simply 'committed to the faith' of the person addressed. Augustus, however, caused some individual *fideicommissa* to be enforced by the consuls, and they later became generally actionable before a *praetor fideicommissarius* (first appointed under Claudius) by *cognitio extraordinaria*. The original purpose of *fideicommissa* was to benefit a person who was legally unable to be an heir or a legatee (e.g. a peregrine, or a woman debarred by the *Lex Voconia* (q.v.)), but most such persons were excluded during the first two centuries A.D., and a *fideicommissum* became in most respects a formless legacy. It could, however, effect a transfer of the entire inheritance from the heir to some other person, either immediately or at some future date, and could therefore be used to create a 'family settlement' lasting several generations or even indefinitely. Hadrian, however, forbade *fideicommissa* in favour of uncertain (including unborn) persons. Justinian revoked this prohibition but restricted the duration of such settlements to four generations.

The formalities of *legata* were abolished in A.D. 339, and Justinian removed all distinctions between different types of *legatum* and almost all distinctions between *legata* and *fideicommissa*. See also INHERITANCE, LAW OF.

G. Grosso, *I legati nel dirritto romano²*. (1962). B. N.

**FIDENAE,** modern *Castel Giubileo*, the first station on the Via Salaria (q.v.). In early Latium it frequently fought Rome, which controlled a rival Tiber crossing 5 miles downstream. After 390 B.C. Fidenae dwindled to unimportance. Its quarries supplied stone for the Servian Walls of Rome. In A.D. 27 an amphitheatre collapsed there causing great loss of life.

E. Panaitescu, *Ephemeris Dacoromana* 1924, 416 f. E. T. S.

**FIDES,** the Roman personification of good faith. Although her temple (on the Capitol, near that of Jupiter, with whom she is closely connected) is no older than 254 B.C. (see Platner–Ashby, 209), her cult is traditionally very old, said to have been founded by Numa (Livy 1. 21. 4). Livy also gives details of her ritual; the *flamines* (q.v.), meaning probably the *flamines maiores*, drove to her shrine in a covered carriage drawn by two beasts, and the sacrificer must have his hand covered with a white cloth. A pair of covered hands is indeed her symbol, as often on coins commemorating the *fides* of the Augusti, the legions, etc., in imperial times. Since giving the hand is a common gesture of solemn agreement, the symbolism is natural.

Wissowa, *RK* 133 f.; Latte, *RR* 237. H. J. R.

**FIMBRIA,** GAIUS FLAVIUS (*PW* 88), son of a *novus homo* (consul 104 B.C.) and friend of Marius. He supported Cinna and killed some eminent men after his return (87), trying to assassinate or prosecute Scaevola (q.v. 4) after the death of Marius who had protected him. Sent to Asia in 86 as legate of Valerius Flaccus (q.v. 6), he killed him in a mutiny and assumed his command. Ruthless but successful, he nearly captured Mithridates, whom Lucullus (q.v. 2) allowed to escape. After his peace with Mithridates, Sulla attacked Fimbria with overwhelming superiority, forcing him to commit suicide. (85). E. B.

**FINANCE, GREEK AND HELLENISTIC.** Conclusions on the revenue and expenditure of the Minoan and Mycenean kings are at present only guesswork based on excavations or disputed Linear B lists and treasury accounts. Homeric finance was simple. The kings had comparatively high expenses for household, wars, and hospitality; their revenues came from the royal estate (*temenos*), from gifts (*dotinai*), personal services and customary contributions (*themistes*) of the people, from piracy, presents of foreign merchants and other foreigners, tributes and war-booty.

2. Sparta kept many Homeric characteristics up to the Classical period. No regular taxes existed, except a small contribution in kind to the kings. The helots paid nothing to the State, but gave a share of their crops to their Spartan landlords. The *perioikoi* may have paid a small tribute in kind to the kings, who also had a privileged share of the spoils. Irregular war revenue was derived from the enemy, from contributions of allies, or primitive collections within the community.

3. Exceptional expenses for court and bodyguards, public works, colonization, and wars were characteristic of the finances of the Greek tyrants, and it was, as a rule, impossible for them to pay all these out of the ordinary taxes. Confiscations, irregular levies, monopolies, the undemocratic poll-tax on free citizens, and even extortions had to be introduced to fill the always empty treasuries of such governments.

4. The financial system of the Greek cities, democratic and oligarchic, was more developed. Athens took the lead and was very often the model for smaller communities. The usual expenditure was concerned with police, army, navy, fortifications, ambassadors, palaestrae, gymnasia, education (a Hellenistic innovation), sacrifices, religious festivals, public works (those of Pericles were famous), distribution of money (*see* THEORIKA), grain, and other foodstuffs, salaries of State officials and of citizens entrusted with official duties (e.g. the Councillors, Dicasts, and *ekklesia* of Athens), honorary distinctions (e.g., entertainment in the Prytaneum at Athens), and the maintenance of orphans, invalids, and crippled soldiers.

5. The State revenues of Greek cities were varied. Most towns had a considerable income from state property, especially mines (e.g. the famous silver mines of Laurium in Attica), quarries, houses, and state domains. Court fees and fines at Athens and other towns were another important source of revenue. Direct taxes were, as a rule, only paid by foreigners, non-citizens, and despised professions (e.g. by *metoikoi*, freedmen, *hetairai*, certain craftsmen, and traders). The indirect taxes brought a greater return. The custom dues of Attica at the beginning of the fourth century B.C. amounted to 2 per cent on both exports and imports (during the fifth century, perhaps, only to 1 per cent). Of like importance were the customs of the Bosporus and Black Sea ports during the Classical period, of Rhodes and the Egyptian ports during the Hellenistic. Treaties made by Athens and other towns, many of which are preserved, provided for delivery, under favourable conditions, of grain and materials for army and navy.

6. Excise duties existed, at least in the smaller cities of Greece. They may have been influenced, in some cases, by the practice of Hellenistic monarchies. The so-called *eponia* represented *ad valorem* gate tolls, auction taxes, and taxes on sales. They were in some places varied for real estate, slaves, cattle, bread, wheat, wine, etc. Another group of excise duties was called *enkyklia*, a Greek term which may be rendered as 'taxes on transport'. Belonging to this group of indirect taxes were harbour rights and dues, fishing rights in lakes and in the ocean, ferry taxes payable from shippers, pasturage taxes, duties for the use of public scales, and for the use of temple precincts for business purposes. In addition,

there were a few land and cattle taxes during the Hellenistic period, and Classical as well as Hellenistic monopolies (q.v.). Certain liturgies (q.v.) had to be performed regularly too.

7. An important item of the Athenian Empire's budget in the fifth and fourth centuries, as well as of other hegemonic States, consisted in tribute and contributions from allies and subject States. The *phoros* of Aristides amounted to 460 talents, a sum which was subsequently increased. A certain amount of external revenue was derived from lands in the cleruchies (q.v.) of Athens and other powerful towns which belonged to the ruling State and were rented out as in the mother country. The regular revenues of Athens, the richest town of Classical Greece, were not always sufficient to meet expenditure. Irregular sources of income included *eisphora* (q.v.), *epidoseis*, and other endowments, sale of state property, public loans (often compulsory), selling of political rights and honours, tampering with the coinage, war booty, and financial expedients. The Athenian Empire and the temple States of Delphi and Olympia were able to collect large state treasures in times of peace.

8. Remarkable financial systems were developed in the Ptolemaic and Seleucid Empires, Syracuse, Hellenistic India, and other Hellenistic monarchies. The best-known of these, the Ptolemaic organization, may be described as typical. A planning economy regulated the Empire's budget. Attic and other city-state institutions were imitated. The expenditure was similar to that of the tyrants, but on a much larger scale. Monopolies (q.v.) were most important for the revenues. The whole country-side was farmed out as State land under rigorous State control of agriculture. The Greek poll-taxes, *eponia* and *enkyklia,* were used on a wider scale than in the *poleis*. The Ptolemaic control of agriculture, banking, commerce, and industry of Egypt's administrative units reminds us of the planning economies of the eighteenth and twentieth centuries A.D. As Greek *polis* economy has influenced all later public financial organization in countries with free economy, so most later tendencies to planned economy from Byzantium and Hellenistic India to modern times seem to show a clear connexion with such Hellenistic systems.

*See* AGRICULTURE, ANTIDOSIS, ARISTIDES (1), BANKS, BOULE, COINAGE (GREEK), DICASTERIES, ECCLESIA, EISPHORA, ENDOWMENTS, EUBULUS, INDUSTRY, LAURIUM, LITURGY, LYCURGUS (3), METICS, MINES, MONEY, MONOPOLIES, PRYTANIS, SITOPHYLAKES, SOLON, SYMMORIA, THEORIKA, TRIERARCHY. Cp. with extensive earlier bibliography F. M. Heichelheim, *Wirtschaftsgeschichte des Altertums* (1939), index, s.v. 'Staatswirtschaft'; *An Ancient Economic History* i (1958), 280 ff., 522 ff. *passim*; ii (1964), 118 ff., 133 ff., 222 ff., 238 ff.; *Handwörterbuch der Sozialwirtschaften* (1956, 1962, 1963), art. 'Geld- und Muenzgeschichte I', Stadt II', 'Wirtschaftsgeschichte II, 1, 2 A'; *Kl. Pauly*, s.vv. 'Agio', 'Bank-Wesen', 'Bergbau', 'Darlehen', 'Eikoste', 'Finanz', 'Writschaft', 'Hekatoste', 'Hektemoroi', 'Hemiolion', 'Kredit'; M. I. Finley, *Land Credit in Ancient Athens* (1951); M. Th. Lenger, *Corpus des ordonnances des Ptolémées* (1964); Cl. Préaux, *L'économie royale des Lagides* (1939); Rostovtzeff, *Hellenistic World*.
F. M. H.

**FINANCE, ROMAN.** The management of Roman public finance formed a part of the general administration of public business; decisions relating to financial matters were made in the Republic by the Senate and in the Empire by the Emperor. The quaestors, and later other officials, in charge of the *aerarium* (q.v.) came to the post as a stage in a senatorial career, and had the duty of making payments when instructed and of preserving the cash and documents kept there, but had no responsibility for financial decisions or policy. Very little is known of the functions of the *a rationibus*, later *rationales*, employed by the Emperor. Only in the fourth century A.D. do we find the office of the Praetorian Prefect making up something resembling an annual budget, to determine the level of the *indictiones* (q.v.), or exactions in kind. Throughout Roman history there is little or no evidence of interest either in the technicalities of public accounts or budgeting, or even (except with the systematic reform by Diocletian) in the general structure of State finance or the principles of financial policy. Cicero's speeches *de lege agraria*, however, emphasize the importance of the *ager publicus* as a source of revenue and a reserve of wealth for the State. In the speech, directed to the conditions of the early third century A.D., which Cassius Dio (q.v. 2) puts into the mouth of Maecenas in book 52 of his *Roman History*, he proposes that public properties derived from confiscation should be sold, and the proceeds loaned to landholders; the needs of the State, which should be carefully calculated, should be met primarily from the revenue from mines and other properties; only then should taxes, direct and indirect, be levied. The anonymous author of the treatise *de rebus bellicis*(q.v.), probably written in the second half of the fourth century, makes proposals designed to decrease the burden of taxation and allow agriculture to flourish, specifying fraud at the mint, the corruption and excessive exactions of governors and tax-collectors, and the superfluous size of the army as the evils to be dealt with.

If serious analyses are lacking in our sources, so also are extended financial documents comparable to those of classical Athens. Only the two main inscriptions of Trajan's *alimenta* (q.v.) give substantial quantities of information on the workings of a financial operation—itself one which was quite unrepresentative of normal financial business. Frontinus' *De aquae ductu* includes some details of the expenditure on and revenue from the aqueducts of Rome.

Our earliest evidence for the general structure of Roman public finance comes from the sketch of the Roman constitution in the sixth book of Polybius, reflecting conditions in the mid second century B.C. The *aerarium* was managed by two urban quaestors; but all decisions as to payments from it were made by the Senate. On setting out on campaign a consul could draw funds on his own responsibility. But further payments, for the supplies, clothes, or pay of the army, had again to be authorized by the Senate. The Senate also made a quinquennial grant to the censors (q.v.), on the basis of which they let out contracts for building and repairs of public buildings in Rome and the *municipia* and *coloniae* of Italy, and for the exploitation of public properties—rivers, harbours, gardens, mines, and land. Ultimate control of the contracts, for instance in altering the terms, again lay with the Senate.

The acquisition, from the third century onwards, of provinces outside Italy led to two main developments, not included in Polybius' sketch, the raising of tribute (*see* TRIBUTUM) in cash or kind, collected by *publicani* (q.v.) whose greatest period of influence covered the last century and a half of the Republic; and the establishment of provincial governors, who were made a grant, again by the Senate, for the expenses of themselves and their staff, and thereafter were responsible, with the provincial quaestor (q.v.), for revenue and expenditure in the province (the system is most fully illustrated by Cicero's *Verrines*. On his return the governor presented his accounts (*rationes*) to the *aerarium*; it is evident that these could be very perfunctory (see *Verr*. 2. 1. 36) and afforded no real check on the disposition of the funds. A stricter procedure was laid down by Julius Caesar, in accordance with which one copy of the *rationes* had to be left at each of two cities in the province, and a third deposited at the Aerarium.

The *aerarium* was the central depository of the State, for both cash and documents; the question of to what extent cash was physically transferred to it from the provinces remains, at all periods, quite obscure. Plut. *Cat. Min.* 16 is the best evidence for the functions of the quaestor, and his relations with the *aerarium* scribes. The *aerarium* contained the documents relating to the finance of the state, but its officials did not compile them into any sort of budget. The earliest examples of general accounts of the public funds are the *rationes imperii* published by Augustus, Tiberius (until A.D. 26), and Gaius, and the *breviaria* prepared by Augustus in 23 B.C. and A.D. 14. No *rationes* appear to have been published after the reign of Gaius; but the existence, from Tiberius onwards, of the post *a rationibus*, first held by imperial freedmen and later by *equites*, seems to indicate that *rationes* continued to be prepared. Precise evidence about the functions of the *a rationibus* is not abundant. Statius, *Silv*. 3. 3. 85–110, gives valuable details of the revenues and expenditures with which he was concerned; an inscription (*CIL* ix. 2438) shows an *a rationibus* of Marcus Aurelius concerned with protecting imperial flocks in Italy.

The establishment of the Empire meant the transfer from the Senate to the Emperor of the effective power of decision in financial matters, although the Senate retained the function of making routine votes of funds, especially for expenditures in Rome. The *publicani* ceased, finally, to collect taxes (q.v.) but continued to collect indirect taxes (*see* VECTIGAL) until replaced in the second century by imperial procurators (q.v.). A complication was introduced in the pattern of State finance by the appearance of the imperial treasury or *fiscus* (q.v.) whose origins, legal nature, and revenues remain in dispute. The first three centuries saw also the steady accretion of landed property (some of it from confiscation or inheritance) in the hands of the Emperor; the importance of revenue from such property is likely to have been considerable, but cannot be accurately assessed. From c. A.D. 200 documents reveal officials of two apparently separate types of imperial property, the *patrimonium* (q.v.) and the *res privata*; the distinction between them remains obscure. What is certain is that a considerable role in expenditure on public needs was played by the private funds of the Emperor; this is most fully attested at the very beginning of the Empire, in the *Res Gestae* of Augustus. By the third century little real distinction remained between public funds and properties and those of the Emperor.

The third century saw the culmination of two developments, the increasing strain of maintaining a permanent regular army without significant quantities of booty to compensate (in the Empire only Trajan's conquest of Dacia in 105–6 produced booty in large amounts), and the depreciation of the currency; the third century also witnessed a rapid inflation of prices. The result was a decline in the importance of the fixed cash tribute of the provinces (partly compensated for by ever more frequent demands for *aurum coronarium*, q.v.) and a tendency for the State to demand instead supplies in kind for payment to troops and officials. Under Diocletian the irregular requisitions in kind of the third century were put on a regular basis; censuses were taken throughout the Empire and payments assessed by units of population (*capitatio*) and of land (*iugatio*). The principles and workings of this system, which certainly varied from area to area, are still subject to debate. But it seems to have produced a more equitable assessment of capacity to pay and provided a measure of stability for the finance of the later Empire.

This period saw the full development of various tendencies manifest in the finance of the Principate. The Prefects of the *aerarium* are attested until the middle of the fourth century but were of no importance in the finance of the Empire as a whole. This was managed by three departments, the *res privata* which dealt primarily with imperial property, the *sacrae largitiones*, which controlled mines, mints, and State factories, collected taxes and levies in cash, and paid donatives to the troops, and the most important of the three, the office of the Praetorian Prefects, which was responsible for the rations of soldiers and officials, for the maintenance of the *cursus publicus* and of most public buildings, and for calculating annually the required rate of the indiction to produce the supplies in kind.

J. Marquardt, *Römische Finanzverwaltung*² (1884) = *Organisation Financière* (1888); Frank, *Econ. Survey* i and v; Jones, *Later Rom. Emp.*, 411 ff. F. G. B. M.

**FIRE.** That the central importance of fire was widely recognized is shown by its prominence both in myth (esp. Prometheus) and in cosmological speculation. Since until recent times its kindling required considerable effort, the easiest way to ensure the availability of fire was to have a flame or glowing embers (ζώπυρα) always burning. The ubiquity of perpetual fires, both in public ritual and in private houses, may have been largely due to this, although there are indications that some 'everlasting' fires (e.g. that of Vesta) were rekindled annually. Similarly, banishment was traditionally *aquae et ignis interdictio*. If the fire went out and could not be relit from a neighbour's hearth, the most primitive way of restarting it was to rub two pieces of wood together until the friction generated sufficient heat. The usual πυρεῖον (*igniarium, ignitabulum*), however, was a kind of 'drill', consisting of a τρύπανον (*terebra*), for which laurel wood was thought best, and an ἐσχάρα (*tabula*), preferably of ivy-wood, in which it was rapidly rotated, usually with the aid of a thong or a bow-like contrivance. But side by side with this it was known, by the fifth century B.C. or earlier, that sparks could be struck from pyrites or flint with a second stone or with a piece of iron or steel to set alight tinder (*fomes*) of dry leaves, fungus, or similar material (later sometimes sticks dipped in sulphur). Finally, it was known also, at least by Aristophanes' time, that the rays of the sun could by refraction in a suitably shaped piece of glass or rock-crystal (or even in drops of oil or water) be sufficiently concentrated to kindle tinder placed at the focal point. But this method of fire-lighting was probably very rare, and the use of reflection from a concave (metal) mirror was almost certainly even rarer. Yet Archimedes may well have known the theory of kindling fire at a distance by so arranging a group of mirrors that they reflect the sun's rays to a common focus; but the story that he set fire to the Roman fleet in this way must be apocryphal.

Theophrastus, *de Igne*. M. H. Morgan, *Harv. Stud.* 1890, 13 ff. (with sources). L. A. M.

**FIRMICUS MATERNUS,** JULIUS, of Syracuse, wrote (A.D. 334–7) an astrological treatise, *Mathesis*, in eight books, the first containing an apologia for astrology. Firmicus urges the highest moral integrity on the astrologer. The conflict between destiny and freedom of will he resolves on Stoic lines: the soul, being divine, can triumph over the stars. Firmicus shows small technical knowledge; his merit, if any, is rhetorical and stylistic. Later, converted to Christianity, he wrote a fanatical *De errore profanarum religionum*—of great interest to the student of religion—urging Constantius and Constans to eradicate paganism. Dom Morin's attribution of *Consultationes Zacchaei et Apollonii* (ed. 1935) to this author has not gained universal acceptance.

TEXTS. *Mathesis*, Kroll–Skutsch–Ziegler (1897–1913). *De errore*, K. Ziegler (1953, trans., 1953); with comm., G. Heuten (also trans., 1938), A. Pastorino (1956). L. R. P.; A. H.-W.

**FIRST FRUITS.** The rite of bringing first fruits to the gods is not strongly characterized in ancient Greece. It is comprised under the rite known as *panspermia*, the bringing of a mixture of fruits at various festivals, some-

times cooked in a pot (at the Thargelia and the Pyanopsia). Θαλύσια are, according to the lexicographers, *aparchai* (q.v.) of the fruits and also the first loaf baked after the threshing. The opinions have been advanced that the offering of first fruits represents the breaking of the taboo imposed upon the unripe fruits and that it serves to enhance the power of the remaining crop; in the opinion of the Greeks themselves they were brought in order to ensure fertility; they were also called εὐετηρία, i.e. a Good Year. They survive in ecclesiastical usage today under the ancient name κόλλυβα.

Nilsson, *GGR* i². 127 ff. M. P. N.

**FISCUS** originally meant 'basket' or 'money-bag' and thence came to be used, in relation to private persons, like 'pocket' ('ex suo fisco', Val. Max. 6. 2. 11), or, in an administrative context, to mean the public funds held by a provincial governor (Cic. *Verr.* 2. 3. 197; Suet. *Div. Aug.* 101). Its most important use came to be that of denoting the funds of the Emperor, as opposed to the public *aerarium* (q.v.).

The question of the origins, legal nature, and revenues of the imperial *fiscus* remains in dispute. The principal views are:

1. The *fiscus* was the property of the Emperor; its income was formed principally by the revenues of the imperial provinces (Mommsen, *Röm. Staatsr.* ii³. 998 ff.). On this view the distinction between *fiscus* and *aerarium* was a product of the 'dyarchy' of Emperor and Senate, and of the division of the provinces.

2. 'Fiscus' was used originally only of the private funds of the Emperor (Sen. *de ben.* 7. 6. 3), by extension from the usage relating to private persons. Its revenues came at first from properties, gifts, and inheritances, plus probably *aurum coronarium* (q.v.) and *manubiae* (q.v.), and its steady acquisition of wider sources of income represents an encroachment of the Emperor on the public domain.

3. The *fiscus* was in part the property of the Emperor, but the word is also used, by extension from the usage relating to the funds held by proconsuls, to refer to the public funds held by the Emperor, principally in his capacity as governor of the imperial provinces.

It is clear that by the end of the first century, if not before, the *fiscus* was a recognized legal entity. Nerva appointed a praetor to hear cases between the *fiscus* and *privati* (*Dig.* 1. 2. 2. 32), while Hadrian instituted the post of *advocatus fisci* to represent the *fiscus* in such cases. The legal writers of the late second and third centuries indicate that the *fiscus* has a number of important privileges in litigation; in this period such cases were normally judged by imperial *procuratores* (q.v.).

A number of other *fisci* (*fiscus Asiaticus, fiscus Alexandrinus, fiscus frumentarius, fiscus castrensis, fisci transmarini*) are known only from inscriptions of the imperial *liberti* attached to them; nothing is known of their nature or of their relationship to the *fiscus*. The *fiscus libertatis et peculiorum* presumably received the payments made by imperial slaves for manumission, and the property which reverted to the Emperor from his slaves and *liberti* on death.

The *fiscus Iudaicus* received the special poll-tax of two *denarii* p.a. paid by all Jews after the revolt of 66–70. Cases relating to this payment were heard by a *procurator* (Suet. *Dom.* 12) and *ostraka* and a papyrus recording payment of the tax are known from Egypt.

O. Hirschfeld, *Die kaiserlichen Verwaltungsbeamten* (1905), 29 ff., 48 ff.; S. Bolla, *Die Entwicklung des Fiskus zum Privatrechtssubjekt* (1938); H. Last, *JRS* 1944, 51 ff.; C. H. V. Sutherland, *AJPhil.* 1945, 151 ff.; A. H. M. Jones, *JRS* 1950, 22 ff. (= *Studies in*

Roman Government and Law (1960), 99 ff.); F. Millar, *JRS* 1963, 29 ff.; P. A. Brunt, *JRS* 1966, 75 ff. *Fiscus Iudaicus*: Tcherikover and Fuks, *Corpus Papyrorum Iudaicarum* ii (1960), 111 ff. F. G. B. M.

**FISH, SACRED.** Fish were held sacred by various Oriental peoples. The Egyptian priests abstained from fish (Hdt. 2. 37) and there were local taboos on particular species. The Syrian reverence for fish early impressed the Greeks (Xen. *An.* 1. 4. 9); the temples of Atargatis (q.v.) regularly contained a pool for them, and a *lex sacra* from Smyrna (*SIG* 997 = Sokolowski, *Lois sacrées de l'Asie mineure*, 1955, 17) deals with their care. Atargatis punished with illness eaters of fish (Menand. fr. 544, Kock), and the taboo may have originated in the unwholesomeness of the local species. Her priests, however, ate them daily in a ritual meal (Mnaseas, *FHG* iii. 155), and they were a sacred food also in Thracian and Samothracian mystery cults, perhaps through Oriental influence; Julian (*Or.* 5. 176 d) says they were sacrificed in certain mystic rites (*and see* VOLCANUS). The early Christian symbolism of Ἰχθύς may be in part connected with their sanctity in Syria, but its popularity was enhanced by its equation with the formula Ἰ(ησοῦς) Χ(ριστὸς) θ(εοῦ) υ(ἱὸς) σ(ωτήρ), which constituted a convenient confession of faith. *See* BRIZO.

F. Cumont, *PW*, s.v. 'Ichthys'; F. J. Dölger, *IXΘYC* 1910, 1928–43; C. Andresen, *Die Religion in Geschichte und Gegenwart³* (ed. H. Gunkel and L. Zscharnack, 1956–62), s.v. 'Fisch'. F. R. W.

**FLACCUS** (1), QUINTUS FULVIUS (*PW* 59), as consul I (237 B.C.) fought against the Gauls in north Italy; censor (231); consul II (224) he temporarily subdued the Boii; *praetor urbanus* in 215 and again *extra ordinem* in 214 to guard Rome; *magister equitum* (213). As consul III (212) he captured Hanno's camp near Beneventum, thus cutting off supplies from Capua, which he then besieged and captured as proconsul (211); proconsul in Campania and dictator to hold the elections (210); consul IV (209), he won over some Lucanian hill-towns. He served again as proconsul (208/7), opposed Scipio's African expedition (205), and died soon afterwards. H. H. S.

**FLACCUS** (2), QUINTUS FULVIUS (*PW* 61) (*cos.* 179 B.C.), son of (1) above, was curule aedile in 184. As praetor in Spain in 182 he opened the campaigns against the Celtiberians (182–180) which led to the settlement of Ti. Sempronius Gracchus. Consul in 179 in Liguria, he became censor in 174, repatriating Latins in Rome and controlling the *equites*. In 173 he dedicated a temple to Fortuna Equestris, after despoiling the temple of Hera Lacinia in Croton. He committed suicide in 172. It is doubtful whether he built the Via Fulvia. A fine general and conservative senator, his career marks the Fulvian predominance after Scipio Africanus.

Scullard, *Rom. Pol.* 149, 190 ff. A. H. McD.

**FLACCUS** (3), MARCUS FULVIUS (*PW* 58), supporter of Ti. Gracchus (q.v. 3) and agrarian commissioner from 130 B.C. When the commission was prevented from applying the Gracchan limits on public land to the Italians (*see* SCIPIO 11), he proposed to offer them the citizenship to obtain the land, thus introducing the 'Italian question' into Roman politics. Elected consul (125) on this platform against Optimate opposition, he was circumvented by the Senate, which ordered him to assist Massilia against the Salluvii. Returning to triumph (123), he stooped to a tribunate (122) to aid C. Gracchus (q.v. 4) in carrying out an amended version of his policy and shared in his defeat and death (121). Cicero's description of him as a scholar (*Brutus* 108) helps to reveal the distortion that his picture has suffered in hostile sources.

E. Badian, *Foreign Clientelae* (1958), 176. E. B.

**FLACCUS** (4), LUCIUS VALERIUS (*PW* 173), the friend and colleague of Cato, curule aedile (201 B.C.), praetor in Sicily (199), was consul with Cato in 195, defeating the Boians and Insubrians (195–194). Legate at Thermopylae (191), he was triumvir in 190–189, reinforcing Placentia and Cremona and founding Bononia. Censor with Cato (184), he became *princeps senatus* on the death of Scipio Africanus; he died in 180. Capable but not outstanding, he maintained a conservative traditionalism against Hellenism in Rome.

Scullard, *Rom. Pol.* 124, 137, 153 ff. A. H. McD.

**FLACCUS** (5), LUCIUS VALERIUS (*PW* 176), *flamen Martialis*, was prosecuted *repetundarum* (101 B.C.?) after his praetorship (Cic. *Div. Caec.* 63). Consul in 100 with Marius, he was, according to Rutilius (q.v. 1), 'more his slave than his colleague'. As censor (97) with Antonius (q.v. 1), he apparently helped to enrol Italians generously as citizens. Made *princeps senatus* by Marcius Philippus (q.v. 4) and Perperna (q.v. 2) in 86, he worked for accommodation with Sulla; he joined him in time and (as *interrex*, late 82) secure him a vote of indemnity and election to the dictatorship, becoming his *magister equitum*. He seems to have died soon after, as he is not mentioned again. E. B.

**FLACCUS** (6), LUCIUS VALERIUS (*PW* 178), was unsuccessfully prosecuted after his aedileship (98 B.C.) by Decianus; he governed Asia after his praetorship. As suffect consul succeeding Marius (86) he was given the command against Mithridates in 86, passed a law cancelling three-quarters of all debts, and left for Asia, which he reached without a clash with Sulla. But he was murdered in a mutiny brought about by Fimbria (q.v.), who assumed his *imperium*. E. B.

**FLACCUS** (7), LUCIUS VALERIUS (*PW* 179), son of (6), served under his father and on the latter's death fled to his uncle Gaius in Gaul. He was military tribune under Servilius (q.v. 1) Vatia in Cilicia, quaestor in Spain under Piso (q.v. 4), legate of Metellus (q.v. 8) in Crete, then perhaps under Pompey. As urban praetor (63) he assisted Cicero against the Catilinarians and, after governing Asia (62–61), was successfully defended by him *repetundarum* in a largely extant speech (59). Legate of Piso (q.v. 5) in Macedonia, he died *c.* 54. E. B.

**FLACCUS** (8), VERRIUS, a freedman, the most erudite of the Augustan scholars and teacher of the grandsons of Augustus. His works (now lost) included *Libri rerum memoria dignarum* (freely used by Pliny the Elder), *De obscuris Catonis*, *Libri rerum Etruscarum*, and *De orthographia*. The *Fasti Praenestini* (*CIL* i²) were also drawn up by him. But he is best known for his lost *Libri de significatu verborum* in which he quoted freely from the earlier republican authors. His material he arranged in alphabetical order and devoted several books to each letter. From the epitome made by Festus (q.v. 2) we can gain some idea of the richness of learning contained in this work of Verrius Flaccus, which was a quarry for the scholars of the immediately succeeding generations.

Schanz-Hosius, §§ 340–1a. J. F. M.

**FLACCUS** (9), AULUS AVILLIUS (*PW* 3), schoolfellow of C. and L. Caesar (q.v. 6, 7) and a friend of Tiberius and Macro (q.v.). In A.D. 29 he prosecuted Agrippina (q.v. 2). As prefect of Egypt (32–8) he was friendly to the Greek elements there, and so anti-Jewish. Philon (q.v. 4) wrote Εἰς Φλάκκον against him. In 38 he was unexpectedly arrested, condemned at Rome, perhaps on a charge of plotting with Tiberius (2) Gemellus and Macro, banished to Andros, and later put to death on Gaius' instructions.

Philo, *In Flaccum* ed. H. Box (1939); J. P. V. D. Balsdon, *The Emperor Gaius* (1934), 129 ff.; A. Stein, *Die Präfekten von Ägypten* 1950), 26 f.                                                   A. M.; T. J. C.

**FLAMINES.** The word *flamen* appears to mean 'priest' or 'sacrificer', cf. Old Icelandic *blót*, 'sacrificial feast', etc. (Walde, *Lat. etym. Wort.*[2] (1910), s.v.). In Rome the *flamines* were a group of fifteen priests, three *maiores* and twelve *minores*, forming part of the *collegium pontificum*. Each was assigned to the cult of one god, though he might on occasion take part in the worship of some other; e.g. the flamen Quirinalis conducted the ritual of the Robigalia, Ov. *Fasti* 4. 910; Varro, *Ling.* 5. 84, Cic. *Leg.* 2. 20. The three *maiores* were the flamen Dialis, of Jupiter; Martialis, of Mars; Quirinalis, of Quirinus (Gaius 1. 112). The first of these was obliged to observe an amazingly elaborate system of taboos, all designed to keep his extremely holy person from any pollution or bad magic (list, with authorities, Marquardt–Wissowa, *Staatsverw.*[2] iii. 328 ff.); it is probable that the observances of the other two were, at least originally, hardly less complicated. It is further highly likely that the Dialis represented an ancient king, see Rose, *Roman Questions of Plutarch*, 111. Of the twelve *minores* we know the following ten: Volturnalis, Palatualis, Furinalis, Floralis, Falacer, Pomonalis (these seem to have been the last six, Festus, 144. 12 ff. Lindsay; all six in Ennius ap. Varr. op. cit. 7. 45); Volcanalis (Varr. op. cit. 5. 84), Cerialis (*CIL* xi. 5028), Carmentalis (Cic. *Brut.* 56), Portunalis (Festus, 238. 9 Lindsay), but the order of precedence of these four is unknown. Their deities were respectively Volturnus, Pales, Furrina, Flora, Falacer, Pomona, Volcanus, Ceres, Carmentis, and Portunus. The Divi, from Julius Caesar in 42 B.C., were regularly assigned special flamines.

Latte, *RR* 36, 404.                                          H. J. R.

**FLAMININUS** (1), TITUS QUINCTIUS (*PW* 45) *cos.* 198 B.C., the victor of Cynoscephalae, was military tribune under Marcellus (208 B.C.), propraetor *extra ordinem* at Tarentum (205–204), and for his philhellenism and diplomatic address became consul in 198, not yet thirty, to win the support of Greece against Philip V in the Second Macedonian War. After Cynoscephalae (197) he confined Philip in Macedonia, rejected Aetolian claims in Thessaly, and in 196 at the Isthmian Games proclaimed the freedom of Greece; in 195 he forced Nabis to surrender Argos. In 194 he evacuated Greece, and the Greek cities honoured him as deliverer. In 194–193 he upheld against Antiochus' envoys the Roman guardianship of Greek autonomy in Asia Minor, and in 193–192 suppressed Nabis, but failed to check the pro-Syrian policy of Aetolia. After Thermopylae (191) he procured a truce in Greece. Censor in 189 with M. Marcellus, his liberal policy appears in the restoration of the Campanians' census rights. In 183 he demanded the surrender of Hannibal from Prusias. He died in 174; a son was consul in 150 and a grandson consul in 123. Ambitious and idealistic, he was in his philhellenism and policy a rival rather than a protégé of Scipio Africanus, and this, with his diplomacy and generalship, made him the Senate's best instrument in establishing a protectorate over an autonomous Greece.

Polyb. bks. 17–18; Livy, bks. 32–36; 38. 28 and 36; 39. 51; Plut. *Flam.* G. Colin, *Rome et la Grèce* (1905), 82 ff.; L. Homo, *Rev. hist.* 1916, 241 ff.; 1916, 1 ff.; De Sanctis, *Stor. Rom.* iv. 1. 76 ff.; A. Aymard, *Les Premiers Rapports de Rome et de la confédération achaienne* (1938); F. W. Walbank, *Philip V of Macedon* (1940); Scullard, *Rom. Pol.* 97 ff., 119, 175. Coin-portrait: C. Seltmann, *Greek Coins*, 225 f.                                                                  A. H. McD.

**FLAMININUS** (2), LUCIUS QUINCTIUS (*PW* 43), *cos.* 192 B.C., curule aedile (201 B.C.), praetor (199), commanded the Roman fleet in Greece in 198–194 for his brother T. Flamininus. Consul in 192, he was guilty of oppression in Gaul, for which on moral grounds Cato expelled him from the Senate in 184.                                          A. H. McD.

**FLAMINIUS** (*PW* 2), GAIUS, a *novus homo* who reached the consulship in 223 B.C. and was the greatest popular leader before the Gracchi to challenge the senatorial government. *Tribunus plebis* in 232 B.C., despite bitter senatorial opposition he carried a timely measure to distribute to poor Roman citizens the *ager Gallicus* (?*et Picenus*), recently confiscated from the Senones. A hostile aristocratic tradition (preserved by Polybius and probably reflecting Fabius Pictor) alleges that this caused the beginning of 'the demoralization of the people' and, by annoying the Gauls, hastened the Gallic invasion of 225; further, it was alleged that his own father opposed Flaminius. As praetor in 227 he was the first to hold that office in Sicily: his governorship was popular. Consul I (223), he led the first Roman army across the Padus disregarding a senatorial order to return to Rome. He defeated the Insubres: accounts which assign the victory to the legions' efficiency in spite of their general's rashness are suspect. He celebrated a triumph at the people's wish despite senatorial objection. He was *magister equitum* to his enemy Q. Fabius Maximus (221). As censor (220) he built the Via Flaminia (q.v.) and the Circus Flaminius. The reform of the Comitia Centuriata, which Mommsen assigned to his censorship, is probably earlier. Alone of the senators, he supported the *Lex Claudia* (see CLAUDIUS 7). His election to a second consulship in 217 was a popular criticism of the Senate's conduct of the Hannibalic war. He guarded the Western Apennines at Arretium; when Hannibal passed, he hastened south (probably to join his colleague Servilius with whom it was alleged he refused to co-operate) but fell into Hannibal's ambush at Lake Trasimene, where his army was destroyed and he himself met a hero's death, a fate which hostile tradition attributed to his disregard of the customary religious ceremonies.

K. Jacobs, *Gaius Flaminius* (1938; written in Dutch); F. Cassola, *I Gruppi politici romani nel III sec. a. C.* (1962), 209 ff. (unorthodox: cf. *JRS* 1963, 185 f.); Z. Yavetz, *Athenaeum* 1962, 325 ff. H. H. S.

**FLAVIUS** (1, *PW* 15), GNAEUS, son of a *libertus* of Appius Claudius (q.v. 4) Caecus, whose secretary he became. Pomponius (q.v. 6) relates that he purloined a MS. of Appius' containing the *Legis actiones* (see LAW AND PROCEDURE, ROMAN II. 2) and published it (but perhaps Appius in fact instigated his act). This publication (known as *Ius civile Flavianum*) was supposedly the first to give the people knowledge of the forms of procedure, which had been the monopoly of the pontiffs. For this service Flavius became *tribunus plebis*, senator, and *aedilis curulis* in spite of his humble origin. In his aedileship (304) he exhibited in the forum the calendar of court-days on which the *legis actio* was admissible.

F. Schulz, *History of Roman Legal Science* (1946), 9 ff. (criticizing this traditional account); A. K. Michels, *The Calendar of the Roman Republic* (U.S.A. 1967), 108 ff.                                  A. B.; B. N.

**FLAVIUS** (2) **FELIX**; his verses, often unclassical in quantities, are preserved with Florentinus' verses in the *Anthologia Latina* (ed. Riese, 254).

**FLEVO LACUS,** the Zuyder Zee. In Roman times it was a lake (whose name is preserved in *Vlieland*), with an island of the same name; most of the Frisian Islands were then part of the mainland. The waterways of this region were used by the Roman fleets in the wars of Drusus, Tiberius, and Germanicus; and Drusus canalized the Vecht for navigation from the Rhine to the sea. Knowledge of the shape and size of the Zuyder Zee in the Roman period may be considerably affected by current studies on relative sea-level in the North Sea region.                                    O. B.; P. S.

**FLORA** (Oscan *Flusia*: Conway, *Ital. Dial.* nos. 46; 175 a; L 24), an Italian goddess of flowering or blossoming plants. The antiquity of her cult in Rome is proved by the existence of a *flamen Floralis* (cf. FLAMINES), but her festival is not in the 'calendar of Numa' (*see* CALENDARS), and therefore was movable (*conceptiuae*). In 238 B.C., by advice of the Sibylline books, she was given a temple (Pliny, *HN* 18. 286; cf. Platner–Ashby, 209 f.). Its dedication day was 28 Apr., and games (*ludi Florales*) began to be celebrated then annually in 173 B.C. (Ov. *Fast.* 5. 329 f.). These included farces (*mimi*) of a highly indecent character (Ov. ibid. 331 and Frazer, ad loc.). Foreign, probably Greek influence accounts for this non-Italian feature (Aphrodite Ἀνθεία?).

Wissowa, *RK* 197; Latte, *RR* 73.                    H. J. R.

**FLORENTIA**, the modern *Florence*, probably was not an Etruscan foundation. It may have been in existence by the time of the Civil Wars (Florus 2. 8: text doubtful and certainly exaggerated), and possibly received a colony under the Triumvirs (*Lib. Colon.* 213). In Tiberius' reign a Florentine mission to Rome asked that the Clanis be not diverted into the Arnus (Tac. *Ann.* 1. 79). Otherwise Florentia played no recorded part in history until late imperial times. In the fifth century it was a considerable fortress (Procop. *Goth.* 3. 5. 6); by Lombard times apparently the capital of a duchy.

L. A. Milani, *Mon. Ant.* 1896; E. Pucci, *Short History of Florence* (Florence, 1939); G. Maetzke, *Florentia* (1941); C. Hardie, *JRS* 1965, 122 ff.                    E. T. S.

**FLORIANUS**, MARCUS ANNIUS (*PW* 46), praetorian prefect of the Emperor Tacitus—of whom he was wrongly said to be the brother. On the death of Tacitus at Tyana he seized the Empire and was recognized everywhere except in Syria and Egypt, which set up Probus. Probus took the field against him at Tarsus and, by cleverly delaying the campaign, tired out and demoralized Florianus' troops. Florianus was put to death by his own men (autumn A.D. 276).                    H. M.; B. H. W.

**FLORUS** (*PW* 9) (*Lucius Ann(a)eus F.* in Cod. Palat. 894 and most editions, *Julius F.* in Cod. Bamberg.) is generally held to be identical with Florus the poet-friend of Hadrian and with P. Annius Florus, author of the imperfectly preserved dialogue *Vergilius orator an poeta* (*see infra*). The dialogue states that he was born in Africa and in boyhood took part unsuccessfully in the Capitoline competition under Domitian; he afterwards settled at Tarraco in Spain, but returned to Rome in Hadrian's time. His chief work is entitled *Epitome bellorum omnium annorum DCC.* He states (Introd. § 8) that he is writing 'not much less than 200 years after Caesar Augustus'; if these words mean the beginning of Augustus' principate (27 B.C.), '200 years' is a considerable exaggeration.

WORKS. The *Epitome* is an abridgement of Roman history with special reference to the wars waged up to the age of Augustus. Some manuscripts describe it as an epitome of Livy; but it is sometimes at variance with Livy. The author also made use of Sallust, Caesar, and in one passage (i. Intr. 4–8) probably the Elder Seneca; and there are reminiscences of Virgil and Lucan. It is planned as a panegyric of the Roman people. Of the two books the first traces the rise of Rome's military power, the second its decline, the former containing wars of conquest down to 50 B.C., the latter covering civil wars from the time of

the Gracchi and going down to the wars of Augustus, with the suggestion that the latter had brought peace to the world.

Of the dialogue only a fragment of the introduction survives. It was probably written about A.D. 122 (F. Schmidinger, 'Untersuchungen über Florus', *Neue Jahrb. f. Philol.* xx, Supplement 6, 781 ff.; E. Woelfflin (*Arch. für latein. Lexikogr.* vi (1889)) shows that its diction closely resembles that of the *Epitome*.

*Poems.* The lines on Hadrian beginning 'Ego nolo Caesar esse', had the honour of a retort from him (S.H.A. *Hadr.* 16. 3). Other fragments are preserved (Riese, *Anth. Lat.* i. 1, nos. 87–9 and 245–52). They are not sufficient to enable judgement to be passed on the author's poetry and hardly justify the theory that the famous *Pervigilium Veneris* is his work (H. O. Müller, *de P. Annio F. poeta et Pervig. Ven.* (1855); E. K. Rand, *Rev. Et. Lat.* 1934, 83 ff.

Florus in the *Epitome* shows a certain literary gift marred, however, by a strong tendency to rhetoric. His brevity often entails obscurity, though he sometimes produces a felicitous epigram. He has irritating habits of inserting exclamatory remarks and repeating favourite words. As an historian he is often inaccurate in both chronology and geography, but the work as a whole achieves a limited success as a rapid sketch of Roman military history. It was a favourite school-book in the seventeenth century.

LIFE AND WORKS. Schanz–Hosius, § 537 ff.; Teuffel–Schwabe–Kroll–Skutsch, *Geschichte der römischen Literatur* (1913–20), § 348; J. Wight Duff, *Lit. Hist. Rome, Silver Age²* (1960), 513 ff.; P. Monceaux, *Les Africains* (1894), 193 ff.; F. Eyssenhardt, *Hadrian u. Florus* (1882); F. Schmidinger, *Untersuch. über Fl.* (1894); O. Hirschfeld, *Anlage u. Abfassungszeit d. Epitome d. Fl.* (1899); S. Lilledahl, *Florusstudien* (1928); E. Malcovati, *Athenaeum* 1937, 69, 289; 1938, 46, 68.

TEXTS. E. Malcovati (1938). (*Epitome and Dialogue*) O. Jahn (1852), C. Halm (1854), O. Rossbach (1896). (*Poems*) L. Mueller, *Rutilii de Reditu* (Teubner, 1870), 26–31.

COMMENTARIES. Salmasius and Gruter (1609); Freinsheim (1632); Graevius (1680); Duker (1744); Seebode (1821).

TRANSLATIONS. *Epitome*: E. S. Forster with text (Loeb, 1929). *Poems*: with text (Duff, *Minor Lat. Poets* 426 ff.).
                                        E. S. F.; G. B. T.

**FOEDUS** means a treaty, solemnly enacted, which established friendly association, *pia et aeterna pax*, and alliance between Rome and another State or States for perpetuity. *Foedus* is distinct from *indutiae*, which ended a state of war and were limited in duration up to a century. It might be *aequum* or *iniquum*. The former kind set both parties on equality, and provided for military assistance in defensive wars. The latter marked out Rome as *in foedere superior*, the second party being bound to assist Rome in offensive wars also, and to respect the dignity of Rome, *maiestatem populi Romani comiter conseruare*. This attempt to express the spirit of the law in the letter indirectly limited the allies' sovereignty, placing them in the relationship of client to patron (*see* SOCII). Special conditions were not normally added to the treaty, being out of place in *foedus aequum* and unnecessary in *foedus iniquum*, until the later Republic. Treaties were usually limited to establishing the general alliance, with arrangements for agreed alterations and the usual sanctions. The earliest known *foedus aequum* is the treaty of Spurius Cassius (q.v. 1). *Foedera iniqua* were commonest in Italy and stressed the Roman hegemony (*see* SOCII). Fetiales (q.v.) or consuls usually officiated, but other military commanders also could make treaties, which then needed ratification at Rome. They were published on bronze and kept on the Capitol. Exceptional forms appear in the first two Carthaginian treaties, which are of non-Roman type, and the *foedus Gabinum* which mediated the incorporation of Gabii in Rome (6th c. B.C.).

For bibliography *see* SOCII.                    A. N. S.-W.

**FOLK-SONGS, GREEK.** The Greeks, like other peoples, had their folk-songs, though it is impossible to give dates to them or to construct a history. They may be roughly classified as follows: (1) to gods (*Carm. Pop.* 5, 8, 14, 25, 26); (2) ritual songs (ibid. 2); (3) occupational (ibid. 3, 23, 28); (4) averting songs (ibid. 13); (5) love-songs (ibid. 7, 27).

TEXT. Page, *Poet. Mel. Gr.* 450–61; J. M. Edmonds, *Lyra Graeca* (Loeb) iii, 488 ff.                                                    C. M. B.

**FOLK-TALES.** Only one *märchen*, told as such, has come down to us from antiquity, and that in a literary form, Apuleius' story of Cupid and Psyche (*Metam.* 4. 28 ff.; this is Stith Thompson C 421). Tertullian names two more, *adv. Valent.* 3. But numerous folk-tale themes are to be found scattered up and down classical legends, though the chronological question whether the theme or the legend is the older often cannot be decided. Examples are the external soul (Meleager 1, q.v.); the husband who returns just in time to stop his wife, who supposes him dead, marrying another (Odysseus, q.v.); the unwitting killing by Aëdon (q.v.) and Themisto (*see* ATHAMAS) of their own children (essentially the story of Tom Thumb and the ogre); Home-Comer's Vow, the tale of the man who, like Jephtha, vows to sacrifice the first thing which meets him on his return, or otherwise to destroy or dispose of it, and is met by his own child. This is told of Idomeneus (q.v. 1). At least one Greek tale, that of Odysseus and Polyphemus (*see* CYCLOPES), is found as far away as Lapland (see Qvigstad, *Lappiske Eventyr og Sagn* ii (1928), 448 f.). The vast popularity of Homer made it no wise incredible that we have here simply Homer's story (source unknown). That several of the longer cycles of story, as the legends of Perseus and of the Argonauts (qq.v.; see S. Hartland, *Legend of Perseus* (1894–6), and Halliday, op. cit. *infra* (2), 21 ff.), are packed with details found in various folk-tales in and out of Europe is common knowledge.

For one common form of (Oriental?) folk-tale, the beast-fable, Greece has been a great distributing centre, owing to the collections popularly associated with the name of Aesop (q.v.). From earlier oral or written versions (see Halliday (1), 101 ff.; (2), 143 ff.) these apologues have spread, first into Latin (Phaedrus, 'Romulus', etc.), thence into modern languages, meanwhile never ceasing to be repeated among the later Greeks themselves. In all cases it is necessary to remember the reciprocal action between literary and popular compositions. Supposing, for example, what is likely in itself, that the beast-fable was originally popular and oral, we find it at very varying levels. It is used by serious authors to point grave morals (Hes. *Op.* 202 ff.; Pind. *Pyth.* 2. 72 ff.; Aesch. fr. 139 Nauck). It was a popular form of after-dinner story (Ar. *Vesp.* 1259 f.). It was used as edifying reading for children (Babrius, *praef.*), and for first exercises in composition (Quint. *Inst.* i. 9. 2). Finally, it became a popular chap-book, and so found its way back into oral or quasi-oral circulation. Thus the simple, popular tale may always be a worn-down form of the elaborate and literary one, not its predecessor. Caution is therefore necessary in tracing connexions such as those suggested above.

W. R. Halliday, *Greek and Roman Folklore*, U.S.A. 1927 ('Halli-day (1)'); *Indo-European Folk-Tales and Greek Legend*, Cambridge, 1933 ('Halliday (2)'); Rose, *Handbook of Greek Mythology*, ch. 10, where some further references are given. Nilsson, *GGR* i². 17 ff. *See also* FABLE.                                                                  H. J. R.

**FOLLIS,** the bag in which coins were collected for large payments; then the coins themselves.

*Follis* seems to be applied only to coins of bronze or silvered bronze, but not to be restricted to any continu-ously unchanged denomination. Under Diocletian it may have denoted the common 'Genio Populi Romani' piece.

Under Julian six *folles* are the price of a pound of pork. St. Augustine knows the *follis* as a tiny fraction of the *solidus*. In Byzantine times the *follis* was pre-eminently the piece of 40 *nummia*. The *Historia Augusta* is very doubtful authority for the use of the word in the third century A.D.

E. Babelon, *Traité des monnaies grecques et romaines* (1901) i. 615 ff., 761 ff.; A. H. M. Jones, *JRS* 1959, 34 ff.; L. Ruggini, *Rend. Linc.*, 1961, 306 ff.; A. Cameron, *Num. Chron.* 1964, 135 ff.          H. M.

**FONTEIUS** (*PW* 12), MARCUS, began his career under Cinna (q.v. 1), but joined Sulla. He served in Spain and Macedonia and, after his praetorship, governed Trans-alpine Gaul (probably 74–72 B.C.), enthusiastically exact-ing men, money, and grain for the wars in Spain and elsewhere. Accused *repetundarum*, he was defended by Cicero in a speech which is partly extant, and probably acquitted.                                                          E. B.

**FOOD AND DRINK.** The Greeks and Romans were in general notably frugal in their diet. The austerity of the Spartans, the 'greed' of the Boeotians, and even the much-condemned luxury of imperial Rome must be viewed in the context of the standard set by this general simplicity.

The diet was based on corn, oil, and wine. Cereals were the principal source of carbohydrate, and at all times provided the staple food, so that σῖτος and *frumentum* often denoted food generally. For details *see* CORN. When wheaten bread had become common it was sometimes flavoured with or accompanied by cheese, honey, etc., and many varieties of cake (πλακοῦς, *placenta*) were also known.

Fats were derived mainly from olive-oil (q.v.), while wine (q.v.), usually diluted with water, was the only important beverage. The drinking of beer and to a large extent that of milk (q.v.) ranked as marks of barbarians; and there were no infused or distilled drinks. For sweeten-ing, honey was used instead of sugar.

Among the 'things eaten with bread (or other cereal food)', for which the Greeks used the generic term ὄψον, fish, which might be fresh, dried, or pickled, occupied a prominent place. Many species were known (cf. D'A. W. Thompson, *A Glossary of Greek Fishes*, 1947), and at Athens fish was ὄψον *par excellence*. In Rome lampreys, mullets, and oysters came to be reared in fishponds by and for the wealthy.

Poultry, game, and eggs played a large part in Roman cookery, but there was comparatively little butcher's meat, except for pork and occasionally veal. Wild birds (pheasants, partridges, quails) were also eaten; but the appearance of peacocks, flamingoes, cranes, etc., on the tables of the rich must have been largely due to the mere search for novelty.

For ordinary folk, however, vegetables (especially the pulses, but also onions, radishes, marrows, beet, garlic, etc.) provided the most important addition to the 'basic three'; and in the eyes of imperial Roman writers a 'simple' diet is often vegetarian in the strictest sense. Among fruit, figs and grapes played a leading part, but apples, pears, mulberries, and dates (the latter of Phoenic-ian origin) were also eaten widely; and by Roman times peaches, apricots, and cherries had been naturalized in Italy. (Potatoes, tomatoes, oranges, and bananas were un-known, and most berries were not cultivated.)

Sauces (especially the Roman fish-sauce *garum*, *liquamen*) and condiments and herbs (including the famous silphium) were popular throughout; and the Romans in particular seem to have disliked the natural taste of most cooked foods. This partiality for flavourings, which still gives much Mediterranean cooking its special character, is one of several features of the ancient diet of which survivals are discernible in the diet of present-day Greece and Italy. Cf. *also* COOKERY, MEALS.

J. André, *L'Alimentation et la cuisine à Rome* (1961); M. A. Levi, *La Grecia antica* (1963), 33 ff., *Roma antica* (1963), 81 ff., with bibliography; J. I. Miller, *The Spice Trade of the Roman Empire* (1969).
L. A. M.

**FORDICIDIA** (this is the pure Latin form; Sabine *Hordicidia*, cf. Conway, *Ital. Dial.* i. 385): Roman festival of Tellus on 15 Apr., when a *forda* (cow in calf) was sacrificed to her (Ov. *Fasti* 4. 630 ff.). It and the Fornacalia (q.v.) were the only festivals which in historic times were organized on the basis of the Curiae (q.v.). See further Frazer, *Fasti of Ovid* iii. 317; add Pausanias 2. 11. 4 (pregnant ewes sacrificed to the Eumenides).
H. J. R.

**FORGERIES, LITERARY.** I. GREEK. Forgeries differ from other *pseudepigrapha* (works wrongly attributed to authors) in two respects. With a true forgery the attribution must be made by the real author himself, and there must be intention to deceive. On both points we are frequently left in doubt. If Lobon (q.v.) wrote the *Hymn to Poseidon* attributed to Arion, Lobon is not necessarily responsible for the attribution; and the authors of the later *Theognidea* certainly took no pains to pass off their work as that of Theognis. Again, the *Anacreontea*, though they bear the superscription of Anacreon, and often refer to his darling Bathyllus as living, make no serious claim to be Anacreon's work (cf. 1, and 60 B τὸν Ἀνακρέοντα μιμοῦ). The poems are only fathered on the old poet by a fanciful pretence, not even consistently maintained. Similarly, we cannot say that the composers of letters attributed to eminent Greek authors or personages (e.g. the famous Epistles of Phalaris) meant in every case to deceive the public (*see* LETTER). On the other hand, it is certain that from desire for gain, fame, or a *cachet* for philosophical doctrines some deliberate forgeries were perpetrated, e.g. the *Orphica* of the neo-Pythagoreans and much Jewish-Greek literature. Heraclides Ponticus, according to Aristoxenus, wrote tragedies which he attributed to Thespis; and *pseudo-Democritea* (see Diels's *Vorsokratiker*) are numerous. The music to part of Pindar's first *Pythian*, published by Kircher in 1648, is an almost certain example of forgery by a modern scholar. The invention of sources, e.g. by Ptolemaeus Chennus (*and see* DIONYSIUS (12) SCYTOBRACHION), may also be mentioned here.
J. D. D.

II. LATIN. Forgeries should be distinguished from pseudepigraphic literature (q.v.) by the author's calculated attempt to have the works attributed to someone other than himself. Suetonius in his life of Horace told of such work: *venerunt in manus meas et elegi sub titulo eius et epistula prosa oratione quasi commendantis se Maecenati: sed utraque falsa puto, nam elegi volgares, epistula etiam obscura, quo vitio minime tenebatur.* Suetonius could detect the elegy and the letter attributed to Horace as forgeries by their style. Not all critics (not even he) were always so perceptive, and the *Culex* (among other forgeries in the *Appendix Vergiliana*—q.v.) was accepted as a very early work of Virgil by Lucan, Statius, Martial, and even Suetonius. The first half of the first century A.D. seems to have been particularly interested in such productions. It seems likely that in this period the *Epistulae ad Caesarem senem* were carefully composed in the very distinctive style of Sallust (and are still deceiving scholars). The *Invectiva in Ciceronem*, though certainly a forgery and probably of the same time, differs in that its author was not so concerned or else not so successful in reproducing Sallustian style: the intention was, however, to produce a fake. Another clear example of a forgery, prob-

ably produced also in the same period, is the so-called *Commentariolum Petitionis*, ostensibly a treatise on how to attain the consulship written by Quintus to his brother Marcus Tullius Cicero in the year 64 B.C. (but it is really a farrago, composed in an imitation of Ciceronian style, from the speeches of Cicero—including speeches now lost—of 63 B.C.). It is preserved in the correspondence *ad Quintum fratrem.*

G. L. Hendrickson, *The* Commentariolum Petitionis *attributed to Q. Cicero* (1904); E. Fraenkel, *JRS* 1952, 2 ff. (= Kl. Beiträge ii. 181 ff.); R. Syme, *Sallust* (1964), Appendix II.
G. W. W.

**FORMIAE,** modern *Formia*, reputedly the home of Homer's Laestrygones (q.v.), Volscian town on the Via Appia (q.v.) below Tarracina (q.v.). It obtained Roman citizenship early (*sine suffragio*, 338 B.C.; full franchise, 188 B.C.). Its fine climate and surroundings made it a fashionable resort where prominent Romans had villas: e.g. Mamurra (q.v.) and Cicero, who was murdered nearby. Ancient ruins include Munatius Plancus' tomb.
E. T. S.

**FORNACALIA,** a movable festival, celebrated not later than 17 Feb. (Quirinalia), which day was hence called also *stultorum feriae*, because, as Ovid explains (*Fast.* 2. 531–2; from Verrius Flaccus, cf. Festus, 304. 5 ff.; 418. 33 ff.; 419. 5 ff. Lindsay), those who were too stupid to know to what *curia* they belonged kept the festival then instead of on the proper day, proclaimed by the *curio maximus* (Ov. ibid. 527–8). It was, then, celebrated by the *curiae*, not the people as a whole; it consisted of ritual either to benefit the ovens, *fornaces*, which parched grain, or to propitiate the doubtful goddess Fornax who presided over them, ibid. 525.

See Frazer, ad loc.; Wissowa, *RK* 158, 399; Latte, *RR* 143.
H. J. R.

**FORTIFICATIONS** in the Mediterranean area were from the first closely related to physical conditions. 'Praeruptis oppida saxis' are generally typical. In the Aegean region, the successive stages of Troy (q.v.), and, in the Late Bronze Age, the cyclopean walls of Mycenae, Tiryns, Athens, and Gla (on Lake Copais) well represent this acropolis type. But small fortified towns also occur, e.g. Early Cycladic Khalandriani (on Syros), having a main wall with frequent semicircular towers and a lower outer wall. Particular attention was paid to protection of gates by enfilading bastions (e.g. Mycenae; cf. Troy I) and tactical plan (e.g. Gla, courtyard gate), and to safeguarding the water supply (Mycenae). (For corresponding developments in the Near East, see Y. Yadin, *The Art of Warfare in Biblical Lands*, 1963.) The simple yet robust brick walls of Old Smyrna (900–600 B.C., *BSA* 1958/9, 35 ff.) illuminate the somewhat obscure position in the Dark Age and archaic period. Extensive town-walls of masonry or brick began to develop in the sixth and, especially, fifth centuries B.C., while the systems of Long Walls (q.v.) show how large-scale fortifications were used for strategic ends. Fourth-century improvements in siegecraft (q.v.) and the introduction of artillery (q.v.) created increasing problems. Fortification-designers steadily responded to the challenge. Towers increased in number (e.g. Mantinea; Latmian Heraclea) and, from Messene (369) onwards, in height (e.g. tall towers at Aegosthena, Perge). Their upper chambers were embrasured for defensive catapults. Walls, occasionally casemated for artillery (Perge; Side; Rhodes), became thicker and higher. A ditch (Poseidonia) or ditches combined with outworks (Syracuse; Selinus) hampered the approach of powerful Hellenistic siege-engines. Defences sometimes included numerous sally-ports to facilitate active resistance. Philon (q.v. 2) Byzantinus (*c.* 200 B.C.;

cf. Vitr. i. 5) admirably summarizes the full, relatively sophisticated Hellenistic defensive technique.

The Italic tradition had an early development partly akin to that of Greece, but was less dependent upon the acropolis, being early modified by dissociation of the fortified bank, or *agger*, from hillsides, as at Ardea or at Rome itself (*murus terreus*, Varro, *Ling.* 5. 48), and the revetment of such earth-banks in stone, creating earth-filled walls. The progressive development of such a wall has been traced at Pompeii (*Mon. Ant.* 1930, pt. 2), beginning in 520–450 B.C.; it was enlarged in Italic style, as a revetted *agger* with rearward slope, in the fourth and third centuries B.C., and only hellenized, by the addition of towers, in 120–89 B.C. Meanwhile Rome had been experimenting with a masonry wall of partly Hellenistic type (*see* WALL OF SERVIUS), such as she found already existing round her colony at Paestum (Poseidonia) and adopted in her colonies of Ostia, Minturnae, and Cosa (qq.v.). But Hellenistic practice was not introduced wholesale until Sulla's day, as at Tarracina and Ostia II, though artillery casemates, as at Perusia and Rome, had been introduced somewhat before this. Another strain in Roman military architecture had already been introduced by military field-work, developed on a scale hitherto quite unknown, and predominant in all frontier provinces until the latter half of the first century A.D. There are notable works in earth and timber at Xanten, Haltern, Oberaden, and Alteburg in lower Germany, at Margidunum and Fendoch in Britain. This tradition of military building, combining simplicity and strength, was not ousted until the Flavian period in legionary fortresses, and under Trajan on the frontiers. Thenceforward masonry building takes first place, though never completely deserting the earthwork tradition. The fortified frontier, in which a wall, rampart, or palisade, patrolled from watch-towers, connected a chain of forts, is also a Roman invention (*see* LIMES). The town-walls of the later Roman Empire and occasional forts, like Altrip, culminating in the double walls and artillery defences of Constantinople, combine the best Greek theory with Roman resource, and remained unsurpassed until the invention of gunpowder created entirely new defensive problems.

A. W. Lawrence, *Greek Architecture* (1957); R. L. Scranton, *Greek Walls* (1941); F. G. Maier, *Griechische Mauerbauinschriften*, 2 vols. (1961); F. Krischen, *Die Stadtmauern von Pompeji und griechische Festungsbaukunst in Unteritalien und Sizilien* (1941); W. Fischer, *Das römische Lager* (1914); for Haltern, *Mitteilungen d. Altertums-Komm. für Westfalen*, 1909, 1 ff.; I. A. Richmond, 'Trajan's Army on Trajan's Column', *PBSR* 1935, 1 ff.; 'The Agricolan Fort at Fendoch', *Proc. Soc. Ant. Scot.* 1939, 'Das römische Kastell in Altrip', *Neue deutsche Ausgrabungen, Deutschtum und Ausland*, Heft 23/4 (1930); I. A. Richmond, *City Wall of Imperial Rome* (1930); A. Blanchet, *Les Enceintes de la Gaule romaine* (1907).

I. A. R.; E. W. M.

**FORTUNA** or **FORS** (Ennius ap. Cic. *Off.* 1. 38), in full Fors Fortuna (Ter. *Phorm.* 841), an Italian goddess identified in classical times with Tyche (q.v.). There is, however, good evidence that she was in the native cult not a deity of chance or luck, but rather the 'bringer', as her name signifies (*ferre*), of fertility or increase. She is praised by gardeners (Columella 10. 316), and her ancient temple in the Forum Boarium at Rome (see Platner–Ashby, 214; ibid. 212 ff., for her other Roman shrines) had the same dedication-day as that of Mater Matuta (*see* MATUTA), viz. 11 June (Ov. *Fasti* 6. 569). These facts suggest a deity potent for the fruits of the earth and the life of women, cf. her titles Muliebris (Festus, 282. 21 Lindsay; this shrine was 4 miles from Rome, and only women living in a first marriage might approach the goddess) and Virgo (Varro ap. Non. 189. 19). However, her titles are so numerous (see especially Plut. *Quaest. Rom.* 74, and Rose ad loc.) that too much should not be made of these.

It is regularly said that her cult was introduced into Rome by Servius Tullius (Plut. ibid., and many other passages), and this is true in the sense that she has neither a *flamen* nor a feast-day belonging to the oldest list. How old her cult is in other parts of Italy is unknown, but certainly older than at Rome, whither it came from some place outside. Of the other Italian centres of her worship, one of the most interesting is Praeneste, where a number of archaic inscriptions throw light on the cult. One is a dedication 'nationu cratia', 'for offspring' (*CIL* xiv. 2863), which furthermore calls the goddess 'Diouo filea primocenia', i.e. 'Iouis filia primigenia', the one instance in Italian cult which makes one deity the child of another, unless, as suggested in Rose, *Roman Questions of Plutarch* (1924), 83 f., a very old error underlies the title. Equally interesting is the fact that she had an oracular shrine there. The method of consultation was for a boy to draw at random one of a number of billets of oak-wood (*sortes*), inscribed with sentences (one was 'Mars shakes his dart', at a similar oracle at Falerii, Livy 22. 1. 11) which the consultant might apply to his own case (Cic. *Div.* 2. 85–6, and Pease ad loc.). A temple was built to the Praenestine goddess on the Quirinal (Livy 29. 36. 8; 34. 53. 5). This was in 194 B.C. At Antium a plurality of Fortunae was worshipped (Macrob. *Sat.* 1. 23. 13), and these also gave oracles, apparently by movements of the statues (Macrob. ibid.). Cf. NORTIA.

Wissowa, *RK* 256 ff.; Drexler in Roscher's *Lexikon* i. 1503 ff. (exhaustive account of her titles, identifications, representations in art, etc.); Latte, *RR* 176 ff., with references to excavations at Praeneste (q.v.). The temple of Fortuna in the Forum Boarium is probably to be identified with one of the two temples excavated at Sant'Omobono; of the early fifth century, it was preceded by an open-air sanctuary: see E. Gjerstad, *Early Rome* iii (1960), 378 ff.; Nash, *Pict. Dict. Rome.* i. 415 ff.
H. J. R.

**FORTUNATAE INSULAE** ('Blessed Islands') were originally, like the 'Gardens of the Hesperides', the mythical winterless home of the happy dead, far west on Ocean shores or islands (Hom. *Od.* 4. 563 ff.; Hes. *Op.* 171; Pind. *Ol.* 2. 68 ff.). They were later identified with Madeira (Diod. 5. 19–20; Plut. *Sert.* 8), or more commonly with the Canaries, after their discovery (probably by the Carthaginians). The Canaries were properly explored by King Juba II (*c.* 25 B.C.–*c.* A.D. 23), who described apparently six out of the seven. From the meridian line of this group Ptolemy (*Geog.* passim) established his longitudes eastwards.

Cary–Warmington, *Explorers* 52 ff.; (Pelican) 69 ff.; Thomson, *Hist. Anc. Geog.* 184, 262; Hyde, *Greek Mariners* 150 ff.; J. Delgado, *Archivo Español de Arqueologia* 1950, 164 ff.
E. H. W.

**FORUM AUGUSTUM** or **AUGUSTI,** dedicated in 2 B.C., is the vast precinct (110 metres by 83 metres) of Mars Ultor in Rome, vowed by Octavian at Philippi. The octostyle temple, of the Corinthian order, stood upon a lofty podium at the north end; the interior of the cella was flanked by columns and terminated in an apse, housing colossal statues of Mars and Venus. Caesar's sword was kept there. The apse was set against the high precinct wall of fire-resisting peperino, irregular in plan owing to rising ground and the difficulties of buying out private property in the populous Subura. The temple lies between broad walks, leading from the Subura by flights of steps and spanned by triumphal arches, dedicated to Drusus and Germanicus in A.D. 19. The Forum area was flanked by porticoes in two stories, the upper decorated with Caryatids copied from the Erechtheum at Athens. Behind the porticoes were big semicircular *exedrae* in which stood statues of mythical figures, *viri triumphales*, and others. Laudatory inscriptions from the bases of the statues survive. In this *Forum* youths were admitted to manly estate, here provincial governors ceremonially departed or returned. Behind the northern *exedra* a group of apartments, centred upon an *atrium*, may have housed the Salii, priests of Mars.

G. Lugli, *Roma antica* (1946), 258 ff.; Nash, *Pict. Dict. Rome* i. 401 ff.; G. Fiorini, *La Casa dei Cavalieri di Rodi al Foro di Augusto* (1951), 10 ff. I. A. R.; D. E. S.

**FORUM CAESARIS or IULIUM,** dedicated by Julius Caesar in 46 B.C., on land bought eight years earlier for 60 million *sesterces* (Cic. *Att.* 4. 16. 8). The Forum (approximately 160 metres long by 75 metres wide) had long colonnades on the east and west sides and a series of *tabernae* behind the eastern colonnade. The main entrance was at the southern end and by the south-west corner lay Caesar's new *curia* (q.v. 2) and appendages. At the north end stood the octostyle temple of Venus Genetrix, mythical foundress of the Julian *gens*, with an equestrian statue of the Dictator in front of it. The temple was completely rebuilt after a fire and rededicated between A.D. 108 and 113 (*Not. Scav.* 1932, 201).

G. Lugli, *Roma antica* (1946), 245 ff.; R. Thomsen, *Opusc. Arch.* (1941), 195 ff.; Nash. *Pict. Dict. Rome* i. 424 ff. I. A. R.; D. E. S.

**FORUM IULII,** modern *Fréjus*, presumably founded by Julius Caesar as a market town (*forum*). A colony was settled here probably by Augustus, who dispatched here the warships captured at Actium, so that Forum Iulii became a naval base as well (*Colonia Octavanorum Pacensis Classica*). The fleet was still here in A.D. 69, but the harbour, now quite dry, was perhaps already silting up. Very extensive remains of the port and colony survive. **Forum Iulii was the birthplace of Cn. Julius Agricola and probably of C. Cornelius Gallus.**

A. Donnadieu, *Fréjus* (1927); Grenier, *Manuel* i. 298 ff.; *Carte arch. de la Gaule rom.* ii. 1 ff.; O. Brogan, *Roman Gaul* (1953), 94 ff. C. E. S.

**FORUM NERVAE or TRANSITORIUM,** 120 metres long by 45 metres wide, was built in Rome by Domitian and dedicated by Nerva in A.D. 97. It converted the Argiletum, which approached the *Forum Romanum* between *Forum Augustum* and *Forum Pacis*, into a monumental avenue: hence the name *Forum Transitorium*. At its east end, against the south *exedra* of *Forum Augustum*, stood a temple of Minerva, Domitian's patron goddess; reliefs illustrating her cult and legends decorated the marble frieze and attic of the peperino precinct wall, which is divided into fifteen shallow bays by detached marble columns. Alexander Severus placed here colossal statues of the *Divi*. At the east end traffic from the Subura entered on the south side of the temple only; at the west end, towards the *Forum Romanum*, were twin monumental gates.

P. H. von Blanckenhagen, *Flavische Architektur und ihre Dekoration untersucht am Nervaforum* (1940); Nash, *Pict. Dict. Rome* i. 433 ff. I. A. R.

**FORUM PACIS or VESPASIANI** was the precinct of the Temple of Peace at Rome, dedicated by Vespasian in A.D. 75. The area, 145 metres long by 100 metres wide, was laid out with ornamental flower beds and surrounded by an enclosure wall of peperino and marble porticoes. The Temple of Peace, which housed the treasures from Jerusalem, was in the centre of the east side, flanked by other buildings, including the *Bibliotheca Pacis*. The Severan Marble Plan was attached to a building, almost certainly the library, on the south of the Temple, which was later converted into the church of St. Cosmas and Damian. After the fire of Commodus the Forum was restored by Severus, and the Marble Plan shows traces of a Diocletianic restoration.

A. M. Colini, *Bull. Com.* 1937, 7 ff.; G. Carettoni, *Forma Urbis Romae* (1960), 177 ff.; Nash. *Pict. Dict. Rome* i. 439 ff. I. A. R.; D. E. S.

**FORUM ROMANUM,** the chief public square of Rome, surrounded by monumental buildings, occupied a swampy trough between the Palatine, Oppian, Quirinal, and Capitol. The edges of the marsh, of which Lacus Curtius was a survival, were covered with cemeteries of early Iron Age settlements, until the area was drained in the sixth century B.C. by the Cloaca Maxima (q.v.). The establishment of the Forum as the centre of Roman civic life dates from this time; the Regia, Aedes Vestae, and Lacus Iuturnae were traditionally associated with this period. The earliest dated monuments are the temples of Saturn (497 B.C.: Livy 2. 21), Castor (484 B.C.: Livy 2. 20, 42), and Concordia (336 B.C.: Plut. *Cam.* 42). The *rostra* (q.v.) were decorated by Maenius (338 B.C.), whose civic sense gave balconies (*maeniana*) to the *tabernae veteres* and *argentariae novae*, the latter associated with the shrine of Venus Cloacina, and decorated in 310 B.C. with Samnite *clipei*. Butchers and fishmongers were relegated to the *macellum* and *forum piscarium*. *Basilicae* were introduced in 184 B.C. by Cato (Livy 39. 44), and of this stage in the Forum's development Plautus (*Curc.* 468–81) gives a racy sketch. Cato's work was soon imitated by the *basilica Aemilia* (179 B.C.) on the north side behind the *tabernae novae*, and *basilica Sempronia* (170 B.C.) on the south screened by the *tabernae veteres*.

The growing official importance of the *Forum* is emphasized by the transfer thither of the *comitia tributa* in 145 B.C., with the consequent change in direction of the *rostra*. In 121 Opimius restored the temple of Concord, and built a new adjacent *basilica*, while the first triumphal arch, to Fabius Maximus Allobrogicus (*CIL* vi. 1303–4), spanned the Sacra Via. The temple of Castor was rebuilt in 117 (Cic. *Scaur.* 46). Much of the present setting, however, is due to Sulla (*JRS* 1922, 1 ff.), who planned the erection of the Tabularium (q.v.), new *rostra*, and a new *basilica Aemilia*, paving much of the area and altering many minor monuments to suit his new plan.

Caesar, working through Aemilius Paulus (Cic. *Att.* 4. 16. 14), rebuilt the *basilica Aemilia* and planned a new *basilica Iulia*, to replace the old *basilica Sempronia*, which, like the *curia* (q.v.) was finished by Augustus. His repaving of the *Forum* is marked by the series of galleries (*cuniculi*) below it. After Caesar's assassination a column was erected to mark the site of his pyre and later (29 B.C.) replaced by the *aedes divi Iuli*. Caesar's *rostra* were also rebuilt by Augustus, who received a triumphal arch in 30 B.C., replaced by another arch in 19 B.C. Many old buildings were rebuilt at this time by *viri triumphales* and others: the Regia (36 B.C.), the *Basilica Aemilia* (14 B.C.), and the temples of Saturn (*c.* 30 B.C.), Castor (A.D. 6), and Concord (A.D. 10). Minor Augustan monuments were the *porticus Iulia*, the *milliarium aureum*, the repair of *fons Iuturnae*. Under Tiberius came an *arcus Tiberii* (A.D. 16), another repair of *basilica Aemilia*, the *templum divi Augusti*, and the *schola Xantha* (*CIL* vi. 30692).

The Flavians made their impression on the *Forum*. The temple of Vespasian (*CIL* vi. 938; 1019) was built in 81, and Domitian also restored the *curia* and the temple of *divus Augustus*. His equestrian statue occupied the centre of the open space in 91.

Later monuments were the Hadrianic sculptures from the *rostra*, commemorating *alimenta* for Italy and taxation-reliefs for the provinces, the *templum divae Faustinae* (A.D. 141: *CIL* vi. 1005), the *arcus Severi* (A.D. 203: *CIL* vi. 1003), the Diocletianic columns in front of *basilica Iulia* (*Röm. Mitt.* 1938), the columns for the *decennalia* and *vicennalia* (*CIL* vi. 1203; 1204), the *templum divi Romuli* (A.D. 307), the *basilica* of Maxentius, completed by Constantine, the *equus Constantini* (*CIL* vi. 1141), the *statio aquarum* at *fons Iuturnae* (*CIL* vi. 36951). Last of all come the monuments to Stilicho (*CIL* vi. 1187), the *rostra Vandalica*, and the column of Phocas (*CIL* vi. 1200).

G. Lugli, *Roma antica: il centro monumentale* (1946), 55 ff.; E. Gjerstad, *Early Rome* iii (1960), 217 ff.; Nash, *Pict. Dict. Rome* i. 446 ff. Platner–Ashby.                                    I. A. R.; D. E. S.

**FORUM TRAIANI or ULPIUM.** Of all *fora* in Rome this huge colonnaded square, of which the fourth side is occupied by the Basilica Ulpia, most resembles provincial *fora*, though on the vaster scale paid for by Dacian spoils. The *Forum* was completed for Trajan by the architect Apollodorus of Damascus in A.D. 113. It lies between the Capitol and Quirinal, impinging upon the slopes of both by immense *exedrae*. It has a single portico to the south, where its main entrance, adorned by a triumphal arch in A.D. 116, faced the *Forum Augustum*; the lateral porticoes were double. The *basilica*, with broad nave, double aisles, and two very large apsidal *tribunalia*, occupied the north side of the *Forum*. Behind it lay Greek and Latin libraries, flanking a colonnaded court, modified to contain Trajan's Column, 38 metres high. The column was decorated with a spiral frieze of reliefs illustrating the Dacian Wars; Trajan's statue surmounted it, and it contained his and Plotina's ashes. The inscription on the column seems to assert that its purpose was to show the height of the cutting required for the *Forum*: this refers to the scarping of the Quirinal, where the elaborate *exedra*, separated from the *Forum* by firewall and street, screens a terraced rock-face ingeniously adapted to streets and staircases and crowned by an interesting market-hall. The libraries and column originally marked the end of the group of buildings, but Hadrian added the *templum Divi Traiani* beyond them.

G. Lugli, *Roma antica* (1946), 278 ff.; Nash, *Pict. Dict. Rome* i. 450 ff.                                                      I. A. R.

**FOUR HUNDRED, THE,** were a revolutionary oligarchic council set up to rule Athens in 411 B.C. The movement started in the fleet at Samos in summer 412, when Alcibiades (q.v.) offered to win Persian help for Athens if an oligarchy were established. Peisander (q.v. 2) was sent to Athens in the winter to prepare the way, and secured an embassy to negotiate with Persia. Though the oligarchs soon discarded Alcibiades and the Persian negotiation failed, it was then too late to stop. In the spring the oligarchic clubs (*hetairiai*, q.v.) murdered prominent democrats and intimidated the Council and the Assembly. So far the published programme was 'moderate': financial economy and the restriction of the franchise to 5,000, those 'able to serve the state in person or with their wealth'. But after Peisander's return to Athens in May 411 a meeting of the Assembly, summoned to hear the proposals of a constitutional commission, was persuaded or terrorized into electing five men who, indirectly, selected 400 to act as a *boule* with full powers to govern. The supporters of the original 'moderate' programme were overwhelmed by the extremists of the 400, who never summoned the 5,000. But the democrats recovered control over the fleet at Samos; and when the Peloponnesians attacked Euboea, the squadron hastily sent by the 400 was completely defeated. Theramenes (q.v.) now came out for the moderates, the 400 were overthrown (Sept. 411), and the 5,000 were instituted; but after the victory at Cyzicus (spring 410) full democracy was restored. *See also* ANTIPHON (1).

Thuc. bk. 8 (probably closest to the actual course of events); Arist. *Ath. Pol.* chs. 29–33 (based on documents, reformers' drafts rather than measures actually passed, which seriously distort the narrative). Hignett, *Hist. Athen. Const.*, ch. 10 and app. xii.   A. A.

**FRANKS,** a name ('freemen') assumed in the third century by a coalition of German tribes on the middle and lower Rhine. They are prominent in attacks on Gaul and Spain between A.D. 253 and 276. A violent

incursion in 355 was subsequently defeated by Julian, who granted the Salian Franks a large area for settlement (Toxandria). Frankish relations with the Empire were fairly good after this, and Franks (e.g. Count Arbogastes) rose to high positions in the Empire. About 425, however, the Salians under Chlodio broke out from Toxandria, and the Franks of the middle Rhine crossed into Gaul. Both were checked by Aetius, but succeeded after his death in extending their power southward and westward. With the defeat of Syagrius in 486 or 487 by the Salian Clovis at Soissons, the last remains of Roman power in Gaul disappeared, and in the ensuing century the Merovingian house of the Salian Franks made itself supreme in the whole area of modern France (*Francia*).

L. Schmidt, *Geschichte der Deutschen Stämme*[1] (1938) ii. 433 ff.; J. B. Bury, *Invasion of Europe by the Barbarians* xii, xiii (1928).
C. E. S.

**FRATRES ARVALES,** an ancient priestly college in Rome, mentioned under the Republic only by Varro, *Ling.* 5. 85, and restored by Augustus before 21 B.C. We owe our detailed knowledge of this brotherhood to the survival of substantial remains of their records (*Acta Fratrum Arvalium*) in inscriptions, some found in various places in Rome, but most on the site of the sacred grove of the brethren at the fifth milestone on the *Via Campana* outside the *Porta Portuensis* (now the settlement *La Magliana* on the Rome–Pisa railway, near the station). The first in a long series of discoveries was made there in 1570; systematic excavations carried out in the years 1867–71 almost doubled the number of fragments.

The college consisted of twelve members chosen from the most distinguished senatorial families by co-optation; the reigning Emperor was always a member. The president (*magister*) and his assistant (*flamen*) were elected annually. The most important ceremony of the brotherhood took place in May in honour of the goddess Dea Dia to whom the grove was dedicated. The rites of this agricultural cult belong to an early stage of Roman religion. The Acts of the year A.D. 218 have preserved the famous song of the Arval Brethren, the *Carmen Arvale* (q.v.), which originated in the fifth century B.C., and traces of Greek influence have been seen in its construction and form.

While the brotherhood's worship was directed to Dea Dia and other traditional deities, divus Augustus was added after his consecration, and one of the explicit intentions of that worship was the well-being of the imperial house. Numerous events in the history of that house received commemoration, and these commemorations, being dated, are a very important source for the chronology of the Empire. The preserved records begin in 21 B.C. and end in A.D. 241 (*ILS* 9522), but the cult still existed in 304 (*Not. Scav.* 1919, 105 f.). *See also* AMBARVALIA.

For the history of Latin script in Rome the *Acta Fratrum Arvalium* are of unique significance.

FUNDAMENTAL EDITIONS. W. Henzen, *Acta Fratrum Arvalium* (1874); *CIL* vi. 2023–119, 32338–98, 37163 f. The edition by E. Pasoli (1950) is worthless.
NEW FRAGMENTS. *Not. Scav.* 1914, 464 ff.; 1919, 100 ff.; 1921, 49–51; *Bull. Com. Arch.* lv (1927/8), 275 ff.; *Epigraphica* 1945, 27 ff.; *Athenaeum* 1946, 188 ff.; *Bull. Comm. Arch.* lxxviii (1961/2), 116 ff.
SELECTIONS. H. Dessau, *ILS* 229–30, 241, 451, 5026–49, 9522. For the *Carmen Arvale* see Ed. Norden, 'Aus altrömischen Priesterbüchern', *Acta Reg. Soc. Hum. Litt. Lund.* 1939, 109 ff. A new edition of the *Acta* is being prepared by H. Bloch.   H. B.

**FREEDMEN.** Roman *libertini* and *liberti* appear to have been far more numerous than Greek ἀπελεύθεροι and ἐξελεύθεροι because (1) little survives of Greek legislation and there was virtually no Greek juristic writing; (2) many Roman freedmen became citizens and were therefore much discussed in politics and literature; and (3) the *liberti Caesaris* were for a time at the centre of political conflict. The fact is that we have no figures at all, absolute or relative. The freedman of great wealth or political influence was rare, but he was also notorious, leading to the illusion that there were many more like him.

As a general rule an owner was free to manumit a slave whenever and however he pleased. The legislation of Augustus restricting the number who could be manumitted by testament and introducing a few other controls (Gai. *Inst.* 1. 13–47) was altogether exceptional and will not bear the weight of sweeping reform that has been imposed on it. The form in which a manumission was completed did not often matter substantially, though there might be later legal complications (*see* LATINI IUNIANI). Many were accomplished informally, others by testament, by fictitious sale to a god (as at Delphi), or by some other formality designed to provide the freedman with legal proof if challenged.

The law bound a freedman in certain ways to his manumittor, now his *patronus* (q.v.). How far these obligations extended in practice beyond *obsequium* and *reverentia* is not clear, other than, in Rome, such claims as a patron had on any client (q.v.), and the patron's right to inherit if the freedman died childless and intestate. The not infrequent Greek practice, surviving to the end of antiquity, whereby an ex-owner explicitly retained a claim to specified services, suggests that otherwise, in a society without the institution of *clientela*, the freedman's obligations were more formal than practical.

Most freedmen were humble people. In Greece they merged with the other free non-citizens (*see* METICS), though some communities imposed special restrictions on them, such as residence in specified localities. In Rome, however, they normally acquired the political status of their manumittor, even Roman citizenship. The state therefore had to take cognizance of them, for example, in allocating them to voting tribes during the Republic, in excluding them from the legions and the curule magistracies, or, under Augustus, in excluding criminals from citizenship and even Latin status (*see* DEDITICII). Children born to a freedman after his manumission were free from all special restrictions.

The policy begun by Augustus of using his own *familia* in the administration led under Claudius to the rise of a few freedmen to great power and wealth (*see* PALLAS 3, NARCISSUS 2, NYMPHIDIUS). After Nero they were soon reduced to the lower echelons of the service. *See also* SLAVERY.

A. Calderini, *La manomissione e la condizione dei liberti in Grecia* (1908); A. M. Babakos, *ΣΧΕΣΕΙΣ ΟΙΚΟΓΕΝΕΙΑΚΟΥ ΔΙΚΑΙΟΥ ΕΙΣ ΤΗΝ ΝΗΣΟΝ ΚΑΛΥΜΝΟΝ* (1963); A. M. Duff, *Freedmen in the Early Roman Empire* (reissue 1958); C. Cosentini, *Studi sui liberti* (1948–50); M. Kaser, 'Die Geschichte des Patronatsgewalt über Freigelassene', *Sav. Zeitschr.* 1938, 88 ff.; on *liberti Caesaris*, P. R. C. Weaver, *Proc. Camb. Phil. Soc.* 1964, 74 ff.; *Hist.* 1964, 188 ff.; *CQ* 1963, 272 ff.; *Past and Present* 1967, 3 ff.; S. Treggiari, *Roman Freedmen during the Late Republic* (1969). M. I. F.

**FREGELLAE,** modern *Opri* near *Ceprano*, on the River Liris (q.v.) below Sora (q.v.). Establishment of a Latin Colony here (328 B.C.) provoked the Second Samnite War. Staunchly loyal to Rome against Pyrrhus and Hannibal, it revolted against her in 125 B.C. and was destroyed. Fabrateria Nova, a new foundation some miles away, replaced it.

G. Colasanti, *Fregellae* (Rome, 1906). E. T. S.

**FRENTANI,** Oscan-speaking people between Marrucini and Apulia (qq.v.) on Italy's Adriatic coast. Chief settlements: Ortona, Histonium, Buca, Anxanum (*see too* LARINUM). A tribally organized State, they sided with Rome, after initial hostility, in the Second Samnite (q.v.) War and remained her loyal allies until the Social War when they joined the insurgents. They were romanized rapidly thereafter.

E. T. Salmon, *Samnium and the Samnites* (1967), see index E. T. S

**FRISII,** a Germanic people, who lived on the North Sea coast where the Frisians still live, but extended eastwards to the Ems. Overrun by Drusus in 12 B.C., they paid the Romans taxes of ox-hides but revolted in A.D. 28 owing to the extortionate exaction of the hides by a centurion named Olennius. They maintained their freedom until 47, when Corbulo subjugated them; but in 69–70 they were active in the rebellion of Civilis (q.v.). In the third century, however, *cunei Frisionum* (*ILS* 2635, 4761) served in Britain. Like the Bructeri and the Chauci, they were divided into two sections called *maiores* and *minores*, but the significance of this is unknown; nor do we know their precise relationship with the Franks, who ruled their part of the world at a later date. E. A. T

**FRONTINUS,** SEXTUS JULIUS (*PW* 243), c. A.D. 30–104 *praetor urbanus* in 70 and *consul suffectus* in 74 (?); after his consulate he was appointed governor of Britain (probably 74–8), where he subdued the Silures (q.v.). He was probably the founder of the legionary camp at Isca (q.v.).

Frontinus' writings are essentially practical, dealing with professional subjects in a straightforward style admirably suited to his purpose. Of his two-volume work on land-surveying, published under Domitian, only excerpts survive. A theoretical treatise on Greek and Roman military science (*De re militari*), used by Vegetius (1. 8; 2. 3), has perished; but the *Strategemata*, also of Domitian's reign, a more general manual of historical examples illustrating Greek and Roman strategy for the use of officers (book 1, *praef.*) survives in four books. The first three are closely related (stratagems before, during, and after battle; during sieges); but book 4, where critics detect differences of style and structure, collects instances more ethical in character (Discipline, Justice, etc.) and has been attributed to a later 'Pseudo-Frontinus'. Its authenticity remains doubtful.

Appointed *curator aquarum* by Nerva (A.D. 97), Frontinus began for his own and his successors' guidance a two-volume account of the water-supply of Rome (*De aquis urbis Romae*), completed under Trajan. This describes the aqueducts and their history, with complete technical details as to quantity and distribution of supply, and examines the regulations governing the system and its public and private use. The sources include personal inquiry, engineers' reports, State documents and plans, and senatorial decrees, as well as previous technical writers.

He was again suffect consul in 98, and *ordinarius* in 100 with Trajan.

CAREER. Frere, *Britannia*, 101 ff.
WRITINGS. Texts. Surveying: excerpts in C. Lachmann, *Röm. Feldmesser* (1848); C. Thulin, *Corpus Agrimensorum Rom.* i. 1 (1913). *Strategemata*: G. Gundermann (1888); G. Bendz, *Index verborum* (1939): *Textkrit. u. interpr. Bemerkungen* (1943). *De aquis*: F. Bücheler (1858); F. Krohn (1922). Text and translation: *Strat.* and *De aq.*, C. E. Bennett, M. B. McElwain (Loeb, 1925); *Les aqueducs*, P. Grimal (Budé, 1944–61).
On *De aquis*: R. Lanciani, *Topografia di Roma antica; i commentarii di Frontino intorno le acque e gli acquedotti* (1880); C. Herschel, *The Two Books on the Water-supply . . . of . . . Frontinus²* (1913); T. Ashby, *Aqueducts of Ancient Rome* (1935).
On 'Pseudo-Frontinus': C. Wachsmuth, *Rh. Mus.* 1860 (bk. 4 spurious); P. Esternaux, *Die Kompos. v. Frontins Strategemata* (1899) (bk. 4 authentic); G. Bendz, *Die Echtheitsfrage des vierten Buches der Frontinschen Strategemata* (1938) (convincing defence). G. C. W.

**FRONTO,** MARCUS CORNELIUS (*PW* 157) c. A.D. 100– c. 166, born at Cirta, Numidia, became the foremost Roman orator of his day. After passing through the *cursus honorum* (*CIL* viii. 5350) he was *consul suffectus* in 143.

Some years earlier he had been appointed tutor in Latin rhetoric to the future Emperors M. Aurelius and L. Verus, and he continued in their service till his death in 166 or soon after.

In the pages of Aulus Gellius Fronto makes several appearances as the centre of a philological coterie. Later writers speak highly of his oratory, mentioning him in the same breath with Cato, Cicero, and Quintilian; the author (Eumenius?) of the *Panegyricus Constantio dictus* (14) even calls him 'Romanae eloquentiae non secundum sed alterum decus'. Except for a doubtfully ascribed treatise *De Differentiis Vocabulorum* there was no basis for testing these judgements till early in the nineteenth century, when palimpsests at Milan and Rome were found to contain the greater portion of his correspondence with M. Aurelius and others. Its publication so disappointed the expectations of historians that Fronto became the victim of much intemperate criticism. The correspondence has indeed little bearing on history, though it does something to rehabilitate the characters of Verus and of the Elder and Younger Faustina, and clearly pictures the bourgeois home life of the Antonines. It is, however, of considerable interest as a personal record, as a literary by-product, and as a document for the study of rhetoric and language. The mutual affection of Fronto and M. Aurelius is unquestionably sincere, and is the more remarkable since the author of the *Meditations* so obviously preferred philosophy to rhetoric and Greek to Latin. They write to each other as close friends, with just that touch of self-consciousness which is inevitable between master and pupil, but with no thought of having to run the gauntlet of posterity. Much of their correspondence is the merest small-talk, but it is also largely concerned with the study of rhetoric, and Fronto's views on this subject are amply documented, though it remains impossible to estimate his achievement in oratory either from his precepts or from the few rhetorical exercises which survive with the correspondence. As a teacher Fronto employed the traditional rhetorician's technique, and reposed an excessive faith in similes. His favourite prose reading consisted of Cato, C. Gracchus, Sallust, and Cicero's letters; of Seneca he speaks slightingly. He deprecated the purism which would confine literary Latin to the vocabulary of Cicero's orations, and by drawing partly on early poets and partly on the *sermo cotidianus* he devised the *elocutio novella*. This euphuistic attempt to revitalize a decaying language is best illustrated in his own writings and those of his fellow countryman Apuleius, but it left its mark on most of the Latin prose written after his time.

TEXT. M. P. J. van den Hout (Leiden, 1954). With translation: C. R. Haines (Loeb, 1919–20).
Critical essays, text and translation of selected letters, and full bibliography to date: M. D. Brock, *Studies in Fronto and his Age* (1911). Critical (but over-enthusiastic) study: F. Portalupi, *Marco Cornelio Frontone* (1961). See also R. Marache, *La Critique littéraire de langue latine et le développement du goût archaïsant au IIe siècle de notre ère* (1952). Date of death: G. W. Bowersock, *The Sophists in the Roman Empire* (1969), App. iii.                              R. G. C. L.

**FRONTONIANI** (Sid. Apoll. *Ep.* 1. 1. 2), followers of Fronto (q.v.) in his archaizing theories of a style, *elocutio novella* (q.v.), calculated to displace both Silver Age mannerisms and Quintilian's veneration for Cicero by a return to the old-fashioned and largely discarded language of Ennius, Cato, and the Gracchi as models. *See* ARCHAISM.

M. D. Brock, *Studies in Fronto and his Age* (1911); E. S. Bouchier, *Life and Letters in Roman Africa* (1913), ch. 5.             J. W. D.

**FRUSINO,** modern *Frosinone*, on the Via Latina (q.v.). It participated in, and indeed instigated, the revolt of some Hernici against Rome in 306 B.C. and lost much territory in consequence. Although reduced to a *prae-fectura*, it remained reasonably prosperous. Today it is a large town with negligible traces of antiquity.     E. T. S.

**FUCĬNUS LACUS,** a large lake at the centre of Italy. It lacked a visible outlet, but legend stated that the river Pitonius from the Paeligni country traversed it without their waters mingling, the Pitonius reappearing near Sublaqueum to supply the Aqua Marcia (Pliny, *HN* 2. 224; 31. 41; Lycoph. *Alex.* 1275). The lake sometimes overflowed (Strabo 5. 240: exaggerated). Claudius, employing 30,000 men for eleven years, executed Caesar's plan to drain the lake: an *emissarium* was excavated 3½ miles through a mountain ridge to carry the lake waters to the Liris (q.v.) (Suet. *Iul.* 44; *Claud.* 20 f.; 32). But Claudius's efforts were not entirely successful. Even repairs to his *emissarium* by Trajan and Hadrian proved vain (Dio Cass. 60. 11. 33; Dessau, *ILS* 302; S.H.A. *Hadr.* 22). Drainage attempts recommenced in A.D. 1240, but were unsuccessful until the nineteenth century, when practically the whole lake-bed was reclaimed.

E. Agostinoni, *Il Fucino* (1908).                    E. T. S.

**FUFIUS** (*PW* 10) **CALENUS,** QUINTUS, assisted Clodius (q.v. 1) as tribune in 61 B.C., supported Caesar as praetor (59), and some years later served under him in Gaul and in the Civil War (especially in Greece), becoming consul in 47 (not elected till September) with Vatinius (q.v.). After Caesar's death he supported his friend Antonius (q.v. 4) against his enemy Cicero. He held part of Italy during the Philippi campaign, and then governed Gaul for Antony with eleven legions, which, on his death (40), his son handed over to Octavian.     E. B.

**FULGENTIUS,** FABIUS PLANCIADES, *c.* A.D. 467–532, *vir clarissimus*, known as the *Mythographus*, is probably identical with the famous bishop of Ruspe. (A summary of the question in K. Polheim, *Die lateinische Reimprosa* (1925), 287 ff. Critical of the identification, G. Krüger in *Harnack-Ehrung* (1921).) Fulgentius was born at Thelepte in Byzacene, Africa, of a rich family, received a good education, including Greek, and became *procurator* in his native town. The collection of writings usually grouped together under his name (*Mitologiarum Libri tres, Expositio Virgilianae Continentiae secundum Philosophos moralis, Expositio Sermonum antiquorum, De aetatibus mundi et hominis,* and the *Super Thebaiden* (Bischoff, *Byz. Zeitschr.* 1951, ascribes the last to the 12th or 13th c.)), with their bizarre style, their searching after unusual words, their strange etymologies and stranger allegorizing, probably belong to an earlier period of Fulgentius' life. All of them, but especially the *Virgiliana Continentia*, were widely read in the Middle Ages. Apuleius and Martianus Capella (qq.v.) were Fulgentius' models. He uses the dialogue form, by means of which Calliope unravels the meaning of the myths, and Virgil the allegory underlying his *Aeneid*. The *De Aetatibus mundi* is a summary of world history, sacred and secular. Besides his highly rhetorical sermons modelled on Augustine, and theological works, there is an alphabetical 'psalm', against the Arian Vandals, which closely follows the pattern of Augustine's 'psalm' against the Donatists.

After years of monastic life, Fulgentius became bishop of Ruspe in 507. The Vandal King Thrasamund twice banished him to Sardinia, finding him too able a champion of the Catholic faith.

*Opera*, ed. R. Helm (Leipzig, 1898); theological works, Migne, *PL* lxv; two 'new' sermons, J. Leclercq, *Revue Bénéd.* 1945/6; Fulgentius' *Commonitorium*, A. Souter, *JTS* 1913: Psalm, C. Lambot, *Revue Bénéd.* 1936. G. Lapeyre, *S. Fulgence de Ruspe* (1929); O. Friebel, *Fulgentius der Mythograph und Bischof* (1911); P. Courcelle, *Les Lettres grecques en Occident de Macrobe à Cassiodore* (1948: pp. 206–9 for bibliographical references in notes); bibliography in *Clavis Patrum Latinorum*, ed. E. Dekker (1961).          F. J. E. R.

**FULLING.** In the ancient world the fuller (κναφεύς, *fullo*) was employed both in the finishing processes of cloth and in the cleaning of soiled garments that could not be washed at home (mainly, though not exclusively, those made from wool). In the absence of soap, the cloth was first washed by treading it in ditches (πλυνοί, *lacunae*) or tubs (*pilae fullonicae*) with water and soda (νίτρον) or some other alkaline detergent (often human or animal urine). It was then beaten with wooden sticks or mallets to close up its texture, washed again to clean and shrink it, dried, brushed with special tools or teasel burs to raise the nap, bleached with sulphur, dressed with fuller's earth or some similar substance, and finally 'shorn' (to remove uneven fibres) and pressed in special presses. Fullers' workshops (one with wall paintings illustrating the processes) have been found at Pompeii and elsewhere. Fullers' guilds were well established in Ptolemaic Egypt, and in imperial Rome the 'collegium aquae' was of considerable importance.

Pliny, *HN* 35. 196–8. H. Blümner, *Technologie der Gewerbe und Künste* i² (1912), 170 ff.; Forbes, *Stud. Anc. Technol.* iv². 82 ff.
L. A. M.

**FULVIA** (*PW* 113), the rich daughter of M. Fulvius Bambalio and Sempronia, both from disappearing noble families, was wife successively of Clodius (q.v. 1), Curio (q.v. 2), and (by 45 B.C.) Antony. The stories of her cruelty in the proscriptions are suspect, but she was certainly ambitious and strong-minded, and took a prominent part in the political campaign of 41 which led to the Perusine War (*see* ANTONIUS 6). Thereafter (early 40) she escaped to Greece, where she shortly died, her spirit broken by Antony's reproaches. To Clodius she bore a son Publius (later praetor) and a daughter Claudia who became Octavian's first wife (he dismissed her untouched during the dissensions of 41), to Curio a son executed by Octavian after Actium, and to Antony Antyllus and Iullus (*see* ANTONIUS 7 and 8).

Syme, *Rom. Rev.*, see index; E. Malcovati, *Le donne di Roma antica* i (1945); C. L. Babcock, *AJPhil.* 1965, 1 ff. (speculative).
T. J. C.

**FUNDANIUS,** GAIUS, unrivalled in witty comedy according to Horace, *Sat.* 1. 10. 40–3 (cf. Porphyr. ad loc.). Belonging to Maecenas' circle, he is imagined to describe Nasidienus' dinner (*Sat.* 2. 8. 19).

**FUNDANUS,** MINICIUS (*PW* 13) or MINUCIUS, *cos. suff.* A.D. 107, had a wide circle of friends who included the Younger Pliny and Plutarch. As proconsul of Asia (in 122–3: cf. *AE* 1957, 17) he received Hadrian's rescript about procedure concerning Christians. A copy of this was later attached to the end of Justin Martyr's *First Apology* (*c.* 150).
H. H. S.

**FUNDI,** modern *Fondi*, interesting for its walls and ancient street plan, Volscian town on the Via Appia near Tarracina (q.v.). It obtained Roman citizenship early (*sine suffragio*, 338 B.C.; full franchise, 188 B.C.) and became a prosperous *municipium*, whose chief official Horace ridicules (*Sat.* 1. 5. 34). Its territory produced the choice Caecuban wine.

G. Lugli, *La tecnica edilizia romana* (1957), 152 ff.; Castagnoli *Stud. urb.*, 71 ff.
E. T. S.

**FURIAE,** Latin equivalent of Erinyes (q.v.), perhaps a translation ( *furere* = ἐρινύειν, to rage like an Erinys). There is no proof of their existing in cult or unprompted popular belief; sometimes they are identified with the obscure goddess Fur(r)ina (q.v.), as Cicero, *Nat. D.* 3. 46.
H. J. R.

**FURIUS** (1, *PW* 34) **ANTIAS** (i.e. of Antium), AULUS (fl. 100 B.C.), friend of Q. Lutatius Catulus (Cic. *Brut.*

132), epic poet influenced by Ennius and in turn influencing Virgil, cf. his 'pressatur pede pes' with Verg. *Aen.* 10. 361. From his *Annales*, a national poem in at least eleven books, Gellius (18. 11) quotes six hexameters.

Baehr. *FPR*; Morel, *FPL*.
J. W. D.

**FURIUS** (2, *PW* 78) **PHILUS,** LUCIUS, friend of Scipio (q.v. 11) Aemilianus, whose cultural interests he shared (*see* SCIPIONIC CIRCLE). As consul in 136 B.C. he was closely concerned with the affair of the *foedus Mancinum* (Cic. *Rep.* 3. 28; *see* MANCINUS), and under his supervision Mancinus was offered to the Numantines. This Furius may be the author of a work which included two sacral formulae used against besieged cities (Macrob. *Sat.* 3. 9. 6). Cicero, who introduced him into his *De Republica*, reports the excellent Latinity and educated style of his speeches.

Malcovati, *ORF*² 137; A. E. Astin, *Scipio Aemilianus* (1967).
A. E. A.

**FURNITURE.** Very little furniture has survived from the Minoan and Mycenaean Palaces. At Cnossos there was some wooden furniture and furniture of gypsum and coloured marbles. The Treasury of Atreus is reported to have had marble tables, and part of a table of rosso antico was found in the megaron at Mycenae. The Palace at Pylos yielded a variegated marble table top inlaid with red stone and the remains of wooden thrones, chairs, and footstools. Very gaudy and elaborate furniture is recorded in the Pylos furniture tablets, and these records, together with fragments found in excavations, show that Homer's references to bedsteads, chairs, and footstools with inlays of gold and silver and ivory preserve an authentic Mycenaean tradition.

The forms of classical Greek furniture are known mainly from representations in art. Most of the furniture was carved wood, turnery being introduced in the sixth century B.C. The principal forms were: the throne (θρόνος), a high-backed chair for occasions of state; the chair (κλισμός) of lighter build, without arms, in general domestic use; the stool (δίφρος), four-legged, boxed, or folding (δίφρος ὀκλαδίας); the footstool (θρῆνυς), which might be square or oblong; the table (τράπεζα), always small and portable, on three legs and oblong or circular (τρίπους); the couch (κλίνη), used for dining as well as for sleeping; and the chest (κιβωτός, λάρναξ), in which clothes and bedding were stored. Rugs were used on the couches; in the fifth century their use as floor-coverings was considered effeminate, though the practice was known to Homer and became common in Hellenistic times. Utensils were piled on the floor or hung on the walls; lamps stood on shelves or in niches. The general effect to our eyes would be one of bareness and simplicity.

The Greek types are the basis of Etruscan and Roman furniture, and the greater luxury of these nations is evinced more in costliness of material than in novelty of form. Etruria introduced a new type of chair with rounded back resembling the modern arm-chair, and high candelabra of metal on which clusters of candles could be placed. Rome adapted these as lamp-stands. The Roman throne (*solium*), chair (*cathedra*), and stool (*sella*), follow Greek models; the couch (*lectus*) was either of Greek shape or was provided with a back, like a sofa. Sideboards and cupboards with drawers, sometimes used as book-cases, appear in imperial times, together with new forms of the table (*mensa*) which was the typical object of domestic ostentation: Cicero gave a million sesterces for a table of citron wood.

G. M. A. Richter, *The Furniture of the Greeks, Etruscans and Romans* (U.S.A. 1966); W. Deonna, *Délos* xviii: *Le Mobilier délien* (1938); *A History of Technology* (ed. C. Singer, 1956) ii. 221 ff.
F. N. P.; D. E. S.

**FURRINA** (preferable to **FURINA**), a divinity belonging to the earliest stratum of Roman religion; she possessed a grove, an annual festival (*Furrinalia*, 25 July), and a *flamen*, but by the last decades of the Republic her very name was largely forgotten. The interpretation as *Furia* (despite Altheim, *History of Roman Religion* (1938), 116 f.) rests upon a false analogy; the term *Nymphae Furrinae* appears to be late, although Furrina may have been a divinity of a spring or of springs. The location of her grove, on the slopes of the Janiculum near the Pons Sublicius, is indicated by the account of the death of C. Gracchus in 121 B.C. (Plut. *C. Gracch.* 17; Auctor, *De Vir. Ill.* 65; less precisely, Oros. 5. 12. 8), and fixed by epigraphical and other discoveries (P. Gauckler, *Le Sanctuaire syrien du Janicule*, 1912); these have established the existence of springs and the fact that under the Empire the traditional worship became almost totally ousted by Oriental cults. Cicero (*QFr.* 3. 1. 4) mentions another shrine near Arpinum.

S. M. Savage, 'The Cults of Ancient Trastevere', *Am. Ac. Rome* 1940, 35 ff. A. W. VAN B.

**FURTUM** (theft) is defined in Justinian's *Digesta* (q.v.) as 'contrectatio ["handling"] rei fraudulosa lucri faciendi gratia. . .' (*Dig.* 47. 2. 1. 3). The *res* must, however, be movable: land could not be stolen. This, and the probable etymology of 'furtum' ('fero'), suggest that a carrying away was necessary, but, at least in the developed law and in the majority opinion, this was not so. Nor need the thief intend permanently to deprive the owner (e.g. when a borrower uses the thing in an unauthorized way—the so-called *furtum usus*). The owner could himself be liable for theft (e.g. from a pledgee—the so-called *furtum posses-*

*sionis*). By the XII Tables a thief who came by night, and any thief who used a weapon, might be killed out of hand. A *fur manifestus* (caught in the act) was scourged and subjected to the plaintiff by *addictio*, but the praetor substituted a penalty of fourfold the value of the thing. For *furtum nec manifestum* the penalty was, and remained, twofold. The plaintiff was the owner or other person, such as a usufructuary (*see* SERVITUTES) or a pledgee, having a sufficient interest. These distinctions and penalties were preserved by Justinian, but it is probable that already in the classical law the normal proceeding was by criminal prosecution. The owner might also claim restitution of the thing by *vindicatio* (q.v.) or compensation for its loss by *condictio furtiva*.

P. Huvelin, *Études sur le furtum* i (1915); H. F. Jolowicz, *Digest* xlvii. 2, *De Furtis* (1940); B. Albanese, *Annali del seminario giuridico Palermo* 1953, 1956. B. N.

**FUSCUS**, CORNELIUS (*PW* 158), of a senatorial family, adopted the equestrian career, 'quietis cupidine', though of a dashing and adventurous character (Tac. *Hist.* 2. 86). He was a partisan of Galba in A.D. 68 and was rewarded by him with the procuratorship of Illyricum, in which function he actively helped the Flavian generals to invade Italy. Later, as Prefect of the Guard, he was entrusted with the conduct of the war against the Dacians; he crossed the Danube and penetrated into Dacia (86 or 87), but met with a signal defeat and lost his life (Dio 67. 6; Jordanes, *Getica* 13. 76). The altar at Adam-Klissi (q.v.) has been connected with him, without much reason (cf. *CAH* xi. 670); and the problem of his *colonia* of origin (perhaps Narbonensian) arouses some interest.

R. Syme, *AJPhil.* 1937, 7; *Tacitus*, 623; 683 f. R. S.

# G

**GABII,** an ancient Latin city whose site has been excavated 12 miles east of Rome. Prehistoric finds do not contradict the story of its foundation by Alba Longa (q.v.) (Verg. *Aen.* 6. 773). Its resistance to Tarquin (q.v. 2), separate treaty with Rome, and special role in augural practices prove its early importance (Livy 1. 53 f.; Dion. Hal. 4. 53; Varro, *Ling.* 5. 33). After 493 B.C. Gabii appears as Rome's ally but was possibly sacked in the Latin War (Livy 3. 8; 6. 21; Macrob. *Sat.* 3. 9. 13). By 50 B.C. it had become a village (Cic. *Planc.* 23. Record of Sulla's colony is suspect: *Lib. Colon.* p. 234). Nevertheless the poets exaggerate its desolation. Under the Empire Gabii was a prosperous *municipium* with celebrated baths and ornate Hadrianic buildings (*ILS* 272). Although still a bishopric in the ninth century, today only a temple (third century B.C.) remains. The Romans reputedly derived from Gabii the *cinctus Gabinus*, a particular mode of wearing the *toga* which was used in certain ceremonial rites (Serv. on *Aen.* 7. 612; Livy 5. 46).

T. Ashby, *PBSR* 1902, 180 ff.; A. Alföldi, *Early Rome and the Latins* (U.S.A. 1965), 378 ff. E. T. S.

**GABINIUS** (1, *PW* 6), AULUS, the grandson of a slave, served under Metellus (q.v. 3) in Macedonia in 148 B.C., and as legate in 146 warned the Achaeans against war. Tribune in 139, he introduced the secret ballot in elections. A. H. McD.

**GABINIUS** (2, *PW* 11; cf. 10), AULUS, as tribune 67 B.C. transferred Bithynia and the legions of Lucullus (q.v. 2) to the consul Glabrio, and then carried the law giving

Pompey (q.v.) command against the pirates, threatening to depose Trebellius, a fellow tribune who attempted veto. It was also probably now (rather than in his consulate) that he forbade the lending of money to provincials in Rome. He served Pompey as legate in the East and in 58 as consul, when he incurred Cicero's lasting hatred by scorning his appeals for help. Clodius had bribed him with the province of Syria, which he administered competently, reorganizing Judaea and setting Antipater in power. But in 55 he restored Ptolemy Auletes, for a large bribe; in return for this, and for his alienation of the *publicani* (perhaps through his leniency to the provincials —Cic. *Prov. Cons.* 10), he had to face three prosecutions on his return in 54. Cicero called his acquittal for *maiestas* a 'lex impunitatis', but next month was shamefacedly defending him for *repetundae*; this time, however, Gabinius was condemned and went into exile, a third charge, for *ambitus*, being dropped. Recalled by Caesar, he fought for him in Illyricum (winter 48/7), but was besieged by barbarian tribes in Salonae, where he died.

He seems to have reached the consulate late, since he is probably identical with the Gabinius who was military tribune under Sulla in 86 and his legate in Asia in 81. See E. Badian, *Philol.* 1959, 87 ff. G. E. F. C.

**GADES** (τὰ Γάδειρα, from Phoenician Gadir; now *Cádiz*), on the Spanish coast north-west of Gibraltar. The traditional foundation by Phoenicians of Tyre *c.* 1100 B.C. is accepted by some; others lower the date to the eighth or seventh century. It was often confused with Tartessus (q.v.). Before Herodotus, the adjacent island was the legendary seat of Geryon; Heracles-Melqart and Saturn-Baal were long worshipped in Gades. It was Hamilcar Barca's first Spanish base, and kept Punic letters on its coins down to Augustan times. It went over to Rome in 206 B.C. and received favourable terms; Julius Caesar, after other acts of patronage, gave it Roman municipal status; it added Augustus' name to its title. In social prestige it ranked with the Roman colonies; in wealth it was next to Rome and Patavium, having 500 men of equestrian census. Always a trading-post, it was long unrivalled in the West for commercial shipping; both busy and gay, Gades iocosae also had the best dancing-girls. In the second century A.D. it was eclipsed by the traffic of Hispalis (q.v.), and by the fourth century it was decadent or derelict. It had been the home of the Cornelii Balbi, Columella, and Hadrian's mother.

For temple and cult of Hercules, see A. Garcia y Bellido, *Archivo Español de Arqueologia* 1963, 70 ff. M. I. H.

**GAEA** (*Γαîα*) or **GE** (*Γῆ*), the Earth, conceived as a vaguely personal goddess. It may be that in the earliest times she, like Tellus (q.v.), was simply the power or *mana* resident in that parcel of earth which the particular group of worshippers tilled or otherwise used; but as far back as our records go she is the Earth in general, or a goddess resident in and governing it. Her cult can be traced in a number of places, though in most of them she has been superseded by a more definitely personal power, chthonian or other. At Delphi she was the original holder of the oracular shrine (Aesch. *Eum.* 2), a statement which there is no reason to doubt, as it is supported by sundry other traditions and by the fact that Apollo is said to have killed Python, a serpent and therefore a creature of earth (he actually gave the oracles, Hyg. *Fab.* 140. 1), before he could take over the holy place; cf. APOLLO. Her well-supported identity or close connexion with Themis (q.v.; Aesch. loc. cit. and *Prom.* 209–10) is to be explained by that goddess's original nature as simply 'the fixed or firm one' and not an abstraction (see Farnell, op. cit. *infra* 12 ff.). For more or less probable identifications of her with other figures, see ibid. 19 ff. One of her most characteristic functions is as a witness to oaths (as *Il.* 3. 278), because she must know what is done on her surface.

In mythology she is the offspring of Chaos, or at least comes into being after it. Heaven (*Οὐρανός*) is her child and husband, and their offspring, besides such things as seas and mountains, are the Titans, Cyclopes, and Hecatoncheires (qq.v.). After her separation from Uranus (cf. KRONOS) she bore the Erinyes and Giants (qq.v.), being fertilized by the blood from his mutilation; later she produced Typhon (q.v.), whose father was Tartarus (Hesiod, *Theog.* 117 ff.; 820 ff.). This is a systematized account of the wedding of Sky and Earth; there are many legends ultimately to the same effect, e.g. the union of Zeus and Semele (see DIONYSUS) and many more children of Earth, as Erichthonius (see ATHENA), and Python in some accounts.

Apart from actual cult of Earth as a goddess, antiquity had its share of beliefs concerning her, as, e.g., the source (probably) of the life of new-born children, hence the Roman custom of placing them on the ground; the author of the potency ascribed to sundry herbs, and so forth. See, in general, A. Dieterich and E. Fehrle, *Mutter Erde*[3] (1925); for herbs, A. Delatte, *Herbarius*[2] (1938).

Farnell, *Cults* iii. 1 ff. (cult); Drexler in Roscher's *Lexikon*, s.v. (mythology, etc.); for a critical view, largely discounting her cult, Nilsson, *GGR* i[3]. 456 ff. H. J. R.

**GAISERIC**, king of the Vandals and Alans (qq.v.) from A.D. 428 to 477. In 429 he transported the Vandals from Spain to Africa, and in 439 occupied Carthage and de-

clared himself an independent ruler owing no allegiance to Rome. In 431, 441, and 467 he heavily defeated East Roman attempts to overthrow him. He was the only German king to build a fleet, and with this fleet he controlled the western Mediterranean throughout his reign. His most famous exploit was the capture of Rome in June 455. For a fortnight his men occupied the city and carried off many valuable works of art, including the treasures which Titus had taken from the Temple at Jerusalem. He died undefeated in 477.

See C. Courtois, *Les Vandales et l'Afrique* (1955). E. A. T.

**GAIUS** (1), the Emperor, 'Caligula' (GAIUS JULIUS (*PW* 133) CAESAR GERMANICUS; A.D. 12–41), son of Germanicus and Agrippina, born at Antium on 31 Aug. A.D. 12. In 14–16 he was on the Rhine with his parents and, because of the military boots which he wore, was nicknamed Caligula ('Baby Boots') by the soldiers. In 18–19 he was with his parents in the East and, after Germanicus' death in 19, lived in Rome with his mother until her arrest in 29, then successively with Livia and Antonia Minor, until 32, when he joined Tiberius on Capreae. After the death of his brother Drusus in 33 he was the only surviving son of Germanicus and, with Tiberius (q.v. 2) Gemellus—Claudius' claims not being considered seriously—next in succession to the Principate. He was elected *pontifex* in 31 and was *quaestor* two years later, but received no other training in public life. Tiberius appointed Gaius and Tiberius Gemellus joint heirs to his property, having already indicated in language typically obscure that he expected Gaius to succeed to the Principate. Strongly supported by Macro (q.v.), prefect of the Praetorian Guard, Gaius was acclaimed Emperor (16 March 37), Tiberius' will being declared invalid by the Senate, so that Gaius might inherit the whole of his property. In the early months of his rule Gaius honoured the memory of his mother, father, and brothers and spoke abusively of Tiberius. Antonia, a restraining influence, died on 1 May 37. In October Gaius was seriously ill, and it is possible that Philo (*Leg.* 14; 22) is right in thinking that his mind was unhinged as a result (see, however, Balsdon, op. cit. *infra* 212 ff.). On recovering he executed, some time before 24 May 38, both Macro and Tiberius Gemellus. In Jan. 39 Gaius quarrelled seriously with the Senate, revised his attitude to Tiberius' memory, and became more autocratic. The autumn and winter of 39–40 he spent in Gaul and on the Rhine; at Moguntiacum he forestalled a conspiracy against his life, whose leader, Cn. Cornelius Lentulus Gaetulicus, was executed. It is possible that at this time two new legions were raised (XV and XXII Primigeniae) and that Gaius intended to invade Germany or Britain. The intention, if serious, was abandoned, either because of military indiscipline or because of Gaius' instability of character (Suet. 24. 3; 39; 43–9; Dio Cass. 59. 21–3; 25. 1–5; cf. Balsdon, op. cit. 58–95 and *JRS* 1934, 13–18). After his return to Rome (in ovation, on 31 Aug. 40) Gaius was in constant danger of assassination, governed with much cruelty, and was murdered in the Palace on 24 Jan. 41. His (fourth) wife, Milonia Caesonia, and daughter (his only child) were also murdered.

The government of Gaius was more autocratic than that of earlier emperors. He was consul four times, in 37 (suffect), 39, 40 (sole consul), 41; on the first occasion for two months, on the last two for a few days only. In many respects he appears to have deserted the Augustan form of principate in favour of monarchy of the Hellenistic type; this, at least, is the easiest explanation of his treatment of his sisters, especially Drusilla, with whom he was suspected of committing incest and whom he consecrated after her death. For himself he accepted extravagant honours, which came close to deification, and, though in face of opposition he desisted from his intention to set up a statue of himself in the temple at Jerusalem, he was responsible for serious unrest among the Jews both in Alexandria and in Judaea.

ANCIENT SOURCES. Bks. 7 and 8 of the *Annals*, in which Tacitus described the principate of Gaius, being lost, we depend on Suetonius, *Gaius Caligula*, Dio Cassius, bk. 59, and Josephus, *AJ* 18. 6. 8. 205-19. 2. 5. 111 (with a detailed account of the murder of Gaius and an estimate of his character and principate, probably derived from Cluvius Rufus: see M. P. Charlesworth, *Camb. Hist. Journ.* 1933, 105 ff.). For detailed knowledge of Gaius' relations with the Greeks and Jews of Alexandria we have contemporary evidence in Philo, *Contra Flaccum* (edited by H. Box, 1939), *Legatio ad Gaium* (edited by E. M. Smallwood, 1961) (Philo was himself a member of the embassy to Gaius which he describes), and from papyri (H. A. Musurillo, *The Acts of the Pagan Martyrs : Acta Alexandrinorum*, 1954). See also, on the sources, A. Momigliano, *Rend. Linc.* 1932, 293 ff.

MODERN LITERATURE. J. P. V. D. Balsdon, *The Emperor Gaius (Caligula)* (1934); E. Koeberlein, *Caligula und die ägyptischen Kulte* (1962); J. A. Marner, *A Commentary on C. Suetoni Tranquilli Vita C. Caligulae Caesaris, 1-31* (U.S.A. 1949). J. P. B.

**GAIUS** (2, *PW* 2) (2nd c. A.D.), one of the most renowned Roman jurists, though nothing certain is known of his personality. His gentile name and cognomen are unknown, likewise his origin (perhaps a Greek province) and studies. Born perhaps under Trajan, he evidently lived at some period at Rome and wrote extensively, without having the *ius respondendi* or any public office. An adherent of, and perhaps a teacher in, the Sabinian School (*see* SABINUS 2), he sometimes rejects their point of view, and takes into consideration opinions of the opposite school. It is a striking fact that he was never cited by his contemporaries or by later jurists, not even by Paulus (q.v. 1) and Ulpianus (q.v. 1) who must have known and used his works. In post-classical times, however, he was popular and his authority was officially established by the Law of Citations (A.D. 426) which gave his writings equal authority with those of Papinianus (q.v.), Paulus, Ulpianus, and Herennius (q.v. 2). Justinian seems to have had a special predilection for Gaius, for he frequently calls him 'Gaius noster', and by his order Gaius' students' textbook, the *Institutes*, which was already the basis of first-year studies in the Eastern law-schools, was used as the basis for the composition of the imperial *Institutiones* (q.v.).

WORKS: *Ad edictum provinciale*, a long commentary in thirty-two books, which is one of the grounds for the suggestion that he was a provincial; *Ad edictum praetoris urbani*; *Ad legem XII tabularum*; *De verborum obligationibus*; *Res cottidianae sive Aurea*; *Liber singularis regularum*; and several monographs. His principal work was his *Institutionum commentarii quattuor*, probably completed soon after 161. Until they were discovered (1816) on a codex rescriptus at Verona (probably of the 5th c.), the *Institutes* were known only by a score of fragments in the *Digest* and an epitome in two books in the *Lex Romana Visigothorum*. The Veronese MS., containing the fourth book of the *Institutes* (till then unknown), furnished quite new details on the *legis actiones* and formulary procedure (*see* LAW AND PROCEDURE, ROMAN II). In spite of attacks by some radical critics, the Veronese text is generally held to be substantially genuine. The new fragments of the *Institutes* found in Egypt in 1933 on a few parchment sheets, and belonging apparently to the fourth century, supported this view, although they revealed the omission of a passage dealing with the obsolete *societas ercto non cito* (*see* COMMUNIO).

Opinions differ as to the merits, and in particular as to the originality, of Gaius. The arrangement of his *Institutes*, with its division of the law under the headings *personae, res, actiones*, and its further sub-divisions, achieved, through the medium of Justinian's *Institutes*, immense influence in later legal thought, but it may not have been originated by him. His work indisputably, however, has the qualities of clarity, simplicity, and economy, and his style, judged by the standards of his time, is plain and good. His historical explanations are sometimes erroneous, but he stands almost alone among the jurists for his interest in such things. Moreover, even if his merits are less than they are, his *Institutes* would still be of the greatest importance as being the only classical legal work to have come down to us in substantially its original form.

Editions of the *Institutes*: G. Studemund and P. Krüger (1923); E. Seckel, B. Kübler, 8th ed. (1939); F. de Zulueta (1946), with commentary (1953); M. David and H. L. W. Nelson (1954- unfinished). On the new fragments (*PSI* xi. 1182), see F. de Zulueta, *JRS* 1934, 168 ff., 1935, 19 ff., 1936, 174 ff. A. M. Honoré, *Gaius, A Biography* (1962), on which see F. Wieacker, *Sav. Zeitschr.* 1964, 401; and see bibliography s.v. JURISPRUDENCE. A. B.; B. N.

**GALATEA** (Γαλάτεια, perhaps 'milk-white'), name of a sea-nymph, first in Homer (*Il.* 18. 45); her legend was apparently first told by Philoxenus (see Bergk, *PLG*⁴ iii. 609 ff.). Polyphemus (*see* CYCLOPS) loved her, and wooed her uncouthly; the story is a favourite especially with pastoral writers (Theocr. 11; cf. 6. 6 ff.; Bion, fr. 12 Wilamowitz-Moellendorff; Ἐπιτάφιος Βίωνος, 58 ff.; Verg. *Ecl.* 9. 39 ff.; cf. 2. 19 ff.; 7. 37 ff.; but particularly Ov. *Met.* 13. 738 ff.). In this, the earliest surviving passage which adds anything important to the story, Galatea loved a youth, Acis, son of Faunus (Pan ?) and a river-nymph. Together they listened in hiding to Polyphemus' love-song, but when he had finished he rose to go and caught sight of them. Galatea dived into the sea, but Polyphemus pursued Acis and hurled a huge rock at him. As it fell on him and crushed him, Galatea turned him into a river, which bore his name ever after. The whole may well be a local Sicilian tale. The resemblance between Galatea's name and Γαλάτης, a Gaul, seems to underlie a less-known version in which she finally accepted Polyphemus' attentions and had by him a son, Galas or Galates, ancestor of the Gauls (see App. *Ill.* 2)—mere pseudo-historical or pseudo-mythical aetiology. H. J. R.

**GALATIA** is used, when applied to territory in the East, in two senses. (1) As the name of a territory in central Asia Minor, comprising parts of what was formerly Phrygia and Cappadocia, occupied and settled by a Celtic people which crossed the Hellespont in 278 B.C., and after much raiding and plundering were finally penned in an area stretching from the Sangarius to east of the Halys by Attalus I of Pergamum in 230. Here they continued to harass their neighbours; after the battle of Magnesia Rome sent Manlius Vulso to subdue them, and afterwards used them as a check on Pergamum. In the Mithridatic Wars they remained faithful to Rome. Their territory was organized on the Celtic tribal basis, the three tribes Tolistobogii, Tectosages, and Trocmi occupying separate areas around their respective capitals Pessinus, Ancyra, and Tavium, and each tribe being divided into four parts under tetrarchs. The council of the three tribes met at a place called Drynemetum, and tried cases of murder. The Galatians maintained their Celtic character throughout the imperial period, and when visited by St. Jerome were still speaking a Celtic language.

(2) As the name of a Roman province, formed in 25 B.C., incorporating the kingdom of Amyntas, which comprised besides Galatia proper parts of Phrygia, Lycaonia, and Pisidia, and possibly Pamphylia. Other territories in Paphlagonia and Pontus were afterwards added to the province, which was normally governed by a praetorian *legatus* until about A.D. 72, when Cappadocia and Armenia Minor were united with Galatia, and the combined province was put under a *legatus* with consular rank. Galatia was reduced in size, and again put under a praetorian *legatus*, by Trajan, and still further diminished about A.D. 137. Under Diocletian the province shrank

to the size of Galatia proper, with a strip of Lycaonia. The two principal cities of the province Galatia were Ancyra (the metropolis) and Pisidian Antioch.

It is disputed whether the 'Galatia' of St. Paul's Epistle to the Galatians refers to Galatia proper (the 'North-Galatian theory') or to the province Galatia, in whose Lycaonian and Phrygian regions St. Paul founded the churches mentioned in Acts (the 'South-Galatian theory').

F. Stähelin, *Geschichte der kleinasiatischen Galater*[2] (1907); Jones, *Cities E. Rom. Prov.*, ch. 4; Magie, *Rom. Rule Asia Min.* 453 ff.; R. K. Sherk, *The Legates of Galatia* (1951): cf. G. Pflaum, *Hist.* 1955, 119 ff.                                                                 W. M. C.

**GALBA** (1), the Emperor (SERVIUS SULPICIUS (*PW* 63) GALBA, *c.* 3 B.C.–A.D. 69), son of C. Sulpicius Galba and Mummia Achaica, was adopted by Livia Ocellina, second wife of his father. He was highly esteemed by Augustus and Tiberius, and was a favourite of Livia, as afterwards of Gaius and Claudius. Governor of Aquitania, consul (A.D. 33), legate of Upper Germany, proconsul of Africa (45), and from 60 governor of Hispania Tarraconensis, he had an exceptionally brilliant record to his credit, when in 68 Vindex (q.v.) invited him to replace Nero. He made his troops proclaim him only a legate of the Senate and of the Roman people. He had one legion and enrolled another of provincials (afterwards VII Gemina). The dangers inherent in the fall of Vindex were removed by Nero's death (*see* VERGINIUS (2) RUFUS). Nymphidius (q.v.) Sabinus with the praetorians declared for Galba, who took the title of Caesar and marched slowly to Rome with Otho (q.v.), governor of Lusitania, entering the city in early October. Threats from Nymphidius Sabinus and Clodius (q.v. 2) Macer were removed; but Galba incurred odium for massacring a body of marines outside Rome. Galba had the mind of an honest, but suspicious, administrator: 'omnium consensu capax imperii nisi imperasset'. His parsimony was notorious. He did not pay the donative promised to the soldiers. A commission was appointed to recover Nero's presents. He was unwise in sending his Spanish troops to Pannonia. Early in Jan. 69 the troops of the Rhine declared against him (*see* VITELLIUS 1). He adopted a certain L. Calpurnius Piso (q.v. 11) Frugi Licinianus as his successor, and offended Otho, who had hoped for that position. Otho organized a conspiracy among the praetorians, and Galba was killed on 15 Jan. 69.

SOURCES. Tac. *Historiae* i (ed. H. Heubner, 1963); Suet. *Galba* (ed. G. W. Mooney, 1930); Plut. *Galba* (ed. E. G. Hardy, 1890); Dio Cass. bks. 63–4. Tacitus, Suetonius, Plutarch mainly follow the same author (the usual identification with the Elder Pliny is not certain, but see G. B. Townend, *AJPhil.* 1964, 337 ff.).
MODERN LITERATURE. Syme, *Tacitus*, esp. 150 ff., 204 ff.; E. Koestermann, 'Das Charakterbild Galbas bei Tacitus', *Navicula Chiloniensis* (1956), 191 ff.; G. E. F. Chilver, 'The Army in Politics, A.D. 68–70', *JRS* 1957, 29 ff.; M. Fuhrmann, 'Das Vierkaiserjahr bei Tacitus', *Philol.* 1960, 250 ff.                          A. M.; G. E. F. C.

**GALBA** (2) **MAXIMUS**, PUBLIUS SULPICIUS (*PW* 64), was elected consul for 211 B.C. without having held any curule magistracy. He defended Rome against Hannibal's surprise attack. As proconsul (210–206) in Greece he conducted the First Macedonian War against Philip of Macedon, leading the first Roman fleet into the Aegean, where he captured Aegina (210); he achieved little else, and the main burden of war was gradually transferred to Rome's Greek allies. He was dictator in 203, probably to hold the elections. As consul II (200) he conducted the Second Macedonian War. Landing at Apollonia he planned to invade Macedonia from the west. He worsted Philip at Ottolobus and forced the pass of Banitza, but retired to Illyria for the winter (199); this campaign, though marked by no great military success, led the Aetolians to support Rome. Galba served as legate to Flamininus (197), as one of the ten senatorial

commissioners appointed to help Flamininus settle Greece (196), and later as ambassador to Antiochus (193).

N. G. L. Hammond, *JRS* 1966, 42 ff. (for campaign of 199).
                                                                        H. H. S.

**GALBA** (3), SERVIUS SULPICIUS (*PW* 58), military tribune in 168 B.C., opposing Aemilius Paullus' triumph in 167, was praetor in 151 in Further Spain, where in subduing the Lusitanians he treacherously massacred a number who had sued for peace (151–150). A prosecution against him in 149, supported by Cato, failed. He was consul in 144. His oratory set new rhetorical standards in emotional effect.

Livy 45. 35 ff.; *Per.* 48–9; App. *Hisp.* 58–60; Cic. *Brut.* 22. 86. Scullard, *Rom. Pol.* 234 ff., 269 ff.; Malcovati, *ORF*[2] 109.
                                                                        A. H. McD.

**GALBA** (4), GAIUS SULPICIUS (*PW* 51), son of (3) above, in 143 B.C. married Licinia, the elder daughter of Crassus (q.v. 1) the father-in-law of Gaius Gracchus. He probably served on a land-commission in Africa *c.* 121–119 (see Degrassi, *ILLRP* n. 475) and conceivably also on the Gracchan agrarian commission (so Cichorius, *Röm. Stud.* 113 ff., but see M. Gelzer, *Gnomon* 1929, 656 f.). Though possibly an augur, he was condemned by the Mamilian commission (110) for corruption in the Jugurthine war; the peroration (*Epilogus*) of his defence was a choice specimen of oratory to be committed to memory in Cicero's boyhood (*Brut.* 127).                     H. H. S.

**GALBA** (5), SERVIUS SULPICIUS (*PW* 61), probably grandson of no. 4, was a *legatus* in Gaul under C. Pomptinus (62–60 B.C.) and Caesar (58–56), and praetor in 54. In 50 he stood unsuccessfully for the consulship. In the Civil War he apparently took Caesar's side (Cic. *Att.* 9. 9. 3; Tac. *Hist.* 1. 15 ?) but in 44 joined in his assassination. In 43 he fought against Antony in the battle of Forum Gallorum, which he described to Cicero in a letter (*Fam.* 10. 30). He was condemned for Caesar's murder under the law of Pedius (q.v. 1).            T. J. C.

**GALBA** (6), GAIUS SULPICIUS (*PW* 52), son of (5) and grandfather of the Emperor Galba, wrote an historical work cited by Juba.

Peter, *HRRel.* ii. 41; *FGrH* 92.

**GALEN** of Pergamum (A.D. 129–? 199) in a spectacular career rose from gladiator-physician in Asia Minor to court-physician in the Rome of Marcus Aurelius. Well educated in his native town, he travelled later, studied in Greece and Alexandria, started practising in Pergamum in 157, and went to Rome in 162. He had become very famous when he left there in 166, only to return again from Pergamum in 169. He then stayed in Rome until his death. Writing all his life, he began with philosophical treatises and ended with medical books.

As philosopher and as physician Galen was an eclectic dogmatist. Plato and Hippocrates were his gods; Aristotle he held in sincere respect. But in spite of his belief in authorities he was anxious to form his own judgements, and his personality, therefore, takes the foreground in all his actions and writings. His knowledge was equally great in theory and practice; he excelled in diagnosis and prognosis and was a remarkably good teacher. His system is the ambitious effort to comprise the whole of medicine, the usual specialization of that time being rejected. Yet Galen realized that the physician has to deal with individuals, and that medicine can never be expressed adequately in general statements.

Galen was particularly productive as anatomist and physiologist. Performing dissections carefully in all their details, he collected and corrected the results of earlier generations and added many new facts. His physiological research based on experiment was masterly, particularly in the field of neurology; he proved that the arteries as well as the veins carry blood. His pathology was founded on the doctrine of the four humours; here he was most strongly influenced by speculative ideas. His pharmacological and dietetic doctrines were the codification of what had been accomplished in these fields.

Galen's monotheistic views, his ardent belief in teleology, his religious attitude—even anatomy to him was praise and veneration of God—foreshadow the coming Middle Ages. Yet his dominant influence on later generations, comparable only to that of Aristotle, is rather based on his two greatest achievements as a scientist, and in establishing a sect of medicine, which was above all sects; he had overcome the dissension characteristic of all earlier science and had laid the basis for the modern concept of a *scientia aeterna*, a science in which all scientists equally share and on which all of them unanimously agree.

TEXTS. *Opera omnia*, C. G. Kühn, i–xx (1821–33), the only complete edition, unreliable text. Published by Teubner: *Scripta minora* i–iii (1884–93); *Institutio logica* (1896); *De victu attenuante* (1898); *De temperamentis* (1904); *De usu partium* (1907–9); *Historia Philosophica* in Diels, *Doxographi Graeci* (1879). Modern editions of various writings in dissertations etc. listed, F. Ueberweg-K. Praechter, *Die Philosophie d. Altertums* (1926), 558, and A. Rehm-K. Vogel, *Exakte Wissenschaften*, Gercke–Norden ii. 5 (1933). A. Lesky, *Geschichte der griechischen Literatur* (1963²), 953; E. Wenkebach, *Optimus medicus philosophus*; H. Schöne, *De septimanis, Quell. u. Stud. z. Gesch. d. Naturw. u. d. Med.* (1933); for *De septimanis*, cf. R. Walzer, *Riv. degli Studi orient.* (1935); E. Wenkebach, *Protrepticus, Quell. u. Stud. z. Gesch. d. Naturw. u. d. Med.* (1935) and *De parvae pilae exercitio, Archiv f. Gesch. d. Medizin* (1938); Mau, *Galen, Einführung in die Logik* (Berlin, 1960); E. Orth, *Einführung in die Logik* (Rome, 1938); S. P. Kieffer, *Galen's Institutio Logica* (U.S.A. 1964). List of works published in *CMG*, K. Deichgräber, *Deutsche Akademie der Wissenschaft* (1957); *Schriften Sektion ür Altertumswissenschaft*, Heft 8 (1957). Fragments, Kühn i, p. clxxii. Translation from Arabic into German cf. Rehm–Vogel, loc. cit.; besides M. Meyerhof–F. Schacht, 'Über die medizinischen Namen', *Berl. Abh.* (1931); cf. also *Galen on Medical Experience*, ed. and tr. R. Walzer (1944). For Arabic MSS., R. Walzer, 'New Light on Galen's Moral Philosophy', and 'A Diatribe of Galen' in *Oriental Studies* i (1962); on Jews and Christians (1949); *Compendium Timaei Platonis* (1951).
TRANSLATIONS. With text, *On Natural Faculties* (A. J. Brock, Loeb). Ch. Daremberg, *Œuvres anatomiques, physiologiques et médicales* i–ii (1854–6); Ch. Singer, *Galen, De anatomicis administrationibus* (1956).
WORKS. List of writings, Christ–Schmid ii⁶ (1925), s.v. 'Galen'; cf. H. Diels, *Sitz. Berl.* 1908. In Arabic: R. Walzer, *Sitz. Berl.* 1934. Spurious books, Kühn i, p. clviii); M. Meyerhof, *Sitz. Berl.* 1928. Epitome of works, J. R. Coxe, *The Writings of Hippocrates and G.* (U.S.A. 1846). Chronology of writings, J. Ilberg, *Rh. Mus.* 1889 and 1897.
LITERATURE. General: J. S. Prendergast, *Enc. Brit*¹⁴. s.v. 'Galen'; J. Mewaldt, *PW* vii. 578; W. A. Greenhill, *Dict. of Greek and Roman Biography and Mythol.* (1846), s.v. 'Galen'. Life, M. Meyerhof, *Arch. f. Gesch. d. Med.* 1929; K. Deichgräber, *Sitzb. D. Akad. Klasse für Sprachen, Lit. und Kunst* (1956/3). Galen's position in the history of science, L. Edelstein, *Journal of the History of Ideas* 1952; *Scientific Change*, ed. A. C. Crombie (U.S.A. 1963), 28 ff. General survey, G. Sarton, *Galen of Pergamon* (U.S.A. 1954). Influence on G.'s writings, J. Walsh, *Annals Med. Hist.* 1927 f. G. as critic, L. O. Bröcker, *Rh. Mus.* 1885. G.'s philosophy, Ueberweg-Praechter (1926), 177 ff. Medical views, T. C. Allbutt, *Greek Medicine in Rome* (1921). Anatomy, F. Ullrich, *Die anatomische u. vivisektorische Technik d. G.*, Diss. Leipz. (1919). Physiology, Th. Meyer-Steineg, *Arch. f. Gesch. d. Med.* 1911; T. C. Allbutt, *CR* 1917. Biology, H. O. Taylor, *Greek Biology and Medicine* (1922), Ch. Singer, *A Short History of Biology* (1931). Gynaecology, J. Lachs, *Abh. z. Gesch. d. Med.* (1903). Laryngology, Gordon Holmes, *History of Laryngology* (1885). Practice, J. Ilberg, *Neue Jahrb.* 1905. *See also* G. W. Bowersock, *The Sophists in the Roman Empire* (1969), ch. 5.        L. E.

**GALERIUS** (1), the Emperor (GAIUS GALERIUS VALERIUS MAXIMIANUS, *PW* 2), was chosen as Caesar of the East by Diocletian in A.D. 293 and put away his wife to marry Diocletian's daughter, Valeria. Born about A.D. 250 at Serdica, the son of a peasant, he had risen from the ranks in the army. Tough and uneducated, he was entirely loyal to Diocletian. In 294 he engaged the Sarmatians on the Danube frontier and in 295 the Carpi, many of whom he settled in Pannonia. In 297 he was called East to a greater task, the defence against Narses of Persia. Defeated at first near Carrhae, he was given opportunity to repair his

error. With reinforcements from the Balkans, he invaded Armenia, and gained a complete victory over Narses; a peace entirely favourable to Rome followed (298). Diocletian is said to have discountenanced the large annexations that Galerius was disposed to make.

Galerius' religious views were similar to those of Diocletian; but being of a less prudent temperament than the latter he may have been the leading spirit behind the persecution of the Christians which began in 303. On Diocletian's abdication, Galerius became Augustus of the East (1 May 305), nominally second to Constantius, actually superior, as both Caesars, Severus and Maximinus Daia, were his men. When Constantius died (306) Galerius reluctantly accepted Constantine as Caesar of the West, but declined to recognize Maxentius who rebelled the same year, and sent Severus, now Augustus of the West, against him. After the defeat and capture of Severus, he himself invaded Italy, but was forced to beat an ignominious retreat. Summoning Diocletian from his retirement, he made a new settlement of the Empire at Carnuntum (308), appointing Licinius Augustus and declaring Maxentius a public enemy. But Constantine and Daia refused the offered rank of 'filii Augustorum' and assumed the full imperial title in 310. Falling ill in 311 Galerius relented so far as to issue an edict of partial toleration to the Christian Church. He died shortly afterwards, leaving the Church on the edge of triumph and the system of Diocletian on the brink of dissolution.

C. H. V. Sutherland, *RIC* vi, 15 ff.        H. M.; B. H. W.

**GALERIUS** (2, *PW* 8) **TRACHALUS** (*cos.* A.D. 68), a recent orator mentioned by Quintilian. He had an impressive appearance and his lofty and lucid style were enhanced by a voice and delivery 'that would have done credit to the stage' (*Inst.* 10. 1. 119; 12. 5. 5 and 10. 11). Tacitus says that it was generally believed that Otho made use of his ability in civil matters and some thought that he employed him to write the speech referred to in *Hist.* i. 90. He was proconsul of Africa.

J. W. D.; G. B. A. F.

**GALINTHIAS** (Γαλινθιάς, Anton. Liber. 29), or **GALANTHIS** (Γαλανθίς, Ov. *Met.* 9. 307), in mythology, a friend or servant of Alcmene (q.v.). When the latter was bearing Heracles, Eileithyia (and the Moirai) sat with hands clasped (and knees together), magically preventing delivery. Galinthias, perceiving this, ran out crying that Alcmene had borne a son; the goddess(es) leaped up in surprise and the charm was broken. In anger, they turned Galinthias into a lizard (Ovid) or weasel (Ant. Lib.).        H. J. R.

**GALLIC WARS** is the name usually given to the campaigns by which Caesar (q.v. 1) completed the Roman conquest of Gaul (58–51 B.C.). It is uncertain whether this conquest had been premeditated by Caesar; but appeals for his intervention on behalf of one Gallic tribe against another, or against German intruders, involved him in campaigns beyond the existing Roman province in south Gaul, and drew him as far as the Rhine (*see* AEDUI, ARIOVISTUS, HELVETII). At the end of 58 Caesar took up winter-quarters in north-east Gaul, an act foreshadowing a permanent Roman occupation of all Gaul. In 57 accordingly he had to meet preventive attacks by the tribes of northern Gaul (*see* BELGAE, NERVII); by his victories over these he brought northern France and Belgium under Roman control. In 56 Caesar had evidently resolved on the complete subjugation of Gaul, for in this year he forced the submission of the peoples on the Atlantic seaboard (*see* VENETI 1). It is uncertain whether the tribes of central Gaul at this time came to terms with him; but these were now ringed off within the Roman area of occupation, and Caesar at this stage considered the pacification of Gaul as complete.

In this belief Caesar spent the campaigning seasons of 55 and 54 in Germany and Britain. But sporadic revolts in northern Gaul kept him occupied throughout the winter of 54/3 and the following summer, and in 52 he was confronted by a formidable coalition of tribes in central Gaul under the leadership of Vercingetorix (q.v.). The duel between Caesar and Vercingetorix was the most critical event in the Roman conquest of Gaul. After repeated marches and counter-marches across central Gaul the issue still remained undecided, when Vercingetorix allowed Caesar to invest him in the fortress of Alesia (q.v.). The reduction of Alesia by famine and the capture of Vercingetorix finally broke Gallic resistance, and the local rebellions which flared up here and there in 51 strained Caesar's patience more than his resources.

The conquest of Gaul was accomplished by Caesar at a surprisingly low cost of men. The Gauls lost heavily in men and in treasure; but the estimate of Plutarch (*Caesar*, ch. 15), that their casualties amounted to one million killed and two millions captured, need not be taken literally. For the results of the conquest *see* GAUL.

For bibliography *see* CAESAR (1) *and* GAUL; T. Rice Holmes, *Caesar's Conquest of Gaul*[2] (1911); C. E. Stevens, 'The *Bellum Gallicum* as a Work of Propaganda', *Latomus* 1952, 3 ff. and 165 ff.; G. Walser, 'Caesar und die Germanen', *Hist.* Einzelschr. 1956.

M. C.

**GALLIENUS,** PUBLIUS LICINIUS (*PW* 84) EGNATIUS, son of Valerian, appointed Augustus with him in A.D. 253. While his father lived, he commanded in the West and fought a series of successful campaigns against German tribes on the Rhine. In 258 he checked an invasion of Italy by the Alamanni at Milan. After the capture of Valerian by the Persians (260), he faced continual invasions and internal revolts. The defence of the Eastern provinces was left to the care of surviving officers and to Odaenathus of Palmyra, while Gallienus successfully crushed two rebels, Ingenuus and Regalianus, in Pannonia (260). The revolt of Postumus, probably in the same year, detached Gaul and the West; Gallienus could make no headway against him. There was also unrest in Africa. At the end of the year Macrianus revolted in the East, but was defeated in 261 by Aureolus in Thrace, and Odaenathus then defeated Quietus and Ballista in Emesa. After the failure of an attempt on Gaul in 263/4, Gallienus tacitly recognized the rule of Postumus. In the East, Odaenathus received the title of *dux c.* 262 and loyally defended the Roman cause; counter-attacks were launched on Persian territory which perhaps twice (262 and 266) penetrated as far as Ctesiphon. The chronology of further barbarian attacks on the Balkans and Asia Minor is obscure, but in 267 the Goths and Heruli made a particularly destructive raid, sacking Athens and other Greek cities. While marching against them, Odaenathus fell victim to a domestic plot. A substantial victory over the invaders may perhaps be attributed to Gallienus. In 268 he defeated Aureolus who had been proclaimed Emperor at Milan, but was then murdered by his staff officers, who proclaimed Claudius his successor.

Later tradition is uniformly hostile to Gallienus, probably because he excluded senators from military commands; this policy was dictated by the need to have professional rather than amateur generals. Modern scholarship has tended to rehabilitate his reputation; another fruitful military development was the creation of a substantial cavalry corps. He was tolerant toward the Christians, reversing his father's policy. In general, he successfully preserved the essential unity of the Empire in a time of great danger.

G. Walser and Th. Pékary, *Die Krise des römischen Reiches* (1962), 28 ff.

B. H. W.

**GALLIO,** LUCIUS ANNAEUS (*PW* 12) NOVATUS, brother of the philosopher Seneca, was adopted by the orator and senator L. Junius Gallio, by which name he was then known. As proconsul of Achaea *c.* A.D. 52 (*SIG* ii[3]. 801) he refused to consider the case put by the Jews against St. Paul (Acts xviii. 12). He was consul at some unknown date. Seneca dedicated some works to him. After his brother's ruin he was compelled to commit suicide.

F. Jackson and K. Lake, *Beginnings of Christianity* v (1933), 462; E. Groag, *Röm. Reichsbeamten von Achaia* (1939), cols. 32 ff.; Syme, *Tacitus*, 589 ff.

A. M.

**GALLUS** (1), GAIUS LUCRETIUS (*PW* 23), praetor commanding the Roman fleet against Perseus in 171 B.C., destroyed Haliartus and captured Thisbe. He oppressed the Greek allies, e.g. Chalcis, and requisitioned corn, e.g. from Athens. Returning to adorn Antium with spoil, he was convicted and fined.

A. H. McD.

**GALLUS** (2), GAIUS SULPICIUS (*PW* 66), the Roman astronomer, as military tribune under Aemilius Paullus, predicted the eclipse of the moon on 21 June 168 B.C., before Pydna. Consul in 166, in Liguria, he was envoy to Pergamum in 164. He wrote, or adapted, an astronomical work from Greek sources (Pliny, *HN* 2. 53 and 83).

De Sanctis, *Stor. Rom.* iv. 1. 369.

A. H. McD.

**GALLUS** (3), GAIUS CORNELIUS (*PW* 164), poet, general, and friend of Augustus and Virgil, was born *c.* 69 B.C. at Forum Iulii (q.v.), possibly of a native Gallic family, and rose to equestrian rank. Concerned in the settlement of veterans in Cisalpine Gaul (41), he is said to have saved Virgil's farm for him. In 30, as a *praefectus fabrum* (*see* FABRI) of Octavian, he took over the Antonian forces in Cyrenaica from the renegade L. Pinarius Scarpus, advanced against Egypt, occupied Paraetonium, defeated Antony's attempt to retake it, helped in the capture of Cleopatra, and—as he recorded on an ancient obelisk, now in front of St. Peter's in Rome—laid out a 'forum Iulium' in an Egyptian town, perhaps the Nicopolis founded by Octavian near Alexandria. Octavian made him the first *praefectus* of the new province of Egypt. He easily crushed local rebellions at Heroonpolis and in the Thebaid, advanced beyond the First Cataract, formally received the king of Ethiopia (q.v.) into Roman protection, and appointed a ruler for the buffer-district of Triakontaschoinos. He celebrated these achievements in a boastful trilingual inscription at Philae (*see* ELEPHANTINE) dated 15 Apr. 29 (*ILS* 8995) and in inscriptions on the pyramids, and set up statues of himself all over Egypt. For this and other obscure reasons Augustus apparently recalled him, and formally renounced his friendship; moves to prosecute him (for treason?) were made, and he committed suicide (26). That Virgil, on Augustus' instructions, now rewrote the latter half of his fourth *Georgic*, replacing a long eulogy of Gallus which had stood in the first draft (Serv. *Ecl.* 10. 1; *Georg.* 4. 1), is unlikely.

His poetry, of which one pentameter survives (Morel, *FPL* 99), included four books of love-elegies which were widely read (Prop. 2. 34. 91 f., Ov. *Am.* 1. 15. 29). Entitled *Amores*, they were addressed to his (once Antony's) mistress, the actress Cytheris, under the pseudonym of Lycoris. Virgil, in his tenth *Eclogue*, of which Gallus the poet and disappointed lover is the theme, included lines (43–49?) based on some of Gallus' own (Serv. ad loc.). Besides elegies, Gallus apparently also wrote *epyllia* including one, on Apollo's shrine at Gryneum, cf. Verg. *Ecl.* 6. 64–73). Euphorion (q.v.) was his principal Greek model (Verg. *Ecl.* 10. 50), and his friend Parthenius (q.v.) supplied him with suitable love-themes. For his place in Roman literary history, *see*

ALEXANDRIANISM, LATIN; ELEGIAC POETRY, LATIN; EPYLLION.

H. Volkmann, *Zur Rechtsprechung im Principat des Augustus*(1935), 115 ff.; R. Syme, *CQ* 1938, 39 ff., and *Rom. Rev.*, see index; A. Stein, *Die Präfekten von Aegypten* (1950), 14 f.; L. Winniczuk, *Eos* 1959/60, 127 ff.; for the obelisk inscription, E. Hartman, *Gymnasium* 1965, 1 ff., and H. Volkmann, ibid. 328 ff.; Schanz–Hosius ii. 169 ff.; H. Bardon, *La Littérature latine inconnue* ii (1956), 34 ff.; W. Richter, *Vergilii Georgica* (1957), 106 ff.; J.-P. Boucher, *Gaius Cornelius Gallus* (Paris 1966). T. J. C. and G. W. W.

**GALLUS** (4), AELIUS (*PW* 59), Prefect of Egypt after Gallus (3) above and before C. Petronius. Influenced by prevalent and exaggerated reports of the wealth of Arabia Felix, Augustus instructed him to invade that land. The expedition, which lasted two years (25 and 24 B.C.), was a complete failure; the blame was conveniently laid upon the treachery of the Nabatean Syllaeus. Aelius Gallus wrote upon medical topics and was a personal friend of Strabo the geographer. It is highly probable that he adopted the son of the distinguished Roman knight L. Seius Strabo (*see* SEJANUS).

S. Jameson, *JRS* 1968, 71 ff. R. S.

**GALLUS** (5), GAIUS ASINIUS (*PW* 15), son of C. Asinius Pollio (q.v.), was consul in 8 B.C. and proconsul of Asia two years later. He had married Vipsania (*see* AGRIPPINA 1) when Tiberius was forced to divorce her in 12 B.C., and there were five sons of the marriage. A friend of Augustus, who judged him ambitious enough to aim at the principate (Tac. *Ann.* 1. 13), he angered Tiberius, whom in the Senate he went out of his way to offend, and, at the age of 71, was arrested in A.D. 30 and died of starvation after three years' imprisonment. His book *A Comparison of Cicero and my Father* evidently contained intemperate criticism of Cicero's style.

For coin-portrait see M. Grant, *From Imperium to Auctoritas* (1946), 387. J. P. B.

**GALLUS** (6), AULUS DIDIUS (*PW* 6) (*cos. suff.* A.D. 36), a prominent Claudian senator. When legate of Moesia *c.* A.D. 46 he conducted an expedition to the Cimmerian Chersonesus and established Cotys as king of Bosporus, for which service he received the *ornamenta triumphalia*. He was also *curator aquarum* and proconsul of Asia or Africa. Legate of Britain from 52 to 58, Didius made no noteworthy advance, though interfering with the Brigantians, and was able to maintain the conquests of his predecessors. The fragmentary inscription *ILS* 971 (Histonium) may be referred to him (see also *AE* 1947, 76; 1949, 11, Athens). He was the adoptive parent of Fabricius Veiento (q.v.). R. S.

**GALLUS** (7), APPIUS ANNIUS (*PW* 49), *consul suffectus* between A.D. 62 and 69, was dispatched as general by Otho against the Vitellians in 69. In 70 he was legate of Germania Superior against Civilis. A. M.

**GALLUS** (8) CAESAR (FLAVIUS CLAUDIUS CONSTANTIUS, *PW* 5), reigned in Antioch, A.D. 351 to 354. Born in Etruria (*c.* 325) he was the half-brother of Julian. His lonely upbringing left him harsh and tactless, and his reign at Antioch is described as oppressive and bloody. He put down revolts in Palestine and in Isauria, but was recalled by Constantius II and executed near Pola (354). E. A. T.

**GAMES.** One of the earliest games played in Greece, if we may believe Athenaeus, was marbles. According to his story the suitors of Penelope shot their alleys in turn against another marble, which represented the queen; the first one to hit had another turn, and if he were successful again he was considered to be the presumptive bridegroom. A favourite game at Athens was draughts (πεσσοί). The board was divided into thirty-six squares, and on them the oval pieces were moved; the centre line was called ἱερὰ γραμμή, perhaps because when you crossed it you were on the enemy's ground. A tablet somewhat resembling a backgammon board has been found in the Palace of Cnossos. More popular still was the 'Wine-throw' (κότταβος), especially at the end of dinner. The players, reclining on their left elbow, had to throw with their right hand the last drops of wine from their cups into a basin set in the middle, so that none was spilt. This was the simplest form; alternatively the basin was filled with water on which saucers floated, and the game was to sink the saucers with the wine; in a third variety the wine had to fall into a scale suspended over a small figure—Manes—so that the two came into contact.

At Rome the two favourite games were 'Twelve Lines' (*duodecim scripta*) and 'Robbers' (*ludus latrunculorum*). The first resembled our backgammon or race-game. The other, also played on a board, had pieces of different value, *calculi, latrones, mandrae*, and the object was either to take or check—*ad incitas redigere*—your opponent's pieces. There were also two games, common to Greeks and Romans, whose names explain themselves, 'Odd and Even', and 'How many fingers do I hold up?' *See also* ASTRAGALUS, ATHLETICS, BALL-GAMES, DICING, LUDI.

Athenaeus 15. 2–7; *Panegyricus in Pisonem* 180–200. F. A. W.

**GANYMEDES** (Γανυμήδης: probably not Greek, but suggesting to a Greek ear γάνος or a cognate, cf. *Etym. Magn.* s.v.; older Latin *Catamitus*). Son of Tros (*Il.* 5. 265; 20. 232; later authorities, from the *Little Iliad* on, make him son of one of the other Trojan princes), carried off by the gods to be Zeus' cup-bearer, his father being given in exchange a marvellous breed of horses (*Il.* loc. cit.) or a golden vine (*Little Iliad* ap. schol. Eur. *Or.* 1392, *Tro.* 821). The older authorities say nothing definite of the manner of his carrying off, though the reason given is his beauty, and Zeus, who gives the horses or the vine, is clearly the prime mover. In the *Homeric Hymn* to Aphrodite it is a storm-wind, ἄελλα, which takes him (208), but at some unknown date, probably not early, it was said that he was snatched up by an eagle (Verg. *Aen.* 5. 255), or Zeus himself in that shape (Ov. *Met.* 10. 155 ff.). The eagle, in the former version, was turned into the constellation Aquila, Ganymedes himself becoming Aquarius (Homil. *Clement.* 5. 17; [Eratosth.] 26; 30). The earlier versions also imply simply that the gods wanted a handsome cup-bearer; the later ones (from Theognis 1345) make him Zeus' minion. His childishly pretty figure is a favourite in Hellenistic and later literature and art. For examples see Drexler in Roscher's *Lexikon*, s.v. H. J. R.

**GARDENS.** Minoan and Helladic pottery, wall-paintings, and artistic objects, evincing manifest pleasure in decorative flowers, anticipate the Homeric appreciation of wild and planted flora, notably trees (cf. *Il.* 6. 419; *Od.* 5. 64), including the imported date-palm (*Od.* 6. 162), and prepare for palace gardens like that of Alcinous (*Od.* 7. 112 ff.). The emphasis, however, is upon vegetables and fruit. Cultivated roses are first mentioned in 648 B.C., though the appreciation is much older in Homeric epithets. Evidence has been discovered in recent excavations for the formal layout of shrubs and trees in the area of the Agora at Athens. Royal parks (παράδεισοι) derive from Persia, and Hellenistic examples are described in the *Geoponica*, a work containing extracts from earlier writers compiled by Cassianus Bassus in the tenth century A.D. (10. 1; 11. 23; 3. 13), by Longus (4. 2), and Achilles Tatius (1. 15). Closely connected are the sacred groves (ἄλσοι), as at Antioch-Daphnae. A wide range of plants is mentioned by Theophrastus (*passim*), while private gardens occur in Alciphron (fr. 6. 1–9).

In Rome also the *hortus* is old, but primarily a kitchen garden, part of the *heredium*. Flower-gardens, however, soon grew up in the *xystus* or *viridarium* of the courtyard house. But the word for gardener (*topiarius*) is of the late Republic, and so is the formal garden, with topiary work (Pliny, *HN* 12. 13) and *ambulationes* of given sizes (*CIL* vi. 29774, 29975). Wall-paintings give a vivid picture of the scope of Roman gardening, from formalism to landscape-gardening (cf. *Röm. Mitt.* 1890, 783 ff.; *JDAI* 1904, 103 ff.). Much attention was paid to irrigation. Large pleasure gardens are very late, the earliest in Rome being the *horti Lucullani*, and they always remained the privilege of emperors, aristocrats, and wealthy freedmen. Sacred groves were no less frequent than in Greece.

D. B. Thompson, *Garden Lore of Ancient Athens* (U.S.A. 1963); P. Grimal, *Les Jardins romains* (1943); M. M. Gabriel, *Livia's Garden Room at Prima Porta* (1958). For Fishbourne *see* B. Cunliffe. *Ant. Journ.* 1967, 55 ff.                                    I. A. R.

**GARGANUS MONS:** promontory projecting from Apulia (q.v.) into the Adriatic to form the 'spur' on the Italian boot. Its forested mountain rises over 5,000 feet. It is the *Matinus* celebrated by Horace (*Odes* 1. 28. 3; 4. 2. 27; *Epod.* 16. 28), but otherwise seldom appears in ancient literature.                                           E. T. S.

**GARGILIUS MARTIALIS,** QUINTUS, wrote on gardens (*De hortis*), probably in the third century A.D.; Galen is already quoted by him. The remnants preserved in late excerpts do not allow a judgement about the book as a whole; they show, however, that Gargilius relied on his own experience as well as on a carefully discriminating study of the literature. The book apparently was very famous, since Servius, in commenting on Virgil (*G.* 4. 147–8): 'haec... praetereo atque aliis post me memoranda relinquo', tersely remarks: 'aliis: Gargilium Martialem significat'. Cassiodorus recommended Gargilius' work, like those of Hippocrates and Galen. If this Gargilius is identical with the Gargilius who wrote on the diseases of oxen, both treatises may have been part of a book on agriculture. The identification with the otherwise unknown historian Gargilius who wrote about Alexander Severus (S.H.A. *Alex. Sev.* 37. 9) is as uncertain as is that with the Gargilius of an inscription of A.D. 260 (*ILS* 2767).

TEXT. V. Rose (Teubner, 1875), together with Plinius Secundus, *De Medicina*; *Curae Boum*, in Vegetius, E. Lommatzsch (Teubner, 1903); other fragments, V. Rose, *Anecdota Graeca* ii.
MODERN LITERATURE. A. Thomas, *Rev. Phil.* 1907; Gargilius source of Palladius (?), M. Wellmann, *Hermes* 1908.                    L. E.

**GAUL** (Transalpine). Geographically, the territory bounded by the Alps, the Rhine, the Ocean, the Pyrenees, and the Mediterranean forms a unity, and most of its history has been a sequence of unifying cultural developments, followed by catastrophes. Such a cultural unity was achieved in respect of religious feeling in the neolithic period (*c.* 2000 B.C.), when megalithic tombs are found spread over the area, and maintained itself more or less till disrupted by the invasions of the Celts across the Rhine. Commencing perhaps as early as 900, these spread with varying thickness a layer of Celtic culture over the country, represented from *c.* 500 by the artistic style of La Tène. An 'erratic' in this picture is the Phocaean colony of Massilia, founded *c.* 600, which established trading-posts along the Mediterranean, and spread Hellenism in the hinterland.

**2.** Rome's interest in Transalpine Gaul was at first confined to the security of communications with Spain, and these were guarded by her old ally Massilia. When Massilia, however, was threatened by a Celtic coalition,

Rome intervened (121) and annexed a belt of territory between the Cévennes and the Alps. Threat to the *status quo* in the shape of Helvetian and German inroads led to the campaigns of Julius Caesar (58–51), by which all Transalpine Gaul was annexed (*see* GALLIC WARS).

**3.** Formal settlement came with Augustus. The earlier conquests, called Gallia Narbonensis from their capital Narbo (q.v.), became senatorial; the remainder (Gallia Comata) became imperial, and was eventually divided into three provinces, cutting deliberately across ethnological divisions.

**4.** Narbonensis (the *provincia* above all others, its inhabitants 'provinciales') had an Italian air. There were five military colonies; the important native towns enjoyed Latin rights, and eventually the name, and, in some cases at least, the full privileges of a Roman colony. Throughout the country *tria nomina* (the badge of citizenship) are as normal as they are rare in Gallia Comata, and legionary soldiers with Narbonensian domiciles are numerous.

**5.** In Gallia Comata, Lugdunum, Augusta (*Augst*), Noviodunum (*Nyon*), and subsequently Cologne are the only Roman colonies. Native towns enjoying at later date the title of colony are also rare (e.g. Trier, Avenches), as is possession of the citizenship or entry into the legions. Under Claudius Aeduan nobles were admitted to the Senate (A.D. 48). Local government was based on the old tribes (now *civitates*) with their subdivisions of *pagi* and *vici*.

**6.** Romanization proceeded apace with construction of new towns in place of hill-forts, public buildings (temples, theatres), and roads; the expense of the process indeed provoked local revolts (A.D. 21), which were easily suppressed by the troops of the Rhine. Here eight legions with auxiliaries were stationed in two commands, intended as much to overawe Gauls as to repel Germans; and a rebellion in 68 against Nero was similarly suppressed by them; while a national movement started by the Treveri under cover of disturbances in the frontier garrisons (69–70) failed not least owing to the lukewarmness of the Gauls, who were realizing the advantages of the Roman connexion.

**7.** Roman ideas were introduced by the application of Roman names to native gods, which often maintained, however, extraordinary shapes (e.g. horned, cross-legged Cernunnus); and by the imperial cult, which may have been utilized to supplant Druidism (suppressed by Claudius). The centres of worship were Narbo and the river-junction below Lyons, itself the financial centre of the Comata. To the latter the sixty Celtic *civitates* sent deputies to form a provincial parliament.

**8.** Gaul developed a vigorous if somewhat upstart culture, and was famous for good foodstuffs (and good eating). Its pottery industries, undertaking orders of thousands of mass-produced pieces, competed successfully even in the Italian market. Inroads on capital wealth and a series of devastating barbarian invasions (notably 253 and 276) crippled its prosperity, which was but partially restored in the fourth century. Studded with fortresses and posts connected with state supplies, with its towns huddled into a fraction of their former area behind walls made of the debris of temples, with brigands (Bagaudae) abroad, Gaul had a sad look. Christianity, however, which was becoming important in the second century, had firm hold by the fourth, and was responsible, incidentally, for extinguishing the Gaulish language: its development stimulated the Gallic taste for story-telling (Sulpicius Severus) and vigorous rhetoric (Hilary of Poitiers, Salvian). The later Empire shows a veritable Indian summer of interesting if rather mediocre literary figures (Ausonius, Paulinus of Nola, Sidonius).

**9.** The withdrawal of Roman garrisons in the fifth

century and the slow development of federate barbarian settlements into independent kingdoms, mark the end of the Roman Empire in Gaul. But though there are decisive dates (e.g. the cession of Auvergne in 475, the victory of Clovis in 486 or 487), the process was gradual. Of formal movements of independence there were virtually none; indeed, even the 'regnum Galliarum' (260–70) was a device of military expediency rather than a separatist movement. Gaul through all its history remains a document of the success of romanization.

INSCRIPTIONS. Latin: Narbonensis, *CIL* xii and E. Espérandieu, *Inscriptions romaines de la Narbonnaise*; Comata, *CIL* xiii and P. Wuilleumier, *Inscriptions latines des trois Gaules* (1963). Greek: G. Kaibel, *Inscriptiones Graecae Siciliae et Italiae*, 2427–547. Celtic: C. Dottin, *Langue gauloise* (1920).

SCULPTURE. E. Espérandieu, *Recueil général des bas-reliefs, statues et bustes de la Gaule romaine* (1907–55). Illustrations in M. Pobé, *The Art of Roman Gaul* (1961).

COINS. A. Blanchet, *Traité des monnaies gauloises* (1905); R. Forrer, *Keltische Numismatik* (1908).

NOMENCLATURE. A. Holder, *Altceltischer Sprachschatz* (1891– ).

MAP. A. Blanchet and others, *Carte archéologique de la Gaule romaine* (in progress).

BIBLIOGRAPHY. C. E. Ruelle, *Bibliographie générale des Gaules* (1880–6); R. Montandon, *Bibliographie générale des travaux paléthnologiques et archéologiques* (in progress); R. de Lasteyrie and others, *Bibliographie générale des travaux historiques et archéologiques publiés par les sociétés savantes de France* (in progress). Yearly summaries in *Revue des études anciennes* (C. Jullian and A. Grenier); *Pro Alesia* (J. Toutain) and *Revue celtique* (J. Vendryès); *Gallia 1943–* (R. Lantier). See also R. Lantier, 'Roman Gaul, 1940–44', *JRS* 1946, 76 ff.; P.-M. Duval, *Hist.* 1956, 238 ff. (excavations 1941–55).

GENERAL WORKS. J. Déchelette, *Manuel d'archéologie* (1911–14), E. Desjardins, *Géographie de la Gaule* (1886–93); A. Grenier, *Manuel d'archéologie gallo-romaine* (in progress); 'Gaul' in Frank's *Economic Survey*, vol. iii; C. Jullian, *Histoire de la Gaule* (1908–26); O. Brogan, *Roman Gaul* (1953); J. J. Hatt, *Histoire de la Gaule romaine²* (1967); J. P. Clébert, *Provence antique* I, *Des origines à la conquête romaine* (1966). C. E. S.

**GAVIUS** (1) **BASSUS,** contemporary with Cicero, wrote *De Origine Verborum et Vocabulorum* and other works quoted by Gellius and Macrobius.

H. Funaioli, *Gram. Rom. Frag.* 486 ff.

**GAVIUS** (2) **SILO,** an orator to whose eloquence in pleading cases Augustus testified when he heard him at Tarraco in 26 B.C. (Sen. *Controv.* 10 *praef.* 14).

**GAZA,** an ancient city of the Philistines with harbour on the coast of southern Palestine in a key position on the route from Egypt to Syria and Mesopotamia. For long an ally of the Assyrians it was later a Persian garrison town. In the Persian period its coins reflect trade connexions with Greece, although its main economic links were always with the lands to the south. It was stormed by Alexander after a lengthy siege in 332 B.C. but continued to be an important city, obliged to submit to Ptolemies and Seleucids in turn, throughout the Hellenistic period. It was captured and destroyed by the Jewish ruler, Alexander Jannaeus, in 96 B.C. and lay deserted for a generation, but Pompey declared it a free city (hence its era, dated from autumn 61) and Gabinius rebuilt it on a new site, like the former site some 13 miles inland from the harbour. It was granted to Herod in 30 B.C. but after his death reverted to the province of Syria, in which it flourished for centuries. Its coins cease with Gordian, who, like Hadrian before him, was honoured by the city as a benefactor. Later it acquired the status of a Roman colony. It was for long a centre of Hellenistic culture, with a famous school of rhetors. Pagan cults survived until the end of the fourth century. In 635 it was conquered by the Arabs under Omar.

Benzinger, *PW* s.v.; G. F. Hill, *B.M. Coins, Palestine* (1914), lxvi f., 143 f.; Jones, *Cities E. Rom. Prov.*, ch. 10. E. W. G.

**GELA** (Γέλα—modern *Gela*, until 1927 *Terranova*) on the south coast of Sicily was founded in 688 B.C. by

Cretans and Rhodians, itself colonizing Acragas (q.v.) a century later. Commanding the fertile plain of the River Gelas, it spread its influence inland to native settlements such as Butera (Omphake?) and Monte Bubbonia (Maktorion?). Its tyrants Cleander and Hippocrates (q.v. 1) made it temporarily Sicily's strongest state; but on Gelon's (q.v.) removal to Syracuse many Geloans were compelled to accompany him, and Hieron (q.v. 1) exiled many others. Repopulated after 466, Gela prospered, refounding Camarina (q.v.) in 461 and supporting Syracuse in 427–424 and 415–413. Abandoned by Dionysius I (q.v.) in 405 it never fully recovered. A revival under Timoleon (q.v.) was frustrated by Agathocles (q.v.), who slaughtered 4,000 Geloans (311). In 280 Phintias of Acragas removed Gela's inhabitants to his new foundation Phintias (*Licata*); the Mamertini subsequently destroyed the vacated city. The surviving stretch of the Timoleontean fortifications is one of Sicily's most remarkable monuments.

Bérard, *Bibl. topogr.* (1941), 53 f.; Dunbabin, *Western Greeks*; P. Orlandini, Κώκαλος 1962, 69 ff.; P. Griffo and L. von Matt, *Gela* (1963). A. G. W.

**GELIMER,** the last Vandal king of Africa (A.D. 530–4), was a great-grandson of Gaiseric (q.v.). He deposed his pro-Roman cousin Hilderic in 530, but in 533 an East Roman army led by Belisarius (q.v.) landed in Africa and occupied Carthage. Gelimer, who mishandled the campaign and was utterly defeated, was taken prisoner (534) and was sent to Constantinople. He was given an estate in Galatia but refused to abandon his Arian Christianity. E. A. T.

**GELLIUS** (1, *PW* 4), GNAEUS, the Gracchan annalist, whom Cato attacked in defence of L. Turius, wrote *annales* from the origins of Rome to at least 146 B.C., reaching the Sabine Rape in book 2, the year 389 in book 15, and the year 216 in book 33 (or 30); a reference to book 97 is incorrect. His work is fuller than the previous annals; the reason is probably the publication of the *annales maximi* and the first use of rhetorical methods in elaborating source material. Dionysius used his work.

Peter, *HRRel.* i², cciv, 148; Beloch, *Röm. Gesch.* 103 f.; M. Gelzer, *Kl. Schr.* iii (1964), 102, 220 ff. A. H. McD.

**GELLIUS** (2, *PW* 17) **POPLICOLA,** LUCIUS, probably related to the Valerii Messallae, studied oratory under C. Carbo (q.v. 1). *Praetor peregrinus* in 94 B.C., he governed an eastern province as proconsul afterwards and, while passing through Athens, offered—not altogether seriously—to reconcile the rival schools of philosophy. Consul in 72 with Lentulus (q.v. 3), he acted against Verres (q.v.), passed a law enabling Pompey to confer citizenship for valour, and was defeated by Spartacus (q.v.). Censor (again with Lentulus) in 70, he severely purged the Senate. He served under Pompey against the pirates, supported Cicero against Catiline, and lived on, amid domestic troubles, until the late 50s. E. B.

**GELLIUS** (3, *PW* 2), AULUS (*c.* A.D. 130–*c.* 180), wrote the *Noctes Atticae* in twenty books (we now lack the beginning and the end, and all book 8 except for the chapter headings). There is no indication of his place of birth, nor are the dates of his life securely known. He was still at school when Erucius Clarus (d. A.D. 146) was *praefectus urbi*; hence his birth must come around A.D. 130. E. Castorina (*Giorn. Ital. Filol.* 1950, 137 ff.) argues from 19. 12. 1 that his work cannot have been published much before 180. As a youth he studied literature at Rome, above all with Sulpicius Apollinaris, and knew Fronto. Thereafter he went for further work in Athens for at least one year, attending the lectures of Calvenus Taurus and visiting Herodes Atticus. His work contains many delightful pictures of his student days at Athens. It was possibly after his return from Athens that he was appointed a *iudex* to try private cases (14. 2. 1), for which the minimum age at this time was probably 25 (*Digest* 42. 1. 57; 50. 4. 8). There is no evidence whatsoever to lead us to believe that he continued his interest in legal practice in later life. His preface also tells us that he married and had children.

The *Noctes Atticae* is a collection of mainly short chapters dealing with a great variety of topics: philosophy, history, law, grammar, literary criticism, textual questions, and many others. He began collecting his material during the winter nights in Attica (*praef.* 4), and assembled it later in life (*praef.* 23–4), with the specific purpose of entertaining and instructing his own children (*praef.* 1).

The writer of the *Noctes* reveals himself to us as a man of great enthusiasm for learning, although he lacks a keenly critical mind. His work, he tells us (*praef.* 2), is in a deliberately haphazard arrangement, but individual chapters are usually carefully worked out, often with picturesque (if fictitious) settings to enliven the discussion. Most of his information is clearly obtained at second-hand, but the investigation of his sources is often difficult or impossible (cf. Hosius, *praef.* xvi–lix). The work has a distinct charm of its own, but the great usefulness of the *Noctes* is derived from the preservation of countless fragments of earlier writers. Many hundreds of quotations are given from both Greek and Latin literature. He was widely used by later writers (list in Hertz, *ed. maior* ii. ii–xlvii), especially by the compilers Nonius Marcellus and Macrobius. His popularity in the Middle Ages is attested by a number of twelfth-century anthologies of his work.

His Latinity is a strange mixture of an attempt at classical purity and an affectation of archaism, but is by no means as peculiar as that of his contemporaries Fronto and Apuleius. His literary tastes reflect the general feeling of his time, with a heavy leaning towards the archaic writers, but he has the good sense to appreciate Virgil as well as Ennius in verse, and Cicero as well as Cato in prose.

TEXTS. M. Hertz (ed. maior 1883–5); C. Hosius (Teubner, 1903); P. K. Marshall (O.C.T. 1968).
COMMENTARY. H. M. Hornsby (1936), bk. 1 only.
TRANSLATION. J. C. Rolfe, with text (Loeb, 1927).
LIFE. L. Friedländer, *Sittengeschichte Roms*[7] (1908–13), appendix lx; P. K. Marshall, *CPhil.* 1963, 143 ff.
SPECIAL STUDIES. R. Marache, *La Critique littéraire de langue latine et le développement du goût archaïsant au IIᵉ siècle de notre ère* (1952); R. Marache, *Mots nouveaux et mots archaïques chez Fronton et Aulu-Gelle* (1957); M. D. Brock, *Studies in Fronto and his Age* (1911). P. K. M.

**GELLO** (Γελ(λ)ώ), a female daemon that steals children, in ancient, medieval, and modern Greek belief, from Sappho (fr. 178 Lobel–Page) on. According to the *Suda*, s.v. Γελλοῦς παιδοφιλωτέρα, she was a woman who died untimely, ἄωρος, notoriously a dangerous kind of ghost.

Leo Allatius, *De Graec. hodie quorundam opinationibus*, 3; B. Schmidt, *Volksleben der Neugriechen*, 139 f.; P. Perdrizet, *Negotium Perambulans in Tenebris* (1922). H. J. R.

**GELON** (Γέλων) (*c.* 540–478 B.C.), son of Deinomenes. Cavalry-commander under Hippocrates (q.v. 1), tyrant of Gela, he became guardian to his sons, whom he dispossessed (*c.* 490), assuming the tyranny himself. He fulfilled Hippocrates' ambitions by seizing Syracuse, under cover of reinstating the exiled Syracusan aristocrats, and transferred his seat of power thither (485 B.C.), leaving his brother Hieron (q.v. 1) at Gela as viceroy. Syracuse thus inherited the Geloan supremacy in eastern Sicily and prospered to such an extent that it was acknowledged as the greatest Hellenic power of the time. In the next two years Gelon destroyed Camarina and Megara Hyblaea (qq.v.), removing their inhabitants to Syracuse. Envoys

of the Hellenic alliance sought his aid against Persia, but drew back when, as the price of assistance, he claimed the supreme command (Hdt. 7. 157–62). In any event, a Carthaginian invasion had been imminent since 483, but Gelon was well prepared. In alliance with Theron (q.v.) of Acragas he defeated at Himera a great Carthaginian army under Hamilcar, whose expedition landed at the time of, if not in concert with, Xerxes' attack on Greece (480 B.C.). Gelon lived two years after his greatest triumph, a great and popular ruler much (perhaps exaggeratedly) respected in later tradition.

Dunbabin, *Western Greeks*, 410 ff.; A. Schenk, Graf von Stauffenberg, *Trinakria* 1963, 176 ff.; A. G. Woodhead, *The Greeks in the West* (1962), 76 ff. A. G. W.

**GEMINUS,** writer of elementary textbooks on mathematical subjects (? *c.* 70 B.C.). His only extant work is *Introduction to Astronomy* (εἰσαγωγὴ εἰς τὰ φαινόμενα), which gives a factual but non-mathematical account of basic concepts of astronomy, mathematical geography, and the calendar (important as a source for Greek knowledge of Babylonian astronomical parameters). He also wrote a treatise on the scope of the mathematical sciences entitled Περὶ τῆς τῶν μαθημάτων τάξεως or θεωρίας, in at least six books, citations from which are made by various writers, especially Proclus (q.v.) and the scholiasts on Euclid book 1, including the Arabian an-Nairīzī (*c.* A.D. 990), whose knowledge of it comes from Simplicius. The treatise included a classification of the mathematical sciences, arithmetic, geometry, mechanics, astronomy, optics, geodesy, *canonic* (musical harmony) and *logistic* (practical calculation), an examination of the first principles, definitions, postulates, axioms, and of the whole structure based upon them (book 6 dealt with conic sections). Geminus also classified 'lines' (including curves), from 'simple' lines (straight lines and circles) to higher curves, e.g. the conics, the cissoid, 'spiric' curves, and the cylindrical helix; so also with surfaces. Geminus gave a proof of the special property of 'uniform' lines (the straight line, the circle, and the cylindrical helix). Simplicius (*in Phys.* 291–2 D.) quotes from an epitome by Geminus of Posidonius' *Meteorologica*.

Edition of the εἰσαγωγή by Manitius (Teubner, 1898), with German translation.
COMMENT. K. Tittel, *De Gemini Stoici studiis mathematicis* (Leipzig, 1895, with index of references to his lost work). Heath, *Hist. of Gk. Maths.* ii. 222 ff.
On the optical part of the work see *Damianos' Schrift über Optik, mit Auszügen aus Geminos* hrsg. von R. Schoene (1897).
T. H.; G. J. T.

**GEMS.** Precious stones were valued in antiquity as possessing magical and medicinal virtues, as ornaments, and as seals when engraved with a device. Such engravings (intaglios) in soft mediums like steatite or ivory are found in Early Minoan days (*see* SEALS); the use of hard stones dates from the Middle Minoan Age. Late Minoan and Mycenaean gems have a rich repertory of human and animal designs; the favoured shapes are the lenticular (round) and glandular (sling-stone). In sub-Mycenaean and Geometric times the art of working hard stones was largely lost. A revival in the seventh century B.C. is usually associated with the island of Melos, and the commencement of classical gem engraving in the sixth century is marked by the introduction of the scarab (beetle) form of seal from Egypt. This was soon abandoned in Greece for the scaraboid, which omits the beetle-back. The late fifth and fourth centuries mark the climax of Greek gem engraving. In Hellenistic times the choice of subjects grows restricted, but excellent work was done in portraiture. In Italy the Etruscans used the scarab until the third century; gems of the later Roman Republic show a wide range of subjects, combined with clumsiness of execution. With Augustus begins the large series of 'Graeco-Roman' gems with few local characteristics. A period of decadence in the middle Empire is succeeded by a revival under Constantine.

Cameos, in which the design is in relief, are for ornament only, and the finest are of the early Empire.

Several gem-engravers are recorded in literature, e.g. Pyrgoteles, who worked for Alexander the Great; others are known from their signatures on extant stones, though many signatures are false.

Engravers of gems used the drill and the wheel. These had to be coated with powdered emery (of which Naxos was and is an important source), except for working softer stones such as steatite, which was consequently often used in the earlier periods. The stones most favoured for engraving in view of their durability, moderate hardness, and absence of grain were quartzes, especially those of the crypto-crystalline variety such as agate, plasma, jasper, carnelian, and most popular of all, sard. Red garnet, amethyst, lapis lazuli were much prized in jewellery. Cameos in which design and background were in contrasted colours were made of layered stones such as onyx and sardonyx. Of the hardest stones, emeralds, aquamarines, and sapphires were rarely engraved, while the diamond, probably unknown before the first century A.D., was not even cut. The diamond-point, however, was sometimes used for engraving other stones. Imitations of gems in paste (see GLASS) were apparently much in demand; in the British Museum collection they even out-number sards. Imitations of rock crystal and red garnet were considered particularly convincing.

C. W. King, *Antique Gems* (1866); A. Furtwängler, *Die antiken Gemmen* (1900); H. B. Walters, *Catalogue of the Engraved Gems and Cameos, Greek, Etruscan, and Roman, in the British Museum* (1926); R. A. Higgins, *Greek and Roman Jewellery* (1961).
F. N. P.; D. E. E.

**GENETHLIACON**, a birthday poem. We do not know of such poems at Rome before the last century of the Republic. Though there were Greek antecedents in the conception of the δαίμων, in the rhetorical handling of natalician themes, and in epigrams of the Anthology, yet the typical birthday poetry of Rome was so intimately associated with the worship of the Genius, that as a separate genre it made one of the original features in Latin literature. Virgil's fourth Eclogue stands apart as a mystical herald of an expected birth. The birthday poetry of Tibullus and in the *Corpus Tibullianum* shows more independence of Hellenic mythology than Propertius does, and more devotion to Roman religious tradition. Propertius' single example (3. 10) greets Cynthia with an anticipation of banquet and festivity. In him and in Horace (*Carm.* 4. 11, invitation to Phyllis to celebrate Maecenas' birthday) there is formal excellence, but a sincerer human note marks Tibullus and Ovid. Ovid pours out his personal feelings: *Tr.* 3. 13 deplores the melancholy birthday of an exile for whom there is no white robe or altar ceremony; and 5. 5 expresses his sympathy with his innocent wife on her birthday.

Persius in his second *Satura* turns birthday congratulations into a homily on praying aright; and Statius in *Silv.* 2. 7, addressed to Lucan's widow on the dead poet's anniversary, blends birthday elements with those of the *laudatio funebris* and *consolatio*. Martial proves the importance attached to birthdays: he celebrates a friend's anniversary, which he loves like his own (9. 52; cf. 10. 24; 12. 60); he sends three epigrams to Lucan's widow recalling *his* anniversary (7. 21; 22; 23); another is on Virgil's (12. 67), which Pliny (*Ep.* 3. 7. 8) says Silius kept more strictly than his own birthday; others are bantering pieces, on being passed over for a birthday feast, on being asked for the day after, on a man of 'no birth' who entertains the highest society on his birthday, on one who, as he does not want gifts on the day, might oblige

Martial with a gift instead (7. 86; 11. 65; 10. 27; 8. 64; 9. 53). The last pagan poem in this class is Ausonius' address to his grandson entering his sixteenth year (*Idyll* 5), where the Genius no longer counts. Christian poets break the ancient tradition by their faith that death is a new birthday, though in structure poems of the sort by Sidonius Apollinaris, Ennodius, and Julianus are indebted to classical rules (see Menander Rhetor ap. Spengel, *Rhet.* iii, 368 ff.).

E. Cesareo, *Il carme natalizio nella poesia latina* (1929). J. W. D.

**GENIUS**, literally 'the begetter', cf. *ludius*, 'player'. In classical Latin the attendant spirit of every man, a sort of guardian angel, but originally his inborn power whose activities were apparently directed largely towards fostering the natural desires and their satisfaction; 'suom defrudans genium' (Terence, *Phorm.* 44) means living very parsimoniously; 'genio indulgere' is to enjoy oneself. Although in common parlance every male, bond or free, seems to have a *genius*, in family cult only one *genius* was honoured in each household, that of the *paterfamilias*, particularly on the occasion of his marriage, as Festus, 83. 23 Lindsay ('genialis lectus, qui nuptiis sternitur in honorem genii'), but also in the ordinary worship at the *lararium*, see, e.g., G. K. Boyce in *Am. Ac. Rome* 1937, plate 17. 1 (one large serpent, bearded and therefore male, a well-known art-convention, underneath a scene of sacrifice); 18. 1 (two such serpents, one beardless, i.e. female, presumably the *iuno* of the *materfamilias*, cf. JUNO). It is quite conceivable (see Rose, *CQ* 1923, 57 ff.) that originally the *genius* is the life-force of the family or clan, always in the guardianship of the *paterfamilias* for the time being and passing on at his death to his successor.

Be that as it may, in classical times the *genius* seems to have been thought of as exactly equivalent to the ἴδιος δαίμων (cf. BIRTHDAY); Horace even says that it is mortal (like its possessor: *Epist.* 2. 2. 188), though adding 'in unum quodque caput', which might imply that it passes to another person on the death of the first one. By a curious extension, gods are said to have a *genius* (first in 58 B.C., *CIL*¹ i. 166 = Bruns 90, line 16). It is more understandable that corporations and places are said to have each its *genius* (Wissowa, 178). Through the practice that slaves venerated the *genius* of their master developed in imperial times the cult of the Emperor's *genius*. The fact that occasionally the *genius* of a dead person is mentioned (examples in De-Marchi, 71) is certainly Greek; cf. the occasional dedications to the *daimon* of the departed. It is the divine guardian who still watches over him in another world.

A. De-Marchi, *Il culto privato di Roma antica* i (1896), 69 ff.; Wissowa, *RK* 175 ff.; Latte, *RR* 103, 306. H. J. R.

**GENOS** (γένος, in some States πάτρα or πατριά), a family, in the sense of a group of persons claiming descent in the male line from a single ancestor; narrower than a phratry (q.v.), of which it might form a part, it could itself comprise a number of branches (οἶκοι). Its members were γεννῆται (or πατριῶται). We naturally hear most of noble families, supposedly of heroic, ultimately divine ancestry and usually bearing names in patronymic form. Such families were to be found in most, probably all, Greek States. Like phratries, *gene* were organized corporations whose specific activity was the worship of the supposed ancestor. In some states the advance of democracy involved the establishment of artificial γένη or πάτραι forming the lowest tier in a new classification of the citizen-body.

At Athens the noble, i.e. named *gene* appear to correspond with the Eupatridai (q.v.). About sixty such *gene* are known; most have patronymic names. That the lower classes were organized in *gene* is at best doubtful: the tradition that the whole citizen-body at an early date comprised 360 *gene* of thirty men each, distributed equally between the twelve phratries and four *phylai* (q.v.), so as to correspond with the days, months, and seasons of the year (Arist. *Ath. Pol.* fr. 3), is quite unreliable; and, whatever may have been the position in early times, it is hard to see how the new citizens accepted by Solon (q.v.) and Cleisthenes (q.v. 1) can have been admitted into existing *gene* or given new *gene* of which we hear nothing. That some citizens were not *gennetai* is implied by the law obliging *phrateres* to accept both *orgeones* (q.v.) and ὁμογάλακτες (said to be an old synonym for *gennetai*); and the evidence of the fourth-century orators makes it pretty clear that while all citizens had *phrateres* and, potentially, συγγενεῖς (relations on the father's and mother's side: *see* ANCHISTEIS), some did not have *gennetai*. Hence the widely accepted view that the Athenian *gene* were throughout aristocratic in character.

Like the phratries they had a definite constitution and elected officials, including an ἄρχων. Besides the eponymous ancestor, they worshipped Zeus Herkeios and Apollo Patroos, the tutelary deities of all Athenians. They met at least once a year to elect officials, pass decrees, and enrol new members, who had to be sons of existing members born in lawful wedlock or formally adopted. Acceptance seems to have carried unquestioned acceptance in the phratry also; rejection might be contested in the courts. *Gennetai*, like *phrateres*, συγγενεῖς, and *demotai* (*see* DEMOI) were called on in the courts to bear witness to status.

The Athenian aristocratic *gene* were probably formed in post-Mycenaean times and dominated public life till Solon. Not only was the archonship reserved to them (*see* EUPATRIDAI), but individual families had an exclusive right to certain priesthoods; e.g., the Eumolpidae and Kerykes (*see* EUMOLPUS) supplied priests for the Eleusinian Mysteries (q.v.). Solon deprived the *gene* of their monopoly of office, and though Cleisthenes did not legislate against them directly (Arist. *Ath. Pol.* 21. 6), his reorganization of the citizen-body (*see* DEMOI, PHYLAI), must further have diminished their political power. While some *gene* gave their names to demes, which perhaps indicates that they were still locally concentrated and continued to wield local influence, others, already dispersed, are found split between several demes. But their priestly privileges remained intact (ibid.); they continued to provide leading men; and though some were wiped out in the wars (Isocr. 8. 88), they remained a prominent feature of Athenian life and long outlived the phratries, some surviving into the third century A.D.

Greek writers on Roman affairs used γένος to translate *gens* (q.v.).

J. Töpffer, *Attische Genealogie* (1889); C. Lécrivain in Dar.-Sag., s.v. (1896); W. S. Ferguson, *CPhil.* 1910, 257 ff.; R. Dahms, *PW* vii. 2, 2867 ff.; Busolt–Swoboda, *Griech. Staatsk.³*, see indexes; D. P. Costello, *JHS* 1938, 171 ff.; Hignett, *Hist. Athen. Const.*, see index; A. Andrewes, *BSA* 1957, 30 ff.; *JHS* 1961, 1 ff.; N. G. L. Hammond, *JHS* 1961, 76 ff. T. J. C.

**GENS** (etymologically related to *gignere*) indicates a Roman clan, or a group of families linked together by a common name and their belief in a common ancestor. Beside this, purity of blood, personal liberty, descent from freeborn parents, and freedom from any shameful punishment implying *deminutio capitis*, were held the essential claims to membership of a *gens*. Theories that the *gentes* existed before the State, or were set up by law, or originated from an artificial partition of the community, have been refuted by anthropologists and historians, who have rightly emphasized how the rapid economic improvement of the wealthier classes in a predominantly agrarian State would soon lead to a marked distinction

between upper and lower classes, and later to the establishment of an order with a narrow family organization. Yet the *gentes*, despite their political and social importance, never fulfilled any specifically public or political duties, apart from superintending several cults and ceremonies. The privacy of the *gentes* and the fact that their members (*gentiles*) neither recorded nor worshipped their founders confirms their relatively late origin. A further proof that the gentile assemblies were not regarded as legally capable of passing resolutions binding on the whole community is that the annalists never mention any public enactment carried in these assemblies, although they often record measures taken by the *gentes* (cf. Livy 6. 20. 14). Although the *gentes* played little part in Roman constitutional and political history they greatly influenced the development of law and religion, even after the prohibition of intermarriage between the orders, which caused the early collapse of several patrician *gentes*, had been abrogated by the *Lex Canuleia* (*see* CANULEIUS). When social equality was attained, the wealthiest plebeian families had already organized themselves on the model of the patrician *gentes*, to which some of them probably gained admission. This, rather than a supposed original difference of race, settlement, or nationality, explains best the existence of both plebeian and patrician families within the same *gens*, and both *minores* and *maiores gentes*.

If a member of a *gens* died intestate, his *gentiles* inherited all in default of direct agnates; this fact supports the view that in early times land-property was based on the principle of family, rather than individual, ownership. The gentile assemblies dealt with questions concerning testaments and bequests, *adrogatio*, adoption, emancipation, guardianship of minors, and appointment of *curatores* for insane or spendthrift members; their resolutions had to come twice a year before the *comitia calata* which also had to ratify resolutions referring to the *detestatio sacrorum* and the consequent *transitio ad plebem*. Clients and servants of the *gentiles* shared in their worship, and ceremonies, and were often buried in their masters' family tombs. These *sacra gentilicia* mainly consisted in honouring the guardian divinities of the *gens*. They frequently came to be worshipped by the whole community; so, for instance, faith and flattery transformed Apollo, the 'private god' of the *gens Iulia* and of Augustus, into the most honoured god of imperial Rome.

Mommsen, *Röm. Staatsr.* iii³. 9 ff.; A. H. J. Greenidge, *Roman Public Life* (1911), 9 ff.; De Sanctis, *Stor. Rom.* i. 229 ff.; P. de Francisci, *Primordia Civitatis* (1959), 162 ff. P. T.

**GENUA,** the modern *Genoa*, although presumably always Liguria's chief town, is not mentioned until 218 B.C. when already under Roman control (Livy 21. 32). After its destruction in the Hannibalic War Rome restored Genua and used it as a base against the Ligurians (q.v.) (Livy 30. 1; 32. 29; Val. Max. 1. 6. 7). A boundary quarrel between Genuates and Veiturii Langenses was settled by Roman adjudicators in 117 B.C. (*ILS* 5946). Although an important harbour and road-centre, ancient writers seldom mention Genua. For its exports and imports see Strabo 4. 202. E. T. S.

**GENUCIUS** (*PW* 5), LUCIUS, tribune of the plebs in 342 B.C., is credited with three laws of which only the first has historical foundation: (1) forbidding the lending of money on interest as a temporary measure (which was soon disregarded) to relieve social troubles, caused by debts, usury, and a military rebellion; (2) fixing a ten-year interval before a second tenure of the same office (this was seldom observed and its attribution to Genucius is doubtful); (3) according to Livy (7. 42. 2) allowing both onsuls to be plebeian, or more probably making one lebeian consulship obligatory.

G. Niccolini, *Fasti dei tribuni della plebe* (1934), 66 ff.　　P. T.

**GEOGRAPHY** (γεωγραφία, 'delineation of land'). It was the Greeks who created geography as a science (the Romans being merely their pupils). The Greeks based their geography on fewer adjunct sciences than modern geographers, and throughout they lacked good technical appliances, and therefore could not obtain technical accuracy. Their knowledge of the globe covered but a fraction of the Old World; and scientific study merged with imaginative speculation and *a priori* deduction about the unknown. Within these limitations, however, their achievements in mathematical and descriptive geography were considerable.

**2.** In Homer and Hesiod the earth was a round ocean-girt plane, symmetrically vaulted by heaven above and Tartarus below. In the following centuries the gradual discovery of the Mediterranean basin and of the adjacent lands not only gave wider knowledge of geographical details, but stimulated the Ionian philosophers (from *c.* 625 B.C.) to investigate the real causes of the earth's structure and to map the earth and heavens more systematically. The Pythagoreans (after *c.* 525 B.C.) put forward the theory that the earth was a sphere, and Aristotle proved it. Heraclides Ponticus (*c.* 388–315) declared that the earth revolved round its axis, Aristarchus of Samos *c.* 310–230) stated that it might also be revolving round the sun. But only the theory of the earth's sphericity won general acceptance, and after 450 the 'universal' geography of the Greeks tended to be replaced by a more narrow study of the οἰκουμένη or inhabited land-mass of the earth.

**3.** Geographic elucidation of the οἰκουμένη, progressing continually with geographic discovery, was expressed in a literature comprising the following classes:

A. WORKS ON PARTICULAR REGIONS. (*a*) Reports of discoveries. These were partly official, e.g. the reports of Hanno on north-west Africa, and of Nearchus (embodied in Arrian's *Indica*) on the Asian coast from Indus to Euphrates. Some of Caesar's chapters are geographical, e.g. *BGall.* 5. 12–13, 6. 25. A surviving unofficial specimen is the *Periplus of the Erythraean Sea* (*see* PERI-PLOI).

(*b*) Reports of surveyors. Of this class we possess fragments from Alexander's surveyors in Asia, and the *Parthian Stations* of Isidorus of Charax. These were in the nature of road-books, giving the important halts on the routes described.

(*c*) Manuals for travellers, sometimes based on first-hand information. A large proportion of these consisted of coastal descriptions for practical navigators (περίπλοι, παράπλοι, ἀνάπλοι). Fragments of an early example *c.* 500 B.C.) are reproduced in Avienius; an almost complete specimen survives in the so-called 'Periplus of Scylax' (*c.* 350). We also have large pieces of Arrian's *Periplus of the Euxine Sea*, and of the *Stadiasmus Maris Magni* (3rd c. A.D.), detailing landmarks, harbours, and waterpoints of the Mediterranean coasts, with distances in stades. To this class also belong the surviving Itineraries (q.v.).

(*d*) Maps (q.v.), issued in connexion with the above works, or published independently.

B. GENERAL TREATISES OF DESCRIPTIVE GEOGRAPHY. These comprised comprehensive surveys (γῆς περίοδοι or περιηγήσεις), with or without maps, coupled with descriptions of separate lands and land-groups (χωρο-γραφίαι), or of particular places (τοπογραφίαι). They sometimes included physical geography and ethnography. The Γῆς περίοδος of Hecataeus (*c.* 510–490) described towns and peoples as well as geographic

features; the geographic insertions in Herodotus' *History* contain much ethnological material. Of two fourth-century historians who included geography Ephorus attempted ethnography and historical geography, and devoted entire books to descriptive geography. Timaeus dealt largely with the general geography of western Europe. The contemporary historians of Alexander contained much useful geographical material. The description of India by Ctesias (*c.* 400) was overloaded with fable, but that of Megasthenes (*c.* 295) gave a good description of the Ganges valley, of which he had personal knowledge.

The opening up of the Near East by Alexander's successors was reflected in Agatharchides' description of the Red Sea coasts (*c.* 110—partly extant), and in the geographical chapters of Diodorus Siculus (*c.* 100–20), that of western Europe by the Romans in the geographical excursuses of Polybius and of Posidonius. A general resumptive work on Mediterranean and Near Eastern geography was composed by Artemidorus (*c.* 100). This was eclipsed a century later by the treatise of Strabo, which includes topography, physical, historical, political, and also mathematical geography. The only other descriptive geography of scientific value was the *Descriptio Orbis* of Agrippa, containing a commentary to his map of the world. Other works of this class were books 2–6 of the *Natural History* of Pliny (little more than a gazetteer); a description of Africa by Juba II (25 B.C.–*c.* A.D. 24); a versified description of the whole known world by Dionysius Periegetes (Hadrianic?); and school primers like that of the versifier miscalled 'Scymnus' (*c.* 100 B.C.?) and of Pomponius Mela (*c.* A.D. 43).

C. MATHEMATICAL GEOGRAPHIES. Scientific analysis of the earth's surface and a more accurate plotting of maps became possible when Aristotle demonstrated the earth's sphericity, Eratosthenes made a reasonably exact measurement of the earth's circumference, and latitudes were determined by means of shadow-sticks or by calculation from the length of a solstitial day. Aristotle introduced the general principle of dividing the globe into zones. Dicaearchus (*c.* 310) laid down a basic line of latitude from Gibraltar to the Himalayas; Eratosthenes drew several parallels of latitude and longitude to a main line of latitude and a meridian intersecting at Rhodes; Hipparchus (*c.* 150) divided Eratosthenes' main parallel of latitude into 360 degrees, drew parallels of latitude computed from the duration of the longest day, and proposed to plot all places on the map by latitude and longitude. A comprehensive attempt to apply the principles of mathematical geography was made in the Γεωγραφικὴ ὑφήγησις of Ptolemy (*c.* A.D. 150–60). Though the greater part of his geographical data was not actually determined by astronomical observation, he systematically expressed them in reference to curved lines of latitude measured northwards from the Equator, and curved meridians measured eastwards from the Canary Islands. Unfortunately the works of the mathematical geographers and of Strabo did not command the attention which they deserved; the erroneous beliefs of older writers were preserved by tradition, and the authors of later date than Ptolemy were for the most part mere compilers from variegated and incongruous sources. *See also* ITINERARIES, MAPS, PERIPLOI, and articles on the persons mentioned above.

E. H. Bunbury, *History of Ancient Geography* (1879, 1883, and 1959); H. Berger, *Geschichte der wissenschaftlichen Erdkunde der Griechen*[2] (1903), H. F. Tozer, *History of Ancient Geography*[2] (1935); Cary–Warmington, *Explorers*; Thomson, *Hist. Anc. Geog.*; P. Sykes, *A History of Exploration*[3] (1950); Gisinger, *PW* Suppl.–B. iv. 521 ff.; H. E. Burton, *The Discovery of the Ancient World* (1932), a concise account with sources. E. H. Warmington, *Greek Geography* (1934). C. van Paassen, *The Classical Tradition of Geography* (1957); A. Diller, *Isis* 1949, 6 ff.; O. Neugebauer, *Isis* 1949, 240 ff.; and his *The Exact Sciences in Antiquity* (1942), 220 ff.　　E. H. W.

**GERASA,** later Antiochia on the Chrysorhoas and modern *Jerash* in Jordan, was a Seleucid foundation, probably by Antiochus IV. Held by Alexander Jannaeus (102–71 B.C.), it remained in Jewish hands untilPompey assigned it to Roman Syria and the Decapolis. Henceforth its prosperity, which largely depended on caravan trade with the Nabataeans and others, increased, particularly later when Trajan annexed Arabia Nabataea. Gerasa was visited by Hadrian and enjoyed a 'golden age' under the Antonines. Though a colony in the third century A.D., the city and its trade steadily declined until a revival under Justinian; then followed capture by Persians (614) and Arabs (635) and an earthquake in 746. Extensive ruins of many buildings survive and the cityplan is clear: an arch, stadium, forum, colonnaded avenue, temples of Zeus and of Artemis (with Propylaea), theatre, open reservoir, and several Christian churches.

M. Rostovtzeff, *Caravan Cities* (1932), 62 ff., *Roman Empire²*, see index; C. H. Kraeling, *Gerasa* (U.S.A. 1938); G. L. Harding, *The Antiquities of Jordan²* (1967); R. O. Fink, 'Jerash in the first century A.D.', *JRS* 1933, 109 ff.; J. W. Crowfoot, *Churches at Jerash* (1931).
H. H. S.

**GERGOVIA,** modern *Gergovie* (*Merdogne* till 1865), an *oppidum* of the Arverni (q.v.) successfully held by Vercingetorix against Caesar in 52 B.C. Caesar's camps here were located by Stoffel for Napoleon III and more recently the hill-fort itself has been excavated. Occupation before 52 appears to have been slight, but thereafter a small Gallo-Roman town persisted until well into the first century A.D., despite the foundation of Augustonemetum (*Clermont-Ferrand*) only 4 miles to the northwest, while a temple remained in use still longer.

Caes. *BGall.* 7.4.2 and 34–53. C. Jullian, *Hist. de la Gaule* iii (1909), 465 ff.; Grenier, *Manuel* i. 198 ff.; E. Desforges and P. Balme, *Gergovie* (1943); O. Brogan and E. Desforges, *Arch. Journ.* 1940, 1 ff.; J. J. Hatt et al., *Gallia* 1943, 97 ff., 1947, 27 ff., 1948, 31 ff., 1950, 14 ff.
A. L. F. R.

**GERMANI.** The earliest home of the German race was south Scandinavia, Jutland, and the north German coast from the Weser to the Oder. In the long period from the last glaciation to the Iron Age many different immigrant groups arrived from south-west, south, and east. From *c.* 1000 B.C. Germans expanded southwards and westwards, so that by 600 there were Germanic elements in the lowlands around the lower Rhine mixing with the peoples already established there. As the Germans moved southwards they came into contact with the Celts, who held the belt of highlands from the Ardennes to Bohemia against them for some centuries to come. In the third century German pressure became serious, and a fresh horde crossed the lower Rhine, while others pushed into the Westerwald and Taunus region of the middle Rhine and crossed to the Moselle, where they brought a Germanic strain into the Treveri. A new invasion west of the lower Rhine brought in the *Germani cisrhenani* known to Caesar, and some of the mixed population was driven down into the Marne–Aisne basins (*see* BELGAE). The migration of the Cimbri and Teutones followed shortly after 120, and the Helvetii south of the Main, already suffering from the pressure of tribal movements, retreated into Switzerland. This general falling-back of the remaining trans-Rhenane Celts was hastened when early in the first century B.C. a new German host, the Suebi, moved south-west to the Main and Rhine.

Corresponding expansion took place among the Germans to the East. Those of the Baltic coast had spread over a wide area before the second century B.C. but were pushed away from the sea by the arrival of successive tribes from Scandinavia (q.v.), Vandals from Jutland, Burgundians from Bornholm, the Langobardi from Gotland, the Rugii from south Norway, and the Goths from south Sweden. The vanguard of the east Germans

were the Bastarnae, who appeared on the borders of Thrace *c.* 200 B.C. By the first century A.D. the Vandals, with the Lugii, occupied Silesia, the Burgundians were behind them astride the Warthe, and the Langobardi had moved in the wake of the Cimbri and Teutones to the lower Elbe, leaving the Rugii on the Pomeranian coast, while the Goths held the lower Vistula.

The origin of the name *Germani* is explained in Tacitus, *Germania*, 2. One of the tribes or tribal groups taking part in the great offensive along the lower Rhine of the third century B.C. had been called *Germani*, and this name was adopted by the Gauls to designate the whole race (cf. the analogous case of *Alemanni* and *Allemands*).

The Germans themselves believed that they were descended from the god Tuisto, born of the earth; his son Mannus (Man) had three sons, the ancestors of the three west German groups, Ingaevones (northern and north-western tribes), Istaevones (Westphalian and Rhenish tribes), Herminones (Suebi, Chatti, Cherusci, etc.). The absence of the east Germans from this classification points to its originating in a period before they became differentiated. They worshipped Woden (Mercury), Donar or Thor (Hercules), Ziu or Tiu (Mars). Goddesses were as a rule less important, though notable exceptions like Nerthus and Tamfana are known, both the central deities of important religious federations. Though there were no temples in the classical sense, there were from an early age places—most commonly sacred groves—set apart for the worship of the gods. (*See* RELIGION, GERMANIC.)

The Germans in the time of Tacitus were pastoralists who also engaged in agriculture. Among some tribes there were permanent chiefs, but among others special leaders were elected for special campaigns. The final decision on all matters of importance was taken by the warriors in their assembly; but the business of the assembly was considered first by a council of *principes*, whose manner of appointment is unknown. Whether the *notae* mentioned by Tacitus (*Germ.* 7) were a form of runes is still a matter of dispute.

Tac. *Germ.*, ed. Anderson (1938); E. A. Thompson, *The Early Germans* (1965); Much, *PW*, *Suppl.* iii, s.v., L. Schmidt, *Geschichte der deutschen Stämme²* (1934–41).
O. B.; E. A. T.

**GERMANIA.** For the Romans Germania long remained an undefined area east of the Rhine. After Caesar's campaigns the river became a frontier of the Empire. Augustus (q.v.) abandoned his plans to conquer western Germany and to advance the frontier eastwards from the Rhine to the Elbe (cf. also GERMANICUS), although he established the Danube as a frontier line against the German tribes to the north. Thereafter the Rhineland became a military area, controlled by eight legions under two consular 'legates of the armies in Upper and Lower Germany' (with the point of division at Vinxtbach); civil administration belonged to the governor of Gallia Belgica. Under the Flavians some districts east of the Rhine, namely the Agri Decumates (q.v.) and the Taunus Mountains area, were annexed (*see* VESPASIAN) and *c.* A.D. 90 Domitian (q.v.) formally established two provinces of Germania Superior in the south and Germania Inferior in the north under *legati Augusti pro praetore*, although their financial administration was still linked to Belgica under a *procurator provinciae Belgicae et utriusque Germaniae.* The reduction of the legions to four under Trajan indicates general pacification. With Hadrian and Antoninus (1) (qq.v.) the frontier system was reorganized (*see* LIMES). After the loss of the Agri Decumates and other transRhenane territory (*c.* 263), Diocletian named Germania Inferior Germania Secunda, while Superior became Prima and Maxima Sequanorum, all three belonging to the diocese of the Gauls and under the *praefectus praetorio Galliarum* at Trier.

E. Stein, *Die kaiserlichen Beamten und Truppenkörper im röm. Deutschland unter dem Prinzipat* (1932); E. Ritterling, *Fasti des röm. Deutschland unter dem, Prinzipat* (1932); *Germania Romana: ein Bilder-Atlas²* (1924); C. B. Rüger, *Germania Inferior* (Köln, 1968); G. Alföldy, *Die Hilfstruppen d. röm. Provinz Germ. Inf.* (1968).
H. H. S.

**GERMANICUS JULIUS** (*PW* 138) **CAESAR** (before adoption NERO CLAUDIUS GERMANICUS?), elder son of Drusus (q.v. 3), and Antonia (3), was born 24 May 15 B.C. and adopted in A.D. 4 by his uncle Tiberius. Since the latter was immediately adopted by Augustus, Germanicus thus became a member of the Julian *gens*, standing in the direct line of succession, and his career was presently accelerated by special dispensations. He served under Tiberius in Pannonia (7–9), and Germany (11). In 12 he was consul, and in 13 was sent out again as proconsul and commander-in-chief in the Gallic and German provinces. By now he was an established popular figure. Like his father, he was held to entertain republican sentiments, and his affability was contrasted with the dour reserve of Tiberius. But, though by no means incapable, he was over-emotional and his judgement was unsteady. When, on the death of Augustus, the legions of Lower Germany mutinied, his loyalty was proof against the suggestion that he should supplant Tiberius, but his handling of the awkward situation lacked firmness: he resorted to theatrical appeals and committed the government in Rome to the acceptance of the mutineers' principal demands.

Eager to emulate his father and conquer a large part of Germany, before the end of 14 he led the repentant legions against the Marsi. In the spring of 15 he campaigned against the Chatti (q.v.), Cherusci (q.v.), and Marsi, and rescued the pro-Roman Cheruscan Segestes from Arminius (q.v.). In the summer he attacked the Bructeri (q.v.), reached the Saltus Teutoburgiensis (q.v.), and paid the last honours to Varus (q.v. 2): after an indecisive battle with the Cherusci, led by Arminius, his forces suffered heavy losses on their way back. For the main campaign of 16 a great fleet was prepared and the troops were transported via his father's canal and the lakes of Holland to a station on the Ems, whence they proceeded to the Weser and defeated Arminius in two battles at Idistaviso (near Minden) and somewhat to the north; the fleet suffered considerable damage from a storm on its homeward journey.

Although Germanicus believed that one more campaign would bring the Germans to their knees, Tiberius judged that the positive results so far achieved did not justify a continuation of the drain on Roman resources, and called him to Rome to celebrate a triumph (26 May 17) and to take up a new command over all the eastern provinces, with *maius imperium*. Germanicus entered on his second consulship (18) at Nicopolis (q.v. 3), crowned Zeno, son of Polemo (q.v.), king of Armenia and reduced Cappadocia and Commagene (qq.v.) to the status of provinces. In 19 he offended Tiberius by travelling, out of romantic curiosity, to Egypt, which Augustus had barred to senators. On his return to Syria the enmity between him and Cn. Piso (q.v. 7), whom Tiberius had unhappily appointed governor of Syria with the intention of controlling him, became intolerable, and he ordered Piso to leave his province. Presently, however, he fell mysteriously ill, and on 10 Oct. died at Antioch (q.v. 1), convinced that Piso had poisoned him. His death—compared by some with that of Alexander—provoked widespread demonstrations of grief and in Rome some suspicion and resentment also; many honours were paid to his memory (*see* TABULA HEBANA); his ashes were deposited in the mausoleum of Augustus at Rome.

Germanicus married Agrippina (2), the daughter of Agrippa (3) and Julia (2). She bore him nine children, among whom were Nero (d. 31), Drusus (d. 33), Gaius (later Emperor), Agrippina (3), Drusilla (q.v.), and Julia (4). Eloquent and studious, he wrote comedies in Greek (all lost) and Greek and Latin epigrams; he also translated into Latin the *Phaenomena* of Aratus (q.v. 1), bringing it up to date and adding further matter on the planets and the weather.

G. Kessler, *Die Tradition über G.* (1905); K. Christ, *Drusus und G.* (1956); C. Questa, *Maia* 1957, 291 ff.; E. Koestermann, *Hist.* 1957, 429 ff.; 1958, 332 ff.; J. van Ooteghem, *LEC* 1959, 241 ff.; D. C. A. Shotter, *Hist.* 1968, 194 ff. Children. Mommsen, *Ges. Schr.* iv. 271 ff.; Schanz–Hosius ii. 437 ff. Iconography. L. Curtius, *Röm. Mitt.* 1934, 119 ff.; *MDAI* 1948, 68 ff.; J. P. V. D. Balsdon, *JRS* 1936, 152 ff.; S. Füchs, *Röm. Mitt.* 1936, 212 ff.; A. W. Byvanck, *Mnemos.* 1947, 238 ff.; E. Hohl, *Arch. Anz.* 1948/9, 255 ff.; V. Poulsen, *Claudische Prinzen* (1960).
A. M.; T. J. C.

**GEROUSIA,** the Council of Elders at Sparta, consisting of twenty-eight γέροντες of over 60 years of age drawn from a restricted circle of aristocratic families, together with the two kings. Elected similarly to the ephors (q.v.), by acclamation of the citizens (a childish system, Arist. *Pol.* 2. 1271ª), the *gerontes* held office for life, but at some later date the office was made annual, and under the Roman Empire re-election became a frequent practice. Possessing both deliberative and judicial functions, they considered questions of public policy and prepared business for the assembly (*see* APELLAI 1), whose wishes they were in some circumstances competent to ignore. They heard cases involving death, exile, or ἀτιμία, and could try even the kings; when the ephors laid charges before them they joined them in passing sentence. But representing as they did a largely unchanging aristocratic élite the effect of their prestige alone would go far beyond anything given to them by specific powers.

Gerousia was also a common name for city councils of an aristocratic or plutocratic type, whether survivals of the Homeric Councils of Elders, or new creations, as in the Greek towns of Asia Minor in Hellenistic or Roman times.
A. M. W.; W. G. F.

**GESORIACUM (Bononia** under the later Empire), modern *Boulogne-sur-Mer*, and almost certainly the Portus Itius (i.e. 'channel harbour') of Caesar; under the Empire the normal port of embarkation for Britain and station of the *Classis Britannica*. Its lighthouse was constructed by Caligula. Carausius' fleet was blockaded here in A.D. 292.

A. E. E. Desjardins, *Géographie hist. et admin. de la Gaule romaine* (1875–93) i. 346 ff.; T. Rice Holmes, *Ancient Britain²* (1935), 552 ff.; J. Heurgon, *Rev. Ét. Anc.* 1948, 101 ff.
C. E. S.

**GESSIUS FLORUS,** from Clazomenae, married Cleopatra, a friend of Poppaea (q.v.), and thus gained the favour of Nero who in A.D. 64 appointed him procurator of Judaea which Gessius proceeded to govern ruthlessly. Although Josephus' account of his villainies may be exaggerated, he certainly inflamed Jewish feeling (e.g. a demand for 17 talents from the Temple treasury led to rioting and bloodshed) and helped to precipitate the great insurrection of 66.

A. H. M. Jones, *The Herods of Judaea* (1938), 235 ff.       H. H. S.

**GESTURES.** Since the peoples of southern Europe notoriously make more use of gesture than the northerners, it is not surprising that gesticulation was frequent and lively among the ancients. (*a*) The natural signs of the emotions were less restrained than with us. Thus, to jump for joy would appear to be no mere metaphor nor confined to children and excitable young people; Q. Cicero says he did it on receiving good news (*Fam.* 16. 16. 1). Angry or troubled people bite their nails or their fingers (Hor. *Epod.* 5. 48; Pers. 5. 162). Achilles, disturbed by bad news, smites his thighs (*Il.* 16. 125), and so do many after him, but it was too violent a gesture for an orator till Cleon introduced it (Quint. *Inst.* 11. 3. 123). One or two gestures are strange to us, as the angry or perplexed scratching of the ear or cheek (Apul. *Met.* 6. 9; Heliodorus 2. 8 (p. 44. 29 Bekker)). (*b*) Orators and actors naturally made a study of gesture. The former were at first very restrained, particularly at Athens, where it was not good form till after Pericles to withdraw the hand from under the mantle (Aeschin. 1. 25); later they elaborated, keeping, however, within narrower limits than those of the stage (Quint. loc. cit., 89; see the whole passage for oratorical usage). Concerning actors we are not so well informed, especially for tragedians of the classical Greek period, who cannot have gesticulated freely in their heavy costume. Of New Comedy we can say a little more, owing to the descriptions by characters of their own movements, e.g. Plaut. *Capt.* 794 ff., where Ergasilus runs about the stage, shouldering through an imaginary crowd. In farce and pantomime much could be conveyed by gesture (e.g. Suet. *Nero* 39; Lucian, *Salt.* 37 ff.). (*c*) Religious and magical gestures: the most common gesture of prayer was to look up, or down, according as a celestial or infernal power was invoked, holding the hands palm upwards, or downwards (*Il.* 3. 275; 24. 307; Picard in *Rev. Hist. Rel.* 1937, 137 ff.). In the latter case the ground might be struck or stamped upon (as *Il.* 9. 568; Cic. *Tusc.* 2. 60), which perhaps is why the latter is not very common as a mere sign of irritation. Kneeling or prostration were not usual in Greece (Theophr. *Char.* 16. 5, where see H. Bolkestein, *Theophrastos' Charakter der Deisidaimonia*, quite common in Rome. Kissing statues was common (Cic. *Verr.* 2. 4. 94), also blowing kisses to them (Min. Fel. *Oct.* 2. 4). In human relationships a friend kissed the face, a suppliant the hand (Sittl, op. cit. *infra*, 79, 166); handshaking was more solemn. The most common magical gesture (to avert the evil eye, etc.) was to hold the hand so as to imitate the *pudenda* of one or the other sex, Sittl, 101 ff.

It is not surprising that there grew up a sign-language, ranging in signification from rudeness (Pers. 1. 58–60) to arithmetical calculations and even a sort of deaf-and-dumb alphabet (Bede, *De computo vel loquela digitorum*; critical text in Sittl, 256 ff.).

C. Sittl, *Die Gebärden der Griechen und Römer* (1890). T. Elworthy, *The Evil Eye* (1895), *Horns of Honour* (1900), contain much but inaccurate and unsystematic information. G. Neumann, *Gesten und Gebärden in der griechischen Kunst* (1965); R. Brilliant, *Gesture and Rank in Roman Art* (U.S.A. 1963). H. J. R.

**GETA** (1), LUCIUS SEPTIMIUS (*PW* 32), younger son of Septimius Severus and brother of Caracalla, became Caesar in A.D. 198 and Augustus in 209. During the Scottish campaigns he was left as governor of Britain at York. The mutual hatred of the two brothers was intensified after their father's death. On their return to Rome they lived in different parts of the Palace. After some vain attempts at reconciliation by their mother, Geta was assassinated by his brother in 212. See AURELIUS (2).
H. M. D. P.

**GETA** (2), GNAEUS HOSIDIUS (*PW* 6), perhaps the subject of an acephalous inscription from Histonium (*ILS* 971), in A.D. 42 as propraetorian legate in Mauretania fought against the Moor Sabalus. Afterwards he (if Γναῖος is read for Γάιος in Dio Cass. 60. 9. 1), or his brother, served as legionary legate on Plautius' staff during the invasion of Britain and distinguished himself at the Medway battle. He was later suffect consul (*c.* 45).

R. Syme, *AJPhil.* 1956, 270. H. H. S.

**GETA** (3), HOSIDIUS (2nd c. A.D.), contemporary with Tertullian (*De praescr. haeret.* 39), patched together

from lines or phrases of Virgil a cento (q.v.) to form dialogue and choruses of a tragedy *Medea*, probably identical with that in *Anth. Lat.* (codex Salmasianus).

TEXT. Baehr. *PLM* iv. 219 ff.; Riese, *Anth. Lat.²* i. i. 61 ff.; with metrical English translation J. J. Mooney (1919); with notes P. Burman Younger, *Anth. Vet. Lat. Epigr. et Poem.* (1759), 149 ff. See J. O. Delepierre, *Tableau de la littérature du centon* (London, 1874–5) i. 37 ff. J. W. D.

**GETAE,** a Thracian tribe who had settled by the fourth century B.C. on the lower Danube to the south and east of the Carpathians (*see* THRACE). Greek writers tended to confuse them with the Dacians (*see* DACIA) while later writers applied their name to the Goths, with whom they had nothing in common. J. J. W.

**GIANTS,** a mythological race of monstrous appearance and great strength. According to Hesiod they were sons of Ge (Earth) from the blood of Uranus which fell upon earth; he describes them as valiant warriors (*Th.* 185). Homer considers them a savage race of men who perished with their king Eurymedon (*Od.* 7. 59). The prevailing legend of the fight of the gods and the giants was formulated in archaic epics and was embroidered by many later writers. A substantial account is given by Apollodorus (1. 6. 1.). When the gods were attacked by the giants they learned that they could win only if they were assisted by a mortal. They called in Heracles, who killed the giant Alcyoneus and many others with his arrows. Zeus, who led the gods, smote with his thunderbolt Porphyrion who attempted to ravish Hera; Athena killed Pallas or Enceladus; Poseidon crushed Polybotes under the rock that became the island of Nisyrus (Strabo 489); Apollo shot Ephialtes; Hermes slew Hippolytus; Dionysus killed Eurytus and many other giants besides who were caught in his vine; and Hephaestus aided the gods, throwing red-hot iron as missiles. The giants were defeated and were believed to be buried under the volcanoes in various parts of Greece and Italy, e.g. Enceladus under Aetna. Bones of prehistoric animals were occasionally believed to be bones of giants.

The Gigantomachy was one of the most popular myths in Greece and accordingly the names of participants and the episodes of the battle vary from writer to writer and from representation to representation. Zeus, Heracles, Poseidon, and later Athena, are the usual protagonists. In its early stage the myth seems to represent a variation of the popular motif of the tribe that attempted to dethrone the gods; in a more advanced stage of culture the myth was interpreted as the fight of civilization against barbarism.

In art the giants are first shown as warriors or wild men (Hanfmann, *Art Bull.* 1937), later as snake-legged monsters (Waser, *PW* Suppl. iii, s.v. 'Giganten'). The most famous sculptural renderings are found on the archaic treasury of the Siphnians and on the Hellenistic altar of Pergamum.

F. Vian, *La Guerre des Géants* (1952); A. van Windekens, *BN* 1956, 59; W. Havers, *Sprache* 1958, 23; M. Delcourt, *History of Religions* (1965), 209 ff. G. M. A. H.

**GILDAS** (died *c.* A.D. 570), a British cleric and author of the *De excidio et conquestu Britanniae* (written *c.* 540), a work of moral exhortation which includes a short history of Britain. Full of imaginative errors though this is, it yet can yield valuable information on the chronology and culture of the Dark Age, and was used as a source by Bede, who thus perpetuated some of Gildas's chronological mistakes, notably in relation to the coming of the Saxons.

Collingwood–Myres, *Roman Britain*; Frere, *Britannia*, 379 ff.; Myres, 'Adventus Saxonum' in W. F. Grimes, *Aspects of Archaeology in Britain and Beyond* (1951), 221 ff.; C. E. Stevens, 'Gildas Sapiens', *Eng. Hist. Rev.* 1941, 353 ff.; J. Morris, 'Dark Age Dates', in M. G. Jarrett and B. Dobson, *Britain and Rome* (1966), 150 ff. S. S. F.

**GLABRIO** (1), MANIUS ACILIUS (*PW* 35) (*cos.* 191 B.C.), *novus homo*, tribune in 201 B.C., plebeian aedile in 197, rose under the aegis of Scipio Africanus to the praetorship in 196, crushing an Etruscan slave revolt, and became consul in 191 in the Syrian War. He defeated Antiochus at Thermopylae and began operations against the Aetolians; he extended the Delphic sanctuary. After triumphing (190) he stood for the censorship, but withdrew under a charge of peculation supported by Cato in opposition to the Scipionic group. In 181 his son dedicated a temple to *Pietas* vowed at Thermopylae. The *Lex Acilia de intercalando* may belong to his consulship.

G. Daux, *Delphes au IIᵉ et au Iᵉʳ siècle* (1936), 225; R. Flacelière, *Les Aitoliens à Delphes* (1937), 356; Scullard, *Rom. Pol.* 28 n. 3, 81, 25, 131 n. 1, 137 ff.; A. K. Michels, *The Calendar of the Roman Republic* (U.S.A. 1967), 101 ff. A. H. McD.

**GLABRIO** (2), MANIUS ACILIUS (*PW* 37), grandson of (1), born *c.* 155 B.C., son-in-law of Scaevola (q.v. 3); augur and friend of C. Gracchus (q.v. 4); as his colleague as tribune (122) he passed a *lex Acilia repetundarum* changing procedure in the *repetundae* (q.v.) court to make it more severe and providing for juries consisting of *equites* (q.v.). He died soon after. The law is almost certainly that preserved (in part) on bronze tablets now in Naples and Vienna (Riccobono, *FIRA* 7; transl. E. G. Hardy, *Roman Laws and Charters*, 1).

E. Badian, *AJPhil.* 1954, 374. E. B.

**GLABRIO** (3), MANIUS ACILIUS (*PW* 38), son of (2), as *praetor repetundarum* (70 B.C.) presided at the trial of Verres (q.v.); consul in 67; as proconsul he fought ineffectually against Mithridates until superseded under the law of Manilius (q.v. 2). E. B.

**GLABRIO** (4), MANIUS ACILIUS (*PW* 40), consul with the future Emperor Trajan in A.D. 91, when he was compelled to fight in the arena and was exiled. In 95 he was executed. The cause is uncertain (Christian faith?). He or his family is connected with the catacombs of Priscilla.

Dio Cass. 67. 14. P. Styger, *Die römischen Katakomben* (1933), 100 ff.; F. Cabrol–H. Leclerq, *Dict. d' Arch. chrétienne* vi. 1259; K. Friedmann, *Atene e Roma* 1931, 69 ff. A. M.

**GLADIATORS.** Gladiatorial combats, held at the funerals of dead warriors in Etruria, were introduced to Rome (perhaps by way of Samnium and Campania) in 264 B.C., when three pairs fought at the funeral games in honour of D. Brutus Pera. They were held on an increasingly lavish scale—Julius Caesar exhibited 320 pairs in 65 B.C.—by private individuals, at first always as or on the pretext of being) games in honour of a deceased male relative until in 46 B.C. Julius Caesar's games were in part not commemorative at all, in part commemorative of his daughter Julia (q.v. 1). Five thousand pairs fought in eight different games given by Augustus (*Res Gestae* 22. 1), and the same number in a single series of games given by Trajan to celebrate the conclusion of the Dacian war in A.D. 107. Gladiators were of four types: the Mirmillo, with a fish for crest on his helmet, and the Samnite, both heavily armed with oblong shield, visored helmet, and short sword; the Retiarius, lightly clad, fighting with net and trident; and the Thracian with round shield and curved scimitar. They were prisoners of war, condemned criminals, slaves bought for the purpose, or volunteers who had signed on for a fee and bound themselves by oath, *auctoramentum gladiatorium* (a practice which Marcus Aurelius tried by legislation to prevent). They were trained in gladiatorial schools (mainly in Campania) under a *lanista* (who was sometimes a retired gladiator) and were an investment which attracted even the prudent Atticus (q.v. 1). After Domitian gladiatorial games could only be given by emperors in Rome; outside Rome they

required official sanction. In Italy and the provinces they were given in amphitheatres or theatres by rich individuals or local magistrates or priests (often as a result of strong public pressure) or by entrepreneurs, who charged for admission. Though the life of a defeated combatant was often spared by the audience's wish, these games (approved by the Younger Pliny, *Pan.* 33) were condemned by sensitive pagan as well as by Christian writers.

Friedländer, *Roman Life and Manners* (E.T. 1908–13) ii. 41 ff.; iv. 166 ff.; 190 ff.; Dar.–Sag. and *PW* Suppl.-B. iii. 760, s.v. 'Gladiatores'; P. J. Meier, *Gladiatura Romana* (1881); F. Weege, *Arch. Jahrb.* 1909, 134 (claiming Campanian origin); A. Piganiol, *Recherches sur les jeux romains* (1923); L. Robert, *Gladiateurs dans l' Orient grec* (1940); H. M. Colini and L. Cozza, *Ludus Magnus* (1962); M. Grant, *Gladiators* (1967). Illustrations: *Bull. Mus. Civ. Rom.* 19 (1956–8), 37; S. Aurigemma, *I mosaici di Zliten* (1926), 131. J. P. B.

**GLANUM** (Γλανόν), a Greek and Roman town south of St.-Rémy-de-Provence, under excavation since 1921. The earliest element was a Ligurian shrine, but in the second century B.C. a considerable Massaliote settlement grew up. Structures uncovered include several Hellenistic houses and a possible *bouleuterion*, and the town struck its own coins.

Romanization began, after a break, in the time of Marius, but the town seems to have suffered with Massalia in 49 B.C. Thereafter, as Glanum Livii, it was re-established, with massive public buildings, and enjoyed Latin rights (Pliny, *HN* 3. 37). To the north stands a monumental arch and a mausoleum (*Les Antiques*); though the latter has been claimed as a cenotaph for Gaius and Lucius Caesar (qq.v. 7 and 8), a date *c.* 48 B.C. now seems probable for both. After the destruction of Glanum by barbarians (*c.* A.D. 270) the site was abandoned and a new walled town built at St.-Rémy itself.

H. Rolland, *Fouilles de Glanum* i (1946), ii (1958) (supplements to *Gallia*); G. C. Picard, *Les Trophées romains* (1959), 195 ff. A. L. F. R.

**GLAPHYRA** (1), a hetaera, met Antony in 41 B.C. and supposedly induced him to make her son Archelaus king of Cappadocia (q.v.) *c.* 36. T. J. C.

**GLAPHYRA** (2), daughter of Archelaus, king of Cappadocia (q.v.), was wife first of Alexander, son of Herod (q.v. 1), then of Juba II (q.v.), and finally of Alexander's half-brother Archelaus (q.v. 4), ethnarch of Judaea.

T. J. C.

**GLASS** (ὕαλος, *vitrum*). The art of producing a vitreous surface on stone, powdered quartz (faience), or clay was known in predynastic Egypt and passed to Crete, where plaques and figurines from the Palace of Cnossos illustrate the high level attained in the second millennium B.C. Glazed objects are common on Greek sites of the archaic period, some of them Egyptian imports, others probably made locally. In Hellenistic and Roman times Egypt and Asia Minor were centres of fabrication, and St-Rémy-en-Rollat in southern France produced vases during the Early Empire.

Objects composed entirely of glass paste begin to appear in Egypt about 1500 B.C., when two allied processes seem to have been in use: modelling molten glass about a core of sand, and pressing it into an open mould. The chief Mycenaean glass is dark blue imitating lapis lazuli, used for beads, inlays, and architectural ornaments. In the sixth century small vases made by the sand-core process became known in Greece; they have opaque blue or white bodies decorated with polychrome bands formed by fusing coloured threads rolled round the body, and zig-zag patterns were produced by means of a comb or spike. Their place of origin is unknown. In the Hellenistic period bowls made in moulds come into fashion; these were produced mainly in Egypt. Here the tradition of opaque polychrome glass was continued far into Roman times with the *millefiori* bowls, in which polychrome patterns were formed by fusing glass canes of various colours and pressing them into moulds. In the same tradition are the vases in two layers of which one is carved like a cameo: the Portland Vase in London is the best-known example.

The invention of glass-blowing in the first century B.C. (probably in Syria) wrought a profound change in the glass industry, which, hitherto limited to luxury articles, now became capable of cheap mass production. Under the Roman Empire glass largely replaced pottery for domestic use and funeral furniture. Foundries have been located in many provinces; like the *terra sigillata* potteries, the manufacture tended to move away from the Mediterranean towards the borders of the Empire. Thus in the later Empire, Belgic Gaul and Germany had taken the place of Italy and southern Gaul. In Britain also there were glass works, e.g. at Wilderspool, near Warrington. The vases, even when plain, show much variety of form, and there are several styles of decoration—tooling or applying relief ornament to the surface when warm, cutting or engraving or painting when cold. Window glass, made by a primitive process of rolling, was known at Pompeii, and later became common; in the late Empire also begins the use of glass for mirrors. Gemstones were imitated, often skilfully, in glass paste at all periods from the seventh century B.C. onwards. Burning-glasses were used, and these may conceivably have been used as magnifying glasses by gem engravers. There is, however, no evidence that spectacles were known in antiquity.

A. Kisa, *Das Glas im Altertume* (1908); M. L. Trowbridge, *Philological Studies in Ancient Glass* (U.S.A. 1930); Forbes, *Stud. Anc. Technol.* v; D. B. Harden in *History of Technology*, ed. C. Singer, etc., ii (1958), 311 ff. F. N. P.

**GLAUCIA**, GAIUS SERVILIUS (*PW* 65), of low (i.e. equestrian?) birth, but a witty popular orator. His career is obscure; but he was quaestor before 102 B.C., when Metellus (q.v. 6) Numidicus, as censor, wanted to expel him from the Senate. As tribune (101) and praetor (100) he co-operated with Saturninus (q.v. 1), and, in one of those years (probably), passed a law on the *repetundae* (q.v.) court, restoring the court to the *equites* (q.v.), whose support he was seeking. He hoped to be consul for 99, after the assassination of Memmius (q.v. 1), but his candidature was disallowed and he died with Saturninus.

J. P. V. D. Balsdon, *PBSR* 1938, 98 ff.; E. Badian, *Hist.* 1962, 206 ff. E. B.

**GLAUCUS**, in mythology, (1) a Lycian, son of Hippolochus, second in command of the Lycian contingent before Troy (*Il.* 2. 876 and often). He encounters Diomedes (q.v. 2), and exchanges armour with him in sign of friendship when told that they are hereditary ξένοι, getting the worse of the bargain, since his is gold and that of Diomedes bronze (*Il.* 6. 234–6; proverbial later). Wounded by Teucer (12. 387–8), healed by Apollo (16. 527 ff.), he rallies the Lycians after the death of Sarpedon. Killed, over the body of Achilles, by Aias son of Telamon (Quint. Smyrn. 3. 278 ff.), Apollo caused the winds to snatch his body from the pyre and take it to Lycia, where the Nymphs made the river of like name to spring up about his grave (ibid. 4. 4 ff.). (2) Of Anthedon in Boeotia. He somehow (Ov. *Met.* 13. 920 ff. is but one of several versions; see Drexler in Roscher's *Lexikon* i. 1679–80) became immortal by a magic herb (or a magic bath, schol. on Pl. *Resp.* 611 c) and then for some reason leaped into the sea and became a sea-god. He was renowned for his prophecies (schol. ibid. and often); vainly wooed Scylla (q.v. 1; Ov. ibid.). (3) Of Corinth (*Il.* 6. 154), son of Sisyphus and father of Bellerophon (qq.v.), therefore great-grandfather of Glaucus (1)

(Bellerophon–Hippolochus–Glaucus). His most famous legend is connected with Potniae in Boeotia, where he kept a stud of mares and fed them on human flesh (or they ate a herb which drove them mad, or Aphrodite was angry with Glaucus because he would not let them mate) till they devoured him at the funeral games over Pelias whereupon he became a Taraxippos (horse-frightener) which scared the teams at the Isthmus (Verg. *G.* 3. 267, Servius and 'Probus' ad loc., Pausanias 6. 20. 19; *Etym. Magn.* 685, 41). That the name belongs to these and some dozen other persons (Drexler, op. cit.) is due to its being (*a*) an epithet of the sea, (*b*) an adjective appropriate to the 'bright' eyes of a vigorous man. H. J. R.

**GLAUCUS** (4) of Chios (or Samos, according to some late authors), to whom is ascribed the invention of welding iron (σιδήρου κόλλησις; not of soldering iron which is a modern process), made for Alyattes of Lydia (reigned 617–560 B.C.) a stand of iron, supporting a silver bowl; this was for Herodotus (1. 25) 'worth seeing above all the other offerings at Delphi'. In the time of Pausanias (10. 16. 1) the bowl had disappeared, but the stand remained, tower-shaped with an upward taper, the sides of openwork with crossbands, and decorated with figures and animals (Ath. 5. 210 c). F. N. P.

**GLAUCUS** (5) of Rhegium (*c.* 400 B.C.) wrote an important work *On the Ancient Poets and Musicians* (used by [Plut.] *De mus.*), which began the ancient study of the history of lyric poetry. His comments on Homer and his discussion of the plots of Aeschylus may have formed part of this work. The name Glaucus has been thought to be a pseudonym of the sophist Antiphon.

*FHG* ii. 23 f.; E. Hiller, *Rh. Mus.* 1886. J. F. L.

**GLEVUM**, Roman *Gloucester*, was founded as the fortress of Legio XX Valeria in A.D. 49 when Ostorius (q.v.) was moving against the Silures; *cohors VI Thracum* had earlier occupied an adjacent fort at Kingsholm as an outpost of the frontier of Plautius (q.v. 4). Legio XX is thought to have moved to Viroconium (q.v.) in 66, and Glevum was probably then held by Legio II Augusta until *c.* 74 when it was advanced to Isca (q.v. 3). In 96–8 the vacant fortress was settled as a *colonia* under Nerva (*ILS* 2365). Little is known of its subsequent history: the town never expanded as did Lindum (q.v.), and was perhaps overshadowed by the prosperity of Corinium (*Cirencester*). Colonial tile-works are attested by stamps reading R(ei) P(ublicae) G(levensium) and sometimes mentioning magistrates. The town fell to Ceawlin and the West Saxons in 577.

I. A. Richmond, *Arch. Journ.* 1946, 68 ff. S. S. F.

**GLITIUS ATILIUS AGRICOLA**, a *novus homo* from Augusta Taurinorum, was one of Trajan's generals, and is known only from epigraphical evidence (*ILS* 1021, 1021a: *CIL* v. 6980). His career: military tribune in Moesia and quaestor under Vespasian; after his praetorship, *iuridicus* in Hither Spain, commander of Legio VI Ferrata in Syria, legate of Gallia Belgica (A.D. 95?–96/97), suffect consul under Nerva (97), governor of Pannonia under Trajan (100/1–3), consul suffect II (103), and *praefectus urbi*.

Syme, *Tacitus*, see index. H. H. S.

**GLOSSA, GLOSSARY** (Greek). In Greek literary criticism γλῶσσαι meant any words or expressions (not being mere neologisms or metaphors) ἃ οὐδεὶς ἂν εἴποι ἐν τῇ διαλέκτῳ (Arist. *Poet.* 1458ᵇ32), i.e. belonging not to the spoken language familiar to the critic (1458ᵇ6), but to a dialect, literary or vernacular, of another region or period (1457ᵇ4). The interpretation of Homeric γλῶσσαι, misunderstood already by Hesiod, fell, no doubt, from the first, to schoolmasters (cf. Ar. *Daitaleis*) and rhapsodes, and it appealed to sophistic interest in language: cf. Democritus, Περὶ ʽΟμήρου ἢ ὀρθοεπείης αἰ γλωσσέων. The living dialects were early used for the purpose (cf. Arist. *Poet.* 1461ᵃ12), but, apart from Aristarchus, Alexandrian commentators, no less than the Pergamenes, usually preferred to explain by etymology, as did Neoptolemus of Parium in Περὶ γλωσσῶν ʽΟμήρου. Interest in dialects was fostered by fifth-century linguistic speculations, and in the next two centuries by Peripatetic studies, not least in natural history and its vocabulary, and by monographs based on personal knowledge of local dialects before the levelling operation of the κοινή. The spirit of Alexandrianism in literature further encouraged search for linguistic oddities. Sometimes literary glosses were collected with only sporadic dialectal illustration, as the Homeric Glosses of Philetas and Simmias. Some specifically dialectal collections were devoted to Homer, Alcman, the Old Comedy, etc.; others were not so related to particular authors or styles, e.g. the Φρύγιαι φωναί of Neoptolemus, the ʼΕθνικαὶ λέξεις of Zenodotus (perhaps not the Alexandrian), and the Αἰολικαὶ γλῶσσαι of Antigonus of Carystus. The Ὀνομαστικόν, often with dialectal variants, also became common: e.g. Callimachus compiled names of winds, fishes, and months; Dionysius Iambus had a chapter on fishermen's terms, and Eratosthenes other vocational vocabularies. Aristophanes of Byzantium excelled all in the scope and diversity of his lexicographical labours (cf. Ael. *NA* 7. 47). In his footsteps followed his pupil Artemidorus (on Doric, and cookery), Philistides (on names of family relationships), and many others, notably, in the first century B.C., Cleitarchus of Aegina, who proved a fertile source of dialect glosses under the Empire. The Περὶ τῶν ὑποπτευομένων μὴ εἰρῆσθαι τοῖς παλαιοῖς of Aristophanes is a prototype of the 'Atticist' lexica which were common in the first century A.D. and still more in the following centuries. The first professed Atticist lexicographer was Eirenaeus of Alexandria (end of 1st c. A.D.), and the ultimate sources of most later Atticists are also Alexandrian. As to glosses of all kinds, in the first century B.C. compilation largely displaces independent research, and almost exclusively prevails under the Empire; to the latter period, down to Constantine, the extant scholiasts and lexicographers are directly or indirectly indebted; but the sources thus absorbed have generally perished. The many glossaries and word-lists surviving in papyri show the importance of such aids to reading in an age when the literary and spoken languages diverged considerably. Some of these are mere jejune lists; others are works of scholarship in which entries are supported by quotations. Some are general alphabetical lists, others limited to the vocabulary of a particular dialect or a particular craft.

K. Latte, *Philol.* 1925, 136; R. Reitzenstein, *Geschichte d. Gr. Etymologika* (1897); R. A. Pack, *The Greek and Latin Literary Texts from Greco-Roman Egypt*² (1965), 1658 ff.; *see also under* GRAMMAR, ETYMOLOGY. P. B. R. F.; R. B.

**GLOSSA, GLOSSARY** (Latin). The need for marginal or interlinear interpretations of difficult or obsolete words (γλῶσσαι) is coincident with the serious study of literature. The earliest reference to Latin glosses is in Varro (*Ling.* 7. 10: ' "tesca" aiunt sancta esse qui glossas scripserunt'). Some of the work of republican scholars like Opilius and Ateius was of a glossographical kind, and Verrius Flaccus was indebted to collections of glosses on Plautus, Ennius, Lucilius, etc.

The extant Latin glossaries (generally named from their first item, e.g. Abstrusa, Abavus, or from the home of their chief MS., e.g. St. Gall, Erfurt) cannot be traced back further than the sixth century A.D. They arose from the needs of monastery teachers who in the first instance gathered together (as *glossae collectae*) and arranged in a roughly alphabetical order the trivial marginalia from copies of the Bible, Terence, Virgil, Orosius, etc., in their own or neighbouring libraries; only rarely did such marginalia contain any scholarly comment, and few glossary compilers had access to e.g. Festus or the *Etymologiae* of Isidore from which to borrow. Copies of a glossary thus constructed sometimes had a wide circulation and formed the basis for larger derivative compilations; for example, Abstrusa (which contained material from a good Virgil commentary) and Abolita (which contained Festus items and Terence and Apuleius glosses) form the foundation for Abavus, Affatim, etc., and above all for the huge (early 9th c.?) encyclopaedic *Liber Glossarum* or *Glossarium Ansileubi* (which also includes long passages from Jerome, Ambrose, Gregory, Isidore, etc.). The value of such glossaries is threefold: (a) their interpretations sometimes contain or provide evidence for Late Latin or Early Romance words; (b) they sometimes contain latent evidence for readings in the text of an author; (c) occasionally they transmit some fragment of ancient learning.

Amongst later collections of glosses the best known are those of Salomon (10th c.) and Papias (11th c.), both of which rely on the *Liber Glossarum*.

Of bilingual glossaries may be mentioned: (a) the (6th-c.?) Cyrillus glossary (Greek with Latin interpretations) wrongly attributed to the fifth-century patriarch of Alexandria and not yet fully published; (b) the Philoxenus glossary (Latin with Greek interpretations) wrongly attributed to the consul of A.D. 535; (c) the *Hermeneumata* (Greek with Latin interpretations) wrongly attributed to Dositheus; (d) glossaries with Anglo-Saxon, Celtic, or Germanic interpretations.

J. Tolkiehn, s.v. 'Lexikographie', and G. Goetz, s.v. 'Glossographie', in *PW*; Schanz–Hosius, § 1119; W. M. Lindsay and H. J. Thomson, *Ancient Lore in Medieval Latin Glossaries* (1921); J. F. Mountford, *Quotations from Classical Authors in Medieval Latin Glossaries* (1925). Vol. i (1923) of the *Corpus glossariorum latinorum* (ed. G. Goetz), entitled *De origine et fatis glossariorum latinorum*, consists entirely of prefatory material; vols. ii–v give apographs of the oldest MS. of the chief early medieval glossaries (with readings of other MSS. in the app. crit.): ii (1888) contains Latin–Greek (= Philoxenus) and Greek–Latin glossaries; iii (1892) contains the pseudo-Dositheus *Hermeneumata*; iv (1889) contains Abstrusa + Abolita (under the name *gloss. cod. Vat. lat. 3321*) and short derivative glossaries; v (1894) contains the Placidus glossary, excerpts (only) from the *Liber Glossarum*, etc.; vols. vi and vii (1899–1901), entitled *Thesaurus Glossarum Emendatarum*, present the items of vols. ii–v in alphabetical and corrected form. The series *Glossaria Latina* (ed. W. M. Lindsay and others) gives critical editions of the chief glossaries and (where possible) indications of the source of each item: vol. i (1926) contains the purely glossary material of the *Lib. Gloss.* in its entirety; vol. ii (1926) contains the Arma, Abavus, and Philoxenus glossaries; vol. iii (1926) contains Abstrusa and Abolita; vol. iv (1930) contains Placidus (and an ed. of Festus based on glossary material); vol. v (1931) contains the Abba and AA glossaries. Of Latin–Anglo-Saxon glossaries, the Leyden glossary has been edited by J. H. Hessels (1906), the Corpus glossary by W. M. Lindsay (1921). Latin–Celtic glossaries were edited by Whitley Stokes and John Strachan, *Thesaurus Palaeohibernicus* (1901–3), two vols. with *Supplement* (1910); cf. R. Thurneysen, 'Irische Glossen', *Zeitschrift für Celtische Philologie* xxi; and Latin–Germanic by E. Steinmeyer and E. Sievers (*Die Althochdeutschen Glossen*, 4 vols. 1879–98).
J. F. M.

**GLYCON** (1), poet of unknown date and place to whom the Γλυκωνεῖον or glyconic metre is attributed by Hephaestion (33. 12). Nothing else is known about him. The epigram in *Anth. Pal.* 10. 124 on the unreason of the universe is thought to be by a different poet of later date, since it appears with other late poems.
S. Leichsenring, *De metris graecis quaestiones onomatologicae* (1888). C. M. B.

**GLYCON** (2), sculptor, of Athens; known from signature of Farnese Heracles (Winter, *KB* 333. 4) in Naples. The statue was found in the baths of Caracalla, and is proved by the ancient inscription on another example in

Florence to be a copy of a Heracles by Lysippus (q.v. 2) Nothing in the copy suggests a date later than the first century B.C.

G. Lippold, *Kopien und Umbildungen* (1923), 56.     T. B. L. W.

**GNATHIA,** near modern *Fasano* on the Adriatic coast of Apulia (q.v.), which gives its name to a curious type of polychrome pottery. Its history is unknown, but inscriptions from its recently excavated site reveal that Messapii (q.v.) once lived there. Horace (*Sat.* 1. 5. 99) rightly ridicules the story of volcanic activity here (cf. Pliny, *HN* 2. 240).     E. T. S.

**GNIPHO,** MARCUS ANTONIUS, a scholar of the Ciceronian age. He taught in the home of Julius Caesar and had a school of his own. His lectures on rhetoric were attended by Cicero during his praetorship (66 B.C.). He is said (by his pupil Ateius Philologus) to have composed only two books *De sermone latino*; but there is evidence that he wrote a commentary on the *Annales* of Ennius.
                                                         J. F. M.

**GNOME** (γνώμη). From the root-meaning 'expression of opinion' various specialized meanings spring, one of which is 'pregnant utterance', the pithy expression of a general thought. The sense is something like 'epigram' (in the commonest modern sense of that word), or, when the epigram has become current coin, 'proverb'. Man must have begun to think of gnomes almost as soon as he was capable of making general propositions. At any rate we meet them on the threshold of Greek literature; for Homer's αὐτὸς γὰρ ἐφέλκεται ἄνδρα σίδηρος (*Od.* 16. 294) is a gnome. The famous γνῶθι σεαυτόν and μηδὲν ἄγαν are unsurpassable for brevity. Hesiod is full of gnomes, and so, centuries later, is Euripides, in whose day the cult of the gnome in intellectualist circles is satirized by Aristophanes (see LSJ, s.v. γνωμίδιον, γνωμοτυπέω, and cognate words). In prose, the gnomic tendency is strongly marked in Heraclitus (q.v., and e.g. fr. 43), and even more so in Democritus (q.v.). The use of the gnome as not merely an ingredient in poetry or prose but as a literary form in itself can be traced back to Phocylides and Theognis (1) (qq.v.) in the middle of the sixth century B.C., and Democritus (*c.* 460–370 B.C.) himself talks of his works as γνωμέων (fr. 35). For the collection of gnomic sayings into anthologies, *see* CHREIA. *See also* SENTENTIA.

*PW.* Suppl. vi (1935), 74 ff. (Horna and v. Fritz).     J. D. D.

**GNOSTICISM** is a generic term primarily used of theosophical groups which broke with the second-century Christian Church. A wider, imprecise use of the term describes a syncretistic religiosity diffused in the Near East, contemporaneous with and independent of Christianity. Many ingredients of second-century Gnosticism are pre-Christian. But there is no evidence of a pre-Christian religion or cultic myth resembling Christianity as closely as the systems of Basilides, Valentinus, and Manichaeism (q.v.), all of which owed the essentials of their beliefs to Christianity, or even as the doctrine of Simon Magus which provided a rival religion of redemption with a redeemer replacing Jesus.

The principal characteristics of the second-century sects are (1) a radical rejection of the visible world as being alien to the supreme God and as incompatible with truth as darkness with light; (2) the assertion that elect souls are divine sparks temporarily imprisoned in matter as a result of a pre-cosmic catastrophe, but saved by a redeemer, sent from the transcendent God, whose teachings awake the sleep-walking soul to a consciousness of its origin and destiny, and also include instructions how to pass the blind planetary powers which bar the soul's

ascent to its celestial home. The first proposition has close affinities with late Jewish apocalyptic; for the second the Gnostics claimed, with some reason, large support in the dialogues of Plato. The characteristic theosophical claim is also made, viz. to present a religion that is at once esoteric and universal, satisfying the quest for an exclusive mystery while also claiming that all religions offer equally valid symbolic myths about the human condition. To explain how humanity came to need such drastic redemption, many Gnostics expounded Genesis i–iii as an allegory of the fall of a female cosmic power, an accident which led to the making of this visible world by an incompetent, perhaps malevolent creator. So the natural world betrays nothing of a beneficent creative intention. The cosmogony provided the ground for an ethic which in most sects was rabidly ascetic, but in a few groups (especially Carpocrates') produced a religion of eroticism, supported by an antinomian interpretation of St. Paul's antithesis of law and grace and by an extreme predestinarianism.

The principal sources of Gnosticism are the Platonic dualism of spirit and matter in which matter is invested with quasi-demonic properties by an evil world-soul (*Leg.* 896 e, *Tht.* 176 e), hellenized forms of Zoroastrian dualism (chiefly attested in Plutarch's interpretation of Isis and Osiris), Mithraism with its theme of the soul's ascent through the seven planets (modified to form part of the Ophite Gnostic system as described in Origen, *contra Celsum* vi), Judaism which, besides the book of Genesis, contributed the apocalyptic themes of the conflict between angelic powers and of the deliverance of the elect from this evil world, and above all Christianity to which Gnosticism was like a diabolical Doppelgänger. The evidence of the Pauline epistles (esp. Galatians, 1 Corinthians, Colossians) shows St. Paul using language often close to that of Gnosticism and at the same time strenuously resisting Gnostic tendencies in his churches. The fact that some of the proto-Gnostic elements in the Pauline epistles can also be found in Philo suggests that extreme liberalizing Judaism was a material cause of Gnostic origins. Nevertheless, the Jewish element is not strong in all the systems, and in many there is an anti-semitic spirit. From the second century, attitudes closely resembling Gnosticism appear in pagan texts, especially in Plutarch's theosophical tracts, 'Hermes Trismegistus', Numenius of Apamea, the Chaldean Oracles (qq.v.), and alchemists like Zosimus. It is entirely possible that some Gnostic influence passed from Numenius to Plotinus and Porphyry. Plotinus' passionate attack on the Gnostics (2. 9) is the work of a man who not only had to purge his own circle but felt within himself the power of Gnostic infiltration; and the theurgy of the later Neoplatonists is near to some of the grosser forms of second-century Gnosticism combated by the Church.

In Christianity Gnosticism produced a sharp reaction against its rejection of the doctrines of the goodness of the creation and the freedom of man. The capacity of individual sects for survival was also weakened by the syncretistic acceptance of all religious myths as valid and true. Nevertheless, Gnosticism had a strikingly successful future in Manichaeism (q.v.). One early sect still survives in the Mandeans of Iraq.

SOURCES. Original Gnostic documents survive mainly in Coptic, esp. forty-four documents in thirteen codices found at Nag-Hammadi, Upper Egypt, in 1946, in process of publication: see J. Doresse, *The Secret Books of the Egyptian Gnostics* (1960); W. C. van Unnik, *Newly Discovered Gnostic Writings* (1960). Earlier discoveries: C. Schmidt, *Koptisch-gnostische Schriften* (1905). Fragments of Heracleon, Marcion, and Valentinus are preserved in quotations made by orthodox critics (esp. Irenaeus, Tertullian, Clement of Alexandria, Hippolytus, Origen).
LITERATURE. E. de Faye, *Gnostiques et Gnosticisme*[2] (1925); F. C. Burkitt, *Church and Gnosis* (1932); W. Bousset, *Hauptprobleme der Gnosis* (1907); H. Jonas, *The Gnostic Religion* (1958); R. M. Grant, *Gnosticism and early Christianity* (1959); *Gnosticism, an Anthology*

(1961); K. Rudolph, *Die Mandäer* (1960–5, 3 vols.); H. C. Puech, 'Gnosis and Time', *Papers from Eranos Yearbooks, Man and Time* (1958); A. D. Nock, 'Gnosticism', *Harv. Theol. Rev.* 1964, 255 ff.; A.-J. Festugière, *La Révélation d'Hermes Trismégiste* (1949–54, 4 vols.); U. Bianchi (ed.) *Origins of Gnosticism* (1967). H. C.

**GOLD** (χρυσός, *aurum*). Gold is a rare metal in Greece, and the source of the rich treasures found in tombs of the Bronze Age (Mycenae, etc.) is unknown. The island of Siphnos prospered in the sixth century B.C. by its gold production; later the mines were flooded. Mines on Thasos, opened by the Phoenicians, were working in Thucydides' day, but have not been found. Macedonia and Thrace had a large auriferous area, where the mines of Mt. Pangaeus were working before 500 B.C. More fruitful than the home supplies were probably those from overseas. Nearest at hand were Mysia, Phrygia, and Lydia; their fame as gold-bearing lands is attested by the stories of Midas, Croesus, and the river Pactolus. Electrum (ἤλεκτρον), a natural alloy of gold and silver, was panned in the rivers of Asia Minor, and was used for the earliest coins and for jewellery. Colchis also furnished gold, and Scythians brought supplies from inner Asia. Yet there was a scarcity of gold in Greece until the conquests of Alexander made available the hoards of Persia.

Early Etruscan tombs show a wealth of gold furniture comparable to that of Bronze Age Greece. Traces of early mining are found in several districts of Italy, in particular the Pennine Alps. At Rome the metal long remained rare; it probably first became common through war indemnities. Under the late Republic and early Empire the main source of supply was Spain, where the north-west and Baetica yielded immense quantities. Gold was also mined in southern France and dredged from rivers in other parts of Gaul; there are also workings in south Wales. After the first century the western gold-fields were largely superseded by those of the Balkans, Noricum, and Dacia. When the supply from these fell off during the third century a shortage of the metal appears to have been generally felt.

O. Davies, *Roman Mines in Europe* (1935); M. Rosenberg, *Geschichte d. Goldschmiedekunst* (1910–25); R. A. Higgins, *Greek and Roman Jewellery* (1961); G. Becatti, *Oreficerie antiche* (1955). F. N. P.

**GORDIAN I** (MARCUS ANTONIUS (*PW* 61) GORDIANUS), Roman Emperor, A.D. 238. When proconsul of Africa he was at the age of 79 invited to become Emperor by some young nobles who had revolted at Thysdrus out of resentment at Maximinus' fiscal policy. He made his son, GORDIAN II, his colleague. The Senate, possibly forewarned, acknowledged him, but Capellianus, governor of Numidia, remained loyal to Maximinus. Gordian II opposed his legionary army with a volunteer militia, and when he was killed his father committed suicide after a reign of twenty-two days (238). See R. A. G. Carson, *Centennial Publication of the American Numismatic Society* (1958), 181 ff.

GORDIAN III (*PW*, Antonius 60), son of Gordian I's daughter Maecia Faustina, was, after the murder of Balbinus and Pupienus (*see* BALBINUS) in A.D. 238, saluted Emperor by the Praetorians at the age of 13. The conduct of affairs was at first in his mother's hands, but in 241–4 it passed to the praetorian prefect Timesitheus. A major campaign began in 242 in reply to a Persian attack the previous year (the Alamanni and Carpi took advantage of troop movements to raid across the northern frontiers). There were substantial Roman successes before Timesitheus died (243). In his place Gordian appointed an Arab called Philippus, who soon showed his imperial aspirations. Profiting by a food shortage he appealed to the soldiers who wanted a man, not a boy, as their ruler. Gordian was murdered at Zaitha in 244 (*see* PHILIPPUS I).

A. T. Olmstead, *CPhil.* 1942, 241 ff.; P. W. Townsend, *YClS* 1955, 49 ff. H. M. D .P.; B. H. W.

**GORDIUM,** capital of ancient Phrygia, situated at the point where the River Sangarius is crossed by the main route westward from the Anatolian plateau to the sea, that of the 'Royal Road. The site was occupied in the Early Bronze Age and Hittite period, and Phrygian settlement began probably in the tenth century B.C. at the latest. Gordium became capital of Phrygia in the eighth century, at the end of which it reached its height under King Midas. The city had massive fortifications and impressive buildings, and around it many tumuli were built in the eighth to sixth centuries containing richly furnished tomb chambers. Gordium was destroyed by the invading Cimmerians in the early seventh century; it recovered, but passed under Lydian and then, after a further destruction, under Persian domination. It was visited by Alexander the Great (333), who cut or untied the 'Gordian knot'. From the mid third century it was a Galatian village, abandoned in 189 B.C. In the time of Strabo there was a village at the site.

*See* PHRYGIA; G. and A. Körte, 'Gordion', *JDAI* 1904; R. S. Young, Excavation reports in *AJArch* 1955–60, 1962, 1964, 1966; *Proc. Amer. Phil. Soc.* 1963, 348 ff. D. J. B.

**GORDYENE,** a small Hellenistic kingdom (remnant of the Seleucid Empire), originally the land of the Kardouchoi, east of sources of Tigris, bordering Armenia (Strabo 16. 1. 8 and 24). It was a vassal kingdom of Tigranes (q.v. 1) the Great, who enlarged it at the expense of Parthian Adiabene. Its last king, Zarbienus, was executed for plotting with Lucullus (Plut. *Luc.* 29), who later looted its treasures. Pompey resisted Parthian claims, sent Afranius to overrun it, and restored most of it to Tigranes (Cass. Dio 37. 5. 4). Occupied by Trajan but regularly part of the Parthian and Sassanid Empires, it was finally ceded to Persia by Jovian (Ammian. 25. 7. 8 f.).

Baumgartner, *PW* vii, s.v. Γορδυηνή; U. Kahrstedt, *Artabanos III* (1950), 59 ff. E. W. G.

**GORGIAS** (1) of Leontini (*c.* 483–376 B.C.), one of the most influential of the sophists (q.v.), principally a teacher of rhetoric (cf. Pl. *Grg.* 449 a). His visit to Athens as an ambassador from his home town in 427 is a landmark in the history of rhetoric (q.v., § 1). Later writers attribute philosophical doctrines to him, especially the thesis that 'nothing exists, and if anything did we could not know about it'; but it seems likely that this was a paradox maintained as a *tour de force* rather than a serious position. Gorgias' main contribution to literature is in style; the extant *Encomium of Helen* (notable especially for the praise of λόγος, §§ 8–14) and *Defence of Palamedes*, and also the *Epitaphios* fragment (6 Diels–Kranz), illustrate clearly the seductions of his antithetical manner, with its balancing clauses and rhymes: antithesis, homoeoteleuton, and parisosis became known as σχήματα Γοργίεια. His influence can be seen in Antiphon and Thucydides, as well as in his great pupil Isocrates. Plato treats him with some respect; but Agathon's speech in *Symposium* 194 ff. is a vigorous parody.

FRAGMENTS. Diels, *Vorsokr.*⁵ 82 (76); L. Radermacher, *Artium Scriptores* (1951), B. vii. *Helena*, ed. O. Immisch, 1927. See G. B. Kerferd, *Phronesis* i (1955/6), 3 ff.; E. R. Dodds, ed. of Plato's *Gorgias* (1959), 6 ff.; Norden, *Ant. Kunstpr.* 63 ff.; J. D. Denniston, *Greek Prose Style* (1952), 8 ff.; G. A. Kennedy, *The Art of Persuasion in Greece* (1963), 61 ff. D. A. R.

**GORGIAS** (2) (1st c. B.C.), a rhetor, who taught Cicero's son at Athens in 44 B.C. He was best known for a treatise in four books Περὶ σχημάτων (cf. Quintil. 9. 2. 102 ff.), of which a Latin abridgement by Rutilius Lupus is extant (Halm, *Rhet. Lat. min.* 3–21).                          D. A. R.

**GORGO** or **MEDUSA,** a terrible monster in Greek mythology. Gorgo was the daughter of the marine deities Phorcys and Ceto. She had a round, ugly face, snakes instead of hair, a belt of the teeth of a boar, sometimes a beard, huge wings, and eyes that could transform people into stone. She had two immortal sisters, who in art are also shown in the shape of Gorgons, Sthenno ('the Strong') and Euryale ('the Wide Leaping'), with whom she lived in the far West, where Poseidon loved her. Perseus went in search of Gorgo, killed her with the aid of Athena, and escaped (Hes. *Theog.* 270). Her head adorned the aegis (q.v.) of Zeus and also that of Athena (*Il.* 5. 738). From the body of Gorgo blood sprang forth; from one vein blood that Asclepius used to revive the dead, from the other blood which he used to harm men (Apollod. 3. 10. 3). In the moment of her death Gorgo-Medusa gave birth to Pegasus and Chrysaor.

The myth of Gorgo-Medusa as known in classical Greece contained religious and folkloristic elements of diverse origin. The head of Gorgo, buried under the Agora of Argos (Paus. 2. 21. 5), seems to indicate that the Gorgoneion was originally an independent embodiment of apotropaic power. Medusa again may have been originally an independent earth goddess (L. Malten, *JDAI* 1914, 184; 1925, 121 ff.). In art, Perseus killing Gorgo and pursued by Gorgons is a popular subject during the archaic period; Gorgo alone, a running winged daemon, is also frequently shown, especially in Corinthian art. In the classical period Gorgo is humanized, and Hellenistic representations develop a definitely beautiful type of head for the dying maiden Gorgo (cf. Cic. *Verr.* 4. 124). Her head always remained a popular apotropaic symbol.

C. Hopkins, *AJArch.* 1934; H. Besig, *Gorgo und Gorgoneion* (1937); J. M. Woodward, *Perseus* (1937); C. Hulst, *Perseus and the Gorgon* (1947); T. Howe, *An interpretation of the Perseus-Gorgon myth in Greek literature and monuments through the classical period* (1952); I. Serrailler, *The Gorgon's Head* (1961); B. Goldman, *A Snake Goddess, in Asiatic Demonology, and the Gorgon* (1961); C. Hopkins, *The Sunny Side of the Greek Gorgon* (1961); W. Hermann, *MDAI(R)* 1963, 1; E. Kunze, *MDAI(A)* 1963, 74; M. O'Brien, *AJPhil.* 1964, 13.                    G. M. A. H.; J. R. T. P.

**GORTYN,** one of the most important towns of Dorian Crete and capital of the Roman province, was situated in the southern central plain of the island. Many ruins have been excavated, and many inscriptions found, among them the famous 'Code of Gortyn', containing large parts of a supplementary codification (probably *c.* 450 B.C.). It included many older laws, or referred to them; some of these are also preserved in other inscriptions. The code contains rules of civil law only, but some facts of public law are mentioned. The laws, lacking systematic order, deal with the family and family property, with slaves, surety, donations, mortgage, procedure in trials, and other items. The code of Gortyn is a mixture of primitive and developed regulations. Most interesting is the position of the slaves, who had certain rights for their protection; they were also allowed to have their own property, and even to marry free women. There was a clear distinction, especially in matters of hereditary right, between family and private property. There were detailed and rather liberal regulations on adoption and sole heiresses. Criminal law was still closely connected with family law, but in many cases money penalties had replaced previous forms of punishment, and frequently the fines were payable to the State. Self-defence was forbidden. Witnesses and compurgators, and the oath of the party, served to establish a case; but the judge decided at his own discretion. On the whole, the laws of Gortyn are the most important source of pre-Hellenistic Greek law, and reveal rather a

high standard of juristic conceptions, though it is not certain how far this code was valid even among Cretan states.

J. Kohler and E. Ziebarth, *Das Stadrecht von Gortyn* (1912); R. Dareste, B. Haussoullier, Th. Reinach, *Recueil des inscriptions juridiques grecques* (1891) i, 352 ff. cf. Tod, no. 36; V. Ehrenberg, *The Greek State* (1960); D. Levi, *Ann. scuola d'Atene* 1955–6. Date: M. Guarducci, *Riv. Fil.* 1938, 264 ff.; R. F. Willets (ed.), *The Law Code of G.* (1967).                    V. E.

**GOTHS,** a Germanic people, who left their original homes in southern Scandinavia about the beginning of the Christian era, and settled around the lower Vistula, where Tacitus knew of them. In the period A.D. 150–200 they migrated to the lands north of the Black Sea, and in 238 at latest began to raid the Roman Empire. In the mid third century they launched heavy attacks on the provinces of Asia Minor and the Balkans, but were checked by the victories of Gallienus and Claudius (2) Gothicus (qq.v.). A section of them, the Visigoths, occupied the province of Transdanubian Dacia, from which Aurelian (q.v.) withdrew the Roman army and administration (*c.* 275). The remainder, the Ostrogoths, built up a huge empire in the Ukraine, which they held until the Huns overran them *c.* 370. Escaping from Hun rule in 455, they lived in the Balkan provinces until 489 when they marched to Italy under the leadership of Theodoric the Great (q.v.). As for the Visigoths, the Huns drove them across the lower Danube in 376; and on 9 Aug. 378, led by Fritigern, they defeated and killed the Emperor Valens in the great battle of Adrianople. After living as Federates in Lower Moesia (382–95), they then, under the leadership of Alaric, devastated Greece, migrated to Italy, and in Aug. 410 sacked Rome. Thereafter they moved to Gaul and Spain, and in 418 settled as Federates between the mouths of the Garonne and the Loire with their capital at Toulouse; but in 475 King Euric threw off the overlordship of Rome and proclaimed an independent kingdom. His son Alaric II was defeated and killed by Clovis and the Franks at the battle of Vouillé in 507, and the Visigoths were driven from most of Gaul. They retreated to Spain, much of which had been conquered by Euric. In Spain the Visigothic kingdom survived until it was overrun by the Muslims in 711. Ulfila (*c.* 311–83) translated the Bible into Gothic and was responsible for the conversion of the Visigoths to Arian Christianity late in the fourth century. They became Catholics under King Reccared in 589.

L. Schmidt, *Die Ostgermanen²* (1942), 195 ff.; E. A. Thompson, *The Visigoths in the Time of Ulfila* (1966).
E. A. T.

**GRACCHUS** (1), TIBERIUS SEMPRONIUS (*PW* 51) curule aedile (216 B.C.) and *magister equitum* to Junius Pera after Cannae, commanded two legions of *volones* slaves enrolled after Cannae. As consul I (215) he thwarted Hannibal at Cumae, as proconsul (214) near Beneventum he defeated Hanno who was trying to join Hannibal from south Italy. Consul II (213); as proconsul in 212 he was surprised and killed probably in Lucania.                    H. H. S.

**GRACCHUS** (2), TIBERIUS SEMPRONIUS (*PW* 53), the censor, was augur in 204 B.C., accompanied the Scipios to the East in 190, negotiating with Philip V, and as tribune at the time of the prosecution of L. Scipio saved him from imprisonment. Envoy to Greece in 185, he became curule aedile in 182, and as praetor in 180 succeeded Q. Fulvius Flaccus in Spain. Here he completed the reduction of the Celtiberians by systematic operations and a liberal settlement (180–179), founding Gracchuris and giving peace for a generation. Consul in 177, he ruthlessly subjugated Sardinia (cf. Livy 41. 28. 8–10,

Censor in 169, with C. Claudius Pulcher, he intervened in the levies, opposed the *publicani*, and restricted the rights of freedmen; his austerity became famous. He served on embassies to the East (165, 162), was again consul (163), and died in 154. A man of high character and liberal thought, a fine strategist and great colonial governor, he dominated the policy of foreign consolidation and internal restoration towards the middle of the century. He married Cornelia, daughter of Scipio Africanus, and his twelve children included Tiberius and Gaius Gracchus.

Livy 37. 7; 38. 52 ff.; 39. ʰ24 and 33; bks. 40–5; Polyb. bks. 25 and 31–2; App *Hisp.* 43; Gell. 6. 19; Cic. *Prov. Cons.* 8. 18. De Sanctis, *Stor. Rom.* iv. 1, 240, 440, 463, 596, 611; J. Carcopino, *Autour des Gracques* (1928), 47; Scullard, *Rom. Pol.* 143, 204 ff., 282, 294 ff.; E. Badian, *Foreign Clientelae* (1958), 121 ff.; D. C. Earl, *Tiberius Gracchus* (1963), 49 ff.                                    A. H. McD.

**GRACCHUS** (3), TIBERIUS SEMPRONIUS (*PW* 54), son of (2) and Cornelia (q.v. 1), was cousin and brother-in-law of Scipio (q.v. 11) Aemilianus, under whom he served in 146 B.C. As quaestor (137) in Spain, he used his father's connexions and reputation to save Hostilius Mancinus' (q.v.) army by a treaty, which the Senate, on Scipio's advice, disowned. Embittered against Scipio for undermining his *fides*, he married a daughter of Ap. Claudius (q.v. 9) and, as tribune in 133 in Scipio's absence, proposed—on the advice of Claudius, the consul P. Scaevola (q.v. 2) and Crassus (q.v. 1) Mucianus—an agrarian law designed to solve the main social and economic problems of the day in a way profitable to this faction. The law reaffirmed the statutory (but long ignored) limit of 500 *iugera* of public land per person, allowed an extra 250 per child to make this more acceptable, and instituted a commission (to which he, his brother (4) and Claudius were appointed) to confiscate the surplus land—with power to judge on disputed boundaries—and distribute it in small holdings to poor citizens. The purpose of the bill was probably both to alleviate poverty (thus Plutarch) and to increase the number of men with sufficient property for military service (thus Appian). No doubt at the suggestion of his advisers (two of them eminent lawyers), he tried to short-circuit delaying tactics in the Senate (cf. LAELIUS 2) by putting the bill straight to the People—which was legal, but contrary to *mos maiorum*. It was vetoed by Octavius (q.v. 2)—who, persisting in opposition, was deposed by popular vote—and then passed in a harsher form. This deposition struck at the foundations of Roman constitutional practice and alarmed many hitherto uncommitted. Tiberius next took advantage of the death of Attalus III (of which, through inherited connexions with Pergamum, he had heard first) to propose that Attalus' property, left to Rome, should be used to equip the new allotment-holders. This prejudged the important question of whether to accept the bequest and struck a blow at the Senate's traditional (though not legally established) control of foreign affairs and finance. When he sought re-election in order to see his programme through, he aroused fears of tyrannical power even among some of his previous supporters. When his friend Scaevola refused to use force against a tribune, Scipio (q.v. 12) Nasica led a mob of senators and their clients against Tiberius. Taken by surprise, he and some of his adherents were killed on the Capitol. In 132 Popillius (q.v. 2) punished many of those surviving; but the land commission continued its work, for the moment unhampered, and Tiberius' opponents tried to claim the credit for moderate reform.

Tiberius' tribunate marks the introduction of murder into Roman politics and the beginning of the disintegration of the ruling oligarchy under the blows of Populares in its own ranks.

D. C. Earl, *Tiberius Gracchus* (1963). For further bibliography see next article. The sources on Tiberius Gracchus (3) are bedevilled by his brother's propaganda and by rival ancient interpretations.   E. B.

**GRACCHUS** (4), GAIUS SEMPRONIUS (*PW* 47), younger brother of (3), served under his cousin Scipio (q.v. 11) Aemilianus at Numantia (134/3 B.C.) and on his return to Rome made it his main aim to avenge Tiberius' death and continue his programme. A member of the agrarian commission from the start, he supported the plans of Fulvius Flaccus (q.v. 3) in 126, but was sent to Sardinia as quaestor. Returning in 124, despite obstacles raised by his enemies, he was elected tribune for 123 and again for 122. After laws meant to avenge his brother and secure himself against a similar fate, he passed a programme of radical reform, aided by friendly tribunes. The most important measures were: (1) a law assuring citizens of wheat at a reasonable (normally subsidized) price; laws founding colonies—including one on the site of Carthage which, early in 122, Gaius himself went to establish— and reviving land distributions; laws regulating army service and providing for public works throughout Italy —all these both to relieve poverty and to gain the support of the plebs; (2) a law to have contracts for the *decuma* (q.v.) of Asia sold by the censors in Rome; and two laws (one probably passed by M. Iunius Silanus and one by Acilius Glabrio (q.v. 2)) establishing a new procedure for *repetundae* (q.v.) trials and taking juries for them, finally, from the wealthiest non-senators (*see* EQUITES)—these to protect provincials from senatorial extortion, provide a sounder basis for budgeting, and set up men assumed to be uninterested in politics to control politicians; (3) finally, in 122, he proposed (but could not pass) a bill to give citizenship to Latins and Latin status to other Italians—probably still chiefly for economic reasons (*see* FLACCUS 3), but also to protect them against increasing oppression by Roman magistrates.

In 123 he found little opposition. In 122 Fannius (q.v.), for whom he had secured the consulship, and the noble tribune Drusus (q.v. 1) combined to defeat him on the citizenship bill, building up the common people's reluctance to share their privileges—a policy that ultimately led to the Social War. Gaius and Fulvius failed to secure re-election for 121. When their policies were attacked in that year, they resorted to violence and, after the Senate's first use of the so-called *senatus consultum ultimum* (q.v.), died in a riot. The consul Opimius (q.v.) severely punished many of their supporters.

Gaius was more gifted and more far-seeing than his brother. A proud aristocrat himself, a good orator and skilled at using the political system, he saw the need for radical reform, though not always the right way to achieve improvement. Aiming at the relief of poverty and the protection of citizens and allies from oppression; at the improvement of budgeting and administrative efficiency; above all, at the creation of a politically responsible senatorial class, subject to constitutional checks in its control of the state (which he did not intend to take from it); he in fact created, in the *equites* (q.v.), a new exploiting class, more oppressive than the Senate and not restrained by a tradition of public service or the exercise of political responsibility. Thus he ultimately reinforced the worse and neutralized the better characteristics of Senate rule. However, it was his enemies' final success that prepared the way for disaster.

Our chief sources on the Gracchi (apart from numerous passing references in Cicero) are Appian, *BCiv.* i and Plut. *Tiberius and Gaius Gracchus*. On the tribunates, see Broughton, *MRR* 1. 493, 513, 517. Recent treatment with bibliography and discussion of sources, in H. H. Scullard, *From the Gracchi to Nero*² (1963), ch. ii. See also E. Badian, *Hist.* 1962, 200 f. (bibliography 233 f.); R. J. Rowland, *TAPA* 1965, 361.                                    E. B.

**GRAECINUS**, JULIUS, entered the Senate under Tiberius and reached the praetorship. He is quoted by Columella (e.g. 1. 1. 14; 4. 3. 6) for his work on vines; possibly son of the Graecinus addressed by Ovid, *Am.* 2. 10, *Pont.* 1. 6, and father of Julius Agricola (Tac. *Agr.* 4), whose name may allude to farming tastes. Agricola's father was executed A.D. 39 or 40 (*AE* 1946, n. 94).

J. W. D.; G. B. A. F.

**GRAIAE** (*Γραῖαι*), in mythology, daughters of Phorcys and Ceto, by name Pemphredo, Dino, and Enyo, sisters of the Gorgons (Hes. *Theog.* 270 ff.); they were three (Aesch. *PV* 794 ff.). They are an incarnation of age, grey-haired from birth (Hesiod), with one eye and one tooth left (Aesch.). Perseus (q.v. 1) stole their eye and so made them tell him the way to the Gorgons (Pherecydes ap. schol. Ap. Rhod. 4. 1515); or threw it away (Aesch. ap. [Eratosth.] 22) and left them blind and unable to help their sisters.                                                    H. J. R.

**GRAMMAR, GRAMMARIANS** (Greek). Linguistic analysis and classification begin, in Greece, with the fifth-century sophists. Their phonetic studies are reflected in the title of a lost work of Democritus 'On euphonious and cacophonous letters', and in a fragment of Euripides' *Palamedes* *ἄφωνα καὶ φωνοῦντα συλλαβὰς τιθείς* .... Plato (*Cra.* 424 c; cf. *Tht.* 203 b) mentions a classification of the alphabetic sounds as (*a*) voiced (the vowels), (*b*) *ἄφωνα* but not *ἄφθογγα* (the *ἡμίφωνα* of Aristotle), and (*c*) *ἄφωνα καὶ ἄφθογγα* (the largest class): the last are the *ἄφωνα* of the Alexandrians, who followed Aristotle in dividing them into *δασέα*, *ψιλά*, and *μέσα* (*χ θ φ*, *κ τ π*, and *γ δ β*), and used *σύμφωνα* (consonants) to include both second and third classes, (*b*) and (*c*) above.

**2.** Plato notices two distinctions of accentual intonation, 'acute' and 'grave' (*Cra.* 399 b), Aristotle also a third, intermediate, our circumflex (*Poet.* 1456ᵇ33). In ps.-Arcad. at p. 186—probably a sixteenth-century interpolation—Aristophanes of Byzantium is said to have invented signs for the accents (and other marks); but earlier work in this subject was eclipsed by that of Aristarchus.

**3.** Grammatical classification of words begins with Protagoras, who first distinguished *γένη ὀνομάτων* as *ἄρρενα*, *θήλεα*, and *σκεύη*. Aristotle has the same terms, but sometimes uses *μεταξύ* for *σκεύη*, and notes that many *σκεύη* are *ἄρρενα* or *θήλεα*. By the first century B.C. *οὐδέτερον* (neuter) came into use, and *κοινόν* (common) was added, and *ἐπίκοινον* (i.e. of one gender but used of both sexes).

**4.** Plato (*Soph.* 261 d) makes a practical discrimination between examples of two classes of words, *ῥήματα* and *ὀνόματα*, distinguished by their potential functions as predications and designations respectively, in a sentence. Aristotle (*Poet.* 20) names and defines *ὄνομα*, *ῥῆμα*, *σύνδεσμος*, and *ἄρθρον*; but as to the two last the text is disputed as to both definitions and examples. These four, however, with *στοιχεῖον*, *συλλαβή*, *πτῶσις*, and *λόγος* (composite statement—possibly without verbs) Aristotle calls parts of speech. He includes under *πτώσεις* all forms of the noun (which comprises also our pronoun, adjective, and adverb) other than the *κλῆσις*, our nominative, and all verb-forms except the present indicative (*ῥῆμα* in the narrowest sense). These flexions, whether nominal or verbal, have no separate names. Subject and predicate are distinguished as *ὑποκείμενον* and *κατηγορημένον*.

**5.** The stages leading up to Stoic grammar are obscure. There is evidence that Chrysippus discriminated *τὰ προσηγορικά*, perhaps as a class of noun. Diogenes Babylonius recognized five parts of speech—Aristotle's with the addition of *προσηγορία* (common noun). His pupil, Antipater of Tarsus, added a sixth, named by him *μεσότης* (as allied to noun and verb), by others *πανδέκτης*, but excluded from the final Stoic classification, which was the same as that of Diogenes. The terminology of inflexion—as of most phenomena—was greatly developed

by the Stoics. In Chrysippus, *On the Five Cases*, the fifth was almost certainly the adverb (cf. Aristotle); for the Stoics did not reckon the vocative a case. The nominative they called *ὀρθή* or *εὐθεῖα*; the others (*πλάγιαι*, oblique) were *γενική*, indicating a *γένος*, *δοτική*, used after verbs of giving, and *αἰτιατική*, denoting the *αἰτιατόν*, the result caused. A tense (*χρόνος*), present (*ἐνεστώς*) or past (*παρῳχημένος*), might be *ἀτελής* (sometimes called *παρατατικός*), imperfect, or *τέλειος* (or *συντελικός*), perfect; a past tense might be described as *ἀόριστος*, undefined in respect of this distinction. The future tense was named *ὁ μέλλων* (*χρόνος*). Predications by finite verbs (*κατηγορήματα* or *συμβάματα*, while *ῥῆμα* is, in contrast, restricted to the infinitive) were classified as active (*ἐνεργητικά*), passive (*παθητικά*, including reflexives, *ἀντιπεπονθότα*), and *οὐδέτερα* (neuter, e.g. *ζῶ*); or, on another basis, as complete (our intransitive) and incomplete (our transitive —requiring an object), with other refinements as to *παρασυμβάματα* (e.g. *μέλει μοι*).

**6.** From their predecessors the Alexandrians adopted *ὄνομα* (but not, as an independent part of speech, *προσηγορία*), *ῥῆμα*, *σύνδεσμος*, and *ἄρθρον*; also the adverb (including our interjections), under a name, *ἐπίρρημα*, the history of which is obscure. To these they added *ἀντωνυμία* (personal and possessive pronouns only) and *πρόθεσις*—a term which Chrysippus used, but in what sense does not appear; the later Stoics had a class of *προθετικοὶ σύνδεσμοι*. The eighth part was created by separating the *μετοχή* (participle) from the verb; and some proposed, in vain, to give the infinitive and possessive adjective a like status. These eight were known to Aristarchus, and were standardized by the text-book of his pupil, Dionysius (q.v. 15) Thrax. Thus far Greek grammar was descriptive. With the Atticist movement we find prescriptive grammar coming to the fore. One of the results of this change is the growth of false forms, known only to grammarians and those who followed them.

**7.** Systematic syntax made little progress until the first century A.D. (*see* HABRON *and* THEON 1): the next century saw, however, the great and original work of Apollonius (q.v. 13) Dyscolus.

For the history of kindred studies, *see* GLOSSA (GREEK) *and* ETYMOLOGY. It should be noted that *γραμματική* is much wider in meaning than 'grammar'. Of the six elements in Dionysius Thrax's (q.v.) definition of *γραμματική* only two belong to 'grammar'; the rest fall under lexicography or literary criticism.

J. E. Sandys, *Hist. of Class. Schol.* i (1903); H. Steinthal, *Geschichte d. Sprachwissenschaft b. d. Gr. und Römern* (no index). G. Murray, *Greek Studies* (1946), 171 ff. R. H. Robins, *Ancient and Mediaeval grammatical theory in Europe* (1951); Christ-Schmid-Stählin. The most important Greek grammarians have been, or are to be, published in Teubner's *Grammatici Graeci* and *Lexicographi Graeci*.
P. B. R. F.; R. B.

**GRAMMAR, GRAMMARIANS** (Latin). The Romans' interest in formal grammar was stimulated, even if not first aroused, by Crates of Mallos (c. 169 B.C.). The Greek influence on Roman grammatical theory was permanent and is clearly indicated by the Latin terminology, e.g. *casus* (*πτῶσις*), *accentus* (*προσῳδία*), *coniugatio* (*συζυγία*). It was the doctrines of the Stoic scholars of Pergamum in their *τέχνη περὶ φωνῆς* (a part of the theory of *διαλεκτική*), and not (as is sometimes asserted) the work of Dionysius Thrax, which afforded the model for Roman grammatical treatises. The short school grammar, no less than the large comprehensive expositions, had three essential sections: (*a*) on *vox*, *littera*, *syllaba*, with an introduction defining *ars* and *ars grammatica*; (*b*) on the parts of speech with details of declensions, conjugations, etc.; (*c*) on the *vitia* and *virtutes orationis*.

When fully expanded, section (*b*) treated each of the eight *partes orationis* according to their *accidentia*: thus, nouns (including adjectives) were subdivided according to *qualitas* (*propria* or *appellativa*), *genus* (= gender), *figura* (*simplex* or *composita*, as *felix* : *infelix*), *numerus*, and *casus*; verbs according to *qualitas* (as *perfecta*, *inchoativa*, etc.), *genus* (*activum*, *passivum*, *neutrum*, *deponens*), *figura* (*simplex* or *composita*, *persona*, *numerus*, *modus*, *tempus*, *coniugatio*. Section (*c*) included discussions of *barbarismus*, *soloecismus*, *cetera vitia* (e.g. *pleonasmus*, *tapinosis*), *tropi* (e.g. *metaphora*, *onomatopoeia*), *metaplasmus*, *schemata lexeos*, and *schemata dianoeas*. Syntax was treated incidentally in sections (*a*) and (*b*), but sometimes (as in Priscian) a further section *de constructione* was appended. The later grammars frequently included other sections: *de orthographia*, *de differentiis*, *de idiomatibus* (i.e. divergences between Greek and Latin usage, e.g. *sequor te* : σοι ἕπομαι), *de metris* (in which all metres were frequently derived by *additio* and *detractio* from the dactylic hexameter and the iambic trimeter); but these topics were often the subjects of separate treatises.

2. Interest in grammatical matters is first attested in the ninth book of Lucilius. In the second century B.C. Aelius Stilo, in the first century B.C. Gnipho, Opilius, Cosconius, Ateius, Nigidius Figulus, and Santra are known as writers on grammar; but it is Varro's grammatical system (included in book I of his lost *Libri disciplinarum* and implicit in his *De Ling. Lat.*) which is the earliest we can reconstruct with any fullness. He distinguished only four parts of speech: nouns (including adjectives and pronouns), verbs, participles, and particles (including adverbs). The genitive, dative, and ablative cases he called *casus patricus*, *casus dandi*, and *casus sextus* (the last of which persisted for centuries alongside of *ablativus*); and nouns he grouped according to the ending of the nominative singular. The terms *declinatio* and *modus* were apparently not used by him, nor were the conjugations clearly defined.

3. No complete grammatical work of the first century A.D. is extant (if we except the very interesting sketch in Quint. 1. 4–8), but the *Ars* of Remmius Palaemon, known to Quintilian and quoted by later writers, was clearly a work of great importance. Planned on a large scale, it brought a new clarity into grammatical exposition. The eight parts of speech are now satisfactorily differentiated, the ending of the genitive singular becomes the basis for classification into declensions, and the four conjugations (I, II, III *correpta*, III *producta* [= IV]) are distinguished by the final syllable of the second person singular present active indicative. Furthermore, the practice of illustrating points by quotations from standard authors is firmly established.

4. Except for the *De Orthographia* of Velius Longus and a similar work of Terentius Scaurus, nothing remains of second-century A.D. grammatical work, though both these writers, like Flavius Caper, seem to have written comprehensive grammars. Of the third-century writers, Julius Romanus is known only by fragments, and the relatively short work of his contemporary Sacerdos (which omits the *vitia et virtutes orationis* and includes a section on metre) remains as our oldest extant Latin grammar. Possibilities of originality and innovation were apparently exhausted by the fourth century; for, apart from short grammars of the school-book type (e.g. Aelius Donatus), authors either boldly copied out with minor modifications large sections of their predecessors' work (e.g. Charisius) or fashioned a minute mosaic of borrowed phrases and ideas (e.g. Diomedes); in either case they achieved a fictitious novelty by their combination of sources and their illustrative quotations. To this century belong, besides those mentioned, Albinus,

Cominianus, Marius Victorinus, Servius (who expanded the *ars* of Donatus), and the bilingual Dositheus. From the fifth century have been preserved the treatises of Asmonius, Cledonius, Consentius, Phocas, Pompeius, and Rufinus, none of which is of major importance; but the early sixth century witnessed the publication of the vast grammar of Priscian (in eighteen books) which remained a standard work of reference for grammatical matters in the Middle Ages.

H. Keil (and others), *Grammatici Latini*, 8 vols. (1855–78), contains all the extant treatises from the third to sixth centuries A.D. (but for Charisius the standard ed. is now that of Karl Barwick, 1925; for Dositheus, that of J. Tolkiehn, 1913); G. Funaioli, *Grammaticae Romanae Fragmenta* (1907), gives the remains of republican and early imperial grammarians. A. Gudeman, s.v. 'Grammatik' in *PW*; K. Barwick, *Remmius Palaemon und die römische ars grammatica* (1922; = *Philologus*, suppl. xv, ii), especially 215 ff.; J. E. Sandys, *History of Classical Scholarship* i² (1906).                J. F. M.

**GRAMMAR, GREEK.** There are two fundamental reference works:

1. R. Kühner, *Ausführliche Grammatik der griechischen Sprache*, 3rd ed., I (Phonology and Morphology) by F. Blass (1890–92); II (Syntax) by B. Gerth (1898–1904).

2. E. Schwyzer, *Griechische Grammatik* (in I. von Müller's *Handbuch*), 3 vols. (1939–53).

Kuhner–Blass–Gerth is primarily a synchronic descriptive grammar, while Schwyzer's treatment is diachronic. Schwyzer contains full bibliographical material.

For Hellenistic and New Testament Greek the indispensable reference work is:

3. F. Blass, *Grammatik des neutestamentlichen Griechisch*, 10th ed. by A. Debrunner (1959).

The history of the Greek language is treated by:

4. A. Meillet, *Aperçu d'une histoire de la langue grecque*[7] avec bibliographie mise à jour et complétée par D. Masson (1965).

5. O. Hoffmann and A. Debrunner, *Geschichte der griechischen Sprache*, 2 vols. (1953–4). N.B. This work does not take account of the decipherment of the Linear B tablets.

The dialects of ancient Greek are treated exhaustively n two works:

6. A. Thumb, *Handbuch der griechischen Dialekte*, 2nd ed., vol. i by E. Kieckers (1932), vol. iii by A. Scherer (1959).

7. F. Bechtel, *Die griechischen Dialekte*³, 3 vols. (1963).

A briefer treatment of the dialects with select texts is found in:

8. C. D. Buck, *The Greek Dialects* (U.S.A. 1955).

A detailed descriptive treatment of Classical Greek syntax is given by:

9. W. W. Goodwin, *Syntax of the Moods and Tenses of the Greek Verb*, rewritten and enlarged (1912 and reprints).

The most complete treatment of the particles is given by:

10. J. D. Denniston, *The Greek Particles*² (1954).
R. B.

**GRAMMAR, LATIN.** There are two fundamental reference works:

1. R. Kühner, *Ausführliche Grammatik der lateinischen Sprache*. New ed. by F. Holzweissig and C. Stegmann, 3 vols. (1912–14).

2. M. Leumann, *Lateinische Laut- und Formenlehre* (1963); J. B. Hofmann and A. Szantyr, *Lateinische syntax und Stilistik* (1965) (both in I. von Müller's *Handbuch*). Leumann–Hofmann–Szantyr is more diachronic in treatment than Kühner–Holzweissig–Stegmann.

The history of the Latin language is treated in broad outline by:

3. L. R. Palmer, *The Latin Language* (1954).

For detailed discussion of historical phonology and morphology reference should be made to:

4. W. M. Lindsay, *The Latin Language* (1894).

5. F. Sommer, *Handbuch der lateinischen Laut- und Formenlehre³* (1948).

6. R. G. Kent, *The Sounds of Latin³* (U.S.A. 1945).

7. R. G. Kent, *The Forms of Latin* (U.S.A. 1946).

The most complete treatment of morphology, on a synchronic basis, is to be found in:

8. F. Neue, *Formenlehre der lateinischen Sprache*, 3rd ed. by C. Wagener, 4 vols. (1892–1905).

A modern survey of Latin syntax is given by:

9. E. C. Woodcock, *A New Latin Syntax* (1959).

A fuller, historical discussion of many aspects of Latin syntax is given by:

10. E. Löfstedt, *Syntactica²*, 2 vols. (Lund, 1933–42).

The evidence for the spoken Latin underlying the literary language is discussed by:

11. J. B. Hofmann, *Lateinische Umgangssprache²* (1936).

A good introduction to later Latin both literary and non-literary is:

12. E. Löfstedt, *Late Latin* (Oslo, 1959).

On vulgar Latin, the ancestor of the Romance languages see, in addition to 3 above,

13. C. H. Grandgent, *An Introduction to Vulgar Latin* (U.S.A. 1907).

14. V. Väänänen, *Introduction au latin vulgaire* (1963).

R. B.

**GRAMMATEIS**, secretaries, of various kinds; generally not responsible magistrates, though like them elected (mostly by lot), and serving for a year only. They are found in most Greek States (sometimes called γραμματισταί or γραφεῖς). In Athens the *grammateus* of the *boule* was, until *c.* 367 B.C., an elective official; but he served for a prytany only. After this the *boule* had two secretaries, both elected by lot (but not from the *bouleutai*) and serving for one year. The γραμματεὺς τῆς βουλῆς performed the general secretarial duties. The γραμματεὺς κατὰ πρυτανείαν supervised the copying, registering, and preserving of all State documents, and (at first) arranged for their publication when this was ordered; his name was normally put at the head of a published document as a guarantee of its accuracy. The γραμματεὺς τῷ δήμῳ or τῆς πόλεως read out dispatches, etc., to the *ekklesia*. The *prytaneis* (q.v.) also had a *grammateus* (one of their own number); and collegiate magistracies, as the Eleven, the *Hellenotamiai*, the *Thesmothetai*, had theirs—the last chosen from the *phyle* not represented by the nine archons, and performing some duties for his *phyle*.

A more important official, though serving for a year only, was the γραμματεὺς τοῦ κοινοῦ or τῶν συνέδρων of Federal States, such as the Aetolian and Achaean Confederacies. He generally ranked next after the higher military officers.

A. W. G.

**GRAMMATICUS** in rhetoric has a wider meaning than 'grammarian', and implies a professor of literature, who carried on the elementary work of the *litterator* and trained a student for advanced rhetoric or even trenched on its province (Quint. *Inst.* 2. 1. 4–6). The Greek γραμματικός supplanted the Latin *litteratus*: *grammatici* were *poetarum explanatores* (Cic. *Div.* 1. 116) and expounders of a still more extensive field of knowledge (Cic. *De Or.* 187). Suetonius (*Gram.* 4) gives an instructive summary. See EDUCATION, IV. 6.

J. W. D.

**GRANIUS** (*PW* 13) **LICINIANUS** wrote a handbook of Roman history in annalistic arrangement going back ultimately to Livy, but including antiquarian material,

e.g. signs and wonders, anecdotes, and curiosities. The remains, preserved in a London palimpsest, come from books 26 (?), 28, 33 (?), 36, referring to events of 165, 105, 78 B.C. The work, which shows archaism in style, an interest in Sallust, and the aim of school use, was written after Hadrian's completion of the Olympieum in Athens, at earliest in the Antonine period.

EDITIONS. G. Camozzi (1900); M. Flemisch (1904). O. Dieckmann, *De Gran. Lic. fontibus et auctoritate* (1896); M. Flemisch, *Gran. Lic.* (1898).
A. H. McD.

**GRAPHE** (γραφή) in Athenian law was a type of prosecution, the commonest kind of public case. The name seems to imply that when this procedure was instituted its distinctive feature was that the charge was made in writing, whereas in other procedures the charge was made orally. It may perhaps have been introduced by Solon early in the sixth century B.C. By the fifth century charges in other cases also were put in writing, but the name *graphe* continued to be used for ordinary public cases, excluding special types like *apagoge* or *phasis*.

Sometimes the term was used more loosely, either to refer to any type of public case, or to refer to the written charge in any case, public or private.

*See* DIKE, GRAPHE PARANOMON.

J. H. Lipsius, *Das attische Recht und Rechtsverfahren* (1905–15), 237 ff.; G. M. Calhoun, *The Growth of Criminal Law in Ancient Greece* (1927).
D. M. M.

**GRAPHE PARANOMON** (γραφὴ παρανόμων) in Athens was a prosecution (*see* GRAPHE) for the offence of proposing in the assembly or council a law or decree which was contrary to an existing law in form or content. As soon as the accuser made a sworn statement (ὑπωμοσία) that he intended to bring a *graphe paranomon* against the proposer, the proposal, whether already voted on or not, was suspended until the trial had been held. The case was tried in a lawcourt (*see* DIKASTERION) under the presidency of the *thesmothetai* (q.v.). If the jury condemned the proposer, his proposal was annulled and he was punished, usually by a fine; if a man was convicted three times of this type of offence, he suffered disfranchisement (*see* ATIMIA). If more than a year had elapsed since a law had been passed, its proposer could no longer be prosecuted, but the law could still be attacked and annulled by a similar procedure.

It is not known when this type of prosecution was instituted, but the earliest known cases are the prosecution of Speusippus by Leogoras in 415 B.C. (And. 1. 17) and the prosecution of Demosthenes the general at about the same time (Plut. *Mor.* 833 d). At that period ostracism (q.v.) had recently fallen out of use, and in its place a *graphe paranomon* became a popular method of attacking prominent politicians; the fourth-century politician Aristophon (q.v.) boasted that he had been acquitted on this type of charge seventy-five times. The most famous example is the prosecution of Ctesiphon by Aeschines (q.v. 1) for his proposal to confer a crown on Demosthenes; the surviving speeches of Aeschines *Against Ctesiphon* and Demosthenes *On the Crown* were written for this trial. Other extant speeches composed for such cases are those of Demosthenes *Against Leptines*, *Against Androtion*, *Against Aristocrates*, and *Against Timocrates*, and Hypereides *Against Philippides*.

J. H. Lipsius, *Das attische Recht und Rechtsverfahren* (1905–15), 383 ff.; Hignett, *Hist. Athen. Const.* 210 ff.
D. M. M.

**GRATIAN**, FLAVIUS, Roman Emperor (A.D. 367–83), was the son of Valentinian I. Most of his reign was spent in the defence of Gaul. An earnest Catholic he was much influenced by St. Ambrose. He was the first Emperor to omit the words *pontifex maximus* from his titulature; and despite the protests of Symmachus he ordered the statue of Victory to be removed from the Senate House in Rome. He was overthrown by Magnus (q.v.) Maximus and was murdered at Lyons in 383.

A. Cameron, *JRS* 1968, 96 ff. E. A. T.

**GRATTIUS 'FALISCUS'** (less correct 'Gratius', Buecheler, *Rh. Mus.* 1880, 407: *CIL* vi. 19–117 ff.; his connexion with Falerii, based on 1. 40 and the epithet 'Faliscus' reported from a lost MS., are not universally accepted), Augustan poet contemporary with Ovid before A.D. 8 (*Pont.* 4. 16. 34), has left one work in about 540 hexameters, the *Cynegetica*. In it he treats of the chase and especially the management of dogs for hunting. It is difficult to decide whether he owes anything to Xenophon (or pseudo-Xenophon) and Plutarch; for his list of breeds of dogs he may have used an Alexandrian source. The Latin influence most operative upon him is that of Virgil's *Georgics*; but he also borrowed from the *Aeneid* and from Ovid (Verdière i. 33–57). Authorities differ as to his influence on the similar poem by Nemesianus (q.v.).

The earlier part of his work, after a proem, deals with equipment for capturing game (nets, snares, spears, and arrows); the remaining and longer part (150–541) deals with huntsmen, dogs, and horses. Here, the allotment of nearly 300 lines to dogs (their breeding, points, and ailments) justifies his title. Fortunately for a reader's interest, Grattius diversifies his theme by the introduction of episodes. There is pleasant relief in these digressions—a eulogy on the chase, the accounts of two clever huntsmen (Dercylus and, considerably later, Hagnon), the homily on the deleterious effects of luxurious fare on human beings (somewhat amusingly juxtaposed with plain feeding for dogs), and two descriptive passages, a Sicilian grotto and a sacrifice to the huntress deity Diana. The concluding portion on horses is mutilated. Grattius' diction and versification are Augustan, but he does not always express himself lucidly. How far his inadequacies are to be ascribed to his exiguous MS. tradition (Vindob. 277 is the sole independent witness) is uncertain.

TEXTS. M. Haupt, *Ovidii Halieutica, Gratii et Nemesiani Cynegetica* (1838); E. Baehrens, *PLM* i (1879); G. Curcio, *Poet. Lat. Min.* (1902); J. P. Postgate, *CPL* ii (1905); F. Vollmer, *PLM* ii. 1 (1911). Cf. also J. A. Richmond, *The Halieutica ascribed to Ovid* (1962), 1 ff.

EDITIONS (C = commentary, T = translation). P. J. Enk (C) (1918); Duff, *Minor Lat. Poets* (T); R. Verdière (C, T, bibliography) (1964).

SPECIAL STUDIES. M. Fiegl, *Des Gr. Cynegetica, seine Vorgänger u. seine Nachfolger* (1890). J. W. D.; E. J. K.

**GREECE** (*Geography*). Greece with the Aegean basin is a section of the great mountain zone, a product of tertiary earth-movements, running from the Himalaya to the Alps; a section tilted and sunken towards the east, where the Cyclades are the mountain-tops of a land submerged. A volcano remains active in Thera. The breach between the Cyclades and the eastern Aegean islands, off Asia Minor, is ancient enough to be marked by significant differences in the native flora.

2. To west and south, the Aegean basin has a high rim. The many-folded ranges of Pindus, with some peaks exceeding 8,000 feet in height (Parnassus is just 8,000), run NNW.–SSE. from Albania (Illyria) to the Corinthian Gulf. Their line is continued in the ranges of Parnon (6,427) and Taÿgetus (7,895 feet), dropping to the southern capes of Malea and Taenarum (Matapan) respectively. Turning east, the 'rim' reappears in the mountains of Crete, where Ida and the White Mountains slightly exceed 8,000 feet. The greatest sea-depths in the Mediterranean are found off the west coast, with 2,000 fathoms west of Cephallenia and more west of Crete. None of the above mountains, nor any other in Greece, approaches

the height of Olympus (9,750 feet), which towers above its neighbours in the coastal range and the northern frontier range of Thessaly.

3. The mountains, whose slopes formerly carried much oak and beech forest, a protection against the terrible later denudation, are mainly of blue-grey tertiary limestone; in a few places, as in Crete and Cephallenia, cretaceous rocks appear. In places, where the limestone has been metamorphosed under great pressure, it has become crystalline; hence the famous white marbles of Paros, Naxos, Thasos, and of Mount Pentelicus in Attica, and the coloured marbles, valued in the Roman Empire, of Tenos, Scyros, Euboea, and Thessaly. Other valuable minerals are rare. The gold and silver mines of Siphnos were worked out or flooded in late archaic times, and the chief source of gold in the Aegean area was now in the Pangaean massif in Thrace; but the silver mines of Laurium in Attica and iron-ores in Laconia played a considerable part in the rise to power of Athens and Sparta.

4. Rain falls in the Mediterranean mainly in winter; in Greece from mid May to late August there is normally none. The mountains intercept the rain-bearing westerly winds, producing a disparity in rainfall between west and east: Corfu has 45 inches in an average year, Attica about 16. The west coast of Asia Minor is again well-watered, and fertile; hence the early power of the Ionian cities, cut short only through their exposure to enemies inland. Summer temperatures can reach 40° C. (104° F.) in Athens, and more in mountain-girdled Thessaly; but the dry air and north winds of summer (a constant factor in Aegean sailors' calculations) render the climate of Athens one of the most bracing in the world. Agricultural work is intense in late spring, with harvest in May, and autumn, with ploughing and sowing after the first rain, vintage and the long business of olive-picking, but slack in winter and summer; an alternation of work and leisure, in which some have found one of the keys to an understanding of the Greek achievement.

5. But the vital factor determining the course of ancient Greek history, the struggles of the city-states, was the scarcity, and the distribution in scattered pockets among the mountains, of arable land. The chief alluvial plains of the peninsula—those of Laconia, Messenia, 'hollow' Elis and Argos; of Agrinium in Aetolia; of Eleusis, Athens, the 'midland' and Marathon in Attica; the plain of Thebes and the Boeotian Cephisus valley, its adjacent hill-sides studded with the cities of Boeotia and Phocis; the Spercheius valley and even the wide plains of Thessaly (qq.v.)—all together make up only a small part of the land area. In the highlands and islands, such land is still scarcer. Where it occurs, it is tolerably fertile, though better for olives (between which corn is grown) and vines than for the essential grain; and the difference between its quality and that of the hill-foot land, to which peasants perforce expanded, tended to deepen the gulf between them and the old 'best families' in the plains (*see* PEISISTRATUS). The hill-country between the chief centres of population, and the abundance of strong citadels, helped to confirm autonomy at the city level; the success of Sparta, controlling Taÿgetus, in conquering Messenia, was exceptional, and fateful. Expansion overseas and the import of food were the only solution (*see* COLONIZATION).

6. To the traveller northward-bound, the change of scenery in Thessaly and still more in the plains of Macedonia is striking; but precisely here, the characteristic ways of life of the city-state did not take root. Only the colonies in the Chalcidic peninsula played some part in the affairs of Greece proper (*see* OLYNTHUS). Sicily and Magna Graecia (qq.v.) were as an America to Greece's Europe; but the Greek heart-land remained in the

peninsula, 'rough', as Odysseus said of Ithaca, 'but a good mother of men'.

M. I. Newbigin, *The Mediterranean Lands* (1924); E. C. Semple, *Geography of the Mediterranean Region* (1932); Cary, *Geographic Background*; Sir John Myres, *Geographical History in Greek Lands* (1953).

A. R. B.

**GREECE** (*History*). Greek history begins not with the first occupation of the peninsula and islands which we call Greece but with the arrival, several millennia later, of those Greek-speaking invaders whose language has been dominant over all comers of whatever race down to the present day. The Hellenes, as the Greeks of classical times called themselves, traced their ancestors back to Thessaly, then ruled by Deucalion's descendants 'Hellen, the war-loving king, and his sons Dorus, Xuthus, and Aeolus', and to southern Macedonia where 'Magnes and Macedon, delighting in horses, lived in the area of Olympus and Pieria'; and they saw Jason, Perseus, Heracles, Laius, and many others as Greek heroes living in Greece before the Trojan War, that is before the last phase of the Bronze Age. The decipherment of Linear B has provided a *terminus ante quem* Greek was written on the mainland and in Crete, whether that terminus is dated *c.* 1400 B.C. or *c.* 1250 B.C. (*see* MINOAN SCRIPTS). Extensive excavation has shown that the mainland experienced large-scale invasions *c.* 2000–1700 B.C.; thereafter settled conditions enabled Mycenaean civilization (q.v.) to develop and flourish. It is generally agreed that these invasions marked the coming of the first waves of Greeks, their dialects being Ionic (Ion being son of Xuthus) and Aeolic, and in the following centuries Greek dominated the languages of the earlier races of the mainland. The last wave of Greeks, those represented by the ancestor Dorus, entered Greece in the century *c.* 1125–*c.* 1025, their dialects being Dorian and north-west Greek. As they came from the areas of Epirus and Western Macedonia, it seems likely that the reservoir of Greek-speaking peoples from which these waves of invasion spread was situated *c.* 2000 B.C. in Albania and in western and southern Macedonia.

Mycenaean civilization resulted from a fusion of the Greek genius and the skills of their predecessors on the mainland, of Minoan culture in Crete (*see* MINOAN CIVILIZATION) and of inspiration from the Near East (kings such as Danaus, Cadmus, and Pelops having come from overseas, according to the Greek tradition). One Greek element was love of war; it enabled the Mycenaeans to capture Crete and the southern islands, to carry Mycenaean arms and trade to the Levant and to Sicily and Italy, and finally to sack Priam's city, Troy. The legends and the physical remains show that wealth and power were concentrated in the citadels of the kings and their noble retainers, champions in battle, armed with bronze weapons and equipped with horse-drawn chariots, an élite as remote as the medieval knights from the commoners. Love of war was one of the factors which weakened the Mycenaean world in the last century and a half of its existence. Many citadels were strengthened by even more massive fortifications; Thebes was sacked by its rival Argos; the palace at Pylos was destroyed, perhaps by its neighbours, perhaps by pirates from the Adriatic Sea. Although the Greek kings combined to capture Troy, they returned to an even more troubled Greece. As we learn from the Nostoi (*see* HOMER *and* EPIC CYCLE), from Thucydides (1. 12), and from the results of excavation, internal revolution and inter-state warfare caused widespread destruction. The annihilation of Troy, the weakening of her allies, and the deterioration of the Mycenaean world opened the way for invaders from the north. Hordes overran Asia Minor early in the twelfth century and set up waves of migration which threatened Egypt. Invasions of central Greece were followed by the so-called Dorian invasion which overthrew Mycenaean power in the Peloponnese for ever (*c.* 1125 B.C.) and set up waves of migration overseas. The Iron Age started in chaos and in poverty, so far as Greek lands and the eastern Mediterranean were concerned.

Our knowledge of the Late Bronze Age is being constantly enlarged by excavation and by the decipherment of inscribed tablets but mainly in matters of economic and material life. Greek mythology which was concerned to a remarkable extent with the last century and a half of the Mycenaean world gives us some idea of the beliefs and motives of men at that time. The epic poems of Homer and the Epic Cycle (qq.v.) *may* supply a much fuller and a generally authentic picture of Greek life towards the end of the first great age of Greek achievement. As these poems were composed from 800 B.C. onwards in the form in which they have survived and as even the earliest of them, the *Iliad*, was at least four centuries later than the events in the Trojan War which it describes, some scholars regard them as almost wholly fictitious. The Greeks of the classical period thought otherwise, and the results of archaeological investigation have gone far to justify their credence. For example, the poems describe the Greeks not as Hellenes or Dorians but as *Akhaioi* and *Danaoi*, and these names have appeared on Hittite and Egyptian documents which were contemporary with the period of the Trojan War. The Catalogue of Greek allies (*Iliad* 2. 485–760) provides a map of political power which was at variance with the situation *c.* 800 B.C. but has been strikingly vindicated through excavation as true of the Late Bronze Age. The evaluation of poetic evidence is a fascinating problem in Greek history.

The invasions of *c.* 1125–1025 B.C. were on a more massive scale than those of *c.* 2000–1700 B.C.; for they brought a completely new population to many parts of the mainland. Sometimes the invaders expelled the earlier inhabitants, sometimes they held them in serfdom, sometimes they merged with them. Attica and Arcadia alone preserved their independence and became centres for refugees from other Mycenaean countries: Attica because she preserved the unity, centred on Athens, which Theseus had brought about, and she was attacked only when the forces of invasion were spent, and Arcadia because the mountaineers were as tough and vigorous as the invaders. Peoples displaced from Thessaly and countries to the south, speaking the Aeolian dialect, went overseas to occupy Lesbos and the northern sector of western Asia Minor. Peoples displaced from the Peloponnese and the Isthmus and led by refugees who had been adopted by Athens occupied the islands of the central Aegean and the central sector of western Asia Minor; they and the Athenians spoke Ionic dialects. Dorians, who pressed on after capturing most of the Peloponnese, occupied Melos, parts of Crete, the southern islands, and the southern sector of western Asia Minor. The north-western islands and mainland were swamped by the rearguard of the invading peoples who came from further north. The map of classical Greece was largely drawn by 900 B.C.—a map entirely different from that of Mycenaean Greece—and the newcomers together with people of Mycenaean origins were destined to produce a second age of great achievement, markedly different from its predecessor except in one respect, love of war.

This was not apparent in 1125–900 B.C. The unit of organization was the village in most of the mainland and in Crete, but the villages were split by tribal and family feuds, and in Dorian areas by the gulf between the masters and the serfs. The first development was the partnership of several villages which was known as the *polis* (q.v.; Arist. *Pol.* 1252b28), small, compact, based on race and initially self-sufficient. The earliest-known *poleis* of this kind were formed in Crete, Sparta, Corinth, and Megara, all Dorian states in which the masters alone had the franchise. At Sparta the creation of the *polis* made possible the reduction of the Dorian villages in Laconia and later in 720 B.C. the annexation of Messenia, two achievements which laid the economic basis for Sparta's greatness. But it was the organization of the Spartiates within their *polis* which was most remarkable (*see* SPARTA): State education, military mess-life for men to the age of 60, equality of the franchised in politics and in agricultural property, free use of State-owned serfs (Helots) and the brigading of the franchised for political and military purposes not by racial tribes but by residential qualifications. The constitution had the same elements as in other primitive *poleis*—King, Council, and Assembly—but gave more power to the Assembly of 'Equals', which elected the councillors and made final decisions on the Council's proposals, and less power to the two kings (for Sparta had two royal families), who were members of the Council (called the Gerousia); later, when the Assembly's powers declined, its elected magistrates (the Ephors) represented its interests. Thucydides attributed the power of Sparta to this organization and constitution, which he dated to the late ninth century (1. 18. 1); his attribution is generally accepted, though many scholars lower his date.

Cultural revival came from the east, where the Ionian school of Epic poetry reached its zenith in the Homeric poems and the skill of the Phoenicians in seafaring, art, and writing (*see* ALPHABET) inspired Greek traders. One effect of political development and cultural revival was the ability to launch the colonizing movement (*see* COLONIZATION, GREEK), which was led by seafaring commercial states, such as Miletus, Paros, Chalcis, Megara, and Corinth, and planted hundreds of small independent *poleis* on the seaboards of the Black Sea, the northern Aegean, the north-west mainland, Italy, Sicily, southern France and Spain, and Cyrenaica, generally within the period 750–550 B.C. Corinth alone retained some political influence over her colonies; she was able to apply sanctions because she controlled the porterage on a runway (*diolkos*) across the Isthmus for trade between the Aegean basin and the western Mediterranean and she held the lead in naval construction. Aegina too benefited from the expanding trade which resulted from the colonizing movement; her wealth enabled her to be the first State of the western Aegean to adopt coinage (invented in Lydia; *see* COINAGE, GREEK) soon after 650 B.C.

Another beneficiary was Athens. A large but loosely organized State, it had launched the Ionian migration but had since then shown less energy and initiative than the young Dorian *poleis*. Wealth and privilege were still concentrated in the leaders of the familial units—clans, phratries, and tribes. They held the archonships (which had replaced the monarchy and its officers) and formed the Areopagus Council; and their power was such that the State authorized them to hold bankrupt debtors on the land in a form of serfdom and (where the debtors were not landowners) sell their victims as slaves. This chaos was ended in 594 B.C. by Solon (q.v.), the founder of the progressive Athenian State. He abolished serfdom and enslavement of Athenians by Athenians, established a people's court (Heliaea) to safeguard the equality of all Athenians before the law, classed the citizens not by racial qualifications but by financial resources, and directed the Athenian economy towards the commercial field alongside Corinth. His constitutional reforms were directed towards making the Assembly effective but controlled; to this end he established as its steering committee a Council of 400, nominated from the three higher classes. The magistrates were now answerable to the Heliaea as well as to the Areopagus; candidature for office was restricted to certain classes, members of the fourth and lowest class being excluded. The purposes of Solon were thwarted by prolonged faction but were fulfilled in part by an enlightened party leader, Pisistratus, who seized power, ruled as tyrant (546–527 B.C.), and was succeeded by his sons (527–510 B.C.). Many wealthy States had already experienced the rule of tyrants (Corinth, for instance, from c. 657 B.C. to c. 582 B.C.), capable men who put an end to faction, promoted the prosperity of the State but left a legacy of political animosity (*see* TYRANNY).

Inter-state relations were facilitated by the religious centres and festivals (*see* DELPHI, OLYMPIA, DODONA, DELOS, NEMEA, ISTHMIA) and by the common bond of aristocratic oligarchy, which prevailed in the archaic period. The tyrants too were aristocrats and favoured dynastic and military alliances. Wars tended to be between rival States—Sparta and Argos, or Chalcis and Eretria—and rules of warfare were laid down by the religious league (*see* AMPHICTIONIES). The first State to initiate a system of lasting alliances was Sparta c. 550 B.C. She attracted other States because her constitution was stable, her army was incomparable, and her territorial ambitions were satisfied, and in the sixth century she overthrew the last tyrant in several States. The alliances were defensive alliances between Sparta and an individual state, but they each contained two clauses in Sparta's interest: that she commanded the allied forces and that her allies helped her against the Helots. Before the end of the century Sparta and her allies created a machinery for the formation of policy: the Spartan State deliberated independently, the assembly of allied representatives—each State casting one vote—deliberated independently, and a joint policy was formed by agreement of the two chambers. Under this bi-cameral system Sparta as military commander (*hegemon*) had an equal say with the sum of her allies, and the organization was known as 'The Lacedaemonians and their allies', οἱ Λακεδαιμόνιοι καὶ οἱ σύμμαχοι. It has been called by modern scholars 'the Peloponnesian League' and more correctly, because it was a military coalition called into existence only if a defensive alliance was invoked, 'the Spartan Alliance'.

In 510 B.C. 'the Lacedaemonians and their allies' included most Peloponnesian States but not Argos; Aegina; and several central Greek States, including Athens which had been liberated with Spartan aid from her last tyrant. However, the dominance of Sparta was repugnant to Ionian Athens. Faction broke out again, and despite Spartan intervention Athens broke away under a democratic leader, Cleisthenes, defeated Boeotia and Chalcis when they attacked her, and held off a third enemy, Aegina. The surprising success of Athens was due to the foresight of Solon and the policy of the Pisistratids, which had placed her ahead even of Corinth in commercial prosperity, and to the brilliance of Cleisthenes (q.v. 1), who united and inspired the relatively large Athenian State by his democratic reforms. He destroyed an important source of aristocratic power, which worked through the clan system, by establishing ten new tribes recruited on a territorial basis from *demes* (q.v.) or small wards. The new tribes and their constituent demes had their own religious and political activities; and they each provided by a system of election in demes and sortition in tribes a group of fifty State councillors annually. The ten groups made up the democratic Council of 500, each group sitting in permanent committee for a tenth of a year (*see* PRYTANEIS) and the whole Council meeting regularly as a steering committee for the Assembly and as an organ of administration. Replacing the Solonian Council of 400, it acted alongside the Council of the Aeropagus, which remained guardian of the constitution. In 501/0 B.C. the people elected one *strategos* (q.v.) from each tribe to command the armed forces for one year.

The expansion of Greece and the maturing of the city-states had taken place when their neighbours were unaggressive or backward. But the sudden rise of Persia changed the situation. When Darius crossed the Bosporus *c.* 514 B.C., his empire extended from the Indus valley to the Mediterranean coast and included the Greek States in Asia Minor; and although discomfited by the Scythians he controlled the north Aegean coast and some islands off the Asiatic coast. The presence of this colossus did not stop the Greek States of the mainland from warring with one another; but it alarmed Sparta, which opposed Persia in diplomacy, and it tempted Argos, Athens, and other States to intrigue with Persia. In 499 B.C. a Persian force intervened at Naxos, in the centre of the Aegean. Its lack of success led to a revolt by the Ionians, which was supported at first by Athens and Eretria. Although the revolt spread to other Greek States on the Asiatic coast, to Caria, and to Cyprus, the Persian armies proved too strong and its final sea-battle at Lade Greek disunity brought disaster. A Persian expeditionary force destroyed Eretria but was defeated by Athens and Plataea at Marathon in 490 B.C., and a huge army and a large fleet invaded the Greek mainland from the north in 480 B.C. (*see* PERSIAN WARS). The unexpected victories of the Greeks were due to the superior equipment and fighting power of the hoplites, to the new Athenian fleet, to the seamanship and ramming tactics of the trireme crews (*see* TRIREMES), and to the co-ordination of operations on land and at sea; in a wider sense to the formation of a Greek League (similar to the Ionian League in that each State had one vote) and its election of Sparta to command on both elements; and in the widest sense to the libertarian spirit and vigorous intelligence of the Greek States. In the West the same qualities enabled the Greeks of Sicily (q.v.) to defeat the Carthaginians decisively.

The expansion of the Greek world and the defeat of Persia and Carthage were the greatest achievements of the Greek city-states in terms of foreign policy. They were due in the main to the well-directed dynamism of the city-states and to their ability to combine in a crisis. The sense of direction or purpose in the city-state of this period sprang from a solidarity of feeling among the citizens who found a common focus in the religion of tribe and clan and in the worship of the gods and goddesses of the State; we can see this sense of purpose in the poetry of Tyrtaeus, Solon, Pindar, and Aeschylus (qq.v.). One factor in their ability to combine was a Panhellenic feeling, which contrasted Greek and barbarian ways and found religious expression in the worship of the Olympian gods and in the festivals of Delphi, Olympia, Nemea, and the Isthmus (qq.v.); it inspired a large number of states to resist foreign aggression in a spirit which was not found in later centuries. After the Persian Wars the forces of traditional corporate religion began to ebb; rationalism, humanism, and individualism in inter-State relations and in social conduct within the State gained ground, bringing to birth unparalleled intellectual and artistic achievements but a diminution of creative political power in the Greek world. In the aftermath of victory over Persia Sparta lost her power of leadership because she sought only her own advancement in refusing to let Athens rebuild her defences and in restricting the scope of Greek actions against Persia. Athens stepped into her place; she was prepared to act with vision, to liberate the Ionian States and their neighbours from Persia, and to carry the war into the enemy's camp. She organized her supporters in the so-called Delian League (q.v.), which was in origin and in name an Athenian Alliance; for each ally was an ally of Athens and conceded to Athens the hegemony or command in war. The allies as a group had their own treasury and their own Synod or meeting of delegates at Delos, the religious centre of the islanders. Athens

and her allies had at first a common purpose in expelling Persia from the Aegean area and safeguarding Greek maritime trade; and this purpose was acceptable also to Sparta and the mainland States, who had opted out of the war against Persia. The rapid success of Athens was achieved under the leadership of Cimon (q.v.).

In 462/1 B.C. an advanced democracy was established at Athens under the leadership of Ephialtes (4) and Pericles (qq.v.). Its foreign policy was marked by aggressive action against both Persia and Sparta and by exploitation of the allies, and the energy and the courage of the democrats were such that Athens achieved a favourable peace with Persia, a stalemate with Sparta, and the conversion of her alliance into an empire. This position was recognized in the Thirty Years Peace of 445 B.C. which marked the division of the Greek States into two armed camps but produced a cessation of hostilities for fourteen years. These years were those of Athens' acme as the acknowledged ruler of an empire, the leading sea-power in the Mediterranean and the centre of the artistic and intellectual life of the Greek world, and those of Athens' unrivalled statesman, Pericles, who set his own stamp on the culture of his city. His aim for Athens was expressed in the Parthenon and the Propylaea and in the Funeral Speech which Thucydides included in his history. But it was an aim which had no place for passivity; he planned to remove Sparta from his path, and his diplomacy produced a situation in which the risk of war was obvious. Sparta took up the challenge. The Peloponnesian War (q.v.) resulted in the complete overthrow of Athens and the dissolution of her empire; in the limited victory of Sparta which included the alienation of her allies and the invocation of Persia; and in the revival of Persian influence in Greek political affairs. In Sicily too the strain of war weakened Syracuse and the Sicilian States, and they were almost engulfed by Carthage in 405 B.C. (*see* SICILY). More sinister was the spread of *stasis*, the revolutionary struggle within a State between extremist parties which aimed at annihilating one another; Thucydides described its effects in a famous passage (3. 82–3). While the internecine wars of the Greek States made combination and even peace unlikely, the onset of *stasis* revealed the breakdown of communal spirit among the citizens, the animosity between the rich and the poor, and the deterioration of political aims. The victor of the Peloponnesian War, Sparta, tried to unite the Greek States against Persia but Thebes and Athens rose against her; Sparta then sold the liberties of the Greek States in Ionia for Persian help and imposed her rule on the States of the mainland by authoritarian methods (*see* AGESILAUS). In 379 B.C. Thebes and Athens rose again. Thebes, led by Epaminondas (q.v.), defeated the Spartan army decisively at Leuctra in 371 B.C., and Athens drove the Spartan navy from the seas. Thebes formed the Boeotian Confederacy on a democratic basis, whereby a federal union of States was drawn tighter by a sovereign Assembly of all Boeotian citizens, and through her influence similar federations developed in Acarnania, Aetolia, Thessaly, Arcadia, and Achaea. Athens formed the Second Athenian League (q.v.) in which explicit guarantees of independence were given to the contracting States; its immediate success showed the Greek States' need of liberal leadership in pursuit of peace and liberty. But Athens and Thebes, once in positions of power, quarrelled with one another and pursued imperialistic policies which failed utterly in the Social War 357–355 B.C. (q.v.) and in the Sacred War 356–346 (q.v.). In Sicily union had been imposed after 405 B.C. by a tyrant using mercenary troops and ruthless methods, Dionysius (q.v. 1); he defeated Carthage, held southern Italy, and allied himself with Sparta, but his son and successor was expelled in 355 B.C. and anarchy ensued in Syracuse and in Sicily.

This century of political turmoil in which the Greek States damaged no one except themselves was a period of intense intellectual and artistic activity which set the highest standards for ensuing ages in drama, architecture, history, oratory, philosophy, and sculpture. Greek society was moving towards a common form and outlook which rose above the limitations of city-state nationalism. Capitalism was fully developed; banking, insurance, and legal procedures were standardized (see BANKS *and* FINANCE). Slavery provided relatively cheap methods of production; seaborne trade flourished throughout the Mediterranean area, including the Black Sea; and the Greek way of life was spreading into barbarian lands and creating new markets.

Where the city-states had failed, Macedonia succeeded. Philip II (q.v.), having demonstrated the solidarity of the Macedonian State and the superiority of its military power over that of Thebes and Athens, persuaded the Greek States to enter into a federal union, known as 'The Greeks', with full guarantees of autonomy, collective security, and stable government, and then to ally themselves with the Macedonian State in a joint war against Persia in which the military command was vested in the king of Macedon. The Macedonian State was a monarchy with feudal institutions, entirely distinct from the city-state and fully conscious of its distinctness; but Philip and his successor Alexander (q.v. 3) the Great appreciated Greek culture and Greek capitalism. When Alexander overthrew the Persian Empire and advanced to the Indus valley, he opened up a vast field for Greek enterprise and founded numerous urban communities which practised a Greek way of life and spread Greek culture far and wide. But in Greece itself many city-states maintained resistance to Macedon, both before and after Chaeronea (q.v.); the leader was Demosthenes (q.v. 2) of Athens, and after the death of Alexander a war conducted by Athens and the Aetolian League in 323–322 B.C. ended in the capitulation of Athens and the suicide of Demosthenes. Thereafter the fortunes of the city-states depended upon the strength of the Macedonian kingdom. They were involved in the Wars of the Successors (see DIADOCHI) who divided up the great empire of Alexander, between 320 and 275 B.C. Then the Antigonids gained and held the Macedonian throne, Antigonus (q.v. 2) Gonatas defeated Athens and Sparta, when they combined against him and took subsidies from Egypt 267–263 B.C. He and his successors faced stronger powers in the Aetolian Confederacy (q.v.), which expanded until it contained most of central Greece by 224 B.C., and the Achaean Confederacy (q.v.) which, led by Aratus (q.v. 2), gained adherents from the Peloponnesian States except Elis, Messenia, and Sparta, the last being revolutionized by Cleomenes III (q.v.) in 227 B.C.

In 229 B.C. Roman forces gained control of part of the Illyrian coast and of Corcyra. Their proximity to Macedonia led Philip V (q.v.) to ally himself with Carthage in 215 B.C. Rome raised his Greek enemies against him in 212 B.C. and defeated him decisively in 197 B.C. at Cynoscephalae with the help of the Aetolian and Achaean Leagues, Athens, Rhodes, and Pergamum. Rome was now involved in the rivalries of the Hellenistic kingdoms as well as in those of the Greek States. When Antiochus (q.v. 3) of Syria entered Greece at the invitation of the Aetolian Confederacy, Rome drove him back into Asia, defeated him at Magnesia in 189 B.C., and extended her protectorate over the Greek city-states in Asia Minor. The Aetolian Confederacy was reduced to impotence. In 171 B.C. Rome ordered Perseus (q.v. 2) to disband his forces; he refused and was crushed at Pydna in 168 B.C. The Macedonian kingdom was split into four republics. In 167 B.C. Molossia in Epirus was sacked for its support of Perseus, and in 146 B.C. the Achaean Confederacy and

its allies in central Greece were crushed and Corinth was razed. Rome's regulations were thenceforth to be obeyed; the liberties of the Greek States were at an end.

The outer Greek world had grown enormously with the conquests of Alexander both in extent and in prosperity. The Hellenistic kingdoms, established by the Successors, were ruled by Macedonian dynasts and relied to a great extent upon Greek personnel and Greek civilization. The Ptolemies (see PTOLEMY I *to* PTOLEMY XV) harnessed the productivity of Egypt by highly efficient administration and capitalist methods formed on the Greek model; their foreign policy was directed against the kingdoms of Syria and Macedonia; they controlled Cyrenaica and traded along the coasts of East Africa and Arabia. The last of the Ptolemies, Caesarion, son of Cleopatra and Julius Caesar, was executed on the order of Octavian (later Augustus) in 30 B.C. The Seleucids (see SELEUCUS, ANTIOCHUS, *and* SYRIA) founded many Greek cities in their realm and ruled through district governors, but the onslaughts of Egypt, Rome, and Parthia reduced the kingdom to a small area which was annexed by Pompey in 62 B.C. Many smaller Hellenistic kingdoms grew up in the period between Alexander's conquests and the expansion of Rome to the east; they ranged from those of Bactria (q.v.) in Afghanistan and western Pakistan to the kingdom of Lysimachus (q.v.) in Thrace or that of Pyrrhus (q.v.) in north-western Greece and southern Illyria. Monarchies of a similar kind ruled in the Crimea (see SPARTOCIDS) and in Syracuse. Some kings, e.g. Hiero II of Syracuse and Attalus I of Pergamum, joined the Roman cause and survived; others were reduced to the status of client kings; others were suppressed. But under their care the Hellenization of the eastern Mediterranean and of some countries in the east as far as Afghanistan was completed. The Greek genius flowered for many centuries in this wider world. It gave cultural vitality to the Roman Empire and to the Byzantine Empire, and it brought enlightenment to Italy and the west in the Renaissance.

Specialist bibliographies will be found under separate headings, e.g. ATHENS, COINAGE, EPIGRAPHY, PERSIAN WARS. A brief general bibliography is given here.

(a) SOURCES. M. N. Tod, *Greek Historical Inscriptions* i² (1946), ii² (1948); C. Seltman, *Greek Coins²* (1955); G. F. Hill, *Sources for Greek History between the Persian and the Peloponnesian Wars³*, rev. by R. Meiggs and A. Andrewes (1951).

(b) GENERAL HISTORIES. G. Grote, *History of Greece* (1888 ed.); G. Busolt, *Griechische Geschichte²* (1893–1904); E. Meyer, *Geschichte des Altertums* (1901–2 and 1928–37); K. J. Beloch, *Griechische Geschichte²* (1916–27); *Cambridge Ancient History* i–ix (1923–32) and i–ii³ (in progress); G. Glotz et al., *Histoire grecque* (1925–38); G. De Sanctis, *Storia dei Greci* (1939); H. Bengtson, *Griechische Geschichte²* (1960); J. B. Bury, *History of Greece³*, rev. by R. Meiggs (1951); F. Schachermeyr, *Griechische Geschichte* (1960); N. G. L. Hammond, *History of Greece²* (1966).

(c) SPECIAL PERIODS. E. Vermeule, *Greece in the Bronze Age* (1964); D. L. Page, *History and the Homeric Iliad* (1959); G. S. Kirk, *The Songs of Homer* (1962); C. G. Starr, *Origins of Greek Civilization 1100–650 B.C.* (1961); T. J. Dunbabin, *The Western Greeks* (1948); A. Andrewes, *The Greek Tyrants* (1956); A. R. Burn, *The Lyric Age of Greece* (1960) and *Persia and the Greeks* (1962); C. Hignett, *Xerxes' Invasion of Greece* (1963); M. L. W. Laistner, *A History of the Greek World³ 479–323 B.C.* (1957); W. W. Tarn, *Alexander the Great* (1948); W. W. Tarn and G. T. Griffith, *Hellenistic Civilization³* (1952); M. Cary, *A History of the Greek World 323–146 B.C.²* (1951); M. Rostovtzeff, *The Social and Economic History of the Hellenistic World* (1941); S. Accame, *Il dominio romano in Grecia dalla guerra achaica ad Augusto* (1946).

(d) SPECIAL TOPICS. M. Cary, *The Geographic Background to Greek and Roman History* (1949); F. M. Heichelheim, *An Ancient Economic History* i (1958), ii (1964); M. I. Finley, *Slavery in Classical Antiquity* (1960); H. I. Marrou, *History of Education in Antiquity* (1956); A. W. Gomme, *The Population of Athens in the Fifth and Fourth Centuries B.C.* (1933); J. Boardman, *The Greeks Overseas* (1964); J. M. Cook, *The Greeks in Ionia and the East* (1962); A. G. Woodhead, *The Greeks in the West* (1962); A. K. Narain, *The Indo-Greeks* (1957); G. L. Huxley, *Early Sparta* (1962); C. Hignett, *History of the Athenian Constitution to the End of the Fifth Century B.C.* (1952); F. W. Walbank, *Philip V of Macedon* (1940); W. S. Ferguson, *Hellenistic Athens* (1911); F. E. Adcock, *Greek and Macedonian Art of War* (1957). N. G. L. H.

**GREGORY** (1) **I,** the Great, *c.* A.D. 540–604, was born of a patrician Roman family. Before becoming Pope (590) he had a career as civil administrator (*praefectus urbi* 573), then as monk and for six years Roman nuncio in Constantinople (579–85). His correspondence is a rich source both for church affairs and for the political and social situation in Italy under the Lombard conquests. He never learnt Greek properly and distrusted the court and patriarch at Constantinople. In Italy he acted with astonishing freedom in relation to both the Emperor and his exarch at Ravenna, and negotiated with the Lombards independently. The Papacy's gaze was turning towards the barbarian kingdoms, a policy expressed in his mission to the Anglo-Saxons. Several letters were written to accompany gifts of wonder-working relics to barbarian kings, and his *Dialogues*, partly modelled on Sulpicius Severus (q.v. 5) exemplify his vivid faith in prodigies. His relation to classical culture is not simple. One bishop is rebuked for teaching pagan mythology, 'inappropriate even for a religious layman' (*ep.* 11. 34). The story that he burnt the Palatine library, so shocking to Machiavelli and humanists since, is legend first reported in John of Salisbury's *Policraticus* (1159). He despised pedantry and preciousness, but not clear grammatical prose. He seems to have found Pliny's *Natural History* and the *Physiologus* (q.v.) helpful in explaining strange beasts in Job. But most of his letters concern administrative questions, and are written with the polished formality of a high official, without classical allusions or rhetorical turns. The attribution to Gregory of the institution of the Roman *schola cantorum* and the invention of 'Gregorian chant' rests on the ninth-century 'Life' by John the Deacon.

Ed. Migne, *PL* lxxv–lxxviii; Letters, ed. P. Ewald and L. M. Hartmann (*MGH* 1891–9); *Dialogi,* ed. U. Moricca (1924). F. H. Dudden, *Gregory the Great* (1905); E. Caspar, *Geschichte des Papsttums* 2 (1933). H. C.

**GREGORY** (2) **OF NAZIANZUS,** A.D. 329–89, later entitled 'the theologian'. His father (not he) was bishop of Nazianzus in Cappadocia. With his friend Basil (q.v.) of Caesarea he shared an Athenian education and subsequent enthusiasms for Origen (q.v. 1) and for asceticism. Basil mistakenly forced him to become nominal bishop of the village of Sasima (372); he never went there. At Constantinople (379–81) he helped Theodosius' expulsion of Arianism, and during the council of Constantinople (381) became, briefly, bishop of the capital. His impractical policies raised a storm to which he was unequal. Too thin-skinned for politics, he retired to Cappadocia and wrote a self-pitying autobiography in iambic trimeters. Recognition and applause meant much to him. His greatness lay in rhetoric. His orations and letters, full of neatly turned phrases and classical allusions, put Christian content into traditional forms with exemplary skill. His theological verses and epigrams are not great poetry but show a mastery of school models put to as good a use as in any contemporary pagan. He understood the classical tradition as well, or as indifferently, as Julian (q.v.), whose edict excluding Christians from education he resented and against whom he published two invectives.

Ed. Migne, *PG* xxxv–xxxviii; Letters, ed. P. Gallay (1965– ); Epigrams in *Anth. Pal.* 8. J. Quasten, *Patrology* 3 (1960), 236 ff.; M. M. Hauser-Meury, *Prosopographie zu G.* (1960); R. R. Reuther, *Gregory of N.* (1969). H. C.

**GREGORY** (3) **OF NYSSA,** *c.* A.D. 330–*c.* 395, younger brother of Basil (q.v.) of Caesarea who made him bishop of Nyssa (371). Despite Basil's complaints of his political ineptitude, which gave him an inferiority complex, he played a worthy role from 379 to 380 in assisting Theodosius' suppression of Arianism. A superior thinker to his brother, he achieved an intimate synthesis of Christianity and Plotinian mysticism, expressed in, e.g., his commentary on the *Song of Songs* or his *Life of Moses* whose ascent to Sinai's darkness symbolizes the soul's beatific union with God. Against Plato, Gregory denies the soul's pre-existence and inherent immortality. Through moral purification and a contemplation of its true destiny made possible by divine grace, the soul, created in God's image and akin to its maker, seeks for salvation in a knowledge of God which is infinite advance unthreatened by satiety. His criticims of Plotinus and Origen (1) (qq.v.) do not hide the extent of his debt to both. He held Origen's belief in the final salvation of all souls, which he cautiously expresses in a tract 'on the soul and resurrection' largely modelled on Plato's *Phaedo*.

Ed. W. Jaeger and others (1952– ). J. Quasten, *Patrology* 3 (1960), 254 ff. W. Jaeger, *Early Christianity and Greek Paideia* (1962). H. C.

**GREGORY** (4) **THAUMATURGUS,** A.D. *c.* 213–*c.* 275, was born of noble family at Neocaesarea, Pontus. He went to study law at Berytus, but when visiting Caesarea (Palestine) was converted to Christianity by Origen (q.v. 1). His parting panegyric of gratitude describes Origen's methods of instruction. On returning to Pontus he successfully preached Christianity. His memory was venerated a century later by Basil (q.v.) of Caesarea and Gregory (q.v. 3) of Nyssa. The latter wrote a 'Life' on the basis of Pontic folk-traditions which ascribed to him extraordinary prodigies as 'the wonderworker'.

*Panegyric,* ed. P. Koetschau (1894). J. Quasten, *Patrology* 2 (1953), 123 ff. H. C.

**GRILLIUS** (5th c. A.D.), grammarian. Extracts from his *Commentum in Ciceronis libros de inventione* are extant (ed. Halm, *Rhet. Lat. Min.* 596–606).

Schanz–Hosius, § 1122.

**GROMATICI,** Roman land-surveyors. Earlier and commoner names are *mensores, agrimensores*. The later name comes from their instrument, the *groma* (derived, through Etruscan, from γνώμων or γνῶμα). This had a cross which fitted into a pivot on top of a curved bracket; from each arm of the cross hung plumb-lines. It was used to take bearings on a system of squares (*limitatio, centuriatio*): *see* CENTURIATION. References were made by means of *cardines* and *decumani* (*see* TOWNS, II), e.g. SD I = first road to left (*sinistra*) of *decumanus maximus*; VK II = second beyond *cardo maximus* (*ultra kardinem*). A surveying instrument more accurate than the *groma* was the *dioptra*, perfected and described by Heron (q.v.); among others was the *chorobates*, a levelling instrument about 20 feet long. A surveyor's workshop with tools was found at Pompeii in 1912.

The land-surveyors formed a special profession, to which we find reference made as early as Plautus (*Poen.* 48 f. *finitor*). Their services were used for the plotting of camps (q.v.; *castrametatio*), the division and assignation of *ager publicus* (q.v.), the planning of colonies (*see* COLONIZATION, ROMAN), the measurement and division of estates, and the assessment of land tax. They also produced plans (*formae*) and several types of register, and acted as arbitrators or assessors in private land-disputes. During the land assignations of the last century of the Republic the demand for surveyors was probably met by private enterprise. An example of their activity under the early Empire has survived in the fragments from Arausio (q.v.). Under the later Empire official surveyors formed a highly organized branch of the civil service. Military surveying, which in Caesar's army was done by the centurions, became a specialized profession, and inscriptions show that each legion had *mensores* attached. The combination of mathematics, practical advice, and law which we find in Roman writings on this subject does not occur in Greece, although the mathematical basis is Greek.

The technical literature of the profession is represented by a collection of miscellaneous treatises ranging widely in date, and dealing with such subjects as the technique of mensuration, boundary-marking and map-making, and the rules of land-tenure as they concern the surveyor. The collection has come down to us in an edition of the sixth century A.D., in which the original matter has suffered much from corruption and interpolation. Besides excerpts from Frontinus (q.v.), embedded in a commentary by Agenius Urbicus, it contains works ascribed to Hyginus (2), Balbus (5), Junius (3) Nipsus, Siculus Flaccus, and Innocentius (qq.v.), *libri coloniarum* (q.v.), notes on geometry, and extracts from registers and laws. The wide differences in date between the parts are reflected in their latinity; the writing is crabbed, often to the point of obscurity, and devoid of literary merit. MSS. of the corpus at Wolfenbüttel and Rome contain well-preserved coloured miniatures of the sixth–seventh and ninth centuries.

The only complete edition is *Die Schriften der römischen Feldmesser*, by F. Blume, K. Lachmann, and A. Rudorff (2 vols. 1848, 1852, repr. 1962); vol. ii contains essays by Lachmann, Rudorff, and Mommsen which are still valuable. The Teubner *Corpus Agrimensorum Romanorum* (i. 1 ed. C. Thulin, 1913; no more appeared) contains Frontinus, Agenius Urbicus, Hyginus, and Siculus Flaccus. A. Schulten, *Die römische Flurteilung* (1898); H. Stuart Jones, *Companion to Roman History* (1912), 15 ff.; M. della Corte, 'Groma', *Mon. Ant.* 1922, 5 ff.; F. Castagnoli, 'Le *formae* delle colonie romane e le miniature dei codici dei gromatici', *Atti Accad. Ital.* (*Mem. Linc.* 7th ser.) iv (1943), 83 ff., and *Le ricerche sui resti della centuriazione* (1958); J. Bradford, *Ancient Landscapes* (1957), 145 ff.; A. Piganiol, *Les Documents cadastraux de la colonie romaine d'Orange, Gallia*, Suppl. 16 (1962); O. A. W. Dilke, 'The Roman Surveyors', *Greece & Rome* 1962, 170 ff.; 'Illustrations from Roman Surveyors' Manuals', *Imago Mundi* (1968).       C. J. F.; O. A. W. D.

## GUARDIANSHIP. (a) GREECE.

The development of the law of guardianship in Greece and Rome was influenced by the change in the conception of guardianship itself, which began as a right of preserving and protecting the ward's property in the interest of the whole kin (as contingent heir of the ward), but became gradually a duty of the guardian in the interest of the ward himself. This explains the restrictions imposed upon the guardian with regard to his control over the child's property, and the increasing supervision of public authorities over his activity as guardian. The Greek guardian was either ἐπίτροπος of boys and girls until their majority—18 years in the case of boys— and registration in the citizen list, or κύριος of women for lifetime or until marriage. Guardians were appointed by the father's will; failing testamentary appointment the next relatives (brother or uncle), being the most likely successors, were entitled to claim the guardianship; in the absence of these an official (the Chief Archon in Athens) appointed the guardian. The guardian had to provide for the ward's education, attend to all his interests, and represent him in legal transactions; in general he was required—as Plato, *Leg.* 11. 928 recommends—to act on his behalf with the same solicitude as for a child of his own. The administration of property by the guardian, especially of landed property, was submitted to the control of magistrates. Action for damages caused by the guardian might be brought against him by the ward within five years of the end of the guardianship. The principles of guardianship of women were analogous; but a woman could dispose freely of objects of lesser importance, without the help of her κύριος.

**2.** (b) ROME. Roman law distinguished between *tutela* and *cura* as types of guardianship of persons *sui iuris*, i.e. not subject either to *patria potestas* or *manus* (qq.v.). *Tutela* concerned children below the age of puberty (*impuberes*: eventually boys under 14, girls under 12) and women; *cura* comprehended *puberes* under 25 (*minores*), lunatics (*furiosi*), and spendthrifts (*prodigi*).

**3.** The original conception of guardianship (above)

can be seen in the rule which gave *tutela* of an *impubes* on the death of the *paterfamilias* to the nearest agnate (*tutor legitimus*), as being the person who would succeed to the property of the ward (*pupillus*) in the event of his death (*see* INHERITANCE, LAW OF). But already in the XII Tables the father was allowed to appoint someone else by will (*tutor testamentarius*). In later times, if there were neither a *tutor testamentarius* nor a *tutor legitimus*, a magistrate would appoint one (*tutor dativus*). *Tutela* of males ended with puberty, when the ward was capable of begetting an heir who would exclude the agnate from the inheritance and therefore from any interest in the *tutela*. But a female could have no such heir (her children would be heirs to their father), and *tutela* of women was therefore in principle lifelong. In the classical law, however, it had become for the most part an empty form, except, significantly, in the case of *tutela legitima*.

**4.** The shift in the nature of *tutela* from a valuable right to a burden can be seen in the evolution of the tutor's liability for misconduct. In early law he was liable only for fraudulent misappropriation, but in the later Republic he could be required (by *actio tutelae*) to account for his conduct according to the principles of good faith. There thus grew up a body of rules which required him to act conscientiously in the interest of the ward. This in turn led to the evolution of a list of grounds (public office, age, ill health, etc.) on which a *tutor testamentarius* or *dativus* (but not a *tutor legitimus*) might be excused.

**5.** The tutor's concern was with the property of the child, not with his custody or upbringing. In regard to the property he could act either directly, by administering it himself, or indirectly by validating the acts of the ward. The former method suffered from the disadvantage that in principle his acts only affected himself and therefore the ward might repudiate them on coming of age. In the classical law some inroads had been made on this principle, but the indirect method remained the more effective. So long as a child was incapable of reason (strictly, of speech—*infans*: fixed in A.D. 407 at 7 years) he could do no legal act. Thereafter he could act, but (until puberty) if the act might make his position worse (i.e. cause him to relinquish rights or incur duties) he required the express oral approval (*auctoritas*) of his tutor. It was by giving or withholding *auctoritas* that the tutor exercised his control.

**6.** *Cura minorum* grew out of the Lex Plaetoria (*c.* 200 B.C.) and the Praetorian remedy of *in integrum restitutio*, whereby transactions with a *minor sui iuris* might be impugned if advantage had been taken of his inexperience. This made dealings with *minores* risky, and the practice grew up of calling in an independent adult to approve the transaction. This practice eventually, in the Principate, hardened into the institution of a *curator* appointed by a magistrate on the request of the *minor*. In Justinian's law *cura* and *tutela* have been largely, but not entirely, assimilated.

(a) GREECE. O. Schulthess, *Vormundschaft nach griechischem Recht* (1886); Beasley, *CR* 1906, 249 ff.; J. H. Lipsius, *Attisches Recht und Rechtsverfahren* ii. 2 (1912); L. Mitteis, *Grundzüge der Papyruskunde* (1913), 248 ff.; A. R. W. Harrison, *Law of Athens, Family and Property* (1968), 97 ff.

(b) ROME. S. Solazzi, *La minore età* (1913); 'Tutele e curatele' (*Rivista ital. per le scienze giuridiche*, 1914); *Istituti tutelari* (1929); R. Taubenschlag, *Vormundschaftsrechtliche Studien* (1913); P. Bonfante, *Corso di diritto romano* i (1925); O. Lenel, *Sav. Zeitschr.* 1914; *See also* LAW AND PROCEDURE, ROMAN, I.       A. B.; B. N

**GYGES,** king of Lydia (*c.* 685–657 B.C.), founded the Mermnad dynasty by murdering King Candaules and marrying his widow; attacked Miletus and Smyrna, captured Colophon, and sent offerings to Delphi. He sought protection from Assyria against the Cimmerians, but lost it later by helping Psammetichus of Egypt, and was killed in a new Cimmerian invasion. He coined in gold (Pollux 3. 87) and his tomb was famous (Hipponax fr. 24); it has been identified at Bin Tepe and was excavated recently (*Arch. Rep.* 1964–5, 40). His son Ardys succeeded him.

Hdt. i. 8–12; Plato, *Resp.* ii. 359 d. G. Radet, *La Lydie* (1893), 151 ff.; P. N. Ure, *Origin of Tyranny* (1922), 127 ff.
P. N. U.; N. G. L. H.

**GYLIPPUS,** Spartan general, was sent in 414 B.C. to help Syracuse against Athens. His very arrival won Sicel support and gave heart to the Syracusans, whose resistance he organized with skill and courage. He succeeded in regaining the initiative for Syracuse and eventually defeating the Athenians. Returning to Sparta after the war, he was convicted in 405 B.C. of embezzling public funds, but fled into exile.

Thuc. bks. 6–7; Diod. 13. 106; Plut. *Nicias.* A. G. W.

**GYMNASIARCHOS.** This official appears in Egypt under the Ptolemies as a functionary of Greek type, charged with the supervision of gymnasia in towns or villages where there was a hellenized community; the office was probably a voluntary one. The Roman authorities seem to have allowed an organization of the Graeco-Egyptian population to subsist under officials with Greek titles, of whom the gymnasiarch ranked as the chief; his duties, judged by the evidence of papyri, were extended from the gymnasia to all kinds of public works. The office thus became in practice a liturgy. At first the normal tenure was apparently a year; as the impoverishment of the Graeco-Egyptian class increased two men might share the burden; in the third century several are found acting together or for short periods. As even children are named as gymnasiarchs, the title would seem

to have been given to any person of means who could be asked for money. The only place where the gymnasiarchs played a part of more than local importance was Alexandria; in the time of Strabo they were not of sufficient standing there to be named as city officers, but half a century later they were the leaders of the Nationalist opposition to Rome, and reappeared as such on occasion till the end of the second century.

B. A. van Groningen, *Le Gymnasiarque des métropoles de l'Égypte romaine* (1924); Jones, *JEg.Arch.* 1938, 65 ff.; J. Delorme, *Gymnasium* (1960), index, s.v. J. G. M.

**GYMNASIUM.** The Greek γυμνάσιον was a sports ground, usually outside the city walls; a public institution, and open to all citizens. Its main feature was a running-track, but it usually also contained a *palaestra* (q.v.). The site was often a sacred grove beside a stream, as was the case with the three gymnasia at Athens, the Lyceum on the banks of the Cephisus, the Academy and the Cynosarges by the Eridanus and the Ilissus. The two first of these were large enough for riding lessons and cavalry parades, and besides the running-track there were jumping-pits and ranges for throwing the discus and javelin. The buildings included bathrooms, undressing-rooms, an oil store, a dust-room where the athletes powdered themselves before exercise, a room for ball games, and a room for practising boxing with hanging punch-balls of different sizes. The gymnasia were especially frequented by the *epheboi* (q.v.). At Athens they were managed by a board of ten *Sophronistai*, in other cities by an honorary magistrate, the gymnasiarch, who employed and paid professional trainers, the *gymnastai* and *paidotribai*. See EDUCATION, IV.

E. N. Gardiner, *Athletics of the Ancient World* (1930), 72 ff.; J. Delorme, *Gymnasion* (Paris, 1960). F. A. W.

# H

**HABRON,** of Phrygia and Rhodes (1st c. A.D.), a Greek grammarian at Rome. His Περὶ ἀντωνυμίας is cited, sometimes with approval, by Apollonius Dyscolus.

FRAGMENTS. R. Berndt, *B. phil. Woch.* 1915.

**HADES** (Ἅιδης, Epic Ἀίδης, 'the Unseen'), one of the sons of Kronos (q.v.), lord of the lower world, 'the House of Hades'; the name is always that of a person, never of a place, in classical Greek, the dead going ἐς Ἅιδου. He has next to no mythology, except the story of his wedding with Persephone (*see* DEMETER). Personally, he is represented as grim, unpitying, a severe punisher of wrongdoers (in those pictures of the lower world which find room for a Hell or a Purgatory), but never as evil; Greek mythology has no Satan. Nor does he appear as the actual tormentor of the wicked dead, that being the business of the Erinyes (q.v.).

Under his own name he has almost no cult, the one exception being his precinct at Elis (Paus. 6. 25. 2). But under various titles he is heard of here and there. Of these the best known is Pluton (Πλούτων), i.e. the Rich One, obviously connected with Plutus (q.v.). For example, at Byzantium there was a temple of Pluton (Dionysius Byzant. fr. 9 Müller; *GGM* ii. 23). For others *see* CLYMENUS, EUBULEUS; more examples in Farnell, op. cit. *infra* 281 ff. He is quite often called Zeus, with some distinguishing title. It seems reasonable to recognize three motives at work: (*a*) reluctance to name anyone so ill-omened as the god of the dead, to which may be added a feeling that he has little to do with the living,

save in so far as they are solicitous for the condition of their dead kin; (*b*) confusion of such a god, as lord of the depths of the earth, with deities concerned with its fertile surface (cf. DEMETER); (*c*) comparatively developed theological ideas, which extended the activity of Zeus beyond his proper sphere of the sky and air.

Farnell, *Cults* iii. 280–8 and refs. H. J. R.

**HADRIAN:** PUBLIUS AELIUS (*PW* 64) HADRIANUS, Roman Emperor A.D. 117–38, was born in 76, probably at Italica in Baetica. He was son of P. Aelius Hadrianus Afer and of Domitia Paulina of Gades; his paternal grandfather (a senator) had married Ulpia, aunt of Trajan (q.v.). Left fatherless in 85, Hadrian became the ward of Trajan and of Attianus (q.v.) and entered Trajan's childless household. He became tribune successively of Legio II Adiutrix, probably at Aquincum (95), V Macedonica in Lower Moesia (96), and XXII Primigenia under L. Julius Ursus Servianus in Upper Germany (*ILS* 308). Thence, in 99 he accompanied Trajan (now Emperor) to Rome where he married Vibia Sabina (q.v.) in 100. He became imperial quaestor (101); staff-officer in the First Dacian War (101–2); senatorial archivist; plebeian tribune (105); commander of Legio I Minervia in the Second Dacian War (105–6), and simultaneously praetor (106); governor of Lower Pannonia (107); *cos. I suff.* in June 108; and a member of priestly colleges. He was in high favour with Trajan and Plotina and friendly with the chief court officers. However, he had received no special position to suggest that Trajan envisaged him as successor and also he was perhaps unpopular with some f Trajan's more senior generals. Nevertheless, in 111 r 112 he was elected archon of Athens—a significant honour—and in 114 (less probably 117) he was appointed governor of Syria (S.H.A. *Hadr.* 4. 1) during Trajan's Parthian war. He was designated *cos. II* in 117 for 118.

2. Trajan died at Selinus in Cilicia on 8 Aug. 117. On the 9th it was announced at Antioch that he had adopted Hadrian as his successor, and on the 11th (Hadrian's *dies imperii*) that he was dead. The circumstances were unfortunate, even ambiguous. Trajan had not advertised his dynastic intentions (but see, for a now lost gold *aureus* with the reverse legend HADRIANO TRAIANO CAESARI, B.M. *Coins, Rom. Emp.* iii. lxxxvi, 124); men like Neratius (q.v.) Priscus and Servianus (q.v.) were senior in experience; Plotina (q.v.) was known to favour Hadrian; Trajan's sudden death in a remote and isolated town encouraged doubt of the validity of Hadrian's adoption and claim to the succession. The ancient biographers regarded the 'adoption' as fictitious, forgetting that Hadrian had been given the key position in Syria during Trajan's absence in the East—the culmination of a life of intimacy and advancement under Trajan, who would hardly leave the succession a matter for armed contention, still less for senatorial decision. The death-bed adoption may probably be accepted.

3. Hadrian at once communicated Trajan's death and his own proclamation by the troops to the Senate, with a promise to respect senatorial privileges. The Senate, despite doubts, voted to him the imperial powers. Hadrian returned to Rome only in 118, when he held a Parthian triumph in Trajan's name. Called quickly to Moesia, he subdued the Sarmatae and Roxolani, and gave unified command of Dacia and Pannonia to Turbo (q.v.). He had already removed Lusius (q.v.) Quietus from Judaea. Thus he brought to a head the disaffection of the 'old guard', in the 'conspiracy of the four consulars': Quietus, A. Cornelius, Palma (q.v.), L. Publilius Celsus, and C. Avidius (q.v. 2) Nigrinus were said to have plotted against Hadrian's life, and were swiftly executed in different Italian towns by the Senate in his absence. Returning to Rome (still in 118), Hadrian attributed responsibility for the executions to Attianus, now praetorian prefect, and by such favours as an extra public largesse, remission of accession gifts for Italy, a week's gladiatorial show, reform in the postal services, grants to the *alimenta*, financial assistance to poor senators, and especially a ceremonial cancellation of 900,000,000 HS. worth of debts to the State, he sought to placate a suspicious public opinion. Senatorial circles, however, cannot have relished his prompt abandonment of Trajan's imperialist policy in the East. But senatorial prerogative was not sensibly diminished (S.H.A. *Hadr.* 8; Dio 69. 5. 7).

4. Various reasons prompted Hadrian to tour the provinces: military organization and defence; administrative co-ordination; the need to recognize—and guide—provincial aspirations by showing himself as their common symbol; and his own desire to observe provincial conditions, especially in the hellenized areas. He deliberately advertised his policy by coins (cf. *B.M. Coins, Rom. Emp.* iii. clxxi ff.). In 120 or 121 he travelled to Gaul, and thence to the Rhine, where, living a simple soldierly life, he instituted stricter regulations for legionary discipline. Crossing from Holland to Britain in 121 or 122 (cf. *CIL* iii. 4279; a previous detour by Raetia and Noricum is very unlikely), he established the triple *limes* (see WALL OF HADRIAN). Returning to Gaul, where he commemorated Plotina's death by a temple at Nîmes, he reached Spain in 122; his personal intervention in the Mauretanian campaign (S.H.A. *Hadr.* 12. 7) is very doubtful. In 123 he sailed to the East from Spain, and toured Asia, the Troad, Propontis, and Phrygia, founding or restoring or favouring communities. In 125, he went to Greece, and

finally, in 127, returned via Sicily to Rome, after an absence of about seven years. In 128 he visited Africa, to review the troops (*CIL* viii. 2532, 18052) and to revise conditions of land-tenure on imperial domain lands (ibid. 10570). After a few weeks in Rome, he left late in 128 to winter in Athens, where he dedicated the Olympieum (q.v.), and himself—called in the East a new Zeus Panhellenios—accepted the title *Olympius*. In 129 he travelled to Caria, Cilicia, Cappadocia, and Syria; in 130 he journeyed up the Nile (there to lose Antinous; q.v. 2), and only returned to Rome in 131.

5. These travels influenced a foreign policy which aimed at peaceful economy and secure defence, witness the restoration of the Flavian *status quo* in the East, the building of the British 'sentry-walk' (the Wall of Hadrian; q.v.), the consolidation of Dacia (the contemplated destruction of the Danube bridge deserves no credence), and the demarcation of a customs palisade on the German–Raetian frontier. Risings in Britain and Mauretania called for purely punitive measures. Only in Judaea was his policy questionable: the building of a shrine to Jupiter Capitolinus on the site of the Temple at Jerusalem (itself renamed *Colonia Aelia Capitolina*), with or without the prohibition of circumcision, precipitated a revolt in 132–5, which perhaps drew Hadrian to Antioch for a time. After a siege of Jerusalem and widespread repressive measures, Judaea became *Syria Palaestina*, under a consular legate with two legions; and the new colony and temple were established. This final denationalization of Judaea meant that the Jews became 'homeless' (see JEWS B), and definitely divorced the nascent Christian Church from dependence on its original nucleus in Jerusalem (see CHRISTIANITY). To Christianity as such Hadrian's attitude was, like Trajan's, tolerant so far as consistent with the maintenance of good order.

6. His general administrative policy was perhaps less innovating than is sometimes held. He made regular (but not absolute, as implied by S.H.A. *Hadr.* 22. 8; cf. *Epit. de Caes.* 14. 11) the appointment of equestrians instead of freedmen (q.v.) to the chief secretaryships in the imperial bureaucracy. There was reorganization in the army; the *alimenta* (q.v.) continued in Italy; Trajan's institution of municipal *curatores* (q.v.) was developed to supervise local finance; provincial extortion was rare; and conditions of slavery were ameliorated. In jurisdiction there was real progress, of which the appointment of four consular circuit judges (*IVviri consulares*) to administer law in Italy was a symptom. The *consilium principis* (q.v.) was established on a more regular basis, with jurisconsults (perhaps salaried) as members. About 131, the Praetors' Edict (see EDICTUM) was given a definitive text by L. Salvius Julianus (q.v. 2); thereafter this text could be altered only by the Emperor. This put an end to legal innovation (*ius honorarium*) by magistrates. Hadrian also made the unanimous opinions of authorized jurisprudents binding on courts (Gaius, *Inst.* 1. 7; Pomponius in *Dig.* 1. 2. 2. 49). It may be noted that Hadrian allowed no treason charges.

7. Spanish born and Greek inspired, intellectual critic and connoisseur, littérateur, accomplished executant in music and the arts, Hadrian enjoyed from 131 to 138 the mature pleasures of peaceful life at Rome. He erected important buildings in Athens and in Rome, notably the Pantheon (q.v.), the Temple of Venus and Rome, and his mausoleum (the Castel San Angelo), as well as a vast villa below Tibur (q.v.). All of these embody significant architectural innovations. Government was enlightened centralization, in which his debt to the gods was plain (cf. *B.M. Coins, Rom. Emp.* iii. clxiv f.). The succession must be made clear, especially if plotting now began: Servianus and his grandson Fuscus were

both executed in 136. Hadrian, weakening in health, in the same year adopted L. Aelius (q.v. 2); after Aelius' death (138) he turned to Antoninus (q.v. 1) Pius. In 138, consumptive and dropsical, he died, aged 63, at Baiae (q.v.), reputedly with a versified farewell to his soul on his lips. Buried in the Mausoleum which he had built, he was deified at the insistence of Antoninus by a Senate perhaps alienated, perhaps apathetic.

ANCIENT SOURCES. *Literary*: the garbled biography in the *Historia Augusta* contains a few statements from Hadrian's lost Autobiography and from Marius (q.v.) Maximus. Cf. also fragments of Dio Cassius bk. 69, with a critique in F. Millar, *A Study of Cassius Dio* (1964), 60 ff.; brief references in Aurelius Victor and Eutropius.
*Coins: B.M. Coins, Rom. Emp.* iii (1936); Strack, *Reichsprägung* i (1931), 230 f., for the *aureus* of Hadrian as *Caesar*; ii (1938), throughout.
MODERN LITERATURE. *Diz. Epigr.*, s.v. 'Hadrianus'; B. W. Henderson, *Life and Principate of the Emperor Hadrian* (1923); Syme, *Tacitus*; Wegner, *Herrscherbild* iii. 3 (1956); J. A. Crook, *Consilium Principis* (1955), 56 ff.; H. G. Pflaum, *Essai sur les procurateurs équestres, etc.* (1950), 58 ff.; for equestrian secretaries, M. Hammond, *The Antonine Monarchy* (1958), 468 n. 37; for the *edictum perpetuum*, H. F. Jolowicz, *Hist. Introd. to the Study of Roman Law*[3] (1952), 366 ff.; for Hadrian's buildings in Rome, Nash, *Pict. Dict. Rome* (1961/2); on his travels, G. W. Bowersock, *The Sophists in the Roman Empire* (1969), Appendix II; for the succession, J. Carcopino, 'L'Hérédité etc.', *Rev. Ét. Lat.* 1949, 262 ff.; H. G. Pflaum, 'Le Reglement successoral d'Hadrien', *Hist.-Aug.-Colloquium* (1963), 95 ff.; M. Yourcenar, *Memoirs of Hadrian* (1954), end note; see also Bengtson, *Röm. Gesch.* 327 ff.; E. M. Smallwood, *Inscriptions Illustrating the Principates of Nerva, Trajan, and Hadrian* (1966). Bibliography: A. Garzetti, *L'impero da Tiberio agli Antonini* (1960), 676 ff.; A. Piganiol, *Hist. de Rome*[2] (1962), 304 f., 580 f.
C. H. V. S.; M. H.

**HADRUMETUM** (modern *Sousse*), a seaport 60 miles south of Carthage founded by the Phoenicians probably in the sixth century B.C. Hannibal made Hadrumetum his base for the Zama campaign. It joined the Romans in 146 B.C., and was made a *civitas libera et immunis*. In 46 B.C. it opposed Caesar; his plan for a colony there was probably carried out in 42–40. Under Trajan it was entitled *Colonia Concordia Ulpia Traiana Frugifera*. Hadrumetum grew very prosperous from agriculture, horse-breeding, and shipping. Under Diocletian's reorganization it became capital of the province of Byzacena. It was an important Christian centre with extensive catacombs.

L. Teutsch, *Das Städtewesen in Nordafrika* (1962), 144 ff.; L. Foucher, *Hadrumetum* (Paris, 1964). W. N. W.; B. H. W.

**HAEMON** (*Αἴμων*), (1) eponym of Haemonia, i.e. Thessaly, and father of Thessalus (Rhianus, fr. 25 Powell). (2) Grandson of Cadmus (q.v.): leaving Thebes on account of homicide, he came to Athens, and his descendants went successively to Rhodes and Acragas; Theron, tyrant of the latter city, claimed him as an ancestor (schol. Pind. *Ol.* 2. 16). (3) Son of Creon (q.v. 3). For his legend as usually told *see* ANTIGONE; but according to Apollodorus (3. 54) he was killed by the Sphinx (cf. the *Oedipodia* ap. schol. Eur. *Phoen.* 1760). Homer makes him father of Maeon, one of the Thebans who ambushed Tydeus (*Il.* 4. 394). H. J. R.

**HALICARNASSUS,** a Greek city of Caria commanding the sea route between Cos and the Asiatic mainland. Founded perhaps *c.* 900 B.C. from Troezen in the Argolid, it is said by Herodotus (himself a Halicarnassian) to have been one of the cities that participated in the Dorian festival at Triopion; but in classical times its culture was Ionic, and a high proportion of its citizens had Carian names. It was the capital of a minor dynasty which included the Artemisia who fought on the Persian side at Salamis in 480. Joining the Delian League, it served as an Athenian naval station after the revolt of the allies in 412. Mausolus, dynast of Caria, made his capital at Halicarnassus *c.* 370 and incorporated into it a number of native villages. Thereafter, with its great wall circuit, closed harbour, dockyard, public buildings, and the

funerary temple of the dynasty (the Mausoleum), Halicarnassus was one of the spectacular cities of the ancient world. Captured by Alexander after an arduous siege in 334, it was in turn subject to the dowager Ada, Asander, Antigonus, Lysimachus, and the Ptolemies (until 197), then in 129 B.C. came under Roman rule. Nothing remains in position of the superstructure of the Mausoleum, but carved marble pieces, mostly recovered from the castle of the Knights of St. John, are now preserved in the British Museum.

C. T. Newton, *Halicarnassus, Cnidus and Branchidae* (1863); G. E. Bean and J. M. Cook, 'The Halicarnassus Peninsula', *BSA* 1955. J. M. C.

**HALIRRHOTHIUS,** in mythology, son of Poseidon; for the usual legend about him *see* ARES. There is, however, another account, according to which he was sent by his father to cut down Athena's sacred olives, but his axe missed the trees and mortally wounded him (schol. Ar. *Nub.* 1005, cf. Servius on Verg. *G.* 1. 18). H. J. R.

**HALTERES** (*ἁλτῆρες*) were pieces of iron or stone shaped and gripped like our dumb-bells. They normally weighed between 3 and 5 pounds. Competitors in the long jump always used them, one in each hand, thereby effectively improving their performance. They were also employed in various gymnastic exercises and in musical drill. F. A. W.; R. L. H.

**HALYS** (the 'Salt River', so called from the salt springs in its upper course), the longest river in Asia Minor (about 650 miles in length), now called Kızılırmak, the 'Red River'. It rises near the Armenian border and flows in a great loop from south-west to north-east to join the Euxine west of Amisus. In the time of Croesus it divided the Lydian Kingdom from the Persian Empire; hence 'Croesus by crossing the Halys destroyed a great empire'. There was a bridge across it in the fifth century (Hdt. 1. 75), of which the position has not been conclusively determined. Herodotus (5. 52), probably in error, made the Royal Road from Sardes to the Cilician Gates cross the Halys. W. M. C.; G. E. B.

**HAMILCAR** (1) (5th c. B.C.), Carthaginian general, son or grandson of the great Mago (q.v. 1). He commanded a large army and fleet against the Sicilian Greeks. At the hard-fought battle of Himera he was completely beaten by Gelon (q.v.) and killed (480 B.C.). Diodorus, probably based on Timaeus (q.v. 1), is here a better informed source than Herodotus.

Hdt. 7. 165 f.; Diodorus 11. 20 ff. V. E.

**HAMILCAR** (2) **BARCA** (probably = Semitic Bārāq, 'lightning'), commanded the Carthaginian fleet and ravaged the coast of Bruttium (in 247 B.C.). Landing in Sicily he seized Heircte (q.v.), where he held the Romans at bay by frequent skirmishes, again raiding the Italian coast as far as Cumae. In 244 he advanced to Mt. Eryx (q.v.), but failed to relieve the siege of Drepana. After the Punic defeat at Aegates Insulae he negotiated the terms of peace, and his command terminated. When attempts to suppress the subsequent revolt of the mercenaries failed, Hamilcar was reappointed commander-in-chief (241). He thrice defeated the mercenary leader Spendius; then, co-operating with Hanno, his old enemy, he defeated the other leader Matho and reduced Utica (238), thus ending the revolt. In 237 he was sent to Spain with his young son, Hannibal. Based on Gades he conquered southern and eastern Spain, advancing the frontier to Cape Nao and building a fortress at Acra Leuce (Alicante). To a Roman protest, prompted by Massilia, he replied that his conquest was designed to secure money to pay his country's war indemnity (231). While withdrawing from the siege of Helice (? Ilici, modern *Elche*) he was drowned (229/8). The anti-Barcid tradition, found in some Roman writers, that he conquered Spain against the will of the Carthaginian government, is tendentious and designed to shift the responsibility of the Hannibalic war on to the Barca family and to represent it as a personal war of revenge not countenanced by the home government. The immediate purpose of Hannibal's conquest was to add the mineral wealth and man-power of Spain to his country's empire, which had lost Sicily and Sardinia; whether he hoped ultimately to invade Italy is uncertain, but each of his three sons, Hannibal, Hasdrubal, and Mago, attempted this adventure. H. H. S.

**HANNIBAL,** the great Carthaginian general, born in (late) 247 B.C., was the eldest son of Hamilcar (q.v. 2) Barca. After making Hannibal swear eternal hatred to Rome Hamilcar took him in 237 to Spain, where he served until he assumed command in 221 on the death of Hasdrubal (q.v. 1). Although he married a Spanish princess from Castulo, he reverted to his father's warlike policy by attacking the Olcades (Upper Guadiana). In 220 he advanced Carthaginian arms beyond the Tagus, defeating the Vaccaei and Carpetani. He then besieged Rome's ally, Saguntum, which fell after an eight months' blockade (219). Although his action may have broken no formal agreement with Rome, he knew that it involved the risk of war.

2. Hannibal intended to win the war, which he had precipitated, by a bold invasion of Italy before Rome was prepared. He would sacrifice his base in Spain, cross the Alps recruiting *en route*, and seek a new base on the northern plain of Italy, where he could encourage the Italian allies of Rome to revolt. Leaving Carthago Nova in Apr. 218 with some 35,000–40,000 men he reached the Rhône. Thence by a heroic effort, made more difficult by early autumn snow, he crossed the Alps (somewhere between the Little St. Bernard and Mt. Genèvre passes: the perennial problem of the exact route does not admit of a definite solution) and reached Turin, but with only 26,000 men. After defeating P. Scipio in a cavalry engagement at Ticinus, he won a great victory at Trebia over the combined forces of Scipio and Ti. Sempronius Longus, thanks to his outflanking tactics combined with an ambush (Dec. 218). In May 217 Hannibal crossed the Apennines, ravaged Etruria, and entrapped the army of Flaminius (q.v.) in a defile between the hills and lake of Trasimene: nearly two Roman legions were destroyed. But as no towns revolted to him Hannibal marched to Apulia and then into Campania, where he failed to force Fabius (q.v.) to an open battle and was thus compelled to retire to Apulia for the winter. In 216 at Cannae (q.v.) he inflicted on the Romans the worst defeat they had known. Capua and many towns in Campania and south Italy went over to him, but as the Romans refused to acknowledge defeat and central and northern Italy remained loyal to them, he had to devise a wider strategy to force them to dissipate their strength (*see* PUNIC WARS), while in Italy he vainly tried to provoke another pitched battle.

3. While the Romans held the line of the Volturnus Hannibal wintered in Capua, where it was alleged (falsely?) that luxurious quarters undermined the discipline of his troops. The failure of his attacks from Mt. Tifata on Cumae, Nola, and Puteoli (215–214), which were parried by Marcellus, Gracchus, and Fabius (qq.v.), forced him to abandon his offensive in Campania. He won over Tarentum and other Greek cities in 213, but after failing to force the Romans to relax their siege of Capua (started in 212) by a vain march against Rome itself (211), he retired to Apulia. Ever pressed further south, Hannibal suffered a setback in the Roman capture of Tarentum

(209), while his hope of reinforcements was sadly diminished when his brother Hasdrubal (q.v. 2) was defeated at Metaurus (207). Forced to withdraw, unaided and undaunted, to Bruttium, he lost Locri in 205 and held on desperately like a lion at bay until ordered to return to Africa to defend Carthage (autumn 203). After sixteen years in enemy country he withdrew his unconquered army and advanced to final defeat by Scipio (5) Africanus at Zama (qq.v.) in 202. He escaped to Carthage and counselled peace.

4. As suffete (between 197 and 195; probably 196) Hannibal weakened the power of the oligarchs at Carthage by constitutional reforms; he also reorganized the revenues and encouraged commerce and agriculture. His political enemies replied by telling Rome that Hannibal was intriguing with Antiochus of Syria. When a Roman commission of inquiry arrived in Carthage, Hannibal fled, ultimately to Antiochus, whose hostility to Rome he is alleged to have encouraged. He was ready, it was said, to stir up the Carthaginians against Rome and even to invade Italy if given an army by Antiochus. In fact he took only a small part in the subsequent war: he was defeated in a small naval engagement off Side in Pamphylia by the Rhodian fleet under Eudamus (190). After Antiochus' defeat at Magnesia Hannibal fled to Crete and then to Prusias of Bithynia whom he supported against Eumenes of Pergamum (184). He took his own life to avoid a Roman extradition order (183 or 182).

5. Adjudged by common consent one of the world's greatest soldiers, Hannibal was the disciple of Alexander and Pyrrhus as well as of his father Hamilcar. He developed the Hellenistic system of combining infantry and cavalry till he could surround and annihilate the enemy. But beside extraordinary tactical skill and a wide and bold conception of strategy he possessed a capacity for leadership which commanded the loyalty of mercenary troops amid danger and defeat. His strategical plans and his reforms at Carthage should win for him the name of statesman. Above all it is his character (which remains unsullied despite accusations of perfidy and cruelty deriving from Roman propaganda) that counts and that has given to the Hannibalic war its epic quality and invested his name with an undying glamour (see, e.g., Polyb. 9. 21–26, 10. 32–33, 11. 19, 23. 13 and Livy 21. 4).

For bibliography *see* PUNIC WARS; fundamental for his campaigns are the works of J. Kromayer and G. De Sanctis there cited (cf. De Sanctis in *Enc. Brit.*, s.v. Hannibal). See also Walbank (1929), *passim*; G. Charles-Picard, *Hannibal* (Paris, 1967). For his statesmanship: E. Groag, *Hannibal als Politiker* (1929). For his coin-portraiture see E. S. G. Robinson in *Essays in Roman Coinage presented to H. Mattingly* (1956), 39 ff. H. H. S.

**HANNO** (1), Carthaginian, sent to west Africa before 480 B.C., founded Thymiaterium (*Mehedia*), Carian Fort (*Mogador*), Acra (*Agadir*), etc., beyond Soloeis (*C. Cantin*), and river Tensift. After staying by river Lixus (*Draa*) and founding Cerne (*Herne?*), Hanno reached river Chretes (*Senegal*), the Guanches, and C. Verde, river Gambia, West Horn (*Bissagos Bay*), God's Chariot (*Mt. Kakulima?*), S. Horn (*Sherbro Sound*), where gorillas (dwarfs? apes?) were caught, and Sierra Leone. Of his report, written in Punic, a Greek version survives. The original Punic may have had intentional gaps and obscurities (so Carcopino believes); or the Greek writer of a later date may have been influenced by Herodotus' style (so G. Germain).

*GGM* i. 1–14 (later refs. to H. are confused); A. Diller, *The Tradition of the Minor Greek Geographers* (1952), esp. 188; L. del Turco, Ἄννωνος Περίπλους [sic], *Coll. Melagrano* 1958; J. E. Casariego, *El Periplo de Hannon de Cartago* (1947); J. Lacarrière, 'Périple d' Hannon' in *Découverte du Monde* (1957), 271 ff.; Cary-Warmington, *Explorers* 47 ff. (1963, Pelican) 63 ff.; E. Warmington, *Greek Geography* (1934), 72 ff. Cf. also J. Carcopino, *Le Maroc antique* (1943), 73 ff., and (on this) G. Marcy, *Hespéris* 1935, 21 ff. and in *Journ. asiatique* ccxxxiv (1943–5), 1 ff.; G. Germain, *Hespéris* 1957, 205 ff.;

R. Mauny in *Comptes rendus de la I<sup>ere</sup> Conférence Internat. des Afri-canistes de l'Ouest* ii. 511 ff.; O. von Seel, *Antike Entdeckerfahrten* (1961); R. Hennig, *Terrae Incognitae*² (1950), 70 ff.; Thomson, *Hist. Anc. Geog.* 73 ff. etc.; Hyde, *Greek Mariners*, 141 ff.; P. Schmitt, 'Connaissance des Îles Canaries dans l'antiquité', *Latomus* 1968, 362 ff. E. H. W.

**HANNO** (2), called 'the Great', led the anti-Barcine faction at Carthage. He raised supplies in Africa for the First Punic War. A good organizer, but a poor general, he helped after failures and quarrels with Hamilcar Barca to crush the rebel mercenaries (241–238 B.C.). He represented the landed nobility who wished to maintain good relations with Rome and to develop the Carthaginian land empire in Africa rather than to pursue foreign conquest in the interests of the trading class. He thus disapproved of the Hannibalic War and argued for peace after Cannae (216). He may be identified with a Hanno who participated in the peace negotiations after Zama. H. H. S.

**HARBOURS.** The first steps in harbour improvement must be connected with the increase of commerce during the Greek age of colonization and the development of trade routes centring on certain cities. Beginning with Delos in the eighth century, the more prosperous communities guarded their natural harbours with moles of rough stone and built quays, to which ships, now larger, tied up. Harbour works increased steadily in magnitude, carefulness, and complexity. Whereas the earlier port had often been some distance from the city, to assure neutrality of commerce and to protect the city itself (cf. Arist. *Pol.* 7. 5), by the fifth century the importance of commerce and of the grain trade demanded that the urban walls should contain at least one harbour, and many cities possessed two. The moles were fortified and ended in lofty towers, the ancestors of the lighthouse (q.v.), between which chains could be strung to close the entrance. Within the harbour were storehouses for warcraft, and the market, with a sales hall, grain hall, and other buildings. Such a complex as the Piraeus (q.v.), with its three harbours, Cantharus, Zea, and Munychia, all enclosed by walls and connected by the famous Long Walls with Athens itself, possessed a greater unity and self-sufficiency than our modern harbour.

The new ports of the Hellenistic period were built on a more regular plan which took less account of natural protection. In the Roman Empire military and commercial harbours were separated for the first time, and architects gained complete independence of nature. The great Claudian harbour at Ostia, measuring over 170 acres—the largest in antiquity—was constructed on a bare shore by extensive excavation and the sinking of a large ship as artificial island breakwater.

Strabo 17. 1. 6–10 (Alexandria); Pliny, *Ep.* 6. 31 (Centumcellae). K. Lehmann-Hartleben, 'Die Antiken Hafenanlagen des Mittelmeeres', *Klio*, Beiheft 14 (1923). C. G. S.

**HARMOST** (ἁρμοστής) the title of a Spartan military governor or commander abroad, first attested in 412 B.C. (Thuc. 8. 5. 2) but probably already used at Heraclea Trachinia in 426 (Thuc. 3. 92). Harmosts became common in occupied cities after the fall of Athens in 404, occasionally with wider commands, e.g. Thibron and Euxenos in Asia Minor (Xen. *Hell.* 3. 1. 4; 4. 2. 5), Teleutias in Chalcidice (ibid. 5. 2. 18 and 37). One is attested in Cythera (*IG* v. 1. 937, ? 4th c. B.C.); but it is unlikely that such officials regularly governed the towns of the *perioikoi* (q.v.).

H. W. Parke, *JHS* 1930, 37 ff. W. G. F.

**HARPALUS** (*c.* 355–323 B.C.), a Macedonian noble of the princely house of Elimiotis and a close friend of Alexander from earliest youth. A cripple, and hence no

soldier, he accompanied Alexander to Asia as paymaste but gave early evidence of his unreliability by a sudde flight to Greece, of which the occasion is unknown. Alex ander reinstated him, and later (331) entrusted him wit the central treasury of the Empire at Babylon. Durin Alexander's absence in India (327–5) Harpalus was guilt of gross extravagance and malversation, if not of positiv treason, and when Alexander returned he decamped wit money and soldiers. He sought refuge in Athens, an probably bribed various Athenian politicians, includin Demosthenes; but failing of his purpose he took his forc to Crete, where he was killed by one of his officers.

Berve, *Alexanderreich*, no. 143; E. Badian, 'Harpalus', *JHS* 196 16 ff. G. T. C

**HARPALYCE,** in mythology, (1) *see* ALASTOR, CLYMENUS (2) Daughter of Harpalycus, king of the Amymonei i Thrace. Her mother dying, her father brought her u as a warrior, and on one occasion she saved his life i battle. After his death she became a brigand, but at las was caught and killed. At her tomb rites were celebrate which included a sham fight (Hyg. *Fab.* 193; Servius o *Aen.* 1. 317). Cf. Verg. loc. cit. (earliest mention); hi Camilla is modelled upon her. H. J. R

**HARPOCRATION,** VALERIUS, of Alexandria, lexico grapher. His date is not known: some identify him wit the teacher of Verus named by Capitolinus. His *Collec tion of florid expressions* (Συλλογὴ ἀνθηρῶν) is lost, bu elements of it survive in later rhetorical lexica. Hi *Lexicon of the Ten Orators* is preserved in an earl abridgement and in a longer form, closer to the origina but not free from corruptions. It is designed as an aid t reading, not to composition. It is based mainly on work of the imperial age, e.g. by Didymus, Dionysius o Halicarnassus, and Dionysius son of Tryphon, but cite also Aristophanes of Byzantium, Aristarchus, οἱ γλωσσο γράφοι, and many historical and antiquarian source such as Hecataeus, Hellanicus, Theopompus, Ister, an Apollodorus. The contents are words (including prope names) and phrases, mainly from the Orators, in alpha betical order, generally assigned to their sources, wit explanations of points of interest or difficulty. Some o the entries are drawn from non-oratorical literature, an in his explanations throughout Harpocration quotes from time to time, nearly every important Greek write from Homer downwards. Besides stylistic details he ha valuable notes on architectural, religious, legal, constitu tional, social, and other antiquities.

EDITIONS. I. Bekker, 1833; W. Dindorf, 1853. C. Boysen, *De H lex. fontibus*, 1876; G. Kalkoff, *De cod. epitomes Harpocrationea* (1886); *FGrH* 244, 208 ff.; M. Naoumides, *TAPA* 1961, 384 ff. P. B. R. F.; R. B

**HARPYIAE, HARPIES** (Ἅρπυιαι), supernatura winged beings, apparently winds in origin, wh 'snatch', as the name implies, and carry off various person and things. They have at the same time some charac teristics of ghosts, and, as the ideas of wind and spiri are closely allied (cf. the etymology of the words ir Greek, Hebrew, Latin, and other tongues), it is perhap most correct to say that they are spirit-winds. Thei names are Aello, Ocypete, and Celaeno (Hes. *Theog.* 267 who says that they and Iris, q.v., are daughters o Thaumas and Electra, daughter of Ocean). They appea in *Od.* 20. 77 as carrying off the daughters of Pan dareus, apparently to the other world, since they ar given as servants to the Erinyes (q.v.). Much later (Ap Rhod. 2. 188 ff.) they plague Phineus (q.v.) by carrying off his food and defiling what they leave with thei excrement. Whence this detail comes is not known; i is an ingenious suggestion (W. R. Dawson, *Bridle o Pegasus*, 1930 (1), 27) that Apollonius had heard of th voracious and filthy fruit-eating Indian bat. Virgil (*Aen.* 3. 210 ff.) follows Apollonius in part, but describes them as birds with women's faces.

They appear (named) on an Attic vase of about 600 B.C. Here, and in pictures of their pursuit by the Boreads from the sixth century on, they are shown as winged women, not woman-headed birds, the type used for Sirens; though death-spirits in this form have given its modern name to the 'Harpy Tomb' from Xanthos (Brommer, *Vasenlisten*², 351). H. J. R.; C. M. R.

**HARUSPICES.** This word, variously spelled (*haru-, aru-, hari-, ari-, are-*) and probably cognate with χορδή, Latin *hira*, etc. (Walde–Hofmann, *Lat. etym. Wörterb.*³ s.v.) and the root of *specio*, was applied to diviners imported into Rome from Etruria (where an *haruspex* was called *netśvis*; *CIL* xi. 6363). Appearing, according to Livy 1. 56. 4–5, in the reign of Tarquinius Superbus, *haruspices* increased in importance from the Second Punic War, and though long regarded as barbarous (Cic. *Nat. D.* 2. 11), gradually encroached upon the field of the augurs. From the late Republic on they formed an *ordo haruspicum LX*, headed by a *summus, primarius,* or *maximus haruspex*, while others served in Italian municipalities. The art was practised to the time of Theodosius (*Cod. Theod.* 16. 10), and still seriously discussed as late as Laurentius Lydus (6th c.) or later. The principles were contained in priestly books (Cic. *Div.* 1. 72), which legend derived from Tages (q.v.; also Cic. *Div.* 2. 50 and Pease's note), and some of which were translated into Latin by Tarquitius Priscus (C. Thulin, *Ital. sakrale Poesie u. Prosa* (1906), 1–5).

This *Etrusca disciplina* sought to interpret three types of phenomena (Cic. *Div.* 1. 12, 2. 26): *exta, monstra* (*ostenta, portenta, prodigia*), and *fulgura*. Significant for the *exta* were the size, shape, colour, and markings of the vital organs, especially the livers and gall-bladders of sheep, changes in which were believed by many races to arise supernaturally (cf. Pl. *Tim.* 71 a ff.; Cic. *Div.* 1. 118; Iambl. *Myst.* 3. 16) and to be susceptible of interpretation by established rules. Models of the liver—e.g. from Piacenza (Etruscan), Boghazkeui (Hittite), and Babylonia—were probably intended for instruction in extispicy. *Monstra* (from *moneo*) or prodigies (*see* PRODIGIA) included teratological or otherwise unusual births or growths and abnormal meteorological phenomena. *Fulgura* were interpreted by their frequency, the precise one of the sixteen Etruscan divisions of the heavens in which these were seen, and by their physical effects. Of these three types of divination that through the *exta* was deliberately sought (*impetratiuum*), but those by *monstra* or *fulgura* were considered divinely sent (*oblatiua*) and hence usually demanding some expiation (*procuratio*). *See also* RELIGION, ETRUSCAN.

For bibliography *see under* DIVINATION. A. S. P.

**HASDRUBAL** (1), a popular leader in Carthage and son-in-law of Hamilcar (q.v. 2) Barca, whom he accompanied to Spain (237 B.C.). Later he reduced a Numidian rising in Africa, and according to the anti-Barcine tradition used by Fabius Pictor (Polyb. 3. 8) he schemed to overthrow the Carthaginian constitution. He succeeded to the command in Spain on Hamilcar's death (229) and achieved more by diplomacy than force of arms. He married an Iberian princess and founded Carthago Nova (q.v.), whence he advanced to the Ebro, which was later recognized as the boundary of Carthaginian and Roman spheres of influence in a treaty with Rome (226). In 221 he was murdered by a Celtic slave. The view of Fabius that Hasdrubal ruled as viceroy in Spain

independent of his home government is improbable (cf. Walbank, *Polybius*, I. 310 f.).

For a possible coin-portrait, see E. S. G. Robinson in *Essays in Roman Coinage presented to H. Mattingly* (1956), 37 f. H. H. S.

**HASDRUBAL** (2) (BARCA), son of Hamilcar (q.v. 2) and younger brother of Hannibal, was left in command in Spain (218 B.C.). Repulsed by Cn. Scipio (218), he launched a combined land and sea attack which terminated in a naval defeat off the Ebro (217). Reinforced and with his rear secured by his defeat of the Turdetani (216), Hasdrubal took the offensive with the hope of ultimately joining Hannibal in Italy, but was defeated at Ibera on the Ebro owing to the failure of his enveloping tactics (215). Recalled to Africa, where he crushed the rebellious Syphax, he returned to Spain (212) and defeated Cn. Scipio at Ilorci (211), so that Carthaginian control was extended to the Ebro. Tactically outwitted by P. Scipio (q.v. 5) at Baecula, he withdrew his army from complete defeat and reached Gaul through the western Pyrenees (208); crossing the Alps, perhaps by the pass used by Hannibal, he raised his forces to 30,000 and moved south to join Hannibal (207). Unexpectedly faced by two consular armies through the arrival of Claudius Nero (q.v. 2) he could not force the coast road and so withdrew along the Metaurus (q.v.) valley by a night, either to retire to north Italy or more probably in a desperate attempt to reach central Italy. Overtaken and defeated in a decisive battle, he died fighting. A good organizer and a fairly competent soldier, his generalship did not match his courage (Polyb. 11. 2). H. H. S.

**HASDRUBAL** (3) (son of Gisgo) commanded a Carthaginian army in Spain 214–206 B.C. With Mago he compassed the destruction of P. Scipio (211), but later was driven from his base Orongis (? Jaen) to Gades (207) and was completely defeated with Mago at Ilipa by Scipio Africanus (206). He fled via Gades to Africa, where as commander-in-chief he relieved the siege of Utica (204), but his camp was burnt by Scipio and his newly raised army was defeated at Campi Magni (203). After some guerrilla warfare he was accused of treason and committed suicide before Zama. H. H. S.

**HASDRUBAL** (4), commanded the Carthaginian forces against Masinissa (q.v.) and was defeated in 150 B.C. Although condemned to death, he escaped and was reinstated in his command at the outbreak of the Third Punic War. He organized resistance at first in the countryside (149), twice repulsing the Romans at Nepheris, and then, on the arrival of Scipio Aemilianus, in Carthage itself during the siege (148–146). In this he showed more ability than Polybius' unflattering characterization might suggest (38. 1–2), but when the city was doomed Hasdrubal surrendered, later to grace Scipio's triumph, while his wife and children preferred death to capture. H. H. S.

**HATĒRIUS,** QUINTUS (*cos. suff.* 5 B.C.), Augustan orator and declaimer, of senatorial family, noted for facility of improvisation and fluency of delivery (Tac. *Ann.* 4. 61; Sen. *Ep.* 40. 10) which caused Augustus to remark 'What he needs is a brake' (Sen. *Controv.* 4. *pr.* 6–11). He died A.D. 26, nearly 90 years old.

Syme, *Tacitus*, 323 f., 580. C. J. F.

**HATRA** (modern *al-Ḥaḍr*), a city in Mesopotamia *c.* 50 miles south of Mosul. It first comes into notice in A.D. 117, when it successfully withstood a siege by Trajan. Septimius Severus twice failed to take it (201–200) after its ruler, Barsemius, had supported his rival, Niger. It was ruled by a dynasty of Aramaic origin and owed its rise to the increasing importance of the overland trade route between northern Syria and the Persian Gulf. Because of Parthian obstruction or negligence the merchant caravans opened up a new desert route through upper Mesopotamia and past Hatra. In its last years an ally of Rome, Hatra was finally captured (c. 241) by the Sassanid Sapor I (q.v.) and thereafter was gradually abandoned by its inhabitants. Its decline was parallel with that of Palmyra and due to loss of trade caused by the increasing frequency of frontier wars. In 363 Jovian's army found it a ruin.

Its extensive ruins date mainly from the last period of Parthian rule. Its walls, nearly 4 miles in circuit, are strengthened by some thirty rectangular towers and within them is a vast palace complex of buildings and temple-remains, in process of excavation in 1965. The syncretistic religion, art, and architecture of Hatra reveal the cultural influence of its more powerful neighbours on what was essentially an Arab city and population.

W. Andrae, *Hatra* i, ii (1908–12); A. Stein, *Journ. Royal Asiatic Soc.* 1941, 299 ff., on trade route; J. Ingholt, *Parthian Sculptures from Hatra* (1954); A. Maricq, *Syria* 1955, 273 ff.; ibid. 1957, 288 ff.; J. Walker, *Num. Chron.* 1958, 167 ff., on coinage; D. Homès-Fredericq, *Hatra et les sculptures parthes* (1963); J. Teixidor, *Syria* 1966, 93 f.   E. W. G.

**HEATING** for cooking or warmth was primarily supplied in the classical world by charcoal stoves: hence the importance of charcoal-burning. The stoves took the form of chafing-dishes, gridirons, or braziers, elaborated in the Hellenistic world into jacketed vessels heated by fire or boiling water, of which magnificent examples for table use have been discovered at Pompeii. Equally old is the oven, extending from baker's shop to field-army, without a flue and heated by blazing wood withdrawn upon exhaustion of the air within. The use of hot water for bathing is as old as Homer (*Od.* 8. 249, 253) and precedes him at Cnossos, while Herodotus (4. 75) mentions sweat-baths, traditionally assigned to Sparta (Strabo 3. 154; Mart. 6. 42. 16) and warmed with heated stones, as in Lusitania. In Italy, where public bathing was widely introduced by the third century, heating was revolutionized by the introduction of the heated floor or hypocaust (q.v.). *See* BATHS.   I. A. R.

**HEBE** (Ἥβη, i.e. adolescence, youthful beauty), daughter of Hera (q.v.) and Zeus, sister of Ares and Eileithyia (qq.v.) (Hesiod, *Theog.* 922). She is unimportant in cult (temple at Phlius, Paus. 2. 12. 4; 13. 3, where she had been anciently called Ganymeda, cf. GANYMEDES), but occasionally associated with other deities (Heracles at Cynosarges, Paus. 1. 19. 3; Aphrodite, Farnell, *Cults* ii. 624, 744). In mythology she is the cup-bearer of the gods, as *Il.* 4. 2 and often later. Heracles has her to wife from *Od.* 11. 603 (a doubtfully genuine passage) onwards, and she appears now and again in a scene of Olympian domesticity, e.g. she bathes Ares after his encounter with Diomedes (*Il.* 5. 905), as a sister might an earthly brother in Homeric society. She intervenes to make the aged Iolaus young again, Eur. *Heracl.* 349 ff.; according to Ovid (*M. et.* 9. 401–2) Heracles induced her to make him young again. See von Sybel in Roscher's *Lexikon*, s.v.   H. J. R.

**HECALE** or **HECALINE**, a goddess worshipped with Zeus Hecalos in the deme Hecale; said to have been an old woman who entertained Theseus.

Callim. *Hecale* (see CALLIMACHUS 3); Plut. *Thes.* 14; L. Deubner, *Attische Feste* (1932), 217.

**HECATAEUS** (1), son of Hegesander, of Miletus, one of the earliest Ionian logographers, advised against the Ionian revolt in 500 B.C., but Aristagoras (q.v. 1) rejected his advice (Hdt. 5. 36, 124–6). He was familiar with the strength of the Persian Empire thanks to travels in Asia and Egypt, where Herodotus followed in his footsteps (2. 143) and borrowed much from him, as later critics pointed out (Euseb. *Praep. Evang.* 10. 3). Like Anaximander (q.v.) he made a map, perhaps the map of the world which Aristagoras showed to Cleomenes in Sparta (Hdt. 5. 49). He wrote a *Periegesis* or Περίοδος Γῆς, a 'guide' or 'journey round the world', to illustrate his map, a description of the countries and peoples to be encountered on a coastal voyage of the Mediterranean and Black Sea, with some diversions into the interior, ranging as far as India, Persia, and Scythia. There are over 300 fragments of this work, but many are brief citations in Stephanus of Byzantium, mentioning that a certain city or people occurred in the first book, 'Europe', os the second, 'Asia' (which included Africa). Callimachus (q.v. 3) as librarian of Alexandria would not accept the copy of 'Asia' known to him as the work of Hecataeus, but the grounds for his decision are unknown. Herodotus made use of the *Periegesis*, perhaps quite extensively, but he never mentions it and professes to scorn makers of maps (4. 36).

Hecataeus also wrote a mythographic work, cited variously as Γενεηλογίαι, Ἱστορίαι or Ἡρωολογία. The fragments of this work are less numerous, but they show that he dealt with the legends of Heracles and Deucalion and their descendants, as with other families that claimed heroic or divine origin—including, apparently, his own (Hdt. 2. 143). Some fragments show a rationalistic interpretation, and in his opening sentence (fr. 1) he shows a dogmatic attitude: 'I write what I believe to be the truth, for the Greeks have many stories which, it seems to me, are absurd.'

Fragments and testimonia in *FHG* i. 1–31, iv. 627b; *FGrH* i, no. 1; G. Nenci, *Hecataei Milesii Fragmenta* (1954). H. Diels, *Hermes* 1887, 411 ff.; F. Jacoby, *Griechische Historiker* (1956), repr. from *PW Hekataios*; W. A. Heidel, *Mem. Amer. Acad. of Arts and Sc.* 18. 2 (1935), 53 ff.; L. Pearson, *Early Ionian Historians* (1939), ch. 2 (bibliography 106 ff.). *See* GEOGRAPHY, HERODOTUS, LOGOGRAPHERS.   L. P.

**HECATAEUS** (2) of Abdera. His history of Egypt (Αἰγυπτιακά) under Ptolemy I, c. 300 B.C., popularized the theory of Egypt as the source of civilization, and was the basis of Manetho's more official account.

*FGrH* iii. 264.

**HECATE,** an ancient chthonian goddess (a kind of fish, τρίγλη, is sacrificed to her, Apollodorus ap. Ath. 325 a, and fish are a typical offering to under-world powers, cf. F. J. Dölger, *Ἰχθύς* (1928–43), *passim*), probably of Carian origin, as suggested by Nilsson (*GGR* i², 722 ff.). She is frequently confused with Artemis (q.v.), whose functions overlap to some extent with hers, also with Selene, the theory that she is a moon-goddess being supported also by many modern authors, though without justification, as no cult of the moon is to be found in Greece; however, a goddess of women, such as she was, tends to acquire some lunar features. Her associations with Artemis are so close and frequent that it is not always easy to tell to which of them a particular function or title belongs originally (Farnell, *Cults* ii. 516 ff.).

Hecate is not mentioned at all in Homer, but comes into sudden prominence in a sort of hymn to her in Hes. *Theog.* 411 ff., a passage whose genuineness has been much disputed. There she is granddaughter of Coeus and Phoebe, other authors giving other genealogies in a way which suggests that her connexion with Greek, or even pre-Greek and Titanic, deities was precarious. Zeus honours her exceedingly, giving her power and honour on earth and sea and also in the heavens, and taking away none of her original rights. If a man invokes her, she can benefit him in all manner of ways, for she is powerful in courts of law and in assemblies, can grant victory in war and athletics and success in horsemanship, in fishing, and cattle-breeding; she is also a nurturer of children (κουροτρόφος, a title likewise of Artemis). No other passage rates her so high, and this one must reflect the enthusiasm of a strong local cult, Boeotian or other, of which no more is known. Generally she is associated with uncanny things and the ghost-world. For this reason she is worshipped at the cross-roads (typically a place where a side path joins a main road), which seem to be haunted the world over. Here the notorious 'Hecate's suppers' were put out monthly for her (Ar. *Plut.* 594 ff. with schol.). It was a rite of purification, and one of its common constituents was dogs' flesh (Plut. *Quaest. Rom.* 290 d); cf. EGG. Hecate is herself a formidable figure, Ἀνταία (see Hesychius, s.v.), i.e. a bogy which 'meets' and frightens wayfarers. Hence it is not remarkable that she is associated with sorcery and black magic, from at least the tragic Medea (Eur. *Med.* 394 ff.) onwards. Thus we find her invoked to go away and take an obsessing spirit with her (Sophron, new frag.; see Festa in *Mondo classico* ii. 476 ff. for recent text); to help a dangerous love-charm which may bring destruction on the person it is aimed at (Theoc. 2. 12 ff.); and very often in magical papyri, etc. However, a more respectable cult of her seems also to have continued, see Farnell, *Cults* ii. 501 ff., 596 ff., and Nilsson, op. cit. and vol. ii *passim* for references to her cult in late periods.

Alcamenes was said to be the first to show her with three bodies (Paus. 2. 30. 2). Apart from the little Roman 'Hecataia' which may echo his statue, she is rarely re-presented in art. On a vase of the time of the Parthenon she lights Persephone from Hades; and other figures with torches may be meant for her rather than Persephone or Demeter.

T. Kraus, *Hekate* (1960); at cross-roads, see Roscher in his *Lexikon* i. 1904 ff., to which add *Hymn. Magic.* 5. 22 Abel (in his *Orphica*); Preisendanz, *PGM* iv. 2817 f.; Lydus, *Mens.* 3. 8, p. 41. 20 Wünsch, for her fourfold aspect. H. J. R.; C. M. R.

**HECATOMNUS** of Mylasa, son and successor of Hyssaldomus, satrap of Caria after the fall of Tissaphernes. He commanded the fleet in the Persian operations against Cyprus in 390 B.C. After his death in 377 his children (Mausolus and Artemisia, Idrieus and Ada, Pixodarus) ruled in succession as satraps and despots in south-western Asia Minor. J. M. C.

**HECATON** (Ἑκάτων) of Rhodes, a Platonizing Stoic, pupil of Panaetius, wrote chiefly on ethics, and was, next to Panaetius and Posidonius, the most influential member of the middle Stoic school.

WORKS: Περὶ ἀγαθῶν, Περὶ ἀρετῶν, Περὶ παθῶν, Περὶ παραδόξων, Περὶ τελῶν, Περὶ τέλους, Χρεῖαι, Περὶ καθήκοντος. Cicero preserves some of his arguments with regard to conflict of duties, from which he seems to have been interested in casuistry.

H. Gomoll, *Der stoische Philosoph Hekaton* (1933); M. Pohlenz, *Die Stoa*² ii (1955), 123 f. W. D. R.

**HECATONCHEIRES**, hundred-handed monsters, Cottus, Briareos, and Gyes, sons of Heaven and Earth (Hes. *Theog.* 147 ff.); aided Zeus against the Titans (713 ff.). Briareos (called Aegaeon by men) was brought by Thetis to protect Zeus against Hera, Poseidon, and Athena (*Il.* 1. 396 ff.).

**HECTOR**, in mythology, eldest son of Priam and Hecuba (qq.v.), and the bravest of the Trojan champions; husband of Andromache (q.v.) and father of Astyanax (*Il.* 6. 394 ff.). His name appears to be Greek ('holder', 'stayer'), and it is possible that he is the invention either of Homer or of some earlier poet. In the *Iliad* he first appears leading the Trojans out to battle (2. 807 ff.); he reproaches Paris for avoiding Menelaus (3.

38 ff.), and arranges the truce and the single combat between the two (85 ff.). He takes a prominent part in the fighting of books 5 and 6, but in the latter leaves the field for a while to advise the elders to make offerings to the gods. He thus sees Andromache for the last time and returns with Paris to the battle. In book 7 he challenges any Greek to single combat, and is met by the greater Aias, who has somewhat the better of it; they part with an exchange of gifts. In the next book he drives the Greeks back to their camp and bivouacs with his army on the plain. In the long battle of books 11-17 he takes a prominent part, leading the chief attack on the fortification of the camp and being struck down with a stone by Aias (14. 409 ff.), but restored by Apollo at the command of Zeus (15. 239 ff.). He dispatches Patroclus (16. 818 ff.). After the appearance of Achilles at the trench he again bivouacs in the open, against the advice of Polydamas (18. 249 ff.). After the rout of the following day he refuses to enter Troy (22. 35 ff.), but waits for Achilles, despite the entreaties of his parents. At Achilles' approach he flees, but after a long chase halts, deceived by Athena into thinking that Deïphobus has come to his aid. In the subsequent fight he is killed and his body dragged behind Achilles' chariot to the ships. After the burial of Patroclus, Priam ransoms his body (24. 188 ff.), and his funeral ends the *Iliad*. Later poets add nothing of importance to Homer's account.

Hector had a hero-cult in several places, notably at Troy and at Thebes, his supposed bones having been brought to the latter city at the bidding of an oracle (Julian, *Ep.* 79 Bidez–Cumont; Lycophron, 1205 ff. and schol. there; Paus. 9. 18. 5). See Halliday in *Liverpool Annals* xi, 3 ff.

In art he is shown from the early sixth century setting out to fight, or in combat with Aias or another, and especially meeting his death at Achilles' hands. The dragging and ransom of his body are also shown (Brommer, *Vasenlisten*², 257 ff., 279, 288 ff.).

Farnell, *Hero-Cults* 328 f. H. J. R.; C. M. R.

**HECUBA** (Ἑκάβη, Lat. *Hecuba*), in mythology, chief wife of Priam (q.v.), daughter of Dymas king of the Phrygians (*Il.* 16. 719; but later writers, as Eur. *Hec.* 3, call her father Cisseus). Who her mother was posed a problem to mythologists in Tiberius' time (Suet. *Tib.* 70). She was the mother of Hector (q.v.) and eighteen others of Priam's fifty sons (*Il.* 24. 495-7), the most noteworthy being Paris (q.v.).

In Homer she is a stately and pathetic figure, coming only occasionally into the foreground, as in the lament for Hector (*Il.* 24. 747 ff.). In Tragedy she is more prominent. Euripides (*Hecuba*) tells the following story of her last days. Her son Polydorus (q.v. 2) had been murdered by the Thracian Polymestor, to whom he had been entrusted; the discovery of his body came as a final blow to Hecuba after the sacrifice of her daughter Polyxena (q.v.). By a desperate appeal to Agamemnon, she got permission to revenge herself and, enticing Polymestor into her tent, she and her women killed his children and blinded him. He then foretold that she should turn into a bitch before her death, the place Cynos Sema getting its name from her tomb. In Eur. *Tro.* 969 ff., she so convincingly accuses Helen that Menelaus promises to kill her on reaching home, one of Euripides' curious departures from tradition. In several plays no longer extant, e.g. Ribbeck, *TRF, incert.* 5, from some Greek model, she was represented as dreaming, while carrying Paris, that she brought forth a torch, which burned all Troy (Apollod. 3. 148). All these legends appear in numerous variants, with rationalizations, more or less fanciful additions, and so forth, as is usual with much-handled themes. H. J. R.

**HEDYLUS** (fl. 280 B.C.), Greek epigrammatist, came from a family of Athenian poets and lived in Samos and Alexandria. He has a few gay poems in the Greek Anthology (q.v.) and others are cited by Athenaeus: drink and feasting are his main themes. He worked closely with Asclepiades (2) and Posidippus (2) (qq.v.) but his tone is coarser.

Gow and Page, 1825 ff. W. and M. Wallace, *TAPA* 1939; T. B. L. Webster, *Hellenistic Poetry and Art* (1964), ch. 2.          G. H.

**HEGEMON** of Thasos, parodist, described 'by some' as a poet of Old Comedy (Ath. 1. 5 b. But Ath. 15. 699 a γέγραφε δὲ καὶ κωμῳδίαν εἰς τὸν ἀρχαῖον τρόπον ἦν ἐπιγράφουσι Φιλίνην suggests a later date for him). For Aristotle (*Poet.* 2. 1448ª12) Hegemon is ὁ τὰς παρῳδίας ποιήσας πρῶτος, in that Hegemon raised Parody (already cultivated by others, *see* PARODY) into an independent genre with a separate place of its own in competitions. A passage of Hegemon (21 vv.) is quoted by Athenaeus (15. 698 f.) from Polemon: Hegemon's verses claim for his performance 50 drachmae, the second prize, and Polemon attests the victory of Hegemon at Athens with his *Gigantomachia* and other parodies.

For two verses of the *Philine* see *CAF* i. 700. Brandt, *Corp. poes. ep. Graec. lud.* 37 ff.; *FCG* i. 214 f.          W. G. W.

**HEGESANDER** of Delphi (2nd c. B.C.) wrote at least six books of *Memoirs* (Ὑπομνήματα: Ath. 162 a), an ordered collection of unreliable anecdotes concerning Hellenistic kings, parasites, courtesans, philosophers, etc.; references mainly in Athenaeus (*FHG* iv. 412–22).

**HEGESIAS** (1) of Cyrene, head of the Cyrenaic school between Paraebates and Anniceris in the time of Ptolemy Soter (who died 283 B.C.); nicknamed Πεισιθάνατος because in his Ἀποκαρτερῶν he advocated suicide. He was expelled from Alexandria because of the scandal caused by his lectures.

G. Giannantoni, *I Cirenaici* (1958); E. Mannebach, *Aristippi et Cyrenaicorum Fragmenta* (1961).          W. D. R.

**HEGESIAS** (2) of Magnesia (3rd c. B.C.), historian and orator. Some fragments of his *History of Alexander* survive (*FGrH* 142). All ancient judgements of his style are hostile; as the typical 'Asianist' (*see* RHETORIC, GREEK § 3), he was the *bête noire* of classicizing writers from the time of Cicero onwards (see, e.g., Cic. *Brutus* 286; Dion. Hal. *de compositione verborum* 4. 28; 'Longinus' 3. 2). His fragments show strongly rhythmical short cola, eccentric expression, and 'Gorgianic' figures.

Norden, *Ant. Kunstpr.* 134 ff.          D. A. R.

**HEGESIPPUS** (1) (c. 390–c. 325), Athenian statesman, contemporary with Demosthenes, nicknamed κρωβύλος ('top-knot') from his old-fashioned hair style, an obscure but not unimportant figure. He was already a man of note in the 350s, and in 355 proposed the decree of alliance with Phocis. In the 340s he became prominent as a vigorous opponent of Philip, and appears to have been one of the very few Athenian statesmen who opposed the making of the Peace of Philocrates (Schol. ad Dem. 19. 72). In 344/3 he played a decisive part in obstructing the offer of Philip, brought by Python of Byzantium, to turn the Peace into a Common Peace of all the Greeks. With Demosthenes' support, Hegesippus persuaded the Athenians to send him on an embassy to renew their claim on Amphipolis, which they had renounced in 346; as was to be expected, he was unceremoniously received by Philip, and, when in early 342 Philip made the offer again, Hegesippus exerted himself to secure its final rejection. The speech *de Halonneso* ([Dem.] 7) is now generally agreed to be his contribution to the debate on that occasion (Dionysius of Halicarnassus, who accepted it

as Demosthenic despite strong contrary indications of style, was not followed by Libanius). The speech is misleadingly titled from the first topic with which it deals; it is really concerned to answer a letter from Philip περὶ τῆς ἐπανορθώσεως τῆς εἰρήνης (§ 18 ff.) and manifests a complete refusal to assent to the decisions of 346. His policy was, in short, like that of Demosthenes, to seek a renewal of the war (cf. Plut. *Mor.* 187 e and Aeschin. 2. 137). He was still active in politics after Chaeronea, but was not one of the demagogues whose surrender Alexander demanded in 335.          G. L. C.

**HEGESIPPUS** (2), New Comedy poet, who, like others in this period, mentions Epicurus (fr. 2). In fr. 1 a vainglorious cook expatiates upon his art.

*FGG* iv. 479 ff.; *CAF* iii. 312 ff.

**HEGESIPPUS** (3) (fl. 300 B.C.), a professional writer of epigrams: eight of his poems are in the *Greek Anthology*, most of them authentic inscriptions for tombs and votive tablets. His language is noticeably formal, archaic, and impersonal.

**HEIRCTE** (Εἵρκτη, Ἑρκταί, Ἑρκτή), a mountain near Panormus (*Palermo*) in Sicily, seized and held by Hamilcar Barca (247–244 B.C.) in order to strike at the rear of the Roman armies besieging Drepana and Lilybaeum and to threaten Panormus. Its identification with *Monte Pellegrino* has been maintained by De Sanctis (*Stor. Rom.* iii. 1. 181) against J. Kromayer (*Antike Schlachtfelder* iii (1912), 1), who identifies it with *Monte Castellaccio* north-west of Palermo.

Polyb. 1. 56 (cf. Walbank, *Commentary* ad loc.).          H. H. S.

**HEKTEMOROI** (ἑκτήμοροι), 'sixth-part men', a class of peasants in Attica before Solon (q.v.). Exactly what they were and what Solon did for them was not clearly remembered and is much disputed. Most probably they were in origin free small-holders who in difficult times had borrowed corn from wealthier neighbours. These, in default of repayment, progressively took over their land, planting on it markers of wood or stone (ὅροι) as a sign of ownership, but allowed them to continue to farm it as serfs, on condition they handed over one-sixth of the produce. If they failed to do this, they and theirs were apparently liable to be sold into slavery. Solon cancelled their debts and restored their land to them, removing the markers.

N. G. L. Hammond, *JHS* 1961, 76 ff.; A. French, *Hist.* 1963. 242 ff.; *Growth of the Athenian Economy* (1964), 10 ff.; F. Cassola, *PP* 1964, 26 ff., with full bibliography; also E. Will, *Rev. Ét. Anc.* 1957, 5 ff.; G. Ferrara, *PP* 1960, 20 ff.; R. J. Hopper in *Ancient Society and Institutions* (1966), 139 ff.          A. W. G.; T. J. C.

**HELEN** (Ἑλένη), daughter of Zeus and Leda, or Nemesis (qq.v.). She is one of the most plausible examples of a 'faded' goddess, i.e. one whose original deity has been forgotten, and who has been consequently made into a mortal woman in mythology. This is not proved by her having had a cult at Sparta and elsewhere (Farnell, *Hero-Cults*, 323); we may compare, for instance, the much more widely spread worship of Heracles (q.v.). But her non-Greek name, her association with trees (Δενδρῖτις at Rhodes, Paus. 3. 19. 10, with a story that she was hanged on a tree, cf. Artemis Ἀπαγχομένη, ibid. 8. 23. 6–7; 'Helen's tree' at Sparta, Theoc. 18. 43 ff.), and her connexion with birds (she is born from an egg and Zeus takes bird-form to visit her mother; cf. Nilsson, *Minoan-Mycenaean Rel.²*, ch. 10, for epiphanies of Minoan gods in bird-shape) all fit an ancient, pre-Hellenic goddess, probably connected with vegetation and fertility, better than a dimly remembered princess, or even a purely imaginary human member of an ancient royal family. It is in no wise impossible that an old deity traditionally worshipped by the pre-Dorian population of Laconia had been taken, long before Homer, for an ancestress of their kings. Even in Homer she has something daemonic about her, e.g. the mere fact of being her husband is Menelaus' passport to Elysium (*Od.* 4. 569). Also, as Nilsson (*GGR* i², 475) has stressed, the legends of her being carried off fit a goddess of vegetation.

In the *Iliad* and *Odyssey* she is the human wife of Menelaus, who has been carried off to Troy by Paris (q.v.). She is, while at Troy, Paris' wife, not his mistress, but feels deeply the anomalous position of being the legal wife of two different men in different places (see *Il.* 3. 139–40, 443 ff.; 24. 763 ff.). Her sympathies are on the whole with the Greeks, but on occasion she is decidedly pro-Trojan, as *Od.* 4. 274 ff. There seems to have been no difficulty about a reconciliation between her and Menelaus after the war, and in the *Odyssey* she is living happily with him at Lacedaemon. Her carrying off by Paris is the cause of the war (*Il.* 3. 87 and often).

Later authors, not realizing that Agamemnon was overlord of Mycenaean Greece, elaborate the reasons for the war. Besides the original plan of Zeus (cf. NEMESIS, and add Hesiod, fr. 96. 58 ff. Rzach), she was wooed by the noblest men in Greece, and they all swore to support the rights of her husband, whoever he might be (authorities and variants in Rose, *Handb. Gk. Myth.* 249, note 7). Others tell the story of her earlier and later life. She was carried off when a mere child by Theseus (Plut. *Thes.* 31 and elsewhere; cf. DIOSCURI). At the sack of Troy Menelaus was at first disposed to kill her (see Robert, *Bild und Lied* (1881), 76 ff.; cf. HECUBA). She never went to Troy at all, but Paris carried off a phantom of her, (Stesichorus; J. Vürtheim, *Stesichoros' Fragmente* (1919), 64 ff.). She appears as St. Elmo's fire (schol. Eur. *Or.* 1637, Pliny, *HN* 2. 101). *See also* ACHILLES.

Her chief appearances in art, from the sixth century, are: her abduction by Theseus; her wedding to Menelaus; her flight with Paris; the wedding to Paris in Troy; Helen with Paris; her recovery by Menelaus (who sometimes attacks her with drawn sword). On some late fifth- and fourth-century vases we find her hatching from the egg; and Agoracritus showed her on the base of his Nemesis at Rhamnus being presented to Nemesis by Leda.

Farnell, *Cults* ii. 675; *Hero-Cults* 323 ff.; and the dictionaries and handbooks of mythology. In art, Brommer, *Vasenlisten²*, 168 f., 291 ff., 311, 320, 326, 362 f.; Ghali-Kahil, *Les enlèvements et le retour d'Hélène* (1955). H. J. R.; C. M. R.

**HELENUS**, in mythology, son of Priam, warrior and prophet. In the *Iliad* he gives prophetic advice to Hector (6. 76, 7. 44), and is wounded by Menelaus at the battle of the ships (book 13). Captured by Odysseus, he prophesied the fall of Troy if Philoctetes was brought there with his bow (Soph. *Phil.* 604–13). After the fall of Troy he was carried off by Neoptolemus, who gave him Andromache as his wife (Eur. *Andr.* 1243). They settled in Epirus and made 'a little Troy'; there they were visited by Aeneas, to whom Helenus prophesied his future wanderings (Verg. *Aen.* 3. 294–505). C. B.

**HELIAIA** (ἡλιαία) seems originally to have meant just 'assembly', but in Athens the term was used specifically for an assembly of citizens meeting to hear appeals against magistrates' verdicts, or to impose penalties above certain limits, according to the procedure instituted by Solon (q.v.). When this function was taken over by juries, *heliaia* was sometimes used to mean the whole body of jurors, and ἡλιαστής was a word for 'juror', synonymous with δικαστής. But more often *heliaia* was used as the name of one particular court, the court of the *thesmothetai* (q.v.).

*See* DIKASTERION and the bibliography there. D. M. M.

**HELICON**, the largest mountain of Boeotia (5,868 feet), between Copais and the Corinthian Gulf; and particularly the summit behind Thespiae, which contained the sanctuary of the Muses in a glen. There are remains of an Ionic temple, theatre, and statues of the Muses; games were held every fourth year in their honour. On its slopes lay Ascra, the home of Hesiod. The spring Hippocrene, struck by Pegasus' foot from the rock, the inspiration of poets (Prop. 3. 3; legend and function are Hellenistic), is a little below the summit.

Paus. 9. 28–31; Bölte, Mayer, and Fiehn, *PW* viii. 1 ff., 1853 ff.; xvi. 696 ff., 821; P–K, *GL* I. ii. 434 ff. *See also* THESPIAE.
T. J. D.; R. J. H.

**HELIODORUS** (1) of Athens wrote (*c.* 150 B.C. ?) Ἀναθήματα (title varies), fifteen books on artistic works on the Athenian Acropolis, with historical and other digressions.

Ath. 6. 229 e; 9. 406 c; 2. 45 c (?); Pliny *HN* 1. 34–5; *FGrH* iii. 373.

**HELIODORUS** (2), a metrist who flourished in the middle of the first century A.D. He gave Aristophanes' comedies a colometry (division of the text into cola), adding metrical signs (σημεῖα) and a continuous metrical analysis. Much of his labours is preserved in the scholia to Aristophanes. He was the principal authority used by Juba (q.v. 3).

J. W. White, *The Verse of Greek Comedy* (1912), 384 ff. K. J. D.

**HELIODORUS** (3), a popular surgeon of the time of Juvenal (who lived *c.* A.D. 60–140; cf. Juv. 6. 373), probably from Egypt. He belonged to the pneumatic school.

WORKS: (1) Χειρουργούμενα (principal work, chiefly known from Oribasius); (2) ? Περὶ ἄρθρων πραγματεία or Ἐπιμήχανος; (3) Περὶ ὀλισθημάτων πραγματεία; (4) Περὶ ἐπιδέσμων (on bandages); (5) Περὶ μέτρων καὶ σταθμῶν; (6) *Epistula phlebotomiae* (Lat. transl.). *See* SURGERY, § 6.
W. D. R.

**HELIODORUS** (4), Greek romancer, author of the *Aethiopica*, the longest and best constructed of the Greek novels extant. His floruit is generally put (Münscher) at A.D. 220–50, on the basis of admittedly treacherous stylistic comparisons with other romancers and authors. Whether he is to be identified with the Heliodorus who became a Christian bishop (Socrates, *Hist. Eccl.* 5. 22) is doubtful. Heliodorus was from Emesa in Syria, as he says (*Aeth.* 10. 41), calling himself 'son of Theodosius, of the race of the Sun', which seems to point to some family connexion with the Helios cult established in that town. The environment did not fail to influence our author, whose work is penetrated with sincere religious piety, pervaded by an edifying tone and free from licentiousness. Heliodorus' syncretistic faith is deep: Helios (identified with Apollo) holds the personages (often through his priests) in leading-strings. The story is that Charicleia, the daughter of the queen of Aethiopia, having been born white and consequently exposed by her mother for fear of the king's suspicions, had been brought up by priests and became herself a priestess of Apollo in Delphi, where she meets, and falls in love with, a noble Thessalian by the name of Theagenes. After innumerable adventures and much wandering the enamoured couple are finally married, in the very presence, and with full approval, of the Aethiopian royal couple. The scheme of the plot is evidently the traditional one in the genre (the triumph of two lovers over all difficulties; there are, of course, battles, abductions, pirates, robbers, tortures, voyages, all the compulsory ingredients). Language and style, too, are very much in accordance with the genre: Heliodorus follows the canons of the sophistic *apheleia*, his diction is pure Attic (although vulgarisms escape him now and then), there are excursuses on natural phenomena, descriptive *ekphraseis*, letters. The author's literary pretentions are evident in the use of excessively daring metaphors and recherché expressions; unlike Achilles Tatius, he often indulges in ample sentences with frequent use of participles, in harmony with the amplitude of his work. Heliodorus' characterization is weak, as Byzantine critics did not fail to note: this is another point which he has in common with the other romancers. He is lacking in sense of humour, and his—fortunately rare—*argutiae* are frigid. On the other hand, the author's literary knowledge was unusually wide, as appears from his frequent and often apt quotations and allusions. What makes Heliodorus excel over the other Greek romancers is, however, his skilled and unsurpassed technique of narration: he superbly masters the development of the plot, which, in spite of its amplitude and complexity, never becomes confused. The novel brings us *in medias res*: our interest is immediately, and for ever, captivated. Through 'flash-back', appropriate concatenation of the many accessory episodes, 'surprises' intervening at the right moment, the tension is never relaxed: he mentions himself some elements of his technique in *Aeth.* 10. 39. The Byzantine critics particularly admired Heliodorus for the skilled oikonomia of his narration and his edifying tone; their admiration was inherited by the Renaissance. Scaliger praised him very highly, and so did Tasso, who modelled the early life of one of his heroines (Clorinda, in *Gerusalemme Liberata* 12. 21 ff.) on that of Charicleia. Calderon's *Los hijos de la Fortuna* and Cervantes' *Persiles y Sigismunda* are modelled upon Heliodorus' romance. After the appearance of the editio princeps (1534) and Amyot's French translation (1547) innumerable translations in modern languages were published (German, Italian, Spanish, English, Dutch).

EDITIO PRINCEPS. Basel, 1534 (Opsopoeus).
STANDARD EDITIONS. Colonna (Rome, 1938); Rattenbury–Lumb–Maillon (Paris, 1935–43, 3 vols., with excellent introduction and preface on text, style, etc.; repr. 1960).
COMMENTARY. Coraes (Paris, 1804, in modern Greek).
CRITICISM. Münscher, *PW*, s.v. Heliodoros 15; Rohde, *Griech. Roman* 453 ff.; Christ–Schmid–Stählin ii. 2⁶, 820 ff.; A. Lesky, *Gesch. d. griech. Litt.²* (1963), 922 ff.; J. Fritsch, *Der Sprachgebrauch des ... Heliodor und sein Verhältnis zum Atticismus* (1901–2) (2 parts); M. Oeftering, *Heliodor und seine Bedeutung für die Literatur*, (1901); H. Dörrie, H. Rommel, see biography under ACHILLES TATIUS; V. Hefti, *Zur Erzählungstechnik in Heliodors Aethiopica* (Diss. Basel, 1950); M. SchnePf, *De Imitationis ratione, quae intercedit inter Heliodorum et Xenophontem Ephesium* (Progr. Kempten, 1887); P. Neimke, *Quaestiones Heliodoreae* (Diss. Halle, 1889).
DATE: late fourth century: R. Keydall, *Polychronicon für F. Dölger* (1966), 345 ff.                                                              G. G.

**HELIOPOLIS** (modern *Baalbek*) was the religious centre of the Ituraean tetrarchy (q.v.), after whose dissolution it received a Roman colony (*c.* 16 B.C.). The huge temple of Jupiter-Hadad (1st. cent. A.D.), its two courtyards (completed under Philip the Arab), the adjacent temple of Bacchus (Antonine period), and another small circular temple are among the most impressive monuments of the Syrian school of Hellenistic architecture.

T. Wiegand, *Baalbek* (1921–5); O. Eissfeldt, *Tempel und Kulte syrischer Staedte* (1941); P. Collart and P. Coupel, *L'Autel monumental de Baalbek* (1951).                                    A. H. M. J.; H. S.

**HELIOS**, the Sun-god. The general attitude towards the heavenly bodies in Greece seems to have been that although undoubtedly gods (cf. the indignation at Athens over Anaxagoras' announcement that the sun was a material body, Diog. Laert. 2. 12; and Nilsson's com-

ments, *Harv. Theol. Rev.* 1940), they were no concern of mankind, or at most were beings to be saluted with due reverence on occasion (Pl. *Leg.* 887 e), not to receive a regular cult, as did those gods who dwelt in the cities or country-side, like Athena or the Nymphs, or at farthest on hill-tops, like Zeus. Hence the traces of sun-cult in Greece proper are few and often uncertain (see Farnell, *Cults* v. 419 f.). Rhodes, however, had a vigorous cult of Helios, which is one of several non-Greek features in its classical culture. He appears to have been the chief national god (Diod. Sic. 5. 56. 4), and the local legend (Pind. *Ol.* 7. 54 ff.) makes the island his peculiar property, chosen by him before it rose to the surface of the sea, and his sons its chief early inhabitants, after whom the leading towns were named; their mother was the eponymous nymph of the country, Rhodos. His festival was the Halieia (Nilsson, *Feste* 427); it was celebrated with much splendour and included important athletic contests, though never rising to the level of the Great Games. Outside of actual cult, Helios is often appealed to as a witness of oaths and the like, as *Il.* 3. 277, because, as there stated, he sees and hears everything.

He has not much mythology; for the most interesting story about him *see* PHAETHON. He is regularly conceived as a charioteer, who drives daily from east to west across the sky. The question how he got back again during the night was evidently discussed very early, and the quaint solution evolved that he floated around the earth by the stream of Ocean in a huge cup (references collected in Athenaeus, 469 c ff.).

In later times the theological importance of Helios increased considerably, owing to the growing tendency to identify him with other gods. In the case of Apollo (q.v.), this is as early as the fifth century B.C., and doubtless the allegorizing tendency of the Stoics, who very commonly sought a physical explanation of myths, made its contribution a century or so later; but the strongest impetus in this direction was given by the late imperial increase of actual cult of the Sun, culminating in making him in some sense the principal god of the Empire from Aurelian on. The *locus classicus* is Macrobius, *Sat.* 1. 17. 2 ff., where by a series of ingenious arguments the proposition is supported that all the gods, 'dumtaxat qui sub caelo sunt', i.e. with the omission of the transcendental powers outside the material universe, are powers or activities ('uirtutes', 17. 4) of the sun; but Macrobius' own quotations, beginning with Verg. *G.* 1. 6, show that the theory had been long growing.

Farnell, *Cults* v. 417 ff.; Rapp in Roscher's *Lexikon*, art. 'Helios'; Cumont, *Rel. or.*, see index, s.v. 'Soleil'; Nilsson, *ARW* 1933, 141 ff.; Cumont, *Mélanges Bidez* (1934), 141 f. For the developments in late periods, see Nilsson, *GGR* ii. 486 ff.          H. J. R.

**HELLANICUS** of Lesbos was a contemporary of Herodotus who outlived him and was still writing in 406 B.C. (Schol. Ar. *Ran.* 694); since the name Ἑλλά-νικος appears to commemorate a 'Greek victory' one tradition held that he was born on the day of Salamis (*Vit. Eurip.* 2). He was a prolific writer, and fairly extensive fragments survive which mention twenty-four separate titles. His work falls into three groups:

(1) Mythographic works, which attempted to bring order into the contradictions of mythology, often with bold innovations. *Phoronis*, *Deucalioneia*, *Atlantis*, and *Asopis* offered systematic accounts of heroic families; *Troica* continued the story after the fall of Troy and brought Aeneas to Italy. These works were used extensively by Dionysius of Halicarnassus in his *Roman Antiquities* and in Apollodorus, *Bibliotheca*.

(2) Regional history or ethnography, e.g. *Lesbiaca*, *Boeotiaca*, *Aegyptiaca*, *Persica*, *Scythica*, Βαρβαρικὰ νόμιμα.

(3) Local history and chronology, e.g. *Atthis*, the first

history of Athens from earliest times (*see* ATTHIS), cited by Thuc. 1. 97 for its inadequate chronology of the fifth century; a chronological table based on lists of *Priestesses of Hera in Argos* (cf. Thuc. 2. 2.); and a list of *Carnean victors*.

His style is said to have been undistinguished (Cic. *De Orat.* 2. 12. 53).

*FHG* i. 45–69; *FGrH* i (ed. 2 1957), no. 4, iii B. 40–50, iii b Suppl. 1–57; Jacoby, *Gr. Historiker* (1956), 262 ff. (repr. of *PW*), *Atthis* (1949); L. Pearson, *Early Ionian Historians* (1939), ch. 5, *The Local Historians of Attica* (1942), ch. 1; A. Lesky, *History of Greek Literature* (Engl. Transl. 1966), 330 ff. L. P.

**HELLANODIKAI** were the judges of the Olympian Games (q.v.). They were chosen from the ruling families of Elis, to whom also the revenues of the festival accrued. Dressed in purple robes, they had special seats, presented the victors with their crowns, and presided over the banquet which ended the festival. They exercised disciplinary authority over the athletes and imposed fines for breaches of their rules. F. A. W.

**HELLEN** (Ἕλλην), eponymous ancestor of the Hellenes, son or brother of Deucalion (q.v.; Thuc. 1. 3. 2; schol. Pind. *Ol.* 9. 68). His sons were Dorus, Xuthus (*see* CREUSA 1) and Aeolus (q.v. 2) (Hesiod, fr. 7 Rzach); i.e. the Dorians, Ionians, and Aeolians have a common ancestry. This is not mythology, but early ethnological theory cast in the traditional mythological form of a genealogy. H. J. R.

**HELLENES** (Ἕλληνες), the national name of the Greeks. Originally it was confined, as well as the territorial name of Hellas, to a small tribe in south Thessaly (Hom. *Il.* 2. 683 f.). Perhaps these were in some way related to the Selloi or Helloi of Dodona (though these were a priesthood, not a tribe); the surroundings of Dodona were called Hellopia (cf. Arist. *Mete.* 1. 352ᵃ 31 ff.). The name of 'Hellenes' wandered southwards, probably in connexion with the migration of the Dorians and the western tribes. We do not know how the name spread further. 'Panhellenes' was earlier than 'Hellenes' (*Il.* 2. 530, Hes. *Op.* 528, Archil. 54 D), but was nothing but an extended tribal name. Homer calls the Greek people Achaeans, Argives, or Danai. The name 'Hellenes' for the Greek people in general is probably not older than the seventh century B.C. For their eponymous ancestor, Hellen, father of Dorus, Aeolus, and Xuthus (whose sons were Ion and Achaeus), see the preceding article. The name of the judges at the Olympian Games (*Hellanodikai*, q.v.) may indicate that the name of Hellenes was first used at the Games. In calling the treasurers of the Delian League *Hellenotamiai* (q.v.) it was made clear that they were not State officials; at the same time, there may have been the implicit idea of a Hellenic league.

*Entretiens Hardt*, vol. 8; V. Ehrenberg, *The Greek State* (1960). V. E.

**HELLENOTAMIAI** ('Treasurers of the Greeks') were the financial overseers of the Delian League, with their office in Delos from 477 to 454 B.C., thereafter in Athens; from the first, however, they were Athenian officials, elected at Athens, and they were ten in number. After 454 they were elected perhaps by vote, normally one from each *phyle*, and received, through the *apodektai* (q.v.), the tribute from the cities of the League, subject to audit by the *logistai* (q.v.). They had general management of the tribute for the year, paying out sums on the instruction of the *ekklesia*, chiefly to *strategoi*, sometimes for other purposes (such as the Acropolis buildings). After 411 they received wider powers (*see* KOLAKRETAI); with the fall of the Athenian Empire in 404 the office was abolished.

A. G. Woodhead, *JHS* 1959, 149 ff. A. W. G.

**HELLESPONT,** the narrow strait dividing Europe from Asia at the final exit of the waters of the Black Sea and Marmara into the Aegean—the modern Dardanelles. It was crossed by the Persian army under Xerxes between Sestos and Abydos, at the narrowest part near the modern Nagara Point. It was again crossed by Alexander the Great in 334 B.C. A strong current runs out from the Hellespont into the Aegean. Callipolis (*Gallipoli*), Lampsacus, Sestos, and Abydos are on its shores, with the sites of Troy and Dardanus on the Asiatic side. All cities alike derived much of their wealth from the fisheries, and from the passage of people and armies from Europe to Asia and vice versa. The name Hellespont is connected with the legend of Phrixus and Helle (*see* ATHAMAS).

J. Boardman, *The Greeks Overseas* (1964), 275 ff. S. C.

**HELOTS.** Some Greek States had servile populations who were not proper, privately owned slaves (q.v.) but stood 'between the free men and the slaves' (Poll. *Onom.* 3. 83). Unlike slaves, they were not imported from outside but were subjected *en bloc* in their own territories, either during the 'dark age' in early Greece and Crete or during the later Greek expansion, western and eastern. They were engaged chiefly in agriculture and pasturage and in domestic service, and their historical importance was primarily in the less urbanized States. Very little is known about any of them other than the helots of Sparta (q.v.) and it is therefore convenient to group them under this rubric, without, however, implying that they were all in precisely identical positions. Much of the surviving information comes from the lexicographers, who were attracted by their curious names and the opportunity for fanciful etymological play: the *penestai* of Thessaly, the *gymnetes* of Argos, the *korynephoroi* of Sicyon, the *Mariandynoi* of Heraclea Pontica, the *Kyllyrioi* of Syracuse, and the various odd names in Crete. 'Helots' were probably more widespread, at one time or another, in Sicily, Asia Minor, and what are now Rumania and Russia, than this mere collection of names might suggest.

The helot system in Laconia (q.v.) presumably originated during the migrations and resettlement following the Mycenaean breakdown, and it was then extended to Messenia (q.v.) by conquest. Actual figures are unavailable (the 7:1 ratio implied by Hdt. 9. 10, 29 is unacceptable), but the helots clearly outnumbered the Spartans and perhaps even the total free population of Laconia, a balance unknown in communities with a genuine slave population. Unlike slaves, too, helots maintained genuine family, and even community, relations. They were a self-perpetuating body who survived, without recruits from outside, in Messenia until Thebes freed them in 369 B.C., in Laconia until King Nabis (q.v.) early in the second century B.C. They were 'owned' by the State (Strabo 8. 5. 4), who had the sole power to manumit, exercised only exceptionally, in particular when, from the Peloponnesian War on, manpower shortage compelled the enrolment of surprisingly large numbers in the hoplite ranks. After manumission helots became *Neodamodeis*, a status about which hardly anything is known.

The main responsibility of helots to their individual Spartan masters was the provision of a fixed quota of supplies (keeping the surplus for themselves) and some domestic service, including that of batman on campaign. The extent to which individual Spartans could dispose of their helots by gift, dowry, or possibly even sale, is unclear, nor is it known if and how the State replaced anyone's depleted stock (e.g. as the result of enrolment in the army). Control and punishment were exercised both by individuals and by the State (*see* KRYPTEIA).

Greek writers stressed Spartan brutality towards the helots (e.g. Thuc. 4. 80). If helot revolts are attributed chiefly to that, the difficulty arises of explaining their employment in the army or the fact that the great revolts were restricted to the Messenian helots. Probably the emphasis should rather be on 'national' cohesion, the element lacking in the large slave concentrations (who did not revolt). Aristotle noted (*Pol.* 1272ᵇ16) the quiescence of the servile population in Crete and explained the difference in behaviour by the absence of foreign intervention. Some support comes from the Argive revolt (Hdt. 6. 83), probably, in 494 B.C., in conjunction with the invasion by Cleomenes (q.v. 1), possibly from the Sicel revolt under Ducetius (q.v.), and perhaps from the Crimean revolt under the Scythian Saumacus at the time of Mithridates VI (q.v.).

D. Lotze, *ΜΕΤΑΞΥ ΕΛΕΥΘΕΡΩΝ ΚΑΙ ΔΟΥΛΩΝ* (Berlin, 1959), and 'Zu den Φοικέες von Gortyn', *Klio* 1962, 32 ff.; M. I. Finley, 'The Servile Statuses of Ancient Greece', *Rev. Int. des Droits de l'Antiquité* 1960, 165 ff.; R. F. Willetts, *Aristocratic Society in Ancient Crete* (1955), chs. 5-6; 'The Servile Interregnum at Argos', *Hermes* 1959, 495 ff.; D. M. Pippidi, *Epigraphische Beiträge zur Geschichte Histrias* (1962), ch. 5; C. Mossé, 'Le Rôle des esclaves dans les troubles politiques . . .', *Cahiers d'histoire* vi (1961), 353 ff.; B. Shimron, 'Nabis of Sparta and the Helots', *CPhil.* 1966, 1 ff. M. I. F.

**HELVETII,** a Celtic tribe originally located in south Germany, which migrated gradually *c.* 200 B.C. to an area between the Rhine, the Jura, and the lake of Geneva. Part of it joined the Cimbri *c.* 111, and a migration (probably not, as Caes. *BGall.* 1. 29. 1, *en masse*) in 58 was defeated by Caesar, who sent the remnants home, allowing them, however, the privilege of a *foedus*. Under Augustus they formed part of *Gallia Belgica*, later of *Germania Superior*, with the normal organization of a cantonal senate at the capital, Aventicum (q. v.: *Avenches*), and *pagi*. The region paid dearly for opposition to Vitellius (A.D. 69); Vespasian, however, restored Avenches with the title of colony, and a period of prosperity began. From *c.* A.D. 260, when the *Limes* was abandoned, the region was exposed to the attacks of Alamanni and was heavily fortified. By 460 it was under the control of Burgundians and Alamanni.

F. Stähelin, *Die Schweiz in römischer Zeit³* (1948); Grenier, *Manuel* i. 350 ff.; ii. 375 ff., 593 ff.; G. Grosjean, 'Die röm. Limitation um Aventicum', *Jahrb. d. schweizerischen Gesellschaft für Urgeschichte* 1963, 1 ff. C. E. S.

**HELVIDIUS PRISCUS,** son of a *primipilaris* from Samnium, was *tr. pl.* A.D. 56, praetor 70. In early youth he studied philosophy seriously, and about 55 married (as his second wife) Fannia, daughter of Thrasea (q.v.) Paetus, whose political doctrines he shared. Exiled after his father-in-law's condemnation, he returned under Galba; and though earlier a friend of Vespasian, he took a critical attitude towards the Flavian regime from the start (Tac. *Hist.* 4. 6-8, 43). Later his attacks on the Emperor became violent, and he was exiled and subsequently executed (? 75). If Tacitus was right in ascribing Stoic principles to him, the δημοκρατία which Dio Cassius (65. 12) says he preached can hardly have been rule by the people: it was probably the old aristocratic ideal of *libertas* not necessarily Republicanism, but perhaps including strong opposition to Vespasian's conception of an hereditary principate.

Helvidius' son by his first marriage, a friend of Tacitus and Pliny the Younger, became consul under Domitian but was executed *c.* 93.

D. R. Dudley, *A History of Cynicism* (1937), 132 ff.; Rostovtzeff, *Roman Empire²*, 114 ff.; Syme, *Tacitus*, see index. G. E. F. C.

**HEMITHEA,** in mythology a daughter of Staphylus, was established by Apollo as a healing deity at Kastabos in the Carian Chersonese (Diod. 5. 62-3). Her sanctuary has been identified on a spur of the Eren Dağ. The temple, in the Ionic order with 6 by 12 columns, was built in the late fourth century, and the cult was at its height in the following period of Rhodian domination.

J. M. Cook and W. H. Plommer, *Sanctuary of Hemithea at Kastabos* (1966). J. M C.

**HENDEKA.** The Eleven (οἱ ἕνδεκα) were Athenian officials, appointed by lot, who had charge of the prison and executions. They took into custody persons accused of theft or certain other crimes. If an accused man admitted guilt, they executed him without trial; if he denied it, they presided over the lawcourt which tried him. They also carried out the confiscation to the State of the property of an executed criminal.

*See* DIKASTERION, DIKE (2).

Arist. *Ath. Pol.* 52. 1. J. H. Lipsius, *Das attische Recht und Rechtsverfahren* (1905-15), 74 ff.; U. E. Paoli, *Rev. Int. des Droits de l'Antiquité* 1957, 151 ff. D. M. M.

**HENIOCHUS,** Middle Comedy poet. One of his plays was named Πολύευκτος, not necessarily after the well-known partisan of Demosthenes: it was a common name. From the prologue of a piece (fr. 5), perhaps entitled Πόλεις, eighteen verses are spoken by a deity or abstraction who introduces the assembled States (did they form the chorus?); they have come to Olympia to make thank-offerings for freedom, but the disturbing influence of Δημοκρατία and Ἀριστοκρατία thwarts their purpose. This perhaps refers to the time of the Corinthian alliance under Philip, 338 B.C.

*FCG* i. 421 f., iii. 560 ff.; *CAF* ii. 431 ff. W. G. W.; W. G. A.

**HEPHAESTION** (1) (*c.* 356-324 B.C.), son of Amyntor, a Macedonian noble, became a friend of Alexander the Great from childhood, and remained his closest companion. His military career after 330 was distinguished, and he was evidently a competent commander, though probably not the equal of Craterus or Ptolemy (or others who proved themselves later). His value to Alexander, however, apart from personal affection, lay in his sympathetic understanding of his dearest plans for the empire. Alexander revived for him the Persian office of 'chiliarch' (vizier), which, with other honours, marked him out as his first subordinate (324). Hephaestion seems to have been of an arrogant and possessive nature, and he was not liked by all, but his sudden death caused Alexander great grief, and he was mourned extravagantly.

Berve, *Alexanderreich*, no. 357. G. T. G.

**HEPHAESTION** (2), metrist, probably to be identified with the tutor of Verus (A.D. 130-69). His treatise Περὶ μέτρων, originally written in forty-eight books, was reduced by successive abridgements to an ἐγχειρίδιον in one book, in which form it is extant. Ancient commentaries on Hephaestion sometimes enable us to reconstruct the earlier, fuller, versions; and parts of the extant treatise appear to belong to one of these versions, not to the final abridgement (Π. σημείων and Π. παραβάσεως), while others may not come from Hephaestion at all (Π. ποιήματος, Π. ποιημάτων). The work is divided into the following parts: (1) on long and short syllables; (2) on συνεκφώνησις (synizesis); (3) on feet, in general; (4) on catalexis; (5)-(13) on the various feet, including the antispast (∪–-∪); (14) on cola composed of heterogeneous feet; (15) on ἀσυνάρτητα (combinations of two cola separated by diaeresis, e.g. the Archilochean dicolon); (16) on πολυσχημάτιστα (cola which assume varying forms). There follow appendices dealing with the building of a poetic structure out of lines and cola (Π. ποιήματος, Π. ποιημάτων) and with notation for elucidating that structure (Π. σημείων). Besides the *Encheiridion* various other works on metre are ascribed to Hephaestion in the *Suda*.

Hephaestion belonged to the school of metrists who

sought to explain metre by analysing it into its primary elements (μέτρα πρωτότυπα), that is, the feet, as opposed to others who derived all metres from the Homeric hexameter and the iambic trimeter. His treatment of lyric metre is almost confined to solo lyric and comedy, and he rarely tries his hand on the more difficult measures of choral poetry and tragedy. His procedure is extremely mechanistic, and we learn little from him directly of the true nature of Greek metric. But he has preserved many fragments of lost poems which are of great value to metrical science.

TEXT. M. Consbruch (Teubner, 1906). J. D. D.

**HEPHAESTUS** (Ἥφαιστος), god of fire and especially of the smithy fire. It is, however, extremely unlikely that this was his original character. Examination of the distribution of his cult (facts in L. Malten, s.v. 'Hephaistos', in *PW*) shows that it spreads from the volcanic regions of Asia Minor via Lemnos, which is also volcanic. This decidedly indicates that he was originally an Asianic deity of volcanic fire; that he is associated with volcanoes in Greek mythology (his forge is under Aetna, or one of the neighbouring islands, Callim. *Dian.* 47; Verg. *G.* 4. 170 ff., *Aen.* 8. 416 ff.) is less cogent, as such a notion might have grown up independently, to explain the eruptions of the mountain, considered as a huge chimney. But there is no doubt that for the Greeks he was a craftsman's god and himself a divine craftsman; hence the distribution of his cult in Greece itself, where it is practically confined to the most industrialized regions, being particularly prominent at Athens and partly displacing the old native worship of Prometheus.

His mythology is what might be expected from his development into a smith-god, which had taken place before Homer. Indeed his worship has been inferred from a tablet at Cnossos. He is lame (in an early community a lame man with strong arms would naturally become a smith, being handicapped for farming, fighting, or hunting), and consequently awkward in his movements and somewhat ridiculous (*Il.* 1. 597 ff.). He is constantly employed in making marvellous works of all sorts (as *Il.* 18. 373 ff.; *Od.* 7. 91 ff.), clearly magical (a smith is often a magician also). He makes various famous objects, as Achilles' armour, Harmonia's necklace (*see* CADMUS), Agamemnon's sceptre (*Il.* 2. 101 ff.). His workmen are the Cyclopes (q.v.), though not in Homer (see Callimachus and Virgil, locc. cit. *supra*). He makes Pandora, the first woman (Hesiod, *Op.* 70 ff.), or mankind in general (Lucian, *Hermot.* 20); cf. PROMETHEUS. His parents are Zeus and Hera (Homer), or Hera alone (Hes. *Theog.* 927), but he was cast out of heaven by Hera, because he was misshapen (*Il.* 18. 395 ff.), or by Zeus, because he defended Hera against him (*Il.* 1. 590 ff.). A comic story of his return was told by Epicharmus in his Κωμασταί (see Hyg. *Fab.* 166 and Rose ad loc.) and can be traced much earlier in archaic art. His wife is Charis (*Il.* 18. 382) or more usually Aphrodite (as *Od.* 8. 266 ff.), which is little more than an allegory, Craftsmanship allied to Grace or Beauty.

From the first half of the sixth century Hephaestus' return to Olympus is a favourite subject in vase-painting. He is also shown helping Zeus to give birth to Athena and in gatherings of Olympians; and from the fifth century delivering Achilles' arms to Thetis.

Malten, op. cit.; Rapp in Roscher's *Lexikon*, s.v.; Farnell, *Cults* v. 374 ff.; M. Delcourt, *Héphaistos ou la légende du magicien* (1957). H. J. R.; C. M. R.

**HERA** (Ἥρα, Epic Ἥρη), an ancient, pre-Hellenic goddess. Her Greek name seems to be a title, 'lady', fem. of ἥρως; her native name is unknown. She is regularly said to be wife of Zeus, his numerous connexions with other goddesses being explained away by making

them either former wives or mistresses. But the natural suggestion that she is the earth, a common consort of the sky-god, lacks cogent evidence (see Farnell, op. cit. *infra*, 181 ff.). She is rather a deity of marriage and of the life, especially the sexual life, of women. Her connexion with Zeus is perhaps best explained by supposing that the Greeks on arrival found her cult too strong to be suppressed or ignored, supposing that they wished to do so, and made room for her by making her the wife (and sister) of their own principal god. It seems conceivable that the persistent stories of the quarrels of the divine pair (e.g. *Il.* 1. 540 ff.) reflect a faint memory of a time when the two cults were not fully reconciled. That in pre-Hellenic belief she should be very prominent and have either no male partner or none of any importance is quite in accord with what is known of early religion. She is associated with Zeus on a tablet from Pylos.

Mythologically, she is one of the children of Kronos and Rhea (e.g. Hes. *Theog.* 454); later versions differ only in details, as Hyg. *Fab.* 139, where Hera has not been swallowed by her father (cf. KRONOS) and saves Zeus from him. She is the mother of Ares, Eileithyia, Hebe, Hephaestus, and, in one account, of Typhon (qq.v.). Beyond these points her story consists mainly of her hostility to Troy, and consequently in later authors, such as Virgil, to Aeneas (q.v. 1), and generally her bitterness against her numerous rivals and their offspring, *see*, e.g., LETO, SEMELE. In the story of the Argonauts (q.v.) she appears in all accounts as the friend and helper of Jason (q.v.). For her part in the Judgement of Paris, *see* PARIS.

Her most ancient place of worship seems to be Argos (q.v. 2), hence her very common title of Ἀργεία. But Samos (q.v.) certainly worshipped her from very early times also (references in Farnell, 253 f.), and there is abundant evidence for cults of her, many certainly old, all up and down the Greek world, both alone and with Zeus. Perhaps her most characteristic rite is the sacred marriage (q.v.), whereof more or less clear evidence can be had for eight places (Farnell, 185). She is also connected with the ritual of ordinary human marriage, as at Ceos (Callim. *Aet.* 3, fr. 1. 4 Mair), at least in legend. To her functions as marriage-goddess several of her titles refer, as Zygia, Gamelia, and so forth; for her remarkable surnames at Stymphalus see EPITHETS, § 2. She is also frequently connected with birth and the nurture of children; not only is she mother of Eileithyia (q.v.), but she is called Eileithyia herself (Hesychius s.v. (Argos), Farnell, 247, n. 28 c (Attica)).

At some places, especially Argos and Samos, she rises to the status of a city-goddess, a not unnatural development, considering the vital importance of increase to any State; but not many of her titles bear witness to a civic side of her activities (Farnell, 196 f.).

Associations with deities other than Zeus are occasionally to be found; for example, she is paired with Aphrodite (q.v.) (Paus. 3. 13. 9; Sparta, where an ancient statue of her was called Hera Aphrodite), and once or twice elsewhere.

Her ritual for the most part is not remarkable; at Argos she is connected with the ancient ceremonial of the Shield. At her festival, the Heraia, a shield was the prize at the athletic contests which took place, and an armed procession was a prominent feature. A detailed discussion of this somewhat unusual proceeding for the cult of a goddess (I. R. Arnold, *AJArch.* 1937, 436 ff.) would associate it with the Minoan-Mycenaean sacred shield and shielded goddess.

Hera was commonly identified with Juno (q.v.), occasionally with other foreign goddesses. She appears in archaic and classical art as a queenly figure with sceptre and diadem (in archaic sometimes a *polos*): alone; with

Zeus; in Olympian gatherings, fastened to the magic throne in pictures of Hephaestus' return.

Farnell, *Cults* i. 179 ff.; M. P. Nilsson, *Minoan-Mycenaean Religion³* (1950), index, s.v.; Roscher in his *Lexikon*, s.v.
H. J. R.; C. M. R.

**HERACLEA** (*'Ηράκλεια*) (1), modern *Policoro*, a Tarentine foundation in Lucania (432 B.C.), which replaced Siris (q.v.). Here Pyrrhus (q.v.) won his first costly victory over Rome, 280 B.C. By granting Heraclea an exceptionally favourable treaty Rome detached it from Tarentum *c.* 278 B.C. (Cic. *Balb.* 21 f.; *Arch.* 6 f.). The so-called *Lex Iulia Municipalis* (*see* LEX, LEGES) was found here (Dessau, *ILS* 6085).

For bibliography *see* MAGNA GRAECIA.                        E. T. S.

**HERACLEA** (2) (*ή πρὸς Λάτμῳ*), a Carian city on the slope of Mt. Latmus (famous for the legend of Endymion) at the head of the gulf east of Miletus. Originally called Latmus it was refounded (perhaps by Mausolus) with the new name, and may have been the Heraclea occupied by Pleistarchus, brother of Cassander, *c.* 300 B.C. The fortifications are excellently preserved.

F. Krischen, *Milet* iii. 2 (1922).                        J. M. C.

**HERACLEA** (3) **PONTICA,** a Megarian and Boeotian colony founded *c.* 560 B.C. among the Mariandyni, whom the colonists reduced to serfdom, but agreed not to sell outside the city territory. Heraclea at one time controlled much of the coast as far as Cytorus; it founded two colonies, Callatis and Chersonesus, and was active in Euxine trade, its people being among the chief navigators there in the days of Xenophon. Civil discord led to tyranny, which lasted eighty-four years (until 280 B.C.), and is said, when at its height, to have been the town's best period. Clearchus, a pupil of Plato and Isocrates, who seized power in 364/3, was murdered in 353/2. He was succeeded by his brother Satyrus and then by his two sons Timotheus and Dionysius. Dionysius, who ruled 337/6–305, extended his dominions in 334, supported Antigonus I, and finally took the title king. He was succeeded by his widow Amastris (a Persian princess and former wife of Craterus); she married Lysimachus of Thrace (302) who soon abandoned her for Arsinoe, daughter of Ptolemy I. She returned to Heraclea and founded a city named Amastris, but was murdered by her sons. Lysimachus resumed control of Heraclea but on his death (280) democracy was re-established. The rise of the Bithynian and Pontic kingdoms and the settlement of the Galatians in the interior steadily weakened the city and reduced its territory. Allied to Rome soon after 188, it was forced to join Mithridates in 74. Taken and sacked by the Romans in the Third Mithridatic War, it finally lost its prosperity, and the colony which Caesar founded there did not endure. Heraclea became a metropolis of the Pontic *Koinon* in the second century A.D.

Memnon, *FGrH* no. 434; Xen. *An.* bks. 5–7; Strabo 12. 3. 4 ff. Magie, *Rom. Rule Asia Min.* 307 ff. and index; C. Roebuck, *Ionian Trade and Colonization* (1959), 123; W. Hoepfner, *Herakleia Pontike* (1966).                        T. R. S. B.

**HERACLEA** (4) **TRACHINIA,** a Spartan colony founded in 426 B.C. in a strong position about 5 miles from Thermopylae, as a halting-place for armies marching to the north and also as a naval base. Owing to misgovernment by Spartan officials and raids by local tribes the colony scarcely fulfilled expectations. In the Corinthian War Heraclea was captured by Boeotians and Argives, who expelled the Peloponnesians. After a brief revival of Spartan control, Jason of Pherae dismantled the fortifications and handed the city over to the Oetaeans.

Heraclea was forced to join the Aetolian League in 280 and was sacked by the Romans in 191.

Thuc. 3. 92–3. Y. Béquignon, *La Vallée du Spercheios* (1937).
H. D. W.

**HERACLES** (*'Ηρακλέης, 'Ηρακλῆς*). Many details must remain obscure for us concerning this, the most popular and widely worshipped of Greek heroes. In the first place, we have lost all the older continuous accounts and also Plutarch's 'Life' of him, which no doubt contained much valuable information, and are reduced to patching together many scattered references, with such late documents as [Apollodorus] 2. 61 ff., Hyginus, *Fab.* 29–36 as our basis. However, the following conclusions may be accepted as fairly certain.

2. He is a hero, not a god, although occasionally worshipped as a god (Farnell, op. cit. *infra*, 97; on his cult see also Ch. Picard, *BCH* 1923, 241 ff., H. Seyrig, ibid. 1927, 185 ff. and 369 ff.), for his name is theophoric, and no Greek deity is thus named from another. Heracles (cf. 'Diocles'), 'Hera's glory', i.e. probably 'glorious gift of Hera (to his parents)', is a typically human name. Behind all the rest of the story, then, must lie a man, real or, less likely, imaginary, the son of a Hera-worshipping people. This fits excellently with the constant tradition that he was an Argive, or rather a Tirynthian, apparently of a younger branch of the Perseid dynasty (cf. *Il.* 19. 105), related to Eurystheus of Argos, for whom he performed the Labours. If the real Heracles was prince or baron of Tiryns, the king of Argos (or Mycenae) might well have been his overlord, and it seems possible that distinguished service in some forgotten war or other exploit may have laid the first foundations of his vast reputation for strength and courage, though the stages by which he rose to his unique position in popular favour remain unknown. But his Argive nationality is supported by the geography of his Labours, six of them belonging to the Peloponnesus. By all accounts, these were (1) The Nemean Lion. For authorities see Rose, *Handb. Gk. Myth.* 211, n. 113; it may be remarked that in the earliest versions the beast was apparently not invulnerable (O. Berthold, *Die Unverwundbarkeit*, 1911, 2 ff.). (2) The Hydra of Lerna. (3) The Boar of Erymanthus.(4) The Hind of Ceryneia. (5) The Birds of Stymphalus. (6) The Stables of Augeas (authorities, Rose, ibid., n. 117 ff.). Nor are the other six Labours inconsistent with Argive origin and residence. The seventh, the Cretan Bull, and the eighth, the Horses of Diomedes (q.v. 1), are in or near the Greek world, but the other four are quite outside it, and so about equally remote wherever we suppose Heracles' home to have been; they are (9) The Girdle of the Amazon (q.v.), (10) Geryon, (11) Cerberus, (12) The Apples of the Hesperides. All these last three are variants of one theme, the conquest of Death. The hero must go to an island in the extreme west, Erytheia (q.v.), and there overcome a triple-bodied monster, Geryon, and his attendants and take his cattle; or he must descend to the House of Hades and steal the infernal watch-dog; or, finally, he must pluck the golden apples from the dragon-guarded tree at the world's end (further details and references in Rose, op. cit. 214 ff.). All these are manifestly more elaborate forms of the simple and ancient tale that on one occasion Heracles met Hades and worsted him (*Il.* 5. 395 ff., cf. Pind. *Ol.* 9. 33). The fact that they are variants of one another indicates that the cycle of the twelve Labours is artificial, made up to the round number, familiar anywhere in the wide region which used the Babylonian sexagesimal counting, by including duplicates.

3. But the story is complicated by an attempt on the part of Thebes (already known to Homer, *Il.* 19. 99) to acquire Heracles; cf. ALCMENE, AMPHITRYON. The only

legend of his birth and early adventures which we have is laid in Thebes, and in this connexion we must notice that he is often called Alcides, a name explained by that of the father of Amphitryon, Alcaeus (Apollod. 2. 50). As a matter of fact, Ἀλκαῖος and Ἀλκείδης are variants, respectively Boeotian, as we may suppose, and a translation from it into a more normal Greek patronymic, of a name which meant no more than Valiant; and it is a reasonable guess that this Alcaeus was a Theban hero, with whom Heracles became identified by local zeal. To Alcaeus we may attribute the little group of Boeotian adventures, the conquest of Orchomenus (Apollod. ibid. 67 ff.), the killing of the lion on Mt. Cithaeron (ibid. 65), which suspiciously resembles the Nemean labour, and the episode of the daughters of Thespius, all fifty of whom the hero enjoyed while the guest of their father (ibid. 66).

4. Finally, an attempt was made by the Dorians to acquire him, with some success, since it was for a time a dogma of modern researchers that he was a Dorian hero. *See* AEGIMIUS, HERACLIDAE.

5. The Athenians were content to model their national hero upon him; *see* THESEUS.

6. So far we have dealt with him simply as a hero; it is to be noted that he was on occasion identified with foreign gods. The story that he was sold into slavery to Omphale, queen of Lydia (Soph. *Trach.* 252; Apollod. ibid. 131–3), probably has behind it some myth of an Oriental goddess and her inferior male consort. At the other end of the Mediterranean the famous temple of 'Heracles' at Gadeira (*Cadiz*), in a region under Carthaginian influence and with its Semitic-sounding taboo on swine (Silius Italicus 3. 22–3), is no doubt a shrine of Melqart (cf. Arrian, *Anab.* 2. 16. 4). In Egypt, Herodotus identifies him with one of the native deities (2. 43). The ancients themselves had noticed the diversity of these identifications, and early evolved a theory that Heracles was not one person but several (Herodotus and Arrian, locc. cit.).

7. Outside the cycle of the Labours, the chief events of his life, as generally told, are as follows. Hera pursued him from childhood with implacable enmity; here we may see a stock feature of the myths of Zeus' children imported into a legend where, to judge by the hero's name, it is little in place. She first attempted to destroy him by sending serpents to attack him in his cradle (Pind. *Nem.* 1. 39 ff., and many later passages). These he strangled. Later, when for his services to Thebes he had been given Megara, daughter of Creon (q.v. 2), to wife and she had borne him children, he murdered (her and) them in a fit of madness sent by Hera (Eur. *HF*, which puts this after the Labours; Apollod. ibid. 72 makes them the penance prescribed by Delphi for his purification). In addition, incidentally to the Labours, he had a vast number of other adventures, traditionally classified into the πράξεις, or independent exploits, and the πάρεργα, which merely happened as incidents in the Labours proper. Of these only a few examples can be given. For the former, we may instance his dealings with Laomedon king of Troy, whom he killed and sacked his city, sparing, however, his son Podarces, later known as Priam (q.v.). This arose out of a πάρεργον; on his return from the ninth Labour, bringing the girdle of Hippolyte, queen of the Amazons, he touched at Troy and found the city in distress as a result of Laomedon's treacherous dealings with Apollo and Poseidon, whom he cheated of their wage when they built the wall of his city. A sea-beast was ravaging the country and must be appeased by the sacrifice of Hesione, Laomedon's daughter. Heracles promised to kill the monster and save her if Laomedon would give him his famous horses; he fulfilled his part of the bargain, but Laomedon would

not keep his, hence the campaign later (see Apollod., ibid. 103–4, 134–6). For his second marriage and death *see* DEIANIRA; it is noteworthy that the manner of his death, by burning on a pyre on Mt. Oeta, when he found Nessus' poison overcoming him, is an interpolation into his original story, though an early one, due to the desire to find an *aition* for the ancient fire-ceremony there (Nilsson, *Hist. Greek Rel.* (E.T. 1949), 63 f.; to the refs. there add *Nordisk Tidskrift* (1923), 125). He is an intruder into the Argonautic story, hence perhaps the dropping of him early in the adventure, cf. HYLAS. One of the most singular ramifications of his legend is the story of Heracles the Dactyl (Paus. 8. 31. 3, statue at Megalopolis; 5. 7. 6 ff., foundation of the Olympian Games by him and not, as generally said, by Heracles son of Alcmene). No plausible connexion between the hero and this gnome-like being has ever been suggested.

8. Something has incidentally been said of his cult. Details are given in Farnell, ch. 5. It is interesting that, especially in private worship, he was commonly appealed to as warder-off of evils and victor over them (ἀλεξίκακος, καλλίνικος). Naturally, his sundry identifications with other deities and his ambiguous status (mostly worshipped as a hero but occasionally as a god) led to very great local variations in his ritual. The Cynic and Stoic schools seized on his reputation for hardiness, simple living, and valour in the service of mankind to idealize him into the exemplar of the follower of their doctrines.

9. Heracles is popular in all forms of archaic and classical art. His equipment of lion-skin, club and bow becomes canonical during the sixth century. In archaic and early classical art he is sometimes beardless when confronting the lion, otherwise bearded; later often youthful. The twelve labours first appear as a set in the metopes of the temple of Zeus at Olympia (*c.* 560 B.C.), which perhaps fixed the canon.

*See also* AMALTHEA, ANTAEUS, STONES, SACRED.

Farnell, *Hero-Cults*, 95 ff.; Preller–Robert, *Griechische Mythologie*⁴ (1894), ii. 422 ff. In art, F. Brommer, *Die zwölf Taten des Herakles in antiken Kunst und Literatur* (1953); id., *Vasenlisten*², 1 ff.

H. J. R.; C. M. R.

**HERACLIDAE** ('Ηρακλεῖδαι). The Dorians, who seem to have little mythology of their own, having tried to make Heracles (q.v.; cf. AEGIMIUS) a kind of connexion of theirs and his eldest son Hyllus a Dorian by adoption, formed the adventures of his sons into a legend legitimizing their conquest of the Peloponnesus by making their kings descendants of the Perseidae. After sundry adventures, in which the sons of Heracles were persecuted by Eurystheus and defended by Athens (Eur. *Heracl.*), they inquired of Delphi when they might return, and were told to do so at 'the third harvest'. Hyllus supposed this to mean the third year, but failed and was killed in single combat against a Peloponnesian champion at the Isthmus. A hundred years later his descendant Temenus again inquired, and got the same reply, which was now interpreted for him as meaning the third generation. The Dorians therefore tried again, in three companies, led by Temenus, Cresphontes, and the sons of Aristodemus, Eurysthenes, and Procles. They entered by Elis, taking, again by oracular advice, the 'three-eyed man' for their guide; he turned out to be Oxylus of Aetolia, whose mule, or horse, had but one eye. Conquering the Peloponnesus, they divided it into three parts, whereof Cresphontes took Messenia, Temenus Argos, and the sons of Aristodemus Lacedaemon, thus founding the dual kingship of Sparta. In the fighting Tisamenus, son of Orestes and grandson of Agamemnon, was killed, thus ending the line of the Pelopidae.

See Apollod. 2. 167 ff.; Paus. 1. 41. 2; 3. 1. 6; 5. 3. 5 ff.; 8. 5. 1; Hdt. 9. 26. 4 ff.                    H. J. R.

**HERACLIDES** (1) **PONTICUS,** academic philosopher of the fourth century. Born of a wealthy and aristocratic family in Heraclea on the Black Sea (Pontus), he came to Plato's Academy in Athens as a pupil of Speusippus, although he also attended Aristotle's lectures. He was placed in temporary charge of the Academy during Plato's third visit to Sicily (361/360) and after the death of Speusippus (338) he was a candidate for the leadership. Defeated by only a few votes, Heraclides returned to Heraclea where he possibly opened his own school. He was still alive in 322.

The fragments of Heraclides' writings, mostly dialogues, reveal the wide variety of interests—ethical, political, physical, historical, and literary—characteristic of the fourth century. Diogenes Laertius (5. 86–8) gives an incomplete list of titles of his works, including those on logic and metaphysics which are completely lost.

Heraclides' significance for posterity lies in four directions: in the distinctive form of his dialogues; in physics, particularly astronomy; in his eschatology; and in his contribution to the Pythagorean legend. His dialogues were famous for their elaborate proems, their colourful use of historical personages, and the seductive quality of their anecdotes and myths. They influenced both Cicero, whose *De Re Publica* may give some indication of their characteristics, and Plutarch. In astronomy, ancient authorities credit him with (i) the hypothesis of the earth's axial rotation; (ii) an attempt to explain the apparent movement of Venus in relation to the sun, in which some scholars have seen a theory that both Venus and Mercury revolve around the sun, and the sun around the earth: hence a step towards the Tychonic system (Heath, 255 ff.; against, Frank, 212); (iii) a vague adumbration of the heliocentric theory. Clearly Heraclides took part in the lively astronomical debate of his time, but the importance of his contribution is difficult to gauge. In physics, Heraclides proposed a theory of 'loose-jointed particles' (ἄναρμοι ὄγκοι), i.e. molecules, which he probably developed from Plato's *Timaeus* as an attempt to account for elemental change. In a way typical of fourth-century philosophy, Heraclides combined this interest in science with an interest in eschatology and in such shamanistic figures, real or invented, as Empedotimus, Abaris, Pythagoras, and Empedocles. In the vision of Empedotimus (Fr. 96 and 98 Wehrli), the soul was described as substantial light, having its origin in the Milky Way. By his use of Empedocles and Pythagoras as dialogue figures, Heraclides influenced the biographical tradition; in particular, he may be responsible for Academic coluring in the Pythagorean legend.

Heraclides has been seen alternatively as a highly original thinker, and as a dilettante. Perhaps the answer lies in his literary ability. Without great powers of scientific invention himself, he was in close and intelligent touch with the most fertile thought of his day, which he was able to present in an attractive form to succeeding centuries.

Diog. Laert. v. 86–93; fragments and testimonia newly collected and discussed by F. Wehrli, *Herakleides Pontikos* (Basel 1953), though O. Voss, *De Heraclidis Pontici vita et scriptis* (Diss. Rostock 1896), is still very useful; *PW* viii. 472 ff.; Ueberweg-Praechter, *Grundriss* 345; Zeller, *Phil. d. Gr.* ii/1. 1034 ff.; R. Hirzel, *Der Dialog* (1895) i; T. L. Heath, *Aristarchus of Samos* (1913), 249; E. Frank, *Plato und die sogenannten Pythagoreer* (1923), 209 ff.; J. Bidez, *Eos, ou Platon et l'orient* (1945), 52 ff.; P. Boyancé, *Rev. Ét. Anc.* 1934, 321 ff.; I. M. Lonie, *Phronesis* 1964, 156 ff. and *Mnemos.* 1965, 126 ff.; *PW* Suppl. xi. 675 ff.     I. M. L.

**HERACLIDES** (2) of Cyme, author of a Persian history (Περσικά) written *c.* 350 B.C. One of Plutarch's sources for the life of Artaxerxes II.

*FGrH* iii. 689.

**HERACLIDES** (3) **LEMBUS** of Callatis or Alexandria became an Egyptian civil servant at Oxyrhynchus, and was living at Alexandria in 170 B.C.

WORKS: (1) 'Ιστορίαι, a mythological ΅and historical commonplace-book, only known by five fragments; (2) Λεμβευτικὸς λόγος, perhaps about Homer. (3) The Epitome of the 'Lives' of Satyrus, and (4) the Epitome of the Διαδοχή of Sotion. These two collections of biographies of the Greek philosophers were much used by Diogenes Laertius. (5) A 'Life' of Archimedes in Eutocius, *In Arch. circ. dim.*, may be by him. (6) A selection from Aristotle's Πολιτεῖαι.

Fragments in Müller, *FHG* iii. 167.     W. D. R.

**HERACLIDES** (4) of Tarentum (fl. *c.* 75 B.C.), physician. He was trained in the Herophilean school, but later became more empirical in his methods and, indeed, the most important empirical physician of antiquity. He is highly praised by Galen for his technical skill and for his objectivity in the pursuit of truth. He seems to have practised dissection of human bodies, and this makes it probable that he worked in Alexandria. The names of fourteen works by him are known, and fragments of some of them are preserved in Galen; his most important work was done on pharmacology, therapeutics, and dietetics.     W. D. R.

**HERACLIDES** (5) **PONTICUS the Younger,** grammarian, from Heraclea Pontica, pupil of Didymus, later taught at Rome under Claudius and Nero, and wrote three books in Sapphic hendecasyllables (Ath. 649 c) called Λέσχαι, which may have influenced Statius' *Silvae.* These were erudite and obscure (*Etym. Gud.* 297, 50, Artem. 4. 63) in the style of Lycophron. He also wrote epic poems and *Pyrrichae* of which nothing is known.

Susemihl, *Gesch. gr. Litt. Alex.* ii. 196.     C. M. B.

**HERACLITUS** ('Ηράκλειτος), son of Bloson of Ephesus, probably came of royal blood and surrendered the (nominal) kingship voluntarily to his brother. He is said instead of publishing his treatise (written *c.* 500 B.C. and surviving in brief but numerous fragments) to have deposited it in the temple of Artemis.

Heraclitus' book opened by assigning the traditionally divine attribute of eternity not (like the Milesian philosophers) to a primary substance but to the universal Logos, which men can but do not understand, although their experience (like all occurrences) is governed by it. Following Anaximander he conceived the universe as a ceaseless conflict of opposites regulated by an unchanging law, but he found in this law the proper object of understanding; it is the Logos which spans but could not exist without the cosmic process:'people do not understand how what is at variance accords (has one logos) with itself, an agreement in tension as with bow and lyre' (fr. 51). This Logos Heraclitus equated with transcendent wisdom and the elemental fire. So 'God is day–night, winter–summer, war–peace, satiety–famine', and when we are aware of one opposite of any pair, our standpoint is partial and perceptual, our linguistic activity one of using 'names' not 'discourse' or logos (fr. 67). Hence in politics 'the people must fight for the law as for a wall' (fr. 44), for 'all human laws are nourished by the divine which is one' (fr. 114). Unlike his predecessors Heraclitus disbelieved in the genesis of the universe in time and the Stoics were wrong in thinking he believed in a periodic world-conflagration. In the perpetual stream of creation 'all things are an exchange for fire and fire for all things, as goods for gold and gold for goods' (fr. 90), but 'the world-order (κόσμος) was not made by any god or man but was, is, and will be everliving fire being kindled in measures and quenched in measures' (fr. 30).

Heraclitus' challenge to mankind is to learn to understand (ξυνιέναι) the discourse of nature, i.e. to know the 'natural' way to discourse and act. Wisdom lies not in much learning (fr. 40) but in the awakening of the entire soul from the slumber of its private wants and opinions to awareness of the 'common' world-order. Thus all knowledge is self-knowledge ('I sought for myself' fr. 101). 'The dry soul is wisest' (fr. 118), for it approximates more to the divine fire. Nevertheless, compared with God man is a child in wisdom, his speech at best a lisping version of the divine discourse (fr. 79). Accordingly Heraclitus writes consciously in the oracular style of Delphi, aiming 'neither to say nor conceal but to indicate' the truth (fr. 93).

Heraclitus' physics and astronomy are elementary. His achievement is that he is the first Greek writer to inquire what discourse is and how it can be true and to find the intelligible principle of the universe not only in an external order (like Anaximander), but primarily in the depths which the philosophic soul discovers within itself and cannot fathom because it itself deepens them (frs. 45, 115).

I. Bywater, *Heracliti Ephesii Reliquiae* (1877); Diels, *Vorsokr.*[8] i. 139–90. Burnet, *EGP* 130 ff.; O. A. Gigon, *Untersuchungen zu Heraklit* (1935); G. S. Kirk, *Heraclitus. The Cosmic Fragments* (1954); Kirk–Raven, *Presocratic Philosophers*, ch. 6; Zeller–Mondolfo, *La filosofia dei Greci* i. iv (1961); Guthrie, *Hist. Gk. Phil.* i. 403 ff.; *PW* Suppl. x. 246 ff.                    A. H. C.

**HERALDS** (κήρυκες) in Homeric times were important aids of the kings used for a multiplicity of tasks such as maintaining order in meetings, making proclamations, and bearing messages. They were under the protection of Hermes, were inviolable, and carried a herald's staff as a symbol of authority. In later Greece they retained much of their importance, assisting magistrates in assemblies and lawcourts and bearing messages to other States. In this capacity they are to be distinguished from ambassadors, who were authorized not only to transmit messages but also to negotiate. Heralds could circulate freely even during wars and so at times were sent to open negotiations and request permission to send ambassadors. The Roman public crier (*praeco*) was a more humble attendant of magistrates. *See also* WAR, RULES OF.

J. A. O. L.

**HERCULANEUM** was built on a spur projecting from the lower slopes of Vesuvius, *c.* 5 miles from Naples, on the coast road to Nuceria Alfaterna; it covered *c.* 26 acres. Strabo (5. 4. 8) says that it was settled, like Pompeii, successively by Oscans, Etruscans, Pelasgians, and Samnites; but the Greek character of the town-plan suggests Greek colonization (6th c.?) and the influence of Naples. During Samnite occupation Herculaneum was in the league headed by Nuceria, but Roman intervention in Campania (326–307 B.C.) brought the town into the Roman confederacy. In the great Italian rebellion Herculaneum joined the rebels, was reduced in 89 B.C., and became a Roman *municipium*; her *meddix tuticus* was superseded by *duoviri*. Though small (*c.* 4,000) the town was wealthy; in the early Empire her public buildings were richly ornamented, and her upper classes lived elegantly. The earthquake of A.D. 63 did serious damage (Seneca, *QNat.* 6. 1. 2); the eruption of Vesuvius in A.D. 79 was fatal. Herculaneum was buried deep under heavy volcanic ash; the covering solidified to a form of tufa. As a result the buildings have collapsed more completely than at Pompeii, but having been more completely sealed, their furnishings are better preserved.

In the eighteenth century excavation began in search of works of art. By shaft and tunnel the theatre and, later, the basilica were reached and robbed. In the nineteenth century tunnelling was abandoned in favour of complete excavation; systematic work on the site was resumed in 1927.

Herculaneum differs profoundly from Pompeii. The Greek town-plan is completely regular. The streets show no signs of heavy traffic, there are no stepping-stones for pedestrians, no painted notices on the walls; shops are less obtrusive. Herculaneum was a residential, not a commercial town, the main industry being fishing. The houses show great variety in construction and plan, more modern than Pompeii. The principle of lighting from inner court and windows is freely used; upper stories are built with confidence. Most of the houses show taste and refinement as well as wealth, notably those that overlook the sea, with their terraces and gardens. In contrast is the *Casa a graticcio*, lightly built of rubble in a timbered frame, with small apartments separately accessible.

Luxurious villas were common in the neighbourhood, and the Villa of the Papyri, north-west of the town, excavated in the eighteenth century, yielded numerous statues and an Epicurean's library of papyrus rolls, mainly the work of Philodemus of Gadara. Recent excavations on the north of the site have revealed the lower side of the colonnaded forum, and on the east part of an unusually grand palaestra.

INSCRIPTIONS. *CIL* x. 156–70. M. Ruggiero, *Storia degli scavi di Ercolano*; J. Beloch, *Campanien* (1890), 214 ff.; E. R. Barker, *Buried Herculaneum* (1908); A. Maiuri, *Ercolano*[5] (1959); id., *I nuovi scavi di Ercolano* (2 vols., 1959); R. Carrington, *Pompeii* (1936), 180 ff.; Comparetti and de Petra, *La Villa Ercolanesi* (1883); V. Catalano, *Storia di Ercolano* (1953).                    R. M.

**HERCULES,** Roman pronunciation of Heracles (q.v.). His is perhaps the earliest foreign cult to be received in Rome, the Ara Maxima (see Platner–Ashby, 253), which was his most ancient place of worship, being within the *pomerium* of the Palatine settlement. It was probably desired to make the Forum Boarium, in which it stood, a market-place under the protection of a god better known than the local deities. The theory of some ancients (as Propertius 4. 9. 71 ff.) that he is identical with Semo Sancus Dius Fidius (q.v.), although revived in modern times by Preller (Preller–Jordan, *Römische Mythologie*[3] (1881–3) ii. 272 ff.) is untenable, and seems ultimately to rest on nothing better than the interpretation of *Dius Fidius* as *Iovis filius*. His cult had become very popular with merchants, no doubt because of his supposed ability to avert evil of all kinds (*see* HERACLES) and the long journeys involved in his Labours and other exploits. It was common to pay him a tithe of the profits of an enterprise (see, e.g., Eliz. C. Evans, *Cults of the Sabine Territory* (U.S.A. 1939), 70 ff.); this was not confined to commercial dealings but included spoils of warfare.

His worship at the Ara Maxima had some interesting features. No other god was mentioned (Plut. *Quaest. Rom.* 90, citing Varro); no women were admitted (Propert. ibid. 21 ff.); dogs were excluded (Plut. loc. cit.). The ritual was originally in the hands not of the Pontiffs but of two *gentes*, the Potitii and Pinarii, of whom the former were senior (Plut. ibid. 60, Veranius ap. Macrob. *Sat.* 3. 6. 14); in the censorship of Appius Claudius Caecus, 312 B.C., it passed to the State (Asper ap. Macrob. ibid. 13). It was performed in Greek fashion (Varro ap. Macrob. ibid. 17). The exclusion of women is found also in his cult at Lanuvium (Tert. *Ad nat.* 2, 7).

For his numerous other places of worship at Rome, see Platner–Ashby, 251 ff.; Nash, *Pict. Dict. Rome* i. 462 ff. The most important, after the Ara Maxima, are a sanctuary of Hercules Cubans within Caesar's Gardens, temples of Hercules Custos near the Circus Flaminius (probably *c.* 221 B.C.), of Hercules Invictus near the Porta Trigemina, of Hercules Musarum near the Circus Flaminius (erected by Fulvius Nobilior *c.* 187 B.C.), of

Hercules Pompeianus near the Circus Maximus, of Hercules Victor (dedicated by Mummius in 142 B.C.), and of Hercules Victor (Invictus), a round temple in the Forum Boarium decorated with frescoes by Pacuvius.

Identification or comparison with Hercules was common among the later emperors, as Commodus (S.H.A. *Comm.* 1. 8. 5), Maximinus (*Maxim.* 18. 4. 9; 6. 9).

Wissowa, *RK* 271 ff.; J. Bayet, *Les Origines de l'Hercule romain* (1926); Latte, *RR* 213 ff.; D. van Berchem, 'Hercule Melquart à l'Ara Maxima', *Rend. Pont.* 32 (1959/60), 61 ff.     H. J. R.

**HERCYNIAN FOREST,** German mountains, properly the wooded heights of Thuringia and Bohemia. Originally put near the Pyrenees (schol. ad Dionys. Per. 286) or among Celts (schol. Ap. Rhod. 4. 640) near the Northern Ocean (Diod. 5. 21, etc.), Aristotle (*Mete.* 1. 13) placed it in north Europe, Timaeus found the Danube's sources in it ([Arist.] *Mir. Ausc.* 105). The name came to be used for all the wooded mountains extending from the Rhine to the Carpathians. Caesar (*BGall.* 6. 25) heard that it was more than nine days' journey wide, sixty days' travel long from the Black Forest along the Danube's northern bank, and thence turned north. Strabo (7. 290) extends it from Lake Constance and Danube sources to the north frontier of Bohemia and Moravia. After the exploratory conquests of Tiberius and Drusus the Hercynian Forest was clearly distinguished from the Alps and was identified with the heights extending round Bohemia and through Moravia to Hungary (Pliny, *HN* 4. 80, 99–100; Tac. *Germ.* 28, 30). In Ptolemy (*Geog.* 2. 11. 7) the name is restricted to a range between the Sudetes and the Carpathians.     E. H. W.

**HERDONIAE** (*Herdonia, Erdonia, Erdoniae*), a town in Apulia which overlooked the Carapelle near modern Ordona 11 miles south-east of Foggia. The surrounding Daunian cemeteries attest its early importance. In the late Republic it received a wall circuit (still partially visible) and grew in importance when it became a stage on the Via Traiana. Recent excavations have uncovered many of the internal streets and buildings. Centuriation systems based on twenty *actus* grids occupy the land to east and west of the town.

*CIL* ix. 64 ff.; T. Ashby and R. Gardner, *PBSR* 1916, 148 ff.; F. Johnson, *The Farwell Collection*; J. Mertens, *Ordona*, 2 vols. (Brussels, 1965–7).     G. D. B. J.

**HERENNIUS** (1, *PW* 44) **SENECIO,** a native of Hispania Baetica, was its quaestor and afterwards supported Pliny the Younger in the prosecution of Baebius Massa, an oppressive governor of Baetica (A.D. 93). He wrote the 'Life' of Helvidius Priscus and was put to death by Domitian. His memory was attacked by M. Aquilius Regulus.     A. M.

**HERENNIUS** (2, *PW* 31) **MODESTINUS,** one of the last classical Roman jurists. A pupil of Ulpianus (q.v. 1), he was *praefectus vigilum* at some time between 226 and 244, and an apparently recent *responsum* of his is cited in a rescript of 239, but little else is known of his life. He was one of the five jurists singled out as authoritative in the 'Law of Citations' (426), but this is perhaps attributable more to his late date than to any outstanding merits. His works seem to have been mainly handbooks for students and practitioners, but they included an extensive collection of his *Responsa* (nineteen books). He cites previous jurists rarely (imperial constitutions more often) and he seems to have relied mainly on Ulpian and Paulus (q.v. 1), his few citations of earlier jurists being perhaps at second hand. He wrote a monograph in Greek on the grounds of exemption from guardianship, and this has been adduced as evidence that Greek was his mother tongue, but it is at least as

likely that the work was intended for those who had recently been made citizens by the *constitutio Antoniniana* (*see* CITIZENSHIP, ROMAN).     B. N.

**HERILLUS** of Carthage, pupil of Zeno of Citium and founder of a separate Stoic sect. He seems to have treated knowledge as the supreme end, the life of moral virtue as a subordinate end (ὑποτελίς), and to have added that the subordinate end differs in detail for different men according to their circumstances; the natural goods of life, in distinction from knowledge and virtue, he treated as strictly indifferent. The sect of the 'Ηρίλλειοι seems not to have survived 200 B.C.

Testimonia in von Arnim, *SVF* i. 91–93.     W. D. R.

**HERMAGORAS** of Temnos (fl. *c.* 150 B.C.), the most influential rhetor of the Hellenistic period, author of an elaborate system of rhetoric which we know in fair detail from later writers, especially Quintilian and Hermogenes. His most important work concerned εὕρεσις; he did little for the theory of style. By discussing not only themes involving particular situations (ὑποθέσεις) but also general themes (θέσεις, e.g. 'should a man marry?'), he helped to extend the scope of rhetorical education to cover moral and philosophical subjects. His complex and subtle classification of the στάσεις (*status*, 'issues') of cases was decisive for later theory (*see* RHETORIC, GREEK, § 4), and it is this for which he was mostly remembered.

D. Matthes, *Hermagorae Temnitae Testimonia et Fragmenta* (1962); id., *Lustrum* 1958, 58 ff.; G. A. Kennedy, *The Art of Persuasion in Greece* (1963), 303 ff.     D. A. R.

**HERMAPHRODITUS** or **Aphroditus.** The concept of this bisexual divinity is perhaps due originally to certain marriage rites in which the sexes exchange clothing; the god was then fashioned to fit and explain the rite. Aphroditus (Hesych. s.v.; Macrob. *Sat.* 3. 8. 2) is found at Amathus in Cyprus. A unique dedication, of the early fourth century B.C., attests the cult of Hermaphroditus in Attica (*Ath. Mitt.* 1937, 7 f.; cf. Theophr. *Char.* 16. 10; Alciphr. *Epist.* 3. 37). Fourth-century art portrayed Hermaphroditus as a beautiful youth with developed breasts; later art as an Aphrodite with male genitals. Ovid (*Met.* 4. 285–388) relates the myth of the union in one body of Hermaphroditus, son of Hermes and Aphrodite, and the nymph Salmacis.

Nilsson, *Feste* 369 ff.; M. Delcourt, *Hermaphrodite, Mythes et rites de la bisexualité dans l'antiquité classique* (1958, Engl. transl. 1961).     F. R. W.

**HERMARCHUS** of Mytilene, Epicurean, studied under Epicurus in Mytilene before the school was moved to Lampsacus in 310 B.C., and in 270 he succeeded Epicurus as head of the school. Epicurus' will enjoins his heirs to put part of the revenues of his estate at Hermarchus' disposal for the maintenance of the school, and bequeaths to him the whole of Epicurus' library. With Epicurus, Metrodorus, and Polyaenus, Hermarchus was treated as representing the authoritative form of the Epicurean doctrine.

WORKS: Πρὸς Πλάτωνα, Πρὸς Ἀριστοτέλην, Ἐπιστολικὰ περὶ Ἐμπεδοκλέους, Περὶ τῶν μαθημάτων, all of them polemical works.

K. W. G. Krohn, *Der Epikureer Hermarchos* (1921).     W. D. R.

**HERMES** (1) ('Ερμείας, 'Ερμῆς), one of the younger gods in myth, though in reality he is probably one of the oldest and most nearly primitive in origin. His name may occur on a tablet from Pylos. The most plausible explanation of his name is that it is connected with ἕρμα, and signifies the daemon who haunts or occupies a heap of stones, or perhaps a stone, set up by the roadside for some magical purpose (examples of such in Frazer, *GB*, see index s.v. 'Stones' and art. STONES, SACRED, herein). Tradition and cult facts combine to make him Arcadian; he was son of Zeus and Maia daughter of Atlas, born on Mt. Cyllene on the fourth day of the month (*Hymn. Hom. Merc.* 19; four is Hermes' number). He was cunning from birth, and on the first day of his life invented the lyre, stole Apollo's cattle, impudently denied the theft, and was reconciled to his elder brother. The merry tone of the hymn is characteristic. Hermes never had much concern with the higher moral or philosophical developments of religion: the writings ascribed to Hermes (q.v. 2) Trismegistus have nothing to do with the Greek Hermes but are the result of fathering on the Egyptian Thoth, who was identified with him, certain late mystical philosophizings. For the most part, Hermes has a subordinate part in myth, being rather a messenger of the greater gods, and especially of Zeus, than an independent actor. Hence the shape he takes when represented in fully human form is that of a herald, equipped for travelling with a broad-brimmed hat and a stout pair of sandals and carrying the *kerykeion* (Lat. *caduceus*) or herald's staff (to be distinguished from the magic wand which also he bears on occasion, see de Waele, *The Magic Staff*, The Hague, 1927). But he was from early times shown, and continued to be so represented, as a mere stock or stone, a herm, having generally a human head carved at the top and a phallus half-way up it. The latter is, indeed, a characteristic emblem of this god, who was always interested in fertility; which perhaps is why we find him occasionally united with a goddess connected with fertility, Aphrodite (mother by him of Hermaphroditus, Ovid, *Met.* 4. 288; of Priapus, q.v., see Hyginus, *Fab.* 160, cf. H. Herter, *De Priapo*, 64), Hecate (q.v.), or Brimo (schol. Lycophron, 1176, cf. Propert. 2. 2. 11–12), Herse daughter of Cecrops (Ovid, *Met.* 2. 708 ff.). One of his most striking functions may also derive in part from his connexion with fertility, though his occupation as messenger probably has something to do with it. He is the Guide of Souls, from Homer (or at least *Od.* 24. 1 ff., be that genuinely Homeric or not) onwards. In this respect he is unique among the gods, unless we count the Dioscuri (qq.v.) as originally divine; for the others belong either to the upper or the lower world, the peculiar position of Persephone, for whom *see* DEMETER, not constituting a real exception. It is in this connexion especially that his magic wand (see above) becomes prominent (e.g. Verg. *Aen.* 4. 242 ff., where see the further material collected by Pease ad loc., and add Wilamowitz-Moellendorff, *Glaube der Hellenen* (1921) ii. 147, n. 2). Such a wand is the characteristic implement of a necromancer. It is not particularly remarkable that he is the god of merchants and others who use roads, including thieves, though the latter characteristic illustrates his non-moral nature (for illustrations see Ar. *Plut.* 1155, with schol., Plut. *Quaest. Graec.* 55, with Halliday's note). In Crete we find him associated with a piece of ritual topsy-turvydom, for which cf. KRONOS, SATURNUS. At the Hermaea there (city not specified) masters waited on their slaves as they feasted (Ath. 639 b). For a deity with chthonian associations he has very little to do with divination and oracles; Apollo grants him an obscure minor form of divining, in the Homeric Hymn, 550 ff., and he had an oracle at Pharae (Paus. 7. 22. 2–3). Here the consultant, after paying his respects to the god, stopped his ears till he got beyond the market-place where the temple stood; the first words he heard when he unstopped them were the answer to any question he had asked of Hermes. This is no more than a systematization of one of the most usual forms of omen, the κληδών or unintentionally significant utterance.

Two other functions show a longer development from the old daemon of the roadside, if that is what he originally was. A herald must of course state his business plainly and on occasion plead the cause of those who sent him. Hence from a fairly early date Hermes is associated with oratory. When to this is added the invention, already told, of the lyre, we can see how he became in time a general patron of literature, Horace even calling those who follow it 'Mercuriales uiri' (*Carm.* 2. 17. 29–30). It is less evident why he is constantly regarded, in classical times, as the patron of young men and their exercises, and himself represented in statuary as a young man. The stages are perhaps as follows: fertility easily passes into the notion of luck or good fortune; luck is needed by those who engage in athletic contests (cf. HECATE); but the most regular practitioners of such things are the younger men, whose athletic training formed an important part of their education in every normal Greek State.

Hermes is popular in archaic and classical art, often escorting heroes, with herald's wand, winged cap, and boots (later sandals). In archaic art he is bearded and clad in a short chiton, later often naked and, apart from archaizing heads of phallic herms, young. His adventures as a baby are found on some archaic vases.

Farnell, *Cults* v. 1 ff., for his worship generally; Nilsson, *Feste* 388 ff., for his non-Attic, L. Deubner, *Attische Feste* (1932), 217, for his (unimportant) Attic cult; K. Kerényi, 'Hermes, der Seelenführer', *Albae Vigiliae* i (1944); J. Duchemin, *La boulette et la lyre*. *Recherches sur les origines pastorales de la poésie*, 1. *Hermès et Apollon* (1960).                                                          H. J. R.; C. M. R.

**HERMES (2) TRISMEGISTUS**, a clumsy translation of Egyptian 'Thoth the very great', with the adj. emphasized by repetition (W. Scott, *Hermetica* i. 5, note 1). When so named, Thoth is the reputed author of the philosophico-religious treatises known collectively as *Hermetica* (*see* GNOSTICISM), also of sundry works on astrology, magic, and alchemy. These are invariably late, Egyptian in the sense of being produced in Egypt by men of Greek speech, and (except for the astrological books: Nock, *Gnomon* 1939, 359 ff.) contain little or nothing of native Egyptian doctrine or custom. Their attribution to the Egyptian god of letters is a result of the then prevalent enthusiasm for the supposed ancient wisdom of Egypt and of the older Oriental cultures generally.

W. Scott–A. S. Ferguson, *Hermetica* (1924–36); edition by A. D. Nock and A. J. Festugière i–iv (1945–54); A. J. Festugière, *La Révélation d'Hermès Trismégiste* i–iv (1944–54).                    H. J. R.

**HERMESIANAX** of Colophon, probably born *c.* 300 B.C., was a pupil of Philetas (schol. Nic. *Ther.* 3). His mistress's name, which he took as title for his collection of elegies, was Leontion (Ath. 13. 597 b).

WORKS. The *Persica* (schol. Nic. *Ther.* 3) may have contained the story of Nanis and Cyrus (Parth. 22 = fr. 6). The *Leontion* was in three books. One line describing Polyphemus gazing out to sea is definitely cited from book 1. This suggests a treatment of the Polyphemus–Galatea story, cf. fr. 7. 69–74, and two other bucolic love-stories (frs. 2 and 3) may have been narrated in this book. Book 2 contained the tale of Arceophon and Arsinoe, the rejected suitor and the callous maid, who is punished by being turned into stone (Ant. Lib. *Met.* 39), possibly also the story of Leucippus' incest with its tragic sequel (Parth. 5). From book 3 Athenaeus (13. 597 b) has preserved a 'catalogue of love-affairs'. In the manner of contemporary Peripatetic biographers, e.g. Chamaeleon, Hermesianax details the loves, unrequited or otherwise unlucky, of a series of poets, starting with Orpheus and ending with Philetas, and of philosophers (Pythagoras, Socrates, Aristippus). Three times in the fragment the poet addresses Leontion herself, but it is unlikely that he used this device throughout the poem. Of the remaining fragments (8–11) one is cited from an 'Elegy on the Centaur Eurytion'.

The loss of most early Alexandrian poetry has given to the long fragment from the *Leontion* an importance which it hardly merits. It is true that Hermesianax illustrates many features found in later representatives of that poetry, e.g. a fondness for 'glosses', an interest in love, especially if it be unhappy, and in aetiology, but, though he is a tolerable metrist despite his monotonous habit of ending the first half of a pentameter with an adjective and the second with the substantive which it qualifies, he possessed, to judge by what remains of his poetry, a very mediocre brain. Thus Homer is made the lover of Penelope and Hesiod of Eoia, a name taken from a poem attributed to him; Alcaeus and Anacreon are rivals for the love of Sappho, and Socrates is the lover of Aspasia! If this is meant to be comical, the humorous element is not made evident.

TEXTS. Powell, *Coll. Alex.* 96–106; Diehl, *Anth. Lyr. Graec.* II², fasc. vi, 56–64.
GENERAL LITERATURE. Heibges, 'Hermesianax (2)', in *PW* viii. 823 ff.
E. A. B.; C. A. T.

**HERMIAS** (1), tyrant of Atarneus (in Mysia, opposite Lesbos) *c.* 355 B.C. A former student of the Academy (though he never met Plato), he introduced a more moderate regime, admitting the Platonists Erastus and Coriscus of Scepsis to a share in his power and encouraging them to found a new philosophical school at Assos. There they were joined on Plato's death (348) by Aristotle, Xenocrates, and Callisthenes, and later by Theophrastus. Aristotle became an intimate friend of Hermias and married his niece and adopted daughter Pythias. Hermias possessed a formidable naval, military, and financial power, and was virtually independent of the Persian Empire. He negotiated, with Aristotle's assistance, an understanding with Macedonia. In 341, however, he was treacherously arrested at a conference with Mentor, and sent captive to the Great King, who vainly tried to coerce him into revealing Philip's plans and executed him. He was a recipient of Plato's sixth epistle and is said to have written on the immortality of the soul.

W. Jaeger, *Aristotle* (1934), 105; D. E. W. Wormell, *Yale Studies in Classical Philology* v (1935).
D. E. W. W.

**HERMIAS** (2), choliambic poet, of Curion, not before the third century B.C., reviled the Stoics (Ath. 563 d).

Powell, *Coll. Alex.* 237; G. A. Gerhard, *Phoinix von Kolophon* (1909), 213.

**HERMIONE,** in mythology, daughter of Menelaus and Helen (qq.v.; *Od.* 4. 14 and often in later authors). Possibly she was originally a goddess, as her name occurs as a title of Demeter and Persephone (Hesychius, s.v.). She was at various times (details differ in different authors, see Weizsäcker in Roscher's *Lexikon*, s.v.) betrothed to Orestes and Neoptolemus (1) (qq.v.). According to Eur. *Or.* 1655 Neoptolemus never married her, but in Eur. *Andr.* he did so, was murdered by Orestes while at Delphi inquiring why Hermione was childless, and she was carried off by Orestes. All authors, save schol. Pind. *Nem.* 10. 12, citing Ibycus, who says she married Diomedes, agree that she became Orestes' wife and mother (Paus. 2. 18. 6) of his son Tisamenus.

**HERMIPPUS** (1), Athenian comic poet and brother of Myrtilus (q.v.), won at least one victory (435 B.C.) at the City Dionysia and four at the Lenaea, the first *c.* 430 B.C. (*IG* ii². 2325. 57, 113, *Hesperia* 1943, 1 ff.). We have ten titles and 100 fragments. Ἀρτοπώλιδες, in which Hyperbolus and his mother were ridiculed (cf. Ar. *Nub.* 551 ff. cum schol.), must belong to the period 421–416.

Fr. 46 (from an unnamed play) refers to Cleon's attack on Pericles in 431 or 430; fr. 63 (from Φορμοφόροι) is of interest because it names (with jokes interspersed) the characteristic imports to Athens from various Mediterranean countries *c.* 430–420 B.C., and fr. 82 (play unnamed) represents Dionysus giving his opinions on different wines. Several of Hermippus' titles indicate mythological burlesque.

*FCG* ii. 380 ff.; *CAF* i. 224 ff.; *FAC* i. 284 ff.
K. J. D.

**HERMIPPUS** (2) of Smyrna (fl. 3rd c. B.C.), Peripatetic biographer and follower of Callimachus, wrote a vast work (descending to his own time) on famous writers, philosophers, and law-givers, which Plutarch used. Hermippus deliberately falsified history, revelling in sensationalism, particularly in death scenes. Fragments in Diog. Laert. Perhaps Hermippus also wrote Φαινόμενα.

*FHG* iii. 35–54; additional frs. listed by Heibges, *PW*, s.v.
F. W. W.

**HERMIPPUS** (3), grammarian of the time of Trajan and Hadrian, from Berytus (a village of the interior, not the harbour-town, according to the *Suda*). By birth a slave, he became a pupil of Philon (q.v. 5) of Byblos. His works include Ὀνειροκριτικά in five books; Περὶ ἑβδομάδος; and Περὶ τῶν παιδείᾳ διαπρεψάντων δούλων.

*FHG* iii. 35; Schmid–Stählin ii, 2, 868.

**HERMOCRATES** (d. 407 B.C.), Syracusan statesman and general, much (perhaps exaggeratedly) admired by Thucydides, who saw in him a Sicilian Pericles. He urged a pan-Siceliot front against Athenian intervention at the conference of Gela (424), and as leader of the moderates in 415, contrasted with the demagogue Athenagoras, he organized resistance to Athens' great expedition. Next year he was unsuccessful as general, but the arrival of Gylippus (q.v.) reinvigorated the defence, and Hermocrates' tactics helped to bring about the Athenian disaster.

Hermocrates commanded the Syracusan squadron sent to assist Sparta in 412. The more radical democracy under Diocles (q.v. 1) exiled him *in absentia*, but after Cyzicus (410) he continued in Spartan service as a mercenary captain. Returning to Sicily in 408, he raided Carthaginian-held territory, and with moderate democracy, perhaps even with tyranny, as his aim he made an attempt on Syracuse in the course of which he was killed. Dionysius I (q.v.) married his daughter.

Thuc. 6–8; Xen. *Hell.* 1; Diod. Sic. 13. H. Wentker, *Sizilien und Athen* (1956); K. F. Stroheker, *Dionysios I* (1958); H. D. Westlake, *Bull. Rylands Libr.* xli (1958/9), 239 ff.; F. Grosso, Κώκαλος 1966. 102 ff.
A. G. W.

**HERMOGENES** (1) (*c.* 200 B.C.), a Greek architect. His only known works are the temple of Dionysus at Teos and the temple of Artemis Leucophryene at Magnesia-on-Maeander, both in the Ionic Order. From these, and from his books about them, Vitruvius (q.v.) derived some of the principles of proportion included in his own book. But the remains of the two temples do not exactly agree with the precepts he attributes to Hermogenes; nor was the octastyle pseudodipteral type of temple invented by Hermogenes as he states. He also includes Hermogenes among those architects who objected to the use of the Doric Order in sacred buildings because of the complications arising from the spacing of the triglyphs. Strabo praises the Magnesian temple, and it is probable that Hermogenes' influence on Roman architecture of the Augustan period was considerable. Hermogenes son of Harpalus, mentioned in an inscription of Priene (no. 207), may be the same man.

Vitr. 3. 3; 4. 3; 7 *praef.*; Strabo 14. 1. 40 (c. 647).
H. W. R.; R. E. W.

**HERMOGENES** (2, *PW* 22) of Tarsus (2nd c. A.D.), rhetor. A child prodigy, admired by M. Aurelius, he failed to fulfil his promise as a speaker (hostile account in Philostr. *VS* 2. 7); he did, however, write a comprehensive set of textbooks which were much used and annotated in Byzantine and Renaissance times. We have two works which are certainly authentic: Περὶ τῶν στάσεων (*see* HERMAGORAS) and Περὶ ἰδεῶν. A set of progymnasmata (q.v.) is of doubtful authenticity; Περὶ μεθόδου δεινότητος is spurious, as is also Περὶ εὑρέσεως, though Hermogenes did write on these subjects. The most significant of his works is Περὶ ἰδεῶν, which deals with seven qualities of style, all to be seen as ingredients in the perfection of Demosthenes: σαφήνεια, μέγεθος, κάλλος, γοργότης, ἦθος, ἀλήθεια, δεινότης. These ἰδέαι derive from the ἀρεταὶ λέξεως found, e.g., in Dionysius of Halicarnassus, and traceable to Theophrastus (J. Stroux, *De Theophrasti virtutibus dicendi*, 1912); a similar scheme is to be found in the τέχνη ascribed to Aristides (q.v. 5).

The text in Spengel, *Rhet.* ii, was superseded by H. Rabe (1913). Byzantine commentaries in C. Walz, *Rhetores Graeci* (1832–6), vii. D. Hagedorn, *Zur Ideenlehre des Hermogenes* (1964).          D. A. R.

**HERMOGENIANUS** (*PW* 2), a Roman jurist of the time of Diocletian, and one of the two post-classical writers excerpted in Justinian's *Digesta* (q.v.). (The other is Arcadius Charisius, a *magister libellorum* of approximately the same period, who is represented by only a few fragments). Hermogenian's only work, *Iuris Epitomae* (six books), is relatively generously represented, and can be seen as characteristic of its period—an anthology of summarized (and unattributed) extracts from the legal literature of the Classical period. He may be the author of the Codex Hermogenianus (*see* CODEX, LEGAL), and was perhaps *praefectus praetorio* under Maximian.

D. Liebs, *Hermogenians Iuris Epitomae* (1964); A. Cenderelli, *Ricerche sul Codex Hermogenianus* (1965).          B. N.

**HERMOPOLIS** (modern *Ashmunein*) in Graeco-Roman times marked the boundary between Middle and Upper Egypt, where dues were collected on goods passing along the Nile. The mounds there have yielded many papyri, but the buildings described by Jomard (*c.* 1800) have almost disappeared. Recent excavations have disclosed important religious and sepulchral structures in the western quarter, with interesting Graeco-Egyptian wall-paintings and inscriptions. The papyri give useful information about the organization of the town under the Romans.

E. Jomard, *Description de l'Égypte, Antiq.* ch. 14, pl. 50–2; G. Méautis, *Hermoupolis-la-grande* (1918) (chiefly on papyri); S. Gabra, *Rapport sur les Fouilles d'Hermoupolis Ouest* (Cairo, 1941); A. J. B. Wace and others, *Hermoupolis Magna, Ashmunein, The Ptolemaic Sanctuary and the Basilica* (Alexandria, 1959).     J. G. M.

**HERMS** were marble or bronze pillars surmounted by a bust and given a human semblance by the addition of genitals in the case of the male. Usually two beam-shaped projections near the shoulders were added to hold wreaths. Originally herms represented only the god Hermes, but later they served also for other deities. Alcamenes (q.v.) made a famous herm of Hermes Propylaeus at the entrance of the Acropolis of Athens. Herms stood in large numbers in the streets of Athens and other cities. Their mutilation in 415 B.C. was a sacrilegious act which led to the banishment of Alcibiades (q.v.). The use of the herm for portraits apparently began in the Hellenistic period and became particularly common with the Romans, who in their copies converted the original Greek portrait statues into the abbreviated forms of herms and busts.          S. C.; G. M. A. R.

**HERMUS**, now *Gediz Çayı*, the largest river on the west coast of Asia Minor after the Maeander, is mentioned by Homer (*Il.* 20. 392). Herodotus (i. 80, cf. Strabo 626, Pliny *HN* 5. 119) says it rises on the holy mountain of the Dindymene Mother in Phrygia (now *Murat Dağı*) and enters the sea by Phocaea. This is also its present course; but at some unknown time it left its bed and turned to the south after passing the gorge west of Magnesia ad Sipylum and ran into the Gulf of Smyrna. In 1886, to save the gulf from becoming silted up, the river was diverted back into its ancient bed. Among its tributaries are the Hyllus and the gold-bearing Pactolus.
          G. E. B.

**HERNICI** inhabited the Trerus valley and hills north of it in Italy (Strabo 5. 231: inaccurate). Their treaty with Rome in regal times is possibly apocryphal (Dion. Hal. 4. 49; Festus, 476 L.). But they certainly signed a defensive alliance with Rome *c.* 486 B.C., and in the subsequent wars against Aequi and Volsci (qq.v.) fought staunchly (Dion. Hal. 8. 64 f.; Livy 2. 41, etc.: untrustworthy). Later, in 387 and 362, the Hernici opposed Rome but renewed the old alliance in 358 (Livy 6. 2 f.; 7. 6 f.). After remaining loyal in the Latin War the Hernican cities, except Ferentinum, Aletrium, and Verulae, were led into war against Rome in 306 by Anagnia (qq.v.), but were easily conquered and granted partial, later full, citizenship (Livy 9. 42 f.; Festus, 262 L.). Hernican territory became part of Latium and the Hernici were so completely latinized that their own language cannot be discovered. Possibly it was a Latinian dialect, but their name meaning 'men of the rocks' (Festus, 89 L.) looks Oscan (q.v.).

G. Devoto, *Gli Antichi Italici* (1951), 127 f.          E. T. S.

**HERO** (Ἡρώ) **and LEANDER** (Λέανδρος), a pretty love-story of apparently Alexandrian origin (earliest surviving authorities Ov. *Her.* 18 and 19, where see Palmer's note, and Verg. *G.* 3. 258 ff.). Hero was priestess of Aphrodite at Sestos; Leander lived at Abydos, saw her at a festival, fell in love with her, and used nightly to swim the Hellespont to see her until a storm put out the light by which she guided him across and he was drowned; she threw herself into the sea after him. Cf. Strabo 13. 1. 22.          H. J. R.

**HERO-CULT**, the worship, as being superhuman, of noteworthy dead men and women, real or imaginary, normally at their actual or supposed tombs. The nature of the cult did not differ appreciably from that given to other chthonian powers (black victims, generally not shared by the worshippers, evening or night rather than day for the ritual, blood and other liquids poured into a trench, hearth, or low altar, ἐσχάρα, rather than the high Olympian altar, βωμός), except that it was seldom practised at more than one place, or if at more, usually because several places claimed to possess the bones of the hero or heroine. The most noteworthy exception, Heracles (q.v.), was on his way to become a god and, indeed, received divine honours in some places. Hero-cult must be distinguished from the ordinary tendance of the dead, i.e. the performance of certain rites, including offerings of food and drink, intended to make them comfortable in the next world, for this did not involve worship.

Hero-cult is not found in Homer, where the word ἥρως means simply 'gentleman, noble'; *Iliad* 2. 550–1, supposing it genuine, is proof rather that Erechtheus (q.v.) was regarded as a god than that hero-worship was then practised. But excavation has repeatedly shown that Mycenaean tombs were the site of cult continuously into the historic period (see Nilsson, *GGR* i². 378 ff.). In classical and post-classical literature mention of it is exceedingly common, and its typical objects are the traditional ἥρωες of Homer and other writers of saga, though this is not the only category (see below). It is therefore likely that it began after the Dorian migration, when the ancient chieftains had become legendary figures, idealized because native and not belonging to the new invading aristocracy. Whatever its origin, it spread to include many persons who had never existed save in the imagination of their worshippers.

These imaginary figures may be considered as a class in themselves; for more elaborate classification, see Farnell (op. cit. *infra*). It includes the so-called 'faded gods', that is to say figures originally divine, which for one reason or another had come to be considered dead men, and their places of worship tombs. Many such are of course doubtful, *see* ASCLEPIUS, HELEN, IPHIGENIA, for example. Others are practically certain, as Hyacinthus (q.v.), Trophonius, and Agamedes (*see* TROPHONIUS), who, although they have a characteristic folk-tale told of them concerning their prowess as master-builders and master-thieves (Paus. 9. 37. 5 ff.), have no other existence except that the former is the possessor of a famous oracle. Generally the following characteristics may be looked for in a 'faded' figure. The name often, if Greek, is significant of something directly connected with the ritual; Trophonius seems to be the 'feeder', a natural enough name for a chthonian power, but odd for a human being. The legend, if one exists, is generally irrelevant to the cult altogether, as in the case of Hyacinthus, or explains some detail of it only, as with Glaucus (q.v. 3), whose connexion with the Taraxippos at the Isthmus is obviously secondary. The connexion with a genealogy is non-existent, fluctuating, or artificial (Hippolytus may be a case in point, see Farnell, 64 ff.; Aeneas, perhaps an offshoot of Aphrodite to begin with, becomes an ancestor by suspicious processes, cf. Farnell, 55, and *Cults* ii. 638 ff.). Finally, the ritual generally contains something alien to normal worship of the dead, as the curious performances connected with the Delphic 'heroine' Charila (Plut. *Quaest. Graec.* 12).

The more normal heroes, i.e. those who, if they ever really existed, were human, are simpler. Many naturally are worshipped by their descendants or former subjects; indeed, this is the ordinary case, as with Theseus (q.v.) at Athens and the Tritopatores (q.v.) in the same city. Many, again, are characters from the epic poems, and here ancestral connexion, although desirable (presumably the alleged fetching by the Spartans of Orestes' bones from Tegea, Hdt. 1. 67. 3 ff., had to do with their adoption of the house of Agamemnon as in some sense theirs), was not necessary; the Thebans who imported the bones of Hector (q.v.) did not claim to be descended from him, nor the Athenians from Oedipus (q.v.); the mere presence in the land of the bodies of such men was a blessing, however they came there. Others, though regarded as ancestors, are transparent inventions, made up from the name of the city or its people, as Messene (see Farnell, 360). Finally, a considerable number were fully historical, heroized because of some notable action or even mere strangeness, as Brasidas at Amphipolis (Thuc. 5. 11. 1) and the homicidal lunatic Cleomedes at Astypalaea (Paus. 6. 9. 6 ff.). (*See also* EUTHYMUS.)

Theological speculation busied itself with the possibility of heroes ultimately becoming gods (see Plutarch, *De def. or.* 415 b), not the least interesting part of the common Hellenistic and later belief that men could turn into gods if sufficiently virtuous.

See also RELICS. Older standard work E. Rohde, *Psyche* (1907); completest, with many references to ancient and modern literature, Farnell, *Hero-Cults*. On the ritual see W. S. Ferguson and A. D. Nock, *Harv. Theol. Rev.* 1944. *See* CITY-FOUNDERS, RIDER-GODS.

H. J. R.

**HEROD** (1) **THE GREAT** (*c.* 73–4 B.C.) was the son of the Idumaean Antipater (q.v. 6) and a Roman citizen from 47. By 41 Herod had risen to a high position in Judaea, and when Hyrcanus was captured by Parthian invaders in 40, he escaped to Rome, where Antony nominated him king of Hyrcanus' ethnarchy together with Idumaea. His throne was not secure, however, until a Roman force stormed Jerusalem for him in 37. Despite the intrigues of Cleopatra, who coveted his kingdom, he kept Antony's favour, and in 30 Octavian confirmed his position and restored to him most of the cities freed by Pompey in 63. In 23 and 20 he added large parts of the tetrarchy of Ituraea (q.v.). Herod was an able administrator and a skilful financier. He developed the economic resources of the country, building a new port, Caesarea (q.v. 2). Spiritual and temporal power were henceforth separated; the High Priesthood, now in Herod's gift, ceased to be hereditary or life-long, the Sanhedrin lost much of its power to a royal council on Hellenistic lines, and the old aristocracy was replaced by a new nobility of office, including Greeks. As a secular king Herod tried to promote Hellenization: games were held even in Jerusalem; his sons received Greek education; the imperial cult was introduced among his non-Jewish subjects; several cities were founded or refounded on Greek lines within his kingdom; and lavish gifts, mostly of buildings, were bestowed on many cities outside it. This policy was unpopular with his Jewish subjects, and neither his championship of the rights of the Dispersion nor his magnificent new Temple won him their affection. Rather their hatred for their semi-foreign king steadily increased, and late in his reign there was opposition from the Pharisees, previously acquiescent. His power was based on his chain of fortresses (including the Antonia in Jerusalem, q.v.), his gentile mercenary army, his secret police, and a centralized bureaucracy, with which he ruthlessly and effectively fulfilled a client king's function of maintaining order. By steadfast loyalty to Rome he retained Augustus' confidence for many years, but he eventually lost it through his high-handed conduct in a dispute with Nabataea and his savagery towards his family, intrigues in which caused him to execute his favourite wife, Mariamne I, in 29, her two sons in 7, and his eldest son in 4. Serious disturbances requiring Roman intervention followed his death, and his kingdom was then divided between his sons Antipas, Archelaus, and Philip (qq.v.).

Josephus, *BJ* 1. 203–673; *AJ* 14. 158–17. 199. W. Otto, *PW* Suppl. ii, 1 ff.; A. H. M. Jones, *The Herods of Judaea* (1938), 28 ff.

E. M. S.

**HEROD** (2) **ANTIPAS,** on the death of his father Herod the Great (q.v.), was appointed tetrarch of the central part of his kingdom, Galilee, where he rebuilt the city of Sepphoris and founded Tiberias (q.v.), and Peraea, where he rebuilt Betharamphtha as Livias (later renamed Julias). When he was in Jerusalem for the Passover (A.D. 30 or 33) Pilate tried unsuccessfully to transfer to him the responsibility for trying the Galilaean Jesus. In 36 Tiberius trusted him with a share in the negotiations between Rome and Parthia. During or before John the Baptist's ministry Antipas had divorced his wife, a daughter of Aretas IV of Nabataea, in favour of his niece Herodias, and in 37 Aretas took revenge by invading Peraea and defeating Antipas; Roman reprisals on Aretas were called off on Tiberius' death. In 39, at Herodias' instigation, Antipas asked Gaius for the title of king, but he was deposed on a charge of treason trumped up by his nephew Agrippa I (q.v.), who inherited his tetrarchy.

Josephus, *BJ* 2. 94–5; 167–8; 181–3; *AJ* 18. 27; 36–8; 101–5; 109–24, 240–55. *PW* Suppl. ii. 168 ff.; A. H. M. Jones, *The Herods of Judaea* (1938), 176 ff., 195 f.

E. M. S.

**HERODAS** (Herondas?), a third-century B.C. writer of *mimiambi*, literary mimes in iambic scazons. Questions of time and place are debatable, and even the correct form of his name is uncertain. Only a few quotations were extant until 1891, when a papyrus acquired two years previously by the British Museum was published by F. G. Kenyon. This edition contained Mimes 1–7 and the first three lines of 8. Additional fragments were pieced together later. The mimes are short, subtle, realistic presentations of typical mime-themes, perhaps intended for solo performance. 1. *The Bawd*. Metriche, whose lover (husband?) has gone to Egypt, is visited by old Gyllis, who urges her to transfer her affections to a young athlete, Gryllus. She refuses with refreshing firmness and politely dismisses Gyllis with a cup of wine. 2. *The Pimp*. Battarus delivers a harangue in court against a trader for house-breaking and attempted abduction of one of his slave-girls. The vulgar, unctuous, menacing yet entirely mercenary pimp is perhaps the author's masterpiece. There is much parody of legal forms. 3. *The Schoolmaster*. The voluble Metrotime, exasperated by poverty and the pranks of her incorrigible son Cottalus, brings him to the dry schoolmaster, Lampriscus, for a flogging, which is duly administered. 4. *The Women Worshippers*. Cynno, her friend Coccale, and the maid (mute) bring their humble offering to the temple of Asclepius at Cos. The matter-of-fact, short-tempered mistress Cynno, the naïve Coccale, lost in admiration at the temple-statues, and the oily sacristan are effectively portrayed. 5. *The Jealous Mistress*. Bitinna, furious at discovering the infidelity of Gastron, her slave-paramour, orders him off for flogging, in spite of his entreaties; then she hastily sends her maid Cydilla to fetch him back for branding; finally Cydilla wheedles her into granting a provisional pardon. 6. *The Private Conversation*. Metro calls on Coritto to ask for certain information, and the two dear friends converse with admirable cynicism. 7. *The Shoemaker*. Metro introduces some prospective lady-customers to the fashionable shoe-maker Cerdon, an outstanding portrait of the salesman, alternately oily and truculent. 8. *The Dream*. A farmer (clearly Herodas himself) relates his dream of how his goat was torn limb from limb by certain worshippers of Dionysus, and how, in the subsequent contest, he won the prize. Herodas is evidently referring to the harsh treatment of his works by his critics (perhaps Callimachus and his circle), and his hopes of ultimate recognition as the successor of Hipponax. 9. *Women Breaking a Fast*. Only a fragmentary introduction survives. Guests are greeted; and slaves seem to be scolded somewhat in the manner of the opening of Theocritus 15.

ANNOTATED EDITIONS. J. A. Nairn (1904); W. Headlam and A. D. Knox, with translation (1922); O. Crusius (2nd ed., by R. Herzog, 1926); A. D. Knox (Loeb, with Theophrastus' *Characters*).
W. B.; D. E. E.

**HERODES** (1), Ti. Claudius (*PW* 71) Atticus (d. *c.* A.D. 137), the wealthy father of Herodes (q.v. 2) Atticus, received *ornamenta praetoria*, and was legate of Judaea (99/100–102/3?). He became *cos. suff.* (?104) and, according to Philostratus, again under Hadrian. ἀρχιερεύς τῶν Σεβαστῶν at Athens (between 97 and 102), where he had a seat of honour in the theatre (*IG* ii. 3². 5090), he was honoured throughout Greece.

P. Graindor, *Un Milliardaire antique, Hérode Atticus* (1930), 20 ff.; for dates, E. M. Smallwood, *JRS* 1962, 131 ff. H. H. S.

**HERODES** (2) ATTICUS (L. Vibullius Hipparchus Ti. Claudius Atticus Herodes), *c.* A.D. 101–77, Athenian of the deme Marathon, consul at Rome 143. A sophist of great wealth, generously used in building and benefaction, he combined a career as a Roman senator with literary activity that won him primacy among coevals

and comparison with the classics. His style was straightforward, elegant, and restrained, recalling Critias and influencing a wide circle of pupils. A friend of Hadrian, Antoninus, and Aurelius, he was responsible for the teaching of the last and of L. Verus. His works included letters, διαλέξεις and ἐφημερίδες: only a Latin translation of a *fabula* survives (Gell. 19. 12) apart from a sym-bouleutic speech with the superscription Ἡρώδου περὶ πολιτείας whose attribution is contested.

Philostr. *VS* 2. 1; ['Ηρώδου] περὶ πολιτείας ed. Drerup (1908) cf. Wade-Gery, *CQ* 1945; W. Schmid, *Der Atticismus* (1887), vol. i; P. Graindor, *Hérode Atticus et sa famille* (1930); G. W. Bowersock, *Greek Sophists in the Roman Empire* (1969), ch. 7. E. L. B.

**HERODIAN**(1)(Aelius Herodianus), son of Apollonius Dyscolus, of Alexandria, grammarian at Rome under M. Aurelius. He wrote works on the accentuation of the *Iliad* and *Odyssey*, and of Attic. These he afterwards included in his Καθολικὴ προσῳδία, reviewing the accentuation of (it is said) some 60,000 words. It was in twenty-one books: 1–19 contained rules of accentuation, the 20th dealt with quantities and breathings, and the last with enclitics, synaloepha, and some other points concerning words in combination. This immense work survives only in later citations, and in extracts such as those by Theodosius and ps.-Arcadius. It was largely based on Aristarchus and his successors in this field. Two of Herodian's other works are extant—Περὶ μονήρους λέξεως (on anomalous words) and Φιλέταιρος, a short Atticist lexicon. He disagrees, however, with his father's extreme doctrines of ἀναλογία, expressly repudiating such forms as ἱμῦ (see APOLLONIUS (13) DYSCOLUS). Of his many other works the titles of about thirty survive, together with extracts and quotations by later scholars: they cover many departments of grammar, including, e.g., treatises on various parts of speech, figures, declensions, conjugations, defective verbs, and some anomalous words such as ὕδωρ. Herodian ranks with his father as one of the greatest, as he is the last, of original Greek grammarians. A number of later compilatory works are falsely attributed to him.

EDITIONS. Φιλέταιρος: A. Dain, 1954; Π. μον. λέξ.: Dindorf, 1823; Π. μον. λέξ., Π. 'Ιλιακῆς προσῳδίας, Π. διχρόνων, Lehrs, 1848. *Herodiani Reliquiae* (much conjectural reconstruction), Lentz in Teubner's *Gramm. Gr.*; cf. also H. Erbse, *Beitr. zur Überlieferung d. Iliasscholien* (1960), 311 ff. P. B. R. F.; R. B.

**HERODIAN** (2) of Syria, a subordinate official in Rome early in the third century A.D., wrote Τῆς μετὰ Μάρκον βασιλείας ἱστορίαι in eight books from M. Aurelius to Gordian III (A.D. 180–238). Moralizing and rhetorical, his work is superficial, although his value increases with his contemporary knowledge.

TEXTS. L. Mendelssohn (1883); K. Stavenhagen (1922); F. Cassola, *Erodiano* (1968), text with Italian transl. A. H. McD.

**HERODICUS** of Babylon (perhaps late 2nd c. B.C.), author of Κωμῳδούμενοι (persons satirized in Comedy, see AMMONIUS 1), Σύμμικτα ὑπομνήματα, and Πρὸς τὸν φιλοσωκράτην.

M. Müller, *De Seleuco Homerico* (1891), 10 ff.; J. Steinhausen, *Κωμῳδούμενοι* (1910); A. Dittmar, *Aischines von Sphettos* (1912), 56 f. J. D. D.

**HERODOTUS** (1), son of Lyxes, of good family in Halicarnassus, and related to Panyassis, a 'reviver of epic', was born 'a little before the Persian War, and lived till the Peloponnesian War' (Dion. Hal. *Thuc.* 5). In civil strife at Halicarnassus Panyassis was killed by the tyrant Lygdamis, grandson of Artemisia (q.v.), and Herodotus withdrew to Samos. By 454 Halicarnassus was pacified and a Delian tributary; but if Herodotus returned, he did not remain; for he had travelled, and lectured in Greece, and visited Athens, before he joined the Athenian colony at Thurii (founded 444/3). Biographers who dated his birth in 484 (Aul. Gell. 15. 23) may have simply counted back forty years from this central event of his life. Lucian, *Herodotus*, represents him as giving lectures in various cities, but it is hard to believe that he was paid 10 talents for a lecture or reading in Athens (Plut. *De malign. H.* 826 b), however highly he may have flattered Athenian pride. His history was known in Athens in 425, when it was parodied by Aristophanes (*Ach.* 513 ff.), but there is no clear proof of any return after 443. He mentions Greek events of 430, but none later, and is presumed to have died in Thurii before 420; a tomb, with an epitaph in verse (Steph. Byz. s.v. Θούριοι) was shown there in later years, but there was also a tradition that, like Euripides, he died at Pella.

**2.** TRAVELS. Besides acquaintance with Samos (3. 60), Athens (5. 77), and south Italy (4. 15. 99), Herodotus records travels—(*a*) in Egypt, to Elephantine, during the Nile flood and ebb, after the Persian reconquest (449), perhaps also before the revolt of 460–454; (*b*) to Gaza (3. 5), Tyre (2. 44), and down the Euphrates (1. 185) to Babylon (1. 178–83); (*c*) in Scythia, to Olbia (4. 16) and up the Borysthenes (4. 81), and in the north Aegean from the Bosporus (4. 87) to Thasos (6. 47). Though he has much to say of Persian customs, he never indicates a visit to Persia; but Cyrene (4. 156–203), like Crete, is a likely stopping place on a voyage to Egypt. It has been conjectured that he travelled as a merchant, but there is nothing in the text to suggest it; on the contrary, he sometimes says that he went to places expressly to seek information (2. 3, 44). What he saw with his own eyes (ὄψις) is contrasted with what he heard (ἀκοή). Sometimes, especially in Egypt and at Delphi, he tried to corroborate traditions by examining monuments and questioning priests and temple attendants. Silence about western journeys suggests that the main motive was not geographical but historical, and that the visit to Athens was a crisis in life and outlook: acquaintance with Sophocles, who wrote him verses (Plut. *Mor.* 785 b), interest in Pericles and Alcmaeonid house-lore, in Cimon's ancestors (4. 137–8; 6. 34 ff., 103 ff.), and in topographical details (5. 77, 8. 53) enhance the significance of his eulogy and vindication of Athenian aims and achievements (7. 139). This does not mean that he started to write his history or conceived it in any coherent form before going to Thurii.

**3.** OTHER SOURCES. Besides his own travels and inquiries Herodotus has wide geographical, historical, and literary knowledge. He quotes Homer and Hesiod, discusses the authorship of the *Cypria* (2. 117), notes suspect or misapplied oracles (7. 6; 8. 20; 9. 43), and defends genuine ones (8. 77); dissents from current Ionian theories (2. 15, 20; 4. 36), and expressly criticizes and derides Hecataeus (2. 143; 6. 137), from whom, however, he borrows freely. Other literary sources, lost or unknown to us, have been suspected, e.g. accounts of oracles (R. Crahay, *La Littérature oraculaire chez H.* (1956)), memoirs written by Dicaeus, an Athenian exile in Persia (8. 65, P. Trautwein, *Hermes* 1890, 527 ff.), as well as the work of logographers like Charon and Xanthus (*see* LOGOGRAPHERS). But apart from Hecataeus Herodotus mentions no contemporary prose writers and his frequent references to national sources, e.g. a Samian version, as contrasted with a Spartan (3. 47), probably indicate oral information as a result of inquiry (ἱστορίη).

**4.** TEXT. There are a few lacunae, and the account of the Pyramid kings (2. 124–36) should follow 2. 99. An unfulfilled reference to Ἀσσύριοι λόγοι (1. 184) indicates that a Mesopotamian counterpart to the description of Egypt has been lost, or was not written.

**5.** PLAN AND SCOPE. The plan of the *History* is stated in its opening words (1. 1). Great deeds have value in retrospect, whether done by Greeks or by others (and Herodotus' portraits of Persians are masterly), and it is reasonable to ask, of the Great War, 'what they fought each other for'. Blame for the clash of Persians with Greeks is put on Croesus, whose headstrong attack on Cyrus ruined Lydia (1. 6). The story of that 'middle kingdom' (1. 7–94) is interrupted characteristically by a pair of digressions (1. 59–68), explaining why neither Athens nor Sparta helped Croesus. The rise of the Medes, their subjection by Cyrus, and a sketch of him and his Persians (1. 95–140) lead to his conquest of the Asiatic Greeks (1. 141–77). The story of the Empire under Cyrus, Cambyses, and Darius (1. 178 to 5. 27) includes a long account of Egypt (book 2), formally motivated by Cambyses' invasion of the country. The accession and reforms of Darius (3. 61–87, 150–60) are interleaved with his first oversea success, against Polycrates of Samos (3. 39–60; 120–49), and followed by pendent narratives of his aggressions in Thrace and Scythia (4. 1–144; 5. 1–27) and in Libya (4. 145–205). After all this retrospect comes the Ionic Revolt (5. 28–38), its suppression (5. 97–6. 42), and the consequent Marathon campaign (6. 94–120), similarly alternated with events in Greece, involving Sparta (5. 39–54; 6. 51–84) and Athens (5. 55–96; 6. 85–93, 121–40) in resistance to Persia. In books 7, 8, 9 the accession of Xerxes and his choice between policies (7. 1–19) lead to pendent narratives of preparation, Persian (7. 20–131) and Greek (7. 131–75). Then the sea-fight at Artemisium (7. 175–95) and the land-battle at Thermopylae (7. 196–239), with their sequels (8. 1–23, 24–39), prepare for the crucial struggle at Salamis (8. 40–112) and its aftermath, the return of Xerxes (8. 113–32), and the winter parleys (8. 133–44). Finally, the land-battle of Plataea (9. 1–89) and the naval operations at Mycale (9. 90–106) are the counterpart of Artemisium and Thermopylae.

**6.** The *History* has been regarded as unfinished; but the brief epilogue (9. 107–22) elaborately displays Persian demoralization, contrasted with initial hardiness. If Herodotus meant to go beyond the capture of Sestus (9. 117–21), it would mean a fresh 'account' of new aims and events; and it is where our text of Herodotus ends that Thucydides begins his retrospect (1. 89) of τὰ μετὰ τὰ Μηδικά. The clumsy division of the work into nine 'Muses' is some librarian's fancy: Herodotus himself cross-refers to this or that λόγος.

**7.** LITERARY ART. Within this broad design the main story is clearly distinguished from 'additions' (προσθῆκαι 4. 30; παρενθῆκαι 7. 171) large and small, some composed for their place, some utilizing earlier drafts. Such digressions have epic precedent, and those of Herodotus—for which he apologizes, e.g. 2. 123—are deliberate. His literary art must be compared with Pindar's notions of relevance, and with the tragedians' use of choral odes, annotating rather than interrupting the development of the plot. Like the dramatists, too, Herodotus chooses a hero—Croesus, Polycrates, Cleomenes, Mardonius—and traces his response to events and persons, in success and in disaster. Through *peripeteia* and *catastrophe* the question—δι' ἣν αἰτίην—answers itself: only rarely need Herodotus intervene, chorus-like, to point a moral; for his public, like the audience of a tragedy, knew the outline of the story. Hence economy of detail, significant hearsay without guarantee of veracity; Aeschylean word-painting, Pindaric allusiveness, Aristophanic humour, above all, Sophoclean irony; a new literary art and expository skill, applied in lucid prose to a fresh field of research—the causes of 'men's deeds'—which establish Herodotus as the 'Father of History'.

**8.** HISTORICAL METHOD. Herodotus professes to record things seen and heard. His book results from his journeys; yet it is no mere περίοδος γῆς or ἐπιδημίαι, but ἱστορίης ἀπόδεξις, the outcome of research. What he has seen (ὄψις 2. 99, 147; 4. 81; cf. 5. 59), heard (ἀκοή 2. 99–106; 6. 82; 7. 35), and read (in poets, Ionian travellers, and theorists) is supplemented and verified by inquiry (ἱστορίη 2. 19, 44, 75, 113, 118; 4. 96) and criticized by common sense (γνώμη 2. 24; 5. 3). He states alternative versions and views with discreet reticence (2. 3, 46–7), and reserves judgement or offers conjecture (εἰκασίη 2. 24; 4. 11–12; 8. 22) when evidence fails. Ethnographical and historical interests have outrun (but not extinguished) physical and geographical. Historical facts have intrinsic value and natural meaning. Patriotic pride and religious belief are tempered by comparison of regimes and customs, and by respect for age-long Oriental experience. In Egypt he believed that he had received mystic teaching; but he reveals nothing, because 'all men know equally about divine things' (2. 3).

**9.** PERSONALITY. His personality is written in his book. Explorer, observer, and listener, he combines encyclopaedic interest and curiosity—about deeds rather than ideas—with humane sympathy and goodwill. Childlike, he loves wonders and secrets, enjoys a tale and a joke, and tells them vividly. Devoid of race-prejudice and intolerance, he venerates antiquity and is fascinated by novelties; and in these things trusts informants overmuch. Without linguistic skill, he extracts information from all; without military insight, he has recorded a great war. For a philosophy he has common sense, moral honesty, and piety. In a world regulated by fate (μοῖρα), but deranged by chance (τύχη), the gods uphold righteousness and punish wrong-doers. They can warn, but they do not prevent, though they intervene to punish arrogance. Amid these external forces, and with the guidance of law and usage, man, using experience and reason, has freedom of choice and is responsible (αἴτιος) for his acts.

**10.** Of such work, criticism was immediate and persistent. Herodotus himself replies to critics (6. 43); Thucydides (1. 20) challenges statements (6. 57; 9. 53); Aristophanes parodies the preface (*Ach.* 513 ff.); Plutarch (*De Malignitate Herodoti*) imputes unfairness and perversion of facts, thinking him disrespectful of tradition and φιλοβάρβαρος. Christian writers make charges of plagiarism, which Sayce (1883) has repeated and amplified. But closer study and better acquaintance with the resources, equipment, and literary custom of ancient writers have restored Herodotus' reputation for industry and honesty, while noting mistakes and omissions. J. L. M.

**11.** Herodotus' style probably owes little to the early logographers, whose scanty fragments hardly reveal any style at all—an impression confirmed, on the whole, by Dion. Hal. *Thuc.* 5 and 23. To Homer he undoubtedly owes much, in cast of thought as well as in language (Norden, *Ant. Kunstpr.* i. 40). What other literary influences may have gone to the moulding of him it is hard to say. Nor is it easy to analyse the surpassing beauty of his prose, for Herodotus has no mannerisms. Sometimes it is traceable to a subtle disposition of long and short words, as in the majestic proem (comparable, in this respect, to the openings of Sappho's *Ode to Aphrodite* and Lucretius' poem) and in 1. 45, ad fin.; sometimes to other technical means (1. 119, unobtrusive word-echoes; 1. 45, loc. cit., hyperbaton; 1. 32, asyndeton and initial assonance). But hardly a single technical device can be said to be characteristic of Herodotus. Each is used when, and when only, it is needed, as the period, for example, is reserved for great moments (e.g. 1. 45, 86). The first book is peculiarly rich in noble passages: Solon and Croesus (29–33, with the unforgettable solemnity of τὸ θεῖον πᾶν ἐὸν φθονερόν τε καὶ ταραχῶδες and πᾶν ἐστι ἄνθρωπος συμφορή, and 86–90); Harpagus eating

his children's flesh (119, with the master-stroke at the close, where the historian is transformed into the hushed, yet curious, spectator). Such passages are the perfection of tragedy, as Don't-care Hippocleides pirouetting on his head is the perfection of comedy. They reveal a side of Herodotus not always perceived by modern readers or by ancient critics, who praise his sweetness and beauty, but find him lacking in emotional power (e.g. Cic. *Orat.* 39 'quasi sedatus amnis fluit'; Quint. *Inst.* 10. 1. 73 'dulcis et candidus et fusus Herodotus'; Dion. Hal. *Pomp.* 3 and *Thuc.* 23 (comparisons with Thuc.); Ath. 3, p. 78 e (μελίγηρυς)). Hermogenes, however (*Id.* 2, p. 421), does recognize his grandeur and emotional power. Herodotus has suffered the fate which befell Mozart. His charm, wit, and effortless ease have diverted attention from the note of profound sadness and pity sounded not seldom in his History.

TEXTS. J. C. E. Bähr (1856); H. Stein (1856–1901); C. Hude (O.C.T. 1908; 1927); Ph. E. Legrand (Budé) 1932–54, with introd. and essays.
COMMENTARIES. G. Rawlinson (1858; 1876²); H. Stein (1869; 1901⁶); A. H. Sayce (bks. 1–3, 1883); R. W. Macan (bks. 5–6, 1895, bks. 7–9, 1908); W. W. How and J. Wells (1912; 1928²).
TRANSLATIONS. G. Rawlinson (1858; ed. A. W. Lawrence, 1935, ed. W. G. Forrest, 1966; G. C. Macaulay (1890); A. D. Godley (Loeb, 1921); J. E. Powell (1949); A. de Sélincourt (1954).
INDEXES AND LEXICA. J. E. Powell, *Lexicon to H.* (1938); Ph. E. Legrand (in Budé ed., 1954), *Index analytique.*
LANGUAGE AND STYLE. Ph. E. Legrand (Budé ed. introd., 1932); H. B. Rosen, *Laut- u. Formenlehre d. Herod. Sprachform* (1962).
HERODOTUS IN EGYPT. Bk. 2 ed. A. Wiedemann (1890), ed. W. Waddell (1939); H. Sourdille, *La Durée et l'étendue du voyage d'H. en Égypte* (1912); W. Spiegelberg, *Die Glaubwürdigkeit d. H. Beschr. v. Aeg.* (1926, Engl. transl. A. M. Blackman, 1927).
LITERARY, HISTORICAL, AND GENERAL. A. Kirchhoff, *Entstehungs-zeit d. H. Geschichtswerkes* (1878); A. Bauer, *Enst. d. H. Gesch.* (1878); A. Hauvette, *Hérodote* (1894); E. Meyer, *Forschungen z. alt. Gesch.* i–ii (1892–9); G. B. Grundy, *The Great Persian War* (1901); F. Jacoby, *Gr. Historiker* (1956) repr. from *PW, Herodotos; Gr. Geschichtschreibung, Die Antike* 2 (1926), 1 ff.; T. R. Glover, *Herodotus* (1924); M. Pohlenz, *Herodot* (1937); J. E. Powell, *The Hist. of H.* (1939); J. L. Myres, *Herodotus, Father of History* (1953); K. Latte, *Die Anfänge d. gr. Geschichtsschreibung,* in *Entretiens Hardt* 4 (1956); A. de Sélincourt, *The World of H.* (1962); F. Chatelet, *La Naissance de l'histoire* (1962); H. R. Immerwahr, *Form and Thought in H.* (1966).
SURVEYS OF LITERATURE. *CAH* v. 520 ff.; P. MacKendrick, *Classical World* 1954, 145 ff., 1963, 269 ff.; W. Krause, *Anzeiger d. Altertums-wissenschaft* 1961, 26 ff.; W. Marg (ed.), *Herodot; eine Auswahl aus der neueren Forschung* (1962). J. D. D.; L. P.

**HERODOTUS** (2), pupil of Agathinus and adherent of the pneumatic school of medicine, in the Flavian period (A.D. 70–96), wrote Ἰατρός and Περὶ βοηθημάτων (lost); Διάγνωσις περὶ τῶν ὀξέων καὶ χρονίων νοσημάτων (extant).

**HERON** of Alexandria, mathematician and inventor (fl. A.D. 62), was known as ὁ μηχανικός. The following works are associated with his name: (1) *Metrica*, 3 books, on the measurement of surfaces and bodies, and division of them in a given ratio. (2) *Definitions* (ὅροι), defining geometrical terms and concepts. (3) *Geometrica*, (4) *Stereometrica*, and (5) *On Measures* (Περὶ μέτρων), all works of practical mensuration. (6) *Pneumatica*, on the construction of devices worked by compressed air, steam, and water. (7) *On Automata-making*, mostly on the construction of θαύματα ('miracle-working' devices used especially in temples). (8) *Mechanica*, 3 books (extant only in Arabic), a treatise on how to move weights with the least effort, containing (book 1) the foundations of statics and dynamics, (book 2) the five simple machines, (book 3) the building of lifting-machines and presses. (9) *Dioptra*, on the construction and use of a sighting-instrument for measurement at a distance (with additions describing unrelated instruments, e.g. a hodometer). (10) *Catoptrica* (extant only in Latin translation), on the theory and construction of plane and curved mirrors. (11) *Belopoeica*, on the construction of war-catapults. Some of these, notably (3), (4), and (5), can hardly be by Heron in their present form, but all may well be based on treatises by him.

Other works by Heron no longer extant include a commentary on Euclid's *Elements* (substantial remains in an-Nairīzi's commentary on Euclid, ed. Curtze, *Euclidis Opera Omnia Supp.*, Leipzig, 1899); βαρουλκός, description of a machine for lifting huge weights by means of a combination of gear-wheels (parts are incorporated into *Mechanica* i. 1 and *Dioptra* 37); *On Waterclocks* (Proclus, *Hypotyp.* 120); and perhaps *Cheirobalistra*, another type of artillery weapon (only fragmentarily preserved). The *Geodaesia* and *Liber Geeponicus* are later compilations, largely extracts from the *Geometrica* and other mensurational works.

Heron, though very adept at both mathematics and applied mechanics, was probably not very original in either. But his mensurational works are of great importance as our main source for practical mathematics in the Greco-Roman world. While classical 'Euclidean' mathematics aimed at constructing theorems, 'Heronic' mathematics was directed towards solving practical problems, if necessary by approximation. Thus, Heron gives examples of approximations to irrational square- and cube-roots. He also solves quadratic equations arithmetically, and gives the formula for the area of a triangle, $\Delta = \sqrt{\{s(s-a)(s-b)(s-c)\}}$. The roots of this type of mathematics lie in Mesopotamia. In pneumatics, mechanics, and the other sciences too, though Heron often discusses theoretical matters, his purpose is utility and amusement; hence we get detailed descriptions, with figures, of devices such as siphons, a self-regulating lamp, a water-organ, pulley-systems, and a variety of 'mechanical toys'. Though the discovery of the principles behind these, and perhaps many of the devices too, were due to Heron's predecessors, such as Archimedes and Ctesibius (q.v.), here too he is of major importance as a source. *See also* PHYSICS. §§ 5, 6

EDITIONS. (1) to (10) in *Heronis Opera*, 5 vols. ed. W. Schmidt and others, Leipzig (Teubner), 1899–1914 (with German translation and fragments). See also Hultsch, *Heronis Alexandrini geometricorum et stereometricorum reliquiae* (Berlin, 1864). *Belopoeica*, ed. H. Diels and E. Schramm, *Abh. Berlin. Akad.* 1918, 2 (Phil.-hist. Kl.) (with German translation). For an attempted reconstruction of the *Cheirobalistra* see V. Prou, *Notices et Extraits des Manuscrits* xxvi. 2 (1877).
COMMENT. Heron's mathematics: Heath, *Hist. of Greek Maths.* ii. 298 ff. *et al.*
PNEUMATICA. A. G. Drachmann, *Ktesibios Philon and Heron* (Copenhagen, 1948).
MECHANICA AND BELOPOEICA. A. G. Drachmann, *The Mechanical Technology of Greek and Roman Antiquity* (Copenhagen, 1963).
DIOPTRA. A. G. Drachmann in *A History of Technology* 3 (ed. Singer, 1957), 609 ff., also O. Neugebauer, *Kgl. Danske Vid. Selsk., Hist.-fil. Med.* xxvi. 2, 1938 (for date of Heron).    G. J. T.

**HEROPHILUS** of Chalcedon, one of the leading dogmatic physicians, lived in Alexandria in the first half of the third century B.C.; his school was still flourishing at the end of the first century B.C. Herophilus stressed the importance of experience no less than that of reasoning. Though a great scholar, his work seems primarily determined by the practical task of the physician; health he went so far as to consider the indispensable foundation of all physical and intellectual happiness. His greatest original contributions were his anatomical inquiries based on the human cadaver; he probably wrote a systematic outline of anatomy (particularly famous was his study of the brain—to him the organ of the soul—of the liver, the eye, the sexual organs). He discovered the rhythm of the pulse and formulated a mathematical law of its systole and diastole. Much interested in the aetiology of diseases, he explained their origin through humours. In therapy he paid careful attention to prognostics and used drugs abundantly; but he was also an authority on dietetics and gymnastics. Through his books, in which practical questions were emphasized, he exercised a considerable influence. *See* ANATOMY AND PHYSIOLOGY, § 7.

TEXT. Fragments: K. F. H. Marx (1838); Marx, *De vita, scriptis*, etc. (1842). On Herophilus as the discoverer of both sensory and motor nerves see F. Solmsen, *MH* 1961, 185 ff. List of writings: Susemihl i. 787.
TRANSLATION AND COMMENTARY. J. F. Dobson, *Proceedings of the Royal Society of Med.*, Section Hist. of Med. (1925), indispensable for interpretation of the more important fragments.
LITERATURE. The handbooks on history of medicine; F. Kudlien, 'Herophilus und der Beginn der Medizinischen Skepsis', *Gesnerus* 1964, 1 ff., assumes an influence of Pyrrhon's scepticism on Herophilus, especially on the preference he gives to the study of phenomena. But this trait and the sceptical overtones of Herophilus' theory seem to derive from the emphasis and scepticism of the late Peripatos (see L. Edelstein, *Bulletin Inst. Hist. Medicine* 1935, 235 ff., on the development that led to human anatomy of which Herophilus is one of the founders). Tradition unanimously regards Herophilus as a Dogmatist; a turn to academic scepticism is responsible for the rise of the Empirical School which grew out of that of Herophilus (s.v. Philinus). Pupils of Herophilus: H. Gossen, *PW* viii. 1104.    L. E.

**HERULI,** a Germanic people, who were expelled from Scandinavia by the Danes. In the later third century A.D. some of them appear on the Rhine and others in the Black Sea region. The former were of little importance, but the latter in 267 sacked Athens, Corinth, Sparta, and Argos. One of the most primitive of the Germanic peoples, they still practised human sacrifice in the sixth century.    E. A. T.

**HESIOD,** one of the oldest known Greek poets, often coupled or contrasted with Homer as the other main representative of early epic. Which was the older of the two was much disputed from the fifth century B.C. on (Xenophanes ap. Gell. 3. 11. 2, Hdt. 2. 53, Ephorus fr. 101 J., etc.): Homer's priority was carefully argued by Aristarchus, and generally accepted in later antiquity. Hesiod's absolute date is now agreed to fall not far before or after 700 B.C. Of his life he tells us something himself: that his father had given up a life of unprofitable sea-trading and moved from Aeolian Cyme to Ascra in Boeotia (*Op.* 633–40); that he, as he tended sheep on Mt. Helicon, had heard the Muses calling him to sing of the gods (*Th.* 22–35, a celebrated passage); and that he once won a tripod for a song at a funeral contest at Chalcis (*Op.* 650–60). For his dispute with Perses see below (2). He is said to have died in Hesperian Locris (Thuc. 3. 96, etc.), but his tomb was shown at Orchomenus (Arist. fr. 565, *Certamen* 14, Paus. 9. 38. 3). The story of his meeting and contest with Homer was probably an invention of the sophist Alcidamas (see *Certamen Homeri et Hesiodi*). The poems anciently attributed to him are as follows (only the first three have survived complete, and only the first two have a good claim to be authentic):

1. The *Theogony* (Θεογονία). The main part of the poem, which is prefaced by a hymn to the Muses (1–104; cf. the Homeric Hymns), deals with the origin and genealogies of the gods (including the divine world-masses Earth, Sea, Sky, etc.), and the events that led to the kingship of Zeus: the castration of Uranos by Kronos, and the overthrow of Kronos and the Titans, the 'former gods' (424), by the Olympians. This 'Succession Myth' has striking parallels in Akkadian and Hittite texts, and seems originally to have come from the Near East. Hesiod's version shows some stylistic awkwardness and inconcinnity, but is not without power. Interlaced with it are the genealogies, which run smoother. The first powers born are Chaos, Earth, and (significantly) Eros (116–22). From Chaos and Earth, in two separate lines, some 300 gods descend; they include personified abstracts, whose family relationships are clearly meaningful. There is an interesting passage in praise of the unhomeric goddess Hecate (411–52), further myths, notably the aetiological tale of Prometheus (521–616), and a detailed description of Tartarus (720–819). The

poem ends with the marriages of Zeus and the other Olympians, and a list of goddesses who lay with mortal men. This last section, which refers to Latinus (1013) and led on to the *Catalogue* (below, 4), is agreed to be post-Hesiodic, though opinions vary as to where the authentic part ends.

2. The *Works & Days* (Ἔργα καὶ Ἡμέραι). This poem, apparently composed after the *Theogony* (cf. 11–24 with *Th.* 225), would be more aptly entitled 'the Wisdom of Hesiod'. It gives advice for living a life of honest work. Hesiod inveighs against dishonesty and idleness by turns, using myths (Prometheus again, with the famous story of Pandora, 42–105; the Five World-Ages, 106–201), parable (202–12), allegory (286–92), proverbial maxims, direct exhortation, and threats of divine anger. The sermon is ostensibly directed at a brother Perses, who has bribed the βασιλῆες and taken more than his share of his inheritance (37–9); but Perses' failings seem to change with the context (cf. 28 ff., 275, 396), and it is impossible to reconstruct a single basic situation. Besides moral advice, Hesiod gives much practical instruction, especially on agriculture (381–617, the year's 'Works'), seafaring (618–94), and social and religious conduct (336–80, 695–764). There is a fine descriptive passage on the rigours of winter (504–35). The final section, regarded by many as a later addition, is the 'Days' (765–828), an almanac of days in the month that are favourable or unfavourable for different operations. The poem as a whole is a unique source for social conditions in early archaic Greece. It has closer parallels in Near Eastern literatures than in Greek, and seems to represent an old traditional type. (Virgil's *Georgics*, though much influenced by Hesiod, are shaped by the Hellenistic tradition of systematic treatment of a single theme (*see* DIDACTIC POETRY).)

It has always been the most read of Hesiodic poems. There was even a 'tradition' that it was Hesiod's only genuine work (Paus. 9. 31. 4); but he names himself in *Th.* 22, and links of style and thought between the two poems confirm identity of authorship. Both bear the marks of a distinct personality: a surly, conservative countryman, given to reflection, no lover of women or of life, who felt the gods' presence heavy about him.

3. The *Shield* (Ἀσπίς) is a short narrative poem on Heracles' fight with Cycnus, prefaced by an excerpt from the fourth book of the *Catalogue* giving the story of Heracles' birth (1–56). It takes its title from the disproportionately long description of Heracles' shield (139–320), which is based partly on the shield of Achilles (*Il.* 18. 478–609), partly on the art of the period c. 580–570 (R. M. Cook, *CQ* 1937, 204·ff.; this proves that Aristophanes of Byzantium was right in denying the poem to Hesiod). Disproportion is characteristic of the work; the Homeric apparatus of arming, divine machination, brave speeches, and long similes is lavished on an encounter in which two blows are struck in all. Parts of the description of the shield betray a taste for the macabre.

4. The *Catalogue of Women* (Γυναικῶν Κατάλογος) or *Ehoiai* (Ἠοῖαι) was a continuation of the *Theogony* in five books, containing heroic genealogies with many narrative annotations. Numerous citations and extensive papyrus fragments survive. The poem was accepted as Hesiod's in antiquity, but seems not to antedate the sixth century.

5. Other lost poems. (*a*) Narrative: Μεγάλαι Ἠοῖαι (genealogical), Μελαμποδία (in at least three books; stories of famous seers), Κήϋκος Γάμος, Ἰδαῖοι Δάκτυλοι, Αἰγίμιος (in at least two books; alternatively ascribed to Cercops of Miletus). (*b*) Didactic: Χείρωνος Ὑποθῆκαι (addressed to Achilles), Ἀστρονομία (risings and settings—and myths?—of principal stars), Μεγάλα Ἔργα, Ὀρνιθομαντεία (appended to the *Works & Days* in some ancient texts). A few fragments of most of these poems survive.

6. The Κάμινος or Κεραμεῖς (Hom. *Epigr.* 14) was ascribed to Hesiod by some (Pollux 10. 85).

GENERAL. Schmid–Stählin I. i; H. Fränkel, *Dichtung und Philosophie*² (1962), ch. 3; F. Solmsen, *Hesiod and Aeschylus* (1949); B. A. van Groningen, *La Composition littéraire archaïque grecque* (1958). Lost works: J. Schwartz, *Pseudo-Hesiodeia* (1960).
TEXTS. Rzach, 1902 (ed. maior with full testimonia), 1913 (ed. minor², Teubner). (*Op.*:) Colonna, 1959. (Fragments:) Merkelbach–West, 1967.
COMMENTARIES WITH TEXT. (*Th.*:) West, 1966. (*Op.*:) Mazon, 1914; Wilamowitz, 1928 (omits *Days*); Sinclair, 1932. (*Shield*:) Russo², 1965. (*Catalogue*, papyri:) Merkelbach, 1957.
TRANSLATIONS. Mair, 1908; Evelyn-White², 1936 (Loeb); Lattimore, 1959.
LANGUAGE. Rzach, *Der Dialekt des Hesiodos* (1876); J. Paulson, *Index Hesiodeus* (1890); I. Sellschopp, *Stilistische Untersuchungen zu Hesiod* (1934); F. Krafft, *Vergleichende Untersuchungen zu Homer und Hesiod* (1963).
EASTERN PARALLELS. F. Dornseiff, *Antike und alter Orient*² (1959); P. Walcot, *Hesiod and the Near East* (1966). (*Th.*:) F. M. Cornford, *The Unwritten Philosophy* (1950); H. G. Güterbock, *AJArch.* 1948, 123 ff.; G. Steiner, *Der Sukzessionsmythos* (1958).                M. L. W.

**HESIONE** (Ἡσιόνη), in mythology, (1) an Oceanid, wife of Prometheus (Aesch. *PV* 560). (2) Wife of Nauplius and mother of Palamedes (q.v.), Oeax, and Nausimedon (Apollod. 2. 23). (3) Daughter of Laomedon (q.v.; ibid. 3. 146). After her rescue from the sea-monster by Heracles (q.v.), she was taken prisoner by him when he captured Troy, given as the prize of valour to Telamon, and granted leave to save any prisoner she chose; she therefore bought (ἐπρίατο) her brother Podarces for a nominal price, and he was henceforth called Πρίαμος. By Telamon she became mother of Teucer (q.v.; Apollod. 2. 136; 3. 162).                H. J. R.

**HESPERIDES,** the daughters of Night and Erebus (Hes. *Theog.* 215) or, in later versions, of Hesperis and Atlas (q.v.; Diod. Sic. 4. 27. 2) or of Ceto and Phorcys (schol. in Ap. Rhod. 4. 1399), were guardians of a tree of golden apples given by Earth to Hera at her marriage. From the same tree came the apples thrown down by Hippomenes (or Melanion) in his race against Atalanta (q.v.). The garden of the Hesperides was popularly located beyond the Atlas mountains at the western border of the Ocean. The number of the sisters, renowned for their sweet singing, varies from three to seven. Names attributed to them include Aigle, Erytheia, Arethusa, Hespere, and Hesperethusa. In some accounts they were associated with the Hyperboreans (q.v.). Heracles (q.v.) succeeded in taking the apples after slaying Ladon, the dragon who guarded the tree.

**HESPERUS** (Ἕσπερος, Lat. *Vesper, Vesperugo*), the Evening Star; shown in art as a boy carrying a torch. Early tradition makes him the son of Astraeus (or Cephalus) and Eos (see Hyg. *Poet. Astr.* 2. 42) but later he was associated with Atlas (q.v.) as his son or brother (Diod. Sic. 3. 60; Serv. in Verg. *Aen.* 1. 530, 4. 484). He disappeared from Mt. Atlas in a whirlwind after climbing up to observe the stars. As father of Hesperis, he was grandfather of the Hesperides (q.v.).

**HESTIA,** goddess of the hearth, etymologically identical with Vesta (q.v.), and not unlike her in cult, though less important and not having her virgin priestesses. In early times, when it was a difficult and slow process to make fire, to keep a hearth burning continually was very advisable, and it would seem that in communities of that age, both in Greece and in Italy, the hearth of the chief or king was especially important, probably for practical reasons and certainly also from magico-religious motives; it seems to have been considered in some sense the life of the people (the equation 'fire = life' is very widespread). Hence the cult of the communal or sacred hearth was apparently universal, but the goddess never developed, hardly even achieving anthropomorphization. She therefore has next to no mythology. Homer never mentions her, the word ἱστίη meaning simply a fire-place; Hesiod and later authors after him make her daughter of Kronos (q.v.) and Rhea (*Theog.* 454), and the *Homeric Hymn to Aphrodite* says (21 ff.) that she 'liked not the works of Aphrodite', and so refused to marry either Poseidon or Apollo, but swore to remain a virgin, and Zeus accordingly granted her sundry honours, especially to 'sit in the midst of the house taking the fatness'. The brief *Hymn* to Hestia (24) was evidently composed for the eternal fire in the temple of Apollo at Delphi. Of her private cult not much is known; swine or, on occasion, cows were offered to her, no doubt according to the means of the household (Ar. *Vesp.* 844 and schol.; Callim. *Cer.* 109). At the Amphidromia (Plato, *Tht.* 160, schol. there and lexicographers s.v.), when the 5-days-old child was received into the family and named, part of the ceremony was to run with it around the hearth, but it does not appear that the goddess was thought present in any personal way. Publicly, she has 'the town halls (*prytaneia*) for her portion' (Pind. *Nem.* 11. 1), confirmed by the public hearth in the *prytaneia* of many cities (Farnell, op. cit. *infra* 348). Since the Senate-house often had a sacred hearth also, Hestia is not infrequently called Βουλαία, 'she of the Senate'. She commonly received the first of the sacrifice, or a preliminary sacrifice for herself, was named first in prayers and first or nearly so in oaths (Preuner in Roscher, 2616 ff.; Farnell, 346, 349; Rose in *Harv. Theol. Rev.* 1937, 172.

Farnell, *Cults* v. 345 ff.; Preuner in Roscher's *Lexikon*, s.v. (cf. his *Hestia-Vesta*, 1864); Diehl, *Anthologia lyrica*¹ ii. 301 f. (hymn of Aristonous at Delphi). H. J. R.

**HESYCHIUS** of Alexandria, lexicographer. If the Eulogius to whom he addresses the introductory epistle of his lexicon is Eulogius ὁ σχολαστικός, Hesychius (like Eulogius) probably belongs to the fifth century A.D. The comprehensive scope of his design is indicated both in that epistle and in the title, Συναγωγὴ πασῶν λέξεων κατὰ στοιχεῖον. The work, Hesychius says, was based on the specialist lexica (*see* GLOSSA, GREEK) of Aristarchus, Heliodorus (1st c. B.C.), Apion, and Apollonius, son of Archibius (pupil of Apion), and on Diogenianus and Herodian; Hesychius seems to have added the interpretations of a number of proverbs which are included. The lexicon is known only from a fifteenth-century MS., badly preserved, and in many places interpolated (even obliterated) by expansions and other notes made by the first editor, Marcus Musurus (1514). Bentley showed that the Biblical Glosses in Hesychius are interpolations; less successful attacks have been made on the Latin and Atticist items. The original, as Hesychius says, included the sources of the rare words listed. The sources, however, have disappeared in the severe abridgement which has reduced the lexicon to a glossary, copious though that remains. Hesychius often preserves correct readings for which easier synonyms have been substituted in our extant MSS. of Greek literature. His dialectal items are sometimes imperfect: he writes ϝ either as Β (less often Υ) or as Γ (less often Τ), as, e.g., Γοῖδα· οὐκ οἶδα [*sic* cod.], Γισγόν [*sic* cod.]· ἴσον. Nevertheless, he is of the greatest value for the study of Greek dialects, the interpretation of inscriptions, and the criticism of poetic texts.

EDITIONS. Alberti, 1746–66; Schmidt, 1858–68; ed. minor, 1867; K. Latte, i: *A–Δ* (1953), ii: *E–O* (1966); A. von Blumenthal, *Hesychiosstudien* (1930). P. B. R. F.; R. B.

**HETAIRAI.** Although Archilochus and Sappho were familiar with the phenomenon, the name first occurs in Herodotus (2. 134). Despite modern and ancient arguments to the contrary (e.g. Ath. 571–2), it is simply the Attic euphemism for those women, slave or free, who traded their sexual favours for long or short periods outside wedlock (Dion. Hal. 1. 84. 4; *Suda*, s.v.), whether

they were streetwalkers, the inmates of civic or private brothels, or accomplished and expensive courtesans (μεγαλόμισθοι). They were unknown in the heroic period and at Sparta, and our earliest references point to their existence in Ionia and Egypt in the sixth century. By Solon's time they were established in Athens and no doubt elsewhere in mainland Greece (Plut. *Vit. Sol.* 23. 1). The social protection they offered as an alternative to adultery ensured their continued toleration until the growth of Christianity. They enjoyed legal safeguards in most cities as well as certain social and civil disadvantages, such as taxation (πορνεῖον τέλος). Certain towns, especially ports, were notorious for the number and quality of their *hetairai*, among them Athens, Comena, and Corinth, which boasted also sacred prostitutes (ἱερόδουλοι ἑταῖραι) and high prices. *Hetairai* often had other professions and might double as hostesses, entertainers, and musicians; the most attractive and talented of them (e.g. Phryne, Lais, Neaera, Thais, and Leontion) sometimes became the mistresses of men of political, philosophical, or artistic distinction. It is from the late fifth to the third century, the great age of *hetairai*, that the most famous names and stories come down to us: an extensive literature sprang up about them, and real and fictitious members of the profession figured in New Comedy (e.g. Machon q.v.), where attitudes towards them varied from the cynical to the romantic. It is at this period that we find attempts made to distinguish the better class of *hetairai* from the lowly πόρνη or slave prostitute. Their social danger lay in their frequent rapacity and the ruinous infatuation they could inspire in the young or foolish, an aspect stressed in New (and Roman) Comedy, although the depiction is lightened by tales of *hetairai* with hearts of gold and reluctant *hetairai* of respectable origins. Our best source of information other than Comedy is Athenaeus Book 13, but Lucian (*Dial. Meretr.*) and Alciphron offer convincing and amusing sketches of their psychology and methods.

Dar.–Sag. s.v. *Meretrices*; K. Schneider, PW: H. Herter, 'Die Soziologie der antiken Prostitution', *Jahrb. f. Antike u. Christentum* 1960, 70 ff. J. P. S.

**HETAIRIAI** (ἑταιρίαι, -εῖαι), associations of 'comrades' (ἑταῖροι). In some, perhaps most, Cretan cities the citizens were grouped in *hetairiai* as part of the military system; each had its table in the city's *andreion* or common mess (cf. the Spartan *phiditia*). For the 'Companions' of the Macedonian kings, see the next article. There is some evidence for the use of the words ἑταῖρος and ἑταιρία by associations of a wholly private character, as professional guilds (*see* CLUBS, GREEK); but the *hetairiai* best known to us are political factions, i.e. more or less temporary associations of partisans under a leader or leaders. They are sometimes called συνωμοσίαι, from the oaths of loyalty which might be required. They are attested for many cities and for all periods of Greek history from the archaic to the Roman, and were formed for the maintenance or overthrow of the existing regime, the furtherance of the personal ambitions of their leaders, and for mutual assistance in the law courts or at elections. At Athens most political leaders from Cylon (q.v.) onward organized such a following; Aristides (q.v. 1) was said to be an exception. After the establishment of the democracy, its opponents worked through *hetairiai*, and these helped to bring about the usurpations of the Four Hundred (q.v.) and of the Thirty Tyrants (q.v. 1). A law against subversive *hetairiai* cited by the orators may have been passed on the restoration of the democracy.

G. M. Calhoun, *Athenian Clubs in Politics and Litigation* (1913); Busolt–Swoboda, *Griech. Staatsk.*³, see indexes; E. L. Minar, *Early Pythagorean Politics* (1942), 19 f.; G. Schreiber, *Zur Gesch. der Hetairien in Athen* (Diss. Vienna, 1948); F. Sartori, *Le Eterie nella vita politica ateniese* (1957); *Iura* 1958, 100 ff.; *Hist.* 1958,

157 ff.; R. Sealey, *Hist.* 1960, 155 ff.; C. Talamo, *PP* 1961, 297 ff.; G. J. Stagakis, *Institutional Aspects of the Hetairos Relation* (Diss. Wisconsin, 1962; *Hist.* 1968, 385 ff. T. J. C.

**HETAIROI** (ἑταῖροι, Companions), first applied to the 2,500 Myrmidons of Achilles in the *Iliad*, this title in classical times was peculiar to Macedonia. Anaximenes (fr. 4 Jacoby *FGrH*) ascribed the institution of *hetairoi* and *pezetairoi* to Alexander. Probably the *hetairoi*, as Cavalry-Companions, had existed for centuries before the *pezetairoi* or Infantry-Companions were formed; since Macedonia was not economically emancipated until the fourth century, the *pezetairoi* system may be ascribed to Alexander II (369–368 B.C.). By adopting the nobles of Upper Macedonia and able Greeks into the Companions, Philip II welded together his expanding State on a military basis. The *hetairoi*, to whom Philip granted estates of conquered land, numbered 800 c. 340 B.C. (*FGrH* 115 F 225). Alexander the Great increased their number, and late in his life enrolled Asiatics even in the royal bodyguard who served as his Council. In war the *pezetairoi*, equipped by Philip with *sarissa* and *pelta*, formed the defensive phalanx, and the *hetairoi*, equipped with a thrusting spear, delivered the offensive, usually from the right wing; they formed the core of the invincible army led by Alexander the Great. After his death Seleucus commanded the survivors of the *hetairoi* in one hipparchy, which later split up among the Successors. Further references in Arrian, *Anab*. N. G. L. H.

**HIATUS,** the gap that occurs when a word ending with a vowel is immediately followed by a word beginning with a vowel.

I. HIATUS IN GREEK VERSE

For hiatus at end of line or colon *see* METRE, GREEK. I (4).

Hiatus within line or colon, (1) without shortening of the first vowel, (2) with shortening:

(1) Hiatus without shortening is common in Homer, at certain points in the line, and, after certain words, in Comedy. Elsewhere it is rare, except that post-Homeric poets allow themselves some epic freedom in hexameters. Broadly speaking, the post-Homeric examples fall into the following classes:
(i) Where the second word is digammated (e.g. ἄναξ, ἔπος, ἴον), hiatus cannot be truly said to exist in the case of poets (e.g. Alcman, Pindar, Bacchylides, Epicharmus) for whom the digamma was a living letter. Further, the precedent of epic and lyric makes tolerable such juxtapositions as δέ οἱ (dative) in Sophocles. Hiatus is also tolerated (ii) before certain proper names in lyric poetry (e.g. 'Ἰσθμός, Pind. *Isthm.* 1. 9 and 32); (iii) often in drama after, or between, exclamations: e.g. ἐλελεῦ ἐλελεῦ (Aesch. *PV* 877), αἰαῖ, ἱκνοῦμαι (Soph. *El.* 136), ὦ 'Ἡράκλεις, often in Comedy. Even in tragic trimeters, ὦ οὗτος (Soph. *OC* 1627). Similarly with quasi-interjectional expressions: ἴθι ἴθι (Soph. *Phil.* 832), παῖ, ἠμί, παῖ (Ar. *Ran.* 37); (iv) after τί, occasionally in tragic trimeters, very frequently (and also after ὅτι, ὅ τι) in Comedy, especially in such phrases as τί ἐστι; τί οὖν; (v) εὖ οἶδα (ἴσθι, ἴστε) very occasionally in tragic, more frequently in comic, trimeters; (vi) in Comedy often after περί, occasionally after πρό and μέχρι (ἄν); (vii) οὐδέ (μηδέ) εἰς (ἕν), occasionally in Old Comedy, very often in Middle and New Comedy; (viii) in the phrase μὴ ὥρας, ὥρασι (Comedy).

It will be noticed that in drama hiatus is mainly found within a more or less closely unified word-group, where the *concursus vocalium* seemed hardly more objectionable than within a single word (e.g. ἄοκνος). Perhaps, therefore, the freer toleration of hiatus (as of crasis) in Comedy is a consequence of a delivery more rapid, and less articulated, than that employed in Tragedy.

(2) Hiatus with shortening, sometimes called 'Epic correption' because of its commonness in epic (and elegiac) verse, is found in the dactylic cola of the early lyric poets (e.g. Sapph. fr. 116 οἶον τὸ γλυκύμαλον ἐρεύθεται ἄκρῳ ἐπ' ὕσδῳ), and is frequent in the dactylo-epitrites of Pindar and Bacchylides. In the lyrics of Tragedy, Sophocles uses it far more frequently (e.g. *El.* 162–70) than Aeschylus or Euripides (who in his later plays almost banishes it). It is found in the anapaestic dimeters of Tragedy and Comedy (in the resolved arsis as well as in the thesis), and in the catalectic anapaestic tetrameters of Comedy (much more often in earlier than in later Aristophanes). A monosyllabic thesis does not admit correption; consequently all cases in dochmii, and the few cases in lyric iambics, occur in resolved arses (e.g. Soph. *Aj.* 349 μόνοι ἐμῶν). The shortened syllable is much more frequently a diphthong (especially, perhaps, an accentually short diphthong in -αι or -οι) than a single vowel.

See J. Descroix, *Le Trimètre iambique* (1931), 26 ff. and for bibliography see E. Kalinka in *Bursian Jahresb.* 250, 402 ff.
J. D. D.

II. HIATUS IN GREEK PROSE

*Theory*. Isocrates (Τέχνη) deprecates hiatus generally; Hermogenes and Longinus accept this ruling (Walz iii. 289; vi. 102–3; ix. 560). [Arist.] *Rh. Al.* 1435[ab] probably concerns ambiguous elision, not hiatus. Dionysius distinguishes: the austere style (Thucydides) allows hiatus freely; the middle style (Demosthenes) allows a little; the smooth style avoids it carefully—Isocrates and Theopompus too carefully (*Comp.* 22–3; *Dem.* 4, 38, 40, 43; *Isoc.* 2; *Pomp.* 6). Plutarch satirizes Isocrates' scrupulousness (*Mor.* 350 e). Demetrius thinks marked hiatus desirable in the grand style, but too dignified for the simple style (*Eloc.* 68–74, 207, 299–301). Cf. also Cic. *Orat.* 77, 150–2, *De Or.* 3. 171–2; Quint. 9. 4. 33–7.

*Practice*. Marked avoidance of hiatus first appears in Thrasymachus, then in Gorgias (*Pal.*) and Alcidamas (*Soph.*); there is moderate avoidance in Antisthenes and Lysias; little in Andocides; none in Antiphon. (Benseler assumes that pre-Isocratean writers cannot have avoided hiatus, and rejects as spurious those works which show avoidance.)

Isocrates is the pattern of the technique of avoidance, in securing which he relies little on crasis, elision, or pauses, but much on word-order and word-choice; hence some hyperbaton and such plurals as ταῖς ἀληθείαις, σεμνότησιν. His few licences are chiefly before ἄν, οὖν, and after καί, περί, πρό, ὤ. He avoids long vowels in hiatus (especially η) more strictly than short. His judicial speeches show rather more freedom than the rest.

Demosthenes, though careful, allows hiatus also before ὡς and after εἰ, ἤ, ὅτι, μή, and the article; at pauses within and after sentences; and with proper names and set phrases (ἐν τῷ ἐμῷ ὕδατι εἰπάτω). He often elides.

Further, hiatus is avoided carefully: by Lycurgus, Dinarchus, Demades, Theopompus, Polybius, Philodemus; by Isaeus and Plutarch sometimes; by Plato in his late works; by Aristotle in *Pol.* and *Metaph.* 1. It is tolerated by Aeschines and Hyperides, and freely allowed by Herodotus, Thucydides, and Xenophon.

G. E. Benseler, *De hiatu in oratoribus Atticis* (1841; detailed, dogmatic); F. Blass, *Attische Beredsamkeit*[2] (1887–98); S. Skimina, *Études sur le rythme de la prose grecque I* (1937).
W. H. S.; K. J. D.

III. HIATUS IN LATIN VERSE

There are three groups of fairly homogeneous cases:
(1) 'Epic correption' *in or before Greek words* from Cicero to Horace: *etesiäe* Cic. *Aratea* (*Phaen.*) fr. 24

(marked by himself, *Orator* 15. 2) and Lucr. 6. 716, *Peliŏ Ossam* Verg. *G.* 1. 281 (imitated—Ov. *Met.* 1. 155), *insulae Ionio Aen.* 3. 211; cf. *Ecl.* 6. 44, *G.* 1. 437, 4. 461, *Aen.* 5. 261, Ov. *Am.* 2. 13. 21. *Without a Greek word*: *valě* Verg. *Ecl.* 3. 79 (imitated—Ov. *Met.* 3. 501); cf. *lectulŏ* Catull. 57. 7. This licence is of Greek origin and conditioned by metrical necessity.

(2) Hiatus without shortening is not infrequent in Virgil, e.g. *pecori,* | *apibus G.* 1. 4, *dea.* | *ille Aen.* 1. 405 (cf. Hor. *Epod.* 5. 100, *Carm.* 1. 28. 24). In some of these cases Greek technique is obviously imitated, e.g. *Glauco* | *et Panopeae G.* 1. 437, *castaneae* | *hirsutae Ecl.* 7. 53 (cf. Hor. *Epod.* 13. 3, Ov. *Met.* 3. 184, 5. 625).

(3) Cases like *qui a(mat), dum ab(est)* = ⌣⌣(○). They are frequent in dramatists (especially Plautus) and Lucretius (see Munro on 2. 404), and occur sporadically in Catullus (55. 4), Virgil (e.g. *Ecl.* 8. 108), Horace (*Satires*), etc., but not in Ovid or later. This phenomenon is not of Greek origin and its prosodical character is doubtful, disyllabic and monosyllabic pronunciation being both possible.

Apart from these three groups there are some hundreds of cases of hiatus in Plautus, many of them complicated by problems of prosody or textual criticism. Some scholars think that hiatus in the caesura is legitimate in Plautus; but it has not yet been proved that hiatus is more frequent in the caesura than it would be if it was legitimate at any place in the line.

Luc. Mueller, *De re metr.*² (1894), 368 ff.; B. Maurenbrecher, *Hiatus u. Verschleifung im alten Latein* (1899); J. Pelz, *Der prosodische Hiat* (1930); Kalinka, *Bursian Jahresb.* 1935, 407 ff.

P. M.

**HIBERNIA** ('Ἰέρνη), Ireland, first known to the Greeks through Massiliote mariners (*c.* 525 B.C.) as being 'five days' sail from Brittany, near the Albiones' island'. Eratosthenes (*c.* 235), probably through Pytheas' circumnavigation of Britain (*c.* 310–306), placed Ireland correctly on his map. Strabo (4. 201) says that, oblong in shape, it lay near and *north* of Britain and contained greedy incestuous cannibals. Mela (3. 6. 53) makes Ireland nearly as large as Britain, oblong, with pastures that caused the cattle to burst, and savage untrustworthy husbandmen. Pliny gives as its area 800 × 100 miles. Agricola may have reconnoitred Ireland. Ptolemy (*Geog.* 2. 2) shows fair knowledge of the whole coast, giving sixteen peoples of counties Wicklow, Kildare, Waterford, Wexford, Kerry, Dublin (Eblana, south of the mouth of the River Bubinda—the Boyne), Connaught province; rivers Shannon, Barrow, Lagan, Avoca, Boyne, Liffey. Solinus added the detail that Ireland has no snakes. The older tendency to place Ireland between Britain and Spain was due probably to early direct voyages from Spain.

Cary–Warmington, *Explorers* 29 ff.; (Pelican) 43 f., 59 f.; Orpen, *Journ. R. Soc. Antiqu. of Ireland,* June 1894 (Ptolemy); MacNeill, *New Ireland Rev.,* Sept. 1906; S. P. O'Ríordáin, *Proc. Royal Irish Academy,* section liC, 1948, 35 ff.; R. E. M. Wheeler, *Rome beyond the Imperial Frontiers* (1955), 16; J. J. Tierney, *JHS* 1959, 132 ff.; Thomson, *Hist. Anc. Geog.* 54, 144, 194, 235, 236 f. (Ptolemy's map), 334, 357 f.

E. H. W.

**HICETAS** of Syracuse, Pythagorean, probably the teacher of Ecphantus and younger than Philolaus, is said to have been the first to teach that the earth moves in a circle (also ascribed to Philolaus). His view probably was that the earth rotates on its own axis while the heavenly bodies are at rest.

Testimonia in Diels, *Vorsokr.*¹¹ i. 441–2.

W. D. R.

**HIEROCLES**, Stoic of the time of Hadrian (A.D. 117–38), wrote (1) an 'Ηθικὴ στοιχείωσις (*Elements of Ethics*) which may have been an introduction to (2) a work on ethics, fragments of which are preserved in

Stobaeus. The former was a scientific work dealing with the instinct of self-preservation (πρώτη οἰκείωσις) as the starting-point of the Stoic ethics, and with self-consciousness as the foundation of this instinct. The latter was a work of edification dealing with duties, Περὶ καθηκόντων. The teaching in both works followed the orthodox doctrine of the early Stoics.

Ed. H. von Arnim, *BKT* 4 (1906).

W. D. R.

**HIERODOULOI**, a relatively late term (first in 3rd-c. B.C. papyri), though temple-slaves, performing the menial tasks, existed from early times in Greece as elsewhere (cf. Martiales at Larinum, Cic. *Clu.* 43). The word *hierodouloi* can designate such chattels of a god; it can also bear certain special connotations. In Ptolemaic Egypt the *hierodouloi* take minor roles in the ceremonies, tend the sacred cats (*PSI* 440), or collect temple revenues (*PHib.* 35). In Asia Minor they may be the serfs, rather than actual slaves, attached to the great temple estates (Strabo, books 11–12, *passim*). The religious prostitutes of Comana Pontica (Strabo 559) and Corinth (Athen. 573–4; Strabo 378) are called *hierodouloi*, and the term has hence been mistakenly applied to all sacred prostitution (q.v.). In Oriental cults a devotee might consider himself the slave of a divine master (cf. δοῦλος τοῦ θεοῦ in Christian inscriptions); the κάτοχοι of Egypt (cf. SARAPIS) and some of the ἱεροί in Anatolia may fall in this category. In the Hellenistic period arose the custom of manumitting slaves through a fictitious sale (or occasionally dedication) to a god, who thus became the guarantor of their freedom; persons thus freed were occasionally called *hierodouloi* (A. Cameron, *Harv. Theol. Rev.* 1939, 154 f., cf. 149).

*See* METRAGYRTES.

F. R. W.

**HIEROMNEMONES**, religious officials, found in many Greek States. Aristotle (*Pol.* 1321ᵇ) classifies them with the civil registrars of public and private documents, and temples frequently served as record offices. Their functions varied widely: some appear as archivists, others as financial officers, some managed the festivals or controlled temple properties, and in several cities, e.g. Issa and Byzantium, they were the eponymous magistrates. They usually formed a college, and the position was one of responsibility and honour. Best known are the *hieromnemones* who represented their States in the Delphic-Pylaean Amphictiony. Their number was normally twenty-four, but varied considerably under the Aetolian domination (*c.* 290–191 B.C.). Their exact relationship to the other delegates, the *pylagorai* (in the Aetolian period called *agoratroi*), is not clear. The duties of the *hieromnemones* are set forth in a law of 380 (*IG* ii². 1126). Their tenure of office varied from State to State: in the fourth century the Thessalian *hieromnemones* served for several years, the Athenians one year, while the Malians sent different *hieromnemones* for each of the semi-annual meetings; a Chian decree of 258–254 (*SIG* 443) stipulates that their delegate should serve one year and be ineligible for reappointment. For ἱερομνάμονες ἐπὶ θησαυρῶι and ἐπὶ τῶι σίτωι at Locri Epizephyrii see *Klearchos* 1961–2; for *hieromnemon* as a functionary of a private cult association see *AJArch.* 1933, 254. The term was sometimes used to translate the Latin *pontifex*.

F. R. W.

**HIERON** (1) **I** was appointed ruler of Gela when his brother Gelon (q.v.) became master of Syracuse. He succeeded to the Syracusan tyranny in 478 B.C., overcoming the counter-claims of his brother Polyzelus. He sought to rival by intervention in Italy Gelon's Carthaginian triumph, in 477 helping the Sybarites against Croton and deterring Anaxilas (q.v. 1) of Rhegium from an attack on Locri. Etruscan pressure on Cumae required his assistance further north, and he destroyed Etruscan sea-power by a great victory in 474 (for dedicated helmets see *SEG* xxiii 252/3). A short-lived colony on Ischia was a further devlopment of his Italian policy. He strengthened his power in Sicily by refounding Catania under the name Aetna with 10,000 new settlers (475). After a breakdown of his alliance with the Acragantines, his victory over Acragas contributed to the overthrow of the tyranny there (472). His court was open to poets and philosophers, while his victories in the Games extended his prestige. He died in 467/6.

Ancient reff. assembled in G. F. Hill, *Sources for Greek History between the Persian and Peloponnesian Wars*[2] (1951), 361 f. A. Schenk, Graf von Stauffenberg, *Trinakria* (1963), chs. 14, 15, 17, 18; H. Berve, *Die Tyrannis bei den Griechen* i (1967), 147 ff.; on the chronology, R. van Compernolle, *Étude de chronologie et d'historiographie siciliotes* (1959), 319 ff. A. G. W.

**HIERON** (2) **II** (*c.* 306–215 B.C.), of an unimportant Syracusan family, first appears as a lieutenant of Pyrrhus (q.v.), then (in 275 B.C.) as independent commander of the Syracusan army. In this capacity he seized power in Syracuse. Severely defeated by the Mamertines (q.v.) in 270, he won a great victory in the following year at the river Longanus and was hailed as king. Now claiming descent from Gelon and Hieron I (qq.v.), he reigned for fifty-four years—years of wealth and prosperity for Syracuse even though initially his political misjudgements involved the city in difficulties.

When the Romans seized Messana in support of the Mamertines, Hieron defied tradition and allied himself with Carthage. Driven back by Roman forces he concluded a peace with Rome (263) by which he became Rome's ally, remaining so till his death (Polyb. 1. 16. 10). He provided ships, supplies, and facilities for Rome during the Punic Wars, and paid 100 talents as indemnity —25 immediately and the rest in annual payments. The latter were remitted on the renewal of the alliance in 248, when additions were made to Syracusan territory.

Relying thereafter on Roman protection, Hieron maintained a good fleet and employed Archimedes to improve the city's defences. The *Lex Hieronica* formed an equitable basis for taxation under a system of tithes, later taken over by the Roman provincial government. His son Gelon predeceased him, and he was succeeded by his grandson Hieronymus.

*See also* SICILY, SYRACUSE, THEOCRITUS.

J. Carcopino, *La Loi de Hiéron* (1919); A. Schenk, Graf von Stauffenberg, *König Hieron II von Syrakus* (1933); H. Berve, *König Hieron II* (*Abh. Akad. München*, 1959); id., *Die Tyrannis bei den Griechen* i (1967), 462 ff. A. G. W.

**HIERONYMUS** (1) of Cardia, the contemporary and trustworthy historian of the period from the death of Alexander (323 B.C.) to the death of Pyrrhus (272) or perhaps as far as 263, the year of the treaty between Antigonus Gonatas and Alexander of Epirus. He appears first in the service of Eumenes of Cardia, fighting for him against Perdiccas and Antigonus until Eumenes' execution by the latter after the battle of Gabiene (316). Hieronymus entered the service of Antigonus, was present at the battle of Ipsus (301), and was appointed harmost of Boeotia (293) by his son Demetrius Poliorcetes. He retained the friendship of Antigonus Gonatas until his death (*c.* 250). His account of this period, for which he became the accepted authority, was entitled Αἱ περὶ Διαδόχων Ἱστορίαι and was the most important source behind Arrian (Τὰ μετὰ Ἀλέξανδρον) and Diodorus (books 18–20). The work was known to Pompeius Trogus and Pausanias and was used by Plutarch for his lives of Eumenes, Pyrrhus, and Demetrius. The relatively few fragments do not allow the distribution of the subject-matter to be assessed.

*FGrH* ii B. 154. T. S. Brown, *Amer. Hist. Rev.* 1947, 684 ff.; R. H. Simpson, *AJPhil.* 1959, 370 ff. G. L. B.

**HIERONYMUS** (2) of Rhodes, philosopher and historian of literature, lived at Athens *c.* 290–230, under the protection of Antigonus Gonatas. Trained in the Peripatetic school, he left it when it was declining under Lycon's headship, and founded an eclectic school.

WORKS: Περὶ ἐποχῆς; Περὶ μέθης; Συμπόσιον; a work on ethics; Περὶ ἀοργησίας; Περὶ ποιητῶν; Ἱστορικὰ ὑπομνήματα; Σποράδην ὑπομνήματα; Περὶ Ἰσοκράτους; Ἐπιστολαί. The extant fragments illustrate his love of literary gossip.

F. Wehrli, *Die Schule des Aristoteles* x (1959). W. D. R.

**HIEROPHANTES,** head of the Eleusinian cult, was the most revered priest in Attica. He was chosen for life from the hieratic family of the Eumolpidae (*see* EUMOLPUS). He was distinguished by a head-band (στρόφιον) and a long purple-dyed robe ornamented with embroideries. His principal duty was to preside over the Mysteries. Before the celebration he sent forth *spondophoroi* to proclaim truce for the period of the Mysteries. He opened the ceremonies with a proclamation that barbarians, murderers, and those defiled must keep away, and he had the right to refuse admittance to others. To the initiates he revealed the secrets of the Mysteries; for this purpose it was necessary that a man of impressive voice should be selected for the office. He was assisted by the *daduchos* (δᾳδοῦχος, torch-bearer) and two *hierophantides* (ἱεροφάντιδες). He also took part in other State festivals and had several minor public duties. In the imperial period his only legal name was Hierophantes; on entering office he performed the ceremony of casting his old name into the sea.

P. Foucart, *Les Mystères d'Éleusis*, (1914) 168 ff.; G. Méautis, *Les Mystères d'Éleusis* (1934), 35 f.; G. E. Mylonas, *Eleusis and the Eleusinian Mysteries* (1961), 229 ff. See F. Cumont, *AJArch.* 1933, 243 f., on the use of this title in the cults of Dionysus. J. E. F.

**HILARY** (*Hilărius*) of Poitiers (d. A.D. 367), after receiving the complete pagan education, in which he failed to find satisfaction for his soul, was converted by Scripture study. As bishop (*c.* 353), he became a protagonist in the conflict with Arianism. Being banished to Asia, he used the opportunity to increase his knowledge of Greek literature. He wrote commentaries on Matthew and on the Psalms, and a 'liber mysteriorum', but the greatest of his works is his *De Trinitate* (in twelve books). He was also the author of three Latin hymns, the earliest we have.

Ed. Migne, *PL* ix–x; partly in *CSEL* xxii, lxv; tr. E. W. Watson, *Post-Nicene Fathers* (1899); A. S. Walpole, *Early Latin Hymns* (1922). C. Borchardt, *H.'s Role in the Arian Struggle* (1966). A. S.

**HILDESHEIM TREASURE,** a collection of Roman silver plate found in 1868 at Hildesheim in south Hanover and now in Berlin; assigned to the Augustan age and possibly booty from the camp of Quinctilius Varus in the Saltus Teutoburgiensis (A.D. 9). The principal piece is a mixing-bowl covered with floral relief resembling that of the Ara Pacis; there is also a series of drinking-bowls with embossed designs of Minerva, Hercules and the snakes, reliefs of Cybele and Men-Attis, and Bacchic emblems.

E. Pernice and F. Winter, *Der Hildesheimer Silberfund* (1901). F. N. P.

**HIMERA** (Ἱμέρα), on the north coast of Sicily, was founded *c.* 649 B.C. by the Zanclaeans, helped by the clan of the Myletidae, exiled from Syracuse. Stesichorus (q.v.) was its most famous citizen. In the early fifth century it was controlled by a tyrant Terillus who, on his expulsion by Theron (q.v.) of Acragas, appealed to Carthage. The Carthaginian expedition was decisively defeated at Himera (480 B.C.), where a fine Doric temple celebrated the triumph of Gelon (q.v.) and Theron. Independent of Acragas after 461, Himera was obliterated by Carthage in 409 as an act of revenge.

In 408/7 the Carthaginians founded Thermae Himeraeae (*Termini Imerese*) 7 miles westward, where the Himeraean refugees settled. Although in Carthaginian territory, it was completely Greek—even sometimes referred to as Himera, and was the birthplace of Agathocles (q.v.). Within the Roman province of Sicily after 241 B.C., it became a *colonia* under Augustus.

Bérard, *Bibl. topogr.* 57 f.; Dunbabin, *Western Greeks*; P. Marconi, *Himera* (1931). *Thermae Himeraeae*: G. Giacomazzi and G. Corrieri, *Termini Imerese* (1965). A. G. W.

**HIMERIUS** (*c.* A.D. 310–*c.* 390), Greek rhetorician. Born in Prusias in Bithynia, he studied in Athens, where he spent most of his life as a successful teacher of rhetoric. He was a younger contemporary and rival of Proairesius (q.v.). He visited Constantinople, Thessalonica, Nicomedia, and Antioch, among other places. Of his eighty speeches Photius (q.v.) read seventy-two, but there survive now only twenty-four, with excerpts from ten others. Six are declamations on themes from Athenian history, the rest deal with contemporary subjects, and include addresses to high Roman officials, inaugural lectures and other ceremonial orations in connexion with his school, and a funeral oration on his son. Unlike Themistius (q.v.) and Libanius (q.v.), Himerius has no interest in politics; he is equally untouched by philosophy. His eloquence is an end in itself, like poetry. His style is marked by wealth of imagery, care for euphony, avoidance of the concrete, and frequent quotations from classical poetry. Though the school orations are of some interest, Himerius in the main displays a talent for saying nothing gracefully and at length. Among his pupils were Gregory (2) of Nazianzus and St. Basil (qq.v.).

SOURCE. Eunapius, *Vit. Soph.* 95 Boiss.; Photius, *Bibl.*, cod. 165. EDITION. A. Colonna (1951). R. B.

**HIMILCO** (1), Carthaginian navigator who explored northwards four months from Gades but not beyond Brittany (probably before 480 B.C.). His complaints about calms, shoals, tangled seaweeds, which held ships back, have been taken to indicate that he reached also, or was blown up to, the Sargasso Sea. But he may never have gone out of sight of Spain and France. Whether he ever visited Britain is unknown.

See Pliny 2. 169; Avienius, *Ora Maritima*, 114–34, 380–9, 406–15. Cary–Warmington, *Explorers* 31 ff.; (Pelican) 45 ff.; Warmington, *Greek Geography* (1934), 75 ff.; Thomson, *Hist. Anc. Geog.* 54 f.; Hyde, *Greek Mariners*, 121 ff. E. H. W.

**HIMILCO** (2), a Carthaginian general. Signatory of an agreement between Carthage and Athens in 407/6 B.C., he commanded the forces which in 406 conquered and sacked Acragas, Gela, and Camarina (qq.v.). Next year, when Syracuse seemed at his mercy, disease in his army forced him to conclude a peace which nevertheless confirmed Carthaginian power in Sicily. In 397 Dionysius I (q.v.) renewed the war. Himilco, returning to the island, reconquered the north coast in 396, advancing once more to the gates of Syracuse. His blockade, strengthened by a naval victory, was again broken by the onset of plague, and the Syracusans completely defeated his demoralized troops. By agreement with Dionysius Himilco saved the Carthaginian citizen-soldiery; after returning home he committed suicide.

Diod. Sic. 13–14; *SEG* x. 136, xiv. 10, xxi. 56, and reff. there. K. F. Stroheker, *Dionysios I* (1957), chs. 2–3. A. G. W.

**HIPPALUS**, a Greek merchant who discovered the full use of monsoon-winds to and from India. Mortimer Wheeler (as cited below) forcefully argues that complete use of these winds was known before the death of Augustus in A.D. 14. Becoming aware of the general shape of the Arabian Sea and the southward projection of India and the existence of regular winds between Aden Gulf and north-west India, one summer Hippalus sailed across from Ras Fartak to the Indus. This resulted in cross-sea voyages even to south India and back by Greeks and vast increase in commerce with India. Hippalus' name was given to the south-west monsoon, to an African cape, and to part of the Arabian sea.

*Peripl. M. Rubr.* 57; Pliny 6. 100–6, 172; Ptolemy, *Geog.* 4. 7. 12; *It. Alex.* 110. Warmington, *Indian Commerce*, 44 ff.; W. W. Tarn, *The Greeks in Bactria and India* (1938, 2nd ed. 1951), 369; J. Thiel, *Eudoxus van Cyzicus* (in Dutch, 1939); W. Otto and H. Bengtson, *Abhandlungen d. bayerischen Ak. d. Wissenschaften, philosophisch-historische Klasse* 1938, 194 ff.; Thomson, *Hist. Anc. Geog.* 176, 298 f.; R. E. M. Wheeler, *Rome beyond the Imperial Frontiers* (1955), 154 ff. E. H. W.

**HIPPARCHUS** (1), younger son of Pisistratus of Athens by his first wife; constantly associated with his elder brother Hippias, under whom he acted as patron of literature and art. Anacreon and Simonides came to Athens at his invitation, and the artistic movements of Pisistratid Athens, which included the first great developments of red-figured vase-painting and corresponding activities in sculpture and architecture, owed much to this frivolous and amorous but cultured prince. His personal vices led to his murder by Harmodius and Aristogiton in 514 B.C. Hipparchus planned the temple of Zeus Olympius at Athens with a double peristyle of the Ionic order.

For bibliography, see PISISTRATUS. P. N. U.

**HIPPARCHUS** (2) (fl. *c.* 260 B.C.), New Comedy poet and (probably) actor. In frs. 1 and 3 foreign drinking-cups (κόνδυ, λαβρώνιος) are mentioned, and in Ζωγράφος, fr. 2, the painter praises professional skill.

*FCG* iv. 431 f.; *CAF* iii. 272 ff.

**HIPPARCHUS** (3), astronomer (*c.* 190–after 126 B.C.). Born at Nicaea in Bithynia, he spent much of his life in Rhodes; his recorded observations range from 162 to 126. His only extant work is the *Commentary on the Φαινόμενα of Eudoxus and Aratus*, in three books, containing criticisms of the descriptions and placings of constellations and stars by those two (qq.v.), and a list of simultaneous risings and settings. Though it is a comparatively early and slight work, valuable information on Hipparchus' own star co-ordinates has been extracted from it. Most of our knowledge of Hipparchus' other astronomical work comes from the *Almagest* of Ptolemy (q.v. 4), whose solar and lunar theory is only a modification of his predecessor's.

Hipparchus was the first to construct a theory of the motion of sun and moon which was properly based on observational data. The theory of the epicyclic/eccentric system which he adopted had already been worked out by his predecessors, probably Apollonius (see ASTRONOMY). His contribution was to combine his own systematic observations with the Babylonian eclipse-records going back to the eighth century which were available to him, and to extract accurate estimates of the mean motions of sun and moon, and the length of the tropical year (which he put at $365\frac{1}{4} - \frac{1}{300}$ days). He is most famous for his discovery of the precession of the equinoxes, which he did by comparing his own observation of the distance of the star Spica from the autumnal equinox with that of Timocharis about 160 years before (*Almagest* 7. 2). He investigated the problem of parallax, and thus came to devise the first practical method for determining the sizes and distances of the sun and moon; his estimate for the latter was close to the truth (Pappus, *Comm. in Alm.* v, 11 ed. Rome, 66 ff.). He was a paradigm of the practical astronomer: to accuracy of observation (he improved observational techniques) he joined great critical acumen in selecting observational data and in distinguishing what was relevant to his ends. His scientific spirit is shown in his refusing to attempt to construct a planetary theory because of the insufficiency of the data; he was content to record his own and previous observations and to show that they contradicted existing theories (*Almagest* 9. 2). He displayed considerable mathematical ability in applying observational results to determine the numerical parameters of his geometrical schemata for the movements of the heavenly bodies. He is the first person known to have made systematic use of trigonometry (he compiled a *Table of Chords in a Circle*, the ancient equivalent of a sine-table). He was probably the inventor of stereographic projection (Synesius, *Opusc.* ed. Terzaghi 2, 138).

His geographical work was a polemic against the *Geography* of Eratosthenes (q.v.), criticizing descriptive and especially mathematical details. Hipparchus' work was important in the development of mathematical geography, as it laid down the rules for the essential observational foundations for a scientific treatment of the subject (*see also* GEOGRAPHY).

Among other works were some on astrology and weather signs.

EDITIONS. *Comm. in Arat.*, ed. Manitius (Teubner, 1894, with German translation). *Geographical Fragments* ed. D. R. Dicks (1960, with introduction and translation).
LIFE AND WORKS. Dicks, op. cit. 1 ff.
COMMENT. General: Tannery, *Histoire de l'astronomie ancienne* (1893), esp. chs. 8–13. Most of what has been written about the *star catalogue* (e.g. Boll in *Bibl. Math.* 3F. 2 (1901), 185 ff.) misrepresents our knowledge of what it was really like. Most useful is H. Vogt in *Astronomische Nachrichten* 24 (1925), nr. 5354–5, cols. 17–54, which is based on the data in the *Comm. in Arat.* Use of Babylonian parameters: A. Aaboe in *Centaurus* 1955, 122 ff., O. Neugebauer, *Notes on Hipparchus* in *Studies presented to Hetty Goldman* (U.S.A. 1956), 292 ff. Geography: Dicks, op. cit. Astrology: Several texts edited in *CCAG.* Boll, 'Die Erforschung der antiken Astrologie', *N. J. f. Kl. Alt.* 21 (1908), 106, n. 4. Neugebauer, op. cit.          G. J. T.

**HIPPASUS** of Metapontum, an early Pythagorean later regarded as having founded the branch of the school called μαθηματικοί (*see* PYTHAGORAS 1), and as having been punished for revealing a mathematical secret: later sources disagree both on the punishment (expulsion, shipwreck) and on the secret (irrational magnitudes, construction of the dodecahedron). Aristotle couples him with Heraclitus as having identified the source of the world with fire.

Testimonia in Diels, *Vorsokr.*[11] i. 107–10. M. T. Cardini, *I Pitagorici* i (1958); W. Burkert, *Weisheit und Wissenschaft* (1962); Guthrie, *Hist. Gk. Phil.* i. 320 ff.          G. E. L. O.

**HIPPEIS** (ἱππεῖς), cavalry. The use of cavalry in Greek warfare dates from the decline of the war-chariot (obsolete by *c.* 700 B.C.), and was never on a large scale except in areas suitable for horse-breeding, such as Thessaly and Boeotia. After hoplites (q.v.) had become the standard troops, those who could afford horses often used them merely as a means of proceeding expeditiously to and from battle. The Athenians first instituted a regular cavalry-force after the Persian Wars; the original strength of 300 had been raised to 1,000 by 431. As the men provided their own horses, it was a rich men's corps, with corresponding political sentiments (Ar. *Eq.* 225–7). At Sparta there was a long-established body of 300 *hippeis*, but by the early fifth century it had become an élite of infantry. Regular cavalry was instituted in 424, when a force of 400 was raised; in the fourth century it numbered 600. Cavalry was an important element in the armies of Alexander and the Hellenistic kings. *See* ARMIES, GREEK AND HELLENISTIC, *and* WAR, ART OF (GREEK).

In most States the rearing and possession of horses was a mark of the upper class, and, where and when strongly established, favoured the maintenance of oligarchical government (Arist. *Pol.* 1297[b]18–32, 1321[a]7–11). In some States the ruling oligarchs were actually known as Hippeis, as at Eretria; cf. the Hippobotai at Chalcis. At Athens, too, Hippeis was one of the names for the uppermost class (*see* EUPATRIDAI), until Solon (q.v.) gave it to the second of his census-classes, which comprised men with an estimated annual income of between 300 and 500 *medimnoi* of corn, or the equivalent in other produce or money. As the minimum qualification was not high, most of the citizens of this class probably served as hoplites.

W. Helbig, *Les Ιππεῖς athéniens* (1904); Busolt–Swoboda, *Griech. Staatsk.*[3], see indexes; J. Kromayer–G. Veith, *Heerwesen . . . d. Griechen u. Römer*, (1928), see index. J. K. Anderson, *Ancient Greek Horsemanship* (1961).          A. W. G.; T. J. C.

**HIPPIAS** (1), tyrant of Athens 527–510 B.C., eldest son and successor of Pisistratus (q.v.), was at first a mild ruler; he reduced taxation and came to an understanding with some leading clans, whereby Cleisthenes (1) and Miltiades (qq.v.) held the eponymous archonship, while his brother Hipparchus favoured the arts and included recitation of Homer in the Panathenaic festival. But his rule became harsher as conditions worsened with the advance of Persia. He lost his outpost at Rhaecalus and his revenues from mines at Mt. Pangaeus (q.v.), and a group of exiled nobles, based upon Leipsydrium, made an unsuccessful attempt to oust him. Hipparchus was assassinated in 514 B.C. (*see* ARISTOGITON). The Spartans, supported by the Alcmaeonidae (q.v.) and egged on by Delphi, invaded Attica and were defeated by Hippias and his Thessalian allies. But a further invasion forced him to capitulate. He and his family escaped to Sigeum and later went to the court of Darius. He was with the Persian forces at Marathon.

Bibliography: *see* PISISTRATUS.          N. G. L. H.

**HIPPIAS** (2) of Elis, sophist, a younger contemporary of Protagoras (who lived *c.* 485–415), is vividly depicted in Plato's *Hippias Major* and *Hippias Minor*. He acquired great fame and wealth by travelling all over Greece as a teacher and orator, claiming competence in mathematics, astronomy, grammar, poetry, music, and the history of the heroic age, as well as in various handicrafts, and was frequently employed on State business by his native city. That his claims had a solid basis is indicated by the fact that he can probably be identified with the Hippias who discovered the *quadratrix*, the first curve other than the circle to be recognized by the Greek geometers. It was probably discovered in the attempt to solve the problem of trisecting the angle, but was subsequently used in the attempt to square the circle. Of his immense output, the following works are known by name: an elegy on the drowning of a chorus of boys from Messenia; a συναγωγή (probably archaeological in its contents); a Τρωικὸς λόγος; an Ὀλυμπιονικῶν ἀναγραφή; Ἐθνῶν ὀνομασίαι.

Testimonia and fragments in Diels, *Vorsokr.*[11] ii. 326–34.
          W. D. R.

**HIPPIATRICI** are veterinarians, more strictly those who treat animals of the farm (Varro, *Rust.* 2. 7. 16: 'De medicina vel plurima sunt in equis et signa morborum et genera curationum . . . itaque ab hoc in Graecia potissimum medici pecorum ἱππιατροί appellati'). The *Hippiatrici* gave medical and surgical treatment in more difficult cases; ordinary diseases were handled by the farmers themselves. The so-called *Corpus Hippiatricorum Graecorum*, collected in the ninth century A.D., has preserved only excerpts dealing with horse-medicine, hardly any of them earlier than the Christian era. The authors mentioned (Apsyrtus, Eumelus, Theomnestus, Anatolius, Hierocles, etc.) are only names. Of older books nothing is known. The treatise of the Athenian Simon (5th c. B.C.) and Xenophon's Π. ἱππικῆς are written by gentlemen-amateurs, interested in horse-breeding or the selection of horses; Ps.-Aristotle, *Historia Animalium* 8. 21 f., treats of animal diseases from a more theoretical point of view.

Within the *Corpus Hippiatricorum* the semeiotics of diseases plays an important part; for 'animals cannot speak'. Cures consist in drugs and diet; the prevention of diseases is considered even more important than their treatment. Magical remedies are rejected, at least by physicians (for farmers cf. *Geoponica* xvi). All these features are reminiscent of human medicine; in fact, conclusions based on the observation of men seem valid for animals and vice versa. The great achievement of veterinary art is certainly dependent on the fundamentally agrarian character of ancient life and the resulting close contact with animals, but also on the fact that animal anatomy had been practised continuously since the fifth century B.C.

TEXTS. *Corpus Hippiatricorum Graecorum*, E. Oder–C. Hoppe (Teubner, 1924–7). Latin translation, *Mulomedicina Chironis*, E. Oder (Teubner, 1901), the original written about A.D. 400; MSS., G. Björk, *Rev. Ét. Grec.* (1935).
MODERN LITERATURE. General survey, Sir Fr. Smith, *The Early History of Veterinary Literature* i (1919), antiquated in its literary data; survey on literature, G. Sarton, *Isis* (1937). Date of collection not tenth century, as formerly assumed, Hoppe, op. cit. ii, xv; relative chronology of authors, ibid. vi; cf. Björk, *Uppsala Universitets Årsskrift* 1932, 1944, who also proves that Heraclides Tarentinus (2nd c. B.C.) did not write on veterinary medicine. *PW* viii. 1713. L. E.

**HIPPO REGIUS** (near modern *Bône* in Algeria), a seaport no doubt first used by the Carthaginians; it already existed by the end of the fourth century B.C. As its name implies it was later a residence of Numidian princes. It became a *municipium* under Augustus, and later acquired colonial rights. In the late second century it became the centre of activity of one of the three *legati* of the proconsul of Africa. Augustine was bishop from 395 to 430, and died while the city was being besieged by the Vandals.

H. van M. Dennis, *Hippo Regius* (U.S.A. 1924); E. Marec, *Hippone* (Algiers, 1950); *Monuments chrétiens d'Hippone* (1958); L. Teutsch, *Das Städtewesen in Nordafrika* (1962), 163 ff. B. H. W.

**HIPPOBOTUS** (fl. late 3rd c. B.C.) wrote a philosophico-historical Περὶ αἱρέσεων and Φιλοσόφων ἀναγραφή, used by Diog. Laert. (Frs. catalogued by v. Arnim, *PW*, s.v.).

**HIPPOCOON** ('Ἱπποκόων), in mythology, son of the Spartan or Amyclaean hero Oebalus, and elder brother of Tyndareos (q.v.). He and his many sons drove out Tyndareos and his other brother Icarius from Sparta (Apollod. 3. 124). Later Heracles, offended at some action of Hippocoon, attacked and killed him and his sons (Alcman fr. 15 Bergk). H. J. R.

**HIPPOCRATES** (1), tyrant of Gela, succeeded his brother Cleander c. 498 B.C. Within seven years, by conquering most of eastern Sicily, he created a Geloan Empire which he ruled as autocrat, prototype of the great Sicilian tyrants. He temporarily won for Gela a primacy among Sicels and Siceliots like that later enjoyed by Syracuse. Ruthless and cynical in war and political intrigue, he signally defeated the Syracusans at the river Helorus, but was restrained by Corinthian and Corcyrean diplomatic intervention from occupying Syracuse itself.

He fell in battle c. 491/90 B.C., fighting against Sicel Hybla.

Hdt. bk. 7. Dunbabin, *Western Greeks*, 376 ff.; A. Schenk, Graf von Stauffenberg, *Trinakria* (1963), 157 ff. See ANAXILAS (1).
A. G. W.

**HIPPOCRATES** (2), the Asclepiad of Cos, a contemporary of Socrates (469–399), though the most famous Greek physician, is yet the one least of all known to posterity. That he was of small stature, that he travelled much, that he died at Larissa is probable; more about his life and his personality cannot be ascertained.

According to Plato, Hippocrates claimed that one cannot understand the nature of the body without understanding the nature of the whole. That means, Plato adds, that one must ask whether the body is simple or multiform and, whatever the answer, then determine what is its power of acting on or being acted upon by other things. Thus, Hippocrates considered the body an organism; medical practice he based on the knowledge resulting from the comprehension of the scattered particulars into one concept and the division of the whole in turn into its natural species, or, to use Platonic language, on dialectic. Diseases he explained, as Aristotle's pupil Meno relates, by assuming that if food is not digested air is excreted from the remnants, invades the body, and causes illness.

Such a conception of medicine is not to be found in any of the so-called Hippocratic books, though these writings, dealing with all subjects of medicine, with prognostics, dietetics, surgery, pharmacology, with health and diseases, show the most widely different attitudes towards medicine. Being inconsistent in themselves they were never attributed to Hippocrates in their entirety; moreover, there is not a single book the authenticity of which was not disputed already in antiquity. Only fractions, and always different fractions, were ascribed to Hippocrates by later centuries according to their constantly varying conception of Hippocrates as a philosopher or a mere practitioner, a dogmatist, an empiric, a sceptic, a believer in the four humours or in the pneuma-theory, a surgeon or a theoretical scientist.

It seems likely that none of the books preserved under the name of Hippocrates is genuine. Their content does not agree with the pre-Alexandrian testimonies. Moreover, the authenticity of hardly any of them seems to be attested by good tradition; in this case one would expect unanimity of the critics at least in regard to one or a few books. It is probable rather that the writings came to Alexandria as the remnants of medical literature which had circulated in the fifth and fourth centuries, but that they were anonymous, as technical literature of that era commonly was. Philological criticism then attributed them to Hippocrates on the basis of what was considered Hippocratic doctrine in the various periods. But since the proof of genuineness depended on logical argument alone, not on tradition or testimonies, no general agreement could be reached.

All that can be said of the identity of Hippocrates, then, is that he is a physician whose works are lost, though he is not a mere name; his method and doctrine are known; he is the founder of scientific medicine in the Platonic sense; moreover, his fame has been recognized since Plato's time. If one asks what Hippocrates meant to the Greeks, the Middle Ages, the Renaissance, what he means even today, the answer is that by a complicated historical process he has become the embodiment of the ideal physician. *See also* ANATOMY and PHYSIOLOGY, § 3, MEDICINE II, IV–VII, SURGERY §§ 2, 3.

TESTIMONIES. Plato: *Phaedrus* 270 c–d; *Anon. Lond. ex Aristotelis Iatricis Menoniis et aliis medicis eclogae*, ed. H. Diels, *Suppl. Arist.* iii. 1 (1893), v. 35 f. The meaning of these testimonies is much disputed. The above interpretation is maintained by L. Edelstein, *Problemata* iv (1931); *PW*, Suppl. vi, 1317. The opposite theory: K. Deichgräber, *Abh. Berl.* (1933); H. as representative of meteorological medicine, pneuma-theory, M. Pohlenz, *Hippokrates* (1938); reviewed L. Edelstein, *AJPhil.* 1940. Concerning the interpretation of the *Phaedrus* passage see H. Cherniss, *Plato* (1950–7), *Lustrum* iv (1959), no. 700 ff.

All more recent attempts to identify any of the Hippocratic writings as genuine have failed to find general acceptance. As for the origin of the Corpus Hippocraticum, it has been suggested that it constitutes the library of the medical school of Cos, H. Diller, 'Stand und Aufgeben der Hippokrates-Forschung', *Jahrb. Akademie der Wissenschaften und der Literatur* (1959). Disregarding the fact that the existence of such a library remains conjectural, one would surely expect at least one or two books to have been included in the collection which could certainly be attributed to the greatest of the Coan physicians.

WORKS. Corpus Hippocraticum, *Œuvres complètes d'H.*, E. Littré, i–x (1839–61); Opera omnia i–ii, J. Ilberg–H. Kühlewein (Teubner, 1894–1902), not complete; I. L. Heiberg, *CMG* i. 1 (1927); *CMG* to be continued. Separate editions and commentaries: H. Gossen, *PW* viii. 1811. Besides, Περὶ καρδίης, F. C. Unger, *Mnemosyne* (1923); Περὶ σαρκῶν, K. Deichgräber–E. Schwyzer, *Hippokrates, Über Entstehung u. Aufbau d. menschlichen Körpers* (1935); Ὅρκος, W. H. S. Jones, *The Doctor's Oath* (1924); L. Edelstein, *The Hippocratic Oath*, (U.S.A. 1943); A. J. Festugière, *Hippocrate l'ancienne médecine* (1948). Ἐπιστολαί, W. Putzger (Gymnasium Wurzen, 1914), cf. H. Diels, *Hermes* 1918.

TRANSLATIONS. French: with text, E. Littré. Ch. Daremberg, *Œuvres choisies d'Hippocrate* (1855). English: with text, *Selected Works*, i–iv (Loeb); F. Adams, *The Genuine Works of Hippocrates*, i–ii (1849). German: R. Kapferer, *Die Werke des Hippokrates* (1934 f.).

LITERATURE. Introductions to editions of Littré, Daremberg, Loeb Series. Ch. Singer, *Enc. Brit.*[14], s.v. H.; cf. also Ch. Singer, *Greek Biology and Greek Medicine* (1922). J. Hirschberg, *Vorlesungen über Hippokratische Heilkunde* (1922). More recent literature collected in A. Rehm–K. Vogel, *Exakte Wissenschaften*, Gercke-Norden ii. 5 (1933); H. Diller, *Hermes* 1956; J. H. Kühn, *Hermes*, Einzelschriften, Heft 11 (1956). L. E.

**HIPPOCRATES** (3) of Chios (*c.* 470–400 B.C.), mathematician, the first person to compose a book of *Elements of Geometry*; his work anticipated much of Euc. book 3, as well as some later parts of Euclid. He succeeded in squaring three out of the five 'lunes' which can be squared by means of the straight line and the circle; and he contributed to the problem of doubling the cube by reducing it to the finding of two mean proportionals.

Heath, *Hist. of Greek Maths.*, ch. 6. W. D. R.

**HIPPODAMUS** of Miletus was the most famous Greek town-planner. He was born probably about 500 B.C. He did not invent or introduce to Greece the typical rectangular or 'gridiron' type of planning, but he seems to have shown skill and ingenuity in adapting the elements of the Greek city to this scheme (*see* TOWNS). Ancient authorities speak of his *nemēsis* or allocation of sites. Towards the middle of the fifth century he planned Peiraeus for the Athenians, and boundary stones found there are probably evidence of his work (*IG* i². 887 ff.; cf. *Hist.* 1964, 138). In 443 B.C. he went with the colony to Thurii (q.v.) and he may well have been responsible for its rectangular plan. Strabo (14. 2. 9) records a tradition that 'the architect of Peiraeus' planned Rhodes (q.v.), which was founded in 408 B.C. Most modern authorities reject this on the ground that the date is too late for Hippodamus, but it is not impossible. Aristotle (*Pol.* 2. 5) speaks of Hippodamus' foppish appearance, and his political theories, and notes that he thought that the ideal size for a city was 10,000 (i.e. probably citizens).

For bibliography *see* TOWNS; and F. Castagnoli, *Ippodamo di Mileto e l'urbanistica a pianta ortogonale* (1956). R. E. W.

**HIPPOLYTUS** (1) (Ἱππόλυτος, i.e. 'loosed horse', wild driver or rider?), in mythology, son of Theseus by the Amazon Hippolyte (cf. AMAZONS). Hippolyte being dead, Theseus married Phaedra daughter of Minos (q.v.). Her character varies in Tragedy. Apparently in the (lost) Ἱππόλυτος καλυπτόμενος of Euripides and certainly in the *Phaedra* of Seneca she was a lustful and wholly unscrupulous woman; in the surviving *Hippolytus* of the former she is much more interesting, having intense

natural desires but a strong sense of modesty. Theseus being long absent (on his journey to the lower world, according to Euripides), Phaedra conceived a passion for Hippolytus, but he, being honourable (Euripides makes him anti-sexual), repulsed her. She thereupon hanged herself, leaving behind a letter which accused him. Theseus returned, read the letter, and would not believe Hippolytus' protestations of innocence. He banished Hippolytus and used one of the three wishes which his father (Poseidon, in this version; cf. AEGEUS) had given him in asking for his death. Poseidon sent a sea-monster which frightened Hippolytus' horses as he was driving away, and he was thrown from his chariot and dragged to death; Theseus learned the truth from Artemis too late.

In cult Hippolytus is associated with Aphrodite, who had a shrine ἐφ' Ἱππολύτῳ on the Acropolis at Athens; while at Troezen, the place of his death, he had a ritual including laments for him and offerings of hair from girls about to marry (Eur. op. cit. 1423 ff., Paus. 2. 32. 1); the local legend said that he did not die as above described but became the constellation Auriga, but this clearly is not early. Whether he was originally god or hero is disputed (Farnell, *Hero-Cults* 64 ff.).

The story that Asclepius restored him to life is as old as the *Naupactica* (Apollod. 3. 121); it led to his identification with Virbius (*see* DIANA) at Nemi (see Verg. *Aen.* 7. 765 ff., and Servius on 761).

W. S. Barrett, Introduction to Euripides, *Hippolytus* (1964). H. J. R.

**HIPPOLYTUS** (2), *c.* A.D. 170–*c.* 236, Roman presbyter and (probably) rival bishop to Callistus of Rome (217–22) whom he regarded as compromised by heresy because of his opposition to Hippolytus' Logos doctrine. He died in exile in Sardinia under Maximinus' persecution. In 1551 a statue representing him in philosopher's dress was found at Rome (now in the Vatican Library). It gives a list of his writings and his table for calculating Easter. His chief work, *Refutation of all Heresies*, is planned to show how heresies are the offspring of Greek philosophical systems; it transcribes Sextus (q.v. 2) Empiricus and doxographic works, and has valuable fragments of Heraclitus (q.v.) and others. His chronicle of history from Creation to 234 (like his commentary on Daniel) was in part intended to quench apocalyptic expectations of the imminent end of the world.

*Elenchos*, ed. P. Wendland (1916); *Chron.*, ed. A. Bauer (1929). J. Quasten, *Patrology* 2 (1953), 165 ff. H. C.

**HIPPON**, also called **HIPPONAX**, natural philosopher of the Periclean age, probably came from Samos. He treated water or the moist as the principle of all things, reasoning chiefly from observation on the semen of animals. He considered the soul (seated in the brain) to be derived from the semen and to be itself moist, and devoted special attention to the development of the human body from the embryonic state to maturity. Aristotle describes him as a second-rate thinker, probably because of his materialistic bias. He was lampooned as an atheist by Cratinus and this became his stock epithet in later writers.

Testimonia and fragments in Diels, *Vorsokr.*[11] i. 385–9. W. D. R.

**HIPPONAX** (fl. 540–537 B.C.; Pliny, *HN* 36. 11), iambic poet, of Ephesus, whence he was banished and went to Clazomenae. By making the iambic trimeter end with a spondee he invented the σκάζων or χωλίαμβος, and in this metre he wrote satirical, colloquial verse. Some of his fragments are concerned with his love for Arete (frs. 15–22), others with his quarrel with the two sculptors Bupalus and Athenis. The story was that they made a statue which caricatured him and were so distressed by his lampoons that they committed suicide

(Pliny, loc. cit., cf. frs. 1, 13, 15, 20). He also fell foul of the painter Mimnes (fr. 45). Polemon credited Hipponax with the invention of parody (Ath. 698 b), and frs. 77–8 show the existence of a poem in mock-heroic verse on the adventures of the glutton Eurymedontiades. Hipponax has a vivid, terse style and drew for his vocabulary on contemporary speech and at times on foreign words in Lydian and Phrygian.

TEXT. E. Diehl, *Anth. Lyr. Graec.* i. 3, 74 ff.; with commentary, O. Masson, *Les Fragments du poète Hipponax* (1962).　　　C. M. B.

**HIPPOTHOON**, in mythology, son of Poseidon and Alope daughter of Cercyon (Hyg. *Fab.* 187, who calls him Hippothous); eponym of the Attic tribe Hippothoontis (Paus. 1. 5. 2; Harpocration, s.v. Ἀλόπη; Hesychius, s.v. Ἱπποθοώντειον).　　　H. J. R.

**HIRTIUS** (*PW* 2), AULUS (*cos.* 43 B.C.), since *c.* 54 B.C. an officer of Caesar, who sent him as envoy to Pompey in Dec. 50. In the Civil Wars he served in Spain, was possibly *tr. pl.* in 48, and was at Antioch in spring 47; in 46 he was praetor and next year governed Transalpine Gaul. After Caesar's murder he was consul designate, and Cicero induced him to take arms against Antony (43). With Octavian he raised the siege of Mutina, but was killed in the victory, receiving with his colleague Pansa (q.v.) a public funeral. Hirtius added to Caesar's *De Bello Gallico* an eighth book, and probably also wrote the *Bellum Alexandrinum* (q.v.); his correspondence with Cicero, published in nine books, and the draft for Caesar's *Anticato* have not survived. A notorious epicure, Hirtius was also a fluent and reasonably painstaking writer: his military competence was probably not as low as Quintus Cicero later pretended (Cic. *Fam.* 16. 27. 2). G. E. F. C.

**HISPALIS** or **HISPAL** (modern *Sevilla*), on the lower Baetis (*Guadalquivir*), is not mentioned before Caesar's Civil War. A ship-building and trading port, it received a modest colony of veterans from Caesar. A double colonization should not be inferred from its title Julia Romula, nor from the alternative names *Hispalenses* and *Romulenses*; the colony was, however, reinforced by Otho, and the town grew in size and importance. In the second century A.D. it rivalled Corduba (q.v.), and eclipsed the old port of Gades (q.v.). Lying on reaches navigable by the largest ships, close to some of the busiest mines, it handled the exports of the richest province of the West. Imperial procurators and agents of the *praefectus annonae* operated there. It had a bishop from the early fourth century or before, and later became the metropolitan see, occupied in the seventh century by St. Isidore (q.v.).　　　M. I. H.

**HISTIAEA**, a city on the north-west coast of Euboea, with a rich plain facing Thessaly. It was said to have been founded from Thessaly by Ellopians, and in the Catalogue of Ships is characterized as rich in vines. It was sacked by the Persians after their defeat at Artemisium and subsequently joined the Athenian League. For their part in the Euboean revolt the Histiaeans were expelled by Athens in 447/6, and 2,000 cleruchs were established in the new colony, Oreioi, a deme of Histiaea; but the city with the new name was not demonstrably on a different site. The Histiaeans returned after the Peloponnesian War. They remained suspicious of Athens and supported Sparta until the Euboean War and after 357/6 they rejoined the Athenian League. The Macedonians took an early interest in this part of the island. The city was taken by Attalus II and the Romans in 199 and sacked. It later served Roman fleets. There are scanty Bronze-Age finds from the acropolis by the sea, slight Classical remains, and a Byzantine circuit wall.

L. H. Sackett and others, *BSA* 1966, 39 f.　　　J. B.

**HISTIAEUS**, tyrant of Miletus, rendered service to Darius during the Scythian campaign (*c.* 512 B.C.). He was presented with Myrcinus on the important coastal road near the later city of Amphipolis, but Darius growing distrustful invited him to Susa, where he held an honourable post as one of the 'King's Councillors'. Meanwhile his son-in-law Aristagoras (q.v. 1) ruled Miletus. They both seem to have co-operated in preparing the Ionian Revolt. After the destruction of Sardes (498) he was sent on his own request to pacify Ionia, but distrusted by both sides he was unsuccessful. He settled at Byzantium as a kind of pirate, and fought on his own account on the islands and in Asia Minor. In 494 or 493 he was captured and crucified. He probably was no more than an ambitious adventurer, though Herodotus' story relies too much on sources hostile to Histiaeus.

Hdt. bks. 4–6. A. Blamire, *CQ* 1959, 142; A. R. Burn, *Persia and the Greeks* (1962); M. Lang, *Hist.* 1968, 24.　　　V. E.

**HISTORIA AUGUSTA.** Title given by I. Casaubon (1603) to a collection of biographies of Roman Emperors, Caesars, and usurpers from A.D. 117 to 284 (Hadrian to Carinus and Numerianus). The present text is not complete, as there is a lacuna for the years 244–59. Though the work is modelled on Suetonius' lives of the XII Caesars there is no cogent reason to believe that it was a direct continuation of Suetonius and therefore originally included the lives of Nerva and Trajan. According to the complex manuscript tradition (which includes a family of MSS. (Σ) with interesting variants) the biographies were written by six different authors who lived in the time of Diocletian and Constantine. Some of the biographies are dedicated to Diocletian or Constantine, others to private persons. Four of the authors—Aelius Spartianus, Iulius Capitolinus, Vulcacius Gallicanus, Aelius Lampridius—say that they have written more biographies than those appearing in our present compilation. Only two authors—Trebellius Pollio and Flavius Vopiscus—do not profess to have written more than the extant biographies. The *Scriptores Historiae Augustae* (as the six are normally called) claim to have used many literary sources, only a few of which, such as Herodian, are extant. Furthermore, they quote about 130 documents (letters by Emperors, *senatus consulta*, inscriptions, etc.) which are unevenly distributed among the biographies. Lives of little-known Emperors and usurpers are filled with documents, whereas there is no document in the lives (which altogether appear more reliable) of Hadrian, Antoninus Pius, Marcus Aurelius, and Septimius Severus. This would be enough to raise suspicions. Indeed the *Historia Augusta* has never enjoyed great authority among scholars, although it is our only continuous account for the history of the Emperors of the second and third centuries. More radical criticism, however, was expressed for the first time by H. Dessau in *Hermes* 1889, 337, and his paper opened up a new era in the study of the *Historia Augusta*. Dessau contended that the *HA* was not written in the time of Diocletian and Constantine, but in the time of Theodosius, and that there was only one author behind the six names of the alleged biographers. One of his many impressive arguments was that the life of Septimius Severus, chs. 17–19, copies Aurelius Victor, *De Caesaribus* 20 (written in A.D. 360) and that the life of Marcus Aurelius 16. 3–18. 2 depends on Eutropius 8. 11–14 (written in A.D. 369). Since Dessau the so-called problem of the *HA* has involved five questions: (1) how many authors wrote the *HA*? (2) when was the *HA* written? (3) did the original text of the *HA* undergo later changes? (4) what was the purpose of the writer or writers of the *HA* in composing this work? (5) how many literary references and documentary quotations of the *HA* are forgeries?

Scholars of the last seventy-five years have been sharply divided in their answers to the first four questions, while they have been fairly unanimous in considering the literary references and documentary quotations as invariably suspect, where not altogether false. Whereas Mommsen suggested that an original text which had been written under Diocletian and Constantine was substantially revised under Theodosius I, some scholars (e.g. G. De Sanctis) have defended the Diocletianic-Constantinian date of the entire work. Other scholars have followed Dessau in the notion of a total forgery, but have proposed different dates: under Constantius II (H. Stern), under Julian (N. H. Baynes), in A.D. 394 (W. Hartke), in the early fifth century (O. Seeck, J. Straub), even in the late sixth century (A. von Domaszewski), though the last date is made very improbable by the fact that the *HA* seems to have been used by Q. Aurelius Symmachus (quoted in Jordanes, *Getica* 15. 85) towards the end of the fifth century. The problem of the alleged plurality of authors is also still unsolved, though recent research has emphasized the uniformity of style in all the lives. There is continued disagreement about the aims of the writer or writers. The *HA* displays pro-senatorial sympathies and does not approve of hereditary monarchy (though it shows great admiration for the descendants of Claudius Gothicus) nor of interference by the army in politics. But this is not enough to explain the work as a whole, especially if one regards it as a major forgery. Some scholars incline to think that the *Scriptores Historiae Augustae* were simply trying to entertain the reader by sensational and unscrupulous writing; others feel that the *HA* is a Pagan attack on Christianity. The theory that the author of the *HA* concealed his personality and time of writing in order to attack Christianity and to present Paganism as more tolerant has been developed by A. Alföldi and J. Straub and has received considerable support.

Best critical edition by E. Hohl (1927 with later reprints). Loeb text by D. Magie (1922–32). J. Casaubon's and Cl. Salmasius' notes are still invaluable. Cf. Th. Mommsen, *Hermes* 1890, 228 ff.; G. De Sanctis, *Riv. St. Ant.* 1896, 90 ff.; F. Leo, *Die griechisch-römische Biographie* (1901), 268 ff.; E. Hohl, *Klio* 1911, 178 ff.; O. Seeck, *Rh. Mus.* 1912, 591 ff.; A. v. Domaszewski, various papers in *Sitz. Heidelberg. Ak.* 1916–20; N. H. Baynes, *The H.A., its date and purpose* (1926); W. Hartke, *Geschichte und Politik im spätantiken Rom, Klio* Beiheft 45 (1940); H. Stern, *Date et destinataire de l'H.A.* (1953); E. Hohl, *Wien. Stud.* 1958, 132 ff.; A. Momigliano, *Secondo contributo alla storia degli studi classici* (1960), 105 ff.; J. Straub, *Heidnische Geschichtsapologetik in der Christlichen Spätantike* (1963); *Atti del Colloquio Patavino sulla Historia Augusta* (1963); *Historia-Augusta-Colloquium Bonn 1963* (1964) with bibliography (cf. the review of the last three titles by A. D. Cameron, *JRS* 1965, 240 ff.; A. D. Cameron, *Hermes* 1964, 363 ff.; P. White, *JRS* 1967, 114; R. Syme, *Ammianus and the Historia Augusta* (1968). A. M.

## HISTORIOGRAPHY, GREEK.

The discovery of inscribed tablets in Crete, at Pylos and elsewhere, and the decipherment of the so-called Linear B (*see* MINOAN SCRIPTS) prove that the habit of listing objects and recording events goes back in Greece (both on the islands and in mainland Greece) to the last centuries of the second millennium B.C. (at the latest). There is therefore no longer any need to argue at length about the likelihood of historical and chronographic material having been collected and listed by the priests at the main Greek shrines and by the authorities of the Greek city-states from an early date, however much one may doubt or dispute the accuracy and historical value of the lists and kindred material which have survived. Yet it was not from annalistic sources that Greek historiography arose. Historical writing only came into being with the awakening of the Greek mind under the influence of science and rationalism. Following the example of the Ionian physicists and geographers, the so-called *logographoi* (prose writers, as opposed to epic poets) assumed a critical attitude towards the traditions of poetry and mythology, and thus created historical science. The greatest of the *logographoi* to our knowledge, the Milesian Hecataeus, was the first to submit tradition to the test of reason.

**2.** The followers of Hecataeus (Xanthus, Hellanicus, Scylax, etc.) either confined themselves to local history, or wrote general history (not Greek history exclusively) from a Persian standpoint. A noticeable exception was a contemporary of Hecataeus, Antiochus of Syracuse, who wrote a history of the Greek colonies in southern Italy and Sicily. Herodotus also may be styled a disciple of Hecataeus. He felt such admiration for the achievements of the Persian kings that he planned to write both a history of the wars they had waged and a geographical survey of their empire. Only at a later stage, when he fell under the spell of the Athenian democracy, did he realize the greatness of the victory of Greece over Persia, and made this the chief subject of his narrative. Even so, his account showed so much sympathy with the vanquished that later Greek writers, probably influenced by Isocratean panhellenism, did not hesitate to brand Herodotus as a friend of the barbarians.

**3.** The immediate success of Herodotus was great; but his history was too discursive to satisfy the literary taste of succeeding generations, and seemed remote from the problems of party politics and of Athenian imperialism which soon took the place of the Persian Wars as the centre of Greek political interest. These problems produced two new kinds of historical writing: (1) a 'scientific' account of the Peloponnesian War by Thucydides; (2) a violently biased propaganda, chiefly on the part of Greek conservatives, who cast their programmes into the mould of an idealized or merely fictitious past, and published pamphlets against the Athenian democracy (Pseudo-Xenophon) and its leaders (Stesimbrotus), as well as schemes of oligarchic constitutions (Critias, Theramenes, etc.). Meanwhile, a new branch of historical writing, the memoir, was created by Ion of Chios and others.

**4.** In the fourth century Greek historiography was influenced by the prevailing dissatisfaction with public life, the growing detachment from politics, and a renewed interest in foreign Powers (Persia and, later, Macedonia) which showed signs of becoming the deciding factor in Greek politics. It was the Asiatic Greek Ctesias who was chiefly responsible for the revival of interest in Persian history and civilization. Thucydides himself had prepared the way for these tendencies, for in the final draft of his *History* he had emphasized the bearing of moral ideas on history, and had shown that the subject of historical writing could not be confined to politics alone. His continuators, however, neglected his method of research and his accuracy and obeyed new masters, Socrates, Plato, and Isocrates. The latter, besides imposing new rules of style, taught the principles of panhellenism, while both Socrates and Plato laid down principles of morality as standards of political judgement. Xenophon, Theopompus (both of whom started at the point in the Peloponnesian War where Thucydides had left off), and Ephorus combined the two methods and created a new form of historical writing. Xenophon inaugurated a literary fashion in associating historical memoirs and romance (in the *Anabasis* and the *Cyropaedia*); his political partisanship and eulogistic rhetoric appealed to every class of reader and secured for his *Hellenica* a wide, though not wholly merited influence. Ephorus envisaged the history of the Greek peninsula as a unity, and was the first to write a complete account from the mythical age down to Philip of Macedon. The success of his work, which was to become the 'vulgate' of Greek history, is best attested by the fact that it was never repeated. In his principal work, the *Philippica*, Theopompus accomplished something equally unique in

Greek historical writing. Psychological insight into his protagonist, Philip, whom he saluted as the creator of a new age, moral and political discussions, geographical digressions in which he boasted that he had surpassed Herodotus, made of the *Philippica* perhaps the crowning achievement of classical and certainly the forerunner of Hellenistic historiography.

5. A more scientific if less ambitious school of historiography was founded in the fourth century by Cleidemus and Androtion, who wrote local histories of Attica (Ἀτθίδες) based on documentary evidence, and by Aristotle and Philochorus, who also collected and published records of public and religious institutions, games, and literary competitions. These research historians laid the foundations of Hellenistic scholarship and antiquarianism. But the principal historians of the Hellenistic age, disregarding documentary evidence and the technique of historical writing, aimed, as a general rule, not at being accurate and learned, but readable. The political and military accounts of the expedition of Alexander the Great written by official authors such as Aristobulus, Nearchus, and Ptolemy (on whom Arrian is chiefly dependent) were soon superseded by the highly rhetorical and romantic stories of Callisthenes, Onesicritus, and Cleitarchus, who founded the 'vulgate' tradition represented by Diodorus and Plutarch, as well as by Justin and Curtius.

6. In the third and second centuries the field of historiography was similarly divided between men of political and military experience, such as Hieronymus, Aratus, and Polybius, and writers who sought to entertain or to excite their readers by a pathetic or realistic style of narrative (Duris, Phylarchus). The latter school was more generally read; because of the prominence which it gave to outstanding personages, it was largely utilized by biographers and ultimately became the chief source of Plutarch.

7. Since no Hellenistic historian, with the exception of Polybius, survived the change in Greek taste and mentality towards the end of the first century B.C., Plutarch is indisputably the author who provides the best survey of the methods, peculiarities, and defects of Hellenistic historiography. Plutarch established the principle that history is the product, not of dry abstractions, such as economics, parties, climate, environment, etc., but of the will and the passions of individuals. Another feature of Plutarch's biographies, the equal measure of importance which he attached to Greek and to Roman personages, illustrates the readiness with which Hellenistic historians perceived the significance of the Roman conquests and influenced Roman culture and historical writing. Greek authors were the first to realize the problem and importance for world-history of the Roman Empire, and through them the Romans became conscious of the mission they were called on to fulfil. A far-sighted interest in the beginnings of Roman history was shown by Timaeus, a Sicilian Greek of the early third century, who coupled the history of his native island with that of Greece and Italy. Polybius, taking up the story where Timaeus left off, at the beginning of Rome's Punic Wars, made it the object of his work to bring home to his compatriots the military, political, and moral advantages which gave the Romans their victory and guaranteed its permanence. The providence of God had imposed on Rome the task of building an empire, and this empire was actually working out to the material and moral benefit of its subjects. This idea Polybius' continuator, Posidonius, also sought to convey; in his view, apparently, the commonwealth of God was reflected in the world-wide Roman Republic, and the unity of history was realized in the unity of the Roman Empire. The immense influence exerted by Posidonius is attested

by the revival of historical feeling which he promoted. Not only did he become the model and the chief source of universal historians and epitomizers, such as Diodorus and Nicolaus of Damascus, and of geographers such as Strabo, but he also suggested inquiries into less familiar fields. It was under his spell that interest in primitive or non-European races was felt and satisfied. In the Augustan age the literary critic, Dionysius of Halicarnassus, turned to explore the origins and early history of Rome. In a similar spirit Flavius Josephus, proceeding along the path paved by Philo, wrote under the Flavians a history of the Jews, in order to show the similarity of their civilization with that of the Greeks and Romans.

8. Hitherto Greek historians had merely tried to vie with their Roman counterparts. The Greek historians of the second century A.D. took advantage of the post-Neronian resurgence of the Hellenized East and gave their contemporaries a new knowledge of their past and a new stimulus to study contemporary problems. There thus came about a revival of interest in 'classical' authors, some historical criticism of them even by mere *littérateurs* such as Aelius Aristides, Herodes Atticus, etc., and eventually Libanius, and a renewed study of the methods and techniques of historical writing as practised by Thucydides and Polybius. There is evidence of this in Lucian's treatise 'How to write history'. Arrian recounted the story of Alexander the Great and his successors in the manner of a Herodotus or a Xenophon and in conscious opposition to the 'vulgate' of the romancers, such as Callisthenes and Cleitarchus, and the 'biography' of Plutarch. Above all Greek historians turned to Rome no longer to justify her origins and her sway, as Dionysius, Nicolaus of Damascus, Strabo, and others had done, but to record the wars of the Republic (so Appian of Alexandria) or to supply a sort of *pendant* to Livy by relating in Greek the whole course of Rome's history down to the era of the Severi (so Cassius Dio). These developments marked the entry of the Greeks and their culture into the Roman Empire, gave their interpretation of Roman history, and helped to preserve not only the records of the past but also the consciousness of a common bond in cultural affinities which was still felt by Byzantine scholars (e.g. Procopius). Through them, and sometimes through Latin authors such as St. Augustine and Orosius, who were the chief Western heirs of the Oriental and Hellenistic tradition of the cyclical succession of Empires, the methods of Greek historiography were transmitted to Christianity and played a part in forming the new conception of history which was required by Christian belief.

See the articles on individual historical writers.

TEXTS. The fragments of the lost Greek historians are collected in C. Müller, *Fragmenta historicorum graecorum* (*FHG*), 5 vols. (with a Latin translation, 1841 ff.), and F. Jacoby, *Die Fragmente d. griech. Historiker* (*FGrH*) (with German and eventually English introductions, commentary, and notes, 1923 ff. in progress). The papyrus fragments (with the exception of the Hellenica Oxyrhynchia—*see* OXYRHYNCHUS HISTORIAN) have been collected by F. Bilabel (1923).

GENERAL LITERATURE. C. Wachsmuth, *Einleitung in das Studium der alten Geschichte* (1895); U. v. Wilamowitz-Moellendorff, *Greek historical Writing* (1908; the revised and enlarged German text republished in *Redenu.Vorträge* ii⁴,1926); J. B. Bury, *The Ancient Greek Historians* (1909); B. Croce, *Theory and History of Historiography*; R. G. Collingwood, *The Idea of History* (1946); Ed. Schwartz, *Charakterköpfe aus der Antike³* (1950), 35 ff., 76 ff.; P. Scheller, *De hellenistica historiae conscribendae arte* (1911); B. Lavagnini, *Saggio sulla storiografia greca* (1933); M. Braun, *History and Romance in Graeco-Oriental Literature* (1938); G. De Sanctis, *Studi di storia della storiografia greca* (1951); *Ricerche sulla storiografia siceliota* (1958); *Storia dei Greci* ii (1939); F. Jacoby, *Griech. Historiker* (the PW articles in book form) (1956); *Atthis* (1949); *Abhandlungen z. griech. Geschichtsschreibung* (1956); *Histoire et historiens dans l'antiquité* (*Entretiens Hardt* iv, 1958); M. Platnauer, *Fifty Years of Classical Scholarship* (1954), ch. 6 (G. T. Griffith); L. Pearson, *The Early Ionian Historians* (1939); *The lost Historians of Alexander the Great* (1960; cf. E. Badian, *Studies in Greek and Roman History*, 1964, 250 ff.); W. W. Tarn, *Alexander the Great* (1948) ii. 3 ff.; B. L.

Ullman, *TAPA* 1942; H. Bloch in *Harv. Stud.* (Ferguson) 1940; G. Avenarius, *Lukians Schrift zur Geschichtsschreibung* (1956); Walbank, *Polybius* i; H. Bengtson, *Einführung in die alte Geschichte* (1962), 81 ff.; P. Pédech, *La Méthode historique de Polybe* (1964); A. Momigliano, *Studies in Historiography* (1966). **P. T.**

**HISTORIOGRAPHY, ROMAN.** The beginnings of Roman historical writing lie not solely in the pontifical tradition but in Hellenistic historiography. The first Roman historians, Fabius Pictor, Cincius Alimentus, Postumius Albinus, and C. Acilius, wrote in Greek to glorify Rome's foundation and justify her institutions and policy to the Hellenistic world. Their work thus comes under the class not of annalistic chronicles but of the Hellenistic histories. Political writers, not professional historians, *narratores*, not *exornatores rerum*, they fell short of Cicero's rhetorical standards (*De Or.* 2. 51–2; *Leg.* 1. 5), but their quality is reflected in the ἐπιστόλια of Scipio Africanus (Polyb. 10. 9) and Scipio Nasica (Plutarch, *Aem.* 15 ff.). Their tradition inspired Polybius to analyse and set in its perspective the imperial rise of Rome, and their work was continued in Latin, in its same form, by Cato in his *Origines* (see ANNALS).

**2.** It was Cato, after Ennius, who inspired national historiography in Rome. The 'early' annalists, Cassius Hemina and Calpurnius Piso, began the systematic reconstruction of Roman history; and the study of pontifical law, cult and constitutional antiquities, public and private law, reflects the growth of historical consciousness, influenced by Stoic thought, which led to the publication of the *annales maximi* (*c.* 123 B.C.). This definitive work of documentary reconstruction and formal arrangement founded the annalistic historiographical γένος; the influence of Hellenistic theory furthered its development. Cn. Gellius probably first applied the rhetorical Isocratean methods to elaboration of the records; the immediate post-Sullan annalists, Valerius Antias and Claudius Quadrigarius, by free legalistic reconstruction and conventional rhetorical elaboration, fully established the literary form, which was accepted by Livy and adapted by the imperial annalists and Tacitus.

**3.** In contemporary historiography Polybius' work was continued by Posidonius, and his methods followed by Sempronius Asellio. Aemilius Scaurus and Rutilius Rufus wrote autobiography, Catulus and Sulla left ὑπομνήματα. Coelius Antipater introduced the historical monograph and Asianic style; Hellenistic biography grew on the tradition of the *laudatio funebris* (q.v.). It may be said that all the Hellenistic historiographical γένη were established in Rome, with increasing literary independence, by the time of Sulla.

**4.** Sisenna practised the dramatic 'Peripatetic' art of Cleitarchus in his work on Sulla. Annalistic history continued with Macer, the democrat, and Tubero, the Caesarian. Contemporary history is represented by names from Cn. Aufidius to Tanusius Geminus. Antiquarian studies flourished with Nigidius Figulus and Varro, and Cornelius Nepos shows the advance of biography. Caesar's *Commentarii* represent the Hellenistic military ὑπομνήματα in Latin. The Caesarian and anti-Caesarian writings, the *Catones* and *Anticatones*, mark the maturity of political propaganda.

**5.** It is in this setting that Sallust wrote and Cicero defined the tasks of Roman historiography. Sallust represents political analysis, associating Catonian archaism with Thucydidean *severitas*, and joining to rhetorical device the syntactical aggressiveness of his style. Cicero held the Hellenistic view that history, an 'opus oratorium maxime', should be based on the rhetorical Isocratean canons represented by Timaeus. These theoretical principles reflect their different historical purpose, Cicero justifying the tradition with dignity, Sallust attacking present corruption against the principles

of traditional morality. The issue in thought and in mode was defined, and Livy's Augustan idealism could follow Cicero, Tacitus draw inspiration from Sallust.

**6.** Augustan historiography marks the balance of Roman tradition and Hellenistic influence. Memoirs dealing with the end of the Republic are common, from Augustus himself to Tiro. Asinius Pollio practised independent criticism. Livy, on the one side, glorified the Republican tradition; Pompeius Trogus, on the other, set Rome in her Hellenistic perspective. To the Isocratean rules Livy adds elaborate rhetorical and dramatic effects, practising the fine psychological interpretation which had come to maturity in Rome from Hellenistic studies. Poetical colour makes his opening books the prose epic of Rome; the later books enshrine the annalistic tradition and adapt the form to contemporary history. Trogus avoided direct rhetoric.

**7.** The Augustan achievements were final in their own field. Fenestella might add antiquarian interest, L. Arruntius Sallustian style to the annalistic tradition, but Livy was followed, after Velleius Paterculus, only by the Epitome and its dependent writers. Trogus, unchallenged, was joined by Curtius Rufus, but Thallus, L. Cornelius, Bocchus, and Vibius Maximus led merely to Justin's Epitome. After the Republican work of Cremutius Cordus, however, the imperial annalists appear: Aufidius Bassus, the Elder Pliny continuing his work, the Elder Seneca, and Bruttedius Niger; then Cluvius Rufus, Vipstanus Messalla, and Fabius Rusticus. Imperial rule increased biography, not only of the emperors but of their administrators, and memoirs were common. *Exempla* were published by Valerius Maximus and Hyginus. Ethnography and geography became popular, while rhetorical theory developed in declamation.

**8.** Thus the Roman historiographical γένη held their place in the first century, and Tacitus adapted them in unity of conception and stylistic mastery. Historical in his treatment of rhetorical theory, biography, and ethnography, he pressed these in their turn into the service of history. Roman in his central theme, traditional in his political judgement, he strove for dramatic concentration and psychological depth; to the annalistic conventions and rhetorical effect he added the *severitas* and syntactical aggressiveness of Sallust. Drawing on historical tradition and historiographical technique, he created a work of original genius.

**9.** Imperial biography attained its highest point with Suetonius, but after Marius Maximus it degenerated to the *Historia Augusta*. Roman historiography entered the age of epitome and chronicle: the handbooks of Ampelius and Julius Obsequens, chronographical work, the *breviaria* of Florus, Granius Licinianus, Aurelius Victor, Eutropius, and Festus. Ammianus Marcellinus alone shows historical quality in his continuation and imitation of Tacitus, but his technique and style, for all their power, betray his historiographical isolation. Meanwhile Julius Africanus had added Jewish to Hellenistic and Roman history in order to establish a Christian chronicle, and Eusebius made this work definitive as well as creating ecclesiastical history. Thus, Roman historiography passed to Hieronymus (Jerome) and Orosius, and supported Augustine's *City of God*, as it were, *sub specie aeternitatis*.

See ANNALS and the various writers mentioned; and HISTORIOGRAPHY, GREEK, for Hellenistic influences.

A. Rosenberg, *Einleitung und Quellenkunde zur röm. Geschichte* (1921); E. Norden, *Die Antike Kunstprosa* (2nd ed. 4th reprint, 1923); W. Kroll, *Studien zum Verständnis der röm. Literatur* (1924), 331 ff.; T. Frank, *Life and Literature in the Roman Republic* (1930), 169 ff.; M. Gelzer, *Kl. Schr.* iii. 51 ff.; M. Platnauer (ed.), *Fifty Years of Classical Scholarship* (1954), ch. 13 (A. H. McDonald); A. Momigliano (ed.), *Conflict between Paganism and Christianity in the fourth century* (1963), ch. 4 (A. Momigliano); T. A. Dorey (ed.), *Latin Historians* (1966). **A. H. McD.**

**HOMER.** The Greeks, with insignificant exceptions, believed that both the *Iliad* and the *Odyssey* were composed by Homer, but they had no certain or accepted facts about his life. His date was very variously given, as contemporary with the Trojan War (Tzetz. *Chil.* 12. 183), soon after it ([Plut.] *Vit. Hom.* A 5), at the time of the Return of the Heraclidae (? Crates Theb. ap. Tatianum *Ad Gr.* 31), at the time of the Ionian wandering (Philostr. 194. 9), in the middle of the ninth century (Hdt. 2. 53), and 500 years after the Trojan War (Theopomp. Hist. ap. Clem. Al. *Strom.* 1. 117). This great divergence indicates that external evidence was lacking and that the Greeks knew little more than we do. If we try to date the poems by internal evidence, some facts emerge. Archaeology gives ambiguous results, but forbids an early date, since the sitting statue of *Il.* 6. 302–3 cannot be earlier than the eighth century, the shield of Agamemnon in *Il.* 11. 19 ff. may be even later, and the use of the phalanx in warfare (*Il.* 13. 131 ff.) may be later still. Even if we regard these passages as later corrections or additions, the *Iliad*, though it contains echoes of much earlier times in some matters, certainly does not describe the culture of the Mycenaean age as a contemporary document should. Literary evidence gives at least a *terminus ad quem* in the seventh century, when Terpander is said to have recited Homer at Sparta and echoes of him are to be seen in Tyrtaeus (frs. 6–7, 21–8 from *Il.* 22. 71–6, fr. 8. 29–34 from *Il.* 16. 215–17), Semonides (fr. 29 from *Il.* 6. 146), and Alcman (fr. 1. 48 from *Il.* 9. 124, fr. 73 from *Il.* 3. 39). Archilochus seems also to give variations on Homeric phrases at fr. 65 (*Od.* 22. 412), fr. 41 (*Od.* 14. 228), fr. 38 (*Il.* 18. 309), and though the date of Hesiod is not known, he seems to be later than Homer, since *Op.* 159–60 may owe something to *Il.* 12. 23 and *Th.* 340 ff. to *Il.* 12. 20 ff. We may then perhaps place Homer before 700 B.C., though we must admit that there is always a possibility of his text having been altered and the indications of date being additions.

**2.** His place is a matter of dispute in antiquity. Of the different possibilities Chios and Smyrna are best supported. Chios was regarded as his home by Semonides of Amorgos (fr. 29), and it was there that the Homeridae lived and maintained his memory (schol. Pind. *Nem.* 2. 1), while Smyrna was supported by Pindar (fr. 279). The predominance of Ionic elements in Homeric language points to Ionia as Homer's home, and this is supported by hints in the poems, notably by similes which mention the Cayster (*Il.* 2. 459 ff.), the Icarian Sea (ibid. 144 ff.), and a Maeonian or Carian woman (*Il.* 4. 141–2), and by a certain geographical acquaintance with the Troad, the weeping Niobe on Sipylus (*Il.* 24. 614 ff.), and the towns of the Aeolic peninsula. Since in certain places (*Il.* 9. 4–5, 11. 305–8) he implies a shore facing west, he may have the Asiatic coast in his mind. On the other hand, in the *Odyssey* there is certainly some, not always exact, information about the islands round Ithaca and the Peloponnese, which may be due to personal acquaintance or more probably to hearsay. He seems on the whole to have lived in Ionia, since his apparent ignorance of the Dorians in the Peloponnese indicates that he knew little of it.

**3.** Other traditions of his life, embodied in the ancient *Lives*, are almost without value. The episodes in them are usually to be traced back to episodes in the *Iliad* and *Odyssey*. The tradition that he was blind is better founded, since bards were often blind and the Homeric *Hymn to Apollo* 172 speaks of a blind poet in Chios and may refer to him. His condition may well have resembled that of the bards in the *Odyssey* who earned a livelihood by singing lays at the courts of princes. In the *Iliad* and *Odyssey* the poet says next to nothing about himself. This may imply that he was of a social position inferior

to that of his patrons, and belonged to the class of δημιοεργοί (*Od.* 17. 383). His tastes may to some extent be seen in his similes, which are drawn from contemporary life and show an interest in humble people quite unlike the heroes and heroines of his poems, in handicrafts and agricultural pursuits, in animals and birds.

**4.** Our ignorance of Homer's date, place, and life has led to scepticism about his existence. It has been thought that the poems are collections of lays put together from different sources, or original poems much expanded and altered, or single examples of poems of which many different variants existed. The early arguments for such views, based on the belief that no man could have composed poems of such a length before writing was known, have now been dispelled by our knowledge of what memory can do when writing is not familiar. Other arguments, such as the presence of repetitions and inconsistencies, are less powerful when we realize that such poems were meant not to be read but to be heard, and that in such conditions the poet cannot be so exact about details as he can when he is helped by a written text. Still other arguments based on the varying treatment of the gods, of moral questions, of history and mythology, do not necessarily prove variety of authorship, since it is at least possible that Homer belonged to an old tradition which provided him with a very mixed collection of materials, on which he drew freely and not always critically.

**5.** On the other hand, the *Iliad* and the *Odyssey* each shows in itself the marks of a controlling and unifying poet. In the *Iliad* the whole poem hangs on the wrath of Achilles, and though many other episodes are introduced, this gives a unity to the whole. The last book picks up the themes of the first and shows the end of the wrath with which the poem began. The *Odyssey* shows what Ithaca was before Odysseus returned and then his return with his triumphant conduct of it. In each poem the characters are admirably consistent, convincing, and even elaborated—a trait unlikely if many hands have been at work. In each poem the language, rich, complex, and traditional though it is, seems to show no real differences between one section and another. The use of abstract nouns, of the digamma, of Aeolic forms, of patronymics, all seem to be spread equally through the whole work. Any extensive omission of a long passage from either poem in the belief that it is a later addition seriously impairs the structure and makes the plot less easy to understand. In both poems devices such as similes are used on a consistent plan, revealing the individual tastes of the poet and providing a variety where it is most needed in the narrative. Each poem shows that it is a whole and suggests that even if many hands have gone to its making, most of the poets preceded the actual author, who made use of their work but harmonized it according to his own ideal of composition.

**6.** These considerations do not prove that the *Iliad* and *Odyssey* were necessarily composed by the same poet. This has been doubted even by some who believe that each is itself the work of a single man. The Alexandrian grammarians who held this view were known as the 'Chorizontes'. There are certainly differences between the two poems, though not all are equally important. Much may be explained by differences of theme and of setting. The *Iliad* deals with war, the *Odyssey* with peace; therefore the social structure of life at Troy is different from that at Ithaca. The *Iliad* with its long accounts of battles is more monotonous than the *Odyssey*; therefore it uses many more similes to diversify its narrative. Many words appear in one poem and not in the other, but that is to be expected from two stories so different. The *Odyssey* has an element of fairytale almost lacking in the *Iliad*, but that is natural in telling of a man's wanderings at the ends of the world. It places its emphasis on wits, while the *Iliad* places its on courage, but that does not mean that the poems were written in different ages; for a heroic age may well admire cunning as much as bravery, and in any case the cunning of Odysseus is already manifest and admired in the *Iliad*.

**7.** The *Odyssey* certainly looks as if it were composed to be a sequel to the *Iliad*. The events which fall between the two stories, the Wooden Horse, the sack of Troy, the returns of the Achaeans, the murder of Agamemnon, are all introduced, so that we have in effect a continuous narrative. Important characters of the *Iliad* who have no essential part in the story of Odysseus—Helen, Menelaus, Nestor, even Achilles and Aias—appear at one point or another, before or after death, in the *Odyssey*. The *Odyssey* closes with a second Νέκυια in which the great ghosts of Troy make their last bow on the stage as if to make a finale to both poems. Moreover, these characters preserve their individuality from one poem to the other; Odysseus, though depicted on a far greater scale, is recognizably the same man that he was in the *Iliad*, Nestor is no less garrulous and reminiscent, Helen still shows wisdom learned in suffering. Both poems, too, are similar in structure, though the *Odyssey* shows an advance in its treatment of events which take place contemporaneously. In both we find similarities of technique, such as the way in which an action is first suggested and then postponed, the abrupt transition from one episode to another, the rapidity with which the final crisis comes when it comes, the slackening of tension after the crisis, and the quiet end. In both we find repeated lines and even passages which suggest that the poet, well instructed in his formulae, felt no qualms about using them when they suited his need. Compared even with Hesiod or the *Homeric Hymns* the *Iliad* and *Odyssey* seem to belong to a world of their own and suggest that they are the work of a single poet.

**8.** On the other hand, there are, undeniably, serious differences between the two poems. The *Odyssey*, at least in its second half, seems to lack the rapidity and force of the *Iliad*. The poet does not lead to his crisis with the same directness, and in the handling of it there is not the same immediacy of effect. The difference may of course be due to advance of years; Homer may have begun to fail in his later poem (as [Longinus] suggests, *Subl.* 9). Again, in the *Odyssey* the gods are not what they were in the *Iliad*. Certain episodes show the old gay touch, but their position is, on the whole, different, and in the relations between Odysseus and Athene we may perhaps see a new view of the ways of the gods with men. Finally, the *Odyssey* seems to take a different view of life from the *Iliad*. The Suitors are lower characters than anyone except Thersites, and their end, deserved though it may be, is conceived in a harsher and less tragic temper than that in which Achilles revenges the death of Patroclus on Hector. These differences can be explained either as the result of passing years on a single poet or as the work of a second poet who admired and imitated the poet of the *Iliad* but did not see eye to eye with him on all points. The first alternative seems more likely because the differences are outweighed by the similarities and are at least explicable if we assume the *Odyssey* to be the later of the two poems.

**9.** Even if we admit that a single poet composed both poems, we must also admit that he owed a very great deal to tradition. The extent of his debt may be seen in the many stories which he mentions but does not elaborate, showing that they were already known, in his use of standard epithets for his characters, who have often grown beyond them, in his inconsistent treatment of the gods, now as real moral forces, now as figures of comic relief, in the episodic character of his narrative, a

survival from the method of short narrative lays, in his language, which was never a spoken tongue, but, being drawn from different dialects and full of archaisms, artificial lengthening, synonyms, and alternative forms, shows the marks of many years given to its making. Above all, this traditional character is apparent in the important fact that Homer composes not with words but with groups of words or formulae. In almost every line we find a set of words that occurs elsewhere, often many times. This technique belongs to improvised verse. The poet who improvises must learn formulae before he can practise his art, and though there is no reason to believe that the *Iliad* and *Odyssey* were ever improvised, it is clear that their technique was derived from improvisation. Of these formulae many must have existed before Homer, and at times we may see traces of his indebtedness when a phrase is not perfectly suited to its context. But such formulae were no doubt altered and new formulae invented, and there is no reason to think that Homer took over all his from other poets. In fact the success of many parts of his poetry is unthinkable if he confined himself entirely to traditional phrases. So, too, in his plots we may find hints of an earlier treatment which is not his. In the poems which lay behind the *Iliad* Achilles seems actually to have mutilated Hector, but Homer avoids this and makes his hero give back the dead body to Priam. In the stories of Odysseus there must have been variants of the means by which he was recognized; in the *Odyssey* these are combined and worked into a single story. These earlier versions were obliterated by Homer and quite forgotten, but it seems next to certain that he used them and improved on them.

**10.** Even if Homer composed the *Iliad* and *Odyssey*, we cannot assume that we have them just as he left them. There are certainly interpolations in them. Some are not serious; others, like passages in *Od*. 11, may easily be detected. But it is quite possible that there are still others, though there is no sure way to mark them. The language, too, has certainly been altered from its first appearance, notably by the substitution of Attic forms due to the recitation of the poems at Athens and to the fact that Athens was the centre of the Greek book-trade. Other changes are due to the misunderstanding of archaic words and their distortion or replacement by others. And the text may have suffered more than this. If it was preserved, as is possible, in the oral tradition of the Homeridae, it cannot but have suffered seriously in the centuries between Homer's death and the appearance of the first texts in the time of Pisistratus. Even if it was written down much earlier and preserved with reverence as a sacred book, it may still have suffered serious changes. In any case it is not as we have it that the author left it, and we cannot confidently restore it to its original purity.

**11.** Whatever our views may be on the authorship of the Homeric poems, there is no doubt of their astonishing quality. They combine legends of a very distant past with a lively sense of the living scene, and though their characters are heroes and heroines, they are remarkably real. The story is told with a great simplicity, but this makes its episodes more dramatic, and in their greatest moments they contain some of the greatest poetry in the world. The plot moves with an unusual speed and the climaxes in both poems make an overwhelming impact. The rich, traditional language is ready for every occasion and, despite its richness, helps to maintain the essential simplicity. The poems are variously exciting, humorous, pathetic, and dramatic, and despite their fantastic elements never far from common humanity. The similes present a whole world of contemporary people and things which lie outside the actual heroic tale, and the description of the shield of Achilles is surely the poet's vision of his own world as he knew it in war and peace. The poet or poets fully deserve their place at the beginning of European literature, since they have marked out for succeeding generations what the poetry of action and suffering ought to be.

For the allegorical interpretations of Homer, see ALLEGORY.

TEXT. *Iliad*, ed. T. W. Allen (1931), with prolegomena and full apparatus; *Odyssey*, ed. T. W. Allen (O.C.T., 1906).
COMMENTARY. *Iliad*, W. Leaf (1900–02); *Odyssey*, W. B. Stanford (1947).
CRITICISM. F. A. Wolff, *Prolegomena ad Homerum*[2] (1876); K. Lachmann, *Betrachtungen über Homers Ilias*[3] (1874); P. Cauer, *Grundfragen der Homerkritik*[2] (1921–3); E. Drerup, *Das Homerproblem in der Gegenwart* (1921); U. von Wilamowitz-Moellendorff, *Die Ilias und Homer* (1916); J. A. Scott, *The Unity of Homer* (U.S.A. 1921); C. M. Bowra, *Tradition and Design in the Iliad* (1930); W. J. Woodhouse, *The Composition of Homer's Odyssey* (1930); M. Parry, *L'Épithète traditionelle dans Homère* (1928); M. Nilsson, *Homer and Mycenae* (1933); H. L. Lorimer, *Homer and the Monuments* (1950); T. B. L. Webster, *From Mycenae to Homer* (1958); D. L. Page, *History and the Homeric Iliad* (1959); A. J. B. Wace and F. H. Stubbings, *A Companion to Homer* (1962); G. S. Kirk, *The Songs of Homer* (1962); A. Lesky, *PW* Suppl. xi, 687 ff.          C. M. B.

**HOMERIDAE,** a guild devoted to reciting Homer's poetry (Pind. *Nem.* 2. 1, Pl. *Phdr.* 252 b) and telling stories about his life (Pl. *Resp.* 599 e, Isoc. 10. 65; the extant 'Lives of Homer' must ultimately derive from this source). Ordinary rhapsodes (q.v.) looked up to them as authorities and arbiters. They flourished in Chios, and it is said that they were originally Homer's descendants (Harp., s.v. Ὁμηρίδαι, quoting Acusilaus and Hellanicus), but later admitted others, who foisted much of their own work on Homer (schol. Pind. *Nem.* 2. 1; *see* CYNAETHUS). It was on them that Chios based its claim to Homer (Strabo 645, *Certamen* 13–15).

T. W. Allen, *Homer, the Origins and the Transmission* (1924), 42 ff.
M. L. W.

**HOMONOIA,** agreement or concord between the members of a community. The bitter experience of faction in Greek States led to much theoretical praise of concord, also from early Hellenistic times to a certain amount of cult (altar at Syracuse, Livy 24. 22. 13; at Olympia, Paus. 5. 14. 9; inscriptional dedications, see Stoll in Roscher's *Lex.* i. 2701, 30 ff.), also quite common occurrence on coins (ibid. 2702, 31 ff.), which may or may not connote actual cult in the States issuing them. Hence the cult was occasionally projected into remote antiquity, as Ap. Rhod. 2. 717 ff., where the foundation of a shrine of Homonoia is ascribed to the Argonauts (q.v.). No doubt some of the dedications, etc., refer at least equally to Concordia (q.v.).

See in general Eiliv Skard, *Euergetes-Concordia* (1932), 67 ff.; W. W. Tarn, *Alexander the Great and the Unity of Mankind* (1933); and various references in the index to Nilsson, *GGR* ii.      H. J. R.

**HONESTIORES.** The Romans made a broad distinction, which was at first social but acquired in the Principate and thereafter an increasing number of legal consequences, between an upper class usually termed *honestiores* and a lower class of *humiliores*. No legal definition of the two classes is found, and the allocation of an individual to one or the other was probably at the discretion of the court. The legal consequences lay in part in the private law, but were most marked in the criminal law, *honestiores* being subject to milder penalties than *humiliores* (rarely the death penalty, never death by crucifixion or *bestiis obicere*; *relegatio* (q.v.) *in insulam* in place of forced labour in the mines, etc.). The distinction is not the same as that drawn in the later Empire between *potentiores* and *tenuiores*. The legal relevance of the latter distinction lies not in privileges conferred on the *potentiores*, but on the contrary in the restrictions which the legislator attempted to impose on their abuse of their wealth or position.

G. Cardascia, *Rev. Hist. de Droit* 1950, 305 ff., 461 ff.      B. N.

**HONESTUS** of Corinth, author of ten epigrams in the Greek Anthology and some others discovered on stone near Thespiae, was apparently contemporary with Tiberius. His poems lack all but historical interest.

Gow and Page, 2400 ff. Cichorius, *Röm. Studien* viii. 11; H. Dessau, *Hermes* 1912; E. Preuner, *Hermes* 1920.      G. H.

**HONEY** (μέλι, *mel*), the chief sweetener known to the ancients, who understood apiculture (cf. Varro, *Rust.* 3. 16) and appreciated the honey-producing qualities of flowers and localities. Hymettus honey was famed for pale colour and sweet flavour; Sicilian (particularly Hybla) as proverbially good; Corsican, harsh and bitter; Pontic, poisonous, inducing madness. Honey was used in cookery, confectionery, and medicine, and valued for its preservative qualities. Its religious associations derive from the notion that it is a *ros caelestis*, which bees gather in the upper air as well as from flowers (cf. Arist. *Hist. An.* 5. 22, 553[b]29). Poets repeat the fancy that it dripped from trees in the Golden Age. As celestial it possesses mystic virtues, was used in libations for the dead (see S. Eitrem, *Opferritus* (1915), *passim*), and in literature is given to infants to impart numinous qualities, as wisdom or eloquence (see H. Usener, *Kl. Schr.* iv (1913), 398 ff.). Bees fed the infant Plato with honey (Cic. *Div.* 1. 78: cf. A. S. Pease, ad loc.), and Zeus was called Melissaios from a similar legend of his Cretan birth.

W. H. Roscher, *Nektar und Ambrosia* (1883); W. Robert-Tornow, *De apium mellisque apud veteres significatione et symbolica et mythologica* (1893); W. Telfer, *JTS* 1927, 167 ff.; W. Michaelis in Kittel's *Theologisches Wörterbuch zum Neuen Testament* iv. 556–7 (1942); and W. F. Arndt and F. W. Gingrich in *The Greek–English Lexicon of the New Testament* (1957). *See also* BEE-KEEPING, MELISSA. W. T.

**HONORIUS,** FLAVIUS, West Roman Emperor (A.D. 393–423), born in 384, was the younger son of Theodosius I (q.v.), who elevated him to the rank of Augustus in 393. He became sole ruler of the West when his father died in 395; but the effective ruler until 408 was Stilicho (q.v.). The main events of his reign thereafter were the sieges of Rome in 408–10, a period which Honorius spent safely in Ravenna, the occupation of Spain by the Vandals and other barbarians in 409, and the loss of control in Britain. In addition, numerous usurpers rose and fell. Honorius died without issue (423). He was one of the feeblest of all the Roman Emperors, and when he did intervene in politics his interventions were usually calamitous.      E. A. T.

**HONOS** and **VIRTUS.** These abstractions, representing bravery in battle and its due reward, had three temples in Rome; one outside the Porta Collina (Cic. *Leg.* 2. 58), to Honos; one *ad portam Capenam*, dedicated originally to Honos by Q. Fabius Maximus Verrucosus in 234 B.C., then enlarged into a double temple to both by M. Marcellus (Livy 25. 40. 2–3; 27. 25. 7–9; 29. 11. 13), because two deities could not be worshipped in one *cella*; one somewhere near the Capitolium, built by Marius after defeating the Cimbri and Teutones.

Platner–Ashby, 259; Wissowa, *RK* 149 ff.; Latte, *RR* 235 ff.; M. Bieber, *AJArch.* 1945, 25 ff.      H. J. R.

**HOPLITES** (ὁπλῖται) were the regular type of heavy-armed infantry in the Greek city-states. Citizens who could not maintain horses, yet had sufficient property to equip themselves with full personal armour, were required to serve as hoplites. In the later fifth century at Athens the hoplite qualification was regarded as equivalent to the old Solonian class of the *zeugitai* (q.v.).

The body-armour of the hoplite consisted of a helmet with nasal and cheek pieces, a breastplate, and greaves of bronze. The heavy bronze shield was his chief defence; it was circular or elliptical in shape and was usually secured on the left arm and hand by a central metal arm-band and a handgrip on the inner rim. The iron sword was short and straight; the spear, some 9 feet long, was held in the hand for thrusting. When in proper formation on their appropriate terrain hoplites were able to sustain effectively the assaults of archers or cavalry. But they were slow and heavy in attack, and when in difficult country or scattered they were easily defeated in detail.

J. Kromayer and G. Veith, *Heerwesen und Kriegführung der Griechen und Römer* (1928), 50 ff.; H. L. Lorimer, 'The Hoplite Phalanx', *BSA* 1947, 76 ff.; A. N. Snodgrass, *Arms and Armour of the Greeks* (1967).                                        H. W. P.

**HORAE,** goddesses of the Seasons in Greek mythology. In Homer the Horae roll aside the veil of clouds from the gate of Olympus (*Il.* 5. 749; 8. 393), which is perhaps a mythological expression of the belief that they could give rain or heat. Hesiod (*Th.* 901) makes the Horae daughters of Justice and gives to them individual names, *Eunomia* (Good Government), *Dike* (Right), and *Eirene* (Peace). Commonly they are, however, regarded as goddesses who come with the changes of seasons and make flowers and plants grow. Their names and number vary from region to region. In Attica these names were *Thallo, Karpo,* and perhaps *Auxo,* referring to growth, flowering, and ripeness of vegetation (C. Robert, *Comment. in hon. Mommsen,* 143). These Horae of fertility had a place on the lips of peasants (Ar. *Pax* 1168). The Hesiodic Horae, who stand for ethical and political ideas, are mentioned in some later inscriptions (Kaibel, *Epigr. Gr.* 1110). Because they have the power to make things and beings grow and because the gifts of the Horae are pleasant, they are wel-come guests at marriages and births of Olympians and heroes (Hes. *Op.* 75; *Hymn. Hom. Ven.* (vi), 5; Pind. *Pyth.* 9. 60; Paus. 2. 13. 3; Moschus 2. 164). When Hellenic religion develops to a more unified and intel-lectual state, the Seasons, whether three or four, are also called *Horae.* Spring, Summer, Autumn, Winter all bring their proper blessings and are depicted in art with appropriate attributes. The regularity of seasons was a favourite argument of Greek philosophers for the exist-ence of a divine world order (Plato, *Epin.* 977 b; von Arnim, *SVF* i, no. 499; cf. Aratus, *Phaen.* 550). Seasons appear in Roman houses and on Roman tombs (F. Cumont, *Rev. Arch.* 1916, ii, p. 1). The Horae are associ-ated with many deities, e.g. Demeter, Kore, Pan, Apollo, Dionysus, Aphrodite, and Helios, but only as subordinate companions. Philochorus describes some details of the cult of the Horae in Athens (ap. Athen. 2. 38; 14. 656). They were worshipped also in Argos and Olympia. In art, Horae are first shown on the François vase, without any individualizing attributes, whereas the later Season-Horae are carefully distinguished from each other by attributive plants and animals.

P. Herrmann, *De Horarum figuris* (1887); J. A. Hild in Dar.–Sag., s.v.; A. Merlin, *Monuments Piot* 1934, 133; M. P. Nilsson, *Primitive Time Reckoning* (Lund, 1920); Farnell, *Cults* v, 426; F. Schroeder, *Gymnasium* 1956, 57.                                        G. M. A. H.

**HORATII** were, according to a popular tradition (pro-bably independent of Greek literary influence), three Roman brothers in the time of Tullus Hostilius. Two of them were killed in combat with the Curiatii, three Alban brothers, while the survivor was tried, but ac-quitted on appeal, for the murder of his sister Horatia, betrothed to one of the Curiatii. An ancient ritual cele-brated at the *Tigillum sororium* and traditionally explained as a commemoration of Horatia probably gave rise to the story, unless it was invented as a precedent for the insti-tution of the *provocatio ad populum* (*see* PROVOCATIO).

Ogilvie, *Comm. Livy 1–5,* 109 ff.                                        P. T.

**HORATIUS** (1, *PW* 9) **COCLES,** a Roman who tradi-tionally held back the Etruscan army of Porsenna (q.v.) from the wooden Sublician bridge until it could be de-molished, and then, despite his wounds, swam across the Tiber to safety. Polybius, however, records (6. 55) that Horatius was drowned. The story is probably an aetio-logical myth. Opposite the Sublician bridge, in the area consecrated to Vulcan, there stood an ancient statue of a lame, one-eyed man, erected traditionally to Horatius. In fact, however, it represented not the wounded Horatius but Vulcan (one-eyed as a sun god, and lame like the Greek Hephaestus, or rather because the primitive sculp-tor could not express the movement of the legs). The earliest allusion to the story is probably in Callimachus' *Aetia* (4. 107 Pf.).

G. De Sanctis, *Riv. fil.* 1935 (*contra,* G. Pasquali, *Terze pagine stravaganti* (1942), 96 ff., and Walbank, *Polybius* i. 740 f.); Ogilvie, *Comm. Livy 1–5,* 258 ff.                                        P. T.

**HORATIUS** (2) **FLACCUS,** QUINTUS, was born at Venusia (*Venosa*) in Apulia in Dec. 65 B.C. (*Epist.* i. 20. 26 f.); the day was the eighth (*Vita*). He died on 27 Nov. 8 B.C. (*Vita*). Horace says that his father's family was of servile origin, and that his father was an auctioneer, with a small-holding (*Sat.* i. 6). His father took him all the way to Rome for schooling under Orbilius (*Sat.* i. 6; *Epist.* ii. 1. 69 ff.). Horace then went to the university at Athens, and there was enticed by Brutus to serve under him as *tribunus militum* until the defeat at Philippi in 42 B.C. He returned to Italy to find his father's house and land gone in the confiscations; then, as he says with humorous exaggeration, *paupertas impulit audax ut versus facerem* (*Epist.* ii. 2. 41 ff.). But just as his education suggests more paternal wealth than Horace implies, so here humour conceals the reality: he obtained a pardon for his political indiscretion and purchased the post of *scriba quaestorius,* a keeper of records to the quaestors (*Vita*). Yet there is an important truth in the humour: Horace's poetical activity caught the attention of Maecenas to whom he was introduced by Virgil (*Sat.* i. 6). From this time (perhaps about 38 B.C.—*Epod.* i. 25–32; *Sat.* ii. 6. 53 ff.), Horace became an increasingly important member of a circle of writers who, through Maecenas, were collected under the patronage of Augustus. He frequently mentions his Sabine farm which was an early benefit of this patronage. He was able to refuse a request from Augustus to become his secretary, and the *Vita* preserves fragments of surprisingly jocular letters from the *princeps* to Horace: these facts are a measure of Horace's success in winning the confidence of the most powerful man in Rome. A less surprisingly warm relationship existed between Horace and Maecenas whose will contained the words (addressed to Augustus) *Horati Flacci ut mei esto memor.* As long as Maecenas was the intermediary between poets and Augustus this affection is reflected in the many poetic addresses to him; in Horace's later work, however, there is only one brief reference to Maecenas (*Carm.* iv. 11. 19). This need reflect no cooling of affection; poetic addresses, how-ever friendly, were formalities, and, since Horace now addresses Augustus directly, the simplest explanation is that soon after 20 B.C. Augustus no longer felt the need of a patronage–secretary relationship between himself and certain carefully selected writers. Horace was successful with the great and he rose above his humble birth: he expresses pride in both achievements, but a cautious reader will note that an unflattering description of his own personal appearance follows (*Epist.* i. 20. 19 ff.). Horace's self-revelation is often illusory.

WORKS

**Epodes.** Seventeen poems (eleven in iambics and six in a combination of iambics with dactyls) in professed imitation of Archilochus. Eight are invectives (3, 4, 5, 6, 8, 10, 12, 17), but only the joking attack on Maecenas (3) for giving Horace garlic concerns a real person (the identification by Porphyrio of Canidia in 5 and 17 as a Gratidia is both dubious since it could be an invention, and unhelpful since nothing is otherwise known of her). The feigned bitterness and ferocity, combined at times with obscenity (especially in 8 and 12), derive from Archilochus (e.g. with 10 cf. frs. 79 and 80 D.) or Hipponax (mentioned by Horace in 6). A poem of Archilochus seems to be the model for 2 (fr. 22 D.), sixty-six lines of which praise the joys of the country and then a surprise ending of four lines reveals that Alfius the moneylender has been speaking. The rest of the *Epodes* look forward to the *Odes*: 11 and 15 are on love (treated rather amusingly), 14 explains to Maecenas that a love-affair has delayed publication of the *Epodes* and 13 makes preparations for a symposium. 1, 7, 9, and 16 are political, and, while they seem to have analogues in Archilochus (with 16 cf. Arch. frs. 52 and 54 D.), they represent something quite new in Roman poetry which Horace gradually evolved through the *Epodes* and *Odes*. Since 1 and 9 concern the battle of Actium, while 16 depends on Verg. *Ecl.* 4 (see *Hermes* 1938, 237 ff.), the *Epodes* range between 40 and 31 B.C. and were published about 30 B.C. Despite Horace's claim to have introduced the iambics of Archilochus to Rome (*Epist.* i. 19. 23 ff.), the composition and style of the *Epodes* display polished techniques derived from Hellenistic Greek poetry and particularly epigrams. The actuality of Archilochus is absent (as Horace says, loc. cit.), and, in this respect, Horace differed from Catullus who might otherwise be claimed as a predecessor (though Catullus, in spite of apparent similarities, is unlikely to have regarded Archilochus as his model).

**Satires.** Horace called the work *satirae*, but sometimes referred to the genre (especially together with the *Epistles*) as *sermones.* i. 5 (*iter Brundisinum*) refers to an event of 37 B.C. and this is the only firm date. Book ii was published in 30 B.C. since ii. 6. 53–5 refer to events of late 31 B.C. Each book is formally homogeneous: in book i the author speaks and presents his views; in book ii all of the satires but one are written in the form of a dialogue. Book i contains ten satires (a fashionable number, cf. Virgil's *Eclogues*); book ii contains 8, no doubt because some of the satires are long and the bulk is about the same as that of book i (and of the twenty epistles in *Epist.* i and of *Epist.* ii if the *Ars Poetica* is added). Though Ennius and Pacuvius had written *satirae*, the Horatian form of the genre was the invention of Lucilius (q.v.). Horace's dependence on him extended to subjects and motifs (e.g. the *iter Brundisinum* i. 5 corresponds to Lucilius' *iter Siculum*), but Horace's greatest debt was the autobiographical form: every aspect of the composition proceeds from and reflects the poet's own life—opinions, ideas, adventures, food, family, friends, literary criticism, and, particularly, views on morality. Horace's own view of Lucilius' work can be shown to develop, and the most adequate expression of it (ii. 1. 30 ff.) most closely corresponds to Horace's own method. The two satires (i. 7 and 8) which appear least autobiographical (though 8 contains Canidia: cf. *Epodes* 5 and 17) are perhaps earliest. The characters criticized are often traditional or invented (e.g. Gallonius, Maenius); or, again, unimportant or dead or both ('Tillius, Priscus, Tigellius). Sustained biting satire of the Juvenalian type

is absent, and vicious personalities against the living, if present at all, are very rare. In this respect Horace differs from Lucilius, as also in the polished skill of his style and metre. The metre is a careful informalizing of the epic hexameter, which, like the style, is infinitely varied between the extremes of high epic and conversational laxity. Such a degree of stylistic flexibility is unknown outside the *Satires* and *Epistles* of Horace, and it is the product of careful artistry. Most characteristic of the composition is a fund of stories (αἶνοι), skilfully and pointedly told, that break and illustrate the flow of ideas. Perhaps most disconcerting and surprising is the humour that enlivens every subject, concealing the real mind of the writer, playing with equal ease over obscenities as over the pomposities of philosophers, and mocking the writer no less than his world.

**Odes** (*Carmina*). Books i–iii were published as a unit, framed between i. 1 in which Horace hopes to be placed in the canon of lyric poets and iii. 30 where he claims an immortal lyric achievement. The earliest datable ode is i. 37 (after Cleopatra's death in 30 B.C.) and the collection was probably published about 23 B.C. The collection was addressed to Maecenas. Horace claims the early Greek lyric poets, Sappho and Alcaeus, as his model, and he claims to be the first Roman to introduce their style and rhythms into Latin (the two highly idiosyncratic poems of Catullus 11 and 51 impair that claim no more than the slight similarities between Archilochus and Catullus impair Horace's claim in respect of the *Epodes*). In spite of this his stylistic debt to the polished techniques of Alexandrian poets is very great (as a comparison, e.g., of i. 10 with Alcaeus fr. 308 L. and P. will show), and odes like i. 5, 28, 30; iii. 22, 26 clearly owe much to the technique of Hellenistic epigrams. The scholiast Porphyrio says that i. 45 was modelled on Bacchylides, and the poem is unique among the *Odes* in treating an epic theme in straight narrative. The ode i. 12 is modelled fairly closely on Pindar, *Ol.* 2 and iii. 4 on *Pyth.* 1; while i. 23 is related to a fragment of Anacreon (fr. 39 D.). These odes are not truly lyric either in an ancient or a modern sense (*see* LYRIC POETRY, LATIN). Mostly, in imitation of early Greek lyric, they address individuals and are given a personal point of reference (sometimes highly contrived as in iii. 11 and 27); exceptions like i. 2 or iii. 6, which are closer to the technique of the *Epodes* (where Horace was prepared to address his countrymen in general), may be relatively early. There are eighty-eight poems in the collection, with the widest conceivable range of mood and topic. Some are hymnic in form or contain hymnic elements, like i. 10, 17 (combined with invitation), 21, 30, 32, 35; iii. 11, 13, 18, 21, 22, 26, 30. Others have the form of invitations or give orders for preparations for a symposium; this must have been a traditional poetic form (cf. Catullus 13) but Horace extended it and adapted it to accommodate serious reflections on life and politics in a great variety of ways: e.g. i. 7, 9, 17, 20, 26, 27, 28; ii. 3, 7, 11, 14, iii. 8, 14, 17, 18, 21, 28, 29 (in all of these—though in very different ways and with a great variety of tone—the occasion and structure are provided by the idea of a symposium). Another form is that of the *recusatio* (going back to Callimachus' refusal—prologue of *Aitia*—to write an epic poem): Horace made this into a poetic form in which, while explaining that he could not treat great political themes in his poetry, he treated them by a form of *praeteritio*: e.g. i. 6; ii. 1, 9 (where Horace urges Valgius to join him in praising the deeds of Augustus), 12. Horace's love-poems are (usually amusing) essays in a form of poetic composition rather than expressions of a human experience: i. 5, 8, 11, 13, 17, 19, 22, 23, 25, 30, 33; ii. 4, 5, 8; iii. 7, 9, 10, 15, 26, 27, 28. When addressing others his tone is teasing: when speaking of himself there is no attempt to convey self-revelatory experience. Horace's most striking innovation was to introduce serious political statement into non-epic Roman poetry: such statements pervade all his poetic forms (not simply the so-called Roman Odes iii. 1–6) and the novelty may be characterized by comparing Catullus 34 with i. 21 which is modelled on it: Catullus concentrates on the traditional Greek hymnic forms and the actual prayer is the bald *Romulique . . . bona sospites ope gentem*. Horace concentrates his prayer on Apollo and the whole final stanza summarizes hopes for the present political situation. Many of the odes are complex, either combining several themes (e.g. i. 7, 9, 12; iii. 6, 11, 14, 24, 29) or making demands on the reader with a dramatic setting only gradually revealed by hints (e.g. i. 27, 28; iii. 8, 19). Horace's themes are often criticized as commonplace—life and death, etc. The criticism is too easy: it misses originality of treatment (e.g. i. 24 where the *consolatio* has a new vivid, almost colloquial, form) and originality of expression, in which usage, choice (including borrowings from prose: see Axelson in Bibliography), and order of words produce novelty in Roman poetry. The *Odes*, like all Horace's work, abound in illustrative αἶνοι and portraits which are often the poetic core of an ode: e.g. iii. 5 (Regulus), iii. 6 (the modern girl and the young Italian of an earlier century), iii. 25 (the Bacchante), iii. 29 (the Tiber in flood), i. 4 (simply a series of pictures), i. 25 (the old prostitute). A similar effect, on a smaller scale, is often achieved by a mythological reference, made with great economy (e.g. i. 28. 7 ff.), or a name that conjures up the great past of Rome or the sense of a far-off region or a loved and familiar place: these are often the more effective for their very lack of precision and detail (e.g. i. 12. 33 ff.; ii. 1. 25 ff.; iii. 14. 17 ff.; i. 22. 5 ff.; ii. 20. 17 ff.; iii. 4. 14 ff.; iii. 29. 5 ff.). Care and polish (*limae labor et mora*, *AP* 291) and technical excellence were Horace's ideals, but the effect of the *Odes* is seldom laboured.

Horace ceased writing lyrics after the publication of *Odes* i–iii; he resumed when he was commissioned by Augustus to write the *Carmen Saeculare* (a choral lyric in Sapphic metre to be performed by a choir of twenty-seven boys and twenty-seven girls) for the *ludi saeculares* in 17 B.C. The great marble inscription recording the ceremonies and the part played by Horace was found in 1890 (*ILS* 5050). The ode is addressed to Apollo, Diana, and the Capitoline deities; in the form of a prayer to them, the achievements of Augustus are reviewed. Horace continued writing lyrics, and *Odes* iv was the result; the latest datable ode is 6 (return of Augustus in 13 B.C.). There are fifteen odes and the collection is addressed to Paulus Fabius (q.v. 9) Maximus (aristocratic friend, almost relative, of Augustus). Some of the odes are similar to the earlier compositions: 7 (on Spring, cf. i. 4); 8 and 9 (on the power of poetry); 10 and 13 (love); 11 and 12 (invitations); 2 and 15 (*recusationes*). But serious treatment of political themes predominates, and the *Vita* says that 4 and 14 (*epinikia* for Tiberius and Drusus) were specially requested by Augustus. The style of writing and composition is more elevated, more nearly Pindaric, than the odes of i–iii; apart from this, what has been said of books i–iii applies also to iv. Of the 103 odes in the four books, 37 are composed in Alcaic stanzas, 25 in Sapphic, and 34 are in various forms of Asclepiad (the remaining 7 are mainly isolated examples). *See* METRE, LATIN III.

**Epistles.** The first book of *Epistulae* was probably published in 20 B.C. (i. 20. 26 ff.), if the reference to the Spanish victory of Agrippa (i. 12. 26) can be referred to a beginning of the campaign in 20 B.C. None is demonstrably earlier than 23 B.C. (13 refers to the presentation of *Odes* i–iii to Augustus), but some may have been written while *Odes* i–iii were still being composed (cf. *Satires* and *Epodes*). Letters in verse had been written before, especially by Lucilius; but the *Epistles* of Horace are an original creation, a form of poetic composition which enabled him to treat any subject from a personal and subjective point of view. In i. 1 to Maecenas, Horace jokingly claims to have given up poetry in favour of the far more important philosophy; but such 'philosophy' as is found in the *Epistles* is of a very homespun, untechnical sort: how to get on with great men, the dangers of avarice, the excellence of the simple life, town versus country life, etc. None can be shown to be addressed to a fictitious person (but to Maecenas, Lollius, Aristius Fuscus, Tiberius, Horace's bailiff, Manlius Torquatus, Tibullus, etc.) and the epistolary form is often only casually indicated (most often by the mere geographical separation of Horace from his addressee, but sometimes by formal indications: e.g. 5. 30; 9, *epistula commendaticia*; 10. 1 ff., 49–50; 16. 4)—20 is an address to the book itself as if it were a slave for sale. The element of reality probably ceases here, and the occasion of each epistle is fictitious, a dramatic setting for the composition (e.g. i. 5 is an invitation and closely comparable to the examples of the form in the *Odes*): that is, the reader is never required by Horace to believe that he is reading a real letter, sent on a particular occasion and personal to the addressee, and Horace is at no pains to create such an illusion. The value of the form was that it provided Horace with a framework for informal, conversational composition; full expression could be given to the writer's personality and the writing has all the humour and lively variety of the *Satires*, with an equal fund of illustrative stories and portraits but with more stylistic polish and refinement.

*Epist.* ii. 1 to Augustus was written after 17 B.C. (132–7 seem to refer to *Carm. Saec.*) and probably after Drusus' Alpine victories of 15 B.C. (cf. 252 with *Carm.* iv. 14. 11 f.) but before the publication of *Carm.* iv. *Epist.* ii. 2, to Florus, was probably written in 19 B.C. while Tiberius was still in Armenia. Both are long (270 and 216 lines) and concern literature: ii. 2 is close to i. 1 and asserts Horace's reasons for concerning himself with philosophy, not lyric poetry; ii. 1 is about poetry in the context of the Augustan regime and surveys the earlier, still admired, literature of Rome in its relationship to society, asserting the merits of contemporary poetry. The conversational technique and the consequent absence of a strict logical framework combine to obscure the movement of thought in both these *Epistles*, a difficulty scarcely found in the shorter, less complicated *Epistles* of book i.

**Ars Poetica:** this is another *epistle*, addressed to a Piso and his two sons, but by the time of Quintilian it had been given the more formal title (*Inst.*, *Ep. ad Tryph.* 2, viii. 3. 60); it is not attached to the *Epistles* in the MSS. Its date and the identity of the Pisones are unknown (Porphyrio says he was the consul of 15 B.C.). If any weight can be given to the joking lines 301–9, they would most naturally suggest the context of *Epist.* i. 1 and ii. 2, i.e. about 19 B.C. and before 17 B.C. It is a most puzzling work and, despite its skill and humour, little is said about poetry that seems worthy of Horace. It concentrates heavily on the traditional literary genres of epic and drama, and it is hard to believe that what Horace says was intended to have relevance to the contemporary literary scene, except for the general exhortations to care and polish in style. Porphyrio says of it: *. . . congessit praecepta Neoptolemi* τοῦ Παριανοῦ *de arte poetica, non quidem omnia sed eminentissima*. Fragments of the fifth book of Philodemus' Περὶ ποιημάτων were found at Herculaneum, and they preserve some account, at second-hand, of the views of Neoptolemus. Various attempts have been made to show that Horace followed Neoptolemus and that the structure of the *Ars Poetica* depends on him. In spite of this, it remains most probable that Horace constructed the work himself with the same informality and lack of framework as the other *Epistles*. It is impossible to estimate his debt to Neoptolemus, and statements of ancient commentators on such matters are apt to be untrustworthy. The work belongs to a context in which literary studies were still dominated by the work of Aristotle and by his exclusive interest in epic and drama: Horace adopted that point of view and what is original to him is the lively epistolary style and the humorous treatment.

BIBLIOGRAPHIES. E. Burck in Kiessling–Heinze⁹ (1957), in 3 vols. (very complete bibliographies); R. J. Getty, on work published 1945–57, *Classical World* 1959, 167 ff., 246 ff.
TEXTS. E. C. Wickham and H. W. Garrod (1912: does not contain *Vita*); O. Keller and A. Holden² (1899–1925); F. Klingner² (1950).
SCHOLIA. Porphyrio: A. Holden (1894), Pseudo-Acron: O. Keller (1902–4).
COMMENTARIES. D. Lambinus (1561); R. Bentley (1711: repr. ed. K. Zangemeister, 2 vols. 1869, with full *Index Verborum*); Orelli–Baiter–Hirschfelder–Mewes, 2 vols. (1886–92); Kiessling–Heinze⁹, 3 vols. (1957); E. C. Wickham, 2 vols. (1891–6); *Odes* and *Epodes*, F. Plessis (1924); *Satires*, A. Palmer (1883), P. Lejay (1911); *Epistles*, A. S. Wilkins (1892), *Ars Poetica*, A. Rostagni (1930, repr. 1946); *Odes I*, M. Hubbard and R. G. M. Nisbet (1970).
O. Keller, *Epilegomena zu Horaz* (1878–80); A. W. Verrall, *Studies in Horace* (1884); W. Y. Sellar, *Horace and the Elegiac Poets* (1892); E. Courbaud, *Horace, sa vie et sa pensée à l'époque des Épîtres* (1914); J. F. D'Alton, *Horace and his Age* (1917); A. Y. Campbell, *Horace* (1924); various essays by R. Heinze collected in *Vom Geist des Römertums* (1938, repr. 1960); B. Axelson, *Unpoetische Wörter* (1945), 98 ff.; L. P. Wilkinson, *Horace and his Lyric Poetry²* (1951); E. Fraenkel, *Horace* (1957—fundamental for all aspects of Horace); C. O. Brink, *Horace on Poetry* (1963). L. Cooper, *Concordance of Horace* (1916).     G. W. W.

## HORSE AND CHARIOT RACES.

In the four Panhellenic Festivals there were races both of driven and of ridden horses, and Pindar gives us the name of one racehorse, Pherenikos, belonging to Hieron of Syracuse, which won the race for single horses both at the Olympian and at the Pythian Games. This race, however, was only a sprint of under 6 furlongs, and was held of far less importance than the four-horse chariot-race which was the chief event of the day. The Hippodrome was a long rectangle of about 600 yards, with pillars at each end round which the horses turned. The chariots were light two-wheeled cars with a rail in front and at the sides; the driver wore a long white robe girt at the waist, and held a whip in his right hand, the reins in his left. In later times the fields were large, forty teams sometimes starting, but the distance was twelve laps, nearly 9 miles, and as accidents at the turning-points were frequent it is probable that few teams finished.

From the Greeks chariot-races passed on to the Romans, who found an ideal site for a race-course in the centre of Rome in the level space between the Palatine and Aventine hills. This *Circus* (q.v.) *Maximus* they gradually surrounded with permanent stands, which in the fourth century A.D. could hold over 200,000 spectators. Down the length of the course there ran a low wall—*spina*—ornamented with two obelisks, seven stone dolphins, and seven stone eggs. At one end were the twelve closed stalls—*carceres*—from which the chariots started when the presiding magistrate gave the signal; at the other was a wide semicircle where the chariots turned, the race being usually seven laps, and twenty-four races forming a full day's programme. The chariots were drawn by two, three, or four horses, the most important horse being that in the left-hand traces. The driver wore a short tunic, with the reins fastened round his body and a knife in his girdle to cut them in case of need, together with a cap bearing the colour of the faction which he represented. These factions were a Roman development; in Greece chariot-racing had been possible only for rich men, in Rome it passed into the hands of companies. There were four of these, distinguished by their colours,

white, red, blue, and green, the last two of which gradually absorbed the others. The Roman onlooker displayed his favourite colour and betted on it, and the rivalry between the blues and the greens became so intense that at Constantinople it led to the famous Nika riot.

Friedländer ii. 19–40. For other literature *see* ATHLETICS.
    F. A. W.

**HORSES.** The horses of classical antiquity were derived from animals domesticated upon the northern steppes and brought into south-west Asia and the Mediterranean region from the early second millennium B.C. onwards. Zoologists now question the distinction between the western and eastern (Przewalski) wild horses and consider that ancient breeds differed because separate strains developed in different environments. Horse-bones are reported from Early-Bronze-Age sites in Macedonia, a Middle Helladic site in Messenia, and from Troy VI. Representations of horses were found in the Shaft Graves of Mycenae. The horse was brought to Anatolia probably by the Hittites and to Egypt perhaps by the Hyksos, and later reached Libya. Its arrival in Italy is not documented, but horse-bits are common in Villanovan graves. Horses were both ridden and driven in the second millennium B.C. The replacement of chariots by cavalry in war (early first millennium in the Levant; after 700 B.C. in Greece and Italy; later in Western Europe and North Africa) was made possible by severer bits as well as by better horses. The small, fine-headed horses portrayed in Greek and Etruscan art later degenerated, while the horses of North Africa and Illyria retained their primitive qualities. The large Persian horses noted by Herodotus appear at Persepolis as low, massive, heavy-headed animals. Roman cavalry horses are illustrated on Trajan's Column. The statue of Marcus Aurelius on the Capitol is mounted on a magnificent charger. Mosaics illustrate other types of horses, including race-horses and hunters. No heavy draught horse was developed in antiquity, and the horse remained a rich man's possession, used for war, sport, and travel, but not for agriculture.

G. Nobis, 'Beiträge zur Abstammung und Domestikation des Hauspferdes', in *Zeitschrift für Tierzüchtung und Züchtungsbiologie*, Bd. 64, Heft 3 (1955), 201 ff.; F. Hančar, *Das Pferd in prähistorischer und früher historischer Zeit* (1955); W. A. Heurtley, *Prehistoric Macedonia* (1939); J. K. Anderson, *Ancient Greek Horsemanship* (1961) (for classical references); J. M. C. Toynbee, 'Beasts and their names in the Roman Empire', *PBSR* 1948, 24 ff.     J. K. A.

**HORTENSIUS** (1, *PW* 7), QUINTUS, was appointed dictator in 287 B.C., despite his obscure descent, to reconcile the Orders after debts and usury had provoked the final secession of the *plebs* to the Janiculum. He carried a *Lex Hortensia* by which *plebiscita* were to be binding on the whole community and the Senate had to recognize such measures as legal before they were put to the plebeian assembly. Another *Lex Hortensia* (probably 287) provided that lawsuits should take place on the *nundinae*, when the peasants, taking advantage of the country-holiday, came to Rome on business.

Mommsen, *Röm. Staatsr.* iii³. 153, 372 f.; G. W. Botsford, *The Roman Assemblies* (1909), 313 ff.; E. Costa, *La 'lex Hortensia de plebiscitis'* (1912); V. Costanzi, *Riv. fil.* 1914; A. K. Michels, *The Calendar of the Roman Republic* (U.S.A. 1967), 103 ff.     P. T.

**HORTENSIUS** (2, *PW* 13) **HORTALUS**, QUINTUS, born in 114 B.C., was a son-in-law of Catulus (q.v. 2) and boyhood friend of Lucullus (q.v. 2) and Sisenna (q.v.), with whom he shared cultural interests and a love of luxury. One of the leading orators under Cinna (q.v. 1) and Carbo (q.v. 2) (associated with the latter in defending Pompey), he joined Sulla in time and was supreme in the lawcourts in the 70s B.C., using a florid and theatrical 'Asianic' style (then new and exciting) and resorting to shameless bribery. Defeated by Cicero in the case of his friend Verres, he still remained an eminent orator and, after his consulship (69), a man of high standing among the Optimates. He opposed Pompey's special *imperia* and joined Cicero in many political cases (especially those of Rabirius (q.v. 1), Sulla (q.v. 2), and Sestius (q.v.)), but looked down on him as a *novus homo*. Cicero, who distrusted him in his lifetime, after his death (50) paid him many tributes in his rhetorical and philosophical works, especially in the *Brutus*.

Malcovati, *ORF*² 310 ff. E. B.

**HORUS,** usually called **Harpocrates** (Horus the child) by the Greeks, was originally a god of lower Egypt. His characteristics and his unique qualities as they were known to the Greeks came almost entirely from his role in the myth of Osiris. The myth is given in a late, hellenized form by Plutarch in his essay concerning Isis and Osiris. After the murder of Osiris Isis gave birth to a son, Horus, who, after many trials, succeeded in punishing the wicked Set (Typhon). Egyptian mythology dealt at length with the obstacles which the untried youth had to overcome, and, in later times, Horus the child drew the affections of the Greeks and Romans. There are a few dedications to Horus outside Egypt, and he is sometimes represented as a mounted warrior with the head of a hawk. In unnumbered instances, however, he appears as Harpocrates and is represented as a chubby infant with his finger held to his mouth. He is frequently represented within Egypt and outside as a baby being suckled by his mother Isis, less frequently as a youth with pomegranate or a child on a lotus flower. Harpocrates is usually found as a member of the cult of the Egyptian deities, along with Isis and Sarapis, his mother and father. Representations of him are almost innumerable, from rings and amulets to life-size statues of him as a youth. In his various forms he is at times identified with Heracles, Eros, and Apollo.

A. Erman, *Die Religion der Ägypter* (1934); P. Roussel, *Les Cultes égyptiens à Délos* (1916); Cumont, *Rel. or.*; G. Lafaye, *Histoire du culte des divinités d'Alexandrie* (1884); P. Perdrizet, *Terres cuites de l'Égypte gréco-romaine* (1921); W. Weber, *Die ägyptisch-griechischen Terrakotten*, 2 vols. (1914). T. A. B.

**HOSTIUS,** an epic poet, wrote about the *Bellum Histricum* of 129 B.C. Perhaps he dealt with contemporary events (as Naevius and Ennius had). There were at least three books and scanty fragments survive.

Morel, *FPL* 33 f.; Schanz–Hosius, § 61a.

**HOUSES, GREEK.** The houses of the archaic period and of the fourth and fifth centuries were simple in form and construction. The usual material was unbaked brick, often lime-washed externally, on a stone socle, with timber of course and terracotta tiles for the roof (though flat terraced roofs were also sometimes used, and thatch in early times). The poorest houses consisted of a mere couple of rooms; but usually there was a small courtyard (*aule*), which tended to be on the south side, giving the main part of the house a southward aspect. The courtyard was entered from the street by way of a porch (*prothyron*), and sometimes displayed an altar, of Zeus Herkeios. The arrangement of the rooms around it was informal and variable, without any attempt at symmetry. Greek houses presented a plain façade to the streets, broken by the door and a few small windows. Architectural interest was concentrated in the interior. In the better houses the courtyard might have a simple colonnade (*prostoon*) on one or more sides; complete peristyles are mostly Hellenistic, though there are several earlier examples at Olynthus. In a commodious house the rooms might include the *andron* (the main dining-room, more handsomely decorated than most), work- and store-rooms; a kitchen; a small bathroom; and a room or rooms set apart for the women (*gynaikonitis*). Many houses had a second story (hardly more), often no doubt with a balcony; here one would find the bedrooms, and perhaps the *gynaikonitis*. Sometimes a room or a couple of rooms formed a separate unit, opening on the street, and serving as a shop. The same basic house-type could do duty not only as a dwelling but also as an inn, a factory, or warehouse for a family business, an elementary school, or a farmhouse. Country houses could be allowed a somewhat more spacious layout (see J. E. Jones, L. H. Sackett, and A. J. Graham, *BSA* 1962, 75 ff.).

Floors at ground level were of hard earth, except in a few important rooms. Walls might be plastered and painted in simple schemes, but were often left in bare brick. Water was provided by wells and underground rain-water cisterns, which supplemented the fountains built in the public places of the city. Efficient sanitation was non-existent. Heating was by means of hearths built of stone slabs set in the floor, and movable braziers. The smoke escaped by holes contrived in the roof, though in some Olynthian houses there is evidence of a flue-like arrangement. Furniture, even in the houses of the well-to-do, was sparse and simple by modern standards (see *Hesp.* 1956, 210, 212).

Olynthus (q.v.) in north Greece now provides the most plentiful evidence for houses of the fifth and early fourth centuries. On the South Hill was the older quarter, with irregular streets and small houses. On a plateau to the north an extensive new town was laid out in the latter part of the fifth century (see TOWNS), and here the houses were uniform and square (about 56 feet), in blocks of ten, though in interior arrangement there was still great variety and individuality. A constant feature is the *pastas*, a long room extending east-to-west across the whole width of the house, or nearly the whole, and opening southwards through pillars on the courtyard. A series of rooms opened on the *pastas* from the north. There was no single important room forming a nucleus as at Priene. A number of fifth- and fourth-century houses have recently been found on the fringes of the agora at Athens (*Hesp.* 1951, 135 ff.; 1959, 98 ff.; 1966, 51 ff.); these have a very general similarity to the Olynthian houses, but are simpler and more irregular.

More elaborate types appear in the Hellenistic period. The houses of Priene (q.v.) were more monumental in construction, with a greater use of stone. Most distinctive is a feature which may be a survival or revival of the ancient *megaron* (see TEMPLES), a dominant room opening on to the court from the north through a handsome columnar porch. The houses of wealthy merchants at Delos (q.v.) exhibit a greater degree of luxury, with elegant peristyle courts and elaborate mosaics in the chief rooms. Simpler houses stand side by side with these at Delos—there is no evidence that the residential segregation of classes was carried far in Greek towns; in some an external stairway led to a separate apartment on the upper floor.

There was no place for anything which could be called a palace in the normal Greek city of the fifth and fourth centuries. A curious example occurs at Larisa on the Hermus in north-western Asia Minor (cf. A. W. Lawrence, *Greek Architecture* (1962), fig. 138). Presumably the residence of a local ruler, it has several megaron-like units opening on to a court. In Hellenistic times more truly palatial residences appear. Houses recently excavated at Pella (q.v.), the capital of Macedonia, show on a splendid scale the features noted in the more elegant Delian houses; they were presumably occupied by very important persons. Another fine Macedonian palace was excavated at Palatitza several years ago; it has extensive suites of rooms grouped around a peristyle with sixteen columns on each side (plan, see *JHS* 1957, *Arch. Rep.* 1956, 18; *AJArch.* 1957, 285). Hellenistic 'palaces' were essentially variations of a vastly extended and highly elaborate form of a Greek type—the peristyle house. (*See also* PERGAMUM.)

Vitruvius (6. 7) describes a 'Greek house' which has two courtyards; in one, the *gynaikonitis*, the intimate life of the household goes on; another, the *andronitis*, is much more splendid, and contains dining-rooms. There are also suites of guest-chambers, gardens, and other amenities. This is no doubt based on a late Hellenistic type, and contrasts strongly, as far as our limited evidence goes, with the houses of the time of Pericles and Demosthenes.

B. C. Rider, *The Greek House* (1916); D. M. Robinson, *Excavations at Olynthus*, vol. viii (with J. W. Graham; U.S.A. 1938), *The Hellenic House*, and vol. xii (1946) (see vol. x for content and equipment of houses); *see also* books noted under ARCHITECTURE, DELOS, PRIENE, TOWNS.                                                        R. E. W.

**HOUSES, ITALIAN.** In historical times, two types of town-house coexisted in Italy, the *insula* and the *domus*. The former was an apartment block, large, high, housing many families: the latter generally the home of a single family. The former was essentially an urban growth: the latter seems to have had its origin in quite different conditions, probably rural.

**2.** *Insula*. The *insula* was a natural growth from a row of shops or workshops lining a street, with living-quarters behind or above them. Cost of land drove first the humble, later the well-to-do (Cic. *Pro Caelio* 17), to build upwards rather than outwards. The use of timber and sun-dried bricks made for cheapness, though not for stability. The *insulae* acquired an unsavoury reputation as overcrowded (Mart. i. 117), unsightly, and insecure (Strabo 235). Until Augustus limited their height and Nero improved their building standards (Tac. *Ann.* 15. 43), the risk of fire and collapse was ever-present. However, the use of brick-faced concrete led to a vast improvement after Nero. In Rome of the fourth century A.D., the *insulae* outnumbered the *domus* by more than twenty-five to one. Actual remains in Rome are fragmentary, though plans are preserved in the *Forma Urbis Romae*. To see the *insula* in its varied character one must look to Ostia, where it developed later than in Rome though under Rome's influence. At least three types are found, viz. (i) a row of shops facing the street, with living-quarters behind or above. Such a row is found at Pompeii in the Sullan age (Via della Fortuna), and at Ostia in the late republican and early imperial age; such rows reached an imposing dignity, having upper balconies or porticoes over the pavement of the street; (ii) a double row of shops built back to back (Via delle Corporazioni at Ostia); (iii) rows of rooms or shops surrounding a central area. The rooms might face on the street or might be in a double series, one facing outwards, the other facing into the courtyard (Casa del Triclinio at Ostia). Many of the Ostian apartments are spacious, many-roomed, and well-lighted, in strong contrast to the picture of those in Rome painted by Martial and Juvenal.

**3.** *Domus*. Originally the *domus* had as its main feature an *atrium*, i.e. an unroofed or only partially roofed area with rooms round about, which were lighted from it and arranged along a central axis in a more or less stereotyped order (viz. the *tablinum* and its flanking rooms at one end, the *alae* separating the *tablinum* end from the rest, and small rooms on each of the sides and also flanking the door, which lay opposite the *tablinum*). The origin of the *atrium* is uncertain. The triple division of the *tablinum* and its flanking rooms may be related to the triple division of the *cella* of an Etruscan temple, and the whole house may derive from the Etruscans. The purpose of the *alae* is not clear: possibly under different conditions of life they were entrances, since in a number of Campanian *villae rusticae* entrances are found in this position. The earliest extant examples of *atrium*-houses

are found at Pompeii, e.g. Casa del Chirurgo (fourth to third centuries B.C.). This house, when first built, had no *impluvium* (a basin in the floor designed to catch rainwater). This feature is not found earlier than the second century, but thereafter became normal. In the absence of an *impluvium*, it is not known if the *atrium* of the Casa del Chirurgo was roofed. A century later a more imposing design is found in the Casa di Sallustio at Pompeii. The *atrium* had an *impluvium*, which implies that except for the *compluvium* (a rectangular opening in the centre of the roof) the area was roofed. The darkening of the *atrium*, caused by the roofing, was offset by large windows in the *tablinum* and adjoining rooms, which opened on a portico and overlooked a garden. The rooms on the street side were converted into shops, an innovation doubtless inspired by the plan of the *insula*.

**4.** *Foreign Influence.* Neither the *domus* nor the *insula* remained untouched by foreign influence. In the *domus* the most striking importation was the Hellenistic peristyle in the second century B.C. (a garden surrounded by a portico), which either was incorporated as an additional feature behind the *atrium* (Casa di Pansa, etc.), or superseded the *atrium* altogether. In the Ostian *insulae* Greek influence is suggested in type iii above (e.g. Casa di Diana). Behind façades of shops lies an open area with entrances from the street, surrounded by narrow corridors on several floors with rooms opening off them and on one side a large, high room, sometimes with two columns supporting the lintel—an arrangement which can be paralleled from fifth to third centuries B.C. from the Palace at Vouni, from Olynthus, Priene, and Delos.

At Ostia during the late Empire the independent *domus*, which had passed out of favour in the crowded conditions of Ostia's heyday, came into use once more; not, however, in the stereotyped form of the old *atrium*, but with new architectural features (stylized capitals, arches springing direct from columns) that looked forward to the Byzantine age and to the Middle Ages.

**5.** *Palaces.* The imperial palace in Rome began modestly under Augustus (Suet. *Aug.* 72) with a traditional *domus*, the remains of which may be seen near the Palatine; but it did not long remain on this simple scale. After the fire of A.D. 64 had cleared the ground, Nero built his fantastic *domus aurea* (q.v.) between the Palatine, Caelian, and Esquiline, artificially landscaped, with a central lake on the site of the future Colosseum. Remains of its lower stories survive and indicate rows of marble-lined rooms opening into colonnades, of inner chambers decorated with stucco paintings, of an octagonal room with vaulted ceiling, flanked by apsed chambers—an important architectural development. The Domitian palace on the Palatine was more compact in plan but no less grandiose in conception, with throne-room, peristyle, triclinium in the state apartments, all on a stupendous scale, repeating in an adjoining room the octagonal shape and double apse already mentioned, and an interesting series of private apartments, turned inwards for seclusion but with two stories of windowed galleries overlooking the Circus Maximus along the shallow arc of the façade. Next, chronologically, came Hadrian's villa at Tivoli, rambling for a mile over the lower Apennine slopes, an epitome in its architectural fancies of its builder's world-wide travels, out-vying Nero's *domus aurea* in its architectural richness, but with learning and intellect revealed in every contrivance. Finally, just outside the bounds of Italy, the palace of Domitian at Spalato, on the coast of Yugoslavia, a fortified camp in outline with barracks for the imperial guard, and the palace proper in place of the headquarters—throne room flanked by arches which spring direct from capitals and herald the romanesque, basilica, banqueting hall, temple, octagonal mausoleum, and, facing the sea, a great gallery running the entire width with corbelled columns supporting an entablature. Here Roman palatial architecture said its last word. *See also* HYPOCAUST.

*Insula.* G. Calza, *Mon. Ant.* 23 (1914), 541 ff., and 'Le origini latine dell'abitazione moderna', *Architettura e arti decorative* (1923-4); A. Maiuri, 'Contributi allo studio dell'ultima fase edilizia pompeiana', *Atti del Primo Congr. Naz. di Studi Romani* (1929), 161; A. Boethius, 'Remarks on the Development of Domestic Architecture in Rome', *AJArch.* 1934, 158 ff.; 'Appunti sul carattere razionale e sull'importanza dell'architettura domestica di Roma imperiale', *Scritti in onore di B. Nogara* (1937), 21 ff.; P. Harsh, 'The Origins of the *Insulae* at Ostia', *Amer. Acad. Rome* (1935), 9 ff.; D. S. Robertson, *Greek and Roman Architecture* (1943); R. Meiggs, *Roman Ostia* (1960), ch. 12.
*Domus.* G. Patroni, *Rend. Linc.* 1912, 260 ff.; R. C. Carrington, *Antiquity* 1934, 261 ff.
*Palaces.* K. M. Swoboda, *Römische und romanische Paläste* (1924); A. Bartoli, *Domus Augustana* (1938); H. Kähler, *Hadrian und seine Villa bei Tivoli* (1950); A. Boethius, *Roman and Greek Town Architecture* (1948), *The Golden House of Nero* (1960); R. E. M. Wheeler, *Roman Art and Architecture* (1964), 137 ff. R. C. C.

**HUNS,** a nomadic pastoralist people whose early history is unknown. They appeared in south-eastern Europe *c.* A.D. 370, destroyed the kingdom of the Ostrogoths in the Ukraine, and drove the Visigoths of Transdanubian Dacia into the Roman provinces in 376. Early in the fifth century they advanced into central Europe driving other barbarians into Italy and Gaul (*see* VANDALS); but details of their history in this period are lacking. They were ruled *c.* 430 by a certain Rua, who in 434 was succeeded by Attila (q.v.) and Bleda. After Attila's death (453) their vast empire was divided between his sons, who were defeated in 455 by a coalition of their subjects. The Huns were of little historical significance thereafter. In their heyday they were superb but not invincible horsemen— Aetius (q.v.) defeated them in Attila's lifetime (451)— and exploited their subjects mercilessly. They exacted enormous quantities of gold from the Eastern Empire, but failed to win any of its territory.

E. A. Thompson, *A History of Attila and the Huns* (1948); F. Altheim, *Attila und die Hunnen* (1951). E. A. T.

**HUNTING** (κυνηγεσία, *venatio*) was practised by the Greeks and Romans, but, except in Homeric times, not in a very sporting spirit. In Homer the animals hunted have a fair chance of escape and the hunter incurs a certain amount of danger, as Odysseus did when faced by the wild boar (*Od.* 19. 429–46). But in classical Greece the hunter ran little risk; hunting, as Xenophon tells us, meant chiefly pursuing hares on foot, with dogs and nets placed to catch the quarry, which was then dispatched with a club. In hunting the roe deer nets were used and snares in the form of a wooden clog, which caught the deer's foot and hindered its escape; another method was to catch a fawn and to entice the dam into the open—'that is the moment to set the hounds on and ply the javelins'. In hunting the wild boar caution comes first: 'Provide yourself with Indian, Cretan, Locrian, and Laconian hounds, boar-nets, javelins, spears, and caltrops; also a company of hunters, for the task of capturing the beast is no light one.' The Romans followed the same methods; but under the Empire the hunting of big game for the arena became an important business. (*See* VENATIONES, DOGS.)

Xenophon, *Cynegeticus*; Oppian, *Cynegetica*; Nemesianus, *Cynegeticus*. A. J. Butler, *Sport in Classic Times* (1930); D. B. Hull, *Hounds and Hunting in Ancient Greece* (1964); J. Aymard, *Essai sur les chasses romaines* (1951). F. A. W.

**HYACINTHUS,** a pre-Hellenic god worshipped at Amyclae. In historical times his cult was subordinate to that of Apollo, and a story was told that he was a beautiful boy whom the god loved, killed accidentally with a discus (in one version Zephyrus, who was Apollo's rival, blew the discus aside so that it struck Hyacinthus on the head), and mourned for, in token of which the flower of the same name, a sort of iris, sprang from the boy's blood and is marked αἰαῖ ('alas, alas!'; cf. AIAS 1). But the ritual of the festival, the Hyacinthia (Ath. 139 d ff.), the representation in local art of Hyacinthus as bearded (Paus. 3. 19. 4), the name of Artemis Ἰακυνθο-τρόφος, and the pre-Greek -*nth*- of the name, all point to the truth. Various Dorian cities had months named after Hyacinthus.

See Rose, *Handb. Gk. Myth.* 142, 160; Farnell, *Cults* iv. 125, 264 ff., *Hero-Cults* 22, 27; Nilsson, *Minoan-Mycenaean Religion*[2] (1950), 485 ff. Machteld J. Mellink, *Hyakinthos*, diss. 1943. Chief ancient references, besides those already given: Nic. *Ther.* 902 ff. and schol.; Apollod. 1. 16–17; 3. 116; Palaephatus 46 (47). H. J. R.

**HYADES** (Ὑάδες, 'the rainers'), a group of five stars in Taurus, so named because their acronychal rising and setting (respectively 17 Oct. and 12 Apr. according to Eudoxus) are at rainy times of the year; absurdly called Suculae in Latin, as if from ὗς. Mythologically they were nurses of Dionysus (q.v.; see Hyg. *Fab.* 182. 2 and Rose ad loc.); but the story, which seems to go back to Pherecydes, is very confused in the forms which we have. Another account (Hyg. *Poet. Astr.* 2. 21; schol. *Il.* 18. 486; Eustath. 1155. 45 ff.) is that they are sisters who cried themselves to death when their brother Hyas was killed hunting. H. J. R.

**HYGIEIA** (Ὑγίεια), personified Health, usually said to be daughter of Asclepius (q.v.), and associated with him in cult. She is the most important of his attendants, having a cult at Titane (Paus. 2. 11. 6), apparently almost as honoured as his. In the Hippocratic oath her name follows immediately on his and before that of Panacea (Kühn, 1), and Licymnius (fr. 4 Diehl) addresses her as 'mother most high', curiously, for she is usually said to be virgin. The word occurs also as a title of Athena (q.v.; Plut. *Pericles* 13), earlier than the introduction of Asclepius to Athens. For further references see Nilsson, *GGR*, s.v. H. J. R.

**HYGINUS** (1), GAIUS JULIUS; a Spaniard (according to another account, an Alexandrian brought to Rome by Caesar), a freedman of Augustus, appointed by him librarian of the Palatine Library (Suet. *Gram.* 20). A pupil of Alexander Polyhistor, he was himself a teacher and was a friend of Ovid, who addresses him in *Tr.* 3. 14. His writings, now lost, covered a wide range of scholarship: (*a*) a treatise *De Agricultura*, perhaps including the *De Apibus* cited by Columella; (*b*) a commentary on Virgil, cited by Gellius and Servius, apparently both exegetical and critical; (*c*) historical and archaeological works—*De familiis Troianis*, *De origine et situ urbium Italicarum*, *De vita rebusque illustrium virorum, exempla*; (*d*) works on religion—*De proprietatibus deorum, De dis penatibus*.

See Peter, *HRRel.*; Funaioli, *Gramm. Rom. Frag. See also* SCHOLARSHIP, LATIN, IN ANTIQUITY. C. J. F.

**HYGINUS** (2), *gromaticus*, of Trajan's time; author of treatises (1) on boundaries, (2) on types of land-tenure, (3) on land-disputes. He refers to another work not extant, a handbook of imperial land-regulations. A treatise *De limitibus constituendis* to which his name is attached is generally assigned to a later author. *See* BIBLIOGRAPHY *under* GROMATICI. C. J. F.

**HYGINUS** (3). Two extant Latin works are attributed to a Hyginus who cannot be identified with Augustus' freedman or with the *gromaticus*.
(*a*) *Genealogiae*, a handbook of mythology, compiled from Greek sources, probably in the second century A.D. The work was abbreviated, perhaps for school use, and has suffered later accretions; its absurdities are partly due

to the compiler's ignorance of Greek. The usual title *Fabulae* is due to the *editio princeps* of Micyllus (Basle, 1535), now the only authority for the text; the manuscript which he used is lost. *See* MYTHOGRAPHERS (ad fin.). Critical ed.: H. J. Rose, Leiden 1934.

(*b*) A manual of astronomy, based on Greek sources, possibly by the same author. C. J. F.

**HYGINUS** (4). To Hyginus Gromaticus there has been falsely attributed the incomplete treatise *De munitionibus castrorum*, a handbook of castrametation on a basis more theoretical than practical. Its date is disputed, and has been assigned to the later years of Trajan, to the first half of the second century, to the age of Septimius Severus, and to the third century. Of these the third-century date appears the most probable. *See* CAMPS.

EDITIONS. Lange (1848); Gemoll (1879); A. von Domaszewski (1887). G. R. W.

**HYLAS.** Theiodamas king of the Dryopes attacked Heracles because the latter had seized and eaten one of his plough-oxen. After a desperate struggle in which even Deianira took part, Theiodamas was defeated and killed. Heracles spared his young son Hylas and made him his page. They went together on the voyage of the Argonauts (q.v., § 2), till the landing at Cios. There Hylas went to fetch water, found a spring, and was pulled into the water by its nymphs, who were in love with his beauty. Heracles stayed to look for him and the rest, after some discussion, went on without him; cf. DIOSCURI. It would seem that this story connects with a local custom, for Apollonius says (1354) that in his day the people of Cios still looked for Hylas. Ritual search for a deity, perhaps of vegetation, is not unfamiliar in the Greek world, see Athenaeus, 619 f (Bormos among the Mariandyni, Rose, *Handb. Gk. Myth.* 118 (Britomartis). See Ap. Rhod. 1. 1177 ff. and schol.; Theocr. 13. H. J. R.

**HYLLUS**, in mythology, eldest son of Heracles (q.v.) by Deianira (Soph. *Trach.* 55, etc.) or Melite (schol. ibid. 54). *See* HERACLIDAE.

**HYMENAEUS.** It was customary at Greek weddings to cry Ὑμὴν Ὑμέναι᾽ ὦ or ὦ Ὑμὴν Ὑμέναιε (Ar. *Pax* 1334 ff.; Catull. 61. 4, etc.; 62. 5, etc.). Rightly or wrongly, this was understood as an invocation of a being called Hymen or Hymenaeus, and various stories were invented of him, all to the effect that he was a very handsome young man who either married happily or had something happen to him on his wedding-day. See Sauer in Roscher's *Lexikon*, s.v. H. J. R.

**HYMNS.** A ὕμνος is any metrical address to a god, originally sung. The word is of doubtful origin, possibly non-Greek. It occurs once in Homer (*Od.* 8. 429), and a choral hymn to Apollo is described in *Il.* 1. 472–4. Hesiod speaks of winning a prize for a ὕμνος (*Op.* 651 ff.). Hymns were both lyric and hexametric, and Callim. *Lav. Pall.* may be based on earlier elegiac models. Although all choral lyric poetry seems religious in origin, and hymns were written by the well-known early lyrists (e.g. Alcaeus), the hexameter was in antiquity considered the earlier form. (Cf. esp. Pausanias, who knows of Olen, Pamphus, Orpheus, Musaeus, and Homer as hymn-writers.) The content was usually an accumulation of names and epithets of the god (suggesting an original element of magical compulsion), and recital fo his deeds, followed by a short prayer. Hymns written to invoke a local god on special occasions must have existed from very early times. An example survives in the Elean invocation of Dionysus (Diehl, *Anth. Lyr. Gr.* ii. 206). Hexametric hymns mentioned by Pausanias

have the same local and ritual nature, and were sometimes written for private mystical groups, e.g. the Lycomid *genos* (Paus. 9. 30. 12). The Homeric Hymns (8th to 6th cc.) are literary rather than devotional, and the myth is the chief feature. The ascription to Homer suggests the aristocratic epic tradition, and they were probably delivered in competition by professional rhapsodes at festivals (cf. *Hymn. Hom. Ven.* (vi) 19). Geographically they are widely scattered. Lyric hymns tended to displace the hexametric (cf. Pindar's Ὕμνοι and Παιᾶνες, and in the sphere of cult the paean to Asclepius found in four copies, J. U. Powell, *Coll. Alex.* 137 f.), but the hexameter survived for purposes of cult. (For ritual hymns in the classical period see also F. Adami in *Jahrb. f. cl. Phil.* Suppl. xxvi (1901), 215 ff.) Hymns were sung at Symposia (Pl. *Symp.* 176 a), as—according to his accusers—was Aristotle's paean in honour of Hermias (Diehl I². i. 117–19; for its literary genre see C. M. Bowra in *CQ* 1938, 182 ff. The Hellenistic period provides the hymns of Callimachus together with many cult-hymns from inscriptions, e.g. the paean of Isyllus to Apollo and Asclepius (Wilamowitz, *I. von Epidauros*, 1886; cf. Powell and Barber, *New Chapters*, 46 f.). Some found at Delphi have musical notation, a valuable addition to the scanty evidence for Greek music. Epigraphical material increases in the Graeco-Roman age, especially from Asia Minor, telling, e.g., of guilds of ὑμνῳδοί and their performances. The Palaikastro hymn to the Cretan Zeus, with interesting magical element (Diehl ii. 279 f.), recorded in a copy made not earlier than A.D. 200, but reproduces a Hellenistic or earlier composition. In a series of pregnant prose sentences, which were reworked by later writers into hexametric and iambic form, the goddess Isis recounts her own virtues (W. Peek, *Der Isis-Hymnos von Andros und verwandte Texte*, 1930), illustrating the age's craving for revelation. From imperial times we have the prose hymns of Aristides, the directions of the rhetorician Menander for the writing of such compositions, and the hexametric hymns of 'Orpheus' (ed. E. Abel, 1885, and W. Quandt, 2nd ed. 1955), syncretistic and with a flavour of popular Stoicism, which were almost certainly written for a cult-society on the coast of Asia Minor (O. Kern in *Hermes* 1911, 431 ff.).

From Cleanthes onwards appears the philosophico-religious hymn, beloved of the Neoplatonists. Finally, the growth of superstition brought back the magical hymn in elaborate forms.

R. Wünsch, *PW*, s.v. 'Hymnos'; E. Norden, *Agnostos Theos* (1913), and, for early Roman hymns, *Aus altrömischen Priesterbüchern* (1939, including, 217 ff., a discussion of the Palaikastro hymn). W. K. C. G.

**HYPATIA,** lady learned in mathematics, astronomy, and philosophy (d. A.D. 415). Daughter of the mathematician Theon (q.v. 1) of Alexandria, she revised the third book of his *Commentary on the Almagest*. Commentaries by her on Diophantus and Apollonius are lost. Influential in Alexandria as a teacher of the pagan Neoplatonist philosophy, she was torn to pieces by a mob of Christians at the instigation of their bishop (later Saint) Cyril.

Edition of the *Commentary on the Almagest* by A. Rome, *Studi e Testi* 106 (Rome, 1943). See introduction, cxvi–cxxi. Socrates Scholasticus 7. 15. See also the letters of Synesius, her pupil. Gibbon, *Decline and Fall*, ch. 47. R. Hoche, *Philol.* 1860, 435 ff. G. J. T.

**HYPERBOLUS** (d. 411 B.C.), Athenian demagogue of humble origin. During the Archidamian War he was a prominent member of the radical war-party and became its leader after the death of Cleon. In 417 (according to some, in 415) an ostracism was held by which Hyperbolus expected to secure the removal of Alcibiades or Nicias, but they secretly allied against him, and he was himself ostracized. He went to Samos, where he was murdered by oligarchical revolutionaries. He is condemned by Thucydides in unusually violent terms (8. 73); but, since he was the constant butt of comic poets, his influence must have been considerable. **H. D. W.**

**HYPERBOREANS.** A legendary race of Apollo-worshippers living in the far North, highly revered by the Greeks. (Earliest mention is Hes. *Cat.* fr. 49 Trav.; for their blessed existence see esp. Pind. *Pyth.* 10.) In Delphic legend Apollo spent the winter months with the Hyperboreans. Offerings from them arrived at the Delian shrine (Hdt. 4. 33), not brought by the Hyperboreans themselves (a myth gives the *aition* for this), but passed 'from city to city' until brought to Delos by the men of Tenos. The name has been variously interpreted as 'beyond the North wind', 'beyond the mountains', and 'carriers round or over' (cf. the περφερέες, officials at Delos, Hdt. loc. cit.). **W. K. C. G.**

Various historical substrata to the legend of the Hyperboreans have been sought by modern scholars. Some have suggested that the line of stations by which the offerings of the Hyperboreans reached Delos was an actual trade route for amber in Herodotus' day. But we know from Callimachus that the offerings were ears of wheat (*Del.* 283–4). A different theory is that the wheat was sent as firstfruits to Apollo by some lost Greek colony in the cornlands of the lower Danube (C. T. Seltman, *CQ* 1928, 155). But the route by which the offerings travelled cannot be traced back beyond Epirus; their place of origin must remain conjectural.

J. Bolton, *Aristeas of Proconnesus* (1962). **M. C.**

**HYPERIDES** ('Υπερείδης) (389–322 B.C.), son of Glaucippus, an Athenian of good family, who was uncompromisingly hostile to Macedon and was one of those originally demanded by Alexander in 335. At first a professional speech-writer, he made a name later as a prosecutor in public trials, beginning in 362 with an attack on Aristophon. In the 340s he sympathized with Demosthenes, and in 343 successfully prosecuted Philocrates. As a delegate to the Amphictionic Council he staunchly supported the claim of Athens to the presidency of the temple of Apollo on Delos. After Chaeronea he proposed extreme measures, including the manumission of slaves, for the public safety, and was impeached by Demades for illegality. Shortly before this he had proposed a decree to honour Demosthenes, but later he was one of the prosecutors of Demosthenes in the affair of Harpalus (q.v.), 324 B.C. After the death of Alexander, Hyperides was chiefly responsible for the Lamian War, and pronounced the funeral oration on the Athenian dead. The general Leosthenes, who was among the fallen, was his personal friend, and the speech deals mainly with him. After the battle of Crannon, Antipater demanded that Hyperides, together with Demosthenes and others of the war-party, should be surrendered to him. Hyperides was arrested and put to death (322).

Works. Although in antiquity of the seventy-seven preserved under the name of Hyperides no less than fifty-two were regarded as genuine, except for a few fragments Hyperides' work was unknown to the modern world until 1847. Between that year and 1892 papyri were discovered containing several of his speeches, in whole or in part, the most interesting being the all too fragmentary *Against Demosthenes*.

Hyperides was a pupil of Isocrates, whose influence may be traced in the exalted style of the *Epitaphios*, but in general tone he is more akin to Lysias. He borrowed words and phrases from Comedy, thus bringing his language into touch with the speech of everyday life. Linguistically his speeches have been studied in relation to the rise of the κοινή. [Longinus] *On the Sublime* draws attention to his wit, his suavity and persuasiveness, his tact and good taste. He can be sarcastic and severe without becoming offensive; his reproof often takes the form of humorous banter. He speaks with respect of his adversaries, and avoids scurrilous abuse. Ancient opinion ranked him second only to Demosthenes as an orator.

For general bibliography *see* ATTIC ORATORS.
TEXT. O.C.T. (Kenyon, 1907); Teubner (Jensen, 1917).
TEXT AND TRANSLATION. Colin (Budé); Burtt, *Minor Attic Orators* ii (Loeb).
SPECIAL STUDIES. D. Gromska, *De Sermone Hyperidis* (1927); U. Pohle, *Die Sprache des H. in ihren Beziehungen zur Koine* (1928). INDEX. H. Reinhold (in Teubner text). **J. F. D.**

**HYPERION,** a Titan, husband of his sister Theia and father by her of the Sun, Moon, and Dawn (Hes. *Theog.* 371 ff., cf. 134 f.). Often the name is used as an epithet of the Sun himself, as *Od.* 12. 133.

**HYPNOS,** the god of sleep in Greek mythology. Hypnos is fatherless, son of Nyx and brother of Thanatos (Hes. *Theog.* 211, 756). According to Hesiod he lives in the underworld and never sees the sun, but in contrast to his brother he comes softly and is sweet for men. In Homer, however, Hypnos lives on Lemnos and gets from Hera the Charis Pasithea as wife. He is human at first, but changes into a bird of the night before he makes Zeus fall asleep (*Il.* 14. 231 ff.). Throughout antiquity Hypnos was usually thought of as a winged youth who touches the foreheads of the tired with a branch (Verg. *Aen.* 5. 854) or pours sleep-inducing liquid from a horn. Myths about Hypnos are few: he helps to bury Sarpedon (*Il.* 16. 672) and is said to have fallen in love with Endymion whom he made to sleep with open eyes (Ath. 13. 564 c). He had a cult in Troezen (Paus. 2. 31. 3). In art, Hypnos carried by Nyx was shown on the Chest of Cypselus; on vases, he and Thanatos carry Memnon, Sarpedon, and human warriors to the grave. A beautiful Hellenistic statue known through several copies shows Hypnos gliding over the ground and pouring sleep-bringing liquid from his horn.

B. Sauer in Roscher, *Lex.*, s.v.; Paus. ed. Frazer, iii, 600; H. Schrader, *Winckelmannsprogramm Berlin* 1926; E. Pottier, 'Étude sur les lécythes blancs', *Bibl. Éc. Franç.* 1883; D. Jones, *CR* 1949, 83; Y. Jeannin, *Revue archéologique de l'Est et du Centre-Est* 1963, 118 ff. **G. M. A. H.**

**HYPOCAUST** (ὑπόκαυστον, *hypocaustum*), a raised floor heated from below by a furnace (ὑπόκαυσις), a device applied *c.* 100 B.C. to baths (Val. Max. 9. 1. 1; Pliny, *HN* 9. 168) and occurring also in private houses by the time of Vitruvius (5. 10). During the first century A.D. box-tiles (*tubuli*) were introduced into walls and roof, permitting the development of Roman bathing from the simple Greek sweat-bath (*laconicum*) to an elaborately graded system (Celsus, *Med.* 1. 4; 2. 17). Heat was conveyed by radiation, the floors being carried upon many thin pillars, while walls were continuously jacketed (Sen. *Ep.* 90. 25; Pliny, *Ep.* 2. 17. 9 and 23). The furnace might also carry hot-water boilers (*ahena*, Vitr. 5. 10). A second type, the channelled hypocaust, employed charcoal to heat large masses of masonry intersected by channels. While Pliny's Italian villa boasted few hypocausts, they were common in colder lands for heating living-rooms ('diaetarum hypocaustarum', *Dig.* 32. 1. 55).

See Macdonald, *PSAS* lxiii (1928–9), 446 ff.; *Arch. Ael.* ser. 4, viii (1931), 219 ff.; G. Fusch, *Über Hypokausten-Heizungen und mittelalterliche Heizungsanlagen* (1910); E. D. Thatcher, *Amer. Acad. Rom.* 1956, 167 ff.; J. B. Ward-Perkins and J. M. C. Toynbee, *Archaeologia* 1949, 165 ff.; D. Krencker and E. Krüger, *Die Trierer Kaiserthermen* (1929). **I. A. R.; S. S. F.**

**HYPOTHESIS** (Greek). (1) Prefixed to plays. Nearly all Greek dramas have an introductory note giving an outline of the plot and often other information; a number of them are in verse. They are of three main types, though they have become much confused in the course of transmission. Far the most important are those which are based on the introductions which Aristophanes of Byzantium seems to have prefixed to each play in his edition. These consist of a terse note on the subject-matter and of information on the production, etc., of the play derived from Alexandrian scholarship, especially the *Pinakes* of Callimachus, and so ultimately from Aristotle's *Didascaliae*. No complete hypothesis of this type survives, but it can be seen that the following information was given in the case of tragedy: treatment of subject, if any, by other poets; the scene of action; the identity of the chorus and first speaker; the number of the play in chronological order; the date of production, success in the competition and names of competing plays; name of choregus. Sometimes critical judgements are added. The second type is of Byzantine origin and mainly for school use; they are verbose, full of elementary information, and many of those belonging to comedies contain garbled history. The third type is associated especially with Euripides. Each contains a competent summary of the plot keeping to the past tense throughout and supplying names for characters who are nameless in the play. These seem to have been intended as substitutes for the plays rather than as introductions and form a sort of mythological compendium. In addition to those which occur in the MSS. of the plays considerable fragments of the collection have been recovered on papyrus (*POxy*. 27. 2455, 2457; *PSI* 1286) grouped by initial letters in the same sort of quasi-alphabetical order as is found in the list of plays on the Piraeus stone *IG* ii. 2. 992 and as is indicated by the numerals attached to plays in the Laurentian MS. of Euripides. They are a valuable source of information on lost plays. Since their date is probably of the first century B.C. they cannot be the same as those produced by Dicaearchus for Sophocles and Euripides (Sext. Emp. *Math*. 3. 3), which appear to have contained also investigations into the origin of the poet's subject-matter.

The hypotheses of comedies are on the whole better supplied with didascalic information. A number of them are the work of an atticizing writer, perhaps Symmachus, of early imperial times and they are similar to the hypothesis of Cratinus' *Dionysalexandros* (*POxy*. 4. 663). The portions of the hypotheses of Menander's *Hieraiai* and *Imbrioi* (*POxy*. 10. 1235) seem to be part of a complete set comparable to the Euripides hypotheses, but in the case of Menander in addition to the opening line of the play didascalic information is supplied.

Verse hypotheses, rare for tragedy, seem to have been regularly prefixed to comedies. Those of Aristophanes are all of ten lines, the two that survive for Menander, *Dyscolos* and *Heros*, are of twelve. The date of the papyri shows they are not Byzantine, but whether their language is Hellenistic is doubtful. The frequent ascription to Aristophanes of Byzantium carries no weight.

Cohn in *PW* ii. 908 f.; Körte, *Hermes* 1904, 481 ff. (on the Cratinus hyp.); Achelis, *Philol.* 1913–14; Radermacher, *Aristoph. Ran.* (Vienna, 1954), 74 ff.; Zuntz, *Political Plays of Eur.* (1963), ch. 6; Michel, *De fabularum Gr. argumentis metricis* (Giessen, 1908).

D. W. L.

(2) Hypotheses to the speeches of Demosthenes written by Libanius for the proconsul Montius, an enthusiastic admirer of Demosthenes.

(3) A particular case propounded for discussion in rhetorical schools, contrasted with a general question (θέσις) discussed in dialectical schools. The distinction is, however, not always observed.

H. Thom, *Die Thesis* (1932), 61 f.      J. D. D.

**HYPSICLES** of Alexandria, mathematician and astronomer (fl. *c.* 150 B.C.), wrote: (1) 'Book 14' added to Euclid's *Elements*. This contains interesting propositions and historical information about relationships between the regular dodecahedron and eicosahedron inscribed in the same sphere. (2) *On Rising-times* (ἀναφορικός), which adapts what is now known to be a Babylonian arithmetical scheme for computing the times taken by the individual signs of the zodiac to rise to the latitude of Alexandria. It is the earliest extant Greek work containing the division of the ecliptic into 360 degrees (μοῖραι). Diophantus (ed. Tannery I, 470) quotes a definition of a polygonal number from a lost work of Hypsicles. Also lost is a work on the harmony of the spheres (Achilles, *Eisagoge*, ed. Maass, *Comm. in Arat.* 43).

EDITIONS. Elements Bk. 14 in Heiberg, *Euclidis Opera Omnia* v (Lepizig, 1888). ἀναφορικός, ed. V. de Falco and M. Krause, *Abh. Ak. Wiss. Göttingen, Phil.-hist. Kl.* 3 F, nr. 62 (1966), with German transl.
COMMENT. Elements Bk. 14, Heath, *Hist. of Greek Maths.* i. 419 f. The rising-times, O. Neugebauer, *Exact Sciences in Antiquity*[2] (1957), 158 ff. and Introduction to de Falco's edition.    G. J. T.

**HYPSICRATES** (probably 1st c. B.C.), historian, may be identified with the grammarian Hypsicrates of Amisus; he may have served Caesar, who freed Amisus in 47 B.C., as Theophanes served Pompey. His work was perhaps rather a history of the times than a local chronicle or Ποντικά, and was possibly Strabo's source for Bosporan affairs.

*FGrH* ii B, 923; BD, 618.      A. H. McD.

**HYPSIPYLE.** The women of Lemnos having neglected the rites of Aphrodite, the goddess plagued them with a foul odour. Their husbands left them in disgust and took to themselves concubines from Thrace; whereat the women planned to murder all the males on the island. The massacre was successful; but Hypsipyle, daughter of King Thoas the son of Dionysus, hid her father and managed to convey him out of the country. She governed Lemnos and received the Argonauts (q.v.) when they came. She and her women now mated with them (nothing more is heard of Aphrodite's curse), and Hypsipyle had two sons (*see* EUNEOS) by Jason. Some time after their departure she was captured by pirates and sold to Lycurgus king of Nemea, whose wife employed her as nurse to her child Opheltes or Archemorus. For the sequel, *see* ADRASTUS.

AUTHORITIES. Eur. *Hyps.*; Ap. Rhod. 1. 609 ff., and schol. there; Stat. *Theb.* 4. 715 ff.; 5. 28 ff.; Apollod. 1. 114 f.; 3. 64 f.; Hyg. *Fab.* 15; 74.      H. J. R.

**HYPSISTOS** was, like Hypatos, a not uncommon title in Greece of Zeus as the supreme god, or as a mountain or sky god; it was popular in Macedonia. Theos Hypsistos seems generally to have been an unofficial synonym for Zeus Hypsistos. In the Orient Hypsistos was applied under the Empire to various native gods of Asia Minor and to the local Baals of Syria, many of whom were mountain divinities. Numerous bilingual inscriptions of Palmyra equate Zeus Hypsistos and the anonymous god 'whose name is blessed forever'. This cult was pagan but shows clear signs of Jewish influence (H. Seyrig, *Études syriennes* (1934–8), i. 98 f. = *Syria* 1933, 249 f.). The epithet is frequent in Hellenistic Judaism, and hellenized Jews and Gentile sympathizers could meet in a common cult of Theos Hypsistos, as at Gorgippia and Tanais. A Jewish background appears also in dedications and prayers for vengeance to Theos Hypsistos at Delos. But except where Jewish influence is indicated, its presence need not be assumed, and in general the term implies only a tendency to exalt one god to a pre-eminent position.

Cook, *Zeus* ii, Appendix B; C. Roberts, T. C. Skeat, A. D. Nock, *Harv. Theol. Rev.* 1936.      F. R. W.

# I

**IACCHUS** (Ἴακχος). A minor deity (τῆς Δήμητρος δαίμονα, Strabo 10. 3. 10) associated with the Eleusinian deities and probably in origin a personification of the ritual cry ἴακχ' ὦ ἴακχε (Ar. *Frogs* 316); cf. Hymenaeus (q.v.). The deity, the song of which these words apparently formed the refrain, and the day (Boedromion 19) on which his image was fetched to Athens from Eleusis with other holy things were all called by the same name, Ar. op. cit. 320, Hesychius, s.v. Ἴακχος; cf. MYSTERIES, PROCESSION. Iacchus was variously said to be the son of Demeter, of Persephone, and of Dionysus, or the consort of Demeter (refs. in Höfer, see below); in art he is seen torch in hand (cf. Ar. op. cit. 340 ff.) conducting the mystics, Deubner, plate 5. 1 (pinax of Ninnion). But, owing to the resemblance between his name and Βάκχος, the title of Dionysus, he is often identified with the latter, not only in literature (e.g. Eur. *Cyc.* 69, Verg. *G.* i. 166, Strabo, loc. cit.), but to some slight extent in cult; at the Lenaea, when the daduchus said 'Invoke the god' the congregation answered Σεμελήι' Ἴακχε πλουτοδότα (Schol. on Ar. op. cit. 479). In Italy he was on occasion identified with Liber (q.v.), as in the temple of Ceres on the Aventine, where Ceres Liber and Libera are Demeter Iacchus and Kore.

L. Deubner, *Attische Feste* (1932), 73 f.; Höfer in Roscher's *Lexikon*, s.v. 'Iakchos'; Nilsson, *GGR* i. 599 ff.　　　H. J. R.

**IALMENUS,** in mythology, son of Ares and Astyoche; leader, with his brother Ascalaphus, of the contingent from Aspledon and Orchomenus at Troy (*Il.* 2. 511 ff.).

**IAMBIC POETRY, GREEK.** The word ἴαμβος, of unknown but probably Asiatic origin, is first used by Archilochus (fr. 20) and seems to refer to his own satirical verse written in the iambic metre. It is possible that he was not the first so to use it, since Aristotle (*Poet.* 4) regards the Homeric *Margites* as the first work in which it appeared. He considers that its use for such purposes as satire and ridicule was due to its nearness to common speech. Archilochus' debt to the *Margites* may be seen in his use of a line from it (fr. 103), but he certainly developed iambic satire in his own way and used it especially to portray his own likes and dislikes. So, too, he used iambic epodes and the trochaic tetrameter for similar purposes. He probably influenced Semonides of Amorgos, who used the simple iambic trimeter, and seems both to have shown less personal spite and to have been more dependent on traditional fables than Archilochus was. Hipponax, however, follows the Archilochean tradition in giving full vent to his hatreds and in using everyday language. His chief innovation was the substitution of the σκάζων for the true iambic, but this did not alter his essential similarity to Archilochus. Satirical iambics were also written in the sixth century by Anacreon, though his fundamental good nature does not seem to have left him except in his lines on Artemon (fr. 54) which are not strictly iambic in metre, though their temper is violently satirical. These poets all belong to Ionia, and iambic verse, as they practised it, was characteristic of free Ionian life. Elsewhere it took rather different forms. In Syracuse the ἰαμβισταί were a choir who carried *phalli* in honour of Dionysus (Ath. 181 c) and may have sung abusive songs, while the use of trochaics by Epicharmus in his early dramatic pieces indicates that he may have owed something to this tradition, while it must be to him and his kind that Attic comedy owed its use of iambic and trochaic verse. In

Athens the iambic and trochaic measures were used from about 600 B.C. by Solon to answer his critics and justify his political decisions. He shows little rancour or abuse, and his temper is quite unlike that of the Ionian iambic poets, but he probably owed the form to them. It was the best means available for personal controversy, and that, no doubt, was why he used it. His example does not seem to have inspired many followers in Athens, and though such work is attributed to Euenus of Paros, its real influence is to be seen in Comedy. A possible follower of Solon is Chrysogonus (fl. 408 B.C.), whose poem Πολιτεία was wrongly ascribed to Epicharmus (Ath. 648 d).

In the Hellenistic age the satirical iambic was revived with some success. Some oddities appeared, like Castorion's *Hymn to Pan*, in which each dipody in the trimeter ended with the end of a word (Ath. 454 f), and the riddles attributed to Panarces (Diehl, *Anth. Lyr. Graec.* i. 3. 70), but the traditional use may be seen in Alcaeus of Messene's political diatribes against Philip of Macedon (Euseb. *Praep. Evang.* 10. 3. 23) and the philosophical invectives of Timon of Phlius, Heraclides Ponticus, and Hermeias of Curion. In this kind the most important practitioner was Callimachus, who wrote iambic, choliambic, and trochaic verses in the character of a new Hipponax, into whose mouth some of the verses are put. But he is less bitter than his predecessor, and the remains indicate that his *Iambi* were quite mild and humorous, with plentiful fables and discursions on varied topics. He seems to have widened the scope of topics for which the iambic metre was used, and his influence may be seen on Cercidas, whose scazons deal with topics of popular morality and make fun of pretentious speculations, and on Phoenix of Colophon, who wrote on such different matters as Ninus and the song of beggars in Rhodes. More primitive were the verses of Sotades, which belong essentially to this tradition and were famous for the scurrility and impropriety of their abuse. A new turn was given to iambic verse by Menippus of Gadara, who is best known through Varro's Latin adaptations and wrote criticisms of all manner of men and things, set his situations in fantastic backgrounds, and mixed verse with prose. In the Roman period iambic verse was put to new uses, some of them instructive, as when 'Scymnus' wrote his geography, Diodotus about plants, and Simylus about literature.

TEXTS. Diehl, *Anth. Lyr. Graec.*; J. M. Edmonds, *Elegy and Iambus* (Loeb, 1931).　　　C. M. B.

**IAMBIC POETRY, LATIN.** The use of iambic metres for personal invective and the censure of contemporaries is not widespread in Latin poetry, where the spirit of Archilochus and Hipponax is most often enshrined in Phalaecean hendecasyllabics and elegiac couplets (cf. Catullus, Ovid's *Ibis*, and Martial). The iambic senarius of the republican dramatists (cf. METRE, LATIN) was, indeed, used occasionally for non-scenic purposes, as by Pacuvius and others for epitaphs and by Volcacius Sedigitus for literary criticism; yet Lucilius (like Horace, Persius, and Juvenal) preferred the dactylic hexameter for satire and included senarii in his 28th and 29th books only. In the first half of the first century B.C. Cn. Matius introduced the scazon (limping iambic) in his *mimiambi* (in imitation of Herodas), and Laevius in his *Erotopaegnia* experimented with iambic dimeters, scazons, hendecasyllabics, and other metres; Varro also achieved a mastery of the iambic trimeter in his *Menippeae*. The scazon found some favour with Catullus, Cinna, Calvus, and Bibaculus; and of the eight poems of Catullus in this metre, all except no. 31 contain some personal criticism or abuse. Horace avoids the metre, but it occurs twice in the *Appendix Vergiliana* (*Catal.* 2 and 5, both critical of *rhetores*) and occasionally in the salacious *Priapea*. Martial was not strongly attracted to the metre, though he employed it in seventy-seven of his poems with epigrammatic effect. The iambic trimeter appears in Catullus in three poems only—nos. 4 (not scurrilous), 29, and 52; and when (in hendecasyllabic poems: nos. 36, 40, 54, and fr. 1) he mentions his 'iambi', he probably has in mind the critical spirit of his attacks rather than the exact metres (trimeter or scazon) in which a few of them were made. Horace's claim (*Epist.* 1. 19. 23) to have been the first to introduce *Parii* (= Archilochean) *iambi* into Latin is therefore not unjustified; for all his *Epodes* (in which abuse, friendship, moralizing, and patriotism provide the themes) have iambic elements used in the manner of Archilochus; in nos, 1–10 the couplets consist of a trimeter followed by a dimeter, 11–16 show iambic and dactylic elements variously combined into couplets, and 17 is entirely in trimeters. In this type of poetry Horace had no real successor. In the *App. Verg.* three poems (*Catal.* 6, 10, and 12) are in trimeters and one (no. 13) in iambic couplets; all except no. 10 (a parody of Catullus 4) are vituperative. In the first century A.D. Phaedrus used iambics for his fables; but his 'trimeters' (like those of the maxims of the mimographer Publilius Syrus, 1st c. B.C.) admit spondees in the 2nd and 4th feet and so are nearer to the dramatic senarius than to the stricter forms employed by Horace. Seneca, who in his tragedies uses elegant trimeters in the dialogue and some dimeters in the lyric parts, is far removed from the spirit of the ἴαμβος; Martial, who might have made powerful use of iambics, almost entirely neglects the dimeter and trimeter; and the apotheosis of the iambic metres (especially the dimeter) is found in Christian poets such as Prudentius (*Cathemerinon* and *Peristephanon*) and the author of 'Veni creator spiritus'.

Texts of minor authors and fragments in: E, Baehrens, *PLM*; W. Morel, *FPL*; F. Bücheler, *Carmina Lat. Epigraphica* (in A. Riese's *Anthologia Latina*).                                    J. F. M.

**IAMBLICHUS** (1) (fl. *c.* A.D. 160–80), Greek writer of Syrian origin, author of a novel entitled *Babyloniaka* or *Rhodanes and Sinonis*. The work (whose length is disputed: 16, 35, or 39 books) is now lost, but an abstract of it made by Photius (*Bibl.*, *Cod.* 94) and a few fragments preserved by the *Suda* suggest that the story presented all the compulsory ingredients of the genre (a couple of lovers are separated by events, and after going through innumerable hazards are at last reunited). The plot seems to have been richer in the adventurous element and more disjointed in structure than is the case with the extant novels; the language and style conformed to the canons of the Sophistic; characterization was poor.

Text. E. Habrich, *Jamblichi Babyloniacorum Reliquiae* (Teubner, 1960).
Criticism. Rohde, *Griech. Roman*, 388 ff.; Christ–Schmid–Stählin ii. 2⁶, 817 ff.; F. Altheim, *Literatur u. Gesellschaft im ausgehenden Altertum* (1948–50), i. 48 ff. (U. Schneider-Menzel); A. Lesky, *Gesch. d. griech. Lit.²* (1963), 921 ff.          G. G.

**IAMBLICHUS** (2) (probably *c.* A.D. 250–*c.* 325), Neoplatonist philosopher, born at Chalcis in Coele Syria, studied under Porphyry in Rome or Sicily; later he founded his own school in Syria (? at Apamea). Extant writings: (1) Περὶ τοῦ Πυθαγορικοῦ βίου (*Vit. Pyth.*); Λόγος προτρεπτικὸς εἰς φιλοσοφίαν (*Protrept.*); and three treatises on mathematics (see bibliography: the authorship of Θεολ. ἀριθμ. is disputed). These five formed part of a semi-popular encyclopaedia of Pythagoreanism. *Protrepticus* is a *catena* of extracts from earlier writers, and valuable as a source-book. (2) The 'Reply of Abammon to Porphyry's *Letter to Anebo*', a defence of ritualistic magic, generally known as *De mysteriis*, is attributed in our best MS. to Iamblichus, on the authority of a lost work of Proclus. The ascription, which Zeller doubted, is probably right (C. Rasche, *De I. libri . . . de myst. auctore*, 1911). Though ill-written and philosophically worthless, the book is a curious guide to the superstitions of its age. Iamblichus' lost writings include a Περὶ ψυχῆς (excerpts preserved in Stobaeus); a Περὶ θεῶν, used by Macrobius and Julian; an elaborate exposition of 'Chaldaean' theology; and a number of highly tendentious commentaries on Plato and Aristotle, much quoted by Proclus.

Iamblichus' extant works are superficial; but his successors credit him with important contributions to the architecture of the Neoplatonic system. On the other hand, he corrupted Plotinus' teaching by introducing theosophical fantasies from alien sources; and his tendency is to substitute magic for mysticism, θεουργία for the Plotinian θεωρία.

Texts. *Vit. Pyth.*, L. Deubner (1937); *Protrept.*, H. Pistelli (1888); Περὶ τῆς κοινῆς μαθηματικῆς ἐπιστήμης, N. Festa (1891); Εἰς Νικομάχου ἀριθμητικὴν εἰσαγωγή, H. Pistelli (1894); Θεολογούμενα τῆς ἀριθμητικῆς, V. de Falco (1922); *De myst.*, text and transl. E. des Places (Budé, 1966). Germ. transl. and comm. Th. Hopfner (1922).
Ideas and Influence. K. Praechter in *Genethliakon Robert* (1910), 108 ff.; J. Bidez, *Rev. Ét. Gr.* 1919; E. R. Dodds, *Proclus' Elements of Theology* (1933), xix ff.; P. Merlan, *From Platonism to Neoplatonism²* (1960); A. C. Lloyd in *Cambridge History of Later Greek and Early Medieval Philosophy* (1967), 294 ff.; cf. bibliography under NEOPLATONISM.                        E. R. D.

**IAMBULUS,** author of a narrative now lost, excerpts of which are preserved in Diodorus (2. 55–60). Nothing is known about him, except that his name is Syrian. His work belongs, as Rohde has emphasized, to the genre 'Reisefabulistik' rather than to the novel proper, in so far as it does not seem to have contained any erotic element at all. It is a fantastic description of a journey, made by the author, through Aethiopia to a happy Island of the Sun (vaguely located in the South) whence, after a seven years' sojourn amongst the natives, Iambulus was expelled, finally to return home (Syria?) via India. The detailed description of the island (improbably identified by various scholars with Java, Bali, Ceylon, etc.), its inhabitants, and their customs, seems partly inspired by utopistic theories (of Euhemeristic-Cynic origin) then current (common property of women and many 'communistic' social features are noted by Iambulus as established amongst the natives) and partly reflecting purely fabulous motifs which had been circulating amongst the Greeks since times immemorial (cf. the Hyperboreans, the *Insulae Fortunatae*, the Hesperides) and which were stimulated by the increased contacts with the East after Alexander's conquest.

Rohde, *Griech. Roman*, 241 ff.; R. von Pöhlmann, *Gesch. d. sozialen Frage...in d. antiken Welt³* (1925), ii. 317 ff. (cf. also Register, s.v. Jambulos). Cf. Tarn, *Alexander* 411 ff., for possible influence on the Sun-State (Heliopolitai) which Aristonicus (q.v.) promised his followers (but see D. R. Dudley, *JRS* 1941, 96 f.).          G. G.

**IAMUS,** legendary son, by Apollo, of Evadne (q.v. 1). She bore him while alone and left him in a bed of (?) gillyflowers (ἴα, hardly violets, for they were yellow and red, Pindar, *Ol.* 6. 55). Aepytus, her guardian, learning at Delphi what had happened, had the baby searched for, and found that he had been fed with honey by serpents. From the flowers he was called Iamus. Coming to young manhood, he prayed to Poseidon and Apollo, and the latter bade him go to Olympia; there he became a prophet and ancestor of the clan of the Iamidae, which continued at Olympia well into the third century A.D. (L. Weniger, *ARW* 1915, 53 ff.).          H. J. R.

**IAPETUS,** in mythology, son of Earth and Heaven, father by Clymene the Oceanid of Prometheus, Epimetheus, Atlas, and Menoetius (Hes. *Theog.* 134, 507 ff.). His name yields no plausible Greek etymology, and it is far from unlikely that it is to be connected with that of Japhet son of Noah, both probably going back to some very old figure of Asianic mythology, variously handled by Greek and Hebrew tradition. H. J. R.

**IAPYGIA,** name given by Greek writers to the 'heel' of Italy, the region the Romans called Calabria (q.v.). Roman poets sometimes employed the name in imitation of the Greeks. Often Iapygia was used to include Apulia (q.v.) as well. The inhabitants of the region were collectively called Iapyges. E. T. S.

**IASUS, IASIUS.** These names seem to be etymologically identical, are perpetually confused, and occasionally are confounded with Iasion, Demeter's lover (*see* DARDANUS, DEMETER). Apart from Dardanus' brother, they are borne by a number of persons, all totally insignificant and uninteresting, e.g. two early kings of Argos, Arcadian and also Boeotian heroes, etc.; list given by Höfer in Roscher's *Lexikon* ii. 88 f. H. J. R.

**IAZYGES,** a Sarmatian nomadic people, originally lived near the Lower Danube (Ov. *Pont.* 1. 2. 7 f.) but during the first half of the first century A.D. they migrated westward to occupy the plain between the Danube and Theiss (Pliny, *HN* 4. 80). Domitian campaigned at least once against them (A.D. 89); under Trajan they became Roman allies, but later joined in the Marcomannic Wars against Rome. Wars also occurred in 283, 284, and 358. J. J. W.

**IBERIA,** (1) one of the ancient names for Spain (q.v.); (2) the name of the mountain-girt land (roughly coincident with modern *Georgia*) south of the Caucasus, northeast of Armenia, between the Black Sea and the Caspian. Its chief river was the Cyrus (*Kur*). The Greeks, after Pompey's exploration in 65 B.C., knew four entrance-passes: from Colchis by Scharapani; from the north by the Caucasian Gates (*Darial Pass*); from Albania by Derbent Pass; from Armenia through Kars. The people, organized in four classes (chiefs, priests, fighter-tillers, slaves), were subject probably to Persia and certainly to Mithridates VI. They were not included in the Roman Empire except occasionally as 'clients'.

Strabo 11. 491–2, 497, 500–1, 528; Ptol. *Geog.* 5. 9. 27 ff.; 8. 18. 2; 19. 1. 5. Cary, *Geographic Background*, 177. E. H. W.

**IBYCUS,** son of Phytius, of Rhegium, lyric poet of the sixth century B.C., whose *floruit* is given by the *Suda* as 564–561 B.C. and by Eusebius–Jerome as 536–533 B.C. He seems to have begun by writing lyrical narratives in the style of Stesichorus, and fragments indicate that he told of the Sack of Troy (fr. 22), the Calydonian boar-hunt (fr. 9), and the birth of Athene (fr. 17). He also wrote about Ortygia (fr. 40) and told Sicilian stories (Ael. *NA* 6. 51). He left Sicily because, it was said, he refused to become a tyrant (Diogenian. 1. 207) and went to Samos, where he worked at the court of Polycrates (*Suda*, s.v. *Ἴβυκος*). To this period may belong his most striking fragments, notably those about love when he is getting old (frs. 5 and 6), and the lines to Euryalus (fr. 7). *POxy.* 3 (fr. 1) has been attributed to him, since it mentions Polycrates, but this has been questioned. If it is his, it is more probably concerned with the tyrant's son than with the tyrant himself, and seems to be a playful leave-taking of his earlier manner for the erotic poetry in favour at Samos. His works were collected in seven books and seem to have consisted largely of choral poems, of which some

were *encomia*, and personal love-songs, written in a great variety of metres. He has a rich and brilliant style, a vivid imagination, a great capacity for describing the emotions, especially love, and a real love of nature (frs. 33, 34, 36). He is said to have been killed by robbers, who were brought to justice by birds who saw the murder (Plut. *Garr.* 14; Antip. Sid. ap. *Anth. Pal.* 7. 745), and was buried at Rhegium (*Anth. Pal.* 7. 714).

TEXT. Page, *Poet. Mel. Gr.* 144–69.
CRITICISM. U. von Wilamowitz-Moellendorff, *Sappho und Simonides* (1913), 121 ff.; C. M. Bowra, *Greek Lyric Poetry*² (1962), 241 ff. C. M. B.

**ICARIUS** or **ICARUS** (but the latter name is usually that of Daedalus' son (*see* DAEDALUS)), in mythology, (1) an eponym of an Athenian deme who received Dionysus hospitably when he came to Attica, and was given the vine. He made wine and gave some to his neighbours, who on feeling the effects concluded that they were poisoned and killed him. His daughter Erigone was guided by their dog Maera to his body and hanged herself for grief. In memory of her the festival of the Aiora was instituted, in which swinging played a part, and Aristaeus propitiated the shade of Icarius; in consequence, a pestilence on Ceos which had followed their reception of the murderers of Icarius ceased. Icarius became the constellation Boötes; Erigone, Virgo; the dog, Canicula (Procyon). See schol. *Il.* 22. 29; Hyg. *Fab.* 130 and Rose ad loc.; *Poet. Astr.* 2. 4. (2) Father of Penelope (q.v.; *Od.* 1. 329 and often). Tyndareus induced him to give Penelope to Odysseus in return for the latter's good advice to make Helen's wooers take the oath (*see* HELEN). Icarius tried to induce them to remain with him in Lacedaemon, but, on the choice being left to her, she indicated that she would follow her husband to Ithaca (Apollod. 3. 132; Paus. 3. 20. 10). H. J. R.

**ICENI,** a British tribe in Norfolk and Suffolk whose coins suggest a Belgic aristocracy ruling an indigenous population. The following pre-Roman rulers are attested on the coinage: *Cans-duro, Anted, Ecen, Aesu, Saemu,* and *Subidastu.* Under pressure from the Catuvellauni, the tribe voluntarily made a treaty with Claudius, but in 47 rebelled against forcible disarmament. Prasutagus was established as client-king until his death in 60 when the attempted suppression of independence by Roman officials caused the rebellion of the tribe under his wife Boudicca (q.v.). After the harsh suppression of this outbreak (from which economic recovery was slow) a self-governing *civitas* was created with *caput* at Venta (Caistor by Norwich) (*It. Ant.* 474. 6; 479. 10; *Rav. Cosm.* 103). The town remained small (35 acres within its third-century walls). Apart from a considerable local pottery industry, the *civitas* was agricultural with some evidence for wool production in the fourth century, but few villas. In the third century the coast was protected by a series of forts (Saxon shore), and there is evidence for Germanic settlements from early in the fifth.

R. R. Clarke, *Arch. Journ.* (1939); *East Anglia* (1960), chs. vi–viii; D. F. Allen, in *Iron Age in S. Britain* (coinage); C. F. C. Hawkes, *Arch. Journ.* 1949, 62 (Caistor); A. L. F. Rivet, *Town and Country in Roman Britain*² (1964), 156 f. S. S. F.

**ICILIUS** (*PW* 2), LUCIUS, a plebeian hero, though probably of patrician descent, betrothed to Verginia and leader of the second secession, has little claim to historical existence, but the *Lex Icilia de Aventino publicando* (traditionally dated 456 B.C.), the text of which was still preserved in Augustus' time in the Aventine temple of Diana (Dion. Hal. 10. 32. 4), is indisputably a genuine document of *c.* 450. The law provided allotments on the Aventine to the *plebs* either as agricultural or (very probably) as building land. It was later attributed to Icilius merely because of his renown as a popular hero.

Ogilvie, *Comm. Livy 1-5*, 446 f. P. T.

**ICTINUS** was one of a number of fine architects who worked at Athens in the time of Pericles, under the general direction of the sculptor Phidias (q.v.; cf. Plut. *Per.* 13). He designed the Parthenon (q.v.) in collaboration with Callicrates (q.v. 1), and with a certain Carpion, otherwise unknown, as co-author, wrote an account of it (Vitr. *Pref.* 7)—it was not unusual for architects to write about their work from this time onwards. He was also the architect of the temple of Apollo at Bassae (q.v.) in Arcadia. In spite of Pausanias (8. 41. 7-9), who implies a date in the 420s, Dinsmoor (*Architecture of Ancient Greece* (1950), 148, 154 ff.) believes that the temple was designed and begun before the Parthenon, about 450 B.C., though it was not completed till much later. Ictinus was also one of a series of architects—Coroebus, Ictinus, Metagenes—who worked at Eleusis (q.v.) on the Telesterion, the great hall in which the performance of the mysteries took place; the plan of the hall, with its rows of columns supporting the roof, was repeatedly modified.

R. E. W.

**ICTIS**, probably *St. Michael's Mt.* by Penzance. Identification with the Isle of Wight (even Thanet has been suggested) is not favoured. Diodorus (5. 22. 2, 4) records that the people of Belerium (*Land's End*) brought tin in wagons at ebb-tide to the adjacent island Ictis. Pliny (4. 104 from Timaeus) puts Ictis six days' sail inwards from Britain, perhaps confusing it with Vectis (*Isle of Wight*) or the Isles of Scilly.

Thomson, *Hist. Anc. Geog.* 145 f., 403. E. H. W.

**IDAEAN DACTYLS** (Δάκτυλοι Ἰδαῖοι), literally the Fingers of Ida, but whether the Phrygian or the Cretan Ida and whether their name refers to craftsmanship, dwarfish size, or something else, the ancients were in doubt. The oldest mention surviving is in the *Phoronis*, ap. schol. Ap. Rhod. 1. 1129, which says they were called Celmis, Damnameneus, and Acmon, that they were big and powerful, wizards, servants of 'Adresteia of the mountains', presumably the same as Cybele or Rhea, Phrygians, and inventors of smithcraft. But Apollonius (ibid.) says they were Cretans, sons of a nymph Anchiale, who grasped handfuls of dust in her birthpains, or (the language is ambiguous) produced them by throwing handfuls of dust. More and divergent accounts of them in the schol., ibid., and still more collected by Lobeck, *Aglaoph.* 1156 ff.; von Sybel in Roscher's *Lexikon*, s.v. 'Daktyloi'. For their dwarfish size cf. Paus. 8. 31. 3, and for their connexion with Heracles *see* HERACLES. *See also* MAGIC, § 4. H. J. R.

**IDAEUS**, 'connected with Ida', and so (*a*) a title of Zeus (*Il.* 16. 605 (Trojan) and on Cretan coins and (usually in a dialect form) inscriptions); (*b*) a stock name for sundry little-known Trojans or Cretans (list in Stoll in Roscher's *Lexikon* ii. 95). (*c*) Magic name for a finger, perhaps the index (*PMG* iv. 455). H. J. R.

**IDAS**, in mythology, son of Aphareus and brother of Lynceus. He was 'the strongest of men' (*Il.* 9. 558), and drew his bow against Apollo (ibid.). The reason, according to later authorities (Chest of Cypselus in Paus. 5. 18. 2; Apollod. 1. 60-1), was that after he had won his bride Marpessa from her father Euenus, son of Ares (add Bacchylides 19), Apollo in turn carried her off; Idas fought him and Zeus made peace by giving Marpessa her choice between them; she preferred Idas. He was one of the Argonauts (q.v.; Ap. Rhod. 1. 152 and often),

valiant but hot-tempered. He also took part in the Calydonian boar-hunt (Apollod. 1. 67), as was natural, for Meleager (q.v. 1) was his son-in-law (*Il.* 9. 556). Though his final encounter with the Dioscuri (q.v.) is variously told, Pindar (*Nem.* 10. 60) makes Idas kill Castor, while Lynceus, whose sight was preternaturally sharp, looks out for the approach of the twins. H. J. R.

**IDMON**, 'the knowing one', name of several skilful persons, especially a seer, son of Apollo or Abas (Ap. Rhod. 1. 139 ff. and schol.), who accompanied the Argonauts (q.v.) although he foreknew he would not return alive (ibid. and 2. 815 ff.); he was killed by a boar in the country of the Mariandyni. H. J. R.

**IDOMENEUS** (1), in mythology, leader of the Cretan contingent before Troy (*Il.* 2. 645); of distinguished valour although older than most of the warriors (13. 210 ff., 361 ff.). He was of Minos' race and one of Helen's suitors (Hesiod, fr. 96. 16 ff. Rzach). The story of Homecomer's Vow (Stith Thompson, S241) is told of him (Servius on *Aen.* 3. 121); in a storm he vowed to sacrifice to Poseidon the first thing which met him on his return. This was his son; fulfilling or trying to fulfil the vow he was forced to leave Crete for Italy because a pestilence broke out. H. J. R.

**IDOMENEUS** (2) (*c.* 325-*c.* 270 B.C.), biographer and politician of Lampsacus, and friend of Epicurus (cf. Usener, *Epicurea*, frs. 128-38).
WORKS (*FGrH* 338). (1) Περὶ τῶν Σωκρατικῶν (Diog. Laert. 2. 20): fragments on the Socratic Aeschines. (2) Περὶ δημαγωγῶν in at least two books; fragments in Plutarch and Athenaeus concern leading Athenian politicians (3) Ἱστορία τῶν κατὰ Σαμοθράκην, cf. *Suda* s.v. 'Idomeneus'. Following the Peripatetic, anecdotal method, Idomeneus reproduced much unreliable scandal, perhaps attacking politicians whose ideas he disliked; after Hermippus he was not used. F. W. W.

**IDUMAEA** was the arid country south of Judaea occupied by the Edomites in the fourth century B.C. when they were pushed westwards by the Nabataeans. Soon after 129 B.C. it was annexed by John Hyrcanus (*see* JEWS) and the inhabitants forcibly converted to Judaism. Adora and Marisa, both prominent Idumaean commercial centres since the third century B.C., were organized as cities and freed from Jewish control by Pompey (63: cf. ANTIPATER 6). In 40 Idumaea as a whole was incorporated in the kingdom of Herod (q.v. 1) the Great as a toparchy, and an attempt by an Idumaean noble, Costobar, in collaboration with Cleopatra to regain independence (*c.* 34) failed. After Herod's death Idumaea formed part of the ethnarchy of Archelaus (q.v. 4), which became the Roman province of Judaea in A.D. 6. Despite the Idumaeans' firm adherence to Judaism, they were not fully accepted by the Jews, who resented Rome's appointment of the Idumaean Herod as their king.

E. M. S.

**IGUVIUM**, modern *Gubbio* in Umbria. Although infrequently mentioned in ancient literature, Iguvium is famous for the Tabulae Iguvinae (q.v.). Constituting the largest corpus of liturgical texts from pre-Christian Europe, they are written in Umbrian, a language they reveal to be closely related to Oscan (q.v.). (*See* UMBRIANS.)

J. W. Poultney, *Bronze Tables of Iguvium* (U.S.A., 1959). E. T. S.

**ILERDA** (modern *Lérida*), Iberian city of the Ilergetes in Catalonia, north-west of Tarraco (q.v.), on a steep rise over the Sicoris (*Segre*); a Roman *municipium* under Augustus. The Iberian and early Latin coinage displays a wolf; the municipal coins adapt its sex to the she-wolf of Rome. Here, in 49 B.C., Caesar defeated Pompey's legates Afranius and Petreius (Caes. *BCiv.* 38–87). The city was largely ruined by the Frankish invasion of the third century. M. I. H.

**ILIAS LATINA** (*Homerus Latinus*), a version of the *Iliad* in 1,070 hexameters. The ascription of the work (entitled merely 'Homerus') to Silius Italicus on the grounds of two acrostics (at the beginning and end) is untenable; but the author may be a Baebius Italicus. The allusion to the Julian house in 899 ff. precludes a date of authorship later than A.D. 68. Though important for its perpetuation of the *Iliad* during centuries ignorant of Greek, the work is in general a meagre epitome devoid of artistic merit, characterized by free and uneven treatment, a straightforward style thickly embellished with Virgilian and Ovidian echoes, and by heavy and monotonous versification.

TEXTS. *PLM* ii². 3; F. Plessis (1885). J. Tolkiehn, *Homer u. die römische Poesie* (1900). A. H.-W.

**ILIONA** ('Ἰλιόνη), in mythology, eldest daughter of Priam and Hecuba (qq.v., Verg. *Aen.* 1. 653–4). Wife of Polymestor (*see* HECUBA), she saved the life of Polydorus by passing him off as her son, Polymestor thus murdering his own child (Hyg. *Fab.* 109, cf. Pacuvius, frs. of *Iliona*). H. J. R.

**ILIUM,** an Aeolian foundation, established in the seventh century B.C. on the site of ancient Troy. Its importance derived from the famous temple of Athena (visited by Xerxes and Alexander), the centre, from the fourth century onwards, of a religious synedrion. The landing of Livius Salinator (190) inaugurated cordial relations with Rome (though Ilium was sacked by Fimbria's unruly troops in 85); and the Emperors followed Julius Caesar's example in patronizing Ilium and its temple, because of the legend that the founders of Rome were of Trojan origin.

A. Brückner, in Dörpfeld's *Troia und Ilion* (1902), ii. 549. D. E. W. W.

**ILLYRICUM,** the territory of the Indo-European Illyrians. Their attacks on Adriatic shipping brought Roman intervention in the First and Second Illyrian Wars (228–9; 219 B.C.): *see* TEUTA, DEMETRIUS, 6. During the Second Punic War the Illyrian kingdom acted as a buffer State between Rome and Macedon, and at the peace after Cynoscephalae (197 B.C.) the Illyrians under Pleuratus II (206–180) were awarded some Macedonian territories. Under his successor Gentius (*c.* 180–168), however, piracy was revived and as an ally of Perseus of Macedon they suffered ignominious defeat from the praetor L. Anicius Gallus in 168 B.C. (Livy 44. 30–2). The settlement, by which the kingdom was divided into three parts, did not lead to a permanent Roman administration in Illyricum, and thereafter only sporadic campaigns by consuls or proconsuls are attested, chiefly against the Delmatae (*see* DALMATIA). In 59 B.C. Illyricum was allotted to Caesar along with Cisalpine Gaul and during the winters between his campaigns in Gaul he administered his province from Aquileia (Caes. *BGall.* 2. 35; 5. 1–2). During the Civil War the Illyrians sided with the Pompeians while the coastal settlements of Roman citizens (*conventus civium Romanorum*) supported Caesar. His legates were defeated more than once but during Caesar's dictatorship P. Vatinius made headway against the Delmatae. Later Octavian undertook limited campaigns in the area, mainly for propaganda and military reasons, against the Iapudes and Pannonians in 35 B.C., and against the Delmatae in 34–33 B.C. (cf. W. Schmitthenner, *Hist.* 1958, 169 ff.). After 27 B.C. Illyricum remained a senatorial province until Roman

control was advanced along the Save valley to the Danube during the Bellum Pannonicum of 13–9 B.C. by Tiberius. The institution of Illyricum as an imperial province probably took place in 11 B.C. (Dio 54. 34. 4; for a list of legates 8 B.C.–A.D. 6 cf. R. Syme, *JRS* 1934, 130). In A.D. 6 the Breuci of the Save valley and the Daesitiates of Bosnia revolted, carrying with them the rest of Illyricum. Reconquest was achieved by Tiberius, in the Save valley in A.D. 6–8, in the southern interior in A.D. 9. It was probably in A.D. 9 that Illyricum was divided into two imperial provinces, known earlier as *Illyricum superius* and *inferius*, later Dalmatia and Pannonia (qq.v.). Under the Empire all the Danubian provinces (Raetia, Noricum, Pannonia, Dalmatia, Moesia, and Dacia) were grouped in a single customs-area, *portorium Illyricum*. From Diocletian onwards Illyricum denoted two dioceses, *Illyricum orientale* or *dioecesis Moesiarum*, *Illyricum occidentale* or *dioecesis Pannoniarum*.

M. Fluss, *PW* Suppl. v, s.v. 'Illyrioi'. R. L. Beaumont, *JHS* 1936, 159 ff. on Greek trade and settlement.
ROMAN CAMPAIGNS. G. Zippel, *Die römische Herrschaft in Illyricum bis auf Augustus* (1877); E. Badian, *PBSR* 1952, 72 ff. = *Stud. Gr. Rom. Hist.* 1 ff.; C. Patsch, *Sitz. Wien*, 214 i (1932); E. Koestermann, *Hermes* 1953, 345 ff.; N. G. L. Hammond, *JRS* 1966, 39 ff.; 1968, 1 ff; H. J. Dell, *Hist.* 1967, 344 ff.
PORTORIUM. A. Dobó, *Publicum portorium Illyrici* (Diss. Pann. II. 16, 1940). J. J. W.

**ILLYRII,** a large group of related Indo-European tribes, who occupied in classical times the western side of the Balkan range from the head of the Adriatic Sea to the hinterland of the Gulf of Valona and extended northwards as far as the Eastern Alps and the Danube and eastwards into some districts beyond the Balkan range. The name was properly that of a small tribe between Scodra and the Mati river, and it was applied by the Greeks and later by the Romans to the other tribes with which they had regular contact. Thus Illyris meant to the Greeks the southern part of the area, that neighbouring Macedonia, Epirus, and the Greek cities on the Adriatic coast and islands, and Illyricum meant to the Romans the whole area from the Eastern Alps to the hinterland of the Gulf of Valona. The earliest signs of Indo-European penetration into Illyris have been found at Pazhok in Central Albania, where chieftains of a 'Kurgan' culture were buried in mortuary chambers in large tumuli in the latter part of the third millennium, and there is ample evidence of seafaring and traffic in the southern Adriatic Sea in the second millennium, when piratical groups made settlements in Corcyra and in Leucas. The southwards expansion of Illyrian peoples into what is now Central Albania occurred probably in the tenth century. Later, people of a similar culture reached Vergina in the Haliacmon valley. Greek colonies were planted on the Albanian coast at Epidamnus (later called Dyrrachium (q.v.)) in the late seventh century, Apollonia (q.v.) in the early sixth century, and later at Lissus, and on the islands at Corcyra Nigra (*Korčula*), Issa (*Vis*), and Pharos (*Hvar*). Enlivened by Greek trade and ideas the Illyrian tribes, which were always warlike on land and sea, exerted continual pressure on Macedonia and Epirus and raided far into the Mediterranean Sea. Individual tribes became very powerful—in particular the Liburni, Dardani (q.v.), Ardiaei, and Autariatae—but they enslaved their neighbours and never created an effective combination of tribal states against a common enemy. When Macedonia became strong under Philip II (q.v.) and Epirus under Pyrrhus (q.v.), they occupied the southern part of Illyris. When the power of Macedonia and of Epirus declined, the Illyrians pressed southwards by land and by sea, and in particular the Ardiaean kingdom, based on the southern Dalmatian coast, expanded southwards to Scodra and Lissus under Pleuratus I (*c.* 260 B.C.) and under his son Agron. On the death of the latter his widow Teuta (q.v.) was acting as regent for Pinnes when the first clash with Rome occurred. See ILLYRICUM.

H. Krahe, *Die Sprache der Illyrier* (1955); A. Mayer, *Die Sprache der alten Illyrier* i (1957), ii (1959); M. Fluss, *PW* Suppl. v, s.v. 'Illyrioi'; R. L. Beaumont, *JHS* 1936, 159 ff.; Selim Islami and Hasan Ceka, *Studia Albanica* 1964, 1 (Tirana); F. Papazoglou, *Hist.* 1965, 143 ff.; Hammond, *Epirus*; *BSA* 1967, 239 ff.; *JRS* 1968, 1 ff.    N. G. L. H.

**ILUS,** in mythology, (1) son of Dardanus (q.v.; Apollod. 3. 140). (2) His grand-nephew, son of Tros and father of Laomedon (q.v.). He founded Ilium, being guided to the site by a cow (cf. CADMUS) and received the Palladium from heaven (ibid. 141–3).

**IMAGINES.** The wax masks of Romans who had held curule office were kept in cupboards in the atrium or *alae* of the family house with inscriptions beneath them, arranged and connected so as to form a family-tree. They received religious cult, and, on the death of a member who had held similar office, were worn by actors in the funeral procession. The custom lasted until well into the Empire, having acquired ethical and social significance. It helped in the formation of the *nobilitas* (q.v.). In the first century B.C. it was disputed whether all *gentiles* or only immediate descendants were entitled to keep masks. Condemned criminals seem to have lost the *ius imaginum*, active or passive (see, e.g., Cic. *Sulla* 88; Suet. *Nero* 37. 1). *See also* PORTRAITURE, ROMAN.

Polyb. 6. 53; Pliny, *HN* 35. 6 f. *PW*, s.v. 'Imagines maiorum'; E. Bethe, *Ahnenbild und Familiengeschichte bei Römern und Griechen* (1935).    E. B.

**IMMUNITAS** was the exemption of a community or an individual from obligations to the Roman State or of an individual from obligations to a local community. As regards Roman taxation, *civitates foederatae* or *civitates* declared *immunes* by a *lex* or *senatus consultum* were in theory permanently immune, though in practice, especially under the Empire, both statuses could be removed at will by Rome. Grants of immunity intended to be permanent were rare under the Empire; one example is Nero's proclamation of the *libertas* and *immunitas* of Greece—which was revoked by Vespasian. Temporary grants of immunity from taxation in special circumstances were not uncommon; they might be made either by the Emperor (*AE* 1916, 42) or by the Senate (Tac. *Ann.* 12. 61–3).

Immunity for life from Roman taxation could also be granted to individuals by *lex*, *senatus consultum*, or imperial decree (*SEG* ix. 8. iii) and might sometimes apply to the person's descendants in perpetuity (*CIL* i². 588). Immunity from other State services—military services, forced labour, the provision of supplies to officials or soldiers, could also be granted, as by the edict of Octavian as Triumvir on the privileges of veterans (*FIRA* i². 56).

Equally important was the question of immunity from local *munera*, to which adult male citizens and *incolae* of communities were normally liable (see *Dig.* 50. 5–6). *Immunitas* might be granted either by Rome or by the community. Apart from personal grants, there was general exemption under the Empire for such groups as shippers supplying corn to Rome, *conductores* (q.v.) and *coloni* of imperial estates, and local *philosophi*, *rhetores*, and *medici*.

In the Roman army *immunes* were soldiers promoted from the ranks and released from ordinary duties to perform certain skilled tasks (*Dig.* 50. 6. 7).    F. G. B. M.

**IMPERATOR** (αὐτοκράτωρ), a generic title for Roman commanders, became a special title of honour. After a victory the general was saluted *imperator* by his soldiers. He assumed the title after his name until the end of his magistracy or until his triumph. Sometimes the Senate

seems to have given or confirmed the title. The origin of this form of honour is unknown, but some religious meaning is possible (cf. the formula *Iuppiter imperator*). The first certainly attested *imperator* is L. Aemilius Paullus in 189 B.C., as the evidence about Scipio Africanus is uncertain. The title was assumed especially by proconsuls and gained new importance through Sulla before he was appointed dictator. The increasing influence of the army in the late Republic made *imperator* the symbol of the military authority. Sulla occasionally stated (and Pompey emphasized) that he was saluted *imperator* more than once. Caesar first used the title permanently, but it is doubtful whether in 45 B.C. he received from the Senate a hereditary title of *imperator* (as Dio Cass. 43. 44. 2 states). Agrippa in 38 B.C. refused a triumph for victories won under Octavian's superior command and established the rule that the *princeps* should assume the salutations and the triumphs of his legates. Henceforth, apparently, Octavian used *imperator* as praenomen (*imperator Caesar*, not *Caesar imperator*), perhaps intending to emphasize the personal and family value of the title. Thus the title came to denote the supreme power and was commonly used in this sense. But, officially, Otho was the first to imitate Augustus. Vespasian definitively converted the name *imperator* into a praenomen of the *princeps*. The formula *imperator Caesar* was sometimes extended to members of the family of the *princeps* who were associated with him in power. On the death of a *princeps*, or during a rebellion, the *salutatio* of a general as an *imperator* by an army indicated that he was the candidate of that body for the imperial dignity.

The use of the praenomen did not suppress the old usage of *imperator* after the name. After a victory the Emperor registered the *salutatio imperatoria* after his name (e.g.: Imp. Caesar . . . Traianus . . . imp. VI). From the second half of the third century the Emperor was deemed to receive a *salutatio* every year. The number of the salutations became practically identical with the number of the years of the reign.

Theoretically, governors of senatorial provinces, having their own *auspicia*, could assume the title of *imperator*. But the last instance of such a *salutatio* is that of Junius Blaesus (q.v. 2), proconsul of Africa in A.D. 22 (Tac. *Ann.* 3. 74).

D. McFayden, *The History of the Title Imperator under the Roman Empire* (U.S.A. 1920); M. A. Levi, *Riv. Fil.* 1932, 207 ff.; G. De Sanctis, *Studi in onore di S. Riccobono* (1936), ii. 57 ff.; J. Carcopino, *Points de vue sur l'impérialisme romain* (1934), 127 ff.; J. Stroux, *Die Antike* 1937, 197; H. Nesselhauf, *Klio* 1937, 306 ff.; A. v. Premerstein, *Vom Werden und Wesen des Prinzipats* (1937), 245 ff.; E. Peterson, 'Christus als Imperator', in *Zeuge der Wahrheit* 1937, 54 ff.; M. Grant, *From Imperium to Auctoritas* (1946); K. Kraft, *Jahrb. f. Numism.* 1952–3, 65 ff.; A. E. Raubitschek, *JRS* 1954, 65 ff.; R. Syme, *Hist.* 1958, 172 ff.; D. Kienast, *Sav. Zeitschr.* 1961, 403 ff.; F. de Martino, *Storia della costituzione romana* iv (1962), 188 ff.; L. Lesuisse, *Ant. Class.* 1961, 415 ff.; R. Combes, *Imperator* (Paris, 1966).    A. M.

**IMPERIUM** was the supreme administrative power, involving command in war and the interpretation and execution of law (including the infliction of the death penalty), which belonged at Rome to the kings and, after their expulsion, to consuls, military tribunes with consular power (from 445 to 367 B.C.), praetors, dictators, and masters of the horse. It was held later in the Republic by members of certain commissions (e.g. boards for the distribution of land, Cic. *Leg. Agr.* 2. 28) and by proconsuls and propraetors, who were either ex-magistrates or *privati*, on whom a special command had been conferred. Its application was increasingly restricted; first, when two consuls replaced the king, by the principle of *collegium*. Secondly, by the *Leges Valeriae*, traditionally assigned to 509, 449, and 300 B.C., and the *Leges Porciae*, probably of the second century B.C., magistrates were not allowed to execute Roman citizens at Rome without trial, a prisoner at Rome having the *ius provocandi ad populum*. This right of appeal was extended, probably by convention and not by legal enactment, to Roman citizens on service with the armies and in the provinces. Thirdly, the *imperium* of pro-magistrates was generally restricted to the bounds of their *provinciae* (*see further* PROVINCIA). *Imperium* needed ratification by a *lex curiata*—a convention which persisted to the end of the Republic (Cic. *Leg. Agr.* 2. 26; *Fam.* 1. 9. 25). To a pro-magistrate or a *privatus cum imperio*, *imperium* was granted for a year at a time, or until his commission was achieved. Grants of *imperium* for a specified term of several years occur only at the end of the Republic, the earliest being the grant of *imperium* to Pompey for three years by the *Lex Gabinia* of 67 B.C.

**2.** Under the Republic, in the case of conflict, the *imperium* of a consul, who held twelve *fasces* (q.v.), could probably override that of a praetor, who held six. As between consuls and proconsuls, each of whom held twelve *fasces*, the consul could override the proconsul by virtue of the *auctoritas* of his office. Conflict in the same territorial sphere between proconsuls first arose in 67 between Pompey (in pursuit of pirates) and Metellus, proconsul of Crete; so in 57 B.C. the question of allowing Pompey, in virtue of his corn commission, to override other proconsuls was mooted, and Brutus and Cassius were actually granted *imperium maius* in the East by the Senate in 43 (Livy, *Per.* 122).

**3.** Octavian held *imperium, pro praetore* and later as consul, in 43, as triumvir from 42 to 33 B.C., and as consul in 31–23 B.C. (and, from 27, as proconsul of a large number of provinces). When in 23 he resigned the consulship and the *auctoritas* that went with it, his *imperium* was made *maius*, and could be exercised from within the city of Rome. This entitled him to interfere with authority in the public provinces (those of which he was not himself proconsul), as the Cyrene edicts (*JRS* 1927, 34 ff., 42 ff.) conclusively prove. By this same enactment or, if Cassius Dio 54. 10. 5 is right (as A. H. M. Jones has argued, *Studies in Roman Government and Law*, 1960, 3 ff.), by a further bill in 19 B.C., Italy was included within the field of his *imperium*. *Imperium* was granted to him for ten-year periods in 27 and 8 B.C. and A.D. 3 and 13, and for five-year periods in 18 and 13 B.C. It was voted to succeeding emperors at their accession by the Senate (Dessau, *ILS* 229, at Nero's accession), though the senatorial decree was probably ratified formally by a *lex curiata* (Gaius, *Inst.* 1. 5, 'lex de imperio').

**4.** This *imperium* should be dissociated from the *praenomen imperatoris*, which was used by Augustus; though refused by Tiberius, Gaius, and Claudius, it appears frequently in inscriptions, and from the Flavian period onwards it was in common use. It is probable that this *praenomen* was inherited by Augustus from Julius Caesar, who used *Imperator* (q.v.) as *cognomen*.

**5.** *Imperium* was recorded in a different sense in the titles which followed the emperor's name. Under the Republic a general, after winning a victory and being saluted by his troops, adopted the official title *Imperator* (q.v.) until he celebrated his triumph. Under the Empire the whole army fought under the Emperor's *auspicia*, and he, rather than the general who was his deputy (*legatus*), was accorded the *salutatio*. Emperors therefore recorded, among the titles which followed their names, the number of salutations which they had received, the first being the acclamation at the time of their accession. Claudius, for example, at the end of his life was *Imperator xxvii*.

**6.** *Imperium maius* was sometimes conferred on others besides the Emperor, for the creation of a single military command—in this way it was granted to Germanicus in the East in A.D. 17 (Tac. *Ann.* 2. 43) and to Corbulo in A.D. 63 (Tac. *Ann.* 15. 25). If given for no such specific purpose, its recipient was indicated as a suitable successor to the Principate; in this sense it was granted to Agrippa in 18 B.C. (Cassius Dio 54. 12) and to Tiberius in A.D. 13 (Vell. Pat. 2. 121; Tac. *Ann.* 1. 3).

Mommsen, *Staatsr.*; A. H. J. Greenidge, *Roman Public Life* and *Legal Procedure in Cicero's Time* (1901), 410 ff.; M. Grant, *From Imperium to Auctoritas* (1946); H. M. Last, 'Imperium Maius', *JRS* 1947, 157 ff.; V. Ehrenberg, '*Imperium Maius* during the late Republic', *AJPhil.* 1953, 113 ff.; E. S. Staveley, 'The Constitution of the Roman Republic, 1940–54', *Hist.* 1956, 74 ff. (with bibliography), and 'The *Fasces and Imperium Maius*', *Hist.* 1963, 458 ff.; K. M. T. Atkinson, ' "Restitutio in Integrum" and "Iussum Augusti Caesaris" in an Inscription at Leyden', *Rev. int. d. Droits de l'Antiquité*, 1960, 228 ff.
J. P. B.

**INACHUS,** an Argive river and river-god, father of Io (q.v.). He was made judge between Poseidon and Hera when both claimed Argos, and decided in favour of Hera, whose cult he introduced (Apollod. 2. 13; Paus. 2. 15. 4–5); Poseidon therefore dried up his waters. He is often represented as a mortal, ancestor of the Argive kings, and therefore the earliest figure in Greek legend.
H. J. R.

**INCUBATION** denotes the practice common among the Greeks and Romans of sleeping within the precincts of a temple for the purpose of receiving a dream vision of the healing god, who would reveal a remedy for the sleeper's sickness or trouble. All gods could speak in dreams, but not all were thought capable of being induced by specific means to give an answer or perform a function. Some deities profoundly impressed visitors with their powers. At the oracle of Trophonius at Lebadea, for instance, one received a memorable emotional experience by descending into the earth and visiting the god (Paus. 9. 39). The technique of incubation was generally used for producing cures, although it could be used to regain lost articles or to receive desired information. The technique was akin to magic in that ritual acts coerced the deity to perform his healing function. Incubation was most widely used in the temples of Asclepius. The practice is attested for the cult of this deity at Epidaurus (*IG* iv². 121–7); Pergamum and Smyrna (Aristides, *Sacred Orations*); Rome (*CIG* 5980); Lebene (Hamilton, *Incubation* 69); Cos (Pliny, *HN* 29. 4, Strabo 14. 2. 19). The cult of Amphiaraus (q.v.) also fostered the practice, especially at Oropus (*Hermes* 1886, 91 ff. = *IG* vii. 235; Paus. 1. 34); Strabo (14. 1. 44) mentions the practice at the three Plutonia in Asia Minor; Ino had an incubation shrine near Thalamae in Laconia (Paus. 3. 26. 1), and the closely related Hemithea had one at Carian Castabus (Diod. 5. 63). Isis was credited with healing powers, and Sarapis was widely acclaimed as a deity who communicated cures in dreams. Before sleeping in a healing god's temple or *temenos* the incubant performed prescribed rituals designed to purify him and to ascertain the god's disposition. At Oropus he sacrificed a ram and slept that night on the victim's hide; Asclepius' clients apparently offered cakes and fruits, and slept on mattresses. Votive offerings frequently testify to cures produced by dream-revelations, and long inscriptions were set up which detailed at some length the miraculous cures that the deity performed. In some temples (in the temple of Sarapis at Delos for instance) there were official interpreters of dreams as well as aretalogists whose duty it was to sing the praises of the god. Many of the dreams and the miracles which resulted from them had no connexion whatever with cures or disease, though there must have been many cures recorded, especially cures of nervous ailments and mental complaints (*see* MIRACLES).

ANCIENT SOURCES. Notices and testimonies of incubation shrines of Asclepius are conveniently assembled in Edelstein, *Asclepius* i (see *infra*); see also A. D. Nock, 'A Vision of Mandulis Aion', *Harv.*

*Theol. Rev.* 1934; P*Oxy.* 1381; P. Roussel, *Les Cultes égyptiens à Délos* (1916).

MODERN LITERATURE. L. Deubner, *De Incubatione* (1900); Mary Hamilton, *Incubation* (1906); E. J. and L. Edelstein, *Asclepius: A Collection and Interpretation of the Testimonies*, 2 vols. (1945); A.-J. Festugière, *Personal Religion among the Greeks* (1954), ch. 6.
T. A. B.; J. E. F.

**INDIA.** This country had early trade connexions with east Africa; but it remained unknown to Mediterranean peoples until the extension of the Persian Empire to the Indus and the voyage of Darius' admiral Scylax down the Kabul and Indus rivers and round Arabia to Suez (Hecataeus, frs. 244–9 Jacoby; Hdt. 3. 98 ff.; 4. 44). Even so, India remained a land of fable and wonders (as in the *Indica* of Ctesias, *c.* 400 B.C.); it was believed to lie in the Farthest East, yet Indians were confused with Ethiopians, and in popular belief India and Ethiopia formed one country. The conquests of Alexander (327–325) brought accurate knowledge of north-west India as far as the river Hyphasis (*Beas*), and vague information about the Ganges valley and Ceylon; and the voyage of Nearchus (q.v. 2) opened up a sea connexion with the Persian Gulf. Seleucus I perhaps penetrated to the river Jumna, but in 302 he relinquished India to the Mauryan king Chandragupta. He kept a resident named Megasthenes at Chandragupta's court in Patna, who published much detail about India (*see* MEGASTHENES, PALIBOTHRA); and King Asoka (264–227) sent embassies to the Hellenistic kings. In the second century north-west India was reoccupied by the Greco-Bactrian rulers (*see* DEMETRIUS (9), MENANDER (2)); but the rise of the Parthian Empire separated India from the Greek lands, and invaders from Central Asia (*c.* 80–30 B.C.) obliterated the Greek principalities in the Indus valley. In the first century A.D. Chinese silk reached the Roman dominions through India, but land-communications with India remained irregular. The chief routes to India were (1) via Meshed and the Bolan or Mula passes, (2) via Merv, Balkh, Kabul, and Peshawar. For Roman connexions with Pakistan and Afghanistan, and especially on Sirkap (the old Taxila) and Begram, see R. E. M. Wheeler, *Rome beyond the Imperial Frontiers* (1955), 183 ff., and 'Roman contact with India, Pakistan and Afghanistan' in *Aspects of Archaeology*; A. C. Soper, 'The Roman style in Gandhara' in *AJArch.* 1951, 311.

Sea communications between India and the Persian Gulf were probably maintained by the Seleucids, but were interrupted under Parthian rule. Direct travel from Egypt to India was impeded for long by the Arabs of Yemen, whose monopoly of trade was not seriously challenged by the Ptolemies, and the voyages of Eudoxus (q.v. 3) to India proved abortive. The Arab obstruction was removed by the imperious appetite of Rome for Eastern luxuries in the prosperous days of Augustus, and by the discovery of open-sea routes from Africa to India. In the first century B.C., or soon after, the periodicity of the monsoons in the Indian Ocean and the right seasons for navigation were discovered by Hippalus (q.v.), and direct crossings to various points of the western coast were subsequently established (Pliny 6. 96–100). Augustus received Indian envoys (Dio Cass. 54. 9), and Greek merchants organized a regular trade from Egypt. In Augustus' day 120 ships sailed to India every year, and under his early successors the drain of Roman money to pay for Indian imports caused passing anxiety (Pliny 6. 101; 12. 84), the main goals of visitors from the Roman world being the Chera, Pandya, and Chola kingdoms of Tamil south India. The principal imports to Rome were perfumes, spices (especially pepper), gems, ivory, pearls, Chinese silk. The Romans exported linen, coral, glass, base metals, 'Arretine' table-ware, wine in amphorae, etc., and also sent much gold and silver (and later copper) coin, of which large hoards have been found

in south India. Imitations (usually in terracotta for ornaments) of Roman coins have turned up, mostly in places included in the old Andhra Empire. Articles and remains of Roman origin have been found not only at the modern *Arikamedu* (see below), but also in the central Deccan plateau—at *Brahmagiri*, *Chandravalli*, *Maski*, and *Kondapur*; and at *Amaravati Sisupalgarh*, *Nasik*, *Nevasa*, *Kolhapur* (or near it), *Akota*, and *Karvan*.

The chief marts on the west coast were Barbaricon (*Bahardipur*) and Barygaza (*Broach*) and, above all, the Tamil towns Muziris (*Cranganore*) and Nelcynda (*Kottayam*). Beyond Cape Comorin the Greeks visited Colchoi (*Kolkai*), Camara (*Kaviripaddinam*), a trading-station now called *Arikamedu* two miles south of *Pondicherry* (R. E. M. Wheeler in *Ancient India* 2, July 1946, 17 ff.; J. M. Casal, *Fouilles de Virampatnam-Arikamedu*, 1949; Wheeler in *Aspects of Archaeology*, 1951, 354 ff.), Poduce (*Pondicherry?*), and Sopatma (*Madras*); a few reached the Ganges mouth and brought news of Burma, Malaya, and of the Thinae or Sinae (in S. China—*see* SERES). Greek traders figure in Tamil literature as residents in many of the inland centres (A.D. 70–140). The Maldives and Laccadives were now discovered, Ceylon was circumnavigated (*see* TAPROBANE), and one Alexander, taking advantage of the Bay of Bengal monsoon, sailed past Burma and Malaya to Cochin China and even to China proper (Ptolemy 7. 1–2). See, e.g., *Bull. de l'École française d'Extrême-Orient*, xlv, fasc. 1, 1951, 75 ff., on excavations at *Oc-eo* in Indo-China; and *Aspects of Archaeology* 361, on discoveries made 40 miles up the river Mekong. Nevertheless, Greek geographers always underrated the extent of India's southward projection and exaggerated the size of Ceylon. From *c.* A.D. 200 direct Graeco-Roman trade declined, communications with India passed into the hands of intermediaries (Arabians, Axumites, Sassanid Persians), and India again became a land of fable to the Mediterranean world. The founders of Christian settlements in India were mostly Persians.

V. A. Smith, *The Early History of India* (1924; embodying Indian records); H. Rawlinson, *Intercourse between India and the Western World* (1926); Warmington, *Indian Commerce* (1928); A. K. Narain, *The Indo-Greeks* (1957); W. W. Tarn, *The Greeks in Bactria and India* (1938, 1951²); Wheeler, op. cit. 141 ff., and 'Roman contact with India, Pakistan, and Afghanistan' in *Aspects of Archaeology* (*Essays presented to O. G. S. Crawford*), ed. W. Grimes, 1951; M. P. Charlesworth, 'Roman Trade with India; a re-survey' in *Studies in Roman Economic and Social History* (in hon. of Allan Chester Johnson, ed. P. Coleman-Norton, 1951); Cary, *Geographic Background* 200 ff.; J. Vogel, 'Ptolemy's Topography of India . . .' in *Archaeologica Orientalia in mem. E. Herzfeld* (ed. G. C. Miles, 1952); J. I. Miller, *The Spice Trade of the Roman Empire* (1969).   E. H. W.

**INDICTIO** under the Principate meant the compulsory purchase of food, clothing, and other goods for the army and the court. Owing to the inflation of the mid third century the payments made for such purchases became derisory and were finally abandoned. From the time of Diocletian the term *indictio* was applied to the annual assessment of all levies in kind made by the praetorian prefects: the *indictio* declared the amount of each item (wheat, barley, wine, oil, clothing, etc.) payable on each fiscal unit (*caput*, *iugum*, etc.). From 287, indictions were numbered serially in cycles of five years, from 312 in cycles of fifteen years. The number of the indiction was regularly used for dating financial years (which began on 1 Sept.) and sometimes for dating other documents.

Jones, *Later Rom. Emp.* 448 ff.   A. H. M. J.

**INDIGETES** or **-ITES, INDIGITAMENTA.** Both words, also the corresponding verb *indigitare*, are fairly common and there is no doubt that they mean respectively a class of Roman gods, a list of gods and their titles, and to address by the proper name or title.

Concerning their more exact meaning and relation to one another three views have been held. (1) Peter in Roscher's *Lexikon*, s.v., explains the *indigetes* as the *di minuti* (*Sondergötter*), deities of extremely limited function, as Cunina, who looks after the child in the cradle, Cinxia, who sees to the bride's girdle, etc. (2) G. Wissowa, *Ges. Abh.* 175 ff., refuted this. The *indigitamenta* contain names of other gods, including Apollo (Macrob. *Sat.* 1. 17. 15) and the Bona Dea (q.v.; ibid. 12. 21). Furthermore (Wissowa loc. cit. 304 ff.), the lists of the *di minuti* show many features suggesting late grammatical learning, not early priestly lore. He explained the *di indigetes* as native gods, from *indu* + rt. *gen*, an impossible etymology, but the latter half of the word could be explained (Th. von Grienberger, *Indogerm. Forsch.* xxiii. 337 ff.) as from root of *agere*, 'dwell'. *Indigitamenta* Wissowa supposed to be from *indu* + rt. *agh*, 'say'. Modifications of Wissowa's view are proposed by E. Goldmann (*CQ* 1942, 43) and H. Wagenvoort (*Roman Dynamism*, 1947, 99 f.). Both understand *indiges* as 'active within', though they interpret this differently. (3) C. Koch, *Gestirnverehrung im alten Italien*, 1933, 78 ff., points out the absence of any sort of proof that the *indigetes* were native as distinct from foreign gods, or even an important class of deities. Starting from the cult of Sol Indiges he takes the epithet to mean 'ancestral' (but his proof is very unconvincing, see Rose, *Harv. Theol. Rev.* 1937, 165 ff.) and makes *indigitare* mean 'treat as an *indiges*', i.e. worship, *indigitamenta* the formulae of address in such worship. At present *indiges* seems of doubtful meaning, but the connexion of it with the other two words likely.

For recent discussion see Latte, *RR* 43. H. J. R.

**INDUSTRY** (Greek and Roman). Craftsmanship in wood, bone, shell, earth, stone, and leather, as well as use of colour for painting and of fire for cooking purposes, and the preparing of primitive tools are palaeolithic, craftsmanship in textiles, pottery, architecture, flint-mining, and ship-building neolithic. Metal-work and glass production began with the Bronze Age, and rationalization of craftsmanship by written prescriptions, exact measures, and weights in the Ancient Oriental towns. The Indo-European and Semitic tribes of the Neolithic and Cuprolithic Ages had wandering craftsmen who performed the more difficult work of larger households. The crafts of smiths originated in the Bronze Age, representing the first village artisan, with his own workshop in some places. The Ancient Oriental, the Minoan, and Mycenaean metal-workers, potters, ship-builders, brewers, weavers, leather-workers, artists, and doctors occupied more often special workshops, mostly provided for them by kings, temple-rulers, and wealthy owners.

2. Homer and Hesiod mention a considerable variety of craftsmen. But only the smiths had their own workshops, a standard which was gradually reached by potters and, perhaps, ship-builders in Corinth, Athens, and other towns during the eighth and seventh centuries B.C. The money economy of the sixth century produced the *ergasterion*, a workshop able to produce for the needs of expanding markets, with a number of slaves and free workers under the control of foremen. *Ergasteria* of potters, leather-workers, and smiths are known from paintings of sixth-century Attic vases. Many other branches of craftsmanship followed during the fifth and fourth centuries, primarily those producing for export and the military and naval requirements of the Athenian Empire and other States. Craftsmanship in metal, leather, wood, bone, and pottery therefore reached a higher economic and social standard, and was specialized to a higher degree. Craftsmen of the branches of leather manufacture (Cleon, Anytus, Lysias father of Iphicrates), pottery (Hyperbolus), and of work in metal, wood, and

bone (Cleophon, the fathers of Sophocles and of Demosthenes) could reach political and social honours in democratic Athens. Here we find shops with at least 20 to 30 slaves (owned by Demosthenes' father), yielding annually from c. 15 to 30 per cent of the investe dcapital. Division of labour is known in *ergasteria* which produced metal-work and from potters' shops, but was not usual everywhere. The craftsmen of Athens and other big towns seem to have sold more of their products to merchants and traders than to private customers. Only a few wandering craftsmen may have existed still in rural districts of Greece during the Classical period, the only exception being artists who roamed from town to town and from court to court. On the other hand, there existed wandering Greek metal-workers in the Persian Empire, in South Russia, Italy, and the Alps, who immigrated for longer or shorter periods and produced Greek merchandise on the spot. Specialized crafts of metal- and leather-workers, potters, dyers, musicians, and *fabri* (primitive all-round craftsmen), are ascribed by tradition to Rome under the kings. These craftsmen were organized in *collegia*, which were originally institutions with military obligations, but later of political and economic importance as well.

3. The Hellenistic age, and that of the later Roman Republic, produced a growth of the Greek *ergasterion* system which spread throughout the whole civilized world, and was introduced into textile and food production. Glass-blowing was invented c. 30 B.C.; several glass producers of the first century B.C. and a potter, Aristion, of c. 200 B.C., seem to have had workshops in more than one town. The Ptolemaic Empire combined the craftsmanship of the whole of Egypt in its industrial enterprises. The baths of Egypt, the production of papyrus scrolls, oil, perfumes, textiles (perhaps not woollen goods), and beer became government monopolies. The craftsmen of these trades became State employees, who were controlled by tax-farmers and government officials, received salaries and, in the oil production, a share of the profit for their work. The State issued a production schedule each year and provided the workshops with tools and raw materials. Privileges were granted to temples and to distinguished owners who combined large estates with commercial, industrial, and banking enterprises; but State control was even there not completely removed. Large enterprises for fish-curing, for the production of metal-work and of bricks, also belonged to the Ptolemaic State, which might be considered the greatest trust organizer in the Ancient World.

4. Craftsmanship in republican Rome developed on Greek lines during the second and first centuries B.C., periods of a considerable specialization and expansion of slave *ergasteria* throughout the whole of industry. The petty craftsmen often combined general retail trade with the sale of their own products. Another characteristic of Roman craftsmanship was the prevalence of great capitalistic enterprises which united different branches of industry with banking, commerce, and agriculture, and gave their slaves and freedmen the necessary capital for half-independent workshops. Among persons of this type we need mention only the Elder Cato, the publisher Pomponius Atticus, and Rabirius Postumus with his big *terra sigillata* workshops.

5. Organizations of craftsmen were more common during these centuries than in the Classical period. Those of the city-states had almost exclusively social and religious intentions. They were tools of the Ptolemaic Government for orders and concessions throughout the Egyptian countryside. The Roman *collegia* mixed so much in politics that they had to be dissolved or strictly controlled (*see* CLUBS).

**6.** The period of the Roman Principate saw craftsmanship of the Greek and Roman type with its specialization, *ergasteria*, and great capitalistic enterprises, spreading over the provinces of the Empire. The Egyptian monopolies were broken up or changed into monopolistic concessions for small districts farmed out to independent craftsmen. Nevertheless, remains of controlled economy were found throughout the whole Empire as a Hellenistic heritage, especially in mining districts, temples, and public domains. Gradually the craftsmen of public and private estates began to furnish the local markets of provincial districts with bricks, coarse pottery, cheap leather- and metal-work, *terra sigillata*, cheap textiles, etc., and even to supersede town craftsmen. A regulated economy began to grow in many small regions from the second century A.D. Finally, the State built up its own workshops for the needs of army, court, and administration, or commandeered private corporations of craftsmen for State purposes, and used them for the farming out of concessions and monopolies. During the crisis of the third century A.D. the craftsmen of whole regions became dependent on orders of the administration.

**7.** The Late Roman period, which begins with Diocletian, made this organized compulsion final. It did not mean a breakdown of technical knowledge; but the number of independent workshops decreased everywhere, and estate workshops and union between craftsmen and traders became the rule in the countryside of the Late Roman world. The State provided for its own requirements by establishing factories in all provinces and by regulating the more important *collegia* of craftsmen throughout the Empire. Sons had to follow their father's trade, and large taxes in merchandise had to be paid collectively by the corporations, which thus gained a new economic unity. Gradually they received privileges (especially during Justinian I's reign), which enabled them to influence prices, to buy raw materials cheaply for all members, to regulate production and sale, workshop capacity, and the number of their members. The guilds of Byzantium, which are known from the tenth century A.D. and preserved a fundamental nucleus of Graeco-Roman technique and craftsmanship, originated directly from these earlier corporations, and the Christian, Jewish, and Islamic guilds of the Middle Ages are doubtless either in historic connexion with Byzantine institutions or, what is more likely in some cases, with Late Roman and similar Sassanian corporations of the periods before the Germanic and Arabic conquests in West and East. *See* ARCHITECTURE, DYEING, FULLING, METALLURGY, MILLS, MINES, MONOPOLIES, POTTERY, SPINNING, WEAVING.

M. N. Tod in *CAH* v, ch. 1; T. Frank, ibid. viii, ch. 11; F. Oertel, ibid. x, ch. 13; xii, ch. 7; H. Francotte and H. Gummerus, *PW*, s.v. 'Industrie und Handel'; H. Bluemner, *Technologie und Terminologie der Griechen und Roemer* i², ii–iv (1879–1912); H. Bolkestein, *Economic Life in Greece's Golden Age*² (1958), ch. 3; V. Ehrenberg, *The People of Aristophanes*³ (1962), chs. 5, 6, 7; M. I. Finley, *Studies in Land and Credit in Ancient Athens* (1951), index, s.v. workshops; Forbes, *Stud. Anc. Technol.* i–ix; H. Francotte, *L'Industrie dans la Grèce ancienne* i, ii (1900–1); T. Frank, *An Economic History of Rome*² (1927), chs. 7, 13, 14; *Econ. Survey* i–v (index); G. Glotz, *Le Travail dans la Grèce ancienne* (1920), pts. i, chs. 3, 1; 5; ii, chs. 6; iii, chs. 4; 9; iv, ch. 5; J. Hasebroek, *Griechische Wirtschafts- und Gesellschaftsgeschichte bis zur Perserzeit* (1931), pts. i, chs. 5, iv; 6, c, iii; iii, ch. 3 iv; F. M. Heichelheim, *Wirtschaftsgeschichte des Altertums* (1938), index, s.v. 'Handwerk'; *Historia Mundi* iv (1956), 407, 420 f., 443 ff., 470 ff.; *An Ancient Economic History* i (1958), 261 ff., 510 ff.; ii (1964), 93 ff., 207 ff.; *Kl. Pauly*, s.vv. 'Berufsvereine', 'coactor', 'collatio', 'fiscus', 'Freigelassene', 'Industrie'; Jones, *Later Rom. Emp.*, ch. 21; Michell, *Econom. Anc. Gr.*, ch. 5; G. Mickwitz, *Die Kartellfunktionen der Zuenfte* (1936), chs. 5–8; Cl. Préaux, *L'Économie royale des Lagides* (1939); Rostovtzeff, *Hellenistic World*; *Roman Empire*² (indexes). F. M. H.

**INFAMIA** as a legal term embraces a variable number of disabilities (the common one being an incapacity to act or appear for another at law—*postulare pro aliis*) imposed in a variety of circumstances. It is at root social, involving loss of *fama* or *existimatio*, but is given legal content by *leges*, *senatusconsulta*, imperial constitutions, or by the Praetor's Edict in specific situations, such as condemnation in ordinary criminal prosecutions, condemnation in civil actions for delict and in other civil actions in which the defendant was guilty of a breach of faith (partnership, guardianship, mandate, etc.), engaging in certain disreputable occupations. In classical law there is no single concept of *infamia* (or *ignominia*—the earlier word: see Gai. *Inst.* 4. 182), but in the law of Justinian there appears to be an attempt to generalize.

A. H. J. Greenidge, *Infamia in Roman Law* (1894) (out of date but still useful); M. Kaser, *Sav. Zeitschr.* 1956, 220. B. N.

**INHERITANCE, LAW OF.** (*a*) GREECE. In Greek law (as at Athens and Gortyn) intestate succession was favoured. The sons and male descendants of the deceased came first in order of succession. In default of them his brothers and their descendants inherited, and in the third place the sons of his grandfather and their male descendants. Ascendants were excluded if their descendants were living: a brother of the deceased excluded the father, an uncle the grandfather. Adoptive sons were treated on the same footing as natural ones. The claims of sons and male descendants could not be set aside by testamentary dispositions. In general, males excluded females in the same group of kinship. A daughter inherited only if no sons or male descendants of predeceased sons existed; she was obliged to marry the man to whom her father had destined her either in his lifetime or by will. Failing such disposition the next collateral could claim the daughter, together with her father's fortune. But if a son remained, the daughter had no right to succeed and could demand only a dowry, to be determined at her brother's discretion.

**2.** Wills (introduced into Attic law, according to tradition, by Solon) were allowed only when the testator had no sons; disherison was possible only in the father's lifetime by solemn declaration. Before Solon adoptions were used to achieve some of the purposes of a will; they continued to be common and were treated to some extent like wills. Wills were normally in writing and witnessed. Legitimate sons could take possession of the inheritance without any formality, and they had no right to refuse it; other relatives needed an official authorization.

**3.** (*b*) ROME. Roman law recognized a will as early as the XII Tables, and intestacy was in historical times considered reprehensible. The essential of a Roman will was the nomination of an heir (*heres*), or several jointly, on whom the assets and liabilities of the dead man should devolve as a whole (universal succession). Only then could other dispositions, such as legacies, take effect. The earliest will (obsolete before the end of the Republic) was a public act in the *comitia* (q.v.) *curiata* or before the army in battle array. The earliest private will (*testamentum per aes et libram*; probably after the XII Tables) was in form a *mancipatio* (q.v.) *inter vivos* of the estate to a friend (*familiae emptor*) with directions as to its disposal on the death of the 'testator'. In the classical law the *mancipatio* was a pure formality, the only effect of which was to give validity (but only after death) to the directions, now on wax tablets, which in fact constitute the will. (The *familiae emptor* is a man of straw.) The Praetor (*see* EDICTUM) went further, and in effect dispensed with the *mancipatio* by giving possession of the estate (*bonorum possessio*: cf. LAW AND PROCEDURE, ROMAN, II. 11) to anyone named *heres* in tablets sealed by seven witnesses (derived from the five witnesses and the *libripens* of the *mancipatio*, with the *familiae emptor*). Until Antoninus Pius this 'praetorian will' could be upset by a person entitled on intestacy, but thereafter it was fully effective.

In post-classical times *mancipatio* went finally out of use, and in A.D. 439 Theodosius II added to the Praetorian requirement of the seals of seven witnesses the further requirement that the testator should 'subscribe' the will. There was also a public will (Greek in origin), entered in the records of a court or deposited in the imperial archives, and (in certain circumstances) a holograph will (i.e. in the testator's own writing).

4. There was also a contrast between civil and praetorian law on intestacy. By the civil law only agnates (*see* PATRIA POTESTAS) were entitled: in the first place, *sui heredes* (i.e. those persons in the *patria potestas* of the deceased who became *sui iuris* on his death, males and females equally); secondly, if there were no *sui heredes*, the nearest agnates (e.g. brothers, sisters); finally, in early law, members of the *gens* (q.v.). The Praetor recognized the claims of cognates (blood relations), and gave *bonorum possessio* to categories of person neglected by the civil law, such as emancipated sons, cognates up to (usually) the sixth degree. Moreover, if those in one class or degree refused, those in the next class or degree could claim, whereas by the civil law this was possible only if there were no members of the earlier class or degree. Lastly, when no other entitled person existed or all of them had refused, *bonorum possessio* was given to the wife (or husband), by contrast with the civil law by which a wife was only entitled if in *manus* (q.v.) and therefore classed as a daughter. After various subsequent innovations, the law was radically reformed by Justinian (*Novels* 118 and 127) (*see* CODEX), who established an order of succession of descendants, ascendants, and collaterals on the cognatic principle.

5. The claims of some relatives were recognized even against the testator's will. By the civil law *sui heredes* must either be appointed heirs or formally disinherited in the will (and the Praetor extended this to emancipated sons, etc.), but if they were formally disinherited they had no claim. In the Principate, however, the court of the *centumviri* (q.v.) developed an additional remedy (*querela inofficiosi testamenti*) whereby certain close relatives, if they would have been entitled on intestacy and had without out just cause been passed over or given less than a quarter of what they would have obtained on intestacy (*legitima portio*), could wholly or partially upset the will. They would thus usually obtain more than the *legitima portio*. Under Justinian's law, however, the complainant was in most cases allowed only his *legitima portio*. *See also* LAW AND PROCEDURE, ROMAN, I; FIDEICOMMISSUM; ADOPTIO.

(*a*) GREECE. F. Schulin, *Das griechische Testament* (1882); K. Hermann–Th. Thalheim, *Lehrbuch der griechischen Rechtsaltertümer* (1895); L. Beauchet, *Histoire du droit privé de la république athénienne* iii (1897); J. H. Lipsius, *Attisches Recht und Rechtsverfahren* ii, 1 (1912); L. Gernet, *Droit et société dans la Grèce ancienne* (1962); A. R. W. Harrison, *Law of Athens, Family and Property* (1968), 122 ff.
(*b*) ROME. C. Fadda, *Concetti fondamentali di diritto ereditario romano* i–ii (1900, 1907); V. Scialoja, *Diritto ereditario romano* (1914); S. Solazzi, *Diritto ereditario romano* i–ii (1932, 1933); P. Voci, *Diritto ereditario romano* i–ii² (1960, 1963). A. B.; B. N.

**INIURIA** in Roman law, apart from more general meanings (*Inst. Iust.* 4. 4. pr.), is either a delict in itself or an element in another delict (*see* DAMNUM INIURIA DATUM). As a delict in itself, it originates in the XII Tables (q.v.) which provided for retaliation (*talio*) for severe bodily harm (*membrum ruptum*), unless the aggrieved party accepted a money composition, and for money penalties for lesser injuries. By the later Republic the fall in the value of money had made these penalties derisory (Gell. *NA* 20. 1. 13) and the Praetor (*see* EDICTUM) intervened to grant a new action (*actio iniuriarum*), not for a fixed penalty but for damages. Thereafter further actions were introduced into the Edict to enable plaintiffs to obtain damages for a variety of acts, such as public insults, affronts to the modesty of a woman, and, more generally, any attack on the reputation of another which might cause him to suffer *infamia* (q.v.). By the end of the Republic the jurists had held that these actions were merely particular applications of a general principle implicit in the original *actio iniuriarum*, that any wilful affront to the dignity of the individual was actionable. From this generalization grew the classical delict which embraced almost any contumelious disregard of another's rights or personality, and of which *Dig.* 47. 10 provides many illustrations. In the later law a criminal prosecution could also be brought. For assault and for forcible entry into a house a *Lex Cornelia* of Sulla (q.v. 1) had earlier introduced a (probably) alternative action, which was criminal in that it was tried by a *quaestio* (q.v.) but private in that it could be brought only by the person wronged.

G. Pugliese, *Studi sull'iniuria* (1941); D. Daube, *Atti cong. int. dir. rom.*, Verona (1948), iii. 418; D. Simon, *Sav. Zeitschr.* 1965, 132.
B. N.

**INNOCENTIUS,** *gromaticus*. An *agrimensor* of this name is known in A.D. 359 (Amm. Marc. 19. 11. 8), but the treatise said to be extracted from the work *De litteris et notis iuris* by Innocentius is of later date (probably 5th–6th c.). Commonly known as *casae litterarum*, it differentiates between thirty-nine types of estate (*casa = villa* or *fundus*); each is given a letter of the Latin or Greek alphabet, and the diagrams incorporate these letters together with distinguishing features of each estate. The language is of interest for the development of vulgar Latin.

A. Josephson, *Casae Litterarum: Studien zum Corpus agrimensorum Romanorum* (1950); *Casae Litterarum*, ed. A. Josephson (1951). Each of these contains text, apparatus criticus, and German translation. O. A. W. D.

**INNS, RESTAURANTS.** In primitive times hospitality towards strangers was universal. It remained common throughout antiquity, and men of social standing had guest-friends (ξένοι, *hospites*) in most places that they were likely to visit. In the Hellenistic and Roman world, with greatly increased travel (q.v.), these relations were very widespread. But as early as the fifth century B.C. there is evidence of the common existence of inns in cities and by the roadside. Standards varied enormously: in the cheapest, travellers had to provide their own food and linen, and even physical safety could not be taken for granted. Though hotels for better-class people existed—ambassadors might have to use them for purposes of state (Dem. 19. 158)—inns in general had a reputation for bedbugs, discomfort, rough-houses, and prostitution. Famous shrines in due course provided public accommodation, run either by the host city or by other cities for their own citizens—not always to their satisfaction. Herodotus (5. 52) was impressed with the government-controlled Persian posting-inns along the Royal Road. Classical Greece had no elaborate restaurants, but knew the κάπηλος, who sold wine and snacks and was proverbial for dishonesty.

In the Roman world conditions were similar. Men of standing tried to avoid using inns and were never seen in taverns or restaurants. They had their own *deversoria* along roads which they travelled frequently (e.g. to their country estates), or could use those of their friends. When they travelled further, they could expect hospitality (private or public) and, under the Empire, sometimes use the facilities of the postal service (q.v.). Yet—as in Greece—anyone might have to stop at an inn on a long journey (e.g. Horace's to Brundisium); and though innkeeping was classed among disgraceful trades, good and even luxurious establishments existed. Taverns were universally popular among the lower classes, many of whom had no adequate cooking facilities at home, and became centres of their social life, often noisy and dangerous to public order. Various emperors passed legislation restricting the sale of prepared food and wine and, by building baths, provided alternative attractions.

In Pompeii taverns, restaurants, and inns (some with accommodation for animals) were common. The inns clustered near the gates and the town centre and were mostly kept by Orientals. In better-class places conditions would be pleasant, with *triclinia* (q.v.) perhaps set out in a garden and musical entertainment and good food provided: archaeological evidence bears out the *Copa* (*Appendix Vergiliana*). The best hotels in Pompeii were converted upper-class mansions. In lesser places, a colourful inn-sign might go with two or three dingy rooms, and customers had to eat sitting on stools and sleep on hard and bug-infested beds. Female company— no doubt of varying standards—was universally provided if required. This accounts for the fact that innkeepers are classed with *lenones*.

PW, s.vv. 'Καταγώγιον', 'Πανδοκεῖον', 'Κάπηλος'; T. Kleberg, *Hotels, restaurants et cabarets dans l'antiquité romaine* (1957); W. F. Jashemski, *CJ* 1964, 337 ff. E. B.

**INSTITUTIONES** were elementary textbooks of Roman law. The most renowned work of this kind is the *Institutiones* of Gaius (q.v. 2). Justinian took Gaius' book as the basis of his own *Institutiones*. This work, though primarily intended, like its model, as a students' manual, was given legislative validity from the same day as the *Digesta* (q.v.) (30 Dec. 533). It was compiled by Tribonianus (q.v.) and two of his collaborators in the *Digesta*, the professors Theophilus and Dorotheus. Apart from passages which record post-classical changes in the law (mainly by Justinian), it is a compilation of classical writings, the principal identifiable sources (apart from Gaius' *Institutes*) being Gaius' *Res cottidianae* and the *Institutes* of other jurists (Marcianus q.v., Florentinus, Ulpianus, q.v. 1).

C. Ferrini, *Opere* (1929), vol. i; A. Zocco-Rosa, *Justiniani Institutionum Palingenesia* (2 vols., 1908); S. Sangiorgi, *Ann. Sem. Giur. Palermo* 1959. B. N.

**INSUBRES** lived north of the Po. The most powerful people in Cisalpine Gaul (q.v.), they frequently exercised dominion over the neighbouring Taurini, Salassi, etc. Their capital was Mediolanum (q.v.) (Strabo 5. 213). Livy (5. 34) represents them as Aedui (q.v.) who entered Italy via the Mont Genèvre Pass; but his account is untrustworthy. These Gauls, however, certainly established themselves about the Ticinus c. 400 B.C., and were henceforth called Insubres—probably a pre-Celtic name. About 232 B.C. they clashed with Rome. At Clastidium (q.v.) (222) Marcellus stripped the *spolia opima* from their king. In 218 the new Latin colony at Cremona (q.v.) and Hannibal's arrival incited them to fresh efforts, until finally they were subjugated in 194 (Polyb. 2. 17 f.; Livy, books 21–34). Subsequently they disappeared as a separate nation. Insubrian districts obtained Latin rights in 89, full citizenship in 49 B.C. For bibliography *see* CISALPINE GAUL. E. T. S.

**INTERAMNA,** modern *Terni*, in Umbria near the confluence of the Velinus and Nar (whence its inhabitants were called Nahartes). The *municipium* prospered amid its fertile surroundings and the Via Flaminia (q.v.) was diverted to serve it. E. T. S.

**INTERAMNA LIRENAS,** modern *Pignataro*, in Latium (q.v.) near the confluence of the Liris and *Rapido*. A Latin colony here (312 B.C.) helped contain the Samnites (q.v.). E. T. S.

**INTERAMNIA,** modern *Teramo*, in southern Picenum at the confluence of the *Vezzola* and the *Tordino*, town of the Praetuttii, whose name survives in *Abruzzi*.
E. T. S.

**INTERCESSIO** was the right of a Roman magistrate to veto a motion carried by another magistrate, provided the former was invested with *maior* or *par potestas*. It arose from the idea of magisterial collegiality, and was reputed to be a necessary precaution against any abuse of their power by magistrates. Only a dictator could not be obstructed by the *intercessio* of an official magistrate, since he had no equal or superior. The same principle was later applied to municipal administration. The tribunes of the *plebs*, as equal colleagues, also had the right of *intercessio* against one another; but their veto of magisterial decrees, comitial enactments, and senatorial *consulta* was of a special kind and is unlikely to have had any basis in law. Like the 'right' of *auxilium*, the tribune's veto derived ultimately from the inviolability of his person and his consequent freedom to resist magisterial authority with impunity. General recognition of it as a tribunician prerogative probably accompanied or followed the absorption of the plebeian offices into the framework of a united State in the late fourth century. Annalistic references to its use in earlier times are therefore anachronistic. *Intercessio* was valid only within the sphere of civil legislation and within Rome, and fell into disuse when it was conferred upon the emperors, as a part of their *tribunicia potestas*. See also COLLEGIUM.

Mommsen, *Röm. Staatsr.* i³. 258 ff.; ii³. 290 ff. P. T.; E. S. S.

**INTEREST, RATE OF.** The rate of interest in Greece and Rome is known from the fifth century B.C., throughout which the temple of Delos gave loans at 10 per cent. The Roman Republic fixed interest at 8⅓ per cent (*fenus unciarium*) in the XII Tables and in c. 357 B.C. A *Lex Genucia* of perhaps 342 forbade usury completely; but this law, though re-enacted several times during the fourth, third, and second centuries, fell into disuse because it defied the laws of economics.

During the fourth century the interest on town mortgages in Athens amounted to c. 8 per cent, and on country mortgages to c. 6–12 per cent. Other loans brought from 10 to 33⅓ per cent, and on the average c. 12 per cent. A contemporary Delphic law fixed the interest of normal loans at 9 per cent, of small short-term loans at perhaps 25 per cent. In Persian Babylonia and Egypt, however, interest up to 40 per cent was paid during the fifth and fourth centuries, a rise of 100 per cent compared with the second millennium B.C. Safe investments in the Greek motherland brought 6 to 10 per cent during the third century, 24 per cent in the Hellenistic East of the same period, from 5 to 10 per cent in Egypt during the later second century.

The maximum rate of interest introduced by Lucullus and Cicero for their Asiatic provinces was 12 per cent. Nevertheless, 'political' interest rates of up to 48 per cent were asked for in Achaea, Asia, and Cilicia during this period. Sulla decreed in 88 B.C. a maximum of 8⅓ per cent, and the Roman Senate in 51 B.C. 12 per cent, a regulation valid throughout the Roman Empire for centuries. Interest in Rome during the first century B.C. and probably the first and second centuries A.D. was normally c. 6 to 10 per cent for safe investments, while loans in kind brought up to 50 per cent. Alexander Severus reduced the interest maximum for senators to 6 per cent. But business switched now to the unregulated loans in kind of 50 per cent and more.

The maximum rate of interest was increased to 12⅓ per cent during the fourth century A.D. More capital seems gradually to have accumulated during the following centuries, and Justinian I was able to fix the ordinary interest at below 6 per cent, that for trade investments at 8 per cent, for foreign trade and loans in kind at 12½ per cent, and that which senators were permitted to demand at 4 per cent. Bottomry loans (q.v.) were excepted from these and earlier regulations.

H. Billeter, *Geschichte des Zinsfusses im griechisch-roemischen Altertum bis auf Justinian* (1898); H. Bolkestein, *Economic Life in Greece's Golden Age*² (1958), 63; H. E. Finck, *Das Zinsrecht der graeko-aegyptischen Papyri*, Jur. Diss. Erlangen (1962); M. I. Finley, *Studies in Land and Credit in Ancient Athens* (1951), index; Frank, *Econ. Survey* i–v, index; G. Glotz, *Le Travail dans la Grèce ancienne* (1920), index; E. Grupe, *Sav. Zeitschr.* 1926, 26 ff.; F. M. Heichelheim, *Wirtschaftsgeschichte des Altertums* (1938), index, s.v. 'Zins'; *Historia Mundi* iv (1956), 404, 411, 453 f., 460 f.; *An Ancient Economic History*² i (1958), 219 f., 481 f.; ii (1964), 26 ff., 167 f.; *Handwörterbuch der Sozialwissenschaften* (1963), s.v. 'Geld- und Münzgeschichte'; J. Herrmann, *Journal for Jur. Papyrology* 1962, 23 ff.; Jones, *Later Rom. Emp.* i–iii, index; W. Kroll, *Die Kultur der ciceronischen Zeit* i (1933), 93 ff.; Magie, *Rom. Rule Asia Min.* i, ii, index, s.v. interest rate; Michell, *Econom. Anc. Gr.* 342 ff.; 347 ff. Cl. Préaux, *Chronique d'Égypte* 1950, 281; Rostovtzeff, *Hellenistic World*; *Roman Empire*² (indexes, s.v. 'interest', 'rate'). F. M. H.

**INTERPRETATIO ROMANA,** literally, 'Roman translation' (Tac. *Germ.* 43. 3); the use of a Latin divine name, as Mercurius, to signify a foreign god, as Odin. This is merely a particular case of the assumption that all peoples worshipped the same gods; thus the Greeks regularly call Minerva Athena, and the Romans speak of Zeus as Iuppiter. Foreign divine names were hardly used unless no native equivalent could be found, as Apollo in Rome, or a foreign cult (e.g. Isis, Mithra) was adopted.

G. Wissowa, *ARW* xix (1916–19), 1 ff.; cf. H. J. Rose, *Roman Questions of Plutarch*, 53 ff. H. J. R.

**INTERREX** was originally the individual appointed by the senators on the death of a king to exercise provisional authority. Later, in the event of the death or resignation of both consuls before the conclusion of their year of office, *interreges* were successively appointed from each of the senatorial *decuriae* for five days each until the auspices were taken and the new consuls elected. The first of a series was debarred from conducting the elections. The *interrex* had to be a patrician and a senator. He exercised all the functions of the consulship, and was escorted by twelve lictors. The last known example of *interregnum* occurred in 43 B.C. *Interreges* also held temporary office in cities of Latin Italy until the dawn of the imperial age.

Mommsen, *Röm. Forsch.* i. 218 ff.; *Röm. Staatsr.* i³. 647 ff.; E. S. Staveley, *Hist.* 1954, 193 ff. P. T.

**INVULNERABILITY.** Such stories of invulnerable men or beasts as are found in classical mythology mostly conform to the Sigurd type, in which there is one vulnerable spot (*see* ACHILLES, AIAS 1), or the Balder type, in which there is one thing which can wound (Nemean lion; own claws, Theoc. 25. 277. Caeneus, q.v.; (?) wooden pikes, Hyg. *Fab.* 14. 4 and Rose ad loc.).

O. Berthold, *Die Unverwundbarkeit* (1911); *and see* MESSAPUS. H. J. R.

**IO,** in mythology, priestess of Hera at Argos; usually said to be daughter of Inachus (q.v.). Zeus loved her, but to conceal her from Hera gave her the shape of a heifer. Hera asked to be given the heifer, which Zeus could hardly refuse; she set Argos (q.v. 1) to watch her. On his being killed by Hermes Hera plagued Io with a gadfly, which drove her out of the country. After long wanderings she came to Egypt, where Zeus restored her with a touch of his hand; hence the son which she bore him was called Epaphus (from ἐφάπτειν). For his descendants *see* DANAUS. See especially Aesch. *PV* 561 ff.; Ov. *Met.* 1. 583 ff.; Apollod. 2. 5 ff. Io was identified with Isis (q.v.; Apollod. 9); this is in turn due

to Isis' identification with Hathor, who has bovine shape. Rationalizations of the story were current early, as Hdt. 1. 1. 4–5 (she was kidnapped by Phoenicians); Ephorus ap. schol. Ap. Rhod. 2. 168 (she was kidnapped and the Egyptians sent Inachus a bull for compensation). It has been suggested that she was originally a moon-goddess (hence the cow-horns), or a form of Hera (q.v.); see Engelmann in Roscher's *Lexikon* ii. 269; Farnell, *Cults* i. 200; Eitrem in *PW* ix. 1732 ff. H. J. R.

**IOLCUS,** a city of Thessalian Magnesia, situated on the northern shore of the Bay of Volo, where it was sheltered by Pelion (q.v.). It was celebrated in mythology as the home of Jason (q.v. 1) and the starting-point of the Argonauts (q.v.). Recent excavation has proved that Iolcus, with its harbour at Neleia, was the centre from which Mycenaean influence spread inland over most of Thessaly. A settlement there, which existed from the Early Helladic period, evidently developed and prospered throughout the Late Helladic period. Its principal building, covering a considerable area and presumed to have been a palace, was destroyed by some disaster in the first half of the twelfth century and was never replaced. The rest of the settlement, however, after being abandoned for a short time, soon revived, and the prevalence of Mycenaean influences suggests that some former inhabitants returned, doubtless reinforced by newcomers. Iolcus remained moderately prosperous in the Protogeometric period, but it lost its links with inland Thessaly, which had been overrun by northern invaders. Subsequently, though continuing to exist, it became an insignificant village, being overshadowed by Pagasae (q.v.).

V. R. d'A. Desborough, *The Last Mycenaeans and their Successors* (1964), esp. 127 ff. H. D. W.

**ION** (1), eponymous ancestor of the Ionians; his legend as we have it seems to be Attic in all its forms. He is the son of Creusa (q.v. 1), but his father, in the tradition followed by Euripides, is Apollo (Patroös); elsewhere, as in Apollod. 1. 50, he is Xuthus, son of Hellen (q.v.). After the death of Erechtheus, Xuthus, Ion, and his brother Achaeus (q.v. 1) have adventures which vary from author to author and obviously have more to do with early ethnological theory than real tradition (see Stoll in Roscher's *Lexikon*, s.v., for particulars), but regularly Ion settles sooner or later in Athens and divides the people into the four traditional Ionian tribes, Hopletes, Geleontes, Argadeis, and Aigikoreis (named after his four sons, Eur. *Ion* 1575 ff.). For his use in religious propaganda by Athens in the fifth century, see J. P. Barron, *JHS* 1964, 37 ff. H. J. R.

**ION** (2), of Chios, but equally at home in Athens, Greek poet, was probably born about 490 B.C. He was on friendly terms with Cimon, whom he met, with Themistocles, at a dinner party in Athens about 475, and whose sociability he contrasted with the aloofness of Pericles; and in 462 he heard Cimon speak in the Assembly in favour of assisting Sparta when hard-pressed by her neighbours (Plut. *Per.* 5, *Cim.* 9, 16). Anecdotes record his meeting with Aeschylus at the Isthmian Games (Plut. *De prof. virt.* 8), with Sophocles at Chios in 441–440 when the latter was a general in the Samian War (Ath. 13. 603 e), and possibly with Socrates (Diog. Laert. 2. 23). He was fond of his wine and other pleasures—the satyric element which, as he said, virtue, no less than tragedy, needed to complete it (Plut. *Per.* 5). He died before 421 (Ar. *Pax* 835 and schol.). His first appearance as a tragic poet was about 451 B.C. (*Suda*, s.v.); in 428 he was defeated by Euripides when the latter produced the *Hippolytus* (Arg. Eur. *Hipp.*), but on another occasion he won the first prize at the Great Dionysia for both tragedy and dithyramb, and in his delight made a present of Chian wine to every Athenian citizen (Ath. 1. 3 f.). The number of his plays was variously given as 12, 30, or 40 (*Suda*, s.v.). The known titles include, from the Heraclean cycle of legend, *Alcmene, Eurytidae*, and the satyric *Omphale*; from the Trojan, *Agamemnon, Laertes, Teucer, Φρουροί* (dealing with Odysseus'ι entry into Troy as a spy); and besides these, *Argivi, Phoenix* or *Caeneus*, and *Μέγα Δράμα* (a title unparalleled for a Greek tragedy); but fragments are few and insignificant (*TGF* 732–46). The Alexandrian critics admitted him to the *Canon*— their select list of outstanding tragic poets (Cramer, *Anecd. Par.* 4. 197, etc.); Aristarchus and Didymus wrote commentaries on his plays (Ath. 14. 634), and Baton (2nd c. B.C.) a monograph on him (Ath. 10. 436). In the treatise *On the Sublime* (33) he is described as a faultless and perfectly finished writer in the 'smooth style', but without the force and fire of Pindar and Sophocles. In addition to his tragedies he composed elegiac poems, epigrams, encomia, paeans, hymns, scolia, possibly a comedy, at least one cosmological work in prose, the *Τριαγμός*, in which he showed on Pythagorean principles the triadic structure of the cosmos, a history of the foundation of Chios (of which Pausanias 7. 4. 8 made use), and memoirs. These last are to us the most interesting of his works, especially on account of the long quotation given by Athenaeus 605 e in which he describes with lively detail an evening spent by Sophocles in Chios. No other Greek before Socrates is presented so vividly. The title *Ἐπιδημίαι* probably refers to the visits of distinguished characters to the island. Whether it is identical with the *Συνεκδημητικός* Pollux 2. 88 and the *Ὑπομνήματα* schol. Ar. *Pax* 835 is uncertain. Ion appears to have had no immediate imitators in the genre that he had invented.

See A. von Blumenthal, *Ion von Chios* (1939); T. B. L. Webster, *Hermes* 1936, 263 ff.; F. Jacoby, *CQ* 1947, 1 ff., *FGrH* 392.
A. W. P.-C.; D. W. L.

**IONIAN SEA** ('*Ιόνιος, Ἰώνιος κόλπος*), a name used as an alternative to 'Adriatic Sea' for the waters between the Balkan Peninsula and Italy; no clear line of demarcation can be drawn between the two seas. The name 'Ionian', like that of 'Adriatic', was sometimes extended to include the sea to east of Sicily.
M. C.

**IONIANS** ('*Ιωνες, Ἰάϝονες*), a section of the Greek people mentioned but once by Homer (*Il.* 13. 685, Ἰάϝονες ἑλκεχίτωνες), but important later, after the central part of the west coast of Asia Minor (still non-Greek in Homer) had become known as Ionia.

Ionia was colonized, according to early traditions, by refugees from the Greek mainland, flying before the Dorians and other tribes from north-west Greece (Mimnermus in Strabo, 634; Hdt. 1. 145–8; Thuc. 1. 12). Herodotus (1. 146–7) speaks of the mixed blood of the colonists, and adds that some of them took the women of the conquered Carians. All were, however, reckoned as Ionians 'who trace their descent from Athens and keep the Apaturia' (q.v.).

The claim of Athens to be the mother-city of all Ionians will not hold, as Herodotus himself says; and the eponymous ancestor Ion (q.v. 1) could only artificially be worked into the Athenian genealogies, themselves extremely artificial. But the Athenian claim to be the 'eldest land of Ionia' was as old as Solon, and long preceded any Attic claims to political predominance (Arist. *Ath. Pol.* ch. 5); and it receives confirmation from the appearance of some of the four ancient 'tribes' of Attica—the Aigikoreis, Hopletes, Geleontes, and Argadeis—in inscriptions of Delos, Teos, Ephesus, Perinthus (a Samian colony), Cyzicus and Tomi (Milesian colonies).

There may be some truth in the Athenian claim to have organized expeditions to Ionia.

The Ionic dialect, first known to us from Homer, was spoken (with local variations) in a compact region comprising the Cyclades, Ionia proper, Euboea, and Attica. The fact that inscriptions from Chios show some forms akin to the adjacent Aeolic and the surviving Aeolicisms in Homer—mostly *metri gratia* (εἶος, λαός, for ἕως, λεώς, etc.), but also gratuitously (e.g. Ναυσικάα, ὁρᾶτο) —suggest that Ionic arose *after* the migrations, among the states whose culture-centre was at Delos. Its area was subsequently expanded by colonization.

A mixed race, descended in part from the Mycenaean peoples, and highly 'selected' amid the turmoil of the migrations, the Ionians, from about 750 B.C., developed precociously (see the brilliant picture in the *Hymn to the Delian Apollo*). Indeed, the whole initiation of Greek colonization (q.v.) and Greek rationalism belongs to them and to those neighbouring Greeks who came within their orbit. Throughout the East 'Yawani' (Javan: Genesis x. 2) became the generic term for 'Greek' (cf. 'Frank' later). They were, however, exposed to attack from the Lydian and Persian monarchies, and the effort to throw off Persian rule, exercised through Greek 'tyrants', ended in ruin after a struggle of six years (494). Then came Athenian overlordship and the unmerited depreciation of Ionians as unmanly (Hdt. 1. 143; 5. 69; Thuc. 5. 9; 6. 77; 8. 25). To fifth-century Greek theory 'Dorian' and 'Ionian' corresponded to 'Nordic' and 'Mediterranean' in modern Europe (Hdt. 1. 56). The generalization that credited the former with more steadfastness, the latter with more intelligence, is in each case open to numerous exceptions: contrast the sobriety of Ionian Olbia or Massilia (Strabo 179–80; Dio Chrys. *Borysthenite Discourse*) with the unstable brilliance of Dorian Syracuse and Tarentum in Thucydides and Livy.

J. M. Cook, *The Greeks in Ionia and the East* (1962); G. L. Huxley, *The Early Ionians* (1966). *See also* CHIOS, EPHESUS, MAGNESIA, MILETUS, PHOCAEA, PRIENE, SAMOS.
A. R. B.

**IOPHON**, son of Sophocles, competed with frequent success, sometimes with his own tragedies, sometimes, it was suspected, with his father's (or at least with his father's help) (Ar. *Ran.* 73 ff. and scholia). He won the first prize *c.* 435 (cf. *Hesp.* 1943) and second prize in 428, Euripides being first and Ion third (Arg. Eur. *Hipp.*). The story that he tried to obtain control of his father's property by accusing him of senile decay, and that Sophocles disproved the charge by reading from the *Oedipus Coloneus*, is very doubtful (*Vit. Soph.*, etc.). He wrote an epitaph for his father's monument after his death (Val. Max. 8. 7. 12). He was credited with fifty plays (*Suda*, s.v.).
*TGF* 761.
A. W. P.-C.

**IPHICLES**, in mythology, twin brother of Heracles (q.v.), also called Iphiclus. He was Heracles' companion on some exploits and father of Heracles' better-known companion Iolaus. Two other children of his were killed by Heracles in his madness (Apollod. 2. 61 ff.; schol. on Lycoph. 38 and *Od.* 11. 269; Nic. Dam. fr. 13 Jacoby).
H. J. R.

**IPHICRATES** (*c.* 415–353 B.C.), Athenian general. A man of humble origin, he first won fame by commanding a company of peltasts who annihilated a Spartan division (390). During the Corinthian War he led successful raids from the Isthmus, and afterwards (386) took service as a mercenary commander in Thrace, where he married Cotys' daughter, and in Syria against the Egyptian rebel kings. After returning to Athens (373) he was sent to relieve Corcyra from a Spartan invasion. He succeeded, but caused dissatisfaction by failing to prevent Epaminondas from invading the Peloponnese (369). He led the Athenian attempts to recover Amphipolis (367–364), but on his failure ceased to be στρατηγός and retired to Thrace. With his son Menestheus he commanded the Athenian fleet at Embata (355), and was afterwards prosecuted by his colleague, Chares, but acquitted. Two forensic speeches, now lost, were cited under his name (Dion. Hal. *Lys.* 12).

Iphicrates was notable as the general who first established the importance of peltasts (q.v.). He also had a reputation for strictness of discipline and the ingenuity of his stratagems.

Xen. *Hell.*, and Diod. bks. 14–16 (*passim*); Nepos' 'Life' (poor); C. Rehdantz, *Vitae Iphicratis.* etc. (1845); *Prosop. Att.* 7737.
                                                                H. W. P.

**IPHIGENIA** ('Ιφιγένεια), perhaps a by-form of Artemis (A. Iphigeneia at Hermione, Paus. 2. 35. 1; 'Ιφιγένεια· ἡ Ἄρτεμις, Hesychius) (q.v.), but in mythology a daughter of Agamemnon. For some reason he was obliged to sacrifice her, either because he had vowed to sacrifice the fairest thing born in a particular year, and she was born then, or because he had offended Artemis by an impious boast (Eur. *IT* 20 ff., cf. IDOMENEUS; Soph. *El.* 569, whereon see Jebb). She enforced this by delaying the fleet at Aulis with contrary winds until the sacrifice was made (Aesch. *Ag.* 184 ff. and elsewhere; the story is from the *Cypria*). Iphigenia was therefore sent for to Aulis, under pretext that she was to be married to Achilles before the fleet sailed (*Cypria*; Eur. *IA*), and led to the altar. Aeschylus (loc. cit.) implies that she was actually killed; but the story in the *Cypria*, followed by Euripides, *IT*, is that Artemis snatched her away, substituting a hind for her, and brought her to the country of the Tauri. There, according to the version followed by Euripides, she was Artemis' priestess, and by the local rite she had to superintend the sacrifice to the goddess of all strangers caught in the country. At length Orestes (q.v.) came there with Pylades, having been instructed that he could finally get rid of the Erinyes if he brought to Greece the Taurian image of Artemis. Both were taken prisoner, but during the preparations for sacrifice Iphigenia discovered who they were and under pretence of purificatory rites got them and the image away from the temple to the sea-shore, whence they escaped with the help of Athena. The image was duly brought to Halae in Attica (cf. ATTIC CULTS), where Iphigenia continued to be priestess, the goddess was given the title of Tauropolos, and a pretence of human sacrifice (a slight cut made in a man's throat) was kept up.

The local legend of Brauron said that the sacrifice of Iphigenia took place there, and that a bear, not a hind, was substituted for her (schol. Ar. *Lys.* 645, an interesting example of adaptation of a Panhellenic story to particular purposes; for the rite which it purports to explain, *see* ARTEMIS). Antoninus Liberalis, 27, says the surrogate was a calf, and that Iphigenia finally was made immortal and married to Achilles (q.v.) on Leuce.

P. Clément, *Ant. class.* 1934.                    H. J. R.

**IPHIS**, in mythology, (1) father of Eteoclus, one of the Seven against Thebes, and of Euadne, wife of Capaneus (q.v.). (2) A young Cypriot, who loved Anaxarete, a noblewoman of that island. She would have none of him, and he finally hanged himself at her door; she looked, unmoved, from her window, and was turned by Aphrodite into stone. The resulting image was called Aphrodite *prospiciens* (ἐκκύπτουσα?).

See Ovid, *Met.* 14. 698 ff., cf. Ant. Lib. 39 (from Hermesianax).
                                                                H. J. R.

**IRENAEUS** (*c.* A.D. 130–*c.* 202), sometimes called the first systematic Christian theologian, was born in Asia

Minor, had contacts as a boy with Polycarp of Smyrna, but spent most of his active life in Gaul, becoming bishop of Lyons *c.* 178. He was thus an important link between East and West, and intervened at Rome on behalf of the Montanists (*see* MONTANISM) at Lyons (177/8), and the Quartodecimans of Asia (190) who observed Easter (the Christian Passover) on Nisan 14 rather than the following Sunday. Only two of his numerous works survive, the vast anti-Gnostic *Adversus haereses* (mainly in a Latin translation) and the short *Proof of the Apostolic Preaching* (in an Armenian translation). His constructive exposition of Christian theology developed out of his critique of Gnostic systems, and was characterized by stress on the traditional elements in Christianity.

TEXTS. Ed. A. Stieren (Leipzig, 1848–53), W. W. Harvey (Cambridge, 1857), F. M. M. Sagnard and A. Rousseau (Paris, 1952– ).
                                                                J. N. D. K.

**IRIS**, the goddess of the rainbow, and for the most part hardly distinguishable from the natural phenomenon itself. She appears to have had no cult at all, being simply, when thought of as in human form, a messenger of the greater gods, presumably because the rainbow seems to touch both sky and earth. In Hesiod (*Theog.* 266 ff.) she is daughter of the Titan Thaumas and Electra the Oceanid, and sister of the Harpyiae (q.v.). According to Alcaeus (fr. Z 3, Lobel–Page; Plut. *Amat.* 765 e) she is the mother by Zephyrus of Eros, a conceit which means no more than that in moist spring weather men feel amorous; a few later writers catch it up. As messenger of the gods she is specialized to Hera in many of the later poets, e.g. Callim. *Del.* 228 ff., where she sleeps under her throne like a dog; Homer represents Zeus as her usual employer.

In her earliest appearances in art (François vase and other early sixth century Attic vases) she is wingless and dressed like Hermes in short *chitōn* and winged boots. Later her dress may be long or short but she is always winged. She carries the herald's staff. As a lone traveller she is sometimes beset by satyrs or centaurs. Already on the Parthenon frieze she stands close by Hera.
                                                    H. J. R.; C. M. R.

**IRON.** The earliest specimens are mainly of meteoric origin, though smelted iron belonging to the third millennium has been found in Mesopotamia. Probably meteoric iron was used for Mycenaean jewellery, and Homer mentions it as a valuable metal. It normally contains much nickel. In the thirteenth century it was mined in Hittite territory, though it is unknown if the later famous Chalybes (q.v.) were its discoverers. It appears suddenly as the material for weapons in Greece in perhaps the eleventh century. The change was probably due to the failure of bronze-supplies, as in other countries the replacement was gradual. It was hardly an advance, as early iron was of uncertain quality. Homer speaks of an iron knife, but has no explicit reference to iron swords.

Greece possesses small iron-deposits, but the main sources in classical times were Elba and the Chalybes country behind Trapezus. The manufacture of iron articles was concentrated at Athens and the Isthmus States. As geographical knowledge extended, other sources became available. The magnetite sands of Thrace were used at an early date. Spanish iron was prized under the Roman Republic, and from about 40 B.C. Rome drew on the deposits of Noricum. The mines of inner Dalmatia are of later date. In many parts of Gaul are enormous slag-heaps, and British iron was used locally. Indian iron is mentioned, but cannot have been of economic importance. Egypt did not obtain iron before contact with Assyria; thence iron-working reached Meroe in the later centuries B.C. and was diffused fairly rapidly through barbarian Africa.

The furnaces of the ancients could not normally produce cast iron. Statues were made by chasing pure wrought iron. Weapons were of mild steel, which was produced without understanding the reactions involved. Quenching to harden is known as early as Homer, and certain waters were thought (without real reason) to be particularly suitable. The Romans understood intentional carburization and annealing, and by complicated dama-scening they produced blades which would not snap. They did not use water-power, and all iron-working was by hand. Semi-nomadic natives often reduced the ore in the mountains, and sold the blooms at cities or at military forts, where they were forged into tools.

O. Davies, *Roman Mines in Europe* (1935); Forbes, *Stud. Anc. Technol.* ix; E. Hulme, *Trans. Newcomen Soc.* xviii (1937–8), 181.
O. D.

**ISAEUS** (1) (*c.* 420–350 B.C.). Nothing is known with certainty about the life of this orator; it is even doubtful whether he was an Athenian by birth, and some ancient authorities call him a Chalcidian. Traditionally he was a pupil of Isocrates and a teacher of Demosthenes. His political views, if he had any, were never allowed to intrude into his speeches, which were all composed for delivery by others. All the extant speeches are concerned directly or indirectly with questions of inheritance. The earliest of these, if we follow Jebb (*Attic Orators* (1875) ii. 350), is *Or.* 5, which he assigns to the year 390 B.C., but a later date (372) is possible, in which case the earliest is 377. The date of the latest is *c.* 353.

WORKS. Of fifty speeches which the biographer (Ps.-Plutarch) considered genuine we possess eleven and the fragment of a twelfth. Six deal with disputed inheritance. Three refer to prosecutions for false witness in testa-mentary cases. *On the estate of Hagnias* throws light on the Athenian law of collateral succession. In the *Euphi-letus* the speaker appeals to have his name restored to the roll of his deme. Dionysius quotes a fragment from the *Eumathes* for comparison with the style of Lysias.

Isaeus is our chief authority for the laws of inheritance, in which he was an expert. In addition to his minute legal knowledge, he possessed a singular skill in stating a case, so that the most complicated pleadings assume, under his treatment, the appearance of lucidity. His language is comparable to that of Lysias for simplicity, but he uses a certain number of words which have a poetical association, and some few colloquialisms. Dionysius considered him artificial in comparison with Lysias, but the examples which the critic gives do not make this statement obvious. His efficiency is beyond question; to read his speeches is a fine intellectual exer-cise; but he makes no appeal to the senses.

For general bibliography *see* ATTIC ORATORS.
TEXT. Teubner (Thalheim, 1903).
COMMENTARY. W. Wyse (1904).
TEXT AND TRANSLATION. E. S. Forster (Loeb); P. Roussel (Budé).
INDEX. W. A. Goligher and W. S. Maguinness (1964).
J. F. D.

**ISAEUS** (2) (1st c. A.D.), Syrian rhetor, famous in Trajan's time at Rome for improvisation and for impas-sioned and epigrammatic utterance (Pliny, *Ep.* 2. 3; Juv. 3. 74).

**ISAGOGIC LITERATURE** denotes didactic com-positions addressed to particular recipients and intended as an introduction (εἰσαγωγή) to the knowledge of a science or to the practice of an art or of an activity, administrative or political. It seems to be a form of writing first used by the Stoics. The word is used in Latin under its Greek form or latinized, *isagoga* (Gell. 1.

2. 6; 14. 7. 2; 16. 8. 1). Sometimes it is rendered by *institutio* or *introductio*. An author occasionally employs the method of question and answer, and often divides his work into two principal parts, *ars* and *artifex*: e.g. Quintilian books 2–11, *ars oratoria*; book 12, *orator*. But it is now impossible to make a clean distinction between εἰσαγωγαί and actual handbooks, τέχναι, *artes*. Works which have been assigned to the former category may well belong to the latter: Cato, Varro, Columella, their treatises on agriculture; Cicero, *Partitiones oratoriae*; [Q. Cicero], *Commentariolum petitionis*; Horace, *Epistula ad Pisones*; Vitruvius, *De Architectura*; Celsus, *De Medicina*; Frontinus, *De Aquis*; Quintilian, *Institutio oratoria*; Vegetius, *Epitoma rei militaris*.

L. Mercklin, *Philol.* 1849; Jahn, *Ber. Sächs. Ges. Wiss.* 1850; E. Norden, *Hermes* 1905, 508 ff.; C. O. Brink, *Horace on Poetry* (1963), 22 ff.
C. F.; G. W. W.

**ISAURIA.** A small and wild country on the north face of Mt. Taurus. The Isaurians first appear about 325 B.C., when they murdered the Macedonian governor Balacrus. For this they were punished by Perdiccas; Diodorus (18. 22) speaks of their 'city' (Isaura) as full of silver and gold, 'as if it had long been prosperous'. Subsequently they maintained their independence as a community of villages, living largely by banditry, till they were subdued in 76–75 B.C. by Servilius (q.v. 1) Vatia, who thus acquired the cognomen Isauricus. Included first in the province of Cilicia (q.v.), then in that of Galatia, the country re-mained backward; of its two chief towns, Isaura Vetus and Nova, the former achieved the rank of a city under the early Empire, the latter not until the fifth century.
G. E. B.

**ISCA,** British river-name, hence applied to sites on rivers so called:

(1) Ptolemy's Isca (2. 3. 3), where he fixes the Second Legion (ibid. 14), is apparently a site on the Axe (Bradley, *Archaeologia* xlviii. 390).

(2) Modern Exeter on the Exe was occupied as a civil settlement under Claudius and became a walled town (earth-bank *c.* 150, stone wall *c.* 200), the capital of the Dumnonii, with trading connexions (A. Fox, *Roman Exeter* (1952)).

(3) Modern Caerleon on the Usk was probably from *c.* A.D. 75 the fortress of Legio II Augusta. Originally consisting of timber buildings surrounded by a clay bank, it was gradually rebuilt in stone, and its bank fronted with a stone revetment from 99/100 (*JRS* 1928, 211). During periods of reduced occupation in the second century its buildings decayed; but a complete overhaul occurred under Severus and his successors; a partial rebuilding is recorded 254–60 (*ILS* 537). The legion left Isca towards the end of the century. Christian martyrs Aaron and Julius may be realities (Gildas, 10), but an archbishopric is fabulous. Administrative build-ings (including a hospital?), barrack-blocks, and, of extra-mural works, an amphitheatre and baths have been excavated.

*Archaeologia Cambrensis* lxxxiv–lxxxvii (1929–32), xc (1935); *Archaeologia* lxxviii (1928), 111 ff. (amphitheatre); V. E. Nash-Williams, *The Roman Frontier in Wales* (1954), 18 ff.
C. E. S.

**ISCHIA,** ancient Pittekoussai (Pithecusae) and Aenaria (Inarime in Virgil and other poets), the largest island in the Gulf of Naples. It was settled, prior to the foundation of Cumae, by Chalcidians and Eretrians, presumably as a centre of trade with Etruria and as a port of call on the route to the metal-rich region of north-west Tuscany. The acropolis of the Greek town of Pittekoussai, on Monte Vico, was in use continuously from the eighth to the first century B.C., and had previously been inhabited in the Bronze and Iron Ages; sixth–fifth century Greek temple terracottas have been found there. The eighth and seventh century tombs, revealed in the excavations started in 1952 in the Valle San Montano cemetery at the foot of Monte Vico, near Lacco Ameno, have produced vases and other objects imported from Corinth, Athens, Euboea, north Syria, Phoenicia, Egypt (a Bocchoris scarab may be compared to the Bocchoris vase from Tarquinii, q.v.), Etruria, and Apulia, including a vase (c. 730–720) inscribed with Greek verses mentioning the Homeric king Nestor, and another, depicting a shipwreck (the first example of Greek Geometric figurative painting found in Italy). Ischia was subject to volcanic outbursts and noted for its medicinal warm springs. Its clay, from the hills above Casamicciola, was the best available to the potters of Campania, and remained in general use on the island until after the Second World War.

G. Buchner and A. Rittmann, Origine e passato dell'isola d'Ischia (1948); G. Buchner, Atti e Mem. Soc. Magna Grecia 1954, 3 ff.; id.; Röm. Mitt. 1953–4, 37 ff.; id. and C. F. Russo, Rend. Linc. 1955, 215 ff.; D. L. Page, CR 1956, 95 ff.; S. Bosticco, PP 1957, 215 ff.; S. Brunnsåker, Opusc. Romana 1962, 165 ff.; G. Buchner, Atti III Com. Studi Magna Grecia 1963, 263 ff.; H. Metzger, Rev. Ét. Anc. 1965, 310 ff.; G. Buchner and J. Boardman, JDAI 1966, 1 ff.
                                                                      D. W. R. R.

**ISIDORUS** (1), a Greek of Charax, near Tigris mouth, wrote c. A.D. 25 on Parthia and its pearl-fisheries (Ath. 3. 93 d), and, to judge from Pliny, a general geographical work, a portion perhaps of which is the extant Σταθμοὶ Παρθικοί, a meagre description of 'stations' from Zeugma on the Euphrates through Seleuceia, Ecbatana, Rhagae, Caspian Gates, Hyrcania, Parthia, etc., to Alexandria (Kandahar). The suggestion that he had been sent out by the Emperor Augustus to get information about Arabian coasts, and about Parthia for young C. Caesar (who was killed in Armenia in A.D. 4), rests on the assumption that Pliny in 6. 141 calls Isidorus 'Dionysius' by mistake.

GGM i. lxxx ff., 244 ff.; FGrH 781; W. Schoff, The Parth. Stations of I. of C. (1914).                                          E. H. W.

**ISIDORUS** (2) **HISPALENSIS**, bishop of Seville (c. A.D. 602–36), one of the most important links between the learning of antiquity and the Middle Ages. His chief works were: (1) Chronica Majora, a history extending to his own times; (2) Historia Gothorum, preserved in two editions; (3) De natura rerum, (4) Differentiae, in two books, (5) Quaestiones in vetus Testamentum; (6) Etymologiae or Origines (now divided into twenty books), a widely used encyclopaedia which deals not only with the seven liberal arts but also with geography, law, medicine, natural history, prodigies, gems, foods, drinks, etc. (See ENCYCLOPAEDIC LEARNING.) Though Isidore does not often mention his sources, it is clear that he gathered his information from a wide range of authorities (including Pliny and Suetonius).

Migne, PL lxxxi–lxxxiv; Etymologiae, ed. W. M. Lindsay (2 vols., 1911). M. Manitius, Geschichte der lat. Lit. des Mittelalters (1910–11), i. 52 ff.; J. Fontaine, Isidore de Séville (1959).   J. F. M.

**ISIGONUS** of Nicaea (1st c. B.C. or 1st c. A.D.), a writer of paradoxa (see PARADOXOGRAPHERS), who probably drew to some extent on Varro, and was himself drawn upon by Pliny the Elder.

A. Westermann, Paradoxographi (1839), 162 f.; FGrH iii. 674.

**ISIS**, in Egyptian religion, was the wife of Osiris and the mother of Horus. In addition to her position as a national deity in Egypt, Isis acquired in the Hellenistic age a new rank as a leading goddess of the Mediterranean world. Her worship was established in Piraeus by the fourth century by Egyptians residing there. Most of the foundations of her cult in the Aegean area during this period, however, included her as a member of the new Hellenistic cult of the Egyptian deities (q.v.) along with Sarapis, Harpocrates, and Anubis (qq.v.). Many of these cults in the Greek cities soon became public ones and were managed by priests who were magistrates of the State. Yet one finds attached to some of these public cults such groups as the melanephoroi, a fact which indicates that there probably was some sort of periodic ritual or ceremony carried on. The cult of these gods was highly Hellenized, at least in externals: the statues and temples are frequently Greek in design and execution, the priests, in Greece at least, are usually civic functionaries, and the language of the cult is Greek. The practices of the cult, such as incubation, the interpretation of dreams, festive banquets, and cult societies, have a Hellenic character, though there are Egyptian analogies for many of them. Herodotus had identified Isis with Demeter, but in the early Hellenistic age she is identified, via Hathor, with Aphrodite, with Arsinoë II the wife of Ptolemy II, and with later Ptolemaic queens. The plastic representation of her in Greece is almost uniformly Hellenic in character, portraying her with the ancient Egyptian head-dress, in a long garment with a characteristic knot of drapery on the breast. In her most Hellenic form she is shown with serene, ideal, and typically Greek features, with no head-dress, but a curl or braid of hair hanging down each side of her face. Isis came more and more to mean all things to all men. In the great hymns which celebrate her manifold accomplishments, virtues, and miracles, she is addressed as 'O Thou of countless Names', and is identified with many and varied goddesses. Although the cult of Isis had, in many instances in Greece, the external appearance of a typical public city-state cult, it had also, to some extent in Greece and in the West, the characteristics of a mystery cult as well. The range of experience involved in participation in the cult runs all the way from individual initiatory rites to the elaborate cult drama which celebrated the old myth of the death and resurrection of Osiris. At Rome, Pompeii, near Corinth, and probably at other places the elaborate mysteries of Isis were carried out. At the numerous other temples of Isis which we know in the Graeco-Roman world it is frequently difficult to say just what form the ritual of the cult assumed. Prominent among the characteristics of the cult of Isis which distinguished it from ordinary Greek and Roman cults were the appearances of an Egyptian professional priesthood, the regular ritual, the use of sacred water from the Nile, elaborate processions, penitents, dances, and the use of musical accompaniments. Certain festivals were of especial importance, one of the most significant being the Ploiaphesia which marked the opening of the season of navigation. That these Mysteries and their attendant ritual could awaken a deep religious emotion is testified by the conversion of Lucius which Apuleius describes (Met. book 11). Of all the temples of Isis known to us, the one at Pompeii is most perfectly preserved. Here we find at the top of a flight of steps a high platform upon which sacred rites were performed, a cistern for holding Nile-water, homes or cells for the priests, and many of the other arrangements necessary for the celebration of the worship. Although Sarapis and other deities of the group associated with Isis were worshipped in her temples, it is she who appears as the chief deity, occupying the place that Sarapis had frequently held in the public cults of Greece. The goddess Isis as she was presented in the Mysteries, however, must have drawn a more devoted and significant type of worship than was ever inspired by a civic deity. Not only are the statues and monuments of her worship found in all parts of the Roman Empire and her symbols quite commonly used on rings, gems, pins, and other jewellery, but many grave reliefs and tombs show representations of her symbols, particularly the sistrum and the *situla*. The deceased, if a woman, was frequently portrayed on the funeral monument in the costume characteristic of the deity.

ANCIENT SOURCES. W. Peek, *Der Isishymnus von Andros und verwandte Texte* (1930). For the Iseum at Pompeii see Mau–Kelsey, *Pompeii*[2] (1902), 168 ff. For other sources *see under* SARAPIS *and* EGYPTIAN DEITIES.

MODERN LITERATURE. In addition to the literature cited under SARAPIS and EGYPTIAN DEITIES the following are important: A. Erman, *Die Religion der Ägypter* (1934); W. Drexler, 'Isis' in Roscher's *Lexikon*; A. D. Nock, in *CAH* xii; R. Merkelbach, *Isisfeste in griechisch-römischer Zeit* (1963).                    T. A. B.

**ISOCRATES** (436–338 B.C.), Athenian orator of central importance. Although he lacked the voice and the confidence ever to address a large audience and so played no direct part in the affairs of the State, his written speeches, which presumably were of some influence on public opinion, provide us with a most valuable commentary on the great political issues of the fourth century. His system of education in rhetoric exercised a profound effect on both the written and the spoken word: his many pupils included the historians Ephorus and Theopompus (3), the atthidographer Androtion, and the orators Hyperides and Isaeus (1) (qq.v.). Judgements of his importance have variously treated him as the prophet of the Hellenistic world, and as the specious adulator of personal rulers, but, admired or contemned, he cannot be neglected in the study of his age.

1. LIFE. As son of a rich man, he studied under Prodicus, Gorgias (1) in Thessaly, Tisias, and the moderate oligarch, Theramenes. He was also a follower of Socrates (1) (qq.v.). Thus, while the Peloponnesian War was destroying both his father's fortune and his city's, he was receiving his education from teachers who included the critics of democracy and empire, and the effect was lasting.

In the 390s he turned his theoretical training to account and wrote speeches for others to use in the courts. Orations 16–21 belong to this early phase. Soon discontented with the profession of *logographos*, he began to train others in rhetoric. In *Against the Sophists* he advertised his principles, and of the early writings the *Helen* and *Busiris* displayed his skill on themes already treated by others. It was perhaps in this period before the King's Peace that he opened a school on Chios. The *Panegyricus*, published in 380 after ten years of composition, was his version of a conventional subject celebrated by Gorgias and Lysias; its demand that the Greeks unite under the shared hegemony of Athens and Sparta was familiar, and the long period of composition suggests that it was intended to be an enduring masterpiece of its kind, not, as some have supposed, a topical plea for the establishment of the Second Athenian League. One of Isocrates' most distinguished pupils was Timotheus (q.v. 2) whom at some stage Isocrates had accompanied on campaign and served by writing his dispatches to the Athenian people, and as a result of Timotheus' successes Athens was able in 375 to make the peace which embodied the principle of the shared hegemony. Dspite the fact that Persia's position in the peace was unchanged, Isocrates lauded it, perhaps partly on personal grounds, and began to address pleas, very similar in form to the *Philippus* of 346, to eminent individuals begging them to assume the lead against Persia, first Agesilaus, then Dionysius I, then Alexander (5) of Pherae (qq.v.) (cf. Speusippus' *Letter to Philip* 13) and later perhaps Archidamus (cf. *Epistle* 9, of doubtful authenticity). Their reaction is not recorded, nor that of other Greeks, but the ambitious proposals of Jason (q.v. 2) of Pherae suggest that Isocrates' pleas were to some not wholly impracticable.

In 373 when Thebes seized Plataea, he composed the *Plataicus* purporting to be a speech to the Athenian assembly urging reprisals, and this may have been a

sincere manifestation of antipathy to Thebes as a disruptive rival to Athens and Sparta. Likewise the *Archidamus* (366), the imagined speech of the future Spartan king about the Peace of 366/5, may reflect Isocrates' own inclinations. But other writings in this period can hardly be much more than rhetorical exercises, viz. the orations *To Nicocles* (*c.* 372), *Nicocles* (*c.* 368), and *Evagoras* (*c.* 365).

The failure of Athens in the Social War and the perilous financial position of the State in 355 stirred Isocrates to denounce in the *De Pace* the war policy of the imperialists as the way to bankruptcy, and to demand, in place of the limited peace being made with the allies, a Common Peace and the solution of economic difficulties by the foundation of colonies in Thrace: on the question of a Panhellenic crusade the speech is strikingly silent; the Persian ultimatum of 355 had ruled it out for the moment. The speech is a companion piece to the *Poroi* of Xenophon (q.v. 1); both writings illuminate the financial and foreign policy of Eubulus (q.v. 1). Shortly after in the *Aeropagiticus* Isocrates advocated return to a sober constitution under which the Areopagus (q.v.) would exercise its ancient general supervision of all aspects of life: although some would ascribe the speech to the period before the Social War, it probably belongs to 354 when the supporters of Chares (q.v. 1) were beginning to raise their heads again, and in view of the impending prosecution of Timotheus Isocrates may have been in a gloomy mood about the future of Athens under its existing constitution. The treatise must have made a curious impression on his countrymen. Certainly by 353 Isocrates was very much on the defensive. By then he had amassed wealth unprecedented for his profession, and by the law of Periander (? 357) he had become liable to frequent trierarchies; challenged in 354/3 to an antidosis (q.v.), Isocrates had emerged from the court unsuccessful and, imagining himself as a second Socrates, felt moved to write his apologia in the *Antidosis* of 353, in which he criticized his rivals and gave some account of what he himself professed. This is the chief source of our knowledge of his system of education.

In 346 he published his most important treatise, the *Philippus*. Written between the voting of the Peace of Philocrates and Philip's intervention in Phocis, it expounded afresh the programme of the *Panegyricus* and called on Philip προστῆναι τῆς τε τῶν Ἑλλήνων ὁμονοίας καὶ τῆς ἐπὶ τοὺς βαρβάρους στρατείας (§ 16) and to relieve the misery of Greece by planting colonies in the western satrapies of the Persian Empire (§ 120). In the following year, when Philip instead of beginning the crusade had got himself wounded in war against northern barbarians, Isocrates sent a further letter (*Epistle* 2) urging Philip to begin the campaign against Persia and so acquit himself of slanderous accusations about his real intentions; there is no suggestion here that Isocrates thought of a League of Corinth as the necessary instrument for Philip's *prostasia* of 'the concord of the Hellenes'. We do not know how Isocrates reacted to Philip's proposal to extend the peace brought in 344 by his old pupil Python, but shortly after the collapse of this diplomatic initiative in early 342, he began the last of his great treatises, the *Panathenaicus*, the completion of which was delayed by illness until 339. It was in part personal apologia, in part a comprehensive comparison of Athens and Sparta greatly to the glory of the former. Nowhere did he manifest any further interest in the great theme of the *Panegyricus* and the *Philippus*. Events had disappointed him and the epistles *To Alexander* (? 342) and *To Antipater* (? 340) were purely personal. One last effort remained. After discussion with Antipater (q.v. 1), when after Chaeronea he came to negotiate, Isocrates wrote an appeal to Philip (*Epistle* 3) to set about the programme of the *Philippus*. The Peace of Demades was the answer, and at the time of the annual burial of the dead in autumn 338 Isocrates starved himself to death.

2. SIGNIFICANCE. In the realm of political ideas large claims have been made for Isocrates as the man who inspired Philip with the idea of attacking Persia, who envisaged not only the form of Hellenic league that established concord and defined the relation of Greece and the Macedonian kings but also the flowering of Greek culture in the Hellenistic world. These claims cannot be substantiated. The various writings addressed to Philip probably helped Philip to form a clearer idea of the nature and strength of the Panhellenist movement the support of which he needed, but that they did more is a conjecture against which Isocrates' own words in *Epistle* 3 (§ 3) contend. His ideas about the partnership of Philip and the Greeks appear from the treatises to have been very imprecise, and the fact that he was said to have sent substantially the same epistle to Philip as to Agesilaus suggests that he sought little more than a good general for the campaign. As to the role of the new colonies, he appears not to have thought of a dispersion of Greeks beyond Asia Minor and far from the leavening of barbary he spoke as if Greek cities would form separate free entities surrounded by barbarians, ruled as barbarians had to be ruled. For the colonies were to effect merely the removal from Greece of the impoverished, and he had no vision of the prosperity that could and did flow from the creation of new trading areas. On the other hand, Isocrates did provide answers to the two great problems of his age, viz. the discord within cities due to poverty and the discord between cities due to petty ambitions and rivalries, and one has only to compare the views of Plato and Aristotle to see that, naïve as Isocrates seems, he was by far the most practical; neither of the philosophers explained how cities were to be kept from destroying each other and their plans for ensuring concord within the city by controlling the growth of population contrast unfavourably with Isocrates' proposals to settle in prosperity those whose poverty was the source of revolutionary violence.

Much has been made of the somewhat imprecise proposals for curing the ills of democracy in the *Areopagiticus*. It is to be noted that these proposals are part of a long tradition deriving from his early master, Theramenes, and found fulfilment in the arrangements of Demetrius (q.v. 3) of Phalerum: Isocrates was not alone. In his other writings the tone is very different, and this outburst may have been occasioned largely by the serious condition of Athens after the Social War.

In the history of education Isocrates has an important place. The details of his system remain somewhat obscure, but it would seem that his pupils received under his personal supervision a course of instruction which was neither purely speculative nor a mere training in rhetoric. His relation to Socrates and Plato remains matter for debate.

3. WRITINGS. Of the sixty orations extant under his name in Roman times, twenty-five were considered genuine by Dionysius (q.v. 7), and twenty-eight by Caecilius (q.v. 4). Twenty-one survive today; six are court speeches. Of the nine letters extant the authenticity of 1, 3, 4, and 9 has been questioned but never disproved.

The works of Isocrates represent Attic prose in its most elaborate form. Dionysius (*Comp.* 23) compared it to 'closely woven material', or 'a picture in which the lights melt imperceptibly into shadows'. He seems, in fact, to have paid more attention to mere expression than any other Greek writer. He was so careful to avoid hiatus that Dionysius could find no single instance in the whole of the *Areopagiticus*; he was very sparing even in the elision of short vowels, and crasis, except of καὶ

and ἄν, occurs rarely. Dissonance of consonants, due to the repetition of similar syllables in successive words, and the combination of letters which are hard to pronounce together, is similarly avoided. These objects are attained without any perceptible dislocation of the natural order of words. Another characteristic of the style is the author's attention to rhythm; though avoiding poetical metres, he considered that prose should have rhythms of its own, and approved of certain combinations of trochee and iambus. His periods are artistic and elaborate; the structure of some of the longer sentences is so complex that he overreaches himself; he sacrifices lucidity to form, and becomes monotonous. His vocabulary is almost as pure as that of Lysias, but while the simplicity of Lysias appears natural, the smoothness of Isocrates is studied.

For general bibliography *see* ATTIC ORATORS. Valuable brief account in G. Kennedy, *Art of Persuasion in Greece* (1963), 174 ff. Fairly full bibliography in E. Mikkola, *Isocrates, seine Anschauungen im Lichte seiner Schriften* (Helsinki, 1954), 297 f. Recent work on I. is reviewed by U. Albini in *Atene e Roma* 1961, 193 ff.
TEXT. Teubner (Benseler–Blass, 1879), with app. crit. E. Drerup (vol. i, 1906).
TEXT AND TRANSLATION. Norlin and van Hook, 3 vols. (Loeb); Mathieu and Brémond, 4 vols. (Budé).
SPECIAL STUDIES. *Les Idées pol. d'I.*, G. Mathieu (1923); N. H. Baynes, *Byzantine Studies and other Essays* (1955), 144 ff.; P. Cloché, *Isocrate et son temps* (1963); and for his place in the history of education see W. Jaeger, *Paideia* iii (Engl. transl. 1945), and H. I. Marrou, *Histoire de l'éducation dans l'antiquité*[6] (1965).
INDEX. S. Preuss (1904).                                    G. L. C.

**ISOPOLITEIA** is a term that probably originated in the practice of granting citizenship to new citizens on terms of equality with older citizens and thus means practically the same as *politeia*. The word was used frequently in grants to individuals but also became a technical term, used both in documents and literature, for grants to the entire citizen body of a State and particularly for reciprocal grants between two States. This use of the term occurs first in the second half of the third century, though the institution existed earlier; a unilateral grant occurs as early as 405/4 B.C. (Athens to the Samians), and there were several reciprocal grants in the fourth century. Cities connected by *isopoliteia* were not merged but remained distinct; in fact *isopoliteia* is included in several treaties of alliance. Instead, the citizens of one State became potential citizens of the other; to become active citizens it was necessary to establish residence and be registered. For the others there were such privileges as *enctesis* (the right to own land), *epigamia* (the right to contract a marriage), and the right to trade without paying import and export duties. *Isopoliteia* was used extensively by Miletus and the Aetolians.

ANCIENT SOURCES. Examples of documents: *SIG* 116, 172, 421, 472, 522, 633; *GDI* 4940, 5039–40, 5075, 5183–5; *Milet* i, pt. 3, nos. 136–7, 141–3, 146.
MODERN LITERATURE. C. Lécrivain in Dar.-Sag., s.v.; E. Szanto, *Das griechische Bürgerrecht* (1892), ch. 2; G. Busolt, *Griechische Staatskunde*[3] (1920–6), index; V. Ehrenberg, *Greek State* (1960), 106 f.; J. A. O. Larsen, *Greek Federal States* (1968), 262 ff.
                                                            J. A. O. L.

**ISTER** was the name given by the Greeks to the lower Danube. From a knowledge of its estuary, where they established a colony before 600 B.C. (*see* ISTRIA 1), the Greeks drew conclusions as to the size of the Danube. Hesiod mentioned it as one of the four great streams of the world (*Theog.* 337). Herodotus regarded it as the largest river of Europe and a northern counterpart to the Nile (4. 47–51). He correctly stated that it had a constant volume of water, but mistakenly assumed that its last bend was to the south and was quite in the dark as to its source. In the third and second centuries the Greeks probably ascended as far as the Iron Gates, but they remained ignorant as to the river's upper course; perhaps misled by a vague inkling of the river Save, and by the name of the Histri in the hinterland of Trieste, they imagined that the Ister threw off an arm into the Adriatic. This error was corrected by the Roman advance from Italy into the Danube basin after 200 B.C.; the identity of the Ister with the Danuvius was probably established during Octavian's Illyrian campaign in 35 B.C. (Sall. *Hist.* fr. 79). *See also* DANUVIUS.

M. C.

**ISTER** of Cyrene (*c.* 250–200 B.C.), pupil of Callimachus. His chief work was concerned with the mythical period of Attica in at least fourteen books, quoted under various titles, Συναγωγὴ τῶν Ἀτθίδων, Ἀττικά, etc. Contrary to the practice of the other atthidographers, Ister in none of the fragments refers to the historical period, and there is no trace of any chronological arrangement. He was concerned with the earlier period of Attic history which in Androtion and Philochorus had receded into the background. Accounts of festivals and cults appear in widely different books, which suggests a subject system, perhaps by kings or localities. It was a compilation from the earlier atthidographers dealing only with the mythical period, and the last in the series of Ἀτθίδες. Another work (Ἄτακτα) in four to five books also dealt with matters of interest in Attic history.

*FGrH* iiiB. 334.

G. L. B.

**ISTHMIA.** The Isthmian Games were athletic competitions held at Corinth in honour of Poseidon, the prize being a crown of wild celery. According to one legend they were founded by Sisyphus, king of Corinth, to commemorate his kinsman the sea-god Melicertes Palaemon. The Athenians preferred the story that they were established by Theseus after he had killed the robber chief Sinis. This was one reason why the Athenians especially patronized the Isthmian Games, but there were others: the journey was easily made, Corinth was the pleasure city of Greece, and, although there was less parade, there were more amusements at the Isthmian than at the other three festivals. It was at the Isthmian Games in 412, when Athenians as well as Peloponnesians and others were present, that the Athenians heard of the trouble that was brewing in Chios (Thuc. 8. 10). They were definitely organized, as an international festival held in every second year, in 581 B.C.      F. A. W.; R. L. H.

**ISTRIA** (1) or **ISTRUS**, a Milesian colony, situated on a promontory (or island) south of the Danube estuary. Founded in 657 according to Eusebius, but late seventh-century material is the earliest revealed to date by the considerable excavations. These excavations, together with the inscriptions and coins, make Istria one of the best-known colonies of the Pontus. It traded extensively from the sixth century with most Greek commercial centres, notably Miletus, Rhodes, Samos, Chios, Thasos, and Sinope. It sent Greek goods, especially wine and oil, far into the interior, all over the Dobruja, up the Danube and beyond the river to the north. Its independence was ended by M. Lucullus, who brought it under Roman rule in 72 B.C. The city was occupied till early in the seventh century A.D.

J. Boardman, *The Greeks Overseas* (1964), 257 ff.; V. Canarache, *Importul Amforelor Stampilate La Istria* (1957).      A. J. G.

**ISTRIA** (2) or **HISTRIA**, a peninsula at the north-eastern extremity of the Adriatic, lying between Venetia and Illyricum and extending inland towards the Julian Alps. The Illyrian Istri inhabited the peninsula, eastward to the plateau of the Cicceria and Monte Maggiore, and to the river Arsia; the western strip of the Istrian peninsula was inhabited by the Liburni. The Istri were known

as pirates (Livy 10. 2. 4), but Rome did not interfere before 221 B.C., when the Istri seized a ship carrying corn. How far they were subdued then is not known, since the Second Punic War must have hindered the Romans from establishing their power in Istria. As the Istri showed a hostile attitude when Aquileia was founded, the Romans conquered them after capturing their chief settlement (178–177); however, they did not cease to threaten Aquileia thereafter, e.g. in 171 (Livy 43. 1. 5). In 129 B.C. the Istri were among a number of tribes in the north-east of Italy who surrendered to C. Sempronius Tuditanus (*Inscr. Ital.* xiii. 3. 90. Cf. *Ann. épigr.* 1953, 95). In 52 the Istri attacked Tergeste (*Trieste*), to whose aid Caesar sent troops (Caes. *BGall.* 8. 24); this was probably their reason for siding with Pompey in the Civil War. In the west their territory must once have reached the Timavus (Strabo 5. 9, 215 c), but the Formio was made the frontier in the first century B.C., no doubt because the Celtic Carni occupied the territory round Tergeste. Istria, which was part of Illyricum during the Republic, became part of Italy under Augustus and with Venetia formed *regio* X. The boundary with Illyricum was the river Arsia.

H. Nissen, *Italische Landeskunde* ii. 1 (1902), 237 ff.; A. Gnirs, 'Forschungen über antiken Villenbau in Südistrien', *JÖAI* 1915, 99 ff.; A. Gnirs, *Istria praeromana* (1925); archaeological reports in *Not. Scav.*; A. Degrassi, 'Istria archeologica (1918–32)', *Aevum* 1933, 279 ff.; 'Notiziario archeologico' in *Atti e Mem. d. Soc. Istriana d. Arch. e Stor. patria* 1928 ff.; A. Degrassi, *Il confine nord-orientale dell'Italia romana* (1954); for inscriptions, *Inscr. Ital.* iv, fasc. 1–4 (1934–51).      F. A. W. S.; J. J. W.

**ISYLLUS** of Epidaurus, author of six poems found inscribed at Epidaurus in a hand of about 300 B.C. Nos. I and III are dedications, the first in trochaic tetrameters, the other in an elegiac couplet followed by three hexameters. II is a hexameter poem in which the poet praises himself for the introduction of a procession to Phoebus and Asclepius to Epidaurus. IV is a paean to Apollo and Asclepius, and V a hymn in hexameters to Asclepius, in which the poet thanks the god for defending Sparta from the attack of King Philip, and which may refer to the war of 338 B.C. The poems have little poetical merit.

Powell, *Coll. Alex.* 132–6.      C. M. B.

**ITALICA** (modern *Santiponce* near Seville) was founded by Scipio Africanus as an outpost against the Lusitanians (206 B.C.). It received municipal status, probably from Augustus, possibly before; and it was the ancestral home of three emperors, Trajan, Hadrian (who made it a titular colony and largely rebuilt it), and Theodosius I. Its wealth is attested by the remains of the fourth largest amphitheatre of the Roman world, and by its coins, statues, mosaics, etc. (Seville Museum). The magnitude of its oil exports is indicated by the fragments of amphorae from Italica in the Monte Testaccio at Rome.

Conde de Aguiar, *Italica* (1929); A. Garcia y Bellido, *Colonia Aelia Augusta Italica* (Madrid, 1960).      J. J. VAN N.

**ITALY.** The name *Italia*, probably a graecized form of Italic Vitelia (= 'calf-land'), was originally restricted to the southern half of the 'toe' but was gradually extended. By 450 B.C. it meant the region subsequently inhabited by the Bruttii (q.v.) (Theophr. *Hist. Pl.* 5. 8); by 400 it embraced Lucania (q.v.) as well (Thuc. 6. 4; 7. 33). Campania (q.v.) was included after 325, and by Pyrrhus' day Italia as a geographical expression meant everything south of Liguria and Cisalpine (q.v.) Gaul (Zonar. 8. 17); this area, however, only acquired political unity after the Social War. Cisalpine Gaul was not officially incorporated until Augustus' time when, accordingly, Italy reached its natural Alpine frontiers. Unofficially, however, whatever the administrative divisions, the whole country south of the Alps has been called Italy from Polybius' time onwards. The Augustan poets also call Italy *Hesperia* (= 'the western land'), *Saturnia* (= strictly Latium), *Oenotria* (= strictly SW. Italy), *Ausonia* (= 'the land of the Ausones', *Opica* to the Greeks: strictly Campania).

2. Italy's greatest length is roughly 700 miles; the greatest breadth of the peninsula proper is some 150 miles. Its long coast-line possesses comparatively few, mostly indifferent, ports, Genoa, Spezia, Naples, Tarentum, Brundisium, Ancona, and Pola being noteworthy exceptions. In compensation, however, Italy could exploit its central position to build a Mediterranean empire. Mountains, valleys, and plains in juxtaposition feature the Italian landscape. On the north are the Alps, a natural but not impassable frontier: the Carnic Alps pass is not formidable and the Brenner from time immemorial has been used by invaders attracted by Italy's pleasant climate, fertility, and beauty; the Alps actually are steeper on the Italian side. Between Alps and Apennines lies the indefensible North Italian plain watered by the Padus (q.v.). The Apennines (q.v.) traverse peninsular Italy, impeding but not actually preventing communications; the ancients' belief that they abounded in minerals was erroneous, since Italy only possessed some alluvial gold, copper (Etruria), iron (Elba), and marble (Liguria).

3. Despite fertile upland valleys the mountain districts usually permitted only a frugal existence. The plains, however, were amazingly productive, being enriched partly by volcanic activity (Euganean district in the north, Alban Hills in Latium (q.v.), Mons Vultur in Apulia (q.v.), the still-active Vesuvius in Campania), partly by fertilizing silt carried down by numerous rivers which in winter contained adequate amounts of water. (Northern Italy also possessed important lakes, but not central and southern Italy apart from Trasimenus, Fucinus, and water-filled craters like Albanus and Avernus.) Italy's natural products were consequently abundant and varied: olives, various fruits, cereals, timber, etc., even though some typically Italian products of today, e.g. oranges, were unknown in antiquity. The variety is explained chiefly by the varied climate, which is temperate if not cold in the mountains and northern Italy and warm if not hot in southern Italy. Possibly the ancient climate was slightly more equable; malaria was certainly less prevalent. Italy contained excellent pasturage; in many districts ranching supplanted agriculture. Also its seas abounded in fish.

4. Italy was thus well adapted to support human life and attract invaders, and actually did so from very early times. Traces of Neanderthal not to mention palaeolithic man have been found, while remains of neolithic people, chalcolithic *terramaricoli* (*see* TERRAMARA), and iron-using Villanovans (q.v.) are copious. Long before the rise of Rome Italy was well populated and civilized from end to end. On the east coast were Illyrian immigrants: Veneti (?), Picentes, Messapii (qq.v.); these occasionally penetrated to the west. Hardy Sabelli (q.v.) and the related Umbrians and Volsci (qq.v.) held and tended to expand from the mountainous central regions. The southern coast-lands comprised Magna Graecia (q.v.). In the north Gauls began to settle *c.* 400. Various peoples inhabited the west: Ligurians, who were possibly of neolithic stock and originally held a wider area; Etruscans; Latini and the related Falisci and Hernici (qq.v.); Aurunci-Ausones and Oenotri (= Sicels?). These various peoples differed greatly from one another in race, language, and civilization, and Italy's mountainous configuration accentuated and perpetuated their mutual divergencies.

5. But ultimately they were united under the hegemony of Rome. Her political unification of Italy, however, was a protracted task finally accomplished only in Augustus' day. The romanization of Italy took much longer and, indeed, was never fully achieved.

6. After unifying Italy Augustus divided it into eleven administrative districts:

  i. Latium, Campania, Picentini district.
  ii. Apulia, Calabria, Hirpini district.
  iii. Lucania, Ager Bruttius.
  iv. Region inhabited by Samnites, Frentani, Marrucini, Marsi, Paeligni, Aequiculi, Vestini, Sabini.
  v. Picenum, Praetuttii district.
  vi. Umbria, Ager Gallicus.
  vii. Etruria.
  viii. Gallia Cispadana.
  ix. Liguria.
  x. Venetia, Istria, Cenomani district.
  xi. Gallia Transpadana.

This arrangement lasted almost unaltered until Constantine's time, when the islands were customarily included in Italy.

ANCIENT SOURCES. Strabo's detailed description (bks. 5 and 6) is good; *inter alia* it corrects Polybius' assertion (2. 14) that Italy is triangular. Pliny's account (*HN* 3. 38–132) is based on Augustus' *Commentaries*. Pomponius Mela (2. 58–73), Ptolemy (bk. 3), and the *Liber Coloniarum* are less important. Amongst others Varro (*Rust.* 1. 2. 1 f.), Virgil (*G.* 2. 136 f.), Dionysius of Halicarnassus (1. 36 f.), Propertius (3. 22. 17 f.), Pliny (*HN* 37. 201 f.), and Rutilius Namatianus (2. 17 f.) extol Italy's beauty and fertility. Roads are described in the Itineraries (q.v.), especially the Antonine Itinerary (4th-c. copy of a work of *c.* A.D. 212) and Peutingerian Table (q.v.) which is probably based on Castorius' world-map of A.D. 366. See, too, the separate articles: VIA APPIA, etc.

For epigraphic finds, see *CIL* xi and *Inscriptiones Italiae* (Italy: 1932– ); for archaeological, *Notizie degli Scavi, Monumenti Antichi*, and *Forma Italiae* (1928– ).

MODERN LITERATURE. (i) *General.* H. Nissen, *Italische Landeskunde* (2 vols., 1883, 1902); F. Sabin, *Classical Associations of Places in Italy* (U.S.A. 1928); D. S. Walker, *A Geography of Italy* (1958); V. Ussani–F. Arnaldi, *Guida allo studio della civiltà romana* (1959) i. 13 ff.

(ii) *Special.* Economics: A. Sambon, *Monnaies antiques de l'Italie* (1903); Frank, *Econ. Survey*, vols. i, v (documented). Ethnography: J. Whatmough, *Foundations of Roman Italy* (1937; documented). Maps: *Edizione archeologica della carta d'Italia* (1 : 100,000). Maps of Istituto Geografico Militare (Florence). Bibliographies for Italian cities: Mau–von Mercklin–Matz, *Katalog der Bibliothek des deutsch. arch. Inst. in Rom* (1914–32). *Italia romana: municipi e colonie* (1939– ). R. Thomsen, *The Italic Regions from Augustus to the Lombard Invasions* (Copenhagen, 1947).     E. T. S.

**ITHACA** ('Ιθάκη) is one of the loveliest islands in Greece. Deep bays cutting into steep hills provide scenery which might well inspire a poet. The English excavations have shown not only that Ithaca was more important than her neighbours in both Homeric and Odyssean times, but that she was the staging post for Corinthian trade to Italy, up to and perhaps even after the foundation of the colonies. The Northern Museum houses striking Early Bronze Age vases from the settlement near Stavros. A fallen-in cave at Polis Bay was occupied from Bronze Age to Roman times. Inscriptions to Athena, Hera, the Nymphs, and Odysseus show its religious nature. There were some Mycenaean vases, much Protogeometric material, and bits of twelve splendid Geometric tripods, one on wheels, which must recall the tripods brought by Odysseus (*Od.* 13. 13, 217, 363 ff.). A Mycenaean house was found nearby, and there were Mycenaean sherds all round the slopes of the bay along with Corinthian graves. The Museum at Vathy contains the finds from another rich shrine on the shoulder of the hill Aetos. W. A. Heurtley called the piles of stones and Protogeometric sherds 'cairns'. No human bones were found, the sherds were not burnt, and the patches of black earth beside them were barren of offerings; so probably they were fallen roofs. Many of the vases were too grand to belong to huts, and as Protogeometric sherds were also scattered round the archaic *temenos*, a Protogeometric temple seems a possible solution. One still wonders why the shores round the excellent harbour of Vathy are devoid of antiquities and why Ithaca played no part in Classical Greece.

Excavation reports in *Archaeologia* xxxiii (1849); *BSA* xxxi, xxxiii, xxxv, xlii, xliii, xlviii (1930–53); P-K *GL* 2. 2. 491 ff.     S. B.

**ITHOME,** a prominent and easily fortified mountain rising isolated in the Messenian plain (2,646 feet), was the rallying point of the Messenians in their struggles for independence against Sparta. In the first Messenian War they held it for twenty years; on its fall they lost their freedom. In the rising of the helots against Sparta in the fifth century it was fortified and became a chief centre of resistance. Epaminondas founded the town of Messene on its west side, fortifying it with some of the finest extant Greek walls, which include part of Ithome as an acropolis.

Tyrtaeus; Thuc. I. 101–3. F. Kiechle, *Messenische Studien* (1959), 72 ff., 82 ff.; G. L. Huxley, *Early Sparta* (1962), 34 ff. For problems of chronology, N. G. L. Hammond, 'Studies in Greek Chronology. (i) 'The Third Messenian War', *Hist.* 1955, 371 ff.; D. W. Reece, *JHS* 1962, 111 ff.     T. J. D.; R. J. H.

**ITINERARIES,** dealing with land routes after the manner of *periploi* (q.v.) i.e. giving distances along roads, with varying amounts of information, were common in the Roman Empire: copies were kept in libraries and sections exhibited on stone. Some survive in fragments, but few written itineraries are known, chief of them the *Itinerarium Antoninianum*, which may be a late third-century collection of routes used for troop movements, proceeding by *mansiones* (see ANNONA *and* POSTAL SERVICE). An *Itinerarium Maritimum* is preserved together with it. The *Ravenna Cosmography* (c. A.D. 700) includes an itinerary following a geographical disquisition, all based on earlier sources (see *Bonner Jahrb.* 1963, 238 ff.) The Peutinger table (q.v.) is a map based on an itinerary. The fourth-century *Bordeaux* (or *Jerusalem*) *Itinerary*—it treats the journey between the two places—is one of many guides for Christian pilgrims; written in descriptive form, it gives annotation as well as distances.

*Itineraria Romana*, 1 (ed. Cuntz, 1929), 2 (ed. Schneitz, 1940); *PW*, s.v. 'Itinerarien', 'Karten'; D. van Berchem, *L'Annone militaire* (1937), 166. For a new find *see* A. Deman, *Das Altertum* 1965, 115 f.     E. B.

**ITINERARIUM EGERIAE (PEREGRINATIO AETHERIAE),** an account by a nun, Egeria (or, less probably, Aetheria), of her pilgrimage to the East, including Constantinople, Asia Minor, Palestine, Sinai, Egypt, and Edessa, written in the East for the nuns of her own convent, perhaps in Spain. It is generally agreed that its date is round about A.D. 400, with a few years margin on either side. The sole MS., apart from fragments, was discovered in Arezzo, and published in 1887. It had been written in Monte Cassino in the second half of the eleventh century. It is incomplete, but it is important for the information given about liturgical practices at the Holy Places as well as for the account of biblical sites and of the writer's visits to the churches and tombs of Eastern martyrs. It is of great value to philologists as a source of Late and Vulgar Latin. Its language does not represent any specific dialect.

Ed. O. Prinz, Heidelberg (1960); A. Francheschini and R. Weber, *Corpus Christianorum* (1958). W. van Oorde, *Lexicon Aetherianum* (Amsterdam, 1930); A. A. R. Bastiaensen, *Observations sur le vocabulaire liturgique dans l'Itinéraire d'Egérie, Latinitas Christianorum Primaeva* xvii (1962) (full bibliography); E. Löfstedt, *Philol. Kommentar zur Peregrinatio Aetheriae* (1936).     F. J. E. R.

**ITURAEA.** The Ituraeans, a predatory Arab people, occupied the Libanus, Antilibanus, and Hermon, and the Massyas, where lay Chalcis their capital and Heliopolis (q.v.) their religious centre. In the early first century B.C., under their tetrarch and high-priest Ptolemy, they almost captured Damascus, having conquered most of the country north and south of it. Ptolemy was confirmed by Pompey (64); his son Lysanias was killed by Antony (35), who granted his dominions to Cleopatra. The tetrarchy was restored by Octavian (30) to Zenodorus, who was, however, soon deprived of most of it owing to his depredations (24). Parts were granted to Berytus, Sidon, and Damascus; part became the tetrarchy of Abilene; Batanaea, Trachonitis, and Auranitis went to Herod, who on Zenodorus' death in 20 received Paneas and Gaulanitis also. Herod's Ituraean dominions passed to his son Philip (4 B.C.–A.D. 34), Agrippa I (37–44), who from 41 also ruled Abilene, and Agrippa II (53–c. 93), who ruled Abilene and in addition Arcene, an Ituraean tetrarchy in northern Libanus which had never belonged to the main principality. Chalcis formed a kingdom for Herod, brother of Agrippa I (41–8) and Agrippa II (50–3). The Ituraeans were gradually broken of their predatory habits, but remained a primitive people, living in villages. Famed as archers, they contributed three cohorts and an *ala* to the imperial army.

A. H. M. Jones, *JRS* 1931, 265 ff.; *Cities E. Rom. Prov.* 255 ff.     A. H. M. J.

**IUDEX.** In the Roman civil procedure (*see* LAW AND PROCEDURE, ROMAN, II), with its bipartite arrangement in two stages, *in iure* and *apud iudicem*, the *iudex* was a private person taken from the higher social classes (senators and, later, *equites*). No special juridical education was legally required; only persons with physical defects, women, and *minores* were excluded. The choice of the judge lay with the parties, and was normally, but not necessarily, made from a panel of qualified persons (*album iudicum*). The plaintiff usually proposed a name, but the defendant had the right of refusal. It is uncertain what happened if the defendant refused every name in the *album* (choice by lot, or treatment of defendant as *indefensus?*). The parties' choice was approved by the magistrate *in iure*. The *iudex* was unable to refuse the commission conferred upon him by the magistrate's *iussum iudicandi*, except on recognized grounds such as old age, a numerous family, or a privileged profession (philosopher, physician, rhetorician). For the proceedings *apud iudicem* see the article quoted above. The functions of the *iudex*, assisted, if he wished, by advisers (*consilium*), ended with the verdict pronounced by him orally in the presence of the litigants. He could, however, refuse to give a verdict if he was in doubt (Gell. 14. 2); the trial was then repeated before another *iudex*. In classical times the *iudex* had full discretion in appraising the evidence and was not bound by previous decisions in similar cases. Nevertheless, decided cases (*res iudicatae*) probably acquired some authority in later times (*Dig.* 1. 3. 38). The XII Tables are said (Gell. 20. 1. 7) to have punished by death the judge convicted of bribery; the praetorian edict (*see* EDICTUM) introduced a special civil remedy against the careless or corrupt judge (*qui litem suam fecit*).

The judge might be an *arbiter* rather than a *iudex*. In early law there may have been a substantial difference, but in historical times *arbiter* seems merely to have been an alternative word for *iudex* in those suits in which the judge had a wide discretion. (It also may denote an arbitrator to whom the parties may privately agree to submit their dispute: *Dig.* 4. 8.) The *iudex* sat alone (*unus iudex*), but there were also courts composed of several persons, *recuperatores*, *centumviri* (qq.v.), and *decemviri stlitibus iudicandis* (*see* VIGINTISEXVIRI).

In the *cognitio extra ordinem* the judge was appointed, independently of the parties, by the official before whom the case first came. He was now called *iudex datus*, *pedaneus*, or *specialis*, and his competence (final decision or only a partial cognition of the case) depended on his commission. Under the late Empire the use of the term *iudex* became much larger: any official endowed with jurisdictional or administrative power was so called. Therefore '*iudex*' was often interpolated in classical texts in place of judicial magistrates. Justinian's constitution *Cod.* 3. 1. 14. 1 demonstrates the wide application of the term.

For bibliography, *see* LAW AND PROCEDURE, ROMAN, II. J. Mazeaud, *La Nomination du iudex unus* (1933); P. Collinet, *Le Rôle des juges* (Recueil d'études F. Gény i, 1935); G. Broggini, *Iudex arbiterve* (1957). A. B.; B. N.

**IUDICIA POPULI**, trials before the *comitia* (q.v.) *centuriata* at Rome. The XII Tables (q.v.) provided (Cic. *Leg.* 3. 4. 11) 'de capite civis nisi per maximum comitiatum . . . ne ferunto'. According to the long-accepted view of Mommsen, this meant that (in normal times) a citizen could never be sentenced to death except after such a trial and that therefore any death sentence was subject to revision by the *comitia* (*see* PROVOCATIO). The proceedings were peculiar in that the investigation (*anquisitio*) by the magistrate was made *in contione*, i.e. before the assembled people, who subsequently judged by what they heard, there being no repetition of the evidence. The people had no option but to confirm or quash the magistrate's sentence; a magisterial acquittal was final.

In recent years a different view has been propounded. According to this view the XII Tables rule did not forbid the sentencing to death of a citizen by ordinary criminal process; it provided merely that the only popular assembly which might impose such a sentence was the *comitia centuriata*. Moreover, *iudicia populi* were used only for political offences, not for ordinary crimes, and *provocatio* was confined to acts of administrative *coercitio* (q.v.). In a *iudicium populi* the proceedings *in contione* were an investigation by the magistrate as prosecutor, and his 'sentence' was only a proposal made by him in the same capacity.

Mommsen, *Röm. Strafr.*; C. H. Brecht, *Sav. Zeitschr.* 1939, 261 ff.; W. Kunkel, *Untersuchungen zur Entwicklung des röm. Kriminalverfahrens* (1962). A. B.; B. N.

**IURIDICUS** was a judicial functionary of praetorian rank in Italy (except Rome and its environs), nominated by the emperor. The first mention of *iuridici* is in A.D. 163. By introducing them Marcus Aurelius imitated the *consulares* created by Hadrian but abolished by Antoninus Pius. The field of their competence (confined to civil cases) was one or more districts, *regiones*; the procedure was *cognitio extra ordinem*. The *iuridici* disappear under Diocletian; later uses of this title (as in the *Digest*) are to be referred to the *iuridicus Alexandreae*, a high jurisdictional officer in Egypt, known also from the Greek papyri as δικαιοδότης. In other imperial provinces there were *legati iuridici* (called in some inscriptions simply *iuridici*), also appointed by the Emperor, with a limited jurisdictional competence. A. B.

**IUS CIVILE.** This term derives its meaning from its context. By contrast with *ius gentium* (q.v.) in the 'theoretical' sense it is the law of a particular State, and usually, unless otherwise qualified, the law of Rome. By contrast with *ius gentium* in the 'practical' sense it is that part of the law of Rome which is applicable only to Roman citizens. By contrast with *ius honorarium* (*see* EDICTUM) it is law derived from statute and 'common law' as interpreted by the jurists (*see* JURISPRUDENCE). It was also used in a still narrower sense to denote only the product of the jurists' interpretation. B. N.

**IUS GENTIUM.** This term has three main senses. (1) In a 'practical' sense it denotes that part of Roman

law which was open to citizens and non-citizens alike. Originally commercial and other relations between Romans and foreigners were based merely on reciprocal trust, since the institutions of the old *ius civile* (q.v.) and the procedure of *legis actiones* were accessible only to Romans, in accordance with the general principle of the ancient world that law was 'personal' (i.e. that a man lived by the law of his own State). The growth of international trade made it necessary to recognize some institutions which could be applied by Roman courts to relations between foreigners and between foreigners and citizens. The course of development of this *ius gentium* is conjectural. No doubt the establishment in 242 B.C. of the office of *praetor* (q.v.) *peregrinus* played a part, but there must have been other factors, since in the classical law *ius gentium* was not regarded as a praetorian creation, and it was applicable also to relations purely between citizens. It included even some institutions which were part of the old *ius civile* (notably *stipulatio*, q.v., except in the form using 'spondeo'). It had thus come to include the most flexible and commercially significant parts of Roman law. The law of the family and of succession on death remained for the most part 'personal', but the historically important institutions of the rest of the law, and especially of the law of contracts, belonged to the *ius gentium*. After the *constitutio Antoniniana* (*see* CITIZENSHIP, ROMAN), when the same law was applied to Romans and *peregrini*, the distinction between *ius gentium* in this sense and *ius civile* was only an historical reminiscence.

(2) In a more 'theoretical' sense the term is used as a synonym for the philosophical *ius naturale*, conceived as an ideal and universally valid set of precepts. Gaius (q.v. 2) contrasts it with the *ius civile* of each individual State: 'quod vero naturalis ratio inter omnes homines constituit, id apud omnes populos peraeque custoditur vocaturque ius gentium, quasi quo iure omnes gentes utuntur' (*Inst.* 1. 1). The term 'ius naturale' looks to the origin of this law in natural reason, 'ius gentium' to its universal application. This is strictly a confusion of thought, since *ius naturale* is law which ought to be universally applied, and *ius gentium* is law which is in fact so applied, but the Romans never made this sharp distinction. Only in the case of slavery did they differentiate between *ius naturale*, according to which all men were born free, and *ius gentium*, by which they might be slaves. Though without direct practical consequences, these concepts of *ius gentium* and *ius naturale* were indirectly important in fertilizing and developing the law.

(3) *Ius gentium* also sometimes denoted legal rules governing relations between States, corresponding to modern 'public international law'.

G. Lombardi, *Ricerche in tema di ius gentium* (1946); id., *Il concetto di i.g.* (1947); G. Grosso, *Rev. int. des droits de l'antiquité* ii (1949); E. Levy, *Stud. et Doc. Hist. et Iuris* xv (1949); and literature on history and sources under LAW AND PROCEDURE, ROMAN, I. B. N.

**IUS ITALICUM** represents the legal quality of Roman territory in Italy: the land is free from *tributum soli* and can be possessed in full ownership *ex iure Quiritium*; the inhabitants are not liable to *tributum capitis*. The distinction arose when Roman colonies were founded outside Italy, from which such privileges might be withheld. Under the Empire this was the highest privilege obtainable by a provincial municipality. Augustus only gave it to genuine citizen colonies, mostly his eastern foundations. Later it was granted along with colonial rights to Roman municipalities, but, for fiscal reasons, sparingly. Severus, however, distributed it not only to three municipalities of Africa, his native province, but, after their co-operation in the Civil War, to several Greek cities. This development typified the assimilation of East and

West, which the *Constitutio Antoniniana* completed (*see* CITIZENSHIP, ROMAN).

J. Triantophyllopoulos, 'Ius Italicum personnel', *Jura* 1963, 109 ff., *and see* COLONIZATION, ROMAN.     A. N. S.-W.

**IUS LATII.** The Latin rights of the Empire were a continuation of the rights enjoyed by the Latin Name (*see* LATINI) of the Republic, which were derived from the social and political ties existing between the original *populi Latini*. Latins after 338 B.C. shared *conubium* and *commercium* (q.v.) with Rome, and possessed the *ius mutandae civitatis* together with the closely associated *ius exsilii*. Hereby individual Latins settling permanently in Rome acquired the Roman citizenship, and vice versa. Later, when this encouraged the depopulation of the Latin States, the more limited *ius civitatis per honorem adipiscendae* was substituted for it (*c.* 150 B.C.?). This gave Roman citizenship to Latins holding the magistracies of their local communities. Latins temporarily resident in Rome also possessed a limited right of voting in the tribal assemblies. The *ius provocationis* was possibly added in 122 B.C. There were no different kinds of Latin rights, although sometimes special regulations might be included in the charter establishing a Latin colony or group of colonies. In 89 B.C. Latin rights were conferred *en bloc* upon the Transpadane Gauls. Their communities were remodelled on the pattern of the earlier Latin colonies, adopting Latin language and law. In 49 B.C. the Transpadanes received Roman citizenship, and in the following century *ius Latii* was extended to many communities of Gallia Narbonensis, Hispania Ulterior, and Africa. It became an intermediate stage in the promotion of individual *peregrini* to Roman citizenship, and some Latin municipalities acquired the full status of *municipia civium Romanorum*. Under Hadrian *Latium maius* appeared, whereby *decuriones* (q.v.), as well as magistrates, received the citizenship *per honorem*.

For bibliography, *see* LATINI.     A. N. S.-W.

**IUS LIBERORUM.** The Augustan marriage legislation (*lex Iulia de maritandis ordinibus* and *lex Papia Poppaea*) gave certain privileges to the parents of three children (four for *libertini*). In particular this *ius trium* (*quattuor*) *liberorum* freed the mother from *tutela* (*see* GUARDIANSHIP). It also gave the father a prior claim to magistracies. The privilege came also to be granted as a favour by the Emperors (e.g. by Trajan to Pliny the Younger) regardless of the number of children.     B. N.

**IUS PRIMAE RELATIONIS.** When in 23 B.C. Augustus ceased to hold the consulship, certain compensatory rights and powers were voted to him by the Senate in order that his position might not be weakened, among them the *ius primae relationis* (Dio Cass. 53. 32. 5). His *tribunicia potestas* gave him the right to introduce business in the Senate: the *ius primae relationis* either allowed him to submit proposals to the Senate in writing (so Mommsen, *Staatsr.* ii (3), 899) or, far more probably, gave him, for one piece of business at each meeting of the Senate, the prior right of reference that would otherwise have belonged to the consuls (so H. F. Pelham, *Essays in Roman History* (1911), 74 ff.). This right is specified as 'relationem facere' in the *Lex de imperio Vespasiani* (Dessau, *ILS* 244). Later the number of items of business for which the Emperor was given precedence was raised as high as five (*Vita Alexandri* 1).     J. P. B.

**IUSIURANDUM.** An oath was used in several ways in the stage before the magistrate (*in iure*) in classical Roman civil proceedings. (i) In almost every action either party might exact from the other, on pain of losing the case, an oath that he was proceeding in good faith

(*iusiurandum calumniae*). Justinian made this oath compulsory for both parties and for their representatives. (ii) In a few actions only the plaintiff might invite the defendant to swear to the validity of his claim (*deferre iusiurandum*); the defendant might then either swear and win the case, or refuse and lose, or invite the plaintiff to swear instead, with the same alternatives before him (*referre iusiurandum*), or, finally, might invite the plaintiff to swear a *iusiurandum calumniae*. (iii) Either party in any action (or at any stage of any dispute) might invite the other to swear an oath of this kind; the other might either swear and win or refuse with impunity. These last two oaths are distinguished by the modern names of *iusiurandum necessarium* and *voluntarium* respectively.

In the proceedings *apud iudicem* an oath served only as evidence or (*iusiurandum in litem*) for the assessment by the plaintiff of the value of the thing in issue in certain actions.     B. N.

**IUSTITIA**, Roman equivalent of Dike (q.v. 1); mostly in poetry, but had a temple from 8 Jan. A.D. 13 (Ov. *Pont.* 3. 6. 25, *Fasti Praen.* under 8 Jan.; see further Wissowa, *RK* 333). In inscriptions she sometimes has the title Augusta.     H. J. R.

**IUSTITIUM** (from *iuris stitium* = *ius sistere*), temporary suspension of all jurisdictional activity of magistrates, *iudices*, and courts, in civil and criminal matters, on account of events disturbing the whole of public life, as in the case of great national calamities, riots, and the like. A *iustitium* could be proclaimed by the Senate; it produced immediate suspension of *iurisdictio* and inhibition of *iudicia* (Cic. *Har. Resp.* 26. 55).     A. B.

**IUVENES** (or **IUVENTUS**—i.e. *Equestris ordinis iuventus*, Val. Max. 2. 2. 9). When, usually at the age of fourteen, a Roman boy adopted the *toga virilis*, he became a *iuvenis*. At the age of seventeen those who intended to follow an equestrian or a senatorial career started the military service which Augustus made a necessary preliminary to those careers. In the interval the *iuvenes* of fourteen to seventeen years of age who were *equites* (whose number included the sons of senators) served at Rome their *tirocinium*, a preparation for military service. They practised physical exercises and riding, paraded at great festivals, and held their own games, the *ludi sevirales* (the *lusus Troiae* being celebrated by those who were still *pueri*). This institution, which had precedents in the Roman Republic (Cic. *Cael.* 11), was thoroughly organized by Augustus, with a view to invigorating the youth of the upper classes at Rome (cf. Maecenas' speech, Dio Cass. 52. 26). It was extended also, for freeborn youths, to the *municipia* of Italy and, by the second century A.D., had spread widely through the western provinces of the Empire. Nero held games called *Iuvenalia* and organized a body of picked youths, perhaps known as *Iuvenes Augustiani*. A *collegium iuvenum Augustianorum* was established, perhaps by Domitian.

*Iuventus* was also used in a wider sense to indicate at Rome the whole body of *equites equo publico* (i.e. *equites* under the age of 35 who were still 'iuniores' technically, and sons of senators under the age of 25 who had not yet held a senatorial magistracy), organized in six *turmae* and parading, for inspection by the Emperor, under the *seviri equitum* at the *recensio equitum*. This is the sense of *iuventus* in the courtesy title 'Princeps Iuventutis' (q.v.).

M. Rostovtzeff, 'Römische Bleitesserae', *Klio*, Beiheft iii (1905), 59 ff.; M. Della Corte, *Iuventus* (1924) and *Not. Scav.* 1939, 239 (inscriptions and graffiti of the great palaestra at Pompeii); S. L. Mohler, 'The Iuvenes and Roman Education', *TAPA* 1937. 442.     J. P. B.

**IUVENTAS,** goddess, not of youth or youthful beauty in general, but of the *iuvenes*, or men of military age (contrast HEBE). She had a shrine in the vestibule of Minerva's *cella* in the Capitoline temple (Dion. Hal. *Ant. Rom.* 3. 69. 5), and is said to have been there before the temple was built, she and Terminus (q.v.) refusing to leave (ibid. and Livy 5. 54. 7; but see Latte, *RR* 256). When any young man took the *toga virilis*, a contribution was made to her temple chest (Dion. Hal. 4. 15. 5).

Wissowa, *RK* 135 f. H. J. R.

**IVORY.** Bronze-Age Greece first learnt ivory working from Egypt, and later obtained ivory from Syria. There were distinguished Minoan schools making statuettes and in the later Mycenaean period furniture was often decorated with ivory plaques. Fresh inspiration from the East came in the eighth century, together with the material and techniques, although the Syrian herds of elephant probably did not survive that century. There were orientalizing schools in the Peloponnese and east Greece but the finds became sparse after the seventh century when supply became more difficult. Ivory was used for the flesh parts of cult statues like Phidias' chryselephantine Parthenos and Zeus at Olympia, and for minor works it could be carved in low relief or with incised patterns which might be gilt or painted. In the Hellenistic and Roman period, when Indian sources were available, its use was mainly confined to decorative plaques for furniture and toilet articles.

R. D. Barnett, *JHS* 1948; H. Payne, *Perachora* ii (1962); R. M. Dawkins, *Artemis Orthia* (1929); B. Freyer-Schavenburg, *Elfenbeine aus dem samischen Heraion* (1966). J. B.

**IXION,** the Greek Cain, the first to murder one of his kin (Pindar, *Pyth.* 2. 31 f.); as other accounts (e.g. schol. Ap. Rhod. 3. 62, quoting Pherecydes) make the victim his father-in-law Eïoneus, whom he killed to avoid paying bride-price, either Pindar is speaking loosely or Eïoneus was also his blood-relation. Zeus purified him, but he attempted the chastity of Hera; consequently he was first deceived with a cloud-image of her, on which he begat the Centaurs (q.v.) or their father, and afterwards attached to a revolving wheel. Pindar, ibid. 21 ff.; scholiasts on Pindar and Apollonius (above).

Weizsäcker in Roscher's *Lexikon* ii. 766 ff.; Cook, *Zeus* i. 198 ff. H. J. R.

**IYNX** (*ἴυγξ* 'wryneck') was in legend a nymph, daughter of Peitho or Echo, who by magic spells won the love of Zeus for herself (or for Io), and was turned to a bird by Hera. The legend may be due to the use of the wryneck, spread out on a wheel, as a love-charm, which Pindar says (*Pyth.* 4. 214) Aphrodite invented to enable Jason to obtain the love of Medea. The iynx used by Simaetha in Theoc. *Id.* 2 was probably a simple wheel, pierced with two holes, and threaded with string, the twisting of which caused the wheel to rotate (see R. Gow, *JHS* 1934, 1 ff.). For further discussion of the iynx-wheel as a solar symbol, see Cook, *Zeus* i. 253 ff. C. B.

# J

**JANICULUM,** the prominent ridge on the west bank of the Tiber at Rome, some 3½ miles long. The name was anciently connected with Janus, but the only trace of his cult on the hill is the shrine of his son Fons or Fontus. The place was early a defensive outpost (Livy 1. 33) and was later enclosed in a great salient of Aurelian's Wall. Here lay the Lucus Furrinae, scene of the death of C. Gracchus and later occupied by the temple of the Syrian cults favoured by Commodus and the Severi and restored by Julian.

The district was primarily industrial, with mills driven by the Aqua Traiana (*CIL* vi. 1711), and nurseries for sacred fish fed from the same source.

P. Gauckler, *Le Sanctuaire syrien au Janicule* (1912); F. Cumont, *CRAcad. Inscr.* 1917, 275 ff.; Darier, *Les Fouilles du Janicule à Rome* (1920). I. A. R.

**JANUARIUS NEPOTIANUS,** author of a loose and imperfect epitome of Valerius (q.v. 8) Maximus before the sixth century A.D. It was inferior to that by Julius Paris.

**JANUS.** The word properly means a gate or barbican (Livy 1. 19. 2 and often); especially the monument there named, the *Ianus geminus* in the Forum 'ad infimum Argiletum', though other structures of a like kind were so called also. They were mostly free-standing, not part of a city or other wall, and used originally for ceremonial purposes, and it is very probable that such *iani* as that in the Forum were used for the formal setting-out of an army or other party, to make sure that they began in the proper way. (There is a right and a wrong way to march out through a gate (Livy 2. 49. 8); the Fabii go out to war 'infelici uia, dextro iano [arch] portae Carmentalis'.) Hence *ianua*, the outer door of a house, and the god Janus, who is the *numen* of both

it and the arch. But to enter house or city one must pass through the gate or the door; hence Janus tended to become a god of beginnings. He is named at the beginning of any list of gods in a prayer, even before Jupiter (as Livy 8. 9. 6); the first month of the reformed calendar, Ianuarius, is his and his festival comes in it (*see* AGONIUM). His priest is the *rex sacrorum*, his proper offering a ram, and the place the Regia (Varro, *Ling.* 6. 12; Ov. *Fasti* 1. 318)—perhaps some ancient piece of ritual connected with the king's door, but if so it is the only instance of Janus' ritual being connected with a door. All this seems to have given rise to the notion that he was a very great god ('diuom deus', hymn of the Salii ap. Varro, op. cit. 7. 27), and finally a sky-god or cosmic god (e.g. Ov. ibid. 101 ff., where see Frazer's note for modern adaptations of this theory). When represented otherwise than by the gate, his symbol was a double-faced head, a very old art-type, sometimes awkwardly joined to a body. The closing of the *Ianus geminus* signified peace (i.e. no need for war-magic).

Wissowa, *RK* 103 ff.; Latte, *RR* 132 ff.; L. A. Holland, *Janus and the Bridge* (1961). For the temple in Forum Holitorium (dedicated by Duilius after the victory of Mylae in 260 B.C.), shrine in Forum (Janus Geminus), and arch in Forum Boarium (Janus Quadrifrons), see Platner–Ashby, 275 ff.; Nash, *Pict. Dict. Rome* i. 500 ff. H. J. R.

**JASON** (1) (*'Iάσων*), in mythology, son of Aeson and leader of the Argonauts (q.v.). Apart from his adventures on the voyage the chief events in his life are as follows. On the usurpation of Pelias his parents smuggled him out of Iolcus, under cover of a mock funeral and a report of his death, and gave him to Chiron to bring up. On reaching young manhood he returned to claim his heritage, and arrived in the city with but one sandal, having lost the other in crossing a torrent. Pelias, who knew that the man with the one sandal was to be fatal to him (or in general, that one of the Aeolidae should overthrow him), managed to induce him to go for the Golden Fleece (Pind. *Pyth.* 4. 71 ff., for earliest surviving account). The episode of the lost sandal is variously explained, the most interesting story being that Hera disguised as an old woman met him and asked to be taken across the river, in struggling through which he lost his shoe in the mud. It seems possible that originally Pelias did not neglect to sacrifice to her (Ap. Rhod. 1. 14) but refused to carry her across. See in general Apollonius, loc. cit. and schol.; Γένος Ἀπολλωνίου; Hyginus, *Fab.* 12 and 13. After the return from the voyage the chief incident is his desertion of Medea (q.v.; cf. CREON 1); thereafter there is nothing interesting save the manner of his death (foretold Eur. *Med.* 1386–7, whereon see schol.): as he slept under the stern of the Argo, part of it fell on him and killed him.　　　　　　　　　　H. J. R.

**JASON** (2), tyrant of Pherae *c.* 385–370 B.C., probably son of Lycophron. He sought to gain control of all Thessaly, and finally gained his object in 374 by winning over Pharsalus. Elected *tagos* (q.v.), he modernized the organization of the Thessalian State and extended his influence over northern Greece. He maintained friendly relations with Athens and allied himself to the Thebans, who summoned him to Leuctra immediately after their victory (371). He refused to use his well-trained mercenaries on their behalf and negotiated an armistice between them and the Spartans. In 370 he caused alarm in Greece by mobilizing the entire Thessalian army at the time of the Pythian Games, but he was assassinated before the completion of his preparations, and their object remained unknown.

The success of Jason in uniting a potentially strong people, long weakened by inter-city feuds and external intervention, affords proof of his ability. His ambition to establish a Thessalian hegemony over Greece remained far from accomplishment, but his methods foreshadowed, and may in some degree have suggested, those adopted by Philip of Macedon.

Xen. *Hell.* 6. 1. 2–19 and 4. 20–32 (who had excellent sources); Diod. bk. 15. H. D. Westlake, *Thessaly in the Fourth Century* B.C. (1935), chs. 4–6; M. Sordi, *La lega tessala* (1958).　　H. D. W.

**JASON** (3), a hellenized Jew of Cyrene, wrote a history of the exploits of Judas Maccabaeus in five books, of which 2 Maccabees is an epitome; he was probably a contemporary (2 Macc. ii. 23).

*FGrH* ii. 182.

**JAVELIN, THROWING THE.** The javelin (ἄκων) was a spear about 8 feet long, probably with a metal point. Round the middle was bound a thong with a loop through which the athlete placed his first finger, or first and middle fingers, when throwing. As he let go the javelin he held on to the loop of the thong which, as it unwound, gave a spinning motion to the javelin. This, together with the extra leverage given by the use of the thong, added distance and accuracy to the throw.　R. L. H.

**JAVOLENUS PRISCUS,** GAIUS (or LUCIUS) OCTAVIUS (*PW* 59) TIDIUS TOSSIANUS, a prominent Roman jurist, born before A.D. 60, died after 120. After commanding two legions, he was *iuridicus* of Britain, *cos. suff.* (86), governor of Germania Superior (90) and Syria, and proconsul of Africa. He enjoyed a high reputation among his contemporaries, was a member of Trajan's *consilium* and head of the Sabinian School (*see* SABINUS 2); but posterity did not cite him very frequently. This may be explained by the fact that his literary production consisted mainly of epitomes of the works of earlier jurists, in which his

own opinions are manifested only by short phrases of approval or dissent (*libri ex Cassio, ex Plautio, ex Posterioribus Labeonis*). His most mature and most important work is his *Epistulae* (in fourteen books), freely excerpted by Justinian's compilers. The *Epistulae* reveal fine, independent legal thought, and prove that he was a sagacious respondent and not merely a critical and judicious epitomator. The great Salvius Julianus (q.v. 2) acknowledged him as his teacher.　A. B.; B. N.

**JAXARTES,** Asiatic river (*Syr Darya,* flowing into the Aral Sea). Though known perhaps to Herodotus by repute, it was discovered by Alexander, who founded Alexandria Eschate (*Khodjend?*) on it. The Greeks thought that it flowed into the Caspian (which perhaps was once true—*see* CASPIAN SEA), and sometimes confused it with the Araxes (*Aras*). Ptolemy gives geographical details of tribes on its banks.

Strabo 11. 507 ff.; Ptol. *Geog.* 6. 12–14. Thomson, *Hist. Anc. Geog.* 85, 127 f.　E. H. W.

**JEROME,** EUSEBIUS HIERONYMUS (*c.* A.D. 348–420), is the most important to the classical student of all the Fathers. Born at Stridon, in Dalmatia, he was taken early to Rome; it was his good fortune to be taught by the greatest teacher in that age, Aelius Donatus (q.v. 1). The best training in rhetoric followed. There he was baptized, but this did not prevent him from indulging in immorality. After his studies he proceeded to Trèves (Trier), and dedicated himself to religion. Later, at Antioch, he laid the foundations of his theological training, and mastered Greek. The ascetic life had a growing attraction for him, and he visited the Chalcis desert (375 to 378), where he learned Hebrew with great difficulty. The theological disputes of Antioch brought him no peace. He decided to return to Rome. He received priest's orders from the Bishop of Antioch. On his way westwards, at Constantinople, about 381, he made the acquaintance of the great Greek theologian Gregory (q.v. 2) of Nazianzus. His stay in Rome lasted from 382 to 385. It was then that Pope Damasus compelled him to revise the old Latin texts of the Gospels, in view of the variety of such texts then in existence. The revision took two directions: first, the Latinity was made more literary; second, the underlying Greek texts were brought into accord with the type of Greek text closely related to that in the Codex Sinaiticus, now in the British Museum. Several ladies of the Roman nobility found in him a valued religious adviser. The death of Damasus (384) made things difficult for Jerome, as he was suspected of aspiring towards the papal chair. He left Rome, Aug. 385, and travelled by Antioch to Jerusalem, then to Egypt to see ascetic life at close quarters, and subsequently with some like-minded friends to Palestine and Bethlehem. There, 389, he founded a religious house and spent his days in study and writing. He died 30 Sept. 420.

Of all Christian Latin writers Jerome most closely approaches the standard of classical purity, when writing his best. He had so absorbed Cicero, Virgil, Horace, and other Latin writers that we hear constant echoes of them in his works. Though he tried hard to 'declassicize' himself, he could not succeed. His pagan master was Cicero; his Christian was Origen. His most important works are his *Chronicle* (partly based on Suetonius) translated from Eusebius and expanded (380–1), a leading authority for dates of ancient historical events; *De Viris Illustribus* (392), short notices of 135 Christian writers; his revision and translation of the Latin Bible (called since 9th c. *Vulgata: see* VULGATE), and his correspondence, full of interest to students of Scripture and to historians of morals. His controversial works are characterized by the foulest abuse. His reputation is due to his immense services to the study of Scripture in the West rather than to saintliness of character.

Migne, *PL* xxii–xxx; newly discovered works, ed. G. Morin, *Anecdota Maredsolana*, vol. iii (3 parts) (Maredsous, 1895–1903); *Chronicle* (J. K. Fotheringham, 1923; R. Helm, 1913). See H. Goelzer, *Étude lexicographique et grammaticale de la latinité de Saint Jérôme* (1884); 'Lives' by G. Grützmacher and F. Cavallera. A. S.

**JERUSALEM** ('Ιεροσόλυμα) was reoccupied by the Jews in 538 B.C. after the Exile, and the second Temple was dedicated in 516, though the walls were not rebuilt until 445. Palestine came into Alexander's Empire after Issus, but his visit to Jerusalem is legendary. Jerusalem became a city, temporarily called Antioch, during a Hellenizing movement in the reign of Antiochus IV, who in 167 dedicated the Temple to Olympian Zeus and built and garrisoned a new citadel, the Acra, dominating it. The Maccabean revolt resulted and the Temple was reconsecrated to Yahweh in 164. From 152 the Hasmonaean (Maccabean) High Priests ruled in Jerusalem, and with the surrender and demolition of the Acra in 142 the country achieved independence. In 63 Pompey, supporting Hyrcanus against Aristobulus, captured Jerusalem and dismantled the walls, which were rebuilt with Caesar's permission in 47. In 37 the city was again stormed by a Roman force under C. Sosius, now supporting the appointment of Herod the Great as king. Herod's buildings in Jerusalem were many: a theatre, hippodrome, and amphitheatre; a palace defended by three massive towers named after Mariamne, Phasael, and Hippicus (the lower courses of Phasael survive in the present 'Tower of David'); the fortress of Antonia, of which the paved courtyard, the cisterns, and some substructures survive under the convent of the Dames de Sion; and the third Temple, of which parts of the platform and surrounding wall, including the 'Wailing Wall', survive. Agrippa I began to fortify the northern suburb Bezetha. Jerusalem, the centre of resistance in the revolt of A.D. 66–70, was destroyed by Titus after a long siege. The rabbinic schools were transferred to Jabneh (Jamnia) and Jerusalem became the camp of Legio X Fretensis. After the revolt of 132–5, during which it was reoccupied by Bar Cochba (q.v.), it was rebuilt by Hadrian as Colonia Aelia Capitolina (without *ius Italicum*), a pagan city which no Jew was allowed to enter. The east gate of Aelia survives, known since the Middle Ages as the 'Ecce Homo Arch'. Though ruling a large territory, Aelia did not flourish until the Christian pilgrim traffic developed.

G. A. Smith, *Jerusalem* (1907–8); H. Vincent and F.-M. Abel, *Jerusalem* (1912–26); M. Join-Lambert, *Jerusalem* (1958); K. M. Kenyon, *Jerusalem* (1968). E. M. S.

**JEWISH GREEK LITERATURE.** By the beginning of the second century B.C. the Greek language and Greek civilization were widely diffused over Judaea, and continued to flourish there up to the fall of Jerusalem. The revolt of the Maccabees against the extreme hellenization attempted by Antiochus Epiphanes (175–164 B.C.) stopped the spread of Greek religion, but not that of Greek culture; and Herod the Great (37–4 B.C.) was an enthusiastic Philhellene. But the Jews of the Diaspora were naturally more influenced by Hellenism than the Jews of Judaea. Jews were numerous in Egypt, particularly in Alexandria, the centre of Hellenistic-Judaic literature. Here the Septuagint (q.v.) translation of the Bible was made in the third and second centuries B.C. for the benefit of the Jews of the Diaspora, to whom Hebrew was largely an unknown tongue, and formed the foundation of Hellenistic-Judaic literature. This literature was largely apologetic and propagandist in aim, being designed to show that the Jews possessed all that was

most valuable in Greek thought, an orientation which inevitably led to a certain hellenization of Jewish ideas.

The literary forms were sometimes Jewish (Hebraic histories, collections of wise sayings, prophetic books, etc.). At other times they were taken over from the Greeks—philosophy (see PHILON 4 and ARISTOBULUS 2), sometimes in dialogue form, imaginary letters, epic, and tragedy, but no comedy. The first writer of Jewish history in Greek was the Jew Demetrius (end of 3rd c. B.C.), who wrote simply and did not hellenize the great figures of Jewish history. Eupolemus (q.v.) was freer in his treatment of the biblical tradition. The greatest of these historians were Josephus and Justus of Tiberias (qq.v.). See also JASON (3) and *FGrH* 722–37.

Three Jewish authors treated themes from Jewish history in the forms of Greek poetry. Philo the Elder (? *c.* 200 B.C.) wrote an epic, Περὶ τὰ Ἱεροσόλυμα, of which 24 lines in an obscure style survive (A. Ludwich, *De P. carmine graeco-iudaico*, 1900); Theodotus (date unknown) a Περὶ Ἰουδαίων, another epic of which 47 lines in a clear and simple style survive (A. Ludwich, *De T. carmine graeco-iudaico*, 1899). Ezechiel (date unknown) wrote a drama Ἐξαγωγή, describing the Exodus from Egypt; 269 trimeters survive, in simple Euripidean Greek (A. Kuiper, *Mnemos.* 1900, 237 ff.). Among *pseudepigrapha* (see PSEUDEPIGRAPHIC LITERATURE) may be mentioned the fictitious letter of Aristeas about the Septuagint translation (Engl. Transl. H. St. J. Thackeray, 1917) and the *pseudo-Phocylidea*, probably of the first century A.D. (M. Rossbroich, *De pseudo-Phocylideis*, 1910). See in general, E. Schürer, *Geschichte des jüdischen Volkes im Zeitalter Jesu Christi* iii⁴ (1909). J. D. D.

**JEWS** (in Greek and Roman times). A. PALESTINE. Palestine was under Persian rule from 538 B.C. until its annexation by Alexander in 332. During the third century it was under the rule of the Ptolemies, for whose administration the Zeno papyri (see APOLLONIUS 3) provide much information. In 200 Palestine passed into Seleucid hands. Early in the reign of Antiochus IV the Hellenizing party in the priestly aristocracy, led by Jason who usurped the high-priesthood from his brother Onias, attempted to convert Jerusalem into a Greek city, and in 167 the king's answer to the resultant disturbances was to install a garrison, to dedicate the Temple to Olympian Zeus, and to attempt to suppress Judaism. This caused a popular revolt, led by Judas Maccabaeus, a priest of the house of Hashmon, and the emergence of the party later known as the Pharisees into prominence. The Temple was reconsecrated to Yahweh in 164, but the Hellenizers remained in power, and the revolt continued as a struggle for political freedom, led after Judas' death in 160 by his brother Jonathan, whom Alexander Balas appointed High Priest in 152 and governor of Judaea in 150 as a reward for military help. After Jonathan had been killed by Tryphon in 143, his brother Simon expelled the Seleucid garrison in 142, and was confirmed as High Priest by a national assembly. For the next eighty years the Jews were independent under the rule of the hereditary Hasmonaean High Priests, except for a few years of subjection to Antiochus VII.

2. Territorial expansion, begun under Jonathan and Simon, proceeded rapidly. Simon's son, John Hyrcanus (134–104), conquered the Samaritans and Idumaeans, forcibly converting the latter to Judaism. John's sons, Aristobulus (104–103), who took the title of king, and Alexander Jannaeus (103–76), annexed and forcibly judaized the southern Ituraeans, Galilee, and Peraea, and conquered many Greek cities in Transjordan and on the coast. But as the dynasty grew in military strength, it became secularized, relying on the aristocratic Sadducaean party and losing popular support. John Hyrcanus

quarrelled with the Pharisees, and Jannaeus faced a serious revolt. His successor, however, his widow Alexandra Salome (76–69), regained the Pharisees' support and reigned peacefully. After her death her two sons quarrelled. The younger, Aristobulus, supported by the discontented military leaders, expelled his brother Hyrcanus, who, incited by an Idumaean noble, Antipater (q.v. 6), fled to Aretas III of Arabia. Aretas was besieging Aristobulus in Jerusalem in 63 when Pompey intervened, stormed the city, and appointed Hyrcanus High Priest and ethnarch of Judaea, Samaria, Galilee, and Peraea, although he deprived him of all the conquered Greek cities. In 57 Gabinius split the ethnarchy into five autonomous communes, leaving Hyrcanus only his spiritual powers. Hyrcanus relied heavily on his minister Antipater, who in 48 gave important aid to Caesar at Alexandria; in recompense Hyrcanus was reinstated as ethnarch, and granted Joppa. When Cassius (q.v. 6) exacted money from Judaea, Antipater and his sons, Phasael and Herod (q.v. 1), co-operated. Antipater was murdered in 43, and after Philippi Phasael and Herod secured from Antony positions as tetrarchs under Hyrcanus, who continued as ethnarch. In 40 Antigonus, son of Aristobulus, was installed in Jerusalem by the Parthians, who had invaded Syria. Hyrcanus was carried off to Babylonia, Phasael committed suicide, but Herod escaped to Rome, whence he returned as client king. For his reign and those of his successors see HEROD (1) THE GREAT, HEROD (2) ANTIPAS, ARCHELAUS (4), *and* PHILIP (4).

**3.** In A.D. 6 Judaea, Samaria, and Idumaea were annexed as the Roman province of Judaea and administered by procurators. A census in that year aroused opposition and led to the foundation of a nationalist party (perhaps to be identified with the Zealots), which aimed at recovering political independence. Despite Rome's official protection of Jewish religious liberty there was much unrest and discontent, especially under Pontius Pilate (26–36). In 39–40 Gaius almost provoked a rebellion by attempting to have his statue placed in the Temple, and in 41 Claudius thought it wise to put the province under Agrippa I (q.v.). On Agrippa's death in 44 his whole kingdom was annexed. Under the subsequent series of procurators, who were apparently even more tactless and inefficient than their predecessors, discontent increased, now aggravated by famines and manifesting itself in pseudo-messianic risings and in brigandage which eventually developed into guerrilla warfare led by the terrorist organization of the *sicarii*. In 66 this culminated in an open rebellion, despite the efforts of the priestly aristocracy and Agrippa II at pacification. It was crushed by Vespasian and Titus, who in 70 destroyed Jerusalem and the Temple. The two-drachma tax paid by all adult Jewish men to the Temple funds was diverted to Jupiter Capitolinus and paid into the new *fiscus Iudaicus*, and its incidence was widened to cover women and children.

**4.** From 70 the province was governed by legates and Legio X Fretensis was stationed in Jerusalem. The synagogues now replaced the Temple as the focus of Jewish religion, the rabbis replaced the priests as leaders, and Jabneh (Jamnia) became the centre of rabbinic learning and the seat of the Sanhedrin. The revolt of the Diaspora in 115–18 caused disturbances in Palestine, which were quelled by Lusius Quietus. The second great Palestinian revolt of 132–5, led by Bar Cochba (q.v.), was perhaps the culmination of years of unrest. Its immediate causes were Hadrian's prohibition of circumcision and his proposal to found a pagan city on the site of Jerusalem. Apart from Jewish legends, little is known of the course of the revolt or of its suppression by Julius Severus (*see* BAR COCHBA). The devastation and loss of life were very heavy. From 135 the name of the province was Syria

Palaestina, Legio VI Ferrata was stationed in Galilee, and Jerusalem was rebuilt as the pagan city of Colonia Aelia Capitolina, from which the Jews were excluded. But unrest continued. Although Antoninus Pius exempted the Jews from Hadrian's ban on circumcision, which was retained after the suppression of Bar Cochba's revolt, a further revolt, of which no details survive, occurred during his reign. The Jews are said to have supported Avidius Cassius. And a revolt under Septimius Severus is recorded, perhaps associated with the rising of Pescennius Niger. Economic conditions were poor in the second century as a result of repeated wars, but there seems to have been some improvement early in the third, especially in Galilee, to which the centre of learning had shifted, and this is perhaps to be connected with Septimius' visit in 199. There is little evidence for friction between the Jews and the Romans during the third century, but the province felt the effects of the anarchy.

Although Greek was widely known in Palestine, the Jews there retained their own language through centuries of Greek and Roman domination, and their post-biblical literature was written in Aramaic.

MAIN ANCIENT SOURCES. 1 and 2 Maccabees; Joseph. *BJ*; *AJ*, bks. 12–20.

MODERN ACCOUNTS. S. Dubnow, *Weltgeschichte des jüdischen Volkes* ii (1925) and iii (1926); F.-M. Abel, *Histoire de la Palestine depuis la conquête d'Alexandre jusqu'à l'invasion arabe* (1952); V. A. Tcherikover, *Hellenistic Civilization and the Jews* (1959) pt. i.; M. Avi-Yonah, *Geschichte der Juden im Zeitalter des Talmud* (1962); S. W. Baron, *A Social and Religious History of the Jews* i and ii (1952).

A. H. M. J.; E. M. S.

**B. THE DIASPORA.** The Dispersion of the Jews began in 586 B.C., when Nebuchadnezzar took the inhabitants of Jerusalem into captivity. Many of them did not return when permitted by Cyrus in 538 but remained voluntarily in Babylonia, where flourishing communities existed for centuries and from the third century A.D. became the chief centres of rabbinical learning. During the Hellenistic period many Jews migrated from Palestine and Babylonia to the eastern Mediterranean lands, where Syria and Egypt in particular attracted large settlements; the Alexandrian community became one of the most important, comprising about a third of the city's population by the first century A.D. This movement was fostered by some kings, who found the Jews industrious subjects and good soldiers and encouraged settlement by granting privileges. Expansion to Italy and the West began later, but the community in Rome was established by the mid second century B.C. The frequent wars and disturbances in Palestine gave additional impetus to emigration, and Jews taken prisoner and sold into slavery swelled the numbers of the Diaspora.

The Jews of the Diaspora were not absorbed into the races among which they lived, but preserved their national identity and religious beliefs and practices, with the Temple in Jerusalem, to which, until A.D. 70, they paid their annual tax, as their spiritual focus. But their exclusiveness and refusal to be assimilated and their attitude towards paganism made them unpopular, and anti-Semitic literature appeared from the third century B.C. Julius Caesar and Augustus sponsored legislation to protect Jewish religious liberty throughout the Empire: the synagogues, which were classified as *collegia*, were exempted from the general ban on such associations; the rights to hold meetings and to collect and transmit the Temple-tax were granted; Sabbath-observance was safeguarded; and gentile attacks on the synagogues were punishable as sacrilege. Judaism was thus established as a *religio licita*, and the Jews' religious privileges and civic rights were vindicated by Rome when necessary against gentile infringements. The legal status thus granted to Judaism was not affected by the revolt of 66–70, although the Diaspora suffered with Palestine the indignity of having to pay the erstwhile Temple-tax to Jupiter; and Hadrian's prohibition of circumcision is the only known repressive action of Rome against Jewish religion. But while Rome had no objection to the practice of Judaism by Jews, she disapproved of proselytism, whether full conversion involving circumcision, or the adoption of certain Jewish tenets only for which there was a fashion from the late Republic, and made spasmodic attempts to check it. Three expulsions of the Jews from Rome are recorded—in 139 B.C., in A.D. 19, and during Claudius' principate. The offence on each occasion seems to have been proselytizing activities, although disorder caused by the arrival of Christianity may have helped to provoke the last. Domitian attacked converts to Judaism and Christianity. Antoninus Pius' continuance of Hadrian's ban on circumcision in the case of gentiles was probably an attack on proselytism. Septimius Severus explicitly forbade *Iudaeos fieri*.

The Diaspora communities whose history is best known are those in Egypt and Alexandria, for which papyri provide information on social and economic conditions to supplement the literary evidence. In Alexandria, as at Berenice in Cyrenaica and most probably in other Greek cities also, the Jews formed a πολίτευμα, a civic organization independent of the host city. Friction developed after the Romans annexed Egypt between the Greeks, who resented their domination, and the Jews, who benefited from coming under their protection, and this was apparently aggravated by the aspiration of some Jews to admission to the Greek citizen body. It was here that anti-Semitism took its most active form. The tension flared up in A.D. 38 into a violent anti-Jewish riot, in which synagogues were desecrated or destroyed, many Jews were massacred, and a ghetto was temporarily instituted. Claudius re-established the Jews' civic position and rights but refused them Greek citizenship. Feelings continued to run high for nearly a century and to cause recurrences of trouble, including a sanguinary clash in 66—a time when the Palestinian revolt inspired anti-Semitic outbursts in Antioch, Damascus, and other Syrian cities. Finally, when the Jews in Cyrenaica attacked both Greeks and Romans there in 115, the rising rapidly spread to Alexandria, most of Egypt, and Cyprus, and developed from a racial quarrel into a serious rebellion against Rome. It was particularly dangerous because it coincided with, and was no doubt encouraged by, the revolt of Trajan's new provinces in 116, in which the Babylonian Diaspora played a considerable part. Marcius Turbo was put in charge of the suppression, which was probably not completed until 118. The Jews were then excluded from Cyprus, and in Egypt and Cyrenaica they never recovered in numbers or prosperity.

From an early date Greek was the language of the Diaspora in the eastern Mediterranean. During the second century B.C. the Septuagint (q.v.) translation was made for the benefit of the Egyptian Jews who could no longer read their Scriptures in Hebrew. Even in Italy Greek predominates over Latin in Jewish inscriptions, especially in epitaphs from the six Jewish catacombs in Rome; only a small minority are in Hebrew or Aramaic.

J.-B. Frey, *Corpus Inscriptionum Judaicarum* i (1936), ii (1952); V. A. Tcherikover and A. Fuks, *Corpus Papyrorum Judaicarum*, 3 vols. (1957-64). J. Juster, *Les Juifs dans l'Empire romain* (1914); V. A. Tcherikover, op. cit., pt. ii; H. J. Leon, *The Jews of Ancient Rome* (1960). E. M. S.

**JORDANES (JORDANIS)**, an historian who lived c. A.D. 550. According to his own declaration he had been a notary to the Gothic chief Gunthigis Baza prior to an unspecified 'conversion' (to Catholicism from Arianism or to monastic life). He was probably a Goth himself, born somewhere on the lower Danube. About A.D. 551, when Cassiodorus was still alive, he summarized the latter's *Gothic Histories* in his *Getica*. He used a MS. which came from the household of Cassiodorus himself. Immediately afterwards he concluded the composition of a summary of Roman history (known as *Romana*) which seems to be mainly derived from the lost history of Aurelius Memmius Symmachus. It has been suggested that Jordanes is to be identified with his namesake, bishop of Croton in Italy. It is also disputed whether Jordanes wrote his books in Italy or in Constantinople and whether the final chapters of the *Getica* (which were written in the hope of a permanent reconciliation between the Gothic royal family and the Roman imperial family) were inspired by Cassiodorus or independently added by Jordanes. *See* CASSIODORUS.

Crit. ed. by Th. Mommsen, in *MGH*. Engl. transl. of the *Getica* with commentary by Chr. Mierow (1915). Important study and commentary (in Russian) of the *Getica* by E. C. Skržinskoj (1960). W. Ensslin, *Sitz. Bayer. Ak.* 1948, n. 3; Wattenbach–Levison, *Deutschlands Geschichtsquellen* i, 1952, 75 ff.; A. Momigliano, *Proc. Brit. Acad.* 1955, 207 ff.; D. R. Bradley, *Riv. Cultura Class. Med.* 1963, 366 ff. A. M.

**JOSEPHUS**, FLAVIUS (b. A.D. 37/8), was a Jewish priest of aristocratic descent and a Pharisee. Though a zealous defender of Jewish religion and culture, politically he was pro-Roman and without sympathy for extreme Jewish nationalism. A visit to Rome (c. 64) impressed on him the futility of resistance, and when the Sanhedrin put him in command of Galilee early in the Jewish revolt, he tried unsuccessfully to curb the extremists. In 67 he was besieged in Jotapata and captured, but saved his life by prophesying that Vespasian would become emperor. When this prediction came true, he was released but remained with Titus until the fall of Jerusalem. He then settled in Rome, where he received Roman citizenship and a pension. His first work was a history of the war written in Aramaic for the Mesopotamian Jews, of which a Greek translation, the extant *Bellum Judaicum* in seven books, appeared between 75 and 79. The first one and a half books are introductory, sketching Jewish history from the Maccabean revolt to A.D. 66. The narrative of the war is based largely on Josephus' own notes and memories, probably supplemented by the *Commentarii* of Vespasian and Titus. His next work, the *Antiquitates Judaicae* in twenty books (published in 93/4), is a history of the Jews from the Creation to immediately before the outbreak of the war, giving a fuller account of the period from the Maccabees to A.D. 66 than that in the *BJ* and showing a more hostile attitude to Herod the Great. The principal sources were the Old Testament for the early history, and the writings of Nicolaus (q.v.) of Damascus for the period 175 B.C. to the death of Herod, together with 1 Maccabees in books 12-13. Josephus' last works were his *Vita*—not a full autobiography but an answer to the allegations of Justus (q.v.) of Tiberias about his conduct in Galilee—and his apologia for Judaism in two books (*Contra Apionem*), in which he attacks the ignorant or malicious mis-statements of anti-Semitic writers from the third century B.C. to Apion (q.v.).

TEXTS. B. Niese (1887-9, repr. 1955); S. A. Naber (1888-96). TEXT AND TRANSLATION (Loeb). H. St. J. Thackeray, R. Marcus, A. Wikgren, and L. H. Feldman (1926-65). R. Laqueur, *Der jüdische Historiker Fl. J.* (1920); H. St. J. Thackeray, *J. the Man and the Historian* (1929); F. J. Foakes Jackson, *J. and the Jews* (1930); R. J. H. Shutt, *Studies in J.* (1961); H. Schreckenberg, *Bibliog. zu Fl. J.* (1968); K. H. Rengstorf, *Concordance to Fl. J.* (forthcoming). A. H. M. J.; E. M. S.

**JOVIAN**, FLAVIUS, Roman Emperor in A.D. 363-4, was born c. 331 in Singidunum (*Belgrade*). He took part in the Persian campaign of Julianus (q.v. 1), and on the death of the latter was elevated by the army. He immediately made an unpopular peace with the Persians, surrendering to them all the territory which Diocletian had won in the East along with the cities of Nisibis and Singara. Before reaching Constantinople he died at Dadastana (364). He was an earnest Catholic.   E. A. T.

**JUBA** (1), son of Hiempsal II of Numidia, was notorious for cruelty and arrogance. Offended by Caesar in his youth and, after his accession, by Curio (q.v. 2), he joined Pompey in the Civil War, and defeated and killed Curio (49 B.C.). Ceasing to behave as a client king, he began to aim at the annexation of Roman Africa. He assisted Cato (q.v. 5) and Metellus (q.v. 11) Scipio, but was distracted by an attack by Sittius (q.v.) and Bocchus II. Promised Africa by Scipio (it was said), he rejoined him, escaped after Thapsus (46) and, hated and rebuffed on all sides, died in a suicide pact with Petreius (q.v.).
   E. B.

**JUBA** (2) **II,** king of Mauretania and son of Juba (1) of Numidia, was led in Caesar's triumph in 46 B.C. when still an infant, and brought up in Italy; he received the Roman citizenship, apparently from Octavian, and accompanied him on campaigns. Perhaps first reinstated in Numidia (q.v.), in 25 he received from Augustus the kingdom of Mauretania (q.v.), to which parts of Gaetulia were added in compensation for the annexation of Numidia. About A.D. 6 the Gaetuli rebelled and were put down with the help of a Roman proconsul, Cossus Lentulus (*cos.* 1 B.C.); and in 17 Juba seems to have taken part in the defeat of Tacfarinas (q.v.). He married first (by 20 B.C.) Cleopatra Selene, the daughter of Antony and Cleopatra (q.v. VII), and secondly Glaphyra (q.v. 2). He died *c.* A.D. 23 and was succeeded by Ptolemy, his son by Cleopatra.

Juba was above all a man of learning, who sought to introduce Greek and Roman culture into his kingdom. His capital at Iol, refounded as Caesarea (q.v. 3), and in the west Volubilis (q.v.), where he may have had a second residence, became fine cities. His artistic collections were remarkable. He developed the production of the 'Gaetulian' purple, perhaps prepared by his invention from orchil (*see* DYEING, PURPLE). He wrote many books (now lost) in Greek: works on Libya, Arabia, and Assyria; a history of Rome; researches into language, drama, and painting; a treatise on the plant euphorbia, which he discovered and named after his doctor Euphorbus, brother of Antonius (q.v. 10) Musa; and Ὁμοιότητες, a comparative study of antiquities, mainly Greek and Roman. Pliny the Elder and Plutarch were among the authors who used his writings.

S. Gsell, *Hist. anc. de l'Afrique du Nord* viii (1928), 206 ff.; P. Romanelli, *Storia delle prov. rom. dell'Africa* (1959), 156 ff. Gaetulian territory: J. Desanges, *Rev. Ét. Lat.* 1964, 33 ff. Purple: J. Desjacques and P. Koeberié, *Hespéris* 1955, 193 ff.; J. Gattefossé, *Hespéris* 1957, 329 ff. Literary works: Christ–Schmid– Stählin ii. 401 ff.; Jacoby, *FGrH* 275. Iconography: G. M. A. Richter, *Portraits of the Greeks* (1965), 280 f.   A. M.; T. J. C.

**JUBA** (3), of Mauretania (2nd c. A.D.), wrote a treatise (now lost) on metric which was based on the Greek Heliodorus (q.v. 2) and was used by later Latin grammarians.

Schanz–Hosius, § 606.   J. F. M.

**JUGURTHA,** grandson of Masinissa (q.v., but illegitimate), served at Numantia under Scipio (q.v. 11) Aemilianus, hereditary patron of the Numidian royal house, and, on his recommendation, was adopted by King Micipsa and given pre-eminent rank in the succession. When his two brothers and joint heirs challenged this after Micipsa's death (118 B.C.), Jugurtha had one of them murdered and attacked the other (Adherbal), who fled to Rome and appealed for aid. A mission under Opimius (q.v.) divided Numidia, giving the western and more primitive part to Jugurtha. In 112 he again attacked

Adherbal, besieged him in Cirta and, despite two Roman embassies (one under Scaurus, q.v. 1), captured the city and killed him. Some Italian businessmen died in the sack of Cirta (which they had helped to defend), and this aroused anger in Rome and led to agitation for war by Memmius (q.v. 1). In 112 the consul Bestia (q.v.) invaded Numidia, but soon gave Jugurtha a tolerable peace—perhaps through the efforts of the king's Roman friends, but also in order to avoid a long colonial war. There was widespread discontent at this; Jugurtha was summoned to Rome under safe-conduct, but a tribune (C. Baebius) vetoed his interrogation and he left hurriedly after having a pretender murdered (*see* BOMILCAR).

In Numidia, war started in earnest, but was waged incompetently by the consul Postumius (q.v. 4) Albinus and his brother, who had to capitulate. After an outcry in Rome, which led to the commission of Mamilius (q.v. 3), the consul (of 109) Metellus (q.v. 6), in two campaigns, achieved considerable success (including a major victory at the Muthul), but got little nearer finishing the war. His legate Marius (q.v. 1), profiting by this, gained the consulship 107, promising a quick end to the war. Despite army reforms, including the admission of *proletarii* (q.v.), he failed to provide this and thus caused a short reaction in favour of the Optimates (*see* CAEPIO 1, METELLUS 6). But the war was ended when Sulla persuaded Bocchus (q.v.) to surrender Jugurtha to Marius. He was executed after Marius' triumph (1 Jan. 104).

The Jugurthine War, as Sallust saw, marks an important stage in the decline of the oligarchy, showing its political vulnerability and, through Marius and his army reform, preparing the way for the use of the army in politics.

Sallust's *Jugurthine War* is the chief source; see R. Syme, *Sallust* (1964), chs. 10 and 11 (with extensive bibliography). For the chronology and strategy of the war see also M. Holroyd, *JRS* 1928, 1 ff.
   E. B.

**JULIA** (1, *PW* 547), daughter of Caesar and Cornelia, born *c.* 83 B.C., was betrothed to Q. Servilius Caepio, but married in Apr. 59 to Pompey, whom her affection bound more strongly to her father. In 55 the sight of Pompey returning from the *comitia* bespattered with blood caused a miscarriage; and next year she died in childbirth, the child dying a few days later. On the people's insistence, she was buried in the Campus Martius, and in 46 Caesar held magnificent shows over her tomb.

On the possibility that Caepio was M. Brutus (q.v. 5), the tyrannicide, see F. Münzer, *PW* xiii. 497 f.   G. E. F. C.

**JULIA** (2, *PW* 550), only daughter of Augustus and Scribonia (q.v.), was born in 39 B.C. and betrothed in 37 to M. Antonius (q.v. 7) 'Antyllus' and later, according to Antony, to Cotiso, king of the Getae (q.v.). She was brought up strictly by her father and stepmother Livia (q.v.). In 25 she married her cousin M. Marcellus (q.v. 7) and in 21 Agrippa (q.v. 3), to whom she bore C. and L. Caesar (6 and 7), Julia (3), Agrippina (2), and Agrippa (4) Postumus. Her third marriage, to Tiberius (in 11), is said to have been happy at first, but estrangement followed, and her licentious conduct may have contributed to Tiberius' decision to retire from Rome in 6. In 2 B.C. Augustus at last learned of her adulteries (e.g. with Iullus Antonius, q.v. 8) and banished her to Pandateria; in A.D. 4 she was allowed to move to Rhegium. Scribonia voluntarily shared her exile. Augustus forbade her burial in his mausoleum, and Tiberius kept her closely confined and stopped her allowance, so that she died of malnutrition before the end of A.D. 14. Macrobius (*Sat.* 2. 5) speaks of her gentle disposition and learning, and gives anecdotes attesting her wit.

Syme, *Rom. Rev.*, see index; E. F. Leon, *TAPA* 1951, 168 ff.; P. Sattler, *Studien aus dem Gebiet der alten Geschichte* (1962), 1 ff. J. Carcopino, *Passion et politique chez les Césars* (1958), 83 ff.; R. A. Bauman, *The Crimen Maiestatis* (1967), 198 ff.

ICONOGRAPHY. C. Hanson and F. P. Johnson, *AJArch.* 1946, 389 ff.; H. Rolland, J. Carcopino, *Bull. Soc. Nat. Ant. France* 1950/1, 221 ff.
G. W. R.; T. J. C.

**JULIA** (3, *PW* 511), daughter of Agrippa and Julia (2), was born *c.* 19 B.C. and married (*c.* 4 B.C.) L. Aemilius Paullus (q.v. 5). After her husband's fall Augustus relegated, then recalled, and finally (A.D. 8) banished her permanently for adultery to the island of Trimerus off the Apulian coast, where she died in 28.

Syme, *Rom. Rev.*, see index.
T. J. C.

**JULIA** (4, *PW* 575), sometimes called Livilla, youngest daughter of Germanicus and Agrippina (2), born in A.D. 18. In 33 she married M. Vinicius (grandson of Vinicius (1), and consul in 30 and 45). After the accession of her brother Gaius she received special honours like her sisters Agrippina (3) and Drusilla (qq.v.), but in 39 was relegated to the Pontian islands for adultery with her brother-in-law, M. Lepidus. Claudius restored her, but Messallina (q.v. 1) presently accused her of adultery with Seneca (q.v. 2) and she was again banished and shortly killed (42?).

F. Giancotti, *Rend. Linc.* 1953, 52 ff.
T. J. C.

**JULIA** (5), FLAVIA (*PW* 552), daughter of Titus (q.v.) by his second wife, was born *c.* A.D. 65 just before her parents' divorce. She married her cousin Flavius Sabinus (q.v. 4), and after his execution (*c.* 84) lived with her uncle Domitian (q.v.) as his mistress. She died in 91, and was deified.
G. E. F. C.

**JULIA** (6, *PW* 566) **DOMNA**, sister of Julia (7) Maesa, a Syrian by birth, was the second wife of the Emperor Septimius Severus. According to some accounts she collected about her a large coterie of men of learning (e.g. Galen and Philostratus), and was not undeservedly called ἡ φιλόσοφος ᾿Ιουλία. Intelligent and ambitious, she was eclipsed from *c.* 200 to 205 by Severus' praetorian prefect Plautianus but regained influence on his fall. After Septimius' death she tried unsuccessfully to reconcile her sons Caracalla and Geta. She died or committed suicide at Antioch in 217 on hearing of the death of Caracalla.

J. Réville, *La Religion à Rome sous les Sévères* (1885); *B.M. Coins, Rom. Emp.* v. cxxxvi, cxcv f.; G. W. Bowersock, *The Sophists in the Roman Empire* (1969), ch. 8. *See also* SEVERUS (1).
H. M. D. P.; B. H. W.

**JULIA** (7, *PW* 579) **MAESA**, daughter of Julius Bassianus of Emesa and sister of Julia (6) Domna, was the wife of Julius Avitus, a Syrian of consular rank, by whom she had two daughters, Julia (8) Soaemias and Julia (9) Mamaea. After Caracalla's death she returned from Rome to Emesa. She assisted in the proclamation of Elagabalus and accompanied him to Rome, becoming Augusta and 'mater castrorum et senatus'. Later she induced Elagabalus to adopt his cousin Alexianus. She died in 226.

COINS. Mattingly–Sydenham, *RIC* iv. 2. 62, 101.
A. M.; B. H. W.

**JULIA** (8, *PW* 596) **SOAEMIAS BASSIANA**, daughter of Julia (7) Maesa, and wife of Sex. Varius Marcellus, a knight of Apamaea in Syria. In A.D. 218 she and her mother procured the elevation of her son Elagabalus and the death of Macrinus. Lacking her mother's intelligence she, with Elagabalus, flouted opinion in Rome and the two were killed by the praetorians in 222.
B. H. W.

**JULIA** (9, *PW* 558) **AVITA MAMAEA**, younger daughter of Julia (7) Maesa, was married to Gessius Marcianus, a knight of Arca Caesarea in Syria. With her mother she procured the removal of Elagabalus and the elevation of her son Alexianus, subsequently known as Severus Alexander, in A.D. 222. From the death of Maesa

(226) she dominated Alexander, who was only 13 on his accession. Although her influence was prudently exercised, and she cultivated good relations with the Senate, this unwarlike regime ultimately alienated the army and led to the murder of herself and her son (235; *see* SEVERUS (2) ALEXANDER).

R. A. G. Carson, *RIC* vi. 39 ff.
B. H. W.

**JULIANUS** (1, *PW* 26), FLAVIUS CLAUDIUS ('Julian the Apostate'), born in A.D. 332, was the son of Julius Constantius, half-brother of Constantine, and Basilina. In 337 his father was lynched in a mutiny promoted by Constantius II. Julian was brought up with his half-brother Gallus in a remote fortress in Cappadocia. The brothers were given a pious Christian education and were even ordained as readers, but Julian acquired from his tutor, the eunuch Mardonius, a passion for the classics and for the old gods. In 351 he was allowed to complete his education at Ephesus where he fell under the influence of the celebrated pagan philosopher Maximus, and later at Athens. From here he was summoned to the West by Constantius II, who on 6 Nov. 355 proclaimed him Caesar, placing him in charge of Gaul and Britain. Julian quickly made himself the idol of his troops by sharing their hardships, and displayed his powers as a general by defeating the Alamanni at Argentoratum. In a series of campaigns (356–9) he reduced the Franks and Alamanni to obedience and restored the Rhine frontier. Meanwhile during the winters he reformed the fiscal administration, despite the opposition of the praetorian prefect, Florentius, reducing the tax from 25 to 7 *solidi* per *caput*.

Constantius II (q.v.), becoming jealous and fearful of Julian's success, demanded that he should send some picked troops to the East, but when Julian gave the order the troops mutinied and proclaimed him Augustus (Feb. 360). Julian accepted the title and paid the customary donative, but failed to reach a compromise with Constantius. He therefore marched East (361), but before he reached Constantinople Constantius died.

Julian had openly professed his paganism directly he became Augustus. He now proclaimed general toleration for all religions, reinstituted the pagan cult, restored the lands to the temples, and rebuilt such as had been demolished. He also appointed pagan high priests of provinces and cities to supervise and stimulate pagan worship and granted them subsidies to distribute in charity. The churches lost their imperial subsidy and the clergy their immunities. There was no persecution, but pagans were favoured and promoted, and the troops were glutted with sacrificial meat and encouraged to offer incense on pay days. In religious disorders Julian was sharper in punishing Christians than pagans. His most criticized anti-Christian measure was to forbid Christian professors to teach the classics.

Julian also carried through a number of vigorous reforms and economies, drastically reducing the overgrown palace staff and palatine offices, such as the notaries, the *agentes in rebus*, and the *protectores*. He reduced the burden on the post by instituting a strict control of postal warrants. He restored their lands and revenues to the cities and brought the city councils up to strength.

After five months at Constantinople Julian moved to Antioch to prepare his Persian campaign. The temple of Daphne was burnt down during his stay, a famine occurred in which the city council sabotaged his relief measures, and the Christian populace insulted him. He replied by publishing the *Misopogon*, a satirical defence of his actions.

On 5 Mar. 363 he marched eastwards. He defeated the Persian army outside Ctesiphon, but did not attack the city. His march to meet a reserve force, which he had sent via Armenia to Assyria, was continually harassed by the Persians, and in one of the battles he was mortally wounded.

Julian's religious beliefs were the Neoplatonist monotheism expounded by his friend Sallustius. He was superstitious, believing in oracles and miracles and devoutly practising the ancient rituals. He was by temperament and in principle highly ascetic. He was an immensely hardworking and conscientious emperor.

Julian's surviving works include eight orations, the *Misopogon*, the *Convivium* or *Caesares*, a comic account of Constantine's reception on Olympus, and about eighty letters, including the Letter to the Athenians, which recounts his life up to the death of Constantius.

WORKS. G. F. Hertlein (Teubner, 1879), and W. C. Wright (Loeb, 1913–23). J. Bidez, *La Vie de l'empereur Julien* (1930); W. E. Kaegi, 'Research on Julian, 1945–1964', *Cl. Weekly* 1965, 229 ff. A. H. M. J.

**JULIANUS** (2) **SALVIUS** (*PW* 14) (L. OCTAVIUS CORNELIUS P. SALVIUS JULIANUS AEMILIANUS) (*c.* A.D. 100–*c.* 169), a Roman jurist, perhaps born at the village of Pupput near Hadrumetum, disciple of Javolenus (q.v.), and the last recorded head of the Sabinian School; *see* SABINUS (2). Even as a young man he enjoyed a high authority among his contemporaries, as is shown by the fact that before he was 30 years old he was entrusted by Hadrian with the revision and rearrangement of the praetorian edict (*see* EDICTUM). This work procured him a wide reputation, and Justinian praised him for it in the highest terms. He combined great distinction as a jurist with an outstanding career in public life, the main stages of which are recorded in an inscription (*ILS* 8973) discovered at Pupput (see above). He was: *decemvir stlitibus iudicandis* (*see* DECEMVIRI), *quaestor* (q.v.) of Hadrian (and given double the usual salary because of his learning), one of the *tribuni plebis* (q.v.), *praetor* (q.v.), *praefectus* both of the *aerarium Saturni* and of the *aerarium militare* (*see* AERARIUM), consul in 148, *pontifex* (q.v.), *curator* (q.v.) *aedium sacrarum*, governor of Lower Germany under Antoninus Pius, of Nearer Spain under Marcus Aurelius and Verus, and of Africa (168/9); and he was a member of the *consilium principis* (q.v.) under Hadrian and Antoninus Pius. His principal work was his *Digesta* (in ninety books), a systematic, richly casuistic treatise on civil and praetorian law, partly following, as was usual in works of this kind, the arrangement of the *edictum* (q.v.) *perpetuum*. Justinian's *Digesta* (q.v.) include a large number of excerpts from this and other works, and a still larger number of citations of him by later classical jurists. Many of his *responsa* were published by his pupil Caecilius Africanus (q.v. 2).

Julian is perhaps the most remarkable representative of Roman jurisprudence. It may justifiably be claimed that Roman legal science reached in him the height of its development. The Severan jurists, Ulpianus (q.v. 1), Papinianus (q.v.), and Paulus (q.v. 1), surpassed him in the volume and encyclopedic character of their writings, but he had the greater originality and creative power, and exercised a more formative influence on the law.

H. Buhl, *Salvius Julianus* (1888); L. Boulard, *Salv. Julianus* (1902); A. Guarino, *Salv. Julianus* (1946): repr. *Labeo* 1964; W. Kunkel, *Iura* 1950; F. Serrao, *Atti III cong. int. epigrafia* (1959); A. Guarino, *Labeo* 1959. *And see* bibliography s.v. JURISPRUDENCE. A. B.; B. N.

**JULIUS** (1, *PW* 363) **MODESTUS**, freedman of Julius Hyginus (Augustus' *libertus*), followed his patron's broad treatment of grammar (Suet. *Gram.* 20).

**JULIUS** (2, *PW* 167) **CANUS** or **KANUS**, a philosopher whose uncompromising reproaches offended Caligula and led to his execution (Sen. *Dial.* 9. 14. 4–9).

**JULIUS** (3, *PW* 184) **CEREALIS**, epic and pastoral poet, friendly with Martial (11. 52. 1 and 16–18).

**JULIUS** (4, *PW* 254) **GABINIANUS**, SEXTUS, mentioned in Suetonius' list of rhetors, was an eminent teacher in Gaul in the Flavian age (Hieron. *Ab. Abr.* 2092 = A.D. 76; Tac. *Dial.* 26. 11).

**JULIUS** (5, *PW* 511–2) **TIRO** (full name *CIL* ii. 3661 *C. Iulius C. f. Gal. Tiro Gaetulicus*), given in Suetonius' list of rhetors next after Quintilian's name (Reifferscheid wrongly emended to *M. Tullius Tiro*). Pliny mentions a case about his will (*Ep.* 6. 31. 7).

**JULIUS** (6, *PW* 434) **ROMANUS** (3rd c. A.D.) wrote an extensive grammatical work entitled Ἀφορμαί, of which considerable fragments are preserved by Charisius (q.v.).

Schanz–Hosius, § 603. J. F. M.

**JULIUS** (7, *PW* 520) **VALERIUS ALEXANDER POLEMIUS** (3rd–4th c. A.D.) composed a Latin version of a Greek novel on Alexander the Great by 'Aisopos' or 'pseudo-Kallisthenes'. His style is artificial and checkered.

Edited by B. Kübler (1888). See C. Fassbender, *De Iulii Val. sermone quaest. sel.* (1909).

**JULIUS** (8, *PW* 532) **VICTOR**, GAIUS (4th c. A.D.), author of an *ars rhetorica* largely and closely based on Quintilian.

Halm, *Rhet. lat. min.* 373.

**JUNIUS** (1, *PW* 68) **CONGUS**, a friend regarded by Lucilius as a reader to whom he would have his satires appeal (595 f. Marx). It has been maintained that a satire in book 26 was addressed to him. Some identify him with Marcus Junius Gracchanus, author of a work *de potestatibus*. J. W. D. ; G. B. A. F.

**JUNIUS** (2, *PW* 108) **NIPSUS**, MARCUS (perhaps 2nd c. A.D.), *gromaticus*; author of treatises on mensuration, replacement of boundaries, and surveying of rivers.

Ed. K. Lachmann, *Die Schriften der röm. Feldmesser* i (1848), 285 ff.

**JUNIUS** (3, *PW* 113) **OTHO**, rhetor, praetor A.D. 22; formerly an elementary schoolmaster, he owed his advancement to Sejanus (Tac. *Ann.* 3. 66). He was master of innuendo, and wrote four books of *colores*, 'complexions to be put on cases' (Sen. *Controv.* 2. 1. 33).

**JUNO**, an old and very important Italian goddess, in functions resembling Hera (q.v.), with whom she was anciently identified. There is no doubt that she was closely connected with the life, especially the sexual life, of women (hence indirectly with the moon, and therefore theorists ancient and modern have made her a moongoddess; see Roscher in his *Lexikon* ii. 578 ff., cf. *Juno und Hera* (1875), i ff.). This is shown among other things by the fact that she either assimilates the minor deities Lucina, who makes the child see the light of day, Opigena, who brings help to women in childbirth, Cinxia, *numen* of the bride's girdle, Iterduca, who brings her to her new home, and several other such vague figures, or else these are titles of hers which tended to assume independent existence as goddesses attendant on women (references in Roscher, *Lex.* 579 ff.). But she developed wider functions and became a great goddess of the State (probably for the same reason as Hera), notably at Lanuvium, where she was worshipped as Sospita or Sispes and shown armed and wearing a goatskin cloak, and, under the Etruscan kings, at Rome also, where as Juno Regina she forms one of the Capitoline triad with Jupiter and Minerva (qq.v.); see Wissowa, *RK* 187 ff., and Latte, *RR* 166 ff. Concerning her origin there is much doubt. Wissowa (ibid. 181) would derive her name from the root of *iuvenis, iunix*, etc., with the meaning 'young woman', 'bride', and her functions from the individual *iuno* who is to a woman what the *genius* (q.v.) is to a man ('iuno mea', Petron. *Sat.* 25. 4; cf. Lygdamus 6. 48; Sen. *Ep.* 110. 1). Others, notably J. Whatmough (as in *Foundations of Rom. Italy* (1937), 159 f.), suppose the individual *iuno* secondary and late and support a derivation of the name from the same root as that of *Iuppiter*, despite the difficulty that no such forms as *\*Diuno, \*(D)iouno* ever occur, as would be expected. The views are not wholly exclusive of each other; the *numen* which watches over women and their functions might from the beginning have been thought of now as appearing in each individual woman, now as forming a great reservoir of power on which all women drew, and these have developed respectively into the individual *iunones* and the great goddess.

Her most interesting festival is the Nonae Caprotinae, *see* CAPROTINA. It was commonly alleged in antiquity that she was connected with the Lupercalia (see Wissowa, op. cit. 185, but *contra*, Rose in *Mnemos.* 1932, 389 f.). The Kalends of every month were sacred to her (Macrob. *Sat.* 1. 15. 18), and in the old ceremony of announcing at the new moon the date of the Nones (Varro, *Ling.* 6. 27, whereon Goetz and Schoell ad loc., and Latte, *RR* 43) she was addressed as Juno Covella, showing some connexion with the moon. An important festival was the Matronalia of 1 Mar., also the foundation-day of the temple of Juno Lucina (Wissowa, ibid.). Cf. MONETA.

H. J. R.

**JUPITER** (*Iuppiter*), the Italian sky-god, *Diou-pater*, the first member of the name being etymologically identical with that of Zeus (q.v.), and the god himself an inheritance from pre-ethnic days among the Wiro-speaking population. Primitively it would appear that he was simply the power (*numen*) of the sky, manifesting itself in various ways. As Iuppiter Lapis (see Gell. 1. 21. 4; Livy 1. 24. 8, cf. FETIALES; 30. 43. 9; Festus, 102. 11 Lindsay; Rose in *Custom is King* (1936), 56 ff.) he was incorporated in one or all of sundry stones used in taking oaths and presumably supposed to be thunderbolts; they were probably neolithic implements. As Iuppiter Feretrius he appears to have been a holy tree (Livy 1. 10. 5–7; Dion. Hal. *Ant. Rom.* 2. 34. 4; Rose, op. cit. 54 ff.). How old his association with the Ides of every month may be (Macrob. *Sat.* 1. 15. 15) we cannot say, but it probably is very ancient; he is naturally worshipped at the time of full moon, when the light from the sky is most powerful. Like Zeus he is also associated with rain (Iuppiter Elicius originally, perhaps, see Wissowa, *RK* 121, but regularly spoken of as connected with the ritual of thunderstorms, see Valerius Antias, fr. 6 Peter; Ov. *Fasti* 3. 291 ff.). It is also as sky-god that he was worshipped at the Vinalia (Rustica) on 19 Aug., when the flamen Dialis (*see* FLAMINES) offered a ewe-lamb to him and cut the first grapes 'inter exta caesa et porrecta' (Varro, *Ling.* 6. 16). His development into a personal and to some extent anthropomorphic god seems to have been more complete in the rest of Italy than in Rome, and it is also outside Rome that signs are to be found of an early association with Juno (q.v.), and of connexions with the underworld (cf. Zeus Chthonios, etc.); see C. Koch, *Der römische Juppiter* (1937), and cf. Rose in *Gnomon* 1938, 255 ff. In Rome, apart from Greek and Etruscan influence, he remains almost purely a sky-god and not very sharply personal.

**2.** His festivals, besides the Vinalia, not only Rustica but Meditrinalia on 11 Oct., where his connexion with the goddess Meditrina is obscure (see Varro, ibid. 21; Festus, 110. 21 Lindsay; *Fasti Amiternini* on 11 Oct.; Wissowa, op. cit. 115), and Priora, 23 Apr. (Varro 16; Pliny, *HN* 18. 287; Ov. *Fasti* 4. 863 ff., whereon see Frazer), include the *nundinae* or market-days, when the flaminica Dialis sacrificed a ram to him (Macrob. *Sat.* 1. 16. 30); also the very obscure Poplifugia on 5 July (see Rose in *CQ* 1934, 157) and an unnamed festival on 23 Dec. (Macrob. 1. 10. 11 and *Fasti Praenestini* on that date), apparently because the winter solstice occurs about then. His oldest associates in Roman cult are Mars and Quirinus, e.g., 'Numa' ap. Festus, 204. 13 ff. Lindsay; the first *spolia opima* go to Jupiter, the second to Mars, the third to Quirinus.

**3.** The Etruscan kings introduced (shortly before their fall according to tradition, supported by the fact that the oldest calendar-festivals do not include those of the Capitol) the cult of Iuppiter Optimus Maximus, i.e. the best and greatest of all Jupiters, in which the god, in his Capitoline temple, built in the Etruscan manner and with three *cellae*, was associated with Juno and Minerva (qq.v.), apparently a purely Etruscan grouping. From then on his cult became more splendid. The oldest games, *Ludi Capitolini* (15 Oct., Plut. *Rom.* 25; see, further, Wissowa, ibid. 117), are indeed connected with Iuppiter Feretrius and have peculiarities in their celebration which may be pre-Etruscan; but the *Ludi Romani* (which seem to have originated from games celebrated on the occasion of a triumph; see below) of 4–19 Sept., the *Ludi Plebei* of 4–17 Nov., and the attendant *epula Iouis* (cf. EPULONES) were among the greatest feasts of the year. To this temple also came the triumphs (q.v.), in which the general, in the full costume of a king (and so in that of Jupiter, whom he did not impersonate) drove at the head of his army to do honour to the god (see Marquardt, *Staatsverw.* ii². 582 for references).

**4.** In the moral and political sphere Jupiter was associated not only with war but with treaties and oaths of all kinds, a development, as the cult of Iuppiter Lapis shows (see above), from his functions as sky-god and wielder of thunderbolts, wherewith he can punish the perjurer; cf. ZEUS, and *see also* FETIALES. Hence it is that he seems to be connected in some way with Fides (q.v.); cf. also SEMO SANCUS.

**5.** For his Roman temples and shrines see Platner–Ashby, 291 ff.; Nash, *Pict. Dict. Rome* i. 518 ff. (and for his Capitoline temple, E. Gjerstad, *Early Rome* iii (1960), 168 ff.). Outside Rome, but within her sphere of influence in historical times, his most noteworthy solemnity was the *feriae Latinae*, celebrated yearly, but not on a fixed date, on the Alban Mount. Here he bore the title Latiaris, in his capacity of god of the Latin League. The ritual was in some respects archaic, milk and not wine being used for libation (Cic. *Div.* 1. 18, whereon see Pease for further details); the chief Roman magistrate for the time being was in charge, and representatives of all the cities of the League were present to claim their share of the sacrificial meat (*carnem petere*) and take part in the ritual, which as usual must be exactly observed (Livy 41. 16. 1–2).

Jupiter is the *interpretatio Romana* (q.v.) of a number of foreign sky-gods.

Latte, *RR* 79 ff. and elsewhere.

H. J. R.

**JURISPRUDENCE.** Until the third century B.C. at Rome knowledge of the law and its procedure was a monopoly of the patrician *pontifices* (q.v.), but thereafter the line of lay jurists (*iurisprudentes, iurisconsulti, iurisperiti*) begins (*see* FLAVIUS I *and* CORUNCANIUS I). The jurist was the central figure in the Roman legal system, since statute law was relatively unimportant in the private law, and neither magistrate nor judge was necessarily or normally learned in the law (*see* EDICTUM, IUDEX). The jurist influenced the law at every point. He assisted the private citizen by drafting legal forms for legal transactions, wills, etc. (*cavere*), advising on the conduct of litigation (*agere*), and giving opinions on questions of law submitted to him (*respondere*). His wider influence lay in his advice to magistrates, and especially to the urban praetor, on the formulation of their edicts and the granting of remedies in individual cases, in his advice also to *iudices* in the making of their decisions, in his teaching, and above all in his writing. But though he was an adviser, a teacher, and a writer, he was not normally an advocate (*see* ADVOCATUS). And he was usually a man of standing, whose activity in the law was only one facet of a public career. Until the last years of the Republic, the leading jurists came from senatorial families and held high office. Thereafter, they came from a wider class, but were still, for the most part, prominent public men, and in the later Principate were more and more to be found among the highest officials in the emperor's service. The Republican jurist is typified by Quintus Mucius Scaevola (q.v. 4), the jurist of the late period by Papinianus (q.v.), Paulus (q.v. 1), and Ulpianus (q.v. 1), while Javolenus (q.v.) and Salvius Julianus (q.v. 2) represent the transitional period. Others, however, such as Pomponius (q.v. 6) held no public office.

Though Roman legal writing came inevitably under Greek influence, for example in its use of the dialectical method, it is substantially an original creation of the Roman mind, and one which has had immense influence in medieval and modern Europe. Its principal forms were: commentaries, particularly on the Praetor's Edict (*see* EDICTUM), and, of a rather different kind, commentaries on the works of earlier jurists (e.g. those of Sabinus (q.v. 2)); collections of opinions (*responsa*) and of discussions of hypothetical or actual cases (*Quaestiones* or, when more general and systematic, *Digesta*), monographs; and some expository textbooks, of which the *Institutiones* (q.v.) of Gaius (q.v. 2) are the most famous example. The method is usually markedly casuistic, even in works, such as commentaries, which are not ostensibly of that kind, and frequent reference is made to the opinions of other jurists. It is this casuistic character which gives to Roman law its richness of detail. By far the greatest part of the surviving literature is known only through Justinian's *Digesta* (q.v.).

The extent to which *responsa* were binding on a *iudex* is obscure, and controverted. Pomponius says that Augustus gave to some jurists the 'ius respondendi ex auctoritate principis', but it is quite uncertain what the effect of this was. It is unlikely that Augustus took so radical a step as to make *responsa* of privileged jurists formally binding. More probably he wished simply to mark out certain jurists as especially eminent. It is uncertain also whether authority attached to such *responsa* generally and in perpetuity or only for the case for which they were given. An obscure passage of Gaius (*Inst.* 1. 7) suggests that by the time of Hadrian the authority was general and that the problem therefore presented itself of possible conflicts of authoritative *responsa*. It is also uncertain who had the *ius*: it is directly attested only for Sabinus (q.v. 2). Nor did it certainly continue to be granted after Hadrian.

In the Republic the young man learned his law by attaching himself to a jurist. In the Empire, however, there emerge two 'schools', the Sabinians and the Proculians, which evidently had some teaching functions, but no details are known. *See* SABINUS (2).

The line of jurists breaks off in the middle of the third century A.D. (*see* HERENNIUS 2), and thereafter decay sets in. A revival of legal science comes in the fifth century from the law schools of the Eastern part of the Empire, especially that of Berytus; but it was essentially a classicizing revival rather than a new life, and its importance lies in its contribution to the codification of Justinian (*see* TRIBONIANUS). *See further* LAW AND PROCEDURE, ROMAN, I: 10, 11. For individual jurists see special articles.

(*a*) SOURCES. For the *Digest, see* DIGESTA. The fragments are restored to their original order in O. Lenel, *Palingenesia Iuris Civilis* (1889; repr. with suppl. 1960). For the literature surviving independently of Justinian: Riccobono, *FIRA* ii; Huschke, *Iurisprudentiae anteiustinianae reliquiae⁶*, ed. E. Seckel, B. Kübler, 3 vols. (1908–27). (*b*) GENERAL WORKS. S. Riccobono, *Jurisprudentia* (Novissimo Digesto Italiano viii); H. Fitting, *Alter u. Folge d. Schriften röm. Juristen²* (1908); P. Krüger, *Gesch. d. Quellen u. Litteratur d. röm. Rechts²* (1912); F. Schulz, *History of Roman Legal Science* (1946); W. Kunkel, *Herkunft und soziale Stellung der römischen Juristen* (1952); A. M. Honoré, 'The Severan Lawyers', *Stud. et Doc. Hist. et Iuris* 1962; 'Julian's Circle', *Tijdschr. voor Rechtsgesch.* 1964; W. Kalb, *Roms Juristen nach ihrer Sprache dargestellt* (1890); id. *Das Juristenlatein²* (1888); id. *Wegweiser in die röm. Rechtssprache* (1912). *And see* works on *History and Sources*, and on *Transmission of texts* under LAW AND PROCEDURE, ROMAN, I.                                       B. N.

## JUSTIN MARTYR

**JUSTIN MARTYR** (*c*. A.D. 100–65), a Christian apologist, flourished under Antoninus Pius and died a martyr in Rome in 165 after his condemnation as a Christian by the *praefectus urbis* Q. Junius Rusticus. He tells us at the outset of his account of his debate with the Jew, Trypho, at Ephesus (*c*. 135), that he was born at Flavia Neapolis, the ancient Schechem in Samaria, of pagan parents. Never, it seems, attracted to Judaism, for some years he led a peripatetic life searching for truth successively in Stoicism, Aristotelianism, Pythagoreanism, and finally Platonism. While a Platonist he came into chance contact with an aged Christian at Ephesus, but was converted to Christianity by his admiration at the constancy of Christian confessors (ii. *Apol.* 12). After his debate with Trypho he moved to Rome where he set up a small Christian school. He wrote two Apologies (nominally directed to the emperor, but in fact to the liberal provincial public), one (*c*. 155) providing a general defence of Christians and their faith against current pagan calumnies (*see* CHRISTIANITY) and the second (*c*. 162) in which he is more concerned with specific acts of persecution resulting from the denunciation of Christians to the authorities. He himself is said by his disciple Tatian to have been the victim of the jealousy of the Cynic philosopher Crescens.

Justin believed that Christianity was the true philosophy, and though he was endowed with no great philosophical skill attempted to harmonize current philosophy, principally Platonism, with Christianity. In his belief that truth had been moving gradually towards its final revelation in Christ and that all men shared in the 'generative' or 'germinating' Word (λόγος σπερματικός) he anticipates Clement and the Alexandrian school. In his relatively optimistic views of Church–State relations he is in line with the thought of Melito of Sardis (*c*. 175) and also anticipates the philosophy of history of Origen and Eusebius. His life and thought illustrate the attraction which Christianity was beginning to exercise on thoughtful provincials in the eastern part of the Empire in the Antonine period. Despite the Jewish-Christian imprint apparent in the *Dialogue with Trypho*, he foreshadows the philosophical interpretation which was to be given to the Christian message under the influence of these Gentile converts.

EDITIONS. P. Marin, O.S.B. (Paris, 1742), J. C. T. Otto (3 vols. Jena, 1842–8 and 5 vols. 1876–81), and Migne, *PG* vi.
MODERN WORKS. A. von Harnack, 'Judentum und Judenchristentum in Justin Dialog mit Trypho', *Texte und Untersuchungen* xxxix (Lg 1913); E. R. Goodenough, *The Theology of Justin Martyr* (Jena, 1923); W. Schmid, 'Die Textüberlieferung der Apologie des Justin' *Zeitschr. f. N.T. Wissenschaft* xl, 1941, 87 ff.; H. Chadwick, 'Justin

Martyr's Defence of Christianity', *Bull. Rylands Libr.* 1965, 275 ff. and *Early Christian Thought and Classical Tradition* (1967). H. Scott Holland, *DCB* iii. 560 ff.; G. Hardy, *DTC* viii. 2. 2228 ff and *ODCC* 756 f.; L. W. Barnard, *Justin Martyr* (1967). W. H. C. F.

**JUSTINIAN** (FLAVIUS PETRUS SABBATIUS JUSTINIANUS) was born *c.* A.D. 482 at a village near Naissus. His original name was Petrus Sabbatius; he took the name Justinianus on his adoption by his uncle Justin. When Justin became emperor (518), Justinian was rapidly promoted to be *comes* and then *magister militum praesentalis*, becoming consul in 520. In 522 he married the actress Theodora. They were a devoted couple until her death (548) and she did much to hearten him in difficult times, notably during the Nika rebellion of 532, when circus riots at Constantinople developed into a movement to make Hypatius, a nephew of Anastasius, Emperor. She also inspired some of his reforms, but there is no evidence that she exercised undue influence on appointments or policy, though on the major religious issue she was sharply opposed to her husband, being a strong monophysite.

Justinian was crowned as Augustus on 4 Apr. 527 and succeeded on his uncle's death on 1 Aug. He had a deep sense of the past greatness of the Roman Empire and was determined to restore it, by recovering the lost provinces of the West, by reforming its administrative abuses, and by codifying and rationalizing its legal system. He was also a strongly religious man, who believed that the greatness of the Empire depended on God's favour, which he was resolved to win by suppressing heresy and paganism. He chose able generals and ministers to carry out these projects. The chief military tasks were assigned to Belisarius, Germanus, and Narses. His legal expert was Tribonian, his financial and administrative expert John the Cappadocian, diplomacy was entrusted to Peter the Patrician.

Justinian had no ambitions on the eastern frontier, but was forced to conduct long campaigns there by the aggressive attitude of the Persian kings. After five years' fighting (527–32) he secured an Eternal Peace at the price of 11,000 lb. gold. In 540 Chosroes broke the Peace and the war continued with intervals of partial truce until another treaty was signed in 562. Meanwhile in the West Belisarius (q.v.) reconquered Africa from the Vandals (533), and Italy from the Ostrogoths (535–40). The latter, however, were not finally crushed until 553 (*see* NARSES). In 551 part of southern Spain was conquered from the Visigoths.

On 13 Feb. 528 a commission was appointed to codify all imperial constitutions from Hadrian up to date which were still valid; the first Codex Justinianus was issued on 7 Apr. 529, and on 15 Dec. 530 a second commission was appointed to excerpt and codify the works of the classical jurists; the *Digest* was published on 16 Dec. 533. On 16 Nov. 534 a second revised edition of the Codex Justinianus was issued. Justinian subsequently issued over 150 novels; many were administrative, others reformed or codified topics of law.

Justinian carried out many reforms of the provincial administration; in particular he tried to root out corruption and extortion by abolishing the sale of offices and by raising the status and salaries of governors. He reorganized the system of appeals to speed up justice and to prevent minor cases coming up to the capital. Since his wars were very expensive he made many economies, such as reducing the public post, and tried to eliminate peculation and waste by strict audit of municipal and military accounts. It nevertheless proved necessary to introduce a supplementary land tax (the *aerikon*) and later to institute many monopolies.

Justinian carried out an active building programme throughout the Empire, erecting fortresses and churches and restoring aqueducts and other public buildings. His supreme achievement was S. Sophia at Constantinople.

In the religious field Justinian drastically reinforced the penal laws against pagans, Jews, and heretics, and made persistent efforts to heal the quarrel between the Chalcedonian and Monophysite parties. In an attempt to placate the latter he issued in 543–4 an edict of Three Chapters condemning certain works of Theodoret and Ibas and Theodore of Mopsuestia, and in 546 carried Pope Vigilius off to Constantinople and made him confirm the edict. Vigilius later retracted, but Justinian in 553 summoned a general council at Constantinople which ratified the edict and Vigilius yielded next year. The Monophysites, however, remained obdurate and established a rival hierarchy. In 564 Justinian declared the aphthartodocete doctrine orthodox, but he died in 565 and the edict was ignored.

C. Diehl, *Justinien et la civilisation byzantine au VIème siècle* (1901); B. Rubin, *Das Zeitalter Iustinians* i (1960). A. H. M. J.

**JUSTINUS**, MARCUS JUNIAN(I)US (*PW* 4) (Justin), made an epitome in Latin of Pompeius Trogus' *Historiae Philippicae*, probably in the third century A.D. It is an unequal work, but preserves the main lines of the original (cf. the report of Mithridates' speech in 38. 4–7). The epitome was widely read in the Middle Ages.

EDITIONS. F. Ruehl (1886), E. Pessonneaux (1903) with notes, M. Galdi (1923), O. Seel (1935). L. Castiglioni, *Storie Filippiche di Giustino* (1925); M. Galdi, *L'epitome nella lett. lat.* (1922), 108. A. H. McD.

**JUSTUS**, a leading citizen of Tiberias (q.v.), was an opponent of Josephus (q.v.) when the latter was in command in Galilee in A.D. 66–7. After helping to instigate the revolt of Tiberias, he fled to Agrippa II (q.v.), who saved him from punishment by Vespasian and later appointed him his secretary. After Agrippa's death he published a history of the war (possibly part of his history of the Jews from Moses to Agrippa II entitled Ἰουδαίων Βασιλέων τῶν ἐν τοῖς στέμμασι). Josephus criticizes it severely in his *Vita* for inaccuracy, but his own picture of Justus may well be distorted by personal antagonism.

Joseph. *Vit.* 336–67, 390–3; Phot. *Bibl.* 33. H. Luther, *Josephus und Justus von Tiberias* (1910). E. M. S.

**JUVENAL** (DECIMUS IUNIUS IUVENALIS), the last great Roman satiric poet, was (unlike Horace and Persius) reticent about himself and was little known during his lifetime. Since the ancient 'biographies' are largely fictitious, no detailed account of his career is possible: any reconstruction must be tentative. He came from Aquinum (3. 319). When he published his first extant satires (between A.D. 100 and 110), he was middle-aged (*Sat.* 1. 25, cf. 3. 26–28): thus he was born between 50 and 65. (For a slightly later dating see Syme.) He was still writing in A.D. 127 (*Sat.* 13. 17, 15. 27). Like his friend Martial (Mart. 7. 24 and 91, 12. 18), he was for some time miserably poor and lived in Rome as a dependant of the rich (*Sat.* 1, 3, and 5); but in time he acquired a small competence (11. 64–182). No extant contemporary except Martial ever mentioned him. His work was scarcely known until the fourth century, when Lactantius quoted him by name and Ausonius and others imitated him. Then, after 352 and before 399, his satires were edited and published with a commentary—perhaps through the influence of Servius (q.v. 2)—and at once became popular.

Several ancient sources say he was banished for lampooning a court favourite. His terror of satirizing living persons (1. 147–71), his penetrating hatred of Domitian, and the mildness of his later work make it likely that Domitian (if anyone) exiled him. Since his property would be confiscated, when he returned after Domitian's murder he would be as poor as he appears in his early poems. On a votive tablet from Aquinum (*CIL* x. 5382) the broken name '. . . nius Iuuenalis' was found. If the poet dedicated it, he was once an important magistrate of Aquinum and a knight in the imperial service. Possibly his failure to obtain promotion caused him to write the lampoon that ruined him. In any case the chief impetus behind his satires was a bitter sense of failure and injustice: focused on Domitian's principate, it gradually faded in intensity with advancing years.

Juvenal left sixteen hexameter satires, grouped in five books which run from 662 to nearly 1,000 lines in length and are apparently arranged in the order of publication. The books differ considerably in tone, the fourth and fifth being markedly gentler than the rest.

In book i (after A.D. 100, cf. 1. 49–50), 1, the introduction, explains that Juvenal cannot help writing satire when he sees the corruption of Rome, but that for safety he will attack only the dead; 2, beginning with gibes at hypocritical Stoics, broadens into a savage polemic against sodomy; in 3 Juvenal's friend Umbricius explains he is leaving Rome, where honest men cannot make a living and poverty entails scorn, discomfort, and danger; 4 tells how Domitian summoned his cringing cabinet to discuss the cooking of a giant turbot; 5 describes a client's dinner at his patron's home, where insolent servants bring him cheap food while his host laughs to see him squirm.

Book ii (*c.* A.D. 116, cf. 6. 407–12) consists of satire 6, a vast, ruthless denunciation of affected and immoral wives.

Book iii (after A.D. 118, cf. 7. 1–3, 20–6) opens with 7, which compliments Hadrian as a friend of literature and exposes the misery of intellectuals lacking generous patrons; 8 reproaches the aristocrat who thinks nobility superior to virtue; in 9, a witty but repulsive dialogue, a male prostitute describes the troubles of his profession.

Book iv (without indication of date) contains 10, a magnificent declamation on the folly of men in desiring hurtful things instead of courage, health, and sanity; 11, an invitation to dinner, contrasting decent moderation with contemporary extravagance and archaic austerity; and 12, relating a friend's escape from shipwreck, with reflections on the nature of true friendship.

In book v (in or after A.D. 127) satire 13 is a mock consolation to a friend cheated of some money; 14 discusses the influence of parents' sins upon children, emphasizing the danger of greed; 15 describes a case of cannibalism and mob-violence in Egypt, adding reflections on man's inhumanity to man; 16 (whose end was evidently lost in antiquity) is a fragment ironically expounding the advantages of a soldier's life.

Although Juvenal speaks as a moralist, he poses not as a philosopher but as an ordinary man (1. 30, 79–80; 13. 120–3) who feels his world is out of joint, and writes satire as a protest rather than a remedy. His denunciations of folly, avarice, vulgarity, vice, and crime gain great force from the fascinated accuracy with which he describes their practitioners and victims. His bitterness often seems to be dictated by literary fashion, over-

emphasized by rhetoric, or exaggerated by personal rancour. Yet (despite Tac. *Ann.* 3. 55) there can have been no great change in the morality of the Roman upper class since it was attacked by Seneca on similar charges. Martial's callous frankness and the moral crusades of Domitian and M. Aurelius show that Juvenal told the truth, even if he confined himself to its darker side.

He retained in his poems the variety characteristic of satire, adding a more lofty and sustained tone of invective. His memorable epigrams have seldom been surpassed, and he is an amusing though cruel parodist. In his large vocabulary colloquialisms and queer foreign words jostle the grand phrases of epic and oratory. His poems, often condemned for structural laxity, have at their best quite as clear a pattern as is compatible with the quasi-improvisatory tone of his medium. He is the last Roman poet to use the full range of the hexameter, which he constantly varies with brilliant effects of sound and rhythm. He was much admired as a thinker in the Middle Ages, and he became the model for many satirists in and after the Renaissance.

TEXTS. A. E. Housman (1931²); U. Knoche (Munich, 1950); O.C.T., W. V. Clausen (with Persius, 1959).

COMMENTARIES. J. E. B. Mayor (2 vols., 1880–1²; omits 2, 6, and 9); L. Friedlaender (Leipzig, 1895); J. D. Duff (1898; omits 2, 9, and passages elsewhere).

STUDIES. R. Schütze, *J. ethicus* (Greifswald, 1905), content; J. de Decker, *J. declamans* (Ghent, 1913), style and content; U. Knoche, *Die Überlieferung J.'s* (1926) and *Handschriftliche Grundlagen des J.-Textes* (Philol. Suppl. 33, 1940), text; P. de Labriolle, *Les Satires de J.* (1950), general; F. Gauger, *Zeitschilderung und Topik bei J.* (1936), content; G. Jachmann, *Studien zu J.* (1943), text; G. Highet, *J. the Satirist* (1954), general; A. Serafini, *Studio sulla satira di Giovenale* (1957), general; Syme, *Tacitus*, appendices 74 and 75, date and prosopography; W. S. Anderson, *J. and Quintilian*, *YClS* 1961, 3 ff., general.

INDEX VERBORUM. L. Kelling and A. Suskin (U.S.A. 1951). SCHOLIA vetustiora ed. P. Wessner (Leipzig, 1931).

For fuller bibliography see Highet (1954) and the penetrating analysis of Juvenalian literature 1941–61 by M. Coffey, *Lustrum* 1963, 161 ff. G. H.

**JUVENCUS**, GAIUS VETTIUS AQUILINUS, a Spanish priest of noble birth, apparently the first Latin poet to aim at providing a Christian substitute for the traditional poetry of paganism, *c.* A.D. 330 composed an epic, *Evangeliorum libri IV*, in hexameters, utilizing an early Latin translation and closely following the Gospel narrative (especially Matthew). The work shows strong Virgilian influence and some skill in versification.

TEXT. J. Huemer, *CSEL* xxiv. N. Hansson, *Textcritisches zu J.*, mit vollständigem Index verborum (1950). A. H.-W.

**JUVENTIUS** (*PW* 16) **LATERENSIS**, MARCUS, of a Tusculan family with a consul in the second century B.C., served in Bithynia and Cyrenaica. In 59 B.C. he abandoned his tribunician candidature to avoid taking an oath to preserve Caesar's legislation. He helped Cicero during his exile. In 55 he prosecuted Cn. Plancius (q.v.) for *ambitus*; but Cicero defended him and secured his acquittal. Praetor in 51, he is hardly heard of until 43, when he tried to keep Lepidus (q.v. 3) loyal to the Republic and, after failing, committed suicide. E. B.

# K

**KAIROS,** personified Opportunity. He had an altar at Olympia (Paus. 5. 14. 9), and Ion of Chios (cited there) called him the youngest son of Zeus (i.e. opportunity is god-sent) in a hymn possibly composed for this cult. That he was a little more substantial than most personifications is perhaps indicated by Antimachus, fr. 32 Wyss, where Kairos is one of Adrastus' horses. He has no mythology, but was a favourite subject in art, especially from Lysippus onwards. Then or later he was shown with a long forelock, but bald behind (Posidippus in *Anth. Plan.* 4. 275; see Sauer in Roscher's *Lexikon,* s.v.). Hence, by a gross mistranslation of his name, our phrase 'to take time by the forelock'.

Material in Cook, *Zeus* ii. 859 ff. H. J. R.

**KANEPHOROI** (κανηφόροι) were usually young women who bore baskets or vessels (κανᾶ) in religious processions. In the Panathenaic procession the young women were chosen from noble houses, and were required to be of good family (Harpocration, Photius, Hesychius, s.v.), unmarried, and of unsullied reputation; hence 'to be fit to carry the basket' is to live chastely (as Men. *Epit.* 221 Allinson), and to reject a candidate was a grave insult (Thuc. 6. 56. 1). They were dressed in splendid raiment; hair and garments were decked with gold and jewels; they were powdered with white barley-flour and wore a chain of figs (ἰσχάδων ὁρμαθός). They carried vessels of gold and silver, which contained all things needed in the sacrificial ceremony: firstfruits, the sacrificial knife, barley-groats (ὀλαί), and garlands. Erichthonius was said to have introduced Kanephoroi at the Panathenaea. Certainly the institution was very old, and its·object was doubtless to secure the efficacy of the sacrificial materials by letting them touch nothing that was not virginal and therefore lucky and potent.

Kanephoroi are also found in other Attic cults, e.g. those of Apollo, Dionysus, and Isis, and in the cult of Zeus Basileus at Lebadea.

E. Pfuhl, *De Atheniensium pompis sacris* (1900), 20 ff.; Mittelhaus, *PW* x. 1865 f.; L. Deubner, *Attische Feste* (1932), 25; and numerous references in Nilsson, *GGR* ii, s.v. J. E. F.; and H. J. R.

**KASIOS** (Κάσιος, less correctly Κάσσιος), **ZEUS.** An oriental god, possibly Semitic, but the etymology of the name is uncertain. He is plainly connected with Casius, a mountain near Antioch on the Orontes, and also one near Pelusium, on both of which he had a cult. He was also worshipped (owing to the similarity of the names?) at Cassiope in Corcyra. The evidence for his worship, which is Hellenistic and imperial, is largely archaeological, and his original nature is conjectural. He may have been a mountain- or weather-god, thus leading to his identification with Zeus.

See further Roscher, *Lex.* ii. 970 ff.; *PW* x. 2265 ff.; Cook, *Zeus* ii. 906, 981, 1191. H. J. R.

**KERES,** malignant spirits, the bringers of all sorts of evil. They pollute and make unclean (Pl. *Leg.* 937 d, like the Harpies), cause blindness (Eur. *Phoen.* 953), other diseases (Soph. *Phil.* 42), old age and death (Mimnermus fr. 2. 5 f. Diehl), spiritual blindness (ἄτη), misfortune, and troubles in general (cf. Emped. fr. 121 Diels, Semon. 1. 20 Diehl). In its most frequent sense of death or death-bringer Ker is used almost as a common noun. Sometimes it must be rendered 'fate', as when Achilles is given the choice between two Keres (*Il.* 9. 411), but it is never neutral or favourable in sense.

Keres can also mean the souls of the dead, as in the cry at the all-souls festival (end of the Anthesteria, q.v.) θύραζε κῆρες, οὐκέτ' Ἀνθεστήρια (the only certain instance— but see R. Ganszyniec, *Eranos* 1947, 100 ff.: the weighing of Keres in *Il.* 22. 210 ff. may reflect an earlier weighing of souls (Malten, *PW,* Suppl. iv. 895; M. P. Nilsson, *Homer and Mycenae* (1933), 267 f., fig. 56)). From this use earlier writers (Crusius, Rohde) posited 'ghosts' as the original meaning of Keres, but this is convincingly denied by Malten (*PW,* Suppl. iv, s.v.). Malten concludes that Keres is originally a predicative word (like θεός, Wilamowitz, *Platon* (1948) i. 348) meaning harmful (√ κηραίνειν, ἀκήρατος). See also Nilsson, *GGR* i. 206 ff. As to their form, literary descriptions suggest birds of prey, similar to Harpies or Sirens; it is hard to identify any figures on monuments as Keres.

W. K. C. G.

**KEYS AND LOCKS.** The primitive Greek door-fastening was a horizontal bolt working in staples behind the door (μοχλὸς θύρας, ὀχεύς, sera, claustrum). From the outside the bolt was drawn by a strap passing through a hole in the door; it was withdrawn by inserting through a second hole a bar (κλείς, clavis) bent twice at right angles, so that its end engaged in a groove in the bolt. This bar is the 'temple key' of Greek art. Subsequently a slot was cut in the bolt, into which a vertical peg (βάλανος) fell as the bolt moved forward; then a βαλανάγρα had to be employed to hook up the peg before the bolt could move back. This seems to be the 'lock of Penelope' (*Od.* 21. 46); it remained long in use, with growing complexity of the slots and correspondingly of the prongs of the key. The 'Laconian key', with three teeth (Ar. *Thesm.* 421, Plaut. *Mostell.* 404), is probably one of these variants. The modern form of lock in which the key rotates the bolt on a pivot is not found before Roman times, but is then common, as are movable padlocks. The key in art is often a symbol of power, as when Hecate holds the key of Hades (κλειδοῦχος, clavigera); to give or take back the household keys was a Roman form of divorce.

*British Museum Guide to Greek and Roman Life,* s.v. 'Keys'; R. Vallois, Dar.-Sag., s.v. 'Sera'; *PW,* s.v. 'Schlüssel'; Singer *et al., Hist. of Technology* ii (1956), 415 f. F. N. P.

**KOLAKRETAI** (κωλακρέται) were Athenian officials in charge of the State treasury. The date of their institution is not known, but they existed at least as early as the time of Solon (q.v.) (Arist. *Ath. Pol.* 7. 3). References in Aristophanes and in inscriptions show that they still had charge of public money at the time of the Peloponnesian War and paid the fees of jurors (*see* DIKASTERION) and others who performed services for the State. But they are not heard of after 411 B.C., and were probably abolished in that year. Some, perhaps all, of their functions were taken over by the *hellenotamiai* (q.v.).

*ATL* iii. 359 ff.; F. Jacoby, *FGrH* iii b Suppl. (1954), commentary on 324 F 5. D. M. M.

**KRONOS,** youngest son of Heaven and Earth and leader of his brethren the Titans (q.v.). By advice of his mother he castrated his father, who therefore no longer approached Earth but left room for the Titans between them. Kronos then married his sister Rhea, and there were born to them Hestia, Demeter, Hera, Hades, Poseidon, and Zeus, all of whom (or all the males), save the last, he swallowed, because he was fated to be overcome by one of them. Rhea, by counsel of her parents, wrapped a stone in swaddling-clothes when Zeus was born and hid him away in Crete (cf. CURETES, ZEUS); Kronos swallowed the stone, thinking it to be his son. Later, by the contrivance of Earth, Kronos vomited up all those he had swallowed, and was overcome by them after a desperate struggle (Hes. *Theog.* 137–8, 154 ff., 453 ff., and many later authors, who differ only in minor details).

This story is so extraordinary and so unlike normal Greek mythology that it is pretty certainly pre-Hellenic; Andrew Lang long ago pointed out (*Myth, Ritual and Religion* (1887), ch. 10) its resemblance to the Maori myth of Tane Mahuta; for legends of swallowing see Stith Thompson, F 913. Since E. Forrer ('Eine Geschichte des Götterkönigtums aus dem Hattireiche', *Mél. Cumont*, 1936, 687 ff.) first published the documents, it has become clear that the legend of Kronos is largely derived from Asia Minor. Another group of stories represents Kronos as king of the Golden Age (ὁ ἐπὶ Κρόνου βίος; Hes. *Op.* 111) or of a distant wonderland (ibid. 169, if genuine; Pind. *Ol.* 2. 70; Plut. *De def. or.* 420 a, etc.). Hence, through his identification with Saturnus (q.v.), his position as civilizer of Italy.

Before the discovery of the Hittite documents, a usual interpretation was that Kronos was a god of the pre-Hellenic population, but it would now be admitted that he was mainly a mythological figure, whose cult was localized in a few places. His festival, the Kronia, was celebrated at Athens and elsewhere (L. Deubner, *Attische Feste* (1932), 152 ff.; Farnell, op. cit. *infra*, 20) at harvest-time, masters and slaves feasting together; here and there, as at Olympia (Paus. 6. 20. 1), we find him with a priesthood and a sacrifice. Where references to a cult occur after the period of Roman influence the worship of Saturn seems to have led to modifications. At all events he had a somewhat grim reputation, leading to his being identified with foreign gods of formidable character (e.g. [Plato], *Minos* 315 c, Dion. Hal. *Ant. Rom.* 1. 38. 2).

Cult: Farnell, *Cults* i. 23 ff. Mythology: M. Mayer in Roscher's *Lexikon*, art. 'Kronos'; M. Pohlenz, *PW*, s.v. 'Kronos'. Nilsson, *GGR* i³. 501 ff., for recent literature and discussion
H. J. R.; H. W. P.

**KRYPTEIA,** the Spartan secret police, in which selected young Spartiatae were, among other things, authorized by the ephors to patrol the remoter parts of Laconia and to murder secretly any supposedly dangerous helots (q.v.). It probably represents the formalization of some old initiation rite. Aristotle (quoted by Plut. *Lyc.* 28) ascribes it to Lycurgus (q.v. 2) but Plutarch dates its institution to the period after the helots' revolt of 464 B.C., and quotes the murder of 2,000 helots in 424 B.C. (Thuc. 4. 80) as typical of its methods.

Xen. *Lac. Pol.* 4. 4; Plut. *Cleom.* 28. 4. H. Jeanmaire, *Rev. Ét. Grec.* 1913, 121 ff.
A. M. W.; W. G. F.

# L

**LABEO** (1), MARCUS ANTISTIUS (*PW* 34) (d. A.D. 10 or 11), one of the most prominent Roman jurists. Of plebeian extraction, he was by political conviction a republican; his official career ended with the praetorship, for he refused the consulate offered to him by Augustus. In his legal work he showed great independence of mind and was a bold innovator ('plurima innouare instituit', *Dig.* 1. 2. 2 (*fin.*) ). His learning was enormous: besides mastering his special branch of knowledge, to which he was introduced by his father (who was also a jurist), and by other teachers, including Trebatius (q.v.) Testa and some of the disciples of Servius Sulpicius (q.v. 2) Rufus, he was expert in dialectics, in the history of Latin language and grammar, and in philosophy. Gellius (13. 10. 1) emphasizes his knowledge of ancient Roman literature. Labeo was a voluminous writer: it was his practice to spend six months in every year with his pupils in Rome, and to devote the remainder of the year to writing in the country. He is said to have written about 400 volumes. We know from citations by other jurists the titles of the following works: *Pithana* (collection of decisions on individual cases); *Responsa*; *Epistulae*; a large treatise *De Iure Pontificio* (fifteen books); a commentary on the Praetor's Edict. After his death his *Libri posteriores* (at least forty vols.) were published. These are known only by quotations in other jurists, and by a large Epitome made by Javolenus (q.v.) and freely excerpted by the compilers of the *Digest*.

He was a contemporary of Ateius Capito (q.v. 2), and if Pomponius' account is true (*see* SABINUS 2), it was the political and personal antagonism between them which originated the schools of jurists named later *Sabiniani* and *Proculiani*. Labeo enjoyed a high reputation not only with his contemporaries but also with later jurists.

A. Pernice, *M. Antistius Labeo* i (1873). *See also under* JURIS-PRUDENCE.
A. B.; B. N.

**LABEO** (2), ATTIUS (1st c. A.D.), an unscholarly ('indoctus') translator of both *Iliad* and *Odyssey* into Latin hexameters (Pers. 1. 4 and 50 with the scholia).

**LABERIUS,** DECIMUS (c. 115–43 B.C.), together with Publilius Syrus, elevated to literary standards the popular southern Italian *mimus* (q.v.), in Rome called also *fabula riciniata*. The surviving forty-three titles and 155 lines (Ribbeck, *CRF*) do not offer enough material for understanding, since the fragments were preserved to illustrate unusual words. Women acted in his plays for the first time in Rome. Macrobius (*Sat.* 2. 7) records a story of Caesar and Laberius.

G. Malagoli, *Atene e Roma* 1905, 188 ff.; H. Reich, *Der Mimus. Ein litterarentwickelungsgeschichtlicher Versuch* (1903).
R. M.; G. W. W.

**LABIENUS** (1, *PW* 6), TITUS (c. 100–45 B.C.), served under Servilius (q.v. 2) as *tribunus militum* in Cilicia (c. 78–74). In 63 as *tribunus plebis* he conducted the prosecution of C. Rabirius for *perduellio*, and obtained the re-enaction of the *Lex Domitia* sanctioning election to priesthoods (*see* LEX, LEGES). Appointed *legatus* of Caesar, he acted as his principal subordinate in Gaul (58–51), taking full command in his absence, and he was entrusted with the independent conduct of important operations (e.g. against the Treveri 54–53 and Parisii 52—the latter a strategical and tactical masterpiece). Caesar may have intended him for consul in 48 (a very doubtful inference from *BGall.* 8. 52. 2), but at the beginning of 49 he deserted to Pompey. There is reason to believe that Labienus was always a partisan of Pompey, also of Picenian origin (R. Syme, *JRS* 1938, 113 ff.). He fought at Pharsalus and in the African campaign, and died in the final campaign of Munda.
C. E. S.

**LABIENUS** (2, *PW* 5), QUINTUS, son of (1) above, was sent to Parthia by Cassius in winter 43/2 B.C. to solicit help against the Triumvirs. Philippi marooned him in Parthia, but in winter 41/40 he and the king's son Pacorus led Parthian troops into Syria and defeated Antony's governor Decidius (q.v.) Saxa; then, with Saxa's army, which went over to him, Labienus overran part of Asia Minor, and put on his coins the shameful title 'Parthicus imp(erator)'. In 39 he was defeated and killed by Ventidius (q.v.). W. W. T.; T. J. C·

**LABIENUS** (3, *PW* 8), TITUS, Augustan orator who combined an older eloquence with a modern vigour in furious invectives which earned him the nickname of 'Rabienus' (Sen. *Controv.* 10. *praef.* 4 ff.). He also wrote history. When his books, like those of Cassius (q.v. 9) Severus, were burned by senatorial decree, Labienus refused to survive them. Caligula restored their works to circulation (Suet. *Cal.* 16). J. W. D.

**LABRANDA**, great religious centre in Caria, famous for the cult of Zeus Labraundos or Zeus Stratios, clearly a deity of native origin. It lay on a remote hillside 8 miles north of Mylasa, and was approached thence by a Sacred Road. The earliest traces of occupation are archaic, and the earliest temple dates probably from the fifth century, but Labranda only gained importance through the patronage of the Hecatomnids, who probably had a palace there.

Mausolus (q.v.) and Idrieus rebuilt the sanctuary on a large scale; the temple was small, but there were imposing *oeci* and *androns* on a series of terraces, and entrance *propylaea* at the lowest corner. There was little further building activity except in the Julio-Claudian period, and the main buildings were apparently destroyed soon after A.D. 350.

A. Laumonier, *Les Cultes indigènes en Carie* (1958) 45–101; *Labraunda, Swedish Excavations and Researches*, vol. i. 1: K. Jeppesen, *The Propylaea*, (1955); i. 2: A. Westholm, *The Architecture of the Hieron* (1963); ii. 1: P. Hellström, *The Pottery of Classical and Later Date, Terracotta Lamps and Glass* (1965). D. J. B.

**LABYRINTH** (λαβύρινθος, probably derived from a pre-Greek word), a building of complicated plan, constructed by Daedalus for King Minos of Crete, from which nobody could escape. The original labyrinth was located at Cnossos (Cleidemus in Plut. *Thes.* 19), perhaps suggested by the ruins of the Bronze-Age palace, but some later writers identified it with a quarry near Gortyn. The Minotaur lived in the labyrinth and was killed there by Theseus (Catull. 64). By extension Greeks called all kinds of architectural mazes labyrinths, especially, in Egypt, the funeral temple of Amenemhet III (Hdt. 2. 148; H. Kees in *PW* xii. 324). An inscription found in Rome records the construction of a labyrinth in the reign of Septimius Severus (Kaibel, *Epigr. Gr.* 920).

A dance with complicated figures performed in Delos and at Cnossos in memory of the delivery of Athenian youths and maidens from the Minotaur is said to have been an imitation of the labyrinth (Plut. *Thes.* 21).

The labyrinth is represented on coins of Cnossos, on Greek vases, and in Roman mosaics (L. Shear, *AJArch.* 1923). Even on the walls of a house in Pompeii we find a graffito of the labyrinth inscribed: 'hic habitat Minotaurus'.

R. Eilmann, *Labyrinthos* (1931); W. F. J. Knight, *Epic and Anthropology* (1967). G. M. A. H.

**LACHARES**, Athenian general after Ipsus (301 B.C.), friend of Cassander. He used his mercenary troops to crush an attempted usurpation by his colleague Charias, but in 300 employed them to make himself tyrant, though until 299/8 he maintained the forms of constitutional

government. He abolished compulsory military service at Athens and stripped the gold from Athena's statue to pay his troops. His opponents rallied against him in the Piraeus and in 296/5 besieged Athens with the aid of Demetrius Poliorcetes. After a determined resistance he fled to Boeotia, leaving Athens in Demetrius' hands (295). Of his later adventures nothing certain is known.

G. De Sanctis, *Riv. fil.* 1928 (= *Scritti minori* i, 349 ff.), 1936; W. S. Ferguson, *CPhil.* 1929 (chronology as above). F. W. W.

**LACONIA** ('Η Λακωνική [γῆ or χώρα] and *Laconica* are the usual forms, derived from Λάκων, a short and unofficial version of Λακεδαιμόνιος), the south-eastern district of the Peloponnese, bounded on the north by Argolis and Arcadia, on the west by Messenia, and on the south and east by the Aegean Sea.

It is a mountainous limestone-region, comprising in the eastern portion the chain of Mt. Parnon, which rises to nearly 6,000 ft. near the Argive frontier, and runs south-south-east from there towards Cape Malea; in the western portion Mt. Taygetus, which runs nearly north to south and forms a high ridge (summit *c.* 7,800 ft.) overlooking the plain of Sparta. It continues southward at a lower elevation to form the promontory ending in Cape Taenarum (*Matapan*). Between Parnon and Taygetus is the valley of the Eurotas, which flows into the Laconian Gulf; its principal tributary, the Oenus, joins it from the north-east, just above Sparta, and smaller streams flow from Taygetus through the Spartan plain to join it further south.

A flourishing Mycenaean kingdom (*see* MENELAUS 1) was destroyed in the twelfth century (*see* DORIANS), and by 950 new Dorian settlements had appeared. By 700 B.C. one of these, Sparta (q.v.), on low hills to the north of a fertile plain between Taygetus and the Eurotas, had annexed the rest of the Eurotas valley down to the sea, the adjoining coastal plains, and a fertile region west of Gytheum, which became the harbour and arsenal of Sparta. This formed the territory of the *Spartiatai*, cultivated for them by their helots (q.v.). The remainder of Laconia, whose northern frontier was fixed by about 540 B.C. after long disputes with Argos and Arcadia, belonged to technically independent *perioikoi* (q.v.) who occupied smaller fertile areas both coastal and inland. But Spartan domination was complete, with some temporary local exceptions, until, after the fall of Nabis (q.v.), Sparta herself with much of Laconia came under the Achaean Confederacy (q.v.). A league of Laconian cities seems to have grown up again after 146 B.C. under some Spartan influence, but this was transformed by Augustus into the Κοινὸν τῶν Ἐλευθερολακώνων, independent of Sparta; it comprised twenty-four members, which had dwindled to eighteen by the Antonine age (Paus. 3. 21. 7).

Paus. bk. iii. For excavations *see* SPARTA and the survey by H. Waterhouse and R. Hope-Simpson, *BSA* 1965, 67 ff.; 1966, 114 ff. A. M. W.; W. G. F.

**LACTANTIUS** (L. Caelius (? Caecilius) Firmianus qui et Lactantius, c. A.D. 240–c. 320), a native of North Africa, pupil of Arnobius (q.v.), Christian apologist. Under Diocletian he was officially summoned to Nicomedia to teach rhetoric there: it is uncertain when he was converted to Christianity, but he was a Christian by 303, and lost his position when persecution began in that year. He remained in Nicomedia till 305, and then moved to the West; in extreme old age he was tutor (c. 317) to Crispus, eldest son of Constantine.

Lactantius wrote numerous works on various subjects, but only Christian works survive. He commenced to write these after persecution began. The *De Opificio Dei* (303–4) is a demonstration of providence from the construction of the human body. The *Divinae Institutiones* (303–13), begun as a reply to attacks on Christianity by a philosopher and a high official (Hierocles), was intended to be a refutation of all opponents, past, present, and future; later (317?) Lactantius produced an *Epitome* of this work. The *De Ira Dei* (314?) demonstrates, against certain philosophers, that anger was a necessary element in the character of God. The *De Mortibus Persecutorum* (318?) is a pamphlet designed to show how all persecutors, particularly those of his own times, came to an evil end. The doubts long cast on its authorship have now been allayed. One poem by Lactantius, *The Phoenix*, also survives. At the Renaissance Lactantius, became known as 'the Christian Cicero'. He is the most classical of all the early Christian Latin writers, and also makes much use of Latin authors, particularly of Cicero. He shows little philosophic knowledge or ability, and has little of importance to say on Christian doctrine or institutions. But the last point may be due to his apologetic method, because he was chary of using Christian sources to refute those who did not believe in them.

Ed. S. Brandt and G. Laubmann, *CSEL* xix, xxvii; J. Moreau, *De la Mort des Persécuteurs*, Sources chrétiennes, 39 (1956); H. Kraft and A. Wlosok, *De Ira Dei* (Darmstadt, 1957); E. H. Blakeney, *Epitome* (1950); R. Pichon, *Lactance* (1901); A. Wlosok, *Laktanz u. die philosophische Gnosis* (1960). Jas. S.

**LACYDES** of Cyrene succeeded Arcesilaus as head of the Middle Academy in 241/40, B.C., and held the position till at least as late as 224/3, after which the headship was probably in commission till Carneades became head; Lacydes died in 206/5. He is sometimes described as founder of the New Academy, but in truth he simply emphasized the scepticism which was already well developed in Arcesilaus. He seems to have made no important contribution to philosophy. W. D. R.

**LAELIUS** (1, *PW* 2) (**MAJOR**), Gaius, a *novus homo* who owed his political advancement to his commander and friend Scipio Africanus. In Spain (210–206 B.C.) he commanded the fleet at New Carthage and fought at Baecula and Ilipa. He shared in Scipio's African campaign (204–202), defeating Syphax (q.v.), capturing Cirta, and commanding one wing at Zama. He was plebeian aedile (197), praetor in Sicily (196), consul with L. Scipio (190), proconsul in Gaul (189), and ambassador to Perseus (174) and to some Celtic tribes (170). He lived to meet Polybius (160), to whom he was a valuable source of information about Scipio Africanus, since he shared so much of his life. H. H. S.

**LAELIUS** (2, *PW* 3), Gaius, the closest friend of Scipio (q.v. 11), Aemilianus whose cultural interests he shared (*see* SCIPIONIC CIRCLE). As Scipio's *legatus* he led the decisive assault on Carthage in 146 B.C., and as praetor in 145 he won some successes in Spain. Either in that year or as consul in 140 he sponsored an abortive proposal for some kind of agrarian resettlement. In 132 he assisted the consuls (*see* RUPILIUS *and* POPILLIUS 2) in the persecution of the Gracchans. His nickname *Sapiens* probably refers to his sagacity. Later generations judged him one of the ablest orators of his day. He is the central figure in Cicero's *De Amicitia* and appears also in the *De Republica*.

Malcovati, *ORF²* 115. H. H. Scullard, *JRS* 1960, 62 ff.; A. E. Astin, *Scipio Aemilianus* (1967). A. E. A.

**LAELIUS** (3) **ARCHELAUS,** a friend of Lucilius, who, like Vettius Philocomus, lectured and commented on Lucilius' satires.

Suet. *Gram.* 2.

**LAESTRYGONES,** a race of cannibal giants encountered by Odysseus (q.v. *and see* ANTIPHATES). In their country the night is so short that men going out with the flocks to pasture meet those coming back (*Od.* 10. 82 ff.), apparently a vague echo of some traveller's tale of northern conditions in summer (cf. Crates in schol. ibid. 86). Their city, Laestrygonia, is described as the 'lofty town of Lamos', a name suggesting Lamia (q.v.), i.e. their royal family is descended from King Bogey. The ancients, as usual, tried to locate the country in the neighbourhood of Magna Graecia, either in Sicily (Thuc. 6. 2. 1) or at Formiae (Cic. *Att.* 2. 13. 2), when they did not suppose it completely fabulous, as it is. H. J. R.

**LAEVINUS,** Marcus Valerius (*PW* 211), praetor in 227 B.C. and again in 215, commanded a fleet on the Illyrian coast against Philip V in 214, and in 212/11 entered into alliance with the Aetolians and Attalus of Pergamum in the First Macedonian War. Consul in 210, he captured Agrigentum, completing Marcellus' work in Sicily, which he governed for three years; in 208 he defeated a Punic fleet. In 205 he brought the Magna Mater from Pessinus to Rome. He died in 200. The record of a consulship in 220 suggests faulty election; a command in Greece in 201 (Livy 31. 3) is uncertain. A. H. McD.

**LAEVIUS** (the cognomen Melissus depends on a conjectural identification with a person named by Suetonius, *Gram.* 3) wrote *Erotopaegnia*, playful lyrics on amatory themes, probably in the early years of the first century B.C. Other known titles (*Adonis, Helena, Alcestis, Io, Sirenocirca, Protesilaodamia*) probably refer to parts of that collection: the surviving fragments suggest a fanciful, sentimental, and romantic treatment of the love-stories of mythology. He experimented with a variety of metres (scazon, iambic dimeter, ionic, anapaests) and indulged in bizarreries of language—picturesque compounds, affective diminutives, novel forms of words—which attracted the attention of later grammarians. In the *Phoenix* he seems even to have reproduced the Hellenistic conceit of the technopaignion, in which the length of the lines was contrived to make a shape. An obscure figure who is never mentioned in the succeeding two centuries and only emerges in the *literati* of the second century A.D., Gellius, Fronto, and Apuleius, who were attracted by his idiosyncrasies, he is of importance as a pioneer, both in technique and in matter, of Alexandrianism in Latin poetry.

Fragments in Morel, *FPL*. C. J. F.

**LAMACHUS** (d. 414 B.C.), Athenian general. He was *strategos* as early as *c.* 435 and must have become well known for his military leadership by 425, when he was caricatured as a blustering soldier in the *Acharnians* of Aristophanes. In 415 he was appointed with Alcibiades and Nicias to conduct the expedition to Sicily. He advocated an immediate attack on Syracuse, but failed to convince his colleagues. The rapid progress of the Athenian blockade in 414 seems to have been largely due to his energetic leadership; it terminated abruptly when he was killed in a skirmish. Aristophanes in later plays pays tributes to his heroism.

Thucydides, bk. 6. H. D. W.

**LAMBAESIS** (modern *Lambèse*), a Roman camp in Numidia north of the Aurès range, is attested in A.D. 81 (*AE* 1954, 137; cf. *Libyca* 1953, 189 ff.). Under Trajan the Legio III Augusta there controlled the route which led north from the Sahara through Vescera (*Biskra*) and Calceus Herculis (*El Kantara*). Military roads enabled the legate to reinforce the auxiliaries in Numidia and the Mauretanias. Hadrian visited Lambaesis (A.D. 128); his address to the troops was inscribed on a column, and much of it survives (Dessau, *ILS* 2487 and 9133–5). The legion was disbanded by Gordian III (238), but Valerian restored it to its old quarters (253).

Lambaesis is the finest example of a Roman fortified camp extant. It contains an *arcus quadrifrons* (usually called the *praetorium*), legionary headquarters, offices, storerooms, chapels, messrooms, baths, and latrines. Platforms along the walls served as artillery emplacements, and at the four corners are rounded re-entrant towers. An amphitheatre was built outside the walls, and married-quarters were erected after Septimius' army reforms; these grew into a substantial town with its own baths, arches, and temples. W. N. W.

**LAMIA** (1), a child-stealing nursery bogey, Ar. *Vesp.* 1035 = *Pax* 758 (where she is apparently bisexual) and often. The schol. on *Pax* says she was daughter of Belus and Libya (*see* DANAUS), whose children Hera destroyed because Zeus was her lover, whereat she became savage with grief; more refs. in Roscher's *Lexikon* ii. 1819. For a later conception of her see Philostr. *VA* 4. 25. H. J. R.

**LAMIA** (2), the principal city of Malis, commanding the chief route from Thessaly to central Greece. It did not exist, or was an insignificant village, until the close of the fifth century. Thereafter it became increasingly important, especially after Spartan control of Heraclea (q.v. 4) terminated. During the Greek rising against Macedonia after the death of Alexander an army under Antipater was besieged at Lamia. Its strong fortifications helped him to resist the Greeks throughout the winter of 323/2. In the third century the city reached the height of its prosperity under Aetolian hegemony, but in 190 it was sacked by Acilius Glabrio.

Y. Béquignon, *La Vallée du Spercheios* (1937). H. D. W.

**LAMPADIO**, GAIUS OCTAVIUS, a Roman scholar of the second century B.C., prompted by the influence of Crates of Mallos to take a literary interest in early Latin poets (Suet. *Gram.* 2). He arranged in seven books the *Bellum Punicum* of Naevius.

**LAMPOON** (GREEK). The tradition of abusive and satirical verse seems to have been indigenous to the Greeks. An early example can be seen in the verses with which Archilochus assailed Lycambes, or later those with which Hipponax attacked Bupalus. The form was recognized by the word ἴαμβος, used for any poetry which abused (cf. Procl. ap. Phot. *Bibl.* 321 a 28, Ael. *VH* 3. 40, Poll. 2. 54). Hence it was applied to the satirical verses of Xenophanes and Timon. *See also* ALCAEUS (3) OF MESSENE. C. M. B.

**LAMPROCLES** (early 5th c. B.C.), Athenian musician and poet, teacher of Damon (schol. Pl. *Alc.* 118 c), exponent of the mixo-Lydian mode (Plut. *De mus.* 16), composer of dithyrambs (Ath. 491 c) and of a famous hymn to Athene quoted by Aristophanes (*Nub.* 967).

TEXT. Page, *Poet. Mel. Gr.* 379 f.
CRITICISM. U. von Wilamowitz-Moellendorff, *Textg. d. gr. Lyr.* (1900), 84 f. C. M. B.

**LAMPS** (λύχνος, *lucerna*) were used not only to illumine interiors and shop exteriors, but as votive offerings to deities and as tomb-furniture. The commonest materials were bronze and clay, and olive oil the usual fuel (*see* LIGHTING). Middle and Late Minoan clay and stone lamps are plentiful, usually having unbridged nozzles, and certain handled, open vessels from Mycenaean sites have been described as lamps, but recognizable lamps

appear only on the fringes of the Mycenaean world, in places, like Cyprus, close to the lamp-using countries of the East. Homer has only a single reference to lamps (*Od.* 19. 34), and after the Bronze Age there are no identifiable lamps in Greece until the early seventh century B.C. when 'cocked-hat' lamps of Athenian manufacture are found, deriving from Eastern examples, the production of which, in Palestine, continued with only cultural breaks, from about 2000 B.C. In Italy outside the Greek cities the use of lamps, apart from some isolated Etruscan examples, does not begin before the third century. The more efficient bridged nozzle was introduced, probably in Asia Minor or the Islands, towards the end of the seventh century. Thereafter the Greek wheel-made lamp has a tendency to become less open and shallow. Athens would appear to be the main innovator of new forms; these products were exported and copied over much of the Greek world. Mould-made lamps, with greater possibilities for different shapes and decorative features were introduced at the beginning of the third century B.C. Hellenistic moulded lamps, decorated on their wide shoulders, died out in the first century A.D. when the new Italian lamps, with dished tops bearing relief pictures, swamped the market and were copied everywhere. Elaborate specimens with many nozzles are not uncommon, while the forms of the metal lamps are extremely varied. Clay lamps modelled in a great variety of plastic forms are found from the third century B.C. through to the later Empire. In the second and third centuries A.D. there was a revival of high-quality lamps in Corinth and Athens, and the Italian lamps degenerated. From the fourth century the finest lamps were produced in North Africa, probably near Carthage, and Christian symbolism becomes common. After the sixth century few lamps of good workmanship were produced, except in Palestine and Egypt.

H. B. Walters, *British Museum Catalogue of Lamps* (1914); O. Broneer, *Corinth* iv. 2 (1930); S. Loeschcke, *Lampen aus Vindonissa* (1919); R. H. Howland, *Athenian Agora* iv (1958); J. Perlzweig, *Athenian Agora* vii (1961). D. M. B.

**LAMPSACUS,** a Phocaean foundation in the northern Troad with a good harbour. Its strategic position guarding the eastern entrance to the Hellespont explains the city's economic prosperity and historical significance. Hence, too, sprang its attempt to check the elder Miltiades' domination of the Chersonese. In the sixth and fifth centuries Lampsacus passed successively under Lydian, Persian, Athenian, and Spartan control. It was assigned by Artaxerxes I to Themistocles, whom it supplied with the wine for which it was famous. Its tribute of twelve talents as a member of the Delian League, and its gold coinage in the fourth century, attest its commercial well-being. Attempts to assert its independence against Persia and Athens were quickly repressed, but in the fourth century Lampsacus enjoyed long periods of self-government. Its prosperity continued during the Hellenistic age and under the Roman Republic (Cic. 2 *Verr.* i. 24. 63) and Empire.

W. Leaf, *Strabo on the Troad* (1923), 92. D. E. W. W.

**LANUVIUM,** modern *Lanuvio*, an ancient Latin city in the Alban Hills (Cato fr. 58 P.; Strabo 5. 239). In 338 B.C. Rome dissolved the Latin League, granted Lanuvium Roman citizenship, and officially adopted its famous cult of Juno Sospes (Livy 8. 14; Cic. *Nat. D.* 1. 83: for ancient remains, G. Bendinelli, *Mon. Ant.* 1922, 292). Although it suffered in the Civil Wars (App. *BCiv.* 5. 24), Lanuvium, unlike many Latian towns, continued to flourish even in imperial times (however, reject *Lib. Colon.* 235). Milo, Roscius, and Antoninus Pius were born there (Cic. *Mil.* 27; *Div.* 36; S.H.A. *Ant. Pius* 1;

*Comm.* 1). Lanuvium was often confused with Lavinium (q.v.): hence its medieval name *Civita Lavinia*.

G. B. Colburn, *AJArch.* 1914; A. E. Gordon, *Cults of Lanuvium* (U.S.A. 1938). E. T. S.

**LAOCOÖN,** a legendary Trojan prince, brother of Anchises and priest of the Thymbraean Apollo or (in some accounts) of Poseidon. Of his story as it was told by Arctinus in the *Iliupersis*, by Bacchylides, and by Sophocles in a tragedy bearing his name we know little. According to the generally accepted tale (Verg. *Aen.* 2. 40–56, 199–231; Apollod. *Epit.* 5. 17–18), he protested against the proposal to draw the Wooden Horse within the walls of Troy, and two great serpents coming over the sea from the island of Tenedos killed him and his two sons (in Arctinus one son, in Quint. Smyrn. 12. 444–97 Laocoön himself escaped). According to Hyginus (*Fab.* 135. 1) the serpents were sent by Apollo to punish him for having married in spite of his priesthood, in Quint. Smyrn. and Virgil, by Athena on account of his hostile attitude to the Horse. The story is famous not only from the dramatic pathos of Virgil's rendering, but as the subject of one of the most famous examples of ancient sculpture, the marble group now in the Vatican which depicts father and two sons in their death-agony. This, a masterpiece of the Pergamene school, was the work of three Rhodian sculptors, Agesander, Polydorus, and Athenodorus, of the second half of the first century. In Roman times it was exhibited in the palace of the Emperor Titus, and in Pliny's view (*HN* 36. 37) surpassed all other works of painting and sculpture. Lessing made it the text for his famous essay of 1766 on the difference between poetry and the fine arts.

H. Kleinknecht, *Hermes* 1944, 66 ff. R. A. B. M.

**LAODICE** (1), in mythology, a stock name for women of high rank, meaning 'princess' (cf. CREON, CREUSA), e.g. (*a*) a daughter of Priam, *see* ACAMAS, DEMOPHON, (*b*) a daughter of Agapenor (q.v.); she founded the temple of Paphian Aphrodite in Tegea (Paus. 8. 53. 7, cf. 5. 3); (*c*) daughter of Agamemnon (*Il.* 9. 145), later replaced by Electra (q.v. 3). H. J. R.

**LAODICE** (2), probably a niece of Antiochus I (q.v.), married her cousin Antiochus II (q.v.), by whom she had two sons and two or three daughters. Antiochus repudiated her and her children in favour of Berenice (daughter of Ptolemy II), whose son (b. 251 B.C.) became heir-apparent. The result, when Antiochus died, was a war of succession, in which Egypt supported Berenice's son ('Third Syrian', or 'Laodicean War', 246–241), though Ptolemy III's expedition in Asia did not prevent mother and son from being killed by Laodice's supporters. Tradition gives Laodice a share in inspiring and organizing the resistance (especially in Asia Minor) which enabled her elder son to succeed as Seleucus II.

W. W. Tarn, *CAH* vii, 715 ff.; W. Otto, *Beiträge zur Seleukidengeschichte des 3. Jahrhunderts v. Chr.* (1928), 48 ff. G. T. G.

**LAODICEA AD LYCUM** (Λαοδίκεια ἐπὶ Λύκῳ, also called Λ. τῆς Ἀσίας), a city founded by Antiochus II (261–246 B.C.) and called after his wife Laodice (q.v. 2). It occupied the site of an older city on a flat hill overlooking the valley of the Lycus a few miles east of its junction with the Maeander; its territory was bounded by the rivers Λύκος and Κάπρος, symbolized as Wolf and Boar on its coins. It lay on a great trade-route and was one of the most prosperous cities in Asia; it was the head of a *conventus* and one of the 'Seven Churches' of the Apocalypse. Diocletian made it the *metropolis* of the province of Phrygia. W. M. C.

**LAOMEDON,** legendary king of Troy, for whose genealogy *see* DARDANUS. For his relations with Heracles *see* HERACLES; for his dealings with Apollo and Poseidon *see* ibid. Apart from this he has little place in mythology, the most interesting feature of his legend being the story of his grave, which lay over the Scaean Gate and ensured the safety of the city so long as it was undisturbed (Servius on *Aen.* 2. 241, cf. Plaut. *Bacch.* 955; see W. F. J. Knight in *CJ* 1933. 257 ff., cf. the tomb of Aitolos in Elis, Paus. 5. 4. 4). This undoubtedly refers to some kind of magical precaution, whether or not originally associated with Troy.

**LARCIUS ( ? LARGIUS) LICINUS** (1st c. A.D.) wrote a *Cicero-mastix*. Its reprehensible audacity in criticizing the orator is coupled by Gellius (17. 1. 1) with that of Asinius Gallus.

**LARES** (older **LASES,** Arval hymn; Henzen, *Acta Arualium*, cciv. 33). The etymology and consequently the connexion, if any, with the names Larentia (Acca, q.v.), Larunda, Lara, and Etruscan Lasa and Larth are very uncertain (Boehm, op. cit. *infra*, 806 f.). As to their origin there are two principal theories, supported respectively by Samter and by Wissowa, W. Warde Fowler, and K. Latte.

(1) They are the ghosts of the dead. Samter starts from the *Lar familiaris*, and supposes him closely connected with the cult of the dead, because (*a*) if a bit of food falls on the floor during a meal, it is proper to burn it before the Lares (Pliny, *HN* 28. 27; see X. F. M. G. Wolters, *Antique Folklore* (1935), 96 ff., but *contra*, Rose, *Gnomon* 1936, 390). Now the floor is a notorious haunt of ghosts; the food, therefore, has gone to the ghosts' region and so is formally given to the ghosts. (*b*) At the Compitalia, or festival of the cross-roads (cross-roads being again a favourite place for ghosts, cf. HECATE), it was the custom to hang up a male or female puppet for each free member of a household, a ball for each slave (Festus, 272. 15 Lindsay, cf. 108. 27; 273. 7), that the Lares, says Festus, might spare the living and take these surrogates instead. This is a quite reasonable precaution against ghosts. (*c*) The connexion, which he assumes, with Larentia and the Larentalia definitely connects them with chthonian ritual.

(2) Wissowa points out that the Roman dead are honoured not in the house but at their graves; the hearth is the place of Vesta and the *di Penates* (qq.v.), and the *Lar* (*familiaris*), a later intruder. The ceremonial at the cross-roads is easily enough explained when it is remembered that a *compitum* is properly and originally the place where the paths separating four farms meet (Gromatici, 302. 20 ff., Lachmann; schol. Pers. 4. 28). This has no ghostly associations, but it regularly had a chapel of the Lares, and Latte would explain the rite as a purification, not a sacrifice. That the *Lar familiaris* (Lar of the servants, rather than of the household generally, in origin) was brought into the house by the farm-slaves is likely, cf. Warde Fowler, *Roman Essays* (1920), 61.

The Lares, then, are originally deities of the farm-land. From this, and from the secondary cult in the houses, they expand (apart from purely theoretical developments of the use of their name to signify ghost or *daimon*) (1) into guardians of any cross-way, including one in a city. Hence grew up in Rome the *collegia compitalicia*, associations of humble people, mostly freedmen, who tended the shrines, and their festival. These were restored by Augustus, with the addition of his own Genius (q.v.; Ov. *Fasti* 5. 145, Suet. *Aug.* 31. 3 with Latte, op. cit. 307); (2) into guardians of roads and wayfarers, *Lares uiales*, including travellers by sea, *Lares permarini*; (3) into guardians of the State in general, *Lares praestites*; see especially Wissowa, *Ges. Abh.*, 274 ff.; Ovid, ibid. 129 ff., and Frazer thereon.

Like all Roman deities the Lares have no mythology. Ovid (*Fasti* 2. 599 ff.) has a story of their begetting by Mercurius on Lara, manifestly a late invention and quite possibly his own. For another alleged mother *see* MANIA. In one version (Pliny, *HN* 36. 204) of the wonderful birth of Servius (q.v. 1) Tullius his father is the *Lar familiaris*; a late anthropomorphizing (for a different one see Ovid, *Fasti* 6. 627) of an old folk-tale, that he or some other remarkable person was born of a woman fertilized by the fire.

Since the cult of the *Lar familiaris*, whatever its origin, became universal (see for many examples in popular art G. K. Boyce in *Amer. Acad. Rome* 1937), *lar* or *lares* is used like *penates*, by metonymy for 'home', 'house'; *lararium* is 'private chapel'.

Latte, *RR* 90 ff.  H. J. R.

**LARINUM,** town near the Adriatic immediately north of Apulia (q.v.): modern *Larino*. The Larinates were ethnically identical with, but politically independent of, the neighbouring Frentani (q.v.). A wool trading centre, Larinum witnessed several of the Hannibalic War operations, but is chiefly celebrated for its notorious cases of murder (*see* CLUENTIUS).  E. T. S.

**LARISSA,** the principal city of Thessaly, dominating the fertile plain of Pelasgiotis, with an acropolis on a low hill protected by the river Peneus. It was the first Thessalian city to strike coins, and its earliest issues, struck on the Persian standard, reflect both the medism of the Aleuadae (q.v.) and their influence over the Larisseans. In the second half of the fifth century the city was weakened politically by conflicts between rival factions but apparently continued its economic prosperity. From the end of the fifth century, although it formed the centre of aristocratic opposition to the tyrants of Pherae, its efforts were seldom successful without external support. Jason won Larissa before 374, but it resisted his successors by enlisting aid first from Thebes and later from Philip of Macedon. This policy led to the Macedonian annexation of Thessaly, and Larissa remained in Macedonian hands until liberated by Rome in 196, after which it became the capital of the new Thessalian Confederacy and enjoyed considerable prosperity.

F. Stählin, *Das hellenische Thessalien* (1924), 94 ff.  H. D. W.

**LĀRUNDA,** an extremely obscure Roman goddess, said to be Sabine (Varro, *Ling.* 5. 74, cf. E. C. Evans, *Cults of the Sabine Territory* (1939), 227 ff.), and generally supposed to be chthonian (Wissowa, *RK* 234). She was honoured with an annual sacrifice on Dec. 23 at an altar in the Velabrum. The quantity of the first syllable (known from Ausonius, *Technop.* 8. 9 (p. 161 Peiper), 'nec genius domuum, Larunda progenitus Lar') suggests a possible connexion with Acca Larentia (q.v.). The ancients equate her with Lāra, said by Ovid (*Fasti* 2. 599 ff.) to be mother of the Lāres (see Frazer ad loc.; Lactantius, *Div. Inst.* 1. 20. 35). The quantity, however, is against this. Probably this identification is meant by Philoxenus, 225 (LA 66), Lindsay–Laistner, *Larunda*: δαιμόνων μήτηρ, cf. [Placidus], 66 (L 15) Lindsay–Pirie, 'Larunda: quam quidam Maniam dicunt', but the reading is doubtful. If right, cf. Varro, *Ling.* 9. 61, 'uidemus enim Maniam matrem Larum dici'. For the Mother of the Lares cf. Henzen, *Act. Arval.* 145, and add Dessau, *ILS* 9522, on which see L. R. Taylor in *AJArch.* 1935, 299 ff.; E. Tabeling, *Mater Larum* (1932). The most probable explanation of the occurrence of this un-Roman genealogy in a sacral document is that it had been affected

by the theories mentioned above. On the whole question, see Latte, *RR* 92.  H. J. R.

**LASUS** (b. *c.* 548–545 B.C., *Suda*), son of Charminus, of Hermione, lived at the court of Hipparchus, where he disclosed the forgeries of Onomacritus (Hdt. 7. 6). Rival of Simonides (schol. Ar. *Vesp.* 1410), he composed hymns (Ath. 467 a, 624 e) and dithyrambs, of which he was a pioneer in Athens (schol. Pind. *Ol.* 13. 25; schol. Ar. *Av.* 1403; Clem. Al. *Strom.* 1. 16).

TEXT. Page, *Poet. Mel. Gr.* 364 ff.  C. M. B.

**LATIFUNDIA.** It was a characteristic of ancient Oriental large estates that commercial, industrial, and lending enterprises were interrelated with agriculture. The primitive serf estates of Linear B Hellas and of archaic Greece and Italy were broken up, except in backward countries like Thessaly, as a consequence of democratic movements. Imitation of the *ergasterion* (*see* INDUSTRY), however, led to a new slave estate in classical Greece, which was larger than the normal peasant holdings, used scientific handbooks on agriculture, and produced with a view to high profit. The Hellenistic large estates and the Italian *latifundia* originated in a blending of Oriental and Greek estate systems in Hellenistic and, probably, Carthaginian territories. The division of labour and the wide economic activities of Oriental estates were preserved, and very cheap labour became most important. Hellenistic estates like the *dorea* ('concession') of Ptolemy II's minister Apollonius (q.v. 3) used more free workmen than slaves, in spite of being actively engaged in the slave trade. The West exploited cheap slave labour with an unrivalled mercenary spirit and cruelty.

The Roman *latifundium* originated in distributions of the *ager publicus* in the early second century B.C., as soon as the wealth of the Roman upper class had sufficiently increased to imitate Eastern landlords. The *villa* with its slave *familia* was much stronger economically than the surrounding peasants, because only large owners had capital for introducing new crops and breeds. In consequence, a large number of peasants in Italy and even in the provinces lost their homesteads. *Latifundia*, with *villa urbana*, *villa rustica*, *instrumentum vocale* (= slaves), *semivocale* (= cattle), and *mutum* (furniture and implements) became characteristic of all Roman provinces.

A change came as soon as slave labour ceased to be cheap, and the *familia* gave way to the *colonus*, who learned all the methods of *latifundium* agriculture useful to him. A new type of large estate arose after A.D. 100 or so, the *patrocinium*, which later became a model for the Middle Ages. Most of the soil was in the hands of *coloni*, who cultivated small tracts in accordance with the teachings of Cato (1), Varro (2), and Columella (qq.v.), as far as the economic situation permitted. Enterprises in trade, craftsmanship, and banking, as well as small garrisons, remained on the estates. These Late Roman estates, together with State and Church institutions, remained as islands of classical culture culture and experience during the difficult times of the Germanic, Slavic, and Islamic conquests. *See* AGER PUBLICUS, AGRICULTURE, COLONUS, GRACCHUS (3, 4), PASTURAGE, VILLA.

F. M. Heichelheim, *Kl. Pauly*, s.vv. 'Bauernstand', 'Collatio'. 'Grundbuch', Hektemoroi, 'Idios Logos', 'Indictio', 'Leges Agrariae'.  F. M. H.

**LATIN, CHRISTIAN.** The notion that the early Christian communities of the Roman world brought into being a distinct category of Latinity, which subsequently passed into general current usage, was put forward by Mgr. J. Schrijnen of the University of Nijmegen in his *Charakteristik des altchristlichen Latein* (1932). His pupils, notably Professor Christine Mohrmann, of the Nijmegen School of Christian Latin Studies, have done much to propagate Schrijnen's theory by publishing an extensive series of monographs on the language of the Church Fathers.

However, the term 'Christian Latin' must be used with some reserve. The early Christians were charged by their antagonists with being a *latebrosa et lucifuga natio, in publicum muta, in angulis garrula* (Min. Fel. *Oct.* 8). Such remarks may be regarded as hostile propaganda. The Christians were also suspect because of their weekly assemblies (Pliny, *Tra.* 96) which appeared to violate the ban on *collegia*. But to argue from this that the Christians formed closed communities, living apart from their non-Christian neighbours, is unrealistic. They belonged largely to the lower orders, among whom they had to pursue their daily tasks, while many of them were slaves for whom segregation from the rest of the *familia* was clearly impossible.

It is therefore rash to maintain that Christian Latin was a *Sondersprache*, if this is meant to have syntactical or even merely stylistic implications. Much has been made of the Grecisms prevalent in the language of the Christian writers. It is true that the Latin versions of the Scriptures have many echoes of the Greek (as also of the Hebrew) originals and that these were the only reading which many Christians permitted themselves (the style of the authoress of the *Itinerarium Egeriae* (q.v.) is completely dominated by the Scriptures); but this would not make for a Latin markedly different from the Graeco-Latin of say the freedmen in Petronius' *Cena Trimalchionis*. There is no evidence that the speech of the unlettered majority of Latin speakers converted to the new Faith was anything but the *sermo plebeius* of imperial times, which already had a strong admixture of Greek, especially as regards vocabulary.

In fact, the researches of the Nijmegen School are largely concerned with lexicology, and it is upon this that their *Sondersprache* rests. 'Christian Latin' owes what specific character it possesses to the large number of loan-words from the Greek Bible and from the Greek technical language of liturgy and exegesis (*angelus, diabolus, episcopus, ecclesia, presbyter*) and also to a number of Latin words which acquired new, specifically Christian meanings, like *orare* ('to pray'), *gratia* ('grace'), *sacramentum* ('sacrament'), *saeculum* ('the world'), *caritas* ('love').

The Church Fathers, even those well acquainted with the pagan classics, like Augustine, Jerome, Ambrose, and Lactantius, could on occasion write a Latin close to the popular idiom, while the language of the Vetus Latina and Vulgate versions shows morphological and syntactical phenomena such as change of gender and conjugation, increased use of prepositions to combat the breakdown of case endings, extensive compounding of nouns, verbs, adjectives, and adverbs, replacement of the accusative and infinitive by *quod, quia, quoniam*, etc., all of which are found equally in the pagan writers and mark the evolution of the living Latin towards Romance.

See J. Schrijnen, *Charakteristik des altchr. Latein* (Nijmegen, 1932); Chr. Mohrmann, *Études sur le latin des Chrétiens* i–iii (Rome, 1961–5); also the series *Latinitas Christianorum Primaeva*, Nijmegen (some twenty fascicles since 1932); numerous articles in *Vigiliae Christianae* and *Revue Bénédictine*; L. R. Palmer, *The Latin Language* (1954), ch. 7.                                                    P. B. C.

**LATIN LANGUAGE.** Latin was originally the language of the city of Rome and the Latian plain, and it was only as Rome's power extended that her language spread itself over the ancient Western world. It belongs to the Italic branch of the Indo-European family of languages and is thus akin to Greek, Germanic, Celtic, etc.; within Italy its nearest relative is Faliscan, and next

are the Italic dialects proper, Oscan and Umbrian (qq.v.). When and whence Italic came into Italy cannot be stated exactly, but it presumably came over the Alps and Apennines from somewhere in Europe before the eighth century B.C. Besides the numerous Italic dialects there were in Italy also Greek in the south and on the coast, Celtic in the north, and the non-Indo-European language of Etruria. All these exerted more or less influence upon Latin. Borrowings from Celtic were confined to a few words, e.g. *petorritum, gaesum, carrus*, and the Greek influence, though considerable, did not come in till late. From Etruscan came names such as *Sulla, Casca*, and many with an -*n*-suffix, e.g. *Perpenna, Sisenna, Maecenas*. Etruscan also are technical terms such as *histrio, subulo, persona, puteal, camillus*, and perhaps even such common words as *urbs* and *amare* (infinitive). The substitution of breathed for voiced sounds in words like *sporta* (< σπυρίδα), *catamitus* (< Γανυμήδης), the aspirate in names like *Gracchus, Cethegus*, and the weakening or disappearance of syllables which resulted from the shifting of the word-accent as in *Pollux* (< Πολυδεύκης) are probably due to Etruscan. This theory receives support from the Etruscan names of the old Latin tribes, *Ramnes, Tities, Luceres* (cf. *lucumo*), and it is now generally accepted that the Latin alphabet is derived not directly from Greek but is partly of Etruscan origin.

**2.** Outside Italy the Italic group (including Latin) has its closest affinity with Celtic, and the number of morphological innovations which both groups share gives much plausibility to the theory that their pre-ethnic speakers must have lived in close association after the separation of the Indo-European peoples. Both groups show

(a) extension of the abstract-noun stems in -*ti*- by an -*n*-suffix, e.g. *men-ti-on-em*;

(b) superlative formation in -*sṃmos*, e.g. *aegerrimus* (< *aegr-isṃmos*);

(c) genit. sing. of -*o*-stems in -*ī*: e.g. *filī*, OIr *magi*;

(d) medio-passive formation in -*r*: *sequitur* = Ir. *sechedar*;

Both Celtic and Italic are divided into two sub-families, a Goidelic and Brythonic, and an Oscan-Umbrian and a Latin-Faliscan respectively, which differ in the same way in their treatment of Indo-European *q*. Thus Latin has *quod, quinque* while Oscan has *pod, pompe*: Irish has *coic* (five), Welsh *pump*; Gaelic has *Mac* (e.g. MacDonald), Welsh *Ap* (e.g. Powell < Ap Howell).

**3.** The most striking feature of Latin is its accentuation. In Indo-European the accent was predominantly *musical* and was unrestricted. In the historical period of Latin, while remaining *musical*, it was restricted by the trisyllabic law dependent on the quantity of the penult. In the intervening period, however, it became strongly *stress* and shifted to the first syllable of the word. This resulted in the transformation of words by

(a) syncope: *ardere, audere* (cf. *aridus, avidus*);

(b) umlaut: *teneo, capio* (cf. *retineo, retentum; incipio, inceptum*);

(c) iambic shortening: *benĕ, vidĕ* (cf. *rectē, audē*).

Thus all short vowels in open position in medial syllables either disappeared or were narrowed to *i* or *ĕ*, and diphthongs became monophthongs, e.g. *caedo, claudo* (cf. *occido, exclūdo*).

**4.** Other vocalic changes were the reduction of (accented) diphthongs *ai, ei, oi, eu*, e.g. *aedes* (αἴθω), *dico* (δείκνυμι), *ūnus* (οἶνη), *iumentum* (ζεῦγος).

**5.** Of the consonants original *i* and *u* were lost very early, the former between any two vowels (e.g. *tres* < *treies*), the latter between two similar vowels if the first was accented, e.g. *audiī* < *audīvi* (but not in *amāvi* or *avārus*). Where *i* occurs between vowels it equals *ij*, e.g. *Maia*. Initially *du*- became *b*-, e.g. *bis* (cf. *duo*). In the second century A.D. Latin *v* (pronounced *w*) came to be sounded like English *v* (cf. *vox*, Fr. *voix*), and Latin *b* in certain positions developed the same sound (cf. *habere*, Fr. *avoir*). Hence late spellings like *Bictorinus, birtus*. Between 450 and 350 B.C. intervocalic *-s-* became *-r-*, e.g. *gero*: *gestum*. Therefore, words such as *rosa, miser* are non-Latin, while in *causa, fisus* there was originally not *-s-* but *-ss-*.

6. The chief innovations in morphology are:
(*a*) loss of the dual number;
(*b*) new forms of genitive singular and nominative plural in *-o-* and *-ā-* stems;
(*c*) new adverbial forms in *-ē-*, *-m*, *-iter*;
(*d*) rise of the so-called 5th declension;
(*e*) confusion of consonantal stems with stems in *ĭ-* and the disuse of the *u* declension in adjectives, e.g. ἡδύς but *suavis*;
(*f*) confusion of primary and secondary personal terminations in the verb;
(*g*) almost complete disappearance of non-thematic conjugations;
(*h*) fusion of aorist and perfect forms and of active and middle endings in what we call the perfect;
(*i*) complete fusion of conjunctive and optative into one mood.

7. Latin syntax has restricted case-usage more sharply than Greek except in the ablative, which combined ablative, locative, and sociative-instrumental uses from which developed the characteristically Latin ablative absolute. In the verb there is a great extension of the subjunctive, particularly in dependent clauses, and a very complex and strict system of *oratio obliqua* and sequence of tenses.

8. As a vehicle of literature Latin, unlike Greek, appears at first as crude and unpolished in both verse and prose. The pioneer efforts of Ennius, however, to graft on Latin the artistic excellences of Greek were ably seconded by Lucretius and Catullus and culminate in the full glory of Latin poetry in the *Aeneid* of Virgil and of prose in the resonant periods of Cicero and the rich smoothness of Livy. The rhetorical style reaches its height in the Ovidian elegiac and the brilliant epigram of Tacitus. In the hands of the greatest masters Latin was shown to be the worthy vehicle of the thought of a great imperial race.

A. Meillet, *Esquisse d'une histoire de la langue latine*⁴ (1938); Stolz–Schmalz, *Lateinische Grammatik*, 5th ed. by Leumann–Hofmann (Müller's Handbuch, 1928); J. Marouzeau, *Le Latin*² (1927); L. R. Palmer, *The Latin Language* (1954).      P. S. N.

**LATIN, SILVER.** The period of Silver Latin is broadly from A.D. 17 to 130, but the literary decline which marks it began even before Livy's death. The loss of political liberty and the practice of barren declamation led to a striving after novelty in which forced expression, exaggerated emphasis, antithesis, and epigram were cultivated for the express purpose of winning applause. Though the diction of Seneca is still fairly classical, all these faults abound in his works, and thereafter the same vein of rhetoric runs through the literature, reaching its height in Tacitus, the greatest of Silver writers. Quintilian has well summarized its faults when he says (book 8 proem) 'nihil iam proprium placet, dum parum creditur disertum, quod et alius dixisset' and 'tum demum ingeniosi scilicet, si ad intelligendos nos opus sit ingenio'. The chief features of Silver Latin are:
(1) words borrowed for prose from the poets, especially Virgil;
(2) words in new (frequently poetical) meanings;
(3) new formations of agent-nouns in *-tor*, *-sor*, and abstracts in *-sus*, *-ura*, *-mentum*;
(4) as in poetry, use of simple instead of compound verbs;

(5) freer use of cases, e.g. dative of purpose, ablative of separation without preposition, ablative of duration of time, instrumental ablative even of persons, etc.;
(6) present and perfect subjunctive in *oratio obliqua* after secondary tenses;
(7) subjunctive of indefinite frequency and its extension to relative conjunctions;
(8) interchange of *quin* and *quominus*;
(9) *quamvis, quanquam* with subjunctive even when denoting facts;
(10) *tanquam, quasi, velut* to express, not comparison, but alleged reason.      P. S. N.

**LATIN, SPOKEN.** Colloquial Latin (*sermo cotidianus*) means the easy everyday Latin of cultured people in which, as Quintilian says, 'cum amicis, coniugibus, liberis, seruis loquimur'. The plays of Plautus and Terence are written mostly in this style, just as in a modern comedy of manners the language is the ordinary speech of polite society. Thus Cicero tells us that the speech of nobly born Roman ladies, e.g. Laelia, was strongly reminiscent of the language of Plautus, and Terence has always been considered a model of familiar, but elegant, latinity. Particularly important are the letters of Cicero, especially those written to his 'second-self' Atticus, or, e.g., to Paetus, to whom he says: 'Quid tibi uideor in epistulis? nonne plebeio sermone agere tecum? epistulas uero cotidianis uerbis texere solemus.' Characteristic features of this style are (1) the frequency of diminutives; (2) interjections; (3) very free syntax; (4) use of Greek words and tags, as we nowadays use French; (5) wide use of forms intensified by *per-* or weakened by *sub-*, e.g. *subinuidere*. The same style in verse is found in Horace's *Satires* and *Epistles*, and there are occasional lapses into colloquialism in other writers, e.g. Catullus. On a somewhat lower level are the *Bellum Africanum* and *Bellum Hispaniense*, while in the *De Architectura* of Vitruvius we have what might be called the Latin of business life. Very important, too, is the *Satyricon* of Petronius with its descending scale of urbanity from the cultured familiarity of Encolpius to the coarse vulgarity of Echion and Habinnas.

J. B. Hofmann, *Lateinische Umgangssprache*, 1925 (2nd ed. with additions 1936); L. R. Palmer, *The Latin Language* (1954).      P. S. N.

**LATIN, VULGAR.** Vulgar Latin is that form of the Latin language which was used by the uneducated classes in Italy and the provinces. We know it from (1) inscriptions, (2) a few texts such as the *Satyricon* of Petronius, *Itinerarium Egeriae*, *Mulomedicina Chironis*, *Appendix Probi*, and (3) the early development of the Romance languages. It differs from classical Latin mainly in a disregard of seemingly unnecessary distinctions, a desire for greater regularity in word-form, and a striving after emphasis. Vowels are slurred and confused, final *-m*, *-s*, *-t* are dropped, *b* is confused with *v*, *s* with *x*; hence forms like *oli, plevis, milex*. Analogy creates *nura, aprus, acrum*, and syncope *veclus, oclus, virdis, frigda*. *Caelus* and *caelum* are pronounced *caelo*, whence confusion of gender (e.g. *vinus, fatus*); and the break-up of declension leads to a greatly increased use of prepositions (e.g. *ab + ante*, *de + intus*). The infinitive and accusative construction disappears in favour of clauses with *quia, quoniam, ut*; and new perfect and future tenses are formed by auxiliary verbs, *habere, debere*, e.g. *qui nasci habent* (= *nascentur*). There is great activity in word-composition, especially diminutives of nouns (e.g. *ossucula, oricla, audaculus*) and frequentatives and intensives of verbs (e.g. *ausare, contenebricare*). Many common words become obsolete and are replaced by others, e.g. *magnus*, *ĕdere, ludus, senex, ignis, ferre, emere* by *grandis, manducare, iocus, vetulus, focus, portare, comparare.* Finally, the word-order of Vulgar Latin is simpler and more rational, e.g. 'Haec est autem vallis ingens et planissima, in qua filii Israhel commorati sunt his diebus, quod sanctus Moyses ascendit in montem Domini' (*Itinerarium Egeriae,* 2. 2).

V. Väänänen, *Le Latin vulgaire des inscriptions pompeiennes* (Berlin, 1958); G. Rohlfs, *Sermo vulgaris latinus* (Tübingen, 1956); L. R. Palmer, *The Latin Language* (1954). P. S. N.

**LATINI.** The inhabitants of the plain of Latium—a people of mixed stock, predominantly 'cremators' but including a late wave of 'inhumators'—lived originally in numerous small communities, *populi*, which gradually coalesced or were forcibly amalgamated between the sixth and fourth centuries B.C. into larger States, the greatest of which was Rome. The *populi* formed confederations for religious purposes. The largest was the cult-group of Jupiter Latiaris on the Alban Mount, the presidency of which passed early to Rome but was of no political significance. The 'league of Ferentina', based on a shrine of Diana in the territory of Aricia, was from the sixth to the fourth century the political centre of all Latium, where the representatives of the independent *populi* deliberated on equal terms, elected federal officers, and decided on joint policy. These conditions, interrupted by the partial ascendancy of the Etruscan kings of Rome, were reaffirmed by the Cassian treaty (*see* CASSIUS 1) and continued during the troubled period of the fifth century till, in the fourth, Rome began to encroach seriously on her neighbours. Eventually, in 338, Rome incorporated the smaller States and reduced the larger to subject allies. The characteristics of the later Latin Name were fixed in this early period by the continuous tradition of social and political equality between the Latins. Even the establishment of federal colonies drawn from all the Latin peoples, and the sharing of booty won in federal wars, persisted unchanged after 338 (*see* IUS LATII, COMMERCIUM). Henceforth the Latin Name consisted of the few remaining *populi Latini* and an ever-growing number of Latin colonies, of which the man-power was increasingly drawn from Rome. These colonies were autonomous States subject to Rome only in foreign policy, but dependent for their existence upon the Roman law establishing them. This autonomy remained unchallenged even when Rome in the second century assumed the supervision of all Italy, since her edicts were only advisory. The Latin Name provided Rome with numerous troops *e formula togatorum*, and garrisoned Italy at strategic points with loyal colonies. The Latins by their origin and special social position formed an intermediate category between Romans and the foreign *socii Italici* (*see* SOCII), and were commonly associated by Rome in many material privileges with Roman citizens. Though in 209 twelve colonies objected to the strain of continuous military service and were later punished (but not by diminution of civic rights), the Latins remained continuously loyal till the abuse by Roman commanders of their *imperium* at the expense of individual Latins led to a demand for the *ius provocationis*, which, after the rebellion of Fregellae (125), may have been granted by the tribune Drusus in 122; for the Latins took no major part in the Social War, accepting the Roman citizenship by the *Lex Iulia*. After 89 B.C. *Latium* became a purely legal concept (*see* IUS LATII).

ANCIENT SOURCES. Livy and Dion. Hal. *Antiquities, passim,* are basic, but misleadingly retroject Roman supremacy to earliest period. Scattered references in Cato, Cicero, Gellius, Pliny *HN*, Varro, etc. Also Gaius, *Digest.*
MODERN LITERATURE. (a) Republic: K. J. Beloch, *Der italische Bund* (1880); *Röm. Gesch.* (1926); De Sanctis, *Stor. Rom.*; M. Gelzer, 'Latium' in *PW*; Mommsen, *Röm. Staatsr.* iii. 1, for legal

aspects; E. T. Salmon, *Phoenix* 1953, 93 ff., 123 ff.; A. Alföldi, *Early Rome and the Latins* (U.S.A. 1965); E. T. Salmon, *JRS* 1936, 47 ff., A. H. McDonald, *JRS* 1944, 11 ff., for second century; A. Rosenberg, *Hermes* 1919; A. N. Sherwin-White, *The Roman Citizenship* (1939); J. Göhlen, *Rom und Italien* (1939); E. T. Salmon, *Roman Colonization* (1969). (b) Empire: E. G. Hardy, *Six Roman Charters*; Hirschfeld, *Kl. Schr.* (1913) xxii. *See also* MUNICIPIUM. A. N. S.-W.

**LATINI IUNIANI.** By a *Lex Iunia* (*Norbana*?) of either 17 B.C. or A.D. 19, a slave of a Roman citizen manumitted informally or in violation of certain rules of Augustus (*see* FREEDMEN) became not a Roman citizen but a *Latinus*, a status now wholly divorced from nationality (*see* IUS LATII; LATINI). There is no way of knowing how numerous the *Latini Iuniani* were, nor is it clear why the status was established in the first place. The *Lex Iunia* gave the benefit of full statutory sanction to informal manumissions, previously protected only by praetorian action, while at the same time lowering the status of a man so freed. His chief civil disability was that on his death his property reverted to his former master, and that is what preoccupied the legal writers on the subject. He could still acquire citizenship in one of several ways, for example, once he had a one-year-old legitimate child. Justinian abolished *Latinitas Iuniana* in 531.

For alternative views, see A. Steinwenter, *PW* xii. 1; A. M. Duff, *Freedmen in the Early Roman Empire* (reissue 1958), 75 ff., 210 ff. M. I. F.

**LATINUS,** eponymous hero of the Latini (q.v.). Hesiod (*Theog.* 1011–16) makes him the son of Circe and Odysseus and king of the Tyrrhenians. Timaeus first connects him with Aeneas, whose daughter Rhome Latinus married and had as sons Rhomus (in Roman tradition Remus) and Romulus, founders of Rome. Cato's version (probably also that of Naevius and Ennius) is that Latinus betrothes his daughter Lavinia to Aeneas; Turnus, to whom she was formerly promised, makes war with Latinus on Aeneas, Latinus is killed, and Aeneas becomes king of the Latins. In Livy's version (1. 2) Latinus is killed fighting with Aeneas against Turnus. Virgil (*Aen.* books 7–12) in the main follows Cato's version, but makes Latinus son of Faunus and the nymph Marica. Latinus, a weak and vacillating character, takes no part in the war and only emerges from his palace to propose concessions to Aeneas (book 11) and to arrange the single combat of Turnus and Aeneas (book 12). C. B.

**LATIUM,** lying between the Apennines and the Tyrrhenian Sea in western Italy, originally was a small area about the Albanus Mons (q.v.). By 500 B.C., however, it stretched from the Tiber to the Circeian promontory (*Latium Vetus*). Subsequently Latium embraced Volscian, Auruncan, and Hernican territories, and by Strabo's time included Mons Massicus and Sinuessa (*Latium Adiectum*). Augustus amalgamated Latium with Campania, and after A.D. 292 the name Campania prevailed; consequently Latium is still called *Campagna*. Eastern Latium (the Apennine slopes and Trerus valley) and Central Latium (an undulating plain embracing the Alban Hills and Pomptine Marshes) supported large herds; subterranean drainage channels, excavated apparently in pre-Roman times, aided flourishing agricultural operations. Western Latium contained extensive forests. Latium was well watered and possessed sulphur springs, abundant volcanic building-materials (tufas, travertine, basalt, pozzolana), and a road network (ultimately developed into Viae Latina, Appia, etc.). The earliest inhabitants, the prehistoric Aborigines, (= Ligurians? or Sicels? Ciaceri identifies the two) apparently did not speak Latin. In historical times Latium was peopled by Latini, traditionally a mixed race and presumably an amalgam of the prehistoric population and various

Bronze and Iron Age invaders: 'Southern Villanovans' (q.v.) (who probably introduced Latin into Latium), Sabelli, and apparently Picenes (= Illyrians). The Latini inhabited mutually independent settlements on knolls or mountain slopes, but from early times grouped themselves together for religious, and ultimately for political, purposes. There were several Latin federal sanctuaries (at Albanus Mons, Ardea, Aricia, Lavinium, and elsewhere) and therefore perhaps several Latin Leagues, although tradition is explicit about only one—that led by Alba Longa (q.v.). When Rome destroyed Alba (c. 600 B.C.) she allegedly succeeded her as leader of this league. However, when the Roman monarchy fell (508 B.C.) the Latini (led apparently by Tusculum, Aricia, Lanuvium, Cora, Tibur, Pometia, Ardea: Cato, Orig. fr. 58 P) threw off any predominance Rome possessed, but failed to subordinate her to themselves (see REGILLUS LACUS). In 493 B.C. Rome and the Latin League signed a defensive alliance (foedus Cassianum) against threatening Volsci and Aequi. For Rome's subsequent relations with the Latini see LATINI, IUS LATII.

Depopulation of Latium began c. 300 B.C., caused chiefly by the centripetal pull of Rome, various wars (Pyrrhic, Hannibalic, Civil), the growth of latifundia, and malaria (which, however, reached its full virulence much later). The Augustan poets mention, and exaggerate, the desolation of Gabii and other places; Pliny, significantly, records towns that had utterly disappeared. Other towns (e.g. Tibur, Praeneste, Antium) undoubtedly became fashionable resorts, and in imperial times Latium contained numerous opulent villas. In general, however, its towns failed to revive. Pasturage ousted agriculture (Pliny, Ep. 2. 17) and, after the Barbarian Invasions, Latium assumed that derelict appearance which it bore until recently.

ANCIENT SOURCES. Livy, bks. 1–8; Dion. Hal. bks. 1–11; Diodors Römische Annalen, ed. Drachmann; Verg. Aen. bks. 7–12; Strabo 5. 228 f.; Pliny, HN 3. 54 f.; Mela 2. 4. 70.
MODERN LITERATURE. M. Zoeller, Latium und Rom (1878); T. Ashby, Roman Campagna in Classical Times (1927); T. Frank, Economic History of Rome² (1927); G. Lugli, I santuari celebr. del Lazio antico (1932); G. Säflund, Opuscula Archaeologica i (1934); A. Blakeway, JRS 1935. 129; H. Rudolph, Stadt und Staat im römischen Italien (1935); J. Whatmough, Foundations of Roman Italy (1937); E. Ciaceri, Le origini di Roma (1937); A. N. Sherwin-White, Roman Citizenship (1939); B. Tilly, Vergil's Latium (1947); A. Alföldi, Early Rome and the Latins (U.S.A. 1965, with good bibliography). See also LATINI.
E. T. S.

**LAUDATIO FUNEBRIS,** the funeral oration, originally part of the rites of the Roman patrician gens, developed into a public laudatio, pronounced by a magistrate, later over women as well as men, e.g. Catulus' mother. It retained its traditional character, linking praise of the deceased with glorification of his ancestors, covering public and (probably) private life, and describing outstanding events. The encomiastic treatment, when the laudationes were published, tended to falsify history (Livy 8. 40. 4; 27. 27. 13; Cic. Brut. 16. 62). In Roman biography—as in Roman portraiture—the funeral rites added emphasis, especially on the political side, to the Hellenistic technique from the later Peripatetic school which had been accepted in Rome (see BIOGRAPHY, ROMAN).

Polyb. 6. 53–4. F. Vollmer, Laud. fun. Rom. historia et rel. editio (1892); F. Leo, Die griech.-röm. Biographie (1901), 225 ff.; D. R. Stuart, Epochs of Greek and Roman Biography (1928), 209 ff.
A. H. McD.

**LAUREA,** MARCUS TULLIUS, one of Cicero's freedmen, wrote an epigram on the hot springs which burst out at Cicero's villa soon after his death (Pliny, HN 31. 7–8).

Baehrens, FPR 316; Morel, FPL 80.

**LAURENTUM,** on the Tyrrhenian coast of Latium immediately below the Tiber mouth, where Aeneas found King Latinus reigning (qq.vv.). Although separately mentioned in the Latin War, it had dwindled to insignificance by imperial times, when its inhabitants formed one community with those of nearby Lavinium. Ruins still exist of the Younger Pliny's celebrated Laurentine villa (Epp. 2. 17).

B. Tilly, Vergil's Latium (1947). E. T. S.

**LAURIACUM,** modern Lorsch near Enns on the Danube, was a Celtic and Roman settlement in Noricum. An earth and timber military station occupied from the first century A.D. was superseded under Marcus Aurelius by a legionary fortress occupied by the newly raised Legio II Italica. Lauriacum was destroyed in 405 by the Ostrogoths. J. J. W.

**LAURIUM,** a hilly district in south Attica near Cape Sunium, was one of the largest mining areas in the Greek world, famed for production of silver from galena. The deposit was discovered probably in the early Iron Age. Exploitation was at first limited to surface operations with little or no burrowing. However, with impetus supplied by the tyrant Pisistratus and by the increasing demand for coined silver, more sophisticated techniques and a growing understanding of the basically simple geological formation led to the finding of rich beds of ore lying deep below the surface, particularly at Maronea c. 483 B.C. (Arist. Ath. Pol. 22. 7). The mines flourished in the fifth century until the latter part of the Peloponnesian War, and they did not revive fully until the second half of the fourth century; in the third they suffered under the low prices of silver, but were exploited ruthlessly in the second until the revolt of the slave workers in 103. A few tailings were reworked in the first century A.D., and the mines closed soon after. An attempt was made to reopen them in the fourth century. Throughout the district there are copious remains from the mining industry: buildings, shafts, cisterns, and washing tables. The mines were considered the property of the State and were rented out to private citizens by the poletai (q.v.). Fragments of those leases have been found in the Athenian Agora.

E. Ardaillon, Les Mines du Laurion (1897); G. M. Calhoun, 'Ancient Athenian Mining', J. Econ. Bus. Hist. 1931, 333 ff.; M. Crosby, 'The Leases of the Laureion Mines', Hesp. 1950, 189 ff.; Forbes, Stud. Anc. Technol. viii, 193 ff. C. W. J. E.

**LAUS PISONIS,** a panegyric in 261 hexameters on a Calpurnius Piso, possibly the conspirator of A.D. 65 (cf. Tac. Ann. 15. 48; Σ Vallae ad Juv. 5. 109 is based on L.P. and has no independent value). The style is correct but diffuse. Efforts to identify the poet have been fruitless.

TEXT, TRANSLATION, AND BIBLIOGRAPHY. Duff, Minor Lat. Poets; R. Verdière, T. Calpurnii Siculi De Laude Pisonis, etc. (1954). E. J. K.

**LAVINIUM:** modern Pratica di Mare, where Aeneas (q.v.) landed in Latium (q.v.), a town of the Latin League, whose federal sanctuary it became in the sixth century B.C.: thirteen large archaic altars survive in situ. The Romans revered Lavinium for its Trojan associations, its Venus temple common to all Latins, its cults of Vesta and Penates, and its loyalty in the Latin War. It dwindled to a village, however. In imperial times, if not in primitive (see Livy 1. 14), Lavinium apparently formed one community with Laurentum (q.v.), Laurolavinium, whose aristocrats were styled Laurentes Lavinates (Dessau, ILS 1371).

A. Alföldi, Early Rome and the Latins (U.S.A. 1965), 246 f. (with bibliography). E. T. S.

**LAW AND PROCEDURE, ROMAN.** I. CIVIL LAW. The beginning and the end of the historical development of Roman law are marked by two legislative works, both unique in universal legal history, though different in origin, nature, and structure—the XII Tables (q.v.) and Justinian's codification (*see* DIGESTA, TRIBONIANUS, CODEX, INSTITUTIONES). In the intervening thousand years the Romans produced no codification; the XII Tables were never repealed and remained formally effective, though in a considerable part obsolete, down to the time of Justinian. Though probably no more than a publication of the most important rules of the existing customary law, they were for the Romans, and still are for us, the starting-point of the history of Roman law. Four periods may be distinguished in that history: (*a*) the period of the primitive law, ending with the third century B.C.; (*b*) the formative period of the last two centuries B.C.; (*c*) the classical period of the first two and a half centuries A.D., or, more narrowly, of the century from *c*. 130 to *c*. 230 (*see* JULIANUS 2, EDICTUM, JURISPRUDENCE); (*d*) the post-classical period, in which the law, particularly in the Western Empire, is 'vulgarized', but which culminates in the East in a classical revival and the codification of Justinian. The great bulk of the sources for our knowledge of the private law comes from the extracts of the writings of the jurists of the classical period (in the narrower sense) preserved, and to an uncertain extent altered, in Justinian's *Digesta* (q.v.).

2. The most characteristic mark of the primitive law was its rigorous formalism: both in legal transactions and in litigation solemn oral forms were required; the will of the parties was without effect unless clothed in these forms. In this respect Roman law resembles other primitive systems. It differs from them in the simplicity of the forms, and in its 'economy' in their use: a very small number of forms serves a wide variety of purposes (*see* MANCIPATIO, EMANCIPATIO, ADOPTIO, MANUS, NEXUM, STIPULATIO). And like other early systems it was exclusive: the small rustic community excluded foreigners from participation in its own *ius Quiritium* (*see* IUS GENTIUM). The Roman family preserved its exclusive organization and its central place (*see* PATRIA POTESTAS).

3. In the last two or three centuries B.C., however, the expansion of Rome's commerce and Empire over the Mediterranean world made it impossible to maintain the formalism and exclusiveness of the old *ius civile* (q.v.). New, informal institutions appear, resting on the intentions of the parties and not on the observance of external forms, notably the 'consensual' contracts (*see* CONTRACT, ROMAN LAW OF), which provide for the principal commercial transactions. These new institutions were open to foreigners and citizens alike (*see* IUS GENTIUM), and so also now was the central contract of *stipulatio* (q.v.). Special courts of *recuperatores* (q.v.) had early been set up for disputes with non-citizens, and *c*. 242 B.C. a special *praetor* (q.v.) *peregrinus* was created with jurisdiction over such litigation. In the same period the old formalistic procedure for the trial of suits between citizens (*legis actiones*) gave way to the informal and flexible formulary procedure (see below, II). All this was accompanied and made possible by a first flowering of legal thought and writing, stimulated by contact with Greek culture but essentially Roman in character (*see* JURISPRUDENCE). Owing to the sparsity of direct contemporary evidence the details of much of this development are obscure, but it is plain that in this period the foundations were laid both of the flexible system which was capable of satisfying the needs of a great Empire, and of the legal literature which has influenced legal development ever since.

4. A factor which contributed vitally to the release of the law from its early rigidity was the development of the *ius honorarium* (*see* EDICTUM). The introduction of the formulary procedure did more than simplify procedure. It gave the controlling magistrate (and especially the *praetor* (q.v.) *urbanus*) the power, in effect though not in

form, to reform and develop the law. Under the system of *legis actiones* a claim could be instituted only in one of a limited number of ritual modes recognized by statute. The praetor's function was to administer but not to alter this system. With the introduction of the formulary procedure, however, he acquired the power to grant new remedies (by way of action, defence, etc.) and thereby to 'support, supplement, and correct the civil law' (*Dig.* 1. 1. 7. 1). He supported it by giving more effective remedies to enforce existing rights (*see*, e.g., INIURIA); he supplemented and corrected it by enforcing claims which the civil law did not recognize and barring those which it did. This supplementing and correcting power produced a dualism between the old *ius civile* and the newer *ius honorarium* in some fields, especially in the law of inheritance (q.v.) and of ownership (*see* DOMINIUM).

5. Legislation (*see* COMITIA) played only a minor part in the development of the private law during the Republic. Such statutes as there were dealt usually with details of existing institutions. The *Lex Aquilia* (*see* DAMNUM INIURIA DATUM) is a notable exception. *Senatus consultum* (q.v.) likewise played little part in the private law. It was not recognized as having independent legal validity until perhaps the second century A.D. (Gai. *Inst.* 1. 4), and it was then largely an expression of the imperial will.

6. *Senatus consultum* can indeed be seen as a transitional legislative form between Republic and Empire, which cloaked the growing fact of the Emperor's power. The *lex* and *plebiscitum* (qq.v.) of the Republic became rare after the time of Augustus (*see* LEGES IULIAE) and disappeared altogether in the course of the first century A.D. By the middle of the second century it was accepted that pronouncements of the Emperor had the force of law (Gai. *Inst.* 1. 5). These pronouncements might take various forms, either openly legislative or ostensibly judicial (*see* CONSTITUTIONES), but after the codification of the praetor's edict by Julian (*see* EDICTUM, JULIANUS 2) had brought to an end the innovatory power of the *ius honorarium*, the Emperor emerged as the sole direct legislative force. Indirectly the jurists continued to play a large part—in one sense indeed larger than before, since they were increasingly to be found among the leading officials of the Emperor (*see* JURISPRUDENCE). It is to the activity of the jurists in elaborating and co-ordinating in a vast legal literature the developments of the preceding centuries that the period of the Principate, and especially the later Principate, owes its description as 'classical'.

7. A factor which tended to break the pattern of the earlier law was the development of the new procedure by *cognitio extra ordinem* (see below, II), which at first existed side by side with the formulary procedure but eventually, by the early fourth century, entirely superseded it. Out of this came institutions, especially *fideicommissum* (q.v.) which cut across the old line between *ius civile* and *ius honorarium*.

8. New problems arose from the conquest of provinces to which the Romans conceded from the first the right of organizing their legal life according to their own laws. Only persons upon whom Roman citizenship was conferred (individually, regionally, or by groups) were obliged to observe in their legal relations the Roman *ius civile*. Differences between the various legal systems gave rise to misunderstandings which were submitted to the decision of the Emperor, who decided not infrequently in favour of the provincial law. The general bestowal of Roman citizenship by Caracalla (A.D. 212) (*see* CITIZENSHIP, ROMAN) simplified the legal situation, but unavoidably some conceptions of local law penetrated the law of the Empire. This penetration of the imperial law by local law was to be an important factor in the post-classical period.

**9.** The end of the classical period is marked by the disappearance of the independent jurist. With the shadowy exceptions of Hermogenianus (q.v.) and Arcadius Charisius, both probably of the early third century, Herennius (q.v.) Modestinus is the last of the named jurists. The next three centuries are a period of almost complete anonymity and absence of original legal writing outside the imperial chancery—and after the time of Constantine the standard of legal thought even inside the chancery is low. Apart from wider reasons for the decline of Rome in this period, the disappearance of the old type of jurist was foreshadowed in the careers of the great jurists of the Severan age. Men such as Ulpianus (q.v. 1), Papinianus (q.v.), and Paulus (q.v. 1) influenced the law both from inside the chancery and from outside it, by their writings. Their successors were confined to the chancery. The *responsa* of the jurists were now wholly replaced by the rescripts of the Emperor (*see* CONSTITU-TIONES).

**10.** Modern opinion distinguishes three stages within the post-classical period. The first, until the reign of Constantine, is a time in which the classical law was still known (the rescripts of Diocletian's chancery are notable for their insistence on the old distinctions and the old rules—though the need for the insistence is significant), and in which the classical writings were probably subjected, especially c. 300, to editing and abridgement. It is probable that many of the interpolations (*see* DIGESTA) in the excerpts of the classical books contained in Justinian's *Digest*, which until recently were attributed to Justinian's compilers, or at least to their immediate predecessors, were in fact made in this period. Certainly the small amount of literature which survives from this time outside the compilation of Justinian consists of epitomes or anthologies (*see* ULPIANUS (1) for the *Epitome Ulpiani*, and PAULUS (1) for *Pauli Sententiae*), or collective works (*Fragmenta Vaticana*).

**11.** The period after Constantine is now seen as the period of the Vulgar Law. No doubt even in the classical period the Roman law applied among Roman citizens in the provinces often failed to live up to the standard of the metropolitan jurisprudence. Now that, on the one hand, everyone was a Roman citizen, and on the other, the standards of legal learning even at the centre had fallen, this vulgar law tended to swamp the imperial law. The careful distinctions and the elaborate constructions of the classical jurists were blurred and misunderstood. The great works of the classical period were too complex for current use (but the *Institutes* of Gaius (q.v. 2) now came into their own as an elementary work, though even they were eventually epitomized). In the western part of the Empire this vulgar law was continued in the compilations (*Lex Romana Visigothorum, Lex Romana Burgundionum*) made by the successors of the Roman emperors for their Roman subjects, and in this way a shadowy form of Roman law survived. In the East the tide was turned back by a classical revival in the later fifth century. This classical revival, which is a matter of inference more than of observation, seems to have been centred on Berytus, where there had been a law school ever since the middle of the third century, and to a lesser extent on Constantinople, where a law school was in being in the early fifth century. It was evidently in the law schools that the old literature was studied once again and a knowledge of the old law recovered. It is this revival which is now seen as making possible the codification of Justinian (*see* DIGESTA, TRIBONIANUS, CODEX, INSTITU-TIONES). For this codification now appears not as the terminus of a gradual development from the classical law, but rather as a reaction against the vulgarization of the intervening period. Against this background the debate over the extent to which the law of Justinian was

influenced by the ideas and practices of the Greek East takes on a new appearance. Some individual institutions of Greek origin there certainly are, and some of the old institutions, especially those of a formal character, have disappeared, but the purpose of the whole compilation is a revival of the old law. In some fields, again, the influence of Christianity can be seen—in the law of marriage, for example, or in the treatment of slaves. But here it is perhaps the smallness of the influence which is notable. The law remains markedly Roman.

For particulars on sources *see* CODEX, CONSTITUTIONES, DIGESTA, EDICTUM, INSTITUTIONES, IUS CIVILE, IUS GENTIUM, JURISPRUDENCE, TRIBONIANUS, TWELVE TABLES; for the private law: COMMUNIO, CONTRACT, DAMNUM INIURIA DATUM, EMPHYTEUSIS, FIDEICOMMISSUM, GUARDIANSHIP, INHERITANCE, INIURIA, MANCEPS, MANCIPATIO, MARRIAGE, NEXUM, POSSESSIO, SECURITY, SERVITUTES, SLAVERY, STIPULATIO, VINDICATIO. *See also below,* II. 'Civil procedure'.

(*a*) SOURCES. For Justinian's compilation *see under* DIGESTA, CODEX. For the surviving pre-Justinian sources *see* JURISPRUDENCE.
(*b*) HISTORY AND SOURCES OF LAW. H. F. Jolowicz, *Hist. Intro. to the Study of Roman Law*² (1952); W. Kunkel, *Röm. Rechtsgesch.*⁴ (1964), transl. J. M. Kelly, *Introduction to Roman Legal and Constitutional History* (1966); V. Arangio-Ruiz, *Storia del dir. rom.*⁷ (1957); and the monumental work of L. Wenger, *Quellen d. röm. Rechts* (1953); *and see under* JURISPRUDENCE.
(*c*) GENERAL TEXTBOOKS. The fundamental modern work is M. Kaser, *Röm. Privatrecht* i (1955), ii (1959). Others: W. W. Buckland, *Textbook of Roman Law*³ (1963, but in substance 1932); F. Schulz, *Classical Roman Law* (1951); V. Arangio-Ruiz, *Istit. di dir. rom.*¹³ (1957); E. Volterra, *Istit. di dir. priv. rom.* (1961); P. Bonfante, *Corso di dir. rom.* i, ii, iii, vi (1925–30); S. Perozzi, *Ist. di dir. rom.*² (1928); R. Monier, *Manuel élém. de droit romain* i⁶ (1947), ii⁴ (1948); B. Nicholas, *Intro. to Roman Law* (1962); J. Crook, *Roman Law and Life* (1967).
(*d*) WORKS OF CHARACTERIZATION. F. Schulz, *Principles of Roman Law* (1936); F. Wieacker, *Vom röm. Recht*² (1961).
(*e*) VULGAR LAW AND LATE LAW. L. Mitteis, *Reichsrecht u. Volksrecht in den östl. Provinzen des röm. Kaiserreichs* (1891); E. Levy, *West Roman Vulgar Law, The Law of Property* (1951); *Weström. Vulgarrecht. Das Obligationenrecht* (1956); J. Gaudemet, *La Formation du droit séculier et du droit de l'église aux IVᵉ et Vᵉ siècles* (1957). And see Kaser (under (*c*) above) ii.
(*f*) TRANSMISSION OF TEXTS. F. Wieacker, *Textstufen klassischer Juristen* (1960); F. Schulz, *History of Roman Legal Science* (1946); M. Kaser, *Sav. Zeitschr.* 1952. A. B.; B. N.

II. CIVIL PROCEDURE. The Roman civil trial from earliest times showed a characteristic feature: the division into two stages. The first took place before a magistrate, *in iure* (*ius* signifies here the place of magisterial jurisdiction), and its purpose was to define and formulate the issue (i.e. the limits of the dispute between the parties). This stage culminated in *litis contestatio* (joinder of issue), an acceptance by the parties, under the magistrate's supervision, of the issue as formulated and of the *iudex* authorized by the magistrate. It was the *iudex* who presided at the second stage (*apud iudicem*), at which the case was heard and argued. He was a private person empowered by the magistrate's order to give judgment (*iussum iudicandi*) (*see* IUDEX). This bipartite division of the trial (whose origin is much disputed) was an ingenious combination of official jurisdiction and private arbitration, from which it differs in that the *iudex* was obliged to accept the commission conferred upon him by the magistrate and the litigants, and was bound by their agreed definition of the matter in dispute. Only in the first stage, *in iure*, were certain formalities observed; the second stage, *apud iudicem*, was conducted without any prescribed form. Two systems are to be distinguished in the proceedings before the magistrate: *legis actiones*, the earlier one, and *formulae*.

**2.** *Legis actio* was a solemn procedure of a rigidly formal character, wherein the plaintiff (*is qui agit, actor*) and the defendant (*is cum quo agitur, reus*) had to assert their rights in oral forms prescribed by law or custom. This system existed in the time of the XII Tables, as has been confirmed by the new fragments of Gaius (q.v. 2).

There were five types of *legis actiones* (Gai. *Inst.* 4. 11 ff). The most usual, applicable to claims of ownership (*see* VINDICATIO) and to claims originating in obligations, was the *legis actio sacramento*, involving in historical times a formal wager (*sacramentum*, q.v.) between the parties, who both deposited a fixed sum of money (also called *sacramentum*). The winner (the party whose assertion was declared right by the judge) received his *sacramentum* back, while the loser's *sacramentum* was forfeited to the State. The other types were (1) *per iudicis postulationem* for claims based on *stipulatio* (q.v.) or for disputes about the division of property belonging to several persons; (2) *per condictionem* (of later date) for recovery of *certa pecunia* or *certa res* in particular cases. These were of greater simplicity and did not require a *sacramentum*. The last two *legis actiones* were methods of execution: the one (*per manus iniectionem*) against the person of the condemned debtor, the other (*per pignoris capionem*) against his property.

3. *Legis actiones* were supplanted by the formulary system (Gai. *Inst.* 4. 30 ff.), in which the matter in dispute was defined in a written document (*formula, concepta verba*) in place of the oral forms of the *legis actio*. Moreover, the number of *formulae* was in principle unlimited and depended on the discretion of the praetor in the formulation and administration of his *edictum* (q.v.). Whereas each *legis actio* was appropriate to a number of causes of action (see above), the principle of the formulary system was that each cause of action had its appropriate *formula*. Thus in the contract of sale (*emptio venditio*: *see* CONTRACT, LAW OF) the buyer had the *actio empti* and the seller the *actio venditi*. But while the *formula* varied from action to action, its structure was based on some permanent essential parts: the *intentio* (concise formulation of the plaintiff's claim) and the *condemnatio*, by which the judge was authorized to condemn the defendant if he found after hearing the evidence and the arguments that the plaintiff's case was good, otherwise to discharge him. To suit the complexities of each case the *formula* might be extended by additional clauses, e.g. by a *demonstratio*, which served to determine more precisely the matter at issue when the *intentio* was indefinite (*incerta*); or by an *exceptio*, a clause on behalf of the defendant excluding his condemnation, if he should prove a fact recognized by the praetor as making such condemnation unjust (e.g. that the plaintiff had been guilty of fraud: *exceptio doli*; or that the plaintiff had agreed not to sue the defendant: *exceptio pacti*). Model *formulae* for all recognized actions, defences, etc., were published with the edict. The principle that each cause of action had its appropriate *formula*, coupled with the praetor's power to create new *formulae* either generally in the edict or on the facts of a particular case, lay at the root of the *ius honorarium* (see above, I. 4).

4. The origins of the formulary system are obscure. Gaius (4. 30) says only that the *legis actiones* were replaced by the *formula* by a *lex Aebutia* (probably after 150 B.C.) and by two *leges Iuliae* (17/16 B.C.), but the part played by each of these pieces of legislation is conjectural. It is probable that the formula originated well before the *lex Aebutia* in proceedings between peregrines (to whom the *legis actiones* were not open) under the jurisdiction of the *praetor* (q.v.) *peregrinus* (first created 242 B.C.) or in the provinces. In either case the proceedings would depend entirely on the *imperium* (q.v.) of the magistrate authorizing them and would therefore be free of the restrictions imposed by statute on suits between citizens by *legis actio*. It is also likely that the *formula* was admitted before the *lex Aebutia* in suits between citizens arising out of the newer, flexible institutions open to citizens and peregrines alike (see above, I. 3). If this is so, the *lex Aebutia* would for the first time have allowed the formu-

lary procedure as an alternative to the *legis actio* in cases involving the old *ius civile*, and the *leges Iuliae* would have abolished the *legis actiones* altogether, except for proceedings before the centumviral court (*see* CENTUMVIRI).

5. The formulary system was the ordinary procedure of the classical period. But from the time of Augustus there developed beside it various other forms of procedure in particular contexts. These other forms are commonly called *cognitio extra ordinem* (sc. *iudiciorum privatorum*) or *extraordinaria*. Their common characteristic is that the whole proceeding takes place before an official appointed by a magistrate or by the Emperor (*iudex datus, pedaneus*). There is no division of proceedings *in iure* and *apud iudicem*, and no private *iudex*. This procedure is used in Rome for cases in certain fields singled out by the Emperor, such as *fideicommissa* (q.v.) and later the claiming of *honoraria* for services performed by members of the upper classes (*see* CONTRACT, ROMAN LAW OF; ADVOCATUS), and more widely in the provinces. The procedure in appeals, which from the beginning of the Empire were probably admissible even from decisions under the formulary procedure, was also by *cognitio*. The formulary procedure finally (*see* APPELLATIO) disappeared in the early fourth century. The *cognitio* procedure of the Late Empire was more akin to the modern process than to the voluntary submission to a non-professional judge of the classical and earlier law. It is appropriately called the bureaucratic procedure.

6. Roman juridical language had two expressions for a civil lawsuit: *actio* and *iudicium*. Both terms originally had separate meanings, which were enlarged by the development of the procedure, so that from early times they overlapped, particularly when used to indicate a special kind of action by its technical name (e.g. *de dolo mandati, tutelae, communi dividundo, in factum* and so on. *Actio* probably signified originally the activity of the plaintiff who initiated the trial, but subsequently came to denote the whole proceedings, and especially their first stage *in iure*. But *actio* had also a material sense. A famous definition (*Dig.* 44. 7. 51) qualifies *actio* as 'ius quod sibi debetur, iudicio persequendi', where the difference between the material *actio* and the formal *iudicium* is evident. *Iudicium* signifies generally the second stage of the classical lawsuit, before the *iudex*, but it may indicate either the entire trial or only its final act, the judgement; frequently it refers to the written *formula*. In the language of Justinian's compilers *iudicium* acquired a very wide application and was often interpolated in the place of classical mentions of the first stage, *in iure*, after the bipartition had been abolished.

7. The classical trial began with an extra-judicial private act, *in ius vocatio*, by which the plaintiff personally summoned the defendant to follow him before the magistrate. The XII Tables contained detailed provisions for cases in which the defendant disobeyed the summons on grounds of physical disability. It is noteworthy that they began merely by stating the absolute duty of the party summoned to go with the plaintiff immediately: 'si in ius uocat, ito.' The only manner of avoiding an immediate appearance before the magistrate (which could be procured by force in case of resistance) was for the summoned party to give a guarantor (*vindex*). In the formulary system summons remained a mere private act, the plaintiff being obliged to announce to the defendant the claim and the form which he wished to apply against him. In the extraordinary procedure the summons was issued in writing with the assistance of an official. Finally the summoning was performed exclusively by a judicial functionary without any co-operation of the plaintiff.

8. The magistrate began by trying some preliminary questions such as the competence of the court, the

personal capacity of the litigants, and their legitimation to be plaintiff or defendant in the intended lawsuit. A negative result of this examination made further litigation superfluous; *denegatio actionis* by the magistrate put an end to the trial. Other cases where the litigation was finished *in iure* were: acknowledgement of the plaintiff's claim by the defendant (*confessio*) or, in certain cases, the swearing of an oath by one or other party (*see* IUS-IURANDUM). Normally, however, the stage *in iure* was devoted to defining the issue (see above). In the formulary process there might often be long discussions about the composition of the *formula*, especially when the case and the appropriate form were not provided in the praetor's edict and the plaintiff tried to obtain the grant of a new form adapted to the particularities of the case (*actio in factum*). *Litis contestatio* required the co-operation of both the parties, but neither of them could frustrate the achievement of this act by repeated refusal of the other's proposals, the plaintiff being exposed to *denegatio actionis*, the defendant to an executive measure applied by the magistrate on behalf of the plaintiff (*missio in possessionem*).

**9.** The *litis contestatio*, as the name declares, was performed in the presence of witnesses. In the developed formulary system it probably referred to the witnessed document embodying the *formula*. After its completion another trial on the same claim was debarred; and the judge's sentence was determined by the condition of the case at the moment of the *litis contestatio*, especially in regard to the fruits or the alienation of the object at issue and the like.

**10.** The second stage of the trial was in the control of the private *iudex*. It was occupied by the pleadings of the parties and their advocates (*see* ADVOCATUS), and the submission of evidence, the assessment of which depended wholly on the discretion of the judge. If the defendant lost the case, he was obliged to carry out his obligations under the judgment within a fixed term (thirty days according to the XII Tables; various in later development; extended to a maximum of four months by Justinian). But, although until the end of the Republic there was no appeal (see above), a sentence could be annulled by an extraordinary remedy such as *restitutio in integrum*. If the condemned debtor did not carry out the terms of the sentence the creditor could proceed to a forcible execution of his rights. Personal execution (*manus iniectio*) was the rule; real execution on objects forming part of the property of the debtor (*pignoris capio*) was admitted only for distraints of a sacral or public character. Real execution eventually became prevalent, but not exclusive. The formulary procedure comprised a special *actio iudicati* for execution of the sentence, wherein a contumacious debtor risked a condemnation in double value of the object in dispute and an immediate authorization of the creditor to seize his property. The *cognitio extraordinaria* softened the rigid earlier forms of execution by restricting it to single objects instead of the whole property.

**11.** A strange procedural institution, partly of administrative character, was provided in classical Roman law by the *interdicta*. These were orders or prohibitions issued by the magistrate without long investigations and addressed as a rule to a particular person. Their object was to give immediate protection to menaced or violated interests of the plaintiff. If the defendant ignored the interdict, or disputed the plaintiff's right to it, a procedural wager enabled the matter to be litigated by an ordinary action. A variety of private interests were protected in this way, but the most important were *possessio* (q.v.) and the praetorian rights of inheritance created by grant of *bonorum possessio* (*see* INHERITANCE, LAW OF). Interdicts also protected rights of a public character,

such as public rights of way. After the disappearance of the formulary procedure the distinction between *interdictum* and *actio* was effaced.

*See* ADVOCATUS, APPELLATIO, CENTUMVIRI, EDICTUM, IUDEX, IURIDICUS, IUSIURANDUM, IUSTITIUM, RECUPERATORES, SACRAMENTUM, TESTIMONIUM, VINDICATIO.

M. Kaser, *Das röm. Zivilprozessrecht* (1966); G. Luzzatto, *Procedura civile romana* i–iii (1946–50); G. Pugliese, *Processo civile romano* i (1961), ii. 1 (1963)—. O. Lenel, *Edictum Perpetuum³* (1927) (*see* EDICTUM). P. Collinet, *La Procédure par libelle* (1935), *La Nature des actions, des interdits et des exceptions dans l'œuvre de Justinien* (1947); V. Zilletti, *Studi sul processo civile giustinianeo* (1965); J. M. Kelly, *Roman Litigation* (1966). A. H. J. Greenidge, *The Legal Procedure of Cicero's Time* (1901) is out of date but still useful.    A. B.; B. N.

III. CRIMINAL LAW AND PROCEDURE. In the evolution of Roman criminal law we can distinguish three phases governed by different fundamental ideas not unknown in criminal law of other ancient nations. The older phase is characterized by the principle of private revenge; then followed the period of composition between offended and offender, first voluntary and sporadic, later obligatory. But even in this phase the beginnings of a new system can be observed: intervention of the State in punishing some crimes, especially those directed against the structure or existence of the community (a characteristic feature of the last phase). The State now takes in its hands the repression of offences, not only those which menace the public order or interest directly, but also those affecting private property or interests. The separate systems cannot be distinguished by exact dates, as none of them was completely replaced by the next one, but generally speaking the first phase falls in the Regal period, the XII Tables represent a combination of the first two systems, while in the advanced Republic the intervention of the State, hitherto exceptional, becomes more and more common. Under the Principate it gains dominance, and under the Late Empire and Justinian it becomes exclusive, having absorbed nearly the whole field of private criminal law. A survival of the idea of vengeance is found in the *noxae deditio*, the surrender of the wrongdoer (slave or child under *patria potestas*) to the person wronged (*see* PATRIA POTESTAS).

**2.** The Romans did not create an organic body of statutes relating to criminal law. The XII Tables are, as the fragmentary remains of Tables VIII and IX show, a mosaic of various penal provisions but not a code. They were restricted to such criminal matters as interested a primitive peasant community, and therefore could not suffice for the State in its further development. The copious legislation of the Republic did not solve the problem, as these *leges* dealt only with single crimes, and it is noticeable that some offences were even treated by several *leges* voted within a relatively short period of time, e.g. the *crimen repetundarum* (*see* REPETUNDAE) or *ambitus* (q.v.). The various *Leges Corneliae* (of Sulla) and *Iuliae* (of Caesar and Augustus; it is not always certain which of them was the author) with their different courts and proceedings for particular crimes were as far from a systematic treatment or a coherent code as the later legislation of the Empire, which, though creative in particular details, made no attempt to codify. Extensive interpretation of earlier statutes to cover new facts (wherein the Senate co-operated as long as it remained active), or modification of penalties in the direction of greater or lesser severity, constitutes all the legislative activity of these times in substantive criminal law. The procedure *extra ordinem*, it is true, caused the introduction of new ideas into the general doctrines of penal law; and imperial constitutions applied some novel conceptions; but all these, being sporadic and exceptional, did not give an impulse to systematic and comprehensive elaboration.

**3.** The jurists of the second century A.D.—the best

period of classical jurisprudence—contributed to the development of criminal law far less than to that of civil law. A compilation analogous to the *Edictum* (q.v.) *perpetuum* in civil law would certainly have roused their interest in criminal matters; and it is noticeable how fertile was their contribution to doctrines of private delicts, with which the praetorian edict dealt (cf. the excellent elaboration of *iniuria*, *Dig.* 47. 10), in comparison with their modest part in public criminal law. The effect of the interpretative work of all these more or less authoritative elements (imperial rescripts and edicts, *senatus consulta*, practice of *cognitio extra ordinem*, jurisprudence) was that offences quite different from those which were described and made punishable in Republican statutes were subjected to the statutory penalties. Thus (1) Sulla's *Lex Cornelia testamentaria* (*nummaria*, called also *de falsis*), which originally dealt with falsification of wills and of coins, was extended not only to the forgery of documents and the assumption of false names, titles, or official rank, but even to corruption in litigation, as when a juror, accuser, witness, or advocate was bribed, in which case both giver and receiver were punishable. Even a juror who *constitutiones principum neglexit* was punished according to this statute. (2) The penalties of the *Lex Cornelia* against murderers and poisoners were extended in later times to magistrates, jurymen, and witnesses who contributed to an unjust capital sentence. (3) The *Lex Iulia de ambitu* was applied to cases of pressure exercised on a juryman by the accuser or the accused, though the original field of the statute was electoral corruption.

**4.** Under the Late Empire criminal legislation is directed more to penalties than to the doctrinal treatment of offences. The punishableness of some delicts varied under the influence of political or religious points of view; the creation of new categories of crimes in this long period is restricted to abduction and offences against the Christian religion after its recognition by the State. The profession of Christianity had at one time been prosecuted as *crimen maiestatis* (*see* MAIESTAS). Justinian's legislative compilations show the first endeavour to collect the scattered provisions of public and private criminal law into a systematic whole. The *Digest*, books 47–9, and the *Code*, book 9, give a well-arranged design of criminal law, procedure, and penalties. The compilers, of course, found some help in works of the latest classical jurists, who in just appreciation of the difficulties created by this fluctuating and uncertain state of criminal legislation dealt with these matters in monographs: *de iudiciis publicis* (Marcianus, Macer, Paulus), *de poenis* (Paulus, Saturninus, Modestinus), *de cognitionibus* (Callistratus). But all these and similar works, though doubtless meritorious and useful, aimed rather at collecting material than at creative criticism or presentation of new ideas. Even the terminology distinguishing different categories of offences does not show that stability and precision which is so excellent a feature of Roman legal language. The terms most used are *crimen*, *delictum*, *maleficium*; but it can hardly be affirmed that these expressions had a particular exclusive sense, though generally *crimen* indicates more serious offences directed against the State or public order, whilst *delictum* is rather used for delicts against private property or personal integrity and of no great harmfulness. The meaning of *maleficium* as a general term is even less technical, especially as it was used for designating sorcery and magic arts. All endeavours to bring order into classical texts by allotting to these terms an exclusive technical sense and removing all inconvenient texts as interpolated break down because of the indiscriminate use of these terms.

**5.** For the distinction between public and private offences we likewise lack any precise definition or statement of distinguishing marks; and yet it was of fundamental importance for Roman criminal law. This distinction rested upon a practical rather than a doctrinal differentiation of offended interests, and found its visible consequences in the fields of procedure and penalties, which differed greatly in the two spheres. The Roman jurists dealt more with the distinction between *iudicia publica* and private *actiones poenales* than with that between the interests violated as public or private, and the post-classical and Justinian classification into *delicta privata*, *crimina extraordinaria*, and *iudicia publica* (*Rubr. Dig.* 47. 1; 47. 11; 48. 1) was also made from a procedural point of view.

**6.** The private delicts form a group apart: the wrongdoer is exposed to an action under the ordinary civil procedure (see above, II) by the person wronged, the effect of which is that he must pay a pecuniary penalty to the plaintiff (to be distinguished from another *actio* by which the restitution of the *res* or compensation is claimed—*rei persecutio*). The State as such did not show any interest in the prosecution of these offences, but the proceedings had a punitive character. By contrast with other civil proceedings (i.e. for *rei persecutio*) they did not lie against the heir if the wrongdoer died before he had been sued, and each of several wrongdoers was liable for the whole penalty. The principal forms were theft (*furtum*, q.v.); robbery (*rapina*, theft combined with violence); damage to property (*see* DAMNUM INIURIA DATUM); assault, and in general all affronts to the plaintiff's dignity and personality (*iniuria*, q.v.). The praetor also made other wrongs actionable, such as threats (*metus*), deceit (*dolus*), malicious corruption of other people's slaves, and the like. Praetorian law also introduced a category of actions for misdemeanours which affected public interests, e.g. damage to the *album* (q.v.) of magistrates, violation of sepulchres, and pouring liquids or throwing things out into the streets. In such cases anyone, *quivis ex populo* (hence the name *actiones populares*), could be plaintiff and claim the penalty. Proceedings for private delicts were in later times greatly restricted in favour of the criminal *cognitio extra ordinem* (see below).

**7.** The special domain of criminal law is, however, the second group of crimes prosecuted by public organs in *iudicia publica*. The oldest law knew the intervention of the State, as avenger of offences against its security or against public order, only in exceptional cases such as treason (*perduellio*, q.v.), desertion to the enemy, or special forms of murder (*parricidium*, q.v.). For the evolution of this group the series of criminal *leges* of the last century of the Republic (*Corneliae*, *Iuliae*, see above) were of the greatest importance. They instituted special criminal courts for particular crimes, extending in large measure the competence of the State to the prosecution and punishment of criminal acts. A survey of the various kinds of crimes allotted to the *quaestiones perpetuae* shows that they comprehended not only offences against the State, its security and organization, or public order in the widest sense of the word, but also the more serious offences against life, personal integrity, private interests (falsification of wills and documents, serious injuries), and morality (adultery). (For the procedure before these courts *see* QUAESTIO.)

**8.** However, even with the help of the Senate, imperial constitutions, and the jurists, this legislation covered only part of the offences needing repression. Furthermore, the *quaestiones* operated only at Rome and tried Roman citizens only (not women or slaves or *peregrini*). Augustus introduced juries into some provinces (*see* CYRENE, EDICTS OF), but they had no jurisdiction over Roman citizens. These and other deficiencies were made good by a new kind of procedure called *extra ordinem*, as not being subordinated to *ordo iudiciorum*.

The trials in these *iudicia publica extra ordinem* were always conducted by public officials. Jurisdiction was exercised—apart from political offences and senatorial matters reserved for the Senate—chiefly by the Emperor and the prefects, in the provinces by *praesides* and *procuratores* as his delegates. The sphere of *cognitio extra ordinem* became, thanks to the Emperor's policy, more and more extensive and superseded the *quaestiones*, which are not mentioned after Alexander Severus. On the strength of new legislative provisions new forms of offences arose (called later *crimina extraordinaria*), e.g. fraud (*stellionatus*), participation in illicit corporations, displacing of boundary stones, special types of theft (*fures balnearii, nocturni*). Whilst in *quaestiones* only the penalty laid down by the statute could be pronounced, the imperial judges had discretion in grading the penalty according to their appreciation of all the facts of the case. From the earliest times the intention of the wrongdoer was taken into consideration; even the legendary law of Numa on parricide (*see* PARRICIDIUM) required that the murderer had acted *sciens dolo*; the analogous expression in Republican laws was *sciens dolo malo*.

9. More adequate differentiation between different states of mind was developed in the practice of the *cognitio extra ordinem*, influenced also by imperial constitutions. In appreciating the atrocity of the act and depravity of its author the judge considered the intensity and persistence of the delinquent's will (*dolus*), the question whether the act had been committed with premeditation or on sudden impulse, whether it had been provoked by a moral offence (e.g. murder of an adulterous wife when caught in the act) or was due to drunkenness ('per uinum'). A late classical jurist, Claudius Saturninus, known only by a treatise on penalties, distinguished seven points to be taken into consideration in determining the punishment: reason, person, place, time, quality, quantity, and effect (*Dig.* 48. 19. 16). Judicial liberty, however, gave occasion for arbitrariness: the third century, with the decline of imperial authority, brought anarchy into criminal jurisdiction. Under the Late Empire fixed penalties—now more severe than formerly—were restored, the discretion of the judge in the infliction of punishment having been abolished. But in contrast to the trial before *quaestiones*, appeal was admitted *extra ordinem*. A distinction was made between *honestiores* (q.v.) and *humiliores*, the latter being punished more severely than distinguished persons. There is no further trace of the old Republican principle of equality of all citizens in the eyes of the criminal law which had been expressed in the rule 'priuilegia ne inrogato' ascribed by Cicero to the XII Tables.

10. The magistrates invested with *imperium*, acting personally or by delegates, were in general the organs of criminal justice. From early times their power of punishment was restricted by the rule that a sentence *de capite civis* could be passed only by decision of the people assembled in *comitia* (for an alternative view *see* IUDICIA POPULI). The magistrate could, however, apply by informal procedure coercive measures (*coercitio* in a narrower sense) against disobedient or recalcitrant citizens, e.g. prison, castigation, and fines (*multae*); foreigners, slaves, and women were also subjected to *coercitio*. The oldest stage of criminal proceedings before the magistrate was governed by the inquisitorial principle: the magistrate initiated the prosecution at his discretion; he controlled the investigation and production of evidence, he passed the sentence. During the struggle of the orders the jurisdiction of *tribuni plebis* in criminal matters was established especially for political offences and abuses committed by patrician magistrates. Sulla's reform, however, aimed at superseding the jurisdiction of *comitia* and plebeian tribunes and completed the new system of *quaestiones*. This procedure was a compromise between the former criminal proceedings (the jury now representing the popular element) and principles of civil procedure, as the accused had a voice in the choice of jurymen. But the criminal trial preserved its own forms, distinct from the bilateral, contractual character of civil proceedings. The *quaestiones* brought about a restriction of the magistrates' prerogatives, because the prosecution depended now upon the necessary intervention of an accuser. This accusatory system was, however, abolished in the trials *extra ordinem*, where the imperial jurisdictional official regained the full initiative in prosecuting criminal acts and conducted the trial from beginning to end. Accusation was sometimes admitted and even, when successful, rewarded, but the accuser was simply an informer without any substantial procedural rights.

11. The Roman penal system was peculiar in its distinction between public and private penalties, reflecting the division into public and private offences. The private penalty was originally a substitute for private vengeance and retaliation (*talio* = infliction on the delinquent of the same injury as that done by him: *see* INIURIA). Pecuniary composition between the parties (*pacisci*), always permissible, had become compulsory. The private penalty consisted in payment of a sum of money to the person wronged, and is to be distinguished from *multa*, a fine inflicted as a coercive measure by a magistrate and paid to the State. The public penalty originated, as in other primitive systems, in the idea of public revenge, or religious expiation for crimes against the community, or religious conceptions ('sacer esto'), and could not be other than the death of the delinquent. The death-penalty (*poena capitis*), known already in the XII Tables for several crimes, was inflicted in different ways, varying with the times: decapitation (with *gladius*, applied to military persons), gallows (crucifixion, *furca*), burning (in case of arson; application of the *talio*-principle), drowning in a sack (*culleus*), precipitation *de saxo Tarpeio*, and the like. The most severe form, *bestiis obicere*, was practised under the Empire till Justinian. In the republican times the execution (and even the sentence) could be avoided by voluntary exile of the wrongdoer (*see* EXSILIUM). Banishment was later applied as an independent penalty in various forms: *relegatio* (q.v.), *deportatio*, and condemnation to heavy work in mines (*metalla*) or public works (*opus publicum*) or to the gladiatorial training-schools (*in ludos*). These penalties were normally combined with loss of citizenship; *damnatio in metalla* (considered as *morti proxima*), with loss of liberty and flagellation; an accessory penalty was the total or partial confiscation of property. It is noticeable that the Romans applied imprisonment only as a coercive or preventive measure, not as a penalty (*see* PRISON): the Roman conception of penalty laid more stress upon its vindictive and deterrent nature than on correction of the delinquent.

For particular topics *see* ADULTERY, AMBITUS, AMPLIATIO, APPELLATIO, DAMNUM INIURIA DATUM, DIVINATIO, EXSILIUM, FURTUM, HONESTIORES, INFAMIA, INIURIA, IUDICIA POPULI, PARRICIDIUM, PERDUELLIO, PRISON, QUAESTIO, RELEGATIO, REPETUNDAE, TORTURE.

Mommsen, *Röm. Strafr.* (1899) (French transl.: *Ler Doit pénal romain* (1907)); W. Kunkel, *Untersuchungen zur Entwicklung des röm. Kriminalverfahrens in vorsullanischer Zeit* (1962) (Bay. Akad. d. Wissensch., Phil.-Hist. Klasse, N.F. 56); C. Ferrini, *Diritto penale romano* (1899); J. L. Strachan-Davidson, *Problems of the Roman Criminal Law* i, ii (1912); M. Wlassak, 'Anklage und Streitbefestigung im Kriminalrecht der Römer', *Sitz. Wien* 1917; 1920; E. Costa, *Crimini e pene da Romolo a Giustiniano* (1921); E. Levy, 'Röm. Kapitalstrafe' (*Sitz. Akad. Heidelberg*, 1930–1); M. Lauria, 'Accusatio-Inquisitio', *Atti Accad. Napoli* lvi (1934); H. Siber, *Analogie, Amtsrecht und Rückwirkung im Strafrecht des röm. Freistaates* (1936); E. Albertario, 'Delictum e crimen'² in *Studi di dir. rom.* iii. 141 ff. (1936); M. Lauria, *Studia et documenta historiae et iuris* 1938, 182 ff.; U. Brasiello, *La repressione penale in dir. rom.*

(1937); E. Levy, 'Gesetz und Richter im kaiserlichen Strafrecht', *Bull. Ist. Dir. Rom.* 1938; J. M. Kelly, *Princeps Iudex* (1957); J. Bleicken, *Senatsgericht u. Kaisergericht* (1962); C. Dupont, *Le Droit criminel dans les constitutions de Constantin* (1953); F. M. de Robertis, *Studi di dir. pen. rom.* (1942); id. *La variazione della pena nel dir. rom.* (1950); J. Crook, *Roman Law and Life* (1967).          A. B.; B. N.

**LAW, INTERNATIONAL.** Under this heading law must be taken in its widest sense to include customary, religious, and moral law. Some approach to statutory law can be seen in the Amphictionic laws, the decrees of the Congress of Plataea of 479 B.C., and the King's Peace, not to mention that the relations of States to each other were regulated by treaties. Nevertheless, international law remained essentially customary and, in contrast to the laws of individual States, which also had once been customary, was never officially recorded or codified. The importance of religion is seen in the Amphictionic oath, the *fetial* rites, and the practice of ratifying treaties by oath.

2. Public international law was relatively well developed by Homeric times, when heralds and ambassadors were considered inviolable and the sanctity of sworn agreements was recognized. Similar evidence is supplied for early Italy by the *fetial* code with its demand that every war be a just war. Greek law was soon expanded by the Amphictionic oath and the truces for the Panhellenic Games.

3. In both countries treaties were negotiated at an early date. The Greek treaties (σπονδαί, ὅρκοι, συνθῆκαι) obviously were descended directly from the compacts of Homeric times, while the Roman organization of Italy indicates extensive use of treaties relatively early. Omitting armistices, the chief classes were treaties of peace, of alliance, and of friendship. The lack of treaties need not mean hostility. Thus, though Rome had treaties of friendship (*amicitia*) with several States, friendly relations often existed without such a treaty. Though permanent treaties probably were made at an early date, the oldest Greek treaties preserved in detail were made for a limited period, and treaties 'for all time' did not become the rule before the fourth century. The short-term treaties of peace probably were not looked upon as interrupting a natural state of war by a temporary rest, but as imposing additional obligations for the period of their duration. Many Greek treaties contained clauses providing for the arbitration of disputes, and even in their absence arbitration was frequently offered. The system was used with some success and continued to be used under Roman supervision in the second and first centuries B.C.

4. Private international law developed more slowly. At first piracy, private seizure, and enslavement of foreigners were common. In fact, the theory of the complete absence of rights for foreigners not protected by special arrangements was retained by Roman jurists (*Dig.* 49. 15. 5). The foreigners in question are not enemies, so that the theory does not involve the doctrine that all strangers are enemies. On the other hand, there was a high regard for the sanctity of suppliants and for hospitality. Out of this grew hereditary exchanges of private hospitality and later the institution of *proxenoi*, to which the Roman *hospitium publicum* roughly corresponded. Outright piracy soon was widely condemned, and the feeling developed that private seizure should be used only as a reprisal for wrongs suffered. Its use sometimes was further regulated and limited by treaties. Courts, too, began to give protection to foreigners, sometimes when no treaties existed, but probably more frequently on the basis of commercial treaties (σύμβολα). These, at least at Athens, were ratified by a jury-court and so probably were regarded as contracts of a less sacred nature—but not less binding—than other treaties. More extensive rights were granted through treaties of

*isopoliteia* (q.v.). Related to this for Rome was the frequent grant of *commercium*.

5. The regard for what was customary or morally right applied to many points not so far mentioned, for instance to the rules of war. Such a basis for law meant that the standards varied from time to time and from place to place. Everyone is familiar with the lowering of standards which, according to Thucydides, resulted from the Peloponnesian War, while the accusation of piracy constantly made against the Aetolians implies that their standard was lower than those of other States. Nor were all foreigners treated alike, but barbarians were shown less consideration than closely related States. Yet there was always a line which could not be overstepped without incurring censure.

6. Roman expansion, at first glance, seems to leave less scope for development of international law in the Roman Empire than in Greece. It must not be forgotten, however, that Rome's early organization of Italy was based on international law and that the existence of free and allied cities also outside Italy and the control of States not formally annexed caused the Roman Empire to be governed for long largely by a modified form of international law.

See also AMPHICTIONIES; ASYLIA; FETIALES; HERALDS; ISOPOLITEIA; POSTLIMINIUM; PROXENOS; SYMBOLON; SYMMACHIA; WAR, RULES OF.

C. Phillipson, *The International Law and Custom of Ancient Greece and Rome* (1911); F. E. Adcock, 'Some Aspects of Ancient Greek Diplomacy', *Proc. Class. Ass.* 1924; M. N. Tod, *International Arbitration amongst the Greeks* (1913); E. Täubler, *Imperium Romanum* (1913); A. Heuss, *Die völkerrechtlichen Grundlagen der römischen Außenpolitik in republikanischer Zeit* (1933), and his discussion of treaty-making in *Klio* 1934; V. Martin, *La Vie internationale dans la Grèce des cités* (1940); E. Bickerman, 'The Greek Experience of War and Peace', *Conference on Science, Philosophy, and Religion,* iv (1944).          J. A. O. L.

**LEAD.** Metallic lead was discovered early, but little used in primitive cultures. Even at Laurium (q.v.) much was thrown away; but the Romans needed for water-pipes all that they produced. Lead was extensively used for desilvering pyritical ores and for alloying with copper to save tin, both processes being known in pre-Roman times.

Lead mines were mainly exploited for silver, the lead being regarded as a by-product. Of the various deposits in Greece the most important were at Laurium. There were extensive workings in Anatolia. Of pre-Roman origin are the mines of Sardinia and Etruria. Spain, Gaul, and Britain were exploited actively by the Romans, and many stamped Roman pigs have been found there. In the Late Empire mines were opened in the Balkans; the workings in Africa are of doubtful date.

E. Ardaillon, *Les Mines du Laurion* (1897); W. Gowland, *Archaeologia* lxix (1917–18), 121; M. Besnier, *Rev. Arch.* 1919, 31; 1920, 211; 1921, 40; G. C. Whittick, *JRS* 1931, 256; O. Davies, *Roman Mines in Europe* (1935).          O. D.

**LECTISTERNIUM.** A Roman version of the Greek customs of κλίνη and θεοξένια (q.v.). A god or gods were made guests at a meal, couches being prepared for them as for human banqueters. This might be (*a*) in a private house (e.g. Varro ap. Serv. on *Aen.* 10. 76); (*b*) at some shrine, when the *lectus* may but need not be identical with the *pulvinar* (q.v.; Agnes H. Lake in *Quantulacumque* (1937), 243 ff.); (*c*) simultaneously for several gods, first in 399 B.C. (Livy 5. 13. 6). The gods might be represented by statues or *capita deorum,* i.e. bundles of herbs (Festus, 56, 12; 473, 4 (cf. 410, 6) Lindsay; H. Wagenvoort, *Roman Dynamism* (1947), 21.

Latte, *RR* 242.          H. J. R.

**LEDA,** in mythology, daughter of Thestius king of Aetolia, wife of Tyndareus, and mother of the Dioscuri and Helen (qq.v.), but see below. Zeus approached her in the shape of a swan (a very favourite subject in art, see Höfer–Bloch in Roscher's *Lexikon* ii. 1925 ff.) and begat Helen and Polydeuces (Apollod. 3. 126); Castor was begotten by Tyndareus the same night (ibid.). Hyginus (*Fab.* 77) adds Clytaemestra (*see* CLYTEMNESTRA), whose name has perhaps fallen out of the text of Ps.-Apollodorus; but the whole story is told in a number of different ways, Helen being regularly daughter of Zeus (but of Tyndareus, Hyg. 78. 1), the Dioscuri both his sons in Homer. The most noteworthy variant (Apollod. ibid. 127) is that Helen was daughter of Zeus and Nemesis; both parents having been transformed into birds, Nemesis (q.v.) laid an egg, of which Leda took care; when Helen was hatched out from it she passed for Leda's daughter. This is obviously a reconciliation of two conflicting stories. Leda is everywhere mother of Clytaemestra, and frequently, as [Eur.] *IA* 49–50, she has a third daughter, called there Phoebe, Timandra in Apollod. loc. cit. and elsewhere, even a fourth (Apollodorus), Phylonoe, who was made immortal by Artemis. Again, Helen was hatched from an egg laid by Leda, not Nemesis (Eur. *Helena*, 257–9, a doubtfully authentic passage, but the earliest mention surviving, if genuine). The egg is, indeed, a central feature in the story, and was alleged to be preserved in Sparta down to Pausanias' time (Paus. 3. 16. 1); it may therefore be conjectured to go back to some very old tale of deities in bird-shape (Minoan-Mycenaean? cf. Nilsson, *Minoan-Mycenaean Religion*, ch. 10). It may well be older than Homer and the lack of mention of it in his poems due to his dislike of the grotesque; later Greeks disbelieved the story (Eur. *Hel.* loc. cit.) or made fun of it (Cratinus in Athenaeus, 373 e). H. J. R.

**LEGATI.** During the late Republic *legati* were senatorial members of a provincial governor's staff, and were used by Caesar in particular as commanders of individual legions or detachments. This served as a precedent for the reorganization of the army by Augustus.

In the imperial army of the first two centuries each legion (except those in Egypt) was commanded by a *legatus legionis*, normally of praetorian rank. Where there was only one legion in a province, its commander was also the provincial governor and had the title *legatus Augusti pro praetore*. An exception was Africa, where at first the legion was under the command of the proconsul: from the time of Caligula, however, it came under the command of a *legatus*, while the proconsul remained in charge of the civil administration. Where there was more than one legion in a province, the governor held the supreme command and the *legati* of individual legions served under him. The legions of Egypt were commanded by equestrian *praefecti legionum*, as were the three legions raised by Septimius Severus.

*Legati Augusti pro praetore* was also the title of commissioners appointed by the Emperor to perform special tasks, or, especially in the second century, to act as his advisers when he took the field in person.

A. von Domaszewski, *Die Rangordnung des römischen Heeres* (1908); Parker, *Roman Legions²*; G. Iacopi, *Diz. Epigr.* (1949), s.v. 'Legatus'. G. R. W.

**LEGION. 1. EARLY REPUBLIC.** The early history of the legion is very uncertain. A 'Romulean' legion of 3,000 men may have been doubled in size in the later Regal period and then divided into two on the establishment of the Republic. The first trustworthy account is that of Polybius (6. 19 ff.), which reflects the conditions, supposedly of the Second Punic War, but more probably of his own time. The *dilectus* is still based upon a property-qualification, now of 4,000 *asses*: it had earlier been 11,000,

and this seems evidence of some proletarianization of the army before Marius. The legion was drawn up in three lines of *hastati*, *principes*, and *triarii*, with the youngest and poorest forming the *velites*, or light-armed troops. The tactical unit was the maniple, of which there were thirty to the legion, ten to each of the three lines. The maniple had a *signum*, was composed of two centuries, and was commanded by the senior of its two centurions. *See* MANIPULUS, VELITES.

**2. MARIUS TO CAESAR.** By the Marian reforms (*a*) eligibility for service was extended to the *capite censi*, and the legions became largely volunteer forces of semi-professional soldiers; (*b*) each legion, now standardized at 6,000 strong, received an *aquila*; (*c*) the cohort permanently superseded the maniple for tactical purposes; (*d*) the legionary cavalry and the *velites* were replaced by *auxilia*. *See* AUXILIA, MERCENARIES (ROMAN).

**3. THE PRINCIPATE.** Out of the forces of the triumvirs Augustus established a standing legionary army. In 15 B.C. the number of legions, each comprising some 5,000 foot-soldiers and 120 mounted men, was 28, which, by the loss of 3 in A.D. 9, was reduced to 25. In the next two centuries additions were made and losses sustained, but the total did not exceed 30 until Septimius Severus raised three new legions. Each legion bore a number, which was not infrequently duplicated, and a title honorific to itself or its creator.

The commander was a senatorial *legatus*, except in Egypt, where an equestrian *praefectus* was employed. This latter practice was extended by Severus to his new legions, and under Gallienus *praefecti* became general. *See* LEGATI, PRAEFECTI.

In the beginning the legions in the West were recruited mainly from Italy and Gallia Narbonensis. As citizenship became more widely extended recruitment became more and more provincial, till by the late second century local recruitment had become the rule. The period of service was fixed by Augustus first at 16 and then at 20 years *sub aquila*, with an additional 4 and 5 years respectively in a veteran corps *sub vexillo*. The Flavians abolished the veteran corps and made 25 years the total legionary service. The legionary received pay of 225 *denarii* a year in the basic grade under Augustus, which was increased to 300 by Domitian. Further increases were made by Severus and Caracalla. The legionary received also donatives and a gratuity on discharge. *See* DONATIVUM, STIPENDIUM.

**4. CONSTANTINE.** Diocletian considerably increased the number of legions, the majority of which remained (with new units added) under the Constantinian reorganization. The legions of the field army, composed entirely of infantry, were only 1,000 strong. (Some had their origin in existing vexillations, which had regularly been of this size since the second century.) They were commanded by *tribuni*. The legions of the *limitanei*, however, commanded by *praefecti*, which were the rumps of the former frontier legions, may have remained at two-thirds or half their original strength. *See also* CENTURIO, COHORS, COMITATENSES, DONATIVUM, LIMITANEI, PALATINI, PRIMIPILUS, SACRAMENTUM, SIGNA MILITARIA, TRIBUNI MILITUM, VEXILLUM, WAR (ART OF, ROMAN). H. M. D. P.; G. R. W.

**5. THE INDIVIDUAL LEGIONS.** Legio I: perhaps re-formed from an earlier I *Augusta* which disgraced itself in Spain in 19 B.C. Stationed at Cologne after disaster of Varus: perhaps previously at Mainz. Moved to Bonn, probably under Caligula. Disbanded after revolt of Civilis, and perhaps incorporated with VII *Galbiana* to form VII *Gemina* (q.v.). On one inscription (*CIL* xii. 2234) called I *Germanica*.

Legio I *Adiutrix*: a force raised from marines by Nero,

made *iusta legio* by Galba. Fought at Bedriacum for Otho, capturing the eagle of XXI *Rapax*, and posted by Vitellius to Spain. Transferred to Mainz (Germ. Sup.) in 70. Moved to Danube *c.* 85; granted title *pia fidelis* by Trajan; perhaps garrisoned Dacia from 107 to *c.* 113. Probably taken by Trajan on Parthian campaign; returned with Hadrian to Danube. Thereafter stationed at Brigetio (Pann. Sup.).

Legio I *Italica*: raised by Nero in 67; sent to Gaul in 68. Supported Vitellius, defeated and sent to Moesia. Thereafter stationed at Novae.

Legio I *Macriana liberatrix*: raised by Clodius Macer in Africa in 68; disbanded by Galba.

Legio I *Minervia*: raised by Domitian in 83 as I *Flavia Minervia*, and stationed at Bonn. For loyalty in 89 granted title of *pia fidelis Domitiana.* (*Flavia* and *Domitiana* dropped after Domitian's death.) Served in Trajan's Dacian Wars and in the Parthian War of M. Aurelius: Bonn remained permanent station.

Legio I *Parthica*: raised by Severus *c.* 197 and stationed at Singara in Mesopotamia.

Legio II *Adiutrix pia fidelis*: created by Vespasian from men of Ravenna fleet; became *iusta legio* 7 Mar. 70. After opposing Civilis went with Cerealis to Britain, and stationed at Lincoln. At Chester under Frontinus and Agricola. Transferred to Danube *c.* 87, possibly to Singidunum; by 114 was in a permanent station at Aquincum (Pann. Inf.).

Legio II *Augusta*: raised by Octavian and in Spain till disaster of Varus, when it moved to Germany, perhaps near to Mainz. From 17 at Argentorate (*Strasbourg*). With invasion force to Britain in 43 (*see* GLEVUM). Eventual permanent station at Isca Silurum, first under Frontinus.

Legio II *Italica*: raised *c.* 165 by M. Aurelius. Stationed at *Albing* (Noricum) from *c.* 176; under Commodus moved to Lauriacum. Early names are II *Pia* and II *Italica pia*; called II *Italica pia fidelis* before end of century.

Legio II *Parthica*: raised by Severus *c.* 197. On return from the East stationed at Albanum near Rome from 202. As the Emperor's personal legion saw service all over the Empi.e. Became *pia fidelis* under Elagabalus.

Legio II *Traiana fortis*: raised by Trajan, possibly for Dacian Wars, but early history obscure; later in Syria. Transferred to Egypt *c.* 125 and stationed at Nicopolis near Alexandria.

Legio III *Augusta*: probably a legion of Octavian. Stationed in Africa, first at Ammaedara and later at Theveste; from end of first century at Lambaesis except for period 238–53. Suffered *damnatio memoriae* in 238; restored by Valerian.

Legio III *Cyrenaica*: perhaps a legion of Lepidus. In the early reign of Augustus stationed in Upper Egypt; when the garrison was reduced to two legions (after A.D. 6?) it shared the double camp at Nicopolis with XXII *Deiotariana*. Moved to Bostra (Arabia), probably after the Jewish Revolt of 132–5.

Legio III *Gallica*: a legion of Antony, perhaps of Caesarian origin. Consistently part of the Syrian command. Transferred to Oescus (Moesia) by Nero in 68; returned to Syria in 70, perhaps to Raphaneae, its second-century station. Still there as garrison of Phoenice after Severus divided Syria. Suffered *damnatio memoriae* for opposing Elagabalus *c.* 219: restored after his fall. Moved to near Damascus in 231/2.

Legio III *Italica*: raised by M. Aurelius *c.* 165. Stationed at *Regensburg* (Raetia), where it remained till end of Roman occupation. In the early period called III *Concors*.

Legio III *Parthica*: raised by Severus *c.* 197; stationed in Mesopotamia, perhaps near Resaina.

Legio IV *Flavia felix*: reorganized by Vespasian in 70

from former IV *Macedonica* (q.v.); replaced XI *Claudia* at Burnum (Dalmatia). Probably transferred to Moesia in 85/6; its stations may have been Viminacium (86–9?) and, possibly, Ratiaria (89–100?), before it became part of the first garrison of Dacia (107–13?). From the time of Hadrian, at least, it was at Singidunum.

Legio IV *Macedonica*: a legion of Octavian which was in Spain during the Early Empire; transferred to Upper Germany *c.* 43, probably to replace XIV *Gemina* at Mainz. Supported Vitellius, surrendered to Civilis, disbanded by Vespasian.

Legio IV *Scythica*: early history obscure, garrisoned Moesia after A.D. 9. In 55 or soon after transferred to Syria, where it remained.

Legio V *Alaudae*: raised by Caesar in Narbonensis. In Spain at beginning of Principate: transferred to Rhine possibly before 17 B.C., when it may have lost its eagle (Vell. Pat. 2. 97), and in A.D. 14 was stationed at Vetera (Germ. Inf.). A Vitellian legion defeated at Cremona, it was sent to Moesia, and was probably destroyed in the disaster of Cornelius Fuscus in Dacia in 86.

Legio V *Macedonica*: probably transferred to Moesia from the East in A.D. 9. Stationed, at least since Claudius, at Oescus. Moved to Armenia *c.* 62; afterwards took part in Jewish War. Returned to Oescus in 71, where it remained as garrison of Moesia Inf. on division of Moesia *c.* 85/6. During or after Trajan's second Dacian War it moved to Troesmis. After Marcomannic War stationed at Potaissa (Dacia). On abandonment of Dacia north of the Danube in 274/5 returned to Oescus as garrison of new province of Dacia Ripensis.

Legio VI *Ferrata*: an Antonian legion stationed under Augustus in Syria, perhaps at Raphaneae. Fought under Corbulo. Marched west with Mucianus, but soon returned. Probably at Samosata from 72. Probably annexed Arabia in 106, and at Bostra till Jewish Revolt of 132–5. Then transferred to Caparcotna in Galilee as part of garrison of new province of Syria Palaestina. Granted title of *fidelis constans* for supporting Severus.

Legio VI *Victrix*: a Caesarian legion which fought for Octavian. Stationed in the early Principate in Spain. Transferred to the Rhineland in winter of 69/70; repaired and occupied the camp at Novaesium (Germ. Inf.). Rewarded with title of *pia fidelis Domitiana* for loyalty in 89. Moved to Vetera *c.* 93. Transferred to Britain *c.* 119. Stationed at York thereafter.

Legio VII: a Caesarian legion whose early history is obscure. The occasional cognomen *Macedonica* suggests an early station in Macedonia, perhaps from *c.* 12 to 1 B.C. From A.D. 9 at Delminium (Dalmatia). Rewarded with title of *Claudia pia fidelis* for its loyalty in 42. Transferred to Moesia *c.* 57, and stationed at Viminacium probably from the beginning, certainly from Vespasian onwards.

Legio VII *Gemina*: raised by Galba and apparently at first called VII *Galbiana*. Accompanied Galba to Rome; then sent to Carnuntum to replace X *Gemina*. Under its legate Antonius Primus it fought for Vespasian. Changed name to VII *Gemina*, perhaps by incorporation of former leg. I (q.v.). Rewarded with title *felix*, perhaps after campaigns of Clemens in Upper Germany in 72/3. Returned to Spain *c.* 74, probably to Legio (*Leon*), where it is attested later. Under Severus became VII *Gemina pia felix*.

Legio VIII *Augusta*: a Caesarian legion whose early history is obscure: perhaps in Moesia before A.D. 6. After A.D. 9 in Pannonia, probably at Poetovio. Transferred to Moesia *c.* 45, and under Nero stationed at Novae. Sent to the Rhine in 70, where its station became Argentorate (*Strasbourg*) in Upper Germany.

Legio IX *Hispana*: Caesar's old Ninth, which may have acquired its cognomen from a period in Spain.

Before 13 B.C. it had probably left for Illyricum; after A.D. 9 it remained in Pannonia. Transferred in 20 to Africa to fight Tacfarinas, it returned to Pannonia in 24. Took part in Claudius' invasion of Britain in 43; within a few years was stationed at Lincoln. In the early years of Vespasian it moved forward to York. Its end is obscure; it was probably not destroyed in Britain c. 119, but moved to Nijmegen c. 121, and later to the East. Perhaps it was finally destroyed in Palestine in the Jewish War of 132–5, or even in Armenia in 161.

Legio X *Fretensis*: Caesar's Tenth. Probably stationed in Syria from the beginning of the Principate; from A.D. 17 at least it was at Cyrrhus. Moved to Alexandria in 66 for the projected campaign against Ethiopia, but employed instead in the Jewish War, and subsequently stationed at Jerusalem. Near the end of the third century moved to Aelana on the Red Sea.

Legio X *Gemina*: the name implies a composite unit; perhaps it was descended partly from Caesar's Tenth and partly from some other legion. Stationed in Spain from the beginning of the Principate, it was transferred to Carnuntum in 63. Returned to Spain in 68. Sent to Lower Germany in 70; stationed first at Arenacum and then at Noviomagus. Rewarded with title *pia fidelis Domitiana* for its loyalty in 89. Transferred to Pannonia c. 103, first at Aquincum(103–13?) and then at Vindobona.

Legio XI: a legion of Octavian whose early history is obscure. By A.D. 9 was at Burnum (Dalmatia). Rewarded with title *Claudia pia fidelis* for its loyalty in 42. Slow to join the other legions supporting Vespasian, it marched with them to Rome, and in 70 was ordered to Germany, where it remained at Vindonissa (Germ. Sup.). Transferred to the Danube c. 101, first at Brigetio (101–5?) in Pannonia and then at Durostorum (Moes. Inf.).

Legio XII *Fulminata*: a Caesarian legion which may have been in Africa or Egypt during the early years of Augustus. By the time of Tiberius it was in Syria, probably at Raphaneae. Disgraced in the campaign of 62 and the surrender of Rhandeia, it was sent back to Syria. Took part in the Jewish War in 66 and lost its eagle (perhaps temporarily). Transferred in 70 to Melitene in Cappadocia. The legend of the miraculous storm of rain which helped XII *Fulminata* in the campaign against the Quadi of 172, if not apocryphal, may refer to a vexillation.

Legio XIII *Gemina*: probably constituted by Octavian from an amalgamation of two legions. Apparently in Illyricum before A.D. 9, when it moved to the Rhine, where its headquarters eventually became Vindonissa (Germ. Sup.). Transferred to *Poetovio* (Pannonia) c. 50. Moved forward to Vindobona under Domitian. Took part in Trajan's Dacian Wars and remained at Apulum thereafter. On the abandonment of Dacia in 274/5 moved to Ratiaria in the new province of Dacia Ripensis.

Legio XIV *Gemina*: another composite legion formed by Octavian. Probably in Illyricum before A.D. 9, then at Mainz. Took part in the invasion of Britain in 43, and within a few years was at Viroconium (*Wroxeter*). Rewarded with title *Martia Victrix* for its part in the defeat of Boudicca. Recalled in 67 for Nero's projected Eastern campaign; returned by Vitellius to Britain. Recalled to fight Civilis; then stationed once more at Mainz. Supported Saturninus in 89; transferred to Pannonia in 92/3, perhaps first at Aquincum (93–101?), and then Vindobona, before it settled finally (at least by 114) at Carnuntum.

Legio XV *Apollinaris*: a legion of Octavian. Stationed in Illyricum at the beginning of the Principate; moved forward to Carnuntum c. A.D. 14. Sent to the East in 62; fought under Corbulo, and then in the Jewish War. Returned to Carnuntum in 71. Went east again for Trajan's Parthian War, and thereafter was stationed in Cappadocia at Satala.

Legio XV *Primigenia*: raised by Gaius in 39 for his projected German campaign or by Claudius in preparation for the invasion of Britain. Originally at Mainz, soon after at Bonn, and later at Vetera (Germ. Inf.). Destroyed in the revolt of Civilis.

Legio XVI: raised by Octavian before 30 B.C.; early history obscure but the name XVI *Gallica* on a few inscriptions may be significant. Perhaps in Raetia before A.D. 9; subsequently in Upper Germany at Mainz. During reign of Claudius transferred to Novaesium in Lower Germany. Surrendered to Civilis, disbanded by Vespasian, and reconstituted as XVI *Flavia Firma* (q.v.).

Legio XVI *Flavia Firma*: created by Vespasian on disbandment of XVI. Its first province was probably Cappadocia, and it was stationed perhaps at Satala, but Trajan's Parthian War caused its transference to Syria. Subsequently it was stationed in Commagene at Samosata.

Legiones XVII, XVIII, XIX: legions of Octavian which by A.D. 6 at the latest were based on what was later Lower Germany. In A.D. 9 they were annihilated in the Teutoburgian Forest and their commander, Varus, committed suicide. Their numbers were never reused. The eagle of XIX was recovered from the Bructeri in 15, the others in 16 and 41 from the Marsi and, probably, the Chauci.

Legio XX *Valeria Victrix*: probably a legion of Octavian. Perhaps originally in Spain, but later part of the army of Illyricum. Transferred to Lower Germany in A.D. 9 and stationed at Cologne. Sometime during Tiberius' reign moved to Novaesium and stayed there till 43, when it took part in the invasion of Britain. It played a key part in Agricola's campaigns and probably built and occupied Inchtuthil from c. 84 to 86. On the withdrawal of II *Adiutrix* it retired to Deva (*Chester*), where it was to remain for the rest of the Roman occupation.

Legio XXI *Rapax*: raised by Augustus probably soon after 25 B.C., certainly before 8 B.C. It may have been serving in Raetia in A.D. 6. Transferred to Vetera (Germ. Inf.) after the Varian disaster of A.D. 9. Moved to Vindonissa (Germ. Sup.) in 43. After the campaign against Civilis remained in Lower Germany at Bonn. Returned to Upper Germany to Mainz c. 83. Supported Saturninus in 89 and was transferred to the Danube, where it was probably destroyed in 92.

Legio XXII *Deiotariana*: originally a legion of Deiotarus which was taken over by Augustus on the death of Amyntas in 25 B.C. Became a *iusta legio* soon after, i.e. after formation of XXI *Rapax*. Served in Egypt probably from the start (attested at Alexandria in 8 B.C.). The legion's end is uncertain, but probably occurred in the Jewish revolt of 132–5.

Legio XXII *Primigenia*: raised at the same time as XV *Primigenia* (q.v.). Originally at Vetera (Germ. Inf.) but transferred to Mainz (Germ. Sup.) c. 43. Supported Vitellius; after his defeat sent to Danube, probably Pannonia. By 71 back on Rhine, but now in Lower Germany at Vetera. Rewarded with title *pia fidelis Domitiana* for its loyalty in 89. When XIV *Gemina* was transferred to the Danube c. 92, XXII *Primigenia* returned to Mainz.

Legio XXX *Ulpia Victrix*: raised by Trajan, probably after, not before, II *Traiana*. After the Dacian Wars was stationed at Brigetio (Pann. Sup.). Transferred in 119 to Vetera (Germ. Inf.) to replace VI *Victrix*, which had left for Britain.

E. Ritterling and W. Kubitschek, PW, s.v. 'Legio'; A. Passerini, *Diz. Epigr.*, s.v. 'Legio' (1950); Parker, *Roman Legions²*; Kromayer–Veith, *Heerwesen und Kriegführung der Griechen und Römer* (1928); R. Syme, *JRS* 1928, 41 ff., 1933, 14 ff., *Laureae Aquincenses* 1938, 267 ff.; E. Birley, *JRS* 1928, 56 ff., *Roman Britain and the Roman Army* (1953), esp. 20 ff.; R. E. Smith, *Service in the Post-Marian Army* (1958); Jones, *Later Rom. Emp.*, ch. 17; J. E. Bogaers, *Studien zu den Militärgrenzen Roms* (1967), 54 ff. G. R. W.

**LELEGES** (Λέλεγες), a tribe mentioned, *Il.* 10. 428, 21. 86, as allied with Troy and occupying Pedasus in the Troad. Later writers give them a wide distribution. In Herodotus (1. 171) Carians 'formerly called Leleges' occupied the Islands and manned King Minos' navy. Philip of Theangela (in Caria) says that Leleges were to Carians as helots to Spartans (Ath. 6. 272). Hesiod located Leleges as aborigines in Locris, and Aristotle in Acarnania, Aetolia, Boeotia, and Megaris (Strabo 321–2). Pausanias (3. 1. 1) makes 'Lelex' the first king of Laconia. Archaeology and place-names do, in fact, confirm that the earliest agriculturalists in Greece came from Asia Minor. A. R. B.

**LEMNOS,** an island of the north-east Aegean. The lava from its volcano (reputed to be the forge of Hephaestus, but extinct in historical times) gave it high fertility, and it grew considerable wheat crops. An important Bronze Age culture has connexions with Troy. In the *Iliad* it figures as a victualling centre for the Achaeans at Troy. From the eighth century on, the island became thoroughly hellenized, but it is doubtful whether it had a Greek population before the sixth century. According to ancient writers its early inhabitants were 'Pelasgians' and 'Tyrsenoi' from the mainland, and there is an undeciphered inscription (*IG* xii. 8. 1; probably of the 6th c.), which seems to have affinities with Etruscan. Lemnos received Athenian colonists after its seizure by the Younger Miltiades in his capacity as ruler of the Thracian Chersonese, *c.* 500 B.C. It was organized as an Athenian cleruchy *c.* 450, and after a brief period of Spartan domination (404–393) was recovered by Athens. From the time of Philip II of Macedon it passed occasionally into the possession of various Hellenistic dynasts, but it was again in Athenian hands from 307 to 295 and from 281 to 202. In 166 it was definitely attached to Athens by the Romans.

P-K, *GL* iv. D II (c); *IG* xii. 8; D. Mustilli, *Annuario* 1932–3 (Hephaestia cemetery); Brea, *Poliochni* i– (1964– ; prehistoric).
M. C.; J. B.

**LEMURIA,** 9, 11, 13 May, on which days apparently kinless and hungry ghosts, *lemures* (Wissowa's doubts, *PW*, s.v. 'Lemuria', col. 1932, that such a word originally existed seem unjustifiable), were supposed to prowl about the houses. Ovid (*Fasti* 5. 419 ff.) describes the ritual of feeding and getting rid of them, but his assertion (443) that they were addressed as *manes paterni* is incredible.

H. J. Rose *Univ. of California Publ. Class. Phil.* 1941, 89 ff.; Latte, *RR* 99. See also AFTER-LIFE, § 8. H. J. R.

**LENAEA,** a Dionysiac festival celebrated in Athens on the 12th day of the month Gamelion (Jan.–Feb.), which in other Ionian calendars is called Lenaeon. The name is derived from λήνη, maenad. The official Athenian name, Διονύσια τὰ ἐπὶ Ληναίῳ, proves that it took place in this sanctuary, which is believed to have been situated west of the Acropolis. Very little is known of the rites. There was a procession and it is said that the *dadouchos* of Eleusis officiated in the Lenaean ἀγῶνες. The chief importance of the festival lies in the dramatic performances; it seems that originally comedy was preferred to tragedy. Much has been written on the so-called Lenaea vases; this still forms a controversial subject.

M. P. Nilsson, *Studia de Dionysiis atticis* (1900), 109 ff.; L. Deubner, *Attische Feste* (1932), 123 ff.; A. W. Pickard-Cambridge, *Dramatic Festivals of Athens²* (1953), 68 ff. M. P. N.; J. H. C.

**LENAEUS,** POMPEIUS, a learned freedman of Pompey, taught in Rome and, loyal to his patron's memory, attacked the character and style of Sallust who had described Pompey as 'oris probi, animo inuerecundo' (Suet.

*Gram.* 15). Pompey caused him to translate into Latin Mithridates' writings on pharmacology (Pliny, *HN* 25. 5 and 7). J. W. D.

**LENTULUS** (1), LUCIUS CORNELIUS (*PW* 188), served under Scipio Africanus in Spain, where he remained from 206 to 201 B.C. as a *privatus* with proconsular imperium, which was constantly prolonged, despite his election as curule aedile for 205. He claimed a triumph in defiance of precedent, but received an *ovatio*. He served in north Italy as consul (199) and proconsul (198). In 196 he was sent on an ineffective diplomatic mission to Antiochus III to mediate on behalf of Egypt. H. H. S.

**LENTULUS** (2), PUBLIUS CORNELIUS (*PW* 202), legate in Greece (172–171 B.C.), curule aedile (169), envoy to Perseus after Pydna, became praetor in 165, reorganizing the *ager Campanus*, and consul *suffectus* in 162. In 156 he negotiated with the kings of Asia Minor. *Princeps senatus* from 125, he opposed C. Gracchus. A. H. McD.

**LENTULUS** (3) **CLODIANUS,** GNAEUS CORNELIUS (*PW* 216), a fair orator, perhaps fought under Sulla in the East and returned to Rome with him. Consul in 72 B.C., he co-operated closely with his colleague Gellius (q.v. 2), taking action against Verres and validating grants of citizenship made by Pompey. He then fought disastrously against Spartacus (q.v.) and (again with Gellius) exercised a stern censorship (70), ejecting sixty-four senators. A legate of Pompey against the pirates, he supported the law of Manilius (q.v. 2) and died soon after. E. B.

**LENTULUS** (4) **SURA,** PUBLIUS CORNELIUS (*PW* 240), disgraced himself as quaestor (81 B.C.); *praetor repetundarum* (74) and consul (71), he was expelled from the Senate by the censors of 70. Praetor again in 63, he joined Catiline (q.v.), negotiated with the Allobrogan envoys and was arrested on their evidence; forced to abdicate, after the senatorial debate he was executed. He was buried by his stepson Antonius (q.v. 4). E. B.

**LENTULUS** (5) **SPINTHER,** PUBLIUS CORNELIUS (*PW* 238), an agreeable aristocrat, lavish in his aedileship (63 B.C.) and praetorship (60), was active as consul (57) in promoting Cicero's recall. Next year Cicero vainly tried to preserve for Spinther as governor of Cilicia the right, procured during his consulate, of restoring Ptolemy Auletes. Before leaving Cilicia in 53 Spinther was saluted *imperator*, and he triumphed in 51. In 49 he fled from Asculum before Caesar's advance, and surrendered at Corfinium with Domitius; he abused Caesar's clemency and was executed after Pharsalus. G. E. F. C.

**LENTULUS** (6) **MARCELLINUS,** GNAEUS CORNELIUS (*PW* 228), a fair orator, as a patron of Sicily (being a descendant of Marcellus, q.v. 1) supported Cicero against Verres. He was a legate of Pompey against the pirates, one of the prosecutors of Clodius (q.v. 1) in 61 B.C., praetor (60), and proconsul in Syria. As consul (56) he opposed Clodius and proposals for armed intervention in Egypt and reproached Pompey and Crassus over their renewed alliance with Caesar. He died soon after. E. B.

**LENTULUS** (7) **CRUS,** LUCIUS CORNELIUS (*PW* 218), praetor 58, was consul 49 B.C., and a determined anti-Caesarian. Later in 49 he administered Asia, and thence brought two legions to Dyrrhachium; after Pharsalus he fled to Egypt, and arrived to meet his death the day after Pompey's. It is possible (though *see* BALBUS 3) that, after fighting against Sertorius, Lentulus gave Balbus Roman citizenship and his name Cornelius; in any case they were close friends, and Balbus persistently begged Lentulus to keep the peace. But Lentulus, according to Caesar, was made desperate by debt; and all authors, including Cicero, whom he had befriended in 58 and 49, describe him as lazy, luxurious, and pretentious. G. E. F. C.

**LENTULUS** (8), GNAEUS CORNELIUS (*PW* 181), consul 14 B.C., known as 'Augur' to distinguish him from Cn. Lentulus, consul 18 B.C. (*PW* 180). Poor to begin with, he received a grant from Augustus, and became extremely rich (Sen. *Ben.* 2. 27. 1 f.). He was proconsul of Asia (2/1 B.C.), was still alive in A.D. 22 (Tac. *Ann.* 3. 59), and died under Tiberius, whom he made his heir (Suet. *Tib.* 49. 1). He, and not his namesake, is very probably the Cn. Lentulus referred to by Tacitus (*Ann.* 1. 27, 2. 32, 3. 68, 4. 29, 44) as victor over the Getae (q.v.) under Augustus and a close friend of Tiberius who accompanied Drusus to Pannonia in A.D. 14, was ridiculously accused *de maiestate* in 24 (cf. Dio 57. 24. 8), and died in 25, very rich after earlier poverty.

*PIR²* C 1379; R. Syme, *JRS* 1934, 112 ff. and *Tacitus* 750; R. S. Rogers, *Class. Weekly* 1948/9, 91 f. T. J. C.

**LENTULUS** (9) **GAETULICUS**, GNAEUS CORNELIUS (*PW* 220), was consul in A.D. 26 and legate of Upper Germany, possibly in succession to his brother, in 30–9. As a lax disciplinarian he was popular with his own army and also with the Lower German legions, commanded by L. Apronius, his father-in-law. An attempt to indict him in 34 as an associate of Sejanus failed. In 39 he appears to have led a conspiracy by which the Emperor Gaius was to be murdered at Moguntiacum. Gaius was forewarned of the plot and Gaetulicus was executed. He was an erotic poet, regarded by Martial (1 *praef.*) as one of his models. Nine epigrams in the *Greek Anthology* may be by him.

Baehr. *FPR* 361. J. P. B.

**LEO** (1) **I**, the Great, Pope A.D. 440–61. Ninety-six sermons and 143 letters survive. They speak with the voice of the institution in which he had merged his personal identity. In a disturbed age he tried to bring order by centralization, persuading metropolitans to send him reports and then writing them answers like imperial rescripts. He won from Valentinian III recognition of Roman ecclesiastical jurisdiction over all western provinces. Though ignorant of Greek, he was drawn into the eastern theological controversy and in 448 issued a theological manifesto, the *Tome*, which rejected the monophysite Christology of Eutyches. Its orthodoxy was acutely criticized by the monophysite Egyptians, but was recognized by the council of Chalcedon (451). Leo welcomed the doctrinal decisions of Chalcedon, but attacked the council's decree conceding the dignity of Constantinople as the second see of Christendom 'because it is new Rome'. In 452 he persuaded Attila to withdraw from Italy, and in 455 dissuaded the Vandals from massacring the defenceless population of Rome, though he could not prevent systematic plunder. He was a crucial figure in the development of the ideology of papal primacy.

Ed. Migne, *PL* liv–lvi; Letters, ed. Schwartz, *Acta Conciliorum Oecumenicorum* ii. 4 (1932). E. Caspar, *Geschichte des Papsttums* i (1930). H. C.

**LEO** (2) **I**, Eastern Roman Emperor (A.D. 457–74), a Thracian by birth, planned a vast expedition to overthrow the Vandal kingdom in Africa. But his army, said to number 100,000 men, was utterly outwitted by Gaiseric (q.v.) and failed even to reach Africa. At home his strength depended mainly on the support of soldiers from Isauria. E. A. T.

**LEOCHARES,** sculptor, probably Athenian. Pliny places his *floruit* in 372 B.C., but Leochares is mentioned in a letter of Plato written after 366 as 'young and good' (*Ep.* 13, 361 a).

SELECTED WORKS: *dated*, (1) Isocrates, dedicated by Timotheus presumably before his banishment in 356 (the surviving bust (Winter, *KB* 317. 5) derives from a later statue). (2) Signature from the Acropolis, about 350. (3) West side of Mausoleum, after 351. Slabs 1020, 1021 of the Amazonomachy (Winter, *KB* 304. 2) with tall, slim, dramatic figures are probably by Leochares. (4) Gold and ivory group of Philip, Alexander, Amyntas, Olympias, and Eurydice in the Philippeum at Olympia, dedicated after Chaeronea, 338. (5) (with Lysippus, q.v.) Alexander's lion hunt, bronze, after 321. *Undated*, (6) Ganymede. Pliny's description of the eagle 'parcentem unguibus etiam per uestem puero' (*HN.* 34. 79) fits the marble group in the Vatican (Winter, *KB* 299. 1), which must therefore be the basis of attribution to Leochares. *Attributed*, (7) Apollo Belvedere in the Vatican (Winter, *KB* 299. 2–4), Roman adaptation of fourth-century original (Leochares made an Apollo in Athens). (8) Artemis of Versailles (Winter, *KB* 312. 3). (9) Hypnos (Winter, *KB* 299. 6). Nos. 3, 6–9 are all theatrical compositions of tall, slim figures. B. Ashmole, however, starting *not* from the Ganymede but from the Alexander on the Acropolis (Acr. no. 1331), which he gives to Leochares, associates with it the Demeter of Cnidos and Mausoleum slabs 1013–16, which others have given to Bryaxis.

Overbeck, 508. 1177–8, 1301–16, 1491; F. Winter, *JDAI* 1892, 164; P. Wolters and J. Sieveking, *JDAI* 1909, 171; O. Deubner, *Hellenistische Apollogestalten*, 46; Lippold, *Griech. Plastik* 268 ff.; B. Ashmole, *JHS* 1951, 13; J. Charbonneaux, *Monuments Piot* 1963, 9. T. B. L. W.

**LEON** (1) of Byzantium, prominent as one of the leaders of his city who claimed Athenian support against Philip of Macedon. He conducted the successful resistance to Philip's siege, 339 B.C., but when the city later made terms Philip secured his death. If he died *c.* 338 various historical works on Philip, the Sacred War, and Alexander should probably be assigned to a later Leon (fl. *c.* 300 B.C.) who was a pupil of Aristotle.

*FGrH* ii B. 132. G. L. B.

**LEON** (2) of Pella (? late 4th c. B.C.), wrote a book on the Egyptian gods, in the form of a letter from Alexander the Great to his mother, in which the gods are represented as in origin human kings, the discoverers of agriculture and other means of human subsistence.

*FGrH* iii. 659.

**LEONIDAS** (1), king of Sparta, succeeded on the mysterious death of his half-brother Cleomenes (q.v. 1), whom the family had fettered as insane. He married Cleomenes' daughter Gorgo. In 480, while his countrymen were celebrating the Carneia, he marched to Thermopylae with his royal guard of 300 (selecting 'men who had sons living' Hdt. 7. 205. 2) and volunteers picked up *en route*, and secured the pass with some 7,000 hoplites, in time to make possible the massive Artemisium naval operation (*see* PERSIAN WARS). He repelled assaults for two days, but when his Phocian allies failed to stop a Persian move by the Anopaea path (*see* THERMOPYLAE), his flank was turned. Leonidas then secured the retreat of his main body, remaining with 1,100 Boeotians, some helots, and his own guard and, after counter-attacking fiercely, fell with all his Spartans. A fifth-century warrior-statue, found at Sparta, may be from his monument.

Hdt. 7. 204–39; to which Diod. (11. 3–11) and Plut. (*Apophth.*, 'Leonidas') add fulsome and unreliable embellishments. A. R. Burn, *Persia and the Greeks* (1962), 273, 378 ff., 403 ff. A. R. B.

**LEONIDAS** (2) of Tarentum, the greatest Greek epigrammatist of the Alexandrian era, led a poor vagabond life (*Anth. Pal.* 7. 715) in the first half of the third century B.C. The Greek Anthology (q.v.) contains about a hundred of his epigrams—some dedications (mainly genuine), some real or imaginary epitaphs, the rest very varied in subject and tone. He is a pessimist of almost tragic intensity (*Anth. Pal.* 7. 472). He does not (like his contemporaries Asclepiades and Posidippus) write of love or feasting, but evokes the life of the poor (*Anth. Pal.* 6. 226, 296, 355), among whom he counts himself (6. 300, 6. 302, 7. 736). In this he resembles certain Hellenistic sculptors of old fishermen (*Anth. Pal.* 6. 4) and decrepit women. But his verse is highly finished, full of baroque compounds and odd technical terms set out in complex sentences. Sometimes his epigrams end in a sharp point, which for his time is unusual. Many later poets, both Greek (e.g. Antipater (q.v. 3) of Sidon) and Roman (Propertius 3. 13. 43–6 ~ *Anth. Pal.* 9. 337), admired and imitated him.

C. M. Dawson, *AJPhil.* 1950; J. Geffcken, *Neue Jahrb.* Suppl. 1897; A. S. F. Gow, *CQ* 1958; B. Hansen, *De L. Tarentino* (1914); L. A. Stella, *Cinque poeti dell'Antologia Palatina* (1949); T. B. L. Webster, *Hellenistic Poetry and Art* (1964), ch. 10; Wilamowitz, *Hell. Dicht.* 1. 139 ff.; Gow and Page, 1955 ff. G. H.

**LEONIDAS** (3) of Alexandria, an astrologer turned poet, wrote in the time of Nero and Vespasian. He is the earliest known author of isopsephic poems, so composed that the letters in each couplet, if read as numbers ($a = 1$, $\beta = 2$, etc.), make the same sum. Thirty such are in the Greek Anthology, with other poems imitative of his predecessors.

Cichorius, *Röm. Studien* viii. 12; P. Perdrizet, *Rev. Ét. Grec.* 1904; K. Radinger, *Rh. Mus.* 1903. G. H.

**LEONNATUS** (c. 358–322 B.C.), a Macedonian noble related to the royal house, accompanied Alexander to Asia, became one of his personal 'Bodyguard' in 332 and (after 328) a prominent general, distinguishing himself in an independent command on the return from India. As satrap of Hellespontine Phrygia (323) he reinforced Antipater in the Lamian War; but he was defeated and killed in Thessaly by the Greek insurgents. His character lacked moderation and stability, and he would probably have fared badly against cooler heads in the age of the 'Successors'.

Berve, *Alexanderreich*, no. 466. G. T. G.

**LEONTINI** (modern *Lentini*, though the excavated remains of the south gate, walls, and tombs are at *Carlentini*), founded from Naxos (q.v. 1) in 729 B.C. on a commanding hillside position south of the Piana di Catania. Flourishing in the sixth century (its ruler Panaetius being the earliest Sicilian tyrant), it was captured by Hippocrates (q.v. 1) c. 494 B.C., and thereafter was usually dominated by Syracuse, with intervals of precarious freedom. Its alliance with the Athenians (renewed in 433/2 B.C.; see *IG* i². 52) was implemented in 427 when its most famous citizen, the orator Gorgias (q.v. 1), led its delegation to Athens. Hieronymus, successor of Hieron II (q.v.), was murdered there in 215 B.C. and after further provocations Leontini was sacked by the Romans who then besieged Syracuse. A *civitas decumana* under Roman rule, it suffered in the Servile War (104) and its inhabited area contracted in later antiquity.

Good description in Polyb. 7. 6. Bérard, *Bibl. topogr.* 59 ff.; Dunbabin, *Western Greeks*; recent excavations, G. Rizza, *Not. Scav.* 1955, 281 ff. A. G. W.

**LEOSTHENES** (d. 322 B.C.), an Athenian, general at Athens in 324/3, having probably served as captain of mercenaries in Asia previously. With acute political insight he organized the return and maintenance at Taenarum of mercenaries disbanded by Alexander's satraps (324), and presumably organized (by means unknown) their feeding and payment till the time should come to employ them in an anti-Macedonian war. The Lamian War (323–322) was his opportunity. He commanded the Greek army and inspired its devotion, and his death at the siege of Lamia was a heavy blow to the Greek cause.

Berve, *Alexanderreich*, no. 471; E. Badian, 'Harpalus', *JHS* 1961, 27, 36 ff. G. T. G.

**LEOTYCHIDES**, king of Sparta c. 545–469 B.C., succeeded the exiled Demaratus (c. 491 B.C.) with aid of Cleomenes I (q.v.). In the Aeginetan War he apparently secured the granting of a truce to Athens and delivery of hostages by Aegina. In 479, as commander-in-chief of the allied fleet, he fomented the revolt of Chios and Samos, and decisively defeated the Persians in a land and sea battle at Mycale. He led another combined Greek force on a punitive expedition against the medizing aristocracies in Thessaly (c. 477). He took Pagasae and perhaps Pherae, but failed to capture Larissa. He was tried at Sparta on a charge of bribery (probably c. 476), but he escaped condemnation by retiring to Tegea. An earlier namesake (with whom Leotychides has often been confused) subdued Messenia in the Second Messenian War (*see* MESSENIA).

Beloch, *Griech. Gesch.*² i, pt. 2, 179 ff.; ii, pt. 2, 190 ff.; J. Johnson, *Hermathena* 1931; J. Kroymann, *Sparta und Messenien*, 3 ff. (1937); L. R. Shero, *TAPA* 1938, 516 ff. P. T.

**LEPCIS** (or **LEPTIS**) **MAGNA** (neo-Punic *Lpqi*). One of the Phoenician Emporia between the Syrtes, perhaps founded before 600 B.C. (*see* TRIPOLIS 1). Its prosperity came from its olive-bearing hinterland and from the trans-Saharan trade. Lepcis became a colony under Trajan, and Septimius Severus, a native of the city, gave it the *ius Italicum* and adorned it with splendid buildings, including a forum, basilica, and colonnaded street leading to his newly built harbour. It had bishops in the third century. New city walls (late third or early fourth century) saved Lepcis from the Austuriani who in 365 devastated its territory (Amm. Marc. 28. 6). Thereafter it declined and its Byzantine walls enclosed only a fraction of the former city. The ruins of Lepcis, excavated since 1920, are exceptionally fine. Besides the Severan buildings, the Augustan forum, under which remains of the early settlement have been found, the theatre, amphitheatre, Hadrianic baths, and Hunting baths are of outstanding interest.

·P. Romanelli, *Leptis Magna* (1925); T. H. Carter, 'Western Phoenicians at Lepcis', *AJArch.* 1965, 123 ff.; R. Bartoccini, *Il porto romano di Leptis Magna* (1958); G. Caputo and E. V. Caffarelli, *Buried City* (1966); M. Squarciapino, *Leptis Magna* (1967). *See also* bibliography s.v. TRIPOLIS. O. B.

**LEPIDUS** (1), MARCUS AEMILIUS (*PW* 68), the censor of 179 B.C., appears first on the embassy to Greece, Syria, and Egypt in 200, delivering the Roman ultimatum to Philip V. Curule aedile (193), praetor in Sicily (191), he became consul (187), constructing the Via Aemilia, and as triumvir (183) founded Mutina and Parma. Pontifex Maximus (180) and censor (179) with M. Fulvius Nobilior, he reformed the Comitia Centuriata and carried out a large building programme, including the Basilica Aemilia. Consul again (175) in Liguria, he was decemvir for land settlement there (173). From his censorship to his death in 152 he was *princeps senatus*. Well-born and handsome, combining liberal culture with observance of tradition, he was pre-eminent in the Senate, and his name marks the pacification of Cispadane Gaul.

F. W. Walbank, *Philip V of Macedon* (1940), 134, 313 ff.; H. H. Scullard, *Rom. Pol.* 135, 180, 233, 237; H. Mattingly, *Roman Coins*² (1960), 70. A. H. McD.

**LEPIDUS** (2), MARCUS AEMILIUS (*PW* 72), descendant of (1), whose Gallic connexions he inherited and used. Military tribune under Pompeius (q.v. 3), probably aedile under the *Cinnani*, he joined Sulla—divorcing his wife (related to Saturninus, q.v. 1)—and amassed wealth in the proscriptions. Elected consul for 78, with Pompey's support, he agitated—perhaps even before Sulla's death —for the overthrow of his constitution, against the opposition of his colleague Catulus (q.v. 2). Given Gaul as a province, he held Cisalpina through his legate Brutus (q.v. 4), stirred up trouble in Transalpina, and made contact with Sertorius (whom his supporters later joined) in Spain, then marched on Rome (77), where the emergency decree was passed. But lacking experience of command, he was defeated by Catulus and fled to Sardinia, where he was defeated by Triarius (q.v.) and died (we are told) of grief over his divorce (Pliny, *HN* 7. 122). The first to realize the resources and strategic importance of Gaul, he lacked tactical ability to match his strategic grasp, but showed the way to others. Caesar watched him with interest and later secured an amnesty for his supporters (Suet. *Iul.* 3; 5).

**LEPIDUS** (3), MARCUS AEMILIUS (*PW* 73), the Triumvir, younger son of (2), as praetor in 49 B.C. supported Caesar, then governed Nearer Spain (48–47), intervening in the dissensions in Further Spain (*see* CASSIUS 5) and returning to triumph. He was consul (46) and Caesar's *magister equitum* (46–44). On Caesar's death he gave armed support to Antony, who in return contrived his appointment as *pontifex maximus* in Caesar's place. He then left to govern the provinces assigned him by Caesar, Gallia Narbonensis and Nearer Spain. When, after the war of Mutina, Antony retreated into Gaul, Lepidus assured Cicero of his loyalty to the Republic but on 29 May 43 joined forces with Antony and was declared a public enemy by the Senate. At Bononia in October he planned the Triumvirate with Antony and Octavian, accepting Further Spain with his existing provinces as his share of the Empire; and demanding (or conceding) the proscription of his brother Paullus (q.v. 3). After triumphing again 'ex Hispania' he held a second consulship (42) and took charge of Rome and Italy during the campaign of Philippi. After their victory his colleagues deprived him of his provinces, on the pretext of a rumour of collusion between him and Sextus Pompeius, but nothing serious was proved; and after helping Octavian ineffectively in the Perusine War he was allowed to take over Africa instead (40). He played an independent part in the campaign of 36 against Sextus, and laid claim to Sicily, but Octavian won over his army and compelled him to leave the Triumvirate and retire into private life, retaining only his office of *pontifex maximus*. Lepidus, who died in 13 or 12 B.C., lacked the character and energy to use the opportunities which high birth and Caesar's favour placed in his way. His wife Junia was a sister of M. Brutus.

Cic. *Letters* and *Philippics*; Vell. Pat. 2. 63–7, 80; Plut. *Ant.*; App. *BCiv.* 2–5; Cass. Dio 41–54. Syme, *Rom. Rev.*, see index.
G. W. R.; T. J. C.

**LEPIDUS** (4), MARCUS AEMILIUS (*PW* 74), son of (3) above, plotted in 30 B.C. to assassinate Octavian on his return to Rome, but was detected by Maecenas and executed. His wife Servilia, perhaps the Servilia once betrothed to Octavian, committed suicide. Either he or another son of the Triumvir had earlier been promised to Antonia (1).

Münzer, *Röm. Adelsparteien*, 369 f.; Syme, *Rom. Rev.*, see index; E. Hohl, *Würzb. Jahrb.* 1948, 107 ff. T. J. C.

**LEPIDUS** (5), MARCUS AEMILIUS (*PW* 75), younger son of Paullus (4) and Cornelia, was consul in A.D. 6, then served under Tiberius in Pannonia, receiving *ornamenta triumphalia* in 9. In 14 he was governor of Nearer Spain; in 21 he prudently declined the proconsulship of Africa in favour of Blaesus (q.v.), uncle of Sejanus; later (probably 26–8) he was proconsul of Asia. In 22 he repaired the Basilica Aemilia. He died in 33. Augustus, on his death-bed, had adjudged him 'capacem (imperii) 'sed aspernantem', Tac. *Ann.* 1. 13 and he is one of the more prominent senators of Tiberius' reign; Tacitus stresses his wisdom and moderation. His children included Lepida, who married Drusus (q.v. 5), helped to bring about his fall in 30, and committed suicide when accused of adultery in 36; perhaps also Lepida, wife of Galba (1), and Marcus, last of the family, who married Drusilla (q.v.), was promised the succession by Gaius, but conspired against him in 39 with Lentulus (q.v. 9) and was executed.

R. Syme, *JRS* 1955, 22 ff. (reading 'Manium' for 'Marcum' in Tac. *Ann.* 3. 32, and keeping the MS. 'M.' in 1. 13; 3. 11, 35, 50; 4. 20, 56; 6. 5, 27). T. J. C.

**LEPIDUS** (6), MANIUS AEMILIUS (*PW* 63), probably a grandson of the Triumvir and also of Faustus Sulla (3) and Pompeia (cf. Tac. *Ann.* 3. 22), was consul in A.D. 11, defended his sister Lepida in 20, and was appointed proconsul of Asia (21/2) despite objections on the score of his poverty and inactive disposition.

R. Syme (cited under the preceding). T. J. C.

**LESBONAX.** The author of three extant Atticizing declamations, set in fifth- and fourth-century B.C. situations: perhaps to be identified with the writer of μελέται and ἐρωτικαὶ ἐπιστολαί mentioned in the scholia to [Lucian] Περὶ ὀρχήσεως 19. Probable date: second century A.D.

TEXT. Bekker, *Oratores Attici* (1823–8); Kiehr (1907). Norden, *Ant. Kunstpr.* 390. D. A. R.

**LESBOS,** the largest of the islands off the coast of Asia Minor, lying athwart the entrance to the Gulf of Adramyttium, roughly triangular in shape, but with two landlocked bays cutting deep into the hills on the southern side. The fertile soil and mild climate supported five cities: Mytilene (overshadowing but never completely dominating her neighbours), Methymna, Eresus, Antissa, and Pyrrha. An important Bronze-Age settlement at Thermi has close connexions with Troy. The Aeolian immigrants, who formed the chief element in the population, turned to the sea, as well as to agriculture, for a livelihood, as their secondary colonization on the coast of the Troad and their participation in founding the Hellenium at Naucratis show. This widening of horizons must have helped to stimulate the intense intellectual and cultural life among the aristocratic classes during the Golden Age of the late seventh and early sixth centuries B.C., represented by the poets Arion, Sappho, and Alcaeus, and the statesman Pittacus, and the construction of 'Aeolic' (or 'proto-Ionic') temples at Mytilene and Nape. Lesbos later had a distinguished philosophical tradition: Theophrastus came from Eresus, and in the fourth century Aristotle and Epicurus, in the first century Cratippus, resided for a time on the island. *See also* MYTILENE.

P-K, *GL* iv. E I; *IG* xii. 2; Longus, *Daphnis and Chloe* (a vivid picture of life on Lesbos in the third century A.D.); R. Koldewey, *Die ant. Baureste der Insel Lesbos* (1890); W. Lamb, *Thermi* (1936). D. E. W. W.; J. B.

**LESCHES** of Mytilene (? 7th c. B.C.), epic poet, to whom the *Ilias Parva* is almost universally attributed. *See* EPIC CYCLE.

*EGF* 3, 36–43.

**LETO** (Λητώ, Lat. Latona), a Titaness, daughter of Coeus and Phoebe, 'gentle to men and to the deathless gods' (Hes. *Theog.* 404 ff.). She is one of the few Titans who have a cult in historical times, although generally it is together with her children (see Sauer in Roscher's *Lexikon* ii. 1966 ff.), and some of her temples had pious legends connected with them, see Semos of Delos in Athenaeus, 614 a (the Letoön on Delos), Nicander in Ant. Lib. 17, cf. LEUCIPPUS (2) (the Letoön at Phaestus). The etymology of her name is quite obscure, though Wilamowitz-Moellendorff (cf. APOLLO) would connect it with Lycian *lada*, 'woman' (*Apollo* (1908), 31). It is almost certainly not Greek. (For her cult in Lycia, cf. W. H. Buckler, *JHS* 1935, 78; in Phrygia, L. Robert, *Villes d' Asie mineure* (1935), 128.) But her chief importance is as mother of Apollo and Artemis (qq.v. *and see* DELOS). Homer (*Il.* 24. 605 ff.) and Hesiod (*Theog.* 918–20) merely say she bore them and give no details; we may conjecture that many famous shrines of one or both deities claimed to be the birthplace, but for some reason, perhaps not unconnected with the great 'Homeric' hymn to the Delian Apollo, Delos imposed its claims on nearly the whole Greek world, other legends, such as those of Tegyra in Boeotia (Plut. *Pel.* 16), Zoster in Attica (Semos in Steph. Byz. 611, 5 Meineke, cf. Paus. 1. 31. 1), and Ephesus (Tac. *Ann.* 3. 61), fading into obscurity.

According to the Hymn Leto was delivered of Apollo (but not Artemis, 16) 'leaning against Cynthus' mountain' in Delos (26; her gigantic size needed this huge prop), or more usually described as grasping the sacred palm-tree (116 with Allen, Halliday, and Sykes' note). None of the other islands dared to let so terrible a god be born in it, and even Delos was afraid till reassured by an oath of Leto (83 ff.) that Apollo would make his temple there. But Leto was in labour nine days and nights, because Hera would not let Eileithyia go to her (97 ff.) till the other goddesses sent her word and promised her a great fee; she then came without Hera's knowledge or consent and Leto was delivered. Callimachus in his fourth Hymn follows a somewhat different account; Hera forbade any land to afford Leto refuge and set Ares and Iris to see that they did not, but at last Delos ventured to disobey (202 f.), and was forgiven because she was once the nymph Asteria (q.v.). A later story (Hyg. *Fab.* 160. 3) makes Poseidon overreach Hera; the waves were washing over Delos, therefore it was not land.

A curious legend is preserved by Aristotle (*Hist. An.* 580ᵃ15 ff.). Leto, as mother of the 'wolf-god' (cf. APOLLO), took the form of a she-wolf to deceive Hera, and so journeyed from the Hyperborean country to Delos in twelve days. Therefore there are but twelve days of the year in which she-wolves bring forth.

Leto appears with Apollo and Artemis already in the art of the early seventh century (bronze statuettes from Dreros in Crete), and they are commonly shown together from the later sixth. Two groups of the three are recorded by Praxiteles, as well as a statue of Leto alone.

Besides the literature cited in the text see the art. 'Leto' in PW (Suppl. v. 555), and Nilsson, *GGR* i². 500, 562.

H. J. R.; C. M. R.

**LETTERS, GREEK.** For the sake of convenience Greek letters may be roughly divided into six classes:

(1) Private letters, almost exclusively represented by papyri. These are valuable both as evidence of the language commonly spoken and written in Hellenistic and later periods and as documents illustrating contemporary social and economic conditions in Egypt. Of the great number of those already published many have now been re-edited in separate collections.

(2) Official letters by means of which representatives of the government communicated with each other or with their subjects and subordinates. The most interesting of these are to be found in the official correspondence of the Hellenistic kings.

(3) 'Literary' letters contained in the authentic collections of the great fourth-century epistolographers, e.g. Julian, Libanius, St. Basil, St. Gregory of Nazianzus, St. John Chrysostom, and Synesius, many written with a view to subsequent publication.

(4) Letters employed as a medium for the exposition of ideas, e.g. on philosophy by Epicurus, on science by Archimedes and Eratosthenes, on literary criticism by Dionysius of Halicarnassus; the epistles of St. Paul belong to this class, as do the long 'hortatory' letters of Isocrates (*Or.* 2 and 3), at least from one point of view.

(5) Letters, for the most part spurious, attributed to persons of note, which owe their survival to the general interest of their contents or the reputations of their supposed authors. The spurious letters are sometimes real forgeries; more often they are school exercises or inventions intended to illustrate the characters of famous men. The deliberate forgeries belong for the most part to the last two centuries B.C. and may have been partly due to the eagerness of the Attalids and Pergamids to acquire additions to their libraries; the second sort is chiefly the product of the period 100 B.C.–A.D. 200, amongst these those of Anacharsis (which imposed on Cicero), Hippocrates, and Diogenes the Cynic. The famous letters of Phalaris, exposed by Bentley after a long and celebrated controversy, may be as late as fifth century A.D.

The most important surviving collections are those of Isocrates, Plato, and Demosthenes: some at least of these have strong claims to authenticity, the majority are almost certainly spurious. We know also of collections by Theophrastus, Epicurus, Arcesilaus, and Carneades, the practice of collecting letters being specially characteristic of philosophical schools; those of Aristotle, even if the six printed in Hercher are not genuine, were much admired in antiquity.

(6) 'Imaginative' letters, designed to entertain readers by recreating the lives and manners of real or imaginary persons of a bygone age. The master of this style is Alciphron but also worthy of mention are Aelian, Aristaenetus, and Philostratus, who in this respect at least may be said to have anticipated the historical novel and such works as Richardson's *Pamela* and *Clarissa* and Rousseau's *La Nouvelle Héloïse*.

The theory of epistolography first began to interest the Greeks themselves in the Hellenistic period. The earliest name known to us in this connexion is that of Artemon, who is said to have edited the letters of Aristotle but cannot be identified with any certainty; others who expounded the subject were Apollonius of Tyana, Dionysius and Theon of Alexandria, Philostratus of Lemnos, and St. Gregory of Nazianzus. Practical handbooks which have survived are the Τύποι ἐπιστολικοί of Demetrius, written as an excursus to his Περὶ ἑρμηνείας and the Περὶ ἐπιστολιμαίου χαρακτῆρος of Proclus, which is probably an earlier edition of the 'Επιστολιμαῖοι χαρακτῆρες attributed to Libanius. It can be argued that it is possible to detect a certain degree of continuity of form and even of phraseology throughout the history of Greek letters, whatever the class into which they happen to fall.

PRIVATE AND OFFICIAL LETTERS. D. Brooke, *Private Letters, Pagan and Christian* (1929); W. Döllstädt, *Griechische Papyrusbriefe in gebildeter Sprache* (1934); G. Ghedini, *Lettere cristiane* (1923) (cf. Cavassini, 'Lettere cristiane', *Aegyptus* 1954, 266 ff.). R. Herzog, 'Griechische Königsbriefe', *Hermes* 1930, 455 ff.; A. S. Hunt and C. Edgar, *Select Papyri* i (Loeb, 1952); B. Olsson, *Papyrusbriefe aus der frühesten Römerzeit* (1925); A. Salonius, *Zur Sprache der griechischen Papyrusbriefe* (1927); C. B. Welles, *Royal Correspondence in the Hellenistic Period* (1934); S. Witkowski, *Epistulae privatae graecae*² (Teubner, 1911).
LITERARY AND OTHER LETTERS. R. Bentley, *A Dissertation upon the Epistles of Phalaris* (1699); R. Blass, *Die attische Beredsamkeit*² (1887–98), pt. iii, 439 ff. (Demosthenes); R. Hackforth, *The Authorship of the Platonic Epistles* (1913); J. Harward, *The Platonic Epistles*

(1932); R. Hercher, *Epistolographi graeci* (1873); R. C. Jebb, *The Attic Orators*[2] (1893), ii. 239 ff. (Isocrates); A. Mayer, *Theophrasti Περὶ λέξεως fragmenta* (Teubner, 1910); M. Plezia, 'De Aristotelis epistulis observationes criticae', *Eos* 1951, 77 ff.; J. Sykutris, *Die Briefe des Sokrates und der Sokratiker* (1933); U. von Wilamowitz-Moellendorff, 'Unechte Briefe', *Hermes* 1898, 459 ff.
HISTORY AND THEORY. K. Dziatzko, 'Brief' in *PW* iii. 836 ff.; A. Brinkmann, 'Der älteste Briefsteller', *Rh. Mus.* 1909, 310 ff.; F. X. J. Exler, *The Form of the Ancient Greek Letter* (1923); H. Hinck, 'Die *Ἐπιστολιμαῖοι χαρακτῆρες* des Pseudo-Libanios', *Neue Jahrb. f. Philologie u. Pädagogik* 1869, 537 ff.; C. W. Keyes, 'The Greek Letter of Introduction', *AJPhil.* 1935, 28 ff.; H. Koskenniemi, *Studien zur Idee und Phraseologie des griechischen Briefes bis 400 n. Chr.* (1956); J. Sykutris, 'Proklos Περὶ ἐπιστολιμαίου χαρακτῆρος, *Byz.-Neugriech. Jahrb.* vii (1928/9), 108 ff., and 'Epistolographie', *PW* Suppl. v. 185 ff.; A. Westermann, *De epistularum scriptoribus Graecis* i–viii (1850–4); V. Weichert, *Demetrii et Libanii qui feruntur Τυπ. ἐπ. et Ἐπ. χαρ.* (1910); F. Ziemann, *De epistularum graecarum formulis sollemnibus quaestiones selectae* (1910). R. H.; B. R. R.

**LETTERS, LATIN.** Letter-writing was, next to Satire, Rome's most distinctive legacy to the world's literature. In the self-contained communities of independent Greece there was comparatively little need or scope for correspondence; but as Rome became the hub of the Mediterranean world written communication gained in importance. Landowners visiting their estates in Italy, senators on military or administrative service in the provinces, merchants and tax-farmers, students and exiles, all needed to be kept in touch with the capital, and every traveller went laden with letters he had been asked to deliver, often in return for letters of introduction to influential persons (*epistulae commendaticiae*), such as are found among Cicero's extant correspondence (*Fam.* 13). Men of wealth and position in Cicero's time had among their slaves couriers (*tabellarii*) who could cover fifty Roman miles a day, and the companies of tax-farmers had their own postal service (*publicanorum tabellarii*). Later Augustus, in order to maintain close contact with his provincial governors, instituted a system of post-couriers along the main routes of the Empire, but there was still no organized postal system for private correspondence (*see* POSTAL SERVICE).

2. Letters were normally written with a reed pen (*calamus*) and ink (*atramentum*) on papyrus (*charta*). Pages were pasted together, as in the case of books, to form a roll which was tied with thread and sealed. Notes written off-hand to persons at no great distance were sometimes scratched with a *stilus* on wax-covered folding tablets (*codicilli*), the recipient could erase the message and use the same tablets for his reply (Cic. *Fam.* 6. 18. 1; Pliny, *Ep.* 6. 16. 8). To Atticus, his most intimate friend, Cicero generally wrote in his own hand ('suo chirographo') unless for some special reason (*Att.* 2. 23. 1, 8. 13. 1); but it was usual for persons of rank to employ an amanuensis (*librarius* or *servus ab epistulis*). Cicero's secretary, Tiro, appears to have kept copies of letters dictated to him (*Fam.* 7. 25. 1), and to have pasted together in rolls (*volumina*) those which Cicero thought best worth keeping. It is no doubt to this practice that we owe the preservation of Cicero's *Epistulae ad Familiares*, though his intention, expressed in 44 B.C. (*Att.* 16. 5. 5), of revising and publishing a selection of letters remained unfulfilled. His letters to Atticus and to his brother Quintus were preserved by their recipients, and the former probably remained unpublished for a century after his death (*see* CICERO 1).

3. Cicero himself (*Fam.* 2. 4) classified letters under three heads, news-letter, 'genus familiare et iocosum', and 'genus seuerum et graue'. To the first of these categories belong his letters to Atticus, which, more than any other document of antiquity, show history in the making, and discuss with absolute frankness all that is in the writer's mind; also the vivid and somewhat cynical letters of M. Caelius Rufus, seventeen of which are preserved (*Fam.* 8). The second type is well represented by Cicero's letters to C. Trebatius Testa, M. Fadius Gallus,

and L. Papirius Paetus (*Fam.* 7. 6–27, 9. 15–26); the third perhaps best of all by the letter of condolence addressed to Cicero, on the death of his daughter Tullia, by Sulpicius Rufus (*Fam.* 4. 5). This last, together with such letters as those in which Cicero asks the historian Lucceius to immortalize his consulship (*Fam.* 5. 12), or expresses his distaste for the *Ludi* exhibited by Pompey in 55 B.C. (*Fam.* 7. 1), may be taken as representing the type of letter which was to serve as a model for the Younger Pliny. Close on a hundred letters from other correspondents are preserved along with Cicero's; of these perhaps the most distinctive in character and style are those of Q. Metellus Celer (*Fam.* 5. 1), M. Cato (*Fam.* 15. 5), M. Antonius (*Att.* 10. 8 a), P. Vatinius (*Fam.* 5. 9–10), C. Asinius Pollio (*Fam.* 10. 31–3), and C. Matius (*Fam.* 11. 28), and the letter in which Cicero's son, writing to Tiro, gives a glimpse of student life at Athens (*Fam.* 16. 21).

4. The correspondence of Augustus was extant in the time of Suetonius (*Aug.* 71, 76; *Claud.* 4, etc.), and Macrobius (*Sat.* 1. 24. 11) quotes a letter of Virgil. But the Augustan age has left us only the verse epistles of Horace and Ovid, and from the Claudian and Flavian dynasties we possess only the *Epistulae Morales* of the Younger Seneca (q.v.). With these authors the epistolary form is a mere literary convention, and although Seneca was undoubtedly influenced by the *Epistulae ad Atticum*, his letters to Lucilius are essentially the ramblings of a philosopher; their ancestry should be sought rather in the epistles of Epicurus.

5. That life under the Empire afforded neither the material nor the freedom of expression for letter-writing in the true Ciceronian tradition is evident even when we come to the second great collection of Latin letters, published under the liberal rule of Trajan. The letters of Pliny the Younger (q.v.) resemble Cicero's in that they cover a wide range of topics and reflect the life, interests, and personality of their author; but they do so deliberately and selectively. Their writing belongs, not to the urgent business of living, but to the tranquil detachment of literature. The tenth book, consisting of letters exchanged between a responsible official and his emperor, stands alone as representing the practical side of Pliny's activities. Certain of Statius' *Silvae* are poetical epistles.

6. The correspondence of Fronto (q.v.) with Marcus Aurelius and others owes nothing to the literary tradition of Seneca or Pliny. Much of its subject-matter is purely academic, but the affectionate exchanges of gossip between master and pupil have something of the unselfconscious intimacy of Cicero's letters to Atticus, and their style and diction, quaintly compounded of colloquialism and pedantry, add both to their interest and to their charm.

7. The literary epistle reappears in the fourth century with Symmachus, last of the pagan prose-writers, and Ausonius, first of the Christian poets, some of whose *Epistles* are in prose. In a long list of letter-writers extending through the two following centuries the outstanding names are those of Ambrose, Jerome, Paulinus of Nola, Augustine, Sidonius Apollinaris, and Cassiodorus.

Cf. H. Peter, *Der Brief in d. röm. Lit.* (1901); Sykutris, *PW*, Suppl. v, s.v. *Epistolographie*; D. R. Shackleton Bailey, *Cicero's Letters to Atticus* i (1965), 59 ff. R. G. C. L.

**LEUCAS,** an island of the Ionian Sea, opposite the coast of Acarnania. It derived its name from the white limestone cliffs on its west coast. Its south-west promontory, C. Leucatas, has a sheer drop of 2,000 ft.; suspected criminals were hurled from it, and if they survived the ordeal were rescued in boats (Strabo 10. 452). The shallow waters between its north-east coast and the mainland were liable to be closed to navigation by the formation of a sand-bar. The early Corinthian colonists cut through this spit (Strabo, ibid.), but in the fifth century ships had to be hauled across it (Thuc. 3. 81, 4. 8).

Leucas took its culture from the mainland in prehistoric times, but it was subject also to occasional influences from the north, which are indicated by the occurrence of 'barbotine' pottery late in the Early Neolithic period and by interesting groups of tombs under tumuli of Early Helladic and Middle Helladic date. In the Mycenaean period it was on the fringe of the Greek world and is to be identified with the Homeric Dulichium rather than, as Dörpfeld argued, with the Homeric Ithaca. The history of the island in classical times begins with the arrival of Corinthian colonists *c.* 625 B.C., who soon dominated the native population and remained loyal to their mother-city.

In the Persian Wars Leucas furnished contingents to the Greek fleet at Salamis and to the army at Plataea, and gave active assistance to Corinth in the Peloponnesian War. After a brief alliance with Athens against Philip of Macedon it passed into the hands of various Hellenistic rulers (Cassander, Agathocles, Pyrrhus), but *c.* 250 it joined the Acarnanian Confederacy, of which it became the capital. The Romans besieged and captured it in 197; in 167 they detached it from Acarnania and constituted it a free city.

P-K, *GL* ii. 2, 460 ff.; *IG* ix. 1; W. Dörpfeld, *Alt-Ithaka* (1927).
M. C.; N. G. L. H.

**LEUCE COME** (*Λευκὴ Κώμη*, 'White Village'), on the Red Sea, probably *Sherm Wehj*, possibly *El Haura*. Nabataean Arabs here received in small ships Eastern wares for Petra and the West. A due (25 per cent; *Peripl. M. Rubr.* 19) was levied there (perhaps under Roman control: in 25 B.C. Aelius Gallus, on an expedition to S. Arabia, landed there). It seems to have declined after Nabataea became a Roman province (A.D. 106). It may be Ptolemy's *Aὔαρα*.

Strabo 16. 780–1; *Peripl. M. Rubr.* 19; Plut. *Ant.* 51; Cosmas 2. 143. Warmington, *Indian Commerce*, 16, 334 f.; Thomson, *Hist. Anc. Geog.* 284.
E. H. W.

**LEUCIPPUS,** 'person who keeps white horses', hence 'rich man, noble'. Name of fifteen mythological characters, see Stoll in Roscher's *Lexikon*, s.v., but especially (1) father of Hilaeira and Phoebe, cf. DIOSCURI; (2) a young Cretan, turned from a girl into a boy by a miracle of Leto (Ant. Lib. 17).

**LEUCIPPUS** (3), originator of the atomic theory in the second half of the fifth century B.C. His birthplace is reported to be Elea, Abdera, or Miletus (D.L. 9. 30), but all of these may be inferences from affinities between his work and that of philosophers known to come from these places; Miletus is slightly more probable than the others. He wrote later than Parmenides, and almost certainly later than Zeno and Melissus. Epicurus is said to have denied his existence (D.L. 10. 13), but this is not to be taken seriously, in the face of Aristotle's frequent mentions of him.

WORKS. Of the Democritean works collected by Thrasyllus (D.L. 9. 45–9), two are sometimes attributed to Leucippus: *The Great World System* (*Μέγας διάκοσμος*), and *On Mind*. Both attributions appear to stem from Theophrastus and may well be right.

For the atomic theory, *see* DEMOCRITUS of Abdera. Various attempts have been made to separate Leucippus' contribution from that of his more prolific pupil Democritus, but none is sufficiently convincing.

ANCIENT SOURCES. Diels–Kranz, *Vorsokr.*[11]
MODERN LITERATURE. *See* DEMOCRITUS. D. J. F.

**LEUCON,** writer of Old Comedy who lived during the Peloponnesian War (*Suda*). In his *Φράτερες* he attacked Hyperbolus (fr. 1)—probably as a *βάρβαρος* who had no clansmen (*φράτερες*).

*FCG* ii. 749–50; *CAF* i. 703–4.

**LEUCOS LIMEN** (*Λευκὸς Λιμήν*, 'White Haven'), *Kosseir*, Egyptian port on the Red Sea, was connected with Coptus on the Nile by a track with stations and intervisible beacons, but was less important in Oriental trade than Berenice and Myos Hormos (qq.v.).

**LEUCOTHEA** (probably 'white goddess', perhaps 'runner on the white [foam]'), a sea-goddess identified early (*Od.* 5. 333–5) with Ino daughter of Cadmus, for reasons unknown. For her story *see* ATHAMAS. It is an old suggestion (see Farnell, *Cults* ii. 637) that she has Semitic connexions (through the 'Phoenician' Cadmus) and her son Melicertes is Melqart; but this is unproved and unnecessary, for his name may be Greek, 'Honey-cutter', i.e. a minor deity of bee-keeping. He is also called, or identified with, Palaemon ('the Wrestler'), again for uncertain reasons. Children are said to have been sacrificed to him (schol. Lycoph. 229).

Eitrem in *PW*, s.v.; Farnell, *Hero-Cults*, 35 ff. H. J. R.

**LEX** (1) (cf. *ligare*, to bind), signifies an agreement binding on the contracting parties. *Lex privata* means a contract signed by private individuals. *Lex publica* is an agreement between two parties of whom at least one is invested with magisterial authority and represents the State. Two types of *lex publica* must be distinguished according to the procedure followed and the authority enacting the law: a *lex rogata* results from the co-operation of the magistrate and the people, a *lex data* proceeds from the unilateral action of the magistrate. The *leges regiae*, of which the extant fragments are in all likelihood forgeries of the Republican age, were probably *leges datae*, but the laws of the early Republic were indisputably *leges rogatae*, despite the small share of the lower classes in legislation. *Plebiscita*, too, were formally in the same category as *leges rogatae*, since they were passed in assemblies summoned and presided over by a plebeian magistrate, although in practice they could hardly be regarded as the equivalent of laws until the right of the plebeians to legislate for the whole community was recognized. After the *Lex Hortensia* (*c.* 287 B.C.) (*see* HORTENSIUS 1) the terms *lex* and *plebiscitum* were used indiscriminately in common parlance, although the jurists continued to define the *lex* as a contract to which the entire *populus*, inclusive of patricians, was party (*see* PLEBISCITUM). The *lex rogata* was divided into four categories: (1) a *lex perfecta* invalidated an act prohibited by the terms of the law itself; (2) a *lex minus quam perfecta* penalized any person performing an act which the law forbade, but did not invalidate; (3) a *lex plus quam perfecta* both invalidated an act which it prohibited and penalized the offender; (4) a *lex imperfecta* neither invalidated an act which it prohibited nor punished the offender.

**2.** In order to be valid a *lex rogata* had to pass through three stages: (1) *legislatio* or public announcement by a magistrate of the draft of the *lex* (*promulgatio*), and the summoning by him of an assembly to debate it at a date not earlier than a *trinundinum* (q.v.) after the *promulgatio*; (2) *rogatio*, or the polling in the assembly, where debate, not amendment, was allowed; (3) *publicatio*, or the publication of the Bill in due form and time. Copies of laws enacted had to be kept in the *aerarium* (q.v.), engraved on wooden, and later bronze, tablets. Any enactment could be legally abrogated by subsequent legislation.

**3.** A *lex data* was issued by a Roman magistrate, and depended on his authority only, provided that senatorial approval was previously secured. It generally concerned either aliens (individuals and communities), or statutes issued by the Roman Republic, which the new law was intended to amend. In Republican times *leges datae* were mainly concerned with provincial administration and municipal statutes. They were issued by magistrats *cum imperio*, appointed to organize a province, or to reform its administration (*see* PROVINCIA), or as municipal statutes granted (also by a magistrate *cum imperio*) to cities both inside and outside Italy.

4. The unlimited power conferred upon the dictator or on the triumvirs *rei publicae constituendae* enabled them to legislate without the people's co-operation or approval. Moreover, they were exempted from the obligations and restrictions of ordinary legislation. Their exceptional legislative measures therefore mark an intermediary stage between Republican and Imperial legislation. The theory and practice of the Hellenistic monarchies, and the political philosophy of Cicero and his age, tended to make belief in leaders and emperors as the living source of law widespread. Consequently the emperors were regarded as *legibus soluti* and as alone competent to give laws to their subjects. From Tiberius onwards the *comitia* were seldom summoned for legislation (the last known law was passed under Nerva), and the distinction between *lex data* and *lex rogata* thus ended. The imperial constitutions finally covered all the field originally covered by the *leges datae* (grants of citizenship, municipal statutes, founding of new cities, enfranchisement of slaves, etc.).

5. *Lex* also indicated a contract between the State and a private individual (e.g. a middleman) to whom the State leased the exploitation of public land (e.g. a mine, estate), or the collection of the provincial taxes, etc. Similarly the regulations affecting a locality, or building, reputed to be holy (e.g. a wood, common, temple, altar) were termed *leges*.

Mommsen, *Röm. Staatsr.* iii³. 308 ff.; É. Cuq, in Dar.–Sag. iii. 1107 ff.; G. Barbieri and G. Tibiletti, *Diz. Epigr.* iv. 702 ff.; A. C. Johnson, P. R. Coleman-Norton, and F. C. Bourne, *Ancient Roman Statutes* (1961), transl. and commentary.          P. T.

## LEX (2), LEGES.

Individual Roman laws are generally treated in this work under the name of the magistrate who introduced them. The following list contains crossreferences and occasional explanation. For a detailed list and discussion see G. Rotondi, *Leges publicae populi Romani* (1912).

ACILIA
  (1) *de intercalando* (191 B.C.), *see* GLABRIO (1).
  (2) *de repetundis* (123 B.C.), *see* GLABRIO (2).
  (3) (*Acilia*) *Calpurnia de ambitu* (67 B.C.) imposed perpetual incapacity to hold office as a penalty for electoral corruption.

AEBUTIA
  (1) *de magistratibus extraordinariis* (? 154 B.C. or post-Gracchan) prohibited the election to an extraordinary magistracy of the man who had proposed its institution.
  (2) *de formulis* (*de legis actionibus*), *see* LAW AND PROCEDURE, ROMAN, II. 4.

AELIA
  (1) *Aelia et Fufia* (c. 150 B.C.?), two separate but similar laws of uncertain content. They regulated the use of auspices by magistrates, establishing or more probably confirming the right of magistrates and tribunes to obstruct the holding of all (or only legislative) assemblies through the announcement of unfavourable auspices (*obnuntiatio*). They probably forbade the holding of legislative assemblies in the interval between the announcement of consular elections and the elections themselves.

See W. F. McDonald, *JRS* 1929, 164 ff.; S. Weinstock, *JRS* 1937, 215 ff.; L. R. Taylor, *JRS* 1962, 22 ff.; G. V. Sumner, *AJPhil.* 1963, 387 ff. (who dates them to 132 B.C.); A. E. Astin, *Latomus* 1964, 421 ff. (dates c. 147/6).; A. K. Michels *The Calendar of the Roman Republic* (U.S.A.1967), 94 ff.
  (2) *Aelia Sentia* (A.D. 4) regulated the manumission of slaves and completed the work begun by the *Lex Fufia Caninia* (*see* SLAVERY). It also established registration of births; F. Schulz, *JRS* 1942, 78 ff.

AEMILIA of M. Aemilius Scaurus (consul 115 B.C.), of uncertain content, which concerned the distribution of freedmen among the tribes. See L. R. Taylor, *Voting Districts of R. Rep.* (1960), 141 ff.

AGRARIAE. Laws concerned with the distribution of public land (*ager publicus*, q.v.), such land being distributed in allotments to individuals or allocated to colonies of Roman citizens. Over forty agrarian laws of republican date are known, e.g. those of Flaminius and the Gracchi (qq.v.). An agrarian law of 111 B.C. has been partially preserved on a bronze tablet: *see below under* THORIA.

ANNALES. Laws regulating qualifications (e.g. minimum age) for magistracies. *See* CURSUS HONORUM, VILLIUS. Cf. A. E. Astin, *The Lex Annalis before Sulla* (1958).

ANTONIA
  (1) *de Termessibus* of a tribune C. Antonius and his colleagues (71 or 68 B.C., cf. Broughton, *MRR* i. 141) concluded an alliance between Rome and the Pisidian city of Termessus. It is partly preserved: Dessau, *ILS* 38; Riccobono, *FIRA* 135.
  (2) *leges Antoniae*, a variety of measures passed by the triumvir M. Antonius (q.v. 4), included laws to abolish dictatorship, to readjust provincial commands (*de permutatione provinciarum*), to confirm Caesar's *acta*, and to grant *provocatio* to those convicted *de maiestate* and *de vi*.

APPULEIA: various *leges* of Saturninus (q.v. 1) in 103 and 100 B.C.

AQUILIA, *de damno, see* LAW AND PROCEDURE, ROMAN, I. 5

ATERNIA-TARPEIA (454 B.C.) fixed the maximum fine which magistrates could impose (Gell. 11. 1).

ATINIA, *de tribunis plebis in senatum legendis* (before 102 B.C., possibly in 149) made tribunes regular members of the Senate (Gell. 14. 8. 2; Livy, *POxy.* 50).

AUFEIA, a tribunician (?) measure to settle Asia after the war with Aristonicus, probably 124 B.C. It was opposed by C. Gracchus.

AURELIA
  (1) *de tribunicia potestate* (75 B.C.), *see* COTTA (1).
  (2) *iudiciaria* (70 B.C.), *see* COTTA (3).

BAEBIA, *de praetoribus* (? 181 B.C.), enacted that four and six praetors should be elected in alternate years (Livy 40. 44. 2); it was not long observed. Cf. De Sanctis, *Stor. Rom.* iv. 504 ff.

BANTINA, *see* TABULA BANTINA.

CAECILIA DIDIA (98 B.C.), *see* DIDIUS (1) *and* COMITIA.

CALPURNIA
  (1) *de repetundis* (149 B.C.) established a permanent court to try cases of extortion. Cf. W. S. Ferguson, *JRS* 1921, 86. See REPETUNDAE *and* PISO (1).
  (2) *de civitate sociorum* (90 B.C.), of uncertain content,

probably added two new tribes and empowered generals to grant citizenship for bravery (Sisenna, frs. 17, 120 Peter). For date and Calpurnius see Broughton, *MRR*, Suppl. 13.

(3) *de ambitu, see* LEX ACILIA, no. 3, *above.*

CANULEIA, *de conubio patrum et plebis* (445 B.C.). *See* CANULEIUS.

CASSIA
(1) *tabellaria* (137 B.C.), of the tribune L. Cassius Longinus, introduced vote by ballot in the *iudicia populi*, except in cases of *perduellio. See* VOTING *and cf.* LEX COELIA *below.*
(2) a tribunician measure of 104 B.C. which expelled from the Senate men condemned or deprived of their *imperium* by the people. It was aimed at Caepio (q.v. 1).
(3) *de plebeis in patricios adlegendis* (44 B.C.) empowered Caesar to create patricians (Tac. *Ann.* 11. 25). *See* PATRICIUS.

CENSORIAE were the conditions imposed by censors in contracts with tax-collectors (*see* PUBLICANI) and in sales and auctions when State property was alienated or leased.

CICEREIA *de sponsu*, probably second century (173 B.C.?), required a creditor to state publicly, before a surety (*sponsor*) committed himself, the amount of the debt and the number of sureties. See J. Triantaphyllopoulos, *Lex Cicereia* (1957–9).

CINCIA, *de donis et muneribus* (204 B.C.), of the tribune M. Cincius Alimentus, forbade gifts which might defeat justice and certain donations above a given amount. *See* ADVOCATUS, PATRONUS.

CLAUDIA, *de nave senatorum* (218 B.C.). *See* CLAUDIUS (7).

CLODIAE: various *plebiscita* proposed by P. Clodius (q.v. 1), tribune in 58 B.C.

COELIA, *tabellaria* (107 B.C.), of the tribune C. Coelius Caldus, extended vote by ballot to cases of *perduellio* which had been excepted in the *Lex Cassia.*

COLONIAE GENETIVAE IULIAE or LEX URSONENSIS, generally considered a *lex data*, contains the charter granted by Julius Caesar to the colonia Genetiva Iulia at Urso (modern *Osuna*) in southern Spain which was organized for him by Antony. Our knowledge of it derives from four bronze tablets, found in 1870–3; a few more fragments of the inscription were found about 1940. The surviving portion deals with jurisdiction, priests, games, etc. See *ILS* 6087; Riccobono, *FIRA* 177 ff.; frs. *Emerita* 1941. Bibliography, *Diz. Epigr.* iv (1957), 727 f. Translation, E. G. Hardy, *Three Spanish Charters* (1912), 7 ff.

CORNELIAE
(1) Various *leges* passed by Sulla (q.v. 1). *See also* LAW AND PROCEDURE, ROMAN, III. 3.
(2) Cornelia Pompeia. Laws, e.g. *de comitiis centuriatis et de tribunicia potestate*, carried by Sulla and his fellow consul in 88 B.C. (App. *BCiv.* 1. 59; Livy, *Epit.* 77).
(3) Laws of Cinna (q.v. 1), consul in 87 B.C.
(4) Measures of the tribune Cornelius (q.v. 1) in 67 B.C.

DIDIA *sumptuaria* (143 B.C.) extended the application of *lex Fannia* to all Italy (Macrob. *Sat.* 3. 17. 6). *See also* LEX CAECILIA-DIDIA.

DOMITIA, *de sacerdotiis* (104 B.C.) of Cn. Domitius (q.v. 3). It was abrogated by Sulla, but renewed by a *lex* of Labienus in 63 B.C.

DUODECIM TABULARUM, *see* TWELVE TABLES.

FANNIA, *sumptuaria* (161 B.C.), limited the sums to be spent on entertainments.

FLAMINIA, *agraria. See* FLAMINIUS.

FRUMENTARIAE, laws concerned with the distribution of grain. *See* GRACCHUS (4), ANNONA, etc.

FUFIA CANINIA, *de manumissione* (2 B.C.), limited the number of slaves a master might liberate by will. Cf. *CAH* x. 432. *See* SLAVERY, § 7. *See also* EX AELIA (2) *above.*

GABINIA
(1) *tabellaria* (139 B.C.) *See* GABINIUS (1).
(2) Various *leges Gabiniae* (67 B.C.) of the tribune Gabinius (q.v. 2), which included the establishment of a command against the pirates (for Pompey), the forbidding of the lending of money to provincials in Rome, and *de senatu legatis dando*, which fixed February as the month of audience for foreign *legati* to the Senate.

GELLIA CORNELIA, of the consuls of 72 B.C., validated grants of citizenship by Pompey in Spain.

GENUCIAE, *see* GENUCIUS.

HADRIANA, *see* LEX MANCIANA.

HIERONICA was not strictly a *lex. See* HIERON II.

HORTENSIA, *see* HORTENSIUS (1).

ICILIA, *see* ICILIUS.

DE IMPERIO VESPASIANI (A.D. 69/70) is the name given to the content of a bronze inscription (*ILS* 244) of which only the end survives. It is part of an enactment which conferred powers on Vespasian. Although the phrasing suggests a *senatus consultum*, it is a *lex rogata*; the People who passed it into law allowed the formation of the prior *S.C.* to stand. The surviving fragment enumerates specific privileges. The problem is to deduce what the missing part contained, whether it conferred on Vespasian (*a*) *imperium*, i.e. is a *lex de imperio* (Ulpian records that Vespasian received his *imperium* by a *lex regia*), (*b*) *tribunicia potestas* (this is unlikely), (*c*) all his powers (the jurists of the second and third centuries conceived that all imperial power had been bestowed on Augustus by a single enactment), or (*d*) 'a consolidated grant of miscellaneous rights additional to those which formed the main basis of the imperial position', i.e. the right to do what Vespasian's predecessors had done by virtue of either special enactment or their own *auctoritas* (so H. Last, *CAH* xi. 404 ff.). A survey of modern views is given by G. Barbieri, *Diz. Epigr.* iv (1957), 750 ff.

IUDICIARIAE were laws dealing with the organization of the courts and judicial procedure. *See* QUAESTIO.

IULIAE. It is doubtful whether certain *leges Iuliae* were enacted by Caesar or by Augustus.
(1) *de civitate Latinis et sociis danda* (90 B.C.), *see* CAESAR (2).
(2) *Leges* of Julius Caesar (q.v.) in 59 B.C. (*agraria, de publicanis Asiae, de actis Pompeii, de Ptolemaeo Aulete, de pecuniis repetundis* (cf. *PW* xii. 2389), *de provinciis*), and in 49–44 B.C. measures which included *de pecuniis mutuis* (to relieve debtors);

*de civitate Transpadanis danda*; *frumentaria* (reducing the number of recipients of free corn); *de collegiis* (*see* CLUBS, ROMAN); *iudiciaria* (*see* TRIBUNI AERARII); *sumptuaria*; *de maiestate* (*see* MAIESTAS); *de re pecuaria* (that at least one third of Italian herdsmen should be freemen); *de provinciis* (limiting provincial promagistracies to one year for ex-praetors, to two years for ex-consuls); *Lex Iulia municipalis* (so-called; also known as Tabula Heracleensis because a bronze tablet containing part of the law was found at Heraclea). It was probably a collection of various statutes, drafted by Caesar and later incorporated in one general bill and carried by Antony. Part of the text refers to Rome (comprising regulations for, e.g., corn supply, building, traffic), the other part to municipalities and colonies (e.g. qualifications for local magistrates and Senate). Text: *ILS* 6085; Riccobono, *FIRA* 140. Transl. E. G. Hardy, *Roman Laws and Charters* i. 136 ff. Modern views discussed by G. Barbieri, *Diz. Epigr.* iv. 725 ff.

(3) *Leges* of Augustus included *de maiestate* (*see* MAIESTAS *and* PERDUELLIO); *de vi*; *de ambitu* (18 B.C.; excluding from office for five years men convicted of bribery; *see also* LAW AND PROCEDURE, ROMAN, III. 3); *de adulteriis coercendis* (18 B.C.; cf. *CAH* x. 443 ff.; *see* ADULTERY); *de maritandis ordinibus* (18 B.C.; cf. *CAH* x. 448 ff.; *see* MARRIAGE); *de senatu*; *de vicesima hereditatum* (A.D. 6; levied a 5 per cent tax on legacies which was paid into the *aerarium militare*); *de magistratibus* (12 B.C.); *de collegiis* (*see* CLUBS, ROMAN); *de tutela*; *de iudiciis privatis* (*see* LAW AND PROCEDURE, ROMAN, II. 4); *de iudiciis publicis* (A.D. 7; *see* QUAESTIO).

(4) *Iulia Papiria* (430 B.C.) is said to have introduced payment for fines in bronze instead of in sheep or oxen. *See* COINAGE (ROMAN), § 1.

IUNIA
(1) *de peregrinis* (126 B.C.) of the tribune M. Junius Pennus, expelling non-citizens from Rome.
(2) *de manumissione* (? 17 B.C. or A.D. 19), *see* LATINI IUNIANI, SLAVERY § 7.
(3) *Iunia Licinia* (62 B.C.) ordered the deposition in the Aerarium of a copy of promulgated laws.
(4) *Iunia Petronia* (A.D. 19) enacted that in trials about manumission the judgement should be for liberty if the jurors were equally divided.
(5) *Iunia* (123 B.C.), *see* REPETUNDAE.

LICINIA
(1) *sumptuaria* (between 143 and 102 B.C.).
(2) *Licinia Mucia* (95 B.C.), proposed by L. Licinius Crassus and Q. Mucius Scaevola, set up a *quaestio* on aliens who were illegally claiming to be citizens. *See* CRASSUS (3).
(3) *Liciniae Pompeiae*, two measures passed by Crassus and Pompey: (*a*) *de tribunicia potestate* (70 B.C.), which restored full competence to the tribunate, and (*b*) *de provincia Caesaris* (55 B.C.), which effectively prolonged Caesar's Gallic command for five more years (until ? 13 Nov. 50 or 1 March 49).
(4) *Liciniae Sextiae* (367 B.C.), *see* STOLO.

LIVIAE, *see* DRUSUS (1) and (2).

LUTATIA *de vi* (78/7 B.C.), perhaps directed against sedition and specifically in relation to Lepidus. *See* VIS.

MAENIA, *de patrum auctoritate* (q.v.).

MALACITANA. The grant of Latin rights to the whole of Spain by Vespasian entailed a long process of re-

organization (some 400 new charters were needed). Parts of the text of municipal charters granted (as *leges datae*) to Malaca and Salpensa were found near Malaga. They belong to *c*. A.D. 82–3 and contain regulations for the municipal government and constitution of the two towns. For Malaca the surviving portions concern municipal magistrates, elections, and finance, for Salpensa magistrates, manumission of slaves, and legal guardians. For text of Lex Malacitana, *ILS* 6089, Riccobono, *FIRA* 208 ff. Cf. E. G. Hardy, *Three Spanish Charters* (1912), 61 ff. Lex Salpensana, *ILS* 6088, Riccobono, 202 ff., Hardy, 83 ff.

MAMILIA
(1) *de coniuratione Iugurthina* (109 B.C.) established a court of inquiry. *See* MAMILIUS (3).
(2) *Mamilia Roscia Peducaea Alliena Fabia* (Riccobono, *FIRA* 138 ff.) hardly belongs to Caesar's land legislation of 59 B.C. but is more probably a later supplement to it (55 B.C.). Its attribution to the tribune Mamilius (109 B.C.) is improbable. Cf. Broughton, *MRR* ii. 220; *Diz. Epigr.* iv. (1957), 722 f.

MANCIANA. A measure known as the lex Manciana of uncertain date (Flavian?) and called after a certain Mancia, either an imperial agent or a landowner. It is concerned with the administration of imperial and private estates in North Africa, conferring certain rights upon cultivators and regulating their relations with the proprietors or their agents (*conductores*). Its scope was extended by Hadrian, in the so-called *lex Hadriana*, which aimed at developing waste land by permanent tenants. Texts: Riccobono, *FIRA* 484 ff., 493 ff. Cf. Rostovtzeff, *Roman Empire²*, 368 f: R. M. Haywood in Frank, *Econ. Survey* iv. 89 ff.

MANILIA, *see* MANILIUS (2).

MARIA, a *lex tabellaria* introduced by C. Marius as tribune in 119 B.C., included the narrowing of gangways (*pontes*) along which voters passed, in order to reduce intimidation.

METALLI VIPASCENSIS. An ordinance for the administration of the imperial mines at Vipasca in Spain (early 2nd c. A.D.?). These local rules, which were published by procurators of individual mining districts, derived from regulations sent out to the provinces from Rome where a general order (a *lex data*) had been drawn up (under Vespasian?) to regulate the exploitation of different types of mine. The inscription contains detailed instructions about leasing the mines to private contractors. A second inscription, part of a letter to the local *procurator metallorum*, transmits part of imperial rules for the actual exploitation of the mines. Texts: Riccobono, *FIRA* 502 ff., 498 ff. Cf. J. J. van Nostrand, in Frank, *Econ. Survey* iii. 167 ff.

MINUCIA, *de liberis* (before 90 B.C.), established that sons of parents who had not *conubium* should take the status of the inferior parent.

MUNATIA AEMILIA (42 B.C.) authorized the Triumvirs to grant citizenship and exemption from taxes (Riccobono, *FIRA* 310, l. 10).

OCTAVIA, *frumentaria* (? *c*. 120 B.C.), modified the *Lex Sempronia frumentaria* by raising the prices.

OGULNIA, *see* OGULNIUS.

OPPIA, *see* OPPIUS (1).

ORCHIA, *sumptuaria* (182 B.C.), limited the number of guests at entertainments.

OVINIA, *see* OVINIUS.

PAPIA (65 B.C.) was designed to stop illegal exercise of citizen rights by expelling from Rome all foreigners who resided outside Italy.

*Papia Poppaea* (A.D. 9) completed the *Lex Iulia de maritandis ordinibus*.

PAPIRIA

(1) *tabellaria* (131 B.C.), of Carbo (q.v. 1).

(2) *semunciaria* (89 B.C.) of the tribune C. Papirius Carbo, made the *as* semiuncial.

PETRONIA

(1) *de praefectis iure dicundo* (? Augustan) provided for the appointment of *praefecti* in municipalities when regular magistrates were lacking.

(2) *Petronia* (?A.D. 61), forbade masters arbitrarily to send their slaves to fight wild beasts.

PINARIA FURIA (472 B.C.) regulated the quadrennial period of intercalation.

PLAETORIA, protected minors from fraud (c. 193–192 B.C.), *see* GUARDIANSHIP.

PLAUTIA

(1) *iudiciaria* (89 B.C.), *see* PLAUTIUS (1) *and* QUAESTIO.

(2) *de vi* (between 78 and 63 B.C.), *see* VIS.

(3) *de reditu Lepidanorum*, restored citizenship to the followers of Lepidus. For the date (70 B.C. ?) see Broughton, *MRR* ii. 130.

(4) *Plautia Papiria* (89 B.C.), *see* PLAUTIUS (1).

POETELIA, *see* POETELIUS.

POMPEIA

(1) *de Transpadanis* (89 B.C.). *See* POMPEIUS (3) STRABO.

(2) various *leges* of Pompeius Magnus, which included *de parricidio* (q.v.); *iudiciaria* (55 B.C. ?; limiting the magistrate in the choice of *iudices*); *de vi* (52 B.C., simplifying the procedure and increasing the penalty of the *lex Plautia*); *de ambitu* (52); *de provinciis* (52, prescribing a five-year interval between a magistracy and a provincial command); *de iure magistratuum* (52, renewing the obligation for candidates to register in person). *See also* LEGES LICINIAE POMPEIAE, *above*.

PORCIAE, *de provocatione* or *de tergo civium*. Three laws— see A. H. McDonald, *JRS* 1944, 19.

(1) The tribune P. Porcius Laeca extended the right of *provocatio* in capital cases to Roman citizens in Italy and the provinces (199 B.C.).

(2) M. Porcius Cato, as praetor (198) or less probably as consul (195), prohibited the scourging of citizens without appeal.

(3) Military officers were deprived of the right of summary execution by the consul L. Porcius Licinus (184) or more probably later (c. 150–135).

PUBLILIAE, *see* PUBLILIUS (1) and (2) *and* PATRUM AUCTORITAS.

PUPIA, *de senatu diebus comitialibus non habendo. See* SENATUS, § 1 *b*.

QUINCTIA: proposed by T. Quinctius Crispinus, consul 9 B.C., for the preservation of aqueducts (Riccobono, *FIRA* 152 ff.).

REMMIA, *see* LIBEL § 3.

REPETUNDARUM, *see* REPETUNDAE.

ROMANAE BARBARORUM are codes promulgated by Germanic kings in the territory of the former Western Roman Empire where they established themselves. Thus the *Lex Romana Visigothorum* was promulgated in A.D. 506 by Alaric II for the use of his

Roman subjects, and the *Lex Rom. Burgundionum* (c. 500) for Burgundian and Roman subjects of King Gundobad.

ROSCIA

(1) *theatralis* (67 B.C.), *see* ROSCIUS (2).

(2) *de civitate Transpadanorum* (49 B.C.) mentioned in *Tabula Atestina*; its content is uncertain (*see* LEX RUBRIA (2), below).

RUBRIA

(1) A bill to found a colony at Carthage carried by a tribune Rubrius in 123 or 122 B.C. The date is controversial; see G. Tibiletti, *Athenaeum* 1953, 5 ff.; E. Badian, *AJPhil.* 1954, 374 ff. and *Hist.* 1962, 206. An attempt to repeal it in 121 led to disorder and C. Gracchus' death; it was repealed soon afterwards.

(2) A *plebiscitum* mentioned twice in, and usually (but not universally) identified with, a *lex de Gallia Cisalpina* which is partly preserved on a bronze tablet found at Veleia near Piacenza: Riccobono, *FIRA* 169 ff. It belongs to the years 49–42 B.C. and deals with the conduct of a variety of civil cases in the courts of Cisalpine Gaul. See E. G. Hardy, *Six Roman Laws* (1911), 110 ff.; *Diz. Epigr.* iv. 730; M. W. Frederiksen, *JRS* 1964, 129 ff. It is uncertain whether another fragment found at Ateste, the so-called Tabula Atestina (Riccobono, *FIRA* 176 ff.), is part of the same law. See *Diz. Epigr.* iv. 723 f.

RUFRENA, probably 42 B.C., enacted the setting up of statues to the dead Julius Caesar, Divus Iulius, throughout Italy. See *ILS* 73.

RUPILIAE, *de iure Siculorum, de re frumentaria*, etc., were *leges datae* of the proconsul P. Rupilius, regulating the condition of Sicily in 131 B.C.

SACRATAE were laws which, if violated, made the offender *sacer*, an outlaw. Thus the sacrosanctity of the tribuni plebis (q.v.) was upheld.

SAENIA, *see* PATRICIUS.

SALPENSANA, *see* LEX MALACITANA.

SATURAE (*per saturam*) were statutes which dealt with varied subject-matter in one bill. They were forbidden by the lex Caecilia Didia: *see* DIDIUS (1).

SCRIBONIAE, *rogationes* of Curio (q.v. 2), tribune 50 B.C.

SEMPRONIAE of Tiberius and Gaius Gracchus. *See* GRACCHUS (3) and (4).

*Sempronia de pecunia credita* (193 B.C.), of M. Sempronius Tuditanus, extended to *socii* and the *nomen Latinum* the laws about loans (Livy 35. 7).

SERVILIA

(1) *iudiciaria, see* CAEPIO (1).

(2) *de repetundis, see* GLAUCIA.

(3) *rogatio Servilia agraria, see* RULLUS.

SULPICIAE of Sulpicius (q.v. 1) Rufus (88 B.C.).

TABELLARIAE were laws dealing with voting in the popular assemblies with tablets (*tabellae*). *See* LEX CASSIA, GABINIA, MARIA, PAPIRIA.

TARENTINA. A municipal charter (*lex data*) of Tarentum, dating between 89 and 62 B.C. The part preserved in an inscription (Riccobono, *FIRA* 166 ff.) gives provisions about the responsibilities of local magistrates, building regulations, etc.

TARENTINUM (FRAGMENTUM) *de repetundis*. The fragment of a law found at Tarentum and published in 1947

(*Epigraphica* 1947, 3 ff., 1948, 159). It has been identified with the law of Servilius Glaucia (e.g. by Piganiol) or of Servilius Caepio (by Tibiletti, *Athenaeum* 1953, 38 ff.), but the question remains open.

TERENTIA
(1) *de libertinorum liberis* (189 B.C.), *see* CULLEO.
(2) *Terentia Cassia frumentaria* (73 B.C.), *see* LUCULLUS (3).

THORIA, *agraria*. Sp. Thorius was, according to Appian (*BCiv.* 1. 27, MSS. Θόριος), the author of a measure (of 119 B.C.) which (*a*) abolished the land commission established by the Gracchi, (*b*) granted perpetual tenancy to *possessores* of *ager publicus*, and (*c*) reimposed rent on this. More probably Thorius was the author of an agrarian law of 111 B.C. (Cic. *Brut.* 36, 136) which has been partially preserved on the back of a bronze tablet which has the *Lex Acilia* on its other side; this laid down (*a*) that all public land should become the private property of its occupants, (*b*) the abolition of rent, (*c*) all colonies and municipia were given security of tenure in *ager publicus* which had been granted to them, (*d*) the system of *possessio* was abolished, (*e*) lands in Africa and at Corinth were dealt with. For this law see Riccobono, *FIRA* 102 ff.; E. G. Hardy, *Roman Laws and Charters* (1912), 35 ff. (translation); *Diz. Epigr.* iv (1957), 717 ff. (bibliography). For other interpretations of the three laws of Appian and of the lex Thoria, see E. Badian, *Hist.* 1963, 211 ff.; A. E. Douglas, ed., *Cicero, Brutus* (1966), 247 ff.

TITIA, *de IIIviris reipublicae constituendae* (27 Nov. 43 B.C.). *See* TRIUMVIRI.

TREBONIA, *de provinciis consularibus* (55 B.C.), *see* TREBONIUS.

TULLIAE of Cicero in his consulship (63 B.C.).
(1) *de ambitu* forbade anyone to exhibit a public show for two years before he was a candidate, and extended the penalty established by the *Lex Calpurnia* to ten years.
(2) *de legationibus liberis* limited the privilege of *libera legatio* to one year.

URSONENSIS, so-called, *see* LEX COLONIAE GENETIVAE.

VALERIAE
(1) of Valerius Poplicola (509 B.C.), *see* VALERIUS (1).
(2) *Valeriae Horatiae* (449 B.C.), *see* VALERIUS (2).
(3) *de provocatione* (300 B.C.) of the consul M. Valerius Corvus. *See* PROVOCATIO.
(4) *de aere alieno* (86 B.C.), *see* FLACCUS (7).
(5) *Valeria Cornelia* (A.D. 5) dealt with electoral procedure. *See* DESTINATIO.

VARIA, *de maiestate* (90 B.C.), *see* VARIUS (1).

VATINIAE of the tribune P. Vatinius (q.v.) in 59 B.C., including the conferring on Caesar of the Gallic command.

VIBIAE. The consul C. Vibius Pansa (43 B.C.) carried some *leges* (confirming Caesar's *acta*, founding colonies, and abolishing the dictatorship) to replace similar laws of Antony which had been abrogated.

VILLIA, *annalis* (180 B.C.), *see* VILLIUS.

VISELLIA (A.D. 24) granted full citizenship to *Latini Iuniani* (q.v.) who served in the *Vigiles* for six years and debarred all who were not *ingenui* from gaining municipal magistracies unless supported by the Princeps.

VOCONIA, *de mulierum hereditatibus* (169 B.C.), limited the right of inheritance by women, and restricted individual legacies to less than the portion of the heir(s) instituted in the last will. H. H. S.

**LEX CURIATA** (frequently and perhaps inaccurately termed *lex curiata de imperio*) was a measure in favour of Roman consuls, praetors, and other holders of *imperium* commonly carried immediately or soon after their election. Its purpose and content are the subject of controversy. Hints in Cicero that it was conceived in his day as peculiarly essential to the exercise of military command (cf. *Leg. Agr.* 2. 30) lend weight to the view that there was a necessary connexion between the *lex curiata* and *imperium*. Yet the fact that a parallel measure was carried in favour of censors, albeit in a centuriate rather than a curiate assembly, appears to belie this theory. Indeed, the fact that all known beneficiaries of such a measure were *magistratus maiores* (i.e. magistrates who held the *auspicia maxima*) suggests that there may be more truth in the alternative tradition of Cicero that the *lex curiata* was carried 'for the sake of the auspices'. Possibly the *lex curiata* (or in the case of censors the *lex centuriata*) conferred on the magistrate the right to take auspices in the name of the people. In this case it will have been a prerequisite not of the tenure of *imperium*, but only of its undisputed and efficient exercise. The *lex curiata* is unlikely to have dated from earlier than the institution of magistracy, and it soon became a formality, the full curiate assembly being replaced by thirty representative lictors. It appears to have assumed political significance only in the last century of the Republic, when personal and factional conflict dictated attempts to obstruct its passage. *See also* AUSPICIUM, COMITIA, IMPERIUM.

Mommsen, *Röm. Staatsr.* i³. 609 ff.; K. Latte, *Gött. Nachr.* 1934, 59 ff.; U. v. Lübtow, *Sav. Zeitschr.* 1952, 154 ff.; E. S. Staveley, *Hist.* 1956, 84 ff. E. S. S.

**LEXICA SEGUERIANA**, so named from a former owner of the MSS. (now cod. Paris, Coislin 345 and 347), or Bekkeriana, from the editor (*Anecd. Bekk.* i), are I, Phrynichus the Atticist (excerpts); II, Anonymus Antatticista; III, Περὶ συντάξεων; IV, Δικῶν ὀνόματα; V, Λέξεις ῥητορικαί; VI, Συναγωγὴ χρησίμων λέξεων. Of the last Bekker prints only *A*: Bachmann adopts this and edits the rest (*B*, etc.) in his *Anecd.* i (1828).

P. B. R. F.; R. B.

**LIBANIUS**, born at Antioch (A.D. 314), died there (*c.* 393), was a Greek rhetorician and man of letters who embodied in his work many of the ideals and aspirations of the pagan Greek urban upper classes of late antiquity. He belonged to a wealthy Antiochene curial family, and after a careful education at home was sent to study in Athens (336–40). Thereafter he taught rhetoric successively at Constantinople (340/1–346) and at Nicomedia. Recalled to Constantinople by Constantius he was offered but declined a chair of rhetoric at Athens; in 354 he accepted an official chair of rhetoric in Antioch, where he passed the rest of his life. His pupils numbered many distinguished men, pagan and Christian alike. John Chrysostom and Theodore of Mopsuestia were almost certainly among them, Basil and Gregory of Nazianzus probably, and Ammianus Marcellinus possibly.

In his later years Libanius became a literary figure of renown throughout the Greek world, and was in correspondence with many of its leading figures, e.g. the Emperor Julian, for whom he had an unbounded admiration, and whose death was a bitter blow to him. In spite of his adherence to paganism, which for him was uncomplicated by Neoplatonist speculations, he enjoyed considerable influence under Theodosius I, who granted him the honorary title of praetorian prefect.

His sixty-four surviving speeches deal with public or municipal affairs, educational and cultural questions. Many are addressed to emperors or high government officials, with whom he intervenes on behalf of the citizens or the curials of Antioch (e.g. after the riot of 382). Some of these were never actually delivered, but were sent to their addressees and published. Other speeches include his funeral oration on Julian (*Or.* 17), his encomium of Antioch (*Or.* 11), and the autobiography which he composed in 374 (*Or.* 1). There also survive some 1,600 letters, fifty-one school declamations, numerous model rhetorical exercises and minor rhetorical works composed in the course of his teaching. The speeches and letters are a mine of information on social, political, and cultural life in the eastern half of the Empire in the fourth century A.D.

Deeply attached to old values, and seeing the rapidly changing world about him through the distorting lens of a pedantic and snobbish literary tradition, Libanius was vain, petty, and wrapped in finicking antiquarianism. Yet his sincerity, his freedom from vindictiveness, his never-failing readiness to use his eloquence to combat injustice, and a certain warmth of character which breaks through the restraints of classicizing purism make him attractive to the patient reader. He writes an atticizing Greek which is always the result of painstaking labour, and often tortuous and difficult. He was much esteemed as a model of style in Byzantine times.

LIBANII OPERA, ed. R. Foerster, 12 vols. (1909–27); *Or. I* (Autobiography), ed. A. F. Norman (1965) and *Selected Works* i (Loeb, 1969). L. Petit, *Libanius et la vie municipale à Antioche au IVᵉ siècle après J.-C.* (1956, with a full bibliography). R. B.

**LIBEL and SLANDER** in Rome: **1.** LAMPOONS: The legislation of the XII Tables (see § 3 below) shows that these were as common in ancient Rome as in medieval Italy. The form of extra-legal self-help, referred to by words cognate with *flagitare* (cf. Plaut. *Pseud.* 357–69, Catull. 42, and Usener in bibliography), was a related phenomenon. The first-known use was the lampoon which Naevius (q.v.) caused to be uttered from the stage against the Metelli and which, with others of a like kind (later scholars, knowing the fact, searched his works for hidden allusion and absurdly found one to the great Scipio—Gell. 7. 8. 5), resulted in his imprisonment. The poetry of Lucilius (q.v. 1) contained personal attacks which would fall under this head. Many of the poems of Catullus are obviously lampoons (with Bibaculus he was mentioned by Tacitus, *Ann.* 4. 34. 8, as notorious for such compositions). Octavian wrote them, e.g. on Antony and Fulvia (Mart. 11. 20) or on Pollio (Macrob. *Sat.* 2. 4. 21). Much of the writing of Martial and Juvenal has a lampooning intention, except that the objects are normally dead (the lampoon which Juvenal was alleged to have written about Paris and the exile which it was supposed to have earned him are probably later fictions). A real-life lampoon in trochaic tetrameters was found at Pompeii (*Carm. Epigr.* 231).

**2.** INVECTIVE: The study of Greek literature brought the rhetorical invective to the attention of Romans—Thrasymachus, for example, was a great expert in such ψόγοι (Pl. *Phdr.* 267 d). Invective is easily found even in the fragments of early Roman orators, e.g. Cato, fr. 213 *ORF²*, Scipio Aemilianus, fr. 17, C. Gracchus, frs. 43, 58, Titius, fr. 2. Cicero brought the form to a high point in speeches like *in Pisonem*. Caesar's *Anticatones* (Suet. *Jul.* 56. 5) are a different form of the same genre, and the pamphlet-literature of the Empire, including forgeries like the pseudo-Sallust *invectiva in Ciceronem*. A stock series of inventions, suitable for such compositions, can be traced from the fourth century in Greece to the fifth century A.D. in Rome. (On all this, see especially R. G. M. Nisbet's edition of Cicero's *in Pisonem*, 192 ff.)

**3.** THE LAW: One of the XII Tables provided execution for libel and slander (Cic. *Rep.* 4. 11). At a much later stage came the praetorian edict: *ne quid infamandi causa fiat, si quis adversus ea fecerit, prout quaeque res erit, animadvertam* (O. Lenel, *Das Edictum Perpetuum³* (1927), Titulus 35. 193). This is dated by Daube (see bibliography) between 200 and 100 B.C. It is put in a peculiarly cautious form, since libel-legislation is very open to abuse. Daube considers that this edict was concerned with *infamia* in the narrow technical sense and that it was later (from about the second half of the first century B.C.) assimilated to the general edict for *iniuriae*. The question is highly complex and difficult. It is not known under what procedure Naevius was imprisoned; it was probably under a form of the law in the XII Tables. But, in spite of the meagre evidence, it is not reasonable to reject the story of his imprisonment, from which he was rescued by tribunician action (Gell. 3. 3. 15, who adds the further explanation that he expiated his sin by two plays written in prison—no doubt an attempt to harmonize the romantic fiction of the prison-plays with the meagre report of the legal circumstances). He was forced to leave Rome by the Metelli (not necessarily by legal proceedings). There is no justification for talking of Naevius attacking 'the Government', or of 'the State' taking action against him. At most it was a matter of sectional family-politics. The next cases known are of success by Accius and failure by Lucilius to obtain a trial against a writer of mimes under the *actio iniuriarum* for mention by name from the stage (which shows with what caution the praetors allowed trials in such cases). There was no distinction between libel and slander, and Lucilius' ability to escape impeachment for his lampoons should not be attributed simply to their being in written documents (for Catullus also escaped), which would be an uneasy distinction to make in Roman literature; the explanation lies more in the social status of men like Lucilius and Catullus. Reply would be in like kind (see Pollio's reply to Octavian, Macrob. *Sat.* 2. 4. 21). There would be many reasons for not attempting a libel action (in ancient times or in modern), and one would be the influence (i.e. *auctoritas*) and friends of one's opponent. Another would be that such compositions, within limits, were recognized types of literary composition in which criteria of truth and falsehood were known to be inapplicable. The same consideration would apply to speeches like *in Pisonem*, with, perhaps, in addition something analogous to the concept of a privileged occasion, which attached to meetings of the Senate. Horace in *Sat.* 2. 1 has an amusing discussion of libel with the great lawyer Trebatius who advises against it as liable to prosecution. The imperial system introduced the added complication of *maiestas* (q.v.), and Augustus is usually credited with subsuming libel under this procedure (cf. Tac. *Ann.* 1. 72), but in *Ann.* 4. 34, Cremutius is made to express a different view of Augustus. Curiatius Maternus in the *Dialogus* of Tacitus was clearly getting away with a great deal of dubious political comment in his tragedies, and the action of Augustus should not be credited with too much precision. A rather different aspect of the law was dealt with by the *lex Remmia* (date unknown) *de calumnia* (more or less on malicious prosecution): little is known about its working and the difficulty of proof will have restricted actions under it (see Landgraf on Cic. *pro Rosc. Am.* 55).

A. H. J. Greenidge, *Infamia* (1894); H. Usener, *Rh. Mus.* 1900, 1 ff. (= *Kl. Schr.* 4. 356 ff.); E. Fraenkel, *Gnomon* 1925, 105 ff. (= *Kl. Beiträge* ii. 397 ff.); L. Robinson, *Freedom of Speech in the Roman Republic* (1941); A. Momigliano, *JRS* 1942, 121 ff.; D. Daube, *Atti del congresso internaz. di diritto romano, 1948* iii. (1951), 413 ff. (very important and not known to the next two authors); R. E. Smith, *CQ* 1951, 169 ff.; H. B. Mattingly, 'Naevius and the Metelli', *Hist.* (1960), 414 ff. (a rather violent treatment of the evidence); R. G. M. Nisbet, *Cicero, in Pisonem* (1961), esp. 192 ff.
G. W. W.

**LIBELLUS** was a petition to the Emperor by a party to a judicial suit at Rome. It was answered by a *subscriptio* appended to it, which the Emperor himself signed (S.H.A. *Comm.* 13). The official who dealt with *libelli* was the *a libellis*, who was a personal secretary of the Emperor. The post of *a libellis* no doubt existed from the time of Augustus, but it is prominent first under Claudius, when it was held at first, perhaps, by Polybius (Sen. *Consolatio ad Polybium* 6. 5) and then by Callistus. It was in the hands of freedmen until the reign of Hadrian, after which its holders were *equites* (S.H.A. *Hadr.* 22). The jurists Papinianus and Ulpianus (1) (qq.v.) held the post.
                                                     J. P. B.

**LIBER PATER,** Italian god of fertility and especially of wine, commonly identified with Dionysus (q.v.). Concerning his origin and relation to Jupiter (I. Liber) divergent views have been held, see Wissowa, *RK* 138; Altheim, *Hist. Rom. Rel.* 125, 149. But it is certain that he was an independent god when the festival calendar was completed, for it contains his feast, the Liberalia of 17 Mar. He had, however, no temple, or none of any importance, in Rome (see Platner–Ashby, 316, 321). This may be explained by the fact that his feast would be chiefly rustic and have little to do with the city. According to Verg. *G.* 2. 385 ff. it was a merry occasion, and characterized by crude songs, doubtless traditional, and the use of masks, which apparently were hung on trees; they may have been intended to scare away evil influences.

Liber had, however, an important cult in Rome along with his partner Libera as associate of Ceres on the Aventine (cf. CERES); but we have too little information about the ritual there to say anything definite about the manner of his worship. It appears to have been Greek in origin, like everything about that temple. By a sort of play on words (*Liber—liberi*) the Liberalia became a favourite day for boys to put on the *toga virilis* (Ov. *Fast.* 3. 771). It was a day of feasting (Wissowa, op. cit. 299), but the native and Greek elements are not easily dissociated.

He has no mythology of his own, simply taking over that of Dionysus.

A. Bruhl, *Liber Pater* (Paris, 1953).             H. J. R.

**LIBERTAS,** the personification of personal liberty, the condition of a free man. She was given a temple in or about 238 B.C. by Ti. Sempronius Gracchus, consul in that year, on the Aventine (Livy 24. 16. 19); it was restored by Augustus (*Mon. Ancyr.* 4, 6; 10, 11 of the Greek version). Here, as commonly, she was associated with Jupiter, like Liber (q.v.): (*aedem*) *Iouis Libertatis* (Augustus ibid., but cf. Platner–Ashby, 296 f.). How old her cult is we do not know, but certainly later than the 'calendar of Numa', which contains no mention of her. Under the Empire *libertas* comes to mean political liberty, not only in republican declamations, as Lucan 7. 432 ff., but in official language, to signify constitutional government, especially as opposed to usurpation or tyranny (for a full discussion, see Ch. Wirszubski, *Libertas as a Political Idea at Rome* (1950).    H. J. R.

**LIBITINA,** Roman goddess of burials, which were registered at her grove; Dion. Hal. *Ant. Rom.* 4. 15. 5, cf. Plut. *Quaest. Rom.* 23. Both identify her with Venus (q.v.), a mere confusion with Lubentina.

See Latte, *RR* 138 and 185, n. 2.

**LIBRARIES.** I. GREEK. In the article on BOOKS it is noted that writing was available well before the date of composition of the Homeric poems, but that the earliest books probably existed only for the use of rhapsodists, actors, singers, and the like. There is no trace of a reading public until about the end of the fifth century. Athenaeus (1. 4) names Polycrates of Samos and Pisistratus as traditional owners of collections of books, but he may be gratuitously crediting them with the habits of the cultured Hellenistic despot. Euripides owned books (ibid.), and Socrates refers to the accessibility of books (Pl. *Ap.* 26 d, *Phd.* 97 b, 98 b; Xen. *Mem.* 1. 6. 14), but evidently reading and the ownership of books were far from common, and provided the basis of Aristophanic jests at 'highbrows' (Denniston, *CQ* 1927, 117). In the fourth century Aristotle (*Rhet.* 1413ᵇ12) recognizes the existence of authors whose works were intended to be read (ἀναγνωστικοί) rather than recited, naming the dramatist Chaeremon and the lyric poet Licymnius.

Strabo's statement (13. 1. 54) that Aristotle was the first collector of books and taught the kings of Egypt how to arrange a library can only mean that a carefully organized library, essential to the methods of Aristotelian research, was first set up in the Lyceum, and that this provided a model for Alexandria. It is significant that Athens had to wait till the second century B.C., and for the munificence of a Ptolemy for its first public library (*IG* ii². 1009+*Hesperia* 1947, 170). Beyond doubt the foundation of the Library at Alexandria marks an epoch in bibliographical history. It appears to have been founded, in connexion with the Museum, by Ptolemy I, under the direction of Demetrius of Phalerum, but greatly extended by Ptolemy II, whom some regarded as the real founder. It is variously said to have contained from 100,000 to 700,000 volumes (Aristeas, ed. Thackeray ap. Swete, *Introduction to the O.T. in Greek*, 520; also ed. P. Wendland (Teubner) and Meecham (1935); Tzetzes ap. Ritschl, *Opusc.* i. 8, *Die alexandrinische Bibliotheken*; Gell. 6. 17; Amm. Marc. 22. 16); but book-counting is notoriously an inexact science. At its head were placed a series of distinguished scholars, Zenodotus, Eratosthenes, Aristophanes of Byzantium, Aristarchus; Callimachus and Apollonius Rhodius worked there, but were apparently not chief librarians. It became the great centre of literature in the Hellenistic world, and the practice of its copyists was probably decisive in the forms of book-production. Classified catalogues (πίνακες) of its contents were drawn up under the direction of Callimachus, and no doubt continued by his successors. A second, smaller library was established at the Serapeum.

According to Plutarch (*Caes.* 49) the great library was burnt when Caesar was besieged in Alexandria. Dio Cassius (42. 38), however, says only that the 'store-houses of corn and books' were so destroyed. Later legend magnified this into the total destruction of the great Library, or of both libraries (Sen. *Tranq.* 9; Oros. 6. 15; Gell. 6. 17); but this is very improbable.

The chief rival of the Alexandrian Library was that of Pergamum, founded by Eumenes II (*see* BOOKS). This is said to have contained 200,000 volumes when Antony presented it to Cleopatra (Plut. *Ant.* 58). Perseus of Macedon had a library (Plut. *Aem.* 28); and no doubt there were also libraries in the other principal Hellenistic towns.

Of private libraries there is little mention. The discoveries of literary papyri in Egypt are proof of private collections of books; but no particulars are on record. A third-century papyrus from the Fayum contains a fragment of an inventory of a library, comprising 132 rolls of philosophy (100 opisthograph) and 296 of medicine (*Arch. Pap.* 11. 277). With the beginning of the Hellenistic age the habit of reading set in, and libraries, public and private, seem to have become common. Specialist libraries were attached, e.g., to the medical school at Cos and to the Asclepieion near Pergamum; synagogues and later churches had their own libraries (as did gymnasia), the latter being the genesis of the great monastic libraries.

II. LATIN. At Rome, apart from archives of official documents, there is no trace of libraries before the first century B.C. Lucullus is recorded to have possessed a large library, which he made freely accessible, especially to Greeks (Plut. *Luc.* 42). Atticus and Cicero had considerable collections of books. Caesar commissioned Varro to assemble a library for him (Suet. *Iul.* 44), but the project was not consummated. The first public library in Rome was founded by C. Asinius Pollio (Pliny, *HN* 7. 30. 115; 35. 2. 10); but the decisive impulse was given by Augustus, who founded two libraries, one (the Porticus Octaviae) in the Campus Martius, the other on the Palatine. Both were connected with temples and comprised separate Greek and Latin libraries and a hall or reading-room in which conversation was possible (Gell. 13. 19). This model was generally followed. Tiberius, Vespasian, and Trajan built libraries in Rome, and Hadrian at Athens, all in connexion with temples. Eventually there are said to have been twenty-six in Rome alone, and the gift of a library to a provincial town was a recognized form of public munificence. The Younger Pliny gave one to Comum (*Ep.* 1. 8. 2), and remains of libraries, also the result of private benefactions, have been found at Ephesus and Timgad.

Private libraries also became so fashionable that Seneca (*Tranq.* 9) declares that a library is considered as essential to a house as a bath, and that the idlest people fill their houses with books from mere ostentation. The *Suda* (s.v. 'Epaphroditus') mentions a private library of 30,000 volumes. A specimen of a private library was found in the excavation of Herculaneum in 1752. It was a room about 12 ft. square, lined with bookcases ornamented with inlaid woods. In the middle was a table for readers. In the presses (*plutei, armaria*) of such libraries the rolls lay on shelves or in pigeon-holes (*nidi, foruli*), or stood in boxes (*capsae, scrinia*) with projecting *tituli*. Portraits of authors were often inserted in the woodwork of the presses, or stood as busts upon them. The Younger Pliny had a bookcase let into the wall of his bedroom (*Ep.* 2. 17. 8), a fashion afterwards followed in medieval monasteries.

J. W. Clark, *The Care of Books* (1909), ch. 1; Dziatzko in *PW*, s.v. 'Bibliotheken'; W. Schubart, *Das Buch bei den Griechen u. Römern²* (1921); C. Wendel in *RAC* ii, s.v.          F. G. K.; C. H. R.

**LIBRI COLONIARUM** (or *libri regionum*). Two lists of regions and colonies in Italy, the first also including a chapter on Dalmatia, are preserved in the *corpus gromaticorum* (see GROMATICI). They contain historical, legal, and agrimensorial information; much of the history is incorrect or doubtful, so that some of the rest too has come under suspicion. Recently, however, the section on Apulia has been shown by air photography and ground survey to be substantially true.

T. Mommsen, *Hermes* 1883, 173 ff.; E. Pais, *Storia della colonizzazione di Roma antica* (1923).          O. A. W. D.

**LIBURNI**, an Illyrian people on the east coast of the Adriatic, once occupied a large part of the coast of Illyricum (Strabo 6. 2. 4) but by the Roman period they were confined to the sector between the R. Arsia (modern *Raša*) on the west side of Istria and the Titius (*Krka*), where the territory of the Delmatae began. The Liburni were famous as seafarers, especially as pirates (Livy 10. 2. 4), and invented the *liburna* (or *liburnica*), a warship adopted by Octavian at Actium.          J. J. W.

**LIBYA** was in Homer (*Od.* 4. 85–9) merely a narrow piece of land west of Egypt; but later it became the Greek name for the modern continent of Africa. The relation of Libya to Asia was at first in dispute. Until *c.* 500 B.C. it was regarded as part of Asia; when it came to be regarded

as a separate continent its frontier was drawn along the Nile, or to west of Egypt, but after Herodotus it was fixed at Suez.

The north coast was opened up by the Phoenicians, and a Carthaginian, Hanno (q.v. 1; *c.* 490?), followed the Atlantic coast to Sierra Leone (or perhaps Kamerun). The east coast was known to the early Egyptians as far as Somaliland; in the first two centuries A.D. Greek pioneers sailed to C. Delgado. The story that Phoenicians had circumnavigated Libya (Hdt. 4. 42) found little credence, and the attempt by Eudoxus (q.v.) to sail round ended in failure.

Inland exploration was carried on under the Ptolemies by way of the Atbara and Blue Nile to Abyssinia; some Roman soldiers under Nero reached the swamps of the White Nile to the south of Khartoum. But these obstructed further advance, and it was probably by journeys from the east coast that knowledge was obtained of the 'Mountains of the Moon' (Kilimanjaro and Ruwenzori?) and lakes (Victoria and Albert Nyanza) of central Africa, and of the Nile's sources. The Sahara was traversed *c.* 500 B.C. by some natives from Tripoli, who found the Niger near Timbuctoo (Hdt. 2. 32–3); a Roman officer, Julius Maternus (*c.* A.D. 100?), reached the Sudanese steppe, probably near Lake Chad. But there is little evidence of trans-Saharan trade before the Middle Ages.

There was, until at least Alexander's time, a strange but widespread belief that east Africa outside the Red Sea was joined to north-west India (*see* NILE). After Alexander's explorations had disproved this idea, better informed people believed that Africa continued indefinitely southwards. But in the general opinion of the Greeks Libya was a right-angled triangle (with the right angle at Suez); it lay wholly north of the equator (its southernmost parts being too hot to inhabit), and it was water-girt. But later exploration of the east coast suggested the theory (accepted by Ptolemy) that east Africa joined by land to SE. Asia.

Cary–Warmington, *Explorers* 45 ff., 62 ff., 86 ff., 165 ff., (Pelican) 61 ff., 110 ff., 202 ff. For the Romans in Algeria and Libya see especially J. Baradez, *Fossatum Africae* (1949); R. G. Goodchild and J. B. W.-Perkins, *JRS* 1949, 81 ff., and Goodchild, *JRS* 1950, 30 ff.; also *Mon. Ant.* 1951; R. E. M. Wheeler, *Rome beyond the Imperial Frontiers* (1955), 119 ff.          E. H. W.

**LICENTIUS,** of Thagaste, friend and (probably) relation of St. Augustine, to whom (A.D. 395) he addressed 154 hexameters, declaring himself unable to understand Varro's encyclopaedia without St. Augustine's guidance, and asking for a copy of the latter's work *De Musica*. The poem is preserved with St. Augustine's reply (Aug. *Ep.* 26 g). It hardly justifies St. Augustine's description of Licentius as 'poeta paene perfectus', its language being unoriginal and often obscure; its prosody, however, is fairly correct (shortening of final *o*, as is usual in late poetry; actual mistakes 'Pelŏpum', 'Maeŏtidum'), and the hexameter is built with care (no spondee word in the first foot, etc.).

See Baehrens, *FPR* 413–19; M. Zelzner, *De carmine Licentii* (diss. Breslau, 1915); G. Bardy, *L'Année théol.* 14 Aug. 1954, 55 ff.          O. S.

**LICINIUS** (1, *PW* 31a), VALERIUS LICINIANUS, born of peasant stock in (new) Dacia, a comrade-in-arms of Galerius. At the conference of Carnuntum in A.D. 308 he was created Augustus of the West to replace Severus, killed by Maxentius. He made no effort to remove the latter or to contest Constantine's assumption of the title of Augustus in Gaul, and thus controlled only the Illyrian provinces. On the death of Galerius in 311 he prepared to contest the inheritance of the eastern provinces with Maximinus, but concluded peace on the Hellespont on the basis of *uti possidetis*. In 312 he formed a close alliance with Constantine, marrying his sister, Constantia, and, after Constantine had destroyed Maxentius, himself conquered Maximinus (313). In 314 or 316 he quarrelled with Constantine, lost a sharp but indecisive war, ceded part of Illyricum, and allowed his nominee, Valens, to fall. In 317 his infant son, Licinius, was made Caesar with Constantine's sons Crispus and Constantine II. From c. 320 new difficulties arose. Licinius withdrew his favour from the Christians, which he had agreed upon with Constantine at Milan in 313, and revived the persecution. In 324 Constantine attacked and won decisive victories on land and sea. Licinius was sent into retirement at Thessalonica, then accused of plotting, and put to death. His colleague, Martinian, fell with him.

P. M. Brunn, *RIC* vii, 64 ff. H. M.; B. H. W.

**LICINIUS** (2) **IMBREX**, Latin poet, called by Gellius 'an old writer of comedies', whose *palliata* entitled *Neaera* he cites (13. 21. 16; 15. 24).

**LICTORES** were attendants, ranking higher than the *viatores* and lower than the *scribae* (*see* APPARITORES) and *accensi*, who formed part of the *apparitio* of Roman magistrates, priests, and certain other persons. The main body was that of the *lictores qui magistratibus apparent* who formed a corporation divided into several decuries each under the presidency of ten men. Lictors drawn from this body accompanied holders of *imperium* at all times in and out of Rome, proceeding before them in single file and each bearing a bundle of *fasces* (q.v.) on his left shoulder. Their function was to announce the approach of the magistrate, clearing everyone except Vestals and *matronae* from the path, and to implement his right of arrest, summons, and in early times execution. Their number varied according to the nature of the magistrate's *imperium*. In the late Republic lictors were also provided from the same body for such men as *privati* holding public games and travelling senators, but they are unlikely to have carried *fasces*. Lictors drawn from a separate decury of *lictores curiatii* attended certain religious officials and were responsible for the summoning of the *comitia curiata*, while in the imperial age those from a third group—the *lictores populares denuntiatores*—attended at the games of the *magistri vicorum* (*see* VICUS). The institution of lictors was of Etruscan origin. They were normally citizens of low birth. Their traditional dress was a toga in Rome, a red coat (*sagum*) out of Rome and in the triumphal procession, and a black mourning-dress at funerals.

Mommsen, *Röm. Staatsr.* i³. 355 ff., 375 ff. *See also* bibliography under FASCES. E. S. S.

**LICYMNIUS** (1), in mythology, brother of Alcmene and uncle of Heracles (q.v.). He was the only son of Electryon to escape the Taphii (*see* AMPHITRYON), and when Amphitryon and Alcmene left for Thebes he accompanied them (Apollod. 2. 55. 57). He met his death when an old man at the hands of Tlepolemus *Il.* 2. 661–2). The reason is variously given. Pindar (*Ol.* 7. 27 ff.) says Tlepolemus struck him in anger 'as he came from the bowers of Midea', whether that means the town or his mother, Electryon's concubine; the reason for the quarrel is not given. Others, as Diod. Sic. 5. 59. 5, say it was an accident; but all agree that Tlepolemus left for Rhodes, where he founded the Dorian settlement, led his people before Troy (Homer, loc. cit.), and was killed by Sarpedon (*Il.* 5. 628 ff.). H. J. R.

**LICYMNIUS** (2), of Chios, dithyrambic poet and rhetorician, teacher of Polus (Pl. *Phdr.* 267 c). Aristotle says that his works were better to read than to hear (*Rh.* 1413ᵇ14). Also wrote on language (ibid. 1414ᵇ15).

Page, *Poet. Mel. Gr.* 768–73.

**LIGARIUS** (*PW* 4), QUINTUS, one of three brothers of undistinguished family from Sabinum, was *legatus* in Africa under C. Considius Longus in 50 B.C. Left in charge of the province, he surrendered it in 49 to the Pompeian P. Attius Varus (q.v. 1), helped him to keep out L. Aelius Tubero (q.v. 1) who had been appointed governor by the Senate, and apparently remained with the Pompeians in Africa till 46, when Caesar captured him at Hadrumetum. Cicero and Ligarius' two brothers, who had supported Caesar in 49, pleaded for his recall, but Q. Aelius Tubero (q.v. 2), piqued by his father's humiliation in 49, accused him before Caesar as a stubborn foe. Cicero defended him and he was restored. In 44, however, he joined the conspiracy against Caesar. His brothers perished in the proscriptions; his own fate is unknown.

Cicero, *Lig.* Schanz–Hosius i. 439 f.; G. Walser, *Hist.* 1959, 90 ff.; R. A. Bauman, *The Crimen Maiestatis* (1967), 142 ff. T. J. C.

**LIGHTHOUSES.** Although the Piraeus had been indicated at night by open fires on columns in the fifth century B.C., and the use of towers as day beacons began in the Hellenistic age, the first true lighthouses seem a result of the growing commerce in the Roman Empire. The Pharos at Alexandria bore a lantern by the reign of Nero, and subsequently towers at the mouths of numerous harbours and on some dangerous coasts, as at Sestos, were crowned by lanterns or open fires within a wall. The largest such tower, the Alexandrian Pharos, built about 300–280 B.C. by Sostratus of Cnidos (Strabo 17. 1. 6) 'for the safety of sailors', rose 300 feet to the top of the crowning statue, and was composed of three stories, respectively square, hexagonal, and round. Other lighthouses, apart from the Colossus at Rhodes, imitated this arrangement to some extent. The stump of a Roman lighthouse may be seen inside Dover Castle.

H. Thiersch, *Der Pharos von Alexandria* (1909); M. de Asin and M. L. Otero, *Proc. Brit. Acad.* 1933, 277 ff., with four plates. C. G. S.

**LIGHTING.** The ancients knew two methods: the burning of oil in a lamp (*see* LAMPS) and the combustion of a solid substance. In Minoan and in classical times lamps were preferred for indoor illumination, and in the Roman Empire they were sometimes employed for streets and on exteriors of buildings. The torch (λαμπάς) was more generally used out of doors and also for interiors during the early Iron Age. The Greek torch was generally of wood (δαΐς), a branch or a bundle of twigs (δετή). The Italians preferred candles of tallow (*candela*) or wax (*cereus*), and the abundance of these materials explains the late adoption of the lamp in Italy. Lanterns were also freely used, candles or lamps enclosed within horn or (in imperial times) glass. Torches were also used for signalling in warfare.

Forbes, *Stud. Anc. Technol.* vi. F. N. P.

**LIGURIANS.** Mentioned from Hecataeus onwards as the indigenous neighbours of the Greeks at Massilia. Their territory is first defined clearly (by Polybius and Livy) for the time of Roman expansion in northern Italy during the third century B.C. They were then allies of the Celts and occupied lands adjacent to them: along the coast from the Rhône to the Arno and inland as far as the Durance and the mountains south of the Po. Roman campaigns between 238 and 117 B.C. reduced to submission Ligurian tribes throughout this area. After Ligurian support of Mago (q.v. 2) c. 205–203, the most important Roman successes were against the Cisalpine Ingauni and Apuani in 181 and 180 (40,000 Apuani were deported to Samnium), against the Alpine Statielli in 173, against the Deciates and Oxybii around Nice in 154 (after Massilian appeals for help against Ligurian pirates), and against the

'Celtoligurian' Salluvii and their allies near Aix in 123, after further Massilian appeals for help. This marked the major Roman success: only lesser Ligurian tribes remained unconquered and the Roman Province was established. By this time, the western Ligurians at least had become thoroughly Celticized and Strabo (4. 6. 3) refers to the Salluvii and other tribes near Massilia as Celtoligurian or simply Celtic.

Liguria formed one of the Augustan *regiones* of Italy. The history of the Ligurians before the third century B.C. is obscure. Contemporary classical writers simply mention them in passing and the traditional account in later works (most notably Justin 43) is semi-mythical. Few ethnographic details are given by early or late authors. The principal account in Diodorus Siculus (5. 39) insists on the toughness of the Ligurians, both male and female, and of their environment.

Despite claims that some words or place-names (e.g. those ending in -*asco*, like *Giubiasco*) are diagnostically Ligurian, the existence of any Ligurian language is still hypothetical.

Relevant archaeological evidence is scanty and imprecise, and it is not possible to equate any archaeological culture with the historical Ligurians. However, Urn-field traditions, like those of neighbouring Alpine and Villanovan groups, are prominent throughout the Ligurian area at the beginning of the Iron Age, with influences from the Greek colonists and from the La Tène culture north of the Alps appearing later. There is little evidence to support theories of a persisting Mediterranean Neolithic tradition in the area.

A. Berthelot, *Rev. Arch.* 1933, 72 ff.; 245 ff. *Revue d'Études Ligures* (Bordighera), *passim*. F. R. H.

**LILYBAEUM**, the westernmost point of Sicily, was the site of a fruitless attempt at colonization *c*. 580 B.C. by Cnidians under Pentathlus (Diod. 5. 9). A small Carthaginian settlement later grew up there, but Diodorus' reference to it in 454 B.C. (11. 86) is probably mistaken. Its real importance began in 396, when the Carthaginians established it as a city to replace Motya (q.v.), sacked by Dionysius I (q.v.). It became a flourishing port and important Punic stronghold. Pyrrhus failed to take it (276), and it withstood a long siege by the Romans (250–241); cf. Polyb. 1. 41–59. After 241 it formed part of the Roman province of Sicily as a *civitas decumana* and the headquarters of a quaestor; Cicero resided there in that capacity and thought it a 'civitas splendidissima' (*Verr.* V. 5. 10). It became a *municipium* under Augustus and a *colonia* under Pertinax or Severus. The harbour was blocked in the sixteenth century, and modern *Marsala* covers only part of the extensive ancient city.

TOPOGRAPHY. G. Schmiedt, Κώκαλος 1963, 49 ff., with good photographs; recent excavations: G. A. Ruggieri, *Archaeology* 1957, 131 ff. A. G. W.

**LIMES** originally meant a pathway, especially the strip of open land along which a column of troops advanced into enemy territory. Hence, it came to mean a military road, with fortified posts and signal-towers, and finally a frontier. While Roman expansion continued, there was no thought of static frontiers. As expansion slackened and finally ceased the provincial garrisons gradually formed continuous frontier lines to facilitate control. After the conquest of the Wetterau Domitian constructed a series of wooden signal-towers along the Taunus. Physical barriers are first certainly attested under Hadrian: a palisade in Raetia and Upper Germany, stone walls in Britain and Numidia. Elsewhere, close-spaced structures along rivers (lower Rhine, middle and lower Danube, upper Euphrates) or, in deserts, along a frontier road (Red Sea to Euphrates, controlling cross-frontier nomadic migration); in Dacia and Mauretania Tingitana, networks of forts without apparently strictly delimited frontier lines. In Upper Germany part of the line was advanced by Antoninus Pius, in Mauretania Caesariensis a more southerly line was occupied under Severus. The attempt to advance into Scotland, begun under Antoninus Pius, was abandoned under Caracalla. In Upper Germany the palisade was reinforced, probably under Caracalla, by an earth bank and ditch (*Pfahlgraben*), in Raetia it was replaced by a stone wall (*Teufelsmauer*). On river frontiers legionary fortresses (*castra*) stood on the frontier line itself, elsewhere they lay back, usually with fortified road-communications to the frontier. The *limes* itself was held by auxiliary units and *numeri*, stationed in forts (*castella*) with subsidiary posts (*Zwischenkastelle*, mile-castles) and signal-towers between. Patrols along the line secured intelligence, signalled information, prevented petty raids, ensured customs collection but above all imposed political control, preventing contact between hostile outsiders and dissident elements within the Empire. The Walls in Britain, Germany, and Africa were not fighting platforms (there were no projecting towers to give enfilading fire); the enemy was met, wherever possible, in the open. The market created by frontier garrisons had a considerable economic effect. Settlements of traders grew up at legionary fortresses (*canabae*, q.v.) and auxiliary forts (*vici*), reinforced increasingly by the families of soldiers and by settlement of veterans (the latter officially promoted by land-grants from the early third century, to encourage hereditary enlistment). Garrisons became less and less mobile in practice, and failed to stem barbarian invasion in the mid third century. The Upper German and Raetian frontiers were abandoned under Gallienus, Dacia under Aurelian. The frontiers were greatly strengthened under Diocletian and Constantine, but nevertheless imperial defence thereafter depended mainly on the mobile Field Armies. For the late developments of frontier defence *see* LIMITANEI.

G. Forni in Ruggiero, *Diz. Epigr.*, s.v. For Germany, O. Brogan, *Arch. Journ.* 1935, 1 ff.; W. Schleiermacher, *Der römische Limes in Deutschland* (1961), with bibliography. For Syria, A. Poidebard, *La Trace de Rome dans le désert de Syrie* (1934). For N. Africa, J. Baradez, *Fossatum Africae* (Paris, 1949). For Britain *see under* WALL OF HADRIAN, WALL OF ANTONINUS. For new research, see especially reports of Congresses of Roman Frontier Studies—*The Congress of Roman Frontier Studies 1949* (ed. Eric Birley, Durham, 1952); *Carnuntina* (*Römische Forschungen in Niederösterreich* iii, ed. E. Swoboda, Graz, 1956); *Limes-Studien* (*Schriften des Instituts für Ur- und Frühgeschichte der Schweiz*, 14, ed. R. Laur-Belart, Basel, 1959); *V Congressus Internationalis Limitis Romani Studiosorum* (ed. G. Novak, Zagreb, 1963); *Studien zu den Militärgrenzen Roms* (Vorträge des 6. internationalen Limeskongresses in Süddeutschland, 1967). A. M.; J. C. M.

**LIMITANEI** (or *riparienses*, *ripenses*) was a generic name for the frontier army of Constantine and his successors. It comprised cavalry (*cunei equitum*, *equites*, *alae*), and infantry (*legiones*, *cohortes*, *auxilia*), and was commanded by *duces*. Its units were normally static, but on occasion they could be converted into regiments of the field army as *pseudocomitatenses*, or even sometimes upgraded into *comitatenses*. It is therefore unwise to dismiss it as a mere peasant militia. See COMITATENSES.

R. Grosse, *Römische Militärgeschichte* (1920), 63 ff.; Jones, *Later Rom. Emp.* 98 ff., 649 ff.; *PW*, Suppl. xi, 876 ff. G. R. W.

**LINDUM** (*Lincoln*) lay in the territory of the Coritani, whose capital was Ratae (*Leicester*) (q.v.). It began as a fortress for Legio IX Hispana perhaps a little before A.D. 60 (Collingwood and Wright, *RIB* 254–7, 260) and its *munimenta* may be referred to by Tacitus (*Ann.* 14. 32). Soon after 71 this legion was advanced to Eburacum (q.v.) and Lindum seems to have been held by Legio II Adiutrix perhaps till *c*. 76 (*RIB* 253, 258). Within the Flavian period and perhaps *c*. 90 a colonia was founded at Lindum (*CIL* xiii. 6679). The new town, with colonnaded main streets, small insulae, a piped aqueduct, and notable sewers, occupied the site of the fortress, but later doubled its area. A wall with monumental gates was provided perhaps early in the third century. The town was an important road centre and enjoyed good water communications (Car and Fosse dykes, R. Witham); in the fourth century it was the seat of a bishopric and perhaps the capital of Flavia Caesariensis.

I. A. Richmond, *Arch. Journ.* 1946, 26 ff., 64 ff.; G. Webster, *JRS* 1949, 57 ff.; F. H. Thompson, ibid. 1956, 22 ff.; *Arch. Journ.* 1954, 106 ff.; D. F. Petch, ibid. 1960, 40 ff.; J. C. Mann, *Antiquity* 1961, 316 ff.; Frere, *Britannia, passim.*      I. A. R.; S. S. F.

**LINUS** (*Λίνος*). An old and apparently mournful-sounding song (*Il.* 18. 570, which shows that it was not always sung on mournful occasions, for there it is at a vintage; but it may be a lament for the 'death' of the grapes, a custom widely paralleled, see Frazer, *GB* vii. 216 and the whole chapter) contained the sounds *αἴλινον*, interpreted as meaning 'alas for Linus'. The song was called a Linus (Homer, ibid.), and the question was asked who Linus was and why he should be bewailed. Argos said he was a son of Apollo and Psamathe, a local princess; she exposed him, he was devoured by dogs, and the city plagued by Apollo till satisfaction was made (Paus. 1. 43. 7–8). In central Greece, Linus was son of Amphimarus and Urania, killed by Apollo for saying he was as good a singer as the god (Paus. 9. 29. 6). A third variant made him Heracles' music-teacher, whom his pupil killed with a blow from a cithara (Apollod. 2. 63). A favourite modern explanation (Frazer, loc. cit.) is that *αἴλινον* is Phoenician, *ai lanu*, 'woe to us!' This is not impossible, cf. LITYERSES.      H. J. R.

**LIRIS**, river of central Italy, called *Garigliano* below Interamna Lirenas (q.v.). Rising near the Fucinus Lacus (q.v.) it flows SSE. to Sora, turns sharply SSW., cascades picturesquely at *Isola del Liri*, and enters the Tyrrhenian through marshy country at Minturnae. Chief tributaries: Fibrenus (Cicero's natal stream: *de leg.* 2. 6), Trerus, Melpis, *Rapido.*      E. T. S.

**LITERARY CRITICISM IN ANTIQUITY.** The arts of formal speech played a great part in ancient life, both in business and in pleasure. Instruction in oratory was provided by rhetoric (q.v.), and rhetorical teaching soon became influential in the work of historians and poets as well as speakers. Most ancient criticism is a by-product of rhetoric. Hence it is concerned with literature as producing an effect on an audience, not as the self-expression of an author. The idea, variously interpreted, that the poets 'teach' is seldom absent. With the notable exception of Aristotle's *Poetics*, there is little general aesthetic theory. It is a very different thing from most modern criticism.

**2.** The early poets made pronouncements on their profession. The art of Homer and Hesiod was a gift of the Muses, who inspired their poet, knew all things, and could tell false tales as well as true (*Il.* 2. 484–92, *Od.* 8. 479 ff., Hes. *Theog.* 1–104). Pindar is the *προφήτης* of the Muses (fr. 137 Bowra), his *σοφία* is the product of endowment (*φυά*), not mere technique (C. M. Bowra, *Pindar* (1964), ch. i). Hesiod and Pindar criticize the falsehoods of the epic (*Theog.* loc. cit., *Nem.* 7. 20 ff.); so, with much more trenchancy, do the philosophers (e.g. Xenophanes, fr. 11). Allegory (q.v.) helped for the defence. The notion of inspiration (cf. Democr. fr. 18, 21) and the tendency to find fault with myth, usually on moral grounds, are the two main critical attitudes to poetry which Plato's generation inherited, though the paradox of Gorgias on the *ἀπάτη* of tragedy ('the deceived is wiser than the undeceived . . .': Plut. *De glor. Ath.* 348 b–c) and the saying of Simonides that 'poetry is silent painting' (ibid. 346 f)

perhaps indicate different lines of reflection. The contest between Aeschylus and Euripides in Aristophanes' *Frogs* contains not only a moralizing element, but the essentials of the distinction between 'high' and 'low' styles which became an important tool of later critics (F. Wehrli in *Phyllobolia für P. von der Muehll* (1946), 9 ff.).

**3.** Plato devalued inspiration (*Ion, Meno, Phaedrus*); he also (*Republic, Laws*) developed the educational criticism of poetry and music. He thought that the spectacle of degrading emotion nourished the same emotion in the hearer. He severely criticized the amoral technicalities of contemporary rhetoric (q.v. § 2). His superb quality as a critic is shown most clearly by his gift of parody (*Symposium, Phaedrus, Menexenus*), in which Aristophanes is his only rival.

**4.** Aristotle's *Poetics*, the fountain-head of most later criticism, is in part an answer to Plato; this is the point both of the improved and very important analysis of *μίμησις* (imitation) and of the much-debated doctrine that tragedy effects the *κάθαρσις* of pity and fear. Aristotle does not theorize without detailed observation, and though he hardly gives the impression of an instinctively sensitive judge, he is an extremely acute one. His discussions of *ἁμαρτία*—the tragic hero's mistake or flaw—*περιπέτεια* ('reverse'), and *ἀναγνώρισις* (recognition) touch fundamental principles of dramatic construction. The contrast (1459b15) between the *Iliad* as a poem of emotion (*παθητικόν*) and the *Odyssey* as a poem of character (*ἠθικόν*), moralized and realistic, is of great significance for later criticism (compare and contrast 'Longinus' 9. 13–15). Few texts of the length have been so much debated; and this is a tribute to the seminal quality of the thought even more than to the difficulties of interpreting a book which must be in some sense a set of lecture notes.

**5.** Throughout the Hellenistic and Roman periods, with their various swings in taste and the running battle between classicism and modernism (*τὸ καινόσπουδον*, 'Longinus' 5), criticism retained its rhetorical character. Theophrastus' remark (fr. 64 Wimmer) that *λόγος* directed *πρὸς τὰ πράγματα* is the pursuit of philosophers, while poets and orators are both concerned with *λόγος* in its relation to the audience, is fundamental. Conviction is the poet's aim as well as the orator's. It follows that the form of his work may be judged apart from its content; like the orator, he may have a good case but not know how to present it. Rhetoricians indeed used poets freely as examples; they treated them as having more freedom, in language and in invention, but as playing essentially the same game.

**6.** It was therefore natural that the main achievement of this long period should be new refinement in the discussion of style. (i) The contrast between 'high' and 'low' (cf. *Frogs*) developed, under Theophrastus or soon after, into a system of three types (*χαρακτῆρες*). The intermediate type, originally thought of as a golden mean, was identified with the smooth, flowing style of Isocrates, with the result that the three *χαρακτῆρες* (*ἰσχνός, γλαφυρός* or *ἀνθηρός, μεγαλοπρεπής*: *genus tenue, floridum, grande*) came to form a descriptive rather than a normative scheme. All kinds of writing could be classified on this principle: e.g. the representative historians were Xenophon, Herodotus, Thucydides. The system dominates later criticism; a locus classicus is Cicero, *Orator* 75–90. There were many variations and adaptations. Dionysius (q.v. 7) uses an analogous scheme to classify *ἁρμονίαι* (types of word-arrangement); Demetrius (q.v. 17) has a four-style system which may be original; in 'Longinus' (q.v.), the most congenial and, after Aristotle, the most influential of the Greek critics, *ὕψος* ('the Sublime') is described largely with the help of the traditional accounts of the high or grand style, though it is clearly a concept which does not fit into the scheme. (ii) There was also the doctrine of the ἀρεταὶ λέξεως, *virtutes dicendi*. These had been enumerated by Theophrastus, following up Aristotle's *Rhetoric*, as ἑλληνισμός (good Greek), σαφήνεια (clarity), τὸ πρέπον (appropriateness), and κατασκευή (elaboration, *ornatus*); in Dionysius (e.g. *Epistula ad Pompeium* 3) these are reinforced by additional (ἐπίθετοι) excellences, most of which are appropriate to one or other type of writing rather than to writing in general (e.g. τὸ μέγα καὶ θαυμαστόν, ἰσχύς, ἡδονή (charm)). (iii) A conflation of χαρακτήρ-language with ἀρετή-language produced the elaborate system of ἰδέαι of the later rhetoricians (*see* HERMOGENES 2). The critical interest of all this lies partly in the delicate metaphorical vocabulary developed, and partly in the application of theory to examples (so also with the figures, *see* RHETORIC, GREEK, § 4: see, e.g., 'Longinus' 17–29 for a group of traditional examples sensitively treated).

**7.** Philosophers and scholars, as well as rhetors, contributed to Hellenistic criticism. (i) The Stoics (Ariston, Diogenes of Babylon) viewed poetry primarily as educational, and in a sense continued Plato's moralizing approach. Plutarch's *de audiendis poetis* is in this tradition. (ii) Epicurean theory is known mainly from Philodemus Περὶ ποιημάτων, book 5, extant on papyrus; he strongly criticizes the didactic approach. (iii) Alexandrian scholarship owed much to Aristotle (e.g. to *Poet.* 25). The great scholars used aesthetic as well as historical arguments in the discussions of authenticity which were among their main concerns. Dionysius is in the same tradition in the sense that his historical interests combined fruitfully with his rhetoric in the criticism of the orators. Many extant commentaries and scholia, all the way down to Eustathius (q.v.), contain critical judgements of interest.

**8.** The Roman contribution is not a mere appendage to Greek criticism; it has its own value and originality. In the great period of Latin literature (as in the days of the Old Comedy) criticism appears in topical writing in quite unacademic contexts; in Lucilius and Horace (as later in Persius and Petronius) it is an ingredient of satire. Horace (*Sat.* 1. 4, 1. 10, 2. 1; *Epist.* 1. 19, 2. 1, 2. 2) defended his own literary position, expounded literary history and finally (*Ars Poetica*) built an epistle combining a poet's personal experience with the Peripatetic theory of Neoptolemus of Parium, known also from Philodemus. The *Ars* mingles traditional precepts on the drama and views on the poet's place in society with much individual wisdom and humour. It set a fashion followed in the Renaissance by Vida, Boileau, Pope.

**9.** Cicero's achievement as a judge of oratory (*see* RHETORIC, LATIN, § 2) is unequalled by any Greek. Political oratory died with him; the age of the declaimers and rhetorical schools which followed produced critics of a different cast. The Elder Seneca (q.v.) makes many shrewd points in commenting on his favourite declaimers (*see* DECLAMATIO); to many in the first century A.D. the sophisticated declamatory style was a symptom of decadence. Seneca's son (*Epist.* 114) and Tacitus (*Dialogus*) reflect interestingly on the moral, political, and intellectual causes of decline. With Quintilian, there is a return to Cicero's ideals: the famous chapter (10. 1) in which Quintilian catalogues the authors to be read by the budding orator both summarizes traditional teaching Περὶ μιμήσεως and shows a capacity for independent judgement.

**10.** The writers of the second century—Gellius and Fronto—represent a further change in taste. They often prefer early poets and pre-Ciceronian prose-writers to the Ciceronian and Augustan classics. From now on, Latin literature becomes, as Greek had long been, backward-looking and archaistic. In the Late Empire scholia and commentaries on the classical writers (e.g. Servius on Virgil, Donatus on Terence) preserve the traditions of rhetoric and criticism and enshrine many interesting and valuable judgements.

In general, see the articles on the authors mentioned. Early texts are usefully collected in G. Lanata, *Poetica pre-Platonica* (1963).
Aristotle's *Poetics*. I. Bywater's commentary (1909) remains valuable, his text is superseded by R. Kassel's (1965). See also A. Rostagni's edition (1945) and the useful short interpretation by H. House, *Aristotle's Poetics* (1956). New commentary by D. W. Lucas (1968). Many translations: e.g. Bywater (1909), G. M. A. Grube (1958); Longinus, *On the Sublime*, ed. D. A. Russell (1964).
On Plato, see P. Vicaire, *Platon critique littéraire* (1960). On Horace (and Neoptolemus and Philodemus), C. O. Brink, *Horace on Poetry* (1963).
GENERAL SURVEYS. G. Saintsbury, *History of Criticism* i (1900); J. W. H. Atkins, *Literary Criticism in Antiquity* (1934); E. E. Sikes, *The Greek View of Poetry* (1931); J. D. Denniston, *Greek Literary Criticism* (anthology, in translation) (1924); J. F. D'Alton, *Roman Literary Theory and Criticism* (1931); G. M. A. Grube, *The Greek and Roman Critics* (1965).     D. A. R.

**LITERATURE, GREEK. 1.** W. Schmid and O. Stählin, *Geschichte der griechischen Literatur* (in I. von Müller's *Handbuch*). The latest volumes are:
7th ed.: I. i. *Die griechische Literatur vor der attischen Hegemonie* (1929). I. ii. *Die griechische Literatur in der Zeit der attischen Hegemonie vor dem Eingreifen der Sophistik* (1934). I. iii. *Die griechische Literatur zur Zeit der attischen Hegemonie nach dem Eingreifen der Sophistik*, Erste Hälfte (1940). I. iv. ibid., Zweite Hälfte, Erster Abschnitt (1946). I. v. ibid., Zweite Hälfte, Zweiter Abschnitt (1948).
6th ed.: II. i. *Die nachklassische Periode der griechischen Literatur*, Erste Hälfte: *Von 320 vor Christus bis 100 nach Christus* (1920). II. ii. *Die nachklassische Periode der griechischen Literatur*, Zweite Hälfte: *Von 100 bis 530 nach Christus* (1924). 'Schmid–Stählin' is essentially a reference work, and does not lend itself to continuous reading. It contains full bibliographies.
**2.** T. Sinko, *Literatura grecka*, 3 vols. in 6 parts (Cracow, 1931–54). This Polish work is on a scale comparable to Schmid–Stählin. Volume iii, dealing with Greek literature in the Roman and early Byzantine period, offers the most up-to-date treatment of its subject. The extensive bibliographies may be consulted by those unable to read Polish.
**3.** F. Susemihl, *Geschichte der griechischen Literatur in der Alexandriner-Zeit*, 2 vols. (1891–2). Still fundamental as a reference work, though its bibliographical information is out of date.
**4.** K. Krumbacher, *Geschichte der byzantinischen Literatur von Justinian bis zum Ende des oströmischen Reiches* (527–1453)² (1897), in I. von Müller's *Handbuch*. Still the essential reference work on Byzantine Greek literature. For theological literature it is now supplemented by
**5.** H. G. Beck, *Kirche und theologische Literatur im byzantinischen Reich* (1959), in I. von Müller's *Handbuch*, and for historical literature by
**6.** Gy. Moravcsik, *Byzantinoturcica*², vol. i (Berlin, 1958).
**7.** A. Lesky, *Geschichte der griechischen Literatur*² (1963) and Engl. Transl., *A History of Greek Literature* (1965), is an eminently readable and authoritative shorter study, with up-to-date bibliographical information. There are many shorter histories of Greek literature in English. The most informative is probably
**8.** H. J. Rose, *Handbook of Greek Literature from Homer to the age of Lucian*⁴ (1957). For the period after Lucian reference can still profitably be made to
**9.** F. A. Wright, *History of Later Greek Literature from the death of Alexander in 323 B.C. to the death of Justinian in A.D. 565* (1932).     R. B.

**LITERATURE, LATIN. 1.** M. Schanz, C. Hosius, G. Krüger, *Geschichte der römischen Literatur* (in I. von Müller's *Handbuch*). The latest volumes are:

4th ed.: I. *Die römische Literatur in der Zeit der Republik* (1927). II. *Die römische Literatur in der Zeit der Monarchie bis auf Hadrian* (1935).

3rd ed.: III. *Die Zeit von Hadrian 117 bis auf Constantin 324* (1922).

2nd ed.: IV. i. *Die römische Literatur von Constantin bis zur Gesetzgebungswerk Justinians.* Erste Hälfte: *Die Literatur des vierten Jahrhunderts* (1914). IV. ii. ibid., Zweite Hälfte: *Die Literatur des fünften und sechsten Jahrhunderts* (1920). 'Schanz–Hosius–Krüger' is essentially a reference work, unsuitable for continuous reading. It contains full bibliographies.

2. W. S. Teuffel, *Geschichte der römischen Literatur*, 6th/7th ed. by W. Kroll and F. Skutsch, 3 vols. (1913–20). On a somewhat smaller scale than 'Schanz–Hosius–Krüger', this too is suitable for reference rather than reading.

3. M. Manitius, *Geschichte der lateinischen Literatur des Mittelalters*, 3 vols. (1911–31), in I. von Müller's *Handbuch.* Essential for study of medieval Latin literature, but rather a collection of monographs than a unitary history. The most extensive treatment of Latin literature in English is offered by

4. J. Wight Duff, *Literary History of Rome from the Origins to the Close of the Golden Age* (1909; 3rd ed. 1953, with corrected impression, 1960, by A. M. Duff); and

5. id. *Literary History of Rome in the Silver Age, from Tiberius to Hadrian* (1930). There are many shorter studies in English, of which the most generally useful is probably

6. H. J. Rose, *Handbook of Latin Literature*[3] (1954). On the Latin literature of late antiquity and the Middle Ages the best shorter history is

7. M. Hélin, *A History of Mediaeval Latin Literature*, transl. by J. C. Snow (U.S.A. 1949). A longer, and most sensitive and perceptive survey of medieval Latin literature is given by

8. J. de Ghellinck, *Littérature latine au moyen âge*, 2 vols. (1939), and

9. id. *L'Essor de la littérature latine au XII^e siècle*, 2 vols. (1946). Fundamental for the study of late and medieval Latin poetry are

10. F. J. E. Raby, *A History of Christian-Latin Poetry*[2] (1953), and

11. id. *A History of Secular Latin Poetry in the Middle Ages*[2], 2 vols. (1957).      R. B.

**LITERNUM,** Roman citizen colony on the northern coast of Campania (q.v.), founded in 194 B.C. but soon derelict (Livy 34. 45): excavations near *Lago di Patria.* The disillusioned Scipio Africanus Maior retired and possibly was buried there (Livy 38. 52, 53, 56; Sen. *Ep.* 86). Later the Via Domitiana (q.v.), like the modern railway, somewhat increased its importance.      E. T. S.

**LITIS AESTIMATIO,** the assessment, made by the *iudex* (q.v.), of the amount of money which the unsuccessful defendant in a Roman civil action must pay to the plaintiff. In the formulary procedure (*see* LAW AND PROCEDURE, ROMAN, II) all actions, except those intended only to settle a preliminary question (*actiones praeiudiciales*: Gai. *Inst.* iv. 44), necessarily led to a *condemnatio* for a money sum (Gai. *Inst.* iv. 48). There could be no order for specific performance or for the restitution of a thing, though it was open to the defendant to do so before judgment (Gai. *Inst.* iv. 114), and in some actions the *condemnatio* was made conditional on his not doing so, the plaintiff making his own assessment of the value (*see* VINDICATIO). In an action concerning title to property, if the defendant paid the *litis aestimatio*, the title thereby passed to him.      B. N.

**LITURGY.** At Athens in the fifth and fourth centuries B.C. certain public functions were compulsorily conferred upon the richer citizens and metics. Of these liturgies some, like the trierarchy (q.v.), were occasional, others were imposed regularly, according to a fixed order of rotation. These included the *choregia* (q.v.: the production of a chorus at the musical and dramatic festivals), the gymnasiarchy (*see* GYMNASIUM), ἑστίασις (the provision of a banquet for a tribe at festivals), ἀρχιθεωρία (the leadership of a public delegation to a foreign festival), ἱπποτροφία (the maintenance of a horse by a knight). To some liturgies nominations were made by a magistrate, e.g. by the archon to the tragic *choregia*, to others by the tribes, e.g. to the cyclic *choregia* and ἑστίασις. A person nominated might challenge another whom he considered better able to bear the expense, and the latter might either undertake the liturgy or exchange properties with his challenger, or appeal to the courts (*see* ANTIDOSIS). A liturgy involved the holder both in personal service (though he might employ a deputy) and in expense. In some cases the State made an allocation, but this did not by any means cover the costs.

In the Hellenistic age no clear line was drawn between ἀρχαί and λειτουργίαι. Both were filled by popular election; neither imposed any obligatory expenditure in theory, but both in fact often involved a heavy personal outlay; both might in the last resort be compulsorily imposed. Immunity was in this age often granted, not only from liturgies, but from magistracies, and the term 'liturgy' came to denote minor offices, which were onerous but did not carry much authority.

In Roman municipal law a sharp distinction was drawn between *honores* and *munera*; *honores* qualified their holder for a seat on the council; the *immunitas* conferred by the Roman government meant exemption from *munera.* These rules were also applied in the Greek East, and offices must therefore have been definitely classified into ἀρχαί and λειτουργίαι. In time the distinction became blurred; immunity (ἀλειτουργησία) by the early third century included exemption from magistracies. By this time the most important and onerous liturgies were imperial, such as the collection of tribute.

In Egypt a liturgy meant a compulsory State office. Compulsion was little used in the Ptolemaic or early Roman period, but from the latter part of the first century A.D. became commoner, till every post below the rank of στρατηγός or βασιλικὸς γραμματεύς became a liturgy. Qualified persons were nominated by the scribes of the *metropoleis* and villages to the *strategoi*, who themselves appointed to lower posts, and for higher posts submitted the names to the *epistrategos*, who drew lots between them. When councils were instituted in the *metropoleis*, many of the more important officers were elected by them.

V. Thumser, *De civium Atheniensium muneribus eorumque immunitate* (1880); J. Oehler, *PW*, s.v. 'Leitourgia'; F. Oertel, *Die Liturgie, Studien zur ptolemäischen und kaiserlichen Verwaltung Aegyptens* (1917).      A. H. M. J.

**LITYERSES.** 'Some say that he was a son of Midas, and that he challenged all and sundry to a contest in reaping, and maltreated those who were overcome by him. But, encountering a stronger reaper, he met his death. Some say that it was Heracles who killed him' (Pollux 4. 54, who says that Lityerses is the Phrygian reapers' song). His source is uncertain, cf. Crusius in Roscher's *Lexikon*, s.v. It would seem, therefore, to be a traditional song with a story to explain it, cf. LINUS.      H. J. R.

**LIVIA** (*PW* 37) **DRUSILLA,** daughter of M. Livius Drusus Claudianus (adoptive son of Drusus 2?) and Alfidia, was born 30 Jan. 58 B.C. and in 43 or 42 married Ti. Claudius Nero (q.v. 3), whom she accompanied on his flight after the Perusine War and to whom she bore Tiberius, the future emperor, and Drusus (3). In 39 Nero divorced her so that she could marry Octavian (Augustus), whose affection and esteem she retained throughout, although they did not have the children he longed for. She ruled his household with old-fashioned propriety, and her beauty, dignity, intelligence, and tact well fitted her for the high position which she presently filled as the consort of a monarch. Augustus valued her counsel, and was believed to have shown clemency to conspirators at her instance (*see* CINNA 4). Under his will she was adopted into the Julian *gens* and renamed Julia Augusta. After this her position was less happy; a desire to continue to exert influence seems to have caused some discord between her and Tiberius, and he was even supposed to have retired from Rome in A.D. 26 chiefly to be away from her. When she died in 29 he refused to execute her will or to allow her to be deified: the former omission was repaired by Gaius, the latter by Claudius. Though she was generally popular with the Senate for her many kindnesses to individuals, there were always those who assigned to her the character of a ruthless intriguer (Gaius called her 'Ulixes stolatus') and believed her to have had a hand in the deaths of Marcellus (q.v. 7), C. and L. Caesar (qq.v. 6 and 7), Agrippa (q.v. 4) Postumus, and Germanicus (q.v.), and even to have hastened the end of Augustus himself. But, while her influence may well have helped Tiberius to power, it does not appear that these graver imputations rested on any solid evidence.

Syme, *Rom. Rev.* and *Tacitus*, see indexes; J. Carcopino, *Passion et politique chez les Césars* (1958), 65 ff.; T. P. Wiseman, *Hist.* 1965, 333f. Iconography. W. H. Gross, *Iulia Augusta* (1962).

G. W. R.; T. J. C.

**LIVILLA (CLAUDIA LIVIA JULIA?** *PW* Livii 38), daughter of Drusus (3) and Antonia (3), born *c.* 13 B.C., was married to C. Caesar (q.v. 7) and then to Drusus (q.v. 4). In 25 Sejanus (q.v.) asked Tiberius for her hand, but was refused. In 31 Tiberius was informed that she had been Sejanus' mistress and had helped him to have Drusus poisoned; she was put to death.          T. J. C.

**LIVIUS (1) ANDRONĪCUS,** LUCIUS. Accius (q.v.), whose chronology was at fault, said that Livius came from Tarentum, and there is no reason to think this false. He came to Rome as prisoner of war (perhaps after the surrender of Tarentum in 272 B.C.); on manumission he took his owner's name. The first performance of a play (probably a tragedy) was in 240 B.C. (Cic. *Brut.* 72—relying on the *liber annalis* of Atticus, who based his work on Varro's researches). In 207 B.C. Livius was commissioned to compose a παρθένειον in Greek style after the Sibylline books were consulted (Livy 27. 37. 7—previously done in 217 B.C., Livy 22. 1. 16, when the author is unknown, and later in 200 B.C., Livy 31. 12. 5, when the author was P. Licinius Tegula—presumably Livius was dead). In honour of this work of Livius the temple of Minerva on the Aventine was set aside as a place where writers and actors could meet and could make dedications (Festus, s.v. *scribas*). The lengthy account in Livy 7. 2. 3–12 which traces the origin of Roman drama from dramatic *satura*, with anecdotes about Livius, is untrustworthy and probably a construction, on Greek analogies, made about 100 B.C.

*Plays*: the titles of some eight tragedies are known and indicate Sophoclean and Euripidean originals, but the fragments are very scanty. There is one fragment (20–22 R.) from the *Equos Troianus* in cretics which is most plausibly identified as coming from a speech of Sinon: if so, Livius must have invented the practice of dispensing with the Greek choral odes and producing *cantica* of his own from trimeter monologues (this practice

was transferred then to comedy: *see* NAEVIUS, ENNIUS, PLAUTUS, CAECILIUS (1) STATIUS). Even less is known of his comedies but enough to show that, in contrast to Greek practice, he used the same pattern of senarius for both tragedy and comedy.

*Odyssia*: this 'translation' of Homer's *Odyssey* became famous and influential. It was composed in Saturnians, a poor substitute for the hexameter (cf. Ennius, *Ann.* 213 ff. V.), but it was clearly a work of great skill and some force. It was no 'translation' in fact: it was a Roman adaptation of Homer, with many happy inventions, e.g. the Muses became *Camenae* (fountain goddesses), μοῖρα (*Od.* 3. 238) becomes *Morta* (a mysterious Italic goddess of death); the Roman use of patronymics adds a touch of solemnity, e.g. Μοῦσα (*Od.* 8. 481) becomes *diva Monetas filia*, Apollo becomes *filius Latonas*, etc. The high-flown effect of Homeric language is imitated by the use of archaisms, but Livius seems to have avoided the temptation to invent compound adjectives (e.g. πολύτροπος becomes *versutus*). Horace's characterization (*Epist.* 2. 1. 166) of early Roman poetry *nam spirat tragicum satis et feliciter audet* applies to Livius; what was clearly lacking was the easy flow and grace of Homeric composition.

E. H. Warmington, *Remains of Old Latin* ii (1936), 2 ff. (with transl.). PLAYS. Ribbeck, *TRF³*, *CRF¹*; Klotz, *Scaen. Rom. Fr.* i. 19 ff. (tragedies).
    *Odyssia.* Morel *FPL* (1927), 7 ff. Leo, *Gesch. d. röm. Lit.* (1913), 55 ff. E. Fraenkel, *PW* Suppl. v, 598 ff. S. Mariotti, *Livio Andronico e la traduzione artistica* (1952).          G. W. W.

**LIVIUS (2,** *PW* 9), TITUS (Livy) (59 B.C.–A.D. 17 or 64 B.C.–A.D. 12), the Roman historian, was born in Patavium (Padua) at the height of the old Venetic city's prosperity and fame; thus he grew up under the influence of stern Italian morality. We know little of his life. His daughter married a rhetorician, Magius, and his son may have been a writer, followed by Pliny. He himself wrote philosophical dialogues, historical in tendency, and his advice on rhetoric to his son (Quint. 10. 1. 39) shows his place in the Ciceronian tradition. At Rome he gave readings of his work, and won Augustus' interest in his historical task (4. 20. 7) and respect for his republican sentiment (Tac. *Ann.* 4. 34); he encouraged Claudius in his historical studies (Suet. *Claud.* 41). He must have spent most of his time at work in Rome or in Padua, where he died.

The history of Rome (*ab urbe condita libri*) was composed in 142 books. Books i–v covered from the origins to the Gallic sack of Rome, vi–xv reached the beginning of the Punic Wars, xvi–xx treated the First Punic War, xxi–xxx the Second Punic War, xxxi–xlv the Macedonian and Syrian Wars. As the work grew under his hand the pentad and decade arrangement had to be modified. The destruction of Carthage appeared in book li, Ti. Gracchus in lvii, the defeat of the Cimbri in lxviii, the opening of the Social War in lxxi, Marius' death in lxxx, Sulla's death in xc, Caesar's consulship in ciii, Pharsalus in cxi, Caesar's death in cxvi, Actium in cxxxiii, the death of Drusus (9 B.C.) in cxlii. Books cix–cxvi were entitled *belli civilis libri*.

The proemium reflects the situation at Augustus' accession to sole power; book i. 19. 3 was published after 27 B.C. and before 25 B.C.; book xxviii. 12 presupposes Agrippa's Spanish campaign of 19 B.C. Book lix followed Augustus' quotation of Metellus' speech on marriage in 18 B.C. If book cxxi was published after Augustus' death (A.D. 14), it may have been accompanied by the subsequent books; for books cxxxiv–cxlii (from 28 B.C. to Drusus' death in 9 B.C.) could well be deferred in publication.

Of this immense work only thirty-five books are extant: i–x, xxi–xlv. For the lost books we have a palimpsest fragment of book xci, cited fragments and excerpts, and the epitomized, perhaps slightly 'contaminated' tradition of the *Periochae* (q.v.) and the Oxyrhynchus Epitome of books xxxvii–xl, xlviii–lv; also, in basis, the work of Florus, Granius Licinianus, Aurelius Victor, Eutropius and Festus, Orosius and Cassiodorus, Julius Obsequens.

Livy stood at the peak of annalistic historiography, and was able to develop the work of the immediate post-Sullan annalists. Valerius Antias from the beginning, and Claudius Quadrigarius from the Gallic sack (book vi), appear to have provided the basis of composition; they are cited regularly. The set annalistic arrangement allowed easy transition from source to source and the incorporation of episodic material; in books i–x Licinius Macer, Aelius Tubero, and (indirectly) Fabius Pictor and Calpurnius Piso, in books xxi–xxx Coelius Antipater and Polybius, in xxxi–xlv Polybius, supplement Valerius Antias and Claudius Quadrigarius; afterwards Posidonius, and perhaps Sulpicius Galba, Sisenna, Caesar, and Augustus' *Memoirs*, among others, were used in the same way.

In accordance with contemporary historiographical practice, Livy does not cite his authorities, except in cases of dispute or doubt, and often, e.g. in the comparison of casualty figures, this may be conventional. As a rule he adapted the source material with scarcely more than literary and stylistic elaboration, apparently without 'contamination', if we may judge from his reproduction of Polybius and the common inconsistency of the annalistic narrative. There is always a certain negligence in his treatment of context, with obvious discrepancies, repetitions, and chronological divergences; this is most striking in his use of Polybius, where the Olympiad yearly divisions are forced within the narrative based on the Roman year. The reason appears to lie in his undue dependence upon narrative form in constructing his work. This acceptance of the annalistic tradition in both matter and form largely explains his lack of source criticism; the authority of the *annales maximi*, persisting in its literary development, limited criticism to detail, and Livy remained the rhetorical writer.

Yet, even if we grant this, he falls short in critical method. His defective treatment of the problem of Cossus' *spolia opima* (4. 19), his neglect of the *libri lintei* when two sources cited the same passage differently (4. 23), not to mention again the inconsistencies in his narrative, reflect his subservience to written authority. Livy had little knowledge of Roman institutions. His inexperience in military matters affects his description of battles: his ignorance of the phalanx, for example, is unpardonable; he is, however, better on ships. He does not falsify events, but his literary elaboration often makes his narrative conventional and misleading. His ignorance of conditions in early Rome and in the East leaves blemishes on his historical reconstruction. There is little reason to believe that he improved his methods in the later books, once he had chosen his main sources, or that he applied sharp historical interpretation even where the circumstances of the Late Republic required it—and still less so for the dubious events since Caesar's death.

Livy's purpose in the first instance was not to analyse the process of history in the light of its political discordance. He set himself to give Rome a history that in conception and style should be worthy of her imperial rise and greatness, and challenge his generation to resume the responsibilities of their position. As a sober Italian he felt closer to the true traditions of Rome than the sophisticated politicians of the capital, and nourished the hopes of the early Augustan period. Thus he depicted the life and character, the policies and personalities of the past and the later decay of discipline; in particular, the social morale of early Rome, the 'integra atque immobilis virtus' against Hannibal, the policy of Republican freedom against the Hellenistic monarchies, and the consequences of luxury and avarice in the later age. He failed to see the radical consequences of imperial expansion, social change, and political rivalry; yet he had faith in the moral qualities which should maintain what had been gained and so nearly lost.

Livy's genius lay in his power of vivid historical reconstruction, visualizing scenes and people. His natural feeling developed under the influence of Hellenistic psychological interpretation, and his literary talent was trained in rhetorical expression; the annalistic tradition gave him material and form. Cicero had defined his task, and his patriotic hopes of Augustus gave life to his early writing. In his first books his narration, fitting the subject-matter, has poetical colour and style: it is the prose epic of Rome, ranking with the *Aeneid*. The later books take on a more regular prose form, but show equally brilliant description of men and events. The feeling for atmosphere, as well as the principle of variation, allowed the set appearance of formal notices and prodigy tables.

In detail Livy's composition followed the Isocratean canons of brevity, economy, and verisimilitude, with the devices of literary elaboration, characterizing speeches, and dramatic technique. The style conformed to the Ciceronian requirements of 'varietas colorum, collocatio verborum', and 'tractus orationis lenis et aequabilis' in historical narration (e.g. for the sake of homogeneity, Livy (27. 37) would not quote Livius Andronicus); but composition and style had their own varying character, suitable to the different elements in the annalistic tradition. Livy's 'clarissimus candor' and 'lactea ubertas' reflect the lucidity and continuity of his thought, but the style is not purely periodic: it corresponds to the mode of the passage, poetic or formal, elaborate or plain, expository or rhetorical. Even stylistic irregularity or strained word-usage may occur to convey a nuance, departing from the pure Latinity of the capital. This may justify the charge of 'Patavinitas', if Pollio's gibe was not directed at the moral and romantic tone of Livy's work.

The command of his theme and its expression, and his deep seriousness and wide humanity give life to Livy's history. It is Augustan, with the faults as well as the merits of the time, and it falls below modern critical standards. Yet it reproduces tradition faithfully, without the defective rationalization practised in both ancient and modern times; thus modern criticism may be grateful.

His success was immediate and lasting. His work was used by historians and epic poets; an epitome had appeared for common use by the time of Martial (14. 190); his speeches were collected. In the Middle Ages, Dante praised 'Livio che non erra'. The Renaissance saw him in high favour, and printing made him a popular author. Machiavelli discoursed on the First Decade. Niebuhr and Lewis began the critical examination of his early tradition, and historical study has continued it.

EDITIONS. A. Drakenborch (1738–46; 1820–8); J. Th. Kreyssig (xxxiii; 1839); C. F. S. Alschefski (i–x, xxi–xxiii; 1841–6); M. Hertz (1857–64); A. Luchs (xxvi–xxx; 1879; xxi–xxx; 1888–9); W. Weissenborn–M. Müller–W. Heraeus (2nd ed. 1860; 1881 ff. Teubner); A. Zingerle (1883–1908); J. N. Madvig–J. L. Ussing (1861 ff.; 4th ed., 1886 ff.); R. S. Conway–C. F. Walters–S. K. Johnson–A. H. McDonald (i–x; xxi–xxxv; 1914–65, O.C.T.); C. Giarratano (xli–xlv; 1933); P. Bayet (i–v, Budé, 1940–54); J. Heurgon (i, Érasme, 1963). *Periochae*: O. Jahn (1853); O. Rossbach (1910).

COMMENTARIES. W. Weissenborn–H. J. Müller–O. Rossbach (2nd ed. 1867 ff.); R. M. Ogilvie, i–v (1965).

TRANSLATIONS. W. M. Roberts (1912–24); B. O. Foster–E. T. Sage–A. C. Schlesinger–R. M. Geer (1919–59); A. de Sélincourt (i–v, 1960).

LEXICONS. A. W. Ernesti, *Glossarium Liv.* (1827); F. Fügner, *Lex. Liv.* i (A–B, 1897); D. W. Packard, *A Concordance to L.* (1969). SOURCE CRITICISM. H. Nissen, *Krit. Unters. über die Quellen der IV. und V. Dekade des L.* (1863); H. Hesselbarth, *Hist. krit. Unters. zur III. Dekade des L.* (1889); W. Soltau, *Livius' Geschichtswerk* (1897); G. De Sanctis, *Storia dei Romani*, vols. i–iv, pt. 1 (1907–23);

U. Kahrstedt, *Gesch. der Karthager* (Meltzer, vol. iii, 1913); *Die Annalistik von L., B. 31–45* (1913); M. Zimmerer, *Qu. Claudius Quadrigarius* (1937), 22; A. Klotz, *Livius und seine Vorgänger* (1940–1); R. M. Ogilvie, *JRS* 1958, 40 ff.
HISTORICAL AND LITERARY CRITICISM. H. Taine, *Essai sur T.-L.* (1856; 8th ed. 1910); K. Witte, *Rh. Mus.* 1910, 270, 359; W. Kroll, *Stud. zum Verständnis der röm. Literatur* (1924), 351; R. Ullmann, *La Technique des discours dans Salluste, T.-L. et Tacite* (1927); R. Heinze, *Vergils epische Technik*[4] (1928), 333; *Augusteische Kultur* (1930); T. Frank, *Life and Lit. in the Roman Republic* (1930), 169; G. De Sanctis, *Problemi di storia ant.* (1932), 225; H. Bornecque, *Tite-Live* (1933); E. Burck, *Die Erzählungskunst des T. L.* (1934); Istituto di Studi Romani, *Studi Liviani* (1934); K. Latte, *CPhil.* 1940, 56 ff.; W. Hoffmann, *Hermes*, Einzelschriften, Heft VIII (1942); F. Klingner, *Röm. Geisteswelt*[3] (1956); R. Syme, *Tacitus* (1958), 136, 366; *Harv. Stud.* 1959, 27 ff.; P. G. Walsh, *Livy* (1961); R. M. Ogilvie, *Comm.* i–v, Introd. (1965).
STYLE AND LANGUAGE. E. Wölfflin, *Liv. Kritik und liv. Sprachgebrauch* (1864); L. Kühnast, *Die Hauptpunkte der liv. Syntaxe*[3] (1871); O. Riemann, *Études sur la langue et la grammaire de T.-L.*[2] (1885); S. G. Stacey, *Die Entwicklung des liv. Stiles* (Archiv. für lat. Lex. x, 1898, 17), cf. K. Gries, *Constancy in Livy's Latinity* (1947); R. Ullmann, *Étude sur le style des discours de T.-L.* (1929); E. Löfstedt, *Syntactica* ii (1933), 294 ff.; A. H. McDonald, *JRS* 1957, 155 ff.
RENAISSANCE. G. Billanovich, *JWI* 1951, 151 ff.; B. L. Ullman, *Studies in Italian Renaissance* (1955), ch. 4. A. H. McD.

**LOBON** of Argos (perhaps 3rd c. B.C.) was a literary forger, author of a work (perhaps in verse) on poets (Diog. Laert. 1. 34. 112), in which he ascribed verses fabricated by himself to the Seven Sages and works in prose to early poets, e.g. Aristeas, Semonides, Pindar. His treatise seems to have been extensively, though indirectly, used by the *Suda*. J. F. L.

**LOCRI EPIZEPHYRII** (Λοκροὶ Ἐπιζεφύριοι), a Dorian city in the 'toe' of Italy, was founded *c.* 700 B.C., apparently by Opuntii (East Locrians), although its settlers probably included Ozolae (West Locrians), fugitive slaves, and Lacedaemonians. Oenotri (= Sicels?) previously inhabited the site. Locri's oligarchy, The Hundred Houses, reputedly governed excellently: the town possessed Europe's earliest written legal code (attributed to Zaleucus, q.v.). Locri defeated Croton at the Sagras battle (6th c.), founded its own colonies (Hipponium, Medma; before 450), and usually was friendly with Syracuse who supported it against its rival Rhegium (q.v.). Bruttian, Pyrrhic, and Hannibalic Wars caused some decline, but Locri was still a considerable town, allied to Rome, in Polybius' day; Polybius knew it intimately (12. 5 f.). Apparently Saracens finally destroyed it.
Strabo 6. 259 f.; Pindar, *Ol.* 10 and 11; *Pyth.* 2; Thuc. bks. 3–8; Diod. bks. 12 and 14; Justin 20. 2; Livy, bks. 22 and 29. J. Bérard, *Bibliogr. topogr.* (1941), 62; A. G. Woodhead, *The Greeks in the West* (1962), 57 f.; A. de Franciscis, *Archaeology* 1958, 206 ff. E. T. S.

**LOCRIS.** Eastern Locris, comprising the mainland coast of the Euboean Straits from Thermopylae to Larymna, and Western Locris, comprising the valley of Amphissa and the northern coast of the Corinthian Gulf from Naupactus to near Crisa, were separated from one another by Doris and Phocis, probably the results of an invasion through an early Locrian State occupying central Greece. As late as the fifth century B.C. the two divisions of Locris, known as 'Opuntian' and 'Ozolian', possessed a joint franchise. Their territory being mainly infertile and hemmed in by stronger States, the Locrians played little part in history. Opuntian Locris united round a centre at Opus, where the assembly of the Thousand drawn from noble families met, founded Locri in south Italy, and began to coin in the fourth century B.C. But Ozolian Locris remained backward and without unity (Thuc. 1. 5). Both areas were curtailed by their neighbours, Opuntian Locris losing Thermopylae to the Thessalians and Daphnus to the Phocians, whereby Eastern Locris split into Hypocnemidian and Opuntian Locris, and Ozolian Locris losing Naupactus to Athens. The valley of Amphissa, traversed by the

route from Doris to the Corinthian Gulf, was of strategic importance and became involved in the Sacred Wars (q.v.).
P–K, *GL* 1. 2. 339 ff., for Eastern Locris, and L. Lerat, *Les Locriens de l'Ouest* (1952), for Western Locris. N. G. L. H.

**LOCUSTA (LUCUSTA)**, a noted poisoner of Gallic origin, was employed by Agrippina to poison Claudius and by Nero for Britannicus. Nero took with him on his flight a poison prepared by her. Galba executed her. A. M.

**LOGIC**, the science of valid argument-forms, developed among the Greeks as a result of their interest in arguments of all kinds, not only those occurring in philosophy and mathematics but also the arguments of politics and the lawcourts. The comparison of valid and invalid arguments leads first to the abstraction of *logical form* from many arguments of a similar verbal pattern and then to the analysis of *logical constants*, i.e. the propositional connectives such as 'not', 'if', and 'or', and the quantifiers, 'every' and 'some'. Both processes may be observed within the context of philosophical argument in many of Plato's dialogues, e.g. the *Parmenides* and the *Sophist*. Aristotle at the end of the *Sophistici Elenchi* claims to have been the first to study the technique of argument (dialectic) systematically, and it can be seen in this work and in the *Topics* how the study of argument-forms is gradually disengaged from the practical study of argument-winning.

Aristotle's main contributions to logic are his theory of the four forms of general statement and the relations between them, developed in the *De Interpretatione*, and the doctrine of the syllogism, presented in the *Prior Analytics*. Two features distinguish the latter as the first great work of formal logic: the use of letters as *term-variables*, which immensely simplifies the presentation of formal argument, and the development of syllogistic *as a system*. By the doctrine of reduction the syllogistic moods are shown to be interconnected, so that all can ultimately be reduced to two, later called *Barbara* and *Celarent*. A literal translation of Aristotle's formula for *Barbara* is 'If A belongs to every B and B belongs to every C, then A belongs to every C'. Aristotle also made a beginning in the study of modal logic, i.e. the logic of propositions expressed by the use of the words 'necessary', 'possible', etc., but his technical equipment was insufficient for this task and his treatment is generally recognized to be unsatisfactory. The discovery of the syllogism was so brilliant an achievement that it appeared as something final to Aristotle's followers, and his successors did little more than introduce minor improvements. Theophrastus, without complete success, attempted to render the theory of modal syllogisms consistent by what came to be known later as the *peiorem* rule.

The Megarian-Stoic school of logic developed independently of the Aristotelian. Two prominent early members, Eubulides and Diodorus Cronus, were contemporary with Aristotle, and Philo of Megara was slightly younger. According to the judgement of his successors, the greatest logician of the school was the Stoic Chrysippus. His works are unfortunately lost and Stoic logic has, for the most part, to be reconstructed from fragments. The interest of the Megarians and the Stoics was concentrated on the propositional connectives, whereas syllogistic is essentially a logic of the quantifiers. Philo anticipated some modern logicians by giving a truth-functional definition of 'if . . . then . . .' and other connectives, but Chrysippus preferred to give them a stronger, modal sense. Both Megarians and Stoics also worked on modal logic. The Stoics used variables, but the values of their variables were propositions, not terms, and the signs they employed were ordinal numbers, not letters. They also elaborated their logic as a deductive system with five indemonstrable moods (ἀναπόδεικτοι τρόποι) as basic. The first of these (later called the *Modus Ponens*) was expressed as follows, 'If the first, then the second; but the first; therefore the second'. They differed from Aristotle in presenting logic as a system of argument-forms, whereas he formulated his syllogistic moods in general conditional statements. It is probable, however, that he would not have recognized the difference; for the Stoics seem to have been the first to recognize clearly the distinction between a valid argument and a true conditional statement. They were also aware of the Principle of Conditionalization, i.e. that to every valid argument there corresponds a true conditional statement.

It was unfortunate for the development of logic in antiquity that the two systems were regarded as alternatives, whereas they are in fact complementary, the Stoic logic of propositions being required as a substructure for the Aristotelian logic. Thus the Stoic theorem, 'If the first and the second, then the third: but not the third; on the other hand the first; therefore not the second', is presupposed in Aristotle's indirect reduction of the second-figure mood *Baroco* to *Barbara*.

An attempt to synthesize the two traditions seems to have been made by Galen in the second century A.D. but his major work is lost so that we cannot say how successful he was. Some conflation, or perhaps, confusion, did, however, certainly occur in later antiquity and some Stoic elements are to be found in Boethius (470–524), although he writes in general as an Aristotelian.

Inductive logic was comparatively little developed in antiquity. Aristotle discusses ἐπαγωγή in the *Topics* and in the *Posterior Analytics*, but he seems generally to mean by this term what was later called intuitive induction. There is, however, some attempt to formulate principles of scientific research in the Hippocratic writings, and the Epicureans developed a theory of inductive inference under the title σημείωσις.

C. Prantl, *Geschichte der Logik im Abendlande*, 4 vols. (1855–70), still a valuable source-book, although the text is all but worthless; I. M. Bochenski, *Formale Logik* (1956), a collection of texts with commentary; *A history of Formal Logic*. Engl. transl of the above by I. Thomas (U.S.A. 1961); W. and M. Kneale, *The Development of Logic* (1960); J. Łukasiewicz *Aristotle's Syllogistic from the Point of View of Modern Formal Logic*² (1952); B. Mates, *Stoic Logic* (U.S.A. 1959); G. Patzig, *Die Aristotelische Syllogistik* (1959); P. H. and E. A. De Lacy, *Philodemus on Methods of Inference* (U.S.A. 1941). M. K.

**LOGISTAI** (λογισταί) in Athens were the public auditors. In the fifth century B.C. there were thirty, but in the fourth century there were only ten, perhaps because they had less to do after the Athenian Empire came to an end. They were appointed by lot by the members of the *boule* (q.v.) from among themselves (unless, as some have thought, the statement to this effect in Arist. *Ath. Pol.* 48. 3 refers to a different board of auditors). Their chief function was their part in the procedure called *euthyna* (q.v.): with the assistance of ten advocates (συνήγοροι) they examined the accounts of every magistrate who had handled public money, and brought him before a lawcourt for trial. In the time of the Athenian Empire they also performed various duties in connexion with the accounts of the tribute.

J. H. Lipsius, *Das attische Recht und Rechtsverfahren* (1905–15), 101 ff. D. M. M.

**LOGOGRAPHERS.** The word λογογράφος, as used by the contemporaries of Demosthenes, commonly means a speech-writer for litigants in the courts, or else a writer of prose, as distinct from a poet (cf. Arist. *Rh.* 2. 11. 7 with the note in Cope's edition). Modern practice, however, has followed Thucydides (1. 21) in applying the term to the predecessors and contemporaries of Herodotus who were the pioneers of history-writing. Early writers of narrative prose are called λογοποιοί, 'tellers of tales', by Herodotus (2. 134, 143). But like the early philosophers and natural scientists, those who claimed to offer a faithful account of human activities considered their task as an investigation (ἱστορία), as scientific rather than poetic. If we grudge the title of historian to the predecessors of Herodotus, it is largely because they wrote of gods and heroes as well as of men and some of them professed to offer a true and correct version of mythology as well as of history.

No MSS. of these authors have survived, but there are numerous references to them and occasional direct quotations in later Greek writers. Some later writers (e.g. Strabo 11. 6. 2, 12. 3. 21) have a low opinion of their accuracy and accuse them of fabricating names and incidents; others stress their lack of critical judgement; all agree that they wrote in simple style and language (cf. esp. Dion. Hal. *Thuc.* 23). It would be easier to estimate their talents and their value as historical sources if Herodotus had been more explicit in recording his obligations to them. *See* HERODOTUS (1).

Many of them came from Ionian cities. Two supposed Milesians, Cadmus and Dionysius, are often given as the earliest logographers; but they are very uncertain figures, and the references to them in later literature are probably not to be trusted (Hellenistic writers were quite capable of fabricating their sources). Hecataeus of Miletus, on the other hand, is a well-attested historical figure, mentioned several times by Herodotus; he was active politically in Miletus as early as 500 B.C. (Hdt. 5. 36, 125), and much can be learnt from surviving fragments about the range and character of his literary work. Acusilaus, Charon (2), Damastes, Euagon, Hellanicus, Pherecydes (2), Scylax, and Xanthus (2) (qq.v.) can all be considered contemporaries of Herodotus, though there is much uncertainty about precise dates.

The work of the logographers may be classified under various heads:

1. Mythographic treatises, which involved attempts to rationalize and systematize Greek mythology, and to trace the genealogies of families who claimed descent from a god or hero.

2. Geographical works, often in the form of a Periegesis or Periplous, describing the peoples and areas met with on a coasting voyage and the neighbouring peoples inland.

3. Accounts of the customs and history of non-Greek peoples.

4. Local histories, especially accounts of the Founding of Cities (κτίσεις).

5. Chronological works, which might include tables based on lists (real or apocryphal) of kings, magistrates, priests, or priestesses.

Herodotus combines the various strains of the logographers' work, and was the first to provide a coherent history, which had for its main theme the contest of Greek and barbarian that culminated in the Persian Wars.

For fragments and testimonia see *FGrH* (index auctorum, iii B, 767). L. Pearson, *Early Ionian Historians* (1939), with bibliography; J. O. Thomson, *Hist. Anc. Geog.*, ch. 2; G. T. Griffith in *Fifty Years of Classical Scholarship* (ed. Platnauer, 1954), 150 ff.; A. Lesky, *Hist. Gk. Lit.* (Engl. transl. 1966), 218 ff. L. P.

**LOGOS** combines in its meaning both speech and reason. Its first use to signify the intelligible law of the universe has been attributed to Heraclitus (Diels frs. 1, 2, 45, 50, 72, 115), but this may be doubted; and the origin of the metaphysical meaning must probably be sought in Stoic teaching. According to this, the whole natural order was pervaded by ὀρθὸς λόγος (to be identified, if need be, with Zeus: Zeno, von Arnim fr. 162), and this rational purpose prompted the regular motions of the heavenly bodies and the exact functioning of natural objects. Within at least the wisest of men there is a λόγος σπερματικός and man's duty and distinction is to live κατὰ λόγον; for in this way (according to Posidonius) he 'is akin to, and has a like nature with the power governing the whole cosmos'. The consistency of earlier Stoic teaching was later modified, especially in the schools of Alexandria, by the adoption of the cosmogony of Plato's *Timaeus*, so that transcendental monotheism was combined with an original pantheism. Hellenistic-Jewish teachers adopted language appropriate to the Stoic λόγος for the divine Wisdom (as in Wisd. Sol. vii. 22–viii. 1), and their tradition influenced writings as diverse as the cosmogony of Poimandres and the philosophy of Philo. The Logos in Philo can be the divine pattern of which the material world is a copy, the divine power immanent in the cosmos, the divine purpose or agent in creation, an intermediary between God and the world (*Quis r. d. heres?* 205 f.) and, hence, never wholly personal nor impersonal. The prologue of St. John's Gospel draws on a similar range of ideas, though treating them very differently: it asserts that in Christ, as the unique Son of God, the cosmological λόγος was incarnate. According to the second-century Apologist, Justin Martyr, the divine Logos appeared in its fulness in Christ; but every man possesses the λόγος σπερματικός. In so far as the philosophers lived according to reason they were Christians before Christ; but after Christ's coming, Christians have the whole and undiluted truth (*I Ap.* 46; *II Ap.* 8, 13).

M. Heinze, *Die Lehre vom Logos in der griechischen Philosophie* (1872); A. Aall, *Der Logos. Geschichte seiner Entwickelung in der griechischen Philosophie und der christlichen Literatur* (2 vols., 1896–9); W. R. Inge, *ERE*, s.v.; H. Kleinknecht and G. Kittel in *Theologisches Wörterbuch zum Neuen Testament* iv (1942), 76 ff., 131 ff.; T. F. Glasson, 'Heraclitus' alleged Logos doctrine', *JTS* N.S. 1952, 231 ff.; E. Bevan, *Stoics and Sceptics* (1913); C. H. Dodd, *The Bible and the Greeks* (1935), 115 ff.; J. Lebreton, *Les Théories du Logos au début de l'ère chrétienne* (1907); E. Bréhier, *Les Idées philosophiques et religieuses de Philon d'Alexandrie²* (1925); E. R. Goodenough, *An Introduction to Philo Judaeus²* (1962); M.-J. Lagrange, 'Vers le Logos de S. Jean' and 'Le Logos de Philon', *Revue Biblique* 1923, 161 ff.; C. H. Dodd, *The Interpretation of the Fourth Gospel* (1953), 263 ff.; E. R. Goodenough, *The Theology of Justin Martyr* (1923). K. G.

**LOLLIA** (*PW* 30) **PAULINA** was granddaughter of M. Lollius (q.v.) and very wealthy. She was forced to abandon her marriage with P. Memmius Regulus (q.v. 3) in order that she might marry the Emperor Gaius in A.D. 38. Divorced by him in the following year, she was an unsuccessful candidate for the hand of Claudius after Messalina's death in 48. Agrippina secured her banishment (on the charge of consulting astrologers) in the following year, and she was driven to suicide. J. P. B.

**LOLLIUS** (1, *PW* 21) **PALICANUS**, MARCUS, 'a Picene of humble origin' (hence an adherent of Pompey), 'loquacious rather than eloquent' (Sall. *Hist.* 4. 43); father-in-law of Gabinius (q.v. 2). As tribune (71 B.C.) he was Pompey's main political agent, helping to formulate his policy on *Popularis* lines. Praetor in 69, he was not allowed to rise to the consulate. E. B.

**LOLLIUS** (2, *PW* 11), MARCUS (*cos.* 21 B.C.), a *novus homo* and prominent partisan of Augustus, praised by Horace (*Carm.* 4. 9. 33 ff.) for conspicuous integrity, but described by Velleius as crafty, corrupt, and rapacious. He was the first legate of Galatia (25), active in Macedonia, probably as proconsul (*c.* 19–18) and then in Gaul, where German raiders inflicted a defeat, capturing the eagle of a legion, but hardly causing a serious disaster. In 1 B.C. he was chosen to be counsellor and overseer of C. Caesar in the East. A bitter enemy of Tiberius, he influenced the young prince against the exile. As a result of quarrel or intrigue, however, he fell from favour, was accused of taking bribes from the Parthian king, and died before

long, perhaps by suicide (A.D. 2). Lollius left enormous wealth.

Syme, *Rom. Rev.*, see index; *Hist.* 1964, 118 ff. R. S.

**LOLLIUS** (3) **BASSUS** of Smyrna has about a dozen epigrams in the Greek Anthology. *Anth. Pal.* 7. 391 is a pompous comment on the death of Germanicus (A.D. 19); *Anth. Pal.* 10. 102 looks like an adaptation from Horace (*Carm.* 2. 10), and 11. 72 is a joke in the manner which Lucillius (q.v. 1) was to perfect later.

Gow and Page, 1587 ff. Cichorius, *Röm. Stud.* viii. 4. G. H.

**LOLLIUS** (4, *PW* 28) **URBICUS**, QUINTUS, governor of Britain from A.D. 139 until after 142 (*JRS* 1922, 66) and formerly legate of Legio X Gemina and governor of Lower Germany, built the Wall of Antoninus (q.v.) (S.H.A. *Pius* 5. 6; Collingwood-Wright, *RIB* 2191, 2192). Inscriptions commemorating the erection of buildings under Lollius come from Corstopitum (*RIB* 1147, 1148), and from High Rochester (*RIB* 1276). He later became governor of Africa (Apul. *Apol.* 2) and *praefectus urbi* (*CIL* viii. 6705, 6706). I. A. R.

**LOMBARDS,** a Germanic people whose original home appears to have been in the island of Gotland. By the time of Tacitus, who regards them as few in number but warlike and audacious, they lived east of the lower Elbe. After the Roman defeat in A.D. 9 they spread to the west of that river. Conquered by Maroboduus and the Marcomanni they joined Arminius in A.D. 17 and lived in freedom thereafter. The chief event in their history was their settlement in A.D. 568 in northern Italy, where they maintained themselves for two centuries. E. A. T.

**LONDINIUM** (perhaps denoting 'place of Londinos', 'the fierce one') originally stood on the eastern of two hillocks bounding the Walbrook at the mouth of the Thames. Tacitus states that at the time of Boudicca's revolt (A.D. 60) it was an important trading-centre. (*Ann.* 14. 33) and that at the principal towns, Londinium, Verulamium, and Camulodunum, 70,000 persons perished. Early vestiges have been found, but authority inclines against a pre-Roman origin for this considerable community.

Perhaps after 60 it became the financial centre of the province (*CIL* vii. 30 and *JRS* 1936, 264 f.), and eventually the capital, probably of Britain, and is mentioned as a key-point in official activities. In *c.* 290–326 and 383–8 it was the seat of a mint, and a treasury official was stationed there (*Not. Dign. Occid.* xi. 37). The Council List of Arles calls it a 'ciuitas' and assigns it a bishop. It received at an unknown date (? 326–65) the title of Augusta. Of its local divisions, a *vicinia* is known (*CIL* vii. 20).

The principal remains are subsequent to Boudicca's destruction, after which the settlement spread to the western hill. About 80 a vast *basilica* (500 feet long) and *forum*, enclosing perhaps an official temple, were built, and about the same time a stone fort, *c.* 10 acres in area, was built in what was to be the north-west re-entrant (Cripplegate) of the town wall; this was built of squared stones and brick-bonders with bank and ditch (*c.* 200). It enclosed an area of *c.* 330 acres, making Londinium the fifth largest town in the west. Traces of stone and timber foundations, mosaics, etc., are found with frequency within the walls, and there was a suburb on the south bank connected by a bridge. A serious fire seems to have occurred *c.* 120–30, and at various dates bastions were added to the town wall (some may even be Saxon), the river section of which was built (or rebuilt). A Mithraeum (*see* MITHRAS) close to the east bank of the Walbrook was discovered in excavations after bomb-damage and left open for view. It dated from the end of the second and was abandoned in the fourth century. It has yielded important statues and inscriptions.

How far Londinium survived the Saxon invasions is still a matter of great uncertainty; 'The period remains blank' (Grimes). Londinium was certainly a town without a bishop in the seventh century (Bede, *Hist. Eccl.* ii. 3) which is hardly credible if significant town life had existed.

Royal Commission on Historical Monuments, London (Roman) (1928) is complete to its date, though its conclusions are often (e.g. on date of town wall) obsolete. For subsequent discoveries, see *JRS* and W. F. Grimes, *The Excavation of Roman and Medieval London* (1968).
C. E. S.

**LONG WALLS, THE** (τὰ μακρὰ τείχη or σκέλη), were built between 461 and 456 B.C. to connect Athens with her ports, Phalerum and Piraeus. About 445 the Phaleric wall was replaced by a third, parallel to the north or Piraeus wall. They were destroyed by the Spartans to flute music in 404, rebuilt by Conon in 393, but allowed to fall into a half-ruined state by 200 (Livy 31. 26. 8). The walls to Piraeus were about 4 miles long and c. 200 yards apart; the traces visible a century ago have now almost entirely disappeared. The course of the Phaleric wall is uncertain. The main road from Piraeus to Athens lay outside, the road inside being primarily military. The Long Walls were used in the Peloponnesian War to make Athens into an isolated fortress, in which most of the population of Attica could live on sea-borne provisions. The example of Long Walls was followed elsewhere, notably at Megara.

W. Judeich, *Topographie von Athen*² (1931), 155 ff. (his course for the Phaleric wall is improbable); T. Lenschau, *PW* xix, 88 f.; R. L. Scranton, 'The Fortifications of Athens at the opening of the Peloponnesian War', *AJArch.* 1938, 525 ff.; 'Ι. Τραυλός, Πολεοδομικὴ ἐξέλιξις τῶν Ἀθηνῶν (1960), 48 ff. T. J. D.; C. W. J. E.

**'LONGINUS'.** The literary treatise Περὶ ὕψους, *On the Sublime*, of which about two-thirds survives, is ascribed by the medieval tradition to 'Dionysius Longinus' or 'Dionysius or Longinus'. Until the early nineteenth century, it was generally believed to be by Cassius Longinus (q.v.). Internal evidence, especially the chapter on the decline of oratory (44), points, however, to an earlier date, some time in the first century A.D. The writer sets out to answer Caecilius (q.v. 4) of Calacte, who had given what 'Longinus' holds to be an inadequate account of ὕψος ('elevation', 'grandeur', 'sublimity'), failing in particular to give due weight to the emotional element (πάθος).

*On the Sublime* is a work of the first importance. In discussing the quality of thought and style which marks writing as ὑψηλόν, the author breaks free of the rhetorical tradition within which he works, and throws real light on what constitutes literary greatness. He wrote in an archaizing age, and his own style is a product of great sophistication; but his concern with the moral function of literature and his impatience with pedantry give a clear impression of a serious and original mind. The period of his greatest influence extends from Boileau's translation (1674) to the early nineteenth century; but as a stimulus to critical thought and to the understanding of ancient literature he has permanent value.

EDITIONS. O. Jahn–J. Vahlen⁴, 1910; W. Rhys Roberts (with notes and translation)², 1907; D. A. Russell (with notes), 1964.
TRANSLATIONS. W. Smith (1739, etc.), A. O. Prickard (1906), G. M. A. Grube (1957), D. A. Russell (1966), many others.
INTERPRETATION. W. Bühler, *Beiträge zur Schrift vom Erhabenen* (1964).
INFLUENCE. S. H. Monk, *The Sublime* (1935); J. Brody, *Boileau and Longinus* (1958). D. A. R.

**LONGINUS,** CASSIUS (c. A.D. 213–73), rhetorician and philosopher, who taught at Athens (see J. Bidez, *Vie de Porphyre* (1913), ch. 4) and, in the last few years of his

life, became the principal adviser of the rulers of Palmyra, Odenathus and Zenobia; he was executed when the city fell to Aurelian (Gibbon, *Decline and Fall*, ch. 11, gives the classic English account). Plotinus (*Vita* 14) spoke of Longinus as φιλόλογος, φιλόσοφος δ' οὐδαμῶς; though he wrote on philosophical subjects (Περὶ ἀρχῶν, commentary on *Timaeus*), he was much more celebrated for his critical and rhetorical work; Eunapius (*Vitae Sophistarum* 4) calls him 'a living library and walking Museum'. For the attribution to him of Περὶ ὕψους, see 'LONGINUS'.

Fragments in J. Toup's edition of Περὶ ὕψους (1778); rhetorical fragments in A. O. Prickard's (O.C.T. 1906). D. A. R.

**LONGUS,** Greek writer, creator of the pastoral romance, and author of *Daphnis and Chloe*. Nothing is known about him: even his name has been suspected. He was perhaps from Lesbos, since his descriptions of the island seem to betray autopsy; his *floruit* is most uncertain, because our conjectures depend only upon stylistic comparisons with other romancers and authors, an admittedly hazardous criterion which has caused him to be assigned by scholars to every century A.D. from the second to the sixth. His work is a bucolic idyll in prose, adapted into the traditional framework of Greek romance, and narrates how Daphnis and Chloe, two foundlings brought up by shepherds in Lesbos, gradually became enamoured of each other and finally married. The difficulties traditionally hindering lovers in the genre (such as abductions) are severely reduced in number and bearing: what interests the author is really to describe how the passion of love developed in the two protagonists, from the first naïve and confused feelings of infancy to full sexual maturity. Longus' work is, in this respect, the prototype of the modern *Entwicklungsroman*: his psychological analysis is penetrating and felicitous, and stands out in sharp contrast to the poor characterizations of the other Greek romancers. His style has been described as 'a triumph of sophistic *apheleia*': short sentences are neatly arranged in isocolic structures (*antitheta* and *parisa*), which aim perhaps at reflecting the symmetric structures of Alexandrian bucolic poetry: in his diction he is, as the laws of the genre 'romance' required, a pure atticist, although vulgarisms appear, together with poetic words and a few baroque metaphors. The general tone of his romance is dictated by *glykytes*, which was prescribed by ancient critics for the bucolic genre: this sweetening of pastoral life appealed very much to the critics of the eighteenth and early nineteenth centuries, when 'bergeries' were the fashion (Bernadin de S. Pierre, with his *Paul et Virginie*, and S. Gessner, with his pastoral idylls in rhythmical prose, are the most illustrious imitators of Longus, whilst Corot is one of his most famous admirers) but is today very variously judged. In spite of his artificiality in language and style, his ecphrastic descriptions of nature (gardens, the alternating of seasons, landscapes) testify to a notable love of nature, which was highly praised by Goethe (in his *Gespräche mit Eckermann* the poet recommends the reading of *Daphnis and Chloe* once a year). Even Longus' detractors (like Wilamowitz, who blames in the author 'die Naturschwärmerei des Salonmenschen') cannot deny that the general structure of the romance is well woven and laudably compact (four books, without inharmonious parts) and that the atmosphere of pastoral *naïveté*, if recognizable as artificial by the more perspicacious critics, is so dexterously created as to appear natural and convincing to most readers.

EDITIO PRINCEPS. 1598 (Giunta, Florence), preceded by Amyot's famous French translation, which contributed enormously to making the romance popular (Paris, 1559).
STANDARD EDITIONS. Dalmeyda (Paris, 1960², with French translation and excellent Introduction); Schönberger (Berlin, 1960; highly commendable).
COMMENTARY. Villoison (Paris, 1778, still useful); Seiler (Leipzig, 1843),

CRITICISM. Schissel von Fleschenberg, *PW*, s.v. Longos; Rohde, *Griech. Roman*, 531 ff.; Christ–Schmid–Stählin ii. 2⁶. 823 ff.; G. Valley, *Über den Sprachgebrauch des Longos* (Diss. Uppsala, 1926); L. Castiglioni: *Rend. Ist. Lomb.* 1928, fasc. i–v; H. Dörrie: see bibliog. s.v. ACHILLES TATIUS; H. Reich, *De Alciphronis Longique aetate* (Diss. Königsberg, 1894): although controversial, contains much useful material on the 'Schöpfung des bukolischen Romans auf Grundlage des bukolischen Mimus'.

ENGLISH TRANSLATIONS. Thornley (1657, rev. by J. M. Edmonds in his Loeb edition of Longus), R. Smith (in Bohn's Classical Library). G. G.

**LOTOPHAGI,** a fabulous people, living on the lotus (flower?), the effect of which is to make the eater forget his own country and desire to live in Lotus-land (*Od.* 9. 82 ff.).

**LUA MATER.** Cult-partner of Saturnus, Gellius 13. 23. 2 (Luam Saturni; cf. SATURNUS). Her name may be connected with *lues* and mean something like 'baneful'; she is one of the deities to whom captured arms may be dedicated and burned (Livy 8. 1. 6; 45. 33. 2). H. J. R.

**LUCA,** modern *Lucca*, in Liguria (later incorporated in Etruria) on the river Ausar (Strabo 5. 217). Both notices of the town before 100 B.C. are suspect (Livy 21. 59; Vell. Pat. 1. 15: preferably read Luna (q.v.) in each case). A border town of the Cisalpine province, Luca became famous when Caesar and Pompey met there for their conference in 56 B.C. (Suet. *Iul.* 24, etc.). Under the late Republic Luca was a *municipium* (Cic. *Fam.* 13. 13), under the Empire a *colonia* (Pliny, *HN* 3. 50). But, although a fairly important station on an extension of the Via Clodia (q.v.), it is rarely mentioned until late imperial times. E. T. S.

**LUCAN** (MARCUS ANNAEUS LUCANUS, A.D. 39–65) was born at Corduba (modern *Cordova*), 3 Nov. A.D. 39. His father, M. Annaeus Mela, was a Roman knight and a brother of the philosopher Seneca. Mela migrated to Rome when his son was about eight months old. There Lucan received the ordinary liberal education, ending with the school of rhetoric, where he was a great success; there is also good reason to believe that he studied philosophy under the famous Stoic Cornutus. He continued his studies at Athens, but was recalled by Nero, who admitted him to his inner circle and conferred on him the offices of quaestor and augur. In A.D. 60, at the first celebration of the games called Neronia, he won a prize with a poem in praise of Nero. In 62 or 63 he published three books of his epic on the Civil War. Growing enmity between him and Nero, for which various reasons are given, finally caused the emperor to debar him from further exercise, or at least from public display, of his literary talent. Lucan recklessly joined the conspiracy of Piso, and on its disclosure was compelled to put an end to his life (30 Apr. 65). The story that he sought to win leniency by accusing his mother of complicity in the plot is probably a malicious fabrication (see F. Plessis, *La Poésie latine* (1909), 547 ff.).

WORKS. Lucan was a voluminous writer from early years. The titles of many of his works, both in prose and in verse, have come down to us, but nothing more than a few lines remains of any of them except the *Bellum Civile* (the title *Pharsalia* is due to a misunderstanding of 9. 985). It is in ten books, the last being unfinished. Beginning with the causes of the war between Caesar and Pompey, it carries the story beyond the death of Pompey until it breaks off with Caesar's occupation of Pharos in Egypt. The battle of Pharsalus is related in book 7. In all probability Lucan intended to continue the narrative to the death of Caesar, if not further. His principal historical authority was undoubtedly Livy, but he probably consulted others, including Caesar. It is not his purpose to give a full account of the war. Several events are omitted, others receive only a brief perfunctory mention. He dwells at length on particular episodes, not solely for their intrinsic importance, but largely because they appealed to his emotions or offered scope for a display of his powers. There are a few glaring departures from historical truth, as when he makes Cicero, who was not present at Pharsalus, deliver a harangue to Pompey on the eve of the battle; but apart from instances of carelessness, his perversions of the facts consist mostly of a false colouring due to his Stoic and Republican bias. On the other hand, he shows some notable instances of penetrating insight.

Recent history is ill suited to be the subject of a sustained epic poem, and Lucan, by discarding (wisely, it is true) the traditional apparatus of divine interventions, made his task doubly hard. All the resources of rhetoric are enlisted to impress the reader; vehement declamation and brilliant epigrammatic utterances (*sententiae*) are everywhere in evidence. There are numerous digressions, many of them making a display of curious learning. In book 6, for example, we find 80 lines on Thessaly and 136 on witches, in book 9, 115 lines on serpents and their bites, in book 10, 138 lines on the Nile. In general Lucan shows an excessive fondness for the purple patch. There is much exaggeration, often absurd; bizarre effects and far-fetched paradoxes abound. Nevertheless, the poet's feeling is strong and sincere. The horrors of civil war stirred his heart, and as the poem proceeded (and especially after his estrangement from Nero) his detestation of Caesarism and of its founder became a ruling passion. But with all his prejudice he cannot entirely conceal, even from himself, the greatness of Caesar, and the attempt to exalt the unheroic Pompey above such a colossus was foredoomed to failure; he does, however, succeed in making Pompey a truly tragic figure and in evoking sympathy both for him and for his cause. The portrayal of Cato, the unflinching Stoic, arouses at best a qualified admiration without much appeal to the heart. The language of the poem, though not without vigour and occasional novelty, lacks the richness and colour of Virgil. The verse is deficient in flexibility and variety; the comparative rarity of elision and the great fondness for the 'hephthemimeral jerk' are conspicuous features. But with all its faults the work is a remarkable achievement for so young a writer. Permeated though it is, and often marred, by rhetoric, it soars at times to those higher regions where poetry and oratory meet, where vision, imagination, and emotion commingle and find noble utterance. Even where this has not been achieved, there are many passages whose stirring trumpet-tones vibrate in the memory and whose unsurpassed epigrams, incisive and often strangely thrilling, have become part of the world's literary heritage. Lucan had a great vogue in the Middle Ages, and his influence is often seen in the poetry and drama of the seventeenth century. In later times he has found more critics than admirers, but Shelley drew inspiration from him, and, like Southey, at first preferred him to Virgil. Macaulay considered him one of the most remarkable men that ever lived. W. B. A.

CRITICAL TEXTS by Hosius (³1913) and Housman (²1927). COMMENTARIES by C. E. Haskins, with useful introduction by W. E. Heitland (1887); R. J. Getty (Book 1) with important introduction (²1955). TRANSLATION by J. D. Duff (Loeb, 1928). SOURCES AND TECHNIQUE. R. Pichon, *Les Sources de Lucain* (1912); H. P. Syndikus, *Lucans Gedicht vom Bürgerkrieg* (diss. Munich, 1958); M. P. O. Morford, *The Poet Lucan* (1967). CRITICISM. H. E. Butler, *Post-Augustan Poetry* (1909), ch. 4; O. S. Due, *Class. et Med.* 1962, 68 ff.; J. Brisset, *Les Idées politiques de Lucain* (1964), with bibliography. E. J. K.

**LUCANIA,** a mountainous region of southern Italy; recently its ancient name has replaced the medieval *Basilicata*. Its earliest recorded inhabitants are Oenotri

(= Sicels?) and Chones (= Illyrians). About 700 B.C. Greeks commenced colonizing its fertile coastlands. About 420 Sabelli (q.v.), the pugnacious Lucani, began to subjugate the Greeks; by 390 they held all Lucania and were partly hellenized (Polyaenus 2. 10; Diod. 14. 91–102; Strabo 5. 253 f.). Lucanian communities had an official known as *meddix*; a generalissimo led their confederation in war (Strabo 6. 254). In the fourth century Tarentum was their chief enemy; apparently their decline began after her mercenary captain Alexander defeated them (326). Thereupon they prudently sought a Roman alliance (Livy 8. 24, 27; 10. 11; Diod. 20. 104). Later, however, Lucani opposed and were conquered by Rome in the Pyrrhic, Hannibalic, and Social Wars. These struggles completely ruined Lucania; malaria appeared and is only now being eradicated (Zonar. 8. 3 f.; Livy 22. 61; App. *BCiv.* 1. 90 f.). Sulla massacred both Lucani and Samnites, and the Lucani as a separate nation disappeared. Chief towns: coastal Greek colonies and Grumentum, Atina, Potentia, and perhaps Bantia.

E. Magaldi, *Lucania romana* (1947); E. Vetter, *Handbuch der ital. Dialekte* (1953), i. 119 ff. E. T. S.

**LUCCEIUS** (*PW* 6), Lucius, as praetor (67 B.C.) and friend of Pompey (q.v.) quarrelled with the consul Glabrio (q.v. 3). In 64, when Caesar, in charge of the murder court, encouraged prosecutions of those who had killed men proscribed by Sulla, Lucceius accused Caesar's friend Catiline (q.v.), forcing Caesar to stop. He supported Cicero in 63. In 60 he joined Caesar (now Pompey's ally) in canvassing for the consulship (he provided the money for both), but was defeated by Bibulus (q.v. 1). In the 50s he wrote a history of the period 90–81, and Cicero (*Fam.* 5. 12) unsuccessfully asked him to glorify the suppressor of Catiline next. By 49 he was one of Pompey's most trusted advisers. After Pharsalus he returned to Rome and in 45 wrote to Cicero on the death of his daughter. E. B.

**LUCERIA**, modern *Lucera*: town on the borders of Samnium and Apulia (qq.v.). Inhabited since prehistoric times, it is not certainly recorded until 315/14 B.C. when it was a Samnite-controlled strongpoint, which the Romans captured and made a Latin Colony. Its strategic importance was repeatedly demonstrated and it has remained a large town. E. T. S.

**LUCIAN** (Λουκιανός) of Samosata (b. *c.* A.D. 120), author of some eighty pieces, chiefly in Dialogue form. For details of his career we have to depend largely on his writings. Though his mother-tongue was not Greek, but probably Aramaic, he received a sufficiently good education to become, first a pleader (*Suda*), and later a travelling lecturer; he practised the art of Sophistic rhetoric as far afield as Gaul (Δὶς κατηγορούμενος 27). About the age of 40 ('Ερμότιμος 13), when he moved to Athens, he deserted rhetoric for 'philosophy'. From then onwards he proceeded to develop the special variety of Dialogue which made him famous. He later resumed the habit of public recitation and accepted a post under the Roman administration in Egypt. He died later than A.D. 180 (Ἀλέξανδρος 48).

Of his writings, certain μελέται, or exercises on set themes (e.g. Φάλαρις), probably belong to his early period; so also his first essays in Dialogue (e.g. Θεῶν διάλογοι). His προλαλίαι ('introductions') and certain epideictic pieces (Μυίας ἐγκώμιον, Περὶ τοῦ οἴκου) may belong to any part of his career. The strongest influence in his development was the Cynic humour of Menippus of Gadara (Δὶς κατ. 33); it was supplemented by that of the Mime, Attic Comedy (notably the Old) with which he shares a robust sense of humour, and in his later works

the Platonic Dialogue. In his typically Menippean period he aimed his satire at such objects as popular religious ideas ('Ικαρομένιππος, Θεῶν ἐκκλησία), human vanity (Χάρων, Νεκρικοὶ διάλογοι), and philosophic pretensions (Βίων πρᾶσις). Contact with the Platonic Dialogue produced a series of pieces, some late in his life, in which he introduces himself as Λυκῖνος ('Ερμότιμος, Πλοῖον, Εἰκόνες). Beside the Dialogue form he adopted the epistolary, either direct (Πῶς δεῖ ἱστορίαν συγγράφειν), or as a setting for Dialogue (Νιγρῖνος). Notable among his productions in this style are Περεγρῖνος and Ἀλέξανδρος, the castigation respectively of a religious maniac and of a charlatan. His most famous narrative is Ἀληθὴς ἱστορία; the authorship of Λούκιος ἢ ὄνος is questioned.

Lucian compares favourably with his contemporaries, not merely in the variety of his literary resources and in his skill in handling them, but in the reality of his objects. He uses his Atticism, in which he yields to none of them, as a means rather than as an end. He illustrates contemporary life and manners, and criticizes many of the received ideas of his time; his comments on art, in particular, are more helpful than those of some professed critics. He cannot, however, be called either a great original literary artist or a profound thinker. His stock of ideas, except when he is dealing with topical subjects, is drawn either from classical literature or from the popular philosophy of the preceding age; he has no genuine philosophic position, but is essentially an opportunist, σπουδαῖος ἐς τὸ γελασθῆναι (Eunapius). At the same time, though he derived his forms from earlier models, the Satiric Dialogue as he ultimately developed it is a worthy addition to Greek literature of the second rank. A certain adroitness of appeal to the less reflective side of human nature has preserved his work in spite of contemporary disregard. There are scholia dating from late antiquity and the Middle Ages, including those of Arethas of Caesarea.

ANCIENT SOURCES. *Suda*; Eunap. *VS prooem.* 9; Photius, *Bibl.* cod. 128.
EDITIONS. J. Sommerbrodt (1886–99); C. Jacobitz (1896); Nils Nilén (1907– ); A. M. Harmon and others (Loeb, 8 vols. published, 1921–67).
SCHOLIA. H. Rabe (1906).
COMPLETE STUDIES. R. Helm, *L. und Menipp.* (1906); M. Caster, *L. et la pensée religieuse de son temps* (1938); J. Bompaire, *L. écrivain* (1958); H. D. Betz, *L. von Samosata u. das Neue Testament* (1961) (esp. bibliography 215 ff.).
ARTICLES and NOTICES. R. C. Jebb, *Essays and Addresses* (1907); E. J. Putnam, *CPhil.* 1909. Norden, *Ant. Kunstpr.* (style). W. Schmid, *Atticismus* i (1887) (language); G. W. Bowersock, *The Sophists in the Roman Empire* (1969), ch. 9. W. M. E.; R. B.

**LUCILIUS** (1), GAIUS: the date of birth is unknown but he died an old man in 102/1 B.C. at Naples. He was born in Suessa Aurunca on the edge of Campania, a Roman citizen, of a rich and noble family; his brother was a senator (perhaps his father too), and his niece was the mother of Pompey. He owned large estates. He did military service in Spain from 139 B.C. and was at the siege of Numantia (134/3 B.C.). He may, like Terence and Accius, have gone on an educational trip to Athens. He was a friend and equal of the greatest men in Rome. Horace gives several accounts of him: *Sat.* 1. 4 (excessive emphasis on Aristophanic element); *Sat.* 1. 10; and 2. 1 (this last is the best and most comprehensive). No poet's personality before Catullus makes such an impact, even through the meagre fragments. Lucilius invented a new literary genre, of which the outstanding characteristic is the personal autobiographical form (*omnis . . . vita senis*): all that he says is coloured by his personality, his feelings, his views—he is the real subject of his satire. Here his social position gave him a unique advantage. The earliest books are xxvi–xxx (perhaps written 132–125 B.C.), the first two in trochaic septenarii, the next two mixed hexameters, trochaics, and senarii, then xxx in hexameters alone—and this metre he retained for all the rest of his writing; except that xxii–xxv contain traces of elegiac couplets—perhaps epigrams and epitaphs. Book i contained (on the precedent of Ennius' scene in *Ann.* 1) a *concilium deorum* which carried an attack on Cornelius Lentulus Lupus (who died *c.* 123 B.C.: Lucilius had attacked him before). Book ii contained an account of the trial of Q. Mucius Scaevola (*cos.* 117 B.C.), accused by Albucius of maladministration in Asia: this gave Lucilius the opportunity to contrast tellingly two styles of rhetoric. Book iii contained the *iter Siculum*, the model for Horace, *Sat.* 1. 5. Book iv contained a contest of gladiators. Book v contained a letter reproaching a friend for not visiting him when ill. Book vi, Scipio Aemilianus meets a wretched bore (cf. Hor. *Sat.* 1. 9). Books vi–vii seem to have contained satirical matter on sex. Book ix contained grammatical ideas, including an attack on Accius' (q.v.) orthographical theories. Book x, perhaps on literary and stylistic questions. Book xi anecdotes about contemporaries. Book xv on philosophy. About many of the books little can be said since the fragments are so meagre, and the context of many important fragments cannot be known. It is clear that sheer invective played only a minor role in Lucilius' conception of satire—though, by its very freedom, it impressed later readers disproportionately; Horace himself started from this view, but as his own satire developed so did his view of Lucilius, to whom no doubt he owed far more than can now be traced. Lucilius established the hexameter as the metre of this new genre, and, as he wrote it, it was the hexameter of Ennius. His style appears uneven, at times almost careless, and he was prepared to mix Greek words with Latin; but its power, vigour, and flexibility are unmistakable—a reflection of his own turbulent genius—and they conceal a serious regard for Alexandrian canons of style.

F. Marx, *C. Lucili Carminum Reliquiae* (1905; text and commentary); E. H. Warmington, *Remains of Old Latin* iii (1938), 2 ff. (with transl.). C. Cichorius, *Unters. zu Lucilius* 1908; M. Puelma Piwonka, *Lucilius und Kallimachos* (1949); I. Mariotti, *Studi Luciliani* (1960)—especially useful on Lucilius' style. G. W. W.

**LUCILIUS** (2, *PW* 26) **IUNIOR**, GAIUS, friend of Seneca (2) and the recipient of the *De Providentia, Quaestiones Naturales,* and *Epistulae Morales,* was born in Campania, perhaps at Pompeii or Neapolis (Sen. *Ep.* 49. 1; 53. 1; 70. 1), without wealth or prospects (*QNat.* iv. *praef.* 14–15; *Ep.* 19. 5). He was some years younger than Seneca (*Ep.* 26. 7). Talent, literary style, and distinguished connexions brought him into prominence (*Ep.* 19. 3). His own energy made him an *eques Romanus* (*Ep.* 44. 2). He was loyal to the memory and friends or relatives of Lentulus (q.v. 9) Gaetulicus after the latter's execution under Gaius, and to victims of Messallina or Narcissus under Claudius (*QNat.* iv. *praef.* 15). Under Claudius and Nero he held procuratorships in Alpes Graiae, Epirus or Macedonia, Africa, and Sicily (*Ep.* 31. 9; 45. 2; 79. 1; *QNat.* iv. *praef.* 1). The date of his death is unknown.

Lucilius had an inquiring mind; many of Seneca's letters start from some question he has put—generally philosophical, but sometimes literary, linguistic, or social (*Ep.* 9, 29, 39, 43, 71, 72, 106, 108, 109, 111, 113, 114, 117). In spite of business (*Ep.* 17, 19, 22, 24), travel (*Ep.* 69, 84, 104), ill health (*Ep.* 78, 96), and a tendency to grumble (*Ep.* 21, 28, 44, 45, 60, 96, 103) he was a philosopher, probably an ex-Epicurean Stoic. On one occasion Seneca delightedly says to him 'meum opus es' (*Ep.* 34. 2). Lucilius wrote a philosophical treatise, warmly praised by Seneca (*Ep.* 46).

Lucilius was a poet too (*QNat.* iv. *praef.* 14 and ch. 2. 2). Four Latin lines of his (two iambics and two hexameters) are preserved by Seneca (*Ep.* 8. 10; 24. 21; *QNat.* iii. 1. 1). It is unlikely that he is the same as the

Luci*ll*ius (q.v.) of the Greek Anthology; but one Greek epigram of twelve lines (*IG* xiv. 889 = *Epigr. Gr.* 810), inscribed on stone in Sinuessa with the genitive heading 'Ιουνίωρος may well be his. From the passage Sen. *Ep.* 79. 5–7 Wernsdorf and others have attributed the pseudo-Virgilian *Aetna* (q.v.) to Lucilius; but the wording suggests a poem including a description of Aetna rather than one devoted to Aetna *per se.*

See preface to Seneca *QNat.* iv and his *Epp.* (*passim*—esp. 19, 31, 79); L. Delatte, 'Lucilius, l'ami de Sénèque', *LEC* 1935, 367 ff., 546 ff.; J. H. Waszink, *Mnemos.* 1949, 224 ff., supports the attribution of *Aetna* to Lucilius. A. M. D.

**LUCILLA**, ANNIA (*PW* 123), for whom *CIL* viii. 27777 shows also the names *Aurelia Galeria*, was a daughter of Marcus Aurelius and Faustina (2) the Younger (qq.v.), born *c.* A.D. 148. She was married (*c.* 164) at Ephesus to L. Verus (q.v.), co-emperor with Marcus, and given the title *Augusta*. On Verus' death in 169, Marcus immediately married her—an unwilling bride—to Ti. Claudius (q.v. 15) Pompeianus. About 182 she conspired unsuccessfully against her brother Commodus (q.v.); she was exiled by him to Capri and subsequently put to death.

*Diz. Epigr.* i. 945; Wegner, *Herrscherbild* (1939) ii. 4. 74 ff.; *B.M. Coins, Rom. Emp.* iv; F. Grosso, *La lotta politica al tempo di Commodo* (1964). *See also under* AURELIUS (1), MARCUS, *and* VERUS.
C. H. V. S.; M. H.

**LUCILLIUS** (Λουκίλλιος), a Greek epigrammatist of Nero's time, is credited with over a hundred poems in the Greek Anthology (q.v.). Most are quasi-satirical jokes about eccentric or repulsive individuals, e.g. the thief who stole everything including the detective (*Anth. Pal.* 11. 177) and the thin man who had to wear a sinker when diving (11. 100); the rest are mostly occasional pieces written to amuse guests at parties. His language is colloquial but cultivated. He was the first epigrammatist to specialize in bringing his poems to a sharp humorous point in the last line, and in mocking contemporaries. Much of his work is reminiscent of Petronius and of the *Apocolocyntosis*: it strongly influenced Martial.

F. J. Brecht, *Motiv- und Typengeschichte des griech. Spottepigramms* (1930); Cichorius, *Röm. Stud.* viii. 13; A. Garzya, *Giornale Italiano di Filologia* 1955; K. Prinz, *Martial und das griech. Epigramm* (1914); P. Crupi, *L'epigramma greco di L.* (1964). A. Linnenkugel, *De Lucillo Tarrhaeo* (1928), and H. Usener, *Kl. Schr.* ii (1913), identify him with a grammarian of Tiberius' reign. G. H.

**LUCRETIA**, the wife of Tarquinius (q.v. 3) Collatinus, according to legend was outraged by Sextus, son of Tarquinius Superbus; after telling her husband, she took her own life. This incident resulted in a popular rising led by Junius Brutus (q.v. 1) against the Tarquins, and their expulsion from Rome. While the story of Lucretia probably arose from popular poetry, independent of Greek literary influence, her father Lucretius (q.v. 1) was invented by Roman annalists who elaborated the legend. The Greek character of the Lucretia (as well as of Verginia) story is overstressed by Ogilvie, *Comm. Livy* 1–5, 218 ff. P. T.

**LUCRETIUS** (1, *PW* 30) **TRICIPITINUS**, SPURIUS, the father of Lucretia (q.v.). When the annalists associated her with the fall of the monarchy, they placed Lucretius amon gthe founders of republican freedom by alleging that he had been appointed prefect of Rome by the last king, and had retained that office under the Republic. The tradition that he was consul in 509 is disproved by Livy (2. 5).

Ogilvie, *Comm. Livy* 1–5, 228 ff. P. T.

**LUCRETIUS** (2) (TITUS LUCRETIUS CARUS), poet and philosopher, probably 94 to 55 B.C. Jerome gives the date of his birth as 94 and says that he died in his 44th year, i.e. in 51 or 50. Donatus in his 'Life' of Virgil states that Virgil assumed the *toga virilis* on 15 Oct. 55, and adds that 'it happened that on that very day Lucretius the poet died'. Cicero (*QFr*. 2. 9. 3), writing in 54, implies that both he and his brother had read the poem, but it is clear from its unfinished state that it was not published till after the poet's death. His death should therefore probably be placed in 55; if Jerome is right as to his age, he was born in 99.

Of Lucretius' life almost nothing is known. It is natural to assume that he was a member of the aristocratic Roman family of the Lucretii, whose names occur in the Fasti as holders of magistracies. This view has lately been contested on the ground that Carus was not a cognomen of noble families, but of slaves and freedmen, and was possibly a romanized version of a Celtic name; Lucretius would then be a freedman attached to the house of the Lucretii. But inscriptions show Carus as a cognomen of free men. A more recent theory is that Lucretius was a Campanian—a landowner near Pompeii —and learned his Epicureanism at Naples, but the evidence is slender.

The only certain fact of his life is that he was a friend—or possibly dependant—of the aristocrat C. Memmius, the patron of Catullus and Cinna, to whom the poem is dedicated. A 'Life' prefixed to the Editio Veneta in the British Museum and written in the hand of Girolamo Borgia, secretary of Pontanus, states that he was intimate with Atticus, Cicero, Cassius, and Brutus, but this 'Life' is of doubtful authority. Jerome makes the famous statement that Lucretius was poisoned by a love-philtre, wrote the poem in his lucid intervals, and ultimately committed suicide. The attack on the passion of love in book 4 might be held to support this, but the poem itself does not show signs of insanity. Jerome also says that Cicero 'emended' the poem, and this probably means that he edited it for posthumous publication.

Lucretius' only work is the *De Rerum Natura*, a didactic poem in six books, in which the poet expounds the physical theory of Epicurus (q.v.) with a view to abolishing superstitious fears of the intervention of the gods in the world and of the punishment of the soul in an after-life. This he accomplishes by demonstrating that the world is governed by the mechanical laws of nature ('foedera naturai') and that the soul is mortal and perishes with the body. The bulk of the poem is occupied in setting out in detail the atomic view of the universe, which Epicurus adopted with modifications from the Atomists Leucippus and Democritus (qq.v.). Lucretius also touches from time to time on Epicurus' moral theory that pleasure is the end of life, and his thought is regulated throughout by Epicurus' rules of procedure (*Canonica*), which are to some extent expounded in book 4. The root-idea is that of atoms infinite in number moving in space infinite in extent and by their combinations bringing about the creation of things. Lucretius' philosophy is thus purely material, but not, like that of Democritus, deterministic; for he postulates free-will for man and, analogous to it, a certain spontaneity of movement in the atoms (2. 216–93).

5. Book 1, after an introductory address to Venus as goddess of creation, starts from the principle of the permanence of matter and demonstrates the existence of matter in the form of 'first-bodies' or particles, and of void as empty space. Lucretius then shows that the first-bodies are 'atoms', solid, indivisible, and eternal. In a digression he refutes the rival physical systems of Heraclitus the monist and Empedocles the pluralist, and the homoeomeria of Anaxagoras; and in conclusion shows that the universe and its components, the atoms and space, are infinite.

Book 2 opens with a poem on the blessings of philosophy and deals first with the motions of the atoms, then with their shapes and the effects of difference in their shapes on compounds. Lucretius then argues that the atoms do not possess secondary qualities, colour, heat, sound, taste, and smell, or sensation, and concludes with a section on the many worlds and their formation and destruction.

Book 3 deals with the soul. After a preliminary laudation of Epicurus, Lucretius discusses the atomic formation of the soul and its relation to the body. There follows a long series of proofs of its mortality, drawn from its atomic structure and from the phenomena of disease and its cure. The book ends with a triumph-hymn on the mortality of the soul and the folly of the fear of death.

Book 4, which opens with a picture of Lucretius' mission, treats mainly of the psychology of sensation and thought. Lucretius demonstrates that sight is effected by means of 'images' coming off from things and entering the eye. He then discusses the nature of sensation and thought, and deals with false inferences of the mind based on sensation, which is itself infallible. In the end of the book he treats of certain functions of the body and especially of the passion of love, which he violently condemns.

Book 5 is devoted to the phenomena of our world. After another hymn of praise to Epicurus and an attack on the theological view, he shows that the world had a beginning and will have an end, describes its formation, and discusses certain problems of astronomy. He then speaks of the origin on the earth of vegetable and animal life, of the creation of man and the early development of civilization.

Book 6, whose proem is once more a laudation of Epicurus, deals with miscellaneous phenomena, celestial and terrestrial. Among the former Lucretius discusses thunder, lightning, and thunderbolts, waterspouts, clouds, and rain; among the latter earthquakes, volcanoes, the Nile, infected lakes and hot springs, the magnet, and pestilences. The last leads to a description of the plague at Athens, with which the poem closes.

Lucretius regarded himself primarily as a philosopher and only secondarily as a poet (1. 931–4); but the sheer logical architecture of the poem is an extraordinary accomplishment. As a thinker he followed in the steps of Epicurus, but he seems to have made a far-reaching shift of emphasis so that the aim to relieve mankind of the fear of death has become central and paramount (there is also evidence that he avoided some of the more abstruse of his master's discussions). Modern editors have, however, erred in endeavouring by transposition, lacuna, and the assumption of passages written by the poet but not adjusted to their place, to establish a dryly logical sequence in the poem. He adorned the dry exposition of Epicurus with a wealth of illustration and imagery, derived from a vivid observation of the world, which shows him as the true poet. Cicero (*QFr*. 2. 9. 3) recognized in him both 'high lights of genius' ('lumina ingenii') and 'artistry' ('ars'), and both elements are abundantly evident. In style Lucretius owed far more to the influence of Ennius and other early Roman poets than his Alexandrianizing contemporaries. He used alliteration and assonance, archaic forms and constructions, and many compound adjectives; verbs fluctuate between conjugations and substantives between declensions. He complains of the poverty of his native tongue and does not hesitate to invent words as he wants them. His hexameters, judged by the standard of Virgil, are rough and sometimes clumsy, and exhibit certain licences which later taste spurned. As philosopher he accomplished an amazing feat in expounding atomism in verse, and as poet his lines have a weight and majesty, and often a depth of passion and feeling, which have caused critics to rank him as the equal of Virgil, if not his superior.

C. Gordon, *A Bibliography of Lucretius* (1962).

EDITIONS. C. Lachmann (1850, 1855, showed the superiority of the MSS. O and Q—and laid the foundation of all modern criticism of the text); H. A. J. Munro (1860, 1886); A. Brieger (Teubner, 1894, 1909); C. Giussani (1896–8); C. Bailey (O.C.T. 1898, 1921); W. A. Merrill (U.S.A. 1907, 1917); A. Ernout (Budé, 1920); H. Diels (1923); J. Martin (Teubner, 1934); C. Bailey (1947).

COMMENTARIES. Munro, Giussani, Merrill, Ernout, and L. Robin (1925); C. Bailey (1947); W. E. Leonard and S. B. Smith (1942); C. Pascal (bk. 1, 1904, revised by L. Castiglioni 1928); R. Heinze bk. 3, 1897); M. Patin (bk. 5, 1884).

TRANSLATIONS. Verse: W. E. Leonard (U.S.A. 1916); Sir R. Allison (1919); A. S. Way (1933); R. C. Trevelyan (1937); A. D. Winspear (U.S.A. 1955). Prose: Munro; Bailey (1910, 1921); W. H. D. Rouse (Loeb, 1924); T. Jackson (1929).

*Index Lucretianus*: J. Paulson (1911).

LIFE AND POEM. Munro; Mewaldt (*PW*); O. Regenbogen, *Lukrez, seine Gestalt in seinem Gedicht* (1932); G. della Valle, *Tito Lucrezio Caro e l'Epicureismo Campano* (1933).

CRITICISM. Giussani, *Studi Lucreziani* (1896); C. Martha, *Le Poème de Lucrèce* (1869); C. Pascal, *Studi critici sul poema di L.* (1903); J. Masson, *L., Epicurean and Poet* (1907, 1909); E. E. Sikes, *Lucretius* (1936); N. W. de Witt, *Epicurus and his Philosophy* (1954); A. J. Festugière, *Epicurus and his Gods* (trans. C. W. Chilton, 1955); P. Boyancé, *Lucrèce et l'Epicurisme* (1963); *Studies in Latin Literature and its Influence: Lucretius*, ed. D. R. Dudley (1965).

SPECIAL STUDIES. Life: F. Marx, *Neues Jahrbuch* 1899; G. Giri, *Il suicidio di L.* (1895). Composition: J. Mussehl, *De Lucretii Libri Primi Condicione ac Retractatione* (1912); K. Büchner, *Beobachtungen über Vers und Gedankengang bei Lukrez* (1936); F. Giancotti, *Il preludio di Lucrezio* (1959); U. Pizzani, *Il problema del testo e della composizione di* de rerum natura *di Lucrezio* (1959).

GRAMMAR. F. G. Holtze, *Syntaxis Lucretianae Lineamenta* (1868); A. Cartault, *La Flexion dans Lucrèce* (1898).

INFLUENCE. G. D. Hadzsits, *L. and his Influence* (U.S.A. 1935).
C. B.; G. W. W.

**LUCRINUS LACUS,** shallow lagoon near Baiae (q.v.), which a narrow spit separated from the Bay of Naples. Its oysters were famous. Agrippa (q.v. 3) converted it temporarily into a naval anchorage by cutting canals that linked it with Lake Avernus (q.v.) on the one side and open sea on the other. Today the Lucrine Lake has largely disappeared beneath *Monte Nuovo*, a hill upheaved by an earthquake in 1538.　　　　E. T. S.

**LUCULLUS** (1), LUCIUS LICINIUS (*PW* 102), first consul of his house (151 B.C.), tried to enforce the levy for troops for Spain so harshly that he was temporarily imprisoned by the tribunes. When he reached Spain and found that peace had been made with the Celtiberians, he treacherously attacked the Vaccaei and Cauci. As proconsul, he joined Galba (q.v. 3) in an attack on Lusitania. He later built a temple to Felicitas. Scipio (q.v. 11) Aemilianus served under him as military tribune.

H. Simon, *Roms Kriege in Spanien* (1962), see index.　　E. B.

**LUCULLUS** (2), LUCIUS LICINIUS (*PW* 104), grandson of (1), nephew of Metellus (q.v. 6), for whose return from exile he pleaded. He served in the Social War under Sulla and, as quaestor (88 B.C.), was the only officer who supported his march on Rome. As proquaestor in the East, he was Sulla's most reliable officer, charged with diplomatic missions, collecting ships and money, and letting Mithridates escape from Fimbria (q.v.) in accordance with Sulla's policy. Aedile (79) with his brother (3), he gave splendid games. Praetor in 78, he became Sulla's literary executor and guardian of Faustus Sulla (q.v. 3), and then governed Africa. As consul in 74, he opposed tribunician agitation and, worried by the threats of Pompey, sent him generous supplies to Spain; after complicated intrigues (*see* CETHEGUS), he secured an *imperium* against the pirates for Antonius (q.v. 2) and the command against Mithridates for himself.

He won over envoys of Sertorius (q.v.), relieved Cotta (q.v. 2) and Cyzicus, invaded Pontus and occupied much of it, forcing Mithridates to flee to Armenia; and he asked for a Senate commission to settle Asia Minor. When negotiations, through Ap. Claudius (q.v. 12), with

Tigranes (q.v. 1) failed, he invaded Armenia and occupied its capital (69). But he failed to end the war: Parthia threatened intervention, Mithridates and Tigranes collected fresh forces, and Lucullus' troops—kept under strict discipline—began to mutiny. His fair settlement of Asian finances (ensuring order and prosperity there for a generation) had offended many senators and equites, and he came under heavy attack in Rome, with his old enemy Pompey preparing to profit. When the campaign of 68 failed, his brother-in-law Clodius (q.v. 1) incited further mutinies and Marcius Rex (q.v. 2) in Cilicia refused assistance. The army almost disintegrated and Pompey finally took it over under the law of Manilius (q.v. 2). Lucullus had to wait for a triumph until 63, was prominent in opposing Pompey's demands, but after unpleasant experiences in Caesar's consulate (59) retired to live in refined luxury and lapsed into insanity before his death.

He was an able soldier and administrator, an Epicurean, a lover of literature and the arts, and a generous patron. But he lacked the easy demagogy that was needed for success in both war and politics in his day.

Plut. *Luc.*, and references in Dio and Cicero are the chief sources. For the war, see also App. *Mith.* J. van Ooteghem, *Lucius Licinius Lucullus* (1959), with bibliography.　　E. B.

**LUCULLUS** (3), MARCUS TERENTIUS VARRO (*PW*, 'Licinius' 109), younger brother of (2), adopted by a Varro. Quaestor under Sulla *c.* 87 B.C., legate in the *bellum Sullanum*, aedile with his brother (79), he was praetor in 76. As consul (73), with his colleague C. Cassius Longinus, he passed a *lex Terentia Cassia* providing for a supply of a moderate quantity of cheap grain to the city *plebs* (see R. Rowland, *Acta Antiqua Acad. Sc. Hungariae* 1965, 81). As proconsul in Macedonia, he extended Roman control in Thrace up to the Danube and the Black Sea, triumphing in 71. Harassed (with his brother) in the 60s, he supported Cicero against both Catiline and Clodius and died soon after his brother.
　　　　E. B

**LUCUS FERONIAE,** sanctuary dedicated to the Italic woodland goddess Feronia (q.v.) at *Scorano*, south of Soracte (q.v.) in Etruria. The town which grew around its annual festival became a *colonia* in imperial times. Excavations have confirmed Livy's statement (26. 11. 8) that Hannibal plundered the sanctuary (211 B.C.). Another less important Lucus Feroniae existed near Tarracina (q.v.).

Hor. *Sat.* 1. 5. 24–6. G. D. B. Jones, *PBSR* 1962, 191 ff.
　　　　E. T. S.

**LUDI.** The chief uses of the word touch diverse fields of Roman culture:

1. Formal sports and representations, generally with religious origin, motivation, and sanction, and counting as religious rites just as did sacrifices and processions; commonly annual, sometimes *ad hoc*. First, *L. Circenses*: the evolutions of the contestants suggested, eventually if not originally, the movements of the planets about the centre of the heavens—a form of sympathetic magic conceivably thought to promote the orderly progress of the seasons. Then, the gladiatorial and other displays in the fora and amphitheatres, a survival from the funeral games of the Etruscans and Campanians—whether their original purpose was to send the spirits of the brave as companions to the souls of the deceased, to satisfy the craving of the departed spirit for blood, or to release a high degree of emotion in replenishment of the vitality of the dead man, or perhaps something more vague or confused. Further there were priestly games like the dances of the Salii (q.v.), and these constituted an older type under the control of priests as contrasted with others, including the *Circenses*, which were under the control of

magistrates. *L. Scaenici* were associated with literature, music, and the dance; they were held especially at the Apollinare in the Prata Flaminia (*L. Apollinares*, from 208 B.C.) and at the temple of the Magna Mater on the Palatine (*L. Megalenses*, from 191 B.C.), but every city in the Empire possessed at least one theatre as well as an amphitheatre. *Ludi*, part sport, part pre-military drill, entered into the routine of the Juventus (*see* IUVENES), probably an early Italic institution for the training of youth, revived by Augustus; they included the *Lusus Troiae* (Verg. *Aen.* 5. 545–603; E. Norden, *Aus altrömischen Priesterbüchern* (1939), 188 f.). There were eventually over forty different varieties of *ludi* in Rome itself, religious, votive, or commemorative, with specific names: *Magni* (regularized as *Ludi Romani*), *Florales* (regularly from 173 B.C.), etc.

2. Informal games, of which the Romans had fully as many varieties as the moderns, retaining the practice of some of them even in mature years; the Campus Martius contained a 'multitude of those exercising themselves with ball and hoop and in the sports field' (Strabo 5. 236). They are attested by numerous toys, dice, tablets, etc., in the museums; also by 'gaming-boards' scratched upon ancient pavements. The games of chance led to grave abuses, as the Church Fathers realized.

3. Schools of instruction, also training-schools for gladiators (q.v.). Grammatical and literary instruction was largely in the hands of Greeks; training for the law and politics was acquired through apprenticeship until the schools of rhetoric replaced the old tradition (Quintilian; Tac. *Dial.*).

4. Buildings for housing *ludi* in the third sense: a school building has been identified with probability at the north-west end of the forum of Pompeii, scratched inscriptions testify to school-teaching in a hall adjoining the Forum of Julius Caesar in Rome, and the *L. Magnus* and *L. Matutinus* in the Third Region of Rome served for the practice of the gladiators who were to perform in the Amphitheatre.

*See also* SECULAR GAMES, LUDI SCAENICI, GLADIATORS.

Wissowa, *RK* 449 ff.; Habel, *PW* Suppl. v. 608 ff. A. M. Colini and L. Cozza, *Il Ludus Magnus* (1962). A. W. VAN B.

**LUDI SCAENICI,** theatrical shows, first added to the *Ludi Romani* in 240 B.C. (*see* LIVIUS (1) ANDRONICUS); in 200 the *Stichus* was produced at the *Plebeii*; in 194–191 the scenic *Megalenses* were instituted; in 169 the *Thyestes* was performed at the *Apollinares*; in 160 the *Adelphoe* was performed at the funeral games of Paullus. Under the Empire performances chiefly consisted of mime and pantomime. The cost was usually shared between State and presiding magistrates. Admission free; certain seats reserved; women and slaves admitted (Prologue, *Poenulus*).

Dar.-Sag., s.v. 'Theatrum'; A. Piganiol, *Recherches sur les jeux romains* (1923). W. B.

**LUGDUNUM.** (1) *Colonia Copia Claudia Augusta Lugdunum*, modern *Lyon*, was founded 43 B.C. by L. Munatius Plancus (q.v. 1) and was the birthplace of the Emperor Claudius. Its position led to its becoming the centre of Agrippa's road system in Gaul, the capital of the Augustan province of Lugdunensis and the financial centre of Gallia Comata, with a mint (*see* COINAGE, ROMAN) and a *cohors urbana* to protect it. Despite a disastrous fire in A.D. 66 and constant disputes with its neighbour Vienna (q.v.), which reached their height in the troubles of 68–9, Lugdunum flourished in the first and second centuries. A Christian community developed early and a full record of its persecution in 177 is preserved (Eus. *Hist. Eccl.* 5. 1). But the city suffered severely in the revolt of Albinus (197) and in the Late Empire its primacy was usurped by Augusta Treverorum

(q.v.), Lugdunum being merely the capital of Lugdunensis Prima. It became the centre of the Burgundian kingdom *c.* 460.

The Colonia occupied the hill of Fourvière, west of the confluence of Rhône and Saône. Between the rivers (*ad confluentem*, Gallic Condate, q.v.), on ground overlooked by the Colonia, Drusus established in 12 B.C. the altar of Rome and Augustus, the centre of the Imperial Cult for the Tres Galliae, around which the Concilium Galliarum developed. On the cult site only a fragment of the amphitheatre survives, though numerous important inscriptions have been found. In the Colonia the most notable monuments are the theatre and odeon, but the four aqueducts, involving extensive use of syphons, are especially interesting, while the museum contains the bronze tablets of Claudius' speech on the admission of Gauls to the Senate (*ILS* 212).

P. Wuilleumier, *Lyon, Métropole des Gaules* (1953); id. *Fouilles de Fourvière à Lyon* (1951, Suppl. to *Gallia*); Grenier, *Manuel* iii. 220 ff. (general), 685 ff. (amphitheatre), 786 ff. (theatre and odeon), iv. 118 ff. (aqueducts); G. de Montauzon, *Les Aqueducs antiques de Lyon* (1909).

(2) *Lugdunum Convenarum* (*St. Bertrand-de-Comminges*), a town in Aquitania, to which Herod (q.v. 2) Antipas was banished in A.D. 40. In 72 B.C. a hill-fort on the site of the *haute-ville* became the nucleus for Pompey's resettlement of assorted survivors of the Sertorian wars, whence the quasi-tribal name of Convenae (Strabo 4. 190). Under the Empire a considerable town developed in the plain between the hill and the Garonne. Excavation has uncovered much of its plan, including forum, temples, baths, theatre, amphitheatre, market, and a fourth-century Christian church; extensive use was made of marble from the quarries at St. Béat, 10 miles to the south. In the later Empire the hill was fortified with a wall which largely survives, but the town was sacked by Vandals in 409 and came under Visigothic control in 418. According to Strabo (4. 191) the Convenae enjoyed *ius Latii*, but Ptolemy's application of *Colonia* to Lugdunum (2. 7. 13) is probably due to confusion with Lyon.

R. Lizop, *Les Convenae et les Consoranni* (1931); B. Sapène, *St. Bertrand-de-Comminges—Lugdunum Convenarum* (1961).

(3) A town of the Batavi, near modern *Katwijk* (not Leyden).

Holwerda, *Nederlands vroegste Geschiedenis*² (1925), 190. A. L. F. R.

**LUNA,** Roman moon-goddess. Varro (*Ling.* 5. 74) names her among a number of deities introduced by Titus Tatius and therefore of Sabine origin. The latter statement may be doubted, but the existence of an early cult of Luna remains likely, though Wissowa (*RK* 315) objects that no trace of it is to be found. This may be mere accident; in historical times she certainly had a cult with a temple on the Aventine, first mentioned in 182 B.C., and another on the Palatine (ibid. 316; cf. C. Koch, *Gestirnverehrung im alten Italien* (1933), 27; Latte, *RR* 232. H. J. R.

**LUNA,** a town in Liguria on the river Macra, the boundary with Etruria, a district still called *La Lunigiana* (Strabo 5. 222). The Romans early used its harbour (= the Bay of Spezia? or the mouth of the Macra?), but the first certain reference to a town is in 177 B.C., a Roman citizen colony, which in 168 quarrelled with Pisae (q.v.) over boundaries (Livy 34. 8; 41. 13; 45. 13; Ennius fr. 1, 2 Steuart). Subsequently Luna became a *municipium* (derelict by 49: Lucan 1. 586). The triumvirs colonized it anew (*Lib. Colon.* 223), but it never became a place of consequence. The neighbouring Carrara marble quarries were extensively worked under the Empire.

L. Banti, *Luni* (1937). E. T. S.

**LUPERCALIA,** a Roman festival held on 15 Feb. After the sacrifice of a goat or goats and a dog, a rite generally in ancient and commonly in modern times thought to be directed to the god Faunus, at the Lupercal, a cave below the western corner of the Palatine, youths, naked except for girdles made from the skins of the victims, ran about the bounds of the Palatine settlement, striking those whom they met, especially women, with strips of the goat-skins, a form of fertility magic combined with the ritual beating of the bounds and with purificatory rites. Their name, *Luperci*, suggests aversion of wolves or propitiation of a wolf god, and the whole ceremony reflects the needs of a small pastoral community. It is described by Dion. Hal. 1. 80. 1; Ov. *Fasti* 2. 19–36, 267–452 (see Frazer's commentary); Plut. *Ant.* 12, *Rom.* 21, *Caes.* 61. At the Lupercalia of 44 B.C. the consul Marcus Antonius, being one of the Luperci, offered an enwreathed diadem to Caesar. Augustus added dignity to the ceremony (Suet. *Aug.* 31; Mommsen, *Staatsr.* iii. 566 f.).

L. Deubner, *ARW* 1910, 481 ff.; H. J. Rose, *Mnemos.* 1933, 385 ff.; for another view, F. Altheim, *History of Roman Religion* (1938), 206 ff.; Latte, *RR* 84 ff.                          A. W. VAN B.

**LUSCIUS LANUVINUS** (? LAVINIUS), Latin poet (attacked in prologues by Terence, whom he blamed for departing from Greek models and for 'contaminatio'— fusion of several plots into one), translated Menander's *Phasma* and (Menander's ?) *Thesaurus*.

Ribbeck, *CRF*[2] 83 (3rd ed. Teubner). (Ter. *Ad.* 1; *An.* 15; *Eun.* 9–10; *Haut.* 16; *Phorm.* 1.)                          E. H. W.

**LUSITANIA,** a region of western Spain named from the Ibero-Celtic ethnological group of Lusitani. They were mobilized into a coalition against Rome by Viriathus (q.v.), defeated in 139 B.C., and overrun by D. Junius Brutus (q.v. 2) in 137, but again mobilized in rebellion by Sertorius (q.v.). Though they were reduced to submission by Pompey in 73–72, the provincial organization of Farther Spain did not extend north of the Tagus, and most of the old province was assigned to the Senate in 27 B.C. (see BAETICA). Augustus proceeded to conquer the north of the peninsula, and at some date created a separate province of Lusitania including the southern region west of the Anas (*Guadiana*), stretching north to the Durius (*Douro*) and eastward beyond his road from Emerita (q.v.) to Salmantica (*Salamanca*). It was divided into the *conventus* of Emerita, Pax Julia, and Scallabis, and was governed by a praetorian *legatus* without legionary troops. It developed slowly but steadily; under Trajan some of its towns built the great bridge of Alcántara; it was prosperous in the later Empire. Its chief products were horses, pigs, wood, and metals; the harbour of Olisipo (*Lisbon*) and the coast had little importance before medieval times.                          M. I. H.

**LUSIUS** (*PW* 9) **QUIETUS,** a Libyan Moor, was *praefectus alae Maurorum* under Domitian (q.v.), by whom he was dismissed. He volunteered with his Moorish cavalry for Trajan's Dacian wars and served with such distinction that Trajan (q.v.) enrolled him in the Senate with praetorian rank and made him *cos. suff.* at an uncertain date, possibly as late as 117. In the Parthian war, Lusius captured Singara, repelled the Parthians from northern Mesopotamia, and *c.* 116 ruthlessly quelled a revolt of Mesopotamian Jews. He then became legate of insurgent Judaea. He was un-Roman, impetuous, and cruel, but a capable commander and loyal to Trajan's policy of expansion. When Hadrian, on his accession, reversed this policy, he removed Lusius from Judaea and deprived him of his Moorish cavalry detachment. In 188 Lusius was put to death for alleged parti-

cipation in the 'conspiracy of the four consulars' (*see* HADRIAN).

Lambrechts, *Sénat*, no. 87; J. Carcopino, *Istros* i (1934), 5 ff.; A. Iordanescu, *Lusius Quietus* (*Bibl. d'Istros* iii, 1941); Syme, *Tacitus,* see index.                          C. H. V. S.; M. H.

**LUSTRATION.** A *lustrum* is a purificatory ceremony conducted every five years by the censors (q.v.) at Rome: *lustrare* is to perform this or a like ceremony and *lustratio* is the performance of such ritual. The ultimate etymology of the words is uncertain, especially the connexion (defended by C. Koch, *Gestirnverehrung im alten Italien* (1933), 25 f.) with *lustrare*, to illuminate. In all cases the general form of the ceremonial seems to have been the same, whether the object to be purified was a body of people (*lustratio exercitus, populi*), a piece of land (*see* AMBARVALIA), a city (*see* AMBURBIUM), or some other object. Plautus (*Amph.* 775–6) clearly knows of a like process for ridding a mad person of his disease or possession: 'quin tu istanc iubes pro cerrita circumferri?' The essential was to carry or lead materials having supposedly magical virtues around the object to be benefited; the speaker, believing Alcumena ('istanc') to be insane, proposes that this should be done to her.

Normally such a process would require a procession of some kind, small or great; hence the not uncommon use of *lustrare*, to move slowly around something, like a procession (Warde-Fowler, *Anthropology and the Classics*, 169 ff.; *Rel. Exper.* 209; qq.v. for his discussion of the words and ideas involved). This is shown by the passages quoted s.v. AMBARVALIA, especially by Verg. *G.* 1. 345 ff.; the farmers go around the farm (or *pagus*), taking with them a *felix hostia*, that is a beast proper to be sacrificed to the gods and so full of good luck; they accompany this by a loud invitation to Ceres to come into the barn. In Cato, *Agr.* 141, the victims are three, *suouetaurilia*, and the prayer is to Mars (q.v.) to keep away all manner of evil from the land and its inhabitants. Ceres might fittingly be invited into a place thus made pure and lucky. In the case of the censors' *lustratio populi* it is not unlikely that the ceremony concluded with the burial or other disposal of the materials used; cf. the phrase *lustrum condere*. In an *amburbium*, the State clergy formed the procession (Lucan 1. 592 ff.); this could be reinforced by sacrifices at the gates, as at Iguvium (*tab. Iguvin.* vi A f.; i A f.; see I. Rosenzweig, *Ritual and Cults of pre-Roman Iguvium*, 26 ff., and *see* TABULAE IGUVINAE). The Lupercalia (q.v.) were an early and peculiar expression of the like idea (see Rose, *Mnemos.* 1932, 385 ff.). In all cases the ceremonial keeps evil out and puts good in.                          H. J. R.

**LUTETIA** (or **Lutecia**), modern *Paris*. Originally a marshy island (*c.* 25 acres) in the Seine, and capital of the Parisii, it was burnt by them in Labienus' campaign (52 B.C.). Under the Empire it spread up the Mont Ste Geneviève on the S. bank, where vestiges of important public buildings still exist. The town was laid out in irregular *insulae*. In the third century the island alone was inhabited, surrounded by a wall of reused stones. It was a favourite residence of Julian, who was proclaimed Augustus here in 360. Lutetia (from the 3rd c. called Parisii) fell to Clovis *c.* 493.

P.-M. Duval, *Paris antique* (1961).                          C. E. S.

**LUXORIUS** of Carthage (early 6th c. A.D.), grammarian and poet, wrote epigrams in imitation of Martial, mostly in hendecasyllables, elegiacs, and hexameters.

TEXTS. Baehrens, *PLM* iv; Riese, *Anth. Lat.* i[2]; with transl. and comm. M. Rosenblum (1961).                          A. H.-W.

**LYCANTHROPY.** It was occasionally believed in antiquity that a man might turn into a wolf. Herodotus encountered the belief in Scythia that the Neuri changed annually into wolves, but refused to accept it (4. 105). Plato (*Resp.* 565 d) knows a story that in the worship of Zeus Lycaeus a man is sacrificed and whoever tastes of his flesh becomes a wolf (cf. SACRIFICE). Pliny (*HN* 8. 34) has a circumstantial tale of a whole clan, one of whose members in each generation becomes a wolf for nine years. A sorcerer could turn himself into a wolf (Verg. *Ecl.* 8. 97; Petron. *Sat.* 61–2). *See also* LYCAON (3). Wolves are among the shapes into which Circe (q.v.) changes men (Verg. *Aen.* 7. 18).

R. P. Eckels, *Greek Wolf-Lore* (U.S.A. 1937), 32 ff.; Nilsson, *GGR* i². 399.　　　　　　　　　　　　H. J. R.; H. W. P.

**LYCAON**, in mythology, (1) Son of Priam (q.v.) and Laothoe; killed by Achilles (*Il.* 21. 34 ff.). (2) Father of Pandarus (q.v.; *Il.* 2. 826–7). (3) Son of Pelasgus (q.v.), king of Arcadia, first mentioned in Hesiod, fr. 44 Rzach. According to Apollodorus (3. 96 ff.), who seems to follow Acusilaus, he had fifty sons, but accounts vary, partly owing to attempts to provide Arcadian towns with founders going back to remote antiquity (e.g. Halipherus and Mantineus, eponyms of Haliphera and Mantinea, in Apollod.; Phigalus, of Phigalia, Paus. 8. 3. 1). His character is an odd mixture of piety and extreme impiety. He founded the cult of Zeus Lycaeus (Paus. ibid.), but sacrificed a child on his altar, and therefore was turned into a wolf (for this story cf. R. P. Eckels, *Greek Wolf-Lore* (U.S.A. 1937), 49 ff.). He tried to murder Zeus, also to trick him into eating human flesh (Ov. *Met.* 1. 222 ff.), thus provoking the deluge, cf. DEUCALION.

Nilsson, *GGR* i². 597 ff.　　　　　　　　　　　　　H. J. R.

**LYCAONIA.** The original home of the Lycaonians was the mountainous country around Laranda (on the north side of Mt. Taurus), but they were already under Persian rule raiding and settling in the plain to the north, which came to be called Lycaonia. Subdued by Perdiccas in 322 B.C., they were subject to the Seleucids (280–189) and Attalids (189–133). Lycaonia became, it is uncertain when, a *conventus* of the province of Cilicia; the southern mountainous area was, however, ruled by a dynast, Antipater (50–36 at least). The plain, with Iconium as capital, was granted by Antony to Polemon in 39, and in 36 was transferred to Amyntas, who conquered Antipater. From 25 B.C. the plain was part of Galatia and Cappadocia-Galatia. The mountainous country was probably ruled by Archelaus I and II, and certainly by Antiochus IV, till A.D. 72, when it (Lycaonia Antiochiana) joined Cappadocia–Galatia. Trajan on dividing this province probably allotted the plain to Galatia, Antiochiana to Cappadocia. Under Antoninus Pius most of Lycaonia (excluding Iconium and Laodicea) was added to Cilicia, within which it was a κοινόν. The Lycaonians were a backward people, still speaking their native language in the first century A.D. Most of their cities issued no coins till Antoninus Pius' reign.

Sir W. M. Ramsay, *BSA* 1901, 243, *JÖAI* 1904, Beiblatt 57; Jones, *Cities E. Rom. Prov.*, 124 ff.　　　　　　　　A. H. M. J.

**LYCIA.** A mountainous country in the south-west of Asia Minor. According to Herodotus (1. 173) the Lycians came there direct from Crete under Sarpedon, and at that time were called Termilae; the name of Lycians they took from the Athenian Lycus son of Pandion. In fact a tribe called Lukka appears in the Hittite records; on the other hand, the name Termilae (in the form Trm̃mili) is used in the epichoric inscriptions of the fourth century. Another tradition said that Sarpedon came from Crete to Miletus; it has been suggested that the passage of the Lycians from there to the south coast is marked by the recurrence of the syllable *mil* in Miletus, Mylasa, Milyas (Termilae). The Lycians fought at Troy as allies of Priam; at that time they already occupied the classical Lycia (*Il.* 2. 876–7). Their chieftains Sarpedon and Glaucus are among the more notable of the minor heroes in the *Iliad*.

In 546 B.C. Lycia was overrun by the Persians after a heroic resistance at Xanthus. Liberated by Cimon *c.* 468, the Lycians were temporarily included in the Delian League (appearing in the tribute lists for a single year 446), but quickly fell back under Persia. Included for a while in the Hecatomnid dominions (*see* MAUSOLUS), Lycia submitted readily to Alexander, and after his death passed into the hands of the Ptolemies. The country was conquered in 197 B.C. by Antiochus III, upon whose defeat at Magnesia it was granted in 189 by the Romans to Rhodes. The Lycians bitterly resented and resisted the Rhodian rule, and in 169 were given their freedom by Rome. This freedom was not revoked until A.D. 43, when Claudius established the province of Lycia-Pamphylia, under a praetorian legate.

The Lycians had an unusual capacity for collaboration and federation. Even in the fourth century, when the cities were ruled, under the Persians, by their own dynasts, the uniformity of their coinage indicates some kind of confederation. At some time in the Hellenistic period, perhaps even before 200 B.C., a regular Lycian Confederacy (κοινὸν τῶν Λυκίων) was established. The east coast cities of Olympus and Phaselis (q.v.) were now for the first time included in Lycia, and in 83 B.C. three cities of the Cibyratis were added. In the federal Council and Assembly the individual cities were represented proportionally to their size and importance (Strabo 14. 664–5). In the two centuries following 169 B.C. the Confederacy performed all the functions of a Sovereign state; under the Empire it continued to exist with limited authority. Federal coinage was struck, of a uniform type generally bearing a lyre, in the names of the various cities, which at the same time issued their own individual types. The lyre represents Apollo, the principal deity of the Lycians.

The Lycian language and script continued in use down to the end of the fourth century. Greek appears in the inscriptions, side by side with Lycian, from about 400, and soon after 300 supplants it entirely. The language is largely *sui generis*, but exhibits certain Indogermanic features; it is still only imperfectly understood. The alphabet contains twenty-nine letters, rather more than half of which are of Greek form; of some of the others the phonetic values are still uncertain.

Herodotus' statement (1. 173) that the Lycians alone of all men reckoned descent through the female side receives no support from the oldest inscriptions; none of these, however, is quite as early as Herodotus' time.

O. Treuber, *Geschichte der Lykier* (1887); G. Fougères, *De Lyciorum Communi* (1898); Jones, *Cities E. Rom. Prov.* 96 ff.; *Tituli Asiae Minoris* vols. i–ii (1901–44); Magie, *Rom. Rule Asia Min.*, ch. 22; on the Confederacy, J. A. O. Larsen, *Greek Federal States* (1968), 240 ff.　　　　　　　　　　　G. E. B.

**LYCO** (*PW* 14) (*c.* 302/298–*c.* 228/224 B.C.), son of Astyanax of Troas, pupil of Strato of Lampsacus and his successor as head of the Peripatetic school (q.v.) which he directed for forty-four years. The sources for his life, mostly derived from a lost biography by Antigonus (q.v. 4) of Carystus, show that he was a man of the world, a friend of kings and statesmen, a benefactor of the people, a lover of pleasure and luxury of all kinds—all but a great philosopher or scientist like his predecessors. He was a fluent and interesting speaker (φραστικός), but had little to teach (Cicero, *Fin.* 5. 13, calls him 'oratione locuples, rebus ipsis ieiunior'), and with him began a long period of decline in the history of the Peripatetic school. At his death he left some writings, but only a few fragments, and no titles, have survived.

Diog. Laert. 5. 65–74. Wilamowitz, *Antigonos von Karystos* (1881), 78 ff.; F. Wehrli, *Die Schule des Aristoteles* vi (1952), 9 ff.　　J. G.

**LYCOPHRON** (1), tyrant of Pherae *c.* 406–390 B.C. He may have established his tyranny by championing a democratic element against the aristocracy, for he was opposed by the nobles of Larissa and other cities, whom he defeated in 404. He allied with Sparta and in 395 fought against Medius of Larissa, who, with support from Boeotia and Argos, may have won a temporary advantage over him. In a period of violent struggles between Thessalian cities and factions he played a prominent part, but so little evidence has survived that it is impossible to determine the extent of his success or to assess his ability as a military and political leader. His ambition to dominate Thessaly was achieved by Jason (q.v. 2), probably his son.     H. D. W.

**LYCOPHRON** (2) (b. *c.* 320 B.C.), of Chalcis in Euboea, as a young man frequented the philosopher Menedemus at Eretria. *Circa* 285–283 he went to Alexandria and was entrusted by Ptolemy Philadelphus with the *diorthosis* (preliminary sorting-out) of the comedies collected for the Library. He was included in the *Pleiad* of Tragic Poets. According to Ovid, *Ibis* 529–30, Lycophron was killed by an arrow.

WORKS. (1) *Verse*: Tzetzes credits Lycophron with 64 or 46 tragedies, and the *Suda* gives the titles of 20. The *Cassandreis* must have been historical and based on recent events, since Cassandreia was founded *c.* 316. The only fragment (4 lines) is from the *Pelopidae* (*TGF* 818). Lycophron's satyric drama, the *Menedemus* (*TGF* 817–18), depicted the high thinking and low living of Menedemus' circle. The *Suda* further credits Lycophron with 'the *Alexandra*, the obscure poem'. This survives, a dramatic monologue in 1474 tragic iambics, in which the slave set to watch Alexandra (Cassandra) reports her prophecies to Priam. Apart from prologue (1–30) and two epilogues (1451–74) the poem falls into three sections, 31–364 Destruction of Troy and crime of Ajax, 365–1282 Return of the Greeks, 1283–1450 Struggle between Europe and Asia. At one time or another the poem touches on nearly all the themes of the Epic Cycle, but the central idea, the Greek sufferings as compensation for the Trojan, was probably suggested by Euripides' *Troades*. In 365–1282 the author devotes most space to early Greek and Trojan colonization of the West and here draws extensively on Timaeus. In 1226–80 Cassandra foretells Aeneas' arrival in Latium and the future glories of Rome. This passage and 1446–50, where the precise reference is disputed, raised doubts even in antiquity (cf. the scholia on 1226) whether Lycophron, the tragic poet, was the author of the *Alexandra*. Since the two passages show no stylistic differences from the rest of the poem, excision is unjustified. Some see a reference to Pyrrhus in 1446–50 and attribute the recognition of Rome's power to her victory in the Tarentine war. On this view the poem was composed by the tragedian Lycophron, probably *c.* 273, when the Romans sent an embassy to Alexandria. Others refer 1446–50 to T. Quinctius Flamininus, who defeated Philip V at Cynoscephalae in 197. These date the poem not long after that event and suppose the author to have been a namesake, perhaps descendant, of the tragedian. General grounds favour the later dating. The obscurity of the *Alexandra* exceeds that of any other Greek poem. This is due to the recondite material, to the blending of inconsistent myths, but above all to the language. Of about 3,000 words used in the *Alexandra* 518 are found nowhere else and 117 appear for the first time (Scheer). Of the rest many are 'glosses' from Epic and Tragedy, especially Aeschylus. Neologisms too are frequent, and there are some modernisms and vulgarisms. The syntax is characterized by extravagant use of the figures of speech and rhetoric. The real names of gods and men occur rarely, and, when they do, usually refer to another

character, e.g. Zeus means Agamemnon and vice versa. Normally the gods appear under some obscure cult-title, the heroes under the names of animals or disguised by a riddling periphrasis. Countries are indicated by some little-known town, mountain, or river situated in them. In metre the author is strict. There are few resolutions and the rule of the final cretic is uniformly observed. The explanation of the numerous coincidences between the *Alexandra* and the poems of Euphorion depends on the dating of the former. The first explicit reference to the poem is in Statius (*Silv.* 5. 3. 157), but soon after this Clement of Alexandria, Lucian, and Artemidorus all mention it, and later the lexicographers and Stephanus of Byzantium cite it frequently. Theon (fl. *c.* 40 B.C.) wrote a *hypomnema* on the *Alexandra*, and some of the material contained in the scholia and in the commentary of Tzetzes probably goes back to this scholar.

(2) *Prose*: The only known work of Lycophron is a lexical compilation Περὶ κωμῳδίας in at least nine books (Ath. 11. 485 d). This treatise, presumably a by-product of his labours in the Library, was much criticized by later workers in this field.

TEXTS. E. Scheer, *Lycophronis Alexandra*, i, Text (1881); ii, Scholia (1908); C. von Holzinger, *Lykophron's Alexandra* (1895); A. W. Mair, in *Callimachus, Lycophron, Aratus* (Loeb, 1921).

GENERAL LITERATURE. K. Ziegler, 'Lykophron (8)', *PW* xiii. 2316–81 and Suppl. xi, 888 ff.; G. W. Mooney, *The Alexandra of Lycophron* (1921); A. Momigliano, *JRS* 1942; *CQ* 1945.    E. A. B.

**LYCORTAS**, father of Polybius and friend of Philopoemen, represented with these the Megalopolitan policy of Achaean independence in a unified Peloponnese with Egyptian support. Hipparch in 192/1 B.C., he defended Philopoemen's pressure on Sparta before the Senate (189/8), and after visiting Egypt (186), renewed alliance with Ptolemy Epiphanes as General in 185/4. General *suffectus* in 182, after Philopoemen's death, he suppressed the Messenian revolt and received Sparta again into the League. Possibly General in 182/1, he was prevented by Epiphanes' death from going to Egypt in 180. Against the pro-Roman Callicrates he failed to gain Achaean neutrality in the Third Macedonian War or help for Egypt against Syria in 168.

Polyb. bks. 22–4; 28–9; Livy, bks. 38–9. G. Colin, *Rome et la Grèce* (1905), 203; A. Aymard, *Les Premiers Rapports de Rome et de la confédération achaïenne* (1938).    A. H. McD.

**LYCURGUS** (1), a mythological personage, according to Homer, *Il.* 6. 130 ff., a son of Dryas, who attacked Dionysus (q.v.), driving him and his nurses before him till the god took refuge in the sea; thereafter Lycurgus was blinded and died soon. This is vaguely placed on Mt. Nysa. Later, as in Aeschylus (Nauck, *TGF* 19 ff.), he is an Edonian; he and others elaborate the story in various ways. Apollodorus (1. 35) and Hyginus (*Fab.* 132) say Dionysus drove him mad, and further embroider the story of his sufferings and death; their sources are uncertain. For details, see Rapp in Roscher's *Lexikon*, s.v., Marbach in *PW*, s.v.; Nilsson, *GGR* i². 580.    H. J. R.

**LYCURGUS** (2), the traditional founder of the Spartan constitution, social and military systems, and consequently of the *eunomia*, the 'good order', which they created. The earliest surviving mention of him is in Herodotus, where he is guardian of the Agiad king Leobotes (*c.* 900 B.C.); most later writers attached him, directly or by implication, to the Eurypontid Charillos (*c.* 775 B.C.) but there are also traces of other traditions.

Modern opinion sees much of his social system (the ἀγωγή) as a survival of primitive tribal customs, much of Sparta's later character (e.g. her austerity) as a gradual development conditioned by her peculiar economic and political position, many of his other reforms (e.g. a ban on coinage) as later accretions, and this, with ancient doubts about his date and life and the obvious elements of romance in the tradition, has led many to doubt his existence. Pointing to the quasi-divine honours which he received by the fifth century they explain him away as the god under whose protection the new regime was placed.

But the basic structure of this regime was established, or at least defined, at some one moment, though probably not as early as 775 (*see* SPARTA), and no compelling argument forbids the belief that this was the work of one great legislator.

Hdt. i. 65–6; Plut. *Lyc.* J. Wells, *Studies in Herodotus* (1923), 44 ff.; V. Ehrenberg, *Neugründer des Staates* (1924), 1 ff.; W. G. Forrest, *Phoenix* 1963, 157 ff.      W. G. F.

**LYCURGUS** (3) (*c.* 390–*c.* 325/4 B.C.), Athenian statesman, of great importance after Chaeronea. The principal evidence about him is the 'Life' in [Plut.] *Lives of the ten Orators* and the appended honorific decree of 307/6, the original of which is partially preserved (*IG* ii². 457). Clearly he played the major part in the control of the city's finances for a period of twelve years, raising the revenue to perhaps 1,200 talents a year, and financing projects by raising capital from individuals (προδανεισμοί); scattered epigraphic evidence attests the wide range of his activities (note esp. *SIG*³ 218, *IG* ii². 1627 and 1672, ll. 11 and 303). The powers by which he did it all are obscure. Some have inferred from Hyperides fr. 118 and other passages that he was given a general but extraordinary commission to supervise the city's finances, but the manner of Aristotle's allusions to the financial officers in the *Ath. Pol.* tells against such a theory: the passage in Hyperides *in Dem.* (col. 28) frequently taken to describe Lycurgus' position should be referred to Demosthenes' powers as Theoric Commissioner. Probably he occupied different offices including the position of ταμίας τῶν στρατιωτικῶν and controlled the whole by personal influence (cf. Plut. *Mor.* 841 c), which manifests itself to us in the varied decrees which he proposed. Whatever his powers, it is certain that he carried through a diverse building programme including the completion of the Skeuotheke begun by Eubulus (q.v. 1), the rebuilding of the theatre of Dionysius, the construction of docks, and the improvement of the harbours. The substantial increase in the navy in this period is ascribed to him. He also concerned himself with the arrangements for processions and festivals, and had statues of the three great tragic poets erected and an official copy made of their works (later borrowed by Ptolemy Philadelphus (q.v.) for the library of Alexandria and never returned). The common belief that Lycurgus instituted, or reformed, the corps of *epheboi* (q.v.) is ill grounded. In politics he was bitterly suspicious of Macedon and was one of those at first demanded by Alexander in 335. He prosecuted Lysicles who had been a general at Chaeronea and any who after the battle seemed to show signs of defeatism, and, when the revolt of Agis III (q.v.) in 331/30 put the city in turmoil, Lycurgus used the occasion to attack Leocrates, who had been absent from the city from 338 to 332 but probably not illegally, and very nearly had him condemned for treachery. The fragments of his speeches attest the wide range of his prosecution of corrupt practices. He died shortly before the Harpalus (q.v.) affair. According to a story contained in a letter ascribed to Demosthenes he was accused by his successor Menesaechmus of having left a deficit; his sons were condemned to repay the money, and were imprisoned when unable to do so. They were released on the appeal of Demosthenes. By 307/6 his great services were generally recognized.

WORKS. Of fifteen speeches regarded as genuine by Caecilius, the only one extant is *Against Leocrates*. The ancient opinion that Lycurgus was mercilessly severe in his prosecutions is supported by the study of this speech. His literary style was influenced by that of Isocrates, but he is a much less careful writer, being often negligent in the matter of hiatus, and inartistic in the composition of his sentences. Evidently he cared more for matter than style. His disregard of proportion is shown by his inordinately long quotations from the poets.

GENERAL LITERATURE. *See* ATTIC ORATORS.
TEXT. Blass (Teubner ed. maior 1899; ed. minor 1912).
COMMENTARIES. A. Petrie (1922), P. Treves (1934), E. Malcovati (1947); N. C. Konomis, 'Notes on the fragments of L.', *Klio* 1961, 72 ff.
TEXT AND TRANSLATION. F. Durrbach (Budé, 1932); J. O. Burtt, *Minor Attic Orators* ii (Loeb, 1954).
INDEX. *See* ANDOCIDES.      G. L. C.

**LYCUS** of Rhegium (fl. 300 B.C.), second in importance to Timaeus for his history of Sicily (Περὶ Σικελίας), and one of Timaeus' sources. The history of Libya ('Ιστορία Λιβύης) was a separate work.

*FGrH* iii. 570.

**LYDIA** was a territory in the west of Asia Minor, centred in the lower Hermus and the Caÿster valleys, bordered on the north by Mysia, on the east by Phrygia, on the south by Caria; the Phrygian and Carian borders were indeterminate, and the coastal cities (Cyme, Smyrna, Ephesus, etc.) were reckoned sometimes to Lydia, sometimes to Aeolis or Ionia. Lydia contained much natural wealth, and lying astride and along the two main routes from the coast to the interior of Asia Minor it was an entrepôt of trade and lay open both to Greek and to Anatolian influences, which are united in its civilization, art, and cult. Under the Mermnad dynasty (*c.* 700–550 B.C.) Lydia was a powerful kingdom which by the time of its last king Croesus had incorporated all the plateau of Asia Minor up to the Halys (q.v.). After his defeat, Lydia became the chief Persian satrapy in the West, with its headquarters at Sardes; this satrapy was in close political relations with the Greek States throughout the Persian period. The conquest by Alexander threw Lydia open to Graeco-Macedonian settlement; after the battle of Magnesia in 189 it became Attalid territory and passed to Rome with the rest of the Attalid kingdom in 133. It remained part of the province Asia till Diocletian made it a separate province, with Sardes as *metropolis*.

Lydian civilization and art were influenced by and reacted on Greece; Lydia was the first realm to use coined money and was an innovator in music. The Lydian language, though obscure, seems to belong to the Anatolian group of Indo-European; it survives on about fifty inscriptions of the fourth century B.C. excavated from the temple of Artemis—in Strabo's day it was still spoken on the border of Lycia.

G. Radet, *La Lydie* (1893); L. Bürchner and J. Keil, *PW*, s.v. 'Lydia'.      W. M. C.; J. M. C.

**LYDIADAS** (d. 227 B.C.), son of Eudamus (*SIG* 504), was Megalopolitan commander against Sparta in 251 (Paus. 8. 10. 5) and assumed the tyranny *c.* 243. Threatened by Achaea, he abdicated, brought Megalopolis into the Achaean Confederacy (235), and was elected general in 234, 232, and 230. He was a constant rival of Aratus and disobeyed his orders in the battle of Ladocea against Cleomenes III, when he charged with the cavalry and was killed (227). He was ambitious and generous, but was eclipsed by Aratus.

Plut. *Aratus, Cleomenes.* Beloch, *Griech. Gesch.* iv; F. W. Walbank, *Aratos of Sicyon* (1933).      F. W. W.

**LYDUS**, IOANNES LAURENTIUS. Greek writer of the sixth century A.D. He talks about himself in *De magistratibus* 3. 26–30 and elsewhere. He was born in 490 in Philadelphia in Lydia (hence his name), and went to Constantinople in 511 to learn philosophy. A protégé of his countryman the praetorian prefect Zoticus, he soon entered the *officium* of the praetorian prefect as *excerptor*. He ended his career forty years later with the highest rank of *cornicularius*, notwithstanding the hostility of John the Cappadocian. For some years he also taught Latin philology in Constantinople. Bribes and perquisites made him a rich man. After his retirement in 551 or 552 he (probably) wrote *De mensibus* and *De ostentis* and (certainly) composed his most important work, *De magistratibus populi romani*. He wrote them in Greek, though he was a great champion of the Latin language and altogether a representative of that revival of interest in old Roman customs and institutions which is characteristic of Justinian's reign. His works go back directly or indirectly to the authoritative antiquarians of the first century B.C. and of the first two centuries A.D.—perhaps they owe most to Suetonius' lost works (but further research on their sources is needed). The *De magistratibus* is a very unusual attempt to trace the development of Roman institutions, beginning with the monarchic period. The section on the *officium* of the praetorian prefect is of great importance, and also elsewhere Lydus provides good evidence for his own time.

De mensibus (only partially preserved), ed. R. Wünsch (1898); De ostentis, ed. C. Wachsmuth (1897); De magistratibus, ed. R. Wünsch (1903). Bibliography in B. Rubin, *Das Zeitalter Justinians* i (1960), 427 ff., and Latte, *RR* 7. A. Klotz, *PW*, s.v. Lydos, 7; A. H. M. Jones, *JRS* 1949, 51 ff.; E. Stein, *Histoire du Bas-Empire* ii (1949), 729 and 838; G. Moravcsik, *Byzantinoturcica* i² (1958), 328.　A. M.

**LYGDAMUS**, the author of six smooth but wooden elegies transmitted with the poems of Tibullus. His derivative and tedious poems are addressed to a Neaera. Both names may be pseudonyms, and the poems give no real clue to the status of either; 4. 85 ff. compare Neaera's parents favourably with the Chimaera, Cerberus, and Scylla, but this hardly justifies the inference that she was of good family. No attempt to identify Lygdamus himself carries any conviction, and the preservation in the Tibullian corpus of a poet who apparently pretends to be Ovid (5. 18) is a puzzle.

Text in editions of Tibullus; commentary in the older editions by Heyne and Dissen; see also G. Némethy, *Lygdami Carmina*, etc. (1906); Postgate, *Selections from Tibullus*² (1910); A. Cartault, *Tibulle et les auteurs du Corpus Tibullianum* (1909); Kirby Smith, *The Elegies of Albius Tibullus* (1913). Cf. Schanz–Hosius ii § 282.　M. E. H.

**LYRIC POETRY, GREEK.** Lyric poetry, in the sense of song accompanied by a musical instrument which is normally but not necessarily the lyre, must have existed both as monody and as choral song from an early age in Greece. Homer hints at monody in the Linus Song which a boy sings (*Il.* 18. 570), and he knows of several kinds of choral song which were later to be practised by known poets, notably the Dirge (*Il.* 18. 50–1, 314–16, 24. 746–7), the Paean (ibid. 1. 472–4), the *Hymenaeus* (ibid. 18. 493), the *Hyporchema* or song accompanied by mimetic dancing (*Od.* 13. 256–65), and the Maiden-Song (*Il.* 16. 182–3). In all these the procedure seems to be the same; there is a choir and a leader, each belongs to a definite occasion, and each is accompanied by music and dancing. These characteristics survived for centuries, and the different types of song known to Homer were standard parts of Greek life. Poets wrote words and music for them, so that all five kinds are, for instance, included in the different types of poetry written by Pindar. The earliest example of such a poem comes from Alcman's Maiden-Song (fr. 1), written in the seventh century. Its

chief characteristics belong to its kind and lasted long after it. First, there is the attention paid to the gods at whose festival it is sung. Secondly, there are the moral maxims which the poet makes. Thirdly, there are remarks about the persons who take part in the festival. Fourthly, there is the myth or story, from which, in this case, the poet draws an emphatic moral. These main elements are to be found in Pindar and Bacchylides and seem to be essential to the choral ode as such. Of them the only one that needs some comment is the myth. In origin its presence must have been due to the song's being sung in honour of some god, and no doubt the myth told something about him. But even in Alcman the connexion of the myth and the festival is not clear, and in Pindar the myth might be introduced for different reasons, though often it gave an example of some law about god and man which the poet wanted to emphasize.

**2.** Another early type of choral song was the *Prosodion* or Processional Song. Homer does not mention this, but it was already in existence in the middle of the eighth century, when Eumelus of Corinth wrote one for the Messenian choir which was sent to Delos (Paus. 4. 4. 1). Only a little later came the Dithyramb, which, after being an unorganized song to Dionysus, was reduced to order by Arion and made like other choral songs in the seventh century. It is possible that some of Stesichorus' poems and a fragment of Alcman (fr. 56) were also of this kind, though its heyday came when it was made a subject for competition at Athens in the last quarter of the sixth century, and was written by Lasus, Simonides, Pindar, and Bacchylides. Later than this came songs which were addressed not to gods but to pre-eminent men. Their development probably belongs to the age of the tyrants, and an early example may perhaps be seen in Ibycus' lines to Polycrates (fr. 1), in which all centres on the boy whom the poet wishes to honour. *Encomia* were written for distinguished persons like Scopas by Simonides, Hieron and Xenophon of Corinth by Pindar, Alexander of Macedon by Bacchylides. Similar to the *Encomium* in origin was the Epinician, a song written for a victor in one of the great games. This might be sung at the place where he won or at his home after his return. It came into prominence under Simonides, who seems to have treated it in a light-hearted way, but its real exponent was Pindar, who gave to it most of the characteristics of the formal hymn by writing for occasions when the victor was welcomed at the feast of some god in his home. It may be doubted whether earlier Epinicians had this religious character.

**3.** These different types survived into the middle of the fifth century, and even later, since Euripides wrote an Epinician for Alcibiades and Sophocles a Paean for Asclepius. But with the rise of tragedy and the decay of the Greek aristocracies the choral hymn seems to have declined. The best poets seldom wrote them, and the occasions which required them were no longer as important as before. The only popular choral poetry of the later fifth and the fourth centuries was the Dithyramb, which underwent considerable changes, becoming less formal than before, more concerned with music than with words, more artificial in its language. Closely allied to it was the *Nomos*, an astrophic composition, like Timotheus' *Persae*, which aimed at sensational effects in words and music.

**4.** Outside this main stream of development other types may be observed. Monody grew to great distinction c. 600 B.C. in Lesbos, where Sappho and Alcaeus produced a personal poetry concerned with the emotions and interests of their own lives; they were followed a generation later by Anacreon in Ionia, and the example of all three may have helped Athenian aristocrats to produce their σκόλια or drinking-songs at the turn of the sixth and fifth centuries. But this art, like that of choral poetry, declined as the fifth century advanced, and σκόλια seem to have ceased to be composed. Quite separate from these was the poetry written by women for women in different parts of Greece. Corinna in Boeotia, Telesilla in Argos, and perhaps Praxilla wrote a special kind of traditional verse which in simple language told of local myths.

5. In the fourth century the old divisions of forms began to be confused. Aristonous wrote a Paean (proper to Apollo) to Hestia, Philodamus to Dionysus; Aristotle used the form of the Paean as a memorial hymn for his dead friend Hermias and addressed it to the abstract power Ἀρετά. This confusion persisted into the Hellenistic age, when Paeans were addressed to human beings, and the form of the folk-song was used by Hermocles for the entry of Demetrius Poliorcetes into Athens. But the lyric tradition survived both in the real Paeans which were still composed for Apollo and in other new types of monody, of which the most distinguished are the Serenade, the Lovers' Dialogue from Marisa (Powell, *Coll. Alex.* 184), simple songs of work like that of the Nile Boatmen (ibid. 195), while more elaborate forms existed like Mesomedes' hymns to Nature and Isis, and the beautiful anonymous *Teliambi* (ibid. 197). There were still imitations of earlier poets like the Aeolic poems of Theocritus based on Alcaeus, and the sapphics of Melinno, who seems to have lived in south Italy and used the form of personal monody to praise the grandeur of Rome.

TEXT. Page, *Poet. Mel. Gr.*; J. M. Edmonds, *Lyra Graeca* (Loeb). COMMENTARY. H. W. Smyth, *Greek Melic Poets* (1900). CRITICISM. C. M. Bowra, *Greek Lyric Poetry from Alcman to Simonides*² (1962); D. A. Campbell, *Greek Lyric Poetry* (1967).
C. M. B.

**LYRIC POETRY, LATIN.** Greek lyric poetry, on a reasonably workable definition produced by Alexandrian scholars, was distinguished by its musical accompaniment. This definition has no relevance whatever to Latin lyric poetry. No Latin lyric poet sang his compositions to the accompaniment of the lyre although Horace often self-consciously speaks as if he did. Equally the modern notion of lyric poetry as brief, personal, and subjective in tone will not apply to Latin lyric—it will apply to some Latin lyric poems, but by no means to all. The only way by which Latin lyric poetry may be defined is by its metres: such a test will admit some of the very fragmentary predecessors of Catullus and poems 11, 30, 34, 51, and 61 of Catullus himself (it will be noticed that the poems of Catullus which a modern judgement would be most ready to call lyric are excluded); it may be extended to include not only the *Odes* of Horace, but also the *Epodes*, and Statius, *Silvae* 4. 5 and 7. The definition in Greek which allowed the choral odes of tragedy to be considered in the genre of lyric poetry may in Latin allow the choral odes which Seneca composed for his tragedies. Beyond that there are some fragments of the first century A.D., perhaps Hadrian's poem to his soul, then Ausonius and the Christian hymns of Prudentius and Ambrose.

2. The Romans are usually represented as allergic to the lyric spirit, and Cicero's scathing remark is quoted (Sen. *Ep.* 49. 5) that, even if he had a second lifetime, he would not find time to read the lyric poets. Seneca adds the explanation that they make a business of trivialities. Quintilian (10. 1. 96) considered Horace pretty well the only lyric poet worth reading, but his educational aim was cramping to the free range of literary perception. These opinions should not be taken alone: in *Orator* 183 Cicero shows a technical acquaintance with lyric poetry, and in *Dialogus* 10 Tacitus makes Aper list *lyricorum quoque iucunditatem* among the branches of literature which he considers worth while.

*See* articles on ALEXANDRIANISM and on the authors mentioned above; *also* METRE, LATIN, III.　　G. W. W.

**LYSANDER** (d. 395 B.C.), Spartan general and statesman. Appointed admiral for 408/7, he restored the efficiency of the Peloponnesian fleet, gained the friendship and support of Cyrus, and won a victory at Notium which caused the withdrawal of Alcibiades (q.v.). After the battle of Arginusae he resumed command, and, transferring his fleet to the Hellespont, destroyed the Athenian navy at Aegospotami (405). He conducted the blockade of the Piraeus and after the surrender of Athens (spring, 404) supported the establishment of the Thirty. In most of the cities hitherto allied to Athens he set up 'decarchies' of his oligarchical partisans, reinforced by Spartan harmosts. Soon, however, he became estranged from the Spartan government, which reversed his policy by assisting in the restoration of the Athenian democracy and modifying his system of decarchies. Attempts to regain his autocratic position proved unsuccessful: his plot to introduce an elective monarchy at Sparta miscarried, and after he had secured for Agesilaus the kingship and supreme command in the war against Persia he found himself discarded by his protégé. At the outbreak of the Corinthian War he invaded Boeotia from Phocis, but before he could establish contact with Pausanias he was surprised and killed at Haliartus. He made himself unpopular by his arrogance and his unscrupulous pursuit of personal aggrandisement, and this unpopularity is reflected in the unsympathetic attitude of the literary authorities. He was, however, among the ablest of all Spartan leaders.

Xen. *Hell.*, bks. 1–3; Diod. bks. 13–14; Plut. *Lys.*　　H. D. W.

**LYSANIAS** of Cyrene (fl. 2nd c. B.C.), Alexandrian philologist, taught Eratosthenes, wrote Περὶ ἰαμβοποιῶν and Homeric studies (fragments listed by Gudeman, *PW*, s.v.).

**LYSIAS** (c. 459–c. 380 B.C.), son of Cephalus (a Syracusan whom Pericles persuaded to settle in Athens), went, with his brothers Polemarchus and Euthydemus, to Thurii, where they lived for some years. Returning to Athens in 412, they carried on a prosperous business at the Piraeus as manufacturers of shields. The evidence of Plato (*Resp.* i ad init.) makes it clear that they moved in the best intellectual society at Athens. In 404 they were proscribed by the Thirty, partly on the ground of their democratic sympathies, but chiefly because of their wealth; Lysias was arrested, but escaped to Megara; Polemarchus was put to death, and their funds were confiscated. While in exile Lysias still showed himself a true friend of the democracy and on his return in 403 the *ekklesia* conferred on him the rights of citizenship. Owing to some informality this decree was pronounced illegal and Lysias lost his new privilege. Between this time and his death he is said to have composed over two hundred forensic speeches. As a *metoikos* he could not appear in court himself, but he could appeal to a far wider audience by his *Olympiac* speech of 388 B.C., which contained a solemn warning against the dangers of internal discord.

2. WORKS. In addition to the *Olympiacus*, an *Epitaphios*, and a fragment (*Or.* 34) of a deliberative speech, the following are preserved:

(i) *Speeches in public causes*: *Or.* 20, on a charge of subverting the democracy, which, if by Lysias, is his earliest extant work (c. 407 B.C.); 27, 28, and 29, dealing with embezzlement and the betrayal of Greek cities in Asia; 21, a charge of taking bribes; 30, negligence in performing public duties; 22, prosecution of the public corndealers for making excessive profits; 16, 25, 31, cases concerning δοκιμασία; 1, 12, 13, murder-charges, of which 12 (*Against Eratosthenes*) provides first-hand evidence about the reign of terror under the Thirty, and 1 (*On the Murder of Eratosthenes*) throws an interesting light on the domestic life of the middle classes; 3 and 4, charges of malicious wounding; 5 and 7, sacrilege; 14 and 15, charges of (*a*) desertion, (*b*) evasion of military service, against the son of the great Alcibiades; 17, 18, 19, claims on confiscated property; 9, non-payment of a fine; 24 (*For the Cripple*), an excellent speech in defence of a man charged with receiving a state-pension under false pretences.

(ii) *Speeches in private causes*: Or. 32 against Diogiton, a dishonest guardian, is admirable for its character-drawing, its clear exposition of a complicated story, and the dramatic touches which enliven the narrative; 10 is in an action for defamation; in 23 the charge is not stated; 8 is a trivial declamatory exercise; 6 (*Against Andocides*) is probably spurious.

3. Lysias, by his exceptional mastery of idiom, turned the spoken language of everyday life into a literary medium unsurpassed for its simplicity and precision. He possesses a felicity of expression which is based on art skilfully concealed. He avoids rare and poetical words, striking metaphors, and exaggerated phrases, with the result that at times he may seem to lose in force what he gains in smoothness. His blameless style and unimpassioned tones may seem monotonous to some readers who would prefer a diction that rises above the level of conversation; to others his smoothness may seem more telling than the vigour of Antiphon or the solemnity of Demosthenes. Even when his own personal feelings are deeply concerned he is always moderate. The character of the Thirty is brought out by the calm narration of their actions rather than by denunciation. In the structure of sentences he passes without effort from a running style to the use of the period, which he employs with skill and moderation.

4. Lysias did not, any more than other orators, vary his language to suit his characters, but he succeeds, by subtle nuances of thought rather than of language, in suggesting their personality. We cannot fail to sympathize with the young Mantitheus (*Or.* 16)—ambitious and unaffectedly pleased with himself, he seems to have some ground for his harmless conceit; the 'Cripple' (*Or.* 24) strikes us as a plausible rogue. In the construction of his speeches Lysias is no less simple than in his language: they regularly consist of preface, narrative, proof, and epilogue—a form approved by Isocrates, but seldom adopted with such regularity as by Lysias. It is noted, as a proof of his versatility and good taste, that he never used the same exordium twice, nor borrowed from current collections of Prefaces (*see* PROOEMIUM).

TEXTS. O.C.T. (Hude, 1912); Teubner (Thalheim; ed. maior 1913; ed. minor 1928); with transl., Gernet and Bizos (Budé); Lamb (Loeb).
COMMENTARY. E. S. Shuckburgh, *Select Orations* (1882).
INDEX. D. H. Holmes (1895).
GENERAL. K. J. Dover, *Lysias and the Corpus Lysiacum* (1968). *See also* s.v. ATTIC ORATORS.　　　　J. F. D.

**LYSIMACHUS** (c. 360–281 B.C.), companion and 'successor' of Alexander. His father was probably a Thessalian Greek who migrated to Macedonia. He was one of Alexander's bodyguards, and in one of Alexander's lion-hunts he killed a beast at close quarters, though wounded himself. (This feat gave rise to the absurd story that Alexander had caged him with a lion.) After Alexander's death he received a province consisting of Thrace and the north-west of Asia Minor. In 315 he joined the coalition of Cassander and Ptolemy against Antigonus, but was mainly occupied with the consolidation of his power in Thrace, where he founded a new capital at

Lysimacheia (on the neck of the Thracian Chersonese). In 306 he assumed the royal title. Four years later he drew Antigonus into Asia Minor and held him on successive prepared lines until Seleucus, coming from the eastern provinces, could join hands with him. In 301 he helped Seleucus to defeat Antigonus at Ipsus, and received northern and central Asia Minor as his share of the spoil. Crossing the Danube in 292, he was captured by a Thracian chief, but obtained his speedy release. In 285 he won Macedonia and Thessaly from Demetrius and thus became the strongest of the 'successors' in manpower. But he was disliked for his high-handed administration and oppressive taxation, and was distracted by family quarrels. In 281 he was attacked by his former ally Seleucus and completely defeated in a battle at Corupedium (near Magnesia ad Sipylum), where he fell fighting. His kingdom was broken up after his death.

G. B. Possenti, *Il re Lisimaco di Tracia* (1901); Berve, *Alexanderreich*, no. 480; G. Saitta, Κόκαλος 1955, 62 ff.　　　M. C.

**LYSIPPUS** (1), poet of Old Comedy. Won prizes in 435 and 410–409 B.C. (*IG* xiv. 1097). His Βάκχαι contained an attack on the seer Lampon (fr. 6).
*FCG* ii. 744 ff.; *CAF* i. 700–3.

**LYSIPPUS** (2), sculptor, of Sicyon; Pliny places his *floruit* in 328 B.C. (because of Alexander). Athenaeus connects him with the founding of Cassandreia (316). Selected works:

*Dated*: (1) Troïlus, Olympic victor, 372. (2) Coridas, Pythian victor, probably in 342. (3) Statues of Alexander, from about 340. Alexander allowed Lysippus alone to figure him because he preserved his lion-like and manly look as well as the turn of his neck and the softness of his eyes. Herm of Alexander in the Louvre has ancient inscription attributing it to Lysippus (Winter, *KB* 334. 1–2); bronze statuette in the Louvre (Winter, *KB* 334. 3) and head in the British Museum are near in style. Bronze statuette in Grado best fits Plutarch's description of Alexander with spear. (4) Agias of Pharsalus, epigram and signature preserved. The epigram without signature recurs under the Agias (Winter, *KB* 331. 3) of a group erected at Delphi by Daochus, tetrarch of Thessaly, 338–334; this Agias is probably a contemporary marble copy of the Pharsalus Agias. (5) Equestrian group, commissioned by Alexander after Granicus, 334. (6) Socrates, probably erected by Lycurgus, 338–326. Has been reconstructed by combining the Louvre bust (Winter, *KB* 317. 1) with seated body in Copenhagen. (7) Signatures from Corinth and Thermon, about 330. (8) Chilon, who fell at Lamia, after 322. (9) (with Leochares, q.v.) Alexander's lion hunt, erected by Craterus' son after his death in 321. Reflected in relief in the Louvre (Winter, *KB* 334. 8). (10) Seleucus, probably after 312. (11) Signature from Megara, about 300. Probably not from base of Zeus and Muses.

*Undated*: (12) Colossal bronze Zeus at Tarentum. (13) Chariot of the Sun for Rhodes. (14) Eros at Thespiae. Lysippan Eros survives in copies (Winter, *KB* 332. 2). (15) Satyr in Athens. Borghese satyr may be copy (Winter, *KB* 343. 1). (16) Kairos in Sicyon. Reproduced on reliefs and gems. (17) Colossal bronze seated Heracles at Tarentum, later in Rome and Constantinople. Described by Nicetas. (18) Heracles Epitrapezius. Statuette derived from this described by Statius (*Silv.* 4. 6) and Martial (9. 44). Copies are preserved. (19) Heracles at Sicyon. Original of Farnese Heracles by Glycon (q.v. 2) (Winter, *KB* 333. 4). (20) Polydamas, Olympic victor. Base has been discovered. (21) Apoxyomenos. Copy in the Vatican (Winter, *KB* 331. 1–2).
*Attributed*: from likeness to 18, 22, seated Hermes (Winter, *KB* 333. 1); from likeness to 19, 23, Satyr with

infant Dionysus in the Louvre; from likeness to 21, 24, athlete tying sandal (Winter, *KB* 332. 1).

Lysippus was famed for the new and slender proportions of his figures (although he called the Polyclitan Doryphorus his master), his representation of momentary appearance, the precision of his detail. The tridimensionalism of the Apoxyomenos is in advance of any earlier statue. His influence lasted into the Hellenistic period through his pupils, e.g. Eutychides (q.v.).

Overbeck, 903, 954, 1443–1516; F. P. Johnson, *Lysippus* (1927); F. Poulsen, *Delphi* (1920), 265; *Iconographic Studies* (1931), 31; F. von Lorentz, *Röm. Mitt.* 1935, 333; Lippold, *Griech. Plastik*, 276 ff.; E. Sjöqvist, *Opuscula Atheniensia* i (1953), 87 ff.; J. Marcadé, *Rev. Ét. Anc.* 1963, 351.                                T. B. L. W.

**LYSIS** (1) of Tarentum, a Pythagorean who migrated to Achaea and then to Thebes and became the teacher of Epaminondas. It is uncertain whether he wrote anything.

Testimonia in Diels, *Vorsokr.*⁵ i. 420–1. PW xiv. 64.

**LYSIS** (2) (fl. *c.* 300 B.C.), originator of λυσιῳδία, and probably from Magnesia in Ionia, like his predecessor Simus, inventor of σιμῳδία. *See* MAGODIA.

**LYSISTRATUS**, Greek sculptor, brother of Lysippus (q.v. 2), active in the second half of the fourth century B.C. A native of Sicyon (Pliny 35. 153). According to Pliny (ibid.), 'he was the first person who modelled a likeness

in plaster of a human being from a living face, and established the method of pouring wax into this plaster mould and then making final corrections in the wax cast' (transl. H. Rackham); and that 'he introduced the practice of making exact likenesses (*similitudines*) whereas before him the object was to make a portrait as beautiful as possible'. From this passage one can deduce that Lysistratus was especially interested in realistic portraiture, and for this end took impressions from living models—a perfectly possible proceeding. Pliny furthermore states that Lysistratus 'invented the taking of casts from statues (*de signis effigies exprimere invenit*), a method which advanced to such an extent that no figures or statues were made without a clay model' (*crevitque res in tantum ut nulla signa statuaeve sine argilla fierent*). This interesting passage, if credible, suggests that the making of casts from statues was invented as early as the late fourth century B.C. Plutarch's anecdote (*De Soll. An.* 984 b) in which he refers to 'taking an impression of' (ἀπομάξασθαι) a statue of Kore for Ptolemy I Soter would supply another instance of the 'casting' of a statue in the late fourth century B.C.; but its credibility has been doubted (cf. A. D. Nock, *Conversion* (1933), 50 ff. with notes).

Two signatures of *c.* 300 B.C. with the name Lysistratus have been found in Thebes and Tanagra (*IG* vii. 553, 2463; there read Histiaios), and may refer to the same sculptor, though the ethnic there given is in one case Athens, in the other Thebes.                       G. M. A. R.

# M

**MACAR**, sometimes called Macareus (q.v.), in mythology a Lesbian king (*Il.* 24. 544), but usually a son of Helios and so a Rhodian (schol. Pind. *Ol.* 7. 135); for various accounts of his parentage and adventures, see Schirmer in Roscher's *Lexikon*, s.v. His name, very strange for a mortal because a stock divine epithet, has been interpreted as corrupted from Melqart. H. J. R.

**MACAREUS**, when not identical with Macar (q.v.), is usually the name of a son of Aeolus (q.v. 2, for his incestuous love of his sister Canace). Several minor figures have the same name, e.g. a son of Lycaon (q.v.; Apollod. 3. 97); a Lapith (Ov. *Met.* 12. 447).  H. J. R.

**MACEDONIA.** By its geographical position Macedonia forms the connecting link between the Balkans and the Greek peninsula. Three important routes converge on the Macedonian plain: from the Danube via the Morava and Vardar (Axius) valleys, from the Adriatic via Lake Ochrida, and from Thrace via Mygdonia. In climate Macedonia is intermediate between Europe and the Mediterranean. Contact with the south is made by sea or by the narrow vale of Tempe into Thessaly. Macedonia proper consisted of the coastal plain of the Thermaic Gulf, which has been formed by the rivers Haliacmon, Lydias, and Axius; these rivers, draining the wide plateaux of Upper Macedonia, cut the mountain-ring of the Macedonian plain at Beroea, Edessa, and the defile of Demir Kapu respectively. Of the cantons of Upper Macedonia Orestis occupied the upper and Elimiotis the middle Haliacmon valley, Lyncus the upper valley of the Erigon (tributary of the Axius), Paeonia the upper valley of the Axius, and Eordaea the basin of Lake Ostrovo west of Edessa. The Macedonian plain comprised Bottiaea between the lower Haliacmon

and Axius, Pieria south of the Haliacmon mouth, Almopia in the upper Lydias valley, Mygdonia in the Lake Bolbe basin leading towards the Strymon valley, Krestonia and Anthemus north and south respectively of Mygdonia. Upper Macedonia is girt by high mountain-ranges traversed mainly by the three important routes mentioned above; when united, it had strong natural defences. The Macedonian plain is vulnerable from the sea and from Mygdonia, but the defiles leading into Upper Macedonia are easily defensible. The natural products were horses, cattle, sheep, crops, wine, fruit, timber, and silver (at Mt. Dysoros between Krestonia and the Strymon valley), the last two being exported in antiquity.

Prehistoric Macedonia, occupied continuously from early neolithic times, possessed a uniform culture in the Bronze Age, little influenced by Mycenae, and was invaded *c.* 1150 B.C. by a northern people, who may also have provoked the Dorian invasion. Of the Dorian peoples some known as Macedni (Hdt. 1. 56) came from south-west Macedonia; a remnant of these perhaps formed the nucleus of the classical Macedonians. In the centuries after the Dorian invasion many new peoples came into Macedonia; one of them, perhaps deriving from Illyria, left a remarkable burial ground with tumuli at Vergina in the middle Haliacmon valley ("Εργον 1958, 81 ff., and following vols., and Ἀρχ. Δελτ. 1961/2, 1. 218 ff.). The tradition of the royal house of Macedon, the Argeadae (Hdt. 8. 137 f.; Thuc. 2. 99 f.), suggests that from the upper Haliacmon valley they conquered Eordaea, occupied Aegae, and captured the Macedonian plain *c.* 640 under Perdiccas I, the first in the Macedonian list of kings. While these Macedonians were probably of Dorian blood, the tribes of Upper Macedonia appear to have been composed of Greek, Illyrian, and Thracian elements.

Until the reign of Philip II Macedonia struggled with the semi-independent principalities of Upper Macedonia, the Illyrians, the Odrysian kingdom in Thrace, the Greek States in Chalcidice, and Persia, Athens, and Sparta. Hellenization began with Alexander I (q.v.), who claimed descent from Argos and issued State coinage, and urbanization followed in the fourth century B.C.

When Philip II incorporated Upper Macedonia and annexed the Strymon valley and Chalcidice, he created a State superior in military and economic strength to any Greek city-state; the military genius of Philip and Alexander raised Macedonia to a world power, but imposed a severe strain upon the nation, which was accentuated by the Wars of the Successors, and resulted in its collapse before the expanding power of Rome (167 B.C.). Disintegrated into four republics by Rome, Macedonia was annexed as a province in 146, and its history merged with that of the Roman Empire.

During its acme, Macedonia, a national territorial State with an enlightened monarchy, was the intermediary between Greek and Hellenistic culture, being herself a fusion of Greek and barbarian elements and transmitting a fused culture which long survived under the Roman Empire.

W. A. Heurtley, *Prehistoric Macedonia* (1939); R. J. Rodden, in *Balkan Studies* 1964, 109 ff.; S. Casson, *Macedonia Thrace and Illyria* (1926); F. Geyer, 'Makedonien bis zur Thronbesteigung Philipps II.' (*Historische Zeitschrift*, Beiheft 19, 1930); P. Cloché, *Histoire de la Macédoine jusqu'à l'avènement d'Alexandre le Grand* (1960). N. G. L. H.

**MACEDONIAN CULTS.** There are two distinct elements in the religion of early Macedonia. The first is the pre-existing cults of the regions successively conquered by the Argead kings; the second is the original worship of the dominant Μακεδόνες.

(1) Cults, largely Thracian, indigenous to the regions occupied by the Argead Macedonians were received and preserved. Such was the βέδυ, the water-air spirit which gave its name to Edessa, an old town famous for its springs situated near Aegae, the earliest residence of the Macedonian kings. Sileni (σαυάδαι) and Bacchae (Κλώδωνες and Μιμαλλόνες) illustrate the prevalence of Dionysus-Sabazius worship (*see* SABAZIUS). Deities such as Ζειρήνη (equated with Aphrodite) and Artemis Γαζωρία, both stated to be Macedonian, were in fact Thracian and took their names from localities east of the Strymon river first conquered by Philip II. In western Macedonia Illyrian elements appear.

(2) The religion of the Μακεδόνες themselves was Hellenic, as is proven by the names of the Macedonian months. Cults of most of the chief Greek deities are sufficiently attested for the early period. To Zeus, father of Μακεδών, the eponymous ancestor of the folk (Hesiod fr. 5 Rzach; *FGrH* nos. 135–6, fr. 13), and to Heracles the progenitor ('Η. προπάτωρ) of the Argead clan as also of the later Antigonid dynasty the Macedonians were particularly devoted. Notable are the cults of Zeus 'Εταιρίδης, who presided over the relationship of the Argead kings with their aristocratic Companions (ἑταῖροι) and whose epithet gave its name to the festival of the *Hetairideia*, and Heracles Κυναγίδας, the patron of hunting, a sport to which the Macedonians were passionately attached, who presided over the Royal Huntsmen (βασιλικοὶ κυνηγοί) and the game preserves of the kings. Established custom (νόμος) required the king personally to conduct innumerable rites and sacrifices. Among these two of the most important were the formal purification of the army performed each year at the festival of the *Xandica* held in the early spring at the beginning of the campaigning season (Polyb. 23. 10. 17; Livy 40. 6. 1–5), though this purification could be performed at other times as well (Curt. 10. 9. 11–12), and

the most solemn responsibility of the kings themselves to oversee the ceremonial interment of the Macedonian combat dead (Curt. 5. 4. 3; Livy 31. 34. 1–2).

The Hellenistic and Roman imperial periods show few developments peculiar to Macedonia. By the end of the third century B.C. the Egyptian gods (q.v.) had been widely received, and the cult of the Syrian Goddess is found at Beroea. The documents do not as yet attest the worship of Zeus "Υψιστος before the second century, but the cult may well be earlier and at any rate achieved real popularity. In the Roman period, above all at Thessalonica, a most successful cult was that of the Dioscuri-Cabiri derived from Samothrace (*see* CABIRI). Ma of Cappadocia is found at Edessa in the third century A.D. And from the late Hellenistic period down to the triumph of Christianity the Thracian Rider ("Ηρων or "Ηρως) was the object of widespread devotion, particularly in connexion with the burial of the dead.

W. Baege, *De Macedonum sacris* (1913); C. Edson, *Harv. Stud.* 1934, 226 ff., and 1940, 125 f.; *Harv. Theol. Rev.* 1948, 153 ff.; J. N. Kalléris, *Les anciens Macédoniens* i (1954); O. Hoffmann, *Die Makedonen, ihre Sprache und ihr Volkstum* (1906), 92 ff.; A. D. Nock, *Harv. Theol. Rev.* 1936, 60 ff. C. F. E.

**MACER** (1), GAIUS LICINIUS (*PW* 112), the Roman annalist, tribune in 73 B.C., when he agitated for popular rights (cf. Sallust, *Hist.* 3. 48), praetor in 68, was convicted of extortion in 66 and committed suicide. His history of Rome, in at least sixteen books, began with the origins; Pyrrhus appeared in book 2; its closing point is unknown. It reflected democratic and family bias (Livy 7. 9. 5) and was rhetorically composed. At the same time, it rationalized legends and quoted original authorities, particularly the *libri lintei* (Livy 4. 7. 12; 4. 20. 8; 4. 23. 2), in order to reinterpret the old political institutions. Livy and Dionysius used his work.

Peter, *HRRel.* i². cccl, 298; Beloch, *Röm. Gesch.* i, 105; Ogilvie, *Comm. Livy 1–5*, 7 ff. A. H. McD.

**MACER** (2), AEMILIUS, of Verona, was an Augustan poet, older than Ovid (*Tr.* 4. 10. 43–4). A few lines of his didactic poems *Ornithogonia*, *Theriaca*, and *De Herbis* remain (Morel, *FPL*). Ovid mentions him first amongst recent 'bards' (*Tr.* 4. 10. 41–56); and Quintilian (10. 1. 56, 87; 12. 11. 27) couples his name with that of Virgil and Lucretius. R. M.

**MACHAON** (Μαχάων) and **PODALIRIUS** (Ποδαλείριος), sons of Asclepius (q.v.), *Iliad* 2. 731–2, where they are described as physicians, but also as leaders of the contingent from Tricca, Ithome, and Oechalia. Whatever may be the character of their father, their names have no hieratic meaning; Machaon is 'Warrior', Podalirius apparently 'Lily-foot'. Machaon heals Menelaus (4. 200 ff.), but is also active as a fighter and is wounded by Paris (11. 505 ff.); Podalirius is too busy in the battle to tend Eurypylus (11. 836). Their further adventures consist mostly of healing (Machaon, or both, cure Philoctetes (q.v.), Soph. *Phil.* 1333, where see Jebb) and fighting (Machaon killed by Eurypylus, *Little Iliad*, fr. 7 Allen; Podalirius survives the war and settles in one of several places, see Türk in Roscher's *Lexikon* iii. 2588–9). They had a cult, both separately (Machaon at Gerenia, Paus. 3. 26. 9; Podalirius at Drion in Daunia, Strabo 6. 3. 9, 284) and together, generally with their father (references in Farnell, *Hero-Cults*, 420). There seems no reason for supposing them originally gods.

H. J. R.

**MACHON** (Μάχων), New Comedy poet and raconteur, born at Corinth or Sicyon and resident in Alexandria, where he staged his comedies about the middle of the third century B.C. From his epitaph by Dioscorides (Ath. 6. 241 f, *Anth. Pal.* 7. 708)—'O city of Cecrops, sometimes on the banks of the Nile too the pungent thyme has grown in the garden of the Muses'—it has been inferred that he revived the keen invective of Old Comedy in Alexandria (cf. fr. xxi Gow), but the two extant comic fragments belong to the type of Middle or New Comedy, which was not devoid of δριμύτης (pungency).

In another genre Machon composed a book of anecdotes (Χρεῖαι: *see* CHREIA) in iambic verse of the sayings and doings of notorious Athenian courtesans, parasites, etc. (462 verses, mainly scurrilous, preserved by Athenaeus, book 13).

Edited with introduction and commentary by A. S. F. Gow (Cambridge Classical Texts and Commentaries, 1, 1965). W. G. A.

**MACRIANUS,** TITUS FULVIUS (*PW* 82) JUNIUS, Emperor A.D. 260–1, son of (Fulvius) Macrianus, a staff officer of Valerian. On the latter's capture by the Persians, the Elder Macrianus refused the imperial title on account of his age, but allowed the elevation of his two sons, Macrianus and Quietus. The former marched west with his father against Gallienus, but both were killed in battle in Thrace. Quietus was besieged and killed at Emesa by Odaenathus of Palmyra. B. H. W.

**MACRINUS,** MARCUS OPELLIUS (*PW* 2), a native of Africa, became praetorian prefect under Caracalla and from motives of personal safety contrived his assassination (A.D. 217). Saluted Augustus by his troops, he was the first Roman Emperor who was not a senator. He ended Caracalla's Parthian war on somewhat inglorious terms. His subsequent retrenchments in pay and the retention of the European legions in Syria made the army regret the death of Caracalla. Through the agency of Julia (q.v. 7) Maesa the story was put about that her grandson Bassianus was Caracalla's natural son. The soldiers of Legio III Gallica saluted him Emperor (218), and Macrinus was routed in a battle near Antioch and subsequently captured and put to death (*see* ELAGABALUS 2).

Herodian 4. 14–5. 4; Dio Cassius bk. 78; S.H.A. *B.M. Coins, Rom. Emp.* v. ccxiii, 494 ff. H. M. D. P.

**MACRO,** Q. NAEVIUS CORDUS SUTORIUS (*PW* 21), came from Alba Fucens and, as Prefect of the Vigiles, was in A.D. 31 Tiberius' agent in the overthrow of Sejanus (q.v.), whom he succeeded as sole commander of the Praetorian Guard. Predominating in Roman politics during the remainder of Tiberius' principate and influential in securing Gaius' accession, he was appointed Prefect of Egypt but then—leaving money for an amphitheatre to his native city—forced, with his wife Ennia, to commit suicide. Much of this knowledge (including his correct name) we owe to an inscription (*Ann. Épigr.* 1957, 250). J. P. B.

**MACROBIUS** (*PW* 7), AMBROSIUS THEODOSIUS, 'uir clarissimus et illustris' (so the MSS. give his rank), has variously been identified with Macrobii named in the Codex Theodosianus (16. 10. 15; 8. 5. 61; 11. 28. 6; 6. 8. 1) as *vicarius Hispaniarum* (399), or as *proconsul Africae* (410), or as *praepositus sacri cubiculi* (422). He was foreign to Italy (*Sat.* i. praef. 11, 12, where he admits that his style is deficient in *nativa Romani oris elegantia*), and may have been African; his works show no trace of Christianity.

WRITINGS. (1) *De differentiis et societatibus Graeci Latinique uerbi*: fragments in Keil, *GL* v. 599 ff. (excerpts made by Iohannes Scottus, 9th c.; cf. Manitius, *Gesch. d. lat. Lit. des Mittelalters* i. 331, 338).

(2) *Commentarii in Somnium Scipionis*, a Neoplatonist exposition of Cicero's *Somnium*, the text of which appears

with the *Commentarii* in some MSS.: thus, through Macrobius in the first instance, the 'Dream' was known to the Middle Ages when other parts now extant of Cicero's *De republica* were still undiscovered. In all probability the *Commentarii* largely depend on Porphyry's commentary on Plato's *Timaeus*, either directly or through a Latin intermediary; they exercised much influence on medieval philosophic writings.

(3) *Saturnalia*, an academic symposium in seven books, in form and manner recalling Athenaeus and Gellius (who is much drawn upon, though nowhere named); among the imaginary speakers in the pretended 'dialogue' are Avienus, Symmachus, and the young Servius. Macrobius compiled it as a *scientiae supellex*, a *noscendorum congeries* (i. praef. 2, 4) for his son's education as a gentleman, an ancient 'Sandford and Merton': the topics are arranged methodically (contrast Gellius), and are fascinatingly rich in philological, historical, antiquarian, and scientific lore, throwing a clear light on the interests and taste of the period. But this miscellany of discussions (on, e.g., fishes, indigestion, dancing, drunkenness) is a mere framework: the central theme (books 3–6) is Virgilian criticism. Mainly by means of parallels, relentlessly adduced, from Homer, Ennius, Lucilius, Lucretius, and many others, the critics steadily develop a build-up of Virgil as the Complete Rhetorician, the omniscient, infallible, unique scholar-poet; opposition is provided by the villainous stooge Euangelus, whose views are duly demolished. The whole section is of great importance, both for the history of early Virgilian scholarship and for the medieval conception of Virgil, which it significantly foreshadows.

TEXT. J. Willis (Teubner, 1963), with very full bibliography. T. R. Glover, *Life and Letters in the Fourth Century* (1901), ch. 8; P. M. Schedler, *Die Philosophie des Macrobius* (1916); T. Whittaker, *Macrobius, or philosophy, science and letters in the year 400* (1923); K. Mras, *Macrobius' Kommentar zu Ciceros Somnium* (*Sitz. d. preuß. Akad. d. Wiss.*, Phil.-Hist. Kl. vi, 1933); D. Comparetti, *Virgilio nel Medio Evo* (rev. G. Pasquali [1937]), i. 77 ff. (tr. E. F. M. Benecke, 63 ff.); P. Courcelle, *Les Lettres grecques en occident de Macrobe à Cassiodore²* (1948); W. H. Stahl, *Macrobius' Commentary on the Dream of Scipio* (U.S.A. 1952); A. Cameron, 'The Date and Identity of Macrobius', *JRS* 1966, 25 ff.; Teuffel–Schwabe, *Gesch. d. römisch. Lit.⁶* (1913–20) iii. 383 ff.; Schanz–Hosius IV. ii. 189 ff.

*Macrobius and Servius.* Ribbeck's Virgil, *Prolegomena* (1866), 104 ff.; E. Thomas, *Essai sur Servius* (1880), 134 ff.; Thilo–Hagen, *Servius* i, praef. xxii ff. (1881); H. Nettleship, in Conington–Nettleship's Virgil, i⁵ (rev. Haverfield, 1898), xxix ff., xcv ff.; Teuffel–Schwabe, loc. cit. 304; Schanz–Hosius, loc. cit. 195. R. G. A.

**MADAUROS** (modern *Mdaourouch*) in Numidia was ruled successively by Syphax and Masinissa (qq.v.). It was occupied by the Romans to dominate the powerful Musulamii. Under the Flavians its Berber-Phoenician population was supplemented by time-expired legionaries, and it received colonial rank. It was noted for its olives and its schools. Apuleius was born at Madauros; Augustine received part of his education there, and paganism flourished till late times. Substantial remains of Byzantine fortifications survive and an exceptional number of important inscriptions have been found.

S. Gsell and C.-A. Joly, *Khamissa, Mdaourouch, Announa* (1914–22). W. N. W.; B. H. W.

**MAEANDER** (Μαίανδρος), a river which rises in several sources, including the Marsyas, in and near Celaenae-Apamea in Phrygia, and flows through the Peltene plain to engage itself first in a narrow valley and then in a canyon 1,500 feet deep, sunk in the western flank of the Anatolian plateau, whence it emerges to join the Lycus near Colossae, Laodicea, Hierapolis, and Tripolis. Thence to the Sinus Latmius it flows through a flat-bottomed, fertile valley, here dividing Lydia from Caria, and passing among other cities Tralles and Magnesia ad Maeandrum. In this part of its course it winds much, and the Greeks described it as σκολιός and used its name to describe a winding pattern. Flowing past Priene in antiquity, the river eventually made a bar across the mouth of the Latmic Gulf, so that the harbours of Miletus and the island of Lade (scene of the naval battle of 494 B.C.) are now landlocked. W. M. C.; J. M. C.

**MAECENAS,** GAIUS, probably from Arretium (q.v.), a scion of the ancient Etruscan aristocracy and a Roman knight, was the trusted friend, counsellor, and diplomatic agent of Octavian (Augustus). He accompanied him on the campaign of Philippi, negotiated his marriage with Scribonia (q.v.), represented him in the discussions which led to the pact of Brundisium (40 B.C.), undertook a diplomatic mission to Antony (38), and in 37 helped to negotiate the pact of Tarentum (*see* NERVA 2). His luxurious habits and apparent indolence concealed a capacity for vigilance and firmness, and though he never held public office he was more than once entrusted by Octavian with the management of affairs in Rome and Italy when he was absent abroad—alone (36–33) and in company with Agrippa (31–29); in 30 he detected the conspiracy of Lepidus (q.v. 4). Of great importance to the Augustan Principate was his influence as a patron of letters; in addition to Virgil, Horace, and Propertius his circle of poets included his freedman C. Melissus (q.v. 2), L. Varius (q.v. 2) Rufus, and Domitius (q.v. 7) Marsus. He himself wrote prose works of uncertain scope (e.g. *Prometheus, Symposium, De Cultu Suo*, and *In Octaviam*; *Dialogi* was perhaps a generic title) and verses. His affected style was much criticized. Few fragments survive. He married Terentia, sister of Varro (q.v. 4) Murena. She frequently quarrelled with him and was unfaithful to him with Augustus, who, possibly because of this, ceased to make use of his services during his last years. That there was a serious rift is not clear; at all events when Maecenas died, in 8 B.C., he left all his extensive property to the Emperor, including a magnificent house and gardens on the Esquiline. Maecenas was his *nomen*; 'Cilnius' (Tac. *Ann.* 6. 11) may have been his mother's.

Syme, *Rom. Rev.*, see index; A. Fougnies, *Mécène* (1947); A. Dalzell, *Phoenix* 1956, 151 ff.; K. J. Reckford, *TAPA* 1959, 195 ff.; Schanz–Hosius ii. 17 ff., 116 f.; R. Avallone, *Mecenate. I Frammenti* (1945). G. W. R.; T. J. C.

**MAECIANUS,** LUCIUS VOLUSIUS (*PW* 7), a Roman jurist of the second century A.D. His official career is fully known from two inscriptions discovered in 1930 at Ostia (*CIL* xiv. 5347–8). Some of his official posts (*procurator bibliothecarum, praefectus vehiculorum, adiutor operum publicorum, praefectus fabrum*) are not known to have been held by any previous jurist. He was also *praefectus annonae, a libellis et censibus* under Antoninus Pius, and *praefectus Aegypti* about 161. He instructed Marcus Aurelius when he was heir to the throne, and was a member of the imperial *consilia* under Antoninus Pius and the *divi fratres*. From the *Digest* we know the following works of Maecianus: a voluminous treatise on *fideicommissa* (16 books), *De iudiciis publicis* (14 books), and a monograph written in Greek on the *Lex Rhodia*. A booklet entitled *Assis distributio* and dedicated to Marcus Aurelius is preserved almost complete; it contains the terms used to denote fractions, particularly with reference to inheritance.

BEST EDITION OF *Assis distributio*, E. Seckel and B. Kübler, in Huschke, *Jurispr. anteiust.* i⁶ (1908). A. B.

**MAELIUS** (*PW* 2), SPURIUS, a rich plebeian, was alleged to have relieved a food shortage and courted popularity by distributing corn at his own expense (440–39 B.C.); suspected of aiming at a tyranny he was killed (? by C. Servilius Ahala, q.v.). Many modern critics have questioned his historicity and undoubtedly many features are late Republican inventions, but the story was told by

Cincius (q.v.) Alimentus and is thus of the pre-Gracchan period when there was less reason to invent it, while the circumstances of the corn-shortage cannot easily be rejected (*see* MINUCIUS 1).

Cf. Ogilvie, *Comm. Livy 1–5*, 550 ff. H. H. S.

**MAENADS,** also **Bacchae** or **Thyiades,** women inspired to ecstatic frenzy by Dionysus. Wearing fawn or panther skins and wreaths of ivy, oak, or fir they carry snakes or bunches of grapes, wave wands or torches and celebrate the power of Dionysus in song, music, and dance. They roam through mountains and woods, oblivious of all human concerns, conventions, and fears. Dionysus inspires them with strength so that they can uproot trees and kill strong animals. They also hunt animals and devour their raw flesh, a characteristic feature of the Dionysiac *omophagia* (*see* DIONYSUS).

In mythology Maenads accompany Dionysus in his triumphal journey from Lydia or Phrygia to Thrace and Greece. The women of Thebes who followed Dionysus also became Maenads (Eur. *Bacch.* 915, 1021). They destroy his enemies Pentheus (ibid. 1114) and Orpheus (Ov. *Met.* 11. 22; M. P. Nilsson, *Harv. Theol. Rev.* 1935, 190). Maenads form a contingent in the army of Dionysus during his campaign in India. But they are also associated with the peaceful aspect of Dionysus as inventor of wine and are frequently shown gathering grapes or preparing wine.

In literature Aeschylus (q.v.) had given a powerful picture of Maenads in his lost plays *Edonoi, Bassarides, Xantriai,* and *Pentheus,* but the classic description of Dionysiac ecstasy of Maenads was drawn by Euripides in the *Bacchae.* This was the model of later accounts by Lycophron, Accius, Pacuvius, Ps.-Theocritus (26), Ovid (*Met.* 3. 511), and Nonnus.

From the middle of the sixth century B.C. onwards Maenads are distinguished in art from other Dionysiac female figures. They wear the long χιτών, rarely the short, and are seldom naked. Greek vase-painters delight in depicting their revelries in the *thiasos* or *komos* (T. B. L. Webster, *Greek Theatre Production,* 1956). Their amorous meeting with satyrs and sileni (H. Jeanmaire, *Mélanges Picard,* 1949), their nocturnal dances, their sacrifices to Dionysus, and their assaults on Pentheus and Orpheus. In classical and later art they are sometimes shown in more subdued mood with Aphrodite and her circle, with Eirene, and even with Muses. Two fine types of statues show dancing Maenads. The first (Dresden) is commonly assigned to Scopas, the other is a Hellenistic creation. The Maenads of tragedy and myth are an idealized reflection of human Bacchantes modelled on the behaviour of women in the orgiastic worship of Dionysus in Thrace. More than any other figure of the Dionysiac worship they represent the complete liberation from conventions of daily life, the awakening of primeval instincts, and the union with nature achieved in the cult of Dionysus.

Ps.-Theoc. 26; Catull. 63. 24; Verg. *Aen.* 7. 373; Ov. *Met.* 3. 511, 11. 1; Nonnus 45. 273; Ps.-Eratosth. 24, ed. Robert; E. R. Dodds, *Harv. Theol. Rev.* 1940; T. B. L. Webster, *Greek Art and Literature 700–530 B.C.* (1959); E. R. Dodds, *The Bacchae of Euripides*² (1960); M. W. Edwards, *JHS* 1960; R. Goodchild, *Lib. Ant.* i (1964), 121. G. M. A. H.; J. R. T. P.

**MAENIUS** (*PW* 9), GAIUS, the only Maenius to reach the consulship. As consul (338 B.C.) he conquered the Latins and the fleet of Volscian Antium (q.v.); his statue was erected in the Forum, and the captured ships' beaks (*rostra*) adorned the speaker's platform (henceforth called rostra) (Livy 8. 13 f.). The *columna Maenia* in the forum, however, probably did not celebrate him; apparently it was a column of the Basilica Porcia supporting a projecting balcony (*maenianum*) erected by a descendant (M. Lehmann-Hartleben, *AJPhil.* 1938, 290). Later Maenius was censor (318) and the first certainly attested plebeian dictator (314). An earlier dictatorship (320: *Fasti Cap.*) is apocryphal. E. T. S.

**MAEOTIS** was the ancient name for the *Sea of Azov*. Greek colonists from Miletus and other Ionian towns were attracted by the fisheries at its mouth (the 'Cimmerian Bosporus'), and here founded Panticapaeum (q.v.). They subsequently founded a city named Tanais (q.v.) at the upper end of the sea, but they do not appear to have explored its interior systematically. Greek geographers (Herodotus, Scylax, Strabo, Ptolemy) greatly exaggerated its size and were very hazy about the river Tanaïs (q.v.). But they noted the shallowness of the sea and prophesied that it would eventually be silted up. M. C.

**M(A)EVIUS** belonged to a group of poetasters who criticized Horace and Virgil and incurred their contempt and enmity (*Ecl.* 3. 90). Horace wrote the tenth Epode against him.

E. Fraenkel, *Horace* (1957), 24 ff.

**MAGIC** is a complex of practices through which man exercises power on the world around him by irrational means. It is based upon a mental attitude that is called 'primitive' in this sense that it knows no clear-cut distinction between the natural and the supernatural; but the word 'primitive' should not be taken in a chronological sense, as the magical attitude forms a substratum to all human thought and experience. In it, man does not see the world as an object, but he participates in it as it does in him; he transfers the outward world into himself and dominates it from within. In this aspect of participation magic is a religious phenomenon. On the other hand, it is often opposed to what is usually called a religious attitude, as the latter does not use prayers of constraint, but in devotion, submission, and hope. Magic uses the word of power (spells, charms, curses, etc.) and the act of power (imitative rites, *infra* under 8), cf. the *legomena* and *dromena* at Eleusis (*see* MYSTERIES).

2. As the intellectual adventure of Greek civilization is precisely the discovery of the world as an object of rational contemplation, the magical elements were more and more suppressed. Nevertheless traces remain at all levels. This applies equally to 'black' (i.e. harmful) and to 'white' (i.e. harmless or beneficial) magic. In a time when secularization prevailed in the higher social levels, the fourth century B.C., there was a conspicuous outburst in the lower (E. R. Dodds, *The Greeks and the Irrational* (1951), ch. 6).

3. Our earliest examples of Greek magic come from Homer, but we may presume that the Greek invaders a long time before had taken over much pre-Greek magic (connected, e.g., with agriculture, navigation, and useful arts). An incantation can stop the flow of blood from the wounded Odysseus (*Od.* 19. 457). Circe effects the most wonderful transformations by means of potions, salves, and a magic wand (which we also find in the hands of Hermes and Athena); she is also able to teach Odysseus how to summon the ghosts from the nether world. In the Homeric epics the great Olympian gods generally do not practise any witchcraft. Hermes, however, still preserves traits which remind us of the old magician; he presents the 'moly' to Odysseus, who by this means is able to outdo Circe. In Hesiod's *Opera et Dies* we get glimpses of agricultural and everyday usages, and his *Theogony* contains a unique glorification of Hecate (q.v.), elsewhere the protectress of all witches, as the greatest and most beneficent of all deities.

4. Greek myth affords still more material. We hear of the Telchines (q.v.; perhaps pre-Greek), skilful but malignant smiths, hostile to gods and fearful to men, well versed in magic; cf. the Curetes (q.v.) and Dactyli (*see* IDAEAN DACTYLS), the latter especially known as masters of medical charms and music (the same combination recurs in Chiron). Orpheus the magician, Musaeus, Melampus, Autolycus (Hesiod fr. 136 Rzach) are other well-known names; but the female sex seems in literature as elsewhere to predominate, the most renowned enchantress through all antiquity being Medea. She commands all nature, puts the dragon at Colchis to sleep, makes warriors invulnerable and old men young. She also has the Evil Eye, terrible to all living things (*see* TALOS). Magic brings her victory, but love is her tragedy (*see* MEDEA); so far she remains a prototype for the jilted witch of later literature (cf. Canidia in Horace). The Thessalians claimed that she had lost her box of drugs on their fertile soil, and their wonder-working plants were just as widely known as their witches (see the equally brilliant *Metamorphoses* of Ovid and Apuleius).

5. Later literature gives us further evidence of the interest taken in magic and magicians by poets and writers, Greek as well as Latin. New fragments of Sophron give a vivid picture of a piece of Hecate-magic (the prototype of Theoc. 2), but we are still waiting for more of Sophocles' 'The female Herbalists' and Menander's 'Thessalian Woman', where the popular Thessalian feat of 'drawing down the moon' was mentioned. The dramatists on the whole were fully alive to the scenic possibilities of a *necyomantia*, the first description of which we find in Homer's *Odyssey* (cf. Aeschylus' *Persae*, Aristophanes' *Frogs*, Seneca's *Oedipus*). Lucian used it as a welcome satirical theme. Virgil and Horace have a specialist's insight into love-charms, popular—and feared—in their time, and Lucan in his epic gave an illustration of Thessalian witchcraft which for completeness and gruesome description remains unrivalled. The keen interest felt in the theme is excellently illustrated by Apuleius' *Apologia*.

6. A clear insight into the whole magical technique of a syncretistic character, its practices, prayers, and faith in demons and demonic powers is furnished by the many finds of magical papyri in Egypt, collected by Preisendanz, *Papyri Graecae magicae*. Thus we can now also measure the distance between ancient witchcraft in real life and the literary treatment of the subject.

7. Sociologically, magic, both of positive ('white') and negative ('black') *mana* is divided into *official* and *private* practices, but their mutual interpenetration is evident. A number of official Greek and Roman festivals, concerned with, e.g., the fertility of soil and man (*hieros gamos*: *see* MARRIAGE, SACRED), rain-making (weather-charms), war (e.g. the Roman fetiales), where public welfare is at stake, have preserved their old magic character. On the other hand, many apotropaeic ceremonies to purify and avert, having an obviously magical character, were used in a public and in a private way; so likewise prayers (cf. HYMNS, PAEAN) and curses (*see* CURSES); even sacrifices offered to the gods on behalf of the State or the single family were magical in much of their ritual (cf. the use of fire and water, circumambulation as in the Roman *lustratio*), still more so the offerings to the dead. All the main events in man's life (birth, marriage, death, etc.) and the emotional force of such events called for supernatural help and defence.

8. Theoretically the division into 'sympathetic' 'homoeopathic' (*similia similibus*) and 'contagious' magic (*pars pro toto*) is of great help. You make an image of a person whose love you desire or whose death you wish, you melt it at a fire, you pierce it with nails, etc., and the person in question suffers correspondingly—this is a homoeopathic procedure (cf. Pl. *Leg.* 933 b, Theoc. 2, Verg. *Ecl.* 8, Ov. *Her.* 6. 91). If, when burning the image, you throw some of the victim's hair or a bit of his cloak

(Theoc. 2. 53 ff.) or anything else that has been his (Verg. *Aen.* 4. 494 ff.) into the fire, you simultaneously make use of contagious magic. The combination naturally gives you a stronger hold upon the victim. Further we may call the transmission of disease into another person or beast (e.g. when stung by a scorpion you whisper into the ear of an ass: 'A scorpion has stung me', Pliny, *HN* 28. 155) *direct* magic, as contrasted with the *indirect* where gods, demons, or spirits are at work (cf. *devotio*). Direct are, e.g., the apotropaeic efficacy of rings and crowns of amulets (the phallus, *fascinum*, vulva, the Gorgoneion on wine-cups, etc.), the 'binding' practices (δέω σε, *ligo te*; κατάδεσις, *defixio*, *see* CURSES), the use of the wryneck (ἴυγξ) in homoeopathic love magic, a host of medical charms, preserved, e.g., in Cato, *Agr.* 160, and in so many works of popular medicine (Marcellus, *De medicamentis*, Aëtius, Alexander of Tralles, etc.), innumerable concoctions, incantations (ἐπῳδαί) and formulas to be found in the papyri (in Egyptian and Greek), magical sounds and tunes, finally the power of the spoken word and the name, the 'great name', of god or demon. We find an early example of *indirect magic* in the Homeric description of a *necyomantea*, the evocation of the spirits of the dead (*Od.* 11, cf. the witch of Endor (1 Sam.xxviii, 3 ff.) and the definition of γοητεία in Cramer, *Anecd. Ox.* iv. 240). The necromancers (ψυχαγωγοί) were a definite class of magicians (popular also in Etruria), and corresponding official oracles existed, cf. the incubation (q.v.), officially sanctioned at Asclepiea and elsewhere. Compare also the ὀνειραιτητά of *PGM*. The introduction of foreign demons (and rites), characteristic of ancient magic from early times, culminated in the 'syncretistic' period after Alexander the Great. A wider outlook on all sorts of magic and on the powers of the supernatural world now made possible the synthesis of magic and *theurgia* which the Alexandrian philosophic speculation attempted (cf. the magico-religious Gnostics: *see* GNOSTICISM). Accordingly, the prescriptions for consecration and prayer, for the material to be used (e.g. plants, stones, extensive use of lead), and for the ritual fitness of the persons became more and more complicated.

9. As civilization developed, the lawgivers in Greece as in Italy (where the Marsi and Paeligni were famous indigenous magicians) became more and more interested in repressing magic (so far the division into beneficent and mischievous witchcraft often materially coincides with public and private magic). Already in Ancient Egypt a magician could be prosecuted, and the Homeric hymn to Demeter (228) contains a hit at witchcraft. Plato wants the abuse of magic (φαρμακεία) to be punished (cf. also [Dem.] 25 *contra Aristog.* 79 f.), and the Roman *decemviri* really did so. New laws under the Roman emperors repressed the new growth of magical influence (cf. Julius Paulus, *Sent.* 5. 23, 14 ff.; *Cod. Theod.* 9. 10; 16. 10; *Cod. Iust.* 9. 18). *See* AMULETS, ASTROLOGY, CURSES, DIVINATION, SACRIFICE.

J. G. Frazer, *GB³* i–ii; G. van der Leeuw, *Phaenomenologie der Religion²* (1956), ch. 83 (= *Religion in Essence and Manifestation* (1938), ch. 82); Nilsson, *GGR* i². 51 ff.; ii². 520 ff.; 696 ff.; W. K. C. Guthrie, *The Greeks and their Gods* (1950), 270 ff.; S. Eitrem, 'Magische Papyri' (*Münchener Beitr. z. Papyrusforschung* xix (1933), 243 ff.); Warde Fowler, *Rel. Exper.*, ch. 3; C. Bailey, *Phases in the Religion of Ancient Rome* (1932), ch. 1; E. Massonneau, *La Magie dans l'antiquité romaine* (1934).                S. E.; J. H. C.

**MAGISTER EQUITUM,** or the master of the horse, was a subordinate official, nominated by every dictator on appointment, originally to control the cavalry, but, in later practice, to represent the dictator either on the field of battle or at Rome. He held derivatory *imperium* from the dictator and ranked with the praetors. His commission ended with that of his dictator. A notable but unsuccessful attempt was made in 217 B.C. to equate

the *magister equitum* with the *dictator* as a colleague (*see* MINUCIUS 2). A similar though permanent magistracy is found in the municipalities of Italy, known as *magister iuventutis* or *magister iuvenum*. *See also* MAGISTER MILITUM.

For bibliography *see* DICTATOR.                A. N. S.-W.

**MAGISTER MEMORIAE** was the most important of the imperial secretaries in the third century A.D., acting as legal adviser and foreign minister, but when Constantine created the *quaestor* and *magister officiorum* (q.v.) he lost these functions but continued to deal with petitions and write rescripts to them (*adnotationes*). From the late fourth century he was *spectabilis*. He had under him the *scrinium memoriae* (sixty-two clerks).                A. H. M. J.

**MAGISTER MILITUM.** Constantine deprived the praetorian prefects of their military functions, and left them with purely administrative duties. To command the army he appointed two new generals, the *magister peditum* and *magister equitum*; the former was the senior officer. Later, with the division of the field-army into local groups, the number of *magistri* was increased, and the limitation of command to a particular arm was removed. The *magistri* who commanded that part of the army which was attached to the Emperor's headquarters were styled *in praesenti* or *praesentales*.

R. Grosse, *Römische Militärgeschichte* (1920), 180 ff.; Jones, *Later Rom. Emp.* 608 ff.                H. M. D. P.; G. R. W.

**MAGISTER OFFICIORUM,** an official created by Constantine. He originally held the rank of tribune, was *spectabilis* under Valentinian I and *illustris* by the end of the fourth century; he was also a *comes primi ordinis consistorianus*. He controlled the imperial couriers (*agentes in rebus*, q.v.) and the inspectors of the post (*curiosi*) drawn from them, and issued postal warrants (*evectiones*). He exercised disciplinary control over the secretariats (*sacra scrinia*) which served the quaestor and the *magistri memoriae*, *epistolarum* and *libellorum*, the *scrinium dispositionum*, the *officium admissionum*, the *decani*, *cancellarii*, *lampadarii*, *mensores*, and the interpreters who translated for foreign ambassadors. He was also commander of the imperial guard (*scholae palatinae*). From the end of the fourth century he also controlled the armament factories (*fabricae*) throughout the Empire, and in 443 he became inspector general of the *limitanei* (q.v.) in the Eastern Empire. The *magister officiorum*, as controlling audiences with the Emperor, was a very influential minister, and virtually foreign secretary. He also had an extensive jurisdiction over palatine civil servants. His *officium* was drawn from the *agentes in rebus*.

A. E. R. Boak, *The Master of the Offices in the Later Roman and Byzantine Empires* (1924).                A. H. M. J.

**MAGISTRACY, GREEK.** Magistracy in Greek city-states was the heir of the old monarchy which survived in a few States only (Sparta, Cyrene). According to Greek tradition, which, however, sometimes tends to over-emphasize the regularity of the process, firstly one or a few magistrates, elected by the ruling class, governed the State for life. At an early stage military, judicial, and religious functions were separated, part of the religious duties being transferred to an official who preserved the royal title. Next the duration of office became limited, and official power was distributed among several colleagues. By a procedure which varied in each city the leaders of the State gradually became mere executive instruments. The number of officials increased. Besides the leading political and military magistrates there were officials needed for special tasks, e.g. finance or public works. But it was never usual to elect men with special qualifications, except to military offices. Officials were generally elected by the full-citizens out of their own body. They received no salary and some magistracies were open to men of great wealth only. All officials had to undergo a test (*dokimasia*), confirming legal birth and family cult as well as fulfilment of certain civic duties. In democracies the number of magistracies underwent a large increase, and their power accordingly diminished. Boards of three, five, or more colleagues were far more common than single officials. Their term of office never exceeded one year and they could usually not be re-elected. One official (or priest) gave his name to the year (*eponymos*). Some technical offices excepted, election was by lot (*see* SORTITION), a fact that made the elective offices more powerful; only their holders could exercise political leadership. All officials had to render account (εὔθυναι) after their terms of office. Most of the lower officials received small daily salaries. In general, Greek magistracy expressed the participation of all citizens in politics, and their equality; there existed no hierarchy or 'cursus honorum'.

In the Hellenistic monarchies magistrates were on a quite different footing. They were professionals, paid by the king in money, natural products, or gifts of land. The higher magistracies were occupied by Macedonians or Greeks, the lower mostly by natives, who did not rise to high positions before the second century B.C. Greek was the official language. The members of the central government resided in the chief city, but there were numerous higher and lower officials in every part of the realm. The most important provincial officials were generally called *strategoi*. The administration was strictly centralized in Egypt, but decentralized in the Seleucid Empire. In all cases there was a firm hierarchy, well organized and rather bureaucratic, nowhere more than in Egypt. Lower officials were often personally dependent on the higher, as the higher were on the king.

F. Leifer, *Klio*, Beiheft 23 (1931); U. Kahrstedt, *Untersuchungen zur Magistratur in Athen* (1936); Bengtson, *Strategie* I–III; V. Ehrenberg, *The Greek State* (1960). V. E.

**MAGISTRACY, ROMAN.** Magistracy was one of the three basic elements of the Roman Republic, the other two being the Senate and the people. In the regal period all power was embodied in the person of the king, and the other executive officials were merely his representatives. But under the Republic it rested with magistrates who were regarded as the representatives of the *populus Romanus*, and who were invested with rights, duties, and executive power (*potestas*) by the joint authority of the Senate and the people. During the fifth century a new board of plebeian officials who were commonly called *magistratus plebeii* was created in opposition to the senatorial magistrates, but it soon lost its revolutionary character, since a process of compromise, beginning as early as 450 B.C., led by the middle of the third century to the large-scale admission of plebeians to all the official magistracies and to the absorption of the plebeian offices within the sphere of authority of the Senate. Even earlier, however, excessive magisterial power had been successfully checked by several limitations. The *imperium* (q.v.) was restricted to the military sphere (*imperium militiae*), and thus was exercised only beyond the walls of Rome (*extra pomerium*); while the *imperium domi*, although, like the *imperium militiae*, it still included *iurisdictio* and *coercitio*, was considerably limited by the right of appeal (*provocatio*). Moreover, the principle of collegiality always made it impossible for a magistrate to start any revolutionary movement (until the age of Sulla and Caesar, when magistrates came to be commanders in chief of professional, mercenary armies). Magistrates became

progressively more dependent on the Senate, with whom they were compelled to collaborate, especially when the Senate became a closed assembly of magistrates and ex-magistrates, from whose ranks alone the candidates for magistracies were mostly taken. As Polybius observed, it was this compromise between the Senate, conceived as the administrative power, and the magistrates invested with the executive, that assured the stability and continuity of the Roman constitution. To maintain the correct balance, measures were taken to guarantee the regular succession of magistrates, and the alternate and balanced exercise of authority by colleagues. The *leges annales* determined both the age-limits required for candidature and the intervals of time between the tenure of magistracies: this *certus ordo magistratuum* remained essentially undisturbed from 180 B.C. (*Lex Villia*) until the Augustan age (*see* VILLIUS, CURSUS HONORUM). Similarly the principle, emphatically maintained by Cicero, that public office and service was a civic duty, was observed until the end of the Republic. Since public service was never regarded as a profession, no remuneration was given to Roman magistrates, except for journeys, special celebrations, military commands and expenses, etc. This purely honorary aspect of magistracy was confirmed by regulations concerning the escort of lictors (q.v.) and their number, the dress to be worn, the use of the *sella curulis* (q.v.), different forms of homage due to magistrates, etc. These formalities were observed even under the Empire, at least down to the end of the fourth century A.D., when magistracies lost any independence and political significance. Imperial magistrates, being appointed by the emperor, were in fact reduced to the condition of civil and military subordinates.

Mommsen, *Röm. Staatsr.* i³ (abridged in *Abriss d. röm. Staatsrechts*, 1893, 82 ff.). P. T.

**MAGISTRI.** A common title for the head of a religious or semi-religious organization in Rome was *magister*. This official was primarily not a priest, though he generally had some sacral duties, but rather a president (see De-Marchi, *Culto Privato* ii. 146 f.). Thus the *fratres Aruales* elected a *magister* annually to serve from one Saturnalia to the next (e.g. *Acta Arualium* for 19 May, 87, cxix 30, Henzen; at the same time a different person was made *flamen*, ibid. 32). When Augustus restored the worship of the Lares Compitales (*see* LARES), he apparently organized it under *magistri uicorum*, perhaps on the analogy of the *magistri pagorum* or presidents of the rural districts (see De-Marchi, i. 230; cf. Marquardt–Wissowa, *Römische Staatsverwaltung*² (1881–5), iii². 204 ff.).

For other uses of the term, and in particular for that revealed in J. Johnson, *Excavations at Minturnae* ii (Rome and Philadelphia, 1933), see A. D. Nock, *AJPhil.* 1935, 86 ff. H. J. R.

**MAGNA GRAECIA,** the collective name for the Greek cities of southern Italy. Cumae (q.v.) was the oldest, Heraclea (q.v. 1) the youngest. The inhabitants of Magna Graecia, the so-called Italiotes, developed an amphictiony, Olympic champions, schools of philosophy, etc. Fertile surroundings and foreign commerce brought prosperity, but political instability proved fatal. The total destruction of Sybaris (q.v.) by Croton (q.v.) illustrates the mutual animosities of the cities. After 400 decline began: hostile Italian neighbours, Sicilian tyrants, and possibly malaria accelerated it. By 300 most cities needed Roman protection: Tarentum (q.v.), however, relied on Greek *condottieri* (*see* PYRRHUS). Pyrrhic and Hannibalic wars completed the ruin of Magna Graecia. See, too, CAULONIA, ELIA, LOCRI, METAPONTUM, NEAPOLIS, PAESTUM, RHEGIUM, SCYLACIUM, SIRIS, THURII.

Dunbabin, *Western Greeks*; F. Sartori, *Problemi di storia costituzionale Italiota* (1953); A. G. Woodhead, *The Greeks in the West* (1962). E. T. S.

**MAGNENTIUS**, FLAVIUS MAGNUS, usurping Roman Emperor (A.D. 350–3), was a pagan. Elevated at Autun he murdered the Emperor Constans (q.v.) and ruled over the West. He was defeated by Constantius II at the great battle of Mursa (351) and committed suicide in Gaul two years later.                                                    E. A. T.

**MAGNES** is treated by Aristotle (*Poet.* 1448ᵃ34) as one of the two earliest Athenian comic poets. He won eleven victories at the City Dionysia, one of them in 472 B.C. (*IG* ii². 2318. 8, 2325. 44, Anon. *De Com.* 6). We have eight titles, but the plays ascribed to him in Hellenistic times were of very doubtful authenticity (Anon. ibid., Ath. 367 e and 646 e); the titles include *Dionysus*, *Lydians*, *Fig-flies*, *Frogs*, and *Birds*, of which the last three may possibly be only inferences from Ar. *Eq.* 520 ff., where Magnes is described as πτερυγίζων . . . καὶ ψηνίζων καὶ βαπτόμενος βατραχείοις.

  *FCG* ii. 9–11; *CAF* i. 7–9; *FAC* i. 8 ff.                K. J. D.

**MAGNESIA AD MAEANDRUM** (Μαγνησία πρὸς (or ἐπὶ) Μαιάνδρῳ), a city of Ionia on a tributary of the Maeander, inland from Ephesus. Colonized by the Magnetes (q.v.), it and Magnesia ad Sipylum (q.v.) both commanded rich inland valleys. Successively subject to Lydia and Persia, it was presented by Artaxerxes to Themistocles, whose female relatives were priestesses of the local goddess Artemis Leucophryene. The temple (a work of Hermogenes), together with public buildings of the city, which was refounded by the sanctuary in 399, has been excavated. Like Magnesia ad Sipylum it sided with Rome against Mithridates, and was made a *civitas libera* by Sulla when he reorganized the province of Asia.

  K. Humann, *Magnesia am Maeander* (1904). W. M. C.; J. M. C.

**MAGNESIA AD SIPYLUM** (Μαγνησία πρὸς Σιπύλῳ), a city of Lydia lying in the fertile Hermus valley at the point where the roads from the interior and the Propontis converge on the way to Smyrna, the scene of the decisive battle between Antiochus and the Scipios in 190 B.C. *See also* MAGNESIA AD MAEANDRUM.

**MAGNETES**, a tribe occupying the mountain-systems of Ossa and Pelion on the eastern border of Thessaly. Their long coastline on the open sea was harbourless, and their chief towns, Meliboea, Homolion, and Rhizus, were very small. They became *Perioikoi* to the invading Thessalians and had to surrender the coastal district round Pagasae, but they retained their two votes on the Amphictionic Council. Pagasae was restored to the Magnetes when Philip expelled the tyrants of Pherae, but they lost the limited autonomy which they had previously enjoyed and became subjects of Macedonia. In 293 Demetrias (q.v.) was founded through a 'synoecism' of the Magnetes.                                                    H. D. W.

**MAGNUS** (1), of Carrhae, accompanied Julian on his Persian expedition in A.D. 363 (*see* JULIANUS 1) and wrote an account of it, of which a paraphrased passage is quoted by Malalas. The view that Magnus' narrative was used by Ammianus and Zosimus has been rejected by E. A. Thompson.

  *FGrH* 225. E. A. Thompson, *The Historical Work of Ammianus Marcellinus* (1947), 28 ff.                H. H. S.

**MAGNUS** (2) **MAXIMUS**, Roman Emperor (A.D. 383–8), was a Spaniard who rose to the command of the troops in Britain, where he fought successfully against the Picts and Scots. Elevated by the army in Britain, he at once crossed to Gaul and overthrew Gratian (q.v.). He was recognized as Emperor by Theodosius I and controlled Gaul and Spain as well as Britain. He successfully

invaded Italy but was decisively defeated by Theodosius in battles fought near Siscia and Pola, and was executed in 388. Maximus was a Catholic and persecuted Priscillian and his followers.                                                    E. A. T.

**MAGO** (1), fl. 550–520 B.C. The founder of a family which held quasi-monarchical power at Carthage from *c.* 550 to 450 B.C. He fought in Sardinia to consolidate the power of Carthage in the island, and changed the basis of the Carthaginian army; previously a citizen levy, it was subsequently a mercenary force, officered and led by Carthaginians.

  B. H. Warmington, *Carthage* (1960), 40 ff., 121.                B. H. W.

**MAGO** (2) was youngest brother of Hannibal, under whom he served in Italy (218–216 B.C.), fighting at Trebia and Cannae. He fought in Spain from 215 till his defeat at Ilipa (206). After failing to seize Carthago Nova and to re-enter Gades he attacked the Balearic Isles (Mahon in Minorca perpetuates his name) and in 205 landed in Liguria. After lengthy recruiting he advanced into the Po valley, where he was defeated by the Romans (203). He successfully re-embarked his army for Africa, but died of wounds on the voyage.                                                    H. H. S.

**MAGODIA**, a type of low-class mime or lyric, subliterary (like *hilarodia*, *simodia*, and *lysiodia*), about which the ancient tradition (Ath. 14. 620 d, Strabo 14. 648) is far from clear. *Magodia* is defined as ὄρχησις ἁπαλή (Hesych.); the actor, accompanied by kettledrums and cymbals, represented usually in comic style the drunken lover and other low characters. Possible libretti are the παρακλαυσίθυρον found on an Egyptian papyrus of the second century B.C. and a lament for a lost cock (texts in Powell, *Coll. Alex.* 177 ff., 182 ff.; see also Page, *GLP*, no. 75).

  Maas in *PW*, s.v. σιμῳδοί.                W. G. W.; W. G. A.

**MAHARBAL**, Hannibal's chief cavalry officer, defeated a Roman cavalry squadron near Assisi after the battle of Lake Trasimene (217 B.C.). After Cannae (216) he is alleged to have urged Hannibal to march on Rome ('for in five days you shall dine in victory on the Capitol'), and when Hannibal wisely refused he added 'uincere scis, Hannibal, uictoria uti nescis' (Livy 22. 51. 4).                H. H. S.

**MAIA**, (1) Μαῖα, mother of Hermes (q.v.) by Zeus and daughter of Atlas; she is one of the Pleiads (*Od.* 14. 435, where she is called Maias; Hes. *Theog.* 938, fr. 275, 3 Rzach). Her name means simply 'mother' or 'nurse' (cf. M. P. Nilsson, *AJPhil.* 1938, 392 on the Attic sacrifice mentioned in a text published by W. S. Ferguson, *Hesperia* 1938, 5, 65 f.), and apart from her son she has little existence. (2) A Roman goddess, associated with Volcanus (Gell. 13. 23 (22). 2); on 1 May the *flamen Volcanalis* sacrificed to her (Macrob. *Sat.* 1. 12. 18), further confirming the association, which, however, is quite unexplained, since he is undoubtedly a fire-god (*see* VOLCANUS), while her name appears to come from the root *mag* and signify growth or increase; cf. the by-form Maiesta (Piso in Macrob. ibid.) and the month-name, appropriate to a time of year when all plants are growing. By a natural confusion with (1) she was associated with Mercurius (q.v.) and worshipped also on 15 May, the *natalis* of his temple, apparently under the title of *inuicta* ('Maiae inuict.', *Fasti Antiates* on that date).

  Wissowa, *RK* 229, 304; Latte, *RR* 130, 163.                H. J. R.

**MAIESTAS**, technically *maiestas minuta*, was 'treason', thus defined by Cicero: 'Maiestatem minuere est de dignitate aut amplitudine aut potestate populi aut eorum quibus populus potestatem dedit aliquid derogare' (*Invent.*

*Rhet.* 2. 17. 53). Established as a crime by the Lex Appuleia of 103 B.C. (*see* SATURNINUS 1), it virtually replaced the earlier *perduellio* (q.v.). Saturninus was provoked by the incompetence and corruption of Roman generals in the wars against the Cimbri and Teutones. Sulla's *lex maiestatis* of 81 B.C., establishing a permanent *quaestio*, was an important part of his attempt to re-establish senatorial government, and survived the Republic. Its prime purpose was to curb the dangerous initiative of proconsuls by making it a crime for them to take an army outside their provinces except under instruction of the government in Rome—'iniussu senatus populique Romani'. (Caesar's invasion of Italy in 49 was the most startling imaginable violation of the law.) Proconsuls, however, were not the only objectives of the law, for the ex-tribune Cornelius was accused under it in 66 B.C. for disregarding the veto of a fellow tribune. Already under the Republic it was sometimes difficult to know what could legitimately be construed as treason (Cic. *Fam.* 3. 11. 2).

The *lex Iulia maiestatis* of Julius Caesar or Augustus (*Dig.* 48. 4) revised Sulla's law. The Emperor came to control foreign policy, and the very existence of a *princeps* inevitably widened the application of the law to include conspiracy against his life, libel and slander against him, and, after the exposure of Julia (q.v. 2), adultery with a member of his family. The law was never redrafted to take precise account of such offences and, where conspiracy was concerned, Domitian was to observe sagely that 'the only time that anybody believed an Emperor's statement that he had detected a conspiracy was when the conspiracy had succeeded and he was dead' (Suet. *Dom.* 21; cf. Tac. *Ann.* 4. 70. 7). Prosecutions for *maiestas* might now be brought before the *quaestio maiestatis*, the Senate sitting as a consular-senatorial court, or before the Emperor himself (see Tac. *Ann.* 3. 10–12 for these three possibilities in the trial of Cn. Piso in A.D. 20). Information was laid and prosecutions were brought by individuals (informers, *delatores*, *quadruplatores*) who, if they secured a condemnation, received a quarter of the accused man's property, for a condemned man's property was confiscated to the Treasury; he was increasingly liable to the death sentence (with no opportunity given to retire into exile) and he suffered *damnatio memoriae* (q.v.). Only if he committed suicide before the charge was formally laid against him could he escape these indignities.

Charges of *maiestas* were increasingly frequent under Tiberius, many on seemingly trifling grounds, and after A.D. 23 disfigured his administration. Their background from 23 to 31 was the increasing power of Sejanus at the expense of Agrippina (q.v. 2), her sons, and friends; from 31 to 37 the determination of Sejanus' enemies to be avenged on his surviving friends. The virulent hatred of one faction of the Senate for another was in the tradition of the late Republic and the civil wars. Cn. Piso was rightly condemned in 20; but there is no certain evidence, even in the case of Sejanus, of a real conspiracy against Tiberius' life. Tiberius did nothing to encourage the evil; but he did nothing to repress it.

There were condemnations for *maiestas* under Gaius, Claudius, and Nero, yet all three Emperors were confronted by dangerous conspiracies, and the horror of Tiberius' Principate was not re-enacted until the last years of Domitian's rule, when the property of the condemned passed to the Emperor himself; indeed Domitian was accused of instigating prosecutions to rescue himself from his extensive financial embarrassments.

J. E. Allison, C. D. Cloud, 'The Lex Julia Maiestatis', *Latomus*, 1962, 711; Mommsen, *Röm. Strafr.*; C. W. Chilton, 'The Roman Law of Treason under the Early Principate', *JRS* 1955, 73; K. M. T. Atkinson, *Hist.* 1960, 440 ff., and D. Stockton, ibid. 1965, 18 ff., on the trials of M. Primus and Varro Murena; E. Koestermann, 'Die Majestätsprozesse unter Tiberius', *Hist.* 1955, 72. Cases under Tiberius are listed in R. S. Rogers, *Criminal Trials and Criminal Legislation under Tiberius* (1935). J. P. B.

**MAJORIAN,** JULIUS, Western Roman Emperor (A.D. 457–61), was elevated by Ricimer (q.v.). He tried to improve the administration of his realm. His planned expedition against the Vandals of Africa was completely defeated at Carthago Nova; he was obliged to make a humiliating peace with Gaiseric (q.v.), and was shortly afterwards put to death by Ricimer. Sidonius Apollinaris addressed a panegyric to him. He was the last Western Emperor of any ability. E. A. T.

**MALACA** (modern *Malaga*), a Phoenician foundation on the southern coast of Spain, was noted by Artemidorus as an emporium for the opposite African shore and kept a Phoenician look. Its trade and industry (chiefly fish-curing) were not interrupted when it became an ally of Rome. With the other Spanish communities, it received the *ius Latii* (q.v.) from Vespasian. The extant parts of its charter and that of Salpensa are important sources for Latin municipal status in imperial times.

Dessau, *ILS* 6089; Bruns, *Font.* (1919) 147, no. 30
J. J. VAN N.; M. I. H.

**MALALAS,** IOHANNES, a Greek rhetorician and historian who lived in Antioch *c.* A.D. 491–578 (the name Malalas means 'rhetor' in Syriac). We have under his name a universal chronicle (*Chronographia*) in eighteen books from the creation of the world to A.D. 565. The only continuous text of it is preserved in the Oxford MS. Bodl. Baroccianus 182 of the twelfth century, but fragments are extant in other MS. sources, including the *Excerpta* by Constantinus Porphyrogenitus. Even the Oxford MS. (apart from lacunae) shows clear traces of abridgement of the original text: this is confirmed by a Slavonic translation of the tenth to eleventh century, which is preserved in excerpts. The chronicle had great influence on Byzantine, Slavonic, and Oriental historiography. In the first seventeen books and at the beginning of book xviii Antioch is at the centre of the narration; and the author shows monophysitic sympathies. The second part of book xviii gives prominence to Constantinople and displays orthodoxy. Some modern critics explain the difference by postulating a different author for book xviii. Others think that the author moved to Constantinople late in life and modified his convictions. It has even been suggested that Iohannes Malalas should be identified with Iohannes III, Patriarch of Constantinople 565–77, who was of Antiochian origin. Malalas' direct or indirect sources have not yet been established with certainty: they must have included official records and local chronicles of Antioch together with general histories and universal chronicles. Uncritical, confused, and often childish, Malalas preserves many otherwise unknown facts and is, of course, of special importance for his own time. His popular language, his interest in local traditions, and his desire to appeal to the semi-educated Christian are in themselves extremely significant.

A critical edition is available only for books ix–xii in A. Schenk von Stauffenberg, *Römische Kaisergeschichte bei Malalas* (1931) with important commentary, discussed by W. Ensslin, *Phil. Woch.* 1933, 769 ff. The standard ed. remains L. Dindorf (1831): also Migne, *PG* xcvii (1865). The proemium first published by A. Wirth, *Chronographische Späne* (1894), 3. Part of the Slavonic version translated into English by M. Spinka–G. Downey (1940). Cf. W. Weber, *Festgabe A. Deissmann* (1927), 20 ff.; E. Bikerman, *Byzantion* 1951, 63 ff.; G. Moravcsik, *Byzantinoturcica* i² (1958), 329 ff.; G. Downey, *A History of Antioch* (1961), 38, for other bibl. A. M.

**MALCHUS** (1), a Carthaginian general (fl. 580–550 B.C.?). The form of the name is uncertain; possibly it is a misunderstanding of *melek*, king. He extended the overseas empire of Carthage. He strengthened Punic control of western Sicily, was perhaps checked by Phalaris of Acragas, and then set off to conquer Sardinia where he was defeated by the natives. He was 'exiled', that is perhaps ordered to stay with his men (as colonists ?) in Sardinia, but the troops insisted on returning home. He seized Carthage, but was soon overthrown and executed. His career represents the first-known threat of a general and army to the civil government of Carthage. He was succeeded in power by Mago (q.v. 1).   H. H. S.

**MALCHUS** (2), king of the Nabataeans (q.v.), 47–30 B.C. He sent cavalry to Caesar for the Alexandrine war (47). He refused to receive Herod (q.v. 1) when he was driven from Palestine by the Parthians (40). For his help to the Parthians he had to pay Ventidius a fine, while Antony gave part (but not all) of his territory to Cleopatra who skilfully sowed seeds of discord between Malchus and Herod. Herod was later ordered by Antony to attack Malchus who was defeated (31).   H. H. S.

**MALCHUS** (3), a Byzantine historian (*c.* A.D. 500) from Syrian Philadelphia. He recorded the story of at least the years 474–80 in seven books, thus starting where Priscus (q.v.) left off. He relied not on literary sources, but on personal knowledge gained during his stay in Byzantium. He is also well informed about the Ostrogoths. The *Suda* and Photius approved of his style. The majority of the surviving fragments of his history are preserved in Constantine Porphyrogenitus' *De legationibus*.

See Müller, *FHG* iv (1851), 111 ff.; Dindorf, *Hist. Gr. Min.*[1] (1870), 383 ff.; C. De Boor, *Excerpta de Legationibus* (1903), 155 ff., 568 ff.   H. H. S.

**MALEA**, south-eastern promontory of Laconia, and of the whole Peloponnesus, a dangerous corner for shipping, chiefly because of the sudden veering of the winds off a harbourless coast. It was denounced on this account from Homer down to Byzantine writers. But in part this perilousness was a literary tradition, and there was always much traffic through the narrow strait between Malea and Cythera.   V. E.

**MALLIUS THEODORUS** (*cos.* A.D. 399) wrote a *De metris* (ed. Keil, *Gramm. Lat.* 6. 585–601). His philosophical and astronomical works are lost.

Schanz–Hosius, § 1085.

**MAMERTINES**, a body of Campanian (i.e. Oscan) mercenaries, whom Agathocles had settled in Syracuse, after his death treacherously seized Messana between 288 and 283 B.C. Calling themselves *Mamertini* (Mamers is the Oscan form of Mars), they dominated and plundered north-east Sicily, although temporarily checked by Pyrrhus, until defeated near the Longanus river by Hieron of Syracuse (? 265). At their request Carthage installed a protective garrison in Messana, but at the same time or soon afterwards they also asked Rome for help, thereby precipitating the First Punic War. When Rome accepted the alliance, they ejected the Carthaginian garrison and called in Appius Claudius (q.v. 5) Caudex, who drove back both Carthaginians and Hieron.

M. Särström, *A Study in the Coinage of the Mamertines* (Lund, 1940). For the few inscriptions see Conway, *The Italic Dialects* i (1897), 1 f.   H. H. S.

**MAMILIUS** (1, *PW* 4) **TUSCULANUS**, OCTAVIUS, said to have been the son-in-law of Tarquinius (q.v. 2) Superbus, and to have assisted the exiled king in his attempt to return to Rome by force. At the battle of Lake Regillus, in which he commanded the army of the Latin League, he was defeated and killed. Though Livy's

account of him (2. 18. 3 ff.) ultimately may depend on popular ballads, this does not disprove his historical character.

Ogilvie, *Comm. Livy 1–5*, 198.   P. T.

**MAMILIUS** (2, *PW* 1), LUCIUS, dictator of Tusculum, is praised by tradition for the voluntary help which he brought to the Roman Republic when its safety was menaced by the Sabine Appius Herdonius, who had entrenched himself on the Capitol (460 B.C.). Mamilius is said to have been rewarded with the Roman citizenship (458), which is likely to be a historical fact.   P. T.

**MAMILIUS** (3, *PW* 7) **LIMETANUS**, GAIUS, as tribune in 109 B.C. set up a commission of 'equestrian' *iudices* (with Scaurus (q.v. 1) as one of the chairmen) to investigate the mishandling of relations with Jugurtha. Those condemned included Bestia, Cato (2), Galba (4), Opimius, and Postumius (4) (qq.v.). He also passed a law (necessitated by the agrarian legislation of 133–111) to settle boundaries, thus getting his *cognomen*.   E. B.

**MAMURRA** of Formiae, *praefectus fabrum* under Caesar in Spain (61 B.C.) and Gaul, where he accumulated great wealth. His extravagance aroused ill feeling, and Catullus (29, 41, 43, 51), who had personal reasons for disliking him, coupled his name scandalously with Caesar's.

For a possible identification with Vitruvius, see VITRUVIUS.   C. E. S.

**MANCEPS** has several meanings. Most commonly it denotes the successful bidder in an auction of contracts for the sale or leasing of State lands or for public works (*see* CONDUCTOR). Festus and others associate this with the raising of the hand in bidding. But this is etymologically unconvincing, and Festus also gives a quite different meaning, 'quod manu capiatur', which is presumably related to *mancipatio* and connected words and perhaps refers to *res mancipi* (*see* MANCIPATIO), *manceps* being a person with the power of *mancipium* or *manu capium* (*see* PATRIA POTESTAS). The original meaning of *manceps* in this context is, however, much disputed (cf. Plaut. *Curc.* 515, where *manceps* is evidently the person making a *mancipatio*, the *auctor*).

The *manceps* in State contracts normally acted on behalf of associates—in the late Republic of a *societas publicanorum* (*see* PUBLICANI), but the details are obscure. He is sometimes, but not always, the *magister* of the *societas*. In the late Empire, when the functions of the *publicani* have become public duties discharged by guilds (*collegia*), *manceps* is a person charged with an obligatory public function (e.g. *mancipes salinarum et thermarum* for the salt monopoly and the public baths).

M. Kaser, *Das altröm. ius* (1949), 135 ff.; P. Meylan, *Studi de Francisci* (1956) i. 65 ff.; F. Kniep, *Societas publicanorum* (1896).   B. N.

**MANCINUS**, GAIUS HOSTILIUS (*PW* 18), *praetor urbanus c.* 140 B.C. As consul in 137 he was defeated by the Numantines. His quaestor Ti. Gracchus (q.v. 3) secured a peace that saved the army; but it was disowned by the Senate at the suggestion of Scipio (q.v. 11), and Mancinus, with his own consent, was surrendered in expiation. When the Numantines refused to accept him, he returned, was readmitted to citizenship and again became praetor.   E. B.

**MANCIPATIO** was a solemn transaction with copper and scales (*per aes et libram*), mentioned already in the XII Tables. In historical times it was a symbolic sale (Gaius calls it 'imaginaria venditio'), but it originated, no doubt, as a real sale, the scales being for weighing out the price. As we know it, it served as a conveyance of ownership of *res mancipi*, and also for the transfer of rights akin to ownership over persons (*see* DOMINIUM, PATRIA POTESTAS, MANUS, ADOPTIO, EMANCIPATIO, NEXUM, SECURITY, INHERITANCE—LAW OF, § 3). *Res mancipi* included the most important objects in a primitive agricultural economy, such as land (*solum Italicum*), slaves, and beasts of draught and burden. In a set form of words (Gaius 1. 119) the recipient asserted his ownership of the property, and struck the scales with the copper; the act acquired a kind of publicity by the presence of five citizens as witnesses and the *libripens* holding the scales (*see* TESTIMONIUM). A. B.; B. N.

**MANDURIA,** principal town of the Sallentini in the 'heel' of Italy. Its Messapic remains (extensive town-walls, necropolis, etc.) are of exceptional interest. The Tarentine mercenary, Archidamus III (q.v.), of Sparta possibly fell here, 338 B.C. (Plut. *Agis* 3. 2, emending *Mandonion*). A curious fountain described by Pliny (*HN* 2. 226) still exists at modern Manduria.

G. B. Arno, *Manduria*² (1954). E. T. S.

**MANES,** the spirits of the dead. The most generally accepted derivation is that from the old Latin adjective *manus*, 'good'; the appellation may be euphemistic (but see Latte, *RR* 99, n. 3). (i) In early times the dead were thought of as an undifferentiated mass with a collective divinity expressed in *Di Manes*; Cicero (*Leg.* 2. 9. 22) quotes the ancient ordinance 'deorum manium iura sacra sunto'. Graves were dedicated to them in the formula DIS MANIBUS SACRUM, and they were worshipped at the festivals of the Feralia, Parentalia, and Lemuria (qq.v.). From this primary sense there are two derivatives: (*a*) *manes* is used by the poets in a topographical sense for the realm of the dead (e.g. Verg. *Aen.* 11. 181). (*b*) *Manes* was applied to the Graeco-Roman underworld gods, Dis, Orcus, Persephone, etc. (e.g. Verg. *Aen.* 10. 39). (ii) Later in a special, though still collective sense, the *Di Manes* were identified with the *Di Parentes*, the ancestors of the family (e.g. Ov. *Met.* 9. 407). (iii) Still later *manes* came to be used of the soul of individual dead persons. The first recorded instance is Cic. *Pis.* 16 'coniuratorum manes', and in Augustan writers the usage is frequent (e.g. Livy 3. 58. 11 'manes Verginiae'); and so in the famous line of Virgil, *Aen.* 6. 743, 'quisque suos patimur manes'. From the beginning of the Empire it became customary on grave inscriptions to add to DIS MANIBUS SACRUM the name of the dead person in the genitive or dative case (see Latte, *RR* 99, n. 4, for the inscriptional evidence). *See also* AFTER-LIFE, § 8. C. B.

**MANETHO** (fl. 280 B.C.), Egyptian high-priest in Heliopolis under the first two Ptolemies, who dedicated to Ptolemy II a history of Egypt (Αἰγυπτιακά) from mythical times to 323. His claim to have consulted the lists of kings (ἱερὰ γράμματα) implies that his version was more official than that of Hecataeus of Teos. The three-fold division of the thirty-one dynasties corresponds with the recognized division into old, middle, and new kingdoms. Frequently used by Jewish and Christian writers to establish biblical chronology.

*FGrH* iii C 609; Manetho, ed. W. G. Waddell (Loeb; with Ptolemy, *Tetrabiblos*, ed. F. E. Robbins). G. L. B.

**MANIA,** Roman goddess of whom nothing certain is known except her name. This apparently means 'the good one', cf. *manes*, and may be a euphemism for a death-goddess. By way, it would appear, of the theory that the Lares (q.v.) are ghosts, ancient speculation made Mania their mother (Varro, *Ling.* 9. 61), and this affects

late cult (Henzen, *Acta Arvalium* (1874), 145; add Dessau, *ILS* 9522).

F. Altheim, *Hist. Rom. Rel.* 117 f., 133. H. J. R.

**MANICHAEISM,** a developed form of gnosticism (q.v.) founded by the Syriac-speaking Babylonian Mani (A.D. 216–77). At first influenced by a gnostic sect like the Mandaeans (some of whose hymns the Manichees used), he left the sect after two visions convinced him that he was a manifestation of the Paraclete promised by Jesus. After visiting India he returned to the Sassanid Empire, where he enjoyed friendly relations with Sapor I (q.v.); but Mazdean opposition under Bahrâm I led to his death. He left tracts, sermons, and hymns. A systematic catechism (*Kephalaia*), preserved in Coptic, was edited in his name. His doctrine was a religion of redemption in which dualistic myth provided a rationale for an ascetic ethic. A precosmic invasion of the realm of light by the forces of darkness had resulted in the present intermingling of good and evil, the divine substance being imprisoned in matter. In Jesus the Son of God came to save his own soul, lost in Adam. The Elect, to whom all worldly occupations and possessions were forbidden, participated in redemption and were destined for deliverance from transmigration. The community also included an inferior order of Hearers who by keeping simple moral rules could hope for rebirth as one of the Elect.

Proscribed in the Roman Empire by Diocletian (297: his edict is preserved) and later Emperors, it was attacked by Neoplatonists (Alexander of Lycopolis *c.* 300, Simplicius *c.* 540) and Christians (Hegemonius, Titus of Bostra, Serapion of Thmuis, Ephraem Syrus, Epiphanius, Augustine, cf. Rylands papyrus 469). Nevertheless, it spread rapidly in the West; Augustine (q.v.) was a Hearer for nine years. Eastwards, the advent of Islam drove it across central Asia to survive in China till the fourteenth century. Important texts and paintings were found (1895–1912) at Turfan in Chinese Turkestan, and many Coptic papyri in Egypt in 1933. In the medieval West its legacy passed to the Paulicians and Bogomils.

H.-C. Puech, *Le Manichéisme* (1949); G. Widengren, *Mani und der Manichäismus* (1961, E.T. 1965). Bibliography, *CAH* xii. 773 ff.
H. C.

**MANILIUS** (1, *PW* 12), MANIUS. After a not very successful praetorship in Spain (154 B.C., or 155) Manilius as consul in 149 commenced the siege of Carthage in the Third Punic War, his colleague L. Marcius Censorinus co-operating by sea. After two expeditions to Nepheris (south-east of Tunis) had been saved from disaster by Scipio Aemilianus, Manilius was superseded in 148. In 133 he urged Tiberius Gracchus to submit his dispute with Octavius to the Senate. He was introduced by Cicero as one of the speakers in the *De Republica*. He was a famous jurist, one of three who 'fundauerunt ius ciuile' (Pomponius). His works included *Monumenta*, presumably consisting of *responsa*, and a collection of *formulae* (precedents for contracts, wills, and pleadings, etc.). A few of his *actiones* and *responsa* survive (see Huschke, *Iurisprud. anteiust. Reliquiae*⁶ 1. 5–7). H. H. S.

**MANILIUS** (2, *PW* 10, cf. 23), GAIUS, on the last day of 67 B.C. carried as tribune a law distributing freedmen through all the tribes; this the Senate annulled next day for non-observance of the *trinundinum*. Manilius then (66) conferred on Pompey the command against Mithridates and Tigranes, with *imperium* over all the provinces of Asia Minor. On laying down his tribunate he was prosecuted for *repetundae* by Pompey's enemy Cn. Piso, but the case was dropped amid the disturbance of Jan. 65, to which date Cicero, praetor for 66, had postponed it.

But Manilius was soon prosecuted for *maiestas* and condemned.

Asconius 53, 57 ff.; Schol. Bob. *Cic. Mil.* 284 Or.; Dio 36. 42. 4; Plut. *Cic.* 9. G. E. F. C.

**MANILIUS** (3, *PW* 6), MARCUS, author of the *Astronomica*, a didactic poem on astrology, wrote under Augustus and Tiberius. (Book 1. 899 mentions Varus' defeat in A.D. 9, while in 384–6, etc., Augustus (who died in August A.D. 14) is still alive, as he is in 2. 508–9; in 4. 763–6 and 773–7 Tiberius is the reigning *princeps*.) Of the man himself we know nothing else whatever. Of his work we have five books. Book 1 (926 lines) describes the creation, the arrangement of the starry heavens, and the circles which mark them out; book 2 (970 lines) the signs of the zodiac, their characteristics, mutual aspects, and subdivisions; book 3 (682 lines) their division into twelve *sortes*, methods of determining the place of the horoscope, etc.; book 4 (935 lines) their influence on men born under them, their divisions as combined in decads, and other technicalities; book 5 (745 lines) the risings of the other signs and their effects on children born on each occasion. Thus many essential parts of the subject are omitted, for instance any discussion of the movements and influence of the planets; but whether the work is incompletely preserved or was never finished we cannot tell. Manilius writes as an enthusiast for his subject, anxious to make converts and to provide practical instruction for their use, but his poem even if complete would not serve as a technical treatise. He is not seldom inaccurate and sometimes appears to have misunderstood his sources; what these were is unknown, for much of what he tells us appears nowhere else. He is not a great poet, but his literary gifts are by no means negligible. If sometimes feeble or obscure, his language is correct, often forcible, and sometimes eloquent, and he writes with an easy mastery of the technique of hexameters; his skill in doing sums in verse is worthy of Ovid. Much of the poem is condemned by its subject to find few readers, but the non-technical books 1 and 5, and the proems to the others, deserve to be better known. To students of Latin he will always appeal as the object of some of the best work of three great latinists, Scaliger, Bentley, and Housman.

*See also* ASTROLOGY.

TEXT AND COMMENTARY. A. E. Housman, 5 vols. 1903–30 (with Latin notes); text only, 1932. Book 2 (with English notes and translation) H. W. Garrod, 1911. D. R. Shackleton Bailey, *CQ* 1956, 81 ff.; W. Bühler, *Hermes* 1959, 475 ff. (with full bibliography of recent work). R. A. B. M.

**MANIPULUS.** With the introduction, perhaps during the fourth century B.C., of the *pilum* or throwing spear, the legion ceased to be a phalanx and was organized for open-order fighting. It was subdivided into thirty maniples, which in the Polybian period varied in strength from 120 to 200 men. Each maniple comprised two centuries, was commanded by the centurion of the right-hand century, and had its own standard (*signum*). For tactical purposes the maniples were normally drawn up in three lines with the rear units covering off the intervals in the line in front. After the introduction of the cohort as a tactical unit the maniple gradually lost its importance.

Parker, *Roman Legions*, 11 ff. H. M. D. P.

**MANLIUS** (*PW* 51), MARCUS, according to Roman tradition defeated the Aequi as consul in 392 B.C., held the Capitol against the Gauls, and repulsed a night attack after being awakened by the cackling of the sacred geese (387); hence he was surnamed *Capitolinus*. It is not unlikely that he or his kinsmen rendered distinguished service against the Celts, but the above story in its present form is probably an aetiological myth invented to explain the surname *Capitolinus* borne by a branch of the Manlii,

because they lived on the Capitol even before the sack of Rome. In the crisis that followed the Gallic catastrophe Manlius, though a patrician, probably supported the poor against Camillus (q.v. 1), and may have made an abortive attempt at revolution, in which he fell. The traditional account was greatly elaborated by late annalists, who read back into the story of Manlius the aims and policy of the *plebs* in and after the Gracchan period.

Mommsen, *Röm. Forsch.* ii. 179 ff.; Ogilvie, *Comm. Livy 1–5*, 694, 734 f. P. T.

**MANTINEA** lay in a plain of south-east Arcadia, to the north of Tegea (q.v.). The two States were constantly at war over boundaries and the control of the swallow-holes which drained the plain (Thuc. 5. 65); their rivalry often prevented the Arcadians from uniting against Sparta. Mantinea was synoecized from five villages (Strabo 337), probably *c.* 500 B.C., when its coinage began. It became a moderate democracy *c.* 450 B.C. (for date of synoecism and democracy, not necessarily related, see *PW* xiv. 1318 ff.). Mantinea withdrew from the anti-Spartan movement after the Persian Wars (Hdt. 9. 35) and supported Sparta in the helot revolt (Xen. *Hell.* 5. 2. 3) (see also, on fifth-century Arcadian–Argive–Spartan relations, W. G. Forrest, 'Themistokles and Argos', *CQ* 1960, 221 ff., and A. Andrewes, 'Sparta and Arcadia in the Early Fifth Century', *Phoenix* 1952, 1 ff.); but under the democracy it grew in power and joined Sparta's enemies in 420. It was the scene of a decisive Spartan victory in 418. After the peace of 387 the Spartans obliged the Mantineans to dismantle their walls and live in villages, but after the battle of Leuctra (371) the city was restored. In 362 Epaminondas won his last victory over the Spartans here. The city was destroyed by the Achaean League in 223 and refounded under the name of Antigonea. Unlike most fortified Greek cities, Mantinea stood in the middle of a plain.

*IG* v. 2, 46 ff. G. Fougères, *Mantinée et l' Arcadie orientale* (1898); Bölte, *PW* xiv. 1290 ff.; W. J. Woodhouse, *King Agis of Sparta* (1933) (battle of 418 B.C.). T. J. D.; R. J. H.

**MANTUA,** modern *Mantova*, town of (presumably) Etruscan origin between Cremona and Verona in Cisalpine Gaul (q.v.), situated amid the sluggish waters of the River Mincius. Seldom mentioned in ancient literature, Mantua is famous as the town near which Virgil was born and whose territory the Second Triumvirate confiscated. E. T. S.

**MANUBIAE** (or *manibiae*, as in inscriptions. From *manus* and *habeo*, or rather perhaps from an old verb *manuo* = to grasp). The original meaning of this term has been variously defined, (1) (Mommsen) as the revenue raised from the public sale of booty (Gell. 13. 25. 28: 'pecunia per quaestorem populi Romani ex praeda uendita contracta'), or, (2), more probably (Karlowa), as the portion of the booty reserved for the victorious general, which he could dispose of at his discretion (Ps.-Asc. in Cic. *Verr.* 2. 1. 54: 'manubiae . . . sunt praeda imperatoris pro portione de hostibus capta'). Although legally he could not be prosecuted for any use to which he put his share of the booty, the commander generally devoted it to works of public utility (temples, roads, forums, theatres, etc.), or, to avoid popular resentment, he shared it or the proceeds of its sale with his officers and men. Thus the distinction between *praeda* and *manubiae* was easily forgotten or ignored, especially when the Emperors compelled their officials to contribute a certain amount of their *manubiae* to the Emperor's privy purse.

Mommsen, *Röm. Forsch.* ii. 443 ff. (cf. J. Marquardt, *Röm. Staatsverw.*, ii. 277 f.); O. Karlowa, *Röm. Rechtsgesch.* (1885–1901), ii. 1, 5 (cf. Ph. Fabia, Dar.-Sag. iii. 2, 1582 ff.). P. T.

**MANUS** was the power (akin to *patria potestas*, q.v.) which a husband might have over his wife. Entry into *manus* (*conventio in manum*) took place in three ways. *Confarreatio*, the earliest form, was a religious ceremony in the presence of ten witnesses (requiring the assistance of a pontiff and the utterance of formal words); it was necessary for, and perhaps confined to, the members of certain priesthoods. *Coemptio*, evidently a survival of marriage by purchase, was a *mancipatio* (q.v.) of the wife to the husband. In the absence of these two forms, marriage by itself did not result in *manus*, but would do so by prescription (*usus*) if the partners lived together as man and wife uninterruptedly for a year. By a rule of the XII Tables if the wife was absent for three successive nights, the *usus* was interrupted. The legal effects of *conventio in manum* were similar to those of *adoptio* (q.v.), the wife being *filiae loco* to her husband.

Marriage with *manus* was evidently uncommon by the end of the Republic. *Usus* was obsolete by the second century A.D., and *coemptio* was perhaps only used as a collusive device (*coemptio fiduciae causa*) to enable a woman to escape from *tutela* (*see* GUARDIANSHIP). *Confarreatio* may have lasted as long as the old religion. *See also* MARRIAGE, LAW OF. B. N.

**MAPS** (πίνακες). For measuring distances the Greeks and Romans counted the steps of a pedestrian or estimated the length of a sea-journey on a basis of 500 stades (*c.* 55 statute miles) by sea. Lacking the compass, they determined direction by the sun or stars. For latitude they used sticks that projected their shadow into a bowl (πόλοι, introduced from Babylon by Anaximander). For longitude they were reduced to guesswork, since their sand- or water-clocks were useless for synchronizing. In spite of this primitive equipment, the Greeks achieved considerable proficiency in cartography. Their first world-maps, constructed in the sixth century by Anaximander and Hecataeus (1) (qq.v.), showed a plane landmass of circular contour round the Mediterranean basin. Herodotus (esp. 4. 36-40) derided these 'compass-drawn' maps and had a rudimentary idea of meridians. Local maps had become familiar in the fifth century (Ar. *Nub.* 200 ff.).

The foundations of scientific cartography were laid when Aristotle (*Cael.* 293ᵇ ff., *Mete.* 362ᵃ ff.) confirmed the sphericity of the earth (previously assumed by Pythagoras) and defined more closely the five zones of Parmenides. Parallels of latitude were established by Pytheas (q.v.), and Dicaearchus (q.v.; *c.* 310 B.C.) laid down a median line from Gibraltar to the Himalayas. Eratosthenes (q.v.; *c.* 200) made a scientific and accurate computation of the earth's circumference, and drew two main axes of latitude and longitude intersecting at Rhodes, with corresponding parallels. His world-map was the first to achieve tolerable accuracy. Hipparchus (q.v. 3; *c.* 140) divided Eratosthenes' main parallel of latitude into 360 degrees and drew 12 parallels of latitude (with details of longest days), dividing the land-mass into 'climata' or zones. Crates constructed a large globe (with three imaginary land-masses besides the known one).

The results of Greek cartography were combined with data from Roman road-makers by Artemidorus, and especially by Agrippa (Pliny, *HN* 3. 17; R. Mauny, *Hespéris* 1949, 47 ff.), who set up a large globe at Rome. Strabo discussed the principles of map-making on plane and sphere (3. 116-17, 120). Lastly, Ptolemy (q.v. 4) constructed a plane world-map, using a modified method of conical projection (with curved lines of latitude and longitude), and furnished delusively accurate calculations of latitude north of the Equator and of longitude east of the Canaries. Copies of his map survive in his manuscripts. Other extant maps are a street-plan of Rome (*Forma*

*Urbis Romae*) *c.* A.D. 200; the Peutinger Table (q.v.); and various road-maps (*see* ITINERARIES). *See also* GEOGRAPHY, PEUTINGER TABLE.

E. H. Bunbury, *History of Ancient Geography* (1879, 1883, 1959), with maps; E. H. Warmington, *Greek Geography* (1934), 234 ff.; H. Berger, *Geschichte der wissenschaftlichen Erdkunde der Griechen* (1903); W. Kubitschek, *PW* x. 2022 ff.; and Suppl. vi. 31 ff. Thomson, *Hist. Anc. Geog.*, index s.vv. maps, Eratosthenes, Hipparchus, Strabo, Ptolemy, etc.; A. Libault, *Histoire de la cartographie* (1959); R. M. Bentham, *The Fragments of Eratosthenes* (1948; Univ. of London; unpublished but very important); D. R. Dicks, *The Geographical Fragments of Hipparchus* (1960), 204 ff. (stereographic projection); 146 ff. (circumference of the earth); cf. Dicks, *CQ* 1955, 248 ff. (κλίματα); O. Neugebauer, *The Exact Sciences in Antiquity* (1942), 220 ff.; A. Diller, *Isis* 1949, 6 ff. E. H. W.

**MARATHON,** a large Attic deme on the north-east coast, with its centre near Vrana, although the scanty remains there do not justify a positive identification. It commanded part of a long, fertile plain lying beside a deep bay sheltered at its northern end, and was a member of an ancient religious confederacy of neighbouring communities called the Tetrapolis. Partly because it was connected to Athens by a main road running south of Mt. Pentelicus, the plain was the scene of two hostile landings, the first by Pisistratus *c.* 545 B.C. when he recovered Athens for the last time, the second by the Persians in 490 when the Athenians helped by the Plataeans became the first Greeks to defeat Persia. Of the sons of Marathon perhaps Herodes (q.v. 2) Atticus was the most famous.

W. K. Pritchett, *Marathon* (1960); E. Vanderpool, 'The Deme of M. and the Herakleion, *AJArch.* 1966, 319 ff.; 'A Monument to the Battle of M.', *Hesp.* 1966, 93 ff.; N. G. Hammond, *JHS* 1968. C. W. J. E.

**MARBLE.** Under μάρμαρος, *marmor*, the ancients included granites, porphyries, and all stones capable of taking a high polish.

In the third millennium B.C. the white marbles of the Greek Islands were used for Cycladic sculpture. The Minoans employed coloured marbles and breccias for vases and furniture and in architecture for facings and column bases. The Mycenaeans also used coloured marbles including green porphyry and rosso antico for furniture and in architectural decoration. Neither the Minoans nor the Mycenaeans used marble as a building stone or for sculpture.

The fine white marbles of Greece and the Greek Islands were widely used for architecture and sculpture from the seventh century B.C. onwards. Grey Naxian and white Parian were the best of the island marbles; Attic marbles were the fine-grained Pentelic used in the Parthenon and other fifth-century buildings, and the inferior Hymettian. Coloured marbles for use especially in interior decoration came into fashion in Hellenistic times.

In Italy the Etruscans made little use of marble and the famous quarries at Luna (*Carrara*) were not opened commercially until the middle of the first century B.C. by the Romans. Augustus employed marble, specially Luna marble, extensively in his programme of rebuilding the city of Rome. Throughout the Empire public buildings were often constructed of marble, but more commonly the marble was used as a facing for brick and concrete construction. A wide variety of coloured marbles was popular; they were used for columns as well as interior decoration. For statuary the Romans used Luna marble, most of the Greek marbles, and some coloured marbles. A flourishing marble trade was carried on throughout the Empire, the main quarries being in imperial control under a special office, the *ratio marmorum*. The storehouses of foreign marbles have been discovered by the Tiber in Rome.

Pliny, *HN* 36. *Enciclopedia dell'arte antica*, s.v. marmo; J. B. Ward-Perkins, *JRS* 1951, 89 ff. D. E. S.

**MARCELLINUS** (1) (probably 2nd c. A.D.), author of an extant work Περὶ σφυγμῶν, borrowed very largely from Hippocrates.

Ed. H. Schöne, *Festschrift zur 49. Versammlung deutscher Philologen und Schulmänner* (1907).

**MARCELLINUS** (2), biographer of Thucydides (text in Jones and Powell's ed. of Thuc., 1938). His 'Life' contains three sections, of which A (ch. 1–45) is probably the 'Life of Thucydides' from [Proclus'] *Chrestomathia*, worked over by a schoolmaster, and B (ch. 46–53) by a contemporary of Dion. Hal. (perhaps Caecilius), whose main interest was Thucydides' style. To these Zosimus (5th c. A.D.) added C (ch. 54–8) to make the introduction to his edition of scholia on Isocrates, Demosthenes, and Thucydides. Marcellinus was probably the scholar, who, shortly after Justinian, isolated the Thucydidean scholia and gave the composition his name. Its main value lies in the biographical parts, where the deductive method is employed to reach sound conclusions. F. W. W.

**MARCELLUS** (1), MARCUS CLAUDIUS (*PW* 220), served in the First Punic War and was augur, aedile, and praetor. As consul (222 B.C.) he campaigned successfully against the Insubres, relieving Clastidium and winning the *spolia opima* (q.v.) by killing the Gallic chief Viridomarus in single combat; he celebrated a triumph. As praetor II he thwarted Hannibal's attack on Nola (216). He was appointed *consul suffectus* for 215, but abdicated when the augurs objected to two plebeian consuls and declared his election invalid. In 215, with proconsular *imperium*, and as consul III in 214 he followed a Fabian strategy from his base at Castra Claudiana near Suessula, whence he parried two further thrusts by Hannibal on Nola; in 214 he stormed Casilinum. From the autumn until 211 he served in Sicily. He sacked Leontini, commenced the blockade of Syracuse by land and sea (213), stormed Epipolae (212), and finally took Syracuse despite the engineering skill of Archimedes (211). After routing a Carthaginian force near Himera he returned to Rome and celebrated an *ovatio*. As consul IV (210), proconsul (209), and consul V (208) he skirmished cautiously but successfully against Hannibal until he was killed while reconnoitring near Venusia. Named the Sword of Rome, he had shown an energy which set him above most of his contemporaries, while the exaggerations which embellish the annalistic accounts of his exploits against Hannibal are a tribute to his vigorous personality. His faith was exemplified in his dedication of temples to Honos and Virtus, his appreciation of Greek culture by the artistic treasures which he shipped from Syracuse to Rome. For his appearance see coin, *CAH*, Pl. IV, 57. H. H. S.

**MARCELLUS** (2), MARCUS CLAUDIUS (*PW* 222), eldest son of (1), tribune (204 B.C.), curule aedile (200), praetor in Sicily (198), became consul in 196, crushing the Insubrians near Comum; he was legate in Gaul (193). Censor in 189 with T. Flamininus, he restored census rights to the Campanians. He died in 177. A. H. McD.

**MARCELLUS** (3), MARCUS CLAUDIUS (*PW* 225), tribune in 171 B.C., was praetor in 169, when, after intervening in the levies, he commanded in Spain (169–168); he became consul in 166 in Liguria. He was consul again in 155 in Liguria, and for a third time in 152, within the ten years' interval, on account of the war in Spain. He subdued the Celtiberians and negotiated a peace in the liberal tradition of Sempronius Gracchus (152–151); the Scipionic tradition (in Polybius) depreciates his achievement. He was drowned in 148 on an embassy to Africa.

H. Simon, *Roms Kriege in Spanien, 154–133 v. Chr.* (1962), 30 ff.; R. L. Calvert, *Athenaeum* 1964, 11 ff. A. H. McD.

**MARCELLUS** (4), MARCUS CLAUDIUS (*PW* 229), consul 51 B.C., proposed a motion, declared illegal by the Caesarians, probably to recall Caesar on 1 Mar. 50. Pompey resisted this, but in October Marcellus carried various resolutions which, though some were vetoed, ensured that the question be discussed on the ensuing 1 March. He also declared invalid the *Lex Vatinia* on Novum Comum, and flogged a citizen of Comum to prove that he was not a Roman. After Pharsalus Marcellus retired to Mytilene, but in Sept. 46 Caesar allowed his return; Cicero in gratitude delivered the *pro Marcello*. But in May 45 Marcellus was murdered at the Piraeus, and Caesar, unjustly according to Cicero, was suspected of complicity.

SOURCES. (a) The *Relatio* of 51: [Hirtius], *BGall.* 8. 53. 1; Suet. *Iul.* 28; Dio 40. 59. 1; App. *BCiv.* 2. 25; Cic. *Att.* 8. 3. 3; (b) the flogging: E. G. Hardy, *Problems in Roman History* (1924), 126 ff. G. E. F. C.

**MARCELLUS** (5), GAIUS CLAUDIUS (*PW* 216), first cousin of (4), was consul in 50 B.C. Frustrated in his efforts to procure Caesar's recall, he called on Pompey to take command of the two legions stationed at Capua and to raise more troops (2 Dec.). After the outbreak of war, however, he remained in Italy and obtained Caesar's pardon. He took no part in the dissensions of 44–42 and died in 40. By his wife Octavia (2) he had three children, Marcellus (7) and two daughters: the elder Marcella married, c. 28 B.C., Agrippa (3) and, after being divorced by him in 21, Iullus Antonius (8); the younger Marcella, born in 40, was married to a M. Valerius Messalla (*cos.* 12 B.C.), and to Paullus (4 or perhaps 5).

Syme, *Rom. Rev.*, see index. G. W. R.; T. J. C.

**MARCELLUS** (6), GAIUS CLAUDIUS (*PW* 217), brother of (4), was consul in 49 B.C. He supported Pompey and crossed over to Greece with him; in 48 he was joint-commander of the Rhodian section of his fleet. He probably died before the battle of Pharsalus. T. J. C.

**MARCELLUS** (7), MARCUS CLAUDIUS (*PW* 230), son of (5) above and of Octavia (2), sister of Augustus, was born in 42 B.C. His betrothal in 39 to a daughter of Sextus Pompeius (q.v. 6) was brief. In 25 he and Tiberius served in Spain under Augustus, whose preference for Marcellus was shown by his marriage in the same year to Julia (q.v. 2); and in 24 a more rapid anticipation of the normal *cursus* was decreed for Marcellus than for Tiberius. In 23, as aedile, Marcellus gave exceptionally magnificent games. He began to be thought of as a rival to Agrippa (q.v. 3) for the position of heir to the monarchy, but he died late in 23. He was buried in Augustus' own mausoleum; Octavia named a library after him and Augustus a theatre. His death was lamented by Virgil (*Aen.* 6. 860–86) and Propertius (3. 18).

Syme, *Rom. Rev.*, see index.
LIBRARY AND THEATRE. Platner–Ashby, 84 f., 513 ff.; Nash, *Pict. Dict. Rome* ii. 254 ff., 418 ff.
ICONOGRAPHY. V. H. Poulsen, *Acta archaeologica* 1946, 12, 22 ff.; L. Fabbrini, *Arch. Class.* 1961, 152 ff. A. M.; T. J. C.

**MARCELLUS** (8), MARCUS POMPONIUS (early 1st c. A.D.), grammarian, notorious for pedantic purism in diction. Nothing of his work remains.

Schanz–Hosius, § 475 a.

**MARCELLUS** (9) of Side, physician and poet, lived under Hadrian and Antoninus Pius and wrote forty-two books of 'Ιατρικά in heroic metre (lost); Περὶ λυκανθρώπου; a poem Περὶ ἰχθύων (fragments preserved); *Epigrammata* written in A.D. 160 for Herodes Atticus' *Triopion*.

Ed. M. Schneider, *Commentationes philologae quibus O. Ribbeckio . . . congratulantur discipuli* (1888), 115. M. Wellmann, *Marcellus von Side als Arzt* (1934).

**MARCELLUS** (10), ULPIUS (*PW* 4), a Roman jurist of the second half of the second century A.D., a member of the *consilium* of Antoninus Pius and Marcus Aurelius. An acute, independent thinker, he criticizes effectively the opinions of earlier jurists (even those of Julianus, q.v. 2), and is cited with predilection by his successors. His main work was the *Digesta* (thirty-one books), a partly casuistic, partly dogmatic treatise, which was extensively used by later jurists (particularly by Ulpianus (q.v. 1) in his commentary on the Edict), and was also discussed in special commentaries by Ulpianus and Scaevola (q.v. 5). Marcellus also wrote *notae* to the *Digesta* of Julianus and to Pomponius' *Regulae*, and besides this a collection of *Responsa*, a commentary *Ad legem Iuliam et Papiam*, and five books *De officio consulis*.

A. B.; B. N.

**MARCIA,** a freedwoman, was mistress of Quadratus and, after his execution, of Commodus (q.v.). Friend and helper of the Christians, she co-operated in the murder of Commodus. She later married Eclectus and was killed by Didius Julianus. H. M. D. P.

**MARCIANA,** ULPIA, older sister of Trajan (q.v.), was born at latest by A.D. 48 and probably married C. Salonius Matidius Patruinus (d. 78), by whom she had one daughter, Matidia (q.v.). Pliny (*Pan.* 84) speaks of her closeness to Trajan and Plotina. Indeed Trajan named for her two new settlements: *Colonia Ulpia Marciana Traiana* (Thamugadi, q.v.). and *Marcianapolis* in Lower Moesia (Provadiya). Though Marciana at first refused the title *Augusta*, she had accepted it by 105 (*ILS* 288). On her death in 112, she was consecrated (*Fasti Ost.*, s.a.) and in 119 Hadrian apparently flanked a temple to Matidia in Rome with halls commemorating both Marciana and Matidia.

COINS. *B.M. Coins, Rom. Emp.* iii (1936); Strack, *Untersuchungen I* (1931), 41, 201 Katalog.
I. Rubel, *Z. für die öst. Gym.* 1916, 488 ff.; L. Vidmann, *Fasti Ost.* (1957), 64; Platner–Ashby, 81; Wegner, *Herrscherbild* ii. 3 (1956). M. H.

**MARCIANUS,** AELIUS (*PW* 88), one of the last classical Roman jurists, was active in the period after Caracalla. He was the author of voluminous manuals (*Institutiones, Regulae*) and some monographs, chiefly in the domain of criminal procedure, and perhaps addressed to the new citizens created by the *Constitutio Antoniniana* (see CITIZENSHIP, ROMAN) for the purpose of instructing them in Roman Law. He cites numerous rescripts, especially from the period 198–211. This has led some to conjecture that he held office in the imperial chancery. His writings are elegant, clear, well-arranged, and not unoriginal.

W. W. Buckland, *Studi Riccobono* i (1932). *And see under* JURIS-PRUDENCE. A. B.; B. N.

**MARCIUS** (1, *PW* 9), ANCUS, traditionally the fourth king of Rome (642–617 B.C.), is probably a historical figure and not an annalistic reduplication of the portrait of Numa. To surmise, from the connexion of Marcius' name with Mars, that he was a god, or that his acts are mere duplications of achievements by members of the *gens* Marcia, is quite gratuitous. He did not build the Aqua Marcia (cf. REX 1) or capture and colonize Ostia (q.v.), but indubitably he seized from the Etruscans a territory near the salt-pits at the Tiber mouth, he enlarged Rome, and he built the Pons Sublicius.

Ogilvie, *Comm. Livy 1–5*, 125 ff. P. T.

**MARCIUS** (2, *PW* 97) RUTILUS, GAIUS, consul in 357, 352, 344, and 342 B.C., was the first plebeian dictator (356) and censor (351). His repulse of an Etruscan invasion in 356, for which despite patrician opposition Marcius

was granted a triumph, led to the foundation of the first Roman settlement at Ostia. By a natural confusion this settlement was subsequently attributed to King Ancus Marcius (q.v. 1). P. T.

**MARCIUS** (3) is the eponymous author of a number of miscellaneous oracular sayings current in Rome in early days. During the Punic Wars certain *carmina Marciana*, similar to the Sibylline oracles, succeeded in obtaining sufficient authority to give rise to the Ludi Apollinares celebrated in 212. This may have been due partly to war-time conditions, and partly to the collection of scattered oracular sayings and prophecies ordered to be made by the Senate in the previous year. There seem to have been two diverging views about their authorship. According to Cicero (*Div.* 1. 115; 2. 113), whose view is supported by Servius in his commentary on *Aeneid* 6, there were *Marcii fratres*, men of noble birth, who wrote prophecies and oracular sayings. According to Livy, however, and several later writers, there was one only, *vates Marcius*; and it seems impossible to determine the truth more exactly.

Of an ancient collection of *praecepta* under the name of Marcius three Saturnian quotations survive, which may be dated at latest as of the second century B.C. It is uncertain whether they have any connexion with *Marcius vates*.

See Morel, *FPL* 63. A. L. P.

**MARCOMAN(N)I** (Stat. *Silv.* 3. 3. 170 scans Marcomǎni), a West-German (Suebic) tribe, the name meaning inhabitants of a border country, are first mentioned by Caesar. Stirred up by the Cimbri and Teutones, the Marcomanni left Saxony and Thuringia (*c.* 100 B.C.) and settled down on the upper and middle Main; they joined Ariovistus' expedition against Gaul. Attacked by the elder Drusus (9 B.C.), they emigrated to Bohemia (*c.* 8 B.C.). There Maroboduus (q.v.) established a powerful kingdom, which Augustus considered a danger and wanted to destroy, but was hindered by the Pannonian-Illyrian revolt. Weakened by a war against Arminius, Maroboduus was expelled by Catualda (A.D. 19), who in turn was overthrown by Vibilius (20), the following kings being more or less dependent on Rome. After wars under Domitian and Nerva peace prevailed till the great Marcomannic wars (166–72; 177–80) under M. Aurelius. The Marcomanni must have played their part in the subsequent wars on the middle Danube, though they are not very frequently mentioned. After 500 they left Bohemia and occupied Bavaria.

J. Klose, *Roms Klientel- und Randstaaten am Rhein und an der Donau* (1934); R. Heuberger, *Klio* 1931, 89 ff.; L. Schmidt, *Geschichte der deutschen Stämme bis zum Ausgang der Völkerwanderung. Die Westgermanen²* (1938); W. Zwikker, *Studien zur Markussäule* i (Amsterdam, 1941). F. A. W. S.

**MARDONIUS,** the brilliant young nephew and son-in-law of Darius, took over command in Ionia *c.* 492, immediately after the great Ionian Revolt, and removed one major cause of discontent by abolishing government through 'tyrants' and permitting democracies. He *may* have served during the Revolt, under Datis at Lindos (*Lind. Tempelchronik*, ed. Blinkenberg (1915), 38). He then restored Persian authority in southern Thrace, despite storm damage to his fleet off Mount Athos, and being himself wounded by the Brygians. Herodotus makes him the moving spirit of Xerxes' invasion. Left in command in Greece after Salamis, he vainly attempted to detach Athens from the Greek alliance by offers of favourable terms. Withdrawing from Attica in 479 in face of the Greek land-forces, he gave battle near Plataea and was defeated and killed (*see* PERSIAN WARS).

Hdt. 6. 43–5; 7. 5, 9; 8, 9, *passim*; Beloch, *Gr. Gesch.* ii². 8₃ ff. A. R. B.

**MARINUS** (*c.* A.D. 130), anatomist, often mentioned by Galen, perhaps lived in Alexandria.

WORKS: (1) Ἀνατομικαὶ ἐγχειρήσεις; (2) an Anatomy in 20 books; (3) a book on the roots of the nerves; (4) an Anatomy of the muscles; (5) a commentary on aphorisms.
W. D. R.

**MARIUS** (1, *PW* 14, Suppl. vi), GAIUS, born *c.* 157 B.C. near Arpinum (q.v.), of an equestrian family apparently not of long standing, but with good Roman connexions (including the Metelli). Serving under Scipio (q.v. 11) Aemilianus at Numantia, he attracted his attention and thus won an elective military tribunate (perhaps 129, before Scipio's death). Quaestor *c.* 123, he was helped to a tribunate by the Metelli (119), but—in an anti-Optimate atmosphere—carried a law impeding Optimate intervention in comitial voting procedure, and threatened Metellus (q.v. 5) who opposed it. Disliked for this, he failed to gain an aedileship, but became praetor (115), barely securing acquittal (through his 'equestrian' connexions) when prosecuted for *ambitus*. His year passed quietly, and as proconsul in Spain he showed aptitude at guerrilla warfare. On his return he brought off a *coup* by marrying a patrician Julia (later aunt of Caesar, 1). In 109 Metellus (q.v. 6), impressed with his promise, forgave his past and took him to Numidia as his senior legate. There Marius began to aim at a consulship. Insulted by Metellus over this, he intrigued against him in Numidia and Rome and secured election for 107; by a special law he superseded Metellus. In enrolling troops he remedied the long-standing manpower shortage by admitting *proletarii* (q.v.), thus creating—without realizing it—a new type of client army, bound to its commander as its patron.

After fighting against Jugurtha (q.v.) with varying success, he finished the war through the diplomacy of his quaestor Sulla (q.v. 1) and triumphed on 1 Jan. 104, having already been elected consul again to oppose a threatened German invasion of Italy. Consul each year until 101, he enrolled a new army and—building on the work of Rutilius (q.v. 1)—improved its organization, equipment, and training (*see* ARMIES, ROMAN); he finally defeated the Teutones (q.v.) at Aquae Sextiae (102) and with Catulus (q.v. 2) the Cimbri (q.v.) at the Vercellae (probably near Rovigo, in the Po valley) (101). He thus built up immense *auctoritas*, attracting nobles who hoped for his favour (*see* CATULUS 2), retaining the support of *equites* and *plebs*, and securing the clientship of his Numidian veterans through land grants passed for him by Saturninus (q.v. 1). Voted a sixth consulship (100) without serious opposition, he hoped for similar aid for his German army and gladly co-operated with Saturninus in bringing about Metellus Numidicus' exile. But when he saw Saturninus building up independent power, he joined the Optimates in defending the Republic against him. He thus alienated Saturninus' supporters, but offended the Optimates by refusing to agree to Metellus' return; and when this was brought about, he had to admit defeat and left for Asia Minor (where he met Mithridates, q.v. 6), giving up hope of a censorship.

He returned when the award of an augurate in his absence restored his *dignitas*, and during the 90s he parried attacks launched on his friends (*see* AQUILLIUS (3), NORBANUS (1)) and on his *auctoritas* (e.g. by the prosecution of T. Matrinius (Cic. *Balb.* 48 f.), to whom he had given the citizenship); yet he seems gradually to have lost many of his noble friends as his importance faded. Seizing an opportunity in 92, he reasserted his links with the *equites* and showed his power in the prosecution of Rutilius (q.v. 1). Though he had favoured Italian enfranchisement, especially as a reward for military service, he probably opposed Drusus (q.v. 2),

who wanted to bring it about with the greatest benefit to his own faction; in co-operation with L. Marcius Philippus (q.v. 4) Marius mobilized his Italian clients against him. In 90 he commanded with fair success, on part of the northern front in the Social War, but failed to secure a special commission to save the State and retired offended, especially as the Optimates now embraced Sulla, who sought for advancement at the expense of Marius.

With war in the East imminent, Marius hoped for another consulship for 88 and violently opposed the attempt of his former friend Caesar (3) Strabo to gain it. In this he co-operated with Sulpicius (q.v. 1) Rufus; and when Sulla gained the consulship and command, Sulpicius, his Drusan plans rebuffed by the Optimates, joined Marius and, in return for political support, passed a law transferring the command to him. Sulla replied by armed usurpation; Marius, unprepared for this, had to flee (in dramatic circumstances, later much embroidered) and finally found security among his African veterans. After the expulsion of Cinna (q.v. 1) he landed in Etruria, collected an army among his veteran clients, imposed himself on Cinna as an ally, sacked Ostia, and brought about the capture of Rome. He and Cinna became consuls 86 and he was voted the Eastern command. His enemies—particularly treacherous friends like Antonius (1), Catulus (2), Caesar (2), and Crassus (2) (qq.v.)—were cruelly punished, until Cinna stopped the slaughter. Marius' health now gave out and he died before he could take up his command.

A typical *novus homo* (q.v.), like Cato (q.v. 1) before him and Cicero (q.v. 1) after, Marius wanted to beat the nobles at their own political game, substituting self-made support for their inherited connexions. It did not occur to him—as it did to some nobles from the Gracchi through Sulla to Caesar—that the rules of the game could be changed. Though connected with the *equites* by birth and interests, and favouring the welfare of soldiers (including Italians), he had no positive policies or solutions for basic problems. Yet he marks an important stage in the decline of the Republic: creating the client army (which Sulla taught him how to use), he was the first to show the possibilities of an alliance of a military leader with demagogues and a noble faction. His noble opponents, on the other hand, in their attitude both to him and to Sulla, revealed their lack of political principle and loss of power and cohesion.

Marius, after his death, remained a hero to the Populares 'and a villain to their opponents. Cicero (also a *novus homo* from Arpinum) uneasily admired him. The sources are conflicting and difficult to evaluate. They are fully treated in the modern works; see esp. T. F. Carney, *A Biography of Gaius Marius* (1961). Cf. also E. Badian, *Hist.* 1962, 214 ff. (with bibliography); J. van Ooteghem, *Gaius Marius* (1964).
E. B.

**MARIUS** (2, *PW* 15), son of (1) and of a Julia (aunt of Caesar, q.v. 1), born *c.* 110 B.C., shared his father's flight and return (88–87). Made consul of 82 (to his mother's horror) with Carbo (q.v. 2), who hoped to exploit his name against Sulla (1), he was defeated by Sulla at Sacriportus; besieged in Praeneste, he died during its capture by Ofella (q.v.).
E. B.

**MARIUS** (3, *PW* 42) **GRATIDIANUS**, MARCUS, nephew, both by birth and by adoption, of (1) and second cousin of Cicero (q.v. 1). As tribune (87 B.C.) he supported Cinna (q.v. 1) and after his return to Rome prosecuted Catulus (q.v. 2), who killed himself. Praetor twice, he announced as his own a plan evolved by the praetors and tribunes to improve the coinage and, in gratitude, received heroic honours (Cic. *Off.* 3. 80 f.); but he was not allowed to become consul. After Sulla's victory he was cruelly killed by his brother-in-law Catiline (q.v.) at the request of Catulus (q.v. 3), and his head was thrown into Praeneste.

The scheme for the coinage probably involved having coins tested by expert slaves or freedmen (in private employ) and sealed in bags authenticated with a marked bone tab (see *PW*, s.v. 'Nummularius'). This became standard practice.                               E. B.

**MARIUS** (4, *PW* 28), SEXTUS, was a very wealthy owner of mines in Spain. He was accused unsuccessfully in A.D. 25, but in 33 he was charged with incest and thrown from the Tarpeian rock. His mines became imperial property.

**MARIUS** (5, **MAXIMUS,** a biographer of the Emperors from Nerva to Macrinus or Elagabalus, a 'continuator' and imitator of Suetonius. His work does not survive. He is probably the Marius Maximus who had a long senatorial career, governed Syria, Africa, and Asia, and was *praefectus urbi* in A.D. 217 (*ILS* 2935). He was a source of the 'Historia Augusta', in which his entirely uncritical attitude is reproduced, though the authors of the work complain of his verbosity and unreliability. Most of his material was concerned with the scandals of the imperial court and the city of Rome, and the biographies were arranged in topics as in Suetonius. He included direct quotations from documents, but chiefly from the unreliable *acta urbis*. He was still read in the time of Ammianus Marcellinus, who deplored this.

Schanz–Hosius iii². 82 ff.; G. Barbieri, *Riv. Fil.* 1954, 36 ff., 262 ff.                                          B. H. W.

**MARMARICA,** a district on the coast of North Africa, being the eastern part of Cyrenaica extending from Derna in the west to the Egyptian border in the east. It roughly corresponded to the Late Roman province of *Libya Inferior* or *Libya Sicca*. The native inhabitants were collectively called Marmaridae and frequently troubled the few towns on the coast.          B. H. W.

**MARMOR PARIUM,** an inscribed marble stele, originally about 6 ft. 7 in. high, 2 ft. 3 in. broad, and 5 to 6 in. thick, set up at Paros. Two fragments survive, one of which, brought from Smyrna to London in 1627, is now preserved in the Ashmolean Museum, Oxford (save the upper part, which perished during the Civil War), while the other, discovered at Paros in 1897, is now in the Museum there. The compiler of the inscription, whose name is lost, claims to have 'written up the dates from the beginning, derived from all kinds of records and general histories, starting from Cecrops, the first king of Athens, down to the archonship of Astyanax (?) at Paros and Diognetus at Athens', i.e. 264/3 B.C. The text is written continuously, but comprises a number of items (80 on the first fragment, 27 on the second), each containing one or more events, dated by the number of years separating it from 264/3 and by the name of the Athenian king or archon then in office; the first fragment covers the period from 1581/80 to 355/4; the second that from 336/5 to 299/8. The events commemorated form a curious medley, drawn chiefly from political, military, religious, and literary history.

The best editions are those by F. Jacoby, *Das Marmor Parium* (1904), and *FGrH* ii B, D, no. 239; and by F. Hiller von Gaertringen, *IG* xii (5), 444 and 315, xii Suppl. 110. Cf. Jacoby, *Rh. Mus.* 1904, 63 ff.; Tod 205; G. Pfohl, *Die inschriftliche Überlieferung der Griechen* (1964), 33 f.                              M. N. T.

**MAROBODUUS,** a prince of the Marcomanni, persuaded his tribe to migrate from southern Germany to Bohemia (soon after 9 B.C.), where he built up a kingdom and extended his power over the Germans of Saxony and Silesia. His army was large and well trained. Confronting Roman armies of invasion from the west and from

the south in A.D. 6, he was saved from destruction by the outbreak of the great rebellion in Illyricum. He refused to help Arminius three years later. In A.D. 19, however, as the result of troubles fomented by the Romans, Maroboduus was expelled from his kingdom, sought refuge on Roman territory, and was interned at Ravenna, where he lived on for eighteen years, 'multum imminuta claritate ob nimiam vivendi cupidinem' (Tac. *Ann.* 2. 63).   R. S.

**MARON,** a legendary priest of Apollo, son of Euanthes, of Ismarus in Thrace, who gave Odysseus the wine with which he made Polyphemus drunk (*see* CYCLOPES), along with other presents, for sparing him and his family (*Od.* 9. 197 ff.). His name links with the Thracian place-name, Maroneia. Later writers connect him with Dionysus, e.g. Euanthes is Dionysus' son (schol. *Od.* ibid.).

                                                  H. J. R.

## MARRIAGE, LAW OF. I. GREEK

**1.** Greek marriage was monogamous; indeed, monogamy was believed to be a distinguishing feature of Greek as opposed to barbarian usage (Eur. *Andr.* 172 ff.). The oldest form of contracting marriage was the purchase of the bride from her κύριος (father or nearest male relative); her consent was not necessary, for she was the object of the sale. On this occasion the bridegroom gave to the father a consideration (ἔδνα), which, after having been originally a real purchase-price, became later a fictitious one, since the father delivered it to the wife, or the husband gave it directly to her without intervention of the father. In classical Attic law the conclusion of a marriage, with handing over (ἔκδοσις) of the bride (or of the protection over her), was necessarily preceded by an act of betrothal (ἐγγύη) between the κύριος and the bridegroom. The legal nature of this ἐγγύησις is debated. In Hellenistic times ἐγγύη and ἔκδοσις disappear and marriage becomes simply a matter of fact, usually but not necessarily identified by the giving of dowry (προίξ) and the making of a written marriage contract.

**2.** Greek marriage, being a mere matter of fact, could be dissolved by simply terminating the facts—in the case of the husband by expelling the wife. In principle the wife likewise could simply leave the home, but in order to establish the husband's duty to return the dowry it was usual for her to give written notice of divorce in court.

## II. ROMAN

**3.** According to the celebrated definition of Modestinus (q.v.), Roman marriage was 'coniunctio maris et feminae et consortium omnis vitae, divini et humani iuris communicatio' (*Dig.* 23. 2. 1), though this is rather an ideal than a legal definition. No formalities were necessary for the inception of a marriage: the ceremonies which normally accompanied it had no legal character. All that was necessary was the living together of a man and a woman with the intention of forming a lasting union (*affectio maritalis*) to which should attach the social consequences of marriage (*honor matrimonii*). The ceremonies, and in particular the customary *deductio in domum mariti*, would provide the normal evidence of this intention. Moreover, the intention was necessary not merely at the beginning of marriage but throughout; hence if the intention ceased, the marriage was in principle at an end (see below). Subject to this factual character, Roman marriage was essentially monogamous.

**4.** Marriage in the ancient world was a matter of personal law (*see* IUS GENTIUM), and therefore a full Roman marriage (*iustae nuptiae, iustum matrimonium*) could exist only if both parties were Roman citizens or had been granted *conubium* (right to contract a Roman marriage; *see* COMMERCIUM), either generally (e.g. *Latini*, q.v.) or individually. Only such a marriage could place the children in the *patria potestas* (q.v.) of the father and create rights of succession, etc. Further, parties might have *conubium* in this sense but still be incapable of marrying each other (lack of so-called relative *conubium*). Impediments of this kind varied through the centuries, but the principal were: (1) Difference of social rank: patricians could not marry plebeians until a *Lex Canuleia* (445 B.C.); nor could any free person marry a freedman or freedwoman, until the marriage legislation of Augustus (*Lex Iulia de maritandis ordinibus* of 18 B.C. and *Lex Papia Poppaea* of A.D. 9) limited the restriction to persons of senatorial rank. (2) Considerations of morals or public policy: e.g. the Augustan legislation forbade the remarriage of an adulteress, and unions between free persons and women of ill-repute; later, provincial officials were forbidden to marry women of their province (to preserve the impartiality and loyalty of the administration); and soldiers, at least in some circumstances, were forbidden to marry at all. (3) Relationship, by blood, adoption, or marriage, within certain degrees. Also, although 'nuptias non concubitus sed consensus facit', the parties must be physically capable (limit of age eventually 14 years for males, 12 for females).

**5.** The Augustan restrictions on marriage gave new importance to the already existing institution of *concubinatus*, a permanent union similar to marriage, but because of these restrictions or for social reasons, lacking *honor matrimonii*. It had no legal consequences, but was a tolerated method of satisfying the father but not the substance of the restrictions. It was not, however, necessarily an alternative to marriage: a man might have a wife and a concubine, or more than one concubine. Under the influence of Christianity concubinage was subjected to restrictions, and in particular became exclusively a monogamous alternative to marriage, permitted only within the same limits of age and relationship.

**6.** Marriage was usually, but not necessarily, preceded by a betrothal, *sponsalia*. In the early law this reciprocal promise of marriage was made on behalf of the future consorts by their fathers in the solemn form of a *sponsio* (*see* STIPULATIO) (hence the nomenclature *sponsalia*, *sponsus*, *sponsa*); later it became informal and was not binding, and even a *stipulatio poenae* in case of breach was without effect. In course of time some secondary legal effects, similar to those of marriage (e.g. creation of an impediment to marriage with a relative of the betrothed) were ascribed to the *sponsalia*. In the fourth century A.D. an institution of oriental origin, the *arrha sponsalicia*, or earnest money in guarantee of the fulfilment of the promise of marriage, came into use.

**7.** Except where accompanied by *manus* (q.v.), marriage made no difference to the status or property rights of the wife. She remained either in the *patria potestas* of her father or *sui iuris*, as before, and retained unfettered ownership of her property, if any. This entire separation of the property of husband and wife was, however, considerably modified by the institution of dowry (*dos*). *Dos* was not legally necessary, but it was considered to be a moral duty so to endow a daughter. *Dos* could be constituted either by an actual conveyance of the property, or by a promise (either in the old special form of *dotis dictio*, a unilateral declaration in formal words, or merely by *stipulatio* (q.v.)). In the early law the husband acquired full ownership of the *dos*, considered as a contribution to the expenses of the joint household, but the wife, or whoever provided the *dos*, could stipulate for its return at the end of the marriage. With the increase of divorce in the late Republic there developed an *actio rei uxoriae*, by which the return of the *dos* could be required, even if there had been no *stipulatio*. In this way the husband was required to account, subject to any special agreement (*pactum dotale*), for his management of the property; he could also retain fixed proportions of it in certain circumstances, especially in the event of divorce by fault of the wife. His powers were subsequently still further reduced, and under Justinian he had in substance only a usufruct.

**8.** It necessarily followed from the factual character of Roman marriage that it could be brought to an end by the free will of either or both. As with the formation of marriage, so also with its termination, all that was needed was some evidence of intention, though in the case of unilateral divorce (*repudium*) a communication by intermediary (*per nuntium*) or later by letter was common. Augustus in his marriage legislation required a declaration before seven witnesses, but probably only where *repudium* was for adultery by the wife, the purpose being to exclude the possibility of the husband's being prosecuted as a *leno* (*see* ADULTERY). If the wife were *in manu* it was necessary also to terminate the *manus*, either by *mancipatio* (q.v.) to a fiduciary, who then made a manumission, or, if *manus* had been created by *confarreatio*, by a reversal of that process (*diffareatio*). Divorce was rare in the earlier Republic, but by the last century B.C. had become common, almost the only material deterrent being the rules governing retention or return of *dos* (above). The Christian Emperors imposed penalties for divorce on grounds not recognized by the legislator, but did not deprive it of effect. Divorce by mutual consent remained unpenalized until Justinian forbade it, but the ban was lifted within five years of his death.

GREECE. J. H. Lipsius, *Attisches Recht* ii. 2 (1912), 468 ff.; W. Erdmann, *Die Ehe im alten Griechenland* (1934); H. J. Wolff, *Beiträge zur Rechtsgeschichte* (1961) (reprinted from *Traditio* 1944); *Sav. Zeitschr.* 1950; *Tijdschr. voor Rechtsgeschiedenis* 1952; M. I. Finley, *Seminar* xii (1954); W. K. Lacey, *The Family in Classical Greece* (1968). A copious literature exists on the law of marriage in Graeco-Roman papyri, especially on the very controversial matter of γάμος ἔγγραφος and ἄγραφος, cf. F. Bozza, *Aegyptus* xiv (1934); W. Erdmann, op. cit.; R. Taubenschlag, *Law of Greco-Roman Egypt*² (1955). A. R. W. Harrison, *Law of Athens. Family and Property* (1968), 1 ff.

ROME. H. F. Jolowicz, *Roman Foundations of Modern Law* (1957); P. Bonfante, *Corso di dir. rom.* i (1925); R. Orestano, *La struttura giuridica del matrimonio romano* (1951); E. Levy, *Hergang der römischen Ehescheidung* (1925); P. E. Corbett, *The Roman Law of Marriage* (1930); H. J. Wolff, 'Zur Stellung der Frau im röm. Dotalrecht', *Sav. Zeitschr.* 1933; S. Solazzi, 'Studi sul divorzio', *Bull. Ist. Dir. Rom.* 1925; M. Lauria, 'La dote romana', *Atti Accad. Napoli* 1938; E. Volterra, *La Conception du mariage d'après les juristes romains* (1940); H. J. Wolff, 'Written and unwritten Marriages in Hellenistic and Post-classical Roman Law' (*Amer. Philol. Assoc., Philological Monographs* ix, 1939). A. B.; B. N.

**MARRIAGE CEREMONIES.** GREEK. The favourite time was said to be winter, in the month of Gamelion. Sacrifice (προτέλεια γάμων) was made to the θεοὶ γαμήλιοι, primarily Zeus and Hera, and a lock of the bride's hair might be dedicated. The bride took a ritual bath (in Athens it would appear popular to have the water brought from the spring Kallirhoe). A wedding feast was held, generally at the house of the bride's father: the bride was present, veiled, with other women, but they sat apart from the men. In the evening the bridegroom took her, veiled, from her father's house, on a carriage (ἄμαξα); he sat on one side of her and his best friend (παράνυμφος or πάροχος) on the other. A torchlight procession went ahead singing the wedding-cry of Hymen. At the bridegroom's house, the bride was conducted, still veiled, into the bridal chamber, and the epithalamium was sung outside the closed door. This is an outline account of high-society wedding ritual inferred from Athenian literature. It is formalized and idealized.

K. F. Hermann-Blümner, *Lehrb. d. griech. Privataltertümer*³ (1882), 268 ff.; W. Erdmann, *Die Ehe im alten Griechenland* (1934), 250 ff.

**2.** ROMAN. The favourite season was June. Usually on the previous day the bride put away her *toga praetexta*— she had come of age. Her dress and appearance were ritually prescribed: her hair was arranged in six locks (*sex crines*), with woollen fillets (*vittae*), her dress was a straight white woven tunic (*tunica recta*) fastened at the waist with a 'knot of Hercules', her veil was a great flame-coloured head-scarf (*flammeum*) and her shoes were of the same colour. Friends and clients of both families gathered in the bride's father's house: the bridegroom arrived, words of consent were spoken, and the matron of honour (*pronuba*) performed the ceremony of linking bride's and bridegroom's right hands (*dextrarum iunctio*). This was followed by a sacrifice (generally of a pig), and (in imperial times) the marriage contract (involving dowry) was signed. Then the guests raised the cry of *feliciter*. There followed the wedding feast, usually at the expense of the bridegroom. The most important part of the ceremony then took place: the bride was escorted in procession to the bridegroom's house (*deductio*), closely accompanied by three young boys, whither the bridegroom had already gone to welcome her. The bridegroom carried her over the threshold to avert an ill-omened stumble; in the house she touched fire and water, was taken to the bedchamber and undressed by *univirae* (women who had known only one husband), and the bridegroom was admitted. Meanwhile an epithalamium might be sung. Such is a generalized account of a society wedding as it appears in literature. There could be many variations of detail and there could be different forms of marriage (*see* MARRIAGE, LAW OF, II).

A most important source is Plutarch, *Quaest. Rom.*: see the edition by H. J. Rose (1924), nos. 1, 2, 6, 7, 9, 29, 30, 31, 65, 85, 86, 87, 105, and 107. Marquardt *Privatleben* (1886), 39 ff.; H. Blümner, *Röm. Privataltertümer* (1911), 349 ff.                           G. W. W.

**MARRIAGE, SACRED** (ἱερὸς γάμος), the sexual union of two persons, both divine or one divine and the other human but in some way sacral. The supposed result would appear to be increase of fertility, animal or vegetable, or of prosperity in general. An interesting example is the union on the day of the Choes (*see* ANTHESTERIA) of Dionysus with the wife of the Basileus at Athens (cf. DIONYSUS). Here one partner only is divine, there being no sufficient reason to suppose that an Attic queen was regarded at any date as other than human. No doubt, however, while the monarchy lasted both she and her husband had some priestly functions. Both partners are divine at the Daedala (references under BOEOTIA, CULTS), viz. Zeus and Hera; for a main feature of it was the bringing of a wife for Zeus. She was represented by a wooden image and came on a carriage, like a Boeotian bride (cf. Plut. *Quaest. Rom.* 29), accompanied by a brideswoman (νυμφεύτρια, Paus. 9. 3. 7).

Nilsson, *GGR* i². 121 ff.                           H. J. R.

**MARRUCINI,** a small tribe on the Adriatic coast of central Italy. Chief town: Teate (modern *Chieti*). They spoke an Oscan-type dialect and had very close ties with the Marsi, Paeligni, and Vestini (qq.v.). Allied with Rome before 300 B.C. they remained loyal until they joined the Social War insurgents under Herius Asinius, grandfather of Asinius Pollio (q.v.). Their rapid romanization ensued.                           E. T. S.

**MARS (Mavors, Mamers,** Etr. **Maris;** reduplicated **Marmar),** next to Jupiter (q.v.) the chief Italian god. Months were named after him at Rome (Martius, mod. Engl. March), Alba Longa, Falerii, Aricia, Tusculum, Lavinium, and among the Hernici, Aequiculi, Paelignians, and Sabines (Ov. *Fasti* 3. 89–95, presumably from Verrius Flaccus). At Rome his festivals came in March and October, with the exception of the first Equirria (27 Feb.). They were the *feriae Marti* on 1 Mar. (old New Year's Day), second Equirria (14 Mar.), *agonium Martiale* (17 Mar.), Quinquatrus (19 Mar.; after-

wards extended to five days and supposed to be a festival of Minerva, q.v.), and Tubilustrium (23 Mar.). All these may be reasonably explained, so far as their ritual is known, as preparations for the campaigning season, with performance of rites to benefit the horses (Equirria), trumpets (Tubilustrium), and other necessaries for the conduct of war. On 1, 9, and 23 Mar. also, the Salii, an ancient priesthood belonging to Jupiter, Mars, and Quirinus (Servius on *Aen.* 8. 663), danced a sort of wardance in armour of the fashion of the Bronze Age and sang their traditional hymn, addressed apparently to all the gods, not to these three only. This is intelligible as further preparation for war. In October the Equus October came on the Ides (15th). A horse-race (q.v.) took place in the Campus Martius; the off horse of the winning team was sacrificed and his head contended for by the inhabitants of the Sacra Via and the Suburra. On the 19th was the Armilustrium, presumably the purification of the soldiers' arms before putting them away for the winter. In this month again the Salii performed their dances ('arma ancilia mouent', the *ancilia* being archaic shields shaped like the figure 8). Before commencing a war the general shook the sacred spears of Mars in the Regia, saying 'Mars uigila'; it is most probable that these were the original embodiments of the god. His priest is the *flamen Martialis* (*see* FLAMINES) and his sacred animals the wolf and woodpecker (see Wissowa, *RK* 141 ff., 555 ff.). It is therefore not remarkable that he is usually considered a war-god and was equated with Ares (q.v.). But it has been pointed out (summary in Bailey, *P. Ouidi Nasonis fastorum lib. iii*, 33 ff., cf. Frazer, *Fasti of Ovid* iii. 1 ff.) that he has agricultural functions also (Cato, *Agr.* 141. 2 ff.; hymn of Arval Brethren, Henzen, *Acta Arvalium*, cciv), and that some at least of his feasts (see above) can be interpreted as agricultural from their date and the ceremonial. Four explanations seem possible. (*a*) He was originally a war-god, and therefore called upon to guard the fields of his worshippers from enemies physical and spiritual. (*b*) He was a god of the wild, and therefore was worshipped either to protect the fields or when his territory was crossed on campaign. (*c*) He was originally a chthonian deity, hence a god of death and hence of war (cf. ARES), though originally connected with the fertility of the soil. (*d*) He was the high god, little differentiated as to function, of a people often engaged in war and having agriculture for their staple industry and food-supply. All of these have been maintained by various scholars.

His mythology is almost entirely borrowed from Ares, the only exception being the comic tale of how he was deceived into marrying Anna Perenna (q.v.; Ov. ibid. 675 ff.), probably a folk-tale applied (by Ovid?) to deities treated after the Alexandrian manner. Under Augustus he obtained an important new title, Ultor, in recognition of the victory over Caesar's assassins (Nash, *Pict. Dict. Rome* i. 401 ff., and Platner–Ashby, 329 f., for his other places of worship in Rome).

Latte, *RR* 114 ff.                           H. J. R.

**MARSI** inhabited mountains and strategic passes in central Italy near the Fucine Lake. Their chief town was Marruvium (Strabo 5. 241). They probably spoke an Oscan-type dialect, but their early latinization makes proof of this impossible. They were allied, ethnically and politically, with Marrucini, Vestini, and Paeligni (qq.v.), but from early times were friendly to Rome (cf. App. *BCiv.* 1. 46). In 340 B.C. they gave Roman troops passage through their territory and remained friendly in the Second Samnite War (Livy 8. 6, 29; 9. 13; Diod. 20. 44, 101. Records of Marsic hostility are suspect: K. J. Beloch, *Röm. Gesch.* 403; Livy 9. 41, 45; 10. 3 probably confuses Marsi with Aequi). The Marsi were loyal against Hannibal (Livy 28. 45) but took the initiative in demanding Roman citizenship in the Social War (hence often called Marsic War: Vell. Pat. 2. 21). When this demand was granted, the separate nation of Marsi disappeared. Marsic magicians were famous for miraculous snake-bite cures. A grove, sacred to Angitia, Italic goddess of healing, stood on Marsic territory (whence modern *Luco ne' Marsi*).

G. Devoto, *Gli Antichi Italici* (1951), 125 f.                E. T. S.

**MARSYAS** (1), a satyr or silenus, generally associated with the river of that name, a tributary of the Maeander, but also with other streams (Jessen in Roscher's *Lexikon* ii. 2439, s.v. for the legend and its representation in art). He was a musician and inventor of a form of music for flute or oboe, the μητρῷον αὔλημα, Paus. 10. 30. 9, which passage also shows that at Celaenae he was the subject of local myths and regarded as a guardian deity. He is therefore pretty certainly a Phrygian or at all events Asianic figure. In the Greek handling of his story, the origins of which are obscure, he is associated with Athena and Apollo (qq.v.) as follows. Athena, having invented the oboe (αὐλός), threw it away because it distorted her face to play it. Marsyas picked it up and soon learned to play on it (*Frag. Trag. Adesp.* 381 Nauck; Melanippides and Telestes in Ath. 616 e ff.; and later authors). He now challenged Apollo to a contest in music; Apollo, having defeated him, took advantage of an agreement that the winner should do as he liked with the loser and flayed him alive (Apollod. 1. 24). The river sprang from his blood or the tears of his mourners.

The picking up of the discarded flutes was shown by Myron in the mid fifth century in a bronze group on the Acropolis, and this and the contest with Apollo on Attic vases of the second half and in later works. The punishment was shown by Zeuxis and appears in fourth-century vase-painting and in a famous Hellenistic statuary group.

In art, J. Boardman, *JHS* 1956, 18 ff.; C. W. Clairmont, *YClS* 1957, 161 ff.                                        H. J. R.; C. M. R.

**MARSYAS** (2) of Pella, relative and afterwards admiral of Antigonus I, wrote on Alexander.

*FGrH* ii. 135.

**MARTIAL** (MARCUS VALERIUS (*PW* 233) MARTIALIS), born at Bilbilis in Spain *c.* A.D. 40 (1. 61. 12), died *c.* 104. His cognomen records his birth on 1 Mar. (9. 52; 10. 24 and 92. 10; 12. 60). H. Lucas (*CQ* 1938) argues against taking this literally; but references to other birthdays seem to mark actual anniversaries rather than adjacent kalends (e.g. 3. 6; 11. 65). Educated in Spain, he went in 64 to Rome, where intimacy with his fellow Spaniards Seneca and Lucan was soon cut short by their fate in the Pisonian conspiracy. Celebrating at Rome his 57th birthday (10. 24. 4), he had spent thirty-four years there (10. 103. 7–10, i.e. in a poem probably of A.D. 98, but this depends on whether it belongs to the first or second edition of book 10). Before his *Spectacula* (80) we know little of his career. It was one mainly of poverty-stricken dependence on patrons not over-generous in return for complimentary verses. For a time he had to be content with a three-storey-high lodging in the sweltering city (1. 117. 7); acquisition of a small farm at Nomentum afforded a welcome relief. By degrees his social influence, but not his wealth, increased. He received an honorary military tribunate and, though he never married, the *ius trium liberorum* (q.v.) (3. 95. 5). Brought into contact with all classes from Emperor and court downwards, he chronicled succinctly every sort and condition of men and women. With his chief literary contemporaries, except Statius, he had friendly relations. These included Frontinus, Juvenal, Silius Italicus, Quintilian, and the

Younger Pliny. His early works attracted notice, but his real fame rests on the amazing versatility which marks his epigrammatic depiction of life in the volumes issued from 86 (books 1, 2) to 98 (book 11). Then, under Nerva, he recognized that indecency and flattery were no longer acceptable. The Younger Pliny paid for his return to his never entirely forgotten homeland, and he settled on a rural property presented by a patroness Marcella. Three years later his final book was complete and in a letter which can be dated *c.* 104 Pliny regrets his recent death.

WORKS. A.D. 80. *Liber Spectaculorum* commemorated the opening by Titus of the Flavian Amphitheatre ('Colosseum'). Its 33 surviving pieces record contests in the arena without as yet full mastery of style.

A.D. 84–5. (*a*) *Xenia* (now book 13), mottoes for 'guest-gifts', 127 pieces, all except three in elegiac couplets, and, with four exceptions, on eatables and drinkables —an extended list indicative of Roman dinners like the fuller *menus* in some of Martial's invitations (10. 48; 11. 52). (*b*) *Apophoreta* (now book 14), mottoes for 'gifts to take home', 223, all, except two, couplets, originally perhaps paired to suit the purse of rich and poor alternately, and forming an instructive catalogue of presents.

Of his twelve *Epigrammaton libri* most appeared at intervals of about a year from 86, when he issued a revised edition of books 1 and 2 together. Book 3 came out during a temporary retreat to Cisalpine Gaul. From books 10 and 11 he made for Nerva an expurgated anthology. Book 12 occupied him for three years after he left Rome in 98. The division into books was his own (2. 93; 5. 2 and 15; 7. 17, etc.). Prose prefaces of literary significance are given to books 1, 2, 8, 12, and a few lines of prose introduce the poem prefixed to book 9.

Of his 1,561 poems the most by far, 1,235, are in elegiac metre, where Ovid's influence unites with that of Catullus; 238, hendecasyllabic; 77, choliambic; a few are in iambics and hexameters. His three chief metres are frequently, though not exclusively, used satirically; but he can employ limping iambics for telling description or personal grief (3. 58, a farm; 10. 30, beach at Formiae; 5. 37, lament for Erotion: cf. the beautiful one in elegiacs 5. 34); while hendecasyllables can be realistic, as in 4. 64 (a view), or semi-personal, 4. 55 (pride in Spain). Martial regards as his Latin exemplars Catullus, Domitius Marsus, Pedo Albinovanus, and Gaetulicus (2. 77; 5. 5. 6). The last-named may be the Γαιτυλικός of the *Greek Anthology*, and recalls its influence, which Martial never mentions. But Greek epigrams contributed to his literary skill and some (e.g. those by Lucillius, q.v.) suggested subjects, though Martial's great repertory lay in the Roman world around and though his fame was largely won by the suspension of point or sting to the close of an epigram—a feature comparatively rare in Greek.

Martial's predominant interest centred in his fellow human beings: 'hominem pagina nostra sapit' (10. 4. 10). He denounces mythology as remote from life (4. 49); and in his pictures of Roman society, high and low, rich and poor, virtuous and vicious, he is a spectator writing with a sort of Spanish detachment. His *métier* was no deep system of thought, but extraordinarily keen observation and sharply condensed expression. Much of his work is therefore that realism in a nutshell which fits Coleridge's definition of an epigram as 'a dwarfish whole: its body brevity and wit its soul'. He often calls his poems *nugae* or *ioci*, yet he maintains they are not mere flippancies. They reflect life as in a mirror (10. 4. 8). Conscious of contemporary fame (5. 15; 6. 60; 7. 88), he is sure that he will survive, and no century, medieval or modern, has failed to remember him.

Where Martial most repels is in his undisguised mime-like obscenity, parallel to the naked licence of the Floralia, and in that grotesque adulation of Domitian which tempts him into artificial conceits foreign, as a rule, to his genius. The method in his satiric epigrams is one of concealed personalities, using invented names (2. 23), 'to spare the sinner but denounce the sin' (10. 33. 10). He thus regards his sportive attacks as harmless ('ludimus innocui', 7. 12), but recognizes that, to avoid insipidity, epigrams need a drop of gall (7. 25). His poems of friendship and of mourning over young lives cut short are a winning testimony to the warm affections of the most many-sided of all epigrammatists. Privations rather than any theoretical Stoicism taught him endurance as a health of soul. He has little sympathy for the theatrical exit from the world affected by some Stoics (1. 8. 5–6): 'contempt for life is easy in distress' (11. 56. 15). Without profound philosophy, he yet had the roots of his writings in his manifold experience of life and penetrating insight into humanity.

*See also* EPIGRAM.

LIFE AND WORKS. L. Friedländer's ed. (*infra*), introd.; *Sittengeschichte Roms* (ed. 9, posthumous, by Wissowa) iv. 209 ff.
TEXTS. W. Heraeus (1925); W. M. Lindsay, O.C.T. (1929).
COMMENTARY. L. Friedländer, *Martialis Epigrammaton Libri* (1886).
TRANSLATIONS. The Bohn translation (prose) adds many examples of verse translations including some by W. Hay, 1755. W. C. A. Ker (prose with text; Loeb, 1919–20). J. A. Pott and F. A. Wright, *Twelve Books* (London and New York, 1926). J. W. D.

**MARTIANUS CAPELLA,** of North African origin and a proconsul, composed between A.D. 410 and 439 a didactic treatise, addressed, in accordance with literary convention, to his son, in the mixture of prose and verse inherited from the Menippean Satire. Its usual title is *De Nuptiis Mercurii et Philologiae*, and the first part describes in a fantastic setting and in a style influenced by Apuleius, the ascent to heaven of Philologia, accompanied by her handmaids the seven Liberal Arts, to be married to the god of *Eloquentia*, Mercury. This extravagant fantasy was the model for subsequent allegories involving heavenly ascents. The remainder of the work is a compendium of elementary and superficial information about the Seven Arts, and as such it appealed to the later Carolingians and the twelfth-century school of Chartres, especially on account of its cosmographical information. Martianus was a mere compiler, an adherent of paganism, well grounded in Greek.

Most of the numerous MSS. have been examined and described by C. Leonardi (*I codici di Marziano Capella*, 1959) and much work has been and is still being done on the medieval commentaries.

EDITIONS. F. Eyssenhardt (Teubner, 1866); A. Dick (Teubner, 1925); J. Willis is preparing a new Teubner text, and W. H. Stahl and R. Johnson an English translation. For the results of latest research and bibliographical references, W. H. Stahl, *Speculum* 1965, 102 ff. F. J. E. R.

**MARULLUS.** At his rhetorical academy the Elder Seneca and Porcius Latro were fellow students (Sen. *Controv.* 1 praef. 22).

**MARZABOTTO,** 17 miles south-west of Bologna, is near the site of an Etruscan city (Etr. ? *Misa*) on the floodplain of the Reno, which by a subsequent change of course has partially destroyed it. The city, which gives us a unique picture of the ancient appearance of an Etruscan city, was laid out as a carefully oriented rectangular grid divided into two halves by a wide north–south road crossed at right angles by secondary roads, the northernmost of which connects the urban complex with a row of temples on a higher terrace. The quarters of the city are divided into *insulae* of city-dwellings separated by party walls and similar in plan to certain chamber-tombs at Caere (q.v.). The earliest finds belong to the last quarter of the sixth century, and there is a preponderance of material from the second half of the fifth. In the fourth

century the area was invaded by Gauls, who left a cemetery.

E. Brizio, *Mon. Ant.* i, cols. 249 ff.; P. Ducati, *Atti e Mem. Dep. St. Patria Romagne* 1923, 69 ff.; P. E. Arias, ibid. 1953, 223 ff.; Scullard, *Etr. Cities*, 205 ff.; J. B. Ward-Perkins, *Town Planning Review* 1955/6, 133 ff.; G. A. Mansuelli, *MDAI(R)* 1963, 44 ff.; P. Saronio, *Stud. Etr.* 1965, 385 ff. D. W. R. R.

**MASADA** is a small isolated plateau rising 1,300 feet sheer above the western shore of the Dead Sea. A small fort was built there by either Jonathan Maccabaeus or Alexander Jannaeus. Herod the Great (q.v.) used Masada as a refuge for his family during the Parthian invasion of 40 B.C., and later developed it as a sumptuous residence and the most southerly of the chain of fortresses controlling his kingdom. Recent excavations have supplemented Josephus' description of his buildings. The plateau was surrounded by a casemate wall with towers, except at its northern tip, where natural rock terraces were used to form a three-tiered palace. At the western edge of the plateau there was a much larger palace on a magnificent scale, and other buildings included a garrison-block, baths, storage rooms for vast quantities of food and weapons, and (probably) a synagogue. Other parts of the plateau may have been cultivated. Enormous cisterns were supplied by aqueducts from two wadis and by the infrequent rain. On the east the fortress was accessible only by the tortuous and precipitous 'Snake path'. The easier western approach was guarded by a tower.

Early in the revolt of A.D. 66 the Jewish extremists, the zealots or *sicarii*, captured the fortress from its Roman garrison and held out until three years after the fall of Jerusalem. In May 73, after a siege of six months, Masada fell to a force of some 7,000 legionaries and auxiliaries under Flavius Silva, who surrounded the rock with eight siege camps and a circumvallation (still clearly visible), and built an earth ramp (still standing), crowned with a stone platform on which artillery was mounted, against the lowest part of the cliffs on the west. When the wall was breached, the garrison, less than 1,000 strong, set fire to the buildings and then, with the exception of two women and five children, committed suicide. The fortress was reoccupied by Roman troops until early in the second century.

Finds at Masada, mostly of the Zealot period, include numerous domestic objects, ostraca, coins, remains of food and clothing, and scrolls containing fragments of Old Testament books and a liturgical document of the Qumran sect.

Joseph. *BJ* 7. 252–3; 275–406, and scattered references elsewhere. Excavation reports in *Israel Explor. Journ.* 1957, 1 ff. and forthcoming vols. I. A. Richmond, *JRS* 1962, 142 ff.; Y. Yadin, *Masada* (1967). E. M. S.

**MASCHALISMOS** (μασχαλισμός), a practice adopted by man-slayers, literally to prevent the ghost from walking or otherwise manifesting itself. The hands and feet of the corpse were cut off and tied under the armpits (μασχάλαι). See Aesch. *Cho.* 439; Soph. *El.* 445, with schol. there, which, however, is confused; Jebb's note and appendix ad loc. quote the other authorities, all apparently going back to Aristophanes of Byzantium, and analyse them usefully.

Nilsson *GGR* i². 92, 99. H. J. R.

**MASINISSA** (so Latin writers; Polybius gives Μασσανάσσης) (c. 240–148 B.C.), son of Gaia king of the eastern Numidian Massyles, was brought up at Carthage and served with the Carthaginians against the Romans in Spain from 212 until 206, when he was won over by the diplomacy and friendship of Scipio (q.v. 5). Dynastic troubles following Gaia's death forced Masinissa to flee from his kingdom, which was partially overrun by Syphax (q.v.). After many adventures Masinissa joined the Romans when they landed in Africa (204), and fought in the night attack on the enemy's camps and at Campi

Magni, after which he defeated Syphax and reoccupied Cirta, where he met Sophonisba (q.v.) in 203. He was then publicly hailed as king by Scipio, according to Livy (30. 15. 11). His cavalry played a decisive part in Scipio's victory at Zama (202). Thereafter as Rome's faithful ally Masinissa was complete master of all Numidia, while Carthage was by treaty unable to resist when he gradually advanced his frontiers at her expense, filching the Emporia on the Syrtis and finally (c. 155) Tusca near Campi Magni. To Carthaginian complaints of this naked aggression Rome merely replied by sending out boundary commissions which decided in Masinissa's favour or left the question unsettled (e.g. in 193, 182, 174, 172, 153). Finally, helped by a party within Carthage, Masinissa goaded the Carthaginians to break their treaty with Rome by attacking him; he defeated them (150). When the Roman army arrived he was treated somewhat coldly by the Romans, who feared his ambitions (see PUNIC WARS). He died soon afterwards (148), and his kingdom was divided between his sons.

Of great physical strength even in extreme old age, Masinissa was a brave soldier, a skilful diplomatist, and a creative statesman. He not only extended his empire until it embarrassed Rome, but he energized its economic and social life, making 'nomads into farmers and welding them into a State' (Strabo 17. 833), and turning local dynasts into feudal barons owning large estates and loyal to the throne; Punic art, language, and culture permeated inner Numidia, urban life was encouraged, and Masinissa, following the pattern of Hellenistic monarchy, became Numidia's greatest king. He united his country and by widening the basis of Punic civilization enabled it to survive to influence the Africa of the Roman Empire.

J. Mazard, *Corpus Nummorum Numidiae Mauretaniaeque* (1955), 30 ff.; G. Camps, *Masinissa* (= *Libyca* viii, 1960); P. G. Walsh, *JRS* 1965, 149 ff. H. H. S.

**MASSALIA (MASSILIA** in Roman writers), modern *Marseille*, was founded *c.* 600 B.C. by settlers from Phocaea (q.v.), who obtained the site, on the excellent harbour of Lacydon (*Vieux-Port*) from the Ligurian Segobriges. Though preceded in the area by Rhodian and other traders, the Massaliotes eventually dominated the coast from Nicaea (q.v. 2) to Emporiae (q.v.), with outposts further west at Hemeroscopium, Alonae (near *Cape Nao*), and Maenaca (near *Malaga*). This last, founded for trade with Tartessus (q.v.), was soon lost to the Carthaginians though Massaliote venturing beyond the Straits of Gibraltar is reflected in the anonymous sixth-century *Periplus* (*see* AVIENIUS) and in the works of Pytheas (q.v.) and Euthymenes, who explored the west African coast. In Gaul and eastern Spain the Greek presence had profound effects. Trade up the Rhône, especially in the sixth century, contributed to the evolution of the La Tène culture of the Celts, while among the Ligurian and Iberian tribes of the coast all excavated hill-forts have yielded quantities of imported pottery and many show Greek influence in their fortifications, architecture, and art; occasionally, as at St. Blaise and Glanum (q.v.), a native settlement was actually taken over. The introduction of the vine and olive completed the picture of *Gallia in Graeciam translata* (Just. *Epit.* 43. 4. 2). Despite Massalia's remoteness and the failure of the Phocaean expedition to Corsica (q.v.), relations with Greece were maintained with a treasury at Delphi. Renowned for the stability of her own aristocratic constitution (Strabo 4. 179; Cic. *Flac.* 26. 63), she was not involved in wars with other Greek cities, but victories over the Carthaginians are recorded in the sixth and fifth centuries. She early enjoyed Rome's *amicitia* which later developed into formal alliance; Massaliote ships helped Rome in the Second Punic War. In 125 B.C. constant aggression by the Salluvii

(q.v.) prompted an appeal to Rome, which led ultimately to the formation of the Provincia. Having supported Pompey, the city was taken by Caesar in 49 B.C. Thereafter, though retaining federate status and a high reputation for Hellenism, Massalia gradually declined. The city wall was rebuilt under Nero by the doctor Crinas, and Maximian (q.v.) defended himself here in 307. Excavations since 1945 have revealed many details of both Greek and Roman phases, including a Greek theatre, temples, agora, docks, town walls, and pagan and Christian cemeteries.

M. Clerc, *Massalia* (1929); F. Villard, *La Céramique grecque de Marseille* (*VIe–IV*° *siècle*) (1960); Grenier, *Manuel* i. 284 ff., ii. 476 ff.; *Gallia* 1947, 155 ff., 1948, 207 ff., 1950, 116 ff., 1953, 100 ff., 1954, 426 ff., 1955, 88 f., 1960, 286 ff., 1962, 587. A. L. F. R.

**MASSICUS MONS,** mountain spur projecting from the Apennines (q.v.) towards the Tyrrhenian and separating Latium from Campania (qq.v.). It is not lofty but very fertile; grapes from its slopes produced some of the choicest wine in Italy. Sinuessa (modern *Mondragone*) controlled the narrow gap between its western extremity and the sea. E. T. S.

**MASTARNA,** a legendary hero of Etruria, was identified with Servius (q.v. 1) Tullius by the Emperor Claudius or his authority (Dessau, *ILS* 212; A.D. 48). According to another, purely Etruscan, version (attested by the famous wall-paintings from Vulci), Mastarna came to power at Rome after rescuing his comrade Caeles Vibenna, and murdering a king Tarquinius. He must therefore be identified not with the Servius Tullius of the Roman tradition, but with the Servius Tullius of the Etruscan version, or with Porsenna (q.v.), or with both. In any case, although he may be a purely mythical figure, Mastarna represents an Etruscan king of Rome.

G. De Sanctis, *Klio* 1902, 96 ff.; L. Pareti, *Stud. Etr.* 1931, 154 ff.; A. Momigliano, *Claudius*² (1961), 12 ff., 85 ff.; A. Alföldi, *Early Rome and the Latins* (1964), 212 ff. P. T.

**MATHEMATICS.** Our knowledge of the origins and early development of mathematics among the Greeks is negligible. In Mesopotamia an advanced mathematics had existed since at least the time of Hammurapi (*c.* 1700 B.C.). Characteristic of this were problems in arithmetic and algebra, but many facts of elementary geometry were known, e.g. 'Pythagoras' theorem' and the mensuration formulas for a variety of plane and solid figures. It is highly probable that much of this knowledge reached the Greek world at some time, but the nature of our sources makes it impossible to say what came when, particularly as independent discovery can rarely be ruled out. Greek doxographic tradition ascribed the invention of geometry to the Egyptians, whence it was made known to the Greeks by Thales (q.v.) in Ionia or Pythagoras (q.v. 1) in Magna Graecia. However, there was little to learn from Egypt beyond elementary mensuration formulas, and since neither Thales nor Pythagoras left writings there could be no foundation for the tradition. The most we can say on the positive side is that it is probable that fifth-century 'Pythagoreans' such as Philolaus (q.v.) discussed the properties of numbers in the semi-mystical way imitated by Speusippus in the fourth century (in *Theol. Arith.* 82. 10 ff. de Falco).

2. The first concrete evidence we have concerns the mathematical activity of Hippocrates (q.v. 3) of Chios in the late fifth century. While investigating the problem of squaring the circle (already considered a typical mathematical problem, as is shown by Aristophanes, *Av.* 1005) he produced some ingenious theorems on the quadrature of lunes. The *content* of these is reasonably certain, but our knowledge of the *form* is derived via two intermediaries, Eudemus (q.v.) and Simplicius (*Comm.*

*in Phys.* 60. 22 ff. Diels), and it may have been very different from the Euclidian cast in which we have it. However, these theorems exhibit the concept of proof, the most notable distinguishing characteristic of Greek mathematics. Clearly there was a geometrical tradition before Hippocrates; but how old, and of what kind, we shall never know. It is possible that the arguments of Zeno (q.v. 1) of Elea in the mid fifth century, showing that infinite division involved self-contradiction, were in part directed against current mathematical procedures. It is certain that the logical difficulties he raised influenced the later course of Greek mathematics in its avoidance of infinitesimals. That this was a difficulty in the early stages is shown by Democritus (q.v.) asking whether the two contiguous faces of a cone cut by a plane parallel to the base are equal or unequal (Plut. 1079 e). Another difficulty at this period was the existence of irrationals, specifically the incommensurability of the diagonal of a square with its side. Both arise only when one deals with continuous magnitudes (geometry), not with discrete (arithmetic in the Greek sense). Hence perhaps the statement of Archytas (q.v.) in the early fourth century that arithmetic can provide proofs where geometry fails (B 4 D–K). But these logical difficulties did not inhibit the practice of geometry, as is shown by Archytas' own ingenious solution to the problem of finding two mean proportionals (which Hippocrates had already shown to be equivalent to the problem of 'doubling the cube'), and by the work of his contemporary Theaetetus (q.v.), who made important discoveries about irrationals and the five regular solids.

**3.** The difficulties were solved, or at least circumvented, by Eudoxus (q.v.), *c.* 360. He formulated a general theory of proportion including both commensurable and incommensurable magnitudes, and also invented the method of approach to the limit which became the standard Greek way of dealing with problems involving infinitesimals. Euclid's formulation of this is found in Book 10, Prop. 1 : 'If from the greater of (any) two unequal magnitudes more than its half is subtracted, and from the remainder more than its half, and so on, there will be left a magnitude less than the smaller of the original two.' Archimedes (*Quadr. Parab.* int.) quotes another formulation: 'The amount by which the greater of two unequal areas exceeds the smaller can, by being added continuously to itself, be made to exceed any given finite area.' He says that 'the earlier geometers' used this to prove among other things that pyramid and cone are one-third of prism and cylinder respectively with equal base and height. Since he tells us elsewhere (*Method* int.) that Eudoxus was the first to prove these theorems (though Democritus had stated them), it is likely that the second formulation is Eudoxus'. We may guess that Eudoxus, with his interest in logical rigour, was also chiefly responsible for the axiomatization of geometry as we find it in its classical form (Euclid). The great interest and progress in strict deductive logic during the fourth century is best seen in the logical works of Aristotle (q.v.).

**4.** From Proclus' summary of the early history of mathematics extracted from Eudemus we know many names of mathematicians active in the fourth century, but very few details of what they did. However, Eutocius (*Comm. in Arch.*[2] 78 ff. Heiberg) preserves an account of a solution by Menaechmus (mid 4th c.) to the problem of finding two mean proportionals which is the first use of conic sections. Aristaeus wrote a textbook on these not very much later.

**5.** With the *Elements* of Euclid (*c.* 300 B.C.) we come to the first extant mathematical treatise (apart from the slight work of Autolycus (q.v. 2). This, though an introductory textbook, reflects the sophistication of contemporary geometry in both form and content, but the axiomatic method of exposition necessarily obscures the historical development. A particular problem is raised by propositions concerning the 'application of areas'. 6. 28 gives a general solution of which a particular case can be derived from 2. 5 (see Heath's translation, 383): 'To a given straight line (*b*) to apply a rectangle which shall be equal to a given area (*A*), and fall short of the rectangle formed by the straight line and one of its own sides by a square figure'. In algebraic terms this is $xy = A, x + y = b$ (in other words the quadratic equation $bx - x^2 = A$ is to be solved). This is exactly what one would arrive at if one were to transform the 'normal forms' of Babylonian numerical problems involving a quadratic equation into geometric terms, and it is likely, though not demonstrable, that this 'algebraic geometry' is just such a transformation. If so, some knowledge of advanced Babylonian mathematics had reached Greece in the fourth century. As well as plane and solid geometry, the *Elements* comprises elementary number theory; but the latter, and the branches of mathematics treated in Euclid's other works (some lost), had not reached the same level of systematization as pure geometry. However, some remarkable results were reached, such as the proof that there are an infinite number of primes (*Elements* 9. 20).

**6.** This deficiency was supplied in the case of conics by Apollonius (q.v. 2), who completely transformed the approach to the field by extending the algebraic 'application of areas' to include it. His elder contemporary Archimedes (q.v.) created new branches of mathematics by applying the axiomatic approach to statics and hydrostatics, but systematization was not his main interest. Most of his surviving work is in higher geometry, where he proves by traditional methods many theorems that would now be proved by the integral calculus. But his *Method* shows that he could use infinitesimals to achieve the same results. This is only one of the ways in which his thought was so far ahead of his time that it had no effect in antiquity: thus the concept of a numerical system implicit in the *Sand-reckoner* has no echo in surviving literature. However, many of his results, such as the formula for the volume of a sphere and his approximation to $\pi$, became mathematical commonplaces.

**7.** The third century was the great period of pure geometry. After this most creative mathematics was done in other fields. Several of these were connected with the study of astronomy. For instance, the necessity of determining the time of day accurately led to the development of the theory of sundials. Though the sundial itself goes back to at least the fifth century in Greece, the mathematical treatment of it known by the ancients as 'analemma' (an application of descriptive geometry) does not seem older than Diodorus (q.v. 4), of Alexandria, first century B.C. The most elegant example is found in Ptolemy's *Analemma*; earlier but cruder methods are found in the works of Heron (q.v.) and Vitruvius. There is evidence that the related technique of stereographic projection was used by Hipparchus (q.v. 3) about 150 B.C. for mapping circles of the heavenly sphere on to a plane in order to solve certain astronomical problems. The same problems led to the development of spherical trigonometry, probably by Menelaus (q.v. 3) about A.D. 100. Hipparchus himself had used plane trigonometry, for his 'Table of Chords' had the same function as a modern sine table.

**8.** It is in later Greek mathematics too that we find the non-axiomatic, numerical, and algebraic techniques which are typical of Babylonian mathematics. But it is accidental that they first occur as late as the work of Heron (q.v.), *c.* A.D. 60, for we cannot doubt that they are directly descended from Mesopotamian sources in a continuous tradition, which did not hesitate to borrow from the works of the classical mathematicians, though apparently ignored by them. It is also found in mathematical papyri, and was evidently a 'popular' mathematics (in Heron it is mostly 'practical'). A different branch of the same tradition is found in Diophantus (q.v.). This is the work which comes nearest to the modern conception of algebra, though it is not a textbook on the solution of equations but rather groups of similar problems, mostly of indeterminate equations. Though the roots of this lie in Babylon, much of the content is probably original, and the form of exposition owes much to the Greek tradition.

9. Even in late antiquity there were still competent mathematicians such as Theon (q.v. 4) and Eutocius to edit and comment on the classical works, and even an original one (Pappus, q.v.) to add his own extensions. But the real revival of Greek mathematics came in sixteenth-century Europe, when the works of Archimedes began to have effect. Even in the seventeenth century a mathematician of the calibre of Descartes could be inspired by reading Pappus' account of lost works of higher geometry, and Fermat by Diophantus.

For special studies see the articles on the ancient authors referred to. A detailed general account is in Heath, *Hist. of Greek Maths.* See also O. Neugebauer, *The Exact Sciences in Antiquity*[2] (U.S.A. 1957), and B. L. van der Waerden, *Science Awakening*[2] (Groningen, 1954).                                                                G. J. T.

**MATIDIA** (*PW* 28; ? *Salonia*) the Elder was the only child of Marciana (q.v.) and hence niece of Trajan (q.v.). Born at latest by A.D. 68, she married an otherwise unknown L. Vibius (? Sabinus), by whom she had two daughters, (Vibia) Sabina (q.v.), wife of Hadrian (q.v.), and (Vibia) Matidia the Younger (*ILS* 327), who survived, apparently unmarried, into the 160s. Matidia the Elder was, like her mother, close to Trajan and Plotina; on her mother's death (112) she received the title *Augusta* (*Fasti Ost.*, s.a.) and in 117 she, Plotina (q.v.), and Attianus (q.v.) brought back Trajan's remains from Cilicia to Rome (S.H.A. *Hadr.* 5. 9). On her death in 119 Hadrian pronounced her funeral oration (*CIL* xiv. 3579), deified her (*Acta Fr. Arv.*), and erected a commemorative temple in Rome with attached halls named for her and Marciana; she was probably the first *diva* to have her own temple in Rome.

COINS. *B.M. Coins, Rom. Emp.* iii (1936); Strack, *Untersuchungen* i (1931), 41; ii (1933), Katalog.
I. Rubel, *Z. für die öst. Gym.* 1916, 497 ff.; L. Vidmann, *Fasti Ost.* (1957), 64; Nash, *Pict. Dict. Rome* ii (1962), 36; Wegner, *Herrscherbild* ii. 3 (1956).                                                      M. H.

**MATIUS** (1), GNAEUS, in Sulla's time translated the *Iliad* into Latin hexameters. Gellius admired his learning. He introduced scazons into Latin light verse from the *mimiambi* of Herodas.

Baehr. *FPR* 281; Morel, *FPL* 48.

**MATIUS** (2, *PW* 1), GAIUS, a learned friend of Cicero and partisan of Caesar, helped the former in his relations with the latter, especially in 49 and 48 B.C. In 44 he shared in the management of the games which Octavian exhibited in July in honour of Caesar. Cicero's letter to him about his devotion to Caesar, and his reply, written later in 44 (*Fam.* 11. 27 f.), are of outstanding interest. Augustus' friend and assistant, C. Matius (*PW* 2), an *eques* and expert on arboriculture (q.v.) and gastronomy, has been identified with Cicero's friend, but seems to belong to the next generation.

A. Heuss, *Hist.* 1956, 53 ff.; 1962, 118 ff.; R. Combès, *Rev. Ét. Lat.* 1958, 176 ff.; B. Kytzler, *Hist.* 1960, 96 ff.; *Philol.* 1960, 48 ff.; Schanz–Hosius i. 604 f.                                        A. M.; T. J. C.

**MATRIS** of Thebes (3rd c. B.C.?), rhetor, who wrote an Ἐγκώμιον Ἡρακλέους with Asianist characteristics.

**MATRON** of Pitane (late 4th c. B.C.), parodist, wrote a poem called Δεῖπνον Ἀττικόν, quoted by Athenaeus

(4. 134–7), beginning Δεῖπνά μοι ἔννεπε, Μοῦσα, πολύτροφα καὶ μάλα πολλά.

*Corp. poes. ep. Graec. lud.* i. 53–95.

**MATUTA, MATER,** a Roman goddess of growth (Varro ap. August. *De Civ. D.* 4. 8: '[praefecerunt frumentis] maturescentibus deam Matutam'). Lucretius (5. 656), followed by many moderns, makes her a goddess of dawn, but this is hardly possible, since she is a figure of cult, not poetry or myth, which the dawn seems never to be. For her temple in the Forum Boarium see Platner–Ashby, 330 f.; Nash, *Pict. Dict. Rome* i. 411. Her festival, the Matralia, 11 June, is included in the 'calendar of Numa'. The ritual was conducted by women, apparently *uniuirae* (Tert. *De Monog.* 17), and they prayed only for their sisters' children (Ov. *Fasti* 6. 559; Plut. *Quaest. Rom.* 267 e, *De frat. amor.* 492 d, the ultimate source being probably Verrius Flaccus). This being both well attested and absurd, it seems probable that they prayed for *pueri sororii*, i.e. adolescent children; Rose, *CQ* 1934, 156 f.                                                    H. J. R.

**MAURETANIA,** the land of the Moors, stretching from the Ampsaga to the Atlantic and embracing the western half of the Atlas range. Most of the country is high and rocky, supporting sheep and producing a little wine; corn and olives grew on the coast, in the Mulucha valley, and on the plains of Volubilis (q.v.) and Sala. The chief exports were ebony, precious woods, and purple dyes.

There seems to have been communication with Spain from early days, binding Europe and Africa by piracy and colonization. The bulk of the population belonged to the Moorish branch of the Berber race; there was an admixture of negro blood in the south, and numerous Phoenician trading-stations were established on the Mediterranean and Atlantic coasts.

By the second century B.C. the small Moorish tribes had formed kingdoms; their rulers, Bocchus and Bogud (qq.v.), played important parts in the Jugurthine and Civil Wars. Roman law and Greek art spread during the reign of Juba II. The murder in Rome of Ptolemy, his son and successor (A.D. 23–40), led to disturbances. Mauretania was pacified by Suetonius Paulinus (41–2) and Hosidius Geta. Before 44 Claudius constituted two Mauretanian provinces, ruled by procurators with capitals at Tingi and Caesarea (q.v. 3). Moorish cavalry served in the Roman armies, and the Moor Lusius Quietus won distinction under Trajan. A number of *coloniae* were founded in the first century, and there was a certain amount of Italian immigration; romanization was also spread by the auxiliary units which defended the country. Large tracts of country remained under Moorish chieftains; there were serious rebellions in the late third and fourth centuries. Mauretania Tingitana was attached to the diocese of Spain by Diocletian.

L. Chatelain, *Inscriptions latines du Maroc* (1942) and *Le Maroc des Romains* (1944); R. Roget, *Index de topographie antique du Maroc, Publicat. du service des antiquités*, fasc. 4 (1938); J. Mazard, *Corpus Nummorum Numidiae Mauretaniaeque* (Paris, 1953); S. Gsell, *Histoire ancienne de l'Afrique du Nord*, esp. vol. viii (1928); J. Carcopino, *Le Maroc antique*[2] (1947); for early Roman settlements, L. Teutsch, *Das Städtewesen in Nordafrika* (1962), 190 ff.                        W. N. W.

**MAUSOLEUM,** the Tomb of Mausolus (q.v.), satrap of Caria, built of white marble by his widow, Artemisia *c.* 353 B.C. at Halicarnassus, the architect being Pythius (q.v.). An earthquake caused its collapse before the fifteenth century. In 1857 the site was excavated by Sir C. Newton, who brought many pieces to the British Museum, including some fine friezes and the colossal statues of Mausolus and Artemisia, and many subsidiary figures, human and animal. The monument was regarded as one of the seven wonders of the ancient world. Four leading sculptors contributed to its decoration—Scopas, Bryaxis, Timotheus (3), and Leochares (qq.v.) (Vitruvius, no doubt wrongly, includes Praxiteles). The architect himself, Pythius, added the great chariot group, according to Pliny. Vitruvius mentions a second architect, Satyrus of Paros (Pref. 7. 12–13; cf. 2. 8. 12).

The foundation cutting measured about 100 by 127 feet. On a high base stood a colonnade of thirty-six Ionic columns, above which rose a pyramid-like structure, reaching a height of about 134 feet. Pliny's description (36. 30–1) and the remains give plenty of scope for theoretical reconstructions, of which scores have been produced, differing widely in such matters as the arrangement of the columns and the position of the sculpture.

W. R. Lethaby, *Greek Buildings represented by Fragments in the British Museum* (1908); *PW* xxiv, Halbbd. 47, 372 ff., s.v. *Pytheos* (reconstructions, 383 ff.); for some reconstructions see H. Law, *JHS* 1939; F. Krischen, *Die Griechische Stadt* (1938), Taf. 1 and 37 (cf. R. Lullies and M. Hirmer, *Greek Sculpture* (1957), fig. 10); W. B. Dinsmoor, *Architecture of Ancient Greece* (1950), pl. lxiii (cf. 257 ff., 376).             T. F.; R. E. W.

**MAUSOLUS,** satrap of Caria 377/6–353 B.C. in virtual independence of Persian control. His early relations with the Great King were cordial and in 365 he co-operated with Autophradates in suppressing Ariobarzanes. Subsequently, however, he embarked on an expansionist policy symbolized by the substitution of Halicarnassus for Mylasa as the seat of government, and in 362 he became involved in the Satraps' Revolt, though he diplomatically deserted the losing side at the right moment. Left in undisturbed possession of his satrapy, he resumed his advance at the expense of Lycia and Ionia. The conflict of his interests with those of Athens resulted in the Social War of 357, when Rhodes, Cos, Chios, and Byzantium revolted on a promise of support from Mausolus. Athens' attempts at reasserting her control proved unsuccessful, and Rhodes and Cos became appendages to his kingdom. His marriage to his sister Artemisia, the fortress-like palace with its private harbour at Halicarnassus, his philhellenic patronage of literature and the arts, and the monumental tomb (*see* MAUSOLEUM) which he planned but did not live to complete, foreshadow the rule of the Ptolemies.

W. Judeich, *Kleinasiatische Studien* (1892), ch. 6.    D. E. W. W.

**MAVORTIUS** (perhaps not the consul of A.D. 527) wrote two Virgilian centos, *Iudicium Paridis* and *De Ecclesia* (Baehr. *PLM* iv. 198 f., 214 ff.; K. Schenkl, *CSEL* xvi).

**MAXENTIUS** (*PW* 1), MARCUS AURELIUS VALERIUS, son of Maximian (q.v.) and Eutropia, was passed over in A.D. 305 when Diocletian and Maximian abdicated and Galerius and Constantius succeeded as Augusti, and was living in retirement at Rome when Constantius died (306) and Constantine, son of Constantius, who had also been passed over, was irregularly proclaimed emperor by the army in Britain. The Praetorian guard and the city of Rome, both bitter over lost privileges, then elevated Maxentius to the throne, and he called his father from his retirement in Lucania to assist him. Severus, the new Augustus of the West, marched against Rome, but was driven to surrender after retreating to Ravenna, while Maximian went to Gaul and won over Constantine. Galerius, invading Italy, was likewise forced to retire, and when Maximian tried to depose his son he failed and fled to Constantine. Declared a public enemy at Carnuntum (308), Maxentius yet maintained himself for some years in Italy; he was recognized in Spain *c.* 308, though this was lost to Constantine in 310. More serious was the revolt of Africa (308–11) under its *vicarius* Domitius Alexander, which created famine at Rome. In 312 Constantine invaded Italy with a small but experienced army and destroyed Maxentius at the battle of the Mulvian Bridge. Maxentius' reputation was assiduously blackened by the victor. He was certainly no soldier but there is little evidence to support the various charges. He granted toleration and restitution to the Christians and his 'persecution' of the Roman Senate was fiscal in character. His chief significance is as the champion of the old privileges and the old faith of the capital.

C. H. V. Sutherland, *RIC* vi. 15 ff.      H. M.; B. H. W.

**MAXIMIAN** (MARCUS AURELIUS VALERIUS MAXIMIANUS, *PW* 1), called by Diocletian in A.D. 285 to assist him as his Caesar. Born *c.* A.D. 240 near Sirmium of peasant parents, he had a solid military career under Aurelian and Probus. Uneducated and rather stupid, he was an excellent general and completely loyal to Diocletian, his old comrade in arms. Sent against the Bacaudae in Gaul, he soon dispersed their irregular bands and was promoted to be Augustus, early 286. Against Carausius, who revolted to escape punishment for neglect of his duties against the pirates, Maximian was less successful. A first expedition by sea failed and Carausius was left in peace for some years.

Maximian, charged with the defence of Italy and the West, was heavily engaged on the lower Rhine and in Raetia between 288 and 292. He acted in close accord with Diocletian whom he met in 289 and 290/1. In 293, under Diocletian's tetrarchic system, he received Constantius, formerly his praetorian prefect, as his Caesar, and gave him his daughter Theodora in marriage. Constantius took charge of a new attack on Carausius. He took Boulogne, and, after the death of Carausius, recovered Britain from his murderer Allectus in 296. Maximian came up in person to secure the Rhine frontier. In 296 and the following year he was in Africa where there was a revolt by the Quinquegentanei and other Mauretanian tribes, and later visited Rome where he began the building of the Baths of Diocletian. The persecution of the Christians (303–5) was enforced with some severity in North Africa where they were numerous. He abdicated with Diocletian on 1 May 305.

Maximian returned from retirement in Lucania to support the rising of his son, Maxentius (306). He forced Severus to surrender at Ravenna and then won over Constantine, giving him his daughter, Fausta, in marriage. In 307, after the failure of Galerius against Rome, Maximian tried in vain to depose his son and fled to Gaul. Required to abdicate again at Carnuntum (308), Maximian could not settle down to a life of honourable inactivity. He led a revolt against Constantine, but was captured at Massilia and died by his own hand (310).

C. H. V. Sutherland, *RIC* vi. 15 ff.      H. M.; B. H. W.

**MAXIMINUS** (1), GAIUS JULIUS (*PW* 526) VERUS (Roman Emperor A.D. 235–8), a Thracian peasant who had been promoted centurion by Septimius Severus because of his physical strength. He had held a number of equestrian military appointments when saluted Emperor at Mainz (Mar. 235) in the mutiny which overthrew Alexander Severus. An energetic soldier, he ravaged Germany and won a victory in a swamp in Württemberg (235). After two years' fighting on the Danube a rebellion in Africa led to the proclamation of Gordian I and his son (qq.v.) as Emperors (Apr. 238). They were recognized by the Senate, who feared the uneducated Maximinus. The latter invaded Italy, but his progress was arrested by the stout resistance of Aquileia. His troops became disheartened, till the soldiers of II Parthica sought an end of civil war by murdering him with his son (*see* GORDIAN 1–3; BALBINUS).

Herodian, bks. 7–8; S.H.A. G. M. Bersanetti, *Studi sul imperatore Massimino il Trace* (1940); E. Hohl, *Maximini duo Julii Capitolini* (1949). H. M. D. P.; B. H. W.

**MAXIMINUS** (2, *PW*, s.v. Daia), GAIUS GALERIUS VALERIUS, originally named *Daia* (or *Daza*), son of a sister of Galerius, received rapid promotion in the army through his uncle's interest, was adopted by him and made Caesar when Galerius became Augustus on the abdication of Diocletian, 1 May 305. Entrusted with the government of Syria, Egypt, and the south of Asia Minor, Maximinus served Galerius faithfully but, in 310, when the tetrarchic system was breaking down, refused the offered title of 'filius Augusti' and assumed the rank of Augustus, already conferred on Licinius. When Galerius died in 311, Maximinus occupied Asia Minor up to the Hellespont, but made peace with Licinius, who contested the crossing to Europe. Maximinus now drew closer to Maxentius, to balance the alliance of Constantine and Licinius; after the fall of Maxentius, anticipating an attack on his own territory, he took Byzantium and Heracleia. He was then defeated near the latter by Licinius and after fleeing through Cappadocia died, a fugitive, at Tarsus (autumn 313).

Maximinus was a noted persecutor—in some ways the most interesting of them all. Not content with repression of the Christians, he tried to revive and reform the paganism of his subjects. He encouraged cities to petition against the Christians, and strove to improve the organization and raise the morale of the pagan priesthood.

C. H. V. Sutherland, *RIC* vi, 15 ff. H. M.; B. H. W.

**MAXIMUS** (1), SEXTUS QUINCTILIUS (*PW* 24) VALERIUS, born in Alexandria Troas, received the *latus clavus* from Nerva (*ILS* 1018), and is probably identical with an Epicurean friend of Pliny the Younger, who served as *legatus Augusti ad corrigendum statum liberarum ciuitatium* in Achaea, probably not after A.D. 108–9.

M. N. Tod, in *Anatolian Studies presented to W. H. Buckler* (1939), 333 ff.; E. Groag, *Die röm. Reichsbeamten von Achaia* (1939), cols. 125 ff.; Syme, *Tacitus*, 84 n. A. M.

**MAXIMUS** (2) of Tyre (*c.* A.D. 125–85), sophist, the author of forty-one extant Διαλέξεις (lectures), lived the life of an itinerant lecturer; he is known to have lectured in Athens, and the extant lectures were delivered in Rome, apparently in the reign of Commodus (180–92). He was well read in Greek literature, but apparently not in Greek philosophy except in Plato, of whom he claimed to be a follower. His lectures show no philosophical originality, and are simply eloquent exhortations to virtue decked out with quotations, chiefly from Plato and Homer; he belongs to the same genus as the sophists, though his views have no affinity with theirs, being borrowed from Cynicism and Platonism.

Ed. H. Hobein (1910). W. D. R.

**MAXIMUS** (3) (probably 2nd c. A.D.), author of the extant astrological poem Περὶ καταρχῶν, part of which later passed under the name of Orpheus. The *Suda* calls the author an Epirote or Byzantine, but identifies him with Julian's teacher Maximus (q.v. 4), who came from Ephesus; this, however, seems improbable, as the poem is quite unphilosophical.

Ed. A. Ludwich (1877). W. D. R.

**MAXIMUS** (4) of Ephesus (d. A.D. 370), Neoplatonist philosopher. A pupil of Aedesius, who was himself a pupil of Iamblichus (q.v. 2). Maximus followed his master's tendency to emphasize theurgy and magic at the expense of the more serious side of Neoplatonism.

Maximus' own most distinguished pupil was the future Emperor Julian, to whom he was recommended by Aedesius. He is said to have foretold Julian's subsequent elevation to the throne, a prophecy which could readily be made without supernatural knowledge, and he no doubt encouraged the young prince in his abjuration of Christianity. In 361 Maximus was invited by Julian, now Emperor, to join his court at Constantinople, and remained with him until his death during his Persian campaign, for which he had prophesied a fortunate outcome. For some time he enjoyed the confidence of Valens, but fell into disfavour and was imprisoned in 364. His release was due to the intervention of Themistius. In 370 he was put to death for complicity in a plot to assassinate Valens. He is not the author of an astrological poem in hexameters sometimes attributed to him. Maximus is a typical member of the group of self-assured near-charlatans who exercised so harmful an influence on the brilliant but weak young Emperor.

Eunapius, *VS* vii (pp. 40–56 Giangrande); Julian, *Ep.* 26, 190, 191, Bidez–Cumont; Libanius, *Or.* 5, 12. J. Bidez, *Vie de l'empereur Julien* (1930), 11–12. R. B.

**MEALS.** The times and names of meals in Greece varied at different periods. In early times breakfast (ἄριστον) was taken soon after sunrise, followed by a main meal (δεῖπνον) in the middle of the day and supper (δόρπον) in the evening. In classical Athens two meals—a light lunch (ἄριστον) in the forenoon and dinner (δεῖπνον) in the evening—appear to have been usual; but from the fourth century B.C. onwards an earlier breakfast (ἀκράτισμα) was again added (or, among frugal people, substituted for lunch).

Among the Romans, too, dinner (*cena*) was in early times eaten in the middle of the day, with a light supper (*vesperna*) in the evening; but in course of time an evening *cena*, often beginning in the late afternoon, became usual; and lunch (*prandium*), consisting of fish or eggs and vegetables together with wine, was eaten towards midday and took the place of supper. These meals were preceded by a very light breakfast (*ientaculum*), which might consist of only bread and salt and rarely included more than a piece of bread and some fruit or cheese.

The *cena*, at least among the wealthy (to whom most of our information relates), consisted of three parts. A *gustatio* of eggs, shell-fish, or salad, taken with honeyed wine (*mulsum*), was followed by the *cena* proper. This often included several (up to seven) successive *fercula*, with one chief item (*caput cenae*), which might be a roasted animal served whole, preceded and followed by smaller, but still very substantial courses (e.g. lampreys, turbot, roast peacock, roast veal). The meal ended with *mensae secundae*, consisting of sweetmeats and fruit.

Such elaborate meals, however, must always have been the prerogative of a minority. But even among ordinary people the consumption of fish and meat gradually increased, and the early *cena*, of porridge and vegetables with only occasional meat, came to be regarded as characteristic of pristine simplicity. It may have been this development that caused dinner to be eaten, as it still is in many southern countries, at an hour when the day's work was done.

*PW*, s.vv. Cena (iii. 1895 ff.), Kochkunst (xi. 944 ff.), Mahlzeiten (xiv. 524 ff.); v. Müller–Bauer, *Griech. Privat- u. Kriegsaltertümer*[2] (1893), 118 ff.; Blümner, *Röm. Privataltertümer* (1911), 160 ff.; Carcopino, *Daily Life in Ancient Rome* (1956), 262 ff. L. A. M.

**MEALS, SACRED.** To eat together is everywhere a sort of communion, varying in different cultures from a mere mark of friendliness to a close and binding connexion. If a god is present at the meal, it becomes sacred, and the human participants are his hosts or guests and so in association with him. Hence every meal in an ancient household which kept up the old customs was sacred, for the household gods were present (cf. CHILDREN, WORSHIP, HOUSEHOLD; 'sacrae adsistere mensae', Juvenal 6. 365. O. 4, is to be present at a family meal). This is true also of the normal Olympian sacrifice, where the god and the sacrificers both partake of the victim, and equally of such rites as the *lectisternium* (q.v.), at which the god is a guest. It is most of all true of those rites in which the god himself is devoured (*see* DIONYSUS). In the Hellenistic mystery-cults this idea seems to have been strongly developed, ritual feasts, at which apparently the bond between god and worshippers was renewed, being a regular feature of them. These also served to mark the tie uniting initiates of a common cult; see for examples Cumont, *Rel. or.*[4] 37, 65, 192, with 219, note 43; dining-rooms formed a regular part of Syrian temples, 256, note 52. It is therefore natural that such feasts were imagined as the portion of the blessed hereafter (ibid. 57, 61, 202 f.; 309, note 51). More examples will be found by consulting Cumont's index, s.vv. 'Banquet', 'Festin', 'Repas'. Nock in *Essays on the Trinity and the Incarnation* (1928), 124 ff., *Harv. Theol. Rev.* 1936, 77 ff.; Nilsson, *GGR* i[2]. 47, 144, 337. *See also* BIRTHDAY, EPULONES, THEOXENIA. H. J. R.

**MEASURES.** I. MEASURES OF LENGTH. **1.** Measures of length were based primarily on parts of the human body, with the foot as unit both for fractions like finger and palm and for multiples like pace and arm-span. Pylos tablets designate tables as six-footers (*we-pe-za*) or nine-footers (*e-ne-wo-pe-za*); whether this is a measure or description of supports is uncertain. Homer is acquainted with the foot-standard, but the length of his foot is unknown. In historic Greece many standard feet are found, the absolute values for which are derived from surviving stadia (preserved with starting and finishing lines), calculated basic units of various buildings, and literary evidence providing correspondences with the Roman foot (296 mm), of which ancient examples survive. Of the two feet most generally used in Greek buildings the shorter (294–6 mm) approximates the Roman foot, the longer (326–8 mm) approaches the *pes Drusianus* of Gaul and Germany in the first century B.C. (330 mm). Compare also the Olympic foot of 320 mm, the Pergamene of 330 mm and the so-called Aeginetic of 333 mm. Subdivisions of the foot are taken from the fingers: thus

| 2 finger-breadths, δάκτυλοι | = 1 κόνδυλος, middle joint of finger |
|---|---|
| 4 ,, ,, | = 1 παλαστή (Homeric δῶρον), palm |
| 8 ,, ,, | = 1 διχάς or ἡμιπόδιον, half-foot |
| 10 ,, ,, | = 1 λιχάς, span of thumb and first finger |
| 12 ,, ,, | = 1 σπιθαμή, span of all fingers |
| 16 ,, ,, | = 1 πούς, foot. |

**2.** Higher dimensions are taken from the arms; thus

| 18 δάκτυλοι | = 1 πυγμή, short cubit, elbow to start of fingers |
|---|---|
| 20 ,, | = 1 πυγών, short cubit of Homer and Herodotus, elbow to end of knuckles of closed fist |
| 24 ,, | = 1 πῆχυς, normal cubit, elbow to tips of fingers. |

For longer distances:

| 2½ feet | = 1 βῆμα, pace |
|---|---|
| 6 feet | = 1 ὄργυια, fathom, stretch of both arms |
| 100 feet | = 1 πλέθρον, breadth of the γύης, acre. |

Beyond this Homer uses phrases such as the cast of a stone or quoit or spear. The later Greek unit, the στάδιον, originally the distance covered in a single draught by the plough, contained 600 feet, no matter what the length of the foot might be, and its exact length is therefore often doubtful. The παρασάγγης of 30 stadia was adopted from Persia.

**3.** The Roman foot (*pes*) of 296 mm was generally divided into 12 inches, corresponding to the division of the *libra* into 12 *unciae*; the names of the subdivisions are the same and are given under WEIGHTS. There was also a division into 16 *digiti*, similar to the Greek system and possibly derived from it.

For higher distances:

| 5 *pedes* | = 1 *passus*, pace |
|---|---|
| 125 paces | = 1 *stadium* |
| 1,000 ,, | = 1 mile, about 95 yards less than the English mile. |

**4.** II. MEASURES OF AREA. Measures of area in both Greece and Rome were based on the amount ploughed in a day by a yoke of oxen. The Greek unit is the πλέθρον, measuring 100 × 100 = 10,000 square feet. Another unit, the μέδιμνος, found in Sicily and in Cyrenaica, represented the amount of land that could be sown by a *medimnus* of wheat. (Similarly, Mycenaean land measures seem to have been expressed by volumes of grain.) The Romans employed the *actus quadratus*, a square of 120 feet, two of which formed the *iugerum* of 28,800 square Roman feet = 5/8ths of an acre. Two *iugera* formed a *heredium*, 100 *heredia* a *centuria*.

**5.** III. MEASURES OF CAPACITY. Measures of capacity fall into two divisions, dry and wet (μέτρα ξηρά, μέτρα ὑγρά), corresponding to the primary products, corn and wine, of ancient agriculture. In the Mycenaean system the two divisions share the same symbols and ratios for the smaller measures; absolute values are not certain. In historic Greece the *kotyle*, which is basic to both wet and dry, is made up of six *kyathoi* or four *oxybapha*; its absolute value in various local systems ranges from 0·21 litre to more than 0·33 litre, the most usual being 0·24 and 0·27 litre. The dry measures are:

| 4 *kotylai* | = 1 χοῖνιξ, at Athens a day's corn ration for a man |
|---|---|
| 8 *choinikes* | = 1 ἑκτεύς |
| 6 *hekteis* | = 1 μέδιμνος. |

For liquid measures the table continues:

| 6 *kotylai* | = 1 ἡμίχους |
|---|---|
| 12 ,, | = 1 χοῦς |
| 12 *choes* | = 1 μετρητής. |

**6.** The basic unit in the Roman system is the *sextarius* (0·546 litre), which is equivalent to the Greek *dikotylon*; its components are:

| 48 *cochlearia* |
|---|
| 12 *cyathi* |
| 8 *acetabula* |
| 4 *quartaria* |
| 2 *heminae*. |

For dry measures the higher denominations are:

| 8 *sextarii* | = 1 *semodius*, nearly an English gallon |
|---|---|
| 16 ,, | = 1 *modius*. |

For liquid measures:

| 12 *heminae* | = 1 *congius* |
|---|---|
| 8 *congii* | = 1 *amphora* |
| 20 *amphorae* | = 1 *culleus*, tun of 120 gallons. |

The *amphora*, or quadrantal, by which the burden of ships was determined, was the volume of a cubic Roman foot, 25·79 litres.

M. Ventris and J. Chadwick, *Documents in Mycenaean Greek* (1956); W. B. Dinsmoor, *The Architecture of Ancient Greece* (1950); O. Viedebantt, 'Forschungen zur Metrologie des Altertums' (*Abh. d. phil.-hist. Klasse der k. sächs. Ges. Wiss.* xxxiv, iii) (1917); P. Tannery, Dar.–Sag. s.v. 'Mensura'; F. Hultsch, *Reliquiae Scriptorum Metrologicorum* (1882). F. N. P.; M. L.

**MEDDIX** *tuticus* or *summus*, assisted by a *meddix minor*, was the senior magistrate among the Oscan-speaking peoples. His authority differed from that of the Romano-Latin *praetura*, to which some communities, notably Bantia (q.v.), tended to assimilate the office, in being non-collegiate and yet lacking the absolute character of *imperium* (q.v.), though supreme in jurisdiction and administration. The relation of *m. minor* to *m. tuticus* recalls that of *magister equitum* to *dictator* (q.v.).

A. Rosenberg, *Staat der alten Italiker* (1913); J. Whatmough, *The Foundations of Roman Italy* (1937); G. Camporeale, *Atti d. Acc. Tosc.*, 1957, 91 ff. A. N. S.-W.

**MEDEA** (*Μήδεια*), 'the cunning one', in mythology, daughter of Aeetes king of the Colchians and his wife Eidyia ('the knowing'), grand-daughter of Helios and niece of Circe (q.v.). She is universally said to have been a witch, but shows a certain tendency to pass into a goddess (*ἀθανάτου στόματος*, Pind. *Pyth.* 4. 11, meaning the mouth of Medea; cf. Athenagoras, *Leg. pro Christ.* 14, a corrupt passage but sufficient to show that according to him she was worshipped somewhere). In the story of the Argonauts (q.v.) as we have it she plays a prominent part; when Aeetes sets Jason a seemingly impossible task, Medea, being in love with him, helps him to perform it by magic. In other words, she is that common figure of folk-tale, the Ogre's Daughter (Stith Thompson, G 530. 2). But the Argonauts have in many cases highly specialized characteristics, as wonderful sight (Lynceus), extraordinary speed (Euphemus), power of flight (the Boreadae) (Ap. Rhod. 1. 153, 182, 219); hence it is clear that there was another form of the story, whether older or not, in which they and not Medea helped Jason (cf. Grimm, *Kinder- u. Hausmärchen*, no. 246). Her love is elaborately motivated by Ap. Rhod. 3. 7 ff., but this would not be original, though it may belong to the earliest literary form of the story (cf. Pind. *Pyth.* 4. 213 ff.). Having helped Jason, Medea escapes with him in all known variants, and is regularly pursued; either her brother Apsyrtus leads the pursuit and she contrives his murder (so Ap. Rhod. 4. 410 ff.), or he is a child whom she takes with her, kills, and scatters his limbs in the way of Aeetes, thus delaying him (Cic. *Leg. Man.* 22, and elsewhere). Returning to Iolcus, she renewed the youth of Aeson, Jason's father, by boiling him with virtuous herbs (fullest description in Ov. *Met.* 7. 162 ff., but earliest reference in *Nostoi*, fr. 6 Allen). This done, she persuaded the daughters of Pelias to attempt the like on their own father, but was careful to give them inefficacious herbs, thus rendering them guilty, technically, of his death. This story is as old as the fifth century (Pind. *Pyth.* 4. 250 calls Medea Pelias' slayer, cf. Pherecydes in the schol. there, and both Sophocles and Euripides wrote on it, respectively in the *'Ριζοτόμοι* and the *Peliades*), but doubtfully part of the oldest form of the legend, since Hesiod (*Theog.* 997 ff.) represents her and Jason as settled in Iolcus and her child Medeus as born there.

Her connexion with Corinth seems due to the Corinthian school of epic poets, who traded on the ambiguity of the name Ephyra (a town in Thesprotia where Jason and Medea lived, schol. *Od.* 1. 259, or Corinth). For her dealings with Creon see s.v. (1); after the murder of him, his daughter, and her children, she took refuge with Aegeus (q.v.) in Athens. After her banishment from that city, a late story (Hyg. *Fab.* 27) represents her as bringing about the death of Perses, Aeetes' brother and enemy, with the help of her son by Aegeus, Medus; the country was thereafter called Media.

The tricking of the daughters of Pelias is found on vases from the late sixth century. To the mid fifth and later belong some with Medea, Aegeus, and Theseus; to about 400 some with the capture of Talos. The slaughter of the children appears on fourth-century Italiote vases and was the subject of a famous late Hellenistic picture by Timanthes, which may be echoed in Roman paintings and gems (Brommer, *Vasenlisten*², 163, 348).

*See also* MAGIC, § 4. H. J. R.; C. M. R.

**MEDIA,** the mountainous country south-west of the Caspian Sea which was for a century the centre of the Median Empire. The Medes, an Indo-European people ethnologically and linguistically akin to the Persians, appear as a group of tribes, some nomadic, some settled in fortified villages, against whom the Assyrians waged war. They were possibly in the neighbourhood of L. Urmia as early as the beginning of the first millennium B.C.

Deioces, whom Herodotus (1. 96–100) accounts the founder of the Median Empire, appears in the Assyrian records only as a local chieftain. The real unifier of the Medes seems to have been Phraortes (Khshathrita, *c.* 675–653 B.C.). His son Cyaxares (Uvakhshtra, 625–585 B.C.) conquered neighbouring territories and, in alliance with Nabopolassar of Babylon, defeated the Assyrians; Nineveh fell in 612 B.C. His empire included most of Iran, the northern territory once subject to Urartu, and Cappadocia as far as the river Halys. Of its organization little is known. Astyages (Ishtumegu, 585–549 B.C.) extended his boundaries at the expense of Babylonia, but was defeated by his vassal Cyrus, and the Median Empire passed to the Persians.

E. G. Klauber, *Politisch-religiöse Texte aus der Sargonidenzeit* (1913); F. W. König, *Älteste Geschichte der Meder und Perser* (1934); J. V. Prášek, *Geschichte der Meder und Perser* (1906–10); I. M. Dyakonov, *Istoriya Midii* (1956); W. Culican, *The Medes and Persians* (1965). *See also* PERSIA. M. S. D.

**MEDICINA PLINII,** an extant compilation made (probably A.D. 300–50) from Pliny's account, in books 20–32 of the *Naturalis Historia*, of the plants and animals used for medicinal purposes. Marcellus Empiricus describes it as being the work of a second Pliny. This work has to be distinguished from a work commonly but falsely ascribed to Plinius Valerianus, of which the first three books are a garbled version (6th or 7th c.) of the earlier work, while the last two books come from a different source.

A. Önnersfors, *In Medicinam Plinii studia philologica* (Lund, 1963). W. D. R.

**MEDICINE. I. NON-RATIONAL ELEMENTS.** Historians of Greek Medicine rightly stress its scientific character. This goes far back, for there are traces of science in the medical practice of the Homeric poems and the very earliest scientific works are medical. Nevertheless throughout antiquity and in every part of the ancient world other and lower types of Medicine were prevalent. Indeed, it is a remarkable fact that certain forms of non-rational medicine flourished more than ever at about the time that saw the rise of scientific medicine. No cultural element is so transmissible as irrational beliefs and practices concerning disease. These are susceptible neither of logical arrangement nor of true historic treatment, nor can their sources be entirely separated from each other. Such material can only be discussed under artificial headings based on mere convenience.

(*a*) References to practices on a very low anthropological level are scattered through the literature of classical antiquity. Sympathetic, contagious, and imitative magic, the influence of rulers, priests, and the dead upon disease, and the various elements with which folklore deals are all represented. They were long ago collected and analysed by Sir J. G. Frazer in *The Golden Bough*.

(b) Peculiar rites and beliefs are associated with the gathering of herbs in both early and late literature. There are collections of them attached to the *Inquiry into Plants* of Theophrastus and embedded in the *Natural History* of Pliny. Some of these customs are comparable to those in the Sanskrit Vedas. A fair case can be made for the existence of a stream of Indo-Germanic Medicine associated specially with herb remedies. Some of these practices persist among European peasants. (*See* BOTANY, THEOPHRASTUS, PLINY THE ELDER.)

(c) The Medicine of the New Testament is mainly that of possession by evil spirits. There is only a trace of demonism in the Old Testament and it is not prominent in classical writings until Christian times. Its presence often indicates Persian contacts. It is well illustrated in the writings of Philostratus. Its main source is probably Mesopotamian. (*See* POSSESSION.)

(d) All deities, both Chthonic and Olympian, had healing powers. There was also, among the Greeks and later among the Romans, a tendency to the formation of cults ascribing such powers to deceased physicians. The most prominent of these cults was that of Asclepius. A whole family of supernatural healers became associated with him. His history has an extraordinarily close parallel in Egyptian civilization. (*See* ASCLEPIUS.)

(e) Essential to Asclepian rites was 'Incubation', the temple-sleep and its accompanying dream. This, however, neither originated with nor was peculiar to the cult. Throughout antiquity advice concerning disease and preservation of health was drawn from dreams which were held to be sometimes curative. The *Oneirocritica* of Artemidorus (2nd c. A.D.) is an exposition of this. (*See* INCUBATION.)

(f) Dedication of votive models of affected parts, especially in Asclepian shrines, was a common practice. The model may bear a representation of the disease or an invocation to the deity or an indication of the remedy desired. Similar votives are found in all civilizations. Modern votives are often indistinguishable from ancient. (*See* VOTIVE OFFERINGS.)

(g) Amulets and periapts, inscribed with prayers, invocations, charms, or signs of power, were suspended or tied to the person to ward off evil or effect cure. Specially common in the Western Empire was the ocular cachet—an inscribed clay tablet to be applied to the diseased eye. Identical practices still persist. (*See* AMULETS.)

(h) Magical incantations of syncretic origin were used against disease. Characteristic of these is the inclusion of foreign words of power, especially names of foreign divinities. Most records come from the later classical period. (*See* MAGIC.)

(i) A peculiarity in Roman practice, not easily paralleled, was the association of bodily parts and even sensations, symptoms, and diseases with their own specific deities. These tutelary beings needed propitiation according to the part or function affected.

(j) There is an important body of herb-lore that is irrational but unassociated with 'superstitious' practices. Such is the drug list of Dioscorides. Only a minute percentage of his hundreds of herbs have the activities he ascribes to them. Yet these drug lists remained in use for centuries and generated the ancient herbals and the medieval and modern pharmacopoeias. (*See* BOTANY, DIOSCORIDES 2.)

(k) Apart from superstitious practices, Medicine in classical antiquity retained throughout certain relations to the current higher religion. (See § II.)

II. 2. RELATION TO RATIONAL RELIGION AND PHILOSOPHY. Celsus calls Hippocrates 'the first who separated medicine from philosophy'. In fact the works of the Hippocratic Collection that date from the fifth and fourth centuries B.C. have definite philosophical affinities. This is true even of works which were written expressly in order to combat the function of philosophical presupposition in medical thought and practice.

3. Among the ancients there were many who took the 'practical' scientific attitude towards phenomena, regarding them as explicable without recourse to divine powers. It is true that some of the ancient philosophers, scientists, and physicians occasionally used language borrowed from religious terminology; but their modes of explanation nevertheless remained rational and scientific. They excluded divine caprice from natural processes and insisted on the uniformity of nature. However, the fact that there is an overlap between the terminologies of religious, philosophical, and scientific discourse is one reason, among others, why a translation into a modern language of the terminology of Greek Medicine is liable to be sometimes misleading.

4. Greek scientific medicine was singularly free from magical and superstitious practices and beliefs. But although it was thus proof against the danger of religious influence there were other dangers against which it was not so well protected. It is ironically significant that these dangers were the result of the insistent and radical rationality of Greek medicine. Like other forms of Greek science it was constantly prone to the temptation to produce an axiomatic system based on first principles from which the body of the science could then be deductively derived. Early Hippocratic and later medical literature contains, in addition to clinical treatises, a good number of discussions on methodological problems. It is clear from these that in all periods of the history of Greek medicine the doctors had to argue against the adoption of philosophical presuppositions in their medical work. These discussions ranged from the fifth century B.C. treatise *De Vetere Medicina* to the works of obscure authors in very late antiquity. It is interesting to note that even those doctors who most vigorously argued against the introduction of philosophical postulates and methods into what ought to be an empirical science themselves too failed to resist the lure of *a priori* hypotheses; thus, the author of *De Vetere Medicina* is only one amongst many who, while arguing against *a priori* methods, introduced at the same time theoretical presuppositions such as the humoral theory which can be shown to be closely linked with other physical-philosophical notions such as those of the four elements.

5. Greek Medicine also suffered from two other drawbacks: (a) the exaggerated authority accorded to their predecessors by the ancient doctors. This is as true of the earlier period as it is of Galen and indeed of the inheritors of Greek medicine in the Middle Ages. (b) The attempt both in early and in later times to represent the doctrines of different doctors as belonging to unitary schools.

6. There was no unity of outlook among the earlier physicians, no 'primitive Hippocratic doctrine', for which historians of Greek Medicine, following Galen, have vainly sought. From Hellenistic times, however, the philosophic differences that divided the medical world, though no more profound than before, are certainly more clearly visible. They are conventionally and somewhat artificially treated under four 'schools', known as the Dogmatists, Empirics, Methodists, and Pneumatists, corresponding roughly to the philosophic sects Stoics, Epicureans, Sceptics, and Eclectics respectively.

7. Galen (129–99), summator of ancient Medicine, borrowed ideas from all four medical schools and all four philosophic sects, inclining most to the Dogmatists and Stoics. Since he was not only a selective but also an extremely voluminous writer, it is not surprising that he was not always consistent. His inconsistency did not, however, lessen his influence and in his *Uses of the bodily*

*parts of man* he reached conclusions that determined medical thought for nearly a millennium and a half. He claims in that work that the organs are so well constructed, and in such perfect relation to the functions to which they minister, that it is impossible to imagine anything better. Following Aristotle's dictum that 'nature makes naught in vain' (*Cael.* 271ᵃ33, 291ᵇ13), he seeks to justify the form and structure of all the organs, and of every part of every organ, with reference to the functions for which he believes they are destined. Moreover, he considers that he can discover the end served by every part and requiring it to be constructed as it is.

**8.** Galen was the last active scientific intellect of antiquity. His teleological message, delivered in a world of Stoic determinism, carried the implication of the worthlessness of research. His doctrine demanded *a priori* solutions of all the problems of physiology. Galen himself was among the most important proponents of this teleological view. It seemed that, according to it, the world was worth exploring only to verify the hypothesis. He explored it, but his theory removed the motive for further exploration (*see* ANATOMY AND PHYSIOLOGY). His view fitted well with the Christian attitude and works by Galen were studied and respected throughout the Dark and Middle Ages.

**9.** The writings of the ancient physicians before Galen had no association with the lower religious elements. This cannot be said for all the derivative works which appear after him. But there was one earlier cult which had a general relation to the practice, if not to the theory, of Medicine. It was by no accident that Asclepius became god of doctors as well as of patients. His worship, in its best presentation, had certain affinities with rational religion. It contained a psychological element that was of great value to rational practice. The physician's attitude to Asclepius and that of Asclepius to Medicine is indicated in the famous Hippocratic *Oath*. It is not misleading to say that the normal relation of Medicine to the best side of the Asclepian cult was fairly near what it is to the current practice of religion in a settled modern society.

III. **10.** MEDICAL STATUS AND ORGANIZATION. The status of the Greek physician was at first not much above that of the higher craftsman. He carried his skill from town to town, establishing in each a workshop or surgery (ἰατρεῖον). As nurses and assistants he had pupils bound by agreement, one form of which is the Hippocratic *Oath*. This was not a legal but a private contract; for there was no licenciation. Medical status was raised by the Alexandrian school, where for the first time there was systematic instruction. At Rome Medicine was originally the work of slaves or subordinates. In 46 B.C. Julius Caesar gave citizenship to all who practised there. Thus status rose further and way was made for such physicians as Galen, the friend of emperors.

**11.** The earliest scientific teacher in Rome, who founded the first regular school there, was Asclepiades (q.v. 3) of Bithynia (*c.* 40 B.C.). But schools, at first mere personal followings, combined at the beginning of the Christian era in the use of a meeting-place on the Esquiline. State-paid professors with public *auditoria* were available at Rome from the time of Vespasian (70–9). Subsidiary teaching centres were founded in other Italian towns and later in such transalpine centres as Marseille, Bordeaux, Arles, Nîmes, Lyon, and Saragossa.

**12.** State physicians existed in the time of Herodotus. We know little of their terms or duties. District physicians were early appointed in Italy and the custom spread to the provinces, beginning with the army and associated first with military *valetudinaria*. Inscriptions show that such men were held in respect. In the army itself, however, the medical staff had status equivalent only to that of higher non-commissioned officers.

**13.** From the military *valetudinarium* it was no great step to the construction of similar institutions for the numerous imperial officials and their families in the provinces. Motives of benevolence came in and public hospitals were founded in many localities. The idea passed to Christian times. The pious foundation of hospitals for the sick and outcast in the Middle Ages is to be traced back to the Roman *valetudinaria*. The first charitable institution of this kind concerning which we have clear information was established at Rome in the fourth century by a Christian lady of whom we learn from St. Jerome.

IV. **14.** CLINICAL THEORY. There are sufficient common features in the practice of antiquity to make possible a general sketch, despite differing individual doctrinal allegiances throughout, and changes in the different periods.

**15.** First of all, and without any theory, there comes to every physician the duty of observation. His first question must be 'How ill is this patient?' We see the ancient physician at this task of observation in his records of actual cases. The most remarkable of these are the forty-two in the Hippocratic Collection, evidently from a practitioner's day-to-day note-book (*Epidemics*). They are models of succinct record, and are without any attempt at diagnosis or prognosis. Among them the modern physician can discern clearly a case of diphtheria, and examples of the 'typhoid state', and of 'Cheyne-Stokes breathing'. All forty-two cases were gravely ill and the majority died.

**16.** An outstanding feature of ancient Medicine is stress on foreknowledge of the course of the sickness. 'It is most excellent for a physician to cultivate *pronoia*. Since he foreknows and foretells the past, present, and future . . . men would have confidence to entrust themselves to his care. . . . By an early forecast in each case he can tend aright those who have a chance to survive and by foreseeing who will die . . . he will escape blame' (*Prognostic*). *Pronoia* is not quite our prognosis, which, however, it includes. It means knowing things about a patient without being told them. A great *pronoia* is the description of the signs of death, known still as the *Hippocratic facies*:

'The physician should observe thus in acute diseases. First, the face of the patient, if it be like to those in health, and especially to itself, for this would be the best of all; but the more unlike to this, the worse; such would be these: sharp nose, hollow eyes, collapsed temples; ears cold, contracted, and with their lobes turned out; skin about the face rough, distended, and parched; colour greenish or dusky. If it be so at the beginning and if this cannot be explained by other symptoms, inquiry should be made whether he has been sleepless; whether he be purged; whether he is suffering from hunger. If any of these be admitted the danger may be reckoned so far the less and it may be judged in a day and a night if the appearance proceed from these. But if none of these exist and the symptoms do not subside in that time, be it known for certain that death is nigh' (*Prognostic*).

**17.** After his *pronoia* the physician must consider the nature of the condition he is to treat. Most ancient medical works pass lightly over theories of disease. Nevertheless treatment to be rational must have some theoretical basis. The usual doctrine was simple. Just as matter was made of the four elements, so the human body was made of their surrogates, the four cardinal fluids or humours, Blood, Phlegm, Yellow Bile, and Black Bile (melancholy). Health meant that the humours were blended harmoniously; sickness that they were in disharmony. A determinant of health was the *innate heat*, which was greatest in youth, when most fuel is needed, and declined with age. Its abdication is death. The supporter of the innate heat is the pneuma (or pneumata) which circulate(s) in the vessels. (*See* ANATOMY AND PHYSIOLOGY.)

18. Disease must be treated by rectifying any disharmony of the humours. Happily these have a natural tendency to equilibrium and, left to themselves, are likely to reach that state. This is the 'Hippocratic' doctrine of *Nature as the healer of diseases*, νούσων φύσις ἰητρός, the *Vis medicatrix naturae* of the later Latin writers and of the present day. It was ridiculed by the more active—and more dangerous—practitioners as a 'meditation on death'.

19. The actual process by which the humours come into harmony is *pepsis* (Latin *coctio*, later elaborated as a series of 'digestions'). The turning-point at which *pepsis* is complete is the *crisis*, a term which still bears some of its original medical meaning. The crisis was expected on certain days. The physician must bring his remedies to bear especially at the critical time.

V. 20. TREATMENT. Disturbance in the balance of the humours was, however, only the immediate cause of disease. There were more remote factors which the physician needed to study. Injudicious modes of life, exposure to climatic changes, and the like could be directly corrected. For such disturbances as could not be healed on these preventive lines various therapeutic measures were available.

21. After rest and quiet the central factor in treatment is dietetics, concerning which there are exceedingly elaborate details. An entire book is devoted to the preparation and uses of barley-water! The general principles of dietetics, especially related to fevers, are substantially those of the present day. The physician also had at his disposal a variety of physical remedies—baths, inunctions, clysters, etc. He employed cupping and bleeding too frequently.

22. Until later times the ancient physician was no great user of drugs except, we may note, in the treatment of diseases of women; from works on these the greater part of the 300 constituents of the pharmacopoeia of the Hippocratic Collection are derived. At first drugs were given by themselves—they were 'simples'. From Alexandrian times onward prescriptions were liable to become very elaborate. The prescription of a Theriac by Andromachus, physician to Nero and the first to bear the title *Archiater*, was one of the longest on record. About one-third of the herbs employed in a modern pharmacopoeia bear names known to the Greek physicians.

23. The general line of treatment—surgery excepted—was not very unlike that of an intelligent and rather conservative English country practitioner of about a century and a half ago. (For surgical resources of the ancients *see* SURGERY.) The ancient physician was, perhaps, a little less confident than his eighteenth-century successor, a little more cautious, a little more conscious of his helplessness.

24. Few medical works have had the influence of the great *Aphorisms*, a series of very brief generalizations by a highly experienced physician many of whose conclusions have been confirmed by later ages, some passing into medical commonplaces, others becoming popular proverbs. The work is included in the Hippocratic Collection but cannot be even approximately dated. The meaning of the first Aphorism is misrepresented by its usual truncated quotation. In depressing completeness it runs: 'Life is short and the Art long, the occasion urgent, experience deceptive, and decision difficult; yet not only must the physician be ready to do his duty but patient, attendants, and circumstances must co-operate if there is to be a cure.'

VI. 25. MATERIAL AND LITERARY SOURCES. Of material remains the most impressive are Asclepian sites excavated at Epidaurus, Cos, Pergamum, Athens, Rome, and elsewhere. There is a doctor's house and nursing-home at Pompeii. Numerous instruments have been found at Pompeii and at many other places. Vase-paintings have yielded much information, especially for hygiene, bathing customs, athletics, etc. Sanitation is superbly represented by the aqueducts, water-supply, and drainage-systems of Rome. There are remains of military hospitals in the Empire, of which the best known are those at Novaesium and Vetera (*Neuss* and *Xanten* on the Rhine frontier) in lower Germany and at Aquae Helveticae (*Baden* in Switzerland). In the latter numerous instruments were found. Many inscribed stone stamps used for impressing ointments, especially for diseases of the eyes, with name of maker and directions for use have been found in the western provinces.

26. The fund of Greek manuscripts is very large and is inadequately explored. Latin manuscripts containing versions and translations from Greek also yield information. The papyri are disappointing, but among them is a substantial fragment of the otherwise unknown historical work of Menon, pupil of Aristotle, giving views of some early doctors. There are also papyri illuminating the herbal tradition. Information is accumulating of works lost in the original but surviving in versions in Arabic, Hebrew, and Syriac manuscripts.

27. Light is cast on practice by innumerable allusions in literary texts. Here we consider only technical literature, which is so extensive that no one would claim to have studied the whole closely; there are modern critical editions of only about a half. Best explored is the Hippocratic Collection, but it is complete in no edition after Littré's (1839–61) and for many of its members we still depend on this. Of Galen's writings and pseudepigrapha only a small percentage is critically edited, and we still depend substantially upon an inferior edition completed in 1833.

28. For the earliest stratum of rational Medicine we have only the fragments of the pre-Socratic philosophers, notably those of Pythagoras, Alcmaeon, Heraclitus, Empedocles, Anaxagoras, and Democritus. For the fifth century there are several works in the Hippocratic Collection and fragments of several other medical writers. For the fourth century there is the bulk of the Hippocratic Collection, one work in which can be ascribed to Polybus, son-in-law of Hippocrates. There are also many relevant passages in the works of Plato, Aristotle, and Theophrastus. Specially interesting are fragments of the physician Diocles, contemporary with or a little older than Aristotle.

29. Of the earlier Alexandrian period there are fragments of Herophilus and Erasistratus, the poems on drugs by Nicander, and fragments of a number of herbalists and others. The later Alexandrians are more happily represented by Celsus *On medical matters* (in Latin from a Greek original), by finely illustrated texts of the herbal of Crateuas (*c.* 80 B.C.), of a commentary on the *Dislocations* of the Hippocratic Collection (*c.* A.D. 50), of Dioscorides *On materia medica* (*c.* A.D. 60), and of Soranus *On fractures and bandaging* and *On obstetrics* (*c.* 2nd c. A.D.). There are also fragments of the first Greek practitioner in Rome, the 'methodist' Asclepiades (q.v. 3) of Bithynia, and others.

30. Writers after Galen were numerous and mostly inferior. Important historically are the fourth- and fifth-century Latin translations of Dioscorides and of works both of the Hippocratic and of the Galenic corpus. Interesting for the soundness of its physiology is Nemesius, Bishop of Emesa, *On the nature of man* (*c.* 400). Solid derivative source-books are those of Oribasius (325–403), Aëtius (*c.* 550), Paul of Aegina (625–90), and Alexander of Tralles (525–605). The last still shows some spark of originality but much superstition.

**31.** Of Latin works that *On acute and chronic diseases* by Caelius Aurelianus, a Numidian of the fifth century, is interesting both linguistically and as the only complete 'methodist' work. Among the more bizarre survivals are the medical verses of Quintus Serenus Sammonicus which introduce that word of power *Abracadabra*; the popular, irrational but also non-superstitious herbal of 'Apuleius Platonicus Madaurensis' known in scores of early illustrated manuscripts; and the disgusting Sextus Placitus Papyriensis *On drugs from animals*. On the lowest level is Marcellus Empiricus of Bordeaux (*c.* A.D. 400), whose semi-insane assembly of folly and superstition is a happy hunting-ground for folklorists.

**VII. 32.** MODERN CRITICISM. Nineteenth-century scholarship produced an account of the origin and course of ancient Medicine that accorded substantially with the views of the ancient physicians from the third century onward as to the history of their art. The ancient tradition was modified but not fundamentally altered. Despite the difficulty in identifying the 'genuine' works of Hippocrates it was persistently held that from the older elements in the Hippocratic Collection a fairly coherent doctrinal system could be deduced, which was treated under the (sometimes admittedly conventional) name of 'Hippocrates'. The figure and part of the personal history of the 'Father of Medicine' were substantially retained.

**33.** Work of the last few decades calls for a fundamental change in this attitude. A middle way is impossible. The controversy turns primarily on the figure of Hippocrates (*c.* 400 B.C.) and upon the question of his share in the so-called 'Hippocratic Collection', which took its first form in the third century B.C. (*See* HIPPOCRATES.)

**34.** The 'Hippocratic' works, even of the older stratum in that collection, contain differences in outlook as great as those between Socrates and Anaxagoras. Parts of the 'Collection' are separated from each other by centuries in time and were written under widely different social and geographical conditions. To attribute all or many of their doctrines, or of the works that contain them, to a conventionalized 'Hippocrates' conserves nothing but confusion. Moreover, archaeological, textual, and historical investigation combine to render untenable the traditional account of the life of the 'Father of Medicine' even in a greatly modified form.

**35.** It has been assumed in this article that scientific Medicine did not take shape first with Hippocrates; that it was not originally connected with Cos or with the cult of Asclepius either at Cos or elsewhere; that we know almost nothing of Hippocrates except the approximate period of his life, and that he was regarded by his immediate successors as one—but only one—of several distinguished physicians of his age; that we have no evidence of the existence of any work by Hippocrates, and that we have some evidence that no work by him exists. These are negative conclusions; the positive are incorporated in §§ III, IV, and V. This critical attitude affects neither the value of the Greek picture of the ideal physician, nor the view that such qualities were to be found among the ancients, nor the inspiration and beauty of the 'Hippocratic' mode of life.

For the complete Hippocratic Collection and Galenic writings the reader must still rely on the editions of E. Littré (10 vols., 1831-62) and C. G. Kühn (20 vols., 1821-33). The collection of general information on Greek Medicine in F. Adams, *The Seven Books of Paul of Aegina* (3 vols., 1844-7), is still unexcelled. The best modern Hippocrates, by W. H. S. Jones and E. T. Withington (Loeb Library, 4 vols., 1922-31), is imperfect, as is H. Kühlwein and J. Ilberg, *Hippocratis Opera Omnia* (2 vols., 1894-1902). The *Corpus Medicorum Latinorum* contains several useful volumes. The progress of the *Corpus Medicorum Graecorum* is negligible. Works of other individual authors are given in the article under their names.

Charles Singer, *Greek Biology and Greek Medicine* (1922); Werner Jaeger, *Diokles von Karystos* (1938). Arturo Castiglioni, *A History of Medicine²* (1958); H. E. Sigerist, *A History of Medicine* vol. ii (1961);

M. R. Cohen and I. E. Drabkin, *A Source Book in Greek Science²* (1958); L. Edelstein, *Greek M. Sel. Papers* (1967).

L. Edelstein, 'Greek Medicine in Relation to Religion and Magic', *Bull. of the Inst. of Hist. of Med.* v (U.S.A. 1937), 201, and 'Hippocrates' in *PW*, Suppl. vi (1935), 1290 ff.; W. A. Heidel, *The Heroic Age of Science* (U.S.A., 1933); M. Neuburger, *History of Medicine* (2 vols., 1910-25); O. Weinreich, *Antike Heilungswunder* (1909); E. J. and L. Edelstein, *Asclepius* (2 vols., U.S.A., 1946). See also references and bibliography under HIPPOCRATES (2), etc.

T. Meyer, *Geschichte des römischen Aerztestandes* (1907).

Ch. Daremberg, *La Médecine, histoire et doctrine* (1863) and *Histoire des sciences médicales* (1870). T. Clifford Allbutt, *Greek M. in Rome* (1921); A. J. Brock, *Greek M.* (1929); J. Scarborough, *Roman M.* (1969).

Important communications between 1911 and 1919 are listed by F. E. Kind in Bursian, *Jahresb.* 1919, and after that in the bibliographies of *Isis* and the *Mitteilungen zur Gesch. der Med. und der Naturwissenschaften*. Miriam Drabkin, 'A Select Bibliography of Greek and Roman Medicine', *Bull. Hist. Med.* 1942, 399 ff.

The Greek MSS. are indexed in H. Diels, *Die Handschriften der antiken Aerzte* (2 vols., 1905-6).

§ VII. Max Pohlenz, *Hippokrates und die Begründung der wissenschaftlichen Medizin* (1938). L. Edelstein, ΠΕΡΙ ΑΕΡΩΝ *und die Sammlung der hippokratischen Schriften* (1931); O. Temkin, 'Geschichte des Hippokratismus' in *Kyklos* iv. 1, 19. C. S.; A. W.

**MEDIOLAN(I)UM,** modern *Milan*, founded *c.* 396 B.C. on or near the site of Etruscan Melpum (Pliny, *HN* 3. 125) by the Insubres (q.v.), came under Roman control temporarily in 222, permanently in 194 B.C. (Polyb. 2. 34; Livy 5. 34; 34. 46). It obtained Latin rights in 89, Roman citizenship in 49 B.C. Under the Empire, as *municipium* and later as *colonia*, it grew steadily. The principal north Italian road-centre, Mediolanum ultimately became the capital of the Western Empire. The frequent presence of the imperial court, especially in the fourth century, contributed to its prosperity; but, centrally situated in the fertile plain of Cisalpine Gaul (q.v.), it was independently important. After 300 Mediolanum was the seat of the governor of Liguria, the praetorian prefect, and the vicar of Italy. Attila (452), Odoacer (476), Theodoric (493), Uraia who sacked it (539), and Alboin (569) successively captured Mediolanum. Its famed bishop Ambrose (374-97) established its ecclesiastical independence. The Emperors Didius Julianus and Geta were born there.

Strabo 5. 213; Eutrop. 9. 27; Aur. Vict. *Caes.* 39; Procop. *Goth.* 2. 8. A. Colombo, *Lombardia Romana* (1939). E. T. S.

**MEDON** (Μέδων), name of several mythological persons, the only one of importance being the herald in the *Odyssey*, who warns Penelope of the suitors' plot against Telemachus (4. 677 ff.) and is spared by Odysseus (22. 357 ff.).

**MEFITIS,** Italian goddess of sulphurous vapours arising from the ground (Verg. *Aen.* 7. 84 and Servius there); hence her temple at Cremona was outside the walls (Tac. *Hist.* 3. 33), though in Rome her grove was on the Esquiline (Varro, *Ling.* 5. 49). There are indications that her cult extended throughout Italy, but especially in the central (the most volcanic) regions.

Wissowa, *RK* 246; Latte, *RR* 190.

**MEGACLES,** son of Alcmaeon, of the family of the Alcmaeonidae (q.v.) at Athens. He was the successful suitor of Agariste, daughter of Cleisthenes (q.v. 2), tyrant of Sicyon (perhaps in 575 B.C.). Later he appears as head of the faction known as the *Paraloi*, in opposition to the *Pedieis*, led by Lycurgus, and the *Hyperakrioi* or *Diakrioi*, newly formed by Pisistratus (q.v.). These factions were named after regions of Attica, the Paralia or south, the Pedion or plain of Athens, and the Diakria or north-east, but the extent of the connexion is not agreed. When Pisistratus made himself tyrant (*c.* 560), Megacles combined with Lycurgus to expel him, but presently, worsted in renewed strife with Lycurgus, helped him to a second tyranny, in return for a promise to marry his daughter Coesyra. The marriage, however, led to a further quarrel and Pisistratus again retired before a combination of the other two factions (*c.* 556). Nothing later is recorded of Megacles: if he survived till Pisistratus' third and final usurpation (*c.* 546), he was then banished with the rest of his family. He was father of Cleisthenes (q.v. 1) and Hippocrates, the father-in-law of Xanthippus (q.v. 1) and grandfather of Pericles.

R. J. Hopper, *BSA* 1961, 189 ff.                                    T. J. C.

**MEGALOPOLIS** (ἡ μεγάλη πόλις: the compound form is Latin) was founded by Epaminondas between 370 and 362 B.C. as the centre of the Arcadian Confederacy. Most of the Arcadians (excluding the NE. and E. Arcadian towns) and the Scirites of the Laconian borderland became its citizens; forty villages were completely or partially abandoned (Paus. 8. 27. 3–4). It lay in a plain, through which the headwaters of the Alpheus and Eurotas flow, and was therefore a centre of communications. It was one of the largest cities of Peloponnesus, and many of its buildings have been excavated, including the Thersilion, where the Arcadian federal assembly met, and a large theatre.

Megalopolis was often hard pressed by Sparta, and suffered from the lukewarmness or hostility of other Arcadian cities and the centrifugal tendencies of the mountaineers. It consistently took the Macedonian side in the fourth century. In 235 its tyrant Lydiadas (q.v.) abdicated and introduced Megalopolis into the Achaean Confederacy (Polyb. 2. 44. 5), in which it subsequently played a leading part under Philopoemen. The last great Megalopolitan was Polybius the historian. In Roman times Megalopolis became an ordinary provincial town (Strabo 388).

Paus. 8. 27. 30–2; Diod. 15. 72. P–K, *GL* III. i. 288 ff. *Excavations at Megalopolis*, 1890–1 (British School at Athens); E. Fiechter, *Das Theater in Megalopolis* (1931).                T. J. D.; R. J. H.

**MEGARA** was a town on the isthmus of Corinth, situated in a fertile but narrow plain between Mts. Geranea, Cithaeron, and Cerata, which separated it from Corinthia, Boeotia, and Attica respectively. Its communications with the Corinthian Gulf were difficult, but it had good harbours on the Saronic Gulf, and it was of some importance as a land of passage between Peloponnesus and central Greece. See Hammond, *BSA* 1954, 103 ff., 'The Main Road from Boeotia to the Peloponnese through the Northern Megarid'.

It was held in antiquity that Megara had once been part of the heritage of the rulers of Attica, until after the death of the Athenian king Codrus, when Megara was 'Dorized' to form one State from a number of villages. Between 730 and 550 B.C. Megara displayed considerable colonizing activity. On this problem, the relations of Megara and Corinth, and the process of Dorization, see Hammond, ibid. 92 ff., 'The Heraeum at Perachora and Corinthian Encroachment'. Its chief daughter-cities were Megara Hyblaea in Sicily, Chalcedon and Byzantium on the Bosporus, and Heraclea Pontica in Bithynia. To this period we may also assign the rise of its extensive woollen industry. But *c.* 600 B.C. it came under the rule of a tyrant (*see* THEAGENES 1). The large fountain-house associated with his name has recently been excavated, *BCH* 1958, 688 ff. Megara subsequently fell a prey to domestic strife. Consequently it lost its western region, the Peraea Chora, to Corinth, and Salamis to Athens. Shortly before 500 it joined the Peloponnesian League, and it played its full part in the Persian Wars. After 460 it became a bone of contention between Athens and Corinth, and an attempt by Pericles to starve it into surrender by the 'Megarian Decree', which laid an embargo upon its Aegean and Pontic trade (432), was an important contributory cause of the Peloponnesian War.

In the fourth century it generally contrived, despite its position, to remain detached from the inter-city warfare of the period, and it recovered its early prosperity. It allied itself with Athens against Philip, but in the Hellenistic period it relapsed into obscurity. Megara was the temporary seat of the Socratic school of philosophers and is commonly believed to have been the home of the poet Theognis (q.v. 1). For the Megarian school of sculptors in the fourth century, see C. Picard, *Manuel d'archeologie grecque* iii (1948).

P–K, *GL* I. iii. 940 ff. E. L. Highbarger, *The History and Civilisation of Ancient Megara* (U.S.A. 1927).

M. C.; R. J. H.

**MEGARA HYBLAEA,** on the east coast of Sicily some 14 miles north of Syracuse, was founded by Megarian colonists who had previously failed to establish themselves at Trotilon and Thapsos nearby. The traditional foundation-date, 728 B.C., has been called in question by the discovery of pottery remains supposedly earlier than the earliest Syracusan material, and the alternative 750 B.C. has been proposed.

The city's proximity to Syracuse conditioned its history. After flourishing for some 250 years, during which time it colonized Selinus (q.v.), it was destroyed by Gelon (q.v.) in 483 B.C. (Thuc. 6. 4. 1–2). The firm date is a valuable *terminus ante quem* for the archaeology of Greek Sicily. Restored under Timoleon, to whose generation remains of a small Doric temple (? of Aphrodite) may be attributed, Megara prospered in the third century but was again destroyed in 214 B.C. by Marcellus (q.v. 1: Livy 24. 35). Some occupation continued, however, at least to the end of the republican period.

Bérard, *Bibl. topogr.* 65 ff., for earlier literature; J. Bayet, *Études d'archéologie classique* i (1955–6), 23 ff.; G. Vallet and F. Villard, *Mégara Hyblaea* ii (1964), iv (1966). Excavation reports: Villard and Vallet, *Mélanges d'arch.* 1951–64, *BCH* 1952, 289 ff.; see also Κώκαλος 1958, 100 ff.                A. G. W.

**MEGARIAN SCHOOL, THE,** founded at an uncertain date by Eucleides (q.v. 1) of Megara, the companion of Socrates and a somewhat older contemporary of Plato's. It is not known what form the school took, but it seems probable that it was not a corporate body and it does not appear to have survived as a school for long after the immediate successors of Eucleides. It adopted the doctrines of Parmenides and the Eleatics. Its members seem to have used this doctrine primarily as a basis for criticism of other schools. They developed a reputation for their skill in dialectical argument and were known for the invention of some ingenious sophisms. There are some indications also of contributions to ethical theory, but the exact nature of these is uncertain.

*See* LOGIC. G. C. Field, *Plato and his Contemporaries* (1930), ch. 12; W. and M. Kneale, *The Development of Logic* (1962).      G. C. F.

**MEGASTHENES** (*c.* 350–290 B.C.), an Ionian who served on several embassies, 302–291, sent by Seleucus I to the court of the Indian king, Chandragupta (known to the Greeks as Sandrocottus), founder of the Maurya Empire in north India. Following a treaty between the two kingdoms in 302 Megasthenes paid several visits to Chandragupta's capital, Pataliputra, and acquired a knowledge of the districts between the Indus and the Ganges. This first-hand experience of Indian culture and topography was embodied in a history (Ἰνδικά) in four books; book 1 dealt with the geography, including peoples and cities, books 2 and 3 the system of government, the functional classification of the citizens and religious customs, and book 4 the archaeology, history, and legends. Megasthenes' work appeared at a time when Western interest in India had been stimulated by the campaigns of Alexander and his successors. Despite a credulous acceptance of fables and inaccuracy of observation it provided the fullest account of India so far known to the Greeks, and together with the lesser works of the historians of Alexander's expedition was the source for many centuries of the Western world's knowledge of that country. It was extensively used by Strabo and was the chief source of Arrian's 'Ινδικά; and its contents were handed down to later geographers and historians.

FGrH iii C. 715; *Cambridge History of India*, vol. i (1922), esp. ch. 16. G. L. B.

**MEIDIAS,** potter, in Athens, late fifth century B.C. The 'Meidias painter' who painted for him has a sweet, rich style, often used white for flesh, and added gold for ornaments.

J. D. Beazley, *Attische Vasenmaler* (1925), 459; W. Hahland, *Die Vasen um Midias* (1930).

**MELA** (1), POMPONIUS (*PW* 104), of Tingentera (near Gibraltar), wrote under Gaius (A.D. 37–41) or early in Claudius' reign, a geographical survey in Latin of the inhabited world (*De Chorographia*) in three books. He describes (book 1) the earth's division into north and south hemispheres, and five zones (two habitable, the southern being an island of *Antichthones*); then the relative positions and boundaries of the three continents, surrounded by Ocean, which indented it by four seas, the Caspian (erroneously regarded as connected with the Northern Ocean), Persian Gulf, Red Sea, Mediterranean; then countries, Gibraltar Straits–Egypt, Palestine–Euxine; (book 2) Scythia, Thrace, Macedonia, Greece, Italy; south Gaul, Spain; then all the Mediterranean islands; then (book 3) the outer coasts of Spain, Gaul, Germany, unknown north Europe, and east Asia; British Isles, Thule, India, Persian Gulf, Red Sea; Ethiopians; west Africa. Inner Europe is neglected, so is inner though known Asia. Africa is all north of the equator. The work was a popular summary, with lists of names, but no mathematical details or distances, though there are some details of physical nature, climate, and customs of lands. Mela's idea of the known world is roughly that of Strabo.

TEXT. C. Frick (1880). Cf. E. Bunbury, *Hist. Anc. Geog.* (1879), ii. 352 ff.; Thomson, *Hist. Anc. Geog.* 225 f. E. H. W.

**MELA** (2), LUCIUS (?) ANNAEUS, youngest son of Seneca the rhetorician, and father of Lucan, was *eques* and financier. Claiming Lucan's property after his death in the Pisonian conspiracy of A.D. 65, he was himself implicated and committed suicide (Tac. *Ann.* 16. 17).

E. P. B.

**MELAMPUS** (Μελάμπους) (1), prophet, using the voices of birds and reptiles for divination, missionary of Dionysus (post-Homeric tradition), and ancestor of the prophetic clan of the Melampodidae. Three principal stories are told of him. (*a*) Serpents licked his ears, and he became able to understand the speech of all creatures (schol. *Od.* 11. 290; Eustath. 1685, 25). (*b*) His brother Bias wished to marry Pero, whose father Neleus demanded as bride-price the cattle of Iphiclus son of Phylacus, which had been taken by him from Neleus' mother Tyro. Melampus undertook to get them, was caught and imprisoned, but so impressed his gaoler by foreseeing the fall of a roof, which he had heard of from the wood-worms, that Iphiclus, hearing of it, promised him the cattle if Melampus could discover why he was childless. By questioning a vulture, Melampus discovered that Iphiclus' father had unwittingly worked a charm of impotence against him. All was thus settled satisfactorily (*Od.* 11. 287 ff. and scholia). (*c*) He cured the daughters of Proetus (q.v.) of their madness.

See further Wolff in Roscher's *Lexikon*, s.v., Pley in *PW*, s.v., and art. DIVINATION. H. J. R.

**MELAMPUS** (2), (3rd c. B.C.), author of two extant works on divination, Περὶ παλμῶν μαντικῆς (ed. H. Diels, *Abh. Berl. Akad.* 1907) and Περὶ ἐλαιῶν τοῦ σώματος (ed. J. G. F. Franz, *Scriptores Physiognomoniae Veteres*, 1780).

**MELANIPPIDES,** dithyrambic poet, of Melos. The *Suda* distinguishes two poets of the name, but there was probably only one, who was active from *c.* 480 B.C. to his death at the court of Perdiccas of Macedon (*Suda* s.v. Μελανιππίδης). His fame is attested by Xenophon (*Mem.* 1. 4. 3). He altered the structure of the Dithyramb by introducing ἀναβολαί, or lyric solos, instead of the antistrophe (Arist. *Rh.* 3. 9) and is mentioned by Pherecrates (fr. 145) as the first corrupter of the art of music (*see* MUSIC, § 10). His scanty remains are of a *Danaides*, a *Marsyas*, in which Athena flings away her flute in disgust because of its effect on her cheeks (fr. 3), and a *Persephone*. Meleager included some poems of his in his *Garland* (*Anth. Pal.* 4. 1. 7) and calls them Hymns.

TEXT. Page, *Poet. Mel. Gr.* 392–5.
CRITICISM. Pickard-Cambridge–Webster, *Dithyramb²*, 39 ff.
C. M. B.

**MELANIPPUS,** in mythology, one of the Theban champions opposed to the Seven (cf. ADRASTUS; Aesch. *Sept.* 414 and often). He was one of the Sparti (cf. CADMUS) by descent (ibid.): in Aeschylus he defends the Gate of Proetus against Tydeus (q.v.). His father was Astacus. He succeeded in wounding Tydeus mortally, but the latter with a final effort killed him and, in dying, asked for the head of his opponent. This was brought him by Amphiaraus, who hated him, or Capaneus, and he gnawed it. Thereupon Athena, who had intended to make him immortal for his valour, turned away in horror and Tydeus died. The scene, with Athena leading the personified Athanasia by the hand, is found on two mid-fifth-century Attic vases (see J. D. Beazley, *JHS* 1947, 1 ff.).

See Apollod. 3. 75–6; Stat. *Theb.* 8. 716 ff. For Melanippus' cult see Farnell, *Hero-Cults*, 335. H. J. R.

**MELANTHIUS** (1) (5th c. B.C.), a minor tragic poet of Athens, who wrote an elegiac poem in honour of Cimon (Plut. *Cim.* 4). The comic poets attack his gluttony, effeminacy, and other defects (Ath. 8. 343 c). One of his plays was a *Medea*.

TGF 760. A. W. P.-C.

**MELANTHIUS** (2) (4th c. B.C.), painter. Pupil of Pamphilus (q.v. 1), whom he probably succeedeed as head of the Sicyonian school. The picture of Aristratus in his victorious chariot was painted by 'all those about Melanthius' including Apelles; no other work by him is mentioned. Apelles admitted his superiority in composition. He wrote on painting, and said that works of art, like characters, should show a certain stubbornness and harshness (in contrast to Apelles' boasted 'charm').

T. B. L. W.

**MELANTHIUS** (3) (*c.* 350–270 B.C.) is known from a quotation in the lexicon of Harpocration to have published an Atthis in two or more books towards the end of the third century. He also wrote, perhaps as an exegetes, a special work on the Eleusinian mysteries.

FGrH iii B. 326. G. L. B.

**MELEAGER** (Μελέαγρος) (1), in mythology, son of Oeneus (q.v.), or of Ares (Hyg. *Fab.* 14. 16; 171. 1), and the former's wife Althaea. His story is told in two different forms, the Homeric and the non-Homeric; the former is typical epic, the latter typical folk-tale with the motif of a life-token (Stith Thompson, E 765. 1. 2). In the former he is a valiant warrior, whose aid is desperately needed when the Curetes (q.v.) attack Calydon. Being angry with his mother, who had cursed him 'for the slaying of her brother' (*Iliad* 9. 567; see the whole passage), he refused to defend the city, till at last he yielded to the entreaties of his wife Cleopatra, daughter of Idas (q.v.) and Marpessa. Homer also says (ibid. 533 ff.) that Oeneus forgot to sacrifice to Artemis, and she therefore sent a great wild boar to ravage the country; Meleager then gathered huntsmen and hounds from many cities and killed the boar. Elsewhere (*Il.* 2. 642) it is mentioned in passing that he was dead by the time of the Trojan War, but nothing is said of the manner of his death. In the *Ehoiai* (fr. 135, 12 Rzach) Meleager is killed by Apollo in battle with the Curetes; the text is very fragmentary, but cf. Paus. 10. 31. 3. This, then, continues the Homeric or normal heroic tradition. The other story cannot be traced further back than Phrynichus (q.v. 1) the tragedian (fr. 6 Nauck, from Paus. ibid. 4). As told by later writers (e.g. Apollod. 1. 65 ff.; ultimately from Euripides' *Meleager*?) it runs thus. When the boar-hunt began, Atalanta (q.v.) was the first to wound the beast. Meleager, who loved her, adjudged her the spoils when he himself killed the boar. His mother's brothers tried to take them from her and Meleager killed them. Althaea then had recourse to her power over his life. Shortly after his birth, the Moirai had come to the room and said that he should live until a brand then on the fire burned away; this is a theme which might be found in a modern Greek story, the belief in these spirits of birth being still prevalent. Althaea quenched the brand and put it in a chest; now, hearing of the death of her brothers, she took it out and burned it, and Meleager died.

Bacchylides (5. 93 ff.) combines the two versions; the Curetes and Aetolians fought over the boar's spoils (as in Homer, op. cit. 547 ff.); in the mêlée Meleager accidentally killed his uncles, but Althaea did not reflect that it was an accident, and so brought about his death by means of the brand.

Since the name of the guinea-fowl, μελεαγρίς, suggests that of Meleager, a story grew up (see Thompson, *Gloss. Gk. Birds*[2] (1936), 199) that his sisters turned into them.

The hunt of the Calydonian boar, with Meleager in the lead, is a favourite subject of archaic and classical art. It appears in the east pediment of Scopas' Temple of Athena Alea at Tegea; and a statuary type of Meleager as a young huntsman has been associated with Scopas (Brommer, *Vasenlisten*[2], 235 ff.). H. J. R.; C. M. R.

**MELEAGER** (2) (fl. 100 B.C.), poet and philosopher, came from Gadara in Syria, lived in Tyre, and retired to Cos in old age. His poems on himself (*Anth. Pal.* 7. 417–19) show that he was trilingual, speaking Greek, Syrian, and Phoenician. His Menippean satires, Cynic discourses in prose mingled with verse, are lost. He was also a master of the epigram. He compiled the first large critical selection of poetic epigrams, calling it his *Garland* and likening each poet to a flower (*Anth. Pal.* 4. 1). The Greek Anthology (q.v.) contains about a hundred of his poems, nearly all about love. Many are adaptations of the work of earlier epigrammatists (especially Asclepiades, q.v.). They infuse erotic feeling into the traditional forms of epitaph and dedication, combining remarkable technical adroitness with apparently genuine emotion. Meleager's language is sometimes flamboyant in the manner of 'Asian' rhetoric, but his metre is controlled by fastidiously precise rules.

*See* ANTHOLOGY; CYNICS; *and* EPIGRAM.

Gow and Page, 3926 ff.; D. L. Page in *Miscellanea . . . Rostagni* (1963); K. Radinger, *M. von Gadara* (1895); L. A. Stella, *Cinque poeti dell'Antologia Palatina* (1949); W. and M. Wallace, *TAPA* 1939; T. B. L. Webster, *Hellenistic Poetry and Art* (1964), ch. 9;

A. Wifstrand, *Studien zur griech. Anthologie* (1926). J. Hubaux, *Mus. Belge* 1921, shows Virgil adapting his poems in *Ecl.* 8. G. H.

**MELETUS** (1) (5th c. B.C.), an Athenian tragic poet, attacked by contemporary comic poets for his dullness (*Suda*, s.v., schol. Ar. *Ran.* 1302, etc.), his immorality, and his starveling appearance, composed a tetralogy on the Story of Oedipus (schol. Pl. *Ap.* 18 b, quoting the Διδασκαλίαι of Aristotle); probably the father of the accuser of Socrates in 399 B.C. A. W. P.-C.

**MELETUS** (2), probably son of (1) above; the titular accuser of Socrates in 399. But he was then quite young, and was probably the tool of Anytus, who was Socrates' real opponent. The story that he was later put to death by the Athenians is doubtful. He is apparently not identical with the Meletus who in 399 accused Andocides of impiety. W. D. R.

**MELINNO,** authoress of a poem in five sapphic stanzas on the world-power of Rome, quoted by Stobaeus (3. 7), who calls her a Lesbian. Her dialect is Doric, and it is more likely that she came from some town of Magna Graecia which had been conquered by the Romans. Her date is much disputed. Some think that the similarity of her sentiments to those of Horace and the cult of 'Roma aeterna' point to the imperial age, while others claim that the absence of any mention of a *princeps* points to republican Rome, even so early as the Punic Wars. The first half of the second century B.C. seems the most likely date. There is no need to assume that she was influenced by Latin poetry.

TEXT. Diehl, *Anth. Lyr. Graec.* ii. 315–16.
CRITICISM. F. G. Welcker, *Kl. Schr.* (1845) ii. 160 ff.; C. M. Bowra, *JRS* 1957, 21 ff. C. M. B.

**MELISSA** (Μέλισσα, Bee). Like its Hebrew equivalent Deborah, this is occasionally found as a proper name, also as a title, especially of priestesses of Demeter (according to schol. Pind. *Pyth.* 4. 104); of Artemis (Aesch. fr. 87 Nauck); of Rhea (Didymus quoted below), besides the Asianic cult of the Ephesian Artemis, whose regular symbol is a bee; that, however, her priestesses were called *melissai* is not quite certain, see Ch. Picard, *Éphèse et Claros* (1923), 183 f. One or two minor heroines of mythology are so named, the least unknown being the sister of Amalthea (q.v.); both were daughters of Melisseus king of Crete, who was the first to sacrifice to the gods. While her sister fed the infant Zeus with milk, she provided honey for him, and was afterwards made the first priestess of the Great Mother, meaning presumably Rhea (Didymus in Lactant. *Divin. Inst.* 1. 22, from his commentary on Pindar, the source probably of the above scholion). Columella (*De Re Rust.* 9. 2. 3) mentions a 'very beautiful woman Melissa whom Iuppiter turned into a bee', generally taken to refer to the same story. *See* HONEY.

H. J. R.

**MELISSUS** (1) of Samos commanded the Samian fleet which defeated the Athenians in 441 B.C. He was the last important member of the Eleatic school of philosophy (q.v.), agreeing with Parmenides in making reality changeless and single but differing from him in describing it as boundless and allowing it a past and a future. He held that it was 'full', without any void, but denied it the solidity of a physical body. Fragments of his book show him defending Eleaticism against philosophical theories of change, those of Anaximenes and Diogenes of Apollonia (rarefaction and condensation), Empedocles (rearrangement in a plenum), and probably the atomists (motion in a vacuum).

Testimonia and fragments in Diels, *Vorsokr.*[11] i. 258–76. G. E. L. O

**MELISSUS** (2), GAIUS, Maecenas' freedman, invented a form of light drama in the *fabula trabeata*, whose characters were equestrian. He compiled a book of jests (*ineptiae*, Suet. *Gram.* 21) and was possibly the Melissus quoted several times by Pliny on natural history.

**MELISSUS** (3), AELIUS, contemporary with Gellius, who cites his *De loquendi proprietate* (18. 6. 1).

**MELITA,** modern *Malta*, a strategically situated island between Sicily and Africa with important megalithic monuments and excellent harbours. Phoenicians had colonized Melita by the seventh century, and it was in Carthage's hands by the fifth, but lost in 218, when Melita became a Roman ally administered by the governor of Sicily. Subsequently, although Phoenician was still spoken, Melita acquired Roman citizenship. Despite its barren and waterless condition Melita has always enjoyed industrial and commercial prosperity.

Pliny, *HN* 3. 92; Diod. 5. 12; Livy 21. 51; Cic. *Verr. passim.* A. Mayr, *Die Insel Malta im Altertum* (1909); T. Zammit, *Malta* (Malta, 1926); L. Viviani, *Storia di Malta* (2 vols., 1933–4); J. D. Evans, *Malta* (1959).
E. T. S.; J. B.

**MELITENE,** a city in Cappadocia near the Euphrates (modern *Eski Malatya*). The ancient Hittite metropolis, Milid, gave its name to the district Melitene and this in turn appears as the name of the city when it became an important garrison town and road junction, part of the eastern frontier defences of the Roman Empire. For Strabo (12. 537) the district of Melitene contained no *polis*. Melitene controlled the important crossing of the Euphrates to Tomisa in Sophene, a district east of the river assigned by Pompey to the client king of Cappadocia and still ruled by a client of Rome in A.D. 54 (Tac. *Ann.* 13. 7). In *c.* A.D. 70 the Legio XII Fulminata was installed and soon the town was given city status by Trajan. After Diocletian's reorganization it became part of Armenia. Later Justinian renewed its walls (Procop. *Aed.* 3. 4).
E. W. G.

**MELITO,** bishop of Sardis (d. *c.* A.D. 190), addressed a defence of Christianity to Marcus Aurelius (only fragments extant) in which he sees as providential the coincidence of Christ's birth with Augustus' establishment of the *pax Romana*. A sermon on the Pascha (preserved in three Greek papyri, a Coptic papyrus, some Syriac fragments, a Georgian version, and a Latin epitome) is written in a rich rhetorical style, with many parallels to the florid manner of Maximus (q.v. 2) Tyrius, making much use of the isocolon with anaphora and homoioteleuton.

B. Altaner, *Patrology* (1960), 133 ff.; M. Testuz, *Papyrus Bodmer XIII* (1960); O. Perler, *M. sur la Pâque* (1966).
H. C.

**MELOS,** with Thera, the most southerly of the Sporades. The island was celebrated in neolithic times for its monopoly of obsidian, which was exported all over the Aegean area. There was a rich deposit at Phylakopi, where successive sites were occupied from the Early Minoan period; the examination of these sites has thrown most light on the early history of the Cyclades. It had very close connexions with Minoan Crete from the seventeenth century, and with the later Mycenaean world. In the Dorian migration it was colonized from Laconia. In the later seventh century it was an important artistic centre for vases, jewellery, and gems. In 480 the inhabitants sent a contingent of ships to Salamis. They were not, however, members of the Delian League, and remained neutral at the outbreak of the Peloponnesian War. Nicias attacked them in 426, and ten years later they were brutally enslaved by the Athenians, who established a cleruchy on the island.

P–K, *GL* iv. cvii (d); *IG* xii. 3; C. Smith, etc., *Excavations at Phylakopi in Melos* (1904), *BSA* 1897–8; cf. ibid. 1910–11, 1 ff.; J. Boardman, *Island Gems* (1963).
W. A. L.

**MEMMIUS** (1, *PW* 5), GAIUS, attracted the censure of Scipio (q.v. 11) at Numantia. As tribune (111 B.C.) he attacked the nobles who had had dealings with Jugurtha (q.v.), but was prevented by the veto of his colleague Baebius from interrogating Jugurtha. He was a vigorous prosecutor before the commission of Mamilius (q.v. 3). Praetor *c.* 104, he was later accused *repetundarum*, but acquitted, despite the testimony of his enemy Scaurus (q.v. 1). Competing with Glaucia for the consulship of 99, he was killed in a riot.
E. B.

**MEMMIUS** (2, *PW* 8), GAIUS, married Sulla's daughter Fausta. In 66 B.C., apparently as tribune, he attacked the Luculli and succeeded in delaying L. Lucullus' triumph. As praetor in 58 he was hostile to Caesar. In 57 he went as governor to Bithynia. In 55 he divorced Fausta, now married Milo (q.v.), and in 54 stood for consul with Caesar's support; but his chances were ruined by an electoral scandal which he himself revealed (*see* CLAUDIUS 12); eventually condemned *de ambitu*, he went into exile in Athens (52). In 50 he had hopes of restoration: we do not know if they were realized. He died before 46. His son Gaius was perhaps the *consul suffectus* of 34. Memmius was something of an orator and poet, and a literary patron; Catullus and Helvius Cinna (q.v. 3) accompanied him to Bithynia, and Lucretius dedicated his *De Rerum Natura* to him; hence he has attracted more attention than his life and character may be thought to deserve.

Schanz–Hosius i. 276, 310 f.; A. Biedl, *Wien. Stud.* 1930. 98 ff., 1931, 107 ff.; G. della Valle, *Rend. Linc.* 1939, 737 ff.; *ORF²* 401 ff.; B. Farrington, *Anales de filologia clasica* 1959, 13 ff., *Lucretius* (ed. D. R. Dudley, 1965) 19 ff.
T. J. C.

**MEMNON** (1), a mythical king of Ethiopia, was the son of Eos and Tithonus. He went to Troy to the aid of his uncle Priam, killed Antilochus, and was himself slain by Achilles, after which Zeus rendered him immortal. The legend of Memnon was probably first set forth in the *Aethiopis*, one of the lost poems of the Trojan cycle. The myth is mentioned in the *Odyssey* and by Hesiod, Alcman, and Pindar. Several of the dramatists treated the legend in plays now lost, and other writers refer to it frequently. Aeschylus associates Memnon with Susa, as does Herodotus, while Diodorus (using Ctesias) relates that Memnon was sent by Teutamus king of Assyria with a force of Ethiopians and Susans to the aid of Priam. Strabo and Pausanias likewise, following Herodotus, regard Susa as the city of Memnon. On his march to Troy Memnon was said to have left several great *stelai* along his route, and Herodotus notes that this has caused him to be confused with Sesostris. In spite of reference to Susa and the 'Ethiopians of Asia', there are unmistakable traces of Memnon's being localized in Egypt and Ethiopia. There was a Memnoneion in Thebes which gave its name to a part of the city, and another at Abydos, the latter really a temple built for Osiris by Seti I. During the Ptolemaic period incubation was practised in the Memnoneion at Abydos and *katochoi* attached to the worship of Isis and Sarapis resided there. In Roman times a peculiar cult and oracle of Bes had its location there. The colossi of Memnon whose stones, before the restoration of the statues, were said to sing at dawn, once stood before the temple of a king and are inscribed with the name of Amenhotep III. There have been many attempts to interpret the legend of Memnon. Several modern authorities believe him to have been a Hittite leader.

His final combat and his body carried away by his

mother are favourite themes in archaic and classical vase-painting. He is given regular heroic features, but often has negro squires in attendance, as he had also in Polygnotus' Underworld.

R. Holland, art. 'Memnon' in Roscher's *Lexikon*; P. Perdrizet, G. Lefebvre, *Les Graffites grecs du Memnonion d'Abydos* (1919); A. Widemann, *Herodots Zweites Buch* (1890). Inscriptions of colossi: A. and E. Bernand, *Les Inscriptions grecques et latines du Colosse de Memnon* (1960). Vase-paintings, Brommer, *Vasenlisten²*, 259 ff., 290.
T. A. B.; C. M. R.

**MEMNON** (2), a Rhodian of the fourth century B.C., began his career as a mercenary leader with his elder brother Mentor (q.v. 2). After the failure of Artabazus' revolt (353 B.C.) Memnon stayed with Mentor, and after his death he married his widow Barsine (later Alexander's mistress) and succeeded him as Persian general in Asia Minor. In 336 he fought successfully against Philip's generals. In 334 his ingenious plan to retire before Alexander, to waste the country, and to fight on sea, was rejected by the satraps. He took part in the battle of Granicus and escaped. Appointed commander-in-chief by Darius, he organized the maritime war and occupied several Greek islands, hoping to make the Greeks revolt (333). He died suddenly, a severe loss for Persia.

Arr. *Anab.* bks. 1 and 2; Diod. bks. 16 and 17. H. W. Parke, *Greek Mercenary Soldiers* (1933); Berve, *Alexanderreich* ii, no. 497.
V. E.

**MEMNON** (3) of Heraclea Pontica, after Caesar and probably before Hadrian, wrote the history of his city in at least sixteen books, perhaps following Nymphis; books 9–16 are substantially preserved by Photius. Book 13 had a long digression on the rise of Rome, and in general the wider issues in which the city was involved were treated. The remains allow study of the methods and style of Hellenistic local chronicle.

*FGrH* iii B, 336; b, 171.
A. H. McD

**MEMOR,** ? SCAEVA (? *Scaev(i)us*), a writer of tragedies (lost), contemporary with Martial, who composed an elegiac distich on his statue. His brother Turnus was a well-known satirist (Mart. 11. 9 and 10).

**MEMPHIS,** the traditional centre of Lower Egypt, was naturally the scene of Alexander's installation; it continued populous till the Roman conquest, being ranked by Strabo second to Alexandria. The fortification of Babylon, across the river, as a legionary camp under Augustus probably started its decline, and it sank to a provincial metropolis. Its importance under the Ptolemies was due largely to the cult of the Serapeum, which the religious policy of Augustus would not favour. There are few remains of Graeco-Roman buildings; the walls of the camp of Babylon stand amongst the houses of Old Cairo.

J. Ph. Lauer and Ch. Picard, *Les Statues ptolémaïques du Sarapieion de Memphis* (1955); U. Wilcken, 'Das Serapeum von Memphis', *Urkunden der Ptolemäerzeit* i. 7; A. J. Butler, *Babylon of Egypt* (1894).
J. G. M.

**MEN** (Μήν), a Phrygian god, worshipped throughout Anatolia (cf. Strabo 557, 577, 580). He frequently bears a crescent moon behind his shoulders, or the crescent alone may represent him. The native form of his name was Man(n)es, and his lunar associations, if not original, may be due to a confusion with the Greek μήν. In some respects he seems merely the counterpart of Attis. Both celestial (Οὐράνιος) and chthonic (Καταχθόνιος), he was invoked also as Lord (Τύραννος) and by numerous titles, such as M. Ἀσκηνός, M. Κάρου, M. Φαρνάκου, M. Τιάμου (perhaps = Καταχθόνιος), found chiefly in restricted localities. He was a healing god, a protector of tombs, and a giver of oracles. Metics or slaves worshipped Men in Attica from the fourth or third century

B.C., but elsewhere in Greece only isolated inscriptions of Rhodes, Delos, and Thasos attest his cult. At Rome and Ostia a series of inscriptions to Attis Menotyrannus have been found.

In addition to the general articles (s.v.) in Roscher, *Lex.* and *PW*, see the accounts of the shrine at Pisidian Antioch in *JHS* 1912 and *JRS* 1913 and 1918.
F. R. W.

**MENAECHMUS** (fl. *c.* 350 B.C.), pupil of Eudoxus and friend of Plato, discovered the three conic sections and with the help of two of them solved the problem of doubling the cube. None of his works is extant.

**MENANDER** (Μένανδρος) (1), 342/1–293/89 B.C., by later consensus the leading writer of New Comedy (q.v.), although less successful than Philemon (q.v. 2) with his own contemporaries. An Athenian of good family, he was for a time a pupil of the philosopher Theophrastus, and had some association with Demetrius (q.v. 2) of Phalerum, the prop of the anti-democratic regime of 317–307 B.C. Making his début in 321 B.C. with *Orge*, he wrote over 100 plays, many of which must have been intended for country festivals or perhaps foreign performance. Nearly 100 titles are known, but some may be alternatives; when a play was revived, as frequently happened with Menander's after his death, it was sometimes renamed.

Menander's plays were lost in the 'Dark Age' of the seventh and eighth centuries A.D.; but in modern times numerous finds of papyri, attesting his popularity in antiquity, have so far brought to light one complete play, *Dyskolos* (*The Curmudgeon*), victorious in 317 B.C., and large enough parts of six others to allow of some literary judgement: these are *Epitrepontes* (*The Arbitrants*, named after a brilliantly written scene, and apparently a work of his maturity), *Perikeiromene* (*Cropped*, of which nearly half survives and the plot is clear), *Samia* (mostly preserved) and *Aspis* (the first half), *Sikyonios* (470 lines, of which 160 are more or less complete), and *Misoumenos* (tantalizing remains of a popular and dramatic play). There are smaller but still important fragments of *Dis Exapaton*, *Georgos*, *Heros*, *Theophoroumene*, *Kitharistes*, *Kolax*, *Phasma*, and two unidentified plays, *Fabula Incerta* and *Comoedia Florentina*, now known to be *Aspis*, and mentioned above. Scraps of *Karchedonios*, *Koneiazomenae*, *Perinthia*, and a play first but falsely identified as *Misogynes* are less instructive. Some interesting fragments of unknown authorship may be by Menander, notably *P. Ghôran* II, *P Antinoop.* 15, and the Didot papyrus (but see W. Bühler, *Hermes*, 1963, 345).

Ancient authors preserve over 900 quotations, ranging from a single word to sixteen lines, mainly for grammatical interest or sententious value. These give a false impression, as Menander used gnomes dramatically, and often with irony, more than for their own sake. Still less is to be learned from the collections of one-line gnomes (Μονόστιχοι) ascribed to Menander; of a total of over 800 lines thus known only a few originated with him (W. Görler, Μενάνδρου Γνῶμαι (Berlin 1963)).

Before the papyrus finds had revealed Menander's style there was little basis for guessing how far his work had been modified by his Latin adaptors Plautus and Terence: *Aulularia* from an unidentified play, *Bacchides* from Δὶς Ἐξαπατῶν, *Cistellaria* from Συναριστῶσαι, *Stichus* from Ἀδελφοί α', *Adelphoe* from Ἀδελφοί β', *Andria* from Ἀνδρία and Περινθία, *Eunuchus* from Εὐνοῦχος and Κόλαξ, and *Heauton-Timorumenos* can now be used with caution to supplement the picture of Menander's technique and achievement.

The plays are always set in contemporary Greece, usually in Athens or Attica, and although the characters are not unaware of a wider world, the plots treat their private domestic problems. These often have features traditional on the stage but unusual in real life: foundling children, kidnapped daughters, and scheming slaves cannot have been the experience of many Greek households. Menander was praised for 'representing life'; this means that his characters are lifelike, not that he was an unselective reporter. His plays always contain a love-interest: the range of situation is wide, extending from a young man's passion for a *hetaira* to crises of married life. But love is often the occasion rather than the subject of the drama, e.g. Knemon and his misanthropy are at the centre of *Dyskolos*, and *Adelphoe* is concerned with the right relations between father and son. The more of Menander's work is recovered, the more diverse it appears in theme and treatment.

Menander was a skilful maker of plots and a master of variety and surprise. He wrote for the theatre; the audience was implicated by direct address and long narrative speeches gave scope for the virtuosity of actors. Terence changed this in the interest of realism, which he also pursued by eliminating prologues spoken by divinities. These, sometimes postponed until after an opening scene that whetted the appetite, gave the audience facts as yet unknown to the characters, enabling them better to understand the significance of the events that passed on the stage.

Menander's handling of verse (itself non-realistic) is masterly: his trimeters give the illusion of colloquial speech, while subtle variations of rhythm express the speaker's feelings or character, and the verse-form reinforces the natural emphasis. In his earlier plays at least he introduced variety by using, both for lively and for serious scenes, the trochaic tetrameter with its insistent rhythm. The last scene of *Dyskolos* (iambic tetrameters) even had a flute accompaniment.

Although there is in general an over-all unity of style, each character speaks in an appropriate way (Plut. *Mor.* 853 d). Thus in *Samia* Demeas and Nikeratos, in *Dyskolos* Getas and Sikon, Gorgias and Sostratos are contrasted in language as in character. Some of the non-Attic usages with which Menander was later reproached may have been deliberate pieces of characterization. The occasional use of tragic diction (stichomuthia in *Perikeiromene*, many lines in *Sikyonios*) is sophisticatedly ambiguous, neither simple parody nor completely serious.

Menander's characters range through the whole of society: rich and poor, young and old, slave and free. They include traditional figures, e.g. the soldier and the cook, but though these may retain hints of the traits that were caricatured in Middle Comedy, they become credible and individual human beings like the rest. He attempts no profound psychological insights and may leave to the audience the pleasure of deducing, as in real life, emotions and motives. The dialogue often proceeds so quickly that it requires an alert hearer to grasp all the implications. The same phrase may forward the action, describe a character, and illuminate the speaker. Contrast is a much used device; in *Bacchides* six men form seven contrasted pairs. Typically the persons are portrayed with mingled irony and sympathy, and although the dramatist is primarily an entertainer, he quietly inculcates the lesson that understanding, tolerance, and generosity are the keys to happiness in human relationships.

TEXTS. A. Körte, *Menander, Reliquiae* i³ (1938 and, with supplement by A. Thierfelder, 1957), ii (1959, ed. A. Thierfelder); vol. i contains finds on papyrus or parchment, vol. ii fragments quoted in other authors. Later discoveries: *Dyscolus*, ed. P. H. Lloyd-Jones (1960), J. M. Jacques (1963); *Sikyonios*, ed. R. Kassel (1965) *Oxyrhyncus Papyri* xxiii (1968), with some of the frags.; *Dis Exapaton*, ed. E. W. Handley, *BICS*, Suppl. 22; the supposed *Misogynes*, ed. J. W. Barns, *Antinoopolis Patyri* ii, no. 55. Doubtful fragments, Page, *GLP*, Lloyd-Jones and Barns, *JHS* 1955; H. J. Mette, *Lustrum*, 1966/7.

TEXTS WITH COMMENTARIES. *Das Schiedsgericht [Epitrepontes]*, by Wilamowitz (1925); *Samia*, by C. Dedoussi (1965); *Dyskolos*, by E. W. Handley (1965); *Menandri fabularum reliquiae*, by J. van Leeuwen (1919); E. Capps, *Four Plays of Menander* (1910).

TRANSLATIONS. In Loeb series by F. G. Allinson (1921), probably to be replaced; in Penguin Classics by P. Vellacott (1967); of *Dyskolos*, W. G. Arnott, J. H. Quincey; *Epitrepontes* and *Perikeiromene* translated and completed by G. Murrary under the titles *The Arbitration* (1945) and *The Rape of the Locks* (1942).

CRITICISM. G. Murray, *Aristophanes* (1933); A. W. Gomme, *Essays in Greek History and Literature* (1937); T. B. L. Webster, *Studies in Menander²* (1960).                    F. H. S.

**MENANDER** (2), Milinda of Buddhist tradition (*Milinda Pañho*), born in the village Kalasi near Alasandā (identified with Alexandria of the Caucasus), greatest king of the Indo-Greeks, ruled *c.* 155–130 B.C. He led an expedition into the Ganges valley, reaching Pataliputra (Patna), but returned without annexing any part to his kingdom. He embraced Buddhism after a discussion with Nagasena, a Buddhist scholar-priest. Traditionally associated with the origin of the Buddha image and construction of stupas, he issued a copper coin with the Buddhist *Dharma-Chakra* (Wheel of the Law). His main coin-types, however, show Pallas on the reverse. He adopted the titles of 'Soter' and 'Dikaios'. A Kharosthi inscription is dated from his fifth regnal year and perhaps one of the reckonings used in later Kharosthi inscriptions starts from the first year of his reign. According to Buddhist tradition he handed over his kingdom to his son and retired from the world, but according to Plutarch he died in a camp and 'the cities celebrated his funeral as usual in other respects but in respect to his remains they put forth rival claims and only with difficulty came to terms, agreeing that they should divide the ashes equally and go away and should erect monuments to him in all their cities'.

W. W. Tarn, *Greeks in Bactria and India²* (1951); A. K. Narain, *Indo-Greeks* (1957).                    A. K. N.

**MENANDER** (3) of Ephesus compiled from native records, which he translated into Greek, 'the actions which took place under each of the kings [of Phoenicia?] among both the Greeks and the barbarians'. His Tyrian history is cited by Josephus (*AJ* 8. 144–6, *Ap.* 1. 116 ff.).

*FGrH* iii. 783.

**MENANDER** (4, *PW* 16) of Laodicea (3rd c. A.D.) wrote commentaries on Hermogenes (2) and Minucianus (qq.v.). Two treatises Περὶ ἐπιδεικτικῶν pass under his name; the first (Spengel, *Rhet* iii. 329 ff.) deals with hymns, prayers, encomia of countries and cities, etc.; the second (ibid. 368 ff.), by a less polished but livelier writer, gives rules for ceremonial addresses to the emperor and other officials, various forms of λαλιά ('talk'), epithalamia, etc. Both books deal with a branch of rhetoric which has its interest for the student of ancient poetry as well as oratory, and provide useful material for the interpretation of propemptica (q.v.), epithalamia (q.v.), and other forms.                    D. A. R.

**MENDES,** a he-goat represented usually on monuments as a ram, and identified by Herodotus and other Greeks with Pan, was worshipped in the Egyptian city of Mendes. The cult attained national prominence in the Ptolemaic period. The great Mendes stele (*Zeitschrift für ägyptische Sprache und Altertumskunde* xiii (1875), 33–40) refers to Ptolemy II 'son of the great living goat of Mendes' as having visited the temple 'as the kings before him had done'. The deceased queen Arsinoë II is called 'Arsinoë Philadelphus beloved by the goat', and her deification throughout the land is described. The stele also notes that the province of Mendes paid no taxes to the king but used its revenues for the worship of the god. The completion of the temple and the attendant celebration, the discovery of a new sacred animal, and various feasts and processions are mentioned.

Erman, *Religion der Ägypter* (1934), 362 ff.;                    T. A. B.

**MENECRATES** (1) of Xanthus, a fourth-century writer of the history of Lycia (Λυκιακά) in Ionic.

FGrH iii. 769.

**MENECRATES** (2) of Ephesus, probably born *c.* 340, wrote a didactic poem called *Erga* in imitation of Hesiod, and probably another poem on apiculture (*Melissurgica*).

TEXTS. H. Diels, *PPF* (1901), 171–2.

**MENEDEMUS** (1) of Eretria (*c.* 339–*c.* 265 B.C.) was sent by his city to Megara on military service. He was there won over to philosophy (perhaps after a visit to the Academy in Athens), and studied under Stilpo. He moved to Elis and joined the school founded by Phaedo; he became leader of it and transferred it to Eretria. He involved himself in politics and attained high office, but was forced into exile by political opponents. He took refuge at the court of Antigonus Gonatas in Macedonia and died there. As a philosopher he was called an eristic, and his positive contributions, if any, are unknown.

Diog. Laert. 2. 125–44. D. J. F.

**MENEDEMUS** (2), Cynic philosopher of the third century B.C., from western Asia Minor, first a pupil of Colotes the Epicurean, later of Echecles the Cynic, both of Lampsacus. He is best known from Colotes' polemic against him.

**MENELAUS** (1) (Μενέλαος, Μενέλεως), younger brother of Agamemnon (q.v.) and husband of Helen (q.v.). In all literature, beginning with Homer, Paris' kidnapping of his wife causes the Trojan War. In the *Iliad* he appears prominently in 3. 21 ff. (Paris avoids him, 96 ff.; he agrees to settle the dispute by a duel with Paris, defeats him, but is prevented by Aphrodite from killing him). In 4. 86 ff. Athena instigates Pandarus (q.v.) to wound him, in order to prevent the war from ending; he is slightly hurt, but cured by Machaon (q.v.). In 17. 1 ff. he distinguishes himself in the fighting over the body of Patroclus; elsewhere he is usually rather in the background, being inferior to Agamemnon in prowess and deliberately holding back (10. 121 ff.) so as not to seem to thrust himself before his greater brother. In the *Odyssey* he is seen safe at home with Helen after a long series of adventures on his return (4. 1 ff.) and is promised Elysium (4. 561 ff.).

Post-Homeric accounts supply details of his life before and after the period covered by the Homeric poems. He had previously met Paris (q.v.) at Delphi, and the oracle had warned them, but they had not understood (schol. *Il.* 5. 64). He was in Crete when Helen was carried off, and was warned by Iris of what had happened, (*Cypria* Photius). For his reunion with Helen after Troy fell see the same source. In Euripides' *Helena*, which follows Stesichorus' version of the story, Menelaus comes with the phantom Helen to Egypt, is shipwrecked, and meets the real one outside the palace of Theoclymenus, son of Proteus, who has been humanized into a Pharaoh. She has taken refuge at Proteus' tomb to avoid being forced to marry Theoclymenus. After a half-comic scene in which Menelaus realizes the situation, they plot with Theonoë, Theoclymenus' sister, to escape. Helen tells the king Menelaus is drowned, and gets the use of a ship to perform funeral rites at sea. Menelaus' men overpower the crew and sail away with him and her, the Dioscuri forbidding Theoclymenus to pursue.

For his cult as hero and occasionally as god see Farnell, *Hero-Cults*, 322 f. H. J. R.

**MENELAUS** (2), sculptor, working in the first century A.D. Known from signature on group of Orestes and Electra in the Terme (Winter, *KB* 394. 4), for which he has adapted motives of the fourth century B.C., but Orestes wears his cloak Roman fashion. He called himself

pupil of Stephanus, who signed a statue of a youth in the style of the early fifth century (Winter, *KB* 394. 3). Stephanus was the pupil of Pasiteles, a south Italian Greek sculptor who became a Roman citizen in 89 B.C. and wrote a book on notable works of art. Menelaus has been identified with M. Cossutius Menelaus who signed a lost statue. The Cossutii had a workshop of long standing in Paros, and another of their freedmen, M. Cossutius Cerdo, made the two Polyclitan Pans in the British Museum.

G. Lippold, *Kopien und Umbildungen* (1923), 40; id. *Griech. Plastik*, 386; O. Rubensohn, *JDAI* 1935, 56; Bieber, *Sculpt. Hellenist. Age* 182. T. B. L. W.

**MENELAUS** (3, *PW* 16) of Alexandria, mathematician and astronomer, is dated by astronomical observations made by him at Rome in A.D. 98 (reported by Ptolemy, *Almagest* vi. 3), and was known to Plutarch (*de facie in orbe lunae* 17). Of his works only the *Sphaerica*, in three books, is extant (in Arabic translation). It is a textbook of spherical geometry, and contains the earliest known theorems on spherical trigonometry. Book I gives the definition of a spherical triangle (τρίπλευρον), and develops theorems about it modelled on Euclid's for the plane triangle. Book II is concerned with the solution of problems important for spherical astronomy in a more elegant way than such predecessors as Theodosius (q.v. 4). Book III treats the elements of spherical trigonometry. Prop. 1 is 'Menelaus' Theorem', which was used by subsequent ancient astronomers (e.g. Ptolemy) to solve spherical triangles. It is probable that much of Menelaus' work was original, and superseded earlier methods of solving spherical problems by, e.g., stereographic projection.

Other works by him included one on chords in a circle in six books (Theon, *Comm. in Alm.* 1st ed. Rome, 451) and another on the elements of geometry in three books (al-Bīrūnī, *Das Buch von der Auffindung der Sehnen im Kreise*, tr. Suter, Bibl. Math. 3 F. 11, 31 f.).

Arabic text of *Sphaerica*, with German translation, ed. M. Krause, *Abh. d. Ges. d. Wiss. zu Göttingen*, Phil.-hist. Kl. 3 F. nr. 17 (1936). Latin translation by Ed. Halley, *Menelai Sphaericorum Libri III* (Oxford, 1758).
COMMENT. A. A. Björnbo, *Studien über Menelaos' Sphärik, Abh. z. Gesch. d. Math.* 14, 1902; Heath, *Hist. of Greek Maths.* ii. 260 ff. For history of text and editions see Krause and Björnbo, opp. citt., and *Isis* 1938, 417 ff. G. J. T.

**MENENIUS** (*PW* 12) **AGRIPPA,** consul in 503 B.C. A plebeian, Menenius reputedly appeased the plebeians and brought them back to Rome after the first secession by telling the parable of the Belly and the Limbs (494 B.C.). The story is fictitious, but it is difficult to explain its origin and date (dates of the fourth, third, and first centuries have been suggested); it is either a fable common to the peoples of Aryan stock or the adaptation of an allegorical tale elaborated by Greek sophists.

Ed. Meyer, *Kl. Schr.* i² (1924), 358 ff.; Ogilvie, *Comm. Livy 1–5*, 312 ff. P. T.

**MENESTOR,** a Greek writer on botany much quoted by Theophrastus. He applied the Pythagorean theory of the opposition of the warm and the cold to plants, dividing these into those which by their warm nature can grow even in water or in the cold parts of the earth, and those which from their cold nature need a warm climate. It has been much discussed whether his explanation of evergreenness by the doctrine of 'warm plants' or that of Empedocles by means of pores is the older, but on the whole it seems that he can be dated between Empedocles and Theophrastus. He may fairly be called the first Greek who made an inductive study of plants.

Testimonia in Diels, *Vorsokr.*¹¹ i. 375–6. W. D. R.

**MENEXENUS** of Athens, pupil of Socrates, was one of those present at the conversation in prison related in

Plato's *Phaedo*. He plays a considerable part in the *Lysis*, and a less prominent one in the dialogue called after him.

**MENIPPE,** name of a Nereid in Hesiod, *Theog.* 260, and of two or three insignificant heroines, as the mother of Eurystheus (schol. *Iliad* 19. 116, which also gives her several other names); the mother of Orpheus (q.v.), generally a Muse (Tzetzes, *Chil.* I. xii. 306).

**MENIPPEAN SATIRE,** distinguished by Quintilian (*Inst.* 10. 1. 95) as a separate sort of satire. Ultimately founded on Menippus (q.v. 1), it was characterized by its mixture of prose and verse. In Latin it is represented by Varro, Seneca, and Petronius, and descends to the pedantic fantasia by Martianus Capella (5th c.) and to the French *Satire Ménippée*.

J. Wight Duff, *Roman Satire* (1937), ch. 5. J. W. D.

**MENIPPUS** (1) of Gadara (first half of 3rd c. B.C.), a slave at Sinope, became pupil of the Cynic Metrocles, bought his freedom, and acquired the Theban franchise. Originator of the serio-comic style (σπουδογέλοιον), in which humorous expression was given to philosophical views. His works include Νέκυια (in which he imitated Crates), Διαθῆκαι, Ἐπιστολαὶ κεκομψευμέναι ἀπὸ τοῦ τῶν θεῶν προσώπου, Διογένους πρᾶσις, Συμπόσιον. His prose was interspersed with verses, whether quoted or original is uncertain. He influenced Meleager of Gadara and Lucian, and Varro's *Saturae Menippeae* are adapted from him. *See* IAMBIC POETRY, GREEK.

Diog. Laert. 6. 29, 95, 99–101; *Corp. poes. ep. Graec. lud.* ii. 78–85; R. Helm, *Lucian und Menippus* (1906). J. D. D.

**MENIPPUS** (2) of Pergamum (fl. *c.* 20 B.C.), Greek author of Περίπλους τῆς ἐντὸς θαλάσσης (Mediterranean), abridged, corrected, and augmented by Marcian. Book 1, Euxine, Sea of Marmora; 2, Mediterranean, north side; 3, south; Palestine, Asia Minor. It gave chiefly names and distances.

*GGM* 1. cxxxv ff., 563 ff.; A. Diller, *The Tradition of the Minor Greek Geographers* (1952), 147 ff.; 188. E. H. W.

**MENO,** pupil of Aristotle, author of a doxographical compendium of the older Greek medicine—Ἰατρικὴ συναγωγή. A selection from it is contained in a London papyrus; ed. H. Diels (1893).

**MENODORUS** or **MENAS** was a freedman of Pompey and perhaps previously a pirate. In 40 B.C. he captured Sardinia from Octavian for Sextus Pompeius. In 39 he advised Sextus not to make the Pact of Misenum with Antony and Octavian, and was said to have suggested making away with them at the subsequent celebration. In 38, having aroused in Sextus suspicions of his fidelity, he restored Sardinia to Octavian, was rewarded with equestrian rank, and fought in the naval war against Sextus under L. Calvisius (q.v.). In 36 he returned to Sextus, but failed to recover his trust and again deserted to Octavian. He was killed in Octavian's Illyrian campaign of 35, at the siege of Siscia (q.v.).

G. W. R.; T. J. C.

**MENODOTUS** (1) of Perinthus, author of a history (Ἑλληνικαὶ πραγματεῖαι) probably beginning *c.* 217 B.C. as a continuation of the histories of Psaon of Plataea or Phylarchus.

*FGrH* ii. 82.

**MENODOTUS** (2), Samian Greek (? identical with Menodotus (1), Diod. Sic. 26. 4), wrote (i) Τῶν κατὰ τὴν Σάμον ἐνδόξων ἀναγραφή and (ii) Περὶ τῶν κατὰ τὸ ἱερὸν τῆς Σαμίας Ἥρας.

*FGrH* iii. 541.

**MENODOTUS** (3) of Nicomedia (fl. probably *c.* A.D. 120), follower of Pyrrhon, pupil of Antiochus of Ascalon, and leader of the empirical school of medicine. He was a voluminous author, and is often referred to by Galen.

**MENOECEUS** (Μενοικεύς), in mythology, (1) father of Creon (q.v. 3; Soph. *Ant.* 1098 and elsewhere). (2) Creon's son, whose story is best known from Eur. *Phoen.* 905 ff. Tiresias revealed that Thebes could not survive the assault of the Seven unless atonement were made for the killing of the dragon by Cadmus (q.v.); the victim must be one of the Sparti, and unmarried, and no other was available. Menoeceus, despite his father's attempts to save him, killed himself over the dragon's lair. H. J. R.

**MENOETIUS** (Μενοίτιος), father of Patroclus (q.v.; *Il.* 9. 202 and elsewhere). Of what country he was seems to have been uncertain even to Homer: see *Il.* 11. 765–6; 23. 85.

**MENS,** personified right thinking ('Mens Bona', Propertius 3. 24. 19 and elsewhere; it was her title at Paestum, Wissowa, *RK* 314). She was vowed a temple, by advice of the Sibylline books, in 217 B.C. after Trasimene (Livy 22. 9. 10; 10. 10; cf. Platner–Ashby, 339); it was dedicated two years later (Livy 23. 32. 20). A cult of Bona Mens became popular among slaves and freedmen in imperial times.

Latte, *RR* 240. H. J. R.

**MENTHE** (μένθη) or **MINTHE** (μίνθη), i.e. mint. According to Strabo 8. 3. 14, 344 (more authorities given by Peter in Roscher's *Lexikon*, s.v.) she was Hades' mistress (a Naiad, daughter of Peitho, Photius s.v.), and Persephone trampled her underfoot, whereat she became the plant named after her, which smells the sweeter when trodden upon. H. J. R.

**MENTOR** (1), in mythology, an old Ithacan, friend of Odysseus, who left his household in his charge (*Odyssey* 2. 225 ff.). Athena takes his shape to help Telemachus (ibid. 401 and elsewhere; cf. 24. 548).

**MENTOR** (2), Rhodian mercenary leader, brother-in-law of the satrap Artabazus (q.v.), whose service he and his brother Memnon (q.v. 2) entered. He married his niece Barsine, Artabazus' daughter. Both brothers took part in the Satraps' Revolt (362–360 B.C.) and received some territory in Troas. In 353 they fled with Artabazus. Mentor went to Egypt, entered again the king's service, and was general at the conquest of Egypt (343). He rose high in Persian service and was ordered to quell the dynasts of Asia Minor. Among them was Hermias (q.v. 3), whom he put to death (342). He had previously obtained the recall of Artabazus and Memnon. He probably died soon after.

Dem. 23. 150 ff.; Diod. 16. 42 ff. H. W. Parke, *Greek Mercenary Soldiers* (1933). V. E.

**MERCENARIES (GREEK AND HELLENISTIC).** (1) *From the earliest times till the Peloponnesian War* (431 B.C.) mercenaries play a small part in Greek warfare, being few in number and not clearly distinguishable from voluntary helpers. They are most frequently mentioned as forming the bodyguards of tyrants. But the early tyrants were often content to enrol citizens and, except in Sicily, did not maintain large armies of professional soldiers. Before the Persian conquests Greek mercenaries were employed to some extent in Egypt and Mesopotamia; afterwards they were mainly used as bodyguards for the satraps of Asia Minor and were largely recruited from Arcadia.

(2) *Till the King's Peace* (386 B.C.). During the Peloponnesian War there grew a demand for auxiliary troops to supplement the ordinary hoplite. These were drawn especially from the backward parts of Greece and from Thrace. The end of the war released many soldiers for professional service, from whom Cyrus raised an army of more than 10,000 hoplites for his attempt on the Persian throne. In the Corinthian War Iphicrates (q.v.), leading a force of peltasts (q.v.), achieved such success that this type of soldier was established as an independent unit. Meanwhile in Sicily Dionysius I was founding an outstandingly powerful tyranny on a large professional army.

(3) *Till Chaeronea* (338 B.C.). The possibilities of using mercenaries were now fully exploited. The Persian satraps hired large armies to oppose the Great King, who replied by employing the same material. In Greece the city-states used mercenaries in their struggles with each other or remodelled their citizen-armies on a professional pattern. Many tyrants of a militaristic type arose, and in the Third Sacred War (356–346) Phocis showed how even a small State could be dominant so long as it had large financial resources. Philip II of Macedon, however, relied on mercenaries only as a supplement to the main body of his citizen-army.

(4) *Till Ipsus* (301 B.C.). Alexander employed mercenaries mostly for garrison duty and settlement abroad, and on separate expeditions away from his main column. The Persians until Arbela formed the bulk of their heavy infantry from Greeks. The Diadochi made the nucleus of their armies out of Macedonians, but the bulk of the troops were mercenaries, who were ready to change sides according to the fortunes of war.

(5) *Till Pydna* (168 B.C.). Warfare gradually depended less on foreign soldiers. In the Hellenistic kingdoms a small standing army of professional soldiers was maintained, but newly hired mercenaries were not used to form the main phalanx. In time of need they could reinforce it in other directions. Even barbarians were thus employed with their native equipment.

H. W. Parke, *Greek Mercenary Soldiers from the earliest times to the Battle of Ipsus* (1933); G. T. Griffith, *The Mercenaries of the Hellenistic World* (1935); M. Launey, *Recherches sur les armées hellénistiques* (1949, 1950). H. W. P.

**MERCENARIES (ROMAN).** Contact with foreign powers such as Carthage and Macedon exposed Rome's weakness in cavalry and light-armed troops. This deficiency she remedied by obtaining contingents outside Italy which, in contrast with the Italian *socii*, were called *auxilia*. Some came from independent allies like Masinissa (q.v.), others were raised by forced levies or paid as mercenaries. Gallic *auxilia* served in the First Punic War, 600 Cretan archers fought at Lake Trasimene, Numidian cavalry turned the scale at Zama. During the next two centuries the number and variety of *auxilia* increased. Spain was a favourite recruiting-ground because of the superiority of the native over the Roman weapons, while Caesar obtained his cavalry from Gaul and Germany, and his archers and slingers from Crete and the Balearic Islands. Under the Principate the *auxilia* became part of the standing army. *See* AUXILIA.

G. Veith, in Kromayer–Veith, *Heerwesen und Kriegführung der Griechen und Römer* (1928), 311 ff. H. M. D. P.

**MERCURIUS (Merqurius, Mirqurios, Mircurios),** the god of traders, Roman equivalent of Hermes; indeed, it is highly probable that he is Hermes (q.v.) introduced under a name, or title, suggestive of his commercial activities (cf. *merx, mercari*). He does not appear in the 'calendar of Numa', nor has he a flamen or any other

indication of primitive Roman (or Italian) cult. On the other hand, his temple is *extra pomerium*, being on the Aventine overlooking the Circus Maximus (see Platner–Ashby, 339); he is worshipped there with a goddess who is in essence the Greek, not the Roman Maia (q.v.), and its dedication day, 15 May, became a festival of merchants (Festus, 135, 4 Lindsay). From all this it is generally supposed that his cult is an early example of Greek, or hellenizing, commercial influence, comparable to that of Ceres, Liber, and Libera (*see* CERES); the date of the temple is 495 B.C., see Latte, *RR* 162. Altheim, however, seeks by an ingenious combination to prove that he is an old Graeco-Etruscan deity comparable in functions to the Genius (q.v.; *Griechische Götter* (1930), 39 ff.), and supposes the connexion of the name with *merces* to be a false etymology. It is generally agreed that his ultimate origin is Greek, by whatever route and under whatever circumstances his cult reached Rome; his connexion with trade is equally undoubted. Under the Empire he, like many gods, sometimes takes the title Augustus (see Steuding in Roscher's *Lexikon* ii. 2818; cf. also A. D. Nock, *JHS* 1928, 33 f., 41 f.). His identifications with foreign gods (Steuding, 2826 ff.; *see* RELIGION, CELTIC) result from his equivalence with Hermes, also his mythology, save for one or two tales, probably Latin literary inventions. H. J. R.

**MEROBAUDES,** FLAVIUS, a Spaniard, distinguished as soldier and poet. His works include, besides thirty hexameters in praise of Christ, fragments of a prose panegyric on the second consulship of Aetius (A.D. 437) and of a verse panegyric on his third consulship (446), and a *genethliacon* modelled on Statius, *Silv.* 2. 7.

TEXT. F. Vollmer, *MGH, AA* xiv (1905). A. H.-W.

**MEROË,** the 'island' between the junction of the Bahr-el-Abiad with the true Nile and that of the Atbara with the Nile. The city Meroë (*Bakarawiga*), the southern and later the sole capital of the Kings and Queens of Napata, was known by hearsay to Herodotus. In the time of Ptolemy II the kingdom became partly hellenized. There were queens named Candace ruling there until the fourth century of the Roman Empire. In spite of ravages by the Abyssinians, the town was important until the seventh century. By the third century B.C. the Greeks knew the Nile well as far as Meroë. But despite further exploration of the Nile in Ptolemaic and Roman times (*see* NILE), even Ptolemy the geographer of the second century A.D. knew little beyond Meroë and falsely made the land a true island.

For excavations at Meroë see: E. Budge, *Egyptian Sudan* (1907) and *History of Ethiopia* (1928); J. Garstang, *Meroe* (1911); P. L. Shinnie, *Meroe* (1967); Thomson, *Hist. Anc. Geog.* 10, 66 f., 138, 273. E. H. W.

**MEROPE** (Μερόπη), in mythology, (1) a Pleiad, wife of Sisyphus (q.v.); she is the nearly invisible star of the group, for she hides her face for shame at having married a mortal, while all her sisters mated with gods (see Apollod. 1. 85; Hyg. *Fab.* 192. 5). (2) Wife of Cresphontes king of Messenia; *see* AEPYTUS. (3) Wife of Polybus of Corinth, Oedipus' foster-father (Soph. *OT* 775); *see* OEDIPUS. (4) Daughter of Oenopion (*see* ORION; Apollod. 1. 25). For more Meropae see Stoll in Roscher's *Lexikon*, s.v. H. J. R.

**MERULA,** LUCIUS CORNELIUS (*PW* 272), was made consul suffect (87 B.C.) by Octavius (q.v. 3) after the illegal deposition of Cinna (q.v. 1), chiefly because, as *flamen Dialis*, he could play no active part in war or politics. After Cinna's return he committed suicide, first piously resigning his priesthood, in which he was succeeded (briefly) by Caesar (q.v. 1). E. B.

**MESATOS.** Fifth-century tragic poet who was third in the contest in the year, very possibly 463 B.C., when Aeschylus was victorious with his *Danaid* Trilogy and Sophocles was second, (*POxy.* 20. 2256). His existence was previously attested only by Schol. Ar. *Vesp.* 1502, and was widely doubted, but Wilhelm had conjectured rightly that his was the name in seven letters ending in *-τος* which occurs in the Victor-List between Sophocles, victorious in 468, and ? Aristias; he won either two, three, or four victories.

H. Lloyd-Jones, Appendix to Loeb Aeschylus, vol. ii (1957), 595 ff.
D. W. L.

**MESENE,** a kingdom at the head of the Persian Gulf, at the mouths of Tigris and Euphrates, also called Characene from its chief city, Charax. This was founded by Hyspaosines, who created an independent kingdom out of part of the Babylonian satrapy after the death of the Seleucid king Antiochus VII in 129 B.C. Coins dated by the Seleucid era begin with Hyspaosines and give names of thirteen kings down to A.D. 112. Thereafter coins have no longer Greek but Aramaic legends and give no dates. Names of kings are predominantly Iranian, as was that of Hyspaosines himself. Its inaccessibility enabled the kingdom to enjoy in practice independence of Parthia and it established direct trade relations with Palmyra and the trading cities of the Roman East, relations attested by Palmyrene inscriptions (especially frequent in the second century A.D.). But in *c.* A.D. 224 Ardashir conquered Mesene and made it a Sassanid province.

Pliny, *HN* 6, 136 f., 145 f. S. A. Nodelman, *Berytus* 1960, 83 ff.; G. F. Hill, *B.M. Coins, Arabia, etc.* (1922), cxciv f.; G. le Rider, *Syria* 1959, 259 f.
E. W. G.

**MESOPOTAMIA,** the country between the Tigris and the Euphrates. The name is generally used to include the whole alluvial country south of the mountains, and the deserts on either side, i.e. the ancient kingdoms of Assyria and Babylonia, modern 'Iraq. Classical writers usually regarded Mesopotamia as excluding Babylonia.

As an important political and commercial link between Syria and Babylonia, Mesopotamia was colonized extensively by the Seleucids. It was a frequent battle-ground of Roman and Parthian armies, and the prosperity of the Greek cities diminished under the Arsacids. Mesopotamia was overrun by Trajan (114–17) (his *Provincia Mesopotamia* was promptly abandoned by Hadrian) and **again** overrun by L. Verus (162–5) and Septimius Severus (197–9) but was not permanently occupied. Part of Upper Mesopotamia, however, became Roman after the campaigns of Verus and was formed into a separate province, 'Mesopotamia', by Severus. *See also* ASSYRIA, OSROËNE.

V. Chapot, *La Frontière de l'Euphrate* (1907); Jones, *Cities E. Rom. Prov.*, ch. 9; L. Dilleman, *Haute Mésopotamie et pays adjacents* (1962).
M. S. D.; E. W. G.

**MESSAL(L)A**(1), MANIUS VALERIUS (*PW* 247) MAXIMUS, as consul in 263 B.C., reduced the district around Aetna and drove back Hieron (q.v. 2), who then deserted the Carthaginian for the Roman cause. For having freed Messana, Valerius received the cognomen Messalla, which his predecessor Claudius (q.v. 5) may equally have deserved. He celebrated a triumph and decorated a wall of the Senate-house with a painting of his success. He was censor in 252.
H. H. S.

**MESSAL(L)A** (2), MARCUS VALERIUS (*PW* 266, 268), name of two cousins, distinguished as 'Niger' and 'Rufus', born *c.* 102 B.C. and 100 B.C. respectively. Of patrician, but not recently prominent, family, they gained the favour of Sulla, who, as Dictator, married a Valeria (probably Rufus' sister) and made Niger Pontifex and

Rufus Augur. Both passed quickly through the lower offices and Niger became consul in 61. Rufus, delayed by the troubles of the 50s and involved in a bribery scandal (54), finally reached the office in 53. (Niger, *interrex* three times (*ILS* 46), perhaps presided at the elections.) As censor (55), Niger, with his colleague Servilius (q.v. 1), regulated the Tiber (*ILS* 5922). He was a friend and ally of Cicero and an active barrister until his death (*c.* 50), father of a great orator (see 3) and father-in-law of a famous jurist (SULPICIUS 1). Rufus, prosecuted for bribery (51), was defended by his uncle Hortensius (q.v. 2) and acquitted, but fined on another charge. Offended by Pompey, he fought for Caesar in the Civil War, and after Caesar's death devoted himself to writing books on history and religion that were widely read by ancient scholars but have perished. He died in 26.

Cichorius, *Röm. Stud.* 233; R. Syme, *JRS* 1955, 156.
E. B.

**MESSAL(L)A**(3) **CORVINUS,** MARCUS VALERIUS (*PW* 261) (64 B.C.–A.D. 8), soldier, orator, statesman, and patron of letters, first distinguished himself at Philippi (42 B.C.) as supporter of Brutus and Cassius. Declining command of the Republican army after that disaster, he transferred his allegiance to Antony; but, disgusted with Antony's conduct, he joined Octavian (how soon, however, is not clear). He fought for Octavian against Sextus Pompeius (36) and in the Illyro-Pannonian War (35–34), subdued the Alpine Salassi (34–33), and as consul with Octavian (31) took part in the battle of Actium. After service in the East, as proconsul in Gaul he conquered the Aquitani, celebrating a triumph in 27. In *c.* 25 B.C. he was made *praefectus urbi* but resigned after a few days, 'incivilem potestatem esse contestans' according to Jerome, 'quasi nescius exercendi' according to Tacitus (*Ann.* 6. 11. 4). Already member of the College of Augurs, he became the first permanent *curator aquarum* in 11, and it was he who proposed the title of *Pater Patriae* for Augustus (2 B.C.). He reconstructed part of the Via Latina and several public buildings, gained fame as orator and historian, dabbled in poetry and philosophy, and was the patron of a literary circle—Tibullus, Lygdamus, Sulpicia, and the author of the *Panegyricus Messallae* (q.v., and *see* PASTORAL POETRY, LATIN, § 2). Titles of several of his grammatical and stylistic treatises have survived.

HISTORICAL FRAGMENTS. Peter, *HRRel.* ii. lxxviii ff. and 65 ff.; grammatical, H. Funaioli, *Gramm. Rom. Frag.* i. 503 ff.; rhetorical, Malcovati, *ORF*² n. 176. See also J. Hammer, *Prolegomena to an Edition of the Panegyricus Messallae* (U.S.A. 1925); R. Kuthan, *De duabus Messalae expeditionibus* (1923); Syme, *Rom. Rev.*, see index.
J. H.; M. E. H.

**MESSAL(L)A**(4) **MESSALLINUS,** MARCUS VALERIUS (*PW* 264) (*cos.* 3 B.C.), son of (3) above, and a person of some distinction and oratorical talent but not to be compared with his parent. Legate of Illyricum in A.D. 6 and present with Tiberius on the campaign against Maroboduus, he was sent back to deal with the rebellious Pannonians and Dalmatians and reached Siscia after fighting a battle; he received *ornamenta triumphalia*. Later Messallinus spoke in the Senate on several occasions during the principate of Tiberius. His election as one of the *quindecimviri* in charge of the Sibylline books is celebrated in the longest poem (2. 5) of Tibullus, who enjoyed the patronage of Messallinus' father.
R. S.

**MESSAL(L)A**(5), VIPSTANUS (*PW* 6), a military tribune in A.D. 69, took temporary command of a legion at the battle of Cremona. He was perhaps a source for the account of the campaign in the *Histories* of Tacitus who names him twice (*Hist.* 3. 25, 28). Tacitus introduced him as a speaker in the *Dialogus*, as a defender of the classical orators against more contemporary fashions. Messalla defended his half-brother Aquilius Regulus (q.v. 3) when he was attacked by Eprius (q.v.) in 70. He probably died young. **H. H. S.**

**MESSAL(L)INA** (1), VALERIA (*PW* 403), granddaughter of Octavia (q.v. 2) on her father's and mother's sides, in A.D. 39 or 40 married at 14 her second cousin Claudius (q.v. 1), then 48 years old, and bore him two children, Octavia (q.v. 3) and Britannicus (q.v.). Claudius alone was blind to her sexual profligacy (which Juvenal travestied in Satires 6 and 10), whose climax was reached when in 48 she went through the formalities of a marriage service with C. Silius (q.v. 1). The freedman Narcissus (q.v. 2) turned against her and, while Claudius was in a state of stunned incredulity, ensured that she was put to death. **J. P. B.**

**MESSAL(L)INA** (2), STATILIA (*PW* 45), third wife of Nero (A.D. 66), who put to death her fourth husband Iulius Vestinus Atticus, was great-great-granddaughter of Augustus' partisan T. Statilius (q.v.) Taurus and probably daughter of T. Statilius Taurus (*cos.* 44). She received some divine honours. After Nero's death she maintained a brilliant position, and is said to have been noted for her eloquence and literary culture as well as for her beauty. Otho contemplated marriage with her.

Suet. *Nero* 35. 1, *Otho* 10. 2; scholiast on Juvenal 6. 434. **A. M.**

**MESSANA** (modern *Messina*) was founded as *Zancle* c. 725 B.C., first by Cumaean ληιδταί and then by a contingent from Chalcis. An association with Naxos is apparently erroneous. Colonies were sent to Mylae (*Milazzo*) c. 717 B.C. (?) and to Himera (q.v.). Despite its position on the straits bearing its name, the city though prosperous was not of major political importance, and was overshadowed by Rhegium (q.v.), whose tyrant Anaxilas seized it in 490/89 B.C. (*see* ANAXILAS 1 for details). It received Samian and, later, Messenian immigrants who changed its name to *Messene*. After 461, when coins show the Doric form *Messana* in use, the city's population was further mixed by a settlement of ex-mercenaries from Syracuse and elsewhere. Becoming independent of Rhegium it supported Syracuse in 427–424 and 415–413. In 396 the Carthaginians destroyed it; Dionysius I rebuilt it, and on the fall of Dionysius II it had its own tyrants until it again formed part of the Syracusan system under Timoleon and Agathocles. In 288 the latter's Campanian mercenaries, calling themselves 'Mamertini' (men of Mars), seized it, seeking Roman and Carthaginian aid when Hieron II (q.v.) tried to suppress them. Both responded, and the ensuing imbroglio provoked the First Punic War (*see* MAMERTINES). After 241, Messana became a prosperous *civitas foederata*. Remains of antiquity on the site are meagre, thanks partly to the devastating earthquake of 1908.

Bérard, *Bibl. topogr.* 67 f.; Dunbabin, *Western Greeks*; G. Vallet, *Rhégion et Zancle* (1958). **A. G. W.**

**MESSAPII** immigrated into Calabria (q.v.) in the Early Iron Age. Probably they were Illyrians, not Cretans (despite M. Mayer in *PW* xv. 1175 f.). They undoubtedly spoke an Illyrian language: over 200 inscriptions, written c. 450–50 B.C. in a Tarentine-Ionic alphabet, survive (J. Whatmough, *Prae-Italic Dialects* (1933), ii. 258 f.). The civilized Messapii, strictly neighbours of Tarentum, are scarcely distinguishable from the Calabri (who dwelt near Brundisium) and Sal(l)entini (who inhabited the 'heel' proper); the Apulian Peucetii ( = Poediculi) and Daunii, although they supported Tarentum against the Messapii (Strabo 6. 281), also spoke Messapic. These peoples were collectively called Iapyges (Polyb. 3. 88). In 473 B.C. the Messapii defeated Tarentum (Hdt. 7.

170) and in 413 under King Artas supported Athens against Syracuse (Thuc. 7. 33). In 338 they helped to defeat Tarentum's mercenary, Archidamus, but in the Pyrrhic War supported Tarentum and were consequently subjugated by Rome (266: *Acta Triumph.*). Although only casually mentioned thereafter, they were never completely assimilated. Chief towns: Uria, Rudiae, Caelia, Brundisium, Uzentum.

J. Whatmough, *Foundations of Roman Italy* (1937), 111 (with bibliography); O. Haas, *Messapische Studien* (1962). **E. T. S.**

**MESSAPUS,** (1) eponym of Messapia in south Italy (Strabo 9. 2. 13). (2) Son of Neptune, an Etruscan, invulnerable to fire and steel, one of Turnus' allies (Verg. *Aen.* 7. 691 ff.; cf. 9. 523; 12. 128).

**MESSENE** was founded in 369 B.C. to be the capital of Messenia (q.v.). Situated on the western slopes of Mt. Ithome in the lower Messenian plain, its natural strength was reinforced by city-walls (largely preserved) which furnish the finest example of fourth-century fortification on the Greek mainland. Extensive remains of Hellenistic and Roman public buildings have been excavated below the modern village of Mavromati (*BCH* 1964, 737 ff.) around an extensive Agora: theatre, propylaea, and synedrion on the east; portico with staircases on the north; a temple of Artemis and elaborate columned niches on the west. Attacked unsuccessfully by Demetrius (q.v. 7) of Pharos (214 B.C.), by Philip V of Macedon, and by Nabis of Sparta, it was captured by the forces of the Achaean Confederacy under Lycortas (182 B.C.) in revenge for the Messenians' execution of Philopoemen (q.v.). It retained considerable importance under the Roman Empire. **A. M. W.; R. J. H.**

**MESSENIA,** the south-west region of Peloponnesus, bounded on the north by Elis, along the lower course of the river Neda, and Arcadia, and on the east by Laconia, where the frontier follows at first the main ridge of Taygetus, but further south runs to the west of it, and terminates at the river Choerius a few miles south of the head of the Messenian Gulf. Whilst west Messenia is a bleak, mountainous region, dominated by Mt. Aegaleos, with its few settlements along the coast (Cyparissia, Coryphasion-Pylos, Mothone, Asine, Corone), the central and eastern region watered by the river Pamisus and its tributaries was more populous, and the lower plain, Μακαρία, was renowned for its fertility.

The earlier prehistory of Messenia is represented particularly by the excavation of Malthi (possibly the Dorion of Paus. 4. 33. 6–7) overlooking and commanding the Messenian gap, the main east–west communication of the upper Messenian plain. It was a settlement of irregular house-blocks and winding lanes dating onwards from the Neolithic but developed and heavily fortified in the Middle Helladic period (M. N. Valmin, *The Swedish Messenia Expedition* (Lund, 1938)). In general it is clear that, despite the relatively unpromising terrain of western Messenia (from which Elean Triphylia can hardly be separated), this area developed very considerably from the end of the Middle Bronze Age to c. 1200 B.C. In saga Messenia was the kingdom of Aphareus who welcomed Neleus as a refugee from Thessaly (Paus. 4. 2. 5); on the death of Idas and the extinction of the Apharetid line Nestor inherited the greater part of the territory from both (Paus. 4. 3. 1). The bounds of the Neleid kingdom are set far to the north: in the Catalogue of the Ships Nestor (*Il.* 2. 592) possesses Θρύον, Ἀλφειοῖο πόρον (cf. 11. 711–12: Θρυόεσσα, . . . τηλοῦ ἐπ' Ἀλφειῷ νεάτη Πύλου ἠμαθόεντος (*see* PYLOS)). The disturbance called the Return of the Heraclidae drove Neleids into exile and gave new kings to Athens; also a basis in political mythology for Athens' claim to be mother city of the Ionians among whom Neleids also reigned. The same Athenian connexion is implied (a late development?) in the Andania Mysteries (see below) and the coming of Lycus son of Pandion into exile to Messenia (Paus. 4. 3. 6). Abundant Bronze Age remains underline the importance and population of the region: as well as the palace at Ano Englianos (*see* PYLOS in Messenia) there may be mentioned the very early tholos tomb near the north end of the Bay of Navarino, the extensive discoveries at Tragana and sites to the east of Pylos, and especially the tholos at Routsi with inlaid daggers and other finds (*ILN* 6. 4. 1957). These date from the beginning of the Mycenaean period and later. To the north, in the region of modern Kyparissia and on the borders of Triphylia discoveries have been made at Mouriatadha (tombs and 'palace') which may be Nestor's Amphigeneia, and at Peristeriá (near the village of Moira) a very large tholos and other structures which may be Helos in his kingdom. Of great interest is the possible closer connexion than elsewhere with Crete (pottery baths, and the double axe at Peristeriá, cf. *The Delphic Hymn to Apollo*, 391 ff.; also with the Lipari Islands and regions beyond (British (?) spacer beads of amber at Peristeriá).

After the Dorian conquest Messenia came under Cresphontes, whose youngest son Aepytus evicted and slew the usurper Polyphontes and gave his name to the Messenian royal line. After the First and Second Messenian Wars in the eighth and seventh centuries, associated with the heroic but unavailing leadership of Aristodemus (1) and Aristomenes (1) respectively (qq.v.), such inhabitants as had not left the country were, apart from a few communities of *perioikoi*, reduced to the status of helots, and their lands occupied by the Spartan nobility. The Third Messenian War, after the great earthquake of 464 B.C., terminated, like the first war, in the surrender of the stronghold of Ithome after a long siege. Granted a safe-conduct, many of the survivors (of the *perioikoi* only?) were settled by the Athenians at Naupactus (455). During the Peloponnesian War the Messenian helots were encouraged to sporadic revolts by the Athenian garrison established at Pylos after the victory at Sphacteria (425), in which Messenians from Naupactus played a decisive part. In 369 Messenia recovered its independence with the help of the Theban general Epaminondas. Its subsequent history is bound up with that of its new capital Messene (q.v.). It remained prosperous for a century or more. Later (in the second century) it became a pawn of greater powers until the Romans assumed full control.

Of special interest is the ancient town of Andania in the north-east on the borders of Arcadia and Elis, where Mysteries were celebrated in honour of a group of divinities, and claimed connexion with Attica and the Eleusinian Mysteries (cf. the inscription *IG* v. i. 1390 of 91 B.C.; Paus. 4. 1. 5 and 33. 4).

W. A. McDonald (on communications) in *Mycenaean Studies* (U.S.A. 1964), 217 ff.; M. N. Valmin, *Études topographiques sur la Messénie ancienne* (1930); R. Hope Simpson, 'Identifying a Mycenaean State', *BSA* 1957, 231 ff.; P-K, *GL* III. 2. 371 ff.; C. A. Roebuck, *A History of Messenia from 369 to 146 B.C.* (U.S.A. 1941); G. L. Huxley, *Early Sparta* (1962), *passim*; F. Kiechle, *Messenische Studien* (1959). A. M. W.; R. J. H.

**MESSENIA (CULTS AND MYTHS).** Since the Messenians were in a condition of serfdom between the Third Messenian War and 369 B.C., their religious and mythical traditions were disturbed to a very considerable extent. In their capital the cults as seen by Pausanias suggest partly foreign influence, partly deliberate attempts at revival. He found (4. 31. 6 ff.) temples of Poseidon and Aphrodite, such as any Greek city might have; a cult of Artemis Laphria, imported from Naupactus; shrines of Eileithyia, the Curetes (to whom holocausts of all manner of victims were offered), Demeter, Asclepius, and the local eponymous heroine Messene; also of the national hero Aristomenes, while Zeus was worshipped on Mt. Ithome under the local title Ithomatas. Some of these cults had peculiar legends connecting them with the country and polemizing against myths which claimed them for other regions. Outside the capital the most famous cult, which, however, is of Hellenistic date, is the Mysteries of Andania (Kern, *Relig. der Griechen* iii. 188 ff., and refs.; Nilsson, *GGR* i². 478, ii. 93 ff.). For a list, with references, of other cults, see Reincke in *PW* xv. 1241 (also ATARGATIS for cult of Syrian goddess).

Most of the legends of the country have come down to us in an excerpt by Pausanias of Rhianus' (q.v.) epic on the Messenian Wars (Paus. 4. 6. 1), mingled with material from other authors, as Myron of Priene (ibid.) and inquiries of his own. It is thus impossible to say how much of what he tells us is really Messenian tradition and how much Rhianus' learned imagination or the conjectures of some antiquarian. The central figure is Aristomenes, and the historical kernel nearly undiscoverable. H. J. R.

**METAGENES,** Athenian comic poet, won two victories at the Lenaea in the last decade of the fifth century B.C. (*IG* ii². 2325. 128). We have fragments of four plays; in *Thurio-Persians* Thurii is eulogized fantastically as a land of abundance (*see* CRATES 1 *and* PHERECRATES); *Ὅμηρος ἢ Ἀσκηταί* mentions (fr. 10) the betrayal of Naupactus to the Spartans in 400 (Diod. Sic. 14. 34. 2).

*FCG* ii. 751 ff.; *CAF* i. 704–10; *FAC* i. 838 ff. K. J. D.

**METALLURGY.** After extraction from the mine ore must be crushed. The use of grooved stone hammers was common in the west in early Roman times, though iron hammers replaced them slowly. Socketed stone hammers were too fragile for rough work. The broken pieces of rock were roughly sorted, all poor and sterile material being rejected. If washing was practised, the ore had to be finely milled. From Egypt there are stone rollers operated on saddle-querns, and the latter occur in Wales and the Balkans; more common and of later date are rotary millstones. Sieves were used to reduce the particles to equal size. Ore, especially when markedly denser than the gangue, can be profitably enriched by washing. This applies especially to gold, whether from placers or veins, and to lead-ore, but was used for ochre and is feasible for pyrites. Washing was often carried out in wooden bowls or cradles. Gold may be caught on rough cloth or fleece, a method attested on the Rhine, and in Colchis, where it gave rise to the Golden Fleece legend. The washing-tables at Laurium (q.v.) were well built and cemented, with several tanks to catch the ore. The washing process would normally be repeated several times. In northern Spain auriferous sediments were broken down by large volumes of water, and the washing must have been done in very large sluices, probably of wood.

Sulphide and hydrated ores are best roasted before smelting. Direct evidence for roasting has seldom been found, but certain furnaces are too large for smelting and may have served this purpose. The most primitive smelting-furnaces were banked-up bonfires or holes in the ground. The blast was at first introduced over the rim, but in Gaul some bowl-furnaces have a hole near the base and their height was raised by courses of stones round the lip. This led to the shaft-furnace, a structure often partially sunk in the ground. Vase-paintings of Greek smithies show a high-built shaft whence the bloom was extracted at the base, while the blast was introduced at the back. The shaft-furnace spread fairly rapidly through the west; some in the Jura are thought to be pre-Roman. They probably did not reach England until after the Roman period. Most shaft-furnaces have only one hole at the base, for blast and tapping, though a few in central Europe have six. Whereas in a bowl-furnace only one charge can be smelted at a time, a shaft-furnace admits of continuous production. Fuel and ore can be added down the chimney, and the metal and slag can be tapped at the base. In fact, however, they were probably cooled and demolished frequently. Slag, unless fluxes are skilfully added, will clog the tapping-hole. Only those metals which were liquefied could be tapped. An iron-bloom could be extracted only by destroying the furnace, and the great number of furnaces at some sites shows that each was used only once. The fuel was charcoal, occasionally coal or peat. The blast was by hand; water-driven bellows were an invention of the Middle Ages.

After smelting, iron had to be purified by reheating and hammering. During this process it would become slightly steeled. For weapons it was specially forged: the Romans knew how to weld bars of softer and harder steel to secure toughness without brittleness, and how to give extra hardness only to the cutting edge. Lead would be cupelled to extract silver; the Romans knew bone-ash cupels, though the more primitive method of skimming the oxidized metal from the surface was used earlier. From perhaps the sixth century B.C. gold was freed of silver by cementation with salt, and rather later with some metallic sulphide. Copper would be purified and then alloyed and cast from crucibles into the forms required.

O. Davies, *Roman Mines in Europe* (1935); U. Täckholm, *Studien über den Bergbau der römischen Kaiserzeit* (1937); C. Zschocke and E. Preuschen, *Das urzeitliche Bergbaugebiet von Mühlbach-Bischofshofen* (1932); H. Blümner, *Terminologie und Technologie* iv. 140, 222–7, 330; *Archaeologia* 1900, 113; R. J. Forbes, *Metallurgy in Antiquity* (Holland, 1950) = *Stud. Anc. Technol.* vol. viii, ix² (1964); C. Singer (ed.), *Hist. of Ancient Technology* ii² (1965), i. 2.   O. D.

## METAMORPHOSIS.

Though the word itself is not early, it describes a kind of tale quite common in Greek from Homer on, that of a magical or miraculous transformation into a new shape. The origin of such stories, which have their analogies elsewhere, e.g. in Celtic literature, may perhaps be sought partly in real or fancied resemblances between inanimate and animate objects (e.g. the snake which in *Iliad* 2. 319 turns to stone may have as its origin a stone which looked like a snake, perhaps a fossil of some kind), partly in resemblances between the movements or cries of a bird or beast and those of human beings (the nightingale's song, for instance, *see* AËDON, PHILOMELA). An aetiological story would then grow up around it. Magicians, moreover, are very commonly supposed to be able to change their own shapes and those of others, and for a like power to be ascribed to gods is quite natural. In some cases we can point to the actual object which started the legend: Pausanias (1. 21. 3) says he has seen the Niobe (q.v.) of Mt. Sipylon (apparently a rock-formation, but see Frazer ad loc.) mentioned in *Il.* 24. 614 ff.; cf. also Paus. 8. 2. 7. Collections of such legends seem to have become popular in Alexandrian times; we know, for instance, of the Ἑτεροιούμενα of Nicander, several times quoted by later writers, and Ovid's surviving *Metamorphoses* draws almost entirely on Greek sources. Hence in the later versions of many legends (*see*, for instance, AIAS 1) a metamorphosis of some kind is added of which earlier accounts have no trace.

Cf. S. Eitrem, *PW* vi A. 893 ff.   H. J. R.

## METAPONTUM (or METAPONTIUM),

early Achaean colony, just west of Tarentum (q.v.). Once large and prosperous, it survived various vicissitudes until ruined in the Second Punic War. It never fully recovered. Its site, malarial and deserted until recently, is now fertile and boasts remains of Greek temples and a modern museum. Pythagoras was buried here.

A. G. Woodhead, *The Greeks in the West* (1962).   E. T. S.

**METAURUS,** a river in Umbria flowing into the Adriatic Sea, famous as the site of a victory which was Rome's Crowning Mercy of the Hannibalic War (207 B.C.). In this valley Hasdrubal (q.v. 2), who had hoped to join his brother Hannibal, was forced to fight by the Romans, who rolled up his line.

Polyb. 11. 1–3; Livy 22. 46–9. Kromayer–Veith, *Antike Schlachtfelder* iii (1912), 424 ff.; Walbank, *Polybius* ii. 267 ff.   H. H. S.

**METANIRA** (Μετάνειρα), in mythology, wife of Celeus, king of Eleusis; she received Demeter hospitably, but spoiled her plan to make Metanira's child immortal by screaming when she saw him laid on the fire; *see* DEMETER. She had a cult in Eleusis (Paus. 1. 39. 2) near the well where Demeter sat; cf. Athenagoras, *Leg. pro Christ.* 14.

**METELLA** (1), CAECILIA (*PW* 'Caecilius' 134), daughter of L. Metellus Delmaticus (*cos.* 119 B.C.), and wife of Scaurus (q.v. 1), to whom she bore three children. After his death she married Sulla (1), to whom she bore twins, Faustus Sulla (q.v. 3) and Fausta (later wife of Milo). In 86 she escaped with them from Rome and joined him in Greece. In his dictatorship (81), when she was dying of a disease that she had perhaps caught from him, Sulla divorced her and had her carried out of his house, to avoid ritual contamination.   E. B.

**METELLA** (2), CAECILIA (*PW* 136), known only from her tomb on the Via Appia near Rome. The epitaph (*ILS* 881) calls her daughter of Creticus (i.e. Metellus 8) and wife of Crassus, probably Marcus elder son of Crassus (4).   T. J. C.

**METELLUS** (1), LUCIUS CAECILIUS (*PW* 72) (*cos.* 251 B.C.), thwarted a Carthaginian attack on Panormus, capturing the dreaded enemy war-elephants (250). The elephant was commonly portrayed on coins struck by the Metelli. Metellus was *magister equitum* in Sicily (249), consul II (247), Pontifex Maximus (243–221) and dictator to hold elections (224). He was blinded when saving the Palladium from the burning Temple of Vesta (241) and died in 221.   H. H. S.

**METELLUS** (2), QUINTUS CAECILIUS (*PW* 81), son of (1), served as consul (206 B.C.) against Hannibal in Bruttium. In 205 he was dictator to hold the elections, and in 204 championed Scipio against Fabius in the Pleminius (q.v.) scandal. He served on the land commission for African veterans (201–200) and on embassies to Greece (185) and the Peloponnese (183). He was an enemy of Naevius (q.v.) and an orator of note (Malcovati, *ORF*² 9 ff.).   H. H. S.

**METELLUS** (3) **MACEDONICUS,** QUINTUS CAECILIUS (*PW* 94), *cos.* 143 B.C., praetor in 148, he suppressed Andriscus (q.v.), and in 146 opened the campaign against the Achaean Confederacy. He was awarded a triumph, but secured the consulship only at the third attempt. In 143 and 142 he suppressed all the rebellious Celtiberians except the inhabitants of Numantia (q.v.) and Termantia. In 133 he was a severe critic of Tiberius Gracchus (q.v. 3), and for much of his career he was hostile also to Scipio (q.v. 11) Aemilianus. As censor in 131 he delivered a famous speech urging compulsory marriage in order to stimulate the birth-rate. In 121 he participated in the attack on Gaius Gracchus (q.v. 4). He was eloquent, a capable general, a stern disciplinarian, and he did much to make his family outstanding in the political life of the next generation. When he died in 115 three of his four sons had already achieved the consulship. His public buildings included the Porticus Metelli.

Malcovati, *ORF*² 106; H. Simon, *Roms Kriege in Spanien* (1962), 102; De Sanctis, *Stor. Rom.* iv. 3. 124, 234; A. E. Astin, *Scipio Aemilianus* (1967).          A. E. A.

**METELLUS** (4) **BALIARICUS**, QUINTUS CAECILIUS (*PW* 82), son of (3), as consul (123 B.C.) and proconsul conquered the Baleares, and settled 3,000 Italians in Palma and Pollentia. He triumphed in 121 and was censor in 120 with Piso (q.v. 1).          E. B.

**METELLUS** (5) **DELMATICUS**, LUCIUS CAECILIUS (*PW* 91), grandson of (2), consul in 119 B.C., opposed the law of Marius on election procedure. He attacked and defeated the Delmatae (*see* DALMATIA), triumphing in 117 and rebuilding two temples from the spoils. As Pontifex Maximus he tried three Vestals accused of unchastity, acquitting two (114—*see* CASSIUS 4). His daughter Metella (q.v. 1) married Scaurus (q.v. 1) and later Sulla (q.v. 1).          E. B.

**METELLUS** (6) **NUMIDICUS**, QUINTUS CAECILIUS (*PW* 97), brother of (5). Elected consul (109 B.C.) to finish the war against Jugurtha (q.v.), he won two battles (one at the river Muthul) and stormed several towns (including Zama and Thala) with the help of his legates Marius (q.v. 1) and Rutilius (q.v. 1), but made little progress in guerrilla war. Marius, asking leave to stand for a consulate, was insulted by him and intrigued against him among officers and businessmen in Numidia and *equites* in Rome, until he was finally elected consul (107) and, by a special law, appointed to succeed him. In Rome, Metellus met great hostility, was put on trial (but acquitted), and finally triumphed when public feeling veered round in 106. Censor in 102, he tried to expel Saturninus (q.v. 1) and Glaucia (q.v.) from the Senate, but was prevented by his colleague and cousin, Metellus Caprarius (*cos.* 113). In 100, manœuvred into being the only senator to refuse the oath to observe Saturninus' agrarian law, he had to go into exile. Attempts to recall him after Saturninus' death were opposed by Marius and his friends, but supported by the widespread Metellan family (led by his son (7)) and were ultimately successful. He returned in glory (99 or 98), but was never again prominent.

On his exile, E. S. Gruen, *Latomus* 1965, 576 ff.          E. B.

**METELLUS** (7) **PIUS**, QUINTUS CAECILIUS (*PW* 98), son of (6), acquired a name from his *pietas* in working for his father's return from exile. As praetor (89 or 88 B.C.), he enrolled enfranchised Italians, including his friend Archias (q.v.); he then served in the Social War, defeating Poppaedius (q.v.). Unable to defend Rome against Cinna (q.v. 1), he went into exile in Africa (87), retaining his *imperium*, and after Cinna's death collected a private army there. Defeated by the governor, he joined Sulla, thus giving him the formal approval of the Optimates, and conquered most of northern Italy for him. Made Pontifex Maximus and consul as Sulla's colleague (80), he was next sent to fight against Sertorius (q.v.) in Spain, where his movements can be traced in places named after him: Metellinum (*Medellin*), Castra Caecilia (near *Cáceres*), and Vicus Caecilius (north of the Tagus). Unsuccessful until joined (against his will) by Pompey, he then won several victories, founded settlements, and acquired many clients, but offended opinion by excessive luxury and display. Returning (71), he—unlike Pompey— dismissed his army, triumphed, then lived in retirement until *c.* 63.

**METELLUS** (8) **CRETICUS**, QUINTUS CAECILIUS (*PW* 87), grandson of (3), perhaps praetor in 74 B.C. as colleague of Verres (q.v.), whom (with other Metelli) he supported in 70. Consul in 69 (with Hortensius, q.v. 2), he was next sent to Crete to eradicate piracy (*see* ANTONIUS 2). He fought successfully and captured many Cretan towns until Pompey tried to replace him under the law of Gabinius (q.v. 2). Having equal *imperium*, he ignored Pompey, who was soon called away to succeed Lucullus (q.v. 2). Crete became a province, but Metellus' triumph was delayed until 62 and he led the opposition to Pompey. He died in the late 50s.          E. B.

**METELLUS** (9) **CELER**, QUINTUS CAECILIUS (*PW* 86), grandson of (4), and husband of Clodia (q.v.), was legate of his brother-in-law Pompey (66 B.C.); as praetor (63), he took a leading part in the farce of the trial of Rabirius (q.v. 1) and was given Cisalpina and a special command against the Catilinarians at the request of Cicero, yet he supported his brother (10) against him (see Cic. *Fam.* 5. 1–2). Consul (60), he turned against Pompey (who had divorced Mucia, q.v.) and in 59 opposed Caesar. He died before he could go to his province (Transalpina).          E. B.

**METELLUS** (10) **NEPOS**, QUINTUS CAECILIUS (*PW* 96), brother of (9), was legate of Pompey in 67 B.C. and perhaps until 63, when he was elected tribune for 62. He harassed Cicero and, with the support of Caesar, tried to win a special command against Catiline for Pompey; when he and Caesar were suspended from office, he fled to Pompey. He was praetor (60) and perhaps governor of a Gallic province. Consul (57) with Lentulus (q.v. 5), he proposed Pompey's *cura annonae*, did not oppose Cicero's return from exile, but protected Clodius (q.v. 1). Proconsul in Hither Spain, he called in at the Luca meeting on the way. He died soon after his return to Rome.          E. B.

**METELLUS** (11) **PIUS (SCIPIO)**, QUINTUS CAECILIUS (*PW* 99), consul in 52 B.C., was son of Nasica (pr. 93; for the family see Cic. *Brut.* 211–12). He was adopted by Metellus (q.v. 7) Pius, possibly by will. Tribune in 59, and probably praetor in 55, he was (although now a plebeian) *interrex* in 53, and then became candidate for the consulate of 52. The elections were abortive, and Pompey (q.v.), who had recently married Scipio's daughter (widow of P. Crassus, q.v. 8), became sole consul: but he rescued his father-in-law from a bribery charge and made him his colleague in July. Thenceforward Scipio led the attack on Caesar and proposed the decisive motion in Jan. 49. The Senate granted him Syria, whence in 48 he brought two legions to Thessaly; he commanded the centre at Pharsalus. He escaped to Africa and became supreme general in the Bellum Africum. Caesar tried to bribe Scipio before Pharsalus, but detested him, and wrote a bitter passage on his activities in Syria (*BCiv.* 3. 31–3). Cicero despised him as a man ignorant of his family tradition (*Att.* 6. 1. 17). But his dying words in reply to the Caesarian soldiers who sought him out after Thapsus, 'Imperator se bene habet', passed into 'Republican' legend (cf. Livy, *Epit.* 114).          G. E. F. C.

**METEOROLOGY.** Although nature and natural phenomena had already been considered at length by the pre-Socratic philosophers, and though the word μετεωρο-λογία occurs in Plato (*Phdr.* 270 a), it was left to Aristotle to give an exact definition of what was comprised in the subject. In his four epoch-making books on meteorology he distinguished the respective spheres of meteorology and general natural science with great accuracy, confining the term meteorology to the study of the processes, conditions, and phenomena of the atmosphere. Aristotle's work was continued by Theophrastus and the Epicureans, to whom Lucretius is greatly indebted in the meteorological sections of his poem. Lucretius also made extensive use of Posidonius, who, looking upon meteorology as the doctrine of the structure of the outer and upper world, had fitted it into a system of thought uniting harmoniously matter, mind, and spirit. It is still possible to reconstruct Posidonius' meteorological system, since his book was the main source of the two most important contributions to post-Aristotelian meteorology that have survived, namely Seneca's *Naturales quaestiones* and the poem *Aetna*. After the first century A.D. students of meteorology confined themselves to summarizing and popularizing the discoveries of their forerunners, which, through the Graeco-Byzantine commentators on Aristotle, came to be known to, and to exercise a beneficent influence upon, the scientific achievements of the Arabs.

TEXTS. Aristotle, *Meteorologicorum Libri quattuor*, ed. F. H. Fobes (1919); *Aetna*, ed. S. Sudhaus (1898); Alexander Aphrodisiensis' and Johannes Philoponus' commentaries on Aristotle, ed. M. Hayduck (1899, 1901). Useful selections are given in T. L. Heath, *Greek Astronomy* (1932).

GENERAL LITERATURE. O. Gilbert, *Die meteorologischen Theorien des griech. Altertums* (1907); W. Capelle, *PW* Suppl. iv. 315 ff.; H. Strohm, *Untersuch. z. Entwicklungs-Gesch. d. aristot. Meteorologie* (1935); G. Bergsträsser, *Neue meteor. Fragm. d. Theophrast* (*Sitz. Heidelberg*, 1918). P. T.

## METICS.

In Greek States metics (μέτοικοι) were resident aliens who had acquired a definite status distinguishing them from other foreigners and giving them a recognized place in the community. There were commonly three groups of foreigners: temporary visitors, more permanent residents who had not attained the status of metics, and metics. Among the latter, in turn, some were distinguished by grants of special privileges. Metics were found in many States, but those of Athens are best known. There each metic must have a citizen as sponsor (*prostates*), must be registered in the deme in which he resided, and must pay an annual head tax (*metoikion*) amounting to twelve drachmas for a man and six for a woman not a member of the household of a husband or son. They could also be called on to assume liturgies—though not the trierarchy—and contributed to the *eisphorai*, probably more in proportion than citizens. Metics could not contract legal marriages with citizens and could not own houses or land unless they had received *enktesis* through a special grant. In return they had a share in the life of the community and received the protection of the courts, though the exact role of the *prostates* in court procedure remains a matter of dispute. Metics served in the army in separate divisions and were also used as oarsmen in the fleet. The privileges sometimes granted included *enktesis*, remission of financial burdens, equality with citizens in financial matters, and the right to serve alongside of citizens in the army. Metics were important chiefly in commerce and industry.

A. E. Zimmern, *The Greek Commonwealth*[5] (1931), index; M. Clerc, *Les Métèques athéniens* (1893), and *De la condition des étrangers domiciliés dans les différentes cités grecques* (1898); G. Busolt, *Griechische Staatskunde* (1920–6), 292 ff.; A. H. M. Jones *Athenian Democracy* (1957), index; V. Ehrenberg, *The Greek State* (1960), 38 *et passim*. J. A. O. L.

## METIS

(Μῆτις), counsel personified. She was the consort of Zeus (Hesiod, *Theog.* 886 ff.) and wisest of gods and men. By the advice of Earth and Heaven Zeus beguiled her into letting him swallow her when she was pregnant, since he knew she would first bear Athena and then another child, very mighty, who would become ruler of the universe. Having swallowed her, he had her always with him to advise him, and Athena (q.v.) was in due time born from his head (924 ff.). The story would seem to be an early and crude blend of myth and allegory. H. J. R.

## METON

(Μέτων), Athenian astronomer (5th c. B.C.), cited (with Euctemon) for observations of the summer solstice including one in 432 B.C., the reliability of which was questioned by both Hipparchus and Ptolemy (*Almag.* iii. 1). Meton also suggested a system of regular intercalation over a period of nineteen years (the Metonic cycle so-called) to bring the lunar month into correlation with the solar year; this cycle contained 235 lunar months (seven of which were intercalary) and 6,940 days, and gave a mean lunar month about 2 minutes too long and a solar year of $365\frac{5}{19}$ days ($6,940 \div 19$). Thus every seventy-six years the moon and the sun would be out of step by one day; 100 years later this was corrected by Callippus, who combined four Metonic cycles less one day into a new cycle of seventy-six years or 27,759 days. According to Geminus (*Isag.* ch. 8), who mentions Euctemon but not Meton in connexion with the nineteen-year cycle, of the 235 months 110 were 'hollow', i.e. of 29 days each, and 125 'full', i.e. of 30 days each. There is no evidence that the Metonic cycle ever came into regular use for the civil calendar of Athens; its purpose was to provide a fixed system of reckoning for dating astronomical observations, and it was soon superseded by the Callippic cycle which is regularly used by Hipparchus and Ptolemy. Meton appears as a character in Aristophanes' *Birds* (992 ff.) as a comic 'town-planner'. D. R. D.

## METRAGYRTES

(Μητραγύρτης), a mendicant servitor of Cybele. *Metragyrtai* travelled in bands, begging, dancing, and prophesying. They were known to fifth-century Athens, and Cicero (*Leg.* 2. 22 and 40; cf. Dion. Hal. *Ant. Rom.* 2. 19) implies that these *famuli* were tolerated at Rome. They were generally eunuchs (q.v.), the Galli. Similar *agyrtai* (cf. Pl. *Resp.* 364 b) existed in other cults, chiefly oriental, and Apuleius (*Met.* books 8–9) gives a lively picture of those of the *dea Syria*. An inscription of Syria (*BCH* 1897, 59, no. 68) records the collections made on his travels by one such δοῦλος of Atargatis (cf. *SEG* vii. 358, 801). *See* ANATOLIAN DEITIES.

H. Graillot, *Le Culte de Cybèle* (1912), ch. 8; L. Ziehen, *Leges Graecorum Sacrae* ii (1906), 301 ff., no. 116. F. R. W.

## METRE, GREEK

I. GENERAL PRINCIPLES

(1) The ancient metricians, of whom Hephaestion (q.v. 2) is the chief, do not help us greatly towards an understanding of Greek metric, and it is unlikely that they represent a tradition dating back to the classical period. We are thus mainly dependent on what we can ourselves discover from the poetry. A full appreciation of the Greek metres is rendered extremely difficult for us by the fact that we are accustomed in English verse to rhythms based on stress (which is solely determined by the sense), the differentiation between long and short syllables being virtually obliterated. Greek verse, on the other hand, whether it contained an element of stress or not (see below), is based principally upon a precise differentiation of time values, without the least relation to the sense of the words; and for this there are parallels in the verse of eastern nations. It is very doubtful if our ears, accustomed from childhood to stressed verse, are capable of being trained to a full appreciation of quantitative verse. Further, in two fundamental matters we are left in uncertainty. (a) Was there a verse stress (*ictus*)?* (b) To what extent, if any, were the time values

* In Greek metric long elements, *longa* ('syllables' is an unsuitable term, since we are concerned with the parts of a verse-form, not with the parts of a word), usually alternate with short elements, *brevia*, or with pairs of *brevia* (sometimes, as in the dactylic hexameter and anapaestic dimeter, fused into single long elements, — — or ∪∪ or ∪∪—), or with elements in which either a short or a long syllable is allowed, *ancipitia* (e.g. the first element of the iambic metron ×—∪—). In the ionic (∪∪——) and dochmius ∪——∪—) two *longa* are juxtaposed. In many cases a *longum* may

inherent in the syllables altered by the music in lyric (sung) verse?

(2) *Ictus.* The case for ictus is mainly based on (a) the alleged inconceivability of verse—particularly verse associated with dancing, marching, and other movements of the body—without ictus, (b) the alleged difficulty of differentiating between –∪∪ dactyl and –∪∪ anapaest and between long, or between short, elements in a series of longs or of shorts, without ictus, and (c) the fact that certain lengthenings of short syllables occur in Homer far more often in 'arsis' than in 'thesis'. The opponents of ictus answer that verse without ictus is found in certain Eastern literatures, and that (b) may be disposed of by assuming slight variations in the values of long and of short elements. They also point out that there is no evidence in ancient theory for ictus, since this and other terms denoting striking (e.g. *percussio*) were used simply for the marking off of the parts of a verse by beating time, and they infer from this that ictus did not exist—an argument *ex silentio* which is hardly conclusive. Kalinka (Bursian, *Jahresb.* 250. 332–9) sums up the evidence. It is impossible to decide with any certainty between the contending views.

(3) In lyric iambics and trochaics a short element often seems to be omitted, ∪–∪– appearing alongside of –∪– or ∪–– and –∪–∪ of –∪– or –∪–∪; e.g. Aesch. *Ag.* 385 βιᾶται δ᾽ ἁ τάλαινα πειθώ; Eur. *Phoen.* 1025 χαλαῖσί τ᾽ ὠμοσίτοις. Sometimes this occurs in two consecutive feet, so that we have –– instead of either ∪–∪– or –∪–∪; e.g. Eur. *Phoen.* 1039 βροντᾷ δὲ στεναγμός (––∪–∪). Similarly, by omission of the last long element, we find ∪∪–– among minor ionics (∪∪––). This dropping of an element ('syncopation') is particularly common at the close of a colon, where it is termed 'catalexis' (e.g. –∪–∪ ∪––and –∪–∪ –∪–). Ancient metricians spoke also of 'brachy-catalexis' when two elements are omitted (e.g. what they analysed as ∪–∪– –– and –∪–∪ ––). Catalexis is common in spoken, as well as in sung, iambics and trochaics. Further, the anapaestic dimeter ∪∪–∪∪– ∪∪–∪∪– has its catalectic form ∪∪–∪∪– ∪∪––, in which *two* short elements are omitted.

Was the time value of the suppressed short element, or elements, actually missing? Or was it supplied by the compensatory lengthening of the following, or preceding, long element? In general, to what extent, if any, did the music alter the time values? These questions cannot be answered with certainty. The remains of ancient Greek music (*see* MUSIC, §§ 11–13) almost all have metrical as well as pitch signs, but they are extremely scanty, and only one, the music to a few dochmiacs from Euripides' *Orestes*, may go back to the fifth century B.C. This records no musical alterations of the metrical values. On the other hand the Seikilos inscription (not earlier than 2nd c. B.C.) provides clear examples of long elements protracted after† missing shorts both in catalexis and earlier in the colon, and the hymns attributable to Mesomedes (early 2nd c. A.D. ?) give similar evidence as regards catalexis. (The Berlin paean goes much further in altering the metrical values of the elements.) State-

be 'resolved' into two *brevia*, and substitution of this *biceps* for *anceps* and *breve* is sometimes allowed (e.g. ∪∪– for ×– or ∪– in iambics). The Lesbian poets, Sappho and Alcaeus, do not allow the resolution of *longa* or the fusion of *brevia* except in dactylic hexameters.

This question has often been asked with reference to the 'arsis'. That term, applied to the *longa*, originally (probably) signifies the lifting of the foot, 'thesis', applied to the elements (*brevia* or *ancipitia*) between the *longa*, its placing on the ground. Arsis should therefore mean the weak beat, thesis the strong beat—if such a distinction existed. The modern terminology has inverted the meanings of the two terms. Wrong as it is, it has (at least in England) become canonical.

† It may be noted that protraction *after* a missing element is alien to our modern rhythmic instinct. We rhythmize 'A captain bold from Halifax, who dwelt in country quar-ar-ters', not 'quarter-ers'.

ments of ancient metrists about protraction after missing short elements are thus corroborated for the first century A.D. We have no proof, though the assumption is a reasonable one, that protraction was employed in the fifth century B.C. and earlier.

(4) *Line and colon.* Modern verse is built up of a succession of 'lines', the ending of a line being marked by the end of a word. Greek epic and elegiac verse and the spoken metres of tragedy and comedy are constructed on the same principle. The last element of the line is always a *longum.* For the pause at the end of the line makes the prosodic length of the final syllable indifferent, and thus a short syllable can fill a long element (*syllaba brevis in elemento longo*).

Greek lyric verse, though sometimes built on the repetition of a line (κατὰ στίχον composition, see IV), far more often consists of a varied combination of shorter entities termed 'cola', which are nevertheless long enough (about eight elements) to possess a definite character as metrical entities. These cola sometimes consist of homogeneous parts (e.g. two iambic metra or four dactyls), sometimes of heterogeneous parts (e.g. the glyconic). In places they are divided off from each other by hiatus or *syllaba brevis in elemento longo*, which clearly mark a pause in the rhythmic flow. In other places they are linked together by 'enjambement', the run-over of a word from one colon into the next. In many places there is only diaeresis,* which may or may not indicate a pause. If we are to use the word 'line' at all in such cases, we can only use it of the whole series of cola between one pause and the next; and modern texts of Pindar are in fact printed in such long 'lines'. In the lyrics of drama, where a metrical system is seldom repeated more than once, we have often not sufficient data on which to determine the pauses and to divide up the structure into its lines. (These pauses do not invariably coincide with the ends of sentences or clauses, which in fact often end in quite different places in strophe and antistrophe; and the view that the tolerance of hiatus is in any way dependent on punctuation is untenable.) See further under IV.

## II. The Metres of Epic, Elegiac, and Dramatic Dialogue

The lines are divided at fixed places by word-endings, either caesura or diaeresis.

(1) The dactylic hexameter, used by epic, didactic, and pastoral poets, consists of six feet,† the last of which must be a spondee. The first four are either dactyls or spondees, and the fifth, while almost always a dactyl, is occasionally a spondee. The line is divided by caesura somewhere near the middle. The commonest caesuras are (i) 'penthemimeral' (after 5/2 feet, μῆνιν ἄειδε, θεά: (ii) after the trochee of the third foot, ἄνδρα μοι ἔννεπε, Μοῦσα. (iii) The 'hephthemimeral' caesura (after 7/2 feet), ὅς κε θεοῖς ἐπιπείθηται, is rarer. Diaeresis after the fourth foot (which then must be a dactyl) is particularly characteristic of the pastoral poets, and is hence termed 'bucolic'. The ending of a word after the third foot without caesura in that foot is strictly avoided. After the trochee of the fourth foot it is rare in Homer and Hesiod and nearly excluded afterwards.

(2) The elegiac couplet consists of a dactylic hexameter followed by a dactylic pentameter (or rather 2 × 2½ metra, i.e. two *hemiepe*; see III. 5). The first half of the pentameter allows, the second does not allow, the

* Diaeresis means division between words at the end of a foot or colon; caesura, division within a foot.

† In dactyls the *metron*, or unit of measurement, is the foot; in iambics, trochaics, and anapaests it is the dipody, consisting of two feet. The term 'foot' is somewhat misleading when applied to these last three metres, implying as it does that there is a division after the second element; but its use is convenient for practical purposes.

substitution of spondees for dactyls. Diaeresis is invariably observed between the two halves.

(3) The iambic trimeter is used by the iambographers and is the main metre of dramatic dialogue. It consists of 6 feet (3 metra). There is normally caesura either in the 3rd foot (Soph. *Ant.* 8) or in the 4th (*Ant.* 1). In tragedy spondees are allowed in the 1st, 3rd, and 5th feet, tribrachs (resolved iambi) in the first four and occasionally in the 5th, dactyls (resolved spondees) in the 1st and 3rd, and anapaests (sparingly) in the 1st. Resolved feet become increasingly common in Euripides' later plays. Where a word ends before – ∪ – at the end of the line the preceding syllable is always (or almost always) short (Porson's law), but, e.g., αὖθίς μοι φράσον (Eur. *Hel.* 471) and ἐκ δεμνίων (Eur. *Tro.* 495) are allowed, since in the former case the enclitic μοι looks back, in the latter the preposition looks forward. The comic trimeter allows anapaests in all feet but the last, and is not bound by Porson's law. The *scazon* ('Limper') or *choliambus* is a form of iambic trimeter used by Hipponax and other iambographers, having a spondee in the last foot.

(4) Occasionally, especially in moments of excitement (e.g. Aesch. *Ag.* 1649–73), tragedy employs the trochaic tetrameter catalectic (see I. 3), – ∪ – × – ∪ – × – ∪ – × – ∪ –, which, according to Arist. *Poet.* 1449ᵃ21, was the original metre of dialogue. It is also employed in comedy. Always in tragedy, usually in comedy, there is diaeresis after the second metron.

The dialogue metres of comedy are more numerous, and looser, than those of tragedy. The following are peculiar to comedy.

(5) Iambic tetrameter catalectic, × – ∪ – × – ∪ – × – ∪ – ∪ – –, usually with diaeresis after the third dimeter. Closely connected with this is the *Pnigos* ('Suffocator', a patter metre), of iambic metra, ending with a catalectic dimeter; e.g. Ar. *Ran.* 971–91, following catalectic tetrameters. There is often enjambement between dimeters (Ar. *Eq.* 911–40).

(6) The anapaestic tetrameter catalectic, ∪∪ – ∪∪ – ∪∪ – ∪∪ – ∪∪ – ∪∪ – ∪ ∪ – –, is a dignified metre. The Just Argument and 'Aeschylus' use it (*Nub.* 961 ff., *Ran.* 1006 ff.), while the Unjust Argument and 'Euripides' use the less noble iambic tetrameter catalectic (*Nub.* 1036 ff., *Ran.* 907 ff.). Spondees, and also dactyls, can take the place of anapaests; but anapaest following dactyl (producing ∪∪∪∪) is avoided. Diaeresis occurs after the second metron.

(7) The eupolidean consists of a 'polyschematist' choriambic dimeter, ∘∘ – × – ∪∪ – (see III. 12. ii), followed by ∘∘ – × – ∪ –.* See J. W. White, *Verse of Greek Comedy* (1912), §§ 508, 528; e.g. Ar. *Nub.* 518–62. This appearance of polyschematism in spoken verse is certainly remarkable.

(8) Anapaestic dimeter, ∪∪ – ∪∪ – ∪∪ – ∪∪ – –. Spondee and dactyl may be substituted for anapaest, but only very rarely does an anapaest directly follow a dactyl, producing a series of four shorts. Diaeresis separates the metra. At frequent intervals the series of acatalectic dimeters is broken by a catalectic one, ∪∪ – ∪∪ – ∪∪ – –, called a 'paroemiac' because proverbial expressions (παροιμίαι) are often contained in cola of a similar type. Only after a paroemiac is 'pause' (see I. 4) allowed.

### III. THE METRES OF LYRIC VERSE

Some Greek lyric metres are, like the metres discussed under II, formed by the regular repetition of a single measure, iambic, dactylic, etc.; others, e.g. the glyconic and choriambic dimeter, by the combination of diverse entities within the limits of the colon. In some, e.g.

* ∘∘ means – ∪ or ∪ – but not ∪ ∪.

the archilochean dicolon and dactylo-epitrites, the basis of the rhythm is formed by two diverse cola.

The principal metres of Greek lyric poetry are as follows.

(1) *Iambics*. At times dimeters and trimeters are well defined. At others, the iambics run on continuously for a considerable stretch without obvious breaks (e.g. Aesch. *Ag.* 768–70). Resolutions are allowed, as in spoken iambic trimeters, producing tribrachs and dactyls. The anapaest is rare in lyric iambics, but should perhaps be recognized, e.g. at Soph. *Phil.* 141. Syncopation (see I. 3) is common in tragedy, e.g. Aesch. *Supp.* 138–40 ∪ – – – ∪ – ∪ – ∪ – – – ∪ – ∪ – –. Certain combinations of syncopation are frequent, e.g. the trimeter ∪ – – ∪ – ∪ – (Aesch. *Ag.* 376, etc.). At *El.* 504–15 Sophocles produces a beautiful effect by combining resolutions and syncopations. Often a choriamb (– ∪∪ –) is substituted for an iambic metron ('choriambic anaclasis'), e.g. Aesch. *Supp.* 783.

(2) *Trochaics* are frequent in the lyrics of comedy (e.g. Ar. *Ran.* 589–604), rare in tragedy. The catalectic dimeter goes back to Alcman's *Partheneion*, and is called 'lecythion' because identical (in its resolved form, – ∪ ∪͡∪ – ∪ – ∪ –) with ληκύθιον ἀπώλεσεν (Ar. *Ran.* 1208 ff.): series of lecythia at Eur. *Phoen.* 239–245. The brachycatalectic dimeter (see I. 3) is termed *ithyphallic* – ∪ – ∪ – –). Aesch. *Ag.* 160–6 and Eur. *Hel.* 348–59 illustrate resolution and syncopation (– – ∪ and – – for trochaic metron). Cf. also Eur. *Cyc.* 608–23.

(3) *Cretics* are common in comedy (e.g. Ar. *Eq.* 304–10, with first paeon*), rare in tragedy. But Aeschylus turns the fourth paeon to magnificent account at *Eum.* 328–9, and for the first paeon cf. *Supp.* 418–22. Two hymns of the second century B.C. (Diehl, *Anth. Lyr. Graec.* ii. 303–9) are written in cretics and paeons.

(4) *Anapaests*. Lyric anapaests, sometimes called 'threnodic', but not confined to lamentation, differ from the normal anapaests of II. 8 in the frequency of paroemiacs, the preponderance of long syllables, and the occasional neglect of diaeresis between metra. Ar. *Ran.* 372–7 (a slow march); Eur. *Ion* 859–922 (a lament). Resolution of the long syllable (giving ∪ ∪ ∪ ∪, 'proceleusmatic') is allowed.

The close combination of iambics with trochees (e.g. Pind. *Ol.* 2. 1 ∪ – ∪ – – – ∪ – –) and with anapaests (Eur. *El.* 586, 588, 590) is sometimes found. The swing from iambics to trochaics is capable of charming effects (Eur. *Hel.* 361–3) and humorous ones (Ar. *Ran.* 209–68).

(5) *Dactyls*. Continuous hexameters are occasionally found (e.g. Sappho's *Epithalamia*, frs. 104 ff., Soph. *Trach.* 1010–14, Ar. *Ran.* 1528–33). Cratinus and other comic poets often use them for burlesque. But the tetrameter is far commoner. (As in the hexameter, an admixture of spondees is allowed.) Alcman and Anacreon wrote 'whole strophae and songs' in tetrameters (Heph. cap. 7; cf. Alcm. fr. 17), and Sophocles loves them, constantly mixing them with other metres with beautiful effect (*El.* 124–36). Pentameters and dimeters (called *adonei*, from the cry ὦ τὸν Ἄδωνιν) are found, also catalectic cola of varying lengths. For the trimeter see *hemiepes* below. Aeschylus frequently composes dactyls in a continuous stream, with no perceptible division into cola (e.g. *Pers.* 852–907, with many ithyphallic and related clausulae). Purely, or mainly, dactylic systems are Aesch. *Ag.* 104–21, Soph. *OT* 151–8, Eur. *Phoen.* 784–800. For the association of dactyls with iambics, cf. Archil. fr. 104, Eur. *Hipp.* 1120–30; with trochaics, Eur. *Cyc.* 608–23, Ar. *Lys.* 1279–90, and *Eccl.* 1168 ff. (the salad song).

* The paeon is a cretic with one long syllable resolved. The 'first' paeon is – ∪∪∪, the 'fourth', ∪∪∪ –. The 'second' and 'third' exist in theory only.

'Aeolic', or 'lesbian', dactyls (Sappho, Alcaeus) have a free first foot of two syllables and a cretic close: e.g. the 'fourteen-syllable sapphic' in which Sappho wrote her second book (Heph. cap. 7. 23), × × –⏑⏑–⏑⏑ –⏑⏑–⏑–.

The 'ibycean', –⏑⏑–⏑⏑–⏑–, is perhaps to be explained as a dactylo-trochaic tetrapody catalectic (Ibyc. fr. 5. 1–3, followed by normal dactylic tetrapodies). But in the lyrics of drama the same combination of elements is probably nothing else than a glyconic with dactylic opening.

The dactylic trimeter catalectic and acatalectic, –⏑⏑–⏑⏑– and –⏑⏑–⏑⏑– –, or *hemiepes*, often occurs in dactylic systems, and forms one of the two parts of the dactylo-epitrite (see below). It is sometimes repeated in a series, either one form being used throughout, or the two in combination: Aesch. *Pers.* 584–90; Soph. *Trach.* 113–15; Eur. *Tro.* 1094–8.

(6) The placing of ⏑, –, or ⏑⏑ before the two types of hemiepes, as a spring-off, produces ⏓⏓ –⏑⏑–⏑⏑– and ⏓⏓ –⏑⏑–⏑⏑– –, sometimes called *prosodiac* and *enoplion* (but these terms are not used consistently by modern metricians, nor are they confined to the two cola cited here). For ⏑⏑ in the first and second dactyls, – and ⏑ are sometimes substituted. *Rhes.* 895–8: *Med.* 435–7, cf. 849–53.

(7) The *dochmius* ('slanter'), of which the basic forms are ⏑– –⏑– and –⏑⏑–⏑–, is rarely found before the tragedians, by whom it is much used in agitated lamentations (e.g. Aesch. *Sept.* 78–180). The first and fourth elements may be long (– – – –) among spondaic anapaests, Eur. *Hec.* 182, 190, 193). Resolutions are frequent, but the rhythm can be felt through all the multiplicity of the transformations. Dochmiacs are often associated with iambics, anapaests, and cretics (Aesch. *Ag.* 1156–66, *PV* 574–88, Eur. *Ion* 1445–67). ⏑– – – (Eur. *Hel.* 657, 680–1) is perhaps a syncopated dochmius (⏑–[⏑]–). –⏑–⏑– (Soph. *OT* 1208–10, Eur. *Or.* 992–4) is possibly to be interpreted as a *hypodochmius* or 'anaclastic' dochmius, inverting the first two elements.

(8) *Glyconics* are first found in Sappho, Alcaeus, and Anacreon. The metre is × × –⏑⏑–⏑–. The catalectic form, *pherecratean*, × × –⏑⏑– –, usually comes after every few glyconics. (But at Ar. *Thesm.* 359–66 there is a long series of glyconics, at Aesch. *Sept.* 295–300 a series of pherecrateans. The metre may perhaps be, in origin, a form of aeolic dactyls, manifesting the same freedom in the first foot. Pindar has many glyconics. In drama Aeschylus has few (apart from short stanzas at the end of a system, e.g. *Ag.* 381–4), Sophocles, Euripides, and Aristophanes have many (e.g. Soph. *OC* 1211–18, Eur. *Andr.* 501–14, Ar. *Eq.* 973–84). The penultimate syllable is occasionally long (e.g. Eur. *Hipp.* 141). At the opening, ⏑⏑ is not used in drama; ⏑⏑⏑ is rare in Sophocles, common in Euripides.

(9) The *telesilleion*, or 'acephalous' glyconic, is a glyconic docked of its first element* (Telesilla, fr. 1, Soph. *OC* 1044–6, Ar. *Av.* 1731–4). An acephalous pherecratean (⏓ –⏑⏑– –) forms the metre of the Rhodian *Swallow Song*, ἦλθ᾽ ἦλθε χελιδών (*Carm. Pop.* 2), and is common in Pindar and drama. It is sometimes called a *reizianum* after the German scholar Reiz, and the same name is applied to the acephalous choriambic dimeter (see (12)) catalectic ([–] ⏑⏑– ⏑––). For the two forms cf. Eur. *Alc.* 908–10. The term *reizianum* has also been stretched to include the colon × –⏑– –.

(10) The glyconic may be extended* to various lengths. The *hipponacteum* (Eur. *Bacch.* 902, 904, 906) has one extra

---

* This is a convenient way of putting the matter. It cannot, however, be assumed as by any means certain that the 'acephalous' cola described in this section actually came into existence through such a process of decapitation, or the longer cola by a process of extension.

---

element at its end. The *phalaecean hendecasyllable* adds ⏑ – – to the glyconic: e.g. the first two lines of the Harmodius skolion metre, ἐν μύρτου κλαδὶ τὸ ξίφος φορήσω (*scol. anon.* 12) and Soph. *Aj.* 697, 700. This ⏑ – – is probably a syncopated iambic metron: cf. Soph. *Ant.* 816 glyc. + spondee. Sometimes, again, a full iambic metron follows or precedes the glyc. (Alc. fr. 357, Soph. *Aj.* 600–1, 624–5).

(11) The minor asclepiad (× × –⏑⏑– –⏑⏑–⏑–, e.g. Alc. fr. 350. 1 ἦλθες ἐκ περάτων γᾶς ἐλεφαντίναν) has sometimes been explained on the assumption that a glyconic is × × plus –⏑⏑– plus ⏑–, and that therefore an extra choriamb can be inserted in the middle. A more natural method is to explain it as a fusion of two short cola which are often found, o o –⏑⏑– and –⏑⏑ –⏑–. But some colour is lent to the first view by the existence of the major asclepiad, or 'sixteen-syllable sapphic (× × –⏑⏑– –⏑⏑– –⏑⏑–⏑–, e.g. Alc. fr. 94, Soph. *Phil.* 175–6), which is not easy to explain except on the assumption that *two* choriambs are inserted.

(12) The *choriambic dimeter* assumes, broadly speaking, two forms:

(i) A strict form, in which the first or the second half is a choriamb, the other an iambic metron (Soph. *Trach.* 116–21, Ar. *Eq.* 551–8: cf. Anacr. fr. 54).

(ii) A free form, styled 'polyschematist' ('of many shapes'), in which the first half usually consists of four elements (o o – ×), sometimes increased to five or six by resolutions of long elements, while the second half is a choriamb. This form of dimeter is probably to be explained as dactylo-trochaic, the first half being a trochaic metron –⏑– ×, with free variations of quantity in the first two elements as in the glyconic and in aeolic dactyls. It is already found in Pindar, also in Sophocles (*El.* 121–2, *Phil.* 204–8) and in Corinna. Euripides has a great liking for it, combined with glyconics, and Aristophanes probably parodies this in the cento at *Ran.* 1309–22. Not infrequently the first half consists of only three elements. Systems consisting mainly of glyconics and polyschematist dimeters are found, e.g., at Eur. *Hel.* 1301–18, *Phoen.* 202–13.

The characteristic features of the metres described in §§ 8–12 are the juxtaposition of dactyl and trochee and (in most of them) free variation in the quantities of the first two elements. They are generally known as 'aeolic', owing to their prominence in the poetry of Aeolian Lesbos (Sappho and Alcaeus).

(13) The *minor ionic* (metron ⏑⏑– –) is found in the lyric poets (Alcman, Sappho, and Alcaeus wrote whole songs in it, Heph. cap. 12, 37–38, cf. Alcm. fr. 46, Sapph. fr. 135) and is particularly associated with certain dramas (Aesch. *Supp.* 1018 ff., and *Pers.* 65 ff.; Eur. *Supp.* 42 ff., and *Bacch.* 64 ff.; Ar. *Ran.* 324 ff.). The syncopated form (⏑⏑ –) is frequent, e.g. *Pers.* 100–1. The *anacreontic* (⏑⏑–⏑–⏑– –) is often combined with ionics (e.g. Anacr. fr. 50) and is the metre of the late *Anacreontea*. The view (Heph. cap. 12, 39. 15) that the anacreontic is derived from the ionic dimeter by the interchange of the final long of the first metron with the opening short of the second ('anaclasis') does not account for cola of the form ⏑⏑– – –⏑– – (e.g. Ar. *Ran.* 330). The alternation of iamb. dim. cat. and anacreontic in Sapph. fr. 102 suggests that the anacreontic may be in origin an iamb. dim. cat. with anapaestic opening.

The *major ionic* is – –⏑⏑. According to Hephaestion (cap. 11, 36. 15) one form of it, the Αἰολικόν, was much used by Sappho. He cites frs. 82a+91 × –⏑⏑ – –⏑⏑ – –⏑⏑ –⏑– – (where, as with minor ionics, we have the metron –⏑⏑ – –). But here, as often in other places in lyric and tragedy where major ionics have been detected, choriambic scansion, with a jumping-off element ('anacrusis') at the start (– – ∪ ∪ –, etc.) is possible. Major ionics are far less well attested than minor ionics.

(14) The *archilochean dicolon* consists of enoplion and ithyphallic. Archilochus fr. 107 Ἐρασμονίδη Χαρίλαε, χρῆμά τοι γελοῖον. It is not infrequent in tragedy. Sometimes (Heph. cap. 15, 47. 16) the division is × – ∪ ∪ – ∪ ∪ – ‖ × – ∪ – ∪ – – (prosodiac and iamb. dim. cat.).

(15) *Dactylo-epitrites* are formed of dactylic cola (hemiepes, – ∪ ∪ – ∪ ∪ –) and cretics, which may be separated, preceded, or followed by *anceps* (normally *longum*). The term 'epitrite' is owed to the frequency of the sequence – ∪ – –, a ratio of 3:4, λόγος ἐπίτριτος, taking the length of a *breve* as the standard. There are many variations in the expansion and contraction of the dactylic ingredient. The metre is first found in Stesichorus, and is very often used, in a strictly regularized form, by Pindar and Bacchylides. It occurs in tragedy, especially in certain plays (Aesch. *PV* 526 ff., 887 ff., Eur. *Med.* and *Andr.*), even in comedy (Ar. *Eq.* 1264 ff.). It is one of the easiest Greek metres to grasp.

Common cola of this type are the *iambelegus* (× – ∪ – – – ∪ ∪ – ∪ ∪ –) and the *encomiologicum* (– ∪ ∪ – ∪ ∪ – × – ∪ – –), and the *praxilleion* (– ∪ ∪ – ∪ ∪ – ∪ ∪ – ∪ –) is of related type. The *archebulean* is a praxilleion preceded by one or two short elements or one long one ( ⏔ – ∪ ∪ – ∪ ∪ – ∪ ∪ – ∪ – –).

## IV. The Architecture of Greek Lyric Verse

The principal building materials have been described above. It remains to consider how these are combined into organized structures. In modern verse we are familiar with the stanza form of, say, four lines. Such stanzas play a relatively small part in Greek verse. The following deserve mention.

(1) *Sapphic stanza*, – ∪ – × – ∪ ∪ – ∪ – – (possibly = polyschematist dimeter plus ∪ – –) twice, followed by the same colon plus – ∪ ∪ – – (*adoneus*).

(2) *Alcaic stanza*, × – ∪ – × – ∪ ∪ – ∪ – (probably × plus trochaic metron plus the colon – ∪ ∪ – ∪ –, for which see III. 11) twice: × – ∪ – × – ∪ – – (× plus troch. dim.): – ∪ ∪ – ∪ ∪ – ∪ – – ('Alcaic ten-syllable'), a colon often used, especially as a clausula, in the lyrics of tragedy).

(3) *Skolion metre* (e.g. the Harmodius Song, *Carmina Convivialia* 10), phalaecean hendecasyllable twice: an enigmatical colon, ∪ ∪ – ∪ ∪ – – (perhaps a form of choriambic dimeter, with anapaest for iambus at the opening): – ∪ ∪ – ∪ – twice.

Sappho, Alcaeus, and Anacreon constructed their solo songs for the most part either (1) by the repetition of a single metrical unit, composition κατὰ στίχον (e.g. Sappho's second and third books were written in the '14-syllable' and '16-syllable sapphic' (see III. 5 and 11) respectively, and cf. Alc. frs. 347, 357: or (2) in stanzas, sapphic or alcaic, and cf. Sapph. frs. 94, 96, Alc. fr. 70, Anacr. fr. 13: Anacr. fr. 12 is a little more elaborate in structure, but equally simple in its constituents. There is, broadly speaking, no enjambement (contrast Anacreon's way of writing glyconics with Ar. *Eq.* 973–96). The colon is usually a line, in the modern sense of the term, and a modern reader feels that he is treading familiar ground. In contrast, choral lyric is, from the first, more complicated. Alcman's *Partheneion* (fr. 1) is a highly organized, though readily intelligible, structure: lec. + enopl. four times, 2 troch. trim., 2 troch. dim., dact. tetr., alc. 10-syll. or dact. tetr. cat. Hiatus and *syllaba brevis in elemento longo* occur frequently, while enjambement is eschewed.

Pindar's odes are extremely elaborate. The general character of the dactylo-epitrites is easily grasped, but the remainder, which are virtually all written in 'aeolic' metres (see III. 12, ad fin.), present numerous and formidable difficulties. The constituent cola, among which the shorter forms (o o – ∪ ∪ – and reizianum) are prominent, are interspersed with shorter entities (iambic monometers, cretics, etc.) and with non-aeolic cola. A colon is seldom repeated in juxtaposition. The whole structure has the elaborate intricacy of a tessellated pavement. The 'lines', marked by the presence of hiatus or *syllaba brevis in elemento longo*, occasionally consist of a single colon, but are normally longer, though seldom more than some 25 elements. *Pyth.* 1 str. 6 (dactyloepitrites) runs to 30 elements. The contrast between short and long lines is well illustrated by *Ol.* 1 str. 3–6, where three separated cola are followed by a long combination at 6. Cf. also *Nem.* 2 str. 1 and 4.

In tragedy we find long lines e.g. at Aesch. *Pers.* 882–5, Eur. *Heracl.* 615–17, *Hipp.* 771–5, *Bacch.* 383–6. The dramatists, unlike Pindar, tend to repeat the same colon many times in succession; and they do this in such a manner that the cola are in one place linked, in another separated; e.g. Aesch. *Supp.* 171–4, where 171–2 are linked, 173–4 separated; Soph. *OT* 1202–3, *OC* 1215–18; Ar. *Thesm.* 360–4. The division of a passage into its constituent cola (colometry, κωλισμός) is often subject to doubt, particularly in aeolic systems. Where, as often, diaeresis coincides in strophe and in antistrophe, it is natural to take this as a guide. On this principle Soph. *OC* 668–80 = 681–93 would be regarded as constructed of a great variety of aeolic cola, while alternatively it can be analysed into more homogeneous elements if we assume frequent enjambement between cola.

On the whole, the lyrics of tragedy stand between the complexity of Pindar and the simplicity of Lesbian solosong. Ionic and dochmiac systems are, it is true, very regular in character; and there are many homogeneous iambic systems (e.g. Aesch. *Ag.* 238–47, and often in the *Oresteia*; Soph. *Trach.* 132–40; Eur. *Tro.* 551–67). Other simple systems are Soph. *OT* 1186–96 (tel., glyc., pher., with reiz. clausula), *Trach.* 113–21 (hemiep. and chor. dim.), Eur. *Heracl.* 608–17 (dactyls), *Andr.* 501–14 (glyc., pher.), *Supp.* 971–9, and *Phoen.* 226–38 (glyc., pher., and chor. dim.). Against these we may set the elaboration of some of the lyrics in the *Alcestis*, and the great difficulty of *Bacch.* 135–67 and 576–603. The metres of comedy are in general far simpler than those of tragedy: e.g. Ar. *Eq.* 1111–30 and *Pax* 1329–57 (tel. and reiz.), *Av.* 1553–64 (troch. dim. and lec.), *Ran.* 1251–60 (glyc. and pher.); though even in comedy complicated systems are to be found (e.g. Ar. *Lys.* 1247–70 and, naturally, many parodistic passages). The beginner will be well advised to start with Sappho, Alcaeus, and Anacreon, and feel his way through the early plays of Aristophanes and the dactylo-epitrite poems of Pindar to the complexities of tragedy.

## V. Strophic Responsion

Most Greek choral poetry is 'strophic'. That is to say, a metrical system is repeated, the first occurrence being termed 'strophe', the second 'antistrophe'. In tragedy there is only one repetition, in satyric drama and comedy sometimes more (Eur. *Cyc.* 495 ff., Ar. *Pax* 346 ff.). The oldest extant piece of Greek choral poetry, Alcman's *Partheneion*, repeats the system many times, as does Pindar in his more elaborate odes. Pindar adds an epode to strophe and antistrophe, and then repeats the whole 'triadic' structure. (Triadic structure is already clearly present in Ibyc. fr. 1. There is no good ground for importing it into Alcman's *Partheneion*. The *Suda*, s.v. τρία Στησιχόρου, ascribes its invention to Stesichorus.) Epodes are also often found in drama (e.g. Aesch. *Pers.* 897–906, Soph. *Ant.* 876–82). In the κομμός in the *Choephoroe* (315–475) the structure is highly elaborate, and the antistrophes do not immediately follow the strophes: cf. Soph. *Trach.* 1004–42. Some passages are 'astrophic', the system not being repeated (e.g. Soph. *Trach.* 205–24, Eur. *Hel.* 515–27; particularly in the monodies and duets of Eur.'s later plays). In an *ephymnion* (refrain) words, as well as metrical form, are repeated: e.g. Aesch. *Supp.* 117–75, *Ag.* 1455–1550.

Strophic responsion is usually very close, and often undeviatingly precise, syllable by syllable, for long stretches. The main divergencies from strictness are the responsion of – and ◡ in many metres. A syncopated iambic metron probably sometimes corresponds to a full metron (e.g. Eur. *El.* 1185 = 1201). A few surprising responsions occur, notably that between polyschematist dimeter and glyconic (Corinna, fr. 5, *passim*, and several times in Euripides, e.g. *El.* 146 = 163). For loose responsion in comedy see Wilamowitz, *Verskunst*, 470–86.

The two works of fundamental importance are U. v. Wilamowitz-Moellendorff, *Griechische Verskunst* (1921), and P. Maas, *Greek Metre* (revised, and translated, with additional notes, by H. Lloyd-Jones, 1962). O. Schroeder analysed all the lyric passages of drama in *Aeschyli Cantica²* (1916), *Sophoclis Cantica²* (1923), *Euripidis Cantica²* (1928), and *Aristophanis Cantica²* (1930); the metrical schemata in B. Snell's Teubner editions of Pindar and Bacchylides are valuable. See also A. M. Dale, *The Lyric Metres of Greek Drama* (1948), especially for discussion of the most difficult passages in dramatic lyric. On particular metres: E. Fraenkel, 'Lyrische Daktylen', *Rh. Mus.* lxxii (1917–18), 161 ff., 321 ff.; J. Descroix, *Le Trimètre iambique* (1931); J. D. Denniston, 'Lyric Iambics', in *Greek Poetry and Life* (1936); N. C. Conomis, 'The Dochmiacs of Greek Drama', *Hermes* 1964, 23 ff.                    J. D. D.

**METRE, LATIN.** With the possible exception of the Saturnian metre (q.v.), all Latin metres were borrowed from Greek (not necessarily through literature: cf. the trochaic 'versus quadratus' used in popular songs—e.g. *rex erit qui recte faciet, qui non faciet non erit*). This borrowing was complicated by three important differences between the two languages: (1) the sequences of long and short syllables inherent in Latin words and terminations (cf. Cic. *Orat.* 189) were not always readily adaptable to foreign metres, and the poet's choice of diction was consequently fettered (e.g. Impĕrātor is impossible in dactylic verse); (2) it is virtually certain that stress, not pitch, predominated in the Latin accent, and therefore the relation between word-accent and rhythmical beat (ictus) created problems unknown apparently to Greek; (3) the phonetic tendency of 'breuis breuians' (q.v.) in popular Latin speech made possible a limited degree of prosodical flexibility, especially in the less formal kinds of verse. As in Greek, attenuation ('elision', synaloepha) of a final vowel before the initial vowel of a succeeding word was the common practice, and syllables ending in *-m* were similarly treated; but whereas Latin elides long final vowels more freely than Greek (yet not unrestrictedly), it rarely halves their quantity (e.g. an quī amant, Verg. *Ecl.* 8. 108). Hiatus is tolerated only at fixed places in certain metres, for special effects (e.g. femineō ululatu, *Aen.* 9. 477), or as a bold licence (e.g. Neptunō Aegaeo, *Aen.* 3. 74). Obsolete quantities are occasionally revived by later poets (e.g. velīt, labōr); a few lengthenings are due to Greek models (e.g. liminaquē laurique dei, *Aen.* 3. 91). In republican poets final *-s* after a short vowel was frequently neglected before a following consonant (e.g. rationis potestas, Lucr.). In dactylic and lyric metres the Romans often subject themselves to stricter rules than did the Greeks. The development of accentual metres in late Latin falls outside the scope of this article.

I. Metres of republican drama, introduced by Livius Andronicus, are fully represented in the comedies of Plautus and Terence; fragments of the tragedians are meagre. In general, these metres have three common features: (1) popular pronunciations based on 'breuis breuians' (e.g. bŏnĭs as ◡ ◡) or synizesis (e.g. eōrum) are freely admitted; (2) word-accent and ictus often coincide, and it is possible that the effects of enclisis (e.g. patér-

meus) may have made such coincidences more frequent than appears from a printed text; (3) where two short syllables are used as the resolution of one long, the first short syllable is usually an accented one; this principle embraces and may be the basis of many minor 'rules'. (A) Dialogue metres: (i) The iambic senarius is the commonest (e.g. nunc huc | ad Vĕnĕ|ris fa|num uĕnĭ|o ui|sere, Plaut. *Rud.* 94). Unlike the Greek comic trimeter, which allowed spondees (and dactyls) for ◡ ◡◡ only in the first, third, and fifth feet, the Latin line admitted × – (= ◌◌ ◡◡) in every foot except the last (◡ –); hence the line is felt to be not three *metra* but six feet (cf. Hor. *Ars P.* 251–62). There is caesura usually in the third foot, sometimes in the fourth; at the caesura hiatus is admitted (rarely in Terence). 'Porson's law' (cf. METRE, GREEK, II. 3) does not operate. As in other dialogue metres, resolutions of any long syllable are common (especially in comedy), but proceleusmatic feet (◡◡ ◡ ◡) are restricted in use. (ii) The iambic septenarius (a catalectic tetrameter, sometimes called 'laughing metre') is confined to comedy (e.g. nam quom | modo ex|ibat | foras || ad por|tum se ai|bat i|re, Plaut. *Rud.* 307). The seventh foot is generally a pure iambus and must be so if a monosyllable follows. The fourth foot must be iambic if, as usually happens, diaeresis follows. All other feet are × –. Hiatus is permitted at the diaeresis; failing diaeresis, there is caesura in the fifth foot. (iii) The iambic octonarius has a pure iambus as its last foot; its fourth foot is also pure if, as is usual, diaeresis follows. The other six feet are × –. Hiatus is found at the diaeresis; failing diaeresis, there is caesura in the fifth foot. (iv) The trochaic septenarius (or catalectic tetrameter) is widely used (e.g. exi e | fano | natum | quantumst || hŏmĭnum | săcrĭle|gissu|me, Plaut. *Rud.* 706). It keeps only its seventh foot pure (– ◡) and so differs from the Greek metre, which kept the first, third, and fifth feet also pure. Diaeresis (with hiatus permitted, though not in Terence) is common after the fourth foot; failing diaeresis, there is caesura in the fourth foot. (B) The metres of *cantica* (i.e. lyrical monodies or duets, rare in Terence) are mainly iambic, trochaic, anapaestic, bacchiac, and cretic dimeters and tetrameters (catalectic and acatalectic); choriambic, glyconic, and ionic metres are occasionally used; to these must be added the *colon reizianum* (× ⏌ × ⏌), which, when preceded by an iambic dimeter, gives the *versus reizianus*. The relation between word-accent and ictus, the extent to which popular pronunciations, resolutions, and hiatus are used, and the admission of impure feet differ with the metre employed. For example: conflict of accent and ictus is usual in anapaests, though shortening by 'breuis breuians' is common; in bacchiacs and cretics popular pronunciations are avoided, but accent and ictus generally coincide; in bacchiacs the first part of the foot may be ◡, or ◡ ◡, or –, but it is rare for both long syllables of a foot (× – –) to be resolved; yet cretics normally have the form ◌◌ ◌◌, rarely ◌◌ × ◌◌. Some cantica are composed in a single metre. In others the metre changes with the emotions expressed or when a new topic is introduced; in such passages the division into cola is sometimes uncertain. In a number of cantica it is possible to discern a metrical structure of strophe and antistrophe, especially when a general theme is followed by a particular application (e.g. Plaut. *Amph.* 633–44).

II. Dactylic verse, introduced by Ennius. (i) The hexameter is used with considerable variety of treatment as the metre of epic, narrative, didactic, and satiric poetry, and forms the first line of the elegiac couplet. Its first four feet may be dactyls or spondees, its fifth is regularly a dactyl, its sixth a spondee or trochee. A spondaic fifth foot (an Alexandrian mannerism) is frequent only in Catullus (but cf. cara de|um subo|les, mag|num Iouis | incre|mentum, Verg. *Ecl.* 4. 49). Except for some cretic words in Ennius, no use is made of shortening by 'breuis breuians' and synizesis is rare. Ennius, Ovid, and imperial poets are sparing with elisions; Lucilius, Lucretius, and Virgil (especially in *Aen.*) employ them more frequently. The commonest caesura is after the long syllable of the third foot (penthemimeral); it is often accompanied by another masculine caesura in the fourth foot (hephthemimeral) or in the second foot (trihemimeral), or by both; if there is not a masculine caesura in the third foot, both hephthemimeral and trihemimeral are usual (e.g. o pas|si graui|ora, da|bit deus | his quoque | finem, Verg. *Aen.* 1. 199). The comparative infrequency of a feminine caesura in the third foot is a striking contrast to the Greek hexameter. In the fifth foot, however, feminine caesuras are more frequent than masculine. Monosyllables are avoided where they would create diaeresis near a main caesura. After Ennius they are progressively less frequent at the end of a line (where a disyllabic or trisyllabic noun, verb, or adjective is preferred); in Virgil they are used only for special reasons (e.g. restituis rem, *Aen.* 6. 846, imitating Ennius); in Horace's *Satires* conversational tone is achieved by final monosyllabic adverbs and particles. Diaeresis with a clear break in the sense at the fourth foot (the so-called 'bucolic caesura') is a conspicuous but not common mannerism (e.g. Pollio et | ipse fa|cit noua | carmina: || pascite ¦ taurum, Verg. *Ecl.* 3. 86). In general, there is conflict between word-accent and ictus in the first half of the hexameter, harmony in the second. Whether Latin poets sought this alternation and arranged their caesuras to ensure it, or whether it is the inevitable result of their preference for certain masculine caesuras, is a matter of controversy. It is also disputed whether the Romans read hexameters with normal prose accentuations, neglected them in favour of ictus, or in some way made both audible. By skilfully varying their caesuras, elisions, and sense pauses, and employing all the delicate resources of alliteration and assonance, the great Roman poets made the hexameter a sonorous but flexible instrument for the expression of all human emotions. (ii) The pentameter consists of two catalectic dactylic cola (*hemiepes*, $- \cup \cup - \cup \cup -$) separated by diaeresis. In the first colon spondees may be substituted for either dactyl, but not usually for both; no spondees are permitted in the second colon. A monosyllable before the diaeresis is avoided unless another monosyllable or a pyrrhic ($\cup \cup$) word precedes; the final syllable is usually long. Ovid and later writers normally end the line with a disyllable (though 'es' and 'est' are allowed), but earlier elegists admit polysyllables. Except in Catullus elision is restricted and is generally avoided at the diaeresis, in the second half of the line, and especially in the last dactyl. A symmetrical arrangement of words (e.g. aspicio *patriae* tecta relicta *meae*, Ovid) is a common feature of the best writers, and each couplet is normally complete in sense.

III. *Lyric metres.* Latin lyric verse is smaller in quantity and less complicated in form than Greek. The chief writers are Catullus, Horace, Martial, and Seneca (in his tragedies). Apart from iambic, trochaic, dactylic, and anapaestic lines of various lengths, the principal metres are glyconics, pherecrateans, asclepiads, phalaecean hendecasyllabics, scazons (limping iambics), and the elements of the sapphic and alcaic stanzas (cf. METRE, GREEK); ionics (e.g. Hor. *Carm.* 3. 12) and the controversial galliambic (in Catull. 63) are rare. Popular pronunciations are virtually excluded and there is considerable strictness in matters of caesura, elision, and liaison (synaphea) between successive lines (for details see standard editions). The iambic and trochaic lines of lyric (excluding the 'trimeters' of Publilius Syrus and Phaedrus) are metrically purer than those of comedy,

since they are based on dipodies of the forms $\cup - \cup -$ and $- \cup - \cup$; resolutions of long syllables also are comparatively fewer, though Seneca admits them in his iambics more freely than Horace. Some of the metres (e.g. iambic dimeters and trimeters, hendecasyllabics, asclepiads) are used in continuous passages; but more frequently lines of different length or metre are combined into couplets (e.g. Hor. *Carm.* 1. 7; *Epod.* 16) or four-line stanzas. Horace is especially fond of the alcaic and sapphic stanzas and combinations of asclepiads, glyconics, and pherecrateans, in all of which he restricts himself by rules unknown to Greek (e.g. in sapphics and alcaics he uses an epitrite ($- \cup - -$) where Greek may have a ditrochee ($- \cup - \cup$)).

W. M. Lindsay, *Early Latin Verse* (1922); W. A. Laidlaw, *Prosody of Terence* (1938); E. Fraenkel, *Iktus und Akzent* (1928) and 'Die Vorgeschichte des Versus Quadratus' (*Hermes* 1927, 357 ff.); H. Drexler, *Plautinische Akzentstudien* (2 vols., 1932); O. Skutsch, *Prosodische u. metrische Gesetze der Iambenkürzung* (1934); F. Crusius, *Römische Metrik* (ed. Rubenbauer, 1959) and 'Die Responsion in den Plautinischen Cantica' (*Philol.* Suppl. xxi. 1, 1929); E. Norden, *Aeneis Buch VI* (Anhänge) (1926); A. W. de Groot, 'Wesen u. Gesetze der Caesur (*Mnemos.* 1935, 81 ff.); L. Müller, *De re metrica* (1894); J. P. Postgate, *Prosodia Latina* (1923); W. R. Hardie, *Res Metrica* (1920); F. Vollmer, 'Römische Metrik' in Gercke–Norden's *Einleitung* i, 8; W. Meyer, *Gesammelte Abhandlungen zur mittellat. Rhythmik* (3 vols., 1905–36); W. J. W. Koster, *Traité de métrique grecque suivi d'un précis de métrique latine*² (1953); H. Holtorf, *Grundzüge der römischen Metrik* (1956); L. Nougaret, *Traité de métrique latine classique* (1956); W. Beare, *Latin Verse and European Song* (1957); J. Halporn, M. Ostwald, T. Rosenmeyer, *The Meters of Greek and Latin Poetry* (1963); D. S. Raven, *Latin Metre* (1965).
J. F. M.

**METRODORUS** (1) of Chios, pupil of Democritus, lived in the fourth century B.C. His Περὶ φύσεως seems to have combined Atomism with the attempt to apply the Eleatic denial of change to the universe as a whole. He occupied himself mainly with the explanation of meteorological and astronomical phenomena. He also wrote historical works—a Τρωικά and perhaps also an Ἰωνικά.

Testimonia and fragments in Diels, *Vorsokr.*¹¹ ii. 231–4.
W. D. R.

**METRODORUS** (2) of Lampsacus (331/330–278/7 B.C. was one of the four καθηγεμόνες of Epicureanism, and the most important after Epicurus; Epicurus dedicated to him his *Eurylochus* and his *Metrodorus*, besides writing letters to him and mentioning him often in his works. He reckoned him not among original thinkers, but as first among those who could reach the truth with the help of others, and ordered that Metrodorus' memory as well as his own should be celebrated on the 20th of every month. The list of Metrodorus' writings is a long one, and considerable fragments remain, largely occupied with polemic against other schools, and confirming Epicurus' judgement as to his lack of originality.

Ed. A. Körte, *Jahrbücher für Classische Philologie*, Suppl. 17. 529 (1890); *Papyrus Herculanensis* 831 ed. A. Körte, ibid. 571 ff.; R. Westmann, *Plutarch gegen Kolotes* (1957).
W. D. R.

**METRODORUS** (3) of Stratonicea, an adherent first of the Epicurean school, then of that of Carneades (Diog. Laert. 10. 9, Cic. *De Or.* 1. 45).

**METRODORUS** (4), of Scepsis in Mysia, enjoyed the friendship of Mithridates but later (*c.* 71/70 B.C.) supported Tigranes and fell foul of Mithridates who may have been responsible for his death (Plut. *Luc.* 22). Mentioned several times by Cicero, he was celebrated for his powers of memory and his hatred of Rome. He wrote a book on Tigranes, a *History* (?), on gymnastic training (Περὶ ἀλειπτικῆς), and perhaps a Περιήγησις. He is to be distinguished from an older homonymous philosopher of Scepsis.

*FGrH* 184.
H. H. S.

**METRONOMOI,** overseers of weights and measures in Athens; five for the city, five for the Piraeus, elected by lot for one year. In other States their duties were carried out by the *Agoranomoi* (q.v.).

**METROPOLIS,** (*a*) the mother-city of a colony; (*b*) in Roman times an honorary title granted usually to the capitals of provincial κοινά, sometimes to other important cities; (*c*) in Egypt the administrative capital of a *nomos* (q.v.). Under the Ptolemies the *metropoleis*, though they usually had many Greek residents, possessed no official communal organization. Augustus placed on a special register the hellenized residents of the *metropoleis* (οἱ ἀπὸ μητροπόλεως), and these henceforth formed a hereditary class, paying poll-tax at a lower rate. He also established in each metropolis a body of magistrates (ἄρχοντες), who managed the gymnasium and the ephebic training, the market and corn supply, and the Greek temples. These were chosen—in theory probably by popular election from a hereditary class styled ἡ ἀπὸ γυμνασίου. Septimius Severus established in each metropolis a council (βουλή), which co-opted its members and nominated the magistrates and the principal officials of the *nomos* except the στρατηγός and βασιλικὸς γραμματεύς (who were appointed by the prefect). The *metropoleis* officially became cities probably in A.D. 297, perhaps ten years later.

P. Jouguet, *La Vie municipale dans l'Égypte romaine* (1911); Jones, *Cities E. Rom. Prov.*, ch. 11.          A. H. M. J.

**METTIUS POMPUSIANUS** (*PW*, s.v. L. Pompusius Mettius, but the identification is very doubtful) was consul under Vespasian. He was executed by Domitian because he possessed an imperial horoscope and had made a volume of extracts of royal speeches from Livy.

Suet. *Vesp.* 14; *Dom.* 10. 3; Dio Cass. 67. 12.          G. E. F. C.

**MEZENTIUS,** king of Caere in Etruria, whose aid was invoked by Turnus against the invading Aeneas. According to the earlier story, told in Cato's *Origines*, Turnus and Aeneas alike fell in the subsequent conflict, and Mezentius was later killed or forced to submit in single combat with Ascanius. (Some authorities, e.g. Ovid, *Fasti* 4. 877–900, say he demanded payment to himself of the first-fruits of the vintage.) Virgil in *Aen.* books 7–10 develops him into a full-blooded, atheistical tyrant, killed by Aeneas after the death in his defence of his attractive son Lausus.          R. A. B. M.

**MICON** (Μίκων) (5th c. B.C.), painter and sculptor, of Athens. He painted (1) in the Theseum (soon after 475): Theseus and Minos; probably also Amazonomachy and Centauromachy. (2) In the Stoa Poikile (soon after 460) Amazonomachy. The Amazonomachies and Centauromachy are reflected on vases; one Amazon is named Peisianassa after Peisianax, who built the Stoa; one Centauromachy is very like the centre of the west pediment at Olympia, on which Micon *may* have worked as sculptor. (3) In the Anakeion: Argonauts. He painted Butes (in the Amazonomachy?) so that only head and eye appeared above a hill; analogies can be found on contemporary vases. His painting was closely connected with Polygnotus, but Polygnotan ἦθος is never attributed to him. He made a statue in Olympia of Callias, victor in 472; the Mariémont warrior may reproduce an original by him.

Overbeck, 1058, 1080–93; Pfuhl, 688, 716, 732; J. D. Beazley, *AJArch.* 1933, 366; F. Dornseiff, *Der sogenannte Apollon von Olympia* (1936); Rumpf, *Malerei u. Zeichn.* 94.          T. B. L. W.

**MIDAS** (1), a legendary Phrygian king, of whom several stories are told, the most famous being the following.

Midas had a garden which a Silenus or satyr used to visit. Midas had a curiosity to learn his wisdom, and so mixed wine with the water of a spring in the garden; the Silenus was thus made drunk and caught. What he told Midas seems to have been a subject for learned conjecture; according to Aristotle ap. [Plut.] *Cons. ad Apoll.* 115 b, he said that life was a penance and it was a misfortune to be born; Aelian (*VH* 3. 18) puts into his mouth a lecture on geography. The place of the garden also varies: see Hdt. 8. 138. 4 (somewhere in Macedonia), Xen. *An.* 1. 2. 13 (near Thymbrium in Cilicia), Bion in Athenaeus 45 c (name given as Inna, between Thrace and Paeonia).

Having to judge a musical contest between Apollo and Pan (or Marsyas, q.v. 1, Hyg. *Fab.* 191. 1), Midas voted against Apollo, who therefore bestowed ass's ears on him. He managed to hide these from most people with his head-dress, but was obliged to tell his barber; the latter, bursting with the secret, found relief by whispering it into a hole in the ground; reeds grew over this when he refilled it, and whispered the tale whenever the wind blew through them (Ov. *Met.* 11. 153 ff.).

Midas was very hospitable to a Silenus, whom his people had found wandering drunk and captured (a variant of the first story, probably). Dionysus therefore offered him anything he wished; he asked that all he touched might become gold. Soon after, he found that this applied to his food and prayed to lose the gift; by Dionysus' advice he bathed in Pactolus, which ever since has had golden sands (Ov. ibid. 90 ff.).

Whether any facts of cult or history lie behind the story of Midas is doubtful.          H. J. R.

**MIDAS** (2), an historical king of Phrygia 738–696 B.C. (Eusebius). He was the first barbarian king to make presents to Delphi (Hdt. 1. 14); married the king of Cyme's daughter, who first struck coins in her native city (Heraclides, *FHG* ii. 216, Pollux 9. 83); and drank bull's blood when the Cimmerians overthrew his kingdom (Strabo 1. 61). In Assyrian records he appears as Mita, joins a confederacy against King Sargon (717), but becomes his vassal (707). His story anticipates that of the Lydian Gyges (q.v.).          P. N. U.

**MIDDLE PLATONISM.** The Platonism of the period between Antiochus of Ascalon (d. *c.* 68 B.C.) and Plotinus (b. A.D. 205), characterized by a revulsion against the sceptical tendency of the New Academy and by a gradual advance, with many individual variations, towards a comprehensive metaphysic, often including elements drawn from Stoicism, Aristotelianism, or Neopythagoreanism. *See* ALBINUS (1), APULEIUS, CELSUS (4), PLUTARCH.          E. R. D.

**MILESTONES.** The earliest surviving Roman milestone (*ILS* 5801) dates from *c.* 250 B.C. Under the Republic they bear the names of consuls or other officials concerned with the building or repair of roads. In the Principate the full names and titles of the Emperor usually appear—occasionally nothing more. They may attest the date of new roads (e.g. *ILS* 208, 5834), or methods of financing reconstruction (e.g. *ILS* 5875). On trunk roads in Italy the distance given is often that from Rome, in the provinces from the provincial capital; but in most cases the distance is from the city on whose territory the milestone stood—often useful for the delimitation of those territories. In the Three Gauls and Germany from the time of Trajan distances were measured in *leugae* (1,500 paces). Milestones were usually cylindrical, about 6 feet high.

*ILS* 5801 ff. Schneider, *PW*, Suppl. vi, s.v. 'miliarium'.          G. H. S.; J. C. M.

**MILETUS,** southernmost of the great Ionian cities of Asia Minor, claimed partly Cretan origin; the successive strata of Minoan and Mycenaean settlement uncovered on the site lend colour to this claim, as also to the equation with Milawanda (acknowledged in the Hittite records to have belonged to the king of Aḫḫijava). In Homer the people of Miletus were Carians who fought against the Achaeans at Troy; and in the later Greek prose tradition the Ionic settlers, under their Codrid founder Neleus, seized Miletus from Carians (whose women they took to wife). During the seventh and sixth centuries Miletus founded many colonies on the Black Sea and its approaches (including Abydos, Cyzicus, Sinope, Panticapaeum, Olbia, Istrus), led the way in Greek penetration of Egypt (Milesians' Fort and Naucratis; Necho's offering to the temple at Didyma after Megiddo, 608 B.C.), and had close contacts with Sybaris till its destruction in 510.

Miletus' sea-power and colonies were partly cause, partly result of her long struggle with the kings of Lydia. Alyattes made terms with Miletus (then under a tyrant Thrasybulus, the friend of Periander), which apparently kept a privileged position when Croesus subdued Ionia and when Persia conquered Croesus' dominions c. 546. In 499 Miletus, instigated by its ex-tyrant Histiaeus and Aristagoras (1) (qq.v.), started the Ionian revolt. After the naval disaster at Lade the city was captured, the temple at Didyma was burnt, and Miletus was left desolate (494).

Lade ended for Miletus a long period of great prosperity, interrupted by intervals of party struggles; to this period belong the Milesian philosophers Thales, Anaximander, and Anaximenes, the chronicler and map-maker Hecataeus, and the seated statues from Didyma (British Museum, *Catalogue of Sculpture* 1. i, plates vi–xv). How far the archaic pottery generally known as Rhodian was really Milesian remains uncertain. Milesian woollen goods and furniture were world-famous.

After the Persian defeat at Mycale (479) Miletus joined the Delian League, but in the mid fifth century (perhaps after a revolt) the Athenians imposed a garrison and imperial controls on the city. In 412 Miletus revolted from Athens, only to fall under the Persian satrap. In the fourth century it came under the shadow of Mausolus, the ruler of Caria. Among Milesians of this period were Aspasia of Periclean fame, Hippodamus, town-planner of the Piraeus, and the dithyrambic poet Timotheus (c. 447–357). Miletus was captured and liberated by Alexander.

Delivered from the rule of Asander in 312, Miletus maintained friendly relations with the Hellenistic kings, by whom some of the buildings uncovered in the great German excavations were donated. It made treaties of isopolity (interchange of citizen rights) with its neighbours and colonies, and there was a large Milesian element resident in Athens. After becoming part of the Roman province of Asia (129 B.C.) Miletus lived on its past glories. St. Paul visited it (A.D. 51); Apollo performed a miracle at Didyma when the Goths besieged the city in A.D. 263; but its decline was assured by the silting up of its harbour.

Strabo 14 C 632–5. T. Wiegand, *Milet, Ergebnisse der Ausgrabungen und Untersuchungen seit 1899*. A. G. Dunham, *History of Miletos* (1915); J. P. Röhlig, *Handel von Milet* (1933).
P. N. U.; J. M. C.

**MILK** (γάλα, *lac*) in its fresh form was, if only for climatic reasons, not very important in the diet of the Greeks and Romans, though they knew of (and sometimes admired) 'milk-drinkers' among the northern barbarians. Cows' milk and butter (βούτυρον = 'cow-cheese'), in particular, found little favour; and the milk that was consumed—normally in the form of curds (ὀξύγαλα) or cheese—was usually that of goats or sheep. The medicinal value of milk was well known; and the physicians recommended the internal or external use of fresh and curdled milk or whey (including also human and donkeys' milk) for numerous complaints, sometimes with the addition of water, salt, flour, or honey. Milk was used also for cosmetic purposes; and in religious ceremonies, where it is a natural first-fruit or drink offering, it always retained a place, especially in conservative rustic cults, though in many cases its early use was, as in the human diet, later superseded by that of wine.

*PW*, s.v. Milch (xv. 1569 ff.), with references. L. A. M.

**MILLS.** The early 'saddle-quern', in which grain is rubbed between a fixed flat lower stone and a smaller upper stone held in the operator's hands, continued in use for many centuries; but in the fifth century B.C. an improved version became current, with an enlarged upper stone containing a rudimentary hopper and operated by means of a pole pivoted behind the lower stone. Rotary grain-mills (which alone make working by animals, water, or wind possible) are not securely attested before the early second century B.C., but from then on both the small hand-quern and the 'hour-glass' animal-mill of which numerous examples have been found (especially at Pompeii) became very common. Geared water-mills (described by Vitruvius 10. 5. 2) were invented soon afterwards and gradually established themselves. In the absence of water, geared mills were sometimes driven by animals. (The windmill is a medieval invention.) Originally a household occupation, milling developed into an industry as mills became more complicated; and in imperial Rome the guild of miller-bakers (*pistores*) was of considerable importance.

L. A. Moritz, *Grain-Mills and Flour in Classical Antiquity* (1958).
L. A. M.

**MILO,** TITUS ANNIUS (*PW* 67), of Lanuvium, tribune 57 B.C. Originally Pompey's man, he actively promoted Cicero's recall and organized gladiators against those of Clodius (q.v. 1). Their riots, which continued over five years, were varied by prosecutions for *vis*: in 57 Milo twice sued Clodius, who escaped by being elected aedile; in 56 a prosecution of Milo was also dropped, and he became praetor in 55. Late in 54 he inaugurated, with games costing 1,000,000 HS, a candidature for the consulate of 52 against Hypsaeus and Metellus (q.v. 11) Scipio; but disorder was still preventing the elections when Milo murdered Clodius near Bovillae 18 Jan. 52. Pompey then became sole consul and had Milo prosecuted before a court so heavily guarded that Cicero did not dare to speak (his *Pro Milone* was written and sent to Milo after the condemnation). Milo retired to exile at Massilia, thanking Cicero that his reticence allowed him to enjoy the mullets there. But in 48 he answered Caelius' appeal to re-create disorder and was captured and executed at Cosa.

In 54 he married Fausta, daughter of Sulla and divorced wife of C. Memmius (q.v. 2). G. E. F. C.

**MILON,** an athlete from Croton of the later sixth century B.C.; six times victor in wrestling at the Olympian Games, six times at the Pythian. He is said to have carried a heifer down the course, killed it with one blow, and eaten it all in one day. Trying to rend a tree asunder he was caught in the cleft and eaten alive by wolves.
F. A. W.

**MILTIADES** (c. 550–489 B.C.) belonged to the noble Athenian family of the Philaïdae, and was sent c. 524 by Hippias to continue the policy of Athenian hegemony in the Thracian Chersonese which Miltiades' namesake and paternal uncle had inaugurated under Pisistratus

(c. 555) and probably at his prompting. Miltiades ruled as absolute king over the natives, but he encouraged Athenian settlers and, after freeing Lemnos from Persia in the early years of the fifth century, he handed it over to Athens. He had previously been a vassal of Darius and accompanied him on the Scythian expedition (c. 513), but his claim to have proposed the destruction of the Danube bridge is disproved by the fact that Darius left him unmolested. He married Hegesipyle, daughter of the wealthy Thracian king Olorus, who bore him Cimon. His other children (including the notorious Elpinice) were by a previous marriage with an Athenian lady. After a short exile caused by a Scythian invasion Miltiades was restored by the Thracians (496). At the end of the Ionian Revolt, in which he had participated, he fled from the Persians and returned to Athens (493). Here he survived a trial for 'tyranny' in Thrace and became the most influential politician in spite of the opposition of the Alcmaeonidae. As one of the generals in 490 he won the support of Callimachus (q.v. 1) and most of his colleagues for engaging the Persians at Marathon (q.v.), where he won a decisive victory. Inaugurating a policy of naval expansion, he led an expedition to Paros (early spring 489), which he was unable to capture. On the accusation of Xanthippus (q.v. 1) Miltiades was fined 50 talents for having deceived the people, and soon afterwards succumbed to a wound incurred at Paros.

W. W. How, *JHS* 1919; J. Wells, *Studies in Herodotus* (1923), 112 ff.; E. Cavaignac, *Rev. Phil.* 1929; A. Passerini, *Milziade e l'occupazione di Lemno* (1935); H. Berve, *Miltiades* (1937); V. Ehrenberg, *Polis und Imperium* (1965), 224 ff.; H. Bengtson, *Sitz. der Bayrischen Akademie, philos.-historische Abt.*, 1939, Heft 1. For Miltiades' plan in 490 B.C., cf. C. Hignett, *Xerxes' Invasion of Greece* (1963), 55 ff. and N. G. L. Hammond, *JHS* 1968, 26 ff.; K. Kinzl, *Miltiades-Forschungen* (1968). P. T.

**MIMNERMUS,** elegiac poet and musician (Strabo 643) of Colophon (ibid.) and Smyrna (Paus. 9. 29. 4). His *floruit* is given as 632–29 B.C. by the *Suda*; this suits his interchange with Solon (fr. 6 and Sol. fr. 22). The eclipse of the sun to which he referred (Plut. *Mor.* 931 e) gives no help, as it may be either 648 or 585 B.C. His elegies were collected in two books (Porph. ad Hor. *Epist.* 2. 2. 101), one of which was called *Nanno* after the flute-girl he is said to have loved (Hermesianax ap. Ath. 597 f, Strabo 643). This seems to have been a collection of poems on very different themes, such as mythology about Tithonus (fr. 4), the Sun's magic bowl (fr. 10), and history about the foundation of Colophon (fr. 12, Strabo 633). The same book may have contained his account of the war between Smyrna and Gyges (fr. 13, Paus. 9. 29. 4). His other fragments are concerned largely with the pleasures of youth and the horrors of old age (frs. 1–3). But he tempers his hedonism with a respect for truth (fr. 8) and for warlike qualities (frs. 12–13). He seems to have written a *Smyrneis*, or historical poem on Smyrna, which may have been contained in the *Nanno*. He is remarkable for his musical use of the elegiac, his brilliant sustained images, the directness of his emotional appeal, and his love of pleasure.

TEXT. E. Diehl, *Anth. Lyr. Graec.* I. i. 50–7.
COMMENTARY. T. Hudson-Williams, *Early Greek Elegy* (1925), 90 ff.; D. A. Campbell, *Greek Lyric Poetry* (1967), 222 ff.
CRITICISM. U. von Wilamowitz-Moellendorff, *Sappho und Simonides* (1913), 276 ff.; C. M. Bowra, *Early Greek Elegy* (1936), 17 ff; *PW* Suppl. xi. 935 ff. C. M. B.

**MIMUS** (μῖμος), an imitative performance or performer.
I. GREEK. In Greece, as elsewhere, the instinct for imitation found its expression in the mimetic dance. From early times solo performers, by play of gesture, voice, and feature, gave imitations of neighing horses, etc. (Pl. *Resp.* 396 b), and small companies, called in Sparta δεικηλίκται (? 'masked men'), elsewhere αὐτοκάβδαλοι ('improvisers') or in Italiot towns φλύακες,

presented short scenes from daily life (e.g. 'The Quack Doctor') or mythology, probably on a hastily erected stage in the market-place or in a private house; such performers belonged to the social class of acrobats, etc. Xenophon (*Symp.*) tells of a mime 'of Dionysus and Ariadne', danced at a private banquet by a boy and girl; we note the connexion with Syracuse, the musical accompaniment, the use of dialogue, and the fact that the girl is also a sword-dancer and the concubine of the Syracusan dancing-master. In the fifth century Sophron of Syracuse wrote 'men's' and 'women's' mimes in Dorian rhythmic prose; the language was popular and included frequent proverbs; the surviving titles (e.g. 'The Old Fishermen', 'The Women Quacks', 'The Women Visitors to the Isthmia') indicate stock mime themes. Of the mimes of Sophron's son, Xenarchus, virtually nothing is known. In the third century the taste for realism brought the mime to the fore; Theocritus dressed traditional themes in his courtly hexameters (Idyll 2: the deserted heroine resorts to magic; 15: two Syracusan women visit the festival of Adonis in Alexandria; 21 (probably by an imitator of Theocritus): two old fishermen converse; 14 is also dramatic in form); these pieces, like those of the more realistic Herodas (q.v.), were probably intended for semi-dramatic recitation. Meanwhile the popular mime invaded the theatre; it now took the form either of παίγνια (? slight, often vulgar, performances) or of ὑποθέσεις, 'plots' (Plut. *Quaest. conv.* 7. η'. 4, 712 e), taken over from drama proper and presented in mimic fashion by the μαγῳδοί (Ath. 621 c) or μιμολόγοι (the meaning of the various terms for performers, whether they suggest spoken or musical delivery, is uncertain); cf. the third-century Athenian lamp with its representation of three maskless performers and the inscription 'Mimologi; hypothesis: Mother-in-law'. The 'Alexandrian erotic fragment' is perhaps a sung mime: theme, the deserted heroine. In *POxy.* 413 we have (a) a farce in prose, based on the plot of *Iph. Taur.* (?): a Greek girl, named Charition, aided by her brother, escapes from an Indian king and his followers by making them drunk; the barbarians speak pseudo-Indian; there is a low clowning part; (b) a prose mime: theme, the jealous mistress (cf. Herodas v), who tries to poison her husband and make love to her slaves; there are six or seven short scenes and seven roles, all unimportant except that of the archimima; here, as always, the interest of the mime is in character and situation rather than in action. In the Marissa wall-inscription we have a song-dialogue between a hetaera and the *exclusus amator* (see MAGODIA).

TEXTS. Herodas, ed. Crusius, 1914.

II. ROMAN (known also as *fabula riciniata*). Before the end of the third century B.C. the barefooted *planipes* appeared on the stage at Rome. The undatable epitaph of Vitalis (Duff, *Minor Lat. Poets*; Loeb, 636–9) points to solo, maskless displays; Cicero refers to extempore troupe performances of improbable themes like 'The Beggar turns Millionaire' (*Phil.* 2. 65). A popular feature at the Floralia was the appearance of the *mimae* (alias *meretrices*) naked. Sulla patronized the mime; soon it rivalled the *Atellana* as an after-piece; Dionysia received 200,000 sesterces yearly, and we read of a company of 60 *mimi* under an *archimimus*. Associated with Julius Caesar were the mime-writers Laberius, Syrus, and Matius. Favoured by the emperors, beloved by the rabble, still topical, farcical, and indecent, the mime (with the pantomime) practically monopolized the stage; a typical *mimus* was the close-cropped fool, dressed in the patch-work *centunculus*. Domitian had a real crucifixion inserted in a mime; Heliogabalus ordered mimic adulteries to be performed realistically; in the person of

Theodora a *mima* reached the throne. Unsubdued by their losing battle with the Church and even by the barbarian invasions, the strolling companies, it is claimed, have survived as the wandering *jongleurs* of the Middle Ages.

H. Reich, *Der Mimus* (1903); *PW* (1932), s.v. 'Mimos'; J. R. A. Nicoll, *Masks, Mimes and Miracles* (1931; well illustrated). W. B.

**MINDARUS,** Spartan admiral, 411/10 B.C. Exasperated by the duplicity of Tissaphernes (q.v.), he transferred the main Peloponnesian fleet from Ionia to the Hellespont, where Pharnabazus (q.v.) was willing to support him whole-heartedly. The Athenians defeated his fleet off Cynossema and again off Abydos (autumn, 411), thereby safeguarding the passage of their corn-ships. Early in 410 Mindarus recaptured Cyzicus, but he was there surprised by a superior fleet under Alcibiades and died in a vain attempt to save his ships from capture. Determined to end the stagnation of the campaign in Asia, he displayed energy and enterprise. It was his misfortune that while he was in command the Athenian forces were exceptionally well led.

Thuc. 8. 99–107; Xen. *Hell.* 1. 1. 2–18; Diod. 13. 38–51. H. D. W.

**MINERALOGY.** Greek mineralogy embraced bold theorizing and shrewd observation, but the two seldom coalesced. Plato in the *Timaeus* (60 b–c) was the first to propound a theory about the formation of stone, although to what extent he meant this and similar speculations to be taken seriously is questionable. According to him, stone is formed when earth is filtered through water and compressed by the air into which the water is transformed. Aristotle at the end of *Meteorologica* 3 derives certain minerals from the action of the dry exhalation. Scarcely any evidence is adduced. Stones are cited from time to time in *Meteorologica* 4, which is concerned with the solidification, dissolution, and physical properties of 'homoeomerous' bodies in general.

The physical properties of stones and mineral earths form the main theme of Theophrastus' monograph Περὶ λίθων, a work which, brief as it is, traverses a wide range of topics, many of them for the first time. We find a digression on the combustibility of coal and other minerals, and references to the ease or difficulty of working various stones, the behaviour of fluxes in smelting, the burning of lime, the mining of ruddle and Samian earth, the nature of glass, and the preparation of white lead, verdigris, and quicksilver. Although there are descriptions of many stones and several mineral earths, these are mostly introduced in order to illustrate a point: the work is not intended to be an exhaustive survey. The opening paragraphs contain a summary of a theory concerning the formation of earths and stones. Thanks partly to its dependence on Platonic and Aristotelian concepts, and partly to its exploitation of simple concepts derived from artificial processes, this theory can be reconstructed in some detail. Certain facts presented in the body of the work bear upon it, and others seem to do so. Here, for once, theory and observation were allied. There is one surprising omission. No attempt is made to explain the action of the lodestone, a problem which elicited theories from Empedocles, Plato, Democritus, and the Epicureans, amongst others.

Theophrastus' outstanding work was perhaps too sober and allusive to exert much influence on speculative thought, although Juba (q.v. 2) and the Elder Pliny at least used its factual descriptions. In the Hellenistic period, writers such as Sotacus, Sudines, and Bolus (q.v.) of Mendes concentrated on the supposed magical and medicinal properties of gemstones, a tendency which is only too apparent in Pliny. Theoretical speculation was

correspondingly affected by mystification if we can judge from a theory intended to explain the formation of gemstones, traces of which, perhaps derived from Posidonius, can be found in Pliny and Seneca.

However, Pliny, uncritical though he was, preserves much that is of value. One need only mention as an example his account of amber, the true origin of which he presents for the first time. Other writers of the Roman period make their contribution. Vitruvius discusses the qualities of Roman building stones and describes in detail the preparation of pigments. Dioscorides in book 5 of the *Materia medica* has good notes on a number of minerals and is particularly enlightening on coral. Strabo provides interesting material, including digressions on the Aswan granite outcrops and the dangers of realgar-mining. Galen characteristically interrupts his descriptions with a note on the gender of λίθος. The frustration and long-delayed success of his efforts to witness the ceremony of preparing Lemnian earth was an experience which could even now bedevil a visit to a Greek island. Solinus and Isidore of Seville summarize Pliny, although Solinus has information from elsewhere on topics such as sapphires, Whitby jet, and the coal burnt in the temple of Sulis at Bath.

Several books on stones are cited in [Plutarch], *De Fluviis*, but these are probably part of an elaborate fiction.

GENERAL. C. E. N. Bromehead, 'Geology in Embryo', *Proc. Geolog. Assoc.* 1945, 85 ff.; Forbes, *Stud. Anc. Technol.*, vol. vii. TEXTS. Aristotle, *Meteorologica*, with translation by H. D. P. Lee (Loeb, 1952); Theophrastus, *On Stones*, with translation and commentary by E. R. Caley and J. F. C. Richards (1956): another edition by D. E. Eichholz (1965); Vitruvius, with translation by F. Granger (Loeb, 1931–4); Pliny, *HN* 36–7, with translation by D. E. Eichholz (Loeb, 1962); Dioscorides, edited by M. Wellmann, vol. iii (1914); Galen, vol. xii, Kühn, 165 ff. D. E. E.

**MINERVA** (archaic **Menerva**), an Italian goddess of handicrafts, widely worshipped and regularly identified with Athena (q.v.). Altheim (*PW*, s.v.; cf. *Hist. Rom. Rel.* 235 and note 34; *Griechische Götter* (1930), 142, note 4) believes her actually to be Athena, borrowed early through Etruria; but most scholars think her native, and connect her name with the root of *memini*, etc. At all events there is no trace of her cult in Rome before the introduction of the Capitoline Triad, where she appears with Jupiter and Juno (qq.v.) in an Etruscan grouping. Apart from this she was worshipped in a shrine on Mons Caelius under the name of Minerva Capta, after the taking of Falerii in 241 B.C. (Ov. *Fasti* 3. 835 ff., where see Frazer; cf. Platner–Ashby, 343 f.). A much more important cult lay *extra pomerium* on the Aventine (Platner–Ashby, 342), but its age is unknown; it was the headquarters of a guild of writers and actors during the Second Punic War (Festus, 446, 26 ff. Lindsay) and seems to have been generally the centre of organizations of skilled craftsmen. Minerva's worship spread at the expense of Mars (q.v.) himself, the Quinquatrus coming to be considered her festival, apparently because it was the *natalis* of her temple (Ov. ibid. 812); it was also extended to five days, from a misunderstanding of the meaning ('fifth day after' a given date; see Frazer ad loc.). 13 June was called the *Quinquatrus minusculae* and was the peculiar feast-day of the professional flute-players (*tibicines*; cf. Ov. *Fasti* 6. 651 ff., and Frazer ad loc.).

Latte, *RR* 163 ff. H. J. R.

**MINES.** Though ore had been extracted (both opencast and underground) at other places much earlier, systematic exploitation was first developed at Laurium. The simple geological strata there made it easy to learn to prospect where no indications appeared on the surface. This experience was utilized by the Romans, who were able to test dipping veins, though complex problems such as faulting defeated them.

Ancient shafts and galleries are normally small, as they were cut with hand-tools and it was desirable to obviate propping. Siliceous rocks were broken by fire-setting, a method known in the Bronze Age in Austria. Placer-mines were worked by panning, and for large-scale enterprises (in Spain and at Dolaucothy in Wales) water was brought by aqueducts for hushing (i.e. breaking down of softer beds by rush of water). Iron tools were normal in classical times, though stone hammers survived in many districts for crushing ore.

The miners were mainly slaves, both in the larger Greek mines and in the centralized workings of the Roman Empire. Overseers and engineers also were slaves; in the Empire legionaries were sometimes used. Later, criminals were employed at a few mines and quarries. The Romans sometimes kept their workmen permanently below ground. Some mines the Roman Government exploited directly; at others small concessions were leased, but both technically and socially the mining community was controlled by a procurator. Large lessees, individuals and companies, subject to little control, were common in the Republic but rare later, save at iron-mines. At Laurium concessions were leased to citizens; they were usually large enough to employ several slaves, but sometimes the lessee would himself work underground. In Egypt state-exploitation was the rule.

A developed mining-royalty never existed, though the State claimed dues from miners and authorized mining on other men's property. In earlier times the State *de facto* owned most mines. The idea of royalty was probably developed by the German kingdoms.

The chief difficulties of ancient miners were ventilation and drainage. The former was poor owing to narrow galleries and the use of naked lights, and the various artificial improvements were seldom successful. The best was to drive intercommunicating adits at different levels. The influx of water often caused mines to be abandoned. The Romans used various drainage-machines, such as the screw-pump and perhaps the chain-pump (1st c. A.D.), the water-wheel (2nd c.), and the suction-pump (late Empire); but these devices, being worked by human power, were expensive, and could be used only where the ore was profitable. Batteries of water-wheels superimposed to a depth of 75 metres have been found at Ruda (in Rumania). No machines were sufficiently powerful to reclaim a mine once abandoned. Where the ground-formation permitted, drainage was secured by adits, which were sometimes driven through a mile of sterile rock. The ore was hauled to the surface on trays or in sacks, often by boys who could move quickly in narrow galleries.

ANCIENT SOURCES. Scattered references in Pliny, Strabo, etc. TECHNIQUE. O. Davies, *Roman Mines in Europe* (1935); U. Täckholm, *Studien über den Bergbau der römischen Kaiserzeit* (1937); C. E. N. Bromehead, *Antiquity* 1942, 193 ff.; Forbes, *Stud. Anc. Technol.* vii; detailed studies in E. Ardaillon, *Les Mines du Laurion* (1897), C. Zschocke and E. Preuschen, *Das urzeitliche Bergbaugebiet von Mühlbach–Bischofshofen* (1932); C. Singer (ed.), *History of Ancient Technology* ii² (1965), i. 2 (C. N. Bromehead).
LEGAL POSITION. *Lex Metalli Vipascensis* (Dessau, *ILS* 6891), and references in *Codex Theodosianus*; E. Schönbauer, *Beiträge zur Geschichte des Bergbaurechts* (1929).
MINING PERSONNEL. Inscriptions quoted in general works; the most informative Christian source is *Passio IV Coronatorum.*
DRAINAGE-MACHINES. E. Treptow, *Beiträge zur Geschichte der Technik und der Industrie* viii (1918), 155; R. E. Palmer, *Trans. Institution of Mining and Metallurgy* 1926/7, 299; *Archaeologia Cambrensis* (1936), 51; T. A. Rickard, *Engineering and Mining Journal* 1927, 917. Fire-setting: Holman, *Trans. Institution of Mining and Metallurgy* 1926/7, 219.                    O. D.

**MINOAN CIVILIZATION.** The Bronze Age civilization of Crete (*c.* 3000–1000 B.C.) was thus named by Sir Arthur Evans after Minos (q.v.). It was divided by him in

1905 into nine periods, Early, Middle, and Late Minoan (E.M., M.M., L.M.), each with three divisions, and further subdivisions have since been made using letters and Arabic numbers (e.g. L.M. I A, L.M. I B, L.M. III A 1, L.M. III A 2). Sixteen or more successive chronological periods can be defined in terms of changes in the shapes and decoration of the pottery within the framework of the Minoan civilization. Other classifications proposed, notably by D. Levi (*PP* 1963, 81 ff.) and N. Platon (Zervos, *L'Art de la Crète* (1956), 509 ff.), as yet lack definition.

This high civilization, the earliest on European soil, was not revealed until 1900 when Crete became independent of Turkish rule. The chief sites are: (1) Cnossos (Κνωσσός, Κνώσος), with the largest city and palace, excavated by Evans from 1900 onwards. It lies on the west side of the Kairatos valley about 3½ miles from the sea, in the centre of the north coast of the island, and dominating the wide expanse of fertile rolling hills between the Lasithi Mountains (Dikte) to the east and Ida to the west. The palace was built on top of a 'tell' formed by the debris, some 20 feet deep, of a Neolithic settlement (*BSA* 1964, 132 ff.). The city round it may have covered half a square mile. (2) Phaestus with its city and palace occupied a hill at the west end of the Mesara plain in the south of the island. As at Cnossos the palace was built on the site of a Neolithic settlement. *Ayia Triadha* with a small palace 1½ miles west of Phaestus may have been its harbour town, although the sea is today 2 miles distant. Other important cities with palaces were at *Mallia* on the north coast east of Cnossos, and probably at *Khania* (ancient *Cydonia*) in the west. Towns with smaller palaces have been excavated at *Gournia* and *Zakro* (*Ergon* 1961, 221 ff., 1962, 159 ff., 1963, 159 ff., 1964, 134 f., 1965, 127 ff., 1966, 119 ff.), in the east, at *Kanli Kastelli* south of Cnossos (*Ergon* 1955, 104), and at *Monastiraki* west of Ida (Matz, *Forschungen auf Kreta, 1942* (1951), 27 ff.). Other important town sites include *Tylissus, Arkhanes* and *Nirou Khani* all in the Cnossos area, and *Mochlos* and *Palaikastro* in the east.

The Early Minoan period (*c.* 3000–2200 B.C.) was preceded by a long Neolithic, best known at Cnossos. Copper tools were already in use by the end of the Neolithic there (*PM* ii. 14). But the pottery of E.M. I is so different in its shapes (spouted jugs) and style of decoration ('Pirgos' ware with pattern burnish, 'Ayios Onoufrios' ware with linear designs in red paint on a light ground) as to suggest the presence of a new people arriving from W. Anatolia or from further afield in Syria or Palestine. In E.M. II the arts of stone vase making, seal engraving, and writing seem to have made their first appearance. There is much evidence (stone vases, seal-stones, amulets) of contact with and influence from the direction of Egypt during this phase which corresponds to the end of the Egyptian Old Kingdom and First Intermediary Period. In pottery 'Vasiliki' Ware with mottled red and black surfaces, and small goblets with 'egg-cup' feet, are characteristic of E.M. II.

The flourishing period of the Minoan civilization lasted from M.M. I to L.M. I (*c.* 2200–1450 B.C.). This seems to have been a comparatively peaceful time, although defence walls are attested at Mallia (*Études Crétoises* xi (1959), 4. Cf. *Gnomon* 1961, 827). The island was heavily populated, with cities centred on palaces, with towns, villages, hamlets, and isolated farms. More ambitious 'villas' like Sklavokampos (*AE* 1939–41, 69 ff.) and Vathipetro (*PAE* 1949–56) may have controlled large estates. Writing was practised in hieroglyphic (on stone seals) and linear scripts (Linear A, on clay tablets and stone libation vessels). Two clay cups from Cnossos assigned to M.M. III have Linear A inscriptions written in ink inside them.

What Evans called E.M. III at Cnossos is in effect a phase there which was transitional between E.M. II and M.M. I A. Goblets with low 'egg-cup' feet are taller and narrower than those of E.M. II. In M.M. I A the finer vases at Cnossos begin to be decorated with bichrome designs in red and white on a dark (black or shades of brown and red) lustrous wash. The material assigned to E.M. III in other, notably the eastern parts of the island, appears to be much of it contemporary with M.M. I A at Cnossos: but vases are decorated in white alone. During or at the end of M.M. I A the first great palaces were built at Cnossos and Phaestus, whether owing to a natural evolution of society (Schachermeyr), or by invaders (Luwians) from Anatolia (Huxley). This inaugurated the period of the First Palaces (M.M. I–II).

In M.M. I B, corresponding to the early part of the XII Dynasty in Egypt (c. 2000–1900), the fast potter's wheel came into general use, and vases of great refinement were made including 'eggshell' ware, which imitated metal in fabric and shape. Some of the finest vases have polychrome decoration in dark red, orange, and white.

In M.M. II, contemporary with the late XII and XIII Dynasty in Egypt (c. 1900–1700), the art of the potter reached its highest perfection (Royal Pottery Stores at Cnossos, First Palace at Phaestus). During this period the great palaces at Cnossos and Phaestus were destroyed, whether in war or through natural causes such as an earthquake is uncertain.

The palaces were entirely rebuilt, inaugurating the period of the Second or Later Palaces, i.e. M.M. III–L.M. III A (c. 1790–1375 B.C.). The fine arts of gem engraving, jewellery (Aegina Treasure), metal working (Vaphio cups), and faience (Cnossos Temple Repositories), now reached their highest perfection. It seems that the earliest true pictures ('frescoes'), as opposed to mere decorative designs, painted on the plaster walls of palaces and houses date from this time (M.M. III) and not earlier. But the art of the potter declined, and fine decorated clay vases became rare in M.M. III, due to the increasing use of metal (copper, silver, gold) for table ware. Towards the end of M.M. III a fashion for decorating vases in 'dark on light' (black or brown paint on a light surface) developed at the expense of the earlier tradition of 'light on dark' (decoration in white and red on a black or brown wash). At first the new style of decoration was largely confined to irregular parallel stripes ('Tortoise Shell Ripple'). It reached its highest development in the next period (L.M. I), and especially towards the end of it (L.M. I B) with a rich and varied repertory of flower and marine designs (Plant and Marine Style).

Destruction occurred at Cnossos and some other sites in L.M. I A c. 1500 B.C.; this may have been due to an earthquake accompanying the eruption which overwhelmed the volcanic island of Thera (modern Santorin) about this time. Soon afterwards it seems Thera exploded, involving Crete, especially the eastern parts, in a general destruction which may have been followed by conquest from abroad (in L.M. I B c. 1450 B.C.) (see MYCENAE). After this disaster only the palace at Cnossos appears to have continued to exist as such. For Cnossos the succeeding period, L.M. II (c. 1450–1400 B.C.), was evidently one of prosperity with richly furnished 'Warrior Graves'.

In L.M. II vases including large 'amphorae' were decorated in an elaborate, but stiff and somewhat debased 'Palace Style'. The pottery of this period is thought to show some influence from Mainland Greece. A new script (Linear B) was now in use, but in Crete it is hardly attested as yet outside Cnossos, though it is known from several Mainland sites. The language of Linear B may be different from that of the earlier scripts; it has been interpreted as a form of Greek (see MINOAN SCRIPTS), but this is contested.

The final destruction of the 'Last Palace' at Cnossos was dated by Evans c. 1400 B.C. But much if not most of the pottery which he attributed to a subsequent 'Reoccupation' of the palace site appears to belong to the period of its destruction; this may therefore be dated on the basis of the fine decorated vases to the beginning of the Amarna period in Egypt (L.M. III A, c. 1375 B.C. or not much later). From then onwards (L.M. III B–C) there was a marked decline in the arts of vase decoration and seal-engraving. No fresco paintings are attested after the time of the destruction of Cnossos in L.M. III A.

At some point in L.M. III the inhabitants of many of the coastal sites retreated to high defensible hills ('Kastri' at Palaikastro, Karfi in Lasithi (BSA 1937–8, 57 ff.; 1960, 1 ff.)). But at Cnossos at least there is evidence of continuous occupation till the end of the Bronze Age and into the Early Iron Age (Sub-Minoan and Protogeometric) c. 1000 B.C.

*Architecture.* Palaces and houses were two or more stories high, with walls of rubble on 'megalithic' foundations of great blocks. For outside walls carefully squared stone was often used. The upper parts of walls were normally built of mud or mud brick. Walls were often strengthened by an elaborate timber framework. Square stone pillars, and round wooden columns, straight or tapering towards the bases, helped to support flat roofs and upper floors. The great palaces (Cnossos, Phaestus, Mallia) were built round large rectangular central courts, and had many staircases, together with smaller courts which might be surrounded by colonnades (peristyle), and 'light wells' for admitting light and air.

*Religion* centred upon a goddess, or group of goddesses, whose attribute was a double axe, with male deities in a subordinate role. The palaces themselves were in some sense sanctuaries, with many cult rooms. There were also numerous Sacred Caves and Peak Sanctuaries on the tops of high hills (Platon, *Kretika Khronika* 1951, 96 ff.). 'Horns of Consecration' served to mark places of cult. No great temples like those of contemporary Egypt have been recognized, but the town of Gournia had a small shrine with large clay cult statues in it. All such clay cult statues have been assigned to L.M. III (Alexiou, *Kretika Khronika* 1958, 179 ff.), but some including those at Gournia may be earlier (M.M. III–L.M. I). Dancing and bull-leaping probably formed part of religious or magical ceremonies.

*Burial.* At first (E.M.–M.M.) members of each community were buried together in caves, or in built tombs which might have rectangular rooms, but which were often circular and evidently beehive-domed ('tholos tombs') like the primitive round houses known in Cyprus (Khirokitia) and further east (*Antiquity* 1960, 166 ff.). Bodies might be placed in large store jars (*pithoi*) or oval clay coffins. In time a fashion for small family tombs or individual graves developed, especially after the catastrophe of L.M. I B. Burials in L.M. III were often in rectangular clay coffins (*larnakes*) or bath tubs. What may be royal tombs have been identified at Cnossos (Temple Tomb, Isopata Royal Tomb). Inhumation was the rule, but one or two cremations are attested at Cnossos in M.M. III–L.M. I, others elsewhere in L.M. III.

(a) GENERAL. A. J. Evans, *The Palace of Minos at Knossos* i–iv and index (1921–36, repr. 1964); J. D. S. Pendlebury, *The Archaeology of Crete* (1939, repr. 1963); S. Marinatos and M. Hirmer, *Crete and Mycenae* (1960); R. W. Hutchinson, *Prehistoric Crete* (1962); F. Matz, *Minoan Civilization. Maturity and Zenith* (*CAH*², chs. 4 (b) and 12); F. Schachermeyr, *Die minoische Kultur des alten Kreta* (1964).

(b) SITES. (1) *Cnossos.* A. Evans, *The Palace of Minos* and reports in *BSA* 1900–5, *The Prehistoric Tombs of Knossos* (1906), *The Tomb of the Double Axes* (1914); J. D. S. Pendlebury, *A Handbook to the Palace of Minos* (new edition, 1954); S. Hood, *Archaeological Survey*

*of the Knossos Area* (no date); *BSA* and *Archaeological Reports*, for work since 1940. For the date of the destruction of the 'Last Palace' at Cnossos, L. Palmer and J. Boardman, *On the Knossos Tablets* (1963), esp. 93 f.; M. Popham, *AJArch.* 1964, 349 ff., *Studies in Mediterranean Archaeology* v (1964); S. Hood, *Kadmos* 4 (1965), 16 ff.
(c) For special topics see the bibliographies in MINOAN SCRIPTS and *CAH*² ii, chs. 4 and 14.                                    M. S. F. H.

**MINOAN SCRIPTS.** During the second millennium B.C. Crete developed its own form of writing, and a family of scripts is now known under the name Minoan. The earliest, found principally on seal-stones, is called pictographic. The pictorial signs were then simplified so that they could be represented by an outline, and in this form, known as Linear A, the script was widely used throughout Crete during the period approximately 1900–1500 B.C. It was doubtless used also by Minoan colonies overseas, but true inscriptions rather than potters' marks have so far been discovered only on Keos in the Cyclades. Linear A remains undeciphered in 1969, despite many ingenious attempts; but it is evident that the graphic system resembles that of Linear B (see below). The differences between A and B are perhaps broadly comparable to those between the Greek and Roman alphabets. The inscriptions in Linear A are of three kinds: (1) clay tablets, which from the use of ideograms and numerals can be identified as accounting documents; (2) inscriptions on movable objects, some at least of which are of a religious nature; (3) a small number of ill-preserved graffiti.
LINEAR B is the best-known member of the family, represented on more than 4,000 tablets including all fragments. It was first found at Cnossos in Crete and regarded as a special form of Linear A; but subsequent discoveries at Pylos in Messenia, Mycenae, and Thebes show that it is rather the script of Mycenaean Greece. The mainland examples date from the thirteenth century B.C.; those from Cnossos are apparently a little earlier. The script was shown in 1952 by Michael Ventris to be a notation for an archaic form of the Greek language (*see* DIALECTS, GREEK). It is written from left to right. It consists of three elements: (1) a system of about ninety signs, each of which represents an open syllable. There are five vowels corresponding generally to Greek *a*, *ε*, *ι*, *o*, *υ*; length is not indicated. Combined with each of these is a series of twelve consonants. Five of these correspond to letters of the Greek alphabet (δ, ϝ, μ, ν, σ); but the stops are not usually distinguished for voicing or aspiration, thus one series of signs does duty for κ, γ, and χ, another for π, β, and φ, and a third for τ and θ. The liquids (λ, ρ) are represented by a single series of signs. There is a series for the labio-velar stops, eliminated in later Greek (*qʷ*, *gʷ*, *qʷh*); and another for the semi-vowel *y* produced by contact between ι and a following vowel. There are also signs with more complicated values, often a combination of consonant, semi-vowel, and vowel, and a series partially agreeing with Greek ζ. These signs are used to spell words syllabically; extra vowels are inserted to represent consonant clusters, but continuants at the end of closed syllables (λ, μ, ν, ρ, σ, also diphthongal ι) are usually omitted. This has the effect of concealing much of the noun inflexion; but despite its ambiguities the orthography is adequate for making the stereotyped records which are the main function of the script. (2) A collection of ideograms or signs representing objects, including human beings and animals. These vary from accurate sketches which may show the number of handles attached to a vessel to formal patterns bearing little resemblance to the object designated. The ideograms do not stand for Greek words, but were in many cases taken over from Linear A. (3) A numerical system on a decimal base, using upright strokes for units, horizontal bars for tens, circles for hundreds, circles with rays for thousands, and even a sign for ten thousand. Each sign is repeated the necessary number of times up to nine.

The documents in Linear B are mainly tablets of unbaked clay; these are the day-to-day accounts and inventories kept in the Palaces, which although dull and repetitive do cast some interesting light upon economic conditions and the nature of the administration. The study of the language is also of importance for the history of Greek, though largely as confirming the accuracy of predictions made on comparative evidence. There is also a small number of jars with painted inscriptions in Linear B.
CYPRO-MINOAN is the name given to a related script found in Bronze Age Cyprus. It occurs in varying forms at different dates from the fifteenth to twelfth centuries B.C.; and a variant is also known from Ugarit on the coast of Syria. There is still far too little material to permit decipherment; but it is presumed to be the ancestor of the classical CYPRIOTE SYLLABARY.
THE PHAISTOS DISK is an isolated document found in a Middle Minoan context at Phaestus in Crete. It is almost certainly written in a syllabic script from right to left, but its place of origin is unknown, and its relationship to the Minoan scripts doubtful.

M. Ventris and J. Chadwick, *Documents in Mycenaean Greek* (1956); J. Chadwick, *The Decipherment of Linear B* (1958); L. Deroy, *Initiation à l'épigraphie mycénienne* (1963); M. Pope, *Aegean Writing and Linear A*, Studies in Mediterranean Archaeology VIII (1964).                                    J. C.

**MINOS** (Μίνως), a king of Crete; the traditions concerning him preserve faint reminiscences of the might of the civilization now called Minoan (q.v.), and 'Minos' may be a dynastic name or title. See, e.g., Thucydides 1. 4 for a tradition of his sea-power. It is conceivable at least that the evil character given him in Attic legends, but not in the main stream of Greek tradition ([Plato], *Minos*, 318 d–e), has behind it a real contest between prehistoric Attica and Crete; cf. below. The evidence of Linear B for a Hellenic kingship in Cnossos before its fall has raised again the problem whether Minos should be regarded as Greek or not.
In the *Odyssey* he was a king with special association with Zeus (19. 178) and continues to exercise rule among the dead (11. 568). He is consistently said to be son of Zeus and Europa (q.v.), and to have married Pasiphaë, daughter of Helios (Apollod. 3. 7). Her name, 'all-shining', has been interpreted as that of a moon-goddess, which is unnecessary, as it fits a fully human child of the sun-god (cf. Phaëthon); but that both kings and queens of Minoan Crete were regarded as partly or wholly divine is quite possible. To settle the question whether Minos or another should be king, Minos prayed to Poseidon to send a bull from the sea for him to sacrifice. Poseidon did so, thus confirming his right to rule, but the bull was so handsome that Minos would not kill it. Poseidon (or, according to Hyg. *Fab.* 40. 1, Aphrodite) therefore caused Pasiphaë to fall in love with it. By the help of Daedalus (q.v.) she was disguised as a cow and attained her end; consequently she bore a creature half-man, half-bull, 'Minos' bull', Μίνω ταῦρος, the 'Minotaur(us)' of Latin and English. Daedalus constructed a maze, the labyrinth, to hide it in. The word is pre-Hellenic, connected with λάβρυς, a double axe, the well-known Cretan religious symbol; a rite involving the use of a maze may underlie the story; see W. F. J. Knight, *Cumaean Gates* (1936), ch. 8.
Minos made war on Megara and Athens. As regards the former, for the legend of Minos, Nisus, and Scylla, *see* NISUS (1). At Athens he was provoked by the murder of his son Androgeos, and so made peace only on terms of receiving a yearly tribute of youths and maidens, whom he shut up with the Minotaur (Plut. *Thes.* 15; *see* THESEUS).
Minos' death was due to treachery. Daedalus having escaped, he pursued him to Sicily, where he found him

by a stratagem in the house of Cocalus, king of Camicus. He demanded his surrender, and Cocalus pretended to agree, received Minos with show of hospitality, and handed him over to his daughters to be bathed in the Homeric fashion. They killed him by pouring boiling water (or pitch instead of water) on him (Hdt. 7. 170. 1; Apollod. *Epit.* 1. 13–15.

Minos appears occasionally in pictures of the Minotaur story on archaic and classical vases, Etruscan ash-urns of the Hellenistic age, and Roman sarcophagi; as Judge of the dead on a few south Italian vases.

Besides the larger dictionaries s.v., see Cook, *Zeus* ii, 939 ff.
H. J. R.; H. W. P.; C. M. R.

**MINTURNAE,** important town on the Via Appia (q.v.) where it crossed the River Liris (q.v.) near its mouth. Rome reduced its original inhabitants, the Aurunci (q.v.), in the Latin and Second Samnite Wars and in 295 B.C. established a citizen colony alongside and west of the Auruncan settlement, which had consisted of a small rectangular fortification with polygonal-type walls and angle-towers. The near-by marshes, where Marius sought refuge from Sulla's minions (88 B.C.), rendered Minturnae somewhat unhealthy; but after Augustus restored it, the *colonia* lasted well into imperial times. The *capitolium* and *forum* of the republican colony have been excavated. When an imperial *forum* was built the old one became a portico behind the Augustan theatre, while the *capitolium* was eclipsed by three new temples, one embodying manumission records of the Sullan period. The west town-gate (*JRS* 1933, 155 ff.) embodies an aqueduct-*castellum* or distribution-chamber. Remains of an amphitheatre exist. The neighbouring grove and shrine of the sea-goddess Marica, mother of Latinus (q.v.), were greatly venerated from the sixth century B.C. on.

A. Schulten, *Hermes* 1898, 537 ff. (discussion of the *forma* of the field-system); J. Johnson, *Excavations at Minturnae* (U.S.A. 1933), i, ii; A. De Santis, *Gatea, Formi, Minturno* (1955).
I. A. R.; E. T. S.

**MINUCIANUS** the Elder (2nd c. A.D.), rival of Hermogenes, wrote Προγυμνάσματα, a τέχνη (treating of στάσις theory), and a commentary on Demosthenes. The Π. ἐπιχειρημάτων (Spengel, *Rhet.* i. 417–24) is probably by a third-century namesake. In rhetorical theory Minucianus, influenced by Aristotle and Theodorus, stood for philosophic, as opposed to sophistic, rhetoric; and he challenged without success the innovations of Hermogenes.
J. W. H. A.

**MINUCIUS** (1, *PW* 40) **ESQUILINUS AUGURINUS,** Lucius, is said, as *consul suffectus*, to have been rescued by Cincinnatus (q.v.) from defeat by the Aequi on Mount Algidus (458 B.C.), and to have been a member of the two decemvirates. In 439 he dealt with a famine and a revolutionary attempt by Sp. Maelius. Although the traditional account was much elaborated by annalists of the Gracchan period, who invented his *transitio ad plebem* and vested him with a chronologically impossible *praefectura annonae*, Minucius was probably an actual public benefactor during a fifth-century famine. He was recorded in the *libri lintei* in 440/39 as *praefectus* (? *urbi*, rather than *annonae*) and the Senate decreed a statue for his help against Maelius; later (not before the third century) his descendants set up a commemorative column and statue near the Porta Trigemina (or Minucia). He need not be explained away either as a god, corresponding to Hercules μηνυτής, or as the eponymous builder of the Porticus Minucia, which was not built before c. 106 or used for corn distributions until Claudius, while Cincius Alimentus shows that the story of Minucius was known in his time.

A. Momigliano, *Studia et documenta historiae et iuris* ii (1936); Ogilvie, *Comm. Livy 1–5*, 438, 550 ff.
P. T.

**MINUCIUS** (2, *PW* 52) **RUFUS,** Marcus (*cos.* 221 B.C.), helped to reduce the Istri. After the battle of Trasimene (217) he was appointed *magister equitum* to Fabius (q.v. 5) Cunctator by the Comitia, not by the dictator himself as was customary. Minucius disobeyed Fabius' orders and in his absence attacked Hannibal at Gerunium with considerable success. The People then appointed Minucius co-dictator with Fabius, an undermining of the nature of the office. As dictator he made a dedication to Hercules (*ILS* 11). The aristocratic tradition records that only the timely arrival of Fabius rescued him from an attack by Hannibal. He fell at Cannae (216).

For the view that Livy, unlike Polybius, implies that in 217 Minucius was not made co-dictator but only received *imperium* equal to that of a dictator, see T. A. Dorey, *JRS* 1955, 92 ff., whose further view that Minucius was dictator in 220 is rejected by E. Badian, *Gnomon* 1961, 497.
H. H. S.

**MINUCIUS** (3, *PW* 30) **AUGURINUS,** Gaius, a tribune (probably 187 B.C.), who, after the attack of the Petillii (q.v.), accused L. Scipio of refusing to render an account of monies received from Antiochus; he imposed a fine, a demand for surety, and a threat of imprisonment, but was prevented by his colleague Gracchus (q.v. 2) from enforcing his demands.

Scullard, *Rom. Pol.* 142 f., 294 ff.
H. H. S.

**MINUCIUS** (4, *PW* 54) **RUFUS,** Marcus, consul in 110 B.C. and proconsul in Macedonia, triumphed (106) and built the *porticus Minucia*, used under the Empire for grain distributions. He and his brother Quintus, as hereditary patrons of Liguria, settled a boundary dispute there (*ILS* 5946).
E. B.

**MINUCIUS** (5) **FELIX,** Marcus, fl. A.D. 200–40, author of a dialogue in elegant, ironic Latin between a Christian, *Octavius*, and a pagan, Caecilius Natalis of Cirta (perhaps identical with a Caecilius Natalis mentioned in Cirta inscriptions of c. 210–17). The pagan case uses Fronto's discourse against Christianity. The Christian rejoinder uses Stoic matter from Cicero and Seneca, and has a long-disputed relation to Tertullian's *Apologeticum* which must be one of dependence. The target is philosophical scepticism without the *sinceritas* to abandon polytheism.

Ed. J. Beaujeu (1964); C. Becker, *Der Octavius des M. F.* (1967). *PW*, Suppl. xi, 952 ff., 1365 ff.
H. C.

**MINYANS** (Μινύαι), a prehistoric tribe, whose chief branches inhabited the Boeotian Orchomenus (*Il.* 2. 511) and Iolcus in Thessaly (ibid. 712). To the latter belong the legends of Athamas and Jason (1) (qq.v.). There were also families claiming Minyan descent in Laconia (the Aegeids), Thera, and Cyrene; a Minyan tribe round Lepreum, destroyed by the Eleans c. 475 B.C.; and legends of former Minyans in Lemnos, descended from the Argonauts (Pind. *Pyth.* 4; Hdt. 4. 145–8, who combines all these facts and legends into one story).

The fine wheel-made pottery, of 'soapy' surface, known as 'Grey Minyan', was so called by Schliemann because first found at Orchomenus. It first appears c. 1900 B.C., and has no probable connexion with the Minyae of legend. *See* MINYAS.
A. R. B.

**MINYAS** (Μινύας). Founder of Orchomenus and eponym of the Minyae (Pind. *Isthm.* 1. 56); his 'treasury', shown at Orchomenus in Pausanias' time (Paus. 9. 38. 2), was a Mycenaean beehive-tomb, as was proved by Schliemann's investigations. He is also in some sense ancestor of the Argonauts (q.v.), they being commonly called Minyans, as Pind. *Pyth.* 4. 69; the reason given by

Ap. Rhod. 1. 230 ff., that most of them were descended from his daughters, does not agree with the surviving lists but may have with the primitive form of the story. His legend, if ever he had one (the lost epic *Minyas* may have had something to say of him), has vanished, and we know of him chiefly as a member of several genealogies, mutually inconsistent and connecting him with Orchomenus, Thessaly (Iolcus), and several other regions. These are conveniently assembled by Fiehn in *PW* xv. 2015–8; see the whole article for ancient and modern literature. H. J. R.

**MIRACLES.** Wonderful stories of the power of gods were common at all periods of antiquity, and many of them were attached to particular shrines. For instance, there is the very pretty tale of the ugly child miraculously made beautiful by Helen (Hdt. 6. 61; shrine at Therapnae); another local legend told how Poseidon miraculously smote an impious intruder into his temple at Mantinea (Paus. 8. 10. 3). In Rome tales of this sort perhaps clustered most thickly around Vesta. For example, there is the legend of the Vestal Aemilia, during whose service of the goddess the holy fire went out. It being by no fault of hers, she prayed to Vesta to prove her innocence, and flung a strip of her robe upon the altar, which at once blazed to confirm her innocence (Dion. Hal. *Ant. Rom.* 2. 68. 3). One of Martial's flatteries of Domitian is the story of how a man who violated his 'sacred' fishpond was blinded, a regular form of divine punishment (Mart. 4. 30. 8 ff.; cf. F. Sauter, *Kaiserkult bei Martial u. Statius* (1934), 110 f.). The cult of Asclepius (q.v.) produced a vast quantity of miracles of healing, by no means all confined to his shrines (see, e.g., *Suda* s.v. Θεόπομπος). But miracles are more prominent in Hellenistic times, and especially in connexion with foreign gods, such as Isis and Sarapis. Among these international gods there was necessarily competition. Hence many stories of the manifestation of, e.g., Sarapis' power to convince the sceptical, prove his deity, and so on.

A. D. Nock, *Conversion* (1933), index under 'Miracles'. H. J. R.

**MIRRORS** (κάτοπτρον, *speculum*). The Greeks and Romans used disks of highly polished metal, usually bronze, as mirrors. The bronze alloy frequently contained a high proportion of tin.

Mirrors were introduced into the classical world from Egypt; the earliest examples have been found in the Shaft Graves at Mycenae, and there are a number of others from Late Helladic sites in Greece and Cyprus. Mycenaean mirrors usually had a short tang which was fitted into a bone or ivory handle. Mirrors of the Archaic and Classical periods were open disks polished on one side and equipped with decorated bronze handles; standing mirrors were sometimes given an elaborate figure support. Etruscan mirrors from the sixth century onwards were often richly engraved with figured scenes and decoration on the back; the handles were of ivory, bone, or wood. A new type of mirror without a handle and with the reflecting surface protected by a cover fitting over it became popular in Greece at the end of the fifth century B.C. Figures in relief or engraved decoration appear on the covers.

Some mirrors of gilt or silvered bronze were known in the fifth century and silver mirrors, which were coming into fashion in Hellenistic times, became very common in the Roman period. A few small wall-mirrors set in ornamental frames are known. Roman mirrors of the Early Empire are generally open disk mirrors with metal handles; the back of the disk is sometimes decorated with a relief. In later examples the handle is fixed to the back of the disk. Roman mirrors are rectangular as well as round.

The reflecting properties of glass were known to the ancients and there are references to glass mirrors in Roman times. A few surviving examples, which are all small and not very efficient, belong to the Roman period; they consist of little disks or rectangles of glass backed with lead or plaster and have been found on a number of sites. There is no evidence for the silvering of glass mirrors by means of mercury.

W. Lamb, *Greek and Roman Bronzes* (1929); E. Gerhard, *Etruskische Spiegel*, 5 vols. (1840–97); J. D. Beazley, 'The World of the Etruscan Mirror', *JHS* 1949, 1 ff.; W. Züchner, *Griechische Klappspiegel* (1942). D. E. S.

**MISE** (Μίση), an obscure goddess, first mentioned in Hero(n)das 1. 56, where the name of the festival, κάθοδος, suggests chthonian ritual. The forty-second Orphic hymn says she is bisexual and seems to identify her with both Dionysus and Demeter; she may well be Asianic. H. J. R.

**MISENUM,** the northern headland of the Bay of Naples, with a similarly named town and harbour, reputedly the burial place of Aeneas' trumpeter Misenus, a former follower of Hector and drowned by an envious Triton (Verg. *Aen.* 6. 162 ff.). Cumae early used the harbour, but until imperial times Misenum was merely a villa resort (Octavian, Antony, and Sextus Pompeius signed their Treaty of Misenum at Puteoli, 39 B.C.: *Rev. Arch.* 1913, 253). Agrippa made the harbour Rome's chief naval station (31 B.C.), and the town subsequently became a *colonia* (Dessau, *ILS* 6335). The Elder Pliny was stationed here and perished when Vesuvius erupted, A.D. 79 (Pliny, *Ep.* 6. 16. 20). The harbour fell into disuse *c.* 400, and finally the Saracens destroyed Misenum. Remains exist of Marius' villa, later the property of Lucullus and the emperors.

K. Lehmann-Hartleben, *Die Antiken Hafenanlagen des Mittelmeeres* (1923), 176. E. T. S.

**MITHRAS** (Μίθρας, -ης), an ancient Aryan (Indo-Iranian) god of light, truth, and the plighted word. In Persian Zoroastrianism, according to the *Avesta* (an oriental sacred text), he figures as the ally and agent of the good power, Ahuramazda, and as the implacable foe of Ahriman, the evil principle. In the *Avesta* tradition Mithras' titles include 'Lord of Light', 'God of Truth', 'Saviour from Death', 'Giver of Bliss', 'Victorious', and 'Warrior'. These partly explain his attraction for the Roman world, for its army, its merchant class, and the growing numbers in many ranks of its society who hoped for individual immortality and happiness beyond the grave. There is, however, no trace in the *Avesta* of the essential features of Roman Mithraism as a mystery-cult, with secret rites and stages of initiation through which the god's devotees had to pass. Again, although in the *Avesta* Mithras is also hailed as 'Lord of Wide Pastures', there is nothing there about that bull-slaying exploit, the tauroctony, symbol of life through death and of victory over death and evil, which lies at the heart of the Mithraic creed as we know it from the Roman evidence. The first indication that we have of Mithraic mysteries dates from the first half of the first century B.C. and comes from south-east Asia Minor, where, according to Plutarch (*Vit. Pomp.* 24), the Cilician pirates practised τελεταὶ ἀπόρρητοι of Mithras. (Plutarch, incidentally, does not state, as he is often said to do, that the pirates, settled in Italy, brought the Mithraic mysteries to the West: he says that the West was first aware of them among the pirates in Cilicia and that these mysteries were still being celebrated in his own day.) That the Persian Mithras and the Roman mystery-god were one and the same is certain. Mithras normally appears in Roman art as wearing the Phrygian (Persian) cap and Persian trousers; Statius, alluding (*Theb.* i. 719–20) to the tauroctony (of which he must have seen a representation), says that Mithras slew the bull 'beneath the Persian cave', and one of the Mithraic grades was that of *Perses*. But how, when, and where the god of the *Avesta* evolved into the Roman mystery-god is still an unsolved problem. Mithraism is often described as an oriental mystery-cult: but its shrines, most of its art and inscriptions, and the allusions to it in classical and early Christian writers belong essentially to the Roman world.

From the second half of the first century A.D. onwards Mithraism spread through the Roman Empire. The Romano-Parthian city of Dura-Europos (q.v.) had a fine shrine of Mithras; Syria, Asia Minor, and Spain have yielded some Mithraic temples and monuments, Greece proper has revealed extremely few. The areas most prolific in Mithraic finds of all kinds are central Italy, northern Africa west of Carthage, eastern Gaul, and, above all, the western and northern frontier provinces, the Rhine and Danube regions, and the line of Hadrian's Wall in Britain. The cult was also very flourishing in Rome and other great cosmopolitan centres and in the seaports of the western Mediterranean and beyond—Ostia, Puteoli, Aquileia, Carthage, and London. Soldiers and merchants were clearly the leading channels of its propaganda. The cult was exclusively confined to men.

Early Christian writers record the names of the seven Mithraic grades of initiation—Raven (*Corax*), Bride (*Nymphus*), Soldier (*Miles*), Lion (*Leo*), Persian (*Perses*), Courier of the Sun (*Heliodromus*), and Father (*Pater*). They also tell us that the Mithraists practised a form of baptism, a sealing on the forehead, and a ceremonial meal, and that they had to undergo tests and ordeals of some kind. These statements have all been confirmed by archaeology; and indeed the vast bulk of our evidence for the cult is archaeological and epigraphical.

The temples of Mithras are artificial caves (*spelaea*), sometimes partly underground, to recall the cave in which Mithras caught and slew the mystic bull. They are oblong, with a central 'nave' and lateral 'aisles', generally raised above the level of the 'nave' in the form of benches on which the faithful reclined at sacred banquets. Occasionally (e.g. at Dura, Lambaesis, and London) columns or pilasters separate 'nave' from 'aisles'; very rarely (Lambaesis and London) the 'nave' terminates in a rounded apse. At the end of the 'nave', in the place of honour opposite the entrace, was a kind of reredos, normally carved, but sometimes painted (Rome, ancient Capua, Marino), and depicting the tauroctony. Mithras, accompanied by two standing torch-bearers, Cautes and Cautopates, kneels on the back of the bull and averts his gaze as he plunges his knife into the creature's shoulder: a dog and a snake lap up the life-giving blood; corn-ears sprout from the tail of the dying beast; and a scorpion, emblem of evil, seeks to attack its vitals. This tauroctony scene seems to have been modelled on a Hellenistic statuary group of a bull-slaying Nike kneeling on her victim's back (cf. the reverse-type of the ARMENIA CAPTA *aureus* of Augustus struck at an eastern mint). Episodes in the god's saga represented in Mithraic art include his birth from a rock, his hunting expedition on horseback, and his dealings with the Sun-God. Sol is shown kneeling before Mithras, standing and clasping his hand, seated beside him at a sacred meal, and ascending to heaven with him in his chariot. Mithras and the Sun are, in fact, very closely linked and in his dedications the former is frequently addressed as *Sol invictus Mithras*.

There is no need to believe that the astrological elements that feature prominently in Mithraic art—the planetary gods, the signs of the zodiac, etc.—were directly derived from Mesopotamian sources as the worship of Mithras travelled westwards. By the time that Mithraism reached the West, these things had long formed part of the common stock of Graeco-Roman cultus.

A large proportion of those who made dedications in Mithras' honour were members of the well-to-do business classes (e.g. Ostia) and Roman army officers (e.g. Carrawburgh and Rudchester on Hadrian's Wall); there are three dedications by provincial governors (Lambaesis) and one by Emperors (Diocletian, etc., at Carnuntum).

To judge by the relatively restricted size of the temples, the individual Mithraic communities were small in numbers. But the wealth and high standard of culture of some, particularly of those in cities, is attested by two recent and important discoveries. First the Mithraeum found beneath the church of Santa Prisca on the Aventine in Rome. Here the tauroctony at the termination of the 'nave' is in stucco and on the floor immediately below it is a most unusual feature—the reclining stucco figure of a water-deity. On the side-walls of the shrine are two layers of paintings: the upper one, the work of a highly accomplished artist, shows processions of *Leones* with offerings and Mithras and the Sun banqueting. Also on these walls was made another very rare find, that of metrical texts some of which appear to give directions for a way of life, while others are fragments of hymns: one significant line reads: *et nos servasti eternali sanguine fuso*. Secondly the Mithraeum brought to light in 1954 in the Walbrook in London. This is distinguished by its unusual architectural features of apse and colonnades and by the fine works of art deliberately concealed within it in ancient times. These works include heads of Mithras, Minerva, and Serapis, a colossal right hand of Mithras Tauroctonus, a seated figure of Mercury, a Bacchic group, all in Italian (Luna) marble, and a circular, lidded, silver casket richly adorned with hunting scenes in relief. Such objects illustrate very vividly the syncretistic tendencies of Mithraism.

F. Cumont, *Textes et monuments figurés relatifs aux mystères de Mithra* (2 vols., 1896, 1899); *Les Mystères de Mithra*³ (1913); M. J. Vermaseren, *Corpus Inscriptionum et Monumentorum Religionis Mithraicae* (2 vols., 1956, 1960); *Mithras, the Secret God* (1963); M. J. Vermaseren and C. C. van Essen, *The Excavations in the Mithraeum of the Church of Sta Prisca in Rome* (1965); I. A. Richmond and J. P. Gillam, *The Temple of Mithras at Carrawburgh* (1951); J. M. C. Toynbee, *Hibbert Journal*, Jan. 1956 (Mithraism and Christianity); A. L. Campbell, *Mithraic Iconography and Ideology* (1968).    J. M. C. T.

**MITHRIDATES.** The name of six kings of Pontus. It is disputed whether the series begins with Mithridates II of Cius or Mithridates Ktistes. According to an inscription of Chersonesus Pharnaces I used an era beginning in 337/6 B.C. when Mithridates II became tyrant of Cius, but Mithridates V in an inscription of Abonuteichus and Mithridates VI on his coins use one that began in 298 or 297, possibly the year when Ktistes was established in his kingdom. If the series of eight kings, six of whom were named Mithridates, begins with Ktistes, it is necessary to divide the long reign of Mithridates II (c. 250–c. 185) between two kings of that name (see below).

(1) MITHRIDATES II of Cius (I? of Pontus), a Persian noble who claimed descent from Darius the Great or one of his six associates, was tyrant of Cius from 337/6 to 302, when Antigonus I, suspicious of his loyalty, put him to death.

(2) MITHRIDATES I (II?) KTISTES (302–266 B.C.), son or nephew of (1), escaped from Antigonus I to Cimiata of Paphlagonia, and soon won Pontus, making Amaseia (q.v.) his capital. He joined the Northern League against the Seleucid kings, and was instrumental, with Nicomedes of Bithynia, in settling the Gauls in Phrygia. His successor was his son ARIOBARZANES, who gained Amastris, but died c. 250 at a time of Gallic inroads.

(3) MITHRIDATES II (III?), son of Ariobarzanes (see

above), either ruled from c. 250 to c. 185 or, more probably, died c. 220 and was succeeded by (4) his son Mithridates III (?). Despite his marriage with Laodice, sister of Seleucus II, he aided Antiochus (q.v. 8) Hierax to expel Seleucus from Asia Minor. He made gifts to Rhodes after the great earthquake, but an attempt on Sinope by him or his son (220) was defeated with Rhodian aid. *See* PHARNACES I.

(4) MITHRIDATES IV PHILOPATOR PHILADELPHUS succeeded his brother Pharnaces I (q.v.) before 156, with his sister Laodice as queen. He became a friend and ally of Rome and supported Attalus II of Pergamum against Prusias II of Bithynia in 156–154. He probably died c. 150 B.C.

(5) MITHRIDATES V EUERGETES, probably son of Pharnaces I, followed a philo-Roman and hellenizing policy while striving to enlarge his kingdom. He aided Rome against Carthage in 149–146 and against Aristonicus (q.v. 1) in 132–129, and received Phrygia as a reward from Aquilius. He had already gained control of Galatia, was named the heir of Pylaemenes of Inner Paphlagonia, and brought Cappadocia under his influence through the marriage of Ariarathes VI (q.v.) with his daughter Laodice. He was murdered at Sinope, his capital, in 120, and a suspiciously convenient will named his wife Laodice and his two minor children, Eupator and Chrestus, as his successors.

(6) MITHRIDATES VI, EUPATOR DIONYSUS ('the Great') (120–63), son of Mithridates V, fled from his mother and led a fugitive existence for some years, then suddenly captured Sinope, imprisoned his mother, killed his brother, married his sister Laodice (the first member of a large harem), and resumed his father's policy of expansion. He first acquired the north shore of the Euxine, from which he drew large revenues and many soldiers. He then occupied Lesser Armenia, eastern Pontus, and Colchis. Attempts (in alliance or rivalry with Bithynia) to secure control of Inner Paphlagonia and Cappadocia (*see* ARIARATHES VII–IX, ARIOBARZANES I) were foiled by Rome, and an attempt to expel Nicomedes IV (q.v.) from Bithynia was equally unsuccessful. Raids on Pontic territory in 88 by Nicomedes led to the First Mithridatic War. Mithridates occupied most of Asia Minor, where Roman exactions made him welcome as a deliverer, the islands of the Aegean except Rhodes, and (with Athenian help) much of Greece. Sulla's victories drove him out of Greece and led to a reaction against him in Asia, which he met by severe reprisals. He made peace at Dardanus in 85 on Sulla's terms, giving up all conquered territory. He easily repelled the raids of Sulla's lieutenant Murena in 81 (the Second Mithridatic War), and used the next years to tighten his hold on the Pontic coast, to foster close relationships with the pirate leaders, and lay up stores of treasure and supplies. Rome's decision in 74 to annex Bithynia precipitated the Third Mithridatic War. Mithridates occupied Bithynia, but the resistance of Cyzicus enabled Lucullus to cut off his army from supplies and destroy it. He was expelled from Pontus by Lucullus (72–71), and although a mutiny of the Roman army allowed Mithridates to recover much of his territory (68–67), he had not enough strength left to stand against Lucullus' successor Pompey. Defeated at Nicopolis, he fled to Colchis, sending orders for the massacre of his harem, and made his way to the Crimea. Here the sacrifices which he demanded for a new fleet and army raised his subjects in revolt, led by his son Pharnaces. Driven to bay, he found that a diet of prophylactics had made him immune to poison, and died by the sword of a guard at the age of 69. In cunning, courage, and organizing ability Mithridates was Rome's stoutest oriental antagonist, but he failed in the arts of a strategist, and could not keep the loyalty of his subordinates. His portraits show that he copied

Alexander in personal appearance. He was a true representative neither of the Hellenism which he affected nor of the Iranians who formed the most important element among his people.

App. *Mith.*; Plut. *Luc.* and *Pomp.* Th. Reinach, *Trois royaumes de l'Asie mineure* (1888); *Mithridates Eupator* (1895); *L'Histoire par les monnaies* (1903), 127 ff.; Magie, *Rom. Rule Asia Min.*, index.

T. R. S. B.

**MNASALCES** (not 'Mnasalcas'), of the deme Plataeae in Sicyon, seems to have flourished c. 250 B.C. A satirical epitaph for him (perhaps composed while he was alive) by Theodoridas (*Anth. Pal.* 13. 21) refers to him as ὁ ἐλεγηοποιός, which, however, may mean 'epigrammatist', and derides his plagiarisms and bombast. The first charge is to some extent supported by the extant epigrams; the second may refer to lyric compositions now lost. A few of Mnasalces' epigrams, e.g. *Anth. Pal.* 6. 128, 264; 7. 242, justify Meleager's description (*Anth. Pal.* 4. 1. 16) of them as 'the sharp needles of Mnasalces' pine', but most are devoid of originality.

J. Geffcken, 'Mnasalkes (2)', in *PW* xv. 2247 f. E. A. B.

**MNASEAS** (3rd c. B.C.), Greek traveller of Lycia (*POxy.* xiii, no. 1611, 127 ff.), published geographical and antiquarian details uncritically in (i) Περίπλους, (a) Εὐρώπη; (b) Ἀσία; (c) Λιβύη. (ii) Δελφικῶν χρησμῶν συναγωγή.

*FHG* iii. 149 ff.; iv. 659 ff.

**MNESIMACHUS**, a Middle Comedy writer (Ath. 7. 329 d). Victorious at the Lenaea c. 365–360 B.C. (*IG* ii². 2325. 147). Wrote Ἀλκμέων and Βούσιρις (clearly mythological burlesques), Ἱπποτρόφος, Ἰσθμιονίκης, Δύσκολος, and Φαρμακοπώλης (comedies of everyday life), and Φίλιππος (a political play).

*FCG* iii. 567 ff.; *CAF* ii. 436–42; *FAC* ii. 360 ff. M. P.

**MNEUIS**, the sacred bull of the city of Heliopolis, who was worshipped there in the temple of Ra. His cult is similar in most respects to that of Apis at Memphis, although not so important in Greek and Roman religion. The cult of Mneuis was combined with that of Apis in the temple at Memphis.

A. Rusch, *PW*, s.v. Mnevis, cols. 2285 ff.; A. Erman, *Religion d. Ägypter* (1934), 27 f. T. A. B.

**MODERATUS** of Gades (c. A.D. 50–100) wrote Πυθαγορικαὶ σχολαί in eleven books. He tried to derive the main principles of Plato's metaphysics from Pythagorean teaching, and treated the Pythagorean theory of number as a symbolic representation of metaphysical doctrine, the monad being the principle of rest and harmony, the dyad the principle of change and multiplicity. Ancient references show him to have played a great part in the formation of Neoplatonic doctrine.

E. R. Dodds, *CQ* 1928, 135 ff.; J. M. Rist, *TAPA* 1962, 389 ff. W. D. R.

**MODESTINUS** (3rd c. A.D.) has left a short piece in hexameters on Cupid Asleep.

Duff, *Minor Lat. Poets.*

**MOERIS**, an Atticist lexicographer, to be dated (probably) not long after Phrynichus, and author of the extant Λέξεις Ἀττικῶν καὶ Ἑλλήνων κατὰ στοιχεῖον (sometimes called Ἀττικιστής). The work deals with sundry points of grammar (accidence and syntax) and, mainly, with diction—the choice of words and their correct, 'Attic', forms and proper meanings. It was based on Aelius Dionysius, Phrynichus, Philemon, and the *Synonyms* of Herennius Philon of Byblus. Moeris recognizes the distinction between Old and New Attic;

as models he accepts Plato, Aristophanes, Thucydides, Xenophon, the orators, Herodotus, and Homer, but, unlike Phrynichus, none of the tragedians; both reject Middle and New Comedy. In the nature, merits, and limitations of his work he resembles Phrynichus (q.v. 3).

EDITIONS. Hudson, 1712; Pierson, 1759; Bekker, 1833.
CRITICISM. A. Maidhoff in M. Schanz, *Beitr. z. hist. Syntax d. Griech.* 19 (1912). P. B. R. F.; R. B.

**MOERIS,** a lake in a basin on the west of the Nile valley, fed by the floods at high Nile. When Herodotus visited Egypt most of the basin was under water, though some land had been reclaimed in Pharaonic times; Ptolemy Philadelphus built dikes and canals to control the inflow, and so recovered about half the area of the lake. This created the Arsinoite nome, which was largely peopled by foreign settlers and flourished till the decay of the third century A.D. ruined the irrigation system. The lake is now known as the Birket el-Kurûn.

B. P. Grenfell and A. S. Hunt, *Fayûm Towns* (1900); J. Ball, *Contributions to the Geography of Egypt* (Cairo, 1939), 178 ff.
J. G. M.

**MOERO** (or **MYRO**) of Byzantium (*c.* 300 B.C.), epic poetess; mother of the tragic poet Homerus; wrote poems of various kinds, including a *Curses* (Ἀραί), a genre subsequently used by Euphorion and Valerius Cato.

F. Susemihl, *Gesch. griech. Litt. Alex.* (1891–2) i. 381.

**MOESIA** was in the first instance the country of the Moesi, a Thracian tribe situated on the lower Danube in present-day Serbia. Little is heard of the Moesi before 29 B.C., when they were defeated and subdued by M. Crassus (Cass. Dio 51. 25. 1). They were placed for the time being under a *praefectus* and loosely attached to the province of Macedonia or of Illyricum. The date at which Moesia was constituted a separate province is uncertain. The first imperial legate recorded there is A. Caecina in A.D. 6 (Cass. Dio 15. 29. 3), who left his province to defence Sirmium against the Pannonians. It is possible that an earlier legate was P. Vinicius (*cos.* A.D. 2) attested on a dedication at Callatis (*IGRom.* i. 654). The organization of the province in a definite form appears to have taken place under Tiberius (App. *Ill.* 30). Henceforth Moesia extended along the lower Danube from near the river Drinus to the Black Sea; its southern frontier ran roughly along the main Balkan range. The governor of Moesia also had under his supervision the Black Sea coast to the Straits of Kertch, and from the time of Vespasian, if not before, a *Classis Moesica* patrolled its northern waters. Under Domitian (A.D. 85–6) Moesia was split into two provinces, Superior and Inferior, with the river Ciabrus as the boundary, and the defences of the latter province were strengthened by an earthen wall across the Dobrudja. After the Dacian Wars of Trajan Moesia Superior was extended to comprise the plain between the Danube, the lower Theiss, and the Maros; Moesia Inferior was enlarged so as to overlap Dacia on the east bank of the Aluta.

Moesia always remained a military borderland. Apart from the old-established Greek cities on the Black Sea coast and from Naissus on the upper Morava, all its chief towns grew out of the Roman camps on the Danube —Singidunum (*Belgrade*), Viminacium, Ratiaria, Oescus, Novae, Durostorum (*Silistria*), and Troesmis. Under Hadrian or soon after, these places were constituted colonies or *municipia* of Italian pattern. Under the Roman peace the wheat and orchard lands of the lower Danube valley were well developed, and the Latin language obtained a firm hold among the native population, which had received repeated increments by transplantation of Dacians and kindred peoples across the

Danube. During the invasions of the third century Moesia became a principal storm-centre, but its cities at any rate were held until the sixth or seventh century.

R. Syme, *JRS* 1934, 113 ff.; V. Parvan, *Dacia* (1928), *passim*; A. Stein, *Die Legaten von Moesia* (1940); A. Mócsy, *Acta Arch. Acad. Scient. Hung.* 1959, 283 ff. M. C.; J. J. W.

**MOGONTIACUM** (modern *Mainz*) commanded important routes into the heart of Germany, and between 18 and 13 B.C. a fortress was built here to hold two legions, serving as a base for the invasion of Germany. The timber fortress was replaced in stone in the second half of the first century A.D. and the garrison reduced to one legion after the rebellion of Saturninus (89). A large and impressive town grew up between the fortress and the Rhine, and the seat of the governor of Germania Superior was here. From the first century there was a fort on the right bank of the river guarding the head of the important bridge and there is some evidence that this was replaced in the fourth century by a new fort like that at Cologne (*see* COLONIA AGRIPPINENSIS). The legionary fortress was still garrisoned around 300 and possibly later, but in the later fourth century it had been abandoned and part of its area was included within the new town walls. The town seems to have had a flourishing Christian community and was the seat of a bishopric. Mogontiacum was captured and destroyed by the barbarians in A.D. 406.

D. Baatz, in (*Gymnasium*) *Germania Romana: I, Römerstädte in Deutschland* (1960); G. Behrens, *Das frühchristliche und merowingische Mainz* (1950). P. S.

**MOLIONES** (Μολίονε), the twin sons of Molionē (originally 'Siamese' twins, in the opinion of Schweitzer, *Herakles* (1922), 19; see *contra* Farnell, *Hero-Cults,* 208, who makes this form of the legend Hesiodic and so comparatively late). Certainly in Homer (*Il.* 11. 750 ff.) they are normal and mortal, though sons of Poseidon; their names are Cteatus and Eurytus and they are married and have sons (2. 621). In the former passage they are enemies of the Pylians; elsewhere (Apollod. 2. 139–40) they attack Heracles' men and are afterwards ambushed and killed by him. They are often (as in Homer) called Ἀκτορίωνε, Actor being their mother's mortal husband.

H. J. R.

**MOLOSSI,** common name of tribes forming a tribal State (*koinon*) in Epirus, which originated in northern Pindus (including the Orestae, *FGrH* i F 107) and expanded southwards, reaching the Ambraciote Gulf *c.* 370 B.C. The king exchanged oaths with his people in an annual ceremony and commanded the tribal army, and the royal house, 'The Aeacidae', claimed descent from Neoptolemus, son of Achilles. The earliest inscriptions, of the reign of Neoptolemus in 370–368 B.C., mention ten *damiorgoi,* a *prostates,* and a *grammateus,* all named by one of the ten constituent tribes. 'The Molossians and their Allies' formed a military coalition, analogous to 'The Lacedaemonians and their Allies', in which the Molossian king held the command as *hegemon;* Alexander the Molossian demonstrated its potentiality in south Italy in 334–330 B.C. When the State was absorbed into the Epirote Alliance, the Molossian king commanded the army of the Alliance, and in this capacity Pyrrhus (q.v.) won his victories in Italy and Sicily. After the fall of the monarchy *c.* 232 B.C. the Molossian State was a constituent part of the Epirote Confederacy, until it alone sided with Perseus of Macedon in 170 and was annihilated by Rome in 167 B.C.

*Eph. Arch.* 1956, 3 (inscriptions); Hammond, *Epirus.*
N. G. L. H.

**MOMOS** (Μῶμος), fault-finding personified, a literary figure, hardly mythological (though he occurs in Hesiod,

*Theog.* 214, among the children of Night) and quite divorced from cult. Callimachus makes use of him (*Dian.* 113 and fr. 393 Pf.) as the mouthpiece of views which he opposes, while in Lucian (as *Iupp. Trag.* 19 ff.) he amusingly voices the author's satires on the conventional (popular Stoic) theology, or otherwise makes fun of his fellow gods. He is a figure in a fable, also cited by Lucian (*Nigr.* 32; cf. *Hermot.* 20, *Ver. Hist.* 2. 3).

H. J. R.

**MONA** (1) The Isle of Man (Caesar, *BGall.* 5. 13. 3).

(2) Anglesey. As a centre of Druidism it was attacked by Suetonius Paulinus (A.D. 60), who was baulked of success by Boudicca's revolt. It was reduced by Agricola in 78. It shows scant traces of romanization, but copper-mining and the *pax Romana* increased the quality and quantity of its village life. A late Roman fort exists at Holyhead. Welsh tradition speaks of an Irish invasion (5th c.), repelled by Cunedda, whose descendants ruled here.

*Royal Commission on Historical Monuments (Wales), Anglesey,* lxvii–xc; C. Fox, *Find of the Iron Age at Llyn Cerrig Bach* (1946).

C. E. S.

**MONARCHY** (βασιλεία). Greek monarchy includes several entirely separate institutions. The kingdom of 'heroic' times denotes the Mycenaean lordship as well as the Homeric and legendary kingdom. Its core was military leadership, but the Mycenaeans were at the same time priest-kings and heads of an elaborate royal household. In the period of renewed migrations the king was the military chief of the tribe again; the Spartan, and even more the Macedonian, kings were survivals of this type. It was a hereditary kingship, acknowledged by the assembly of the armed people, and its power was limited by other 'kings', i.e. the heads of the aristocracy, and their council. The second type was what the Greeks called tyranny (q.v.), an individual and democratic rulership arising from the aristocratic *polis*. The third species of Greek monarchy was more theoretical. Usually Greeks of the fifth century B.C. knew monarchy only as barbarian despotism. But the political philosophy of the Sophists and the Socratic Schools, fighting against democracy, established the ideal of the rule of the strongest or of the best man, of the ruler 'by nature' (φύσει). Some of the writers of the fourth century, especially Xenophon and Isocrates, became rather impressed by some real attempts to found monarchies, e.g. the younger tyranny in Syracuse, the rules of Jason of Pherae, of the kings of Cyprus, of Mausolus of Caria; and the conflict between the Greek city-states and Philip of Macedon found its reflection in the antithesis of democratic and monarchic ideas. The reigns of Alexander and his successors ended the theoretical controversies, as far as any practical purpose went. Hellenistic monarchy combined the people's kingship of Macedon, the individual ambitions of Greek 'royal men', and oriental traditions of theocratic despotism. Its characteristic features were: rule over a large territory, dynastic government and succession, and ruler-worship. This monarchy was supported by the philosophical idea of the rule of the truly wise man. It exercised a marked influence on Roman monarchy and imperial administration.

V. Ehrenberg, *The Greek State* (1960); L. Cerfaux and J. Tondriau, *Le Culte des souverains dans la civilisation gréco-romaine* (1957); F. Taeger, *Charisma* i (1958); K. F. Stroheker, *Dionysios I.* (1958); H. Berve, 'König Hieron II', *Abh. Akad. Munich* 1959. V. E.

**MONETA**, a title of Juno (q.v.). The name is probably connected with the root of *monere* ('mindful', 'reminder') and hence is used occasionally (Livius Andronicus, in Priscian, 2, 198 Keil; Hyg. *praef. Fab.* 3 and 27) to translate Mnemosyne. There is no indication, however,

that any cult of a goddess so named, independent of Juno, ever existed. Her temple stood on the Arx under S. Maria in Aracoeli (see Platner–Ashby, 289 f.; Nash, *Pict. Dict. Rome* i. 515 ff.), having been vowed in 345 B.C. and dedicated the next year (Livy 7. 4–6), apparently replacing an older shrine where the sacred geese had been kept (Plut. *Cam.* 27). Cicero (*Div.* 1. 101) explains the title by a story that a warning voice was heard from it directing the proper sacrifice after an earthquake. An adjoining building contained the mint of the Roman State for some time (Livy 6. 20. 13; cf. Platner–Ashby, loc. cit. and 345 f.); hence *moneta* came to mean 'mint', and so passed into modern languages. H. J. R.

**MONEY.** In Minoan Crete (as in all Ancient Oriental cultures) metal measured by weight seems to have been used as money. The usage persisted in non-Hellenic Italy until finally superseded by Roman coinage. Cattle were used as money in the early Iron Age (Homeric Greece and Italy). Tools also were passed as tokens, the form and not the weight or metal purity being of importance for exchange. In the time of Homer money chiefly took the form of axes, which occur in finds and (perhaps) in Linear A and B inscriptions. Written sources and finds point to the use in early Greece and prehistoric Europe of tripods, cauldrons, rings, anchors, metal 'cakes', and scales for weighing (the 'talent' of Homer, unless this was a bar of gold). *Oboloi* also (iron spits), which later gave the name to a small Greek coin, are well known, both by tradition and from finds and an early inscription. This primitive 'tool' money was connected with public sacrifices and religion.

A few decades before 600 B.C. the coinage was invented in Asia Minor, where East and West met, and was perfected in the Greek motherland, where small silver coins replaced local 'tool' money. It combined the principle that the exterior of any medium of exchange should be of conventional type and unalterable form, with the Ancient Oriental preference for bars of a given weight and metal content.

Changes in the price of bullion, of course, influenced the policy of Greek and Roman mints. The ratio of silver to gold was 1 : 13 or 13½ in the Lydian and Persian Empires of the sixth century; 1 : 14–17 in the later years of Pericles; 1 : 10 in Athens during the Peloponnesian War; 1 : 11–12 in Greece and Persia in the early fourth century; 1 : 10 from the later years of Philip; 1 : 13½ *c.* 280 B.C.; 1 : 10 *c.* 189 B.C.; 1 : 9 under Sulla; 1 : 12 under Augustus; 1 : 13 under Nero and Vespasian; 1 : 8–11 in the early third century A.D.; 1 : 10 in the early fourth century; 1 : 18 under Constantine the Great; 1 : 16·8 340; 1 : 14·4 397; 1 : 18 from 410 to 422 or so; 1 : 14·4 538; 1 : 6 *c.* 541; 1 : 12·5 in the later sixth century.

The ratio of bronze to silver was 1 : *c.* 110 in the fifth century; 1 : 50–70 from Alexander's time to *c.* 220 B.C.; 1 : 120 from *c.* 220 to *c.* 149 B.C.; 1 : 112 from *c.* 149 to 89 B.C.; 1 : 56 from 89 B.C. to, perhaps, the third century A.D.; 1 : 125 in A.D. 396 and 1 : 100 in A.D. 538. The decline in value of the precious metals during Alexander's campaigns, and their rise in consequence of the economic crisis in the third century A.D., can clearly be seen from these figures.

By a law of Constantine (A.D. 325) the imperial treasury had to accept both minted and unminted gold at the same rate, and gold coins had to be valued according to their actual weight. The Greek preference for coined money was not to the same extent shared by the Late Roman world, which had seen the terrible inflation of the third century A.D. and reverted of necessity to a more primitive currency system. *See* COINAGE (GREEK, ROMAN.)

*Kl. Pauly*, s.vv. 'coactor', 'Giroverkehr', 'Inflation', 'Kalendarion',

'Kredit'; St. Bolin, *State and Currency in the Roman Empire to 300 A.D.* (1958). A. R. Burns, *Money and Monetary Policy in Early Times* (1927). M. H. Crawford, *JRS* 1964, 29 ff. Gl. Downey, *A History of Antioch in Syria* (1961), 540 ff., n. 167. F. M. Heichelheim, *Historia Mundi* iv (1956), 410 ff., 430 ff., 458 ff.; *Handwörterbuch der Sozialwissenschaften* (1963), s.v. 'Geld- und Muenzgeschichte I'; *Wirtschaftsgeschichte des Altertums* (1938), index, s.v. 'Geld'; *An Ancient Economic History* i (1958), 197 ff., ii (1964), 19 ff., 166 ff. Jones, *Later Rom. Emp.*, index, s.v. 'gold', 'silver'. K. Regling, s.v. 'Geld' in *PW* and in Ebert, *Reallexikon der Vorgeschichte* s.v. 'Wertverhaeltnis' in v. Schroetter, *Wörterbuch der Muenzkunde* (1930). L. C. West–A. C. Johnson, *Currency in Roman and Byzantine Egypt* (1944).                                    F. M. H.

**MONOPOLIES.** The earliest Greek State monopolies (for certain crafts in Sparta and Epidamnus) were political rather than economic. A later stage of progress in public administration is represented by the State currency control of the Attic Empire in the fifth century B.C. and of Olbia after 400; monopolies for the production of silphium in Cyrene, of alum in Lipara, and of salt in Rome, as well as others for his import or export of certain products in Athens, Clazomenae, Heraclea, Lampsacus, and Selymbria; of banking in Byzantium; and of trade and craftsmanship in the camp of the Persian satrap Datames (early 4th c.).

Hellenistic monopolies—in striking contrast to the Classical period—were more concerned with the State's own citizens than with foreigners. We find ferry control in Delos and Miletus; salt control in the empire of Lysimachus; control of salt, oil, and perhaps parchment, perfumes, and public baths in parts of the Seleucid Empire. A complete monopoly system in the Ptolemaic Empire covered the production, sale, and import of oils, textiles, beer, leather, perfumes, papyrus, the output of mines and quarries, currency and banking, hunting, fishing, meat sales, goose-breeding, and the management of public baths. This system included gigantic commercial and industrial enterprises, for which schedules regulating production were issued annually, wholesale and retail prices were fixed, and prohibitive customs duties imposed, very few enterprises escaping notice.

The monopolies of the Roman Principate were nothing more than exclusive local concessions to private capitalists. We know of such in Roman Egypt, controlling salt, oil, perfumes, baths, dyeing, kiln-dried bricks, alum, the goldsmith's trade, the wool trade, ferries, some Indian imports from the Red Sea, and (perhaps) beer, papyrus, and painting. Other sources mention control of banks in Mylasa and Pergamum, ferries in Myra, bakeries in Ephesus; a salt-monopoly in Palmyra, a complete regional sales control in Baetocaece (in Syria); a monopoly of balsam in Palestine, of purple in Tyre, of wood in the Lebanon. The *metallum Vipascense*, a mining district in Spain, had public monopolies which covered banking, auctioning, fulling, leather production, baths, and the barber's trade. Late Roman monopolies for salt, silk, purple, production of arms, and the various monopoly experiments of Justinian should also be mentioned. *See* AGRICULTURE, BANKS, COMMERCE, FINANCE, INDUSTRY.

A. M. Andreades, *A History of Greek Public Finance* (1933), index, s.v. E. Bikerman, *Les Institutions des Séleucides* (1938), 106 ff. J. Bingen, 'Papyrus Revenue Laws', *Sammelbuch griechischer Urkunden aus Aegypten.* Suppl. i (1952). Frank, *Econ. Survey* i–v (index). A. van Groningen, *Aristote, le second livre de l'Économique* (1933). F. M. Heichelheim, *PW*, s.v. 'Monopole'; *Economic History* (1938), i ff.; 'Byzantinische Seiden', *Ciba Rundschau* 1949; *An Ancient Economic History* ii² (1964), 139 ff., 161, 238 ff. Jones, *Later Rom. Emp.*, index. J. Karayannopulos, *Das Finanzwesen des frühbyzantinischen Staates* (1958), 234 ff. M. Th. Lenger, *Corpus des ordonnances des Ptolémées* (1964). M. Lichtheim, *Demotic Ostraca From Medinet Habu* (1957), 5 ff. R. H. McDowell, *Univ. of Michigan Studies.* Hum. Ser. xxxvi (1935). Cl. Préaux, *L'Économie royale des Lagides* (1939), 61 ff. M. Rostovtzeff, *YClS* 3 (1932), i ff.; *Hellenistic World. Roman Empire²* (indexes). Walbank, *Polybius* i, 500. S. L. Wallace, *Taxation in Egypt from Augustus to Diocletian* (1938), 181 ff.
                                         F. M. H.

**MONOTHEISM.** Apart from the influence of developed Judaism and Christianity, no such thing as monotheism, i.e. the refusal to use the predicate 'God' of any but one Being, existed in classical antiquity; even theistic philosophers acknowledged the existence of subordinate deities besides the supreme one. Locally it was usual enough to refer to one particular deity as 'the god' or 'the goddess', e.g. Athena at Athens, Apollo at Delphi. But a further tendency towards monotheism may be detected at any rate in Greek popular religion as interpreted by nonphilosophical authors. This takes the form of an increasing supremacy of Zeus. Even in Homer (*Il.* 8. 18–27) he is much stronger than all the other gods put together; later authors tend to use 'Zeus', 'the gods', 'God' indiscriminately, e.g. Hesiod, *Op.* 42 and 47, where the same act is ascribed, first to 'the gods', then to Zeus. To Aeschylus (*Ag.* 160 ff.) Zeus is the supreme moral governor of the universe, though even there the existence of other gods is clearly recognized (169 ff.). Hellenistic writers favour vague phrases like τὸ θεῖον, τὸ δαιμόνιον.

Nilsson, *GGR* i². 220, 421, ii. 546.              H. J. R.; H. W. P.

**MONS SACER,** a hill near Rome just beyond the Anio (q.v.) on the road to Nomentum (q.v.). In 494 and 449 B.C. the plebeians left Rome, returning only when the patricians granted concessions guaranteed by a *lex sacrata.* The Mons Sacer, for obvious aetiological reasons, was represented as the destination of the seceding plebeians (Livy 2. 32; 3. 52; Festus, 422, 423 L.).
                                         E. T. S.

**MONTANISM** was a prophetic movement among the Christians of Asia Minor. It emerged in Phrygia probably *c.* A.D. 172 (cf. Eus. *Chron.* under 12th year of Marcus Aurelius), though Epiphanius (*Haer.* 48. 1) gives 156–7 as the beginning. Montanus was soon joined by two prophetesses, Prisca and Maximilla, and together they proclaimed the approaching descent of New Jerusalem near the Phrygian village of Pepuza. Their message seems to have been purely eschatological and apocalyptic, with a reiterated stress on the glory of martyrdom, the requirement of ritual purity attained by rigorous fasts and penances, and freedom from the encumbrances of daily life. The movement was strongly opposed by the bishops throughout Asia Minor, who denied the validity of prophecy uttered, like Montanus', while the prophet was in a state of ecstasy. Despite the non-fulfilment of the prophet's promises, Montanism gained a firm hold on the country areas of Phrygia, and an important series of Montanist inscriptions openly proclaiming the Christian beliefs of those commemorated have been found in the Tembris valley in northern Phrygia. Dating 249–79, they are the earliest undisguisedly Christian inscriptions outside the Roman catacombs. It became an organized Church with a hierarchy that included the ranks of Patriarch and Koinonos (companion of Christ) as well as bishops, presbyters, and deacons. Though it persisted in Asia Minor until the eighth century its greatest triumph was its spread to Roman Africa where it won the allegiance of Tertullian (q.v.) *c.* 207. Montanism shows how apocalyptic hopes often underlay the apparent calm of rural Asia Minor in the Antonine period. Its immediate success showed also that rural Christianity was likely to take different forms from those accepted in the Graeco-Roman towns.

Euseb. *Hist. Eccl.* 5. 16 f. and Epiph. *Adv. Haer.* 48 preserve fragments of Montanist prophecies and of anti-Montanist works. N. Bonwetsch, *Texte zur Geschichte des Montanismus* (Lietzmann's *Kleine Texte,* no. 129, 1941). See also P. de Labriolle, *La Crise montaniste* (1913); W. Schepelern, *Der Montanismus und die phrygische Kulte* (German transl., 1929); W. M. Calder, *Bull. Rylands Libr.* 1923, 309 ff. and *Anatolian Studies,* 1955, 27 ff.; W. H. C. Frend, *Martyrdom and Persecution . . . in the Early Church* (1965), 290 ff.
                                         W. H. C. F.

**MONUMENTUM ANCYRANUM.** The so-called Monumentum Ancyranum is one of the four documents written by Augustus which were deposited with the Vestal Virgins and were read in the Senate after his death. It was 'a record of his enterprises (*index rerum a se gestarum*), which he wished to be engraved on two bronze tablets placed outside his Mausoleum' (Suet. *Aug.* 101). The proper title is consequently *Index rerum gestarum*. Neither a MS. copy nor the original inscription near the Mausoleum is preserved. But copies were set up in some, if not all, of the provinces. The greater part of the text has been recovered from a copy found in 1555 at Ancyra (q.v.) in Galatia, on the walls of a mosque which had been the temple of Rome and Augustus. It consists of the original Latin text and a Greek translation. Another copy, far more fragmentary, has been found at Apollonia in Pisidia. The Greek translation is here the same as in the text of Ancyra, which proves its official inspiration. A third fragmentary copy of the Latin text was found at Antioch in Pisidia in 1914 (so-called Monumentum Antiochenum). As Antioch was a Roman colony, it was probably considered unnecessary to add a Greek text.

The Monumentum Ancyranum contains four parts: (1) the *honores* received by Augustus (chs. 1–14); (2) a statement of the money spent on public objects from his private means (chs. 15–24); (3) the *res gestae* proper, an account of his victorious expeditions and conquests (25–33); (4) a concluding statement about his position in the Roman State. A short appendix, written after his death, follows.

The document represents itself as composed in Augustus' last year, apparently after 27 June A.D. 14 (cf. chs. 4 and 8), but since the *Res Gestae* were already mentioned in the testament of Augustus, which was written on 3 Apr. A.D. 13, the text obviously has been retouched either by Augustus himself or by the editor. Further, possibly the document was written by Augustus many years before his death and then revised more than once. Yet no certain evidence of successive stages has been discovered.

The document has a clear internal unity. Part I demonstrates Augustus' exceptional position in the State and his fundamental respect for Roman liberty. In parts 2 and 3 Augustus justifies his position by what he achieved with his own private money and under his own military command. The concluding sentences state again that he restored the Republic and consequently obtained a superior authority and the qualification of *pater patriae*. The style is that of the Roman texts concerning triumphs. The content gives us a profound insight into the way in which Augustus wished to be appreciated.

EDITIONS AND COMMENTARIES. By Mommsen (2nd ed. 1883); E. G. Hardy (1923); W. M. Ramsay and A. v. Premerstein, 'Monumentum Antiochenum', *Klio*, Beiheft 19 (1927); J. Gagé (1935; the best); J. D. Newby, *Numismatic Commentary on the Res Gestae of Augustus* (U.S.A. 1938); H. Volkmann (1957); E. Malcovati*, (1962) with full bibliography; P. A. Brunt–J. M. Moore (1967).
H. Dessau, *Klio* 1929, 261 ff.; U. Wilcken, *Sitz. Preuss. Akad.* 1931, 772 ff.; 1932, 225 ff.; W. Ensslin, *Rh. Mus.* 1932, 335 ff. W. Weber, *Princeps* i, 1936 (cf. E. Hohl, *Phil. Wochenschr.* 1937, 374 ff.; id. *Klio* 1937, 323, and W. Kolbe, *Gött. Anz.* 1939, 152 ff.); J. Gagé, *Rev. Ét. Lat.* 1939, 33 ff.; A. Ferrabino, *Augustus. Studi in occasione del bimillenario augusteo* (1938), 48 ff.; H. Bardon, *Les Empereurs et les lettres latines* (1940), 7 ff.; E. Schoenbauer, *Sitz. Wien* 1946; M. A. Levi, *Riv. Fil.* 1947, 189 ff.; E. Hohl, *Mus. Helv.* 1947, 101 ff.; A. M. Lauton, *Wien. Stud.* 1949, 107 ff.; W. Steidle, *Sueton* (1951), 178 ff.; F. E. Adcock, *JRS* 1952, 10 ff.; id. *CQ* 1951, 130 ff.; H. Volkmann, *Hist.* 1954, 81 ff.; W. Seyfarth, *Philol.* 1957, 305 ff.                                   A. M.

**MOPSUS,** two diviners of the same name, for the legend is quite irreconcilable with the mythological chronology. In one set of authorities (e.g. Pind. *Pyth.* 4. 191) he is the Argonauts' prophet and therefore is contemporary with the generation before the Trojan War; he is son of Ampyx or Ampycus (Ap. Rhod. 1. 1083)

and comes from Titaresos (i.e. Dodona); he dies on the journey (4. 1502 ff.), bitten by a serpent in Libya. In another (as Paus. 7. 3. 2) he is son of Manto, daughter of Tiresias (q.v.), by Rhacius the Cretan; he is connected with the oracle at Claros, and there meets Calchas (q.v.) and causes his death by outdoing him in a contest of divination; this was after the Trojan War. He shared with Amphilochus (q.v.) his oracle-shrine in Cilicia. His name occurs in local place-names there, and in the late eighth-century bilingual hieroglyph inscription at Karatepe (e.g. G. L. Huxley, *Crete and the Luwians* (1941), 47 ff.).
H. J. R.; H. W. P.

**MORGANTINA** (Latin *Murgantia*), a city of east-central Sicily long unidentified, can now be certainly located on Serra Orlando, a steep-sided ridge projecting for some 3 kilometres eastwards from Aidone. Its acropolis, still called 'Cittadella', commands a wide expanse of the western part of the Piana di Catania, and is the site of the earliest settlement (early 7th c. B.C.), the Italic affinities of which reflect Strabo's (6. 1. 6) story of the Morgetes. Greek pottery and masonry suggest that settlers, probably from Catana or Leontini, established themselves c. 560, on good terms with the natives. In the fifth century and afterwards the city was within the Syracusan orbit, save for its capture by Ducetius (q.v.) in 459 (Diod. Sic. 11. 78. 5) and its cession by Syracuse to Camarina in 424 (Thuc. 4. 65). Refortified under Timoleon, it was replanned and resettled under Agathocles and Hieron II (qq.v.). The agora on two levels, linked by a monumental stairway, was flanked by a theatre, stoa, and other public buildings. It suffered in the Second Punic War, having supported Carthage, and was handed over for settlement to Rome's Spanish auxiliaries. By the end of the republican period it had lapsed into decay; Strabo refers to it (6. 2. 4) as no longer existing.

E. Sjöqvist, *Atti del settimo congresso internazionale di archeologia classica* ii (1961), 61 ff.; id. *Κώκαλος* 1962, 52 ff.; R. Stillwell, *Κώκαλος*. 1965/5, 579 ff.; E. Sjöqvist and R. Stillwell, excavation reports in *AJArch.* 1957 and succeeding years.                       A. G. W.

**MORMO** (*Μορμώ*; also *Μορμολύκη*, *Μορμών*), a figure like Empusa, Gello, and Lamia (qq.v.), and equated with the last two by schol. on Theoc. 15. 40; he says she was a queen of the Laestrygones (q.v.) who lost her own children and so tries to kill those of others. Her name is sometimes a mere interjection (Theoc. loc. cit.; Ar. *Eq.* 693). See Tamborino in *PW*, s.v.            H. J. R.

**MORPHEUS.** Three of the sons of Sleep, Morpheus, Ikelos or Phobetor, and Phantasos, send respectively visions of human forms (*μορφαί*), beasts, and inanimate objects (Ov. *Met.* 11. 633 ff.).

**MORSIMUS,** son of Philocles and grand-nephew of Aeschylus, oculist and tragic poet, a frigid or uninspired writer, often ridiculed by comic poets of the fifth century (*Suda*, s.v.; Ar. *Pax* 803 and schol.), though he may have had his admirers (Ar. *Ran.* 151).

**MORYCHUS** (*Μόρυχος*). Lexicographers and paroemiographers (q.v.) explain a saying 'sillier (*μωρότερος*) than Morychus, who neglects inside affairs and sits outside' as alluding to a statue of Dionysus in Sicily, surnamed Morychus, which was outside his temple; their authority is Polemon.                                       H. J. R.

**MOSAIC.** The history of mosaic work in the classical world begins c. 400 B.C. with the pavements, showing two-dimensional, mainly white-on-dark, geometric and figured designs, made of natural, unshaped pebbles for the floors of private houses at Olynthus. Somewhat more elaborate pebble pavements, with a more extended use of colour, dating from the late fourth and early third centuries, have come to light in houses at Pella; and northern Greece seems to have been the centre from which this technique passed to other lands—southern Greece, Sicily, Asia Minor, and Alexandria. Recent finds at Morgantina have suggested that it was Sicilian mosaicists of the mid third century B.C. who invented the new technique of making both black-and-white and coloured pavements of marble, stone, and tile tesserae, for abstract patterns, at first irregularly shaped, then squared, and smoothed flat on the upper surface (*opus tessellatum*), and, for three-dimensional figure work, subtly cut and curved and similarly smoothed (*opus vermiculatum*: cf. *emblemata vermiculata* (Lucilius); *vermiculatae ad effigies rerum et animalium crustae* (Pliny, *HN* 35. 2)). We learn from Athenaeus (*Deipnosophistae* 6. 207 c) that Hieron of Syracuse sent to the reigning Ptolemy a luxury ship with floor mosaics in which the whole story of the *Iliad* was represented; and it seems that this type of 'painting with tesserae' spread from Sicily along the trade routes to Alexandria, Delos, Pergamum, and eventually, from the second century B.C. onwards, to Rome and other Italian sites. One of the most famous Hellenistic mosaicists was Sosus of Pergamum, of whom it is recorded (Pliny, *HN* 36. 184, where Sosus' works appear to be classed as examples of *lithostrotum*) that he made a representation of a floor strewn with the unswept debris of a meal (*asarotos oikos*) and a panel (*emblema*) showing doves drinking from a wine-cup: there are Roman mosaic copies extant of both these pictures. Of surviving Hellenistic mosaic pavements, some of the best preserved are in private houses at Delos, dating, for the most part, from the second century B.C.

The Hellenistic *emblema*, with its surround of abstract or geometric patterns, was essentially a picture intended to be seen from a single viewpoint, like an easel or mural painting. It resembled a patterned rug laid in the centre of, or at the entrance to, a room. But in Italy and other western lands, particularly in northern Africa, there soon developed a tendency to regard a mosaic pavement as a carpet covering the entire floor with an all-over design that could be enjoyed from every angle; and under the Early Empire the *emblema* gradually passed out of fashion. In Italy in the later first, second, and third centuries A.D. the favourite type of pavement was the all-over black-and-white one, either composed entirely of geometric and floral motifs or of figure scenes drawn in black silhouette against a white ground. Meanwhile, in the provinces, gay polychrome pavements, both abstract and figured, were immensely popular, on into the fourth century, when they also appeared more frequently in Italy. On eastern sites, such as Antioch-on-the-Orontes, where there has been excavated a splendid series of datable pavements running from *c.* A.D. 100 to the sixth century, the Hellenistic *emblema* tradition persisted till the fourth century, but was then replaced by the Western idea of a mosaic as an all-over carpet design in which the interest is diffused throughout the floor.

Another technique employed for Roman pavements is that of *opus sectile* (distinguished from *opus tessellatum* by Vitruvius (7. 1. 3) and Suetonius (*Div. Iul.* 46)), in which the mosaic consists of relatively large, thin, shaped pieces of coloured marble forming all-over geometric or floral patterns. This technique is found on floors dating from the first century B.C. to the fourth century A.D.; and in the late-antique period it was also used for elaborate figure scenes on walls. The term *musivum opus* occurs in late literary sources as applied exclusively to wall and vault mosaics, of which many more examples dating from before the Christian Empire have survived than was formerly supposed. Wall mosaics made of glass-paste

tesserae are known as fountain and nymphaeum decorations and even as figured panel pictures at Pompeii and Herculaneum; and we have examples of mosaics on the walls and vaults of baths, tombs, etc., of the second, third, and fourth centuries, the Christian mosaics of the mid third century in the Mausoleum of the Julii under St. Peter's in Rome, and the 'neutral' fourth-century vault mosaics in the Church of Santa Costanza, also in Rome, being among the most notable instances. The earliest Christian floor mosaics, such as those in the fourth-century cathedral and house-oratories at Aquileia (q.v.), display an intriguing mixture of pagan and Christian motifs. Church mosaics on walls and vaults of the fourth and fifth centuries featuring exclusively biblical and other sacred subjects lie outside the scope of this article.

D. M. Robinson, *Excavations at Olynthus* v (1933), 1 ff.; Pella: *Archaeology* 1958, 247 ff.; 1964, 74 ff.; Morgantina, etc.: *Art Bulletin* 1960, 245 ff.; Rome 'and Italy: *Amer. Acad. Rome* 1931, 1 ff.; 1936, 67 ff.; 1940, 81 ff.; E. Pernice, *Die hellenistische Kunst in Pompeii* vi: *Pavimente und figurliche Mosaiken* (1938); D. Levi, *Antioch Mosaic Pavements* (1947); Antioch, etc.: *Dumbarton Oaks Papers* xvii, 1963, 179 ff.; K. Parlasca, *Die römischen Mosaiken in Deutschland* (1950); V. von Gonzenbach, *Die römischen Mosaiken der Schweiz* (1961); Gaul and Africa: *Inventaire des mosaïques de la Gaule et de l'Afrique* 1, i (1911), pls. 1911; 1, ii, n. d., pls. 1922; 2, 1910. pls. 1913; 3, 1911. pls. 1925; S. Aurigemma, *Tripolitania i; i monumenti d'arte decorativa*: pte. i: *i mosaici* (1960). J. M. C. T.

**MOSCHION,** tragic poet, probably of the third century B.C., wrote a *Telephus* and two historical plays, the *Themistocles* and the *Men of Pherae*, the theme of which was perhaps the death of Alexander of Pherae. A long fragment on the origins of civilization recalls in some points Aeschylus, *PV* 436 ff., and his style, though uneven, shows greater boldness than that of most of the late tragic poets.

*TGF* 812–16. A. W. P.-C.

**MOSCHUS** of Syracuse, described by the *Suda* as a pupil of Aristarchus, must have flourished *c.* 150 B.C. This agrees with the *Suda*'s further statement that the chronological order of the three Bucolic poets was Theocritus, Moschus, Bion. The same authority calls Moschus a grammarian, but no traces of such activity survive unless we identify him with the Moschus mentioned by Athenaeus (11. 485 e) as author of a work on Rhodian Words.

WORKS. Three extracts (respectively thirteen, nine, and eight hexameters) are preserved by Stobaeus from Moschus' *Bucolica*. The first contrasts the pleasures of the countryman with the hard lot of the fisher. The two others are erotic *paegnia*, having little or no connexion with Bucolic. The three extracts are probably complete, as it were epigrams in hexameters. Similar in kind are two other pieces, twenty-nine hexameters entitled 'The Runaway Love' and an epigram (*Anth. Plan.* 4. 200) on Eros as Ploughman. Finally, several MSS. of the Bucolic Corpus assign to Moschus an epyllion in 166 hexameters with the title *Europa*, in which the Rape of Europa by Zeus is gracefully narrated. The disproportionate space (25 lines) given to the description of Europa's basket is in the Alexandrian manner, as is also the introductory dream. Moschus' style is sometimes too sugared, but he has the merit of using a fairly simple vocabulary. Metrically the fragments and *The Runaway Love* conform to Callimachus' rules, but the *Europa* is less strict, a fact which has led some to dispute Moschus' authorship. He is also credited in some sources with the *Lament for Bion* and the *Megara*. The former must be by some disciple of Bion (q.v.); the latter, a duet in hexameters between Heracles' mother and wife (who gives her name to the piece), in which they vie with each other in bewailing the anxieties caused by his long absence, may be a product of Moschus' muse in a tearful mood, but may equally well belong to some other late Hellenistic poet.

TEXTS. W. Bühler, *Hermes*, Einzelschriften, Heft 13 (1960) (text and commentary of *Europa*); A. S. F. Gow (1952), 132 ff.; U. von Wilamowitz-Moellendorff, *Bucolici Graeci*² (1910), 91, 106, 120, 131, 138; Ph. Legrand, *Bucoliques grecs* ii (1927), 135 ff.

GENERAL LITERATURE. P. Maas, *PW*, s.v. 'Moschos (2)'.

E. A. B.

**MOTYA** (modern *S. Pantaleo*), an islet which an artificial causeway joined to western Sicily, in Elymian territory. Colonized by the Phoenicians in the early seventh century, it became one of the three great military and commercial strongholds of Carthaginian Sicily (Panormus and Soloeis being the others). Nevertheless it underwent a good deal of Hellenic cultural influence. Dionysius I (q.v.) sacked it in 397 B.C. after a memorable siege, and it was not resurrected thereafter, the Carthaginians preferring to colonize Lilybaeum (q.v.) nearby. (Pausanias (5. 25. 5) appears to confuse Motya with Motyca (modern *Modica*) in southern Sicily.)

J. I. S. Whitaker, *Motya* (1921); Dunbabin, *Western Greeks*, esp. 22, 326 ff.; B. S. J. Isserlin *et al. The Annual of Leeds University Oriental Society* 1962–3, 84 ff.; V. Tusa, *Mozia* i–iii (1964–7).

A. G. W.

**MOUNTAIN CULTS.** There is no classical Greek or Italian cult of a mountain as such, but several indications that such cult may once have existed. Mountains are fairly prominent in Greek myths; thus Atlas (q.v.), at once mountain and Titan, although classically placed in Africa (the Atlas range), probably was originally a mountain of Arcadia. Helicon and Cithaeron contend for a prize of song (Corinna, fr. 1 Page), and Helicon is represented by a wild-looking figure (*BCH* xiv, plates ix, x; cf. Kern, *Rel. d. Griech.* 1. 42). Earth brings forth the mountains in Hesiod (*Theog.* 129), though they are not said to be gods but haunts (ἔναυλοι) of the gods. This is in accordance with much that is told of various deities, Pan (*Hymn. Hom.* 19 Allen, 7), the Nymphs (Eur. *Bacch.* 951, and often; the next line mentions Pan also), Rhea (Eur. *Hel.* 1301 ff., where she is curiously identified with Demeter), and above all Zeus, among whose best-known titles are Olympius and Lycaeus. It is quite possible (see Kern, ibid.; cf. 77) that Zeus, who as 'cloud-gatherer' may be seen at work on the tops of hills, absorbed or displaced many ancient cults of mountain gods: for his mountain-cults cf. Cook, *Zeus* ii. 868 ff., and art. HYPSISTOS. Of cults on mountains of gods other than Zeus who are certainly not themselves mountains personified there is abundant evidence from the familiar Cretan representation (see, e.g., Nilsson, *GGR* i², Tafel 18, nr. 1) of a goddess standing on top of a conventionalized hill onwards, as in the case of all the deities mentioned above. *See* TMOLUS.

For Italy, the clearest example of a mountain cult is perhaps Soranus (identified in historical times with Apollo or Dis Pater, Verg. *Aen.* 11. 785; Servius ad loc.), the god of Mt. Soracte; the legend, connected as it is with a cave on the mountain (Servius ibid.) suggests a divine power which actually lives in Soracte and does not simply choose to roam on the sides or summit. See Wissowa, *RK* 238, and contrast Latte, *RR* 148.

H. J. R.

**MUCIA** (*PW* 'Mucius' 28) **TERTIA**, daughter of Scaevola (q.v. 4), sister or cousin of two Metelli (qq.v. 9 and 10), married Pompey (*c.* 80 B.C.) and bore him Pompeius (5) and (6). Unfaithful to him in the 60s, she was divorced by him on his return to Rome—a step that turned the Metelli against him. She later married Scaurus (q.v. 2) and in 39 tried to mediate between her son Sextus Pompeius and Octavian.

E. B.

**MUCIANUS,** GAIUS LICINIUS (*PW* 116 a) (*cos. suff. c.* A.D. 65, *cos.* II *suff.* 70, *cos.* III *suff.* 72). He served under Corbulo in 58 and was governor of Lycia-Pamphylia. Nero appointed Mucianus governor of Syria about the time when he sent Vespasian to Judaea. Reconciled with Vespasian after earlier disagreements, Mucianus encouraged his designs and secured the allegiance of Syria. Leading the Flavian army through Asia Minor and the Balkans, he was anticipated by Antonius Primus in the invasion of Italy and defeat of the Vitellians, but was able on the way to repel a Dacian incursion into Moesia. He arrived in Rome a few days after its capture, repressed the ambitions of Primus, and controlled the government for Vespasian, whose chief adviser he remained. He is said to have urged that Emperor to banish the philosophers from Rome. Mucianus possessed various accomplishments (for a pointed sketch of his character, cf. Tac. *Hist.* 1. 10). He wrote a book of geographical *mirabilia*, largely used by Pliny the Elder. He was dead by 77.

Syme, *Tacitus*, see index.

R. S.

**MULOMEDICINA** is the Latin equivalent for *Hippiatrike*. The subject was dealt with by all agriculturalists (Cato, Varro, Columella, Celsus, Gargilius Martialis, Palladius), but also by poets who wrote on country life (Verg. *G.* 3. 295) and by naturalists (Pliny, book 8). The earliest special treatises preserved are those of Pelagonius and Vegetius (4th c. A.D.).

Latin writers, if physicians, accept semeiotics and cures and reject magic, in accordance with their Greek sources. Yet Latin literature seems not only dependent but also original. The fact that Latin authors were translated into Greek (e.g. Pelagonius) indicates that 'the barbarians' held views of their own. They were interested in veterinary medicine from a business point of view (Varro, *Rust.* 2. 5. 11), cattle being the most valuable property (*pecunia*). The insistence on the segregation of sick animals from the healthy stock, first mentioned by Columella and demanded long before any such segregation of human beings was thought of, may well be Roman; in the time of Vegetius it was under State control. *See also* SURGERY, § 10.

TEXTS. Pelagonius, M. Ihm (Teubner, 1892); Vegetius, E. Lommatzsch (Teubner, 1903); Palladius, bk. 14, J. Svennung (1926); cf. G. Björck, *Mnemos.* 1938.
J. Svennung, *Untersuchungen zu Palladius*, etc. (1935).
*See also* HIPPIATRICI.

L. E.

**MUMMIUS** (*PW* 7 a) **ACHAICUS,** LUCIUS (*cos.* 146 B.C.), commanded as praetor in Spain in 153 B.C. against the Lusitanians, whom after an unsuccessful opening he decisively checked, celebrating a triumph in 152. As consul he succeeded Metellus in command against the Achaean Confederacy, and after crushing Diaeus took Corinth, which he sacked and destroyed, and dissolved the Confederacy. He shipped the treasures of Corinth to Italy, apparently less appreciative of their artistic value than would have been expected from his association with the Scipionic circle. He was censor with Scipio Aemilianus in 142, modifying Scipio's severity.

Livy, *Per.* 52; Polyb. bk. 39; App. *Hisp.* 56–7; Paus. 7. 16; Cic. *De Or.* 2. 66. 268; *Brut.* 25. 94; Vell. 1. 13. 4. G. Colin, *Rome et la Grèce* (1905), 628; H. Simon, *Roms Kriege in Spanien, 154–133 v. Chr.* (1962), 20 ff.

A. H. McD.

**MUNDUS** (etymology unknown), a ritual pit (*see* PITS, CULT). (1) The traditional site in the Comitium where Romulus in founding the city dug a pit, put in first-fruits, and earth from each country from which his followers came, afterwards filling it up and putting an altar upon it (Ov. *Fasti* 4. 821 ff.; Plut. *Rom.* 11). (2) The *mundus Cereris*, a structure of unknown site, vaulted, divided into two parts, and with a cover which was removed on 24 Aug., 5 Oct., and 8 Nov., which days were *religiosi* when the way was supposed open to the lower world (Festus, 144, 145 Lindsay, quoting Cato and Ateius Capito; Varro ap. Macrob. *Sat.* 1. 16. 18). These have only the name in common.

S. Weinstock, *Röm. Mitt.* 1930, 111 ff.; H. J. Rose, *SMSR* 1931, 3 ff.; Latte, *RR* 141 ff. (who revives Warde Fowler's theory that this was in origin a store for seed-corn). H. J. R.

**MUNICHIA (or MUNYCHIA)** was the citadel of Piraeus, a steep hill on its east part (284 ft.) with a small well-fortified harbour below it on the east, and a larger, land-locked harbour to the south-west (Zea). Hippias began to fortify it in 510 B.C. (Arist. *Ath. Pol.* 19. 2). A theatre of Dionysus on its north-west slope was the place of assembly of the hoplites in 411 and of the Athenian Assembly frequently thereafter. It was the scene of street-fighting in 403, when Thrasybulus took Piraeus (Xen. *Hell.* 2. 4. 10–19), and the chief seat of the Macedonian garrison which controlled Athens, with interruptions, from 322 to 229. Its especial goddess was Artemis. *See also* PIRAEUS. T. J. D.; C. W. J. E.

**MUNICHUS** (Μούνιχος), (1) eponym of the Attic harbour Munichia, Photius s.v. Μουνυχία (an inferior spelling of the name), who says he was a king (of Attica). (2) A pious seer, son of Dryas, king of the Molossians. He and his family, attacked by robbers and in danger of being burned alive in their fortress, were changed by Zeus into birds (Ant. Lib. 14). H. J. R.

**MUNICIPIUM.** *Municipium* originally meant an Italian community (*see* SOCII, CIVITAS) which accepted *civitas sine suffragio*. This denoted not an inferior citizenship but a kind of alliance whereby the *municipium* and Rome exchanged social rights, *conubium* and *commercium* (q.v.), much as in the first treaty between Rome and Carthage (506 B.C.). Such *municipes* retained full local autonomy, except in foreign policy, and provided Rome with troops (*see* MUNUS). They became Romans only by settling in Rome. *Municipium* thus resembled *ius Latii*. *Municipia* were liable to occasional, and eventually annual, visits of Roman judicial authorities—*praefecti*—and were sometimes called *praefecturae* (q.v.). The first Italian *municipes*, from Campania and Volscium (*c.* 338 B.C.), were willing allies. Later this status was given to conquered peoples, notably the Sabines and Picenum, and was eventually regarded as a limited, inferior franchise, mediating full incorporation in the Roman State, by the grant of *ius suffragii*, of Italian peoples, which were then called *municipia civium Romanorum* (*see* CAERITES). First the Sabines were thus incorporated (268 B.C.), others later (Arpinum, Fundi, Formiae in 188 B.C.), but some *municipes* remained *sine suffragio* till 90 B.C. Latin States incorporated by Rome, though properly known as *oppida civium Romanorum* before 90 B.C., were sometimes called *pro municipiis*. The magistrates of the early incorporated boroughs were known as aediles, dictators, praetors, or *octoviri*. After 89 B.C. all the communities of Latins and *socii Italici* except the Transpadanes became *municipia civium Romanorum*. A uniform system of *quattuorviri* was substituted for their diverse magistracies. Between 89 and 44 B.C. new and old *municipia* and *oppida civium Romanorum* were assimilated to one another (*see* OPPIDUM). Lands once organized on a village system were combined into artificial *municipia* (*see* CONCILIABULUM, PAGUS, VICUS). Henceforth *municipium* meant any self-governing Italian borough irrespective of origin, apart from colonies (q.v.). In the Principate citizen rights were extended to provincial communities, when sufficiently italianized, in a similar fashion. Latin rights were usually given first (*see* IUS LATII). Thereby a native *civitas* became a *municipium Latini iuris*, with a municipal charter of Roman type. Later it might be granted full citizen rights, though many *municipia* remained 'Latin'. The whole population, both of town and countryside, was affected: a *municipium* was not a purely urban municipality, though life centred in the towns. *Municipia* spread thus throughout the Western Empire, rapidly in the Mediterranean regions—Narbonensis, the Spains, Africa, and Mauretania—slowly in the German and Balkan provinces (except Dacia), still more slowly in northern Gaul and Britain, where *municipia* were exceptional, their place being taken by the non-urban, pre-Roman cantons (*see* CIVITAS). In and after the second century municipal ambition, centred on the imitation of Rome, caused provincial municipalities to apply for colonial rights (*see* COLONIZATION, ROMAN; IUS ITALICUM). Local government rested with the councils (*see* DECURIONES) and the magistrates. The *quattuorviri* introduced in 89 B.C. developed into two *quattuorviri* or *duoviri iuri dicundo* and two *quattuorviri* or *duoviri aedilicia potestate*, or two aediles. The duoviral system prevailed in the provinces. Quaestors sometimes existed for finance, and there were municipal priesthoods. Every five years the upper magistrates, as *duoviri quinquennales*, etc., held a general census for the central government. The municipal system declined in the third and fourth centuries with the general economic collapse of the Empire (*see* DECURIONES).

ANCIENT SOURCES. Cicero; Festus (esp. s.v. *municipium*, *praefecturae*, *vicus*); Pliny, *HN*; Strabo, *passim*; *Digest* esp. 50. Inscriptions: *CIL* and *ILS passim*, esp. *Lex (Rubria) de Gallia Cisalpina*, *Lex Tarentina*, *Tabula Heracleensis*, *Lex Malacitana*, and *Lex Salpensana*.

MODERN VIEWS. (a) Republic: Abbott and Johnson, *Municipal Administration in the Roman Empire*; Beloch, *Röm. Geschichte*; E. G. Hardy, *Roman Laws and Charters*; Z. Z. Konopka, *Eos* xxxii (Origins of *Civitas sine suffragio*); E. Kornemann in *PW*, s.v. 'Municipium', 'Conventus'; *Klio* 1905, 'Πόλις und Urbs'); Mommsen, *Staatsr.* iii. 1; A. Rosenberg, *Staat der alten Italiker* (1913); H. Rudolph, *Stadt und Staat im römischen Italien* (1935, over-schematic); A. N. Sherwin-White, *The Roman Citizenship* (1939); A. J. Toynbee, *Hannibal's Legacy* (1965), i. 3. 6 f., usefully summarizes many modern views. (b) Empire: Above and W. Liebenam, *Städteverwaltung im. röm. Kaiserreiche*; Mommsen, *The Provinces of the R.E.*; J. S. Reid, *The Municipalities of the Roman Empire*; Rostovtzeff, *Roman Empire²*. See particular provincial histories, esp. T. R. S. Broughton, *The Romanization of Africa Proconsularis* (1929); L. Teutsch, *Das römische Stadtwesen in Nordafrika* (1962). A. N. S.-W.

**MUNUS** meant originally the duty of a Roman citizen to the State. The chief *munus publicum* in the Republic was military service. With the introduction of voluntary enlistment this fell into neglect, and the *munus* came to mean simply the obligations of an individual to his municipality, the *munera municipalia*. These were of diverse kinds, and concerned the maintenance of roads, waterworks, and buildings, and especially the payment of taxes. The municipal system worked smoothly as long as the local magistrates saw to it that the *municipes* performed their *munera*, according to their various degrees of liability, which were determined by wealth and position. In the late Empire the *munus publicum* reappeared, in effect, in the liability of the municipal councillors for the imperial taxes, with disastrous results for the municipal system; for the magistracies themselves came to be regarded as burdensome *munera* (*see* DECEMPRIMI, DECURIONES).

For bibliography *see* MUNICIPIUM. A. N. S.-W.

**MURCUS**, L. STAIUS, perhaps of Marsian origin, was a legate of Julius Caesar in Gaul and Africa (48–46 B.C.), and probably praetor in 45. As proconsul of Syria (44/3) he forced, with help from Marcius Crispus, the surrender of Bassus at Apamea, and was acclaimed *imperator*. He went over to the Liberators and was very active in command of a fleet under Brutus and Cassius in 42. In 41 he joined

Sextus Pompeius in Sicily, but was later distrusted and killed by him (40/39). He issued a coinage, with *obv.* head of Neptune, *rev.* a military trophy, MVRCVS IMP (see Sydenham, *CRR*, n. 1315). H. H. S.

**MURENA,** LUCIUS LICINIUS (*PW* 123), served in Asia under his father in the 80s B.C. He was quaestor (*c.* 75), legate of Lucullus (q.v. 2), *praetor urbanus* (65), and then governed Transalpina. Elected consul for 62, he was accused of *ambitus* by Sulpicius (q.v. 2) Rufus, his defeated rival, and by Cato (q.v. 5); he was defended by Crassus (q.v. 4), Hortensius (q.v. 2), and Cicero (in an extant speech) and though perhaps guilty he was acquitted. With his colleague Silanus (q.v. 1), he passed a *lex Licinia Iunia* on the promulgation of bills. He is not heard of again. E. B.

**MURRINA VASA.** According to Pliny, these were cups and bowls made from a soft mineral found in Persia, and especially in Carmania. The mineral showed a variety of pleasing colours, purple and red predominating, but blending into red and producing iridescence at the edge of a cup. This colouring, added to the fact that pieces large enough for carving vessels were rare, made *murrina* extremely valuable in Pliny's time (Pliny, *HN* 37. 18–22). His description suits fluorspar. Some of the material, however, may have been burnt agate from India (*Periplus Maris Erythraei,* 49, μουρρίνη λιθεία). Propertius, who speaks of 'myrrhine cups baked on Parthian hearths' (4. 5. 26), may have confused Persian fluorspar with Indian burnt agate. But possibly he is referring to a practice, used nowadays, of heating the block of fluorspar and then smearing it with pine resin so as to prevent its disintegrating when struck. The pleasant aroma mentioned by Pliny might well have been caused by the resin.

A. L. Loewental and D. B. Harden, *JRS* 1949, 31 ff.; C. E. N. Bromehead, *Antiquity* 1952, 65 ff. D. E. E.

**MUSAEUS** (1), a mythical singer, closely related to Orpheus, by others connected with Eleusis. Aristophanes (*Ran.* 1032–3) makes the distinction that Orpheus taught mysteries and abstinence from flesh, Musaeus taught cures of diseases and oracles. Oracles attributed to him were in circulation, and Onomacritus was driven out by Hipparchus, the son of Pisistratus, for having added a forged oracle to his collection. Plato speaks of him together with Orpheus and calls both descendants of Selene and the Muses (*Resp.* 364 e). Musaeus is a 'descriptive' name; his personality is pale and thoroughly mythical.

On some Attic vases of the second half of the fifth century a youth with a lyre is named Musaeus and shown with Apollo, or with Muses (in the latter case if it were not for the inscription we should inevitably read the figure as Apollo).

M. P. Nilsson, *Harv. Theol. Rev.* 1935, 192; O. Kern, *Orphicorum fragmenta* (cf. index viii). M. P. N.; C. M. R.

**MUSAEUS** (2) of Ephesus (? Alexandria), epic poet; author of a *Perseid* and poems in honour of Eumenes and Attalus I of Pergamum.

**MUSAEUS** (3) **GRAMMATICUS** (? late 5th c. A.D.), epic poet, author of *Hero and Leander*, a Greek poem of some competence and romantic grace, which influenced Marlowe.

TEXT. A. Ludwich (1912). COMMENTARY. K. Kost, *Krit.-exeg. Kommentar zu Musaios* (1966).

**MUSES,** Greek deities of poetry, literature, music, and dance; later also of astronomy, philosophy, and all intellectual pursuits. Throughout antiquity the prevailing conception of Muses follows Hesiod (*Th.* 25 ff.). Muses approach the poet on Helicon and give him sceptre, voice, and knowledge. Hesiod is also responsible for the canonical number of nine (*Od.* 24. 60 may be ambiguous) and the traditional names of the Muses. The frequent appeals to single Muses (W. Minton, *TAPA* 1960, 292) do not, as has been supposed (K. Marót, *Die Anfänge der griechischen Literatur,* 1960) necessarily preclude the existence of others (W. Stanford, note on *Od.* 24. 62). In late Roman times the Muses were differentiated according to their function (*Anth. Pal.* 9. 504, 505). Calliope is Muse of the heroic epic, Clio of history, Euterpe of flutes, Terpsichore of lyric poetry (dance), Erato of lyric poetry or hymns, Melpomene of tragedy, Thalia of comedy, Polyhymnia of the mimic art, and Urania of astronomy. These functions and names vary considerably and names of other Muses are known.

Daughters of Zeus and Mnemosyne, the Muses sing and dance at the festivities of Olympians and heroes, often led by Apollo. They have few myths of their own. The Thracian poet Thamyris, who competed against the Muses, lost his sight and song (*Il.* 2. 594). They were judges in the contest of Apollo and Marsyas (q.v. 1). The Sirens tried once to compete with the Muses; defeated, they lost their wings and jumped into the sea (Steph. Byz., s.v. Ἄπτερα; J. Pollard, *CR* 1952, 60).

The most ancient cults of the Muses were in Pieria and Ascra (A. R. Burn, *BSA* 1949, 323; G. Roux, *BCH* 1954, 22), but smaller cults existed throughout Greece. Horace (*Carm.* 1. 12. 6) was mistaken in associating the Muses with Pindus (A. Fitton Brown, *Greece and Rome* 1961, 22). Pythagoreans, Plato, and Aristotle organized their schools as associations for the cult of Muses (*thiasoi*). Thus Museum (Alexandria) came to mean a place of education and research. An interesting private cult of Muses was established by Epicteta in Thera (*IG* xii. iii. 330). The earliest representation of a Muse in art occurs on a Middle Corinthian kotyle from Ithaca (*BSA* 1948), while Callioppe appears on the François Vase.

The Muses are among the most lovable and most influential creations; personifications of the highest intellectual and artistic aspirations, they yet retained a personal character. Poets, scientists, and philosophers from Homer (*Od.* 8. 488) to Ausonius (App. III) and from Heraclitus to Proclus celebrate the Muses as bringing to humanity the purifying power of music, the inspiration of poetry, and divine wisdom.

P. Boyancé, *Le Culte des Muses chez les philosophes grecs* (1937). O. Bie in Roscher, *Lex.*, s.v. 'Musen'; W. Otto, *Die Musen und der göttliche Ursprung des Singens und Sagens* (1954); K. Marót, *Musen, Sirenen und Chariten* (1958); J. Morrison, *CQ* 1956, 145; G. Luck, *Mel. Wili* 1960, 77 f.; M. Delienne, *Les Muses d'Homère et d'Hésiode* (1960); S. Accaure, *Riv. Fil.* 1964, 129 ff., 257 ff.; M. Alverny, *Studies Ullmann* (1964), ii. 7; B. Snell, *Archiv für Begriffsgeschichte* 1964, 19 ff.; I. Trencsényi-Waldapfel, *Die Töchter der Erinnerung* (1964). G. M. A. H.; J. R. T. P.

**MUSEUM** (Μουσεῖον), originally a place connected with the Muses (q.v.) or the arts inspired by them. Euripides speaks of the μουσεία of birds, the places where they sing. When a religious meaning was attached an altar or a temple was built to mark the spot. But the predominant significance of the word was literary and educational. Thus Mount Helicon had a Museum containing the MSS. of Hesiod and statues of those who had upheld the arts (Ath. 14. 629 a). Almost any school could be called 'the place of the Muses' (Libanius). There was a Museum in Plato's Academy and in Aristotle's Lyceum.

By far the most famous Museum was that of Alexandria, founded by Ptolemy Soter probably on the advice of

Aristotle's famous pupil, Demetrius of Phalerum. It was distinct from the Library. Both were near the palace, but of neither is the exact site clearly identifiable. The Museum housed a band of scholars, who were supported by a generous salary granted by the Ptolemies and later by the Caesars, who appointed a President (ἐπιστάτης) or Priest (ἱερεύς) as head of the institution. Lectures were secondary to research, but there were many discussions in which the kings joined. Dinners or symposia, illuminated by witticisms, epigrams, and the solution of problems, were frequent and characteristic. Learning was held in repute and many literary prizes were given. The papyri show how great was the influence of the Museum on the smaller towns. The buildings, splendidly furnished by the Ptolemies, included a communal dining-hall, an *exedra* for discussions and lectures, a *peripatos* planted with trees.

*Circa* 146 B.C. political upheavals caused learned men, including the great Aristarchus, to flee from Alexandria, which was henceforth rivalled by Pergamum as well as by Athens, Rhodes, Antioch, Berytus, and Rome. The Museum suffered in reputation, but Cleopatra, the last of the Ptolemies, still took part in its discussions. According to a doubtful tradition Mark Antony gave the Pergamene library to Alexandria to make up for loss by fire during Caesar's siege, 47 B.C. Renewed prosperity came under the Pax Augusta. The early emperors visited the Museum and extended its buildings, and Hadrian bestowed special care on it. The Museum was visited by famous litterati like Plutarch, Dio Chrysostom, Lucian, and Galen. In A.D. 216 it suffered under the tyranny of Caracalla. It was destroyed, probably by Zenobia, in 270, but seems to have resumed its activities. It suffered by the foundation of a library at Constantinople, whither many scholars fled to avoid the theological controversies of Alexandria. The *Suda* gives the last member of the Museum as Theon, the father of Hypatia (c. A.D. 400). In the Ptolemaic period the Museum was famous for science and literary scholarship; in the second century for the New Rhetoric; in the third century for Neoplatonism. In the fourth century Ammianus (22. 16) reports scientific activity, but admits a decline.

Müller-Graupe, PW, s.v. 'Museion'. Wilamowitz, Hell. Dicht. i (1924), 160 ff.; G. Faider-Feytmans, Hommages à Joseph Bidez et à Franz Cumont (1949), 97 ff. T. J. H.

**MUSIC. 1.** IN GREEK LIFE. When the embassy from Agamemnon visited Achilles in his tent and found him playing on a lyre and singing lays about heroes (Hom. *Il.* 9. 186–9), they expressed no astonishment that a hardy warrior should seek relaxation in music of his own making. That is symbolic of the Greek attitude to an art which was woven into the very texture of their lives. It was an important feature of many public religious observances, of marriage and funeral rites, and of harvest and vintage festivals; banquets and convivial gatherings were not complete without it. At the Pythian Games, attended by crowds of competitors and spectators from every Greek State, musical contests had been instituted alongside of the athletic ones from the very beginning; and though such contests were not established at the Nemean and Isthmian Games until comparatively late (and apparently never at the Olympic Games), there were many other festivals, such as the Panathenaea at Athens and the Carnea at Sparta, where prizes were offered for singing to the accompaniment of cithara or aulos (κιθαρῳδία, αὐλῳδία) or for instrumental solos (ψιλὴ κιθάρισις, ψιλὴ αὔλησις). The victors in these contests were honoured no less than the athletes (cf. Pind. *Pyth.* 12).

Nearly every form of Greek poetry was, or had at some time been, associated with music: even the poems of Homer were originally chanted or recited to the accompaniment of a stringed instrument (see § 9). In the compositions of the lyric poets the tune was scarcely less essential than the words; poet and composer were one and the same; words and music must often have been conceived together. In choral lyric poetry the dance was a third element in an integrated artistic whole.

This wealth of music was far from being the preserve of professional performers. The more elaborate kinds, especially of instrumental music, were, indeed, left to professional musicians; but in classical times instruction in singing and lyre-playing was a regular part of the education of the freeborn citizen. There thus existed a musically educated public which could not only judge between good and bad performances but could itself take its part in singing hymns, paeans, dithyrambs, and dramatic choruses.

**2.** MUSIC AND THE PHILOSOPHERS. A philosophic sanction was first given to the study of music by the Pythagoreans. The founder of the school is said to have discovered that the chief concordant intervals (συμφωνίαι) could be represented by simple numerical ratios: the Octave (τὸ διὰ πασῶν, sc. χορδῶν) by the ratio 2 : 1, the Fifth (τὸ διὰ πέντε) by 3 : 2, and the Fourth (τὸ διὰ τεσσάρων) by 4 : 3. If a lyre string were stopped midway by a movable bridge, either half would give a note an octave higher than the note of the whole string; if the string were stopped at a point a third of the distance from one end, the remaining two-thirds would give a note a fifth higher than the whole string. It was thus demonstrated that music, more directly than the other arts, brought men into contact with Number, which for the Pythagoreans was the ultimate reality; music, or at least the study of music, was thereby justified in the eyes of serious men.

Plato's attitude to music is that the art is capable not merely of affecting the emotions temporarily but of permanently influencing the character. This point of view is clearly seen in his discussion of the musical education which would be suitable for the virtuous citizens of his ideal State (*Resp.* 398 c–399 d). He rejects styles of music (ἁρμονίαι) which are plaintive (Mixolydian and Syntonolydian) or effeminate (Ionian and Lydian), and leaves only the Dorian and Phrygian, which represent (μιμοῦνται) courage and sobriety. In his later work, the *Laws* (653 d–673 a; 795 a–812 e), his opinion is still unchanged that the training of the young in good and carefully selected music will contribute to the attainment of virtue.

Aristotle also regards music as important and discusses its uses in his *Politics* (8. 1339ᵃ–1342ᵇ). Less puritanical than Plato, he would allow all types of music for purposes of relaxation; but he holds that rhythms and melodies are representations (μιμήματα) of moral qualities and as such have an effect on the soul. For educational purposes, therefore, only the 'most ethical' types of music (ἁρμονίαι ἠθικώταται) should be used. At the same time he criticizes Plato for including the Phrygian, and would himself apparently confine instruction to the Dorian, which for him is the golden mean in music.

It is impossible to pass these opinions over as idle fancies when they are not only attested by two such different minds as Plato's and Aristotle's, but are implicit in many of the references to music in other writers (e.g. Aristophanes). The direct ethical effect of music may, indeed, have been exaggerated, as Aristoxenus hinted (*Harm.* 31) and as the Epicureans and Sceptics contended (cf. the *De musica* of Philodemus, 1st c. B.C.). Quite probably conventions and associations with poetic texts had much to do with the attribution of ἦθος to the modes; but at least it is evident that the Greeks associated their various ἁρμονίαι with distinctive feelings and emotions; and the keenness with which they felt the differences between the modes is well illustrated by the story of Philoxenus (Arist. *Pol.* 8. 1342ᵇ), who tried to compose his dithyramb 'The Mysians' in the Dorian but had to return to the appropriate ἁρμονία, which was the Phrygian. Furthermore, this attitude of respect for the power of music found expression in an artistic conservatism. In Argos, for instance, the purity of music was regulated by law; and at Sparta venturesome innovators are said to have had their instruments destroyed.

3. IN THE ROMAN WORLD. The cultivated classes under the Republic seem to have regarded music with tolerant contempt; Cato adduced as the final proof of the worthlessness of an opponent the fact that he sang ('praeterea cantat'); practical music did not, as in Greece, form part of a gentleman's education. The status of professional actors and musicians was low (they were *infames*), but they gained some protection by organizing themselves into guilds, and we learn from Livy (9. 30) of a 'strike' in 311 B.C. by the *collegium tibicinum*. This story at least shows the importance attaching to the *tibia* in cult, since the absence of the musicians raised a question of *religio* (*see* MUSIC IN WORSHIP). The use of horns and trumpets in the cult of the dead was doubtless due to Etruscan influence, but the armed dance of the Salii and the songs of the Arval Brethren are likely to have been indigenous. In the field of entertainment, there was first an influence from Etruria (Livy 7. 2) and then from Hellenistic Greece, but music played a more important role in the plays of Plautus than in the Greek New Comedy. The Roman army made use of the *tuba*, the *cornu* (a large almost circular horn), and the *lituus*, all of which instruments had been developed by the Etruscans.

From the second century B.C. onwards, Greek and oriental influences were paramount, including the cults of Dionysus, Cybele, and Isis, with their characteristic instruments, which also penetrated into light entertainment. There was an influx of foreign musicians, but talented native amateurs make their appearance under the Empire and include an Emperor in the person of Nero.

Unlike the Greeks, the Romans developed a taste for large instrumental ensembles (Sen. *Ep.* 84. 9–10), but in this they may have been anticipated by the Alexandrians. They seem to have made no specific contribution to musical theory. Subjected first to Etruscan and then to Greek influences, they doubtless borrowed and assimilated much; in the absence of musical documents we are unable to assert or deny that indigenous elements survived. At least we can conclude, from literary and monumental evidence, that music played a considerable part in the popular life of Rome.

4. EVIDENCE FOR GREEK MUSIC. For knowledge of Greek music we may turn to: (i) actual fragments of musical scores; (ii) remains of musical instruments; (iii) later types of music supposed to be descended from the Greek; (iv) ancient treatises. (i) The musical scores are few and fragmentary; only one is claimed to be classical (see § 12). (ii) The few surviving auloi have lost their mouthpieces; despite patient research (e.g. K. Schlesinger, *The Greek Aulos*, 1938) no agreed conclusions have been reached about the scales they were constructed to play. (iii) It is not inconceivable that modern Greek folk-song retains some elements derived from the ancient art, but it is virtually impossible, after so many centuries of foreign influence, to define features which may be due to Greek inheritance. The influence of classical antiquity upon the music of the Eastern and Western Churches may have been much slighter than was formerly assumed. (iv) The most straightforward line of approach is provided by the treatises on music, though theory unchecked by

musical documents can be misleading (see § 7). A fifth possible source of illumination is the use of analogies drawn from other musical cultures, but these are difficult to apply profitably, except on a basis of agreed facts about the ancient music.

Of the theoretical books the earliest is the *Harmonics* (Ἀρχαί and Στοιχεῖα) of Aristoxenus (q.v.), which is of fundamental importance. Part of book 11 and the whole of book 19 of the ps.-Aristotelian *Problems* (Προβλήματα) are concerned with music, and probably include fourth-century material; Euclid's *Division of the Monochord* (Κατατομὴ κανόνος) contains a series of mathematically formulated propositions about musical intervals. A treatise *On Music* (Περὶ μουσικῆς), attributed (wrongly?) by the MSS to Plutarch, contains much historical material, derived partly from Aristoxenus. To the second century A.D. belong the *Introduction to Harmonics* (Εἰσαγωγὴ ἁρμονική) of Cleonides (formerly attributed to Euclid), which gives a valuable outline of Aristoxenian theory; Theon of Smyrna's *Mathematics useful for reading Plato* (Τὰ κατὰ τὸ μαθηματικὸν χρήσιμα), which includes excerpts from Archytas and other reputable authorities; Claudius Ptolemy's *Harmonica* (Ἁρμονικά), in three books, which is indispensable; the *Handbook of Harmonics* (Ἁρμονικὸν ἐγχειρίδιον) of Nicomachus of Gerasa; and the *Introduction to Harmonics* (Ἁρμονικὴ εἰσαγωγή) of Gaudentius. To the third century A.D. probably belong the three books *On Music* (Περὶ μουσικῆς) of Aristides Quintilianus and the *Introduction to Music* (Εἰσαγωγὴ μουσική) of a certain Alypius, which is our chief source of information for the musical notations. To the fourth century A.D. belongs the *Introduction to the Art of Music* (Εἰσαγωγὴ τέχνης μουσικῆς) by an otherwise unknown Bacchius (Βακχεῖος). In Latin the chief works are the *De musica* of Boethius and the ninth book of the *De nuptiis Philologiae* of Martianus Capella.

It is obvious that most of these treatises are far removed in date from classical Greek music; and though much of their doctrine is traditional, we cannot always be sure when the writers are relying upon older authorities. Unfortunately their testimony is not unanimous in a number of important matters and they are silent about some topics on which information is desirable.

5. ANCIENT AND MODERN MUSIC. (i) The most striking difference between the music of the Greeks and that to which western Europeans are accustomed is that the ancient art made use of a large number of scales or modes, which, in the view of most authorities, differed from each other in the sequence of the intervals composing them and (probably) in tonality. It was to these modes that the Greeks attributed the varying ethical effects of music. Our Major and Minor scales are often called modes, but they give only a poor idea of modal music; for though the sequence of intervals is different and the Minor is distinguished from the Major by the flattening of its third and sixth notes, both scales have a common tonic or key note (actually the lowest note of the scale), in relation to which the importance and function of the other notes is determined. A better, though still imperfect, idea of the ancient modes may be obtained from Gregorian music, in which the tonal centre does not occupy the same relative position in every scale.

(ii) The second difference lies in the size of the intervals used in the modes. Our scales consist only of tones and semitones; the semitones (on the pianoforte at least) are made as nearly equal as possible, and twelve of them complete an octave. In Greek music tones and semitones were not all equal and the enharmonic *diesis* (δίεσις, sometimes translated as 'quarter-tone') was smaller than any interval with which we are familiar. Neither modern nor Gregorian music can afford us any example of this wide variety of intervals; we must listen to Indian, Arabian, or Chinese music if we wish to gain some impression of intervals different from our 'tempered' tone and semitone. Indeed, it is very probable that if we could hear a piece of ancient Greek music accurately performed, we should regard it as bizarre, uncouth, and possibly barbaric.

(iii) The third great difference is of a less technical nature: Greek music was predominantly melodic. Choruses sang in unison (or in octaves if men and boys were performing together); to this practice there seems to have been no exception (cf. [Arist.] *Pr.* 19. 18). There is evidence (Plut. *De mus.* 1137 b) that an instrumental accompaniment played by a professional musician did not always follow the melodic line of the vocal part. How wide a liberty was permissible in such an accompaniment (ἑτεροφωνία, cf. Pl. *Laws* 812 d) is unknown; but there is no reason to suppose that the instrument provided more than an embellishment. It is indisputable that neither in vocal nor in instrumental music was there anything like a counterpoint of mutually independent but congruous parts, and no harmonic structure in the sense in which we understand the term. The Greeks did not evolve the prototype of an eight-part motet or of an orchestral symphony.

**6.** THE ARISTOXENIAN THEORY. (*a*) *Tetrachords and systems.* The simplest approach to an understanding of the details of Greek music is from the theoretical expositions of Aristoxenus and his followers (especially Cleonides). As a starting-point we shall take the diatonic tetrachord such as may be found between the notes *E* and *A* on a pianoforte. In ascending order—if we may neglect the downward progression which is generally favoured by the Greek theorists—its intervals are: semitone, tone, tone (S, T, T, or ½, 1, 1). Two such tetrachords could be combined to form a scale or *system* (σύστημα) either (i) by conjunction (συναφή), when the top note of one tetrachord was identical with the bottom note of the other; or (ii) by disjunction (διάζευξις), when an interval of a tone (τόνος διαζευκτικός) was inserted between the two:

Conjunct system: E F G A B♭ C D   *or*   S T T S T T

Disjunct system: E F G A B C D E   *or*   S T T T S T T

There are three particularly important *systems* thus constructed from tetrachords: (i) the Lesser Perfect System (σύστημα τέλειον ἔλασσον), which consisted of three conjunct tetrachords with an added note called *proslambanomenos* (προσλαμβανόμενος, sc. φθόγγος) at the bottom. This *system*, with the technical names of its notes (originally derived from their position on a simple lyre, see § 9 (i)) and of its tetrachords, may be represented as follows (though it should be clearly understood that a pianoforte will give a very imperfect idea of the intervals even of a diatonic scale):

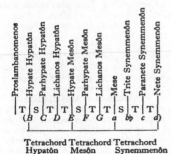

Tetrachord  Tetrachord  Tetrachord
Hypatôn     Mesôn       Synemmenôn

(ii) The Greater Perfect System (σύστημα τέλειον μεῖζον) consisted of the Proslambanomenos and four tetrachords grouped in conjunct pairs:

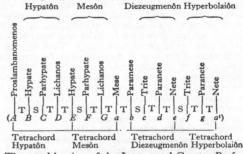

Tetrachord   Tetrachord   Tetrachord    Tetrachord
Hypatôn      Mesôn        Diezeugmenôn  Hyperbolaiôn

(iii) The combination of the Lesser and Greater Perfect Systems gave the Immutable System (σύστημα ἀμετάβολον) which can be regarded as the Greater Perfect System with the addition of the tetrachord Synemmenôn from the Lesser Perfect System.

(*b*) *Octave species.* Within the Greater Perfect System there were seven different types or *species* of octave (εἴδη τοῦ διὰ πασῶν) which could be distinguished by their different interval sequences. Each had its own distinctive name:

Mixolydian: Hypate Hypatôn—Paramese (*B–b*)
Lydian: Parhypate Hypatôn—Trite Diezeugmenôn (*C–c*)
Phrygian: Lichanos Hypatôn—Paranete Diezeugmenôn (*D–d*)
Dorian: Hypate Mesôn—Nete Diezeugmenôn (*E–e*)
Hypolydian: Parhypate Mesôn—Trite Hyperbolaiôn (*F–f*)
Hypophrygian: Lichanos Mesôn—Paranete Hyperbolaiôn (*G–g*)
Hypodorian: Proslambanomenos—Mese (*A–a*) *or* Mese—Nete Hyperbolaiôn (*a–a'*).

(*c*) *Transposition scales, Keys, or Tonoi.* The Perfect Immutable System could as a whole be played at various pitches without any alteration of the internal interval sequence, just as our modern Major or Minor scale can be taken at various pitches. When associated with a given pitch the Perfect Immutable System had a distinctive name and was called a *tonos* (τόνος) or *tropos* (τρόπος). According to Aristoxenus himself there were thirteen such *tonoi*, to which later theorists added two more (the Hyperaeolian and the Hyperlydian). On the commonly accepted equation of Greek and modern pitch the fifteen *tonoi* in ascending order were:

| | | |
|---|---|---|
| Hypodorian | commencing on | F |
| Hypoionian | „ | „ F♯ |
| Hypophrygian | „ | „ G |
| Hypoaeolian | „ | „ G♯ |
| Hypolydian | „ | „ A |
| Dorian | „ | „ B♭ |
| Ionian | „ | „ B |
| Phrygian | „ | „ C |
| Aeolian | „ | „ C♯ |
| Lydian | „ | „ D |
| Hyperdorian *or* Mixolydian | „ | „ E♭ |
| Hyperionian | „ | „ E |
| Hyperphrygian | „ | „ f |
| Hyperaeolian | „ | „ f♯ |
| Hyperlydian | „ | „ g |

It will be noted that the names of the lowest five include the prefix Hypo- (ὑπο-) and the names of the highest five have the prefix Hyper- (ὑπερ-); the middle five have simple ethnic designations. The range from the lowest note of the Hypodorian to the highest of the Hyperlydian was rather more than three octaves, and so corresponded to the combined capabilities of normal male and female voices. Though Aristoxenus is silent on the point, it is reasonable to suppose that the original purpose of the *tonoi* was to bring the various octave *species* within the same vocal range. That is why the pitch order of the *tonoi* is the reverse of the pitch order of the *species* of the same names; and why the terms *tonos* and *harmonia* are equated in some writers. Claudius Ptolemy (*Harm. 2. 9*) points out quite legitimately that since there are only seven *species* of the octave, only seven *tonoi* were really necessary. It is also worth noting that the use of the tetrachord Synemmenôn in the Immutable System provided a means of modulation from one *tonos* to another *tonos* a fourth higher; for the conjunction between the tetrachords Mesôn and Synemmenôn could be treated as if it were the conjunction between the tetrachords Hypatôn and Mesôn of another *tonos*: thus:

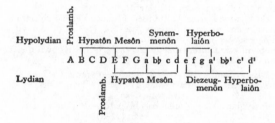

(d) *Genera and 'colours'*. So far we have been concerned only with tetrachords containing no other interval than a tone or semitone. The structure of the tetrachords themselves, however, admitted a number of variations known as *genera* (γένη) and 'colours' (χρόαι). The two extreme notes of a tetrachord were regarded as fixed (φθόγγοι ἑστῶτες), while the position of the two inner notes (φθόγγοι κινούμενοι) was variable; and the two lowest intervals of the tetrachord were together called a *pycnum* (πυκνόν) if their sum was less than the remaining interval of the tetrachord. The *genera* were three in number: the diatonic (γένος διατονικόν), the chromatic (γ. χρωματικόν or χρῶμα), and the enharmonic (γ. ἐναρμόνιον or ἁρμονία). The diatonic itself was subdivided in the Aristoxenian theory into two 'colours', the High (σύντονον) and the Soft (μαλακόν); and the chromatic into three 'colours', the Tonic (τονιαῖον), the Hemiolic (ἡμιόλιον), and the Soft (μαλακόν). If we take the tone as a unit, the intervals constituting the various kinds of tetrachords can be set out as follows:

| | | |
|---|---|---|
| High (σύντονον) diatonic | $\frac{1}{2}$ | 1 | 1 |
| Soft (μαλακόν) „ | $\frac{1}{2}$ $\frac{3}{4}$ | $1\frac{1}{4}$ |
| Tonic (τονιαῖον) chromatic | $\frac{1}{2}$ $\frac{1}{2}$ | $1\frac{1}{2}$ |
| Hemiolic (ἡμιόλιον) „ | $\frac{3}{8}$ $\frac{3}{8}$ | $1\frac{3}{4}$ |
| Soft (μαλακόν) „ | $\frac{1}{3}$ $\frac{1}{3}$ | $1\frac{5}{6}$ |
| Enharmonic | $\frac{1}{4}$ $\frac{1}{4}$ | 2 |

When we make allowances for the fact that this doctrine of *genera* is only a theoretical systematization of the actual practice of musicians, it becomes obvious that a Greek composer had a great wealth of subtle intonations at his disposal, and that Greek melodies must have had a delicacy and fineness of outline to which the melodies of modern music can offer no parallel.

7. THEORY AND PRACTICE. The predecessors of Aristoxenus in musical theory were the Pythagoreans and the Harmonists (ἁρμονικοί). The Pythagoreans, however, were more interested in tracing numerical

relationships in concordant intervals than in establishing a comprehensive theory; and it is significant that the dying Pythagoras was reputed to have adjured his followers to study the monochord, which was a piece of scientific apparatus and not a musical instrument at all. As a whole, the school devoted its attention to the Dorian scale; and intervals whose ratios they evaluated were considered satisfactory only if they conformed to one or other of the favourite Pythagorean formulae, such as $x : nx$ or $x : x+1$. The Harmonists, on the other hand, were much more interested in the practical art; but it is evident from what Aristoxenus himself tells us about their work (*Harm. 2, 6, 36, 37, 40*) that they were not capable of organizing their knowledge into a really homogeneous system of theory. They did not analyse all the scales, but restricted their study to the enharmonic ones whose compass was an octave; they interested themselves in the search for a small unit of measurement (cf. Pl. *Resp.* 531 a), the *diesis*, which they used in the construction of diagrams of close-packed intervals (καταπύκνωσις), without any regard for melodic or unmelodic sequences; and they were at variance with one another in their pronouncements about the order of the *tonoi* and the intervals which separated them.

The homogeneity of the system of Aristoxenus cannot be denied. It seems to provide a means whereby any melody, when reduced to its elements, might be related to a scale whose 'colour', *genus*, *species*, and *tonos* could be defined. But apart from the fact that no theory can profess to give more than the osteology of an art, the Aristoxenian theory, as it has come down to us, is unsatisfying.

(i) Underlying it all is the idea that sound can be regarded as a line, at any point of which the voice could rest (though not at all in succession); and that an interval, since it may be thought of as a linear distance between two such points, can be subdivided exactly into any given number of equal parts. But the Pythagoreans had already laid the foundations of a true acoustic science when they demonstrated that the size of an interval can properly be expressed only by a numerical ratio. There is, in fact, no such interval as a semitone, if by that term we mean an interval which taken twice will produce a 9 : 8 tone, for the ratio involved ($3 : 2 \sqrt{2}$) is irrational. The intervals 18 : 17 and 17 : 16 can be called semitones, and 36 : 35, or 35 : 34, or 34 : 33, or 33 : 32 may be called 'quarter-tones'; but when Aristoxenus speaks of a ἡμιτόνιον or a δίεσις, his vague description does not give us sufficiently precise information about Greek intonations.

(ii) In Plato and Aristotle and other writers we read of ἁρμονίαι most of which had ethnic names: Ionian, Lydian, Dorian, Phrygian. The word itself, when used in this musical sense, is most easily explained by the assumption that each ἁρμονία involved a new tuning of the lyre. Though Aristoxenus (*Harm.* 36) refers to those 'who confined their attention to the seven octave scales (ἑπτὰ ὀκταχόρδων Westphal; ἑπταχόρδων MSS.) which they called ἁρμονίαι', he himself does not use the plural ἁρμονίαι in a technical sense. His octave scales are called *species* (εἴδη τοῦ διὰ πασῶν), and their names are not identical with those used for the ἁρμονίαι. There is amongst them no Ionian or Syntonolydian; and the names of three of them include the prefix Hypo- (ὑπο-) which is not found in earlier writers. Even if we identify the *species* with the ἁρμονίαι and equate, for instance, the Syntonolydian and Lydian of Plato with the Aristoxenian Lydian and Hypolydian respectively, it is quite impossible to believe that the ἁρμονίαι had their origin as *species* within a two-octave scale which itself evidently belongs to a comparatively advanced stage of musical development. It would be worth much to know what modifications, if any, had to take place before the ἁρμονίαι could be theoretically treated as octave *species*.

(iii) A further obscurity, and one of considerable importance, concerns the form of the *species* in the chromatic and enharmonic *genera*. The problem is simple in the case of the Dorian *species* which is bounded by fixed notes (φθόγγοι ἑστῶτες) of the Greater Perfect System; for its enharmonic form would be: $\frac{1}{4}$ $\frac{1}{4}$ 2 1 $\frac{1}{4}$ $\frac{1}{4}$ 2. The enharmonic form of the Lydian, however, which is bounded by movable notes (φθόγγοι κινούμενοι) would appear to be: $\frac{1}{4}$ 2 $\frac{1}{4}$ $\frac{1}{4}$ 2, 1 $\frac{1}{4}$; and it is scarcely credible that such a sequence was ever a musical possibility.

(iv) Nothing is said by Aristoxenus about the tonality either of the Greater Perfect System or of the individual octave *species*. Yet if these *species* were virtually the old ἁρμονίαι or a developed form of them, we cannot understand them fully until we know what note had the function of a tonal centre in each. One of the ps.-Aristotelian *Problems* (19. 20) states that all the best melodies make a frequent use of Mese, and we may conjecture that this note was in fact a tonic. But unfortunately it is not clear whether the writer meant the Mese of the Greater Perfect System (i.e. a Mese κατὰ δύναμιν) or the fourth note ascending (i.e. a Mese κατὰ θέσιν) of any octave *species*.

So far we have mentioned only those deficiencies of the Aristoxenian theory which are evident from an examination of the system itself. Further problems arise when we try to relate it to other evidence. (i) Aristides Quintilianus (21–2) gives an account (possibly derived from some work of Aristoxenus himself) of the six ἁρμονίαι mentioned by Plato in the *Republic*. Of the scales which Aristides describes, only one (the Lydian) is identical with an Aristoxenian *species* (the Hypolydian); the Phrygian and Mixolydian have an internal structure somewhat different from the corresponding Aristoxenian εἴδη; the Dorian has an additional tone at the bottom; and the Ionian and Syntonolydian are less than an octave in compass. Several of them seem to involve a mixture of *genera*. There is no reason to reject in its entirety the evidence of Aristides, which, so far as concerns the Mixolydian, is in part confirmed by a passage of Plutarch (*De mus.* 1136 d); and the truth would appear to be that the old ἁρμονίαι were not parts of a homogeneous musical system. (ii) There is other evidence also for defective and anomalous scales used by Olympus and Terpander and analysed by Philolaus (Plut. *De mus.* 1134 f–1135 b, 1137 b–d; [Arist.] *Pr.* 19. 32; Nicom. 253 Jan.). (iii) In connexion with the older types of music, prominent mention is made (Plut. *De mus.* 1134 f, 1141 b; Aristid. Quint. 28) of intervals called σπονδειασμός (a rise of three *dieses*), ἔκλυσις (a fall of three *dieses*), and ἐκβολή (a rise of five *dieses*). Intervals of these magnitudes have a very unimportant place in the system of Aristoxenus (cf. his μαλακόν diatonic, § 6). (iv) Claudius Ptolemy (*Harm.* 2. 14) has preserved the evaluations for the *genera* made by his predecessors and has added some of his own. He gives the size of the tone as 11 : 10, 10 : 9, 9 : 8, and 8 : 7; he states that the sequence 28 : 27, 8 : 7, 9 : 8, which is also given by Archytas (4th c. B.C.), was the standard diatonic tuning in his day. The smaller intervals of the enharmonic vary from 46 : 45, which is less than a quarter-tone, to 24 : 23, which is larger than a third of a tone; the chromatic intervals vary between 28 : 27 and 12 : 11. Though the enharmonic usually has an interval of ratio 5 : 4 (a major third) at the top, and the chromatic an interval of 6 : 5 or 7 : 6 (a minor third) at that place, in both *genera* the two lower intervals are of varying sizes; and it seems that the distinction between the *genera* is not as clear or as definite as the Aristoxenian theory postulates. (v) Though the widely varying dates (see § 12) of

the fragments of Greek music warn us not to press their evidence too far, it is noteworthy that they exhibit a number of melodic progressions which violate the doctrines of Aristoxenus.

8. THE LIMITS OF DOUBT. Despite the defects of the Aristoxenian system which have just been mentioned and the conflicting evidence from other sources, it would be widely accepted that, in the earlier stages, Greek music made use of a number of modal scales which, because they involved separate tunings of the lyre, were called ἁρμονίαι. As the compass of the lyre and cithara was extended, the relations between the ἁρμονίαι were more clearly apprehended and, at the expense perhaps of the elimination of some apparent anomalies, they came to be regarded as segments of a single two-octave scale based upon homogeneous tetrachords. On the other hand, we know nothing, apart from the evidence of Aristides Quintilianus and Plutarch, about the original structure of the ἁρμονίαι. We cannot say whether each of them had a diatonic, chromatic, and enharmonic form or whether the various *genera* and 'colours' were in practice associated with particular ἁρμονίαι. Nor can we make any positive assertion about the tonality of the ἁρμονίαι or of the octave *species*; the theoretical treatises are almost silent on the point and the musical fragments are not decisive.

9. INSTRUMENTS. Musical instruments (ὄργανα) of many types were known to the Greeks; it was therefore by definite preference that only the lyre and cithara among strings and the aulos among wind-instruments ever attained artistic importance. The lyre or cithara predominated in lyric poetry, though the aulos shared in the accompaniment of Pindar's odes and monopolized the dithyramb and the dramatic choruses; the lyre prevailed in Athenian education, the aulos had its place in social and military life; both were prominent in cult.

(i) *Strings* (ἔντατα). The *lyre* (λύρα), of which the cithara (κιθάρα) was a more elaborate form, was characterized by strings of equal length, vertically strung and sounded by plucking. It thus differed from: (*a*) bowed types, which were unknown to Greece; (*b*) harps, with strings of unequal length, known but not employed in serious music (e.g. ψαλτήριον, τρίγωνον, σαμβύκη). Pitch was regulated by the tension (and perhaps the thickness) of the strings; and, in the absence of a finger- or fret-board, each string would normally provide one note only, by contrast with the lute (πανδοῦρα, ? σκινδαψός), for which there is little or no evidence before the time of Alexander (*JHS* 1965, 62 ff.). We cannot, however, deny the possibility that (*a*) the octave-harmonic was obtained by stopping the string at its middle point (διάληψις); (*b*) the string was shortened by finger-pressure near the cross-bar to raise its pitch by a small interval. The strings (χορδαί, νευραί), of gut or sinew, were stretched from a holder (χορδότονον) fixed to the body over a bridge to the cross-bar (ζυγόν) which joined the two side-pieces, where there was a tuning-apparatus of thongs or pegs (κόλλοπες).

The sound-box of the lyre was formed of the carapace of a tortoise (χελύς), or a wooden structure of similar shape with ox-hide stretched over its concavity (cf. *Hymn. Hom. Merc.* 41 ff.); from it sprung two slender curved side-pieces (πήχεις, κέρατα) of horn or wood. The vaulted wooden body of the cithara was larger and more solidly built, the lower part of the arms constituting a substantial prolongation of the sound-box. The instrument rested against the body of the performer and was supported in position (as also was the lyre) by a belt (τελαμών) attached to his left wrist.

The *barbitos* (βάρβιτος or -ον) was a variety of lyre having longer strings and therefore a lower pitch. The instrument of Sappho and Alcaeus, it is seen in art in convivial contexts. Two varieties of cithara can be distinguished in vase-paintings: the more elaborate flat-based instrument of the professional citharodes, which first appears in the seventh century and can reasonably be associated with Terpander (see § 10), and a simpler instrument with rounded base, to which modern scholars have given the name of 'cradle-cithara'. The latter appears to be descended from a rudimentary cithara seen in artistic representations of the eighth century, to be identified with the *phorminx* or *kitharis* of Homer.

The *phorminx* is shown with from three to five strings (though Minoan and Mycenaean citharas already had seven or more). From the seventh century onward, seven strings become canonical for both lyres and citharas, and in art this number is seldom exceeded; though eight-stringed examples are seen even in the sixth century, we should not put too much trust in the painters' accuracy. There is literary evidence that in the later fifth century innovators such as Phrynis and Timotheus (Timoth. *Pers.* 242; Pherecrates ap. Plut. *De mus.* 1141 f) added strings up to the number of twelve; and this is to some extent confirmed by the monumental evidence. The strings were plucked by the left hand directly (ψάλλειν), by the right hand with the aid of a *plectrum* (πλήττειν), but the respective functions of the two hands are not entirely clear. The left hand probably followed the vocal melody; it may have damped strings as well as plucking them. The right hand may have been used for preludes and interludes and such independent accompaniment as there may have been.

As to the πηκτίς and μαγαδίς, it is uncertain whether they were distinct from one another and whether they belonged to the class of lyre or (more probably) harp. They had many strings, which made playing in octaves possible: hence the term μαγαδίζειν, for doubling a vocal part at the octave.

(ii) *Wind* (ἐμπνευστά). The αὐλός, commonly mistranslated 'flute', was akin rather to the clarinet or oboe. The exact nature of the vibrator is, despite a passage of Theophrastus (*Hist. Pl.* 4. 11. 4), a matter of uncertain inference, but it was probably a double-reed (ζεῦγος, γλῶττα, γλωττίς). This was inserted into a cylindrical or slightly conical pipe, and the extrusion of the reed was partially hidden by one or more bulbs (ὅλμοι). K. Schlesinger, however, in *The Greek Aulos* (a mine of information about the behaviour of reed pipes) maintains that the double-reed gave place at a certain stage to a single-reed. The pipe, of reed, wood, bone, or ivory, was open at the lower end and pierced with lateral holes. Of these the early aulos had probably from three to five, which would seem to provide a very limited range. The Elgin auloi and the recently discovered Brauron aulos (*BSA* 1963), late sixth or early fifth century, have six, one of which may have been a vent-hole. Auloi were generally played in pairs (cf. the Latin *tibiae*), the pipes being often, though not always, held in position by a band (φορβεία) which passed round the cheeks and over the head of the player, assisting him to blow strongly. Since the pipes had each its own reed-mouthpiece, they may have spoken separately and together provided a more extended scale. If they were sounded simultaneously, one may have served as a drone (though there is no positive evidence for this), perhaps a variable drone; in some styles, it is not impossible that there was a rudimentary harmony between the notes of the two pipes (cf. Plut. *De mus.* 1137 b–d). The pipes were not always of the same length: in the Phrygian auloi, the left was longer, with a bell, and consequently lower in pitch. Of such a type, no doubt, were the *tibiae impares* of the Roman *palliata* (illustrations in Fleischhauer, *Musikgeschichte in Bildern*).

In the early period a separate pipe (or pair of pipes) may have been required for each mode (ἁρμονία). Later the potentialities of the instrument were greatly enlarged, particularly by Pronomus and the Theban school of the later fifth century. Length and the number of holes were increased (the longest of surviving auloi has 15 or 16, the shortest 6), and a device was introduced by which the holes not required for a particular scale could be closed by a perforated metal ring operated by a small projection (κέρας). In this way it was possible to play a number of different modes on one pair of auloi; and instruments were no longer classified according to mode, but by general range of pitch. Aristoxenus (ap. Ath. 634 e) distinguishes five types (in descending order of pitch): παρθένιοι, παιδικοί, κιθαριστήριοι, τέλειοι, ὑπερτέλειοι; and he states (*Harm.* 20) that between them they embraced a range of more than three octaves. Furthermore, a practitioner of the highly individualistic art of aulos-playing had at his disposal many professional tricks such as overblowing, cross-fingering, partial obturation of holes, regulation of the reed and of his own breath, whereby he could extend the capabilities of his instrument.

A pipe held horizontally is occasionally seen in later art, and this may be the πλαγίαυλος, whether it was a genuine cross-flute or an aulos in which the reed was introduced obliquely by a lateral tube. The syrinx (σῦριγξ) was blown directly, like a flageolet, and might consist of a single pipe (σ. μονοκάλαμος) or of a raft of pipes (σ. πολυκάλαμος). In Greece the pipes (commonly seven, though more and less are shown) were of equal length, but stopped internally at graduated intervals; the 'stepped' variety is Etruscan and Roman. The pitch was high. The syrinx was doubtless part-ancestor of the water-organ (ὕδραυλις), in which rows of graduated auloi were supplied with air hydraulically. This instrument, invented by Ctesibius of Alexandria in the third century B.C., became popular in the Roman world.

*Brass* instruments (with bone mouthpiece) were primarily employed for military purposes. Both the straight trumpet (σάλπιγξ, *tuba*) and the curved horn (κέρας, *cornu*) were known. The Etruscan-Roman *lituus* was straight in the upper part, but bent back strongly and flared at the extremity.

(iii) *Percussion*. Tambourines (τύμπανα), cymbals (κύμβαλα), and castanets (κρόταλα) infiltrated from orgiastic cult (e.g. of Dionysus and Cybele) into the realm of light entertainment.

10. HISTORY. The history of Greek music overlaps the history of Greek poetry, for the main function of music was to accompany poetic texts. Thus the principal types of musical composition correspond largely to the types of poetry, and our scanty sources mention as leading composers many who are better known to us as poets: Archilochus (evidently an important influence), Sappho, Pindar, Sophocles; unfortunately, no detailed account of the musical side of their work can be given. There are others, however, known primarily as musicians; and we know of types of performance that were primarily musical.

Musical history really begins in the seventh century with Terpander and Archilochus. In the background are folk-song, work-song, song (personal or choral) occasional to the principal events of human life, and above all cult-song. In the background is the epic tradition: a Phemius or Demodocus singing epic verse to the lyre. In the background is also an elusive foreign influence; for Greek music was not racially pure. Recent research into Egyptian, Babylonian, and Palestinian music has shown possible points of similarity; indeed, the Greek tradition itself avowed an influence from the Orient, not only in the names of certain modes, but in the legendary figure of Olympus the Mysian. But the contrast is not a simple one, and Olympus himself is a composite figure, representing a fusion of the Hellenic and the oriental. The instrument with which he is connected, the aulos, first appears in art during the seventh century, but it would be rash to assume that it was previously unknown in Greece; the antithesis of Hellenic lyre and Asiatic aulos needs to be used with great caution, not least because the Greek cithara has itself close connexions with the Orient. Doubtless new styles and techniques were introduced from the East in the early seventh century, but we are not in a position to separate the new from the old.

*Terpander* (mid 6th c.) came from Antissa in Lesbos, but his activity is associated with Sparta. His chief claim to fame is that he first impressed his individuality upon the traditional νόμοι κιθαρῳδικοί so that they were handed down as his personal compositions. Styles, rather than definite melodies, in origin (see Sachs, *Musik d. Altertums* (1924), 64), these νόμοι, which were vocal solos accompanied by the cithara, became the subjects of competition. The texts are said to have been epic, with a prelude written by the composer-executant; the melody was severe and eschewed modulation. About the same time the obscure *Clonas* (of Tegea?) performed the same service for the analogous νόμοι αὐλῳδικοί. But more famous names connected with the aulos are those of *Polymnestus* of Colophon and *Sacadas* of Argos. The former's fame was recognized by Pindar (fr. 178), and Plutarch speaks of him as an innovator who, nevertheless, did not depart from the severe style. Sacadas was the most famous executant of the sixth century. For not only was he singer-composer of νόμοι αὐλῳδικοί, but player-composer of the famous αὐλητικὸς νόμος Πυθικός (a purely instrumental piece, dealing with Apollo's victory over the Python) in which he won in 586 the first of three successive victories at the Pythian Games. The accounts that late authorities give of the structure of this piece reveal an element of 'programme-music'. It is interesting too that purely instrumental music (ψιλὴ αὔλησις) should have won and kept an important place in a Greek festival at all; even solo cithara-playing (ψιλὴ κιθάρισις), which would seem a bleak entertainment, found its way into the Pythian and other festivals.

Doubtless the main triumphs of Greek music in this period were in choral lyric, an indissoluble complex of poetry, melody, and dance, which culminated with Pindar, Simonides, and the early tragedians. To later —and moralizing—theorists this was the epoch of the 'educative' style, in contrast to the 'theatrical' or 'popular' style that developed in the fifth century. The process of transition cannot be traced in detail. An important factor may have been the evolution of the aulos (see § 9), which increased the available range of melody and facilitated modulation. String-players, too, envious of the freedom of their fellows, added strings to the cithara (see § 9). Furthermore, the balance of importance between choir and instrumentalist began to change. The chief factor, however, was mental rather than technical. Individualism was in the air and convention suspect; and the interpreter of a tradition intimately associated with religion became a virtuoso bent upon giving pleasure to an audience. Thus variety (ποικιλία) took the place of simplicity: the melodic range was extended, modulation (and perhaps vocal and instrumental embellishments) cultivated; rhythmical structure became freer; the poetry mattered less in comparison with the melody.

The types of music especially affected were the dithyramb and the νόμος κιθαρῳδικός. The latter was revolutionized by *Phrynis* of Mytilene. The former, under *Melanippides* and *Cinesias*, broke away from strophic structure into free verse (cf. Pickard-Cambridge–Webster, *Dithyramb²*, 38 ff.). *Timotheus* of Miletus (c. 450–360) was a master of both forms; and, indeed, the distinction between them was blurred, for while Timotheus seems to have introduced a choral element into the νόμος, *Philoxenus* (his contemporary) introduced *soli* into dithyramb. The impure poetic style favoured by composers of νόμοι and dithyramb alike can be judged from the *Persae* of Timotheus, a νόμος, which has in great part survived. The rhythms are varied but uninteresting; the diction is turgid, obscure, and undistinguished. But the work is a libretto rather than a poem; and we should not condemn the music unheard, though we may suspect that lack of taste was not confined to the poetic text. How far the new style affected other types of music it is hard to say. Certainly it was not unchallenged in the fourth century; and, when we come to the earliest of our substantial fragments, the Delphic Paeans, we find a strong archaizing tendency. We gather from Polybius (4. 20), however, that the music of Philoxenus and Timotheus had become 'classical' in the Arcadia of the second century B.C.

11. THE NOTATIONS. (i) *Melodic*. To note their melodies the Greeks used alphabetic forms, written, in the case of poetic texts, above the syllables. Two systems of notation for the fifteen *tonoi* are recorded in late authorities (notably Alypius), who also assert that one was used for vocal, the other for instrumental melody (σήματα τῆς λέξεως, τῆς κρούσεως). This is confirmed by the Berlin papyrus, where both notations are so employed. It should be observed, however, that (a), with the possible exception of the *Orestes* papyrus, we have no case of the employment of both in the same piece; (b) the second Delphic Hymn is noted in the instrumental notation, which suggests that, where vocal and instrumental melody were identical, the notations might be employed indifferently.

The history of the notations is obscure and their interpretation controversial. The vocal notation can hardly have preceded the general adoption, towards the end of the fifth century, of the Ionic alphabet on which it is based; the instrumental notation, the origin of whose forms is uncertain, may well be earlier, but, being designed for a system of *tonoi*, it implies a developed theory. That system was not, however, the fifteen *tonoi* of Alypius. For instance, in both notations the signs above Dorian *nete hyperbolaiôn* repeat those an octave below with the addition of an acute accent and probably did not belong to the original scheme; at the lower end the instrumental notation has adapted the forms below Hypolydian *proslambanomenos* from the vocal notation. It would seem, then, that the original scope of the instrumental notation was two octaves and a tone, and that it was designed for a restricted number of *tonoi* with restricted range.

The instrumental notation is characterized by triads, in which the same form appears in three positions (e.g. F ⊔ ⅂), representing the three notes of an enharmonic *pycnum* (see § 6 d). Thus the highest note is a semitone above the lowest, and the highest and lowest notes of the various triads combine to form a semitonal series of fixed pitch. But this notation as applied to the chromatic and diatonic shows some peculiarities: all three *genera* have a common sign for *parhypate*, despite its varying pitch; and, while the sign for diatonic *lichanos* correctly implies an interval of 1½ tones from *hypate*, chromatic *lichanos* is identical with the enharmonic, unless distinguished by a diacritical mark. There were thus two conflicting principles at work, those of absolute pitch and relative function; and it is to this conflict, and to the adaptation of the original enharmonic scheme to additional *genera* and *tonoi*, that many of the much-canvassed anomalies are due: namely, the employment of the same sign with different values, of different signs with the same value. (Sachs, in *Zeitschrift f. Musikwissenschaft* vi, proposing a radically new interpretation, relates the instrumental notation to a pentatonic tuning of the lyre; but see *CQ* 1956, 169 ff.) The vocal notation corresponds to the instrumental note for note, but replaces the triads by a continuous alphabetic series. Most of the letters of the alphabet are employed (in descending order) within the range of the central octave of the Dorian *tonos*; above and below are altered forms of the same series.

(ii) *Rhythmical.* Symbols could be used to elucidate the rhythm. (*a*) The signs ⌐, ⌐|, ⌐|, ⊔ placed over a note indicated that its length was that of two, three, four, and five time-units (or χρόνοι πρῶτοι) respectively. The last two are known from theory only. (*b*) A rest (χρόνος κενός), or a protraction of the preceding note, was indicated by Λ or ⌒, which might be used in conjunction with the signs of quantity: e.g. ⌐. (*c*) Dots (στιγμαί) might be used to distinguish the structure of the metrical foot, and ancient authority states that the function was to mark the *arsis* (ἄρσις). On the whole our fragments confirm this, but the evidence is complicated (see *Symb. Osl.* 1955, 73 ff., *POxy.* (xxv) 117 ff.). (*d*) A subscript curved hyphen might be used to bind together notes sung to the same syllable.

12. THE FRAGMENTS. The following constitute the corpus of surviving Greek melody.

*A. In papyri.* (i) *PRain.* G 2315 (*c.* 200 B.C.). A musical setting of Euripides *Orestes* 338–44 may be Euripidean, since the poet's own score was apparently extant in the time of Dionysius of Halicarnassus (*Wien. Stud.* 1962). (ii) Cairo 59533 (Zenon), *c.* 250 B.C., contains a brief fragment, possibly from a tragedy (*JHS* 1931). (iii) *PBerl.* 6870 (possibly an anthology), written later than A.D. 156, contains: (*a*) twelve lines of a paean in a Hellenistic manner; (*b*) three lines for instrument only; (*c*) four lines in a lyric metre addressed to the suicide Ajax; (*d*) three lines for instrument; (*e*) half a line of lyric. The instrumental pieces have no discernible connexion with the vocal fragments they follow; all five make elaborate use of rhythmical notation (*Sitz. Berlin* 1918). (iv) *POxy.* (xv) 1786, third century A.D., contains a Christian hymn in a rough-and-ready anapaestic metre; melodic and rhythmical notation are Greek, but the antecedents of the melody might be oriental. (v) *POsl.* inv. no. 1413 (an anthology?), second century A.D., contains two short fragments, one anapaestic, one iambic, both probably from Hellenistic tragedies, not obviously connected with one another (*Symb. Osl.* 1955). (vi) *POxy.* (xxv) 2436, second century A.D., contains a fragment perhaps from a satyr-play; the music, if not the text, is post-classical. (vii) *PVienna* G 29.825 a–f. Brief fragments of various dates (*Wien. Stud.* 1962). (viii) G 13763 (*Hermes* 1966). (ix) *PMich.* inv. no. 2958, second century A.D.: contains a fragment, apparently of tragic dialogue (*JEg. Arch.* 1965).

The date of composition, with the possible exception of (i), is in all cases unknown.

*B. On stone.* (x–xi) The most extensive fragments of Greek music that survive are two paeans, both seriously incomplete, found in 1893 during the French excavations at Delphi. The second can be dated 128–127 B.C. and ascribed to a certain Limenius; the first may well have the same date and authorship. Both are written in paeonic or cretic metre, which, in the absence of rhythmical notation, suggests 5/8 time. The second paean is followed by a brief prosodion in an Aeolic metre. Melodically, these two paeans strikingly illustrate the Aristoxenian scale-system, tetrachordal structure being clearly marked and the 'standing-notes' emphasized (see § 6 *d*). (xii) An inscription of the second century B.C. or later, found at Aidin near Tralles, presents us with a brief but intact and attractive melody, commonly known as the 'Epitaph of Seikilos'. The words are a kind of skolion in free iambics, the rhythm being elucidated by notation.

*C. In manuscript.* (xiii–xvi) Four melodies have come down among the manuscripts of the ancient treatises. (xiii–xiv) The Hymn to the Muse should in fact be regarded as two separate pieces, both of uncertain date, but earlier than (xv–xvi). (xv) The Hymn to Nemesis is attributable to Mesomedes, a contemporary of Hadrian. (xvi) Similarity of style suggests the same authorship for the Hymn to the Sun. (xvii) Short snatches of melody occur in Bellermann's *Anonymus* (§§ 97–101, 104). Their apparent purpose is to illustrate types of rhythm.

The melody to the opening lines of Pindar's first Pythian ode, published by A. Kircher in his *Musurgia Universalis* (1650), is under such grave suspicion of being a forgery that its evidential value is negligible (see *CPhil.* 1936, 120 ff.).

13. MELODY, RHYTHM, AND THE GREEK LANGUAGE. Two important principles of composition emerge from a consideration of the fragments. Both in melody and in rhythm a Greek composer had less apparent freedom in setting words than his modern successors. This is explicable from the nature of the Greek language: (*a*) by virtue of its pitch-accent it possessed, even when spoken, an inherent melody—in the phrase of Aristoxenus, λογῶδές τι μέλος; (*b*) it possessed clearly marked long and short vowels, which formed the basis of quantitative metres.

(*a*) In the majority of extant compositions this word or sentence melody is respected: an accented syllable is set to a note which is not lower and is frequently higher than other syllables of the same word (for details see *Symb. Osl.* 1955, 64 ff.). Yet this principle is not observed by all the vocal fragments or by all equally. They fall into three groups: (1) in iii (*a*), v, vi, ix–xiv exceptions are absent or negligible; (2) in i, iii (*c*), vii a–b the accent seems to be altogether disregarded; (3) iv, xv, xvi show the influence of the accent, but with more frequent exceptions. The phenomena of (3) may reflect the gradual breakdown of the pitch-accent which was taking place during the period of their composition. This explanation will not, however, account for (2), which includes the *Orestes* fragment; but it should be observed that i is strophic, v may well be; and, if (as is probable) strophe and antistrophe were sung to the same melody, the accent was then bound to be disregarded.

(*b*) The rhythms of Greek music were practically identical with the metres of Greek poetry; and, where the natural quantities of the syllables are distorted, such a distortion is also a concern of the metrist. Only in the Berlin Paean (where – – – is rhythmized as, e.g., ♩ ♪ ♪) is there a considerable divergence between rhythm and metre. In judging this apparent restriction of the musician's freedom, however, it must be remembered that the Greek lyric metres themselves were elaborate partly because they were musical and choreographic as well as poetic rhythms.

ANCIENT SOURCES. (*a*) *Theoretical Works.* (i) *Collections*: M. Meibomius, *Antiquae Musicae Auctores Septem* (2 vols., Amsterdam, 1652; containing: Aristoxenus, Euclid with Cleonides, Nicomachus, Alypius, Gaudentius, Bacchius, Aristides Quintilianus, Martianus Capella). C. von Jan, *Musici Scriptores Graeci* (1895; containing Aristotelis loci, ps.-Arist. *Problems*, Euclid, Cleonides, Nicomachus, Bacchius, Gaudentius, Alypius). (ii) *Separate Authors*: Aristoxenus, ed. H. S. Macran (1902), R. da Rios (1954); ps.-Aristotelian *Problems*, ed. F. A. Gevaert and J. C. Vollgraf (1903), G. Marenghi (1957); ps.-Plutarch, *De mus.*, ed. H. Weil and Th. Reinach (1900), F. Lasserre (1954), K. Ziegler (² 1959); Theon of Smyrna, ed. E. Hiller (1878); Ptolemy, ed. J. Wallis (1682, and, with the commentary of Porphyrius, in *Opera Math.* iii, 1699), I. Düring (1930); Porphyrius, ed. I. Düring (1932); Aristides Quintilianus, ed. A. Jahn (1882), R. P. Winnington-Ingram (1963), German translation and commentary, R. Schäfke (1937); Philodemus, *De mus.*, ed. J. Kemke (1884), D. A. van Krevelen (1939); Sextus Empiricus, *Adv. musicos*, ed. R. G. Bury (1949), J. Mau (1954). Add also F. Bellermann's *Anonymus* (1841) and H. A. J. Vincent's *Notice sur trois MSS. grecs* (Vol. 16. 2 of *Notices et extraits des MSS. du Roi*, 1847). (*b*) *Fragments of music.* Incomplete collection in C. von Jan's *Musici Scriptores Graeci, Supplementum* (1899). For the Delphic

Hymns add Powell, *Coll. Alex.*; for the Berlin papyrus, R. Wagner, *Philol.* 1929; for the Christian Hymn, Th. Reinach, *Revue Musicale* 1922, R. Wagner in *Philol.* 1923. J. F. Mountford, 'Greek music in the papyri and inscriptions' (in Powell and Barber, *New Chapters* ii).

MODERN LITERATURE. F. A. Gevaert, *Histoire et théorie de la musique de l'antiquité* (1875–81, repr. 1966); R. Westphal, *Theorie d. musisch. Künste d. Hellenen*[3] (1885); A. A Howard, 'The Αὐλός or Tibia', *Harv. Stud.* 1893; D. B. Monro, *The Modes of Ancient Greek Music* (1894); F. A. Gevaert, *La Mélopée antique* (1895); H. Abert, *Die Lehre vom Ethos*(1899); J. F. Mountford, *JHS* 1920; H. Riemann, *Handbuch d. Musikgeschichte*[3] (1923); Th. Reinach, *La Musique grecque* (1926); C. del Grande, *Espressione musicale dei poeti greci* (1932); I. Düring, *Ptolemaios u. Porphyrios über die Musik* (1934); R. P. Winnington-Ingram, *Mode in Ancient Greek Music* (1936); K. Schlesinger, *The Greek Aulos* (1938); O. Gombosi, *Die Tonarten u. Stimmungen der antiken Musik* (1939); C. Sachs, *The History of Musical Instruments* (1940); *The Rise of Music in the Ancient World* (1943); N. B. Bodley, 'The auloi of Meroe', *AJArch.* 1946; M. I. Henderson, 'Ancient Greek Music', and J. E. Scott, 'Roman Music', in *The New Oxford History of Music* i (1957); J. Chailley, *L'Imbroglio des modes* (1960); H. Husmann, *Grundlagen der antiken u. orientalischen Musikkultur* (1961); M. Vogel, *Die Enharmonik der Griechen* (1963); W. D. Anderson, *Ethos and Education in Greek Music* (U.S.A. 1966); G. Wille, *Musica Romana* (Amsterdam, 1967); Dar.–Sag., s.v. 'Lyra', 'Tibia' (Reinach); *Grove's Dictionary of Music and Musicians*[3], s.v. 'Greek Music (ancient)' (Winnington-Ingram); *PW* (W. Vetter); *Musik in Geschichte u. Gegewart* (Vetter, Wegner, Wille). The following works are notably well illustrated: F. Behn, *Musikleben m Altertum u. frühen Mittelalter* (1954); M. Wegner, *Das Musikleben der Griechen* (1949); *Musikgeschichte in Bildern* ii. 4 ('Griechenland' 1963), by M. Wegner, ii. 5 ('Etrurien u. Rom.' 1964), by G. Fleischhauer. Reviews of modern literature: *Bursian* 193 (Abert), 246 (Fellerer); *Lustrum* 1958, 3 (Winnington-Ingram).

J. F. M. & R. P. W.-I.

## MUSIC IN WORSHIP. 

Both in Greece and Italy music, vocal and instrumental, formed an important part of worship at all periods. To begin with Homer, the embassy sent to Chryse in *Iliad* 1. 472–4 spend the whole day after their arrival singing a hymn (παιήων) to Apollo, who is pleased with it. This paean remained typical of his worship, and the quintuple rhythm characteristic of it was named after it. In like manner the dithyramb was appropriated to Dionysus (q.v.). Neither of these, however, was exclusively the property of Apollo or Dionysus; e.g. paeans were composed to Asclepius (see Powell, *Coll. Alex.* 133 ff.). The singing of some kind of hymn (q.v.) appears regularly to have accompanied any formal act of worship, and instrumental music (strings and wind) also is commonly mentioned: cf. SACRIFICE.

Much the same is true for Italy. Hymns are continually met with, some traditional, as those of the Salii (*see* MARS) and Arval Brothers (Henzen, *Acta Arualium*, cciv). Instrumental music was so regular and necessary an accompaniment of ritual (e.g. Cic. *Har. Resp.* 23, the proceedings are vitiated 'si . . . tibicen repente conticuit') that the *collegium tibicinum et fidicinum qui sacris publicis praesto sunt* formed an ancient and important guild with a holiday of its own, cf. MINERVA. One reason for this was doubtless to drown any slight noises which might be of ill omen.

Very little is known of the style of this music, but it is fairly certain that there was no prohibition of the introduction of new forms.

H. J. R.

## MUSONIUS RUFUS, 

GAIUS, of Volsinii, Stoic, seems to have been born before A.D. 30 and to have died before 101/2. About A.D. 60 Rubellius Plautus was banished by Nero to Asia Minor, and Musonius followed him. After Rubellius' death he returned to Rome, but in 65–6, on the discovery of the Pisonian conspiracy, he was banished to Gyaros. He returned to Rome, probably under Galba. He was again banished by Vespasian, but returned again in the reign of Titus. We do not know of his having written books, but many of his apophthegms and discourses have been preserved. Among his pupils were many philosophers (notably Epictetus) and many leading Roman citizens.

Ed. O. Hense (1905); one letter in R. Hercher, *Epistolog. Graec.* 401–4; M. Pohlenz, *Die Stoa*[2] (1955–9); M. P. Charlesworth, *Five Men* (1936), 33 ff.; C. E. Lutz, *YClS* 1947, 3 ff.

W. D. R.

## MUTINA, 

a prosperous wool-trading town in Cisalpine Gaul (q.v.), controlling important roads and passes (Strabo 5. 218); modern *Modena*. Although Boian and possibly Etruscan settlements existed here from early times, Mutina is first mentioned in 218 B.C. when already a Roman stronghold (Polyb. 3. 40—inexact; Livy 21. 25). Rome apparently held Mutina uninterruptedly, making it a citizen colony in 183 which Ligurians sacked in 177; the Romans immediately restored it (Livy 39. 55; 41. 16). Mutina is famous for its successful resistance to Pompey in 78 and to Antony in 43 (the *bellum Mutinense*) (Plut. *Pomp.* 16; App. *BCiv.* 3. 49 f. etc.). Subsequently it is rarely mentioned.

E. T. S.

## MYCENAE 

(Μυκῆναι, Μυκήνη) situated in the north-east corner of the Argive plain in the foothills of Mounts Prophet Elias and Zara, dominated the roads to the north and Corinthia, to the west and central Peloponnesus and, through Tiryns and Argos, the sea-way, some 8 miles away, to the Cyclades and the east. Perseus was its reputed founder, but excavations proved that it was inhabited in the Early Helladic Period (*c.* 2500–1900 B.C.) by people akin to the pre-Hellenic population of the Cyclades and Crete. Then the site was already called by its non-Greek name. In the Middle Helladic period (1900–1660 B.C.) the site was taken over by Greek-speaking Indo-Europeans and towards the end of that period its importance and wealth increased immeasurably, as proved by Grave Circles A and B. The excavation of Circle B in 1952–4 proved that the shaft graves were sepulchres and not depositories as was suggested by Evans.

The Middle Helladic settlement occupied the entire hill. The palace of the rulers, who were buried in the shaft graves, perhaps stood on its summit. No remnants of that palace survive nor traces of an original citadel. Concurrently with the last shaft graves and cists were developed chamber tombs used for the people and tholos or beehive tombs used for royalty; these were produced to the end of the Mycenaean Age.

Phases A and B of the LH III period (*c.* 1400–1200 B.C.) form the great era of Mycenae. Then were constructed the Cyclopean walls and the palace on the summit. Of its first Cyclopean enceinte, built about 1340 B.C., there survive the north and parts of the west and south walls. Grave Circle A was outside the citadel. Well towards the middle of the thirteenth century the citadel was extended to the west and south, the Lion and Postern Gates were erected, Grave Circle A, now included in the citadel, was rearranged, and the palace on the summit was rebuilt, especially its Megaron, the guest room unit. In the last quarter of the thirteenth century the Great Ramp was built, the south-west staircase was added to the palace, and towards the end of the century the north-east extension was built with its subterranean cistern. Storage rooms in the thickness of the north wall were then constructed. Within the citadel were built other structures for officials and for public use such as the granary. Beyond the citadel in LH IIIB times were erected the 'Treasury of Atreus' and the 'Tomb of Clytemnestra', the most perfect examples of tholos tombs. The people lived in the area around the citadel in groups of houses surrounded by the graves of their relatives. The graves especially prove that Mycenae was well-populated and prosperous to the end of the LH IIIB period.

The second half of the thirteenth century B.C. witnessed a number of destructions. The latest, occurring about 1200 B.C., has been attributed to the Dorians or to the so-called Illyrian migration; perhaps they resulted from internal dissension and strife reflected in the stories of murders in the royal family of Mycenae. The destructions resulted in the weakening of the State, in the breaking down of law and order in the country which forced people to emigrate elsewhere, thus bringing about the depopulation of the area indicated by the graves of the LH IIIC period. That period (c. 1200–1120) is characterized by progressive decline culminating in the final catastrophe of Mycenae at the hands of the Dorians c. 1120 B.C.

In Geometric times few people built their homes on the hill and again in the Archaic period the summit was terraced and a temple was constructed from which sculptured fragments survived. A small contingent of Mycenaeans was at Thermopylae in 480 B.C. and its soldiers fought at Plataea in 479 B.C. Some time c. 468 B.C. Mycenae was destroyed by Argos, but in the third century B.C. its walls were repaired by the Argives, a temple was built on the citadel, while its slopes were covered with houses. A lower fortified city was developed and a theatre was built. The town gradually decayed and by the time of Pausanias seems to have been inhabited only by a few shepherds.

H. Schliemann, *Mycenae* (1878); Ch. Tsountas, Πρακτικά (1886); Άρχ. Έφ. 1887, 1888, 1891, 1896, 1897, 1902; Ch. Tsountas and J. I. Manatt, *Mycenaean Age* (1897); A. J. B. Wace, *BSA* xxiv, xxv, xlv, xlviii, xlix, l, li, lii (1919–57), *Chamber Tombs at Mycenae* (1933), *JHS* 1939, *Mycenae* 1949; G. Karo, *Schachtgräber v. Mykenai* (1930); G. E. Mylonas, *Ancient Mycenae* (1957), Άρχ. Έφ. 1958, 1962; *Mycenae and the Mycenaean Age* (1966); E. French, *BSA* 1961, 1963, 1964.
G. E. M.

## MYCENAEAN CIVILIZATION

**MYCENAEAN CIVILIZATION** developed in the mainland of Greece in the Late Bronze Age. It is subdivided into Periods I (c. 1580–1500 B.C.), II (c. 1500–1400), and III (c. 1400–1120), the last of which is considered to be the most characteristic. In essence it is a continuation of the Middle Helladic culture transformed by Minoan influences, which were very strong in Period I, reached their apogee in the first half of Period II, and then declined while native elements reasserted themselves; yet Minoan elements persist to the end.

Graves found at Mycenae, Prosymna, Laconia, West Messenia-Triphylia, etc., constitute the main source of information for Periods I and II. The shaft graves of Circles A and B of Mycenae, forming the transition from MH to Mycenaean, provide evidence of affluence, of advanced techniques in metal and precious stone work sometimes indistinguishable from Minoan. Bronze swords, gold ornaments decorated in repoussé and granulation, objects made of hammered sheets of metal, of gold wire drawn to form spiraliform patterns, miniature engravings on the bezels of gold rings or on gems, articles of rock crystal, including the duck bowl from Grave Omikron, are among the examples of the jeweller, the lapidary, and the metal worker. Especially should be noted swords with engravings on their blades and the inlaid daggers from Circle A with wild life and hunting scenes, the earliest examples of a technique that persists throughout the Age. Sculpture is represented by stelai from Grave Circles; the work is primitive, made probably in imitation of wood carving, but it marks a departure from Minoan practice. Vases of exceptional merit were produced; they exhibit good fabrics, true and pleasant forms, and a geometric and naturalistic plant decoration —spirals, ivy sprays, etc.—in a lustrous paint on a slipped surface. In Period II is developed the Palace style with an exuberant decoration painted on three-handled jars, and the Ephyrean goblets with a restrained decoration mostly of a single element.

Concurrently with the later shaft graves and cists family chamber tombs were made and used for the people and tholos or beehive tombs for royalty. The origin of these tombs is not established, but their development is well defined. Very few tholos tombs have been found even partially intact: the Vaphio and Routsi tombs of

Period II, and the Dendra tombs of IIIA. Chamber tombs with their contents intact are numerous, and they help to establish the burial customs of the people. Inhumation was used universally.

Period III is the era of Mycenaean civilization *par excellence*. Tholos and chamber tombs are the usual types. Of the former the most advanced are the Treasury of Atreus and the tomb of Clytemnestra in Mycenae and the Treasury of Minyas at Orchomenus; all three were erected after 1300 B.C. The construction of citadels and palaces is the most characteristic feature of the period. Mycenae, Tiryns, Gla provide the best-preserved citadels. Their fortification walls, built in Cyclopean style, range from 12 to 45 feet in thickness and perhaps stood to a height of 40 feet. A main and a postern gate gave access to the citadel, but sally ports and other smaller openings were usual. Better known is the Lion Gate of Mycenae, named after the relief placed over its lintel. It dates from c. 1250 B.C.

Palaces are known from Mycenae (cleared by Tsountas), Tiryns (cleared by Schliemann), and Pylos (cleared by Blegen). They exhibit an orderly plan with a megaron forming an important and often the principal constituent. The Megaron, a rectangular roofed structure with one of its short sides open, facing a court open to the sky, is a typical mainland structure with a long history going back to the Neolithic period. In the three examples mentioned it comprises a portico—Homer's *aithousa*, a vestibule—*prodomos*, and a main room—*domos*, with a circular low hearth in its centre. Four columns surrounding the hearth supported the roof, and the throne of the king, placed against the wall to the right of a person entering, added grandeur to the *domos*. Corridors and other compartments, including a bathroom and guest rooms, were arranged around the Megaron all decorated with gay frescoes, similar to those of the Minoan world from which the art was derived, but now are added hunting and war scenes. The artistic merit of furniture is indicated by the Pylos tablets and by fragments of ivories found by Wace, which evidently were applied as inlays. The construction is rubble masonry with timber casings covered with plaster, and the wooden columns were of Minoan type, with shafts tapering downwards. Architectural decoration, exemplified by the facades of the Treasury of Atreus, consists mainly of elongated rosettes, the Mycenaean triglyph, and spirals carved on coloured marble slabs. In general the post and lintel system was used, though the corbel vault was employed in the construction of the tholos tombs and the inverted V arch in the roofing of passages. Subterranean fountains and an elaborate system of roadways characterize the period.

The goldsmiths continued to produce small and larger articles used for adornment and the repoussé and granulation techniques were still in use. Gold beads impressed with a design—rosettes, shells, shields, etc.—were strung together to form necklaces or applied on garments and furnishings. Blue paste and faience were used in making beads and pendants, and glass paste enlivened sculptured motifs; perhaps this paste was Homer's *kyanos*. Ivory carving, already used in Periods I and II, became very popular. The raw material, imported from Syria, was made into pyxides with elaborate carvings, into small rectangular plaques bearing crested griffins and sphinxes carved with exquisite feeling and decorative sense, into mirror handles with figure compositions, into small figured forms—columns, eight-figured shields, small animals—even into female figurines. An outstanding example of ivory carving is the group of two women and a boy found by Wace. Light touches of colour, even gilding, may have enhanced the decorative effect of these ivories. Gems, in smaller numbers than before, continue to be produced, indicating that this art was not abandoned.

The metal workers produce large and small vessels of bronze and lead, swords and daggers, helmets and corselets; a good example of a bronze corselet was found recently in a tomb at Dendra.

The potter's industry now reached its maximum prosperity. Vases produced in IIIB present such uniformity and lack of local variations that the term 'Koine' is applied to their art. The pictorial style, with chariot representations, etc., from Rhodes and Cyprus forms the only exception. Usually the designs are stylized, often placed in a metopic arrangement, and seem to be unimaginative. Their draftsmanship, however, is good and the quality of the vases excellent. Among shapes the stirrup jar, the high stemmed kylix, the deep two-handled bowl, and the crater are popular. In Period III clay figurines covered with a painted decoration become very common. The female figurines fall into three main types: the crescent or $\Psi$ type, the ovoid or $\Phi$, and the kouro-trophos type. Their exact significance is not established to the satisfaction of all, but perhaps they stand for the divinity of blessing (type $\Psi$) and divine nurses (type $\Phi$ and the kourotrophoi). During Periods IIIA and B Mycenaean civilization finds its greatest expansion over the Mediterranean area and commercial activity reaches its apogee. Its products are found from southern Italy to Syria and Palestine and its trading stations from Taranto to Ras Shamra in Syria.

A script known as Linear B, developed from the Minoan Linear A, was used in IIIB. It is not certain whether this script was developed in the mainland or in Crete, whether it was widely used and understood or was the special preserve of a class of scribes and a few officials. We find it incised on clay tablets or painted on stirrup jars especially. Numerous tablets were found at Pylos and Cnossos; limited numbers come from Mycenae and Thebes. Inscribed vases are known from Orchomenus, Thebes, Eleusis, Mycenae, and Tiryns. The inscriptions on the tablets, thanks to the monumental achievement of Michael Ventris, can be partially read with assurance (see MINOAN SCRIPTS). The tablets are inventories, containing accounts of flocks and land, records of assessment, of distribution of materials for production, of commodities produced, and of deliveries. No tablets have been found thus far with literary, judicial, or historical texts. The surviving texts are brief, unimaginative, and dry, but they form a most important source of information for the religious, political, and social structure of the Age. The language of Linear B is Greek; consequently the Mycenaeans were Greek-speaking Indo-Europeans. The political regime at Pylos and Cnossos was an autocratic monarchy with a centralized, bureaucratic administrative system. The *wanax* exercised supreme authority. Next to him was the *lawagetas*, 'the Leader of the Host', who, like the *wanax*, was given a temenos, a slice of land, as a prerogative of his office. Below these we find a number of officials major and minor—*tereta, eqeta, korete, porokorete, qasireu, moroqa*, etc.—whose duties, prerogatives, and relative positions remain uncertain. Land was held by the *wanax*, by individuals, and by the *damos*, the community, and a well-established system of land tenure existed at Pylos. There was a special class of priests and priestesses; artisans were divided into well-defined classes, and slaves were numerous. Whether this political system prevailed at Mycenae, Athens, and Thebes cannot be determined as yet, but their Cyclopean walls and palaces may indicate their rulers' great authority.

Period IIIC, following a series of destructions and the breaking down of law that occurred *c*. 1200 B.C., is one of decline. An early effort at recovery in the Argolid proved short-lived and gradually decay set in which terminated with the destruction of the large citadels of Mycenae and Tiryns *c*. 1120 B.C. by the Dorians, who,

taking advantage of the disintegration of the States, delivered the *coup de grâce* to the Mycenaean world and civilization. The close-style is the best and the granary type the most common pottery produced in IIIC. In some areas of the mainland, i.e. the east coast of Attica, and in the islands of the Aegean prosperity continued, but gradually those areas, too, passed into the less brilliant proto-historic era.

Ch. Tsountas and J. I. Manatt, *Mycenaean Age* (1897); C. W. Blegen, *Korakou* (1921), *Zygouries* (1928), *Prosymna* (1937); G. Karo, *Schachtgräber v. Mykenai* (1930); A. J. B. Wace, *Chamber Tombs at Mycenae* (1933), *Mycenae* (1948); A. Furumark, *The Mycenaean Pottery* (1941), *Chronology of M. Pottery* (1941); G. E. Mylonas, *Ancient Mycenae* (1957), *Mycenae and the Mycenaean Age* (1966). E. L. Bennett, *The Pylos Tablets* (1955); M. Ventris and J. Chadwick, *Documents in Mycenaean Greek* (1956); J. Chadwick, *The Decipherment of Linear B* (1960); L. R. Palmer, *The Interpretation of Mycenaean Greek Texts* (1963); F. H. Stubbings, *CAH²*, fasc. 18; V. R. d'A. Desborough and N. G. L. Hammond *CAH²*, fasc. 13; Desborough, *The Last Mycenaeans and their Successors* (1964); Lord William Taylour, *The Mycenaeans* (1964). G. E. M.

**MYGDON** (Μυγδών). In *Iliad* 3. 184 ff. Priam relates that he went as an ally to a Phrygian army gathered under Mygdon and Otreus to fight the Amazons on the Sangarius. The Coroebus of Verg. *Aen.* 2. 407 was Mygdon's son, [Eur.] *Rhes.* 539. Mygdon is apparently the eponym of the Thracian or Phrygian Mygdones. H. J. R.

**MYIA**, said to have been daughter of Pythagoras, is mentioned in Clem. *Strom.* 4. 19. 121, 224 as a Pythagorean philosopher. A letter purporting to be by her is printed in R. Hercher, *Epistolog. Graec.* 608.

**MYLASA** (Τὰ Μύλασα), modern *Milâs*, the principal non-Greek city of Caria and capital of the country under the Hecatomnid rulers. It is probable (*BSA* 1961, 98 ff.) that the early seat of government was at Peçin Kale, some five miles south of Milâs, and that the city at Milâs was founded by Mausolus. This same ruler later transferred the capital to Halicarnassus. The Hellenistic and Roman city at Milâs continued to be of importance, but its site at the foot of a mountain was considered ill-chosen (Strabo 659). Mylasa had three notable temples of Zeus, namely Zeus Osogos, Zeus Carius, and Zeus Stratius, the last situated in the hills to the east at Labraynda and approached by a paved Sacred Way. After Magnesia in 189 B.C. Mylasa was excepted from the grant of Caria to the Rhodians, and in 167 joined in an uprising of the subjects of Rhodes on the mainland; this was suppressed, but immediately afterwards the Senate revoked its gift of territory to Rhodes (Polyb. 21. 46, 30. 5). In 40 B.C., when Q. Labienus, at the head of a Parthian army, overran Caria the Mylasans were persuaded by Hybreas, a distinguished citizen and rhetorician, to resist him; for this Labienus punished the city savagely, but it soon recovered, probably with help from Augustus (Dio Cass., Dittenberg. *SIG* 768). Strabo's assertion (659) that Physcus was the port of Mylasa is an error: the name of the port (modern *Küllük*) was Passala (Steph. Byz. s.v., cf. *Stadiasmus* 291). Among the ruins at Milâs the most notable are a handsome mausoleum of Roman date and an arched gateway bearing a relief of a double axe, a symbol which also occurs on the coins of the Hecatomnids and of Mylasa itself. G. E. B.

**MYLITTA**, a goddess, certainly akin to Ishtar and perhaps specially concerned with childbirth, worshipped at Babylon, and identified by Herodotus (1. 131) with Aphrodite. In honour of Mylitta every Babylonian woman, once in her lifetime, had to prostitute herself to a stranger: she sat in the temple area, and remained there till accosted by a stranger in the name of the goddess. The fee offered might be of any amount, and was dedicated to Mylitta (Hdt. 1. 199; cf. LXX, *Epist. Jerem.* 42–3 [*c.* 300 B.C.]). *See* PROSTITUTION, SACRED.

F. R. W.

**MYLLUS.** The *Suda* and Zenobius (5. 14) mention him as a writer of Old Comedy. But he may be merely one of the typical figures of farce = 'The Squinter': cf. Cratinus, fr. 89.

**MYOS HORMOS,** 'Mussel-Harbour', *Abu Scha'ar* on the Egyptian coast of the Red Sea, was founded by Ptolemy II (274 B.C.) and connected with Kenah on the Nile by a well-equipped desert-trade. Very important for oriental trade, it was later surpassed by Berenice.

Warmington, *Indian Commerce*, 6 ff.             E. H. W.

**MYRINA** (ἡ Μύρινα), one of the cities of the Aeolian League, situated on the coast north of Cyme at the mouth of the river Pythicus or Titnaeus (now *Koca Çay* or *Güzelhisar Çayı*); supposedly founded by Myrina, queen of the Amazons; of the Greek settlement nothing is recorded. In the Delian League Myrina was assessed at one talent, the highest figure in Aeolis after Cyme. Destroyed by the great earthquake of A.D. 17, the city was rebuilt with Tiberius' help, apparently under the name of Sebastopolis (Pliny *HN* 5. 121). Otherwise Myrina is chiefly remarkable for her possession in imperial times of the ancient temple and oracle of Apollo at Gryneum (temple of white marble in a beautiful grove; Strabo 622, Paus. 1. 21. 7) and for the hundreds of terracotta figurines from the tombs excavated by the French in 1880–2. These tombs are no longer to be seen, and the ruins in general are scanty.

E. Pottier–A. J. Reinach, *La Nécropole de Myrina* (1887); G. E. Bean, *Aegean Turkey* (1966), 106 ff.             G. E. B.

**MYRON,** Greek sculptor, fl. *c.* 480–445 B.C. Native of Eleutherae, on the boundary of Boeotia and Attica. Reputed pupil of Ageladas and rival of Pythagoras (Pliny 34. 57). He was the greatest representative of the period of experimentation in Greek sculpture, and is said to have been much interested in symmetry (Pliny 34. 58). A detailed description by Lucian in his *Eikones*, 4, has made possible the identification of Myron's Discobolus, 'Discus-thrower', in several marble copies of Roman date. The best preserved is a statue formerly in the Lancelotti Palace, now in the National Museum of the Terme at Rome. Its appearance on engraved gems testifies to its fame. Another major work by Myron was a group of Athena and Marsyas, described by Pliny (34. 57) and recognized in representations on Roman coins of Athens, on a red-figured oinochoe in Berlin, on a marble vase in Athens, and in several marble statues. The Marsyas is best represented in a marble statue in the Lateran Collection, the Athena in one in Frankfurt. The contrast between the quietly standing goddess and the agitated Marsyas is well brought out. Of the attributions made to Myron on grounds of style one of the most persuasive is perhaps that of an Anadumenus, 'a youth winding (a fillet) round his head', reconstructed by Amelung from various parts; likewise a standing Heracles in Boston and Oxford. His famous cow has been thought to be reproduced in a bronze statuette in the Cabinet des Médailles.

G. M. A. R.

**MYRONIDES,** Athenian general at least in 458/7 and 457/6 B.C., known by his leadership of 'the oldest and the youngest' (Thuc. 1. 105. 4) in the Megarid against a Corinthian army, and by his victory at Oenophyta over the Boeotians. He is probably not identical with the ambassador Myronides, sent with Cimon and Xanthippus to Sparta in 480, and one of the Athenian generals at

Plataea. Comic poets praised Myronides as a representative of the 'good old times'. Eupolis in his *Demoi* puts him on the stage; he probably died shortly before the performance of this comedy (412).

Ehrenberg, *PW*, s.v., Suppl. vii (superseding vol. xvi); J. M. Edmonds, *Mnemos.* 1939.             V. E.

**MYRSILUS** of Methymna (fl. *c.* 250 B.C.), author of a history of Lesbos (Λεσβικά) who was interested in early folk movements.

*FGrH* iii. 477.

**MYRTILUS,** Athenian comic poet and brother of Hermippus (q.v. 1), won a victory at the Lenaea *c.* 430 B.C. (*IG* ii². 2325. 125). We have two titles, Τιτανόπανες and Ἔρωτες.

*FCG* ii. 418 ff.; *CAF* i. 253–4; *FAC* i. 474 ff.             K. J. D.

**MYRTIS,** Boeotian poetess, said to have been the teacher of Corinna (*Suda*, s.v. Κόριννα) and of Pindar (id., s.v. Πίνδαρος). Corinna (fr. 15) blames her for competing with Pindar. No fragment of her work survives, but Plutarch (*Quaest. Graec.* 40) gives an abstract of her poem on the Boeotian hero Eunostus.

J. M. Edmonds, *Lyra Graeca* (1952), iii. 2–5; Page, *Poet. Mel. Gr.* 371.             C. M. B.

**MYSTERIES** were secret cults which generally include mystic ideas. Their characteristic is that certain initiations were needed for admission. It has been suggested that this is due to the fact that the old mysteries of Greece, at least for a part, go back to an emotional pre-Greek religion which survived in secret societies. In regard to certain mysteries, e.g. those of Eleusis and Phlya, it is also to be taken into consideration that they were family cults to which the head of the family admitted whom he pleased.

The gods with whom the old Greek mysteries are connected were Demeter and Dionysus, and the Eleusinian Mysteries are the most famous of all. In origin they were an agrarian cult, originating in the Mycenaean Age, akin to the Thesmophoria and celebrated in Boedromion (Sept./Oct.) on the occasion of the sowing. After the union of Eleusis with Athens, some time before 600 B.C., the Athenian State took charge of the mysteries. The *mystai* gathered at Athens where an announcement was made excluding murderers and those who spoke a foreign language. The *mystai* bathed in the sea, and the sacred things which previously had been brought to Athens were brought back to Eleusis in the great Iakchos procession (Iakchos may be a personification of the shouts that accompanied it, and was later confused with Dionysus; a Linear B tablet from Cnossos, however, suggests that he is a relic of the Minoan divine child). In the evening the mystery rites began in the mystery hall at Eleusis which was illuminated by many torches. In spite of many ingenious hypotheses the chief rites are unknown. We hear of λεγόμενα, δεικνύμενα, δρώμενα, (1) things recited, from which the Eumolpidae, 'those who sing beautifully', have their name; (2) things shown, from which the chief priest, the ἱεροφάντης (see HIEROPHANTES), has his name; (3) things performed, by the priests or the *mystai* or by both. There were three stages, μύησις, initiation in the Lesser Mysteries at Agra(e) on the Ilissus, τελετή, the preliminary, and ἐποπτεία, the highest rite, to which the *mystai* were admitted the year after; the name indicates that the *epoptai* 'saw' something. The Homeric hymn to Demeter, composed before Eleusis was united with Athens, gives some information concerning the preliminary rites, the fast, the sitting on a chair decked with a ram's skin, the drinking of the *kykeon*. The information concerning the highest rites which is found only in ecclesiastical authors, in particular what relates to sexual symbols by which the *mystes* became a son of the goddess, a matter of which modern scholars have made much, is to be regarded with caution; so is the statement that the highest mystery shown was a corn-ear.

The rape of Kore-Persephone by Pluto is the central subject of the hymn, and it has been suggested that in the mysteries this rape and the bringing back of Kore to Demeter were dramatically represented. There were two pairs of deities: the Mother and the Maid and Pluto and Persephone, who is identical with Kore. Triptolemus, the hero of agriculture, and Eubuleus (q.v.) were also given a certain role. The myth that during four months of the year Kore was absent, dwelling with Pluto, and then was reunited with her mother and dwelt eight months in the upper world is to be referred to the seed-corn which, from the harvest in June to the sowing in October, was stored in subterranean silos and was brought forth at the festival of the sowing: the Corn-maiden was reunited with the Corn-mother. She was also wife of Pluto, the god of the wealth, i.e. the corn store, and Lord of the Underworld. The hymn ends by promising, to those initiated, wealth and a happy life in the Underworld, of which other authors speak confidently: the *Frogs* of Aristophanes proves that this happiness consisted in the continued celebration of the mysteries in the Underworld. Moral notions came to be associated with the mysteries, and righteousness and gentleness were added to ritual purity. At the end of the sixth century B.C. the conception of agriculture as the foundation of a civilized and peaceful life arose; Triptolemus was its hero. Since the end of the fifth century B.C. individual edification came more to the front. The Eleusinian Mysteries had no fixed doctrine; they consisted in rites which might be interpreted variously, provoking various individual experiences and thus they were able to conform to the religious needs of every age. They were so impressive that to the end of paganism they were the most venerated part of Greek religion.

There were other mysteries of Demeter, those at Agrae near Athens (see above under 2), those at Phlya in Attica, which were old but remodelled according to the ideas of a later age, at Pheneus in Arcadia, and at Andania in Messenia which were revived (or instituted) after the liberation of Messenia. The orgia of Dionysus (*see* DIONYSUS) which were celebrated only by women were mysteries in a certain sense. So were the Orphic mysteries (*see* ORPHISM). Dionysiac religion lent itself readily to mystical ideas, but the Dionysiac mysteries mentioned in Greece, e.g. those of Lerna and the Herois at Delphi, seem to be late creations. In the Hellenistic age Dionysiac mysteries developed and flourished; Ptolemy IV regulated them by an edict, and the repression of the Bacchanalia (q.v.) by the Roman Senate is well known. Many Dionysiac mystic cults are recorded from the Roman age. The mysteries of the Phrygian god Sabazius, who was akin to Dionysus, are found at Athens at the time of Aristophanes and at that of Demosthenes, a sign of the growing propensity for foreign and mystic cults: another is the popularity of the mysteries of the Cabiri (q.v.) at Samothrace. The Cabiri were especially venerated as the protectors of seafarers, but we know very little of the cult; in the Cabirion near Thebes it seems to have been influenced by Orphic ideas. The propensity for mystic cults grew in the Hellenistic age and still more in Roman times and was satisfied by cults introduced from the Orient, those of the Great Mother and Attis, Isis and Osiris, Mithras. We cannot here discuss details (see the respective articles), but may note certain general features. These mysteries were in a certain measure bound up with syncretism; the supporters of paganism in its last days were often initiated into various mysteries. Religion was detached from the old ties, the family and the State, and

was individualized; man was able to choose his gods. The adherents of a certain cult (especially foreign) formed associations, sometimes headed by professional priests, an oriental feature. The religious precepts were more detailed and binding than before. There were sacred symbols and rites with magical efficacy, purifications, asceticism, baptisms, sacraments. The adherents were sometimes divided into two classes; sometimes there were several grades of these. The highest promise of the mysteries was a happy after-life. The rise of dualism which considered the corporeal world as evil stressed the need of salvation which was conferred by participation in the mysteries: they promised even the deification of man. The myth was a symbolic expression of the doctrine and the god was the prototype of man, suffering, dying, and rising to a new life. *See also* AFTER-LIFE.

The literature is copious. As regards Eleusis it is summarized and commented upon in the very critical study of G. E. Mylonas, *Eleusis and the Eleusinian Mysteries* (1961); see also Nilsson, *GGR* i². 677 ff.; D. Sabbatucci, *Saggio sul misticismo greco* (1965).
M. P. N.; J. H. C.

**MYTHOGRAPHERS.** Since mythology was much studied in antiquity, at least to the extent of collecting and systematizing the traditional stories, and commenting on them in the light of rather crude and shallow theories (as that the myths were philosophical allegories, or had arisen from misunderstandings of ambiguous phraseology, tendencies exemplified by Heraclitus and Palaephatus respectively, see below), we hear of a number of writers on the subject and the works of a few survive fairly complete. The movement may be said to start with the school of Hesiod (q.v.; *Theogony* and *Ehoiai*). It certainly may properly be taken to include sundry of the early logographi, such as the two or three writers called Pherecydes, Acusilaus of Argos, Hellanicus, and Herodorus (see Rose, *Handb. Gk. Lit.*⁴ (1951), 296 ff.), for although their aim was generally to write history, they used of necessity for the earlier periods the only material available, namely myths. Later, the voluminous writings of Callimachus (b. *c.* 310 B.C.) and other Alexandrian scholars included many treatises more or less purely mythological in content; foreign mythologies also were discussed by Berosus and Philon of Byblos (Rose, *op. cit.* 367).

The composition, however, of compendia of mythology is relatively late, although some semi-philosophical works, such as the absurd treatise of Euhemerus (q.v.) and the rationalizing essay of Palaephatus (Rose, 369), might be considered as types of annotated handbooks of the subject; they are related in their way to Heraclitus' little book on Homeric allegories and Cornutus' Stoic treatise on the inner meaning of myths (ibid. 355, 411). All the surviving works fall not earlier than the time of Augustus, and most are later. One, the *Bibliotheca* of the so-called Apollodorus, of whose personality nothing is known, is valuable for the good information possessed by the author and his not infrequent citations of his sources, direct or indirect. It consists of three books; the rest is lost, though something is preserved in an epitome surviving in two forms. This work was an attempt at a complete mythical history of Greece; the other surviving treatises specialize. Parthenius, the earliest (contemporary and friend of Cornelius Gallus), collects love-stories, primarily as poetic material for Gallus to work up. The Pseudo-Eratosthenes, epitomizing, it would seem, a treatise of the real one (b. *c.* 275 B.C.), is himself much later; his subject is catasterisms, i.e. the metamorphoses of terrestrial persons and objects into constellations. Antoninus Liberalis, whose name shows him not earlier than the second century A.D., collects metamorphoses, but not those into stars. The incompetent author of the *Parallels* which have come down under the name of Plutarch finds, or more commonly invents, Roman stories which are parallel to Greek ones. He is to be dated to the second century A.D.

Latin has not left us many such works, though not a few were written, e.g., by C. Julius Hyginus, Augustus' librarian (Rose, *Handb. Lat. Lit.*³ (1954), 446). The author known as Hyginus who wrote the *Fabulae* (more properly *Genealogiae*) whereof we have a late and bad series of extracts may have been contemporary with the Antonines (ibid.); his so-called *Poetica Astronomica*, if it is his, largely depends on the genuine Eratosthenes, probably not directly. The *Mitologiae* of Fulgentius (three books) may be of about the end of the fifth century; the three miscellaneous collections known as the Mythographi Vaticani (ed. Bode, 1834) are medieval, but contain, amid many blunders, some scraps of material not found elsewhere. H. J. R.

**MYTHOLOGY.** Although etymologically the word means no more than the telling of tales, it is used in modern languages to signify a systematic examination of the traditional narratives of any people, or all peoples, with the object of understanding how they came to be told and to what extent they were or are believed, also of solving various other problems connected with them, such as their connexion with religion, their origin (popular or literary), the relations, if any, to similar stories told elsewhere, and their chronology, relative or absolute. The examination of folk-tales (*Märchenforschung*) is really a branch of mythology, but has grown to such proportions, owing to the abundance of material, that it may be regarded as a separate discipline and will receive only brief mention here.

The most characteristic object of mythological study is the myth proper. This may be defined as a pre-scientific and imaginative attempt to explain some phenomenon, real or supposed, which excites the curiosity of the myth-maker, or perhaps more accurately as an effort to reach a feeling of satisfaction in place of uneasy bewilderment concerning such phenomena. It often appeals to the emotions rather than the reason and, indeed, in its most typical forms seems to date from an age when rational explanations were not generally called for. For example, it was commonly said (Hdt. 7. 129. 5) that the gorge of the Peneus had been created by Poseidon (q.v.) cleaving the mountain-chain which formerly closed in Thessaly on that side. To Herodotus himself this was merely a picturesque way of saying that the gorge had been formed by an earthquake, a solution very like the 'cataclysmic' school of geological theory once popular in modern Europe. But it seems far more probable that the originator of the story had a vivid mental picture of the gorge, which to his eye suggested a great cut, being hewn out by a gigantic and powerful being, and that, finding the picture satisfactory to his imagination, he was not troubled with any question as to its probability. This is not to say that no myth contains intellectual features, for many of them do; to take a crude example, the originator of the quaint tale of the deceiving of Zeus by Prometheus (Hes. *Theog.* 535 ff.) must have asked himself why those parts of a victim which were burned on the altars of the celestial gods were the least valuable. Late myths often show signs of elaborate speculation, e.g., the identification of Virbius (*see* DIANA) with Hippolytus (q.v. 1) in Verg. *Aen.* 7. 761 ff. clearly arises from a sophisticated and learned explanation of the facts that Diana was worshipped at Aricia along with a male being and that horses were not allowed in her grove. The only male associated with and subordinate to Artemis, with whom Diana had long been identified, was Hippolytus; now he had been brought to life by Asclepius

after being killed by his own team; he must therefore be Diana's attendant and the taboo on horses must arise from his, and her, reluctance to have anything more to do with such dangerous creatures.

Myths therefore deal principally with the doings of gods, their ritual and their relationships to one another, or else with natural phenomena in some way striking, and they are characteristically aetiological, having for their aim to furnish an explanation of something. If the main characters of the story are human, or supposedly so, and the tale concerns their doings in battles or other adventures, it is usual to speak, not of myth but of saga or legend. Here the mental process giving rise to the story seems to be different. A real event of some kind, such as a raid or a great and dangerous hunt, impresses those who take part in it and also their contemporaries; it continues to be told from generation to generation, often getting into the hands of a professional maker (finally a professional writer) of such narratives, and so acquiring all manner of additions, modifications, and re-handlings intended to make it a better story. Nevertheless, it regularly has behind it the original fact, which may obtrude itself in curious ways (e.g. in the ballad of Chevy Chase, which springs from the historical Battle of Otterbourne, the Scots are divided into three parts and attack from higher ground, though the rest of the fighting has been changed almost past recognition). Even if the story is pure fiction, it will be modelled upon real semi-historical narratives, and may then be conveniently called pseudo-saga.

The *Märchen* (*see* FOLK-TALES; neither that nor 'fairy-tale' is a wholly satisfactory equivalent) seems always to have been told for pure amusement, with no basis in speculation or fact.

Finally, it must be realized that any two, or all three, of the above forms may be almost inextricably blended in any given story; thus the tale of the Argonauts (q.v.) has manifest elements of *Märchen*, and the adventures of Heracles (q.v.) have also laid myths under contribution.

In order to reach such conclusions as the above, it is necessary to have a sufficient body of material, carefully examined to show its age and origin; else the investigator will perpetually be misled into taking a late or foreign story for the genuine product of the people he is studying, e.g. such a narrative as that in Ovid, *Fasti* 2. 305 ff., either for a genuine part of the Greek tradition concerning Heracles or a native Italian story throwing light on the nature of Faunus, instead of what it is, a typical Alexandrian humorous aetiology, perhaps Ovid's own invention. We may therefore look upon K. O. Müller (1797–1840) as in some sense the father of modern mythology, owing to his consistent emphasis on the historical origins of Greek traditions, i.e. the time and place, so far as they could be discovered, when the earliest form of each tale appeared. With him may be bracketed a slightly earlier investigator, C. A. Lobeck (1781–1860).

Hardly less important for the researcher in any given branch of mythology, e.g. that of Greece, is a knowledge of similar stories told elsewhere, especially among peoples likely to have influenced those he is studying. Here a great service was performed by Max Müller, whose use of Sanskrit material led investigators in the late nineteenth century to examine Greek (and other) material against a comparative background, thus getting a perspective such as earlier researchers had not had. It needed only to widen the scope of comparison, and this was done chiefly by Andrew Lang.

Some account of the progress of the subject is given in any good modern manual of classical mythology, e.g. Nilsson, *GGR* i². 13 ff. For some methodological considerations see Rose, *Modern Methods in Classical Mythology* (1930). For light thrown on Greek myths by art see especially C. Robert, *Bild und Lied* (1881). H. J. R.

**MYTILENE** (or **MITYLENE**; the former was the official form), the chief city of Lesbos (q.v.), situated in the south-east of the island, with a fine double harbour, and facing the Anatolian mainland. The population was predominantly Aeolian—both Sappho and Alcaeus resided in Mytilene. In the sixth century B.C. overseas expansion led directly to war with Athens, indirectly to *stasis*, only relieved by the mediation of Pittacus. Under Persian control Mytilene participated in the forlorn hope of the Ionian Revolt. Its two secessions from the Delian Confederacy (428 and 412) resulted in the loss of its fleet, its fortifications, and much of its land, and brought it to the verge of destruction. During most of the fourth century, however, it was a faithful ally of Athens. In 333 it fell to Memnon, but was soon retaken by the Macedonian fleet. After Alexander's death Mytilene passed successively under Antigonus', Lysimachus', and the Ptolemies' rule. Through tactful diplomacy it kept on good terms with Rome, becoming a favourite holiday resort. Its revolt against excessive taxation following the Mithridatic War led to the storming of the city by Minucius Thermus (80), but Pompey restored its freedom, and this privilege, though suspended by Vespasian, was confirmed by Hadrian.

R. Koldewey, *Die ant. Baureste der Insel Lesbos* (1890).

D. E. W. W.

# N

**NABATAEANS,** a people of north-Arabian caravan-traders, who achieved great wealth by conveying south-Arabian goods to the Mediterranean. In 312 B.C. Antigonus, Alexander's successor, vainly tried to conquer their capital, Petra (q.v.). Their kings also remained independent of the Seleucids. In 169 B.C. Aretas I held Moabitis; in *c.* 96 B.C., Aretas III (q.v.) occupied Damascus, but withdrew before Tigranes in 70; in 66 he besieged Jerusalem, until Scaurus compelled him to leave Judaea. The Nabataeans thenceforward became allies and vassals of Rome under their kings: Obodas II (probably *c.* 62–*c.* 47), Malchus I (q.v. 2: *c.* 47–30), Obodas III (30–9), Aretas IV, q.v. (9 B.C.–A.D. 39), Malchus II (*c.* 40–71), Rabilus (71–106). About 30 B.C., however, they lost their northern possessions around the Hauran. Trajan in A.D. 106 transformed their kingdom into the Roman province of Arabia. Their territory still extended, by that time, over Sinai, the port of Aela, and the coast of the Red Sea to Leuce Come. At this port and at Hejra, the caravanners took over Arabian incense and myrrh, Persian pearls, Indian spices, perfume, and cotton, and Chinese silk. The Nabataeans used Aramaic for their inscriptions. Their main deities were the vegetation-god Dusares, and Allat, a warrior goddess of the morning star. The ruins of Petra are among the most spectacular in the Near East.

A. Kammerer, *Pétra et la Nabatène* (1929–30); R. E. Brünnow and A. von Domaszewski, *Die Provincia Arabia* (1904–9); J. Starcky, in *Biblical Archaeologist* xviii, no. 4 (1955), and *Suppl. au dict. de la Bible* vii (1964), cols. 886 ff.; N. Glueck, *Deities and Dolphins, the story of the Nabataeans* (1966); J. I. Miller, *The Spice Trade of the Roman Empire* (1969), see index.

H. S.

**NABIS,** son of Demaratus, probably descended from the Spartan king of the latter name (q.v.), followed Machanidas in 207 B.C. as guardian of the young Spartan king, Pelops, and on Pelops' death (of which he was accused) seized the crown. Forming a mercenary guard, he drastically restored the revolutionary programme of Cleomenes (q.v. 2) in alliance with the Cretan pirates. In 204–3 he raided Megalopolis, but was in 201 repelled from Messene and in 200 defeated by Philopoemen. In the Second Macedonian War he gained Argos, betrayed to him by Philip V, but went over to Flamininus, only to find himself in 195 charged with tyranny and forced to give up Argos and the Laconian ports. In 193, attempting to regain the ports, he was subdued by Philopoemen and Flamininus. He was assassinated in 192 in an Aetolian *coup d'état* in Sparta. A revolutionary type, his career and policy have suffered unduly in the Achaean tradition of Polybius.

Polyb. 13. 6–8; 16. 13; 16–17; Livy 29. 12; 31–5; Plut. *Flam.*; Phil. J. Mundt, *Nabis, König von Sparta* (1903); De Sanctis, *Stor.* *Rom.* iii. 2, 436; iv. 1. 42, 72, 104, 132; A. Aymard, *Les Premiers rapports de Rome et de la Confédération achaïenne* (1938); F. W. Walbank, *Philip of Macedon* (1940). Coin portrait: C. M. Kraay, *Greek Coins* (1966), Pl. 161, n. 522.

A. H. McD.

**NAEVIUS,** GNAEUS, of Italic stock from the neighbourhood of Capua (Gell. 1. 24), in close contact with Greek cities and Roman colonies. He served in the First Punic War (264–241 B.C.—he himself said so, Gell. 17. 21. 45). In 235 B.C. he was active on the Roman stage. He was outspoken and offended the Metelli (one insult—*fato Metelli Romae fiunt consules*, implying that the Metelli had no ability for high office and showing by its iambic metre that it was delivered from the stage—was long remembered, cf. Cic. *in Verr.* 1. 29). About 204 B.C. (as can be inferred from Cic. *Brut.* 60), he was imprisoned (cf. Pauli Festus s.v. *barbari* with Plaut. *Mil. Glor.* 210 ff.), and later perhaps went into exile, for, under the year 201 B.C., Jerome says that he died at Utica. Later unfounded gossip connected him with the great Scipio Africanus (cf. Gell. 7. 8. 6), but it is the quarrel with the Metelli which is well attested (Caesius Bassus ap. *Gramm. Lat.* vi. 266 knew a public reply by them in Saturnians—*malum dabunt Metelli Naevio poetae*). See LIBEL AND SLANDER in Rome, § 3.

*Tragedies*: very scanty fragments and some six titles (two coincide with titles of Livius Andronicus—perhaps Naevius readapted the same originals). One important fragment from the *Danae* (5 R.) *eam nunc esse inventam probris compotem scis* is a bacchiac tetrameter but, since it reports Danae's disgrace, it must represent a messenger-speech in trimeters—so Naevius, like Livius (q.v. 1), must have produced *cantica* of his own from trimeter speeches. A decisively new step taken by Naevius was the production of original tragedies from Roman material—*fabulae pretextae*. Three examples are known, the *Romulus*, the *Clastidium* (the winning of the *spolia opima* by M. Claudius Marcellus in single combat against the Gaul Virdomarus in 222 B.C.), and the *Lupus* (the story of the twins).

*Comedies*: some twenty-eight titles are known but the fragments are very meagre. One, from the *Tarentilla* (75 ff. R.), describing a girl flirting in a circle of young men, gives some idea of his vigour and liveliness. Otherwise the fragments simply make clear a considerable linguistic debt on the part of Plautus to Naevius.

*Bellum Poenicum*: this was an epic (the division into seven books was the work, a century later, of C. Octavius Lampadio), written in old age (cf. Cic. *de senect.* 50), and regarded as his most important work by later scholars (the epitaph in Gell. 1. 24 refers only to it). The arrangement of the fragments is a matter of controversy, but it seems possible that Naevius began with his account of the First Punic War and that the mythological sections, indicated by the fragments, were introduced in a series of digressions throughout the work. Certainly book iii contained a large part of the 'archaeology'; but scepticism is necessary on details. The most interesting mythological fragments indicate that, to some extent, Naevius was Virgil's predecessor in his account of the wanderings from Troy and that he even brought the Trojans to Carthage to meet Dido (fr. 23 Morel). It is even harder to judge the style of the *Bellum Poenicum* from its fragments than that of Livius Andronicus' *Odyssia*: the metre is the same Saturnian, there is a similar use of elevated archaisms, alliteration emphasizes the solemnity of the style which cannot, however, avoid sometimes giving the impression of bald prosiness, despite the invention of compound adjectives like *arquitenens* and the introduction of a traditional epic theme like the description of a shield (the probable explanation of fr. 19 Morel). Yet, in spite of shortcomings, this was an entirely original venture in Latin, and a long step forward from Livius Andronicus' 'translation' of Homer.

E. H. Warmington, *Remains of Old Latin* ii (1936), 46 ff. (with transl.). E. V. Marmorale, *Naevius poeta²* (1950). O. Ribbeck, *TRF³*, *CRF³*; A. Klotz, *Scaen. Rom. Frag.* (1953), 30 ff. (tragedies). *Frag. Poet. Lat.* (1927), ed. Morel, 17 ff. (*Bell. Poen.*). E. Fraenkel, *PW*, Suppl. 6, 622 ff. L. Strzelecki, *De Naeviano Bell. Pun. carm. quaest. sel.* (1935); S. Mariotti, *Il Bellum Poenicum e l'arte di Nevio* (1955); M. Barchiesi, *Nevio epico* (1962).          G. W. W.

**NAISSUS** (modern *Niš*) in Moesia (after Diocletian in Dardania), first visited by Roman troops in 75/72 B.C., was probably the earliest permanent military camp in Moesia. Though of great strategic importance, little is known of its history: it became a *municipium* under M. Aurelius or later. Here Claudius II decisively defeated the Goths in A.D. 269. Frequently visited by Roman Emperors, especially by Constantine the Great, who was born at Naissus, it was destroyed by the Huns in 441, but was partially restored. Under Justinian Naissus flourished anew, but was seriously threatened by the Slavs. It was destroyed or at least sacked by the Avars in 596, but continued to exist as a Slav town.

F. A. W. S.

**NAMATIANUS**, RUTILIUS CLAUDIUS, the author of the *De Reditu Suo*, an elaborate poetical itinerary, was of Gallo-Roman extraction, probably from Toulouse. An adherent of the old paganism, he yet held under Honorius the offices of *magister officiorum* (A.D. 412) and *praefectus urbi* (414). He had been well trained in the schools of grammar and rhetoric and had a sound knowledge of Greek. Biographical and self-revealing, his poem comes to us in two books, the first of which begins abruptly, while the second is a fragment (68 lines). In Sept. 416 or Oct. 417 (but see Lana in bibliog.) he left Rome to look after his estates in Gaul, which, like Italy, had suffered from barbarian inroads. In two months, by the safer sea route, he reached Luna and here the poem breaks off. He probably reached Gaul, as the poem could not have been composed in its present form during the journey. Besides presenting in rhetorical fashion descriptions of the coastal scenery of Etruria, the poem mirrors both contemporary events and the author's outlook—as well as the minds of the pagan nobility, with whom he shared the belief in Dea Roma and Rome's glorious mission which he celebrates in a long rhetorical eulogy of the *regina pulcherrima mundi* based, perhaps, on a speech by Aelius Aristides on the same theme. He resented the prevailing opposition to paganism. Hence his invectives against Judaism, monasticism, and Stilicho, the barbarian general (then dead), who had burned the Sibylline books; for to Namatianus and his class anti-

paganism and the barbarians were the forces that were undermining ancient institutions and disintegrating the Empire. His lucid, though rhetorical, Latinity and his accomplished elegiacs show that he had studied the best models in Latin literature.

EDITIONS. Ch. H. Keene (1907; English verse translation; commentary); G. Heidrich (1912); V. Ussani (1921); R. Helm (1933 commentary); J. Vessereau and F. Préchac (1933; Fr. transl.); Engl. transl. in Duff, *Minor Lat. Poets*; P. van de Woestijne, Antwerp 1936 (critical edition, with account of MSS. and full *index verborum*) E. Castorina (1967; Ital. transl. and commentary). See R. Pichon *Les Derniers Écrivains profanes* (1906), 243 ff.; E. S. Duckett, *Latin Writers of the Fifth Century* (U.S.A. 1930), 35 ff.; O. Schissel-Fleschenberg, *Claud. Rut. Namatianus gegen Stilicho* (1920). C. Pascal, *Graecia Capta* (Florence, 1905), 163 ff. P. de Labriolle, *Rev. Ét. Lat.* 1928, 30 ff.; J. Carcopino, ibid. 180 ff.; I. Lana, *Rut. Namaz* *iano* (1961), who dates the journey to 415, and Alan Cameron, *JRS* 1967, 31 ff., who dates it to Oct. 417.          F. J. E. R.

**NAMES, PERSONAL. I. GREEK.** Greek personal names exemplify the normal Indo-European pattern. One name was the rule both for men and women, and most names were compounded of two elements and honorific in meaning (Ἀριστο-κράτης, Κλεο-βούλη, cf. Vinda-farna, Vladi-mir, Sieg-fried, Bron-wen). Simple names included shortened forms of compound names (Νικίας) and names indicating personal characteristics (Σίμων), associated circumstances (Δίδυμος), and so on. Many names incorporated the name of a deity (see next article). There was a wide variety of possible terminations. The choice of names was immense and was not restricted by law or rigid custom, though there were tendencies such as that of giving a boy the name of his father's father. In Homer patronymics (Ἀτρείδης, etc.: forms like Ἀτρείων and the Aeolic Τελαμώνιος are less frequent) occur freely with and instead of single personal names, but in classical times they either denote a *genos* (q.v.) or have become personal names without patronymic force; and fathers' names are added, when necessary, in the genitive; this and other determinatives indicating *genos*, deme, or city, though required in particular contexts, were never used in address. Nicknames (Λακκόπλουτος) were not transmitted to descendants. Hellenistic rulers often had both nicknames (Αὐλητής) and honorific (including divine) surnames (Φιλοπάτωρ, Σελήνη). Slaves sometimes had names like those of free persons, but were more commonly given names indicative of origin (Θετταλή), appearance (Ξανθίας), qualities ('Ονήσιμος), etc.

II. ITALIAN. The Romans and other peoples of Italy, including the Etruscans, shared a system of personal nomenclature which differed sharply from the Indo-European pattern in giving every man and (in principle at least) every woman two or more names, and those generally simple and seldom honorific. This system was established before our records begin; and how it grew up, and what traces, if any, of the Indo-European pattern can be discerned in it, are difficult questions. The two basic names were the *praenomen* or personal name and the *nomen* or name of the *gens* (q.v.). Most Roman and many other Italian men had one, sometimes more than one, additional name (*cognomen*). These 'tria nomina' were characteristic of Roman citizens (Juv. 5. 127, Plut. *Mar.* 1).

2. If any of these three types perpetuates Indo-European practice it must be the *praenomen*, and there are perhaps indications that originally it stood alone. Moreover, some *praenomina* contain honorific or divine elements (Serv-ius, Mar-cus). Others indicated, or had once indicated, physical peculiarities (Gnaeus from *naeuus*) or circumstances of birth (Spurius, Quintus). The choice of personal names must originally have been large, but the constant addition of the clan-name and perhaps other factors began early to reduce the number, so that rather less than a hundred male *praenomina* (including Etruscan) are known altogether, and the Roman

upper class used only fifteen or so, with some *gentes* and families restricting themselves to a mere handful. *Praenomina* in common use were regularly written in abbreviated form (L., Q., etc.) except when they occurred alone. Among women, the addition of the clan-name led eventually to a tendency to discard their *praenomina* (of which a fair number are known, including some corresponding to the male ones, as Gaia, Quinta); this tendency was least marked among the Etruscans, but in the Roman upper class, as the literature shows, it amounted to almost complete abandonment.

3. The *nomen*, which as the simple term indicates was presently felt to be the most important name, was generally formed by adding an adjectival suffix (usually -ius, with or without a short connecting element such as -e-, -id-, -il-, -on-; -a, -as, -anus, and -enus are characteristic of the north) to the stem of an existing name. Many are thus formed from *praenomina*: these probably arose as patronymics, Marcius, for example, standing for Marci (filius); the Aeolic patronymics in -ιος (see above) suggest that this development was of great antiquity. Other *nomina* were formed from *cognomina* (Plancius), or from place-names (Norbanus). A very large number of *nomina* are known. One's *nomen* was necessarily that of one's legal father; women, at least in historical times, did not assume their husband's *nomen*.

4. *Cognomina* were primarily extra personal names; most show this by their meanings. They denote physical peculiarities (Naso), mental qualities (Cato), occupations (Pictor), offices (Censorinus), objects associated with the person (Scipio), origin (Camerinus), or adoption (see below). Some are diminutives (Marcellus), some foreign (Philippus). Often, especially in large *gentes*, they were handed down and so came to indicate divisions and even subdivisions of *gentes* (e.g. the Cornelii Scipiones Nasicae). But several plebeian *gentes*, including some distinguished ones (e.g. the Antonii) were never so divided, and personal *cognomina*—distinguished as *agnomina* by the late grammarians—continued to be coined all the time. *Cognomina* were apparently not invented for women in republican times; but they sometimes took the family *cognomen* (Metella).

5. In informal contexts Roman men were addressed or referred to by one name (*praenomen* in the family, *nomen* or *cognomen* among friends); formality required *praenomen* with *nomen* (as when a senator was asked for his *sententia*) or with *cognomen*; the official nomenclature in its fullest form included determinatives indicating descent and tribe (*see* TRIBUS), e.g. M(arcus) Tullius M(arci) f(ilius) M(arci) n(epos) Cor(nelia tribu) Cicero. Women also could add their father's *praenomen* in this way.

6. An adopted son took his adoptive father's full names, but might add a *cognomen* formed by suffixing -anus or -inus to the stem of his original *nomen* (Scipio Aemilianus), or, more rarely, *cognomen* (Lentulus Marcellinus); or (unattested before the first century B.C.) he might retain his original *cognomen* unaltered (Varro Lucullus).

7. Slaves were usually called by their own names, or were given names indicative of origin, etc., as in Greece: the ancient forms Marcipor (Marci puer), etc., fell into disuse as households became large, and in inscriptions of the late Republic servile nomenclature is usually of the form Aphrodisius Ploti G(ai) s(eruus). Freedmen and enfranchised foreigners took their patron's *praenomen* and *nomen*, adding their original name as a *cognomen* (M. Tullius Tiro).

8. The above system underwent various modifications from the late Republic onwards. These included, in aristocratic circles and the imperial family, the revival of old *praenomina* (Faustus Sulla) and use of *cognomina* as

*praenomina* (Germanicus), with the assumption of the *praenomen* Imperator (q.v.) by the Princeps himself; and, generally, a tendency to refer to persons by *nomen* and *cognomen*, sometimes in the reverse order; the inordinate multiplication of names; the use of *signa* or alternative names; and, eventually, the abandonment of the traditional system and reversion to single names.

C. Morel, Dar.–Sag. iv. 1. 88 ff.; *PW*, s.v. Namenwesen (E. Fraenkel), 1611 ff.; F. Solmsen, *Indo-Germanische Eigennamen* (1922). Greek: W. Pape and G. E. Benseler, *Wörterbuch der gr. Eigennamen* (1863–70); A. Fick and F. Bechtel, *Die gr. Personennamen²* (1894); F. Bechtel, *Die historischen Personennamen des Griechischen* (1917); O. Landau, *Mykenisch-Griechische Personennamen* (1958). Italian: E. Forcellini and V. De-Vit, *Totius Latinitatis Onomasticon* (1859–87); Mommsen, *Röm. Forsch.* i. 1 ff.; *Röm. Staatsr.* iii. 200 ff.; J. Marquardt, *Privatleben* 7 ff.; G. D. Chase, *Harv. Stud.* 1897, 103 ff.; W. Schulze, *Zur Gesch. lat. Eigennamen* (1904); K. Meister, *Altitalische und röm. Eigennamen* (1916); B. Doer, *Die röm. Namengebung* (1937); E. Pulgram, *Harv. Stud.* 1948, 163 ff.; A. Pariente, *Emerita* 1949, 247 ff.; R. Syme, *Hist.* 1958, 172 ff.; H. Petersen, *TAPA* 1962, 347 ff.; I. Kajanto, *Latin Cognomina* (1965).

T. J. C.

**NAMES, THEOPHORIC PERSONAL** (GREEK). In all times and places, probably, a majority of Greeks bore names derived from vocabulary words. Distinct from these, personal names derived from names of deities, though a minority, make up the largest unified class of personal names. Usually conscious of the meanings of names, the Greeks discriminated among theophorics. Not only did they exclude deities of ill-omen, such as Plouton, but also deities of insufficient dignity, such as Kourotrophos—although in Athens she received more sacrifices than any other deity. Theophoric names were of two principal kinds, adjectival such as Διονύσιος, verbal such as Ἀπολλόδωρος or Διογένης. Here too there was discrimination: it was all right to be Poseidon-like (Ποσειδώνιος), but no one was *Ποσειδογένης, because his mythological sons were an uncouth lot. Again, it was proper, and common, to be Δημήτριος, but never *Δημητριόδωρος. A boy could be named after a goddess, even Ἀρτεμίδωρος, or a girl after a god.

So many Athenians are known to us by name that the statistics are substantial. Down to 403/2 B.C., only 6·5 per cent had theophoric names; from 403/2 to 30/29 B.C., out of 16,000 names, 15·6 per cent are theophoric; and under the Roman Empire, down to A.D. c. 800, as many as 30·0 per cent are theophoric. These figures doubtless are a reflection of conservatism yielding only slowly. Of deities originally outsiders but admitted to Athens, Asklepios, in 420 B.C., is the chief; as the principal god of cures, his cult soon became strong and perpetual. Yet only six Athenians are known to have been named for him in the fourth century B.C. (none before), again six only in the third century, then fifty-five in the second and first centuries to 30/29 B.C., but 202 under the Empire. The first generation of great change was that c. 150 B.C., when tradition weakened, foreign cults became familiar in Delos, and the ever-working tendency to find new names led to more exotic choices. But even so, no deity of foreign origin had as many persons named for him then as did Asklepios. Sarapis and Isis were the major new Hellenistic cult, yet the names are very modest in number until under the Empire Isis has 301 (Sarapis 48).

Still as judged by personal names, no other cult menaced the Olympians, of whom three led the others. Apollo, with 11 before 403/2, then 258 down to 30/29 B.C., and thereafter 334, had perhaps normal figures. Zeus began with 55 down to 403/2, then 546 in the period to 30/29, but a reduction to 258 under the Empire. What Zeus lost Dionysos gained: he had 13 before 403/2, then 286 in the centuries till 30/29, but 514 under the Empire. It is notable that Aphrodite, with none before 403/2 and only 19 before 30/29, reached 383 under the Empire, of which 108 were Ἐπαφρόδιτος (= felix) *et sim.*

The same conservative forces brought it about that many a Christian bore a pagan theophoric name. Ἰσίδωρος was not alone: the list of pagan theophoric names borne by Christians is a long one, and they continued to be common among Christians at least through the fourth century.

History of the study: E. Sittig, *De graecorum nominibus theophoris* (Diss. Philol. Halenses, vol. xx, pars i, 1911), 1 ff. Sittig takes up the subject deity by deity; table at end. Names in -γεν- and -δωρ-: W. Froehner, *ARW* 1912, 380 ff. Olympian and foreign deities in Athens: S. Dow, *Harv. Theol. Rev.* 1937, 216 ff., 228 f.    S. D.

**NARBO,** modern *Narbonne.* The name, which originally denoted the hill-fort of Montlaurès, appears in Hecataeus (*c.* 500 B.C., *FGrH* 54). It became the centre of a Celto-Iberian kingdom (coins NERONC) which was absorbed by the Volcae. In 118 the *colonia Narbo Martius* was founded in the plain, and Montlaurès was dismantled *c.* 71. Caesar's tenth legion was settled in the new town, which became the capital of Narbonensis, the seat of the imperial cult and an important trading-centre. Enlarged by Claudius, its full title was *Colonia Iulia paterna Claudia Narbo Martius decumanorum.* Damaged by fire in the second century, it declined in prosperity, and apparently lost its position as capital to Nemausus. In 462 it fell finally to the Visigoths.

C. H. Benedict, *A History of Narbo* (U.S.A. 1941); P. Héléna, *Les Origines de Narbonne* (1937); G. F. Hill, *Coins of Narbonensis* (1930); *CIL* xii. 521; Grenier, *Manuel* ii. 483 ff.    C. E. S.

**NARCE,** a Faliscan town, 3 miles south of Falerii, in the valley of the Treia, a tributary of the Tiber. Remains of walls and fortifications are visible, but archaeological exploration has in the main been confined to the numerous cemeteries. The earliest material comes from Iron Age *pozzo*-tombs, the latest from third-century B.C. chamber tombs; it is all in the same general tradition as that from the other sites in the area. *See* FALISCANS.

*Mon. Ant.* iv (1894), *passim*; E. H. Dohan, *Italic Tomb-Groups in the University Museum* (Philadelphia, 1942); M. W. Frederiksen and J. B. Ward-Perkins, *PBSR* 1957, 67 ff.    D. W. R. R.

**NARCISSUS** (1), in mythology, a beautiful youth, son of Cephisus (the Boeotian river) and Liriope, a nymph. He loved no one till he saw his own reflection in water and fell in love with that; finally he pined away, died, and was turned into the flower of like name. The story may arise from the magical danger of seeing one's own image in a mirror (see Frazer, *GB*³ iii. 94), but Ovid gives an explanation (his own?) of it; Narcissus was punished for his cruelty to Echo (q.v.). Hera had deprived her of normal speech because her chatter prevented the goddess catching Zeus at his amours with the other nymphs; she could only repeat what others said. She tried to make love to Narcissus with fragments of his own speech, but he repulsed her and she so wasted away with grief that there was nothing left of her but her voice (Ov. *Met.* 3. 342 ff.). Other explanations, Paus. 9. 31. 7–8; Conon, 24.    H. J. R.

**NARCISSUS** (2). As private secretary (*ab epistulis*) to Claudius, this freedman acquired prodigious wealth (400 million sesterces, it was said) and exercised large political influence. He was even sent to the north of Gaul in A.D. 43 to expedite the embarkation of the expeditionary force to Britain and received *quaestoria ornamenta* in 48 as a reward for the exposure of Messalina (q.v. 1). His power was afterwards eclipsed by that of Pallas and Agrippina, whose marriage with Claudius he had not favoured, and he was unsuccessful in seeking to promote the interests of Britannicus. After the murder of Claudius in 54 he was immediately arrested and driven to suicide.    J. P. B.

**NARNIA** (modern *Narni*), formerly Nequinum, strongly placed Umbrian hill town, which Rome captured and converted into a Latin Colony (299 B.C.). In imperial times it was a flourishing *municipium* on the Via Flaminia with a famous bridge over the Nar (Augustan: one arch survives). The Emperor Nerva was born here.    E. T. S.

**NARRATIO,** rhetorical statement of a case (following the *exordium*), a feature stressed as vitally important by Apollodoreans (*see* APOLLODORUS 5) and by Quintilian (*Inst.* 4. 2).

For three *genera* of *narrationes, Rhetorica ad Herennium* 1. 8. 12; for requisite brevity, perspicuity, plausibility, Cic. *De Or.* 2. 326 ff., *Orat.* 124.

**NARSES,** a Persarmenian general of Justinian, was sent with an army to Italy in A.D. 538 to assist Belisarius (q.v.), with whom he was soon on bad terms; accordingly, Justinian recalled him in 539. But in 550 he was appointed to the supreme command in Italy, where he was brilliantly successful. His major victories were won at the battle of Taginae in 552, where he defeated the Ostrogothic king Totila at Rome, which he captured in the same year, and at the Mons Lactarius, where he defeated and killed Totila's successor Teias. He also defeated the Alamanni, who had invaded Italy, at the battle of Capua, and won numerous lesser engagements. By 554 he had completed the subjugation of Italy, which he administered for the following thirteen years.    E. A. T.

**NAUARCHOS** (ναύαρχος), admiral. The geographical conditions of Greek warfare, with its demand for 'amphibious' operations, discouraged the separation of naval from military commands: thus, Athenian fleets were always commanded by *strategoi* (q.v.). *Nauarchos* was a general term for the commander of a navy, of a squadron however small, even of a single ship. As an official title it appears comparatively late, the outcome of a greater specialization in certain States, mostly such as lacked an established naval tradition. The most important were Sparta (*c.* 430–360 B.C.), Syracuse under Dionysius I and II, Ptolemaic Egypt (and probably Macedonia, Pergamum, and the Seleucid kingdom), the Achaean League, and Rhodes. Everywhere (except perhaps at Pergamum) the *nauarchos* was admiral-of-the-fleet, with no colleague, his tenure varying from the single year (usually) of Greek republican admirals to the long commands of admirals (e.g. in Syracuse and Egypt) who served a monarch.

Strack, *PW*, s.v. 'Nauarchos'.    G. T. G.

**NAUCRATIS,** on the Canopic branch of the Nile, was a Greek 'treaty port' which under Saite Pharaohs became the chief centre of cultural relations between Greece and Egypt. According to Herodotus it was the sole emporium for Greek traders, who received concessions (τεμένη) from Amasis. The chief of these, established jointly by the Ionian cities of Chios, Teos, Phocaea, Clazomenae, the Dorian Rhodes, Cnidos, Halicarnassus, Phaselis, and Aeolian Mytilene, was called the Hellenium and appointed magistrates of the mart; Aegina, Samos, and Miletus had separate concessions. Excavations by Petrie and Gardner (1884–6) and Hogarth (1899, 1903) have produced abundant potsherds (many with dedications to 'the gods of the Greeks' Hera, Apollo, and also Aphrodite and the Dioscuri) dating from the latter years of the seventh century onwards, and show that the history of Greek Naucratis did not begin with Amasis' charter. According to Strabo Naucratis was founded by Milesians who, in the reign of Psammetichus, had founded the 'Milesians' Fort' near the Bolbitine mouth of the Nile. Sappho's brother Charaxus travelled to

Naucratis on business. The city continued to flourish through the classical period.

After Alexander's conquest of Egypt, the trade of Naucratis passed to Alexandria; some references in the correspondence of Zenon suggest that there was still some business done there in the middle of the third century, and inscriptions show that buildings were erected under the earlier Ptolemies; also, about the time of the conquest it struck the only civic silver and bronze coins known in Egypt. It was allowed to retain its Greek constitution by the Romans, and this served as a model for the constitution of Antinoöpolis in the reign of Hadrian. But there is no record of any active life there.

Hdt. bk. 2; Strabo, bk. 17; Sappho (ed. Lobel), 2, 3. W. M. Flinders Petrie and E. A. Gardner, *Naukratis* i, ii (1886–8). *BSA* v (1898), 26 f.; D. G. Hogarth, *JHS* 1905, 105 ff.; E. R. Price, ibid. 1924, 180 ff.; R. M. Cook, ibid. 1937, 227 ff. (with references to earlier literature). F. von Bissing, *Bull. Soc.* [roy.] *arch. Alex.* 1951, 33 ff.; Kienitz, *Polit. Gesch. Ägypt.* 45 ff.; R. M. Cook and A. G. Woodhead, *BSA* 1952, 159 ff. (vase-inscriptions); C. Roebuck, *Ionian Trade and Colonization* (1959), esp. 134 ff.
P. N. U. and J. G. M.

**NAUKRARIAI** (ναυκραρίαι, from ναύκραρος, ship's captain), early local divisions of Attica; according to Aristotle (*Ath. Pol.* 8. 3) there were twelve to each of the four old *phylai* (q.v.). Originally each naucrary will have been responsible for supplying and manning one ship for the Athenian fleet (traditionally fifty ships strong: *Iliad* 2. 556, Hdt. 6. 89); later, perhaps under the tyranny, they were given administrative duties, including the collection of taxes. According to one account Cleisthenes (q.v. 1) raised their number to fifty, to suit his ten new *phylai*: but it is hard to see how a territorial division of Attica into fifty naucraries can have coexisted with that into the thirty *trittyes* (q.v.); and Aristotle (*Ath. Pol.* 21. 5) says Cleisthenes replaced them as administrative units by the *demoi* (q.v.). In any case their replacement for naval purposes by the *boule* (q.v.) and trierarchs (see TRIER-ARCHY) can hardly have been long delayed after the massive enlargement of the fleet begun by Themistocles (q.v.) in 483.

Each naucrary was headed by a *naukraros* who commanded the ship it had provided; and the forty-eight *naukraroi* formed a corporate body with *prytaneis* (q.v.). Herodotus says (5. 71. 2) that in the time of Cylon (q.v.) these administered the State: an exaggeration, but they were doubtless powerful.

Busolt–Swoboda, *Griech. Staatsk*³. (i, 1920; ii, 1926), see indexes; Hignett, *Hist. Athen. Const.*, see index; F. R. Wüst, *Hist.* 1957, 176 ff.
A. W. G.; T. J. C.

**NAUMACHIA.** The word was used for a naval battle, shown as a great spectacle, or for an artificial lake constructed for the purpose, the best known being that excavated by Augustus in 2 B.C. on the right bank of the Tiber (near S. Cosimato), 1,800 feet long and 1,200 wide with an island in the middle, fed with water from a new aqueduct, the aqua Alsietina. Julius Caesar had been the first to give such an exhibition in 46 B.C., on the left bank of the Tiber. Prisoners of war and condemned criminals did the fighting; and some famous sea fight of history (e.g. Salamis, the Athenians at Syracuse, Actium) was re-enacted. Claudius exhibited a great *naumachia*, with 19,000 combatants, on the Fucine lake in A.D. 52 (Tac. *Ann.* 12. 56 f.). Similar displays were sometimes given on private estates and by flooding amphitheatres (the Colosseum at Rome in A.D. 80 and elsewhere, as archaeology shows, e.g. at Capua and at Nîmes).

Friedländer ii. 74 ff.; Platner–Ashby, s.v. J. P. B.

**NAUMACHIUS** (perhaps as early as the 2nd c. A.D.), author of a poem on wifely dutifulness, of which Stobaeus (68. 5, 74. 7, 93. 23) cites portions.

**NAUPACTUS,** in western (Ozolian) Locris, with an excellent harbour and small coastal plain cut off from the interior by mountains, commands the narrowest entrance of the Corinthian Gulf; its least difficult land-contacts are with Amphissa and eastern Greece. A legend, probably derived from the name of Naupactus ('ship-construction'), records that the Dorians crossed into the Peloponnese from Naupactus. Its value as a naval base was appreciated by the Athenians, who seized it and peopled it with exiled Messenians (456 B.C.). During the Peloponnesian War it was the main Athenian station in the west. After Sparta had expelled the Messenians (399), Achaea colonized and held it, until Philip captured it and gave it to Aetolia (338). With the collapse of the Aetolian Confederacy, Naupactus lost its importance.

L. Lerat, *Les Locriens de l'Ouest* (1952), 38 ff.; P–K, *GL* 2. 2. 320 ff. N. G. L. H.

**NAUPLIUS,** (1) eponym of Nauplia; son of Poseidon and Amymone (q.v.). (2) His descendant (Nauplius I–Proetus (q.v.)–Lernus–Naubolus–Clytoneus–Nauplius II, Ap. Rhod. 1. 134–8), father of Palamedes (q.v.) and Oeax. He was an Argonaut (Ap. Rhod. loc. cit.) and plays a part in two other well-known stories. Auge (see TELEPHUS 1) was entrusted to him after her delivery to sell overseas; he gave her to Teuthras, king of Teuthrania, who married her (Apollod. 2. 147). He was instrumental in wrecking the Greek fleet on its return from Troy (his namesake had been a wrecker also, Apollod. 2. 23; indeed, the two are identical, *Nostoi*, quoted there), for to avenge the death of Palamedes he lit false lights at Caphareus in Euboea (Eur. *Hel.* 767 ff., 1126 ff., and many later authors).

Wagner in Roscher's *Lexikon*, s.v. H. J. R.

**NAUSICAA,** daughter of Alcinous (q.v.; *Od.* 6. 15 ff.). The night of Odysseus' landing in Scheria (see ODYSSEUS), she was moved in a dream by Athena to go down to the washing-place at the river-mouth and wash the family linen with her handmaids. Having done so the next morning, she and her maids played ball, and a cry from one of them woke Odysseus. He improvised a loin-cloth from a branch, came out of the hollow under trees where he had spent the night, and appeared before the girls. The maids ran away, but Nausicaa, given courage by Athena, stood her ground. He then made known his wants to her and she gave him food, drink, and clothing and showed him the way to the city, modestly directing him to walk the last part of the distance alone, lest the gossips should see them together and accuse her of husband-hunting. This very charming episode was handled in the lost *Nausicaa* of Sophocles and a few other post-Homeric works; Hellanicus, in Eustathius on Homer, 1796. 42 ff., says she married Telemachus and had by him a son Perseptolis, an obvious next-best to marrying Odysseus, as Alcinous wished on their first meeting (*Od.* 7. 311 ff.). H. J. R.

**NAUSIPHANES** of Teos (b. *c.* 360 B.C.), Atomist, studied under Pyrrhon of Elis, probably while they were fellow soldiers in Alexander's campaigns, and before the end of these campaigns established himself as a teacher at Teos, where Epicurus studied under him *c.* 324. He was essentially a follower of Democritus, and was the channel through which Democritus' physics and theory of knowledge passed to Epicurus. He departed from Democritus' ethical views by insisting that the philosopher should take part in public life, and devoted himself largely to the exposition of a theory of rhetoric, which was later bitterly attacked by Philodemus.

Testimonia and fragments in Diels, *Vorsokr.*¹¹ 2. 246–50.
W. D. R.

**NAUTODIKAI** (ναυτοδίκαι) in the late fifth and early fourth centuries B.C. were Athenian officials who presided over certain trials, primarily ones involving merchants. They were probably instituted in order to relieve other magistrates at a period when Athenian commercial and imperial success had increased the number of such trials.

*See* DIKASTERION.

U. Kahrstedt, *Klio* 1939, 148 ff.; L. Gernet, *Droit et société dans la Grèce ancienne* (1955), 179 ff.                        D. M. M.

**NAVIES** (Greek and Roman). Apart from the Homeric fleets, which served only for transport, the construction of navies followed closely upon the expansion of Greek commerce in the age of colonization. The first recorded sea-battle took place between Corinth and Corcyra in 664 B.C. (Thuc. 1. 13. 4). The new commercial States found warships especially necessary to guard their coasts, to check piracy, and later to assure the free flow of grain and other vital products; also, their growing prosperity permitted maintenance of a fleet more easily. The expense, however, remained an impediment to large-scale, protracted naval operations throughout the Greek and Hellenistic periods, especially when mercenaries replaced citizen rowers (after 400 B.C.). Until the Roman Empire, the peace-time navy of a State consisted usually of a number of hulls, with rigging and oars, laid up in the docks of the harbour (q.v.), from which the galleys were launched only in case of need. Sporadic piracy in consequence flourished; great expeditions in war-time required extra construction and levies of sailors.

The peculiarities of the ancient war galley (*see* NAVIGATION) also influenced the character of naval power. It was impossible to keep up successfully a lengthy blockade, inasmuch as the galleys suffered in storms and furnished but cramped quarters to their crews. Thus, even the most heroic attempt, that of Bibulus to keep Caesar's reinforcements from crossing the Adriatic in the winter of 48 B.C. (Caesar, *BCiv.* 3 *passim*), eventually failed. The simple construction of the warship made it much easier for the so-called naval powers suddenly to be challenged by a State previously without a fleet, as by Sparta at various times in the Peloponnesian War (e.g. Thuc. 3. 26 ff.) and by Thebes under Epaminondas in 364 B.C. (Diod. 15. 78–9). The general object of naval strategy was to protect one's own coast and commerce, to destroy the opponent's fleet and commerce, and to assist land invasions by feints, transport of troops, and acquisition of bases.

Early navies, small in number, were composed chiefly of *pentekonters*, the forty triremes of Polycrates of Samos (Hdt. 3. 44) forming one of the largest squadrons before the fifth century. The Persian Wars brought great changes. Fleets grew in size; the trireme (q.v.) became the standard galley; naval tactics improved greatly. Athens benefited chiefly, under the leadership of Themistocles, who secured the construction of 200 triremes at Athens before 480 (*see* TRIERARCHY); thereafter, apart from a short period after the Peloponnesian War, it remained the pre-eminent naval power in Greece until 322, when its fleet of 170 galleys was destroyed at Amorgos by a Macedonian fleet of 240 ships.

Although navies in the Hellenistic age did not surpass the size of these two fleets, they entailed an immensely greater expense, which lay beyond the resources of the small States. The standard vessel was now the quinquereme (q.v.), with a crew twice as large as that of the trireme, and after the time of Alexander even larger vessels were built. Throughout this period Macedonia generally held the Aegean and Egypt the rest of the eastern Mediterranean, but the balance of naval power shifted frequently. By 188 B.C. all had yielded to Rome.

Although Rome had possessed some previous naval organization (*see* DUOVIRI NAVALES), its first great naval effort came in the First Punic War, during most of which the Romans maintained a fleet of over 200 quinqueremes. Unskilled in naval warfare, they relied upon their soldiery and used boarding tactics exclusively; ships were built in heavy fashion, the number of marines, small on Greek vessels, was increased, and the *corvus*, a grapnel, was extensively used (Polyb. 1. 20 ff.). The classical tactics of manœuvre, with the *diekplus* (q.v.), steadily gave way as the Romans overcame first Carthage, the chief naval power in the western Mediterranean, and then the Hellenistic States.

After 167 B.C. Rome permitted her fleets to decay and, in emergencies, conscripted ships and crews from her Greek allies. In the civil wars the contestants again built up huge squadrons, which were merged at last into the fleets of Antony and Octavian. To the campaign of Actium the former brought 500 warships and the latter 400. After his victory Octavian organized part of these into the first permanent fleet the Mediterranean had known (Tac. *Ann.* 4. 5). Based on Misenum and Ravenna, with auxiliary squadrons off Syria, Egypt, and Mauretania, and on the Black Sea, Rhine, Danube, and English Channel, the Roman imperial navy eradicated Mediterranean piracy for the first and last time previous to the nineteenth century. During the third and fourth centuries this navy vanished, but the Byzantine navy in part perpetuated the Graeco-Roman naval tradition.

ANCIENT SOURCES. Thucydides (1. 13 ff.) and Herodotus (bks. 6 ff.) reveal most clearly the nature of ancient navies.

MODERN LITERATURE. F. W. Clark, *The Influence of Sea-power on the History of the Roman Republic* (U.S.A. 1915); J. Kromayer and G. Veith, *Heerwesen und Kriegführung der Griechen und Römer* (1928); F. Miltner, *PW*, s.v. 'Seekrieg'; H. A. Ormerod, *Piracy in the Ancient World* (1924); W. L. Rodgers, *Greek and Roman Naval Warfare* (U.S.A. 1937); C. G. Starr, *The Roman Imperial Navy* (U.S.A. 1960); W. W. Tarn, *Hellenistic Military and Naval Developments* (1930); J. H. Thiel, *Studies on the History of Roman Sea-power in Republican Times* (Amsterdam, 1946) and *History of Roman Sea-power before the Second Punic War* (Amsterdam, 1954).            C. G. S.

**NAVIGATION.** The Mediterranean, tideless, broken by numerous peninsulas and islands, calm in summer, has always furnished encouragement to the seafarer, and to none more than the Greeks, whose experience became the basis of Graeco-Roman naval knowledge. The progress of navigation, however, was impeded by the lack of instruments for determining direction and distance, such as the compass, sextant, and log. Ships, also, were generally small, and, although they could sail within a few points of the wind, their sails, tackle, and steering apparatus were deficient.

The season of sailing was accordingly limited to the months when visibility was good and the sea mild; when storm clouds veiled the stars, the sailor sought the shore or some harbour. Hesiod (*Op.* 663 ff.) would restrict navigation to fifty days in midsummer, and usual practice placed its limits at March and October. As confidence and experience grew, and ships (q.v.) increased in size and stability, the period of sailing could be extended. Martial (6. 80) mentions Egyptian roses at Rome in winter, and other evidence from the Roman Empire (e.g. Tac. *Ann.* 12. 43) indicates some seafaring in winter by the more hardy travellers.

Although the Romans themselves were not seafarers, the Roman Empire marked the height of ancient navigation. The scourge of piracy was eliminated; traffic by sea increased enormously. Ships, moreover, tended to stand further out from land. As late as 400 B.C. the route from Greece to the west lay by Corcyra and thence to Italy; in like manner, the importance of Rhodes in the Hellenistic period was partly the result of its key situation on the route from Egypt and Syria to the Aegean via Cyprus and Caria. Under the Empire, travellers to the east usually went straight to Alexandria from Puteoli, rather than cross Macedonia as under the Republic (Philo, *In Flacc.* 5. 26–7). Alexandrian merchants at this time, after the discovery of the monsoon winds, voyaged directly to India, but Mediterranean craft never sailed regularly about Spain to Gaul and Britain.

The speed of vessels did not rise greatly in the ancient world. The average speed for cargo ships was approximately three to four knots; voyages of eight days from Puteoli to Alexandria and of six days from Gades to Ostia were records (Pliny, *HN* 19. 3–4). Seasonal winds were often employed, as by the Alexandrian grain fleet under the Empire, which sailed to Puteoli in June and caught the etesian winds back to Alexandria in August. Systematic descriptions of coasts (*Periplus*) appeared in the Hellenistic Age, a period in which physical aids to navigation such as harbours (q.v.) and lighthouses (q.v.) were constructed. This work continued under the Roman Empire.

Acts xxvii–xxviii; Lucian, *The Ship*. L. Casson, *The Ancient Mariners* (U.S.A. 1959); A. Köster, *Das antike Seewesen* (1923); H. J. Rose, *The Mediterranean in the Ancient World* (1933). J. I. Miller, *The Spice Trade of the Roman Empire* (1969). C. G. S.

**NAXOS** (1), the largest and most fertile of the Cyclades (q.v.), famous for its wine and worship of Dionysus. Tradition represents Carians, Thracians, and Cretans as its early inhabitants. It had an important Late Mycenaean settlement. In the archaic period it was important as a source of white marble and of the emery with which it could be worked. Its artists played a leading role in the development of early monumental sculpture and architecture ('Ionic' order) in Greece. Naxos was mistress of the Cyclades in the late sixth century under the tyrant Lygdamis. For its concern with the Ionian revolt the city was sacked by the Persians in 490 B.C. After the Persian wars Naxos joined the Delian League, was the first to revolt (Thuc. 1. 98), and became tributary to Athens, and a cleruchy was established about 450. As a member of the second Athenian League, the island again revolted without success. In the third century Naxos was a member of the Islanders' League; subsequently it was of little importance.

P–K, *GL* iv C V (d); *IG* xii. 5; Welter, *Ath. Mitt.* 1924, 17 f.; Casson, *BSA* 1940, 21 f. W. A. L.

**NAXOS** (2), on what is now *Capo Schisò*, by *Giardini*, was the first Greek colony in Sicily (734 B.C.). Founded by the Chalcidians under Thucles, its sanctuary of Apollo Archegetes was particularly venerated by the Siceliot Greeks. Chiefly important as colonizer of Leontini and Catana (qq.v.), it was not in itself a powerful city. Captured by Hippocrates (q.v. 1) *c.* 495/4 B.C., it formed part of the empire of Gelon and Hieron (who in 476 tried to 'doricize' it). After 461 it was in opposition to Syracuse, allied with Leontini (427) and Athens (415). In 403 Dionysius I (q.v.) captured and destroyed it. Though the site was not wholly deserted, the city was effectively replaced by Tauromenium (q.v.).

Bérard, *Bibl. topogr.* 77 f.; Dunbabin, *Western Greeks*; recent excavation of archaic walls and sanctuary of Aphrodite, P. Pelagatti, *Bollettino d'Arte* 1964, 149 ff., with refs.; coinage, H. A. Cahn, *Die Münzen der sizilischen Stadt Naxos* (1944). A. G. W.

**NEANTHES** of Cyzicus (3rd c. B.C.), historian, pupil of Philiscus of Miletus. His extensive writings included a *Hellenica* ('Ελληνικά) in at least six books, annals of Cyzicus in two works (Τὰ κατὰ πόλιν μυθικά for the legendary period and Ὧροι Κυζικηνῶν for historical times), and a series of biographies (Περὶ ἐνδόξων ἀνδρῶν) notable for the first recorded literary treatment of the life of Timon the misanthrope. His reliability for accurate knowledge is small. The history of Attalus I of Pergamum, 241–197

B.C. (Τὰ περὶ Ἄτταλον), usually ascribed to him, is by a younger Neanthes.

*FGrH* ii A, 84 and ii B. 171. G. L. B.

**NEAPOLIS,** modern *Naples*, was founded in fertile territory by Cumae *c.* 600 B.C. Its early history being unknown, ancient authors invented the tale that its original name was Parthenope. Neapolis became the chief Greek centre of Campania (*c.* 425) and received refugees from Cumae (q.v.) into its suburb Palae(o)polis. In 327 the anti-Roman policies of these Palaeopolitans constrained Rome to capture Neapolis. Palaepolis disappeared; Neapolis became a favoured allied State that furnished Rome naval help and repulsed Pyrrhus and Hannibal. In republican times Puteoli outstripped Neapolis, but by Cicero's day, despite a treacherous massacre of its inhabitants in 82 (App. *BCiv.* 1. 89), Neapolis was a flourishing *municipium* where Virgil and others, seeking beauty or Hellenic culture, sojourned. Subsequently Neapolis became a *colonia* but retained its Greek institutions and language until the late Empire. In the Gothic Wars it suffered severely (Procop. *Goth.* 1 and 3), but was always important. Here Statius was born and Romulus Augustulus, last Western Emperor, virtually imprisoned.

Strabo 5. 246; Livy 8. 22 f.; 35. 16. A. Sambon, *Monnaies antiques de l'Italie* i (1903), 171, 283; Bérard, *Bibl. topogr.* 71; M. A. Napoli, *Napoli greco-romana* (1959). E. T. S.

**NEARCHUS** (1), potter and vase-painter, in Athens. Known from four signatures on small black-figure vases and one on a black-figure plaque of about 550 B.C. and dedication of Antenor Kore (about 530). His sons Tleson and Ergoteles signed 'little master' cups.

G. M. A. Richter, *AJArch.* 1932, 272; A. Rumpf, *Sakonides* (1937), 19; Beazley, *ABV* 82. T. B. L. W. ·

**NEARCHUS** (2) of Crete, Alexander's friend, commanded the fleet which circumnavigated the coast from the Indus to the Tigris. His honest and trustworthy chronicle, written before 312 B.C., was not a history of Alexander, but gave an account of India, which Strabo and Arrian used, and of his voyage, which is reproduced in Arrian's *Indike*. After the death of Alexander Nearchus played a subordinate part under Antigonus I and Demetrius I. He was probably killed at the battle of Gaza (312 B.C.).

*See* ALEXANDER (3), Ancient Sources; and Pearson, *Lost Histories*, ch. 5. W. W. T.

**NECHEPSO,** titular author with Petosiris of a comprehensive astrological work, the basis of the later astrology. He probably invented the astrological significance of the signs of the zodiac, as well as making many other innovations. 'Nechepso and Petosiris' may have been the pseudonym of a single author, and his date may be placed *c.* 150–125 B.C.

Ed. E. Riess, *Philol.* Suppl. 6 (1891–3), 325 ff. W. D. R.

**NELEUS** (Νηλεύς) and **PELIAS** (Πελίας) in mythology, sons of Tyro, daughter of Salmoneus (q.v.) by Poseidon; he approached her in the shape of the river-god Enipeus, whom she loved (*Od.* 11. 235 ff.). Here (237) she is apparently already married to Cretheus (for the relationships *see* AEOLUS 2); later, as in Apollodorus (1. 90), he is her guardian. Apollodorus also says that she exposed the children, who were picked up by a horse-herder. Tyro was ill-used by Sidero, her stepmother, till her sons grew up, recognized her, and pursued Sidero into a temple of Hera, where Pelias killed her at the altar. For the rest of his story *see* JASON, MEDEA. Neleus married Chloris, daughter of Amphion of Orchomenus (*Od.* 11. 281 ff.), who bore Nestor and other sons, also Pero, cf.

MELAMPUS (1). But Heracles attacked Pylos, Neleus' kingdom, because Neleus would not purify him from the blood-guilt of Iphitus (*Il.* 11. 690 ff., Hes. fr. 14 ff. Rzach; schol. *Il.* 2. 336), and killed all his sons save Nestor (q.v. 1). His own death is variously told, see Weizsäcker in Roscher's *Lexikon* iii. 110.     H. J. R.

**NEMAUSUS,** town in Gallia Narbonensis (modern *Nîmes*), originally a Celtic settlement, capital of the Volcae Arecomici. It was probably a *colonia Latina* by 28 B.C. and the seat of an important mint. In 16 B.C. it was laid out with walls enclosing *c.* 550 acres. Very important remains of public buildings exist: amphitheatre, precinct of *Deus Nemausus*, and a temple erected by Agrippa (16 B.C.) and rededicated to C. and L. Caesar (the 'Maison Carrée'). The Pont-du-Gard forms part of its aqueduct. Perhaps in the second century it became the capital of Narbonensis.

Grenier, *Manuel* iii. 143 ff. (general), 393 ff. (temple), 613 ff. (amphitheatre), iv. 88 ff. (aqueduct), 493 ff. (precinct of Nemausus); F. Vittinghoff, *Röm. Kolonisation* (1952), 101 ff.; R. Neumann, *Quellbezirk von Nîmes* (1937); A. C. Balty, *Études sur la Maison Carrée de Nîmes* (1960).     C. E. S.

**NEMEA** was an open valley on the north borders of the Argolid, in the territory of Cleonae. It was the scene of Heracles' encounter with the lion, and of the Nemean Games (q.v.). The fourth-century temple of Zeus, the great altar, palaestra, and gymnasium have been excavated. Nemea is also the name of the river flowing north and forming the boundary of Corinth and Sicyon, the scene of the first battle of the Corinthian War (394; Xen. *Hell.* 4. 2. 13 ff.).

C. W. Blegen, 'Excavations at Nemea', *Art and Archaeology* 1925, 175 ff.; *AJArch.* 1927, 421 ff.; N. Clemmensen and R. Vallois, 'Le Temple de Zeus à Némée', *BCH* 1925, 1 ff.     T. J. D.

**NEMEAN GAMES,** THE, according to one legend were founded by Adrastus of Argos, when he led the Seven against Thebes; according to another by Heracles after he had slain the Nemean lion: but we know little of them until 573 B.C., when they became a Panhellenic festival. They were held in the sanctuary of Nemean Zeus (*see* NEMEA), and were at first managed by the people of Cleonae, afterwards by Argos. The games were conducted on the same lines as those at Olympia, the prize was a crown of wild celery, and they took place every second and fourth year in each Olympiad.     F. A. W.

**NEMESIANUS,** MARCUS AURELIUS OLYMPIUS, from Carthage, late in the third century A.D. composed four pastorals (long ascribed to Calpurnius (1), q.v.), and an incomplete didactic poem in 325 verses on the chase. But he also distinguished himself in poetic contests and meditated an epic on the deeds of the imperial brothers Numerianus and Carinus (S.H.A. *Carus, Numerian. et Carinus*, 11; *Cyn.* 63–78). His *Cynegetica* is best dated between the death of the Emperor Carus, 283, and that of Numerianus, 284. It seems to refer to his pastorals as lighter productions which had preceded (58–62).

WORKS (1) **Eclogae:** these four short poems, 319 lines in all, show the influence of Virgil and Calpurnius. In I the shepherd Timetas' threnody on Meliboeus recalls the praises of Daphnis in Verg. *Ecl.* 5; in III the song demanded from Pan is a parallel to that of Silenus in Verg. *Ecl.* 6. IV (62–72) borrows magical ideas which Virgil in *Ecl.* 8 drew from Theocritus: here too, Nemesianus restores the pleasant music of the refrain which was part of the Theocritean tradition in Virgil. His diction and metre gain by his Virgilian imitations, though his period accounts for shortenings like *laudandŏ, devotiŏ, exercetŏ* (*Ecl.* 2. 80, *Cyn.* 83, 187). From Calpurnius he borrows freely, especially in eclogue III.

(2) **Cynegetica:** 102 lines are introductory; then, departing from the order in Grattius (whom he probably had read), he devotes 223 lines to indispensable preliminaries for hunting—dogs (rearing, training, diseases, breeds), horses, nets, and traps. The poem breaks off on the verge of the chase—'uenemur dum mane nouum'.

(3) **De Aucupio.** Two fragments on birdcatching (28 hexameters) are ascribed to Nemesianus.

His style, though unoriginal, is agreeable. He at least declares his independence of mythology (*Cyn.* 15–47) and certain notes of enthusiasm in him lend colour to the almost conventional claim to be breaking new ground (8–14) in his didactic poem; while in his feeling for pastoral environment there are suggestions of the open air in spite of his book-borrowings. He is rather less inclined to lose himself in details of the essentials for the chase than Grattius is. *See* PASTORAL POETRY, LATIN, § 5.

TEXTS. (*a*) **Eclogues:** E. Baehrens, *PLM* iii; H. Schenkl (w. Calp. Sic.; 1885) and in Postgate's *CPL* (1905); C. H. Keene (w. Calp. Sic., introd., comm.; 1887); C. Giarratano (w. Calp. Sic.; 1910); Turin (Paravia, 1924 and 1939); Duff, *Minor Lat. Poets*. (*b*) **Cynegetica:** E. Baehrens, *PLM* iii; J. P. Postgate, *CPL* (1905); D. Martin (w. comment.; U.S.A. 1917); Duff, *Minor Lat. Poets*; P. van de Woestijne (1937).
SPECIAL STUDIES. M. Haupt, *Opusc.* i. 358 ff. M. Fiegl, *Des Grattius Cynegetica: seine Vorgänger u. seine Nachfolger* (1890) [argues that N. borrowed from G.: supported by Enk (ed. Grattius), opposed by Curcio (ed. Grattius)]; P. Monceaux, *Les Africains: étude sur la littér. latine d'Afrique* (1894); J. Hubaux, *Les Thèmes bucoliques dans la poésie latine* (1930); B. Luiselli, 'Il proemio del Cynegeticon d. Olimpio Nemesiano', *Stud. Ital.* 1958, 73 ff.     J. W. D.

**NEMESIS** (1). One of the most puzzling of Greek goddesses, owing to the wide divergence between her mythology and her position in cult and morals. Her best-known shrine was at Rhamnus in Attica, where she appears to have been a deity of the type of Artemis (q.v.; see Farnell, *Cults* ii. 488 ff.). Zeus pursued her amorously, and to avoid him she took all manner of non-human forms, especially those of fish (*Cypria*, frs. 6 and 7 Allen). Finally (Apollod. 3. 127, continuing what seems to be the same story) she changed into a goose, he into a swan, and so she laid the egg which a shepherd found and gave to Leda (q.v.). This is the sort of story which might be told of almost any minor goddess or nymph. The fact that in Smyrna (Paus. 9. 35. 6) there were statues of the Charites in her temple, of old workmanship ascribed to Bupalus, would suggest that there at least she had something to do with the fertility of the soil.

But in the vast majority of cases she is nothing but retribution or righteous indignation, particularly that of the gods at human presumption, personified. This identification extends to her Attic cult, cf. Catull. 66. 71 (64. 395 seems to make her a war-goddess, but he may mean that she appeared to rouse men fighting in a good cause); and a local worship in Boeotia, apparently of Nemesis Adrasteia, was said to have been founded by Adrastus (q.v.), because of the resentment he felt against the Thebans (Antimachus, fr. 53 Wyss). Adrasteia is certainly the 'unescapable' power before which all must bow (προσκυνεῖν τὴν Ἀδράστειαν, Aesch. *PV* 936, Pl. *Resp.* 451 a). But she in turn is, or is identified with, a goddess of the Phrygian Ida, associated with the Dactyli (*Phoronis* in schol. Ap. Rhod. 1. 1129; *see* IDAEAN DACTYLS). Possibly in this case some accidental resemblance of a foreign to a Greek word has come into play; Nemesis of Rhamnus may have been originally the goddess who deals or distributes, νέμει, appropriate gifts to her worshippers, and was afterwards made abstract, a process like that which Fors Fortuna (q.v.) seems to have undergone. It does not appear that her statue, for which see Rossbach in Roscher's *Lexikon* iii. 153–4 (see the whole art. for good discussion and literature and cf. Herter in

*PW*, s.v.), had the characteristic pose of later representations of her (see Volkmann in *ARW* 26. 296 ff., 31. 57 ff. for this and other points), which are shown spitting into the breast-fold of her robe (cf. Theoc. 6. 39). For her later developments in cult and literature, which last to the days of Theodosius, see Rossbach.     H. J. R.

**NEMESIS** (2) succeeded 'Delia' in the affections of Tibullus (2. 3. 51; 5. 111; Ov. *Am.* 3. 9. 31; Mart. 8. 73. 7).

**NEMĒSIUS**, fl. *c.* A.D. 400, bishop of Emesa in Syria, perhaps identical with the governor of Cappadocia to whom (*c.* 385) Gregory (q.v. 2) of Nazianzus addressed four letters and a protreptic poem inviting him to become a Christian. His essay in Christian Platonism, *On the Nature of Man*, is remarkable not only for its wide reading in medical and philosophical sources, e.g. Galen and Porphyry, but also for its Christian standpoint and its thesis that the spiritual life of man is conditioned by the body's natural limitations.

Ed. Migne, *PG* xl. 508 ff. Translation and commentary by W. Telfer (1955). J. Quasten, *Patrology* 3 (1960), 351 ff.     H. C.

**NENIA.** The derivation from νηνίατον [Φρύγιον] is given by Pollux 4. 79 [80] but it may be an independent Latin onomatopoeia. Usually *nenia* means a dirge containing lamentation and praise of a deceased person (Diomedes, Keil, *Gramm. Lat.* i. 485: 'cum lamentatione'; Festus, 158 Lindsay: 'carmen quod in funere laudandi gratia cantatur ad tibiam'). It was sung to a flute accompaniment by a hired mourner (*praefica*), whose assistants made responses (Serv. ad *Aen.* 6. 216) before the house of mourning, during the funeral procession, and beside the pyre. It never became a literary genre. No example has reached us: we have only an anapaestic parody (Sen. *Apocol.* 12). *Nenia* is also the goddess of the dying; she had a temple at Rome.

From the idea of empty repetition (cf. Plaut. *Asin.* 808 and Cato ap. Gell. 18. 7. 3), it came to mean children's rhymes (Hor. *Epist.* 1. 1. 63), a magical litany, a senseless rigmarole (*nugae*). But it could also signify 'end' (Plaut. *Pseud.* 1278) or *coda* (Hor. *Carm.* 3. 28. 16). In Ausonius it signifies *epicedium* (q.v.); in Sidonius Apollinaris, a metrical epitaph.     C. F.; G. W. W.

**NEOPHRON**, of Sicyon, was said by Dicaearchus and in the pseudo-Aristotelian ὑπομνήματα to have written a *Medea* which was adapted by Euripides in his play of that name (Argum. Eur. *Med.*), but the truth of this is very doubtful and the three extant fragments are almost certainly later than Euripides (see D. L. Page, Euripides, *Medea* (1938), xxx ff.). The *Suda* says that he wrote 120 tragedies and was the first to introduce into his plays '*paedagogi* and the torture of slaves'—perhaps an inference based on his supposed priority to Euripides; such priority is inconsistent with the *Suda*'s further statement that he associated with Alexander the Great, who put him to death with Callisthenes (the *Suda* elsewhere calls Alexander's victim Nearchus).

*TGF* 729-32.     A. W. P.-C.

**NEOPLATONISM**, the revived Platonism—really a new synthesis of Platonic, Pythagorean, Aristotelian, and Stoic elements—which was the dominant philosophy of the pagan world from the middle of the third century A.D. down to the closing of the pagan schools by Justinian in 529, and strongly influenced medieval and Renaissance thought. The following phases may be distinguished in its history. (1) A long period of preparation, extending from the time of Antiochus (d. *c.* 68 B.C.) and Posidonius (d. *c.* 50 B.C.) down to that of Plotinus, during which we can trace the movement towards a comprehensive synthesis. In the work of such second-century writers as the Neopythagorean Numenius and the Middle Platonist Albinus (q.v. 1) there is much that foreshadows Plotinian Neoplatonism. (2) The oral teaching of Ammonius Saccas at Alexandria (early 3rd c.), of Plotinus at Rome (244/5-269/70), and of Plotinus' immediate pupils Porphyry and Amelius. Plotinus' *Enneads* (published posthumously, *c.* 300-5) gave Neoplatonism its abiding shape, and are incomparably its most important philosophical product. *See* PLOTINUS, PORPHYRY. (3) The period of diffusion in the fourth century when Neoplatonism becomes the fashionable creed of the pagan reaction, with its chief teaching centres in Syria and later at Pergamum, while it also begins to influence Christian thought through Gregory of Nyssa and Augustine. To this period belong Iamblichus (q.v. 2); Sallustius, author of the *De diis et mundo*, a curious popular handbook of Neoplatonic religion (ed. and transl. A. D. Nock, 1926); Eunapius, who made out of the lives of his Neoplatonic teachers a pagan hagiology (*Vitae Sophistarum*, ed. and transl. W. C. Wright, Loeb, 1922); and the Latin Neoplatonists Calcidius (Commentary on Plato's *Timaeus*, ed. Waszink, 1962), Marius Victorinus, and Macrobius (q.v.). (4) The Athenian School (Syrianus, Proclus, Simplicius, etc.) and the Alexandrian (Hypatia, Synesius, Olympiodorus, etc.), belonging mainly to the fifth and sixth centuries, fall outside the limits of date of this dictionary; as does the survival of Neoplatonism in writers like 'Dionysius the Areopagite' and John the Scot, and its revival by Psellus at Byzantium in the eleventh century and by Pico and others at the Renaissance.

GENERAL. T. Whittaker, *The Neoplatonists*² (1918); J. Geffcken, *Der Ausgang des griechisch-römischen Heidentums*² (1929); Zeller, *Phil. d. Gr.*⁴ iii. 2; A. H. Armstrong, *An Introduction to Ancient Philosophy*³ (1957). See also bibliography to PLOTINUS, PORPHYRY, IAMBLICHUS. Selections: E. R. Dodds, *Select Passages illustrating Neoplatonism* (text 1924, transl. 1923); C. J. de Vogel, *Greek Philosophy* iii (1959).
ORIGINS. W. Theiler, *Die Vorbereitung des Neuplatonismus* (1930); R. E. Witt, *Albinus and the History of Middle Platonism* (1937); P. Merlan, *From Platonism to Neoplatonism*² (1960); 'Les Sources de Plotin', *Entretiens Hardt* v.
DIFFUSION. W. Theiler, *Porphyrios und Augustin* (1933); P. Henry, *Plotin et l'Occident* (1934); P. Courcelle, *Les Lettres grecques en Occident* (1943).     E. R. D.

**NEOPTOLEMUS** (1), in mythology, son of Achilles and Deidameia; *see* ACHILLES. After his father's death he was sent for to Troy by the Greeks, because his presence was one of the necessary conditions for taking the city (Soph. *Phil.* 114 f., 345 ff.), Odysseus acting as messenger (*Od.* 11. 508-9; Soph. ibid. 344 adds Phoenix). Arrived there, he showed himself a notable warrior and wise counsellor (*Od.* ibid.), killing among others Eurypylus, son of Telephus. He was one of the chosen party who manned the Wooden Horse, and came through that and the other dangers of the war unharmed. So far Homer (Sophocles' details presumably are from some cyclic epic, however); later authors do little more than enlarge and embroider. After the war, Homer says no more of him than that he returned safely and Menelaus sent Hermione to be married to him (*Od.* 3. 188-9; 4. 5 ff.). For the sequel of this marriage *see* HERMIONE. There is, however, a curious double version of the story of his visit to Delphi, which has left its mark on Pindar. In the sixth Paean it is said (100 ff.) that Neoptolemus, having been fetched from Scyros and taken Troy, incurred the wrath of Apollo by killing Priam at the altar of Zeus Herceius (cf. Verg. *Aen.* 2. 513 ff.); the god therefore swore that he should never reach home. Consequently, he was killed at Delphi in a dispute with 'the servants'. (Elsewhere it is explained that this arose from the local practice of the priests of seizing their portion from the sacrifice.) This seems to have given much offence in Aegina; therefore in *Nem.* 7. 33 ff. Pindar retold the tale with a different emphasis. Neoptolemus did go to Delphi and was killed there in a quarrel; but he went with the best of intentions (for details see Farnell's commentary), and the ultimate reason of his death was that one of the Aeacidae must needs enjoy heroic honours at that spot. He never returned to Scyros or Phthia, but, being driven by winds off his course, made his way to the Molossian territory, the kings of which country claimed descent from him through his son by Andromache (q.v.), Molossus; hence the name Pyrrhus borne by the most famous of them, that being the alternative name of Neoptolemus (e.g. *Cypria*, fr. 14 Allen, which says Pyrrhus was his original name; Neoptolemus means 'young warrior'). His cult at Delphi is a historical fact, but it practically dates from the Gaulish invasion, according to Pausanias (1. 4. 4); earlier than that his tomb had been held in no honour, but it was thought that he had been seen fighting alongside the Hyperborean heroes against the attackers.

Neoptolemus is shown on archaic or classical vases leaving Scyros, receiving his father's arms from Odysseus, and especially as the centre of the Iliupersis, killing Priam and Astyanax; also sacrificing Polyxena on Achilles' tomb (Brommer, *Vasenlisten*², 298 f., 313, 323, 331 ff.).

See the larger dictionaries s.v.; Farnell, *Hero-Cults*, 311 ff.; J. E. Fontenrose, *The Cult and Myth of Pyrrhos at Delphi* (1960).
H. J. R.; C. M. R.

**NEOPTOLEMUS** (2) of Parium (3rd c. B.C.; earlier than Aristophanes of Byzantium, probably later than Eratosthenes), Greek writer. His works included poems, literary criticism and philological treatises. His views on poetry, known to us through a summary by Philodemus, are said by Porphyrion to have been adopted in essentials by Horace in the *Ars Poetica. See also* GLOSSA, GREEK; LITERARY CRITICISM IN ANTIQUITY, § 8.

A. Rostagni, *Arte poetica di Orazio* (1930); C. O. Brink, *Horace on Poetry* (1963). J. D. D.; K. J. D.

**NEOPYTHAGOREANISM,** the revived Pythagorean school, or rather direction of thought, which appeared at Rome and Alexandria in the first century B.C. and persisted until it was merged in Neoplatonism. It combined in varying proportions a small amount of early Pythagorean tradition with elements derived from Platonic, Peripatetic, and Stoic sources, the whole being accommodated to contemporary religious tendencies. Neopythagorean writers appear to have been interested mainly in theological speculation, in the symbolism of numbers, and in glorifying Pythagoras as the founder of a way of life and author of a religious revelation. There is little trace of a systematic body of philosophical doctrine held in common by them: some of them were Stoicizing monists, others Platonizing dualists. The historical importance of Neopythagoreanism lies chiefly in the influence which it exercised (*a*) on Neoplatonism, especially in the post-Plotinian period; (*b*) on Jewish thought through Philo and Christian thought through Clement of Alexandria. For individual Neopythagoreans *see* NIGIDIUS FIGULUS, APOLLONIUS (12) OF TYANA, NUMENIUS.

(*a*) ANCIENT SOURCES. Alexander Polyhistor (*c.* 80 B.C.) ap. Diog. Laert. 8. 24 ff. (cf. M. Wellmann, *Hermes* 1919, and A.-J. Festugière, *Rev. Ét. Grec.* 1945); two accounts in Sext. Emp. 10. 261 ff. (Platonizing), 281 ff. (Stoicizing); Photius cod. 249 (cf. O. Immisch, *Sitz. Heid. Ak.* 1919); 'Ocellus Lucanus', ed. R. Harder with Germ. comm. (1926); fragments of Nigidius, A. Swoboda (1889); of Numenius, E. A. Leemans (1937); of other Neopythagoreans, Mullach, *Fragm. Phil. Graec.*
(*b*) MODERN DISCUSSION. Zeller iii. 2⁴; A. Schmekel, *Philosophie der mittleren Stoa* (1892), 403 ff.; A. Delatte, *Études sur la littérature pythagoricienne* (1915); F. Cumont, *Recherches sur le symbolisme funéraire des Romains* (1942). E. R. D.

**NEPET(E),** the modern *Nepi*, a small but strategically important town, 25 miles north-west of Rome, situated on the edge of the territory of the Faliscans (q.v.) and together with Sutrium (q.v.) controlling the road through the Ciminian forest into central Etruria, as well as the direct route to southern Umbria, later the Via Amerina. After the conquest of Veii in 396 B.C. it fell into Roman hands, receiving a Latin colony either in 383 (Livy 6. 21. 4) or in 373 (Vell. Pat. 1. 14. 2). Created a *municipium* after the Social War, it was modestly prosperous under the Empire. In late antiquity (Procop. *Goth.* 4. 35) it became once more of strategic importance, a role which it retained throughout the Middle Ages.

*Not. Scav.* 1910 and 1918; M. W. Frederiksen and J. B. Ward-Perkins, *PBSR* 1957, 89 ff. J. B. W.-P.

**NEPOS,** CORNELIUS (*PW* 274) (*c.* 99–*c.* 24 B.C.), born in Cisalpine Gaul, moved to Rome, but took no part in politics; he was familiar with Cicero, with whom he exchanged letters, and with Pomponius Atticus. Catullus dedicated his book to Nepos in eulogistic verses. Fronto (Loeb ii. 168) tells us that Nepos was also a publisher.

WORKS: 1. *De Viris Illustribus,* in at least sixteen books (Charisius, *Gramm.* 1. 141. 13 Keil), dealing with foreigners as well as Romans. The categories of generals, historians, kings, poets, are certain; and fragments on the Gracchi suggest a section on orators. It was published before the death of Atticus, apparently in 34; before 27 a second edition appeared, including non-Greeks and expanding the *Atticus*. Of this we have *De Excellentibus Ducibus Exterarum Gentium* (see Loeb *Nep.* 357 ff.), and two 'Lives' from *De Historicis Latinis*, besides fragments.

2. *Lost Works: Chronica,* a universal history in three books (Catull. 1); *Exempla,* anecdotes in at least five books (Gell. 6 (7). 18. 11); fuller *Lives of Cato* (Nep. *Cato* 3. 5) and *Cicero* (Gell. 15. 28. 2); a work on Geography, cited by Mela and Pliny. His light verse (Pliny, *Ep.* 5. 3. 6) was probably never published.

Nepos was the writer of the first surviving biography in Latin. The idea of a parallel treatment of foreigners was probably taken from Varro's *Imagines*. His defects are hasty and careless composition (perhaps less marked in his first edition) and lack of control of his material. He is mainly eulogistic, with an ethical aim, but also gives information about his hero's environment. As historian his value is slight; he names many sources, but rarely used them at first hand. His style is essentially plain, but contains colloquial features and many archaisms, not used for artistic effect, but from indifference. His rhetorical training appears in attempts at adornment, neither uniform nor discriminating.

LIFE AND WORKS. Introduction to Commentaries and Translations; Schanz–Hosius i. 351 ff. F. Leo, *Griech.-Röm. Biogr.* (1901), ch. 10; D. R. Stuart, *Epochs of Greek and Roman Biogr.* (U.S.A. 1928), see index; E. M. Jenkinson in *Latin Biography* (ed. T. A. Dorey, 1967), 1 ff.
TEXTS. O.C.T. (Winstedt); Teubner (Halm, Fleckeisen); O. Wagner (Leipzig, 1922); E. Malcovati² (1945).
COMMENTARIES. Staveren (ed. Bardili², 1820); Nipperdey–Witte¹² (1962); Browning–Inge (1887).
TRANSLATIONS. H. Wilkinson (1899); E. O. Winstedt (1904); with text, J. C. Rolfe (Loeb, 1929, with Florus); A. M. Guillemin (Budé, 1923).
STYLE AND DICTION. B. Lupus, *Sprachgebrauch des Corn. Nep.* 1876; Introdd. to Nipp.–Witte, and to Translations.
J. C. R.; G. B. T.

**NEPTUNUS,** Italian god of water (not of the sea, though his identification with Poseidon, q.v., extended his cult in this direction; it was then purely Greek in form, the *exta* being thrown raw into the sea, Livy 29. 27. 5; it is in virtue of this capacity that the absurd identification of Consus with 'Neptunus Equester', i.e. Poseidon Hippios, takes place, Livy 1. 9. 6). The etymology of his name is quite uncertain; in Etruscan it is Neθun(u)s. His festival is of the oldest series (Neptunalia, 23 July); we know concerning its ritual only that arbours, *umbrae*, of boughs were commonly erected (Festus, 519, 1 Lindsay), but it may be conjectured that its object was to obtain sufficient water at this hot and dry time of year. His cult-partner is Salacia (Gell. 13. 23. 2); she may be the goddess of 'leaping', i.e. springing water (*salire*), but was identified with Amphitrite as he was with Poseidon.

For his temples see Platner–Ashby, 360 f.; Nash, *Pict. Dict. Rome* ii. 120 ff. Cf. Wissowa, *RK* 225 ff.; L. Delatte, *Ant. Class.* 1935, 45 ff.
H. J. R.

**NERATIUS** (*PW* 15) **PRISCUS,** Lucius, a considerable Roman jurist of the age of Trajan and Hadrian; born at Saepinum in Samnium. He was *praefectus aerarii Saturni, cos. suff.* 97, *legatus Augusti pro praetore* of Pannonia, and he was at one time, we are told, thought of by Trajan as his successor (and *see under* HADRIAN). Neratius was, with Celsus (q.v. 3), the last head of the Proculian School (*see* SABINUS 2), and was a member of the *consilium* of Hadrian and perhaps Trajan. The excerpts from his writings in the *Digest*, which illustrate well the penetration of his mind, come mainly from his *Membranae*. His reputation as a jurist is evidenced by the frequency with which his opinions are cited by later jurists, and by the fact that Paulus (q.v. 1) wrote a commentary *ad Neratium*.

Syme, *Tacitus*, 762.
B. N.

**NEREUS,** an old sea god, son of Pontus and father by the Oceanid Doris of the Nereids. He lives with the Nereids in the depths of the sea (*Il.* 1. 358; Hes. *Th.* 233 ff.), particularly in the Aegean Sea (Ap. Rhod. 4. 771 f.). Hesiod and Pindar extol his righteousness. To give fair praise to an enemy's achievement is quoted as an advice of a sea god, presumably Nereus, by Pindar (*Pyth.* 9. 94). Like other 'Old Men of the Sea' he has great wisdom and even the gift of prophecy (Hor. *Carm.* 1. 15). These abilities bring him into a strenuous contest with Heracles. Bacchylides (17) and Pherecydes relate that Heracles had to catch Nereus unawares in order to learn the whereabouts of the Golden Apples. Panyassis (Ath. 11. 469 d) makes Nereus give the cup of the Sun to Heracles. When Peleus wrestles with Thetis, Nereus, his future father-in-law, looks on. Later he attends the wedding of Peleus (François Vase) and brings presents. In his contest with Heracles Nereus transforms himself into fire, water, and many other shapes (Apollod. 2. 5. 11). In addition to his fifty or hundred daughters, the Nereids (A. D. Nock, *Mélanges de l'Univ. Saint-Joseph.* 1960–1, 297), he is said by Lucian (*Trag.* 87) to have educated Aphrodite. It is uncertain whether a small cult in Gythium belonged to Nereus or to some other sea god (Paus. 3. 21. 9). The earliest representations of him in art go back to the early sixth century B.C. In an Athenian pediment and on vases he watched Heracles fight Triton. As a dignified spectator Nereus is a great favourite with vase-painters, but sometimes he is also shown wrestling with Heracles (J. Boardman, *BICS* 1958, 6). The only inscription referring to Nereus survives on the famous Hellenistic frieze of Pergamum.

Pind. *Pyth.* 9; *FGrH* i. 65 (Pherecydes). L. Bloch in Roscher, *Lex.*, s.v.; E. Buschor, *Ath. Mitt.* 1921/2, 56.
G. M. A. H.; J. R. T. P.

**NERO** (1) (NERO CLAUDIUS CAESAR, *PW* Suppl. iii, s.v. Domitius 29), Roman Emperor A.D. 54–68, was born 15 Dec. 37 of Cn. Domitius Ahenobarbus (*cos.* A.D. 32) and the Younger Agrippina (q.v. 3). For the circumstances of his accession *see* CLAUDIUS (1).

To strengthen his doubtful claim stories were spread of his miraculous childhood (Suet. *Nero*, 6; Tac. *Ann.*

11. 11), and stress laid on his descent from the divine Augustus. In his inaugural speech he promised to rule 'ex praescripto Augusti' (Tac. *Ann.* 13. 4). He showed modesty by declining an honour with the phrase 'cum meruero', *pietas* by consecrating Claudius and by gratitude to Agrippina ('optima mater'), and clemency by his unwillingness to sign a death-warrant—'quam uellem nescire litteras'. His enthusiasm for art made flatterers hail him as Apollo.

Between artistic son and imperious mother trouble was likely: Otho (q.v.) encouraged Nero to free himself. Agrippina retorted by sympathy for the dispossessed Britannicus (q.v.): Britannicus was poisoned (55), and Agrippina went into retirement. Poppaea (q.v.), Otho's ambitious wife, wishing to marry Nero, planned to eliminate both Agrippina and Nero's wife Octavia. Though Nero preferred literary pursuits or amusement, there was some good legislation (Tac. *Ann.* 13. 51) and able governors—Galba, Suetonius Paulinus, and Corbulo (qq.v.)—were sent to the provinces: here the credit should probably be ascribed to Seneca and Burrus (q.v.), the Prefect of the Praetorians, who apparently controlled serious policy.

But Nero soon became his own master. In 59 he had Agrippina murdered, while the death of Burrus (who was replaced by two Prefects, Tigellinus, q.v., and Faenius Rufus) and the retirement of Seneca (62) left him uncontrolled. Octavia was divorced and murdered. Now Poppaea could marry Nero: in 63 she bore him a daughter who died at four months.

Nero's emancipation meant free rein for his artistic passions. His enthusiasm for art and horsemanship seem genuine enough; he wanted to lead Rome from gladiatorial shows to humaner things. He founded games: the *Juvenalia* (59), where nobles were encouraged to compete, and the *Neronia* (61); he opened a *gymnasium*, and distributed free oil to competitors 'Graeca facilitate'. He eagerly displayed his own powers in public, to the scandal of traditionalists. His voice, 'exigua et fusca' (Suet. *Nero*, 20), hailed by his admirers as divine, may have been passable; his poetry, modernistic and laborious, was probably his own, for Suetonius had seen his notebooks with their erasures (ibid. 52). At Naples his *première* brought thunderous applause from trained Greek bands; Greeks alone deserved to hear him, and he resolved on a Greek tour.

Meanwhile his extravagance, vanity, and fear, coupled with sense of power—'negauit quemquam principum scisse quid sibi liceret' (ibid. 37), made him unpopular. His helpers and associates were low-born, or Greek and Oriental freedmen, avaricious and arrogant. The expense of wars in Britain and Armenia compelled him to depreciate the coinage and rob the rich. The law of *maiestas* (q.v.) was revived (62); wealthy nobles, Faustus Sulla, Rubellius Plautus, and Torquatus Silanus, were executed on suspicion. A fire that ruined one-half of Rome (64) increased his unpopularity, as he seized the opportunity to build himself the colossal *Domus Aurea* (q.v.); rumours circulated that he had instigated the fire, and recited his own poems over the burning city, and Nero tried to make the Christians scapegoats (*see* CHRISTIANITY). By the end of 64 all classes had good reason to hate or fear him.

Hence a conspiracy to assassinate Nero and make C. Calpurnius Piso (q.v. 9) Emperor. The scheme was betrayed (65); Piso and his accomplices, Faenius Rufus, Seneca, Lucan, knights, tribunes, and soldiers were executed. But Nero now suspected all, and more judicial murders followed, including Ostorius Scapula, C. Petronius, *arbiter elegantiae*, and the Stoics Thrasea Paetus and Barea Soranus (qq.v.). Poppaea had died in 65, and next year Nero married Statilia Messallina (q.v. 2). In 66 Tiridates, kneeling, received the diadem of Armenia from him, but a Jewish revolt forced him to send Mucianus to govern Syria and Vespasian to pacify Judaea. By now Nero had left for Greece. The successful general Corbulo was ordered to meet him at Cenchreae and was forced to suicide, probably in Oct. 66; and two popular governors of the Germanies, the 'fratres Scribonii', soon met the same fate (Dio 63. 17). Meanwhile Nero had proclaimed 'Freedom for Greece': 'other emperors have freed cities, Nero alone a whole province' (*SIG* iii. 814). In 67 he toured the country, competing (invincibly) in the great games, collecting works of art, and starting to dig a Corinth canal. Amid the buffoonery executions continued; disaffection grew among the Western provinces and armies; and in Rome there was famine, perhaps because corn ships were being diverted to Greece. In the winter 67/8 the freedman Helius, who had been left in charge at Rome, crossed to Greece to summon Nero urgently home.

He reached Rome in January. In March C. Julius Vindex (q.v.), governor of Lugdunensis, rose against him; Galba (q.v. 1) in Spain declared himself 'legatus S.P.Q.R.', and in Africa Clodius (q.v. 2) Macer revolted. The situation might have been saved by military action, but Nero could only conceive fantastic schemes of revenge or of reducing his enemies to penitent tears by his art (Suet. *Nero*, 43). The Praetorians, bribed by their prefect Nymphidius (q.v.) Sabinus to acclaim Galba, deserted Nero, who fled from Rome and on 9 June 68 committed suicide.

A vicious ancestry and repressed childhood, followed by absolute power, made Nero vain, egotistic, and assertive. Yet his devotion to art was real. Some good he achieved, yet mainly where (as in the solution of the Armenian problem, or the rebuilding of Rome with wider streets) it was grandiose and involved glorification of himself. Jealous fear of all eminence—noble, military, or literary—forced him to persecution and murder; his crimes alienated all, nobles, people, and soldiery, while his phil-Hellenic outlook and theatrical performances shocked Roman sentiment. Greek longing for him is reflected in the mysterious belief that he would 'return'; for the rest the tribune's verdict holds good—'odisse coepi, postquam parricida matris et uxoris, auriga et histrio et incendiarius extitisti' (*Ann.* 15. 67).

ANCIENT SOURCES. Tac. *Ann.* 13–16, supplemented by Suet. *Nero*, and Dio Cass. 61–3. E. M. Smallwood, *Documents illustrating the Principates of Gaius, Claudius, and Nero* (1967).
MODERN LITERATURE. Analysis of sources: E. Ciaceri, 'Claudio e Nerone nelle storie di Plinio', in *Processi Politici* (1918), and A. Momigliano, 'Osservazioni sulle fonti per la storia di Caligola, Claudio, Nerone', *Rend. Linc.* 1932, 293 ff. Works on Nero: A. Boethius, 'The Neronian "nova urbs"', in *Corolla Archeologica* 1932; C. Pascal, *Nerone nella storia aneddotica e nella legenda* (1923); G. Schumann, *Hellenistische und griechische Elemente in der Regierung Neros* (1930); M. A. Levi, *Nerone e i suoi tempi* (1949); F. A. Lepper, 'Some reflections on the "Quinquennium Neronis"', *JRS* 1957, 95 ff.; B. H. Warmington. *Nero* (1969). M. P. C.; G. E. F. C.

**NERO** (2), GAIUS CLAUDIUS (*PW* 246) (*cos.* 207 B.C.), after serving under Marcellus in 214 B.C., took part in the siege of Capua as praetor (212) and propraetor (211). After the defeat of the elder Scipios he was sent to Spain, where he secured the land north of the Ebro (210). He again served under Marcellus in Italy (209). As consul in 207 with his former enemy M. Livius Salinator (q.v.) he took up his command against Hannibal in south Italy. When Hasdrubal's dispatches to Hannibal were intercepted, Nero boldly led part of his army by forced marches (traditionally 240 miles in six days) to join Livius. At the battle of Metaurus the two consuls defeated Hasdrubal, Nero turning the tide of battle by a skilful tactical movement. Nero reported his victory to Hannibal by flinging Hasdrubal's head into his camp. When Nero held the censorship with Livius in 204 the old enmity was renewed. He probably served on the

embassy which delivered the Senate's ultimatum to Philip V in 200. H. H. S.

**NERO** (3), TIBERIUS CLAUDIUS (*PW* 254), Cicero's choice for the hand of Tullia (q.v. 2) in 50 B.C., was quaestor in 48 and commanded Caesar's fleet in the Alexandrian war. In 46 he was entrusted with the settlement of veterans in Narbonese Gaul. In 44, however, he proposed that Caesar's murderers should be rewarded. Praetor in 41, he supported L. Antonius (q.v. 6) against Octavian, and took part in the defence of Perusia. Early in 40 he escaped, attempted in vain to procure a slave-rising in Campania, and joined Sextus Pompeius in Sicily with his wife Livia (q.v.) and infant son Tiberius, the future Emperor. Presently, disagreeing with Sextus, he joined Antony in Achaea, and returned to Rome after the Pact of Misenum (39). Shortly after this Octavian persuaded him to divorce Livia so that he might marry her himself. His second son Drusus (q.v. 3) was born about the time of the marriage. He died in 33.

Syme, *Rom. Rev.*, see index. T. J. C.

**NERO** (4), JULIUS (*PW* 146) CAESAR, the eldest of the three surviving sons of Germanicus and Agrippina, was, after the death of Tiberius's son Drusus in A.D. 23, at the age of 17, next in succession to the Principate. Twice commended to the Senate by Tiberius, he held the quaestorship, probably in 26, but in 29 Tiberius, believing the accusations of Sejanus against him and his mother, denounced him in a dispatch to the Senate. He was deported to Pontia and put to death there in 31. J. P. B.

**NERVA** (1), MARCUS COCCEIUS (*PW* 16), Roman Emperor A.D. 96–8, was grandson of M. Cocceius Nerva (q.v. 4), born at Narnia in Italy, probably in 30. As praetor designate in 65, he received *ornamenta triumphalia* on the suppression of the Pisonian conspiracy. Not discredited by his friendship with Nero, who admired his verses, he was *cos. I ord.* in 71 with Vespasian. He attained distinction as a jurist and became *cos. II ord.* in 90 with Domitian. The report of his temporary exile during Domitian's last years may be doubted.

When Domitian (q.v.) was assassinated on 16 Sept. 96 without leaving an indicated successor, public opinion reacted violently against his autocracy. Whether or not Nerva had been privy to the plot, the Senate regarded him as the best representative of its ideals, since he was a *nobilis* (q.v.), eloquent, peaceful, just, and likely to rule according to its view of the constitution. It therefore bestowed on him the imperial powers, including the title *Pater Patriae*. It also 'damned' Domitian's memory, annulled his official *acta*, ordered his statues to be destroyed, and prosecuted the informers who had been active in his later years. But Nerva failed to check the spirit of vendetta, itself encouraged by his own 'reformist' programme, which abolished treason charges and was reflected in such coin legends as *Libertas Publica, Salus, Aequitas, Iustitia*. Above all, he lacked military support; hence the wishful *Concordia Exercituum* coins. Unrest in the frontier armies was disturbing (cf. Pliny, *Ep.* 9. 13. 11; Philostr. *VS* 1. 7. 1) and the opposition of the Praetorians dangerous. The latter in 97 exacted the execution of Domitian's assassins. To placate both them and the legions, Nerva, who was himself childless and infirm, formally adopted Trajan (q.v.) in Sept. 97, and gave him powers almost equal to his own. On 25 Jan. 98 Nerva died, after sixteen months of morally blameless rule; he was consecrated, and his ashes were placed in Augustus' Mausoleum.

In his brief and inexperienced administration, Nerva sought to be enlightened and progressive, though he chiefly favoured Rome and Italy. But he was hampered by financial difficulties, probably occasioned by Domitian's buildings and campaigns. Nerva himself spent sixty million sesterces on land allotments for poor citizens; he is credited with creating the alimentary system (see ALIMENTA), which Trajan more probably initiated. The cost of postal services in Italy was taken over by the government. In Rome granaries were built; corn distribution and the aqueducts (q.v.) received attention. Legislation was just and humanitarian. Foreign policy was uneventful save for a brief Suebic war (Pliny, *Pan.* 8; cf. *ILS* 2720).

With the pendulum swinging sharply back from autocracy to constitutionalism, *libertas* and *principatus* (*res olim dissociabiles*; Tac. *Agr.* 3. 1) were reconciled, and Augustan ideals of government, the right of free speech, and the principle of dynastic adoption could in some measure be revived. But without military support Nerva could not uphold the complex burden of power—*ruens imperium super imperatorem* (Pliny, *Pan.* 6. 3). *Prouidentia Senatus*, expressed in his accession, required *Concordia Exercituum*, symbolized by the adoption of Trajan, for its fulfilment.

ANCIENT SOURCES. *Literary*: Dio Cass. bks. 67–8; Pliny, *Pan.*, *Epp.*; references in Suet. *Dom.*, Eutropius, bk. 8, Aur. Vict. *Caes.* 12–13, *Epit.* 12.
*Coins*: B.M. *Coins, Rom. Emp.* iii (1936); A. Merlin, *Les Revers monétaires de l'empereur Nerva* (1906); W. Kubitschek, *Anz. d. Akad. d. Wissensch. in Wien* lxx (1933), 4 ff.
MODERN LITERATURE. B. W. Henderson, *Five Roman Emperors* (1927), ch. 8; R. Paribeni, *Optimus Princeps* i (1926), ch. 5; A. Garzetti, *Nerva* (1950); Syme, *Tacitus*, see index; M. Hammond, *The Antonine Monarchy* (1959); for financial difficulties, G. Biraghi, *PP* 1951, 257 ff.; for the Suebic war, refs. in A. Piganiol, *Hist. de Rome⁵* (1962), 580; for his Forum, Nash, *Pict. Dict. Rome* i. 433. Bibliography: A. Garzetti, *L'impero da Tiberio agli Antonini* (1960), 658 ff.; A. Piganiol, *Hist. de Rome⁵* (1962), 303, 580.
C. H. V. S.; M. H.

**NERVA** (2), LUCIUS COCCEIUS (*PW* 12), of undistinguished family, was sent by Octavian to Antony (in Syria) in 41 B.C., returned with him to Italy in 40, and helped to negotiate the Pact of Brundisium. In the spring of 37 he accompanied Maecenas to Brundisium on another diplomatic mission, which led to the Pact of Tarentum. The journey is described by Horace (*Serm.* 1. 5). He was brother of Nerva (3) and probably of C. Cocceius Balbus, *consul suffectus* in 39. He himself is not known to have held any office.
Syme, *Rom. Rev.*, see index.
G. W. R.; T. J. C.

**NERVA** (3), MARCUS COCCEIUS (*PW* 13), supported L. Antonius (q.v. 6) in 41 B.C. Pardoned by Octavian, he held a command in the East, perhaps as governor of Asia 38/7, and was consul in 36. He attended the *ludi saeculares* in 17 B.C. as *quindecimvir sacris faciundis* (q.v.).
Syme, *Rom. Rev.*, see index.
T. J. C.

**NERVA** (4), MARCUS COCCEIUS (*PW* 14), probably grandson of (3), was *consul suffectus* and from A.D. 24 *curator aquarum*. A close friend of Tiberius, he accompanied him into retirement in 26 but in 33, disgusted (it was said) by Tiberius' society and financial policy, he starved himself to death. A distinguished lawyer, he developed the school founded by Antistius Labeo (q.v. 1) and later known as Proculian (see SABINUS 2); his son, Marcus, father of the Emperor, also belonged to it.
O. Lenel, *Palingenesis Juris Civilis* (1889) i. 787 ff.; H. F. Jolowicz, *Hist. Introd. to Rom. Law²* (1952), 388 ff.
T. J. C.

**NERVII,** a Belgic tribe occupying parts of Hainault and Flanders who were defeated by Caesar after a fierce struggle in 57 B.C. Under the Empire they contributed six cohorts to the *auxilia* and were graded as a *civitas libera* (Pliny, *HN* 4. 106). Numerous villas and potteries indicate general prosperity and their capital Bagacum

(*Bavay*) became an important commercial centre. After the barbarian invasions of the third century, however, its forum was converted into a *castellum*; much of the wall of this survives, together with an earlier cryptoporticus.
Caesar, *BGall.* 2. 15–28. C. Jullian, *Hist. de la Gaule* ii (1909), 462 ff.; Grenier, *Manuel* iii. 315 ff.
A. L. F. R.

**NESTOR** (1) (*Νέστωρ*), in mythology, surviving son of Neleus (q.v.), who lived to a great age (he is more than two generations old in *Iliad* 1. 250 ff., i.e. over 60, schol. ad loc., not 200 odd years, as Ov. *Met.* 12. 187 f., makes him), retaining some mental vigour and bodily strength long after his youth was passed. The *Iliad* gives a humorous, kindly portrait of an old and respected but rather ineffective man, full of advice generally either platitudinous or unsuccessful, the really useful counsellors being Odysseus and at times Diomedes (qq.v.). His tactics are archaic (*Il.* 4. 301 ff., cf. Lang, *World of Homer*, 58); he leads the embassy to Achilles with suggestions (9. 179), and when it fails has nothing more to say, except 10. 204 ff., where he advises sending a scout to discover what the Trojans are doing. He is very fond of long narratives of his early successes in war (as 11. 670 ff.) or sport (23. 626 ff.); a particularly delightful touch is his long speech of advice to his son Antilochus (23. 306 ff.), which he himself admits the younger man does not need. In the *Odyssey* (3. 4 ff.) he is safe at home in Pylos (q.v.), and there entertains Telemachus (q.v.). For the death of his son see ANTILOCHUS. His return was due to his realization that things were being ill-conducted after the fall of Troy and disaster impended (*Od.* 3. 165 ff.); at Achilles' funeral he stops the panic of the Greeks at the wailing of Thetis and her attendants (24. 50 ff.). Later works do no more than add details; it is he who settles the dispute over the arms of Achilles by suggesting that Trojan prisoners should be asked whether Aias or Odysseus was more to be dreaded (Quint. Smyrn. 5. 157, cf. 318; cf. schol. *Od.* 11. 547). So far as we know, there was no tradition of when or how he died; his grave was shown in Pausanias' day (Paus. 5. 36. 2).
For a discussion of the topographical problem of identifying Nestor's Pylos, *see* MESSENIA, PYLOS, *and* PYLOS in Triphylia.
H. J. R.

**NESTOR** (2), LUCIUS SEPTIMIUS, of Laranda, lived in the reign of Septimius Severus (A.D. 193–211), and wrote, among other works, an 'Ιλιὰς λειπογράμματος, in each of the twenty-four books of which one letter of the alphabet did not appear, and Μεταμορφώσεις (*Anth. Pal.* 9. 129, 364). Inscriptions show his relations with members of the Roman aristocracy. His son was the epic poet Peisander (q.v. 3) of Laranda.
M. Guarducci, *Riv. Fil.* 1961, 180 ff.; J. and L. Robert, *Rev. Ét. Grec.* 1944, 240; 1951, 204; R. Meiggs, *Roman Ostia* (1960), 346.
J. D. D.

**NEXUM,** a solemn transaction of the oldest Roman law, with copper and scales (*per aes et libram*: see MANCIPATIO), by which a man was reduced to bondage on account of debt. Because of the ambiguity of our literary sources (Varro, Livy), the nature and effects of this institution are obscure. It is disputed whether it was a loan, resulting in immediate execution (without judgement) against the debtor, if he did not repay at the appointed term, or whether it was a kind of self-sale or self-pledge by which the debtor enslaved himself to the creditor to guarantee him the payment of the debt. *Nexum* is mentioned in the XII Tables, but it fell out of use when *Lex Poetelia Papiria* (c. 326 B.C.) prohibited bondage and enchainment for private debts.
Immense literature: see F. de Zulueta, *Law Quarterly Review* xxix (1913) and citations in M. Kaser, *Röm. Privatrecht* i (1955), 148.
A. B.; B. N.

**NICAEA** (1), now *Iznik*, in Bithynia, was founded as Antigoneia by Antigonus (q.v. 1); Lysimachus renamed it Nicaea. Noted as an example of town-planning, it formed an exact square with four gates, the central position being occupied by a gymnasium (Strabo 12. 565–6). The gates, located at the four cardinal points, can be seen from the principal crossroads. Pompey assigned it a vast territory; it became a rival of Nicomedia (q.v.), and remained important under the Roman Empire (Pliny, *Ep.* 10. 39, consulted Trajan about work on its theatre and gymnasium). At the first of two church councils held there the Nicene Creed was formulated (A.D. 325).

Jones, *Cities E. Rom. Prov.*, see index; A. M. Schneider, *Istanbuler Forschungen* 1938, 1943. O. A. W. D.

**NICAEA** (2), now *Nice*, a Greek colony, was founded on Ligurian territory by Massilia, to whose jurisdiction it continued to belong. In 154 B.C., Q. Opimius relieved it and the neighbouring port Antipolis (modern *Antibes*) from attacks by Ligurians. Under the Empire it was overshadowed by its neighbour Cěměnělum (now *Cimiez*), which has substantial remains: an amphitheatre, shops, and baths.

R. G. L. M. Latouche, *Histoire du comté de Nice* (1932); *Carte archéologique de la Gaule romaine, FOR* i (1931), 8 ff., pl. iv. O. A. W. D.

**NICAENETUS** (*PW* 2) (probably second half of 3rd or beginning of 2nd B.C.), of Samos or Abdera (perhaps born at Abdera but migrated early in life to Samos). Athenaeus in quoting from Nicaenetus' *Epigrams* calls him 'the Epic Poet' and refers to his treatment in various works of Samian history. Nicaenetus also wrote a *Catalogue of Women* (Ath. 13. 590 b), and an epyllion called *Lyrkus* (Parth. 1), describing the adventures of that hero. The most attractive of the epigrams is that preserved by Athenaeus (15. 673 b), an invitation to a picnic at Hera's temple in Samos. *Anth. Pal.* 6. 225 is probably a literary reminiscence of Callimachus (fr. 126) and Apollonius Rhodius (*Argon.* 4. 1309, 1323, 1358).

TEXTS. Powell, *Coll. Alex.* 1–4; M. Gabathuler, *Hellenistische Epigramme auf Dichter* (1937), 65. E. A. B.

**NICANDER**, of Colophon. Nicander describes himself as 'reared by the snowy hill of Clarus' (*Ther.* 958), and as 'seated by the Clarian tripods of the Far-Shooter' (*Alex.* 11), and was apparently hereditary priest of Apollo of Clarus (*Vita*, citing Dionysius of Phaselis). His date is variously given. The confusion may be due in part to the existence of another Nicander, son of Anaxagoras, mentioned as an epic poet in an inscription of Delphi (*SIG* 452), which is best assigned to 258. The internal evidence of the two extant poems favours a date in the second century.

WORKS. Two didactic poems in hexameters, the *Theriaca* and *Alexipharmaca*, survive complete. The first is an account of various snakes and other poisonous creatures and the best remedies for their bites. The second enumerates vegetable, mineral, and animal poisons and their antidotes. The matter of both poems is taken from the prose-treatise of Apollodorus the Iologus (early 3rd c.). *Thebaica, Oetaica, Europia* (?), *Sicelia, Cimmerii* were all apparently Epics. Better known is the *Heteroioumena* (Metamorphoses), since it was used by Antoninus Liberalis and Ovid. The *Georgica*, on which Cicero (*De Or.* 1. 69) cites a flattering opinion of the *docti*, had some influence on Virgil. So perhaps had his *Melissurgica* (*On Apiculture*). More in the vein of the two extant poems were the *Prognostica* and *Collection of Cures*. The former was a versification of the (pseudo-) Hippocratean treatise on this subject (the *Suda*). All the above seem to have been in hexameters, but the *Ophiaca* (schol. *Ther.* 377), which recounted legends connected

with snakes, was probably in elegiacs, cf. frs. 31–2, as also was perhaps a poem on Hunting (frs. 97–100). Of three other works, *Aetolica, Colophoniaca*, and *About Poets* or *About Poets from Colophon*, it is not established whether they were in prose or verse. A collection of Glosses and a treatise on Temple Utensils were certainly in prose.

The *Suda* describes Nicander as 'grammarian, poet, and doctor'. The last is probably a false inference from the nature of many of his writings, but the order of the first two is significant. As the *Suda* later puts it, Nicander was a *metaphrastes*, i.e. converter into verse, of any topic that came to hand, whether a medical dissertation or a collection of *paradoxa*. To judge by the *Theriaca* and *Alexipharmaca*, Nicander had little gift and, indeed, little inclination for enlivening his arid themes with flights into real poetry. Digressions are few and similes almost non-existent. But neither was Nicander a scientist. He took over from his sources the bad with the good and thus we find in his poems absurd errors due to popular superstition alongside exact descriptions of plants and medical prescriptions so detailed and precise that the remedy could be made up today. But a grammarian of a sort Nicander undoubtedly was. He describes himself (*Ther.* 957) as *Homereius* and he can at least claim the title as being one of the most diligent seekers after Homeric glosses among the Alexandrians. Like Euphorion and the author of the *Alexandra* he has no scruples about altering the meanings of words nor about playing fast and loose with normal grammar. In metre his handling of the hexameter conforms in general to the rules laid down by Callimachus.

Nicander was read and cited by a certain number of later writers on the subjects with which he had dealt, but he received more attention from professional scholars drawn to him by the obscurity of his language and style. Theon wrote a *hypomnema* on him, as did Plutarch, and the names of other students are mentioned in the Scholia. The result is that the latter, especially those on the *Theriaca*, often contain valuable material.

TEXTS. A. S. F. Gow and A. F. Scholfield, *Nicander* (1953) (text, translation, notes, and general bibliography); O. Schneider, *Nicandrea* (1856).
GENERAL LITERATURE. W. Kroll, 'Nikandros' (10) and (11) in *PW* xvii. 250 ff.; H. Schneider, 'Vergleichende Untersuchungen zur sprachlichen Struktur der beiden erhaltenen Lehrgedichte des Nikander', *Klass. Phil. Stud.* 1962. E. A. B.; C. A. T.

**NICANOR** (1) of Stagira (*c.* 360 (?)–317 B.C.), perhaps shared with Alexander the tuition of Aristotle, whose daughter he later married. He may have commanded Alexander's Greek fleet (334), but he is first identified for certain in 324, when he brought to Greece several rescripts of Alexander, including the decree for the return of exiles. In 319 he commanded Cassander's garrison at Munychia, and from this position he soon secured the Piraeus also. He next commanded Cassander's fleet and defeated Cleitus (q.v. 2) near the Bosphorus (318); but he quarrelled with Cassander, who had him condemned to death for treason by the Macedonian army-assembly.

Diod. 17. 109; 18. 64, 68, 72, 75; H. Berve, *Alexanderreich* ii, no. 557. G. T. G.

**NICANOR** (2) of Alexandria (2nd c. A.D.), wrote on the punctuation of the *Iliad*, of the *Odyssey*, and of Callimachus; also a general work Περὶ στιγμῆς. He recognized three kinds of full stop, three of the comma, and two of the colon. In punctuation he dominates the Homeric scholia as Herodian does in accentuation, Aristonicus in Aristarchan textual criticism, and Didymus in erudition.

FRAGMENTS. Περὶ 'Ιλ. στιγμῆς, Friedlaender (1851); Περὶ 'Οδ. στιγμῆς, Carnuth (1875). P. B. R. F.

**NICARCHUS**, Greek epigrammatist, seems to have been nearly contemporary with Lucillius (q.v.), whom he imitates. The Greek Anthology contains about forty of his poems, some of them very coarse, like the mimes of his period, and some (e.g. *Anth. Pal.* 11. 251) very funny.

F. J. Brecht, *Motiv- und Typengeschichte des griech. Spottepigramms* (*Philol.* Suppl. 22, 1930). G. H.

**NICETA**, bishop of Remesiana (*Bela Palanka*, Yugoslavia) (late 4th c. A.D.), pioneer of Christianity among the barbarians and friend of Paulinus (q.v.) of Nola, wrote an *Explanatio symboli* (an important exposition of the Apostles' Creed) and other treatises; many impute to him the great Church hymn, *Te Deum laudamus*.

Ed.: A. E. Burn, *Niceta of R., Life and Works* (1905). A. H.-W.

**NICIAS** (1) (c. 470–413 B.C.), Athenian politician and general. During the period after the death of Pericles he became the principal rival of Cleon (q.v.) in the struggle for political leadership. He was a moderate and opposed the aggressive imperialism of the extreme democrats, his aim being the conclusion of peace with Sparta as soon as it could be attained on terms favourable to Athens. Elected frequently to serve as *strategos*, he led several expeditions in which, thanks to his cautious competence, he suffered no serious defeat and won no important victory. He was largely responsible for the armistice concluded in 423, and the Peace of 421 appropriately bears his name.

He now favoured a policy of retrenchment and objected to the ambitious schemes of Alcibiades (q.v.) who advocated Athenian intervention in the Peloponnese and later an expedition to Sicily. Despite his disapproval Nicias was appointed with Alcibiades and Lamachus (q.v.) to conduct this enterprise. Alcibiades was soon recalled, and little was accomplished in 415, but in 414 Syracuse was invested and almost reduced to capitulation. The death of Lamachus, the arrival of the Spartan Gylippus, and the inactivity of Nicias, now seriously ill, transformed the situation, and in spite of the efforts of Demosthenes (q.v. 1), who brought reinforcements in 413, the Athenians were themselves blockaded. Nicias, who refused to withdraw by sea until too late, led the vanguard in a desperate attempt to escape by land. His troops were overwhelmed at the river Assinarus, and he was subsequently executed. The narrative of Thucydides, though giving due credit to Nicias for his selfless devotion, shows very clearly that the Athenian disaster was largely due to the inadequacy of his military leadership.

Thuc. bks. 3–7; Plut. *Nicias*. A. B. West, *CPhil.* 1924, 124 ff. and 201 ff.; H. D. Westlake, *Individuals in Thucydides* (1968), chs. vi and xi. H. D. W.

**NICIAS** (2), painter, pupil of Antidotus (pupil of Euphranor), Athenian. Pliny dates 332 B.C. He painted statues for Praxiteles (about 340) and refused to sell a picture to Ptolemy (after 306). His works included Nemea (signed as encaustic), Necyomantea (after *Iliad* book 11), Alexander, Io, Andromeda. The Io and Andromeda are reflected in versions in Pompeii and Rome (Pfuhl, 646–7) which have a similar colour scheme to the fourth-century Alexander sarcophagus (Winter, *KB* 336–7). He advised the choice of large subjects such as cavalry and sea battles (contrast Pausias, q.v.). His treatment of light and shade made his figures stand out. According to Rumpf, 'diligentissime mulieres pinxit' (Pliny, *HN* 35. 130) means that he was the first to represent women plastically; monumental evidence supports this.

Overbeck, 1109, 1726, 1810–26; Pfuhl, 821; A. Rumpf, *JDAI* 1934, 6; *Malerei u. Zeichn.* 143. T. B. L. W.

**NICIAS** (3) of Nicaea, author of philosophic διαδοχαί

('successions' of philosophers), which have been thought to be the basis of Diogenes Laertius' work.

**NICOCHARES**, Athenian comic poet and son of Philonides (q.v.), produced Λάκωνες in 388 B.C. (hyp. 4 Ar. *Plut.*) and in *Galatea* (fr. 3) ridicules the same person as Ar. in *Plut.* 303 f. We have ten titles, several implying mythological burlesque; *Galatea* could possibly be one ancestor of Theoc. 11.

*FCG* ii. 842 ff.; *CAF* i. 700–4; *FAC* i. 926 ff. K. J. D.

**NICOLAUS OF DAMASCUS**, born of distinguished Greek family about 64 B.C. and liberally educated, became the adviser and court historian of Herod the Great, perhaps before 20 B.C., certainly from 14 to 4 B.C., accompanying him twice to Rome. Returning to private life after Herod's death, he re-emerged to represent Herod Archelaus in Rome, but did not resume court life.

Besides dramatic composition (tragedies and comedies) and writings on philosophy and natural science of a Peripatetic character, he published an autobiography, a panegyrical biography of Augustus' youth, and a Universal History in 144 books from the earliest times to the death of Herod the Great. It reached the Persian Empire in seven books (preserved in excerpts), treated the Mithridatic Wars in books 96–110, and with books 123–4, preserved in Josephus' *Jewish Antiquities* 14–17, came to Herod and described in full contemporary events to 4 B.C.; the introduction to Josephus' *Jewish War* is also based upon this work. The early narrative reproduced ultimately, among others, the tradition of Xanthus, Ctesias, perhaps Dinon and Hellanicus, Ephorus, Posidonius, Caesar; the whole work, the greatest World History since Ephorus, followed the rationalistic, rhetorical Ionic historiography of Ctesias, using also, especially in the treatment of Herod's family circumstances, the dramatic technique which marked his biographical writing.

*FGrH* ii A, 324; C, 229. A. H. McD.

**NICOMACHUS** (1), son of Aristotle; to him, according to an ancient account, Aristotle dedicated the *Nicomachean Ethics*; but possibly the name is due to his having edited the work, as Eudemus may have edited the *Eudemian Ethics*.

**NICOMACHUS** (2), New Comedy poet, whom the *Suda* confuses with a tragedian of the same name. Fr. 1 describes a cook magnifying his art.

*FCG* iv. 583 ff.; *CAF* iii. 386 ff.

**NICOMACHUS** (3) of Gerasa (*PW* 21), arithmetician and Neopythagorean (between A.D. 50 and 150), wrote: (1) *Introduction to Arithmetic* (ἀριθμητικὴ εἰσαγωγή), in two books, giving the Pythagorean theory of numbers (classification of numbers, odd, even, prime, etc., 'perfect' and 'friendly' numbers, 'polygonal' and 'pyramidal' numbers, arithmetical and geometrical progressions, means, etc., sum of the series of cube numbers); (2) Ἐγχειρίδιον ἁρμονικῆς (manual of harmony); (3) Θεολογούμενα ἀριθμητικῆς, on mystical properties of numbers. Extracts from this are preserved in the compilation of the same name attributed to Iamblichus (q.v. 2); (4) *Introduction to Geometry* (γεωμετρικὴ εἰσαγωγή, see *Introd. arith.* 2. 6. 1). This is entirely lost.

The *Introduction to Arithmetic* was translated into Latin by Apuleius (Cassiod. in Migne, *PL* lxx. 1208 B). Boethius' *De Institutione Arithmetica* is an adaptation of it. Commentaries on it were written by Iamblichus and Philoponus (6th c.).

EDITIONS. (1) by R. Hoche (Teubner, 1866); (2) in C. Jan, *Musici Scriptores Graeci* (1895); (3) *Theologoumena Arithmeticae*, ed. V. de Falco (Teubner, 1922).

TRANSLATION of (1), with commentary and introduction on life,

etc., by D'Ooge, Robbins, and Karpinski (U.S.A. 1926); Iamblichus' commentary, ed. Pistelli (1894); Philoponus' commentary, ed. R. Hoche (Leipzig, 1864: Bk. I) (Berlin, 1867: Bk. II).
COMMENT. Heath, *Hist. of Greek Maths.* i. 97 ff.　T. H.; G. J. T.

**NICOMACHUS** (4) **FLAVIANUS,** VIRIUS, Roman aristocrat of the fourth century A.D., a member of the Anician house, and a strong champion of the old paganism. After a distinguished public career he whole-heartedly supported the pagan regime of the usurper Eugenius, and on his defeat by Theodosius I committed suicide (A.D. 394). He wrote *Annals* which were possibly used by Ammianus (q.v.). His son, who was *praefectus urbi* for the first time in 393/4, shared in the revision of the text of Livy carried out by the Nicomachi and others; he married the daughter of Symmachus (q.v. 2).

*ILS* 2946-8. H. Bloch, *Conflict between Paganism and Christianity* (ed. A. Momigliano, 1963), ch. 8.　　　E. A. T.

**NICOMEDES,** the name of several kings of Bithynia:
(1) NICOMEDES I (*c.* 279–*c.* 255 B.C.), son of Zipoetes (before 315–*c.* 279), who had taken the royal title in 298, inherited his father's struggle against Antiochus I. He joined the Northern League, purchasing the aid of Heracleia by returning Cierus, invited the Gauls across the Bosporus, and assisted them to settle in Phrygia. He founded Nicomedia *c.* 265, and received honours at Cos and Olympia. At his death his son Ziaëlas (*c.* 255–*c.* 230) seized the throne in defiance of the guardians of his father's will in favour of his minor children, but continued his hellenizing policy.
(2) NICOMEDES II EPIPHANES (149–*c.* 127 B.C.), son of Prusias II (q.v.), cultivated the favour of the Greek cities, and, a faithful ally, aided Rome in the war against Aristonicus (133–129), but his request for territory in Phrygia was refused in favour of Mithridates V of Pontus.
(3) NICOMEDES III EUERGETES (*c.* 127–*c.* 94 B.C.), son of Nicomedes II. His gifts to Greek cities won him the title Euergetes. Yet because of the condition of Bithynia, when Marius requested aid from him against the Cimbri (104) he declared that most of his men had been seized and enslaved by Roman *publicani*, and the Senate decreed that no free man from an allied State should be held in slavery. His attempts to divide Paphlagonia with Mithridates VI of Pontus and to win Cappadocia by marrying Queen Laodice were foiled by Roman intervention (*see* ARIARATHES VII–IX).
(4) NICOMEDES IV PHILOPATOR (*c.* 94–75/4 B.C.), son of Nicomedes III. Mithridates VI of Pontus promptly drove him out in favour of his brother Socrates (*c.* 92), but a Roman commission under M'. Aquillius restored him (90–89). Under pressure from Aquillius and his Roman creditors he raided Pontic territory, and precipitated the First Mithridatic War (88). Restored by Sulla in 85/4, he ruled thereafter in such peace as Roman officials and business men allowed him. Julius Caesar was sent as envoy to him to get ships for the siege of Mytilene (81/80). At his death (late 75 or early 74) he bequeathed his kingdom to Rome.

App. *Mith.*; references in Polybius, Diodorus, and Memnon; *OGI* 340–6. Th. Reinach, *Trois royaumes de l'Asie mineure* (1888); *Mithridate Eupator* (1896); *L'Histoire par les monnaies* (1902), 167 ff.; Rostovtzeff, *Hellenistic World*, see index. Magie, *Rom. Rule Asia Min.* 311 ff. and index; G. Vitucci, *Il regno di Bitinia* (1953).
　　　　　　　　　　　　　　　　　　T. R. S. B.

**NICOMEDES** (5, *PW* 16), mathematician (?*c.* 200 B.C.), was the discoverer of the cochloidal or conchoidal curves, by means of which he solved the problem of trisecting the angle and that of doubling the cube. See especially Eutocius, *Comm. in Arch. de Sph. et Cyl.* (Heiberg[2]), 98 ff.

Heath, *Hist. of Greek Maths.* i. 238 ff., 260 ff.

**NICOMEDIA** ($Nικομήδεια$) was founded by Nicomedes I *c.* 265 B.C. to replace Astacus (on a more northerly site). It became the capital of the kingdom and of the Roman province of Bithynia. In 29 B.C. Augustus authorized a provincial temple to Rome and himself at Nicomedia which became the meeting-place of the provincial assembly. Adorned with splendid buildings, it accumulated titles of honour, and in the third century A.D. was styled 'greatest metropolis, leading city of Bithynia and Pontus, Hadrianic Severianic Nicomedia, twice *neocorus*, sacred asylum, friend and ally of the Roman people'. It suffered from frequent earthquakes, and in 256 or 257 was sacked by the Goths; but it received favours from several Roman Emperors and became the eastern capital of Diocletian. Its prosperity depended on an extensive and fertile territory, a good harbour, and its location on the trunk road from the Danube provinces to the eastern frontier. Nicomedians appear in almost every province of the Empire. In spite of these advantages Pliny's letters and Dio's speeches yield evidence of disordered finances and social discontent.

P. Ruge, *PW*, s.v. 'Nikomedeia'; Rostovtzeff, *Hellenistic World* (see index); Magie, *Rom. Rule Asia Min.* 305 and index.　T. R. S. B.

**NICOPHON,** Athenian comic poet, won one or more victories at the City Dionysia and the Lenaea in the last decade of the fifth century B.C. (*IG* ii[2]. 2325. 67, 131) and produced *Adonis* in 388 (hyp. 4 Ar. *Plut.*). We have six titles, mostly implying mythological burlesque (including *Birth of Aphrodite*; *see* POLYZELUS).

*FCG* ii. 848 ff.; *CAF* i. 775–80; *FAC* i. 934 ff.　　K. J. D.

**NICOPOLIS** was the name of several towns with a Greek-speaking population, built to commemorate Roman victories.
(1) *Nicopolis of Pontus,* the site of Pompey's victory in 66 B.C. over Mithridates, where he settled a mixed colony of veterans, wounded, and natives; the scene also of Pharnaces' victory over Caesar's lieutenant Domitius in 47. Being a strategic point in the system of frontier roads it grew in importance under the Empire, received *ius Italicum*, and finally became the metropolis of Lesser Armenia.
(2) *Nicopolis ad Istrum,* on the main axial road through Thrace from Philippopolis to the Danube, founded by Trajan after the Dacian Wars.
(3) *Nicopolis in Epirus,* on the isthmus of the Bay of Actium. Augustus created this town by sweeping into it the population of the neighbouring Greek communities. It secured much of the former trade of Ambracia and was the scene of the 'ludi Actiaci', a quadrennial festival of equal rank with the Olympian Games, under Spartan stewardship. Its theatre is well preserved.

F. Cumont, *Studia Pontica* ii (1906) 302 ff.; Jones, *Cities E. Rom. Prov.* 152, 172; Magie, *Rom. Rule Asia Min.*, see index. (3) Hammond, *Epirus,* 62.　　　　　　　　　　M. C.; T. R. S. B.

**NICOSTRATUS** (1), Middle Comedy poet, regarded by Apollodorus as a son of Aristophanes. Some of the twenty-one titles known may be of comedies by Nicostratus (2); they are unusually intriguing, e.g. *Hesiod*, $Παρακολυμβῶσα$, $Ψευδοστιγματίας$, but the forty-odd citations give very little away.

*FCG* iii. 278 ff.; *CAF* ii. 219 ff.; iii. 739; *FAC* ii. 28 ff.　K. J. D.

**NICOSTRATUS** (2), New Comedy poet, mentioned in a list of Lenaean victors after Menander, Diphilus, and Philippides, and probably as winner of the second prize at the Dionysia in 311 B.C. (*IG* ii[2]. 2325. 165, 2323a. 43). On a Delian inscription of 280 B.C. (*IG* xi. 107) he is named with two other comic poets, Philemon and Ameinias.

See reference under NICOSTRATUS (1).　　W. G. W.; W. G. A.

**NIGIDIUS FIGULUS,** PUBLIUS (praetor 58 B.C.), scholar and mystic, 'iuxta Varronem doctissimus' (Gellius), friend of Cicero, active supporter of Pompey, died in exile in 45. He displayed an enthusiasm for Pythagoreanism and along with it astrology, and was said to engage in magic. He wrote comprehensive works on grammar (*Commentarii grammatici*), theology (in particular *De dis*), and various branches of natural science. His scholarship was too abstruse to win public esteem and he was eclipsed by his contemporary, Varro (q.v. 2). Fragments of his works survive in Gellius and other writers. *See also* SCHOLARSHIP, LATIN.

TEXT. A. Swoboda, *P. Nigidii Figuli operum reliquiae* (1889). A. della Casa, *Nigidio Figulo* (1963).                     A. H.-W.

**NIKE,** the goddess of Victory in Greek religion. Nike is first mentioned by Hesiod (*Th.* 383) as daughter of the Titan Pallas and of Styx, and as sister of Zelos, Kratos, and Bia (Rivalry, Strength, and Force). With these she was honoured by Zeus because she fought on the side of the gods against the Titans (q.v.). She is here an abstraction or symbol of decisive victory for the gods. The poets of athletic contests see Nike in vivid terms. Bacchylides (11. 1 Kenyon) depicts her standing next to Zeus on Olympus and adjudging the award for 'areta' to gods and men. The victorious athlete sinks into the arms of Nike (Pind. *Nem.* 5. 42). Here Nike is already victory of an athletic, not only a military, contest. She rules over all contests. She is invoked by the chorus of Aristophanes (*Eq.* 581) and on vases she crowns women of victorious beauty or craftsmen of extraordinary skill.

Statues of Nike begin in the archaic period with the famous one from Delos. Some scholars have connected this statue with the base inscribed by Archermus, the sculptor who is said to have first represented Nike as winged (schol. Ar. *Av.* 574). The wooden image in the temple of Athena Nike was unwinged (Paus. 3. 15. 7). The Persian Wars resulted in a great popularity of Nike. The Athenians dedicated her statue in Delphi after the battle of Salamis (Hdt. 8. 121) and she becomes very frequent on vases. She decorates a trophy, writes on the helmet, aids in preparations for the fight, the battle, or the athletic or musical contest, and brings the sacrifice after the victory. She stands on or flies over the chariot of the victorious mortal charioteer (Bacchyl. 3. 5) or serves as charioteer for Heracles on his way to Olympus. The invention of this type of small flying Nike enabled the artists to use her as an attribute. Thus she appeared in Phidias' images of Athena Parthenos and of Zeus of Olympia. These masterpieces are lost as well as the later paintings of Nicomachus and Apelles (Pliny, *HN* 35. 108. 93), but the famous Nike by Paeonius found in Olympia, the balustrade of the temple of Athena Nike in Athens (R. Carpenter, *The Sculpture of the Nike Temple Parapet*, U.S.A. 1929), and the Hellenistic Nike of Samothrace (J. Charbonneaux, *CRAcad. Inscr.* 1950, 262) show the fire and enthusiasm with which Greek artists conceived the goddess.

As befits a race fond of competition the Greeks invoked Nike in most flattering terms and she had cults in Olympia (Paus. 5. 14. 8), Ilion, Tralles, and elsewhere. She enjoyed favour with Hellenistic rulers and as Victoria was worshipped by the Romans. As symbol of Victory over death Nike was a favourite motif of Roman allegorical art.

Baudrillart, *Les Divinités de la Victoire* (1894); H. Bulle in Roscher, *Lex.*, s.v.; G. Oikonomos, 'Αρχ. 'Εφ. 1939–41, 97; L. Alscher, *Die fliegende Nike* (1942); L. Daly, *Studies presented to D. M. Robinson II* (1953), 1124. D. M. Lewis, *BSA* 1955, 1 ff. For Palladas, A. Cameron, *JHS* 1964, 54 ff.  G. M. A. H.; J. R. T. P.

**NILE,** Egypt's river (explored by ancient Egyptians to the Upper Blue Nile and the confluence of the Bahr-el-Gazal with the White Nile), was known to Homer as 'Aegyptos river', to Hesiod first as Νεῖλος. It was opened to westerners after 665 B.C. Cambyses the Persian (*c.* 525 B.C.) reached the desert south of Koroska, but Herodotus knew little beyond Meroë. None knew the cause of summer-time flooding; Anaxagoras' conclusion (melting snows) was good guess-work. Ignorant folk believed that the Nile was joined to the Indus, until Alexander's explorations disproved this. False ideas about the flooding continued, though Aristotle guessed correctly. The foundation of Alexandria and Ptolemaic trading up the river and through the Red Sea changed matters. The White Nile (Astapous), the Blue Nile, and the sources of the Astaboras (*Atbara*) became known, and flooding by waters from Abyssinian heights was confirmed. According to Juba, the Nile rose in Mt. Atlas and emerged in east Sudan after two journeys underground. Explorers sent by Nero passed the confluence of the Sobat with the White Nile, but were blocked by sudd (masses of decayed plants). Later, the Blue Nile was further explored. Lastly, *c.* A.D. 100 a traveller named Diogenes (Ptol. *Geog.* 1. 9. 3–4, etc.) reported from the E. African coast that inland 'Mountains of the Moon', snow-capped, supplied two lakes; from each flowed a stream uniting into the Nile. This vaguely indicates Lakes Victoria and Albert, the Ruwenzori Range, and Mts. Kenya and Kilimanjaro.

Cary–Warmington, *Explorers*, 165 ff.; (Pelican) 202 ff.; E. H. Warmington, *Greek Geography* (1934), index; M. Cary, *Geographic Background*, 207 ff. (but he is wrong about Coptos); Thomson, *Hist. Anc. Geog.*, esp. 275 ff.; Hyde, *Greek Mariners*, 255 ff.    E. H. W.

**NIMBUS,** a circular cloud of light which surrounds the heads of gods, emperors (Serv. *Aen.* 2. 616; 3. 587), and heroes. The belief that light radiates from a sacred or divine person is a common one and the nimbus only a special form which was developed in classical religion and art. Assyrian art, for instance, represents some gods with rays around their shoulders (Th. Dombart, *Journ. Soc. Oriental Research Toronto* 1932, 38) and Greek art shows deities of light, such as Helios, with a radiate crown. Greek vases and Etruscan mirrors of the fifth century afford the earliest examples of nimbus, often combined with the crown of rays; under the Roman Empire the nimbus becomes very common. The temple of the Palmyrene gods in Palmyra has an early dated example (A.D. 32). Almost all pagan gods of any importance are occasionally represented with a nimbus in Pompeian wall paintings, African mosaics, and the painting and reliefs of Palmyra and Dura. In late ancient art emperors, consuls, and other dignitaries, and sometimes even portraits of dead commoners have the nimbus. In Christian art only Christ was represented with nimbus at first, but it was soon extended to the Virgin, the major saints, and angels.

Cabrol–Leclercq, *Dict. ant. chrét.* xii. 1272.    G. M. A. H.

**NINNIUS CRASSUS** (? early 1st c. B.C.), author of a translation of the *Iliad*.

Baehr. *FPR* 283; Morel, *FPL* 51.

**NIOBE** (Νιόβη), in mythology, daughter of Tantalus and wife of Amphion (qq.v.). They had a large family, six sons and six daughters (Hom. *Il.* 24. 604, the oldest mention of her, which seems to imply that the story was already well known and she a stock type of bereavement), or seven of either sex (Ov. *Met.* 6. 182–3); the number varies in different accounts (see for this and other details Apollod. 3. 45 ff. and Sauer in Roscher's *Lexikon*, s.v.). She boasted that she was at least equal to Leto (q.v.), who had borne but two children, Apollo and Artemis. Thereupon the two children of Leto killed all the children of Niobe. According to Homer, Zeus also turned all the people into stone; Niobe lived long enough to eat at least one meal when 'wearied with tear-shedding', and then became a stone which is still on Mt. Sipylon. The gods buried the children on the tenth day. These details, except Niobe's own metamorphosis, do not appear in later accounts. The stone, according to Pausanias (1. 21. 3), was a natural formation looking somewhat like a woman; cf., however, modern opinions in Frazer ad loc. *See* METAMORPHOSIS.

It is fairly evident that the story, the kernel of which must be very old, has been modified in the interests of genealogy. It can hardly be that the daughter of Tantalus of Sipylon was originally married to Amphion of Thebes, of whom Telesilla (ap. Apollod. loc. cit. 47) gets rid again by making him perish with the children. Again for genealogical reasons the pathos is modified by making a son and a daughter survive (ibid. 46 f.).

In art the deaths of the children and the grief of their mother at the sight are a common and favourite subject.

See Roscher's *Lexikon*, s.v. H. J. R.

**NIREUS** (Νιρεύς), in mythology, the commander of a small party (three ships) from Syme (*Iliad* 2. 671 ff.); he was the son of Charops and Aglaia and the handsomest man in the Greek army except Achilles, but a weakling. He was killed by Eurypylus, son of Telephus (Quint. Smyrn. 6. 368 ff.). H. J. R.

**NISIBIS** (modern *Nusaybin*), a city in Mygdonia in north-eastern Mesopotamia. After the end of the Assyrian Empire it disappears from history until the Hellenistic age when Seleucus Nicator settled Macedonians on the old site. Its new name, Antioch of Mygdonia, first appears on coins of Antiochus IV, but soon the city resumed its older name. Nisibis was part of the empire of Tigranes the Great (q.v. 1) when Lucullus' troops stormed it (68 B.C.); later Artabanus III recovered it for Parthia and assigned it to a vassal, Izates of Adiabene. Trajan's ephemeral occupation apart, it first became a Roman city as a result of Verus' campaign. Septimius Severus rewarded it for its loyalty to him by making it a *colonia* (Cass. Dio 75. 3. 2) and it has the title *metropolis* on its coins from Severus Alexander onwards. As a frontier fortress city it suffered many vicissitudes during the wars of the Romans against the Parthians and Sassanid Persians, whose king Sapor II thrice failed to take it (338, 346, and 350). Finally, after Julian's disastrous campaign, Jovian ceded it to Persia, its population, loyal and Christian, preferring to abandon the city rather than live under Persian rule (363) (Amm. Marc. 25. 7–9). It was partly resettled with Persians, although it was the Arab element that gradually became dominant. Never again recovered by Byzantium it fell to the invading Arabs in 640.

Nisibis was always an important centre of trade. In the treaty of 297/8 between Diocletian and the Persian Narses it was specified that Nisibis should be the only Roman market for trade exchanges between the two empires, and fourth- and fifth-century regulations continued to enforce this monopoly (*Cod. Iust.* iv. 63. 4). A school of Syriac literature initiated by Ephraem (q.v.) of Nisibis in the fourth century continued to flourish long after the Arab conquest.

Jones, *Cities E. Rom. Prov.*, ch. 9; G. F. Hill, *BM Coins, Arabia etc.* E. W. G.

**NISUS.** (1) Legendary king of Megara, whose life together with the fate of the city depended on a lock of red hair on his head. His daughter Scylla cut this off and betrayed the city to Minos king of Crete who was besieging it, either for a bribe (Aesch. *Cho.* 613–22) or for love of him (Ov. *Met.* 8. 1–151). Nisus was turned into a sea-eagle, Scylla into a bird *ciris* (see D'A. W.

Thompson, *Gloss. of Gk. Birds²* (1936), s.v.; Hyg. *Fab.* 198. 4 calls it a fish) pursued by him. The story is told at length in the pseudo-Virgilian poem *Ciris*. See also Ov. *Met.* 8. 6 ff., Strabo 8. 6. 13, Stith Thompson, K 976. Cf. AMPHITRYON.

(2) Son of Hyrtacus, hero of a famous episode in Verg. *Aen.* 9. 176–502; also prominent in the foot-race in 5. 286–361.

(3) Roman grammarian of the second half of the first century, used by Suetonius and Velius Longus; his works are now lost. R. A. B. M.

**NOBILIOR**, MARCUS FULVIUS (*PW* 91) (*cos.* 189 B.C.), the victor over Aetolia, was curule aedile in 196, praetor in 193 in Spain, subduing Oretania and Carpetania (193–192), and as consul in 189 defeated the Aetolians, capturing Ambracia and sending its art treasures to Rome. In 188 he won Cephallenia, taking Same, and intervened between the Achaeans and Sparta. He triumphed, despite complaints about Ambracia, building the temple of Hercules Musarum. Censor in 179 with M. Aemilius Lepidus, he reformed the *Comitia Centuriata* and carried out a large building programme. A patron of Greek culture (Ennius accompanied him to Aetolia), he was attacked by Cato. One son was consul in 159, another consul in 153 at Numantia.

De Sanctis, *Stor. Rom.* iv. 1. 210, 456, 605; Scullard, *Rom. Pol.* 141 ff., 180 ff., 266. A. H. McD.

**NOBILITAS.** When the Plebs (q.v.) attained legal equality with the Patricians (q.v.), the magistracies were in theory open to all citizens (cf. Cic. *Sest.* 137). Yet in the lists of magistrates the same families tend to recur, while newcomers always form a slow trickle. Gradually the patrician aristocracy was transformed, largely with its own co-operation, into a new oligarchy increasingly plebeian in composition; though socially patrician status always conferred special distinction. These new rulers were the *nobiles*: men 'known' to all, both by name and even by features, since the masks of their ancestors (*see* IMAGINES) were a common sight in the streets of Rome. These men naturally had an advantage in elections; and it was increased by their network of family and client relationships. Thus they came to have a right to be elected, until by the late Republic the defeat of a *nobilis* by a social inferior might by itself raise a presumption of corrupt practices (see Cic. *Mur.* and *Planc.*).

The word 'nobilis'—never a strict term of law—became increasingly exclusive. As praetorships multiplied, it was only the consulate that gave a family this final distinction: as Sallust says (*Jug.* 63. 7, with tendentious exaggeration), it was regarded as 'polluted' if held by an outsider. In fact, though exclusive, the *nobilitas* never became a closed caste. At all times a proportion of non-noble men of senatorial and occasionally even of non-senatorial birth (*see* NOVUS HOMO) rose to the consulate, usually with the support of noble families (*see*, e.g., CATO 1, CICERO 1). These men were, in general, perfectly absorbed into the oligarchy, thus ensuring its vitality.

Under the Empire the word was purely a social label; it was still chiefly applied to the descendants (on either side) of republican consuls, though sometimes slightly extended. *Nobiles* were raised to (usually harmless) dignity by 'good' Emperors and jealously persecuted by 'bad' Emperors. Most noble families were extinguished by the Antonine period; though the Acilii Glabriones survived to the fourth century A.D.

M. Gelzer, *Kl. Schr.* i (1962), 1 ff. id., *The Roman Nobility* (1969); A. Afzelius, *Class. & Med.* 1938, 40 ff.; 1945, 150 ff. E. B.

**NOLA**, in Campania 20 miles east of Naples. Oscan-speaking Nola came under Roman domination *c.* 313

B.C. It resisted Hannibal, but became a Sabellian stronghold in the Social War (90 B.C.). After 80 B.C. it was thoroughly romanized. Augustus died here (A.D. 14). Destroyed by Vandals (A.D. 455), it recovered and is still a populous town. E. T. S.

**NOMENTUM,** modern *Mentana*: old Latin town on the edge of Sabine territory, 14 miles north-east of Rome. Rome annexed it in 338 B.C. Famed in imperial times for its wine and country villas, it was linked with Rome by the Via Nomentana, which crossed the Anio (q.v.) by a still standing bridge. E. T. S.

**NOMOPHYLAKES** (νομοφύλακες) were a kind of official known to have existed in several Greek cities. In Athens, according to one authority (Philochorus), the office was instituted when Ephialtes (q.v. 1) deprived the Aeropagus (q.v.) of most of its powers in 462/1 B.C.; but this statement is disbelieved by some modern scholars, and even if it is true the office cannot have become permanent, since it seems not to have existed in the time of Demosthenes and Aristotle. But it certainly existed in the late fourth century; it was probably instituted, or reinstituted, in the 320s. At this period there were seven *nomophylakes*. Their chief duty was to attend meetings of the *boule* (q.v.) and the *ekklesia* (q.v.) and veto actions or proposals which seemed to them illegal or contrary to the interests of Athens. They had some kind of power to check magistrates who acted illegally, and they also had some religious functions.

W. S. Ferguson, *Klio* 1911, 271 ff.; F. Jacoby, *FGrH* iii B, Suppl. (1954), commentary on 328 F 64. D. M. M.

**NOMOS** (1) (νομός) was the Greek name for the ancient administrative districts of Egypt; under the Seleucids the term is also found in Palestine, where it was probably introduced by the Ptolemies. The Egyptian *nomoi* probably numbered thirty-six in the third century B.C., but by the third century A.D. had increased to nearly sixty. They were subdivided into toparchies, and these into villages. Each was governed by a στρατηγός, who completely overshadowed the old native governor (νομάρχης). He was assisted by many departmental officials. Of these only the royal scribe (βασιλικὸς γραμματεύς) retained any importance under Roman rule. The *nomoi* were abolished *c.* A.D. 300, becoming the territories of the *metropoleis* (q.v.).

H. Gauthier, *Les Nomes d'Égypte depuis Hérodote jusqu'à la conquête arabe* (1935). A. H. M. J.

**NOMOS** (2). The word νόμος, applied originally to a tune, was applied especially to a type of melody invented by Terpander as a setting for texts taken from the epic (Procl. ap. Phot. *Bibl.* 320 a, 32 ff.). Such νόμοι could be used for the flute or for the lyre. Later the word was used for a choral composition constructed astrophically like Timotheus' *Persae*.

Cf. U. von Wilamowitz-Moellendorff, *Timotheos: Die Perser* (1903), 89 ff.; H. Färber, *Die Lyrik in der Kunsttheorie der Antike* (1936), i. 33 f., ii. 37 ff. C. M. B.

**NOMOTHETAI** (νομοθέται) was a general word for 'law-makers', but in Athens it was used especially for a committee appointed to draft or revise laws. In the fifth and fourth centuries B.C. the following committees are known to have had this title, and there may well have been others on different occasions.

(*a*) In 411 *nomothetai* were appointed in connexion with the drawing up of the constitution of the Five Thousand (Thuc. 8. 97. 2).

(*b*) In 403 *nomothetai* were appointed by the *boule* (q.v.) to draft and publish proposed additions to the laws; and another body of 500 *nomothetai* was elected by the *demoi*

(q.v.) to consider these proposals in conjunction with the *boule* (Andoc. 1. 82–4).

(*c*) In the fourth century the *ekklesia* (q.v.) at the beginning of each year voted whether the existing laws were satisfactory or not, and if it was decided that any were unsatisfactory *nomothetai* were appointed from among the year's jurors (*see* DIKASTERION) to consider proposals for new laws to replace the rejected ones; men were appointed to address the *nomothetai* in defence of the old laws, so that the procedure resembled an ordinary trial by jury (Dem. 24. 20–3).

(*d*) In the fourth century also it was the duty of the *thesmothetai* (q.v.) each year to examine the laws and, if they found any anomalies or inconsistencies, to ask for the appointment of *nomothetai* to deal with them (Aeschin. 3. 38–40). D. M. M.

**NONIUS MARCELLUS** (early 4th c. A.D.), lexicographer and grammarian. The first twelve books of his *De compendiosa doctrina* (ed. W. M. Lindsay, 3 vols., 1903) deal with points of grammar (e.g. *de numeris et casibus*), books 13 to 20 (but book 16 is lost) with miscellaneous information (e.g. *de genere nauigiorum*). The material is arranged with more or less strictness in alphabetical order and each topic is illustrated by quotations. The foundation of the work seems to have been Nonius' own excerpting from a range of authors which included many republican poets. These authors he used in a stereotyped order of his own. In addition he had access to some work like that of Flavius Caper from which he took other citations. For many fragments of early writers, and especially of Varro's poetry, Nonius is our chief authority.

Cf. Schanz–Hosius, § 826; W. M. Lindsay, *CR* 1906, 440; and for Nonius' sources and methods of citation, F. della Corte, *La poesia di Varrone ricostituita* (1938). J. F. M.

**NONNUS** of Panopolis in Egypt (5th c. A.D. ?), the main surviving exponent of an elaborate, metrically very strict style of Greek epic that was popular between the third and sixth centuries. His *Dionysiaca* in forty-eight books is a monotonously lush jungle of mythological learning and sensual description, much influenced by the novel (q.v.) and by epideictic rhetoric. The greater part (books 13–40) is devoted to Dionysus' conquest of India. Nonnus is probably also the author of a curious hexameter version of St. John's Gospel in a similar style.

*Dionysiaca*. TEXT with translation). R. Keydell (1959); W. H. D. Rouse (1940, Loeb).
*Paraphrase of St. John's Gospel*. TEXT. A. Scheindler (1881).
GENERAL. G. d'Ippolito, *Studi Nonniani* (1964). M. L. W.

**NORBA,** on an inaccessible bluff overlooking the Pomptine Marshes (q.v.) south-east of Rome, received a Latin Colony (492 B.C.) to contain the Volsci (q.v.). Although always loyal to Rome, it was destroyed by Sulla (82 B.C.) and never recovered. Fine polygonal walls survive, and stylobates (fourth century B.C. and later).

G. Lugli, *La tecnica edilizia romana* (1957), 137 ff. E. T. S.

**NORBANUS** (1, *PW* 5) (**BALBUS** ?), GAIUS, Popularis with a non-Latin *nomen*, began his career with the tribunate (103 B.C.), in which he successfully prosecuted Caepio (q.v. 1), using force against the intercession of Didius (q.v. 1) and a L. Cotta. Accused of *maiestas* for this (probably 95) by Sulpicius (q.v. 1), in an Optimate attack on the interests of Marius, he was defended by Antonius (q.v. 1), whose quaestor he had been (probably 99), and acquitted (see especially Cic. *De or.* 2. 197 f.). Praetor *c.* 91, he kept Sicily safe during the Social War and defeated a rebel attack on Rhegium (87). Consul (83) with L. Scipio Asiagenus (to symbolize the unity of patrician nobles and *novi homines* behind the government), he was twice defeated by Sulla and Metellus (q.v. 7) in Campania, and as proconsul (82) by Metellus near Faventia. He fled to Rhodes and there committed suicide to escape extradition.

F. Münzer, *Hermes* 1932, 260; Badian, *Stud. Gr. Rom. Hist.*, see index; E. S. Gruen, *CPhil.* 1966, 105 ff.　　　　　E. B.

**NORBANUS** (2, *PW*, s.v. Appius 13), A. LAPPIUS MAXIMUS, *cos. suff.* A.D. 86, *cos. II suff.* 95, as legate of Lower Germany crushed the rebellion of Antonius Saturninus (q.v. 3) in 89, and won great credit for destroying the conspirators' papers before Domitian arrived. Although he won a second consulate, a rare honour in this period, he does not seem to have been employed again by Domitian or by subsequent emperors.

E. Ritterling, *Fasti des römischen Deutschland unter dem Prinzipat* (1932), 24.　　　　　G. E. F. C.

**NORICUM,** a Roman province in the Alps, south of the Danube, between Raetia and Pannonia. The root of the word is Illyrian, as are pre-Roman finds in the interior and the east. This Illyrian element, however, was celticized from the south (3rd/2nd c. B.C.) and from the Danube (2nd/1st c. B.C.). Though the Celtic Taurisci were the chief tribe, Noricum (apparently derived from the Celtic *Norici* dwelling round *Noreia*, the ancient capital) became in the first part of the second century B.C. the name of the Celtic federal State, which had its own coinage. It was of considerable importance in Caesar's time, as shown by the fact that Caesar accepted aid from Noricum in 49 B.C., and that Ariovistus' second wife was the daughter of the king of Noricum. To secure the northern frontier of Italy, the Taurisci north of the Ocra were made tributary (35 B.C.), and then the kingdom of Noricum was peaceably incorporated into the Roman Empire by P. Silius Nerva, governor of Illyricum (16 B.C. or later). Perhaps for some time under a *praefectus civitatum*, Noricum was put under an equestrian governor who resided at Virunum (q.v.) and commanded the *auxilia* and the *iuventus Noricorum*. The first known governor is A. Trebonius (*CIL* iii. 4810; cf. *JÖAI* xxix (1935), Bbl. 261). Owing to the Marcomannic wars the newly raised Legio II Italica was quartered in Noricum (first at Albing, before 191 at Lauriacum), and its commander became the governor of Noricum as a *legatus Augusti pro praetore*, residing at Ovilava; the financial *procurator* remained at Virunum. After Gallienus had eliminated senators from military command, Noricum was put again under equestrian administration (cf. the governor *Ael(ius) Restutus v(ir) p(erfectissimus) a(gens) v(ices) p(raesidis)*, *RLÖ* xi (1910), 151 f., no. 42). Under Diocletian Noricum was divided into two parts under *praesides*: *N. Ripense* on the Danube and *N. Mediterraneum* in the south, the former also having a *dux* as military commander. In the fifth century Noricum was overrun by German tribes and was occupied after 493 by Goths, by Franks (c. 536), by Langobards (568), and shortly before 600 by Slavs and Avars.

INSCRIPTIONS. *CIL* iii (1873–1902) and V. Hoffiller and B. Saria, *Antike Inschriften aus Jugoslavien*, Heft I, *Noricum und Pannonia Superior* (1939).
U. Täckholm, *Studien über den Bergbau der römischen Kaiserzeit* (Uppsala, 1937), 108 ff. On the site of Noreia, see E. Polaschek, *PW*, s.v. For recent research and discussion of problems: E. Swoboda, *Carnuntum, seine Geschichte und seine Denkmäler³* (1964), 221 ff.; G. Alföldy, 'Taurisci und Norici', *Hist.* 1966, 224 ff.　　F. A. W. S.

**NORTIA,** an Etruscan goddess, the native form of whose name is uncertain. Her chief place of worship was Volsinii (Livy 7. 3. 7, cf. Wissowa, *RK* 288, for archaeological evidence). The most remarkable rite was the periodical driving of a nail into the wall of the temple (Livy, loc. cit.). The purpose was certainly not, as Livy there supposes, merely to serve as a record of time, one

nail being driven each year, but rather (cf. ibid. 3–4; Warde Fowler, *Roman Festivals* (1899), 234 f.; Latte, *RR* 154) to nail down evil and make it harmless (here an epidemic; perhaps at Volsinii all the ill of the past year). Another ancient interpretation was that it signified the unchanging fixedness of destiny; hence Nortia was identified with Fortuna (schol. on Juvenal 10. 74), and by implication with Necessitas (Hor. *Carm.* 1. 35. 17 ff.).
　　　　　H. J. R.

**NOSSIS** (fl. *c.* 300 B.C.), Greek poetess from south Italian Locri, has twelve epigrams in the Greek Anthology, mostly inscriptions for votive offerings and for works of art. She praises love like Mimnermus (*Anth. Pal.* 5. 170) and connects herself with Sappho (7. 718), but her quatrains are frail trifles. There may have been more poetic energy in her lyrics, which have not survived.

Gow and Page, 2791 ff. G. Carugno, *Giornale Italiano di Filologia* 1957; G. Luck, *MH* 1954; Wilamowitz, *Hell. Dicht.* i. 135 f.　　G. H.

**NOTITIA DIGNITATUM.** The Notitia Dignitatum is preserved in a copy, made in 1551, of an original MS., now lost, which existed at Speir. It is divided into two parts, covering the Eastern and Western halves of the Roman Empire as it was divided in A.D. 395. Each part contains an index and a series of entries for each of the high offices of State from the praetorian prefects to provincial governors in order of precedence; but for provincial governors (*consulares, correctores, praesides*) one specimen only of each grade is given. The entries give the title and rank of the officer, a brief description of his functions, including a list of his subordinate officers; in the case of military officers a list of units under his command; a list of his *officium*; and in the East the number of postal warrants to which he was entitled. Each entry is accompanied by an illustration, showing the insignia of the office, and in the case of *magistri militum* (q.v.) the shields of their regiments, and in the case of *duces* (see DUX) their forts. Some pages were missing from the archetype, and certain offices, including both *praepositi sacri cubiculi*, are therefore lacking.

The document is clearly the '*notitia omnium dignitatum et administrationum tam civilium quam militarium*' maintained by the *primicerius notariorum*. It is also clearly the copy of the Western *primicerius*, since some chapters of the Eastern half are in an abbreviated form, and the Western half has been corrected to a later date than the Eastern. Neither half can be earlier than 395. The Eastern half is earlier than 413, since it omits the *comes Ponticae dioceseos* (*Cod. Theod.* VI. xiii. 1), and probably not much later than 395, since its army lists contain no unit demonstrably raised after that date and several units raised by Theodosius I are clearly recent additions. The Western army lists on the other hand contain units raised as late as 421. Both halves contain a number of inconsistencies, such as are inevitable in a document which has been subject to piecemeal revision. The inconsistencies are most numerous in the military chapters of the Western half. It may be inferred that the Western half like the Eastern was compiled about 395 and extensively revised in the next twenty-five years.

Edited by O. Seeck, *Notitia Dignitatum* (1876). J. B. Bury, *JRS* 1920, 131 ff.; Jones, *Later Rom. Emp.* iii, app. ii, 347 ff.
　　　　　A. H. M. J.

**NOVAESIUM,** modern *Neuss* on the Rhine. Excavation (H. v. Petrikovits, *Bonner Jahrbücher* 1961) has shown that there was a series of military stations earlier than the stone legionary fortress excavated by C. Koenen (ibid. 1904), starting with an auxiliary-sized fort *c.* 20/10 B.C. and followed by several for forces larger than one legion alone. The stone fortress was evacuated A.D. 92–6 and superseded by a new auxiliary fort which survived till the

Frankish invasions of the third century. Both the legionary and the later auxiliary stations had their attached civil settlements and there was also a separate civil settlement. The walls of the stone fortress were reconstructed in the second half of the third century or the fourth and seem to be those repaired by Julian.                    P. S.

**NOVATIAN(US)**, Roman presbyter, anti-pope (A.D. 251), and founder of the *Novatiani* (or καθαροί), a dissident sect which, persisting for about three centuries, held intransigent views concerning ecclesiastical purity. He apparently suffered martyrdom under Valerian. The first theologian in Rome who wrote in Latin, he composed several works, few of which survive, viz. *De Trinitate* (ed. W. Y. Fausset, 1909; H. Weyer, 1962), two letters to Cyprian (*Ep.* 30 and 36 in the Cyprian collection, *De Cibis Iudaicis* (ed. G. Landgraf and C. Weyman, *Archiv f. lat. Lex.* 1900, 226), and perhaps [Ps.-Cypr.] *De Spectaculis* and *De Bono Pudicitiae* (Hartel, *CSEL* iii. 3). Novatianus was well versed in rhetoric, philosophy (Stoic), and theology, and had an exceptional sense of style.

H. J. Vogt, *Coetus sanctorum, Der Kirchenbegriff des N. und die Geschichte seiner Sonderkirche* (1968).                    A. H.-W.

**NOVEL, GREEK** (Germ. *Roman, Liebesroman*; Fr. *Roman*; Ital. *Romanzo*).

A romantic composition in rhetorical prose, of considerable length (the complete novels extant vary from a minimum of four to a maximum of ten books). Five complete examples, two summaries, and a sizeable number of papyrus fragments are preserved. The authors of the complete novels (Achilles Tatius, Chariton, Heliodorus, Longus, Xenophon Ephesius) are all comparatively late; only Chariton wrote before the second century A.D. Nevertheless Rohde's thesis, according to which the genre Novel was a creation of the Second Sophistic, has been disproved by the papyrus fragments (most important of these is the 'Ninus-Romance'), which have shown that this literary form must have developed in Alexandrian times. The origins of the genre are much debated: according to one school (Rohde, Lavagnini, Giangrande) the Novel is ultimately derived from Alexandrian Love-elegy, whilst another school (Schwartz, followed by Rattenbury and Kroll) derives the Novel from Alexandrian historiography, which 'degenerated' into the 'fabulous'. A third school (Kerenyi, Merkelbach) regards the Novel as the ultimate development, into a lay genre, of religious prototypes. The problem as to the origins of the Greek Novel is made more complicated by the fact that the genre, once established, acted as a literary collecting-basin and admitted features from other genres (e.g. letters (q.v.), from *Epistolography*; sophistic *ekphraseis* (q.v.); short stories, after the example set by writers of the Classical Period, who had admitted 'short-stories' into their works by way of digressions; possibly characters from New Comedy) so that the original nucleus of the literary form under discussion is not easy to identify.

The extant novels, even the *Daphnis and Chloe* of Longus, of which the pastoral setting seems to be an exceptional experiment on the part of the author, show similarities of plot, matter, and style which, with the supporting evidence of the summaries and the papyrus fragments, may be called characteristic. The Novel flourished from the second century A.D. onwards, i.e. as Rostovtzeff and Altheim have emphasized, in the period of mass education: like the modern *feuilletons*, it was chiefly meant for the general public. Hence its poor characterization, compensated by the positive merit of the plots, which, however stereotyped, are ingeniously constructed and developed so as to captivate the interest of the readers of popular fiction. The central figures are

a young man and his betrothed or wife, whose reciprocal faithfulness, moral rectitude, and physical courage are tested by a prolonged series of adventures; the couple invariably overcome all their tribulations, to live happily ever after (the happy-ending feature being very much after the taste of the general public). During their extensive wanderings, the hero and the heroine meet friends and enemies, who, although rather stereotyped, conveniently enable the writer to insert shorter stories into the wider framework of the novel. The erotic element rarely leads to pornography, but the poverty of characterization renders the love-scenes tedious in their artificial sentimentality. *Ekphraseis* after the fashion of the Second Sophistic are often included: these, too, must have been in favour with the novelists' public, who wanted to learn about strange animals and unusual phenomena or—like the modern viewers of 'Westerns'—enjoy the elaborate description of a battle.

The absence of contemporary references to Greek novels as well as the character of their material suggests that they were not esteemed by the intellectuals: the genre, significantly enough, did not acquire a specific name (Photius calls the Novel δρᾶμα; Clitophon in Ach. Tat. i. 9. 1 calls his story μου τὸ δρᾶμα; cf. Ach. Tat. i. 2. 3, μῦθοι ἐρωτικοί, and Long. i. 1. 1, ἱστορία ἔρωτος). On the other hand, the authors of the novels were skilled men of letters, who, like the modern authors of *feuilletons*, wrote for the lower middle classes: not only the writers, but also their readers possessed a notable degree of culture, as is testified by the literary vocabulary and elaborate style in which the novels are composed, as well as by the fair number of unhackneyed literary allusions interspersed in the novels.

As is demonstrated by the comparatively large number of papyrus fragments, the novel enjoyed great popularity in imperial times: this was partly due to the fact that it aptly met the literary needs of the new lower middle classes, and partly to the fact that its adventurous elements (battles, rebellions, etc.) appealed to the public, in so far as they portrayed well the predicament of the private citizen caught, powerless and uncommitted, in the politico-military crises of that period, the age of the absolute Monarchies. The Byzantines admired the Greek novelists; Photius summarized and highly praised several of them, and Byzantine writers continued the genre, not without success. In feudal Western Europe the *Romance of Chivalry* held the field, but in the sixteenth century the newly expanded commercial *bourgeoisie* 'discovered' the Greek Novels, which were then published in French, Italian, Spanish, German, and English translations: the 'bourgeois' character of the Greek novel made them immensely popular, and such popularity lasted down to the Romantic period (Goethe was an enthusiastic admirer of Longus).

TEXTS. For each of the five complete novels the only reliable editions are now those listed under each author; the papyrus fragments are edited by B. Lavagnini, *Eroticorum Graecorum Fragmenta Papyracea* (Teubner, 1922), and by F. Zimmermann, *Griechische Roman-Papyri u. verwandte Texte* (1936, with excellent *Commentary, Grammatical Index, Index Verborum,* and *Bibliography*).
ADVERSARIA CRITICA. H. Richards, *CR* 1906; J. Jackson, *CQ* 1935; G. Giangrande, *Festschrift Teubner* (1964).
CRITICISM. Rohde, *Griech. Roman*[4]; O. Schissel v. Fleschenberg, *Entwickelungsgesch. d. griech. Romans im Altertum* (1913); A. Calderini, *Le Avventure di Cherea e Calliroe, Prolegomeni* (1913); B. Lavagnini, *Studi sul romanzo greco* (1950); R. M. Rattenbury, in Powell, *New Chapters, Third Series,* 211 ff.; S. Gaselee, appendix to the Loeb edition of *Daphnis and Chloe* (1916; repr. 1955, etc.); S. L. Wolff, *The Greek Romances in Elizabethan Prose Fiction* (U.S.A. 1912); J. S. Phillimore, *The Greek Romances,* in *English Literature and the Classics* (1912); Ed. Schwartz, *Fünf Vorträge über den griech. Roman*[2] (1943); R. Helm, *Der antike Roman*[2] (1956); A. Lesky, *Gesch. d. griech. Litt.*[2] (1963), 913 ff.; K. Kerenyi, *Die griech.-orient. Romanliteratur in religionsgeschichtlicher Beleuchtung*[2] (1962); F. Altheim, *Roman u. Dekadenz* (1951); id. *Literatur u. Gesellschaft im ausgehenden Altertum* (1948–50); R. Merkelbach, *Roman u. Mysterium in der Antike* (1962); G. Giangrande, *Eranos* 1962, 132 ff. On the

problem of the 'short-story' in antiquity cf.: B. Lavagnini, *Studi sul romanzo greco* (1950), 185 ff.; W. Aly, Volksmärchen, *Sage und Novelle bei Herodot und seinen Zeitgenossen* (1921); W. Aly, *PW* s.v. Novelle; S. Trenkner, *The Greek Novella in the Classical Period* (1958).

G. G.

**NOVEL, LATIN.** In spite of two great names, there is no continuous tradition of prose fiction among the Romans as there was with the Greeks. We hardly reach fiction, and then only in the form of short stories, before L. Cornelius Sisenna (119–67 B.C.), otherwise known as a historian, translated into Latin the Μιλησιακά of Aristides (2nd c. B.C.), tales with an obscene flavour (Plut. *Crass.* 32; [Lucian], *Amores* 1; Ov. *Tr.* 2. 443).

The adaptations by Terentius Varro (116–27 B.C.) of the satires of Menippus of Gadara (2nd c. B.C.) cannot be regarded as at all close in type to the novel, being rather of the nature of 'character-sketches', but their form, a mixture of prose and verse, reappears in Seneca's *Apocolocyntosis* and in Petronius' (q.v. 3) *Satyricon* (although in Petronius verse is used more for illustrations and plays an unimportant part). The *Apocolocyntosis*, a skit on the Emperor Claudius, may be classed as fiction, but the *Satyricon* is the earliest Latin work which is comparable with the modern novel. Enough of this survives to show that it consisted of a continuous narrative, and it seems to have been of considerable length. It contained at least two Μιλησιακά, the stories of the Widow of Ephesus (chs. 111–12) and of the Pergamene Boy (85–7). As this brilliant work, which is in part a parody on romantic novels, is seldom mentioned in ancient sources it is possible that earlier Latin novels may have existed, whether serious or comic.

Far more use of Μιλησιακά was, however, made by Apuleius (q.v.) about the middle of the second century; his *Metamorphoses* began 'at ego tibi sermone isto Milesio varias fabulas conseram'; and his romance is, indeed, a series of them strung on the thread of a plot—the change of Lucius into an ass and his adventures in animal form—which is sometimes lost sight of for long periods. On the other hand, book 11 (the successive initiations of Lucius into the mysteries) provides a surprisingly elevated ending to the novel. Clodius (q.v. 4) Albinus also wrote Μιλησιακά (S.H.A. *Clod.* 11. 7, 12. 12).

At the very end of the Classical Period we have the anonymous *History of Apollonius, King of Tyre*, perhaps written in Greek in the third century and translated into Latin, christianized, and adapted in other ways about the sixth century; it belongs rather to the tradition of Greek than of Latin fiction, and is chiefly interesting as the ultimate source of Shakespeare's *Pericles, Prince of Tyre*.

Fragments of Sisenna and of Varro's *Menippean Satires* in Buecheler's *Petronius* ed. min.; R. Helm, *Der antike Roman*² (1956); B. E. Perry, *The Ancient Romances* (1967). S. G.; M. S. S.

**NOVENSIDES,** a group of Roman deities of totally unknown function. The view that they are to be etymologized as *nou-en-sides*, the 'newly settled in' gods, i.e. comparatively recent borrowings from non-Roman sources, such as Minerva and Apollo, stands or falls according to what etymology is accepted for *indiges* (s.v. INDIGETES and the second explanation there offered). The *nouensides* seem to be the more important class, to judge from their being mentioned before the *indigetes* in the formula of *deuotio* (Livy 8. 9. 6), where the name is written 'Nouensiles', a characteristic Italian variation of *d* and *l*. Wagenvoort (*Roman Dynamism*, 83) would connect the first syllable with *nuere* and for the suffix compares *utensilis*: hence 'mobile, active' deities. The ancients generally connected the name with *nouem*, occasionally with *nouus*, see Arnobius, *Adv. Gent.* 3. 38–9 (136, 19 ff. Reifferscheid).

Latte, *RR* 45, n. 1. H. J. R.

**NOVIOMAGUS,** a Batavian settlement near Nijmegen (perhaps the *oppidum Batauorum* of Tac. *Hist.* 5. 19). It was destroyed in A.D. 70, and the Romans established a legionary fortress (garrisoned until *c.* 100) near by. The civil population settled on lower ground to the west, where an important commercial town developed, which traded extensively with Britain and the north and was raised to colonial status by Trajan. It suffered badly in the invasions of the third century. Pottery finds persist beyond the fourth century, but by then a new fortified settlement was growing up further east.

W. v. Massow, *Die Grabmäler von Noviomagus* i. ii (1932). O. B.

**NOVIUS** (fl. *c.* 95–80 B.C.: Cicero quotes from him in *De Or.* ii. 255, 279, 285—dramatic date, 91 B.C.), Latin composer of *fabulae Atellanae*, which he and his older contemporary Pomponius (q.v. 1) made literary. Forty-three titles show the stock Atellan characters, country-bumpkins, rustic and other occupations, literary allusions and parodies of tragedy; in popular language with broad jokes. *See* ATELLANA.

FRAGMENTS. O. Ribbeck, *CRF*² 254 (3rd ed. Teubner, 1897). P. Frassinetti, *Fab. Atell. Frag.* 1955), 47 ff. E. H. W.

**NOVUS HOMO,** a term used in the late Republic (and probably earlier) for the first man of a family to reach the Senate, where he normally remained a 'small senator' (cf. *BAfr.* 57), though his descendants might rise higher; and in a special sense for the first to attain the consulate and hence *nobilitas* (q.v.). These two senses must be carefully distinguished. The former feat was not very difficult, provided a man had at least an 'Equestrian' fortune (*see* EQUITES), aristocratic patron, and military or oratorical ability; the latter, despite the exclusiveness of the nobility and the conservatism of the voters who mattered, was far from rare, since noble families—some, like the Valerii Flacci, traditionally more so than others—were always ready to ally themselves with promising men for their mutual advantage. It was in this way that the nobility was constantly reinvigorated. But a man very rarely rose from outside the Senate straight to the consulship. In this sense of the phrase, only about fifteen *novi homines* are attested in the middle and late Republic; though in fact there may have been more. Most of these are men of exceptional ability and ambition, exceptionally fortunate, too, in the time and conditions of their candidature (*see* DENTATUS 2, CATO 1, MARIUS 1, CICERO 1). The ambitious *novus homo* contrasts with those really 'known' (the *nobiles*) as *per se cognitus*; and he has to win his own connexions and *clientelae* to balance their inherited ones. Hence a typical pattern of career and outlook develops. During his rise he prides himself on his *virtus* and tends to compare it with that of the founders of noble families, whose degenerate descendants he denigrates. (See, e.g., Sall. *Jug.* 85; Cic. 2 *Verr.* 5. 180 f.) But he is not a reformer. After attaining the consulship he aims at defending the order in which he has risen and at recognition as an equal by the nobles. Some (e.g. Cato, in part through longevity, and apparently Coelius (q.v. 2) more or less fully succeed in this; others (e.g. Marius and Cicero) are never quite accepted.

Under the Empire men of this sort, at first from Italy, later also from the provinces, can rise high on their own merits, the more so as they generally give the Emperor less cause for jealousy and suspicion.

J. Vogt, *Homo novus* (1926); *and see* NOBILITAS. E. B.

**NUCERIA** (1), large town at foot of peninsula of Surrentum (q.v.): modern *Nocera Inferiore*. Originally peopled by Oscan-speaking Alfaterni, it has regularly changed hands whenever war visited Campania (q.v.). In A.D. 59 it and neighbouring Pompeii (q.v.) staged a bloody riot.

(2) Large town on Via Flaminia (q.v.) in Umbria: modern *Nocera Umbra*. The campaign of Sentinum (q.v.), 295 B.C., probably brought it under Roman control. *See* UMBRIANS.                                    E. T. S.

**NUMA** (*PW* 1) **POMPILIUS,** the second king of Rome (traditionally 715–673 B.C.), is probably a historical figure, although most of the reforms ascribed to him were the result of a very long process of religious and cultural development. He may have been a Sabine who settled on the Quirinal, even though Numa was an Etruscan name. Numa is not the personification of the river Numicius or any other Latin deity. There is no means of deciding whether Numa really organized the priestly colleges and reformed the calendar by fixing the dates of the festivals and adding two months to a primitive ten-month year, or whether he built the Regia (q.v.), which was traditionally assigned to the regal period. Later legends recount that he received counsel from the nymph Egeria and, in defiance of chronology, make him a disciple of Pythagoras (q.v. 1) to account for similarities between early Roman religion and Greek cults in southern Italy.

Ogilvie, *Comm. Livy 1–5*, 88 ff. (with bibliography).     P. T.

**NUMANTIA,** a strategical site on the upper Durius (*Douro*) in Spain, occupied in the Bronze Age, in the Hallstatt period, and by the Celts. Built anew by the Celtiberians *c.* 300 B.C., Numantia played a heroic role in the Celtiberian resistance to Rome, repelling attacks by Cato (195), Q. Fulvius Nobilior (153), Marcellus (152), Q. Pompeius (141), and Popillius Laenas (139–8); the capitulation of Hostilius Mancinus (q.v.) (137) crowned a series of failures and defeats. Finally, after an eight-month blockade Numantia's 4,000 citizens capitulated to the overwhelming forces of Scipio Aemilianus in 133 B.C., a date which marks the end of organized resistance to Rome in Spain. Marius, Jugurtha, and Rutilius Rufus witnessed Numantia's destruction. Thorough excavations have uncovered the city, Scipio's works of circumvallation, and thirteen Roman camps at Numantia or in the neighbourhood (one each of Marcellus and Pompeius, two of Cato and Nobilior, and seven of Scipio). Although reinhabited under Augustus, Numantia gradually sank to the level of a way-station on the Asturica–Caesaraugusta highway.

A. Schulten, *Numantia* (4 vols. and atlas, 1914–31), and a shorter sketch, *Geschichte von Numantia* (1933).          J. J. VAN N.

**NUMBERS, GREEK. I.** GREEK NUMERAL NOTATIONS.
There were two main systems:
(1) The 'alphabetic' or 'Milesian', probably originating in Ionia and the older of the two. It consisted of the ordinary letters of the Ionian alphabet plus ς = 6, ϟ = 90, and ↑ or ⊅ = 900. Thus α to θ represent 1 to 9, ι to ϟ 10 to 90 and ρ to ⊅ 100 to 900. Thousands from one to nine are represented by ͵α to ͵θ, and 10,000 by M. Multiples of 10,000 are written by putting the multiplier above; thus 126,763 is written $M,\varsigma\psi\xi\gamma$.
(2) The 'acrophonic'. Apart from |, the unit, the signs were the initial letters of the numeral words: Γ = πέντε, Δ = δέκα, Η = ἑκατόν, X = χίλιοι, M = μύριοι. Quintuples of the latter four were represented by a combination with Γ; thus Γ⁴, Γ⁵, or Γ^H = 50, Γ^H = 500, Γ^X = 5,000, Γ^M = 50,000. Other multiples were expressed by repetition of the sign; thus 126,763 is written ͰΜΜΜΓ⁵XΓ^HHHΓ^HΔ|||. These signs were frequently used in Attic inscriptions to express sums of money; in that case they represented drachmas, except that Ͱ = 1 drachma and | = 1 obol. C was used for a ½-obol, Ͻ or T for ¼-obol, and T for a talent. The latter sign was

combined with the numerals to express numbers of talents, e.g. Γ^4HX.
On present evidence we may tentatively say that (2) was the system used in all public inscriptions in Attica (with the possible exception of *IG* i². 760) down to *c.* 100 B.C., and sporadically later. It is also the main system used (with local variations) in other Greek States from fifth to third centuries. (1) is found in the earliest Attic vase inscriptions, but from *c.* 480 wide (but not universal) use of (2) is found in Attic private inscriptions. (1) ousted (2) in other Greek States during the third century B.C. It is almost universal in surviving papyri.
A zero sign ō is found in astronomical papyri and MSS. *Fractions*: Like the Egyptians, the Greeks preferred to express fractions as the sum of unit fractions (fractions with 1 as numerator); they expressed the unit fraction by the sign for the number with an accent; thus $\gamma'\delta' = \frac{1}{3}+\frac{1}{4} = \frac{7}{12}$. There were special signs ∟' for ½ and β' for ⅔. However, proper fractions could also be expressed by the word (or the sign) for the numerator and the accented letters for the denominator, e.g. $\delta\acute{v}o\ \mu\epsilon' = \frac{2}{45}$ (Aristarchus), $\theta\ \iota\alpha' = \frac{9}{11}$ (Archimedes), or by expressions like $\delta^{\omega\nu}\varsigma = \frac{9}{4}$, $\nu\ \kappa\gamma^{\omega\nu} = \frac{50}{23}$ (Diophantus). Most convenient was the practice, regular in Diophantus and occasional in Heron, of placing the denominator *above* the numerator, e.g. $^{\phi\iota\beta}_{'\beta\nu\nu\varsigma} = \frac{2456}{512}$ (Diophantus). Sexagesimal fractions are standard in the later astronomical works (e.g. Ptolemy). In this system e.g. $\iota\beta\ \lambda\delta'\nu\varsigma'' = 12+\frac{34}{60}+\frac{56}{60.60}$.

**II.** ARTIFICIAL SYSTEMS
Archimedes, in his lost Ἀρχαί and in the *Sand-reckoner* (*Psammites*), sketched a system for expressing very large numbers going by powers of a myriad myriads (100,000,000 or 10⁸). The first *order* consists of numbers from 1 to 10⁸, the second *order* those from 10⁸ to 10¹⁶, and so on, up to the 10⁸ *order* concluding the first *period*. Other *periods* follow *ad lib.* This system amounts to taking 100,000,000 in place of 10 as the base of a scale of notation. Apollonius of Perga (q.v.) formulated a 'position-value' system going by powers of 10,000, i.e. with 10,000 substituted for 10 as the base (see Pappus I, 8 f.).

Articles by M. N. Tod, *BSA* 1911–12, 1926–7, 1936–7, and *JHS* 1933, give full evidence for the acrophonic system, and in *BSA* 1950 for the alphabetic. On the early vase-inscriptions: R. Hackl in *Münchener archäologische Studien dem Andenken A. Furtwängler gewidmet* (1909), esp. 79 ff. Best general account: G. E. M. de Ste Croix, *Studies in the History of Accounting* (ed. Littleton and Yamey, 1956), 50 ff. See also K. Menninger, *Zahlwort und Ziffer²* ii (1958), 73 ff. *Fractions*: Heath, *Hist. of Greek Maths.* i. 41 ff. In the papyri, E. Mayser, *Grammatik d. gr. Papyri* (1926–38), 52 f. On computation with alphabetic numerals: J. G. Smyly in *Mélanges Nicole* (1905), 513 ff. For the use of α–ω for 1–24 see F. Dornseiff, *Das Alphabet in Mystik und Magie* (1922), 11.          T. H.; G. J. T.

**NUMBERS, ROMAN,** are based on seven signs: I = 1, V = 5, X = 10, L = 50, C = 100, Đ = 500, ∞ (or a recognizable variant) = 1,000 (M was not used as a figure, only as an abbreviation of the words *mille*, *milia*). Of these, I was originally a simple stroke, V perhaps represented a hand, X is V doubled, while L, Đ and ∞ are thought to derive from the aspirated letters of the Greek alphabet, for which early Latin had no use— L from ψ (Chalcidic *chi*) developing through ⋃ and ⊥, ∞ from Φ (Chalcidic *phi*), and Đ from Φ halved, with the medial bar added later to distinguish it from the letter D; C may derive from Θ, the third unused Greek aspirate, acquiring its final form by a combination of the tendency to assimilate figure-signs to letter-forms in current use and the influence of the initial of *centum*, but no early instance survives.
A notation could be constructed on this basis both by the additive method (IIII = 4; XXXX = 40) and by the subtractive (IV = 4; XL = 40) and both methods

were employed, sometimes even in the same document. Inscriptions seem to show a preference for the additive method, especially in official contexts, and this preference is occasionally carried to the extent of ignoring the signs V and L (so IIIIIIviri often for VIviri and such forms as XXXXXX for LX). The rule is that when two figures stand side by side, the smaller, if to the right, is to be added to its neighbour, if to the left, to be subtracted from it (VI = 6; IV = 4); exceptions occur, but are very rare. For numbers above 1,000, for which the additive method might be clumsy, modifications of the basic signs were evolved (so $\mathbb{D}$ = 5,000; $\circledP$ = 10,000) and, later, as an alternative, the use of superscript bars to denote that a figure is to be multiplied by 1,000 ($\bar{X}$ = 10,000), and of superscript bars with dependent verticals at either side to denote that it is to be multiplied by 100,000 ($|\bar{X}|$ = 1,000,000).

From the second century B.C. the figure-signs began to be used also as *sigla* for words or components of words with a numerical reference (so X = *denarius*, IIviri = *duoviri*) and eventually for ordinal adjectives and adverbs and for distributives as well as for cardinal numbers. It was probably to distinguish such usages, in circumstances where confusion with letters or with cardinal numbers might occur, that the practice of using a medial bar was introduced (so $\times$ = *denarius*) and subsequently a superscript bar (so *IIviri* = *duoviri*; $\bar{V}$ = *quinquies*). From the Augustan period onwards this use of a superscript bar was extended, although it never became invariable. In a comparatively small number of cases it appears also above an ordinal number, presumably in error, and creates confusion with the use of the bar to denote multiplication by 1,000.

Cursive forms of the figures are usually recognizable without undue difficulty (cf. $\mathcal{HH}$ = 30), though $\varsigma$ = 6, common especially in Christian texts, is at first sight obscure.

For fractions, a duodecimal system was used. A horizontal stroke was the sign for the unit of $\frac{1}{12}$ (*uncia*) and S, from *semis*, for $\frac{1}{2}$. The appropriate number of horizontal strokes provided the notation for $\frac{1}{12}$ to $\frac{5}{12}$ (= = — is $\frac{5}{12}$) and, when preceded by S, for $\frac{7}{12}$ to $\frac{11}{12}$ (S = = — is $\frac{11}{12}$). For smaller fractions a number of *sigla* were developed; lists may be found in the epigraphic handbooks, *see* EPIGRAPHY, LATIN, bibliography.

E. Hübner, *Exempla Scripturae Epigraphicae* (1885), lxx f.; Th. Mommsen, *Hermes* 1887, 596 f., 1888, 152 f.; J. S. and A. E. Gordon, *Contributions to the Palaeography of Latin Inscriptions* (1957), 166 ff.; B. E. Thomasson, *Opusc. Romana* iii (1961), 179 ff. J. M. R.

**NUMBERS, SACRED.** Most nations have sacred or magical numbers. Some of these are explicable (e.g. seven is the traditional number of the planets), and of others it may be conjectured that they are the last term of some very old and primitive system of counting, or an important term in such a system (e.g., five perhaps because it is the number of the fingers of one hand); others are entirely obscure. For Greece the following may be noted, apart from Pythagorean mysticism and the divinatory calculations given below. Three is very common in all ritual, especially magical; the dead are invoked thrice (Ar. *Ran.* 1175–6); gods are frequently invoked in threes, as Zeus, Athena, and Apollo often in Homer, or grouped in threes, as the Charites (generally); charms are commonly repeated thrice, Theoc. 2. 43; other magical actions, Theoc. 6. 39. Hence nine is of importance (nine Muses usually, sometimes nine Corybantes and nine Curetes), being 3 × 3. Four is Hermes' number, being his birthday (*Hymn. Hom. Merc.* 19), perhaps explaining why it is a holy day (Hes. *Op.* 770). Seven is Apollo's number (see Rose, *Handb. Gk. Myth.*[6] 135, cf. Hes. ibid. 771). This is without doubt oriental;

twelve, though traditionally the number of the signs of the Zodiac, need not be Eastern (twelve gods, see Weinreich in Roscher's *Lexikon*, art. 'Zwölfgötter'; twelve labours of Heracles, q.v.). Finally, there is a tendency to round larger numbers off to fifty (see W. H. Roscher, 'Die Zahl 50 in Mythus', etc., *Abh. sächs. Ges. Wiss.*, 1917). The numerical values of letters of the alphabet are the basis of an elaborate system of divination, see Bouché-Leclercq, *Histoire de la divination dans l'antiquité* (1879) i. 261 ff.; for an attempt to find a like system in early times see Eisler, *Orpheus the Fisher* and *Weltenmantel und Himmelszelt*. Numbers which exceed a familiar 'round' number by one, e.g. 13 (12+1) are occasionally of importance, see O. Weinreich, *Triskaidekadische Studien* 1916; *RGVV* xvi. 1).

In Italy triads of gods are common, not only under Etruscan influence (as the Capitoline triad), but outside it (Jupiter, Mars, and Quirinus are native Roman). Four is of significance (a prayer said four times, Ov. *Fasti* 4. 778); five appears to have had some sacral connotation, see Wissowa, *Gesammelte Abhandl.* 166, cf. Plut. *Quaest. Rom.* 1 and Rose ad loc. Other numbers seem to be Greek.

The references in the text may be supplemented by Keith in Hastings, *ERE* ix. 407 ff., and bibliography, 413; for speculation over numbers in Pythagoreanism, Nilsson, *GGR* ii. 398. H. J. R.

**NUMENIUS** of Apamea (2nd c. A.D.), leading Pythagorean. His works included a treatise *On the Good* and a history of the Academy, designed to show how far it had departed from Plato's (and Pythagoras') teaching; of both these fairly substantial fragments survive. His system combined Greek with oriental elements. He anticipated Plotinus in his doctrine of three gods, and in asserting the potential identity of the human soul with its divine Grounds; he also has ideas in common with Gnosticism (q.v.) and with the *Chaldaean Oracles* (q.v.), and he shows some knowledge of Judaism and Christianity (which he interpreted allegorically). The extent of his influence not only on Plotinus, who was accused of plagiarizing from him, but also on Origen, Porphyry, and later Neoplatonists renders him a significant historical figure.

FRAGMENTS. Ed. E. A. Leemans (1937).
DISCUSSION. H.-C. Puech in *Mélanges Bidez* (1934), 745 ff.; E. R. Dodds in *Les Sources de Plotin* (*Entretiens Hardt* v), 1 ff.; P. Merlan, *Philol.* 1962, 137 ff. E. R. D.

**NUMERI** had a variety of meanings in military terminology. (i) *numerus* was the generic name for any military unit (Tac. *Agr.* 18: 'sparsi per provinciam numeri'); (ii) hence it was frequently used to describe formations which had no normal title, such as the *equites singulares Augusti* or the *frumentarii*; (iii) and in particular as the title for units formed from unromanized tribes which could not easily be assimilated to the normal auxiliary pattern. These 'national' *numeri* are found from the time of Trajan onwards; they were generally employed at some distance from the areas in which they had been raised (e.g. *numeri Brittonum* in Germany). (iv) *numeri* had also the meaning of military roster (*in numeros referre* means 'to enter on the rolls'), in which sense it was supplanted by *matricula* in the fourth century or earlier.

J. C. Mann, *Hermes* 1954, 501 ff.; J. F. Gilliam, *Eos* 1957, 207 ff. G. R. W.

**NUMERIANUS,** MARCUS AURELIUS (*PW* 174), younger son of Carus (q.v.), was appointed Caesar in A.D. 282 and shared in the campaign against Persia. After the death of Carus, July 283, he became Augustus. Having little military talent, he withdrew from the Persian territory occupied by his father. He died in mysterious circumstances on the way to Nicomedia in 284. The army chose Diocles (later Diocletian), commander of the guard, to succeed him, and he struck down Aper, praetorian prefect and father-in-law of Numerian, as being the latter's murderer.                                              H. M.; B. H. W.

**NUMICUS** (or **NUMICIUS**), (modern *Rio Torto?*), the creek near Ardea in Latium where Aeneas allegedly perished. The Romans subsequently venerated him as Jupiter Indiges in a grove on its banks. Near by was another grove, sacred to Anna Perenna.

B. Tilly, *JRS* 1936, 1 ff.                                        E. T. S.

**NUMIDIA,** originally the country of the Numidae or African Nomads, lying west and south of Carthaginian territory. Later the title was given to a Roman province, covering a triangle broadening out from its apex on the Mediterranean coast north of Cirta across the High Plateaux (Atlas Mountains) down to the Saharan *limes*. This Numidia was bounded by Mauretania Caesariensis on the west and the province of Africa on the east. Though not as fertile as the latter, Numidia produced corn, wine, and olives on the plains, and bred horses, cattle, and sheep on the uplands.

The original Berber inhabitants were nomad herdsmen, who sometimes practised a primitive agriculture. Those on the coast came under the influence of Utica, Carthage, and the other Phoenician colonies. By the time of the Second Punic War their small clans had coalesced into the tribal confederacies of the Masaesyli under Syphax and the Massyli under Masinissa (q.v.). Their cavalry were formidable, but disunion made them difficult allies politically. Under Masinissa nomadism was abandoned for agriculture, and town life developed. Masinissa was followed by Micipsa (148–118 B.C.), Adherbal (118–112), Jugurtha (q.v., 118–106), Hiempsal (106–60), and Juba I (60–46). As Numidia supported Pompey (47–46), the native dynasty was overthrown. It was established as the province of Africa Nova (46), then (30–25) made a client kingdom under Juba II (q.v.), and later united with the old province of Africa until separated by Septimius Severus. Christianity spread rapidly in the third century and in the fourth Numidia became the stronghold of the Donatist (q.v.) schismatics.

When the frontiers of Africa Proconsularis were placed on the river Ampsaga (*Rummel*), the Third Augustan legion moved into Numidia under its legate, and was stationed successively at Theveste and Lambaesis (qq.v.). Military colonies were founded at Thamugadi, Madauros (qq.v.), and elsewhere; cereals and olives were cultivated largely; the slave-trade with the Sahara increased. Traffic moved along the great roads which radiated from Theveste to be shipped from Carthage, Hadrumetum, Taparura, and the Syrtic ports. The richest parts of Numidia were in the Tell (*see* ATLAS MOUNTAINS) and round Cirta (q.v.).

On its southern frontier Numidia was protected by the forts of the *limes*, which ran from the Tunisian shotts or salt lakes westward and north-west to Aumale. Between the military roads were districts ruled by native chieftains, who occasionally rebelled. The frontier held till the fifth century when Saharan raiders and Berber tribesmen sacked a number of towns during the Vandal occupation of Africa.

S. Gsell, *Inscriptions latines de l'Algérie* i (1922), ii, ed. H. G. Pflaum (1957); J. Mazard, *Corpus Nummorum Numidiae Mauretaniaeque* (1955); H. G. Kolbe, *Die Statthalter Numidiens von Gallien bis Konstantin* (1962), *and see* AFRICA, ROMAN.                    W. N. W.

**NUMMULARII,** quoted in inscriptions as subordinate officers at the mint, but probably not technical workmen, who are properly called *officinatores*. The *nummularius* of Martial (12. 57. 7) disturbs sleep by thumping the heavy *sestertii* of Nero on his dirty table, in the intervals of business ('otiosus'). He is a money-changer. So was the *nummularius*, whose hands Galba cut off, 'non ex fide uersanti pecunias' (Suet. *Galba* 9); he had cheated over the exchange. This passage shows that the *nummularii* were under official control; they may even have been directly employed by the mint to put on the market the new coin as it was struck.

The passage in Petronius, *Satyricon* 56, where Trimalchio asks 'quod autem putamus secundum litteras difficillimum esse artificium? ego puto medicum et nummularium', does not necessarily imply the meaning of 'moneyer'.                                             H. M.

**NYMPHIDIUS** (*PW* 5) **SABINUS,** GAIUS, son of a court freedwoman, claimed to be the son of the Emperor Gaius (q.v. 1). He probably commanded an auxiliary regiment in Pannonia (*ILS* 1322) and then became a tribune in the guard. In 65 he was given the *consularia ornamenta* by Nero and made *praefectus praetorio* with Tigellinus (q.v.). In 68, by promise of an enormous donative, he induced the praetorians to desert Nero for Galba, but he had designs upon the Principate himself. He forced Tigellinus to resign, and intended to demand from Galba the praefecture for life without colleague. But he met with unexpected opposition from the praetorians, and was killed by them.          R. L. J.; G. E. F. C.

**NYMPHIS** of Heraclea in Bithynia, statesman and historian. Enough remains of his history of Heraclea (in Memnon's epitome) to show how good it was; this and his character as a politician suggest that his lost history of Alexander and his successors (after 247 B.C.) may be a real loss.

*FGrH* iii. B, no. 432. Fragments and Commentary: cf. ibid. no. 434 (Memnon).                                         W. W. T.; G. T. G.

**NYMPHODORUS** (fl. *c.* 335 B.C.), Syracusan Greek, wrote (i) Ἀσίας περίπλους, (ii) Περὶ τῶν ἐν Σικελίᾳ θαυμαζομένων, and possibly (iii) *On strange things in Sardinia* (Ath. 6. 265 c; 13. 588 f, 609 c; Ael. *NA* 16. 34).

*FGrH* iii. 572.

**NYMPHS,** female spirits of nature representing the divine powers of mountains, waters, woods, and trees, and also of places, regions, cities, and States. As the word νύμφη, young unmarried woman, implies, nymphs were thought of as young and fair. Calypso is described as a nymph (*Od.* 1. 14). They like dancing and music and can inspire mortals with poetry and prophetic power. In contrast to gods nymphs are mortal (Ov. *Met.* 8. 771), although Hesiod endows them with extreme longevity. They are daughters of Zeus.

Since nymphs are called after that part of nature in which they dwell, or after their functions, or after the specific geographic locality where they reside, there is an infinite variety of nymphs known. Alseides, Napaeae, and Dryades are nymphs of forests and groves (the last were originally nymphs of the oak but came to stand for nymphs of the woods in general). Hamadryades, the tree nymphs proper, were believed to die when their tree decays (Serv. on Verg. *Ecl.* 10. 62), for the nymph is the life-spirit of the tree. Orestiads are the nymphs of the mountains, Leimoniads those of the meadows. All kinds of waters are inhabited by nymphs, such as the Naiads, the Potameids, the Creneids, and the Hydriads. The difference between these broader classifications of nymphs and the nymphs representing a locality was recognized by the ancients (*Myth. Vat.* 2. 50). Examples of local nymphs are the Acheloids, named after the river Achelous, or the Nysiads, named after the mountain Nysa where Dionysus was born. Many local goddesses are brought under this category of nymphs and married to founders of the cities.

Most of the nymphs are benevolent to mankind. They bring flowers to gardens and meadows, watch with Apollo and Hermes over the flocks, and frequently, as patronesses of healthful springs, aid the sick. Such nymphs are often associated with Asclepius. As goddesses of woods and mountains they give success to hunters. Yet nymphs also partake of the wilder aspects of nature. They are akin to Satyrs (q.v.) and Sileni, and associate with Pan. They range with Artemis over the mountains and take part in the Dionysiac *thiasus*. Folklore tales, similar to those attaching to fairies and mermaids, are told about some of the nymphs. Those of the woods scare travellers. A man who sees nymphs becomes 'possessed by nymphs'. They take mortals whom they love with them as they did Hylas and Bormus (Theoc. 13. 44 and schol. Ath. 14. 619 f). The drowning of a girl in the Nile was associated with them (*SEG* viii. 473). They punish unresponsive lovers as did the nymphs who blinded Daphnis (Diod. 4. 84).

The cult of nymphs was widely spread through Greece from Homeric times on (*Od.* 13. 356; 17. 205), and extended over the Roman provinces under the Empire. The Hill of the Nymphs at Athens is named after an inscription discovered there (M. Ervin, *Platon* (1959), 146). Nymphs were often worshipped in caves; an interesting example is the cave in Vari which was transformed into a sanctuary of the nymphs by their faithful devotee Archedemus (*AJArch.* 1903, 263). In art nymphs are represented on a vase of Sophilus and on the François vase as undistinctive draped females. However, the female partners of padded dancers are naked (M. Edwards, *JHS* 1960). A special type of votive relief for the nymphs was developed in Attica in the late fifth and the fourth centuries B.C. The dancing nymphs are led by Hermes, while Pan and Achelous look on (R. Feubel, *Die attischen Nymphenreliefs* (1935)); sometimes a cave and an altar indicate the rustic sanctuary. Shepherds often dedicated these humble votives.

L. Bloch in Roscher, *Lex.*, s.v. 'Nymphen'; J. E. Harrison, *Prolegomena to the Study of Greek Rel.*³ (1922), 288; E. Paribeni, *Bollet. d' Arte* 1951, 105; A. Carnoy, *Muséon* 1956, 187; A. D. Nock, *Mélanges de l'Univ. Saint-Joseph* 1960–1, 297; K. Schefold, *Antike Kunst* 1965, 87 ff. G. M. A. H.; J. R. T. P.

**NYX.** Naturally enough, Night is frequently personified by the Greek poets as by those of other peoples. But the significance of Nyx in Greek mythology goes far beyond this. She was a great cosmogonical figure, feared and respected even by Zeus (Hom. *Il.* 14. 259). In Hesiod she is born of Chaos and mother of Aether, Hemera, and lesser powers. Frequent touches in the description recall her nocturnal aspect, but this is scarcely seen in the Orphic theogonies, where her influence over creation is immense (cf. ORPHIC LITERATURE, ORPHISM). In the Rhapsodies she is born of Phanes and succeeds to his power. When in turn she hands the sceptre to her son Uranus she continues to advise the younger generations, Uranus, Kronos, and especially Zeus, in the task of world-making. Her influence is due to her oracular powers, exercised from a cave. There are signs that in an earlier Orphic version Phanes was absent and Nyx the primal power. The theogony of the Birds (Ar. *Av.* 693 ff.) makes her prior to Eros (= Phanes), and this supposition suits the awful dignity of Nyx which Homer and 'Orpheus' alike emphasize, and the vague reference of Aristotle (*Metaph.* 1071ᵇ27) to *theologoi* who derive everything from Night. Nyx was primarily a mythographer's goddess, with little cult, but one may mention her connexion with oracles (not confined to Orphic literature, see Plut. *De sera* 22; schol. Pind. *Pyth. Argum.*) and a dedication to her in the temple of Demeter in Graeco-Roman Pergamum (*SIG* 1148, n. 2).

C. Ramnoux, *La Nuit et les enfants de la nuit dans la tradition grecque* (1959; review by H. J. Rose, *CR* 1961, 77 ff.). W. K. C. G.

# O

**OASIS,** derived from an Egyptian word, was the name by which the Greeks called any watered and habitable land in deserts, particularly in north Africa. Though really depressions, oases were regarded as elevations. They were of some importance as trading-stations and sources of alum, and several of them were garrisoned by the Ptolemies, and later by the Romans. The oases of the Sahara were described by Herodotus (4. 181–5) as a chain extending from east to west, about ten days' journey apart. The most renowned of them, near Egypt, were (i) the 'Ammonium' (*El Siwah*), 6 mls. × 3, 20 days from Thebes and 12 from Memphis, famed for springs, salt, old Egyptian temples, and the oracle of Ammon (q.v.); (ii) 'Oasis Magna' (*El Khargah*), 80 mls. × 8–10, 7 days from Thebes, with a Greek and Roman population. (iii) 'Oasis Minor' (*El Dakkel*), south-east of the Ammonium, a source of wheat under the Roman Empire. (iv) 'Oasis Trinytheos' (*El Bakhariah*), north of Oasis Magna, with artesian wells and alum deposits.

For the oasis of Palmyra *see* PALMYRA.

Thomson, *Hist. Anc. Geog.* 69 f., 264. E. H. W.

**OBSEQUENS** (*PW* 2), IULIUS (probably 4th c. A.D.), composed tables of prodigies from 249 to 12 B.C. (extant for 190–12 B.C.; the earlier part and perhaps an introduction lost). Based on the epitomized Livian tradition, further 'contaminated', or on consul lists to which Livian details of prodigies were added, it represents late heathen justification of the forms of the old faith.

Edited by O. Jahn (1853); O. Rossbach (1910), with Livian *Periochae*. A. H. McD.

**OCEANUS** (mythological), son of Uranus (Sky) and Ge (Earth), husband of Tethys, and father of the Oceanids and River gods (Hes. *Th.* 133, 364). In Homer Oceanus is the river encircling the whole world and accordingly is represented as a river by Hephaestus on the rim of the shields of Achilles (*Il.* 18. 607) and Heracles ([Hes.] *Sc.* 314). From Oceanus through subterranean connexions issue all other rivers. Styx, the river of Hades, is part of it (Hes. *Th.* 786). Oceanus begins at the columns of Heracles, borders on the Elysian fields and Hades, and has its sources in the west where the sun sets. Monsters such as Gorgons, Hecatonchires, Hesperides, Geryoneus, and Eurytion, and outlandish tribes such as Cimmerians, Aethiopians, and pygmies, live by the waters of Oceanus (*Od.* 1. 22; 11. 13; *Il.* 3. 3). Those regions of Oceanus are the land where reality ends and everything is fabulous.

In Greek theories of the world Oceanus is conceived as the great cosmic power, θεῶν γένεσις (*Il.* 14. 201, 246, 302; W. Jaeger, *Paideia* i (1939), 149), the water, through which all life grows, and in Greek mythology as a benign old god. Sometimes the elemental, sometimes the personal, aspect is more emphasized. The belief that sun and stars rise and set in the ocean is expressed mythologically in the statement that stars bathe in Oceanus (*Il.* 18. 489), and the Sun traverses it in a golden bowl by night to get back to the East (Mimnermus in Ath. 11. 470 a–b). The rise of rational geographical investigation in Herodotus, Eratosthenes, and others narrowed the significance of Oceanus down to the geographical term of 'Ocean'.

Oceanus never became quite personal enough to accumulate many myths. Pherecydes supplied a humorous sequel to the myth of Sun in the golden bowl: when Heracles set out across the Ocean in the same golden bowl in which the Sun used to cross, Oceanus began to rock. Heracles threatened him with his arrows and Oceanus was frightened (Ath. 11. 470 c).

In art Oceanus appears early (François vase), is represented on the famous Gigantomachy of Pergamum, and becomes really common in Roman times, especially on sarcophagi, with Earth as a counterpart.

P. Weizsäcker, s.v. in Roscher, *Lex.* iii; E. Marec, *Libyca* 1958, 99; B. Ashmole, *JHS* 1967, 4. G. M. A. H.

**OCEANUS** (geographical). Expeditions outside the Straits of Gibraltar by Phoenicians and (after *c.* 630 B.C.) by Greeks, and exploration of the Red Sea and Persian Gulf under Darius I, showed that the Oceanus of mythology (see preceding article) was a salt-water 'ocean' indented with seas (so Herodotus). But erroneous notions persisted. Poets tried to relegate the river Oceanus beyond the newly found Outer Sea. Hecataeus believed that Oceanus flowed from east to west (Hdt. 4. 8), and the Caspian Sea (q.v.) was commonly regarded as one of its inlets. After the voyage of Pytheas (q.v.) in the Atlantic the action of the Ocean tides came to be understood, though the early Roman navigators in Atlantic waters were puzzled by them. As the sphericity of the earth became known (since *c.* 350 B.C.), geographers imagined that eastern Asia might be reached by sailing westward from Europe, and *c.* 120 B.C. Eudoxus (q.v. 3) of Cyzicus attempted the circumnavigation of Africa. But the belief that the Ocean extended all round the inhabited earth was never proved. Some geographers conjectured that the southern Ocean contained another continent, or that it was a vast land-locked sea (so Ptolemy); the northern Ocean was supposed to be frozen or too shallow or glutinous for navigation.

*See also* GEOGRAPHY, HANNO (1), HIMILCO (1), HIPPALUS, INDIA, LIBYA.

F. Gisinger, *PW*, s.v. 'Okeanos'. E. H. W.

**OCELLUS** (or **OCCELUS**) of Lucania occurs in Iamblichus' list of Pythagoreans (testimonia in H. Diels, *Vorsokr.* i. 440–1), but the work Περὶ τῆς τοῦ παντὸς φύσεως bearing his name and known as early as the first century B.C. is undoubtedly spurious. It shows considerable traces of Aristotelian influence, and may probably be dated about 150 B.C.

Ed. R. Harder (Berlin, 1926). W. D. R.

**OCRICULUM**, near modern *Otricoli*, an Umbrian settlement on the left bank of the Tiber, 44 miles from Rome and later on the *Via Flaminia*. It was allied to Rome (308, or 297/95 B.C.) and was sacked in the Social War. Of the later Roman town there survive a theatre, amphitheatre, basilica, and baths. It was known for its pottery industry. Milo (q.v.) had a villa there.

T. Ashby, *JRS* 1921, 163 ff.; C. Pietrangeli, *Rend. Pont.* 1942, 47 ff.; id., *Ocriculum* (1943). H. H. S.

**OCTAVIA** (1, *PW* 95), daughter of Octavius (q.v. 4) and

Ancharia and so half-sister of Augustus, married Sextus Appuleius; their sons Sextus and Marcus were consuls in 29 and 20 B.C. respectively.

Syme, *Rom. Rev.*, see index; M. W. Singer, *TAPA* 1948, 268 ff. T. J. C.

**OCTAVIA** (2, *PW* 96), daughter of Octavius (q.v. 4) and Atia, and sister of Augustus, married (by 54 B.C.) C. Marcellus (q.v. 5). In 40 Marcellus died and, to seal the Pact of Brundisium, she was immediately married to Antony. She spent the winters of 39/8 and 38/7 with him in Athens, and in 37 helped with the negotiations which led to the Pact of Tarentum. When he returned to the East, Antony left her behind. In 35 Octavian sent her to Antony with token reinforcements for his army; Antony forbade her to proceed beyond Athens. She rejected Octavian's advice to leave Antony's house, and though divorced by him in 32 brought up all his surviving children by Fulvia and Cleopatra along with their two daughters and her three children by Marcellus. Her nobility, humanity, and loyalty won her wide esteem and sympathy. She died in 11 B.C.

Syme, *Rom. Rev.*, see index; M. W. Singer, *CJ* 1947, 173 ff.
Iconography. *CAH*, pl. iv. 166 f.; H. Bartels, *Studien zum Frauenporträt der aug. Zeit* (1963), 14 ff.; V. H. Poulsen, *Les Portraits romains* i (1962), 76 f. G. W. R.; T. J. C.

**OCTAVIA** (3), CLAUDIA (*PW* 428), daughter of Claudius and Messallina, was born by A.D. 40. She was betrothed in infancy to L. Junius Silanus, and in 49, after Silanus' repudiation and death, to Agrippina's son L. Domitius Ahenobarbus (Nero), whom she married in 53. Nero, who disliked and neglected her, divorced her in 62 for sterility (a charge of adultery having failed) in order to marry Poppaea (q.v.), and sent her to live in Campania under military surveillance. When a rumour that she had been reinstated provoked demonstrations of popular approval, he contrived fresh charges of adultery and treason, banished her to Pandateria, and presently had her put to death (9 June). For the *praetexta* on her fate, *see below*, OCTAVIA.

Iconography. V. Poulsen, *Opusc. Romana* iv (1962), 107 ff. G. W. R.; T. J. C.

*OCTAVIA*, the one extant *praetexta*, dramatizes in 983 lines the fate of Nero's neglected Empress. Seneca is brought in as a character to protest against the Emperor's barbarity, and Agrippina's ghost comes to foretell Nero's doom in words so true to fact as to show that they were written after the event of A.D. 68. Commonly printed with Seneca's tragedies, it is not by him, but by someone who wrote in his manner soon after Nero died. There is too much melancholy repetition and too little epigram for Seneca, and there are metrical differences.

TEXT. Editions of Seneca's tragedies, e.g. F. Leo. With notes, C. L. Thompson (U.S.A. 1921); C. Hosius (1922); T. H. Sluiter (1949); A. Santoro (1919 and 1955). See R. Helm, *Sitz. Berlin* 1934; M. Torrini, *L'Octavia* (1934); S. Pantzerhielm Thomas, *Symbolae Osloenses* 1945, 48 ff.; F. Giancotti, *L'Octavia attribuita a Seneca* (1954); C. J. Herington, *CQ* 1961, 18 ff.
J. W. D.; G. B. A. F.

**OCTAVIUS** (1, *PW* 17), GNAEUS, curule aedile (172 B.C.?), a member of the embassy assuring Greek allied rights in 169, was praetor in 168, commanding the Roman fleet against Perseus, whom he captured at Samothrace. He celebrated a naval triumph, and from spoil built the *Porticus Octavia*. Consul in 165, he led the embassy to the East in 163/2 which attempted to settle Syria in Roman interests after the death of Antiochus Epiphanes, destroying ships and elephants, and was murdered in a patriotic riot at Laodicea.

B. Niese, *Gesch. der griech. und maked. Staaten* iii (1903), 243. A. H. McD.

**OCTAVIUS** (2, *PW* 31), MARCUS, as tribune 133 B.C. vetoed the agrarian bill of his relative Ti. Gracchus (q.v. 3) and, persisting in opposition, was illegally deposed by a special vote of the assembly. This turned many men, who were not opposed to reform, against Gracchus. C. Gracchus (q.v. 4) in 123 proposed a bill aimed at further punishing Octavius, but withdrew it at his mother's request.

D. C. Earl, *Latomus* 1960, 657 ff.                    E. B.

**OCTAVIUS** (3, *PW* 20), GNAEUS, grandson of (1), failed to gain the aedileship, but became consul in 87 B.C. as a supporter of Sulla. Opposing his colleague Cinna (q.v. 1), he attacked him and his adherents and drove those who escaped death out of the city (thus starting the *bellum Octavianum*). He then had Cinna deposed and the *flamen Dialis* Merula appointed in his place, thus practically seizing sole power. Cinna, collecting an army, with the aid of Marius, Carbo (q.v. 2), and Sertorius (q.v.) besieged Rome; Octavius, despised by his own men, proved unable to defend it and had to call on Pompeius (q.v. 3) Strabo and Metellus (q.v. 7) for help. After Pompeius' death the Senate surrendered the city against his will and he was killed wearing his consular robes.

E. B.

**OCTAVIUS** (4, *PW* 15), GAIUS, from a wealthy equestrian family of Velitrae, rose to the praetorship (61 B.C.) and governed Macedonia with conspicuous ability. He died on his way back to Rome in 58. Velleius (2. 59. 2) sums him up as 'gravis, sanctus, innocens, dives'. By his first wife Ancharia he was father of Octavia (1) and by Atia (q.v. 1) of Octavia (2) and Gaius, the later Augustus.

Syme, *Rom. Rev.*, see index.                    G. W. R.; T. J. C.

**ODAENATHUS**, SEPTIMIUS, a Palmyrene noble of consular rank, on the capture of Valerian assumed the title of king and at the head of local troops inflicted a severe defeat on Sapor (A.D. 260). Gallienus rewarded him with the post of *dux* and, it would seem, *corrector totius orientis*, and Odaenathus on his behalf crushed the usurper Quietus at Emesa. From 262 to 267 he led the Roman army of the East and his own Palmyrene troops against Persia, reconquering Mesopotamia, but failing to capture Ctesiphon; he was rewarded with the title of *imperator*. In 267 he and his eldest son were murdered. Odaenathus' main interest was to protect the Eastern trade of his own city against the Persians, and he was content to acknowledge the suzerainty of Gallienus, since his nominal submission gave him command over the Roman army of the East. He was succeeded by his widow Zenobia (q.v.).

*PW* Suppl. xi, 1242 ff.; J. G. Février, *Histoire de Palmyre* (1931), 70 ff.                    A. H. M. J.

**ODEUM** (ᾠδεῖον), a small theatre or roofed hall for musical competitions and other assemblages. The earlier Athenian Odeum, which according to Plutarch (*Pericles*, 13) was built by Pericles, was a building of a different kind. Plutarch's description, 'many-seated and many-columned', suggests a resemblance to the Telesterion at Eleusis—a square building—and his description of the roof as conical or pyramidal (said to have been copied from the tent of Xerxes) also seems to imply approximate equality of length and breadth. The Odeum abutted on the theatre of Dionysus on the east; it has not been fully excavated and its form and extent have not been precisely determined. Vitruvius (5. 9) states that Pericles ornamented the building with stone columns and with the masts and spars of ships captured from the Persians, and that it was destroyed by fire during the Mithridatic war and rebuilt by King Ariobarzanes.

Pausanias (7. 20. 6) uses the name Odeum for certain theatres of Roman type (*see* THEATRES)—the Odeum of Herodes Atticus, built as a memorial to his wife Regilla, who died in A.D. 160, and a similar building at Patrae, both of which have been largely reconstructed in modern times for the performance of plays. He also mentions an odeum in the Athenian agora (1. 8. 6); this is almost certainly a handsome covered theatre of which remains have been found (*Hesp.* 1950, 31 ff.) and very probably identical with the Agrippeion in which, according to Philostratus (*VS* 2. 5. 4, 2. 8. 3–4), sophists gave rhetorical displays.

W. Judeich, *Topographie von Athen²* (1931), 306, 326; I. T. Hill, *The Ancient City of Athens* (1953), 72 ff., 110 ff.; M. Bieber, *History of the Greek and Roman Theater²* (U.S.A. 1961), 220.
H. W. R.; R. E. W.

**ODOACER,** the first barbarian king of Italy (A.D. 476–93), was a German who served under several Roman commanders before rebelling in 476, when he deposed Romulus (q.v.) Augustulus and was proclaimed king. He recognized the overlordship of the Eastern Emperor Zeno and won the support of the Roman Senate. He ruled Italy capably and, although himself an Arian, he interfered little with the Catholics. He was overthrown in the campaigns of 489–93 by Theodoric (q.v.) the Ostrogoth, to whom he surrendered Ravenna, where he was treacherously murdered (493).                    E. A. T.

A. H. M. Jones. *JRS* 1962, 126 ff.

**ODYSSEUS** ('Οδυσσεύς, Lat. *Vlixes*, a dialect form, not Ulysses), son and successor of Laertes king of Ithaca, husband of Penelope and father of Telemachus (qq.vv.). Like Achilles (q.v.) he comes from a fringe of the Achaean world and is a favourite of Homer. Throughout the *Iliad* he is both brave and sagacious; he gives prudent counsel (e.g. 19. 154 ff.); he is enterprising and so chosen by Diomedes as his companion in the night expedition (10. 242 ff.); he displays great valour in battle, especially 11. 312 ff., where he and Diomedes stop the rout of the Greeks and Odysseus continues to fight after Diomedes is wounded till he himself gets a flesh wound and Menelaus and the greater Aias (qq.vv.) rescue him. He is one of the three envoys sent to carry Agamemnon's offer to Achilles in book 9. In the funeral games of Patroclus he wins the foot race, Aias the Locrian coming in second (23. 778–9); he draws a wrestling match with the greater Aias (708 ff.).

He is the central figure of the *Odyssey*, which, by direct narrative of the poet and his own tale of his adventures in books 9–12, covers his career from the fall of Troy till ten years later. Leaving the Troad, he attacked the Cicones, but was beaten off with loss (9. 39 ff.); he was then caught by a storm, visited the country of the Lotophagi (q.v.), and wandered thence to the land of the Cyclopes (q.v.). Escaping from Polyphemus, he next visits Aeolia, the home of Aeolus (q.v. 1), who gives him a sack containing all the winds save the one which will bring him home. But while Odysseus sleeps his crew untie the sack, a storm arises and blows them from the coast of Ithaca back to Aeolia, where Aeolus refuses to have anything more to do with them (10. 19 ff.); after six days' sailing they reach the Laestrygonians (q.v.), and Odysseus barely escapes with his own ship and crew. He reaches Aeaea, the home of Circe (q.v.), and is told by her that he must, in order to reach home, go to Hades and consult the ghost of Tiresias (q.v.). This he succeeds in doing, sees many of the ghosts, and is told by Tiresias that after reaching home he is to sacrifice to Poseidon in a place where salt is unknown and an oar mistaken for a winnowing-fan, thus appeasing the god's anger for the blinding of his son Polyphemus. He will then find an easy death 'from the sea' (11. 134) in old age. Returning to Aeaea, he is given directions for his further voyage; by means of these he passes the Sirens (q.v.), runs between Scylla and Charybdis (qq.v.) with the loss of six men to the former, and comes to the island where the cattle of the Sun pasture. Here his men insist on landing, but, being windbound and short of provisions, they eat of the cattle. Helios demands revenge, and when they leave the island the ship is caught in a gale and destroyed by a thunderbolt; Odysseus alone escapes, and drifts to the island of Calypso (q.v.). Seven years later she lets him go by order of Zeus (5. 43 ff.) on a boat of his own making, Poseidon wrecks him, he swims ashore at Scheria and there is relieved by Nausicaa (q.v.) and sent home, after munificent entertainment, by Alcinous (q.v.). Meanwhile Telemachus has returned from his search for news of his father; Odysseus, disguised as a beggar by Athena, enters his own palace and disposes of the suitors of Penelope with the help of his son and the two faithful thralls, Eumaeus and Philoetius (21–2). He is reunited to Penelope, and an attempt by the kinsmen of the suitors to take vengeance is stopped by Athena, who makes peace between the two parties after the father of Antinous (q.v. 1) has been killed by old Laertes (24. 523).

The lost *Telegonia* continued the story. Odysseus performs his pilgrimage, meeting with some subsidiary adventures; Telegonus, his son by Circe, sets out to look for him, lands in Ithaca, and starts to plunder it; in the succeeding fight he kills Odysseus. Circe then makes the survivors immortal; she marries Telemachus and Penelope Telegonus.

Later authors, especially the tragedians, tend to blacken Odysseus' character. In Homer he is cunning and lies fluently on occasion; in some of the later legends he is a cowardly rascal. As early as the *Cypria* he tries to avoid coming to Troy, but is outwitted by Palamedes (q.v.), and he and Diomedes murder him (fr. 21 Allen). The same pair steal the Palladium, and Odysseus tries to murder Diomedes on the way back, to get all the credit himself (*Little Iliad*, fr. 9). In the surviving *Philoctetes* of Sophocles and apparently in that of Aeschylus also (see Rose, *Handb. Gk. Lit.* 169) his cunning is contrasted with the straightforwardness of Diomedes, or Neoptolemus, who accompanies him.

Odysseus had occasional worship as a hero in historical times, though, curiously enough, not in Ithaca (see Farnell, *Hero-Cults*, 326). There is no sufficient reason to suppose him other than a real local chieftain originally, though no doubt his actual doings are hopelessly overlaid with details of Homer's imagination or that of later writers. The plot of the *Odyssey* in particular is a folktale, as was pointed out by Nilsson (*Mycenaean origin of Gk. myth.* (U.S.A. 1932), 96; the motif is in Stith Thompson K 1815. 1).

By the most probable theory the scene of his wanderings is outside known territory, however much vague reports of foreign lands may have helped to provide details (see, however, V. Bérard, *Les Phéniciens et l'Odyssée*, 1902–3). But during and after the period of colonization numerous identifications of places in the *Odyssey* with those in or on the way to Italy and Sicily became very popular. Of these perhaps the most plausible is that of Scheria with Corcyra; for some account of this see A. Shewan, *Homeric Essays* (1935), 242 ff. The site of Ithaca itself has been hotly disputed (ibid. 1 ff.), though the traditional place, the modern *Thiaki*, is probably the one Homer means.

The Polyphemus adventure is loved from the seventh century; archaic art also represents Circe, the Sirens, and the quarrel with Aias; in the fifth century and after, the stealing of the Palladium, the death of Dolon, the Nekyia, Nausicaa, Eumaeus, the slaying of the suitors, and other scenes appear. From the later fifth century Odysseus

often wears the conical *pilos*, said to have been first given to him by Apollodorus of Athens (schol. *Il.* 10. 265).

Besides the literature cited in the text, J. Schmidt in Roscher's *Lexikon*, s.v., gives much useful material. For the literary tradition W. B. Stanford, *The Ulysses Theme*[2] (1962). In art, Brommer, *Vasenlisten*[2], 300 ff.  H. J. R.; C. M. R.

**OEA** (neo-Punic *Wy't*; modern *Tripoli*), a Phoenician port between the Syrtes, at the terminus of a trans-Saharan route. Under Rome a city of Africa Proconsularis, it became a *colonia* in the second century A.D. It was visited by Apuleius (*Apol.* 73), had a bishop by A.D. 256, and was the only city of the Tripolis (q.v. 1) to survive into medieval times. In 69 Oea summoned the Garamantes to her aid against Lepcis, and Valerius Festus had to drive them out of the province (Tac. *Hist.* 4. 50). Little remains of ancient Oea except a well-preserved four-way arch of A.D. 163–4.

D. E. L. Haynes, *The Antiquities of Tripolitania* (1956); S. Aurigemma, 'Un sepolcreto punico-romano in Tripoli', *Reports and Monographs of the Dept. of Antiquities in Tripoli* iv (1958).  O. B.

**OEBALUS,** an early Spartan king, who had a hero-shrine at Sparta (Paus. 3. 15. 10). He has no legend, merely a place in several mutually contradictory genealogies, for which see Wörner in Roscher's *Lexikon*, s.v. Hence *Oebalius, Oebalides*, etc., in Latin poetry often mean Spartan, and the name itself is now and then used for some minor character of Spartan or Peloponnesian origin (as Verg. *Aen.* 7. 734).  H. J. R.

**OECLES** (Ὀικλῆς) or **OECLEUS** (Ὀικλέους), in mythology, father of Amphiaraus (q.v.; Aesch. *Sept.* 609 and often). He has neither a consistent place in genealogy nor a legend of the smallest importance.

**OEDIPUS** (Ὀιδίπους, anciently, and probably correctly, taken to mean 'swell-foot'), in mythology, son of Laius king of Thebes and his wife Iocasta (Epicaste in Homer, *Od.* 11. 271 ff.). The story is told there that he married his mother unwittingly, and when it was found out she hanged herself, but he continued to be king. He afterwards fell in battle and had a great funeral feast (*Il.* 23. 679 f.). Hesiod says (*Op.* 162–3) that some men of the heroic age fell before Thebes fighting for the flocks of Oedipus; he may therefore have been killed in warding off a raid. Clearly this is inconsistent with his later story, dating in essentials from the cyclic epics *Thebais* and *Oedipodia* but best known from the tragedians.

Laius had been warned by Apollo that if he begot a son that son would kill him (Ar. *Ran.* 1184–5). This was his punishment for sinning against Pelops (q.v.), who had been his host while he was in exile from Thebes; he had carried off Pelops' son Chrysippus (Soph. *OT*, argument). Nevertheless, he neglected the warning (Aesch. *Sept.* 842; Soph. *OT* 711 ff.); a son was born and Laius exposed him, running a spike through his feet (to prevent his ghost walking?). The infant was found by a shepherd of Polybus king of Corinth, who was herding on the summer pastures of Mt. Cithaeron; Polybus, who was childless, adopted him and passed him off as his own, naming him Oedipus from the state of his feet. But Oedipus, being taxed in young manhood with being a supposititious child, went to Delphi to ask who his parents were. He was told that he would kill his father and marry his mother. Determining never to revisit Corinth, he wandered to Thebes, killing Laius in a chance encounter by the way. Arrived at Thebes, he found the city plagued by the Sphinx, a monster which destroyed those who could not solve a riddle she asked. He guessed it and she killed herself; or he overcame her in fight (Robert, op. cit. *infra*, ch. 2). His reward was the hand of the widowed queen. They had four children, Eteocles and Polynices,

Antigone (q.v. 1) and Ismene (the *Oedipodia*, fr. 1 Allen, made a second wife, Euryganeia, their mother after Iocasta's death). But the secret of the relationship came out; Iocasta hanged herself, Oedipus either blinded himself or (Euripides, fr. 541 Nauck) was blinded by Laius' servants. Thus he ceased to be king, going into exile or retirement. The former is Sophocles' version, the latter that of the lost epics, followed by Euripides (*Phoenissae*) and Statius (*Thebais*). His death is variously told, corresponding to his various cults (see Farnell, *Hero-Cults*, 332 ff.). The Attic version of his disappearance from earth at Colonus is told by Sophocles, *OC*.

But two explanations of the story seem possible. Either Oedipus is a real person, about whom fabulous details had gathered, following on the whole the lines of well-known folktales (so Rose, *Modern Methods in Class. Myth.* (1930), 24 ff.), or he is pure *Märchen*, taken up by epic (so Nilsson in *Gnomon* 1932, 18). See, however, M. Delcourt, *Œdipe ou la légende du conquérant* (1944).

Oedipus and the sphinx (which sits on a column) is a common subject in fifth-century Attic vase-painting, and seems to have been found also in sculpture (see Budde and Nicholls, *Cat. of Greek and Roman Sculpture in the Fitzwilliam Museum, Cambridge*, 20 ff., nos. 40 and 41). Other episodes are occasionally shown—the death of Laius, Euphorbus, and the baby Oedipus (Brommer, *Vasenlisten*[2], 340 ff.).

C. Robert, *Oidipus* (1915). H. J. R.; C. M. R.

**OENEUS** (Οἰνεύς), in mythology, king of Calydon, husband of Althaea and father or reputed father of Deianira and Meleager (1) (qq.v.). The names of husband and wife ('Wine-man' and 'Healer') and the story that Dionysus was the real father of Deianira (Hyg. *Fab.* 129, and Rose ad loc.) suggest that they were originally wine-gods. Oeneus is also connected with Ares, who is his grandfather in Nicander ap. Ant. Lib. 2, Meleager's father in Hyg. *Fab.* 171. 1. Periboea, daughter of Hipponous or Olenus, whom he married after the death of Althaea and who was the mother of Tydeus, is variously said to have been with child by Ares, Oeneus, or a certain Hippostratus (Apollod. 1. 74 f.; Diod. Sic. 4. 35. 1–2). In his old age he was robbed of his kingdom by his brother Agrius, but restored by Diomedes (q.v. 2) or Tydeus (Hyg. *Fab.* 175 and Rose ad loc.; Pherecydes in schol. *Iliad* 14. 120). An obscure story apparently from Ps.-Apollod. (see Wagner's Teubner ed., 186) says that Agamemnon and Menelaus (qq.v.) were put in his charge for a time to escape Thyestes. H. J. R.

**OENOMAUS** of Gadara (*c.* A.D. 120), Cynic philosopher. Works (of which a few fragments remain): Περὶ κυνισμοῦ; Πολιτεία; Περὶ τῆς καθ' Ὅμηρον φιλοσοφίας; Περὶ Κράτητος καὶ Διογένους καὶ τῶν λοιπῶν; Γοήτων φώρα (= Κατὰ χρηστηρίων); Κυνὸς αὐτοφωνία; and tragedies. The fragments of Γοήτων φώρα show it to have been a lively attack on the belief in oracles, an attack resting in part on the belief in freewill. He aimed at a Cynicism which did not follow slavishly either Antisthenes or Diogenes, and defined Cynicism as 'a sort of despair, a life not human but brutish, a disposition of soul that reckons nothing noble or virtuous or good'. W. D. R.

**OENONE** (Οἰνώνη), a nymph of Mt. Ida, loved by Paris (q.v.). When he deserted her for Helen she was bitterly jealous, and on learning that he had been wounded by Philoctetes (q.v.) with one of Heracles' arrows, she refused to cure him. Relenting too late, she came to Troy and found him already dead, whereat she hanged herself or leapt upon his funeral pyre.

Apollod. 3. 154–5; Parth. 4; Quint. Smyrn. 10. 259 ff., all with small variations. H. J. R.

**OENOPIDES** of Chios (fl. *c.* 450–425 B.C.), astronomer and mathematician, discovered the obliquity of the ecliptic, and introduced improvements in elementary geometry; he may have been the first to require that only the ruler and the compasses should be used in the solution of simple problems.

Diels, *Vorsokr.*[11] i. 393–5. W. D. R.

**OFELLA** (thus in the Greek sources), QUINTUS LUCRETIUS (*PW* 25), a Marian leader who joined Sulla and captured Praeneste for him (82 B.C.), sending him the head of Marius (q.v. 2). Persisting (though a mere *eques*) in an attempt to stand for the consulate of 81 despite Sulla's warning, he was killed at Sulla's orders. In the Latin sources the name is 'Afella'.

**OGULNIUS** (*PW* 5) **GALLUS**, QUINTUS (*cos.* 269 B.C.), as tribune of the *plebs* together with his brother Gnaeus, in 300 carried a law (*Lex Ogulnia*), despite the opposition of patricians and Appius Claudius (q.v. 4), by which plebeians became eligible for the highest priesthoods, and gained the majority in the college of the augurs. According to Beloch (*Rom. Gesch.* 350 f.) the *Lex Ogulnia* was passed in 296, when the Ogulnii were aediles. In this year they used fines from usurers for dedications and to set up near the *Ficus Ruminalis* a figure of the she-wolf suckling Romulus and Remus, which was soon commemorated on Rome's earliest silver coinage (Sydenham, *CRR* 2, n. 6). In 292 Q. Ogulnius headed the delegation sent to Epidaurus to bring Asclepius (q.v.) to Rome, which in 293 had been visited by a pestilence. In 273 he was a member of the diplomatic mission to the court of Ptolemy II. P. T.

**OGYGUS** (Ὤγυγος, etymology and meaning uncertain), a primeval king, generally of Boeotia (as Paus. 9. 5. 1), but of Lycia, Steph. Byz. s.v. Ὠγυγία; of Egyptian Thebes, schol. Lycophr. 1206; of the Titans, Theoph. *ad Autol.* 3. 29. The first Deluge was in his time, Euseb. *Praep. Evang.* 10. 10. 7. H. J. R.

**OIL** (cf. OLIVE CULTURE). Olive oil, the widespread use of which is characteristic of the Mediterranean region, was the main source of fat in the diet of Greece and Rome, since butter (βούτυρον = 'cow-cheese') was always considered food for barbarians, while oils and fats from other vegetable and animal sources, though not unknown, were comparatively unimportant. Oil was used as an ingredient of many cooked and baked foods, as fat for frying, and in serving salads and other dishes. Many grades and varieties were distinguished, depending on the kind of olive used, on its degree of ripeness when picked, and on the stage in the extraction process at which the oil was obtained. In this process the aim was to avoid crushing the kernels and to separate the oil from the bitter watery liquid (ἀμόργη, *amurca*) also contained in the fruit, which was fit only for manure and for some of the purposes for which kerosene is used nowadays. The difficulty of achieving this stimulated the invention of special apparatus in which the olives could be crushed after they were gathered (preferably by hand). For this purpose an earlier roller-mill came to be replaced by the *trapetum* (described by Cato, *Agr.* 20–2), in which a pair of stones turning round a solid column could be adjusted to the correct distance from the walls of the basin in which they revolved. After crushing, the kernels were eliminated and the first and best oil (*flos olei*) drawn off. Then the pulp was pressed in a beam or screw press (*torcular, torcularium*), sometimes after being soaked in hot water, to produce more oil (*oleum sequens, oleum cibarium*) of a lower quality. (This pressing was sometimes done in stages, the quality of the oil becoming worse as the pressure was raised.)

Finally, the different grades of oil were transferred to separate settling vats, from which the heavier *amurca* could be drawn off through spouts at the bottom, and stored before use in the *cella olearia*. In addition to its dietary use, oil was commonly employed also in unguents and toilet preparations, in medicine, in lamps, and in religious ceremonies. Its importance in Christian ritual at one time helped to spread its use to parts of Europe not naturally suited to olive culture.

PW, s.v. Oleum (xvii. 2454 ff.); A. G. Drachmann, *Ancient Oil Mills and Presses* (1932); Forbes, *Stud. Anc. Technol.* iii. 101 ff., 131 ff., 146 ff. L. A. M.

**OINTMENTS** served for medical purposes, mere pleasure, and religious ceremonies. The medical application, of course, was determined only by the expediencies of treatment. Half-way between remedy and luxury was the use of ointments in the gymnasium and as stimuli. To the side of luxury belonged, in spite of climatic conditions in the Mediterranean, the use of ointments before, during, and after the bath, at dinner, at almost any time of day or night. Neither the reprobation of the moralists nor governmental restrictions could check this indulgence; people liked ointments, elaborate mixtures, the attribute of Aphrodite, rather than pure oil, that of Athena. Moreover, the use of ointments was a sign of nobility and distinction and therefore was important also in the veneration of the gods and in burial ceremonies.

Material for the fabrication of ointments came from all over the world. Both wholesale trade and retail business were considerable, and hardly of any detrimental effect on the economic life as has been claimed; rather they provided a good tax revenue.

The receptacles in which ointments were kept, vases of various shapes and boxes, are among the most refined objects of art. Dry ointments were also wrapped in papyrus; to serve this purpose was the final destination of many an ancient book.

Hug, *PW* i A. 1851, s.v. 'Salben'; A. Schmidt, *Drogen u. Drogenhandel im Altert.* (1924); J. I. Miller, *The Spice Trade of the Roman Empire* (1969), see index. Economic implications correctly evaluated, Rostovtzeff, *Roman Empire²*. Handbooks on Greek and Roman antiquities. Archaeological material ('Lekythos', 'Aryballos', 'Alabastron', 'Pyxis', 'Plemochoe') surveyed by G. M. A. Richter and M. J. Milne, *Shapes and Names of Athenian Vases* (1935), with bibliography. L. E.

**OKNOS,** delay or hesitancy personified; a figure of Greek folklore. For some reason he is associated with the lower world (Plut. *De tranq. anim.* 473 c; cf. Paus. 10. 29. 1, Polygnotus' picture of Hades). He is always making a straw rope, which an ass eats as fast as he twines it (cf. the futile labour of the daughters of Danaus, q.v.; this may explain his infernal associations). Another version seems to be that he loads the ass with sticks, which fall off as fast as he puts them on (Apul. *Met.* 6. 18); perhaps the rope is to tie them.

See Höfer in Roscher's *Lexikon*, s.v. H. J. R.

**OLBIA,** a colony of Miletus, situated near the mouth of the Hypanis (*Bug*), and within easy reach of the estuary of the Borysthenes (*Dnieper*). It was founded in the late seventh century, and may have been preceded by a settlement on the island Berezan in the outer estuary. It was a fishing-centre and the terminal point of a trade-route up the Hypanis into central Europe; but its main importance lay in its export of wheat from the 'Black Earth' area of south-west Russia, much of which it bought for resale from the Scythian hinterland. Olbia enjoyed its highest prosperity in the sixth century and until the middle of the fifth, at which time it was visited by Herodotus. It apparently had no share in the grain trade with Athens in the later fifth and fourth centuries,

and in the third century it suffered from the growing insecurity of its hinterland (*SIG* 495—a record of frequent danegelds paid to marauding chieftains by a wealthy citizen). It was sacked *c.* 60 B.C. by the Dacian king Burebistas, and the rebuilt city appeared to Dio Chrysostomus (*c.* A.D. 80) impoverished and half-barbarized, though its inhabitants professed a passionate regard for Homer. It recovered some of its prosperity when Hadrian gave it a garrison, but it was destroyed by the Alans in the third century.

E. H. Minns, *Scythians and Greeks* (1913), 451 ff.; *Arch. Rep.* 1962–3, 42 ff.; M. Danoff, *PW* Suppl. ix, 1092 ff. M. C.; J. B.

**OLEN,** mythical epic poet, before Musaeus (q.v.); a Hyperborean or Lycian; said to have brought the worship of Apollo and Artemis from Lycia to Delos, where he celebrated their birth among the Hyperboreans in hymns which continued to be recited there (Hdt. 4. 35; Callim. *Del.* 304–5; Paus. 1. 18. 5; cf. ibid. 8. 21. 3). *See* HYMNS.
W. F. J. K.

**OLIGARCHY,** the 'rule of the few'; on its connexions with the old nobility and its growth out of aristocracy *see* ARISTOCRACY. The chief difference consisted in the replacement of birth by wealth as the decisive qualification: oligarchy was plutocracy. There were many conflicts between the old nobility and the *nouveaux riches*, but finally 'money made the man' (Alcaeus and Theognis, *passim*). This also meant a victory of urban over tribal organization.

In oligarchy political power was confined to a minority of the citizens; the majority had citizenship, but without full political rights. The method of selecting the 'few' varied greatly, according to the economic conditions of each city. In most States the landowners predominated for a long time, but movable wealth was gradually put on an equal level. In addition, the ruling few might be limited to a fixed number which differed in different States, often rising to the 'rule of the Thousand'. Sometimes there was a scale of several citizen classes distinguished by wealth and accordingly by political rights (timocracy). In his classification of oligarchies (*Pol.* 6. 1292ᵃ38 ff., 1293ᵃ11 ff.) Aristotle differentiates between aristocracy and oligarchy rather than between the actual forms of oligarchy. Political power in oligarchies was generally concentrated in the council. In cases where the number of citizens was very small, the assembly could preserve a real activity. It is difficult sometimes to distinguish the assembly from the council, e.g. the 600 in Massilia. Membership of the council was usually by election and expired only at death; sometimes, as in the case of the Areopagus (q.v.), the council was composed of retired high officials formerly elected by the assembly. Some characteristic features of oligarchy appear in Sparta, always its champion. But Sparta represented a particular form of State, and its institutions must not be considered as typically oligarchic.

L. Whibley, *Greek Oligarchies* (1896); G. Glotz, *The Greek City* (1929); V. Ehrenberg, *The Greek State* (1960). V. E.

**OLIVE CULTURE.** We know from finds that olives were grown in the Mediterranean area and Minoan Crete during the Neolithic age. Plantations are mentioned by Homer, and oil was exported from Attica before and after the time of Solon. As soon as it became possible by imports of grain to satisfy most of the requirements of the Greek people, crops such as olives and grapes took the place of grain and were very widely cultivated in Greece during the classical age. There was a similar increase of olive cultivation in Italy after the Second Punic War. From the later first century A.D., exports of oil and wine from Italy being no longer able to compete with the increased local production of the Roman provinces, a more equable cultivation became a characteristic of the Mediterranean areas.

Methods of cultivation were much improved from the classical Greek period to the early Principate, bringing about a world-wide interchange of varieties. Two hundred trees, for example, were exported from Attica to Egypt under Ptolemy II. At least twenty-seven varieties were known, and improved mills and presses increased production. The grafting of olive-shoots on fig-trees and vines was successfully performed, and wild olives were grafted on the cultivated stocks to improve production (*terebratio*). Cheap labour, mostly servile, was used for the harvest. Olives were more remunerative to the large owner than to the small peasant, as it might take fifteen years to ensure a profitable return on an investment in a new plantation.

In Cato's time the average profit was *c.* 6 per cent on the capital invested. A model plantation of 160 acres described by Cato employed a slave overseer, his wife, five slave labourers, three ox-drivers, one ass-driver, a swineherd, a shepherd, with its oil mills, cattle, and working implements. Rome seems to have occasionally restricted cultivation in the provinces to protect Italian growers. Olive cultivation in the ancient world created a tradition in most Mediterranean countries which has never been completely lost even today. *See* AGRICULTURE, OIL.

A. S. Pease, *PW*, s.v. 'Ölbaum', 'Oleum'; J. Hörnle, ibid., s.v. 'Torcular', 'Trapetum'; A. B. Drachmann, 'Ancient Oil Mills and Presses' (*Dansk Videnskab-Selskab, Archeologiske Meddelelser* i, 1932); lamps: Fabrer, *L'Olivier et l'huile dans l'Afrique romaine* (1953). Frank, *Econ. Survey* i–v, index. E. Juengst–P. Thielscher, *Bonner Jahrbuecher* 1954, 32 f.; 1957, 53 f. B. Laum, *Rev. Arch.* 1928, 233 f. Magie, *Rom. Rule Asia Min.*, index. Rostovtzeff, *Hellenistic World. Roman Empire*² (indexes). F. M. H.

**OLYMPIA,** the main sanctuary of Zeus in Greece, was situated in a rich and lovely tract of Elis, in a hollow between the low hills that flank the river Alpheus. Strabo states that its fame was first derived from an oracle of Earth, like that at Delphi, and a pre-Hellenic occupation of the site is proved by the discovery of pottery and houses of the Bronze Age at the foot of Kronos Hill, elsewhere at Olympia, and in the vicinity. There have been numerous finds of Mycenaean material on the lower Alpheus, and at Olympia at the site of the new museum. According to Pindar the Olympic festival was founded by Heracles, and this tradition was also held at Elis; but the local belief was that Pelops originated it after his victory over Oenomaus. The games were said to have started in the ninth century, but the first Olympiad was dated 776 B.C.

The sanctuary of 'Altis' was a walled enclosure, which came into full occupation soon after the Dorian Invasion. The oldest shrine was that of Pelops. There were two temples, that of Hera, dating from the seventh century and originally constructed of wood, and that of Zeus, completed in 457. On the north side, under Kronos Hill, lay eleven Treasuries (q.v.) of various Greek States in a row. The only building on the east side, other than a portico, was the circular 'Philippeum', built by Philip II of Macedon to commemorate himself. Innumerable statues of athletic victors stood in the Altis. Outside it were many large buildings of various dates: the Palaestra, a hostelry known as the Leonidaeum, of fourth-century date, used by officials, a Prytaneum, and a Bouleuterium.

Olympia was excavated by German archaeologists in 1881, although an earlier expedition from France in 1829 had secured parts of the sculptured metopes of the temple of Zeus, now in the Louvre. The German excavators found the remaining metopes and almost 80 per cent of the pedimental sculptures. Among other notable discoveries were the head of Hera (or a sphinx) from the Heraeum, the Victory of Paeonius, the Hermes

and Dionysus, and a bronze head of a boxer attributed to Silanion. Renewed German excavations have revealed a great deal more. It appears that the archaic stadium was replaced by a monumental stadium before mid fifth century. This in turn was superseded about the middle of the fourth century by the stadium still visible which has been restored. The first, mid-fifth-century, monumental stadium extended much further to the West than the later one, projecting into the sanctuary area and forming one unit with it. From these excavations have come an immense number of fine bronzes, including dedicated arms (such as a helmet taken by the Athenians from the Persians) and metal objects of oriental as well as Greek origin, e.g. from Urartu in the Lake Van region of eastern Anatolia. Other excavations on the traditional site of the workshop used by Phidias, when he created the gold and ivory figure of Zeus (Paus. 5. 15. 1), have revealed moulds for hammering metal and casting glass, fragments of ivory, and a mug inscribed with the name of Phidias. The moulds used for hammering out the gold drapery of the Zeus seem to indicate a date (stylistic) in the 30s of the fifth century and establish that the Zeus was made after the Athena at Athens. An edict of the Emperor Theodosius, enjoining the destruction of all pagan shrines, made an end of Olympia as a show-site.

E. N. Gardiner, *Olympia. Its History and Remains* (1925). *Berichte über die Ausgrabungen in Olympia* i–vii (1937–61); *Olympische Forschungen* ii (1950); E. Kunze, *Archaische Schildbänder* iii (1957); F. Willemsen, *Dreifußkessel von Olympia; Neue deutsche Ausgrabungen im Mittelmeergebiet und im vorderen Orient* (1959), for the finds at the 'Workshop of Phidias' (278 ff.). For the earliest remains and history, see *MDAI (A)* 1962, 1 ff. S. C.; R. J. H.

**OLYMPIAN GAMES.** According to tradition the Olympian Games, held once every four years, were founded in 776 B.C., and a list of the winners from that year to A.D. 217, drawn up by Julius Africanus, has been preserved for us by Eusebius. In A.D. 393 they were abolished by the Emperor Theodosius I. At first they were confined to one day and the contests consisted only of running and wrestling; but in the early years of the seventh century B.C., perhaps under the influence of Pheidon, tyrant of Argos, they were reorganized and enlarged, and races for chariots and single horses were introduced. The foot-race, one length of the stadium, always remained the principal event. In early times most of the victors were from Sparta, but as the games attained Panhellenic status Spartan superiority declined and many victors came from Sicily and Italy as well as from other cities of the Greek mainland and islands.

The games were in honour of Olympian Zeus. In his precinct, the Altis, lying between the rivers Alpheus and Cladeus, stood his temple, together with the statues of victorious athletes (*see* OLYMPIA). The first of the five days, to which the games in 472 were extended, was spent in sacrifices and general festivity, while the competitors and judges took the oath of fair dealing. On the second morning the herald proclaimed the names of the competitors, and the day passed in chariot- and horse-races together with the pentathlon competition for men. The boys' contests came on the third day; the men's foot-races, jumping, wrestling, boxing, and pankration on the fourth, the last event being the race for men in armour. On the fifth day there were sacrifices, and in the evening a banquet at which the victors were entertained. The prizes consisted of chaplets of wild olive.

E. N. Gardiner, *Olympia* (1925). For the other literature *see* ATHLETICS. F. A. W.

**OLYMPIAS,** daughter of Neoptolemus of Molossia married Philip II of Macedon in 357 B.C. and bore him two children, Alexander (in 356) and Cleopatra. Passionate and mystical, she gave her son these qualities; but his practical and imaginative mind was not hers. Her relations with the polygamous Philip became strained, but the story that she was his real murderer was only Cassander's propaganda. Devoted as Alexander always remained to her, he wisely refused to let her exercise any power, and he supported his governor in Macedonia, Antipater, against her. In 331 she quitted Macedonia for Epirus, which for years she virtually ruled. After Alexander's death she waged a propaganda war against Antipater's house, until in 317 Polyperchon invoked her help against Antipater's son Cassander in Macedonia. Macedonians regarded Alexander's mother as sacred; she mastered Macedonia without a blow, murdered Philip III, and made her grandson (Alexander IV) sole king. But her unbridled passions, displayed in an orgy of murder, ruined her chances and brought Cassander back; she had to surrender, and Cassander's army condemned her to death. But even so they dared not touch her themselves; she was finally killed by relatives of her victims. Her grave at Pydna was revered.

G. H. Macurdy, *Hellenistic Queens* (1932), 22 ff.; C. F. Edson, 'The Tomb of Olympias', *Hesp.* 1949, 84 f.; *see also* ALEXANDER (3).
W. W. T.

**OLYMPIEUM,** the temple of Zeus Olympius at Athens; begun by Antistates, Callaeschrus, Antimachides, and Porinus, architects employed by Pisistratus, but abandoned after the latter's death, and not resumed until Antiochus Epiphanes employed the Roman architect Cossutius to continue the work. It was completed at the order of Hadrian (Vitr. 7 *praef.*). The Pisistratean building was planned as a Doric temple. Cossutius changed the order to Corinthian, but in general seems to have adhered to the original plan, dipteral at the sides, tripteral at the ends. The cella was of the open-roofed type called 'hypaethral' (Vitr. 3. 2). The stylobate measured *c.* 135 by 354 feet, and the Corinthian columns were nearly 57 feet in height.

The cult was of great antiquity, being founded by Deucalion, according to Pausanias (1. 18. 7-8), and associated with other ancient cults such as those of Ge and Kronos.

The name is also used of other shrines of Zeus such as the large temple at Acragas (q.v.).

W. B. Dinsmoor, *Architecture of Ancient Greece* (1950), 91, 280 f.; R. E. Wycherley, *GRBS* 1964, 161 ff. H. W. R.; R. E. W.

**OLYMPIODORUS** (1) (fl. 307–280 B.C.), democratic Athenian commander, secured Aetolian help against Cassander (*c.* 306), whom he subsequently repulsed from Elatea. He gave support to Lachares (q.v.), but after the recapture of Athens by Demetrius Poliorcetes became virtually tyrant, holding the archonship for two successive years (294–292). In 287 he led an insurrection against Macedon, seizing the Museum; later he helped Demochares to take Eleusis and, perhaps between 280 and 277, temporarily liberated Piraeus (Paus. 1. 26. 3).

W. S. Ferguson, *Hellenistic Athens* (1911); W. B. Dinsmoor, *Archons of Athens* (1931); G. De Sanctis, *Riv. Fil.* 1936; B. D. Meritt, *Hesp.* 1938. F. W. W.

**OLYMPIODORUS** (2) of Gaza, sceptical philosopher, pupil of Carneades (who lived 214–129 B.C.). See Zeller, *Phil. d. Griechen* 3⁴. 1. 544.

**OLYMPIODORUS** (3) of Thebes (Egypt). Greek historian. Born before A.D. 380, he died after 425. We do not know where he lived, but we are informed that in 412 he was sent as an ambassador to the Huns and in 415 he visited Athens. A typical Egyptian 'intellectual' of the late fourth century, he remained a pagan. He gave poetry as his profession, but he is known to us as the writer of twenty-two books of history (or, rather, of memoirs) from A.D. 407 to 425, which he dedicated to Theodosius II.

The work is lost, but was summarized by Photius (*Bibl.* 80) and used by Zosimus and Sozomenus. It contained many references to personal experiences, learned excursuses, details on the life of the contemporary governing class and of the barbarians, and on superstitious beliefs he probably shared. He claimed Homer as his fellow countryman.

Fragments in *FHG* iv. 58, and L. Dindorf, *Hist. Graec. Min.* i (1870), 450. E. A. Thompson, *CQ* 1944, 43 ff.; G. Moravcsik, *Byzantinoturcica²* i (1958), 468 (with further bibl.). A. M.

**OLYMPUS** (1), the highest mountain of the Greek peninsula, situated on the borders of Macedonia and Thessaly. It rises at one point to 9,573 feet, and there are several other heights of over 9,000 feet. Famous as the reputed home of the gods, it was important in religion and mythology and is frequently mentioned by poets. The huge massif covers a large area extending inland from the coast of Pieria, and it therefore served to shield Greece on the north-east: invaders from this direction were compelled, unless prepared to follow very high and difficult tracks, either to force the narrow defile of Tempe (q.v.) or to use the mountain passes of Petra and Volustana to the west of Olympus. It also contributed to the isolation of Thessaly by cutting it off from Macedonia and the Thermaic Gulf. H. D. W.

**OLYMPUS** (2), in Cyprus (modern *Troodos*), rises to 6,403 feet and constitutes the main mountain mass of the south-west part of the island. Heavily wooded, on its lower slopes are modern mines of asbestos, and in antiquity there are said to have been gold-mines. It is today used as both a summer and winter resort. T. B. M.

**OLYNTHUS,** a city north of Potidaea on the mainland of the Chalcidic peninsula. Originally Bottiaean, it became a Greek city after its capture by Persia (479 B.C.) and repopulation from Chalcidice; its position and mixed population made it the natural centre of Greek Chalcidice against attacks from Athens, Macedonia, and Sparta. In 433 the city was strengthened by further migration and received territory from Macedon (Thuc. 1. 58), and it soon became the capital of a Chalcidian Confederacy issuing federal coinage; by 382 the growth of the Confederacy aroused the enmity of Sparta, which reduced Olynthus after a two-year siege and disbanded the Confederacy (Xen. *Hell.* 5. 2. 11 f.). When Sparta collapsed, Olynthus re-formed the Confederacy and resisted Athenian attacks on Amphipolis; when that city fell to Philip II of Macedon Olynthus allied with him against Athens (Diod. 16. 8), expelled the Athenian cleruchy from Potidaea, and received Anthemus from Philip (357–356). Alarmed by the growing power of Philip, Olynthus intrigued with Athens, harboured rivals to the Macedonian throne, and with Athenian assistance defied Philip; the city fell by treachery (Dem. 19. 266 f.) and was destroyed (348). Excavations have revealed the layout of the city.

A. B. West, *The History of the Chalcidic League* (U.S.A. 1919). D. M. Robinson, *Excavations at Olynthus* (U.S.A. 1929–52); M. Gude, *A History of Olynthus* (U.S.A. 1933); F. Hampl, *Hermes* 1935, 177 ff.; J. A. O. Larsen, *Greek Federal States* (1968), 55 ff. N. G. L. H.

**OMPHALE,** in mythology, a Lydian queen, daughter of Iardanus (Apollod. 2. 131, which see for the story, which is much older, perhaps going back to Creophylus and mentioned in Tragedy, e.g. Soph. *Trach.* 248 ff.). Heracles (q.v.), having killed Iphitus son of Eurytus of Oechalia, could find no one to purify him (cf. NELEUS) and applied to Apollo. The god would give him no answer till Heracles started to carry off his tripod, saying he would found an oracle of his own. Zeus stopped the quarrel with a thunderbolt, and Apollo said he could be purified and rid of the madness which afflicted him if he was sold as a slave and the price given to Eurytus. Hermes arranged the sale and Omphale was the buyer. According to Apollodorus, she set him labours of the usual type, against brigands, etc., none of which has a Lydian setting or geography; Alexandrian poets (see, e.g., Ov. *Her.* 9. 53 ff.) make great play with the theme of her setting him to women's work. The length of the slavery varies (one year in Soph., three in Apollod.), and it is commonly said he had a son, Lamus, by Omphale (Ov. loc. cit.).

See further Tümpel and Sieveking in Roscher's *Lexikon*, s.v.; W. R. Halliday, *Plutarch's Greek Questions* (1928), 187.     H. J. R.

**OMPHALOS,** the navel, a name given to objects, especially stones, of navel shape. Such stones were cult-objects in the most primitive religion of the Aegean region. They remained attached to several cults when a higher level of religion had been reached. The most famous omphalos was that in the adytum of Apollo's temple at Delphi (q.v., *and see* APOLLO, § 4). Late authors call it the tomb of Python or of Dionysus; this raises the question of the relation of the omphalos to omphaloid tombs and omphaloid altars. It may be a tombstone in the shape of a beehive tomb. Two omphaloi have been found at Delphi. One is the marble omphalos seen by Pausanias before the temple; its surface is covered with a sculptured network that represents the woollen fillets placed around the omphalos. The other, found down-slope from the temple, may be the true omphalos.

Any centrally located place was called the omphalos of its region, as Phlius of the Peloponnesus. So Delphi's omphalos was thought to mark the centre of the earth. The story was that Zeus, desiring to find the centre of the earth, started two eagles of equal speed at the same moment, one from the eastern edge of the world, one from the western; they met at Delphi. This story led to the placing of two golden eagles beside the omphalos, which were taken by Philomelus in the Sacred War.

ANCIENT SOURCES. Aesch. *Eum.* 40 ff.; Pind. *Pyth. passim*; Varro, *Ling.* 7. 17; Paus. 10. 16. 3; Hesych. *T* 1134; Tatian, *Adv. Gr.* 8.
MODERN LITERATURE. W. H. Roscher, 'Omphalos', *Sächsische Gesellschaft der Wissenschaften, Abh. Phil.-Hist. Kl.* (1913), no. 9; id. 'Neue Omphalosstudien', ibid. (1915), no. 1; J. Harrison, *Themis* (1927), 396 ff.; J. Bousquet, *BCH* 1951, 210 ff.; J. Fontenrose, *Python* (1959), 374 ff. and fig. 28.     J. E. F.

**ONASANDER** ('Ονάσανδρος, the preferable spelling), whom tradition makes a Platonic philosopher, wrote his Στρατηγικός under Claudius. It is a treatise on the duties of a commander, a dull exposition of commonplace military and ethical principles, for which the author disclaims any originality; it was enormously popular during the Renaissance.

A. Köchly, 'Ονασάνδρου Στρατηγικός (1860); Illinois Greek Club, *Onasander* (Loeb, 1923), with full bibliography.     W. W. T.

**ONESICRITUS** of Astypalaea, seaman, Cynic, and Alexander-historian, was with Alexander in India; he steered Alexander's ship down the Jhelum, and was Nearchus' lieutenant on his voyage. He has left a reputation as a liar, but his book did not profess to be history; it was an historical romance resembling Xenophon's *Cyropaedia*, with Alexander as a Cynic hero and culture-bringer. It formed an element in the vulgate, and Strabo and Pliny used it for natural history; but it exercised little direct influence.

Jacoby, *FGrH* 134. T. S. Brown, *Onesicritus* (1949). *See* ALEXANDER (3), Bibliography, Ancient Sources.     W. W. T.

**ONOMARCHUS,** Phocian commander in the Third Sacred War (q.v.). After the Phocian defeat at Neon (354 B.C.) he was elected *strategos autokrator* and em-ployed the temple funds at Delphi to bribe Thessaly into neutrality and to hire mercenaries. Defeating the Locrians and Boeotians, he refounded Orchomenus in Boeotia, and forced Philip II of Macedon to evacuate Thessaly (late 353). All-powerful from Olympus to the Corinthian Gulf, Onomarchus hoped with Athenian and Spartan aid to crush Thebes; but he was drawn north-wards by Philip's invasion of Thessaly. Marching towards his ally, Lycophron of Pherae, probably in co-operation with an Athenian squadron, Onomarchus was defeated and killed at the battle of the Crocus Field (352). An able and unscrupulous individualist, Onomarchus made Phocis a first-class power; gambling on the dwindling assets of Delphian moneys, he came near to success.     N. G. L. H.

**OPHELLAS,** Macedonian officer under Alexander and one of the *hetairoi*; sent by the satrap Ptolemy to subdue Cyrene (322 B.C.). He became governor there; but we know nothing certain of his attitude in the Cyrenean revolt of 313/12, nor whether he was concerned with the constitutional reforms of that period (*see* CYRENE). At any rate, he became almost independent. There is little information about his relations with Carthage. But he took part in Agathocles' (q.v.) campaign to Africa, when, over-estimating his forces, he hoped to subdue Carthage, and to found an African realm. Married to Eurydice of the Philaid family, he was able to induce many Athenians to join him. Having assembled a large body of Greek soldiers and colonists, he lost many of his men during the march through the desert. Eventually the two Greek generals joined forces. But soon after (probably 309), Ophellas was murdered by Agathocles, who took over his troops. Almost all the colonists perished.

V. Ehrenberg, *Polis und Imperium* (1965), 539 ff.     V. E.

**OPHION** ('Οφίων), Orphic god, husband of Eurynome and ruler of the universe before Kronos (q.v.); Ap. Rhod. 1. 503 ff.; Kern, *Orph. frag.* 98, no. 29.

**OPHTHALMOLOGY** was greatly advanced by the Greeks. Twenty operations were devised; until the beginning of the eighteenth century only four were added. The treatment of more than thirty diseases was not essentially changed until the beginning of the seventeenth century. This great achievement, mostly due to the Hellenistic physicians, was closely connected with the development of human anatomy and probably with that of mathematical optics. Other factors may have contributed to a special interest in the subject and there-by to the amazing success: the frequency of eye diseases in the Mediterranean world, the importance of sight for every human being, the valuation of sight peculiar to the Greeks.

As regards anatomy, the fabric of the eye was almost entirely unravelled. Seven membranes were distinguished, the optic nerve was accurately described. The theories of vision were less satisfactory, depending too much on the various philosophical conceptions; Galen assumed that a sight-spirit proceeds from the brain along the nerves, envelops the object seen, and then returns to the crystalline humour, thus completing the act of vision. The explanation of diseases, in spite of all anatomical knowledge, was based mainly on humoral conceptions. The therapy consisted in certain dietetic measures and also in the local application of collyria, the great variety of which is attested by the innumerable seals of Roman oculists. As for surgery, it suffices to refer to the astounding operations for cataract, as described by Celsus and as practised by Antyllus (2nd c. A.D.).

TEXTS. Celsus, bks. 6 and 7; Aetius, bk. 7; the only Greek treatise preserved: Th. Puschmann, 'Nachträge z. Alexander

Trallianus', *Berl. Stud. f. class. Philol. u. Archaeol.* v. 2 (1886). Medieval compilations, probably based on ancient material now lost: P. Pansier, *Collectio ophthalmologica Veterum Auctorum* (1903), (fasc. vii Ps.-Galen, *De oculis*). Fragments of the canon of ophthalmology, written by the Herophilean Demosthenes (1st c. A.D.) and dependent on Herophilus' book on eye diseases, collected J. Hirschberg, *Arch. f. Gesch. d. Med.* (1918–19); concerning a medieval translation of this work, M. Wellmann, *Hermes* 1903. Translation of Antyllus, M. Meyerhof, *Die Antike* 1933.

LITERATURE. General survey, J. Hirschberg, *Gesch. d. Augenheilkunde im Altertum*, *Handbuch der gesamten Augenheilkunde* xii² (1899); cf. also V. Deneffe, *Les Oculistes gallo-romains au III^e siècle* (1896). Galen's theory of vision, H. Cherniss, *AJPhil.* 1933. For other ancient theories of vision see J. I. Beare, *Greek Theories of Elementary Cognition from Alcmaeon to Aristotle* (1906) and G. M. Stratton, *Theophrastus and the Greek Physiological Psychology before Aristotle* (1917). Operations, J. Ilberg, *Arch. Pap.* (1908). Instruments, J. St. Milne, *Surgical Instruments in Greek and Roman Times* (1907). Seals, *CIL* xiii. 3, 10021 (Espérandieu). For the ancients' judgement on blindness, its social implications, and for blinding as self-punishment or punishment of others, see A. Esser, 'Das Antlitz der Blindheit in der Antike', *Janus*, Suppl. iv (1961).          L. E.

**OPIL(L)IUS**, AURELIUS (early 1st c. B.C.), a freedman who wrote on philosophy, rhetoric, and grammar, and was cited as an authority by Varro and Verrius Flaccus. One of his works in nine books was entitled *Libri Musarum*. He interested himself in determining the canon of the genuine works of Plautus, an author whom he frequently cited in his explanations of the meanings of words.

G. Funaioli, *Gramm. Rom. Frag.* 86–95. Schanz–Hosius, § 195. 2.          J. F. M.

**OPIMIUS** (*PW* 4), LUCIUS, as praetor in 125 B.C. crushed the revolt of Fregellae (q.v.), but was not allowed to triumph. As consul (121), with his colleague Fabius (q.v. 8) away in Gaul, he was in charge of Rome; interpreting the so-called '*SC ultimum*' (q.v., then first used) as giving him unlimited powers, he proceeded against C. Gracchus (q.v. 4) and Flaccus (q.v. 3), killing many citizens and in a special *quaestio* condemning (it is said) 3,000. He then dedicated the restored temple of Concordia. Prosecuted by Decius (q.v. 5) in 120, he was defended by Carbo (q.v. 1) and acquitted, thus establishing the '*SC ultimum*' in constitutional practice. Head of a commission that divided Numidia between Jugurtha (q.v.) and Adherbal, he was accused before the tribunal set up by Mamilius (q.v. 3) and went into exile. Cicero saw his tomb at Dyrrhachium.          E. B.

**OPPIAN** of Cilicia (late 2nd c. A.D.), author of Greek hexameter poetry, the *Cynegetica*, for each verse of which Caracalla gave him a piece of gold, and possibly also the *Halieutica*, which may, however, be by another Oppian, of Syria, early third century A.D.; the poems do not contain much new scientific knowledge on their subjects, but have some grace and power of expression.

TEXT. A. W. Mair (Loeb, 1928).          W. F. J. K.

**OPPIDUM** means not a community—*civitas, pagus, municipium*, or *colonia* (qq.v.)—but the town centre of such a community, or else any urban agglomeration in Italy or the provinces to which no territory was juridically attached. In Roman territory before 89 B.C. the chief *oppida* were those of the ex-Latin incorporated States. In them was centred the local administration of their former *territorium*. The towns of the indigenous Romans, known as *fora* and *conciliabula*, had less authority, if any, over the locality. All these *oppida* were, however, assimilated to *municipia* between 89 and 44 B.C., becoming the centre of self-government for the adjacent territory. In the provinces regular communities of Roman citizens (Italian immigrants or enfranchised natives) were at first called *oppida civium Romanorum*, whether administered like villages by boards of *magistri*, or with a fuller constitution. Later these were assimilated to the

Italian *municipia* and adopted the usages of the Italian model.

See bibliography under MUNICIPIUM (Modern Views, (*a*) Republic).          A. N. S.-W.

**OPPIUS** (1, *PW* 8), GAIUS, a tribune of 215 B.C. who carried a war-time sumptuary measure (*Lex Oppia*) forbidding women to own more than half an ounce of gold, wear multi-coloured dresses, or ride in two-horsed vehicles in Rome. It was repealed in 195 despite the fierce opposition of Cato, whose original speech is probably not reflected in that composed by Livy (34. 2–4).          H. H. S.

**OPPIUS** (2, *PW* 9), GAIUS, Caesar's friend of equestrian rank and manager with Balbus (3) of his affairs. He corresponded with Cicero on Caesar's behalf and after Caesar's death helped Octavian. He wrote a number of biographies, certainly of Scipio (5) Africanus, probably of Caesar and Cassius (6); and he also wrote for Octavian (perhaps *c*. 32 B.C.) a pamphlet to prove that Caesarion (q.v.) was not Caesar's son. Some ancient critics wrongly attributed to him the *Bellum Alexandrinum*, *Africum*, and *Hispaniense* (qq.v.).

Peter, *HR Rel.* ii. lxiii f., 46 ff.; Schanz–Hosius i. 350 f.; Syme, *Rom. Rev.*, see index.          A. M.; T. J. C.

**OPRAMOAS** of Rhodiapolis in Lycia is famous for the huge inscription (E. Kalinka and R. Herberdey, *Tituli Asiae Minoris* (Vienna, 1901– ), ii. 905) engraved on his temple tomb, which records the honours decreed to him by the Lycian Confederacy between A.D. 124 and 152, and the letters of the procurators and legates of Lycia-Pamphylia and of the Emperor Antoninus Pius relative to these decrees. He gave more than 600,000 *denarii* to the Confederacy and its constituent cities for games, buildings, distributions, etc., and perhaps hoped by bringing his munificence to the Emperor's notice to achieve senatorial rank. He lived to see his great-grandchildren senators.          A. H. M. J.

**OPS**, Roman goddess, of obscure functions. Her festivals (Opalia, 19 Dec.; Opiconsivia, 25 Aug.) by their dates and the title of the latter suggest association with Consus (q.v.; Consualia, 15 Dec. and 19 Aug.), but the December festival also has a connexion with Saturnus, (q.v.; Saturnalia, 17 Dec.), and, indeed, she is regularly associated with him by the ancients, he being identified with Kronos and she with Rhea. Her oldest place of worship was a small chapel in the Regia (Varro, *Ling.* 5. 21; Festus, 202, 20 Lindsay); for her other shrines, see Platner–Ashby, 372; Rohde, 750 ff. Her titles are Consiva and Opifera, Festus ibid. and *Fast. Arval.* on 23 Aug. (Volcanalia, where she is one of a group of deities receiving sacrifice).          H. J. R.

**OPTATIANUS PORFYRIUS**, PUBLILIUS (4th c. A.D.), poet. From exile he sent (before A.D. 325) a verse panegyric to Constantine and after his recall he became *praefectus urbi*. His poems (ed. E. Kluge, 1926) are full of ingenuities, such as acrostics and deliberate limitations of the kind of words employed; some are arranged to have the shape of altars, water-organs, etc.

Schanz–Hosius, §§ 783–4.          J. F. M.

**OPTIMATES, POPULARES.** Following the model of the Greek upper classes, those at Rome regarded themselves as 'the best .men' combining moral with social superiority. After the end of the 'Struggle of the Orders', in the third century B.C., there is evidence of a move towards a more democratic society. But at the same time the new *nobilitas* crystallized, and the oligarchy emerged triumphant from the Hannibalic War. Until 133 B.C. there was no serious challenge to it. Ti. Gracchus (q.v. 3), starting in part from faction politics, became the first to attack its predominance. With the legislation of his brother Gaius, a new class (*see* EQUITES) emerged, intended to be a check on the oligarchy, whose moral superiority C. Gracchus denied (cf. *ORF²* 48, fr. 17). Henceforth a *Popularis* tradition of challenging the identification of birth with merit was established. It attained its climax in the career of Marius (q.v. 1), but disappeared as a serious factor in politics with his eclipse in the 90s.

The early Populares also established characteristic methods: politically, as defenders of 'liberty' against 'faction', they worked through the People rather than the Senate and extended freedom of voting (q.v.); economically, they sought to relieve poverty and to rally the poor to their support by agrarian, colonial, and grain laws. Against these challenges, which they described as based on sectional interests, harmful to the State, and likely to lead to tyranny (*regnum*), the Optimates (or *boni*) became a conservative political force, based on (but not coextensive with) the traditional oligarchy. They used the word 'popularis' in a derogatory sense (= 'demagogue'); but the tradition of the Gracchi and Marius was cherished by the masses: Cicero, in public speeches, often called himself a Popularis (stressing his non-senatorial birth), and, to discredit opponents like Rullus and Clodius (qq.v.), claimed to be defending the true *Popularis* tradition against them.

This was not pure verbal trickery. In practice, after Sulla, 'popular' methods were generally divorced from serious principle. Drusus (q.v. 1) had shown that they could be used for Optimate purposes, and his son, guided by Crassus (q.v. 3), made this policy acceptable to much of the oligarchy. With some exceptions (e.g. Cornelius, q.v. 1), the Populares of Cicero's generation, many of them aristocrats, traded on the old traditions for their own advancement, trying no longer to improve the system and make it work, but to rise in it and to gain control of it. In the early stages of a noble's career, especially the tribunate (high in popular affection since the Gracchi), 'popular' methods became acceptable behaviour. Violence was used, no longer to counter that of the Optimates (as in the days of the Gracchi and, to some extent, still in those of Saturninus, q.v.), but from set policy, for intimidation. Against this, Cicero, in his political works, tried to redefine the Optimate ideal so as to work out a morally and politically acceptable idea of an élite; see, for a popularized version of it, his exposition in *Sest.* 96 f. (contrasted with 'Populares' in the derogatory sense), which in effect is close to the aim of the earlier Populares, even though (after generations of experience of the Roman mob) he would have given the People less power than they.

Augustus agreed with him (and, even more, with Crassus and Drusus) in recognizing that the People did not want political power; and, like them, he used many of the traditional methods of the Populares to attach the People to a stable regime in which they had no part. But he also saw that, after the Civil Wars, the Optimates were prepared to give up the struggle for political power, if given social eminence and economic security. According each section what it chiefly wanted, and combining Cicero's two opposed programmes, he succeeded in keeping power to himself.

K. Rübeling, *Untersuchungen zu den Popularen* (1958); C. Meier, 'Populares', *PW* Suppl. x. 550 ff.     E. B.

**ORACLES** (*oracula*, μαντεῖα, χρηστήρια). The primary meaning of *oracle* is the response of a god to a question asked him by a worshipper. It may also indicate an oracular shrine. There were many established oracular shrines in the ancient world, several of which had widespread fame. In each the god was consulted by a fixed mode of divination. At the most primitive oracles the god's will was revealed by the casting of lots or by the observation of signs: the movements of objects thrown into a spring, the movements of the god's image when carried, the markings of the entrails of victims sacrificed upon the god's altar, the rustle of the leaves in the god's sacred oak. At healing-oracles, after the performance of preliminary rites, the consultant slept all night in the shrine (*see* INCUBATION) and received a dream-vision. At the most highly developed oracles the god spoke through the mouth of a man or woman. Such was the method at Delphi, where a woman, the Pythia, after a period of preparation, mounted a tripod, heard the consultants' questions, and gave them answers.

At the major oracles the consultants had to go through preliminary rites of sacrifice and purification, and were admitted to consultation only if all signs were favourable. At some shrines their questions were submitted in writing, and the answer was returned to them in writing. At others the consultant approached the god directly. Most authentic responses were either directions to perform some religious act, such as to make sacrifice to a certain god or to found a cult, or sanctions of constitutions, laws, policies, and enterprises. The famous predictions of the future, in clear or ambiguous language, are either not authentic or dubious.

Many of the gods spoke oracles at some of their sanctuaries, but Apollo was most esteemed as an oracular god. He had many oracles of the inspirational type: the world-famous Delphi, Didyma, and Claros, and several shrines in Lycia, Troad, and Boeotia. Zeus, also esteemed as an oracular god, spoke through signs at Dodona and Olympia. Asclepius at Epidaurus, Rome, and elsewhere, and Amphiaraus at Oropus sent healing visions. Trophonius at Lebadea had the most famous of hero-oracles.

Aside from the Egyptian-Libyan oracle of Ammon at the oasis of Siwa in the Sahara, which many Greeks consulted as an oracle of Zeus after 500 B.C., the great oracular shrines were Greek. Oracular temples were rare in Italy. Most popular was the lot-oracle of Fortuna Primigenia at Praeneste. On extraordinary occasions the Roman government or ruler consulted the Sibylline Books, which were kept by the *duoviri* (later *quindecimviri*) *sacris faciundis*.

*See* APOLLO, CLAROS, DELPHIC ORACLE, DIDYMA, DODONA, EPIDAURUS.

ANCIENT SOURCES. (*a*) Cic. *Div.*; Plut. *De Pyth. or.*, *De def. or.*; Euseb. *Praep. Evang.* 3–6; Iambl. *Myst.* 3. 11. (*b*) For a collection of oracles see H. W. Parke, D. E. W. Wormell, *The Delphic Oracle* (1956) ii. For inscriptions containing oracles see Michel, *Recueil*, 840–56; *SIG* 1157–66.
MODERN LITERATURE. A. Bouché–Leclercq, *Histoire de la divination dans l'antiquité* (1879–82); W. R. Halliday, *Greek Divination* (1913); P. Amandry, *La Mantique apollinienne à Delphes* (1950); R. Crahay, *La Littérature oraculaire chez Hérodote* (1956); R. Flacelière, *Devins et oracles grecs* (1961); H. W. Parke, *Greek Oracles* (1967); *The Oracles of Zeus* (1967). See the articles on the individual oracles for further bibliography.     J. E. F.

**ORBILIUS PUPILLUS**, LUCIUS, of Beneventum, teacher and grammarian (Suet. *Gram.* 9), migrated to Rome aged 50 (63 B.C.). His pupils included Horace (*Epist.* 2. 1. 69 ff.), who calls him *plagosus* ('Whacker') from thrashings during lessons on Andronicus' translation of Homer's *Odyssey*. An embittered critic of contemporary characters and conditions, he merits attention as scholar and teacher (J. Collart, summarized in *Rev. Ét. Lat.* 1953, 71).     G. C. W.

**ORCADES**, *Orkney* and *Shetland Islands*, were probably discovered by Pytheas (q.v.), and were visited by the fleet of Agricola (q.v. 1), who temporarily subued them.

Pomponius Mela gave their number as 30–40; Ptolemy mentioned the islands, but placed them incorrectly. Orcas Headland of Britain was the northern end of Scotland—*Dunnet Head* or else *Duncansby Head.*

Mela 3. 54; Tac. *Agr.* 10; Ptol. *Geog.* 2. 3. 31. W. J. Watson, *History of Celtic Place-names in Scotland* (1926), 28; V. Gordon Childe, *Prehistoric Scotland* (1935), 266; *Royal Commission on Ancient Monuments of Scotland, Orkney and Shetland* (1946) i. 7.

E. H. W.

**ORCHOMENUS** (local form Erchomenos), name of cities in Phthiotic Achaea, Boeotia, and Arcadia. Saga seemed to connect Thessaly and at any rate Boeotian Orchomenus, since the legendary Minyae had Thessalian origins and Argonaut connexions (cf. the Thessalian origins of the Neleids of Pylus, who also claimed a special connexion with Poseidon like the Minyae). For the connexion of east Arcadia and Arcadian Orchomenus with Boeotia and Thessaly, see F. Kiechle in *Kadmos* i (1962), 105. The Arcadian Orchomenus appears as πολύμηλος in the Homeric Catalogue of the Ships (*Il.* 2. 65) and with other north-eastern Arcadian towns Αἰπύτιον παρὰ τύμβον manned sixty ships provided by Agamemnon. It was an important city of Arcadia in archaic times and appears on the Serpent Column from Delphi as a participant in the battle of Plataea. More important was Boeotian Orchomenus, of which the wealth is stressed in its personal names (Chryses, Chryse, Chrysogeneia). It is called Μινύειος in the Catalogue (*Il.* 2. 511), and appears to have been the dominant city of Boeotia before the rise of Thebes. It stood on a promontory on the north of the Copaïc plain. It was an important Neolithic and Bronze Age site (see F. Schachermeyr, *Die ältesten Kulturen Griechenlands* (1955) and had a Late Bronze Age palace and beehive tomb. The association in Greek tradition of the Minyans and wealth is taken to imply that the Copaïs was then drained, and indeed this is the implication of the story (Paus. 9. 38. 7) that Heracles temporarily destroyed its drainage system and vindicated the independence of Thebes. On the other hand, the association of Orchomenus with Poseidon and its membership of the Amphictyony of Kalaureia with the worship of Poseidon Kalaureatis might suggest an interest in sea traffic, though Poseidon was not necessarily a sea god. It was among the first Boeotian cities to coin (*c.* 550 B.C.), and appears then not to have belonged to the Boeotian Confederacy. It declined continually, as a result of the hostility of Thebes and the flooding of Lake Copaïs, and was destroyed by the Boeotian Confederacy in 364. None the less the impressive fortifications of mid fourth century or later date, 'among the finest specimens of ancient Greek fortification in existence' (J. G. Frazer, on Paus. 9. 38. 1) underlines its strategic position. The Nymphs were especially worshipped there (Pind. *Ol.* 14).

P-K, *GL* I. ii. 472 f.; H. Schliemann, *Orchomenos* (1881); H. Bulle and E. Kunze, *Orchomenos* i–iii (1907–34); A. de Ridder, 'Fouilles d'Orchomène', *BCH* 1895, 137 ff. (archaic period; cf. Frazer on Paus. 9. 38).

T. J. D.

**ORCHOMENUS.** (1) Eponym of the Boeotian Orchomenus, a vague genealogical figure. He is son of Zeus and the Danaid Isonoe (schol. Ap. Rhod. 1. 230; obviously late, cf. DANAUS) and father of Minyas (q.v.); son of Minyas (Paus. 9. 36. 6 and elsewhere); his brother, and so son of Eteocles (not the Theban) (schol. Pind. *Isthm.* 1. 79). (2) Eponym of the Arcadian Orchomenus (Paus. 8. 36. 1).

H. J. R.

**ORESTES,** in mythology, son of Agamemnon and Clytemnestra (qq.v.). In all accounts he avenged the death of his father, but the story is variously told in authors of different ages.

(1) Homer says that when Orestes reached manhood he killed Aegisthus (q.v.), and implies that he also killed Clytemnestra; it was a most laudable and exemplary deed, for which he won great reputation. No details are given, save that till the vengeance was accomplished Orestes was in exile (he came from Athens, *Od.* 3. 307), as indeed he must have been to escape. It is a straightforward telling of a quite possibly real event, and no regrets are expressed by anyone at his having to kill his mother; she was 'hateful' (*Od.* 3. 310), and in any case Orestes, as head of the family, would be her only possible judge and executioner. See *Od.* 1. 29 ff.; 298 ff.; 3. 310; 4. 546–7; 11. 458 ff.

(2) Stesichorus (we may neglect the shadowy and perhaps fabulous Xanthus of Sicily, Aelian, *VH* 4. 26) told a slightly different and much more elaborate story in his *Oresteia* (see Vürtheim, *Stesichoros' Fragmente und Biographie*, 45 ff.). The scene was transferred to Sparta, an interesting reflection of the political situation; Sparta is Menelaus' kingdom, not Agamemnon's, in Homer. Here Simonides (schol. Eur. *Or.* 46) and Pindar (*Pyth.* 11. 16) followed him. Orestes was apparently a baby when his father was killed, for his nurse rescued him (fr. 8 Vürtheim), whereas in Homer only eight years intervene between the murder and the revenge. Whether Stesichorus said that he was sent to Strophius of Phocis and that the latter's son Pylades became his close friend and helper (Pindar, ibid. 15. 35) does not appear from the scanty remains; but Clytemnestra was put on her guard by a boding dream (fr. 9) and, most important of all, Orestes was haunted after her death by the Erinyes and given a bow by Apollo with which to keep them away (fr. 7). *See further* ELECTRA.

(3) The tragedians elaborate three points especially: the manner of the return, the characters of Orestes and his sister, and the consequences of the deed. In Aeschylus (*Choephoroe*) he returns by strict command of Apollo, gets access to the palace as a stranger, bringing news of his own death, can scarcely bring himself to kill Clytemnestra, and is at once haunted by the Erinyes, of whom he is rid in the sequel (*Eumenides*). Sophocles (*Electra*) brings him into contact with his mother by a like stratagem, but otherwise has a Homeric atmosphere, with no Erinyes and no remorse, only a little natural hesitancy, which Electra does not share. Euripides modernizes the whole setting (*Electra*, *Orestes*) and makes brother and sister hateful monomaniacs. He also, following local legends (cf. IPHIGENIA), makes the ridding of Orestes from the Erinyes (who are purely subjective phantoms of his disordered conscience) a long process, involving a journey to the land of the Tauri (*Iphigenia in Tauris*).

(4) Later and less known versions of the story elaborate sundry minor points and tell parts of the adventures of Orestes and his companions differently. Some of the accounts we have may be due to lost tragedies, while others are local traditions; others are seen, by the date of the vases and other works of art by which we know them, to be old, although our literary authorities say nothing about them. See C. Robert, *Bild und Lied* (1881), 149 ff.; Höfer in Roscher's *Lexikon*, s.v. For example, Pausanias was shown (1. 28. 5) an altar which Orestes set up in commemoration of his being freed from the Erinyes by verdict of the Areopagus (as in Aeschylus), a stone at Troezen (2. 31. 4) on which he had been purified, and another at Gythium where he was cured of madness (3. 22. 1); also a place near Megalopolis in Messene where he had bitten off a finger in his madness and so been cured (8. 34. 1–3). In Hyginus, *Fab.* 122. 3, Orestes kills Aletes son of Aegisthus, but Artemis rescues Aegisthus' daughter Erigone from him. *See also* ANDROMACHE, HERMIONE, NEOPTOLEMUS (1).

Of his death there is no consistent account. His childhood has no real legend, but he is introduced as a subsidiary figure into one or two stories, *see*, for instance, TELEPHUS (1).

The death of Aegisthus occurs on a metope from Foce del Sele before the middle of the sixth century, and is very popular on late archaic and early classical vases (see E. Vermeule, *AJArch.* 1966, 1 ff.). On late fifth- or fourth-century vases appears Orestes' meeting with Electra at the tomb, his purification at Delphi, and the Tauric adventure, which reappears in Roman paintings and sarcophagi (Brommer, *Vasenlisten²*, 321 ff.).

M. Delcourt, *Oreste et Alcméon* (1959), and see references in the text.                                                          H. J. R.; C. M. R.

**ORESTHEUS,** in mythology, a king of Aetolia, grandfather of Oeneus and son of Deucalion (qq.v.). He had a bitch which brought forth a stick; this he buried and from it sprang a vine. From its branches, ὄζοι, the Ozolian Locrians were named, and Orestheus called his son Phytios, 'Plant-man'. Athenaeus, 35 a–b and Pausanias, 10. 38. 1 (= Hecataeus of Miletus). For the connexion of the family with wine cf. OENEUS.                H. J. R.

**ORGEONES** (ὀργεῶνες), celebrants of religious rites (ὄργια). Groups of worshippers already so called existed at Athens in the time of Solon, who guaranteed their rights of association. Another law, variously attributed by modern scholars to Solon, Cleisthenes, and Pericles, obliged *phrateres* (*see* PHRATRIAI) to admit to their number both *orgeones* and *homogalaktes*, i.e. *gennetai* (*see* GENOS). It follows that at this time *orgeones* were Athenian citizens who did not belong to the aristocracy: but it cannot be assumed that they included all such. Solon's law refers also to groups of θιασῶται, and the epigraphic evidence for religious associations, mainly of Hellenistic date, reveals the co-existence of *orgeones*, *thiasotai* (*see* THIASOS), and groups who used neither term. Each group of *orgeones* resembled a *genos* in being an organized corporation with a local shrine or shrines, property, funds, a constitution and officers, and in meeting periodically to worship and feast, to pass decrees, and to enrol new members: but, although membership was to some extent hereditary, the original principle of association was not kinship, and the specific object of worship not a supposed ancestor, but one or more minor local gods or heroes, or foreign deities such as Bendis (q.v.) and the Anatolian mother-goddess (*see* CYBELE), to whose cults alien *orgeones* were admitted. The last *orgeones* known to us worshipped the Semitic goddess Belela, in the early third century A.D. The appellation is little met with outside Attica.

E. Ziebarth, *Das griechische Vereinswesen* (1896), see indexes; F. Poland, *Geschichte des griechischen Vereinswesens* (1909), see index iii; Busolt–Swoboda, *Griech. Staatsk.³*, see indexes; W. S. Ferguson, *Harv. Theol. Rev.* 1944, 61 ff.; A. D. Nock, ibid. 141 ff. Hignett, *Hist. Athen. Const.*, see index; A. Andrewes, *JHS* 1961, 1 ff.; N. G. L. Hammond, ibid. 76 ff. *See also* CLUBS, GREEK.  T. J. C.

**ORIBASIUS** (*c.* A.D. 320–*c.* 400), Greek medical writer. Born in Pergamum, he studied medicine at Alexandria under Zeno of Cyprus, and practised in Asia Minor. He became the personal physician of Julian (q.v.), who took him to Gaul (355). Closely involved in the proclamation of Julian as Emperor (361), Oribasius accompanied him until his death in Mesopotamia (363). Banished for a time to Gothic territory, Oribasius was soon recalled by the Emperor Valens and continued to practise his profession until an advanced age. His principal works are a collection of excerpts from Galen—now lost—and the *Collectiones medicae* ('Ιατρικαὶ συναγωγαί), a vast compilation of excerpts from earlier medical writers, from Alcmaeon of Croton (*c.* 500 B.C.) to Oribasius' contemporaries Philagrius and Adamantius. Both of these works were written at the behest of Julian. Of the 70 (or 72) books of the *Collectiones* only 25 survive entire; but the rest can be in part reconstructed from the *Synopsis ad Eustathium*, and the treatise *Ad Eunapium*, epitomes of the *Collectiones* in 9 books and 4 books respectively made by Oribasius himself, and from various excerpts and summaries, some of which are still unpublished. Oribasius was a convinced pagan, and his medical encyclopedia is a product of the vain effort of Julian and his circle to recall the classical past. For the medical historian its importance lies in the large number of excerpts from lost writers—particularly those of the Roman Period—which it preserves, usually with a precise reference to the source; Oribasius adds nothing of his own. His work was constantly quoted and excerpted by early Byzantine medical writers, the *Synopsis* and the *Ad Eunapium* were twice translated into Latin in Ostrogothic Italy, and Syriac and Arabic translations of portions of Oribasius' work form one of the principal channels by which knowledge of Greek medicine reached the Islamic world.

*CMG* vi; I. Bloch in M. Neuburger and J. Pagel, *Handbuch der Geschichte der Medizin* i (1902), 513 ff.; H. O. Schröder, *PW* Suppl. 7. 797 ff.                                                          R. B.

**ORIENTATION** is the placing of any person or thing so as to front a definite point, generally a quarter of the compass, as north or south. This was not infrequently done in building ancient temples. In Greece they commonly faced more or less due east (e.g. the Parthenon), although examples of other positions are not wanting (e.g. Apollo at Bassae has the long axis N.–S.). This may be a consequence of the east being the lucky quarter, that from which light comes. If so, the same motives were at work in determining the position of a Greek augur, who regularly faced north and counted lucky those omens which appeared on the right (e.g. *Iliad* 12. 237 ff., where 'right' and 'east' are explicitly identified). Contrast, however, Hippocrates, Περὶ διαίτης ὀξέων, 8 (Kühlwein), which says the left is the lucky side in some cases; cf. Psellus (ed. Hercher), *Philol.* 1853, 167, 23 ff. To curse one turned west (Lysias 6. 51), and occasionally the dead were buried facing west (Plut. *Solon* 10; cf. Rose, *CR* 1920, 141 ff., for suggestions). In Italy the common augural position and the correct direction for an Etruscan temple were facing south; for the former, however, there was also an eastward position (Livy 1. 18. 6; cf. Rose, *JRS* 1923, 82 ff.). In general a *templum* had two axes, N.–S. and E.–W. Racial differences may have something to do with this. Sporadic examples of Italian graves apparently oriented have been found (F. von Duhn, *Italische Gräberkunde* i (1924), index under 'Orientierung').                                                          H. J. R.

**ORIENTIUS,** a Gaul of the fifth century A.D. who composed an elegiac exhortation to a Christian life.

**ORIGEN** (1) (ORIGENES ADAMANTIUS) (probably A.D. 185 or 186 to 254 or 255; Euseb. *Hist. Eccl.* 7. 1, Hieron. *De Vir. Ill.* 54) was born at Alexandria of Christian parents. His life is known to us chiefly from Eusebius, who devoted the greater part of the sixth book of his *Ecclesiastical History* to him, collected many of his letters (now lost), and joined with Origen's pupil Pamphilus in writing an *Apology for Origen*, of which one book is extant in a translation by Rufinus (Migne, *PG* xvii. 521–616). Origen received his education from his father Leonides (who perished in 202 in the persecution under Septimius Severus) and later in the Catechetical School of Alexandria under Pantaenus and Clement (q.v.). He became a teacher and was so successful that, though still a layman, he was recognized, at first informally then in 203 officially, as head of the School. In order better to understand pagan thought he attended the Neoplatonic lectures of Ammonius Saccas. He also visited Rome.

Literally applying the precept in Matthew xix. 12, he underwent castration (Euseb. *Hist. Eccl.* 6. 8). His career as a teacher was interrupted in 215 by the massacre of Alexandrians known as the Fury of Caracalla. Origen withdrew to Palestine, but after a time was recalled by his bishop Demetrius. He now engaged in extensive literary work and acquired such personal influence in the Eastern Church as to become its unofficial arbiter. On a journey to Greece in this capacity he allowed himself, without the consent of his bishop, to be ordained priest by the bishops of Caesarea and Jerusalem (*c.* 230). This irregularity caused umbrage to Demetrius, who may also have taken exception to certain elements in Origen's teaching. Origen was banished from Alexandria and deposed from the presbyterate, on what precise grounds is not known; but the decision was disregarded in Palestine, and Origen in 231 settled at Caesarea where he continued his labours. In the Decian persecution (250–1) he was repeatedly tortured. His health gave way and he died at Tyre at the age of 69.

WORKS

Origen's writings were voluminous and their range wide, but only a small proportion has survived. He was a pioneer in textual criticism of the Bible, in exegesis, and in systematic theology.

(1) *Critical.* His chief work in this sphere was the *Hexapla*, begun before 231 and not completed till 244–5. In it were set out in six columns (*a*) the Hebrew text of the O.T., (*b*) the same transliterated in Greek characters, (*c*) and (*d*) the two Greek versions thereof by Aquila and Symmachus, (*e*) the LXX, (*f*) the revision of this by Theodotion. Only a few fragments of the work are extant. Origen's critical work led him into controversy with Julius Africanus; his *Letter to Africanus* survives.

(2) *Exegetical.* He wrote commentaries on the greater part of Scripture. Some of these took the form of scholia on obscure passages; others of homilies on numerous books of the O.T. and N.T., many of which homilies are preserved in the original or in Latin translations by Jerome or Rufinus; others again, τόμοι or volumes, elaborate commentaries on divers books of the O.T., and on the Gospels of St. Matthew and St. John (fragments or considerable parts of some of these are extant). Origen's method of exegesis was allegorical, seeking out a moral as well as a mystical sense in the literal words.

(3) *Doctrinal.* The *De principiis* (Περὶ ἀρχῶν) is a remarkable exposition of Christian dogma written before Origen left Alexandria. Setting out from certain points of doctrine given by the tradition of the Church, he proceeds by speculation to show how these can 'be arranged as a whole by the help either of statements of Scripture or of the methods of exact reasoning' (*DCB* iv. 119). Considerable fragments of the original Greek survive; and the work is preserved in full in a 'translation', frequently adjusted in the interests of orthodoxy, by Rufinus.

(4) *Apologetic.* A certain Celsus, a Platonist and 'an enlightened advocate of the reformed paganism' (Bigg), had, probably in 176, in his Λόγος ἀληθής written an elaborate indictment of Christianity. Origen's reply, *Contra Celsum*, written *c.* 249, which survives, deals with this point by point.

(5) *Devotional.* Two of Origen's works in this category have come down to us, *De Oratione* (Περὶ εὐχῆς) and *Exhortatio ad martyrium* (Προτρεπτικὸς πρὸς μαρτύριον). The former, written probably *c.* 231, treats of prayer in its various aspects. The latter was written *c.* 235 to his friends Ambrosius and Protoctetus, who suffered in the persecution under Maximin.

The *Philocalia* is a collection of excerpts from Origen's writings by Gregory of Nazianzus and Basil. It preserves the original text of many passages known otherwise only in Latin translations and is interesting as showing what in the fourth century were regarded as characteristic points in Origen's teaching.

Origen exerted great influence and left important schools of followers; but the venturesome nature of his speculations aroused controversy, and he himself came repeatedly under ecclesiastical condemnation.

TEXTS. *Opera omnia*, C. de la Rue (Paris, 1733–59); C. H. E. Lommatzsch (1831–48); Migne, *PG* xi–xvii; *Origenes Werke*, in *Die griechischen christlichen Schriftsteller* (1899 ff.). *Origenis Philocalia*, ed. J. A. Robinson (1893). His 'Discourse with Heracleides', discovered in 1941 on Toura papyrus, ed. J. Scherer, *Publications de la Soc. Fouad I de Papyrologie, Textes et documents* ix (Cairo, 1949).
TRANSLATIONS. *Contra Celsum*, H. Chadwick (1953, with introduction and notes); *De Principiis*, G. W. Butterworth (1936); *De Oratione*, E. G. Jay (1954); *Philocalia*, G. Lewis (1911).
GENERAL LITERATURE. Euseb. *Hist. Eccl.* bk. 6; Jerome, *De Vir. Ill.* 54; B. F. Westcott in *DCB*, s.v.; C. Bigg, *The Christian Platonists of Alexandria* (1886, revised 1913); O. Bardenhewer, *Geschichte der altkirchlichen Lit.* ii² (1914), 96 ff.; B. J. Kidd, *History of the Church to A.D. 461* (1922) i, ch. 15; E. de Faye, *Origène, sa vie, son œuvre, sa pensée*, 3 vols. (1923–8); D. Daniélou, *Origen* (Paris, 1948, Engl. Tr. 1955); H. Chadwick, *Early Christian Thought and the Classical Tradition* (1966).

**ORIGEN** (2), Platonist philosopher, third century A.D. Like his Christian namesake and contemporary, he is said to have studied under Ammonius (q.v. 2) Saccas; but Cadiou's reduction of the two to a single person is hard to reconcile with the available evidence. He wrote only two works, both now lost, Περὶ τῶν δαιμόνων and Ὅτι μόνος ποιητὴς ὁ βασιλεύς (Porph. *Plot.* 3. 30); the latter title refers to his refusal to distinguish the Creator from the Supreme God as Numenius and Plotinus did (Procl. *Theol. Plat.* 2. 4).

Zeller, *Phil. d. Gr.* iii. 2⁵, 513 ff.; R. Cadiou, *La Jeunesse d'Origène* (1936), ch. 8; K.-O. Weber, *Origenes der Neuplatoniker* (1962: includes collection of fragments).                    E. R. D.

**ORION** ('Ω(α)ρίων), in mythology, a gigantic hunter, identical, at least in name, with the constellation as early as Homer (*Il.* 18. 486, cf. *Od.* 11. 572–5), an unprecedentedly early star-myth. He was Eos' love and killed by Artemis (*Od.* 5. 121–4); bigger and handsomer even than the Aloadae (q.v.; *Od.* 11. 309–10). A part of his story in later authors is evidently astral; he pursued the Pleiads, or Pleïone their mother (schol. Pind. *Nem.* 2. 16), a clear reference to the relative position of the constellations.

There is some reason for saying that he is Boeotian. A rather late legend (Aristomachus in Hyginus, *Poet. Astr.* 2. 34; see Frazer on Ovid, *Fasti* 5. 494) says that Hyrieus, eponym of Hyriae, asked for offspring from three gods (their names vary) whom he had hospitably received. They made water (οὔρησαν) on a bull's hide and bade him bury it; in time a child was born, which he called Urion, the name afterwards becoming Orion. For more Boeotian legends about him see Rose, *Handb. Gk. Myth.* 116; Küentzle in Roscher's *Lexikon* iii. 1028 ff. He is also connected with Chios. He loved Merope, daughter of Oenopion ('Wine-face'), king of that island, but Oenopion disapproved, made him drunk, and blinded him. He therefore waded through the sea (in one version he is Poseidon's son, and has the power to walk through water) till he came to the furthest east, and there got his sight back from the sun's rays. He was finally killed by Artemis for insulting her, or by a scorpion sent by Earth, because he boasted that he would kill all animals. The story varies greatly in detail; see Küentzle's art., cited above.

Cf. S. Eitrem in *Symb. Osl.* vii. 53 ff.                    H. J. R.

**ORMENUS**, (1) father of Ctesius king of the island Syrie and grandfather of Eumaeus (*Od.* 15. 414). (2) Name of two Trojan warriors, *Il.* 8. 274 and 12. 187. (3) Eponym of the city Ormenion on the Gulf of Pagasae (Demetrius of Scepsis in Strabo 9. 438, cf. *Il.* 9. 448).
H. J. R.

**ORNAMENTA** of a specific magisterial rank (*consularia, praetoria, quaestoria*) were granted sparingly in the late Roman Republic and increasingly in the Empire. To members of the Senate (especially princes of the imperial house) they gave, for voting in the Senate, the status of (but not, as far as their careers were concerned, promotion to) a higher rank (thus differing from *adlectio* (q.v.)). For those outside the Senate—under Tiberius, equestrians; under Claudius, freedmen (Narcissus (q.v. 2) received *quaestoria*, Pallas (q.v. 3) *praetoria, ornamenta*)—they gave, in costume, attendance, and precedence at public festivities and in burial ceremonies, the rights of ex-consuls, ex-praetors, etc. (In the *municipia* (q.v.) similar honorary magisterial distinctions were conferred.) Under the Empire when the triumph (q.v.) was the prerogative of the Emperor, successful generals, to whom *triumphalia ornamenta* were awarded, could on public occasions carry the insignia (e.g. the laurel crown) which belonged under the Republic to those who had celebrated triumphs.                        J. P. B.

**ORODES II** (*c.* 56–*c.* 38 B.C.), son of Phraates III of Parthia and brother of Mithridates III (Dio Cass. 39. 56), with whom he disputed the throne in a struggle lasting many years, and finally gained sole control. In 53, when Parthia was threatened by a Roman invasion, Orodes marched against Rome's ally Armenia, while his general Suren opposed Crassus in Mesopotamia. After the Roman defeat at Carrhae, Orodes' son Pacorus invaded Syria unsuccessfully. During the civil wars the Parthians sided against Caesar and the Caesarians and in 40 B.C. Parthian armies overran Syria, Palestine, and much of southern Asia Minor. Antony's general, Ventidius, however, had defeated and ejected them by 38, killing Pacorus. The inconsolable Orodes was murdered by his son Phraates IV (q.v.) shortly after appointing him his successor.

For Orodes I and III, *see* ARSACIDS.

Coin portraits: Wroth, *B.M.C. Parthia*.    M. S. D.; E. W. G.

**ORONTES** (modern *Nahr el 'Āsī*), chief river of Syria. It rises near Heliopolis (*Baalbek*), flows north-east past Emesa (*Homs*) and Arethusa, bends west past Epiphania (*Hama*) and then, below Apamea, flows due north, and finally south-west through Antioch, to enter the Mediterranean below Seleucia Pieria, after a journey of 170 miles. Strabo's statement (16. 2. 5 ff.) that it flows partly underground and his aetiological story of Orontes, who is said to have bridged it and given it its name, are without foundation. (It appears as A-ra-an-tu on an inscription of Assurnasirpal.) Its valley was renowned for its fertility (Strabo, loc. cit.) and has always been the main route followed by traffic and armies from the north making for Egypt.                        E. W. G.

**OROPUS**, a coastal district on the north-east frontier between Boeotia and Attica with its centre at Skala Oropou, belonged geographically to Boeotia, of which it was originally part. By the beginning of the fifth century it had been annexed to Attica, but not incorporated; it was lost in 412, and changed hands repeatedly later, being most often Boeotian. It was the landward end of the nearest Athenian route for supplies from Euboea (Thuc. 7. 28), a position that favoured the Oropians and probably gained for them their reputation as grasping custom-house officers ([Dicaearchus] fr. 59. 7, in *FHG* ii. 256). In the territory was the Sanctuary of Amphiaraus (q.v.), whose cult and legend were probably brought from Thebes at the end of the fifth century. Oracles were given by the interpretation of dreams and cures effected.

The chief remains are of a temple, stoa (perhaps for incubation), and theatre of the third century.

Paus. 1. 34 and Frazer ad loc.; E. Fiechter, *Das Theater in Oropos* (1930); E. Kirsten and W. Kraiker, *Griechenlandkunde*⁴ (1962), 178 ff.
C .W. J. E.

**OROSIUS**, PAULUS, a Spaniard, presbyter at an early age, fled before the Vandals to Africa in A.D. 414 and became a pupil of Augustine (q.v.). His *Commonitorium de errore Priscillianistarum et Origenistarum* led Augustine to address to him a work on the subject. During a visit to the East, at Jerusalem in 415, he prosecuted Pelagius (q.v.) for heresy. On his return Augustine moved him to write a Christian chronicle, the *Historiae adversum Paganos*, in seven books, from the creation of the world to the founding and history of Rome until A.D. 417. The chronology followed Eusebius and Hieronymus (Jerome); the Roman account drew on pagan sources, including an epitome of Livy, Tacitus' *Histories*, Justin, and Eutropius; the work gave the perspective of Augustine's *City of God*.

Ed. K. Zangemeister (Teubner, 1889); *CSEL* xviii for *Commonitorium*: cf. H. Svennung, *Orosiana* (1922); A. Momigliano, *Conflict between Paganism and Christianity in Fourth Century* (1963), 87 ff., 99.                        A. H. McD.

**ORPHEUS**, the founder of Orphism, generally said to be a Thracian. His fame in Greek myth as a singer is due to the poems in which the Orphic doctrines and myths were set forth. A metope found under the treasure-house of the Sicyonians at Delphi represents him (the inscription reads Ὀρφᾶς) on board the Argo with a lyre in his arms. The first mention in literature is found in Ibycus or perhaps in Alcaeus. Aeschylus and Euripides say that he attracted trees and wild beasts and even stones and was able to charm whom he wished. In vase and wall paintings, even in the Catacombs, he is often represented singing. The Christians referred the representation to the Prince of Peace of whom Isaiah speaks. The best-known myth tells how his wife Eurydice was killed by the bite of a snake, and Orpheus went down to the Underworld and persuaded its lord to allow him to bring her back on the condition that he should not turn round and look at her before he reached the upper world. There may have existed an early version, in which the ending was happy; but the common tradition that he was not able to fulfil the condition existed probably in the fifth century B.C. The myth is probably connected with some Orphic poem called the 'Descent into the Underworld'. Another myth, also represented in vase paintings, tells that Orpheus was killed and dismembered by Thracian women or Maenads. His severed head floated singing to Lesbos. This myth was the subject of Aeschylus' tragedy *Bassarae*. Some scholars think that Orpheus in fact may have been a real personage, the founder of Orphic religion, others take him to be purely mythical. The question must be left undecided.

From the early classical period Orpheus playing to the Thracian men or killed by the Thracian women became popular subjects in Attic vase-painting. Polygnotus showed him in the Underworld, and the subject appears in later art, as does the oracular head. Orpheus charming the beasts is a popular subject in Roman art.

O. Kern, *Orpheus* (1920); M. P. Nilsson, *Harv. Theol. Rev.* 1935, 186 ff.; W. K. C. Guthrie, *Orpheus and Greek Religion*² (1952), 25 ff.; R. Böhme, *Orpheus. Das Alter des Kitharoden* (1953; very speculative). Alcaeus as restored in E. Diehl, *Anth. Lyr. Graec.* i³, fr. 80, 129. In art, Brommer, *Vasenlisten*², 355 ff.    M. P. N.; J. H. C.; C. M. R.

**ORPHIC LITERATURE.** Many poems were in circulation at an early date under the name of Orpheus (q.v.). Euripides and Hippias hint at their existence, Plato is the first to quote verses from them, and Aristotle speaks of the 'so-called Orphic epics'. The fame of Orpheus as a singer is, apart from his mythical reputation, due to these poems. It is said that Onomacritus, who lived at the court of Pisistratus, wrote Orphic poems. A few fragments are preserved. For their content and meaning *see* ORPHISM. A list of Orphic poems and authors, due to an Alexandrian scholar, Epigenes, is preserved in Clement of Alexandria and the *Suda*. The majority of these poems are *pseudepigrapha*. The dates and personalities of the alleged authors are unknown to us and were unknown to Epigenes himself. The most important poem was the *Rhapsodic Theogony*, from which Neoplatonic writers quote many passages. Its age is controversial; most probably it is a compilation, not very much earlier than the authors who quote it, but it may have incorporated earlier elements. Under the name of Orpheus are preserved some late poems: the *Argonautica*, which is dependent on Apollonius Rhodius, the *Lithica* (on precious stones), which has hardly anything to do with Orphism, and a number of Hymns to various gods, probably composed in Asia Minor in the Roman age. The poems are edited together with the fragments by E. Abel, *Orphica* (1885). As regards the fragments this defective edition is superseded by the fundamental work of O. Kern, *Fragmenta Orphicorum* (1922); idem, 'Die Herkunft des orphischen Hymnenbuchs' in *Genethliakon C. Robert* (1910), 89 ff.

M. P. N.

**ORPHISM,** a religious movement originating in the archaic age, the first Greek religion which had a founder (*see* ORPHEUS) and laid down its doctrines in texts (*see* ORPHIC LITERATURE). The early poems being lost, our knowledge of the Orphic system depends on late sources. It comprised a cosmogony and an anthropogony. At the head of the cosmogony was Chronos, the Time which never grows old; of him were born Aither (q.v.), Chaos, and Erebus. Chronos formed an egg in the Aither and from this Phanes (q.v.) sprang forth, the creator and first king of the gods. His daughter Night assisted him and bore to him Uranus and Gaea. Then follows the common myth of Kronos and Zeus. Zeus was praised as the beginning, the middle, and the end of all; the contradiction thus implied to the creation by Phanes was solved by the statement that Zeus swallowed Phanes and all was created anew. By Demeter Zeus had the daughter Kore-Persephone who bore Dionysus, who was also (but not by the specifically Orphic writers) named Zagreus. Zeus wanted to hand over his royal power to the child, but the wicked Titans lured it to them with toys, tore it to pieces, and devoured its limbs. Yet Athena saved its heart and brought it to Zeus, and of him a new Dionysus, the son of Semele, was born. The Titans were struck by the lightning of Zeus and burned to ashes; from the soot man was formed.

The important question is how much of this belongs to the old Orphism of the sixth and even the seventh centuries B.C. in which it spread abroad, especially in Attica and south Italy. Plato quotes an Orphic verse referring to the six generations of Orphic cosmogony, and Aristophanes in his *Birds* (685 ff.) expounds a cosmogony which shows some likeness with that quoted above. It begins with Chaos, Night, Darkness, and Tartarus, adding that neither earth, nor air, nor heaven existed. Black-winged Night bore a wind-egg in the bosom of Darkness and from this emerged Eros (who takes the place of Phanes), gold-winged and like the swift whirlwinds. The high-sounding epithets betray the imitation of hieratic poetry. But significantly the role of Zeus as the second creator is lacking. A little later Isocrates testifies to the fact that Orpheus more than others told crude and immoral stories of the gods. So far Orphism was dependent on old cosmogonic myths, embodying crude folktale motives, and especially on Hesiod, but enlarged them and developed them in a speculative sense.

The anthropogony is in fact the only really original contribution of Orphism to the development of religious thought. The killing of Dionysus-Zagreus is mentioned by Pausanias in a reference to an Orphic poem attributed to Onomacritus; he says that Onomacritus took over the name of the Titans from Homer and instituted orgia for Dionysus and invented the story that the Titans caused the sufferings of Dionysus. The authenticity of this information can hardly be doubted, for Plato speaks of the 'Titanic nature' of man as a proverbial saying in the sense of his innate evil nature, which can only be understood as referring to the crime of the Titans as told by the Orphics. Because man had been formed of the ashes of the Titans who had devoured the Divine Child, he contains within himself something of the divine and something of the evil Titanic nature. Pindar tells that those who can give Persephone atonement for her ancient grief (i.e. the devouring of her child) are reborn to higher life. Further, Plato says that the followers of Orpheus called the body a prison of the soul, and that others with comparable ideas called it ($\sigma\hat{\omega}\mu\alpha$) a tomb ($\sigma\hat{\eta}\mu\alpha$). First it is to be noted that evidently the body is the evil and the soul the divine part of man. Abstinence from killing animals and eating their flesh was the best known feature of Orphic life, noted, e.g., by Euripides and Plato. The reason for this prohibition may be found in the uncleanness of the body or in the crime of the Titans or most probably in the belief in metempsychosis (*see* TRANSMIGRATION). This belief is not expressly ascribed to the Orphics, but it may be inferred from the fragment of Pindar quoted above, and it is to be remembered that Orphism is no isolated religious phenomenon but is in various ways related to the mystic movements and beliefs of the archaic age which it took up and systematized. Plato tells of sorcerers who produced books by Musaeus and Orpheus and through sacrifices according to these and pastimes called initiations promised deliverance and purification from guilt and from pains in the after-life: the righteous were to be rewarded by a symposium in the Nether World. The Orphics had appropriated the belief in punishments in the Underworld. Though it was not peculiar to them it had a special note: whosoever had not undergone the purifications in this life was to lie in the mire in the Nether World; the initiated and righteous were to live in happiness. This belief appealed to the broad public and was important for Orphic practice. In the archaic age there was a tendency, opposed to general Greek ideas, to scorn this life and to attribute a higher value to the other life in which the soul is freed from the fetters of the body. This is consistent with Orphism. Gold leaves from the Hellenistic age, found in tombs in south Italy and Crete, contain verses to be spoken on arrival in the Underworld, in which the dead man presents himself as a child of Earth and Heaven and asks for a drink from the Lake of Memory; it is also said that he has escaped from the sorrowful wheel. These texts may not be specifically Orphic, but at least they belong to a kindred movement.

Although Dionysus is an important Orphic god, there is an apparent hostility between the adherents of Orpheus and those of Dionysus. This is understandable from the fact that the Orphics transformed the central sacred rite of the orgia, the omophagy, into the primeval crime of the Titans. On the other hand, Orpheus is connected with Apollo; he is even sometimes said to be his son. The reason is that both laid stress on purifications and righteousness. The Orphic view of man involved a mental attitude of self-denial and seriousness in religious matters; it required ethics of a high standard. But its high ideas were mixed up with crude myths and base priests and charlatans misused them in practice. In the classical age it was despised; only Pindar and Plato understood its great thoughts. It sank down to rise again with the recrudescence of mystic ideas in a later age. *See also* AFTER-LIFE.

C. A. Lobeck, *Aglaophamus* (1829); W. K. C. Guthrie, *Orpheus and Greek Religion²* (1952, with full bibliography); I. M. Linforth, *The Arts of Orpheus* (1941); Nilsson, *GGR* i³. 678 ff.; L. Moulinier, *Orphée et l'Orphisme à l'époque classique* (1955); Kern, *Orph. frag.*
M. P. N.; J. H. C.

**ORTYGIA,** old name of Delos ('Quail Island'); its nymph was identified with Asteria (q.v.). But as some half-dozen other places were colled Ortygia, it is by no means certain that all references (e.g. *Od.* 5. 123) are to Delos. *See* SYRACUSE.

Höfer in Roscher's *Lexikon*, s.v.

**OSCANS** ('Οπικοί, *Opici, Obsci, Osci*), prehistoric inhabitants of southern Italy. Their original habitat, Campania (q.v.) and much else, gradually shrank. They may be identical with the historical Aurunci (Ausones, with rhotacism and -*co* suffix) (qq.v.). When Sabelli (q.v.) replaced them in Campania and elsewhere, their name survived for the newcomers' language, which the ancients called 'Oscan'. Samnites, Frentani, Campani, Lucani, Bruttii, Mamertini, and Apuli all spoke Oscan, the three first-named writing it in a modified Etruscan alphabet, the others in Greek or Latin characters. The dialects of the central Italian Paeligni, Marrucini, Vestini, Marsi, Sabini, and Aequi (?) resembled Oscan. Many Oscan inscriptions survive, mostly dating from 300 to 90 B.C. Oscan with Volscian and Umbrian forms one group of Italic languages, Latin and Faliscan forming the other. It differs greatly from Latin in sound changes, word forms, and vocabulary, less in syntax (*see* DIALECTS, ITALIC). Official and educated classes in Italy long continued to use Oscan; but the Social War ensured its ultimate displacement by Latin. Strabo (5. 233) makes the astonishing statement that Atellane farces, the only Oscan literary form known to us, were performed in Oscan *at Rome* in his day. Certainly the language was still spoken at Pompeii in A.D. 79 and in country districts survived even longer.

J. Whatmough, *Foundations of Roman Italy* (1937), 110, 301 (with bibliography); E. Vetter, *Handbuch der italischen Dialekte* (1953), 1 ff.; E. Pulgram, *The Tongues of Italy* (U.S.A. 1958). E. T. S.

**OSIRIS** represented the deceased Pharaoh. He died, was brought to a new life, and reigned in the Underworld. He was associated with fertility, and in Herodotus (2. 144) is identified with Dionysus. The Egyptians believed that men (and sacred animals as well) were identified with Osiris, hence Osirified, in the next life. In Hellenistic times, although the name and character of Sarapis indicate his relationship to Osiris, the latter appears sometimes in the cult of the Egyptian deities along with Sarapis, Isis, Anubis, and Harpocrates. In Egypt Osiris remained primarily the god of the Underworld. With the construction of the elaborate mysteries of Isis and their spread throughout the Roman Empire, Osiris travelled along with Isis as a central figure in the liturgical and ritual drama.

ANCIENT SOURCES (Greek and Latin). Th. Hopfner, *Fontes Historiae Religionis Aegyptiacae* (1922–5).
MODERN LITERATURE. A. Erman, *Die Religion der Ägypter* (1934); Cumont, *Rel. or.*; G. Roeder, art. 'Usire' in Roscher's *Lexikon*; H. Kees, *Totenglauben und Jenseitsvorstellungen der alten Ägypter* (1926), 190 ff.; id. *Der Götterglaube im alten Ägypten* (1941), 111 ff.; Frazer, *Adonis, Attis, Osiris* (1906), 209 ff. T. A. B.

**OSROËNE,** kingdom in north-west Mesopotamia, bounded on three sides by the Khabûr and Euphrates, and on the north by Mt. Masius. In the second century B.C. it broke away from Seleucid control and formed a separate kingdom with Edessa (q.v.) as its capital. Its kings bore Semitic names, and the population was mainly Aramean, with an admixture of Greeks and Parthians.

As a Parthian vassal State and a buffer between two empires Osroëne played a prominent and ambiguous role in the struggle between Rome and Parthia. After the campaigns of L. Verus it became a Roman dependency, later a province. Long coveted and more than once overrun by the Sassanids, it was at last conquered by the Arabs (A.D. 638).

A king-list survives in a Syriac chronicle ascribed to Dionysius of Tell-Mahrê (probably *c.* A.D. 800). Of its kings, named Abgar, the following may be noted: Abgar I (94–68 B.C.); II (68–53), the betrayer of Crassus; V (4 B.C.–A.D. 7 and 13–57), famous for his spurious correspondence with Christ; VII (109–16), who entertained Trajan in Edessa; L. Aelius Septimius Abgar VIII (177–212; 212–14 jointly with his son), who became a Christian.

A. von Gutschmid, *Untersuchungen über die Geschichte des Königsreichs Osroëne* (1887); Hill, *B.M.C. Arabia, Mesopotamia and Persia*; A. R. Bellinger, *YCIS* 1935, 142 ff. M. S. D.; E. W. G.

**OSSA,** a mountain of nearly 6,500 feet in Thessalian Magnesia. On the north it is separated from the massif of Olympus by the defile of Tempe (q.v.), but on the south it forms with Pelion an almost unbroken wall which shuts off the interior of Thessaly from the sea.

**OSTIA,** at the Tiber's mouth, some 16 miles from Rome, was, according to the main Roman tradition, the first Roman colony, founded by King Ancus Marcius (q.v. 1), in order to provide salt. The earliest traces of settlement, however, beneath late republican Ostia, are not earlier than 350 B.C., and most scholars have rejected the tradition. But an earlier settlement associated with salt workings would have been outside the Roman Ostia now largely excavated, and the area near the medieval saltbeds has not yet been fully explored.

The earliest Ostia known to us was a rectangular fort of some 5½ acres, protected by strong walls of Fidenae tufa. The plan of straight streets intersecting at right angles was largely preserved through later rebuilding and the Forum of imperial Ostia marked the centre of the fourth-century colony. This colony was probably the first of a series along the western coast of Italy designed to protect the coast against raiders, for Rome had yet no fleet.

The confrontation with Carthage in the third century forced Rome to develop her navy and Ostia became Rome's main naval base; in the Hannibalic War the squadron based on Ostia is frequently mentioned in Livy's narrative. But when Carthage had been crushed the need for maintaining a strong navy seemed to have lapsed and Ostia became more important to Rome as a harbour town providing the essential services for the ships that brought goods from overseas to Rome.

During the second century Rome's defeat of Carthage and eastern victories led to a sharp increase in her imports. The growing population depended increasingly on imported corn and growing wealth increased the appetite for luxuries as well as necessities; the river harbour at Ostia became much busier. Smaller merchantmen could make the journey up river to Rome, combining oars with sail, but the larger merchantmen and particularly the grain carriers had to unload their cargoes at Ostia, where they were stored until they could be sent up-stream in small boats that were rowed or towed. The increase in the shipping that used Ostia's harbour attracted more men to the town, and building extended outside the walls. Between the main street and the river, the area most important to trade, building was controlled and the plan remains orthodox and regular into the Empire; but the area south of the main street remained irregular. The first extension of Ostia was probably on the Rome-side; later the town spread towards the coast and the river mouth.

Ostia's importance to Rome is well illustrated by the fighting between Marians and Sullans. When Marius (q.v. 1) returned from Africa (87) he captured Ostia before advancing on Rome; he knew that by controlling Ostia and the Tiber he could starve Rome. Later (c. 68) Ostia was raided and sacked by pirates. But these setbacks were not lasting. More serious were the unsettled years following Caesar's murder, especially when Sextus Pompeius controlled the western seas. Few towns in Italy can have felt more relief than Ostia when Augustus brought back peace, security, and trade. A reflection of the Augustan revival can be seen in new building. Agrippa (q.v. 3) may have been responsible for Ostia's first permanent theatre, to which was added a large area surrounded by colonnades where local and overseas traders advertised their business. At the north end of the Forum a Capitolium was built. Under Augustus' two successors new building included a temple of Rome and Augustus and an aqueduct which freed the growing population from dependence on wells.

The growth of Ostia was further stimulated when Claudius built a new harbour some 2 miles to the north (see PORTUS). Later Trajan added an inner land-locked basin as the Claudian harbour did not give adequate protection against sudden storms. The great improvement in harbour facilities, and the increased accumulation of wealth in Rome, especially in the emperor's hands, increased Rome's demand for imports and Ostia's population increased to meet the new demands. In the two generations that followed the building of Trajan's harbour Ostia's prosperity reached its peak, and great changes came in the town's architecture and in the composition of her governing class.

The most striking feature of Ostia's rebuilding under Trajan and Hadrian was the domination of tall brick apartment blocks, which replaced the atrium-type 'Pompeian' houses of the late Republic. These blocks, reflecting contemporary housing at Rome, were designed for an expanding population in an area limited by town walls and cemeteries, but they seem to have had little of the squalor that the writers of the period imply for Rome. Individual apartments vary in size but many of them have seven or more rooms. In the three-quarters of the town now excavated there is no recognizable slum area, though the living quarters over the shops, which line nearly every street, were probably overcrowded and badly lit. Independent houses which were not uncommon in the late Republic become much rarer in the second century A.D. and when built they were much more economic in space than the old atrium houses. On the other hand, the number of villas on the sea-shore to the south of the town steadily increased, among the new builders being the Younger Pliny.

Second-century Ostia was more attractive in its private and public buildings and in its amenities than we expect a harbour town to be. The main streets were lined with arcades; in the big blocks the elevations were unspoilt by fussy decoration and relied on the spacing and scale of their windows for their effect. Few houses had their own water supply, but public cisterns fed from the aqueduct were liberally distributed. The drainage system and sanitation were considerably better than England knew before the middle of the nineteenth century. The Forum became an impressive centre when Hadrian built a new Capitolium on a high platform at the north end, facing the Julio-Claudian temple of Rome and Augustus at the south end. Along the west side ran a large basilica. Public baths provided the main recreation, steadily increasing in number until there were at least seventeen sets, the three largest being handsomely equipped with

sculpture and mosaics. There was also a small theatre and an amphitheatre, which has not yet been excavated. Statues of emperors and local dignitaries were to be seen in public gardens as well as public buildings. Ostia's vital importance to Rome ensured the favour of emperors and the growth in trade encouraged public benefactions.

Great changes came over the governing class during the Empire. In the Republic and Early Empire the town seems to have been controlled by a comparatively small group of families whose members could expect to hold the duovirate several times. The wider distribution of wealth from increasing trade broke down social barriers and the second-century records include many new men. Some have come to Ostia from other towns, others are the sons of men who came to Ostia as slaves. It is probable that slaves did most of the hard manual work and they may have accounted for nearly half the population (c. 50,000); but good service could win freedom early and though freedmen were debarred from office they could earn enough money to ensure that their sons entered the Council. They themselves meanwhile could rise to office in the trade guilds, where there was no distinction between freedman and freeborn.

The religious pattern changed no less. From the Republic we have evidence for the cults of Vulcan, Castor and Pollux, Hercules, and other Roman gods. Foreign cults spread quickly and widely in the Empire. Cybele was probably the first to be adopted. Later came the Egyptian gods and, probably not until the Antonine period, Mithras, who eventually could claim no less than fifteen lodges. Of Christianity there is little firm evidence before the third century but we may be certain that in a town so closely linked with Rome there was a Christian community in the second century. There was also very little evidence indeed of Judaism until in 1962 a large synagogue was discovered near the ancient sea-shore. But though oriental cults were popular in second-century Ostia the old temples of Hercules and the other gods of the Roman tradition were kept in repair and attracted worshippers.

Ostia flourished through the Antonine period and Septimius Severus left his mark on the town. But the confusion of the third century, with its rapid succession of brief reigns and contracting trade, led to the decline of Ostia and the shifting of emphasis to Portus (q.v.). There was little new building and much less trade. But by the fourth century the town had acquired a new character. The big apartment blocks were being neglected, and when fires destroyed them they were not rebuilt. By contrast a large number of new independent houses were built in all parts of the town, which show that there were still rich men in Ostia. These houses, which vary considerably in plan, make lavish use of marble and lay great emphasis on the play of water within the house. Lead pipes with the owner's name reveal that among them were Roman senators. When St. Augustine stayed at Ostia with his mother Monica before returning to Africa he could stay with friends, probably known to him by their connexion with Africa. Ostia had become more a residential than a trading town and as at Rome in the Senate so among Ostia's rich men there were keen opponents of Christianity. When the last bid to restore paganism was made in 392 it is significant that the temple of Hercules at Ostia was restored. Some of the Mithraea that have been excavated were violently destroyed. The struggle between Christianity and Mithraism probably continued long after Constantine's conversion.

During the fourth century Ostia could remain a congenial setting for the rich, but the middle class which depended on trade had collapsed, and there was a wide gulf between rich and poor. In the fifth century life became increasingly insecure from invading armies and sea raiders. A much-reduced population hung on until in the ninth century the Pope built and fortified a small new settlement, Gregoriopolis, on the Romeward side of the old town. Ostia was left to become a quarry for builders and treasure hunters until publicly organized excavation started in the nineteenth century.

Ostia's inscriptions are collected in *CIL* xiv and supplement; a second supplement arranges the inscriptions topographically. L. Paschetto, *Ostia: Colonia Romana* (1912); J. Carcopino, *Virgile et les origines d'Ostie* (1919); R. Meiggs, *Roman Ostia* (1960); *Scavi di Ostia*, a series of volumes on different aspects of Ostia, beginning in 1954 and continuing. R. M.

**OSTORIUS SCAPULA**, PUBLIUS, of equestrian family, *consul suffectus* before A.D. 47, when he succeeded Plautius as governor of Britain. He consolidated a frontier for Britain along the Severn, Tees, and Trent rivers with the Fosse Way as a line of communication in the rear, while the hinterland was secured by a *colonia* at Camulodunum (*Colchester*). Attempts at the offensive against Welsh tribes were less successful: an advance to the Irish sea proved premature; and though Ostorius defeated Caratacus, somewhere in the Marches, he was unable to subdue the Silures and Ordovices of Wales, and died worn out in A.D. 52.

Tac. *Ann.* 12. 31–9. Collingwood–Myres, *Roman Britain*, 91 ff.; G. Webster, *Arch. Journ.* 1958, 49 ff.; D. R. Dudley and G. Webster, *The Roman Conquest of Britain, A.D. 43–57* (1965), ch. 5. C. E. S.

**OSTRACA.** Potsherds were not habitually used for writing in Greece, except as voting tablets at Athens. In Egypt such use began after the Greek conquest; the first dated example is of 274 B.C. Nearly all early Ptolemaic ostraca are tax-receipts; later, orders and lists are common, and letters, school exercises, magical spells, and religious texts, pagan or Christian, were inscribed on them. The Thebaid is the most prolific source of ostraca of all periods, especially Thebes itself, with Hermonthis and Crocodilopolis; a fair number have come from Elephantine and Coptos; a single group is recorded from Pselcis in Nubia, another from Tentyra. Oxyrhynchus has produced some hundreds, nearly all Byzantine. In the Fayûm they are rare before Roman times; one lot from Philadelphia is the only considerable find of Ptolemaic date; under the Empire they occur on most town-sites till *c*. A.D. 400. No ostraca have been reported from the Delta. Outside Egypt Latin ostraca have been found near Carthage. Except in the Fayûm, few have been obtained by scientific excavation: they are usually found in ancient rubbish-mounds or in house-ruins.

U. Wilcken, *Griechische Ostraka aus Aegypten und Nubien* (1899); [mainly Thebaid] A. H. Gardiner, H. Thompson, and J. G. Milne, *Theban Ostraca* (1913); P. M. Meyer, *Griechische Texte aus Aegypten* (1916); P. Viereck, *Ostraca aus Brüssel und Berlin* (1922); id. *Ostraka der Bibliothek zu Strassburg* (1923); L. Amundsen, *Ostraca Osloensia* (1933); Claire Préaux, *Ostraca grecs au Musée de Brooklyn* (1935); [Fayûm] B. P. Grenfell, A. S. Hunt, and D. G. Hogarth, *Fayûm Towns and their Papyri* (1900); P. Jouguet, *Ostraka du Fayoum* (1902); P. Viereck and F. Zucker, *Papyri, Ostraka und Wachstafeln aus Philadelphia* (1926); L. Amundsen, *Greek Ostraca in the University of Michigan Collection* (1935); [Oxyrhynchus] E. E. Fund *Arch. Rep.* 1903/4, 16; 1904/5, 15; 1905/6, 14; 1906/7, 9; [Tentyra] J. G. Milne, *Arch. Pap.* vi (1913), 125 ff.; [All districts] J. G. Tait, *Greek Ostraca in the Bodleian Library etc.* i (1930), ii (1955, ed. J. G. Tait, and Cl. Préaux); [Carthage] R. Cagnat and A. Merlin, 'Ostraka latins de Carthage (*Journ. Sav.* 1911, 514). Publications of texts in periodicals are mostly reproduced in Preisigke–Bilabel, *Sammelbuch griechischer Urkunden aus Aegypten.* J. G. M.

**OSTRACISM** (ὀστρακισμός) in Athens in the fifth century B.C. was a method of banishing for ten years a prominent citizen who had become unpopular. Each year in the sixth prytany (*see* PRYTANEIS) the question whether an ostracism should be held that year was put to the vote in the *ekklesia* (q.v.). If the people voted in favour of holding an ostracism, it took place on a day shortly afterwards, probably in the eighth prytany. It was held in the *agora* under the supervision of the *archontes* (q.v.) and the *boule* (q.v.). Each citizen who wished to vote wrote on a potsherd (ὄστρακον) the name of the citizen whom he wished to be banished. The voters were marshalled by *phylai* (q.v.) in enclosures erected for the occasion, to ensure that no one put in more than one *ostrakon*. When all had voted, the *ostraka* were counted, and, provided that there was a total of at least 6,000, the man whose name appeared on the largest number was ostracized. (An alternative view, attributed to Philochorus, *FGrH* 328 F 30, is that the ostracism was valid only if at least 6,000 *ostraka* were cast against one man.) The man ostracized had to leave the country within ten days and remain in exile for ten years, but he did not forfeit his citizenship or property, and at the end of the ten years he could return to live in Athens without any disgrace or disability.

The date of the institution of ostracism has been a matter of dispute. According to the standard account (Arist. *Ath. Pol.* 22) the law about it was introduced by Cleisthenes (q.v. 1) in 508/7, but the first ostracism was not held until 487. Some modern scholars accept this account, and offer various conjectural explanations of the twenty years' interval. Others maintain that the law cannot have been passed until shortly before the first ostracism in 487, and that Cleisthenes therefore was not its author; a statement attributed to Androtion (*FGrH* 324 F 6) has been adduced in support of this view, but there is no general agreement about its interpretation or value. A third view, that the ostracism in 487 was not the earliest, and that Cleisthenes himself was the first victim of his own law (Ael. *VH* 13. 24), is generally rejected.

The man ostracized in 487 was Hipparchus son of Charmus, a relative of the ex-tyrant Hippias (q.v. 1). He was followed in 486 by Megacles, one of the Alcmaeonidae (q.v.), and in 485 by some other adherent of Hippias' family. No doubt these three had all become unpopular because it was thought that they favoured the Persian invaders and the restoration of the tyranny. Xanthippus (q.v. 1) was ostracized in 484, and Aristides (q.v. 1) in 482; but both of these returned from exile in 480, when an amnesty was declared in an attempt to muster the full strength of Athens to resist the invasion of Xerxes. Other prominent men known to have been ostracized are Themistocles (q.v.) about 470, Cimon (q.v.) in 461, and Thucydides (q.v. 1) son of Melesias in 443. Hyperbolus (q.v.) was the last victim of the system; his ostracism is usually dated in 417, though some scholars have placed it in 416 or 415. Ostracism then fell out of use, although the law authorizing it remained in force in the fourth century. The *graphe paranomon* (q.v.) was found to be a more convenient method of attacking politicians.

It is often hard to tell why a particular man was ostracized. Sometimes (as in the cases of Cimon and Thucydides) the Athenians seem to have ostracized a man to express their rejection of a policy for which he stood and their support for an opposing leader; thus an ostracism might serve a purpose similar to that of a modern general election. But no doubt individual citizens were often actuated by personal malice or other non-political motives, as is illustrated by the story of the yokel who wished to vote against Aristides because he was tired of hearing him called 'the Just' (Plut. *Arist.* 7. 7).

Many hundreds of *ostraka* have been found in modern excavations. Most of them date from the period before 480. The names include not only all the men whom we know to have been actually ostracized, but also a considerable number of others. Some are men quite unknown to us, and it may well be that they were not prominent politicians but merely had an odd vote cast against them by some malicious personal acquaintance. Particularly interesting is a find of 190 *ostraka* all inscribed with the name of Themistocles by only a few different hands (*Hesp.* 1938, 228 ff.). Presumably they were prepared for distribution by his opponents. This suggests that he was the victim of an organized campaign, and it illustrates the importance of ostracism as a political weapon in fifth-century Athens.

Ostracism existed also at Argos, Megara, and Miletus. At Syracuse there was a similar system called 'petalism', because the names were written on olive leaves (πέταλα).

A. E. Raubitschek, *AJArch.* 1951, 221 ff., and *CJ* 1952–3, 113 ff.; Hignett, *Hist. Athen. Const.* 159 ff.; F. Jacoby, *FGrH* iii b Suppl. (1954), commentary on 324 F 6 and 328 F 30; R. Werner, *Athenaeum* 1958, 48 ff.; A. R. Hands, *JHS* 1959, 69 ff.; D. Kagan, *Hesp.* 1961, 393 ff. D. M. M.

**OTACILIUS** (*PW* 12) **CRASSUS**, Titus, praetor in 217 B.C., was balked of the consulship for 214 by Fabius Maximus; he received a second praetorship. He served in Sicily 216–211, raiding the African coast (215 and possibly in 211) and commanding a fleet at the siege of Syracuse. His exploits in 212 (Livy 25. 31) and his candidature for the consulship before his death in 211 are doubtful. On the relations of the Otacilii with the Fabii see J. Pinsent, *Phoenix* 1964, 18 ff. H. H. S.

**OTHO**, Marcus Salvius (*PW* 21) (A.D. 32–69), whose father received patrician rank from Claudius, was husband of Poppaea Sabina (q.v.) and friend of Nero. As Nero fell in love with his wife (afterwards divorced), he was sent to Lusitania as governor in 58 and remained there until Nero's death (68). He supported Galba (q.v. 1) and hoped to be his heir. Disappointed, he organized a conspiracy among the Praetorians and was hailed Emperor (15 Jan. 69). He tried to appear as the legitimate successor of Nero. Egypt, Africa, and the legions of the Danube and the Euphrates declared for him. But the legions of the Rhine had already chosen Vitellius (q.v. 1), and their military preparations were far advanced. By early March their advanced guard had crossed the Alps, and an Othonian expedition to southern Gaul achieved little. His generals Vestricius Spurinna and Annius Gallus (7) (qq.v.) held the line of the Po, but his armies from the Danube arrived only gradually. Though defeated in a minor engagement the Vitellians were soon heavily reinforced: yet Otho insisted on a decisive battle before he could oppose equal strength. His troops advanced from Bedriacum, c. 22 miles east of Cremona, and were irretrievably defeated. He committed suicide on 16 Apr. 69.

Otho's profligacy seems not to have impaired his energy or his interest in government. But he was a slave to the Praetorians who had elevated him.

Plutarch, *Otho* (commentary by E. G. Hardy, 1890); Suetonius, *Otho* (comm. G. W. Mooney, 1930). A. Passerini, 'Le due battaglie presso Bedriacum', *Studi di antichità offerti a E. Ciaceri* (1940); F. Klingner, 'Die Geschichte Kaiser Othos bei Tacitus', *Sächsische Sb. Phil.-hist. Kl.* 1940. See also on GALBA (1). A. M.; G. E. F. C.

**OVATIO** was a minor form of triumph (q.v.). It might be granted to a general who could not claim a full triumph, e.g. if his victory had not involved the destruction of a large number of the enemy or if he had handed over his army to a successor. He entered Rome on foot or horseback instead of in a chariot, dressed in a *toga praetexta* and without a sceptre, wearing a wreath of myrtle instead of laurel, and the procession was much less spectacular. For a list of Roman *ovationes* see *PW*, s.v. The last recorded one is in A.D. 47, that of Plautius (q.v. 4). H. H. S.

**OVID** (Publius Ovidius Naso, 43 B.C.–A.D. 17), poet, was born at Sulmo (q.v.) on 20 Mar. The story of his life is told in one of his own poems (*Tr.* 4. 10). He came of an old equestrian family and was intended by his father

for an official career. His studies at Rome under Arellius Fuscus and Porcius (2) Latro (qq.v.; *see also* DECLAMATIO) are described by the Elder Seneca (*Contr.* 2. 2. 8, 9. 5. 17). He visited Athens (*Tr.* 1. 2. 77), probably in the course of a Grand Tour in the company of his friend the poet Macer (*Pont.* 2. 10. 21 ff.). After holding some minor judicial posts (Wilkinson, 15) he abandoned public life for poetry. As one of the group of poets round Messalla (q.v. 3), who had encouraged his first poetical essays (*Pont.* 1. 7. 27 f.), Ovid stood somewhat apart from the main Augustan literary movement which centred on Maecenas. He knew Horace, and Propertius was his friend (*Tr.* 4. 10. 46), but his warmest tribute to a contemporary poet is his elegy on the death of Tibullus (*Am.* 3. 9), like himself a protégé of Messalla. It is possible to overestimate the political significance of these literary groupings, but the point may have some bearing on the problems of his exile (Wilkinson, 294; Thibault, 89 ff.). Ovid was married three times and had one daughter, probably by his second wife. His third wife was connected with the influential Paullus Fabius Maximus, the addressee of a famous Ode of Horace (4. 1; cf. *Pont.* 3. 3). His poetry quickly brought him into prominence, and by A.D. 8 he was the leading poet of Rome. In that year he was suddenly banished by Augustus to Tomis (q.v.) on the Black Sea, for reasons said to be notorious (*Tr.* 4. 10. 99) but not explicitly described by him and never satisfactorily explained subsequently. Two counts against him are repeatedly referred to in the poems of exile: *carmen*, the *Ars Amatoria*; and *error*, an indiscretion whose nature he does not specify, though he insists that it was not a crime (*scelus*). So much is clear, that Augustus took Ovid's offence, whatever it was, as a deep personal affront (*Tr.* 2. 133 f.), but important objections can be made against all the theories hitherto proposed, and the problem, in default of further evidence, must be regarded as insoluble. Augustus' resentment seems to have been reflected in the choice of Tomis as the place of Ovid's exile. It was a superficially hellenized city on the extreme edge of the Roman Empire, subject to periodical attacks from the fierce tribes of the region; the *Tristia* and the *Epistulae ex Ponto* are full of complaints of the dangers of the situation, of the miseries of the climate (these are certainly not exaggerated), and, cruellest of all, of the spiritual and cultural isolation of the place. At Tomis, in spite of repeated appeals to Augustus and later to Tiberius, Ovid passed what remained of his life. The date of his death is uncertain: Jerome gives A.D. 17, a date which it is perhaps hazardous to dispute on the evidence of *Fast.* 1. 223 ff. (cf. Bömer ad loc.).

WORKS (all extant poems written in elegiac couplets except the *Metamorphoses*).

(1) **Amores.** Three books of love poems arranged on the Alexandrian-Augustan principles of artful disorder coupled with formal symmetry (book 1 contains fifteen poems; 2, 20; 3, 15). What we possess is a revised edition published shortly before the *Ars* (*Ars Am.* 3. 343); the original edition in five books may have appeared as early as 20 B.C. (Munari ed. xv). The obvious resemblances to Tibullus and Propertius (Corinna as 'heroine' ~ Delia, Cynthia) should not be pressed: the individual turn which Ovid gave to the genre must be criticized on its merits (cf. Lee). Indeed it may be argued that the 'movement' (cf. W. Marg–R. Harder, *Liebesgedichte*[2] (1962), 168) of the *Amores* from acceptance of love and elegiac poetry (1. 1) to rejection of both (3. 15) is in some sort a criticism, as being almost a *reductio ad absurdum*, of Propertius.

(2) **Heroides** (so called by Priscian, *Gramm. Lat.* ii. 544 Keil; but cf. *Ars Am.* 3. 345 *epistula*. The correct form may have been *Epistulae Heroidum*: G. Luck, *Die*

*röm. Liebeselegie* (1961), 223 f.). These poems fall into two groups. 1–14 (the Ovidian authorship of 15, the *Ep. Sapphus*, is doubtful), published between the two editions of the *Amores* (*Am.* 2. 18), are letters from legendary women to absent husbands or lovers. Ovid may have owed the idea to Propertius (4. 3); in his hands the form is rather that of the dramatic monologue than the epistle, and the influence of his rhetorical training in character-drawing (*ethopoeia*) can be clearly seen. He himself claimed originality for his treatment (*Ars Am.* 3. 346). 16–21, formerly suspected but now generally and rightly attributed to Ovid, are in pairs (the idea apparently suggested by his friend Sabinus, *Am.* 2. 18. 27 ff.), with the girl answering the man. Their date is disputed, but certain metrical features may suggest that they were composed contemporaneously with the *Fasti* (Latta, 2–7). Certainly they are in Ovid's most mature and assured manner, and in the variations given in each pair of letters to the basic theme of romantic love we may also see the influence of the *Metamorphoses*.

(3) **Medicamina Faciei Femineae.** A poem on cosmetics of which only 100 verses survive. It predated the third book of the *Ars* (*Ars Am.* 3. 205 f., also important for establishing the title of the poem).

(4) **Ars Amatoria** (for the title cf. Sen. *Contr.* 3. 7. 2, Eutyches, *G.L.* v. 473 K.). A didactic poem in three books on the arts of seduction and intrigue, published not before 1 B.C. (1. 171 ff.). Books 1–2, for men, were the original extent of the poem; book 3, for women, was added at their request. Ovid almost certainly took the hint for the poem from Tibullus (1. 4), but Roman love-elegy had already shown a didactic tendency (Wheeler, *CPhil.* 1910–11); and the popularity of didactic poetry on frivolous themes is attested by Ovid himself (*Tr.* 2. 471 ff.). The scale and treatment, however, are original: the parody of serious didactic literature, the brilliant vignettes of contemporary Roman society, the occasional note of satire, the mythological illustrations, and the vivacious wit that pervades the whole poem combine to render it unique in ancient literature. Only Pope, in *The Rape of the Lock*, has excelled Ovid in this kind of writing.

(5) **Remedia Amoris.** A mock-recantation, varying in clever and unexpected ways (Prinz, *Wien. Stud.* 1914, 1917) the lessons of the *Ars*. It contains a striking self-vindication (361 ff.) against certain critics of Ovid's outspokenness.

(6) **Metamorphoses.** An epic poem in fifteen books, Ovid's only surviving work in hexameters. Essentially it is a collection of stories from classical and Near-Eastern legend, given formal unity in three ways: (i) every story describes, or at least alludes to, a change of shape; (ii) the stories are linked together in complexes of varying size, and the complexes are themselves linked by elaborate devices of association and contrast; (iii) there is a chronological progression from the great initial metamorphosis of Chaos to Order (Cosmos) to the (from the Augustan standpoint) culminating metamorphosis, the apotheosis of Julius Caesar, the intention being to achieve a continuous poem (1. 4, *perpetuum carmen*). This was the work on which Ovid rested his hopes of immortality (15. 871 ff.), and it is evident that he composed it with unusual care. Both theme and structure were Alexandrian. The idea of transformation had previously been exploited by Nicander, by the obscure Boios or Boio (whose Ὀρνιθογονία was apparently adapted by Macer, *Tr.* 4. 10. 43), and by Parthenius (qq.v.); the obvious model for a long poem formed from originally unconnected stories was Callimachus' *Aetia*, and Callimachean also is the ingenuity with which Ovid links and frames his episodes (criticized by Quintilian, *Inst.* 4. 1. 77; cf. Wilkinson, *Ovidiana*, 231 ff.). For his material Ovid drew freely on the whole

range of Greek poetry, from Virgil (in the latter books), and from many sources now inaccessible. In spite of all these debts the *Metamorphoses* is a highly original poem. Ovid perceived what later epic poets, except Lucan, would or could not perceive, that there could be no question of rivalling Virgil on his own ground; and he had the genius to adapt his apparently unsuitable material to the needs of an Augustan poem. The *Metamorphoses* is a contradiction in terms, a modern epic. It must have been composed contemporaneously with the *Fasti* from *c.* A.D. 2 onwards; it had not received its final revision at the time of his exile (*Tr.* 1. 7. 11 ff.).

(7) **Fasti.** A poetical calendar of the Roman year with a book for each month. At the time of his exile it was incomplete, and only the first six books (Jan.–June) survive. These were partially (1. 3; 2. 15) revised at Tomis. Here too Ovid's models were Alexandrian. His astronomy is indebted to Aratus' *Phaenomena* (*see* ARATUS 1), and his aetiological treatment of Roman history and religion to Callimachus, though a lead had already been given by Propertius (4. 2, 4, 9, 10). The *Fasti* is perhaps Ovid's least successful work. As an attempt at a specifically Roman poem it lacks the spontaneity of his other work, and the elegiac couplet, though employed with astonishing virtuosity, is not a suitable medium for sustained narrative. It is an important source of information on Roman religion.

(8) **Tristia.** Five books of poems addressed to the emperor, Ovid's wife, and other (unnamed) persons at Rome. Book 1 was written on the journey to Tomis and offers more variety and incident than the others; it and book 2 must have been dispatched shortly after Ovid's arrival in A.D. 9. Book 2 is an elaborate defence of the *Ars Amatoria* addressed to Augustus, valuable as a source for ancient literary history but extremely puzzling if seriously intended as an apologia (cf. Marg, *Atti* ii. 345 ff.). Books 3–5 (A.D. 10–12) describe the rigours of his exile and plead for leniency.

(9) **Epistulae ex Ponto.** Four books, distinguished from *Tr.* 3–5 only by the naming of all the addressees (*Pont.* 1. 1. 17 f.). Books 1–3 were put together from poems of various dates (*Pont.* 3. 9. 53) and published in A.D. 13; book 4 probably appeared posthumously (4. 9 written in 16).

(10) **Ibis.** A curse directed at an unnamed enemy, possibly the man referred to several times in the *Tristia* (e.g. 1. 6. 13 f.), published *c.* A.D. 11 (La Penna, vii–xix). The idea for the poem and the name Ibis were borrowed from Callimachus' attack on Apollonius; *Ibis* 53–6 seem to show that the Callimachean original was in elegiacs, but otherwise the relationship between the two poems is obscure. Rhetorical fertility and abstruse mythological learning combine to render the *Ibis* a technical *tour de force*, but it reads more like a literary exercise than genuine polemic.

(11) **Lost and spurious works.** Ovid's tragedy *Medea* (*Tr.* 2. 553) was praised by Quintilian (*Inst.* 10. 1. 98) and Tacitus (*Dial.* 12). Two verses survive. The *Gigantomachia* ostensibly attested by *Am.* 2. 1. 11 ff. is probably a literary fiction (Wilkinson, 48 n.). The fragments of the lost works are collected by S. G. Owen (O.C.T. of *Tristia*, etc.) and F. W. Lenz (Paravia ed.² (1956) of *Halieutica*, etc.). Neither the *Halieutica* (Housman, *CQ* 1907, 275 ff.) nor the *Nux* (Lee, *Ovidiana*, 457 ff.) is by Ovid.

MAN AND POET. Ovid was born too late to be emotionally committed to the Augustan regime, as Virgil and Horace were; his commitment was rather to poetry itself (*Tr.* 4. 10. 41–2; cf. also G. Murray, *Essays and Addresses* (1922), 116). No ancient poet, not even Virgil, can have read more poetry and given back in his own work more of what he read and so made his own: for the fact that much of the experience which he transmutes into poetry is literary experience does not impair its validity (cf. Kenney, 47 n. 1). The raw material of his art is human emotion; the history of his most characteristic work from the *Amores* to the *Metamorphoses* is the history of an exploration, steadily increasing in range and penetration, of the heart and its passions. His early training in the schools of declamation was calculated to encourage his preoccupation with the communication of emotion (*pathos*: cf. S. F. Bonner, *Roman Declamation* (1949), 62 f.). It also stimulated his immense natural fertility of expression. Ovid's astonishing linguistic and metrical dexterity is the product of unobtrusive but far-reaching technical innovation. It is well known that he refined the already strict rules of the Latin elegiac couplet, but the metre has inherent limitations which even Ovid could not transcend. His complete domination of his medium can more profitably be studied in the *Metamorphoses*. His hexameter is not, as it tends to be represented, merely an emasculated version of Virgil's: it is a uniquely suitable instrument created by Ovid for the particular kind of epic he had chosen to write, allowing unobtrusive but effective variations in pace and colour as the tone of the narrative required. Its versatility becomes more apparent where circumstances allow a comparison between hexameter and elegiac versions of the same story (e.g. *Met.* 5. 341 ff. ~ *Fast.* 4. 417 ff.; Heinze, *passim*, Wilkinson, 279 f.). What raises the poem to a position alongside the *Aeneid* (Wilamowitz, *Hell. Dicht.* i. 241) is the transfiguring effect of Ovid's marvellous creative imagination on his stories, whether familiar or recondite, grave or gay, and his ability to extract and illuminate whatever in them in any way contributes to our understanding of humanity. It is in this extraordinary power to isolate the significant moment in each scene or episode that the secret of his influence on later writers and artists must be sought. Ovid's defects are those of his qualities. He was not an Augustan as Horace and Virgil were Augustans: compared with the superbly controlled *Aeneid* the *Metamorphoses* is exuberantly unclassical. *Non ignoravit vitia sua sed amavit*, remarked Seneca (*Contr.* 2. 2. 12); and there are occasions (e.g. *Met.* 13. 789 ff.) when his disregard for the classical canons of restraint and proportion, always in the interest, it should be remarked, of a designed artistic effect, is almost insolent. Well it may be. *Exit in immensum fecunda licentia vatum* (*Am.* 3. 12. 41): this is the freedom of a genius that recognizes no laws but its own. Ovid's poetry invites the reader to an enjoyment of the sensual universe that is uncorrupted by the pessimistic reservations familiar in Greek poetry from the very earliest times. If gaiety on the whole predominates over sadness in his work, that is something that need not be excused: there is *gravitas* enough and to spare elsewhere in Roman literature. It is, however, a mistake to label Ovid an unreflecting hedonist. Other poets surpass him in profundity, but his catholic sensibility has no parallel in the literature of the ancient world.

See ALEXANDRIANISM; ELEGIAC POETRY, LATIN; EPYLLION.

LIFE AND WORKS. E. Martini, *Einleitung zu Ovid* (1933); H. Fränkel, *Ovid: a Poet between Two Worlds* (1945); *L. P. Wilkinson, *Ovid Recalled* (1955); *J. C. Thibault, *The Mystery of Ovid's Exile* (1964).

TEXTS. Teubner (Merkel, Ehwald, Lenz); O.C.T. (Kenney, Owen); J. P. Postgate's *Corpus Poetarum Latinorum*, vol. i (Palmer, Edwards, Davies, Owen, Housman).

EDITIONS (C = commentary, T = translation): Complete works: Heinsius–Burman (C) (1727). Separate works: **Am.** P. Brandt (C) (1911); *F. Munari (T) (²1964). **Her.** A. Palmer (C) (1898). **Medic.** A. Kunz (C) (1881). **Ars Am.** P. Brandt (C) (1902). **Rem. Am.** (+ *Med.*) F. W. Lenz (C, T) (1960). **Met.** P. Magnus (1914); M. Haupt, R. Ehwald (C), rev. M. von Albrecht (1966). **Fasti.** Sir J. G. Frazer (C, T) (1929); F. Bömer (C, T) (1957–8). **Tr.** R. Merkel (+ *Ibis*) (1837); S. G. Owen (1889); book 2: S. G. Owen (C, T) (1924); book 4: *T. J. de Jonge (C) (1951). **Pont.** Book 1: *A. Scholte (C) (1933).

**Ibis.** R. Ellis (C) (1881); *A. La Penna (C) (1957). [**Halieutica** *J. A. Richmond (C) (1962).]

TRANSLATIONS. With text, Loeb and Budé (French) series. Verse translations: **Am.** C. Marlowe (?1598). **Ars Am.** F. A. Wright, *The Lover's Handbook* (1924). **Met.** A. Golding (1567), used by Shakespeare. Greek prose versions by M. Planudes: **Her.** in Palmer's ed.; **Met.** ed. J. F. Boissonade (N. E. Lemaire, vol. 5, 1822). [**Ars. Am., Am., Rem. Am.** P. E. Easterling and E. J. Kenney, *Ovidiana Graeca* (PCPS, Suppl. 1, 1965).]

TEXTUAL CRITICISM, ETC.: **Her.** *H. Dörrie, *Untersuchungen zur Überlieferungsgeschichte von Ovids Epistulae Heroidum* (*Nachr. Akad. Göttingen*, 1960); *B. Latta, *Die Stellung der Doppelbriefe . . . im Gesamtwerk Ovids* (diss. Marburg. 1963). **Met.** D. A. Slater, *Towards a text of the Metamorphoses of Ovid* (1927); K. Dursteler, *Die Doppelfassungen in Ovids Metamorphosen* (diss. Hamburg, 1940); *F. Munari, *Catalogue of the MSS. of Ovid's Metamorphoses* (*Univ. London Inst. Class. Stud. Bulletin*, Suppl. 4, 1957).

LITERARY CRITICISM, ETC.: Fränkel, Wilkinson, opp. citt. E. K. Rand, *Ovid and his Influence* (1926); A. R. Zingerle, *Ovidius und sein Verhältnis zu den Vorgängern* (1869–71); R. Heinze, *Ovids elegische Erzählung* (*Ber. sächs. Akad.* 1919). Individual works: **Am.** Lee, 'Tenerorum lusor Amorum', in *Critical Essays on Roman Literature: Elegy and Lyric*, ed. J. P. Sullivan (1962). **Met.** W. Ludwig, *Struktur und Einheit der Metamorphosen Ovids* (1965); B. Otis, *Ovid as an Epic Poet* (1966). **Tr., Pont.** Kenney, 'The poetry of Ovid's exile', *PCPS* 1965. See also *Ovidiana*, ed. N. I. Herescu (1958); *Atti del Convegno internazionale ovidiano* (1959).          E. J. K.

(* = with bibliography)

**OVINIUS,** as tribune of the plebs, proposed a measure (the *Lex Ovinia* or *plebiscitum Ovinium*) which formulated regulations for the future enrolment of senators. The precise content of the enactment is obscure. That it was responsible for transferring the right to hold a *lectio senatus* from consuls to censors is a pure supposition. All that can be said with assurance is that the censors were required by the law to give precedence in the *lectio* to all worthy ex-magistrates (or possibly ex-curule magistrates). The exercise of excessive personal or factional influence over the composition of the Senate was thus curbed, and for the future a guarantee of a seat in the Senate was afforded by the honourable tenure of high office. The date of the measure is also in doubt, but the opposition aroused by the *lectio* of Appius Claudius the censor in 312 B.C. has been thought to suggest that he was operating the procedure for the first time.

P. Willems, *Le Sénat de la république romaine* i. 153 ff.; i². 668 ff.; Mommsen, *Röm. Staatsr.* ii³. 418 f.; F. Cassola, *I gruppi politici romani* (1962), 140.          E. S. S.

**OXUS** (*Ὦξος*, modern *Amu Darya*). This river was known by name to Herodotus and Aristotle, but was apparently confused by them with the Araxes (q.v.). It was discovered by Alexander, and some Indian merchandise was known to come by it, and thence by the Caspian and the rivers Cyrus and Phasis to the Euxine. But later information about it was from hearsay only, and the belief persisted that it flowed into the Caspian—which may have been true of prehistoric times. Its efflux into the Aral Sea was never located by Greek geographers.

Strabo 11. 514–18; Ptol. *Geog.* 6. 9–18. Warmington, *Indian Commerce*, 26–7, 337, n. 70; Cary, *Geographic Background*, 198 f.; Thomson, *Hist. Anc. Geog.* 80, 85, 126 ff., 172, 294.          E. H. W.

**OXYRHYNCHUS** (*Behnesa*) is now represented only by extensive mounds beyond the Bahr Yusuf to the west of the Nile, which have proved the richest source of papyri in Egypt yet discovered. The first scientific exploration of the site was by Grenfell and Hunt in 1897; since their last campaign there in 1906 other diggers, official and unofficial, have reaped good harvests. The proportion of Ptolemaic papyri is small: most are Roman and Byzantine. Apart from the information derived from these papyri, practically nothing is known of the history of the town.

Kees, *PW*, s.v. Oxyrynchos, cols. 2043 ff.; E. G. Turner, *JEg. Arch.* 1952, 78 ff.; id. *Akten des VIII. Intern. Kongr. für Papyrol.* (1955) 141 ff.; *Oxyrhynchus Papyri*, i–xxxii (1898; in progress).    J. G. M.

**OXYRHYNCHUS, The historian from.** In 1906 some 900 lines of a lost Greek historian were discovered at Oxyrhynchus in Egypt. The writer dealt in considerable detail with events in the Greek world, 396–395 B.C., and was an authority of the first importance. The papyrus indicates a strict chronological arrangement by summers and winters, competent criticism and analysis of motives, a first-hand knowledge of the topography of Asia Minor, and certain details found in no other work on the period. It was probably a continuation of Thucydides beginning with the autumn of 411, was written between 387 and 346, and its elaborate scale suggests that it covered only a short period, perhaps to the battle of Cnidos, 394. Three further fragments (ninety lines) were published in 1949.

Its authorship has been much discussed. Grenfell and Hunt (*POxy.* v. 842) preferred an attribution to Theopompus (q.v. 3), later strongly supported by E. Meyer; the case for Ephorus was ably argued by E. M. Walker, in spite of his previous advocacy of the shadowy Cratippus

(q.v.), and more recently F. Jacoby has argued for Daimachus (q.v.). The close resemblance of the text with Diodorus book 14 coupled with significant divergencies indicates that Diodorus' source, Ephorus, had P, as the editors termed the author of the papyrus, before him for his universal history. Moreover, there is reliable evidence of the use which Ephorus made of Daimachus. However, the question of authorship does not yet admit of a definite solution. Ephorus and Theopompus are now largely discounted, the former on grounds of date and arrangement, the latter for reasons of style. As between Cratippus and Daimachus the evidence points towards the latter even if we reject Jacoby's view that Cratippus was a late Hellenistic writer (disputed by A. W. Gomme, *CQ* 1954, 53).

*FGrH* ii A 66. *Hellenica Oxyrhynchia*, O.C.T.; V. Bartelotti, *Hellenica Oxyrhynchia* (1959); E. Meyer, *Theopomps Hellenika* (1909); E. M. Walker, *The Hellenica Oxyrhynchia* (1913); G. L. Barber, *The Historian Ephorus* (1935), ch. 3; H. Bloch, *Harv. Stud.*, Suppl. Vol. 1940; G. T. Griffith, *Fifty Years of Classical Scholarship* (ed. Platnauer, 1954), 160; I. A. F. Bruce, *An Historical Commentary on the Hellenica Oxyrhynchia* (1967). G. L. B.

# P

**PACUVIUS,** Marcus. Born in 220 B.C. in Brundisium, nephew and successor of Ennius, died aged about 90. The name is Oscan and appears in the original form in an epigram by Pompilius (Varro, *Sat. Men.* 356). Gellius (1. 24) quotes an epitaph, striking in its modesty, perhaps by Pacuvius himself. Pliny (*HN* 35. 19) reports a painting of the poet (who was a painter himself) in the temple of Hercules in the *Forum Boarium*. Only thirteen titles of plays are known and this may reflect a small output (he was the first Roman to confine himself to tragedy, as Plautus had done in comedy): only *Antiopa* indicates an original by Euripides (contrast Ennius and Accius), several indicate Sophoclean originals, while others suggest post-Euripidean originals (cf. Accius). Cicero (*Tusc.* 2. 48 ff.) praises the passage of *Niptra*, where the wounded Odysseus groans in pain, as better than that of Sophocles because Pacuvius has composed more stoically and had more regard for *gravitas*. A certain independence and originality may well have characterized Pacuvius' use of his Greek material: e.g. in *Chryses* a character scorns divination in an un-Sophoclean way but reminiscent of a fragment of the *Chrysippus* of Euripides, which Pacuvius may have imported into the Sophoclean play. Pacuvius composed a *praetexta* with the title *Paullus* (certainly Aemilius Paullus, victor of Pydna in 168 B.C.), but of his *Saturae* nothing is known. His style was characterized by an exuberance of invention: bold coinages, neologisms, Grecisms, and especially compound adjectives (like the infamous 408 R: *Nerei repandirostrum incurvicervicum genus*). Varro and Cicero considered him the greatest Roman tragic poet, the Augustans ranked him with Accius, and later generations (Quint. 10. 1. 97) inferior to Accius.

E. H. Warmington, *Remains of Old Latin* ii (1936), 158 ff. (with transl.). Ribbeck, *TRF³*, Klotz, *Scaen. Rom. Frag.* i. 111 ff. F. Leo, *Gesch. d. röm. Lit.* (1913), 226 ff. M. Valsa, *M. Pacuvius, poète tragique* (1957); I. Mariotti, *Introduzione a Pacuvio* (1960). G. W. W.

**PADUS** (Ligurian *Bodincus*, Greek Ἠριδανός, modern Po): Italy's longest river with numerous tributaries. It rises in the Cottian Alps, flows about 400 miles eastward through Cisalpine Gaul (q.v.), and enters the Adriatic near Ravenna. Its valley was inhabited in pre-

historic times by *terramaricoli* (*see* TERRAMARA), and from Etruscan days dikes have protected its reclaimed riparian lands. In antiquity navigation as far as Turin was possible but hazardous owing to the swift current. Since ancient times floods and the silt carried down have considerably altered its lower course and delta.

Polyb. 2. 16; Strabo 4. 203 f.; 5. 212, 217; Pliny, *HN* 3. 117–22. C. Jacini, *Il Viaggio del Po* (1937) with full bibliography. E. T. S.

**PAEAN.** The Paean seems originally to have been a hymn addressed to Apollo in his role as Healer (*Il.* 1. 473; schol. Ar. *Plut.* 636), but it was early used for other purposes, such as (1) military, as in *Il.* 22. 391, Aesch. *Sept.* 635, schol. Eur. *Phoen.* 1102; (2) sympotic, when all the guests sang it in unison after the libations and before the symposium, as in Alcman fr. 98. 2, Aesch. *Ag.* 247, Ath. 149 c, Pl. *Symp.* 176 a, Xen. *Symp.* 2. 1; (3) on public occasions such as the ratification of peace (Xen. *Hell.* 7. 4. 36; Arr. 7. 11); (4) in the Hellenistic age Paeans were addressed to successful individuals, such as Lysander (Plut. *Lys.* 18) and Titus Flamininus (Plut. *Flam.* 16). Paeans were by no means confined to Apollo, but were also sung to Zeus (Xen. *An.* 3. 2. 9), Poseidon (id. *Hell.* 4. 7. 4), Dionysus, Asclepius, and Hygieia. *See also* HYMNS. C. M. B.

**P(A)ELIGNI,** a central Italian tribe always closely associated with the Marrucini, Marsi, and Vestini (qq.v.). Their language greatly resembled Oscan (q.v.). Allies of Rome before 300 B.C., the Paeligni remained loyal until the Social War, when their principal town, Corfinium (q.v.), became the Italic capital. After 90 B.C. they were rapidly romanized. Ovid (q.v.), born at Sulmo (q.v.), is their most celebrated native son. E. T. S.

**PAEONIUS,** Greek sculptor, native of Mende in Thrace. He is known to us by an original work found in Olympia in 1875—a marble statue of a flying Victory, mounted on a triangular base. The inscription on the latter states that the statue was dedicated by the Messenians and Naupactians and that Paeonius made it. The occasion was evidently the victorious battle of Sphacteria in 424 B.C., a date also suggested by the style of the statue with its transparent drapery and sweeping folds. Replicas of the head are in the Palazzo Venezia and the Vatican. The inscription on the base of the Victory also states that Paeonius made the acroterial figures of the temple of Zeus at Olympia. Pausanias' statement (5. 10. 6) that he was responsible also for the East pediment of that temple must be due to a confusion. It was thought by Pomtow (*PW* Suppl. iv, 1308 ff.) that the lost statue that surmounted a monument, likewise erected by the Messenians and Naupactians, at Delphi, was the bronze prototype of the marble Victory by Paeonius at Olympia. But this seems problematical, for (1) it is not certain that the monument in Delphi was surmounted by a Victory; (2) the inscription does not mention Paeonius as the sculptor; and (3) it was not customary in fifth-century Greece to make exact copies of other statues.

G. M. A. R.

**PAESTUM** (*Ποσειδωνία*), coastal town of Lucania (q.v.), famous for its roses, pottery, well-preserved walls and Doric temples. Founded *c.* 600 B.C. with Doric-speaking colonists by Sybaris (q.v.), it quickly burgeoned. Lucani, who captured it *c.* 390, held it until 273 when Rome made it a Latin colony. Paestum stoutly resisted Hannibal and continued its municipal life under the Empire until spreading marshes rendered its site uninhabitable. The so-called 'Basilica' (mid sixth century) and 'Temple of Neptune' (mid fifth century) were in fact dedicated to Hera, while the 'Temple of Ceres' (late sixth century), lying to the north, was dedicated to Athena. The museum houses interesting paintings from Sabellian tombs and remarkable sixth-century metopes from the Heraeum unearthed near by at the mouth of the Silarus (modern *Sele*).

A. D. Trendall, *Paestan Pottery* (1936); U. Zanotti-Bianco *Heraion alla foce del Sele* (1952); H. Riemann, *PW* (1953), s.v. 'Poseidonia' (with bibliography); F. Krauss, *Die Tempel von Paestum* (1959); P. C. Sestieri, *Paestum*⁴ (1956). E. T. S.

**PAETUS**, LUCIUS CAESENNIUS (*PW* 9), *cos.* A.D. 61, was ordered by Nero in 61 or 62 as legate of Cappadocia to advance to Armenia. His mission failed and he capitulated to the Parthians on disgraceful terms in his camp at Rhandeia. Dismissed, but unpunished, in 70 he was appointed governor of Syria by Vespasian (whose relative he probably was) and in 72/3 annexed the kingdom of Commagene. A. M.

**PAGANALIA**, Roman festival of the *pagi*, or village communities. They were *sacra publica* (Festus, 284, 20 Lindsay), but not *pro populo*, because not on behalf of the people as a whole. They are also called *paganicae feriae*, Varro, *Ling.* 6. 16, who says they were 'agri culturae causa susceptae', and *Paganalia*, Macrob. *Sat.* 1. 16. 6, who lists them among *feriae conceptiuae*, or movable feasts. H. J. R.

**PAGANUS**, an inhabitant of a *pagus* (q.v.). Hence, by imperial times (as Tacitus, *Hist.* 3. 24, where Primus derisively calls the Praetorians *pagani*, cf. Julius Caesar's *Quirites*, Suet. *Divus Iulius* 70; Pliny, *Tra.* 86 b), one who stays at home, a civilian. Hence, in Christian use, one who is not a *miles Christi*, a heathen ( *fides pagana*, Tert. *De Corona* 11, and so often; used also of non-Jews, cf. Augustine, *Retract.* 2. 43, who says it is the usual term for polytheists). But other authors (as Orosius 1, prol. 9, Prudentius, *c. Symm.* 1. 449) imply that this use is derived from the sense of 'rustic', 'uncultured', rather than 'civilian', which is preferred by Latte, *RR* 371. H. J. R.

**PAGASAE,** a Thessalian city situated on the western shore of the land-locked Bay of Volos. After the decline of Iolcus (q.v.) it became the principal harbour-town of this area. It may originally have belonged to the Magnetes (q.v.), but when occupied by the Thessalians it served as the port of Pherae. Since it commanded the only convenient outlet from the Thessalian plain to the sea, it virtually monopolized the export of corn, meat, and slaves, thus contributing largely to the rise of the Pheraean tyranny. Philip captured Pagasae in 353 B.C. and subsequently terminated its dependence upon Pherae. The walls, probably built by Philip, are impressive, but the site was ill chosen, and Pagasae was later supplanted by Demetrias (q.v.).

F. Stählin and E. Meyer, *Pagasai und Demetrias* (1934), a detailed archaeological and historical account. H. D. W.

**PAGUS,** an area of land with its population as distinguished from the *oppidum* or *vicus* (qq.v.) which housed the inhabitants, was the smallest unit of the Italian territorial system. Every community, tribal or urbanized, consisted of a group of *pagi*, which thus persisted after the municipalization of Italy. Within the Roman State before 90 B.C. the *pagi* of those parts where the municipal system was undeveloped were the only intermediaries between the *populus Romanus* and the individual citizens. In the provinces agricultural immigrants from Italy settled in *pagi*, whereas groups of Romans in provincial towns were known as *conventus*. Such *pagi*, which were usually attached to the nearest Roman municipality, assisted the spread of Roman civilization in the neighbouring native *civitas*, whose *oppidum* the *pagus* might share, and with which it was eventually united as a *municipium* or *colonia* (qq.v.). The provincial communities also, especially the great cantons of Gaul, were sometimes subdivided into *pagi*. The administrative powers of a *pagus* varied with its comparative independence. In Italy they had boards of three or four aediles or *magistri*; Roman or peregrine *pagi* in the provinces might form a miniature *res publica*.

For bibliography *see* MUNICIPIUM (Modern views (*a*) Republic). A. N. S.-W.

**PAIGNION,** a title, of which *jeu d'esprit* is a rough equivalent, applied to various very different types of literature. It was used of the satirical poems of Crates the Cynic and of poems of Philetas and Theocritus, and generally of effusions of a light character (LSJ, s.v. *παίγνιον*, III. 3). Gorgias (fr. 11. 21) similarly designates his *Helena*, the prototype of later essays in light-hearted whitewashing and denigration composed by Isocrates (*Helena*) and later by Asiatic rhetoricians; cf. Polyb. 12. 26 b *Ἐγκώμιον Θερσίτου, Ψόγος Πηνελόπης*. *See also* MIMUS *and* TECHNOPAIGNIA. J. D. D.

**PAINTING.** The Mycenaean rulers were inspired by the frescoes of the Cretan palaces to have their palaces decorated with wall-paintings of religious scenes, battle-scenes, scenes of hunting and sport, and decorative motifs. That any of this colourful and conventional art survived even in Athens, which escaped destruction, is perhaps unlikely. Figure-painting starts again in the second half of the eighth century under the impact of imported oriental works (and perhaps of the epic). The scenes on geometric vases are in silhouette with filling ornament; the composition is paratactic and completely disregards spatial relations. From the late eighth century eyes, etc., are reserved, and later the silhouette changes gradually into outline; extreme parataxis is abandoned, but figures are still composed of typical views—head profile with frontal eye, frontal body, profile legs (cf. particularly Proto-Attic and Melian vases). Corinth was early famous for painting; her claim is justified by the clay metopes from Thermon, the elaborate scenes on Corinthian vases (650–550 B.C.) and the Pitsa wooden pictures (late 6th c.). From *c.* 625 B.C. the black-figure style predominates in Athens for vases and plaques; the red-figure style begins *c.* 530 B.C. After 540 B.C. forms are more rounded and clothing more decorative and elaborate (*see* EXECIAS, ANDOCIDES 2). Ionian pictures of *c.* 525 B.C. are echoed by the Caeretan hydriae (Embassy to Achilles, Busiris, etc.). From *c.* 515 B.C. painters experiment with uneven stance, back views, frontal faces, etc., which later become common (*see* EUPHRONIUS, EUTHYMIDES; cf. Pliny on Eumarus of Athens, *figuras omnis imitari ausum*).

In the early fifth century three-quarter faces and varied expressions, ascribed to Cimon of Cleonae, appear on the vases of the Cleophrades painter and his contemporaries; the frontal eye gradually changes into the profile eye. Between 470 and 460 further advances were made by Micon (q.v.) and Polygnotus (q.v.); in their large pictures the surface of the wall was divided by undulating lines representing hillocks, which supported or partly hid the serious figures of men 'better than ourselves', arranged in groups united by a common emotion. The use of perspective was greatly developed by Agatharchus (q.v.), painting *c.* 430, and shading by Apollodorus, *c.* 430. Parrhasius (q.v.), painting from *c.* 450, achieved plastic effects by his outline; he also developed further the painting of facial expression. Aglaophon, *c.* 420, painted in the rich, sweet style, known from the vases of the Meidias painter (*see* MEIDIAS). Zeuxis (q.v.) united the romantic, emotional, and realistic tendencies of the late fifth century, the art which Plato rejected in the *Republic*.

The Sicyonian school in the early fourth century (*see* PAMPHILUS I *and* MELANTHIUS 2) in revolt against the colour effects of Zeuxis, etc., insisted on line, composition, and severity; their art influenced mirrors, ivories, and Attic and Tarentine vases. Aristides (q.v. 2) continued the emotional tradition of Parrhasius, etc.; he 'first painted soul, feelings, and passions'. Encaustic (q.v.), of which Pausias (q.v.) was the first great master, made greater realism possible and he used his technique in painting flowers and garlands; Nicias, who unlike Pausias chose large subjects, made his figures stand out from the canvas (copies of his Io and Andromeda have been recognized). Interiors are first quoted for the late fourth century—Alexander and Roxane by Aëtion (q.v.) and Boy blowing the fire by Antiphilus. A great artist in the late fourth century painted a Battle of Alexander with Darius, of which a mosaic copy survives, a brilliant composition of crowded figures in a shallow strip of space. The Pella mosaics with hunting and mythological scenes are late-fourth-century originals in the Sicyonian tradition.

For later artists literary sources are less informative, and the contributions of different schools are difficult to assess. Art-collecting is attested for Ptolemy III and the Pergamene kings, and copying begins at least in the mid second century. To the third century may be assigned the grave stele of Hediste from Pagasae and the original of the Women at breakfast by Dioscorides (mosaic; *c.* 100 B.C.); both have shallow interior scenes. Hediste is a realistic portrait; the Women at breakfast and its companion, the Komos, are pictures of scenes from New Comedy. The original of the Arcadia and Telephus from Herculaneum should from the subject be Pergamene, second century; the diagonal composition gives the picture considerable depth; the basket of fruit in the foreground is a still life, a descendant of Pausias' flowers, a relative of Sosus' Drinking doves, and an ancestor of small pictures in Pompeii.

A further step—to make landscape or architecture dominate human figures—was apparently taken in the second century (perhaps in Alexandria), although it has only survived in Roman copies from the Esquiline and Boscoreale.

In mainland Greece the mosaic in Delos with Dionysus riding a panther reflects the same neo-classical style as the contemporary sculpture of Damophon (q.v.). Timomachus of Byzantium, the last great painter recorded, painted Medea and Iphigenia in the time of Julius Caesar; reflections in Pompeii show that his figures derived from the fourth century or earlier. The Aldobrandini marriage may also be an eclectic original of *c.* 50 B.C.

Roman Italy was flooded with Greek originals from the early third to the end of the second century B.C., and from the early first century B.C. with Greek artists. Nothing is known of the technique of copying and adapting. The small pictures (like the tragic actor) appear true and good; the large (like the scenes in the Villa of the Mysteries) are coarse and unattractive. The so-called First Style of wall-painting admitted pictures only in narrow friezes, usually at the top of the walls. The Second Style begins in Pompeii, Delos, and Athens early in the first century B.C.; the simple architecture leaves room for large pictures. The painted architecture of the Third Style (20 B.C.–A.D. 20) is elaborate and fantastic, and frames academic groups set against a landscape backcloth. The pictures of the Fourth Style (extending into the Flavian period) are also set in fantastic architecture; and the painting is often impressionistic (cf. the putto in the Catacomb of Domitilla).

The earliest of the Mummy portraits found in Egypt belong to the first century A.D.; the series lasts into the fourth century; most of the portraits (which were cut out of their frames and inserted in the mummies) are in the encaustic technique (q.v.), and many are excellent pictures. After the austerity of the Trajanic period and the softer, more impressionistic style of the late second and third century, they begin to show the hieratic rigidity of Early Christian art, which also appears in contemporary wall-paintings, mosaics, and the best drawings on gold glass.

RECENT WORKS. General: E. Pfuhl, *Malerei und Zeichnung der Griechen* (1923); Rumpf, *Malerei u. Zeichn.*; M. H. Swindler, *Ancient Painting* (1929). Literary sources: J. Overbeck, *Antiken Schriftquellen* (1868); J. J. Pollitt, *The Art of Greece* (1965). Special: M. Robertson, *Greek Painting* (1959); M. Pallottino, *Etruscan Painting* (1958); A. Maiuri, *Roman Painting* (1957); P. Devambez, *Greek Painting* (1962); A. Stenico, *Roman and Etruscan Painting* (1963).
                                                                T. B. L. W.

**PALAEMON,** QUINTUS REMMIUS, a manumitted slave who under Tiberius and Claudius won a reputation for his evil life, arrogance, and unusual learning. Martial (2. 86. 11) pours scorn on his verses. He was the first Roman to write a really comprehensive grammatical treatise (*see* GRAMMAR) which influenced all subsequent writers (e.g. Charisius, Diomedes, Priscian). The extant *Ars Palaemonis* (ed. Keil, *Gramm. Lat.* v. 533; cf. also vi. 206) is apocryphal.

See SCHOLARSHIP, LATIN, IN ANTIQUITY; Schanz–Hosius, § 475; K. Barwick, *Remmius Palaemon und die römische ars grammatica* (1922) = *Philol.* Suppl. xv. 2.                                J. F. M.

**PALAEOGRAPHY** is the science that studies writing upon papyrus, wax, parchment, and paper; it teaches us to read old writings and to observe their changes particularly for criteria of date and place. It is also concerned with the layout of the written leaf and the form of the book. We here confine ourselves to Greek and Latin writing. In both languages the written letters change under the influence of three forces: the first, the desire to make letters with less labour, and the second, the need of being legible, oppose each other; the third, regard for beauty, whether in the individual letter, the line as a whole, or the page, tends to careful work, but sometimes the scribe, forcing the letters into one mould to attain a pleasant regularity, makes them hard to distinguish.

**1.** Writings may be classed as *Book-hands* and *Cursives* or everyday hands: both have existed side by side as far as our documents go back; the book-hand is conservative, but the cursive may change very quickly; its forms tend to invade the book-hand. Hands are also divided into *Majuscules* and *Minuscules*: in Majuscules, comprising *Capitals, Uncials*, and early Cursives, the letters lie in the main between two parallel lines, though, e.g. Φ in Greek or F in Latin Capitals and several letters in Latin Uncials (e.g. h and q) project above and below them. *Uncials* is the name given to the earliest book-hand deviating from Capitals, marked by certain rounded forms. It means 'inch-high', being taken from Jerome's attack upon the elaborate letters in gold and silver on purple parchment fashionable in his day. Later Cursive in both Greek and Latin developed many tall and tailed letters and these passed into the book-hands derived from it. Such hands are called *Minuscules*, scripts in which the bodies of the letters lie between two inner lines but the 'ascenders and descenders' reach out towards two outer lines above and below; only one line is actually ruled, upon which the letters stand, or from which in Greek after A.D. 1000 they hang.

**2.** The *Materials* that receive writing deeply influence its development; as against papyrus and paper, parchment encourages a more careful and heavier style; wax produced in letters special deformations that have left their mark on all subsequent Latin writing, e.g. in d, g, f. Papyrus was the general material from classical times till the fourth century A.D., after which it was, save in Egypt, a mere survival. In the fourth century parchment, hitherto rare though of very ancient use, won a sudden victory. Paper, adopted from China by Islam, spread through Europe in the thirteenth to fifteenth centuries.

**3.** Papyrus (*see* PAPYROLOGY), which did not stand folding well, was mostly used in the form of a roll, the text being in narrow columns; the criss-cross structure of papyrus guided the scribe in keeping these vertical and his lines regular. The bound book arose in Egypt in the second century A.D.; though at first made of papyrus, it suited parchment better; its form was perhaps suggested by that of the wax codex of joined tablets. Its rise was probably associated with the spread of Christianity (*see* BOOKS). Writing on parchment involves elaborate cutting and folding of the double leaves which make up the quires, and laborious pricking and ruling to guide the scribe. The methods of doing this may indicate date and place of writing.

**4.** The *Ink* used on papyrus is finely divided carbon and gum ('Indian ink'), chemically very stable but sensitive to damp. That used on parchment is a solution of oak-galls and iron, not always satisfactory chemically. Pens were of reed and in medieval times of quill. Writing on parchment was often erased and a new text written over it: this is called a *Palimpsest* (q.v.). The older writing may be read by photography under ultra-violet rays. The difficulty of reading manuscripts, apart from bad preservation, is due to the unfamiliar forms of the letters, the non-division of the words, and the use of abbreviations. The first trouble is much increased by the presence under cursive influence of *ligatures*, i.e. combinations in which two or more letters are knotted together and lose their original shapes, e.g. &, a combination of e and t.

**5.** *Abbreviations* are divided into *suspensions*, in which the first letter or the beginning of a word is given but not the ending (sign: a dot or a transverse stroke); *contractions*, giving the first letter, generally some of the middle of a word and always the last letter (sign: a *tittle* or horizontal stroke above); and *specific signs* denoting

particular words, syllables, or letters. These largely go back to ancient shorthand, e.g. in Latin to the *Notae Tironianae* (*see* TACHYGRAPHY). Numerals are marked by tittles, so sometimes foreign words, or by flanking signs, also used for 'quotes'. A letter wrongly written may be dotted above or, more usually, below.

These difficulties tend to increase as time goes on, save that later manuscripts begin to divide the words. Division into paragraphs is at first rare and inconspicuously marked; later it is indicated by the methods still in use. Punctuation too is at first scarce and irregular, and never becomes very helpful.

**6.** A scribe sometimes is good enough, especially in later times, to add at the end of a manuscript a note, called a *colophon*, giving his name with place and date of writing: the Greek era runs from 5508 B.C. We also find *subscriptiones* (q.v.), notes by scribes or correctors, and these are sometimes dated.

The study of the decoration of manuscripts and of miniatures may now help the editor of Renaissance texts, but he must solicit the help of the art historians (e.g. at the Warburg and Courtauld Institutes).

**7.** *Greek Writing* has a simple history: starting with epigraphic capitals it soon adopted rounded shapes for Є, C, ω and made small changes in some other letters. The *Uncial* thus established continued as the only book-hand until the ninth century, the cursive meanwhile developing independently. The uncial changes very little until parchment encouraged scribes to make the vertical strokes thick and gradually arrive at a heavy style (miscalled 'Slavonic') too elaborate for ordinary books. Accents and breathings, hitherto sporadic, and used mostly in difficult texts, now become general. About A.D. 800 scholars in Constantinople got right away from the heavy uncial (which lingered on for another three centuries in liturgical use), and deliberately designed a new book-hand, a *Minuscule*, founded on the cursive: this was the vehicle of Greek literature until the introduction of printing, but it degenerated steadily through the centuries, admitting capricious forms and abbreviations and complicated ligatures combining the letters with the accents; these survived into printing, but have now been eliminated.

**8.** The *Latin Book-hand* until the fifth century shows two varieties, the rare *Square Capital* and the more usual *Rustic* made quickly with a slanting pen. Only school-books and law-books were produced in an easier style with an admixture of cursive forms. This contributed to the Latin *Uncial*, which became the regular book-hand from the fourth to the eighth century, its characteristic letters are ᴀ, ᴏ, ᴇ, ʜ, ʟ, ᴍ, q, ᴜ; it sometimes admits ʙ and d. When more cursive letters, a, ꙅ, m, p, r, f, are used (but ɴ remains), the script is called *Half-uncial*: books written in it are few, but it is the ancestor of the script called *Insular*, developed by the Irish in the fifth and sixth centuries and taught by them to the English and in many monasteries on the Continent. We gave up its use for Latin in the tenth century, but retained it for Anglo-Saxon. The Irish used it for Latin till the fifteenth century and still keep it for their own language.

**9.** Meanwhile from the sixth century the cursive began to be used for books, and by A.D. 800 had been made tolerable in every Latin-using country save 'Insular' Ireland and England; South and North Italy, Spain, Gaul, and Germany each had fair "National" hands labelled *Lombardic, Visigothic*, and *Merovingian*, but they are all still disfigured by ligatures. In the late eighth century book-production was systematized at Tours under Charles the Great; in these books Square and Rustic Capitals, Uncial and Half-uncial, were used for headings, prefaces, initials, etc., and a Minuscule called *Caroline* or *Carolingian*, eliminating most of the ligatures, was designed for the text. Caroline quickly superseded the various forms of Merovingian and the Lombardic in North Italy, and in the eleventh century the Visigothic, but South Italy and Dalmatia retained their beautiful writing, now called *Beneventan*, until the end of the twelfth century. Caroline is the main vehicle of classical literature; manuscripts in capitals are not more than twenty, half of them Virgils: few Uncials are classical; of the other scripts only Insular and Beneventan have any importance for the classics. For most authors a ninth- or tenth-century Caroline manuscript is the best authority; the Caroline scholars copied the ancient manuscripts, which then went out of use and perished (*see* TEXTUAL CRITICISM).

10. Caroline changed very little till the twelfth century; then it developed, first of all in north France, into the angular hand we call *Gothic* or Blackletter; this came to vary greatly in style in different countries; it can be very handsome, but suffers from the letters being very much alike, and from innumerable abbreviations.

In the fifteenth century the Italian scholars revived the Caroline, thinking it to be the writing of the ancient Romans, and used it with singular elegance. Manuscripts and printing in this *Humanistic* or *Roman* hand gradually spread over Europe, and likewise the cursive derived from it. Only Germany retained till recently the Blackletter derived from France.

E. Maunde-Thompson, *Introduction to Greek and Latin Palaeography* (1912); B. Bischoff, 'Paläographie', *Deutsche Philologie im Aufriss* (1956); A. Dain, *Les Manuscrits* (1949).
SCRIBES AND BOOK-MAKING. W. Wattenbach, *Das Schriftwesen im Mittelalter* (1896); T. Birt, *Das Antike Buchwesen* (1882); F. G. Kenyon, *Books and Readers in Ancient Greece and Rome* (1932); B. L. Ullman, *Ancient Writing and its Influence* (1932); F. W. Hall, *Companion to Classical Texts* (1913).
GENERAL SERIES OF FACSIMILES. Palaeographical Society, *Facsimiles of Ancient MSS. and Inscriptions*, Series I and II (1873–94). New Palaeographical Society, Series I and II (1903–29). A. Monaci, *Archivio, Paleografico Italiano* (1881, 10 vols.). G. Vitelli e C. Paoli, *Collezione Fiorentina di Facsimili Paleografici* (1884–97, 2 vols.). A. Chroust, *Monumenta Palaeographica* (1899–1917, 6 vols.).
Manuscripts reproduced in full: *Codices e Vaticanis selecti phototypice expressi* (1899– ); Scato de Vries, *Codices Gr. et Lat. phototypice depicti* (1897– ); *Album Palaeographicum* (1909).
GREEK. B. de Montfaucon, *Palaeographia Graeca* (1708); V. Gardthausen, *Griechische Palaeographie*² (1911–13); P. Maas, 'Griechische Palaeographie' in Gercke–Norden, *Einleitung in die Altertumswissenschaft*, Bd. I, Heft 9 (1924), 69 ff.; R. Devréesse, *Introduction à l'étude des manuscrits grecs* (1954); T. V. Allen, *Notes on the Abbreviations in Greek MSS.* (1889); L. Traube, *Nomina Sacra* (1907, contraction, Greek and Latin).
Facsimiles. W. Wattenbach et A. von Velsen, *Exempla Codicum Graecorum Litteris Minusculis Scriptorum* (1878); W. Wattenbach, *Scripturae Gr. Specimina* (1883); H. Omont, *Facs. des MSS. grecs datés de la Bibliothèque Nationale du Xe au XIVe s.* (1891); id. *Facs. des plus anciens MSS. grecs de la Bibl. Nle. . . . du IVe au XIIe s.* (1892); id. *Facs. des MSS. grecs . . . des XVe et XVIe s. de la Bibl. Nle.* (1887); P. F. de' Cavalieri et J. Lietzmann, *Spec. Codd. Gr. Vaticanorum* (1910); A. Sobolevski et G. Ph. Ts'ereteli, *Exempla Codd. Gr. Litteris Uncialibus Scriptorum* (1913); id. *Ex. Codd. Gr.*, I. *Codd. Mosquenses*; II. *Codd. Petropolitani* (Moscow, 1911–13); K. and S. Lake, *Dated Greek Minuscule MSS. to the year 1200* (U.S.A. 1934–41, 10 vols.).
LATIN. F. Steffens, *Lateinische Palaeographie*³ (1929; in French, 1907–9); H. Foerster, *Abriss der lat. Paläographie* (1949); J. Mallon, *Paléographie romaine* (1952); A. Cappelli, *Dizionario di Abbreviature Lat. ed Ital.*³ (1929); W. M. Lindsay, *Notae Latinae* (1915, abbreviations till about A.D. 900); D. Bains, *A Supplement to N.L.* (1936) (continues to 1100).
Facsimiles. W. Wattenbach et C. Zangemeister, *Exempla Codd. Lat. Litteris Majusculis Scriptorum* (1876–9); E. Chatelain, *Paléographie des classiques latins* (1884–1900); id. *Uncialis Scriptura Codd. Lat. novis exemplis illustrata* (1902); W. Arndt u. M. Tangl, *Schrifttafeln zur Erlernung d. lat. Paläographie* (1904–7); F. Ehrle et P. Liebaert, *Specimina Codd. Lat. Vaticanorum* (1912); E. A. Lowe, *Codices Latini Antiquiores* (1934– , every Latin manuscript to A.D. 800; 10 vols., one to come); J. Mallon, R. Marichal, C. Perrat, *L'Écriture latine de la capitale romaine à la minuscule* (1939).
SPECIAL SCRIPTS. *Uncial.* E. A. Lowe and E. K. Rand, *A VIth Century Fragment of the Letters of Pliny the Younger* (U.S.A. 1922); E. A. Lowe, *English Uncial* (1960).
*Half-uncial.* E. A. Lowe, 'A Handlist of Half-uncial MSS.', *Misc. Ehrle* iv. 34–61 (Rome, 1924); id. *Codices Lugdunenses antiquissimi* (Lyon, 1924).
*Dark-age writing.* L. Traube, *Vorlesungen u. Abhandlungen* (1909–20). W. M. Lindsay, *Early Irish Script, Early Welsh Script*, and

the journal *Palaeographia Latina* (1922–9); *Codex Lindisfarnensis*, Olten (1956–60); F. Henry, *Early Christian Irish Art* (1963).
*Beneventan. Paleografia Artistica di Monte Cassino* (1876–81); E. A. Lowe, *The Beneventan Script* (1914); id. *Scriptura Beneventana* (1929).
*Visigothic.* P. Ewald and G. Loewe, *Exempla Scripturae Visigoticae* (1883); E. A. Lowe, 'Studia Palaeographica', *Sitz. Bayer. Akad., Phil.-hist. Kl.*, 1910 (National Hands). J. M. Burnam, *Palaeographica Iberica* (U.S.A. 1914); Z. G. Villada, *Paleografía española* (1923); R. P. Robinson, 'MSS. 27 and 107 of the Municipal Library at Autun', *Am. Ac. Rome* 1939 (redates early Visigothic).
*Caroline.* E. K. Rand, 'The Vatican Livy and the script of Tours', *Amer. Acad. Rome* 1919. id. 'Studies in the Script of Tours', 1, 3, *Medieval Acad. of Amer.* 3, 20, 3, 1929, 1934. P. Lauer, 'La Réforme carolingienne de l'écriture latine', *Mém. Acad. Inscr. et Belles-Lettres*, 1924 and 1933. L. W. Jones, 'The Script of Cologne', *Med. Acad. of Amer.* 10, 1932.
*Humanistic.* B. L. Ullman, *The Origin and Development of Humanistic Script* (1960); J. Wardrop, *The Script of Humanism* (1963); C. F. Bühler, *The fifteenth-century Book* (1960).
See P. Lehmann, *Erforschung des Mittelalters* (1941–62). T. J. Brown, 'Latin Palaeography since Traube', *Trans. Cambridge Bibliogr. Soc.* 1963, 361 (with references). For catalogues: P. O. Kristeller, *Traditio* vi (1948), ix (1953). E. H. M.; A. H. McD.

**PALAEPHATUS** wrote (? in the late 4th c. B.C.) a Π. ἀπίστων, extant only in an excerpt, in which myths are rationalized. It had considerable influence in the Byzantine period. The name Palaephatus is perhaps a pseudonym.

N. Festa, *Mythographi Graeci* iii. 2 (1902); J. Schrader, *Palaephatea* (1893). J. D. D.

**PALAESTRA** (παλαίστρα), was a low building with a central courtyard in the interior covered with fine sand, and rooms about it for undressing and washing. It was frequently the private property of a schoolmaster, and was especially used by boys, who were there taught the rules of wrestling. *See* GYMNASIUM; BATHS. F. A. W.

**PALAMEDES** (Παλαμήδης, 'the handy or contriving one'), a proverbially (cf. Ar. *Ran.* 1451) clever hero, son of Nauplius (q.v. 2). His chief distinctions are the invention of letters and his cunning while serving with Agamemnon. These respectively bring him into competition with Cadmus and Odysseus (qq.v.). For the former sundry accounts divide the invention of the alphabet between them, e.g. Hyg. *Fab.* 277. 1 (see Rose ad loc.). For the latter, tradition, from the Cypria, makes them rivals and enemies; Odysseus pretended to be mad to avoid going to Troy and Palamedes detected him by a stratagem (see, e.g., Hyg. *Fab.* 95. 2 and Rose ad loc.). In revenge Odysseus forged a letter from Priam to Palamedes, arranging for him to betray the Greeks, and hid a sum of gold in his tent; on this evidence Palamedes was found guilty and put to death by the army (Hyg. *Fab.* 105). He was also credited with having invented draughts (πεσσοί) to while away the Trojan war. See Lewy in Roscher's *Lexikon*, s.v. H. J. R.

**PALATINE**, the chief of the seven hills of Rome, traditionally (Varro, *Ling.* 5. 164; Tac. *Ann.* 12. 24; Dion. Hal. 1. 87; Livy 1. 7, etc.) the site of the oldest settlement there. The etymology is disputed, and the ritual reasons usually given for the early choice of the hill for settlement are probably archaistic inventions, like the legend of *Roma quadrata* (*Phil. Wochenschr.* 1903, 1645). Tradition assigns fortifications to the hill, but their reality is still in need of sound archaeological confirmation. Early settlement is represented by two archaic cisterns and rock-cut post-holes for Iron Age huts near Scalae Caci and elsewhere. Indigenous deities included Aius Locutius (390 B.C.), Viriplaca, Luna Noctiluca, and Febris. Later came the temples of Victoria, near the *clivus Victoriae* (294), the Magna Mater (191), and possibly Jupiter Victor (see *Bull. Com. Arch.* 1917, 84 ff.). The hill was also the seat of many houses, from at least 330 onwards (Livy 8. 19. 4; 20. 8), famous owners being Fulvius Flaccus, Lutatius Catulus, Cicero, Crassus, Milo, P. Sulla, M. Antony, Livius Drusus, and Hortensius. The house of Hortensius was acquired by Augustus (Suet. *Aug.* 72) and became the nucleus of a group of palace buildings in association with the new temple of Apollo (Vell. Pat. 2. 81). The house of Hortensius is generally identified with the so-called House of Livia and the Temple of Apollo with the large temple platform to the south of it (*Att. Accad. S. Luca* i (1951–2), 26 ff.). An Augustan triumphal arch was erected on the *clivus Victoriae* (*AJArch.* 1923, 400). Tiberius built a large palace, *domus Tiberiana* (Tac. *Hist.* 1. 27) on the Cermalus, or north-west summit, to which Gaius added a vestibule contiguous with the temple of Castor. Nero made important additions to the palace buildings both before and after the Great Fire of A.D. 64 (*Not. Scav.* 1949, 48 ff.). Domitian was responsible for the Flavian state-apartments and new residential palace buildings including a monumental garden (*hippodromus*). The architect Rabirius designed the Flavian buildings. Domitian also extended the *domus Tiberiana* towards the *nova via*, as did Hadrian still further. Severus built out towards the south-east, masking his work with the Septizodium (q.v.). The palaces continued to be used until the sixth century, when they were repaired by Theodoric and Athalaric.

G. Hülsen, *Forum und Palatin* (Berlin, 1926, U.S.A. 1928); G. Lugli, *Roma antica* (1946); id. *Mons Palatinus* (1960); E. Gjerstad, *Early Rome* iii (1960), 45 ff.; Nash, *Pict. Dict. Rome* ii. 163 ff.
I. A. R.; D. E. S.

**PALATINI.** In the Late Empire this term referred to two distinct bodies, (i) the higher officials of the various ministries of the *comitatus*, or Emperor's personal staff, who received an increasing number of privileges from Constantine and his successors, (ii) the senior branch of the field army, which, like the *comitatenses*, or junior branch, included *vexillationes* of cavalry and *legiones* of infantry, but contained also infantry formations of a new type, *auxilia. See* COMITATENSES.

Jones, *Later Rom. Emp.* G. R. W.

**PALFURIUS SURA,** an able orator (Suet. *Dom.* 13) and active *delator* under Domitian, is mentioned in Juvenal, 4. 53–5, as an upholder of the Emperor's unlimited claims over property. After Vespasian expelled him from the Senate he turned Stoic.

**PALIBOTHRA** (*Pataliputra,* now *Patna*), situated on the Royal Road from the river Beas down the Ganges valley, was the capital of the Mauryan kings of north India (*c.* 300 B.C.). The Seleucid kings kept Greek residents, Megasthenes (q.v.) and Deimachus, at the court of Kings Chandragupta and Vindusara. In his account of India Megasthenes gave a good description of the city's fortifications, a stockade and a moat. It remained an important royal seat, though little noticed by later Greek or Roman visitors to India.

Strabo 2. 70, 15. 702; Pliny, *HN* 6. 63; Ptol. *Geog.* 1. 12. 9, etc.
E. H. W.

**PALICI** (*Παλικοί*), twin gods of the pool now known as *Lago Naftia* or *Fetia*, more learnedly as *L. dei Palici,* in Sicily, which still sends up a considerable amount of natural gas. Of the bulky ancient literature we have left some extracts in Macrobius, *Sat.* 5. 19. 15 ff., also Diod. Sic. 11. 88. 6 ff., Servius on *Aen.* 9. 581. For some modern writers see Bloch in Roscher's *Lexikon* iii. 1281. Their legend was that a local nymph, Thalia, being with child by Zeus, begged to be swallowed up in the earth to escape Hera; this was granted her, and when she bore twins they made their way up through the pools known as Delloi. The most noteworthy thing about their

worship was that a suspected person might go to the pools and swear he was innocent; if he lied, he lost his life by the power of the gods (the gases are in fact somewhat poisonous); if not, he returned safe and might claim damages from his accuser. H. J. R.

**PALIMPSEST** (*παλίμψηστος*), a term applied to manuscripts in which the original text has been scraped or washed away, in order that another text may be inscribed in its place. As the term properly implies scraping, it must have originally been applied to such materials as leather, wax, or vellum, and only by analogy to papyrus, which could be washed, but not scraped. The term seems to occur first in Catullus (22. 5); cf. Plut. 2. 504 d, 779 c, where it is treated as synonymous with ἔκπλυτος. When vellum was scarce (especially, it seems, about the ninth century) early manuscripts were not infrequently treated thus; and since the removal of the original writing was seldom complete, valuable texts of the Bible, Cicero, Plautus, Gaius, Licinianus, etc., have been recovered from such palimpsests.

V. Gardthausen, *Gr. Paläographie²* (1911) i. 103 ff.; E. M. Thompson, *Introd. to Gr. and Lat. Palaeography* (1912), 64 ff.
F. G. K.

**PALINURUS,** the helmsman of Aeneas who was overcome by the god of Sleep, fell overboard, was washed up on the shore of Italy, and there murdered by Lucanians (Verg. *Aen.* 5. 814 ff.; 6. 337 ff.). Cape Palinurus (*Capo Palinuro* today) between Elea and Buxentum was named after him. Roman fleets were wrecked there in 253 and 36 B.C. A settlement of the sixth/fifth century has been excavated since 1957.

R. Naumann, *Palinuro* (1958); *Atti d. pr. congr. di stud sulla Magna Grecia* (1962), 272 f., 276 ff. H. H. S.

**PALLADAS,** Greek epigrammatic poet, lived in Alexandria in the fourth century A.D. He was a poor schoolmaster with a shrewish wife (*Anth. Pal.* 9. 168 f.); and also, in an era of expanding Christianity, a pagan or an agnostic (cf. *Anth. Pal.* 11. 384). After its long desuetude he revived the art of the poetic epigram. About 150 of his poems—some coldly reflective, some savagely bitter (*Anth. Pal.* 11. 340, cf. 7. 681 f., 11. 292), some hopelessly pessimistic—are in the Greek Anthology. With his bleak frankness, he recalls certain poetic ideals of a vanished 'classical' Greece.

A. Franke, *De P. epigrammatographo* (Leipzig, 1899); L. A. Stella, *Cinque poeti dell' Antologia Palatina* (1949); G. Luck, 'P., Christian or pagan?', *Harv. Stud.* 1958, 455 ff.; C. M. Bowra, 'P. and Christianity', *Proc. Brit. Acad.* 1959; 'P. and the converted Olympians', *Byz. Zeitschr.* 1960, 1 ff.; 'P. and Tyché', *CQ* 1960, 118 ff.; Alan Cameron, *JRS* 1965, 17 ff.; *CQ* 1965, 215 f. G. H.

**PALLADIUM,** an ancient sacred image of Pallas (Athena), said to have been sent down from heaven by Zeus to Dardanus, the founder of Troy (Arctinus ap. Dion. Hal. 1. 69), or to his descendant Ilus (Ov. *Fasti* 6. 419–22). It was believed that the protection of the city depended on its safe custody. Greek legend told that Diomede and Odysseus, at the instigation of Calchas or Helenus, carried off the Palladium and thus made possible the sack of Troy (Serv. ad *Aen.* 2. 166, Sil. Ital. 13. 36–50). Virgil adopts this legend (*Aen.* 2. 162–79), but adds that the theft was followed by the displeasure of the goddess. The more common Roman tradition was that the Palladium was rescued from the fires of Troy by Aeneas, who brought it to Italy, where it was ultimately placed in the *penus Vestae* as a pledge of the safety of Rome (Dion. Hal. loc. cit.; cf. Cic. *Phil.* 11. 24). The Palladium was believed to have saved Rome from the attack of the Gauls in 390 B.C. (Sil. Ital. 13. 79–81), and when the temple of Vesta caught fire in 241 B.C., it was rescued by the Pontifex Maximus, L. Caecilius

Metellus (Ov. *Fasti* 6. 436–54, Cic. *Scaur.* 48). These two legends are clearly inconsistent; Ovid (*Fasti* 6. 433–5) is content not to judge between them, but stories were invented to reconcile them, such as that the image stolen by the Greeks was only a copy (Dion. Hal. loc. cit.), or that Diomede brought the Palladium to Italy and handed it over to Aeneas at Lavinium (Sil. Ital. 13. 51–78). The truth probably is that many cities possessed such talismans, which owing to the fame of the Trojan image all came to be known as Palladia; in Greece Argos and Athens claimed the Palladium, and in Italy not only Rome but Lavinium and Luceria and the Graeco-Roman city of Heraclea in Lucania (Strabo 6. 1. 14).

R. G. Austin, Verg. *Aen.* ii (1964), 83 ff. C. B.

**PALLADIUS** (1), RUTILIUS TAURUS AEMILIANUS (4th c. A.D.), a knowledgeable agriculturalist with estates in Italy and Sardinia, experienced in climatic conditions and soil-variations, wrote a practical manual once thought to contain fourteen books only—an introductory book followed by one for each month of the year, and an appendix 'de insitione' in elegiacs (cf. Columella 10). In 1926 Svennung published the ed. princeps of an extra book *de medicina pecorum*, establishing it as the true fourteenth book (cf. *de insit.* 12; see *CR* 1937, 19). Palladius' prose style is utilitarian, with no 'frills' (1. i. 1 'neque enim formator agricolae debet artibus et eloquentia rhetores aemulari'); his verses are metrically sound, and are conscientious and even ingenious, considering his subject. His sources include Columella, Gargilius Martialis, and others, with various unnamed 'Graeci'; but he constantly quotes from personal experience. Medieval scholars found him useful, notably Albertus Magnus, and a translation into Middle English exists.

TEXT. J. C. Schmitt, Teubner, 1898 (i–xiii, with *de insit.*); J. Svennung, *Eranos* 1926 (*de med. pec.*; cf. *Gnomon* 1937, 382 ff.). J. H. Schmalz, *Glotta* 1915, 172 ff.; H. Widstrand, *Palladiusstudien* (Uppsala, 1926; cf. *Gnomon* 1937, 388 ff.); id. *Eranos* 1928, 121 ff., and 1929, 129 ff. (on *de med. pec.*); J. Svennung, *Untersuchungen zu Palladius* (Uppsala, 1935), important also for many fields of study in Late and Vulgar Latin; G. Bjoerck, *Mnemos.* 1938, 146 ff. (on *de med. pec.*). Teuffel–Schwabe, *Geschichte der römischen Lit.*⁶ (1900), iii. 237; Schanz–Hosius IV². i. 189 ff.; H. Fischer, *Mittelalterliche Pflanzenkunde* (1929). R. G. A.

**PALLADIUS** (2) (*c.* A.D. 364–*c.* 430), a disciple of Evagrius Ponticus and a monk in Egypt and Palestine until Chrysostom made him bishop of Helenopolis (*c.* 400), wrote: (1) *Dialogus de Vita S. Joannis Chrysostomi*, based on personal knowledge (*c.* 408); (2) *Historia Lausiaca*, a collection of biographical notes, one of the chief sources for early monasticism (419–20); (3) Part I of a work on Indians and Brahmins, incorporated into the Alexander Romance.

EDITIONS. (1) P. R. Coleman-Norton (1928, 1958²); (2) C. Butler, 2 vols. (1898–1904). S. L. G.

**PALLAS** (1), Παλλάς, -άδος, title of Athena (q.v.) (apparently by derivation 'maiden'). A late legend, Philodemus, *De piet.* 6 Gompertz, Apollod. 3. 144 (spurious), says she was a friend of Athena whom the goddess accidentally killed and made the Palladium (q.v.) to commemorate her. H. J. R.

**PALLAS** (2), Πάλλας, -αντος, (*a*) a Titan (Hes. *Theog.* 376); (*b*) a giant, killed by Athena (Apollod. 1. 37); (*c*) an Attic hero who with his sons opposed Aegeus and was overcome by Theseus (qq.v.; Plut. *Thes.* 13; Apollod. 3. 206); (*d*) the son of Evander the Arcadian, an ally of Aeneas, killed by Turnus (Verg. *Aen.* 9. 104, 514 ff.; 10. 441 ff.); (*e*) son of Hercules and Evander's daughter (Dion. Hal. *Ant. Rom.* 1. 32. 1). H. J. R.

**PALLAS** (3), freedman of Antonia and financial secretary (*a rationibus*) of her son, the Emperor Claudius. His wealth, success, and arrogant temper made him deservedly unpopular. Devoted to Agrippina and alleged to be her lover, he successfully promoted her candidature in the competition after the execution of Messalina; he also hastened Claudius' adoption of her son. The Senate voted him *ornamenta praetoria* and a sum of money: he refused the money and received public commemoration for virtue and frugality (Tac. *Ann.* 12. 53; cf. Pliny, *Ep.* 7. 29. 2; 8. 6. 1, who indignantly quotes the senatorial decree inscribed on the tomb of Pallas on the Via Tiburtina). After the accession of Nero, Pallas, like Agrippina, was gradually and firmly thrust aside from power. Compelled to resign his office, he stipulated that no questions should be asked, that his accounts be regarded as balanced. Finally, he was put to death by Nero, because of his wealth, it is said (A.D. 62).

S. I. Oost, *AJPhil.* 1958, 113 ff. R. S.

**PALMA FRONTONIANUS,** AULUS CORNELIUS (*PW* 279) was *cos. I ord.* in A.D. 99, governor of Tarraconensis *c.* 101, and governor of Syria *c.* 104. Operating with Legio VI Ferrata, he annexed Nabataea and formed it into a province by 106; the conquest was easy and coins commemorated *Arabia adquisita*. Palma was honoured with *ornamenta triumphalia* and was *cos. II ord.* in 109. Rich and influential, he apparently gave offence to Hadrian in Trajan's lifetime, and was put to death in 118 for alleged participation in the 'conspiracy of the four consulars' (*see* HADRIAN).

Lambrechts, *Sénat.* no. 42. Syme, *Tacitus*, 53, 222 n. 5, 244, 599. C. H. V. S.

**PALMYRA** (Aramaic *Tadmor*) owed its wealth to its position as an oasis between Syria and Babylonia. Owing to the disturbed condition of Mesopotamia in the first century B.C. it captured the trade between these two countries, organizing caravans direct across the desert, which it policed from the Euphrates to Damascus and Emesa. A large number of caravan-inscriptions is preserved. The city was formed by the amalgamation of an ancient Amorite and Aramaic stock with an increasing Arab element, from which the dynasty of Odaenathus (q.v.) was to arise. It was slightly hellenized, Aramaic being regularly used (often with a Greek version added) in the inscriptions, which cover the period from 44 B.C. to the fall of the city. Palmyra was raided by Antony. It was probably annexed *c.* A.D. 17 by Germanicus; Pliny's statement (in Titus' reign) that it was an independent buffer State is an anachronism, for Vespasian built a road from Palmyra to Sura in 75. It retained some independence, however, maintaining its own militia for policing the desert. Septimius Severus made it a Roman colony. Under Odaenathus and Zenobia (q.v.) it ruled the Eastern Empire for a brief space, but after its reduction by Aurelian in 273 it never recovered. The ruins, which include the great temple of Bel, several other shrines, a theatre, colonnaded streets, and a monumental arch, are impressive. The necropolis, with its curious tower tombs, has produced many examples of a markedly oriental school of sculpture. The local civilization, as exemplified by art and costume, is made up of Hellenistic and Parthian elements, borrowed from the Graeco-Iranian metropolis of Seleucia-on-the-Tigris, with which there was a constant exchange of caravans. The cults are almost entirely Semitic, and some of them, in the third century A.D., show an interesting tendency towards henotheism.

HISTORY. J. Starcky, *Palmyre* (1952); M. Rostovtzeff, *Caravan Cities* (1932). MONUMENTS. T. Wiegand, *Palmyra* (1932); I. A. Richmond, *JRS* 1963, 43 ff. A. H. M. J.; H. S.

**PAMPHILA** of Epidaurus, a scholar and historian (of literature) at Rome under Nero. Her chief work,

Σύμμικτα ἱστορικὰ ὑπομνήματα, was summarized by Favorinus.

FHG iii. 520.

**PAMPHILUS** (1) (4th c. B.C.), painter, of Amphipolis. Pupil of Eupompus of Sicyon (contemporary of Parrhasius); teacher of Apelles, Pausias, Melanthius (2) (qq.v.). He painted a 'Battle at Phlius' (probably 367 B.C.) and the Heraclidae, referred to by Aristophanes (*Plut.* 385: before 388 B.C.). His pupils paid him a talent for a course lasting twelve years. He insisted on a knowledge of arithmetic and geometry, and had drawing introduced in Sicyon as a school subject.

Overbeck, 1746–53; Rumpf, *Malerei u. Zeichn.* 132.    T. B. L. W.

**PAMPHILUS** (2) of Alexandria (fl. A.D. 50), lexicographer. He wrote a Τέχνη κριτική, Φυσικά, Περὶ βοτανῶν, and, in ninety-five books, a great lexicon—Περὶ γλωσσῶν ἤτοι λέξεων—which absorbed many previous specialist collections (cf. GLOSSA, GREEK). It was used by Athenaeus, and abridged by a succession of epitomators; the surviving lexicon of Hesychius of Alexandria represents the last stage in this process. Cf. DIOGENIANUS (2).

P. B. R. F.; R. B.

**PAMPHOS**, cited by Pausanias as a pre-Homeric writer of hymns, but judged from the fragments to have been a Hellenistic poet.

Maas, *PW* xviii. 3. 352.

**PAMPHYLIA** was traditionally colonized by a mixed multitude of Greeks led by Amphilochus, Calchas, and Mopsus; the local dialect, which is related to Arcadian, confirms this tradition. The name in early times denoted all the coast from Phaselis to Coracesium, but was later restricted to the plain where lay Magydus, Perga, Sillyum, Aspendus, and Side. Despite Cimon's victory on the Eurymedon these cities remained under Persian rule till they surrendered to Alexander. Though occupied by Ptolemy I and III Pamphylia was generally subject to the Seleucids till 189 B.C. when it was ceded to Rome by Antiochus III; most of the cities were received into the Roman alliance by Cn. Manlius, and the Attalids gained only the strip of coast where they founded Attaleia. Pamphylia was probably part of the province of Cilicia from 102 till c. 44, when it was transferred to Asia. In 36 it was granted by Antony to Amyntas, who coined in Side, and from 25 B.C. was part of Galatia till in A.D. 43 Claudius formed Lycia-Pamphylia. Reattached to Galatia by Galba (the Lycians having been freed), it was reunited to Lycia by Vespasian, remaining a separate κοινόν.

Jones, *Cities E. Rom. Prov.* 124 ff.; R. Syme, *Klio* 1934, 122 ff., 1937, 227 ff.; B. Levick, *Rom. Colonies in S. Asia Minor* (1969).
A. H. M. J.

**PAN** (Πάν), a god native to Arcadia (q.v.). His name, of which a form Πάων also exists, is probably to be derived from the root found in Lat. *pa-sco*, and interpreted 'the Feeder', i.e. herdsman. Since Arcadia was not rich in large cattle the goat was its characteristic beast, and Pan is half-goatish in shape (human body to the loins, goat's legs, ears, and horns). A vague deity, he is not unheard of in the plural, Panes. The ancients regularly associated his name with πᾶς or πᾶν (see *Hymn. Hom. Pan.* 47; Pl. *Crat.* 408 c); hence in late theologizings he becomes a universal god (see Kern, *Relig. d. Griechen* iii. 127 ff.). This, however, has nothing to do with either his native worship or any normal developments of it.

He is regularly son of Hermes, the only other Arcadian deity of importance ('Homer' and Plato, locc. citt., and often); but his mother varies. He has little mythology, hardly more than a couple of late stories of his love affairs, see ECHO, SYRINX; another is that he loved Pitys the nymph of the fir-tree, who ran away from him and changed into her tree-shape (Nonnus, *Dion.* 42. 258 ff.). In general he is amorous, as is natural in a god whose chief business it was to make the flocks fertile. When they did not increase a primitive rite was resorted to of flogging his statue with squills (Theoc. 7. 106 ff., where one of the scholia says it was when hunting was unsuccessful). This was no doubt meant at once to arouse the god and to strike fresh vigour into him. He was also on occasion formidable; it is well to be quiet at noonday (still a haunted time in Greece, see, e.g., Schmidt, *Volksleben d. Neugriechen*, 94), because he is asleep then and will be angry if disturbed (Theoc. 1. 15 ff.). He can induce 'panic' terror (like that of a frightened and stampeding flock or herd) among men, as Polyb. 20. 6. 12 Büttner-Wobst (the actual word is not pre-Hellenistic). He sends nightmares (Artem. 2. 37; 139, 18 Hercher), but not all dreams of him are bad (ibid. 12 ff.). In general, he is thought of as loving mountains, caves, and lonely places (i.e. the regular haunts of flocks in hilly country) and as musical, his instrument being the pan-pipe (still used by shepherds; cf. SYRINX).

He has few relations with other gods. On Mt. Lycaeon he and Zeus both had shrines (Paus. 8. 38. 5). Selene was one of his loves, and he trapped her by attracting her attention to a fine fleece (Verg. *G.* 3. 391 ff., and Servius ad loc.), or bribed her with sheep ('Probus', ad loc.).

His cult began to spread beyond Arcadia early in the fifth century B.C. Pindar, whose piety embraced quite minor deities, wrote him an ode (frs. 85–90 Bowra). Athens adopted him and gave him a cave-shrine on the Acropolis in the year of Marathon, when he was supposed to have promised and given help against the Persians (for the legend of his appearance to the runner Philippides see Herodotus 6. 105. 2–3). There were yearly sacrifices and torch-races in his honour (ibid. 4); L. Deubner, *Attische Feste* (1932), 213, doubts the latter, which, indeed, are hard to connect with Pan. Elsewhere he is not attested before the fourth century (Farnell, op. cit. *infra*, 432).

Of higher developments he has none. Aeschylus (*Ag.* 56) makes him an avenger of wrongs done to beasts; Plato (*Phdr.* 279 b–c) includes him among the gods to whom Socrates prays for inward beauty; pastoral poets make him a kind of divine patron of their literature; but these have nothing to do with his cult.

A creature with man's body and arms, goatish head, legs, and tail, appears on Attic vases and elsewhere from the early fifth century, often in numbers (Panes); he is shown with the nymphs on many late fifth- and fourth-century reliefs. (See Brommer, 'Pan im 5. u. 4. Jhdt. v. Chr.', *Marburger Jahrb. für Kunstwissenschaft* 1949/50.)

Farnell, *Cults* v. 431 ff., and the larger dictionaries s.v. Nilsson, *GGR* i². 235.    H. J. R.; C. M. R.

**PANACEA** (Πανάκεια), 'All-Healer', daughter of Asclepius (q.v.; Pliny, *HN* 25. 30 and often).

**PANAENUS** (fl. 448 B.C., Pliny), painter, brother (or nephew) of Phidias (q.v.), Athenian. He helped Phidias with the colouring of the Olympian Zeus and painted mythical scenes on screens between the legs of the throne. In the temple of Athena in Elis he put on a plaster mixed with saffron (for fresco?), and painted the inside of the shield of Colotes' Athena. The best sources ascribe to him, rather than to Micon or Polygnotus, the 'Battle of Marathon' in the Stoa Poikile (soon after 460); on the left, equal combat, with Miltiades urging on the Athenians and Plataeans; in the centre, Persians fleeing into the marsh; on the right, the fight round the ships with

Cynegeirus and Callimachus; attendant gods and heroes, Theseus rising from the ground.

Overbeck, 696, 698, 1054, 1083, 1094–1108; Rumpf, *Malerei u. Zeichn.* 95. Pfuhl 717. T. B. L. W.

**PANAETIUS** (*c.* 185–109 B.C.), son of Nicagoras of Rhodes, Stoic philosopher. He attended the lectures of Crates of Mallos at Pergamum and then went to Athens, where he became a disciple of Diogenes the Babylonian, then head of the Stoa, and of his successor Antipater of Tarsus. Between 170 and 150 he must have returned to Rhodes for a short time, since he became priest of Poseidon Hippios at Lindus. In about 144 he went to Rome and soon joined the circle which gathered around P. Scipio Aemilianus. About 140–138 he accompanied Scipio on his travels in the Orient. After that he lived alternately in Rome and in Athens. In 129 he succeeded Antipater as head of the Stoa; and he held this position until his death in 109.

In spite of his Stoic creed Panaetius was an admirer of Plato and Aristotle and adopted the Peripatetic doctrine of the eternity of the universe. He tried to adapt Stoic ethics to the requirements of the life of the Roman *grands seigneurs* with whom he associated, by putting into the foreground the more active and brilliant virtues of magnanimity, benevolence, and liberality as against the more passive virtues of fortitude (*not* to be disturbed in danger) and justice (*not* to do wrong), preached by his predecessors. His work Περὶ τοῦ καθήκοντος was used by Cicero in his *De Officiis*.

M. van Straaten, *Panaetii Rhodii Fragmenta*[3] (1962). *Panaetii et Hecatonis fragmenta*, ed. H. N. Fowler (1885); R. Philippson, *Rh. Mus.* 1929, *Philol.* 1930, 357 ff.; B. N. Tatakis, *Panétius de Rhodes* (1931); L. Labowsky, *Die Ethik des Panaetius* (1934); M. van Straaten, *Panétius, sa vie, ses écrits et sa doctrine avec une édition des fragments* (1946); M. Pohlenz, *Die Stoa*[2] (1948–55). K. VON F.

**PANATHENAEA,** an Athenian festival celebrated every year, and every fourth year with much greater pomp (the Great Panathenaea), on the 28th Hecatombaeon (July/Aug.), which was considered to be the birthday of Athena. It comprised a procession, sacrifices, and games. Citizens, maidens carrying sacred implements, youths conducting the sacrificial animals, metics, chariots which were to take part in the contests, and the cavalry figured in the procession. A famous representation is found on the frieze of the Parthenon. An embroidered *peplos*, hoisted on the mast of a ship set on wheels, was brought to the goddess. The flesh of the numerous victims was distributed among the people. The prize of the games was oil from the holy olives, stored in amphorae with a representation of Athena brandishing the spear and of one of several kinds of games.

E. Pfuhl, *De Atheniensium pompis sacris* (1900), 3 ff.; L. Deubner, *Attische Feste*[2] (1959); J. A. Davison, *JHS* 1958, 23 ff.; K. Peters, *Studien zu den panathenaeischen Preisamphoren* (1942); for the Hellenistic and Roman amphorae: G. R. Edwards, *Hesp.* 1957, 320 ff. M. P. N.; J. H. C.

**PANDAREOS** (Πανδάρεως), name of either one or two obscure mythological persons, the father of Aëdon (q.v.), and, if this is not the same Pandareos, the father of two daughters whose story is told in *Od.* 20. 66 ff., whereon see the ancient commentators. Their names were Cleothera and Merope, and they were left orphans (the scholiast says Zeus killed their father and mother because Pandareos had stolen his dog from Crete). Hera, Athena, Artemis, and Aphrodite befriended them, brought them up, and gave them all manner of good qualities; but while Aphrodite was visiting Zeus to arrange their wedding, the Harpyiae (q.v.) carried them off and gave them to be servants to the Erinyes (q.v.). Cf. Roscher, *Lexikon*, s.v. H. J. R.

**PANDARUS,** a Trojan, son of Lycaon (*Iliad* 2. 826–7), and an archer favoured by Apollo. At the instigation of Athena, he broke the truce between the Greeks and Trojans by shooting at and slightly wounding Menelaus (q.v. 1; 4. 88 ff.); wounded Diomedes (5. 95 ff.), and was killed by him (290 ff.). H. J. R.

**PANEGYRIC, LATIN.** The origins of Latin panegyric are to be sought in the ancient institution of the *laudatio funebris* (q.v.). Such speeches of Cicero as the *Ninth Philippic*, the *Pro Lege Manilia*, and the *Pro Marcello* show developments and extensions of eulogy in relation both to deceased and to living persons. The *Pro Marcello* combines *laudatio* and *gratiarum actio*. In the imperial age the *gratiarum actio*, formerly addressed to Senate or People, was delivered in honour of the Emperor. A *senatus consultum* passed under Augustus required newly elected consuls to return thanks publicly to gods and Emperor, but by Pliny's time the Emperor's praise had supplanted that of the gods. This consular *gratiarum actio* provided the model for panegyrics addressed to the Emperor or his representative on various occasions.

A collection of such speeches was found by Aurispa, 1433, in a Mainz manuscript (now lost) under the title of *XII Panegyrici Latini*. Its contents are (numeration according to W. A. Baehrens' ed. 1911): I. Pliny's (q.v. 2) *gratiarum actio* to Trajan on Pliny's elevation to the consulship. II. Latinus Pacatus Drepanius' panegyric to Theodosius. Pacatus (q.v.), a Gaul, had been sent to Rome to congratulate Theodosius on his victory over Maximus. III. Claudius (q.v. 16) Mamertinus' *gratiarum actio* to Julian, at Constantinople, on Mamertinus' elevation to the consulship. IV. Nazarius' panegyric to Constantine (in his absence) on an important imperial anniversary. V. Anonymous Gallic orator's *gratiarum actio* to Constantine, at Trèves, for benefits conferred on Autun. VI. Anonymous Gallic orator's panegyric to Constantine, at Trèves. VII. Anonymous orator's panegyric to Maximian and Constantine, at Trèves, in celebration of Constantine's marriage to Fausta. VIII. Anonymous Gallic orator's panegyric to Constantius, at Trèves, after the death of Allectus and the recovery of Britain. IX. Eumenius' (q.v.) *Pro Instaurandis Scholis Oratio*, in honour of all four Emperors, at Autun, in presence of a provincial governor. X. Panegyric of a Gallic orator (named Mamertinus in the editions) to Maximian, in Gaul (at Trèves?), on Rome's birthday. XI. *Panegyricus Genethliacus* to Maximian by the author of X. XII. Anonymous orator's panegyric to Constantine, at Trèves, after the defeat of Maxentius.

Although Pliny's speech is prefaced to the collection as the model of later panegyrists, the later speeches are much shorter, the longest, by Pacatus, being less than half as long as Pliny's. Otherwise there is considerable similarity, and Pliny's methods of adulation are imitated with progressive exaggeration. Former Emperors, historical and mythological heroes, the gods, and nature herself are disparaged in favour of the Emperor, whose most neutral and even unpraiseworthy actions and characteristics are eulogized with fantastically ingenious artificiality. The authors' outstanding virtue is the purity of their latinity, which is almost Plinian, if scarcely Ciceronian. The speeches are by no means equal in quality: they contain frequent passages of real beauty and eloquence, in spite of their general tawdriness. *Pro Instaurandis Scholis* is a pleasing speech, to whose author some of the anonymous panegyrics have been attributed. The *panegyrici* are of considerable historical interest, and throw much light on fourth-century Gaul.

Examples of panegyric not included in this collection are Ausonius' (q.v.) *Gratiarum Actio* and Ennodius' (q.v.)

*Panegyricus*, addressed to Gratian and Theodoric respectively.

Verse panegyric is represented by the pseudo-Tibullian *Panegyricus Messallae* (q.v.), the anonymous *Laus Pisonis* (q.v.), Statius' *Silvae* 5. 2, and the panegyrics of Claudian and Apollinaris Sidonius (qq.v.). Its methods resemble those of prose panegyric.

TEXTS. Teubner (E. Baehrens, W. A. Baehrens, 1874 and 1911); O.C.T. (R. A. B. Mynors, 1964). Edition: Budé (É. Galletier, 1949–55). Style, diction, etc.: R. Pichon, *Les Derniers Écrivains profanes* (1906); Schanz–Hosius iii (1922; for authorship problems).
W. S. M.

**PANEGYRICUS MESSALLAE,** aptly characterized by Sellar as 'a strange specimen of a fly preserved in amber', a tasteless and bombastic eulogy of Valerius Messalla (q.v. 3) Corvinus in 212 hexameters, which opens the fourth book of the collection of Tibullian poetry. That is why it survives. Fruitless attempts have been made to identify the unknown author with Tibullus, Propertius, and Ovid. Once wealthy, but now vexed by 'the sense of loss', he tries hard, by celebrating Messalla's exploits, to find favour in his eyes—and to secure a reward. The piece was composed between 31 and 27 B.C.

Text in editions of Tibullus; with commentary, in the older editions by Heyne and Dissen; G. Némethy, *Lygdami Carmina, acc. Panegyr. in Messalam* (1906). See F. Hankel, *De Panegyrico in Messallam tibulliano* (1874); H. Hartung, *De Panegyrico ad Messallam pseudo-tibulliano* (1880); R. S. Radford, *TAPA* 1920; (most exhaustive) S. Ehrengruber, *De Carmine panegyrico Messalae pseudo-tibulliano* (1889–99); cf. Schanz–Hosius ii.
J. H.

**PANGAEUS,** a mountain in Thrace (q.v.), lying between the lower reaches of the Strymon and the seacoast; it extends for some twenty-five km. from southwest to north-east, and at its highest point reaches 1956 m. The name first appears in Pindar, *Pyth.* 4. 180, and in Aeschylus, *Persae* 494, and Herodotus (6. 46; 7. 112) mentions the gold and silver mines. Casson concluded, after exploring the mountain, that the bulk of the gold (q.v.) and silver (q.v.) deposits from Pangaeus were found round, and not on, the mountain. Geologically the higher part of the mountain is not of a metalliferous nature, consisting, as it does, of crystalline white marble. There are few traces of mines, and it is clear that the ancients found it easy and lucrative to wash gold fom the streams that discharge from the sides of the mountain into the plain. (Aristotle, *Mirabilia* 45, speaks of gold being brought to the surface by constant rain in Paeonia.) According to Perdrizet, the Scaptesyle mines worked by Thasos (q.v.) were on the eastern slopes of Pangaeus. Probably Athens first took an interest in the mines in the time of Pisistratus (Arist. *Ath. Pol.* 15. 2), and, with the reduction of Thasos in 463 B.C., they passed to Athenian control, which was later strengthened by the foundation of Amphipolis (q.v.) in 437/6 B.C. Possession of the mines passed from Athens to Macedon, when Philip II (q.v.) captured Amphipolis in 357 B.C., and advanced his frontier to the Nestus (Strabo 7. 331, fr. 35; Diod. 16. 8. 6). Under Philip the mines produced 1,000 talents of gold annually. Philippi (q.v.), one of Philip's foundations, was a centre for the mining of Pangaeus (Strabo 7. 331, fr. 34). In Roman times the mines played no great part.

S. Casson, *Macedonia, Thrace and Illyria* (1926), 63 ff., 88 ff.; P. Perdrizet, 'Scaptesyle', *Klio* 1910, 1 ff.; P. Collart, *Philippes* (1937).
J. M. R. C.

**PANIONIUM,** the place where the common festival of the twelve Ionic cities was held and *probouloi* met to discuss common policy in time of need. It was founded after the destruction of the city of Melie (perhaps early seventh century B.C.) and revived in the fourth century at the end of Persian rule. The site lay on the territory of Priene north of Mt. Mycale. Traces of an altar 60 feet long have been uncovered on top of a hill near the sea

(Otomatik Tepe), and of the council chamber on the slope; but nothing remains of the temple of Posidon Heliconius.

Hdt. 1. 143, Vitr. 4. 1. 4–5. G. Kleiner, P. Hommel, and W. Müller-Wiener, *JDAI* Ergänzungsheft 23 (1967).
J. M. C.

**PANKRATION** (παγκράτιον). In this event boxing and wrestling were combined with kicking, strangling, and twisting. It was a dangerous sport, but strict rules were enforced by umpires who closely watched the combatants. Biting and gouging were forbidden, but nearly every manœuvre of hands, feet, and body was permissible. You might kick your opponent in the stomach; you might twist his foot out of its socket; you might break his fingers. All neck holds were allowed, the favourite method being the 'ladder-grip', in which you mounted your opponent's back, and wound your legs round his stomach, your arms round his neck.
F. A. W.

**PANNONIA,** the territory of the Pannonii, a group of Illyrian peoples who had absorbed Celtic influences to varying degrees, lay south and west of the Danube between Carnuntum (q.v.) and Sirmium in the Save valley. In 119 B.C. the Romans campaigned against them, capturing Siscia (q.v.). In 35 B.C. Octavian advanced against them and captured Siscia, where he established a garrison. Fighting broke out in 16 B.C. with a Pannonian invasion of Istria and continued in Pannonia in 14. In 13 M. Agrippa and M. Vinicius advanced eastward down the Save and Drave valleys. After Agrippa's death (12 B.C.) the conquest of the Pannonians, notably the Breuci, was completed by Tiberius and Roman control was extended to the Danube. Pannonia north of the Drave appears to have accepted Roman rule without a struggle, probably owing to fear of the Dacians further to the east. Some fighting is attested under Sex. Appuleius in 8 B.C. but the Pannonians remained more or less peaceful until A.D. 6 when the Breuci joined the Daesitiates in revolt, under two chiefs called Bato (qq.v.). After the end of the war in A.D. 9 Illyricum was divided into provinces known later as Pannonia and Dalmatia (q.v.). The province was governed by *legati Augusti pro praetore* of consular rank. Early under Trajan, probably in 103, Pannonia was subdivided into two provinces, *Superior*, comprising the western part with capital at Carnuntum, *Inferior*, a smaller area in the east with capital at Aquincum (q.v.). *Pannonia Superior* was governed by a consular legate, *Inferior* by a praetorian, the latter being upgraded to consular under Caracalla by a boundary alteration which equalized the strength of the two provincial armies. Following the reforms of Gallienus the senatorial legates were superseded by equestrian *praesides*. Under Diocletian both provinces were subdivided, *Pannonia Superior* into *Pannonia Prima* in the north (capital Savaria) under a *praeses* and a *dux*, *Pannonia Ripariensis* or *Savia* in the south (capital Siscia) under a *dux*; *Pannonia Inferior* into *Valeria* in the north (chief places: Aquincum and Sopianae) under a *praeses* and a *dux*, and *Pannonia Secunda* in the south (capital Sirmium) under a *consularis* and a *dux*. During the fourth century Pannonia suffered greatly from barbarian invasions. The end appears to have come with the incursion of Radagaisus and the Ostrogoths in 405, causing large numbers of Romans to flee to Italy.

A. Mócsy, *PW* Suppl. ix, s.v. Pannonia; P. Oliva, *Pannonia and the onset of crisis in the Roman Empire* (Prague, 1962); A. Mócsy, *Die Bevölkerung von Pannonien bis zu den Markomannenkriegen* (Budapest, 1959); A. Dobó, *Die Verwaltung d. rom. Prov. P.* (1968).
J. J. W.

**PANNYCHIS,** an all-night festival or vigil in honour of a deity, e.g. Demeter at the Haloa (Deubner, *Attische Feste*, 62); Artemis at the Tauropolia (ibid. 208). Since these were on occasion made an excuse for illicit love-affairs (see Menander, *Epit.* 234 ff. Allinson), it is not surprising that Pannychis appears as an attendant of Aphrodite (see Höfer in Roscher's *Lexikon*, s.v.). It was also a common name for a hetaera, as in Lucian, *Dial. Meret.* 9 (name of a speaker). H. J. R.

**PANORMUS** (modern *Palermo*), founded by the Phoenicians early in the seventh century B.C., became the main Carthaginian *point d'appui* in north-western Sicily. Despite its name it was never Greek, and save for a brief capture by Pyrrhus (q.v.) in 276 was continuously in Punic hands until taken by the Romans in 254 (Polyb. 1. 38). It is mentioned sporadically in the sources, usually as a Carthaginian base of operations (e.g. in 480). A *civitas libera et immunis* under Roman rule, it became a *colonia* under Augustus, with recolonization under Vespasian and Hadrian (*Lib. Colon.* 211). Its superb position, with a notable harbour backed by the fertile Conca d'Oro, ensured its importance and prosperity; it became the capital of Arab, Norman, and modern Sicily. But few traces of ancient Panormus now survive.

There is no good ancient description, but cf. Diod. Sic. 22. 10; Callias fr. 2 (*FGrH* no. 564); Silius Ital. 14. 261–3. Foundation date, Rhys Carpenter, *AJArch.* 1958, 42 ff. Geography and antiquities, E. A. Freeman, *History of Sicily* i (1891), 249 ff.; B. Pace, *Arte e civiltà della Sicilia antica* i (1935), *passim. See also* HAMILCAR (2), HEIRCTE. A. G. W.

**PANSA CAETRONIANUS,** GAIUS VIBIUS (*PW* 9), defended Caesar's interests as tribune in 51 B.C., governed Bithynia in 47–46 and Cisalpine Gaul in 45, and was designated by Caesar consul for 43. In March 43 he led four legions of recruits by the Via Cassia to join Hirtius (q.v.) against Antony. He was wounded in a preliminary engagement at Forum Gallorum, 8 miles from Mutina, and after the battle of Mutina he died. Gossip alleged that Octavian had poisoned him. G. E. F. C.

**PANTHEON,** a temple in the Campus Martius, built with adjoining Baths and water gardens by M. Agrippa in 27–25 B.C. It was completely rebuilt early in the reign of Hadrian who preserved Agrippa's name on the frieze (*CIL* vi. 896), and later repaired by Septimius Severus and Caracalla. The building consists of a rotunda (43·30 m in internal diameter) of brick-faced concrete, stuccoed externally to imitate masonry, with a pedimented portico (33·10 m wide and 13·60 m deep) of granite Corinthian columns, eight in front and two groups of four behind. The portico is linked with the rotunda by a rectangular structure as wide as the porch and as high as the rotunda. The rotunda is 43·30 m high with a circular skylight 9 m in diameter at the top of the dome; the cylindrical wall (6·20 m thick) contains four rectangular and three semi-circular recesses with free-standing columns. The door, breaking the circle, is flanked by niched buttresses, a common structural device which also occurs in the body of the wall. The wall itself is converted by semicircular chambers into eight piers built as niches, all vertically linked by a very elaborate system of relieving arches extending to the haunch of the richly coffered dome. The interior was richly decorated in marble with a continuous entablature above the columned recesses and canopied statue-bases, and an attic panelled in marble, a small section of which has been restored to its original form. The ancient bronze doors of the building still survive. The Pantheon had a long rectangular forecourt in front of it and was masked on the east by the Porticus Argo-nautarum and on the south by the Baths of Agrippa.

B. Beltrami, *Il Pantheon* (1898); R. Vighi, *The Pantheon* (1905); L. Crema, *L' Architettura romana* (1959), 375 ff.; W. L. McDonald, *The Architecture of the Roman Empire* (1965), 94 ff.; Nash, *Pict. Dict. Rome* ii. 171 ff. I. A. R.; D. E. S.

**PANTHOUS** (Πάνθοος, Πάνθους), a Trojan elder (*Iliad* 3. 146). Apollo protects his son, Polydamas (q.v.; *Il.* 15. 521–2), whence some said he was a Delphian (schol. ibid.). In Verg. *Aen.* 2. 318 ff. he is a pious priest of Apollo, killed by Aeneas' side at the storming of Troy.

**PANTICAPAEUM,** a colony of Miletus, on the west side of the Cimmerian Bosporus (q.v. 2: *Straits of Kertch*), founded in the late seventh century. It throve on the fisheries of the Straits, on the trade along the river Tanais, and especially on the export of wheat from the Crimea. Dependent foundations in the Straits were at Myrmekion, Tiritaca, and Nymphaeum. It was ruled successively by two dynasties, the Archaeanactids (probably a line of Greek tyrants), and the Spartocids (q.v.), who gained power in 438. The gold coinage of Panticapaeum and the magnificently furnished rock tombs of its chief citizens attest its wealth in the fourth and third centuries. It subsequently (*c.* 115) became the capital of Mithridates VI's territory in south Russia, and was the seat of the local Crimean dynasty founded by his descendants under Roman sovereignty. In the third century A.D. it fell to the Sarmatians and Goths.

E. H. Minns, *Scythians and Greeks* (1913), 503 ff.; M. Danoff, *PW* Suppl. ix. 1119 ff.; E. B. de Ballu, *L'Histoire des colonies grecques du littoral nord de la mer Noire*² (1965), a bibliography of Russian works, 1940–62. M. C.

**PANTOMIMUS,** a dancer who represented traditional themes in dumb show, supported by instrumental music and a chorus. (The apparent meaning is 'one who imitates everything', but the distinctive quality of pantomime was that the chief performer did everything by imitation.) This type of performance (the Greeks called it the 'Italian dance') was introduced at Rome in 22 B.C. by Pylades of Cilicia and Bathyllus of Alexandria. 'To dance the shepherd Cyclops' in tragic mask and buskins was nothing new (Hor. *Sat.* 1. 5. 64: for other antecedents, in particular a παντόμιμος mentioned in an inscription from Priene of *c.* 80 B.C., see *PW*, s.v., 834 ff.); Pylades' innovation, according to himself (Macrob. *Sat.* 2. 7), was to add the orchestra and chorus. Bathyllus seems to have specialized in light themes, akin to comedy or satyric drama, with a rustic setting—e.g. Pan revelling with a satyr (Ath. 1. 20 d–e; Plut. *Quaest. conv.* 7. 711 f.; Sen. *Con. Ex.* 3. pref. 10 and 16; cf. Lucian, *Salt.* 74 and Libanius iii. 392, Reiske); Pylades' style is said to have been 'high flown, passionate' (Ath. 1. 20 e) and more akin to tragedy; but these comparisons with drama look artificial; the immediate origins of pantomime do not appear to have been dramatic; its themes, whether erotic or otherwise, are taken from mythology or (occasionally) remote history as presented by the poets, whether dramatic or epic. It was a highly sophisticated type of entertainment, demanding much from both performers and spectators; though demoralizing, it was not coarse, like the mime.

Performances took place on the public stage or in private houses. The pantomimus, usually a handsome, athletic figure, wore a graceful silk costume (long tunic and cloak, Suet. *Calig.* 54), which allowed of free movement, and a beautiful mask with closed lips (Lucian, *Salt.* 29, A. Baumeister, *Denkmäler des klassischen Altertums* (1885–8), figs. 1351–2). Behind him stood the chorus, the players of flutes, pipes, cymbals, etc., and the *scabillarii*, who beat time by pressing with the foot on the *scabillum*, a wooden or metal instrument fastened underneath the sandal (see Baumeister, fig. 1350). Beside the pantomimus there sometimes stood an assistant—perhaps an actor with a speaking part (ὑποκρίτου εὐφωνίαν, Lucian 68). Lucian tells (83) of a pantomimus who overacted the part of 'mad Ajax': he tore the clothes of one of the *scabillarii*, snatched a flute from an intrumentalist and with it struck the triumphant 'Odysseus' a blow which would have been fatal but for Odysseus' traditional head-dress (the πῖλος); then, springing down into the body of the theatre, he seated himself between two alarmed ex-consuls —all this to the delight of the rabble, who thought it the perfection of acting. Better performers were more subtle: Pylades, when the chorus uttered the words τὸν μέγαν Ἀγαμέμνονα, expressed the monarch's greatness by assuming an air of statesmanlike reflection (Macrob. loc. cit.). The dancer might in one piece have to appear in five different roles, each with its own mask (Lucian 66; change of costume seems unproved; cf. *eodem pallio*, Fronto 157, 3, ed. Naber—but Arnobius, *Adv. Gent.* 7. 33, seems to speak of a special costume for the part of Adonis). To convince an unbeliever, a pantomimus acted single-handed the love-tale of Ares and Aphrodite—Helios bringing his tidings, Hephaestus setting his snare, the gods coming one by one to look at the entrapped lovers, the confusion of Aphrodite, the abject alarm of Ares (Lucian 63; Lucian adds a story of a foreigner from the Pontus on a visit to Rome who, though he could not follow the song of the chorus because of his lack of Greek, found the pantomime's performance so lucid that he wished to take him home as an interpreter). The dancer's power to convey his meaning by steps, postures, and above all gestures (Quint. *Inst.* 11. 3. 88) was aided by certain conventions, e.g. there was a traditional dance for 'Thyestes devouring his children', which one panto-mimus unfortunately performed when wishing to represent Kronos devouring *his* children.

The songs of the chorus were of secondary importance (Libanius 381); such fragments as we possess are in Greek. Lucan and Statius wrote libretti for pantomimes —a degrading (Sen. *Suas.* 2. 19), if lucrative, occupation (Juv. 7. 87). That the chorus also expounded the narrative in recitative, while the dancer was changing for his next role, seems to be merely a guess of Friedländer. The music, like the whole performance, was enervating (Pliny, *Pan.* 54).

For the popularity of the pantomimi (and pantomimae), the faction-fights of their supporters, the effect of their performances on public morality, and the efforts of the government to deal with the problem, see Friedländer, *Roman Life and Manners under the Early Empire* (E.T. 1908–13), ii. 100 ff.                                    W. B.

**PANYASSIS** of Halicarnassus (5th c. B.C.), epic poet, uncle of Herodotus; revived epic poetry; author of a *Heraclea*; classed by some critics second to Homer; discussed by Quintilian (*Inst.* 10. 1. 54); said to have plagiarized a poem of Creophylus.

*EGF* 253–65.                                    W. F. J. K.

**PAPHLAGONIA,** a territory of northern Asia Minor, which included the mountainous coastal region between Bithynia and Pontus and extended inland to the plateau. It was noted for its ship timber and cabinet woods. In social structure it was similar to Pontus. Villages pre-dominated, organized in administrative districts, and temple territories were numerous. Greek settlements dotted the coast from Heraclea to Sinope, but in Persian times the native population remained largely autonomous. After Alexander Paphlagonia was broken up, part falling to Bithynia and part to Pontus; and either then or at the fall of the Pontic kingdom the coastal cities acquired extensive territories. Pompey included the coastal region in the province of Bithynia and Pontus (63–62). From the third century B.C. a portion south of Mt. Olgassys, called Inner Paphlagonia, kept its independence under native kings. Occupied in turn and divided by the kings of Bithynia and Pontus, and entrusted at first by the Romans to various dependent kings, this portion was attached by

Augustus to the province of Galatia (6 B.C.). Diocletian revived Inner Paphlagonia as a province under a *corrector*. The chief town was Gangra-Germanicopolis.

RULERS OF INNER PAPHLAGONIA. Morzius (before 189 to after 179 B.C.). Pylaemenes, c. 132 B.C. (a dynastic name). Pylaemenes, son of Nicomedes III of Bithynia, c. 107 B.C. Attalus Epiphanes, c. 62 B.C. (over a part). Pylaemenes, c. 62 B.C. (over a part). Castor, son of Castor Saocondarius (Tarcondarius), c. 40–37/36 B.C. Deiotarus Philadelphus, son of Castor, 37/36–6/5 B.C. (with the addition of the Amnias valley and Phazimonitis of Pontus).

Strabo 12. 542–4. R. Leonhard, *Paphlagonia* (1915); Jones, *Cities E. Rom. Prov.* 148 ff.; Magie, *Rom. Rule Asia Min.* 186 ff. and index.                                    T. R. S. B.

**PAPHOS,** a city of Cyprus, situated a short distance inland from the west coast near the modern village of *Kouklia*. It has yielded rich Mycenaean remains; and seemingly it received a trading settlement in the four-teenth century B.C., numerous colonists from Mycenaean Greece in the thirteenth. These were led according to tradition by the Arcadian Agapenor. It possessed a famous temple of Aphrodite, believed to have risen from the sea off this coast, and was regarded by Homer as her chief resort. The sanctuary was reputed to have been founded by the 'Eteo-Cyprian' Cinyras, a contemporary of Agamemnon; and his descendants combined the priest-hood of Aphrodite with the royal authority down to the time of the Ptolemies. Nicocles, the last of the Cinyrads, transferred his capital to a site with a good natural harbour some 10 miles to the north. This new Paphos became towards the close of the third century B.C. the capital of Ptolemaic Cyprus; and it remained under the Romans the seat of their proconsuls. The name Paphos was re-served for the harbour town; and the upper city, known as Old Paphos (Παλαίπαφος), was little more than its sanctuary and a place of pilgrimage for all Cyprus.

D. G. Hogarth, *Devia Cypria* (1889), ch. 1. For the temple of Aphrodite see M. R. James, *JHS* 1888, 175 ff.; C. Blinkenberg, *Le Temple de Paphos* (1924); T. B. Mitford, *BSA* 1961, 1 ff.
T. B. M.

**PAPINIANUS,** AEMILIUS (*PW* 105), one of the greatest Roman jurists. His origin (Syria?, Africa?) is uncertain. His official career was brilliant and in A.D. 203 he became *Praefectus praetorio* in which capacity he had both Paulus (q.v. 1) and Ulpianus (q.v. 1) as assessors. He was executed in 212 by order of Caracalla for having dis-approved of the murder of the Emperor's brother Geta.

Papinian was highly appreciated by posterity. Imperial constitutions of the later third century cite him with the greatest respect, and in the Law of Citations (426) his pre-eminence was formally recognized by the provision that, failing a majority of jurists cited on one side or the other, Papinian's view should prevail. Justinian said of him: 'acutissimi ingenii uir et merito ante alios excellens' (*Cod.* 6. 42. 30). His high reputation rested on a relatively small literary output. (Justinian's compilers took six times as much from Ulpian and three times as much from Paul). His principal works were: *Quaestiones* (thirty-seven books), completed before 198, and *Responsa* (nine-teen books), not completed until after 204. Neither of these works conforms exactly to its title: the *Quaestiones*, though predominantly problematic in character, contain also doctrinal discussions, while the other work reduces *responsa* to their most abstract form, and also includes *responsa* of other jurists, decisions pronounced in the emperors' and prefects' *auditoria* and even in imperial constitutions. *Notae* on both these works are attributed to Paul, and on the *Responsa* alone to Ulpian. Other writings of Papinian: *Definitiones, De adulteriis*. He did not publish any comprehensive systematic work.

He is one of the most elegant and instructive of the jurists, though sometimes difficult on account of the conciseness of his style. The independence of his judgement and the sagacity of his mind led him to original solutions which were not governed by technicalities, but left room for equity and for moral considerations. He was capable of changing his opinion when another appeared to him to be right (*Dig.* 18. 7. 6. 1: 'nobis aliquando placebat . . ., sed in contrarium me uocat Sabini sententia').

E. Costa, *Papiniano* (1894–9). On Papinian's language: Leipold, *Sprache des Juristen Aemilius Papinianus* (1891). *And see* bibliography s.v. JURISPRUDENCE.                                   A. B.; B. N.

**PAPĪRIANUS** (5th c. A.D.), grammarian, from whose *De Orthographia* excerpts are preserved by Cassiodorus (ed. Keil, *Gramm. Lat.* vii. 158–66). Schanz–Hosius, § 1108.

**PAPĪRIUS** (1, *PW* 52) **CURSOR**, LUCIUS, Roman hero of the Second Samnite War, consul in 326, 320, 319, 315, 313 B.C.; dictator in 325, 309. The details of his military career, especially in the years immediately after the Caudine Forks (321) disaster (321), are untrustworthy, although it can hardly be doubted that he was a great general, a fit match for Alexander the Great according to Livy (9. 16; 9. 38 f.). Rhetorical accounts are also given of his eating, drinking, and running abilities, while his alleged attempt to execute the other patrician hero of the age, Fabius (q.v. 3) Rullianus, for fighting against orders illustrates his strictness and severity (Livy, books 8 and 9; [Aur. Vict.] *De Vir. Ill.* 31; Eutrop. 2. 8; Zonar. 7. 26). Possibly Cursor was partly responsible for the law which virtually terminated enslavement for debt (H. Last, *CAH* vii. 545).                          E. T. S.

**PAPĪRIUS** (2, *PW* 53) **CURSOR**, LUCIUS, son of (1), twice consul with Spurius Carvilius: in 293 B.C. when he defeated specially consecrated Samnite levies at Aquilonia (Livy 10. 38–42: numbers exaggerated); and in 272 when he ended the Pyrrhic War by subduing Lucani, Bruttii, and Tarentines (Zonar. 8. 6). He erected the first sun-dial at Rome (Pliny, *HN* 7. 213).           E. T. S.

**PAPIUS** (*PW* 12) **MUTILUS**, GAIUS, *imperator*—as a Samnite—of the southern group of rebels in the Social War (*see* POPPAEDIUS), after some successes in Campania was defeated by Caesar (q.v. 2) in 90 B.C. and again by Sulla in 89. Unmolested during the next few years and apparently enrolled as a citizen, he was proscribed after Sulla's return and killed himself. A descendant of his was consul A.D. 9 (*see* LEX PAPIA POPPAEA).

E. T. Salmon, *Samnium and the Samnites* (1967), see index.   E. B.

**PAPPUS** of Alexandria (fl. A.D. 320), a distinguished mathematician, wrote commentaries on (1) Euclid's *Elements*, quoted by Proclus and others; the part on book 10 is extant in Arabic translation: it contains interesting historical information about a lost work of Apollonius on unordered irrationals and about Theaetetus (q.v.); (2) some books of Ptolemy's *Almagest*; the part on books 5 and 6 of this survives; (3) Euclid's *Data*, Ptolemy's *Planisphaerium*, and the *Analemma* of Diodorus (q.v. 4); all are lost. He also wrote χωρογραφία οἰκουμενική, a work of universal geography based on the world-map of Ptolemy (q.v. 4). The extant geography of 'Moses Chorençai' (early Armenian) is based on it. But his great work is the 'Collection' (συναγωγή), a handbook to Greek mathematical sciences. Books iii–viii and part of ii survive. It is invaluable for its accounts of (a) Greek

achievements in higher geometry, notably works (now lost) by Euclid, Aristaeus (2), and Apollonius (2) (qq.v.) belonging to the 'Treasury of Analysis' (τόπος ἀναλυόμενος); (b) astronomical works by Autolycus (2), Theodosius (4), and Menelaus (3) (qq.v.), Euclid's *Optics* and *Phaenomena*, and Aristarchus' *On the sizes and distances of the sun and moon*; (c) various solutions of the problem of two mean proportionals, a method of inscribing the five regular solids in a sphere, Archimedes' spiral, Nicomedes' (q.v. 5) 'cochloids', and the *quadratrix*; (d) Archimedes' semi-regular solids, and the subject of *Isoperimetry*, or the comparison of the areas and volumes of different figures with equal contours and equal surfaces respectively, including the volumes of the five regular solids when their surfaces are equal; (e) works on theoretical and practical mechanics by Archimedes, Philon, Heron, and Carpus. *Pappus'* work is primarily of importance for the historical data it contains, but he supplies many lemmas, etc., to the treatises elucidated, and significant additions of his own, e.g. and extension of Euclid i. 47 ('Pythagoras' Theorem') to *any* triangle, proof of the constancy of anharmonic ratios, measurement of the superficial area bounded by a spiral on a sphere, an anticipation of Guildin's theorem, and 'Pappus' Problem' which was taken up by Descartes.

EDITIONS. *Comm. on Euclid Bk. 10*, ed. Junge and Thomson, with English translation (U.S.A. 1930). *Comm. on Almagest 5 and 6*, ed. A. Rome, Studi e Testi 54 (1931). For the geography see *Géographie de Moïse de Corène*, ed. Arsène Soukry (Armenian text, French translation), Venice, 1881. *Synagoge*, ed. F. Hultsch, 3 vols., Berlin, 1876–8 (with Latin translation). French translation by P. ver Eecke, 2 vols., Bruges–Paris, 1933.
COMMENT. For Pappus' date see Rome, op. cit. x ff.
GENERAL. Heath, *Hist. of Greek Maths.* ii. 355 ff.
PAPPUS' PROBLEM. Descartes, *Géométrie*, ed. and tr. D. E. Smith and M. L. Latham (U.S.A. 1925), 16 ff.          T. H.; G. J. T.

**PAPYROLOGY, GREEK.** Papyrus (*see* BOOKS), a marsh plant that grew abundantly in the Nile valley and elsewhere (though the Egyptian variety alone was manufactured into paper), was the normal writing material of the ancient world from the classical age onwards. Less for this reason than because almost all our papyri come from Egypt south of the Delta, where the rainless climate favours their survival, papyrology is identified with Egypt. The principal exceptions are (a) the Epicurean papyri from Herculaneum; (b) the Hellenistic and Roman documents found, with a few literary texts, at Dura-Europos; (c) the religious and documentary papyri from Qumran and Murabba'at in Palestine, and the Byzantine texts excavated at Aujā-el-Hafīr; (d) the single, charred papyrus, Orphic in character, recently found in a burial at Derveni near Salonica. Of the Egyptian papyri a few have been found placed in tombs or buried in jars, some have been extracted from the wrappings of mummies; but the great majority come from the ruined buildings and rubbish heaps of the towns and villages of Upper Egypt, abandoned when the irrigation level receded; hence the fragmentary condition of so many of our texts. From 1788 onwards miscellaneous papyri (including some rolls of Homer and of the lost speeches of Hyperides) were acquired by travellers and made their way into European collections; excavations of Graeco-Roman sites did not begin till a century later. The most successful of these were carried out by B. P. Grenfell and A. S. Hunt, in particular at Oxyrhynchus (q.v.) which, with the Fayûm, the ancient Arsinoite nome, has proved the most fertile source of papyri.

**2.** We have no papyri certainly anterior to Alexander's conquest of Egypt in 332 B.C., though it is likely that our oldest literary papyrus, the *Persae* of Timotheus, dates from the middle of the fourth century, and the Orphic text from Derveni is only a little later; our earliest dated document is a marriage contract of 311 B.C. from Assuan;

the latest documents extend well beyond the Arab conquest of A.D. 642. Under the first two Ptolemies settlers from all parts of the Greek world flocked into Egypt, and in the first century of Greek rule the country was steadily hellenized. Greek was the official language of the country and remained so throughout the Roman and Byzantine periods; for a large part of the population it was also the language of business and of everyday life. Of this civilization—Hellenistic, Roman, Byzantine— the papyri are the record; of it, thanks to their endless variety, which includes ephemeral matter such as private letters, school exercises, prayers and charms as well as literary texts and public and legal documents, we can form a picture in singular detail. The number of published texts, varying enormously in size, condition, content, and value, is approximately 25,000. The extent of the material as yet unpublished is unknown.

3. Papyrology, which is strictly the decipherment and study of anything written on papyrus, is not a unified subject except in as far as all the papyri represent the different activities of a single civilization. The most obvious division is between literary and documentary texts. We owe the former, over 2,500 in number, but some mere scraps, in part to the fact that a knowledge of the Greek classics, in particular of Homer, was the staple of education throughout the period. Among them the new texts slightly outnumber those already known to us, though in the later centuries new texts become rare; yet the Byzantine papyri have given us a codex of Menander and a poem of Sappho's. The new texts include, besides those mentioned, various fragmentary manuscripts of the lyric poets and Pindar, Bacchylides, much of Callimachus (notably the *Aitia* and the *Iambi*), Herodas, the *Ichneutae* of Sophocles, and many other fragments of the dramatic poets, including Aeschylus, the *Dyskolos* of Menander and much of the *Sikyonioi*, Aristotle's *Constitution of Athens*, and the *Hellenica Oxyrhynchia*, an historical work by an unknown continuator of Thucydides.

4. Of the papyri of extant Greek authors more than half are texts of Homer, the *Iliad* appearing more frequently than the *Odyssey*. The later Homeric papyri add very little to what we know from our medieval manuscripts, but the 'eccentric' papyri of the earlier Ptolemaic period, with their numerous additions and omissions and variant readings, even if the text they present is an inferior one, yet enable us to appreciate the work of the Alexandrian scholars in standardizing the text. For the textual criticism of other authors the papyri have often been of great value. They are almost invariably not only older than the medieval manuscripts (in the case, e.g., of Xenophon or Lysias by as much as 1,000 years) but are also older than the families into which the manuscripts are commonly divided. There are not a few instances of new and improved readings contributed by, a few of emendations confirmed by, the papyri; but on the whole they bear witness to the general soundness of our tradition, by showing that the text as established by Alexandrian scholars and known to the Graeco-Roman world differed little from that we already possess. These papyri are, as a rule, from the standpoint of our medieval manuscripts, 'eclectic'; they agree now with one manuscript, now with another, and not infrequently the readings of the later and less valued manuscripts have been found in papyri. They have thus assisted in dispelling the mirage of an uncontaminated tradition and consequently in undermining the theory that textual criticism should rely, wherever possible, on the testimony of a few ancient MSS. or even on that of a single witness.

5. Besides the strictly literary papyri there are others which may be termed 'quasi-literary'; these include the scientific, in particular the medical, texts, the astrological and the magical; texts of these last two classes are of value for social and religious history. But more important than any of these are the Christian literary texts. Here the papyri of texts already known are hardly, if at all, less important than the new texts; the Chester Beatty papyri, which consist of extensive portions of eleven papyrus codices, and some of the equally important Bodmer papyri take our knowledge of the text of the Greek Bible back to the second century A.D., while the Rylands Library at Manchester has some fragments of Deuteronomy dating from the second century B.C. Here again, in spite of important modifications in the history of the text at various points for which we are indebted to the papyri, its general soundness is confirmed. Among the new texts may be mentioned the Unknown Gospel in the British Museum of the second century and Origen's *Discourse with Herakleides*; the famous Oxyrhynchus *Sayings of Jesus* can be identified as part of the Greek original of the Gnostic *Gospel of Thomas*, now known from a complete Coptic text. There are many other fragments of apocrypha and of liturgical, theological, and hagiological works—of the last class the lengthy *Acta Pauli* is the best representative. Evidence of Christianity can also be found in some of the documents, notably in the *libelli* (certificates of sacrifice) of the Decian persecution and in private letters; of the latter the small archive of letters relating to the Meletian schism (A.D. 330–40) is particularly noteworthy.

6. The great mass of the papyri is roughly classified under the heading of documents—official, legal, and private papers of every description. Their value to the historian lies less in the direct information about events of historical importance which they convey (though texts of this character are extant, e.g. decrees of the Ptolemaic kings, the letter of the Emperor Claudius to the Alexandrians, the imperfect text of the *Constitutio Antoniniana* of A.D. 212 announcing the extension of the Roman *civitas* throughout the Empire) than in the indirect evidence about the historical background; such evidence may be all the more valuable because it was not deliberately selected for the benefit of posterity. Their contribution, apart from that to such specialist studies as metrology and numismatics or chronology, belongs to economic and social history in the widest sense and to the history of Greek and Roman law. In the Ptolemaic period, for example, we can observe in detail the nature and methods of Greek colonization of an Eastern Mediterranean country and its adaptation to the local conditions, and the growth of a bureaucracy which set the precedent for that of Rome; in the Roman age we see at close quarters what the Roman system of government meant to the governed and the exploitation of the country in the interests of Rome; in the Byzantine period there is the change-over to a quasi-feudal system, the growth of the great estates, the decay of Greek culture and its final disappearance before the Arab invaders.

7. The history of Greek culture and education in Egypt is partly to be found in the literary texts, their frequency, their geographical distribution, and their contents, partly in the private letters relating to education, and not least in the language of the documents themselves. Of this language, the Egyptian *Koine*, there is not one variety but many in the documents; not only does the clear, straightforward Greek of the Ptolemaic documents differ from the cumbrous, half-understood periphrases of the Byzantine age, but in a given century the language of the official document will differ from that of a business document or that of a private letter of an educated writer, and these again from the illiterate documents closest to the spoken tongue. The language of the documents has been of the greatest value for the study of the contemporary works of the New Testament in both syntax and vocabulary, and provides a link

connecting the language of the classical age with that of Byzantine and modern Greece.

The best introductory works that deal with the whole subject are W. Schubart's *Einführung in die Papyruskunde* (1918) and E. G. Turner, *Greek Papyri* (1968); for the historical and legal documents the *Grundzüge und Chrestomathie der Papyruskunde* (1912: 4 vols., with briefly annotated editions of 882 texts) of L. Mitteis and U. Wilcken is indispensable; for the legal papyri cf. also P. M. Meyer, *Juristische Papyri* (1917). A complete inventory of the literary papyri, with select bibliography, will be found in R. A. Pack, *The Greek and Latin Literary Texts from Greco-Roman Egypt* (1965); for a survey of the literary texts, new and extant and including the Christian, see J. G. Winter, *Life and Letters in the Papyri* (U.S.A. 1933; includes chapters on social life; text and translation of most of the new verse fragments in Page, *GLP* i.
The list of published volumes of papyri is too long to give here; a useful list is that in H. I. Bell, *Egypt from Alexander to the Arab Conquest* (1948). Of English publications the Oxyrhynchus series (ed. B. P. Grenfell, A. S. Hunt, and others, vols. i–xxxii (1848–1967)) is the most representative. K. Preisendanz, *Papyrusfunde u. Papyrusforschung* (1933), has useful information about excavations, collections, and publications. For a selection of the documents see A. S. Hunt and C. C. Edgar, *Select Papyri* (Loeb, 2 vols., 1932–4). For publication of new books, texts, etc., on all branches of the subject see the annual bibliographies in *Aegyptus* (Milan) and *Chronique d'Égypte* (Brussels). C. H. R.

**PAPYROLOGY, LATIN.** Latin papyri have been found in Herculaneum, Dura-Europos, Palestine (Aujā-el-Hafīr and Murabba'at) as well as in Egypt, but are comparatively rare; for every Latin papyrus there are well over fifty Greek. For this relative scarcity there were cultural and geographical reasons, and where Egypt was concerned, political as well. One consequence of the peculiar situation of Egypt under the Augustan settlement was that no senator and few other Romans were allowed to enter the country, apart from members of the armed forces; and even these became increasingly hellenized in the later first and second centuries. Not surprisingly, few Latin papyri survive from this period; some military archives and some occasional private letters and legal documents (mostly relating to soldiers or veterans) and a handful of literary texts. This situation changed at the end of the third century when Diocletian both made Egypt equal in status to the rest of the Empire and actively encouraged the use of Latin in the Eastern provinces. A knowledge of Latin, and particularly of Roman law, became essential to a successful public career. Latin appears, e.g., in the preamble and subscriptions to all cases heard in courts in Upper Egypt, and is found more frequently in public correspondence. Most of our literary papyri belong to the two centuries following Diocletian's reform; many of them carry the unmistakable stamp of the school, e.g. texts of Virgil and Cicero with Greek word-for-word translations on facing pages. Among the latest Latin texts from Byzantine Egypt is the Juvenal with Greek scholia from Antinoopolis (Cavenaile 37); the latest dated document is a military text of A.D. 548 (Cavenaile 147).

It is noticeable that among literary papyri from the Roman period the historical texts predominate. Among them are a new fragment of Sallust's *Histories* (Cavenaile 28), the *Epitome* of Livy (Cavenaile 33), and a fragment of an antiquarian writer on Servius Tullius (Cavenaile 41). There is a near-contemporary fragment of Cicero's *Verrines* (Cavenaile 20), but, with the exception of a schoolboy's copy of some lines from Virgil, no verse at all. Herculaneum, however, supplies the *Carmen de Bello Aegyptiaco*.

In the Byzantine period, as might be expected, Cicero and Virgil, the favourites of the school, are most frequently found, though by no means all of the MSS. of these authors are scholastic in origin; e.g. the fragments of a splendid *édition de luxe* of the *Georgics* were found in Antinoopolis. These apart, there is a substantial and important text of Terence: *Andria* (*POxy.* xxiv. 2401), the Juvenal mentioned above, and some fragments of

known works of Sallust. There is no Horace, no Ovid. Egypt has not added one new line to the corpus of Latin poetry. In this period the literary texts proper are outnumbered by those of Roman legal writers, no less than thirty-three in all, a superiority that indicates where the importance of Latin studies in Egypt lay. Some of them are provided with Greek glosses and several of them are important evidence on the vexed question of interpolation. Among individual texts pride of place must go to the *Gaius* (Cavenaile 78) from Antinoopolis and some near contemporary texts of Justinian's *Digest* (Cavenaile 89, 99–101).

Christian texts also make their appearance in the Byzantine period, some of them from the Old Latin version of the Bible. The earliest is a liturgical fragment of about A.D. 300 (Cavenaile 45); the oddest is a trilingual conversation book in Greek, Coptic, and Latin for visitors to the monasteries (Cavenaile 281), the most unexpected a fragment of St. Luke with a Gothic translation *en face* (Cavenaile 53). Pagan religion is represented by an important military calendar of an earlier age from Dura-Europos, the *Feriale Duranum* (Cavenaile 324).

Taken together, the Latin texts represent a chapter in the history of Latin culture about which we should otherwise know little. Literary and documentary alike, they are of particular importance for the history of Latin palaeography. The few new texts apart, the literary papyri are also of value for the tradition of Latin scholarship, particularly the Terence and the Juvenal. The interest of the documents may be less obvious, but they have much to contribute, both as a source for the day-to-day life of the Roman army (in particular the texts from Dura) and as a picture of Roman private law in action.

Texts are referred to above by their number in the useful collection of documents as well as of literary texts made by R. Cavenaile, *Corpus Papyrorum Latinarum* (Wiesbaden, 1958); see also U. Wilcken, *Über den Nutzen der lat. Pap.* (Atti del IV Congresso di Pap., 1936, 101 ff.) with references to earlier literature. Facsimiles of most of the literary texts will be found in E. A. Lowe, *Codices Latini Antiquiores.* For military texts, G. R. Watson, *The Roman Soldier* (1969), 220 ff. C. H. R.

**PARADOXOGRAPHERS.** Interest in the marvellous and out-of-the-way, as such (παράδοξα, θαυμάσια), is prominent in the *Odyssey*, the histories of Herodotus, Theopompus, and Ephorus, and other Greek writings. Paradoxography came into existence, as a distinct literary genre, early in the Alexandrian age, and continued to be practised for many centuries. The Seven Wonders of the World (τὰ ἑπτὰ θεάματα, or θαύματα), that is, the temple of Zeus at Olympia, the Colossus of Rhodes, the hanging gardens of Semiramis, the walls of Babylon, the Pyramids, the Mausoleum, and the temple of Artemis at Ephesus (or the Delian altar of Apollo), seem to have been canonized in Alexandrian times. Callimachus' contemporary, Bolus, who wrote Περὶ τῶν ἐκ τῆς ἀναγνώσεως τῶν ἱστοριῶν εἰς ἐπίστασιν ἡμᾶς ἀγόντων, and Callimachus himself, one of whose Ὑπομνήματα was entitled Θαυμάτων τῶν εἰς ἅπασαν τὴν γῆν κατὰ τόπους ὄντων συναγωγή (so the *Suda*), may perhaps be regarded as the founders of paradoxography. Archelaus composed Ἰδιοφυῆ (epigrams on 'peculiarities') for Ptolemy Euergetes (247–221 B.C.), and Antigonus (q.v. 4) of Carystus wrote on similar themes at about the same time. Callimachus' pupil, Philostephanus of Cyrene, wrote, like Archelaus in verse, on Παράδοξοι ποταμοί and κρῆναι. Prominent among the paradoxographers of the Roman period are Isigonus and Phlegon (qq.v.). After Phlegon paradoxography seems to have declined in popularity. But as late as the sixth century A.D. Philo of Byzantium wrote Π. τῶν ἑπτὰ θαυμάτων. The paradoxographers often took some particular country as their field, Sicily, Scythia, etc. Natural phenomena, especially rivers, attracted them greatly. But zoology, history, and social customs also came within their purview.

A. Westermann, *Paradoxographi* (1839); O. Keller, *Rerum naturalium scr. gr. minores* (1877).                    J. D. D.

**PARAGRAPHE** (παραγραφή) in Athenian law was a procedure for objecting that a prosecution was inadmissible, because it was in some way contrary to law. Before the main trial (εὐθυδικία) could proceed, the objection had to be heard at a separate trial, in which the objector (the accused in the original case) spoke first and his opponent replied. If the objector won, the original case was dropped; if he lost, it went to trial. Whoever lost at the hearing of the *paragraphe* had to pay his opponent one-sixth of the sum at stake in the main case (ἐπωβελία); this discouraged the use of *paragraphe* as a device for delaying a trial without justification.

The procedure was instituted under a law proposed by Archinus in 403/2 B.C., permitting *paragraphe* against prosecutions which contravened the amnesty of that year. The first *paragraphe* to be heard under this law was the one for which Isocrates wrote his speech *Against Callimachus*, perhaps in 402. Within a few years the procedure was being used also for objections on other grounds to the admissibility of private cases, but it appears not to have been used for public cases (*see* DIKE).

H. J. Wolff, *Die attische Paragraphe* (1966).          D. M. M.

**PARAKLAUSITHURON,** a serenade or lover's complaint sung at his mistress's door (Plut. *Aem.* 8). A good example comes from a Tebtunis papyrus (Powell, *Coll. Alex.* 177–80).

**PARASITE** (παράσιτος), originally 'guest' or 'fellow diner' with no invidious meaning (cf. Pl. *La.* 179 b συσσιτοῦμεν ... καὶ ἡμῖν τὰ μειράκια παρασιτεῖ). Diodorus of Sinope fr. 2 (*CAF* ii. 421) is the *locus classicus*; cf. CRITO 2, and writers cited by Athenaeus 6. 234 ff. (from Epicharmus onwards).

From contemporary life Comedy early adopted the parasite, 'sponger', or man-about-town, as a regular character. In Eupolis' *Κόλακες*, parasites doubtless form the chorus. Plays of Middle Comedy are entitled Παράσιτος (Antiphanes, Alexis; also, later, Diphilus) from their chief character; and in New Comedy the parasite is the satellite of the swaggering soldier, playing upon his vanity (Menander, *Κόλαξ*: Terence, *Eunuchus*).

Notorious parasites in real life are mentioned in Comedy, e.g. Chaerephon (Menander, *Sam.* 258), to whom a prose δεῖπνον was attributed.

Outside Comedy, but indebted to it, are the studies of parasites in Lucian, Περὶ παρασίτου, and Alciphron, *Epistles*.

See O. Ribbeck, 'Kolax', *Abh. sächs. Ges. Wiss.* 9 (1883).
                              W. G. W.; K. J. D.

**PARENTALIA,** Roman feast of All Souls, on the *dies parentales* (13–21 Feb.), the last of which was a public ceremony, the Feralia (q.v.), while the rest were days reserved for private celebrations of the rites to the family dead (cf. *di parentum*, or *parentes*). They were *dies religiosi* (cf. DIES FASTI) during which the magistrates did not wear the *praetexta*, temples were closed and no weddings celebrated, but not all *nefasti* (Lupercalia, 15th, Quirinalia, 17th, 18th–20th all *comitiales*).

Ov. *Fasti* 2. 532 ff., and Frazer ad loc.          H. J. R.

**PARILIA,** festival of the god and goddess Pales (cf. *Palibus II, fast. Antiates* on 7 July, and the varying gender of the name in literature), held on 21 Apr. As they were the patrons of flocks and herds, their feast was one of purification of the beasts, herdsmen, and stalls.

The Vestals distributed *februa*, in this case ashes of the calf of the Fordicidia, blood of the October Horse (*see* MARS), and bean-straw. The beasts were sprinkled with water at dawn, the stalls swept out and decked with branches and wreaths; sulphur and other purifying agents were used to fumigate the beasts, and bonfires lighted through which the celebrants jumped three times. A prayer to Pales was recited four times, facing east (Ov. *Fasti* 4. 721 ff., with Frazer's notes). For some unknown reason it was supposed by Cicero's time (*Div.* 2. 98; Varro, *Rust.* 2. 1. 9) that it was the foundation-day of Rome (*natalis urbis*).

Wissowa, *RK* 199 ff.; J. Heurgon, *Latomus* 1951, 277 f.   H. J. R.

**PARIS** (Πάρις) or **ALEXANDER** (Ἀλέξανδρος), in mythology, son of Priam and Hecuba (qq.v.). The double name is very unusual in epic (cf. Nilsson, *GGR* i². 476, n. 1). Homer introduces him as a well-known character and merely alludes to his doings before the *Iliad* begins. He had insulted Hera and Athena (24. 28–30), an earlier equivalent of the Judgement (see below); he had carried off Helen from Lacedaemon (3. 443 ff.). He takes part in the fighting with some distinction, especially as an archer, but shrinks from Menelaus (q.v. 1; *Il.* 3. 16 ff.), and though he afterwards challenges him to a duel to decide the war, he gets much the worst of it and is only rescued by Aphrodite (3. 67 ff., 340 ff.). His death is implied but not mentioned in the *Odyssey* (*see* DEÏPHOBUS).

The *Cypria* gave a more detailed account (Proclus, in Photius). After the incident of the 'apple of Discord' (*see* ERIS), Hera, Athena, and Aphrodite are brought by Hermes to Paris to judge which is the most beautiful; bribed with a promise of Helen, he prefers Aphrodite. This incident is not later than the seventh century, see *Artemis Orthia* (*JHS* supp. vol. v, 223 and pl. cxxvii; cf. Reinhardt, *Das Parisurteil* (1938), 6). An ivory from Sparta shows Paris seated, holding the apple, as the goddesses approach him. It is essentially a folk-tale of choice (which is best, kingship, warlike prowess, or love?), comparable to the Hebrew story of the choice of Solomon (1 Kings iii. 5 ff.; wisdom, long life, riches, destruction of enemies). How it came to be attached to the (possibly historical) Paris is not known. As a result, the *Cypria* continued, he built ships by advice of Aphrodite, went to Sparta, and so carried off Helen (q.v.). He was killed, according to the *Little Iliad* (Proclus), by Philoctetes (q.v.); cf. OENONE.

His early adventures cannot now be traced further back than the tragedians, though they may have been told in some quite lost part of the *Cypria*, or other epic. As the tragedies also are lost (Soph. and Eur., *Alexandros*), our remaining sources are the mythographers. Hyginus, *Fab.* 91, says that he was one of the younger children of his parents, and Hecuba while pregnant dreamed that she brought forth a torch from which serpents issued. The dream-interpreters ordered her child to be destroyed, but the servant charged with killing him exposed him instead; he was rescued by shepherds, grew up, and made a pet of a bull which Priam's servants carried off for a prize at funeral games. Paris, to recover it, entered Troy, took part in the games, won all his events, and was recognized and restored. Something like this must have been the plot of the lost plays, especially that of Euripides, see the frs., Nauck 42–64. Apollodorus (3. 148 ff.) makes him the second son, says he was suckled by a she-bear, and omits the incident of the games.

For his slaying of Achilles *see* ACHILLES. He does not appear to have had any hero-cult (correct Farnell, *Hero-Cults*, 412, n. 97; the passage there cited refers to Alexander (q.v. 13) of Abonuteichos).

The Judgement is a favourite theme in art from the

mid seventh century. The Trojan wedding of Paris to Helen is sometimes shown in the sixth; his return to his father's house, his abduction of Helen, and his combat with Menelaus from the early fifth. Paris and Helen together are popular from the late fifth; and there was a famous statue of him by Euphranor in the early fourth.

Türk's art. 'Paris' in Roscher's *Lexikon*. In art, Brommer, *Vasenlisten²*, 298, 326; Clairmont, *Parisurteil* (1951).

H. J. R.; C. M. R.

**PARISI,** a British tribe in east Yorkshire, well known for its La Tène cemeteries. The tribe may have become a self-governing *civitas* under Roman rule (Collingwood and Wright, *RIB* 707). Their only centre to be mentioned by Ptolemy (2. 3. 17) is Petuaria (*Brough on Humber*), where a small town (*c.* 12 acres within its defences) developed in the second century on the site of a fort, and where an aedile of the *vicus* erected a stage-building in the reign of Antoninus Pius (*RIB* 707). Romanization proceeded slowly, villas being late; the mosaic from Rudston is famous for the rustic execution of its classical theme.

A. L. F. Rivet, *Town and Country in Roman Britain* (1958), 157 f.; J. M. C. Toynbee, *Art in Britain under the Romans* (1964), 287–8; P. Corder and I. A. Richmond, *Journ. Brit. Arch. Assoc.* 1942; J. S. Wacher, *Ant. Journ.* 1960, 58 ff.

S. S. F.

**PARIUM** (τὸ Πάριον), now *Kemer*, a city on the European coast of the Hellespont near its entrance to the Propontis. Founded (Strabo 588) by a team of Milesians, Erythraeans, and Parians, from the last of whom it apparently took its name; the date is given by Eusebius as 710 B.C. Its assessment of one talent in the Delian League places it above Priapos and Sestos, but far below Abydos and Lampsacos. It was taken in 302 B.C. by Demetrius from Lysimachus, and later curried favour with the Attalids of Pergamum, by whose permission it annexed a considerable portion of the territory of Priapos. Augustus gave it the rank of a colony under the title Colonia Gemella Julia Pariana, to which Hadrian added Hadriana. Strabo mentions a family of Ophiogeneis at Parium who were said to have the power of curing snake-bites by their touch. An oracular temple of Apollo Actaeus which stood on the neighbouring plain of Adrasteia was pulled down and transferred to Parium, but the oracle ceased to exist (Strabo loc. cit.). There stood also in Parium a great altar of Apollo, designed by Hermocreon, having a length of one stade (Strabo 487); and the city further possessed a famous statue of Eros by Praxiteles. Both of these works of art are shown on the coins. Little is now to be seen on the site beyond a fragment of a Roman aqueduct and the emplacement of the theatre.

W. Leaf, *Strabo on the Troad* (1923), 80–6.

G. E. B.

**PARMA,** on the Via Aemilia (q.v.) south of the Padus (q.v.) in Cisalpine Gaul (q.v.), first recorded as a Roman colony (183 B.C.), which Mark Antony later sacked (43 B.C.). Still a *colonia* in imperial times, it has always retained its importance, but has no ancient remains. E. T. S.

**PARMENIDES** of Elea is said to have been about 65 years old in 450 B.C. (Pl. *Prm.* 127 b) and to have given his city laws (Speusippus fr. 1). His didactic poem in prosaic but trenchant hexameters survives in large fragments. It opens with an allegory describing his chariot-journey through the gate leading from night to daylight, where he is welcomed by a goddess whose address forms the remainder of the poem.

Only three methods in philosophy (ὁδοὶ διζήσιος) are conceivable, viz. (to assume) that (the reality to be studied) necessarily is *or* that it necessarily is not *or* that it both is and is not, comes to be and perishes, changes and moves. The last two methods are excluded by the argument that only what is and cannot not be can be known. The goddess therefore proceeds to a summary deduction of the characteristics of what is; given that it necessarily is whatever it is, it must be ungenerated and imperishable, indivisible, self-identical, unique, motionless, determinate, perfect, and in perfect equilibrium like a solid sphere. It follows that the many things of which mortals speak as being and not being, etc. (i.e. as having a contingent and relative being), exist only in name.

In the remaining and longest part of the poem (of which little remains) the goddess expounds 'mortal beliefs in which there is no true faith'. The cosmology and physics of this section are presented not as a 'way', i.e. as matter of knowledge, but as the most useful analysis of human experience. Expressly rejecting Ionian physical monism Parmenides derives the relativity of the sensible world from its ultimate constitution out of two opposite forms (μορφαί), Light and Dark, which themselves have only a nominal existence. Its speciousness he derives from the possession by each 'form' of characteristics as near as possible to those of the one reality.

Parmenides is the first philosopher to consider the intrinsic meaning of the term 'to be' and to assert that what can be known must 'be' and that nothing else can 'be'. His account of the three ways is the earliest discussion of philosophical method; his rejection of the third way, the earliest formulation of the Law of Contradiction; his notion of a proposition (ὡς ἔστιν) as a way to be followed, the establishment of the method of demonstrative proof in philosophy; his distinction of the object and method of knowledge (νοῦς) from those of belief (δόξα), the separation of philosophy from science.

Diels, *Parmenides Lehrgedicht* (1897); *PPF* 48–73; *Vorsokr.*¹¹ i. 217–46; Burnet, *EGP* 169 ff.; K. Reinhardt, *Parmenides und die Geschichte der griechischen Philosophie* (1914); G. Calogero, *Studi sull'eleatismo* (1932); W. J. Verdenius, *Parmenides* (1942); W. Jaeger, *The Theology of the Early Greek Philosophers* (1947), 89 ff.; G. E. L. Owen, *CQ* 1960, 84 ff.; J. Mansfeld, *Die Offenbarung des Parmenides und die menschliche Welt* (1964); L. Taran, *Parmenides* (1965); Guthrie, *Hist. Gk. Phil.* ii. 1 ff.

A. H. C.

**PARMENION** (*c.* 400–330 B.C.), son of Philotas, a Macedonian noble, became the best general of Philip II, though few details are known of his activities at this time. He accompanied Alexander to Asia as second-in-command of the army, and besides holding independent commands was present at all the great engagements of the first three years; at Issus and Gaugamela he commanded the left (defensive) wing. He was left at Ecbatana to guard the Persian treasure and the lengthening communications when Alexander himself moved east (330); but the trial and execution for treason of his son Philotas made him an obvious danger to Alexander, who promptly had him murdered.

Parmenion was certainly no accomplice to the alleged treason of Philotas. But he was not in sympathy with Alexander's bold ideas for the conquest (still less the government) of the Persian Empire: he represented the older school among the Macedonian officers ('Philip's men'), in contrast to Alexander and his intimates. He was certainly a good general, but the view (Beloch, *Gr. Gesch.²* iv. 2, 290 ff.) that his was the brain directing Alexander's victories is fantastic.

Arrian, *Anabasis*, bks. 1–3; Berve, *Alexanderreich*, no. 606.

G. T. G.

**PARMENISCUS,** pupil of Aristarchus and defender of his texts against Crates of Mallos, wrote Πρὸς Κράτητα, Περὶ ἀναλογίας (recognizing eight noun declensions), and some commentaries.

**PARMENO,** of Byzantium, author of *Iambi*, i.e. choliambi. The fragments exhibit Parmeno as a realist with a turn for moralizing. He was probably contemporary with Phoenix of Colophon, i.e. first half of third century B.C.

TEXTS. Diehl, *Anth. Lyr. Graec.* iii³. 136–7; Powell, *Coll. Alex.* 237–8; A. D. Knox, *Herodes, Cercidas, and the Greek Choliambic Poets* (Loeb, 1929), 272–3.
GENERAL LITERATURE. G. A. Gerhard, *Phoinix von Kolophon* (1909), 211 ff. E. A. B.

**PARNASSUS,** outlying spur of the Pindus range, running south-east and rising to 8,200 feet. It separates the Cephissus valley from that of Amphissa and runs into the Corinthian Gulf at Cape Opus. Its limestone mass is mostly barren, but its lower slopes are well watered; they carry the Phocian towns on its eastern flank and the plain of Crisa with the high valley of Delphi on the south. The best ascent is from Daulis; the passes, which cross its spurs, run from Cytinium to Amphissa and from Daulis to Delphi via the σχιστὴ ὁδός, where the latter is joined by the route from Lebadea. A sacred mountain especially to the Dorians. N. G. L. H.

**PARODY, GREEK** (παρῳδία). A cartoon exaggerates a prominent feature of the subject and presents him in incongruous dress and surroundings. Parody uses the same means, exaggeration and incongruity, either together or singly. Much ancient and modern parody contents itself with describing trivial things in the language of high poetry. The subtler task of bringing into bolder relief, by exaggeration, the salient features of an individual's style was seldom attempted by the Greeks. Aristophanes achieves it brilliantly in the Glyke song in the *Frogs* (1331–63), with a bathetic subject (the stolen cock) to add to the fun; and Plato's parodies, unaided by bathos, are perhaps as near to their originals as Max Beerbohm's Meredith in *Seven Men.* Aristotle (*Poet.* 1448ᵃ12) mentions Hegemon as ὁ τὰς παρῳδίας ποιήσας πρῶτος, but Athenaeus (15. 699 a) says, more precisely, that he was the first to enter τοὺς θυμελικοὺς ἀγῶνας and win contests at Athens for parody. (For similar contests cf. an Eretrian inscription of *c.* 400 B.C., Ἐφημερὶς Ἀρχαιολογική 1902, 98 ff.). Athenaeus (15. 698 b), following Polemon, regards Hipponax as the real inventor of the genre, and quotes from him four burlesque hexameters on a parasite. In the same vein are some of Simonides' iambics on women (fr. 7. 83–93). But we can go further back than any of these poets. The *Margites,* generally attributed to Homer in antiquity, was known to Archilochus (8th–7th c. B.C.). It described the adventures of a Simple Simon, and had iambics mixed up with its hexameters. Virtually nothing of it or of the *Cercopes* remains. The extant *Batrachomyomachia* (*Battle of the Frogs and Mice*), written perhaps during the Persian Wars, is a mildly amusing piece. Athena, impartially detesting the mice who gnaw holes in her Peplus and the frogs who keep her awake in the small hours (178–96), is entertaining, and the dying mouse (65–81) rather pathetic as well. The tradition of Homeric parody runs through comedy from Cratinus to Diphilus, the gastronomists (Matron, Archestratus, etc.), and the Sillographers (*see* TIMON 2).

2. Epicharmus' mythological burlesques must have contained much parody, but little of it survives (frs. 42–3. 10–11, 229). In Old Attic Comedy Hermippus seems to have been fond of parody and in Middle Comedy Eubulus had a flair for it. Fr. 10 (a Euripidean epilogue) is excellent; in fr. 64 even the well-worn theme of the 'Lady of Copaïs in her robe of beet' amuses; and there is freshness in fr. 75. Parody survives sporadically in Diphilus and Menander (Diph. frs. 30, 126; Men. *Pk.* 349 ff., *Sam.* 110 f., 329); but by this time the poet sometimes has to warn his audience that he is parodying.

3. In Aristophanes the rise and fall of style is almost as persistent as in Wodehouse. Noble and ignoble words rub shoulders, 'guts and glory' at *Eq.* 200, 'poniards and piles' at *Vesp.* 1119. *Lys.* 715 descends precipitately to Rabelaisian frankness, set off (as often in Ar., cf. *Eq.* 1242) by the smoothest of tragic rhythm. Mnesilochus-Palamedes, writing his letter (*Thesm.* 781), momentarily forgets the dignity of his role and curses 'that rotten rho'. Often comic tails are appended to well-known passages. *Ran.* 931 'Oft in the stilly night, ere slumber's chain has bound me, I lie wondering what on earth a brown horse-cock is'. *Eq.* 1250–2 the farewell of Cleon-Alcestis. The apostrophe to the soul (Eur. *Med.* 1057) takes unexpected turnings (*Ach.* 450 ff., *Eq.* 1194, *Vesp.* 756). In other passages the contrast is given by two characters talking in contrasted styles, as in the dialogue between Lamachus and Dicaeopolis at the end of the *Acharnians.* In this vein nothing can beat *Thesm.* 808: 'Why live I still?'—'The crows don't know their job.'

4. Sometimes, again, the parody is concerned, not with poetical or tragic style in general, but with some particular feature of tragedy (a prologue, a messenger's speech, a recognition scene), or of religious, political, or forensic procedure (*Eq.* 1316–34, *Vesp.* 892–1008, *Ran.* 738–55, and passages in *Thesm.* 332–432, *Eccl.* 151–65). Then there are parodies of situation, Odysseus under the ram's belly (*Vesp.* 177 ff.), Bellerophon mounted on Pegasus (*Pax* 76 ff.), Palamedes, Helen, and Andromeda (*Thesm.* 769–1135), which give us an idea of what a mythological burlesque was like (*see* COMEDY, OLD, § 5 *and* PHLYĀKES).

5. Aristophanes also parodies the styles of particular authors, especially Euripides. The tragedian's supposed passion for enigmatical epigram is satirized at *Ach.* 397, *Thesm.* 5–8, *Ran.* 1443–4. In the Glyke song (*Ran.* 1331–63) the points are (over and above metrical and musical considerations which are hard to assess) certain idiosyncrasies of diction, such as ὄρφνα and compounds in -φαής (cf. *Ach.* 460, *Vesp.* 1484, *Thesm.* 881, 1075 κλῇθρα χαλάσθω, ἐξώπιος, ὀχληρός), incessant repetitions of words (often parodied elsewhere), and the 'wings of a dove' motif (1352); in the cento (1309–22), excessive affection for the polyschematist dimeter (*see* METRE, GREEK, III. 12), a licentious anapaest (1322), the use of melisma (1314), and perhaps the constant references to animal life. In other places Aristophanes takes off the jargon of philosophical and other cliques (see *CQ* 1927, 113–21, and cf. Damoxenus fr. 2). But many of Aristophanes' poetic flights (cf. *Nub.* 1005–8, *Ran.* 154–7) cannot justly be described as parodistic. They are gay, enchanting lyrics, light as air, which he wrote to delight himself and us. Such parody as they contain consists in the lightest touches, and we are seldom brought down to earth with a bump. Of such a kind are *Eq.* 551–64, 581–94, *Nub.* 563–74, 595–606 (where the Socratic-Euripidean deity Αἰθήρ is possibly meant to sound out of place among the Olympians), and many lyrics in the *Birds.* There is gentle irony in the beauty with which the frogs invest their surroundings (*Ran.* 209–69), but the beauty matters more than the irony. At the same time, the style absorbs a word like κραιπαλόκωμος without incongruity. Aristophanes resembled Shakespeare more than any Greek tragedian in his power to bring homeliness within the compass of beautiful or passionately serious verse (e.g. *Lys.* 1122–61).

6. Plato's parodies are often on a much larger scale than those of the comic poets, and he shows great subtlety and judgement in sustaining the character of the originals without lapsing into absurdity. Agathon's speech in the *Symposium* (194 e–7 e) is a notable example; it is described as being in the style of Gorgias (198 c), and we can compare it with what survives of Gorgias' work. The epideictic speech of Protagoras in *Prt.* 320 c–8 d is

obviously parody, but our limited acquaintance with Protagoras' own work makes assessment of its success difficult. Eryximachus' speech (*Symp.* 185 e–8 e) parodies the grandiloquent generalizations of a type of quasi-scientific literature current in the age of the sophists. The first part of the funeral speech in the *Menexenus* is certainly parody, but the point (and purpose) of transition from the humorous to the serious in that speech remains an enigma. Whether *Phaedrus* 230 e–4 e, purporting to be an epideictic speech by Lysias, is parody or quotation is disputed. Shorter passages of parody in Plato are sometimes identifiable, e.g. *Prt.* 337 a–c, which we can see to be a skit on Prodicus; some may possibly be quotation, e.g. *Grg.* 448 c (Polus); others, again, suggest parody, but we cannot be sure of the original, e.g. *Resp.* 452 d.

7. Lucian's parodies are not on the level of Aristophanes, but his rollicking humour is irresistible. In the *Timon* (9) Zeus' thunderbolt has gone for repairs; he hurled it at Anaxagoras, but missed, and it hit a temple instead. The *Prometheus* has a good lawcourt speech (7–19). There are some clever touches in the *Deorum Dialogi*: 1. 2 Zeus' ignorance of Caucasian geography; 5. 4 Hephaestus, the grubby waiter; 9. 1 Zeus bears children all over his body; 10. 2 the Sun-god, ordered to arrange a Νὺξ Μακρά, grumbles that 'there weren't goings on like this in old Kronos' time; day was day then, and night night'. Best of all is 20, the Judgement of Paris; Zeus is a benign father, Hermes a charming guide, and the three goddesses admirably catty to each other. Ζεὺς Τραγῳδός has some amusing passages; Τραγῳδοποδάγρα and 'Ωκύπους are pretty dull.

H. Täuber, *De usu parodiae apud Aristophanem* (Progr. 1849); W. H. S. Bakhuyzen, *De parodia in comoediis Aristophanis* (1877); A. T. Murray, *On parody and paratragoedia in Aristophanes* (Berlin, 1891); P. Rau, *Paratragodia* (Munich, 1967).　J. D. D.; K. J. D.

**PARODY, LATIN.** The two types of literary parody— (a) pastiche, which caricatures the manner of an original without adherence to its actual words, and (b) parody proper, in which an original, usually well known, is distorted, with the minimum of verbal or literal change, to convey a new sense, often incongruous with the form —are both found in Latin, mostly in verse. Examples of (a) occur sporadically in comedy, when the grandiose language of tragedy is burlesqued. This type is sometimes used as a vehicle of literary criticism; so some lines of Lucilius parody the solemnity of Ennius and the tragic bombast of Pacuvius. Some parts of the poem on the Civil War recited, as a model for epic, by Eumolpus in the *Satyricon* of Petronius (119–24) read like a pastiche on Lucan.

The only extant example of sustained parody of type (b) is the tenth poem of the *Catalepton* (*see* APPENDIX VERGILIANA) in which poem 4 of Catullus, addressed to a yacht, is turned, with remarkable dexterity, into an address to a parvenu magistrate. The *Antibucolica* of Numitorius seem to have been parodies of the 1st and 3rd Eclogues of Virgil, but only the opening lines are preserved by Donatus; in these the point of the parody turns on alleged liberties taken with language by Virgil.
C. J. F.

**PAROEMIOGRAPHERS.** The Proverb (παροιμία), or concise saying in common and recognized use, often summarizing experience or embodying practical wisdom, is a constant feature in Greek literature, both prose and verse, from Homer onwards. It not only provided an ingredient calculated to please the ordinary hearer, but contributed not a little to the formulation of moral philosophy. It might be in prose or metrical form, and gave its name to the Paroemiac (*see* METRE, GREEK, II (7)). Many quotations from literature, and especially from poetry, enjoyed an independent life as proverbs or

gnomes. Paroemiography, or the making of collections of proverbs for specific purposes, may be said to have begun with Aristotle in a work entitled *Παροιμίαι* (Diog. Laert. 5. 26); he was followed in this by his pupil, the Peripatetic Clearchus of Soli, and later by the Stoic Chrysippus; Theophrastus also wrote *Περὶ παροιμιῶν*. So far such collections were made for the purposes of philosophy. In the Alexandrian age collections for literary purposes began to be made by such writers as the antiquarian Demon (*Περὶ παροιμιῶν*, of which a fragment has been recovered); Aristophanes of Byzantium, who made prose and metrical collections; Didymus (thirteen books); and Lucillus of Tarrha (in Crete). The later sophistic movement led to a great demand for the proverb as an ornament of style, as may be seen, for example, in the works of Lucian (W. Schmid, *Atticismus* i. 411) and Libanius. The origins of the existing *Corpus Paroemiographorum* go back to Zenobius, a sophist of the time of Hadrian; he made an Epitome in three books of the collections of Didymus and Lucillus Tarrhaeus (*Suda*, Ζηνόβιος), obliterating their book-divisions in the process; they appear to have been already arranged according to literary genres. The Corpus in its original form, as constituted in the early Middle Ages, consisted of (i) the work of Zenobius, arranged alphabetically for scholastic purposes; (ii) a collection of *Proverbs of Plutarch used by the Alexandrians*, probably deriving from Seleucus of Alexandria (*Suda*, Σέλευκος); and (iii) an alphabetical list of *Popular Proverbs*, derived from the same sources as Zenobius, ascribed to the lexicographer Diogenianus (time of Hadrian), but probably the work of an anonymous writer. A new critical edition of the *Corpus* is much needed. From these were formed later the collections of Gregory of Cyprus (13th c.), Macarius (14th c.), and Apostolius (15th c.). There exist a number of smaller medieval collections of proverbs, published and unpublished, mostly prepared by and for teachers of rhetoric. Some contain proverbs not in the *Corpus*.

EDITIONS. T. Gaisford (1836); E. v. Leutsch and F. G. Schneidewin (1839).
CRITICISM. O. Crusius and L. Cohn, *Philol.* Suppl. 6 (1891–3) (sources and MS. tradition); O. Crusius, *Analecta critica ad Paroem. gr.* (1883); *Paroemiographica, Sitz. Münch. Ak.* 1910; K. Rupprecht, *PW* xviii (1949), 1735 ff.　W. M. E.; R. B.

**PAROS,** the second largest of the Cyclades, a centre of Aegean trade, and famous for its marble. Early in the seventh century the Parians colonized Thasos. In 490 the island furnished a trireme to the Persians under Datis, for which the Athenian Miltiades later besieged the town without success. In 480 the Parians played a double game, and after the battle of Salamis were compelled by Themistocles to pay an indemnity. Paros was a member of the Delian League, also of the second Athenian League, but later revolted, and lost importance before the establishment of Macedonian authority. Here was found the Marmor Parium (q.v.). The Delion sanctuary and a heroon of Archilochus have been excavated.

P-K, *GL* iv. C V (c); *IG* xii. 5; Rubensohn, *Ath. Mitt.* 1900–2; 1917; *Das Delion von Paros* (1962).　W. A. L.

**PARRHASIUS,** painter, son and pupil of Evenor of Ephesus, later Athenian. Pliny dates Evenor 420 B.C. and Parrhasius 397 (with Zeuxis, q.v.); but he made designs for Mys' reliefs on the shield of the Athena Promachus (before 450). He was arrogant and wore a purple cloak and a gold wreath. He painted a 'rose fed' Theseus (i.e. in the rich style; Pliny (*HN* 35. 67) attributes 'elegantiam capilli, uenustatem oris' to him), Demos, 'Healing of Telephus', Philoctetes, 'Feigned madness of Odysseus'. Such pictures displayed the details of expression, 'argutias uoltus', which he discusses with Socrates in the *Memorabilia* of Xenophon. He wrote on painting. He was famed for subtlety of outline (cf. white lecythi, e.g. Pfuhl, figs. 543, 552; Rumpf, pl. 37, 3 and 5); therefore perhaps did not use shading (contrast Apollodorus, q.v. 1). His gods and heroes became types for later artists; his drawings on parchment and wood were used by craftsmen (probably metal workers) in Pliny's time.

Overbeck, 637, 1130, 1649, 1680, 1692–730; A. Rumpf, *AJArch.* 1955, 1 f.; *Malerei u. Zeichn.* 115. T. B. L. W.

**PARRICIDIUM.** The word *paricidas* (whose original meaning is much disputed) first occurs in a law attributed to Numa (Festus, s.v. 'Parricidium') in which it denotes the intentional—*dolo sciens*—murderer of a free man. It was one of the earliest crimes, being placed in the time of the XII Tables in the jurisdiction of special *quaestores parricidii.* In later terminology *parricidium* meant the murder of near relations (e.g. in the *Lex Pompeia de parricidiis, c.* 70 B.C.); it retains this meaning in classical texts and in Justinian's codification, which defines precisely for this purpose the circle of persons considered as near relations (*Dig.* 48. 9). A wider general sense was given to the term *homicidium* (rarely used in earlier texts, but more frequent in the legislation of the later Empire). In ancient times the parricide was drowned in the sea, tied up in a sack (*culleus*). In the later legislation the penalty was differentiated according to the gravity of the act, but the death-penalty remained the normal sanction.

A. Pagliaro, *Studi in onore di L. Castiglioni* ii (1960), 669 ff.; W. Kunkel, *Untersuchungen zur Entwicklung d. röm. Kriminalverfahren* (1962), 37 ff. A. B.; B. N.

**PARTHENIUS** of Nicaea (1st c. B.C.), Greek poet taken prisoner by the Romans during the Third Mithridatic War, was sent to Italy (73 B.C.), where he was freed. He exerted considerable influence on the *poetae novi*, and, according to Macrobius, *Sat.* v. 57, was Virgil's teacher in Naples. It has been said that he acted as 'the prophet of the Callimachean school' in Rome. He was highly esteemed in antiquity for his poetry, mostly elegiac (in *Anth. Pal.* 11. 130 he is placed by Pollianus alongside Callimachus), of which only a few fragments remain. Extant is a collection of prose outlines of love-stories ('Ερωτικὰ παθήματα) culled from Greek poets, antiquarians, and historians. Such skeleton love-stories, which were intended for elaboration into elegies by Cornelius Gallus, the Roman poet, might be described as miniature novels, and are of notable importance for the study of the Greek novel: their relationship with the genre in question, already seen by Rohde, has been brought into focus by Lavagnini and Giangrande. Whereas Parthenius' style was impeccable in his poetic production, he did not eschew occasional colloquialisms in the prose of his 'Ερωτικὰ παθήματα.

TEXT. Martini, *Mythographi Graeci* ii. 1 (Teubner, 1902); S. Gaselee, with English translation (Loeb 1916, several reprints).
COMMENTARY. A. Meineke, *Analecta Alexandrina* (Berlin, 1843); repr. Hildesheim, 1965), 255 ff. (still fundamental for fragments).
CRITICISM. Christ–Schmid–Stählin ii. 1⁶. 322 ff.; A. Lesky, *Gesch. d. griech. Litt.²* (1963), 808 (important for recent discoveries of fragments); E. Rohde, *Der griech. Roman⁴* (1960), 121 ff.; B. Lavagnini, *Studi sul romanzo greco* (1950), 21 ff.; G. Giangrande, *Eranos* 1962, 148 ff.; R. Mayer-G'schrey, *Parthenius Nic. quale in fabularum amatoriarum breviario dicendi genus secutus sit* (Diss. Heidelberg, 1898); R. Reitzenstein, 'Zur Sprache der lateinischen Erotik' (*Sb. d. Heidelb. Akad. d. Wiss., Philol.-hist. Kl.* 1912): still valuable.
G. G.

**PARTHENON.** The Parthenon was the temple of Athena Parthenos (Maiden) built on the highest part of the Acropolis at Athens south of the archaic temple (*see* ATHENS, TOPOGRAPHY). It was begun in 447 B.C.; the temple and cult statue were dedicated in 438, but work continued, notably on the pedimental sculptures, until 432. A temple had been begun on the site before the Persian invasion of 480 B.C., and with modifications its foundations were used for the present building. The architect was Ictinus (q.v.) assisted by Callicrates (q.v. 1) and possibly one Carpion; but the temple formed the principal element of the great Periclean scheme over which the sculptor Phidias (q.v.) had general direction, and the architectural design was affected by the desire to house the great cult statue and exhibit the subordinate sculpture to the best advantage. In the Parthenon the Doric Order (*see* ARCHITECTURE) is seen at its most perfect in proportions and in refined details, though there are some unusual features. The material is fine marble brought at great expense from the quarries of Mt. Pentelicus a few miles north-east of Athens, as in most of the finest Athenian buildings of the Periclean period. The temple measures about 228 by 101 feet on the top step. It has eight columns instead of the more usual six at the ends, and seventeen on the sides. The inner structure has a porch of six columns at each end. The larger eastern room had a two-tiered inner colonnade running not only along the sides but round the western end, behind the great cult statue. The smaller western room opened off the back porch, and had its roof supported by four Ionic columns; it served as a treasury.

The sculpture was more elaborate, more unified in themes, and more relevant to the cult than in most temples. What part Phidias played, besides making the gold and ivory cult statue of the Parthenos, is not clearly defined. But one can see a master mind at work, and it is reasonable to assume that it was that of Phidias. The metopes must have been made first, and then the frieze. The pediments were the latest addition. They showed, in the east, Athena newly sprung from the head of Zeus, and in the west, the contest of Poseidon and Athena for the land of Attica. The figures are carved in the round. The metopes, in high relief, showed the usual mythical combats; on the south side, best preserved, Lapiths and Centaurs, on the east, Gods and Giants, on the west, probably, Greeks and Amazons, on the north—less certainly, since this side is very badly preserved—Trojan scenes. Some of these themes were echoed in the minor decoration of the cult statue. The frieze, in low relief, running high around the cella wall within the colonnade, is unique in showing a contemporary Athenian scene (unless it is some legendary counterpart), the procession at the great festival of the Panathenaea.

The Athenians employed their artistic and financial resources to the full in the Parthenon, and made it a symbol of their piety and strength.

The temple was subsequently converted into a church, of the Virgin, and then a mosque. It remained almost intact, though much defaced, until 1687, when a Turkish powder-magazine in it was exploded by the besieging Venetians. Lord Elgin bought and removed to London much of the sculpture in 1801–12. The outer colonnades have been rebuilt in modern times.

A. Michaelis, *Der Parthenon* (1871); G. P. Stevens, 'The Setting of the Periclean Parthenon, *Hesperia,* Suppl. iii, 1940; W. B. Dinsmoor, *Architecture of Ancient Greece* (1950), 149 f., 159 ff., bibliography 358; C. J. Herington, *Athena Parthenos and Athena Polias* (for the cults) (1955); P. E. Corbett, *The Sculpture of the Parthenon* (1959); F. Brommer, *Die Skulpturen der Parthenon-Giebel* (1963), *Die Metopen des Parthenon* (1967); *Parthenos and Parthenon,* Supplement to *Greece and Rome* 1963 (articles on building, sculpture, cult, etc.; bibliography of sculpture, 58 ff.). R. E. W.

**PARTHENOPAEUS** (Παρθενοπαῖος), in mythology, one of the Seven against Thebes (cf. ADRASTUS). In earlier tradition, he is a brother of Adrastus and an Argive; in later, an Arcadian, son of Atalanta (q.v.). See Wilamowitz-Moellendorff, *Aischylos-Interpretationen* (1914), 100 f., with schol. on Aesch. *Sept.* 547, Soph. *OC* 1320, Eur. *Phoen.* 150 (Antimachus, fr. 17 Wyss). H. J. R.

**PARTHIA** has recently assumed an increasingly important place in the story of Asia. The people whom Greeks and Romans called Parthians were traditionally Parni, members of the semi-nomad Dahae Confederacy north of Hyrcania. Their Greek name is derived from the Seleucid satrapy called Parthia (*Parthava*), which they occupied, traditionally in 247 B.C., the year with which the Parthian ('Arsacid') era begins; later they ruled from the Euphrates to the Indus, with Ecbatana as their capital. They were never more than a land-owning military aristocracy. The king was feudal superior of his nobles, including the seven great Pahlavi families who were almost kings in their territories, Seistan, Atropatene, etc. There were other vassal kingdoms, but Parthia never assimilated Persis (from which emerged a new dynasty, the Sassanids (q.v.), who were to overthrow her early in the third century A.D.), while before the Christian era the Surens (q.v.) in Seistan became independent and gradually created an Indo-Parthian kingdom.

The Parthians spoke Parthian Pahlavi, a north-Iranian dialect akin to Sogdian; they adopted popular Iranian Mazdaism, but tolerated every other religion. They were an easy-going race, fond of hunting, superb horsemen. Their cultural role was largely diffusionist, less creative than syncretistic. They assimilated and began the process of transforming their Seleucid heritage. They utilized Greek science, Greek secretaries, Greek methods of administration and Court titles, wrote on parchment, and had Greeks on their Council; they even flirted with Greek king-worship, and Seleuceia struck their coins for them with Seleucid dating instead of their own Arsacid era. But their architecture reveals important innovations and they developed a 'Parthian' style in their art, which was gradually to merge with the art of the regions on the Parthian periphery as political control weakened at the centre. In warfare they were original and competent: before Carrhae they discarded Greek notions and employed cavalry only; the nobility fought as cataphracts, mailed knights with enormous spears, and their retainers as horse-archers, and they bred the Nesean horses into magnificent chargers for the cataphracts. Their Greek cities had perhaps no less autonomy than under the Seleucids, and there was an outburst of Greek literature in the East; but their Philhellenism was a veneer and they suffered from their inferiority to Rome in political cohesion, diplomatic initiative, and military power.

A change came in A.D. 10 when a collateral branch from Atropatene replaced the old Arsacid line. There was an Iranian reaction against the former Philhellenism; Mazdaism was emphasized; Seleuceia revolted for seven years, whereupon the capital was shifted to Ctesiphon and subsequently Vologasia was founded (near Seleuceia), in an attempt to divert from Seleuceia the increasingly important trade between China, India, and Syria; Parthia realized her lucrative position as middleman and exploited overland communication between East and West. The influence of 'Parthian' art—a revived Iranian art of many branches, which absorbed both Mesopotamian and Greek elements—spread far and is historically interesting.

N. C. Debevoise, *A Political History of Parthia* (U.S.A. 1938); K.-H. Ziegler, *Die Beziehungen zwischen Rom und dem Partherreich* (1964); J. Wolski, *Aufbau und Entwicklung des parthischen Staates* in *Neue Beiträge zur Geschichte der Alten Welt I* (1964), 379 ff.; R. Ghirshman, *Iran, Parthians and Sassanians* (1962); M. A. R. Colledge, *The Parthians* (1967). *See also* ARSACIDS (where the kings are listed). W. W. T.; E. W. G.

**PASION** (d. 370 B.C.) was the wealthiest banker and manufacturer of his time in Athens. He began his career as a slave with a banking firm, becoming a freedman and later an Athenian citizen. We learn much of his business activity from speeches of Demosthenes and the *Trape-*

*ziticus* of Isocrates. The revenue derived from his bank and a shield workshop amounted to 120–60 minae after his death, the bank alone bringing in 100 minae. He left real estate of 20 and a capital of almost 40 talents.

J. C. A. M. Bongenaar, *Isocrates' Trapeziticus* (1933), 45 ff.; M. I. Finley, *Land and Credit in Ancient Athens* (1951), index, s.v.; Michell, *Econom. Anc. Gr.* index; H. Schaefer, *PW*, s.v. 'Pasion (2)' with earlier bibliography. F. M. H.

**PASITELES,** Greek sculptor, born in a Greek city of south Italy, became a Roman citizen in 90/89 B.C. (Pliny 36. 40). He was a contemporary of Pompey (106–48 B.C.: Pliny 33. 30, 156). He made an ivory statue of Jupiter for the temple of Metellus ('Jovem fecit eboreum in Metelli aede'), as well as other statues of which the names have not been transmitted (Pliny 36. 40). He also wrote a book in five volumes on 'the famous works throughout the world'. According to Varro, quoted by Pliny (35. 156), Pasiteles 'never executed any work without first making a model of it', 'qui . . . nihil unquam fecit antequam finxit'. Though no work of Pasiteles has survived, a statue of a youth in the Albani Collection in Rome bears the signature 'Stephanus, pupil of Pasiteles, made it'. It was evidently copied from an earlier work, for the style is that of *c.* 460 B.C., and replicas exist.

From these various records it may be surmised that Pasiteles was one of the sculptors who played a prominent part in the invention of exact copying by the use of casts and the pointing machine, which was introduced at this very period (cf. Furtwängler, *Statuenkopieen im Alterthum* (1896), 20 f.; Richter, *Three Critical Periods in Greek Sculpture* (1951), 44), and soon became widespread (cf. Lucian, *Iupp. Trag.* 33). That, however, Pasiteles also studied from nature is indicated by Pliny's anecdote that while sketching a lion he was almost killed by a panther.

G. M. A. R.

**PASSENNUS PAULUS,** a contemporary *eques* whom the Younger Pliny (*Ep.* 6. 15) praises for his *elegi* as being, like his actual descent, Propertian.

**PASSIENUS** (d. 9 B.C.), Augustan orator, a distinguished representative of the old style (Sen. *Controv.* 3 *pr.* 14, 10 *pr.* 11).

**PASTORAL (or BUCOLIC) POETRY, GREEK** (βουκολικά). Ancient authorities (e.g. *Proleg. scholl. ad Theoc.*; Diomedes, 486 K.; Probus *in Verg. Ecl.* 2. 8 K.; Servius, *praef. in Ecl.*), who derive Bucolic from religious ritual, deserve little credence. Modern theories of the same sort (R. Reitzenstein, *Epigramm und Skolion* (1893), 193 ff.) are equally unconvincing. Pastoral song, accompanied by the flute, doubtless existed in all Greek lands from an early date (cf. *Il.* 18. 525–6), and especially (Diod. Sic. 4. 84) in Sicily, the home of Daphnis, the bucolic hero. This popular origin accounts for certain features, e.g. singing-match, refrain, strophic arrangement, which are found in later bucolic. But the intermediate steps are obscure. Aelian (*VH* 10. 18) makes Stesichorus the founder of bucolic, but probably Stesichorus merely described Daphnis' unhappy love and death. Athenaeus (14. 619 a, b) regards a Sicilian herd, Diomus, as the founder and says that Epicharmus (fr. 105 K.) mentioned him in two plays. Diomus is probably mythical, like Daphnis, but Epicharmus perhaps dramatized bucolic themes, and some of Sophron's *Mimes* dealt with the life of rustics and fishermen. In Greece itself legend (Hermesianax, frs. 2, 3) connects Daphnis and Menalcas, another bucolic figure, with Boeotia and Euboea, and the dimeter (μακραὶ δρύες, ὦ Μενάλκα), repeated by the despairing Eriphanis in search of Menalcas, is assigned by Athenaeus (14. 619 d) to a pastoral song. In literature bucolic matter was handled in satyr-plays (Euripides, *Cyclops*—bucolic touches are even found in tragedy, e.g. Euripides, *Electra* 493 f.), in the dithyramb (Philoxenus, *Cyclops*), and by Peloponnesian epigrammatists (Anyte of Tegea, but this does not wholly explain Arcadia as the later bucolic paradise). The evidence for Philetas' writing bucolic is disputable, but Hermesianax' treatment of bucolic themes is certain. Bucolic love also finds expression in the lyric of Lycophronides (*c.* 350) (cf. Diehl, *Anth. Lyr. Graec.* 2. 1, 157). Whatever its origins, or whatever elements were used by other writers, it is in the rustic idylls of Theocritus that we first find full-blown bucolic or pastoral poetry. In a 'literary' form of the Doric dialect, which may be due to the accident of Theocritus' Syracusan birth, and in a peculiar variation of the epic hexameter (elegiacs are found only in 8. 33–60 and speak against its Theocritean authorship) the poet introduces his pastoral setting. This is on the whole a conventional, closed landscape—there are no sweeping vistas—where water peacefully flows, the foliage of the trees rustles, and the effigies of rustic gods—Priapus, the Nymphs, etc.—appear. There his rustics, cowherds, goatherds, or reapers, converse, quarrel, vie with one another in songs, relate old folk-tales, and strive for the favour of their fair ones; for the erotic element is also preponderant in this type of Alexandrian poetry. The herdsmen of Theocritus, however contrived, are not drawing-room peasants. They have nothing in common with the dainty shepherds of the rococo period. They are lusty rustics, and their behaviour is often quite coarse. In some of the idylls (1, 6, 7, 11) the idealization of bucolic life is more pronounced, whereas in others a more realistic tone is adopted (4, 5, 10). Moreover, songs that originated in urban surroundings are transferred to the rustics (3), and the poet even masks himself and his friends as shepherds (7) in a playful *masquerade bucolique*. It is clear that this bucolic world fluctuates between the contemporary and the mythical. It was the big city life of the Alexandrian era which excited that longing for the tranquillity and the simplicity of country life we find in the bucolic idylls and the bucolic epigrams of the period. Their poets were the true precursors of the Roman *ruris amatores*. Theocritus' successors Moschus and Bion, to judge by the little of their work which has survived, added little to bucolic as such.

The word εἰδύλλιον (Idyll) is a diminutive of εἶδος, and Pindar's lyric odes were called εἴδη, according to some because the εἶδος ἁρμονίας in which they were to be sung was written over each. Hence εἴδη came to mean separate poems (cf. *Suda*, s.v. Σωτάδης) and εἰδύλλια short separate poems (cp. Pliny, *Ep.* 4. 14. 9). The full description in Greek of a pastoral is εἰδύλλιον βουκολικόν.

G. Knaack, 'Bukolik' in *PW* iii. 998 ff.; Christ–Schmid–Stählin ii. 1⁶. 181 ff.; Ph. Legrand, *Étude sur Théocrite* (1898), 141 ff.; R. J. Cholmeley, *The Idylls of Theocritus*² (1919), Introduction; A. S. F. Gow, *Theocritus* (1950), Introduction and Commentary; G. Jachmann, 'L'Arcadia come paesaggio bucolico', *Maia* 1952; J. H. Kühn, 'Die Thalysien Theokrits', *Hermes* 1958; B. Snell, 'Arkadien. Die Entdeckung einer geistigen Landschaft', *Die Entdeckung des Geistes* (1955); E. della Valle, *Il canto buc. in Sicilia e nella Magna Grecia* (1927); R. Merkelbach, *Rh. Mus.* 1956, 97 f.; J.-H. Kühn, *Hermes* 1958, 40 f.                          E. A. B.; C. A. T.

## PASTORAL POETRY, LATIN.

Latin Pastoral poetry, if viewed as extant bucolics on the Theocritean model, consists of Virgil's ten eclogues, Calpurnius Siculus' seven, two Einsiedeln eclogues, and four by Nemesianus (qq.v.). But this is not the full reckoning. Other pastorals, long since lost, were written; and pastoral motifs entered into other genres, especially amatory. Fragments of Roman epigrammatists early in the first century B.C. who introduced pastoral colour into their short poems give cause for regretting their loss. Virgil claims to have been the first to adapt Theocritus to Latin (*Ecl.* 6. 1) but bucolic themes may have been previously used by Latin poets who did not follow the Theocritean norm.

2. The so-called *Elegia in Messallam* (*Catalepton* 9. 13–20), unless with Hubaux we date it as Neronian, indicates that M. Valerius Messalla was a pioneer in Greek imitations of Theocritus which the unknown author of the poem translated into Latin. Among four love-lyrics cited by Antonius Julianus (Gell. *NA* 19. 9) one from Porcius Licinus ('custodes ouium . . .') typically combines bucolic with erotic elements of a sort in favour with Roman literary circles about 90 B.C. The welcome by Lutatius Catulus to young Archias led to the composition of similarly erotico-bucolic epigrams. If the two poems *Dirae* and *Lydia* could be decisively credited to Valerius Cato, their blends of idyll and elegy might be regarded as parallel to Virgil's *Eclogues*. The *Culex*, *Moretum*, and *Copa* of the *Appendix Vergiliana* all contain pastoral ingredients, and the conclusion to be drawn from many pieces of evidence is that there was at Rome a group of bucolic poets of which Virgil was the chief but not the only representative. Fontanus' 'Naids beloved by Satyrs' (Ov. *Pont.* 4. 16. 35) may or may not imply bucolic poetry. Pollio in his 'noua carmina' (*Ecl.* 3. 86) may have affected pastoral themes and recommended them to Virgil (*Ecl.* 8. 11); and the question how far pastoral themes appeared in the poems of Virgil's contemporaries Codrus, Helvius Cinna, Valgius Rufus, Varius, Bavius, Mevius, and others is discussed by Hubaux (*Les Thèmes bucoliques*, 66 ff.). It is likely that Domitius Marsus, continuing the epigrammatic tradition, wrote short poems at once erotic and pastoral.

3. Among extant Latin bucolic poets Virgil reigns supreme in literary power and influence. His debt to Theocritus is deep (*see* VIRGIL, § 7, 2). His shepherds are 'Arcades' (*Ecl.* 7. 4; 10. 31–3), but their Arcadia is mixed with north Italian scenery (*Ecl.* 7. 12–13). Here is an Arcady whose frontiers can be infinitely extended in imagination: from rural surroundings an escape may be made at will into themes of epic dignity, although the Sicilian muses are still invoked (*Ecl.* 4. 1; 6. 1). Or a break-away may be made when the poet's own sufferings from land-confiscations are transposed in the pastoral mode. Virgil's realism depends not merely on his knowledge of the countryside and country life, but on his allusions to contemporary events like the military expropriation of land and to contemporary figures, political or poetical, like Caesar (*Ecl.* 9. 47; but which Caesar? the dictator or Octavian? see Pliny, *HN* 2. 22–3 (89–94)), Pollio, Gallus. Theocritus had given the dignity of the hexameter to themes from Sophron's mimes, and Virgil's pastorals were performed on the stage as mimes (Donatus 27; Serv. on *Ecl.* 6. 11). The call to sing of themes 'paulo maiora' was Virgil's great transformation of bucolic poetry. Theocritus' poetry, perfect in form, had as a rule presented rustics busy with their loves or songs; but Virgil's famous 'Pollio' opened up a world of enchanted hopes; its Age of Gold remained a *locus communis* for subsequent bucolic writers and exerted influence outside the bucolic field on Tibullus and Ovid.

4. Except for the 'Messianic' presages of *Eclogue* 4 Virgil's bucolics turn partly on personal experience (1, 6, 9, and 10), partly on elegiac or erotic motifs, in which 'omnia uincit amor'. Propertius' welcome to the forthcoming *Aeneid* (3. 34. 65 ff.) specially mentions the love-melodies of Virgil's rustics. Their warm feeling and sweet cadences are suggestive now of rural peace, now of poetic learning. Horace (*Sat.* 1. 10. 44) significantly uses one of Virgil's frequent epithets when he stresses his impressionable vivacity ('molle atque facetum'),

implying his openness to beauty around him and his grace of expression.

5. In the Neronian age, Calpurnius Siculus and the Einsiedeln eclogues (qq.v.) have an eye not only for shepherds but also for the times. The Alexandrian notion of a beneficent ruler as a saving deity (σωτήρ, θεὸς ἐπιφανής) was familiar to Virgil, and this soteriological idea reappears in the Golden Age associated with the early part of Nero's reign. The Virgilian and Theocritean sources of Calpurnius are illustrated by E. Cesareo (*La Poesia di Calpurnio Siculo*, 1931). Both influences acted on the pastorals by Nemesianus (q.v.); he was, besides, a sedulous pillager of the text of Calpurnius, but he deserves credit for restoring the music of the Theocritean refrain.

6. Even in Christian poems on pastoral subjects by St. Paulinus of Nola (A.D. 353/4–431) the classic forms of paganism kept their vitality. In Endelechius' (*c.* A.D. 395) *De Mortibus Boum*, where Tityrus has saved his herd from plague by the Sign of the Cross, the elegant asclepiads make an innovation, but the names Aegon and Tityrus and the manner of the dialogue descend from Virgil. The best known of such Christian pastorals, much used in medieval schools, was the so-called *Ecloga Theoduli* (rec. J. Osternacher, Linz, 1902) of 337 lines, probably of the ninth century, though that seems a late date for so elaborate a refutation of long-extinct Graeco-Roman paganism in an exchange of quatrains (like *Ecl.* 7) between the Christian virgin Alēthía and the pagan shepherd Pseustis with Frónēsis (Phronēsis) as umpire.

7. The pastoral allegory, attributed to Virgil by his commentators, was revived, or invented, by Dante Alighieri in his *Eclogue* I of 1319 (though its authenticity has been impugned: Boccaccio attributed the revival of pastoral allegory to Petrarch). The Latin pastorals of Petrarch and Boccaccio are often obscure and harsh. Only later in the Renaissance proper did the Italian poets recall the golden sweetness of Virgil and the charms of Arcadia, idealized as the nostalgic 'image of the Golden Age': e.g. Johannes Baptista Spagnuolo Mantuanus (1448–1516), called by Erasmus 'Christianus Maro', used as a school-book and so quoted by Shakespeare; and Jacopo Sannazzaro (1458–1530) whose *Arcadia* was an antecedent of Sir Philip Sidney's romance, *The Arcadia*. In English, Milton's *Lycidas* is the most famous example of the genre (cf. also his Latin *Damon*).

The phrase 'et in Arcadia ego' (spoken by Death to Arcadian shepherds: 'even in Arcadia there am I') is not classical, but appears first in a painting by Guercino of 1623. Goethe gave it a new turn as 'et ego in Arcadia' ('I too have been in the earthly paradise', i.e. Italy). The pastoral drama was the invention of Torquato Tasso (Aminta, i.e. Amyntas, 1581).

For differences among Virgil's imitators see Calpurnius, Einsiedeln Eclogues, and Nemesianus in Duff, *Minor Lat. Poets.* Cf. J. Hubaux, *Le Réalisme dans les bucoliques de Virgile* (1927); and *Les Thèmes bucoliques dans la poésie latine* (1930); G. Knaack, 'Bukolik', *PW* iii. 998 ff.; H. J. Rose, *The Eclogues of Virgil* (1942); W. Schmid, 'Tityrus Christianus', *Rh. Mus.* 1953, 101 ff.; G. Boccaccio, *Bucolicum Carmen* (16 eclogues) in *Opere Latine Minori*, ed. A. F. Massera (1928), 3 ff.; F. Petrarcha, *Bucolicum Carmen* (12 eclogues), ed. A. Avena (Padua, 1906). Editions of Mantuanus, etc., by W. P. Mustard (U.S.A. 1911– ).
For the idea of Arcadia, E. Panofsky in *Essays . . . E. Cassirer* (1936) and B. Snell in *The Discovery of the Mind* (1953); W. L. Grant, *Neo-Latin Pastoral* (U.S.A. 1965). J. W. D.; C. G. H.

**PASTURAGE.** Cattle was the main source of wealth of the Greek and Roman peasants from earliest times. Horses were reared by the wealthier owners, horned cattle by the less well-to-do, and small cattle by the smaller peasants. Selection in cattle-breeding dates back to archaic Greece and Italy. Stall-feeding is mentioned in Homer (*Od.* 18. 367). The keeping of sheep for milk and wool dates from the earliest times. Poultry-breeding also

flourished during the Classical and Hellenistic periods, and in Italy under the Republic. The horses of Thessaly, the cattle of Epirus, and the Milesian sheep, famous throughout the world, were exported to all countries where scientific agriculture flourished during the period from Alexander to Augustus.

There was not enough natural pasturage for all the cattle of the Mediterranean world. Grazing-grounds were therefore sown by governments and private owners. Many States reserved pasture rights (*epinomia*) for their own citizens; for an alien to receive it was a great honour. Some States (e.g. Delos and Teos) introduced pasture taxes. The Ptolemaic government owned large herds and claimed the right to requisition all cattle in the country for agricultural purposes. For the use of the royal pastures as well as for protection while grazing high fees were imposed.

The Roman *latifundia* developed stock-breeding economy to its highest pitch, often converting grain lands to pasture and so diminishing the population of the countryside. The largest pasture estate mentioned in any ancient source (S.H.A., *Aurelian*, ch. 10) fed 2,000 cows, 1,000 horses, 10,000 sheep, and 15,000 goats, with 500 slaves to work it. Development ended with the breakdown of the ancient slave economy, but the strains developed in ancient times persisted throughout the Middle Ages and are in the main the ancestors of our modern stocks.

For bibliography *see under* AGRICULTURE. Also O. Brendel, *Die Schafzucht im Alten Griechenland* (1933); M. Cobianski, *Aegyptus* xvi (1936), 91 f.; A. Hauger, *Zur römischen Landwirtschaft und Haustierzucht* (1921); A. Hörnschemeyer, *Die Pferdezucht im klassischen Altertum* (1929); O. Keller, *Die antike Tierwelt* i, ii (1909–13); Michell, *Econom. Anc. Gr.* 59 ff.; Cl. Préaux, *L'Économie royale des Lagides* (1939), 207 ff.; Rostovtzeff, *Hellenistic World*. *Roman Empire*[2] (indexes); F. Vincke, *Die Rinderzucht im alten Italien* (1931); H. Winkelstern, *Die Schweinezucht im klassischen Altertum* (1933); K. Zeissig, *Die Rinderzucht im Alten Griechenland* (1934). F. M. H.

**PATAVINITAS,** the provincial smack of Livy's native Patavium declared by Asinius Pollio (Quint. *Inst.* 1. 5. 56; 8. 1. 3) to mark or mar the style of Livy (q.v.). Pollio, as governor of Cisalpine Gaul, might claim to recognize northern expressions in contrast with true Roman *urbanitas*. His charge against Livy excited the indignation of Morhof (1639–91) who retorted on Pollio's 'Asinity' in *De Patavinitate Liviana* (1685).

J. Whatmough, *Harv. Stud.* 1933, 95 ff.; K. Latte, *CPhil.* 1940, 56 ff.; P. G. Walsh, *Livy* (1961), 267 ff. J. W. D.

**PATAVIUM,** a city situated near celebrated springs in a fertile part of Cisalpine Gaul (q.v.) (Strabo 5. 212 f.; Pliny, *HN* 2. 103); modern *Padua*. The Veneti (q.v.), but certainly not Antenor, probably founded Patavium. It became their capital, successfully resisting a Spartan attack in 301 B.C. (Livy 10. 2). By 174 it was subject to Rome, but retained local autonomy (Livy 41. 27). Asinius Pollio (q.v.) temporarily oppressed Patavium, probably because it opposed Antony, 43 B.C. (Macrob. 1. 11. 2; Cic. *Phil.* 12. 10). But in general it prospered. It was a road-centre, and canals connected it with the sea. Its flourishing woollen industries made Patavium the wealthiest north Italian city in Augustus' time. Later Mediolanum and Aquileia (qq.v.) outstripped it, but Patavium always remained important even after Huns (452) and Lombards (601) sacked it. Its most famous sons were Livy, Asconius, and Thrasea Paetus (qq.v.).

C. Foligna, *Story of Padua* (1910); C. Gasparotto, *Padova Romana* (1951). E. T. S.

**PATER PATRIAE.** After the execution of the Catilinarian conspirators in 63 B.C., Cicero was hailed in the Senate as *Parens Patriae* or *Pater Patriae*, and after Munda the title *Parens Patriae* was accepted by Julius

Caesar. Augustus was given the title *Pater Patriae* by 'the Senate, the equestrian order, and the whole Roman people' in 2 B.C. (*Res Gestae* 35. 1). Tiberius consistently refused the title; his successors (down to Pertinax, who accepted it on accession) refused the title at first, but accepted it later (so that short-lived emperors like Galba, Otho, and Vitellius did not hold it at all).          J. P. B.

**PATRAE** (modern *Patras*), situated in Achaea outside the narrows of the Corinthian Gulf, had an unimportant early history though Mycenaean tombs have been found in the region. It supported Athens in the Peloponnesian War (Thuc. 5. 52), took the lead with Dyme in expelling the Macedonians and forming the Achaean Confederacy (*c.* 280 B.C.), but ceased to be inhabited as a city at some date before the Roman occupation. Augustus planted a Roman colony there, attaching to it the neighbouring Achaean towns (Paus. 10. 38. 9). The Roman Odeum is well preserved. As the port where travellers from Italy landed, it attained an importance which it still keeps. *See* ACHAEA.

Paus. 7. 18 ff. W. M. Leake, *Travels in the Morea* (1830), ii. 123 ff.; U. Kahrstedt, 'Die Territorien von Patrai und Nikopolis in der Kaiserzeit', *Hist.* 1950, 549 ff.          T. J. D.; R. J. H.

**PATRIA POTESTAS.** In early Roman law, and to a considerable though diminishing extent throughout, the family was the legal unit and the head of the family (*paterfamilias*) was the only full legal person (*sui iuris*). The family was agnatic, i.e. it included any person, of whatever age, who was directly descended from the *paterfamilias* through the male line by birth *ex iustis nuptiis* (*see* MARRIAGE). It included also those artificially brought in by *adoptio* (q.v.), and likewise the wife if married with *manus* (q.v.), and excluded conversely those made independent by *emancipatio* (q.v.) and those given in adoption, or daughters married with *manus*. On the death of the *paterfamilias* or his *deminutio capitis* (q.v.) there came into existence as many new families as there had been male persons immediately under his *potestas* (e.g. sons, or grandsons whose fathers had died or been emancipated).

The *paterfamilias* had an absolute power (*patria potestas*) over the members of the family which was thought of by the Romans as peculiar to themselves (Gai. *Inst.* 1. 55). It extended to life and death (*ius vitae necisque*), limited only by the restraints of sacred law, by the habit of consulting a family council, and, in case of gross abuse, by the possibility of animadversion by the censors (q.v.). As late as the conspiracy of Catiline (q.v.) a son was put to death by the simple order of his father, and though the power otherwise went out of use in the course of the Principate, it survived in the form of the exposure of infants until well into the Christian Empire. (Exposure was made criminal in A.D. 374, but even then ineffectually.) *Patria potestas* was essentially proprietary in character (*see* DOMINIUM) and in early law differed little from the ownership of slaves (though of course in public law a son (*filiusfamilias*) was a full-citizen and could vote and hold office). Indeed in its widest sense '*familia*' includes all persons and property in the control of the *paterfamilias*. Thus the formalities for *emancipatio* and for the *adoptio* (q.v.) of another's *filiusfamilias* were essentially the same as those for the conveyance and claiming of property. For in early law the father could sell his children as he could sell other property. If sold *trans Tiberim* they became slaves; if sold to a citizen they were *in mancipio* (a status akin to slavery) to the purchaser and if manumitted by him would revert to the *potestas* of the father. The XII Tables, however, provided that if he sold a son three times the son became finally free of his *potestas* (though still of course *in mancipio* to the purchaser until manumission).

Persons *in patria potestate* could (like slaves) own nothing. Whatever they acquired (including rights arising out of contracts into which they entered) they acquired for the father. Likewise they could alienate nothing and could involve him in no liabilities. The praetorian law (*see* EDICTUM), however, allowed a suit against the father on the contracts of his sons (or slaves) in certain circumstances, e.g. when the father had authorized the plaintiff to deal with the son, or when he had allowed the son to have the free administration of a personal fund (*peculium*). The *peculium* remained, however, in law the property of the father, save that Augustus allowed a privilege to soldiers for property which they acquired on service (*peculium castrense*). In its developed form this *peculium* was fully owned by the son, except that if he died intestate it belonged to the father. From Constantine onwards the same privilege was extended to earnings in certain public employments and professions (*peculium quasi-castrense*). At the same time the son was allowed an interest of a different kind in other property—at first in what he inherited from his mother's side and eventually, under Justinian, in any property which he did not derive from his father. In these so-called *bona adventicia* the father's right was then limited to a life interest. In these ways the son's proprietary incapacity was largely removed.

If a son (or a slave) committed a delict the liability was in principle his own, but the action (*actio noxalis*) had to be brought against the father, who had the choice between paying the appropriate penalty and surrendering the wrongdoer to the plaintiff (*noxae deditio*). (The son would then be *in mancipio*—see above.) Since the liability was that of the son or slave, the plaintiff had to proceed against the person with *potestas* over the wrongdoer at the time that the action was brought (*noxa caput sequitur*). If, e.g., the son was given in adoption or the slave was sold after the commission of the delict, the action lay against the adoptive father or the purchaser. Similarly, if the son was emancipated he himself could be sued by the ordinary action. Noxal surrender was finally abolished by Justinian, but had already become obsolete in the fourth century. The principle of noxal liability applied also to animals.

ANCIENT SOURCES. Gaius 1. 55; 2. 86–7; *Inst. Iust.* 1. 9; 2. 9; *Dig.* 1. 6; 49. 17; *Cod.* 8. 46; 6. 61; 12. 30. 36.
MODERN LITERATURE. P. Moriaud, *De la simple famille paternelle* (1909); L. Wenger, 'Hausgewalt und Staatsgewalt im römischen Altertum', in *Miscellanea Fr. Ehrle* ii (1927); P. Bonfante, *Scritti giuridici* i (1916), 64 ff., *Corso di diritto rom.* i (1925), 69 ff.; C. W. Westrup, *Family property and p.p.* (Copenhagen and London, 1936); M. Kaser, *Sav. Zeitschr.* 1938; Micolier, *Pécule et capacité patrimoniale* (1932); F. de Visscher, *Le Régime romain de la noxalité* (1947); J. A. Crook, *CQ* 1967, 113 ff.          B. N.

**PATRICIUS.** Patricians were the privileged class of Roman citizens. Their name is probably connected with *pater*, meaning 'member of the Senate', as exemplified by certain technical phrases such as 'patrum auctoritas', 'auspicia ad patres redierunt'. There is no reason to believe that the patrician *gentes* were the whole citizen body of primitive Rome: indeed, it is a disputed point whether the distinction between patricians and plebeians existed during the monarchy. In the distinction between patrician 'gentes maiores' and 'minores' there is probably a trace of the gradual formation of the patriciate. We have furthermore some hints of the admission of new families in early times: e.g. of the *gens Claudia* at the beginning of the Republic. The same *gens* could probably develop plebeian and patrician branches; this would explain the apparently plebeian names of some of the kings (Hostilius, Marcius), if these kings are not antecedent to the creation of a patriciate (*see* PLEBS).

Until 445 B.C. *patricii* were not allowed to marry plebeians: we do not know when the prohibition, which is codified in the XII Tables, was first introduced.

*Confarreatio* (q.v.) was perhaps a special form of marriage for the patricians. The patricians were the holders of the magistracies and of the most important religious offices. It has been suggested by some modern scholars that they served in the cavalry, and that six centuries were probably reserved to them. The diminution of their political influence (*see* PLEBS) corresponded to a certain extent with the diminution, absolute and relative, of their numbers: about 50 patrician *gentes* are known in the fifth century, 22 (with 81 families) *c.* 367 B.C., only 14 (with 30 families) at the end of the Republic. Only a patrician could become *rex sacrorum, interrex,* and perhaps *princeps senatus*. The *patrum auctoritas* (q.v.) was confined to the patrician senators.

The patricians could renounce their status by a special public act (*transitio ad plebem*) or by simple *adoptio* or *adrogatio*. Caesar (by a *Lex Cassia,* 45 or 44 B.C.) and Octavian (by a *Lex Saenia,* 30) were empowered to admit new members to the patriciate. The later Emperors conferred the rank on the strength of their censorial powers. In the senatorial *cursus* the patricians were *quaestores Augusti* in the quaestorship and passed directly from the quaestorship to the praetorship. The patriciate apparently disappeared in the third century A.D.

The new dignity of *patricius* created by Constantine was a personal title, conferred for faithful service to the Empire.

The chief patrician *gentes* in the mid and later Republic were the Aemilia, Aebutia, Claudia (the Claudii Marcelli were a plebeian branch), Cornelia, Fabia, Furia, Julia, Manlia, Postumia, Papiria, Quinctia, Quinctilia, Sergia, Servilia, Sulpicia, Valeria, Veturia: these 17 *gentes* are known to have had members in the Senate in 179 B.C., but the Aebutii, Furii, and Sergii were not represented in 55 B.C.

Mommsen, *Röm. Forsch.* i (1864), 69 ff.; id. *Röm. Staatsr.* iii (1887), 3 ff.; P. Willems, *Le Sénat de la République romaine²* (1885). A. Alföldi, *Der frührömische Reitesadel* (1952); F. Altheim, *Röm. Geschichte* ii (1953), 429; A. Magdelain, 'Auspicia ad patres redeunt', *Hommages J. Bayet* (1964), 427 ff.; A. Momigliano, Procum Patricium', *JRS* 1966, 16 ff.; 'Patrizi e plebei', *Entretiens Hardt* xiii (1967), 199 ff.; A. Magdelain, *Recherches sur l'imperium, la loi curiate et les auspices d'investiture* (1968). For the patricians under the Empire, C. Heiter, *De patriciis gentibus quae imperii romani saec. I–II–III fuerint* (1909). For the late Empire, O. Hirschfeld, *Kl. Schr.* (1913), 662 ff.; G. B. Picotti, *Arch. Storico Italiano* 1928; W. Ensslin, *Mél. Bidez* (1934), 361 ff.; A. Piganiol, *L'Empire chrétien* (1947), 314 ff. *See also* GENS, PLEBS.                    A. M.

**PATRIMONIUM and RES PRIVATA** were divisions of the property of the Roman Emperors, whose precise nature remains obscure. Equestrian officials with the titles *a patrimonio* or *procurator patrimonii* (eventually of *ducenarius* rank), and slave and freedmen officials (*tabularii, a commentariis, custodes*) of the *patrimonium* are known from the first century onwards. A *ratio patrimonii* is attested for Alexandria in the mid second century (*ILS* 1491) and a *procurator patrimonii* of Narbonensis under Marcus Aurelius (*AE* 1962, 183). From the early third century we have some pottery fragments from the Monte Testaccio in Rome marked *fisci rationis patrimonii provinciae Baeticae* or *Tarraconensis,* and in the third century we have references to local officials of the *patrimonium* in Belgica and the Germanies, Bithynia and areas of Africa.

The *Historia Augusta* (*Sept. Sev.* 12. 4) states that Severus established the *privatarum rerum procuratio.* But a *procurator rationis privatae* is attested under Marcus Aurelius (*AE* 1961, 280). Very early in Severus' reign M. Aquilius Felix was procurator of both the *ratio privata* and the *patrimonium*; the fact that these posts are described in two inscriptions (*ILS* 1387; *AE* 1945, 80) in different terminology suggests that the distinction between them was not yet familiar. The statement in

*Historia Augusta* finds some justification in the fact that between 193 and 235 a considerable number of regional *procuratores rei privatae* appear, especially in areas of Italy, and in Africa and Asia Minor. In this period both terms are used in legal sources (*Dig.* 30. 39. 10; *Cod. Just.* 2. 1. 7) in referring to imperial properties. In the course of the third century the post of *procurator patrimonii* ceases to be attested; the *procurator rationis privatae,* of *trecenarius* rank, develops into the *magister rationis summae privatae,* and in the fourth century into the *comes rei privatae,* head of one of the major financial departments of the Late Empire. In the fourth century *res privata* seems to be the standard term for all imperial property, though *patrimonium* and its cognates are still used (e.g. *Cod. Theod.* 4. 12. 2).

O. Hirschfeld, *Die kaiserlichen Verwaltungsbeamten* (1905), 18 ff., 40 ff.; Jones, *Later Rom. Emp.* 411 ff.                    F. G. B. M.

**PATROCLES,** Greek commander at Babylon after 312 B.C. under Seleucus I, whom he assisted against Demetrius. Under Seleucus and Antiochus I, he governed lands from the Caspian towards India, gathering reliable geographical material including north-west India. About 285 he was sent to explore the Caspian, voyaged up its western and then its eastern sides, learnt about Indian trade down the Oxus, but mistakenly asserted that the Oxus and Jaxartes flowed into the Caspian. His reports confirmed the belief that this sea opened into the supposedly near-by Northern Ocean; and Pliny even states that Patrocles himself sailed by this imaginary route from the Caspian to India.

Strabo 2. 68–70, 74; 11. 508–9; 15. 689. Pliny 2. 167; 6. 36, 58. Cary–Warmington, *Explorers,* 51 f.; (Pelican) 185 f.; Warmington, *Greek Geography* (1934), 67 ff.; W. W. Tarn, *JHS* 1901, 10 ff.; *Greeks in Bactria and India²* (1951), 41, 112 f., 444, 488 ff.; Thomson, *Hist. Anc. Geog.* 127 ff.                    E. H. W.

**PATROCLUS,** in mythology, son of Menoetius (q.v.). Having accidentally killed a playfellow, the young Patroclus took refuge with Peleus (q.v.; *Iliad* 23. 85 ff.). He and his father were kindly received, and Patroclus, who was somewhat older than Achilles (11. 787), was assigned to him as a personal attendant. For the rest *see* ACHILLES.                    H. J. R.

**PATRONAGE, LITERARY. I. IN GREECE.** Literary patronage in Greece is associated chiefly with autocratic rulers. The tyrants of Corinth, Athens, Samos, and the Greek cities of Sicily were notable examples, patronizing such writers as Arion, Alcman, Anacreon, Pindar, Simonides, and Bacchylides. Later Archelaus of Macedonia collected at his court a literary coterie which included Agathon, Timotheus, and Euripides. Later still the Hellenistic monarchs were often literary patrons, especially the Ptolemies, who established and maintained at Alexandria the famous Museum (q.v.) and Library (*see* LIBRARIES). Similar patronage was exercised by the Attalids in Pergamum.

**II. AT ROME.** Literary patronage at Rome was an extension of the ordinary social relationship between *patronus* and *cliens.* Hence the relationship naturally varied in accordance with the social status of both parties and with changing conventions. It not only offered encouragement and economic assistance to writers who were not themselves wealthy, but often provided the main channel by which their work reached a public. Patronage was especially important in the development of poetry and drama, which in the early stages were largely the work of persons of humble origin, e.g. Livius Andronicus, Plautus, Naevius, Ennius, Terence, and Accius; Lucilius was of rather higher social status. Patronage was extended also to Greek writers and scholars, such as Panaetius and Posidonius. In the Principate Augustus and many of his successors acted as patrons, as did Maecenas, the Younger

Pliny and many other wealthy persons. Among the beneficiaries were Virgil, Horace, Statius, and Martial.

See the separate articles on all persons mentioned.

A. E. A.

**PATRONUS,** at Rome, was a man who agreed to protect another person, Roman or non-Roman, by making him his client. Several types of *patroni* may be distinguished.

(1) In the early days of Rome the members of the ruling families attached to themselves a number of poorer citizens to whom they gave financial or legal assistance in return for political services or social deference. The bond between patron and client probably could not be enforced by legal sanctions, but by long custom it acquired a quasi-religious force.

(2) With the growth of slavery and the increasing frequency of emancipation, the relation between a slave-owner and his freedman developed into a special type of patronage which was clearly defined by law (*see* FREED-MEN). The patron retained a certain amount of domestic jurisdiction over his freedmen-clients. Patrons and freedmen were often buried together, and epigraphic evidence (especially since the 2nd c. A.D.) indicates that a genuine feeling of friendship often subsisted between them.

(3) Under the later Republic the function of legal assistance by *patroni* was extended to include cases where practised forensic speakers supported litigants in return for a fee. Though a *Lex Cincia* of 204 B.C. forbade the payment of *patroni*, this statute was frequently circumvented. The forensic *patronus* is to be held distinct from the technical legal adviser or *advocatus* (q.v.).

(4) Roman generals assumed a general patronage over peoples conquered by them, and this patronage was transmitted to their descendants. As early as 278 B.C. C. Fabricius took the Samnites as his clients, while the Claudii Marcelli undertook to look after the interests of the province of Sicily (conquered in 210 B.C. by Claudius Marcellus, q.v. 1). The patronage of Pompey extended widely over the Empire; in 83 B.C. he raised three legions of clients in Picenum and his son Sextus could still get help in Spain and Asia from the clients of his family. It is probable that a patronage of this type was one of the elements that went to make up the *auctoritas* of the Emperors.

(5) A similar form of patronage, which became common under the Empire, originated in the action of Roman municipalities, which appointed one or more influential Romans to defend their interests in Rome and to serve as channels of communication between themselves and the Emperors (cf. the *tabula patronorum* of Canusium—*ILS* 6121).

(6) Under the Roman Emperors many *collegia* or clubs appointed *patroni* similar to those of the municipalities.

(7) Under the Emperors men of wealth kept large numbers of merely parasitic clients for the sake of ostentation. *See* CLIENS.

(8) In the Late Empire powerful men offered protection to individual peasants against the tax-collector and other public obligations in return for money, services, or even the surrender of the ownership of the land. The Emperors' legislation against this type of patronage was hardly successful.

For the patronage over *liberti*, M. Kaser, *Sav. Zeitschr.* 1938, 136 ff.; C. Cosentini, *Studi sui liberti* (1948). For the political *patronatus*, Fuselt de Coulanges, *Histoire des institutions politiques de l'ancienne France* (1892), 205 ff.; M. Gelzer, *Die Nobilität der röm. Rep.* (1912, E.T. 1969), 43; Syme. *Rom. Rev.*: A. v. Premerstein *Vom Werden und Wesen des Prinzipats* (1937). For the *municipia*, Mommsen, *Lex Coloniae Genetivae, Juristische Schriften* i. 188 ff.; A. v. Premerstein, *Sav. Zeitschr.* 1922, 124 ff. For the *collegia*, J. P. Waltzing, *Étude historique sur les corporations professionnelles* i

(1895), 425 ff.; ii (1896), 367 ff. For the Empire, J. Gagé, *Les Classes sociales dans l'empire romain* (1964); L. Harmand, *Le Patronat sur les collectivités publiques* (1957); Jones, *Later Rom. Emp.* ii. 775; R. Rémondon, *La Crise de l'empire romain* (1964), 178 ff. In general, J. Gaudemet, *Institutions de l'antiquité* (1967), 517, 561.          A. M.

**PATRUM AUCTORITAS** was the consent given by the *patres* to the deliberations and to the elections of the popular assemblies in Rome. The conditions under which this consent was given are uncertain. It was probably the prerogative of the patrician senators, not of the whole Senate (Livy 6. 42. 10; Sall. *Hist.* 3. 48. 15; Cic. *Dom.* 14. 38; Gaius 1. 3). As the Senate became mostly plebeian, the *patrum auctoritas* was reduced to a matter of form. A *Lex Publilia* of 339 B.C. (Livy 8. 12) established that it must be given to new laws before the voting of the Comitia. The rule was extended by a *Lex Maenia* of the third century (Cic. *Brut.* 14. 55) to elections. The relevance of the *Lex Hortensia* of *c.* 287 B.C. to the evolution of the *patrum auctoritas* is a disputed point (cf. App. *BCiv.* 1. 59. 266 with E. Gabba's commentary). The *patrum auctoritas* affected the Comitia Curiata and Centuriata and (probably) the Comitia Tributa. There is no clear evidence that it affected also the *Concilium plebis.*

Mommsen, *Röm. Forsch.* i (1864), 233 ff.; id. *Staatsr.* iii. 155 ff., 1036 ff.; P. Willems, *Le Sénat de la république romaine* ii (1885), 33; De Sanctis, *Stor. Rom.* ii (1907), 220 ff.; E. Staveley, *Athenaeum* 1955, 3 ff.; E. Friezer, *Mnemos.* 1959, 301 ff.; E. Meyer, *Röm. Staat und Staatsgedanke*² (1961), 510 for further bibl.; H. H. Scullard, *A History of the Roman World from 753 to 146 B.C.*³ (1961), 433; H. J. Wolff, *Bull. Ist. Diritto romano* 1961, 1 ff.; J. Gaudemet, *Institutions de l'antiquité* (1967), 351.          A. M.

**PAULINUS OF NOLA** (MEROPIUS PONTIUS PAULINUS) (A.D. 353/4–431), born at Bordeaux, and a favourite pupil of Ausonius (q.v.), after embarking on a promising State career, was baptized (*c.* 390) and subsequently, with his wife Therasia, dedicated himself to a monastic life at Nola, where he became bishop (409). A leading figure among the Christian poets, producing over thirty poems, mostly in hexameters, Paulinus did much for the christianization of Latin poetry. He further wrote over fifty letters (1–22 trans. P. G. Walsh, 1966) addressed to various Christian correspondents, including Augustine. The writings of this attractive figure throw an interesting light on contemporary religious life.

TEXT. W. Hartel, *CSEL* xxix and xxx. P. Fabre, *Essai sur la Chronologie de l'œuvre de Saint P. de N.* (1948); N. K. Chadwick, *Poetry and Letters in Early Christian Gaul* (1955), 63 ff.   A. H.-W.

**PAULLUS** (1), LUCIUS AEMILIUS (*PW* 118) (*cos.* I 219 B.C.), brilliantly defeated Demetrius of Pharos in the Second Illyrian War. In 218 he was on the embassy to Carthage opening the Second Punic War. Consul again in 216 he shares, despite the senatorial tradition, in the strategical responsibility for the disaster of Cannae; he fell on the battlefield. Aemilius Paullus (2) Macedonicus was his son; his daughter, Aemilia Tertia, married Scipio Africanus. A distinguished figure, his memory was preserved in the Scipionic Circle and is glorified in Polybius.

J. van Antwerp Fine, *JRS* 1936, 30 ff.; Badian, *Stud. Gr. Rom. Hist.* 17 ff.          A. H. McD.

**PAULLUS** (2) **MACEDONICUS,** LUCIUS AEMILIUS (*PW* 114) (*cos.* I 182 B.C.), curule aedile in 193 B.C., augur by 192, was praetor in 191 in Further Spain, where after initial failure he subdued the Lusitanians (190–189); note the decree for *turris Lascutana* (Dessau, *ILS* 15). On the commission for settling Asia, he opposed the triumph of Cn. Manlius Vulso. Consul in 182, he subjugated the Ligurian Ingauni in 181. In 171 he was patron in the inquiry into extortion in Spain. Consul again in 168, he ended the Third Macedonian War at Pydna; a monument remains at Delphi. His settlement of Greece, including the sack of Epirus, carried out the Senate's policy. Of the spoil he kept only Perseus' library. His triumph was clouded by the death of his two younger sons. Censor in 164, he died in 160; the *elogium* is partly preserved (*CIL* i². 194). His elder sons, by Papiria, were Q. Fabius and P. Scipio Aemilianus; a daughter married Cato's son.

Aemilius symbolizes the union of Roman tradition with Hellenism. Cultured yet conservative, a fine soldier and just administrator, strict in religious observance, he played an honourable and authoritative part in public and private life in Rome.

Livy 37. 46 and 57; 38. 44 ff.; 40. 25–8; 43. 2; 44–5; Polyb. 18. 35; 29–32; Plut. *Aem.* with historical commentary in Dutch by C. Liedmeier (1935). De Sanctis, *Stor. Rom.* iv. 1. 315, 419, 457, 613; Scullard, *Rom. Pol.* 207 ff.; P. Meloni, *Perseo* (1953), 319 ff.
A. H. McD.

**PAULLUS** (3), LUCIUS AEMILIUS (*PW* 81), son of Lepidus (2) and elder brother of Lepidus the Triumvir, accused Catiline *de vi* in 63 B.C. While quaestor in Macedonia in 59 he was absurdly accused by the informer Vettius (q.v. 3) of conspiring to murder Pompey. In 55, as curule aedile, he began to rebuild the Basilica Aemilia. In 53 he was praetor and in 50 consul. Previously a consistent optimate, he was now bought by Caesar for 1,500 talents which he needed for the Basilica, gave him at least passive support in 50, and remained neutral during the ensuing civil war. During the war of Mutina, however, he negotiated for the Senate with Sextus Pompeius and later joined in declaring his brother a public enemy; he was named first in the proscriptions, but allowed to escape. He went to Brutus in Asia, and continued to live at Miletus, though pardoned after Philippi.

Syme, *Rom. Rev.*, see index.
A. M.; T. J. C.

**PAULLUS** (4), AEMILIUS (*PW* 82) LEPIDUS, son of Paullus (3), was proscribed in 43 B.C. and in 42 won Crete for Brutus, but later joined Octavian, whom he accompanied to Sicily in 38. He was *consul suffectus* in 34, proconsul, and censor in 22. He completed the Basilica Aemilia begun by his father. His first wife was Cornelia, daughter of Scribonia (q.v.); her premature death is the subject of a consolatory elegy of Propertius (4. 11); their two sons, Paullus (5) and Lepidus (5), are also mentioned (l. 63). Later he seems to have married Marcella, daughter of Marcellus (5).

Syme, *Rom. Rev.*, see index.
T. J. C.

**PAULLUS** (5), LUCIUS AEMILIUS (*PW* 115), son of Paullus (4) and Cornelia, and husband of Julia (3), was consul in A.D. 1. Towards A.D. 8 he conspired against Augustus and was executed; the engagement between his daughter Lepida and the youthful Claudius was broken off in consequence of this and of Julia's disgrace (later she married a M. Silanus, probably the consul of A.D. 19: for two of their children, 'abnepotes Augusti', see Tac. *Ann.* 13. 1). L. Paullus, replaced as an Arval brother in A.D. 14, may have been his son.

E. Hohl, *Klio* 1937, 339 ff.; Syme, *Rom. Rev.*, see index.
T. J. C.

**PAULUS** (1), JULIUS (*PW* 382) (fl. *c.* A.D. 210), one of the greatest Roman jurists. The place and date of his birth and of his death are unknown. A pupil of Cervidius Scaevola (q.v. 5), he began his juridical activity as a practising advocate, was, together with Ulpian (q.v. 1), assessor of Papinian (q.v.) when he was *praefectus praetorio*, then *magister memoriae*, and member of the imperial *consilium* of Severus and Caracalla. Banished by Elagabalus, he was recalled by Alexander Severus and nominated *praefectus praetorio*, an office which he perhaps held jointly with Ulpian. (It is a remarkable fact that in all their surviving writings they never cite each other.)

Paul was evidently in great demand as a respondent jurist; and he also taught, and wrote *Institutiones* and *Regulae* for students. But these formed only a very small part of his voluminous writings (nearly 320 books). His principal systematic works were a long commentary on the Edict (eighty books) and an exposition of *ius civile* (*Ad Sabinum*, sixteen books); casuistic works included *Quaestiones* (twenty-six books) and *Responsa* (twenty-three books); in addition there were commentaries on the works of older jurists (Plautius, Neratius, Vitellius, Labeo, and Alfenus), notes on Papinian, and a long series of monographs on *leges*, *senatusconsulta*, imperial constitutions, and on various topics in private, criminal, fiscal, and constitutional law. *Pauli Sententiae*, a work which was popular in later centuries and of which part is preserved in the *Lex Romana Visigothorum* and elsewhere, was probably a handy anthology of his writings, compiled about 300 and more than once re-edited.

Paul was highly esteemed in antiquity. His reputation in the nineteenth century was less favourable. He was written down as a clumsy and unoriginal compiler, even a plagiarist, self-importantly reluctant to acknowledge his debts. He is now judged differently (and some of the texts used to found accusations of clumsiness and lack of logic are acknowledged to be interpolated). He is indeed a compiler and a synthesizer, but neither uncritical nor unoriginal, and the width of his interests is remarkable. He is sometimes too doctrinaire, too given to rationalization at the expense of practical considerations, but these are the excesses of an incisive and logical mind. After Ulpian he is the author most frequently excerpted in the *Digest*, more than one sixth of which is taken from his works. But whereas Ulpian was generally taken as the basis, Paul was on the whole used in shorter extracts to amplify and qualify the main theme.

*See* generally bibliography s.v. JURISPRUDENCE. On *Pauli Sententiae*, *see also* bibliography s.v. LAW AND PROCEDURE, ROMAN, I: Vulgar Law and Transmission of Texts. Also E. Levy, *Pauli Sententiae. A Palingenesia* (1945).
A. B.; B. N.

**PAULUS** (2) (d. *c.* A.D. 575), epigrammatic poet, was chief *Silentiarius*, or usher at the courts of Justinian and Justin II. Eighty-one of his poems, doubtless collected by his friend Agathias (q.v.), are in the Greek Anthology: forty deal vividly with love, and twenty sensitively with works of art. He also wrote an elaborate poetical description (*see* EKPHRASIS) of the restored church of St. Sophia: Wilamowitz called this the last triumph of the style of Homeric epic poetry.

P. Friedländer, *Johannes v. Gaza und P. Silent.* (1912); B. L. Gildersleeve, *AJPhil.* 1917; A. Veniero, *Paolo Silenziario* (1916); id. *P. S. Epigrammi* (1963); B. Stumpo, *Rend. Ist. Lomb.* 1924, 241 ff.
G. H.

**PAUSANIAS** (1), son of the Spartan king Cleombrotus I (d. 480 B.C.), and nephew of Leonidas. In 479 he commanded the combined Greek forces at Plataea and was largely responsible for the Greek victory by meeting the Persian onset with a counter-attack. In 478 he captured Byzantium at the head of an allied Greek fleet, but provoked a mutiny by his arrogant behaviour and fell under suspicion of treasonable negotiations with the king of Persia; it was said that he offered to enslave Greece to Persia in return for the hand of a Persian princess. Recalled to Sparta for trial on this charge, he escaped conviction and returned to Byzantium, apparently still with Sparta's approval, since he had a *skytale* or cipher-stick. Expelled by Cimon (*c.* 475) he went to Colonae in the Troad and was believed to be continuing his negotiations with Persia. He was again recalled and tried *c.* 470, only to be once more acquitted. But he now came under further suspicion of fomenting a helot revolt; to escape arrest by the ephors he took sanctuary in a temple, where he was left to starve. At the last moment he was taken out of the sanctuary to expire on unconsecrated ground. Whatever the truth about his earlier plots, it is probable that he finally planned a *coup* against the ephorate.

Hdt. bk. 9; Thuc. 1. 95, 131–4 and Gomme ad locc.; Arist. *Pol.* 1307ᵃ4.                    M. C.

**PAUSANIAS** (2), grandson of (1), Agiad king of Sparta 445–426 and 408–394 B.C. After reigning nominally (as a minor) during the temporary deposition of his father Pleistoanax, he resumed the kingship after his father's death. In 403 he was sent to replace Lysander (q.v.) at the head of the Spartan forces besieging Thrasybulus (q.v.) in the Piraeus. Reversing Lysander's policy, he procured the return of the democrats to Athens and the removal of the remnant of the Thirty Tyrants (q.v. 1). In 395 he was sent to co-operate with Lysander in an invasion of Boeotia, but failed to join hands with him and retired without a battle. For this he was sentenced to death, but fled to exile in Tegea where he wrote a tendentious pamphlet on the Lycurgan constitution (*FGrH* 582).

Xen. *Hell.* 2. 4. 29 ff.; 3. 5. 6. 21–5.         M. C.; W. G. F.

**PAUSANIAS** (3) of Lydia (?) (fl. c. A.D. 150), Greek traveller and geographer, knew Palestine, Egypt, Italy, and Rome, but especially Greece, and wrote Περιήγησις τῆς Ἑλλάδος, 'Description of Greece'. I. Attica, Megara. II. Argolis, etc. III. Laconia. IV. Messenia. V–VI. Elis, Olympia. VII. Achaia. VIII. Arcadia. IX. Boeotia. X. Phocis, Delphi.

Generally, Pausanias sketches the history and then the topography of important cities, and of their surroundings, often including worships and superstitious customs, mythology, and the like. Descriptions of scenery are uncommon, but he dwells on natural phenomena, and in later books we get glimpses of products and social life. He loves all religious and historical remains, as at Olympia and Delphi, the older glories of Athens, and historic battlefields and memorials, but above all, artistic monuments, on which he writes plainly and honestly. His accuracy herein is confirmed by existing remains.

J. G. Frazer, Pausanias' *Description of Greece*, text, translation, and commentary, 6 vols., 1898; W. Gurlitt, *Über P.* (1890); R. Heberdey, *Die Reisen des P.* (1894). Text and transl., W. H. S. Jones (and R. Wycherley), 5 vols. (Loeb); E. Meyer, text, German transl., and notes, 1954; R. Wycherley on Athens in *GRBS* 1959, 21 ff., and 1963, 157 ff.; G. Roux, *Pausanias en Corinthie* (1958); J. Hejnic on Arcadia (Prague, 1961); E. Meyer on Athens (1959). J. Kroymann on the sources for book iv (1943). A. Diller on the MSS., *TAPA* 1957, 169 ff.; O. Regenbogen, *PW* Suppl. viii. 1008 ff.    E. H. W.

**PAUSANIAS** (4) and **AELIUS DIONYSIUS** (q.v. 3) were important Atticists at Rome in the second century A.D. From Aristophanes of Byzantium, Didymus, Pamphilus, and others they compiled Attic Lexica, used by Photius and Eustathius.

FRAGMENTS. H. Erbse, *Untersuchungen zu den attizistischen Lexika* (1950).                    P. B. R. F.

**PAUSIAS** (4th c. B.C.), painter, son and at first pupil of Bryes, then of Pamphilus, a Sicyonian. Restored painting by Polygnotus at Thespiae. According to Pliny was the first to paint ceiling-panels (some, however, survive from the fifth-century Nereid monument). He liked small pictures of boys and flowers (thereby influencing Gnathia vases and later decoration), but also painted a Sacrifice with a frontal view of an ox, painted in black without high light, and Methe (in the Tholos at Epidaurus, about 350 B.C.) drinking from a glass cup through which her face could be seen. Such subjects displayed the encaustic technique (q.v.) of which he was the first

great master. Echoes may be detected in the Pella mosaics and early Gnathia vases.

Overbeck, 1062, 1726, 1760–5; Rumpf, *Malerei u. Zeichn.* 132. T. B. L. W.

**PAUSILYPUS MONS,** named after Vedius Pollio's care-dispelling villa (παύσων λύπην), separates Puteoli from Naples: nowadays *Posilipo*. Two ancient tunnels, one of them badly damaged in World War II, pierce the hill: the *Grotta di Sejano* built c. 37 B.C., and the *Grotta di Posilipo*, near Virgil's reputed tomb, probably built by Claudius.

R. T. Guenther, *Pausilypon* (1913).        E. T. S.

**PAX,** the personification of (political) peace, cf. EIRENE. Scarcely heard of before Augustus, she comes (as Pax Augusta) to represent one of the principal factors which made the imperial government both strong and popular, the maintenance of quiet at home and abroad (cf. Tac. *Ann.* 1. 2. 1: 'cunctos dulcedine otii pellexit'). The most famous, but not the only, monuments of the cult were the Ara Pacis Augustae (q.v.) and the Flavian Templum Pacis, dedicated A.D. 75 (see Platner–Ashby, 386; Nash, *Pict. Dict. Rome* i. 439 ff.; *see also* FORUM PACIS).

Wissowa, *RK* 334 f.                    H. J. R.

**PECULIUM** was property—money, goods, land, slaves (*vicarii*), or claims—assigned for use, management, and, within limits, disposal, by someone who in law lacked the right of property, i.e. either a *filius familias* (*see* PATRIA POTESTAS) or a slave. This device became increasingly important in Roman history (and a comparable one existed in Greek cities), in commercial, financial, and industrial activity. In law, a *peculium* was a purely voluntary grant by the *pater* or master, which involved him in legal responsibility to third parties up to the amount of the *peculium*, but which he was also free to withdraw at any time. In practice, however, the possessor normally had a free hand, and, if a slave, he could expect eventually to buy his freedom with the profits (Plaut. *Stich.* 751) or even to transmit it by a quasi-testament (Pliny, *Ep.* 8. 16). From Augustus on, by law anything a soldier acquired on military service was automatically his *peculium* (the so-called *peculium castrense*).

G. Micolier, *Pécule et capacité patrimoniale* (1932); and the bibliography under SLAVERY.                    M. I. F.

**PEDIUS** (1, *PW* 1), QUINTUS, perhaps of Campanian origin, son of an *eques* and of Julia, Caesar's elder sister (hardly her grandson as Suet. *Jul.* 83. 2 says), served as Caesar's *legatus* in Gaul (58–56 B.C. ?) and supported him in 49. Praetor in 48, he suppressed the rising of Milo (q.v.). In 46 he and Q. Fabius Maximus commanded Caesar's forces in Spain; in 45 they took part in the campaign of Munda and were allowed to triumph. In 44 Pedius inherited one eighth of Caesar's estate but was induced by Octavian to place it at his disposal. In 43 he became consul with him (19 Aug.), carried a law providing for the trial of Caesar's murderers, and was left in charge of the city during Octavian's negotiations with Antony and Lepidus at Bononia. He died of exhaustion after trying to allay the panic caused by the news of the impending proscriptions (Nov.). He married a Valeria Messallina and left a son Quintus who was quaestor in 41.

Syme, *Rom. Rev.*, see index; T. P. Wiseman, *CQ* 1964, 129. G. W. R.; T. J. C.

**PEDIUS** (2, *PW* 3), SEXTUS, a Roman jurist who lived perhaps in the middle of the second century A.D. He wrote a commentary on the praetorian and aedilician Edict, which is often quoted by Paulus (q.v. 1) and Ulpian (q.v. 1), but which is not represented in the *Digest* by any direct excerpt. He was an original thinker who frequently asserted his own doctrines. He wrote also a dissertation *De stipulationibus.* A. B.; B. N.

**PEGASUS** (1), in mythology, winged horse who carries the thunderbolt of Zeus (Eur. fr. 312). The dying Medusa gave birth to him (Hes. *Theog.* 280). When Pegasus was drinking at the fountain Pirene he was caught and tamed by the hero Bellerophontes, with the aid of Athena Chalinitis or of Poseidon (Paus. 2. 4. 1). He helped Bellerophon to fight the Chimaera, the Amazons, and the Solymi (Hes. *Th.* 325, Pind. *Ol.* 13. 86), but when Bellerophon attempted to fly to heaven Pegasus threw him. In another story Bellerophon flung Anteia or Stheneboea from Pegasus (Eur. *Stheneboea*). Pegasus was said to have stamped many famous sources out of the earth with his hoof.

The ending -*ασος* shows that Pegasus is of pre-Greek origin and his legend probably goes back to pre-Greek inhabitants of Asia Minor. Pegasus became early a favourite of Greek artists and poets; proto-Corinthian vases show him in action against the Chimaera (H. Payne, *Necrocorinthia* (1931), 133, cf. pl. 4, 1) and his birth is represented in the early archaic pediment of Corcyra. He also appears on early coins of Corinth, the city with which he is most closely connected by legends (E. Will, *Revue Numismatique* 1952, 239). Pegasus has no connexion with poets in ancient sources beyond the fact that he created Hippocrene (Paus. 9. 31. 3). In Roman times Pegasus becomes a symbol of immortality.

L. Malten, *JDAI* 1925, 138 ff.; J. Aymard, *Mélanges École franç. Rome* 1935, 143 ff.; F. Cumont, *Études syriennes* (1917), 91 ff.; M. Launy, *Mon. Piot* (1935), 32, 47. T. Gericke, *Ath. Mitt.* 1956, 193; B. Shefton, *BCH* 1958, 27; H. Schnur, *Gymnasium* 1963, 573. G. M. A. H.

**PEGASUS** (2, *PW* 4), a Roman jurist, was *consul suffectus* (*c.* A.D. 73) and *praefectus urbi* probably under Domitian; successor of Proculus as head of the Proculian School. He was considered very erudite ('liber, non homo') and was cited by later jurists, but the title of none of his works is known. Whether he is the author of the *senatus consulta* mentioned by Gaius 1. 31 and 2. 254 f. (the latter being called *SC Pegasianum*) is unknown.

Syme, *Tacitus*, 761, 805. A. B.; B. N.

**PEISANDER** (Πείσανδρος) (1) of Cameirus in Rhodes (7th or 6th c. B.C.), epic poet, author of a *Heraclea*, perhaps the most important poem so named; the first to represent Heracles with a club; said to have plagiarized the *Heraclea* from Pisinus; other poems attributed to him were spurious (*Suda*). See QUINTUS (2) SMYRNAEUS.

*EGF* 248–53. W. F. J. K.

**PEISANDER** (2), Athenian politician, *floruit* between 430 and 411 B.C. Often attacked in comedy for corruption and cowardice, and ridiculed for extreme fatness. As a radical democrat he took a principal part in the investigation into the mutilation of the Hermae (*see* HERMS) in 415, but in 412 he revealed himself as an oligarch and showed still more energy in supporting the revolution of 411: the motion in the *ekklesia* which set up the new *boule* of the Four Hundred (q.v.) was proposed by him. On the overthrow of the oligarchs he fled to the Spartans and was condemned for treason in his absence. A. W. G.; A. A.

**PEISANDER** (3) of Laranda (early 3rd c. A.D.), epic poet, author of a long Greek poem on world history under the title Ἡρωικαὶ θεογαμίαι.

**PEITHO** (Πειθώ), persuasion personified, Lat. *Suada*. Although, in the great majority of cases where she is mentioned, she is no more than a poetical or rhetorical figure, she has a slight hold on cult and mythology. Peitho is a cult-title of Aphrodite in a few places (Farnell, *Cults* ii. 664; Fischer, *Nereiden und Okeaninen*, Diss. Halle 1934, 31); it is a curious fact that she is daughter of Ocean in Hesiod, *Theog.* 349 (attempted explanation, Fischer, 32). She is a marriage-goddess in the opinion of the theologians cited by Plut. *Quaest. Rom.* 2. As an attendant on Aphrodite she appears constantly in art and literature; see Weizsäcker in Roscher's *Lexikon*, s.v. H. J. R.

**PELAGIUS**, d. after A.D. 419, either British or Irish, came to Rome as a monk *c.* 400, wrote a commentary on thirteen Pauline epistles and an exhortation to the patrician girl Demetrias which are the earliest extant British literature, and protested against Augustine's prayer *Da quod iubes* (*Conf.* 10. 40) as undermining free will and moral effort. Alaric's invasion brought Pelagius as a refugee to Africa, then to Palestine where he found friends. Against Augustine's and Jerome's overwhelming polemic his cause was elaborated by Julian of Aeclanum, who attacked original sin as Manichee pessimism, and by some seventy extant tracts by anonymous Pelagians. The best of these tracts (attributed without sufficient reason to Pelagius himself by Plinval) are a notable source for social history in a disturbed age.

Pauline commentary, ed. princeps by A. Souter (1922–31); *Ep. ad Demetriadem*, Migne, *PL* xxx. 15 ff. = xxxiii. 1099 ff. G. de Plinval, *Pélage* (1943); J. Ferguson, *Pelagius* (1956); J. Morris, *JTS* 1965, 26 ff.; B. Altaner, *Patrology* (1960), 439; R. F. Evans, *Pelagius* (1968). H. C.

**PELASGIANS** (Πέλασγοι = ? Πελαγ-σ-κοι, Seapeople?), a tribe mentioned by Homer (*Il.* 2. 840; 17. 301) as Trojan allies, 'from Larisa, afar' (apparently in Thrace). In Greece, Achilles' domain includes 'Pelasgian Argos' (*Il.* 2. 684), perhaps named after former inhabitants, and Achilles worships 'Pelasgian Zeus' of Dodona (16. 233). In *Od.* 19. 177 Pelasgi are among the motley population of Crete. In historic times the district round Thessalian Larisa was still called Pelasgiotis. Herodotus (1. 57) records surviving Pelasgian villages east of Cyzicus, and 'beyond the Tyrsenians' at Creston in Chalcidice; they preserved a common non-Greek language.

The Pelasgi seem to have been primarily a North-Aegean people, uprooted (to judge from their scattered distribution) by Bronze Age migrations. The Greeks, however, came to use their name for 'aboriginal' Aegean populations generally (*see* PELASGUS); Herodotus (1. 57) thus uses it, in contrast to 'Hellenic', used of the northern, immigrant elements.

J. L. Myres, *JHS* 1907. A. R. B.

**PELASGUS**, eponym of the Pelasgi (*see* PELASGIANS), the pre-Hellenic inhabitants of Greece. Hence the name is given to mythical ancient princes of various districts whose inhabitants claimed to be autochthonous, or at least of very long residence: Arcadia (Asius in Paus. 8. 1. 4; he was son of Earth); Argos (Aesch. *Supp.* 251; Hyg. *Fab.* 145. 2; contemporary with the rape of Persephone, Paus. 1. 14. 2); Thessaly (schol. *Il.* 2. 681; grandson of Thessalos, eponym of Thessaly). Generally speaking, he is either Peloponnesian (and if so, either Arcadian or Argive), or else Thessalian. H. J. R.

**PELEUS** (Πηλεύς), in mythology, son of Aeacus (q.v.), and therefore an Aeginetan; but as his name seems to mean 'man of Pelion' and his chief adventures are in that neighbourhood, it is highly likely that there has been an early conflation of two genealogies (Achilles is already an Aeacid in Homer), for some reason quite unknown. His transference from one district to the other is explained by the story that he and Telamon killed their half-brother Phocus (Apollod. 3. 160), whereat their father banished them both. Peleus then went to Phthia, was purified by Eurytion, and married his daughter Antigone; but at the Calydonian boar-hunt he accidentally killed Eurytion and was again exiled. This time he reached Iolcus, where Acastus son of Pelias purified him, and he took part in Pelias' funeral games. But Astydameia, Acastus' wife, fell in love with him. As he was unwilling, she sent word to Antigone that Peleus was to marry Sterope, Acastus' daughter, whereat Antigone hanged herself; Astydameia then lied to Acastus much as Phaedra did to Theseus (*see* HIPPOLYTUS 1). Acastus thereupon took him out hunting on Pelion, hid his sword as he slept (for the sword cf. Ar. *Nub.* 1063, and schol. there, who says Hephaestus made it and the gods brought it to Peleus when he was left defenceless), and left him to be attacked by the Centaurs; but Chiron brought him the sword again, he escaped, and took vengeance upon Astydameia, capturing Iolcus and cutting her to pieces (Apollod. 173, who says he led his army between the pieces, a ritual of purification, cf. Livy 40. 6. 1; Plut. *Quaest. Rom.* 290 d). Finally, for his virtue, he was given Thetis (q.v.) to wife; from the Chest of Cypselus on (Paus. 5. 18. 5) he had to win her by wrestling with her, while she took all kinds of shapes (Apollod. 170). She left him because he interfered when she tried to make Achilles immortal by burning his mortality away in a fire (ibid. 171, cf. Lycophron, 178–9). Finally he was reunited to her and made immortal (Eur. *Andr.* 1253 ff.).

His wrestling-match with Atalanta at the funeral games of Pelias; his wrestling with Thetis to win her; his wedding to her; and his bringing the infant Achilles to Chiron, are favourite subjects in sixth- and fifth-century art (the last already in the mid seventh century). He also appears in pictures of the Calydonian boar-hunt (Brommer, *Vasenlisten*², 240 ff.).                H. J. R.; C. M. R.

**PELION** (τὸ Πήλιον ὄρος), a mountain of over 5,300 feet in Thessalian Magnesia. It was the reputed home of the centaur Chiron (*see* CENTAURS). The mountain system of Pelion with that of Ossa cut off the plain of Pelasgiotis from the Aegean. On the east the steeply rising coast was harbourless, but beneath its south-western slopes, which were fertile and enjoyed a mild climate, it sheltered good harbours on the Bay of Volo.                H. D. W.

**PELLA**, capital of Macedonia c. 400–167 B.C., situated on a gentle slope beside the lake of the river Lydias, which was navigable from Pella to the sea (Livy 44. 46; Strabo 7. fr. 20), and at the crossroads where the route down the Axius valley meets the Via Egnatia. Known to Herodotus (7. 123) and Thucydides (2. 100. 4), it became the capital of Archelaus and the largest Macedonian city (Xen. *Hell.* 5. 2. 13), until replaced in importance by Thessalonica in 146 B.C. Pella was later a Roman colony.

A summary of the excavation reports is given in Ἀρχ. Δελτ. 1960, 1. 72 ff. and *Balkan Studies* 1960, 113 ff.                N. G. L. H.

**PELOPIDAS** was born about 410 B.C. of a distinguished Theban family. He must have attached himself prominently to the democratic party of Ismenias before the seizure of the Theban citadel by the Spartans (382), when he took refuge in Athens. He led the *coup d'état* by which the oligarchy was overthrown and the citadel recovered (winter 379/8), and became notable at once as a statesman and general. In 378 he was a Boeotarch, and in the war with Sparta won great fame by his leadership of the Sacred Band (q.v.), especially at Tegyra (375) and Leuctra (371). He accompanied Epaminondas on his first invasion of the Peloponnese (winter 370/69). But after that he turned his attention to Thebes' northern enemies, Alexander of Pherae and Macedon. On his

second expedition (368) he was made prisoner by Alexander, but was rescued by Epaminondas. On an embassy to the Great King he persuaded him to withdraw his diplomatic support from Sparta (367). He defeated Alexander of Pherae at Cynoscephalae, but died in action (364).

Pelopidas' energy and leadership were of great service in the advancement of Thebes. He showed less originality than Epaminondas, but equal capacity.

Nepos' and Plutarch's *Lives*; G. M. Bersanetti, *Athenaeum* 1949, 43 ff.                H. W. P.

**PELOPONNESIAN LEAGUE,** the earliest known, and likewise the most long-lived and influential Greek *symmachia* (q.v.). The name is modern, the usual Greek term being 'the Lacedaemonians and their allies'. In the sixth century B.C. Sparta negotiated treaties of alliance with Peloponnesian States. Some hold that a period of separate treaties with individual States was followed shortly before 500 by the organization of the League as a permanent alliance; others date the organization earlier. Sparta held the command in war and summoned and presided over the assembly of allies. Only after the majority of this body, in which each allied State cast one vote, had ratified a proposal to go to war could Sparta demand the support of all members. She herself probably cast no vote in the Assembly but exercised great influence over its decisions by her power to refuse to call a meeting except to consider proposals that had her own approval. When no League war was in progress, the members were free to carry on separate wars even with other members. Thus the League could not support every allied State in war; even to secure defence against aggression from the League as such it was necessary to convince first Sparta and next the Assembly. Athens, at the time of her surrender in 404, and later other allies, were forced to accept treaties promising complete obedience on questions of peace and war. In other ways, too, a tendency to transform the League into an empire was shown. This process was not completed before the collapse of the power of Sparta and the dissolution of the League in 366 B.C.

ANCIENT SOURCES. Herodotus, Thucydides (especially bk. 1); Xen. *Hell.*

FOR MODERN LITERATURE *see under* SYMMACHIA. The origin and constitution of the League are discussed by Larsen in *CPhil.* 1932, 1933, and 1934. An interpretation differing on many points is given by U. Kahrstedt, *Griechisches Staatsrecht* (1922). In favour of an early date for the origin of the League are H. Bengtson, *Griechische Geschichte*² (1960), 132, and L. Moretti, *Ricerche sulle leghe greche* (1962), ch. i.                J. A. O. L.

**PELOPONNESIAN WAR** (431–404 B.C.). The cause of the war, according to Thucydides, was that the Athenian Empire had destroyed the autonomy of some Greek States and threatened many more. There was a general fear of Athens, particularly on the part of Corinth which was hemmed in on both east and west, and goodwill towards her enemies who were to be the 'liberators of Greece'. Nothing, however, in Thucydides' opinion, would have come of this if Sparta had not feared for her own position. Thucydides, well aware of the economic factor in the *conduct* of the war, does not consider it as a cause. Athens was morally the aggressor, but her enemies began the war. Military victory was therefore a necessity for the Peloponnesians; a draw meant victory for Athens.

**2.** The main lines of strategy were simple. A superior hoplite force was at that time irresistible on land; it could master an enemy's territory, depriving him of supplies, and if necessary besiege the city. But in the absence of effective siege-engines a besieged city could normally be reduced by famine only, and Athens had countered this risk by her Long Walls (q.v.), which provided a refuge space for her country population, and secured her connexion with the sea. On land she could not muster a force half as strong as her enemies (among whom the

Spartans and Boeotians were the finest soldiers in Greece); but she was overwhelmingly strong at sea, in numbers, skill, and morale. She could thus temporarily sacrifice her land without sacrificing her people, and she could neither be taken by assault nor reduced by starvation. At the same time she could harry her enemies' trade (the Peloponnese depending partly on imported food, though not at all to the same extent as Athens) and their coasts. Pericles therefore persuaded his countrymen to transfer themselves and all their movable goods within their walls. The one advantage the Peloponnesians had at sea was that they could concentrate their forces to secure a local superiority; but this was neutralized by their lack of skill and confidence, and by their financial weakness. In available wealth, indispensable for the fleet and for overseas supplies, Athens had a decided advantage.

3. In autumn 433 a quarrel between Corinth and her colony Corcyra gave Athens the opportunity to secure in Corcyra an ally with a considerable fleet and Athenian intervention robbed Corinth of the fruits of a naval victory over Corcyra. In Naupactus she already possessed an important naval base in the Corinthian Gulf. Next year Potidaea revolted from Athens, and Corinth unofficially sent help. In the autumn the Peloponnesian League voted for war. In May 431 war was declared and the Peloponnesians invaded Attica, ravaged the deserted land for about a month, and retired. The first year went according to Pericles' plan: Athens was undamaged and the issue depended on Athenian patience and morale; and so it continued for six years. In 430 a devastating pestilence broke out among the crowded people within the walls (where no proper provision had been made for their housing), and Athens lost more than a quarter of her population, a blow from which she never fully recovered; and Pericles died (429), the one man with enough influence to carry out a consistent policy. But Potidaea was forced to capitulate, Phormion gained two brilliant naval victories over superior forces off Naupactus (429), a revolt in Lesbos was crushed, the Peloponnesian fleet failing to help the island (428–427), and Demosthenes gained a decisive victory over the Peloponnesians in Amphilochia (426). In 425 Pylos on the west coast of Messenia was captured, which gave Athens not only a permanent post in the enemy's country in a vulnerable spot—for helots could be encouraged to revolt—but a number of Spartan prisoners. Sparta was being hemmed in; fearful for her prisoners and of leaving her territory now, she gave up the annual invasions of Attica and sued for peace. Pericles' strategy had triumphed.

4. But the Athenians, at the instance of Cleon, a demagogue who had made capital out of the victory of Pylos, refused the peace. In 424 a brilliant Spartan, Brasidas, first saved Megara from capture by Athens, then slipped through Thessaly, and with support from Perdiccas II of Macedon won over several Athenian dependencies in the Thraceward region, including the important Amphipolis. At the same time an ambitious attempt by Athens to overthrow Boeotia was decisively defeated at Delium. A year's truce was concluded (423); in the autumn of 422 Cleon took a force to Thrace, but after some successes was decisively defeated at Amphipolis; both he and Brasidas fell. Brasidas had been unable to extend his successes; and peace was now made between Sparta and Athens, practically on the basis of the *status quo ante bellum*. This 'Peace of Nicias' was in effect a victory for Athens, the more so because her enemies were divided, Corinth and Boeotia refusing to sign the peace; the united forces of the rest of Greece had been unable seriously to weaken the Athenian Empire.

5. But again the ambition of a politician wrecked the peace and the Assembly failed to follow a consistent or moderate policy. Alcibiades intrigued against Sparta in the Peloponnese, and a coalition was formed against her—Argos, Elis, Mantinea, and Athens; but Athens sent half-hearted help. Sparta recovered herself at Mantinea (418). Athens suddenly attacked and destroyed the unoffending Melos (416), because it was an island not subject to her. She then launched the grandiose expedition to Sicily (415–413), championed by Alcibiades and opposed by Nicias. The finest force that ever left Greek shores went to Sicily; but Alcibiades was soon recalled to answer charges to which his lawless private life had exposed him, and he promptly went over to the enemy; and the irresolute Nicias allowed initial successes to be turned into defeat. Large reinforcements under Demosthenes were sent; but finally the whole force was utterly destroyed (Oct. 413).

6. Meanwhile Sparta had renewed the war in Greece and occupied Decelea in Attica as a permanent base (spring 413). Athens had lost almost all her fleet, and though she began to rebuild she no longer had trained crews. Persia provided money for a Peloponnesian fleet, which crossed the Aegean, and Athens' subject States began to revolt; Athenian food-supplies from the Bosporus and from Egypt were endangered. Further, there was political strife in Athens, ending in the revolution of the Four Hundred and the loss of Euboea (411). But the new fleet, led by Alcibiades, who had been recalled, gained several victories in the Hellespont, secured the food-supply, and recovered many revolted allies (411–408). However, Lysander with Persian help recreated the Peloponnesian fleet. Almost exhausted, Athens won the costly battle of Arginusae (406). But once more politics destroyed what the fleet had saved: a new peace offer was rejected and the victorious generals were tried and executed for failure to rescue the crews of waterlogged ships. In 405 the last Athenian fleet was surprised and destroyed at Aegospotami in the Hellespont. Besieged by sea and land, Athens capitulated in April 404.

7. The Peloponnesian War had been, as Thucydides says, the greatest 'disturbance' in Greek history. Methods of warfare, never gentle in Greece towards prisoners and non-combatants, became more cruel; the only hopeful attempt at Greek unity was defeated; and the old autonomy was not won back, but an incompetent imperialism substituted for an enlightened one. Greece hardly recovered from the war.

ANCIENT SOURCES. For the first twenty years Thucydides is our authority; for the last seven the less adequate Xenophon (*Hellenica*, 1–2. 2). Diodorus' history (12. 30–13. 107; probably only an epitome of Ephorus) covers the whole war, but contains little of value. Of the subsidiary sources, the 'Old Oligarch' (Ps.-Xen. *Constitution of Athens*) gives a right-wing view of the democracy at the beginning of the war, and Aristophanes gives incomparable pictures of Athens in wartime. Several speeches of Antiphon, Andocides, and Lysias throw light on contemporary feeling. Plutarch's *Lives* of Pericles, Nicias, Alcibiades, and Lysander add much biographical detail. For inscriptions see *IG* i (ed. minor, 1924); M. N. Tod, *Greek Historical Inscriptions*[2] (1946), containing a valuable selection of indispensable official documents.
MODERN WORKS. Besides the general histories of Greece, see G. B. Grundy, *Thucydides and the History of his Age*[2] (1948). See also the separate articles on most of the individuals mentioned above.
A. W. G.; N. G. L. H.

**PELOPONNESUS**, 'Isle of Pelops', the large peninsula of south Greece, connected with the mainland only by the Isthmus of Corinth. The name Peloponnesus, mentioned for the first time in the Cypria (fr. xi Allen) and the Homeric Hymn to Apollo, proves that the whole territory was considered an island, a separate part of Greece. Ancient geographers knew about its peculiar shape, comparing it to the leaf of a plane-tree; the medieval name Morea is said to have been taken from the mulberry. It was described, not inappropriately, by Strabo (8. 334), as ἀκρόπολις τῆς συμπάσης Ἑλλάδος.

The area of Peloponnese, including the islands except Aegina and Cythera, amounts to about 8,430 sq. miles (cf. Sicily 9,930, Cyprus 3,580 sq. miles). The number of the population can scarcely be estimated. The civic population may have been about 500,000 or 600,000 in 400 B.C. (1928: 1,053,300).

Although virtually an island, and indented by deep gulfs, Peloponnese had but little communication with the sea. Harbours are relatively few, and except in Argolis and Elis have little or no hinterland. Their lack no doubt made naval operations against the coasts more difficult: hence the importance of Halieis for Athens and Argos when these cities were allied in the mid fifth century (see L. H. Jeffery, *BSA* 1966, 41 ff.) and of Methone (*Modon*) and Pylos (*Navarino*). An 'isthmus' route from the Gulf of Argos to Corinth may account for the importance of Tiryns and Mycenae in Bronze Age Greece. Arcadia, the central, nearly inaccessible district, did not touch the sea at all; the surrounding divisions (Laconia, Messenia, Elis, Achaea, Isthmus, Argolis, qq.v.) were separated from one another by mountains, which also were a great hindrance to intercourse by land.

The parallel mountain chains of central Peloponnesus running to south-south-east once formed part of the huge arc stretching from Albania through middle Greece and Crete to Asia Minor. This original system was destroyed by the subsidence which created the large gulfs and most of the plains in the interior. In the Isthmian province and Argolis the predominant direction of the ranges is west to east, as in the eastern parts of middle Greece. Seen across the Gulf of Corinth from Delphi the great mountains of the Peloponnese, Erymanthus, Panachaïcum, Chelmos, and Cyllene (*Ziria*) seem to present an impenetrable barrier. The western and southern divisions of Peloponnese are characterized by larger plains, forming a kind of counterweight to the smaller closely enclosed plains, as around Tripolis, Mantinea, and Arcadian Orchomenus, Pheneus, and Stymphalus. And as the mountain ranges seem to radiate from Arcadia, the Peloponnese, in spite of its heterogeneous geological formation, gives the impression of a peculiar system, with a centre surrounded by other districts.

There are plains fit for agriculture presenting a certain flourishing aspect even now, and probably far greater in ancient times; by far the largest part of Peloponnese, however, is mountainous, uncultivable, and poor. About 50 per cent of the surface, consisting of chalk and limestone, provides only pasture for sheep and goats, the oak-woods also for swine. Flora and climate depend, of course, upon the geographical and geological conditions, which vary greatly. Arcadia and the east are almost entirely continental, while the western parts are subject to maritime influences.

MOST IMPORTANT SOURCES. Strabo 8. 335–89; Paus. bks. 2–8. E. Curtius, *Peloponnesos* (1851); A. Philippson, *Der Pelonnopes* (1892) (with good maps); P–K, *GL* III. 1. 9 ff. (general); E. Meyer, *Peloponnesische Wanderungen* (1939); *Neue Peloponnesische Wanderungen* (1957). E. Meyer, *PW*, s.v. Area and population: J. Beloch, *Bevölkerung der griech.-röm. Welt* (1886), 109 ff. On the exploration of the Mycenaean Peloponnese, see *BSA* 1957, 231 (south-west), 1960, 67 (Laconia), and W. A. McDonald, 'Overland Communications in Greece during L.H. III', *Mycenaean Studies* (U.S.A. 1964), 217. See also under sites and regions.                    V. E.; R. J. H.

**PELOPS** (Πέλοψ), in mythology, son of Tantalus (q.v.). His chief adventures are: (1) In childhood he was killed and cooked by his father, who served his flesh to the gods to see if they could tell that it was not that of a beast. Demeter inadvertently ate part of his shoulder; the other gods brought him to life again, replacing the lost part by ivory. See especially Pindar, *Ol.* 1. 46 ff. (controverts ordinary account); schol. ibid. 40; Apollod. *Epit.* 2. 3 ff. (2) By favour of his lover Poseidon he became possessed of wonderful horses and great skill in driving.

On reaching manhood he wooed Hippodameia daughter of Oenomaus of Pisa. This king had an incestuous love for his daughter, or had been warned that her husband would kill him (Apollod. ibid. 4). He therefore let it be known that anyone who wished might carry her off, on condition that he might pursue, and spear the suitor if he caught him. Thirteen suitors had already perished when Pelops appeared. He bribed Myrtilus, Oenomaus' charioteer, to take out the linchpins of his master's chariot (the details vary in different authors; see Roscher's *Lexikon*, arts. 'Myrtilos', 'Oinomaos'). Oenomaus was thus thrown and killed and Pelops carried off his bride. But, either because he was ashamed to owe his victory to Myrtilus (Hyg. *Fab.* 84. 5), or because Myrtilus loved Hippodameia and Pelops was jealous (Apollod. ibid. 8), he cast him into the sea which was afterwards called Myrtoan. Myrtilus, or Oenomaus, cursed Pelops in dying, and the curse was efficacious, the more so as they were both sons of gods, Hermes and Ares respectively; see, for the later fortunes of his family, ATREUS, AGAMEMNON. However, for the time being Pelops prospered greatly and had six sons by his wife (various lists in schol. Pind. ibid. 144). But various stories of his offspring were current, see Bloch in Roscher iii, 1872. He was supposed (falsely, for the 'barrow' contained no burial) to be buried at Olympia, where he was worshipped as a hero.

The preparations for the chariot-race are the subject of the East pediment of the Temple of Zeus at Olympia, and these and the race itself are found occasionally in fifth- and fourth-century vase-painting (Brommer, *Vasenlisten*[2], 369 f.).          H. J. R.; C. M. R.

**PELTASTS** (πελτασταί) were Greek soldiers, named from their small round shield (πέλτη). Originally they had no body-armour and their chief weapons were light throwing-spears (ἀκόντια). They are first recorded as derived from Thrace, and were imported into Greece in the later fifth century B.C. to act as skirmishers. Their style of equipment was adopted in Greek armies, and achieved numerous successes, especially under Iphicrates (q.v.) and Chabrias. To Iphicrates are attributed the changes whereby the length of their spears was increased by a half, and the size of their swords almost doubled. The object of these alterations was to enable the peltasts to act as regular troops and not mere skirmishers. After the rise of the Macedonian armies apparently they fell into disuse.

Arist. fr. 498 (Rose), and Diod. 15. 44 (on their equipment). O. Lippelt, *Die griechischen Leichtbewaffneten bis auf Alex. d. Gr.* (1910); J. Kromayer and G. Veith, *Heerwesen und Kriegführung* (1928), 88 ff.; H. W. Parke, *Greek Mercenary Soldiers* (1933), 17 ff. and 79 ff.; A. N. Snodgrass, *Arms and Armour of the Greeks* (1967), 78 f.          H. W. P.

**PELUSIUM**, a city at the eastern mouth of the Nile. Renowned for its flax, it was especially important as a frontier fortress towards Palestine. Near it Cambyses defeated the Egyptians (525 B.C.). In 374 Pharnabazus and Iphicrates were balked here by floods; but the position was carried in 343 by Artaxerxes III, in 333 by Alexander, in 169 by Antiochus IV, in 55 by Gabinius and M. Antonius, and in 30 by Octavian (against Antonius). Under the Roman Empire it was a station on a route to the Red Sea.          E. H. W.

**PENATES, DI**, 'the dwellers in the store-cupboard (*penus*)', cf. *Aquinas, Arpinas*. These guardian *numina* of the family larder were worshipped in close conjunction with Vesta (q.v.), also with the Lares (q.v.), properly the Lar Familiaris. It was the chief private cult of every Roman household, especially in early times. It would seem, however, that the royal *di penates*, like the royal Vesta, were reckoned of especial importance to the community; this at least is the most reasonable explanation of the cult of the *Penates Publici*. This was attached to Vesta's temple (Tac. *Ann.* 15. 41. 1), but there was also a separate shrine, of unknown but fairly early date, on the Velia (see Platner–Ashby, 388). Speculation was rife as to who these Penates originally were, and it was generally supposed that they were the Dioscuri (q.v.). But, since the latter were commonly identified with the Samothracian gods also, and the Penates were called *di magni*, like the Cabiri (q.v.), it was held, not later than Cassius Hemina (see Servius on *Aen.* 3. 12; Cassius Hemina, fr. 5 Peter), that the Roman, and other Italian, *Penates Publici* owed their origin to Samothrace, having been brought by Aeneas (Klausen, *Aeneas und die Penaten*).

Wissowa, *RK* 161 ff.; Latte, *RR* 89; A. Alföldi, *Early Rome and the Latins* (1966), 258 ff.                                       H. J. R.

**PENELEOS** (Πηνέλεως; also Πηνέλαος, *Etym. Magn.* 670. 50 Sylburg, but reading uncertain; Peneleus, Hyg. *Fab.* 81, cf. Πηνέλεον, read by Aristophanes in *Iliad* 13. 92), son of Hippalcimus or Hippalcus (Diod. Sic. 4. 67. 7; Hyg. *Fab.* 97. 8); one of the Boeotian leaders (*Iliad* 2. 494); killed by Eurypylus (Quint. Smyrn. 7. 104); wooed Helen (Apollod. 3. 130); an Argonaut (ibid. 1. 113).                                       H. J. R.

**PENELOPE** (Πηνελόπη, Epic Πηνελόπεια), in mythology, daughter of Icarius, brother of Tyndareos (qq.v.), and wife of Odysseus (q.v.). In the *Odyssey* she faithfully awaits his return, although pressed to remarry one of her numerous suitors, the local nobles. She puts them off for a while by pretending that she cannot marry until she has finished weaving a shroud for Laertes, Odysseus' father. This she unravels every night, so that the work is never finished, but after three years she is betrayed by one of her maids and compelled to complete it (*Od.* 2. 93 ff.; 19. 137 ff.; 24. 128 ff.). At last, ten years after the fall of Troy and twenty after the departure of her husband, she is at her wits' end and determines to give herself in marriage to whoever can bend Odysseus' bow. This is at Athena's prompting (*Od.* 21. 1) and is used by Odysseus to get hold of the weapon and kill the wooers with it. Later writers add very little, save some particulars concerning her father's adventures and the statement (in the *Telegonia*) that she married Telegonus after Odysseus' death.

There is, however, another story of Penelope so different from that of the epic tradition that it seems possible that we have here to do with a different figure (nymph or minor local goddess?) of the same name. This is that she was the mother of Pan. Tzetzes, who mentions the tale that she and Hermes were his parents, is already of this opinion (schol. Lycophron, 772, cf. Apollod. *Epit.* 7. 38). It of course produced sundry reconciliations and rationalizations, the most notorious, that of Duris of Samos in Tzetzes, ibid., being simply an indecent pun. But possibly the whole legend is no more than an etymological fancy, a connexion of Πάν with Doric or Doricized Πανελόπα.

Penelope receiving gifts from the suitors appears on a mid-fifth-century Attic vase. On another, with Telemachus, she sits at her loom, elbow on knee, head on hand. She is shown in the same pose in contemporary sculpture and the type is adapted for other characters.

J. Schmidt in Roscher's *Lexikon*, s.v. In art, Brommer, *Vasenlisten²*, 308, 328.                                       H. J. R.; C. M. R.

**PENIA** (Πενία), poverty personified, a literary figure, perhaps also popular (see Hdt. 8. 111. 3), and so appearing in various allegorical contexts (pleads her cause against Wealth, Ar. *Plut.* 489 ff.; mates with Abundance to

produce Eros, Pl. *Symp.* 203 b f.; humorously said to guard a poor man's house, *Anth. Pal.* 9. 654), not in cult.
                                       H. J. R.

**PENTADIUS** (3rd c. A.D.) has left elegiac poems in 'echoic' verse on Fortune, Spring, Narcissus, besides several epigrams. Text and translation: Duff, *Minor Lat. Poets.*

**PENTAKOSIOMEDIMNOI** (πεντακοσιομέδιμνοι), i.e. 'five hundred bushel men', at Athens, members of the richest of the four census-classes devised by Solon (q.v.), with an estimated annual income of at least 500 *medimnoi* of corn or the equivalent in other produce or money. Under Solon's constitution the *tamiai* and perhaps also the *archontes*(q.v.) were chosen exclusively from this class, and this was still the case with the *tamiai* in Aristotle's time (*Ath. Pol.* 8. 1).                            A. W. G.; T. J. C.

**PENTAPOLIS** (African). The most fertile part of Cyrenaica and the area of intensive Greek colonization in this part of Africa. The five cities were Apollonia, Cyrene, Ptolemais, Arsinoe (Taucheira), and Berenice. In the fourth century A.D. it formed a separate province called *Libya superior* or *Libya Pentapolis*. Synesius was bishop of Ptolemais.

C. H. Kraeling, *Ptolemais* (U.S.A. 1962).                  B. H. W.

**PENTATHLON,** a contest of five events (ἅλμα, ποδώκειαν, δίσκον, ἄκοντα, πάλην, Simonides, *Lyra Graeca* ii, 182 (Loeb)) requiring all-round athletic ability. By some system of scoring or elimination unknown to us the two best competitors in the running, jumping, throwing the discus, and throwing the javelin were selected for the final event, the wrestling. It was one of the contests at the Olympian Games and at many other festivals. *See* ATHLETICS.                                       R. L. H.

**PENTECONTAETIA,** the 'period of fifty years' between the Persian and Peloponnesian Wars, is treated with some surprising omissions by Thucydides, but not so called, in an excursus of his first book, chs. 89–118. It did not comprise exactly fifty years, being the period from autumn 479 (Sestos) until spring 431 (attack on Plataea). The detailed chronology of the Pentecontaetia is highly controversial.

A. W. Gomme, *A Historical Commentary on Thucydides* i (1945); V. Ehrenberg, *From Solon to Socrates* (1968), 187.                  V. E.

**PENTHESILEA** (Πενθεσίλεια), in mythology, queen of the Amazons who came to the aid of Troy after the death of Hector (q.v.), *Aethiopis*, fr. 1 Allen. According to this poem (see Proclus and cf. Quint. Smyrn. 1. 18 ff.) she was daughter of Ares (cf. AMAZONS) and did valiantly until finally overcome and slain by Achilles. She was buried by the Trojans, and Achilles, by a touch of un-Homeric sentimentality, grieved over her so that Thersites (q.v.) reviled him for being in love with her, whereat Achilles slew him and consequently quarrelled with Diomedes (q.v. 2), his kinsman in this version (Thersites was son of Agrius (*see* OENEUS) and so first-cousin once removed to Diomedes, Quint. Smyrn. 1. 770 ff.). The reason for her being willing to help Priam was that after Theseus married Phaedra, Hippolyte (*see* HIPPOLYTUS 1) roused the Amazons against him and in the ensuing battle was accidentally killed by her own comrade Penthesilea. The latter then obtained purification from her blood-guilt at the hands of Priam (Apollod. *Epit.* 5. 1). This is plainly a secondary addition to the story, and in fact Apollod. ibid. gives two other accounts of Hippolyte's death.

Her death at Achilles' hand is often shown in art from the mid sixth century, and was the subject of one of the panels Panaenus painted round Pheidias' Zeus (Brommer, *Vasenlisten²*, 262; D. von Bothmer, *Amazons in Greek Art* (1957), 4 f., 72, 145 ff.). H. J. R.; C. M. R.

**PENTHEUS** (Πενθεύς), in mythology, son of Agave, daughter of Cadmus (q.v.), and her husband Echion. When Dionysus returned to Thebes from his conquests in the East, Pentheus denied his deity and refused to let him be worshipped. But the supernatural strength of the women who had gone out to worship Dionysus was too much for his soldiers, and he consequently (by advice of a mysterious stranger, the god in disguise or another) went out to spy upon them. He was detected and torn in pieces, his mother, who in her frenzy took him for a beast, leading the rest. It is possible that this goes back to some ritual killing, cf. DIONYSUS. See especially Euripides, *Bacchae* (with Dodds's commentary, 1960), whence Ovid, *Met.* 3. 511 ff., Nonnus, *Dion.* 44–6, chiefly derive.

Pentheus torn by maenads is found from time to time in Attic vase-painting from the late sixth century on (Brommer, *Vasenlisten²*, 343). H. J. R.; C. M. R.

**PERDICCAS** (1) I, the first king of Macedon (Hdt. 8. 139), who probably conquered the Macedonian coast *c.* 640 B.C.

**PERDICCAS** (2) II, king of Macedon *c.* 450–413 B.C. By astute diplomacy Perdiccas survived rebellions in Upper Macedonia, invasion by Sitalces (q.v.), and intervention by Athens and Sparta, and succeeded in uniting Macedonia and diminishing the Athenian control of his coast. In alliance with Athens until she founded Amphipolis in 436, he subsequently promoted the revolt of Potidaea and the Chalcidians, whom he advised to concentrate at Olynthus. The Athenians aided by Derdas, prince of Elimiotis, and by Philip, exiled brother of Perdiccas, captured Therme before they came to terms with Perdiccas in order to invest Potidaea. Perdiccas assisted Potidaea until Sitalces negotiated a treaty for him with Athens, who ceded Therme (431); probably Derdas also submitted to Perdiccas. In 429 the invasion of Sitalces was checked by the Macedonian cavalry, and a marriage-alliance was contracted; in 425 Perdiccas allied with Brasidas to oust Athens and to reduce the Lyncestian prince Arrabaeus, but when the campaign in Lyncus failed, allied with Athens (422). Allying in 417 with Sparta and Argos, he allied again with Athens when attacked in 415, and died *c.* 413.

F. Geyer, *Historische Zeitschrift*, Beiheft 19 (1930). N. G. L. H.

**PERDICCAS** (3) (d. 321 B.C.), son of Orontes a Macedonian noble, accompanied Alexander to Asia as 'taxiarch' commanding a brigade of Macedonian infantry. He was promoted 'Bodyguard' (member of Alexander's personal staff; 330), and thereafter often held independent commands. Craterus' return to Europe and Hephaestion's death (324) made him Alexander's second-in-command, and when Alexander died he became in effect, if not in name, regent of the Empire (323–322), an arrangement which alarmed Antipater and Craterus in Europe, and the insubordinate satraps Antigonus (Phrygia, etc.) and Ptolemy (Egypt). In the ensuing war Perdiccas tried to invade Egypt, but Ptolemy's skilful defence and propaganda incited his Macedonians to mutiny, and they killed him. Able, brave, and loyal, but unpopular because of his arrogance, Perdiccas is the type of a Macedonian nobleman and general who just missed greatness.

Berve, *Alexanderreich*, no. 627; W. W. Tarn, *CAH* vi, ch. 15. G. T. G.

**PERDUELLIO** (from *perduellis* = *hostis*) denoted in early Roman law hostile activity against the State. It should perhaps be distinguished from purely military offences of this kind (*proditio*), but it was probably not clearly defined. It was one of the earliest crimes, mentioned in the XII Tables, with the penalty of death, and in early times was subject to the jurisdiction of *duoviri perduellionis*. In the later Republic it was absorbed in the wider offence of *maiestas* (q.v.).

Besides the textbooks on criminal law (*see* LAW AND PROCEDURE, ROMAN, III), E. Pollack, *Der Majestätsgedank im röm. Recht* (1908); F. Vittinghoff, *Der Staatsfeind in der röm. Kaiserzeit* (1936); C. H. Brecht, *Perduellio* (1938); *Sav. Zeitschr.* 1944, 354. B. N.

**PEREGRINI**, meaning the citizens of any State other than Rome, implied membership of a definite community. Some non-Romans were distinguished from *peregrini*, notably the *Latini* (q.v.). The *socii Italici* remained *peregrini* till 89 B.C., and all provincial peoples enjoying any form of local autonomy were *peregrini* (*see* CIVITAS, DEDITICII). They sometimes enjoyed *conubium* or *commercium*, but could not receive the Roman citizenship unless they surrendered their own sovereignty. In practice, however, the grant of Roman status to an individual *peregrinus* meant, by the end of the Republic, that he was automatically freed from liability to the civic duties of his native *civitas*, while enjoying its amenities; for no Roman could be a citizen of two States. This led to abuses, as Roman citizenship spread abroad, which were rectified by a decree of Augustus affirming the liability of such Roman citizens to their local *munera* (q.v.).

For bibliography *see* SOCII; MUNICIPIUM; CITIZENSHIP, ROMAN. A. N. S.-W.

**PEREGRINUS** (with the nickname *Proteus*) of Parium in Mysia (*c.* A.D. 100–65), Cynic. Our knowledge of him comes almost entirely from Lucian Περὶ τῆς Περεγρίνου τελευτῆς. He was suspected of murdering his father, and to avoid the scandal travelled in Palestine, where he became a Christian. For his activities in this connexion he was imprisoned. On being released he returned to Parium, but soon resumed his travels. He quarrelled with the Christian community, and betook himself to Egypt, where he studied under the Cynic Agathobulus. From there he went to Italy, and then to Greece, as a wandering preacher. His reputation became such that by some he was classed with Epictetus, but Lucian has no high opinion of his character. In 165 he committed suicide by throwing himself on the flames at the Olympic Games. W. D. R.

**PERGAMUM**, a city of Mysia, in the fertile Caicus valley *c.* 15 miles from the sea, must have been inhabited from early times, though we hear nothing of it before 401 B.C. Its true history begins only in the third century B.C., when under the so-called Attalid dynasty it became the capital of a Hellenistic kingdom inferior in importance only to Macedonia, Egypt, and the Seleucid realm. For the political history of this development, *see* PHILETAERUS (2), EUMENES (1) and (2), ATTALUS, ARISTONICUS (1–3).

Although the original Greek population of the city cannot have been large, it possessed the constitution of a Greek city-state even under the Attalids, who assumed, however, wide powers of interference at will. They also ruled directly the native population in the surrounding country under their control, and with the expansion of the kingdom and broadening of their political aims, they became increasingly like the great Hellenistic kings, relying on a Greek bureaucracy and a semi-professional army also predominantly Greek, though less elaborate than the Seleucid and Ptolemaic systems based on permanent military settlements. The expansion of Pergamum was due to a skilful exploitation of its natural wealth, which included silver-mines, but also an annual surplus from agriculture (corn) and stock-breeding, with its dependent industries of woollen textiles and parchment. The wealth of the country can perhaps be judged best from its unhappy fate later as the Roman province of Asia.

The Attalids were not founders of cities on the grandest scale, but they made Pergamum itself one of the greatest and most beautiful of all Greek cities. The public buildings, laid out in terraces on a hill-side and culminating in the palace and fortifications of the acropolis, were a splendid example of Hellenistic town-planning. With her famous school of sculpture, her library second only to that of Alexandria, and her kings who were philosophers at least in their spare time, Pergamum became a leader of the Greek world in culture even more than in politics and commerce.

ANCIENT SOURCES. Inscriptions: *Altertümer von Pergamon* viii (M. Fränkel, 1890–5); see also *CAH* ix, bibliography to ch. 19; *Abh. Berliner Akademie*, 1932. For the period 220–168 B.C. Polybius and Livy (bks. 30 ff., using Polybius) are the most important.
MODERN LITERATURE. Hellenistic period: G. Cardinali, *Il regno di Pergamo* (1906); Rostovtzeff, *Hellenistic World*; id. *CAH*, ibid.; Hansen, *Attalids*; Ernst Meyer, *Die Grenzen der hellenistischen Staaten in Kleinasien* (1925), ch. 9; Bengtson, *Strategie* ii. 195 ff.; Magie, *Rom. Rule Asia Min.* i, esp. chs. 1–2 and ii. 725 ff.; L. Robert, *Villes d' Asie mineure²* (1962). Roman period: Jones, *Cities E. Rom. Prov.* 58 ff., 82 ff.                    G. T. G.

**PERGE** (Πέργη), city of Pamphylia on the river Cestrus, founded according to tradition by the 'mixed multitude' of Greeks who wandered across Asia Minor after the Trojan War, led by Calchas, Mopsus, and Amphilochus. Statues of Calchas and Mopsus, qualified by their inscriptions as 'founders', stood with others at the main gate of the city in Roman times. The Pergaeans welcomed Alexander and served him as guides. Later, under the Seleucids, the lower town was fortified with the walls which still stand; the original settlement was on the hill above. The city was famous for the Pergaean Artemis, her chief deity, called Vanassa Preiia in the local dialect; the cult-statue was shown on the coins in the form of a baetyl, originally no doubt a meteoritic stone. The temple, on a height outside the city, has not been found. Perge was visited by St. Paul, and was prosperous under the Empire; in the early second century much fine building was done, largely by the generosity of a certain Plancia Magna. Distinguished Pergaeans were the mathematician Apollonius, a successor of Euclid, and the philosopher Varus the Stork in the second century A.D. The ruins at Aksu have been partially excavated; they include a theatre, a stadium, and a handsome city-gateway. The Hellenistic walls are also well preserved.

Lanckoronsky, *Pamphylien* (1890).                    G. E. B.

**PERIANDER** (Περίανδρος), tyrant of Corinth c. 625–585 B.C., and son of Cypselus (q.v.). He recovered Corcyra, founded Apollonia, which together with Epidamnus exported the goods of southern Illyria, and Potidaea on the western prong of Chalcidice, which exported the goods of Macedonia. He deposed his father-in-law Procles of Epidaurus and seized his dominions; propitiated Delphi and Olympia, had dealings with Thrasybulus of Miletus and Alyattes of Lydia; and arbitrated between Athens and Mytilene in their dispute for Sigeum. Contacts on his part with Egypt are indicated by Egyptian objects found at Perachora and by the Egyptian name of his nephew Psammetichus. Arion the dithyrambic poet came to his court from Lesbos and sailed from it in a Corinthian ship to tour Italy and Sicily. The scene of Plutarch's *Septem Sapientum Convivium* is Periander's court. Arts and crafts, industry and commerce flourished exceedingly under him (witness the ruins of the Apollo temple and the Peirene fountain at Corinth and the Gorgon pediment at Corcyra), and he

laid the *diolkos* or roadway for transporting ships across the Isthmus. The famous Chest of Cypselus at Olympia was probably a dedication of Periander. The potteries increased their output. Periander is said to have built triremes and plied both seas, to have forbidden idleness and luxury, and to have continually found employment for his subjects. His vivid and passionate character left a deep impression, of which we have a picture in Herodotus' dramatic tale of his relations with his son Lycophron. His sons all predeceased him and he was succeeded by his nephew Psammetichus (Cypselus II), whose murder shortly after ended the seventy-three years of the tyranny of the house of Cypselus.

E. Will, *Korinthiaka* (1955); A. Andrewes, *The Greek Tyrants* (1956); *Ergon* 1960, 117 ff. (*diolkos*). See also CYPSELUS *and* CORINTH.
P. N. U.; N. G. L. H.

**PERICLES** (*c.* 495–429 B.C.), Athenian statesman, was the son of Xanthippus (q.v. 1) and of Agariste, niece of Cleisthenes (q.v. 1) and granddaughter of Agariste of Sicyon and Megacles (q.v.). He was *choregos* when Aeschylus' *Persae* was produced in 472; but first came into prominence as one of the State prosecutors of Cimon (q.v.) in 463. In 462/1 he joined with Ephialtes (q.v. 4) in the attack on the Areopagus. According to Plutarch he became popular leader and the most influential man in Athens after Ephialtes' death and the ostracism of Cimon. But little is recorded of him for some years, and we do not know his attitude to the Egyptian war (459–454) and to the campaigns of 457 which resulted in the Athenian domination of Boeotia, Phocis, and Locris. He perhaps initiated the building of the Long Walls (q.v.; 458–456). In domestic politics he proposed payment for the dicasts, and perhaps instituted the *theorika* (q.v.)—in rivalry with Cimon for the popular favour, we are told, and therefore probably after the latter's recall, which he proposed in person. In 451–450 he proposed the law restricting the citizenship to children both of whose parents were citizens. In 454 or 453 he was *strategos* and campaigned in the Corinthian Gulf against Sicyon and Oeniadae. After the truce with Sparta (451 or 450) he led an expedition which restored Delphi to the Phocians (448?). He is said to have opposed the rash expedition of Tolmides which ended in the defeat of Coronea (447) and to have bought off the invading Peloponnesians in 446. He reduced Euboea, which had revolted from the League, to submission; and in the winter of 446–445 he secured Sparta's recognition of the Athenian Empire in the Thirty Years' Peace. In 440–439 Pericles reduced the insurgent island of Samos after a nine months' siege.

Meanwhile his great influence had been shown in other directions. He initiated many cleruchies (q.v.) to strengthen the Empire, especially in the Hellespont, and he established an important colony at Thurii (q.v.) to spread Athenian influence in Italy. He called, perhaps in 448–447, a general congress of all Greek States to consider the rebuilding of the temples destroyed by the Persians, the freedom of the seas for all, and peace—but nothing came of it, owing to the opposition of Sparta. He was building commissioner for the Parthenon (begun in 447) and the other great buildings of this time. His bitter enemy at home in this imperial policy was Thucydides (q.v. 1), son of Melesias, who was at last ostracized in 443; henceforth Pericles had no eminent opponent, and he was elected *strategos* every year till his death. In 437 he founded a colony at Amphipolis (q.v.), and about this time he led an expedition to establish Athenian influence in the Black Sea.

When war with the Peloponnesians threatened, Pericles determined to resist their demands. He doubtless counselled the alliance with Corcyra in 433, and he was the author of the decree against Megara in 432. When war broke out the whole of the Athenian strategy was devised by him (*see* PELOPONNESIAN WAR). The invasion of Attica provoked indignation and excitement in the city, but he remained supreme till the ravages of the pestilence in 430 momentarily broke Athenian morale. He was now driven from office, tried for embezzlement, and fined. Soon after (probably spring 429) he was again elected *strategos*; but he too had been attacked by the pestilence, and he survived only another six months.

Pericles' long eminence was due to his incorruptible character, a consistently intelligent policy, and remarkable powers as an orator. He was reserved and even haughty in demeanour, with nothing democratic about him (unlike Pisistratus, with whom he was often compared). He was intimate with many of the leading philosophers and artists, especially Anaxagoras, Sophocles, and Phidias. His first marriage was unhappy and ended in divorce; but *c.* 450–445 he formed a lasting union with Aspasia (q.v.). Commonplace minds resented his distant superiority; scandalous and ridiculous stories were spread about him; and finally prosecutions were begun against his friends, Phidias and Anaxagoras (qq.v.), and against Aspasia, who was acquitted. These attacks, however, did not affect Pericles' ascendancy.

We have comparatively good and contrasted sources for Pericles' life—Thucydides' detailed account of political events from 433 to 429 and summary of his character and policy (1. 24 to 2. 65), and Plutarch, who adds much biographical detail, mostly from contemporary sources.

G. De Sanctis, *Pericles* (1950); V. Ehrenberg, *Sophocles and Pericles* (1954); L. Homo, *Periclès* (1954); D. Kienast, *Gymnasium* 1953, 210 ff.; F. J. Frost, *Hist.* 1964, 385 ff.          A. W. G.

**PERICLYMENUS,** in mythology, (1) son of Poseidon (and Chloris daughter of Tiresias, schol. Pind. *Nem.* 9. 57, but cf. (2)). Defended Thebes against the Seven, killing Parthenopaeus (q.v.; Eur. *Phoen.* 1157); pursued Amphiaraus (q.v.; Pind. *Nem.* 9. 26). (2) Son of Neleus (or Poseidon, Sen. *Med.* 635) and Chloris daughter of Amphion; Argonaut; killed by Heracles (q.v.) while in the form of a fly, Poseidon having given him power to assume any shape when fighting (Ap. Rhod. 1. 156 ff., and schol.).          H. J. R.

**PERINTHUS,** a Greek city on the shore of the Propontis, founded by the Samians, *c.* 600 B.C. The site lay on a high peninsula, the houses were built along the slopes of a hill, and the city assumed the appearance of an amphitheatre. Perinthus soon encountered the hostility of Megara, whose daughter cities Byzantium and Chalcedon had already been founded in the area, but a Megarian expedition directed against her was defeated by the Samians. Incorporated for a time in the Persian Empire, she became a tributary member of the Delian League, and at the end of the Peloponnesian War became subject to the Spartan harmost of Byzantium. In the fourth century she joined the Second Athenian League, but in 357 revolted along with Byzantium and participated in the Social War. In 355 she was granted autonomy. In 352 she and Byzantium concluded an alliance with Philip II of Macedonia, but refusing in 341/40 to be drawn into hostilities with Athens, she was besieged by Philip. Perinthus was assisted by Byzantium, Athens, and Persia, and Philip, baffled by the natural strength of the place, was obliged to withdraw. In the third century she entered into close relations with Byzantium, and the two cities formed a federation, but in 202 became subject to Philip V of Macedonia. Her freedom was restored by Rome in 196. In 189 she became part of the Attalid kingdom, and at the end of the century

she was subject to the authority of the Roman governor of Macedonia. By the end of the third century A.D. the name Perinthus was changed to Heracleia, preserved today as Erekli. With the foundation of Constantinople, Perinthus-Heracleia declined in importance, but was restored to something of her former splendour by Justinian.

Plut. *Mor.* 303 F.; Hdt. 5. 1; Xen. *Hell.* 1. 1. 21, *Anab.* 7. 2, 7. 4. 7. 62. 4; *IG* ii². 43 l. 84; Diod. 16. 74–6; Dem. 18. 89; Polyb. 18. 2. 4; Livy 32. 33. 7, 33. 30. 3; Procop. *Aed.* 4. 9.          E. I. McQ.

**PERIOCHAE,** the summaries in the Roman epitomizing treatment of long, usually chronographical, works, represent in particular the abridgement of Livy, an epitome of whose history is mentioned by Martial (14. 190). The epitomized Livian tradition appears in the *Periochae* (for all 142 books except 136–7, with two *periochae* of book 1) and in the Oxyrhynchus Epitome (for books 37–40, 48–55), 'contaminated' with further chronological, anecdotal, and antiquarian data, perhaps including *exempla* and reference to Livy's full text.

Ed. O. Rossbach (1910). A. Klotz, *Hermes* 1913, 542 ff.; *Philol.* 1936, 67 ff; M. Galdi, *L'epitome nella letteratura latina* (1922); C. M. Begbie, *CQ* 1967, 332 ff.          A. H McD.

**PERIOIKOI** (περίοικοι, 'those that dwell round about', was the name used to describe neighbouring people frequently constituting groups of subjects or half-citizens, normally with local self-government. They formed parts of or were subject to various Greek States without having a share in their government. *Perioikoi* were found in Argolis, Crete, Elis, Thessaly, and elsewhere, but those of Sparta are best known. These, like the Spartiates, were counted as Lacedaemonians, served in the Lacedaemonian army, were on a par with Spartiates in the payment of taxes, and so were citizens with lesser rights. Nevertheless, though such government never is described, they clearly formed communities with local self-government. Thus the entire complex resembled a federal State with the federal government delegated to the Spartiates, though the emphasis on military service caused it also to resemble an alliance. In Laconia the perioecic towns along the coast and in the mountains roughly formed a circle around the Spartiate land; in Messenia they were less numerous, particularly on the west coast. To them must have fallen what industry and commerce there was, but it seems that the *perioikoi* that served in the army and controlled their communities were landholders. The proportion of Dorians and pre-Dorians among them is unknown and cannot be determined by their dialect, for Spartiates, *perioikoi*, and helots spoke the same language. As in Sparta, so in Crete and Elis, the *perioikoi* appear as citizens with lesser rights, while in Thessaly they are described as subject allies.

G. Gilbert, *The Constitutional Antiquities of Sparta and Athens* (1895), 35 ff.; F. Hampl, *Hermes* 1937; H. Michell, *Sparta* (1952), 64 ff. and *passim*; R. F. Willetts, *Aristocratic Society in Ancient Crete* (1955), 37 ff. and *passim*; F. Gschnitzer, *Abhängige Orte im griechischen Altertum* (1958); V. Ehrenberg, *The Greek State* (1960), 36 f. and *passim*.          J. A. O. L.

**PERIPATETIC SCHOOL.** The Aristotelian school of philosophy in Athens was called after the covered walk (περίπατος) in the buildings which Theophrastus provided for the school. (There was a legend, perhaps invented by Hermippus, Diogenes Laertius 5. 2, that it was so called because Aristotle walked while lecturing.) Aristotle began teaching in the Lyceum about 335/4 B.C., but as a foreigner he could not own real estate, and during his lifetime there was no 'school' in the material sense. Under Theophrastus' leadership, through the influence of Demetrius of Phalerum, the school acquired buildings which were bequeathed in Theophrastus' will to a named group of fellow scholars, including Strato, who succeeded him as Head (c. 287–269). Strato bequeathed the school with its books and furniture to Lyco (Head from c. 269 to 226/4), who in turn left it to a named group, who were to choose a Head from among themselves. (All these wills are preserved in Diogenes Laertius, Bk. 5.) The chosen successor was Ariston of Ceos, who was Head until c. 190. The succession in the second century is obscure; Critolaus was the only Head of any distinction.

During this period the school's achievements became less impressive. In the time of Aristotle and Theophrastus the foundations were laid for systematic, co-operative research into nearly all the branches of contemporary learning. After Theophrastus' death, however, Aristotle's written works were neglected; they may even have been lost, if the story in Strabo 13. 1. 54 is true, according to which Neleus of Scepsis inherited the library from Theophrastus and took it all to his home, where it remained hidden from the world for a century and a half. During this time, Aristotle was known for his 'exoteric' works, mainly dialogues (now lost except for a few fragments), and the Peripatetics narrowed their interests very greatly compared with the immense range of Aristotle and Theophrastus. Strato was the last Head in the great tradition; later members of the school devoted themselves to literary criticism, gossipy biography, and unimportant moralizing.

There was a revival in the first century B.C., under the leadership of Andronicus of Rhodes. The treatises of Aristotle had been rediscovered (they had been sold to Apellicon of Teos and brought by him to Athens, thence taken to Rome by Sulla, passed on to Tyrannion the grammarian and friend of Cicero, and from him to Andronicus; see Strabo 13. 1. 54 and Plutarch, Sulla 26), and Andronicus published an edition of them and wrote some kind of critical commentary. The date of this is uncertain, but since Cicero does not mention it, it was probably after his time. In this period the Peripatos was not sharply distinguished doctrinally from the Academy and the Stoa; the Epicureans were opposed to them all.

In the first two centuries A.D. Aristotle's works were much studied in the school and many commentaries were written, especially on his logic and philosophy of nature. Aristocles of Messana was a member who wrote a history of philosophy; Aspasius wrote several commentaries, of which part of his Nicomachean Ethics survives. Alexander of Aphrodisias is the most important figure. After the third century, very little or nothing is known of the Peripatos itself; the Neoplatonists took over the work of writing commentaries on Aristotle.

Fragments of Dicaearchus, Aristoxenus, Clearchus, Demetrius, Strato, Lycon, Ariston, Heraclides, Eudemus, Phainias, Chamaileon, Praxiphanes, Hieronymus, and Critolaus in F. Wehrli, Die Schule des Aristoteles (1944–59; 2nd ed. 1967– ). K. O. Brink, s.v. 'Peripatos', PW Suppl. vii; I. Düring, Aristotle in the Ancient Biographical Tradition (Studia Graeca et Latina Gothoburgensia 1957). D. J. F.

**PERIPHETES** (Περιφήτης, 'famous', 'notorious'), name of several minor mythological figures, see Höfer in Roscher s.v., and especially of a brigand, also called Corynetes (Κορυνήτης, 'club-wielder'), killed by Theseus (q.v.) on his way to Athens. He was son of Hephaestus and Anticleia, Apollod. 3. 217, who adds that he lived in Epidaurus, was weak in the legs (or feet, πόδας) and killed all passers-by with an iron club. This Theseus took from him and afterwards carried (another resemblance between Theseus and Heracles). Hyginus (Fab. 38. 1) says he was son of Poseidon; no other author mentions his mother. See further Höfer, op. cit., and literature of THESEUS.                                         H. J. R.

**PERIPLOI** (περίπλοι, 'circumnavigations') were (a) reports of navigations by pioneers along unexplored coasts, (b) manuals for the use of navigators, which collected and systematized the information of previous travellers. The term primarily referred to sailings round an enclosed basin like the Mediterranean and Black Seas, but was also applied to continuous navigations along any kind of coast, even a straight coast (thus partially replacing the more appropriate terms παράπλοι, ἀνάπλοι). Some Periploi contained, in addition, descriptions of the adjacent lands and peoples.

Periploi of the former class include (1) an account of the outer coast of Spain, with references to Britain and Ireland, by a Massilian captain (c. 525 B.C.?), quoted by Avienus. (2) A description (extant in Greek) of the west African coast by Hanno (c. 490?). (3) The narrative of Nearchus' cruise from Indus to Euphrates (325–324), reproduced by Arrian. (4) Pytheas' account of his Atlantic voyage (late 4th c.), quoted by Strabo and others. (5) Arrian's extant Periplus of the Euxine Sea (c. A.D. 132).

The Periploi of the latter class comprise (1) the survey of the Mediterranean and Black Seas compiled c. 325 B.C. (?) under the name of Scylax. (2) Agatharchides' description of both Red Sea coasts (c. 110 B.C.), partly reproduced in Diodorus and Photius. (3) The Periplus of the Erythraean Sea (1st c. A.D.), describing the coastal routes from Egypt to India and along E. Africa, with copious information for navigators and traders. (4) The Stadiasmus Maris Magni (4th c. A.D.?), an excellent sailing direction, with details of harbourage and waterspots, and of distances from point to point. (5) Marcianus' description of the 'Outer Sea' (Indian and Atlantic Oceans; c. A.D. 400?), a poor compilation from Ptolemy.

Texts in GGM. Text of the Periplus of the Erythraean Sea by Frisk; translation and notes by W. H. Schoff (1912). On this Periplus see also Hyde, Greek Mariners, 208 ff.; Thomson, Hist. Anc. Geog. 228, 274, 296 f., 301 ff.; J. A. B. Palmer, CQ 1947, 137 ff. (possibly it is a compilation of the 2nd c. A.D.); 1949, 61 ff. 1951, 156 ff. It may even belong to the 3rd c. A.D.: J. Pirenne, Journal Asiatique 1961, 441 ff.; cf. P. L'Évêque, Rev. Et. Grec. 1963, 428 f. F. Gisinger, PW, s.v. 'Periplus'. Cf. also J. E. Casariego, Los Grandes Periplos de la Antigüedad (1949); D. Gernez, 'Les Périples des anciens Grecs', Acad. de Marine de Belgique, Communications, iv, 1947–9, 15 ff.; J. I. Miller, The Spice Trade of the Roman Empire (1969). See also AVIENIUS, HANNO (1), NEARCHUS (2), etc., in the present work.

E. H. W.

**PERPERNA** (1, PW 4), MARCUS, of an Etruscan—but long romanized and probably municipal—family, was the first bearer of a nomen of non-Latin type to become consul (130 B.C.). He succeeded Crassus (q.v. 1) in Asia and captured Aristonicus (q.v. 1), but died soon after and was succeeded by Aquillius (q.v. 2).          E. B.

**PERPERNA** (2, PW 5), MARCUS, son of (1), born c. 148 B.C., was consul in 92 B.C. As censor (86) with Marcius Philippus (q.v. 4), he enrolled the first of the enfranchised Italians. Although he lived on until 49, surviving all but seven of those whom he had put on the Senate list (Pliny, HN 7. 156), he is hardly ever heard of and lacked any known influence.          E. B.

**PERPERNA** (3, PW 6) **VEIENTO**, MARCUS, son of (2), as praetor c. 82 B.C. was sent to Sicily; he refused to join Sulla, but abandoned Sicily to Pompey. He joined the rebellion of Lepidus (q.v. 2) and, after its failure, fled to Sardinia, whence he joined Sertorius (q.v.) in Spain. Resenting Sertorius' ascendancy and his own lack of success, he finally murdered Sertorius at a banquet. Disastrously defeated by Pompey, he offered to surrender Sertorius' correspondence to him; but Pompey refused to read it and executed him (72).          E. B.

**PERRHAEBI**, a tribe occupying a district on the northern border of Thessaly and commanding passes from

Macedonia. Although most of their country was mountainous and sparsely inhabited, their principal towns, Oloosson, the tribal capital, and Phalanna were situated in fertile plains. Neither, however, played any significant role in history. The Perrhaebi, who had been thrust northwards by the invading Thessalians, were reduced to the status of *perioikoi*. Though liable to a war-tax, they enjoyed some degree of autonomy whenever the Thessalian κοινόν was weak, and they held two votes on the Amphictionic Council. With the growth of Thessalian cities in the fifth century they found themselves increasingly dominated by Larissa (q.v.). Philip of Macedon severed Perrhaebia from Thessaly, and it remained under Macedonian control until liberated by Flamininus in 196.

F. Stählin, *Das hellenische Thessalien* (1924), 5 ff. H. D. W.

**PERSAEUS** (c. 306–c. 243 B.C.), son of Demetrius of Citium in Cyprus. He was brought up at Athens in the house of his fellow countryman Zeno, founder of the Stoic school, became his disciple, and later taught philosophy under his guidance. In 277, when Zeno declined the invitation of Antigonus Gonatas to come to his court at Pella, Persaeus was sent in his stead. He became the educator of Antigonus' son Halcyoneus and acquired great political influence. In 244 he was made commander of Acrocorinthus, but lost the town and citadel to Aratus in 243, whereupon he committed suicide. He defended orthodox Stoicism against the heretics Ariston and Herillus, and elaborated on the doctrine of the philosopher king.

WORKS: *On Kingship, Polity of the Lacedaemonians, Dialogues*, and others (cf. Diog. Laert. 7. 1. 36).

Fragments: von Arnim, *SVF* i. 4. 96 ff. K. VON F.

**PERSEPOLIS**, in Persis, residence of the Achaemenid kings. Alexander in 331 B.C. took and looted Persepolis and set fire to the palaces (Diod. 17. 71–2). The royal quarters, built on a hill-terrace, contained two palaces, consisting in either case of a forecourt, a large colonnaded reception-hall which apparently had no outer wall, and a storehouse and armoury.

Excavations on the site have revealed that Darius I levelled the rock-terrace and built the great *apadana* (audience-hall), the main palace-buildings, and the harem. These were completed by Xerxes; Artaxerxes finished the Hall of a Hundred Pillars and built his own palace. Around the whole complex was a fortification wall, and a great gate and stairway led up to the terrace. The bas-reliefs of these palaces are among the finest extant examples of Achaemenid art. The graves of the Achaemenid kings are near by.

E. Herzfeld, *Archäologische Mitteilungen aus Iran* i (1929); *Journ. Royal Asiatic Soc.* 1934, 226 ff.; F. Sarre and E. Herzfeld, *Iranische Felsreliefs* (1910); Erich F. Schmidt, *Persepolis* i (U.S.A. 1953), ii (1957), iii (1966); F. Stolze, *Persepolis; die achämenid. und sassanid. Denkmäler und Inschriften* (1882); R. Ghirshman, *Persia* (1964). D. N. Wilber, *Persepolis* (U.S.A. 1969). M. S. D.

**PERSES** of Thebes, a poet of the later fourth century B.C., has a few sepulchral and dedicatory epigrams in the Greek Anthology, apparently written as real inscriptions (e.g. *Anth. Pal.* 7. 445) but more emotional than similar poems in the classical era (e.g. 7. 730).

Gow and Page, 2859 ff. G. H.

**PERSEUS** (1), a mythological hero. The following, founded on Apollod. 2. 34 ff., is the usual legend; for variants, etc., see the larger works on mythology. Acrisius, brother of Proetus (q.v.), being warned by an oracle that his daughter Danaë's son would kill him, shut her in a bronze chamber. Zeus visited her there in a shower of gold. Acrisius, learning that she had borne a son, whom she called Perseus, put both in a chest and set it afloat. It drifted to Seriphus, where mother and

child were received by the king Polydectes. When Perseus was grown the king contrived to send him to fetch the head of the Gorgon Medusa. This he did by the help of Athena (cf. GRAIAE). After rescuing and marrying Andromeda (q.v.) he returned to Seriphus, where he used the Gorgon's head to turn Polydectes and his followers into stone for persecuting Danaë. He now gave the head to Athena and returned his flying shoes and the wallet in which he had carried the head, also the Cap of Darkness which had made him invisible, to Hermes. With his wife and mother he then came to Argos to see his grandfather, whom he at length found in the Pelasgiotis. Here he contended in some funeral games and, throwing the discus, accidentally struck and killed Acrisius, thus fulfilling the oracle. Leaving Argos to the son of Proetus, he became king of Tiryns and founder of the dynasty of the Perseidae.

The beheading of Medusa and the pursuit by her sisters are favourite themes in art from the seventh century. Perseus is garbed like Hermes and carries a *harpe* and a satchel for the head. From the fifth century the Graiae, the deliverance of Andromeda, and the punishment of Polydectes are found, and he is shown with Danaë.

J. M. Woodward, *Perseus* (1937); J. H. Croon, 'The Mask of the Underworld Daemon', *JHS* 1955, 9 ff.; T. P. Howe, 'The Origin and Function of the Gorgon-head', *AJArch.* 1954, 209 ff.; Brommer, *Vasenlisten²*, 204 ff. H. J. R.; C. M. R.

**PERSEUS** (2), king of Macedon 179–168 B.C., the elder son of Philip V and legitimate heir despite the tradition of slave birth, was born about 213/12. He fought against Rome (199) and the Aetolians (189). Representing his father's Antigonid imperialism against the Roman sympathies and royal aspirations, with Roman favour, of his brother Demetrius, he intrigued against him from 183 until Philip ordered Demetrius' death in 181. Polybius' description, reproducing a partisan version (cf. Livy 41. 23–4), does scant justice to the realities of the political struggle.

Succeeding Philip in 179, he renewed his treaty with Rome, and continued consolidating Macedon, declaring an amnesty. He extended influence in Thrace, Dardania, and Illyria, the northern field of Macedonian imperialism. In Greek diplomacy he married Laodice, daughter of Seleucus IV, gave his sister to Prusias, and was honoured by Rhodes; he influenced the social struggles in Thessaly and Aetolia, subdued Dolopia, and visited Delphi with his army. This challenge to the predominance of Pergamum sent Eumenes to Rome and brought on the Third Macedonian War (171–168). Yet the tradition of his warlike designs against Rome may be discounted; his policy, based on the north, aimed at prestige, not war, in Greece.

His military strategy of defence on the Macedonian frontiers was at first successful. But Roman reinforcements and the collapse of his ally Genthius, opening up Macedonia from the west, forced a decision at Pydna. The charge of the phalanx was his last stroke, failing before Aemilius Paullus' experienced generalship. He was captured at Samothrace, and adorned Paullus' triumph, dying two years later at Alba Fucens.

Vigorous in campaigning, he lacked tactical initiative. His alleged miserliness often rather reflects caution in policy. The charge of cowardice at Pydna is to be rejected. Sound in diplomacy and generalship, he yet lacked in both the virtuosity necessary to reconcile Antigonid aims with the Roman protectorate over Greece.

Livy, bks. 38–45; Polyb. bks. 22, 25, 27–30; Plut. *Aem.*; Diod. bks. 29–31; App. *Mac.* 11–16. P. Heiland, *Unters. zur Gesch. des Königs Perseus* (1913); De Sanctis, *Stor. Rom.* iv. 1. 251, 270; C. F. Edson, *Harv. Stud.* 1935, 191 ff.; F. W. Walbank, *Philip V of Macedon* (1940); P. Meloni, *Perseo* (1953). A. H. McD

**PERSEUS** (3) (2nd c. B.C.), mathematician. Proclus describes him as the discoverer of the sections of the σπεῖρα (tore or anchor-ring).

**PERSIA**, in its widest geographical sense, includes all the great Iranian plateau bounded on west and east by the valleys of Tigris and Indus, and on the north by the Armenian mountains, the Caspian Sea, and the steppes of south Russia—an area of c. 1,000,000 sq. miles. The high mountain ranges lie at the edges of the plateau, so that it resembles a basin. These mountains abound in mineral wealth, gold, silver, copper, lapis-lazuli and other prized stones; the numerous rivers carry down silt and cultivation is possible in the valleys. The interior of the plateau is a waste of salty lakes and marshes, with wide tracts of desert. In spite of this Persia has always had importance as the bridge between east and west Asia, and the ancient trade-routes are still used.

The Aryan Persians probably entered Iran from the north-east; the date at which they reached their final home is unknown. In the ninth century the Assyrians mention Parsua, a northern country adjoining Median territory. If this was for a time their home, they moved southward, for Teispes the Achaemenid was king of Anshan and Parsa, the country later to be known as Persia proper (Persis, modern *Fars*). It was from this southerly kingdom that Cyrus II (or III) set out to conquer western Asia; Susa remained the administrative capital of the Persian Empire.

The organization of this Empire was begun by Cyrus, and completed by Darius. It was a great advance on any previous imperial system, combining local autonomy with the centralization of authority in a supreme controlling power. The country was divided into provinces, each governed by a satrap (q.v.), who might be the local ruler, or a Persian, particularly from one of the six privileged noble families. Within his province the satrap had absolute authority, but the presence of military and civil officials responsible only to the king, and of travelling inspectors, constituted a check on his power. Each satrapy had to contribute a fixed amount to the royal treasury and furnish levies for the army. Local forms of government were preserved as far as possible, e.g. in the Phoenician and Greek city-states religion, language, and local custom were not interfered with. Royal inscriptions are written in the three official languages, Persian, Elamitic, and Babylonian. A universal gold coinage, introduced by Darius, and the building of highways facilitated trade, and a royal messenger post linked the furthest corners of the Empire with Susa.

Religion played an essential part in the life of the Persians. The Achaemenid kings were worshippers of Ahura Mazda, whose vicegerents they regarded themselves (*see* ZOROASTER). The Magian sect, who specialized in ritual observances, acted as the priests of Mazdaism. Popular religion was syncretistic, including the worship of the elements, especially fire, and that of more ancient deities.

Achaemenid art owes much to Babylonia and Assyria, and something to Greece and even Egypt, but it is by no means merely derivative, as the palaces at Persepolis (q.v.) and elsewhere, with their delicate bas-reliefs and impressive architecture, show.

CLASSICAL SOURCES for Achaemenid Persia. Hdt.; Ctesias, *Persica*; Xen. *Cyr.*, *An.*, etc.; Strabo, bks. 11–17.
CUNEIFORM. F. H. Weissbach, *Keilinschriften der Achämeniden* (1911).
ARCHAEOLOGICAL. E. Herzfeld, *Archäologische Mitteilungen aus Iran.*
MODERN WORKS. R. Ghirshman, *Iran* (1954), *Persia* (1964); R. N. Frye, *The Heritage of Persia* (1963). *See also* ACHAEMENIDS, ARSACIDS, SASSANIDS.
M. S. D.; R. N. F.

**PERSIAN WARS.** (1) CAUSES. King Darius' (q.v. 1)

Behistun and other inscriptions, and his reputation as a 'shop-keeper' (Hdt. 3. 89), reveal the character of a born administrator, who also believed that he had a mission from God to impose peace and good order upon the world. To the Persian nation, empire meant increased wealth and, for many, opportunities for a life less laborious than that of upland farmers. Though Cyrus (q.v. 1) is said to have rejected a proposal that the whole people should migrate to a land more opulent than that which they had occupied for the last century, it is evident that many did migrate to enjoy the positions of satraps, soldiers, lesser officials, and landowners. The failures of Cyrus in central Asia, of Cambyses west and south of Egypt, and of Darius himself beyond the Danube had shown that the Empire had reached limits in those directions, beyond which campaigning was unprofitable. But there remained the Greek world, in which Mardonius (q.v.) is said to have dreamed of a princely future as satrap in Europe. The Phoenicians (q.v.), a sea-power in willing symbiosis with the land empire, were also willing to serve against the Greeks, who were aggressive against their trade and colonies in the west; and any chance that Persia might have stopped short at the Aegean was negatived by the fact that a frontier at the coast left some Greeks within the Empire, but most outside. Ionia by 500 B.C. was restive under Persian rule, especially because it was exercised through Greek 'tyrants' in the cities; it was a Greek commonplace that such 'bosses' normally abused their power.

(2) THE IONIAN REVOLT. Its immediate author was the Milesian Aristagoras (q.v. 1), who laid down his 'tyranny' and brought about a general expulsion of tyrants among the cities of Ionia (499 B.C.). The rebel cities formed a league which directed the war and issued a federal coinage. Aristagoras secured a reinforcement of twenty ships from Athens and of five from Eretria, but for one campaigning season only, and he obtained no assistance from Sparta, which shrank from overseas expeditions and was preoccupied with an impending war against Argos; yet success in the revolt depended on support from Greece. In 498 the insurgent army captured and burnt Sardes (thus giving the Persians a good pretext for retaliating upon Greek cities); the fleet spread the rebellion along the coast from Byzantium to Cyprus, and in 497 defeated a Phoenician squadron off Cyprus. But disunion and insubordination among the Greeks allowed the Persians to recover Cyprus despite a naval defeat, and Aristagoras withdrew from the scene of war. Ionia was now invaded and the Greek fleet, weakened by rivalries and treason, was crushed at Lade (494). Miletus and other cities were sacked, but democratic local government was thereafter permitted.

(3) THE CAMPAIGN OF MARATHON. In 492 Mardonius (q.v.) prepared the way for Xerxes' later expedition by the definite reduction of Thrace and Macedonia. In 490 Datis and Artaphernes conducted a punitive expedition by sea against Athens and Eretria. Obtaining the surrender of the Cyclades *en route*, they carried Eretria by treachery and made a landing on Attica at Marathon (probably on the advice of Hippias). An appeal to Sparta for help was conveyed by Pheidippides (q.v.) in record time, but the Spartan forces arrived too late, and the Athenians, some 10,000 strong, with the Plataeans only to assist them, had to encounter the far stronger Persian army. Under the leadership of Miltiades (q.v.) the Athenians routed the Persians with heavy loss (c. 6,400 men) and by a prompt return march to Athens they thwarted an attempt by the Persian fleet to take the city unguarded. The battle of Marathon made Athens safe for democracy and strengthened her alliance with Sparta —and only by a united front could the Greeks hope to resist the main Persian attack, which befell ten years later.

(4) THE EXPEDITION OF XERXES (480). This was planned as a co-ordinated invasion by land (c. 100,000 soldiers?) and sea (1,000 ships?) and, despite the obiter dictum of Aristotle (*Poet.* 23), probably concerted with the simultaneous Carthaginian attack upon the Greeks of Sicily. By a preliminary diplomatic offensive Xerxes won over Thessaly, most of central Greece, Argos, and the oracle of Delphi. But meantime the Athenians had acquired a powerful fleet (*see* THEMISTOCLES), and at a Panhellenic congress held at the Isthmus (autumn 481) they combined with Sparta to resolve internal feuds in Greece and to organize a national league of common defence. Sparta held the chief command, but the plan of campaign was mainly by Themistocles. The Greeks abandoned the Thessalian frontier after a mere inspection, and posted their army and fleet at the interdependent positions of Thermopylae and Artemisium (qq.v.). The Persian fleet, compelled to advance in force down the dangerous coast of Thessaly, lost heavily in late-summer gales but, after three days' fighting, forced the Greeks to withdraw from Artemisium; while the force at Thermopylae was outflanked and its rearguard under Leonidas (q.v. 1) destroyed. All central Greece was now lost, Athens was hastily evacuated, and the Greek fleet withdrew to Salamis. The Peloponnesians now advocated passive defence on the Isthmus of Corinth, but Themistocles, supported by the Spartan commander Eurybiades (q.v.), forced a naval decision in the narrows of Salamis, by which the Greeks gained definite command of the sea. Xerxes now retired to Asia with the remnant of his fleet, but Mardonius was left to winter in Thessaly and to carry on the campaign by land.

(5) THE CAMPAIGN OF 479. After two vain attempts in the next spring to detach Athens with the offer of a separate peace Mardonius fell back to Boeotia, where his superior cavalry forces severely harassed an oncoming army of c. 38,000 Peloponnesian and Athenian hoplites. During a retreat to higher ground near Plataea the Spartan commander Pausanias (q.v. 1) was set upon by the Persians, but repelled and routed them; Mardonius fell, and the remnant of his army evacuated Greece. Meanwhile a Greek fleet under the Spartan king Leotychides (q.v.) cut out and destroyed the remains of the Persian fleet in a land battle off C. Mycale. This victory started a new revolt by the islanders and the Asiatic Greeks.

(6) THE GREEK COUNTER-ATTACK. In support of this rebellion the Greeks cleared the entrance to the Black Sea, and in 478 a fleet under Pausanias started a revolt in Cyprus and captured Byzantium. Friction between Pausanias and the Spartan government led to the recall of the Spartan and Peloponnesian contingents; but the Athenians, assuming command of the liberated Greeks in the Aegean islands and Asia Minor, and enrolling them in the Delian League (q.v.), carried on the war. Their operations (of which little is known) were probably not continuous, but c. 467 Cimon (q.v.) made a bold advance to Pamphylia and Cyprus, and destroyed a Persian army and fleet at the river Eurymedon. He did not follow up this success, but c. 459 Athens sent 200 ships to support a rebellion in Egypt. Difficulties of communication and the outbreak of war in home waters prevented the timely dispatch of reinforcements, and after some early successes, in which the Persians were driven up the Nile, the Greek fleet succumbed to a strong counter-attack and was destroyed near Memphis (c. 454). Another expedition was sent c. 450 to resuscitate the Egyptian rebellion and to safeguard Cyprus against a Persian counter-attack; but in spite of a victory off Cyprian Salamis it abandoned the island, and the death of its commander Cimon left Pericles a free hand to come to terms with Persia. In 449/8 an agreement (whether a formal treaty or simply a non-aggression pact) was negotiated by Callias (q.v. 1), which secured the independence of the Asiatic Greeks (save those of Cyprus) and closed the Aegean to Persian warships.

(7) RESULTS OF THE WARS. Persia had learned to respect Greek military strength. From c. 457 onwards, she used her gold and diplomacy to avert, till Alexander, the threat of Greek attacks; later, increasingly, she employed Greek mercenaries. Greece gained an enhanced consciousness of nationality and conviction of superiority to orientals; Athens rejected Mardonius' terms in the name of 'Greek community of blood and language and religion and ways of life'. Greek internal divisions cut short the golden age; Athenian imperialism was a poor substitute for a Greek common peace. Ionia in the fifth century remained impoverished, and in the fourth fell back under Persian rule. Nevertheless, Athens revealed what Greece could be; the use made of the manpower released by the peace of 449 was in the buildings of Pericles.

SOURCES. By far the most important is Herodotus. For the operations after 479 see Thuc. 1. 93–112. The chief other ancient sources are Diod. bk. 11 (reproducing Ephorus), and Plut. *Themistocles, Aristides, Cimon,* and *De malignitate Herodoti.* These use sources of uneven value. On source-criticism see G. Busolt, *Griechische Geschichte* ii² (1895), 600 ff.

MODERN WORKS. G. B. Grundy, *The Great Persian War* (1901); A. R. Burn, *Persia and the Greeks* (1962); C. Hignett, *Xerxes' Invasion of Greece* (1963); and cf. reviews of these in classical journals, and N. Whatley in *JHS* 1964. See also general histories.

P. T.; A. R. B.

**PERSIUS FLACCUS,** AULUS (A.D. 34–62), the Stoic satirist, was an Etruscan knight, rich and well connected. He knew Lucan (who admired his work), Thrasea Paetus, and other members of what became the Stoic opposition to Nero's rule. The strongest influence on his character was exercised by the Stoic philosopher Cornutus (see *Sat.* 5), who edited Persius' poems for publication after his early death.

His satires form one *libellus* of 650 hexameters and a brief ironic preface in scazons. They are well described as Horatian diatribes transformed by Stoic rhetoric (Villeneuve). (1), the introduction, derides the fashionable admiration for elegant unrealistic poetry and calls for readers with robust taste. (2) attacks the popular conception of prayer, mocking those who ask heaven for external goods rather than virtue. (3) is a quasi-medical diagnosis of the damage done to sick souls by chronic sloth and vice. (4) urges a young statesman to disregard public admiration and examine his own character. (5), eulogizing Cornutus, develops into a pitying indictment of mankind, slaves to vice who could be freed by virtue. (6) is a Horatian preachment on the wisdom of living comfortably, not covetously. Contemporary references are few; but the young statesman of (5) is not unlike Nero, the poetry derided in (1) is in Nero's own vein, and the biographer says the reference to Midas in 1. 119–21 was aimed at Nero and toned down by Cornutus.

Much read in antiquity and the Middle Ages, Persius is now little admired, because his thought, though sincere, is contorted, and his language, though vigorous, is obscure. He strains and even breaks the thread of his argument by digressions, shifts in viewpoint, and abrupt bursts of conversation. Always striving to impress, he writes in a bizarre mixture of cryptic allusions, brash colloquialisms, and forced imagery (e.g. 3. 52–7, 5. 102–4); and he translates his abstract trains of thought into groups of inharmonious pictures like a surrealist montage (1. 126–33, 6. 57–63), so that his work has what he calls 'the taste of bitten nails' (1. 106, cf. *Vita* 41). Yet his effects of sound and rhythm are outstandingly skilful (1. 119–23, 3. 34, 5. 132–9); he uses the language of the common people almost as boldly as Petronius (2. 37–8, 3. 16–18, 3. 94–7); he draws vivid pictures of human predicaments (3. 88–102); and he has many touches of deep sympathy (3. 39–43, 5. 66–9). Donne emulated him, and admirers of Auden might savour his keenly spiced satires.

TEXTS. F. Villeneuve (Paris, 1918); A. Cartault (Paris, 1951³); W. V. Clausen, O.C.T. (1956; with Juvenal, 1959).
COMMENTARIES. J. Conington and H. Nettleship (1893³); J. van Wageningen (2 vols., Groningen, 1911); F. Villeneuve (Paris, 1918). STUDIES. H. Küster, *De A. P. Flacci elocutione quaestiones* (3 parts, Lobau, 1894, 1896, 1897); A. Eichenberg, *De P. saturarum natura atque indole* (Breslau, 1905); F. Villeneuve, *Essai sur P.* (1918); R. C. Kukula, *P. und Nero* (1923); V. d'Agostino, 'D eA. P. Flacci sermone', *Rivista Indo-Greca-Italica di Filologia–Lingua–Antichità* 1928, fasc. 3–4, 11 ff.; 1929, fasc. 1–2, 105 ff.; fasc. 3–4, 21 ff.; 1930, fasc. 1–2, 21 ff.; fasc. 3–4, 75 ff. J. W. Duff, *Roman Satire* (U.S.A. 1937), ch. 6; W. Kugler, *Des P. Wille zu sprachlicher Gestaltung* (1940); E. V. Marmorale, *Persio²* (1956); W. S. Anderson, introduction and notes in W. S. Merwin's translation (U.S.A. 1961); K. J. Reckford, 'Studies in P.', *Hermes* 1962, 476 ff.; R. G. M. Nisbet in *Critical Essays on Roman Literature: Satire,* (ed. J. P. Sullivan, 1963), 39 ff.
BIBLIOGRAPHIES. M. H. Morgan (U.S.A. 1909). V. D'Agostino (1946–57), *Rivista di Studi Classici* 1958, 63 ff.; (1957–62) ibid. 1963, 54 ff.                    G. H.

**PERTINAX,** PUBLIUS HELVIUS (*PW*, Suppl. iii. 895), born A.D. 126. A man of humble origin, he had a long equestrian military career before being adlected to the Senate by Marcus Aurelius; he distinguished himself as a general under Marcus in Raetia and under Commodus in Britain, becoming *cos.* II and city prefect in 192. The Praetorian Guard and its prefect Laetus proclaimed him emperor on 1 Jan. 193 following the assassination of Commodus. During his rule of three months he attempted to restore the principles of government observed by Marcus Aurelius and revived for himself the title of *princeps' senatus*, while refusing the titles of Augustus and Caesar for his wife and son. An excessive eagerness for reform, however, caused discontent in the Senate, and the sale of State offices undermined confidence in his economic policy. His strict discipline aroused the resentment of the Praetorians who now regretted the removal of Commodus, and after an abortive conspiracy to make the consul Falco Emperor, Laetus urged the Praetorians to invade the Palatine. Pertinax, deserted by all his retinue except Eclectus, fell a victim to the spear of a Tungrian soldier (28 Mar. A.D. 193). He was subsequently enrolled among the *divi* by Septimius Severus.

Herodian 2. 1–5; Dio Cass. bk. 73; *B.M. Coins, Rom. Emp.* v, lx. 1–10.                    H. M. D. P.; B. H. W.

**PERUSIA,** modern *Perugia*, an ancient Italian hill city with interesting walls and Etruscan tombs. Originally perhaps Umbrian, Perusia first appears in history as an Etruscan city. In 295 B.C., despite a treaty, it fought against Rome, then submitted and signed a lengthy truce (Serv. ad *Aen.* 10. 201; Diod. 20. 35; Livy 10. 30, 31, 37). Thereafter it remained loyal, e.g. against Hannibal (Livy 23. 17; 28. 45). When Perusia sheltered L. Antonius in 41 Octavian besieged, captured, and plundered it (Perusine War: App. *BCiv.* 5. 32–49). Subsequently called *Augusta Perusia*, Perusia always flourished but is rarely mentioned before the sixth century.

W. Heywood, *History of Perugia* (1910); I. A. Richmond, *JRS* 1933, 161 ff.; C. Shaw, *Etruscan Perugia* (U.S.A. 1939); Scullard, *Etr. Cities,* 159 ff.                    E. T. S.

**PERVIGILIUM VENERIS** is a poem of ninety-three trochaic verses of unknown date and authorship, but written not earlier than the second century A.D. and perhaps nearer to the fifth than the second. The poet, who was a man of culture and learning, combines material for a hymn to Venus with a description of spring; the latter is interrupted with explanation why the coming festival is appropriate at that time, and the festival itself, set in Sicily, is the theme of thirty lines in the middle of the poem which ends on a mysterious

and unexpected note of private sadness introduced by the line: 'illa [the nightingale] cantat, nos tacemus: quando uer uenit meum?' Detailed interpretation is a little difficult because of uncertainty about the proper order of the verses. Whatever may be the exact date of this bright and lively poem, which has as a refrain 'cras amet qui numquam amauit, quique amauit cras amet', the warmth of its description and its delight in passion set it between two worlds and make it the prologue of the Middle Ages.

Edition with introd., text, transl., facsimiles, commentary, full bibliography by Sir Cecil Clementi (1936). The poem has been edited with introd., French translation, and notes by R. Schilling (1944) and is included in I. Cazzaniga's *Carmina Ludicra Romanorum* (1959). D. S. Robertson, *CR* 1938, 109 ff., argues on historical grounds that it was written about A.D. 307 by a poet belonging to the circle of Romula, mother of Galerius. On the poem see also J. Heurgon, *Mélanges . . . offerts à A. Ernout* (1940), 177 ff., and I. Cazzaniga, *Studi Classici e Orientali* 1952, 47 ff. and 1953, 134 ff.                    G. B. A. F.

**PESCENNIUS** (*PW* 2) **NIGER JUSTUS,** GAIUS, came of an equestrian family. After a military career, he was enrolled by Commodus into the Senate, becoming consul and governor of Syria in A.D. 191, where after the murder of Pertinax he was proclaimed Emperor by his legions (April 193). Unable to forestall Septimius' advance upon Rome, he attempted to secure his position from Byzantium, which voluntarily surrendered to him. Although his cause was popular in the East, his troops and his own personal qualities were inferior to those of his rival. Defeated at Perinthus, Cyzicus, and Nicaea (winter of 193/4), he withdrew to Antioch and was routed at Issus. Fleeing towards the Euphrates he was overtaken and executed.

*B.M. Coins, Rom. Emp.* v, lxxvi ff.                    H. M. D. P.; B. H. W.

**PETILLIUS** (*PW* 4, 11). Two cousins named Q. Petillius, *tribuni plebis* in 187 B.C., initiated the attack on L. Scipio (q.v. 7). Livy, following Valerius Antias, wrongly states that they accused Africanus also. One is probably Q. Petillius Spurinus, the praetor who burnt the forged writings of Pythagoras discovered in 181 (Livy 40. 29) and campaigned in Liguria as consul (176).

Scullard, *Rom. Pol.* 142 ff., 171 f., 291 ff.                    H. H. S.

**PETRA** (Aramaic *Selah,* 'the Rock') was the capital of the Nabataeans (q.v.) by 312 B.C. After A.D. 105 it ceased to be the administrative centre but remained the religious metropolis of Arabia. The town lies in a hollow surrounded by mountains; the only access is by narrow gorges. The ruins of the town itself, though extensive, comprising several temples, two theatres, baths, markets, gymnasium, etc., are not impressive. The rock-hewn temples and tombs in the surrounding hills are most magnificent, ranging in style from a primitive blend of Egyptian, Assyrian, and Greek motifs to a highly developed Hellenistic with strong baroque tendencies.

A. Kammerer, *Pétra et la Nabatène* (1929–30); G. Dalman, *Petra und seine Felsheiligtümer* (1908); T. Wiegand, *Petra* (1921); Sir A. Kennedy, *Petra* (1925); J. Starcky, *Suppl. au dict. de la Bible* vii (1964), col. 886 ff.                    A. H. M. J.

**PETREIUS** (*PW* 3), MARCUS, probably son of Cn. Petreius Atinas, a Marian *primipilaris*, was already 'uir militaris' of thirty years' service in 63 B.C. (Sall. *Cat.* 59. 6), when as propraetor in Northern Italy he defeated Catiline at Pistoria. From 55 he governed Hispania Ulterior as Pompey's legate, and in 49 brought his two legions to the Ebro, where he proved more stubborn than Afranius (q.v. 2) in the retreat from Ilerda. In 48 he was in Peloponnesus, but he joined the Pompeians in Africa, where early in 46 he won a success over Caesar.

After Thapsus, by compact with King Juba, he killed the king and then himself.                                   G. E. F. C.

**PETRONIUS** (1, *PW* 24), PUBLIUS, of senatorial family, was *consul suffectus* in A.D. 19 with M. Junius Silanus: they passed the *Lex Iunia Petronia* (q.v.). Petronius was proconsul of Asia (29–35 ?) and *legatus* of Syria (39–42). Commanded to erect a statue of Gaius in the Temple at Jerusalem, he demurred, pleading Jewish opposition. Gaius replied with an order to commit suicide, but the news of the Emperor's death arrived first.            T. J. C.

**PETRONIUS** (2). Courtier of Nero. His praenomen is uncertain (at Tac. *Ann.* 16. 17 *Gaius* is supplied from 16. 18, but it is more likely that a cognomen has fallen out; Pliny, *HN* 37. 20, and Plut. *Mor.* 60 d seem to give the praenomen Titus to the same man, and a T. Petronius Niger is known to have been *cos. suff. c.* A.D. 61). According to Tacitus he had been outstanding for his indolence, though this did not prevent him from being energetic as proconsul in Bithynia and later as consul. For a time he was influential enough to guide Nero in his choice of pleasures, and even when forced by Tigellinus' intrigues to commit suicide he showed himself not merely fearless but also contemptuous of Stoic posturings. Instead of a will full of flattery of Nero or his current favourites Petronius left a document denouncing him in embarrassing detail. Scholars have long ago discarded the notion that this denunciation has anything to do with the *Satyricon*, but it lives on in the attempts to see a significant resemblance between Nero and Trimalchio.        M. S. S.

**PETRONIUS** (3) **ARBITER.** Writer (1st c. A.D.). The main problem about Petronius Arbiter is whether the author of the fragmentary novel is identical with Petronius (2) above, the *arbiter elegantiae* at Nero's court. The style and language of the novel are consonant with the second half of the first century A.D., and arguments designed to bring him to the second or third century, whether linguistic or historical, are unconvincing. (See Browning in bibliography.) Tacitus' description suggests a witty, sophisticated person such as we must suppose the writer of the *Satyricōn* (sc. *libri*) to have been, though he fails to mention that his Petronius had any literary ability beyond what was required to write the scurrilous document (*Ann.* 16. 18). The argument on the identity of the author rests largely, however, on the name Arbiter: the courtier acts as *arbiter elegantiae* for Nero, while the author is given the name Arbiter or Petronius Arbiter in the MSS. of the *Satyricon* and even as early as Terentianus Maurus. The name Petronius was quite common by the first century A.D., but the name Arbiter is very rare indeed. Many have therefore concluded that the author Petronius Arbiter must be the *arbiter elegantiae*. Now the phrase *arbiter elegantiae* in itself looks sufficiently Tacitean, but if it is applied to a man already known as Petronius Arbiter it is reduced to a somewhat feeble play on words. Tacitus might more readily have coined the phrase if Arbiter was merely a nickname, but we cannot rule out the possibility that it was a name given to the author after his death when he was, not necessarily correctly, identified with the *arbiter elegantiae*.

Of his literary work we have fragments of books 14, 15, and 16 of a romance of which we do not know the whole extent, though the *Cena Trimalchionis* is almost intact. The book recounts the adventures, mostly in southern Italy, of the disreputable pair Encolpius (the narrator) and his boy-friend Giton. The choice of Encolpius, a far from admirable character, as his mouthpiece contributes to our uncertainty as to Petronius' main purpose. In view of the fragmentary state of the text it is impossible to reconstruct the plot in any detail. The absurdity of the love-affairs of the three heroes suggests that the work may be in part a parody of the kind of romantic novel known to us from later Greek novels. Literary criticism also finds a place, and a satirical intent is detected by some, particularly in the finest and most complete episode now extant, *Trimalchio's Feast* (this provides valuable evidence on 'Vulgar Latin' (q.v., though Petronius has been highly selective in his reproduction of actual lower-class speech). The form of the work is Menippean, i.e. prose interlarded with occasional verse, and it contains some anecdotes of the type of the Milesian Fables (*see* NOVEL), among which is the famous *Widow of Ephesus* (chs. 111–12). Our remains include two longer poems, a *Troiae Halosis* and a poem on the Civil War. (This latter is not a simple parody of Lucan's *Bellum Civile* since it includes a divine machinery specifically excluded by Lucan.) Apart from the *Satyricon* Petronius has also left to us a small collection of lyric and elegiac poems, but these are inferior to his prose writings.

Petronius' novel seems to have been little known in antiquity: we have bare references to it in Terentianus Maurus and Sidonius Apollinaris. In the Middle Ages he was mainly known from the *Florilegia*, but John of Salisbury (d. 1180) shows an acquaintance with parts of the novel unknown until the discovery of the Codex Traguriensis in the mid seventeenth century. Formerly it was thought that the text of the *Satyricon* was excerpted in the time of Theodosius, but recently Müller (see bibliography) has argued much more convincingly that disjointed remains of the novel were arranged by some Carolingian scholar. He also detects a larger number of interpolations than previous editors, which he ascribes to the Carolingian period.

S. Gaselee, *Trans. of Bibliograph. Soc.* 1910; *Bursian*, vols. 175, 204, 260, 282; *Anz. f. Altertumsw.* 1956, 1 ff.; *Class. Weekly* 1957, 133 ff. and 141 ff.; *Lustrum* 1956 (for verse).
TEXTS. The standard critical text is by K. Müller (1961 revised 1965), but Buecheler (1862) should still be consulted. Few commentaries have been published on the whole work surviving to us; the Variorum editions of Burman (1709, 1743²) remain useful. For the *Cena Trimalchionis*: Friedländer (1891, 1906²), Perrochat (1939, 1962³), Marmorale (1947, 1961²), helpful even if his arguments in favour of a 2nd c. date for P. are rejected; W. B. Sedgwick (1925, 1950²). Poems. *PLM* iv; H. E. Butler in Loeb Petronius; Ernout in Budé edition.
STYLE and DICTION. I. Segebade et E. Lommatzsch, *Lexicon Petronianum* (1898); W. Heraeus, *Die Sprache des Petronius und die Glossen* (1899); W. Süss, *De eo quem dicunt inesse Trimalchionis Cenae sermone vulgari* (1926); D. C. Swanson, *A Formal Analysis of Petronius' Vocabulary* (U.S.A. 1963); Dating. Bagnani, *Petronius Arbiter of Elegance* (1954); R. Browning, *CR* 1949, 12 ff.; K. F. C. Rose, *CQ* 1962 166 ff. General. J. P. Sullivan, *The 'Satyricon' of P.* (1968).                                   M. S. S.

**PETRONIUS** (4, *PW* 75) **TURPILIANUS,** PUBLIUS (*cos.* A.D. 61), succeeded Suetonius Paulinus as governor of Britain. His policy was one of peace. In 63 he was *curator aquarum* in Rome. He contributed to the repression of the Pisonian conspiracy. In 68 Nero entrusted to him the command against the rebels. His conduct is uncertain (Dio 63. 27. 1; Plut. *Galba* 15, 17). He was killed by Galba.                                   A. M.

**PETS.** Animals were kept, inside and outside the house, as pets and for show, from early times. Dogs that fed from their master's table are mentioned by Homer (*Od.* 17. 309) and Penelope found pleasure in watching her flock of geese (*Od.* 19. 536–7).

The commonest pet was the small white long-coated Maltese dog, represented on fifth-century B.C. Attic vases and gravestones. In Aristotle (*HA* 9. 6. 612$^b$10–11), it is used as a comparative standard of size for the marten. Athenaeus says that this dog was especially popular among the Sybarites, accompanying its owner even to the gymnasia (12. 518 f; 519 b). Publius' dog, Issa, was probably a Maltese (Mart. 1. 109). Epitaphs show the affection felt for pet dogs by their owners (*Anth. Lat.* 1176; 1512).

Tamed birds, especially starlings, magpies, ravens, and crows, which could be taught to talk, were popular (Stat. *Silv.* 2. 4. 18–19; Pliny, *HN* 10. 42. 120). Lesbia's 'sparrow' (Catull. 2; 3) was possibly a bullfinch. The more exotic parrot, introduced from India, was rarer (Varro, *Rust.* 3. 9. 17; Pliny, *HN* 10. 42. 117; Ov. *Am.* 2. 6; Mart. 14. 73). Nightingales and blackbirds were kept for their song (Pliny, *HN* 10. 29. 81 ff.; Pliny, *Ep.* 4. 2. 3). Monkeys amused the household with tricks they had been taught (Plaut. *Mil. Glor.* 102; Pliny, *HN* 8. 80. 215). Harmless snakes and the *lagalopex* (long-eared fox) and ichneumon mentioned by Martial (7. 87) were less usual pets. The cat was a late introduction into the Roman house, probably because, being a sacred animal in Egypt, its export from that country was forbidden. But Seneca (*Ep.* 121. 19) and Pliny (*HN* 10. 73. 202) assume their readers' acquaintance with it as a household animal. In earlier times, its function in controlling vermin was performed by the ferret.

Other animals were kept outside the house, more as a hobby and for showing off to visitors. The fishponds of the wealthy contained murenas and bearded mullet which might be trained to eat from their masters' hands (Cic. *Att.* 2. 1. 7; Pliny, *HN* 9. 81. 171). Aviaries and vivaria were fairly common from the late Republic onwards. Here were kept singing birds, doves, pigeons, peacocks, flamingoes, boars, hares, deer, and antelopes (Varro, *Rust.* 3. 3; 12–13; Columella 8. 9. 1; 9. 1. 1). *See* DOGS. S. W.

**PEUCESTAS** (b. *c.* 360 B.C.), son of an Alexander, a Macedonian noble, accompanied Alexander the Great to Asia but held no high command till after the Indian expedition, on which he saved Alexander's life (325). He was then promoted to Alexander's personal staff ('Bodyguard'), and to the important satrapy of Persis (325–324). Alone of the important Macedonians he learned Persian and adopted Persian dress, which pleased Alexander and the Persians greatly, and in equal measure displeased the Macedonian soldiers. In the disorders after Alexander's death he probably took the lead among the eastern satraps, but in the war of Antigonus and Eumenes he chose the losing side, and though his life was spared by Antigonus he disappears from history thereafter (316).

Berve, *Alexanderreich*, no. 634; W. W. Tarn, *CAH* vi, ch. 15; A. Vezin, *Eumenes von Kardia* (1907), 88 ff. G. T. G.

**PEUTINGER TABLE,** a world-'map' of the third or fourth century A.D., copied from a lost original by a monk of Colmar (A.D. 1265) and acquired in A.D. 1508 by a scholar named Peutinger. It is a long narrow strip of parchment, more than 21 feet long, 1 foot wide, in twelve sections, and was intended to serve as a portable road-guide. All distances are greatly elongated (from east to west), and the only features systematically marked on it are rectilinear roads, towns, and the chief mountains and rivers. It extends from Britain to the Ganges mouth, but most of Britain, all Spain, and west Mauretania are missing.

K. Miller, *Die Weltkarte des Castorius* (1888), *Itineraria Romana* (1916, repr. 1962); J. Wartena, *Inleiding op een Uitgave der Tabula Peutingeriana* (1927); Thomson, *Hist. Anc. Geog.* 369, 379 ff.; F. Gisinger, *PW* xix. 2, 1938, 1405 ff. E. H. W.

**PHAEA** (Φαιά, Φαῖα), the name, according to Plut. *Thes.* 9, and other authors, of a monstrous sow (a boar, Hyg. *Fab.* 38. 6, with some support from art, see Höfer in Roscher, iii. 2203, 20), killed by Theseus (q.v.) at Crommyon in Attica (Bacchylides 17. 23 and later writers). Apollod. *Epit.* 1. 1 says that Phaea was the name of the old woman who kept the sow. H. J. R.

**PHAEAX** (Φαίαξ), Athenian politician of noble birth and opponent of Alcibiades (Plut. *Alc.* 13). As ambassador to Italy and Sicily in 422 B.C. he tried to stir up anti-Syracusan feeling (Thuc. 5. 4). According to Theophrastus (Plut. *Nic.* 11) Phaeax, not Nicias, joined Alcibiades in promoting Hyperbolus' ostracism. His oratory is mentioned by Eupolis (fr. 95) and Aristophanes (*Eq.* 1377 ff.). The attribution of the speech *Against Alcibiades* (*see* ANDOCIDES 1, § 4) to Phaeax is improbable (Jebb, *Attic Orators* (1875), i. 136).

*Prosop. Att.* n. 13921. H. H. S.

**PHAEDON** (Φαίδων) of Elis (b. *c.* 417 B.C.), founder of the philosophical school of Elis. He was brought as a slave to Athens but later set free. He became one of Socrates' most devoted pupils, and Plato named after him the dialogue in which Socrates' last hours are depicted. His own teaching seems to have been confined to ethics. Of the dialogues ascribed to him *Zopyrus* and *Simon* were probably genuine. W. D. R.

**PHAEDRUS** (1) of Athens (*c.* 450–400), Socratic philosopher, a character in Plato's *Prt.* and *Symp.* as well as in the *Phdr.* He was a member of the Socratic circle though not precisely a pupil. His personality appears in Plato's dialogues as enthusiastic and rather naïve.

W. D. R.

**PHAEDRUS** (2) (fl. early 3rd c. B.C.), of the deme Sphettus, Athenian statesman, joint leader of the moderate, anti-democratic party after Ipsus (301). He served as general in 296/5 under Lachares, and during the next few years, when Demetrius Poliorcetes held Athens, he occupied various posts including home defence and command of the mercenaries; he also visited Egypt and obtained supplies from Ptolemy I. In Cimon's archonship, as hoplite general, he saved Athens from some unspecified danger. In that of Xenophon he held the same post πρῶτος—which perhaps means first after some suspension of the constitution. The evidence for his life rests on the decree passed in his honour (*IG* ii². 682 = *SIG*³ 409); the later excision of references to Macedonia and the uncertain dates of the archonships mentioned render the reconstruction of his later career uncertain.

W. S. Ferguson, *Hellenistic Athens* (1911); *Athenian Tribal Cycles* (1932); W. B. Dinsmoor, *The Athenian Archon List* (1939). F. W. W.

**PHAEDRUS** (3) (*c.* 140–70 B.C.), Epicurean philosopher, perhaps an Athenian by birth, was in Rome, where Cicero heard him lecture, before 88. He was head of the Epicurean school in Rome for a short time. He appears in Cicero as one of the most respected Epicureans of the time, but perhaps more for his character than for his philosophic ability. Cicero refers to his work Περὶ θεῶν. He is hardly mentioned except by Cicero, and does not seem to have been an independent philosopher.

A. E. Raubitschek, 'Phaidros and his Roman Pupils', *Hesp.* 1949. W. D. R.

**PHAEDRUS** (4) (*c.* 15 B.C.–*c.* A.D. 50), a slave of Thracian birth, received a good schooling perhaps in Italy, became a freedman of Augustus, and composed five books of verse fables. Under Tiberius, through suspected allusions in his fables he offended Sejanus and suffered some unknown punishment. Scarcely noticed by Roman writers (he is not mentioned by either Seneca or Quintilian in their references to fable), he is first named (though identification is uncertain) by Martial (3. 20. 5 'improbi iocos Phaedri') and next by Avianus (*praefat.*). Prose paraphrases of his and of other fables were made in later centuries, in particular the collection entitled 'Romulus', and in the Middle Ages enjoyed a great vogue. The five books are clearly incomplete and thirty further fables

(*Appendix Perottina*), included in N. Perotti's epitome of fables (*c.* 1465) drawn from a MS. now lost, have been shown to belong to them; additional fables deriving from Phaedrus are contained in the prose paraphrases.

Phaedrus' achievement, on which he greatly prides himself, lies in his elevation of the fable, hitherto utilized in literature only as an adjunct, e.g. in satire, into an independent genre. His fables, written in iambic senarii, consist of beast-tales based largely on 'Aesop' as well as jokes and instructive stories taken not only from Hellenistic collections but also from his own personal experience. Philosophic weight is sought by borrowings, sometimes clumsily introduced, from the chreia and diatribe (q.v.). Besides his professed purpose of providing amusement and counsel, Phaedrus sometimes satirizes contemporary conditions both social and also, to an extent difficult to determine, political. His work evidently evoked considerable criticism and retorts to his detractors are frequent. The presentation is, in general, animated and marked by a brevity of which Phaedrus is rightly proud, but which sometimes leads to obscurity; it is not without charm and humour. Eagerness, however, to emphasize the moral, which he sometimes misunderstands, often mars the effect. Departures from his originals are seldom happy. In his outlook he displays a patient resignation rather than the gloomy pessimism sometimes ascribed to him, but offers no profound philosophy. In language he stands in the tradition of Terence: skilfully adapting the *sermo urbanus*, he shows a classical purity (apart from a frequent use of abstract nouns and occasional vulgarisms or other unorthodoxies), clearness, and a simplicity that is in refreshing contrast to the turgid rhetoric of his day. His iambic senarius goes back to the early metre of Comedy and is very regular. Phaedrus is no creative artist; his slight talent does not bear comparison with La Fontaine; yet in the history of fable he occupies an important place. *See also* FABLE.

TEXTS. L. Havet (with notes, 1895); J. P. Postgate, O.C.T. (1919); A. Brenot (with trans., Budé, 1924); B. E. Perry (with trans., Loeb, 1965). L. Hervieux, *Les Fabulistes latins* i²–ii² (1893–4); J. Wight Duff, *Lit. Hist. Rome in Silver Age²* (1960), 107 ff., and *Roman Satire* (1936), 106 ff.; A. Hausrath, 'Zur Arbeitsweise des P.', *Hermes* 1936, 70 ff. Text of 'Romulus' with comm.: G. Thiele (1910); see C. Zander, *Phaedrus solutus* (1921). A. Cinquini, *Index Phaedrianus* (1905, repr. 1964). A. H.-W.

**PHAENIAS** of Eresus (fl. 320 B.C.), a pupil of Aristotle who inherited the Peripatetic interest in literary and historical research. Amongst various writings may be noted Τυράννων ἀναίρεσις ἐκ τιμωρίας, an expansion of Aristotle, *Pol.* 1311ᵃ25, marked by moral judgements characteristic of the period, and Περὶ τῶν ἐν Σικελίᾳ τυράννων. References in Plutarch's 'Lives' of Solon and Themistocles suggest that Phaenias was a valuable addition to Plutarch's sources.

*FGrH* iii B. 493 and 658. G. L. B.

**PHAETHON** (Φαέθων), in mythology, son of Helios (q.v.) and the heroine Clymene. Learning who his father was, he set out for the East to find him, and arriving at his palace, asked him a boon. The Sun granting him in advance anything he liked, he asked to guide the solar chariot for a day. But he was too weak to manage the immortal horses, which bolted with him and were likely to set the world on fire till Zeus killed Phaethon with a thunderbolt. He fell into the Eridanus, and his sisters, mourning for him, turned into amber-dropping trees. See Euripides, fragments of *Phaethon*, with Nauck's notes.

Eur. *Hipp.* 735 ff.; Ovid, *Met.* i. 750 ff. H. J. R.

**PHALANX**, infantry in order of battle. It was used of the common soldiers by Homer, and in the classical period of Greek hoplites generally; but modern usage applies it particularly to the Macedonian infantry after the reform ascribed to Philip II (Diod. 16. 3. 1 f., under the year 359 B.C.; it may really have been earlier). The new phalanx owed its great successes under Philip, and later under Alexander, to its numbers (Macedonia could produce at least 25,000 men for this service), to its unusually long pike (*sarissa*; about 13 feet), to its superior training which made it comparatively mobile and flexible when disposed in depth (up to sixteen deep), and to the splendid cavalry which guarded its flanks and rear, where every phalanx was vulnerable. Inside it the tactical unit was the brigade (*taxis*: about 1,500 men), subdivided into companies (*lochoi*) and sections (*dekades*).

Alexander's conquests made this phalanx, or imitations of it, a primary instrument of Hellenistic strategy, and the problem of manpower became acute. Alexander had planned a mixed phalanx of Macedonians and Asiatics. The 'Successors', unable to get enough Macedonians, used Greeks. The Ptolemies and Seleucids in particular based their army-systems upon military settlers, mostly Greek mercenaries by origin, who received land and became a hereditary soldier class. The Seleucid phalanx lasted well (numerically), mustering 20,000 at a review in 166. Technically, however, the phalanx deteriorated, even in Macedonia, mobility and individual skill being sacrificed to depth and weight and a longer *sarissa* (up to 21 feet). When it met Roman legions it was long past its best (Cynoscephalae, 196; Magnesia, 189; Pydna, 168); and Pyrrhus in Italy (280–275) had few Macedonians.

W. W. Tarn, *Hellenistic Military and Naval Developments* (1930), 1 ff.; J. Kromayer in *Heerwesen und Kriegführung der Griechen und Römer* (1928), especially 95 ff. and 136 ff. F. E. Adcock, *The Greek and Macedonian Art of War* (1957), ch. 2. For Alexander's phalanx, Berve, *Alexanderreich* i. 112 ff.; for Macedonian manpower, M. Launey, *Recherches sur les armées hellénistiques* i (1949), ch. 5. G. T. G.

**PHALARIS**, tyrant of Acragas (*c.* 570/65–554/49 B.C.), established his autocracy a decade or so after the city's foundation, when there was Sican and Phoenician pressure. He conducted successful warfare against the Sicans and by establishing his rule in Himera anticipated the coast-to-coast realm of Theron (q.v.). He became legendary for ingenious cruelty, especially for the hollow brazen bull in which his victims were roasted alive; this practice need not be ascribed to a Phoenician origin. An oligarchy apparently succeeded his overthrow. The letters bearing his name were written by a sophist, perhaps of the second century A.D. (proved by R. Bentley in 1697/9).

E. A. Freeman, *History of Sicily* ii (1891), 64 ff.; Dunbabin, *Western Greeks*, 314 ff.; H. Berve, *Die Tyrannis bei den Griechen* i (1967), 129 ff. A. G. W.

**PHALERON**, the harbour of Athens until the early fifth century (*see* PIRAEUS) was the nearest point to Athens on the coast, at or near the modern Old Phaleron. There is little shelter here; the early port was an open beach. A cemetery of the seventh century on the marshy ground west of Old Phaleron has been excavated.

Σ. Πελεκίδης, Ἀνασκαφαὶ Φαλήρου, Ἀρχ. Δελτ. 2. 13 ff.; J. Day, 'Cape Colias, Phalerum and the Phaleric Wall', *AJ Arch.* 1932, 1 ff.; R. S. Young, 'Graves from the Phaleron Cemetery', *AJ Arch.* 1942, 23 ff. T. J. D.

**PHALLUS**, a model or image of the male organ of generation, used (*a*) in certain rites connected with fertility, e.g. at the rural Dionysia, Ar. *Ach.* 243 (*see* DIONYSIA), cf. 265 ff., for a song in honour of a daimon Phales, a sort of personification of the symbol (Herter, *de dis Atticis Priapi similibus*, 42 ff.); (*b*) as an attribute of some gods, notably Hermes (q.v.) on herms and Priapus (q.v.).

Cf. Nilsson, *GGR* i². 118 ff. and 590 ff. H. J. R.

**PHANES,** a god of the Orphic cosmogony, born from an egg fashioned by Chronos in the Aither, also called Protogonos, the Firstborn. He is the creator of all, bisexual, radiant with light, gold-winged, and has the heads of various animals. His daughter is Night, who bore Gaea and Uranus to him. He is also called Eros, Metis, and Erikapaios. *See* ORPHIC LITERATURE, ORPHISM.

W. K. C. Guthrie, *Orpheus and Greek Religion*² (1952), 80 and 95.
M. P. N.

**PHANOCLES,** Greek poet (place and date of birth unknown). The six fragments from his verse seem all to come from one elegiac poem, the title of which is given by Clement of Alexandria as Ἔρωτες ἢ Καλοί. This was a catalogue-poem and dealt with the affection of gods (e.g. Dionysus) and heroes (e.g. Orpheus, Tantalus, Agamemnon) for beautiful boys. Probably each episode began with a stereotyped ἤ ὥς in the Hesiodic manner, cf. frs. 1 and 3. The longest fragment, in which Phanocles describes the death of Orpheus and its sequel, proves that the author possessed considerable skill in narration. The language is simple and well chosen and the versification melodious, though, like Hermesianax, Phanocles is too prone to the arrangement of the pentameter by which an adjective closes the first half and the noun with which it agrees the second. It is possible that the *Erotes* was intended as a male counterpart to the *Leontion* of Hermesianax, but Phanocles is more interested in aetiology than Hermesianax, cf. frs. 1, 5, 6. A rationalistic interpretation of myth appears in fr. 4. Apollonius Rhodius (*Argon.* 4. 903) seems to imitate an unusual scansion found in Phanocles, fr. 1. 1. If this is correct, Phanocles lived in the first half of the third century B.C. He was perhaps a younger contemporary of Hermesianax.

TEXTS. Powell, *Coll. Alex.* 106–9; Diehl, *Anth. Lyr. Graec.* vi². 71–3.
E. A. B.

**PHANODEMUS** of Athens, born in the first quarter of the fourth century B.C. and probably father of the historian Diyllus. Since his identification by Ad. Wilhelm (*Anz. d. Wien. Akad.* 1895, 45) with the Phanodemus who played a prominent part in the public life of Athens after the Peace of Philocrates (346), we have inscriptional evidence for his activities in four decrees. Three of these (*SIG*³ 227, 287, 298) record the granting of civic crowns as a reward for his services to the *boule* and Demos between 343 and 329, and show his strong interest in the festivals of Dionysus and Amphiaraus. In 329 he was elected to assist in conducting the latter's festival, and a fourth decree (ibid. 296) mentions his appointment as ἱεροποιός to Delphi in 330. He collaborated with Lycurgus, the most important politician in Athens (338–326) and supported the latter's vigorous policy to restore the city's fortunes after Chaeronea. His interest in Attic cults and myths found expression in an Atthis of at least nine books. Whether this account of Athenian history reached his own time is not known; the latest certain date belongs to the period of Cimon. He also wrote an account of the island of Icus of which he may have been commander in the war against Philip. This book was probably one of Callimachus' sources for his Αἴτια.

*FGrH* iii B. 325.
G. L. B.

**PHAON,** a legendary ferryman in Lesbos, made so handsome or given such a potent charm by Aphrodite, that Sappho among others fell desperately in love with him, finally jumping off the Leucadian rock for his sake. The story apparently is a comedian's invention (see Ov. *Her.* 15, with Palmer's notes).
H. J. R.

**PHARMAKOS,** a kind of human scapegoat or embodiment of ill-luck. In Ionia a *pharmakos* was used when some disaster (as famine) befell a community. He was chosen for his ugliness, led to a certain place (presumably outside the city), and there burned in pretence or reality (Tzetzes, *Chil.* 5. 726 ff., with Hipponax, frs. 6 ff. Diehl, quoted there). A like custom existed at Massilia (Petronius in Servius on *Aen.* 3. 57). In Athens, at the Thargelia (q.v.), there were annually two *pharmakoi*, one for the men and one for the women, called also *sybakchoi*; they were sent out of the city, but no one says they were killed (Harpocration and Photius, s.v.). Details are obscure.

See L. Deubner, *Attische Feste* (1932), 179 ff.; V. Gebhard, *Die Pharmakoi in Ionien* (Munich Diss. 1926); Nilsson, *GGR* i². 107 ff.
H. J. R.

**PHARNABAZUS,** satrap of Dascylium *c.* 413–370 B.C. He co-operated with Sparta against Athens at Abydos, Cyzicus, and Chalcedon, but in 408 encouraged the Athenians to open negotiations with Darius, though these broke down through the pro-Spartan sympathies of Cyrus. In 404, at Lysander's request, he caused the refugee Alcibiades to be assassinated. In the war with Sparta which followed Cyrus' downfall Dascylium was ravaged by Dercyllidas (398) and again by Agesilaus, whose famous meeting with Pharnabazus (Xen. *Hell.* 4. 1. 29 ff.) occurred in 395. He strongly supported the revival of Persian sea-power, and shared the command with Conon at Cnidos and in the later naval operations. Recalled to Susa in 392, he was entrusted with the reconquest of Egypt, but failed in two attempts (385–383 and 374), and died shortly afterwards.

J. M. Cook, *Greek Archaeology in Western Asia Minor* (*Arch. Rep.* for 1959–60), 34 ff. describes excavations at Dascylium. For coin-portrait, C. M. Kraay, *Greek Coins* (1966), nos. 623, 718.
D. E. W. W.

**PHARNACES** (1) **I,** king of Pontus, succeeded Mithridates III *c.* 185 B.C. He captured Sinope (*c.* 183) and made war on Eumenes II of Pergamum. He refused to come to terms at the instance of a Roman commission (181), but he was defeated by a combination of kingdoms and cities against him and compelled to surrender most of his conquests (179). However, he kept Sinope and united her colonies Cerasus and Cotyora to form the city of Pharnacia. His diplomatic relations with cities and principalities of south Russia show that he anticipated Mithridates Eupator's dream of a Pontic empire (*IPE* i². 402); and an Attic decree attests his gifts to Athens. He died between 159 and 156.

For bibliography *see* MITHRIDATES. For coin-portrait, C. M. Kraay, *Greek Coins* (1966), no. 770.
T. R. S. B.

**PHARNACES** (2) **II** (63–47 B.C.), son of Mithridates VI Eupator, led the revolt that drove his father to death, and was granted the Bosporan kingdom by Pompey. This he reduced to order and enlarged. During the war between Caesar and Pompey he seized Colchis, Lesser Armenia, and some of Cappadocia, defeated Calvinus, Caesar's lieutenant (48), and overran much of Pontus, but was defeated at Zela by Caesar himself (47), who announced his victory with the words 'Veni, vidi, vici'. He escaped to his kingdom but was killed in battle with the Bosporan rebel Asander.

App. *Mith.*; *Bell. Alex.* Magie, *Rom. Rule Asia Min.*, see index.
T. R. S. B.

**PHARSALUS,** a city of Thessaly, situated on the main road from Larissa to central Greece. It dominated the tetrad Phthiotis (q.v.) and for long periods Achaea Phthiotis as well. A hill overlooking the well-watered plain supplied an impressive acropolis. Apparently several leading families competed for control of Pharsalus, and their rivalries proved a source of weakness. In the struggle between the Pheraean tyranny and the rest of Thessaly,

Pharsalus was several times occupied by a garrison; but thanks to its policy of furthering intrigues of Philip, it became the strongest city of Thessaly under the Macedonian regime, and Pharsalian cavalry served Alexander well in Asia. In the Lamian War, however, the Pharsalians attempted to throw off the yoke of Macedon and paid dearly for their failure.

In the neighbourhood were fought three important battles, the victories of Pelopidas (364 B.C.) and Flamininus (197) at Cynoscephalae, and that of Caesar over Pompey (48).

F. Stählin, *Das hellenische Thessalien* (1924), 135 ff.　H. D. W.

**PHASELIS** (modern *Tekirova*), on the east coast of Lycia, was a Greek colony founded from Rhodes; the traditional date is 690 B.C. Its three harbours, on a coast where good harbours are scarce, gave it an important place in commerce; Phaselis shared in the foundation of the Hellenium at Naucratis. Following Cimon's campaign of c. 468 B.C. Phaselis was included in the Delian League, with a tribute similar to that of Cnidos. In the fourth century the city, still independent, entered into a pact with Mausolus, of which a part is extant (*TAM* ii. 3. 1183). Phaselis welcomed Alexander, who treated it well. Later it came under the Ptolemies, and from 197 B.C. for a short while under Antiochus III. When the Lycian Confederacy was formed (*see* LYCIA) Phaselis was included, though with a lower standing than its less-known neighbour Olympus. In the first century B.C. it ceased to be a member and became instead a headquarters for the pirate chief Zenicetes; for this it was sacked by Servilius Isauricus. Under the Empire it was again a member of the Lycian Confederacy, and was twice visited by Hadrian (A.D. 129, 131).

*TAM* ii. 3. 411 ff.; G. E. Bean, *Turkey's Southern Shore* (1968), ch. 10. For its judicial treaty with Athens c. 450 B.C., see Tod, n. 32. Cf. H. T. Wade-Gery, *Essays in Greek History* (1958), 180 ff.; G. E. de Ste Croix, *CQ* 1961, 100 ff.　G. E. B.

**PHASIS** (modern *Rion*), main river of ancient Colchis (q.v.), flows westward into the south-eastern corner of the Euxine on the south side of the Caucasus mountains, and was often regarded in antiquity as the frontier between Europe and Asia. The pheasant ('phasianus') was brought from the area to Europe.

In the sixth century B.C. the Milesians established a colony of the same name at the mouth of the river. Its exact site has not yet been found. It seems to have been important at first, but had declined to insignificance by the Roman period.

Hippocrates, *On Airs* 15; Arr. *Peripl. M. Eux.* 8–9.　D. J. B.

**PHAYLLUS** (1), an athlete from Crotona in south Italy who gained three victories in the Pythian Games and also fought at Salamis (480 B.C.) in a ship which he fitted out at his own expense. He is presumed to be the athlete of this name who is said in an epigram (*Anth. Pal.*, appendix 297) to have jumped 55 feet.　F. A. W.

**PHAYLLUS** (2), brother of Onomarchus (q.v.) and Phocian commander in the Third Sacred War (q.v.). He was defeated by Philip II of Macedon in Thessaly (353 B.C.), but succeeded Onomarchus upon his death in 352. Realizing Philip's intention to march south, Phayllus united the Phocian people, occupied Thermopylae with a Phocian and mercenary army, and received assistance from Sparta, Achaea, and Athens. After Philip's withdrawal, Phayllus was able to concentrate on the war with Thebes. In 351 he invaded the Peloponnese

to assist Sparta against Thebes. He died of illness, and was succeeded in his command by Phalaecus.

N. G. L. H.

**PHEGEUS** (*Φηγεύς*), in mythology, father of Arsinoë, wife of Alcmaeon (q.v. 1); his sons murdered Alcmaeon when he remarried (cf. CALLIRHOE; Apollod. 3. 87 ff.). An undatable but probably late story (*Certam. Hom. et Hes.* 249 Rzach) says Hesiod stayed for some time at his court and was put to death by his sons, who suspected him of seducing their sister.　H. J. R.

**PHEIDIPPIDES** (so the best MSS. of Herodotus) or **Philippides** was the Athenian courier dispatched to solicit Spartan help upon the news of the Persian landing at Marathon (490 B.C.). He is credited with the exploit (which need not be regarded as fictitious) of having covered the distance (c. 150 miles) in two days. Legend connected him with the establishment of the Athenian cult of Pan.　P. T.

**PHEIDON**, king of Argos, changed the kingship into a tyranny (Arist. *Pol.* 1310ᵇ). He made their measures (*metra*) for the Peloponnesians and interfered at Olympia (Hdt. 6. 127). Later writers add that he struck in Aegina the first Greek coins and dedicated to Hera the spits previously current, and recovered the 'lot of Temenus', the Dorian conqueror of north-east Peloponnesus, from whom they make him variously sixth, seventh, or tenth in descent (i.e. between 900 and 700 B.C.). Pausanias (6. 22. 2) dates the interference at Olympia Olympiad VIII (748), but a plausible emendation proposes XXVIII (668). An earlier date is scarcely possible, and some date him to the sixth century. Herodotus mentions a 'son' of Pheidon c. 575, and even if 'son' is loosely used it favours a date for Pheidon not earlier than early seventh century, the period of the first Aeginetan coins. The statements about Pheidon's striking them are probably genuine tradition, preserved perhaps in the Argive Heraeum, where a bundle of spits has been discovered which may be Pheidon's dedication. For a later date for the introduction of coinage *see* COINAGE, GREEK. Herodotus' story of an occupation of Aegina by Argos that resulted in both adopting the distinctive standard of Aeginetan coins (5. 82–9) may be a distorted version of Pheidon's achievements. He would thus be the immediate predecessor of the tyrant dynasties of Corinth and Sicyon, whose rise c. 660–650 meant his own collapse.

Strabo 8. 358, 376, 355; Marmor Parium, 30; *Etym. Magn.* s.v. ὀβελίσκος. P. N. Ure, *Origin of Tyranny* (1922), 154 f.; *FGrH* 90 (Nic. Dam.) F 41; A. Andrewes, *The Greek Tyrants* (1956); E. Will, *Korinthiaka* (1955), 344 ff.; and for Pheidon's date N. G. L. Hammond, 'An early inscription at Argos', *CQ* 1960, 33 ff.
P. N. U.; N. G. L. H.

**PHEME** (*φήμη*), a rumour of unknown origin which springs up among the people at large; unprompted and unguided popular opinion. It is a god (Hes. *Op.* 763–4) and is never quite in vain (οὐ . . . πάμπαν ἀπόλλυται).

**PHERAE**, a city of Thessaly situated on a hill commanding a fertile district near the southern verge of the plain of Pelasgiotis. It lay close to important land-routes and, alone among Thessalian cities, enjoyed easy access to the sea. When in possession of Pagasae (q.v.), it controlled the export of Thessalian corn. Though prominent in mythology as the home of Admetus, it remained politically insignificant except during the half-century (c. 406–352 B.C.) when it was ruled by the family of Jason (*see* LYCOPHRON (1), JASON (2), ALEXANDER (5)). Philip of Macedon expelled the tyrant-house and established a Macedonian garrison. He also effectively ended the prosperity of Pherae by depriving it of Pagasae.

The walls of the city date probably from the period of the tyrants. A temple, built in the sixth century but reconstructed in the fourth, may be that of Artemis Ennodia, whose head appears on the local coinage.

E. Kirsten, *PW* Suppl. vii. 984 ff. H. D. W.

**PHERECRATES,** Athenian comic poet, won his first victories at the City Dionysia and the Lenaea between 440 and 430 B.C. (*IG* ii². 2325. 56, 122) and produced Ἄγριοι at the Lenaea in 420 B.C. (Pl. *Prt.* 327 d, Ath. 218 d), depicting the fortunes of men who have left civilization (cf. Ar. *Av.*) to live among savages. We have nineteen titles and 250 fragments, which bear out the judgement of Anon. *De Com.* 8 that Pherecrates was εὑρετικὸς μύθων. In *Deserters* the parabasis appears to have been uttered by a chorus of deities (fr. 23; cf. Ar. *Nub.* 607 ff.). In *Miners* the underworld is depicted (fr. 108) as a land of fantastic abundance, and a similar theme appears (fr. 130) in *Persians* (*see also* CRATES 1 and METAGENES). Μυρμηκάνθρωποι contained the story of Deucalion's flood and Zeus' repopulation of the earth by turning ants into men—a conflation of the Flood myth with a story of the origin of the Myrmidons (Hes. fr. 76 Rzach). Τυραννίς may possibly have had a plot similar to that of Ar. *Eccl.* The long and interesting fr. 157 (from what play is not known) is a speech by Music, complaining of her treatment by contemporary musicians.

*FCG* ii. 252 ff.; *CAF* i. 145 ff.; *FAC* i. 206 ff. K. J. D.

**PHERECYDES** (1) of Syros (fl. *c.* 550 B.C.), early prosewriter and author of a cosmogonic myth. His book Ἑπτάμυχος described the origination of the world by one or more of a triad of eternal deities, Zas (sc. Zeus), Chronos or Kronos, and Chthonie or Ge the earthgoddess. Aristotle puts him in a 'mixed' class of theologians who 'do not say everything in the form of myth' (*Met. N* 4), and some scholars discern signs of Ionian rationalism in the scanty reports of his views. Wilamowitz thought 'Pherecydes' a collective name for all anonymous early Ionian prose-writing: see, *contra*, Jacoby, *Mnemos.* 1947.

Diels, *Vorsokr.*¹¹ i. 43–51. Kirk–Raven, *Presocratic Philosophers* 48 ff. G. E. L. O.

**PHERECYDES** (2) of Athens, 'the genealogist' (later confused with (1)), wrote copious *Histories* mythical and genealogical, commended by Dion. Hal. *Ant. Rom.* 1. 13. 1. Eusebius' date is 456 B.C. (*Ol.* 81. 1).

*FGrH* i. 3; cf. iii. 333.

**P[H]ERSEPHONE, PERSEPHASSA or -ATTA** (Περσεφόνη, Φερσ-, Περσέφασσα, -αττα) or **KORE** (Κόρη); in Latin *Proserpina*, a simple mispronunciation, to which a false etymology from *proserpere* came to be attached (Augustine, *De civ. D.* 4. 8, from Varro), with the absurd explanation that she was the deity who made food-plants germinate. The varying forms of the name and the presence in one of the well-known pre-Hellenic suffix -ss- suggest that she is a very old native goddess of the Greek peninsula, taken over by the invaders and identified with the 'virgin daughter' (Kore) of their own corngoddess. For the story of her carrying off by Hades *see* DEMETER.

Another and very remarkable story in which she bears a part is the Orphic myth of Zagreus (cf. ORPHISM and Nilsson, *GGR* i². 686 n., for ancient references). The earliest reasonably certain mention of this is in Pindar (fr. 133 Bergk, 127 Bowra), where the poet states that those in the other world 'at whose hands Phersephona accepts satisfaction for her ancient grief' return in the ninth year to this world and become kings or otherwise distinguished men, later passing to the status of heroes.

The 'grief' seems to mean the death of her child Zagreus (Rose in *Greek Poetry and Life* (1936), 79 ff.). For the story itself see Kern, *Orph. frag.*, nos. 209 ff.; it is fully told only in late authors, as Firmicus Maternus, *De Errore*, 6; Nonnus, *Dionys.* 6. 155 ff. Zeus, in serpent form, approached Persephone and begat Zagreus, to whom he intended to give all power in the universe. But the Titans, incited by the jealous Hera, attracted the child's attention with toys, set upon him, tore him in pieces, and devoured him. Athena saved his heart, which Zeus swallowed, being thus enabled later to beget Dionysus. He destroyed the Titans with thunderbolts, and from their ashes sprang mankind.

In cult Persephone has little place save with her mother, when she is more commonly called Kore (e.g. at Eleusis. For a list of places where the two goddesses are worshipped together see Bloch in Roscher's *Lexikon* ii. 1288 ff. It does not appear (see Paus. 6. 25. 2) that she shared the unique cult of Hades (q.v.) at Elis, although they are continually associated in literature and art (*see* ELEUSIS, MYSTERIES).

In art she often appears with her mother, with or without Triptolemus. Like Demeter she often carries a sceptre or torches, and when alone cannot easily be distinguished from Demeter or Hecate. Her *Anodos* is shown on fifthcentury Attic vases, her abduction by Hades and her wedding on terracotta plaques of the first half of the fifth century from Italian Locri. She is also shown enthroned with Hades. H. J. R.; C. M. R.

**PHIDIAS,** Athenian sculptor, born *c.* 490 B.C. Reputed pupil of Hegias and Hageladas. Among his early works was the so-called Athena Promachos, which, according to a preserved inscription, was erected *c.* 456 B.C. It was about 30 feet high, and the point of its spear and the crest of its helmet were said to have been visible to mariners from Sunium (Paus. 1. 28. 2)—no doubt the golden bronze gleaming in the sunlight. Part of the base survives on the Acropolis. Another statue of Phidias' early period was the so-called Lemnian Athena, a thankoffering by the people of Lemnos (Paus. 1. 28. 2), probably Athenian colonists between 451 and 448 B.C. It has been identified with great probability in a head in Bologna and two statues in Dresden. But the most famous works of Phidias were two cult statues of gold and ivory. The first was the colossal Athena made for the Parthenon. Pausanias (1. 24. 5) gives a long description of it and from it a number of Roman copies have been identified. They consist of statuettes of various sizes, heads, reliefs of the ornaments on the shield, and representations on Roman coins as well as on engraved gems (cf. *Hesp.* 1966, pl. 54). It was finished and in place in 438 B.C. The other colossal chryselephantine statue—the seated Zeus which Phidias made for the temple of Zeus at Olympia—was considered his masterpiece. For its visualization there remain only representations of the head and of the figure on coins of Elis of the time of Hadrian; what seem to be adaptations of it occur on many other coins, for its fame spread throughout the Greek and Roman world. Recently there have been found in Phidias' 'workroom' at Olympia a number of terracotta moulds used for the gold drapery of the statue, in a style suggesting a date around 430 B.C. They have finally shown that the Zeus must have been made after the Athena, that is, after he was exiled by the Athenians for political reasons. It had long been thought by some that the Zeus anteceded the Athena.

Of the other works ascribed by ancient writers to Phidias it has been possible to identify Roman copies of the Amazon which he made for Ephesus in competition with other sculptors; and, with considerable probability, an Anadumenus made at Olympia. More tentatively, based only on style, there have been attributed the Cassel

Apollo, the Athena Medici, the Dioscuri of Monte Cavallo, etc.

Apart from these pale reflections of Phidias' style, there are, however, the sculptures of the Parthenon—the metopes, frieze, and the pedimental figures—for which he must have been responsible (cf. Plut. *Per.* 13. 4). So, though naturally Phidias will not have himself carved these architectural sculptures, he doubtless was the originator of their designs. We have here, therefore, precious originals by which to judge the Phidian style, which had an abiding influence on all Greek sculpture.

The diversity of Phidias' genius is attested by the fact that he was not only a sculptor of colossal and life-size figures, but was also a painter, an engraver, and, in the words of Pliny, opened up new possibilities in metal-work (*toreutice*).

For the indictment of Phidias in connexion with the statue of Athena Parthenos see F. E. Adcock in *CAH* v. 477 ff. and F. J. Frost, *JHS* 1964, 69 ff.    G. M. A. R.

**PHILADELPHIA** (1) (*Φιλαδέλφεια*), in the north-east of the Fayûm, was founded by Ptolemy II Philadelphus in connexion with the reclamation of the Moeris basin. The site, now *Darb Gerze*, was partly excavated for the Berlin Museum in 1908/9; the plan showed the normal Ptolemaic scheme of rectangular *insulae*, mainly of private houses, with a temple and possibly an official bureau. Considerable finds of papyri and small objects were secured by the excavators; others, before and after them, by native diggers, among these being the papers of Zenon (*see* APOLLONIUS 3). The cemetery, lying to the east, has produced many mummy-portraits: one was found in a house. The town seems to have been abandoned in the fourth century.

P. Viereck, *Philadelpheia* (1928), gives a full description and bibliography.    J. G. M.

**PHILADELPHIA** (2) of Lydia, founded in the Cogamis valley by Attalus II Philadelphus (159–138 B.C.). The site is fertile but lies on the edge of the Catacecaumene, and was so constantly troubled by earthquakes that according to Strabo (13. 628) few of the citizens lived actually in the city. Philadelphia struck coins almost from its foundation, and celebrated games in honour of Zeus-Helios and Anaeitis. Wrecked by the disastrous earthquake of A.D. 17, it quickly recovered; under Caligula it added to its name the title of Neocaesareia, and under Vespasian that of Flavia. In the third century it acquired the dignity of a neocorate and the style of metropolis. It was one of the Seven Churches of Asia in Revelation. The ruins at *Alâşehir* are insignificant.    G. E. B.

**PHILAMMON** (*Φιλάμμων*), a musician, either wholly fabulous or so ancient as to be much overlaid with mythical details. Son of Apollo (Hes. fr. 111 Rzach + Pherec. in schol. *Od.* 19. 432); invented maiden choirs (ibid.); first to celebrate the birth of Leto's twins and institute choruses at Delphi ([Plut.] *De mus.* 1132 a), founded the mysteries at Lerna (Paus. 2. 37. 2). H. J. R.

**PHILARGYRIUS**, JUNIUS (5th c. A.D.), a commentator on Virgil; but there is some doubt about his real name (Filagrius?). His *Explanatio in Bucolica* is extant (ed. H. Hagen in Thilo's Servius, III. ii) in a longer and a shorter version, both of which contain Celtic glosses. The Berne scholia to the *Eclogues* and *Georgics* (ed. H. Hagen, *Jahrb. für class. Phil.* Suppl. 4, 1867, 749 ff.) which mention 'Iunilius Flagrius' as one of their sources, and the *Brevis expositio Georgicorum* (ed. H. Hagen in Thilo's Servius, III. ii) probably owe a great deal of their material to Philargyrius.

Cf. G. Funaioli, *Esegesi Virgiliana antica* (1930). Schanz–Hosius, § 248. 6.    J. F. M.

**PHILEMON** (1) (*Φιλήμων*), in mythology, a good old countryman, who lived with his wife Baucis in Phrygia. Zeus and Hermes, coming to earth to test men's piety, were refused hospitality elsewhere but received by them. The gods revealed their deity and warned them to climb a mountain. On arrival near the summit, they saw the district covered by a flood. They then became priest and priestess and finally were turned into trees.

Ov. *Met.* 8. 618 ff.; cf. W. M. Calder, *Discovery* 1922, 207 ff.; J. E. Fontenrose, *Univ. of Cal. Pub. in Class. Phil.* 1945, 93 f.    H. J. R.

**PHILEMON** (2) (b. 368/60 B.C., d. 267/63 B.C.), New Comedy poet from Syracuse (*Suda*) or Soli in Cilicia (Strabo 14. 671), but granted Athenian citizenship before 307/6 (*IG* ii². 3073). In a long life (97 or 99 or 101 years: sources differ) he wrote ninety-seven comedies, of which over sixty titles are known (including *Λιθογλύφος*, not in Meineke or Kock); he won three Lenaean victories, coming immediately after Menander in the victors' inscription (*IG* ii². 2325. 161), while his first victory at the Dionysia is dated to 327 (*Marm. Par.* B 7). Alciphron (4. 18) suggests that Philemon received an invitation to the court of Ptolemy; it is not certain that this was accepted, although another anecdote (Plut. *Mor.* 449 e, 458 a) brings him before King Magas of Cyrene. Accounts of Philemon's death differ, but all agree that he was physically and mentally active to the end.

Most of the titles seem typical of New Comedy; only two (*Μυρμιδόνες*, *Παλαμήδης*) sound like mythological burlesque. Contemporary judgement awarded Philemon frequent victories over Menander, though this verdict was reversed by posterity (Quint. *Inst.* 10. 1. 72; Apul. *Flor.* 16; Gell. *NA* 4. 17. 1). Well over 200 fragments survive, emphasizing the moralizing aspect of Philemon's thought: e.g. fr. 22 (cf. fr. 95), a slave is a human being; fr. 71, peace the only true 'good'; fr. 94, real justice. There are many gnomic lines and couplets, often lacking Menander's terse precision, and Jachmann's attack (*Plautin. und Attisches*, 226 f.) on Philemon's flat-footed, repetitive, and platitudinous verbosity is not altogether unjustified. Of greater interest perhaps are the pompous cook who parodies the *Medea* (fr. 79: see Dohm, *Mageiros* (1964), 122 ff.) and part of a (long-winded?) prologue spoken by Aer (fr. 91).

Of Philemon's technique in complete plays Plautine adaptations furnish some evidence—*Mercator* (from *Ἔμπορος*), *Trinummus* (from *Θησαυρός*), and possibly *Mostellaria* (from *Φάσμα*?). Here the fondness for surprises is probably the most interesting common factor; there is little, however, to make one quarrel with Apuleius' judgement (loc. cit.) that Philemon's plays contained much wit, plots neatly turned, recognitions (or solutions?) lucidly arranged, characters corresponding to reality, maxims agreeing with life, and few seductions.

In Athens Philemon's comedies were revived after his death (*IG* ii². 2323. 101); in the second century A.D. a statue was erected there in his honour (*IG* ii². 4266). But as an index of diminished popularity as compared with Menander, there are far fewer quotations from Philemon, and no papyrus certainly assigned to Philemon has been recovered in Egypt, although several attributions have been made (Page, *GLP*, nos. 61, 64, 69; ostraca in *JHS* 1923, 40 ff., cf. *Hermes* 1924, 362 ff.); of these perhaps the first is the most plausible, in view of the long-windedness of part of the fragment.

FRAGMENTS. *FCG* iv. 3 ff.; *CAF* ii. 478 ff., iii. 749 f.; Demiańczuk, *Suppl. Com.* 71 f.; Page, *GLP*, no. 50.
INTERPRETATION AND CRITICISM. C. A. Dietze, *De Philemone Comico* (1901); E. Rapisarda, *Philemone Comico* (1939); B. Krysiniel-Józefowicz, *De Quibusdam Plauti Exemplaribus Graecis* (1949); Webster, *Later Greek Comedy*, 125 ff.    W. G. A.

**PHILEMON** (3) **the Younger,** son of the celebrated Philemon (2), and himself a New Comedy poet; wrote fifty-four plays (none known to us by name) and won six victories.

FCG iv. 68; CAF ii. 540.

**PHILEMON** (4). A fourth Philemon, whether of the same family as (2) and (3) or not, is known from didascalic inscriptions as author of Μιλησία (CAF ii. 540), 183 B.C.

**PHILEMON** (5). In the middle of the fourth century B.C. lived a fifth Philemon, an actor, mentioned by Aeschines (1. 115) and Aristotle (see ANAXANDRIDES).

**PHILEMON** (6) of Aixonae (an Attic deme) (probably early 2nd c. B.C.), grammarian, edited Homer and compiled Ἀττικαὶ γλῶσσαι.

**PHILEMON** (7) of Athens (c. A.D. 200), an Atticist grammarian, wrote Σύμμικτα and Περὶ Ἀττικῆς ἀντιλογίας (?ἀναλογίας) τῆς ἐν ταῖς λέξεσιν.

**PHILETAERUS** (1), Middle Comedy poet, said by Dicaearchus to be the son of Aristophanes, but this was disputed; however, allusions assign him to the earlier period of Middle Comedy. He won first prize twice at the Lenaea (IG ii². 2325. 143). Of twenty-one comedies (Suda) thirteen titles are preserved; four or five are mythological burlesques, but there are many topical references.

FCG iii. 292 ff.; CAF ii. 230 ff.; FAC ii. 18 ff.
W. G. W.; K. J. D.

**PHILETAERUS** (2) (c. 343–263 B.C.), son of Attalus (a Macedonian?) and a Paphlagonian mother. First an officer of Antigonus (before 302), and next commander of Pergamum for Lysimachus, who kept a large treasure there, he deserted opportunely to Seleucus (282), and henceforth was ruler of Pergamum under Seleucid suzerainty. He may have enlarged his territories somewhat in his last years, but his best work was in defending Pergamum from the Galatian invaders of Asia Minor (278–276), and in founding the Attalid dynasty, which he did by adopting his nephews, one of whom (Eumenes) succeeded him. He was himself said to be a eunuch.

Hansen, Attalids, 15 ff. Coin-portrait, C. M. Kraay, Greek Coins (1966), nos. 737–9.
G. T. G.

**PHILETAS** (rather than **Philitas**) of Cos, son of Telephus, born not later than 320 B.C., became tutor of Ptolemy II Philadelphus (born in Cos 309/8). Other pupils of Philetas were Zenodotus, Hermesianax, and (probably 275–271) Theocritus. His grave seems to have been in Cos, where the Coans put up a bronze statue of him (Hermesianax, fr. 7. 75–8 Powell).
WORKS. (1) Verse. According to the Suda (s.v.) Philetas wrote 'Epigrams and Elegies and other works'. The sources cite five titles: Demeter, Hermes, Telephus, Epigrammata, Paegnia. The Demeter was a narrative elegy, recounting the goddess's wanderings, among them perhaps her visit to Cos (cf. schol. Theoc. 7. 5–9 f.). The Hermes was an epyllion, in which Philetas narrated the intrigue of Odysseus with the Aeolid Polymele (Parth. 2). The emotions of Polymele formed the central theme, but Odysseus told Aeolus the tale of his wanderings, though not in the Homeric order. The Telephus included a reference to the marriage of Jason and Medea. It is uncertain whether Paegnia (frs. 10 and 11) and Epigrammata (frs. 12 and 13) were separate works or alternative titles for one collection. Among the unassigned fragments fr. 22, a reference to the Bougonia of bees, has been thought to prove that Philetas anticipated Theocritus' treatment

(7. 78–89) of the Comatas legend. In any case Theocritus acknowledged Philetas as his master (7. 39–41).
(2) Prose. Thirty fragments survive from a work entitled Miscellaneous Glosses or Miscellanea (Ἄτακτοι Γλῶσσαι, Ἄτακτα). This was a lexical compilation explaining rare words drawn from Homer (Aristarchus wrote a brochure 'Against Philetas') and various dialects, and also technical terms. The book became famous almost at once, being referred to in the Phoenicides of Straton (Ath. 9. 382 c). This passage already figures in a school anthology of c. 220, cf. Guéraud and Jouguet, Un Livre d'écolier du IIIᵉ siècle avant J.-C. (1938). [Strabo] 3. 168 assigns to Philetas a work with the title Ἑρμηνεία (? Interpretation) and quotes from it an elegiac couplet (fr. 17). If this was a prose work, the lines were cited by Philetas as an illustration and need not be by him.
Though Aelian (VH 10. 6) calls Philetas 'the poet of hexameters', it was as an Elegist that he won lasting fame. He was included in the Canon of Elegists and, according to Quintilian (Inst. 10. 1. 58), in the opinion of most came second to Callimachus. Propertius and Ovid several times allude to him as their model in Elegy. In two passages (Tr. 1. 6. 2; Pont. 3. 1. 57–8) the latter refers to one Battis or Bittis as having been sung by Philetas. This is confirmed by Hermesianax, fr. 7. 77–8, where the name is Bittis. It is uncertain whether this lady was Philetas' wife or mistress, and in what kind of verse he celebrated her charms. It is unlikely that Philetas wrote subjective love-elegies in the Roman manner, but tributes to Bittis may have been included in the Epigrams or Paegnia. His great reputation as a poet among his younger contemporaries—besides Hermesianax and Theocritus, Callimachus too mentioned him in the preface to his Aetia, fr. 1 Pf., and probably in fr. 532 Pf.—may have been influenced by his position as the inaugurator of the scholar-poet tradition which the Alexandrians continued. He was also considered by the Callimachean school as a master of the short and highly finished poem (cf. Schol. Flor. Callim. fr. 1. 12–15 Pf.).

TEXTS. Powell, Coll. Alex. 90–6; Diehl, Anth. Lyr. Graec. vi². 49–55; A. Nowacki, Philitae Coi fragmenta poetica (1927); G. Kuchenmüller, Philetae Coi Reliquiae (1928). The last includes the prose fragments.
GENERAL LITERATURE. H. E. Butler and E. A. Barber, The Elegies of Propertius (1933), xxxix ff.xlvi; ff. A. A. Day, The Origins of Latin Love-Elegy (1938), 14 ff.
E. A. B.

**PHILICUS** (not Philiscus), of Corcyra, was one of the 'Tragic Pleiad' under Ptolemy II Philadelphus, also Priest of Dionysus at Alexandria and possibly Eponymous Priest of Alexander (Schubart from PHib. 30. 23). In the procession of 275/4 he marched at the head of the technitai (Ath. 5. 198 c, from Callixenus). The Suda credits Philicus with forty-two tragedies but no certain title or fragment survives (cf. TGF 819). As a lyric poet Philicus claimed in his Hymn to Demeter (Diehl, Anth. Lyr. Graec. vi. 296) to have invented the metrum Philicium (catalectic choriambic hexameters) used in that poem. Fragments from a Hymn to Demeter written in this metre have been published (by M. Norsa in Stud. Ital. N.S. v (1927), 87 ff.) from a papyrus and plausibly identified as belonging to Philicus' poem. The fragments testify to the author's skilful craftsmanship and power of realistic description.

F. Schramm, Tragic. Graec. hellenist. aetatis fragmenta (1929); M. Gabathuler, Hellenistische Epigramme auf Dichter (1937), 16; Powell and Barber, New Chapters, Series I, 107; Series II, 61 f.; Series III, 195 ff.; Page, GLP 402–7; K. Latte, MH 1954.
E. A. B.

**PHILINUS** (1) of Cos (fl. c. 250 B.C.), a pupil of Herophilus, was called, perhaps on insufficient grounds (see SERAPION 1), the founder of the Empirical School of Medicine. He wrote about difficult words in Hippocratic books and rejected any diagnosis based on the pulse—that is all the information which the fragments yield, except a few pharmacological precepts. If Philinus' doctrine is identical with that of his school—and the Empirical system, according to ancient sources, remained essentially unchanged—he must have denounced inquiry into hidden causes, explanation of physiological processes, systematic study of anatomy in dead or living bodies, and general theories concerning diseases. Relying only on his own experience and that of others, and on the conclusions resulting therefrom by analogy, he must have paid attention to factors which evidently influence illness and to the individual differences of people and localities.

FRAGMENTS. K. Deichgräber, *Die Gr. Empirikerschule* (1930). *Galen on Medical Experience*, ed. and transl. by R. Walzer (1944); *see also* L. Edelstein, *The Philosophical Review* (1947) (historical background and philosophical dependence of empiricism); H. Diller, *PW* xix. 2193.                                                                L. E.

**PHILINUS** (2) of Acragas, pro-Carthaginian historian of the First Punic War, writing probably in monograph form, was used by Polybius (1. 13–4) with Fabius Pictor, and perhaps by Diodorus (23–24).

*FGrH* ii. 174. F. W. Walbank, *CQ* 1945, 1 ff.

**PHILIP** (1) **II,** king of Macedon 359–336 B.C., laid the foundations of Macedonia's greatness. Internally, he unified Macedonia by removing the semi-independent principalities of upper Macedonia and incorporating territorial divisions in the army system, by favouring Greek culture, and by promoting urbanization and trade. The capture of Pydna, Methone, and Amphipolis, the exploitation of the Pangaeum mines (yielding 1,000 talents annually), and the alliance with the Chalcidian League favoured the economic growth of Macedonia; by incorporating Thrace, Chalcidice, and Thessaly under the royal mint he created an economic power capable of supporting a standing army and launching the expedition of Alexander. Under the stress of long warfare Philip forged a professional army with national spirit, which became the Grande Armée of Alexander; he developed siegecraft, trained the Macedonian infantry in the novel phalanx formation, employed the tactic of offensive and defensive wings, and bequeathed an able staff to Alexander. At Chaeronea the Macedonian power created by Philip overwhelmed Greece as decisively as it later overwhelmed Persia.

In the rise of Macedon Philip displayed diplomatic genius by exploiting the enmity between Athens and Chalcidice, the Social and Sacred Wars, and the dissension in Thrace and Thessaly. By making peace with Athens in 358 he covered his attack on Amphipolis and Pydna, and by allying with the Chalcidic Confederacy in 356 he captured Potidaea and defeated a Balkan coalition organized by Athens. By marriage alliances with the Molossian royal house and the Aleuadae of Larissa, and by annexing western Thrace he acquired sufficient strength to intervene in the Sacred War. He defeated Onomarchus, organized Thessaly, and penetrated to Thermopylae (352). He invaded and annexed Chalcidice, instigating a revolt against Athens in Euboea to synchronize with it (349–348). After these successes he concluded peace and alliance with Athens, and terminated the Sacred War (346). Invited by Isocrates to lead Greece against Persia, Philip endeavoured to conciliate Athens, until the opposition hardened under Demosthenes' leadership; frustrated at Perinthus and Byzantium by Athenian and Persian help, he used a diplomatic opening offered by the Delphic Amphictiony to force the issue at Chaeronea. He used his victory to give Greece a federal constitution under his leadership as elective Hegemon (the League of Corinth), and to ally it with Macedonia. He was assassin-

ated at the age of 46, when about to lead the forces of Macedonia and Greece against Persia.

Of his contemporaries the nationalist Demosthenes saw in Philip a perfidious despot, the Panhellenist Isocrates and Ephorus a leader of Greece, and the individualist Theopompus the greatest man Europe had known. Modern scholarship, while divided in interpretation of his personality, is unanimous in appreciating his statesmanship, diplomacy, and generalship.

ANCIENT SOURCES. Diod. bk. 16, following Ephorus and Duris (A. Momigliano, *Rend. Ist. Lomb.* 1932), or Ephorus and Diyllus (N. G. L. Hammond, *CQ* 1937–8); Theopompus frs.; Isocrates, *Philippus*; passages in Attic Orators; Polyaenus; Justin, bks. 7–9; Tod, nos. 150 ff.; *'Αρχ. 'Εφ.* 1925/6, 76; Seltman, *Greek Coins²* (1955), ch. 12; West in *Num. Chron.* 1923, 169.
MODERN LITERATURE. A. W. Pickard-Cambridge, *CAH* vi (1933), chs. 8–9; A. Momigliano, *Filippo il Macedone* (1934); U. Wilcken, *Alexander der Große* (Engl. Transl. 1932), ch. 2; J. Kromayer, *Schlachtenatlas* iv, with text 36 f. (1926); N. G. L. Hammond, *Klio* 1938, 186 ff.; F. Hampl, *Der König von Makedonien* (1934); F. R. Wüst, *Philipp II. u. Griechenland 346–338 B.C.* (1938); P. Cloché, *Un Fondateur d'empire, Philippe II roi de Macédoine* (1955).
                                                                N. G. L. H.

**PHILIP** (2) **ARRHIDAEUS** (*c.* 358–317 B.C.), son of Philip II of Macedonia and Philinna of Larissa; became Philip III of Macedonia. Little is known of his life under Philip and Alexander, except that he was feeble-minded, that he married his cousin Adea (Eurydice, q.v.), and that he was at Babylon when Alexander died; presumably Alexander had taken him to Asia in 334 as a precautionary measure. His election as king, jointly with Alexander's posthumous son Alexander IV (323), gave him no real power, but he was steered skilfully through the early struggles of the 'Successors' by Eurydice, his name and authority being used by (successively) Perdiccas, Antipater, Polyperchon, and Cassander. He was ultimately captured and killed by Olympias, who desired the sole succession for Alexander's son.

Berve, *Alexanderreich* ii, no. 781.                             G. T. G.

**PHILIP** (3) **V** (238–179 B.C.), king of Macedon, son of Demetrius II and Phthia (Chryseis), was adopted by Antigonus III, and succeeded in summer 221. The Social War (220–217), in which the Hellenic League opposed Aetolia, Sparta, and Elis, brought him considerable renown, notwithstanding the intrigues of his ministers, headed by Apelles (executed 218), against Achaea. After the Peace of Naupactus (217), instigated by Demetrius of Pharos, he took up arms against Rome in Illyria, first by sea, later, after losing his fleet (214), by land; his treaty with Hannibal (215) defined spheres of operation. His brutal attacks on Messene in 215/14 alienated Achaea. An Aetolian alliance (211) and Attalus of Pergamum's collaboration now gave Roman forces in Greece an advantage; but Philip held out, and when they retired in 207, he sacked Thermum and forced terms on Aetolia (206). The war concluded with the favourable Peace of Phoenice (205). Philip then turned eastward: he employed a pirate, Dicaearchus, to obtain resources, and in 203/2 combined with Antiochus of Syria to plunder the possessions of the infant Ptolemy V. His terroristic methods, however, aroused Rhodes and Pergamum, who in 201 defeated him by sea off Chios, and by alarmist reports persuaded the Senate to declare war on him. This declaration Philip received at Abydos (200), after a campaign against Athens and the Thracian Chersonese; by September a Roman army was in Illyria. After two campaigns in Macedonia (199) and Thessaly (198) the Romans under Flamininus defeated him decisively at Cynoscephalae in Thessaly (197); and the subsequent peace settlement confined him to Macedonia, and exacted 1,000 talents indemnity, almost his whole fleet, and hostages, including his younger son, Demetrius.

Until 189 Philip collaborated with Rome, and having sent help against Nabis (195) and Antiochus and Aetolia (192–189), made acquisitions in Thessaly. For facilitating the Scipios' advance through Macedon and Thrace he had his tribute remitted and Demetrius restored (190). Henceforward he concentrated on consolidating Macedon: finance was reorganized, populations were transplanted, mines reopened, central and local currencies issued. Accusations from his neighbours, however, led to constant Roman interference; and in 185 adverse decisions convinced him that his destruction was intended. In three campaigns (184, 183, 181), therefore, he extended his influence in the Balkans; meanwhile Demetrius' pro-Roman policy led to a quarrel with the crown-prince Perseus, and his own execution for treason (180). In 179, amidst an ambitious scheme for directing the Bastarnae against the Dardani, Philip died at Amphipolis.

A brilliant soldier, Philip was handicapped in politics by his unbalanced temperament. He maintained popular loyalty while combining the protection of his northern frontiers with expansionist programmes elsewhere; but he lacked a consistent constructive policy, hence his main significance is as a figure in the history of Roman expansion.

ANCIENT SOURCES. Polybius; Livy, bks. 23–40; otherwise scattered. MODERN LITERATURE. M. Holleaux, *Rome, la Grèce et les monarchies hellénistiques* (1921); A. H. McDonald and F. W. Walbank, *JRS* 1937; F. W. Walbank, *Philip V of Macedon* (1940); id. *Polybius* i and ii (1957– ).                                          F. W. W.

**PHILIP** (4), on the death of his father Herod (q.v. 1) the Great, became tetrarch of the northern part of his kingdom—Auranitis, Trachonitis, Batanaea, Gaulanitis, and Paneas. When he died in A.D. 34 after an apparently peaceful reign, his territory was administered with the province of Syria until it was put under Agrippa I (q.v.) in 37.                                          E. M. S.

**PHILIPPI**, a city in eastern Macedonia on the Via Egnatia (q.v.), overlooking the inland plain east of Mt. Pangaeus (q.v.). The site, known to the Greeks as Crenides ('springs'), was apparently inhabited by Thracians till 360 B.C., when the Thasians founded a city which they called 'Daton', till then the name for the whole surrounding district. In 356 Philip II of Macedon refounded it under the name of Philippi, and made it the centre for the gold-mines of the region. In 42 it was the scene of the two battles (the second on 23 Oct.) in which Antony defeated Cassius and Brutus. Antony founded a colony for veterans there, and after Actium Octavian added more veterans as well as partisans of Antony evicted from Italy. Philippi was the first European town to hear Christian missionaries (Paul and Silas, c. A.D. 50). It survived at least till late medieval times. There are extensive remains.

App. *BCiv.* 4. 105–31; Cass. Dio 47. 35–49. P. Collart, *Philippes* (1937); P. Lemerle, *Philippes et la Macédoine orientale à l'époque chrétienne et Byzantine* (1945).                                 T. J. C.

**PHILIPPIDES** of Athens, New Comedy poet, who won a victory in 311 B.C. (*IG* ii². 2323a. 41; cf. 2325. 164). Of forty-five comedies (*Suda*) we know fifteen titles. As a friend of Lysimachus, king of Thrace, Philippides possessed great influence; an honorific decree of 285, which records his services to Athens, is still extant (Dittenberg, *SIG* 374, where the inscription is misdated). Fr. 6, Plato's 'good'; fr. 9, the ways of *nouveaux riches*; fr. 18, Euripides quoted for consolation in trouble; fr. 25, a denunciation of the sacrilegious behaviour of Demetrius Poliorcetes.

*FCG* i. 470 ff., iv. 467 ff.; *CAF* iii. 301 ff.          W. G. A.

**PHILIPPOPOLIS**, a city of Thrace, commanding the main road from Macedonia to the Black Sea. It was founded by Philip II of Macedon in 342 B.C., and

reoccupied by Philip V in 183, as a military outpost beyond Mt. Rhodope; but in either case it soon reverted to native rule. Under Roman rule it served as the meeting-place of the provincial parliament of Thrace and as a stronghold against Gothic invaders (A.D. 250–70). From the mixed character of the population which Philip II settled there it obtained the nickname of 'Poneropolis' ('Crookham').

INSCRIPTIONS AND BIBLIOGRAPHY. G. Mihailov, *Inscriptiones Graecae in Bulgaria repertae* III. i (Sofia, 1961), 19 ff.          M. C.

**PHILIPPUS** (1), JULIUS (*PW* 386) VERUS, Roman Emperor A.D. 244–9, a native of Arabia, succeeded Timesitheus as Praetorian Prefect and connived at Gordian's assassination (*see* GORDIAN III). After concluding peace with Persia he reached Rome with his son in 244, where he established good relations with the Senate. A great victory over the Carpi in 247 was followed by the elevation of his son to the rank of Augustus and by the celebrations in the ensuing April of the thousandth birthday of Rome. But in the summer the Goths invaded Moesia and pretenders arose in the Balkans and the East. Decius was appointed to the Danubian command and his popularity with the troops led to his acclamation as Emperor. Despite assurances of loyalty Philip mistrusted Decius' sincerity. He and his son were killed in a battle at Verona.

Later tradition honoured Philip as the first Christian Emperor, but this was certainly false.

Zosimus 1. 19–22; Zonaras 12. 19. A. T. Olmstead, *CPhil.* 1942, 241 ff.; P. J. Parsons, *JRS* 1967, 134 ff. (Philip and Egypt).
H. M. D. P.; B. H. W.

**PHILIPPUS** (2) of Opus (fl. *c.* 350 B.C.), mathematician and astronomer, pupil of Plato. An ancient tradition (D.L. 3. 37) describes him as having transcribed Plato's *Laws* from the wax tablets and written the *Epinomis*. It is still in doubt whether the latter was the work of Plato or of a pupil.

H. C. G. Friedrich, *Stylistische Untersuchung d. Epinomis d. Philippos von Opus* (1927), answered by A. E. Taylor, *Plato and the Authorship of the 'Epinomis'* (1929).          W. D. R.

**PHILIPPUS** (3), QUINTUS MARCIUS (*PW* 79), praetor in Sicily in 188 B.C., as consul in 186 suppressed the Bacchanalian 'conspiracy' and suffered defeat in Liguria in the *saltus Marcius*. In 183 he was envoy in the Peloponnese, checking the Achaean Confederacy. He influenced the preliminaries of the Third Macedonian War, persuading Perseus in 171 to accept a truce which allowed Rome more time for preparations. Consul in 169, he penetrated into Pieria, clearing the way for Aemilius Paullus' Pydna campaign. He was censor with Paullus in 164.

Scullard, *Rom. Pol.* 147, 198 ff.; J. van Ooteghem, *Lucius Marcius Philippus et sa famille* (1961), 58 ff.; J. Briscoe, *JRS* 1964, 66 ff.
A. H. McD.

**PHILIPPUS** (4), LUCIUS MARCIUS (*PW* 75), grandson of (3) and of Claudius (q.v. 9), after a demagogic tribunate (c. 104 B.C.) omitted the aedileship, hence failed to gain the consulship of 93, but succeeded for 91. An enemy of Drusus (q.v. 2) and his faction, and suspicious of his plans to enlarge the Senate and enfranchise the Italians, he led the opposition to him, with the support of Caepio (q.v. 2), the political *equites*, and probably Marius and his Italian clients; after the death of Crassus (q.v. 3), he succeeded in rescinding the laws passed. Not heard of from the Social War to the victory of Cinna (q.v. 1), he perhaps governed a province. Unmolested by Cinna and Marius (who remembered his hostility to the faction of Drusus), he collaborated with the government: as censor in 86 (with Perperna, q.v. 2), he enrolled the Italians—whose enfranchisement he had resisted—according to the restrictive laws then in force and struck his uncle Ap. Claudius (q.v. 10)—who had been banished—off the Senate list. He also joined Carbo (q.v. 2) and Hortensius (q.v. 2) in defending Pompey. Leaving Rome in time, he joined Sulla, conquered Sardinia for him and, as the oldest surviving senator (except for Perperna), became a pillar of the Sullan establishment, leading the opposition to Lepidus (q.v. 2) and proposing Pompey's special *imperium* against Sertorius (q.v.) (as he said) '*pro consulibus*'. Cicero still heard him in the Senate (urging, it seems, the annexation of Egypt) and greatly admired him.

J. van Ooteghem, *Lucius Marcius Philippus* (1961). E. B.

**PHILIPPUS** (5), LUCIUS MARCIUS (*PW* 76), son of (4), was governor of Syria (61–59 B.C.) and consul (56). He took no part in the civil wars. As second husband of Atia (1) he was stepfather to Octavian: in Mar. 44 they both tried to dissuade him from accepting the inheritance of Caesar. In Jan. 43 he went as an emissary of the Senate to Antony. He was still alive in Aug. 43. Philippus (6) was no doubt his son by a marriage previous to that with Atia.

Syme, *Rom. Rev.*, see index; J. van Ooteghem, *Lucius Marcius Philippus et sa famille* (1961), 173 ff. A. M.; T. J. C.

**PHILIPPUS** (6), LUCIUS MARCIUS (*PW* 77), son of (5), was tribune in 49 B.C., *consul suffectus* in 38, and governor of Spain (34–33 ?), whence he triumphed. It was probably he rather than his father who built the Porticus Philippi in Rome. He married Atia (2), younger sister of his father's second wife.

Syme, *Rom. Rev.*, see index; F. W. Shipley, *Amer. Acad. Rome* 1931. T. J. C.

**PHILIPPUS** (7) of Thessalonica, who lived in Rome and may have been a rhetor, published about A.D. 40 a *Garland* of Greek poetic epigrams written since Meleager (q.v. 2). This became one of the sources of the later Greek Anthology (q.v.), in which some eighty of his own poems survive. Most are adaptations of earlier Greek epigrams; a few are interesting for their strangeness, such as a description of Thessalian cowboys 'bulldogging' (*Anth. Pal.* 9. 543).

Gow and Page, 2628 ff. Cichorius, *Röm. Stud.* viii. 9 and 10; E. Hirsch, *Wiss. Zeitschr. Univ. Halle* 1966, 40 ff. G. H.

**PHILISCUS** (1) (*c.* 400–325 B.C.), rhetorician from Miletus, who came to Athens and studied under Isocrates. His works included a Μιλησιακός and an Ἀμφικτυονικός (probably political brochures) and a life of the orator Lycurgus.

*FGrH* iii. 496 F 9.

**PHILISCUS** (2), Middle Comedy poet, to whom the *Suda* assigns six plays (five being mythological burlesques; fourteen lines in a papyrus, *PSI* x. 1175, are doubtfully attributed to Διὸς γοναί).

*FCG* iii. 579 f.; *CAF* ii. 443 f.

**PHILISCUS** (3) of Aegina (4th c. B.C.) came under the teaching of Diogenes of Sinope at Athens and joined the Cynic school. He is said to have taught Alexander the Great, but this is doubtful. Seven tragedies were ascribed to him in antiquity, and the ascriptions may well be correct. W. D. R.

**PHILISCUS** (4) of Thessaly (*c.* A.D. 190–220), rhetorician, professor of rhetoric at Athens under Caracalla.

**PHILISTION** of Locri, physician, a contemporary of Plato (*c.* 427–347), according to Callimachus the teacher of Eudoxus, illustrious in his art according to Plutarch, was the main representative of the Sicilian School of

medicine. Like Empedocles he assumed four elements, fire, air, water, earth, which he equated with the qualities hot, cold, moist, dry, and considered responsible for all bodily processes. Respiration he regarded as the cooling of innate heat. His interest in anatomy may be inferred from the fact that the name ἀετοί for certain veins was attributed to him. In the physiology of drinking he agreed with Plato, as Plutarch relates (2. 1047 c). Diseases he explained by the excess or deficiency of the four elements, by external causes like wounds, climate, nourishment, or by changes in the bodily constitution, especially by difficulties of breathing, which he believed to occur all over the body. His book on dietetics must have been famous (half of the fragments preserved come from it, 9–16).

FRAGMENTS. M. Wellmann, *Die Fragmente d. Sikelischen Ärzte* (1901). Influence of P., Wellmann, *Hermes* 1900. An influence on Plato is often assumed, A. E. Taylor, *A Commentary on Plato's Tim.* (1928), 9, 599, n. 1; F. M. Cornford, *Plato's Cosmology* (1937), 334; W. Jaeger, *Diokles v. Karystos* (1938), 9 f.; 212, n. 1 (P. identical with the Philistion mentioned in the second Platonic Letter?); see also H. Cherniss, *Plato* (1950–7), *Lustrum* 1959, no. 986, 1021; the scarcity of the material makes judgement difficult. The Platonic element in the aetiology of disease in Plato's *Timaeus* is emphasized by H. W. Miller, *TAPA* 1962. For Philistion, as contemporary of Plato in consequence of the new dating of Diocles, see H. Diller, *PW* xix. 2405. L. E.

**PHILISTUS** of Syracuse (*c.* 430–356 B.C.), Sicilian historian who in his youth saw Gylippus rescue Syracuse (414) and took a prominent part for about forty years in supporting Dionysius I and II. He assisted the former to become general and tyrant (405) and served as his counsellor and governor of Syracuse, but later quarrelled with him and was banished for an unknown period. Recalled by Dionysius II he expelled Dion (366) and was appointed admiral. He failed to intercept Dion's expedition from Greece (357) and committed suicide after a naval defeat by Dion (356).

The history (Σικελικά) in thirteen books was written during his exile. The first seven books dealt with Sicilian affairs from the earliest times until 406, a period previously covered by Antiochus of Syracuse; the remainder dealt with contemporary events from Dionysius I onwards. This may explain the classification of the work in two parts by Alexandrine scholars under the titles Περὶ Σικελίας and Περὶ Διονυσίου. Philistus was a competent historian and was regarded by Cicero, Dionysius of Halicarnassus, and Quintilian as an imitator of Thucydides, particularly on grounds of style, though criticized by Dionysius for lack of co-ordination in the arrangement of the work. Philistus became the chief authority for the history of the West in the fourth century. He was sharply attacked by Timaeus on political grounds, but was the latter's main source for the fifth century and the tyrants; and the extensive use of his work by Ephorus is reflected in Diodorus Siculus. The history was popular with Cicero's contemporaries at a time of reaction in favour of Thucydides against the prose style of the Hellenistic period, and was used by Plutarch for his lives of Nicias and Dion.

*FGrH* iii B. 556. G. L. B.

**PHILOCHORUS** of Athens, the most famous and best known of the atthidographers. Born before 340 B.C. of a distinguished family, he held the official positions of μάντις καὶ ἱεροσκόπος in 306. The list of his works contains twenty-seven titles and illustrates his extensive reading and capacity for research. The most important was the *Atthis* in seventeen books which reached 261/60. Philochorus seems to have been executed shortly afterwards by Antigonus Gonatas as a partisan of Ptolemy II Philadelphus.

Philochorus' religious duties implied a close knowledge

of Athenian festivals and cults, and this was linked with an interest in the myths and history of Attica. His large literary output was mostly concerned with books on religious antiquities and customs. These are sparsely represented in the extant fragments almost all of which relate to the *Atthis*. This was mainly based on the *Atthis* of Androtion enlarged by his own knowledge and research, and was arranged on an annalistic framework. Unlike most atthidographers, and perhaps because the material had already appeared in other works, Philochorus dealt summarily with early Athenian history (books 1–2), passed on to the constitutional problems of Solon and Cleisthenes (book 3) and the fifth century (book 4), and with increasing detail devoted some two-thirds of his narrative to a survey of contemporary politics. He took eleven books to record the fifty-five years from the government of Demetrius of Phaleron to the Chremonidean War. The last seven books are almost entirely lost, probably because they had little interest for Alexandrine scholars, who used Philochorus chiefly in explanation of the Attic orators.

The style of the *Atthis* is plain and unattractive, but its chronological arrangement by kings and archons and the evidence of an eyewitness who was also interested in genuine research established Philochorus' position as an historian. His sources included Herodotus, Thucydides, Theopompus, and Ephorus, but his frequent references to authorities are balanced by an independent judgement. His 'Atthis against Demon', a treatise criticizing his predecessor's *Atthis*, should probably be regarded as an earlier work rather than an abridged version of his own *Atthis*.

*FGrH* iii B, 328, *and see* s.v. ATTHIS. G. L. B.

**PHILOCLES**, nephew of Aeschylus, wrote 100 plays and defeated Sophocles on the occasion when the latter produced the *Oedipus Tyrannus* (*Suda* s.v., Arg. Soph. *OT*), but is frequently attacked by the comic poets (e.g. Ar. *Vesp.* 462; *Thesm.* 168; Cratin. fr. 292). His unpleasant style earned him the nicknames Χολή (Gall) and Ἁλμίων (son of Brine). His plays included a tetralogy, the Πανδιονίς, on the story of Tereus (schol. Ar. *Av.* 281).

*TGF* 759–60. U. von Wilamowitz, *Aischylos-Interpretationen* (1914), 238. A. W. P.-C.

**PHILOCRATES**, an Athenian statesman who initiated the peace negotiations with Philip II of Macedon after the fall of Olynthus (348 B.C.). He headed the first peace embassy and secured a place on it for Demosthenes, who had defended him in court (347–346). On the embassy's return Philocrates proposed, and finally carried, a peace and alliance with Philip. He headed a second embassy to obtain Philip's signature, returned to carry a proposal to implement the alliance, despite Demosthenes' opposition, and served on two more embassies to Philip. Prosecuted in 343 for corruption in the peace negotiations, Philocrates absconded and was condemned to death; his prudent policy had become unpopular.

G. L. Cawkwell, *Rev. Ét. Grec.* 1960, 416 ff. N. G. L. H.

**PHILOCTETES**, in mythology, son of Poeas (*Od.* 3. 190) and leader of the seven ships from Methone and other towns of that region (*Il.* 2. 718), but left behind in Lemnos suffering from a snake-bite (ibid. 722–3). Homer says no more of him but that he returned safely from Troy (*Od.* ibid.); the *Cypria* (in Proclus) add that while the Greeks were on their way to Troy they sacrificed in Tenedos and there Philoctetes was bitten and left behind because of the stench of his wound. The *Little Iliad* continues the story. Odysseus captured Helenus, the Trojan prophet, and learned from him that Troy could not be taken unless Philoctetes was present; he therefore

went to Lemnos with Diomedes and brought him. Tragedy (the *Philoctetes* of Sophocles survives, and plays on the subject were written also by Aeschylus and Euripides) gives further details. Philoctetes had the bow and arrows of Heracles (q.v.) given him (Soph. op. cit. 801 ff.) or his father (Apollod. 2. 160) for lighting the pyre on Mt. Oeta. Without these Troy could not fall. He was therefore persuaded or tricked into coming (in Soph. Odysseus' companion is Neoptolemus (q.v. 1), whose honesty produces complications in the Plot), healed on arrival by Machaon (q.v.; *Little Iliad*), and there killed Paris. Since he had hero-cults in more than one place (near Sybaris and at Macella, Lycophron 919 ff., cf. [Aristotle], *Mir. Ausc.* 107) it was naturally said that he had wandered to Magna Graecia after leaving Troy and founded cities there; cf. Apollodorus in Strabo 6. 254. H. J. R.

**PHILODAMUS**, of Scarphea, author of a Paean to Dionysus discovered at Delphi. The poem, of some 150 lines in Aeolic metres, describes the birth and early travels of Dionysus and gives directions for his cult. Date 335–334 B.C.

TEXT. Diehl, *Anth. Lyr. Graec.* ii. 252–7; Powell, *Coll. Alex.* 165–71.
CRITICISM. H. W. Smyth, *Greek Melic Poets*, 525 ff.; Powell and Barber, *New Chapters* i. 42 f. C. M. B.

**PHILODEMUS** (*c.* 110–*c.* 40/35 B.C.), born at Gadara, died probably at Herculaneum; he came to Rome *c.* 75 B.C. as a consequence of the First Mithridatic War and enjoyed there the favour and powerful friendship of the Pisones. One of them, L. Calpurnius Piso (q.v. 5) Caesoninus (*cos.* 58), who was probably his disciple, presented him with a magnificent villa at Herculaneum. Cicero's somewhat ironical praise of Philodemus (*Pis.* 28. 68 ff.) shows that he was already well known in 55 B.C. His connexions with Piso brought Philodemus the opportunity of influencing the brilliant young students of Greek literature and philosophy who gathered around him and Siron at Herculaneum and Naples. In 44/3 B.C. he strongly opposed the policy of Antony, and aroused republican feelings in several of his disciples, as is shown by Varius' *De morte*, Virgil's *Appendix*, and the military career of Horace. Although his prose work was dull and colourless, Philodemus greatly surpassed the average literary standard of the Epicureans. In his elegant but often indecent love epigrams, some twenty-five of which are preserved in the *Anthologia Palatina*, he displays taste and ingenuity worthy of his fellow citizen Meleager. The success of these poems is proved by the allusions to, and imitations of, them in several passages of Horace and Ovid. Although Cicero seems to imply that Philodemus' main activity was poetry, he devoted himself chiefly to the task of popularizing Greek philosophy, which he dealt with systematically and historically (in his treatise σύνταξις τῶν φιλοσόφων, comprising an outline of the doctrines of Greek thinkers viewed from the standpoint of Epicureanism, in ten or more books). His work covered a wide field, including psychology, theology, logic, ethics, aesthetics, and rhetoric. Particularly remarkable was his theory of art, which he conceived as an autonomous activity of the mind, independent of morals and logic, and determined not by its content, but by its aesthetic value. Though scarcely original as a philosopher, Philodemus achieved his great ambition of influencing the most learned and distinguished Romans of his age. No prose work of Philodemus was known until several rolls of papyri, charred but partly legible, containing fragments of his writings, were discovered among the ruins of Piso's villa at Herculaneum.

TEXTS. No complete edition of Philodemus has hitherto been published. His epigrams were edited with a commentary by

G. Kaibel (1885). His prose works, apart from the general editions of the Herculaneum papyri, in part appeared in the Teubner series (Sudhaus, Olivieri, Jensen, Kemke, Wilke), and in part were edited elsewhere by Gomperz (*Herk. Stud.* i–ii, 1865–6), Crönert (*Kolotes u. Menedemus*, 1906), Diels (*Abh. Berl. Akad.* 1915–16), Jensen (1923, Weidmann series), and A. Vogliano in *Epicuri et Epicureorum Scripta* (1928). A lexicon Philodemeum was published by C. J. Vooys (2 vols., 1934).

GENERAL LITERATURE. Suscmihl, *Gesch. Griech. Litt. Alex.* ii. 267 ff.; Ueberweg–Praechter, *Grundriss* i¹². 439 ff.; R. Philippson, *PW* xix. 2444 ff.; W. Crönert, *Memoria Graeca Herculanensis* (1903); Cichorius, *Röm. Stud.* For Philodemus' life and villa, D. Comparetti, *Mélanges Chatelain* (1910), 118 ff.; for his theory of art, A. Rostagni, *Scritti minori* i (1955), 356 ff. and the introductions to Rostagni's (1930) and C. O. Brink's (1963) commentaries on Horace's *Ars Poetica*.

P. T.

**PHILOLAUS** of Croton or Tarentum (b. *c.* 470 B.C.), a Pythagorean, contemporary with Socrates. The authenticity of the 'fragments' is still debated, but there is independent evidence for crediting Philolaus with either the invention or the first published statement of the Pythagorean astronomy which displaced the earth from the centre of the universe in favour of a fire. The legend that Plato's *Timaeus* was plagiarized from a book of Philolaus is probably as early as Aristoxenus (q.v.) but no earlier.

Diels, *Vorsokr*¹¹. i. 398. On the fragments, E. Frank, *Plato und die sogenannten Pythagoreer* (1923), 263 ff.; *contra*, Zeller–Mondolfo, *Filosofia dei Greci* (1938), i. 2. 304 ff., 367 ff. W. Burkert, *Weisheit und Wissenschaft* (1962). G. E. L. O.

**PHILOLOGY, COMPARATIVE**, in British English, denotes that branch of the study of language which, by comparison of different languages, strives to elucidate their (pre)history. The languages thus compared are said to be cognate and descended from a common ancestor, either known from records or unrecorded. The former is the case with the Romance languages whose ancestor is Latin; the latter is the case with most European languages (with the exception of, e.g., Basque, and the Finno-Ugrian languages, e.g. Finnish, Hungarian) and such Asiatic languages as Sanskrit, Persian, and Armenian, whose prehistoric ancestor is the reconstructed Indo-European language (IE).

Considerations of method demand that the comparative study be preceded by the historical study of language; it is essential that the history of a given language, in the case of a classical scholar that of Latin or Greek, should be followed up as far back as possible before any attempt is made to draw comparisons with other languages. In Greek, in particular, there is ample room for a historical study, on account of the wealth of dialect material as well as the exceptionally long period of almost uninterrupted documentation. Such Attic forms as, e.g., γένη, φιλῶν are shown by Homeric Greek to be from γένεα, φιλέων, while τιμῶν is from τιμάων, and dialect evidence reveals that Attic τιμῶσι is from an early τιμάονσι, which itself derives from τιμάοντι. The last form is not directly attested, and philologists indicate the fact that a form is reconstructed, and not actually found, by an asterisk: *τιμάοντι. The beginning of the history of Greek, the earliest document of which had for millennia been Homer, was pushed back by about half a millennium in 1952 when M. Ventris showed that the Linear B tablets were written in a very early form of Greek (*see* MINOAN SCRIPTS). The history of Latin begins about a thousand years later, in the latter half of the third century B.C., although philologists can learn a good deal from the few epigraphic remains scattered over the centuries; but even the earliest, the so-called Praenestine fibula, does not take us back beyond *c.* 600 B.C.

The comparative study and the historical study both require a familiarity with the general characteristics of language, which can only be studied on living languages. Excellent introductions to this study, descriptive linguistics, have been given by Bloomfield, Gleason, Hockett, Robins. They also deal with historical and comparative

linguistics, but for a more specialized treatment see Lehmann, Palmer (1), and Szemerényi (1) in the bibliography below.

**2.** Of these three branches of linguistic study—descriptive, historical, and comparative—only the first was to some extent discovered and practised by the ancients; the results of their studies are still with us in our Greek and Latin grammars. But it is undeniable that the ancients had no *penchant* for a comparative study—although the Greeks could have drawn on such languages as Persian, and even Indian—nor, what is more surprising, for a historical study. Thus when Aristotle (*Poetics* 21. 10) says that Homeric πόληος Πηληιάδεω are lengthened from (his) πόλεως Πηλείδου, or that κρῖ, δῶ, and ὄψ are shortened (from κριθή, δῶμα, ὄψις), he reveals a false, because thoroughly unhistorical, attitude, which persisted down to the last century. A glimmer of a truly historical approach can be seen in Cicero's discussion of *hostis* (*Off.* I. 37), while 'comparison' leads to the (false) derivation of Latin from Greek in the first century B.C.

But modern historical and comparative linguistics owes its being to a closer study of Sanskrit, the literary and scholarly language of India almost down to our own day. After some tentative statements by earlier scholars, and especially after Sir William Jones's paper (1786) asserting the affinity of Sanskrit to the Classical languages, it was Franz Bopp who in his work on the *Verbal Inflection of Sanskrit compared with Greek, Latin, Persian and Germanic* (1816, re-edited in English in 1820) proved by a close comparison of the various verbal forms that the languages mentioned inherited their system from a common ancestor. From this foundation-year of comparative philology almost to the end of the last century research concentrated on comparison, and, after a revolutionary upheaval initiated in the late seventies, found its codification in the still unsurpassed work of Brugmann (1). As a result it was established that the IE group embraced Indian and Iranian (forming Aryan), and Armenian in Asia, Greek, Latin (with Oscan and Umbrian), Celtic, Germanic, Balto-Slavic, and Albanian in Europe; less important and poorly known members are Phrygian, Thracian, Illyrian (with Messapic), and Venetic. The twentieth century brought to light two further groups, unknown before: Anatolian in Asia Minor (Hittite and Luwian being especially important), and Tokharian in Central Asia. The detailed study of all these languages has led to spectacular results in all fields of linguistic study, and the following survey attempts to outline the variety of problems encountered, special regard being had to the classical languages.

**3.** PHONOLOGY. A close study of the word-shapes throughout the centuries has revealed that the ultimate components of words, the sounds, show a regularity in their behaviour which is unparalleled in any other branch of the humanities. If a sound in a given word changes between two points of time, then, as a rule, the sound changes in the same way in all the words in which it appeared. 'Sound laws are without exceptions' was the slogan of the 1870s, and, in spite of the great theoretical and practical misgivings voiced ever since, the thesis has been found correct and indispensable, although the conditions must be stated very carefully. Thus an IE *bh*, preserved in Sanskrit only, invariably appears in Greek as φ (i.e. *p*+*h* in the Classical Period), while in Latin in initial position we find *f*- but internally -*b*-. Cf. Skt. *bhrātar*- 'brother' : Gk. φράτηρ : Latin *frāter*, but Skt. *lubh-yati* 'desires' : Lat. *lubet*. Even more complex is the development of IE *dh* : Greek always presents θ (= *t*+*h*) while Latin has initially *f*- but internally -*d*- and -*b*-, the latter before or after an *r*, after *u* and before *l*. Cf. Skt. *dhūma*- 'smoke' : Gk. θυμός : Lat. *fūmus*; Skt. *madhyas* 'middle' : Lat. *medius*; but Gk. ἐρυθρός : Lat. *ruber*; Skt *ūdhar* 'udder' : Lat. *über*, etc. Conversely, Greek shows a bewildering variety in the representation of the so-called IE labiovelars (velar sounds of the English *k g* type with lip-rounding). In historical Greek they merged with the well-known labial, dental, and velar sounds, but in the Linear B script they still have distinct signs, so that the development must have taken place after the Mycenaean period. To take a simple case, Latin *quis quid* obviously corresponds to Gk. τίς τί, that is to say while Latin preserves an IE *kʷ* as *qu*, Greek changed it to τ. But this occurred only before *i* or *e* (cf. Lat. *-que* : Gk. τε). Before *a* or *o* Gk. shows π, cf. the interrogative forms πόθεν πότε πότερος, etc., from IE *\*kwo-*. This explains the connexion between τίνω and ποινή, so obvious semantically (pay—payment, fine), and so disconcerting when the sounds are compared; yet τι-/ποι- represent the regular developments from IE *\*kwi-* and *\*kwoi-*.

Whereas the consonants, apart from the fairly stable liquids (*l r*) and nasals (*m n*), show a lesser or greater degree of variability, the basic vowels of IE (*a e i o u*, short and long) are fairly faithfully preserved in the classical languages, in Latin in first syllables at least. Cp.

| a | IE *\*agō* | 'I drive' | Gk. ἄγω | Lat. *agō* |
|---|---|---|---|---|
| ā | *\*mātēr* | 'mother' | μάτηρ | *mātēr* |
| e | *\*bherō* | 'I carry' | φέρω | *ferō* |
| ē | *\*plē-* | 'full' | πλή-ρης | *plē-nus* |
| o | *\*oktō* | 'eight' | ὀκτώ | *octō* |
| ō | *\*dō-* | 'give' | δῶρον | *dō-num*, etc. |

Particularly interesting are the so-called sonants of the IE parent language, which in the classical languages develop differently and at first sight show no similarity. In IE, the liquids and nasals could (like the vowels) form the centre of a syllable (could be syllabic or sonant) if they were placed between other consonants; the sounds were similar to the English *-on* in *button*, or *-le* in *bubble*, etc. The IE sonant liquids are preserved in one language, in Sanskrit, where we often find syllabic or sonant *r* (transcribed as ṛ); cp. *mṛta-* 'dead', *kṛp-* 'body', etc. In the classical languages the sonant liquids of IE (*l ṛ*) always develop a vowel, either in front of them (Lat. *ul ur* or *ol or*; Gk. αλ αρ) or after them (Gk. λα ρα). Thus Skt. *ṛkṣa-* 'bear' corresponds with Gk. ἄρκτος but Lat. *ur(c)sus*. The sonant nasals are preserved in no language; their discovery is due to Brugmann (2), and is of particular importance for the classical languages. The Grecian knows that τείνω (τεν-) : τα-τός, κτείνω (κτεν-) : ἔ-κτα-το, etc., are frequent interrelations but he can find no rational explanation for them. The Sanskritist will find similar alternatives in Skt. *tan-* 'stretch' : *ta-tás*, *han-* 'kill': *ha-tás*, etc. Brugmann pointed out that the relation of εἶ-μι : (πρός)-ι-τος, φευγ- : φυκ-τός, showed that the verbal adjective was formed from the weak root which lost its *e* (nil-grade); that τεν- κτεν- were therefore expected to form *tn-tos*, *ktn-tos*, with a syllabic nasal (ṇ) which obviously developed into *a* in Greek (and Sanskrit) but *en* in Latin. This at once explained why the aorist of πενθ- 'suffer' was ἔ-παθ-ον (cf. ἔφυγον). Similarly, the aorist of δέρκομαι was ἔδρακον (from -dṛk-), that of πέρθω, ἔπραθον (from -pṛth-), etc. In contrast to ἄγονται ἄγοντο, the athematic κεῖμαι forms κεῖαται κείατο whose -αται -ατο represents -ṇtai, -ṇto. In IE, the acc. sg. had the ending -*m*, cf. *rosa-m*. But after a consonantal stem, -*m* had to become syllabic (-ṃ) which in Greek gave -α, in Latin -*em*; hence, πόδ-α, but *ped-em*, in contrast to νόμο-ν with -ν from -*m* and *eru-m*. The same applies to δέκ-α: *dec-em*, ἑπτ-ά : *sept-em*, etc.

The most remarkable achievement of research over the last century has been to show that such exact phonetic correspondences can be found between all IE languages. They are often at their clearest between the classical languages.

4. MORPHOLOGY. The same detailed agreement obtains between inflectional patterns of the classical languages, and their cognates. The declension of *familia*, with the old gen. *familiās* (retained in class. *pater familiās*), closely corresponds to that of οἰκία -ᾶν -ᾱς -ᾱι. A most striking agreement exists between *familiārum* and early οἰκιάων (Ionic -έων, Attic -ῶν), in which *-ārum* and *-άων* both represent *-āsōm*. Equally close parallels can be observed in the other declensions, the pronouns, the verbal inflections, etc.

Inflectional patterns also reveal another great force at work in the history of languages: side by side with, and often against, the sound laws work formal patterns, which may produce unexpected results. As we have just seen, the old gen. sg. of Latin *ā*-stems was in *-ās*. But already in Old Latin, the norm is *-ā-ī* (later *-ai*, *-ae*), obviously on the model of the *o*-stem gen. (*domin*)ī. Conversely, the original *o*-stem gen. plural in *-um* which survives into classical times in the prosaic *triumuirum liberum talentum* and poetic *deum diuom*, etc., was replaced on the analogy of the *ā*-stems by *-ōrum*: *deōrum sociōrum* after *deārum*, etc. Analogy is also a potent force in the manifold transformations of the inherited system of numerals. One interesting example is the gradual spread of the ending of *decimus* to all the subsequent ordinals, such as *vīcēns-imus* (instead of *\*vīcēnsus*) *trīcēs-imus* down to *millesimus*; see Szemerényi (2).

For a detailed study of the phonology and morphology of the classical languages, excellent guides are Buck, Meillet–Vendryès; for Latin, Kent (1, 2); for Greek, Lejeune, Chantraine(1); for Homeric Greek in particular, Chantraine (2), Palmer (2). The more ambitious student will have to turn to Leumann–Hofmann and Schwyzer–Debrunner.

5. SYNTAX. The case-system of the classical languages represents a gradual reduction of an earlier richer system of (at least) eight cases, found as such in Sanskrit only. The contraction means that some cases now combine functions that earlier had distinct expressions (syncretism); hence the apparently contradictory functions performed by, e.g., the Latin ablative. One of the exciting discoveries of direct relevance to Greek syntax cleared up the curious Greek rule that after a neuter plural subject the verb is in the singular: φύλλα καὶ ἄνθεα γίγνεται. Although unknown to Latin, the rule was inherited from IE as is clear from its observance in early Indian and Iranian. J. Schmidt showed that its basis was the fact that the neuter plurals were originally collective singulars. The curious rule that unemphatic words (e.g. particles, pronouns) take the second place in the sentence was shown to be a general IE feature in a brilliant paper by Wackernagel (1). Many aspects of the use of moods can only be cleared up by the comparatist, cf. e.g. Gonda.

The elaborate sentence construction of the classical languages, in which hypotaxis seems the dominant feature, can in many cases be shown to be based on a shift of earlier paratactic constructions. Earlier juxtapositions such as *timeo—ne veniat* 'I am afraid—may he not come', *timeo—ut veniat* 'how could he come', were shifted in meaning, rather illogically to our feeling, to 'I am afraid that he might (not) come'; the same explanation applies to φοβοῦμαι μὴ (οὐκ) ἔλθῃ. Similar shifts occur with words clearly indicating dependence, usually from a concrete meaning towards a more abstract one. Gk. ἵνα originally meant 'where' and, depending on the meaning to be conveyed, its verb could be in various moods. With the indicative, ἵνα always retained the original meaning: ἐν ἀγορᾷ . . . ἵνα ὑμῶν πολλοὶ ἀκηκόασι (Pl. *Ap.* 17 c). But with the subjunctive or optative ἵνα assumed a final nuance, which became its main function in classical times. The transition can be seen in, e.g., *Iliad* 3. 130: δεῦρ' ἴθι . . . ἵνα θέσκελα ἔργα ἴδηαι 'come here where you might see . . .' i.e. 'so that you . . .'. Both ἵνα and especially final *ut* are elegantly illuminated by Leumann (1).

For a systematic exposition of the syntax of the classical languages on a historico-comparative basis see Meillet–Vendryès, Wackernagel (2), for both classical languages; Schwyzer–Debrunner ii, Humbert for Greek; Palmer (3, ch. 10), Ernout–Thomas, for Latin.

**6. ETYMOLOGY.** The origin of words has always exercised some speakers at any rate. Greek philosophers at one time hoped to get to the essence of things by a linguistic analysis; Plato's *Cratylus* both illustrates the method and shows its futility. But, even though philosophers felt disappointed, philologists went on for centuries seeking the original, true meaning of any given expression. The ancients' wilful interpretations (e.g. Aelius' derivation of *volpes* from *volat pedibus*, or *lepus* from *leui-pēs* 'light-foot') are of course useless today but only because from the beginning of the last century plentiful material has become available from cognate languages. To be sure, comparatists of the early nineteenth century still hoped to recover the original meaning; thus *pater* was interpreted either as 'protector' (cf. Skt. *pā-* 'protect') or as 'provider, nourisher'. Gradually, however, etymology came to assume its modern meaning: we now strive to recover the earliest form and meaning of a given word, without hoping always to be able to recover the 'original' meaning. Today we know our limitations and are ready to stop when we cannot legitimately go further.

This does not mean that comparative philology has not cleared up many problems which would have remained insoluble within Latin or Greek. The word ποινή, mentioned above, would hardly be analysable in Greek. The comparatist can show that it derives from IE *$k^woi$-nā*, represented also by Lithuanian *kaina* 'price', Slavic *cěna* 'id.', Iranian *kainā* 'punishment'; what is more, he can show that this noun derives from a verbal root *$k^wi$-* 'to pay' which survives in τίνω. The research of a century has succeeded in amassing a vast corpus of firmly established etymologies, conveniently listed in etymological dictionaries (Ernout–Meillet, Walde–Hofmann; Boisacq, Frisk).

It is by paying close attention to phonetic laws, to the implied change of meaning, and to the morphological problems, especially the problems of word-formation that the modern etymologist can hope to get beyond his precursors; see Szemerényi (3–4). Here again, it would be futile to look to cognate languages before clearing up the history of a word or a word-group within the language concerned: historical study must precede the comparative study. In Greek in particular much useful work has been done in this field (e.g. 'the history of κλέος' or 'the verbs of seeing in Greek', etc.), but much remains to be done, especially in Latin.

**7. HISTORY OF THE LANGUAGE.** The prehistory and the history of the phonology and grammar by no means exhaust the problems confronting the student. The study of the lexicon, sketched out in (6), also remains incomplete if it is directed solely to the vocabulary inherited from IE. Every language, of necessity, is exposed to the influence of its environment. This manifests itself most clearly in a number of borrowings. These loan-words are taken over either from an autochthonous population with a high civilization, conquered by the invaders (the Greeks borrowed many words from the Aegean population), or by the autochthonous population from the conquerors whom they manage to absorb (French is Latin with a good many Germanic elements), or from neighbouring populations. The latter is often the case with Latin which absorbed many Greek (Ernout) but also Oscan and Umbrian dialect words. Less easy to pin down is foreign influence affecting the phonology and grammar, although it must be postulated.

Since the classical languages are descended from IE, and IE certainly was not spoken either in the Balkan peninsula or in Italy, it follows that the classical languages were brought there by invaders. This is the first lesson taught by comparative philology, and it is of fundamental importance. Further, since Latin and Greek were brought, in an embryonic state at any rate, from the IE homeland, one might ask whether they had been closely related there. The classicist would be inclined to assume that this must have been the case. But the comparatist can show that Greek has hardly any real agreements with Latin—beyond sharing a common inheritance—while it has many striking features in common with Indian and Iranian, such as the augment, the prohibitive *\*mē*, the more recent comparative formation (-τερο-, Skt. *-tara-*), etc. Latin, on the other hand, shows clear connexions with Celtic and Germanic, but hardly any special agreements with Greek, except perhaps the quite unusual change of the IE mediae aspiratae (*bh dh gh*) to voiceless aspirates (*ph th kh*); see Szemerényi (5, p. 11 f.).

The prehistoric influences between various IE, and perhaps non-IE, groups [Porzig; Palmer (3), ch. i] are merely a prelude to the environmental exposures in the historical habitats. But the internal history of the classical languages, in particular the development of the literary languages in Greece and Rome were just as, if not more, important factors, especially in Greece where the local dialect, in which a genre first took shape, had a lasting hold on that genre. The problems have been given masterly presentations by Meillet (1, 2) and Palmer (3).

The works indicated in the text by the authors' names are here listed in alphabetical order; different works by the same author are distinguished by numbers in brackets.
L. Bloomfield, *Language* (1933); É. Boisacq, *Dictionnaire étymologique de la langue grecque*⁴ (1950); K. Brugmann, (1) *Grundriss der vergleichenden Grammatik der indogermanischen Sprachen* I. ii. 1–3 (1896–1916); (2) *Curtius' Studien* 9 (1877), 285 f.; C. D. Buck, *Comparative Grammar of Greek and Latin*³ (1962); J. Chadwick, *The Prehistory of the Greek Language*, *CAH*³ ii, ch. xxxix; P. Chantraine, (1) *Morphologie historique du grec*² (1964); (2) *Grammaire homérique* i³ (1958), ii (1953); A. Ernout, *Aspects du vocabulaire latin* (1954); A. Ernout–A. Meillet, *Dictionnaire étymologique de la langue latine*⁴ (1959); A. Ernout–F. Thomas, *Syntaxe latine*² (1953); H. Frisk, *Griechisches etymologisches Wörterbuch* i (1960); ii in course of publication; H. A. Gleason, *An Introduction to Descriptive Linguistics* (1955); J. Gonda, *The Character of the IE Moods* (1956); C. F. Hockett, *A Course in Modern Linguistics* (1958); J. Humbert, *Syntaxe grecque*² (1954); R. G. Kent, (1) *The Sounds of Latin*² (1945); (2) *The Forms of Latin* (1946); W. P. Lehmann, *Historical Linguistics: an Introduction* (1962); M. Lejeune, *Traité de phonétique grecque*² (1955); M. Leumann, *Kl. Schr.* (1959), 57 ff.; M. Leumann–J. B. Hofmann–Szantyr, *Lateinische Grammatik* i–ii. 1–2 (1963–4); A. Meillet, (1) *Aperçu d'une histoire de la langue grecque*⁷ (1965); (2) *Esquisse d'une histoire de la langue latine*³ (1948); A. Meillet–J. Vendryès, *Traité de grammaire comparée des langues classiques*² (1953); L. R. Palmer, (1) *An Introduction to Modern Linguistics* (1936); (2) 'The Language of Homer', *A Companion to Homer* (1963), 75 ff.; (3) *The Latin Language* (1954); W. Porzig, *Die Gliederung des indogermanischen Sprachgebiets* (1954); R. H. Robins, *General Linguistics* (1964); J. Schmidt, *Die Pluralbildung der indogermanischen Neutra* (1889); E. Schwyzer–A. Debrunner, *Griechische Grammatik* i–ii (1934–50); iii (indexes by D. J. Georgacas, 1953); O. J. L. Szemerényi, (1) *Trends and Tasks in Comparative Philology* (1962); (2) *Studies in the IE system of numerals* (Heidelberg, 1960); (3) 'Principles of Etymological Research in the IE Languages', *Innsbrucker Beiträge zur Kulturwissenschaft* 1962, 175 ff.; (4) *Syncope in Greek and IE and the Nature of IE Accent* (Naples, 1964); (5) 'The IE mediae aspiratae in Latin and Italic', *Archivum Linguisticum* 4. 27 ff., 99 ff.; 5. 1 ff. (1952–3). J. Wackernagel, (1) 'Über ein Gesetz der indogermanischen Wortstellung', *Indogermanische Forschungen* 1892, 333 ff.; (2) *Vorlesungen über Syntax mit besonderer Berücksichtigung von Griechisch, Lateinisch und Deutsch*² i (1926); ii (1928); A. Walde–J. B. Hofmann, *Lateinisches etymologisches Wörterbuch* i–iii (1930–56).   O. J. L. S.

**PHILOMELA** (Φιλομήλα). Pandion, king of Athens, had two daughters, Procne (Πρόκνη) and Philomela, of whom the former was married to his ally, Tereus, king of Thrace, son of Ares. Tereus, pretending that Procne was dead, asked that Philomela might be sent to him, and on her arrival raped or seduced her and then cut out her tongue to prevent her telling. She contrived to send her sister a piece of embroidery on which she had woven her story. Procne found her and took revenge on Tereus by serving him at a meal with the flesh of his and her child Itys. Finding this out, he pursued the women, but the gods turned him into a hoopoe, Procne into a nightingale, and Philomela into a swallow (a later tradition, represented in Latin authors, reverses these last two).

Apollod. 3. 193 ff.; Ov. *Met.* 6. 424 ff. H. J. R.

**PHILOMELUS,** Phocian commander in the Third Sacred War (q.v.). Elected *strategos autokrator* of Phocis at the threat of war, he seized Delphi (summer 356 B.C.), raised 5,000 mercenaries, defeated the Locrians and Boeotians in the winter, and allied Phocis with Athens and Sparta. In autumn 355, when the Amphictiony declared a Sacred War on Phocis, Philomelus used temple funds to raise 10,000 men; in 354 he defeated the Thessalians and defended southern Phocis until he was defeated and committed suicide near Neon (late autumn 354). An able diplomatist and general, he based Phocian power on mercenaries and the Delphic monies.

N. G. L. H.

**PHILON** (1) of Eleusis (4th c. B.C.), architect. He designed the arsenal at Piraeus, and added a porch to the Telesterion at Eleusis. The former building was destroyed by Sulla, and no vestiges of it have been identified; but we possess a detailed specification (*IG* ii². 1668). His books on the arsenal, and on the proportions of sacred buildings (Vitr. 7 praef.), have not survived.

H. W. R.

**PHILON** (2) of Byzantium (*PW* 48), writer on technology (probably late 3rd century B.C.), was an imitator of Ctesibius (q.v.), and was himself used by Heron (q.v.). He wrote a compendium of technology (μηχανικὴ σύνταξις) in nine (?) books. Of this there are preserved: book 4, βελοποιικά, on the construction of war-catapults; book 5, πνευματικά (in Arabic translation), on the construction of siphons and other devices worked by the action of air and fluids; parts of book 7, παρασκευαστικά, and of book 8, πολιορκητικά, on the construction of offensive and defensive works and other measures to be taken in case of a siege. The lost book 6, on automata-making, is referred to by Heron (*Opera Omnia*, ed. Schmidt, i. 404 ff.). Though not uninterested in theory (see the introduction to the *Pneumatica*), his primary concern is the construction of devices for use or amusement.

Eutocius (*Comm. in Arch. de Sph. et Cyl.* 60–2 Heiberg²) informs us of a solution by Philon to the problem of finding two mean proportionals ('doubling the cube'). It is essentially the same as the solutions by Apollonius and Heron. Philon refers to this (*Belopoeica* 7) as coming from book 1.

EDITIONS. *Belopoeica*, ed. H. Diels and E. Schramm (with German transl.), *Abh. Berl. Akad.* 1918, Phil.-hist. Kl. Nr. 16. *Pneumatica*, ed. Carra de Vaux (with French transl.), in *Notices et extraits des manuscrits* xxxviii. 1 (1903), 27 ff. A medieval Latin partial translation was published by V. Rose, *Anecdota Graeca et Graecolatina* 2 (Berlin, 1870, repr. Amsterdam, 1963), 297 ff., and in *Heronis Opera Omnia* i. 458 ff. *Parasceuastica* and *Poliorcetica*, ed. H. Diels and E. Schramm (with German transl.), *Abh. Berl. Akad.* 1919, Phil.-hist. Kl. Nr. 12.

LIFE AND WORKS. De Rochas and Graux in *Rev. Phil.* 1879, 91 ff.

COMMENT. *Pneumatica*: A. G. Drachmann, *Ktesibios, Philon and Heron* (Copenhagen, 1948), 41 ff. Doubling the cube: Heath, *Hist of Greek Maths.* i. 262 ff. G. J. T.

**PHILON** (3, *PW* 40) **OF LARISSA** (160/59–*c.* 80 B.C.), the last undisputed head of the Academy. (The term 'New Academy' was applied to the sceptical Academy first by Antiochus of Ascalon. 'Middle' and 'Fourth' Academy are later doxographical terms.) Philon studied for eight or nine years in his home town under Callicles, a pupil of Carneades, before he went to Athens at the age of 24 to study under Clitomachus, whom he succeeded as head of the Academy in 110/109 B.C. In 88,

during the Mithridatic wars, he left for Rome, where he numbered among his pupils Catulus, father and son, and Cicero, who became his most devoted pupil and follower. About this time, his controversy with Antiochus of Ascalon led to a break within the school and to Antiochus' assuming the leadership. Philo probably remained in Rome, where he died some time before 79 B.C.

Although Philon published many books, none of them, or their titles, have survived, and we know nothing about their form. Some of his teachings are represented in a long passage in Stobaeus and in Cicero's own speeches in the *Academicus Primus* and *Lucullus*. It is possible that he is the source of book III of Cicero's *De Natura Deorum* and of book IV and part of book V of his *De Finibus*. The attempt to claim him as the source of Cicero's *Tusculans* is unconvincing.

Like his predecessors, Philon was a representative of the sceptical Academy of Arcesilaus in the somewhat milder version of Carneades. Against the Stoic theory of truth he maintained the sceptical principle of ἀκαταληψία (the impossibility of certain knowledge), admitting also the Carneadean modification that some things, though still not certain, are more convincing (πιθανά, *probabilia*) than others. The concept of ἐνάργεια (perspicuity), which he is probably the first to use, is perhaps only a variant on the Carneadean term.

Philon divided moral philosophy into four main parts: (1) προτρεπτικὸς (λόγος)—exhortation to philosophical activities; (2) περὶ ἀγαθῶν καὶ κακῶν—the general nature of good and evil; (3) περὶ τελῶν—on the various philosophical doctrines of the highest good; (4) περὶ βίων—on the various sorts of happy life—the latter subdivided into ἴδιος and πολιτικός—what Aristotle called Ethics and Politics. This, however, is probably not so much a positive doctrine as a general typological study of the various ethical doctrines in existence, not unlike the famous division of Carneades (Cic. *Fin.* 5. 16 ff.).

In Rome, Philon taught some rhetoric (Cic. *Tusc.* 2. 9), but probably concentrated on the philosophical part, the 'topics' rather than on rhetorical techniques (Cic. *De Or.* 3. 110).

Despite modern tendencies to see him as an eclectic with some positive doctrines to teach, there is no clear evidence that Philon was ever anything but a sceptic, who firmly believed in the continuity of scepticism in the Academy ever since Plato himself—though he was probably prepared to admit that some dogmatic teachings are more consistent and 'probable' than others.

SOURCES. *Acad. index Herc.* xxxiii; Cic. *Acad. Pr.* and *Luc. passim*; Stob. *Ecl.* 2. 7. 2; Sext. Emp. *Pyr.* 1. 235; Numen. ap. Euseb. *Praep. Evang.* 14. 8 f.; Augustine, *Contra Academicos* 3. 41. Modern Discussions: Brochard, *Les Scepticques grecs* v. (1887), 189 ff.; Zeller, *Phil. d. Gr.*, iii. 1. 609 ff.; Überweg-Praechter, *Grundriss* (1877–83), 465 f.; 469 f.; 142*; R. Hirzel, *Unters. zu Ciceros Philos. Schriften* iii. 342 ff.; R. Philippson, *Symb. Osl.* 1945, 16 ff. J. G.

**PHILON** (4), commonly known as **Philo Judaeus** (*c.* 30 B.C.–A.D. 45), spent all his life in his native city of Alexandria and became head of its Jewish community, which he represented on the delegation sent to Rome in A.D. 39–40 to ask exemption from the duty of worshipping the Emperor. This is the only incident from the life of Philo of which anything is known; it is related at length in his pamphlet *Legatio ad Gaium*. Here and in his *In Flaccum*, a similar treatise of earlier date, Philo tries to show that God is mindful of His people and punishes with death their persecutors (i.e. the Roman prefect of Egypt and the Emperor). These works exerted a lasting influence upon early Christian literature, e.g. upon the *De mortibus persecutorum*; the latter took over from Philo the idea that persecutors themselves are responsible for evoking the inevitable punishment which, by God's judgement, eventually overwhelms them. Philo cannot, however, be considered as an enemy of Hellenistic and

Roman civilization merely because he was opposed to the worship of the Emperor Gaius; for besides speaking of Augustus and Tiberius in very high terms of praise, and adapting formulas of the Hellenistic ruler-cult to the praise of the Jewish patriarchs, he casts the traditions of judaism into the literary forms of Greek allegory. Modern scholars have often overestimated the extent of Philo's indebtedness to Judaism, esepcially to the Alexandrian school. In fact, he owes far more to Greek philosophy, and his very efforts to demonstrate a substantial similarity between Hellenic and Jewish doctrines are a proof of his Hellenistic character. His main sources were indisputably Plato, Aristotle, and the Stoics, above all Posidonius; the extent of his indebtedness to Neopythagoreanism, although great, is now difficult to estimate. Despite his scanty originality as a philosopher, Philo played a very important role in the history of ancient thought as a mediator between Hellenistic philosophy and both Christianity and Neoplatonism. Not only did the author of the *De mortibus persecutorum* and Plotinus borrow from him, but St. Augustine probably derived from Philo his theory of the two cities, which is merely an application of Philo's dualism to the realm of politics. Nevertheless, Philo did not bridge the gulf between the world of God and the world of matter, since, had matter been created by God, the existence of evil would be inexplicable. To establish an artificial connexion between the two worlds Philo introduced intermediary beings representing the different aspects of God's existence and thought. With these God communicates only through an intermediary, which Philo calls Logos and is careful to distinguish from God himself: the word Logos refers to God in so far as His existence is conceived as pure thought, while the word God merely indicates His essence as pure Being. Man's duty is to conform to the will of God, not only by living according to His law, but by 'seeing' Him. This supreme achievement, the discovery of the essence of God, can be reached only by means of 'ecstasy', which Philo thinks of as an act of grace. But worship and purity of life and mind enable man to succeed in achieving communion with God in His existence as thought. In Philo's system the soul of man is ultimately dependent on the grace of God and cannot enjoy communion with Him by a spontaneous activity of love unassisted by grace.

TEXTS. Best complete edition: Cohn, Wendland, Reiter (*ed. major*, 7 vols., 1896–1930; *ed. minor*, 6 vols., 1896–1915). Ed. T. Mangey (London, 2 vols., 1742). *Œuvres*, ed. R. Arnaldez, C. Mondésert, and J. Pouilloux (1961 ff.). English Translation: Loeb (10 vols., 1929 ff.). Fragments, ed. J. Rendel Harris (1886). The *In Flaccum* edited with an historical commentary by H. Box (1939), *Legatio ad Gaium*, by E. M. Smallwood (1961).
E. R. Goodenough, *An Introduction to Philo Judaeus* (1962); H. A. Wolfson, *Philo*, 2 vols. (U.S.A. 1947). Bibliography (by H. L. Goodhart and E. R. Goodenough) in appendix to E. R. Goodenough, *The Politics of Philo Judaeus* (1938); also, L. H. Feldman, 'Scholarship on Philo and Josephus (1937–59), *Cl. Weekly* liv, 1961, 281 ff., lv. 36 ff., 299 ff. Most important works on Philo: J. Drummond, *Philo Judaeus* (2 vols., 1888); É. Herriot, *Philon le Juif* (1898); J. Martin, *Philon* (1907); É. Bréhier, *Les Idées philosophiques et religieuses de Philon* (1925); T. H. Billings, *The Platonism of Philo* (1919); I. Heinemann, *Philos. griech. u. jüdische Bildung* (1932); M. Pohlenz, *Kl. Schr.* (1965), i. 305 ff. P. T.

**PHILON** (5) of Byblos (A.D. 64–141) composed in Greek a learned work of euhemeristic character in which for the Phoenician religion he cites at length, as he alleges, from the Phoenician Sanchuniathon, who had devoted a treatise in his own language to theogony, cosmogony, and the origins of civilization. Extensive fragments of Philon have been preserved by Eusebius in his *Praeparatio evangelica* (1. 9. 22 ff.) with a parallel in Theodoret. These fragments have now been critically republished, along with translation, extensive essays, and full bibliography, by C. Clemen, 'Die phönikische Religion nach Philo von Byblos', *Mitteilungen d.*

*vorderasiatisch-aegyptischen Gesellschaft* xlii, pt. 3 (1939). Over Philon's alleged translation there has been long dispute, distinguished scholars like Baudissin regarding it as a fraud. But the extraordinary recent discoveries at Ras Shamra, ancient Ugarit, on the Syrian coast north of Laodicea-Latakia, of fourteenth-century B.C. documents, in alphabetic cuneiform script, and of Hebraic language, containing lengthy mythological texts, epic, choric, etc. (published for the most part in *Syria* since 1929), have proved conclusively that Sanchuniathon is doubtless a verity in view of the many correspondences between him and these fresh texts and of the picture of the lush development of Phoenician mythology by the middle of the second millennium.

Philon also wrote a Ῥηματικόν (paradigm of verb-flexions), and a dictionary of synonyms (the probable source of the Byzantine Pseudo-Ammonius). He was much used by Hesychius of Miletus. *See also* SANCHUNIATHON.

FGrH 790. O. Eissfeldt, *Ras Schamra u. Sanchuniathon* (1939), esp. 79 ff.; A. Jirku, *Kanaanäische Mythen u. Epen aus Ras Schamra-Ugarit* (1962). P. B. R. F.

**PHILONIDES,** Athenian comic poet, produced Aristophanes' *Wasps*, *Amphiaraus*, and *Frogs*; we have three titles of his own plays, and he may be the Φιλ[ who won first prize at the City Dionysia c. 410 B.C. (*IG* ii². 2325. 64). It is stated by hyp. 1 Ar. *Vesp.* that he won first prize with Προαγών at the Lenaea in 422 B.C., but Προαγών is everywhere else attributed to Aristophanes.

FCG ii. 421 ff.; CAF i. 254 ff.; FAC i. 564 ff. K. J. D.

**PHILOPAPPUS,** Syrian prince, Roman consul (A.D. 109), and Athenian archon. His sepulchral monument, erected between 114 and 116, stands at Athens on the top of the Museum Hill. His full name was C. Julius Antiochus Epiphanes Philopappus, his grandfather being Antiochus IV, the last king of Commagene.

OGI 409–13. PIR ii¹. 166, 99; ii². 262, 1086. V. E.

**PHILOPATOR,** Stoic, probably of the time of Hadrian (A.D. 117–38). See Zeller, *Phil. d. Griechen* iii. 1⁴. 169, 714.

**PHILOPOEMEN** of Megalopolis (c. 253–182 B.C.), the Achaean soldier and statesman, was trained from his youth in arms and taught by the patriotic Megalopolitan philosophers, Ecdemus and Demophanes. He resisted Cleomenes (223) and won praise from Antigonus Doson at Sellasia. After ten years' mercenary soldiering in Crete, he became hipparch of the Achaean Confederacy in 210/09 and general in 208/7, reforming the army, and in 207 defeated Machanidas of Sparta at Mantinea. General again in 206/5 and 201/200, he repelled Nabis in 202–200. In the Second Macedonian War, favouring neutrality, he lost influence and returned to Crete (199/8). Reappearing after the Roman evacuation to find war with Nabis, he became general (193/2) and blockaded Sparta. Flamininus made a settlement, but on Nabis' assassination (192) Philopoemen incorporated Sparta in the Achaean Confederacy In annexing Messene and Elis (191) and as general in 191/90 or 190/8 9and in 189/8 he dominated policy; finally, in 188, on an ambiguous ruling of the Senate, he demilitarized Sparta and abolished the Lycurgan institutions. General again in 187/6 and 183/2, he was captured during the revolt of Messene and given poison (182). A great soldier and patriot, 'the last of the Greeks', he remained in politics the Megalopolitan, narrow and rancorous, pressing Flamininus' and the Senate's acquiescence in Achaean rights to dominate the Peloponnese, when wider statesmanship was needed to strike a balance with Roman power in Greece.

Polyb. 2. 40; 2. 67–9; bks. 10–11, 16, and 20–4; Livy, bks. 35–9; Plut. *Phil.*; *Flam.* De Sanctis, *Stor. Rom.* iii. 2. 427, 443; iv. 1. 57, 133, 169, 229, 238, 402 ff.; A. Aymard, *Les Premiers Rapports de Rome et de la confédération achaienne* (1938). F. W. Walbank, *Philip V of Macedon* (1940); R. M. Errington, *Philopoemen* (1968). A. H. McD.

**PHILOPONUS,** JOHN, *c.* A.D. 490–*c.* 570, a Christian 'grammarian' who became pupil and virtually literary executor of Ammonius, son of Hermeas. From 517, mainly from notes of Ammonius' lectures, he published commentaries on Aristotle's *Categories, Analytica, Meteorologica, de Generatione, de Anima,* and *Metaphysics* (the last is unprinted). With Philoponus the Alexandrian school thenceforth became Christian. In 529, the year in which Justinian closed the rival school at Athens under Damascius, he published 'On the eternity of the world against Proclus', arguing that Plato's *Timaeus* implies that the world was created in time, though by God's will it continues for ever, and also a (lost) work against Aristotle's doctrine that the circular movement of the heaven is eternal and that the heaven is of a fifth essence. The latter was angrily attacked in Simplicius' commentaries on *de Caelo* and *Physics.* As theologian he applied Aristotelian ideas to defend monophysite Christology and, in a dialogue entitled 'Arbiter' preserved in Syriac (damaging Greek fragments in John of Damascus, Migne, *PG* xciv. 743), he developed the doctrine of the Trinity in a manner open to charges of tritheism. He dedicated to Sergius, monophysite patriarch of Antioch *c.* 546 (?), his *de Opificio Mundi,* attacking Theodore of Mopsuestia's naïve use of scripture as a scientific authority and harmonizing Genesis with Greek cosmology; this work provoked confused polemic from Cosmas (q.v.) Indicopleustes. An attack on the 'two-nature' Christology of the council of Chalcedon, written after 553, is partly preserved in the twelfth-century chronicle of Michael the Syrian; it was known to Photius (q.v.) (*cod.* 55), who also reviewed works now lost on the Resurrection, the Trinity, and against Iamblichus (q.v. 2) on idolatrous images (21, 75, 215). He was not the theologian attacked by Severus of Antioch, *contra impium grammaticum* (as was argued by Gudeman, *PW,* s.v. Ioannes 21).

*Commentaria in Aristotelem Graeca,* 13–17 (1887–1909); *de Aeternitate Mundi,* ed. H. Rabe (1899); *de Opificio Mundi,* ed. G. Reinhardt (1897); *Opuscula Monophysitica,* ed. A. Sanda (1930). B. Altaner, *Patrology* (1960), 612 f. H. C.

**PHILOSOPHY, HISTORY OF.** Aristotle often gives in the introductions to his works a survey of the history of the problem he is going to treat. The scope is more systematic than historical; the treatment is rather polemical. He advised his pupils, however, to write similar works of their own, not as introductions but as separate and autonomous books. Thus Theophrastus wrote a history of Physics and Metaphysics (the fragments and the later history of which are treated in a masterly way by H. Diels, *Doxographi Graeci,* 1879), Eudemus histories of Theology, Astronomy, Geometry, and Arithmetic. In these works history prevails over systematic philosophy, although they follow the order of problems, not of time, and contain some criticism. They are the basis of all later work in this field. In the same generation another Aristotelian, Aristoxenus, became the first writer of philosophical biography.

Scholars in Alexandria found an external principle of unification by arranging the extensive material under 'successors' (διάδοχοι). They made up lineages of teachers, pupils, and pupils of the pupils, many of whom became presidents and successors of their respective schools. This also is the scheme of the only complete ancient history of philosophy which has been preserved,

that of Diogenes Laertius. In this work, as was often the case, biography and doxography are combined.

The standard general work (which takes account of Roman as well as of Greek philosophers) is E. Zeller, *Philosophie der Griechen:* 1⁶ (1919–20), the Pre-Socratics (1881); 2. 1⁴ (1889) (Socrates and the Socratics, 1868, Plato and the Older Academy, 1888); 2. 2⁴ (1921), Aristotle and the Earlier Peripatetics (1897); 3. 1⁴ (1909), Stoics, Epicureans, and Sceptics (1880); 3. 2⁴ (1903), Eclectics (1883). An Italian transl., with extensive addtions, by R. Mondolfo (1932–8), comes down to the Pythagoreans (inclusive). There is a shorter work by Zeller, *Grundriss der Geschichte der griechischen Philosophie*¹³ (1928) (E.T 1892).

A shorter but still fairly full treatment and an excellent bibliography will be found in F. Ueberweg, M. Heinze, and K. Praechter, *Grundriss* ¹² (1926). See too Guthrie, *Hist. Gk. Phil.* (1962– ).

The chief collections of fragments are: Mullach, *FPG* ; Diels, *Vorsokr.*¹¹; von Arnim, *SVF.* C. J. de Vogel, *Greek Philosophy* i–iii (1950–9), is a useful collection of leading passages, with notes. H. Diels, *Doxographi Graeci* (1879), is the standard edition of the Doxographers.

Other books are mentioned under the various schools and philosophers. W. D. R.

**PHILOSTEPHANUS** of Cyrene (3rd c. B.C.), pupil or friend of Callimachus, wrote: (1) geographical works, full of marvels and fables (Ath. 7. 297 f, 8. 331 d; Aul. Gell. 9. 4. 2; Harpocr. s.vv. Βούχετα, Στρύμη; schol. Pind. *Ol.* 6. 77); (2) a mythological and antiquarian treatise *Notebooks* ('Υπομνήματα) (schol. Ap. Rhod. 2. 124); (3) *On Discoveries* (Clem. Al. *Strom.* 1. 308 a). J. F. L.

**PHILOSTORGIUS** (*c.* A.D. 368–430/40), a Cappadocian resident in Constantinople, composed a *Church History* continuing Eusebius to A.D. 425. This is not extant, but Photius epitomized it and fragments survive elsewhere. He writes as a layman and an Arian of the Eunomian school. Though essentially apologetic, his work is a useful corrective and supplement to the orthodox historians, Socrates, etc.

Ed. J. Bidez (Berlin, 1913); further fragments in *Byzantion* 1934–5. S. L. G.

**PHILOSTRATI.** Four members of this family, which was of Lemnian origin, are probably to be distinguished. (1) Verus, a sophistic writer of the second century A.D., none of whose works survives. (2) Flavius Philostratus, son of Verus, born *c.* A.D. 170. He studied at Athens, and later joined the philosophical circle patronized by Septimius Severus and his wife Julia Domna. At her instance he wrote the *Life of Apollonius of Tyana,* a philosophizing mystic of the first century A.D.; the 'Ηρωικός, a dialogue concerned with the cult of Protesilaus, probably belongs to the same period. After returning to Athens he wrote Βίοι σοφιστῶν, chiefly interesting for notices of his contemporaries. He is probably also the author of a few of the Philostratean 'Επιστολαὶ ἐρωτικαί, of the protreptic Γυμναστικός, of the second of the two Διαλέξεις, and of the dialogue Νέρων, wrongly attributed to Lucian. He died in the reign of Philippus Arabs (A.D. 244–9) (*Suda*). (3) Philostratus Lemnius (Βίοι σοφ. 2. 27), born *c.* A.D. 191; a great-nephew of Philostratus (1), and son-in-law of Philostratus (2). He wrote the earlier Εἰκόνες, purported descriptions of pictures in a Neapolitan collection; probably also the second Διάλεξις (*see* LITERARY CRITICISM IN ANTIQUITY, 1. 6). (4) A grandson of Philostratus (3) (*Εἰκ. B, prooem.*), who wrote the later Εἰκόνες.

The *Life of Apollonius* is not uninteresting on account of the mystical and orientalizing tendencies which it illustrates; some have seen in it a counterblast to Christian propaganda: the 'Ηρ. shows similar characteristics. But Philostratus (2) finds his happier vein in the Βίοι σοφ., a work which throws valuable light on the habits and personalities of the Second Sophistic. It is written in the affectedly simple and unmethodical style. The earlier Εἰκ., though they add to our knowledge of Hellenistic art, are hardly, in spite of their subsequent popularity, to be accepted as a serious contribution to criticism; they are exemplary exercises in the art of rhetorical description. It is not certain that the pictures which they purport to describe actually existed. The later *Eik.* are distinctly inferior to them.

The *Suda* (confused notice).
EDITIONS. C. L. Kayser (1844–53; comment.) (1870–1, Teubner); J. Jüthner (1909; *Γυμν.*); O. Benndorf and C. Schenkl (1893; *Eik. A*); C. Schenkl and A. Reisch (1902; *Eik. B*).
TEXT AND TRANSLATION. *Life of Apollonius*, F. C. Conybeare (Loeb, 1912); *Βίοι σοφιστῶν*, W. C. Wright (Loeb, 1922); *Εἰκόνες*, A. Fairbanks (Loeb, 1931). *Letters*, A. R. Benner and F. H. Fobes (Loeb, 1949). Translation. *Life of Apollonius*, J. S. Phillimore, 1912.
CRITICISM. K. Münscher, *Philol.* Suppl. x (1907); F. Solmsen, *PW* xx. 124 ff. (authorship, etc.). W. Schmid, *Atticismus* iv (1896) (P. II, language). See also G. W. Bowersock, *Greek Sophists in the Roman Empire* (1969), ch. 1.                    W. M. E.; R. B.

**PHILOTAS** (c. 360–330 B.C.), a Macedonian noble, son of Parmenion (q.v.), and the commander of the *ἑταῖροι* or Guards Corps in the early campaigns of Alexander the Great. He was distinguished among Alexander's marshals by his gallant bearing and liberality, but gradually became alienated from the king himself. This estrangement may have been due to Philotas' resentment of the disfavour shown by the king to Parmenion, or of Alexander's tendency to disregard Macedonian custom and to adopt oriental habits. In 330 he was accused of conspiracy by Alexander before the Macedonian army, which found him guilty and executed him with a volley of javelins. Philotas was clearly convicted of connivance at a plot against Alexander, but it is uncertain whether he was an active conspirator. The story that under torture he incriminated his father may be dismissed as a later embroidery, perhaps intended to justify Parmenion's execution without trial.

Arr. *Anab.* 3. 26; Plut. *Alex.* 48–9; Curtius Rufus, *Hist. Alex.* vi, *passim*. Berve, *Alexanderreich*, no. 802; E. Badian, *TAPA* 1960, 324 ff.                    M. C.

**PHILOXENUS** (1) of Cythera (436/5–380/79 B.C., *Marm. Par.* 82), dithyrambic poet. He lived at the court of Dionysius of Syracuse, who sent him to the quarries (Ael. *VH* 12. 44). His most famous work was his *Cyclops*, in which the Cyclops sang a solo to the lyre—a great innovation (schol. Ar. *Plut.* 290). The work is parodied in *Plut.* 290 ff. *See* MUSIC, § 10.

TEXT. Page, *Poet. Mel. Gr.* 423–32.
CRITICISM. Pickard-Cambridge–Webster, *Dithyramb²*, 45 ff.
C. M. B.

**PHILOXENUS** (2), author of poem *The Banquet* quoted by Plato Comicus (ap. Ath. 6 d), which described a feast in full dithyrambic language (Ath. 146 f). He may be the same as Philoxenus son of Eryxis (Ar. *Ran.* 932 ff.).

TEXT. Page, *Poet. Mel. Gr.* 433–41.
CRITICISM. U. von Wilamowitz-Moellendorff, *Textgesch. d. griech. Lyr.* (1900), 85 ff.                    C. M. B.

**PHILOXENUS** (3), painter, of Eretria, pupil of Nico-machus (dated by Pliny 330 B.C.). Painted for Cassander (after 306?) a 'Battle of Alexander and Darius'. A mosaic in Pompeii (Pfuhl, fig. 648; Rumpf, pl. 49), prob-ably of the third century, is proved by likeness to the Alexander sarcophagus (Winter, *KB* 336–7) to represent faithfully a fourth-century original; Philoxenus has been suggested as the artist but more recently Apelles' name has been put forward (q.v.).

Overbeck, 1775, 1777; H. Fuhrmann, *Philoxenos von Eretria* (1931); Rumpf, *Malerei u. Zeichn.* 149.                    T. B. L. W.

**PHILOXENUS** (4) of Alexandria (1st c. B.C.) wrote on the text of Homer, accents, metre, verbs, and Atticism, and compiled important (lost) lexica of Homeric and other dialects. *See* ETYMOLOGY.

Funaioli, *Gramm. Rom. Frag.* i. 443 ff.

**PHILUMENUS** of Alexandria, member of the eclectic school of medicine, c. A.D. 180. An excerpt from his work *De Venenatis Animalibus* (on poisonous animals), the basis of the thirteenth book of Aelian, has been edited by M. Wellmann in *CMG* (1908). He also wrote a book on diseases of the bowels (only part extant, in a Latin tr., ed. Michaeleanu, 1910), and one *Περὶ γυναικείων* (on gynaecology, not extant).                    W. D. R.

**PHILYLLIUS,** Athenian comic poet, won the first prize once at the Lenaea at the beginning of the fourth century B.C. (*IG* ii². 2325. 137). We have ten titles, mostly imply-ing mythological burlesque, and thirty-four fragments.

*FCG* ii. 857 ff.; *CAF* i. 781 ff.; *FAC* i. 900 ff.                    K. J. D.

**PHILYRA,** i.e. linden-tree; in mythology an Oceanid loved by Kronos (q.v.), who, being surprised by Rhea while with her, turned himself and Philyra into horses. Her child was the centaur (q.v.) Chiron, and she was so horrified at his monstrous shape that she prayed to change her own form, and so became the tree called after her.

Hyg. *Fab.* 138.                    H. J. R.

**PHINEUS.** The best known of several mythological persons so named was a Thracian king. For some offence, he was plagued by the Harpies (q.v.); since they stole or defiled all his food, he was nearly starved to death by the time the Argonauts arrived at his land (Salmydessus, Soph. *Ant.* 970). He made a compact with them; if they would deliver him from the Harpies, he would prophesy to them the further course of their adventures. The sons of Boreas therefore (*see* CALAIS) attacked them, followed them through the air, and finally meeting Iris, received a pledge through her that Phineus should no longer be troubled. They then turned back from the islands afterwards known as the Strophades (Islands of Turning); Ap. Rhod. 2. 178 ff.

What the offence was is a question variously answered. The best-known account, which does not in all versions lead up to the story of his rescue, and so probably is not originally connected with it, is the following. He married Cleopatra, daughter of Boreas (q.v.), and had sons by her. The marriage coming to an end, by her death or other-wise, he remarried, and the stepmother so slandered her stepsons that Phineus either blinded them himself or let her do so (Soph. loc. cit. and schol. there); the latter records a variant that Cleopatra herself blinded them, in anger at being cast off by Phineus. The name of the second wife, those of the sons, and the reason for their ill-treat-ment all vary in different sources. Another sin attributed to Phineus was betrayal of divine secrets which he had learned through his prophetic powers (Ap. Rhod. loc. cit. 180 ff.); this obviously suits his delivery by the Boreadae much better. For more details and authorities see Jessen in Roscher's *Lexikon*, s.v.

Phineus' banquet, interrupted by Harpies, Boreads driving them off, is found in vase-painting from the later sixth century on (Brommer, *Vasenlisten²*, 351).    H. J. R.

**PHLEGON** of Tralles, a freedman of Hadrian, author of *Olympiades* (a history reaching from the first Olympiad to A.D. 140), *Π. θαυμασίων*, and *Π. μακροβίων*.

A. Westermann, *Paradoxographi* (1839), 197–212; O. Keller, *Rerum natural. script. graec. min.* (1877), 57–105; *FGrH* ii. 257.

**PHLEGYAS,** eponym of the Phlegyae, a Thessalian people, son of Ares (Apollod. 3. 41 and elsewhere; his mother's name varies). He is also represented as living near Lake Boebeis (Pind. *Pyth.* 3. 34), or in Orcho-menus (Paus. 9. 36. 1), while the Epidaurian legend (Paus. 2. 26. 4) brings him to the Peloponnesus. He was father of Coronis, the mother of Asclepius (q.v.; Pind. ibid. and elsewhere); of Ixion (q.v.; Eur. fr. 424 Nauck). Verg. *Aen.* 6. 618, whereon see Servius, puts him in Tartarus.

J. Fontenrose, *Python* (1959), 25 ff., 477 ff. H. J. R.

**PHLYAKES.** Farces (also called ἱλαροτραγῳδίαι) which were performed by 'phlyakes' in south Italy and also perhaps at Alexandria in the fourth and third centuries B.C. The chief authors of these ludicrous scenes from daily life or from mythology are Rhinthon, Sciras, and Sopater of Paphos (qq.v.); vase pictures illustrate an earlier (pre-literary?) stage of the development.

Fragments collected in *CGF* 183–97; Olivieri, *FCGM* ii² (excluding Sopater). See also A. D. Trendall, *The Phlyax Vases, BICS Supp. Paper 8* (with full bibliography). W. G. W.; W. G. A.

**PHOCAEA,** the most northerly of the Ionian cities in Asia Minor, occupying a site with twin harbours midway between the Elaitic and Hermaean Gulfs. She pioneered in the exploration and colonization of the western Mediterranean, though Lampsacus was almost her only contribution to the opening-up of the Euxine. In the sixth century B.C. her trading stations were strung along the route linking Magna Graecia with Spain, where Arganthonius, king of Tartessus, was her friend; and the foundation of Massilia gave the Greeks access to southern Gaul. In 540, when Phocaea was besieged by a Persian army, most of the citizens preferred emigration to submission, and finally found refuge at Elea in Italy. Phocaea never recovered from their loss. Dionysius, the generalissimo of the Greek fleet in the Ionian Revolt, was a Phocaean, but his city contributed only three ships.

Cary–Warmington, *Explorers,* 22; J. M. Cook, *The Greeks in Ionia and the East* (1962); G. E. Bean, *Aegean Turkey* (1966), 117 ff. D. E. W. W.

**PHOCAS** (5th c. A.D.), grammarian, author of an *Ars de nomine et verbo* (ed. Keil, *Gramm. Lat.* v. 410–39) and a *Vita Vergilii* in hexameters (often published, e.g. in Baehrens, *PLM* v. 85). A *De aspiratione* attributed to him (ed. Keil, *Gramm. Lat.* v. 439–41) is apocryphal.

Schanz–Hosius, § 1106. J. F. M.

**PHOCION** (4th c. B.C.), Athenian general and statesman. Although contemptuous of the people's fickleness and of popular leaders, Phocion commanded constant respect and was elected general forty-five times. Making his military reputation in the service of Persia (350 and 344 B.C.), he distinguished himself by campaigns in Euboea (348 and 341), by defending Megara (343) and Byzantium (339), and by repelling a Macedonian attack on Attica in the Lamian War (322). In politics Phocion supported Eubulus, Aeschines, and Demades against Demosthenes and Hyperides. Realizing the military strength of Macedonia, Phocion advised Athens to treat for terms when outmanœuvred before the battle of Chaeronea. After her defeat he assisted Demades in preserving peace with Philip and Alexander, opposed Harpalus, and sought to prevent Athens from joining in the Lamian War, after which he acted as envoy to Antipater and sponsored with Demades the limitation of the franchise at Athens. By an error of judgement he allowed Cassander's general Nicanor to seize the Piraeus. When the democracy was restored, Phocion was condemned to death (318). Prudent, patriotic, and responsible, he controlled Athens by a force of character which is portrayed in Plutarch's *Life of Phocion.* N. G. L. H.

**PHOCIS,** a country of central Greece comprising the middle Cephissus valley and the valley of Crisa, which are linked loosely by passes over the southern spurs of Mt. Parnassus. Both areas were fertile, the former possessing

pasture and agricultural land, and the latter olives, vines, and corn. In the sixth century B.C. Phocis was organized in a strong federation, issuing federal coinage and levying a federal army. Her internal unity enabled her to resist the aggression of her neighbours, who coveted the control of Delphi and of the route to northern Greece via the Cephissus valley and the pass of Elatea to Thermopylae, and she showed skill in her diplomacy. Deprived of Delphi and the Crisaean plain in the first Sacred War (c. 596) and overrun by Thessaly, her ambition was to regain her outlet to the sea; checked from expanding at the expense of Doris by Sparta, the Phocians allied with Athens (457), seized Delphi, and were confirmed in their control by an expedition under Pericles (448), to whom a Phocian alliance was valuable for encircling Boeotia. After the battle of Coronea (447) Phocis joined Sparta, was loyal to her during the Peloponnesian War and in the early fourth century, until Boeotia impressed her into her Central Greek Confederacy. Her bid for independence in the Third Sacred War broke Theban power but exhausted Phocis. *See* PHILOMELUS, ONOMARCHUS.

P–K, *GL* 1. 2. 422 ff. N. G. L. H.

**PHOCUS** (Φῶκος), in mythology, son of Aeacus (q.v.) by the nymph Psamathe, who took the shape of a seal, φώκη; hence the name of her son (Apollod. 3. 158). He proved a distinguished athlete, thus arousing the jealousy of the legitimate sons, Peleus and Telamon (qq.v.); they drew lots to see which should kill him, and Telamon, to whom the task fell, murdered him while they were exercising; Aeacus found out and banished them both (ibid. 160).

H. J. R.

**PHOCYLIDES** (fl. 544–541 B.C., *Suda*), elegiac and hexameter poet of Miletus. His work is of a gnomic character. He sometimes begins his lines with the formula καὶ τόδε Φωκυλίδου, writes about traditional matters such as the virtues of husbandry (fr. 7), the badness of women (fr. 2), the Mean (fr. 12), protecting spirits (fr. 16); he disbelieved in noble birth (fr. 3) and liked club-life (fr. 14).

TEXT. Diehl, *Anth. Lyr. Graec.* i. 1. 58–62. C. M. B.

**PHOEBE** (Φοίβη), a Titaness, daughter of Heaven and Earth (Hes. *Theog.* 136); wife of Coeus and mother of Leto (q.v.; ibid. 404 ff.). She is thus grandmother of Apollo (Phoebus) and Artemis. But her name, 'the bright one', is not infrequently used for the Moon (e.g. Stat. *Theb.* 1. 105), though never in an early author; and therefore also for Artemis and Diana, as identical with the Moon (e.g. Stat. *Silv.* 1. 3. 76). Of several other mythological figures who bear this name, the only well-known one is a daughter of Leucippus, *see* DIOSCURI. The schol. Strozziana on Germanicus, *Aratea,* 175, 3 Breysig, says Hesiod called one of the Heliades Phoebe. H. J. R.

**PHOENICIANS** (Φοίνικες, *Poeni*) are said by Herodotus (1. 1; 2. 44; 7. 89) to have migrated from the Persian Gulf 2,300 years before his time; probably a tradition of the real movements of Mesopotamian conquerors and metal-traders to the north-west. Byblos (*Gebal, Jebail*) was a port known to early dynastic Egypt.

Phoenician sea-faring, however, begins only later. The only Mediterranean sea-traders mentioned on Eighteenth Dynasty monuments (15th c.) are the Keftiu, apparently Minoans. The name 'Phoinix' ('Red'; cf. φοίνιος, φοινός) is Greek, and may first have been applied to any copperskinned Mediterraneans. But the discovery in 1964 of a cache of Babylonian seals among Mycenaean remains at Thebes sheds an unexpected light on the legend that Cadmus (q.v.) was an oriental.

Minoans traded with Syria, notably at Alalakh(*Atchana*)

and Ugarit (*Ras Shamra*). After the disturbances of the Philistine migration (about 1200), the main ports are at island sites, Arvad (*Aradus, Ruad,*) and Tyre, or protected inland, like Tyre again and Sidon, by Mt. Lebanon. Here arose a new, cosmopolitan Phoenicia, its art a mixture of Egyptian, Mesopotamian, and local elements, its hieratic literature, best known in texts from Ugarit, written at first in cuneiform. Probably before 1000, these Phoenicians—Canaanites, Kinahu, Chna (Hecataeus, ap. Steph. Byz. s.v.), as they called themselves—produced their greatest invention, the Alphabet (q.v.). Also, stimulated by the collapse of Aegean carrying-trade and perhaps by Aegean immigrants, they took to the sea.

Homer thus knows Phoenicians well, both as craftsmen and as traders. Sidon is their great city; Tyre is not mentioned (*Il.* 6. 290 f.; *Od.* 13. 272 ff., 14. 288 ff., etc.). Tyre had in fact taken the lead by about 750; but in a Phoenician inscription too (*ClSem.* i. 5, from Cyprus) a king of Tyre about 740 is still called 'King of the Sidonians'.

The Phoenicians traded with Tartessus in southern Spain; probably 'Tharshish', though this word in earlier contexts may have meant Tarsus. That they reached Cornwall, there is no evidence. The dates, 1100 for Cadiz (Gaddir, 'Walled Place', Avienius 265 f.) and 1087 for Utica, accepted by Roman writers (e.g. Velleius 1. 2), may be too early; but archaeology shows them widespread in the West before 900. Most of their settlements were very small, simple trading posts; Carthage (q.v.), founded by political refugees under Dido-Elissa (a historical character; grand-niece of Jezebel) about 814, was exceptional in being from the first a considerable city. The Phoenicians took no land, but were purely traders; hence, unlike the Greeks, they remained on good terms with the natives. Even Carthage paid rent, until after 550, for the very site of the city (Justin 19. 1). They also sailed the Red Sea, by arrangement with Solomon or, much later, with Pharaoh Necoh, for whom about 600 they circumnavigated Africa (Hdt. 4. 42). They were attacked at home by Assyria and then by Babylon; Esarhaddon sacked Sidon about 680; but Tyre remained impregnable and the trade continued. Ezekiel, ch. xxvii, a splendid poem, shows Tyre trading in Asian manufactures for Western tin, silver, etc.; with the hinterland for food (cf. 1 Kings v. 9); and in slaves in both directions (cf. also Amos i. 6; Joel iii. 4 ff.).

With the *pax Persica* the Phoenicians came to terms willingly, and their fleets, serving under their own kings, formed the backbone of the imperial navy. The Persian Wars (q.v.) never lastingly interrupted trade even with Greece, as imports of Attic red-figure pottery show. But in the fourth century there were also revolts. Sidon again suffered severely. Except Tyre, the cities surrendered easily to Alexander (q.v. 3); and with their incorporation in the Hellenistic world, the separate history and culture of Phoenicia come to an end.

SOURCES. In addition to the Greek and Biblical writers, see summary of Phoenician annals from *c.* 970 to 772 in Josephus (*AJ* 8. 5. 3, *Ap.* 1. 17, 18).

MODERN WRITERS. G. Contenau, *La Civilisation phénicienne²* (1949); D. Harden, *The Phoenicians* (1962, with bibliography); S. Moscati, *The World of the Phoenicians* (1968). *See also* CARTHAGE, SIDON, TYRE.
A. R. B.

**PHOENICIDES,** New Comedy poet. Fr. 1 refers to a peace made in 287 B.C. In fr. 4 a ἑταίρα bids farewell to the gay life, describing her experiences with various lovers.

FCG iv. 509 ff.; CAF iii. 333 ff.

**PHOENIX,** in mythology, (1) son of Amyntor king of Hellas (in the old sense of the word), who left home when young on account of a quarrel with his father. The latter had a concubine of whom his wife, Phoenix's mother, was jealous; she induced her son to corrupt the woman

and thus make her lose Amyntor's favour. The old man, finding this out, cursed his son with childlessness, and Phoenix, despite his relations' attempts to stop him, escaped and went to Phthia, where Peleus (q.v.) received him kindly and made him a sort of tutor to the young Achilles (q.v.). He accompanied his charge to the Trojan War, where he was one of the ambassadors sent to bring Agamemnon's offers of reconciliation (*Iliad* 9. 168 ff.); Euripides, in his lost *Phoenix,* followed a version in which Amyntor blinded Phoenix and the latter was finally healed by Chiron (see Nauck, *TGF* 621 ff.).

(2) Son of Agenor and brother of Cadmus (q.v.); like Cadmus, he was sent to look for Europa, did not return home, and founded a people, the Phoenicians, who were named after him (Eur. fr. 819, etc.). He is a shadowy figure whose story, such as it is, varies in different authors, see Türk in Roscher's *Lexikon* iii. 2401 ff.
H. J. R.

**PHOENIX** (3) of Colophon, iambic poet of third century B.C., author of moralizing choliambics and of a poem *Coronistae* based on a Rhodian beggars' song. *See* IAMBIC POETRY (GREEK).

TEXT. Diehl, *Anth. Lyr. Graec.* i. 3. 104–10; Powell, *Coll. Alex.* 231–6.
TEXT AND TRANSLATION. A. D. Knox, *Herodes, Cercidas, and the Greek Choliambic Poets* (Loeb, 1929), 242 ff.

**PHOENIX,** 170 lines (elegiac) on the fabulous bird whose resurrection to life through death made appeal to both pagan and Christian thought. It has sometimes been ascribed to Lactantius (q.v.).

TEXT AND TRANSLATION (with bibliog.). Duff, *Minor Lat. Poets.*

**PHORBAS,** name of several mythological persons, all obscure. (1) A Thessalian (Lapith), son of Lapithes, the eponym of the Lapiths, or of his son Triopas (Paus. 5. 1. 11; *Hymn. Hom. Ap.* 211). His home, according to various accounts, is Thessaly, Elis, Argos, or Rhodes; see Höfer in Roscher's *Lexikon* iii. 2424 ff. This may be the Phorbas who takes part in the fight of the Lapiths and Centaurs (Ov. *Met.* 12. 322). (2) A Phlegyan, living at Panopeus, who challenged pilgrims on their way to Delphi to box with him and so killed them, till he was killed by Apollo in human disguise (schol. *Il.* 23. 660, cf. Ov. *Met.* 11. 414, Philostr. *Imag.* 2. 19; Fontenrose, *Python* (1959), 24 ff.). (3) An Athenian hero, said to have been an attendant on Theseus, schol. Pind. *Nem.* 5. 89. A shrine, the Phorbanteion, belonged either to him or to (4), an ally of Eumolpus (q.v.), killed by Erectheus (Harpocration, s.v. Φορβαντεῖον.
H. J. R.

**PHORCYS,** in mythology, son of Nereus and Earth (Hes. *Theog.* 237). Marrying his sister Ceto, he became father of the Graiae and Gorgons (qq.v.; ibid. 270 ff.). Other children are ascribed to him in various sources, as Thoosa, mother of the Cyclops, Polyphemus (*Od.* 1. 71); the Sirens (q.v.; Sophocles in Plut. *Quaest. conv.* 745 f.). In general he is the father or leader of sea-monsters, such as the Tritons (q.v.; Verg. *Aen.* 5. 824).
H. J. R.

**PHORMION,** Athenian admiral, *strategos* of the *phyle* Pandionis, first mentioned in 440 B.C. before Samos. In the next years he proved an excellent military leader in Acarnania, at Potidaea, and in Chalcidice. In 430 he blockaded Corinth from Naupactus; and next summer, by brilliant tactics, he defeated two superior Peloponnesian fleets, thus restoring Athenian influence in Acarnania. After his return (428), he is said to have been sentenced for peculation (schol. Ar. *Pax* 347). Probably he died at this time.

Thuc. bks. 1 and 2; *Prosop. Att.* 14958. V. Ehrenberg, *AJPhil.* 1945, 119.
V. E.

**PHORMIS** (or **PHORMUS**), Syracusan writer of comedy. Aristotle (*Poet.* 5. 1449[b]6) seems to treat him as a contemporary of Epicharmus. The *Suda* adds that he was tutor to the sons of Gelon (d. 478 B.C.), and attributes to Phormis the invention of long cloaks for his actors and (?) a new form of *skene*. Paus. 5. 27. 1 mentions a notable Arcadian soldier Phormis who fought for Hieron and Gelon; possibly the biographical tradition of the poet Phormis is contaminated.

CGF 148 ;.Pickard-Cambridge–Webster, *Dithyramb*[2], 289. K. J. D.

**PHORONEUS** (Φορωνεύς), a very ancient ancestral figure of Argive tradition. He was older than Deucalion's flood (Pl. *Ti.* 22 a), husband of the Argive Niobe, the first earthly love of Zeus, cf. Hyg. *Fab.* 145. 1, who makes her his daughter. He was son of Inachus (q.v.; ibid. 124, cf. Apollod. 2. 1, where his descendants are given). He has no legend, except that he was one of the judges between Hera and Poseidon for possession of the country (Paus. 2. 15. 5), but he had a cult (ibid. 20. 3). H. J. R.

**PHOSPHORUS** (Φωσφόρος = Ἑωσφόρος; Lucifer), the morning star, personified son of Eos and Astraeus (Hes. *Th.* 381) or Cephalus (Hyg. *Poet. Astr.* 2. 42; cf. Hes. *Th.* 986–91), sometimes represented as a youth bearing a torch. As a cult name Phosphorus was applied to Hecate, Artemis (cf. Diana Lucifera), and, more rarely, to other divinities. The *deus bonus puer Phosphorus* is the Syrian god, Aziz. F. R. W.

**PHOTIUS**, the best of the Byzantine scholars and Patriarch of Constantinople in A.D. 858–67 and 878–86. 'At the pressing intreaty of the Caesar (Bardas), the celebrated Photius renounced the freedom of a secular and studious life, ascended the patriarchal throne, and was alternately excommunicated and absolved by the synods of the East and West. By the confession even of priestly hatred, no art or science, except poetry, was foreign to this universal scholar, who was deep in thought, indefatigable in reading, and eloquent in diction' (Gibbon, ch. 53). His most important work is the *Bibliotheca* (or *Myriobiblion*), 'a living monument of erudition and criticism' (Gibbon, loc. cit.). It is a hastily compiled, ill-arranged critical account (in 280 chapters, with numerous extracts) of 280 prose works read by Photius in the absence of his brother, Tarasius, for whose information, and at whose request, the work was composed, at some date before A.D. 858. Theology and history predominate; oratory, romance, philosophy, science, medicine, and lexicography also come within its scope. Besides its intrinsic value (the criticisms are often felicitous and acute), it has a considerable adventitious importance as the best or sole source of our information about many notable lost works; it mentions some sixty non-theological works not now surviving. The *Lexicon*, which is an earlier work, is a glossary based ostensibly and in fact indirectly upon Aelius Dionysius, Pausanias, and Diogenianus, but immediately drawn from such later compilations as Timaeus' Platonic lexicon, and chiefly from the Συναγωγή (*see* LEXICA SEGUERIANA). The *Lexicon* was long known only from the *Codex Galeanus* at Cambridge, defective at the beginning. Part of the missing portion was supplied by MSS. in Athens and Berlin (R. Reitzenstein, *Der Anfang d. Lexikons d. Photios* (1907)). In 1959 a MS. containing the complete *Lexicon* was found at Zavorda in Macedonia, and an edition is in preparation (L. Politis, *Philol.* 1961, 136 ff.).

EDITIONS. *Bibl.*: Bekker, 1824–5; Migne, *PG* (1860), vol. 103; R. Henry, in progress (1959– ). *Lexicon*: Naber, 1864–5.
CRITICISM. E. Orth, *Photiana* (1928), *Stilkritik d. P.* (1929); K. Ziegler, *PW* xx (1941), 662 ff.; F. Dvornik, *Berichte zum XI. Int. Byzantinisten-Kongreß* (1960), iii. 2. P. B. R. F.; R. B.

**PHRAATES** (1) **IV** (*c.* 38–2 B.C.), king of Parthia. He secured the succession by murdering his father Orodes II (q.v.) and many Parthian princes and nobles (Plut. *Ant.* 37, Dio Cass. 49. 23). He soon had to face a Roman invasion, when Antony penetrated into Media Atropatene, but Phraates' general Monaeses forced him to retire with great loss. From 31 to 25 B.C. Phraates had to contest his throne with the rebel Tiridates (q.v. II). His embassies to Augustus led to better relations between Rome and Parthia, and the standards captured from Crassus and Antony along with surviving captives were restored to Rome in 20 B.C. A few years later he even consigned four of his sons to Augustus for safe keeping. He was assassinated in a harem intrigue. For the other kings named Phraates, *see* ARSACIDS.

Coin portraits: Wroth, *B.M.C. Parthia*. M. S. D.; E. W. G.

**PHRAATES** (2) **V** (**PHRAATACES**) (2 B.C.–A.D. 4), king of Parthia. He was the son of Phraates IV by an Italian slave-girl; Augustus had sent her to the king who later made her his legitimate queen as Thea Urania Musa. She and her son secured the murder of Phraates IV in 2 B.C., and Phraataces succeeded. He drove a certain Artavasdes, who was the nominee of Augustus, out of Armenia in favour of Tigranes III, and tried to take a strong line with Augustus. He soon changed his tune, promised not to interfere in Armenia, and met Gaius Caesar (q.v. 6) on the Euphrates (A.D. 1) where a concordat between Rome and Parthia was reached: Velleius, who was present, called Phraataces *iuvenis excelsissimus* (2. 101. 1). In A.D. 4 Phraataces, who had married his mother Musa in A.D. 2, was deposed by the Parthian nobles who chose Orodes III. The latter survived only until *c.* 6/7, and his successor Vonones I only till 12 (though the latter held the Armenian throne from 12 to 16). Greater stability came with Artabanus II (III) (q.v.). H. H. S.

**PHRATRIAI** (φρατρίαι, with dialectal variations), 'brotherhoods', kinship-groups in Greek cities whose members were φράτερες. They are attested in several of the Greek ἔθνη, and this fact, along with the early replacement of φράτηρ in the sense of 'brother' in all dialects and the existence of similar institutions among other Indo-European peoples (e.g. the *bratstva* of the South Slavs), bespeaks their high antiquity. They are often found as divisions of *phylai* (q.v.) and were themselves composed—at least in theory—of related families (*see* GENOS). Thus they worshipped a common ancestor, and more often than not were called by a patronymic name formed from his. Membership was in principle open only to legitimate sons of *phrateres*, but since in any State the phratries normally covered the whole citizen-body (cf. *Iliad* 9. 63 f.) it became possible for new citizens to be admitted without any hereditary title. The members of any one phratry would long be found in the particular district where their ancestors had settled, and this remained their centre even after many of them had moved away. A phratry was a corporation with a definite constitution. It held regular meetings at least once a year (in Ionian cities, at the Apaturia, q.v.), elected annual officers such as a phratriarch and priest, passed decrees which became part of its 'law' (if conformable to the law of the State), and admitted new *phrateres* after appropriate scrutiny. It could possess property (such as houses and cemeteries) and funds (derived from rent, fines, etc.). Its principal activity was the worship of its tutelary gods, who varied from phratry to phratry and city to city, but usually included Zeus Phratrios (or Patroos). With the growth of democracy phratries tended to be reorganized (cf. Arist. *Pol.* 1319[b]23) and were sometimes replaced by more artificial divisions, e.g. the συννομαί of Rhodes, the χιλιαστύες of Chios, etc., which preserved some of their characteristic features. Under whatever name, they tend to disappear in Hellenistic times, though the phratries of Neapolis survived into the Christian era.

At Argos there were upwards of thirty phratries, at Sparta twenty-seven (perhaps nine to each of the three Dorian tribes). Little is known about them. A long inscription (*SIG*³ 438) gives valuable details of the organization of the Labyadai at Delphi.

Aristotle (*Ath. Pol.* fr. 3) equated the Athenian phratries with the twelve old *trittyes* (q.v.); but although only a handful of names of phratries are known, it is probable that there were far more than twelve. In Draco's time every Athenian belonged to a phratry, and nobles and plebeians might be *phrateres* to one another (*SIG*³ 111. 18 f.). But the noble γένη (*see* GENOS) were doubtless powerful within the phratries and may have tried to make them more exclusive: at all events a law, of uncertain date, obliged *phrateres* to admit both *gennetai* and *orgeones*(q.v.). Down to the time of Cleisthenes (q.v. 1) membership of a phratry was the sole test of citizenship. Cleisthenes introduced a new criterion, that of deme-membership (*see* DEMOI, PHYLAI), but did not disturb the phratries (Arist. *Ath. Pol.* 21. 6), and they continued to register new members as before; though it is not clear whether membership of a phratry remained a necessary feature of citizenship, or became merely normal. Certainly the orators attest the frequent appearance of *phrateres* in the courts as witnesses to status, and foreigners admitted to citizenship were registered in a phratry as well as a deme. Membership of demes and phratries overlapped, though a fair proportion of the members of a phratry would belong to the deme where it had its centre, or to neighbouring demes. Considerable details of admission-procedure in the fourth century are preserved in an inscription of the phratry centred at Decelea (*SIG*³ 921). By this time this and other phratries were divided into small groups called θίασοι (*see* THIASOS) which apparently cut across the distinction between nobles and commoners.

Greek writers on Roman affairs used the word φρατρία to translate *curia* (q.v. 1).

O. Schrader, *Reallexikon der indogermanischen Altertumskunde* (1901), 770 ff.; Busolt–Swoboda, *Griech. Staatsk.*³, see indexes; M. Guarducci, *Mem. Linc.* 1937, 3 ff.; 1938, 65 ff.; A. Andrewes, *Hermes* 1961, 129 ff. Argos: W. Vollgraff, *BCH* 1909, 171 ff.; 1959, 254 ff.; *Mnemos.* 1916, 54 ff. Rhodes: A. Andrewes, *BSA* 1957, 30 ff. Chios: W. G. Forrest, *BSA* 1960, 172 ff. Athens: Wilamowitz, *Aristoteles und Athen* (1893), ii. 259 ff.; W. S. Ferguson, *CPhil.* 1910, 257 ff.; H. T. Wade-Gery, *CQ* 1931, 129 ff. (*Essays in Greek History* (1958), 116 ff.); Hignett, *Hist. Athen. Const.*, see index; A. Andrewes, *JHS* 1961, 1 ff.; N. G. L. Hammond, *JHS* 1961, 76 ff.
T. J. C.

**PHRYGIA,** a country comprising part of the central plateau and the western flank of Asia Minor. The conquest of central and western Asia Minor by the European Phryges took place towards the end of the second millennium B.C., and was still remembered when the Trojan saga was taking shape (*Iliad* 3. 184 ff.); it extended further to the north and west than the Phrygia of the Greek and Roman periods. The limits of the original Phrygian conquest were driven in on the west by the emergence of the Lydian Kingdom, and in the north by subsequent invasions from Europe of Mysians and Bithynians, and, much later, Galatians; in the Roman period the northern boundary of Phrygia lay well south of the northern mountain parapet and far from its early maritime base on the Sea of Marmara. On the east and south the later boundaries still represent the extreme limit of the original Phrygian permanent settlement, which appears not to have crossed the Halys or penetrated beyond Iconium or Pisidian Antioch or south of the Maeander basin.

In Phrygia the European invaders absorbed the older population and founded a kingdom, associated in Greek legend with the names of Midas and Gordius, whose memorials survive in the rock-cities and sculptured façades, some of them inscribed, of the 'Phrygian Monument Country' south of Dorylaeum. After its conquest by Lydia Phrygia never again appears as an independent State; the old warrior stock was merged in the peasant population, and to the classical Greeks 'Phrygian' was equivalent to 'slave'. Phrygia was subject in turn to the Persians, Seleucids, and Attalids; in 116 B.C. the greater part of it was absorbed in the province Asia (q.v.), and in 25 B.C. the remaining eastern portion became a region of the province Galatia. The Phrygian religion, whose male god Papas took his place beside the old Anatolian Mother goddess, and the Phrygian language survived until the early Byzantine period. Diocletian made Asian Phrygia a separate province, which Constantine subdivided into two, Prima or Pacatiana and Secunda or Salutaris, administered from Laodicea and Synnada respectively.

W. M. Ramsay, *Cities and Bishoprics of Phrygia* (1895–7); id. *JHS* 1882, 1884; Perrot–Chipiez, *Hist. de l'art* v (1890); *MAMA* vols. i, iv–vii; A. Gabriel et al. *Phrygie* i–iv (1941–65). W. M. C.

**PHRYNICHUS** (1), Athenian tragic poet, coupled by some ([Plato], *Minos* 320 e) with Thespis as one of the originators of tragedy. His first victory was between 511 and 508 B.C. (*Suda*, s.v.). He produced, probably in 492, with Themistocles as choregus, a play dealing with the taking of Miletus by the Persians in 494, and was fined for reminding the Athenians too vividly of the misfortunes of their friends (Hdt. 6. 21). Another historical play, the *Phoenissae* (probably identical with his Πέρσαι), related to the Persian War just ended; the scene was laid in Persia and opened with a servant setting seats for the Persian nobles (Arg. Aesch. *Persae*). In 476 Themistocles was again his choregus at the Great Dionysia (Plut. *Them.* 5), and this may have been the date of the *Phoenissae*. Among his mythological plays were the *Pleuroniae* (from the story of Meleager and Oeneus); the *Aegyptii* and *Danaides*; the *Antaeus* and the *Alcestis* (possibly a satyric play) which was not without influence on Euripides' play (*Schol. Dan. Aen.* 4. 694, fr. 2), and the *Actaeon*. He was remembered for the beauty of his lyrics (Ar. *Vesp.* 220, *Av.* 748 ff.) and the many varieties of dance which he invented (Plut. *Quaest. conv.* 8. θ. 3); Aristophanes admired him greatly (see also *Thesm.* 165 ff., *Ran.* 1298 f.). He was said (*Suda*, s.v.) to have been the first tragic poet to employ a feminine mask, i.e. to introduce a female character. The few fragments suggest that he employed metaphors freely.

*TGF* 720–5. Pickard-Cambridge–Webster, *Dithyramb*², 63 ff.
A. W. P.-C.

**PHRYNICHUS** (2), Athenian comic poet, produced his first play in 434 (*Suda*) or 429 (Anon. *De Com.* 10); the latter statement probably refers to his first victory—at the Lenaea, where he won two victories (*IG* ii². 2325. 125), his first victory at the City Dionysia being some time after 420 (ibid. 61). He produced Μονότροπος in 414 (hyp. 1 Ar. *Av.*) and *Muses* in 405 (hyp. 1 Ar. *Ran.*). We have eleven titles and 100 fragments; two of the titles, *Connus* and *Revellers*, are also attributed to Ameipsias (q.v.), and this attribution is to be preferred, since it is given by hyp. 5 Ar. *Nub.* and hyp. 1 Ar. *Av.*, the composers of which will have derived their information direct from the διδασκαλίαι. Fr. 58 (play unnamed) refers humorously to the mutilation of the herms (q.v.) in 415.

*FCG* ii. 580 ff.; *CAF* i. 369 ff.; *FAC* i. 451 ff. K. J. D.

**PHRYNICHUS** (3) **ARABIUS,** of Bithynia, Atticist, rhetorician, and lexicographer under M. Aurelius and

Commodus. He compiled Σοφιστικὴ προπαρασκευή, a lexicon of 'Attic' words in thirty-seven books, preserved only in a summary by Photius and in fragments; also Ἀττικιστής (περὶ κρίσεως καλῶν καὶ δοκίμων ὀνομάτων), extant in an abridgement, our Ἐκλογή. They were based on Eirenaeus and Aelius Dionysius. Phrynichus criticizes Pollux (q.v.), his successful rival for the chair of rhetoric at Athens, for his laxity in the choice of words, and, with Moeris, ranks among the strictest of the 'Atticists'. He recognizes different levels of style within 'Atticism'. His models are Plato, the Ten Orators, Thucydides, Aeschines Socraticus, Critias, Antisthenes, Aristophanes, Aeschylus, Sophocles, and Euripides. Nor would he accept the usage of even the best of these without cavil. In the letter to the Imperial Secretary, Attidius Cornelianus, which introduces the Ἐκλογή, he reprobates those who try to justify their diction by citing the impeached words from classical authors: ἡμεῖς δὲ οὐ πρὸς τὰ διημαρτημένα ἀφορῶμεν, ἀλλὰ πρὸς τὰ δοκιμώτατα τῶν ἀρχαίων. Such critical scrutiny, however, if at all possible, would demand a clearer perception than the Atticists ever had of the nature and relations of spoken and literary Attic, and of the diverse sources from which the language of the poets was drawn. Nevertheless, Phrynichus' work contains many acute and accurate observations.

EDITIONS. Σοφ. προπ.: (Summary) Bekker, Anecd. i; (Fragments) J. von Borries, Teubner, 1911. Ἐκλογή: C. A. Lobeck, 1820. W. G. Rutherford (The New P.), 1881; M. Naechster, De Pollucis et Phrynichi controversiis (1908).                                        P. B. R. F.; R. B.

**PHTHIOTIS**, a district of Thessaly. In mythology, when it was the realm of Achilles, and in Roman times it included Achaea Phthiotis and extended from Cynoscephalae to the border of Malis. In the intervening period, however, Phthiotis denoted only the neighbourhood of Pharsalus (q.v.) and formed one of the tetrads of Thessaly proper, whereas Achaea Phthiotis belonged to the Perioecis and owed allegiance to Thessaly, particularly to Pharsalus.

Achaea, a mountainous district including the Othrys range, has a coastal plain on the Bay of Volo. Halus, its chief port, seems to have declined when Pagasae (q.v.) was developed by Pherae (q.v.). The other towns were Phthiotic Thebes, Larissa Cremaste, and Melitaea. The Achaeans rarely enjoyed freedom from external intervention. When liberated from Alexander of Pherae they were forced to join the Boeotian Confederacy, and when Philip detached the Periocis from Thessaly they became subjects of Macedonia. An Achaean Confederacy apparently existed in the third century B.C.

G. Kip, Thessalische Studien (1910), 51 ff.; F. Stählin, Das hellenische Thessalien (1924), 135 ff. and 150 ff.                   H. D. W.

**PHYLACUS**, in mythology, (1) father of Iphiclus, for whose story see MELAMPUS (1), son of Deion and so grandson of Aeolus (q.v.; Apollod. 1. 86). (2) Son of Iphiclus and grandson of (1) (Eust. Il. 323, 42). (3) A local hero of Delphi (Hdt. 8. 39. 1). He appeared with Autonous, another local hero, and helped to drive off the Persian raiders in 480 B.C. (ibid. 38).                              H. J. R.

**PHYLAI** (φυλαί) or 'tribes' were in origin large divisions, based on real or supposed ties of kin, of Greek ἔθνη. They are often found subdivided into the smaller kinshipgroups known as phratriai (q.v.). The best-known phylai are those of the Dorians and Ionians (qq.v.): they appear only as components of their cities, and should therefore be older than their settlement of the oldest of these. The three Dorian phylai, called Hylleis, Pamphyloi, and Dymanes, are found in practically all Dorian cities; where a non-Dorian element existed, in Argos (q.v. 2) and Sicyon (q.v.) and some other cities, it was accommodated in a separate phyle or phylai of its own. The

original four phylai of Athens—Geleontes, Hopletes, Argadeis, and Aigikoreis—recur in some other Ionian cities, together with other phylai for non-Ionians. The territorial divisions of the Aetolians and Arcadians (qq.v.), though usually themselves called ἔθνη rather than φυλαί, were probably in origin kinship-groups which occupied separate districts. We know little or nothing of similar divisions in other ἔθνη.

Phylai were corporate bodies with a hereditary membership and with their own priests and officials (φυλοβασιλεῖς at Athens); they were also administrative and military divisions of the State. For this purpose the old Attic tribes were subdivided into trittyes and naukrariai (qq.v.) as well as phratriai. Colonies were normally equipped with the phylai of the mother-city, with modifications to suit local conditions. When phylai of the ancient type had become politically objectionable, as assisting the continuance of aristocratic rule and the exclusion of new aspirants to citizenship, they were liable to be set aside in favour of new artificial tribes, which took over their administrative and military functions. Artificial phylai were also sometimes devised for new cities formed by synoecism (q.v.), or colonies of mixed origin. The principle of division was usually territorial, but sometimes according to origin.

In Sparta, the three Dorian tribes had, at latest by 600 B.C., been replaced for secular purposes by five local tribes based on the obai or constituent villages of the city; hence the five ephors (q.v.) and five lochoi of the early fifth century army (see ARMIES, GREEK AND HELLENISTIC, § 3). A similar change was made by Cleisthenes (q.v. 1) at Athens. There the old phylai, which had been dominated by the nobles, did not include many of the new citizens admitted under the legislation of Solon (q.v. § 3) and by the tyrants. Cleisthenes created ten new local phylai, allowing the old ones to survive for a few sacred purposes only. To break up not only the old ascendancy of the nobles, but also the more recent domination of the people into Pedieis, Paralioi, and Diakrioi (see MEGACLES, PISISTRATUS), he formed each new phyle from three trittyes (q.v.), one from each of three new territorial divisions of Attica, corresponding only partially with the three older regions. These were 'the town' (τὸ ἄστυ), including Piraeus and Phaleron (qq.v.) and part of the plain of Athens; the Paralia, including most of the old Paralia with the remaining coastal regions; and the 'interior' (μεσόγειος), composed from parts of all the old regions. Each trittys was in its turn divided into demes (see DEMOI). Membership of the demes, carrying with it membership of the new phylai and of the citizen-body, was extended to all free men living in them at the time of the reform. It was not altered by subsequent changes of residence, and was transmitted by descent in the male line. The phylai were not units of local government; each had its headquarters in the city. The new State administration was based on them: most of the magistrates, including the archontes and strategoi (qq.v.) and various committees of the boule (q.v. §§ 4, 5) formed boards of ten, and selection of these, one from each tribe, is in some cases attested and may be generally presumed. Each group of fifty prytaneis (q.v.) within the boule consisted of the councillors from a single tribe. The ten regiments of hoplites and ten squadrons of cavalry (see HIPPEIS), together with their commanders the phylarchoi and taxiarchoi, were likewise drawn from the separate phylai. The phylai were also represented as such by choruses and choregoi in the dithyrambic contests at festivals (see CHOREGIA).

Cleisthenes named his ten tribes after nine Attic heroes and one Salaminian hero; in the official order, they were Erechtheis, Aigeis, Pandionis, Leontis, Akamantis, Oineis, Kekropis, Hippothontis, Aiantis, Antiochis. In Hellenistic and Roman tribes the number was raised by one, two, or three, and the citizens redistributed accordingly, as additional *phylai*, named after powerful princes (Antigonis, Demetrias, Ptolemais, Attalis, Hadrianis), were created and abolished.

Greek writers on Roman affairs used the word φυλή to translate *tribus*.

Busolt–Swoboda, *Griech. Staatsk.*³ (i, 1920; ii, 1926), see indexes; Hignett, *Hist. Athen. Const.*, see index; H. T. Wade-Gery, *Essays in Greek History* (1958), 37 ff. (Sparta); R. Sealey, *Hist.* 1960, 155 ff. (Athens); W. G. Forrest, *BSA* 1960, 172 ff. (Chios); G. Dunst, *Forschung u. Fortschritte* 1961, 272 f. (Miletus); C. Roebuck, *TAPA* 1961, 495 ff. (Ionia); D. Kagan, *Hist.* 1963, 41 ff. (Athens).
                                                                    A. W. G.; T. J. C.

**PHYLARCHUS** of Athens, the most important historian of the period between Pyrrhus' death, 272, and the defeat of Cleomenes by Antigonus Doson, 220 B.C. His history (Ἰστορίαι), one of a number of works, ran to twenty-eight books and drew largely on the history of Duris of Samos. Its arrangement cannot be ascertained, but it was not based on a chronological scheme. The few definite facts of books 6–14 all refer to the East, the remainder to Greece. Phylarchus was Plutarch's chief authority for the lives of Agis and Cleomenes and was one of his sources for the lives of Aratus and Pyrrhus. His moralizing digressions and bias against Macedon throw suspicion on his reliability.

*FGrH* ii A. 81. *PW* Suppl. viii, 471 ff.; xi, 1067 ff.         G. L. B.

**PHYLAS**, name of four minor mythological persons, the least unknown being a king of the Dryopes. He sinned against the shrine at Delphi, and consequently Heracles (q.v.) overthrew him and gave his people to Apollo as serfs. Many of them, either escaping or being sent by Apollo's command, went to the Peloponnesus, where they settled at Asine and other places. Heracles had by Phylas' daughter a son Antiochus, after whom the Attic tribe Antiochis was named (Diod. Sic. 4. 37; Paus. 1. 5. 2; 4. 34. 9–10).                                     H. J. R.

**PHYLE**, an Attic deme and fortress situated on Mt. Parnes astride one of the routes between Athens and Boeotia. Its rocky, isolated character is well brought out in Menander's *Dyscolus*, particularly by Pan, worshipped in a nearby cave. Late in 404, Thrasybulus (q.v.) came from Thebes, seized Phyle, and with a greatly increased following moved on Piraeus early in 403, where he defeated the Thirty Tyrants (q.v. 1). In the fourth century Phyle became a regular frontier post, and the remains of the fortress date from that time.

Xen. *Hell.* 2. 4. 2–22; Diod. 14. 32–3. W. Wrede, 'Phyle', *Ath. Mitt.* 1924, 153 ff.; L. Chandler, 'The North-West Frontier of Attica', *JHS* 1926, 1 ff.; J. Wiesner, *PW*, s.v.; F. Brommer, *PW* (Suppl. viii), s.v. Pan (993 f.).                                  C. W. J. E.

**PHYSICS.** Until the time of Plato and Aristotle physics was a part of philosophy. Occupied with the study of nature and cosmogony, the first philosophers knew only a few isolated facts in physics discovered by experience (cf. Thales on the property of the lode-stone, and Pythagoras' discovery of the musical intervals); they had few general theories, such as those which accounted for change in material substances by rarefaction and condensation (cf. the upward and downward courses in Heraclitus) or by the eternal mixing and unmixing of different elements, combined with the indestructibility of matter. Perhaps the first attempt to state a law was Heraclitus' πάντα ῥεῖ. On the other hand, centrifugal force is postulated by Anaxagoras, and we have Empedocles' declaration that light travels and takes time to pass from one place to another. Anaxagoras and Empedocles both realized the corporeal quality of air; Empedocles, by an experiment with a water-clock, showed that water can enter a vessel only as air escapes. But it

is nevertheless only on rare occasions that we hear of experiments. It is a most important characteristic of Greek physical science that it is axiomatic and deductive and that its procedures are modelled on those of mathematics. Experiments, on the whole, are used not to establish a theory but to illustrate it. Even Democritus whose atomism is so suggestive and so prophetic of modern views did not base his theory on systematic experimentation but on *a priori* reasoning. That we hear of experiments associated with the names of some of the early scientific thinkers is in this context almost irrelevant. On the other hand, another important feature of the scientific attitude, the belief in the uniformity of nature and the inevitability of natural law, is very prominent in Greek physical science. Thus we read the declaration of Leucippus that 'nothing comes into being for nothing; everything happens on a rational ground and by the pressure of necessity'. The earlier monistic thinkers (for whom matter was essentially of one kind) were followed by pluralists who postulated the existence of more than one kind of matter; cf. the four elements of Empedocles, the homoiomeries of Anaxagoras, the atoms of Democritus. The latter was the first to postulate the existence of a void. Atomistic physical doctrines survived in the Epicurean school but were denied by the Stoics whose physics was based on the continuum concept, a concept diametrically opposed to the fundamental teachings of atomism. Atomic theory is based on the atom and the void; the continuum theory on unformed matter and the *pneuma*. The atoms, discrete and solid, move in the void without mixing with it; the Stoics, on the other hand, postulate a total mixture of *hyle* and *pneuma* (cf. on this Samburský, *Physics of the Stoics*). Both atomistic and Stoic physical doctrines have been influential in the formation of modern physical concepts.

**2.** Aristotle made a point, in his treatises, of summarizing all that was so far known in each subject, with a view to adapting it to his own philosophical system. His views on physical subjects are spread over the *Physics, De Caelo, De Generatione et Corruptione*, and the *Meteorologica*. Physics is for him one of the theoretical sciences; it deals with natural bodies having in them a source of movement or rest. Aristotle discusses such things as matter and form, the four causes, three kinds of 'motion' (increase and decrease, change, and locomotion), 'place', and space, the void, the continuous, the infinite, the laws of motion, e.g. the dependence of speed on the weight of the object moved and on the density of the medium through which it moves, natural and forced movement and the prime mover, the application of the theory to the heavenly sphere, the movement of the elements (including the 'aether') to their 'natural places'. Among the things bearing on mechanics we find the germ of the principle of 'virtual velocities' and a statement very like Newton's 'First Law of Motion'; in a void, if a thing is in motion, 'no one can say why it should stop anywhere; for why here rather than there? hence it will either remain at rest or it must move *ad infinitum* unless something stronger prevents it' (*Phys.* 4. 8. 215$^a$20–2). The *Mechanica*, containing mechanical problems, is not by Aristotle, but it retains many ideas which are found in Aristotle's works. It contains the 'parallelogram of velocities' (ch. 2) and the principle of the lever (ch. 3), which it applies extensively to the explanation of many mechanical devices, e.g. the balance, interacting pulleys, etc.

**3.** But, for mechanics, the scientific foundation was laid by Archimedes in his proof of the principle of the lever and his investigation of the position of the centre of gravity in a number of bodies (*Plane Equilibriums* I, II, and the *Method*, in which he makes full use of the 'moment' about a fixed point)—to say nothing of his machines for moving a great weight by a small force (δός μοι ποῦ στῶ, καὶ κινῶ τὰν γᾶν), his water-screw, etc.

4. Archimedes further initiated the whole science of *hydrostatics* (Περὶ ὀχουμένων, *On Floating Bodies*), laying down the principles that a body floating in a fluid will take a position in which its weight is equal to that of the portion of the fluid which it displaces, and that a body weighed in a fluid will be lighter than its true weight by the weight of the displaced portion of the fluid. He further lays it down that the upward force exerted by the fluid on the floating solid will act along the line perpendicular to the surface of the fluid which passes through the centre of gravity of the displaced portion of the fluid. With these principles, Archimedes works out fully the positions of rest and stability of (1) any segment of a sphere and (2) a right segment of a paraboloid of revolution floating in a fluid either way up.

5. On the mechanical side Archimedes' work was continued by Ctesibius, Philon, and Heron. Only Heron's works survive in any completeness, but we find there the recognition of the elasticity of air and the force of steam; his engines include a thermoscope, a forcing air-pump, siphons, a fire-engine, and the first steam-engine, in which the recoil of steam issuing in jets from four tubes, the open ends of which are perpendicular to the tubes, while the tubes issue from a centre, forming a cross (like the *swastika*), makes a ball or a wheel revolve.

6. *Optics*. Until the time of the Atomists it was supposed that sight resulted from visual rays proceeding in straight lines from the eye and impinging on the object seen. The Atomists postulated atoms constantly proceeding from the object and carrying, as it were, copies of it to the eye. Aristotle, too, regards the eye as a receptive organ only; the object acts on the eye through a transparent medium (*De Anima* 2. 7, *De Sensu*, ch. 2). Aristotle gave an explanation of the rainbow and the halo in the *Meteorologica* (3. 2–6). The first systematic treatise on geometrical *Optics* was by Euclid and survives in a version by Theon. The law of reflection was known before Euclid. Heron (*Catoptrica*) bases it on the assumption of a *minimum path*. Ptolemy wrote *Optica*, in which occurs the first attempt to discover a law of *refraction*. The hypothesis of atmospheric refraction appears in Cleomedes (*De motu circulari*, ch. 6).

7. *Acoustics*. The dependence of the musical intervals on numerical ratios was discovered by Pythagoras. There were many writers on harmonics, e.g. Archytas, Aristoxenus, Euclid, Nicomachus, Ptolemy. The κατατομὴ κανόνος included in the *Musici Scriptores* may be partly based on the *Elements of Music* by Euclid.

8. *Electricity and Magnetism*. Thales is said to have known of the attractive power of the lode-stone (Arist. *De An.* 1. 2). Theophrastus mentions the *Lyncurion* as having still stronger force, and notes the necessity of rubbing the lode-stone (Περὶ λίθων, §§ 28–9).

In the Platonic *Ion* 533 we are told that the lode-stone not only attracts bits of iron, but communicates to them the same power: apparently the first hint of magnetic induction.

PW art. 'Physik'; for general concepts, and particularly for concepts of matter, consult histories of ancient philosophy, the fragments of the Presocratic philosophers, the relevant works of Plato, Aristotle, and the later scientific writers. M. R. Cohen and I. E. Drabkin, *A Source Book in Greek Science* (U.S.A. 1958); J. L. Heiberg, *Naturwissenschaft und Mathematik im klassischen Altertum* (1912); H. Diels, *Antike Technik* (1920); B. Farrington, *Greek Science* (1953); M. Claggett, *Greek Science in Antiquity* (U.S.A. 1956); S. Sambursky, *The Physical World of the Greeks* (1956); id. *Physics of the Stoics* (1959); id. *The Physical World of late Antiquity* (1962); C. Bailey, *The Greek Atomists and Epicurus* (1928); L. Robin, *Étude sur la signification et la place de la physique dans la philosophie de Platon* (1919); A. Mansion, *Introduction à la physique Aristotélicienne* (1913); H. Carteron, *La Notion de force dan le système d'Aristote* (1924); E. J. Dijksterhuis, *Archimedes* (Copenhagen, 1956); A. G. Drachmann, *Ktesibios, Philon and Heron. A Study in Ancient Pneumatics* (Copenhagen, 1948); id. *The Mechanical Technology of Greek and Roman Antiquity* (Copenhagen, 1963). T. H.; A. W.

**PHYSIOGNOMONICI**, writers who try to divine the true character of man by comparing him to certain types of animals or races, the moral nature of which they suppose to be known ([Aristotle], *Phgn.* 805ᵇ20), or by inferring a person's idiosyncrasy from movements, gestures of the body, colour, characteristic facial expressions, the growth of the hair, the smoothness of the skin, the voice, conditions of the flesh, the parts of the body, and the body as a whole (ibid. 806ᵃ26). Such observations of necessity result from any social and political contact; they are, therefore, already contained in early Greek literature (Simon. fr. 7); later, after physiognomy, based on the theory of the interdependence of body and soul (Arist. *An. Pr.* 70ᵇ7), had been developed by philosophers, especially by Socratics and Stoics (Posidonius), the results influenced in ever-increasing measure painters, writers, orators, and actors. In medicine physiognomical signs had been valued from the beginning. They were particularly emphasized by the gymnasts of the second century A.D., probably in connexion with the codification of physiognomical studies by Polemon. But at no time in antiquity does physiognomy seem to have been nearly as important as during the Middle Ages and the Renaissance.

TEXTS. R. Förster, *Scriptores Physiognomonici* i–ii (Teubner, 1893), containing Ps.-Aristotle, Polemon (2nd c. A.D.), Adamantius (4th c. A.D.), Anonymi, *De physiognomia, Secreta secretorum* (cf. *Opera hactenus inedita Rogeri Bacon*, ed. R. Steele, fasc. v (1920)). References in Greek and Latin authors collected, Förster ii. 237. Additional material, R. Asmus, *Philol.* 1906; J. Jüthner, *Philostratos über Gymnastik* (1909); R. A. Pack, *AJPhil.* 1935. New MS. readings, Förster, *Rh. Mus.* 1900.
LITERATURE. Förster, i, introduction (history of Ph., tradition. etc.). Best survey, Förster, *Die Physiognomik d. Griechen* (1884); E. Rohde, *Griech. Roman*³, 160; cf. also A. Macalister, *Enc. Brit.*¹¹ s.v. 'Physiognomy'; A. McArmstrong, *TAPA* 1941, on method; E. C. Evans, ibid., on physiognomy in the second century A.D.; *TAPA* 1945, on Galen, *TAPA* 1950, on Seneca; R. A. Pack, op. cit.; J. Schmidt, *PW* xx, s.v. 'Physiognomik'. Brief survey of the whole subject and the most recent literature, R. Megow, *Das Altertum* ix (1963), Heft 4. L. E.

**PHYSIOLOGUS** ('the Naturalist'), a collection of some fifty fabulous anecdotes from natural, mostly animal, history, of a moralizing and symbolical character. The date and place of its production are uncertain; Christian writers towards the end of the fourth century A.D. (more doubtfully Origen and Clement of Alexandria in the third century) knew and used it; in MSS. it is often attributed to Epiphanius of Salamis (d. 403); it was translated into Latin about this time. The subject-matter is largely drawn from traditional allegorizing Christian commentary on Scriptural passages; in general spirit the work may be said to belong to the class of popular descriptions of the marvels of nature, real or imaginary, which tended increasingly to usurp the place of legitimate natural science after Theophrastus. It has much in common with the *Historia Animalium* of Aelian (q.v. 1). The work as it stands appears from internal evidence to have taken shape in Egypt. The *Physiologus* enjoyed great subsequent popularity; it was translated into the principal languages of Europe and the Near East; its material continued to be reproduced in the medieval Bestiaries and to be embodied in medieval art, from sculpture to illuminated initials. Many traditional religious symbols, such as the Pelican and the Phoenix, derive from it.

F. Lauchert, *Gesch. des Physiologus* (Greek text), 1889; M. Goldstaub, *Philol.* Suppl. 8 (1899–1901); M. Wellmann, *Philol.* Suppl. 22 (1930); J. Strzygowski, *Der Bilderkreis des griech. Physiologos* (1899); B. E. Perry, *PW* xx, 1074 ff. W. M. E.; R. B.

**PHYTALUS**, eponym of the Phytalidae, an Attic clan having certain duties in the worship of Theseus (q.v.;

Plut. *Thes*. 23). According to what is no doubt the clan-legend, Phytalus received Demeter in his house when she visited Attica, and she gave him the fig-tree, whereof he is apparently the presiding hero or daimon, hence his name, 'planter', and his descendants welcomed Theseus. Paus. 1. 37. 2 and 4.                                      H. J. R.

**PIAZZA ARMERINA,** a hill-town of south-central Sicily, notable for the remains of a large Roman villa of the fourth century A.D. some 4 miles to the south-west, near the ancient *Philosophiana*. This consists of a vast complex of rooms, many of considerable size, grouped around a large peristyle court. The majority of the floors are paved with rich mosaics of superb workmanship, of which the finest is the 'Great Hunt', extending the length of a 70-yard corridor between peristyle and triclinium. The owner, evidently a magnate concerned with the import of animals for the Roman arenas, is apparently depicted in it. That the villa was an imperial residence of Maximianus, co-Augustus with Diocletian, seems a less likely hypothesis.

G. V. Gentili, *La villa erculia di Piazza Armerina—I mosaici figurati* (1959); B. Pace, *I mosaici di Piazza Armerina* (1955); A. Ragona, *Il proprietario della villa romana di Piazza Armerina* (1962); A. Carandini, *Ricerche sullo stile e la cronologia dei mosaici della villa di Piazza Armerina* (1964).                        A. G. W.

**PICENUM** is situated east of the Apennines between Ancona and the river Sangro. Unlike the Villanovans (q.v.), the warlike Iron-Age inhabitants of the general area of the Marche and the Abruzzi practised inhumation. The inscriptions in the area fall into two groups: northern, from Novilara, Fano, and Pesaro, and southern (the so-called 'Old Sabellic'), which, like the material culture of the region, has strong affinities with the opposite shores of the Adriatic. The extensive use of amber (q.v.) from the Orientalizing period onwards points in addition to commercial contact with the head of the Adriatic. The area was conquered by Rome in the early third century B.C.

D. Randall-MacIver, *The Iron Age in Italy* (1927); J. Whatmough, *The Foundations of Roman Italy* (1937); *Atti II Conv. Stud. Etr.* 1958, *Suppl. Stud. Etr.* xxvi (1959); A. M. Radmilli (ed.) *Piccola guida alla preistoria italiana*² (1965), s.v. 'Marche', 'Abruzzo'.   D. W. R. R.

**PICUS,** properly the woodpecker, sacred to Mars (q.v.), but rationalized into an early king of the Italians (for his identification with Zeus in Diod. Sic. 6, fr. 5, see W. R. Halliday, *CR* 1922, 110 ff.). Ovid (*Met.* 14. 320 ff.) gives an explanation, perhaps his own, of how he came to be changed into bird-form.             H. J. R.

**PIETAS** is the typical Roman attitude of dutiful respect toward gods, fatherland, and parents and other kinsmen (Cic. *Nat. D.* 1. 116: 'est enim pietas iustitia aduersum deos'; Cic. *Inv. Rhet.* 2. 66: 'religionem eam quae in metu et caerimonia deorum sit appellant, pietatem quae erga patriam aut parentes aut alios sanguine coniunctos officium conseruare moneat'). Pietas, personified, received a temple in Rome (vowed 191 B.C., dedicated 181; see Platner–Ashby, 389 f.; Nash, *Pict. Dict. Rome* ii. 418). She is often represented in human form, sometimes attended by a stork, symbol of filial piety; during the Empire, Pietas Augusta appears on coins and in inscriptions. Some Romans adopted as cognomen the term Pius; Virgil's 'pius Aeneas' significantly expresses the Roman ideal in his religious attitude, in his patriotic mission, and in his relations with father, son, and comrades.

Latte, *RR* 238.                                              W. C. G.

**PIGRES,** Carian poet; brother of Artemisia wife of Mausolus; said to have interpolated pentameters into the *Iliad*, and to have written the *Margites*.

*EGF* 65.

**PILUMNUS** and **PICUMNUS.** By Roman custom, when a woman was delivered, three persons kept off Silvanus (q.v.) from her by chopping, sweeping, and pounding with a pestle; the deities Intercidona, Deverra, and Pilumnus were supposed to preside over these actions (Varro in Aug. *De civ. D.* 6. 9). More puzzling is the statement of Varro in Nonius (528 M), which associates Picumnus with Pilumnus as marriage-gods.      H. J. R.

**PINDAR** (*Πίνδαρος*) (518–438 B.C.), lyric poet, of Cynoscephalae in Boeotia, born in the Pythian year of the 65th Olympiad, i.e. 518 B.C. (*Suda*, s.v. *Πίνδαρος*, fr. 183). Nothing is known of his parents, Daiphantus and Cleodice, but they must have belonged to an aristocratic family, since Pindar himself claims to be a member of the Aegeidae, an international clan with high connexions in Sparta, Thera, and Cyrene (*Pyth.* 5. 75, with scholl., cf. Hdt. 4. 149). He learned his craft first from his uncle Scopelinus, later at Athens from Apollodorus and Agathocles, who was also the teacher of Damon (Pl. *La.* 180 d). His earliest known poem is *Pyth.* 10, written in 498 for a young protégé of the powerful Thessalian Aleuadae. In 490 he made the acquaintance of Theron's brother, Xenocrates, and celebrated his chariot-victory with *Pyth.* 6, while *Pyth.* 12, written in the same year for a Sicilian flute-player, is probably due to the same connexion. In 488 he wrote *Ol.* 14, and in 486 *Pyth.* 7 for the ostracized Alcmaeonid Megacles. In the Persian Wars of 480–479 Pindar seems to have accepted the Theban policy of neutrality (fr. 99), but without satisfaction, as *Isthm.* 8, written soon after, shows, while *Isthm.* 5 shows his appreciation of Aeginetan courage at Salamis. In 476 he went to Sicily, where he produced *Ol.* 1 in honour of Hieron's victory in the horse-race and *Ol.* 2 and 3 in honour of Theron's in the chariot-race. *Ol.* 2 is an important and intimate document about life after death, and shows the influence of Orphic ideas, which were prevalent in Sicily. *Nem.* 1 and 9, also written for Sicilian patrons, may belong to the same period. On his return Pindar probably wrote his famous Dithyramb for Athens (frs. 64–5), and it is possible that in *Pyth.* 9 (474 B.C.) he defends himself before a Theban audience against the charge of undue partiality for Athens. *Pyth.* 11 may belong to the same year, but the alternative date of 454 seems on the whole preferable. Though he did not return to Sicily, he maintained his connexion with Hieron. *Pyth.* 3 is a poetical letter, sent probably about 474 as a consolation to the suffering tyrant; it refers to the cult of Pan, for which Pindar wrote a Hymn (frs. 85–90). *Pyth.* 1 celebrates both Hieron's chariot-victory of 470 and the official foundation of his new town of Aetna under his son Deinomenes. *Pyth.* 2, a dark and unhappy poem, may have been written in 468, when Hieron won the chariot-race at Olympia, but asked Bacchylides instead of Pindar to celebrate his victory for him. At the same time Pindar sent a *Hyporchema* (fr. 94) to Hieron. *Ol.* 6, written for a friend of Hieron's, probably belongs to the same year. At this period Pindar numbered patrons in many different parts of Greece. He wrote an Encomium for Alexander of Macedon (fr. 106), a Paean for Abdera (fr. 36), poems for Sparta (frs. 101, 189), *Ol.* 7 for a Rhodian in 464, and *Ol.* 13 and fr. 107 for a Corinthian in the same year. The height of his achievement in these years were *Pyth.* 4 and 5, written for the King of Cyrene in 462–461. In the first of these Pindar enters high politics and appeals to the king to recall his exiled kinsman Damophilus. Before 460 Pindar shows no hostility to Athens, but after it he seems to have been shocked and pained by the policy of the Athenian imperialists. At first he maintained his personal loyalties to Athenians such as Melesias (*Ol.* 8 in 460), but in *Isthm.* 7, which seems to have been composed after Oenophyta (c. 456

B.C.), he combines a quietist attitude in himself with a conviction that the gods punish the presumptuous. His latest known poems are *Pyth.* 8, written in 446 for a young Aeginetan at a time when it seemed possible that Aegina might free herself from Athens, and *Nem.* 11 and fr. 108 for the boy Aristagoras of Tenedos, whose brother Theoxenus is said to have been with Pindar at his death. He died at the age of 80 in 438.

Pindar's works were collected in seventeen books, Hymns, Paeans, Dithyrambs (2), Processional Songs (2), Maiden-Songs (2), other Maiden-Songs Hypor-chemata (2), Encomia, Dirges, and Epinicians (4). The Epinicians have by an accident survived almost complete; despite their peculiar character they are probably typical of all Pindar's work, and new fragments of Paeans and Dithyrambs show little difference of style and thought. Pindar seems to have made the rejoicing over victory a religious occasion on which he demonstrated the power of men to find, temporarily, a happiness like that of the gods by displaying their ἀρετά. This ἀρετά was itself partly inborn and due to men's having divine blood in their veins. His Epinicians are usually choral hymns in which the victor is presented to some god, and they have the traditional characteristics of such hymns—moral maxims, a myth, and praise of the gods. Into this frame the victor's own achievements are fitted, not always easily. In his maxims Pindar sometimes achieves a great beauty and insight. His myths, inserted for varying reasons, tend to stress elements in a story rather than to tell a straight tale. In them Pindar often improves on his originals in the interests of morality, notably in *Ol.* 1, where he rejects the story that Pelops' shoulder was eaten. Sometimes, as in the great Argonautic saga of *Pyth.* 4, the myth is told for its own sake; more often it has a moral, as in *Pyth.* 3 and *Ol.* 1. Some of the shorter Epinicians were sung at the place of victory, notably *Ol.* 11 and *Pyth.* 7, but more usually a longer poem was sung when the victor came home. The other types of poem show a similar high style and temper, though the Maiden-Songs may have been more simple. Pindar's language is an elaborate poetical creation, made of several dialects, with many echoes and variations from Homer. His poems are written in regular stanzas, either in a series of strophes on the same plan or in a series of triads, each consisting of strophe, antistrophe, and epode. Except for *Isthm.* 3 and 4, which may form a single poem, no two poems are the same metrically. Pindar uses three main classes of metre, Dorian or 'dactylo-epitrite', Aeolian built up from such elements as the glyconic, choriambic dimeter, etc., and paeonic as in *Ol.* 2. Pindar was a true conservative in politics, morals, and religion, but the glory of his poetry lies largely in his sense of joy and honour. He was capable of deep emotion and, at times, of a sublimity to which there is no parallel.

TEXT. O. Schroeder, *Pindari Carmina* (1900); C. M. Bowra *Pindari Carmina*[1] (1947); A. Turyn, *Pindari Carmina* (1948); B. Snell, *Pindarus*, 2 vols. (1959 and 1964).
COMMENTARIES. A. Boeckh (1811–32); T. Mommsen (1864); W. Christ (1896); B. L. Gildersleeve, *Olympian and Pythian Odes*[1] (1890); J. B. Bury, *Nemean Odes* (1890), *Isthmian Odes* (1892); L. R. Farnell (1932).
CRITICISM. C. Gaspar, *Chronologie pindarique* (1900); U. von Wilamowitz-Moellendorff, *Pindaros* (1922); F. Dornseiff, *Pindars Stil* (1921); H. Gundert, *Pindar und sein Dichterberuf* (1935); R. W. B. Burton, *Pindar's Pythian Odes* (1962); C. M. Bowra, *Pindar* (1964).

C. M. B.

**PINDARUS,** a name in medieval MSS. for Homerus Latinus (*see* ILIAS LATINA), due perhaps to the possible use of 'Thebanus' as an epithet for Homer.

**PIRACY,** in early antiquity, was not clearly distinguished from trade on the one hand and war on the other. Unless a treaty guaranteed safety and arrangements for legal process had been laid down, owners of ships seized at sea had no easy redress. In Homer (describing conditions after the breakdown of the Cretan thalassocracy) we find piracy accepted as natural; and early Greek cities, having to beware of surprise landings, were usually built away from the coast. Piracy, like brigandage on land, was an easy resource for the hungry, familiar with local tides, currents, and places of concealment. The social conditions of the ancient world, in which (in most periods) starvation and exile were common, provided a constant incentive; and travellers kidnapped could easily be sold as slaves to purchasers who would ask no questions.

Civilized Greek States naturally encouraged orderly trade, and many depended on it. Those claiming thalassocracy (from the legendary Minos—i.e. Minoan Crete—through classical Athens to Alexander the Great) tried to protect at least their own interests at sea, and this would lead to a general decrease in piracy. Yet even their actions, especially in times of war or scarcity, or for political reasons, were sometimes not far removed from semi-legal piracy (*see* SYLE). Polycrates (q.v. 1) used his thalassocracy for open plundering; fifth-century Athens regarded the freedom of the seas as a favour to be conferred on loyal allies (Tod 1². 61, 32 ff.); and the tribute of the Athenian Empire might to many (e.g. Melos) appear indistinguishable from ransom, both in principle and frequently in methods of collection. Ensuring the freedom of the sea, for Athens as for Demetrius (q.v. 4) Poliorcetes (*SEG* 1. 75, 22 ff.), meant ensuring it for oneself and—at a price—for one's allies. War provided constant opportunities for pirates, who would be sought as allies at least by one power and could add profitable blockade-running. This can be seen in the Peloponnesian War, the fourth-century wars, and those of the Successors. On the other hand, since fleets were expensive to maintain, peace (after the end of the Athenian thalassocracy, paid for by reluctant allies) usually led to a running down of naval establishments, to a point where they could not keep the seas safe.

In the western Mediterranean the lack of firm demarcations between trade, piracy, and war appears even more clearly. Etruscans and Carthaginians, on the one hand, and Greeks, on the other, pursued their trade rivalries by methods that often appeared piratical to the other side. The rising Roman State showed little interest in the sea, and the small fleet of the *duoviri navales* (q.v.), combined with the spread of Roman power on land and the establishment of coastal colonies (*see* COLONIZATION, ROMAN), barely sufficed to keep the Italian coasts safe. The people of Antium (q.v.), conquered and colonized (338 B.C.) and ordered off the seas, were engaged in piracy—safely away from the Italian coasts—a generation later, in the time of Demetrius Poliorcetes. The fleets of the Punic Wars were not maintained after the need had passed, and in any case were never used for the general protection of peaceful shipping. The Illyrian Wars led only to the temporary safety of the Ionian Sea—not even (it seems) the Adriatic. In the Aegean, the island power of Rhodes (q.v.), after the decline of the kings' fleets, had tried to police the seas, and did so quite efficiently after 186 B.C., when general peace was secured by Rome and the pirates could find no allies. After the war with Perseus (q.v. 2) the Romans brought about the decline of Rhodian power, and police action at sea—especially in Crete, a favourite pirate base—became too difficult and had to be given up; while the Romans, with no enemy on land, gave little thought to the safety of sea trade and, in the free port at Delos (q.v.), in fact provided an emporium where no questions were asked about the provenance of goods or slaves.

By *c.* 100 B.C., under pressure from Italian traders, the Senate realized that a serious problem existed; especially as Italy's basic food supplies, increasingly imported, were threatened. Efforts were now made to deal with the pirates (see Riccobono, *FIRA* 9—not mentioned in the literary sources and difficult to explain). But these were defeated by two factors: the civil and foreign wars (Mithridates and Sertorius co-operated with the pirates) and the traditional unwillingness to keep a large fleet in being. On the whole, Rome pursued her old-established policy of trying to conquer pirate fleets on land (*see* ANTONIUS 1, SERVILIUS 1, METELLUS 8), concentrating her efforts on Cilicia and Crete, the chief pirate bases, and demanding naval assistance *ad hoc* from provincials and allies. This policy was defeated by the sheer size of the coastline concerned and the difficulty of the terrain: by the 70s, pirates were boldly raiding Italian coasts and coast roads. Constant food shortages, and pressure from Equestrian trading interests (reinforced after Italian enfranchisement) finally led to the law of Gabinius (q.v. 2), for the first time attacking the problem as a whole; and Pompey's success, followed by his defeat of Mithridates, settled the problem for the time being. The civil wars naturally led to a revival of privateering (*see* POMPEIUS 6), and it was Augustus who finally shouldered the burden of a permanent fleet, with provincial detachments that multiplied during the early Empire. In the third century A.D., with the decline of these fleets and the beginning of the barbarian invasions, piracy (like brigandage on land) gained the upper hand and was not again subdued in antiquity.

PW, s.v. 'Seeraub'; H. A. Ormerod, *Piracy in the Ancient World* (1924). And *see* NAVIES. E. B.

**PIRAEUS** (Πειραιεύς) is a promontory 4 miles southwest of Athens, which Themistocles fortified from the time of his archonship (493/2 B.C.) in order to provide the growing Athenian fleet with a strong base instead of the open roadstead of Phaleron (q.v.). It had three harbours, Zea and Munichia (q.v.) on the east, both used for warships, the first having sheds for 196 and some for gear in the famous Arsenal of Philo, and Kantharos or μέγας λιμήν on the west. This last was the biggest, and quickly grew, not only as a naval station, with docks and ship-houses, but also as a thriving emporium, with quays and warehouses. Moles guarded and narrowed the entrances to all three, which could be closed by chains. The city was laid out on a rectangular plan by Hippodamus (q.v.) of Miletus *c.* 450. In the same decade it was joined to Athens by the Long Walls (q.v.). The fortifications were destroyed in 404 by Lysander but rebuilt by Conon in 393. The chief event in its later history was its siege and destruction by Sulla (87–86); the large bronze statues unearthed in 1959 were probably buried then. Considerable parts of the walls remain; also ship-houses in the two small harbours, and the traces of an important Hellenistic theatre near Zea. During the fifth and fourth centuries the inhabitants, many attached by interest to navy and empire, proved the staunch supporters of radical democracy at Athens; they also included many foreigners (e.g. Lysias), who introduced strange cults (e.g. Bendis).

W. Judeich, *Topographie von Athen*² (1931), 144 ff., 430 ff.; E. Fiechter, *Das Theater im Piraeus* (1950); E. Vanderpool, 'News Letter from Greece', *AJArch.* 1960, 265 ff. C. W. J. E.

**PIRITHOUS** (Π[ε]ιρίθοος or -θους), in mythology, a Lapith, son by Zeus of Ixion's wife Dia (*Il.* 14. 317–18; Pherecydes in schol. Ap. Rhod. 3. 62). Homer knows of him as fighting the Centaurs (*Il.* 1. 263 ff.), presumably in the quarrel mentioned in *Od.* 21. 295 ff., and a doubtfully genuine verse (*Od.* 11. 631) mentions him in Hades. In the first and last of these passages he is associated with Theseus (q.v.), whose close friend he is in later authors. Hence, as our mythological tradition is largely Attic, he tends to appear as little more than the pendant of his friend. He is actually an Athenian in schol. *Il.* 1. 263.

One of the few adventures which are his rather than Theseus' is his wedding-feast. Marrying Hippodamia, daughter of Butes (*Il.* 2. 742 and schol. on 1. 263), he forgot, according to one account, to include Ares among his guests (Servius on *Aen.* 7. 304). For that or some other reason (the simplest is that they were very drunk, cf. *Od.* 21. 295, where one Centaur is responsible for the disturbance) the Centaurs abused his hospitality by offering violence to Hippodamia, and a great fight began (Ov. *Met.* 12. 210 ff.; the earlier accounts of a story which the Olympia pediments and Parthenon metopes show to have been well known in the fifth century, if not before, have not survived), ending in the victory of the Lapithae.

For the rest, Pirithous took his share in the carrying off of Helen, the war against the Amazons, and finally Theseus' descent to Hades, which, indeed, in one account (Hyg. *Fab.* 79. 2) was undertaken to get Persephone as wife for Pirithous, in return for his services in the matter of Helen. Theseus in most accounts escapes; Pirithous generally does not (but cf. Hyg. ibid. 3).

The fight of Lapiths and Centaurs appears in early archaic art (François vase and elsewhere) as a pitched battle in armour. The brawl at the feast first appears in the early classical period, in Attic vase-painting, and the West pediment of the Temple of Zeus at Olympia; no doubt also in the picture in the Theseum at Athens probably by Micon. Pirithous is also shown aiding Theseus to abduct Helen, pictured from the mid sixth century. Theseus and Pirithous were shown in the Underworld by Polygnotus, and in a few surviving works from the mid fifth century on.

Weizsäcker in Roscher's *Lexikon*, s.v. In art, Brommer, *Vasenlisten*², 168 ff.; *see also* THESEUS. H. J. R.; C. M. R.

**PISA** was the district round Olympia. Opinions are divided whether there was ever a town of this name; some have suggested that it is represented by a site at Frangonisi (*BSA, Arch. Rep.* 1959–60, 11). The Pisatans were in early times a power independent of the Eleans. After Pheidon's usurpation of the Olympic Games (668 B.C.) they held the presidency until *c.* 580, under the tyranny of the house of Pantaleon. Their claim was revived by the Arcadians in 364 (Xen. *Hell.* 7. 4. 28).

A. Andrewes, *The Greek Tyrants* (1956), 62 f.; H. Berve, *Die Tyrannis bei den Griechen* (1967), i. 35. T. J. D.; R. J. H.

**PISAE,** modern *Pisa* on the Arno, an Etruscan, possibly originally a Ligurian, town (it was certainly not founded from Pisa in Elis: Serv. ad *Aen.* 10. 179; Dion. Hal. 1. 20). Although presumably important earlier, it is first mentioned in 225 B.C. when the Romans used its harbour (Polyb. 2. 16 f.; Livy 21. 39). Pisae served as a frontier fortress for Rome against the Ligurians and in 180 offered territory for a Latin colony (Livy 33. 43, etc.; 40. 43). Apparently this colony never materialized, although in 177 neighbouring Luna (q.v.) received a citizen colony. Later Pisae became a prosperous Augustan *colonia* but, despite its importance, is seldom mentioned (Strabo 5. 222; Dessau, *ILS* 139 f.).

N. Toscanelli, *Pisa nell'antichità*, 3 vols. (1933–4); L. Banti, *Mem. Accad. Pont.* 6, fasc. 4 (1943), 63 ff. E. T. S.

**PISIDIA.** A mountainous region of Asia Minor, between Pamphylia and Phrygia. As it lay off the main routes, its wild and warlike inhabitants were able to maintain their independence of the Lydians and Persians. They submitted to Alexander, but were never effectively controlled by any of the Hellenistic kings. Civilization came late to Pisidia; Selge and Etenna struck silver coins in the fourth century, but otherwise no coinage is known before the first century B.C. Termessus and Sagalassus too were places of some account in Alexander's time.

Nominally included in the province of Cilicia (q.v.), Pisidia was given in 36 B.C. to Amyntas and partially pacified by him; finally (*c.* 6 B.C.?) it was reduced by Sulpicius Quirinius (q.v.) and included in the province of Galatia. To maintain security Augustus established a number of colonies, notably Cremna, Olbasa, and Comama; and under the *pax Romana* the country at last attained a fair degree of civilized prosperity. Of the Pisidian language, mentioned by Strabo (13. 631) as spoken at Cibyra, there are some scanty epigraphical traces.

Jones, *Cities E. Rom. Prov.*, ch. 5; Magie, *Rom. Rule Asia Min.*, chs. 12, 19; G. E. Bean in *Anatolian Studies* 1959, 1960; B. Levick, *Roman Colonies in S. Asia Minor* (1967). G. E. B.

**PISISTRATUS** (Πεισίστρατος), tyrant of Athens, claimed descent from the Neleids of Pylos and Pisistratus, archon 669/8 B.C. His mother was related to Solon. As polemarch (*c.* 565) he distinguished himself in war against Megara. During a period of faction he led a third party called *Hyperakrioi, Diakrioi*, or *Epakrioi* (drawn probably from the hill-country of northern Attica) and added to it citizens who had been recently enfranchised or recently impoverished, and in 561 made himself tyrant with a bodyguard granted him by the Athenian people (*CAH* Plates I. 284). After five years he was expelled by a coalition of the Plain and Coast parties, but an understanding with the Alcmaeonids soon led to his peaceful restoration. (On the story of his restoration by Athena see *PW* xix. 163.) The new *entente* soon broke down. Pisistratus withdrew to Macedonia and the Mt. Pangaeus mining district, where he made money, raised mercenaries, and fostered alliances with Thessaly, Thebes, Eretria, Naxos, and Argos. In 546 he landed near Marathon, defeated his opponents at Pallene, and firmly based his tyranny on mercenaries and money derived partly from the Strymon district, partly from Attica. He remained in power until he died of sickness in 527.

Pisistratus retained the forms of the Solonian constitution, remaining to the end affable and benevolent. He encouraged cultivators of poor land by granting loans and aimed at full employment in the countryside: hence the district judges instituted by him and his frequent journeys about the country. He succeeded in placating many of the nobles. He did not annex or split up their family estates of arable land, and only his bitterest enemies left Attica. Even with these Pisistratus and his sons obtained a temporary reconciliation, as Cimon returned from exile, his son Miltiades was archon in 524/3, and Cleisthenes the Alcmaeonid was archon in 525/4. During the rule of his sons the reconciliation broke down, and the Alcmaeonids at Delphi became the leaders of a powerful group of *émigrés*. The revenues which enabled him to maintain his position were based on a tithe of all produce, which his sons reduced to a twentieth, and on taxes on trade which increased rapidly. Attic black-figured pottery became the foremost fabric in the Greek world, and Attic coinage one of its foremost currencies. His building programme included the Enneakrounos fountain and the temple of Olympian Zeus. At the great festivals of the Panathenaea and Dionysia all Athenians assembled to celebrate the glory of their city.

He fired Athens' ambition by his successful foreign policy, occupying Rhaecalus on the Thermaic Gulf and Sigeum in the Troad, maintaining close alliances with Naxos and Samos, and purifying Delos as the centre of Ionian religion. His long rule weakened the grip of the aristocrats upon their followers, encouraged individualism in many circles, and brought the cultural enlightenment and financial prosperity in which a movement towards democracy became feasible.

P. N. Ure, *Origin of Tyranny* (1922), 32 f., 307 f.; F. E. Adcock, *CQ* 1924, 174 f.; F. Jacoby, *Atthis* (1949), 188 f., on the chronological

problems, N. G. L. Hammond, *CQ* 1956, 49 f. and G. Sanders *Nouvelle Clio* 1955–7, 161 f.; A. Andrewes, *The Greek Tyrants* (1956). P. N. U.; N. G. L. H.

**PISO** (1) **FRUGI**, LUCIUS CALPURNIUS (*PW* 96) (*cos.* 133 B.C.), the Roman annalist, was tribune in 149, carrying his *Lex de pecuniis repetundis* (which established a *quaestio* (q.v.) for cases of extortion), consul in 133, and censor in 120. His *Annales* covered from the origins of Rome to his own times in at least seven books, the year 158 in book 7, the latest date 146; antiquarian and mythological fragments are also attributed to him. He rationalized the legends and, presumably under Cato's influence, set the ancient virtues against contemporary vices. Plain in style, although with lively anecdotes, he did not elaborate his material, and his authority was recognized by Cicero, Varro, Livy, Dionysius, and Pliny; Gellius quoted him for his archaism.

Peter, *HRRel.* i². clxxxi, 120; W. Soltau, *Livius' Geschichtswerk* (1897); K. Latte, *Sitz. Berlin*, no. 7, 1960; Ogilvie, *Comm. Livy 1–5*, 14 ff. A. H. McD.

**PISO** (2), GAIUS CALPURNIUS (*PW* 63), consul in 67 B.C. with Glabrio (q.v. 3), passed a law against bribery. As an enemy of Pompey, he opposed Cornelius (q.v. 1) and Gabinius (q.v. 2) and prevented Lollius (q.v. 1) from being elected consul. Assigned both Gauls as consul and proconsul, he impeded Pompey's recruitment, conquered the Allobroges, and repressed trouble in the Transpadana. (For this he was later prosecuted by Caesar and successfully defended by Cicero.) In 61 he was asked (by his kinsman (4)) to speak first in the Senate, to Cicero's chagrin. He died in the early 50s. E. B.

**PISO** (3), GNAEUS CALPURNIUS (*PW* 69), suspected of complicity in Catiline's 'first conspiracy', was sent to Spain as *quaestor pro praetore*, perhaps during a shortage of commanders, on the motion of Crassus (q.v. 4). Crassus no doubt hoped he would counter the entrenched influence of Pompey there, but he was killed by adherents of Pompey (64 B.C.). E. B.

**PISO** (4) **FRUGI**, MARCUS PUPIUS (*PW* 10), born *c.* 115 B.C., a Calpurnius Piso by birth, was in his youth a promising orator and older friend of Cicero (*Brut.* 236, 240, 310). Marrying the widow of Cinna (q.v. 1), he became quaestor (83), but soon deserted to Sulla and divorced his wife. He failed to become aedile, but was praetor (72 or 71), then governed a Spanish province, triumphing in 69. Giving up oratory (as too strenuous for his health), he took up soldiering, served Pompey as a legate (67–62), and was rewarded by him with the consulship of 61. He supported Clodius (q.v. 1) and opposed Cicero, who in return prevented his obtaining the province of Syria. He failed to secure the ratification of Pompey's *acta* and probably died soon after. E. B.

**PISO** (5) **CAESONINUS**, LUCIUS CALPURNIUS (*PW* 90), in his youth probably served in Greece and rapidly rose to the consulate, which he held in 58 B.C. (with Gabinius, q.v. 2) after marrying his daughter to Caesar (*cos.* 59). He refused to support Cicero against Clodius (q.v. 1), and as a reward was given the province of Macedonia by a law of Clodius. His administration there (57–55) was attacked by Cicero in two speeches (*De prov. cons.* and, after his return, *In Pisonem*). He was censor (50) and remained neutral in the Civil War, which he did his best to prevent. After Caesar's death he again tried to prevent civil war (against Antonius, 4), but died soon after.

An Epicurean and friend of Philodemus (q.v.), he was open to conventional attack as a voluptuary; but he was (at least) no worse than many of his contemporaries, and his political influence was on the side of peace. He was perhaps the owner of a villa in Herculaneum, where Epicurean papyri were discovered in the eighteenth century.

Cic. *Pis.*, ed. R. G. M. Nisbet (1961); Syme, *Rom. Rev.*, see index.
E. B.

**PISO** (6), LUCIUS CALPURNIUS (*PW* 99) (*cos.* 15 B.C.), was called 'the *pontifex*' to distinguish him from the *augur* (8). Born in 48, son of (5) Piso inherited a prudent nature and philhellenic tastes: he was the patron of the poet Antipater of Thessalonica. According to Porphyrio on Horace, *Ars P.* 1, that poem was dedicated to the sons of this Piso. The cognomen 'Frugi' often attached to this Piso derives from two errors in the ancient evidence; and, as concerns the *Ars Poetica*, it is not possible to verify two sons (cf. *JRS* 1960, 20). Attested in Pamphylia in 13 B.C. (Dio 54. 34. 6), presumably as consular legate of the province of Galatia, he was summoned to Thrace to put down a serious insurrection, which task took three years and earned him the *ornamenta triumphalia* (Dio 54. 34. 6 ff.; Vell. Pat. 2. 98). Soon after this he may have been appointed proconsul of Asia (cf. *Anth. Pal.* 10. 25. 3 f.). Piso died in A.D. 32, after having been *praefectus urbi* for twenty years (Tac. *Ann.* 6. 11, if correct). He had enjoyed the unbroken confidence of Tiberius; and his notorious convivial habits impaired neither his efficiency nor his reliability (Sen. *Ep.* 83. 14).

Syme, *Rom. Rev.*, see index; *JRS* 1960, 12 ff. R. S.

**PISO** (7), GNAEUS CALPURNIUS (*PW* 70) (*cos.* 7 B.C.), who inherited from his father (*cos. suff.* 23 B.C.) a republican independence of temper, was appointed governor of Syria in A.D. 17, for the avowed purpose of lending counsel and assistance to Germanicus Caesar when he journeyed to the East. His previous experience had lain in other lands: proconsul of Africa and legate of Hispania Tarraconensis. After reciprocal bickering and open quarrel, Germanicus broke off his 'amicitia' with Piso. Germanicus' death (19) was attributed by his friends to magical devices or poisoning by Piso and his wife Plancina. Returning to Rome, Piso was prosecuted in the Senate, but took his own life before the trial was terminated, protesting his innocence and his loyalty to Tiberius. R. S.

**PISO** (8), LUCIUS CALPURNIUS (*PW* 74), younger brother of (7), and known as *augur* to distinguish him from (6), was consul in 1 B.C. and proconsul of Asia. Like his father and brother a strong-minded man (Tac. *Ann.* 4. 21), in A.D. 16 he spoke out openly in the Senate against the corruption of public life, and brought a suit against Urgulania, a favourite of Livia's; in 20 he defended his brother. He was accused of *maiestas* in 24, but died before trial.

R. Syme, *JRS* 1956, 17 ff. T. J. C.

**PISO** (9), GAIUS CALPURNIUS (*PW* 65), the figurehead of the great conspiracy against Nero (q.v. § 7) in A.D. 65, had been exiled by Gaius, who compelled his wife Livia Orestilla to leave her husband in favour of himself and then accused the pair of adultery (probably A.D. 40). Under Claudius Piso became *consul suffectus*, but he showed no real ambition. He lived in magnificent style and was one of the most popular figures in Rome, with his charming manners and oratorical gifts, which he put at the service of rich and poor alike. Already in 62 he was suspect to Nero's advisers (Tac. *Ann.* 14. 65), but in the actual conspiracy he proved a futile leader and after its betrayal had no thought for any action other than suicide.

His precise relationship to other members of his family is unknown, but his son Calpurnius Galerianus, who was executed in 70, is described as cousin as well as son-in-law of L. Piso (10) (Tac. *Hist.* 4. 49).

R. L. J.; G. E. F. C.

**PISO** (10), LUCIUS CALPURNIUS (*PW* 79), grandson of Piso (7) and son of L. Piso, *cos.* A.D. 27 (Pliny, *Epp.* 3. 7. 12), was consul in A.D. 57 with Nero. In 62 he was made member of an important financial commission; in 69 he was proconsul of Africa. Suspected in 70 of aspiring to the throne, he was murdered by Valerius (q.v. 10) Festus, who was in touch with Mucianus (q.v.) in Rome.

G. E. F. C.

**PISO** (11) **LICINIANUS**, LUCIUS CALPURNIUS (*PW* 100), was adopted by the Emperor Galba (q.v. 1) on 10 January 69 and killed with him in the Forum five days later. Born in A.D. 38, he was son to M. Crassus Frugi (*cos.* A.D. 27), and to Scribonia, daughter of L. Scribonius Libo (*cos.* A.D. 16) and great-granddaughter of Sextus Pompeius: his sister married L. Piso (q.v. 10), the son of her father's consular colleague. This illustrious family had already met disasters under the later Julio-Claudians. Piso's eldest brother, Pompeius Magnus, was married to Claudius' daughter Antonia, but was executed along with both his parents in A.D. 46; a second brother, M. Crassus (*cos.* 64), was forced to suicide during Nero's last years; and Piso himself had been in exile for some time when Galba recalled him in 68. He was perhaps connected with a doctrinaire group in the Senate, and as such was backed for the adoption by Laco the praetorian prefect; but his critics found his personality forbidding, and he was totally unacceptable to the soldiers in the guard. His wife, daughter of Q. Veranius (*cos.* 49), survived him for many years (Pliny, *Epp.* ii. 20).

Tac. *Hist.* i, esp. 14 and 48. The stemma in *PIR²* is in part corrected by R. Syme, *JRS* 1960, 12 ff. G. E. F. C.

**PISO** (12), CALPURNIUS (*PW* 59), a contemporary of the Younger Pliny (*Ep.* 5. 17), chose a Greek title κατασrεριαμοί for his elegiac poem on Constellations. His identification by Mommsen with the consul of A.D. 111 C. Calpurnius Piso (perhaps a grandson of no. 9 above) is possible.

**PITS, CULT.** Apart from a *mundus* (q.v.), pits were dug in ritual for two principal reasons. (*a*) In rites of invocation of the dead, and in their tendance generally, liquid offerings were often poured into a pit, βόθρος, apparently by way of getting them underground into their realm; e.g. *Od.* 11. 517; Lucian, *Charon*, 22. (*b*) Consecrated objects, when worn out or useless (e.g. broken ornaments, bones and ashes of sacrifice, etc.), being still sacred, were often buried in a pit (Lat. *fauissa*) in the temple precincts. H. J. R.

**PITTACUS** of Mytilene (*c.* 650–570 B.C.), statesman and sage. He commanded in the war against Athens for Sigeum, on which Periander of Corinth later arbitrated; helped to overthrow the tyrant Melanchrus, and after further party struggles in Mytilene was elected *aesymnetes* (q.v.) for ten years. He died ten years after laying down office. His best remembered law doubled the penalty for all offences if committed under the influence of drink. A moderate democratic reformer like his contemporary Solon, Pittacus was violently attacked by his younger fellow citizen Alcaeus, whose family had helped to overthrow tyranny but wished to restore the old aristocracy.

Strabo 13. 617; Diog. Laert. 1. 4; *Suda*, s.v. 'Pittacus'; Pl. *Prt.* 26 ff.; Plut. *Conv. sept. sap.* C. M. Bowra, *Greek Lyric Poetry²* (1961), ch. 4. P. N. U.

**PLACENTIA**, a north Italian town near the confluence of Trebia and Padus (q.v.), modern *Piacenza*. Placentia is first mentioned as a Latin colony successfully established despite Boian opposition (218 B.C.). Military mention of Placentia is frequent: it harboured Romans after the

Trebia battle, resisted Hasdrubal, survived Gallic and Ligurian devastations (200–190), and witnessed Civil War battles and Aurelian's Marcomannic defeat (Polyb. 3. 40. 66; Livy 27. 39. 43; 31. 10. 21; 34. 22. 56; 37. 46 f.; App. *Hann.* 7; *BCiv.* 1. 92; Suet. *Otho* 9; S.H.A. *Aurel.* 21). Otherwise, although always a prosperous *municipium* or *colonia* on the Via Aemilia, it is seldom mentioned (Cic. ap. Asc. 3 Cl.; Tac. *Hist.* 2. 19). E. T. S.

**PLACIDIA**, GALLA, daughter of Theodosius I, was born *c.* A.D. 390. Captured by the Visigoths in Rome in 410, she married a Visigothic chieftain called Athaulf. After Athaulf's death she was restored to the Romans (416), and in 417 married Constantius, who later reigned as Constantius III. Her son by this marriage became Valentinian III. She adorned Ravenna (q.v.) and died at Rome in 450. E. A. T.

**PLACIDUS** (1), grammarian of fifth or sixth century A.D. The glossary extant (in several versions) under his name is a compilation from two separate works, one of which (now called Pseudo-Placidus) was based on marginal notes in copies of republican poets. The ed. of J. W. Pirie and W. M. Lindsay (*Glossaria Lat.* iv. 12–70) supersedes that of G. Goetz (*Corp. Gloss. Lat.* v. 3–158).

Schanz–Hosius, § 1120. J. F. M.

**PLACIDUS** (2), LACTANTIUS (6th c. A.D.?), a grammarian under whose name is extant a collection of scholia on the *Thebais* of Statius (ed. R. Jahnke, 1898). He is not identical with the glossographer (1).

Schanz–Hosius, § 408. J. F. M.

**PLAGIARISM.** The charge of plagiarism was freely bandied about by Greek authors. Aristophanes accused Eupolis of 'vilely turning his *Knights* inside-out in the *Maricas*' (*Nub.* 553–4) and other comic poets of stealing his 'images' (ibid. 559), and Phrynichus Comicus was similarly accused (Scholl. Ar. *Av.* 750, *Ran.* 13). Isocrates said that some of his rivals made a living out of copying his writings (12. 16, cf. 5. 94). Among philosophers, Democritus is reputed (Favorinus ap. Diog. Laert. 9. 34) to have charged Anaxagoras with 'filching' (ὑφηρῆσθαι) astronomical theories from someone else. Plato was said to have taken the idea of the *Republic* from Protagoras (Diog. Laert. 3. 37), and Epicurus to have plagiarized from his teacher Nausiphanes (id. 10. 7 and 14). Heraclides accused Apollonius of Perge of appropriating Archimedes' unpublished work on conic sections.

Investigation of plagiarism formed a part of Alexandrian scholarship. Aristophanes of Byzantium wrote Παράλληλοι Μενάνδρου τε καὶ ἀφ' ὧν ἔκλεψεν ἐκλογαί. Such studies enjoyed a great vogue in the first century A.D. *Mimesis*, conscious imitation of good models, was recommended by the Atticists of that period to the aspiring writer, who was urged to say to himself, 'How would Homer, Plato, Demosthenes, or Thucydides have expressed this?' ([Longin.] *Subl.* 14). Such imitation may lead to direct plagiarism, and Longinus (ibid. 13) is careful to distinguish between μίμησις and κλοπή. How freely plagiarism was discussed in the first century A.D. is shown by the list of authors who wrote, mainly in that century, Περὶ κλοπῆς, preserved by Porphyry (ap. Euseb. *Praep. Evang.* 10. 3. 12).

So much Greek literature has been lost that it is seldom possible to say whether the charge is strictly maintainable in a particular case. But it must be remembered that the Greeks laid less stress than we do on originality of material. Originality of style was what mattered in their eyes. Further, in so far as historical works are concerned, writers were unwilling to break the flow of their style by constant references to author-

ities, until the conscientious Aristotle set the precedent, followed by Alexandrian writers, for extensive documentation. Herodotus often uses Hecataeus, but never names him except to disagree. Ephorus uses Herodotus, Plutarch (in his life of Coriolanus) Dionysius of Halicarnassus, without mentioning their sources. But the absence of an acknowledgement is not, of itself, sufficient ground for a charge of plagiarism. The concept of plagiarism, as opposed to originality or imitation, has little relevance to Latin literature.

E. Stemplinger, *Das Plagiat in der griechischen Literatur* (1912). J. D. D.

**PLANCINA**, MUNATIA, was in Syria with her husband, Cn. Calpurnius Piso (q.v. 7), governor of the province, when Germanicus and Agrippina were in the East (A.D. 18–19). By temperament no less domineering than Agrippina, she was, moreover, a friend of Livia. It was inevitable, therefore, that she should quarrel with Agrippina, and when Germanicus died in 19 Agrippina accused her of murder. Livia's intercession saved her life when Piso was condemned in 20. Accused again in 33, she committed suicide. J. P. B.

**PLANCIUS** (*PW* 4), GNAEUS, *eques* from Atina, protégé of the Sentii Saturnini (cf. Saturninus, q.v. 2) of that town, served in Africa, Crete, and (as *trib. mil.*) in Macedonia. As quaestor in 58 B.C. (under a Saturninus) he visited Cicero in his exile. He was tribune (56) and aedile (55?). His election to this office led to a prosecution for *ambitus* by Juventius (q.v.), against which Hortensius (q.v. 2) and Cicero successfully defended him. He fought for Pompey in the Civil War.

Cic. *Planc.* E. B.

**PLANCUS** (1), LUCIUS MUNATIUS (*PW* 30), of senatorial family, served under Caesar in the Gallic and Civil Wars. He was one of the six *praefecti urbi* of 45 B.C., and subsequently proconsul of Gallia Comata (44/3), where he mounted an expedition into Raetia and founded colonies at Lugdunum (q.v.) and Raurica (*Augst*). After frequently protesting to Cicero his loyalty to the Republic, he eventually deserted D. Brutus (q.v. 6) and joined Antony and Lepidus (late summer 43). He procured (or permitted) the proscription of his brother L. Plotius Plancus, and after triumphing 'ex Gallia' became consul with Lepidus (42) and restored the temple of Saturn. In the Perusine War he commanded an Antonian force, escaping with Fulvia (q.v.) to Greece in 40; and governed Asia (40–38?) and Syria (35) for Antony. Opposing Cleopatra's intended participation in the war against Octavian, he went over to him with his nephew M. Titius (q.v. 2) in 32. In 27 he proposed the name Augustus for Octavian; and was censor in 22. He was buried in a monumental tomb at Caieta (see *ILS* 886) and left a son Lucius (*cos.* A.D. 13) and a daughter Plancina (q.v.).

Cic. *Letters* (esp. *Fam.* 10. 1–24); Tyrrell and Purser, *Correspondence of Cicero* vi² (1933), lxxvi ff. Syme, *Rom. Rev.*, see index; G. Walser, *Der Briefwechsel des L. Munatius Plancus mit Cicero* (1957); P. Perrochat, *Rev. Ét. Lat.* 1957, 172 ff.; R. Fellmann, *Das Grab des L. Munatius Plancus bei Gaëta* (1957); *ORF²* 446 f.; Platner–Ashby, 463 ff. G. W. R.; T. J. C.

**PLANCUS** (2) BURSA, TITUS MUNATIUS (*PW* 32), brother of (1), was tribune in 52. He helped Pompey to delay the appointment of an *interrex*, was prominent in the disorders which followed the murder of Clodius, and worked hard for Milo's condemnation. On quitting office he was accused by Cicero *de vi* and, despite Pompey's support, condemned. Caesar provided for him in exile, and restored him in 49, but he held no further office. In 43 he fought for Antony in the war of Mutina and was driven out of Pollentia by Aquila (q.v. 1).

*ORF²* 447 ff. T. J. C.

**PLANTA,** POMPEIUS (*PW* 103), in A.D. 69 fought in the war between Otho and Vitellius. He was procurator of Lycia (*c.* 75 or 76), an *amicus* of Trajan, and Prefect of Egypt (98–100). He wrote an account of the civil war, which Tacitus may have used for his *Histories*.

Peter, *HRRel.* ii. 116. Pflaum, *Les Carrières procurat.* (1960), 140 f.
H. H. S.

**PLANTS, SACRED.** Plants are associated with many deities, the reason being sometimes quite clear. Thus, corn is sacred to Demeter and Ceres alike, it being their province (mythologically the gift of the former; of the latter we have no legends). Similarly, vines belong to Dionysus (q.v.), since he is among other things a wine-god. In other instances we may reasonably conjecture that the plant is associated with the deity because used for some medical or magical purpose which falls within his or her province. Thus, wormwood is called Artemis' herb (*artemisia*), hence in some sense sacred to her; but she is a woman's goddess, and the herb was used to cure some diseases of women (Pliny, *HN* 25. 73), apparently those arising out of childbirth or pregnancy, for it is especially Artemis Eileithyia whom Pliny mentions in this connexion. Laurel had a reputation for purging from other than bodily ills (Festus, 104. 23 Lindsay); hence it is natural enough that Apollo, the divine specialist in purification, should be its patron. It should not, however, be assumed without further examination that the medical or magical use of the plant comes first and the association with the god is secondary, for the reverse may be true. Often the reason for the association is quite unknown and the ancients invented fantastic explanations; thus, no one can tell why the wreaths in Britomartis' festival must be of pine or mastic, and why myrtle (Aphrodite's especial plant) must not be used (Callim. *Dian.* 200 f.).

Cf. J. I. Miller, *The Spice Trade of the Roman Empire* (1969).
H. J. R.

**PLATAEA,** a city in southern Boeotia between Cithaeron and the river Asopos, appealed for and received Athenian protection when threatened by Thebes about 519 B.C. Plataeans joined the Athenian army at Marathon and even Athens' fleet in 480, when the town, like Athens, was sacked. Near it in 479 was won the great victory over Mardonius (q.v.). In 431, after an attack by Thebes, Athens evacuated civilians; the garrison, after a brave defence (429–427) was starved out by the Peloponnesians and its members put to death, except those who had escaped in a daring sortie. Athens granted isopolity to its people until their restoration by Sparta in 386. Destroyed again by Thebes in 373 and restored by the Macedonians, Plataea survived in Roman times, when Plutarch describes the Persian War memorial festival, the Eleutheria, as still celebrated (*Aristides* 21).

Hdt. 6. 108; 8. 1, 41, 50; 9. 25–85; Thuc. 2. 2–6, 71–8; 3. 20–4, 52–68; Isoc. *Plataeicus*; Diod. Sic. 15. 46; Paus. 9. 1. W. K. Pritchett, *Studies in Ancient Greek Topography* (1965), i. 103 ff. A. R. B.

**PLATO** (Πλάτων) (1) (*c.* 429–347 B.C.), son of Ariston and Perictione, both Athenians of distinguished lineage. His writings show the enormous influence that Socrates had upon him both by his life and by his death. He relates in his *Seventh Letter* that the spectacle of contemporary politics, during the ascendancy of his own associates as well as under the democracy, gradually weakened his original intention to become a statesman and drove him to the paradox that there was no hope for cities until philosophers became rulers or rulers philosophers. After the execution of Socrates in 399 he retired for a time to Megara with other Socratics. In the next twelve years he perhaps travelled to many places, including Egypt. At any rate he visited Italy and Sicily

in 387, where he met Dionysius I and initiated lifelong friendships with Dion of Syracuse and the Pythagorean Archytas of Tarentum. On his return he was perhaps captured and ransomed at Aegina. It was probably only a few months later that he began formal and continuous teaching at a place near the grove of Academus about a mile outside the wall of Athens (*see* ACADEMY). This was his chief occupation almost without interruption for the remaining forty years of his life; but he made two more visits to Syracuse. Dionysius I died in 367; and Dion thereupon summoned Plato to try to realize the philosopher-king in the person of Dionysius II, and also to strengthen Dion's declining influence at court. Plato felt bound to try; but the new ruler's suspicion of Dion was soon reinforced by jealousy of his friendship with Plato. He banished Dion and sought to retain Plato. Some years later Plato was obliged to visit Syracuse for the third and last time, because Dionysius had promised to 'do as you wish about Dion' if he came, and to do nothing of the sort if he did not. Dionysius not merely broke his promise, but practically confiscated Dion's money and kept Plato a prisoner until the influence of Archytas procured his release. In 357 Dion re-entered Syracuse by force and expelled Dionysius. A few years later Dion was assassinated by persons who seem to have had something to do with Plato. The *Seventh Letter* was written to Dion's party after his death, ostensibly to urge moderation and constitutional procedure, but more to explain and justify Plato's own part in the whole miserable affair.

**2.** His PUBLICATIONS, which are all preserved, consist of some twenty-five dialogues and the *Apology*. There are also thirteen letters whose genuineness is much debated; but even those who reject them appear to think the *Seventh* reliable in its history. The precise order of these works is unknown; but stylometric and other inferences permit a rough division into three periods, of which the early certainly includes *Apology*, *Laches*, *Charmides*, *Euthyphro*, *Crito*, *Hippias Minor*, the middle certainly includes *Phaedo*, *Symposium*, *Republic*, and the late certainly includes *Sophist*, *Statesman*, *Philebus*, *Timaeus*, *Laws*. (For Plato's poetry *see* ELEGIAC POETRY, GREEK.)

**3.** THE EARLY DIALOGUES aim primarily at portraying a character. Plato's Socrates is ugly in body but magnetic in mind; convivial and erotic, yet Spartan in habits and of enormous physical endurance. The most striking thing about him is his conversation, to which he devotes his whole life. At first appearing absurdly simple and homely, it soon becomes intensely impressive. Its main tone is great moral earnestness, often paradoxically strict; but this is seasoned with paradoxes of another sort (as that pleasure is the only good in *Protagoras*) and with an apparently mischievous treatment of his interlocutor. The main doctrine to which he tends is that virtue is knowledge. He usually does not specify what it is knowledge of, but on the whole seems to mean: of the individual's happiness or good. Hence, since real knowledge is supremely effective in practice, no one willingly does wrong; and so-called incontinence is ignorance. Hence, also, virtue should be teachable; and Socrates wonders why great statesmen have not taught it to their sons. Hence, lastly, Socrates holds it his duty to shatter the false conceit of knowledge wherever it occurs. He asks questions to which there is only one answer; and when these admissions are put together they entail the contradictory of the answerer's original assertion. He explains in Plato's *Apology* that this bewildering elenchus is an essential preliminary to the acquisition of real knowledge and virtue; but neither there nor elsewhere does he justify his sly and mischievous manner of conducting it. The search for knowledge appears to him mostly as a question in the form: 'What is $X$?' When offered examples he says he wants 'not many $X$s but the one $X$', '$X$ itself', the 'form' or 'idea' or 'essence'. He regards this question as prior to all others, and even as answerable apart from any examples of $X$. Yet he cannot himself produce any answer, and all those proffered by others are dissolved by his elenchus. The typical form of an early Platonic work is therefore a dialogue which raises the question 'What is so and so?', refutes all suggested answers, and ends in ignorance.

**4.** The typical work of THE MIDDLE PERIOD is a narration of an earlier conversation, and Plato makes magnificent use of the opportunity to describe the external scene. The elenchus now yields to a blaze of positive doctrine; and the combination of artistic and philosophic excellence thus achieved makes the *Republic* a very great book. Instead of pursuing some particular 'form', Socrates is now represented as concerned about the nature of a 'form' as such, about the whole collection of 'forms' as such, and about the consequences of the hypothesis that there are such entities. 'We are accustomed to posit some one form concerning each set of things to which we apply the same name', *Resp.* 596 a. This form is the very thing itself meant by the name. Being invisible, it is grasped by thought and not by sense. It is absolutely and perfectly what it is, independent of all else, changeless, divine. The 'forms' constitute a second class of existences, more real than the changing animals and things around us. The 'form' of the Good has a unique status among them, being 'even beyond essence'; it has some of the characteristics the Christian ascribes to God, but Plato distinguishes it from God and regards all the 'forms' as quite independent of Him. He leaves the relations between 'forms' and things somewhat vague; but the 'forms' are certainly causes of things, both in that each 'form' causes the things named after it and, apparently, in that the 'form' of the Good helps to cause all things. The relation of a 'form' to its namesake is represented as that of the original to the copy, but also as that of what is shared in to what shares; and Plato apparently thought the two accounts compatible. Modern interpretations of these 'forms' as 'concepts' or 'hypotheses' are wholly mistaken; and even the terms 'substances', 'universals', and 'ideals' can be applied only with careful distinctions and reservations. The 'forms' were 'separate' in that they were independent and self-sufficing and not parts or elements of things; but they were 'unseparated' in that Plato meant his spatial language about them to be taken metaphorically, and in that he really believed that things 'shared' in them and could not have been what they are if there had been no 'forms'.

**5.** As the 'forms' are absolutely distinct from things, so our apprehension of them, which is knowledge, is absolutely distinct from opinion, which is a faculty set over things. There can be no true knowledge of the changing. Opinion is changeable, fallible, irrational, and the result of persuasion; knowledge is enduring, infallible, rational, exact, clear. Knowledge comes from teaching rather than persuasion, but from recollection rather than teaching; it is our recollection of the 'forms' we saw with the mind's eye before the body imprisoned and confused us. The things we see now remind us of the 'forms' they imitate (*Phd.*); and the love of a beautiful person can lead us to the love of wisdom and of the 'form' of beauty itself (*Symp.*). In other places Plato seems to allow no part at all to sense in the creation of knowledge. Knowledge is by nature practical and commanding; for ἐπιστήμη and τέχνη are identical. For the method by which it advances *see* DIALECTIC.

**6.** The hypothesis that there are 'forms' has among its consequences that soul is immortal; and this is elaborately argued in the *Phaedo*. Within the human soul

Plato finds three parts, the natural appetites, the spirit or resolution by which we can if we will resist the appetites, and the reason that determines when we should resist (*Resp.* book 4). Virtue is the proper functioning of these three. The man is wise if his reason decides rightly, brave if his spirit carries out the decision firmly, temperate and just if the better part rules the worse and each confines itself to its own business. Vice is necessarily unhappy because it is disorder and anarchy among these parts. Analogously, the ideal city will separate from the mass a small class of soldiers, living together without private property or family, and rendered by their education completely devoted to the protection of the city. They will perpetuate themselves mostly by procreation, but occasionally by enlisting a common citizen of superior metal. Within this 'spirit' of the city a higher education in mathematics and dialectic, and a series of examinations, will gradually elevate a few philosophic souls to an understanding of the 'form' of the good; and this will give them the duty though not the desire to rule. Plato's main political principle is that government is a science and requires expert knowledge. To this he adds a constitutional love of neatness and order. Both lead him to the strongest condemnations of democracy.

**7.** With the *Parmenides* and the *Theaetetus* Plato's late period approaches. In the latter he explicitly abandons narrated dialogue as cumbrous (143); in the former Socrates is for the first time a subordinate character. The *Parmenides* consists first of an apparently extremely damaging critique of the 'forms', and secondly of a sustained piece of abstract and self-contradictory dialectic. Undoubtedly Burnet and Taylor are mistaken in believing that the first part is really directed against the existence not of the 'forms' but of the sensibles. Undoubtedly also the 'forms' here attacked are those of Plato's own middle dialogues. But beyond this all is uncertain; and interpretations of the second part range from finding it a parody of some fallacious kind of reasoning to finding it an exposition of superrational truth.

**8.** The *Theaetetus*, applying the Socratic question to the concept of ἐπιστήμη, examines three likely answers with great thoroughness and insight. The first, that knowing is perceiving, is developed into an elaborate relativist theory of perception and knowledge, based on Protagorean and Heraclitean notions, before being abandoned because (1) it cannot deal with the undeniable difference between the layman and the expert, and (2) being or οὐσία is grasped by 'the soul herself by herself' and not through the senses. The second, that knowledge is true opinion, is quickly dismissed, but gives occasion for a digression on false opinion, in which Plato compares the mind to a waxen tablet and to an aviary. The third, that knowledge is true opinion with λόγος, allows him to examine the meaning of λόγος, and to consider the theory that knowledge is the analysis of compounds into their unknowable elements.

**9.** The *Sophist*, where the leader is an unnamed Eleatic, is Plato's most intense study in metaphysics. Sophistry entails falsehood, which entails 'not-being', which seems self-contradictory. 'Being' is no better; it raises difficulties alike for pluralists, monists, materialists, and immaterialists; it is neither rest nor motion, yet everything must either rest or move. The solution is the doctrine of 'communication'. Some things communicate with each other, so that we can sometimes truly say '$A$ is $B$'. Some things do not communicate with each other. Some things communicate with everything else; e.g. otherness, for each thing is other than each other thing. Not-being therefore exists and has being as otherness; while being itself 'is not' myriads of things. Using this discovery, Plato finds an explanation for falsehood and error.

**10.** Inquiring about the *Statesman*, Plato reiterates that government like medicine is a job for experts, and infers that the perfect ruler should be completely irresponsible to the people and unfettered by any inviolable constitution. Law is a second-best, useful only when science is lacking. The best constitution is simply the rule of the expert; but, failing that, we have, in order of diminishing goodness, law-abiding monarchy and aristocracy and democracy, and then lawless democracy and oligarchy and tyranny. In this dialogue, and in *Phaedrus*, *Sophist*, *Philebus*, much space goes to the method of διαίρεσις and συναγωγή. Διαίρεσις is occasionally analysis into elements (*Phdr.* 270–1), but oftener distinction, and especially the 'carving' of a 'form' into component 'forms', which seems to be an ancestor of Aristotle's 'genus and species'. By repeated carving until we reach an 'atomic form', Plato expects to reach a definition for any 'form', and also, apparently, to 'demonstrate' its truth. By συναγωγή he understands 'seeing the one in the many', which probably includes both our 'universal in the particulars' and our 'genus in the species' (*Phlb.* 16–18).

**11.** The *Philebus*, weighing the claims of pleasure and knowledge to be the good, and undertaking a close analysis of the former, rejects both, but sets knowledge nearer to that unity of 'beauty and symmetry and truth' which makes a thing good. It is hard to say whether Plato considered this a termination of the *Republic*'s quest for the 'form' of the good.

**12.** The *Timaeus*, devoted to natural science, describes how the creator made the world a single spherical living thing, having both soul and body, modelled upon 'the living creature that truly is', peopled with gods visible and invisible and with men. Tradition declares that this creator is only a mythical device for exhibiting the *rationality* inhering in the world, which has always existed and always will. Plato goes on to exhibit the complementary element, *necessity*. Besides the world and its model there is a third thing, the receptacle in which the copy becomes. The four elements can be analysed into the regular solids. The dialogue then deals at length with man, his various perceptions, the irrational part of his soul, his body, his diseases, and his health. This study, being directed towards things and not 'forms', cannot achieve infallible or even perfectly consistent results (29 c); but it will be as good as possible if we take care always to pursue both kinds of cause, reason and necessity (48 a).

**13.** The *Laws*, Plato's longest and perhaps last dialogue, takes up again the question of the best constitution for a city. Though reaffirming the *Republic*'s doctrine that the ideal is perfect unity achieved through communism (739), Plato now writes in a different temper and plans a different city. Extremes are bad, whether of despotism or of freedom; so let us have a mixed constitution. The citizens shall be 5,040 persons, each supporting his family by the cultivation of two inalienable parcels of land. Trading and teaching shall be practised exclusively by resident foreigners. There shall be an 'Assembly' and 'Council'. A long panel of officers culminates in the thirty-seven 'lawguards', for whom Plato gradually accumulates a multifarious set of duties; their authority, constitutional from the beginning, is further limited in the last book by the institution of 'Examiners' and of a 'Nocturnal Council' to revise the laws. Contrary to the *Republic* and the *Statesman*, this work values law very highly, institutes 'preambles' to the laws by which the legislator adds persuasion to command, and is chiefly remarkable for its immense wealth of detailed enactments, regulating every part of public and private life. Furthermore, dialectic and philosophy, which the *Republic* emphasized as the coping-stones of

the constitution, here yield almost entirely to religion. The reality of the divine can be proved both from the soul and from the stars, which are gods. Plato infers that everyone should be taught astronomy, and that atheists should be converted or killed.

**14.** Aristotle in his *Metaphysics* attributes to Plato doctrines not stated in the dialogues, especially that (1) there is a class of entities intermediate between 'forms' and things, immutable like 'forms' but plural like things, and these are what mathematics studies; (2) the 'forms' are numbers, composed of 'inassociable' units; (3) these number-forms are not ultimate, but result from the action of 'the One' upon 'the indefinite Dyad of the Great and Small'; thus produced, they in turn act upon this Dyad to produce the world of changing things. This report of Aristotle's cannot be wholly mistaken or fictitious; and something of these doctrines was probably delivered in Plato's famous lecture on the Good, for the Good and the One were apparently identical. Plato's view on the inefficiency of writing (*Phdr.* and *Letter* 7) is sufficient explanation of their not being found in the dialogues.

**15.** Burnet's edition of the *Phaedo* (1911) urged that Plato must have meant this dialogue to be essentially a true account of what was said on Socrates' last day. It would follow that Socrates had studied physics in his youth, that he believed in immortality and the 'forms', and that Plato was not the inventor of the 'forms'. Burnet and Taylor subsequently developed this theory into the general principle that Plato aimed at historical accuracy, ascribed to famous persons only the sort of view they had really held, and expressed himself only through such characters as the 'Eleatic stranger'. The extreme consequence, that the *Timaeus* is a minute reconstruction of the state of science several decades earlier, is brilliantly drawn in Taylor's commentary; and it constitutes an adequate disproof of Burnet's hypothesis by reduction to impossibility. R. R.

**16.** Plato's style possesses infinite variety. He can write easy, graceful, charming narrative, lit up with flashes of humour (openings of *Protagoras* and *Republic*, *Symp.* 217 a–21 c) or infused with the noblest pathos (end of *Phaedo*). In another vein he is capable of the gorgeous pageantry of the *Phaedrus* myth (245 c ff.), the passionate religious fervour of the address to the young atheist (*Leg.* 904 e–6 c), and the solemnity of the last paragraph of the *Republic*. Once or twice he recalls the statuesque grandeur of the pre-Socratics (*Phdr.* 245 c–e, *Resp.* 617 d–e), perhaps the only literary influence definitely traceable in him.

His language has a lavish fullness, sometimes amounting to redundancy. In structure he ranges from the simplest λέξις εἰρομένη (*Resp.* 328 b–c) to very long periods, often straggling and anacoluthic (*Resp.* 488 a–e), but sometimes even more powerful than those of Demosthenes, though quite different from them (*Criti.* 120 b–c and the tremendous period at *Leg.* 865 d–e). He fully appreciated the potentialities of a very short clause, closing a period or immediately following it (*Leg.* 727 c βλάπτει γάρ: *Phdr.* 238 c ἔρως ἐκλήθη). His language, as the ancient critics noted, is often deeply tinged with poetry. It is packed with metaphors (sometimes dead metaphors revived), especially from music. He will go back to a metaphor when one thinks he has done with it. Much of the *Sophist* is cast in the form of an extensive metaphor, the elusive Sophist, so hard to define, being represented as a hunted animal eluding chase. In his later years Plato's style shows traces of mannerism—a trick of interlacing the order of words, and some affectations of assonance (*Leg.* 657 d ἡμῖν ἡμᾶς, cf. 659 c; *figura etymologiae*, *Leg.* 868 c), including the pun, which fascinated Plato, though he laughed at it in others. But all in all, from the earliest works to the latest, no other author reveals as Plato does the power, the beauty, and the flexibility of Greek prose.

Dion. Hal. *Comp.* 18, *Pomp. passim*: [Longin.] *Subl.* 12–13, 32. For an admirable discussion of P.'s style and ancient criticisms of it see Norden, *Ant. Kunstpr.* i. 104 ff.                    J. D. D.

The following works, arranged in a probable chronological order, may be confidently accepted as genuine: *Hippias Minor*; *Laches*; *Charmides*; *Ion*; *Protagoras*; *Euthyphro*, *Apology*, *Crito* (comm. J. Burnet, 1924); *Gorgias* (comm. E. R. Dodds, 1959); *Meno* (comm. R. S. Bluck, 1961); *Lysis*; *Menexenus* (*c.* 386); *Euthydemus*; *Cratylus*; *Symposium* (*c.* 384); *Phaedo* (comm. J. Burnet, 1911, R. S. Bluck, 1955, R. Hackforth, 1955); *Republic* (comm. J. Adam, 1902, etc.; tr. A. D. Lindsay, 1908, etc.); *Parmenides* (*c.* 370, tr. A. E. Taylor, 1934, F. M. Cornford, 1939); *Theaetetus* (*c.* 368, comm. L. Campbell, 2nd ed. 1883, F. M. Cornford, 1935); *Phaedrus* (comm. W. H. Thompson, 1868); *Sophist* (360 or later) and *Statesman* (comm. L. Campbell, 1867); *Philebus* (comm. R. G. Bury, 1897); *Timaeus* (A. E. Taylor comm. 1928, tr. 1929; F. M. Cornford, 1937); *Critias*; *Laws* (comm. E. B. England, 1921; tr. A. E. Taylor, 1934; see also G. R. Morrow, *Plato's Cretan City*, 1960).

The following are doubtfully genuine: *Hippias Major* (comm. D. Tarrant, 1928); *Clitopho*; *Epinomis* (comm. F. Novotny, 1960); *Letters* (comm. F. Novotny, 1930; tr. L. A. Post, 1925, G. R. Morrow, 1962).

The following may be confidently rejected as spurious: *Letter* 1; *Alcibiades* 1 and 2; *Hipparchus*; *Amatores*; *Theages*; *Minos*; *De Justo*; *De Virtute*; *Demodocus*; *Sisyphus*; *Eryxias*; *Axiochus*; *Definitions*.

For various aspects of Plato's doctrine and writings, *see also* ACADEMY, AFTER-LIFE, ANATOMY AND PHYSIOLOGY, ASTRONOMY, LITERARY CRITICISM IN ANTIQUITY, §§ 1–3 MATHEMATICS, MUSIC.

LIFE. Pl. *Letter* 7; Diog. Laert. bk. 3. G. C. Field, *Plato and His Contemporaries* (1930); and the general studies below.
TEXT. O.C.T. (Burnet).
SCHOLIA. C. F. Hermann, *Platonis Dialogi*, vol. vi.
COMMENTARIES. Stallbaum–Wohlrab (1836–77); and the special commentaries above.
TRANSLATIONS. B. Jowett, 4th ed. revised by D. J. Allan and H. E. Dale (1953); and the special translations above.
GENERAL STUDIES. G. Grote, *Plato and the Other Companions of Socrates* (1888); C. Ritter, *Platon: Sein Leben, seine Schriften, seine Lehren* (1910–23), esp. for stylometry; J. Burnet, *Greek Philosophy* (1914), 205–351; U. v. Wilamowitz-Moellendorff, *Platon* (1920); A. E. Taylor, *Plato, The Man and His Work*[2] (1927); P. Friedländer, *Platon* (1928–30); P. Shorey *What Plato Said* (1933), esp. for bibliography; I. M. Crombie, *An Examination of Plato's Doctrines*, 2 vols. (1962, 1963).
SPECIAL STUDIES. H. Jackson, 'Plato's Later Theory of Ideas', in *Journ. Phil.* 1882–3, 1885–6; R. Robinson, *Plato's Earlier Dialectic*[2] (1953); Sir David Ross, *Plato's Theory of Ideas* (1951); Sir Karl Popper, *The Open Society*, vol. i, *The Spell of Plato*[3] (1957); Harold Cherniss, *The Riddle of the Early Academy* (1945), and articles in *AJPhil.* from 1932 on.                    R. R.

**PLATO** (2), Athenian comic poet, won his first victory at the City Dionysia *c.* 410 B.C. (*IG* ii. 2325. 63). He produced *Hyperbolus* at some date during 420–416 B.C., *Victories* after 421 (it referred to Ar. *Pax*), *Cleophon* in 405 and *Phaon* (probably) in 391. We have thirty titles and 270 fragments. Many of the fragments refer to people active at various times between 425 and 390 B.C. and known to us from Aristophanes (especially *Av.*) and from historians. The titles show that many of his plays were strongly political, and at least one of them, *Envoys*, belongs to the fourth century, since it mentions an embassy of Epicrates and Phormisius to Persia (fr. 119). Other titles, e.g. Ζεὺς κακούμενος, point to mythological burlesque; *Sophists* ridiculed contemporary artistic (and possibly, though not certainly, philosophical) innovations.

*FCG* ii. 615 ff.; *CAF* i. 601 ff.; *FAC* i. 488 ff.    K. J. D.

**PLATONIUS** (of uncertain date) wrote a work on Old,

Middle, and New Comedy, in which he discussed the characteristics of individual comic poets. The two extant fragments, *On the Difference between Comedies* and *On the Difference between Types*, are brief but valuable.

*CGF* i. 3–6.                    J. F. L.

**PLATORIUS** (*PW* 2) **NEPOS**, AULUS, consul in A.D. 119 and governor of Lower Germany, was legate of Britain from July 122 (*JRS* 1922, 65; 1930, 21) until after Sept. 124 (*CIL* vii. 1195 = xvi. ,64 no. 70). He was a personal friend of and possible successor to Hadrian (S.H.A. *Hadr.* 4. 2; 15. 2) whom he apparently accompanied to Britain (122), bringing Legio VI Victrix from Lower Germany. He built the milecastles (*RIB* 1634, 1637–8, 1666, 1935) and forts (*RIB* 1340, 1427) of Hadrian's Wall (q.v.).                    I. A. R.

**PLAUTIANUS**, GAIUS FULVIUS (*PW* 101) (*cos.* A.D. 203), was probably a native of Lepcis Magna and for this reason favoured by his fellow townsman Septimius Severus. He was appointed Praetorian Prefect in A.D. 197 and came to exercise an almost autocratic power. In A.D. 202 his daughter Plautilla married Caracalla and in 203 he was consul with Geta. His downfall was due to Caracalla, who was disappointed in his marriage and induced his father to believe that the prefect was plotting his assassination (205).

*See* SEVERUS (1). F. Grosso, *Rend. Linc.* 1968, 7 ff.
H. M. D. P.; B. H. W.

**PLAUTIUS** (1) **SILVANUS**, MARCUS, a moderate Popularis of obscure origin, as tribune in 89 B.C. was responsible with C. Papirius Carbo for the *Lex Plautia Papiria* which, supplementing the *Lex Iulia* of 90, offered the citizenship to insurgents who withdrew straightway from the revolt, and to folk not covered by the previous law, in particular to certain persons who, though attached to the *municipia* incorporated in 90 as *adscripti*, were then resident not in their municipality but at Rome or elsewhere in but not outside Italy. Such persons were to apply to the *praetor urbanus* within sixty days.

Plautius also modified the *quaestio Variana*, which was trying the friends of Livius Drusus and other sympathizers with the insurgents, by a *lex iudiciaria* which introduced mixed instead of equestrian juries.

Asc. *Corn.* 79; Cic. *Arch.* 4. 7. A. N. Sherwin-White, *The Roman Citizenship* (1939), 132 ff.; Badian, *Stud. Gr. Rom. Hist.* 75 ff.
A. N. S.-W.

**PLAUTIUS** (2, *PW* 23) **HYPSAEUS**, PUBLIUS, of consular family, was quaestor and proquaestor under Pompey in the East and in 56 B.C. supported his pretensions to an Egyptian command. In 53 he was a candidate for the consulship with Metellus (q.v. 11) Scipio and Milo (q.v.). The campaign, in which he and Scipio were supported by Pompey and Clodius, was corrupt and violent and the elections were repeatedly postponed. After Clodius' death (Jan. 52) the partisans of Plautius and Scipio attacked the *interrex* Lepidus (q.v. 3) in his house in order to force him to fix the election-day. When Pompey had been made sole consul he abandoned Plautius, who was condemned *de ambitu*. He was probably restored by Caesar, since he was in the Senate in Apr. 44.
T. J. C.

**PLAUTIUS** (3, *PW* 43) **SILVANUS**, MARCUS, grandson of a praetor, was consul in 2 B.C., proconsul of Asia, and *legatus* of Augustus probably in Galatia, in which capacity he may have fought the mountaineers of Isauria in A.D. 6. He served with distinction in the Pannonian War under Tiberius and received *ornamenta triumphalia* in 9. He has been identified with the subject of the *elogium ILS* 918 (*see* QUIRINIUS). His mother Urgulania was a friend of Livia's, his daughter Urgulanilla married the future Emperor Claudius.

E. Groag, *JÖAI* 1922–4, Beibl. 445 ff.; R. Syme, *Klio* 1934, 139 ff., *Anat. Stud. Buckler* (1939), 332, and *Rom. Rev.* (see index); L. R. Taylor, *Amer. Acad. Rome* 1956, 7 ff.; K. M. T. Atkinson, *Hist.* 1958, 315 f., 328 f. A. M.; T. J. C.

**PLAUTIUS** (4, *PW* 39), AULUS (*cos. suff.* A.D. 29), governor of Pannonia in 43, when he was appointed by Claudius to command the British expedition. He defeated the sons of Cunobellinus in battle (probably at the Medway and at the Thames), and took the Belgic capital, Camulodunum. Before his departure (47) he seems to have pacified the areas belonging to a wide suzerainty of the Cunobellinus kingdom. On his return he received the honour of an ovation. In 57, 'according to ancient custom', he himself conducted an inquiry into charges of 'externa superstitio' against his wife—and acquitted her.

Dio Cass. 60. 19–21; Tac. *Ann.* 13. 32. Collingwood–Myres, *Roman Britain*, 78–91; E. M. Clifford, *Bagendon* (1961), 57 ff.; D. R. Dudley and G. Webster, *The Roman Conquest of Britain, A.D. 43–57* (1965), ch. 4; Frere, *Britannia* 61 ff. C. E. S.

**PLAUTIUS** (5, *PW* 47) **SILVANUS AELIANUS**, TIBERIUS (*cos. suff.* A.D. 45, *cos.* II 74), is barely known to history save for the long inscription recording his career and exploits, still extant at the Mausoleum of the Plautii near Tibur (*ILS* 986). The precise degree of his relationship to M. Plautius (3) Silvanus is uncertain. Plautius served as a legate in the conquest of Britain, clearly enjoying the favour of the Emperor Claudius (whose first wife, Plautia Urgulanilla (*see* PLAUTIUS 3), belonged to his family). After being proconsul of Asia (*c.* A.D. 57) Plautius was appointed legate of Moesia, in which function he conducted diverse operations, and made the frontier safe, though his army was weakened by the dispatch of troops to the East for Corbulo's campaigns. He prevented a disturbance among the Sarmatians, relieved the siege of Chersonesus, transplanted more than 100,000 natives to the southern bank of the Danube, and sent a copious supply of corn to Rome. For these services, however, he got no honour from Nero; Vespasian subsequently granted him the *ornamenta triumphalia*. After governing the province of Hispania Tarraconensis (70–3 ?), he was appointed *praefectus urbi* by Vespasian.

L. Halkin, *Ant. Class.* 1934, 121; A. Stein, *Die Legaten von Moesien* (1940), 29 ff. R. S.

**PLAUTIUS** (6, *PW* 42) **LATERANUS**, a Roman senator, deprived of his rank in A.D. 48 as a lover of Messalina, was restored by Nero (55). Consul designate (65), he took part in the Pisonian conspiracy and was executed.

For his great palace on the Caelian see Juvenal 10. 15–18; but the Lateranus of Juvenal 8. 146 ff. is not modelled on the real person, who is credited with genuine patriotism by Tacitus, *Ann.* 15. 49. G. E. F. C.

**PLAUTIUS** (7, *PW* 60), a Roman jurist of the later first century A.D., not directly excerpted in the *Digest* and known only through commentaries entitled *ad Plautium* and written by Neratius, Javolenus (qq.v.), Pomponius (q.v. 6) and Paulus (q.v. 1). The existence of these commentaries is evidence of his high reputation. His book seems to have treated of the *ius honorarium* (*see* IUS CIVILE), and to have occupied a position in the literature on that branch of the law similar to that occupied by the work of Sabinus (q.v. 2) in the literature on the *ius civile*. A. B.; B. N.

**PLAUTUS**, TITUS MACCIUS (so in the *Ambrosianus*, but in *Merc.* 10 ambiguously *Macci Titi*, in *Asin.* 11 *Maccus*). Born at Sarsina in Umbria (surprisingly backward region, and perhaps this was a later inference from the joke in

*Mostell.* 769 f.). The biographical details in Gellius (3. 3. 14 f.) are probably later fiction. His death Cicero places in 184 B.C. (*Brut.* 60), but, as always, this probably means the last record of the production of a new play. His work was very popular and 130 plays were attributed to him in the first century B.C. Varro drew up a list of twenty-one plays which were by general agreement by Plautus (before going on to prove others to be Plautine by stylistic analysis —Gell. 3. 3. 3); it seems certain that the corpus of twenty-one plays (the last, the *Vidularia*, fragmentary) which has come down was based on this list and represents a selected edition produced in the second century A.D. The manuscript tradition, consisting of the sixth-century *Ambrosianus* on the one hand, and the Carolingian and later Palatine group on the other, cannot with any certainty be traced beyond the fourth century A.D. (traces of yet a third stem of the tradition can be found in the quotations of Nonius Marcellus).

It is impossible to date the plays absolutely except in two instances: the *didascaliae* have been preserved in *A* for *Stichus* (200 B.C.) and *Pseudolus* (191 B.C.). Otherwise: *Cistellaria* was produced before the end of the Second Punic War (197 ff.); *Miles c.* 204 B.C. (211 f.), if the details of the imprisonment of Naevius (q.v.) and the dating can be trusted; *Truculentus* was a product of his old age (Cic. *Sen.* 50); *Epidicus* was earlier than *Bacchides* (214 f.); *Bacchides* was earlier than *Pseudolus* (which borrows themes from it); *Rudens* was earlier than *Mercator* (225 ff.—see below). No attempt to date the plays on a general hypothesis about development has succeeded: it has been thought, for instance, that Plautus progressed from a stage of few *cantica* to many—but this is based on the early dating of *Miles* which has no *cantica*, and yet *Cist.*, which must be near *Miles* in time, has several very complicated *cantica*.

The poets of the originals are known for some plays: from Menander's Ἀδελφοί came the *Stichus* (didascalia: Menander wrote two plays of that name—*see* TERENCE); *Bacchides* from Menander's Δὶς ἐξαπατῶν (cf. 816 f. with Men. fr. 125 K.); *Cistellaria* from Menander's Συναριστώσαι (cf. 89 ff. with Men. fr. 558 K. and title from quotation in Festus—see *Philologus* 1932, 117 ff.); *Aulularia* from unknown play of Menander (300 f. listed as a trait of Menander's miser Smikrines). From Philemon were 'translated' *Mercator* (9 f.) and *Trinummus* (18 f.) and probably *Mostellaria* (1149); from Diphilus *Casina* (31 ff.) and *Rudens* (32); and from the unknown Demophilos came *Asinaria* (11). None can be proved to be 'translated' from a Middle Comedy original. In a number of the plays can be demonstrated the technique of incorporating material drawn from another play (or else actually invented by Plautus), which Terence's critics condemned as *contaminare* (*see* TERENCE *and* CONTAMINATIO). The technique of Plautus differs sharply from that of Terence who had careful regard for the plot as a whole: Plautus was interested in each scene as it came and inserted material without regard for any resultant incoherence in the plot viewed as a whole: so, e.g., the dream in *Merc.* 225 ff. has been imitated from that in *Rud.* 593 ff.; in *Trin.* IV. 3, lines 1008–27 concern a ring which has nothing to do with the plot of the play. Sometimes Plautus seems to have used material from another part of the same play to construct a new scene of his own, as in *Curculio* 1, sc. 1 and 2, and *Miles* (*passim*: see *Hermes* 1958, 79 ff. and *CQ* 1965, 84 ff.). In other places—these by far the majority—Plautus has used material of his own invention and so imported Roman material into Greek scenes: so, e.g., in *Pseud.* I. 2 and 3, II. 1; *Bacch.* IV. 9, etc. In *Mostell.* I. 3 he expanded the Greek scene with Roman material and a later producer seems to have made provision for drastic shortening of the whole scene (see *JRS* 1958, 22 ff.). The scene *Pseud.* I. 2, the show of the *meretrices*, where the refined Greek *hetaera* is suddenly displayed as the coarse denizen of a low Roman brothel, shows well how Plautus' imagination seized on separate scenes and worked within each one as a unit, not the play as a whole (see Fraenkel, *Plautinisches im Plautus*, 146 ff. = Ital. trans. 136 ff.). This was only one way in which Plautus gave rein to his own imagination, regardless of the Greek play: he also grossly expanded the role of slaves and the part allotted to them, so too that of the parasite as seems clear in *Capt.*, *Curc.*, and *Persa*, and that of the pimp Ballio in *Pseud.* (it is significant that this was the part which the great comic actor of Cicero's time, Roscius, chose for himself). It was of equally little interest to Plautus to preserve coherent characterization and, while he has based his characters on the Greek models, he has felt free to add touches of his own as suited him: what results is usually a person not completely Greek, nor really Roman, but an amalgam of both. He disregarded carefully preserved Greek stage-conventions: e.g. Greek playwrights kept comments made by a speaker concealed from those taking part in the main action on the stage within severe limits; but, when it suited him, Plautus expanded these remarks for their comic effect, cf. e.g. *Capt.* 260 ff. or *Pseud.* 229 ff., 1285 ff. On many occasions he gave a speech a completely new form and tone by parodying some Roman custom: e.g. the custom of the praetorian edict is parodied in *Mil.* 156 ff., *Pseud.* 125 ff., 133 ff.; or the slave in *Bacch.* 925 ff. speaks as if he were a triumphant army commander. For the greatest formal change, Plautus was indebted to his predecessors Livius Andronicus and Naevius (qq.v.): this was to produce great polymetric *cantica* from what will have been trimeter monologues in the Greek originals (the process is quite clear, e.g. in *Most.* I. 2). These *cantica* were probably high points of the performances (like the great *arias* in Mozartian opera) and will have required highly skilled performers. All the plays contain splendid examples, except *Miles* (and here the reason for their absence may have been a lack of suitable performers). Similar in invention are opera-type duets in lyric metres, of minimum dramatic content, but enjoyable in terms of music, rhythm and language: e.g. *Persa*, I. 1, *Pseud.* 243–64, *Rud.* 279 ff., *Stich.* 316 ff., *Trin.* 1059 ff. (The nearest approach Terence makes to such composition is, e.g., *An.* 344 f.—a drastic contrast.) In all of this Plautus shows himself a most versatile and sophisticated master of metrical technique (in Greek and Latin literature perhaps only Aristophanes is in the same class). The prologues of Plautus are curious: five of the plays (*Curc.*, *Epid.*, *Mostell.*, *Persa*, *Stich.*) have no prologue (the opening of *Bacch.* is lost) and of the rest the prologues of *Asin.* and *Trin.* are purely formal and say nothing of the action (the fragment of the prologue of *Pseud.* is similar). The prologues of *Cist.* and *Miles* are postponed (like the prologue, e.g., of Menander's *Heros* or *Perikeiromene*). The most likely hypothesis is that Plautus was moving in the same direction as Terence and dispensed with the Greek prologue as far as possible, consistently with the audience's understanding the action (some parts of the prologues, e.g. *Cas.* 1–20, were clearly written for revival performances after Plautus' death and later compositions may be far more extensive than can now be demonstrated).

The style of Plautus owed much to that of his predecessors (*see* NAEVIUS), but it was nevertheless an original creation. Formally, a Plautine play has three elements: *senarii* (representing ordinary conversation or prose—see *Persa*, IV. 3 which is in trochaic long verse but each time a section of a letter is read out, 501 ff. and 520 ff., the metre shifts to *senarii*), long verse (mainly trochaic *septenarii* and iambic *octonarii*), and *canticum*. The last was sung, the long verse was accompanied by the flute while *senarii* had no music (nothing can now be known

about this music): theoretically the style corresponds to this division—*cantica* have every resource of language lavished on them, while at the opposite extreme *senarii* are in the plainest style. But Plautus could not for long write in a plain style; so the language of the *senarii* varies considerably, and it is essential to note stylistic variations since they are the best clue to the tone of a passage. All the characteristics of artistic composition in Latin can be found in Plautus: dicolon, tricolon, and tricolon crescendo structures, with and without anaphora, structures dependent on the piling-up of synonyms, alliteration, assonance, archaisms, echoes of the language of Roman institutions, *figura etymologica*, etc., and with this a riotous imagination in the creation of metaphors (e.g. *Mil.* 607–8) and their selection from all aspects of human life (military, institutional, legal, religious, slave-punishment), a fantastic application and misapplication of Greek mythology (cf. e.g. *Pseud.* 190 ff., 198 ff.), and an otherwise unparalleled use of personification (cf. e.g. *Amph.* 673, *Asin.* 386, *Curc.* 147 ff., *Mostell.* 266). There is an endless flow of witticism that often totally destroys the pathos of a scene (cf. e.g. *Pseud.* 1–40) and these witticisms sometimes have a characteristic form—a riddling phrase, then an explanation in asyndeton (cf. e.g. *Pseud.* 747 *anguilla est: elabitur* or *Merc.* 361). There is no attempt either in the action of Plautus or in the language at realism: he and Terence stand at opposite extremes—where Terence strives for the natural, the humanly explicable, Plautus gives free rein to fantasy and imagination.

*Act-division.* The act-divisions in editions of Plautus are modern and arbitrary inventions of the sixteenth century. It seems clear that Greek New Comedy relied on a structure of five acts (i.e. four act-divisions), but it is clear that Plautus often ignored this in his adaptation (e.g. the act-division at *Pseud.* 573ª is probably about 200 lines too late). It is somewhat easier to discover the act-division of Terence's plays (Donatus says that they went back to the time of Varro), but he also seems to have written for a different, less sharply divided, performance than his Greek models. (On this complicated question see G. Burckhardt, *Die Akteinteilung in der neuen griech. und in der röm. Komödie* (Diss. Basel, 1927); and a summary with bibliography in G. E. Duckworth, *The Nature of Roman Comedy* (1952), 98 ff.)

*Metre and Prosody.* See METRE, LATIN, I. The metre and prosody of Plautus are too complex and difficult for summary here: the best detailed account in English is given by W. M. Lindsay in the introduction to his edition of Plautus, *Captivi* (1900), 12 ff.

TEXT. Apograph of *Ambrosianus* by W. Studemund (1889); F. Ritschl–Loewe–Goetz–Schoell, 4 vols. (1879–1902)—still indispensable for full information about MSS.; F. Leo, 2 vols. (1895–6; repr. 1958)—the best and most useful text; W. M. Lindsay, 2 vols. (1904); A. Ernout, 7 vols. Budé (1932—with trans.); P. Nixon, 5 vols. Loeb (1928—Leo's text with trans.). Text and commentary in Latin on all plays, J. L. Ussing, 5 vols. (1875–92). Separate commentaries: *Captivi*, W. M. Lindsay (1900), Brix–Niemeyer–Köhler (1930[7]); *Epidicus*, G. E. Duckworth (1940); *Menaechmi*, Brix–Niemeyer (1929[6]); *Mercator*, P. S. Enk (1932); *Miles*, Brix–Niemeyer–Köhler (1916[4]); *Mostellaria*, A. O. F. Lorenz (1886[2]; E. A. Sonnenschein (1907[2]); *Pseudolus*, A. O. F. Lorenz (1876); *Rudens*, F. Marx (1928); *Trinummus*, Brix–Conrad (1931[6]); *Truculentus*, P. S. Enk (1953).
GENERAL. F. Leo, *Plautinische Forschungen* (1912[2]); E. Fraenkel, *Plautinisches im Plautus* (1922: Italian trans. with very important appendices, 1960); G. Jachmann, *Plautinisches u. Attisches* (1931); H. Haffter, *Unters. z. altlateinische Dichtersprache* (1934); K. H. E. Schutter, *Quibus annis comoediae Plaut. primum actae sint quaeritur* (Diss. Groningen, 1952).
PROSODY AND METRE. W. M. Lindsay, ed. of *Captivi* (1900), 12 ff.; F. Leo, *Die plaut. Cantica u. d. hellenist. Lyrik* (1897); E. Fraenkel, *Iktus u. Akzent* (1928); H. Drexler, *Plaut. Akzentstudien* (1932); P. W. Harsh, 'Early Latin Meter and Prosody 1904–55', *Lustrum* 1958, 215 ff.
LANGUAGE. W. M. Lindsay, *Syntax of Plautus* (1907); G. Lodge, *Lexicon Plautinum*, 2 vols. (1924–33).                    G. W. W.

**PLEBISCITUM,** as opposed to *lex* (q.v.), was in theory a resolution carried by any Roman assembly in which no patrician cast his vote. In practice, except perhaps on a few occasions in the late Republic, it was a resolution of a plebeian tribal assembly (*concilium plebis*: see COMITIA (*c*)) presided over by a plebeian magistrate. At first the plebiscite was no more than a recommendation, and it attained the force of law only if re-enacted at the instance of a consul in the full assembly of the *populus*; but from an early date—possibly 449 B.C.—all plebiscites were recognized as universally binding which received the prior sanction of the patrician senators (*patrum auctoritas*, q.v.). By the *lex Hortensia* of 287 B.C. they were afforded unconditional validity, and, with plebeian tribunes being drawn increasingly from within the governing class in the years which followed, they embodied much of the official routine legislation of the middle Republic. In the post-Gracchan period they again became instruments of challenge to senatorial authority. Sulla therefore required in 88, and again in 81 B.C., that all tribunician proposals should be approved by the Senate before being put to the vote. This restriction was removed in 70 B.C.

Mommsen, *Röm. Forsch.* i. 177 ff., *Röm. Staatsr.* iii³. 150 ff.; H. Siber, *Die plebejischen Magistraturen* (1936), 39 ff.; A. Roos, *Comitia Tributa–Concilium plebis, Leges–Plebiscita* (1940); E. S. Staveley, *Athenaeum* 1955, 3 ff.                                      E. S. S.

**PLEBS** was the name given to the general body of Roman citizens, as distinct from the privileged *patricii*; it is perhaps related to πλῆθος. The contrast between it and the *patricii* no doubt arose through the differentiation of certain wealthier and more influential families into a separate class. The modern hypothesis that the *plebs* was racially distinct from the *patricii* is not supported by ancient evidence; and the view of some ancient writers (Cic. *Rep.* 2. 16; Dion. Hal. 2. 9; Plut. *Rom.* 13) that the plebeians were all clients of the patricians in origin can be true only in the sense that the clients were plebeians. The plebeians were originally excluded from religious colleges, magistracies, and perhaps also from the Senate, and by a law of the XII Tables they were debarred from intermarriage with patricians. But they were enrolled in the *gentes, curiae*, and *tribus*; they served at all times in the army and could hold the office of *tribunus militum*. It is very doubtful whether it is legitimate to speak of *plebs* for the period of monarchy. A sharp distinction between the two classes seems to have developed only in early Republican times.

The 'Conflict of the Orders', by which the *plebs* achieved political equality with the patricians, forms part of the general history of Rome. The victory of the *plebs* was essentially due to the fact that it organized itself into a separate corporation, which held its own assemblies (*concilia plebis*), appointed its own officers, the *tribuni* and *aediles plebis* (usually selected from the wealthier members of their order), and instituted its own Record Office (in the temples of Diana on the Aventine and of Ceres). It secured inviolability for the persons of its officers by a collective undertaking to protect them, and at times of special crisis it withdrew *en masse* from Rome (*see* SECESSIO). After two centuries of struggle the *plebs* attained all its political objects by 287 B.C. Under the later Republic the name 'plebeian' acquired in ordinary parlance its modern sense of a member of the lower social orders. In imperial times those who did not belong to the senatorial and equestrian orders, or to the *ordo* of the *municipia*, were often called plebeians.

Mommsen, *Röm. Staatsr.* iii; De Sanctis, *Stor. Rom.* i. 224 ff.; J. Binder, *Die Plebs* (1909); A. Rosenberg, *Hermes* 1913, 359 ff.; H. J. Rose, *JRS* 1922, 106 ff.; F. Altheim, *Lex Sacrata, Die Anfänge der plebeischen Organisation* (1940); H. Last, *JRS* 1945, 30 ff.; P. de Francisci, *Primordia Civitatis* (1959), 777 ff.; E. Meyer, *Röm. Staat und Staatsgedanke* (1961²); A. Momigliano, *JRS* 1963, 117 ff.; *Riv. Storica Italiana* 1967, 297 ff., *Entretiens Hardt* xiii (1967), 199 ff.; J. le Gall, *Mél. A. Piganiol* (1966), iii. 1449 ff.; Z. Yavetz, *Plebs and Princeps* (1969).                                      A. M.

**PLEMINIUS** (*PW* 2), QUINTUS, *legatus pro praetore* in 205 B.C., under Scipio Africanus recaptured Locri from Hannibal. Left in charge of a garrison Pleminius plundered Locri, including the treasury of Persephone. After an inquiry by Scipio he retained his command and continued to oppress the Locrians until they appealed to the Senate. He was arrested by a senatorial commission of inquiry and perhaps held in prison until his death (195 ?).

A. Toynbee, *Hannibal's Legacy* (1965), ii, 613 ff.          H. H. S.

**PLINY (1) THE ELDER** (GAIUS PLINIUS (*PW* 5) SECUNDUS) (A.D. 23/24–79) was born at Comum and probably educated at Rome. His father is not known to have been distinguished, but he had means, and Pliny at the age of about 23 entered upon an equestrian career. He spent the next twelve years mostly with the armies of the Rhine, one of his appointments being the command of a cavalry squadron. One aspect of cavalry tactics was treated by him in a monograph written at this period, but characteristically he found time also to begin a history of the Roman campaigns against the Germans and to write a biography of his patron Pomponius Secundus, a scholar and a writer as well as a man of action, who thus foreshadowed Pliny's own aspirations.

In 57 or 58 Pliny completed his military service and returned to Italy. For the next ten years his official career was interrupted, perhaps because of lack of patronage, but possibly because of his distaste for Nero's regime. He devoted himself to rhetorical and grammatical studies, although these may not have been his only occupation. This may have been the period mentioned by his nephew Pliny the Younger (*Ep.* 3. 5) in which he was active at the bar.

With the accession of Vespasian, Pliny's fortunes changed for the better. He had served in Germany with Titus, a connexion which no doubt helped to bring him the series of procuratorships that he held 'summa integritate' (Suetonius). One of these is known to have taken him to Hispania Tarraconensis (*c.* 73). At this time he was also writing a history in thirty-one books, completed by 77 but published posthumously, and the *Naturalis Historia*, dedicated to Titus in 77. Towards the end of his life Pliny became a counsellor ('amicus') of Vespasian and then of Titus, and was appointed commander of the fleet at Misenum. It was from Misenum that he sailed on 24 Aug. 79 to observe the eruption of Vesuvius from the neighbourhood of Stabiae. There he was overcome by fumes from the eruption and died.

The titles and a rough chronology of Pliny's works are given by the Younger Pliny (*Ep.* 3. 5). Of these only the *Naturalis Historia* survives. The others were:

1. **De iaculatione equestri,** concerning the use of javelins on horseback: see above.

2. **De uita Pomponi Secundi,** in two books: see above.

3. **Bella Germaniae,** in twenty books, a history of all the Roman campaigns fought against the Germans, perhaps extending to A.D. 47. Tacitus made considerable use of this work in the *Germania* and the *Annals*.

4. **Studiosi,** in three books but six rolls, a training manual for students of oratory, containing copious instances of pointed *sententiae* from *controuersiae* (Gell. 9. 16. 1) and thus showing tendencies that Quintilian was to render obsolete.

5. **Dubius Sermo,** on doubtful diction or linguistic forms, completed in eight books, completed in 67 and chosen because it was a safe topic to pursue in dangerous times. It appears that Pliny tried to reconcile the claims of analogy and anomaly (q.v.).

6. **A fine Aufidi Bassi,** a continuation in thirty-one books of Bassus' Roman history. It was written between 71 and 77. The period covered is uncertain (possibly

A.D. 44–71), and attempts to prove that it was extensively used by Tacitus have perhaps been pressed too far.

The **Naturalis Historia,** in thirty-seven books, consists of a Preface and Book 1, which provides an index of topics and authors, followed by: 2, the Universe; 3–6, geography; 7, man; 8–11, other animals; 12–19, botany; 20–7, botany in medicine; 28–32, zoology in medicine; 33–7, metals and stones, including their use in medicine, art, and architecture.

Pliny himself states (*pref.* 17) that the work contains 20,000 important facts obtained from 100 principal authors, but the total of authors and of 'facts, histories and observations' recorded in the index is far higher. Such a compilation was unique in its comprehensiveness, a virtue which is also a vice. And yet, without condoning cases of carelessness in his use of sources, it is all too easy to criticize Pliny for failing to exercise scientific methods for which he had neither training nor time. It is easy also to censure him for his lack of discrimination, for including much that was obsolete or absurd along with so much that was up-to-date and enlightening. Nevertheless, he made good use of his best qualities, his curiosity and his energy, both of which were inexhaustible. A simple example (19. 81–4) will serve to show Pliny at his best and worst: here personal research and personal observation are followed by a gross misreading of a source. His best accounts, for example that of amber (37. 30–46), supersede all others. Being what he was, he was wise to include too much rather than too little. Not the least of his merits is his capacity for making useful mistakes. He may have thought that the *anthracitis* (37. 99) was a precious stone, but his conscientious refusal to suppress material has resulted in an interesting note on coal. To the ancients Pliny's disadvantage lay not in his lack of reliability, but in his diffuseness, his mannered and often tortuous style, and perhaps his forced but powerful imagery, as is shown by the naïve abridgements of Solinus, Isidore (q.v. 2) of Seville, and others. If with all these drawbacks Pliny's work failed to provide the practical benefits for which he hoped, it succeeded—partly in spite of them and partly because of them—in winning a unique place in the tradition of Western culture.

LIFE AND WORKS. *HN*, pref. 1–3; 20; Pliny, *Ep.* 3. 5; 6. 16; fragments of Suetonius' *Vita.* H. N. Wethered, *The Mind of the Ancient World: A Consideration of Pliny's N.H.* (1937); Syme, *Tacitus.*
TEXTS. D. Detlefsen (1866–73); Jan's Teubner text, 2nd ed. (Mayhoff). The modern numbering by short sections is now generally used in references. *Dubii Sermonis Reliquiae,* J. W. Beck (Teubner, 1894).
TRANSLATIONS. Philemon Holland (1601); H. Rackham, etc. (Loeb, 10 vols., 1942–63).
COMMENTARIES. L. Urlichs, *Chrestomathia Pliniana* (1857); K. Jex-Blake and E. Sellers, *The Elder Pliny's Chapters on the History of Art* (1896); K. C. Bailey, *The Elder Pliny's Chapters on Chemical Subjects* (1929–32); *HN* bk. 2, D. J. Campbell (1936); *Histoire Naturelle* (with text and French translation), A. Ernout, etc. (1950– ).
STYLE. Joh. Müller, *Der Stil des älteren P.* (1883); A. Önnerfors, *Pliniana* (1956).
SOURCES. H. Brunn, *De auctorum indicibus Plinianis disputatio isagogica* (1856); F. Münzer, *Beiträge zur Quellenkritik der Naturgesch.* (1897); W. Kroll, *Die Kosmologie des älteren P.* (1930).
                                                                D. E. E.

**PLINY** (2) **THE YOUNGER** (*c.* A.D. 61–*c.* 112), GAIUS PLINIUS CAECILIUS SECUNDUS, is known from his writings and from inscriptions (e.g. *ILS* 2927). Son of a landowner of Comum (q.v.), he was later brought up by his uncle and adoptive father, the literary equestrian Pliny the Elder (q.v.). He studied advocacy in the schools of Quintilian (q.v.) and Nicetes at Rome. After a year's service on the staff of a Syrian legion (*c.* 81) he entered the Senate (*c.* 90) through the influence of highly placed family friends such as Julius Frontinus and Verginius Rufus (qq.v.). He practised successfully in the civil courts

all his life, and conducted several State prosecutions of provincial governors charged with extortion. He held the usual annual offices, becoming praetor in 93 (or less probably 95) and consul in 100, and secured a series of longer administrative appointments as *praefectus aerari militaris* (*c.* 94–6), *praefectus aerari Saturni* (*c.* 98–100), and *curator alvei Tiberis* (*c.* 104–6). He thrice sat as judicial adviser in the cabinet of Trajan (*c.* 104–7), who sent him as *legatus Augusti* to reorganize the disorderly province of Bithynia-Pontus (*c.* 110), where he apparently died in office (*c.* 112). His career, very similar to that of his friend Cornelius Tacitus (q.v.), is the best documented example of the life of a civilian administrator of the Principate, promoted by and loyal to tyrannical and liberal emperors alike, whom he criticized only after their deaths.

Pliny published nine books of literary letters (*epistulae curatius scriptae,* Ep. 1. 1) between 100 and 109 at irregular intervals, singly and in groups of two or three. He and his friends regularly exchanged such letters (*Ep.* 9. 28). They are elegant news-letters about social, domestic, judicial, and political events, or letters of advice, personal introductions, and commendations, interspersed with very short courtesy notes. They resemble short essays, character sketches, miniature histories, and topographies, written with great attention to formal style, and limited either to a single subject treated at appropriate length, or to a single theme illustrated by three examples (cf. *Epp.* 2. 5. 13; 20; 6. 31; 7. 27). But many of the letters, notably those about business affairs (e.g. 3. 19, 8. 2), originated as practical correspondence later edited and expanded for literary publication. Pliny developed the literary letter into something new in Latin literature, akin to the occasional verses of Statius and Martial, whose themes and language he sometimes echoes. In style he uses the devices of contemporary rhetoric, with intricate arrangement and balance of words and clauses in sentences and paragraphs. Intellectually he reveals a scientific accuracy of observation and logicality of argument, especially when discussing natural phenomena—intermittent springs, floating islands, volcanic eruptions. Superstitious and mythological explanations are notably absent.

The letters paint the high society of Rome, both at the capital and in its provincial retreats, observed with a somewhat complacent eye. But Pliny's social origins in the municipal *bourgeoisie* rendered him easily shocked by the sophisticated vices of the capital, and he censures the cruelty of slave masters, the dodges of legacy hunters, and the meanness of the wealthy. He dwells preferably on pleasanter themes, the considerate treatment of wives, friends, and dependants, education, schools, his own forensic activities, and the literary life of Rome. Other letters describe the public life of senatorial debates, elections, and trials, without concealing the weaknesses of senators, and recount, in a manner anticipating Tacitus, heroic episodes of the political opposition to Domitian with which Pliny misleadingly claimed some connexion.

Pliny also dabbled enthusiastically in versification, publishing two volumes in the manner of his protégé Martial, of which he quotes a few indifferent specimens. His surviving speech, the *Panegyricus,* is an expanded version of the original which he delivered in the Senate as consul, using all the tricks of technical rhetoric to contrast the actions of Trajan with the misdeeds of Domitian. The tenth book of letters, written in simpler style than the rest, contains Pliny's official correspondence with Trajan about the administration of Bithynia, and is the only such dossier surviving entire. Each letter concerns a particular problem. Pliny, though fettered by directives that limited his freedom of action, shows, just as in his private letters, a sensible judgement of practical affairs, a quick eye for abuses, and much humanity towards repressed classes such as the Christians. In *Ep.* 10. 96 he gives the earliest external account of their teaching, behaviour, and official repression.

TEXT. *Epistles*, R. A. B. Mynors (O.C.T. 1963); *Paneg.*, M. Durry (Paris, 1938). A.-M. Guillemin, *Pline et la vie littéraire de son temps* (1929); Syme, *Tacitus*, chs. 7–8, appendixes 19–21; A. N. Sherwin-White, *Pliny's Letters, A Social and Historical Commentary* (1966).
A. N. S.-W.

**PLOTINA,** POMPEIA (*PW*, s.v. Pompeius 131), had married Trajan (q.v.) before his accession, but never bore children. She was admired for her simplicity, dignity, fidelity, and virtue. Though she had refused the title *Augusta* in A.D. 100, she finally accepted it in 105. From 112, she was honoured on coins; in particular the type of *Vesta* emphasized the purity of her family life. She was present at Trajan's death in Cilicia in 117 and probably facilitated his adoption (probably genuine rather than pretended by her) of Hadrian (q.v.) as his successor. She had long favoured Hadrian, who later honoured her on coins of 117–18, and at her death *c.* 121/2 consecrated her. She was commemorated by at least two temples, in that of Trajan in his Forum at Rome and independently at Nîmes.

Dio Cass. bks. 68. 5, 69. 1 and 10; S.H.A. *Hadr.*; Aur. Vict. *Epit.* 42. 21; Pliny, *Pan.* 83; Wegner, *Herrscherbild* ii. 3 (1956), 74 ff., 118 ff.; Strack, *Reichsprägung* i. 41; ii. 66 ff., 115 ff.; *B.M. Coins, Rom. Emp.* iii. *See also under* TRAJAN. C. H. V. S.; M. H.

**PLOTINUS** (*Πλωτῖνος*) (A.D. 205–269/70). The main facts of his life are known from Porphyry's memoir (prefixed to editions of the *Enneads*). His birthplace, on which Porphyry is silent, is said by Eunapius and the *Suda* to have been Lyco or Lycopolis in Egypt, but his name is Roman, while his native language was almost certainly Greek. He turned to philosophy in his 28th year and worked for the next eleven years under Ammonius (q.v.) Saccas at Alexandria. In 242–3 he joined Gordian's unsuccessful expedition against Persia, hoping for an opportunity to learn something of eastern thought. The attempt was abortive, and at the age of 40 he settled in Rome as a teacher of philosophy, and remained there until his last illness, when he retired to Campania to die. At Rome he became the centre of an influential circle of intellectuals, which included men of the world and men of letters, besides professional philosophers like Amelius and Porphyry. He interested himself also in social problems, and tried to enlist the support of the Emperor Gallienus for a scheme to found a Platonic community on the site of a ruined Pythagorean settlement in Campania.

WRITINGS. Plotinus wrote nothing until he was 50. He then began to produce a series of philosophical essays arising directly out of discussions in his seminars (*συνουσίαι*), and intended primarily for circulation among his pupils. These were collected by Porphyry, who classified them roughly according to subject, arranged them rather artificially in six *Enneads* or groups of nine, and eventually published them *c.* 300–5. From this edition our manuscripts are descended. An edition by another pupil, the physician Eustochius, is known to have existed (schol. *Enn.* 4. 4. 30); and it has been argued by some scholars (Henry, *Recherches*, etc., see Bibliography) that the extracts from Plotinus in Eus. *Praep. Evang.* are derived from this Eustochian recension. Save for the omission of politics, Plotinus' essays range over the whole field of ancient philosophy: ethics and aesthetics are dealt with mainly in *Enn.* 1, physics and cosmology in *Enns.* 2 and 3; psychology in *Enn.* 4; metaphysics, logic, and epistemology in *Enns.* 5 and 6. Though not systematic in intention, the *Enneads* form in fact a more complete body of philosophical teaching than any other which has come down to

us from antiquity outside the Aristotelian corpus. Plotinus' favourite method is to raise and solve a series of *ἀπορίαι*: many of the essays give the impression of a man thinking aloud or discussing difficulties with a pupil. Owing to bad eyesight, Plotinus never revised what he wrote (Porph. *Vita Plot.* 8), and his highly individual style often reflects the irregular structure of oral statement. Its allusiveness, rapid transitions, and extreme condensation render him one of the most difficult of Greek authors; but when deeply moved he can write magnificently.

PHILOSOPHICAL DOCTRINE. In the nineteenth century Plotinus' philosophy was often dismissed as an arbitrary and illogical syncretism of Greek and oriental ideas. Recent writers, on the other hand, see in him the most powerful philosophical mind between Aristotle and Aquinas or Descartes; and in his work a logical development from earlier Greek thought, whose elements he organized in a new synthesis designed to meet the needs of a new age. These needs influenced the direction rather than the methods of his thinking: its direction is determined by the same forces which resulted in the triumph of the eastern religions of salvation, but its methods are those of traditional Greek rationalism. Plotinus attached small value to ritual, and the religious ideas of the Near East seem to have had little direct influence on the *Enneads*, though Bréhier would explain certain parallels with Indian thought by postulating contact with Indian travellers in Alexandria. To Christianity Plotinus makes no explicit reference; but *Enn.* 2. 9 is an eloquent defence of Hellenism against Gnostic superstition.

Plotinus holds that all modes of being, whether material or mental, temporal or eternal, are constituted by the expansion or 'overflow' of a single immaterial and impersonal force, which he identifies with the 'One' of the *Parmenides* and the 'Good' of the *Republic*, though it is strictly insusceptible of any predicate or description. As 'the One', it is the ground of all existence; as 'the Good', it is the source of all values. There is exact correspondence between degrees of reality and degrees of value, both being determined by the degree of unity, or approximation to the One, which any existence achieves. Reality, though at its higher levels it is nonspatial and non-temporal, may thus be pictured figuratively as a series of concentric circles resulting from the expansion of the One. Each of these circles stands in a relation of timeless dependence to that immediately within it, which is in this sense its 'cause'; the term describes a logical relationship, not an historical event. Bare Matter (*ὕλη*) is represented by the circumference of the outermost circle: it is the limiting case of reality, the last consequence of the expansion of the One, and so possesses only the ideal existence of a boundary.

Between the One and Matter lie three descending grades of reality—the World-mind (*νοῦς*), the World-soul (*ψυχή*), and Nature (*φύσις*). The descent is marked by increasing individuation and diminishing unity. The World-mind resembles Aristotle's Unmoved Mover: it is thought-thinking-itself, an eternal lucidity in which the knower and the known are distinguishable only logically; within it lie the Platonic Forms, which are conceived not as inert types or models but as a system of interrelated forces, differentiations of the one Mind which holds them together in a single timeless apprehension (*νόησις*). The dualism of subject and object, implicit in the self-intuition of Mind, is carried a stage further in the discursive thinking characteristic of Soul: because of its weaker unity, Soul must apprehend its objects successively and severally. In doing so it creates time and space; but the World-soul is itself eternal and transcends the spatio-temporal world which arises from its activity. The lowest creative principle is Nature, which corresponds to the immanent World-soul of the Stoics: its consciousness is faint and dreamlike, and the physical world is its projected dream.

Man is a microcosm, containing all these principles actually or potentially within himself. His consciousness is normally occupied with the discursive thinking proper to Soul: but he has at all times a subconscious activity on the dreamlike level of Nature and a superconscious activity on the intuitive level of Mind; and his conscious life may lapse by habituation to the former level or be lifted by an intellectual discipline to the latter. Beyond the life of Mind lies the possibility of unification (ἕνωσις), an experience in which the Self by achieving complete inward unity is momentarily identified with the supreme unity of the One. This is the Plotinian doctrine of ecstasy. The essays in which he expounds it, on the basis of personal experience, show extraordinary introspective power and are among the classics of mysticism. It should be observed that for Plotinus unification is independent of divine grace; is attainable very rarely, as the result of a prolonged effort of the will and understanding; and is not properly a mode of cognition, so that no inference can be based on it.

Plotinus also made important contributions to psychology, particularly in his discussion of problems of perception, consciousness, and memory; and to aesthetic, where for Plato's doctrine that Art 'imitates' natural objects he substitutes the view that Art and Nature alike impose a structure on Matter in accordance with an inward vision of archetypal Forms. His most original work in ethics is concerned with the question of the nature and origin of evil, which in some passages he attempts to solve by treating evil as the limiting case of good, and correlating it with Matter, the limiting case of reality.

TEXT. P. Henry and H.-R. Schwyzer, editio major (1951– ); editio minor, O.C.T. (1964– ). Pending completion of this critical edition *Enn.* 6 must still be read in Bréhier's text (Budé, 1924–38).
TRANSLATIONS. English, S. MacKenna and B. S. Page³ (1962); selections, A. H. Armstrong (1953). German, R. Harder (1930–7); revised edition with Greek text, 1956– . Italian, V. Cilento (1947–9).
COMMENTARY. R. Harder, R. Beutler, and W. Theiler (1956– ).
MSS. AND HISTORY OF TEXT. P. Henry, *Recherches sur la 'Préparation Évangélique' d'Eusèbe et l'édition perdue des œuvres de P. publiée par Eustochius* (1935); *Les États du texte de P.* (1938); *Les Manuscrits des Ennéades* (1941).
PHILOSOPHY. (*a*) General: E. Bréhier, *La Philosophie de P.²* (1945); W. R. Inge, *The Philosophy of P.³* (1929); M. de Gandillac, *La Sagesse de P.* (1952); P. Hadot, *P. ou la simplicité du regard* (1963). Schwyzer in *PW* s.v. is especially valuable.
(*b*) Special problems: R. Arnou, *Le Désir de Dieu dans la philosophie de P.* (1921); E. Schröder, *P.'s Abhandlung Πόθεν τὰ κακά;* (1916); C. Schmidt, *P.'s Stellung zum Gnosticismus und kirchlichen Christentum* (1901); A. H. Armstrong, *The Architecture of the Intelligible Universe in the Philosophy of P.* (1940); J. Trouillard, *La Purification plotinienne* and *La Procession plotinienne* (1955).
See also bibliography to NEOPLATONISM, and B. Marien, *Bibliografia degli studi plotiniani* (1949).     E. R. D.

**PLOTIUS TUCCA**, a friend of Virgil (*Catal.* 1) and Horace (*Sat.* 1. 5. 40) and a member of Maecenas' literary circle. He assisted Varius (q.v. 2) Rufus as literary executor to Virgil, whose initial instructions to burn the *Aeneid* were rejected, the poem being published at Augustus' command without additions after merely superficial revision (Donat. *Vita Verg.* 39; Serv. *Praef.* 2. 12 Th.).     G. C. W.

**PLOUGHING** is designed (1) to aerate the soil, and to provide crops with a suitable seed-bed: (2) to enable moisture to penetrate the surface. Ploughs vary greatly. The asymmetrical mouldboard ploughs, which cut a slice of earth, invert it in the furrow, and throw it to one side, are post-classical. All classical ploughs belong to the family of *ards*, which are symmetrical in design, and throw up the earth on either side of the furrow.

Hesiod's 'built' plough (*Op.* 427 ff.) is a *sole-ard* (Fr. *araire dental*), which comprises three distinct parts: (1) the

sole or share-beam (ἔλυμα, *dentale*), a horizontal beam shaped to a point, over which could be drawn a share, usually of iron (ὕννις, *vomis*); (2) the plough-beam (γύης, *bura, buris*), a curved pole of strong timber, one end of which was mortised into the front portion of the share-beam, the other end being connected with the pole (ἱστοβοεύς, *temo*), by means of a pegged joint; to the other end of the pole, which is often represented as continuous with the plough-beam, was attached the yoke (ζυγόν, *iugum*); (3) the stilt or ploughtail (ἐχέτλη, *stiva*), a straight piece of wood, mortised into the rear portion of the share-beam, and usually set vertically and at right angles with it. This type of plough, well suited to breaking and stirring the surface of light soils, is still in use in many parts of the Mediterranean region. The operation, which is perfectly illustrated on a well known black-figured *kylix* of the sixth century, now in the Louvre (see Dar.-Sag. s.v. *Rustica Res*, fig. 5968), is quite simple: a pair of oxen, yoked to the pole, draws the share-beam steadily through the ground, the strain being taken by the strong curved plough-beam, while the ploughman keeps the implement on an even keel by pressing down on the handle (Columella, *Rust.* 1. 9. 3) or, if necessary, on the share-beam with his foot. The only surviving description of a Roman plough, that given by Virgil (*G.* 1. 169 ff.), is unfortunately vague. It may be a variety of the beam-ard, a type designed for heavy soils, and common in ancient Scandinavia, but the references to ploughing methods in the Roman agricultural writers presuppose a sole-ard of the type described above. Several ploughings of the fallow between crops were required to retain vital moisture, to keep down weeds, and to provide a suitable seed-bed. The removable ploughshares were of varying sizes and weights to suit different conditions, ranging from mere tips (Columella, *Rust.* 2. 2. 25) to long 'sleeves' covering the entire share-beam (Pliny, *HN* 18. 171). The result of these ploughings and cross-ploughings was a smooth even surface, needing little or no harrowing (Columella, *Rust.* 2. 4. 2). To prepare ridges for sowing on, or to cover the seed, detachable wooden boards (Virgil's *aures* (loc. cit.), Varro's *tabellae* (*Rust.* 1. 29. 2)) were employed. Palladius' *aratrum auritum* (*Rust.* 1. 43. 1) evidently had fixed ridging-boards. Ploughs equipped with a wheeled fore-carriage to enable heavier soil to be worked more easily are mentioned by Pliny (loc. cit.) as a recent innovation in what is now Switzerland: Virgil's *currus* (*G.* 1. 174) is, however, a poetic reference to the whole implement, not to a wheeled plough.

*PW*, s.v. Pflug; H. Behlen, *Der Pflug und das Pflügen* (1904); A. S. F. Gow, *JHS* 1914, 249 ff.; A. G. Haudricourt and M. J.-B. Delamarre, *L'Homme et la charrue à travers les âges³* (1955), 92 ff.; 144 ff.; E. M. Jope, in *A History of Technology*, ed. C. Singer, ii (1958), 83 ff.; K. D. White, *Agricultural Implements of the Roman World* (1967); W. H. Manning, 'The Plough in Roman Britain', *JRS* 1964, 54 ff. For a different view of Virgil's plough see R. Aitken, *JRS* 1956, 97 ff.     K. D. W.

**PLUTARCH** (L. (?) MESTRIUS PLUTARCHUS) of Chaeronea; born before A.D. 50, died after A.D. 120; philosopher and biographer. The family had long been established in Chaeronea, and most of Plutarch's life was spent in his home town, to which he was devoted. He knew Athens well, and visited both Egypt and Italy, lecturing and teaching at Rome. His father, Autobulus, his grandfather, Lamprias, and other members of his family figure often in his works; his wide circle of influential friends included the consulars L. Mestrius Florus, whose gentile name he took, Q. Sosius (q.v. 2) Senecio, to whom the *Parallel Lives* and other works are dedicated, and C. Minicius Fundanus, as well as Greek men of letters like Favorinus (q.v.) and magnates like the exiled Syrian prince Antiochus Philopappus (see COMMAGENE). For the last thirty years of his life, Plutarch was a priest at Delphi. A devout believer in its ancient pieties and a profound student of its antiquities, he played a notable part in the revival of the shrine in Trajanic and Hadrianic times. A late and uncertain story (*Suda*, Eusebius) tells us that Trajan and Hadrian gave Plutarch some office (procuratorship?) in Achaea; whatever exactly lies behind this, he was a man of some influence in governing circles, as he was in his writings an active exponent of the concept of a partner-ship between Greece, the educator, and Rome, the great power and of the compatibility of the two patriotisms.

The 'Catalogue of Lamprias' (an ancient list of works attributed to Plutarch) contains 227 items. Extant are seventy-eight miscellaneous works (including some not in the 'catalogue') and fifty biographies. Among the collections of minor works made in medieval times was one of 'moral pieces' ('Ηθικά, *Moralia*), and this name is now used to cover everything apart from the *Lives*. Plutarch was clearly very prolific in late middle age, but no convincing account of his literary development has been given. In the following list of the most important works, the conventional Latin titles are used: for a com-plete list of titles (Greek and Latin), see (e.g.) any volume of the Loeb *Moralia*.

(i) The group of *rhetorical* works—a sophist's *epideixeis* and declamations—includes *de gloria Atheniensium, de fortuna Romanorum* and (slighter) *de Alexandri fortuna aut virtute* and *aquane an ignis sit utilior*. Plutarch's richly metaphorical and grandly periodic style contrasts with Dio Chrysostom's elegance and clarity and the ingenuity of later sophists; it is a reasonable conjecture that he did not have much success as a rhetorical performer, and that most of these productions belong to an early stage of his career.

(ii) The numerous short treatises on themes of popular *moral philosophy* are derivative in content (Plato, Aristotle, Stoics, Epicureans, 'diatribe') but homogeneous and characteristic in style. Noteworthy examples are *de virtute morali* (Aristotelian, anti-Stoic), *de profectibus in virtute, de superstitione* (piety the mean between super-stition and atheism), *de cohibenda ira, de curiositate, de garrulitate, de tranquillitate animi, de vitioso pudore*. In *praecepta gerendae rei publicae* Plutarch draws both on his historical reading and on his own experience to give advice to a young man entering politics. The warm and sympathetic personality never far beneath the surface appears particularly in *coniugalia praecepta* and *con-solatio ad uxorem* (to his wife on the death of their infant daughter).

(iii) Plutarch used the *dialogue* form extensively and ambitiously. *De sollertia animalium* is a simple school debate—'are water-animals more intelligent than land-animals?'—and the nine books of *quaestiones convivales* are in the same vein of learned table-talk as A. Gellius. *De genio Socratis* is quite different: exciting narrative (liberation of Thebes) combined with philosophical conversation about μαντική, and an elaborate Platonic myth of the fate of the soul after death (for this feature, cf. *de sera numinis vindicta* and *de facie in orbe lunae*). *Amatorius* similarly makes a contemporary love-story the background to a discussion of ἔρως. The Pythian dialogues (*de E apud Delphos, de Pythiae oraculis, de defectu oracu-lorum*; with these should be coupled *de sera numinis vindicta*) have Delphi as their scene, and divination, *daimones*, and divine providence as their subjects. These major dialogues (together with the treatise *de Iside et Osiride*) contain the greater part of Plutarch's philo-sophical and religious speculation, rightly regarded by recent scholarship as the most significant part of his many-sided activity.

(iv) *Technical philosophy*—Plutarch was a Platonist—is represented both by interpretations of Plato (*quaestiones Platonicae, de animae procreatione in Timaeo*) and by

polemical treatises against Stoics (e.g. *de communibus notitiis*) and Epicureans (e.g. *adversus Colotem*).

(v) We possess also important *antiquarian* works (*Quaestiones Graecae, Quaestiones Romanae*: a mine of information about religious antiquities) and some on *literary themes* (*de malignitate Herodoti, comparatio Aristophanis et Menandri, de audiendis poetis*).

(vi) Among the *spuria* which have infiltrated the Plutar-chean corpus, several are of historical importance: *de pueris educandis*, influential in the Renaissance; *Consola-tio ad Apollonium* (see CONSOLATIO); *de fato* (ed. E. Val-giglio, 1964), valuable as a document of Middle Platonism; *vitae X oratorum; placita philosophorum* (see Diels, *Dox. Graec.*); and *de musica* (ed. F. Lasserre, 1954), one of the principal sources of our knowledge of the history of Greek music and lyric poetry.

(vii) Finally, the *Lives*. Of the Caesars, only *Galba* and *Otho* survive; of 'parallel Lives' we have twenty-three pairs, nineteen of them with comparisons (συγκρίσεις) attached. Plutarch clearly distinguished writing βίοι from writing history (*Alexander* 1); his object was to exemplify private virtue (and sometimes vice) in the careers of great men; hence his careful treatment of the education and ἦθος of his heroes, the space given to significant anec-dotes, and the frequent omissions and distortions in the historical narrative. Although Plutarch naturally owed much to earlier biographers as well as historians, his work has a scope and form all its own. Much depends on the sources available to him (e.g. *Alcibiades* is full of attested personal detail, *Publicola* is thin and padded out, *Phocion* and *Cato Maior* are unusually apophthegmatic), but the general pattern (family, education, début, climaxes, μεταβολαί of fortune) is maintained wherever possible. Tantalizing and treacherous to the historian, Plutarch has won the affection of the many generations to whom he has been a main source of understanding of the ancient world by his unerring choice of detail, his vivid and memorable narrative, and his flexible and controlled style, varying in complexity and richness between the reflective passages (which are like the *Moralia*) and the narrative, variously coloured as it is by his various sources.

*Influence*. Plutarch was a popular educational writer in medieval times, and the preservation of so many of his works is due to the efforts of Byzantine scholars (espe-cially Maximus Planudes (*see* ANTHOLOGY, § 5)) to collect them; his influence on the Renaissance, however, was far greater. In France, it dates from Amyot's translation (*Lives* 1559, *Moralia* 1572); in England from Sir T. North's version of Amyot's *Lives* (1579) and Philemon Holland's *Moralia* (1603). Montaigne, Shakespeare, Dryden, Rousseau are among Plutarch's debtors; the *Lives* (especially *Dion, Brutus, Timoleon*) made their contribution to the intellectual climate of revolutionary France. Since 1800, his influence has receded; his lack of historical perspective and his unsophisticated moral attitudes have not recommended him to an age suspicious of anything like *naïveté* in history or morals. He remains a writer of great charm, a mine of information, and a significant figure in the intellectual history of the first century A.D.

See Bursian *Jahresb.* 1921, 1936.
GENERAL WORKS. R. Volkmann, *Leben, Schriften und Philosophie des P.'s von Chaeronea* (1869); R. C. Trench, *Plutarch* (1873); R. Hirzel, *P.* (1912); R. H. Barrow, *Plutarch and his Times* (1967).
TEXTS. D. Wyttenbach (1795–1830), with commentary on part of *Moralia* and Lexicon Plutarcheum (not yet replaced); F. Duebner (Didot, 1846 and later), valuable for Index Rerum. *Moralia*, H. Wegehaupt and others (Teubner, 1925– , now nearly complete; vol. vii, *Fragmenta*, by F. H. Sandbach, 1967; F. C. Babbitt and others (Loeb, 1922– , also nearly complete, recent vols.—vii, ix, xi, xii—particularly valuable). *Vitae*, K. Ziegler and others (Teubner, 1914–35, revision in progress); B. Perrin (Loeb, 1914–26); R. Flace-lière (Budé, 1957– , in progress, important).
SEPARATE WORKS. *Convivium VII Sapientium*, J. Defradas (1954); *Quaestiones Romanae* (trans. and comm.), H. J. Rose (1924);

*Quaestiones Graecae* (trans. and comm.), W. R. Halliday (1928); *de Iside et Osiride*, Th. Hopfner, 1940–1 (incomplete); *de E apud Delphos, de Pythiae oraculis, de defectu oraculorum,* R. Flacelière (1941, 1937 (1962 in *Collection Erasme*), 1947); *de sera numinis vindicta,* G. Méautis (1935); *de tranquillitate animi,* H. Broecker, 1954 (comm. only); *Amatorius,* R. Flacelière (1953); *de facie in orbe lunae,* P. Raingeard (1935, see H. Cherniss, Loeb vol. xii); *adversus Colotem,* see R. Westman, *Acta Philosophica Fennica* 1955. Lives: *Sulla, Nicias, Gracchi, Pericles, Demosthenes, Timoleon, Themistocles,* H. A. Holden (1885–94: useful word indexes); *Aratus* and *Dion,* W. H. Porter (1937, 1940); *Galba* and *Otho,* E. G. Hardy (1890); *Caesar,* A. Garzetti (1954); *Demetrius,* E. Manni (1953); *Cicero,* D. Magnino (1963); *Aristides,* I. C. Limentani (1964); *Gracchi,* E. Valgiglio (1963); *Alexander,* J. R. Hamilton (1968).

TRANSLATIONS. Selection from Philemon Holland in Dent's Everyman Library, which also contains 'Dryden's' Lives; two-volume selection from *Moralia* by T. G. Tucker and A. O. Prickard (1913–18); North often reprinted, esp. parts relevant to Shakespeare (T. J. B. Spencer, *Shakespeare's Plutarch,* 1964).

OTHER BOOKS. W. C. Helmbold–E. N. O'Neil, *Plutarch's Quotations* (1959); C. Stolz, *Zur relativen Chronologie der Parallelbiographien* (1929); N. Barbu, *Les Procédés de la peinture des caractères... dans les biographies de P.* (1934); W. Graf Uxkull-Gyllenband, *P. und die griechische Biographie* (1927); A. W. Gomme, *Commentary on Thucydides* i (1944), 54 ff.; O. Gréard, *La Morale de Plutarque* (1866); R. Hirzel, *Der Dialog* ii (1895); R. M. Jones, *The Platonism of Plutarch* (1916); B. Latzarus, *Les Idées religieuses de Plutarque* (1920); G. Soury, *La Démonologie de Plutarque* (1942); J. P. Mahaffy, *The Silver Age of the Greek World* (1906), 339 ff. See also BIOGRAPHY (GREEK).                                             D. A. R.

**PLUTUS** (Πλοῦτος), Wealth, originally and properly abundance of crops, hence associated with Demeter (q.v.) at Eleusis (see Deubner, *Attische Feste* (1932), 85 f.); he is son of Demeter (q.v.) and Iasion (Hes. *Theog.* 969 ff.). He is thus closely connected in idea with Pluton (cf. HADES), and presumably with the nymph Pluto, mother of Tantalus. Cf. Hesychius s.vv. εὔπλουτον, πλοῦτος. Demeter and Kore send him to those whom they favour (*Hymn. Hom. Cer.* 486 ff.). He appears mostly as a figure in popular, not merely literary, tradition, see especially the *Eiresione* (Ps.-Hdt. *Vit. Hom.* 465), in which he comes with Mirth and Peace to the house which the bearers of the *eiresione* visit. In art he is shown with Demeter in more than one connexion. He is consigned to Tartarus by Timocreon (fr. 5 Diehl), because his blindness makes so much trouble. Aristophanes' *Plutus* takes up this theme, which may very well have been a popular proverb, and describes the curing of his blindness, after which, knowing where he goes, he visits honest men only. Here he is wealth in general, not only agricultural prosperity. *See* EIRENE.

Nilsson, *GGR* i². 421 ff.                                   H. J. R.

**POETELIUS** (*PW* 7) **LIBO VISOLUS,** GAIUS, was consul in 360, 346 and 326 B.C. In 326 he is reputed, with his fellow consul L. Papirius, to have carried a law during the troubled period of the Second Samnite War, as a measure of social appeasement. It prohibited imprisonment for debt, and enacted that loans should henceforward be based on the security of the borrower's property, not on his personal liberty. If the right of personal execution was not abolished until much later in spite of the *Lex Poetelia de nexis,* at least it was mitigated and made dependent on judgement. Varro (*Ling.* 7. 105) placed the Lex Poetelia in 313, when a son of Poetelius was dictator.                                        P. T.

**POETOVIO,** modern *Ptuj* on the Drave, was a Roman military station and city in Pannonia. From Augustus until A.D. 43–5 it was occupied by Legio VIII Augusta, followed by XIII Gemina which remained until 98. In place of the legion Trajan established a *colonia* (*Ulpia Traiana Poetovio*) of legionary veterans, probably the last settlement of this type made in the Empire. J. J. W.

**POLA,** at the southern end of the Istrian peninsula in the northern Adriatic, has always owed its importance to its fine land-locked harbour. This ancient town was probably founded by Illyrians, certainly not by Colchians in pursuit of Argonauts (reject Strabo 1. 46; 5. 215). Presumably it came under the Romans' control when they conquered the head of the Adriatic (178 B.C.: Livy 41. 13). Destroyed in the Civil Wars, Pola was rebuilt by Augustus as the colony *Pietas Iulia* and became a flourishing town whose magnificent Antonine amphitheatre still survives (Pliny, *HN* 3. 129).

A. Degrassi, *Scritti Vari* (1962), 2. 913 ff.            E. T. S.

**POLEMARCHOS** (πολέμαρχος) in Athens was one of the nine *archontes* (q.v.), appointed annually. The name indicates that his original duty was to command the army; presumably the office was created to take over this function from the king. The *polemarchos* Callimachus seems to have been the Athenian commander-in-chief at Marathon (though the account in Hdt. 6 is obscure, and its interpretation has been disputed), but after 487/6 B.C., when the *archontes* began to be appointed by lot, it could not be expected that every *polemarchos* would make a competent military commander, and so this function was handed over to the *strategoi* (q.v.).

The other functions of the *polemarchos* were mainly religious and legal. He conducted certain sacrifices, and he arranged the funeral ceremony for men killed in war (*see* EPITAPHIOS). His legal functions concerned cases involving persons who were not Athenian citizens: in some types of case he was the magistrate responsible for the trial (*see* DIKASTERION), and in other cases he had duties in connexion with arbitration and bail.

Arist. *Ath. Pol.* 58.                                       D. M. M.

**POLEMON** (1, *PW* 2) **I** of Pontus was the son of a wealthy rhetorician, Zeno of Laodicea. With his father he won Roman favour and probably Roman citizenship by defending his city against the Parthians in 40–39 B.C. Antony first made him ruler of Lycaonia and part of Cilicia Tracheia (38), then when he gave Tracheia to Cleopatra (37/6) compensated him with Pontus and later with Lesser Armenia. He accompanied Antony's Parthian expedition, was captured, and held to ransom (36). After Actium Augustus confirmed his title but withdrew Lesser Armenia from him. In 15 B.C. Agrippa awarded him the Bosporan kingdom and assisted him to occupy it. He was killed by Bosporan rebels in 8 B.C. His widow, Pythodoris, succeeded him in Pontus.

Strabo 12. 499, 556, 559. Magie, *Rom. Rule Asia Min.,* see index.
T. R. S. B.

**POLEMON** (2) of Athens, head of the Academy from the death of Xenocrates (314–313 B.C.), who converted him from a dissolute life and whose zealous follower he was, to his own death in 270, when he was succeeded by his pupil Crates. He seems to have been impressive by his force of character, but nothing is known of any original contribution by him to philosophy, and Diogenes Laertius 4. 17 says he attached more importance to conduct than to dialectic.

Zeller, *Phil. d. Griechen* ii. 1⁴. 993 f.; K. von Fritz, *PW* xxi. 2. 2524 ff.
W. D. R.

**POLEMON** (3), a Greek of Ilium (fl. *c.* 190 B.C.), Stoic geographer who collected geographical, epigraphic, and artistic material in Greece, published in Περὶ τῶν κατὰ πόλεις ἐπιγραμμάτων, including especially dedications and monuments at Delphi, Sparta, Athens. In another work Polemon attacked Eratosthenes (Ath. 6. 234 d; 10. 436 d; 442 e etc.).

*FHG* iii. 108–48.                                          E. H. W.

**POLEMON** (4, *PW* 10), MARCUS ANTONIUS, *c.* A.D. 88–144, born at Laodicea in Caria but a citizen and benefactor of Smyrna, was a prominent sophist who enjoyed the friendship of Trajan, Hadrian, and Antoninus.

It was he who was chosen to deliver an oration at the inauguration of Hadrian's Olympieion at Athens (A.D. 130). His oratory was in the grand manner, his delivery passionate and excited. Extant are two short declamations, in which the fathers of two Marathon heroes, Callimachus and Cynegirus, present their sons' claims for the prize of valour. Besides his speeches, he wrote history and on physiognomy (see PHYSIOGNOMONICI).

Philostr. *VS* 1. 25; extant declamations ed. H. Hinck, 1873; see also A. Boulanger, *Aelius Aristide* (1923), 87 ff.; W. Schmid, *Der Atticismus* i (1887), 46 ff.; H. Jüttner, *De Polemonis rhetoris vita operibus arte* (Breslau, 1898, repr. 1967); G. W. Bowersock, *Greek Sophists in the Roman Empire* (1969), see index.　　　D. A. R.

**POLETAI** (πωληταί), or 'sellers', were Athenian officials. The date of their institution is not known, but they already existed in the time of Solon. In Aristotle's time there were ten, appointed annually by lot from the ten *phylai* (q.v.). They conducted the selling or letting of property belonging to the State, including not only land and buildings, but also non-citizens enslaved as a penalty, and goods confiscated from convicted offenders. They also let rights to work mines, to collect taxes, and the like. The method generally used was an auction held in the presence of the *boule* (q.v.). The *poletai* then made out lists of the payments due from purchasers and tenants, for the use of the *apodektai* (q.v.).

Arist. *Ath. Pol.* 7. 3, 47. 2–3.　　　D. M. M.

**POLICE.** The ancient city-state never developed a proper police system. Athens in the fifth century had a corps of Scythian archers (public slaves), probably more decorative than useful, except for keeping order in law-courts and assemblies. (This task was later taken over by ephebes.) Ἀστυνόμοι, whose assortment of duties included what we might call police action, are found in Athens and elsewhere. Secret police (the notorious κρυπτεία) are recorded in Sparta, but only for use against the helots.

We have little information about Hellenistic police outside Egypt. The army of the king could suppress brigandage, and the royal garrison commander or governor (where there was one) could call on troops to restore order and enforce his own judgements and those of the city courts, and so often developed judicial and police powers. Rudimentary city police forces (φυλακῖται of various sorts and perhaps also mounted men) appear sporadically, but are chiefly attested in the Roman period. It is only in the second century A.D. that we regularly find an *eirenarch* (a LITURGY, q.v.), in command of small local forces. Secret police had been freely used in the Persian Empire and were probably available to Hellenistic kings.

In Ptolemaic Egypt there were regular forces of native φυλακῖται, given *kleroi* and commanded by officers (usually Greeks). There was a desert patrol and Alexandria (at least) had a Head of the Night Watch. (In the *metropoleis* he and his force are not attested till well into the Roman era.) Under the Roman Empire, *stationes* of Roman soldiers, as elsewhere, came to play a major part in keeping public order.

In the Roman Republic every magistrate had *coercitio* (q.v.), to enforce obedience through his attendants. Consuls and praetors had *imperium* and lictors (q.v.); but this, in classical times, gave little additional power over citizens, especially in Rome. Roman soldiers kept down brigandage in Italy and the provinces; but they could not be used in the city (except perhaps under a 'senatus consultum ultimum', q.v.): there only the aediles and the *tresviri capitales* (see TRIUMVIRI), with their small personal staffs, were normally available for keeping order. Rome at night was not a safe place; and it was perhaps not only for display that important people never went out without

a crowd of slaves and clients. In the late Republic, armed gangs, used by *populares* for political purposes, were difficult to suppress except—as Milo and Sestius finally did against Clodius (qq.v.)—by arming other gangs against them. When Pompey was asked to move troops in (52), this was a bold step, disapproved of (e.g.) by Cicero.

Augustus made the first serious attempt to arrange for a force to keep order: this became possible only after the loss of *libertas*. It was and remained part of the duties of the *vigiles* (q.v.). Later, the *praefectus urbi* (q.v.)—regularly appointed after Augustus—had wide powers over the lower classes in Rome and much of Italy. He could call on the three (later nine) *cohortes urbanae* (q.v.) of 1,000 men each, and in emergencies on the *vigiles* (q.v.) as well. In major riots in the city the Praetorian Guard was availble for decisive action; but it was sparingly used. All these forces were dissolved in the fourth century.

Urban cohorts were for a time stationed at Ostia and Puteoli; later they were succeeded by *vigiles*. One urban cohort was stationed at Lugdunum by Augustus and a cohort of this type remained there until Septimius Severus. Vespasian also placed an urban cohort at Carthage, and it seems to have been called on for police duties in many parts of the African provinces. But no such cohorts appear in other provincial cities. Centurions or *beneficiarii* (q.v.) with detachments could be sent to cities to keep order, or perhaps stationed (often reluctantly) in important places. In some (e.g. Utica) even praetorians are found. In times of political trouble, these forces often got out of hand. Local police is rarely mentioned in the Western provinces. In the country, the army was generally used for keeping order, and particularly for keeping the main roads clear: *stationes* of legionary detachments, under *beneficiarii* or centurions, were set up at key points along roads, acting as a kind of *gendarmerie*. *Beneficiarii* were particularly convenient to use for police duties in the widest sense, from secret police activities to keeping records of known undesirables. Brigandage remained a constant challenge, especially in the wilder parts, away from main roads; and in the third century it began to gain the upper hand. By then the *stationarii* were probably too busy exacting taxes from reluctant provincials—which, even in the second century, had proved an (originally) unexpected use for them.

In Italy, particularly, the *stationes* came to be taken over by *frumentarii*—a special corps that, at least from the early second century, concealed police duties (including secret ones) under its innocent name, combining them with courier duties in the postal service (q.v.). Dreaded for their abuse of their irresponsible power, they were abolished by Diocletian (q.v.), but soon reappeared under the equally harmless name of *agentes in rebus* (q.v.), and acquired more power than ever. From the third century, Italian *stationes* also were manned by legionaries.

O. Hirschfeld, *Kl. Schr.* (1913), 576 ff.; E. Echols, *CJ* 1957/8, 377 ff., 1961/2, 25 ff.; R. MacMullen, *Soldier and Civilian in the Later Roman Empire* (1963), 50 ff.; *Enemies of the Roman Order* (1967), 163 ff.　　　E. B.

**POLIS** (πόλις), the Greek city-state. Its origin reaches back to the times of Homer and Hesiod, when the old monarchy was disappearing. The Polis arose as an anti-monarchic State, and it remained so, in spite of tyranny (q.v.). It was a State of small size, there being several reasons for political particularism in the Greek world—firstly, the natural division of the country into many separate districts, islands, peninsulas, etc.; further, the division of the Greek people into many larger or smaller tribes, and accordingly of the Greek religion into numerous local cults. Several hundreds of city-states existed, most of them extremely small, many of them colonies founded by mother cities. It seems almost impossible (and this not only for lack of information) to write a general history of all these States. We can only describe the most characteristic features of the type which was to become the Greek State *par excellence*.

The territory of a Polis (in contrast with the 'ethnos', or tribal State) included both town and country (hinterland). There always was only one town, mostly walled round, with the citadel, the original πόλις (later: 'acropolis'), and the agora or market-place. The citizens resided alike in town and country, but the government of the State was entirely concentrated in the town. Membership of the citizen body would depend upon the constitution of each Polis, but in every case the Polis was identical with the totality of its citizens. Therefore the name of the State was taken from the citizens, not from the town or territory: οἱ Ἀθηναῖοι etc.; "ἄνδρες γὰρ πόλις", says Thucydides (7. 77. 7). The citizens were a ruling class, not only in aristocracies and oligarchies (qq.v.), but even in democracies (q.v.); for class differences were never entirely removed; moreover, besides the slaves there always was a population not belonging to the State, e.g. dependent lower classes, resident strangers (metics), inhabitants of surrounding districts (*perioeci*), etc. Even in citizenship (q.v.) there were different degrees, and for a long time the internal development of the Polis was a struggle, especially among oligarchs and democrats, for equality in citizenship and political rights, as well as in social and economic conditions. Civil war (στάσις) was all too frequent, and concord (ὁμόνοια) an ideal rarely achieved.

The State consisted of its citizens, considered less as individuals than as forming smaller communities of kinship, of cult, of locality. Each individual was tied to the life of these communities and of the State. Moreover, the State was not only a political community. To be a citizen meant adherence to the cults of the gods of the Polis, as well as military and economic service to the State, and obedience to its laws. The perfect Greek citizen was Aristotle's ζῷον πολιτικόν, at the same time attached to his Polis, and a free man.

Liberty, autonomy, autarky were the ideals of the Polis, and its chief claim was to be ruled by law (*nomos*). In actual fact government remained a question of power, but the sacred 'nomos' always directed and regulated actual politics. Government was carried on mainly by three institutions: Assembly, Council, magistracies, all derived from earlier times. Each of these preponderated according to the various types of constitution. The Council held the chief political power in aristocracy and oligarchy, the Assembly in democracy. Jurisdiction was performed partly by the Council, partly by special officials, the final court being mostly the people, i.e. the Assembly. In democracies the dicasteries (q.v.) gathered almost all jurisdiction into their hands.

Remembering always that it is wrong to generalize from the institutions of any single Polis, all of which differed in many ways, we may consider the Athenian democracy as having reached (and gone beyond) the highest standard of a Polis; its organization strongly influenced other States. In fifth- and fourth-century Athens democracy as the rule of the people became a reality. The Assembly, although in fact consisting of only part of the people, especially those living in town, was open to any citizen, and was the true sovereign (τὸ κύριον). All foreign policy, all military and naval questions, all legislation, and the control of all executive officials were treated and decided by the Assembly. Its functions and its power were really unlimited. But all matters presented to the Assembly were prepared by a *probouleuma* of the Council. Therefore the decrees (ψηφίσματα) were finally

resolved by Council and people in common (ἔδοξε τῇ βουλῇ καὶ τῷ δήμῳ). But the Assembly could always reject, add, or amend. In addition to its main task of *probouleusis* the Council collaborated authoritatively with the magistracies and controlled public finance. The councillors were elected by lot and not allowed to be re-elected more than once. Thus the majority of those citizens who attended the Assembly were councillors once in their life. The Council formed a committee of the people, its membership changing yearly. It was not a restraining power, as the Areopagus formerly used to be. The magistracies had to execute the people's decrees, but some rights of initiative and command were given to the higher of them. There was no real political power connected with any magistracy, although some of them carried a certain measure of influence.

The great number of independent and self-centred States was the chief reason for the endless wars between the Greek States, and for the weakness of any form of Panhellenism. Attempts at creating either the hegemony of one Polis over another as in the Athenian Empire, or federations of several States, never succeeded in overcoming the ultimate isolation of each Polis. If trade helped to break this isolation, the only real bond was that of common religion, language, and civilization.

The Polis lost its power and function of leadership in Greek politics partly through the corruption of democracy, but more so through the overwhelming power of Alexander's empire and the Hellenistic monarchies. However, it did not vanish, nor even cease to appear politically autonomous. There were still political and economic struggles between the parties of the Polis, and oligarchy was often renewed. Some of the city-states remained centres of cultural or economic life, and in the monarchies of Asia newly founded cities, many of them originally military colonies, became the agents of hellenization of the East. The Hellenistic age owed much of its intellectual life to the traditions of the Polis, not least to the part it played in Greek philosophy. In the fourth century, when the Polis began to decline, Plato designed his immortal picture of the ideal State, and Aristotle created political science. For both of them political theory was theory of the Polis, and even the Stoics considered the world as the unity of 'cosmo-polis'.

G. Glotz, *The Greek City* (1929); A. H. M. Jones, *The Greek City from Alexander to Justinian* (1940); V. Ehrenberg, *JHS* 1937, 147 ff.; *The Greek State* (1960); W. G. Forrest, *The Emergence of Greek Democracy* (1966).                              V. E.

**POLITES,** in mythology, son of Priam (q.v.) by Hecuba (q.v.), a swift runner and consequently employed as a scout (*Iliad* 2. 791 ff., cf. 24. 250). He takes a minor part in the fighting (13. 533; 15. 339). In Verg. *Aen.* 2. 526 ff. he is killed by Neoptolemus (q.v. 1); cf. Quint. Smyrn. 13. 214; source unknown.                              H. J. R.

**POLLIO,** GAIUS ASINIUS (*PW* 25) (76 B.C.–A.D. 4), supported Caesar, as praetor in 45, commanding in Spain in 44, and then joined Antony; in Cisalpine Gaul in 41 he saved Virgil's property from confiscation. Consul in 40, he celebrated a triumph over the Parthini of Illyria in 39; from the booty he built the first public library in Rome. Then, with full honours, he retired from politics to devote himself to literature, organizing the first public recitations.

In youth an associate of Catullus, he later enjoyed the friendship of Horace (*Carm.* 2. 1) and Virgil (*Ecl.* 4). His own work included poetry, tragedy, and oratory in Atticist style, but he was above all an historian. The *Historiae* treated the period from 60 B.C. to the battle of Philippi in 42, analytical, critical, and serious; they were used by Plutarch and Appian. A sharp critic, he corrected Cicero and Caesar, Sallust for archaism, and Livy for provincialism (*Patavinitas*); and he maintained his republican independence even against Augustus.

J. André, *La Vie et l'œuvre d'Asinius Pollio* (1949); E. Gabba, *Appiano* (1956); Syme, *Tacitus*, 136, 569 ff.                    A. H. McD.

**POLLUX,** JULIUS, of Naucratis (2nd c. A.D.), scholar and rhetorician. His *Onomasticon* was composed in the lifetime of Commodus, to whom are addressed epistles prefixed to each of its ten books: that introducing book 8 indicates that the author's appointment to a Chair of rhetoric at Athens (not before A.D. 178) preceded the completion of the work. In books 8–10 he replies to Phrynichus' criticism of points in 1–7. As an example of Atticism and other profitable vices of the age he comes under Lucian's lash in '*Ρητόρων Διδάσκαλος*: cf. ch. 24— *οὐκέτι Ποθεινὸς ὀνομάζομαι ἀλλ' ἤδη τοῖς Διὸς καὶ Λήδας παισὶν ὁμώνυμος γεγένημαι*. Like his other works, the *Onomasticon* in its original form has perished: the extant manuscripts from which it is now known are derived from four incomplete, abridged, and interpolated copies from an early epitome possessed (and interpolated) by Arethas, archbishop of Caesarea, *c.* A.D. 900. The arrangement is topical, not alphabetical. The work partly resembles a rhetorical handbook, e.g. in its collections of synonyms and of subject-vocabularies, in collections of compounds (*ὁμο*- and some others), in the fifty-two terms for use in praising a king, or the thirty-three terms of abuse to apply to a tax-collector. The story of Heracles' discovery of purple is added expressly as a light relief for the student. Wider philological and encyclopedic interests appear in the citations from literature and in the treatment of music and the theatre. Besides these, his subjects include religion, private and public law, human anatomy and ethics, war, the sciences, arts, crafts and trades, houses, ships, husbandry, cookery, children's games, and a host of other matters. The sections on stage antiquities (book 4) and on the Athenian constitution (book 8) are of especial interest to scholars. But the work is predominantly a thesaurus of terms, not of information.

EDITIONS. Bekker, 1846; Bethe, in Teubner's *Lexicog. Gr.* IX. i–iii, 1900–31.                    P. B. R. F.; R. B.

**POLUS** of Agrigentum, Sophist, younger than Socrates (Pl. *Grg.* 463 e), pupil of Gorgias; like his teacher he confined himself in later years to teaching rhetoric. He wrote a rhetorical *Τέχνη*, the beginning of which may perhaps be seen in Pl. *Grg.* 448 c. He is mentioned often by Plato and once by Aristotle.

Zeller, *Phil. d. Griechen* i⁶. 1323.                    W. D. R.

**POLYAENUS** (1) of Lampsacus, one of the chief direct disciples of Epicurus, who turned Polyaenus' attention from mathematics to philosophy. He died before his master.

WORKS: *Περὶ φιλοσοφίας*: *Τὰ πρὸς τὸν Ἀρίστωνα*: *Περὶ ὅρων*.

Zeller, *Phil. d. Griechen* iii. 1⁴. 379–80; W. Crönert, *Kolotes und Menedemos* (1906).                    W. D. R.

**POLYAENUS** (2), a Macedonian rhetorician, in his later years dedicated his collection of *Stratagems*, in eight books, to the Emperors Marcus and Verus, to aid them in Verus' Parthian War (A.D. 162). His examples, true or false, are taken from every people of the known world, gods included. Similar collections of extracts, called *hypomnemata*, on every subject and from all sorts of sources, had been common in Hellenistic literature, and Polyaenus, who produced his book very quickly, did not make his own extracts but utilized earlier compilations; theories about his sources are useless. Some items are historically valuable, others worthless; each one must be judged separately.

TEXT. E. Wölfflin and J. Melber (1887); *FGrH* 639.    W. W. T.

**POLYBIUS** (1) (*c.* 200–after 118 B.C.), the Greek historian of the rise of Rome to world power, son of the Achaean statesman Lycortas (q.v.), was born at Megalopolis, and after a liberal education entered politics. He bore Philopoemen's (q.v.) ashes to burial in 182, was appointed in 180 as envoy to Egypt (the mission was cancelled on Ptolemy V's death), and in 170/69 served as Hipparch of the Achaean Confederation. After Pydna he was among 1,000 eminent Achaeans deported to Rome for political investigation and detained without trial in Italy. He now became friend and mentor to Scipio Aemilianus, remaining in Rome as a member of his circle (*see* SCIPIONIC CIRCLE). He probably accompanied Scipio to Spain (151) and to Africa (meeting Masinissa) and, returning to Italy, crossed the Alps in Hannibal's footsteps. In 150 the Achaean detainees were released. Polybius witnessed the destruction of Carthage in Scipio's company (146), afterwards undertaking an exploratory voyage in the Atlantic. After the sack of Corinth (*see* CORINTH) he helped organize Greece and acted as mediator (146–145). Later he visited Alexandria and Sardes and may have been at Numantia (q.v.) in 133. He died, some time after 118, through a fall from a horse.

His early panegyric on Philopoemen, his *Tactics*, his history of the Numantine War, and a treatise on the habitability of the equatorial region are all lost. Of his *Histories*, containing forty books, books 1–5 are extant, and from the rest excerpts, some substantial, from various collections. His original purpose was to narrate the history of the fifty-three years (220–168), from the Hannibalic War to Pydna, which left Rome mistress of the world. Books 1–2 contain an introduction (*προκατασκευή*, I. 3. 10) covering the years from the First Punic War (264) to 220, following on Timaeus. Later, perhaps after 146, he revised his plan to show how the Romans exercised their supremacy and extended the work down to 146. These later events, which are increasingly assessed from the Roman point of view, are related in books 30–9; book 34 dealt with geography; and book 40 contained a recapitulation and chronological survey. Books 1–6 seem to have been published by about 150; when the rest appeared is unknown.

Polybius conceived a double purpose for history, to train the statesman and to teach the general reader how to face disaster; though he did not exclude pleasure, the main aim was didactic. His subject-matter consisted of political and military events (*πραγματικὴ ἱστορία*) analysed to bring out their causes. From this standpoint he attacks the sensationalism and tragic colouring characteristic of most contemporary historians and exemplified in Phylarchus (2. 56. 7 ff.); here he aimed at new standards. Writers of monographs tended to magnify and write up insignificant material for self-glorification (29. 12. 3). Universal history was preferable, and not only on general grounds; for since the affairs of the whole world had developed into an organic whole, it had become the only historical form adequate to treat Rome's rise to power. The synoptic view reflected the character of history itself. This development Polybius saw as the work of Fortune (Tyche), which since 220 had guided all the world's affairs in one direction (1. 4. 1–2). Normally his references to Tyche merely echo conventionally the Hellenistic phraseology common to several philosophical schools and in general use. But the rise of Rome to world power was envisaged as the handiwork of a real power directing events; and this led him to attribute to the Romans a greater single-mindedness in their imperial expansion and to that expansion an inevitability which are not confirmed by his conscientious narrative of detailed events. Rome was raised up by Fortune because of her merit; this assumption allowed him to maintain the emphasis on causality essential to his didactic purpose. Important factors in Roman success, he believed, were the constitution, the army, and the city's early development. All these were discussed in book 6. His analysis of the mixed constitution, which put a brake on the cycle of political change to which simple constitutional forms are subject, presents many problems but was to exercise noteworthy influence from Cicero down to Montesquieu and the founders of the American Constitution.

Polybius saw the historian's task as the study of documents, acquaintance with the scene of historical events, and personal political experience (12. 25 e)—the last two being the more important. But he used written sources critically, for instance Aratus (q.v. 2) and Phylarchus (q.v.) for Achaean affairs before 220, and Fabius (q.v. 6) Pictor and Philinus (q.v. 2) for the First Punic War. For the main period he employed a variety of writers whom he rarely names—an exception being Zeno (q.v. 4) of Rhodes. He also used private sources such as letters. He consulted the Achaean record office and some Roman official sources, as well as inscriptions (cf. 3. 33. 18). But above all interrogation of eyewitnesses formed a vital part of his technique (12. 4 c. 2–5) and at Rome he could meet men from all over the world.

'Truth is to history,' he wrote (1. 14. 6), 'what eyesight is to the living creature.' Despite this he betrays some prejudice, especially against Aetolia and Boeotia; and he concedes the historian's right to slight patriotic bias (16. 14. 6–10). In particular, his polemic against former historians, exemplified in the long digression on Timaeus and others in book 12, though professing to discuss points of literary or historical interest, sprang partly from personal or political considerations never explicitly stated; similar bias lay behind many of his judgements on individuals and explains the prominence accorded to Scipio Aemilianus. In general, however, he attained a high standard of honesty, and even his speeches (traditionally a field for improvisation) were as accurate as he could make them.

Following Timaeus, he used a chronological system based on a modified 'Olympiad year'. His narrative is lucid and informed; but his style, that of the Hellenistic chanceries, is cumbersome and inelegant and proved unattractive to his successors: no one, said Dionysius, could bear to read him to the end—which may explain why so much of his work failed to survive. This loss is unfortunate, for he brought honesty and illumination to a great theme and to a period for which he remains the main substantial source. *See* HISTORIOGRAPHY, GREEK, § 7.

EDITIO PRINCEPS. V. Opsopaeus (1530, bks. 1–5: Lat. translation, N. Perotti, 1473).
CHIEF EDITIONS. Casaubon (1609); Ernesti (1763–4); Schweighaeuser (1789–95); Hultsch (1867–72, 1888–92); Büttner-Wobst (1889–1904, 1905); Strachan-Davidson, *Selections* (1888).
TRANSLATIONS. E. S. Shuckburgh (1889; U.S.A. repr. 1962); W. R. Paton (1922–7, Loeb).
CRITICISM. R. von Scala, *Die Studien des Polybios* (1890); O. Cuntz, *Polybios und sein Werk* (1902); J. B. Bury, *Ancient Greek Historians* (1909); C. Wunderer, *Polybios* (1927); E. Mioni, *Polibio* (1949); K. Ziegler in *PW* (1952, excellent); F. W. Walbank, *A Historical Commentary on Polybius* (1957– ); *JHS* 1938, 55; *Hist.* 1960, 216; *JRS* 1962, 1; 1963, 1; C. O. Brink and F. W. Walbank, *CQ* 1954, 97; P. Pédech, *La Méthode historique de Polybe* (1964); J. M. Moore, *The Manuscript Tradition of Polybius* (1965).
A. Mauersberger, *Polybios-Lexicon* (1956– ). F. W. W.

**POLYBIUS** (2, *PW* 5), a freedman, one of Claudius' secretaries, particularly concerned with literary matters (*a studiis*) and perhaps also with petitions about lawsuits (*a libellis*: *see* LIBELLUS). He translated Homer into Latin and Virgil into Greek. In A.D. 42 or 43 Seneca (q.v. 2) addressed to him from exile a *Consolatio* (for the death of a brother), hoping that it would be construed as a petition for recall. He was killed in 47 by the contrivance of Messallina.

Sen. *Consolatio ad Polybium* (ed. J. D. Duff, 1915). A. Momigliano, *Claudius²* (1961), 43, 75; V. Scramuzza, *The Emperor Claudius* (1940), 5 f., 84 f.; F. Giancotti, *Rend. Linc.* 1953, 59 ff. A. M.; T. J. C.

**POLYBOEA,** (1) name of several mythological heroines; (2) a goddess, sister of Hyacinthus (q.v.), identified with Artemis and Kore (Paus. 3. 19. 4; Hesych. s.v.).

**POLYBUS,** in mythology, king of Corinth or Sicyon, a figure of some importance in the legends of Oedipus and Adrastus (qq.v.). Being childless, or at all events without sons, he and his wife adopt the infant Oedipus and rear him as their own (Soph. *OT* 1016 ff.). He is sonless again in the version preserved by schol. Pind. *Nem.* 9. 30, cf. Hdt. 5. 67. 4. In this tradition Adrastus is his daughter's son and inherits his kingdom. But he is either an extremely vague figure or a conflation of several persons, for we hear of him also as in Tenea (Strabo 8. 6. 22, 380), Boeotia (schol. Eur. *Phoen.* 28), and Argos (*Etym. Magn.* 207. 41 ff.).

See further Höfer in Roscher, s.v. H. J. R.

**POLYCARP** (2nd c. A.D.), bishop of Smyrna, disciple of St. John, and correspondent of Ignatius of Antioch. The only extant letter warns the Philippian church against apostasy. In the controversy about celebrating Easter (c. A.D. 154–5) he visited Rome to defend the old Asian tradition of keeping the feast with the Jewish passover. His martyrdom at the age of 86 is described in a letter from the Smyrnean church to the church of Philomelium, Phrygia; that the MSS. preserve an interpolated text is probable from Eusebius of Caesarea's quotations (*Hist. Eccl.* 4. 15). The date of the martyrdom can be decided only by a choice between conflicting evidence. Eusebius' *Chronicle* dates it under Marcus Aurelius, 167–8. But a (post-Eusebian) addition to the Smyrnean letter (ch. 21) dates it on 23 Feb. 'in the high priesthood of Philip of Tralles, in the proconsulship of Statius Quadratus'. Quadratus was consul in 142; his proconsulship of Asia, attested in inscriptions and Aelius Aristides (q.v.), can hardly fall later than 155–6. This date makes it easier to accept Irenaeus' evidence of his contact with St. John and to fit in his correspondence with Ignatius, martyred before 117. But the later, Eusebian date remains possible. The fifth-century Life of Polycarp by 'Pionius' is valueless legend.

Ed. J. B. Lightfoot, *Apostolic Fathers* ii² (1889). B. Altaner, *Patrology* (1960), 110 ff. H. C.

**POLYCLITUS** (1) of Larisa, used by Eratosthenes as a geographical source. *See* ALEXANDER (3), bibliography, ancient sources.

**POLYCLITUS** (2), native of Argos, a leading sculptor of the second half of the fifth century B.C., said to have been a pupil of Ageladas. He worked chiefly in bronze, but also in marble, gold, and ivory, and in embossed metalwork. Ancient authors mention a number of his statues of athletes set up at Olympia and elsewhere, and several of their inscribed bases have come to light in the excavations at Olympia. Through Pliny's detailed description (34. 55) it has proved possible to identify in Roman copies his famous Doryphorus, 'youth holding a spear', which became a model for other sculptors. The most complete copy was found at Pompeii and is in the Naples Museum. From it can be sensed in some measure the harmony of the proportions and the careful finish of details, for which Polyclitus was famous. We are told that he wrote a book on rhythm and proportion and embodied his theories in this statue (Pliny 34. 55). Also reliably identified is his Diadumenus, 'youth binding a fillet round his head', of which a number of copies exist. Furthermore, some of his other athletes have been tentatively recognized in various extant statues of Roman date, for instance, the Cyniscus in the Westmacott Youth of the British Museum. The Amazon, which he is said to have made for Ephesus in competition with Phidias and Cresilas (qq.v.), is probably preserved in a type of which several Roman copies have survived—in Berlin, New York, and elsewhere. His most celebrated work, however, was the chryselephantine statue of Hera which he made for the Heraeum at Argos. It is described by Pausanias (2. 17. 4) as colossal, seated on a throne, holding a sceptre in one hand, a pomegranate in the other, and was said to have been comparable to Phidias' Olympian Zeus. Strabo (8. 372) considered Polyclitus' work more beautiful in workmanship ($\tau\acute{\epsilon}\chi\nu\eta$) than the Zeus, but second in size and magnificence ($\pi o\lambda\upsilon\tau\acute{\epsilon}\lambda\epsilon\iota\alpha$). The only copies that have survived of it are the little reliefs on coins of Argos, both of the head and of the figure. G. M. A. R.

**POLYCRATES** (1) seized Samos c. 540 B.C. with his brothers Pantagnotus and Syloson, but soon made himself sole tyrant. He made Samos a great naval power, annexed neighbouring islands (including Rheneia near Delos), and celebrated Delian Games. He formed alliances with Egypt and Cyrene, but later sent a force of disaffected Samians to help Cambyses against Egypt. These sailed back and attacked the tyrant unsuccessfully, though supported by a Spartan force, which Polycrates bought off with a bribe of specially struck false coins. C. 522 Polycrates was lured to the mainland by the satrap Oroetes, who pretended to be plotting against Darius, and there crucified. His piratical thalassocracy suggests a consistent effort, tempered by opportunism, to maintain an unconquered Samos as successor to Miletus (then under Persian rule). Polycrates imported sheep and other animals to improve Samian stock. He attracted craftsmen from other States and patronized artists and poets (Theodorus, Anacreon); but the two most famous public works in Samos, the great temple of Hera and the tunnelled aqueduct bringing water into the city, sometimes attributed to him, were probably begun earlier.

Hdt. bk. 3; Thuc. 1. 13, 3. 104; Arist. *Politics* 1313ᵇ; Ath. 540 d. E. Curtius, *Ath. Mitt.* 1906, 151 f.; P. N. Ure, *The Origin of Tyranny* (1922), ch. 3; M. White, *JHS* 1954, 36 ff.; J. P. Barron, *CQ* 1964, 210 ff. P. N. U.; R. M.

**POLYCRATES** (2) (4th c. B.C.), Athenian teacher of rhetoric; author of an encomium on Busiris, criticized in Isocrates' *Busiris*, a Κατηγορία Σωκράτους (see E. R. Dodds, *Plato: Gorgias*, 28 f.) and other epideictic pieces.

L. Radermacher, *Artium Scriptores* (1951), 128 ff.; J. Humbert, *Polycratès* (1930); A.-H. Chroust, *Socrates, Man and Myth* (1957), ch. 4. D. A. R.

**POLYDAMAS** (Πο(υ)λυδάμας), in mythology, son of Panthoos (Homer, loc. cit. *infra*). In the *Iliad* he takes some part in the fighting, but is chiefly noteworthy for his sage advice, which Hector rejects to his cost (18. 249 ff.). His death is nowhere recorded and he seems to be thought of as surviving the war. H. J. R.

**POLYDORUS** (Πολύδωρος). There are some ten mythological persons bearing this name, the only ones of any importance being: (1) son of Cadmus (q.v.) and Harmonia, a purely genealogical figure, ignored by Euripides (*Bacch.* 43–4), but mentioned, e.g., by Herodotus (5. 59). (2) Youngest son of Priam and Hecuba (qq.v.). When the Trojan War was raging, Priam sent him with much gold to Polymestor, a Thracian king, who murdered him for the gold after the fall of Troy. His ghost speaks the prologue of Euripides, *Hecuba*, and an important part of the

plot is Hecuba's discovery and avenging of the murder. Cf. Verg. *Aen.* 3. 22 ff. H. J. R.

**POLYEIDUS** (1), a seer, one of the Melampodidae, a Corinthian. When Glaucus, son of Minos (q.v.), was drowned in a honey-jar, Polyeidus, after passing a test imposed by Minos, found the body and afterwards restored it to life by using a herb revealed by a snake.

See Hyg. *Fab.* 136; Roscher's *Lexicon*, s.v. H. J. R.

**POLYEIDUS** (2) 'the Sophist' is known only from Aristotle (*Poet.* 16, 17), who refers to the recognition scene in his *Iphigeneia* (if that was the title).

**POLYGNOTUS** (fl. c. 475–447 B.C.), painter, son and pupil of Aglaophon of Thasos; later an Athenian citizen. Friend of Cimon and probably of Sophocles. Pliny dates before 420 B.C. He painted the 'Iliupersis' in the Stoa Poikile soon after 460, the 'Iliupersis' and 'Nekyia' in the Cnidian Lesche at Delphi probably between 458 and 447; according to a very probable emendation he painted in the Theseum soon after 475. The 'Rape of the Leucippidae' in the Anakeion, the 'Suitor-Slaying' in Plataea, the 'Achilles in Scyros' and the 'Nausicaa' (both later in the Pinakotheke) are undated. Contemporary and later vases, particularly the Niobid painter's Argonaut crater (Pfuhl, fig. 492; Rumpf, pl. 28/1 and 2), illustrate Polygnotan grouping and postures, as described by Pausanias, and the transparent drapery and freer treatment of the face, noted by Pliny. Many of the elements of his art had appeared sporadically before, but he combined them to represent men of high moral purpose ($\mathring{\eta}\theta o\varsigma$) and 'better than ourselves', often either taking a decision or in the reaction after the event. For Theophrastus and others he was a primitive (he did not use shading), but still the first great painter.

Overbeck, 380, 614, 1042–79; C. Dugas, *Rev. Ét. Gr.* 1938, 53; Rumpf, *Malerei u. Zeichn.* 91; E. Simon, *AJArch.* 1963, 43 ff.; L. H. Jeffery, *BSA* 1965, 41 ff. T. B. L. W.

**POLYPERCHON** (b. c. 380 B.C.), son of Simmias a Macedonian noble, first appears when promoted 'taxiarch' to command a brigade of Alexander's Macedonian infantry after Issus (333). Under Alexander he rose no higher, and his first independent command was in the Lamian War (321), when he showed some skill. This, with his seniority and want of personal ambition, inspired the regent Antipater to recommend the army to elect him his successor (319); but, lacking Antipater's prestige, he had no chance of controlling the 'separatist' generals. He failed even to hold Macedonia and retain possession of the two kings, and degenerated into a mere general of mercenaries in Greece, employed alternately by Antigonus and Cassander against each other. The date and circumstances of his death are unknown.

Berve, *Alexanderreich*, no. 654; W. W. Tarn, *CAH* vi, ch. 15; Bengtson, *Strategie* i. 81 ff. G. T. G.

**POLYPHRASMON** (so spelt *IG* ii². 2325), son of the tragic poet Phrynichus, wrote a tetralogy on the subject of Lycurgus, presented in 467 B.C., but defeated by Aeschylus' Theban tetralogy and by Aristias (Arg. Aesch. *Sept.*).

**POLYSTRATUS**, perhaps a direct disciple of Epicurus, followed Hermarchus (successor of Epicurus) as head of the school.

WORKS: Περὶ ἀλόγου καταφρονήσεως, frs. ed. C. Wilke, 1905: Περὶ φιλοσοφίας, frs. ed. Crönert, *Kolotes u. Menedemos*, 36.

See Zeller, *Phil. d. Griechen* iii. 1⁴, 318 f.; A. Vogliano, *Epicureorum Scripta* (1928).

**POLYXENA** (Πολυξένη), in mythology, daughter of Priam and Hecuba (qq.v.); not in Homer. In the *Cypria* she is mortally wounded at the fall of Troy and buried by Neoptolemus (fr. 26 Allen). In the *Iliu Persis* and later she is sacrificed to the ghost of Achilles (Proclus); cf. e.g. Eur. *Hec.* 220 ff. Hence the story that Achilles in life was in love with her, e.g. Hyg. *Fab.* 110.
H. J. R.

**POLYZELUS,** Athenian comic poet, won four victories at the Lenaea, the first in the last decade of the fifth century B.C. (*IG* ii². 2325. 130). We have six titles and a dozen fragments; four of the titles indicate theogonic burlesque; a fifth, Δημοτυνδάρεως, is clearly political, but its occasion and point are not known.

*FCG* ii. 367 ff.; *CAF* i. 789 ff.; *FAC* i. 878 ff. K. J. D.

**POMERIUM** was the line demarcating an augurally constituted city, the point beyond which the *auspicia urbana* could not be taken; it was essentially a religious boundary, marked by *cippi* (Varro, *Ling.* 5. 143), and was distinct both from the city-wall and from the limit of actual occupation, though it might coincide with the former and was often understood as the strip inside or outside the wall (cf. Livy 1. 44; Plut. *Rom.* 11). Almost every aspect of the history of the *pomerium* of Rome is debatable; our sources refer to an original Palatine *pomerium*, later extended by Servius Tullius and then unchanged until Sulla's day (sources in Lugli, *Fontes* ii. 125 ff.); but none of the descriptions is reliable (e.g. Tac. *Ann.* 12. 24, seems to describe the Lupercal circuit), although Varro's account (*Ling.* 5. 46–54) of the city of the Four Regions may correspond to the *pomerium* at some early date. Our best evidence for its history from the first century B.C. is probably Gellius, *NA* 13. 14. 4–7, quoting the *augur* Valerius Messalla Rufus (*cos.* 53 B.C.); Gellius mentions extensions by Sulla (cf. Tac. *Ann.* 12. 23—'*auctis p. R. finibus*') and also by Caesar (cf. Cic. *Att.* 13. 20; Dio 43. 50. 1). On the other hand, Augustus' silence in the *Res Gestae* suggests that he did not extend it, despite the explicit statement of Tacitus (loc. cit.). Later extensions were made by Claudius, who was the first to include the Aventine (Tac. loc. cit., Gell. loc. cit., *CIL* vi. 31537 a–d; 37023–4; *Not. Scav.* 1912, 197; 1913, 68) and by Vespasian (*CIL* vi. 31538 a–c; *Not. Scav.* 1933, 241; cf. *CIL* vi. 930. 14–16). The *cippi* dating from Hadrian (*CIL* vi. 31539 a–c; *Not. Scav.* 1933, 241) seem only to be restorations. Aurelian's claim (S.H.A. *Aurelian* 21) is doubtful. The imperial *pomerium*, as loosely defined by the *cippi*, is thought to have coincided on the east with the republican wall, breaking away to include the Aventine and Emporium, the southern half of the Campus Martius and all the Pincian hill, at the last point extending beyond Aurelian's Wall. *See also* AUSPICIUM.

M. Labrousse, *Mélanges d'arch.* 1937, 165 ff.; P. Grimal, ibid. 1959, 43 ff. I. A. R.; J. N.

**POMETIA** (near modern *Cisterna?*), also known as Suessa, gave its name to the Pomptine Marshes (q.v.). Volsci and Romans often disputed its possession in primitive Latium (q.v.). About 495 B.C. Rome obliterated it. It was never rebuilt. Spoils from Pometia enabled Tarquin to found the Capitoline temple at Rome (Livy 1. 53). E. T. S.

**POMONA,** Roman goddess of *poma*, i.e. fruits, especially such as grow on trees, apples, etc. Her flamen (q.v.) was lowest in rank of all, corresponding apparently to the small importance of her province. She had a sacred place, *pomonal*, 12 miles out of Rome (Festus, 296, 15 ff. Lindsay), but no known festival. Ovid (*Met.* 14. 623 ff.)

has a story (unconnected with facts of cult and clearly his own or another comparatively late author's invention) that Vertumnus (q.v.) loved her, pled his own cause in disguised shape, and finally won her. H. J. R.

**POMPEIA** (*PW*, 'Pompeius' 52), granddaughter of Pompeius (q.v. 2) and of Sulla, married Caesar (1) in 67 B.C. and, after the Bona Dea scandal (*see* CLODIUS, 1), was divorced as not above suspicion. E. B.

**POMPEII,** situated on a small volcanic hill, 5¼ miles south-east of Vesuvius, was not a small town by ancient standards (*c.* 160 acres). Its sudden end in the eruption of A.D. 79, described by the Younger Pliny (*Epp.* 16 and 20), struck the imagination of the ancient world as well as the modern. The site, forgotten in the Middle Ages, was rediscovered in 1748, since when intermittent excavation has proceeded. About four-fifths have now been uncovered.

Pompeii served in Strabo's time as a port of Nola, Nuceria, and Acerrae (5. 4. 8). Its commercial and strategic position near the mouth of the Sarnus, one of the gateways of Campania, explains its history. Strabo (ibid.) states that it was occupied successively by Oscans, Etruscans and Pelasgians, Samnites, and Romans.

The Oscans were the descendants of the Neolithic inhabitants of Campania, as appears from their pottery. The town-plan of Pompeii seems to contain an older portion in the south-west (24 acres), and a newer portion added later to north and east. From the eighth century B.C. the inhabitants came under the influence of the Greek colonies of the coast (Cumae), and Greek pottery (geometric, proto-Corinthian, Corinthian) and bronzes appear in their graves. In the seventh century Etruscan influence becomes apparent, issuing perhaps from Capua and Nola, and from this time Greek and Etruscan influence alternated—first, the Greeks of Cumae; then the Etruscans, from *c.* 530 B.C., when they occupied Campania, to their defeat at sea by Hieron of Syracuse in 474 B.C.; finally, the Greeks again, from 474 B.C. to the Samnite invasion *c.* 420 B.C. Traces of all three phases are found in the Doric Temple of the Foro Triangolare and in the Temple of Apollo.

The Samnites invaded Campania in the fifth century, occupying Capua in 432 and Cumae in 420, and their penetration south of Vesuvius must have followed soon. When was Pompeii enlarged from 24 to 160 acres, and by whom? The fortifications of the enlarged town suggest a date in the fifth century B.C., and since the enlargement argues a not inconsiderable increase of population, the Samnites are the most likely candidates, though the influence of Greek or Etruscan town-planning is obvious.

From the end of the fifth century B.C. till the age of Sulla, Pompeii was a Samnite town. Its language was Oscan. Coinage suggests that it belonged to a league of which Nuceria was the head. Its chief magistrate was a *meddix tuticus*, and under him were quaestors and aediles. An assembly (*kombennion*) appears in inscriptions, though it is not known whether it was an assembly of all citizens or a town-council. The period was one of great prosperity, based on agriculture and commerce. Culturally the town passed through two phases, the line between them falling about the middle of the third century B.C. The first (in which local limestone was the chief building material) may be called Italian in the sense that it is a reflection of a more or less homogeneous civilization which was spread widely in south Italy at the time (cf. the Oscan and Lucanian tomb-paintings in the Naples and Capua museums), and had strong Etruscan reminiscences. The second phase (in which a handsome dark tufa was imported from Nuceria) was Hellenistic and received a great impetus from the ever-widening trade connexions of Campania during the second century B.C. Increasing prosperity is reflected in the dignified monuments which date from the third and second centuries B.C. The main Forum, hitherto a rough and unsystematic market-place, was converted into a dignified civic centre. The region of the Foro Triangolare was rebuilt after the manner of a Greek gymnasium, with a large open-air theatre adjoining, to be a centre of the town's cultural life. Bronzes, marble tables, terracottas, and mosaics were imported in large quantities from Hellenistic factories or made by local workmen after Hellenistic designs. A Hellenistic public bath was built and the cult of Isis was introduced. In houses wall-decoration became markedly Hellenistic, and the Greek peristyle was added to the Italian atrium.

In the Social War Pompeii joined the Italians (App. BCiv. 1. 39) and in 89 B.C. was attacked by L. Sulla. The outcome of the siege is unknown, but the war as a whole completely changed the position of Pompeii. With the rest of Italy it received Roman franchise and the citizens were enrolled in the tribus Menenia. As a punishment for resistance to Sulla's army a colony of Roman veterans was planted on the town under the leadership of P. Sulla, the Dictator's nephew (c. 80 B.C., Cic. Sull. 60–2). At this time, except for the incipient use of Latin in place of Oscan as the language of official life, the romanization of Pompeii had not gone far, but hereafter it made rapid strides. The names and functions of the magistrates were brought into line with those of other Roman colonies. The Oscan language was replaced by Latin, and Oscan weights and measures by Roman standards. Houses, wall-paintings, metal-work, and pavements all took on a Roman tinge. Romanization in architecture was indirectly assisted by an earthquake in A.D. 62. Seneca (QNat. 6. 1. 1–2) and Tacitus (Ann. 15. 22) say that it left much of the city in ruins, and this is confirmed by the remains. In the parts that were rebuilt before the eruption the influence of Rome was strong.

Local families and traditions were not, however, entirely swamped by the Roman colonists. Indeed, inscriptions suggest that after initial difficulties the two groups lived amicably side by side. Municipal elections continued to be contested with vigour, and except to deal with irregularities and disorder (e.g. the riot in the amphitheatre of A.D. 59; Tac. Ann. 14. 17) there was little interference from the central government. The remains of the last half-century before the eruption present the picture of a prosperous town—a market for the produce of a rich countryside, a port with wide connexions in the Mediterranean, and an industrial centre producing certain specialities (wines, millstones, fish-sauce, perfumes) for which the demand was more than local.

ANCIENT SOURCES. (a) Inscriptions: CIL iv and x, 787–1079, 8143–57, 8348–61; Eph. Epigr. viii. 86–90, 202; Not. Scav. 1927 ff. passim. (b) Authors: scattered references of which the most important are: Cic. Pro Sull. 60–2; Strabo 5. 4. 3–8; Sen. QNat. 6. 1. 1–2; Tac. Ann. 14. 17 and 15. 22; Hist. 1. 2; Pliny, Ep. 6. 16 and 20; Suet. Tit. 8. 3 ff.; Dio Cass. 66. 21–4.

MODERN WRITERS. For further bibliography, A. W. van Buren, A Companion to the Study of Pompeii and Herculaneum (Rome, 1933). General works: A. Mau, Pompeii, Its Life and Art (tr. F. W. Kelsey, U.S.A. 1899); E. Pernice, Pompeii (1926); R. C. Carrington, Pompeii (1936); A. Sogliano, Pompei nel suo sviluppo storico: Pompei preromana (1937); M. della Corte, Case ed abitanti di Pompeii² (1954); T. Frank, Econ. History of Rome² (1927), 245 ff.; H. H. Tanzer, The Common People of Pompeii: a Study of the Graffiti (U.S.A. 1939); A. Maiuri, Pompeian Wall Paintings (1960); id., Pompeii (1960); P. Ciprotti, Pompei (Universale Studium, Rome, 1962).   R. C. C.

**POMPEIUS** (1, PW 12), QUINTUS, a novus homo attached to Scipio Aemilianus, became consul in 141 B.C. by trickery and against Scipio's will (it was said), and succeeded Metellus (q.v. 3) Macedonicus in the Numantine command, blaming his lack of success on his predecessor. In 140 he was forced to negotiate a treaty, but

repudiated it on his successor's arrival and gained the Senate's approval for this action. Prosecuted repetundarum, in a cause célèbre, by Metellus and other distinguished men, he was acquitted, and in 136 he and Metellus served together as legates in Spain under Furius (q.v. 2). A prominent opponent of Ti. Gracchus, he became censor (131) with Metellus (the first pair of plebeian censors).

H. Simon, Roms Kriege in Spanien (1962), see index; A. E. Astin, Scipio Aemilianus (1967), see index.   E. B.

**POMPEIUS** (2, PW 39) RUFUS, QUINTUS, son or grandson of (1), as tribune (100 B.C.) unsuccessfully worked for the recall of Metellus (q.v. 6) Numidicus and remained closely attached to his family. He was praetor urbanus in 91, and consul in 88 with Sulla, whose daughter married his son. He opposed Sulpicius (q.v. 1) Rufus, his former friend, and was driven from Rome, but then occupied it with Sulla. Sent (by a SC whose validity could be impugned) to supersede his distant relative Pompeius Strabo, he was killed by the latter's soldiers with the commander's acquiescence.

For a coin-portrait see Sydenham, CRR, Pl. 25, no. 908.   E. B.

**POMPEIUS** (3, PW 45) STRABO, father of Pompey, after his quaestorship tried to prosecute his commander. In the Social War he fought in the northern sector, as legate (90 B.C.) and—after a victory over T. Lafrenius—as consul (89). Pompey, Cicero, and Catiline, among others, served under him (Cichorius, Röm. Stud. 144). Capturing Asculum, he ended the northern war and triumphed late in 89, but was perhaps prosecuted in 88 and (if so) contumaciously resumed his command. His distant relative Pompeius (2) was sent to supersede him and was killed, not without Strabo's acquiescence. In 87, asked to defend Rome against Cinna, he behaved ambiguously; he negotiated with Cinna (he probably had connexions with Carbo, q.v. 2) over a joint consulship, excluding both Marius and the Optimates. His death in an epidemic was thought fit punishment and his body was dragged through the streets. He was one of the first, in the light of Sulla's march on Rome, to see the possibilities offered to unscrupulous leaders by the new army (see MARIUS 1, SULLA 1) and the spread of citizenship. As consul, he had given Latin rights to Transpadana and enfranchised some Spaniards on the battlefield (ILLRP 515). In those regions and in Picenum he built up the following later inherited and exploited by his son.

M. Gelzer, Kl. Schr. (1962–3), ii. 106.   E. B.

**POMPEIUS** (4, PW 31), GNAEUS, called MAGNUS after 81, (POMPEY) (106–48 B.C.), served with his father Pompeius (q.v. 3) at Asculum, and brought three legions from his father's veterans and clients in Picenum to win victories for Sulla in 83. He was then sent to Sicily, where he defeated and killed Carbo (q.v. 2), and thence to Africa, where he destroyed Cn. Domitius and King Iarbas. Though he was still an eques, Sulla grudgingly allowed him to triumph (80 or possibly 81); and in 80, after the death of his wife Aemilia, Sulla's stepdaughter, he married Mucia (q.v.), a close connexion of the Metelli, who perhaps accepted him as an ally against Sulla's autocracy. He supported Lepidus (q.v. 2) for the consulship of 78, but assisted Catulus (q.v. 3) to overcome him next year; later in 77 he obtained proconsular imperium to reinforce Metellus (q.v. 7) Pius against Sertorius (q.v.) in Spain. Thence he returned in 71 and co-operated with the reluctant Crassus (q.v. 4) in finishing off the Servile War. Again he triumphed, and extorted from the Senate the consulate, emphasizing the illegality by surrendering his horse with great ceremony to the censors, whose office he now restored; in this year, too, the tribunes recovered their rights, and L. Cotta reduced senatorial representation on the courts to one-third (70 B.C.).

Though now a senator, Pompey took no normal consular province. But from both tribunes and *equites* he reaped his reward: in 67 the *Lex Gabinia* created for him an *imperium* with unprecedented powers against the pirates, whom he destroyed in three months; and Manilius next year added Lucullus' Asiatic provinces and conduct of the Mithridatic War. His eastern campaigns were his greatest achievement. Mithridates was defeated immediately, and though attempts to pursue him over the Caucasus failed, he committed suicide in the Crimea in 63. Further, Pompey founded colonies, annexed Syria, settled Judaea, and laid the foundation of subsequent Roman organization of the East (though he reached no agreement with Parthia).

In 62 he returned, disbanded his army, and triumphed, a *popularis* no longer (Cic. *Att.* 2. 1. 6). He made two requests: settlement of his veterans and ratification of his eastern *acta*. But he had divorced Mucia, allegedly for adultery with Caesar (q.v. 1); and the Metelli, aided by Lucullus and Cato (q.v. 5), frustrated him until in 60 he allied with Crassus and Caesar; he married the latter's daughter Julia (q.v. 1) in 59. His demands were satisfied by Caesar as consul; but his popularity waned, and in 58–57 Clodius (q.v. 1) deliberately flouted him. In 57, after backing Cicero's recall, he received control of the corn-supply for five years; but no military power was attached, nor could he secure the commission to restore Ptolemy Auletes in Egypt next year. In Apr. 56 the 'Triumvirate' was renewed at Luca. Pompey became consul with Crassus for 55, and received Spain for five years; but he governed his province by proxy. After Julia's death in 54 he declined a further marriage alliance with Caesar; and in 52 after Clodius' murder he was appointed sole consul, with backing from extreme *optimates*. His immediate actions—the trial of Milo (q.v.) and his legislation *de vi, de ambitu,* and *de iure magistratuum*—were designed only to restore order in Rome, rather than to injure Caesar; but the prolongation of his *imperium* for five years from this date destroyed the balance of power; and he took as his colleague Metellus (q.v. 11) Scipio, whose daughter Cornelia he had married. Gradually his new alliance led him to support demands that Caesar be recalled before he was sure of the consulate of 48; and in 50, when negotiations with Caesar were breaking down, he accepted from the consul C. Marcellus the command of the Republic's forces in Italy. In 49 he transported his army from Brundisium to Greece and spent the year mobilizing in Macedonia. He met Caesar on his arrival in 48 with a force powerful in every arm, and inflicted a serious reverse when Caesar attempted to blockade him at Dyrrhachium. But later (9 Aug.), perhaps under pressure from his senatorial friends, he joined in a pitched battle at Pharsalus, and was irretrievably defeated. He fled to Egypt, but was stabbed to death as he landed (28 Sept. 48).

The violence and unconstitutional character of Pompey's early career invites comparison with Augustus, whom in his constitutional position he so often resembled: in 67 he had twenty-four *legati*; from 55 he governed Spain through *legati*, and while doing so was made consul in 52. But still more significant was his unofficial power: by 62 in Spain, Gaul, Africa, the East, and parts of Italy, there were colonists and clients bound to him by the relationship of *fides* and surrounding him with a magnificence unsurpassed by a Roman senator hitherto; the climax was reached with the dedication of his theatre in the Campus Martius in 55. He owed much to his military genius, which must have been of the highest order even though other commanders, Metellus, Crassus, Lucullus, often paved the way to his successes. But in politics he showed a mastery which it was easy for clever men to underrate (e.g., for all its brilliance, the epigram of Caelius in Cic. *Fam.* 8. 1. 3). 'Modestus ad alia omnia nisi ad dominationem' (Sall. *H.* 2. 14), by superb skill and timing he rose from his lawless beginnings to a constitutional pre-eminence in which he could discard the use of naked force; and even his final miscalculation was a narrow one. Whether he had disinterested aims in government must remain uncertain, but there are signs that he tried to restore dignity and order in the city, and perhaps also in Rome's relations with her provinces. His private life, too, was of a high standard for such an age, and two women, Julia and Cornelia, married to him for dynastic ends, became deeply attached to him. Cicero, though he never understood Pompey's subtleties (see esp. *Att.* 1. 13–14), remained a devoted admirer; and despite the disappointments of the war years Pompey's death brought from him a heartfelt tribute: 'hominem enim integrum et castum et grauem cognoui' (*Att.* 11. 6. 5).

For the sources *see* CAESAR (1). Various lives by Plutarch (e.g., *Sertorius, Lucullus*) add much information when carefully criticized: Plutarch's *Pompey* is based probably on Nepos. M. Gelzer, *Pompeius* (Munich, 1949); J. van Ooteghem, *Pompée le Grand* (1954); E. Badian, *Foreign Clientelae* (1958), ch. 11.                    G. E. F. C.

**POMPEIUS** (5, *PW* 17), GNAEUS, elder son of Pompey and Mucia (qq.v.), was born 79 B.C. About 54 he married a daughter of Ap. Claudius (q.v. 12). In 49 he secured an Egyptian fleet, with which before the battle of Dyrrhachium he destroyed Caesar's transports. Early in the African War he occupied the Balearics and crossed to Spain, where he was joined after Thapsus by his brother and Labienus, raised thirteen legions, and won most of the southern province. But after manœuvres which drove him south from Corduba he was defeated by Caesar in 45 in the hard-fought battle of Munda, and later captured and executed.                    G. E. F. C.

**POMPEIUS** (6, *PW* 33) **MAGNUS PIUS**, SEXTUS, younger son of Pompey and Mucia, was born probably *c.* 67 B.C. Left in Lesbos with Cornelia (q.v. 2) during the campaign of Pharsalus (48), he accompanied his father to Egypt and after his murder went to Africa; after Thapsus (46) he joined his brother Gnaeus in Spain, and during the campaign of Munda (45) commanded the garrison of Corduba (q.v.). Subsequently he contrived to raise an army, partly of fugitive Pompeians, and won appreciable successes against Caesar's governors in Further Spain, C. Carrinas (*cos. suff.* 43) and after him C. Asinius Pollio (q.v.). In the summer of 44 Lepidus (q.v. 3) arranged a settlement between him and the Senate, under the terms of which he left Spain; but instead of returning to Rome, he waited on events in Massilia with his army and fleet. In Apr. 43 the Senate made him its naval commander, with the title *praefectus classis et orae maritimae*; but in August he was outlawed under the *lex Pedia* (*see* PEDIUS 1), and presently employed his fleet to rescue fugitives from the proscription and to occupy Sicily, at first sharing authority with the governor Pompeius Bithynicus, but later putting him to death; and using the island as a base for raiding and blockading Italy. He repelled an attack by Octavian's general Salvidienus (q.v.) in 42, supported Antony against Octavian in 40 (when his lieutenant Menodorus, q.v., occupied Sardinia) and in 39 concluded the Pact of Misenum (q.v.) with the triumvirs, who conceded to him the governorship of Sicily, Sardinia and Corsica, and Achaea in return for the suspension of his blockade. In 38 Octavian accused him of breaking the pact and again attacked him, but was defeated in sea-fights off Cumae and Messana. In 36 the attack was renewed, and after Agrippa's victory off Mylae, Octavian's defeat off Tauromenium, and Lepidus' occupation of southern and western Sicily, the war was decided by the battle of Naulochus (3 Sept.). Sextus escaped with a few ships to Asia, where he attempted to establish himself, but was forced to surrender to M. Titius (q.v. 2), who put him to death.

Sextus was like his father an able and energetic commander. His brief career was spent entirely in the continuation—symbolized by his adoption of the surname Pius—of an inherited struggle, and left him no time for cultivation of the arts of peace. Despite his long absence from and blockade of Italy, he seems to have been popular in Rome. His wife was Scribonia, daughter of L. Scribonius (q.v. 1) Libo. It was apparently through a daughter of this marriage that M. Scribonius (q.v. 2) Libo Drusus and Cn. Pompeius Magnus, Claudius' son-in-law, traced their descent from Pompey.

M. Hadas, *Sextus Pompey* (U.S.A. 1930); Syme, *Rom. Rev.*, see index.                                    G. W. R.; T. J. C.

**POMPEIUS** (7) **SILO**, rhetor, some of whose arguments are cited by the Elder Seneca.

**POMPEIUS** (8) **SATURNINUS**, orator, historian, poet whose verse, in the manner of Catullus and Calvus, Pliny greatly admired (*Ep.* 1. 8 and 16). Pliny sent him for criticism his speech at the opening of the Como library.

**POMPEIUS** (9) (5th c. A.D.), grammarian, author of a *Commentum artis Donati* (ed. Keil, *Gramm. Lat.* v. 95–312).

Schanz–Hosius, § 1102.

**POMPILIUS** (*c.* 100 B.C.), epigrammatist quoted by Varro.

Baehr. *FPR* 274.

**POMPONIUS** (1), LUCIUS, of Bononia (fl. *c.* 100–85 B.C.), Latin poet, older contemporary of Novius (q.v.), from Cisalpine Gaul. These two made *fabulae Atellanae* literary and tended to fuse them with *palliatae*. Seventy known titles show the stock Atellan characters, various occupations, political satire, religious and mythological themes and burlesque of tragedy; in popular language, with coarseness and farcical scenes. *See* ATELLANA.

FRAGMENTS. O. Ribbeck, *CRF*² 225 (3rd ed. Teubner, 1897). P. Frassinetti, *Fab. Atell. Frag.* (1955), 1 ff.          E. H. W.

**POMPONIUS** (2) **RUFUS** wrote *Collecta* from which Valerius Maximus (4. 4 *ad init.*) quotes 'maxima ornamenta matronis liberos'.

**POMPONIUS** (3, *PW* 103) **SECUNDUS,** [? PUBLIUS CALV]ISIUS SABINUS (Quint. *Inst.* 8. 3. 31; 10. 1. 98), was *cos. suff.* A.D. 44, and a friend of the Elder Pliny who wrote his biography (Pliny, *Ep.* 3. 5) and calls him 'consularem poetam' and 'uatem ciuemque clarissimum' (*HN* 7. 80; 13. 83). Endangered by prosecution under Tiberius, he survived (Tac. *Ann.* 5. 8). He wrote *Aeneas*, a *praetexta*. Under Claudius his verses on the stage drew insults from the mob (ibid. 11. 13). Legate of Upper Germany, he victoriously checked the Chatti in 50 (ibid. 12. 28). Pliny (*HN* 13. 83) mentions having seen the handwriting of the Gracchi, about two centuries old, in his possession. He died either between 51 and 57 (so Otto) or in the late 60s (so Cichorius).

He was stepbrother of Caesonia, Gaius' wife. His brother Quintus (*cos. suff.* A.D. 41) favoured the restoration of the Republic after Gaius' death; as an accomplice of Camillus Scribonianus in 42, he committed suicide or was killed.

Cichorius, *Röm. Stud.* 423 ff.; W. Otto, *Philol.* 1935, 483 ff.; Schanz–Hosius ii⁴. 475; E. Ritterling, *Fasti des röm. Deutschlands* (1932), 15.                                       J. W. D.

**POMPONIUS** (4) **BASSULUS**, MARCUS (? 1st c. A.D.), recorded in an inscription of Aeclanum (*CIL* ix. 1164) as a translator of Menander and writer of original comedies (probably not for performance).

**POMPONIUS** (5) **PROCULUS VITRASIUS POLLIO,** TITUS (*PW*, s.v. Pomponius 67 and Vitrasius 8), a patrician, entered upon a senatorial career under Hadrian. He became *cos. I suff.* before A.D. 157 (perhaps *c.* 150) and thereafter successively governor of Hispania Citerior (*ILS* 1113–1114), of Lower Moesia in 157 (*Ann. Épigr.* 1937, 408, no. 247), and proconsul of Asia at an uncertain date thereafter. He served on the staff of Marcus and Verus in the German campaign (*c.* 168) and of Marcus and Commodus in the Sarmatian (*c.* 174). He became *cos. II ord.* in 176. He married Annia Fundania Faustina, daughter of M. Annius Libo, himself the son of a M. Annius Verus who was also father of Faustina the Elder (q.v.) and of Annius Verus, the father of M. Aurelius (q.v.). Hence Annia was a first-cousin of the Emperor. For his career see *ILS* 1112.

Lambrechts, *Sénat*, no. 462; A. Degrassi, *I Fasti cons. dell'imp. rom.* (1952), 44 n.; A. Stein, *Die Legaten von Moesien* (1940), 72 ff.                                            C. H. V. S.; M. H.

**POMPONIUS** (6, *PW* 107), SEXTUS, a Roman jurist of the time of Hadrian and the Antonines. He held no official post nor (probably) had he the *ius respondendi* (*see* JURISPRUDENCE); he seems to have given his time to literary activity and probably to teaching. He was one of the most productive legal writers (more than 300 *libri*). But though not without critical ability, he is rather a compiler. Roman legal literature owed to him its biggest work: his commentary on the Edict, composed at Hadrian's order, seems to have had over 150 books, as a passage of the 83rd book, preserved in the *Digest*, deals with a subject treated little more than half-way through the Edict. It is curious that the work was not excerpted directly for the *Digest* and is known only from quotations in later commentaries on the Edict (of Paulus, q.v. 1, and Ulpian, q.v. 1). His otherworks are also extensive: two textbooks of *ius civile*, *Ad Sabinum* (36 books) and *Ad. Q. Mucium* (39 books); two (or one?) works of predominantly casuistic character, *Variae Lectiones* (41 books) and *Epistulae* (20 books). In addition, an epitome *Ex Plautio* and monographs on *Senatus consulta*, *Fideicommissa*, and *Stipulationes*. Especially notable is the booklet *Liber singularis enchiridii*, a unique compendium of the history of Roman legal sources, magistrates, and legal science up to the time of Julian (q.v. 2), Pomponius' contemporary; a long extract from it is preserved in *Dig.* 1. 2. 2. It contains a good many mistakes and corruptions, and has no doubt been shortened and deformed by Justinian's compilers or by an intervening epitomator, but it is nevertheless of value, as it gives information preserved nowhere else. Pomponius had a good knowledge of the older legal literature, and he himself is often quoted by later writers. The *Digest* drew extensively on his works; his contribution to it is, after those of Paulus and Ulpian, one of the largest.

A. M. Honoré, *Gaius* (1962), ch. 3. *See also under* JURISPRUDENCE.
A. B.; B. N.

**POMPTINE MARSHES**, a malaria-stricken region, formed by the stagnation of the Ufens and other streams, lying south-east of Rome between Volscian mountains and Tyrrhenian Sea. Pliny's statement that twenty-four cities once flourished here (*HN* 3. 59) is an exaggeration: Suessa Pometia (q.v.), like the lands later assigned to citizens of the Pomptina and Oufentina tribes, lay outside the marshes proper (Livy 6. 21; 7. 15; 9. 20). The Via Appia crossed the marshes, but travellers apparently preferred to use the parallel, 19-mile-long ship-canal, since the marshes included highwaymen among other perils (Strabo 5. 233; Hor. *Sat.* 1. 5. 10 f.; Juv. 3. 307). From 160 B.C. or earlier numerous attempts were made by Cethegus, Trajan, and others to drain them—a task successfully accomplished in the twentieth century.

M. Hofmann, *PW*, Suppl. viii. 1135 ff. E. T. S.

**PONS MULVIUS** carried the Via Flaminia across the Tiber north of Rome; it is first mentioned in 207 B.C. The existing bridge, the modern *Ponte Milvio*, was first built by Aemilius Scaurus in 109 B.C. and there has been much later rebuilding. Of the four main 60-foot arches, only the southern pair are ancient. Above the pointed cutwaters, both up- and downstream, there are arched flood-passages. The road makes a sloping approach on either side. The Allobroges were trapped here during the Catilinarian conspiracy in 63 B.C. and Maxentius was defeated by Constantine in A.D. 312.

R. Delbrück, *Hellenistische Bauten in Latium* i (1907); T. Frank, *Roman Buildings of the Republic* (1924), 141; M. H. Ballance, *PBSR* 1951, 79 ff.; Nash, *Pict. Dict. Rome* ii. 191 ff. I. A. R.; D. E. S.

**PONTIFEX, PONTIFICES.** The word (cf. *artifex, aurifex*) means one skilled in the important magic of bridge-making (see Giuffrida–Ruggeri, *Journ. Roy. Anthropol. Inst.* 1918, 100; Birt, *Rh. Mus.* 1926, 115 ff., but Latte (*RR* 196, n. 1) argues that *pons* originally meant 'way'), and by extension a priest acquainted with the increasingly elaborate ceremonial of public cult (cf. Cic. *Har. Resp.* 18). At Rome, and with local differences no doubt elsewhere, the *pontifices* were originally an advisory board (*collegium*) whose business it was to assist the chief magistrate in his sacral functions; this is strongly indicated by the fact that their normal meeting-place was the Regia (Pliny, *Ep.* 4. 11. 6). Their number seems to have been primitively three (this was the number at Colonia Genetiva Iulia, see *Lex Ursonensis* [Bruns, *Fontes* 27], 67, and colonies were constituted on the model of Rome), but was successively increased to six, nine, fifteen, and finally (under Caesar) sixteen (Livy, *Periocha* 89; Dio Cass. 42. 51. 4). In historical times the original meaning of their name was quite unheeded, and they presided over the State cult generally. Like all the State priesthood, the *pontifices* were originally patricians; but by the *Lex Ogulnia* of 300 B.C. (Livy 10. 6. 6; see Mommsen, *Staatsr.* ii³. 22) half the college was chosen from the plebeians. Their position as an advisory body remained unaltered, at least in theory, and their decisions were *decreta*, i.e. pronouncements on points submitted to them or coming within their competence; they were not laws and had in themselves no executive effect. In practice it does not seem that they were disregarded, but the magistracy, not the pontiffs themselves, must enforce them.

The head of the college was the *Pontifex Maximus*, whose official residence under the later Republic was in the Regia. He appears to have ousted the *Rex Sacrorum* from his control of the State religion. The original manner of his appointment was presumably by choice either of the king or of the other pontiffs; in historical times (before 212 B.C., but the date is uncertain, see Mommsen, ibid. 27) he was elected by vote of seventeen of the thirty-five tribes, chosen by lot, and thus, by a curious compromise, never by a majority of the people, like secular magistrates. He was head of the whole State clergy, exercising disciplinary functions over some at least of them as well as over the Vestal Virgins (Wissowa, *RK* 509 ff.).

The *collegium pontificum* included, besides the pontiffs themselves, the *flamines*, Vestals, and *rex sacrorum*, but not the augurs nor the minor colleges. In imperial times the post of *pontifex maximus* was held by the reigning

Emperor, Gratian being the first to refuse it, *c.* A.D. 375 (Zosimus 4. 36).

Mommsen and Wissowa, locc. citt.; Latte, *RR* 195 ff. and 400 ff. H. J. R.

**PONTIUS** (1), GAVIUS, Samnite general who trapped a Roman army in the Caudine Forks, 321 B.C., and imposed his own peace terms. Patriotic annalists invented the story that Rome immediately repudiated the peace and defeated Pontius (Livy 9. 2 f.; F. E. Adcock, *CAH* vii. 599). Pontius himself is probably no mere annalists' figment modelled on Pontius Telesinus, Sulla's Samnite opponent. But the story that in 292 he defeated Fabius Gurges, whose father Fabius Rullianus then proceeded to defeat, capture, and execute him, is fiction suggested by events of 213, when Fabius Cunctator was his own son's legate (Livy, *Epit.* 11; 24. 4).

E. T. Salmon, *Samnium and the Samnites* (1967). E. T. S.

**PONTIUS** (2, *PW* 21) **TELESINUS,** descendant of (1), Samnite 'praetor' in the Social War, in 82 B.C. tried to relieve Marius (q.v. 2) at Praeneste and, when prevented, marched on Rome. After a fierce day-and-night battle, he was defeated by Sulla outside the Colline Gate and was killed with most of his army.

E. T. Salmon, *Samnium and the Samnites* (1967), 379. E. B.

**PONTIUS** (3) **PILATUS** (*PW* s.v.), prefect of Judaea (A.D. 26–36). On arrival he offended the Jews by bringing images of the Emperor into Jerusalem, and showed himself unsympathetic to their religious scruples on other occasions; they thought him 'inflexible, merciless, obstinate' (Philo, *Leg. ad Gaium* 38). On the other hand, his condemnation of Jesus, probably on a charge of sedition, seems to have been by way of a concession to them. Summoned to Rome by Tiberius, probably late in 36, upon a complaint of the Samaritans to L. Vitellius (q.v. 2), governor of Syria, he arrived shortly after the Emperor's death. Therewith he disappears from authentic history. Eusebius relates that he committed suicide. Christian opinion was not always hostile. Tertullian (*Apol.* 21. 24) estimated him 'pro sua conscientia Christianus', and he is canonized with his wife in the Coptic Church. The large apocryphal literature on him includes several versions of his presumed report to the Emperor on the condemnation of Jesus.

Joseph. *AJ* 18. 35–89, *BJ* 2. 169–77; the Gospels; Tac. *Ann.* 15. 44. G. A. Müller, *Pontius Pilatus* (1888); E. Schürer, *Gesch. d. jüd. Volkes¹* i (1901), 487 ff.; H. Peter, *Neue Jahrb.* xix (1907), 1 ff.; E. Stauffer, *Nouvelle Clio* 1949/50, 495 ff.; E. M. Smallwood, *Journ. Jewish Stud.* 1954, 12 ff.; J. Blinzler, *Novum Testamentum* 1957, 24 ff.; A. N. Sherwin-White, *Rom. Soc. and Rom. Law in the N.T.* (1963), 24 ff.; M. Sordi, *Il Cristianesimo e Roma* (1965). His title, *praefectus*: A. Frova, *Rend. Ist. Lomb.* 1961, 419 ff.; A. Degrassi, *Rend. Linc.* 1964. The legend: A. Harnack, *Gesch. d. altchr. Lit.* i (1893), 21 ff.; ii. 1 (1897), 603 ff.; Christ–Schmid–Stählin ii. 1106 f.; M. Sordi, *Rend. Linc.* 1957, 58 ff.; P. Winter, *Novum Testamentum* 1964, 37 ff. A. M.; T. J. C.

**PONTUS** (Πόντος), the sea mythologically personified; he is son of Earth (Hes. *Theog.* 131–2); father of Nereus, Ceto, and Eurybia (233 ff.); husband of Mare, i.e. Thalassa (Hyg. *Fab., praef.* 5).

**PONTUS,** a region of northern Asia Minor including the south coast of the Euxine between the Halys and Colchis and extending southward to Cappadocia and Lesser Armenia. A series of mountain ranges with deep valleys runs parallel to the coast. Two small coastal plains are formed by the deltas of the Halys and the Iris, which break through the mountains and provide the main lines of drainage and communication. It has but one convenient cross-road, from Amisus to Sebasteia. Pontus is well watered and fertile, with a mild climate at the coast and in the valleys. Olives and other fruits, nuts, pasture, and grain abound near the coast. The coastal range supplies abundant timber for ships, and the mountains are rich in iron (*see* CHALYBES), copper, silver, salt, and alum.

The social and political structure of Pontus resembled that of Cappadocia; the same village population organized in territorial units, the same large temple territories with numerous sacred slaves ruled by priests, and the same feudal iranized nobility. Some mountainous regions in eastern Pontus remained for long uncivilized in tribal territories. The Greek colonies on the coast were simply trading stations with little or no territory.

The centre and strength of the Pontic kingdom was the Pontic territory proper, but the kings continually added to it until it reached its greatest extent under Mithridates VI (*see* MITHRIDATES I–VI, PHARNACES I). They apparently brought the priests and nobility under control, and established a regional administration, but they did little to develop cities. Pompey gave much of the kingdom to princes, Deiotarus of Galatia and the priest of Comana, and divided the rest among various centres, chosen with an excellent eye for natural advantages, which he raised to municipal status and included in the province of Bithynia and Pontus. Besides the coast cities these were Magnopolis, Amaseia, Cabeira-Diospolis, Zela, Megalopolis, Neapolis, Pompeiopolis, and probably Nicopolis. Practically all of these reverted to native rulers under Antony, but in the early Empire they gradually returned, often under new names, to the Roman provincial regime. The western part was known as Pontus Galaticus, with Amaseia as its metropolis. The eastern part remained under the rule of Polemon's (q.v. 1) dynasty, until it was annexed in A.D. 64, and retained the name of Pontus Polemoniacus, with the former royal capital Neocaesarea (Cabeira-Diospolis) as metropolis. Thus Pontus became part of the Galatian-Cappadocian province, and it remained joined with Cappadocia (q.v.) from Trajan until Diocletian, who divided it between his two provinces of Diospontus and Polemoniacus. To the end Pontus kept much of its native character; the cities remained regional and artificial, the feudal aristocracy important, and in the eastern portion the native tribes were only slightly touched by Hellenic civilization.

Th. Reinach, *Mithridates Eupator* (1895); *Trois royaumes* (1888); J. A. R. Munro, *JHS* 1901, 52 ff.; J. G. C. Anderson, F. Cumont, H. Grégoire, *Studia Pontica* i–iii (1903–10); Jones, *Cities E. Rom. Prov.* 148 ff.; Magie, *Rom. Rule Asia Min.* 177 ff., and index.
T. R. S. B.

**POPILLIUS** (1, *PW* 18) **LAENAS**, GAIUS, consul in 172 B.C., when he defended M. Popillius, whose highhanded conduct in Liguria had incurred the Senate's disapproval, was envoy in Greece in 170, and in 168 led the embassy to Egypt which after Pydna forced Antiochus Epiphanes to withdraw his army immediately from Egypt: he demanded a decision before the king stepped outside a circle drawn by Popillius.

Scullard, *Rom. Pol.* 195, 210 ff.
A. H. McD.

**POPILLIUS** (2, *PW* 28) **LAENAS**, PUBLIUS, son of (1), praetor *c.* 135 B.C.; as consul (132) he severely punished supporters of Ti. Gracchus and, under a law of C. Gracchus, had to go into exile, but returned under a law of Bestia (q.v.) after the judicial vindication of Opimius. He built a road in north-east Italy (*see* VIA POPILLIA). If *ILS* 23 refers to him (the name is lost), he was praetor in Sicily, built a road from Rhegium to Capua with a *forum* named after himself, and as consul furthered agrarian reform on behalf of the Optimates. But it seems better to refer the inscription to T. Annius Rufus, *cos.* 128 B.C. (*see* VIA ANNIA 2).

T. P. Wiseman, *PBSR* 1964, 21.
E. B.

**POPLIFUGIA.** A mystery festival recorded in the Roman calendar under 5 July. The form of the name resembles that of the equally puzzling Regifugium (q.v.). As an aetiological legend, it was explained by the flight of the people on the occasion of the death of Romulus (Dion. Hal. 2. 56. 5, Plut. *Rom.* 29). Wissowa (*RK* 102) does not seem to have proved that Jupiter was the deity of the festival. Latte (*RR* 128) may be right in his conjecture that at this ceremony and at the Regifugium some ritual was performed which was supposed to evoke terrible powers whose presence must be avoided.
H. W. P.

**POPPAEA** (*PW* 4) **SABINA,** daughter of T. Ollius (d. A.D. 31), and named after her maternal grandfather C. Poppaeus Sabinus (*cos.* A.D. 9, governor of Moesia 12–35), was married first to Rufrius Crispinus, prefect of the praetorians under Claudius. During her second marriage, to the future Emperor Otho (q.v.), she became (by 58) mistress of Nero (so Tac. *Ann.* 13. 45 f.; another version in *Hist.* 1. 13). It was allegedly at her instigation that Nero murdered Agrippina (q.v. 3) in 59 and in 62 divorced, banished, and executed Octavia (q.v. 3). Nero now married Poppaea, who bore a daughter Claudia (63); both mother and child received the surname Augusta, but the child died at four months. In 65, pregnant again, she died from a kick which Nero gave her in a fit of temper, and was accorded a public funeral and divine honours. The supposition that she was interested in Judaism is dubious.

Syme, *Tacitus*, see index; E. M. Smallwood, *JTS* 1959, 329 ff.; O. Schönberger, *Hist.* 1963, 500 ff. Iconography: see *PW*.
T. J. C.

**POPPAEDIUS SILO,** QUINTUS, friend of Drusus (q.v. 2), then *imperator* of the northern group of rebels in the Social War (*see* PAPIUS). He defeated and killed Caepio (q.v. 2) in 90 B.C. and the consul Cato (q.v. 3) in 89; but, after withdrawing southward and recovering Bovianum, was himself defeated and killed (88), probably by Metellus (q.v. 7) Pius.

E. T. Salmon, *Samnium and the Samnites* (1967), see index.
E. B.

**POPULARES** were Roman political leaders who, working through the People (*populus*) rather than the Senate, challenged the predominance of the ruling oligarchy of nobles, the Optimates. The resultant struggle was a main feature of domestic politics from 133 B.C. onwards. Populares are discussed s.v. OPTIMATES (q.v.).
H. H. S.

**POPULATION** (GREEK). Most Greek States from at least the sixth century (and the development of the common use of writing) kept records of population, it must be assumed, which were generally concerned with citizen status and duties or with financial obligations and benefits: therefore of the free rather than of slaves and of adult men rather than of women and children except in so far as these latter were involved in matters of citizenship. The multiplication of inscriptions from the fourth century onwards shows an increasing stress on records, but these are generally religious, social, or honorific, and it is uncertain how far local figures of population and levies were consolidated and recorded in any permanent fashion. The ultimate preoccupation being with *effectives* the relation of these to over-all totals is often obscure. In general (because of the principal concern of records with duties) there is the difficulty of passing from figures for male citizens to those for total citizen and free population, and from the citizen population of a *polis* to the total population of a geographical area. Calculations based on land areas are highly speculative, like all observations, also, based on the present aspect of Greece; for its character, fertility, and capacity to bear population have undergone extensive changes since antiquity, and indeed in quite recent times (compare the development of the Vardar-Haliakmon region of Macedonia in recent years; or of Lake Copais). Reputations for fertility and for the production of food surpluses have to be conditioned by a consideration of social and political organization (as in Thessaly, with large estates and serfs contrasted with the situation in classical Attica). Air photographs are less likely to yield indications of economic development and settlement than in the case of south Italy. Even in Attica a good deal remains to be done on the interpretation of settlement remains and cemeteries. Bound up with problems of population are questions of birth-rates, infant mortality (natural and artificial), and death-rates, important for the judgement of numbers in age-groups. Ultimately the study of skeletal remains and cemeteries will give more reliable information than comparisons with other times and regions supposedly comparable. It is much to be regretted that before the spread of Christianity grave-inscriptions rarely give ages or causes of death (apart from death in war or at sea). Greek antiquity lacked the factual and statistical studies (even if writers, and especially orators, had been convinced of the value of facts) which are the necessary basis of demographical conclusions.

Apart from calculations based on land areas, the general character of settlement, and the scattered references to military effectives in certain battles between Greek States (for a recent and very superficial account resting mainly on Cavaignac and Jardé, and giving some references to modern literature, see P. Salmon, 'La Population de la Grèce antique', *Bulletin de l'association Guillaume Budé* 1959, 448 ff.), the main body of information is for Athens. As noted above, contemporary documents are limited in numbers and scope, and such promising sources of material as lists of *epheboi* (in effect the 19- and 20-year age classes), *bouleutai* (see S. Dow, *Prytaneis*, *Hesp.* Suppl. i, 1937), and *diaitetai* (in effect the 60-year age group) are defective in almost every case and therefore ambiguous (see Gomme, *JHS* 1959, 65 f.). The excavation of the Athenian Agora has not yielded as much as was hoped. At Athens every boy at 18 was registered in his deme, and the total of deme registers formed the list of those entitled to attend the Ecclesia. Every boy of 18 of zeugite census or over (*see* ZEUGITAI) was also entered in the hoplite ranks of the army, and a list was kept of *thetes* (q.v.) liable for service in the fleet; boys and girls were entered in their phratries (q.v.) also. Metics (q.v.) were registered in their deme of residence; and there was perhaps a poll-tax on slaves. Even so this information has come down to modern times in a fragmentary and garbled form. Other statistics on which population calculations might be based are in worse case: cereal production (figures for one year); cereal imports (also for one year). Calculations based on State payments are too uncertain to be of value. Scope for guesses and conjecture is therefore large (especially when concerned with naval levies and triremes), and even in texts of agreed dependability, such as Thucydides, there are serious problems of interpretation (such as possible liability or exemption in the case of certain duties). Apart from the useful recent account of A. French, *The Growth of the Athenian Economy* (1964), 135 ff., the problems involved are well illustrated in A. H. M. Jones's Appendix (161 ff.) to his *Athenian Democracy* (1957) and Gomme's rejoinder, 'The Population of Athens again', *JHS* 1959, 61 ff. A particularly vexed problem is presented by slave numbers, especially the immense figures given in sources of varying reliability for Corinth, Aegina, and Athens. For a sceptical view of them and for other problems (again of interpretation in some cases, as of the χειροτέχναι of Thuc. 7. 27. 5) see Gomme, 'The Slave Population of Athens', *JHS* 1946,

127 ff. Equally disputed must be questions of increase or decrease of population at various periods, with the complication that an increase of population may be attended by a decline in citizen numbers. Thus it is difficult to say whether the colonizing activity of the archaic period was carried out with or without a lasting reduction of population in Greece. It is commonly asserted that overpopulation was a feature of the fifth century, but it is quite unclear what effect military losses and the establishment of cleruchies had on Athens. What were the effects of mercenary service and Alexander's conquests in the fourth century? Certainly from the time of Alexander decline of citizen numbers and of the *polis* unit did not necessarily mean a decline in the numbers of Greeks (though 'Greek' was now to a considerable extent a cultural rather than an ethnic term) and in the influence of Hellenism. Few of the matters of controversy are likely to be settled, and with this in mind the following should be regarded as reasonable deductions from inadequate information.

**2.** *Separate States.* From the meagre evidence the following rough figures have been estimated for Attica (area, *c.* 2,500 sq. km):

| Date B.C. | Citizens: Men 18–59 | | Citizens: Total | Metics: | | Slaves: Total | Total population of Attica |
|---|---|---|---|---|---|---|---|
| | Hoplites and cavalry | Thetes | | Men 18–59 | Total | | |
| 480 | 15,000? | 20,000? | 140,000? | ? | ? | ? | ? |
| 431 | 25,000 | 18,000 | 172,000 | 9,500 | 28,500 | 110,000 | 310,000 |
| 425 | 16,500 | 12,500 | 116,000 | 7,000 | 21,000 | 80,000 | 217,000 |
| 400 | 11,000? | 11,000? | 90,000 | ? | ? | ? | ? |
| 323 | 14,500 | 13,500 | 112,000 | 12,000? | 42,000? | 106,000? | 260,000 |
| 313 | 12,000 | 9,000 | 84,000 | 10,000 | 35,000 | | |

There must have been far fewer metics and slaves in 480, and again in 400 than in 431; but we have no figures even for a rough estimate. There was considerable emigration to colonies between 480 and 431, less between 400 and 323. Of the total population in 431 perhaps half lived in Athens, Piraeus, and environs (not entirely urban in character)—one-third of the citizens, nearly all the metics, and about two-thirds of the slaves; a hundred years later perhaps three-quarters of the total.

**3.** For other States we have only figures for their hoplite forces and their approximate areas. Argos (1,400 sq. km) had in 400 a citizen population equal to that of Athens, but not as many metics and slaves; Corinth (880 sq. km) in the fifth and fourth centuries less than half the hoplites of Athens in 400, so less than half the population—perhaps 80,000. Arcadia (4,700 sq. km), a poor country from which men were always emigrating, had 6,000–7,000 hoplites in the fourth and third centuries; by comparison with Attica this would mean about 80,000–90,000 citizen population—two-thirds only of its population today—with but few slaves to add; there were probably far more men below the hoplite census. Elis, a much richer land, but rural in character, may have had a population of 80,000. The population of Laconia (8,500 sq. km, of which Messenia had nearly 3,000) is much more difficult to estimate. It had much of the richest land in Greece, but it was thinly populated. The Spartiates of 21–50 years numbered some 3,000, so perhaps 4,000 in all (i.e. *c.* 12,000 total population); the *perioeci* in the army were also about 3,000, but in what proportion to the total of *perioikoi* we do not know. Still less do we know the number of helots, except that they were more numerous relatively to the free population than in any other State with serfs.

**4.** Boeotia (2,600 sq. km) was prosperous and agricultural, with few foreigners and slaves; it put 7,000 hoplites and 1,000 horse in the field in 424, and similar numbers in the fourth century; it had about 10,000 of hoplite rank in all the third century. In 424 there were 10,000 light-armed. This yields c. 25,000–30,000 adult males, 90,000–100,000 citizen population (rather larger than today). Of the islands Corcyra (720 sq. km), parts of Euboea, Thasos (300), Lesbos (1,750), Chios (820), Samos (470), Naxos (450), Andros (400), Paros (200), and Rhodes (1460) were highly developed, and their density of population approached that of Athens in 323; Corcyra probably and Chios perhaps exceeded it, each with large numbers of slaves. Aegina (100 sq. km), before its conquest by Athens, was exceptionally well populated (perhaps 25,000–30,000 persons, nearly half of them slaves). The cities of the Hellespont and Bosporus and those in the Euxine were very prosperous, but we have no figures. Ionia and especially Miletus had declined since their conquest by Persia; Erythrae and Ephesus were the richest of the Ionian cities in the fifth century, but neither half so rich as Byzantium.

5. In the West Syracuse (4,700 sq. km) rivalled Athens in population, and in the early fourth century easily out-distanced it. Acragas (4,300 sq. km) was not far behind, and Selinus, Gela, Himera, Messene were all populous. In all the Greek cities of Sicily (25,500 sq. km) there may have been 700,000–800,000 persons (including numerous slaves). In south and south-west Italy Tarentum became in the fourth century the most populous, not much behind contemporary Athens; Sybaris and Croton had surpassed it in the sixth and fifth centuries. The total Italiote population may have equalled that of the Greeks in Sicily.

K. J. Beloch, *Bevölkerung der griechisch-römischen Welt* (1886), and 'Griechische Aufgebote' (*Klio* 1905–6); A. W. Gomme, *Population of Athens* (1933). A. W. G.; R. J. H.

**POPULATION** (ROMAN WORLD). The earliest information of value for the demographic history of the Roman world comes from surviving census figures. In its original form the Roman census (q.v.) was a survey made for military and fiscal purposes, which seems to have included all male adult citizens. The republican period has left thirty-seven census figures which, although derived from a number of different authors, are sufficiently self-consistent to appear authentic for the most part. The figures for the fifth century B.C. indicate an average of approximately 120,000 male adult citizens at Rome. In the fourth century the number rose above 160,000, almost reaching 300,000 in the mid third century. But the census was not always a thorough record of actual citizen numbers. Under normal practice returns could apparently be made only in Rome itself; and the heavy penalties for failure to register were not enforced consistently enough to ensure that all citizens living at a distance travelled to Rome to make their declarations. As the area under Roman rule grew, the geographical source of omission certainly increased, especially after the abolition of the citizen tribute in 167 B.C., which removed the main fiscal reason for making a thorough count of citizen numbers. Natural demographic trends within the citizen population were further obscured by losses due to war casualties and the removal of Roman citizens to Latin colonies, and by additions to the citizen number through the manumission of slaves and the incorporation of new citizens from other communities.

The effect of external circumstances on the census figures is especially apparent in the sudden jump from the total of 318,823 citizens recorded in 131/30 to the number of 394,736 in 125/4. This rise of 24 per cent in six years, which is too great to be explained by natural increase, has been plausibly attributed to the registration of holdings recently acquired under the Gracchan land-laws by citizens who had neglected to register in any previous census. The increase was sustained in the census of 115/14

B.C., whose total was 394,336. Although Roman citizenship was extended to the whole of Italy south of the Po in 89 B.C., the next census failed to show any commensurate increase in citizen numbers (463,000 in 86/5). The census of 70/69 produced a much higher total (900,000), but returns were apparently still made only in Rome. When in 28 B.C. a full and systematic survey was at last carried out, using the local machinery set up by Caesar, a total of a different order of size emerged: 4,063,000 Because it is so large, this figure has been interpreted by Beloch and others as including women and children; but the terminology of the *Res Gestae* and other considerations imply that the total was one of adult male citizens, as in previous censuses. The discrepancy was probably due mainly to the much greater efficiency with which the new census was carried out. The extension of Roman citizenship to Cisalpine Gaul in 49 B.C. also meant the inclusion of a large number of new citizens of recent date. The geographical implications of the figure are imprecise, because by 28 B.C. Roman colonization overseas was already extensive, and a certain number of the citizens recorded then must have lived outside Italy. Nevertheless, the population of Italy was probably very much higher now than it had been two centuries earlier, when Polybius' figures for fighting strength (225 B.C.) suggest a total free population for the peninsula of about 3 million.

The last three Roman census figures that survive continue to show increase in citizen numbers: 4,233,000 in 8 B.C.; 4,937,000 in A.D. 14; the total in A.D. 47 is given as 5,984,072 by Tacitus but as approximately 6,900,000 by three later writers. Some absolute rise in population under the early Principate is almost certainly indicated; but the concern about the citizen birth-rate shown by Augustus and some of his successors suggests that further enfranchisements of provincials and freedmen may have made an important contribution to the apparent buoyancy of these figures.

The very fragmentary evidence for regional population under the Empire includes statistics for some of the most important cities of the East. A Roman city normally possessed rural territory whose free inhabitants were combined in the local census figure with those who lived in the town proper. Thus the population of the urban nucleus must as a rule have been substantially less than the total figure reported in ancient sources. According to Diodorus, Alexandria (second or third city of the Empire in size) numbered over 300,000 free inhabitants at the end of the Republic. Antioch was not much smaller than this when Strabo wrote under Augustus. A free population of about 140,000 at Pergamum is suggested by Galen in the mid second century A.D. This number was at least equalled at Ephesus, to judge from an inscription of the late second century. A total free population of 117,000 was recorded at Syrian Apamea in the census of A.D. 6/7. Although very large cities were fewer in the West than in the East, Roman Carthage vied with Alexandria for the place of second city of the Empire, and thus can hardly have had less than 300,000/400,000 inhabitants at its height. Direct evidence for imperial Rome is lacking, but most modern estimates place its total population at roughly 1 million. None of the ancient figures so far cited includes slaves (q.v.), though they undoubtedly formed a substantial part of the labour force of the Empire as a whole. Galen suggests that there were as many slaves at Pergamum in his day as there were male citizens of the town.

Any estimate of the over-all population of the Empire is bound to be speculative, as there are no sound statistics for substantial areas which can be used as a basis for general inference. Nevertheless, Beloch's estimated total for the whole Empire of 54 million at the death of Augustus is a plausible indication of the order of size likely at that

**POPULATION** (cont.) date. The population of many areas was probably higher by the 160s, when the first of a series of plagues struck the Empire. A general fall in population by the fourth century A.D. is indicated by contractions in the area of cultivated land and in the occupied area of cities.

K. J. Beloch, Bevölkerung der griechisch-römischen Welt (1886); Frank, Econ. Survey, see index, s.v.; A. H. M. Jones, Ancient Economic History (1948); K. J. Beloch, Jahrbücher für Nationalök. und Statistik, III Folge, xiii (1897), 321; Atene e Roma 1898, 257; Rh. Mus. 1899, 414; Klio 1903, 471; E. Ciccotti, Metron ix. 2 (1931), 111; R. P. Duncan-Jones, JRS 1963, 85; Hist. 1964, 199. On Roman mortality figures, M. K. Hopkins, Population Studies 1966, 245.
R. P. D.-J.

**POPULONIA** (Etr. *Pupluna*), on a promontory overlooking the harbour of Porto Baratti, was the port of the metal-rich (copper, iron, lead, tin) zone of north-west Tuscany, and the smelting-centre for the iron of Elba; in due course it became one of the twelve cities of Etruria in its own right, and the only one to be established directly on the sea. Little is known of the Etruscan town, apart from its polygonal walls; attention has been concentrated rather on the characteristic series of late orientalizing domed chamber tombs, constructed of stone blocks and covered with tumuli surrounded by stone kerbs.

A. Minto, Populonia: la necropoli arcaica (1922); id. Populonia (1943); id. Stud. Etr. 1954, 291 ff.; A. de Agostino, ibid. 1955-6, 255 ff., 1962, 275 ff. and Populonia, La città e la necropoli (n.d.); Scullard, Etr. Cities, 141 ff.
D. W. R. R.

**POPULUS**, a citizen-body: thus *populus Romanus* meant the whole Roman community, independent of classes and social distinctions (excluding minors, women, and slaves). Probably the original meaning was the citizens as a military body, as is shown by the title *magister populi* (*see* DICTATOR). During the struggle of the Orders *populus* indicated the community as distinguished from the *plebs*, and in legal parlance the word continued to be used to denote an electoral or legislative body in which patricians were present. At the time of the crisis of the nobility, *populus* designated the classes supporting the *populares* in their opposition to the Senate. In phrases as *senatus populusque Romanus* and *amicus populi Romani* it represented the people as the sovereign body. It exercised its powers, electoral, legislative, and judicial, through *comitia*, *curiae*, *tribus*, and *centuriae* (qq.v.).

Mommsen, Röm. Forsch. i. 168 ff.; Röm. Staatsr. iii³. 3 ff. P. T.

**PORCIA** (*PW* 28) was daughter of Cato (5) and wife first of Bibulus (1) and from 45 B.C. of Brutus (5). She shared the political ideals of her father and her husbands, insisted on being let into the secret of the plot to murder Caesar, and took part with her mother-in-law Servilia in the conference of Republicans at Antium on 8 June 44. When Brutus sailed for the East she returned to Rome, where she became ill and in the early summer of 43 took her life, perhaps by inhaling fumes from a brazier (Plut. *Brut.* 53, Cic. *ad Brut.* 1. 9. 2, 17. 7). The less good tradition makes her do this on the news of Brutus' death in 42.
T. J. C.

**PORCIUS** (1, *PW* 48) **LICINUS** (fl. probably at the end of the 2nd c. B.C.) wrote a literary history of Rome in trochaic septenarii: we possess two lines which date the coming of the Muse to Latium in the Second Punic War and eleven on Terence and his relations with the Scipionic circle. An elegiac epigram clearly based on a Hellenistic original which Gellius quotes from him represents the beginnings of the influence of Alexandrian poetry in Rome.

Fragments in Morel, FPL. C. J. F.

**PORCIUS** (2, *PW* 47) **LATRO**, MARCUS, Augustan rhetor; born in Spain, contemporary and intimate friend of the Elder Seneca. He was the most distinguished representative of the new rhetoric at Rome, more at home in the schools than in the courts, but critical of its Asianic excesses, and combined a vigorous and natural style with a vast capacity for work (Sen. *Controv.* 1 *pr.* 13–24); among his many admirers was Ovid, who borrowed ideas from him in his verse (*Controv.* 2. 2. 8). He died A.D. 4.
C. J. F.

**PORPHYRION**, POMPONIUS (early 3rd c. A.D.), scholar, whose commentary on Horace is still extant (ed. A. Holder, 1894), though not in its original form. Porphyrion's exposition, intended for school pupils, includes subject-matter, grammar, and style. He incorporated the work of earlier commentators, including Acron (q.v.).

Schanz–Hosius, § 602. J. F. M.

**PORPHYRY** (Πορφύριος) (A.D. 232/3–c. 305), scholar, philosopher, and student of religions. He was born at Tyre (or Batanea in Palestine); originally bore the Syrian name *Malchus*; studied under Longinus at Athens; became devoted personal disciple of Plotinus at Rome, 262–3; edited Plotinus' *Enneads*, after A.D. 300. His extremely numerous and varied writings (seventy-seven titles are listed by Bidez) fall into the following classes. (1) Early philosophico-religious works, written before his conversion to Plotinism: Περὶ τῆς ἐκ λογίων φιλοσοφίας (extensive fragments preserved, containing curious information about theurgic practices); Περὶ ἀγαλμάτων (fragments extant); perhaps Φιλόσοφος ἱστορία, a history of philosophy down to Plato, from which the extant Πυθαγόρου βίος is an excerpt. (2) Later works on philosophy and religion, written from the Plotinian standpoint. The following are completely or partially extant: Ἀφορμαὶ πρὸς τὰ νοητά, a disjointed collection of edifying thoughts, borrowed or adapted from Plotinus; Περὶ ἀποχῆς ἐμψύχων, a treatise on vegetarianism in four books, drawing on Theophrastus, etc.; Πρὸς Ἀνεβώ, a letter on theurgy, strikingly sceptical in tone; Πρὸς Μαρκέλλαν, an *epistola moralis* addressed to his wife. An essay *De regressu animae* is known from quotations in Augustine; the Σύμμικτα ζητήματα mainly from Nemesius. The important treatise Κατὰ Χριστιανῶν, in fifteen books, was condemned to be burnt in 448, but interesting fragments survive, from which we learn that Porphyry used the modern weapon of historical criticism, e.g. to establish the lateness of the Book of Daniel. Elsewhere he similarly proved the 'Book of Zoroaster' to be a forgery. (3) Περὶ Πλωτίνου βίου καὶ τῆς τάξεως τῶν βιβλίων αὐτοῦ: this has the double character of a biography of Plotinus and a preface to Plotinus' edition of the *Enneads*. (4) Numerous philosophical commentaries on Plato, Aristotle, Theophrastus, Plotinus, of which only a school-commentary on Aristotle's *Categories* survives complete. Here belongs also the Εἰσαγωγὴ εἰς τὰς Ἀριστ. Κατηγορίας or Περὶ τῶν πέντε φωνῶν, which became a standard medieval textbook of logic. (5) Philological works include Ὁμηρικὰ ζητήματα, a landmark in the history of Homeric scholarship which Schrader has reconstructed; and the extant Περὶ τοῦ ἐν Ὀδυσσείᾳ τῶν νυμφῶν ἄντρου, a specimen of allegorizing interpretation. Porphyry wrote also on grammar, rhetoric, and the history of scholarship. The Βίος Ὁμήρου falsely included in Plutarch's *Moralia* is sometimes attributed to Porphyry. (6) Extant works on technical subjects are a commentary (incomplete) on Ptolemy's *Harmonica*; an introduction to Ptolemy's *Tetrabiblos*; and a treatise on embryology, Πρὸς Γαῦρον περὶ τοῦ πῶς ἐμψυχοῦται τὰ ἔμβρυα (formerly attributed to Galen but probably by Porphyry).

Though unoriginal and often uncritical, Porphyry is a remarkable polymath, and has the good habit of quoting his authorities by name; he has thus preserved many fragments of older learning. As a thinker he is unimportant: 'in the whole extant work of Porphyry there is not a thought or an image which one can confidently affirm to be his own' (Bidez).

LIFE AND WORKS. J. Bidez, *Vie de Porphyre* (1913: includes collection of ancient sources and full bibliography).

TEXTS. Π. τῆς ἐκ λογίων φιλοσοφίας, G. Wolff (1856); frs. of Π. ἀγαλμάτων and *De regressu animae* in Bidez, op. cit.; Πυθαγόρου βίος, Π. ἀποχῆς, Π. τοῦ ἐν 'Οδ. τῶν νυμφῶν ἄντρου, Πρὸς Μαρκ., and frs. of Φιλοσ. ἱστορία, Nauck, *Porphyrii opuscula²* (1886); 'Αφορμαί, B. Mommert (1907); Πρὸς 'Ανεβώ, A. R. Sodano (1958); frs. of Κ. Χριστιανῶν, A. Harnack, *Abh. Berl. Ak.* 1916 and *Sitzb. Berl. Ak.* 1921; Π. Πλωτίνου βίου in editions of Plot.; works on Arist. in *Comm. in Arist. graeca* iv. 1; 'Ομηρικὰ ζητ., H. Schrader (1880–90); Εἰς τὰ 'Αρμονικὰ Πτολ., I. Düring (Goteborg, 1932); Εἰς τὴν ἀποτελεσματικὴν (Τετράβιβλον) Πτολ., H. Wolf (1559); Πρὸς Γαῦρον, K. Kalbfleisch, *Abh. Berl. Ak.* (1895, Anhang), French trans. and comm., A.-J. Festugière in *La Révélation d'Hermès*, vol. iii; frs. of Σύμμικτα ζητ. with comm., H. Dörrie (1959); frs. of comm. on Plato's *Timaeus*, A. R. Sodano (1964). A complete edition of the fragments by H. Dörrie is in preparation. E. R. D.

**PORSEN(N)A**, probably an Etruscan title misinterpreted by Roman annalistic tradition as the name of a chieftain. The story went that, summoned by the exiled Tarquinius (q.v. 2) Superbus, Lars Porsenna of Clusium vainly laid siege to Rome. Another (and obviously more reliable) version, however, whether deriving from the Etruscan legend of Mastarna (q.v.) or independently of it, asserts that Porsenna conquered the Capitol and ruled over Rome, imposing harsh terms on her citizens. Porsenna and Mastarna are therefore to be considered most probably as the Roman and Etruscan name respectively of the same Etruscan king (either a friend or, more likely, an enemy of his fellow Etruscan Tarquinius), who attained power at Rome towards the end of the sixth century. Later speculation fitted him into the list of the traditional seven kings of Rome by equating Mastarna with Servius Tullius or by connecting the story of Porsenna with the fall and the attempted restoration of the Tarquins. It is a fact, however, that Porsenna belongs to (and represents) the epoch of mutually friendly relations between (Etruscan) Rome and Cumae as well as of the rivalry between Rome and the Latin League, whether the latter arose in self-defence against Porsenna, then Etruscan lord of Rome, or at a later stage, namely after the overthrow (or as the cause of the overthrow) of the monarchy.

G. De Sanctis, *Klio* 1902, 96 ff.; L. Pareti, *Stud. Etr.* 1931, 154 ff.; A. Alföldi, *Early Rome and the Latins* (1964), 51 ff.; Ogilvie, *Comm. Livy 1–5*, 255. P. T.

**PORTICO.** In Roman Italy and the western provinces the functions of the Greek Stoa (q.v. 2) were largely taken over by the Basilica (q.v.), but from at least 193 B.C. (the Porticus Aemilia) colonnaded porticoes (*porticus*) of similar architectural form were a commonplace of Roman public architecture, passing thence also into domestic use. Some were long streetside galleries (e.g. the Porticus Vipsania, and commonly at Ostia). Many more were enclosed rectangular open areas, with or without buildings in the middle (Porticus Metelli, Octaviae, Philippi, Pompei, at Rome; the Piazzale of the Corporations at Ostia; the Forum at Pompeii; the Palaestra at Herculaneum). The colonnaded streets (*viae porticatae*) of the eastern provinces represent a distinctive and widespread development of the idea. J. B. W.-P.

**PORTORIA** were in origin duties on goods entering or leaving harbours, the upkeep of which was a charge on public funds. Such levies were made in Italian harbours under the Republic, though they were temporarily abolished between 60 B.C. and Caesar's dictatorship, and in provincial harbours such as Syracuse (Cic. *Verr.* 2. 185; cf. *ILS* 38. 2. 32 ff.). In the Principate a customs-duty was levied in the provinces on the major traffic-routes and for this purpose several provinces might form a single unit (e.g. the Gallic and the Danubian provinces) in the sense that duty was raised at a uniform rate (often, as in Gaul, 2½ per cent) within the area. There is some evidence that a higher charge was made at the frontiers of the Empire—25 per cent at Leuce Come on the Red Sea, and, probably, at Palmyra (*AE* 1947, 179 f.). Otherwise the *portoria* were levied solely for revenue purposes and were not protective. Their collection was let out to *publicani* (q.v.) during the Republic and the first century of the Principate (Tac. *Ann.* 13. 50–1). In the early second century these were gradually replaced by individual *conductores* (q.v.) and in the late second and early third century these in their turn by imperial *procuratores* (q.v.).

S. J. de Laet, *Portorium* (1949); *Ant. Class.* 1953, 98 ff.; R. Étienne, *Rev. Ét. Anc.* 1951, 62 ff. G. H. S.; F. G. B. M.

**PORTRAITURE** (GREEK). The Greeks were the first to attempt realistic representations of individuals instead of the 'types' that had been current for thousands of years. At first—during the whole of the archaic period—they too made generalized figures of the people they commemorated on tombs and in sanctuaries. But in the first half of the fifth century B.C., when naturalism in the rendering of the human form had been attained, one can note the beginning of an interest in individuality. The famous head of Themistocles found at Ostia in 1938 is a notable example. This interest in realism, observable also in some figures in the vase-paintings of the time, was apparently diverted during the second half of the fifth century B.C. into the more idealistic trend introduced by Phidias and Polyclitus (qq.v.). The portrait of Pericles, which survives in several Roman copies (*see* CRESILAS), shows the mingling of a typical statesman and of the individual Pericles. This generalization, combined with progressive naturalism, continued through the fourth century, until during the Hellenistic period admirably realistic portraits were achieved. The various stages are exemplified by the portraits first of Thucydides, Plato, Aristotle, and Alexander (4th c.), then by those of Demosthenes, Epicurus, Philetaerus, Euthydemus I (3rd c.), and finally by the portraits of the blind Homer and of Pseudo-Seneca, as well as many a small portrait of a Hellenistic ruler on the coinage of the second and first centuries B.C. They form the immediate precursors of the 'veristic' portraits of republican Rome. It is also noteworthy that throughout the Greek period not only were portraits of contemporaries produced, but likenesses were invented of the great personalities of the epochs before real portraiture was practised. A notable example is the portrait of Homer, of whom we have invented likenesses made during the fifth century, the fourth, and the Hellenistic period, all different from one another.

Practically all these Greek portraits survive only in Roman copies, and we owe to the Roman interest in the great Greek personalities the survival of Greek portraiture. In most cases these Roman copies, however, consist only of herms and busts instead of the statues produced in Greek times.

In addition to sculptured portraits the Greeks also had painted ones. One hears of Apelles as a famous portraitist at the time of Alexander the Great. But of these paintings no trace survives, except perhaps for some adaptations in later Roman mosaics.

G. M. A. Richter, *The Portraiture of the Greeks*, 3 vols. (1965). G. M. A. R.

**PORTRAITURE** (ROMAN). The true Roman portrait, that is, the realistic, unidealized likeness of a specific individual as he or she actually appeared, was a legacy during the second century B.C. from late Hellenistic art. But in Rome and Italy immigrant Greek portraitists of the time found a particularly favourable milieu for their craft in the ancient ritual practice of preserving in the home and parading at family funerals *imagines* (q.v.) or masks of ancestors and the newly dead. These *imagines*, originally not death-masks cast from the faces of the deceased, but very generalized representations, now became under Hellenistic stimulus highly individualized and realistic (Polyb. 6. 53). And it was the marriage of these two traditions, that of the late Hellenistic portrait style with that of Roman religious practice, which produced, from the beginning of the first century B.C. onwards, the great array of heads, busts, and statues of Roman subjects, in marble, stone, or bronze, that have come down to us. The outstanding feature of most of these late republican portraits is their 'verism', that is, the faithful, relentless chronicling of all facial details such as lines, wrinkles, creases, and folds of flesh, and even warts and moles. Old age is a favourite subject.

Under the Empire the labelled and often precisely dated coin portraits of emperors, empresses, etc., provide a firm basis for the dating of private portraits, since court fashions in hair- and beard-styles were swiftly adopted throughout the Roman world. Other criteria are changes in general sculptural style and in the bust forms. The bust, which under the late Republic had included little more than head and neck, incorporated the shoulders by Flavian times, and in the early third century had grown into a half-length figure, after which it shrank again. Stylistically, the portraits of Augustus show a strongly idealizing and dignified character, which turns frigid with Tiberius' likenesses, while greater naturalism and an emotional tendency mark the portraits of Claudius and Nero respectively. Republican realism persisted meanwhile in some private portraits and became the official style under the Flavians. Trajanic portraits continue this tradition. Hadrianic iconography combines classical idealism with a more 'baroque' manner: the hair is curled, a beard is worn, and the irises and pupils of the eyes are plastically marked, as they are in all portraits from now onwards. The Antonine Emperors show a distinctive pictorial style, the abundant hair and rich beard being drilled and the marble surfaces polished or left rough to secure effects of light and shade. Under the military Emperors of the third century this picturesque style gave way to simpler treatment. The hair and beard are close-cut and rendered by pitted surfaces; and this manner, after a brief reversion under Gallienus to a more florid type of portraiture, leads to the schematized, non-naturalistic, mainly beardless portraits of the fourth century.

O. Vessberg, *Studien zur Kunstgeschichte der römischen Republik* (1941); B. Schweitzer, *Die Bildniskunst der römischen Republik* (1948); R. West, *Römische Porträt-Plastik* (1933, 1941); Wegner, *Herrscherbild* (1956); B. M. F. Maj, *Iconografia romana imperiale da Severo Alessandro a M. Aurelio Carino* (1958); H. P. L'Orange, *Studien zur Geschichte des spätantiken Porträts* (1933); R. Delbrueck, *Spätantike Kaiserporträts*; H. P. L'Orange, *Apotheosis in Ancient Portraiture* (1947). F. N. P.; J. M. C. T.

**PORTUNUS,** originally the Roman deity protecting doors (*portus*, e.g. XII tables, 2, 3). Later when the meaning of the noun changed to 'harbour', he was thought of as the protector of havens, and was equated with Palaemon, for whom *see* ATHAMAS, LEUCOTHEA (Ov. *Fast.* 6. 547). His festival, the Portunalia, fell on 17 Aug. Either of the two surviving temples (so called Fortuna Virilis and Vesta) in the Forum Boarium in Rome may have been dedicated to Portunus (Nash, *Pict. Dict. Rome* i. 411).

L. A. Holland, *Hommages à A. Grenier* (1962), 817 ff. H. W. P.

**PORTUS** is the name given to the town which grew up round Rome's harbour. Originally Rome had used the Tiber mouth at Ostia (q.v.), but by the end of the Republic the silt carried down by the Tiber was endangering

shipping. Caesar's project of building a new harbour was carried out by Claudius some 2 miles north of Ostia. Part of this harbour was dug out from the land and two moles were built out to sea, enclosing *c.* 160 acres. At the end of the left mole a giant lighthouse was built on a concrete-laden merchantman sunk for the purpose. Owing to the wide expanse of shallow water this harbour did not give complete security against sudden storms; but when Trajan had added a new land-locked inner basin of hexagonal shape (each side measuring nearly 360 metres), even the largest Egyptian corn ships could anchor in safety. The harbours were linked by canal with the Tiber and so with Rome, but while warehouses were built for the storage of goods the bulk of the harbour workers continued to live at Ostia which in the following generation reached the peak of her prosperity. When in the third century Rome's trade sharply declined it was logical that emphasis should shift and that the harbour area should develop its own living-quarters, temples, guilds, and other amenities. By A.D. 300 Portus had her own Christian bishop as well as temples for pagan cults, Roman and foreign. A small town had grown up to the south and east of Trajan's harbour and the main cemetery flanking the road to Ostia covered a considerable area. Constantine recognized realities and made Portus, hitherto controlled from Ostia, an independent town.

During the Late Empire Portus remained vital to Rome, whose corn-supply depended on the effective maintenance and security of the harbours. Strong walls were built, probably early in the fourth century, but the town was captured by Alaric in 410 and sacked by the Vandals in 455. Portus, however, unlike Ostia, recovered and was still busy with shipping in the sixth century, but by the eighth century sand had choked the Claudian harbour. A survey of the diocese of Portus in 1019 mentions six churches, probably dating from the fourth and fifth centuries. Their congregations must have been very small.

G. Lugli and G. Filibeck, *Il Porto di Roma imperiale e l'Agro Portuense*; R. Meiggs, *Roman Ostia* (1960), 149 ff.; O. Testaguzza, *Archaeology* 1964, 173 ff. R. M.

**PORTUS ITIUS,** a harbour of the Morini, used by Caesar (*BGall.* 5. 2 and 5) in the second British expedition (54 B.C.). The words seem to mean 'Channel Harbour', so that Boulogne, the port normally used, is the obvious identification, though there are arguments for Wissant.

T. Rice Holmes, *Ancient Britain*, 552 ff.; *CR* 1909, 77 ff.; J. Heurgon, *Rev. Ét. Anc.* 1948, 101 ff. C. E. S.

**PORUS** (probably Parvataka or Parvatesha of the Indian sources), a contemporary of Alexander, ruled the country between the Jhelum and the Chenab. A brave and powerful king of imposing personality, 'over five cubits in height', Porus fought a heroic battle with Alexander, who was so much impressed by him that he made him an ally and not only reinstated his kingdom but added some more territories to his care. When Alexander left the Panjab, Porus probably joined Chandragupta (Sandracottus, q.v.) in overthrowing the Macedonian yoke.

Tarn, *Alexander*; R. K. Mookerji, *Chandragupta Maurya and his Times²* (1943). A. K. N.

**POSEIDON** (Ποσειδῶν, Doric Ποτειδάν), Greek god of earthquakes and of water, secondarily of the sea, since he appears to be native Greek, not pre-Hellenic, and it is fairly certain that their former habitat was inland, cf. the paucity of Greek names for fishes (examples of non-Greek fish-names in J. Huber, *De lingua antiquissimorum Graeciae incolarum* (1921), 8 ff.). The name is of doubtful etymology, but almost certainly Greek. Some associate the first two syllables with ποταμός, πόσις (drink), etc., but mostly it is interpreted as 'Husband of earth' or 'Lord of earth'. His most significant titles are ἐνοσίχθων or ἐννοσίγαιος, 'earthshaker', and γαιήοχος, 'holder or possessor of earth', meaning probably husband of the earth-goddess. The latter is an appropriate name enough for a deity who, whatever his exact origins, certainly is closely connected with water, which fertilizes the earth; it need not be rain-water, though that is perhaps the most commonly spoken of in such a context (cf., e.g., Aesch. fr. 44 and Eur. fr. 898, Nauck²). In general, the theory (Cook, *Zeus* ii. 582 ff.) that he is 'a specialized form of Zeus', or a sky-god of any kind, has the balance of evidence against it. Being a great god, he has functions not unlike those of his celestial brother, but the Greeks themselves consistently differentiate them. That he causes earthquakes is an idea which possibly reflects some early and crude attempt to explain that phenomenon, cf. the later quasi-scientific theory (Seneca, *QNat.* 6. 6 ff.) that it was due to the action of water in some way.

Mythologically, Poseidon is one of the three sons of Kronos; in Homer he is younger than Zeus (*Iliad* 15. 204); in Hesiod and most later writers (*Theog.* 453 ff.), Zeus is the youngest son. He has but little mythology of his own; he was one of those swallowed by Kronos and afterwards spewed up (ibid. 459), although obscure legends say that Kronos was tricked into swallowing a foal instead (a young horse instead of the young Lord of Horses, see below; Paus. 8. 8. 2, from Arcadia), or that he threw Poseidon into the sea (Hyg. *Fab.* 139. 1). When the three brothers, after the defeat of their father, drew lots for the universe the sea fell to his share (*Il.* loc. cit. 190). It is to be noticed that at least one probably more ancient god, Nereus (q.v.), is thus displaced from the position which it would seem that he once held. His consort is the unimportant Amphitrite, and some legends of little significance are told of his wooing (see Rose, *Handb. Gk. Myth.* 63 f.). Of his various amours, the most interesting is that with Medusa the Gorgon, who became by him mother of Pegasus (q.v.). With Apollo (q.v.) he built the walls of Troy for Laomedon, was cheated of his pay, and in revenge sent a sea-monster to ravage the land (*Il.* 21. 441 ff., where Poseidon alone builds the walls, Apollo herding Laomedon's cattle; cf. AEACUS, HERACLES). For his quarrel with Odysseus, *see* ODYSSEUS. He is commonly the father of strong but rough and brutal men, or monsters such as the giant Antaeus, his son by Earth (Apollod. 2. 115). There are also several tales of his begetting horses, besides Pegasus; for one *see* ARCADIAN CULTS, DEMETER.

In cult he is, of course, prominent as sea-god and worshipped on all occasions connected with the sea and navigation. In addition, as already suggested, he is worshipped as a god of fresh water (Krenouchos, Nymphagetes; see Farnell, 5), and sporadically as god of earthquakes (Strabo 1. 3. 16, 57, the Rhodians found a temple to him on the volcanic island of Thera with the title Asphalios, a by-form of which—Asphalion—is rightly interpreted by Macrobius, *Sat.* 1. 17. 22, as *terram stabiliens*). It is quite natural that a god of water should occasionally be a god of vegetation, Phytalmios, Plut. *Quaest. conv.* 675 f., which says the cult is practically universal in Greece. But it is less obvious why he should be Hippios, Lord of Horses. This cannot arise from a metaphor like Engl. 'white horses' for waves, since no such metaphor is known in Greek, and it is noteworthy that Cornutus (*Theolog. Graec.* 22, 44, 1 Lang) suggests only that it is because we use ships 'like horses', i.e. as means of transport. This is of course absurd, for cult-titles like this do not grow out of poetical figures. The real reason is most probably that he was brought in by the first wave of Indo-European invaders who also brought the first horses. The cult of Poseidon Hippios is

especially Thessalian (Farnell, 23). In general, Poseidon is closely connected with the Minyans in mythical times, the Ionians in historical, though his cult spreads far wider than these parts of the Greek race.

Though popular and held in much reverence (partly because of his worship, as an ancestral god or otherwise, by many noble families; cf. the comparatively respectful handling of him by Aristophanes, whose conservatism is well known), he did not develop with the evolution of higher theological and ethical ideas, thus contrasting with Zeus and even with Hades. One reason for this may be the fact that these ideas were accompanied by a tendency towards monotheism, and hence Zeus hardly left room for another great god, even Hades being on occasion merely identified with him.

Poseidon is frequently shown in archaic and classical art, alone or with other deities. He is bearded, in archaic art robed, later often naked. He carries a trident and often a fish or dolphin. Without attributes he is hard to distinguish from Zeus (the early classical bronze god from the wreck off Cape Artemisium may be either). In the Gigantomachy he shoulders the island of Nisyrus to drop it on Polybotes. His strife with Athena for the land of Attica was the subject of the West pediment of the Parthenon.

Farnell, *Cults* iv. 1 ff., and the relevant arts. in the larger dictionaries; F. Schachermeyer, *Poseidon und die Entstehung des griechischen Götterglaubens* (1950); Nilsson, *GGR* i². 444 ff.

H. J. R.; C. M. R.

**POSIDIPPUS** (Ποσείδιππος) (1), New Comedy poet, born in Macedonia; he won four victories from 289/8 onwards. Fr. 12, a version of the famous story of Phryne's acquittal; fr. 26, a cook instructs his pupils; fr. 28, a Thessalian claims that his dialect is not inferior to Attic.

Posidippus' importance is clear: he is alleged to have introduced slave μάγειροι on to the stage (Ath. 14. 658 f); his Ἀποκλειομένη (which ended with the formula now known to be typical in New Comedy: see E. Vogt, *Rh. Mus.* 1959, 192) was re-acted *c.* 180 B.C.; his work was imitated on the Roman stage (Gell. 2. 23. 1); and his statue (with a reworked head: see H. von Heintze, *Röm. Mitt.* 1961, 80 ff.) is extant.

*FCG* i. 482 ff., iv. 513 ff.; *CAF* iii. 335 ff.; *PHeid.* 184.

W. G. A.

**POSIDIPPUS** (2) (fl. 270 B.C.) was an epigrammatic poet who lived in Samos, working with Asclepiades and Hedylus (q.v.), and later in Alexandria. About twenty of his poems are in the Greek Anthology, some others in Athenaeus. His chief theme is sex, treated with brisk ironic realism. A pathetic elegy, apparently written in his declining years, has been preserved on wooden tablets.

Gow and Page, 3054 ff.; Page, *GLP* 444–9 and 470–5; A. Rostagni, *Poeti alessandrini* (1916), ch. 4; P. Schott, *Pos. epigrammata* (1905); W. Schubart, *Symbolae . . . Danielsson* (1932); C. A. Trypanis, *CR* 1952; W. and M. Wallace, *TAPA* 1939; H. Lloyd-Jones, *JHS* 1963, 75 ff.; T. B. L. Webster, *Hellenistic Poetry and Art* (1964), ch. 2.

G. H.

**POSIDONIUS** (Ποσειδώνιος) (1) of Olbiopolis, sophist and historian, author of a work on the Dniester region, Ἀττικαὶ ἱστορίαι and Λιβυκά, has been identified, though this is uncertain, with the Posidonius who, according to Plutarch (*Aem.* 19), was contemporary with Perseus of Macedon (179–168 B.C.) and described his reign, including the battle of Pydna.

*FGrH* ii. B, 893; BD, 596.

A. H. McD.

**POSIDONIUS** (2) (*c.* 135 to *c.* 51–50 B.C.), born at Apamea on the Orontes, after studying philosophy at Athens under Panaetius devoted several years of his life to scientific research in the western Mediterranean provinces and in North Africa. He then settled down at Rhodes, which became his adoptive country. Towards the end of 87 Posidonius was sent to Rome on behalf of the Rhodians to appease Marius, and he conceived for him an intense dislike, to which he later gave vent in his historical works. In 78 Cicero attended the school of Posidonius, to whom he often pays tribute in his writings, although the philosopher declined to patronize and edit Cicero's Greek account of the conspiracy of Catiline. Another famous visitor of Posidonius was Pompey, who met him twice, after defeating the pirates and on his return from the East. Posidonius was such an enthusiastic supporter of Pompey that he devoted a separate treatise to the narrative of Pompey's eastern campaigns; it was from this that Strabo drew his strongly rationalistic explanation of the work of Moses as a Jewish lawgiver. The wars of Pompey seem to have been dealt with by Posidonius as an appendix to his *Histories*, the fifty-two books of which started from the point where Polybius left off, and included the history of the Eastern and Western peoples with whom Rome had come into contact, from about 146 B.C. to the dictatorship of Sulla. The meagreness of the fragments, which we owe chiefly to the learned curiosity of Athenaeus, makes a reconstruction impossible. But the fact that his work exercised a widespread and lasting influence is sufficient to give us an idea of Posidonius' literary skill as well as of his accuracy and matter-of-factness. Sallust, Caesar, Tacitus, and Plutarch were respectively dependent on Posidonius for the conception of history, for the ethnology of the Gauls and of the Germans (whom Posidonius probably did not distinguish from the Celts), and for the history of Marius and Marcellus; while the so-called universal historians (e.g. Timagenes, Trogus, Diodorus) did not hesitate to borrow even his doctrine of the unity of history, symbolized by the 'cosmopolis', or city of God, in which, ruled ever as it is by His providence, all human beings have a share (*see* HISTORIOGRAPHY, GREEK, § 7). In his *Histories*, which were biased in favour of the *nobilitas*, and consequently strongly opposed to the Gracchi and the equestrian party, let alone the 'independent' Greeks, and their supporter Mithridates, Posidonius aimed at showing that the Roman Empire, embracing as it did all the peoples of the world, embodied the commonwealth of mankind and reflected the commonwealth of God, to which deserving statesmen and philosophers were to be admitted after the fulfilment of their earthly task. This theory Cicero expounds in his *Somnium Scipionis*, which is indisputably based upon the ideas of Posidonius or cognate thinkers. The *Histories* of Posidonius must therefore be considered as the complement and the practical application of his philosophical system. He thus vindicated Roman imperialism, which less civilized peoples were forced to accept, or rather to welcome, for the sake of their own improvement, while at the same time he gave a practical illustration of the doctrine of continual communion and mutual sympathy between the world of God and the world of man. According to Posidonius the end and destiny of the human race are exactly reflected in the vicissitudes of history. Political virtue, therefore, consists in turning humanity back to its state of prehistoric innocence, in which philosophers were the lawgivers and instructors of their fellow men and acted as intermediaries between the world of matter, in which men are compelled to live, and the world of God, from which alone law-abiding morality can spring. Thus politics and ethics are one, and any form of moral or political activity becomes a religious duty, by fulfilling which man frees himself and acquires knowledge of the gifts of the spirit, which enable him to enjoy a superior form of existence after death. Since the God of Posidonius is the creator neither of matter nor of soul, the latter cannot be considered immortal in itself. But since it is composed of the same substance as the heavenly bodies, it escapes from the human prison and returns to the sub-

lime abode whence it originally came. Posidonius, moreover, introduced heroes and daemons as intermediary beings between man and God, in whose eternity they have a share. Their power and influence over earthly creatures is manifested in visions, divination, and oracles. The harmony which Posidonius observed in the world of man he discovered no less in nature. To prove that the same laws and processes were at work in both worlds, he devoted himself to scientific research. His study of primitive cultures led him to establish the principle that the present condition of semi-civilized peoples reflects the original stage of culture among those now civilized. His travels and observations enabled him to prove the connexion between tides and the phases of the moon, and to give an accurate description of the life and currents of the ocean. Nor was he merely a theorist; some important achievements witness his practical skill. For instance, he calculated the circumference of the earth, constructed a sphere, and drew a map. He showed also a lively interest in poetry, rhetoric, lexicography, geometry, etc. *See also* METEOROLOGY.

The contemporaries of Posidonius were more impressed by his personality and the width of his interests than by his system. His influence has often been over-emphasized, but it ought by no means to be underestimated. Although it is uselessly dangerous to attempt to rebuild his system by a mere mechanical spoliation of Lucretius, Cicero, Manilius, Seneca, and Pliny the Elder, it cannot be seriously doubted that they as well as Virgil and the historians were largely dependent upon Posidonius. In the history of ancient thought he can be compared to no one but Aristotle. As Aristotle forms the epilogue of the culture of classical Greece, so Posidonius collected the heritage of the Graeco-Roman civilization, or shaped it afresh, bequeathing to the Renaissance the legacy of the Hellenistic age.

TEXTS. Apart from I. Bake's antiquated edition, no collection of the fragments of Posidonius is available, except for the passages from his historical works, which have been edited, with an exhaustive commentary, by F. Jacoby, *FGrH* ii, no. 87.

MODERN LITERATURE. K. Reinhardt, *Poseidonios* (1921); *Kosmos u. Sympathie* (1926); *P. über Ursprung u. Entartung* (1928); I. Heinemann, *P. metaphysische Schriften* (2 vols., 1921, 1928); G. Rudberg, *Forsch. z. P.* (1918); M. Laffranque, *La Philosophie de Posidonius d' Apamée* (1964); M. Pohlenz, *Kl. Schr.* (1965), i. 140 ff.; H. Strasburger, *JRS* 1965, 40 ff. A detailed bibliography is given in K. Praechter's appendix to Ueberweg's *Grundriss* i¹². 150 ff. and in *PW* s.v. (1953), 559 ff. P. T.

**POSSESSIO.** Classical Roman law made a sharp distinction between ownership (*see* DOMINIUM) and possession. Ownership is the right to a thing, irrespective of whether the owner has any control or enjoyment of it; possession is, essentially, the control of a thing irrespective of whether the possessor has any right to it. A thief therefore has possession. Possession is a 'fact' in the sense that, in principle (though the principle was increasingly stretched), it lasts only so long as the control continues, whereas ownership, which is a right and not a 'fact', may come into existence or continue without any physical control. Possession is a fact, however, to which the *praetor* affords protection by interdicts (*see* LAW AND PROCEDURE, ROMAN, II. 11), though only within narrow limits. The possessor can (broadly) recover or retain his possession against any person interfering with it, provided that he has not himself obtained possession from that person by force, secretly, or by grant at will (*vi, clam, precario*). If therefore a thing is taken from a thief, the thief can recover possession, provided that the taker is not the person from whom the thief himself took it (irrespective of whether that person is the owner or not). If the thing passes from the dispossessor into the hands of a third party, the thief cannot recover possession. For possession is protected only against the immediate dispossessor: against any subsequent holder the claim must be by *vindicatio* (q.v.). (In classical law this is subject to a limited exception in the case of movables.) While possession is essentially the control of a thing, it must (usually) be an exclusive control in the manner of an owner. A tenant (*conductor, colonus*), a borrower, a depositee (see CONTRACT, ROMAN LAW OF), did not have possession; nor did a usufructuary (see SERVITUTES).

The possession considered above (interdict-possession) is usually termed in legal writings simply '*possessio*'. Control not amounting to *possessio* (as by a tenant) is sometimes called '*possessio naturalis*' (more commonly '*possessio*' is avoided by the use of '*tenere*', '*morari in fundo*', etc.). '*Possessio civilis*' (by contrast with interdict-possession which is a product of the *ius honorarium*: see EDICTUM, IUS CIVILE) is that possession which has the other qualities necessary for *usucapio* (see DOMINIUM), though occasionally *possessio civilis* may be in one person and interdict-possession in another (e.g. pledgor and pledgee: see SECURITY).

The interdictal protection of possession probably originated in the case of holding of land, and perhaps of *ager publicus* (q.v.) (cf. Festus, s.v. 'possessiones') or of the land of a great landowner held by grant at will (*precarium*) by a *cliens* (q.v.). Here ownership was impossible or inappropriate, and yet it would be inconvenient to deny to the holder (as to an ordinary tenant) any direct protection against an interloper. (*See also* EMPHYTEUSIS.)

In the post-classical law the distinction between ownership and possession was blurred, but it was restored in the law of Justinian.

P. Bonfante, *Corso di diritto romano* ii. 2 (1928), iii (1933); M. Kaser, *Eigentum u. Besitz im ält. röm. Recht*[2] (1956); M. Lauria, *Possessiones* (1953); E. Levy, *West Roman Vulgar Law, The Law of Property* (1951), *and see under* LAW AND PROCEDURE, ROMAN, I. B. N.

**POSSESSION.** That a human being might become possessed by a supernatural power was a fairly common ancient belief. The effect might be a prophetic frenzy, as in the case of the Pythia (cf. APOLLO); such a person was ἔνθεος. It might also be some terrifying disease, as epilepsy (Hippoc. *De morbo sacro*, especially 592 f. Kühn). Or it might be insanity; the victim was then commonly said δαιμονᾶν, as Aesch. *Sept.* 1001, or κακοδαιμονᾶν, as Dinarchus, 1. 91. Latin called him *larvatus* or *cerritus*, possessed respectively by the Larvae or Ceres, e.g. Plaut. *Men.* 890. Later, under oriental influence (cf., e.g., the numerous references to demoniacs in the N.T.), the belief grew stronger and commoner, and mentions of magical cures and the activity of exorcists, pagan and Christian, are extremely frequent.

Julius Tambornino, 'De antiquorum daemonismo' (1909; *RGVV* vii. 3); T. K. Oesterreich, *Possession* (1930), 150 ff. H. J. R.

**POSTAL SERVICE.** Classical Greece knew no organized postal system. Cities maintained their own ships and messengers (ἡμεροδρόμοι) for official mail. These men (the best known is Pheidippides) were highly trained and probably formed associations. In the Persian Empire (probably following Assyrian precedents) the State maintained a relay service, with couriers and horses stationed at intervals along the royal roads. The system (called by Greeks ἀγγαρήιον) seems also to have been used for the transport of the King and officials, and costs had to be borne, and services provided, by the population (see Rostowzew [= Rostovtzeff], *Klio* 1906, 249). Reorganized by Antigonus I, it continued under the Seleucids and (in the East) under the Romans. The Ptolemies retained the transport system for officials and improved that for mail (Preisigke, *Klio* 1907, 241). There was an express post, arranged in a chain of stations and transporting mail by means of horses provided (as a liturgy, commutable for a tax) by colonists liable for mounted service. For slower mail there were stations employing large numbers of runners, under a postmaster, and a camel service for parcels. All these—maintained by the population—were strictly for public use. Private mail went by private messengers; but officials of the public system tended (despite official fulminations) to entrust their private items to it, and they were not above being 'persuaded' to accept other people's.

**2.** Under the Roman Republic *tabellarii* (q.v.) were employed, and those of the State and of the *publicani* (q.v.) might carry mail for important men. Augustus (see Suet. *Aug.* 49. 3) found a system for the transport of both persons and mail (the two were never clearly separated) in existence in the eastern provinces, particularly in Egypt. In Italy and the West he first organized a relay system of messengers (*iuvenes* of military age), then apparently changed the whole system into one of relay stations providing horses and carriages, no doubt modelled on what he found in the East: in this way a single messenger could cover the whole distance (adding supplementary news by word of mouth). Though the main purpose and organization of the *cursus publicus* was military, it could now also be used for official transport. The population had to bear the cost and provide services. This *vehiculatio* soon proved a major burden (*ILS* 214: Claudius), from which Nerva freed Italy. Trajan (at the latest) created a post *a vehiculis* (later *praefectus vehiculorum*) and Hadrian (S.H.A. 1. 7. 5) relieved local magistrates of personal responsibility for requisitions, of which—under central control—a *manceps* (q.v.) took charge. Under the Severi, with the development of the *annona* (q.v.—a tax in kind), the system was reorganized: the postal service was extended to transport its proceeds, but (at some time, and at least in some provinces) the *vehiculatio* was discontinued. Henceforth the service quickly expanded and officials multiplied. It was used for troop movements, which took advantage of the *mansiones* along the roads, and these were joined to storehouses for the *annona*. The burden on the population on the whole increased, and a postal tax seems to have spread again later. A slower system of heavy transport by ox-drawn vehicles (the *cursus clabularis*) took its place beside the *cursus velox*, and in the Late Empire there was further reorganization.

*Diplomata* (licences) to use the service were strictly controlled. Governors had to justify the use they made of them (cf. Pliny, *Ep.* 10. 120) and equestrian officers were not allowed to take liberties (as young Pertinax found out: S.H.A. 8. 1. 6). But abuses were difficult to prevent, as Claudius (see above) complained. Messages were at first carried by imperial *tabellarii* (organized in military fashion), but in important cases by trusted soldiers, especially the Emperor's *speculatores*. In the second century a related corps, the *frumentarii* (and after Diocletian their successors, the *agentes in rebus*, q.v.), took over the service, combining the carrying of confidential messages with the work of a secret police (q.v.). The *mansiones* were amalgamated with the army guardposts (*stationes*) that had from an early time existed at important points along the roads, and soldiers took over their management from the *mancipes*.

Couriers travelled, on an average, about 50 miles a day; but urgent news could be carried at high speeds: that of the revolt of the Rhine army was carried to Galba in about nine days, i.e. at a rate of over 150 miles a day, over the Alps in mid winter.

*PW*, s.vv. 'Cursus publicus', 'Nachrichtenwesen'; E. J. Holmberg, *Zur Gesch. d. Cursus Publicus* (1933); H. G. Pflaum, *Le Cursus Publicus sous le Haut-Empire romain* (*Mém. Acad. Insc.* 1940). E. B.

**POSTLIMINIUM.** The legal position of a Roman citizen captured by the enemy was similar to that of a slave, but his rights remained in suspense. By virtue of the *ius postliminii*, which was said to be *moribus constitutum*, the captive after his return recovered with his freedom all his former rights just as if he had never been captured by the enemy. The principle applied to rights, but not to 'facts', i.e. to legal relationships which required for their existence some physical manifestation. Such relationships did not revive automatically, but had to be physically resumed. Thus *dominium* (q.v.) revived automatically, *possessio* (q.v.) did not; nor did marriage (but this rule was altered by Justinian). If the *captivus* died in captivity, he died a slave; but a *Lex Cornelia* (of the dictator Sulla) preserved the validity of his will by the fiction that he died a citizen. This so-called *fictio legis Corneliae* was applied to successions on intestacy and further extended in the post-classical law.

The *ius postliminii* was applied also to certain things important in war (slaves, ships, horses used in military service, etc.) and land, which fell into the enemy's hand during war and were subsequently recovered by their owner.

L. Mitteis, *Röm. Privatrecht* (1908), 192 ff.; J. Imbert, *Postliminium* (1944); L. Amirante, *Captivitas e postliminium* (1950); H. Krüger, 'Captivus redemptus', *Sav. Zeitschr.* li (1931), 203 ff.; E. Levy, 'Captivus redemptus', *CPhil.* 1943, 159 ff. (= *Bull. Ist. dir. rom.* 1951). A. B.; B. N.

**POSTUMIUS** (1, *PW* 63) **TUBERTUS**, AULUS, perhaps *magister equitum* in 434, he was appointed dictator in 431 by his son-in-law Cincinnatus, and won a notable and undoubtedly historical victory over the Aequi on the Algidus (traditionally on 19 June), but details of the campaign, which closely resembles that of Cincinnatus in 458, must be rejected. O. Hirschfeld (*Kl. Schr.* 1913, 246 f.) has wrongly assumed that the legend of Cincinnatus grew out of the story of Postumius.

Ogilvie, *Comm. Livy 1–5*, 571 f., 576 f. P. T.

**POSTUMIUS** (2, *PW* 55) **MEGELLUS**, LUCIUS (*cos.* I, 305 B.C.; II, 294; III, 291). The victories over the Samnites, which tradition assigns to his two first consulships, were probably reverses. His alleged triumph 'de Samnitibus Etrusceisque' in 294 is an anticipation of that of 291; he was not in Etruria. In 291 he helped to end the Third Samnite War by storming Venusia. He is said to have 'triumphed' and to have been fined for using military labour on his own land. When sent to Tarentum in 282 to demand restitution, he was insulted.

E. T. Salmon, *Samnium and the Samnites* (1967), 249 ff. H. H. S.

**POSTUMIUS** (3, *PW* 31) **ALBINUS**, AULUS, Roman senator and historian, praetor in 155 B.C., consul in 151, commissioner for the settlement of Achaea in 146, and an enthusiastic philhellene, wrote a history of Rome from its origins, in Greek. Pragmatic in treatment, it belongs to the senatorial tradition. Cato mocked his apology for his Greek (Gell. 11. 8. 2), but Polybius, if grudgingly, recognized his culture and influence (Polyb. 39. 1) and, though his excessive philhellenism and wisdom offended the older Romans, Cicero praises him as 'disertus' (*Brut.* 81). References to a poem and to his *de aduentu Aeneae* may point to one work; Macrobius' reference (3. 20. 5) may, but not necessarily, indicate a Latin version of his history.

Peter, *HRRel.* i. cxxiv, 53; *FGrH* iii C, 881 ff. Scullard, *Rom. Pol.* 238, 249. A. H. McD.

**POSTUMIUS** (4, *PW* 45) **ALBINUS**, SPURIUS, as consul in 110 B.C. renewed the war with Jugurtha (q.v.) after Bestia's treaty and left his brother Aulus in charge when he went to Rome to hold elections. Aulus was defeated and his army was sent under the yoke (early 109). Spurius, returning as proconsul, failed to repair the

disaster, was superseded by Metellus (q.v. 6) and convicted by the tribunal set up by Mamilius (q.v. 3).
E. B.

**POSTUMUS**, MARCUS CASSIANIUS (*PW* 1) LATINIUS, left in military command on the Rhine by Gallienus, when he set out to crush Ingenuus in Moesia, quarrelled with Silvanus, Praetorian Prefect and guardian of the young prince, Saloninus, in Cologne (A.D. 259). He put both guardian and prince to death, and established himself as independent emperor in Gaul; both Spain and Britain adhered to him. He abetted the revolt of Aureolus in 268, but had himself to meet the revolt of Laelianus in Moguntiacum (*Mainz*). He took the city, but was murdered by his own troops when he forbade the sack.

Postumus successfully defended the Rhine frontier against German invasion. His usurpation weakened central authority, but saved the West. H. M.

**POTAMON** (1), a rhetor of Mytilene (*c.* 75 B.C.–A.D. 15), undertook embassies on behalf of his city to Rome to Caesar (47 and 45) and Augustus (26), and was much honoured at Mytilene. He wrote on Alexander, on Samian Horoi, and a Περὶ τελείου ῥήτορος which was perhaps a counterpart to Cicero's *Orator*.

*FGrH* 147. M. Rostovtzeff, *JRS* 1917, 30 ff.; Pearson, *Lost Histories of Alexander*, 248 ff. H. H. S.

**POTAMON** (2) of Alexandria, probably of the time of Augustus (31 B.C.–A.D. 14), founder of the Eclectic school. He attempted without much originality or consistency to combine Platonic and Peripatetic tenets with the Stoic creed (Diog. Laert. *prooem.* 21). The school had little influence.

Zeller, *Phil. d. Griechen* iii. 1⁴. 639–41. W. D. R.

**POTIDAEA**, a Corinthian colony, founded *c.* 600 B.C. for trade with Macedonia and along the line of the later Via Egnatia. It struck coins from *c.* 550 B.C. A strongly fortified port, it withstood a siege by Artabazus (480–479). It joined the Delian League; but its connexion with Corinth, which supplied its annual chief magistrate, rendered it subject to Athens. After an increase of its tribute to fifteen talents (434 B.C.) it revolted (432), but although it received help from Peloponnesus it was reduced in 430. Athenian cleruchs occupied the site until 404, when it passed to the Chalcidians. It was recovered by Athens in 363 and received another cleruchy in 361; but in 356 it fell into the hands of Philip II of Macedon. It was perhaps destroyed in the Olynthian War (348); but it was refounded by Cassander under the name of Cassandreia (*c.* 316).

J. A. Alexander, *Potidaea* (U.S.A. 1963). N. G. L. H.

**POTTERY.** Neolithic pottery, the earliest in Greece, may go back before 5000 B.C., and varieties of it have been found in many parts of Greece, including the Cyclades. The pottery is hand-made, its surface burnished and the colour black or red-brown. On the mainland, painted ware has been found, and in later Neolithic, linear and spiral patterns on white are known. The main Neolithic sites are in northern Greece.

2. In the early Bronze Age the dark clay ware is followed by painted fabrics, dull dark on light ground. In Crete there is a change (*c.* 2300 B.C.) to light-on-dark painted ware, which continues throughout the Middle Minoan period. The potter's slow wheel is introduced, probably from Asia (*c.* 2100 B.C.), soon followed by the quick wheel. In the Late Minoan Age the dark-on-light technique returns, with a naturalistic style embracing floral and marine subjects. The Cyclades and Mainland favour the dark-on-light style throughout. On the Main-

land an intrusive 'Minyan ware' appears *c.* 2000 B.C. of grey clay, wheel-made, the shapes recalling metal work. After 1400 B.C. 'Mycenaean pottery' predominates, with lustrous brown ornament on buff, based mainly on Late Minoan; the pottery, found over a wide area, is remarkably uniform, the main shapes being the kylix, stirrup-jar, and 'Palace style' jar. Later the designs grow stylized, and in the sub-Mycenaean age are reduced to geometric elements.

3. In the twelfth century, Protogeometric pottery, developing from sub-Mycenaean, is made in Athens, austere and precise with concentric circles balanced by areas of black. About 900 B.C. the Geometric style emerges with meander and zigzag pattern in horizontal bands, the shapes well proportioned. Of the local schools which produced this ware, Athens was the most important, and towards the end of the period figured scenes, conventionally drawn, became the focus of the artists' interest.

4. In the late eighth century the Geometric style passes into the Orientalizing, as the result of closer acquaintance with Eastern art. The decorative repertory is enriched by floral patterns, animals, winged monsters, etc., which replace the Geometric patterns in the horizontal bands. Experiments in technique—outline drawing, incised lines, polychromy—are found, the human figure is drawn with increasing naturalism, and mythological representations begin. The local styles are again clearly distinguished; the seventh century sees the high-water mark of the Island and East Greek schools; the chief Mainland fabrics are the Athenian (proto-Attic), proto-Corinthian, and Laconian.

5. By 600 Athenian potters had substantially evolved the Attic black-figured style, and the sixth century sees the gradual assimilation of other local styles to this. The chief shapes are the kylix and the amphora, both syntactically effective. In black-figure the design is laid in dark paint, improved to the brilliant black Attic glaze, on the reddish buff clay; inner markings are made by incised lines; white is used for the flesh of women, red for men's beards and hair, etc. The decorative patterns are reduced, and the field of the vase occupied by a mythological or other subject.

6. About 530 Athens introduces a new technique, the red-figured, in which the decoration is left in the ground-colour and the background filled with black; inner details are rendered in thin glazed lines; accessory colours are sparingly used in the fifth century. In this style greater freedom of drawing was possible, and the artists pass from archaic stiffness to the classic style of the mid fifth and to the free style of the late fifth century. The vases of the fourth century are characterized technically by greater use of accessory colours and gilding. A subsidiary Attic fabric of the fifth century is the 'white-ground' ware, in which the background is white, with designs in black glaze at first, later in matt polychrome; these vases were mainly used for sepulchral purposes.

7. Throughout the Archaic and Classical periods, black and banded vases were produced side by side with figured ware, mainly the same shapes but in different volume. Coarser clay is used for the kettles, ovens, and braziers of Greek homes. Two other classes of pottery are the large jars for transporting wine, and the *pithoi* for storage.

8. By 300 B.C. Attic red-figured vases are no longer made, but the small black vases continue into Hellenistic times as cheap substitutes for metal vases. Painted vases are mainly secondary to those with relief decoration. Sometimes moulded reliefs are added to wheel-made vases; in other fabrics the vase is thrown in a mould, as in the hemispherical 'Megarian bowls', the most widespread Hellenistic fabric. In this period the black ground-colour inherited from Athens is modified in East Greece into red or bronze, and from this develops the *terra sigillata* (q.v.), the standardized fine pottery of Roman times.

9. Italian pottery of the Neolithic and Bronze Ages is mainly of the dark-clay Mediterranean type; painted wares, dark on light, occur sporadically in the south and have been compared with the wares of the Balkan peninsula. In the early Iron Age the hand-made dark-clay ware ('impasto') continues in several local styles; among them the Latin, characterized by its funerary 'hut-urns', and the Villanovan of Tuscany and Bologna, with biconical urns and incised geometric decoration. The 'bucchero' of Etruria (700–500) is also dark-clay ware, but wheel-made, with polished black surface; early decoration is incised, later decoration is in relief. Painted wares imitating the contemporary styles of Greece appear on the west coast about 700, and by 525 the native pottery is largely displaced by Greek (mainly Attic) imported vases and local copies. There are independent schools of pottery in Apulia which, while borrowing the painted technique from Greece, remain barbaric in style. The Italian red-figured style begins in south Italy about 440, perhaps introduced by immigrant Athenian potters. There are five main schools in the fourth century: Apulian, Lucanian, Campanian, Paestan, and Sicilian. Size and elaboration are hallmarks, and production continues into the third century. Etruria gains its main inspiration from Attic models.

. 10. In the Hellenistic period Apulia and Campania are the chief areas of production. Light-on-dark painted ware and vases with applied reliefs are the main fabrics. Alexandria was the principal source of inspiration, and Italy long remained untouched by the East Greek experiments in red glazes and moulded wares; after 30 B.C., however, it took the lead in these with the appearance of Arretine ware (*see* TERRA SIGILLATA).

11. Apart from *terra sigillata*, the pottery of the Roman East is mainly plain earthenware, though moulded vases of the second to third century are not unknown. There is much variety over the Roman Empire, in shape, technique, and decoration, reflecting the intermixture of Roman and native.

Neolithic: F. Schachermeyr, *Das ägäische Neolithikum* (1964). Mycenaean: A. Furumark, *The Mycenaean Pottery* (1941). Greek painted pottery: *see* VASE-PAINTING. Protogeometric: V. R. d'A. Desborough, *Protogeometric Pottery* (1952). Shapes: G. M. A. Richter and M. J. Milne, *Shapes and Names of Athenian Vases* (1935); E. A. Lane, *Greek Pottery* (1948). Uses: B. A. Sparkes and L. Talcott, *Pots and Pans of Classical Athens* (1958). Black and plain: B. A. Sparkes, *Athenian Agora* xii, 1969. Hellenistic: H. A. Thompson, *Hesp.* 1934, 311 ff. Relief wares: F. Courby, *Les Vases grecs à reliefs* (1922). Techniques: G. M. A. Richter, *The Craft of Athenian Pottery* (1923); R. Hampe and A. Winter, *Bei Töpfern und Töpferinnen in Kreta, Messenien und Zypern* (1962); J. V. Noble, *Techniques of Painted Attic Pottery* (1965). Early Italian: T. E. Peet, *The Stone and Bronze Ages in Italy* (1909); *CVA* Heidelberg 2 (23) (1963); Å. Åkerström, *Der geometrische Stil in Italien* (1943). Roman: R. J. Charleston, *Roman Pottery* (1955); H. S. Robinson, *Pottery of the Roman Period, chronology* (*Athenian Agora* v, 1959). Etruscan: J. D. Beazley, *Etruscan Vase-Painting* (1947). General: *Corpus Vasorum Antiquorum* (continuing); *Handbuch der Archäologie* (continuing).
F. N. P.; B. A. S.

**PRAEFECTURA** means an assize-town in Roman territory. When Capua became a semi-citizen *municipium* (q.v.), prefects delegated by the *praetor urbanus* were occasionally sent there to assist in judicial rearrangements consequent upon the grant of *civitas sine suffragio*. The practice spread later to all other *municipia* and also to *oppida* and *conciliabula* in the areas of full-citizens (*see* CITIZENSHIP, OPPIDUM), and became annual. The *praefecti* did not replace but assisted the local authorities of *municipia*; in *oppida civium Romanorum* they were sometimes the only senior judicial authority. In Campania after the abolition of local autonomy following the revolt of 215–211 B.C. a new set of annual *praefecti*, minor magistrates elected at Rome, were instituted to take sole charge of local jurisdiction. Elsewhere the old system prevailed down to the Social War, but was not extended to the municipalities then incorporated. Between 89 and 44 B.C. the surviving *praefecti* were abolished and the *praefecturae* assimilated to *municipia*, though the ancient title sometimes remained in use.

See the bibliography under SOCII, MUNICIPIUM.
                                                    A. N. S.-W.

**PRAEFECTUS.** Before the Social War each *ala sociorum* had six *praefecti*, three of whom were Roman officers. In Caesar's armies *praefecti* were the commanders of cavalry contingents. Under the Principate *praefecti* were officers of equestrian rank. From the time of Nero onwards the regular equestrian career was that of the *tres militiae*—*praefectus cohortis, tribunus militum, praefectus alae.*

*Praefecti* also commanded the Praetorians, *vigiles*, and the imperial fleets of Ravenna and Misenum; the urban cohorts were under the *praefectus urbi*, a senator of consular standing.

The legions in Egypt were commanded by equestrian *praefecti* instead of the normal senatorial *legati*, and Septimius Severus followed this precedent when he raised Legiones Parthicae I–III. Gallienus extended the appointment of *praefecti*.

The post of legionary camp commandant, *praefectus castrorum* (later *praefectus (castrorum) legionis*), was from Claudius onwards regularly held by an ex-centurion who had reached the rank of *primus pilus* and was unlikely to have further promotion. His duties were purely administrative.

*Praefecti* also held extraordinary appointments, e.g. *praefectus levis armaturae*; *praefectus orae maritimae*.

In the Late Empire *praefecti* were commanders in the *limitanei* of legions and detachments of legions, vexillations, *alae, numeri*, and fleets.

*See also* ALIMENTA, ANNONA, FABRI, PRAEFECTUS PRAETORIO, PRAEFECTUS URBI, PRIMIPILUS, VIGILES.

J. Suolahti, *The Junior Officers of the Roman Army in the Republican Period* (1955), 198 ff.; E. Birley, *Roman Britain and the Roman Army* (1953), 133 ff.; G. L. Cheesman, *The Auxilia of the Roman Imperial Army* (1914), 23 ff., 90 ff.; Jones, *Later Rom. Emp.* 640.
                                                    H. M. D. P.; G. R. W.

**PRAEFECTUS PRAETORIO.** The first praetorian prefects were appointed by Augustus in 2 B.C. to command the Praetorians (q.v.). They were regularly two in number (occasionally one or three), and in most cases of equestrian rank (invariably so during the second century). During their term of office, however, they could receive the *ornamenta praetoria*, or, after 69, the *ornamenta consularia* (*see* ORNAMENTA). Though a few were well-known jurists (*see* PAPINIANUS, ULPIANUS I, PAULUS I), the great majority remained military men until the Guard was disbanded by Constantine in 312 and the nature of the office changed. Their positions sometimes gave them great personal influence over the Emperors (*see* SEJANUS, BURRUS, TIGELLINUS, PLAUTIANUS), and occasionally they were able to play a decisive role at a change of Emperor. During the second and third centuries they acquired extensive judicial powers; from the time of the Severi these included appellate jurisdiction from senatorial as well as imperial provinces. In Italy, they had general jurisdiction over cases which arose more than 100 miles from Rome and were beyond the purview of the Praefectus Urbi (q.v.). Praetorian prefects helped to shape imperial legislation as regular members of the Consilium Principis (q.v.). They developed financial functions also, since as chief of staff the praetorian prefect was responsible for the supply of the armed forces. With the growth of the system of requisition in kind the prefects under Diocletian became the most important finance ministers of the Empire. This was the high-water mark

of their power, for under Constantine they lost their military functions. Their areas of responsibility became localized, and these eventually became established as the four territorial prefectures of the Gauls, Italy, Illyricum, and the East.

J.-R. Palanque, *Essai sur la préfecture du prétoire du Bas-Empire* (1933); M. Durry, *Les Cohortes prétoriennes* (1938); A. Passerini, *Le coorti pretorie* (1939); L. L. Howe, *The Praetorian Prefect from Commodus to Diocletian* (U.S.A. 1942); Jones, *Later Rom. Emp.*
                                                    G. R. W.

**PRAEFECTUS URBI.** (1) The temporary deputy in Rome of the absent king or consuls, not often needed after the institution of praetors, except once a year when all regular magistrates attended the Latin festival on the Mons Albanus (q.v.), and so after the institution of (2) known as *praefectus urbi feriarum Latinarum.* The prefect had the *imperium* (q.v.) and was competent to perform all consular functions appropriate to the sphere *domi.* In early times when he had real responsibility he was usually of consular rank; later, men at the beginning of their public career were chosen. L. Caesar (q.v. 4) represents a reversion to the earlier practice. The six prefects of 45 B.C. were unique.

(2) A magistrate instituted by Augustus. After a false start with Messalla (q.v. 3) *c.* 25 B.C., the regular series seems to have begun with L. Piso (q.v. 6) in A.D. 13. The prefect was always a senator, usually of consular rank, and served for a number of years. He was nominally an independent magistrate, with the duty of keeping order in the city, and for this purpose had *imperium* and the command of a standing police force (*see* COHORTES URBANAE). He also presided in his own court of justice which encroached progressively upon, and by the third century practically superseded, those of the regular magistrates, attracting cases originating both inside and outside Rome (excluding, after *c.* 200, those originating beyond the hundredth milestone: *see* PRAEFECTUS PRAETORIO). The office persisted into the later Empire, a separate prefect for Constantinople being added in 359.

Mommsen, *Röm. Staatsr.* i³. 661 ff., ii³. 1059 ff. (*Droit publ. rom.* ii. 340 ff., v. 361 ff.); P.-E. Vigneaux, *Essai sur l'histoire de la Préfecture urbaine à Rome* (1896); J. Blancher, *La Juridiction civile du Praefectus Urbi* (1909); E. Sachers, *PW* xxii (1954), 2502 ff. (Nachträge); G. Vitucci, *Ricerche sulla Praefectura Urbis in età imperiale* (*sec. i–iii*), with a list of prefects (1956); W. Sinnigen, *The Officium of the Urban Prefecture during the Later Roman Empire* (1957), and *Hist.* 1959, 97 ff.; T. J. Cadoux, *JRS* 1959, 152 ff.; A. Chastagnol, *La Préfecture urbaine à Rome sous le bas Empire* (1960), *Les Fastes de la Préfecture de Rome au bas Empire* (1962); W. Schmitthenner, *Hist.* 1962, 83 ff.
                                                    T. J. C.

**PRAENESTE,** modern *Palestrina* with interesting polygonal walls, occupied a cool, lofty spur of the Apennines (q.v.), 23 miles east-south-east of Rome. Traditionally founded in the mythical period (Verg. *Aen.* 7. 678), it enjoyed by 700 B.C. an advanced, etruscanized civilization. It first appears in history in the fifth century B.C. as a powerful Latin city whose strategic site facing the Alban Hills was inevitably attacked by Aequi (q.v.). In the fourth century it frequently fought Rome and, after participating in the Latin War, was deprived of territory and became a *civitas foederata* which still possessed *ius exilii* 200 years later (Polyb. 6. 14) and apparently preferred its own to Roman citizenship (Livy 23. 19 f.). After 90 B.C. Praeneste became a Roman *municipium* devoted to Marius' cause, which Sulla sacked (82), transferred to lower ground, and colonized with veterans. It remained a *colonia* in imperial times, famed chiefly as a fashionable villa resort and seat of the ancient and oracular *sortes Praenestinae* which Roman Emperors, foreign potentates, and others consulted in the huge temple of Fortuna Primigenia, perhaps Italy's largest sanctuary (Polyb. 6. 11). Its impressive remains belong perhaps to the **first** century B.C.: sweeping ramps carry the edifice up **the** hillside in a series of terraces.

Praeneste has yielded the earliest specimen of Latin, whose peculiarities confirm Festus' statement (157, 488 L.) that Praenestine Latin was abnormal, a spectacular marine mosaic (cf. Pliny, *HN* 36. 25), and Verrius Flaccus' calendar; Flaccus probably, and the Greek writer Aelian certainly, were natives of Praeneste. The Anicii were also prominent Praenestines.

Strabo 5. 238; Livy 2. 19; 3. 8; 6. 21, 26 f.; 8. 12 f.; 23. 19 f.; Diod. 16. 45; App. *BCiv.* 1. 65. 94; Cic. *Div.* 2. 41. D. Randall-MacIver, *Iron Age in Italy* (1927); H. Besig, *PW* Suppl. viii (1956), s.v. 'Praeneste'; F. Fasolo and G. Gullini, *Il Santuario della Fortuna Primigenia a Palestrina* (1956); G. Gullini, *Guida del Santuario*, etc. (1956); P. L. MacKendrick, *The Mute Stones Speak* (U.S.A. 1960), 116 ff.      E. T. S.

**PRAEROGATIVA** was the *centuria* in the *comitia centuriata* (q.v.) of the Roman people which had the right of voting first. In early times the eighteen *centuriae* of the knights voted first *en bloc*; but not later than 215 B.C. the right was conferred upon one of the seventy *centuriae* of the first class chosen on each occasion by lot. Even after the introduction of the ballot (*see* VOTING) the decision of the *centuria praerogativa* was made known before the rest of the assembly recorded its vote. According to Cicero its influence upon the final outcome of the voting was very considerable.

Mommsen, *Röm. Staatsr.* iii³. 290 ff., 398.      E. S. S.

**PRAETEXTATUS** (*PW* 1), **VETTIUS AGORIUS** (*c.* A.D. 320–84), a resolute opponent of Christianity and friend of Symmachus (q.v. 2), who held many high State offices and various priesthoods. His epitaph with accompanying poem (*CIL* vi. 1779 = Dessau 1259; *Carm. epigr.* 111) is of interest in showing how a synthesis of pagan cults was attempted in face of the common enemy, Christianity. Like other antichristians, he was attached both to philosophy (cf. Macrob. *Sat.* 1. 24. 21) and to the ancient writers: he produced a Latin version of Themistius' adaptation of Aristotle's *Analytics* and assisted in the purification of the texts of Latin authors.

Th. W. J. Nicolaas, *Praetextatus* (Dutch diss., 1940); P. Lambrechts, *Op de Grens van Heidendom en Christendom. Het Grafschrift van Vettius A. P. en Fabia Aconia Paulina* (1955); A. Momigliano, *Conflict between Paganism and Christianity in the 4th Cent.* (1963).      A. H.-W.

**PRAETOR** (etymologically connected with *prae-ire*, 'to lead', 'to precede') was originally the name borne by the two eponymous Roman magistrates who later (possibly towards the end of the fourth century) officially assumed the name of consul (q.v.). The praetor's close connexion with military affairs is shown by the use of the adjective *praetorius* in such expressions as *praetorium, cohors praetoria*, and *porta praetoria*, and by the Greek translation of *praetor* as στρατηγός. In 366 B.C., however, a further praetor (*praetor urbanus*) was first elected who was not eponymous and who was given special responsibility for the administration of justice in Rome. He enjoyed and sometimes exercised the right of military command and he had the authority to summon *comitia* and initiate legislation; but he was attended by only six lictors, as opposed to the consuls' twelve, was forbidden to leave Rome for more than ten days at a time, and performed the consuls' functions of summoning the Senate and supervising the defence of Rome merely during their absence. The tradition that this new office was one from which plebeians were officially excluded until 337 is unreliable.

Rome's closer relations with foreign Powers led to the creation (*c.* 242 B.C.) of a second praetor, called *praetor qui inter peregrinos ius dicit* (abbreviated to *praetor peregrinus*), who dealt with lawsuits in which either one or both parties were foreigners. The acquisition of overseas provinces greatly enlarged the sphere of the praetors'

activities, so that in 227 B.C. their number was increased from two to four, to provide for the government of Sicily and Sardinia, and to six in 197 B.C., to administer Spain. By exercising the supreme provincial authority, the praetors became once again military magistrates, and in fact the difference of rank and power between them and the consuls decreased progressively, although the *praetor urbanus* was still subordinate to the consuls. In the second century the *praetor urbanus* and *peregrinus* dealt chiefly with the administration of justice. Sulla, who increased the praetors' number to eight, prescribed that all of them should remain in Rome as judges, or presidents of *quaestiones* (q.v.), and should proceed to the governorship of provinces in the following year by prorogation of their office. Sulla's reform, however, was abolished in the Augustan age.

Although the beneficent influence of the praetorship in the domain of law continued to make itself felt under the Emperors (thanks to the edicts in which it was customary for praetors to outline, on entering their office, the main principles of their jurisdiction), the praetorship nevertheless declined rapidly, and its functions were soon reduced to minor jurisdiction, e.g. in matters relating to guardianship, the status of liberty, etc., or financial duties, performed by the *praetores aerarii* from 23 B.C. to A.D. 44. It eventually became a merely honorary appointment, the main feature of which was that the *praetor urbanus* had to superintend the games provided by him on entering his office, to win the favour of the Roman populace.

Mommsen, *Röm. Staatsr.* ii³. 1, 193 ff. For the origins of praetorship see G. De Sanctis, *Riv. Fil.* 1929, 1933; E. S. Staveley, *Hist.* 1956, 90 ff.; Ogilvie, *Comm. Livy* 1–5, 230 f.; A. Momigliano, *Quarto contributo alla storia degli studi classici* (1969), 403 ff.      P. T.; E. S. S.

**PRAETORIANS.** During the last two centuries of the Republic generals commonly had a bodyguard or *cohors praetoria*. A permanent corps of nine cohorts was created by Augustus in 27 B.C. Three of these were billeted about the city, the remainder were quartered in near-by Italian towns. For a time Augustus kept them under direct control, and it was not until 2 B.C. that command was entrusted to two *praefecti praetorio*.

In a sense Sejanus may be called the real founder of the Praetorians. He was made first joint Prefect with his father on the accession of Tiberius, and then sole Prefect (A.D. 16 or 17). By A.D. 23 he had succeeded in concentrating the Guard in one large barracks near the Porta Viminalis. From this event dates the political importance of the Guard and its commanders.

The number of cohorts was raised by Caligula to twelve. In A.D. 69 Vitellius cashiered the soldiers who had supported Otho, and constituted sixteen cohorts, each 1,000 strong, from the German legions. Vespasian, however, reverted to the Augustan figure; a tenth cohort was added, perhaps by Domitian, and this number, apart from a possible reduction by Diocletian, remained unchanged till the Praetorians were disbanded by Constantine in A.D. 312.

The cohorts have generally been thought to have been each 1,000 strong, but Durry argues that they were only half this size, except under Vitellius, till their establishment was increased to 1,000 by Septimius Severus. Each cohort was commanded by a tribune, who from the time of Claudius onwards had regularly been a legionary *primipilus, tribunus vigilum, tribunus cohortis urbanae*. He might next be appointed *primipilus iterum*. The centurions of the Guard were of roughly equal rank, apart from the two senior, who were the *trecenarius* and the *princeps castrorum*.

During the first two centuries, apart from the Vitellian episode, the praetorians were recruited from Italy and the more romanized provinces. A change was made by Septimius Severus, who substituted a new guard recruited mainly from the Illyrian legions.

The Praetorians attended the Emperor and members of his family at home and abroad. Their length of service was fixed in 13 B.C. at twelve years, which was increased in 5 B.C. to sixteen years, but since discharges were made every other year, many soldiers served for seventeen years. Their pay was at first perhaps 375 *denarii* a year, which was increased to 750 *c.* A.D. 13, and to 1,000 by Domitian, and they received large and frequent donatives. On discharge they were granted *diplomata*. (*See* DIPLOMA, DONATIVUM, SIGNA MILITARIA, STIPENDIUM.)

M. Durry, *Les Cohortes prétoriennes* (1938); A. Passerini, *Le coorti pretorie* (1939).											H. M. D. P.; G. R. W.

**PRAETORIUM** denoted a general's tent (Livy 7. 12, 10. 32; Caes. *BCiv.* 1. 76) or his staff or council (Livy 26. 13. 6). Hence comes the *porta praetoria* of Roman castrametation (*see* CAMPS). By an extension of meaning *praetorium* signified the residence of a provincial governor (e.g. *ILS* 2298), a pleasure villa (e.g. Suet. *Tib.* 39), an official road-side rest-house (*CIL* iii. 6123), or an emperor's residence (*CIL* iii. 5050). It is also regularly used for the forces or services of the Praetorian Prefect (*CIL* v. 2837, viii. 9391, etc.). In permanent fortresses or forts it is distinguished from the *principia*, or headquarters building, and clearly refers to the commandant's house, a separate structural entity (Livy 28. 25; Tac. *Ann.* 1. 44; *RIB* 1092, 1685–6, 1912).

Mommsen, *Hermes* 1900, 437 ff.											I. A. R.

**PRASUTAGUS**, client king of the Iceni (q.v.) of East Anglia, was renowned for his wealth (Tac. *Ann.* 14. 31). His death in A.D. 60 precipitated the rebellion of his wife Boudicca, for the king's will dividing his property between his daughters and Nero in the hope of preserving the kingdom was disregarded.											S. S. F.

**PRATINAS** of Phlius (*see* TRAGEDY § 3) is stated by the *Suda* (s.v.) to have been the first to compose satyric plays; and of his fifty plays thirty-two were satyric. He competed at Athens about the beginning of the fifth century B.C., though the abundance of satyrs on Attic vases after *c.* 520 B.C. might suggest an earlier date. A fragment of one of his satyric plays (Ath. 14. 617 b) attacks the growing predominance of the flute accompaniment over the words of the dithyramb. His son Aristias won second prize with a production of his father's plays in 467 B.C. (Arg. Aesch. *Sept.*).

TGF 726. M. Pohlenz, *Das Satyrspiel und Pratinas von Phleius* (1926); Pickard-Cambridge–Webster, *Dithyramb²*, 17 ff., 65 ff.; Fr. Brommer, *Satyrspiele* (1959).							A. W. P.-C.; D. W. L.

**PRAXAGORAS** of Cos (second half of 4th c. B.C.), the teacher of Herophilus, was numbered by Galen among the greatest physicians; the few data preserved do not give a clear picture of his achievements. Praxagoras' anatomy was a strange mixture of correct and false notions. He recognized the connexion of the brain with the spinal cord; on the other hand, he believed that the arteries, coming from the heart, taper away and finally turn into nerves. Respiration he called, though not the cause, yet the re-creating source of the soul, and he considered the arteries as air-channels. The discovery of the arterial pulse was ascribed to him. Diseases he explained by the (eleven) humours, also emphasizing the importance of the pneuma (see Steckerl, op. cit. *infra*); he was particularly interested in fevers. His therapy is almost unknown; his operation on the ileus is mentioned.

TEXT. Fragments, C. G. Kühn, *Opuscula Academica Medica et Philologica* ii (1828), 128 f.; F. Steckerl, 'The Fragments of Praxagoras of Cos and his School', *Philosophia Antiqua* viii (Leiden, 1958), with K. Schubring, *Deutsche Literaturzeitung* 1961, 257 ff. Cf. also *Anth. Plan.* 16. 273.
LITERATURE. E. D. Baumann, *Janus* (1937); K. Bardong, *PW* xxii. 2. 1735. 6 ff. Surgery, K. Sudhoff, *Quellen u. Studien z. Gesch. d. Naturw. u. d. Med.* (1933). Date, about 300 B.C., W. Jaeger, *Diokles v. Karystos* (1938), following from later date of Diocles. Cf. Steckerl, op. cit.; Bardong, 1735. 18 ff. An older and a younger P. (H. Schöne, *Rh. Mus.* 1903, 64), not yet clearly distinguished.											L. E.

**PRAXIDIKAI**, 'the exactors of justice'; goddesses worshipped at Haliartus (Paus. 9. 33. 3). Their temple was roofless (it is common for oaths to be taken in the open air) and they were sworn by, but not lightly. They were daughters of Ogygus, i.e. ancient Boeotian (Dionysius of Chalcis in Photius, s.v.). In the singular an epithet of Persephone (q.v.; *Hymn. Orph.* 29. 5).											H. J. R.

**PRAXILLA** (fl. 451 B.C. (Eusebius–Jerome)), poetess, of Sicyon, wrote dithyrambs (fr. 1), drinking-songs (Schol. Ar. *Vesp.* 1239), and hymns, including one to Adonis, in which a line was proverbial for its silliness (fr. 2, cf. Zenob. 4. 21).

TEXT. Page, *Poet. Mel. Gr.* 386–90.											C. M. B.

**PRAXIPHANES**, Peripatetic philosopher (end of 4th–mid 3rd century B.C.). Probably he was born in Mytilene and worked in Rhodes. At some time he was publicly honoured in Delos (*IG* xi. 613). The few traces of his work remaining suggest that he concentrated on γραμματική and literary criticism. He was involved in controversy with the Epicurean Carneiscus on the subject of friendship, and also with Callimachus, who wrote a book *Against Praxiphanes*.

F. Wehrli, *Die Schule des Aristoteles* ix (1957; frr. and comm.); K. O. Brink, 'Callimachus and Aristotle', *CQ* 1946, 11 ff.; W. Aly, *PW* xxii. 1769.											D. J. F.

**PRAXITELES**, sculptor, probably son of Cephisodotus (q.v. 1), Athenian. Pliny dates 364 B.C., probably by Aphrodite of Cnidos. Selected works, (i) *dated*: 1. Altar of Artemis at Ephesus, after 356. 2. Work on Mausoleum, after 351 (doubtful). 3. Artemis at Brauron, 346. According to Studniczka the bronze original of the Artemis of Gabii (Winter, *KB* 297. 6). 4. Signature from Leuctra, about 330. (ii) *Undated*: 5. Aphrodite of Cnidos. Marble; Lucian describes particularly the face and eyes and the setting which showed the front and back view (cf. copy in open round temple in Hadrian's Villa at Tivoli. Recognized from coins in many copies (ibid. 295. 3–5); fragment in the British Museum is contemporary. Other Aphrodites, including draped Aphrodite of Cos, are recorded. A draped Aphrodite in the Louvre is ascribed by the copyist to Praxiteles; the Aphrodite of Arles (ibid. 312. 2) is attributed on style. 6. Hermes with infant Dionysus in Heraeum at Olympia (ibid. 294. 1–2; 295. 1). Marble; original, not copy as recently suggested. Later than Cnidian Aphrodite, perhaps 343. 7. Apollo Sauroctonus (lizard-slayer). Bronze, known from several copies (ibid. 294. 3). Early, the head nearer Cephisodotus than no. 5. 8. Group of Apollo, Artemis, and Leto with Muses and Marsyas on the base, at Mantinea. Pausanias dates to third generation after Alcamenes. The base has been discovered (ibid. 296. 1–3); dated by parallels on vases not long after 350. 9. Dionysus, Inebriation, and 'the famous satyr'. Bronze, later in Rome. The Dresden satyr (ibid. 297. 7), stylistically near no. 7, may reproduce the satyr. The leaning satyr (ibid. 295. 2) reflects a later original, perhaps Praxiteles' satyr in the street of Tripods. 10. Eros of Thespiae, later in Rome. 11. Eros of Parium, Leto in Argos, Artemis in Anticyra are reproduced on coins. 12. Phryne, Praxiteles' mistress, at Delphi (and Thespiae), gilded or golden. 13. Soldier and horse on grave at Athens. 14. Niobid group, see under Scopas. (iii) *Attributed*: 15. Head from Chios in Boston, original (ibid. 297. 3; attributed from likeness to no. 5 above). 16. Hermes Farnese, copy (ibid. 294. 4; attributed from likeness to no. 6 above). 17. Aberdeen head in British Museum, original; later and heavier than Hermes. 18. Bronze boy from Marathon (Lippold, pl. 96, 3). 19. (Doubtful) Apollo Lyceius, described by Lucian (*Anach.* 7). 20. Women from Herculaneum, copies (Winter, *KB* 394. 1; probably Demeter and Persephone; attributed from likeness to no. 8 above). 21. 'Eubouleus' head (ibid. 297. 2), often considered a Praxitelean original, is probably a copy of Leochares' Alexander (E. B. Harrison, *Hesp.* 1960, 382).

Praxiteles was thought most successful in marble and to excel in representing emotion; he preferred those statues which Nicias (q.v. 2) painted. Intimate feeling can be appreciated in the surviving originals, nos. 6, 15, 17, 18. Nos. 5, 6, 7, 9, 16, 19 are skilfully composed for a single view (no. 5 also for back view). Contrast the tridimensionalism of Lysippus. The assumption of an earlier Praxiteles is uncertain; for Praxiteles' sons *see* CEPHISODOTUS (2).

Overbeck, 525, 1165, 1178, 1180–1, 1188–1300; G. E. Rizzo, *Prassitele* (1932); C. Blinkenburg, *Knidia* (1932); R. Carpenter, etc., *AJArch.* 1931, 249; Lippold, *Griech. Plastik*, 234.  T. B. L. W.

**PRAYER.** Prayer was quite as prominent in ancient as in modern religions, and, then as now, could be formal or informal, accompanied by other acts of worship (in this case generally sacrifice) or used by itself. For the latter our earliest instance is *Iliad* 1. 37 ff., where Chryses prays to Apollo with no more ceremony than going away by himself to a retired place on the sea-shore, this probably for the practical reason that he did not want to be overheard by the men he was asking Apollo to injure. His prayer is formal and contains all the characteristic parts. First he addresses the god by complimentary phrases ('thou of the silver bow', 'thou who protectest Chryse and holy Cilla, mighty lord of Tenedos'), ending with his local title Smintheus. He then reminds Apollo of his own acts of piety and finally makes his petition, that the god shall avenge him on the Greeks. But informal prayers are common also in and after Homer; for instance, in *Iliad* 7. 179 f., all the Greeks pray to Zeus that the lot may fall on one of three leading champions to fight Hector; they say simply Ζεῦ πάτερ and then state their request, using the imperative infinitive, common in prayers (cf. e.g. Ar. *Ran.* 886 ff.; here the prayer is accompanied by an offering of incense). Even liturgies seem to have contained such informal petitions, for example the famous Eleusinian ὗε κύε (Hippol. *Haer.* 5. 7. 34, 87 Wendland), though this might be said to be artificial, even rhetorical brachylogy; cf. Schwenn, op. cit. *infra*, 7 f. Of elaborate formulae belonging to classical liturgies we have none left, the surviving specimens, when not literary or fragmentary, being late and magical; the most famous is that in the great Paris papyrus, *PGM* iv. 486 ff.; cf. A. Dieterich, *Mithrasliturgie* (ed. 3, with addenda by O. Weinreich, 1923); A. D. Nock, *JEg.Arch.* 1929, 231.

For Italy we have a considerable amount of material; that concerning Rome is handily collected by Appel. Perhaps the most outstanding feature of the official prayers is the elaborate accuracy, like that of a legal document, with which they are phrased. Thus, the formula for the *consecratio* of a hostile city (Macrob. *Sat.* 3. 9. 10–11; Appel, op. cit. *infra*, 14) not only invokes the appropriate gods but adds 'or by whatever other name it is lawful to name (you)', and is not content with mentioning the city which is to be destroyed by their help but

goes on with 'which I feel that I am mentioning', lest there should be some other place with the same name. This savours on the one hand of the meticulosity of developed magical formulae, on the other of the exact and legalistic spirit of Roman public institutions generally; like precautions are taken in other prayers. The rest of Italy is represented, in this respect, by the famous *Tabulae Iguvinae* (q.v.; R. S. Conway, *Italic Dialects* (1897), 356 ff.; C. D. Buck, *Oscan and Umbrian Grammar* (1928), 260 ff.). They are hardly less exact and particular as to detail than the Roman formulae. Prayers for individual use were similarly formulaic (Cato, *Rust.* 134. 2).

F. Schwenn, *Gebet und Opfer* (1927); P. J. T. Beckmann, *Das Gebet bei Homer* (1932); Nilsson, *GGR* i². 159, ii. 426. G. Appel, *De Romanorum precationibus* (1909); Latte, *RR* 392. J. Rudhardt, *Notions fondamentales de la pensée religieuse dans la Grèce classique* (1958), 187 ff.; E. des Places, 'La Prière cultuelle dans la Grèce ancienne', *Revue des sciences religieuses* 1959, 343 ff.  H. J. R.

**PRECATIO TERRAE, PRECATIO OMNIUM HERBARUM**, two short iambic litanies to Mother Earth and to All Herbs, probably post-Augustan.

Text with transl., Duff, *Minor Lat. Poets.*

**PRIAM** (Πρίαμος), in mythology, son of Laomedon, (q.v.) and king of Troy at the time of its destruction by Agamemnon. In Homer he is already an old man, father of fifty sons, some by Hecuba (q.v.), the rest by other wives or concubines (*Iliad* 24. 495–7). His non-Greek name (for the popular but absurd etymology *see* HESIONE) and his harem both suggest that some memory at least of a real Oriental prince survives into Epic. He is an amiable character, tender and considerate to Helen, although he disapproves of the war and its cause (*Il.* 3. 162 ff.), respected even by his enemies for his faith and wisdom (ibid. 105 ff., 20. 183), and esteemed by most of the gods, including Zeus (though Hera implacably hates him (4. 20 ff.) and Athena is hardly less hostile), because of his piety. He takes part in the treaty (3. 259 ff.) and has returned to the city before it is broken (305 ff.). He tries to induce Hector to come within the walls after the rout of the Trojans (22. 38 ff.) and after his death goes, encouraged by Iris, to ransom his body (24. 159 ff.), succeeding by help of Hermes (360 ff.) and by the impression which his appearance and words produce upon Achilles.

He did not survive the fall of Troy. The account in the *Iliu Persis*, that he took refuge at the altar of Zeus Herkeios in his own palace and was there killed by Neoptolemus (q.v. 1), remained classical; its best-known telling in surviving literature is Virgil's (*Aen.* 2. 506 ff.). Apart from the above incidents he has no story of any account. His name became almost proverbial for a man who had known the extreme of contrasting fortunes (Arist. *Eth. Nic.* 1101 8ᵃ, Juvenal, 10. 258 ff.).

Neoptolemus killing Priam at the altar is frequent in art from the Corfu pediment of the early sixth century on, as a separate scene or as the centre of a Sack of Troy. It is often associated with the death of Astyanax (Brommer, *Vasenlisten²*, 330 ff.). Priam is also shown coming to ransom Hector's body from Achilles.  H. J. R.; C. M. R.

**PRIAPE(I)A**, poems in honour of Priapus (q.v.). There are Greek poems addressed to him, but the chief Latin collection contains eighty-five poems: two attributed to Tibullus, probably wrongly (Hiller, *Hermes* 1883, 343); three from the *Catalepton* (*see* APPENDIX VERGILIANA); a series of eighty pieces (principally hendecasyllabic and elegiac) composed under Augustus and collected in the first century A.D. The two first of these eighty introduce the collection; the third is by Ovid (Sen. *Controv.* 1. 2. 22), the rest by unknown authors who show signs of Ovid's influence.

The subjects are mainly the shameful chastisements awaiting thieves, the phallus of the god, the offerings presented to him. Clever in versification, lively and sometimes witty in style, they are, with rare exceptions, marked by extreme obscenity.

Other *Priapea*: Catull. fr. 2; Hor. *Sat.* 1. 8; Tib. 1. 4; Mart. 6. 16, 49, 72, 73; Buecheler, *Carm. Epigr.* 193, 1504.

EDITIONS. E. Baehrens, *Poet. Lat. min.* i. 54 ff.; F. Buecheler, ed. minor of Petronius[4], 1904 (86 poems, no. 80 being divided into two). See F. Buecheler, *Rh. Mus.* 1863; C. Cali, *Studi letterari* (1898); R. S. Radford, 'Priapea and Virgilian Appendix' *TAPA* 1921; R. F. Thomason, *The Priapea and Ovid* (U.S.A. 1931); M. Coulon, *La Poésie priapique dans l'antiquité et au moyen âge* (1932); A. E. Housman, 'Praetanda', *Hermes* 1931, 402 ff. C. F., transl. J. W. D.

**PRIAPUS** (Πρίαπος, Πρίηπος), a god of fertility, originally worshipped at Lampsacus on the Hellespont and in that neighbourhood. His symbol was the phallus (q.v.) and indeed he himself may almost be said to have been a phallus provided with a grotesque body. It is clear that his original cult was important, and his local mythology connected him with great deities, for the Greek version of the story is that he was the son of Dionysus, his mother being either a local nymph or Aphrodite (i.e. the Oriental Great Mother) herself (Strabo 13. 1. 12; Paus. 9. 31. 2, who also testifies that he was the god most worshipped at Lampsacus). His local sacrifice was the ass; since this creature was thought of as the embodiment of lust quite as much as stupidity in antiquity, we may suppose that the purpose of the offering was to maintain the god's power of generation (aetiological account of the origin of the sacrifice, Ovid, *Fasti* 1. 391 ff.; an ass once brayed and woke a nymph, Lotis, who in *Met.* 9. 348–9 turns into a lotus-flower to escape him. It thus saved her from his attentions. He therefore hates asses). In any case, the victim is non-Greek, see Frazer on Ovid, *Fasti*, loc. cit.

His cult spread to Greece after Alexander, when interchange of ideas, religious and other, between East and West was common, though Nilsson, *GGR* i². 594 and pl. 33. 1, tries to find evidence for him on a late fifth-century Boeotian vase. It was popular also in the great Hellenistic cities, such as Alexandria, and made its way in due course to Italy. Greece had by that time outgrown most of the more crudely naturalistic worships, and Priapus seems to have been found broadly funny rather than impressive. He was adopted as a god of gardens, where his statue (a misshapen little man with enormous genitals) was a sort of combined scarecrow and guardian deity. For poems in his honour *see* PRIAPE(I)A.

Hans Herter, *De Priapo* (1932). H. J. R.

**PRIENE,** an Ionic city with original Theban connexions, situated by the ancient mouth of the Maeander. It controlled the common sanctuary of the Ionic cities at Panionion; but otherwise it was unimportant and it suffered disastrously in the seventh–sixth centuries at the hands of the Cimmerians, Lydians, and Persians. The city was refounded in the mid fourth century at the foot of Mt. Mycale facing Miletus, on a site dominated by a precipitous spur (the Teloneia) which formed its citadel. The German excavations of 1895–8 were uniquely successful in revealing the layout of a planned city with almost all its essential public buildings, and civic activity there in the Hellenistic age is further illuminated by the archive of inscriptions that came to light; only the harbours remain to be discovered under the accumulation of river silt. Inside the wall circuit, which was skilfully draped round the citadel and town, a grid pattern was laid out to the points of the compass, with level main streets running east–west. The open agora, with the market, was centrally placed; and most of the public buildings were also set in the central panel of the grid, with residential blocks to either flank. Among the interest-

ing buildings fitted into the grid are the theatre, old gymnasium, and indoor council chamber; irregularly sited along the bottom edge of the town was the Hellenistic palaestra (with stadium) which reflects the growing importance of the gymnasium as a civic institution.

T. Wiegand and H. Schrader, *Priene, Ergebnisse* (1904); F. Hiller, *Inschriften von Priene* (1906); M. Schede, *Die Ruinen von Priene* (1934); G. Kleiner, *PW* Suppl. ix, s.v. See also R. E. Wycherley, *How the Greeks built Cities* (1962), *passim*. J. M. C.

**PRIESTS** (ἱερῆς, *sacerdotes*). In no ancient Greek or Italian State was there such a thing as a class or caste of priests, and none was under priestly dominance, as was often the case, for instance, in Egypt. This does not mean that priests had no influence or were not treated with great respect, nor that their office could not be hereditary; it results rather from the absence of any cleavage between the religious and secular life of the community, under normal circumstances at least. Whereas a priest, despite his office, was not generally interdicted from secular activities,[*] a magistrate was usually a priest as a part of his official functions, which is why, in Greek cities, they often wore wreaths, a very common mark of one engaged in religious duties, and in Rome all curule magistrates wore the *praetexta*. The gods were, during the classical epoch, a sort of superior class of citizens, and their servants were not normally cut off from the life of the State as a whole, any more than any other class of persons whose duties were chiefly directed towards some one part of the population, e.g. magistrates who, like Roman aediles and Greek *agoranomoi*, had to do mostly with traders.

Furthermore, the executive powers of a priest were as a rule narrowly defined. He was active chiefly as an expert adviser (cf. PONTIFEX), and was, for example, in sole charge of the conduct of a sacrifice or other piece of ritual which fell within his province. Thus, the priestess of Athena and no one else superintended the annual ritual of the Arrhephoroi (Paus. 1. 27. 3). But the clergy, in spite of responsibilities for sanctuaries, did not draw upon the public funds for the expenses of ritual; the revenues of a temple, usually not very large, were another matter. We have abundant records of the governing body of a State voting the money for sacral purposes, as it might for any other; for instance, in Athens, *IG*¹ i supp. 66, no. 53 a (*SIG* 93) shows us the Council and People, not any sacral body, making the arrangements for some necessary work on a chapel sacred to Codrus and other worthies. *IG* i. 1 (*SIG* 42), though very fragmentary, is enough to show that innumerable details of the Eleusinian Mysteries, though of course not the secret ritual itself, were in the hands of the Athenian Government. At Rome Livy (22. 10. 1) gives the important evidence that according to the highest priestly authority of the day, the then pontifex maximus, a *ver sacrum* (q.v.) could not be vowed save by act of the popular Assembly ('iniussu populi uoueri non posse'); accordingly, the vow was made in the form of a bill proposed to and passed by the Assembly. The chief pontiff did not even give his advice of his own motion, but after consulting his colleagues at the request of a secular magistrate. Even the possessions of a temple, though sacred, were not the absolute property of the deity, in fact at least, though in law they seem always to have been. Thucydides (2. 13. 3–4) represents Pericles as counting among the resources of the Athenian State the treasures of the various temples and even the golden ornaments of the cult-statue of Athena, and there is good inscriptional evidence (e.g. *IG* i. 32, *SIG* 91) that even in times of less stress than those of the Peloponnesian War the State felt at liberty to

[*] In Rome, for example, the flamen Dialis very seldom held a magistracy, cf. Plut. *Quaest. Rom.* 113 and Rose ad loc., but there was no definite prohibition against his doing so; for the pontificate of the Emperors *see* PONTIFEX.

'borrow' from the gods and, if able, to repay, thus re-establishing a reserve fund for emergencies. Since, then, the clergy of a State had neither executive nor economic independence, it is easy to see why they never were supreme.

In private life it seems to have been much the same. The average ancient did, indeed, commingle his religion with his daily occupations to a considerable extent, and hence must on occasion have needed priestly guidance in matters of ritual, for instance that of a professional diviner to tell him the best day for a marriage, or of a priest of some sort to perform the religious rites needed on that and sundry other occasions. But we have only to look at Theophrastus' sketch of the pietistic man (*Charact.* 16, especially §§ 7 and 12) to see that priestly interference in the normal household was slight. This man, whose foible is gross exaggeration of the religious practices in which his more sensible neighbours are moderate, con-sults the *exegetes* (q.v.) and goes monthly to the Orphic specialists to undergo their rites; we may conclude that the ordinary person did such things far less often.

As to the appointment of priests, in some cases the office was in the hands of a clan or family, as the Eumol-pidae at Eleusis, or the Potitii and Pinarii in the cult of Hercules at the Ara Maxima. This presumably is the result of the rites' having been originally domestic or clan-worships. Some priests served for life, while others were chosen to serve for a single year. Normally, a State priest was appointed in some way by the State, often by actual election; in Hellenistic times many priesthoods were publicly sold, e.g. *SIG* 1012 (cf. Nilsson, *GGR* ii. 74). Some were lucrative, but in later times priesthoods were often an expense. The tendency was towards abolish-ing rules which confined eligible candidates to any one class of citizens, although the restrictions remained in the case of some particularly venerable offices (*see* HIERO-PHANTES); thus, the greater flamens at Rome remained patricians. Generally, no ethical tests were imposed, although some few positions were so hedged about with restrictions as to enforce at least an outward respectability of conduct.

Private religious organizations, permitted or tolerated by the State, and cults confined to a family, clan, or other group within the community, had their own rules, but these fall outside the scope of this article. For Roman priesthoods, Latte, *RR* 394 ff. H. J. R.

**PRIMIPILUS.** Under the Principate the centurions of the first cohort were, in order of seniority, *primus pilus* (*primipilus*), *princeps*, *hastatus*, *princeps posterior*, *hastatus posterior*. The *primipilus* commanded the leading century, and for many there was no further promotion except to *praefectus castrorum*; but a *primipilus* who was marked out for higher office could subsequently hold tribunates at Rome, in the order *tribunus vigilum*, *tribunus cohortis urbanae*, *tribunus cohortis praetoriae*, and then be appointed *primipilus iterum*. As such he served on the staff of the *legatus*, ranking immediately below the *tribunus laticlavius*, and was qualified to receive command of the Egyptian legions or a senior procuratorship. *See* CENTURIO.

Domaszewski–Dobson, *Die Rangordnung des römischen Heeres* (1967), 112 ff. H. M. D. P.; G. R. W.

**PRIMUS,** MARCUS ANTONIUS (*PW* 89), born at Tolosa in Gallia Narbonensis *c.* A.D. 20, was a turbulent and ambitious character—'strenuus manu, sermone promptus, serendae in alios inuidiae artifex, discordiis et seditionibus potens, raptor, largitor, pace pessimus, bello non spernen-dus' (Tac. *Hist.* 2. 86). Exiled for his share in the forgery of a will (61), he was restored by Galba and put in charge of Legio VII in Pannonia. In the summer of 69 he declared

openly for Vespasian, won over the other Danubian armies and, spurning a cautious strategy, invaded Italy across the Julian Alps. His dash and vigour carried all before him to victory at the second battle of Bedriacum. He pressed on to Rome, but came too late to save Flavius Sabinus. For a short time he was in supreme control, but after the arrival of Mucianus he was gradually thrust aside. Lapsing into private life, he enjoyed a quiet and happy old age in the city of his birth (Mart. 9. 99; 10. 23). R. S.

**PRINCEPS.** When Augustus selected 'Princeps' as the word which indicated most satisfactorily his own con-stitutional position, he chose, typically, a word which had good republican associations.

It was not an abbreviation of 'Princeps Senatus', though that, also, was a republican title and one which Augustus held. The 'Princeps Senatus', or First Senator, was before the time of Sulla the man who had been placed by censors at the head of the list of members of the Senate, and ranked as the senior member of that body. Augustus in the census of 28 B.C. enrolled himself as 'Princeps Senatus' (Dio Cass. 53. 1; *Res Gest.*, c. 7), and succeeding Emperors held the same position.

'Principes' in the plural, meaning the 'chief men of the State', was a phrase commonly employed by late republican writers, as Cicero, and it continued to be used in the Empire (Suet. *Aug.* 66; *Res Gest.*, c. 12).

It was the singular 'Princeps', however, applied to *one* prominent statesman, especially Pompey, in repub-lican times, which supplied Augustus with something of a precedent (e.g. Sall. *H.* 3. 48. 23 M.; Cic. *Har. Resp.* 46, *Pis.* 25, *Dom.* 66, *Sest.* 84, *Red. Sen.* 5 and 29, *Red. Pop.* 16). Early in 49 B.C. Cornelius Balbus wrote to Cicero (*Att.* 8. 9. 4): 'nihil malle Caesarem quam prin-cipe Pompeio sine metu uiuere.' Cicero used this designa-tion of other statesmen besides Pompey. In 46 B.C. he used it of Julius Caesar (*Fam.* 9. 17. 3). He used it also of himself in connexion with the renown that he won by his action against the Catilinarian conspirators (*Phil.* 14. 17) and by his rallying of the Senate against Antony at the end of 44 B.C. (*Fam.* 12. 24. 2). The phrase 'Princeps Ciuitatis' is also used of the 'Moderator Reipublicae' in Cicero's *De Republica* (5. 7. 9, where the reading is prob-ably sound in spite of the doubts of Dessau, *Gesch. der röm. Kaiserzeit* i. 61, n. 2), though here, almost certainly, he was not thinking of Pompey. In this work Cicero foreshadows a Principate of the Augustan type, a revived Republic, with a statesman in the background strong enough to ensure that it should function properly. Augus-tus' choice of the word 'Princeps' to designate his position was typical of his 'ciuilis animus'; it contrasted strongly with the 'Dictatura' and the suspected monarchical intentions of Julius Caesar and, in indicating an un-questioned but not a narrowly defined or clearly deter-mined primacy, the word suited perfectly Augustus' definition of his own authority in the *Res Gest.*, c. 34: 'Auctoritate omnibus praestiti, potestatis autem nihil amplius habui quam qui fuerunt mihi quoque in magi-stratu conlegae.' *Principatus* was in sharp opposition to *dominatio*, 'Princeps' to 'Dominus', and both Augustus and Tiberius took pains to suppress the use of the title 'Dominus', though it was a conventional form of polite address within the Roman family (Ov. *Fasti* 2. 142; Suet. *Aug.* 53; Dio Cass. 57. 8). The importance of this choice of title was appreciated by Roman historians; cf. Tac. *Ann.* 1. 1: 'cuncta discordiis ciuilibus fessa nomine principis sub imperium accepit'; 1. 9: 'Non regno tamen neque dictatura, sed principis nomine constitutam rem publicam' (cf. 3. 28).

'Princeps' was not an *official* title (like, for example, *Pater Patriae*). It was assumed by Roman Emperors at their accession and not conferred upon them by definite grant of the Senate; nor does it appear in the list of official titles in documents and inscriptions. On the other hand, by itself it might be used in inscriptions (e.g. on the funerary urn of Agrippina: 'Ossa Agrippinae . . . matris C. Caesaris Aug. Germanici principis', Dessau, *ILS* 180). Claudius, in his edict *de Anaunorum civitate*, wrote: 'Gai principatu' (Dessau, *ILS* 206). The Greek form of the word, ἡγεμών, appears in the fifth Cyrene Edict of Augustus (line 86, *JRS* 1927, 36): Αὐτοκράτωρ Καῖσαρ Σεβαστός, ἡγεμὼν ἡμέτερος.

The nuance of the word, chosen by Augustus for its inoffensive character, was soon lost (though the use of the word itself persisted) as the government of the Roman Emperors became more autocratic. It may be doubted whether the Greeks ever appreciated its subtlety; Dio Cassius, for instance, in recording Tiberius' very typical remark (57. 8. 2), 'I am *dominus* of my slaves, *imperator* of my troops, and *princeps* of the rest', loses the point by using, for 'Princeps', not ἡγεμών, but πρόκριτος, which means 'Princeps Senatus'. The title 'Princeps' in Latin survived the reorganization of Diocletian, though such phrases as 'Gloriosissimus Princeps' show that its original significance had been lost.

Further light is thrown on the significance of the word 'Princeps' by the title 'Princeps Iuventutis', meaning Leader of the Equestrian Order, or, more probably, of the 'Iuventus' of that Order (*see* PRINCEPS IUVENTUTIS), which was given in certain cases in the early Empire to princes of the imperial house who might be considered as 'Heirs apparent', the relation of the 'Princeps Iuventutis' to the 'Princeps' being well illustrated by Ovid's words (*Ars Am.* 1. 194): 'Nunc iuuenum princeps, deinde future senum.'

M. Hammond, *The Augustan Principate* (U.S.A. 1933); Mommsen, *Röm. Staatsr.* ii. 2. 3; A. Gwosdz, *Der Begriff des römischen Princeps* (1933); A. von Premerstein, *Vom Werden und Wesen des Prinzipats* (1937); Syme, *Rom. Rev.*² Full bibliography in *PW*, s.v., xxii. 1998.     J. P. B.

**PRINCEPS IUVENTUTIS or PRINCEPS IUVENUM.** The phrase occurs in the Roman Republic (Cicero, *Vatin.* 24, applies it to the younger Curio), but first appears with constitutional significance after the reorganization of the *Iuventus* by Augustus (*see* IUVENES). Probably in 5 and 2 B.C. respectively the *ordo equester* gave silver shields and spears to Augustus' grandsons, Gaius and Lucius, and hailed them as *Principes Iuventutis*. The same honour was paid possibly to Germanicus and Drusus, son of Tiberius; certainly to Tiberius Gemellus, adopted son of Gaius, in A.D. 37; to Nero, after his adoption by Claudius and, much later, to Commodus. The title was retained by these princes when they were no longer *Iuvenes*, and had something of the significance of 'Crown Prince'. This was lost when, occasionally after Domitian, and regularly in the third century, reigning Emperors used the title; its connexion with the *ordo equester* also disappeared in the third century.
     J. P. B.

**PRISCIANUS** (early 6th c. A.D.), grammarian, born at Caesarea in Mauretania, taught in Constantinople. His *Institutiones grammaticae* in eighteen books (ed. M. Hertz in Keil's *Gramm. Lat.*, vols. ii and iii) is the most voluminous work of any Latin grammarian. The first sixteen books deal with the parts of speech in great detail, the last two with points of syntax; but there are no sections devoted specifically to the *vitia et virtutes orationis* or to metre. Priscian made use of Greek grammars, and appears to have been well acquainted with all the more important of his Latin predecessors. His expositions are liberally illustrated by quotations from the standard school authors such as Cicero, Virgil, and Horace; he also drew, especially for books 5 to 10, on sources which afforded him many quotations from Republican writers; and his Greek authorities provided him with Greek examples. During the Middle Ages this work was widely read and commentaries were written upon it. Besides the long treatise, we possess the following shorter works: (*a*) *De figuris numerorum*, (*b*) *De metris fabularum Terentii*, (*c*) *Praeexercitamina rhetorica*, (*d*) *Institutio de nomine et pronomine et verbo*, (*e*) *Partitiones XII versuum Aeneidos*, (*f*) *De accentibus* (of doubtful authenticity), (*g*) *De laude imperatoris Anastasii* (312 hexameters), (*h*) *Periegesis e Dionysio* (1087 hexameters). Of these, (*a*), (*b*), and (*c*) were dedicated to Symmachus (consul 485); (*a*)–(*f*) are in Keil, *Gramm. Lat.* iii. 406–528, (*g*) and (*h*) in Baehrens, *PLM* v. 264–312. *See also* SCHOLARSHIP, LATIN.

Schanz–Hosius, §§ 1111–15.     J. F. M.

**PRISCILLIANISTS.** An ascetic sect holding doctrines seemingly derived from Gnosticism and Sabellianism. Its founder, Priscillian, a Spanish layman, was a Christian of noble birth and well educated. His preaching of a mystical and ascetic form of Christianity (*c.* A.D. 375) attracted the support of bishops Instantius and Salvian, but the opposition of Ithacius of Ossonoba and Idatius of Emerita. However, a Church Council convened at Saragossa (380) failed to condemn the Priscillianists by name, and soon after Priscillian was consecrated bishop of Avila by his friends. Their opponents appealed to Gratian (q.v.) in 381, and forced them to leave Spain and settle in Aquitaine. They failed to win a hearing from Pope Damasus in Rome, but secured a rescript authorizing them to resume possession of their sees from Macedonius, *Magister Officiorum* to Gratian. With Gratian's murder in 383 by Magnus (q.v. 2) Maximus their situation worsened. Maximus wishing to conciliate the Gallic and Spanish clergy convened a new council at Bordeaux at which Priscillian and Instantius were condemned (384). These now foolishly appealed to Magnus Maximus himself. Their enemies Ithacius and Hydatius denounced them as practitioners of magic. Evodius, *Praefectus Praetorio* to Maximus, tried the case and found the accused guilty. Despite the protests of Martin of Tours, Priscillian was executed, while Instantius was banished to the Isles of Scilly (385). The condemnation of clerics by a lay tribunal shocked contemporaries, and Ithacius and Hydatius were forced to resign their sees. Priscillianism now developed into something of a mass movement in Spain. The Council of Toledo (400), however, reconciled the more moderate Priscillianists, but it remained strong in the province of Galicia until *c.* 600.

The difficulty of discovering precisely what Priscillian believed has even been heightened by the publication of eleven treatises found in a MS. under Priscillian's name at Würzburg in 1889. These documents, undoubtedly Priscillianist in origin, show the sectaries denouncing current heresies, Manichaeism and Patripassianism included, but maintaining a sort of Panchristism by which the Trinity would be merged in the person of Christ. This, coupled with vegetarianism, extreme ascetic practices, a reverence for apocryphal gospels, and a secrecy of rite and teaching, suggests that their views stemmed from a tradition of Gnosticism in the West which can be traced back to the late second century (cf. Jerome, *De Viris Illustribus* 121). The movement showed the existence of anti-ecclesiastical as well as non-orthodox trends in the ascetic movement in the West which were to be demonstrated in the Middle Ages by the Albigensians and Adamites.

Würzburg MS. ed. G. Schepps, *CSEL* xviii, 1889. Also, arts. s.v. in *DCB* iv. 470 ff., and *DTC* xii. 391 ff.; E. C. Babut, *Bibl. de l'École des Hautes Études, Sciences historiques et philologiques* clxix (1909); A.

d'Alès, *Priscillien et l'Espagne chrétienne* (1936); B. Altaner, *Patrologie* (1950), 326. W. H. C. F.

**PRISCUS,** Eastern Roman politician and Greek historian of the fifth century A.D. Born in Panium (Thrace) and probably a professional rhetorician (see the article in *Suda*), he accompanied Maximinus in the embassy sent by Theodosius II to Attila in 449. He therefore had the opportunity of observing the court of the king of the Huns at first hand. In 452 he followed the same Maximinus to Arabia and Egypt. Later he became an *adsessor* of the *magister equitum* Euphemius under the Emperor Marcianus. He was in Rome at least once, perhaps in 450. It is uncertain whether he was a Pagan or a Christian. He wrote a *Byzantine History* in seven books, perhaps starting where Olympiodorus (q.v. 3) ended. It included events from at least A.D. 433 to 472: it was probably published after Basilicus' fall (476). The history is lost, but long excerpts of it are preserved in Constantine Porphyrogenitus' *De legationibus* and other Byzantine sources. It was a principal authority for the account of the Huns in Cassiodorus (q.v.) and consequently in Jordanes (q.v.). He wrote as a defender of the interests of the senatorial class and as a critic of the policy of appeasing the barbarians. But he was above all an extremely acute observer of contemporary customs and conflicts both within and without the Roman Empire. His style owed much to Herodotus and something to Thucydides.

Fragments in *FHG* iv. 69; L. Dindorf, *Hist. Gr. Min.* i (1870), 275; and partially, in a better edition, C. De Boor, *Excerpta de Legationibus* (1903), 121 and 575. E. A. Thompson, *A History of Attila* (1948), 9 ff., 103 ff., 184 ff.; G. Moravcsik, *Byzantinoturcica* i² (1958), 479; F. Altheim, *Geschichte der Hunnen* iv (1962), 300 ff. A. M.

**PRISON.** Roman criminal law did not recognize the imprisonment of free persons as a form of punishment. The public prison (*carcer, publica vincula*) served only for a short incarceration applied as a coercive measure (*coercitio*, q.v.) by magistrates for disobedience or recalcitrance to their orders. During inquiry in a criminal trial the accused person could be detained (*custodia reorum*) so as to be at the disposal of the authorities; condemned persons could be imprisoned so as to ensure the execution of the sentence, but as the rules were very lax and no term for such a detention was fixed, the magistrates postponed the arrest of the malefactors in order to give them the chance of going into voluntary exile (*see* EXSILIUM). Private, domestic prisons existed in larger households for the imprisonment of slaves. *See also* TULLIANUM. A. B.

**PROAGON,** a kind of dress-parade in the Odeum of *choregoi*, poets, actors, and choruses a few days before the Great Dionysia and the Lenaea at Athens. Probably the names and subjects of the plays were announced. At the *proagon* next after the death of Euripides, Sophocles appeared in mourning and his actors and chorus did not wear the usual crowns (Aeschin. 3. 66–7 with schol.; Pl. *Symp.* 194 a; *Vit. Eurip.* and schol. on Ar. *Vesp.* 1109). A. W. P.-C.

**PROBA** (4th c. A.D.), poetess, besides an epic on the civil war between Constantius and Magnentius, composed out of Virgilian scraps a cento (q.v.) on parts of the Old and New Testaments.

TEXT. K. Schenkl, *CSEL* xvi (1887).

**PROBOULOI** (πρόβουλοι) was the ordinary word for 'committee', used in many Greek States. The best-known committee with this title is the one appointed in Athens in 413 B.C. It consisted of ten men over 40 years of age;

one of them was Sophocles the tragedian. It was appointed immediately after the failure of the Sicilian expedition, evidently because it was felt that the democratic *ekklesia* (q.v.) and *boule* (q.v.) could not conduct the war efficiently and responsibly. It had some executive powers, but their precise extent is not known; it probably took over some of the functions of the *prytaneis* (q.v.). In 411 the *probouloi* were included in a commission appointed to draft a new constitution; this led to the revolution of the Four Hundred (q.v.), after which they are not heard of again.

Hignett, *Hist. Athen. Const.* 269. D. M. M.

**PROBUS** (1), MARCUS AURELIUS (*PW* 194), born at Sirmium in A.D. 232. His earlier career has become confused with that of Tenagino Probus and is little known. Set up as rival to Florian (q.v.) after the death of Tacitus, he outmanœuvred Florian at Tarsus and became sole Emperor (autumn 276).

The main task of Probus was to consolidate the work of Aurelian which had been interrupted by his death. In Gaul from 277 to 279 he dealt with raids by Alamanni, Franks, and Burgundians and strengthened the Rhine frontier. Then, moving eastward, he defeated the Vandals on the Danube and put down the insurrection of Lydius at Cremna in Pisidia. In Egypt the Blemmyes captured Ptolemais and Coptos, but were defeated by Probus' generals. In 280 he settled the Bastarnae in Thrace. He celebrated a splendid triumph in Rome in 281. In 282 he was at Sirmium, when the troops in Raetia proclaimed Carus, the Praetorian Prefect, Emperor. A corps, sent by Probus, deserted to Carus, and Probus was killed by his own troops.

The rebellions of Saturninus in the East (277–8) and of Proculus and Bonosus in Gaul (280), and an attempt at revolt in Britain, though all successfully quelled, point to serious discontent in the army. The stern discipline of Probus and his employment of troops on the planting of vineyards were both unpopular. The danger of settling barbarians in the Empire was revealed by the exploit of a band of Franks, who made their way home after extensive ravages in the Mediterranean. Probus sought the co-operation of the Senate in government, but did not take the decisive step of putting senators back into military commands.

G. Vitucci, *L'imperatore Probo* (1952). H. M.; B. H. W.

**PRŌBUS** (2), VALERIUS (late 1st c. A.D.), of Berytus, scholar. He interested himself in republican authors and somewhat in the fashion of Aristarchus worked over the texts of Terence, Lucretius, Virgil, and Horace, indicating his views by critical signs. He himself published little (cf. Suet. *Gram.* 24), but communicated his learning in conversation with friends. It is improbable that he wrote full commentaries, but some information about his work on Terence and Virgil is found in scholia to those authors. He is not mentioned in the scholia to Horace. Aulus Gellius and later grammarians quote him with some frequency on points of grammar. The *Libri iuris notarum* (ed. Th. Mommsen in Keil's *Gramm. Lat.* iv. 271–6) attributed to him is not the original work. Other treatises: *Ars catholica, Instituta artium, Appendix Probi, De nomine,* and *De ultimis syllabis* (ed. Keil, *Gramm. Lat.* iv. 3–43, 47–192, 193–204, 207–16, 219–64) are neither genuine notes of Probus nor based on his writings; apocryphal also is the extant commentary on the *Eclogues* and *Georgics* of Virgil (ed. H. Hagen in Thilo's Servius iii. ii). As early as the fifteenth century a 'Younger Probus' was conjured up to account for the false ascription of these works. *See* SCHOLARSHIP, LATIN.

Schanz–Hosius, §§ 477–9. J. F. M.

**PROCESSION.** Processions were very prominent features of Greek festivals. There are various kinds. Best known is that in which people who take part in a festival go in an orderly procession to the temple of the god; so, for instance, in the Panathenaic procession as represented on the Parthenon frieze (cf. PANATHENAEA). The gods are waiting for the procession; certain men look after its order; virgins carry sacred implements, elderly men green branches; youths conduct the sacrificial animals; chariots, which are to partake in the following contest, and the cavalry follow. Later the *peplos* brought to the goddess was hoisted on a ship set on wheels. Everyone's place in the procession was fixed and there was a special building, the Pompeion near the Dipylon gate, where the procession was arranged and from which it started. An inscription from Andania prescribes arrangements in detail (*SIG* 736). Sometimes a procession went to a mountain-top in order to perform a weather ceremony or fire-ritual, e.g. the Daidala to Mt. Cithaeron. Another kind of procession is due to a connexion between two cult-places. The outstanding example is the Iacchus procession, in which the people went to Eleusis in order to celebrate the mysteries. First the sacred things were brought to Athens, on the 14th Boedromion they were taken back to Eleusis together with the image of Iacchus, conducted by the priests, the magistrates, the ephebi, and the great mass of *mystae*. Sometimes a god was brought to visit another temple, e.g. Artemis from the suburb of Mesoa to Patrae; Dionysus was brought from his temple into the orchestra of the theatre in order to be present at the performances. Processions in which a god made his epiphany are peculiar to Dionysus. At the Anthesteria in Athens he was brought into the city on a ship set on wheels. Sometimes the image of a god was brought out to be cleansed; so that of Athena Polias in Athens was taken to the shore of Phaleron. The carrying of the image of a god in procession has always a special reason. In Greece, unlike many other countries, the god was not carried about in procession in order to give blessings and to be venerated. Blessings were distributed by carrying round sacred or rather magical things—the phallus, which was absent from hardly any Dionysiac procession, the 'may' (*eiresione*), the swallow, etc.; the last are rural processions, sometimes conducted by children collecting contributions.

E. Pfuhl, *De Atheniensium pompis sacris* (1900); M. P. Nilsson, *Opusc.* i. 166 ff. M. P. N.

**PROCLUS** (Πρόκλος), Neoplatonist philosopher, A.D. 410 or 412–485. Born in Lycia of wealthy parents, he came as a young man to Athens where, save for a brief period of exile occasioned by his fervent paganism, he spent the rest of his life, at first as the pupil of Syrianus and later as Head of the Academy (whence his title 'Diadochus'). His importance as a creative thinker has sometimes been exaggerated: most of the new features which distinguish his Neoplatonism from that of Plotinus are traceable, at least in germ, to Iamblichus or Syrianus. But he is the last great systematizer of the Greek philosophical inheritance, and as such exerted a powerful influence on medieval and Renaissance thought. His learning was encyclopedic and his output vast. Extant works include the following.

(*a*) Philosophical treatises: *Elements of Theology* (Στοιχείωσις θεολογική, ed. E. R. Dodds[2] with transl. and comm., 1963), a concise summary of Neoplatonist metaphysics; *Platonic Theology* (ed. A. Portus, 1618; new edition by H. D. Saffrey and L. G. Westerink in preparation), a more elaborate account in six books; *Elements of Physics* (Στοιχ. φυσική, ed. A. Ritzenfeld with Germ. transl., 1912), based on Aristotle's theory of motion; *Opus-*

*cula* (ed. H. Boese, 1960), essays on Providence, Fate and Evil, long known only in William of Moerbeke's Latin version but now partially available in the original Greek.

(*b*) Commentaries on Plato's *Timaeus* (ed. E. Diehl, 1903–6); *Republic* (ed. W. Kroll, 1899–1901); *Parmenides* (ed. V. Cousin, *Procli Opera Inedita*[2], 1864, now supplemented by R. Klibansky and C. Labowsky, *Plato Latinus* iii, 1953); *Alcibiades I* (ed. L. G. Westerink, 1954); *Cratylus* (excerpts, ed. G. Pasquali, 1908).

(*c*) Scientific works: *Outline of Astronomical Theories* (Ὑποτύπωσις τῶν ἀστρονομικῶν ὑποθέσεων, ed. C. Manitius with Germ. transl., 1909); commentaries on Euclid, Nicomachus, and Ptolemy.

(*d*) Literary works: *Hymns* (ed. E. Vogt, 1957); *Chrestomathia* (ed. A. Severyns, 1938– , with Fr. transl. and comm.), a handbook of literature extant in epitome only, authorship disputed (*see* EPIC CYCLE); Scholia on Hesiod, *Works and Days* (in Gaisford, *Poet. min. Graec.*, 1823).

LIFE. Marinus, *Vita Procli* (ed. J. F. Boissonade, 1814, repr. in Cousin, *Procli Opera Inedita*[2], 1864).
DISCUSSION. A. E. Taylor, *Philosophical Studies* (1934), 151 ff.; L. J. Rosan, *The Philosophy of Proclus* (1949); E. R. Dodds, introduction to his edition of *Elements of Theology*; *see also* bibliography to NEOPLATONISM. E. R. D.

**PRO CONSULE, PRO PRAETORE.** In 326 B.C. Publilius (q.v. 2) was about to take Naples when his consulate ran out. The people voted that he should retain his *imperium* in place of a consul (*pro consule*). He later triumphed as such. *Prorogatio imperii* (as this was called) was henceforth voted for both consuls and praetors whenever necessary for military purposes and became a routine measure passed by the Senate alone, which relieved the shortage of holders of *imperium* endemic in the original republican system. Quaestors, similarly, could be continued *pro quaestore*.

In 295 B.C., four private men held command *pro praetore*, in at least two (and probably in all four) cases delegated by a consul on his own authority. Such promagistracy by delegation sporadically occurs later; but in the classical Republic it was, on the whole, superseded by the system of *legati* (q.v.) under the Senate's control. *Imperium pro magistratu* was exercised in a *provincia* normally defined by the Senate, and the holder was not allowed to go beyond it. During the Hannibalic War *prorogatio* for long periods became common and several *privati* were given *imperium pro magistratu* by the people (but not, at this stage, allowed to triumph). The former practice became rare and the latter was abandoned at the height of the Senate's authority in the second century, but both were revived (and *privati* like Pompey even triumphed) in the troubles and the shortage of commanders of the last century of the Republic. Quaestors and legates could always be given *imperium pro praetore* if necessary.

After 146 B.C., with the multiplication of provinces, *prorogatio* became an integral part of the administrative system. With the development of the *quaestiones* (q.v.), praetors normally and consuls, if at all, went to a province after their year of office. Sulla made this practice law, except in emergencies. The increase in the number of provinces in the 60s, and the unwillingness of some men (like Cicero) to serve abroad, led to a great increase in long tenures, and this trend was accelerated by the series of emergencies characterizing that period.

Consuls were always prorogued *pro consule*, praetors at first usually *pro praetore*; but both during and after their year of office their *imperium* might be raised to rank *pro consule* (with twelve lictors) when the size of their armies or the importance of their tasks required it. After Sulla, all governors seem to have ranked *pro consule*. Legates of proconsuls holding large commands (e.g. of Pompey and

Caesar) now received *imperium pro praetore* on appointment. The number of their lictors is not certain.

Pompey, in 52 B.C., fixed a compulsory interval between magistracy and provincial government and seems to have tried to limit tenure of pro-magisterial command, in principle, to a year (as had been Sulla's intention), in order to prevent dangerous accumulation of power. This detached the magistracy from the pro-magistracy and regularly bestowed the latter on *privati* chosen by the Senate—a move that Caesar branded as unconstitutional and himself at once abandoned. But Augustus embodied Pompey's idea in his settlement of the 'public provinces' administered by (praetorian or consular) proconsuls with six lictors. After 23 B.C., the Emperor had proconsular *imperium* (defined as *maius* with respect to that of others) and his governors thus ranked as *legati pro praetore* (with five lictors). They would be either ex-praetors or ex-consuls, according to the importance of their command. The Emperor's proconsular *imperium* was probably the original basis of the Emperor's right of coinage and judicial powers. (*See also* PROVINCIA.)

Mommsen, *Röm. Staatsr.*³, see index, s.v.; W. F. Jashemski, *Origin and History of Proconsular and Propraetorian Imperium to 27 B.C.* (1950).                              E. B.

**PROCOPIUS**, Greek historian, born in Caesarea in Palestine *c.* A.D. 500. After a thorough rhetorical and legal education—where he studied we do not know—he obtained by 527 a post as counsellor (ξύμβουλος) and later became assessor (πάρεδρος) on the staff of Justinian's great marshal Belisarius. He accompanied Belisarius on his Persian (527–31), African (533–6), and Italian (536–40) campaigns. By 540/42 he was back in Constantinople, where he probably continued his official career and became Prefect of the City in 562. The date of his death is unknown.

His principal work is his *History of the Wars of Justinian* in eight books. Books 1–2 deal with the first Persian War, 3–4 the war against the Vandals in Africa, and 5–7 that against the Goths; these were probably published in 551. Book 8 contains supplementary material and a short history of the period 551–3. The *History* deals primarily with Justinian's campaigns, but there are many digressions on the political scene in Constantinople and on events elsewhere in the Empire. Procopius, as Belisarius' confidant, had direct and comprehensive acquaintance with military affairs and was favourably placed to interrogate eyewitnesses of what he had not himself seen. These are the main sources upon which his history relies. But he also made use of documents and other written sources in Greek and Latin, and probably also in Syriac. Procopius was a careful and intelligent man, of balanced judgement and sincere in his desire to establish the truth. He has a slight prejudice in favour of his hero Belisarius, and a coolness towards Justinian, Theodora, and the central government. His general attitude is somewhat old-fashioned and backward-looking. The *History* is a most reliable source for the matters of which it treats; but little can be inferred from Procopius' silence.

The *Secret History* (Ἀνέκδοτα), the authenticity of which has often been doubted, but is now generally accepted, covers the same period as Books 1–7 of the *History of the Wars*, but in a very different spirit. It is a virulent, scurrilous, and often scabrous attack upon the whole policy of Justinian, who is blamed for everything from barbarian invasions and financial insolvency to floods and earthquakes. The work rests mainly upon court scandal, and where it conflicts on matters of fact with the *History* it is generally to be rejected. Written about 550, it cannot have been published so long as Justinian was alive. Procopius evidently embodied in it, from private motives and in grossly exaggerated and uncritical form, many of the criticisms of Justinian only adumbrated in his main work.

*On Justinian's Buildings* was composed (*c.* 553–5) at the Emperor's behest, and is panegyric in tone. It is a first-class source for the geography, topography, and art of the period; and Procopius displays an unexpected talent for lucid architectural description.

All the works are written in a classicizing, but generally clear, Greek, with many echoes and reminiscences of earlier historians, particularly Thucydides. Procopius, however, is no imitative epigone, but a historian of the first rank, helped rather than hindered by the literary tradition within which he wrote.

Ed. J. Haury, 3 vols. (1914–40; repr. 1963–4). B. Rubin, *Prokopios von Kaisareia* (1954).                              R. B.

**PROCRIS** (Πρόκρις), wife of the Attic hero Cephalus (q.v.). After sundry adventures, which have come down to us in late forms (Ov. *Met.* 7. 794 ff.; Hyg. *Fab.* 189), she was accidentally killed by him.

**PROCRUSTES** (Προκρούστης; also called **Damastes**, Δαμάστης, Apollod. *Epit.* 1. 4, Plut. *Thes.* 11, or **Polypemon**, Πολυπήμων, Paus. 1. 38. 5, or **Procoptas**, Προκόπτας, Bacchylides 17. 28). All these names refer to his activities. He lived in some part of Attica (see Jebb on Bacchyl. loc. cit.), and having 'overcome' (δαμάζειν) strangers would force them to lie down on one of his two beds. Here he caused them 'much woe' by hammering them out (προκρούειν) to a sufficient length to fit the longer bed (so Bacchyl. and Apollod.) or racking them out with weights (Hyg. *Fab.* 38. 3). If they were longer than the shorter bed he lopped them (προκόπτειν). Theseus (q.v.) killed him in like manner. His father was Poseidon (Hyginus), or is called by one of the names elsewhere given to Procrustes himself (see e.g. Bacchyl.).

See further Höfer in Roscher, *Lex.*, art. 'Polypemonides', and refs. there.                              H. J. R.

**PROCULUS** (*PW* 9a), a prominent Roman jurist of the first half of the first century A.D., of whom little, however, is known. The Proculian School took its name from him (*see* SABINUS 2). Author of *Epistulae*, a collection of opinions and discussions taken from his practice, and of *Notae* to Labeo (q.v. 1), the precursor of the School. He was frequently cited by later jurists.

A. M. Honoré, *Tijdschrift voor Rechtsgeschiedenis* 1962, 472. *And see under* JURISPRUDENCE.                              A. B.; B. N.

**PROCURATOR** signified an agent or, in legal proceedings, representative, and under the Principate came to be the distinctive term for the employees of the Emperor in civil administration. They might be freedmen from the imperial *familia*, but the majority, especially of the holders of the more important posts, were always *equites* (q.v.).

The principal types of procuratorial post were:

(1) The government of minor provinces, such as Judaea, Noricum, Thrace, and the Mauretanias. Such equestrian governors were originally called *Praefecti* (a new inscription, *AE* 1963, 104, shows that Pontius Pilate was called *Praefectus Judaeae*). They were, with very rare exceptions, always *equites*, not freedmen, commanded auxiliary units in their provinces, and exercised full civil and criminal jurisdiction. In the later first and second centuries these provinces tended to be transferred to senatorial *legati pro praetore*, but the Mauretanias, Epirus, and the small Alpine provinces remained under procurators.

(2) Procurators of imperial provinces governed by *legati* performed functions equivalent to those of a provincial quaestor in the senatorial provinces, collecting revenues (Cass. Dio 53. 15) and paying the troops (Strabo 167). *Equites* were more common in these posts, but

Licinus who was exacting excessive tribute from the Gauls in 15 B.C. (Cass. Dio 54. 21) is an early example of a freedman.

(3) Procurators of senatorial provinces were in charge of the properties of the Emperor within the province (Tac. *Ann.* 4. 15; 13. 1). The fact of their connexion with the Emperor tended, however, to give them a wider role; Junius Cilo, the procurator of Pontus and Bithynia, was awarded consular *insignia* in A.D. 49 for escorting Mithridates of the Bosporus to Rome (Tac. *Ann.* 12. 21). They also tended to acquire or usurp the exercise of jurisdiction; this practice was repeatedly forbidden by the Emperors in respect of criminal jurisdiction, but was formally recognized, at least from the end of the second century, in cases between the *fiscus* (q.v.) and *privati*.

Both of these types of procurator might act in place of the senatorial governor of the province. The first-known occasion was in Asia about 88, and this function became increasingly common from the first half of the third century.

(4) Procurators of imperial estates. Their functions are most fully illustrated by the second-century inscriptions from the imperial estates in Africa, which show them issuing regulations about the mutual obligations of *coloni* and *conductores* (q.v.). If the mining area of Vipasca is to be regarded as an imperial property, the inscriptions from there (*FIRA*² i. 104–5) show the wide police and administrative powers of the procurator.

(5) Procurators connected with indirect taxes appear in the first century and more widely in the second (*see* PORTORIA *and* VECTIGAL). Their functions are largely unknown; they may perhaps have judged cases relating to the taxes or have been responsible for collecting them. An anecdote of Suetonius (*Dom.* 12) shows a procurator judging cases relating to the *fiscus* (q.v.) *Iudaicus*.

(6) Throughout the first two centuries there was a steady accretion of procuratorial posts in connexion with such things as the aqueducts, the *annona*, the Mint, and imperial *ludi* or *familiae gladiatoriae*.

Entry to procuratorial posts followed normally on military service, either (for men who were already *equites*, q.v.) the 'tres militiae' (*praefectus cohortis, tribunus legionis, praefectus alae*), or from the rank of *primipilus bis* for men who had risen from the ranks. The first century saw the formation of the 'praetorian cursus', by which a *primipilus* (q.v.) went as tribune of a cohort successively in the three urban units (*vigiles*, Urban, and Praetorian cohorts), went to another legion as *primipilus bis*, and then moved to important procuratorships. In the middle of the first century equestrian procurators began to gain promotion to the major prefectures, Egypt, the *annona*, and the Praetorian Cohorts, and towards the end of the century to the 'secretarial' posts with the Emperor, previously the preserve of imperial freedmen. This process was completed in the reign of Hadrian. Hadrian also created the junior equestrian post of *advocatus fisci*, which served as a non-military point of entry to the equestrian cursus. From the Flavian period onwards it was not uncommon for equestrian office-holders to be adlected into the Senate by the Emperor.

With the steady growth in the number of equestrian posts (182 are attested by the mid third century), they rapidly fell into a regular hierarchy of promotion, which by the mid second century ran (after military service or the post of *advocatus fisci*), from minor procuratorial posts, to provincial procuratorships, equestrian governorships, 'secretarial' posts, and major prefectures. In the later second century came the final formulation of gradations of procuratorial posts by the level of pay—*sexagenarii* (those receiving 60,000 sesterces p.a.), *centenarii* (100,000), *ducenarii* (200,000), and, rarely, *trecenarii* (300,000). Freedmen procurators have been much less

studied, but clearly became progressively less important in the course of the Principate.

In the second half of the third century equestrians steadily replaced senators as provincial governors, a process completed by Diocletian (except for the surviving proconsulates of Africa and Asia); the word *praeses*, increasingly common for both types of governor in the third century, was now universal for equestrian governors. *Procuratores* survived as the officials in charge of imperial mints, mines, factories, and landed properties.

O. Hirschfeld, *Die kaiserlichen Verwaltungsbeamten* (1905); A. N. Sherwin-White, *PBSR* 1939, 11 ff.; H. G. Pflaum, *Les Procurateurs équestres* (1950); *Les Carrières procuratoriennes* (1960–1); A. H. M. Jones, *Studies in Roman Government and Law* (1960), 19 ff.; F. Millar, *Hist.* 1964, 180 ff.; *Hist.* 1965, 362 ff.; P. A. Brunt, *Latomus* 1966, 460 ff. F. G. B. M.

**PRODICUS** of Ceos, a Sophist and a contemporary of Socrates. We have very little reliable information about his life. We learn from Plato that he was employed by his native city on diplomatic missions and that he took advantage of the opportunities these afforded to further his professional interests. He gained considerable repute in his profession and demanded high fees for his courses of instruction. These are described as being concerned with the right use of words and were marked by their subtle discriminations between the precise meanings of kindred terms. Plato represents Socrates as being on friendly terms with him and paying tribute to the value of his teaching, though always with a touch of irony. There are also references to discussions, or perhaps rather exhortations, on moral questions, and he was the author of the famous myth 'The Choice of Heracles'.

Testimonia and fragments in H. Diels, *Vorsokr.*¹¹ ii. 308–19, M. Untersteiner, *I Sofisti* ii (1949). G. C. F.

**PRODIGIA.** A *prodigium* is an event contrary to the supposed or known workings of nature, taken as a sign that the *pax deorum* is broken or in danger of being broken; whereas an *omen* is commonly a natural and ordinary event, observed by a diviner under certain circumstances. Examples are frequent in Livy, and collected by Julius Obsequens, *Prodigiorum liber*, from him. For example, in 136 B.C. (Obs. 25) the town of Rhegium was mysteriously burned, many objects in various places struck by lightning, streams at Puteoli ran blood, and a slave-girl bore a monstrous child. To deal with such things(*procurare*), Etruscan experts were often summoned (cf. HARUSPICES), as in the above instance; by their advice the child was burned and his ashes thrown into the sea. Other examples are mysterious voices of warning (Obs. 24, in 137 B.C.); rains of milk, blood, etc. (ibid. 28, 30, 31, 35, 51, 54); meteors and other like phenomena; the *hastae Martis* or the *ancilia* moving of their own accord (ibid. 44 a, 47); earthquakes and eruptions; statues sweating or weeping (ibid. 6, 28, 52); phantoms of various kinds (ibid. 17, 18, 51). Sacrifices, lustrations, and a *nouendiale sacrum*, or ceremony lasting nine days, were among the commonest forms of *procuratio* (e.g. ibid. 4, 12, 23).

See bibliography to DIVINATION. H. J. R.

**PROEDROI** (πρόεδροι) means 'chairmen'. In the fifth century B.C. in Athens the chair at meetings of the *boule* (q.v.) and the *ekklesia* (q.v.) was taken by the foreman of the *prytaneis* (q.v.), but later this duty was taken over by *proedroi*, presumably because the foreman of the *prytaneis* was thought to be overburdened with responsibilities. The new system was introduced at some date between 403/2 and 378/7 (cf. D. M. Lewis, *BSA* 1954, 31 ff.). At each meeting of the *boule* or *ekklesia*, the foreman of the *prytaneis* picked nine *proedroi* by lot from the other members of the *boule*, one from each of the ten *phylai* (q.v.)

except that to which the *prytaneis* themselves belonged, and then he picked by lot one of these nine *proedroi* to be their foreman (ἐπιστάτης). One man could not be a *proedros* more than once in a prytany, nor foreman of the *proedroi* more than once in a year. The *proedroi* saw that good order was kept at the meeting, brought forward the various items of business in accordance with the agenda, counted the votes, and finally dismissed the meeting.

Arist. *Ath. Pol.* 44. 2–3. D. M. M.

**PROETUS** (Προῖτος), a mythical king of the Argolid, who first appears in Homer, in the story of Bellerophon (q.v.). Later (Apollod. 2. 24 ff.) he and Acrisius are sons of Abas son of Danaus (q.v.); for their quarrel *see* ACRISIUS. The only other legend of importance concerns his daughters. These insulted the statue of Hera, or would not receive the rites of Dionysus (the latter is the Hesiodic story, the former and more probably original from Acusilaus, Apollod. 26). They were driven mad by the offended deity and wandered about the country 'with all manner of unseemliness'. In particular, they fancied themselves cows (Verg. *Ecl.* 6. 48). Melampus (q.v. 1), being asked to heal them, demanded a share of the kingdom; this was refused, and they went madder still and killed their own children. Proetus now agreed to Melampus' terms, although they were raised to include another share for his brother Bias. The women were then caught at Sicyon and cured, except one, Iphinoe, who had died.

H. J. R.

**PROGYMNASMATA**, or preliminary exercises, constituted the elementary stage of instruction in schools of rhetoric. There are extant collections by Aelius Theon, Hermogenes (2), Aphthonius, Libanius (qq.v.), and Nicolaus. The principal exercises were μῦθος (fable), διήγημα (narrative), χρεία (moral anecdote), γνώμη (maxim), ἀνασκευή and κατασκευή (refutation and confirmation), κοινὸς τόπος (*locus communis*), ἐγκώμιον (encomium), σύγκρισις (comparison), ἠθοποιία (piece written in character), ἔκφρασις (description), θέσις (abstract question), νόμου εἰσφορά (introduction of a law). The influence of such textbooks on later literature, including that of the Middle Ages and Renaissance, was considerable.

TEXTS. Theon in Spengel, *Rhet.* ii; Hermogenes, ed. H. Rabe (1913); Aphthonius, ed. H. Rabe (1926); Nicolaus, ed. J. Felten (1913); Libanius, ed. R. Foerster, vol. viii (1915). Kroll, *PW*, Suppl. vii. 1118; D. L. Clark, *Rhetoric in Greco-Roman Education* (1957), 177 ff. D. A. R.

**PRO(H)AERESIUS**, (A.D. 276–367/8). Greek rhetorician. Born in Cappadocia, he studied in Antioch and Athens, where he succeeded his teacher Julianus as professor of rhetoric. He gained an immense reputation through his ability to improvise and his phenomenal memory. Invited by the Emperor Constans to his court in Gaul, he had honours showered upon him both there and in Rome; the Senate set up a statue of him, and offered him a chair of rhetoric in the city, which he declined. Among his students in Athens were SS. Basil and Gregory of Nazianzus and the future Emperor Julian (qq.v.). When Julian in 362 issued his edict forbidding Christians to teach, special exception was made for Proaeresius, who was a Christian; he preferred, however, to resign his chair, but took it up again after Julian's death. None of his speeches survives.

Eunap. *VS* Giangrande 63–79; Jerome, *Chron.* a. 2378. R. B.

**PROLETARII**, as opposed to *assidui*, were the citizens of Rome too poor to contribute anything to the State except their children (*proles*). Originally they were equated with the *capite censi* as persons who paid no tribute and were exempt from military service. In the middle second century B.C., however, direct taxation was abandoned and

the property qualification for military service began progressively to be lowered. It is possible that then the term *proletarii* took on a more specialized meaning, and was used to distinguish those newly eligible for enrolment from those (the *capite censi*) who still remained exempt. In 107 this distinction will have disappeared again, when Marius threw military service open to all.

Although in Ciceronian times the *proletarii* are said to have constituted a majority of the total population, they had virtually no voting strength in the major electoral assemblies. They were collected in a single century, which only voted if the issue was still open after the decision of the centuries drawn from the five property classes had been declared.

Mommsen, *Röm. Staatsr.* iii. 237 f.; G. W. Botsford, *The Roman Assemblies* (1909), 207 f. E. S. S.

**PROMETHEUS** (Προμηθεύς, 'the forethinker'; all other etymologies of his name are merely fantastic; the word is used as a common noun, Aesch. *PV* 86), an ancient and popular demigod, one of the Titans (son of Iapetus, Hesiod, *Theog.* 510, where his mother is Clymene the Oceanid). Originally, his character is entirely non-moral; he is the supreme trickster (cf. the like figure, Coyote or another, in Amerindian mythologies, W. Schmidt, *Origin and Growth of Religion*, 189, citing Kroeber), and as such is on occasion opposed to Zeus, whom he outwits. It would appear that he developed in common belief into a supreme craftsman, and was worshipped as such by craftsmen, particularly in Attica (see L. Deubner, *Attische Feste* (1932), 211 f.). Probably it is in this connexion that he is associated with fire and with the creation of man.

Hesiod has two principal tales of him. The first is that when Zeus hid fire away from man, Prometheus stole it and brought it to earth again (*Theog.* 562 ff.). Zeus would not give fire to the ash-trees for man's use, i.e. prevented the hardwood fire-sticks from being effective when rubbed against the soft ones; Prometheus therefore stole from the gods enough fire to make the pith of a stalk of giant fennel smoulder, and from this men got fire once more. It is a tale of common enough type, see Stith Thompson, A 1415 and references. Hesiod gives it, what probably did not originally belong to it, a preface explaining why Zeus acted so. Prometheus had tricked him with regard to the respective share of gods and men in burnt offerings (*Theog.* 535 ff.); he wrapped all the poorest parts of the victim up in fat, the best parts in another bundle, and bade Zeus choose; the simple-minded god taking the fat, man has ever since kept all the best of the meat for himself. This is a manifest aetiological myth to explain sacrificial usage, and its hero may always have been Prometheus. The story is also given an epilogue. Zeus punished mankind in general by creating woman to their confusion; the first woman was called Pandora, because she had 'all gifts' from the gods (she probably is in reality an earth-goddess, the All-giver); Prometheus' simple brother Epimetheus ('After-thinker') married her despite his brother's warnings, and she let out all evils from the store-jar where they were kept (*Theog.* 570 ff., *Op.* 50 ff.). This tale, for which cf. the part played by Eve in the Hebrew myth, is a piece of satire against women with which Prometheus has no necessary connexion.

The other tale is the vengeance of Zeus on Prometheus. He chained him and sent an eagle to eat his liver, which was as immortal as the rest of him and grew at night as fast as the eagle could devour it by day. In this torment he remained until Heracles released him. In Hesiod the reason for the punishment is the deceit regarding the sacrifices (*Theog.* 534 ff.); in Aeschylus (*PV* 7 ff.) it is the theft of fire. But a further complication is introduced, by Aeschylus himself so far as we know. Prometheus knew the secret regarding Thetis (q.v.), and would not reveal it till, apparently, he at last gave it up as the price of his liberty. Aeschylus also gives Prometheus high moral dignity as the friend of man against the tyranny of Zeus.

Prometheus, as master-craftsman, makes man from clay (Paus. 10. 4. 4) or from clay plus bits of other animals (Hor. *Carm.* 1. 16. 13 ff.).

The punishment of Prometheus and his rescue by Heracles are found in many forms of archaic art from the seventh century, and were shown by Panaenus in his paintings for Pheidias' Zeus at Olympia. He appears on several Attic vases of the second half of the fifth century, carrying fire in a fennel-stalk from which satyrs light torches—evidently illustrating a satyr-play (see J. D. Beazley, *AJArch.* 1939, 618 ff.). The creation of Pandora was shown on the base of the Parthenos, but we do not know whether Prometheus or Hephaestus was there the artificer.

L. Séchan, *Le Mythe de Prométhée* (1951); K. Reinhardt, 'Prometheus', *Eranos* 1956. In art, Brommer, *Vasenlisten*[2], 139 ff.
H. J. R.; C. M. R.

**PRONUNCIATION, GREEK.** The main features of ancient Greek pronunciation may be established through the study of contemporary documents, literary texts, evidence given by grammarians, etc. In many points, however, only approximate phonetic accuracy may be claimed. What follows refers essentially to classical Attic written in the Ionic alphabet (*see* ALPHABET, GREEK).

A. VOWELS AND DIPHTHONGS

Attic had five short vowels and seven long vowels. (1) Three letters indicated both short and long vowels: α, ι, υ. ᾰ and ᾱ were central or, more likely, slightly fronted vowels: [a] (cf. *a* in Northern Engl. *cat*) and [a:]; ῐ and ῑ were close front vowels similar in quality to French *i* and to *ee* in Engl. *see*. In Attic, in part of Ionic, etc., υ probably represented [y] and [y:], i.e. front vowels with lip-rounding, similar to French *u* (in *lune*) and German *ü*. Other dialects used the same sign to indicate [u] and [u:], back vowels similar to German *u* (and to *oo* in Engl. *too*). (2) In Ionic and Attic η = [ε:], long open *e* (as *aî* in French *maître*); [e:], i.e. long close *e* similar in quality to the vowels of French *été*, was represented in the pre-Ionic alphabet by ε, but in the standard Ionic alphabet by the digraph ει (see below). ω = [ɔ:], long open *o*, as in French *fort*; [o:], long close *o* (like the vowel of French *beau*), was expressed first by ο and then by the digraph ου. Later on (*c.* 350??) [o:] was replaced by [u:] still spelled ου. ε and ο indicated short vowels, either similar in quality to ει [e:] and ου [o:] or more open than these, but less open than η [ε:] and ω [ɔ:] respectively. (3) ει, ου. By the end of the fifth century B.C. Attic and Ionic had changed the original diphthongs [ei], [ou] into long vowels: [e:] and [o:]; this is why the digraphs ει and ου were also used for the vowels [e:] and [o:], of similar quality but of different origins. (4) αι, οι, υι were genuine diphthongs [ai], [oi], [yi] (?); in the second century A.D. [ai] changed into [ε:], and later on [oi] into [y:]; similar changes had occurred in Boeotian many centuries before. αυ and ευ remained diphthongs [au] and [eu] throughout the ancient period; their second element was probably [u] and not [y]. (5) ᾱι, ωι, ηι were long diphthongs, and so were probably ᾱυ, ωυ, ηυ. The *i*-element had probably been lost in pronunciation, if not in spelling, by the second or first century B.C. The *iota subscript* is a Byzantine spelling innovation.

*Later developments.* In Modern Greek the phonemic distinctions of quantity have disappeared and phonetically only the stressed vowels may be considered long. ι, η, υ, ει, οι, υι are now pronounced [i]. The second element of the *u*-diphthongs has been changed into a

spirant [f] or [v] according to the environment. Most of these changes were probably complete by the early Byzantine period.

B. CONSONANTS

π, τ, κ and β, δ, γ indicated the voiceless and voiced plosives of the bilabial, dental, and velar series. It is likely that τ and δ were dental and not alveolar like the Engl. *t* and *d*. φ, θ, and χ were voiceless aspirates [pʰ], [tʰ], [kʰ]; cf. the southern English pronunciation of *p* in *pin* and such words as *top-hat*. (2) μ was the labial and ν the dental nasal. A velar variant of the latter (cf. Engl. *ink*) was found before velar sounds and was frequently indicated by γ (as in συγγράφω), which in this use was called ἄγμα by the ancient grammarians. ρ was probably a voiced rolled tip-tongue [r], similar to Italian *r* or to Scottish *r*. Its initial variant (ῥ-) was probably voiceless and accompanied by aspiration. λ was a dental lateral sound [l]. σ indicated a voiceless dental sibilant [s]; cf. French *son* and the alveolar *s* in Engl. *see*. A voiced variant [z] was found before voiced consonants. (3) The *spiritus asper* (ʽ) indicated a breathed glottal fricative (like Engl. *h*) found at the beginning of some words before a vowel; the *spiritus lenis* (ʼ), first used by the Alexandrian grammarians, indicated its absence. (4) The value of ζ is disputed and probably varied from dialect to dialect; it may have indicated a cluster [zd] or an affricate [dz]. However, already in the fourth century B.C., Attic shows signs of a pronunciation [zz] or [z], i.e. of a change into a voiced sibilant. ξ and ψ represented the clusters [ks] and [ps] respectively. (5) Some dialects still knew a voiced semivowel [w], similar to Engl. *w*, which was expressed by the letter ϝ (digamma) and which had disappeared in Attic. A voiceless variant of it may perhaps be indicated by the spelling ϝh found in some inscriptions. (6) The spellings ππ, λλ, etc., probably indicated geminated plosives and continuants [pp], [ll], etc., similar to those of modern Italian. In the case of Attic ττ corresponding to Ionic σσ the real pronunciation, at least for the early period, is disputed.

*Later developments.* Signs of the tendency of the voiced and aspirated plosives to change into continuants may be found very early in Greek documents; the full change, however, took place only in the Imperial and early Byzantine period. φ, θ, χ became [f] (like Engl. *f*), [θ] (like Engl. *th* in *thing*), [x] (like *ch* in Scottish *loch*); β and δ became [v] and [ð] (like *th* in Engl. *other*); [g] (γ) was changed into [ɣ] (the voiced equivalent of [x]) or [j] (cf. *y* in Engl. *yes*). The geminated were changed into the corresponding non-geminated consonants.

C. ACCENT

(1) Much of our information on the nature of the Greek accent comes, directly or indirectly, from the ancient grammarians (*see* GRAMMAR, GRAMMARIANS [GREEK]). The indications are that the early Greek accent was one of pitch, i.e. that the prominence given within the word to the accented syllable was obtained by means of a rise in pitch, while the differences of stress, even if present, were not a relevant factor. It is not easy to establish the date at which the 'musical' or pitch accent was replaced by an accent similar to that of Modern Greek, in which stress is a primary component. It is likely that the change developed over a period of many centuries, but it is usually considered to have been complete by the end of the fourth century A.D.

(2) The Greek inscriptions did not indicate the word accent: for this and for the distinctions among the various kinds of accent we are indebted to the information provided by ancient authors, by some papyri, and by the late MSS. in which accents are marked. The usual signs were first introduced by the Alexandrian grammarians (probably by Aristophanes), but the distinction between

acute and grave is already mentioned in Plato (*Cra.* 399). The acute ' (ὀξεῖα) indicated a high pitch, which, if we believe a much discussed passage of Dionysius of Halicarnassus (*de comp. verb.* 11), differed by a musical fifth from the grave. It could rest on both short and long vowels (or diphthongs): in the second case it is possible, although not generally accepted, that the higher pitch concerned only the second part of the long vowel (⌐ = ◡◝). In the ancient tradition all unaccented syllables were considered to bear a grave ` (βαρεῖα), which therefore indicated a lack of accentuation. The fact that an acute resting on the last syllable of a word was changed into a grave within a phrase (θεοί but θεοὶ ἄλλοι) is variously interpreted by modern scholars (complete loss of accent, partial lowering of pitch, conventional writing, etc.). It should be noticed, however, that this use of the grave is relatively late; the papyri prefer spellings like κἀλὸς ἀνηρ (for καλὸς ἀνήρ), περικλὑτος (for περικλυτός), etc. The circumflex (περισπωμένη) is found only on long vowels or diphthongs and, as indicated by the original sign ∧, represents a higher pitch on the first part of the vowel followed by a lower pitch (Δ = ◡◝); in other words it is a combination of an acute and a grave (ἡ ὀξυβαρεῖα according to another terminology).

(3) In polysyllabic words only the last three syllables could bear the accent, and further limitations depended on the vocalic element of the last syllable. (*a*) If this was short, any of the last three syllables could bear an acute; the penultimate syllable, if long and accented, carried a circumflex in Attic. (*b*) If it was long, the accent could rest on either of the *two* last syllables and the penultimate could bear an acute only. Exceptions to this and rules concerning the behaviour of those words or particles which did not have an independent accent (Enclitics and Proclitics) cannot be illustrated here.

F. Blass, *Ueber d. Aussprache d. Griechischen*[3] (1888; Engl. Transl. W. J. Purton, 1890); E. H. Sturtevant, *The Pronunciation of Greek and Latin*[2] (U.S.A. 1940); E. Schwyzer, *Griech. Grammatik* i (1934), 174 ff.; M. Lejeune, *Traité de phonétique grecque*[2] (1955); J. P. Postgate, *Short Guide to the Accentuation of Ancient Greek* (1924); J. Vendryes, *Traité d'accentuation grecque* (1904, repr. 1945); Ch. Bally, *Manuel d'accentuation grecque* (1945); W. S. Allen, *Vox Graeca* (1968).                                        A. E. M. D.

**PRONUNCIATION, LATIN.** For the pronunciation of Latin various types of evidence are available. Besides the tradition of the schools (inaccurate in several respects) we have numerous phonetic descriptions by Latin grammarians which, though sometimes lacking in clarity, yield valuable information when interpreted by experts. Important evidence is also derived from the forms which Latin loan-words assume in foreign languages, and again from changes in orthodox spelling or departures from that spelling made by people of inferior education who attempted to write as they pronounced. In addition, we have certain evidence furnished by phonetic change within the Latin period and by the development or preservation of Latin sounds in the various Romance languages. It must be remembered that for many of the conclusions thus reached about the pronunciation of a 'dead' language only approximate accuracy can be claimed.

A. VOWELS AND DIPHTHONGS

The vowels *a, e, i, o, u* may be either long or short. It is probable that *a*, long and short, had approximately the same quality as the *a* of Eng. *father*. Between the long and the short forms of each of the other vowels there was a difference of quality. Thus while *ĕ* was open (*ę̆*) like *e* in Eng. *met*, *ē* was close (*ẹ̄*) like *é* in Fr. *été*. *i* was open (*ị̆*) like *i* in Eng. *fit*, while *ī* was close (*ị̄*) like *ee* in Eng. *feed*. Similarly *ŏ* was open (*ǫ̆*) like *o* in Eng. *not*, and *ō* close (*ọ̄*) like *au* in Fr. *faute*. *ŭ* was approximately like the *u* of Eng. *full* and *ū* like the *oo* of *fool*. There was also an 'intermediate' vowel, resembling perhaps a short Germ.

*ü*, which, as in *maximus, maxumus*, was written sometimes as *u*, sometimes as *i*. In educated pronunciation of the classical period *ae* was a diphthong, approximately like *ai* in German *Kaiser*; in Imperial times it became an open long *e* (*ę̄*). *oe* was also a diphthong (like *oy* in Eng. *boy*) in classical times, becoming later close *e* (*ę̄*). *au* was normally a diphthong like *ow* in Eng. *how* throughout the Latin period. Sporadically, however, in vulgar usage *au* got the sound of *ō* and in some words (e.g. *coda* for *cauda*) this seems to have been a very general pronunciation. The rare *eu*, which has no corresponding diphthong in English, combined a short *e* with a *u*; similarly *ui* in *cui* and *huic* seems to have contained the vowel *u* followed in the same syllable by the sound of *i*.

B. CONSONANTS

(1) The voiceless stops *p, t, c* (*k*) and the voiced stops *b, d, g* must have been approximately like the corresponding sounds in English. *c*, even before *e* and *i*, remained a stop during the classical period (i.e. *Cicero* was pronounced *Kikero*) and for long afterwards. Romance developments show that in the late Imperial period it had in this position undergone some degree of assibilation, thereby starting the process of change which led to the pronunciation of *c* in Fr. *cent* and Ital. *cento*. Similarly *g* remained a stop in all positions until about A.D. 500, when before *e* and *i* it developed into a *y*-sound. *b* between vowels became the spirant (bilabial) *v* fairly generally by the third century A.D. (2) *f* was originally a bilabial but later a labio-dental spirant like Eng.*f*. *s* was a voiceless sibilant (like the voiceless *s* in Eng. *past*) in all positions. In contact with voiced stops it caused them to become voiceless, so that a word like *urbs* was pronounced *urps*. (3) *h* was weakly articulated from an early period. Uneducated pronunciation tended to drop it, and in the later Empire it was lost altogether. The reaction against the tendency to omit it caused sometimes an intrusive 'h' in the affected pronunciation of some people (e.g. *hinsidiae* for *insidiae*). This habit is satirized in Catullus 84. (4) *n* before a guttural became the guttural nasal *ŋ* (*ng*); and *g* in *-gn-* probably had the same pronunciation. Thus *anguis* would be pronounced *aŋguis*, and *dignus diŋnus*. Final *m* before an initial vowel in the following word had a reduced pronunciation, of which the exact nature is disputed. Even before initial consonants final *m* eventually weakened and, except in monosyllables, leaves no trace in Romance. (5) *r* was trilled, with the point of the tongue probably against the gum. There were two varieties of *l*, one palatal approximately like Eng. *l*, the other velar or guttural like *ll* in Eng. *all*. Palatal *l* occurred before another *l* and before *i*; *l* final and before *a, o, u* or a consonant (except another *l*) was velar. (6) *i* (written *i*) and *u* (written *u*) were semi-vowels = Eng. *y* and *w* respectively. By the third century A.D. this *u* had become a spirant, either bilabial or labio-dental *v*, except in the combinations *qu, gu*, which continued to be pronounced as in English *queen* and *anguish*.

C. ACCENT

(1) *Early accent.* Most scholars hold that at a period before the beginning of literature the first syllable of every word carried a stress accent or, in other words, was pronounced with greater intensity than the remainder. This theory explains most easily the syncope which many Latin words had undergone (e.g. *quindecim* for *quinquedecem*) and the changes which had affected vowels (e.g. in compounds; *caedo* but *incido, cado* but *incído*). Plautine prosody shows that even in Plautus' period words consting of four short syllables were still accentuated in the old way (e.g. *fácilĭŭs* instead of the classical *facĭlius*).

(2) *Accent of the Classical and later periods.* (*a*) *Position.*
If the above theory is correct, a change must have taken
place in the accentuation of polysyllabic words in the
period before Plautus. Thereafter the position of the
accent is regulated by the Penultimate Law, whereby if
the penult is long by nature or position, the accent rests
on it, but goes back to the antepenult if the penult is
short (*confríngo* but *cóncido*). Apart from some exceptions like *illíc* (for *illíce*), where a final syllable has been
lost, disyllabic words were accented on the first syllable.

(*b*) *Nature.* Descriptions by Latin writers suggest that
during the classical period, and for several centuries
afterwards, the language had a pitch accent whereby the
accented syllable was pronounced on a higher musical
note than the others. The terms employed (*accentus
acutus, gravis, circumflexus*) are all translations of the
Greek musical terminology, and there is no hint in the
Latin accounts that the Latin accent differed in character
from that of Greek. Not until the fourth century A.D.
do we find in the grammarians phraseology which clearly
implies the presence of a stress accent. The form assumed
by Latin words in the Romance languages points unmistakably to the existence of a stress accent in the Late
Latin period.

Scholars differ about the interpretation of these facts.
Some accept the grammarians' accounts at their face
value and believe that the classical accent was musical
but gave way to a stress accent in the late period. Others
hold that the accent throughout was one of stress and
that the evidence of Latin writers is vitiated by an
unscientific dependence on Greek theory. Some, again,
adopt an intermediate position and believe that, while
evidence in the language itself points to a stress accent
having always been predominant, especially in the pronunciation of the lower classes, the influence of Greek
education on the higher classes in the classical period had
brought about a considerable degree of musical accent.

E. Seelmann, *Die Aussprache des Lateins* (1885); W. M. Lindsay,
*The Latin Language* (1894), 13 ff.; Leumann-Hofmann-Szantyr,
*Lateinische Grammatik* (repr. 1963), 50 ff.; E. H. Sturtevant, *The
Pronunciation of Greek and Latin²* (U.S.A. 1940); W. S. Allen, *Vox
Latina* (1965).                                        J. W. P.

## PROOEMIUM. (1) *Verse. See* HOMERIC HYMNS *and*
LYRIC POETRY, GREEK.

(2) *Prose.* With the development of Attic oratory in
the last quarter of the fifth century B.C. the custom arose
of compiling collections of stock openings to forensic and
political speeches (also of perorations, ἐπίλογοι). The
first collection was made by Cephalus (*Suda*, s.v.), others
by Antiphon, Critias, and Thrasymachus. The extant set
attributed to Demosthenes numbers fifty-six, five of
which are identical with the openings of Dem. 1, 4, 14,
15, 16. Blass argues cogently for the authenticity of the
set, often impugned, pointing out that the historical
background, in the few places where it is defined, is
everywhere that of the *first* war against Philip, a restriction only explicable on the supposition that Demosthenes
himself wrote the prooemia between 349 and 346, for his
own use when required (cf. Cicero's practice, *Att.* 16.
6. 4), with the exception that some, including those to
14–16 (354–350), were specially composed for particular
speeches. Ephorus wrote a prooemium to each book of
his history, in which practice he was followed by Diodorus (Diod. Sic. 16. 76. 5). The theory of the prooemium
is discussed by Aristotle (*Rh.* 3. 14), Hermogenes (*Inv.*
1. 1–5, and Apsines (*Rhet.* ad init.).

R. Swoboda, *De Dem. quae feruntur prooemiis* (1887); F. Blass, *Die
attische Beredsamkeit* iii. 1² (1893), 322 ff.; E. Stemplinger, *Das
Plagiat in d. griech. Lit.* (1912), 223 ff.                    J. D. D.

## PROPEMPTIKON (προπεμπτικόν), a composition
wishing a friend a prosperous voyage.

I. GREEK. The earliest extant example is Sappho's

χαίροις ἔρχεο κ.τ.λ. (*Berl. Klassikertexte* 5. 2. 12 f.).
Others are Erinna (?) fr. 2, Theoc. 7. 52–70, and Callim.
fr. 114. Parthenius wrote one. The genre is discussed by
Menander (q.v. 4) Rhetor (Spengel, *Rhet.* 3. 395–9).
                                                      J. D. D.

II. LATIN. The *Propempticon* of Helvius Cinna was
addressed to Pollio in 56 B.C.; only four fragments (containing seven lines) remain and nothing can be known of
its form. The fact that it was so obscure as to need a commentary by Hyginus suggests that it was like the densely
packed travel-poem of Statius to Maecius Celer (*Silv.* 3.
2). The genre as such and its detailed specifications were
probably the invention of Menander (see I. *Greek* above):
at any rate Tibullus 1. 3, Propertius 1. 17, 2. 26, Horace,
*Odes* 1. 3, and Ovid, *Am.* 2. 11, which are sometimes
assigned to the genre, have nothing in common except a
few well-tried commonplaces.

F. Jäger, *Das antike Propemptikon* (1913).          G. W. W.

**PROPERTIUS,** SEXTUS, born between 54 and 47 B.C.,
at Assisi, where his family were local notables (4. 1. 121 ff.).
His father died early, and the family property was much
diminished by Octavian's confiscations of 41–40 (4. 1.
127 ff.); in that revolutionary year a kinsman of Propertius fought and died at Perusia, a fact carefully recalled
at the end of book 1 (1. 22. 6 ff.).

Like others of his class, Propertius rejected the dull
pursuit of office; his rhetorical education was employed
in poetry, not in the courts. Following the example of
Cornelius Gallus (q.v. 3), he celebrated his love for a
mistress to whom he gave the fancy Greek pseudonym of
Cynthia; Apuleius says her real name was Hostia (*Apol.*
10). We need not doubt her reality as we doubt that of
Ovid's Corinna; many of the incidents suggested in Propertius' poems are conventional and tralatician, but
Cynthia is given a consistency of character, or at least of
temper, that convinces us of her actuality.

Book 1 shows Propertius as one member of a coterie
of poets, of which Ovid also claimed membership (*Tr.* 4.
10. 45 ff.). The grander circle of Maecenas was opened
to him after the publication of book 1; but he seems not
to have been intimate with Maecenas' older poets. He
speaks of Virgil with admiration but not as a friend
would, and Horace almost certainly disliked him heartily
(Hor. *Epist.* 2. 2. 90 ff.).

The dates of Propertius' books are uncertain. Book 1
was probably published before Oct. 28 B.C.; the latest
events mentioned in 2, 3, and 4 belong to the years 26,
23, and 16 respectively. There are some grounds for
thinking book 4 was published posthumously. Propertius
was certainly dead by 2 B.C. (Ov. *Rem. Am.* 764). We
may infer that he married and did his duty as an Augustan
citizen, since Pliny's friend, the poet Passennus Paulus,
claimed descent from him (Pliny, *Ep.* 6. 15; 9. 22).

Book 1 was known in antiquity as the *Cynthia mono-
biblos* (Mart. 14. 189) and consists almost entirely of love
poems of remarkable grace and wit. This style is maintained in book 2, though Propertius' association with
Maecenas produced as well some elegant tributes to the
new regime. Book 3 shows a greater diversity of tone and
subject-matter; it is here that Propertius first adopts the
ostentatious pose of the Roman Callimachus that irritated
Horace, and the opening poems, which deal with his own
poetic position, are among its most successful. Some of
the Cynthia poems, notably 8 and 16, show his old comic
power, but others are tedious failures; this switch of
interest is given definition by his rejection of Cynthia at
the end of the book. In many poems he is attempting to
widen his range, but he shows some uncertainty, some
crassness, and some lack of assurance in his new style.
Book 4 is considerably more successful. It consists partly
of the fragments of a Roman *Aetia*, which showed the

way to Ovid's *Fasti* (1, 2, 4, 6, 9, and 10). To these are added poems on various subjects: the two on Cynthia (7 and 8) are among his most brilliant, and though the epicede on Cornelia (11) is often overpraised by people who do not really like Propertius, it is a Roman work.

Some Romans, though not Quintilian, thought Propertius the most *tersus atque elegans* of the Roman elegists (Quint. 10. 1. 93; cf. also Pliny, *Ep.* 9. 22). Polish and refinement are conspicuous in many of his poems, and would no doubt be conspicuous in more if the MSS. tradition were better. In wit, objectivity, and dramatic power and in the thrusting, progressive movement of individual poems he reminds the English reader of John Donne. His obscurity, of which too much has been made, is also like Donne's: much that is puzzling at first sight becomes plain enough when the implied setting and dramatic development are grasped. The really insoluble difficulties are usually not the poet's fault, but a scribe's. Propertius' elaborate and self-conscious artistry, his vivid visual and tactile imagination, and his success in integrating what he derives from Greek literature with Roman feeling and Roman life make him one of the most continuously fascinating of the Latin poets. *See also* ELEGIAC POETRY, ALEXANDRIANISM.

TEXTS. E. Baehrens (1880); A. Palmer (1880); J. P. Postgate, *Corp. Poet.* (1894); M. Schuster (1954); E. A. Barber, 2nd ed. (1960).
COMMENTARIES. K. Lachmann (1816); P. J. Enk (1911); M. Rothstein, i² (1920), ii² (1924); H. E. Butler and E. A. Barber (1933); P. J. Enk (bk. 1, 1946; bk. 2, 1962); D. R. Shackleton Bailey, *Propertiana* (1956); W. A. Camps (bk. 1, 1961; bk. 4, 1965; bk. 3, 1966; bk. 2, 1967). *Selections.* J. P. Postgate (1905).
TRANSLATIONS. J. S. Phillimore (1906); H. E. Butler (1912).
BIBLIOGRAPHIES. Complete to 1940 in P. J. Enk's editio nof bk. 1, extended to 1960 in his bk. 2. See also J.-P. Boucher, *Études sur Properce* (1965). M. E. H.

## PROPHECIES (χρησμοί, *vaticinia*).

Besides the oracles of the greater and lesser shrines, there were in circulation in antiquity a number of prophecies, sometimes nameless, often attached to the name of some inspired person. Of these, the most famous was the Sibyl, or the Sibyls (q.v.); but in addition there were several men, some known to have lived during the historical period. Herodotus (1. 62. 4) mentions Amphilytus, a contemporary of Pisistratus, tyrant of Athens, and preserves the text of an oracle which he was suddenly inspired to give the latter. Such persons were known as χρησμῳδοί in Greek (e.g. [Plato], *Theages* 124 d) or χρησμολόγοι; in Latin, *vates*; for a list of them, with some account of their lives or legends, see A. Bouché-Leclercq, *Histoire de la divination* (1879–82) ii, ch. 2. Naturally, their alleged utterances were particularly rife in times of stress; cf. Thucydides 2. 8. 2, who speaks both of oracular sayings (λόγια) quoted and χρησμολόγοι 'singing' their prophecies at the outbreak of the Peloponnesian War. In 2. 54. 2 he quotes the text of one nameless utterance, ἥξει Δωριακὸς πόλεμος καὶ λοιμὸς (or λιμὸς) ἅμ' αὐτῷ. This craze is a favourite subject for Aristophanes' mockery, particularly in the *Knights*; an especial butt is a certain Bacis (q.v.), whose oracles were extremely popular.

The most celebrated Italian *vates* was perhaps a certain Marcius (q.v. 3), or a pair of brothers, the Marcii (see Cicero, *Div.* 1. 115; 2. 133, with Pease's notes); Cicero also mentions one Publicius. Here again, such effusions were multiplied in times of crisis; Augustus collected and destroyed a number of unauthorized collections (Suet. *Aug.* 31), many of them in Latin, no doubt in large measure a legacy of the Civil Wars. H. J. R.

## PROPHETES (προφήτης),

the title of the mortal who speaks in the name of a god or interprets his will. It is properly used only of seers and functionaries attached to an established oracular shrine; the unattached seer is called *mantis*, etc. (*see* PROPHECIES). Moreover, it is more often used of the officials who presided over oracular shrines (as Didyma) than of the actual receivers of mantic inspiration. At Claros a male prophet remained the direct mouthpiece of the god; but at Delphi and possibly at Didyma a woman who could be described as *prophetis* (προφῆτις) was directly inspired by Apollo. At Didyma the prophet was an annually elected magistrate. At Delphi the title was not used officially; the two magistrates, elected for life, who performed this office had the title of priest (ἱερεύς).

For further information and for bibliography *see* ORACLES; also E. Fascher, *ΠΡΟΦΗΤΗΣ* (1927). J. E. F.

## PROPONTIS (ἡ Προποντίς),

now the *Sea of Marmara*, an intermediate sea between the Aegean and the Euxine, whence its ancient name. Its length, just over 140 miles, and its greatest breadth, hardly 40 miles, are overstated by Herodotus (iv. 85) at 1,400 stades, i.e. 155 miles, and 500 stades, i.e. 55 miles, whereas Strabo (125) gauges the length accurately but exaggerates the breadth absurdly. The Propontis is connected with the Euxine by the deep, narrow, and winding channel of the Thracian Bosporus, and with the Aegean by that of the Hellespont; these waterways were commanded by Byzantium and Troy respectively. The principal cities on its shores are: Byzantium and Chalcedon at the mouth of the Bosporus; Nicomedeia at its eastern extremity; Selymbria, Perinthus-Heracleia, and Bisanthe-Rhaedestus on its Thracian coast; Cius and Cyzicus on its south side. The largest island in the Propontis is Proconnesus, now *Marmara*, meaning 'marble', which has given its modern name to the whole sea. There are other islands, including Ophiusa and Halone, in the same neighbourhood, and at the other end, in full view from Byzantium, are the four small islands now known as the *Princes' Islands* (Demonnesi); their ancient names seem to have been Prote (now *Kinah*), Elaea (*Burgaz*), Chalcitis (*Heybeli*), and Pityodes (*Büyük Ada*). A list of islands is given by Pliny (*HN* v. 151). The rivers Granicus, Aesepus, Macestus, and Rhyndacus enter the Propontis on its south side; on the north side there are no rivers of any consequence. G. E. B.

## PROPYLAEA,

a monumental roofed gateway; preeminently, that on the west side of the Athenian Acropolis (*see* ATHENS, TOPOGRAPHY) designed by Mnesicles, built of Pentelic marble, with some details of black Eleusis stone, *c.* 435 B.C. and still largely intact. The plan, with its deep 'hall', its Doric hexastyle porticoes fronting outwards and inwards, and with its single division-wall pierced by five doorways, is of early origin (cf. the 'South Propylaeum' at Cnossos); but Mnesicles provided wing-buildings of lesser height (the south one being curtailed) projecting from the front, forming loggias with Doric columns and rooms beyond. Larger wing-buildings to the east were intended. An inclined ramp continuing the slope of the natural rock formed the approach, and there were five steps at the four outer doorways. The central avenue had a span of nearly 14 feet and was flanked by Ionic colonnades in the deep outer porch; the ceilings were formed of marble beams and of slabs with deeply hollowed square coffers, richly decorated in blue and gold. The room of the north wing was adorned with wall-paintings by Polygnotus (q.v.) and other artists.

In the Propylaea we have a highly elaborate development of the simple propylon, or gateway with a porch on either side. There are traces of such a Propylon, built before the Persian Wars, on this site (cf. W. H. Plommer, *JHS* 1960, 146 ff.). Bundgaard thinks that the north wing too replaced a simpler archaic building. Mnesicles' design was much curtailed, through lack of resources and deference to adjoining shrines, notably that of Athena

Nike whose little Ionic temple was built a few years later on the bastion to the south-west.

W. B. Dinsmoor, *Architecture of Ancient Greece* (1950), 198 ff.; G. P. Stevens, *The Periclean Entrance Court to the Acropolis* (U.S.A. 1940); J. Bundgaard, *Mnesicles, a Greek Architect at Work* (Copenhagen, 1957).　　　　　　　　　　　　　　　　T. F.; R. E. W.

**PROSCRIPTIO,** the publication of a notice, especially (1) a notice of sale; (2) a list of Roman citizens who were declared outlaws and whose goods were confiscated. This procedure was employed by Sulla (82–81 B.C.) and by Antony, Lepidus, and Octavian (43–42) as a means of getting rid of personal and political opponents and obtaining funds; and in virtue, or anticipation, of special powers of inappellable jurisdiction conferred on them as dictator (q.v.) and *triumviri* (q.v.) respectively. The proscribed were hunted down and executed, not only in Rome, but throughout Italy, by squads of soldiers, and the co-operation of their families and slaves and of the general public sought by means of rewards and punishments.

Sulla's proscription, in part an act of revenge for the Marian massacres of 87 and 82, was said to have named 4,700 persons, including over forty senators and 1,600 *equites*: no doubt many escaped. The lists were closed on 1 June 81. The sons and grandsons of the proscribed were debarred from public life, till restored by Caesar in 49. The impression left was profound, and similar conduct was feared from Caesar or Pompey, whichever should win the Civil War: as it was, Caesar's clemency was made an excuse for the proscription of the triumvirs. Their lists included about 300 senators and 2,000 *equites*; but many escaped, and some of these, including a fair proportion of the senators, were afterwards restored.

Vell. Pat. 2. 28, 66 f.; Plut. *Sull.* 31 f., Cic. 46 f., *Ant.* 20; App. *BCiv.* 1. 95, 4. 5–30; Cass. Dio fr. 109, 47. 3–15. Mommsen, *Röm. Staatsr.* ii². 734 ff. (*Droit publ. rom.* iv. 461 ff.); H. Kloevekorn, *De proscriptionibus anno a. C. n. 43 . . . factis* (1891); Drumann–Groebe, *Gesch. Roms²* (1899–1929), i. 265 ff., ii. 399 ff.; Syme, *Rom. Rev.* 187 ff.; M. Fuhrmann, *PW* xxiii. 2440 ff. (Nachträge).
　　　　　　　　　　　　　　　　　　　　　　T. J. C.

**PROSE-RHYTHM.** By prose-rhythm we mean here the quantitative or accentual arrangement of syllables, articulating the sentence and defining its close. We exclude from discussion: rhythm in general (E. A. Sonnenschein, *What is Rhythm?* (1925); De Groot, *Der Rhythmus*); correspondence of sound and sense (Norden, *Ant. Kunstpr.*); Gorgianic figures. For rhythm emphasized by rhyme *see* ASSONANCE. For *Hiatus in Greek Prose see* s.v.

2. *Ancient theory.* From Thrasymachus onwards, prose-rhythm (ῥυθμός, *numerus*) was a recognized branch of rhetoric. Our chief authorities are Aristotle, Demetrius, Dionysius, Cicero, Caesius Bassus, Quintilian. They are generally agreed that prose-rhythm should be distinct from verse-rhythm, varied, and not too obvious. Cicero adds that sentence-endings (*clausulae*) are rhythmically most important, though the rest of the sentence is not to be neglected. According to him, the last syllable of a clausula is *anceps*; Quintilian disagrees.

3. Extant Greek theory gives few precise details. Aristotle recommends – ∪ ∪ ∪ as an opening rhythm, ∪ ∪ ∪ – as a clausula (he perhaps has Plato in mind; in the *Ethics* – ∪ ∪ ≃ is sought as a clausula and ∪ ∪ ∪ ≃ somewhat avoided). Demetrius and Dionysius are vague, and neglect important contrasts of rhythm in the authors they quote.

4. Latin theorists confuse matters by borrowing from Greek theorists without regard to differences of language. Cicero (whose sources include Aristotle's *Rhetoric* and lost works of Ephorus, Theophrastus, Theodectes, Hieronymus of Rhodes) apparently recommends the clausulae – ∪ ∪ – ≃, – ∪ ∪ – ∪ ≃, ∪ ∪ ∪ ≃, all of which he strongly avoids in practice. However, he also recommends certain of his favourite forms, e.g. – ∪ – – ≃, – ∪ ∪ – ∪ – ∪ – ≃. (See, further, Laurand, *Études*; and *CQ* 1931, 18.) Bassus recommends several Ciceronian clausulae (e.g. – ∪ – – ≃ and its five 'resolutions') together with forms usually avoided. Quintilian prefers – ∪ – – to – ∪ – ∪. Diomedes (4th c. A.D.) is the first theorist to recommend expressly the quite common clausula – – – – ∪ ≃.

5. *Modern research.* To establish the rhythms—clausulae especially—favoured by particular authors, modern scholars have used statistical methods. De Groot has shown that statistics must be *comparative*; since in the structure of any language some rhythms are commoner than others, preference for a clausula is shown, not by its absolute frequency, but by its frequency relative to 'unrhythmical' prose. Cicero's clausula – ∪ ∪ ∪ – ≃ has a low absolute frequency (4·7 per cent); but it has a high relative frequency, for it is about twice as common in Cicero as in unrhythmical prose (2·4 per cent). A supplement to this external comparison is the internal comparison of sentence-rhythm and clausula-rhythm in the same author (De Groot, Skimina, Novotný, Broadhead; and Zieliński in his later work).

6. *Greek quantitative prose.* The Ionians—Heraclitus, Pherecydes, Herodotus—show no distinct clausula.

7. Thrasymachus perhaps initiated a prose-rhythm differing from verse-rhythm; he was certainly regarded as an innovator (Cic. *Orat.* 39. 175), especially in his use of paeonic rhythm (Arist. *Rh.* 3. 1409ª1). We are not told if he cultivated a distinct clausula, and his one short continuous fragment is inconclusive (twelve sentence-endings, of which five are – ∪ – ≃ and one ∪ ∪ ∪ –). Gorgias resembles earlier writers in the verse-rhythms of the sentence, but he has a distinct clausula (– ∪ – – ≃ in *Hel.*, – ∪ – ≃ in *Pal.*).

8. Thucydides is proved by De Groot to be an almost 'unrhythmical' writer, i.e. to depart very little from the natural rhythms of the language. However, he shows some preference for the clausulae – ∪ ∪ – – ≃ and ∪ ∪ ∪ ≃.

9. The sentence-rhythm of Isocrates is too varied for analysis; he seeks as clausulae most forms with a long penultimate (– ∪ ∪ ∪ –, – ∪ ∪ – ∪, – ∪ ∪ – ≃; not – ∪ ∪ – – ≃); is indifferent to – – – ≃; favours final words of four syllables (as does Hyperides).

10. Demosthenes is concerned more with sentence-rhythm than with clausula-rhythm. His only well-defined clausula is – ∪ – ≃. The rhythms – ∪ – – ∪ ≃, – ∪ ∪ – ∪ ≃, – ∪ ∪ – ≃ occur often at the clausula, but oftener throughout the sentence. He avoids series of six or more long syllables. But his most characteristic practice is the avoidance everywhere of series of three or more short syllables ('Blass's Law'). Exceptions to this rule average 5 in 100 lines of Demosthenes (contrast Lysias, 23; Isocrates, 25; Aeschines, 21; Hyperides, 28). His technique here is of word-order rather than word-choice; his exceptions may perhaps be deliberate. Thus, though he continually uses πρότερον without breaking his rule, he has no scruples in 9. 60, 61. He once uses διαγίγνομαι with participle (23. 179, in a form which gives five shorts); but he does not substitute ἐπιβουλευών διαγίγνεται for ἐπ. διατελεῖ (19. 326).

11. Plato's rhythmical preferences show considerable evolution. Throughout his work he favours the clausulae – ∪ – – ∪ ≃, – – – – ∪ ≃, – ∪ ∪ – ∪ ≃, and somewhat avoids – ∪ – ≃. In the earlier books of the *Republic* he seeks – ∪ – ≃, – ∪ – ∪ ≃, – ∪ ∪ ∪ ≃; is indifferent to – – – ≃; avoids ∪ ∪ ∪ ≃ and – ∪ ∪ ∪ – ≃. In the *Laws* he seeks ∪ ∪ ∪ ≃ and – ∪ ∪ ∪ – ≃, avoiding – ∪ – ≃ and increasing his avoidance of – ∪ ∪ – ≃ (*Resp.* 7·0 per cent; *Leg.* 1·3 per cent, probably the lowest figure in Greek). In the sentence his later work shows increasing preference for series of short syllables, and he then

writes κάθαπερ, μέχριπερ, τινα τρόπον for ὥσπερ, ἕωσπερ, τρόπον τινά. His average percentages of exceptions to 'Blass's Law' are: *Cri.*, 18; *Euthphr.* and *Chrm.*, 24; *Resp.* books 2–9, 25; *Resp.* book 1, 29; *Symp.*, 30; *Soph.*, 36; *Ti.*, 46; *Leg.* book 12, 56 (Vogel's statistics). His later preference for the clausula ∪ ∪ ∪ ⊻ is in accord with this; but he does not abandon − − − − ∪ ⊻, and his avoidance of − − − ⊻ is never very marked. The dactylo-trochaic rhythms of *Phdr.* are exceptional in his practice. Lucian's clausulae suggest imitation of Plato.

**12.** The rhythmical practice of other writers is summarized below. Clausulae alone are considered, and only well-marked preference or avoidance recorded.

∪ ∪ ∪ ⊻ Sought by Philo, Plutarch, Chariton, Xenophon Ephesius, Josephus; avoided by Lysias, Aeschines. − ∪ ∪ − ∪ ⊻ Sought by Lys., Alcidamas, Hyperides, Ph., Charit., Xen. Eph., Joseph. − ∪ − ⊻ Sought by Lys., Antisthenes (59·5 per cent), Alcid., Isaeus, Xenophon, Hyp., Antiochus Rex, Ph., Plut., Charit. − ∪ − − ∪ ⊻ Sought by Lys., Alcid., Isae., Aeschin., Antioch. R., Ph., Charit., Xen. Eph. − ∪ − ⊻ Sought by Alcid., Antioch. R., Ph., Charit., Joseph. − ∪ ∪ ∪ − ⊻ Sought by Alcid., Antioch. R., Ph., Plut.; avoided by Lys., Aeschin. − − − − ∪ ⊻ Sought by Lys., Aeschin., Isae., Antioch. R., Ph., Charit., Xen. Eph.; avoided by Alcid., Plut. − − − ⊻ Avoided by Antisth., Ph., Plut., Charit., Xen. Eph., Joseph. − ∪ ∪ − ⊻ Sought by Xen.; avoided by Lys., Antisth., Aeschin., Hyp., Ph., Plut., Charit., Xen. Eph., Joseph.

**13.** *Observations.* Antisth., Plato, Hyp., perhaps others, prefer a long final in certain clausulae. Though classical writers on the whole seek rhythms distinct from verse, a good deal of verse-rhythm remains in Isocrates and Demosthenes; few writers altogether escape iambic sequences (R. A. Pope counts fourteen perfect trimeters in Aeschines). King Antiochus, Philo, Plutarch, and the novelists belong to a Hellenistic school which replaced the variety of classical writers with a small canon of sought and avoided clausulae. Hegesias, an earlier representative of the same school, probably influenced Cicero and his followers. To this period belongs the preference for − ∪ − or − ∪ ∪ before − ∪ − ⊻, as also the general strong avoidance of − − − ⊻ and − ∪ ∪ − ⊻ as clausulae. (Among classical writers − − − ⊻ is little avoided; − ∪ ∪ − ⊻ is sought by Isocrates and Xenophon, and allowed by Demosthenes.)

**14.** *Greek accentual prose.* The origin of the Greek accentual clausula (*cursus*) is still uncertain. There are traces of it in the orator Menander (q.v. 4); it appears fully in Himerius, Procopius, S. Basil, and Byzantine writers generally. The forms most commonly sought have 2 or 4 unaccented syllables between the last two accents: ∠∼∪∼∠, ∠∼∪∼∼∼, ∠∼∼∼∼∠, ∠∼∼∼∼∠ ∼∼. Forms with no syllable between (χρηστὸς ἄνθρωπος) are sought by Procop.; those with 1, by Men. Rh., Him., Procop.; those with 3 or 5 are universally avoided. For details, see Skimina, De Groot.

**15.** *Latin quantitative prose.* Some fragments of C. Gracchus (cf. Cic. *De Or.* 3. 214, Gell. 11. 13) show the earliest traces of quantitative rhythms. Pre-Ciceronian orators (Metellus, Crassus, Titinius, Carbo) seek the clausulae − ∪ − − ∪ ⊻, − ∪ − ∪ ∪ ⊻, − ∪ − − ⊻, − ∪ − ⊻. *Auctor ad Herennium* seeks most Ciceronian forms except − ∪ − − ∪ ⊻, − − − − ∪ ⊻.

**16.** *Cicero* throughout the sentence avoids series of choriambs and dactyls. He has a well-marked system of sought and avoided clausulae. The following are sought as sentence-endings: − ∪ − − ⊻ and its 'resolutions' ∪ ∪ ∪ − ⊻, − ∪ − ∪ ∪ ⊻, ∪ ∪ ∪ ∪ − ⊻, ∪ ∪ ∪ − ∪ ∪ ⊻, − ∪ − − ∪ ⊻, ∪ ∪ ∪ − − ∪ ⊻, − − − − ∪ ⊻, − ∪ − ⊻, often preceded by − − −, − ∪ −, or − ∪ ∪. Commonly avoided, but used for special effects, is − − − ⊻;

strongly avoided are − ∪ ∪ − ⊻, ∪ ∪ ∪ ⊻, − − ∪ ∪ ⊻, − ∪ − ∪ − ⊻, − ∪ ∪ − − ⊻. The preferred clausulae reappear at the end of cola and commata, but with more exceptions; − − − ⊻ is commoner there, and − ∪ ∪ ⊻ less strictly avoided. The variations in Cicero's practice belong to subject-matter rather than chronology (see Laurand); but there is a gradual diminution of the 'Asiatic' clausula − ∪ − ⊻. Cicero shows in the clausula some desire for coincidence of accent and ictus. For ∠ ∪ − ∠ ⊻ there is a coincidence of 60·5 per cent in Cicero as against 54 in unrhythmical prose and 51 in Livy: for ∠ ∪ − ∠ ∪ −, 63·5 as against 49·5 and 40; for ∠ ∪ − ∠ ⊻, 35 as against 31·5 and 29. Broadhead and Zieliński exaggerate the influence of accent.

**17.** We may here group together as a Ciceronian school: Caesar, Nepos, Seneca, Suetonius, Quintilian, the Younger Pliny, Apuleius, Tertullian. Their clausulae are in general Ciceronian, except that − − − − ∪ ⊻ is avoided by most of them, and that − − − ⊻ is tolerated by Caesar and Nepos. − ∪ ∪ ∪ − ⊻ is avoided by Sen. and Nepos. − ∪ ∪ − ⊻ Sought by Xen.; and Tert., and − ∪ − ⊻ by Sen.

**18.** Opposed to Cicero's practice are Brutus ('Attic school'), Sallust, Livy. They seek − ∪ − − ∪ ⊻, but avoid − ∪ − ⊻, − ∪ − ⊻, − ∪ ∪ − ⊻; and they tolerate or seek − ∪ ∪ − ⊻, − − ∪ ∪ ⊻, − ∪ ∪ − − ⊻, and − − − ⊻ (Livy 36·5 per cent). Tacitus in his early work is fairly Ciceronian, but always avoids − ∪ ∪ ∪ − ⊻. In his mature work he is indifferent to most clausulae, only favouring somewhat − ∪ − − ⊻ and − ∪ − − ∪ ⊻.

**19.** The 'Greek' clausulae ∪ ∪ ∪ ⊻, − ∪ ∪ − ∪ ⊻ have little currency in Latin; but ∪ ∪ ∪ ⊻ seems to be sought by Sallust (Cat.), Brutus, Pomponius Mela, Apuleius (*Met.*), − ∪ ∪ − ∪ ⊻ by Sallust (*Jug.*), Brutus, Mela, Apuleius (*Apol. Flor., Met.*).

**20.** *Latin accentual prose.* There is a transitional period when clausulae remain quantitative, but are gradually restricted to forms where (*a*) accent and ictus coincide, (*b*) there are 2 or 4 unaccented syllables between the last two accents. Thus *ésse debétis, ésse confíteor* are retained, but (*núm*)*quam relíquisset, ágere debétis* are avoided. Alone among '3-forms', *ésse vidéatur* keeps a certain prestige, but diminishes. The form *gládio petebátur* passes as a combination of quantitative − ∪ − − ∪ and accentual ∼ ∼ − ∼ ∼ ∼ ∼. These tendencies may be observed in the choice of clausulae recommended by Sacerdos (3rd c.; see Nicolau's commentary) and in the detailed studies of Cyprian–Jerome, Arnobius, Faustus by P. C. Knook, H. Hagendahl, A. G. Elg. For coincidence of ictus and accent compare these percentages with Cicero's: ∠ ∪ − ∠ −, Augustine 78, Arnobius 95, Leo 93. ∠ ∪ − ∠ ∪ ⊻, Augustine 73·5, Arnobius 95·3, Leo 99·5. Much material of this period has yet to be investigated, and unless the works examined are of some length the evidence is apt to be inconclusive; thus it is perhaps impossible to decide whether the rhythms of Niceta's *Te Deum* are purely quantitative or not.

**21.** In the Middle Ages quantity is neglected, and favoured rhythms are practically reduced to the three accentual cursus-forms: ∼ ∼ ∼ ∼ − (*planus*), ∼ ∼ ∼ ∼ ∼ ∼ (*tardus*), ∼ ∼ ∼ ∼ ∼ ∼ − (*velox*)—which are used, e.g., by Gregory of Tours, Bernard of Clairvaux, Héloïse, Dante.

**22.** *Applications.* Study of prose-rhythm has been useful in some questions of chronology (Plato) and authenticity (for Plutarch's Συγκρίσεις, against *Consolatio ad Apollonium*). In textual criticism rhythmical criteria may help to distinguish between MS. variants and to reject mistaken emendations. Original emendation should be very cautious, taking into account not only a writer's preferences but also his margin of exceptions. In *Somnium Scipionis* 12, it is simple to change 'ingeniique tui consiliique' to 'ingenique tui consilique'; it would be rash to change πρὸς ἐμέ to πρός με everywhere in Demosthenes, setting 'Blass's Law' above normal usage.

H. Bornecque, *Les Clausules métriques latines* (1907, fullest collection of Lat. theory). H. D. Broadhead, *Latin Prose Rhythm* (1922, Cicero only). A. C. Clark, *Fontes prosae numerosae* (1909, select theory and texts, Gk.–Lat.). Norden, *Ant. Kunstpr.*; A. W. de Groot, *Der antike Prosarhythmus* (1921, Gk.–Lat.); *La Prose métrique des anciens* (1926, Gk.–Lat.). L. Laurand, *Études sur le style des discours de Cicéron* ii⁴ (1938); *Pour mieux comprendre l'antiquité classique* (1936, Lat. *cursus*). M. G. Nicolau, *L'Origine du 'cursus' rythmique en latin* (1930, also discusses methods). F. Novotný, *Eurhythmie* i (1918, fullest collection of Gk. theory; Czech commentary); *État actuel des études sur le rythme de la prose latine* (1929). W. H. Shewring, *CQ* 1930, 164, 1931, 12 (Gk.–Lat.; criticized by Broadhead, *CQ* 1932, 35, defended by S. 1933, 46). S. Skimina, *État actuel des études sur le rythme de la prose grecque* i (1937, quantitative prose), ii (1930, accentual). T. Zieliński, *Der constructive Rhythmus in Ciceros Reden* (1914). Full bibliographies by Laurand: for Gk., *Mus. Belge* xxv. 133 ff. and *LEC* iv. 237 f.; for Lat., *Rev. Ét. Lat.* 1928, 73 ff., and 1934, 419 ff. W. H. S.; K. J. D.

**PROSPER TIRO** (*c.* A.D. 390–*c.* 455), of Aquitaine, became a monk and may have taken deacon's orders. At Marseille he supported Augustine's doctrine of Grace against more moderate interpretations put forward in John Cassian's *Collationes* (426). In 431 he journeyed to Rome to seek Pope Celestine's support for Augustinianism, and on the accession of Leo I (440) he returned to Rome where he acted as the Pope's secretary. According to Gennadius he drafted Leo's letters against Eutyches.

He was important, first as a protagonist of Augustine in the 'Semi-Pelagian' controversy (427–32), and secondly as the compiler of the Chronicle. Though he did not know Augustine he wrote (427/8) telling him that Pelagianism was rife in Marseille, and after Augustine's death (430) Prosper wrote three books in his defence. He attacked the anti-predestinarian views of John Cassian (q.v.) in a sarcastic work, *Contra Collatorem*, a reference to Cassian's *Collationes*. After the latter's death in 435 his *Expositio super Psalmos* contained more friendly estimates of his views, but also expressed Prosper's distaste for the current misbeliefs of Nestorius, the Donatists, and Pelagians. While at Rome he popularized Augustine's memory in two works of extracts from Augustine's writings, *Liber Sententiarum ex operibus Sancti Augustini delibatarum* and *Epigrammata ex sententiis Sancti Augustini*, the latter in verse.

At Rome he compiled his Chronicle; down to 378 it was based on Jerome's translation of Eusebius' Chronicle, and thereafter to 417 borrowed from Sulpicius Severus and Orosius. He continued it first to 443 and finally to 455. From 417 to 455, Prosper's jejune entries are valuable for contemporary events, e.g. the intrigues which led to the invasion of Africa by Gaiseric (429) and also for the early years of Leo's pontificate. The tendency of the work is heavily anti-heretical. This coupled with vindication of St. Augustine rather than historical accuracy was his main interest.

His lasting memorial lay in the canons of the Council of Orange (529), which were based partly on the *Epigrammata*. His style, often modelled on Cicero, was good and the author's liveliness of spirit survives the rather rigid framework of his subjects.

Critical text of Chronicle ed. Th. Mommsen, *MGH* ix. 341–499. Other works, Migne, *PL* li (Vienna Corpus ed. in preparation). See articles in *DCB* and *DTC*. Also, E. M. Pickman, *The Mind of Latin Christendom* (1937), 418 ff. W. H. C. F.

**PROSTITUTION, SACRED**, existed in two main forms. (1) The defloration of virgins before marriage was originally a threshold rite, whereby the dangerous task of having intercourse with a virgin was delegated to a foreigner, since intercourse was in many, if not all, cases limited to strangers. The custom was observed at Babylon (Hdt. 1. 199) and at Heliopolis-Baalbek (Sozom. *Hist. Eccl.*

5, 10; Soc. *Hist. Eccl.* 1, 18, 48); in Cyprus (Hdt. loc. cit.; Just. *Epit.* 18. 5), in Lydia (Hdt. 1. 93; Ael. *VH* 4. 1), and at Sicca Veneria in Numidia (Val. Max. 2. 6. 15) girls are said thus to have earned dowries. In Acilisene well-born maidens were dedicated to Anaitis as prostitutes for considerable periods (Strabo 532–3), thus constituting a half-way step to (2) regular temple prostitution, generally of slaves, such as existed in Babylonia, in the cult of Ma at Comana Pontica (Strabo 559), of Aphrodite at Corinth (Strabo 378; Ath. 573), and perhaps at Eryx (Strabo 272; Diod. 4. 83), and in Egypt (*PTeb.* 6).

Nilsson would derive all sacred prostitution from the first type, which, he further claims, was originally non-religious, but readily became attached to fertility cults. It might then develop into type 2, or as at Byblus in the cult of Adonis (Lucian, *Syr. D.* 6), where, though the original purpose had been lost, the 'market' was still open only to strangers. The (unfulfilled) vow of the citizens of Locri Epizephyrii to prostitute their virgins (Just. *Epit.* 21. 3), unique in Greek annals, was a desperate measure to secure divine aid in war. The hereditary παλλακαί at Tralles were concubines, and perhaps prophetesses, of the god, not temple prostitutes. The evidence for Thebes in Egypt (Hdt. 1. 182; Strabo 816) is contradictory.

Cumont, *Rel. Or.*⁴ 258 f.; L. R. Farnell, *Greece and Babylon* (1911), 268 ff.; Nilsson, *Feste*, 365 ff. Tralles: K. Latte, *Harv. Theol. Rev.* 1940; L. Robert, *Études anatoliennes* (1937), 406 f.; von Bissing, 'Aphrodision', *Rh. Mus.* 1944, 375 ff. See ANAHITA, HIERODOULOI, MYLITTA. F. R. W.

**PROTAGORAS** of Abdera, one of the earliest and most successful of the Sophists (q.v.). His date is uncertain but his birth cannot be placed much later than 485 B.C., and was probably earlier, while he was about seventy years old at the time of his death. During forty of these he practised the profession of Sophist with great success, probably mainly at Athens. He claimed to teach 'virtue' (ἀρετή), which can perhaps be better expressed as efficiency in the conduct of life. He was evidently a man of high character and generally respected. When Thurii was founded by the Athenians in 444, he was appointed to draw up a code of laws for the new colony. The well-known story of his trial and condemnation at Athens is inconsistent with the statements of Plato and may probably be dismissed as an invention or error of later writers.

His chief significance in the history of thought rests on the doctrine expressed in his well-known dictum 'Man is the measure of all things'. There can be little doubt that this was generally understood in antiquity as being a doctrine of the relativity of all knowledge or opinion to each particular person, and that it involved a complete scepticism about the claims of any science to universal validity. He also adopted an agnostic attitude towards belief in the gods. He does not, however, seem to have extended this scepticism to the claims of morality. Here he apparently adopted conventional moral ideas without much question, and advocated respect by each man for the moral code of his particular community.

Testimonia and fragments in H. Diels, *Vorsokr.*¹¹ ii. 253–71; M. Untersteiner, *I Sofisti* i (1949); A. Capizzi, *Protagora* (1955). Zeller i. 2⁶. 1296 ff.; J. Burnet, *Greek Philosophy, Thales to Plato* (1914), ch. 7; G. Vlastos, pref. to *Plato's Protagoras*, tr. Jowett (1956). G. C. F.

**PROTESILAUS**, in mythology, commander of the contingent before Troy from Phylace and other places in Thessaly. He was killed in landing by one of the defenders (*Iliad* 2. 695 ff.). Homer also states that 'his wife was left mourning and his house half-finished'. From this it is a natural conclusion that he was newly married, whence a touching legend developed, preserved almost solely in Latin authors (Catull. 68. 73 ff.; Ov. *Her.* 13; Hyg. *Fab.* 103 f.). Protesilaus had offended the gods by not sacrificing before he began his house (Catullus); or he knew that the first man ashore was fated to be killed and patriotically took it upon himself to fall (Hyginus). His wife Laodameia grieved so for his loss that the gods granted her prayer to see him again for three hours. At the end of that time she killed herself (Eustathius on the *Iliad*, 325, 23 ff., who makes Protesilaus the prime mover throughout, because owing to Aphrodite's anger he desired his wife even after his death); or she spent so much time with an image of him that her father Acastus burned it and she flung herself on the fire (Hyg. 114, cf. Ov. 151 ff.). The author and date of this legend are unknown.

For his cult see Farnell, *Hero-Cults*, 412, n. 102. H. J. R.

**PROTEUS** (Πρωτεύς), a minor sea-god, herdsman of the flocks of the sea, seals, etc. In Homer (*Od.* 4. 385 ff.) he is an Egyptian daimon, servant of Poseidon, who has the power to take all manner of shapes, but if held till he resumes the true one, will answer questions. Virgil (*G.* 4. 387 ff.) imitates this. But in Herodotus 2. 112 ff., and Euripides, *Helena* 4, he is a virtuous king of Egypt, who takes Helen (q.v.) and her wealth from Paris and keeps them safe till at length Menelaus arrives and claims them. The relation of this to Stesichorus' palinode is not clear.
H. J. R.

**PROTOGENES** (late 4th c. B.C.), painter and sculptor, of Caunus; connected by anecdotes with Apelles, Aristotle, Demetrius Poliorcetes. His pictures included 'Ialysus', 'Resting Satyr', 'Alexander and Pan', 'Paralus and Hammonias' (allegories of the Athenian State galleys), portraits of Aristotle's mother, Antigonus, and Philicus, perhaps copied in the Pompeian tragic poet, Pickard-Cambridge, *Dramatic Festivals of Athens* (1953), fig. 44. He wrote two books on painting. His works showed excessive elaboration, but according to Apelles lacked charm (χάρις).

Overbeck, 1907–36; Rumpf, *Malerei u. Zeichn.* 147. T. B. L. W.

**PROTREPTICUS** (προτρεπτικὸς λόγος), an exhortation (to philosophy), first developed as a genre by the Sophists (q.v.), who thus persuaded students to take their courses in philosophy and various τέχναι, especially those required for politics. No early examples are extant, but Plato's *Euthydemus* includes a protreptic discourse (278 e–282 d), and something similar is found in Isocrates' *Against the Sophists*, *Helen*, *Busiris*, and *To Nicocles*. The most famous example in antiquity was Aristotle's *Protrepticus* (now lost), which was partly imitated by Cicero in his *Hortensius* (lost), and was excerpted, to an extent that remains controversial, by Iamblichus in his *Protrepticus* (extant). A later extant example is Galen's protreptic to medicine (Kuhn, *Med. Graec. Opera* vol. i).

P. Hartlich, *De exhortationum a Graecis Romanisque scriptarum historia* (Leipzig, 1889); K. Gaiser, *Protreptik und Paränese bei Platon* (*Tübinger Beiträge zur Altertumswissenschaft*, 40, 1959); I. Düring, *Aristotle's Protrepticus* (*Studia Graeca et Latina Gothoburgensia* xii, 1961). D. J. F.

**PROVINCIA**, originally the sphere of action of a magistrate with *imperium* (q.v.), later also of quaestors and pro-magistrates. *Provinciae* were normally allotted or assigned by the Senate at the beginning of the year. A law of C. Gracchus (q.v. 4), to prevent consular *provinciae* from becoming the playthings of politics (*see* FLACCUS 3), required the Senate to determine before the consular elections—in a vote exempt from tribunician *intercessio* (q.v.)—which *provinciae* the consuls were to have. Holders of *imperium* were from an early date not allowed to leave their *provinciae* as defined.

Down to the First Punic War all *provinciae* were in Italy. Usually the consuls had to campaign, the praetor

(after his creation) had the *provincia urbana* (chiefly the administration of justice); when a second praetor was created, he normally assumed jurisdiction among aliens. But the consuls and both (in due course all) the praetors could be freely used for different *provinciae*, if the Senate saw fit. When Sicily (except for Syracuse) was conquered, it was at first not organized: some favoured cities remained 'free' (*see* SOCII), the rest paid to Rome the tribute that had gone to Carthage. No more was done for Sardinia (238 B.C.). Only in 227 were two more praetors created, so that the four could normally cast lots for the two new *provinciae* overseas along with the two in the city, which remained superior in standing. During the Hannibalic War Syracuse and parts of Spain were occupied. Sicily was now reorganized under a praetor with two quaestors; Spain, after some time as two *provinciae* of *privati* with special *imperium*, had two praetors created (198/7). No more praetorships were instituted for later 'provinces': Africa and Macedonia-Achaea (146), Asia (133, organized later), Gaul (c. 100). *Prorogatio* became a regular and necessary feature of administration (*see* PRO CONSULE), which avoided multiplying curule magistracies. (The number of quaestors probably went on increasing.) It was a necessary consequence of this that the Senate was unwilling to commit itself to direct administration: not even Numidia was annexed after the defeat of Jugurtha; and Macedonia, Asia, and Transalpine Gaul only after hesitation had shown the military dangers in leaving them free.

The word *provincia*, though still freely used in its traditional sense, now came to mean particularly an administered overseas territory; and a popular etymology (from *pro* and *vincere*) supported this use. After 123 praetors were increasingly needed for *quaestiones* (q.v.) in Rome, and the consuls' presence was desirable for political reasons; hence 'provinces' now normally went to pro-magistrates. Sulla, who added two praetorships and probably two *quaestiones*, apparently intended to formalize this system, with regular annual succession. In the last generation of the Republic, the rise of the *equites* (q.v.), the Populares, and the new army led to a rapid increase in provinces: in particular, Pompey in the East and Caesar in the West added huge territories. (*See* CILICIA, CYRENE, BITHYNIA, CRETE, PONTUS, SYRIA, CYPRUS, GAUL.) This, combined with many men's unwillingness to serve abroad (*see* CICERO, 1), led to the need for long *prorogatio*, especially in periods of civil or major foreign wars; and large *provinciae*, with huge armies, were more and more frequently granted (*see* LUCULLUS 2, ANTONIUS 2, POMPEY, CAESAR 1, CRASSUS 4), either by the People or by the Senate. It also led to increased exploitation of provincials which became a necessary incentive for attracting men into governing provinces. To stop the dangers arising out of this, Pompey (as consul 52), with the Senate's support, fixed an interval of at least five years between magistracy and provincial tenure and probably made acceptance of the latter compulsory (as it had been in the second century) and limited it in duration. This scheme, before the end of the transitional period necessary for it to become fully operative, was upset by the Civil War, but later restored (for public provinces— see below) by Augustus.

A province, under the Republic, was never a large area under uniform administration. Normally organized after a war (and, if not, possibly assimilated to the majority), it owed its status, at least after 150 and probably even before, to a victorious general and a commission of ten senators. The so-called *lex provinciae* was, in law, the general's decree *ex SC*, on the commission's advice (see Cic. 2 *Verr.* 2. 32 and 40). It remained binding unless the Senate superseded or amended it, as it might do (*see* SCAEVOLA 4). Pompey's arbitrary settlement of the East, which he expected to be ratified without scrutiny, was a characteristic piece of arrogance and the cause of genuine anxiety about his intentions. The *lex* would settle local boundaries and constitutions; and it might deal, in greater or less detail, with taxation and other obligations and the administration of justice. It had to take account of numerous free or treaty cities (*see* SOCII) with their own historical relationships with Rome. Inevitably their rights were gradually levelled down: in the late Republic, the free city of Utica was a governor's capital. The *Leges Rupiliae* (q.v.), which probably extended the *lex Hieronica* to all of Sicily not officially 'free', severely limited the 'freedom' of many Sicilian cities; and governors sometimes ignored custom or treaty with impunity, setting up precedents in deterioration.

Within the framework of the *lex*, the governor issued his own edict (q.v.), normally based on his predecessors' tradition and sometimes on that of the urban magistrates, but never strictly binding on a successor or (at least before the law of Cornelius (1)) even on the governor himself. Within the limits of the *lex*, he had absolute authority over provincials, which he could delegate to his quaestor or legates (usually one to three in number) or to other Romans or in part to the cities themselves (as Scaevola (q.v. 4) did in Asia and Cicero in Cilicia); for judicial purposes, he usually drew heavily on his friends (the *cohors*, q.v.), his staff of civil servants (especially *scribae*, q.v.), and provincial Romans (*see* CONVENTUS), who enjoyed a privileged status in law and even more in fact. Supervision from Rome was lax. The money voted had to be accounted for by the quaestor; but this was a mere formality, and it was unusual (by Cicero's day) to declare a surplus; the governor and the *cohors* expected to share it. Arbitrary power gave unlimited opportunities for extortion; and *repetundae* (q.v.) laws, permitting redress only after the governor's return to Rome, could normally be evaded by anyone rich and well-connected. Prosecutions were a major expense to the province and even a conviction (rarely achieved) would not always benefit the provincials (*see* VERRES).

Indirect taxes were always farmed by *publicani* (q.v.). Direct taxes were collected by various methods (*see* DECUMA, TRIBUTUM), normally involving some tax-farmers (Roman or local). Constant warfare (especially in Spain and in the East) led to devastation and an increasing load of debt, which governors would collect on behalf of their senatorial friends, or assist businessmen in collecting, by methods often approaching sheer terror. Spain and Asia duly showed themselves ready to join anyone fighting the Roman government of the moment.

Caesar began the reorganization of the system and Augustus completed it. In 27 B.C. Augustus was given a large *provincia* (originally perhaps Gaul, Spain, and Syria), which he governed—after 23 as proconsul (q.v.)—through *legati pro praetore* (with the finances administered by procurators) and which contained nearly all the legionary forces. The area changed in extent, and the command was renewed from time to time; and by the end of the reign the 'imperial provinces' were an accepted institution. The remaining ('public', in fact senatorial) provinces were governed by proconsuls, with legates and quaestors, as before; but Augustus had *imperium maius*, which we can see him exercising as early as the Cyrene edicts (q.v.). Egypt, made 'subject to the Roman People' (*Res Gestae* 27) by Augustus, was forbidden to senators and governed by an equestrian *praefectus* with legionary forces; and to the natives the Emperor was Pharaoh. Various minor provinces (e.g. Judaea and Noricum) were administered by prefects (later procurators) without legions. Direct taxes were now directly collected: tax farming was limited to indirect taxation and in due course abolished even there.

This system lasted, in essence, until the third century A.D. In the first century, the last 'senatorial' legion (in Africa) was taken over; recognized frontiers were increasingly reached (Domitian began the construction of a *limes*, q.v.); Britain was annexed by Claudius (and later extended), Dacia and Arabia by Trajan (other conquests were of short duration), and various client kings (q.v.) were succeeded by provincial governors. With the multiplication of consuls, an adequate supply of senior men became available for administration and a hierarchy of provinces developed, both in the Emperor's service and in the Senate's. Asia and Africa (both senatorial) were the highest posts in prestige, but the senior imperial commands gave the greatest power and could serve as springboards to the throne. The subdivision of large provinces into more manageable units, begun by Augustus in Gaul, Germany, and Illyricum, was gradually carried further, as was the detailed supervision of local government by the Emperor (*see* CORRECTOR *and* CURATOR REI PUBLICAE). Both these trends culminated in the thorough reorganization of Diocletian (q.v.).

In the provinces themselves, the organization of an imperial cult (*see* RULER-CULT, ROMAN) under Augustus and the Julio-Claudians led to the creation of a *concilium* (q.v.) normally one for each province, under a native high priest (*flamen* or *sacerdos*). These councils, down to the third century, provided a channel through which provincial upper-class opinion could reach Rome. The high priest and even ordinary members often gained citizenship, and their descendants might become Roman *equites* or senators. Within a century after Augustus, the equestrian service and the Senate were freely open to provincials from almost any province though some provinces took longer than others to make their full contribution. While romanization thus spread among the upper class, it was advanced among the lower classes by the army: the legions were soon mainly composed of men of provincial origin, and men in the *auxilia* (q.v.) became citizens on honourable discharge and before long even earlier. Gradually the citizenship and *ius Latii* (q.v.) spread among provincial communities. Thus the provinces were unified into a Roman State.

Mommsen, *Röm. Staatsr.*[3], see index, s.v.; *The Provinces of the Roman Empire* (1909); G. H. Stevenson, *Roman Provincial Administration* (1939); J. R. Hawthorn, *The Republican Empire* (1963, with useful selection of sources on the Republic); F. F. Abbott and A. C. Johnson, *Municipal Administration in the Roman Empire* (1926, with large selection of sources, chiefly documentary). *See also* ACHAEA, AFRICA, ALPS, ARABIA, ARMENIA, ASIA, ASSYRIA, BITHYNIA, BRITANNIA, CAPPADOCIA, CILICIA, CORSICA, CRETE, CYPRUS, CYRENE, DACIA, DALMATIA, EGYPT, EPIRUS, GALATIA, GAUL, GERMANY, ILLYRICUM, JEWS A 3, LYCIA, MACEDONIA, MAURETANIA, MESOPOTAMIA, MOESIA, NORICUM, NUMIDIA, PAMPHYLIA, PANNONIA, PONTUS, RAETIA, SARDINIA, SICILY, SPAIN, SYRIA, THRACE. E. B.

**PROVOCATIO** was an appeal made to the *populus Romanus* by a victim of magisterial *coercitio* (q.v.). It was not until 300 B.C. that a legal right to appeal against a capital sentence imposed by any magistrate within the boundaries of the city was conferred upon every Roman citizen by a *lex Valeria*. (An earlier '*lex Valeria*' assigned by the tradition to the first year of the Republic is now generally dismissed as a fiction, as are the many references to a fifth- and fourth-century *ius provocationis* from which certain magistrates—e.g. dictators and *decemviri*—claimed exemption.) Nevertheless, a formal procedure of *provocatio* which carried no guarantee of admission may well have dated from at least 450 B.C. At that date a law of the XII Tables required that capital cases should be heard only by *comitia centuriata*; and, although this did not rule out summary magisterial jurisdiction, as Mommsen believed, it is unlikely that the plebeians could have been persuaded to comply by abandoning criminal jurisdiction in their own unofficial assembly, had the patricians not made some concession by providing for the

**PROVOCATIO** (continued)

possible use of the *iudicium populi* (q.v.) in cases of appeal from *coercitio*. Before the *lex Valeria* admission of *provocatio* was probably guaranteed solely by the ever-present threat of tribunes to extend *auxilium* in the event of refusal. During the second century the right of appeal was further regulated by a series of three *leges Porciae* (q.v.), one of which extended *provocatio* to citizens in the military sphere (i.e. outside Rome). In the imperial age *provocatio* was superseded by *appellatio* (q.v.).

For Mommsen *provocatio* was the cornerstone of the Roman criminal procedure, all cases tried by *iudicia populi* being theoretically hearings on appeal from a magisterial sentence. In recent years this view has been challenged, and attempts have been made to show that the range of magisterial *coercitio* and consequently of *provocatio* was very limited, and that criminal trials were largely conducted by courts of the first instance. Mommsen's position, however, which rests to some extent upon Cicero, has not been totally discredited, and the issue is still open.

Mommsen, *Röm. Strafr.* 167 f., 473 ff.; C. Brecht, *Sav. Zeitschr.* 1939, 269 ff.; A. Heuß, ibid. 1944, 104 ff.; E. S. Staveley, *Hist.* 1955, 412 ff.; W. Kunkel, *Untersuch. zur Entwicklung des röm. Kriminalverfahrens* (1962). E. S. S.

**PROXENOS.** Since Greek States did not send permanent diplomatic representatives abroad, local citizens served as *proxenoi* to look after the interests of other States in their community. By the beginning of the fifth century this system had developed from earlier practices of hospitality under which some relied on hereditary ties with foreign families and others on the more general respect for strangers and suppliants. Survivals from this were the continued existence of private friends in foreign States (ἰδιόξενοι) and the practice of a few States of appointing *proxenoi* to look after visitors. More commonly States selected their own *proxenoi* in other States and, in return for services already rendered and expected in the future, bestowed honours and privileges upon them. Such appointments were much coveted, and many voluntarily assumed the burdens in the hope of gaining the title. The position usually was hereditary. A *proxenos* must be a citizen of the State in which he served and not of the State he represented. Later, however, when honours were bestowed more freely and had little practical significance, *proxenia* and honorary citizenship frequently were combined in the same grant.

Numerous examples from literature are listed in LSJ, s.v.; examples of decrees, Tod ii, index. Full modern accounts are rare, but see C. Phillipson, *The International Law and Custom of Ancient Greece and Rome* (1911), ch. 6; E. Szanto, *Das griechische Bürgerrecht* (1892), ch. 1. J. A. O. L.

**PRUDENTIUS,** AURELIUS CLEMENS (b. A.D. 348, d. after 405), the greatest of the Christian Latin poets, a native of Spain (Tarraconensis), abandoned an administrative career, in which he attained high distinction, and dedicated himself to Christian poetry. His works are (*a*) lyrical: *Cathemerinon*, 'Hymns for the day', and *Peristephanon*, 'Crowns of martyrdom'; (*b*) didactic: *Apotheosis*, 'The divinity of Christ', *Hamartigenia*, 'The origin of sin', *Psychomachia*, 'Battle of the soul' (an allegory), *Contra Symmachum*, a polemic against paganism based on the events of 384 (see SYMMACHUS 2), and the *Dittochaeon*, hexameter tetrastichs on biblical topics. Prudentius displays remarkable metrical versatility and a profound knowledge of pagan Latin poetry. Described by Bentley as *Christianorum Maro et Flaccus* he achieved a union between the classical poetical form and the spirit and thought of Christianity. A creative artist, he introduced into Christian poetry the literary hymn, allegorical epic, and 'Christian ballad' (*Peristeph.*). The extensive

influence of his work is visible in medieval art as well as poetry.

TEXT. J. Bergman, *CSEL* lxi; M. P. Cunningham, *Corp. Christ.* (*Series Latina* cxxvi (1966)).
TEXT AND TRANSLATION. M. Lavarenne (Budé, 1943–51); H. J. Thomson (Loeb, 1949–53); Guillen-Rodriguez (Madrid, 1950). Concordance. Deferrari–Campbell (1932). Language. M. Lavarenne, *Étude sur la langue de poète Prudence* (1933). A. H.-W.

**PRUSIAS,** kings of Bithynia.
(1) PRUSIAS I CHOLUS (*c.* 230–*c.* 182 B.C.), son of Ziaëlas. He was an energetic and ambitious ruler who used a marriage alliance with Philip V of Macedon and the conflicts of the other powers to enlarge the territory of Bithynia to its greatest extent. He warred with Byzantium (220), defeated Gallic invaders (218), took Phrygia Epictetus and part of Mysia from Attalus I of Pergamum (*c.* 208), received the ports of Cius and Myrleia from Philip V (202), renaming them Prusias and Apameia, and captured Cierus and Tieium from Heraclea. On assurances from the Scipios, he remained neutral in the war with Antiochus III (190–188), but the demand in the settlement at Apameia (188) that he return to Eumenes the former Attalid possessions led to a war (186–184) in which he was defeated, while Hannibal, a refugee at his court, anticipated surrender to the Romans by suicide.
(2) PRUSIAS II CYNEGUS (*c.* 182–149 B.C.), son of Prusias I, joined Eumenes of Pergamum in war against Pharnaces I of Pontus (181–179). His servile attitude toward the Roman Senate after the fall of his brother-in-law, Perseus of Macedon (168), won him contempt. His invasion of the Pergamene kingdom (156–154) ended in defeat, and demand for an indemnity. He sent his son Nicomedes to Rome as an envoy to secure release from this, but the latter, on learning that death would be the penalty for failure, revolted, and with encouragement from Rome and aid from Pergamum, drove him to sanctuary and put him to death (149).

For bibliography, see s.v. NICOMEDES. T. R. S. B.

**PRYTANEIS** (πρυτάνεις) means 'presidents'. In Athens, after the *phylai* (q.v.) and *boule* (q.v.) were reorganized in 508/7 B.C. by Cleisthenes (q.v. 1), the *boule* each year consisted of fifty men chosen by lot from each of the ten *phylai*. Each group of fifty served as *prytaneis* for one-tenth of the year. This period was called a prytany (πρυτανεία); owing to the vagaries of Athenian methods of reckoning a year (see CALENDARS) a prytany might be anything between thirty-four and thirty-nine days in length. It was reduced to one-twelfth of the year when the number of *phylai* was increased to twelve in 307. To decide which *phyle*'s group was to be *prytaneis* next, lots were drawn shortly before the beginning of each prytany except the last by all the groups which had not been *prytaneis* so far that year.

The *prytaneis* were on duty every day. They made arrangements for meetings of the *boule* and *ekklesia*, received envoys and letters addressed to the State, and conducted other day-to-day business. Soon after the Persian Wars an office, called the *tholos* because of its circular shape, was built for them next to the *bouleuterion* (council-chamber) at the south-west corner of the *agora*. There they dined every day at the State's expense.

Each day one of the *prytaneis* was picked by lot to be their foreman (ἐπιστάτης). He remained on duty in the *tholos* for twenty-four hours, with one-third of the *prytaneis*. He had charge of the State seal and of the keys of the treasuries and archives. In the fifth century he also took the chair at any meeting of the *boule* or *ekklesia* held on his day, but in the fourth century this duty was taken over by the *proedroi* (q.v.). No one could be foreman more than once, and consequently a considerable proportion (perhaps half) of the citizens held this position at some time in their lives. The whole system of the *prytaneis* and their foreman, based on lot and rotation, was a means of giving the ordinary citizen a share in the administration of the State, and so was a most important part of Cleisthenes' plan to make Athens democratic.

Arist. *Ath. Pol.* 43–4.                                                    D. M. M.

**PSAON OF PLATAEA,** Hellenistic historian, continuing Diyllus from 297/6 B.C., covered partly the same period as Phylarchus and may have been contemporary with him; his work perhaps extended to Ol. 140 (220–217), where Polybius began, and was continued by Menodotus.

*FGrH* ii A, 158; C, 131.                                          A. H. McD.

**PSELLUS,** MICHAEL (earlier CONSTANTINE), probably of Nicomedia (A.D. 1018–78/9), after studying law at Constantinople held a judicial post at Philadelphia. Under Constantine IX (1042–55) he became professor of philosophy at the newly refounded imperial University in Constantinople. He was now one of the most influential figures in the Eastern Empire and was appointed State Secretary and Vestarch. Apart from a brief period of retirement in a monastery (1054–5), he held high office continuously at Constantinople until the reign of Michael VII (1071–8), under whom he became chief minister. The ingratitude of the Emperor caused him to spend his last days in obscurity.

WORKS. There are many problems of disputed authorship, and many still unpublished works are attributed in MSS. to Psellus. (1) Scientific and philosophical treatises on mathematics, music, astronomy, physics, metaphysics, ethics, theology, alchemy, demonology, medicine, jurisprudence, topography, etc.; e.g. the miscellany *De Omnifaria Doctrina* (Διδασκαλία παντοδαπή), his literary masterpiece *De Operatione Daemonum* (Π. ἐνεργείας δαιμόνων), his discussion of Athenian judicial terminology, and his short account of the topography of Athens. (2) Paraphrases of the *Iliad* and of Aristotle, *Categories*, an abridgement of Porphyry, *De Quinque Vocibus*, a commentary on Aristotle, *De Interpretatione*, a treatise on Plato, *Phaedrus*, and an allegorical study on Homer. Also works in letter-form on rhetoric, and poems on rhetoric, grammar, and Greek dialects. (3) *Chronographia* (Χρονογραφία), a lively and colourful history of the century 976 to 1077, is valuable, though somewhat partisan. (4) Funeral orations, panegyrics, *apologiae* written in a style of persuasive dignity. His letters, of which about 500 survive, are interesting for their picture of Byzantine civilization and of their author himself. (5) Rhetorical exercises and essays on set themes. (6) Occasional verse, satirical and epigrammatic.

Psellus was a man of encyclopedic learning and great literary gifts. At a time when scholarship was at a low ebb, he had a keen though rather self-conscious love of classical and patristic literature and was passionately devoted to Plato and the Neoplatonists. His own style owed much to Plato, Aelius Aristides, and Gregory Nazianzen. More than any other man he laid the foundation of the Byzantine literary and philosophical renascence of the twelfth century.

In his public life he reflects the faults of the age. Amid the atmosphere of palace-intrigue and court-flattery, scruples and sincerity found no place, and his political career was disfigured by servility and unrestrained ambition.

TEXTS. Migne, *PG* cxxii (1864); K. N. Sathas, Μεσαιωνικὴ βιβλιοθήκη iv–v (1874–6); *Scripta minora, I Orationes et dissertationes, II Epistulae*, E. Kurtz–F. Drexl (1936–41); *De Operatione Daemonum*, F. Boissonade (1838); *De Omnifaria Doctrina*, L. G. Westerink (1948); *Chronographia*, E. Rénauld (1926–8); J. Bidez, *Catalogue des MSS. alchim. grecs* vi (1928).

STUDIES. C. Zervos, *Un Philosophe néo-platonicien du XIᵉ siècle* (1920); E. Renauld, *Étude de la langue et du style de M. Ps.* (1920) and *Lexique choisi de Ps.* (1920); K. Swoboda, *La Démonologie de M. Ps.* (1927); J. M. Hussey, *Church and Learning in the Byzantine Empire 867–1185* (1937); G. Böhlig, *Untersuchungen zum rhet. Sprachgebrauch der Byzantiner mit besonderer Berücksichtigung der Schriften des M. Ps.* (1956); Gy. Moravcsik, *Byzantinoturcica*¹ i (1958), 437 ff. (bibliography).                               J. F. L.; R. B.

**PSEUDEPIGRAPHIC LITERATURE.** Antiquity has left us a number of writings which evidence, internal or external, proves not to be the work of the authors whose names are traditionally attached to them. The causes of this seem to be chiefly: (*a*) a tendency to ascribe anonymous pieces to a well-known author of like genre. Thus, the whole Epic Cycle and other hexameter poems were at one time or another ascribed to Homer; in Latin several compositions more or less epic in style, as the *Culex* and *Ciris*, have become attached to the name of Virgil, others, in elegiacs, to those of Tibullus and Ovid. (*b*) Works by the followers of a philosopher tended to be credited to their master; for instance, several short dialogues by members of the Academy bear the name of Plato, and, e.g., the *Problemata*, which are Peripatetic, are preserved as by Aristotle. (*c*) Rhetorical exercises in the form of speeches, letters, etc., supposed to be by well-known persons, now and then were taken for their real works. Thus, no. 11 of our collection of Demosthenes' speeches is a clever imitation of him, said by Didymus, *In Demosth.*, col. 11, 10, to come from the *Philippica* of Anaximenes of Lampsacus. The Epistles of Phalaris are the most notorious work of this kind, thanks to Bentley's exposure of them. (*d*) The existence of deliberate forgeries, made to sell (*see* FORGERIES, LITERARY), is vouched for by Galen (*In Hipp. de nat. hominis* 2. 57, 12 Mewaldt). (*e*) Various mechanical accidents of copying account for a few pseudepigraphies. (*f*) But the most frequent cases are of rather late date and connected with the craze for producing evidence of the doctrines one favoured being of great age. For instance, the numerous Neopythagorean treatises, whereof specimens are preserved chiefly in Stobaeus, are regularly attached to the names of prominent early Pythagoreans, including Pythagoras himself (q.v. 1), despite the fairly constant tradition that he wrote nothing. The Sibylline oracles (*see* SIBYLLA) are an outstanding instance of this; Phocylides (q.v.) is the alleged author of a long set of moralizing verses pretty certainly the work of an unknown Jew and of late date. Christian literature has some glaring examples of this practice, notably the Clementine Recognitions and Homilies, most certainly neither by Clement of Rome nor any contemporary, and the works attributed to Dionysius the Areopagite, really produced some three centuries or more after his death. Cf. also HERMES TRISMEGISTUS.

For a general sketch in Latin Literature, E. H. Clift, *Latin Pseudepigrapha* (U.S.A. 1945); otherwise under the various authors' names.                                                                  H. J. R.

**PSEUDO-CALLISTHENES.** The so-called Alexander Romance, wrongly ascribed in antiquity to Callisthenes (q.v.), is extant in various Greek versions, whose complicated textual relationships—reaching back to about 100 B.C.—have been unravelled by Merkelbach. The work belongs to the genre 'fabulous historiography', which, as Ed. Schwartz has made clear, developed in Alexandrian times; it has, in so far as it does not contain any erotic element at all, little or no relationship with the genre 'novel' (*Liebesroman*).

TEXT. W. Kroll, *Historia Alexandri Magni* (1926); A. Ausfeld, *Der griech. Alexanderroman* (1907).

CRITICISM. R. Merkelbach, *Die Quellen des griech. Alexanderromans* (1954; Zetemata 9); Christ–Schmid–Stählin ii. 2⁶. 813 ff. (useful bibliography); A. Lesky, *Gesch. d. griech. Litt.*¹ (1963), 820 ff.; R. Helm, *Der antike Roman*² (1956), 13 ff.; Ed. Schwartz, *Fünf Vorträge über den griech. Roman*² (1943); id. *Griechische Geschichtsschreiber*² (1959).                                                      G. G.

**PSYCHE,** the soul or, in later usage, the soul as a butterfly, does not appear as a clearly individualized mythological being before the fourth or the fifth century B.C. The notion of the soul occupied the Greeks from very early times. It has been suggested that the soul was first conceived as a bird, on the strength of the passages in Homer where the soul of Patroclus utters a faint noise (*Il.* 23. 101) and the souls of wooers chirp like bats (*Od.* 24. 6). In art a bird is shown flying over the head of a dying hero and birds are often seated on funeral *stelae* (cf. SIRENES). But Homer explicitly depicts the soul as a kind of a double, resembling the dead in 'height, eyes, voice' and wearing the same garments (*Il.* 23. 66), and the archaeological evidence is ambiguous. The Homeric souls, often called *eidola*, disappear like smoke, in the manner of our ghosts, if somebody attempts to touch them (*Od.* 11. 206). They dwell in Hades on the barren asphodel meadow and lack the vitality and memory which they can regain only by drinking blood (*Od.* 11. 25, cf. 24. 1). The Homeric notion remained current down to Plato's times (*Phd.* 81 c, d). On vases we see the soul of Patroclus in full armour watching Achilles as he drags the corpse of Hector; the soul of Sarpedon leaving the body (E. Haspels, *Attic Black-Figure Lekythoi* (Paris, 1936), 51); the souls of Achilles and Memnon weighed by Zeus; and the souls of commoners at a funeral, in the cemetery, and in Hades. On some vases they are shown with Charon, on others with Hermes Psychagogus.

Different notions of the soul were developed by Greek philosophers and poets. The most important change is the elevation of soul from a rather materialistically conceived double to a dematerialized divine being, of a nature totally different from the body. 'The body is the tomb of the soul', said the Orphics (*see* ORPHISM). The inscription honouring the warriors fallen at Potidaea claims that their souls were received by the aether, their bodies by earth (Tod i². 59). The Homeric connexion with the individual had been severed so far that all *Psychai* could be conceived as female. The earliest representation of Psyche in that form, of the late fifth century, appears in south Italy, the home of Pythagoreans and Orphics. It would appear that the type which represents Psyche as a butterfly was evolved approximately at the same time. Plato's inspired version of the chariots of souls in *Phaedrus* presupposes a connexion of Eros and Psyche. Roughly contemporary with Plato are some beautiful bronze reliefs from Asia Minor (Devambez, *Les Grands Bronzes du Musée d'Istanbul*, 1935) on which Eros and Psyche, a maiden, are shown in quiet harmony. They are united in the Hellenistic 'Invention of the Kiss', a marble group which was copied by Romans (E. Strong, *JRS* 1924, 71) and early Christians, perhaps as a symbol of heavenly happiness (F. Cumont, *Syria* 1929, 231). On the other hand, Eros (q.v.), who had before plagued individual victims of love, now turns also on Psyche, since she, the soul, is recognized as the seat of passions. In Hellenistic poetry and art Eros is represented inflicting innumerable tortures upon Psyche (G. Hanfmann, *AJArch.* 1939, 240). In Apuleius (*Met.* 4. 28) the motif of the tormented Psyche is combined with a *märchen* of the Fairy Bridegroom type. The goddess Psyche, who appears in some late writings, is according to Reitzenstein an Iranian goddess in Greek disguise.

E. Rohde, *Psyche* (1907); O. Waser in Roscher, *Lex.*, s.v. O. Weinreich in L. Friedländer, *Darstellung aus der Sittengeschichte Roms* (1921–3), iv. 89; Apuleius, *The Story of Cupid and Psyche*, ed. L. C. Purser (1910); R. Reitzenstein, *Sitz. Heidelberg* 1914 and 1917; A. Dyroff, *Das Märchen von Amor und Psyche* (1941); J. O. Swahn, *Tale of Cupid and Psyche* (Lund, 1955); Nilsson, *GGR*, 194 f.; R. Merkelbach, *Philol.* 1958, 103; R. Helm, *PW* 1959, 1434. G. M. A. H.

**PTAH,** called Φθά or Φθάς and also Hephaestus by the Greeks, was an old deity of Memphis. Originally a god of artisans, a fashioner and maker of things, he acquired later a solar character and became one of the chief deities of Egypt. The temple of Ptah was one of the chief buildings in the complex of structures at Memphis which included the temple of Apis and others. T. A. B.

**PTOLEMAEUS** (1) of Ascalon, of uncertain date, is said by Steph. Byz. to have been a pupil of Aristarchus, and in the *Suda* to have been father (or teacher) of Archibius (a grammarian at Rome under Trajan). Ptolemaeus joined the Pergamenes and disputed the Aristarchan texts of Homer. He also wrote Περὶ διαφορᾶς λέξεων, Περὶ ὀρθογραφίας, and Περὶ μέτρων.

M. Boege, *De Pt. Ascalonita* (1882). P. B. R. F.

**PTOLEMAEUS** (2) **CHENNOS** ('quail') of Alexandria (fl. c. A.D. 100) wrote the *Sphinx*, a mythologico-grammatical work, perhaps in dramatic form (ἱστορικὸν δρᾶμα, *Suda*), though this is disputed; Ἀνθόμηρος, in twenty-four rhapsodies, correcting Homer's errors; Παράδοξος (or Καινὴ) ἱστορία, of which Photius gives an extract. There are no adequate grounds for identifying this Ptolemaeus with the philosopher and biographer of Aristotle (A. Dihle, *Hermes* 1957, 314 ff.).

J. D. D.; K. J. D.

**PTOLEMAEUS** (3) ὁ ἐπιθέτης, grammarian, pupil of Hellanicus the Chorizontist, and a pertinacious opponent of Aristarchus, wrote commentaries on Homer and Bacchylides and kindred monographs.

**PTOLEMAEUS** (4) of Mende, a priest, wrote on the πράξεις of the Egyptian kings in three books; he is scarcely the Ptolemaeus who published a life or history of Herod the Great, soon after 4 B.C.

*FGrH* iii. 611.

**PTOLEMAEUS** (5) of Naucratis (2nd c. A.D.), Egyptian rhetor, uninfluenced by the Second Sophistic, except in style, where he follows Polemon.

**PTOLEMAEUS** (6) **PINDARION** (i.e. commentator on Pindar) (2nd c. B.C.), a pupil of Aristarchus, wrote also on Homeric antiquities and on analogy. *See* CRATES (3) OF MALLOS.

**PTOLEMAIS** (1) **(ACE).** The Phoenician port of Ace was named Ptolemais c. 261 B.C. by Ptolemy II. From Antiochus IV's reign its people, renamed the 'Antiocheis in Ptolemais', issued municipal coins. Claudius made Ptolemais a Roman colony, planting in it veterans from the four Syrian legions. Its famous oracle on Mount Carmel predicted Vespasian's accession (Tac. *Hist.* 2. 78). A. H. M. J.

**PTOLEMAIS** (2) **HERMIOU,** a foundation of Ptolemy Soter, with a substantial Greek population and a Greek constitution, was the centre of Hellenism in Upper Egypt throughout the Graeco-Roman period; Strabo classed it with Memphis in importance, and later it ranked second to Alexandria. Hardly any remains of buildings are visible, but inscriptions have been found recording decrees of the Ptolemaic assembly and council, and references in papyri from other districts show the continued influence of its citizens in Roman times.

G. Plaumann, *Ptolemais in Oberaegypten* (1910); J. Scherer, *BIFAO* 1942, 43 ff.; P. M. Fraser, *Berytus* 1960, 123 ff. J. G. M.

**PTOLEMAIS** (3) **THERON** ('of the Hunts'), on the west coast of the Red Sea, probably at Aquiq (Crowfoot, *Geog. Journ.* xxxvii. 523). Founded by Ptolemy II for elephant-hunts, it was used as a port for a trade-route to Meroe and the Nile.

Agatharchides (*GGM* i. 174); Strabo 17. 768–71. Hyde, *Greek Mariners*, 194. E. H. W.

**PTOLEMY** (1). The name of all the Macedonian kings of Egypt.

PTOLEMY I SOTER (*c.* 367/6–283 or 282 B.C.), son of the Macedonian Lagus and a certain Arsinoe, who was, perhaps, a mistress and not, as was later believed, a second cousin of Philip II. He was exiled as Alexander's friend, recalled after Philip's death, and appointed *hetairos*, *somatophylax*, and *edeatros* ('Companion', 'Life-guard', and 'Seneschal') to Alexander. He fought with distinction during Alexander's campaigns, which he subsequently described in an historical work. He married Artacama, Artabazus' daughter, in 324, divorced her after Alexander's death, and subsequently married Eurydice and (with or without divorce) Berenice I (q.v.). He became satrap of Egypt in late summer 323, executed Cleomenes (q.v. 3), and fought without much success against Antigonus Monophthalmus and Demetrius Poliorcetes (315–301). He declared himself king early in 304, finally conquered Palestine, Cyprus, and many possessions in the Aegean Sea and Asia Minor (*c.* 301–286), but took little active part in government after 285.

He was the originator of the cult of Sarapis (q.v.) and also the founder of Ptolemais Hermiou (q.v.) in Upper Egypt. The legal and military organization of his Empire —the army consisting of military settlers, mercenaries, and native levies—and the main outlines of Ptolemaic administration were due to him (cf. ALEXANDRIA, EGYPT UNDER THE GREEKS AND ROMANS, EPIMELETES, EPISTATES, NOMOS). Registers of land, houses, slaves, cattle, and tax-payers were compiled in the villages, and summaries of these were made for nome registers and the central register in Alexandria, which was used for preparing the State budget. The highest State office was that of the *dioiketes* (= manager) whose *oikonomi* administered the Empire like a royal estate. F. M. H.

Ptolemy I wrote, when king, the best of the histories of Alexander. He used Alexander's official *Journal* and other official material, but much was his own recollection; he was in a better position to know than almost anyone. So far as can be made out his book was a genuine history and not merely a military record; Alexander was a supreme figure, but yet a human man. Probably it was defective on the political side; when he wrote he had long lost sympathy with some of Alexander's ideas. He probably desired to correct current popular history and beliefs, and his silences were part of his criticism; but bad history ousted good, and, but for Arrian, practically all knowledge of his work would have perished. *See* ALEXANDER (3), Bibliography, Ancient Sources. W. W. T.

PTOLEMY II PHILADELPHUS (308–246 B.C.), son of Ptolemy I and Berenice I, was born at Cos, and married Arsinoe I *c.* 289–288. He was made joint ruler with his father in 285, succeeded to the throne in 283–282 and married Arsinoe II *c.* 276–275, uniting her Aegean possessions with the Empire. He conquered important districts in Syria and Asia Minor during the First Syrian War (*c.* 276–271). In the Chremonidean War against Macedonia (266–261) he incurred slight losses; the Second Syrian War (*c.* 260–253) was indecisive, and was concluded by a marriage between Antiochus II and Berenice 'Syra' (q.v.). East African and south Arabian coastal districts received garrisons as outposts for trade.

Ptolemy II and his advisers created most of the scientific system of Ptolemaic financial administration (cf. AGRICULTURE, BANKS, COMMERCE, FINANCE, INDUSTRY, MONOPOLIES, PASTURAGE, VITICULTURE), planted Greek

settlements in Egypt, especially round Lake Moeris (q.v.), and instituted the Ptolemaic ruler-cult with its priests of Alexander and a growing number of deified members of the dynasty. He built the Pharus, the Museum, the Library, and other edifices and institutions of Alexandria as well as a canal from the Nile to the Red Sea.

PTOLEMY III EUERGETES, son of Ptolemy II and Arsinoë I, was born between 288 and 280 and died in 221 B.C. After his (presumable) adoption by Arsinoë II and his succession to the throne in 246 he married Berenice II (q.v.) and united Cyrene with Egypt. In the Third Syrian War (246–241) he acquired important towns in Syria and Asia Minor. Ptolemaic expansion ceased after this, perhaps owing to difficulties in Egypt.

PTOLEMY IV PHILOPATOR (*c.* 244–205 B.C.), son of Ptolemy III and Berenice II, married Arsinoë III (q.v.) in 217. The main events of his reign were: his succession to the throne (221); invasions of Palestine by Antiochus III (221 and 219–217). He gained a decisive victory over Antiochus (q.v. 3) at Raphia (217), but only with the help of the native Egyptians, who revolted for decades afterwards. Almost the whole Thebaid was ruled in consequence by the Nubian kings Harmachis and Anchmachis (208/7–187/6).

PTOLEMY V EPIPHANES (210–180 B.C.), son of Ptolemy IV and Arsinoë III. He was joint ruler with his father from 210; he succeeded to the throne in 205, the death of Ptolemy IV being kept a secret for a considerable time. The official succession (of uncertain date) was followed by revolts throughout two decades, and, from 203 onwards, by plans of the Seleucid and Macedonian kings to partition the outlying Egyptian territories, the consequence of which was the loss of most possessions in the Aegean, Asia Minor, and Palestine, where his troops suffered a final defeat at Panion in 200. The king was declared of full age in 197 and married the Seleucid princess Cleopatra I (q.v.) in 193. His *epistrategos* Hippalus reconquered the Thebaid in 187/6, and the last native revolt of this period in the Delta was quelled in 184/3.

PTOLEMY VI PHILOMETOR, son of Ptolemy V and Cleopatra I, was born in 186 or (perhaps) 184/3 and died in 145 B.C. He succeeded to the throne in 180 in joint rule with his mother, who died in 176; he formally married Cleopatra II in 175/4. In the course of three invasions from Antiochus IV (170, 169, and 168), he established a joint rule with Ptolemy VIII and Cleopatra II from 170 to 164. He defeated native revolts, but fled from Ptolemy VIII, to return as sole ruler in 164/3. His struggle with this brother continued for a decade. After a successful campaign beginning in 150 he was elected Seleucid king in joint rule with Demetrius II, but was killed in a victorious battle against Alexander Balas.

PTOLEMY VII NEOS PHILOPATOR, son of Ptolemy VI and Cleopatra II, was born *c.* 162–161, became joint ruler with his father in 145, sole ruler from his father's death until Ptolemy VIII's return to Egypt, and was killed by his uncle's orders in Aug. 144.

PTOLEMY VIII EUERGETES II (*c.* 182/1–116 B.C.), brother of Ptolemy VI. He was joint ruler with Ptolemy VI and Cleopatra II in 170–164; sole ruler in 164–163; king of Cyrene in 163–145; returning to Egypt in 145. He married Cleopatra II in 144, and took Cleopatra III to wife in 142 without being able to divorce Cleopatra II, who led a successful revolt against him in 132. He reconquered Alexandria in 127, and an amnesty and a peaceful reign with the two queens followed from 124. The king's final testament gave all power to Cleopatra III. An earlier testament during his rule in Cyrene bequeathed his possessions to Rome.

PTOLEMY IX SOTER II (LATHYRUS) (*c.* 141–81 B.C.), eldest son of Ptolemy VIII and Cleopatra III. He was priest of Alexander from 135/4; subsequently became governor of Cyprus and married Cleopatra IV, his sister, during Ptolemy VIII's last years. Elected joint ruler with Cleopatra III against her wishes in 116, he divorced Cleopatra IV and married Cleopatra Selene, another sister. He had to accept his brother Ptolemy X as joint ruler in 110. He reconquered the kingdom, but another revolt of his brother compelled him to flee to Cyprus in 108/7, and from there to Seleucid Syria. Cleopatra Selene divorced him; but he reconquered Cyprus very soon, was victorious in Syria against the Jewish State allied with his mother, and reconquered Egypt in 89–88. Cleopatra Berenice, his daughter, returned from exile as joint ruler in 88, after Ptolemy X's death, and remained sole ruler from Ptolemy IX's death to 80. The Thebaid revolted against the new rule from 88 to 86.

PTOLEMY X ALEXANDER I (c. 140–88 B.C.), younger brother of Ptolemy IX, was governor of Cyprus from 116; was recalled to Egypt by his mother in 110, but resigned after a short joint rule with the title 'king' of Cyprus. Another joint rule in 108 prepared the way for his final joint third rule with Cleopatra III under pressure from the insurgent Alexandrians. After Cleopatra III's (possibly natural) death, the king married Cleopatra Berenice, daughter of Ptolemy IX, a few days later. Expelled from Egypt by a military revolt, he made successive attempts to recover his kingdom by land from Syria and by sea from Asia Minor, and died in a naval battle (89–88).

The framework of events in the reigns of Ptolemy VIII, IX, and X is very uncertain: see the elaborate study of W. Otto and H. Bengtson, *Zur Geschichte des Niederganges des Ptolemäerreiches* (Bayer. Abh. 17, 1938).

PTOLEMY XI ALEXANDER II (c. 100/99–80 B.C.), son of Ptolemy X and his unknown first wife. Sulla made him joint ruler with and husband of his stepmother Cleopatra Berenice (80 B.C.). He murdered her nineteen days after the wedding, and was killed by the Alexandrians, in spite of his being the last legitimate male descendant of the dynasty.

PTOLEMY XII THEOS PHILOPATOR PHILADELPHUS NEOS DIONYSUS (AULETES), son of Ptolemy IX and a mistress, was born between 116 and 108 and died in 51 B.C. He succeeded to the throne in 80, and married Cleopatra V Tryphaena, his sister, in 80/79. His cultivation of friendly relations with Rome led to his expulsion by the Alexandrians in 58, but he was restored by Gabinius in 55.

PTOLEMY XIII, brother of Cleopatra VII (q.v.), was born in 63 and died in 47 B.C. In 51 he married his sister, who became joint ruler with him but was presently expelled by him. After the murder of Pompey by his ministers (48) he was forced by Caesar to share the throne again with Cleopatra. He subsequently made open war against Caesar, was defeated and drowned in the Nile.

PTOLEMY XIV (c. 59–44 B.C.), another brother of Cleopatra VII. Caesar made him king of Cyprus in 48, and joint ruler and husband of Cleopatra in 47. He was murdered by her orders.

PTOLEMY XV CAESAR: see CAESARION.

See APOLLONIUS 3, ARSINOË, BERENICE, CAESARION, CLEOMENES 3, CLEOPATRA.

Wilcken, *PW*, s.v. 'Arsinoe', 'Berenike'; Stähelin, ibid., s.v. 'Kleopatra'; Volkmann, ibid., s.v. 'Ptolemaios'. E. Bevan, *A History of Egypt under the Ptolemaic Dynasty* (1927); A. Bouché-Leclercq, *Histoire des Lagides* i–iv (1903–7); W. Otto, *Abhandlungen der bayrischen Akademie*, Phil.-Hist. Klasse, 1928 no. 1, 1934 no. 11, 1938 no. 17, Sitzungsber. 1939 no. 3; W. Peremans and J. Vergote, *Papyrologisch Handboek* (1942); Rostovtzeff, *Hellenistic World*, passim. Numerous articles in *JHS, JEg. Arch., Arch. Pap.*, and other periodicals. The administration of Ptolemaic Egypt is illustrated by innumerable papyri (Greek and Demotic): see the detailed study by Cl. Préaux, *L'Economie royale des Lagides* (1939), with complete bibliography and an index of important passages. For Ptolemaic dynastic chronology see T. C. Skeat, *The Reigns of the Ptolemies* (1954); A. E. Samuel, *Ptolemaic Chronology* (1962).     F. M. H.; P. M. F.

**PTOLEMY** (2), king of Mauretania (A.D. 23–40), was a son of Juba II (q.v.) and Cleopatra Selene, and thus a grandson of Antony. He shared some responsibility for government in his father's later years. For his help in the war against Tacfarinas (q.v.) he was recognized by Rome as *rex et socius atque amicus populi Romani*; the sceptre and robe that the Senate sent him he displayed on his coinage. In 40 the Emperor Gaius, his cousin, summoned him to Rome and then executed him; whether his offence was his wealth (Dio Cassius), his wearing a purple cloak in public (Suetonius), or a decision to annex Mauretania, is uncertain.

COINAGE. J. Mazard, *Corpus Nummorum Numidiae Mauretaniaeque* (1955), 127 ff.     H. H. S.

**PTOLEMY** (3) of Cyrene revived the sceptical school of philosophy about 100 B.C. (Diog. Laert. 9. 115).

See Zeller, *Phil. d. Griechen* iii. 2⁴. 2.

**PTOLEMY** (4) (CLAUDIUS PTOLEMAEUS, *PW* 66), astronomer, mathematician, and geographer (fl. A.D. 127–48, dates derived partly from his observations in Alexandria). His major work, the *Almagest* (this title is the Arabic form of ἡ μεγίστη sc. σύνταξις: Ptolemy's title is μαθηματικὴ σύνταξις), in thirteen books, is a complete textbook of astronomy as the Greeks understood the term (see ASTRONOMY). The basis of the system it expounds is the eccentric/epicyclic theory developed by Apollonius (2) and Hipparchus (3) (qq.v.), and the calculations are worked out with the aid of the trigonometry created by Hipparchus and Menelaus (q.v. 3). But only in the theory of the sun (book 3) and of eclipses (book 6) did Ptolemy merely repeat Hipparchus' work. He introduced an important correction in the theory of the moon (books 4–5), and himself created the first viable theory of the five planets (books 9–13). The fixed-star table too (books 7–8) is based on fresh observations. The *Almagest* is a masterpiece of clear and orderly exposition by a practising astronomer with considerable mathematical ability and a genius for analysis of observations. It quickly became canonical, and remained so for more than a thousand years, dominating astronomical theory in Byzantium, the Islamic world, and thence Europe of the later Middle Ages. Because of its generous acknowledgement of debt to predecessors, it is also an important source for our knowledge of earlier works which it superseded. Ancient commentaries by Pappus and Theon (4) of Alexandria (qq.v.) survive in part.

2. Other astronomical works by Ptolemy are: (a) φάσεις ἀπλανῶν ἀστέρων, on the times of the risings and settings of prominent fixed stars (only the second of two books survives). (b) ὑποθέσεις τῶν πλανωμένων, book 1 a description of the Ptolemaic system, listing the constants derived in the *Almagest*; book 2 (extant only in Arabic translation) an attempt to translate this geometrical system into physical terms. (c) *Canobic Inscription*, a (MS.) list of astronomical constants (some differing slightly from those of the *Almagest*) supposed to have been set up by Ptolemy on a column in Canopus, where he lived. (d) *Planisphaerium* (extant only in Latin translation from the Arabic), describing the stereographic projection of the celestial sphere from its south pole on to the plane of the equator (the theoretical basis of the astrolabe). (e) *Analemma* (extant only in Latin translation from the Greek, except for a few palimpsest fragments), an application of nomographic techniques to the solution of problems of spherical geometry encountered in the theory of sundials (see MATHEMATICS § 7). (f) Astronomical tables. These are extant only in the revised version of Theon

(q.v. 4) of Alexandria, but Ptolemy's own rules for their use (προχείρων κανόνων διάταξις καὶ ψηφοφορία) survive.

3. (a) *Astrology*. The ἀποτελεσματικά (or *Tetrabiblos*) was almost as influential in its own field as the *Almagest* in its. In it Ptolemy attempts to provide a scientific basis for the various practices of the astrologers. The καρπός (*Centiloquium*) is pseudepigraphic. (b) *Music*. The ἁρμονικά, in three books, is a systematic treatment of the mathematical theory of harmony. (c) *Optics*. The *Optica* is extant only in a Latin translation from the Arabic, from which book I and the end of book 5 are missing. It is greatly advanced in mathematical refinement and representation of physical and physiological reality beyond the crude treatise of Euclid (q.v.). Particularly remarkable are experiments to determine the angles of refraction between various media (5. 5 ff.). *See also* PHYSICS § 6. (d) *Philosophy*. Περὶ κριτηρίου καὶ ἡγεμονικοῦ is a short work on epistemology. (e) *Geography*. See below. (f) *Lost works*. Excerpts from a work on Euclid's 'parallel postulate' are given by Proclus, *Comm. in Eucl.* 191, 362, 365 Friedlein. Simplicius (*in Ar. de caelo*, 9) mentions a work Περὶ διαστάσεως (*On Dimension*), in which Ptolemy 'proved' that there are only three dimensions. *Suda* (s.v.) says that he wrote μηχανικά in three books; this is probably the same as the work Περὶ ῥοπῶν mentioned by Simplicius (*in Ar. de caelo*, 710). Simplicius also mentions a work Περὶ τῶν στοιχείων (*in Ar. de caelo*, 20).

LIFE AND WORKS. F. Boll, 'Studien über Claudius Ptolemäus' (*Jb. f. Cl. Phil.* Suppl. 1894), 51 ff.
*Almagest*, ed. J. L. Heiberg, 2 vols. (Teubner, 1898, 1903). Excellent German translation by K. Manitius, 2 vols. (Teubner, 1912–13, corrected repr. 1963). French translation in the old edition by Halma (Paris, 1813–16, reprinted 1927). Besides the above translations see J. B. J. Delambre, *Histoire de l'astronomie ancienne* (1817), esp. ii. 67 ff. Detailed bibliography in *PW* xxiii. 2. 1799 ff. Other astronomical works are edited by J. L. Heiberg in *Ptolemaei Opera Astronomica Minora* (Teubner, 1907; bk. ii of the ὑποθέσεις in German translation only; Arabic text, including the end of bk. i omitted by Heiberg, published by B. Goldstein in *TAPA* 1967, 3 ff.). This includes the *testimonia* for the lost works. On the φάσεις see H. Vogt, *Der Kalender des Claudius Ptolemäus* (*Sitz. Heidelberg*, 1920). German translation of the *Planisphaerium* by J. Drecker in *Isis* 1927, 255 ff. See also O. Neugebauer, 'The Early History of the Astrolabe', *Isis* 1949, 240 ff. *Analemma*: see P. Luckey, *Das Analemma von Ptolemäus*, *Astronomische Nachrichten* 230 Nr. 5498 (1927), 17 ff. The only edition of Theon's version of the πρόχειροι κανόνες is that of Halma, *Tables manuelles astronomiques de Ptolomée et de Théon*, 3 vols. (1822–5).
The astrological works, and Περὶ κριτηρίου καὶ ἡγεμονικοῦ, are edited in the Teubner edition of Ptolemy's works, vol. iii pts. 1 and 2, by Boll, Boer, and Lammert. For the *Tetrabiblos* see also the Loeb edition by F. E. Robbins, 1940. Much valuable commentary on this will be found in Bouché-Leclercq, *L'Astrologie grecque* (1899, repr. 1963).
The ἁρμονικά are edited, together with the commentary of Porphyry (q.v.) and a German translation and commentary, by Ingemar Düring, *Göteborgs Högskolas Arsskrift* 36, 38, and 40 (1930–4).
*Optica*: edition by A. Lejeune, *L'Optique de Claude Ptolémée* (1956). See also Lejeune's *Euclide et Ptolémée, deux stades de l'optique géometrique grecque* (1948).                     G. J. T.

4. Ptolemy's scientific ideal outstripped his practical application. Adopting Posidonius' estimate of 180,000 stades for the earth's circumference, in preference to Eratosthenes' more correct calculation of 250,000 stades, he systematically underrated the distance between any two positions of longitude, and the errors due to this false graduation accumulated in the outer or eastern portion of his map. Moreover, with rare exceptions, his positions were not really determined by astronomic observation, but by dead reckoning from (often inexact) reports of travellers. Though Ptolemy recognized the danger of this method of computation, he tabulated all his data in exact terms of latitude and longitude, thus giving a delusive appearance of scientific certainty to his deductions. Furthermore, he rejected the theory of a circumfluent ocean round the three continents, and while he left blank the map of the unknown world to west,

north, and east, he assumed the existence of a large sub-equatorial continent.

5. The most conspicuous errors in Ptolemy's map were the extension of the Eurasian land-mass over 180° of longitude (instead of 130°), and the invention of a Terra Australis connecting the east coast of Africa with China and converting the Indian Ocean into a huge lake. Of its innumerable errors and deficiencies of detail the following are most notable. (1) *Europe*. The Atlantic coast of the continent has an almost unbroken north-east trend. Scotland lies on its back in a west–east direction (for a probable reason see J. J. Tierney, *JHS* 1959, 132 ff.). Scandinavia is a small island. Germany, Poland, and central and northern Russia are largely left blank. The Sea of Azov is greatly magnified. (2) *Asia*. The Caspian Sea is correctly conceived as a lake, but is greatly elongated from west to east, and the Persian Gulf is similarly distorted. India is a rectangle with its main axis running from west to east, and Ceylon is magnified fourteen times. The Malay peninsula is determined with fair accuracy, but the Chinese coast curves away to east and south so as to meet Terra Australis. (3) *Africa*. The Mediterranean coast runs almost continuously from west to east. Two unidentifiable rivers, Gir and Nigir, cross north Africa in the same direction. The White Nile is correctly derived from two Central African lakes, but the mountains on either side are connected into a continuous west–east chain ('Mountains of the Moon').

6. But despite its faults, the treatise of Ptolemy was on the whole the most accurate of ancient geographical works, and it was the most comprehensive. It therefore remained standard until modern times.

TEXTS. C. Nobbe (1843–5, text not good); Ch. Müller and C. T. Fischer (bks. 1–3) (1883–1901).
COMMENTARY. E. H. Bunbury, *History of Ancient Geography* (1879), ii. 519 ff.
TEXT, MAPS, AND COMMENTARY. P. J. Fischer, *Cl. Ptolemaei Geographiae codex Urbinas Graecus* 82 (4 folios, 1932); C. L. Stevenson, E.T. and maps (U.S.A. 1932); Hans v. Mžik, *Des Klaudios Ptolemaios Einführung in die darstellende Erdkunde* (1938, *Klotho* 5), German transl. and comm. on *Geography*, bk. 1; W. H. Stahl, *Ptolemy's Geography. A Select Bibliography* (1953); L. Bagrow, 'The Origin of Ptolemy's Geographia', *Geografiska Annaler* 1945, 318 ff. Ptolemy on Germany: A. Schoening, *Germanien in d. Geog. des Ptol.* (1962), and G. Schuette in *Classica et Mediaevalia* 1951, 236 ff. (includes Sogdiana; on Sogdiana: J. Markwart in *Orientalia* 1946, 123 ff.; on the Tarim Basin: W. Haussig in *Zeitschr. d. Morgenländischen Gesellschaft* 1959, 148 ff.; on India: J. Vogel in *Archaeologica Orientalia* 1952; on a southern continent: O. Schulz in *La Nouvelle Clio* 1951, 307 ff. Cf. also Thomson, *Hist. Anc. Geog.* 229 f.; 259 ff. (Africa); 286 ff. (Asia); 232 ff., 245 ff. etc. (Europe); 334 ff.; J. I. Miller, *The Spice Trade of the Roman Empire* (1969), see index.                     E. H. W.

**PUBLICANI.** Since the Roman Republic had only a rudimentary civil service (*see* APPARITORES) and primitive budgeting methods, the collection of public revenue was normally farmed out, i.e. sold as a public contract to the highest bidder, who then reimbursed himself with what profit he could. In addition, as in other States, there were contracts (*ultro tributa*) for public works and supplies (especially for the army), and these tended to be in the hands of the same persons, especially as men of servile birth and (at least by the time of the Hannibalic War) senatorial families were not admitted to either. By investing the money gained on public contracts in purchasing a tax contract (especially the increasing *portoria* (q.v.) and revenues from public land), men could make great fortunes. In the second century B.C., the Senate and censors often carefully scrutinized the activities of these *publicani* and this caused occasional conflicts, which the *publicani* could not hope to win. But C. Gracchus (q.v. 4), by providing for the sale of the Asian tithe by (normally) four-year contracts in Rome, opened a new and lucrative field for them. By transferring the *repetundae* (q.v.) court to the richest non-senators, probably to counter flagrant senatorial corruption, he gave the same class of men immense power in the State. They soon gained full social acceptance (by Cicero's day they were the leading *equites*, q.v.) and, having the greatest wealth and the most obvious common interest within the 'equestrian' class, were the most important pressure group in it, so that *equites* and *publicani*, for political purposes, often seem identified. The huge fortunes made by these men, apart from a (socially necessary) investment in land, were put to work in moneylending and business finance, so that *publicani* and *negotiatores* also came to be largely identical, especially on the highest level.

By the second century B.C., the large capital required for the purpose of the main taxes and for arranging public contracts had led to the formation of public companies for the purpose, with special privileges conferred by law; and in the late Republic these were the biggest and best-organized bodies and the largest employers in Rome. They consisted of *socii* (who put up the main capital) under a *magister* (one of the managing directors), who would act as *manceps* (q.v.) for the contract. Provincial offices were under a *pro magistro* and had a very large staff, from wealthy *equites* in the upper reaches (who could count on the co-operation of the provincial governor) to freedmen and slaves. These offices also could act as bankers to the governor and to other important men visiting the province, and as centres for large-scale financial transactions in their province and adjacent kingdoms. They were particularly wealthy and powerful in Asia, where they collected the main tax. In Rome, shares (*partes*) seem to have been sold to anyone who could afford them, and large numbers of small shareholders, though they had no influence on management, were thus interested in the fortunes of the companies. In the late Republic, senators quite openly held *partes* in the companies and some like Crassus (q.v. 4) were closely connected with them. Competition then seems to have been at best nominal and the companies acted as a monopoly. Thus the main company for Bithynia was owned by all the other *societates*.

Caesar restricted the activities of the *publicani*, depriving them of the Asian *decuma*. Under the Empire, tribute was collected by the government through quaestors and procurators; though on the local level *publicani* might still be called in. Other revenues continued to be collected through them, and the word now acquires the meaning of 'tax-collector'. The New Testament shows their unpopularity. After major complaints, Nero introduced measures to control them, including the compulsory publication of their agreements (*pactiones*) with the local corporations (Tac. *Ann.* 13. 50 f.). In the second century A.D. the place of the companies is taken by individual *conductores* (q.v.).

Bloch–Carcopino, *Histoire romaine* (1950), 75 ff.; *PW* Suppl. xi, 1184 ff.     E. B.

**PUBLILIUS** (1, *PW* 10) **VOLERO,** tribune of the *plebs* in 471 B.C., is traditionally credited with a law that transferred the election of plebeian magistrates from the assembly of the *curiae* to the tribes. As such a concession by the patricians is unlikely at so early a date, the *rogatio Publilia* had better be considered as an anticipation of the *Lex Publilia* (339 B.C.; *see* PUBLILIUS 2).

G. W. Botsford, *The Roman Assemblies* (1909), 270 ff., 300 f.; Ogilvie, *Comm. Livy 1–5*, 373 f.     P. T.

**PUBLILIUS** (2, *PW* 11) **PHILO,** QUINTUS, consul in 339, 327, 320, and 315 B.C. He was the first plebeian dictator (339), and is credited with three laws which were a landmark in the struggle for social equality: (1) censorship to be opened to plebeians; (2) *plebiscita* to be binding on the whole community (an anticipation of the *Lex*

*Hortensia*); (3) the *auctoritas patrum* to be reduced to the formal ratifying of proposals, before they went forward to the centuriate assembly. Publilius was the first plebeian praetor (337), and, as censor (332), helped towards creating the new tribes Maecia and Scaptia. As consul (327) he besieged Naples (Palaeopolis) and was appointed proconsul for 326 (the first known example of *prorogatio imperii*). The tradition which records his triumphs (over the Latins in 339, and over the Samnites and Palaeopolitae in 326) is not altogether trustworthy. He undoubtedly played a leading part in the recovery of Rome after the Caudine catastrophe, and in her expansion in and beyond Campania, but details of his later career (e.g. his alleged implication in the rebellion of Capua in 314) cannot be explained with certainty. There is, however, every reason to maintain that Philo ranked prominently among the so-called 'democrats', i.e. Appius Claudius' opponents chiefly in home affairs, while sharing in and furthering Appius' 'Southern' policy.

G. W. Botsford, *The Roman Assemblies* (1909), 229 ff.; E. S. Staveley, *Athenaeum* 1955, 28 ff.; F. Cassola, *I gruppi politici romani* (1962), 122 ff.     P. T.

**PUBLILIUS** (3, *PW* 28) **SYRUS** (not Publius, Wölfflin, *Philol.* 1865, 439) came to Rome as a slave in the first century B.C., possibly from Antioch (Pliny, *HN* 35. 199). Intellectual ability, psychological discernment, and wit ensured him manumission. He devoted his gifts to the latinized form of the mime, where his one rival was the veteran knight Laberius (q.v.), whom he surpassed in the competition between them ordered by Julius Caesar. Only two of his titles are recorded, *Putatores* and the corrupt *Murmurithon* (Nonius 2. 133; Priscian, *Inst.* K. 2. 532. 25). His clever improvisations suffered through being entrusted to the frail security of actors' copies. The Elder Seneca commended his power of expressing some thoughts better than any other dramatist; and Gellius quotes for their neatness 14 maxims (Sen. *Controv.* 7. 3. 8; Gell. 17. 14). Petronius 55 has wrongly been supposed to cite a passage of 16 lines from Publilius.

In the first century A.D. it was realized that, whatever the harm wrought by the immorality of mimes, the apophthegms uttered by various dramatic personages might well be selected and alphabetically arranged to inculcate in schoolboys a proverbial wisdom founded on human experience. So it came about later that Jerome learned in class the line which he quotes twice, 'aegre reprehendas quod sinas consuescere' (Hieron. *Ep.* 107. 8; 128. 4). The great textual difficulty is to disengage truly Publilian *sententiae* from accretions due to paraphrases of genuine verses, or insertions of Senecan and pseudo-Senecan ideas, or such distortions of the original iambic senarii and trochaic septenarii as induced copyists to mistake them for prose.

There could be no unified ethical standard among maxims spoken by different characters in different scenes. Some are platitudes; some contradict others, as proverbs often do. Many advocate self-regarding behaviour; yet the prevailing terseness of expression is an undeniable attraction.

TEXT. J. C. Orelli, *Publii* [*sic*] *Syri Mimi et aliorum Sententiae* (1822; 791 iambics and 83 trochaics, with Scaliger's Greek verse translations). W. Meyer, *Publii* [*sic*] *Syri Sententiae* (1880; 733 lines); O. Friedrich, *Publilii Syri Mimi Sententiae* (1880); R. A. H. Bickford-Smith, *Pub. Syr. Sent.* (1895; 722 lines).
TRANSLATION. Duff, *Minor Lat. Poets* (734 lines).     J. W. D.

**PUDICITIA,** personification of the chastity or modesty of women. According to Livy (10. 23), she was originally worshipped as Pudicitia Patricia in a small shrine in the Forum Boarium, but in 296 B.C. a rival cult of Pudicitia Plebeia was founded in the Vicus Longus. At first limited to women who had married but once, the cult degenerated and was forgotten.

For criticism see Wissowa, *Ges. Abh.* 254 ff.; Platner–Ashby, 433 ff.; for other cults, see Wissowa, *RK* 334.　　　　H. J. R.

**PULVINAR,** (1) a couch, such as was used for the images or symbols of gods at a *lectisternium* (q.v.; Hor. *Carm.* 1. 37. 3 and often). This seems to be a purely Greek rite, adopted in Rome. (2) A platform on which such objects were placed, either to be adored at a *supplicatio* (q.v.), or for other ritual purposes, see [Acro] on Horace, loc. cit. and literature under SUPPLICATIONES.

Latte, *RR* 224.　　　　　　　　　　　　　　H. J. R.

**PUNIC WARS:** three wars in which Rome gradually superseded Carthage as the dominant power in the western Mediterranean. The early relations of Rome and Carthage had been friendly. The interests of Rome, which were primarily agricultural and confined to Italy, did not clash with those of the Carthaginians, who gained a commercial monopoly in the western Mediterranean. Treaties were negotiated (probably in 509 and 348 B.C.), confirming this Punic monopoly and guaranteeing Italian coast-towns against Carthaginian attack, while the hostility of Pyrrhus to both Rome and Carthage resulted in a supplementary agreement between the two powers (279). But in 264 when the Carthaginians occupied Messana in north-east Sicily a dangerous situation was created, since Rome was now the ally of the Greek cities in south Italy, who saw a threat to their trade or security if Carthage dominated Sicily and the Straits of Messana. When therefore the Mamertines (q.v.) in Messana appealed to Rome for help, the Senate hesitated, foreseeing the possibility of war with Carthage, but the People decided to accept the Mamertine alliance whatever the consequences. When Appius Claudius (q.v. 5) Caudex crossed to Sicily war was declared. In fact both Rome and Carthage had rushed in to secure a key position, but with different motives: defensive imperialism dominated Roman policy; an exploiting commercial imperialism actuated Carthage. Neither side used the Messana affair as an excuse for a predetermined war, but being different in race, culture, and religion, with divergent moral and material interests, Rome and Carthage would gravitate more quickly towards conflict when the minor States between them had been eliminated or assimilated. In the Hellenistic East a common culture held the three great monarchies in a precarious balance of power, which Rome later tried to maintain when she had absorbed something of that culture. In the West dissimilarity made compromise more difficult.

2. THE FIRST PUNIC WAR (264–241) opened with a successful Roman offensive conducted by Appius Claudius Caudex and M. Valerius Messalla (q.v. 1) against the Carthaginians and Hieron in north-east Sicily; this resulted in Hieron entering into alliance with Rome (263). In 262 the Romans won Segesta and, after a siege, Agrigentum, but since Carthage continued fighting they realized that peace could be secured only by driving the Carthaginians completely out of Sicily: this involved challenging their naval supremacy. By a magnificent achievement the Romans built some 160 vessels equipped with grapnels (*corvi*) which helped to thwart their enemy's superior naval skill. The new fleet commanded by Duilius (q.v.) defeated the Carthaginians off Mylae (260). When no decisive result was reached in Sicily, the Romans sent an expeditionary force under Regulus (q.v. 1) to Africa; after the way had been opened by a great naval victory off Ecnomus, it landed in Africa (256), but was defeated in 255. A relieving fleet defeated the Punic navy off the Hermaean Promontory, evacuated the survivors of Regulus' army, but was wrecked by a storm off Pachynus on the way home. In Sicily the Romans captured Panormus

(254), thus confining the Carthaginians to the western end of the island, but a newly raised fleet was wrecked off Cape Palinurus (253). Both sides were exhausted. After L. Metellus (q.v. 1) had repulsed a Punic attack on Panormus (250), the Romans blockaded Lilybaeum and Drepana. A naval attack by Claudius (q.v. 6) Pulcher on Drepana failed, while the rest of the fleet was wrecked off south Sicily (249); the Romans, however, seized Mt. Eryx (q.v.), thus cutting off the land-communications of Drepana. Despite the fresh efforts of Hamilcar (q.v. 2) Barca in Sicily (247–241), the Romans at length raised a new fleet under C. Lutatius Catulus (q.v. 1), who defeated the Carthaginians off Aegates Insulae and negotiated peace-terms, which ultimately included the evacuation of Sicily and an indemnity of 3,200 talents to be paid in ten years.

3. Carthage immediately had to face a serious revolt of her mercenaries (the 'Truceless War'). Scarcely had she crushed this, when the Romans occupied Sardinia in answer to an appeal from some mercenaries there (238). To Carthaginian protests Rome replied by refusing arbitration and declaring war: Carthage had to submit, surrender Sardinia and Corsica, and pay an additional 1,200 talents. The desire to deprive Carthage of an island base against Italy may partly explain this wanton aggression, which embittered relations which were just becoming more friendly. Primarily as compensation for the loss of Sicily and Sardinia the imperialist party at Carthage turned to Spain, which would also furnish abundant natural wealth and manpower in the event of future hostilities with Rome. The conquest of Spain was achieved from 237 to 219 by Hamilcar, Hasdrubal, and Hannibal (qq.v.). By attacking Rome's ally, Saguntum, Hannibal deliberately precipitated the Second Punic War. The question of war-guilt is complicated. Possibly it was not a long-premeditated war of revenge championed by the family of Barca, but when the Romans interfered south of the Ebro (the Punic sphere of influence *de facto* and possibly *de jure*), Hannibal refused to contemplate a recurrence of bullying such as Carthage had suffered in 238: he struck before Rome was ready.

4. THE SECOND PUNIC WAR (218–201). The Romans prepared to send one army to Africa, a second to Spain, but were foiled by Hannibal's bold invasion of north Italy (*see* HANNIBAL *and* SCIPIO 3). They wisely, however, sent an army to Spain where P. and Cn. Scipio (q.v. 4 and 3) prevented reinforcements from reaching Hannibal, won a sea-battle which gave Rome naval supremacy, and took the offensive until their deaths (211); their successor Claudius Nero (q.v. 2) still held the line of the Ebro. Meantime Hannibal had defeated Roman armies at Trebia (218), Trasimene (217), and Cannae (216), but as Rome refused to admit defeat and retained the loyalty of central and northern Italy he attempted to encircle her with a ring of enemies. But this wider strategy ultimately failed: in the west his brother Hasdrubal's offensive in Spain was repulsed (215), while a Carthaginian landing in Sardinia proved abortive (215); in the north the hostile Gauls failed to take decisive action; in the east an alliance was made with Philip V of Macedon, who, however, unaided by the Punic fleet, gradually lost interest in the First Macedonian War (214–205) and negotiated the Peace of Phoenice with Rome (*see* LAEVINUS *and* GALBA 2); in the south Greek cities were encouraged to revolt, but their leader Syracuse was reduced to submission by 211 by Marcellus (q.v. 1). Meantime in Italy Hannibal's strength was being worn down by Fabius (5), Sempronius Gracchus, Marcellus, and Fulvius Flaccus (qq.v.), who avoided further pitched battles and recovered Capua (which had revolted after Cannae) in 211 and Tarentum in 209. Hasdrubal, who at length broke through to Italy from Spain, was defeated at the Metaurus (q.v.) by

Claudius Nero and Livius Salinator (q.v.) in 207, and thereby Hannibal's last hope of receiving reinforcements died, despite the attempt of Mago (q.v. 2). Scipio (q.v. 5) Africanus victoriously drove the Carthaginians from Spain by his final victory at Ilipa (206) and led an expeditionary force to Africa where his successive victories forced the recall of Hannibal from Italy. Thanks to his tactical reforms and the help of Masinissa (q.v.), Scipio defeated Hannibal at the battle of Zama (q.v., 202). In 201 peace was signed: Carthage surrendered her navy and Spain, retained her autonomy and her territory within the Phoenician Trenches (i.e. roughly modern Tunisia), became a dependent ally of Rome, and paid an indemnity of 10,000 talents in fifty annual instalments. But the Romans evacuated Africa. Factors which gave Rome the victory included her superiority by sea and in manpower, the loyalty of the Italian allies, the wisdom of the Senate and the doggedness of the People, the blocking of reinforcements to Hannibal, the defensive strategy of Fabius in Italy combined with the offensive strategy of Scipio, who forged a weapon which drove the Carthaginians from Spain and vanquished Hannibal himself. Against such factors Hannibal's untiring gallantry and genius were unavailing. The war was a turning-point in ancient history; it had profound effects on the political, economic, social, and religious life of Italy, while thereafter for centuries no power could endanger Rome's existence.

5. THE THIRD PUNIC WAR (149–146). Carthage, no longer a great Mediterranean power, made a remarkably quick economic recovery, thanks partly to Hannibal's financial reforms, but she was continually provoked by Masinissa, whose aggression the Romans did little to check. Cato (q.v. 1), from motives of revenge and fear, urged the destruction of Carthage; Nasica (see SCIPIO 10) advocated a more lenient policy. There is little evidence to suggest that Roman policy was dictated by commercial jealousy. Intervention was legally justified when Carthage was goaded into attacking Masinissa, Rome's ally (150). Rome declared war on Carthage (149), and a Roman army under Manilius (q.v. 1) landed in Africa. Carthage surrendered, handed over hostages and arms, and then heard the Roman terms that the city itself must be destroyed. Unexpectedly she refused to comply, and with desperate heroism withstood a Roman blockade until 146, when Scipio (q.v. 11) Aemilianus stormed and sacked the city. Carthage was thus destroyed, and her territory was made into the Roman province of Africa.

ANCIENT SOURCES. *First War*: Polyb. bk. 1 based mainly upon the pro-Roman Fabius Pictor and the pro-Carthaginian Philinus. *Second War*: Polyb. bks. 3 and 7–15 (fragmentary). He drew upon both Roman material (public archives, family records, oral tradition from survivors, and writers as Fabius) and Punic material (the Greek writers Sosylus and Silenus who lived with Hannibal). Livy, bks. 21–30, provides a detailed narrative, based partly upon Polyb., partly upon less trustworthy Roman annalists. *Third War*: Polyb. bks. 36–9 (fragmentary). Appian, *Libyca* 67–135, is based upon Polybius, though contaminated with less reliable annalistic material. Subsidiary authorities add little.

MODERN LITERATURE. Walbank, *Polybius*, is indispensable. G. De Sanctis, *Stor. Rom.*, vol. iii, iv, pt. 3 (1916–64), is of fundamental importance; U. Kahrstedt, *Geschichte der Karthager von 218–146* (1913), contains detailed source criticism. S. Gsell, *Histoire ancienne de l'Afrique du Nord* i–iv (1913–20), esp. vol. iii. For the separate battles J. Kromayer and G. Veith, *Antike Schlachtfelder* iii, iv (1912–31), and *Schlachten-Atlas zur antiken Kriegsgeschichte, röm. Abt.* i, ii (1922). J. H. Thiel, *History of Roman Sea-power before the Second Punic War* (Amsterdam, 1954). *Studies on the History of Roman Sea-power* (1946), ch. ii; H. H. Scullard, *Scipio Africanus in the Second Punic War* (1930); E. Groag, *Hannibal als Politiker* (1929); F. E. Adcock, 'Delenda est Carthago', *CHJ* 1946, 117 ff.; A. E. Astin, *Scipio Aemilianus* (1967). For general background, A. Toynbee, *Hannibal's Legacy* (1965). Cf. also *Studi Annibalici* (Acad. Etrusca di Cortona, 1964); E. G. S. Robinson, 'Carthaginian and other ... coinages of the Second Punic War', *Num. Chron.* 1964, 37 ff.                    H. H. S.

**PUPIUS**, PUBLIUS, contemporary with Horace, who calls his tragedies 'lacrimosa poemata' (*Epist.* 1. 1. 67).

Baehr. *FPR* 348; Morel, *FPL* 112.

**PURPLE.** Of the two main kinds of purple-yielding shellfish described by Pliny (*HN* 9. 125–41), *purpura* and *pelagia* (Greek πορφύρα) correspond to the Linnaean murex, *murex* and *bucinum* (κῆρυξ) to the smaller and less precious purpura haemostoma. In antiquity the purple of Tyre always retained its primacy, but purple dyeing was practised also in the Greek cities of Asia, the Greek mainland and islands, southern Italy, and North Africa. After being gathered or caught in baskets and killed suddenly to preserve the secretion, the molluscs were either opened (esp. the larger) or crushed. The mass was then left in salt for three days, extracted with water, and slowly inspissated to one-sixteenth of its original volume. Impurities were removed during this process, and the liquid was then tested with flocks of wool until the colour was right. Many shades within the violet–scarlet range, and even a bluish green, could be obtained by mixing the dyes from different species and by intercepting the photochemical reaction which gives the secretion its colour. ('Twice-dyed' [δίβαφος] Tyrian purple resulted from consecutive steeping in *pelagium* and *bucinum*.) Less expensive imitation purple dyes, for which several recipes survive, were also made. In Rome, where the use of purple garments was always a mark of rank, purple dyeing became a state monopoly under Alexander Severus.

H. Blümner, *Technologie der Gewerbe und Künste*[2] i (1912), 233 ff.; D'A. W. Thompson, *Glossary of Greek Fishes* (1947), 209 ff.; Forbes, *Stud. Anc. Technol.* iv. 114 ff., 140 ff.                    L. A. M.

**PUTEAL:** literally a well-kerb, but also used of the stone coping put to cover some place which was taboo such as where lightning had struck (*see also* BIDENTAL). The most famous was in the Forum—the *puteal Libonis* or *Scribonianum*; its altar-like well-head is depicted on coins (*B.M. Cat. Rom. Republ.* 1. 419), and its tufa foundation was discovered in 1950 (Nash, *Pict. Dict. Rome* ii. 259 ff.).                    H. W. P.

**PUTEOLI**, modern *Pozzuoli*, a town near Naples (*see* PAUSILYPUS MONS). Samian colonists from Cumae founded Dicaearchia here (c. 521 B.C.). Dicaearchia became Puteoli (date unknown), and Puteoli became a Roman dependency (with Capua in 338?) (Strabo 5. 245 f.; Festus, 262 L.). In the Hannibalic War it was an important military and trading port (Livy 24. 7; 26. 17), and in 194 became a citizen colony which was subsequently recolonized several times (Dessau, *ILS* 5317; Plut. *Sulla*, 37; Tac. *Ann.* 14. 27; Pliny, *HN* 3. 61). As the harbour of Rome, Puteoli became a great commercial entrepôt, by 125 B.C. second only to Delos (Festus, 109 L.). All Rome's eastern imports and exports, including grain, passed through Puteoli (Strabo 3. 145; 17. 793; Pliny, *HN* 36. 70; Sen. *Ep.* 77). Its trade guilds, fire-brigade, imperial post station, its special road (Via Domitiana, q.v.) joining the Via Appia, its lighthouse, artificial harbour-works, and surviving monuments (e.g. amphitheatre), attest a prosperity which survived the rivalry of Ostia. Devastations by Alaric (410), Genseric (455), and Totila (545) finally ruined Puteoli. In its heyday Puteoli was a fashionable villa resort, e.g. of Sulla, Cicero, Hadrian.

K. J. Beloch, *Campanien*[2] (1890); C. Dubois, *Pouzzoles Antiques* (1907); K. Lehmann-Hartleben, *Antike Hafenanlagen des Mittelmeeres* (1923), 163; A. Maiuri, *The Phlegraean Fields* (1957).                    E. T. S.

**PYGMALION**, (1) legendary king of Tyre, brother of Elissa (Dido), whose husband, Acherbas or Sychaeus, he killed in the hope of obtaining his fortune. (See Verg. *Aen.* 1. 343–64, Just. *Epit.* 18. 4, and DIDO.) (2) Legendary king of Cyprus, who having fashioned an ivory statue of a woman fell in love with it. Aphrodite gave it life, and the woman bore Pygmalion a daughter, Paphos, the mother of Cinyras (Ov. *Met.* 10. 243–97), though according to Apollod. *Bibl.* 3. 14. 3 Cinyras was Pygmalion's son-in-law. Philostephanus (*FHG* iii. 31, fr. 13) calls the statue a figure of Aphrodite. Pygmalion was perhaps, like Cinyras (q.v.), a priest-king, associated with the cult of Aphrodite-Astarte (cf. J. G. Frazer, *Adonis Attis Osiris* (1906), i, ch. 3). F. R. W.

**PYGMIES,** dwarfs of ridiculous appearance who live in Africa, or India, or Scythia and are distinct from the Cercopes which annoyed Heracles. They are mentioned and discussed in Greek mythology in connexion with their fight against the cranes. Homer (*Il.* 3. 6) says that the cranes flee before the winter to the (southern) stream of Oceanus and bring death to the Pygmies. Hecataeus of Miletus, who definitely located the Pygmies in southern Egypt, Ctesias, and the writers on India (e.g. Megasthenes) considerably elaborated the story. The Pygmies disguise themselves as rams, or ride on rams and goats. They battle with the cranes to protect their fields, or even conduct operations to destroy the eggs of the cranes. Other mythographers invented explanations for the struggle, tracing the enmity back to a beautiful pygmy girl transformed into a crane (Boeus in Ath. 9. 393 e).

As Herodotus hinted (2. 32. 6) and Aristotle (*Hist. An.* 8. 12. 597ᵃ) confirmed, the dwarfs of Central Africa may have been the origin of the myth (F. Nicolas, *Anthropos* (1956), 551). Modern explorers report that the Akka dwarfs hunt cranes and that the birds vigorously resist. Around this core of fact, possibly conveyed to Greeks through Egyptian sources (R. Hennig, *Rh. Mus.* 1932), grew a solid shell of dwarf folklore (R. Dangel, *SMSR* 1931, 128) and novelistic invention. The geranomachy is often shown in Greek art, the François vase being the earliest instance. In Hellenistic art dwarfs or Pygmies are often used for parodies of mythological and 'genre' scenes, or shown in Nile landscapes (W. B. MacDaniel, *AJArch.* 1932, 260).

E. Wuest, *PW* s.v. 'Pygmaioi'; M. Gusinde, *Kenntnisse und Urteile über Pygmaen* (1962). G. M. A. H.

**PYLAEMENES,** in mythology, king of the Paphlagonian Eneti (*Iliad* 2. 851). He is distinguished chiefly for coming to life in *Il.* 13. 658, cf. 643, after being killed in 5. 576, a slip of Homer's from which most ridiculous consequences have been drawn by ancient and modern critics. H. J. R.

**PYLOS** was the name of three places in western Peloponnese (Strabo 8. 339; cf. Ar. *Eq.* 1059). *Messenian Pylos* lay at the north end of Navarino Bay, on a rocky peninsula (formerly Osmanaga, now called Palaiokhori or Koryphasion) joined by a sandspit to the mainland and separated by a narrow channel from the island of Sphacteria. On the landward side is the so-called 'Cave of Nestor'. There are traces of Mycenaean occupation and also of Hellenistic (houses and walls). Tradition (Paus. 4. 36. 2) placed the house and tomb of Nestor in this vicinity. Uninhabited in 425 B.C., the Athenians fortified it and held it with a Messenian garrison until 409 (Diod. 13. 64). Its subsequent history is obscure. It is surprising that this fertile district, with one of the best harbours of Greece, was not more important in classical times. Its great period of importance is the Mycenaean. For the ever-increasing evidence of Bronze Age cultural development here and elsewhere in the western Peloponnese, *see* MESSENIA *and* ELIS. With Nestor, as ruler of a wealthy State which sent ninety ships to Troy and included Pylos (*Il.* 2. 591–602), has been associated the Mycenaean palace on an acropolis at Ano Englianos, north-east of the Bay of Navarino and near Chora. It is the centre of a region particularly rich in Mycenaean remains (*see* MESSENIA) from late Middle Helladic through to the end

of Late Helladic IIIB (*c.* 1200 B.C.). There is not universal agreement that this is in fact the palace of the Pylian dynasty, established by Neleus from Thessaly (Paus. 4. 36. 1), attacked by Heracles, and visited by Telemachus. The kingdom of Nestor stretches in the Catalogue of the Ships to the Alpheus (*Il.* 2. 592), and the tale of the cattle-raid into Elis told in *Il.* 11. 671–761 (*see* PYLOS in Triphylia) is difficult to understand if the centre of Neleid rule was at Ano Englianos. Excavation of the palace area shows evidence of a lower town to one side of the acropolis, and of earlier palatial structures going back to the beginning of the Mycenaean period. Finds would seem to suggest that the site possessed a fortification wall in early Mycenaean times, and that this was destroyed in Late Helladic IIIA period, but was not restored when the area was levelled and the existing Late Helladic IIIB palace built, which the excavators suggest was the work of Neleus. The circumstances of the destruction of this palace were formerly described as the 'Dorian Invasion', but some uncertainty is now felt concerning the process of destruction of the Late Bronze Age civilization of Greece. The conflagration baked and preserved the great archive of Linear B tablets relating to the business of government immediately before. These tablets appear to indicate not only an elaborate administration but also preparations to repel attack. The site was not subsequently occupied.

Thuc. bk. 4. R. M. Burrows, *JHS* 1896, 55 ff.; 1898, 147 ff.; C. W. Blegen and M. Rawson, *A Guide to the Palace of Nestor* (U.S.A. 1962); F. Kiechle, 'Pylos und der pylische Raum in der antiken Tradition', *Hist.* 1960, 1 ff.; W. K. Pritchett, *Studies in Ancient Greek Topography* i (1965), 6 ff. *See also* MESSENIA. R. J. H.

**PYLOS** in Triphylia, a little south of Samikon, was taken by Strabo (followed by some moderns) for the Homeric town of that name. Rich beehive-tombs of the sixteenth century have been found in this district, near Kakovatos. The region might suit better than Pylos in Messenia (q.v.) the description by Nestor (*Il.* 11. 671–761) of the raid in his youth into Elis, past Samikon (?) to the Alpheus, especially since the discovery of Mycenaean tombs (of L.H. IIIB–C date) at Dhiásela near that river (see *BCH* 1957, 574 ff., and the discussion of the whole episode in relation to the historical background and the site of Kakovatos in *AJArch.* 1948, 115, by H. T. Wade-Gery, 'The Dorian Invasion: What Happened at Pylus').

Strabo 8. 344 ff. W. Dörpfeld and K. Müller, *Ath. Mitt.* 1908, 295 ff.; 1909, 269 ff. T. J. D.; R. J. H.

**PYRAMUS** and **THISBE,** hero and heroine of a love-story almost unknown except from Ovid, *Met.* 4. 55 ff., who says, 53, that it is not a common tale. They were next-door neighbours in Babylon, and, as their parents would not let them marry, they talked with each other through the party-wall of the houses, which was cracked. Finally, they arranged to meet at Ninus' tomb. There Thisbe was frightened by a lion coming from its kill; she dropped her cloak as she ran and the lion mouthed it. Pyramus, finding the bloodstained cloak and supposing her dead, killed himself; she returned, found his body, and followed his example. Their blood stained a mulberry-tree, whose fruit has ever since been black when ripe, in sign of mourning for them. H. J. R.

**PYRENEES** (Πυρήνη, τὰ Πυρηναῖα ὄρη; *Pyrenaeus mons*), the range of mountains between Gaul and Spain. The name was derived from a city, or port of call, frequented by traders from Massilia. Herodotus (2. 33) places near it the source of the Ister (*Danube*). Avienus (559) knew both the town and the mountains, the former near Portus Veneris (*Vendres*). Silius Italicus (3. 414) and Diodorus (5. 35) present other more imaginative derivations. The error of Polybius (34. 7. 4), ascribing a north–south direction for the range, was corrected by Pliny (4. 110), but all classical estimates as to length were excessive. The chief highway (Via Augusta) crossed the mountains near their eastern limit. It was supplemented by a road from Jaca to Pau (*Itin. Ant.* 452. 6), and another from Pamplona to Dax (ibid. 453. 4). Timber, hams, and bacon appear to have been the important contributions of the Pyrenees to the economic life of the peninsula.

Classical references in *PW*, s.v. 'Hispania'. Excellent modern description in M. Sorre, *Les Pyrénées* (1922).     J. J. VAN N.

**PYRGI,** modern *Santa Severa*, was a port of Caere (q.v.) and famous as the site of a wealthy Etruscan sanctuary of Leucothea or Eileithyia (qq.v.), sacked by Dionysius I (q.v.) in 384 B.C. (Diod. Sic. 15. 14). Recent excavations have revealed two Archaic temples: *A* (*c.* 480–470) is typically Tuscan, and *B* (*c.* 500) is a Graeco-Tuscan compromise. Both were destroyed in the third century B.C. Between the two temples were found in 1964 three sheets of gold leaf, one inscribed in Phoenician and the other two (one corresponds generally to the Punic text) in Etruscan. The inscriptions concern a dedication by the 'king' of Caere to the Phoenician goddess Astarte, corresponding to the Etruscan goddess Uni, and demonstrate the close ties that enabled Carthage to influence the internal politics of the cities of Etruria at this time (cf. Arist. *Pol.* 1280ª38 ff.; Polyb. 3. 22. 4–13). A fourth (perhaps earlier) inscription on bronze also concerns Uni. The establishment of a Roman military colony at Pyrgi in the third century B.C. reflects the same naval strategy that prompted the near-contemporary foundations of Castrum Novum (modern *Santa Marinella* nearby), Cosa, and Paestum (qq.v.).

Preliminary reports, etc., first nine seasons: M. Pallottino, G. Colonna *et alii, Arch. Class.* ix–xviii (1957–66); first definitive report: *Not. Scav.* (1959), 143 ff. Inscriptions: M. Pallottino, L. Vlad Borelli, G. Garbini, *Arch. Class.* xvi (1964), 58 ff.; bibliography 1964–6: ibid. xviii (1966), 279 ff.; J. Heurgon, *JRS* (1966), 1 ff.; W. Fischer and H. Rix, *Gött. Anz.* 1968, 64 ff.     D. W. R. R.

**PYRRHON** (*PW* 1) (*c.* 365–360 to *c.* 275–270 B.C.), son of Pleistarchus, of Elis, the founder of Greek scepticism. A painter turned philosopher, he was, according to the sources, first taught by Bryson, son of Stilpo (but chronological considerations make this unlikely), then by the Democritean Anaxarchus, whom he followed to India in the train of Alexander the Great. There he is reputed to have encountered some 'magi', to whose influence tradition ascribes some of his later philosophical views. Returning to his native town, he lived a quiet and modest life, following the precepts of his own philosophy, and was highly respected by his fellow citizens, who elected him their high priest. His chief pupils were Timon (2), Philo (3) of Athens, and Nausiphanes of Teios (qq.v.).

Pyrrhon left no writings, and only a few fragments of his immediate pupils survive. It is difficult to determine how much of the more developed philosophy of the later sceptics derives directly from him. This is made more complicated by the problem of the relations between the Pyrrhonian sceptics and the 'New' Academy of Arcesilaus (q.v. 1) and his followers and successors. It is nowadays believed that, whereas the scepticism of the Academy was metaphysical and polemic (against the Stoics and Epicureans), Pyrrhonian scepticism was essentially an attitude to life, the final aim of it being not so much the theoretical ἐποχή as the more practical ἀταραξία. Using examples from the deceptions inherent in sense perception and from the contradictions found in the teachings of 'dogmatic' philosophers, the Pyrrhonian concludes that no positive knowledge is possible, and his attitude is that of withholding his judgement (ἐποχή) about all things, stating nothing positive (οὐδὲν ὁρίζω), and following in actual life the appearances of things (φαινόμενα), without being committed to any permanent and definite attitude

towards them. This leads the sceptic to the state of imperturbability (ἀταραξία), his final goal in life.

Later sceptics (Agrippa (5), Aenesidemus, qq.v.) produced lists of arguments of general types against the possibility of positive knowledge (the sceptical τρόποι), for refuting the doctrines of the various 'dogmatic' schools. Some of them, in a crude form, may have originated with Pyrrhon himself. But there is no way of deciding on this from our fragmentary evidence. The tendency nowadays to derive some of Pyrrhon's teachings from Democritus (through Anaxarchus), Socrates and the Socratics, and some of the Sophists is based mainly on speculation.

SOURCES: Diog. Laert. ix. 61–108; Eusebius, *Praep. Evang.* xiv. 8; Wilamowitz, *Antigonos von Karystos* (1881), 27 ff.
MODERN DISCUSSIONS: V. Brochard, *Les Scepticques grecs* (1887), 51 ff.; Zeller, *Phil. d. Gr.* iii. 1, 494 ff.; Überweg-Praechter, 461 ff., 140 f.; L. Robin, *Pyrrhon et le scepticisme grec* (1944), 2 ff.; P. Couissin, *Rev. Ét. Grec.* 1929, 373 ff.     J. G.

**PYRRHUS** (319–272 B.C.), the most famous of the Molossian kings of Epirus. After reigning as a minor from 307 to 303 he was driven out and followed the fortunes of Demetrius the Besieger. By the influence of Ptolemy II, whose stepdaughter Antigone he married, and of Agathocles (q.v.), he became joint king with Neoptolemus (297) but soon removed him. Early in his reign he annexed and retained southern Illyria, probably as far as Epidamnus. He tried to emancipate Epirus from Macedonia. By intervening in a dynastic quarrel in Macedonia Pyrrhus obtained the frontier provinces of Parauaea and Tymphaea, together with Ambracia, Amphilochia, and Acarnania. On the death of Antigone he acquired Corcyra and Leucas as the dowry of his new wife, the daughter of Agathocles, and made an alliance with the Dardanian chief Bardylis, whose daughter he also married. Before he could consolidate his kingdom he went to war with Demetrius, now king of Macedon (291–286), obtaining half of Macedonia, Thessaly, and an alliance with Aetolia and Athens; but he was driven back by Lysimachus (283).

Pyrrhus next undertook to assist Tarentum against the Romans, and with a force of 25,000 men and twenty elephants he defeated the Romans at Heraclea (280). He marched close up to Rome, but failed to impose peace. In 279 he again defeated the Romans at Asculum, and then transferred his forces to Sicily, where he met the Carthaginians, at that time the allies of Rome. He almost expelled the Carthaginians from the island, but broke off the war and returned to Italy. After a drawn battle against the Romans at Beneventum (275), he retired to Epirus with one-third of his expeditionary force. In a new attempt to conquer Macedonia he penned up Antigonus Gonatas in Thessalonica but suddenly moved off to Peloponnesus, where he failed in a siege of Sparta and was killed in a street fight at Argos.

A brilliant tactician and adroit opportunist, Pyrrhus impressed his contemporaries but never won a lasting victory except in creating the large and powerful Epirote State. He made Ambracia his capital, built the great theatre at Dodona, and completed the hellenization of Epirus.

Plutarch, *Pyrrhus.* G. Nenci, *Pirro* (1953); P. Lévêque, *Pyrrhos* (1957); Hammond, *Epirus.*     N. G. L. H.

**PYTHAGORAS** (1), son of Mnesarchus of Samos, emigrated *c.* 531 B.C., perhaps to escape the tyranny of Polycrates, to Croton. He was a devotee of Apollo, and the Crotoniates identified him with Apollo Hyperboreus. He wrote probably nothing (though works were later fathered on him) and already in Aristotle's day his life was obscured by legend; but an elegy of Xenophanes (fr. 7 Diels) establishes his belief in metempsychosis, and

Heraclitus (frs. 40, 129), Empedocles (fr. 129), Ion of Chios (fr. 4 Diels), and Herodotus (4. 95) testify to his learning and his claim to reach back in memory to former existences. These and later statements indicate that he believed the soul to be a fallen divinity confined within the body as a tomb and condemned to a cycle of reincarnation as man, animal, or plant, from which, however, it may win release by cultivation of an Apolline purity. The spirit, he held, is purified especially by study; accordingly he taught a 'way of life' (Pl. *Resp.* 600 b), in which the investigation of nature (*ἱστορίη* Heraclitus fr. 129) became a religion. He is reliably said to have discovered the numerical ratios determining the principal intervals of the musical scale, whence he was led to interpret the world as a whole through numbers, the systematic study of which he thus originated (Aristox. fr. 23 Wehrli; Eudem. fr. 142 Wehrli). He is possibly the discoverer (though not in its Euclidean form) of 'Pythagoras' Theorem' (Euc. 1. 47).

In Croton Pythagoras founded a religious society, under the government of which this city rose to supremacy among the Achaean towns in Italy. A conspiracy under Cylon led, however, to Pythagoras' retirement to Metapontum, where he died; and at some date between 460 and 400 the order was almost wholly destroyed. Survivors settled in Thebes (Lysis, Philolaus) and Phleius, some afterwards returning to Tarentum, which became the chief seat of the school till its extinction in the late fourth century B.C. Membership of the order, open to women equally with men, entailed a strict discipline of purity, elements in which were silence, self-examination (*πῇ παρέβην, τί δ' ἔρεξα, τί μοι δέον οὐκ ἐτελέσθη*; Diog. Laert. 8. 22), abstention from flesh, and the observation of precepts originally later interpreted symbolically (*ἀκούσματα, σύμβολα*) and augmented by explicit ethical principles. Fourth-century writers distinguish divergent religious and scientific groups, *ἀκουσματικοί* (*Πυθαγορισταί*) and *μαθηματικοί* (*Πυθαγόρειοι*).

Starting from Pythagoras' discovery of the mathematical basis of the musical intervals, his followers devoted themselves to arithmetic, using a notation consisting probably of patterns of dots; the most important of these was the *τετρακτύς*, which represented the number ten as sum of the first four integers and was traditionally attributed to Pythagoras himself. Pythagorean cosmology was a development of that of the Milesians, which, however, it radically altered by degrading the Infinite from its position as source of the opposites and treating the pair Limit–Unlimited as the primary members of a group of ten pairs, which they regarded as first principles, the Unlimited being inferior in value to the Limit (Arist. *Metaph. A.* 986ª15 f.). They said the universe was produced by the First Unit (the Heaven) inhaling the Infinite (or Void), so as to form groups of units or numbers (Arist. *Metaph. N.* 1091ª15 f., *Phys.* 213ᵇ22 f.), and that all things (even, e.g., opinion, opportunity, injustice, Arist. *Metaph. A.* 990ª22) were numbers and had cosmic position. Probably by about 500 B.C. they had reached the hypothesis that the earth is spherical. Aristotle also attributes to them (*Cael.* 293ª18 f.) an astronomical system presupposing a central fire, around which circle the celestial bodies, including sun, earth (which thus first becomes a planet), and counter-earth (*ἀντίχθων*, intended to account for lunar eclipses). This system, to which the older belief in a 'harmony of the spheres' was accommodated, appears to date at earliest from the late fifth century. *See also* ASTRONOMY, MATHEMATICS.

For Pythagorean writers of independent importance (PHILOLAUS, ARCHYTAS, etc.) and for NEOPYTHAGOREANISM *see* separate articles.

Diels, *Vorsokr.*¹¹ i. 96–113, 440–80; M. T. Cardini, *I Pitagorici* (1958– ); Mullach, *FPG* i. 485–509 (*Pythagoreorum Similitudines*);

R. Hercher, *Epistolographi*, 601 (*Pythagoreorum Epistulae*); Burnet, *EGP* 80 ff., 276 ff.; Heath, *Hist. of Greek Maths.* i. 65 ff., 141 ff.; E. Frank, *Plato und die sogenannten Pythagoreer* (1923); Zeller-Mondolfo, *La filosofia dei Greci* I. ii (1938), 288 ff.; Guthrie, *Hist. Gk. Phil.* i. 146 ff.; K. von Fritz, *Pythagorean Politics in Southern Italy* (1940). A. H. C.

**PYTHAGORAS** (2), Greek sculptor, active *c.* 490–448 B.C. A native of Samos and later resident at Rhegium in Italy, whither he probably emigrated on the fall of Samos in 494 B.C. He is said to have combined a certain advance in naturalism (Pliny 34. 59) with an interest in symmetry and rhythm (Diog. Laert. 8. 46). Several statues by him are cited by Pliny (34. 59) and Pausanias (6. 13. 1), among them an 'Apollo shooting the serpent Python with his arrows'. As this subject is represented on a coin of Croton of *c.* 420–390 B.C., it has been thought that there was some connexion between the two. It has, however, not so far been possible to attribute any extant sculptures to Pythagoras with confidence. G. M. A. R.

**PYTHEAS** (*c.* 310–306 B.C.), Greek navigator of Massalia. From Strabo, Diodorus, and Pliny mostly we learn (upon evidence distrusted by the ancients) that, sailing from Gades (*Cadiz*) past Cape Ortegal, the Loire, northwest France, and Uxisame (*Ushant*), he visited Belerium (*Cornwall*) and the tin-depot at Ictis (q.v.; *St. Michael's Mount*), circumnavigated Britain, described its inhabitants and climate, reported an island Thule (q.v.) (*Norway* or *Iceland*), sailed perhaps to the Vistula, and reported an estuary (*Frisian Bight*?) and an island (*Heligoland*?) abounding in amber. Pytheas calculated closely the latitude of Massalia and laid bases for cartographic parallels through north France and Britain.

Cf. Cary–Warmington, *Explorers*, 33 ff.; (1963, Pelican) 47 ff.; E. Warmington, *Greek Geog.* (1934), 169 ff.; G. E. Broche, *Pythéas le Massaliote* (1936), to be used with caution; H. J. Mette, *Pytheas von Massalia* (1952); J. Casariego, *Los grandes Periplos* (1949), 104 ff.; D. Stichtenoth, *P. ueber das Weltmeer* (1959, 128 pp., one map) and also in *Altertum* 1961, 156 ff.; F. Gisinger, *PW* xlvii 1963, 314 ff.; Thomson, *Hist. Anc. Geog.* 143 ff.; Hyde, *Greek Mariners*, 124 ff.; D. R. Dicks, *The Geographical Fragments of Hipparchus* (1960), 179 ff.; V. Stefansson, *Ultima Thule* (1942) and *Greenland* (1943), to be used with caution; M. Ninck, *Die Entdeckung von Europa durch die Griechen* (1945), 218 ff. Cf. also J. J. Tierney, *JHS* 1959, 132 ff.; E. Davin in *Bull. de l'Assoc. G. Budé* 1954, 2; 60 ff. E. H. W.

**PYTHERMUS** (1), poet, of Teos, wrote drinking-songs, of which one line survives. He composed in the Ionian mode and was mentioned by Hipponax (Ath. 625 c).

Page, *Poet. Mel. Gr.* 910.

**PYTHERMUS** (2) of Ephesus, writing after Antiochus I or II and followed by Hegesandrus (*c.* 150 B.C.), published *Ἱστορίαι* in eight books, treating Hellenistic history.

*FGrH* ii. 80.

**PYTHIAN GAMES.** From early times there had been a festival at Delphi in connexion with the oracle of Apollo, with a musical competition consisting of a hymn to the god—*νόμος Πυθικός*—sung to a cithara accompaniment. This took place every eighth year, but in 582 B.C. the festival was reorganized and placed under the management of the Amphictionic Council. Henceforth it was celebrated in the third year of each Olympiad. The musical competitions—in instrumental music, singing, drama, and recitations in verse and prose—still took the first place, but to them now were added athletic and equestrian contests modelled on those at Olympia. The stadium for the foot-races lay close under Mount Parnassus, the chariot-races were held in the Crisaean plain, where a hippodrome was constructed. The prize was a crown of bay-leaves cut in the valley of Tempe.

The Pythian Games ranked next in importance after the Olympian. F. A. W.

**PYTHIUS** of Priene (4th c. B.C.), architect. He designed the Mausoleum (q.v.) at Halicarnassus and the temple of Athena Polias at Priene, both in the Ionic Order. He held the opinion that architects should be well versed in the arts, and objected to the use of the Doric order in sacred buildings because of the complications arising from the spacing of the triglyphs. His books on the temple and the Mausoleum have not survived. (Vitr. 1. 1; 4. 3; 7, *praef.*; Pliny, *HN* 36. 30–1. It should be noted that the spelling of the name in the MSS. is very confused. One cannot be quite sure that the architect of the Mausoleum and the architect of Priene are one and the same man.) H. W. R.; R. E. W.

**PYTHON** of Catana or Byzantium was said to be author of a satyric play called *Agen*, produced in 324 B.C. in the camp of Alexander the Great on the Hydaspes (in the Punjab); some attributed it to Alexander himself (Ath. 13. 595 d). It contained references to Harpalus, who had recently absconded with Alexander's treasure, and other contemporary persons in the style of the Old Comedy.

*TGF* 810–11. B. Snell, *Scenes from Greek Drama* (1964), chs. v, vi. A. W. P.-C.; D. W. L.

# Q

**QUADI,** a German tribe of the Suebic group, left the Main region (*c.* 8 B.C.) and went to Moravia; they were closely connected with the Marcomanni. Vannius established a kingdom between the March and the Waag, but was overthrown *c.* A.D. 50, his followers being settled by the Romans in Pannonia. After a war against Domitian the Quadi maintained peace till the great Marcomannic Wars. Though overwhelmed by Rome, they remained a permanent danger, and often with Marcomanni or Sarmatae-Jazyges plundered Roman land (e.g. under Valerian and Gallienus and in 282, 358, and 375). Later some of the Quadi joined the Vandals and Alani and went to Spain.

C. Patsch, *Sitz. Wien*, 209 v (1929) and 217 i (1937); L. Schmidt, *Geschichte der deutschen Stämme. Die Westgermanen*² (1938); J. Klose, *Roms Klientel-Randstaaten am Rhein und an der Donau* (1934). F. A. W. S.

**QUADRATUS** (1) **BASSUS,** C. IULIUS, *cos. suff.* A.D. 105, of Pergamum, a *comes* of Trajan. He was praetor (82), served in the Dacian war (86–9), governor of Judaea (*c.* 90–2), *cos. suff.* (105), served as Trajan's *comes* in the second Dacian War, receiving *ornamenta triumphalia*, governor of Cappadocia (*c.* 107–12), of Syria (*c.* 113–17), of Dacia (117/18). He received a public funeral at Pergamum. He is probably to be distinguished from (*a*) C. Antius A. Iulius Quadratus (*cos. suff.* 94, governor of Syria 101–4, *cos. II ord.* 105) and from (*b*) C. Iulius Bassus, the proconsul of Bithynia (101–2) whom Pliny defended on an extortion charge in 103.

*AE* 1933, 268. R. Syme, *JRS* 1946, 162 ff.; id. *Tacitus*, see index. H. H. S.

**QUADRATUS** (2), ASINIUS (*PW* 31), a senator of the Severan age, wrote in Ionic Greek a History of Rome in fifteen books, from the foundation until Severus Alexander, called Χιλιετηρίς, and also Parthica in at least nine books. Possibly of Greek origin, he may be identified with C. Asinius Protimus Quadratus, *cos. suff.* and proconsul of Achaea.

*FGrH* 97; G. Babieri, *L'Albo senatorio* (1952), n. 59. H. H. S.

**QUAESTIONES.** In the earliest Roman law alleged crimes against the State, if too serious for summary action by a magistrate (or on appeal against such action by *provocatio*, q.v.), were tried before the Assembly; though for lower-class citizens, this right was, perhaps, largely theoretical. Crimes against private persons were tried by a magistrate (later normally the praetor) with a *consilium*, under the civil procedure of *sacramentum* (q.v.). Public crimes particularly grave, or needing specially careful investigation, were often turned over to a *quaestio*: an *ad hoc* commission under a magistrate, appointed by the Senate or the People or both (see e.g. Livy 9. 26. 2: 314 B.C.); the Bacchanalia (q.v.) (Livy 39. 14 f.: 186 B.C.); the Silva Sala murders (Cic. *Brut.* 85 f.: 138 B.C.); or the corruption of L. Hostilius Tubulus (Cic. *Fin.* 2. 54). It has been suggested (but not proved) that *sicarii* and *venefici* (armed men and poisoners) were regularly subject to trial by an *ad hoc quaestio* under the praetor or a deputy.

The system was changed by the introduction (by Piso, q.v. 1, in 149 B.C.) of a standing commission (*quaestio perpetua*) of the Senate on *repetundae* (q.v.). At first acting like a civil court, it was converted into a criminal court by C. Gracchus (q.v. 4), who added to it features borrowed from the special *quaestiones*; jurors were drawn from the wealthiest non-senators (*see* EQUITES). In the next forty years, while *ad hoc* commissions on special occasions continued (*see* MAMILIUS 3), several *quaestiones perpetuae* modelled on the *repetundae* court were set up for individual crimes of frequent occurrence: certainly *veneficia* and *maiestas*, probably *ambitus* and *peculatus*. Procedure (including the composition of the juries) probably in general followed the *repetundae* court, with minor individual differences such as we still find later. The composition of the juries was changed by Caepio (q.v. 1), who introduced mixed juries of senators and *equites*; Glaucia (q.v.) restored 'equestrian' juries for *repetundae* and this was certainly followed by the *maiestas* court, possibly by others. After an abortive reform by Drusus, (q.v. 2), Plautius (q.v. 1) introduced juries chosen freely by the individual tribes (which favoured nobles and senators), and Sulla, increasing the Senate to 600, entrusted all the *quaestiones* to senators. He also brought the number of standing courts up to at least seven, possibly more, with a praetor—or, since there were not enough praetors available, a *iudex quaestionis*, normally aedilician —in charge of each. L. Cotta (q.v. 3) in 70, when Sulla's juries had turned out to be clearly unsatisfactory, created three jury panels (*decuriae*) of 300 each, allotting one to senators, one to *equites*, and one to *tribuni aerarii* (q.v.). From these, juries for individual cases (one-third from each *decuria*) were chosen—as probably already since Sulla—by lot (*sortitio*), with prosecution and defence having a limited right of *reiectio*. The size of a jury varied from one *quaestio* to another. The more important (*repetundae* and *maiestas*) perhaps had juries of 75, the less important (like *inter sicarios*) only of 51. Other details of procedure could also vary; thus some allowed *ampliatio* (q.v.), others (like *repetundae*) prescribed *comperendinatio* (a trial in two parts).

There was no public prosecutor at Rome, nor were prosecutions initiated by the magistrate in charge of each *quaestio.* Any private citizen could request authority from such a magistrate to prosecute before his court. If several men wished to bring the same accusation against a person, the magistrate determined in a special *iudicium*, attended by a *consilium* of jurors not on oath, who should be the accuser (though others might then sign the indictment as *subscriptores*); this preliminary inquiry was known as *divinatio*. (Thus Cicero's *Divinatio in Caecilium* sought to show why Cicero rather than Q. Caecilius Niger should be chosen as Verres' accuser.) The authorized accuser then presented the indictment in writing (*nomen deferre*) to the magistrate who entered the charge in the official record (*nomen recipere*), interrogated the accused, and (unless the latter pleaded guilty) fixed the date of hearing. The court for judging each case was constituted from an *album* based on the *decuriae reiectio* with the co-operation of both parties, accuser and accused, who both had a limited right of challenging the composition of the jury. At the end of the trial the jury gave its verdict by a majority vote. The presiding magistrate did not vote, but pronounced judgement and sentence, against which there was no appeal. Where the charge was capital, the condemned man was permitted to go into exile (*see* EXSILIUM). Magistrates and men absent *reipublica causa* could not be prosecuted before a *quaestio*.

After 70, though numerous laws were passed on individual courts (notably *ambitus*, which proved uncontrollable), the system remained basically unchanged. Caesar temporarily suppressed the last *decuria*, Augustus added a fourth (of lower census, for less serious offences), Gaius (1) a fifth—perhaps because by that time senators had practically ceased attending. Special *quaestiones* on the old model continued throughout the Republic: e.g. that on the Bona Dea affair (*see* CLODIUS 1) or that on Caesar's assassins (*see* PEDIUS 1); their juries were normally chosen according to the prevailing system; but some were specially constituted, in attempts to exclude fear and corruption (e.g. those of Pompey in 52).

Augustus reorganized some of the courts and added one on adultery. He also used the *decuriae* for a reform of voting (q.v.) in elections (*see* DESTINATIO). He clearly intended the system to continue; and in fact it remained in use under the early Empire and, to some extent, until the third century A.D. But with the development of imperial and senatorial jurisdiction in important cases (which also made our sources lose interest in the *quaestiones*) and the jurisdiction of the *praefectus urbi* and the *praefectus praetorio* (qq.v.) over the lower classes, the *quaestiones* soon became unimportant and we have little evidence on their working.

Mommsen, *Röm. Strafr.*; W. Kunkel, *Unters. z. Entwicklung d. röm. Kriminalverfahrens in vorsullanischer Zeit* (1962); *see also* REPETUNDAE; LAW AND PROCEDURE, ROMAN. E. B.

**QUAESTOR.** *Quaestores parricidii* are said to have been appointed by the kings. Under the Republic there were two, who prosecuted some capital cases before the People. They fade from our record by the second century B.C.

Financial quaestors (perhaps not connected with them) were at first appointed by the consuls, one by each; after 447 B.C. (Tac. *Ann.* 11. 22) they were elected by the tribal assembly. Two were added when plebeians were admitted (421), to administer the *aerarium* in Rome (hence *urbani*) under the Senate's direction. Four more were instituted in 267 (Tac. loc. cit.; Livy, *Per.* 15), perhaps called *classici* and stationed in various Italian towns, notably Ostia (*see* ANNONA). More (we do not know how many and when) were added as various provinces were organized (Sicily even had two), until Sulla, finding nineteen needed for all these duties, added one for the water-supply and fixed the total at twenty. Caesar doubled this number, but Augustus—proposing to rely less on regular magistrates—returned to it.

The quaestorship was commonly held at the age of 27 to 30 (often—in the late Republic normally—after a military tribunate and/or a civil minor magistracy). It was the lowest of the regular magistracies. By the late second century B.C., ex-quaestors were regularly enrolled in the Senate by the next censors. Sulla made the office compulsory in the *cursus honorum*, fixed 30 as the minimum age, and made entry to the Senate automatic. *Provinciae* of quaestors were normally allotted, but—in a tradition going back to the origins of the office—magistrates could choose a quaestor *extra sortem* for personal reasons. If attached to magistrates or pro-magistrates, quaestors were expected to serve (if necessary *pro quaestore*) until their commander gave up office; and they remained morally bound to him as clients for life. In addition to managing the commander's *fiscus* they had responsible duties (cf. Cic. 2 *Verr.* 1. 40), often commanded military forces, and might have to assume supreme command (*pro praetore*) in their superior's absence.

Augustus and—after a brief restoration by Claudius—Nero removed the quaestors from the Aerarium; but under the Empire the Princeps, as well as each consul, had two quaestors; the *quaestores Caesaris*, chosen by the Emperor himself, were often patricians and always young men of distinction. The actual duties of the quaestors in Italy were gradually taken over by imperial officials, but in the senatorial provinces quaestors retained some financial functions throughout the Principate.

Colonies and *municipia*, and normally *collegia* (q.v.), also had quaestors in charge of their finances.

K. Latte, *TAPA* 1936, 24 ff. (origin). E. B.

**QUEROLUS**, the 'Grumbler', anonymous comedy, also called *Aulularia* because of some resemblance to Plautus' *Aulularia*. It was written in Gaul probably *c.* A.D. 400. Rutilius, to whom it is dedicated, seems to be Rutilius Namatianus (q.v.). Evidence suggesting a later date is flimsy. The play teems with verbal echoes from Plautus and Terence, and their metrical technique is closely followed in the iambic hemistich which, after an initial iambic or trochaic cadence, completes each line.

Ed. G. Ranstrand, Göteborg, 1951. See S. Cavallin, *Eranos* 1951, 137 ff. O. S.

**QUINCTIUS (***PW* 24) **CAPITOLINUS BARBATUS**, TITUS, was consul in 471, 468, 465, 446, 443, and 439 B.C. His main recorded achievement was in 464, when (allegedly as proconsul appointed by a *senatus consultum ultimum*, which is historically nonsense, and makes Livy's source later than and dependent on the events of 121 B.C.), he extricated the consul Furius from a trap set by the Aequi. This bears so close a resemblance to the exploits of Cincinnatus (q.v.), as to suggest that it is a doublet of them.

Ogilvie, *Comm. Livy 1–5*, 398 ff., 516 ff. P. T.

**QUINDECIMVIRI** (originally **Duoviri**, then **Decemviri**, Livy 6. 37. 12, first mentioned as **Quindecimviri** in 51 B.C., Caelius in Cicero, *Fam.* 8. 4. 1) **SACRIS FACIUNDIS**, one of the *quattuor amplissima collegia* of the Roman clergy. They were originally custodians of the Sibylline books (Livy 5. 13. 5–6 and often), but their activities were probably widened to cover the supervision of all foreign cults recognized or tolerated in Rome (Wissowa, *RK* 543) on the authority of these books. They were of course originally patricians, but after 367 B.C., when their number was raised to ten, half of them were chosen from the *plebs*. The method was election, probably as for the *pontifices* (q.v.; Cicero loc. cit.). Caesar increased them to sixteen (Dio Cassius

42. 51. 4), and supernumeraries were common under the Empire (cf. ibid. 51. 20. 3).

Latte, *RR* 397. H. J. R.

**QUINQUEREME.** The standard warship in the fleets of the Hellenistic States and of the Roman Republic was the quinquereme (πεντήρης), a galley accommodating more rowers than the smaller but similar trireme (q.v.) and gaining thus greater force. The crew on a Roman quinquereme numbered 300, in addition to the marines (Polyb. 1. 26. 7). The arrangement of rowers on a quinquereme is even more uncertain than that on a trireme; probably groups of five oarsmen pulled one large oar in the fashion of the medieval Venetian galleys *a scaloccio*. Since the quinquereme did not appear at Athens until 325 B.C., the report that Dionysius of Syracuse introduced the craft is doubtful; possibly it was Phoenician in origin. Expensive to maintain and difficult to man, this vessel lost its supremacy in the first century B.C. but it still found use in the Roman imperial navy. *See* TRIREME.

C. G. S.

**QUINTILIANUS,** MARCUS FABIUS, born *c.* A.D. 30–5 at Calagurris (modern *Calahorra*) in Spain (Auson. *Prof. Burd.* 1. 7). Possibly his father was a rhetor (cf. *Inst.* 9. 3. 73), but his identity with the Quintilianus named by Seneca (*Contr.* 10. *pr.* 2) is pure conjecture. His early education may have been wholly in Rome, though this is disputable, nor is it certain that Remmius Palaemon taught him as is stated by the scholiast on Juvenal 6. 452. As a young man in Rome he attached himself to the orator Domitius Afer, who died in 59 (*Inst.* 5. 7. 7; 10. 1. 86, 118; 12. 11. 3; Pliny, *Epp.* 2. 14. 10). At some period he returned to Spain (possibly he was in Rome in 57 when Cossutianus Capito stood trial, but the reference in *Inst.* 6. 1. 14 does not prove this); Galba brought him back in 68 (Hieron. *Chron.*). He became a famous teacher (cf. Mart. 2. 90): probably he was the first rhetorician to receive a salary from the *fiscus* (under Vespasian, Suet. *Vesp.* 18; the year 88 assigned for this in Hieron. *Chron.* is plainly wrong), and he acquired unusual wealth for one of his profession (Juvenal 7. 186 ff.). He taught, and practised advocacy, for twenty years (*Inst.* 1. *pr.* 1); the Younger Pliny was among his pupils (*Epp.* loc. cit.): he retired with unimpaired powers (cf. *Inst.* 2. 12. 12), presumably in 88, in order to write what would be useful to 'bonae mentis iuuenes'. Domitian made him tutor to his two great-nephews and heirs (*Inst.* 4. *pr.* 2), the sons of Flavius Clemens (q.v.), through whom he gained the *ornamenta consularia* (Auson. *Grat. Act.* 7. 31); it has been hazarded that this brought him into contact with Christianity (Colson, *CR* 1925, 166 ff.). Before retirement he married. His wife died while not yet 19, leaving two little sons; the younger child died aged 5, the elder aged 9, and his overwhelming grief is clear from the preface to *Inst.* 6. The date of his own death is not known; it cannot be inferred from Pliny (*Epp.* loc. cit.) that he died before A.D. 100.

WORKS

(1) *De causis corruptae eloquentiae*, not extant: see *Inst.* 6. *pr.* 3, 8. 6. 76, and cf. 2. 4. 42, 5. 12. 23, 8. 3. 58. It was begun about the time of his younger son's death (6. *pr.* 3; see Colson, introduction to book 1, xix).

(2) A (lost) speech *pro Naeuio Arpiniano*: see *Inst.* 7. 2. 24, where its publication is acknowledged as authentic, in contrast to other speeches circulating under his name. He defended the Jewish Queen Berenice (4. 1. 19), and a woman accused of forging her husband's will (9. 2. 73): these might be the subjects of the unauthorized publications, but there is no proof of the fact.

(3) 'Duo libri artis rhetoricae' (1. *pr.* 7; cf. 3. 6. 68),

unsanctioned publications from lecture-notes, transcribed in faulty shorthand.

(4) *Institutio Oratoria*, written and probably published before Domitian's death in 96 (cf. 10. 1. 91, 3. 7. 4), dedicated to Vitorius Marcellus (1. *pr.* 6, 12. 11. 31; cf. Stat. *Silv.* 4. 4); its composition occupied 'paulo plus quam biennium', after which it was put aside for some time (*Ep. ad Tryphonem*, prefixed to the treatise). It covers the training of an orator from babyhood to the grown man, 'uir bonus dicendi peritus' (12. 1. 1), an ideal that Quintilian had hoped to see realized in his own son (6. *pr.* 1). Book 1 discusses childhood education—practical, humane, fascinating, still of significance. In book 2 the boy enters the school of rhetoric, and here too Quintilian's personality and method are arrestingly clear: note the memorable chapter on the Good Schoolmaster (2. 2. 4 'sumat ante omnia parentis erga discipulos suos animum'). The book continues with an examination of the nature and uses of *rhetoricē*, followed in book 3 by an account of its origin, its parts, and its functions, with a discussion of *status*. Books 4–6 deal with the detailed structure of a speech (valuable in reading Cicero). Book 7 is concerned with arrangement (*dispositio*) and *status*-lore. Book 8 discusses style, under heads such as propriety, ornament, tropes, while in book 9 figures of thought and speech are illustrated, with a chapter on artistic structure and rhythm. Quintilian is conscious that much of this is hard going, but he remembers always that he is dealing with human nature (6. 3, 'de risu', is entertaining and significant), and in all these minutiae his one ultimate aim is to equip the *uir bonus* with the tools needed for successful pleading. Book 10 opens with a critique of Greek and Latin writers, solely from the rhetorical standpoint (this explains what to us seem some strange judgements and unexpected omissions): Quintilian is at pains to show how Latin can stand up to Greek, and many of his dicta are classics of ancient criticism (e.g. on Menander, Thucydides, Sallust, Livy, Ovid, Lucan). The remaining chapters deal with *imitatio* and practical details of composition. Book 11 discusses memory, delivery, gesture, and dress: here the physical side of ancient oratory is fascinatingly illustrated (some of these rules for delivery appear still current in the *Chironomia* and *Chirologia* of John Bulwer, published 1644—see plates in B. L. Joseph, *Elizabethan Acting*[2], 1964). The concluding book shows the Complete Orator in action, a man of highest character and ideals, the consummation of all that is best in morals, training, and stylistic discernment: Roman *grauitas* at its noblest, and a final exposition of oratory as a moral force (cf. M. Winterbottom, *JRS* 1964, 90 ff.).

Quintilian's style is silver-age Ciceronian, vigorous, expansive, often pointed, but sometimes lacking in finish and rather lumbering—practical rather than elegant. The treatise profoundly influenced medieval and Renaissance writers, notably Erasmus and Vives; Ben Jonson drew on it in his *Discoveries*, and Pope admired it (see Colson's introduction to book 1, and P. Lehmann, *Philol.* 1934, 349 ff.).

*See also* LITERARY CRITICISM IN ANTIQUITY, § 9; RHETORIC, LATIN, § 4.

(5) *Declamations. See* DECLAMATIONES PSEUDO-QUINTILIANEAE.

TEXTS. C. Halm (Leipzig, 1868–9); F. Meister (Leipzig-Prague, 1886–7); L. Radermacher (Leipzig, 1907–35, repr. 1959 with additions by V. Buchheit); M. Niedermann (Neuchâtel, 1947), containing the grammatical chapters, 1. 4–8.
COMMENTARIES. G. L. Spalding (Leipzig, 1798–1816, completed by P. Buttmann after Spalding's death in 1811): C. T. Zumpt added a supplementary volume (1829), and E. Bonnell's *Lexicon Quintilianeum* made a sixth volume (1834; repr. Hildesheim, 1963). *Bk.* 1: C. Fierville (Paris, 1890), F. H. Colson (1924), V. d'Agostino (Turin, 1933). *Bk.* 3: J. Adamietz (Munich, 1966). *Bk.* 10: H. S. Frieze (U.S.A. 1865 and 1888), also containing bk. 12; J. E. B. Mayor (1870), incomplete; J. A. Hild (Paris, 1885); W. Peterson (1891). *Bk.* 12: A. Beltrami (Rome–Milan, 1910); R. G. Austin (1948; repr.

with additions, 1954). *Selections*, from bks. 1, 2, 6, 8, 12, by D. M. Gaunt (1952).

TRANSLATIONS. W. Guthrie (1756); J. Patsall (1774); J. S. Watson (1856); H. E. Butler (Loeb, 1921–2); W. M. Smail (1938), containing parts of 1, 2, 12.

SOURCES. J. Cousin, *Études sur Quintilien* (1936), exhaustive and indispensable.

*See also* EDUCATION. R. G. A.

**QUINTUS** (1), anatomist and physician of the eclectic school in Rome, in the age of Hadrian (A.D. 117–38), and pupil of Marinus. He founded an important medical school, to which the teachers of Galen belonged. Later he was banished from Rome and died in Pergamum. He left no written works, but his anatomical teaching had great influence, e.g. on Galen. W. D. R.

**QUINTUS** (2) **SMYRNAEUS** (4th c. A.D.), epic poet, author of a Greek poem, the *Posthomerica*, found in Calabria, headed Ἡ ποίησις τοῦ Ὁμηρικοῦ Κοΐντου, on a manuscript containing also Colluthus, *Rape of Helen* (? 6th c. A.D.). Hence Quintus is sometimes called Calaber, but more often Smyrnaeus, from the single recorded fact about him, that in his youth he lived at Smyrna near the Hermus (Quint. Smyrn. 3. 306–13). The poem, continuing the story of the *Iliad* to the start of the Achaeans for home, shows thorough acquaintance with Homer, but some slight misunderstanding of Homeric Greek, and it may have been meant to form a substitute, in closer agreement with Homer, for the account of the events given in the Epic Cycle (q.v.). The sources are various, some Hellenistic, and one a poem of unknown identity much used by Virgil, possibly the poem indicated by Macrobius (*Sat.* 5. 2) under the name of Peisander. The poetry of Quintus is prolix, never exalted, and sometimes macabre; the parts are greater than the whole, which lacks structural unity; but it has some freedom, competence, eloquence in representing emotion, and pathos, and frequently the similes are attractive.

TEXTS. A. Zimmermann (1891); A. S. Way (Loeb, 1913).
CRITICISM. F. A. Paley, *On Quintus Smyrnaeus and the 'Homer' of the Tragic Poets* (1876); C. A. Sainte-Beuve, *Études sur Virgile* (1891); F. Kehmptzow, *De Quinti Smyrnaei fontibus ac mythopoeia* (1891); G. W. Paschal, *A Study of Quintus Smyrnaeus* (1904); W. F. J. Knight, *CQ* 1932, 178 ff. W. F. J. K.

**QUIRINAL,** the northernmost hill of Rome, traditionally occupied by Sabines, and certainly the site of an early settlement (*Mon. Ant.* 15. 776 ff.) which became one of the Four Regions of Republican Rome. On it were many famous temples, including the age-old *Capitolium vetus* and those of Semo Sancus (466 B.C.), Salus Semonia (311 B.C.), Quirinus (293 B.C.), Honos (*CIL* vi. 30915), Fortuna Publica (204 B.C.), and Venus Erycina (181 B.C.). Later, the hill was the site of houses of famous associations or luxury, as of Atticus, Narcissus, and Martial. Domitian built the *templum gentis Flaviae* on the site of his ancestral home. Constantine erected large *thermae*. The north fringe of the hill was bordered by cemeteries and by the *horti Sallustiani*. I. A. R.

E. Gjerstad, *Early Rome* iv (1966) 49 ff., 182 ff.

**QUIRINIUS,** PUBLIUS SULPICIUS (*PW* 90), *cos.* 12 B.C., a *novus homo* from Lanuvium (on his career cf. Tacitus, *Ann.* 3. 48). Quirinius defeated the Marmaridae (Florus 2. 31), perhaps as proconsul of Crete and Cyrene (? *c.* 15 B.C.). Between 12 B.C. and A.D. 2 he subjugated the Homanadenses, 'Cilician' brigands on the southern borderland of the province of Galatia (Strabo 569). The precise date of this war and the command held by Quirinius are disputed. It has been argued that he must have been legate of Syria at the time; but the war could have been conducted only from the side of Galatia, which province, though normally governed by imperial legates of praetorian rank, might easily have been placed under a consular (cf. L. Calpurnius Piso, *c.* 13 B.C., and M. Plautius Silvanus in A.D. 6). Quirinius prudently paid court to Tiberius at Rhodes, succeeded M. Lollius as guide and supervisor of C. Caesar in the East (A.D. 2), and shortly after married Aemilia Lepida, a descendant of Sulla and Pompey. Legate of Syria in A.D. 6, he superintended the assessment of Judaea when that territory was annexed after the death of Archelaus (Josephus, *AJ* 17. 1 ff., cf. *ILS* 2683; also Acts v. 37, which mentions the insurrection of Judas the Galilaean ἐν ταῖς ἡμέραις τῆς ἀπογραφῆς). In order to reconcile and explain St. Luke ii. 1 and establish a date for the Nativity before the death of Herod the Great (i.e. before 4 B.C.), various attempts have been made to discover an earlier governorship of Syria by Quirinius, and, by implication, an earlier census in Judaea. It is by no means certain that the acephalous elogium from Tibur (*ILS* 918) should be attributed to Quirinius, and, in any case, it cannot prove two governorships of Syria. It is best kept out of the problem.

Quirinius lived to a wealthy and unpopular old age. In 21 he died and was granted a public funeral on the motion of Tiberius, who recounted his meritorious services (Tac. *Ann.* 3. 48).

L. R. Taylor, *AJPhil.* 1933, 120 ff.; R. Syme, *Klio* 1934, 122 ff., and *Rom. Rev.*, see index; A. N. Sherwin-White, *Roman Society and Roman Law in the New Testament* (1963), 162 ff.; B. Levick, *Roman Colonies in Southern Asia Minor* (1967), 203 ff. R. S.

**QUIRINUS,** a god of Sabine origin (Ov. *Fasti* 2. 475 ff., whereon see Frazer), worshipped from very early times on the Quirinal. He appears to have been the local deity of the settlement there before the foundation of Rome. Except that his functions resembled those of Mars and that he had sacred arms (Festus, 238, 9 Lindsay), we know little of him; he regularly forms a third with Jupiter and Mars (qq.v.; e.g. Livy 8. 9. 6); his *ffamen* (q.v.) is the lowest of the three *flamines maiores* and the third *spolia opima* belong to him (Servius on *Aen.* 6. 859). His *flamen*'s activities are known only in the service of other deities (Gell. 7. 77. 7; Ov. *Fasti* 4. 910; Tert. *De Spect.* 5). His festival is on 17 Feb.; his cult-partner is Hora (Gell. 13. 23. 2), of whom nothing is known. The name must mean 'he of *quirium*'; as this is not a possible word for the labializing Sabine speech, the most plausible etymology is that of Kretschmer (*Glotta* 1921, 147 ff.), that it was originally *co-uiri-um*, 'assembly of the men', hence also *Quirites*.

Wissowa, *RK* 153 ff.; Latte, *RR* 113. Cf. ROMULUS. H. J. R.

# R

**RABIRIUS** (1, *PW* 5), GAIUS, an *eques* (later a back-bench senator), was prominent in the action against Saturninus (q.v. 1). Attacked by Populares once or twice before, he was accused of *perduellio* in 63 B.C. by Labienus, with the assistance of Caesar. The aim (as his counsel Cicero says in his extant speech) was probably a challenge to the received interpretation of the *'senatus consultum ultimum'*. Having achieved this, they preferred to leave the issue in suspense and Metellus (q.v. 9) Celer, as praetor, collusively terminated the trial by lowering the flag on the Janiculum—clearly the intended conclusion of the whole archaic procedure. The legal details of the case are obscure.

E. G. Hardy, *Some Problems in Roman History* (1924), 27 ff., 99 ff.
E. B.

**RABIRIUS** (2, *PW* 6) **POSTUMUS**, GAIUS, known unofficially as *Postumus Curtius*, was posthumous son of C. Curtius, adopted under the will of his uncle C. Rabirius (q.v. 1). A banker like his father, he placed loans throughout the Empire, until to recover vast sums from Ptolemy Auletes he took up residence at Alexandria, called himself the king's minister, and requisitioned Egyptian supplies. After the condemnation of Gabinius (q.v. 2) in 54 Rabirius was prosecuted as receiver, but Cicero's extant speech secured his acquittal, mainly on technicalities; the defence of fact was merely that Rabirius was now poor. Caesar assisted him, and by 49 he was a senator, Caesar's ardent partisan, and was employed in the East in 47 and then on commissariat work for the African War; by 45 he had designs on the consulate.

Cf. H. Dessau, *Hermes* 1911, 613 ff.
G. E. F. C.

**RABIRIUS** (3, *PW* 7), GAIUS, epic poet mentioned alongside of Virgil by Velleius (2. 36. 3). Ovid alludes to his 'mighty utterance' (*Pont*. 4. 16. 5). Quintilian (10. 1. 90) says that he deserves to be studied by those who have the time. Some have unjustifiably thought him to be the author of the poem on Actium of which a fragment was recovered in papyrus 817 from Herculaneum. *See* PAPYROLOGY, LATIN.

Morel, *FPL*.
J. W. D.; G. B. A. F.

**RAETIA**, a Roman province in the Alps, including Tyrol and parts of Bavaria and Switzerland. The Raeti were partly Illyrian, partly Celtic, their language having been affected by Etruscan elements (cf. J. Whatmough, *Harv. Stud*. 1937, 181 ff.). After the Camunni and Vennones had been defeated by P. Silius Nerva (16 B.C.) Drusus and Tiberius in a combined operation from the south and from Gaul conquered the Raeti and the Celtic Vindelici, whose territory became a province together with the Vallis Poenina; the latter was disconnected from Raetia after Claudius and before M. Aurelius. At first under the command of the governor of Gaul (who appointed a *praefectus* in A.D. 16–17 after Germanicus had been recalled from the Rhine), Raetia got its own governor, who according to the *communis opinio* was an equestrian procurator with *ius gladii* (Ph. Horovitz, *Rev. Phil.* 1939, 61 ff., tries to prove that until Trajan the governors of Raetia were *praefecti*, and then were replaced by equestrian *procuratores*). The governor, who resided at Augusta Vindelicorum, commanded the troops: 4 *alae* and 11 *cohortes* in A.D. 107 (*CIL* xvi. 55), and 3 *alae* and 13 *cohortes* in 166 (op. cit. 121). During the Marcomannic Wars under M. Aurelius the newly raised Legio III Italica Concors was quartered in Raetia at Castra Regina (q.v.), its commander becoming the provincial governor as a *legatus Aug. pro praetore*. During the Marcomannic Wars Raetia had suffered from barbarian invaders. At least since Gallienus Raetia was again placed under equestrian administration, and was divided under Diocletian for civil administration into Raetia I (capital probably Curia) and Raetia II (capital Augusta Vindelicorum), both provinces being under the military command of the *dux Raetiarum* who resided at Augusta Vindelicorum (on the frontier see R. Heuberger, *Klio* 1931, 348 ff.). Alamannic pressure increased and the Lake of Constance–Argen–Iller–Danube defence-line was given up soon after A.D. 389; the Alamanni occupied the relinquished territory, though temporarily forced back in 430. About 450 the Alamanni and other German tribes again mastered nearly the whole plain. Before 482 the last outposts on the Danube were evacuated and only the Alpine regions remained under control from Italy.

F. Stähelin, *Die Schweiz in römischer Zeit*[3] (1948); R. Heuberger, *Raetien im Altertum und Frühmittelalter* i (1932); id. 'Das ostgothische Raetien', *Klio* 1937, 77 ff.; F. Hertlein–O. Paret–P. Goessler, *Die Römer in Württemberg* i–iii (1928–32). On the *limes Raeticus* see Fabricius, *PW* xiii. 605 ff. On roads see W. Cartellieri, *Philol.*, Suppl. xviii (1926); L. Castelpietra, *Raetia* (1935), 33 ff. (via Claudia Augusta); H. U. Instinsky, *Klio* 1938, 33 ff. (Septimius Severus). Raetia in the Marcomannic Wars: W. Zwikker, *Studien zur Markussäule* i (1941), 76 f.
F. A. W. S.

**RATAE** (*Leicester*), a town of Roman Britain and *caput* of the Coritani (*Rav. Cosm.* 92; Ptolemy, *Geogr.* 2. 3. 20). There may have been a preliminary military phase of occupation under Claudius. Growing to 130 acres within its third-century walls, it possessed distinguished public buildings and was possibly raised to municipal rank in the later second century. The forum is perhaps Flavian; the public baths with exercise-hall (of which the surviving Jewry Wall is part) were built under Antoninus Pius; and at the end of the second century an additional market square with basilica was provided. The town has produced interesting mosaics and painted wall-plaster.

F. Haverfield, *Arch. Journ.* 1918, 1 ff.; G. A. Webster, ibid. 1958, 53, 84; K. M. Kenyon, *Excavations at the Jewry Wall Site, Leicester* (1948); *JRS* 1959, 113 ff.; 1964, 161.
S. S. F.

**RAVENNA**, city of Cispadane Gaul, now some 15 miles from the Adriatic coast, but nearer to the ancient coastline and almost surrounded by watercourses or marsh. Ravenna may be an Etruscan foundation: the name appears to be Etruscan, and an Etruscan inscription has been found in the city. But in historical times the inhabitants were Umbrian. Ravenna, a federate city of Rome in the last century of the Republic, attained Roman citizenship as a *municipium* in 49 B.C. Augustus decided to make it the base of the Adriatic fleet. Much rebuilding was carried out as a result, and a canal was built to carry the waters of a small branch of the Po through the city to the new harbour established at Classis, a suburb on the coast.

The city soon became a flourishing centre of seaborne trade with a cosmopolitan population; shipbuilding, linen manufacture and the export of fish, wine, and asparagus were its staples. The municipal constitution was abnormal, the real power probably lying with the imperial *praefectus classis*. Several prisoners of State, including Arminius' son and Maroboduus, were interned in Ravenna. The Christian community probably dates from the early third century.

In 404 Ravenna was selected as imperial residence by the Western Emperor Honorius because of its security. It continued to be used as a capital by Odoacer and by

Theodoric the Great, who launched an extensive building programme. After the Byzantine reconquest in 540, it became the residence of the Byzantine governor, the exarch of Italy, until it was lost to the Lombards in 751.

The surviving monuments in Ravenna date from the fifth century A.D. or later. To the Western Roman period belong the Orthodox Baptistery and the Tomb of Galla Placidia. The church of S. Apollinare Nuovo with its magnificent mosaics, including a representation of Theodoric's palace, and the Arian Baptistery date from the Gothic period. The Byzantine period saw the building of the churches of S. Vitale, with its mosaic portraits of Justinian, Bishop Maximian and Theodora, and S. Apollinare in Classe. There are many sarcophagi of the same periods decorated in relief. The Gothic and Byzantine archives of Ravenna, which are a valuable source for the economic and social history of late antiquity, are now scattered through a multitude of libraries.

G. E. F. Chilver, *Cisalpine Gaul* (1941), see index; O. G. von Simson, *Sacred Fortress* (1949); G. Bovini, *Ravenna romana, paleocristiana e paleobizantina* (1962); id. *Saggio di bibliografia su R. antica* (1968). R. B.

**REATE,** modern *Rieti*, on the River Velinus in Sabine country 45 miles north-east of Rome. Curius Dentatus brought it under Roman control (290 B.C.). Obtaining full Roman citizenship in 268 B.C. it became and remained a flourishing *municipium*, which reckoned Terentius Varro and the Emperor Vespasian (qq.v.) among its native sons.
E. T. S.

**RECITATIO,** the public reading of a literary work by the author himself. At Rome Crates' lectures suggested the idea of a public reading of the verses of dead poets (Suet. *Gram.* 2), following a Hellenistic practice already adopted by Livius Andronicus and Ennius. But the real creator of the *recitatio* was Asinius Pollio: he was the first Roman to read before an audience his own works (Sen. *Controv.* 4 *praef.* 2). The custom soon spread extraordinarily. It still flourished under Domitian. Afterwards we find fewer allusions to it, although it survives to the sixth century.

Before the construction of Hadrian's Athenaeum, no definite place set apart for *recitationes* existed. Very rarely they took place in a theatre, sometimes at a banquet, oftenest in some hall, hired by the author or lent by a patron; the reader had to supply the necessary furniture (Tac. *Dial.* 9), which cost him dear, as readings did not pay. So starving poets recited anywhere (forum, thermae, circus, etc.).

There were two kinds of *recitationes*: the one meant for a restricted audience, the other for the public (Pliny, *Ep.* 7. 17. 11–12). Invitations were given by the author himself, or by means of short notes (*codicilli*) and programmes (*libelli*). Women were not excluded. From a sort of platform the *recitator*, standing up, first delivered a preamble (*praefatio*), then read seated. Sometimes he preferred to get a freedman to read, supplying gestures himself (Pliny, *Ep.* 9. 34. 2). Readings might extend over several days. They were chiefly of verse (epic, tragic, lyric), more rarely of prose (history, philosophy, discourses). The hearers expressed their approval—with occasional support from hired clappers—by applause and by cries ('effecte', 'euge', 'pulchre', 'sophos', etc.); they might even rise and kiss the reader.

The *recitatio* at first offered genuine advantages: by it an author made his works quickly known, realized whether they were worth publishing, and obtained the criticisms of competent judges. But very soon it degenerated, becoming an end in itself, encouraging the conceit of authors, and exercising on the literature of the Empire the same untoward influences as *declamatio* (q.v.)—love of the showy, of smart sayings, with defects in composition and neglect of depth in favour of form.

Th. Herwig, *De recitatione poetarum apud Romanos* (1864); L. Valmaggi, *Riv. Fil.* 1888; J. E. B. Mayor, *Thirteen Satires of Juvenal* i (1893), 173 ff.; F. Orlando, *Le letture pubbliche in Roma imperiale* (1907); L. Friedländer, *Sittengesch. Roms*[10], Bd. ii (1922), 225 ff.
C. F., transl. J. W. D.

**RECUPERATORES** were jurymen who acted in the second stage of Roman civil proceedings in place of the single *iudex* (q.v.). First established by international treaties for cases involving foreigners (Festus, s.v. *Reciperatio*), they were later extended to proceedings in which both parties were citizens. The advantage of a *iudicium recuperatorium* lay apparently in its celerity (restricted number of witnesses, short limit of time for giving judgement). *Recuperatores* were evidently competent to hear a variety of cases (Gai. *Inst.* 4. 46, 141, 185; and there were others), but no principle is discernible, nor is it known what, or who, determined whether a given case should go before them. In post-classical procedure there was no place for *recuperatores*. In Justinian's *Digesta* (q.v.) the compilers deleted this term and replaced it by *iudices*.

B. Schmidlin, *Das Rekuperatorenverfahren* (1963); G. Pugliese, *Il processo civile romano* ii. 1 (1963), 194 ff. A. B.; B. N.

**REDICULUS.** When Hannibal, attempting to raise the siege of Capua in 211 B.C., made a demonstration against Rome, a shrine was erected to the unknown power which made him go back again, under the name of Rediculus (Festus, 354. 25; 355. 6 Lindsay). It stood outside the Porta Capena, and the deity may have been surnamed Tutanus (Varro, *Sat. Men.*, fr. 213 Buecheler). This connexion, however, and even the association with Hannibal are denied by Latte, *RR* 53. H. J. R.

**RED SEA** ('Ἐρυθρὰ or 'Ἐρυθραία Θάλασσα: *Rubrum Mare*. Derivation of name uncertain, perhaps from 'Red Men' = Phoenicians). This name was extended by the ancients to cover all eastern waters, including the Indian Ocean, but referred specifically, as it does now, to the Arabian Gulf. The Red Sea proper was navigated by the Egyptians, by Israelites and Phoenicians, and by the Persians, through whom it became known to the Greeks. It was mentioned by several of the Attic dramatists, and Herodotus (2. 11; 3. 107 ff.) was acquainted with its shape. In an attempt to circumnavigate Arabia, Alexander sent ships from Suez which sailed as far as Yemen (Theophrastus, *Hist. Pl.* 9. 4. 1). The Ptolemies opened up the Red Sea completely. Under Ptolemy I the west coast was explored; under Ptolemy II forts and stations for elephant-hunts were founded here (*see* BERENICE, MYOS HORMOS, PTOLEMAIS THERON) and the Arabian shore was made known as far as Hedjaz and Al 'Ula; under Ptolemy III piracy was suppressed, and in the first century B.C. a '*strategos* of the Red Sea' makes his appearance. Under the Caesars the Red Sea became an important channel for trade between the Roman Empire and the eastern seas.

*Peripl. M. Rubr.* (translation and notes by W. H. Schoff, 1912); Cary–Warmington, *Explorers*, 67 f., 222; (Pelican) 73 ff., etc.
E. H. W.

**REGIA,** the traditional home of King Numa, was the seat of authority under the Republic of the *pontifex maximus* and contained his archives. It was situated at the east end of the *forum Romanum*, between the Sacra Via and the precinct of Vesta. Its orientation by the cardinal points matched that of the pre-Neronian *Atrium Vestae* and of the *Domus Publica*; foundations of the buildings of the early Republic, 390 B.C. and 148 B.C., still exist. The trapezoidal plan of the main existing structure, an elegant building in marble erected by Calvinus in 36 B.C., reconciles older and newer orientations (F. E. Brown, *Amer. Acad. Rome* 1935, 67 ff.). The view that the *fasti* (q.v.) *consulares* were affixed to its walls is now rejected (cf. A. Degrassi, *Rend. Pont.* 1945–6 and *Inscr. Ital.* XIII. i (1947); L. R. Taylor, *CPhil.* 1946, 1 ff., who attributes them to the adjacent Arch of Augustus). The courtyard contained the *sacrarium Martis*, with *hastae* and *ancilia*, and the shrine of Ops Consiva.

Recent excavations by F. E. Brown (1964–5) have clearly established that the early Regia was built at the end of the sixth or the beginning of the fifth century B.C., in a form very similar to that of later phases of building. (The main rebuilding before 36 B.C. now appears to have been in the latter half of the third century). The excavations have also brought to light, below the Regia, traces of a building that may be dated to the second quarter of the sixth century, and which Brown believes to be a temple. At a still lower level remains of huts have been discovered.

F. E. Brown, *Les Origines de la république romaine = Entretiens Hardt* xiii, (1967), 47 ff.                                    I. A. R.; F. C.

**REGIFUGIUM.** 24 Feb. is marked on the calendars *Q(uando) R(ex) C(omitiauit) F(as)*. The even number indicates that it is not a lucky day; the only other even-numbered festival is the second Equirria (14 Mar.). 24 Mar. and 24 May have the same letters attached, for unknown reasons, but 24 Feb. was called the Regifugium, because the *rex sacrorum* (q.v.) concluded the ritual by running away from the Comitium (Plut. *Quaest. Rom.* 63, where see Rose for suggested interpretations). *See* POPLIFUGIUM.                                    H. J. R.

**REGILLUS,** LUCIUS AEMILIUS (*PW* 127), praetor in 190 B.C., defeated the fleet of Antiochus at Myonnesus, securing the Scipios' passage over to Asia Minor. He celebrated a naval triumph, vowing a temple to *Lares permarini*, which was dedicated in 179.                                    A. H. McD.

**REGILLUS LACUS,** where Rome conquered the Latins *c.* 496 B.C. in a battle allegedly decided by the intervention of Castor and Pollux, is probably the volcanic depression called *Pantano*, south of Gabii (q.v.); it was drained in the seventeenth century.                                    E. T. S.

**REGIO.** (1) At Rome *regio* denoted particularly the city wards, four in number (Livy 1. 43; Varro, *Ling.* 5. 45) during the Republic, and perhaps representing a regal synoecism of the Palatine and Esquiline settlements. By 7 B.C. Augustus had reorganized the whole system, creating fourteen numbered *regiones* (*see* ROME, TOPOGRAPHY) administered by *aediles*, *tribuni plebis*, and praetors chosen by lot (Dio Cass. 55. 8), and divided into *vici* (*see* VICOMAGISTRI). Under Hadrian the administration had passed to libertine *vicomagistri* and one, or two, *curatores* responsible to the *praefectus vigilum* (*ILS* 6073). Fourteen consular *curatores* under the authority of the *praefectus urbi* were instituted by Alexander Severus (S.H.A. *Alex. Sev.* 33. 1, cf. *CIL* xiv. 2078). Each ward possessed a sub-station (*excubitorium*) of the *vigiles*.

(2) *Regio* is also used of the eleven *regiones* of Italy, instituted by Augustus, probably as a basis for the census (*see* ITALY).

For sources, cf. Lugli, *Fontes* i. 75 ff.                                    I. A. R.

**REGNENSES,** a *civitas* of Roman Britain created from the kingdom of Cogidubnus (q.v.). Its *caput* was Novio-

magus (*Chichester*). Romanization was early achieved on an impressive scale under this king as indicated by early villas (Fishbourne, Angmering) and the monuments of Chichester, but thereafter slowed down, for few other towns developed. Apart from the important iron-industry of the Weald, agriculture was the basis of the economy; in the fourth century the Bignor villa, well known for its mosaics, grew to great size.

Collingwood and Wright, *RIB* 89 ff.; A. L. F. Rivet, *Town and Country in Rom. Brit.* (1958), 158 f.; *VCH, Sussex* iii; B. Cunliffe, *Antiquity* 1965, 177 ff. (Fishbourne).                                    S. S. F.

**REGULUS** (1), MARCUS ATILIUS (*PW* 51), as consul reduced Brundisium (267 B.C.). As consul II in 256 with L. Manlius Vulso (q.v. 1) he won the naval battle of Ecnomus, thus opening the way for the invasion of Africa. After Vulso's return Regulus was left in sole command in Africa. He defeated the Carthaginians and captured Tunis, but offered impossibly severe terms. In spring 255 he was defeated on ground chosen by Xanthippus (q.v. 2) and was captured; this disaster ended the African expedition. Later (? 249), it is said, he was sent on parole to Rome to arrange an exchange of prisoners (or to negotiate peace-terms which he urged the Senate to decline) and returned to Carthage, where he died in captivity. The further story of his death by torture on his voluntary return to Carthage became a national epic (Hor. *Carm.* 3. 5), but may have been invented to palliate the action of his widow in torturing some Punic prisoners in Rome. On the Regulus legend see E. Klebs, *PW*, s.v. 'Atilius (51)'; T. Frank (*CPhil.* 1926, 311) defends the story of the peace-mission.                                    H. H. S.

**REGULUS** (2), PUBLIUS MEMMIUS (*PW* 29) (*cos.* A.D. 31), conceivably from Gallia Narbonensis (*Inscr. lat. de Gaule* 633), a 'discovery' of Tiberius, was suffect consul at the time of Sejanus' fall and governed Moesia, Macedonia, and Achaea from 35 to 44. Later under Claudius he was proconsul of Asia. He was consistently influential, in favour under Claudius and Nero, under whom he died in 61, and well spoken of by Tacitus. He was the first husband of Lollia (q.v.) Paulina.                                    J. P. B.

**REGULUS** (3), MARCUS AQUILIUS (*PW* 34), who had been a notorious informer in the Neronian period, was detested by the Younger Pliny as 'the biggest scoundrel on two legs' ('omnium bipedum nequissimus', *Ep.* 1. 5. 14). His hysterical talent ('ingenium insanum', ibid. 4. 7. 4) and effrontery led many to take him for an orator; but for Herennius (q.v. 1) Senecio he was 'uir malus dicendi imperitus', exactly the opposite of Cato's famous definition. Defects notwithstanding, he secured many convictions in trials for *maiestas*. We know of two lost publications of his: (1) a pamphlet satirizing Arulenus (q.v.) Rusticus after his death; (2) a biography of his own dead son, of which he had 1,000 copies made for circulation. Martial mentions him several times in complimentary terms.

Syme, *Tacitus*, see index.                                    J. W. D.

**RELEGATIO** was at first the expulsion of a Roman citizen or a *peregrinus* decreed by a magistrate as a coercive measure. In this application it was a mere administrative act. As a penalty in criminal trials, banishment was applied in different gradations, and terminology is not consistent. The mildest form was merely temporary expulsion, without confinement or death penalty in case of return, and without loss of citizenship or property. The severest form was *deportatio* (introduced by Tiberius), a perpetual banishment to a certain place, combined with confiscation of property and loss of citizenship. *Relegatio* itself consisted either in the exclusion of the *relegatus* from residence in certain places or territories (Rome, Italy, or the provinces), or in his confinement to a particular place. A very common form was *relegatio in insulam* or *in Oasim* (in Upper Egypt). Banishment in all its variations was especially a punishment for the higher classes (*see* HONESTIORES). The lower classes were punished for similar crimes with forced labour (*in opus publicum* or *in metalla*) or even with death.

See bibliography *under* LAW AND PROCEDURE, ROMAN, III; and Z. Zmigryder-Konopka, *Rev. hist. de droit français* 1939, 307 ff.
A. B.; B. N.

**RELICS.** The cult of heroes (*see* HERO-CULT), at their real or supposed graves, had occasionally curious results. Naturally, many of these monuments were not real graves at all, as the Pelopion at Olympia; many places also claimed to possess the buried remains of heroes not native to them, and had legends explaining how they came there (Oedipus at Colonus in Attica, Soph. *OC* 576 ff.; Eurystheus in the deme Pallene, Eur. *Heracl.* 1031; Hector at Thebes, see W. R. Halliday in *Liverpool Annals* xi. 3 ff.). Moreover, unburied remains were venerated here and there, as the 'honoured bones' mentioned by Pausanias at Asopus in Laconia (3. 22. 9), without even a name, and the bones of the Sibyl at Cumae (Paus. 10. 12. 8), in Apollo's temple. But this was not confined to the cult of heroes. The most remarkable instance of such a thing in the cult of a deity was the Hellotia in Crete, a festival of Athena (q.v., cf. Nilsson, *Feste*, 95 f.). Here a very large wreath, called a *hellotis*, was carried and said to contain the bones of Europa (q.v.; Seleucus in Athenaeus, 678 a–b). What the 'bones' really were is unknown. Furthermore, many relics were not bodies or parts of them. Aniconic cult-objects were occasionally explained as relics, as the stone at Delphi said to have been swallowed by Kronos (q.v.; Hes. *Theog.* 497 ff.), cf. the 'sceptre of Agamemnon' at Chaeronea (Paus. 9. 40. 11) and the 'shield of Diomedes' at Argos (I. R. Arnold in *AJArch.* 1937, 436 ff.).

F. Pfister, *Der Reliquienkult im Altertum* (2 vols.; 1909–12); Nilsson, *GGR* i². 189.
H. J. R.

**RELIGION, CELTIC.** Important for the religious concepts and practices of the barbarian Celts is the evidence derived from Classical literary sources, however brief and inaccurate, and from abundant Gallo-Roman iconography and epigraphy. These sources supplement and illumine those forthcoming from archaeological discoveries of prehistoric times, or made in areas beyond the Roman Empire, and also the great body of Irish literary tradition. The cumulative result in the light of comparative studies shows a general Indo-European pattern with anthropomorphic sky and earth deities, ritual observances and vocabulary, and an order of sacred and learned persons. Of chief interest to Greek and Latin writers were these learned men. Beginning with Posidonius, the Druids were credited with philosophical and scientific attainments quite alien to their actual condition and function. Their influence in Celtic politics, and on current events, was none the less potent. Two other groups within the learned order, Seers and Bards, were probably recognized by Posidonius, and are variously mentioned, probably in repetition, by Diodorus (5. 31), Strabo (4. 197), and Julius Caesar (*BGall.* 6. 13–14). Pliny's reference (*HN* 16. 249 ff.) to sacred groves is in accord with other evidence, but his account of the ritual gathering of mistletoe by the Druids is unique. Native Irish tradition generally confirms the names and functions of these three groups of learned persons, as also of a long training in a great body of oral texts (cf. Caesar, *BGall.* 6. 14). Caesar (*BGall.* 6. 17–18) identified with Roman god-names the attributes of Gaulish deities, giving chief place to Mercury, then Apollo, Mars, Jupiter, and Minerva. Gallo-Roman altar

dedications show that in the application of *interpretatio Romana* these Roman gods were variously linked with Celtic gods as in Mars Segomo, Apollo Belenus, and Jupiter Taranucus. A frequent combination in such dedications is a Roman god and a Celtic goddess, as in the case of Mercury and Rosmerta. Alternatively, the monument may be entirely Roman but dedicated to a purely Celtic divine couple such as Sucellus and Nantosvelta. Taranis, Teutates, and Esus, recorded by Lucan (1. 444–6), do not figure at all prominently in Gallo-Roman epigraphy, and it is probable that these are a triad of epithets for a single tribal god, although they may be accounted as appropriate for any of the male deities in the Celtic supernatural whose attributes were all-embracing rather than specialized. The break-up of the old tribal system in Gaul undoubtedly led to the advancement of some gods at the expense of others, and thus to the appearance of specialization equivalent to the Roman system. The original generalization of attributes is also illustrated in Gallo-Roman iconography where symbols such as the hammer, wheel, and serpent occur in different dedicatory groupings, and interpenetrate each other in geographical distribution. The Celtic goddesses were no less important in their way than the gods, but were even more territorially circumscribed. Their function was essentially the fertility of the land and the people; some few whose cult was propagated by devotees in the Roman army enjoyed artificially wide distributions, but these are not to be mistaken for primitively widespread deities (*see* DEAE MATRES, EPONA). Cult practices amongst the Celts included various forms of human sacrifice, and the taking and keeping of heads won in battle. The dedication of booty to the gods was widely observed, and massive votive deposits were placed in lakes and at the sources of rivers. The small square Gallo-Roman temple is now known to have had prehistoric prototypes, and square enclosures, with a deep shaft or well for votive purposes, are a type of cult site newly recognized. Some simple wooden images are known from well or other water deposits in Gaul, but there was no durable Celtic iconography prior to Roman influence and after those fourth-century B.C. stone pillars and heads known especially from the Rhenish area, and of Etruscan inspiration. The sanctuaries at Entremont and Roquepertuse (Bouches du Rhône) with their stonework and sculpture represent a special Celtic adaptation of Graeco-Etruscan monumental possibilities.

J. Zwicker, *Fontes Historiae Religionis Celticae* (Bonn, 1934–5), for all Classical texts. J. J. Tierney, 'The Celtic Ethnography of Posidonius', *Proc. Roy. Irish Acad.* 60 C (1960), 189 ff., is essential for new commentary. A fresh approach to Celtic religion was given by M.-L. Sjoestedt, *Gods and Heroes of the Celts* (1949). J. Vendryès, 'La Religion des Celts', *Mana* II. iii (1948), is comprehensive, and especially useful for epigraphy. M. Dillon, *Proc. Brit. Acad.* 1947, 245 ff., for Celtic oral learning and other Indo-European links. J. de Vries, *Keltische Religion* (1961) is an over-all, if rigid, study with good bibliography. T. G. E. Powell, *The Celts* (1958), ch. 3; A. Ross, *Pagan Celtic Britain: Studies in Tradition and Iconography* (1967); Stuart Piggott, *The Druids* (1968); E. Thevenot, *Divinités et sanctuaires de la Gaule* (1968).
T. G. E. P.

**RELIGION, ETRUSCAN.** Our knowledge of Etruscan religion is based upon funerary and liturgical inscriptions (*see* ETRUSCAN LANGUAGE), archaeological evidence, and references in Greek and Roman authors, who generally interpret genuine material from their own point of view. At the end of the Republic, Roman writers, some of them of Etruscan origin (Tarquitius Priscus, Aulus Caecina, Nigidius Figulus), translated into Latin some of the Etruscan sacred books which enshrined their traditional doctrine: we have only fragments of their work, and they tended to contaminate Etruscan sources with Hellenistic philosophy. Later on, Martianus Capella and Johannes Lydus have handed down to us important, but adulterated information.

Etruscan religion, unlike Greek and Roman, was a revealed religion; semi-divine seers (as Tages, Cacus, and the nymph Vegoia) were said to have taught it to their people, and their teaching, with later accretions, was expressed in a code of religious practices, *Etrusca disciplina*, which included *libri rituales*, *libri fulgurales*, and *libri haruspicini*. The ritual books included 'prescriptions concerning the founding of cities, the consecration of altars and temples, the inviolability of ramparts, the laws relative to city gates, and all other things of this nature concerning war and peace' (Fest. 358 L.). In fact there was nothing either in public or in private life whose course had not been foreseen in the ritual books.

The *libri fulgurales* handled the interpretation of thunder and lightning; thunderbolts were thrown by various gods and portended events in human life. The Etruscan Jupiter, alone or on advice of his counsellors, threw three kinds of thunderbolts either mild or more or less devastating; eight other gods threw one kind each. Johannes Lydus has preserved a 'brontoscopic calendar', translated by Nigidius Figulus, which indicated the significance of thunderbolts for every day of the year (cf. BIDENTAL).

The *libri haruspicini* recorded the experience of the Etruscan people in the practice of scrutinizing the entrails of victims. Their professional *haruspices* won such a reputation in this procedure that the Roman Senate appealed to them whenever unintelligible omens had been announced. The inspection of livers is depicted on Etruscan mirrors and other objects. A bronze model of a sheep's liver, found near Piacenza but probably originating from a priestly college in Cortona (J. Heurgon, *Studi L. Banti*, 1965, 183 ff.), has its convex side divided into forty-four sections, each one marked with names of deities: it shows a reflection of the Etruscan heaven, orientated on the cardinal points, with the seat of all its gods (*templum*). It reflects 'an elaborate belief in the "sympathy" between cosmic and terrestrial life' (S. Weinstock) which also inspired the description of the dwelling-places of the gods given by Martianus Capella; this shows striking though obscure parallels with their distribution on the liver.

We know of a great number of Etruscan gods, but their origin, functions, and relations are difficult to determine. They mostly bear Etruscan names, but from the start they were subjected to oriental and Greek influences, which reflected a complex and somewhat confused divine world of more individualized and anthropomorphized deities. At their head was *tin* or *tinia*, a thundergod like Zeus. With *uni* (Juno), assimilated to the Greek Hera, and *menrva* (Minerva), who took the aspect of Athena, *tin* formed a triad, which was worshipped in tripartite temples (e.g. on the Capitoline hill). But Voltumna = Volturnus or Vertumnus, who was honoured in Rome since the sixth century (*Volturnalia*) and was accompanied by the eagle (*voltur*), was also held to be 'the first of Etruscan gods'. *Turan*, an old Mediterranean goddess, was identified with Aphrodite, *fufluns* with Dionysus, *turms* with Hermes, *seθlans* with Hephaestus etc. The tablets from Pyrgi (q.v.) show the introduction of the Punic goddess Astarte, under the name of *uni-astre*, into a sanctuary of *uni*. Apollo, Artemis, and Heracles kept their Greek names, but *aplu*, *aritimi*, and *hercle* sometimes assumed unexpected features in Etruscan mythology. The Greek Charon, surrounded by a host of other funerary deities, including Tuchulcha, Mantus (cf. the city of Mantua), *calu*, *leθam*, developed into a conspicuous figure, as the torments of the Underworld assumed increasing importance in Etruscan imagination. Some others, *neθuns* (Neptunus), *maris* (Mars), *veive* (Veiovis) reappear in the Roman religion. A great many of them (*cilen*, *caθa*, etc.) remain for us mere names.

Etruscan ceremonies, together with the gods in whose

honour they were held, the sacrifices which were made, and the priests who performed them, are described on the tile from Capua (a funerary ritual) and on the wrappings of the Zagreb mummy (a liturgical calendar), but their detailed interpretation is still under discussion.

Livy called the Etruscans 'a nation more than any other dedicated to religion, the more as they excelled in practising it' (5. 1). This religion in fact imposed on man an overwhelming subjection and a formally codified discipline. It had a deep influence on Roman religion itself, and the *libri Sibyllini* were probably of Etruscan origin. The Christians proclaimed Etruria *genetrix et mater superstitionum* (Arn. 7. 26).

L. R. Taylor, *Local Cults in Eturia* (Rome, 1923); C. Clemen, *Die Religion der Etrusker* (1936); A. Grenier, *Les Religions étrusques et romaines* (1948); M. Pallottino, *Etruscologia*³ (1963), 235 ff.
See also C. O. Thulin, *Die etruskische Disciplin* (1906–9); on *libri fulgurales* S. Weinstock, *PBSR* 1951, 122 ff.; on Nigidius' brontoscopic calendar, A. Piganiol, *Studies A. C. Johnson* (1951), 79 ff.; S. Weinstock, 'Martianus Capella and the Cosmic System of the Etruscans', *JRS* 1946, 101 ff. (cf. M. Pallottino, *Studi Calderini* iii (1956) 223 ff. and *Etruscologia*⁶ (1968), 235 ff.); Capua tile, M. Pallottino, *Stud. Etr.* 1949, 159 ff.; Zagreb mummy, K. Olzscha, 'Interpretation der Agramer Mumienbinde', *Klio Beih.* xl (1939), A. J. Pfiffig, 'Studien zu den Agramer Mumienbinden', *Österr. Akad. d. Wiss.* 1963. J. H.

**RELIGION, GERMANIC.** Written evidence from the Germanic (Teutonic) peoples before their conversion to Christianity is limited to a few Runic inscriptions. Greek and Roman writers supply some information about their heathen religion. Julius Caesar has a little in *De Bello Gallico*, but this is scrappy and appears to be misleading. Our richest source is the *Germania* of Tacitus, who tends to idolize the simple, heroic life of the Germans, and no doubt oversimplifies, but increase in knowledge shows him to be on the whole reliable. He identifies the three chief gods with Mars, Mercury, and Hercules. Beside describing many customs among the various peoples, he gives a celebrated account of the wagon of the goddess Nerthus (cf. ON *Njǫrðr*) journeying through the territories of the tribes in Denmark to bring prosperity. Strabo, Plutarch, Ammianus Marcellinus, and Procopius add a little. Evidence about the heathen period is also found in the Latin histories of ecclesiastical writers of the medieval period, who drew on oral tradition among the different peoples.

Inscriptions on altars and carved stones from territories occupied by the Roman army provide further information. Those to Mars probably represent *Tiwaz* (OE *Tiu*, ON *Týr*), high god and god of war, whose title of Mars Thingsus suggests an association with the Thing or assembly and thus with justice. He may also have been worshipped as *Irmin*, and the sacred pillar of *Irminsûl* of the Saxons must be related to the Jupiter pillars of the Rhineland, based on the conception of a column sustaining the universe, like the World Tree of Scandinavian mythology. Mercury was equated with *Wodan* (OE *Woden*), god of the dead, of magic and inspiration, who gradually replaced Tiwaz as war-god, and became *Oðinn*, ruler of the Scandinavian Asgard. He was the ancestor of German kings, and the horse, spear, and eagle were his symbols. In the first century A.D. the thunder-god *Donar* (OE *Þunor*, ON *Þórr*) seems to have been equated with Jupiter, but later with Hercules, who slew monsters with his club as Donar did with his hammer. These gods took over the days of Mars, Mercury, and Jupiter (Tuesday, Wednesday, Thursday) throughout the Germanic world.

Female deities are also named. Some must be associated with fertility, and like Garmangabi(s) suggest connexion with giving, as do later Scandinavian goddess names such as *Gefion* and *Gefn*. One goddess, *Nehalennia*, had a shrine at Domburg, where carved stones have been found showing her with fruit and corn and sometimes accompanied by a dog or a ship, and it appears that travellers prayed to her for a safe passage to Britain. In the Rhineland there are inscriptions to the *Deae Matres* (q.v.), often shown in threes, established among the Germans as well as the Celts as givers of plenty from the first century A.D. Other female deities were attendants on the war-god, like the *Alaisiagae*, mentioned under various names on stones found at Housesteads on Hadrian's Wall in Britain, predecessors of Valkyries.

Deities remembered vaguely in the North and probably worshipped by the heathen Germans are *Ing*, *Ullr*, and *Forseti*. Ing may have been a predecessor of the Scandinavian *Freyr*, and it is clear that fertility deities were worshipped by the Germans under many names. Wodan's consort *Frija* gave her name to Friday, the day of Venus, and her descendants in Scandinavia are the goddesses *Frigg* and *Freyja*. There is no evidence for worship of *Loki* or *Baldr*. Tacitus mentions the divine founders of the race, *Tuisto* and *Mannus*, and also the twin gods of the Naharvali, the *Alcis*, whose priests wore women's attire, but of these we know little.

Knowledge of Germanic ritual and sacrifice comes partly from Greek and Latin writers, partly from the heroic literature surviving in Anglo-Saxon England and Scandinavia after the heathen period, and partly from archaeological evidence. Much has been learned in recent years from the study of heathen burials, holy places, sacrificial deposits in the peat-bogs of Denmark, Sweden, and north Germany, and from pagan symbols on ornaments and weapons.

J. de Vries, *Altgermanische Religions-Geschichte*[2] (1956); E. A. Philippson, *Germanische Heidentum bei den Angelsachsen* (1929); H. R. Ellis Davidson, *Gods and Myths of Northern Europe* (1964); *Pagan Scandinavia* (1967); H. M. Chadwick, *The Cult of Othin* (1899); A. Houdris-Crone, *The Temple of Nehalennia at Domburg* (1955); R. C. Bosanquet, 'On an altar dedicated to the Alaisiagae', *Arch. Ael.* 1922, 185 ff. H. R. E. D.

**RELIGION, GREEK.** O. Gruppe, *Griechische Mythologie und Religionsgeschichte* (vol. v. 2 of I. von Müller's *Handbuch der klassischen Altertumswissenschaft*. 2nd ed. 1906. Still valuable though replaced by the following work); M. P. Nilsson, *Geschichte der griechischen Religion* (also vol. v. 2 of Muller's *Handbuch*. 3rd ed. vol. i, 1967; 2nd ed. vol. ii, 1961); P. Stengel, *Die griechischen Kultusaltertümer* (vol. v. 3 of Müller's *Handbuch*. 3rd ed. 1920); L. R. Farnell, *The Cults of the Greek States* (1896–1909); id. *Outline History of Greek Religion* (1920); E. Rohde, *Psyche* (Tübingen, 1893: and many later editions, but substantially unchanged); J. E. Harrison, *Prolegomena to the Study of Greek Religion*[2] (1922); U. von Wilamowitz-Moellendorff, *Der Glaube der Hellenen* (1931–2); O. Kern, *Die Religion der Griechen* (1926–38); H. J. Rose, *Ancient Greek Religion* (1946); R. Reitzenstein, *Die hellenistischen Mysterienreligionen*[4] (1927); G. Murray, *The Five Stages of Greek Religion* (1935: originally published as *The Four Stages of Greek Religion* in 1912); W. K. C. Guthrie, *The Greeks and their Gods*[2] (1954); L. Preller-C. Robert, *Griechische Mythologie*[4] (1894); A. Rumpf in H. Haas, *Bilderatlas zur Religionsgeschichte*. 13/14—*Die Religion der Griechen* (1928: a manual of religious art, etc.); A.-J. Festugière, *Personal Religion among the Greeks* (1954).

See also articles on individual deities, festivals, etc.
J. N.

**RELIGION, ITALIC.** The history of a religion needs documents, and those written in the language of the people of whose religious beliefs and practices it is proposed to give an account. The documentary evidence from ancient Italy, other than Latin and Greek, is meagre or, in some cases, imperfectly understood. But it is enough to make certain two facts: (1) the development of religion among the Italic tribes was essentially parallel to what took place at Rome—the differences are differences of detail; (2) hence, as at Rome, so in Italy at large, religion during the period c. 400–90 B.C. (which is the only period in which its activity is attested and also remained comparatively independent) was a composite affair that had received contributions from a very old and persistent stratum of Mediterranean people, from the waves of trans-Alpine immigrants—starting in prehistoric times and including the Gauls—who brought several forms of Indo-European language into Italy, from Illyrian settlers on the east coast, from others on the west (the Etruscans—probably of Anatolian origin), from Greek colonists, and, through them, from the Near East. It was, therefore, especially by the end of that period, ripe for the identification of its deities with those of Rome, to whom many of them were sufficiently akin (e.g. Umbrian *cubrar matrer*, at Fulginia, gen. sing. 'Bonae matris', or Picene *dea Cupra*, cf. the Roman Bona dea), or even identical (e.g. Oscan *diúvei*, i.e. 'Ioui', *mamrt*[*ei*] 'Marti'), as well as for identification with Greek and other deities of the kind that went on in Roman religion. Greek cults are by no means missing from the dialect-records, e.g. Messapic *aprodita* and *damatar*, which interpret themselves; Oscan *apellun*—'Apollo' (Messana, Pompeii), *hereklo*—'Hercules' (Lucania, Campania, Samnium, Vestini, Paeligni, and at Praeneste), *meelikiieis*—'Μειλιχίου' (Pompeii), *euklúi*—'Εὐκόλῳ' (i.e. Hermes, in Samnium); and, in the fastness of Corfinium even, *perseponas* (i.e. Persephonae, gen. sing.), *uranias* 'Οὐρανίας'. If *líganakdíkei* (Samnium) is a translation of Θεσμοφόρῳ rather than an independent compound (quasi \**lignáco-dic-*, qualified by the epithet *entraí*, i.e. 'inmost-forest-revealing goddess'), then a Greek cult-title has been borrowed.

But there is much that is genuinely native, as the enumeration which follows shows (for the *Tabulae Iguuinae* see that article). The fundamental Italic conception of deity, like the Roman, was 'act rather than personality' (e.g. *herentas* 'desire' at Herculaneum and Corfinium, compare the Roman *Venus*, which denoted originally a function or activity of a god (e.g. Jupiter, Ceres; cf. *venerari*); *vezkei*, perhaps 'Lucinae' [?], *patanai* 'Pandae', *genetai* 'Genitae', cf. the Roman Genita Mana Venus, Genetrix—these three all from the *Tabula Agnonensis*, Samnium). The greater part of the beliefs of Italic tribes were concerned with the innumerable aspects of natural order (*diumpais* [cf. *Lumphieis*, Νύμφαις CIL i[2]. 1624, Naples] and *anafriss* 'imbribus' both ibid.— and both with the epithet *kerriío*—'Cerealis', i.e. 'genialis', *cerfu semunu*, Corfinium, gen. pl., cf. Lat. *semunis* acc. pl., *Carm. Arv.*, *Semo Sancus*, and, for *cerfu*, Lat. *duonus cerus*, *Carm. Sal.*, ap. Varr.; cf. also Mefitis) or of human life (Venetic *re·i·tia*, called *sahnat·e·i* 'healer', Ven. *vrota* 'turner', cf. *Postuorta*, *Anteuorta*; or Ven. *lah·v·na*, cf. Messapic *logetibas* dat. pl., Sicel Λάγευσις, Messapic *lahona* dat. sing., perhaps all connected with Gr. Λοχία, and so maieutic; Osc. *ammai*, *Tab. Agn.*, clearly nurturing in function, *maatuís* ibid., cf. *Mater Matuta*).

Then, too, just as in Roman religion, there are gentile cults, proper to certain families, e.g. Raetic *velχanu*, Ven. *Volkanus*; *Diua Plotina* (Ariminum), *Ancharia* (Asculum), *anagtiai diiviai* 'Angitiae Diae' (Samnium, also found among the Marsi and Vestini), and *Pelina* (Paeligni), the last named perhaps already tribal or local, like *Flanatica* (Histri), *Minerua Cabardiacensis* (Travi, Aemilia), *Matronae Vcellasiacae Concanaunae* or *Matronae Braecorium Gallianatium* (Transpadana). From Capua and Cumae comes a large group of inscriptions, which call themselves *iúvilas* (n. pl.), cf. *leima iuvila*, i.e. 'Lima Iouia' (Raetic). Each regularly bears a heraldic emblem and records or prescribes an annual sacrifice to certain tutelary deities, or in honour of the ancestors of the family, on a fixed date. Jupiter 'Flagius' (cf. *Ioui Flazzo, Flazo* at Pozzuoli) is expressly mentioned, and a goddess analogous to the Roman Lucina seems also to be concerned. The wording of these inscriptions is very similar to that of a number of early Theran inscriptions (e.g. *IG* xii. 3 Suppl. 1324, cf. iii. 452), and this interpretation of them is thereby confirmed. During the Social War the confederate Italic tribes represented Italia on coins (*Vttelliú*), just as the Romans had *Roma* long before.

Last we have to note the recognition and worship of certain greater personalized powers, which, again as at Rome, were like enough to some of the Olympian deities to be identified with them, or had been borrowed from them—Jupiter himself, *regenai peai cerie iovia* 'Reginae Piae Cereri Iouiae', Castor and Pollux (Paelignian *puclois iouiois* dat. pl.; *Castorei Podlouqueique Qurois* at Lavinium), Mercury (*Mercui* at Falerii), and Fortuna, originally a goddess of children (*diovo fileia primogeneia* at Praeneste; Antium)—to name no others. Even Juno and Diana appear to have been Latin in the first place rather than Roman. To the most remote times goes back the worship of mother-goddesses, attested by non-epigraphic remains at opposite ends of the peninsula in Liguria and in Malta (compare the later Celtic *Matronae* in Cisalpina, also called *Iunones*), or of mother-earth (Sicel Ἄννα, Messapic *ana*, Osc. *Damia*, with a festival δάμεια at Tarentum, cf. Lat. *damium*, Osc. *damuse* . . . '*Damosia*'), whose cult was extremely ancient all through the Mediterranean basin, or of infernal deities (attested by several Oscan *defixiones*); and not much later is the worship of animals, often disguised subsequently as eponymous ancestors, Messapic *Daunus* (the wolf?), *Hirpus* (Sabini, Hirpini—also the wolf), Messapic *Menzana* (the horse), Sicel 'Ιταλός (the bull), or of natural features such as the mountain-top (Celtic *Penninus* in the Alps, *ocres tarincris* gen. sg., Marrucini), hot springs (Ligurian *Bormo*), or rivers (*Padus pater*). Agricultural deities and festivals, like the Ligurian *Leucimalacus* ('apple-ripener') and *plostralia*, or the Oscan *fiuusasiais* (loc. pl., 'Floralibus'), are a commonplace. There is, in short, every reason to suppose that, together with the same elements (magic, taboo, animism) that are fundamental in early Roman religion, there went, among the Italic communities, the same kind of development of local and functional spirits as at Rome, worshipped in the same way by sacrifice, prayer, lustration, and vow.

The primary sources are collected in R. S. Conway, *The Italic Dialects* (2 vols., 1897), and in R. S. Conway, J. Whatmough, and S. E. Johnson, *The Prae-Italic Dialects of Italy* (3 vols., 1933). J. Whatmough, *The Foundations of Roman Italy* (1937), includes brief surveys of the known facts from all the dialect-areas. A full discussion of the problems of Italic religion, with much theorizing and some questionable assertion, may be had in F. Altheim, *A History of Roman Religion* (1938; to be used with caution). See also H. J. Rose, *Ancient Roman Religion* (1949); Latte, *RR*, esp. 148 ff. For Samnium, E. T. Salmon, *Samnium and the Samnites* (1967), 143 ff.　　　　J. W.

**RELIGION, MINOAN-MYCENAEAN.** As very few finds of religious importance are reported from the Early and Middle Helladic (Bronze Age) periods of the mainland of Greece, our knowledge of the religion of the pre-Greek population of Greece is almost exclusively derived from Crete, where the Bronze Age is called the Minoan Age (*see* MINOAN CIVILIZATION). In the Late Helladic period the immigrant Greeks dominated first the mainland, especially its eastern parts, afterwards also Crete. (We revert later to this period, which is also called Mycenaean.) The cult-places in Minoan Crete were partly natural caves or rock-shelters. Some caves, e.g. at Psychro and Arkalochori, have yielded numerous votives, double axes, bronzes, rings, gems, etc. The cave of

Eileithyia at Amnisus (*Od.* 19. 188) is attested on a Linear B tablet from Cnossos. The rock-shelter at Petsofa is peculiar by reason of its terracottas representing limbs and parts of the body; they cannot, however, be votives to a healing god. There were no great temples, but rustic sanctuaries and small chapels in houses and palaces at Cnossos, Gurnia, etc. Their type of façade is known from wall-paintings and pieces of gold foil; it has three compartments with columns and horns of consecration and is crowned by the same horns. At the back is a raised dais on which idols and vessels were placed, other vessels being placed on the floor. There were altars and several kinds of sacral vessels too. We very often see an object consisting of two hornlike projections united by a common base; it is called 'horns of consecration'. Sacred vessels or branches were put between the horns. 'Horns of consecration' were often used in a purely ornamental way on vase-pictures and buildings, etc. The symbol of Minoan religion is the double axe which is very often depicted on vases and found among votives; the blades are generally curved and so thin that they are useless for practical purposes. Paintings show it crowning a high pole beneath which a sacrifice is performed. Probably it is the sacrificial axe. There is evidence for a cult of pillars, sacred stones (baetyls), and stone-heaps that remind us of the Greek *hermae*. Tree-cult is proved by many gems and especially by the paintings of the sarcophagus from H. Triada, showing a tree in a holy enclosure. Some representations show a dance of an ecstatic kind. The cult idols are female, bell-shaped, and very primitive; they are often found in houses. A few of better workmanship represent the snake-goddess (see under 2), e.g. the faience statuette from Cnossos and the chryselephantine statuette in Boston. Gems and seal-impressions show the epiphany of gods in bird-shape and also in human form, sometimes as small figures hovering down from the air, sometimes full-sized. There is further a great number of daemons, monsters, and fabulous animals.

It is still disputed whether the Minoans believed in a Great Goddess who ruled this world and the Nether World, comparable with the Great Mother of Asia Minor. There is a number of goddesses, prominent among which is the Mountain Mother. They may be local varieties of one general mother- (or Cybele-) type; but it is also possible that they represent individual deities, although the Minoan polytheism never appears as clear-cut as the Hellenic. We can discern a mistress, with beside her a master, of animals who also are gods of hunters, who worshipped the so-called Mother of Mountains mentioned above; a goddess of tree-cult whom the great gold ring from Mycenae shows seated under a tree and approached by votaries; a goddess seated on board a ship; and finally the snake- or household goddess. The snake is to this day, even in Greece, still more venerated in domestic cult than in the cult of the dead. It is therefore clear that the snake-goddess has her origin in the cult of the house-snake. Of the cult of the dead little is known except for the paintings of the sarcophagus from H. Triada which probably represent a deification of the dead man. The heavenly bodies are sometimes represented; it is uncertain whether worship was paid to them. The bull-cult cannot be proved; the bull-ring which gave rise to the Minotaur myth was hardly anything other than a secular sport. On the other hand, the legends of Pasiphaë and Europa give positive evidence. Egyptian influence is apparent in details, Babylonian is less prominent; but, generally speaking, the Minoan religion has a native character of its own.

From the sixteenth century B.C. mainland Greece was strongly influenced by Crete. Mycenaean religion, therefore, culminating in the fourteenth–thirteenth century, seemed, to judge from the monuments above, to have been wholly minoized. Even before the decipherment of Linear B, however, some marked differences were noted (see next paragraph). The male deity known as 'master of animals', now bearded according to the Greek fashion, is more prominent. A forerunner of the Eleusinian triad Demeter–Kore–Plutus occurs on a Mycenaean ivory. The Mycenaean inscriptions have greatly enlarged our knowledge, although much is still disputed. We now know that many familiar Greek deities were already worshipped by the Mycenaeans, both on the mainland and after their settlement in Crete. Some had a Minoan origin; the Cretan vegetation goddess would correspond with Demeter, the household or snake goddess with Athena, the mistress of animals with Artemis. Often these deities receive the epithet *potnia* (a-ta-na po-ti-ni-ja may mean 'the Lady of Athana', the latter being a place-name). Further, the names occur of Zeus (whom the Greeks may have identified with the youthful Cretan god; some think, however, that this was Hermes), Poseidon, Enyalios, Paian, Eileithyia (see above), Hera, and Hermes. The occurrence of Dionysus and some items of the Dionysiac vocabulary has provoked lively discussions (cp. J. Puhvel in *Mycenaean Studies*, ed. by E. L. Bennett (1964)). The predominance of Poseidon over Zeus at Pylus corresponds with this god's role in *Od.* 3.

The Greeks brought with them Zeus from their old home; their State of Gods is, just as always, modelled after the State of men; like the Mycenaean war-king Agamemnon, Zeus is surrounded by vassals, and there is even a popular assembly in which the small gods take part. The Greek State of the Gods corresponds precisely to the feudal organization of the Mycenaean age. There is in Homer a simple belief in Destiny which recurs among other warlike peoples and helps them to brave the risks of warfare; it probably developed during the warring Mycenaean age. Hera probably developed into an Olympian goddess from a local Argive variety of earth-mother. Her name, kindred with Homeric ἥρως, 'Lord', 'Sir', means 'Lady', as much as *potnia*. Plenty of idols are found in Mycenaean tombs and almost none in Minoan, except for the very end of the Minoan age when it was influenced by the Mycenaeans. The Mycenaeans built stately beehive tombs for their kings which have no parallel in Crete, and the dead were buried unburned. Homer, on the contrary, knows only cremation and speaks always of mounds. Cremation began at the end of the sub-Mycenaean age; the question is too difficult to be treated here; but offerings, though not the dead, were sometimes burned in Mycenaean tombs. The beehive tomb was covered by a mound, at least the top of which projected above the surface. A cult was of course given to the dead kings and princes, who when alive were heroes—to use the word as Homer does. The cult of ancestors may, if the people also are devoted to it, survive the extinction of the family and even the forgetting of the name of the dead man. There is evidence that at one Mycenaean tomb the cult was continued down into the historical age—at Menidi (Acharnae), in fact, to the beginning of the Peloponnesian War.

There is other evidence for cult continuity from Mycenaean to historical times; the temple of the city goddess was built on the ruins of the palace of the Mycenaean king at Athens, Mycenae, Tiryns. Thus Minoan religion was transformed by the Mycenaean Greeks and handed down to the historical age. Certain myths of an un-Greek appearance, especially the myth of the birth and death of Zeus, show that Minoan elements were taken over directly. Hyakinthos, whose Minoan origin his name proves, is another representative of the dying and revival of vegetation. The Divine Child abandoned by its mother

and nourished by others represents another Minoan myth which is coupled with the former. Again, the concept of Elysium, or the Islands of the Blest, seems to be a Minoan heritage. The two great antitheses in Greek religion are not, as many say, the Olympian and the Chthonic religion, but the emotional Minoan and the sober Greek religion. Historical Greek religion is a fusion of the two, but the contrast lingered on in the archaic age and gave the mystic movements their force.

M. P. Nilsson, *The Minoan-Mycenaean Religion and its survival in Greek Religion*² (1950); W. K. C. Guthrie, *BICS* 1959, 35 ff.; R. W. Hutchinson, *Prehistoric Crete* (1962), ch. 8; L. R. Palmer, *Mycenaeans and Minoans*² (1965), 130 ff.; W. K. C. Guthrie, *CAH*², ii.

M. P. N.; J. H. C.

**RELIGION, PERSIAN.** The Greeks had, from about the fifth century B.C., a fairly good acquaintance with Persian religion, not always, however, with its native form, but with the mixed beliefs and practices brought about by the extension of Persian influence to Babylonia and elsewhere; hence, e.g., the frequent assertion that Zoroaster (q.v.) was an astrologer; cf. Bidez–Cumont, vi. Further colouring is due either to the general opinion that all barbarians are too stupid, or too sage, to worship any but the natural and visible gods, as heaven, earth, and sun (cf. Ap. Rhod. 3. 714 ff. [Colchians], Caesar, *BGall.* 6. 21. 2 [Germans]), or to the recurrent, but especially Hellenistic, craze for finding deep philosophical learning among Orientals. Hence the numerous statements about Persians worshipping the sun and earth should be read with caution, though some no doubt refer to real cults of Mithras (q.v.) and of a mother-goddess; and such passages as Dio Chrysostom, 36, 39 ff. von Arnim, which put a quasi-Platonic myth into the mouths of the Magi, may be disregarded. Something was known of Persian gods from fairly early times, though the oldest surviving mentions of Mithras and Ahura-Mazda ('Ωρομάσδης, 'Ωρομάζης, 'Ωρομάζης) respectively, Herodotus 1. 131. 3 and [Plato], *Alcib.* 1. 122 a, make the former a goddess, the latter Zoroaster's father. Of surviving authors, Plutarch, *Mor.* 369 d ff., 1026 b, gives a correct account of Ahura-Mazda and Añgra-Mainyu or Ahriman (Ἀρειμάνιος). Other statements substantially correct are, e.g., Herodotus 1. 132 and Phoenix of Colophon, fr. 1 Powell, about the method of sacrifice; Strabo 15. 3. 15 on the holy fire; Cicero, *Leg.* 2. 26, on Persian objection to temples of Greek type, and numerous remarks about the Magi, Hdt. 3. 61. 1 ff. Aristotle's testimony, Περὶ φιλοσοφίας (see J. Bidez and F. Cumont, *Les Mages hellénisés* (1938), ii. 9, 67, n. 26), gives a valuable clue to the evolution of Iranian doctrines. These may have influenced Greek thought as early as the fifth century. Some knowledge of them may be presumed on the part of Hermippus (Pliny, *HN* 30. 4) and those who drew upon him; some were known by name and a certain amount of truth blended with the falsehoods told about them.

For bibliography *see* ZOROASTER, and add C. Clemen, *Fontes historiae religionis Persicae* (*Fontes historiae religionum*, fasc. 1,1920); Nilsson, *GGR* ii. 640 ff.; J. Duchesne-Guillemin, *La Religion de l'Iran ancien* (1962); 'D'Anaximandre à Empédocle: contacts gréco-iraniens', *Atti del Convegno sulla Persia e il Mondo greco-romano* (Rome, 1966), 423 ff.; R. C. Zaehner, *Dawn and Twilight of Zoroastrianism* (1961); I. Gershevitch, 'Zoroaster's own Contribution', *JNES* 1964, 12 ff.

H. J. R.; J. D.-G.

**RELIGION, ROMAN.** J. Marquardt, *Römische Staatsverwaltung*, vol. 3 (3rd ed. revised by G. Wissowa, 1885); G. Wissowa, *Religion und Kultus der Römer* (vol. v. 2 of I. von Müller's *Handbuch der klassischen Altertumswissenschaft*. 2nd ed. 1912. The standard reference book); K. Latte, *Römische Religionsgeschichte* (also vol. v. 2 in Müller's *Handbuch*, but, curiously, not intended to replace Wissowa as a work of reference, 1960); G. De Sanctis, *Storia dei Romani* iv. 2. 1. 121 ff. (1953); W.

Warde Fowler, *The Religious Experience of the Roman People* (1922); id. *Roman Festivals²* (1908); H. J. Rose, *Ancient Roman Religion* (1949); Fr. Altheim, *Römische Religionsgeschichte* (1931–3. 2nd ed. of vols. i and ii, 1956. Engl. transl.: *A History of Roman Religion*, 1938. Very speculative); A. Grenier, *Les Religions étrusque et romaine* (1948); J. Bayet, *Histoire politique et psychologique de la religion romaine* (1957); G. Boissier, *La Religion romaine d'Auguste aux Antonins* (1874); id. *La Fin du paganisme* (1891); J. Toutain, *Les Cultes païens dans l'Empire romain* (i, 1907: ii, 1911: iii, 1925); Fr. Cumont, *Les Religions orientales dans le paganisme romain⁴* (1929); L. Preller–H. Jordan, *Römische Mythologie³* (1881–3); the Fasti Anni Numani et Iuliani have been re-edited with valuable commentaries by A. Degrassi as *Inscriptiones Italiae* 13. 2 (Rome, 1963).

See also articles on individual deities, festivals, etc.

J. N.

**RELIGION, THRACIAN.** This appears to have been crude and barbaric before Greek influences transformed it. There is evidence of primitive animal-worship, human sacrifice, magical ceremonies, orgiastic rites. The earliest evidence, however, shows a belief in a future life. The Thracians brought to their worship powerful religious emotions that were still evident in later times.

Their native gods may have been vaguely conceived until individualized in Greek forms. The chthonian powers were especially favoured. Dionysus (q.v.), or a Thracian deity identified with him, was widely worshipped (but the long-held belief that the Greek Dionysus was Thracian in origin appears no longer tenable). He was a god of vegetation and fertility, worshipped in wild, ecstatic rites. He was closely related to Sabazius (q.v.), whose cult was widespread among Thracians and Phrygians. He was perhaps originally conceived in animal form, and the animals thought to embody the god were, according to tradition, torn to pieces and devoured raw by his worshippers, who thereby filled themselves with the god's power.

Other important Thracian deities are Bendis (q.v.), goddess of the chase and fertility, identified with Artemis; the closely related Cotys (q.v.) or Cotyto; Bedy, a spring and river god; Heros, god of vegetation and the chase, guardian of houses and roads (*see* RIDER-GODS); the closely related Rhesus (q.v.), the mysterious Zalmoxis (q.v.), of whom we know little; water-spirits, identified with the Nymphs; a war-god, identified with Ares; the Cabiri (q.v.). Several Greek gods were worshipped: Apollo, Zeus, Hera, Hermes, Heracles, Helios, Hades, Persephone, Asclepius, Hygieia, Telesphorus. The Thracians had a well-developed cult of the dead, for whom they raised impressive mounds.

P. Perdrizet, *Cultes et mythes du Pangée* (1910); G. I. Kazarow, *Die Denkmäler des thrakischen Reitergottes in Bulgarien* (1938).

J. E. F.

**RELIGION, TERMS RELATING TO.** No word in either Greek or Latin corresponds exactly to English 'religion', 'religious'. In the former language perhaps ὅσιος and εὐσεβής, with their corresponding abstract nouns, come closest. ὁσία seems to mean primitively 'usage', 'custom', hence 'good, commendable, pious usage' or the feelings which naturally go with it. It tends to specialize into meaning that which is proper and lawful with regard to holy things, or to traditional morality; it is, for instance, ἀνόσιον to commit murder. To say that a man is εὐσεβής does not of itself mean that he is what we call pious, unless some such phrase as πρὸς τοὺς θεούς is added; the famous εὐσεβεῖς after whom the εὐσεβῶν χώρα in Sicily was named (see *Aetna*, 623 ff., and R. Ellis ad loc.) were loving and self-sacrificing sons, and so *pii* (see below). Cf. in general J. C. Bolkestein, ῞Οσιος *en*

Εὐσεβής: *Bijdrage tot de godsdienstige en zedelijke Terminologie van de Grieken* (1936). A word belonging essentially to the religious vocabulary in classical times is θέμις, since that which it is or is not θέμις to do is respectively allowed or disallowed by religious law or custom; but the Homeric θέμιστες are traditional laws, not purely religious. ἱερός means properly 'taboo', hence 'consecrated' to some deity, though in Homer it can have a quite secular use (Nilsson, *GGR* i². 70) and a man careful in his religious duties may be called ἱερός, as Ar. *Ran.* 652; ἱερά are religious rites, or materials, especially victims, for them. δεισιδαίμων varies between 'pietistic' and 'pious', but is usually the former, see H. Bolkestein, 'Theophrastos' Charakter der Deisidaimonia' (*RGVV* xxi. 2, 1929). The word ἅγιος so distinctly indicates something belonging to the sacral sphere that it is tempting, despite the difference of breathing, to connect it etymologically with ἄγος, a taboo or the evil state resulting from the violation of one (see E. Williger, 'Hagios, Untersuchungen zur Terminologie des Heiligen', ibid. xix. 1, 1922; and Nilsson, loc. cit.). As regards outward observances, the simple word τιμή is common; a worshipper is often said to 'attend on' or 'serve' the gods, θεραπεύειν and synonyms (never δουλεύειν in a purely Greek context). To be a regular worshipper, e.g. of the gods of a State, is νομίζειν θεούς, which later comes to mean to believe in their existence (see J. Tate in *CR* 1936, 3; 1937, 3). Occasionally θρησκεύειν has the former sense (as Hdt. 2. 64. 1); θρησκεία is a common, though mostly late, word for 'worship'. λατρεία, λατρεύειν are also found (Plato. *Ap.* 23B, *Phaedr.* 244E, Eur. *Ion* 152). A τελετή or τέλος is any rite, though in Hellenistic Greek it tends to mean a mystical rite or even secret doctrine (see C. Zijderveld, Τελετή, diss. Purmerend, 1934; cf. H. Bolkestein, Τέλος ὁ γάμος, *Mededeelingen* lxxvi B, no. 2 (1933)).

In Latin *religio* seems to be properly a bond or restraint of a non-material kind, and so develops into 'sacral or religious observance or scruple'; *religiones*, a complex or system of such restraints, is perhaps the nearest Latin for 'a religion'. Generally, *religio* has a good meaning, though to a materialist, as Lucretius, it is nearly 'superstition', and in Hor. *Sat.* 1. 9. 71 it is something to be slightly ashamed of. *Religiosus* usually means 'pietistic', but denotes a laudable quality in the mouth of an uneducated man (Petron. 44. 18). In its good sense *religio* approaches Hellenistic εὐλάβεια (K. Kerényi in *Byzantinisch-Neugriechische Jahrbücher* 1931, 306 ff.). *Sacer* is almost exactly 'taboo', opposed to *profanus*, that which is used in ordinary life, cf. CONSECRATION. It is thus ambivalent, meaning on occasion 'accursed'. That which is actually *sacer* might also be *profanus*, as a temple or a human being, whereas a god is *sanctus*, as is also a man of venerable life or conduct; the inviolable walls of a city are *sanctae res* (Gaius 2. 8, cf. Plut. *Quaest. Rom.* 27 and Rose, *Rom. Quest. of Plut.* (1924), 181), but a table, which may be used for domestic ritual, is *sacra* (Juv. 6. O 4). *Pius, pietas* correspond fairly closely to εὐσεβής and εὐσέβεια, see above; Virgil's Aeneas is *pius* because he observes right relations to all things human and divine. Outward observances are *ritus*, properly no more than 'customs', *honores*, again by no means a peculiarly religious term, *cura caerimoniaque* (Cic. *Inv. Rhet.* 2. 161, cf. W. Warde Fowler, *Rel. Exper.*, index s.v.), or simply *caerimoniae*. *Sacra* denotes the holy objects and the ritual (*sacra facere*, to perform a religious ceremony).

See Latte, *RR*, under the various Latin words. H. J. R.

**REPETUNDAE.** Cases of alleged abuses of power by magistrates and pro-magistrates in the provinces were originally heard by *ad hoc* commissions of the Senate (e.g. Livy 43. 2). In 149 B.C. the tribune Piso (q.v. 1) passed a law setting up a standing committee (*see* QUAESTIO) under a praetor for this purpose. Its procedure was the *sacramentum* (q.v.) of the civil court, and a verdict of 'Guilty' was probably followed by an assessment of damages (*litis aestimatio*, q.v.) and simple repayment (hence *res repetundae*). C. Gracchus (q.v. 4), finding these courts corrupt and unwilling to convict fellow senators, had two laws passed by fellow tribunes: the first may have been a *lex Iunia* (passed in 123 by M. Silanus, later consul in 109). It provided for a mixed jury of senators and wealthy non-senators (*see* EQUITES). Of the second—probably a *lex Acilia* passed by Glabrio (q.v. 2) in 122—large fragments survive (Riccobono, *FIRA*, no. 7). It established a panel of 450 'Equites' only and laid down a detailed (and largely new) procedure. The law of Caepio (q.v. 1), applicable to all *quaestiones*, probably restored the mixed juries (106) and that of Glaucia (101 or 100) the 'Equestrian' juries. But these lost all credit in the case of Rutilius (q.v. 1) in 92, with the result that Drusus (q.v. 2) and Plautius (q.v. 1) tried various compromises and Sulla finally restored all juries to an enlarged Senate. L. Cotta (q.v. 3), in 70, reintroduced mixed juries for all *quaestiones*, and the old conflict was never renewed, though Caesar, Augustus, and Gaius (qq.v.) made changes in the jury panel. (On all this, *see* QUAESTIONES.)

Piso's law had created what was virtually a special civil court: the only penalty was simple restitution. His law may have been confined to extortion in the provinces, and the oligarchy, while willing to protect its subjects, did not readily do so at the expense of its own members. The *lex Acilia*, while retaining some of the concepts of a civil suit, first made the offence clearly criminal, doubling the amount to be repaid (it was later doubled again), introducing *nominis delatio* and offering public rewards for successful prosecution, including the citizenship for aliens. This offer was apparently restricted later and abolished by Sulla; but rewards for citizens remained. Acilius may have cut down the possibilities of *ampliatio* (q.v.), to avoid infinite delays and Glaucia substituted *comperendinatio* (a trial in two set *actiones* and no more) for it. He also widened the scope by adding a consequential action against senatorial accomplices (*quo ea pecunia pervenerit*); and it was probably he who first linked conviction with *infamia* (including expulsion from the Senate, which had hitherto no doubt been at the censors' discretion). At some time not later than this (and perhaps as early as 122) the law also began to cover illegal enrichment not through extortion in the provinces (e.g. bribery of jurors and collusive prosecution). After Caesar (perhaps even after Sulla) the capital penalty (i.e. in effect exile—which, for various reasons, guilty men had even earlier generally chosen on conviction) could be applied, where the case was serious enough. Caesar's law, comprehensive and severe, remained basic under the Empire.

Augustus, in 4 B.C., procured the *SC Calvisianum* (*FIRA* 68, 409—*see* CYRENE, EDICTS OF), by which provincials complaining of extortion could, with the Senate's permission, have the case investigated by five senatorial *recuperatores* (q.v.) and, if successful, would secure repayment. This return to (practically) civil procedure, by removing the consideration of a penalty, would be more likely to secure them compensation and was less expensive and more convenient. Conviction apparently still carried *infamia*; but intercession with the Princeps could reverse this. Several such cases are known, and it became the normal process under the early Empire. At some stage (quite early, it seems) *equites* also became liable. Cases involving criminal penalties continued alongside this civil process and came to be tried in the Senate, as it developed judicial functions. But senators were reluctant to condemn their peers; and men who enjoyed the Emperor's favour were hard to convict. On the whole,

whatever the merits of the case, *delatores* could secure the conviction (sometimes also on an added *maiestas* charge) of men who had fallen into disfavour, but not of others. As a result, by Trajan's reign, *clementia* was invoked to prevent the punishment even of known offenders. In the later Empire, the Emperor (or Praetorian Prefect) assumed jurisdiction, and the *Codes* give detailed regulations. By then, governors and their staffs were no longer the most serious burden on provincials.

*PW* s.v. 'Quaestio'; J. P. V. D. Balsdon, *PBSR* 1938, 89 ff. A. N. Sherwin-White, ibid. 1949, 5 ff.; *JRS* 1952, 43 ff.; G. Tibiletti, *Athenaeum* 1953, 5 ff.; E. Badian, *Hist.* 1962, 203 ff. (with bibliography); A. H. M. Jones, *PCPS* 1960, 39 ff.; C. Nicolet, *L'Ordre équestre* (1966), 465 ff. The *lex Acilia* is translated in E. G. Hardy, *Roman Laws and Charters* (1912). E. B.

**REPOSIANUS** (3rd c. A.D.), author of a poem in 182 hexameters on the intrigue between Mars and Venus, preserved in one codex only, the Salmasianus.

Text with transl., Duff, *Minor Lat. Poets*. J. Tolkiehn, *Neue Jahrb.* clv. 615 f.; D. Gagliardi, *Le Parole e le Idee* 1966, 184 ff.

**REX,** the Roman word for 'King' (etymologically connected with *regere*, to lead), is in itself evidence for a period of monarchy, the existence of which is postulated by the general process of political development in the Greek and Roman world, and attested by literary tradition, by archaeology, and by juridical and religious survivals. The word occurs in the Lapis Niger inscription in the Roman Forum, though the doubtful date makes it a matter of dispute whether the *rex* referred to is actually a king or the *rex sacrorum* (q.v.). In any case, the name *Regia*, meaning the palace of the supreme pontiff, and such compounds of *rex* as *rex sacrorum* (or *sacrificulus*) and *interrex* would suffice to prove that these republican officials were preceded by kings, whose name and powers they inherited.

That the king had ritual duties is confirmed by the analogous obligations fulfilled by his counterpart in Athens, the (ἄρχων) βασιλεύς. But the question of the power actually held by the king, and the legal foundation of the Roman monarchy, cannot be answered satisfactorily, owing to the lack of contemporary evidence. The only documents mentioned by ancient authorities are an agreement between Tarquin the Elder and Gabii, and an alliance between Servius Tullius and the Latin League. Therefore, annalists and jurists, in setting forth their theory of kingship and in relating the history of the regal period, merely applied the political system of the Republic to the original constitution of the city, substituting for the consuls one magistrate called *rex*, who ruled by virtue of *imperium* and was attended, as were the consuls, by twelve lictors. Although Roman tradition wrongly connected the origins of several Republican functions and customs with the regal period, it seems certain that some of these rights were actually enjoyed, and some of these duties fulfilled, by the kings, especially by those of Etruscan origin—the wearing of a purple robe, the triumphal procession after a victorious campaign, etc. The king administered justice sitting in an ivory chair on a chariot (hence the term *sella curulis*); he made war and peace; in time of war he assumed the chief command and exercised a supreme right of life and death over every soldier and citizen.

Tradition has it that the early Roman monarchs at least did not inherit their throne but were individually elected. They were nominated by an *interrex* (q.v.) and were appointed by Jupiter at the ceremony of the *inauguratio*. Two Tarquins, however, appear in the last three of the traditional list of seven kings; and it is possible that in the sixth century Etruscan influences occasioned the abandonment of the established Latin methods of selection.

The traditional kings certainly represent neither gods nor the personification of the seven hills, but not all of them can be accepted as historical figures. Yet, however many details may be fictitious or retrojections of later events and customs into the past, tradition is indisputably right in dating the fall of monarchy towards the end of the sixth century B.C. (For a brief refutation of the recent attempts, particularly by K. Hanell and E. Gjerstad, to lower the date of the end of the monarchy to the mid fifth century, see A. Momigliano, *JRS* 1963, 103 ff.) It is difficult to say with certainty whether this was due, as traditionally related, to a revolution, or to a gradual evolution, although the fact that legal measures were taken not later than the fourth century to prevent any attempt at the re-establishment of monarchy seems to favour the former alternative, which is also supported by an analysis of the international situation and of the crisis in which both Etruscans and Greeks in southern Italy were involved. Eventually the example and influence of the Hellenistic kingdoms caused at Rome a change of attitude towards both the conception of monarchy and its practice, thus paving the way for the monarchical adventures of Sulla, Caesar, and Augustus. But it was rather in opposition to than in imitation of Hellenistic kingship that the Augustan Principate was set up, and its founder was not called *rex*, but *princeps*.

Mommsen, *Röm. Staatsr.* ii². 1. 4 ff.; Beloch, *Röm. Gesch.* 225 ff.; U. Coli, *Regnum²* (1958) and in *Novissimo Digesto italiano*, s.v. *Monarchia*. On the idea of kingship in the age of Caesar and Augustus, see J. Carcopino, *Les Étapes de l'impérialisme romain* (1961), 120 ff.; J. Béranger, *Recherches sur l'aspect idéologique du Principat* (1953); P. Grenade, *Essai sur les origines du Principat* (1961).
P. T.; E. S. S.

**REX** (1), QUINTUS MARCIUS (*PW* 90), as praetor in 144 B.C. and propraetor built the great Marcian Aqueduct, the first using arches on a large scale.                     E. B.

**REX** (2), QUINTUS MARCIUS (*PW* 92), married to a daughter of Claudius (q.v. 10), was consul in 68 B.C. (alone for much of the year), then sent to Cilicia (chiefly to fight the pirates), then was delayed in Italy by unrest in Transpadane Gaul (*see* CAESAR 1, CRASSUS 4, PISO 2). In his province, instigated by his brother-in-law Clodius (q.v. 1), he refused aid to Lucullus (q.v. 2), and was soon succeeded by Pompey (66). Waiting (vainly) for a triumph, he used his *imperium* against the Catilinarians and died soon after.                                                    E. B.

**REX NEMORENSIS**, the 'king of the grove', i.e. Diana's grove near Aricia. This unique official was an escaped slave who acquired office by killing his predecessor, after a formal challenge in the shape of a violation of the grove by plucking a branch. See Strabo 5. 3. 12, 239; Suetonius, *Calig.* 35; Servius on *Aen.* 6. 136; more in Frazer, *GB* i. 11, note 1. The man was Diana's priest; for attempted explanations of his position see Frazer, op. cit. *passim*; A. Lang, *Magic and Religion*, 206 ff.; Rose, *Roman Questions of Plutarch*, 91; Latte, *RR* 171.
H. J. R.

**REX SACRORUM.** On the expulsion of the kings from Rome, their sacral functions were confided to a priest who bore the title of *rex sacrorum* officially, less formally *rex* simply; Livy (2. 2. 1), which see for the institution, calls him *rex sacrificolus* (not *sacrificulus*). He was subordinate to the Pontifex Maximus (ibid.), but superior to all the flamens (Festus, 198. 30 Lindsay). He was a patrician born of confarreate marriage (Gaius 1. 112), might hold no other post and was chosen for life (Dion. Hal. *Ant. Rom.* 4. 74. 4), and his wife, the *regina*, had certain sacral duties (Festus, 101. 6).

Marquardt–Wissowa, *Römische Staatsverwaltung* (1881–5), iii². 321 ff.; A. Momigliano, *Quarto contributo* (1969), 395 ff.     H. J. R.

**RHADAMANTHYS**, in mythology, son of Zeus and Europa (q.v.); he did not die but went to Elysium (*Od.* 4. 564). There he is a ruler and judge (Pind. *Ol.* 2. 75 ff.). He is uniformly represented as just (id. *Pyth.* 2. 73 f., and often). He is one of the judges of the dead (Pl. *Apol.* 41 a), along with others renowned for their justice, and so often in later authors, e.g. Verg. *Aen.* 6. 566, where he presides over Tartarus. Apart from this he has not much legend; his genealogy varies, Cinaethon ap. Paus. 8. 53. 5 giving Cres–Talos–Hephaestus–Rhadamanthys. His evidently pre-Greek name and the non-Indo-European Elysium have led to many speculations.

Jessen in Roscher's *Lexikon*, s.v.; Nilsson, *GGR* i². 325.
H. J. R.

**RHAMNUS**, one of the remotest of the Attic demes, situated on the north-east coast overlooking the narrow waters between Attica and Euboea. There are extensive remains of a fortress begun in the fifth century and enlarged in the fourth, which, together with that at Sunium (q.v.), constituted the main defence of the east coast and its vital shipping routes. In addition there was a sanctuary containing two classical temples, one to Themis, the other to Nemesis; the cult statue of the latter was created by either Phidias or more likely his pupil Agoracritus (q.v. 2) and judged by Marcus Varro (q.v. 2) to be his favourite work of sculpture.

Paus. 1. 32. 2–8 and Frazer's commentary; Pliny, *HN* 36. 17. H. Plommer, 'Three Attic Temples', *BSA* 1950, 94 ff.; J. Pouilloux, *La Forteresse de Rhamnonte* (1954); W. B. Dinsmoor, 'Rhamnountine Fantasies', *Hesp.* 1961, 179 ff.                    C. W. J. E.

**RHAMPSINITUS**, i.e. Ramses (III?), to whom a folktale (Stith Thompson, K 315. 1) is attached in Herodotus 2. 121. The builder of his treasury left a secret entrance and after his death his two sons stole therefrom. One being trapped, the other beheaded him, avoided capture himself, and at last was reconciled to the king.                                                  H. J. R.

**RHAPSODES** were professional reciters of poetry, particularly of Homer but also of other poets (Ath. 620 a–d, cf. Pl. *Ion* 531 a). The name, which means 'song-stitcher', is first attested in the fifth century (Collitz, *Griech. Dialektinschriften* 5786, Hdt. 5. 67, Soph. *OT* 391), but implies the formulaic compositional technique of earlier minstrels; cf. ῥάψαντες ἀοιδήν 'Hes.' fr. 357 M.–W., ῥαπτῶν ἐπέων ἀοιδοί Pind. *Nem.* 2. 1 (variously explained by schol.). Originally reciters of epic accompanied themselves on the lyre, but later they carried a staff instead (cf. Hes. *Th.* 30 with 95). Both are shown on vases; Plato distinguishes rhapsodes from citharodes, but classes Homer's Phemius as a rhapsode (*Ion* 533 b–c). In the fifth and fourth centuries rhapsodes were a familiar sight, especially at public festivals and games, where they competed for prizes. They declaimed from a dais (ibid. 535 e), and hoped to attract a crowd by their conspicuous attire (ibid. 530 b, 535 d) and loud melodious voice (Diod. 14. 109). They would be likely to own texts of Homer (Xen. *Mem.* 4. 2. 10), but recited from memory (id. *Symp.* 3. 6). They were carefully trained, and preserved a traditional pronunciation of Homer down to Alexandrian times (J. Wackernagel, *Kl. Schr.* (1956), 1094 ff.), probably under the influence of the Homeridae (q.v.), who were looked up to as authorities and arbiters (cf. Pl. *Ion* 530 d). A good rhapsode might be filled with emotion while reciting, and communicate it to his audience (ibid. 535 b–e), and there was felt to be a kinship between him and the actor (ibid. 532 d, 536 a, *Resp.* 395 a; Alcid. *Soph.* 14; Ar. *Rhet.* 1403ᵇ22); but he is not to be confused with the Ὁμηριστής, the low-class actor of Homeric scenes who was later popular (Dem. Phal. ap. Ath. 620 b, Petron. 59, Artemid. 4. 2, Ach. Tat. 3. 20. 4, *POxy.* 519. 4, etc.). Though despised as stupid by the educated (Xen.

locc. citt.) and a byword for unreliability (*Suda*, ῥαψῳδημα· ψεῦσμα. ῥαψῳδία· φλυαρία, etc.), rhapsodes continued to practise their art and compete at games at least down to the third century A.D. (e.g. *SIG*[3] 711 1 30, 958. 35, 959[9], *IG* vii. 1773. 17, 1776. 15). M. L. W.

**RHEGIUM** (*'Ρήγιον*: Regium is probably more correct, the name being pre-Greek), modern *Reggio*, a Greek colony in the 'toe' of Italy opposite Messana, was founded *c*. 720 B.C. by Chalcis (its inhabitants, however, included Messenians, after 600 at least). Originally an oligarchy using the legislation of Charondas of Catana (Arist. *Pol*. 2. 9; 5. 12), Rhegium later became subject to Anaxilas (q.v. 1), who extended its authority, e.g., over Messana (q.v.). But Syracuse, traditional enemy of Chalcidian cities, supported Rhegium's rival Locri and ultimately destroyed Rhegium (387: *see* DIONYSIUS 1). Soon rebuilt, Rhegium, although temporarily held by Campanian mercenaries (280–270), successfully resisted Bruttii, Pyrrhus, and Hannibal. Becoming a favoured and loyal Roman ally, it acquired municipal status after 90 B.C. (Cic. *Arch*. 3) and colonists but not colonial status under Augustus. Despite frequent earthquakes it remained a populous, Greek-speaking city throughout imperial times. The lyric poet Ibycus was born here.

Strabo 6. 257 f.; Hdt. 6. 23; 7. 165, 170; Thuc. bks. 4, 6, 7; Diod. bks. 11–16; Livy 23. 30; 36. 42. F. Cassola, *Gruppi politici romani* (1962), 171 ff.; J. Bérard, *Bibl. topogr.* (1941), 85; G. Vallet, *Rhégion et Zancle* (1958). E. T. S.

**RHENUS** was the Celtic name for the Rhine. This river (cf. Caesar, *BGall*. 4. 10) became the Roman frontier in Caesar's time, and between the river Vinxt and Holland it always so remained, though from the Flavian period until *c*. A.D. 260 the frontier of Germania Superior lay further east. In Classical times, as always, the river, with its important tributaries, was a great channel of commerce, and the Romans maintained a fleet on it from 12 B.C., the *classis Germanica*, with headquarters at Cologne. The stations of the fleet seem to have been concentrated in Lower Germany where river and frontier coincided. As a means of communication the river was of vital military importance, as between units and between the armies of Germany and Britain and during campaigns, e.g. those of Drusus, Germanicus, Tiberius, Corbulo, and Cerealis. Ancient writers generally regarded the Rhine as having two or three mouths, probably the Waal (Vahalis), Old Rhine, and the Vecht (cf. Strabo 4. 193; Pliny, *HN* 4. 101; Ptolemy 2. 9. 1). Drusus canalized the Vecht outlet (*see* FLEVO L.), and he also raised a dike, near the delta, completed by Pompeius Paulinus in A.D. 55 (Tac. *Ann*. 13. 53), to regulate the flow of the Rhine. Civilis cut it in 70 to hinder the Roman pursuit (*Hist*. 5. 19). Corbulo dug a canal, the Vliet, between Rhine and Meuse (*Ann*. 11. 20). Roman bridges existed above Basle and at Mainz, Coblenz, and Cologne; Caesar's bridges were built near Andernach.

C. G. Starr, *Roman Imperial Navy* (1960), 141 ff. For hydrographical detail, see H. J. Mackinder, *The Rhine* (1908); H. Roewer, 'Linksrheinische städtische Siedlung', *Forsch. z. deut. Landeskunde* 1955; D. Gurlitt, 'Das Mittelrheintal', ibid. 1944.

Another Rhenus (*Reno*) flowed into the Po near Bononia, and on an island here the Second Triumvirate was formed in 43 B.C. O.B.; P. S.

**RHESUS**, in *Iliad* 10. 435 ff. a Thracian ally of Priam. On his first night before Troy Odysseus and Diomedes (qq.v.) stole upon his camp, killed him and twelve of his men, and carried off his magnificent horses. Homer makes him son of Eïoneus; [Euripides], *Rhesus*, 279, 393–4, of the river Strymon and a Muse (Euterpe, according to schol. *Il*. loc. cit.). The scholiast on *Iliad* loc. cit. says (cf. Verg. *Aen*. 1. 469 ff., with Servius auctus there)

that if Rhesus' horses had tasted Trojan pasture and he and they drunk of the Scamander, Troy could not have fallen. As the *Rhesus* (962 ff.) says he shall not go to Hades but live on as a demi-god (ἀνθρωποδαίμων) in a cave, he is perhaps originally a Thracian deity. H. J. R.

**RHETORIC, GREEK.** Later antiquity (see Quint. 12. 10. 64) inevitably saw the beginnings of rhetoric in Homer, notably in the descriptions of the oratory of Nestor (*Il*. 1. 247 ff.), Menelaus and Odysseus (*Il*. 3. 212 ff.); the speeches (especially in *Il*. 9) were much admired as models (Quint. 10. 1. 46 ff.). This is fantastic history, but a salutary reminder that people spoke effectively before the rhetoricians, just as they argued logically before Aristotle. In fact, the teaching of the skills of public speech was doubtless first developed (as Aristotle thought) under the pressure of social and political needs in the fifth-century democracies of Syracuse and Athens. The Sicilians Corax (q.v.) and Tisias (q.v.), said to be the first to write handbooks (τέχναι, *artes*), concentrated on forensic speaking, and gave advice on the use of probability (εἰκός) and on how to exaggerate or underplay facts and arguments as required by the case. The spectacular success of Gorgias (q.v. 1) marks the fusion of the native Athenian tradition of political oratory which had produced Pericles with the new technique and style from the West. Gorgias' demonstration pieces (ἐπιδείξεις) impressed by the ingenuity of his thought and by the figures (σχήματα Γοργίεια), which exploited the capacity of Greek for rhyme, assonance, and formal parallelism. Another important teacher of this period was Thrasymachus (q.v.); in the *Tetralogies* of Antiphon (q.v. 1) we have a set of model speeches or exercises, the first in a long history.

2. The brilliant achievements of Attic oratory from Lysias to Hyperides are due to individual genius and political stimulus, not to the influence of rhetorical schools; but behind the great orators stands the mass of average Athenians, dependent for their success in life, and often for their safety, on the exertions of speechwriters (λογογράφοι) on their behalf or on the teaching they could pick up themselves. The *Rhetorica ad Alexandrum* (*see* ANAXIMENES 2) gives an idea of the teaching available at the end of the century; it is much less interesting, and less significant for the future, than the more radical approaches of Isocrates and of the philosophers. (*a*) Isocrates (q.v.) wrote speeches for litigants, perhaps also a τέχνη; but the main achievement of his career from *c*. 390 was educational. His φιλοσοφία was distinct both from the teachings of the Sophists and from the dialectic and mathematics of Plato; he wished to give his pupils the right moral and political attitudes, and his principal method was to make them write about such themes and criticize and discuss his own work (5. 17 ff., 12. 200 ff., 13. 18). This was to moralize rhetoric, hitherto openly or tacitly amoral, and to make a claim for it, under a new name, as an education in itself. (*b*) Plato (q.v. 1) besides criticizing the rhetors and Isocrates (*Gorgias, Phaedrus*) himself outlined (*Phaedrus* 271 c ff.) a 'philosophical' rhetoric, based on an adequate psychology; his hints were followed up by his greatest pupil. (*c*) Aristotle's *Rhetoric*, the product of many years and some changes of mind, deals in its three books with three main topics: (i) the theory of rhetorical, as distinct from philosophical, argument—enthymeme and example; (ii) the state of mind of the audience and the ways of appealing to their prejudices and emotions; (iii) style. Book 3 is perhaps the most interesting and influential part; it introduces the concept of the basic ἀρεταί of style, σαφήνεια (clarity), and τὸ πρέπον (appropriateness), and contains valuable discussions of metaphor and what Aristotle calls ἀστειότης (cf. *urbanitas*). Much of what Aristotle left inchoate (e.g.

ὑπόκρισις, the ἀρεταί) was developed by his pupil Theophrastus (q.v.), whose work was apparently the source of much Peripatetic doctrine which we find in later writers. (*See* LITERARY CRITICISM IN ANTIQUITY, §§ 5–6.)

3. When oratory dried up, rhetoric still continued (cf. RHETORIC, LATIN, § 3). Outliving its original function, it became the principal educational instrument in the spread of Greek culture. The Hellenistic period, however, is, in this as in other fields, obscure. Writers of the Augustan age (*see* DIONYSIUS 7) saw in the immediately post-Demosthenic period a scholastic and perversely ingenious mannerism ('Asianism'), against which they reacted by returning to classical models; but we possess no theory corresponding to this phase. In our knowledge, the achievement of Hermagoras (q.v.) with his doctrine of στάσεις (see below) is the main Hellenistic development. We know also something of Stoic rhetoric (F. Striller, *De Stoicorum studiis rhetoricis*, Breslau, 1886) and we possess, from the end of the period, considerable remains of the Περὶ ῥητορικῆς of Philodemus (q.v.), in which the old question 'whether rhetoric is an art' is discussed, and it is argued that at any rate forensic and epideictic oratory cannot be classed as species of the same activity (H. M. Hubbell, *Transactions of the Connecticut Academy of Arts and Sciences* 1920; translation and notes). The stimulus of Rome produced the earliest extant treatises (RHETORIC, LATIN, § 1); it may well be that the realities of Roman public life roused the whole tradition to new life. The activity of the first century B.C. (*see* APOLLONIUS 9, APOLLODORUS 5, THEODORUS 3) is best understood against a Roman background. With the revival of a more independent Greek literature in imperial times, Greek rhetoric took on a new lease of life; success in the schools might lead to a brilliant future as a sophist. The bulk of the extant *rhetores* are from the imperial and Byzantine periods. The last great systematizer was Hermogenes (q.v. 2); his work and the voluminous later commentaries on it afford the best extant synthesis in Greek, though Richard Volkmann was right to find in the more humane Roman Quintilian the only 'Ariadne's clue' to the labyrinth.

4. A description of the general system of ancient rhetoric, such as Volkmann (and more recently Lausberg: *see* RHETORIC, LATIN, bibliography) gave, is a necessary complement to an account of its development. (i) For practical purposes, rhetorical precepts could well be grouped, as they often were, under the 'parts of a speech' (prooemium, narrative (διήγησις), statement of case (πρόθεσις, προκατασκευή), proofs (πίστεις), epilogue (ἐπίλογος)), or by means of the threefold distinction (cf. Arist. *Rhet.* 1358ᵃ36 ff.) between forensic, deliberative, and epideictic oratory (γένος δικανικόν, συμβουλευτικόν, ἐπιδεικτικόν: see D. A. G. Hinks, *CQ* 1936, 170 ff.). However, these less sophisticated divisions were generally superseded by one which is already implicit in Aristotle: the division into 'invention' (εὕρεσις, essentially Aristotle's πίστεις), diction (λέξις, φράσις) and arrangement (τάξις, οἰκονομία). These, with the two practical appendages, ὑπόκρισις (delivery, *actio*) and μνήμη (mnemonics, *memoria*), form the skeleton of most of the comprehensive manuals (e.g. *ad Herennium*, Quintilian, the *corpus* of Hermogenes). (ii) Under εὕρεσις comes the important subject of στάσεις ('stances', 'issues' by which the problem may be attacked; Lat. *status*, but also *constitutio*). Hermagoras distinguished four: στοχασμός (*coniectura*, e.g. did X kill Y?), ὅρος (*finis*, e.g. was it murder?), ποιότης (*qualitas*, e.g. was it honourable or expedient?), and μετάληψις (*translatio*, e.g. it was all Y's fault?). Such analyses are valuable both for training debaters and advocates and for understanding the art of the great orators; inevitably, they led into barren, scholastic complexities. (iii) Οἰκονομία—not very conspicuous

in ancient treatises—comprised prescriptions for the division of subject-matter within the various 'parts' of a speech and some common-sense advice about arrangement: e.g. 'weakest points in the middle' (see *Il.* 4. 299). (iv) With diction were associated figures, tropes, and σύνθεσις (word-order, euphony, rhythm: see PROSE RHYTHM). This is the department which made most contribution to literary criticism (q.v.). Figures (σχήματα) are, at least in the developed systems (*see* CAECILIUS 4, GORGIAS 2), deviant (παρὰ φύσιν) forms of expression or thought; tropes (τρόποι) are similarly deviant (abnormal, non-literal) uses of words, such as occur in metaphor, metonymy, hyperbole, etc.

5. For the exercises done in schools of rhetoric, which naturally had a more powerful influence on literature than any amount of theory, see PROGYMNASMATA, DECLAMATIO.

(i) C. Walz, *Rhetores Graeci*, 9 vols. (1832–6) contains the fullest collection, including much Byzantine commentary on Hermogenes. L. Spengel, *Rhetores Graeci*, 3 vols. (1853–6, vol. i². revised by C. Hammer, 1894) remains the handiest selection, and includes most of the important works (Apsines, Anonymus Seguerianus, Hermogenes, Alexander Numeniu, etc.). These are not critical texts: some authors (e.g. Aristides, Hermogenes) have been re-edited in the Teubner series by H. Rabe and others (note *Prolegomenon Sylloge* (1931), a collection of ancient 'introductions to rhetoric', some of which contain valuable material).

(ii) Pre-Aristotelian texts: L. Radermacher, *Artium Scriptores* (1951).

(iii) Aristotle: commentary on Rhetoric by E. Cope (1877; *Introduction*, 1867); translations by W. Rhys Roberts (1924) and J. H. Freese (Loeb, 1926). F. Solmsen, *Die Entwicklung der aristotelischen Logik und Rhetorik* (1929); 'The Aristotelian tradition in ancient rhetoric', *AJPhil.* 1941, 42 ff.

(iv) Surveys: W. Kroll, *Rhetorik*, *PW* Suppl. vii, is indispensable; so is the systematic description by R. Volkmann (*Die Rhetorik der Griechen und Römer*² (1885, repr. 1963). Sound and readable modern works: C. S. Baldwin, *Ancient Rhetoric and Poetic* (1928); D. L. Clark, *Rhetoric in Greco-Roman Education* (1957); H. I. Marrou, *Histoire de l'éducation dans l'antiquité* (1950, also É.T.); and especially G. A. Kennedy, *The Art of Persuasion in Greece* (1963), sequel (covering the imperial period) in preparation.

(v) On the early period, see O. Navarre, *La Rhétorique grecque avant Aristote* (1900); V. Buchheit, *Das Genos Epideiktikon* (1960).

(vi) J. C. T. Ernesti's two lexica of technical terms (*Lexicon Technologiae Graecorum* (*Latinorum*) *rhetoricae*, 1795–7, repr. 1962) have not yet been superseded. Recent bibliography: H. Ll. Hudson-Williams, in *Fifty Years of Classical Scholarship and Twelve* (ed. M. Platnauer, 1967), 193 ff.          D. A. R.

**RHETORIC, LATIN.** Oratory at Rome was born early. Rhetoric—speaking reduced to a method—came later, an import from Greece that aroused suspicion. Cato the Censor, himself a distinguished speaker, pronounced 'rem tene, verba sequentur'; and rhetoricians professing to supply the words risked expulsion (as in 161 B.C.). But Greek teachers trained the Gracchi; Lucilius teased T. Albucius for the intricacy of his Graecizing mosaics in words; and Cicero marks out M. Aemilius Lepidus Porcina (*cos.* 137) as the first master of a smoothness and periodic structure that rivalled the Greeks. In the last quarter of the second century prose rhythms based on contemporary Hellenistic practice appear unmistakably in the orators' fragments. Latin rhetorical textbooks soon began to be written; and in 92 B.C. *rhetores Latini* came under the castigation of the censors. But the respectable orator Marcus Antonius (q.v. 1) wrote a *libellus* that showed knowledge of Hermagoras' (q.v.) στάσις-lore. Soon came both the *Rhetorica ad Herennium* (q.v.) and Cicero's *De Inventione*: the former a complete manual, the latter, closely related to it, only partial, but both evidence of the sophistication of Rome's Greek-based rhetoric in the 80s.

2. Cicero never came nearer than this to writing a rhetorical handbook, though his *Partitiones Oratoriae* and *Topica* handled other traditional themes. In his major rhetorical work, the *De Oratore* (55), dialogue form militates against technical detail; moreover, Cicero was concerned to inculcate his idea of the philosophic orator, with the widest possible education, able to speak 'ornate

copioseque' (1. 21) on any topic: and this naturally went with criticism of those who thought that one could become an orator by reading a textbook. Nevertheless, the *De Oratore* contained much traditional material: as did the later *Orator* (46), where Cicero contrasted the 'perfect orator', well-educated and commanding every kind of style, modelled on Demosthenes, and, implicitly, on Cicero himself, with the so-called Atticists, contemporaries who had a narrower and more austere ideal of oratory. Cicero thus was here defending his own oratorical practice (especially in the matter of rhythm); and this practice, no less than the precepts given in his rhetorical works, was carefully studied by later rhetoricians.

**3.** The *Philippics* of Cicero, however, were the last examples of great oratory used to influence political action at Rome. Oratory continued under the Principate, but it had practical effect only in the lawcourt. *Declamatio* (q.v.) dominated the schools, and fascinated even grown men: and it soon gave a new style not only to public oratory but also to literature in general. But this by no means spelt the end of rhetoric. As in the period after the death of Demosthenes, rhetorical theory was if anything encouraged by the newly academic nature of the subject. The dispute of Apollodorus (q.v. 5) and Theodorus (q.v. 3) about the rigidity with which rhetorical rules were to be observed was typical of the new mood: and C. Valgius brought Apollodorus' precepts to Latin readers. The first half of the first century A.D. was marked by the contribution of Cornelius Celsus, whose Encyclopedia went into some detail on rhetoric, and by P. Rutilius Lupus' translation (of which part survives) of a Greek work on figures. A little later the Elder Pliny wrote a long work giving detailed instructions on the education of an orator.

**4.** The massive *Institutio* of Quintilian (q.v.) takes note of this earlier work, if only to reject it; but, more important, it looks back over it to Cicero, and amidst all its detail retains Cicero's enthusiasm for a wide training and his dislike for trivial technicality. There was much in the *Institutio* that reflected contemporary conditions, in its advice to the declaimer and its preoccupation with forensic oratory; but it maintained, in defiance of history, the ideal of the *vir bonus dicendi peritus* (Cato the Censor's phrase), whose eloquence should guide the Senate and people of Rome (12. 1. 26): for a more realistic assessment of the position of oratory under the early Empire we have to look to Tacitus' more or less contemporary *Dialogus*. Despite this, the *Institutio* retained interest, particularly for the Middle Ages and Renaissance, as a handbook on style and a repository of rhetorical wisdom.

**5.** Halm's collection of *Rhetores Latini Minores* (1863: reprinted 1964) may illustrate the ossification and puerility of rhetoric after the first century, in the pat question-and-answer of Fortunatianus and the derivative summaries of Julius Victor. Oratory of this later period is represented by the *Panegyrici Latini* that have come down to us; and the letters of Fronto in the second century reflect the new importance of eulogy. From the schoolroom we have the extravagances of the *Declamationes Pseudo-Quintilianeae* (q.v.). Rhetoricians continued to flourish, and even found themselves celebrated in the poetry of Ausonius; and rhetoric survived to be put to Christian uses in the *Institutiones* of Cassiodorus.

**6.** For a summary of ancient rhetorical doctrine, which was usually Greek in origin but found, on the whole, its best surviving expositors in Latin, see RHETORIC, GREEK, § 4.

M. L. Clarke, *Rhetoric at Rome* (1953), and W. Kroll's article on *Rhetorik* in *PW* Suppl. vii provide the best historical surveys. On details of rhetorical precept R. Volkmann, *Die Rhetorik der Griechen und Römer*² (1885, repr. 1963), and H. Lausberg, *Handbuch der literarischen Rhetorik* (1960): more readable than either, C. Neumeister, *Grundsätze der forensischen Rhetorik* (1964). S. F. Bonner

gives a survey, with extensive bibliography, in *Fifty Years of Classical Scholarship* (ed. M. Platnauer, 1954), 335 ff. *See also* the bibliographies for DECLAMATIO, QUINTILIANUS, and RHETORIC, GREEK.

M. W.

**RHETORICA AD HERENNIUM.** The treatise on rhetoric addressed to C. Herennius (written *c.* 86–82 B.C.) is by an unknown author. Some, interpreting passages of Quintilian, assign it to 'Cornificius'. It is ascribed in the manuscripts to Cicero, and has often been printed with his works; but the Ciceronian authorship, first challenged in the fifteenth century, is no longer accepted. Its relationship to Cicero's *De Inventione* has not been satisfactorily determined. Rhetoric is treated in five divisions: Invention in judicial, deliberative, and demonstrative causes; Arrangement; Delivery; Memory (an important discussion); and, with abundant illustrations, Style (the oldest surviving treatment in Latin). The doctrine is a fusion of Greek systems; the illustrations, terminology, and spirit are Roman. The style is generally clear, and less archaic and 'plebeian' than scholars once maintained.

TEXTS. F. Marx, 1894 (with Proleg. and Index) and 1923, repr. 1964, with addenda by W. Trillitzsch (Teubner); H. Caplan, 1954 (Loeb). H. Cn.

**RHIANUS,** of Bene, less probably of Ceraea, in Crete: a contemporary of Eratosthenes (b. *c.* 275 B.C.), Rhianus began life as a slave and custodian of a wrestling-school. After a belated education he attained fame as a poet and Homeric scholar, probably at Alexandria.

WORKS

*Verse*: Rhianus wrote epic poems and epigrams, but was best known for the former (Ath. 11. 499 d), of which one was a *Heracleias*. Four others, *Thessalica, Achaeica, Eliaca, Messeniaca*, were tribal epics, rich in myth, history, and geography. The last was used by Pausanias (bk. 4, cf. especially 6. 1) as one source for the history of the Second Messenian War. Episodes in the poem seem to have been modelled on Homer or the rest of the cycle. More romantic scenes, e.g. the escape of Aristomenes from prison and the love-affair which betrayed the Messenians, show the influence of a later school of writing. The longest fragment (1) of Rhianus, possibly complete in itself, consists of twenty-one hexameters on the folly of mankind. Most of the epigrams (frs. 66–76) have a paederastic motif.

*Prose*: Rhianus produced an edition of the *Iliad* and *Odyssey*. It was more conservative than that of Zenodotus, and the forty-five readings from it which have survived have led critics to judge it favourably.

To some extent Rhianus falls into line with Apollonius Rhodius against Callimachus and his own contemporary Euphorion. Like Apollonius he preferred epic to epyllia, but his language seems to have been simpler than that of Apollonius. In the extant fragments he uses neologisms, but hardly any 'glosses'. His epics must have been agreeable reading, but it is possible, in view of the numerous citations by Stephanus of Byzantium, that they were too cumbered with geography.

TEXTS. Powell, *Coll. Alex.* 9–21; Diehl, *Anth. Lyr. Graec.* vi². 64–8 (epigrams only).
GENERAL LITERATURE. A. Meineke, *Analecta Alexandrina* (1843), 171 ff.; C. Mayhoff, *De Rhiani studiis Homericis* (1870). E. A. B.

**RHINTHON,** of Tarentum, a potter's son, writer of phlyax-plays (ἱλαροτραγῳδίαι, later known as *fabulae Rhintonicae*: see PHLYĀKES); contemporary with Ptolemy I (early 3rd c. B.C.). He was honoured with an epitaph by the poetess Nossis of Locri in south Italy (*Anth. Pal.* 7. 414): she calls him Syracusan, and claims originality for his 'tragic *phlyakes*', i.e. for raising the crude phlyax-drama by comic treatment of tragic themes. Of thirty-eight pieces attributed to Rhinthon nine titles are known (almost all are burlesques of Euripides), but very meagre fragments (in Doric) survive. One (fr. 10) from 'Ορέστας mentions 'the metre of Hipponax', i.e. scazon: a character in the play (violating dramatic illusion) points out that a curse just uttered will not scan as a tragic iambic trimeter.

E. Völker, *Rhinthonis fragmenta* (1887); *CGF* 183 ff.; Olivieri, *FCGM* ii². 7 ff.                                                            W. G. W.

**RHIPAEI MONTES** ('Ριπαῖα "Ορη), the 'gusty' and ever snowy mountains, imagined from Homer onwards to exist north of the known parts of Europe. From them blew the North Wind; beyond, down to the Northern Ocean, dwelt Hyperboreans (q.v.). Herodotus ignored the Rhipaeans and Strabo denied their existence. Those who believed in them differed as to their location. Aeschylus and Pindar regarded them as the source of the Danube, and Posidonius thought originally that the Alps were meant. On the other hand, Aristotle placed them beyond Scythia, and Roman poets put them in the extreme north. In general, their latitude was moved northward as knowledge increased. Ptolemy, who considered that they were of moderate altitude, located them in Russia (lat. 57° 30'–63° 21'), between rivers flowing into Baltic and Euxine. They remained on maps until modern times.

Ptol. *Geog.* 3. 5, 15, 22; Kiessling, *PW*, s.v. 'Ριπαῖα "Ορη.
                                                                E. H. W.

**RHODANUS,** the *River Rhône*, the name being applied to its whole course from the Alps through the Lake of Geneva to the Mediterranean west of Marseille (530 miles). Flowing between the Alps and the Massif Central it provided a main channel of trade and with its chief tributary the Arar (modern *Saône*) gave access to the Rhineland, to the Seine basin and, by a short portage to the Loire, to north-west France. These routes achieved especial importance in the sixth century B.C. after the foundation of Massalia (q.v.). In Roman times traffic on the Rhône and its tributaries was heavy, conducted by *nautae Rhodanici et Ararici* (*CIL* xiii. 1688 *et al.*) and *nautae Druentici* (*CIL* xii. 731, 982), and in the late Empire there were a *Classis Fluminis Rhodani* and a *Classis Ararica* (*Not. Dign.* [*occ.*] 42). Strabo (4. 189) says that the swift current caused wagons to be used for some northbound traffic, but a relief (Espérandieu ix. 6699) shows *helciarii* operating at least on the Druentia (*Durance*). Silting in the delta caused difficulties and in 104–102 B.C. Marius cut a canal (*Fossae Marianae*, now *Bras Mort*) from the main stream near Grand Passon to the sea west of Fos, where a port was built (now submerged); the canal was handed over to the Massaliotes, but its use contributed to the eclipse of Marseille by Arles. A scheme put forward in A.D. 58 to join the Saône and the Moselle by canal, thus linking the Rhône and the Rhine, came to nothing (Tac. *Ann.* 13. 53). (*See also* ARELATE, LUGDUNUM, VIENNA.)

Strabo, bk. 4 *passim*; Plut. *Mar.* 15. F. Villard, *La Céramique grecque de Marseille* (1960) (Greek trade); Grenier, *Manuel* ii, chs. 12–17 (Roman trade); R. Beaucaire, *Bull. Soc. des Amis du Vieil-Istres* ii, 1949, iii, 1958 (excavations at Fos).       A. L. F. R.

**RHODES,** an island of about 420 square miles, close to the mainland of Caria, was settled by Dorian Greeks who formed three city-states, Ialysus, Lindus, and Camirus. Their development was normal for the time and place—colonization (including Gela, Rhegium, and Phaselis, all Lindian colonies), tyranny, Persian conquest. In the fifth century, till 412–411 B.C., they were members of the Athenian Confederacy, and their constitutions were presumably democratic.

The war with Athens (411–407) combined with internal stresses to produce the union ('Synoecism') of the three cities into one State with a new federal capital *Rhodos*, though the original cities kept the greatest possible local autonomy. The 'Rhodians' remained democrats, perhaps even extremists, till revolutionary disturbances (*c.* 397–388) resulted probably in a moderate democracy which was overthrown only for a period of Persian domination (355–333); its stability later depended on a compromise between the interests of the large citizen proletariat and of the wealthy citizens (see especially Strabo 14. 652).

The prosperity of Rhodes must always have come mainly from the carrying trade, especially of corn. It received a great impetus from the conquests of Alexander, giving unrestricted access to Egypt, Cyprus, and Phoenicia, and in the third century Rhodes became easily the richest of the Greek city-states. Politically, too, the partition of Alexander's empire after 323 enabled it to reassert its independence and steer its own course in foreign affairs. This independent policy provoked the famous siege by Demetrius (305–304); but its survival on this occasion increased its prestige and self-confidence, so that in the third century it successfully avoided subservience to any of the 'great powers'. Like Athens earlier, it stood as a centre of exchange and capital and the enemy of piracy on the high seas. The Rhodian fleet was fairly large and always efficient: it was the 'senior service'—its officers were drawn from the best families, its crews (and the workers in the shipyards) from the poor citizens.

Rhodes (with Pergamum) was largely responsible for the first major intervention of Rome in eastern affairs (201). It co-operated with Rome (not previously an ally) in the wars against Philip V and Antiochus, and was rewarded with territory in Caria and Lycia. But Rome punished the equivocal attitude of Rhodes in the Third Macedonian War by proclaiming Delos a free port (167): this unfair competition, and perhaps an increase in piracy which Rhodes could no longer check, crippled it so severely that in three years its annual harbour revenues fell from a million to 150,000 drachmae. It became an ally of Rome on unfavourable terms, and ceased to be a power in the world. It successfully withstood a siege by Mithridates in 88, but was captured and pillaged by Cassius in 43. Nevertheless, under Roman rule Rhodes remained reasonably prosperous, and enjoyed no small distinction as a beautiful city and a centre of higher education, with Panaetius and Posidonius its greatest savants.

ANCIENT SOURCES. Inscriptions, especially *IG* xii, part 1 (1905), and A. Maiuri, *N:uova silloge epigrafica, Rodi e Cos* (1925); *Clara Rhodos* (1928–40).
LITERARY SOURCES are widely scattered: for the famous siege, Diodorus, book 20. 81–8 and 91–100.
MODERN LITERATURE. H. von Gelder, *Geschichte der alten Rhodier*; M. Rostovtzeff, *CAH* viii. 619 ff. (and bibliography); *Hellenistic World*. P. M. Fraser and G. E. Bean, *The Rhodian Peraea and Islands* (1954); H. H. Schmitt, *Rom und Rhodos* (Münch. Beiträge z. Papyrusforschung, etc. 1957); L. Casson, *TAPA* 1954, 168 ff.
                                                                G. T. G.

**RHODES, CULTS AND LEGENDS OF.** The most noteworthy cult at Rhodes was that of Helios (q.v.); the festival was called Halieia, celebrated yearly with sacrifice of a four-horse team thrown into the sea (Festus, 190, 28 Lindsay) and quadrennially with more elaboration. An ancient cult at Lindos was directed to a goddess identified with Athena; she was, however, plainly chthonian, being worshipped with fireless offerings (Pind. *Ol.* 7. 48); for the remarkable chronicle-inscription of her temple see C. Blinkenberg, *La Chronique du temple lindien*, Acad. royale des sciences et des lettres, Copenhague, 1912, and *Die lindische Tempelchronik* (1915). There were also festivals to Kronos, Poseidon, Apollo (Sminthia), Dionysus, probably the Dioscuri, Heracles and his son Tlepolemus (the Tlapolemeia, an agonistic festival of some importance; cf., for such events in Rhodes, I. R. Arnold in *AJArch.* 1936, 432 ff.). For authorities, see Nilsson, *Feste,* 478. Athenaeus, 360 c, records a custom of Lindos; children in the month Boedromion (presumably Badromios in the local dialect) went about singing a traditional song about the coming of the swallow and collecting contributions from the houses. This was called χελιδονίζειν. Rhodes was the first city to worship Ptolemy I (Diod. Sic. 20. 100. 4) and was from the Hellenistic period a great home of Egyptian cults (Nilsson, *GGR* ii. 117 ff.).

A few legends are known. Helios himself chose the island, which had not then risen above the surface of the sea (Pind. *Ol.* 7. 54 ff.). His children by the nymph Rhodos, daughter of Aphrodite (ibid. 14), were instructed by him to offer sacrifice to Athena the day she was born. In their haste they forgot to bring fire (ibid. 39 ff.), hence the custom of fireless sacrifice (above). The sons of Helios were Lindus, Ialysus, and Camirus, eponyms of the three chief cities of the island (schol. rec. Pind. ibid. 34). Rhodes was also the traditional home of the Telchines (q.v.).

H. J. R.

**RICIMER,** Flavius, patrician and kingmaker in the Western Roman Empire. He compelled the Emperor Avitus to abdicate (A.D. 456), elevated Majorian (q.v.) in 457, deposed and killed him (461), and elevated Libius Severus (461). Severus died in 465, and Ricimer overthrew and killed the Emperor Anthemius in 472, having already elevated Olybrius. He died in 472. As an Arian and a barbarian he could not hope to reign himself.

E. A. T.

**RIDDLES.** A riddle (γρῖφος) in its proper sense may be described as a species of αἴνιγμα or 'dark saying', which in turn belongs to the wider category of αἶνος ('story'). It is essentially designed to baffle or challenge the intelligence of the hearer; its subject-matter may be derived from a variety of sources, e.g. natural phenomena, social custom, or myth. The Oracle, for example, is typically expressed in enigmatic form. Early examples of riddles in Greek literature are Hesiod fr. 160 Rz. (contest of Calchas and Mopsus, perhaps rather to be described as a direct test of intelligence) and Theognis 1229 f.; the later *Certamen Hom. et Hes.* (ad fin.) preserves the traditional story of Homer and the Fishermen. By the fifth century B.C. the propounding of γρῖφοι had become a regular diversion of Greek society, especially at the symposium (Ar. *Vesp.* 20 f.); Aristotle (*Rh.* 1412ᵃ24) mentions τὰ εὖ ἠνιγμένα among the pleasurable seasonings of discourse. The authorship of early collections of riddles was ascribed to Cleobulus of Lindos and his daughter Cleobuline (*Suda*; Wilamowitz, *Textgesch. d. gr. Lyr.* 40. 3; O. Crusius, *Philol.* 1896). The Peripatetic Clearchus of Soli (frs. 61–8 in *FHG* composed a work Περὶ γρίφων, which was used by Athenaeus. Athenaeus himself (10. 448 b–459 b) gives a copious selection of riddles from comedy and other sources. A short collection of metrical examples is contained in *Anth. Pal.* 14. The general tendency to enigmatic expression, not unknown in earlier literature, becomes stronger with the Alexandrians, for example in the *Alexandra* of Lycophron.

Riddles occur sporadically in Latin literature. Aulus Gellius (12. 6) cites a metrical one from Varro; Petronius (58) provides examples of the popular type. The Greek term *aenigma* is habitually employed; Gell. (loc. cit.) gives *scirpus* as the native word. The metrical collection bearing the name of Symphosius (q.v.) (4th–5th c. A.D.) is composed in imitation of the Greek convivial type.

As might be expected from the character of the two peoples, the Greeks liked a riddle—γρῖφος—and the Romans did not. 'The investigation of riddles', said the

philosopher Clearchus, who divided them into seven classes, 'is not unconnected with philosophy: a riddle is a sportive problem, and to find the answer we have to use our intellect.' The most famous riddle was that proposed by the Sphinx and answered by Oedipus: 'What is that which walks on four legs, and two legs, and three legs?' Answer: 'Man.' Another was: 'A man and not a man, with a stone and not a stone, hit a bird and not a bird sitting on a tree and not a tree.' Answers: 'A eunuch, a pumice-stone, a bat, a fennel-stalk.' A third ran: 'What is the strongest of all things?' 'Love: iron is strong, but the blacksmith is stronger than iron, and love can subdue the blacksmith.' The cleavage between appearance and reality characteristic of the thought of late antiquity gave a new lease of life to riddles and other enigmatic and paradoxical modes of expression, which were used to embody and represent serious metaphysical doctrines.

W. Schultz, *PW* i A. 1, s.v. 'Rätsel'; *Rätsel aus d. hellen. Kulturkreise* (1909–12); K. Ohlert, *R. u. Rätselspiele d. alt. Gr.*² (1912); E. Cougny ed. *Anth. Pal.* (1890), 3. 563 (metrical examples from various sources); E. S. Forster, *Greece and Rome* 1945; R. T. Ohl, *The Enigmas of Symphosius* (1928).　　W. M. E. and F. A. W.; R. B.

**RIDER-GODS AND HEROES.** Theriomorphic gods were well known to the Greeks in prehistoric times, witness Poseidon (Hades) and the Dioscuri and their association with the horse; we may add the wind-god Boreas. As the horse was unknown to Minoan civilization, the connexion of these gods with horses may be pure Greek. The god became, after 1000 B.C., when riding was introduced, a rider of a horse (as the dead man, originally represented as a horse, became a rider in the 6th c. B.C.). Epithets (Hippios, Hippia), sacrifices, priesthoods, myths, however, still remind us of the origin. Further evidence is afforded by works of art (cf. the horse's head on the so-called Totenmahl reliefs, on which the dead man is shown on a couch, banqueting). Very widespread is a type of relief on which heroes or gods appear as hunters or riders, e.g. the Dioscuri. We see these also on horseback in the air, approaching the festal table set ready for them (cf. their appearance to the Romans after the battle of Lake Regillus), *see* THEOXENIA. In Thrace and neighbouring countries the type was exceedingly popular during later periods and the Roman age. Copies of the 'Thracian rider' (hunter) were often found in shrines, dedicated 'to the Lord Hero' or to local deities, heroes or heroized dead. In Gallo-Roman art the type of Jupiter on horseback slaying a serpent-footed giant is frequent.

L. Malten, 'Das Pferd im Totenglauben', *JDAI* 1914, 181 ff.; F. Schachermeyr, *Poseidon* (1950); Gawril I. Kazarow, *Die Denkmäler des thrakischen Reitergottes in Bulgarien* (Text und Tafelband, 1938).　　S. E.; J. H. C.

**RINGS** (δακτύλιος, *anulus*) were used in Minoan and Mycenaean times both as signets and as ornaments. They are not mentioned in Homer and are rarely found in Early Iron Age deposits. Since the early sixth century they were in regular use as signets. The practice of wearing rings as ornaments is rare before the fourth century and reaches its height under the Roman Empire. Collections of rings are mentioned at this period. Rings also had special uses at Rome: the gold ring as a military decoration and as a mark of rank, originally limited to *nobiles* and *equites,* extended under the Empire to denote *ingenuitas*; and the betrothal ring, first of iron, later of gold (apparently unknown in Greece).

Pliny, *HN* 33. 8–32. F. H. Marshall, *Catalogue of the Greek, Etruscan, and Roman Finger Rings in the British Museum* (1907); F. Henkel, *Die römische Fingerringe der Rheinlande* (1913). F. N. P.

**RIVER-GODS.** The pre-Hellenic inhabitants of Aegean lands probably had cults of river-gods, since many Greek rivers retained pre-Hellenic names (e.g. Ilissus, Peneius, Enipeus); although the incoming Greeks may have known such cults in their original homeland. The same statement may be made for aboriginal Italy and the incoming Italian peoples.

All rivers, seas, etc., according to Homer (*Il.* 21. 196 f.), are ultimately derived from Oceanus (father of all rivers, Hes. *Theog.* 337 ff.), or they are 'fallen from heaven' (fed by rain; Xanthus in Homer is even 'son of Zeus'). Old legends of river-gods who had children by mortal women gave to the local rivers an exceptional position in Greek genealogies. The river Inachus is, e.g., the father of Io, and rivers are the ancestors of whole tribes and of the oldest heroes (for the offering of hair to rivers as κουρο-τρόφοι see Hom. *Il.* 23. 46, Aesch. *Cho.* 6, Paus. 8. 41. 3; cf. Agamemnon's oath, *Il.* 3. 276 ff.). A vision of rivers is a sign of offspring to the dreamer (Artem. 2. 38). The cults of river-gods, as of other gods produced theophoric names, especially in Boeotia and Attica (Ismenodorus, Cephisodorus, etc.; cf. Bechtel, *Personennamen*, 145 ff. and 529). Yet the river belonged to a lower stratum of polytheism, 'the river power remained only half-personal, an animate nature-power, to whom altars might be erected, but rarely a temple' (Farnell, *Cults* v. 424). A reminiscence of religious primitivism is the ritual of casting victims such as horses and bulls into streams. The bovine nature of rivers is well attested, e.g., by coin-issues of Sicily (river-gods as man-headed bulls or horned youths), but full human shape became conventional, e.g. for Nile and Tiber. There is evidence too for river-gods in the form of horses and snakes. The widespread cult of Achelous, for which the Dodonaean oracle made an intense propaganda, is of special interest.

Farnell, *Cults* v. 420 ff.                                    S. E.; J. E. F.

**ROADS.** I. GREEK. While some stretches of paved road have survived, especially near important sanctuaries such as Delphi, the main traces of ancient roads in Greece are provided by the retaining walls and the bed cut in the limestone rock. The main road from the Peloponnese to central Greece is clearly visible; some three metres wide, it was designed for carts, with well-graded zig-zags and pull-ins for carts to pass one another. Such roads were originally paved, where not on bedrock. The *diolkos* across the Isthmus of Corinth was a roadway designed for transporting ships; it was four metres wide with two parallel channels cut for the wheels of the transporter. The Macedonians built many military roads from the late fifth century onwards, but their roads in the Balkans have not been examined.                        N. G. L. H.

N. G. L. Hammond, 'The main road from Boeotia to the Peloponnese', *BSA* 1954, 103 f.; *Arch. Rep.* 1956, 7 (*diolkos*).

II. ROMAN. From an early date the Romans valued good communications, and their road-system was one of their outstanding achievements. The spread of Roman influence through Italy was consolidated by such roads as the Via Appia (312 B.C.) from Rome to Capua and later to Brundisium, and the Via Flaminia from Rome to Ariminum (268) which in 187 was extended to Bononia as the Via Aemilia. By the end of the Republic all parts of Italy were connected by good roads. In the Principate the main construction was in the provinces, though the Republic had already made the Via Egnatia from Dyrrhachium to Thessalonica and the Via Domitia from the Rhône to the Pyrenees, and the Alps could be crossed easily by the pass of Mt. Genèvre. Augustus made roads across the Great and Little St. Bernard, and his stepson Drusus made one farther east 'from Altinum to the Danube' (*ILS* 208). Much chronological information can be derived from milestones (q.v.): we find, for instance, that Tiberius was specially interested in Dalmatia, Claudius in Gaul, and Hadrian in Africa and the Eastern

Provinces. (Cf. H. S. Jones, *Companion to Roman History* (1912), 40 ff. *See also* VIA AEMILIA, etc.)

Under the Republic the censors were responsible for the roads and let out the contracts for their construction and repair; but even before the Principate *curatores* of particular roads are found (*ILS* 5800, 5892). In 20 B.C. Augustus established a board of senatorial *curatores viarum*, and from the time of Claudius or Nero we find many *curatores* of particular Italian roads (*ILS* III. 1. 359–60), usually of senatorial rank. No *curatores* of provincial roads are known: for them the governors acting through the local authorities were responsible.

The cost of the roads was probably divided between the public treasury (whether *aerarium* or *fiscus* is uncertain), the local authorities, and the owners of the land through which they passed, but the emperors often made large personal contributions. *ILS* 84 records that the Via Flaminia and the most important roads of Italy were repaired at the cost of Augustus. Hadrian added a sum to the contribution of the *possessores agrorum* to the cost of repairing part of the Via Appia, and paid for the bridges on a road in Africa (*ILS* 5872, 5875).

Methods of construction varied with available materials. There is usually a foundation of large stones overlaid by smaller stones and gravel; occasionally the use of cement has been recorded to bind the matrix. Sometimes the surface is cobbled or even paved with large blocks. Always a camber was obtained for drainage, and side-ditches or gutters were normally provided; main roads were often carried on a high *agger*. Engineering is careful: roads run with remarkable directness in open country and in broken country keep to high ground shunning narrow valleys. Their alignments sometimes demonstrate the remarkable accuracy of long-distance survey.

Vegetius (3–6) mentions the military importance of itineraries (q.v.), which also served other public and private purposes. The Antonine Itinerary, Peutinger map, and Ravenna Cosmography are examples of such road-books giving routes and distances; more limited lists are the Bordeaux–Jerusalem itinerary and the Vicarello mugs.

Roman roads had a primary strategic purpose, but their existence did much for trade and social intercourse, thus helping to create a homogeneous civilization within the Empire.

L. Friedländer, *Roman Life and Manners* (E.T. 1908–13), i. 268 ff.; W. Ramsay, 'Roads and Travel in the New Testament' (Hastings, *Dictionary of the Bible*); G. H. Stevenson in *Legacy of Rome* (ed. C. Bailey, 1923), 141 ff.; O. Hirschfeld, *Verwaltungsbeamten* (1905), 205 ff.; H. F. Tozer, *Ancient Geography²* (1935), 299 ff.; Grenier, *Manuel* vi (i); P. Salama, *Les Voies romaines de l'Afrique du Nord* (1951); I. D. Margary, *Roman Ways in the Weald* (1948), *Roman Roads in Britain²* (1967).                        G. H. S.; S. S. F.

**ROBIGUS,** the *numen* of rust in wheat. His festival (Robigalia) was on 25 Apr. (Ov. *Fasti* 4. 905 ff., whereon see Frazer), at the fifth milestone of the Via Claudia (*Fasti Praenest.* on that date). The Flamen Quirinalis offered a dog and a sheep and prayed that rust might not attack the crops. Possibly the original intention was to destroy Robigus (H. J. Rose, *CR* 1922, 17).    H. J. R.

**ROME** (HISTORY)

(*Note.* Separate articles will be found on nearly all the proper names and institutions mentioned in this brief summary. It has not been necessary, therefore, to insert constant cross-references.)

## I. EARLY ITALY AND REGAL ROME

**1.** Long before the emergence of Rome as an influence in Italian affairs a variety of peoples, whose civilization outshone that of nascent Rome, had populated Italy (q.v.). The Terremaricoli and men of the 'Apennine' culture of the Bronze Age and the subsequent Iron Age Villanovans (qq.v.) lived in a period unrecorded by written history: our knowledge of them depends essentially on archaeological evidence. Thereafter the standard of civilized life was gradually raised by Etruscans, Oscans, and Greeks, some of whose activities are dimly reflected in surviving literary sources, and it is particularly against the background of the history of the Greeks in southern Italy and of the Etruscans in the centre and north that the development of early Rome must be set.

**2.** Of the Indo-European peoples in Italy, the Umbrians and Sabellians formed one branch, the Latins another. The latter, who occupied the plain of Latium, soon developed a sense of common origin, from which in time there grew one or more Latin Leagues, and their early hill-top settlements gradually increased in size and influence. One of these shepherds' villages was Rome, traditionally founded as an offshoot from Alba Longa. It quickly surpassed many of its neighbours, thanks to its geographical position near the sea and the centre of Italy, its command of the Tiber-ford, and its control of a primitive salt-route from the Tiber mouth to the central hills. By the beginning of the sixth century the settlements on the different hills had coalesced to form a city (see ROME, TOPOGRAPHY).

**3.** The surviving literary tradition about early Rome, on which we depend for much of our knowledge, is unsatisfactory in many ways, since more than half a millennium elapsed after the traditional date of Rome's foundation before the Romans began to write its history. When towards the end of the third century B.C. Fabius Pictor and then other annalists attempted the task (see HISTORIOGRAPHY, ROMAN), they had some reliable information to draw upon, such as the Annales Pontificum, official lists of magistrates, some documents (as laws, treaties, calendars) and the traditions (oral and written) of many leading families (but probably no ballad poetry, if it had existed, survived), but by this time fact and legend were not easy to distinguish. Further, national pride led the Romans to connect their history with that of the Greek world and to forge links with Greek mythology. Hence were evolved the foundation-stories which attributed a Trojan origin to the Romans through Aeneas, and the founding of the city to his descendants Romulus and Remus (at varying dates: 814, 753, 751, 748, 729 B.C.). Tradition records six kings after Romulus: Numa Pompilius, Tullus Hostilius, Ancus Marcius, Tarquinius Priscus, Servius Tullius, and Tarquinius Superbus, some at least of whom were historical figures. There is no doubt that there were kings in early Rome and that some of them were Etruscan. The king (*rex*) was advised by the Senate, a council of elders (*patres*), representatives of the leading clans (*gentes*), which enjoyed political and religious privileges. The People (*populus*), which included the less privileged classes (how early a sharp division between patricians and plebeians developed is uncertain), were divided into thirty *curiae*. To Servius Tullius are attributed administrative reforms, which in essence are probably his work. He created the *tribus*, which were gradually increased to thirty-five, and divided the people into five *classes* and each class into *centuriae* on the basis of a registration of the citizens and their property (*census*). Gradually a new assembly (Comitia Centuriata) superseded in importance an older assembly of the *curiae* (Comitia Curiata).

**4.** The literary tradition can be supplemented by other evidence, linguistic, religious, and archaeological. Although the earliest Latin inscription at Rome (on the

Duenos vase) belongs only to *c.* 525, it is clear that the inhabitants of early Rome spoke Latin: the survival of three brief graffiti in Etruscan found in Rome and belonging to the sixth century helps to confirm the tradition of a period of Etruscan domination of the city, while at the same time the fact that so few Etruscan words were adopted into Latin demonstrates the transitory nature of Etruscan rule there. Further, some religious ceremonies (Lupercalia, Septimontium, the feast of the Argei), which survived into republican times, reflect different stages in the unification of village settlements into one city, while the religious calendar of the Republic in part indicates customs of the sixth century or earlier. Archaeology in 1960 revealed traces of a Bronze Age ('Apennine') settlement (*c.* 1500 B.C. or later?) near the later Forum Boarium. Evidence for continuity of habitation is lacking, but there is much archaeological evidence for the huts and cemeteries of Iron Age settlements on the hills and in the Forum from the eighth century onwards, some with cremation burials *a pozzo* (in pits, as the Villanovan graves) on the Palatine, others with inhumation *a fossa* (trench graves, as in central Italy) on the Esquiline, and both rites on the Quirinal and in the Forum. These two rites may represent the mingling of Latins and Sabines which the literary tradition records. Further, traces of early buildings and votive deposits, the discovery of archaic architectural terracottas, together with stratigraphic excavation in the Forum, have added much to our knowledge, so that it is possible to trace in general outline the coalescing of the various settlements into an *urbs* or *polis*, not later than *c.* 575 B.C., and to see the advanced state of civilized life that developed, partly under Etruscan influence, during the sixth century when the city was made habitable by drainage and beautiful by the erection of temples such as that of Jupiter on the Capitol. Commerce and industry increased, and the boundaries of the *ager Romanus* were probably extended to include some 350 square miles. But Rome's debt to the Etruscans, though very great, must not be exaggerated. Under the veneer of a dominating Etruscan rule, Rome remained essentially a Latin city, and agriculture continued to be her chief industry.

**5.** Archaeological evidence, both old and new, thus seems to confirm in outline the traditional picture. Some archaeologists, however, including E. Gjerstad, believe rather that the traditional chronology must be modified in the light of it: thus they would move the period of Etruscan rule at Rome from the accepted dates of *c.* 616–510 down to *c.* 530–450. But such a revolutionary change, which puts the foundation of the Republic half a century later than the traditional date, creates what appear to many to be insuperable difficulties. Another challenge to accepted beliefs will probably gain no more supporters, namely that of A. Alföldi who argues that our knowledge of early Rome derives largely from a fiction deliberately devised by Fabius Pictor: knowing that regal Rome was only a lesser Latin city and a vassal of some southern Etruscan States, Fabius attributed to her in the sixth century that strength and predominance over other Latin cities which in fact (according to Alföldi) she gained only in the fifth: in other words Rome's rise to power has been antedated. Such work, together with other views (e.g. that of H. Müller-Karpe who puts the origins of Rome in the tenth century, or of G. Dumézil who tried to bring early Roman institutions into line with primitive Indo-European customs) is at least a testimony to the lively interest which the study of early Rome is provoking.

## II. ROME AND ITALY (509–264 B.C.)

**6.** With the expulsion of Tarquinius Superbus (510) Rome threw off the Etruscan yoke, and despite the efforts at restoration by Lars Porsenna the monarchy was abolished. An aristocratic Republic was established, and two annually elected magistrates, later called consuls, were invested with *imperium*, though in times of national emergency they might temporarily be overshadowed by the appointment of a dictator. The history of the Republic during the next 250 years is marked by two struggles: an internal class-struggle, during which the Republican constitution was hammered out and which ended in a compromise, and an external struggle with surrounding peoples, which ended in the assertion of Rome's supremacy as the head of a confederacy which embraced all Italy.

**7.** The Roman citizens were divided into two classes, patricians and plebeians, perhaps as a result of economic development. Whether or not this division goes very far back in time, the patricians certainly tried to strengthen the barrier after the end of the monarchy. The plebeians suffered grievances which they sought to redress by means of pressure brought by *secessiones* and by virtually creating a separate State within the State. The poorer plebeians sought more land, more liberal laws of debt and personal security against the oppression of patrician magistrates; the wealthier plebeians sought political and social equality with the patricians. During this struggle of the orders the plebeians (*see* PLEBS) established their own officers (tribunes and aediles) and assembly (*concilium plebis*) and gradually forced the patricians to recognize these. Landmarks in the struggle are the *Lex Publilia Voleronis* (471), the appointment of *Decemviri* and the codification and publication of the XII Tables, which formed the basis for the future development of Roman law (451–450), the Valerio-Horatian laws (449), the *Lex Canuleia* (445), the Licinian-Sextian rogations (367), the *Leges Publiliae* (339), the reforms of Cn. Flavius (304), the *Lex Ogulnia* (300), and finally the *Lex Hortensia* (287), which after earlier attempts (449, 339) gave *plebiscita* the force of laws binding on the whole community. Meantime, increase in public business, and, still more, patrician attempts to thwart the plebeian assaults on the patrician monopoly of office, led to the establishment of new magistracies. For many years during the period from 445 to 376 *tribuni militum consulari potestate*, an office open to plebeians, replaced the consuls, some of whose powers were transferred to newly established censors (443). The plebeians gradually gained admission to the quaestorship (421), the restored consulship (366), the dictatorship (356), the censorship (351), and in 337 to the praetorship, which had been established in 366 and led through the praetorian edict to the building up of Roman law.

**8.** Economic problems, such as shortage of food and land and harsh laws of debt, which tended to reduce freemen to serfdom, were attacked by legislators (e.g. Poetelius). Further, the conquest of Italy and the consequent distribution of land and establishment of colonies helped to alleviate economic distress. But while much hardship was lessened, only a small group of plebeian families became sufficiently rich and influential to enjoy the newly gained political privileges, and there grew up a new patricio-plebeian nobility which through the Senate and magistracies exercised a monopoly of government scarcely less exclusive than that enjoyed earlier by the patricians alone. But in theory the sovereignty of the People was at last established and the struggle of the orders was ended; by common sense and compromise the Romans, without bloodshed, had solved a problem which in many Greek States led to unending class-warfare.

**9.** Rome's external history was even more stormy. Following the collapse of Etruscan power in Latium the Romans, after a conflict with the Latins at Lake Regillus (496?), negotiated through Sp. Cassius a new alliance with the Latin League. Union in Latium was necessitated by external danger on all fronts: in the north were Etruscans, in the north-east Sabines, eastwards lay the Aequi, and south-east the Volsci. All these peoples were pressing on the plain of Latium. In the first half of the fifth century, in wars adorned by the exploits of Coriolanus and Cincinnatus, a Triple Alliance of Romans, Latins, and Hernici held their own against Aequi and Volsci; in the second half they moved to the offensive and victory. Then under Camillus' leadership Rome besieged and finally captured the Etruscan outpost, Veii (396), but thereafter a predatory horde of Celts led by Brennus swept down from the north, defeated the Roman army at Allia (387) and sacked the city, although Manlius held the Capitol. Thereafter the city was rebuilt and refortified, while Rome's shaken prestige and power in central Italy were slowly re-established. In 358 the treaty between Rome and the Latin League was renewed on less favourable terms for the Latins, who later fought an unsuccessful war of independence (340–338), saw their League dissolved, and entered into fresh relations with Rome.

**10.** Roman interests were now spreading to Campania, where they became predominant after an alliance with Neapolis (326). This brought Rome into conflict with the Samnite hill-tribes, and bitter struggles ensued. After the (possibly apocryphal) First Samnite War (343–341), the Second lasted intermittently from 326 till Roman victory in 304 and was marked by a major disaster at the Caudine Forks (321). Roman ascendancy in Etruria was extended, and alliances were made with Umbrian cities, the Picenes and Marsi, and with northern Apulia. Early in the third century the Samnites made a new bid for freedom; in alliance with fresh Gallic invaders, Etruscans, and Umbrians they were defeated at Sentinum (295) and finally subdued by 290. Further Celtic tribes and some Etruscan towns gave trouble until the Boii were defeated at Lake Vadimo (283) and again in 282. With the Samnites reduced, Rome was next drawn into southern Italy, where the Greek cities were being hard pressed by Lucanian tribes. When in 282 Rome sent a protective garrison to Thurii at that city's request, Tarentum resented Rome's interference in her sphere of influence, picked a quarrel with Rome, and summoned the help of Pyrrhus of Epirus, who landed in Italy (280). After two 'Pyrrhic' victories at Heraclea and Asculum he withdrew to Sicily (278); after his return (276) he was defeated by Rome (275) and retired to Greece, leaving Rome now undisputed mistress of Italy.

**11.** Rome's conquest of Italy had been achieved not merely by the sword; indeed, Rome was certainly no more aggressive than her neighbours, since the *ius fetiale* forbade wars of aggression. By founding Latin and Roman colonies at strategic points, and by the construction of roads, Rome had bound Italy together. But she had done more: she had created a political confederacy which embraced all Italy except Cisalpine Gaul. By the principle of incorporation Roman citizenship, in whole or part, had been extended to a large area of Italy, while the rest of the peninsula was bound to Rome by alliances of varying type, the most privileged being *ius Latii*. All, citizens and allies alike, were subject to military service, but only the citizens paid direct taxes. Peace was thus at length substituted for war as the normal condition of life in Italy; very gradually, since Rome did not force her civilization on others, local languages, customs, and cults gave place to a common culture based on the Latin tongue and Roman law. Finally, by this political unification of Italy, Rome was no longer merely a Latin city but had become a great military force and a world power, with whom Ptolemaic Egypt entered into friendly relations (*amicitia*) in 273, and whose war with Pyrrhus attracted the pen of a Greek historian, Timaeus. The era to which later Romans looked back as the formative period of their national character, when life was simple and austere, was passing. Rome was now politically linked with the hellenized South and in direct contact with Greek influences.

### III. ROME AND THE MEDITERRANEAN (264–133 B.C.)

**12.** As a world power Rome came into contact with Carthaginian interests in the western Mediterranean and with the Hellenistic world in the East. Her conflicts with Carthage are described under PUNIC WARS; they resulted in the elimination of Carthage from the western Mediterranean and in the acquisition by Rome of overseas *provinciae*, Sicily (241), Sardinia (238), Spain (206, organized 197), Africa (146). The Romans had to face another Gallic invasion of Italy, which was shattered at the battle of Telamon (225). Thereafter the northern frontier was secured by the defeat of the Boii and Insubres (224–220; 200–191), the pacification of Cisalpine Gaul, and the protection of its flanks by the reduction of the Ligurians (197–154), Istrians (178–177), and Dalmatian coast (156–155; 129). Thus Roman authority was extended from near Massilia (*Marseille*) round the sweep of the Alps to Istria and thence down the west coast of the Balkan peninsula.

**13.** Meantime Rome had been drawn into Hellenistic affairs. As a police measure she had suppressed Illyrian piracy in the Adriatic and established a small protectorate in Illyricum (First Illyrian War, 229–228, Second 219; see TEUTA, DEMETRIUS 7). Then she had successfully faced Hannibal's ally, Philip V of Macedon, in the First Macedonian War (214–205: see PUNIC WARS). Thereafter, when Philip launched a career of conquest in the eastern Mediterranean, Rhodes and Pergamum appealed for help to Rome. Actuated by a desire for future security against a possible threat from Philip's fleet or his ally Antiochus III of Syria (a desire which for some may have been strengthened by philhellenic sentiments), the Romans somewhat reluctantly entered upon the Second Macedonian War (200–196), which terminated in the victory of Flamininus at Cynoscephalae. Macedonia was forced to surrender her conquests but survived as an independent State, while Rome proclaimed freedom for Greece; no territory was annexed, and by 194 all Roman troops had evacuated Greece. Rome was next involved with Antiochus, with whom Hannibal had sought refuge. When he invaded Greece he was defeated at Thermopylae by the Romans, who then for the first time crossed to Asia and again defeated him at Magnesia (189). By the treaty of Apamea Antiochus was forced back into Syria, while most of the Seleucid kingdom in Asia Minor was given to Pergamum and Rhodes; Rome annexed no territory. Macedonia remained quiet until the accession of Perseus, who challenged Rome, only to meet defeat at the hands of Aemilius Paullus at Pydna in 168 (Third Macedonian War, 172–168/7). Macedonia was divided into four republics, but after further disorders caused by Andriscus it was at length annexed as a Roman province (147). The Achaean Confederacy was suppressed, and Corinth was destroyed by Mummius (146), not probably from motives of commercial jealousy but as an example to Greece that Roman patience was at an end. For half a century Rome had allowed Greece to enjoy or abuse her freedom: Rome's final intervention brought peace, if not prosperity. Meantime Rome had overawed the Hellenistic kingdoms of Bithynia, Galatia (see VULSO 2), Pergamum, and Rhodes, and had interfered in the politics of Egypt (see POPILLIUS 1) and Syria. In 133 Attalus of Pergamum bequeathed his kingdom to Rome: it was formed into the Roman province of Asia.

**14.** Meanwhile in the west Rome's attempt to administer and protect her provinces of Spain (acquired in 206 and organized in 197) led her into a long series of conflicts with the native tribes of the interior, especially Celtiberians and Lusitanians, which only ended with the destruction of Numantia by Scipio Aemilianus in 133 (*see* NUMANTIA, SPAIN, VIRIATHUS, etc.). Finally, after campaigns against Ligurians, Allobroges, and Arverni (125–121), southern Gaul was formed into the province of Gallia Transalpina or Narbonensis.

**15.** During this period when Rome was establishing an overseas Empire, and more particularly in the latter part of it, economic and social life in Rome and Italy underwent profound changes. In many parts capitalist farming replaced peasant husbandry; with the acquisition of an Empire there was a greater field for industry and commerce, which had relatively little interest for the Roman nobility or influence on Roman policy, but enhanced the importance of the rich business men (*see* EQUITES); slavery increased, both on the land and in the household; women gained greater freedom; life became more luxurious for the privileged classes, and public games increased; the city, adorned with new public buildings, assumed a fresh appearance. From the First Punic War, when Roman soldiers had fought in Grecian Sicily, the floodgates of Hellenism were open. Many nobles, as the Scipios and Flamininus, were ardent philhellenes, while the earliest Roman historians actually wrote in Greek; Cato's attempt to stem the tide was merely temporary. Fresh contacts were made with Greece in the Macedonian Wars, Greek philosophers lectured in Rome (155), while a group of intellectuals, the so-called Scipionic Circle, attempted to reconcile the best aspects of Greek and Roman life. In all spheres, art and architecture, literature and religion, Greek influences prevailed. But despite these profound changes the governing class, drawn from a small number of families, retained many of its old virtues and its general control of public affairs.

### IV. THE FALL OF THE REPUBLIC (133–31 B.C.)

**16.** Rome next had to grapple with many problems of which the solution became urgent. Of imperial problems that of safeguarding the frontiers was the least clamant. More pressing were the consequences of provincial administration, since the institutions of a city-state were ill-adapted to governing an Empire, and the attempts made to modify them were not sufficiently fundamental. The standard of provincial administration fell. Some governors plundered their provinces for private gain, others were corrupted by desire for power. The army began to look rather to its commanders than to the State for the rewards of service, and when led by men of ambition formed a new and dangerous element in Roman life. Rome also faced grave domestic issues, and a struggle developed between Optimates and Populares. Difficulties which might have been settled by compromise were rendered more acute by the rise of ambitious personalities who sought to exploit political power for their own ends. Further, Rome's selfish policy towards her Italian allies, who had helped to win the Empire but were deprived of many of its spoils, led to increasing discontent and ultimately to open war. Finally, there were urgent economic problems. The growth of *latifundia*, the promotion of pasturage at the expense of cereal production, and the system of land-tenure had all combined to drive large numbers of small farmers from the countryside to unemployment in the towns. There was pressing need to re-establish a small peasantry on the land and to rid the cities of idle hands.

**17.** Public attention was focused on many of these problems by the careers of Tiberius and Gaius Gracchus, who as tribunes representative of the sovereign authority of the Roman People challenged the senatorial monopoly of government. Their efforts, and the subsequent agrarian legislation, partially solved some economic problems, while Gaius championed the demands of the allies for Roman franchise and made the *equites* a political force and a Third Estate. Their attempts at reform were followed by a conservative reaction and by the war with Jugurtha (112–105). This was conducted by the Senate with such indolence and probably corruption that at length the People and *equites* demanded energetic action, which was given by Marius in whom the People found a military leader.

18. Unrest in Sicily found expression in two Slave Wars (135–132, 103–101). German tribes were on the move, defeating Roman armies (114, 113), and finally wiped out two consular armies at Arausio (105). In this hour of national crisis Marius held repeated consulships (103–101), and thanks to his military reforms saved his country by defeating the Teutones near Aquae Sextiae (102) and the Cimbri near Vercellae (101). But a new danger was at hand: Marius at the head of an army, which had been raised partly from proletarians by voluntary enlistment and owed more to its leader than to the State, might threaten the Senate in the name of the People. He obtained a sixth consulship (100), but was not prepared to use the army against the Senate's control of government: as a *novus homo* he wanted recognition by, rather than the overthrow of, the existing system. His unhappy temporary alliance with the leaders of the popular party, Saturninus and Glaucia (103–100), was followed by his own temporary eclipse and a brief conservative reaction (99–91) which nearly proved fatal to Rome. The attempted reforms of Drusus (91) and his plan to enfranchise the Italians failed, while his assassination precipitated the revolt of the allies in the Social or Marsian War (91–87), the result of the Senate's selfish policy. Some of the allies fought to win Roman citizenship, others as the Samnites to destroy Roman predominance in Italy. By fighting and by political concessions (*see under* CAESAR 2, POMPEIUS 3, PLAUTIUS 1) the Romans gained victory by conceding the main issue at stake. Italy was now united, and all south of the Po received Roman citizenship.

19. A contention between Marius and Sulla for the command against Mithridates of Pontus led to Sulla's march on Rome at the head of Roman legions (88) and the inauguration of a period of civil war and bloodshed. Thereafter Sulla left for Greece, where he defeated the Pontic army at Chaeronea (86) and settled the East. He returned in 83 to overthrow in civil war the government which Cinna had established in his absence. By 82, after a proscription of his political opponents, he attained a quasi-monarchical position as dictator and attempted to re-establish the authority of the Senate over against the powers of the tribunate and the influence of army commanders by a series of measures which did not long survive his voluntary retirement in 79. Pompey, after defeating Sertorius, who had held Spain against the senatorial government from 80 to 72, enjoyed a joint-consulship in 70 with Crassus, who had suppressed a slave-revolt led by Spartacus in Italy. Backed by their armies these two ambitious leaders, both former lieutenants of Sulla, swept away much of Sulla's legislation. The tribunate once again became a dangerous weapon which might assert the wishes of the Roman People, now mainly the unruly populace of the capital and unrepresentative of Italy as a whole, and those of their unscrupulous and ambitious leaders. Through the tribunate Pompey was given in 67 an overriding command against the pirates, whom he swept out of the Mediterranean, and then against Mithridates, whose renewed aggression had been checked by Lucullus. Though Lucullus had invaded Pontus and defeated Tigranes of Armenia, he had been forced to retire, and thus it was reserved for Pompey to end the Mithridatic

wars and to resettle the East (64–62), where he reorganized the client-kingdoms, established Syria as a Roman province (64), and promoted urbanization throughout Asia Minor. Other recent provincial changes affected Cisalpine Gaul, Bithynia, Cilicia, Crete, and Cyrene.

20. While Pompey was in the East, Crassus and Caesar intrigued in Rome against his return, using a tribune Rullus to further their ends. Catiline led a revolutionary scheme of broken men, which was unmasked by the consul Cicero (63), who began to hope for a *concordia ordinum*, a reconciliation of all moderate elements in the State. But the Senate foolishly withstood the demands of Pompey, who on his return from the East had loyally retired into private life, and also those of Caesar, who in 60 returned from a command in Spain. Pompey and Caesar together with Crassus were thus forced into an unofficial coalition, known as the First Triumvirate (60). In 59 Caesar as consul gained a prolonged command for himself in Gaul, which he added as a new province to the Empire, thus advancing the frontiers to the Rhine and the English Channel (58–50: *see* GALLIC WARS). Meantime, in a period of increasing electoral corruption and public disorder, fostered by gang-leaders as Clodius and Milo and resulting in the temporary exile of Cicero (58–57), the Triumvirate appeared to be breaking up, but was reaffirmed at a conference held at Luca (56). While Caesar made his name and won a devoted army in Gaul, Pompey controlled events in Rome and administered his Spanish province through *legati*. The death of Crassus at Carrhae (53) during a disastrous expedition against Parthia emphasized the rivalry of Pompey and Caesar, who gradually drifted into open conflict, with Pompey somewhat reluctantly supporting the senatorial cause. Caesar defeated the Pompeian army in Spain at Ilerda (49) and Pompey himself at Pharsalus (48); he won further victories in Asia at Zela (47), in Africa at Thapsus, where Cato's suicide exemplified the collapse of the Republican cause (46), and in Spain at Munda (45). Whether or not Caesar intended finally to end the Republic, as dictator he introduced the principle of personal autocracy into the constitution. His beneficial legislative reforms and his plans for safeguarding the Empire by military expeditions against Dacia and Parthia were cut short by his assassination by a group of short-sighted Republican conspirators, led by Cassius and Brutus (44).

21. Instead of a restoration of peace and the Republic another round of civil war followed. At first Octavian, Caesar's heir and avenger, supported by Cicero and the Republican party, struggled against Antony, who had been Caesar's helper. After the battle of Mutina (43) the three Caesarian leaders, Antony, Octavian, and Lepidus, formed an official coalition, the Second Triumvirate. The triumvirs defeated the forces of the Republicans led by Brutus and Cassius at Philippi (42). Gradually Octavian strengthened his hold on Italy and the western provinces, eliminating Sextus Pompeius and Lepidus. Meanwhile Antony had gone to the East, where he met Cleopatra, launched a disastrous expedition against Parthia, and finally became suspect of sacrificing Roman interests to Cleopatra. Thus the scene was set for a final clash between the Roman forces of the East and West which culminated in Antony's defeat by Octavian at Actium (31) and his death at Alexandria (30). The Roman world was reunited under the sole leadership of Octavian and peace was restored when he settled the East and annexed Egypt.

22. Despite civil wars, misgovernment, political corruption, the ambitions of the rival dynasts (*principes viri*), and the collapse of the republican constitution, the Roman world still offered a foundation on which a new

system could be constructed. Further, the political unification of Italy was reflected in the greater unity of Italian civilization. The whole of this period and especially the Ciceronian age witnessed a steady advance of oratory, art, and letters. If Cicero was the dominant literary figure, there were also Lucretius, Catullus, Caesar, Varro, and Sallust. Political instability had not undermined all the productive activities of man.

## V. Augustus and the Julio-Claudian Emperors (31 B.C.–A.D. 68)

**23.** Within the framework of the Republic, which had collapsed through the attacks of military dictators and the lack of an adequate civil service, Augustus, as Octavian was then called, created a new system which endured. His own position as *princeps* (q.v.) made him in fact a disguised constitutional monarch—'auctoritate omnibus praestiti'—with control over legislation, criminal jurisdiction, the army, and to a large extent finance and provincial administration. He shared many of his functions with the Senate, but his power was undivided. The army was reformed and was made the protector instead of a potential destroyer of the State; the frontiers were secured; the provinces were administered with greater care. To secure an adequate supply of civil servants the senatorial and equestrian orders were reorganized; the new executive included boards of *curatores* and *praefecti*, especially the prefect of the newly formed Praetorian Guard, and a *consilium principis*. By new buildings (*see*, e.g., ARA PACIS, FORUM AUGUSTI), by care for the water- and food-supplies (*see* ANNONA), by creating cohorts of *vigiles* to prevent fire and urban cohorts as a police force, Augustus made Rome a worthy capital of the Empire. By renovating the State religion and by less successful legislation designed to encourage marriage and a higher standard of morality Augustus hoped to create a new Roman People, the worthy exponents of that civilization which it was the great achievement of the Empire to spread to the provinces of the West. The Graeco-Roman civilization of the Mediterranean now became one, but the centre of gravity of the Empire was fixed in Italy and the West. True, the pendulum was to swing gradually eastwards during the next 300 years, and the Augustan Empire was radically modified in constitution and finally overrun by the barbarians, but not before it had done its great work of romanizing western Europe. Therein lies to a great measure the debt which the world owes to Augustus and his victory at Actium. Nor could Augustus have accomplished his task alone. He owed much to friends like Agrippa and Maecenas and not a little to writers such as Virgil, Horace, and Livy, who made this the Golden Age of Latin literature.

**24.** Though it was as peacemaker after the long series of civil wars that Augustus derived much of his popularity, he yet added much to the Empire, but for reasons of security rather than from desire for conquest. In the East ambitious plans were abandoned, an agreement was reached with Parthia, and Galatia was made a province (25 B.C.), as was Judaea in A.D. 6. Spain was finally pacified and, like Gaul, was reorganized. Local self-government was encouraged, the growth of towns fostered, and many colonies were founded. In the north Augustus advanced the frontier to the Danube and by the creation of a chain of provinces (Raetia, Noricum, Pannonia, and Moesia) protected the Balkans from invasion by the wild tribes of central Europe. His plan to advance beyond the Rhine to the Elbe was finally abandoned after the defeat of Varus, and the Rhine–Danube formed the frontier. The fostering of provincial *concilia* and the growth of the imperial cult increasingly gave a sense of unity to the Empire. With the frontiers thus secure and a stable central government the Mediterranean world

enjoyed a new era of industrial advance and widespread commerce.

**25.** Not the least difficult problem which faced Augustus was the succession. His efforts to secure it in the direct line of the Julian house were thwarted by the deaths of Marcellus, Gaius Caesar, and Lucius Caesar. At length he made Tiberius co-regent and at his death the Empire was handed on without a hitch. The prestige of his name and the methods which he had adopted determined to a large measure the decisions of his successors.

**26.** The reign of Tiberius (A.D. 14–37) saw the political advancement of the Senate at the expense of the People, but nevertheless the senatorial administration increasingly depended on the will of the *princeps*. The career of Sejanus demonstrated the potential power of the Praetorian Prefect and Guard. Though the reign was marked by the growth of delation and ended in a Terror, the provincial administration was good. Tiberius followed the precept of Augustus not to extend the Empire beyond its existing boundaries, except that Cappadocia was made a province. The interlude of the extravagant reign of Gaius (37–41) emphasized the autocratic tendencies latent in the Principate. Claudius' reign (41–54) was notable for his development of the imperial civil service, in which freedmen were given greater influence, for a more liberal extension of Roman franchise, and for an energetic foreign policy which replaced client kingdoms by provinces, and added the two Mauretanias (42), Britain (43), Lycia (43), and Thrace (46) to the Empire. Nero's reign (54–68) might open well under the guidance of Seneca and Burrus, but his reconciliation with the Senate did not last and he gradually scandalized the aristocracy. Disorder followed in the provinces. In the East Nero adopted a more active policy, which resulted in a clash with Parthia and the defeat of Paetus at Rhandeia (62), although the Armenian problem was settled thanks to Corbulo's display of Roman might. A revolt in Britain was led by Boudicca (61); rebellion spread through Judaea (66–70), while Vindex revolted in Gaul and Galba in Spain. Stoics, aristocrats, army chiefs, and private individuals opposed and hated Nero at home. Thus the Julio-Claudian dynasty collapsed amid rebellion and civil war, but the constructive work of Augustus and Claudius survived the disaster.

## VI. The Flavians and Antonines (A.D. 69–192)

**27.** The 'Year of the Four Emperors' (69) and the period of renewed civil war is important for its revelation that an Emperor could be made elsewhere than at Rome, by the wishes of the armies in the provinces, who recognized, however, that their nominees were still pretenders until approved by the Senate. Galba from Spain was accepted by the Praetorian Guard and Senate, but in 69 the Praetorians acclaimed Otho and killed Galba. The Rhine armies, however, proclaimed Vitellius, on whose behalf Caecina and Valens defeated Otho's forces at Bedriacum. After Otho's suicide Vitellius was accepted as Emperor, but meantime the eastern legions had declared for Vespasian, whose claim was soon accepted on the Danube. Vespasian's cause was led from Pannonia by Antonius Primus, who defeated the Vitellians and captured Rome. In 70 Jerusalem was stormed, the rising of Civilis on the Rhine and the attempt of Classicus to create an Imperium Galliarum were thwarted, and peace was re-established. From the confusion there had emerged a second Augustus, a *restitutor orbis*, who restored peace, founded a new dynasty, and resumed the task of government.

**28.** It was the great achievement of Vespasian (69–79) to restore confidence and prosperity, to prevent the change of the Principate's character from civilian to military, and to minimize the risk of renewed civil war by founding a dynasty and securing the succession of his sons Titus (79–81) and Domitian (81–96). Under the Flavians there was a marked and increasing advance towards absolute monarchy, brought about by the example set by Vespasian of reviving the censorship and holding numerous consulates, and by Domitian's acceptance of semi-divine honours, even though such measures may have been taken primarily to enhance the prestige of the upstart dynasty. The Senate, which by the admission of more provincials became more representative of the Empire, was neglected by Vespasian and slighted by Domitian, who relied more on the *consilium principis*. Wise in the choice of their executive, the Flavians made increasing use of *equites* in place of freedmen. By a prudent economy Vespasian restored the State finances, which withstood Titus' prodigality and Domitian's heavy expenditure. In foreign policy the Flavians aimed at strengthening the existing frontiers, particularly by a valuable consolidation of the Rhine and Danube *limites*, although the rising power of Dacia was given only a taste of Roman might, and an advance was made into Scotland. In general the provinces enjoyed a period of uneventful prosperity, resting on the restored tranquillity of the central government. The Flavians had little to fear from Caecina and Antonius Saturninus, but the obstructive opposition of Stoic and Cynic philosophers (*see*, e.g., HELVIDIUS PRISCUS) was irritating, while after 88 discontented senatorial opposition led to the renewal of delation and charges of *maiestas* and to the Reign of Terror in which Domitian the tyrant perished.

**29.** The reigns of the 'Five Good Emperors', Nerva (96–8), Trajan (98–117), Hadrian (117–38), Antoninus Pius (138–61), M. Aurelius (161–80), culminated in the Indian Summer of the Antonines, that era which Gibbon regarded as the happiest known to man. During this period the Principate underwent considerable modification. Nerva was chosen as the 'best citizen' by the Senate, not by the legions, and he found the armies, especially the Praetorian Guard, difficult to control; he compromised by adopting a soldier, Trajan, and making him co-regent. The next three rulers, none of whom had a son to succeed him, followed Nerva's example of adopting as son and successor a man of tried ability, thus averting further crises at their own deaths. Trajan by his tolerance won from a grateful Senate the title of Optimus Princeps. Hadrian, by his versatility, by his measures for the defence of the Empire and his care for its well-being, and above all by his personal activity in the provinces, won the respect of soldiers and civilians alike and peacefully handed over the reins of government to the senator Antoninus Pius, under whose beneficent influence the Empire entered upon one of the most secure periods of its history, although local self-government gradually weakened under the far-reaching paternalism of the central government. With the accession of M. Aurelius Stoicism was enthroned, and the philosopher manfully shouldered the responsibilities thrust upon him. But an age was passing. The joint rule of M. Aurelius and L. Verus (161–9) foreshadowed the division of imperial power. Further, through danger on the frontiers and a devastating plague the Empire was threatened with the loss of its margin of security and prosperity. When M. Aurelius, by promoting his son Commodus (180–93) to the throne, reverted to the dynastic principle of succession in place of the 'choice of the best', it was an ill day for the Empire. The moral basis of the Principate, emphasized by the recent Emperors, was weakened by the misrule and corruption of Commodus. Gradually, with the swelling tide of eastern religious ideas and with the victory of the military over the civilian conception of the Principate, the way was paved for the Dominate.

**30.** From Nerva to M. Aurelius the Emperors maintained good relations with the Senate, which by the admission of more provincials became yet more representative of the Empire. But if it regained some of its former prestige, it recovered little of its power, although Tacitus might praise Nerva for reconciling *libertas* and *principatus*. From Hadrian's time the administrative civil service, now drawn nearly exclusively from the senatorial and equestrian orders, was organized on a larger and more rigid scale. Honorific titles marked grades of equestrian officials, whose military and civil careers were sharply distinguished. Under Hadrian also there were important changes in the Roman legal system, and here the *consilium principis* played a leading part. The Comitia had died a natural death and its legislative functions were superseded by imperial 'constitutions', which were marked by a spirit of humanity and equity. By careful economy and a modest court the Emperors were able to be liberal in public expenditure, establishing various *alimenta* and *congiaria*, endowing education and planning public works, although under M. Aurelius the *fiscus* began to feel the strain.

**31.** Throughout the provinces urbanization reached its widest extent. Under ruling aristocracies of public-spirited men, who often spent lavishly to endow and maintain their own cities, the municipalities flourished as never before, although occasionally the Roman government was forced to limit their liberties in order to maintain public order or to support their finances, which sometimes became inadequate under the strain of compulsory contributions imposed on the local magistrates and senators (*see* LITURGY, CURATOR). The care which the Emperors exercised in the provinces is well illustrated by the correspondence between Trajan and Pliny or by Hadrian's thorough tours of inspection. Trajan and his three successors, who were all of Spanish or Gallic origin, were naturally liberal in granting Roman franchise.

**32.** There were few extensions of the Empire except under the warrior prince Trajan, who after two wars (101–2, 105–6) defeated Decebalus and annexed Dacia, which was quickly romanized. In the East Trajan annexed Nabataean Arabia in Transjordania and advanced over the Euphrates to wrest from Parthian control the new provinces of Armenia, Mesopotamia, and Assyria. By abandoning his predecessor's eastern conquests Hadrian reached a settlement with Parthia, which was temporarily upset under M. Aurelius. Thus in general Rome still held the line of the Euphrates, but the frontier was strengthened and straightened. Widespread Jewish revolts in 116 were quickly suppressed, while the establishment of a Roman colony in Jerusalem by Hadrian led to a second war in Palestine (131–5) and the ejection of all Jews from Jerusalem, although Hadrian's severe terms were modified by Antoninus. In Britain various attempts were made to secure the frontier: Roman policy led to the evacuation of Scotland and the construction of Hadrian's Wall (122–7); another extension of Roman influence into Scotland was followed by the establishment of the Antonine Wall (142–3). A greater crisis arose when Germanic tribes, the Marcomanni and Quadi, invaded the Danubian provinces and even raided north Italy. By resolute action M. Aurelius repelled the danger and planned to avert its repetition by advancing the frontier to the Carpathians and mountains of Bohemia, but after his death Commodus abandoned the plan. On the Rhine–Danube frontier precautions were taken, such as the rebuilding in stone of earth forts in Upper Germany and Raetia under Hadrian and the construction of an advance line under the Antonines. Administrative changes included the establishment of Upper and Lower Germany as separate provinces under Hadrian, the division of Pannonia into two provinces under Trajan and of Dacia into two and then three under Hadrian.

**33.** Although the Roman army which secured the frontiers was as yet unconquerable, it was undergoing many changes. With Hadrian's system of local recruiting it became less mobile and predominantly provincial. Only the Praetorian Guard retained a Latin tradition; the provincial soldiers, although good fighters, had only a slight acquaintance with Roman political ideas or Graeco-Roman culture, while as a result of the gradual separation of military from civil careers the higher officers, who were still mainly of Italian stock, had little experience of civil government.

**34.** In the latter part of this period the Roman Empire attained its highest economic development with the peace that reigned throughout Mediterranean lands and the extension of the road-system. In agriculture and industry the provinces began to outrun Italy. Commerce extended beyond the bounds of Empire to Scandinavia, overland to China, and through the Indian Ocean to the East. Industry and commerce promoted the growth of cities, while other new towns grew out of the military *canabae*. New buildings at Rome, as the Colosseum, Trajan's Forum, and the Pantheon, found their counterparts in the fora, theatres, amphitheatres, baths, aqueducts, and bridges which now adorned the chief provincial cities. Roman sculpture kept pace with architecture, and imperial ideals often conformed to the artistic traditions of the provinces. Schools and libraries exemplified State interest in education. Literature entered upon its Silver Age with the work of Martial and Juvenal, of Tacitus, Suetonius, and Quintilian, while there was a revival of Greek literature. Christian apologists developed a new branch of literature, and Roman jurisprudence reached its maturity. In every sphere, and especially in the religious, provincial influences spread, and the western stamp which Augustus had set upon the Empire gradually became less clear-cut. Christianity had taken root in Italy, Africa, and Gaul, and was developing that organization which was successfully to challenge the imperial regime. Rome had imposed no uniformity of culture, but had allowed the provincials to retain their varied customs and institutions. The predominantly Latin culture of the West was complementary to the Hellenism of the East. But despite diversity there was a real feeling of unity, and all looked to the Emperor as to a universal Providence by whose unremitting care the *pax Romana* was preserved. True, some problems, such as the social evils of slavery and the pauperization of urban populations or the possibility of a wise policy of decentralization and provincial representation, were not taken in hand. True, the culture of the Empire meant less to the masses in the provinces than to the middle and upper classes for whose benefit the Empire chiefly existed, while there were many foreshadowings of unhealthy changes to come. Nevertheless, the barriers between Rome and the provinces had fallen, and in an age of general serenity and good will, when men had become more humane, the stability of the Empire may well have seemed assured and the 'Aeternitas Populi Romani' more than a pious hope or an empty dream.

## VII. Collapse and Recovery (a.d. 193–330)

**35.** The death of Commodus ushered in a new period of civil war. The attempt of Pertinax to co-operate with the Senate failed through the renewed influence of the Praetorian Guard, which auctioned the Empire to Didius Julianus. Again, as in A.D. 69, provincial armies put forward their candidates for the throne, Clodius Albinus in Britain, Pescennius Niger in Syria, and Septimius Severus in Pannonia. Severus seized Rome, struck down

his rivals, and established a new dynasty. His reign (193–211) was marked by the development of the power of the equestrian order, the reconstitution of the Praetorian Guard and the increased power of its prefect, and by the creation of the *res privata*, but above all by its military aspect: the civilian constitution of the Empire which Augustus had conceived was set aside. Abandoning all pretence of co-operation with the Senate, Severus openly showed that his authority rested on the support of the army. His restoration of order in northern Britain was followed by the evacuation of Scotland. In general the frontier fortifications were consolidated and the provinces were well administered, some being divided into two. His son Caracalla (M. Aurelius Antoninus, 211–17) developed the military tendencies of the father, and by his edict of 212 abolished all distinction between Italians and provincials, so that the Empire legally became a commonwealth of equal members. But Alamanni and Goths were ominously threatening the Danube frontier. After Macrinus' brief reign (217–18), Elagabalus (218–22) gave Rome an unwelcome insight into eastern cult, oriental pomp, and personal corruption. Alexander Severus (221–35), guided by Julia Mamaea, attempted a *rapprochement* with the Senate and gave Rome a few years of comparative peace and tranquillity. But again the military element triumphed over the civil, and Alexander's murder was followed by half a century of military anarchy which nearly led to the final collapse of the Empire.

**36.** Emperors followed one another thick and fast: the Thracian peasant Maximinus (235–8), Gordian I, II, Pupienus, Balbinus (238), Gordian III (238–44), the Arabian Philip (244–9), the Illyrian Decius (249–51), Trebonianus Gallus (251–3), the Moor Aemilianus (253), and Valerian (253–60). While the armies played the game of emperor-making, the security and unity of the Empire were nearly destroyed. In the East the Parthian dynasty of the Arsacids was superseded by the aggressive Sassanidae who overran Syria (256), captured Valerian (259), and invaded Asia Minor. They were checked with the help of the caravan city of Palmyra, which under Zenobia now proceeded to challenge Roman supremacy in the East. In the West a pretender, Postumus, established an independent *imperium Galliarum*, which included Spain and Britain. Franks threatened the Lower Rhine, Saxon pirates ventured into the English Channel, Goths raided the Balkans and the Aegean, Alamanni crossed the Rhine and ravaged north Italy as far as Ravenna. With the Empire thus cracking and being rent asunder under his feet Valerian's son and successor Gallienus (253–68) had also to face a swarm of pretenders and rivals, the so-called Thirty Tyrants (q.v. 2). To his honour he brought the Empire through the crisis without complete disaster and laid the foundations of recovery. The tide was turned by his successors, the Illyrian Emperors, Claudius Gothicus (268–70), who repelled the Gothic peril, and Aurelian (270–5), who, though evacuating Dacia, destroyed Palmyra (273), recovered Gaul, and justly earned the title of *Restitutor Orbis*. The great wall which he constructed around Rome was a bulwark of defence but also a symbol of the vanishing *pax Romana*. But still the army could not agree to a durable government and elevated a succession of Emperors, many Illyrian, who had to fight rivals and barbarians alike: Tacitus (275–6), who defeated some Goths in Asia Minor, Florianus (276), Probus (276–82), who secured the Rhine and Danube frontiers and disposed of the rival Bonosus, Carus (282–3), who invaded Mesopotamia, Carinus (283–5), and Numerianus (283–4). Out of this welter of short-lived Emperors emerged Diocletian, who held power for twenty years (284–305) and then voluntarily laid it aside.

**37.** In order to secure the protection of the Empire and an unchallenged succession Diocletian divided the Empire and imperial power. As joint-Augustus with Maximian he established two junior Caesars, Galerius and Constantius, who should ultimately succeed. But when he insisted on retiring, fresh civil wars followed, in which Constantine by his defeat of Maxentius at the Milvian Bridge gained the Western Empire (312). In the East Licinius won supremacy by defeating Maximinus (313), but was defeated by Constantine in 314 and decisively again in 324, so that the Empire, West and East, was once more united under a resolute ruler. But the centre of gravity was shifting eastwards. The barbarian invasions had left Emperors little time to spend in Rome, and Diocletian had set up his court at Nicomedia in Bithynia. Finally, by 330, Constantine had established at Byzantium a new capital and Christian city, Constantinople or East Rome.

**38.** The Principate was dead; the military had triumphed over the civil aspect. Further, the basis of imperial authority had collapsed and a new sanction must be found. Eastern ideas of the king as the viceregent of heavenly authority were introduced. Thus Aurelian brought back to Rome the Persian worship of the Unconquered Sun, and Diocletian regarded himself as Jovius the earthly representative of Jupiter. The climax came when Constantine took Christianity (q.v.) into partnership with the Empire. The long period of persecution was ended and the struggle, which had gradually assumed the form of State against Church rather than pagan against Christian, was resolved with Constantine reigning as the earthly representative of the Christians' God; thus the way was prepared for a reconciliation between the Christian Church and the culture of the ancient world. Further, the outward form of imperial authority changed no less than its basis, which was legally autocratic after 282, when Carus dispensed with the theory that his power derived from the Senate. In title *dominus* replaced *princeps*. Aurelian (*dominus et deus*) introduced the pomp of oriental absolutism, while Diocletian and Constantine elaborated a court ceremonial in which the 'sacred' person of the Emperor, arrayed in diadem, purple, and gold, demanded prostration on the part of those admitted to audience. The *consilium principis* became a *sacrum consistorium*. The old republican magistracies either died out or were divested of all executive authority. The Senate survived with undimmed prestige, but its authority was reduced to that of a local town council. Under Diocletian military were separated from civilian offices, and under Constantine the senatorial and equestrian orders united. Provincial administration was profoundly modified: the number of provinces rose to 70 and ultimately to 116, the Empire was grouped into prefectures and dioceses, and the officials (*praesides*, *vicarii*, *praefecti praetorio*, etc.) accordingly increased. Municipal patriotism and self-government declined, owing to impoverishment, financial pressure, and the growth of bureaucracy, so that under Constantine the *curiales* became a hereditary caste and the attempt to avoid office and its crushing responsibilities was checked by State action. Thanks to the military reforms of Diocletian and Constantine with frontier forces (*limitanei*) and mobile reserves (*comitatenses*), the Roman army, although profoundly changed, still guarded the frontiers and kept the barbarians at arm's length. But this security was bought at a price. The great increase of the army and the civil service strained both the manpower of the Empire and its financial resources almost to breaking-point: the situation was met by far-reaching economic reforms which involved considerable restriction of personal liberty of movement and employment.

**39.** The mid third century witnessed an economic as well as a political collapse. Rising costs of government led to depreciation of the coinage and the extension of a system of requisitions and compulsory labour. The monetary system was undermined and was partially replaced by payments in kind, although the improvement of the coinage under Diocletian and Constantine led to a slow revival of confidence and a gradual restoration of a money economy: a sound gold and silver currency was established. A new taxation system (*annona*; *indictio*) was developed by Diocletian to remedy the injustices of the arbitrary requisitions which had become more common during the preceding upheavals, while he also extended the system of compulsory corporate responsibility for the collection of taxes and for the performance of other services. Gradually various industrial and commercial guilds were converted into hereditary castes in an attempt to maintain the economic life of the Empire, which had declined seriously in the third century as a result of civil wars and barbarian invasions, increasing difficulties of communication, and above all the general sense of insecurity and lack of confidence. Not all parts of the Empire declined as rapidly as did some, but industry, especially in the west, suffered severely and the total cultivated area and the size of the towns gradually diminished. Finally, through the growth of *latifundia*, some landed gentry in their fortified villas could live securely and at ease in a manner which foreshadowed medieval feudalism, but the tenants (*coloni*) on the large estates gradually to surrender their liberty of movement and sank to a state of serfdom which received legal recognition under Constantine.

**40.** Social life declined in the towns and flourished rather among the country aristocracy. The State educational institutions were not neglected, and letters received some encouragement. After the third-century collapse both Latin and Greek literature enjoyed a mild revival, while Christian literature showed real vigour. Sculpture declined, but architecture maintained a technically high level, and the way was paved for the transition to 'late classical' art. Neoplatonism and Mithraism strove with Christianity for the allegiance of men, while in the countryside paganism still flourished. But the future lay with Christianity (despite Donatist and Arian controversies), and when Constantine, a Roman Emperor, presided at the Council of Christian bishops at Nicaea in 325 an era in man's history was ended and the threshold of the Middle Ages was revealed.

**41.** Diocletian and Constantine had buttressed up the Empire, and their organization of the State and its administration was not much altered by their successors. But Constantine's unerring insight in founding a new Christian capital *in partibus Orientis* could not secure the unity of the whole. After his death and renewed civil war the Empire was temporarily reunited under Constantius and Julian, whose reign witnessed a reaction of paganism against Christianity, and again under Theodosius I (395), whose sons, theoretically joint-rulers of a single Empire, were in practice monarchs of East and West with equal rights; and so it continued for another century, an Emperor usually being succeeded by his eldest son. The *de facto* division was emphasized by the existence of two senates, with hereditary membership, although individual senators in the East did not in general gain the extreme wealth and vast landed estates enjoyed by many of those in the West. The latter numbered some 2,000, and these landed nobles, whose power was increased by the numerous smaller men who attached themselves to them in times of invasion, civil war, and economic difficulty, exercised a feudal sway. Economic and social developments increased the hardships of the curials, of the workers in their trade guilds and state-factories who by law could not change their work, and of the *coloni* and other agricultural labourers. A rigid state control dominated an economy that was theoretically based upon private enterprise. However, among the wealthy, culture survived and even flourished: a revival of letters took place among the pagan nobles of Rome, guided by Symmachus, and Rome's last great historian, Ammianus, flourished. Further, the Church attracted many of the most powerful thinkers: Ambrose, Jerome, Hilary, Augustine, and, in the East, Athanasius, John Chrysostom, Gregory of Nazianzus, and Basil. And the Church, a very different body from the persecuted sect of the days before Constantine, proved in some respects more adaptable than the State. Although at first weakened by heresies, and by monasticism until this way of life was officially regulated, it began to compete with the State for the service of the educated and well-born. A prosperous and powerful Church gradually changed the social balance of the Empire. Bishops might on occasion organize military resistance to the barbarian attacks; they might also seek to convert those federate barbarians who settled within the Empire, thus helping in some degree to romanize them.

**42.** In the East the Byzantine Empire survived until the Mohammedan capture of Constantinople in 1453. It was enabled to ward off the pressure of Persians, Huns, and Goths, and later of Avars, Bulgars, and Arabs, thanks to the impregnability of the capital, the reserves of military manpower that Asia Minor provided, a generally efficient administrative machinery, and fewer economic tensions than existed in the West. If its culture became predominantly Greek, it at any rate produced two of the greatest monuments of Roman law in the codes of Theodosius II and Justinian. East Rome was in fact the direct continuation of the Roman Empire, and to its resolute resistance to the storms of barbarism the modern world owes the preservation of the legacy of the ancient world since much classical literature was continuously studied and thus survived.

The West, separated from the East, could not long survive the storm of barbarian invasion. Picts, Scots, and Saxons overran Britain which the Romans were no longer able to protect and had to leave to its fate. The main German invasions came in waves. First, the Visigoths, fleeing before the Huns, defeated Valens at Adrianople (378), and ultimately, with the Burgundians, occupied the larger part of Gaul as federates, until in 475 Euric in south-west Gaul became independent of the Roman government. A second wave of Vandals, Suebi, and Alani crossed the Rhine in 406; after settling in Spain, some passed on to Africa where they captured Carthage (439) and established a separate State, thus cutting the Mediterranean in two. A third wave followed the collapse of Attila's Empire (453): Ostrogoths settled in Pannonia and threatened Italy. In 410 the Visigoth Alaric had sacked Rome, and although the threat from Attila was averted in 452, Rome was again raided and plundered by the Vandal Gaeseric in 455. Then the German Odoacer advanced and deposed Romulus Augustulus in 476, but although he became master of Rome and in effect its king, he yet acknowledged the authority of the Emperor at Constantinople. Soon, in 493, Odoacer was overthrown by Theodoric who established the Ostrogothic kingdom in Italy, but he too recognized the authority of the Eastern emperors. Conditions naturally varied in the different parts of the West which the Germans, whether federates or independent, had partitioned and occupied, yet the whole picture was not completely changed: the Roman population, which was barred from military service and from intermarriage with the barbarians, was still subject to Roman law and to a Roman civil administration. Roman rule in the West might be ended, but the survival of Roman law and the Latin tongue, the Roman Church,

and the Holy Roman Empire continued to demonstrate the indestructibility of the Roman tradition.

On the sources of Roman history *see* HISTORIOGRAPHY (ROMAN AND GREEK), ANNALS, FASTI, EPIGRAPHY, COINAGE (ROMAN), PAPYRI.

GENERAL HISTORIES. *The Cambridge Ancient History*, edited by S. A. Cook, F. E. Adcock, M. P. Charlesworth, and (vol. xii) N. H. Baynes: vii, *The Hellenistic Monarchies and the Rise of Rome* (1928); viii, *Rome and the Mediterranean, 218–133 B.C.* (1930); ix, *The Roman Republic, 133–44 B.C.* (1932); x, *The Augustan Empire, 44 B.C.–A.D. 70* (1934); xi, *The Imperial Peace, A.D. 70–192* (1936); xii, *The Imperial Crisis and Recovery, A.D. 193–324* (1939). Volumes of Plates, prepared by C. T. Seltman, iii (to vols. vii and viii), iv (to ix and x), v (to xi and xii).

*Methuen's History of the Greek and Roman World*, edited by M. Cary: vol. iv, *A History of the Roman World, 753–146 B.C.*, by H. H. Scullard³ (1961); v, *146–30 B.C.*, by F. B. Marsh³ (1963); vi, *30 B.C.–A.D. 138*, by E. T. Salmon⁵ (1966); vii, *A.D. 138–337*, by H. M. D. Parker² (1958).

M. Rostovtzeff, *A History of the Ancient World*, vol. ii, *Rome* (1927). *European Civilization*, edited by E. Eyre, vol. ii, *Rome and Christendom*, by A. W. Gomme, S. N. Miller, and W. E. Brown (1935). M. Cary, *A History of Rome down to the Reign of Constantine²* (1954). T. Frank, *A History of Rome* (1923). H. F. Pelham, *Outlines of Roman History⁵* (1926). A. E. R. Boak and W. G. Sinnigen, *A History of Rome to A.D. 565⁶* (U.S.A. 1965). H. H. Scullard, *From the Gracchi to Nero²* (1963).

*Histoire ancienne*, edited by G. Glotz. Part III: *Histoire romaine*: I, *Des Origines à l'achèvement de la conquête²*, by E. Pais and J. Bayet (1940); II, *La République romaine de 133 à 44 av. J.-C.*, by G. Bloch and J. Carcopino (1935–6); III, *Le Haut-Empire*, by L. Homo (1941); IV, *Le Bas-Empire jusqu'au 395*: i, *L'Empire romain de l'avènement des Sévères au concile de Nicée*, by M. Besnier (1937); ii, *L'Empire chrétien (325–395)*, by A. Piganiol (1947). A. Piganiol, *Histoire de Rome⁵* (1962).

J. Vogt and E. Kornemann, *Römische Geschichte* in Gercke–Norden, *Einleitung in die Altertumswissenschaft³* iii. 2 (1933). A. Heuss, *Römische Geschichte²* (1964).

L. Pareti, *Storia di Roma* i–vi (1952–62). *Storia d'Italia*, i, *L'Italia antica*, by P. Ducati (1936); ii, *L'Italia imperiale*, by R. Paribeni (1939). *Storia di Roma*: i, *Le origini e il periodo regio* (1954), by R. Paribeni; ii, *Roma nell'età delle guerre puniche* (1938), by G. Gianelli; iii, *Le grandi conquiste mediterranee* (1945), by G. Corradi; v, *L'età di Cesare e di Augusto* (1950), by R. Paribeni; vi, *L'impero da Tiberio agli Antonini* (1960), by A. Garzetti; vii, *I Severi* (1949), by A. Calderini; *Da Diocleziano alla caduta dell'impero d'Occidente* (1941), by R. Paribeni.

EARLY ROME. J. Whatmough, *The Foundations of Roman Italy* (1937). E. Gjerstad, *Early Rome* i–iv (1953–67), with two more volumes to follow, gives the archaeological material. For a brief statement of his historical views (which are very controversial), see *Legends and Facts of Early Roman History* (Lund, 1962). Controversial too are H. Müller-Karpe, *Vom Anfang Roms* (1959), and A. Alföldi, *Early Rome and the Latins* (U.S.A. 1965). For criticism of these views, and his collected papers on early Rome see A. Momigliano, *Terzo contributo alla storia degli studi classici* (1966), 543 ff. and *Quarto contributo* (1969), 273 ff. R. Bloch, *The Origins of Rome* (1960), a sketch. P. De Francisci, *Primordia Civitatis* (1959), for early institutions. H. H. Scullard, *The Etruscan Cities and Rome* (1967). *Les Origines de la république romaine* (Entretiens Hardt xiii, 1967): J. Heurgon, *Rome et la Méditerranée occidentale jusqu'aux guerres puniques* (1969).

THE REPUBLIC. *General*: Mommsen, *History of Rome* (Engl. Transl.). W. E. Heitland, *The Roman Republic* (3 vols., 1909). T. Frank, *Roman Imperialism* (1914). A. H. MacDonald, *Republican Rome* (1966).

*Republic*: E. Badian, *Foreign Clientelae, 264–70 B.C.* (1958), *Roman Imperialism in the Late Republic²* (1968). H. H. Scullard, *Roman Politics, 220–150 B.C.* (1951). A. J. Toynbee, *Hannibal's Legacy*, 2 vols. (1965). E. S. Gruen, *Roman Politics and the Criminal Courts 149–78 B.C.* (U.S.A. 1968). A. H. J. Greenidge, *A History of Rome, 133–104 B.C.* (1904). A. H. J. Greenidge and A. M. Clay (2nd ed. by E. W. Gray), *Sources for Roman History, 133–70 B.C.* (1960). T. Rice Holmes, *The Roman Republic* (3 vols., 1923), covering 70–44 B.C. Chr. Meier, *Res publica amissa* (Wiesbaden, 1966).

A. Piganiol, *La Conquête romaine³* (1967). M. Holleaux, *Rome, la Grèce et les monarchies hellénistiques au iiiᵉ siècle av. J.-C.* (reprint, 1935). G. Colin, *Rome et la Grèce de 200 à 146 av. J.-C.* (1904). K. J. Beloch, *Römische Geschichte bis zum Beginn der punischen Kriege* (1926). F. Münzer, *Römische Adelsparteien und Adelsfamilien* (1920).

G. De Sanctis, *Storia dei Romani*, vols. i–iv (1907–64), down to 133 B.C.). E. Pais, *Storia di Roma* (1927–34), 5 vols. from the regal period until the Gracchan revolution. W. Drumann, *Geschichte Roms in seinem Übergange von der republikanischen zur monarchischen Verfassung*, i–vi, 2nd ed. by P. Groebe (1899–1929).

*Transition to Empire*: F. B. Marsh, *The Founding of the Roman Empire²* (1927). T. Rice Holmes, *The Architect of the Roman Empire* (2 vols., 1928, 1931). R. Syme, *The Roman Revolution²* (1952).

ROMAN EMPIRE. *General*: J. B. Bury, *A History of the Roman Empire from its Foundation to the Death of Marcus Aurelius* (6th impression, 1913). M. P. Nilsson, *Imperial Rome* (1926). J. Wells and R. H. Barrow, *A Short History of the Roman Empire to the Death* of *Marcus Aurelius* (1931). F. Millar, *The Roman Empire and its Neighbours* (1967). M. Grant, *The Climax of Rome* (1968). R. Mac-Mullen, *Enemies of the Roman Order* (U.S.A. 1966).

E. Albertini, *L'Empire romain*² (1939). L. Homo, *L'Empire romain* (1925). P. Petit, *La Paix romaine* (1967).

H. Dessau, *Geschichte der römischen Kaiserzeit* (vols. I, II, i, ii, 1924–30). A. von Domaszewski, *Gesch. der röm. Kaiser*³ (1922). A. Passerini, *Linee di storia romana nell'età imperiale* (1949). S. Mazzerino, *Trattato di storia romana* II (1956).

*The Provinces.* Mommsen, *The Provinces of the Roman Empire from Caesar to Diocletian* (Engl. Transl., reprinted 1909). V. Chapot, *The Roman World* (Engl. Transl. 1928). J. S. Reid, *The Municipalities of the Roman Empire* (1913). F. F. Abbott and A. C. Johnson, *Municipal Administration in the Roman Empire* (1926). A. H. M. Jones, *The Cities of the Eastern Roman Provinces* (1939), *The Greek City* (1940). G. H. Stevenson, *Roman Provincial Administration till the Age of the Antonines* (1939).

*The Later Empire.* E. Gibbon, *The Decline and Fall of the Roman Empire* (ed. by J. B. Bury, 7 vols., 1896–1900). A. H. M. Jones, *The Later Roman Empire, 284–602* (3 vols., 1964), *The Decline of the Ancient World* (1966). J. B. Bury, *History of the Later Roman Empire* (A.D. 395– 565) (1923). F. Lot, *The End of the Ancient World* (Engl. Transl. 1931). F. W. Walbank, *The Awful Revolution* (1969). J. Vogt, *The Decline of Rome* (1967). S. Mazzarino, *The End of the Ancient World* (1967). O. Seeck, *Geschichte des Untergangs der antiken Welt* (6 vols., 1895–1921). E. Stein, *Histoire du Bas-Empire* (284–476), ed. J. R. Palanque (2 vols., 1959). A. Dopsch, *The Economic and Social Foundations of European Civilization* (Engl. Transl. 1938). J. B. Bury, *The Invasion of Europe by the Barbarians* (1928). F. Lot, *Les Invasions germaniques* (1935). *Cambridge Medieval History*, vols. i, ii (1911–13), iv, *The Byzantine Empire* (1965). *Byzantium* (1948), edited by N. H. Baynes and H. St. L. B. Moss. C. N. Cochrane, *Christianity and Classical Culture* (1940). *The Conflict between Paganism and Christianity in the Fourth Century* (1963), edited by A. Momigliano.

CONSTITUTIONAL, ETC. A. H. J. Greenidge, *Roman Public Life* (1901). L. Homo, *Roman Political Institutions* (Engl. Transl. 1929). Mommsen, *Römisches Staatsrecht* (3 vols., 1881–8); *Römisches Strafrecht* (1899). J. Marquardt, *Römische Staatsverwaltung* (3 vols., 1881–5). French translation of Mommsen and Marquardt, *Manuel des antiquités romaines* (19 vols., 1890–1907): i–vii, *Le Droit public romain*; viii, ix, *L'Organisation de l'empire romain*; x, *L'Organisation financière*; xi, *L'Organisation militaire*; xii, xiii, *Le Culte*; xiv, xv, *La Vie privée des Romains*; xvi, *Sources du droit romain*; xvii–xix, *Le Droit pénal romain*. E. Meyer, *Römischer Staat und Staatsgedanke*² (1961). F. de Martino, *Storia della costituzione romana* i–v (1958–67). T. R. S. Broughton, *The Magistrates of the Roman Republic*, 2 vols. and Suppl. (1951–60). J. Crook, *Law and Life of Rome* (1967). D. Earl, *The Moral and Political Tradition of Rome* (1967). M. Gelzer, *The Roman Nobility* (1969).

*See also under* SENATE, COMITIA, PRINCEPS, CONSUL, TRIBUS, CITIZENSHIP, etc.

ECONOMIC AND SOCIAL. *An Economic Survey of Ancient Rome*, edited by T. Frank (5 vols., U.S.A.): i, *Rome and Italy of the Republic*, by T. Frank (1933); ii, *Roman Egypt*, by A. C. Johnson 1936); iii, *Roman Britain, Spain, Sicily and Gaul*, by R. G. Collingwood, J. J. van Nostrand, V. Scramuzza, and A. Grenier (1937); iv, *Roman Africa, Syria, Greece and Asia*, by R. M. Haywood, F. M. Heichelheim, J. A. O. Larsen, and T. R. S. Broughton (1938); v, *Rome and Italy of the Empire*, by T. Frank (1940); *General Index* (1940).

M. Rostovtzeff, *The Social and Economic History of the Roman Empire*² (1957). T. Frank, *An Economic History of Rome*² (U.S.A. 1927). M. P. Charlesworth, *Trade Routes and Commerce of the Roman Empire*² (1926). *Cambridge Economic History of Europe* i, ii (1942–52).

M. Grant, *The World of Rome* (1960). W. Warde Fowler, *Social Life at Rome in the Age of Cicero* (1909). *The British Museum Guide illustrating Greek and Roman Life*. L. Friedländer, *Roman Life and Manners under the Early Empire* (Engl. Transl. of 7th edition, 4 vols., 1908–13; new 11th German edition, 4 vols., 1921–3). S. Dill, *Roman Society from Nero to M. Aurelius*² (1905); *Roman Society in the last century of the Western Empire*² (1899). A. Grenier, *The Roman Spirit* (Engl. Transl. 1926). J. Carcopino, *Daily Life in Ancient Rome* (1940). J. P. V. Balsdon, *Life and Leisure in Ancient Rome* (1969).

Three small introductory books are M. Cary and T. J. Haarhoff, *Life and Thought in the Greek and Roman World* (1940); R. W. Moore, *The Roman Commonwealth* (1942); and H. Grose-Hodge, *Roman Panorama* (1944).

*See also* s.v. AGRICULTURE, COMMERCE, INDUSTRY, etc.

WORKS OF A GENERAL CHARACTER. *A Companion to Latin Studies*, edited by J. E. Sandys³ (1921). H. Stuart Jones, *Companion to Roman History* (1912).

BIBLIOGRAPHIES. Full bibliographies are contained in *CAH*. These may be supplemented by the annual publication *L'Année philologique*.                                                    H. H. S.

**ROME** (TOPOGRAPHY). The Tiber valley at Rome is a deep trough, from ½ to 1½ miles wide, cut into the soft tufa floor of the river's lower basin. The edges of the trough are formed by steep weathered cliffs, seamed and even isolated by tributary streams. Thus were formed the famous hills of Rome, the Capitol, Palatine, and Aventine being cut off from the main hinterland, the Caelian, Oppian, Esquiline, Viminal, and Quirinal as flat-topped spurs. On the valley floor itself the river meanders in an S-shaped curve, the northern or upper twist containing the flat and mephitic Campus Martius and skirting the Vatican plain, the southern curve skirting the Capitol, *Forum Boarium*, and Aventine, and enclosing *Transtiberim*, a smaller plain at the foot of the Janiculan ridge. Just below the middle of the S-curve the river runs shallow and divides at Tiber island, traditionally erected by man upon a natural basis. The ford so made has no fellow between Rome and the sea, or for many miles upstream. Thus, while hills and spurs provided the natural strongholds beloved by primitive communities, traffic across the heavily populated Latian plain concentrated at the Tiber ford, the key to Rome's predominance.

**2.** Archaeology attests widespread primitive settlements on the Palatine, Esquiline, and Quirinal (qq.v.), associated with grave-goods going back to the ninth century B.C. Important cemeteries crowded the edges of the marshy valley of the *Forum Romanum* (q.v.), where burials cease by the sixth century B.C., attesting the synoecism brought about by the kings and coincident with the draining of the valley by the *cloaca maxima* (q.v.) and the creation of the *forum* market-place. The Wall of Servius (q.v.) on the Viminal, and cliffs elsewhere, made Rome a great promontory fortress comparable with Veii or Ardea, while the *pons sublicius* supplanted the ford. Regal ambition made a sacred acropolis of the Capitol, royal acres of the Campus Martius, a religious centre of the Aventine, with temple of Diana and *armilustrium*, and a *circus* (q.v.) of the Velabrum. The Republic kept the monuments, made of the Campus Martius a training-ground, and gradually concentrated civic activities in the Forum. The Palatine became a residential centre. Markets lined the Tiber bank, near the bridge and in touch with river-traffic, or clustered behind the Forum, whence State buildings gradually ousted them. The city became crowded, especially in the valleys which formed the irregular arterial routes, and as early as the third century B.C. tenement houses, which were to become a feature of the capital, attest the overcrowding and squalor which beset the narrow thoroughfares, such as the *Vicus Tuscus*, *Vicus Iugarius*, or *Subura*. Civic pride and family ambition early endowed innumerable temples. The city wall was erected c. 378 B.C., enclosing the *Quattuor Regiones* (*see* REGIO); aqueducts (q.v.) came later, in 312, 272, and 144 B.C.; quays, new Tiber bridges, *basilicae*, and porticoes later still, as in the great outburst of building activity in 184–176 B.C. Sulla was the first of the great dictators or *principes* to systematize large areas, linking the Forum and Capitol as an architectural unit by means of the *Tabularium* (q.v. 1). Pompey set a new fashion in theatres and porticoes, by the famous group of buildings centred upon his theatre and *Hecatostylon*; while of Julius Caesar's grandiose schemes, including Tiber diversion (Cic. *Att.* 13. 33), only the *Forum Iulium* (q.v.) remains, though such buildings as the *basilica Iulia* and the *Saepta* (q.v.) were finished by Augustus.

**3.** Thus the monumental centres of the City had been determined by the Republic upon a basis inherited from the kings. Their surviving outward form, however, owes far more to the Emperors, whose rebuildings or additions transformed or eclipsed the older monuments. Augustus built a new *Forum Augustum* (q.v.), novel in form and dedication, a modest palace on the Palatine, associated with the temple of Apollo, and three new aqueducts (q.v.), while many new monuments in the Campus (q.v.), including the *Mausoleum*, were erected by him or by his *viri triumphales*. It may be claimed that in the Campus he and Agrippa rivalled Pompey. Studied attention was paid to the archaic cult buildings of the

Forum Romanum, in harmony with the religious revival, while the city was divided into fourteen new *regiones* (q.v.). The contributions of Tiberius, the *Castra Praetoria* on the outskirts of the Viminal and the *Domus Tiberiana* on the Palatine (q.v.), are curiously significant of his policy; while the freak building-schemes of Gaius reflect that disregard of public feeling which cost him his life. The only lasting building of Gaius, the *Circus* (q.v.) in *Transtiberim*, was to fix through the martyrs the centre of Christianity. The effect of all these building-schemes was to drive the residential quarters off the Palatine to the villas and parks of the Quirinal, Pincian, and Aventine. To supply these higher sites, Claudius built two sumptuous aqueducts. Nero's parkland palace (s.v. DOMUS AUREA) attests his Hellenistic tastes, as do his *Colossus* and monumental *Via Sacra* (q.v.), the sole street in Rome comparable with the great colonnaded streets of the Roman East or the newer imperial cities of the West. His Baths and Gymnasium are more to Roman taste. The Flavians spent much energy in romanizing the creations of the τύραννος, the *Colosseum* (q.v.), *Forum Vespasiani* (q.v.), and Baths of Titus taking their place. Nerva's *Forum Transitorium* is a curious essay in the monumental approach, linking *Forum Romanum* and *Subura*. Trajan's *Thermae* finally blotted out the *Domus Aurea*, while his monumental *Forum* (q.v.) and market represent the impact of the Syrian Apollodorus upon Roman taste—'in Tiberim defluxit Orontes!' The Aqua Traiana (s.v. AQUEDUCTS) was the first good water-supply in *Transtiberim*. Hadrian replaced the vestibule of the *Domus Aurea* by the temple of Venus and Rome, erected a new *Mausoleum* and the *pons Aelius*, and rebuilt the *Pantheon* and Baths of Agrippa in the Campus.

4. Then followed a pause in building activities: the Antonines could afford to live upon the prestige of their predecessors, adding only triumphal monuments and temples of the *Divi*. Later building-schemes, apart from repairs, take the form of isolated monumental buildings, chiefly of utility. Aurelian's *Templum Solis* is the one notable religious building. The typical erections are the great *Thermae*. But the policy of the Severi is illustrated by their vast extension of the imperial palace on the Palatine (q.v.), with ornamental façade (*see* SEPTIZODIUM) on Via Appia, and the *Castra Equitum Singularium* on the Caelian. It is significant for the overcrowding in the City, as well as for the urgent need of cleanliness, that the sites for the great Baths had to be sought on the fringe, Caracalla picking the low ground outside Porta Capena, Diocletian selecting the Viminal, Constantine choosing the Quirinal. Great fires offered the only chance of rebuilding in the older regions: thus, the *Thermae Alexandrinae* were an enlargement of Nero's Baths in the Campus, while the fire of Carinus in 284 created space for the *basilica* of Maxentius, the noblest experiment in vaulting in the ancient world. The city had now reached the climax of its development, and it is significant that Aurelian had again ringed it with a defensive wall (*see* WALL OF AURELIAN). Further changes belong to the medieval topography.

Platner–Ashby, *Topog. Dict.* (1929); Nash, *Pict. Dict. Rome* i, ii² (1968); C. Hülsen and H. Jordan, *Topographie der Stadt Roms* (4 vols., 1871–1906); R. Lanciani, *Ruins and Excavations of Ancient Rome* (1897); *Forma Urbis Romae* (1893–1901); G. Lugli, *I monumenti antichi di Roma e del suburbio* (vols. i–iii, 1931–8; Engl. Transl., *The Classical Monuments of Rome*, vol. i; vol. i is now superseded by *Roma antica, Il Centro Monumentale* (1946)); Lugli, *Fontes* i–v; O. Gilbert, *Topographie der Stadt Rom* (1883–5); L. Homo, *Rome impériale et l'urbanisme dans l'antiquité* (1951); E. Gjerstad, *Early Rome* i–iv (1953–67); D. R. Dudley, *Urbs Roma* (1967), a source book of translated texts. I. A. R.; F. C.

**ROMULUS** and **REMUS,** mythical founders of Rome. Their legend, though probably as old as the late fourth century B.C. in one form or another (the Ogulnii dedicated a statue of the she-wolf with the twins in 296 B.C.,

Livy 10. 23. 12; see further J. Carcopino, *La Louve du Capitole*), cannot be very old nor contain any popular element, unless it be the almost universal one of the exposed children who rise to a great position. The name of Romulus means simply 'Roman', cf. the two forms *Sicanus* and *Siculus*; Remus (who in the Latin tradition replaces the Rhomos of most Greek authors), if not a back-formation from local place-names such as Remurinus ager, Remona (Festus, 344. 25 and 345. 10 Lindsay), is possibly formed from *Roma* by false analogy with such doublets as Κέρκυρα, Corcyra, where the *o* is short. The part played by a god in begetting children is against all provably Italian tradition; the entire story moves on purely Greek lines, and the idea of having an eponym whose name explains that of a city is itself Greek. However, there is no doubt that the legend was shaped by someone well acquainted with Roman topography and having a not inconsiderable knowledge of Roman religion and custom; contrast the older stories preserved, e.g., in Festus, 326. 28 ff.

In its normal form (Livy 1. 3. 10 ff.; Dion. Hal. *Ant. Rom.* 1. 76. 1 ff.; Plut. *Rom.* 3 ff.; more in Carter, Roscher's *Lexikon* iv. 174. 14 ff., which article is an excellent summary of the whole matter, with relevant literature) the story runs thus. Numitor, king of Alba Longa, had a younger brother Amulius who deposed him. To prevent the rise of avengers he made Numitor's daughter, R(h)ea Silvia, a Vestal Virgin (q.v.). But she was violated by Mars himself, and bore twins. Amulius, who had imprisoned her, ordered the infants to be thrown into the Tiber. The river was in flood, and the receptacle in which they had been placed drifted ashore near the Ficus Ruminalis. There a she-wolf (Plut. *Rom.* 4 adds a woodpecker, both being sacred to Mars) tended and suckled them, until they were found by Faustulus, the royal herdsman (probably a by-form of Faunus, q.v.). He and his wife Acca Larentia (q.v.) brought them up as their own; they increased mightily in strength and boldness, and became leaders of the young men in daring exploits. In one of these Remus was captured and brought before Numitor; Romulus came to the rescue, the relationship was made known, they rose together against Amulius, killed him, and made Numitor king again. The twins then founded a city of their own on the site of Rome, beginning with a settlement on the Palatine; Romulus walled it, and he or his lieutenant Celer killed Remus for leaping over the walls. He opened an asylum on the Capitol for all fugitives, and got wives for them by stealing women from the Sabines, whom he invited to a festival. After a successful reign of some forty years he mysteriously vanished in a storm at Goat's Marsh and became the god Quirinus (q.v.), one of the most obvious Greek touches in the whole story.

For recent discussion see C. J. Classen, *Hist.* 1963, 447 ff.

H. J. R.

**ROMULUS AUGUSTULUS,** commonly known as the last Roman Emperor of the West (A.D. 475–6), was in fact a usurper and was not recognized in the East. He owes his diminutive name to the fact that he was still a child when his father, the patrician Orestes, elevated him at Ravenna (475). But Orestes was overthrown and killed by Odoacer (q.v.), who deposed Romulus, spared him because of his youth, and sent him to live on a pension in Campania. His subsequent fate is unknown.

E. A. T.

**ROSALIA** or **ROSARIA** (generally neut. plur., occasionally fem. sing., plur. **Rosaliae**). The Romans were extravagantly fond of roses and used them especially on all manner of festal occasions, at banquets both official (e.g. *Act. Arval.* ccv, 13 Henzen) and private (e.g.

Martial 9. 93. 5). It is therefore not remarkable that a feast of roses was a common event, although it never became a fixed public festival, except locally. The best-known occasions of this sort were commemorations of the dead, also called *dies rosationis*, when presumably the members of the family met at the grave and decked it with roses. Violets were also used, hence *uiolatio*, *dies uiolares* or *uiolae* (see A. de-Marchi, *Culto privato di Roma antica* i (1896), 201). But quite apart from this, feasts of roses are recorded in a number of documents, none earlier than Domitian, at Capua on 5 May, at Rome on 23 May ('macellus rosa [*sic*] sumat', Philocalus) and 21 May, at Pergamum on 24–6 May, and at various places in northern Italy and central Europe on dates ranging from about 1 June to the middle of July; in other words, at the time of year when roses were to be had abundantly. There is no reason to suppose that all these developed out of the cult of the dead; rather is the reverse true, that the honours done in this manner to the dead were a particular case of inviting them to a feast or other entertainment at which the survivors were also present, or simply a development of the custom, common in antiquity as now, of decking graves with flowers, cf. Nilsson, op. cit. *infra*, 136.

An interesting instance is the *Rosaliae signorum* in the calendar of Dura-Europos which has the entry *pridie kal. Iunias ob rosalias signorum supplicatio*. It seems probable that on that occasion the standards (q.v.) were garlanded with roses. See A. S. Hoey in *Harv. Theol. Rev.* 1937, 15 ff.

M. P. Nilsson, 'Das Rosenfest', *Beiträge zur Religionswissenschaft* ii (1914–15), 134 ff. H. J. R.

**ROSCIUS** (1, *PW* 7), SEXTUS, son of a well-connected man of Ameria. The father was killed in 81 B.C., and two relatives, aided by Sulla's freedman Chrysogonus (q.v.), conspired to enter his name in the proscription lists and divide his property, finally (in 80) accusing his son of the murder. Roscius had many noble patrons, including *adfines* of Sulla; but his defence, involving an attack on Chrysogonus, might be resented by Sulla, and so they did not venture to speak for him. The main speech was entrusted—as his first major case—to young Cicero, who made it an Optimate manifesto, powerfully contrasting the good faith and present impotence of the nobles with the irresponsible power of the freedman. Sulla, who genuinely wished to restore the traditional oligarchy, apparently realized that he must support them: Cicero won his case and nothing further is heard of Chrysogonus.

Cicero, *S. Rosc. Am.* E. Badian, *Foreign Clientelae* (1958), 249. E. B.

**ROSCIUS** (2, *PW* 22) OTHO, LUCIUS, as tribune in 67 B.C. opposed Gabinius (q.v. 2) and tried to gain the support of the *equites* for the Optimates by restoring their right to the first fourteen rows in the theatre—a measure that was unpopular with the *plebs*. It is not known when the right had first been introduced and when abolished; but it was now probably extended to all men of 'equestrian' status. E. B.

**ROSCIUS** (3, *PW* 16) GALLUS, QUINTUS, from Solonium in the *ager Lanuvinus* (Cic. *Div.* 1. 79; cf. *Nat. D.* 1. 79 and 82), the famous actor, was of free birth, being brother-in-law to Quinctius (*Quinct.* 77). Sulla made him a knight (Macrob. *Sat.* 3. 14. 3). Handsome in person (*Arch.* 17), he had a squint (*Nat. D.* 1. 79) and wore a mask (*De Or.* 3. 221). Time moderated his natural vivacity (ibid. 1. 254; *Leg.* 1. 11); supreme in comedy, he also played tragic parts (*De Or.* 3. 102). His name became typical for a consummate artist (*Brut.* 290; *De Or.* 1. 130, 258), his popularity being prodigious (*Arch.* 17). His earnings were enormous (Pliny, *HN* 7. 128; Cic.

*Q Rosc.* 23). He was on intimate relations with Catulus (*Nat. D.* 1. 79), Sulla (Plut. *Sulla* 36), and Cicero, to whom he gave his first important brief (*Quinct.* 77), 81 B.C., and who later (in the *Q Rosc.*) defended him in a private suit. Cicero mentions his death as recent in 62 B.C. (*Arch.* 17). G. C. R.

**ROSTRA.** The earliest *rostra*, or speaker's platform, at Rome lay on the south side of the augurally constituted *comitium* (q.v.); it existed in 338 B.C. when it was adorned with the prows (*rostra*) of ships captured from Antium, later with statues and a sundial. This platform is long, with a straight front, associated with the second level of the *comitium*. When rebuilt, probably by Sulla (*JRS* 1922, 21 ff.), it had a curved front. Caesar planned new *rostra* completed in 44 B.C. at the west end of the Forum. The Augustan *rostra*, which incorporated the Julian core, consists of two parts: the curved steps of access on the west, the so-called hemicycle, and the rectangular platform which was faced with marble and decorated with bronze prows. The Augustan *rostra* were called the *rostra vetera* in contrast with the front of the *podium* of the Temple of Divus Julius (29 B.C.), also treated as *rostra* (Frontin. *Aq.* 129; Dio Cass. 56. 34) with ships' prows from Actium. A rough northward extension of the Augustan *rostra* of about A.D. 470 commemorates a naval victory over Vandals (*Röm. Mitt.* 1895, 59).

G. Lugli, *Roma antica* (1946), 140 ff.; Nash, *Pict. Dict. Rome* ii. 276 ff. I. A. R.; D. E. S.

**ROXANE** (the name may be connected with the hill-state of *Roshan*), daughter of the Bactrian baron Oxyartes, was married in 327 to Alexander, who hoped thus to reconcile the great barons of the north-eastern marches. Beyond the story that after Alexander's death she murdered his other wife Barsine (Stateira), little is heard of her; her son Alexander IV was born after Alexander's death, and she and the boy became pawns in the wars of the Successors till Cassander murdered them both. In Greek and Bactrian legend, however, she became a daughter of Darius III and ancestress, through her (supposed) daughter Apama, of the Seleucid and Euthydemid dynasties.

Berve, *Alexanderreich* ii. 346. W. W. T.

**RUBELLIUS** (1, *PW* 2) **BLANDUS**, from Tibur, as the first *eques* to teach rhetoric, marked the rise in professional status (Sen. *Controv.* 2, *praef.* 5). He trained Papirius Fabianus who in turn taught the Younger Seneca. He is perhaps the historian cited by Servius on Verg. *G.* 1. 103.

Schanz–Hosius, § 336. 9, no. 17.

**RUBELLIUS** (2, *PW* 5) **BLANDUS**, GAIUS, grandson of the above, *consul suffectus* A.D. 18, married Julia daughter of Tiberius' son Drusus in A.D. 33 (Tac. *Ann.* 6. 27. 1). If Juvenal is to be trusted (*Sat.* 8. 39 f.), he had a son of the same name. For his son Rubellius (q.v. 3) Plautus see Tac. *Ann.* 14. 22 and 57–9. M. S. S.

**RUBELLIUS** (3, *PW* 8) **PLAUTUS**, son of C. Rubellius (q.v. 2) Blandus and Julia the granddaughter of the Emperor Tiberius, was an adherent to Stoicism. His imperial descent made some regard him as a possible rival to Nero, and in A.D. 60, on the Emperor's advice, he withdrew to Asia. Two years later, at the instance of Tigellinus (q.v.), he was forced to suicide, though his father-in-law Antistius (q.v. 2) Vetus urged him to disobey the order. G. E. F. C.

**RUBICO** (commonly called **Rubicon**), reddish stream flowing into the Adriatic and marking the boundary between Italy and Cisalpine Gaul: possibly the modern *Pisciatello*. In 49 B.C. Julius Caesar, after some hesitation, precipitated Civil War by crossing it.

Plut. *Caes.* 32; Lucan 1. 213 f.; Suet. *Iul.* 31; App. *BCiv.* 2. 35.
E. T. S.

**RUFINUS** (1), FLAVIUS, was left by Theodosius I on his death (A.D. 395) as the chief adviser of his son Arcadius (q.v. 2). He at once incurred the enmity of Stilicho (q.v.); and the latter sent troops to Constantinople who murdered Rufinus in Nov. 395. The poet Claudian wrote vigorously against him. E. A. T.

**RUFINUS** (2) of Aquileia (*c.* A.D. 345–410), friend and later antagonist of St. Jerome, travelled in Egypt, founded a monastery on the Mount of Olives, and was the author of many translations from the Greek (Eusebius' *Church History* to which he added two books, Origen, Basil, Gregory Nazianzen, etc.), and of several original works.

WORKS. M. Simonetti, *Tyrannii Rufini Opera*, in *Corpus Christianorum, Ser. Lat.* xx (Turnhout, 1961). Biography, etc.: F. X. Murphy, *Rufinus of Aquileia*, Catholic University of America, Studies in Mediaeval History, N.S. vi, Washington 1945. C. P. H.

**RUFINUS** (3) (5th c. A.D.), grammarian. His *Commentarium in metra Terentiana* and his *De compositione et de metris oratorum* are extant (ed. Keil, *Gramm. Lat.* vi. 554–78).

Cf. Schanz–Hosius, § 1104.

**RUFUS** (1), CURTIUS (*PW* 30), of obscure origin and alleged by some to be the son of a gladiator, entered the Senate and won the praetorship, not without encouragement from Tiberius, who remarked 'Curtius Rufus uidetur mihi ex se natus' (Tac. *Ann.* xi. 21). The year of his consulate is unknown (*c.* 43). Legate of Upper Germany in A.D. 47, he employed his troops with digging for silver in the territory of the Mattiaci and was rewarded with the *ornamenta triumphalia*. Later he was proconsul of Africa, thus fulfilling a prediction made to him in his humble beginnings (Tac. loc. cit., Pliny, *Ep.* vii. 27. 2). He was an old man now, and he died there. The obituary notice in Tacitus hits off an unamiable *novus homo*. Identity with Rufus (q.v. 2), the historian of Alexander, has been canvassed. R. S.

**RUFUS** (2), QUINTUS CURTIUS (*PW* 31), rhetorician and historian, wrote probably under Claudius (if so, consul about A.D. 43 ? Cf. RUFUS 1 above), hardly under Augustus, but perhaps under Vespasian. He published a history of Alexander the Great in ten books. Our text begins at book 3 (333 B.C.) and has gaps between books 5 and 6 and in book 10. The portrait of Alexander reflects the Peripatetic view of a tyrant favoured by Fortune, but it contains also varied information, both valuable and dubious, from the general tradition. The description is dramatic, romantic, and rhetorical; we find few technicalities, but emotional presentation, vivid detail, and the introduction of speeches. The style is classic, on the model of Livy, but with contemporary usage in expression.

EDITIONS. J. Mützell (1841), with commentary; E. Hedicke (2nd ed. 1908, ed. minor 1931); Th. Vogel (1881); P. H. Damsté (1897); K. Müller and H. Schönfeld (1954), with German transl. and critical appendix.
W. Kroll, *Studien zum Verstandnis der röm. Lit.* (1924), 331; Tarn, *Alexander* ii. 91 ff. A. H. McD.

**RUFUS** (3), CLUVIUS (*PW* 12), the imperial historian, consul probably before A.D. 41. Nero's herald in the theatre, he became Galba's governor of Hispania Tarraconensis. He first supported Otho, but later declared for Vitellius, defending Spain. His *historiae* may have begun with Gaius and ended with Otho; but in any event its

main part covered the reign of Nero. Tacitus (*Ann.* 13. 20; 14. 2) may have followed him in the *Annals*.

Peter, *HRRel.* ii. clxv and 114; Ph. Fabia, *Les Sources de Tacite* (1893), 171, 376; Syme, *Tacitus*, 178 ff., 293 ff., 675 ff.
A. H. McD.

**RUFUS** (4) of Ephesus, physician under Trajan (A.D. 98–117), probably studied in Alexandria; he knew Egypt well, visited Caria and Cos, and practised in Ephesus, at that time a famous medical centre.

Of numerous writings, mostly on dietetics and pathology, these are preserved: Π. ὀνομασίας τῶν τοῦ ἀνθρώπου μορίων. Ἰατρικὰ ἐρωτήματα. Π. τῶν ἐν νεφροῖς καὶ κύστει παθῶν. Π. σατυριασμοῦ καὶ γονορροίας. Π. τῶν κατ' ἄρθρα νοσημάτων (Latin, *De podagra*).

Rufus was a dogmatist, though of no special creed, a man of great experience and independent mind; in commenting on Hippocrates he did not refrain from criticizing the master. Anatomy he held necessary for sound medical practice. Opposed to general theories, he mostly studied single diseases. He also renounced the usual prognosis and preferred to ask the patient about the history and symptoms of his case. His books, written in a lively and personal style, bear out the judgement of Galen that the objective critic finds nothing missing in Rufus' writings. His influence was greater in the Orient than in the Occident. *See* ANATOMY AND PHYSIOLOGY, § 11.

TEXTS. Opera, Ch. Daremberg and E. Ruelle (1879); not genuine, Ὀνομασίαι τῶν κατὰ ἀνθρωπον α'. Π. ἀνατομῆς τῶν τοῦ ἀνθρώπου μορίων. Π. ὀστῶν. Σύνοψις π. σφυγμῶν. De podagra, H. Mørland, *Symbolae Osloenses* 1933.
MODERN LITERATURE. J. Ilberg, *Abh. Sächs. Akad.* 1930, list of writings, also from Arabic, ibid. 47; cf. M. Wellmann, *Hermes* 1912; for Ephesus, J. Keil, *JÖAI* 1905; 1926. H. Gossen, *PW* i A. 1207; H. Gärtner, 'Die Fragen des Arztes an den Kranken herausgegeben, übersetzt und erläutert', *CMG* Suppl. iv (1962); G. Kowalski, *De corporis humani appellationibus* (Diss. Göttingen, 1960). L. E.

**RULER-CULT.** I. GREEK. The essential characteristic of Greek ruler-worship is the rendering, as to a god or hero, of honour—τιμή—to individuals deemed superior to other men because of their achievements, position, or power. This tendency lies deeply rooted in the Greek mind and is not to be derived from similar practices in the ancient East.

In the aristocratic society of the Archaic Age, as in the classical *polis* of the fifth century, no man could reach a position of such generally acknowledged pre-eminence as to cause the granting of divine honours to be thought appropriate: the only approximation to deification is the posthumous heroization of oecists (*see* CITY-FOUNDERS). Only in the period of disintegration after Aegospotami and through the rise of individualism do we find divine honours given to living men, all persons of admitted superiority, usually due to their political or military achievements.

Ruler-cult in a developed form first appears during the reign of Alexander the Great and is directly inspired by his conquests, personality, and, in particular, by his absolute and undisputed power. Alexander's attempt to force the Greeks and Macedonians in his entourage to adopt the Persian custom of prostration before the king —προσκύνησις (in itself not implying worship)—was an isolated and unsuccessful experiment without consequence. Much more important is his encounter with the priest of Ammon (not as yet generally identified with Zeus) at Siwa in 331. The priest seemingly addressed Alexander as the son of Amon-Ra, the traditional salutation due to any Pharaoh of Egypt, but the prestige which the oracle of Ammon then enjoyed throughout the Greek world had a decisive effect, not only on the Greeks, but also and in particular on the romantic imagination of the young king himself. It is probably the progressive development of these emotions which caused Alexander in 324, together with his order for the restoration of political exiles, to demand and receive formal recognition of his divinity from the Greek *poleis*. Alexander also secured heroic honours for his dead intimate Hephaestion, and it seems clear that his motives were primarily personal rather than political; that is, the desire that his career and personality should receive definite and official recognition from the Greeks.

Alexander demanded honours: they were *voluntarily* granted by the Greeks to his successors and their descendants, and thus the two generations after his death saw the rise of all the characteristic phenomena of Greek ruler-worship. These fall into five categories:

1. Dedications to rulers by individuals are necessarily difficult to interpret; the motives range from sincere devotion to the most interested flattery.

2. Like any oecist, a king was worshipped by cities which he had himself founded—but as a god, not a hero.

3. Rulers were sometimes honoured by having their statues placed in an already existing temple. The king was thought to share the temple with the god (as σύνναος θεός) and thus to partake in the honours rendered to the deity and, on occasion, in the deity's qualities.

4. The most characteristic method of deification was for a Greek *polis*, by legislative enactment, to enrol a king among its official divinities with his own cult and priest. This was a tactful way of honouring a suzerain and could also be an appropriate expression of thanks for the benefactions of a foreign ruler.

5. The Greek monarchies of the east in time created their own official cults. The dynastic cult of the Ptolemies at Alexandria (founded 285–284) in its developed form by the end of the third century consisted of a priest of Alexander, of each pair of deceased rulers, and of the reigning king and queen. In 280 Antiochus I deified his dead father Seleucus and dedicated to him a temple and precinct at Seleuceia in Pieria; it was probably also Antiochus I who established the imperial ruler-cult of the Seleucid Empire with high priests of the living king and his divine ancestors (πρόγονοι) in each province of the Empire. In the later dynastic cult of the Attalids the kings were deified only after death.

Greek ruler-worship is essentially political and is free from any truly religious emotion (there is no known instance of any prayer addressed to a king). It reached full development only in an age when the effective political powers were supranational imperial States. Its prevalence in the Hellenistic period is primarily caused by the fact that it was the only possible method for the expression of loyalty to such States.

E. Bikerman, *Institutions des Séleucides* (1938), 236 ff.; C. Habicht, 'Gottmenschentum und griechische Städte', *Zetemata* 1956; A. D. Nock, *Harv. Stud.* 1930, 1 ff.; Tarn, *Alexander* ii. 347 ff.; U. Wilcken, 'Zur Entstehung des hellenistischen Königskultes', *Sitz. Berl.* 1938, 298 ff. C. F. E.

**RULER-CULT.** II. ROMAN. Hero-cult was not indigenous to Italy. The primitive Romans sacrificed to the ghosts of the dead (*Manes*, q.v.) and conceived of a semi-independent spirit (*genius*, q.v.) attached to living persons. But the myth of a deified founder, Romulus (q.v.), was only invented in or after the fourth century B.C. under Greek influence. From the time of Marcellus' conquest of Syracuse in 212 B.C., Roman officials received divine honours from Greek cities; notable instances are possibly Scipio Africanus (*c.* 200) and certainly the 'liberator' Flamininus (*c.* 191). At Rome such honours are not met with until the beginning of the first century B.C., and then exceptionally, e.g. those offered privately to Marius (101) and popularly to the demagogue Marius (3) Gratidianus (86). Under Stoic influence the idea that worthy

individuals might become divine after death appeared in Cicero's *Somnium Scipionis* (*c.* 51) and in the shrine which he planned for his daughter Tullia (d. 45). Caesar as dictator in 45–44 received divine honours, probably by his own wish and perhaps with a reminiscence of Alexander. After his assassination the triumvirs, supported by popular agitation, secured from the Senate his deification in 42.

Imperial emperor-worship has two aspects, the worship of the living ruler, including his identification with gods, and the apotheosis of the dead one; it occurs at three levels: provincial, municipal, and private. In Egypt Augustus succeeded to the religious position of the Ptolemies. Elsewhere the Greeks continued for him the Hellenistic concept of the divine ruler. And at Rome his titles included *Divi filius* and *Augustus*, which gave him a divine aura if not actual divinity. He also enjoyed a certain sanctity in virtue of his tribunician power and, after 12 B.C., the office of *pontifex maximus* (q.v.). Officially, however, Augustus was usually not worshipped directly but in conjunction with the goddess Roma. He particularly encouraged the cults maintained by the provincial assemblies (κοινά) in the eastern provinces, e.g. for Asia at Pergamum (29 B.C.) and for Galatia at Ancyra. At Rome the poets constantly spoke of him as divine or divinely inspired. In *c.* 12–7 B.C. he joined his *genius* with the *Lares compitales* for the official cults of the 265 wards (*vici*) of the city. Throughout Italy, individuals, groups, and towns spontaneously offered worship to him or to his *genius*. In the western provinces Augustus established altars (not temples) to himself, probably again in conjunction with *Roma*, and assemblies (*concilia*) for Gaul at Lyons (12–10 B.C.), for Germany at Cologne (*c.* 10 B.C.), and perhaps elsewhere. Municipal (e.g. at Narbo) and private worship seems, however, to have been less common in the West than in the East. After his death in A.D. 14, his cult as *divus Augustus* was formally instituted on the Palatine; cities and provinces (e.g. in Tarraco) throughout the Empire dedicated temples to him as *divus Augustus*. His *Res Gestae* have been most fully preserved on such a temple at Ancyra.

Though his 'constitutional' successors, when consulted, deprecated worship of themselves, the Greeks continued to accord it. Of the 'absolutist' Emperors, Gaius and Domitian required worship, but Nero and Commodus probably welcomed rather than demanded divine honours. The Senate rewarded with apotheosis deceased Emperors who had pleased it.

Emperor-worship was not merely a device to lend dignity and superhuman authority to the ruler or to secure the loyalty of subjects; it represented a spontaneous expression of gratitude to one who had saved and benefited his subjects by establishing peace and prosperity, an expression couched in terms of Hellenistic flattery and supported by the prevalent Stoicism. The practice was perhaps at first more widespread in the East than in the West, more sincere in private than in official (municipal or provincial) cult, and more spontaneous under Augustus than under his successors. In general, it probably contributed little or nothing to fill the religious needs of the population of the Empire. However, it acquired increasing political significance. In the towns of Italy the colleges of *seviri* or *Augustales* in charge of the imperial cult afforded an outlet for the ambition of freedmen, to whom public offices were closed. Augustus' hope that the provincial assemblies might become intermediaries between the cities and the Emperor proved vain, but the provincial and municipal priesthoods and the presence of the provincial temple or altar in a city were much sought-after honours. Emperor-worship enhanced the position of the ruler by contributing to court ceremonial and insignia. Either the ruler or his *genius* (in Greek, his 'tyche') might be invoked with the gods to confirm oaths, a practice to be distinguished from oaths of loyalty to the Emperor. The latter were taken, particularly in the army, before a statue of the Emperor. Offenders against the Emperor's divinity laid themselves open to the charge of treason (*crimen laesae maiestatis*). Though Pliny's detection of Christians by their refusal to sacrifice before the statues of the gods and Trajan in Bithynia (*c.* A.D. 112) may not represent a general test, this test or that of refusal to confirm an oath by invoking the emperor had become regular in Tertullian's day (*c.* 200). During the third century, the spread of new oriental 'mystery' cults fostered the view that the emperor was not so much himself divine as especially under divine protection and a channel through which, in a time of temporal and spritual difficulties, divine favour could be secured for the State. Thus Decius demanded sacrifice to the gods, together with offerings in honour of (not to) himself and an oath by his *genius* as evidence of loyalty from everyone, not merely Christians; cf. the Egyptian certificates (*libelli*) of A.D. 250. Finally, when from 312 onwards Constantine (q.v.) and his successors made Christianity more and more the only recognized State religion, the divinity of the Emperor became inconsistent with the dogma that Jesus alone had combined the divine and human. Thus the view that the ruler was especially under divine protection was the only one tenable, and was perpetuated in the medieval theory of the divine right of kings (*rex de gratia*).

General surveys with bibliography, *PW* suppl. iv, s.v. 'Kaiserkult'; L. Cerfaux and J. Tondriau, *Le Culte des souverains* (1957). For the Augustan period, L. R. Taylor, *Divinity of the Roman Emperor* (1931). For the Early Empire, M. Hammond, *The Augustan Principate* (1933), 107 ff., 261 ff., and *The Antonine Monarchy* (1959), 203 ff.; K. Scott, *The Imperial Cult under the Flavians* (1936); further bibliography, A. Piganiol, *Hist. de Rome³* (1962), 332 f., 585; add: *PW*, s.v. 'Messius (9)', for Decius; E. Robert, *Le Culte imp. dans la péninsule ibérique d'Aug. à Diocl.* (1958); A. Roes, *L'Aigle psychopompe, etc.* in *Mélanges Ch. Picard II* (*Rev. Arch.* 1949), 881 ff.; I. Ryberg, *Amer. Acad. Rome* xxii (1955), 81 ff. M. H.

**RULLUS,** PUBLIUS SERVILIUS (*PW* 80), as tribune (63 B.C.) introduced a major agrarian bill, establishing a commission with extravagant powers to redistribute *ager publicus* in Rome and the provinces. It was probably inspired by Crassus (q.v. 4) and was supported by Caesar, and perhaps both the commission and the land were meant as a bargaining counter to hold against Pompey, whose return with a large army was expected. Cicero, presenting himself as a Popularis defending Pompey's interests, secured the withdrawal of the bill by his (largely extant) speeches *De lege agraria*.

E. G. Hardy, *Some Problems in Roman History* (1924), 68; G. V. Sumner, *TAPA* 1966, 569 ff. E. B.

**RUMINA,** an obscure goddess, who, if her name be not Etruscan (Schulze, *Latein. Eigennamen*, 580 f.), is to be connected with *ruma* (breast) and taken to be a *numen* of suckling. She had a shrine and a sacred fig-tree (*ficus Ruminalis*) near the Lupercal, where milk, not wine, was offered.

Varro, *Rust.* 2. 11. 5. Wissowa, *RK* 242; Latte, who believes in the Etruscan connexion, explains her as the deity of Rome (*RR* 111). H. J. R.

**RUPILIUS** (*PW* 5), PUBLIUS, of an eminent Praenestine family of *publicani*, as a friend of Scipio (q.v. 11) reached the consulship (132 B.C.), in which, for a time, he participated in the action of Popillius (q.v. 2) against the adherents of Ti. Gracchus; but he soon went to Sicily, where he put down the slave revolt, capturing Eunus (q.v.). With a senatorial commission he imposed a severe settlement on the province. He died soon after his return. E. B.

**RUSELLAE,** modern *Roselle*, an Etruscan city, stood on a two-crowned hill to the east of the bay that is now the Grosseto plain. Its walls, of polygonal limestone blocks overlaying a seventh-century defence wall of sun-dried bricks, are dated to the early sixth century and are thus the oldest-known Etruscan stone fortifications. The area within them was inhabited from late Villanovan to late imperial times, with particularly flourishing periods between the sixth and fourth centuries, characterized by imported Attic pottery, and in Hellenistic times, when the city attained its maximum expansion. On the south-east hill, a portion of the Etruscan city of Hellenistic date has been revealed, superimposed on remains of the fifth–fourth centuries: this area has produced a well-stratified sequence of bucchero and of local Campana A and B wares. Rusellae was captured by Rome in 294 B.C.

R. Bianchi Bandinelli, *Atene e Roma* 1925, 35 ff.; R. Naumann and F. Hiller, *Röm. Mitt.* 1959, 1 ff., 1962, 59 ff.; excavation reports by C. Laviosa in *Stud. Etr.* 1959–61, 1963, 1965; pottery catalogue by P. Bocci, ibid. 1965, 190 ff.; Scullard, *Etr. Cities*, 134 ff. D. W. R. R.

**RUTILIUS** (1, *PW* 34) **RUFUS,** PUBLIUS, studied philosophy under Panaetius (becoming a firm Stoic), law under P. Scaevola (q.v. 2) and oratory under Galba (q.v. 3); he served under Scipio (q.v. 11) Aemilianus at Numantia. His sister married a Cotta and he was introduced into the circle of the Metelli, with whom he maintained a lifelong connexion. Failing to reach the consulship of 115 B.C., he unsuccessfully prosecuted—and was prosecuted by—Scaurus (q.v. 1) who had defeated him. In 109/8 he served with distinction as a legate of Metellus (q.v. 6) in Numidia, and in 105, as consul, began the reorganization of military training later completed by Marius. As legate of Scaevola (q.v. 4) in 94/3, he assisted him in re-organizing Asia and governed it in his name for three months, offending powerful Roman interests (especially among the *equites*). On his return he was prosecuted *repetundarum* (with Marius active against him) and, seeking Socratic martyrdom, was convicted and went into exile. The trial became notorious and brought about the attempt of Drusus (q.v. 2) and his advisers to reform the *quaestiones* (q.v.). Honourably received in the province, Rutilius became a citizen of Smyrna, where Cicero met him. He wrote a history of his own time, full of acid judgements on contemporaries, which was read by Sallust and underlies much of our tradition on the period. E. B.

**RUTILIUS** (2) **LUPUS,** PUBLIUS (early 1st c. A.D.), rhetorician, abridged in Latin a work on figures of speech by Gorgias, who taught at Athens in the first century B.C. (Quint. *Inst.* 9. 2. 102).

**RUTILIUS** (3, *PW* 19) **GALLICUS,** GAIUS (*cos. suff. c.* A.D. 70, *cos.* II *c.* 85), from Augusta Taurinorum. Apart from the poem, with valuable details of his career, which Statius composed to celebrate Rutilius' recovery from an illness (*Silv.* 1. 4), the only evidence about this eminent senator comes from inscriptions. *ILS* 9499 contains his *cursus* down to the consulate (*inter alia* he had been legate of Galatia for nine years, partly under Cn. Domitius Corbulo). He was governor of Lower Germany in 78 (*ILS* 9052), when he defeated the Bructeri and captured the priestess Veleda (Stat. *Silv.* 1. 4. 89 f.; Tac. *Germ.* 8). By the year 89 he had been appointed *praefectus urbi*, in which post he may have died. R. S.

**RUTUPIAE,** modern *Richborough* (Kent), situated originally on a mainland peninsula of the now silted Thanet channel; a pair of ditches were very probably the defences of a Claudian landing-party (A.D. 43) and the site was used as a stores base for the conquest. About 80–90 a deeply founded structure (trophy+sea-mark?) was built. Rutupiae was the principal landing-place from the Continent, so that in authors 'Rutupinus' = British. About 250 the trophy, itself in ruins, but perhaps replaced by an equally strange cruciform structure, was surrounded by ditches, which were soon replaced by the stone Saxon shore-fort of c. 6 acres (Carausius? c. 290 or a little earlier). Quantities of late coins prove a long, perhaps post-Roman occupation.

J. P. Bushe-Fox, *First, Second, Third, and Fourth Reports of Excavations*, 1926–49. *Fifth Report*, ed. B. Cunliffe, forthcoming 1968.
GENERAL SUMMARY. *VCH*, Kent iii. 24 ff.
COINS. F. S. Salisbury, *Num. Chron.*⁵ vii. 108 ff.; *Ant. Journ.* 1927, 268 ff.          C. E. S.

# S

**SAALBURG,** a site on the Upper German *limes* which commanded a pass across the Taunus mountains, along the outer slopes of which the Roman frontier was established by Domitian. The Saalburg was first occupied during the campaigns against the Chatti (A.D. 83–5) and a fortlet was constructed c. 90 just behind the *limes* proper. A timber fort for an auxiliary cohort was built between A.D. 125 and 128 and given a composite wall of dry stone and timber before 139. This was later reconstructed entirely in stone, probably A.D. 209/13, but the fort was evacuated in the face of the German invasions not later than 259/60 and probably in about 254. The forts and extensive *vicus* have been excavated and the walls and principal buildings of the cohort fort were reconstructed 1898–1907.

*Der obergermanisch-raetische Limes*, B, Bd. ii. 1, no. 11 (ed. E. Fabricius, 1937); H. Schönberger, *Führer durch das Römerkastell Saalburg* (1960).      P. S.

**SABAZIUS** (Σαβάζιος, in Anatolia frequently Σα(o)(υ)άζιος), a Thraco-Phrygian god, regarded by the Greeks now as purely foreign, again as identical with Dionysus. Wherever his place of origin, Phrygia and Lydia were the chief centres of his cult; the Attalid cult of Sabazius at Pergamum (C. Michel, *Recueil d'Inscriptions grecques* (1897–1927), 46, 142–141 B.C.) was a foundation of the Cappadocian princess, Stratonice. Private associations worshipping Sabazius existed at Athens from the late fifth century, and Demosthenes (18. 259–60) derides his purificatory rites, but evidence for the cult is scanty till imperial times. Identification with Jahwe (cf. Val. Max. 1. 3. 2), whether suggested by Σαβαώθ or σάββατον, resulted in some assimilation of Jewish practices, but Jewish influence in the Vincentius frescoes at Rome (Dessau, *ILS* 3961) is disputed. Sabazius' chief attribute is the snake, important also in his mysteries. In art, he appears either in Phrygian costume or, since he was frequently called Ζεὺς Sabazius, with the thunderbolt and eagle of Zeus. Noteworthy are the votive hands, making the 'benedictio Latina' and adorned with numerous cult symbols. *See also* ANATOLIAN DEITIES, HYPSISTOS, MACEDONIAN CULTS.

Eisele in Roscher, *Lex.* s.v.; F. Cumont, *CRAcad. Inscr.* 1906; Nilsson, *GGR* ii. 658 ff.; C. Picard, *Rev. Arch.* 1961, ii.    F. R. W.

**SABELLI** is not synonymous with Sabini (q.v.). It is the Roman name for speakers of Oscan (q.v.). They called themselves *Safineis* and their chief official *meddix* (q.v.). They expanded from their original habitat (reputedly Sabine Amiternum) by proclaiming Sacred Springs and settling in fresh lands (*see* VER SACRUM), where they usually imposed their language and coalesced with the pre-Sabellian populations. Thus originated Samnites, Frentani, Campani, Lucani, Apuli, Bruttii, and Mamertini. (Paeligni, Vestini, Marrucini, Marsi, and Aequi (?), who spoke Oscan-type dialects, presumably had a similar origin). These migrations were still continuing in the fifth century B.C. and later: Sabelli conquered Campania c. 450–420, Lucania c. 420–390; Bruttii appeared c. 356. But the Sabelli were more expansive than cohesive. The Samnites, the most typical Sabelli, had no feeling of political unity with their ancestors the Sabines, nor the Frentani with theirs, the Samnites.

Old Sabellic is the description inaccurately applied to some untranslated inscriptions from Picenum, including the oldest non-Etruscan inscriptions from Italy. The two dialects in question may be Illyrian (J. Whatmough, *Prae-Italic Dialects* ii (1933), 207).

E. T. Salmon, *Samnium and the Samnites* (1967).    E. T. S.

**SABINA,** VIBIA, daughter of L. Vibius Sabinus and Matidia (q.v.) (child of Trajan's sister Marciana, q.v.), was thus Trajan's grand-niece. She married Hadrian (q.v.) in A.D. 100, through Plotina's favour. S.H.A. *Hadr.* 11. 3 describes the childless marriage as unsuccessful and states that the praetorian prefect Septicius Clarus, Suetonius (q.v. 2), and many others were dismissed from service because they were too sympathetic with Sabina. But there is no solid evidence for this view. Sabina remained faithful; she received the honour of coinage with the title *Augusta* in 128. She accompanied Hadrian on his travels; in 130, a companion, Julia Balbilla, had five epigrams cut on the 'colossus of Memnon' in Egypt (*Epigr. Gr.* 988–92). Sabina was consecrated by Hadrian after her death in 136 or 137, and was commemorated on posthumous coins. Groundless scandal subsequently ascribed her death to poisoning by Hadrian, or to compulsory suicide.

S.H.A. *Hadr.*; *Diz. Epigr.* iii. 636 ff.; B. W. Henderson, *Hadrian, etc.* (1923), 22 ff.; Wegner, *Herrscherbild* ii. 3 (1956), 84 ff., 126 ff.; Strack, *Reichsprägung* ii. 23 ff., 116; *B.M. Coins, Rom. Emp.* iii (1930). *See also under* HADRIAN.    C. H. V. S.; M. H.

**SABINI** lived north-east of Rome principally in villages, politically disunited, often unwalled, and usually perched on Apennine hilltops (Strabo 5. 228, 250). Their origin is unknown; ancient writers, observing their bravery and simple morality, thought them Lacedaemonians (Dion. Hal. 2. 49). They probably spoke Oscan (*see* SABELLI; cf. Varro, *Ling.* 7. 28), and were famous for their superstitious practices and strong religious feelings (Festus, 434 L.; Cic. *Div.* 2. 80); many Roman religious institutions reputedly derived from them. Although the Rape of the Sabine Women is fiction, stories connecting Sabines with primitive Rome are not entirely untrustworthy. Peculiarities of the Latin language, duplicated usages in certain Roman religious practices, the double nature of the Roman burial customs, traditions concerning the Quirinal, Esquiline, and Numa Pompilius imply a Sabine element in the Roman population, the result not of Sabine conquest but of amalgamation or gradual infiltration (e.g. the Claudii: Livy 2. 16). Livy and Dionysius record numerous wars against Sabines from regal times until 449 B.C., embellishing them with accounts of the legendary Titus Tatius and victorious Valerii (figments doubtless of Valerius Antias' imagination); probably these were operations against sporadic Sabine bands. In 449 Rome won a resounding victory (Livy 3. 38 f.). Silence envelops the Sabines thereafter until 290, when M'. Curius Dentatus for some unrecorded reason suddenly conquered them (Livy, *Epit.* 11), confiscated some of their territory (T. Frank, *Klio* 1911, 367), and sold some Sabines into slavery, the remainder becoming *cives sine suffragio* (Vell. Pat. 1. 14). However, the fertile *Ager Sabinus* (modern *Sabina*; but its exact ancient limits are unknown) remained Sabine: personal names ending in *-edius* were common there (A. Schulten, *Klio* 1903, 235); *octoviri*, the annual magisterial board (prototype of the quattuorviral constitution of Roman *municipia?*), still administered Sabine towns. Becoming full citizens in 268 (Cic. *Balb.* 13), the Sabines were rapidly romanized and ceased to be a separate nation. Chief towns: Reate, Amiternum, Nursia, and, before 449, Cures, Nomentum, and Fidenae (qq.v.).

A. Schwegler, *Römische Geschichte* i (1853), 243 f.; A. Rosenberg, *Staat der alten Italiker* (1913), 40 f.; H. Rudolph, *Stadt und Staat im römischen Italien* (1935); J. Whatmough, *Foundations of Roman Italy* (1937), 285 f.; E. C. Evans, *Amer. Acad. Rome* 1939; E. T. Salmon, *Samnium and the Samnites* (1967). E. T. S.

**SABINUS** (1), Ovid's friend, who composed imaginary replies to Ovid's letters from heroines (*Heroides*) and modelled a work on the *Fasti*.

**SABINUS** (2, *PW* 29), MASURIUS, a Roman jurist of the first half of the first century A.D. Descended from a relatively poor family, he lived on the contributions of his pupils; in his fiftieth year he obtained equestrian rank, and he received the *ius respondendi* (*see* JURISPRUDENCE), being perhaps the first of this rank to do so. Sabinus was famous for a standard work, an exposition of the *ius civile* in three books, which served posterity as a model for systematic treatises on private law, entitled *Ex Sabino* or *Ad Sabinum* (as following the system and disposition of Sabinus' work). Other works: *Ad edictum praetoris urbani*; *De furtis*; *Responsa*, and some writings not of a juridical character.

Most of the jurists of the imperial period up to the middle of the second century A.D. were adherents of one or other of two jurists' Schools (*scholae, sectae*). The one was called *Sabiniani* after Sabinus or *Cassiani* after his pupil and successor C. Cassius (q.v. 7) Longinus, the other *Proculiani* after its leader Proculus (q.v.), though our main source, Pomponius (q.v. 6) in *Dig.* 1. 2. 2. 47 ff., takes their origins even further back, to Capito (q.v. 2) and M. Antistius Labeo (q.v.) respectively. These two jurists of the Augustan age held opposing views on both law and politics, but no corresponding contrasts of a general character can be traced between the two Schools. There is a long series of points of law on which they were divided, but no consistent doctrinal basis for their disputes can be found. Nor is this surprising in view of the pragmatic character of the jurists and their lack of interest in broad theoretical constructions. Other notable heads of the Sabinians were Javolenus and Salvius Julianus (qq.v.), and of the Proculians, Nerva (q.v. 4), Pegasus (q.v. 2), Celsus (q.v. 3), and Neratius (q.v.) (*see also* POMPONIUS 6 and GAIUS 2). The Schools were evidently more than just 'schools of thought', but of their organization we know nothing. They must have died out in the later second century, since there is nothing to suggest that any of the later jurists, from whom the bulk of the surviving literature comes, were members of either.

O. Lenel, *Sabinus-System* (1892); G. Baviera, *Le due scuole dei giur. rom.* (1898); B. Kübler, s.v. 'Rechtsschulen', in *PW* i A. 381 ff., an exhaustive exposition of the opposing school doctrines; S. di

Marzo, 'Cassiani e Sabiniani', *Riv. ital. per se scienze giurid.* 1919, 109 ff.; *and see* bibliography s.vv. JURISPRUDENCE and LAW AND PROCEDURE, ROMAN, I (History and sources). A. B.; B. N.

**SABINUS** (3), FLAVIUS (*PW* 166) (*cos. suff. anno incerto*), born *c.* A.D. 8, the elder brother of the Emperor Vespasian. He was legate of Moesia for seven years (*c.* 49–56) and *praefectus urbi* for twelve years (Tac. *Hist.* 3. 75, where some suspect the text) under Nero and Otho, though not continuously. When the Flavian forces approached Rome in Dec. 69, he all but completed negotiations for the abdication of Vitellius, when he was set upon by auxiliary troops of the German armies and killed with his friends after a siege on the Capitol, where he had taken refuge. 'Innocentiam iustitiamque eius non argueres; sermonis nimius erat' (Tac. *Hist.* 3. 75). R. S.

**SABINUS** (4), TITUS FLAVIUS (*PW* 169), consul in A.D. 82 with Domitian, was married to Julia (q.v. 5: Titus' daughter, then Domitian's mistress), and was killed by Domitian before the end of 84. His disgrace perhaps involved the banishment of Dio of Prusa.

G. Townend, *JRS* 1961, 54, shows ground for supposing that he and his brother Clemens (q.v.) were not, as has generally been thought, the sons, but the grandsons of Sabinus (3): their father could have been the Flavius Sabinus who commanded Othonian troops and was *cos. suff.* in 69 (Tac. *Hist.* 1. 77, 2. 36). G. E. F. C.

**SABRATHA** (Neo-Punic Ṣbrtn; Greek Ἁβρότονον). A Phoenician port east of the Lesser Syrtis, probably founded in the fifth century B.C., it formed part of the African Tripolis (q.v.) and acquired colonial status in the second century A.D. It enjoyed great prosperity in the Early Empire; the elephant in the mosaic floor of the office of the *Sabratenses* in Ostia may symbolize its trade in African ivory. Sabratha fell into decay in the fifth century and revived briefly under the Byzantines who gave it new walls. Large areas of the city have been excavated, showing the crowded early quarters near the harbour, the Roman civic centre, and a quarter regularly laid out during the second century. Public buildings include the basilica where Apuleius must have been brought to trial (*Apol.* 73), curia, baths, theatre, amphitheatre, temples, including one to Isis, and several churches, among them a Justinianic one with outstanding mosaics (Procop. *De Aedif.* 6. 4. 13).

D. E. L. Haynes, *The Antiquities of Tripolitania* (1956); G. Pesce, *Il tempio d'Iside in Sabratha* (Monografie di Arch. Libica iv, 1953); G. Caputo, *Il teatro di Sabratha* (ibid. iii, 1950). O. B.

**SACADAS**, musician and poet, of Argos (Paus. 9. 30. 2), won three Pythian victories with the flute, composed tunes and elegiac poems set to tunes (Plut. *De mus.* 8), connected with the second establishment of music at Sparta in the first half of the seventh century B.C. Nothing of his work survives. *See* MUSIC, § 10. C. M. B.

**SACAEA** (Σάκαια, Strabo 11. 8. 4–5, 512; Σακέα, MSS. of Athenaeus, 639 c; τῶν Σακῶν ἑορτή, Dio Chrys. *Orat.* 4. 66), a Babylonian festival, perhaps of New Year (S. H. Hooke, *Orig. of Early Semitic Ritual* (1938), 59), kept up by the Persians. It was a time of general licence, feasting, and disguising (Strabo), when slaves ruled their masters (Berosus in Athenaeus) and a criminal was given all royal rights for the five days the feast lasted and then put to death (Dio).

See Frazer, *GB³*, index s.v. H. J. R.

**SACERDOS**, MARIUS PLOTIUS (3rd c. A.D.), grammarian and metrician. The first book of his *Artes grammaticae* (ed. Keil, *Gramm. Lat.* vi. 427–546) deals with the parts of speech and *vitia orationis* (but the introduction is lost); the second with nouns, verbs, and constructions; the third with metres. The three books seem not to have been published as a single work and the second is in essentials identical with the spurious *Ars catholica Probi* (cf. Keil iv. 3–43). This work is the oldest Latin grammatical treatise extant in anything like its entirety.

Schanz–Hosius, §§ 604–5. J. F. M.

**SACRAMENTUM** (LEGAL) signified in the oldest Roman civil proceeding (*legis actio sacramento*) the sum of money deposited *in iure* by both the litigants as a stake. The loser in the hearing before the judge forfeited his deposit to the State. Later *sacramentum* was not deposited but guaranteed by sureties (*praedes*). The opposite assertions of the parties concerning the right claimed by the plaintiff formed a kind of wager, and the judge had to decide (according to Cic. *Caec.* 33. 97) which party's *sacramentum* was *iustum*, and thus indirectly to settle the issue. The amount of the *sacramentum* depended on the value of the object under litigation: 500 *asses* if the value exceeded 1,000 *asses*, otherwise 50. *Sacramentum* has this meaning as early as the XII Tables, but it presumably began as an oath (the literal meaning). Perhaps the sum of money (earlier probably oxen or sheep) originated as an expiation of perjury. We are told that originally the money was paid to the pontiffs and spent on public sacrifices (Varro, *Ling.* 5. 180; Festus, s.v. *Sacramentum*).

For bibliography *see* LAW AND PROCEDURE, ROMAN, II.
A. B.; B. N.

**SACRAMENTUM** (MILITARY), the oath of allegiance, sworn on attestation by a Roman recruit. In republican times this was administered in two stages in order to save time: first came the *praeiuratio*, in which a selected man recited the complete oath, then the remainder came forward in turn and repeated the words 'idem in me'. A similar procedure was probably followed under the Empire whenever circumstances warranted it. At attestation the number of recruits may occasionally have been small enough to justify individual swearing-in, but the shortened version may have been used at the annual renewal of the oath. Up to and including A.D. 69, this annual renewal took place on New Year's Day, but Fink argues that the oath was transferred, either by Vespasian after his defeat of Vitellius, or by Domitian after the rebellion of Antonius Saturninus, to the date of the *vota*, 3 Jan.

A. von Premerstein, *Vom Werden und Wesen des Prinzipats* (1937), 73 ff.; R. O. Fink, *YClS* 1940, 51, 65 ff.; S. Tondo, *Studia et Documenta Historiae et Iuris* 1963, 1 ff. G. R. W.

**SACRED BAND** (ἱερὸς λόχος), the picked corps of Thebans formed by Gorgidas (378 B.C.). It consisted of 300 men who were traditionally grouped as pairs of lovers. To Pelopidas was due the idea of keeping the band together and so fostering their *esprit de corps*. They fought under him at Tegyra (375) and on the attacking wing at Leuctra (371), and were said to have remained undefeated till their heroic annihilation at Chaeronea (338). Their exact equipment is not recorded, but evidently they were shock troops and were largely responsible for the military supremacy of Thebes. A similar corps was formed by the Carthaginians, perhaps in imitation of the Thebans.

Plut. *Pel.* 14 ff.; Ath. 13. 561 e; Polyaenus 2. 5. 1. H. W. P.

**SACRED WARS**, the name of the wars declared by the Delphic Amphictiony against one or more of its members on the ground of sacrilege against Apollo.

The *First Sacred War* arose from a dispute between the Delphians and Cirrha about Cirrha's right to levy tolls on pilgrims. Solon is said to have urged Athens to join in the war, and Cirrha was annihilated *c.* 590 B.C. by the forces of Thessaly, Sicyon, and Athens. Delphi was declared independent, and Thessaly organized the Amphictiony to her interest.

The *Second Sacred War* was precipitated by a Phocian seizure of Delphi. The Spartans restored the Sanctuary to the Delphians. But soon afterwards the Athenians, led by Pericles, reinstated Phocis (448). We do not know when Delphi was again liberated; its independence was affirmed in the Peace of Nicias (Thuc. 1. 112; 5. 18).

The *Third Sacred War* involved most of Greece and ended in the intervention of Philip II of Macedon. During the Theban Hegemony Thebes had controlled the Amphictiony, and in spring 356 B.C. passed through its council a threat of war, unless Phocian separatist leaders paid the fines imposed on them for cultivating the Crisaean plain (between Delphi and Cirrha), which was sacred to Apollo. The separatists, led by Philomelus, seized Delphi and repelled Boeotian and Locrian attacks. The Sacred War was finally begun in autumn 355, when the Thebans obtained an open declaration of hostilities from the Amphictiony. Philomelus, with passive allies in Sparta, Athens, Achaea, and others, raised mercenaries with Delphian funds to face the coalition of Thessaly, Locris, and Boeotia. Defeating the Thessalians, who withdrew from the war, Philomelus defended Phocis successfully but was killed at Neon (354). Onomarchus, his able successor, invaded Boeotia and subdued Doris, Locris, and part of Thessaly, where he twice defeated Philip of Macedon (353). In 352 Onomarchus, despite Athenian assistance, was defeated and killed by Philip in Thessaly; his successor, Phayllus, held Thermopylae with aid from Athens, Sparta, and Achaea, and prevented Philip from entering central Greece. He eventually fell ill and was succeeded by Phalaecus, who pillaged the shrine at Delphi. By 347 Phocis and Thebes were exhausted by guerrilla warfare; Thebes and Thessaly invited Philip to intervene, while a faction in Phocis invited Athens and Sparta; but Phalaecus, regaining power, rebuffed both. Athens then allied with Philip, and Phocis, isolated, surrendered to Philip, who reconvened the Amphictionic Council. The Phocians were disarmed and obliged to receive garrisons and to pay an indemnity. Their Amphictionic votes were transferred to Philip.

For the First Sacred War see W. G. Forrest, *BCH* 1956, 33 f.; H. W. Parke and D. E. W. Wormell, *The Delphic Oracle* (1956), 104 ff. For the chronology of the Third Sacred War see P. Cloché, *Étude chronologique sur la troisième guerre sacrée* (1915); N. G. L. Hammond, *JHS* 1937, 44 ff. N. G. L. H.

**SACRIFICE** (from the Latin *sacrificium*, the performance of a sacred action).

1. A sacrifice, according to Plato (*Euthyphro* 14 c), is a gift to the gods, and this was the current view of antiquity (in which the subject was treated by various scholars, of whom Philochorus is especially noteworthy). Modern comparative method, however, combined with anthropological theory, has sufficiently shown the complexity of the problem. One ancient attempt to classify the confused mass of details is that of Theophrastus, who distinguished offerings of praise, of thanksgiving, and of supplication. We may also distinguish between gods, daemones (heroes), and the dead as recipients of the offerings, and between private and public sacrifices. Finally, we may lay stress on the material of the sacrifice, the difference between vegetable and animal offerings, and on the way in which the offerings were made over to the supernatural powers (communal-sacrificial feast, holocaust, burial, libation, etc.). In view of the prehistoric origin of most of the sacrificial ritual it is for the most part extremely difficult to detect the real source of the ritual in question, which is very often of a purely

magical nature. Only insight into primitive mentality and evolutionary method can here give us a better understanding of the problems; and yet the religious and ethical notions of sacrifice in classical antiquity and in higher religions in general are quite different from those of primitive and savage worshippers.

2. *Bloodless offerings and blood offerings.* (i) Theophrastus and other ancient philosophers believed that man at first knew only vegetarian food and accordingly offered to the gods grass and roots, cereals, vegetables (even blades and leaves), fruits and non-intoxicating liquids (principally milk). Animal food is, however, probably of equal antiquity, but in many Greek cults, especially those of chthonian deities, vegetables were prescribed (all kinds of fruits in the procession for the Sun and the *Horai* at Athens, a dish of beans at the Pyanopsia for Apollo, etc.); in a number of cults cakes (q.v.) were customary (cf. Ar. *Plut.* 661 and schol.). We may add cheese, honey, and oil; and, no doubt, homegrown incense was from the remotest antiquity burnt for the gods (θύω originally means to 'fumigate', later commonly to 'sacrifice', as contrasted with ἐναγίζειν, which is often used of offerings to the dead and heroes).

(ii) *Blood offerings* were the most popular form of ancient sacrifice, public and private. The deity was provided with the same food as the worshipper, meat from domesticated or wild animals and birds, and sometimes fish (q.v.). The meat, specially selected for the deity, was burnt on the altar, wine being simultaneously poured into the flames. Many details, known to us from Homer, may have had a magical character; the sacrificer washed his hands, sprinkled barley-grains, threw some of the victim's hair into the fire, touched the altar (the centre of sanctity), and in a prayer praised the god, thanked him, or begged for his help. The entrails were separately cooked and tasted before the communal sacrificial feast started (on this point Greek and Roman usage agree remarkably). The deity was the honoured guest: this feature was still more prominent at the Theoxenia (q.v.; cf. the *lectisternia*, q.v., of the Romans). Epithets like 'goat-eater' (i.e. Hera), 'bull-eater' (Dionysus) bear witness to the original conception of the deity as really eating of the flesh of the victim. On many inscriptions the necessity of eating the flesh (being sanctified, *tabu*) within the holy precincts is enforced. We may infer that more indifferent worshippers often took it home; in other sacrifices this was quite correct. Concerning Roman ritual it is especially noteworthy that the sacrificer covered his head with his toga during the whole operation. Music (pipes, also lyre) was traditional in Greece as in Rome.

The choice of animals (which ought to be without blemish) was essential and intricate; the rules generally apply to the Greeks as well as the Romans. Male deities usually preferred male victims; bright (celestial) deities demanded light-haired victims, the nether world (and the dead) black victims, but there were many exceptions. The virgins Athena and Artemis sometimes wanted unbroken cattle. A pregnant sow was offered to the earth-goddess in order to intensify her *mana* (her fertility), a cock to the war-god. To some deities animals unfit (or not used) for human food were sacrificed: dogs to Hecate, Eileithyia, Enyalios (Sparta); horses to Poseidon, the Sun (burnt-offering), the Winds (also the river Skamandros into which horses were thrown, according to the *Iliad*; cf. the *equus October* sacrificed to Mars at Rome); asses to Priapus and (at Tarentum) to the Winds. No doubt there existed a mysterious sympathy between these gods and their victims (cf. also the red dog sacrificed to the spirit of the mildew at the Roman Robigalia, *see* ROBIGUS); the gods were formerly believed to appear in the shape of these very animals, as legend and archaeological evidence

still attest (so Poseidon as god of the earth and the underworld in the shape of a horse).

All sacrifices in which the worshippers shared the victim's flesh (or other food-offerings) with the god(s) are communion-feasts. The Bouphonia at Athens was this kind of sacrifice—the sources do not mention fire or cooking of the victim simply because the writers (Andronion ap. Schol. in Ar. *Nub.* 984; Theophr. ap. Porph. *Abst.* 2. 29; Paus. 1. 24. 4, 28. 10) have given their attention to the strange ritual which accompanied the offering. That ox which took a *pelanos* from a cult table at Zeus' festival of the Dipolieia or Bouphonia was killed; the killer dropped the axe or knife and fled; the implement was then brought to trial, convicted, and cast into the sea. After flaying the ox, everyone present tasted its flesh, apparently raw; thereafter, we may suppose (since the words used are θύειν and θυσία), the participants prepared the usual communion-meal. They completed the dramatic ritual by stuffing the victim's hide with grass and yoking the dummy ox to a plough. This sacrifice, it appears, had a preliminary touch of omophagy; but the omophagies of Dionysiac worship belong to legend rather than to reality: we find no trustworthy evidence of Dionysiac omophagy as a contemporary practice.

3. In piacular (propitiatory) and purificatory sacrifices the victim or offering was utterly destroyed. As commonly stated in modern works on Greek religion, heavenly and upperworld gods tended to receive a communion sacrifice made (verb θύειν) upon a βωμός in the daytime; and chthonian deities, heroes, and the dead tended to receive holocausts, made (verb ἐναγίζειν) in the evening on a hearth altar, ἐσχάρα or ἑστία, or in a pit (βόθρος); but such a distinction between heavenly and chthonian worship was far from being invariable and universal, since each cult developed its own customs and practices. Many a chthonian cult had a βωμός and communion sacrifices (especially common in the worship of the dead); Olympian cults occasionally had ἐσχάραι (e.g. in the temple of Apollo at Delphi, who also had an outdoor βωμός); and holocausts could be made to upperworld gods on βωμοί, usually in a time of crisis or fear. Tithes, the firstfruits of herds, flocks, crops, the hunt, and spoils of war (ἀπαρχαί, *primitiae*), were offered in their entirety to either Olympian or chthonian powers. The verbs θύειν and ἐναγίζειν are often used interchangeably, especially in poetry. Some ἐσχάραι, placed over a tomb, had a tube or hole which carried the victim's blood and libations down to the corpse below.

Although Greek heroic legends tell of human sacrifices, as of Iphigeneia at Aulis, there is no trustworthy evidence that the Greeks ever offered human victims. The historical Greeks considered human sacrifice a barbarian practice, unholy (ἀνόσιον) for Greeks (Ps.-Plato, *Minos* 315). Reports of exceptions are very dubious: there is no reliable evidence that human sacrifices were made as late as the second century A.D. or even the fourth century B.C. in the cults of Zeus Lycaeus in south Arcadia, Zeus Laphystius at Halos in Thessaly, and Dionysus Omestes on Tenedos and Chios. We can attribute these reports of exceptional human sacrifices to folk beliefs which circulated throughout Greece outside of the immediate neighbourhoods of these cults, and which probably arose from strangers' misunderstandings of the rites performed. For Italy too there is no sure record of human sacrifice, unless one counts the burial alive of two pairs of foreigners (Gauls and Greeks) in the Forum Boarium (3rd c. B.C.). The piacular killing of a criminal as scapegoat at Massalia and the occasional slaughter of captives of war are hardly evidence of human sacrifice among Greeks and Romans.

4. The oath sacrifice was a magical rite, since an oath is a conditional curse which the oath-taker places on

himself; if he violates the oath, the named penalties are expected to follow automatically. As described in the *Iliad* (3. 268–301, 19. 250–68), the parties to the oath first cut hair from the victims' heads (two lambs in *Iliad* 3, a boar in 19), then invoked the appropriate gods, stated the terms of contract or treaty, cut the victims' throats, poured libations of wine upon the ground, prayed to the gods, and finally either buried the victims or cast them into the sea.

P. Stengel, *Die griechische Kultusaltertümer*[2] and *Opferbräuche der Griechen* (1910); S. Eitrem, *Opferritus und Voropfer* (1915) and *Symb. Osl.* 1938, 9 ff.; A. Loisy, *Essai historique sur le sacrifice* (1920); C. G. Yavis, *Greek Altars* (1949); R. K. Yerkes, *Sacrifice in Greek and Roman Religions and Early Judaism* (1952); S. Dow, D. H. Gill, 'The Greek Cult Table', *AJArch.* 1965, 103 ff. S. E.; J. E. F.

**SACROVIR,** Julius (*PW* 452), a noble of the Aedui (q.v.), whose family had received Roman citizenship, perhaps from Caesar. In A.D. 21 he and Julius Florus of the Treveri (q.v.) led a rebellion against Rome of which the basic cause was the heavy indebtedness of the Gauls to Roman financiers. Sacrovir collected a large army of his countrymen and occupied Augustodunum (q.v.), but was easily defeated by C. Silius, legate of Upper Germany, and committed suicide. The triumphal arch at Arausio (q.v.) probably commemorates the Roman victory.

C. Jullian, *Histoire de la Gaule* iv (1913), 153 ff. A. M.; T. J. C.

**SAEPINUM,** Samnite (q.v.) mountain town south of Bovianum Undecimanorum (q.v.): modern *Terravecchia* near *Sepino*. The Romans stormed and destroyed it in 293 B.C. Tiberius built another Saepinum (modern *Altilia*) in the plain below, athwart a famous sheep-track (c. A.D. 4). The ruins of both Samnite and Roman towns are extensive and are being carefully excavated. E. T. S.

**SAEPTA IULIA,** the voting enclosure for the *comitia tributa*, between the Pantheon and the Temple of Isis in the Campus Martius; it was planned and begun by Julius Caesar (Cic. *Att.* 4. 16. 14) and completed by Agrippa in 26 B.C. The long rectangular voting area, about 300 m × 95 m, lay due north and south, and was flanked by colonnades, the *Porticus Meleagri* on the east and the *Porticus Argonautarum* on the west; the *Diribitorium*, where the votes were counted, closed its southern end. Parts of the building appear on the Severan Marble Plan, and some walls of the *Porticus Argonautarum* and *Diribitorium* survive, dating from a reconstruction after the fire of A.D. 80.

When the building lost its original purpose, it came to be used for gladiatorial contests and other forms of entertainment, and served as a luxury bazaar (Mart. 9. 59).

G. Gatti, *L'Urbe* 1937, fasc. 9, 8 ff.; G. Carettoni, *Forma Urbis Romae* (1860), 97 ff.; Nash, *Pict. Dict. Rome* ii. 291 ff.; L. R. Taylor, *Roman Voting Assemblies* (1966), 47 ff. D. E. S.

**S(A)EVIUS NICANOR** (2nd–1st c. B.C.), grammarian, the first to gain fame by his teaching (Suet. *Gram.* 5), wrote *commentarii*, said to have been mainly borrowed, and a *satura*.

**SAGUNTUM** (later *Murviedro*, now *Sagunto*), a city of the Edetani (or Arsetani; cf. *Arse* on coins) about 16 miles north of Valencia in Spain. It had close trade relations with Massilia. An alliance with Rome, and its subsequent siege and capture by Hannibal (219 B.C.), figured in history as the proximate cause of the Second Punic War. In 217 the elder Scipios moved against it (traces of their camp at the neighbouring Almenara survive) and it fell by 212. The city and its walls were rebuilt by the Romans. Sertorius occupied it, but was driven out by

Metellus and Pompey in 75. It became a *municipium civium Romanorum* under Augustus. It was noted for its cereals, a variety of fig, and a type of pottery. Some of the amphorae in Monte Testaccio at Rome came from Saguntum. There survive traces of the Iberian wall and Punic buildings on the citadel and a Roman theatre.

M. Gonzales Simancas, *Sagunto, sus monumentos y las excavaciones* (1929); *PW* s.vv., 'Saguntum' and 'Zacantha'; for Almenara camp, *Arch. Anz.* 1927, 233; 1933, 525. J. J. VAN N.

**SALACIA,** cult-partner of Neptunus (Gellius 13. 23. 2), probably the *numen* of springing water (root of *salire*; for the suffix cf. *salax*); Neptunus (q.v.) is a deity originally of fresh water.

**SALAMIS** (1), an island in the Saronic Gulf between the western coast of Attica and the eastern coast of the Megarid, closes the bay of Eleusis on the south. In the strait formed by the slopes of Mt. Aegaleus, the island of Psyttaleia, and the promontory of Cynosura on the south and the small island of St. George on the west, the Persian fleet was crushingly defeated (Sept. 480 B.C.). There is an important Early Iron Age cemetery. Though probably colonized by, and originally belonging to, Aegina, and temporarily occupied by Megara (c. 600 B.C.), Salamis shared the fortunes of Athens from the age of Solon and Pisistratus. Declared a cleruchy soon after Cleisthenes' reforms, it was consequently exploited. In 318 it was conquered by Macedonia. Aratus restored it to Athens (c. 230).

P-K, *GL* i. 3. V (b); C. F. Styrenius, *Op. Arch.* 1946; N. G. L. Hammond, *JHS* 1956, 32 f. (the battle). P. T.

**SALAMIS** (2), the principal city of Cyprus, situated on the east coast on a wide, sandy bay. It succeeded an inland settlement at Enkomi which has yielded very rich Mycenaean remains. It appears to have been the first Cypriot city to strike coins; and from these can be recovered a list of kings from the later sixth century onwards. In 411 B.C. King Evagoras began a Hellenic revival against Phoenician encroachment and oriental influences in Cyprus, and became briefly master of nearly all the island. Salamis was the scene of two notable battles: here in 498 B.C. the Persians crushed Cypriot participation in the Ionian revolt, and in 306 Demetrius the Besieger defeated Ptolemy I in a naval action. Capital of Cyprus under the earlier Ptolemies, owing to the silting up of its harbour it was superseded about 200 B.C. by Paphos (q.v.). Under the Romans it remained politically the second city; and supremacy was not restored to it until its refounding by Constantius II as Constantia. In the Roman period, to which all the visible ruins date, it contained until A.D. 116 a large Jewish population.

Excavations. J. A. R. Munro and H. A. Tubbs, *JHS* 1891, 59 ff. Gymnasium and theatre. V. Karageorghis, *BCH* 1963, 380 ff.; id. *Salamis in Cyprus* (1969); *Arch. Anz.* 1963, 574 ff. T. B. M.

**SALAPIA** (modern *Salpi*) was a port at the south end of the Gulf of Manfredonia near Margherita di Savoia in northern Apulia. The area always suffered from silting and the classical coastline now lies over 2 miles inland. The early city, where Hannibal wintered, lay in the area of le Mattone on the edge of the modern salt-pans, 2 miles west of Trinitapoli. Sometime in the last two centuries B.C. this site became so unhealthy through silting and malaria that it was abandoned in favour of another four Roman miles away (Vitr. *De Arch.* 1. 4. 12). This second site is marked by the Roman and medieval remains at Posta di Salpi further west along the coast. G. D. B. J.

**SALARIUM** is a term used in the imperial period to denote regular payments to officials and (from the reign of Vespasian) to doctors and teachers of rhetoric paid either by the Emperor or by local communities (*Dig.* 50. 9. 4. 2). Augustus instituted the making of regular payments to senatorial and equestrian officials in the provinces (Dio 53. 15). The word *salarium* was used (Tac. *Agr.* 42) for the pay of a proconsul, which was 1,000,000 sesterces p.a. (Dio 88. 22); it is not specifically attested for the different sums paid to *procuratores* (q.v.). It is used of the payment by the Emperor to his *quaestor Augusti* (*ILS* 8973), the pay (25,000 sesterces) of a *tribunus semestris* (*CIL* xiii. 3162), payments by an Emperor or a *legatus* to his *comites* (Suet. *Tib.* 46; *Dig.* 1. 22. 4; 50. 13. 1. 8), and the payment by the *aerarium* (q.v.) of the *scriba* of a provincial quaestor (Pliny, *Ep.* 4. 12) and by the *fiscus* (q.v.) to regular *advocati fisci*. A few inscriptions are known in which soldiers, mostly *evocati* of the Praetorian Cohorts, describe themselves as *salarius*.

The rule of classical Roman law that the hire of services could not be the object of *locatio conductio* was waived in the case of *professores*, and by analogy *comites* (*Dig.* 50. 13), who could thus bring actions for the payment of *salaria* by extraordinary proceedings.     F. G. B. M.

**SALASSI,** a Gallic tribe occupying the Val d'Aosta and controlling the Great and Little St. Bernard passes and the mining industry of the valley (gold, iron, and probably other metals). The gold-mines were acquired by Rome in 143 B.C., and the route into the Po valley was controlled from 100 B.C. by the colony planted at Eporedia (q.v.). The tribe was conquered in 25 B.C. by A. Terentius Varro Murena (q.v.), and the colony of Augusta Praetoria (q.v.) founded in the following year.

Strabo, 4, 206 (4.6 . 7); Cass. Dio, 53. 25. G. E. F. Chilver, *Cisalpine Gaul* (1941).     P. S.

**SALII** (from *salire* 'to dance'), an ancient ritual *sodalitas* (*see* SODALES) found in many towns of Italy, usually in association with the war-god. Outside Rome they are heard of at Lavinium, Tusculum, Aricia, Anagnia, and especially at Tibur, where they were attached to Hercules (Serv. ad *Aen.* 8. 285). At Rome they were connected with Mars, though it is possible that of their two companies, each twelve in number, the Palatini and the Collini (or Agonenses), the latter originally belonged to Quirinus; they were required to be of patrician birth and to have both father and mother living. They wore the old Italian war-dress, *tunica picta*, with breastplate covered by the short military cloak (*trabea*), and the conical felt hat known as the *apex* (q.v., see Dion. Hal. 2. 70). A sword was girt by their side; on the left arm they carried the *ancilia*, 'figure of eight' shields, preserved in the *sacrarium Martis* in the Regia and said to be copies of the original *ancile*, which fell from heaven as a gift from Jupiter to Numa (Ov. *Fasti* 3. 365–92); in the right hand they carried a 'spear or staff' (Dion. Hal. loc. cit.). The Salii played a prominent part in the Quinquatrus of 19 Mar. and the Armilustrium of 19 Oct., which marked the opening and closing of the campaigning season. On certain days, too, during each of these two months, marked in the calendar by the note *arma ancilia mouent*, the Salii went in procession through the city. At certain spots they halted and performed elaborate ritual dances (*tripudium*, cf. Plut. *Num.* 13), beating their shields with their staves and singing the Carmen Saliare (q.v.) or *axamenta*, of which some fragments are preserved. In the evening they feasted and resumed their procession on the next appointed day.

Latte, *RR* 115 ff.     C. B.

**SALINATOR,** MARCUS LIVIUS (*PW* 33), was born in 254 B.C.; Livius (q.v. 1) Andronicus was perhaps pedagogue in his father's house. As consul (219) he campaigned against the Illyrians. He celebrated a triumph and served on the commission which delivered the ultimatum to Carthage, but then he was accused of peculation and withdrew from Rome (218). His bitterness and the desertion of his father-in-law, Pacuvius of Capua, to the enemy explain his non-participation in the first part of the Hannibalic War. Recalled by the consuls in 210, he did not speak in the Senate till 208. As consul II (207) he was reconciled in national interests with his colleague C. Claudius Nero (q.v. 2), his former subordinate officer who had witnessed for the prosecution at the trial. Together they defeated Hasdrubal at Metaurus. Salinator celebrated a triumph and was proconsul in Etruria (206–205) and Gaul (204); as censor (204), again with Nero for colleague, he imposed a salt-tax. H. H. S.

**SALLUST** (1) (GAIUS SALLUSTIUS (*PW* 10) CRISPUS) (probably 86–35 B.C.) was born at Amiternum (Hieron. *Chron.* 151 H); not a *nobilis*, he probably derived from the municipal aristocracy. His early career is unknown. The evidence for a quaestorship is late and unreliable (*Invectiva in Sallustium* 15). Our earliest certain information concerns his tribunate in 52, when he acted against Cicero and Milo (Asc. *Mil.* 37, 45, 49 C). He was expelled from the Senate in 50 (Dio 40. 63. 2 ff.); *Inv. in Sall.* 16 alleges immorality but the real grounds were probably Sallust's actions in 52 (ancient gossip about his morals can be dismissed). Ap. Claudius instigated the expulsion; his fellow censor, L. Piso, Caesar's father-in-law, acquiesced, though he shielded the Caesarian Curio. No political connexion is demonstrable between Sallust and Caesar before 50; now, however, he joined Caesar, commanding a legion in 49 (Oros. 6. 15. 8). Elected praetor in 47 (Dio 42. 52. 1 f.), Sallust took part in the African campaign of 46 (*BAfr.* 8; 34) and was appointed the first governor of Africa Nova (*BAfr.* 97; cf. App. *BCiv.* 2. 100. 415; Dio 43. 9. 2). Returning to Rome, he was charged with extortion, allegedly escaping only through Caesar's intervention (Dio, ibid.; *Inv. in Sall.* 19). Malpractice is likely enough. Sallust had no immediate prospect of advancement; before his death Caesar had already promised the consulates of 43–41 to others.

Sallust withdrew from public life—the luxury of the Horti Sallustiani may reflect rather the taste of his heir and grand-nephew—and turned to history writing (*Cat.* 4. 1 f.). His first monograph, the *Bellum Catilinae*, dealt with the conspiracy of Catiline (q.v.), especially memorable 'sceleris atque periculi novitate' (*Cat.* 4. 4); i.e. Sallust accepts, broadly, the assessment of Cicero. But the conspiracy also exemplified the political and moral decline of Rome, begun after the fall of Carthage, quickening after Sulla's dictatorship (*Cat.* 10–14). *Avaritia*, *ambitio*, and *luxuria*, especially of the *nobiles*, are castigated, but Caesar and Cato stand above the wreck of the *res publica*. Yet Caesar is not favoured more than Cato (cf. *Cat.* 53. 6 ff.); and though Cicero may seem but faintly praised, that is in Sallust's manner. The work's prejudices, e.g. against the *nobiles*, issue from his personal experiences rather than any party loyalty. He probably wrote after Cicero's death (Dec. 43); the rivalries of Caesar's day had been superseded.

The second monograph, the *Bellum Iugurthinum*, recounts the venality and incompetence of the *nobiles* over the succession question in Numidia (q.v.) and the advancement of the *novus homo*, C. Marius (q.v. 1). The Roman campaigns in Numidia are narrated patchily, events at Rome more convincingly, especially the opposition to the *nobiles* which, for Sallust, initiated civil strife (*Iug.* 5. 1 f.). The *nobilis* Metellus (q.v. 6), however, is treated favourably, while his political opponent, Marius, is scarcely Sallust's hero (cf. e.g. *Iug.* 64. 4 f.). The prologue probably reflects the Triumviral period, with publication *c.* 40.

Sallust's last work, the *Historiae*, was annalistic, covering events from 78; the last datable fragment, from book 5, concerns the year 67, hardly his chosen terminus. The surviving fragments, including speeches and letters, suggest that his theme was the decline of the *res publica* after Sulla.

The *Invectiva in Ciceronem* ascribed to Sallust in the MSS. and cited as genuine by Quintilian (4. 1. 68; 9. 3. 89) is not appropriate to Sallust in 54 (its ostensible date); its author was probably an Augustan rhetorician. Two *Epistulae ad Caesarem senem*, 'Sallustian' in manner, are transmitted anonymously in a codex (Vaticanus lat. 3864) which includes the letters and speeches from Sallust's works. Convincing objections have been raised against their content, ostensible dates (*c.* 46 and *c.* 50), style, and language. They are probably *suasoriae* of imperial date (*see* DECLAMATIO).

As an historian Sallust has weaknesses: inexact chronology, scant, occasionally inaccurate geography, schematic interpretations, and anti-noble prejudice. Apparent chronological error, however, if not mere carelessness, may sometimes by due to regrouping of material for effect; geographical ignorance was a Roman failing; and hostility to the *nobiles* arose out of the disappointments of a *novus homo*. Sallust was also influenced by his sources: for *Cat.* he must have relied heavily on Cicero's writings, supplemented by oral testimony (cf. *Cat.* 48. 9); in *Iug.* he perhaps used a general history and the autobiographies of Aemilius Scaurus (1), Rutilius Rufus, and Sulla (1) (qq.v.); some geographical notions (but not much more) may derive from Posidonius and Sallust may have consulted contemporary oratory; for *Hist.* he perhaps used Varro's *De Pompeio*, writings on Lucullus (cf. Cic. *Acad. Pr.* 4), and oral tradition.

Sallust is not a philosopher; the prologues to the monographs neatly express philosophical commonplaces. His political thought is essentially moral and traditional, with special attention to *virtus*; his censoriousness and pessimism were compelling. The works are enlivened by speeches, letters, digressions, and character studies. They created a style for Roman historiography, modelled on Thucydides and the Elder Cato. Its features, developing in the course of the works, are noted by ancient writers (*testimonia* in Kurfess, ed. xxvi ff.): archaisms, 'amputatae sententiae et verba ante exspectatum cadentia et obscura brevitas', epigrams, Graecisms, novel vocabulary and syntax, swiftness, 'labor'. Sallust rejects the dominant oratorical style of his day. He won admirers almost immediately and considerably influenced Tacitus.

TEXTS. *Cat.* and *Iug.*: A. Kurfess (3rd. ed., Teubner, 1957); *Hist.* (with comm.): B. Maurenbrecher (1891–3); *Epistulae*, *Invectivae*: Kurfess (6th–4th eds., Teubner, 1962).
COMMENTARIES. *Cat.*, *Iug.*: R. Jacobs (11th ed., Wirz and Kurfess, 1922); *Cat.*: A. M. Cook (1901); *Iug.*: W. C. Summers (1902); *Inv. in Cic.*, *Epistulae*: K. Vretska, 2 vols. (1961).
TRANSLATIONS. J. C. Rolfe (Loeb); A. Ernout (Budé); S. A. Handford (1963).
STYLE AND DICTION. Indexes in eds. of Dietsch (1859), Maurenbrecher (1891–3); *Epistulae*: E. Skard (1930). See also E. Löfstedt, *Syntactica*, vol. 2 (1933), 290 ff.; E. Skard, *Symb. Osl.* 1964, 13 ff.
SPECIAL STUDIES. A. D. Leeman, *A Systematical Bibliography of Sallust (1879–1964)* (1965). Also W. Steidle, *Sallusts historische Monographien* (1958); K. Büchner, *Sallust* (1960); D. C. Earl, *The Political Thought of Sallust* (1961); H. Bloch, 'The Structure of Sallust's *Historiae*' in *Didascaliae: Studies . . . Albareda* (1961); R. Syme, *Sallust* (1964).　　　　　　　　　　　　　G. M. P.

**SALLUSTIUS** (2, *PW* 11) **CRISPUS,** GAIUS, great-nephew and adopted son of the historian, became the chief private counsellor of Augustus and then of Tiberius, remaining an *eques* throughout like his predecessor Maecenas (q.v.). He was privy to the murder of Agrippa (q.v. 4) Postumus in A.D. 14 and in 16 arrested the slave who impersonated him. He owned copper-mines in the Graian Alps (cf. Hor. *Carm.* 2. 2. 1 ff., an Ode addressed to him). He died in 20, leaving his wealth to an adoptive son, C. Sallustius Passienus Crispus, a noted orator who held two consulships (in 27 and 44) and married Nero's aunt Domitia and mother Agrippina (q.v. 3).

Syme, *Rom. Rev.*, *Tacitus*, see indexes; H. W. Benario, *CJ* 1961/2, 321 f.　　　　　　　　　　　　　A. M.; T. J. C.

**SALLUSTIUS** (3, Σαλούστιος), author of a brief manual of Neoplatonic piety known as *De deis et mundo*. He is probably to be identified with the Emperor Julian's friend, Saturninus Sallustius Secundus. His book echoes the language and ideas of Iamblichus and Julian, and seems to have been written during Julian's reign (A.D. 361–3) in the service of the pagan reaction against Christianity.

Ed. A. D. Nock with Engl. transl. and valuable prolegomena (1926); G. Rochefort (Budé, 1960). Translated and discussed by Gilbert Murray, *Five Stages of Greek Religion* (1951).　　E. R. D.

**SALLUVII (or SALYES),** a tribe dwelling north of Massalia from at least the sixth century B.C. (Avienius, *Ora Marit.* 701). Though they were called Ligurians by earlier writers, Strabo preferred 'Celto-Ligurians' and a Celtic element is suggested by their religion, which centred on the cult of the *tête coupée*. The chief shrines were at Roquepertuse (re-erected in Musée Borély, Marseille) and Entremont (north of Aix). This hill-fort was apparently their capital and displays Greek influence in its sculpture, its defences (with bastions), and the lay-out of its streets. The Salluvii constantly opposed the Massaliotes and later the Romans until C. Sextius Calvinus destroyed their capital (123 B.C.). Revolts were crushed in 90 and 83 B.C.

Diod. Sic. 34 frag. 23; Livy 5. 34, *Per.* 60, 61, 73; Strabo 4. 180, 185, 203; Just. *Epit.* 43. 3–5; App. *Celt.* 12. F. Benoit, *Entremont, Capitale celto-ligure des Salyens de Provence* (1957); Grenier, *Manuel* iv, 480 ff.　　　　　　　　　　　　　A. L. F. R.

**SALMONEUS** (Σαλμωνεύς), a son of Aeolus (q.v. 1). In post-Homeric tradition, e.g. Verg. *Aen.* 6. 585 ff., he was king of Elis, and pretended to be Zeus, flinging torches for lightnings and making a noise like thunder with his chariot; Zeus smote him with a real thunderbolt. It is very likely that this story originates in some rite of weather-magic, a mimic storm to make a real one.

Rose, *Handb. Gk. Myth.* 83, and notes 21, 22; O. Weinreich, 'Menekrates Zeus und Salmoneus', *Tübinger Beiträge z. Altertumsw.* 1933, 82 ff.　　　　　　　　　　　　　H. J. R.

**SALONAE** (later **SALONA**) was a city of Dalmatia (q.v.) near *Split* in Yugoslavia. In 118–17 B.C. it served as a base for L. Metellus but had to be recaptured by C. Cosconius in 78–76 B.C. The *conventus civium Romanorum* established there defeated the Pompeian admiral M. Octavius in 48 B.C. (Caes. *BCiv.* 3. 9). Caesar's legate A. Gabinius died there (47 B.C.). Soon afterwards a *colonia* was established there (*Martia Iulia Salona, CIL* iii. 1933) and after A.D. 9 it became the provincial capital of Dalmatia. As the focal point of the newly established road system (*CIL* iii. 3198–3201 and *add.*) it grew very rapidly and prospered. During the Marcomannic Wars in A.D. 170 its walls were repaired by detachments drawn from newly raised legions II Pia and III Concordia (later II and III Italica) (*CIL* iii. 1980). On his retirement in A.D. 305 Diocletian, who was born in the vicinity of Salonae, lived in the palace which he built on the coast a few miles away. When much later Salonae was threatened by Avar and Slav invasions the population retreated within the walls of the palace, which became the nucleus of the medieval town (Spalato).

Date of the *colonia*: G. Alföldy, *Acta Antiq. Scient. Hung.* 1962, 357 ff. Topography and remains: W. Gerber with M. Abramić and R. Egger, *Forschungen in Salona* i (1917), ii (1926). E. Dyggve and others, *Recherches à Salone* i (Copenhagen, 1928), ii (1933). On the palace of Diocletian: F. Bulić, *Kaisar Diocletians Palast in Split* (Zagreb, 1929). J. J. Wilkes, *Dalmatia* (1969), 220 ff.　　J. J. W.

**SALUS,** an old Roman goddess, later often identified with the Greek Hygieia (q.v.), the attendant of Asclepius. The temple to *Salus* (meaning apparently the safety of the State) on the Quirinal is said to have been built in 302 B.C. by the dictator C. Junius Bubulcus. Under the Empire, *Salus publica* and *Salus Augusti* appear often side by side. Where the genitive 'Augusti' appears, *Salus* may be regarded as definitely a 'virtue' of this Emperor, his saving power—not merely his health. An *augurium salutis*, which did not involve any personification of *salus*, was to be taken annually on a day free of all wars: this was an inquiry to ask whether it was permissible to pray for *salus* for the people. The constant wars of the last years of the Republic caused its frequent omission, but it was revived in 29 B.C. and performed on various occasions in the early Principate (Dessau, *ILS* 9337). Prayers 'pro salute Augusti' were commonly offered, as, for example, by the Arval Brethren.

*Salus* very frequently appears on coins, with the type of Hygieia, feeding out of her patera the sacred snake and holding the sceptre of divine majesty. A rarer attribute, ears of corn, may properly belong to the older Roman *Salus*.

Wissowa, *RK* 131 ff., 306 ff., and index; A. S. Pease on Cic. *Div.* 1. 105. For temple, Platner–Ashby, 462.                    H. M.

**SALUTATIO,** a formal greeting; especially at the *levée* (*admissio*) of an eminent Roman. Etiquette required a client (q.v.) to attend in formal dress (*togatus*) at his patron's house at dawn, to greet him (*salutare*) and escort him to work (*deducere*), both for protection and for prestige. Friends of equal or nearly equal standing might also attend, out of special respect or flattery (cf. Cic. *Fam.* 9. 20. 3). A great man—like a Hellenistic king—would admit his visitors in groups, according to class; and his standing to some extent depended on the number and class of those attending him. Under the Empire the clients degenerated into a parasitical claque. The gift of money or food (*sportula*) which they traditionally received in exchange for their services became a standard payment of 25 *asses*; though, as Juvenal shows, they could still expect to be invited to dinner on special occasions.

Dar.–Sag., s.v.                                          E. B.

**SALVIANUS** was born *c.* A.D. 400 probably at Trèves where he witnessed the Franks' attack (418). In 425, with his wife's consent, he joined Honoratus' monastery at Lérins, and *c.* 439 became presbyter at Marseilles till his death (after 470). The German invaders he interpreted as an instrument of divine wrath against the decadent Empire, contrasting Christian laxity with the high morality of the barbarians who erred 'in good faith'. Faced by misery and pauperism he urged that all estates be bequeathed for the poor and denounced inherited wealth. Extant are nine letters, a tract against avarice, and eight books *de Gubernatione Dei* (440).

Ed. F. Pauly (*CSEL* 8). P. Courcelle, *Histoire littéraire des grandes invasions germaniques* (1948), 119 ff.                    H. C.

**SALVIDIENUS** (*PW* 4) **RUFUS,** Quintus, of very humble origin, perhaps from the country of the Vestini, was one of Octavian's associates in 44 and later one of his principal generals. In 42 he was worsted by Sextus Pompeius in a naval battle off Rhegium and in 41 sent to Spain with six legions, but impeded in north Italy by the Antonian commanders and presently recalled for the impending war of Perusia (q.v.) in which he took a prominent part. In 40 he was appointed governor of Gaul and designated consul, though still an *eques*. Later in the year, however, he sent to Antony, then besieging Brundisium, offering to go over to him. Octavian, informed of this by Antony after their reconciliation, summoned

Salvidienus to Rome and denounced him in the Senate, which declared him a public enemy. He either committed suicide or was executed.

Syme, *Rom. Rev.*, see index; T. P. Wiseman, *CQ* 1964, 130.
                                          G. W. R.; T. J. C.

**SAMIAN WARE** was known to Plautus, Martial, and Pliny as a common, inexpensive table-ware. They were probably thinking of a variety of Eastern *terra sigillata* (q.v.), but the name was adopted by antiquaries for the red-coated pottery found in Britain. Despite attempts at rationalization, the name, usually spelt with small initial, remains the standard term in Britain for Gaulish *sigillata*.

The Gaulish industry was founded by Italian immigrants, but soon diverged from the Arretine inspiration. South Gaulish centres at La Graufesenque (Millau) and Montans (near Toulouse) were founded *c.* A.D. 15 and rapidly drove Arretine out of Western markets. By Nero's Principate Gaulish samian sold in Italy and Greece and the industry had reached its apogee technically. South Gaul remained dominant until the end of the first century, but its standards deteriorated and under Trajan and Hadrian Les Martres-de-Veyre and Lezoux, in the Auvergne, captured the provincial trade. By the mid second century there were many potteries nearer the frontiers in East Gaul and the Rhineland, and even a minor one at Colchester, but only Rheinzabern, near Speyer, rivalled the principal Gaulish centres. Export from Central Gaul ended with the second century and the East Gaulish potteries did not survive the troubles of the 260s. Samian was replaced on the table by local fine wares.

Organization in *officinae* is attested in south and central Gaul by potters' stamps, but evidence of slaves is sparse. The immense production is shown by graffiti from La Graufesenque: twenty lists on pots stamped by Castus name thirty-eight workmen in his workshop and record manufacture of half a million pots. Decorative motifs are Classical, never Celtic, but with few exceptions coherent subjects were not portrayed. *Horror vacui* was dominant.

The frequent occurrence of characteristic decoration and of potters' stamps in dated contexts make samian widely useful in dating early imperial sites.

*See* TERRA SIGILLATA. La Graufesenque graffiti: F. Hermet, *La Graufesenque* (1934), 291 ff. Potters' stamps: F. Oswald, *Index of Potters' Stamps on Terra Sigillata* (1931).                    B. R. H.

**SAMNIUM,** Oscan-speaking region in the southern Apennines (q.v.). Its inhabitants, primitive and warlike, lived mostly in agricultural villages, frequently unwalled and unidentifiable. The Samnites were divided into four tribal states (Caraceni, Caudini, Hirpini, Pentri), each administered by a *meddix* (q.v.), but were linked together in a confederation which had a federal diet and possibly an assembly. A generalissimo led the confederation in wartime. (Frentani and other Sabelli (q.v.), although ethnic Samnites, were not members of it.) After their treaty with Rome (354 B.C.) the Liris evidently became their boundary with Latium (q.v.). Shortly thereafter their neighbours sought Roman protection. By granting it the Romans precipitated the Samnite Wars. The First (343–341), often unconvincingly reckoned apocryphal, resulted in Roman control of northern Campania (q.v.); the Second (327–321, 316–304), despite the Samnite success at the Caudine Forks (q.v.), prevented Samnite control of Apulia, Lucania and southern Campania; the Third (298–290) involved and decided the destiny of all peninsular Italy. Samnium, still unbowed, then supported Pyrrhus, but the Romans defeated him and split Samnium apart with Latin colonies at Beneventum and Aesernia. Samnium helped Hannibal and lost both population and territory when the Second Punic War was over. Subsequently depopulation increased; pastoral pursuits gradually replaced agricultural and by 180 Samnium could accommodate transported Ligurians. The Samnites fought implacably in the Social War and in the Civil against Sulla, who slaughtered all he could. The survivors underwent romanization. Chief towns: Aufidena, Bovianum Vetus (q.v.) (Caraceni); Caiata, Caudium, Cupulteria, Saticula, Telesia (Caudini); Abellinum, Aeclanum, Beneventum (q.v.), Compsa (Hirpini); Aesernia, Allifae, Bovianum, Saepinum (qq.v.) (Pentri). The alleged Samnite provenance of *pilum*, *scutum*, and maniple is very questionable.

ANCIENT LITERATURE. Our principal source, Livy (bks. 7–10), depends on annalists more patriotic than trustworthy. Meagre notices in Diodorus (bks. 19, 20) and Polybius (2. 19 f.) supplement him.

MODERN LITERATURE. L. Pareti, *Storia di Roma* (1952), i–iii (for history); E. Vetter, *Handbuch der italischen Dialekte* (1953), i. 97 f., 101 ff., 135 f. (for language); F. Weege, *JDAI* 1909, 98, 141 (for material civilization); G. Camporeale, *Atti Accad. Toscana* 1956, 33 ff. (for constitution). E. T. Salmon, *Samnium and the Samnites* (1967).
E. T. S.

**SAMOS,** an island off western Asia Minor, was occupied in the Early Bronze Age and by Late Mycenaeans. In the Early Iron Age it was settled by Ionians and long preserved a distinctive dialect. Samians settled in Amorgos *c.* 690 B.C., at Perinthos (601), Bisanthe, and Heraion Teichos in Thrace, in Samothrace, at Naucratis, in Cilicia, and perhaps at Dicaearchia (Puteoli), and *c.* 490 at Zancle (Messana). Colaeus of Samos made a famous voyage to Tartessus *c.* 638; Ameinocles of Corinth had built warships for the Samians *c.* 704, Samian ships helped Sparta in the Second Messenian War. The rich landed class (γεωμόροι) continued influential till late in the fifth century (hence the oligarchic reactions in Samian history), but trade and industry flourished, especially in metalwork and woollen products. Sixth-century Samos was the home of notable architects, sculptors, and gem engravers (Rhoecus, Theodorus, Mnesicles), of moralists and poets (Aesop, Ibycus, Anacreon). A Samian engineer, Mandrocles, bridged the Bosporus for Darius. But the greatest of all Samians, Pythagoras, migrated to south Italy. The temple of Hera (built *c.* 560, rebuilding begun *c.* 530) was the largest of its day in the Greek world. The sanctuary has been excavated. Of the town the wall-line, Eupalinos' tunnel, and the Archaic cemetery have been investigated.

The consecutive history of Samos begins with the tyranny of Polycrates (q.v. 1), his steward Maeandrius, and his brother Syloson, the last a vassal of Darius. Samos joined the Ionian revolt, but her ships deserted at Lade (494). When the revolt was crushed the Persians allowed her a democratic government. She fought well for Xerxes at Salamis, but soon turned against the Persians and was an autonomous member of the Athenian League till her revolt in 441 which Pericles himself suppressed. During the oligarchic revolution of the 400 (411 B.C.) Samos was the stronghold of the democracy. For their loyal co-operation the Samians were made Athenian citizens after Aegospotami (405); but the city fell to Lysander in 404. About 394 she had a currency alliance with Ephesus, Cnidos, and Rhodes. In 365 Athens captured the island and planted Athenian cleruchs, who were expelled only after Alexander's death. She was eclipsed by Rhodes in the new Hellenistic world, in which her greatest achievement was to produce the astronomer Conon.

P–K, *GL* iv. E III; E. Buschor, *Altsamische Standbilder* (1935); *Ath. Mitt.* 1929 and successive vols.; Reuther, *Der Heratempel* (1957); *Samos* i (1901), prehistoric; J. Barron, *CQ* 1964, 210 f.; id. *The Silver Coins of Samos* (1966). P. N. U.; J. B.

**SAMOSATA** (modern *Samsât*), a fortified city on the right bank of the Euphrates; the residence of the kings of Commagene (q.v.). Like Zeugma, it guarded an important crossing of the river on one of the main caravan routes from East to West, and it was consequently of considerable strategic and commercial importance. Its formidable defences twice withstood a Roman siege, but in A.D. 72, when the client kingdom of Commagene was annexed, it was forced to surrender, and it was garrisoned henceforth by a Roman legion. Samosata was captured by the Sassanid Sapor I in his invasion of 256 and underwent many vicissitudes during the frontier wars against Persia until in 637 the city was finally captured by the Arabs.

Humann u. Puchstein, *Reisen in Kleinasien etc.* (1890), 181 ff.
M. S. D.; E. W. G.

**SAMOTHRACE,** an island of the north-east Aegean, consisting of a table-like mountain which rises to 5,250 feet, and containing but little cultivable land. Its Greek population was of Samian origin. It formed part of the two maritime confederacies of Athens; in the third century it frequently changed hands among the Hellenistic dynasts; under Roman rule it was a 'civitas libera'. Its chief importance lay in the mystery cult of its twin gods, the Cabiri (q.v.). This cult attained a wide vogue in the Hellenistic age, and its initiates included some Roman notables. The temple of the Cabiri and several Hellenistic buildings have been excavated (here was found the Victory in the Louvre).

P–K, *GL* iv. D I (b); *IG* xii. 8; Conze ,*et al., Untersuch. auf S.* (1875); K. Lehmann, *Guide to Samothrace* (1966); *Samothrace* i– (1958– ). M. C.; J. B.

**SANCHUNIATHON** is cited by Philon (q.v. 5) of Byblos as his ancient Phoenician authority (pre-Trojan War, 14/13th c. B.C.) for his Φοινικικά, including Phoenician mythology. Once suspect as a forgery, his claim is now supported by the evidence of the Ugarit texts, even if the tradition has been transmitted under Hellenistic influence.

*FGrH* iii c, 802. A. H. McD.

**SANDAS** (Σάνδας, Σάνδης, Σάνδων), a god of Tarsus in Cilicia, perhaps of Luwian origin. At his festival a great pyre was erected and burned; the Greeks accordingly equated him with Heracles. Traces of his cult are found in Cappadocia, Lydia, and other nearby lands, but his real nature remains uncertain.

J. G. Frazer, *Adonis Attis Osiris* i, ch. 6. F. R. W.

**SANDRACOTTUS,** the Greek form of the Indian name Chandragupta, was probably a commoner of Kshatriya origin, who founded the Mauryan Empire. In 323/2 B.C., with the help of Chanakya, a Brahmin statesman of great wisdom and experience, who wrote a comprehensive book on Hindu polity and statecraft, he overthrew the Nanda King of Magadha (part of the modern Bihar State), whose power and wealth were such that his renown may have been a factor in the refusal of Alexander's army to advance beyond the river Beas (Hyphasis). According to a Sanskrit drama *Mudra-Rakshasa*, a Prince named Parvataka, who is supposed to be Porus (q.v.), helped Chandragupta. By 305, before Seleucus' encounter with Chandragupta, the latter appears to have been already in the possession of almost the whole of the Indo-Pakistan subcontinent north of the Vindhya mountains. The encounter probably took place in Gandhara, west of the Indus. Seleucus did not succeed in his designs and he ceded to Chandragupta the satrapies of Aria, Arachosia, Gedrosia, and Paropanisadae. A matrimonial alliance between the two royal families was also effected. Chandragupta made a present of 500 elephants and Seleucus sent an ambassador, Megasthenes, to the Mauryan court. Chandragupta is also credited with conquests in south India up to Mysore, where his name survived in the twelfth century in local inscriptions and in the Jain tradition according to which he adopted Jain religion and migrated to the south with his teacher Bhadrabahu and died after a fast. His administration was centrally controlled and strict. He ruled his empire from Pataliputra (*Patna*), with governors at provincial headquarters. Chandragupta reigned for about twenty-four years and died in 299/8 B.C.

R. K. Mookerji, *Chandragupta Maurya and His Times*[3] (1943); K. A. Nilakanta Sastri, *A Comprehensive History of India* ii, ch. 1 (1957). A. K. N.

**SANGARIUS** (modern *Sakarya*), important river of north-west Asia Minor already known to Hesiod and Homer. Rising in Phrygia near Pessinus (Strabo 12. 3. 7; coins, Head, *Hist. Num.*[2] 748) on Mt. Adoreus (Livy 38. 18), it flowed in a winding course through Phrygia Epictetus and Bithynia to enter the Black Sea west of the territory of Heraclea Pontica. The Bithynian section was navigable and rich in fish (Strabo, loc. cit. and Livy, loc. cit.). Its valley provides a line of access from the coast to the plateau, but for part of its course its gorge is a barrier to movements west and east. E. W. G.

**SAN GIOVENALE** takes its name from the medieval castle on the plateau overlooking the river Vesca north of the Tolfa Hills, 16 miles east of Tarquinia. The plateau was inhabited from the Bronze Age, represented by Apennine Culture pottery associated with houses and a fortification wall of large blocks. An extensive Iron Age village of oval huts dates mainly from the eighth to the late seventh centuries and has produced material similar to that of Tolfa and Allumiere. An Etruscan settlement lasted until the beginning of the fifth century. Tombtypes in the zone range from *pozzi* to Etruscan chamber tombs; a late (third-century B.C.) tomb was reused in Hadrianic times. Occupation at Luni, four miles west of San Giovenale, also extends from the Bronze Age to the Middle Ages: the Apennine levels produced five Mycenaean sherds.

E. Berggren and M. Moretti, *Not. Scav.* 1960, 1 ff.; A. Boethius *et al.*, *Etruscan Culture: Land and People* (Malmö, 1962); Scullard, *Etr. Cities*, 94 f.; C. E. Östenberg, *Luni sul Mignone e problemi della preistoria d'Italia* (Skrifte Utgivna 4° xxv, 1967). D. W. R. R.

**SANNYRION**, Athenian comic poet, produced *Danae* after Eur. *Or.* (408 B.C.), to which fr. 8 refers. We have six titles (two of them doubtful) and a dozen fragments. Fr. 1 ('we gods . . . you mortals . . .') shows that at least one deity was a character in *Laughter*.

*FCG* ii. 873 ff.; *CAF* i. 793–5; *FAC* i. 882 ff. K. J. D.

**SANTRA**, a scholar of the Ciceronian age who wrote a *De antiquitate verborum* in at least three books (now lost). He also interested himself in questions of literary history.

Schanz–Hosius, § 196. 1; G. Funaioli, *Gramm. Rom. Frag.* 384–9.

**SAPOR** (*Shapur*), name of Sassanid kings of the Persian Empire (*see* SASSANIDS), of which the most famous was Sapor I (reigned A.D. 241–72). Son of Artaxerxes I (q.v. 4: *Ardashir*) and co-regent with him in 241, he was crowned in 242. He continued with spectacular success his father's policy of aggression against Rome, taking full advantage of the internal crisis in the Roman Empire. Hatra (q.v.) and the Roman outposts in Mesopotamia fell to him at an early date. In 252 he secured control of Armenia, expelling its last Arsacid rulers. Sapor styled himself 'King of Kings of Iran and Non-Iran' as he developed his systematic attacks on his Roman neighbour. The Roman counter-offensive under Gordian III was nullified by the death of Gordian and the concessions made by the usurper Philip; the eastern provinces felt the full weight of Sapor's offensive after his capture of the Emperor Valerian near Edessa in 260. The great cities of

Syria and the provinces of eastern Asia Minor were overrun and pillaged. It was left to Odaenathus (q.v.), dynast of Palmyra (d. 266), to play the major part in forcing Sapor to withdraw from Roman territory. In addition to his military achievements (listed on his great inscription at Naqš-i Rustam, *Res Gestae Divi Saporis*) Sapor was famed for his grandiose building operations (he used the labour of Roman captives) and for his relations with the religious leader Mani (*see* MANICHAEISM), who began his preaching in the Persian Empire soon after 240.

Honigmann et Maricq, *Recherches sur les* Res Gestae divi Saporis (Mém. Acad. Roy. de Belg. 47, fasc. 4, 1953); W. Ensslin, *Zu den Kriegen des Sassaniden Schapur I* (1949) (*Sitz. Bay. Ak. Wiss.*, Phil.-Hist. Kl. Jahrg. 1947, Heft 5). E. W. G.

**SAPPHO**, poetess, daughter of Scamandronymus and Cleis, of Eresus and Mytilene in Lesbos, born *c.* 612 B.C. (*Suda*, s.v. Σαπφώ). As a child, no doubt owing to political troubles, she went into exile in Sicily (*Marm. Par.* 36), though apart from a passing reference to Panormus (fr. 7) no traces of this are left in her fragments. She returned to Mytilene, where she was the centre of some kind of θίασος which honoured Aphrodite and the Muses and had young girls for its members. With these she lived in great intimacy and affection, wrote poems about them, and celebrated their marriages with songs. She married Cercylas and had a child Cleis (*Suda*, loc. cit., cf. frs. 98, 132). Her brother Charaxus angered her by his love for the courtesan Rhodopis or Doricha, whom Sappho is said to have rated (Hdt. 2. 135, Strabo 17. 808, cf. fr. 15). Little else is known of her life, and nothing of her death, since the old story that she threw herself over a cliff in love for Phaon (Ov. *Ep. Sapph.*, *passim*) seems to be an invention of the New Comedy. Her work was collected in nine books. Book 1 contained poems in the Sapphic stanza and included an address to Aphrodite (fr. 1), which may have been written as a hymn for her companions, but seems to be strictly personal to herself, a poem to an unnamed girl, which was probably inspired by seeing her next to her bridegroom and shows the strength of Sappho's feelings for her (fr. 31), a poem wishing her brother a fair voyage home and offering forgiveness for his faults (fr. 5), lines on the beauty of Anactoria (fr. 16), and an invocation to Aphrodite to appear at a festival in the country (fr. 2). Book 2 contained poems in the Aeolic dactylic pentameter, such as lines of great feeling and intimacy to Atthis (fr. 49), and closed with a narrative poem on the wedding of Hector and Andromache, in which the presence of two Attic forms has raised some doubts about its authenticity. Book 3 contained poems in the greater asclepiad, including lines of contempt to an uneducated woman (fr. 55) in which the theme that song confers immortality appears explicitly for the first time. Book 4 contained poems in ionic tetrameters mostly too fragmentary to be intelligible, though fr. 58 seems to have told the story of Tithonus. Book 5 contained poems composed in stanzas of mixed character, especially fr. 96 on a girl who has gone to Lydia and is compared to the moon outshining the stars, and fr. 94, which gives a retrospect of happy days passed with another girl. Of book 6 nothing survives; of book 7 only some lines on a girl who is prevented by love from attending to her weaving (fr. 102)—a theme of folk-song. Of book 8 we have only one mention. Book 9 probably contained wedding-songs of different character in different metres. In the hexameter fragments a bride is compared to an apple (fr. 105 a) and to a hyacinth (fr. 105 c). Fr. 114 gives a dialogue between the Bride and her Maidenhood, another traditional theme. In this book Sappho was more colloquial than usual and showed an element of badinage (Demetr. *Eloc.* 167, cf. fr. 110). Something of her manner may perhaps be seen from

Catullus' imitations of her in his poems 61 and 62. Sappho writes in the vernacular language of Lesbos, except in a small group of poems (frs. 44, 105, 142–3) in which she admits some variations taken from the epic. Her subjects are usually personal; there are few traces of narrative, though some poems (frs. 102, 137) seem to be modelled on folk-songs. She wrote for herself and her friends, gave candid accounts of her and their feelings, had an excellent eye and ear for natural things, a command of verbal melody, and an unequalled directness and power.

TEXT. E. Lobel and D. L. Page, *Poetarum Lesbiorum Fragmenta* (1955), 1 ff.; C. Gallavotti, *Saffo e Alceo* i (1956).
CRITICISM. U. von Wilamowitz-Moellendorff, *Sappho und Simonides* (1913), 17 ff.; G. Perrotta, *Saffo e Pindaro* (1936), 3 ff.; C. M. Bowra, *Greek Lyric Poetry*[2] (1962), 176 ff.; D. L. Page, *Sappho and Alcaeus* (1955), 1 ff.; *PW*. Suppl. xi, 1222 ff.                C. M. B.

**SARAPIS** (usually in Latin **Serapis**), according to Tacitus (*Hist.* 4. 83–4) and Plutarch (*Mor.* 361 f–362 e), was brought to Egypt from Sinope by Ptolemy I. There is another tradition that places Sarapis in Babylon in the time of Alexander, and Tacitus reports that Sarapis was believed by some people to have come from Seleuceia in Syria, while others thought he came from Memphis. It now seems to have been established that the cult of Sarapis arose at Memphis in the temple above the underground chambers where the bodies of the deceased Apis bulls were entombed, and the projection of all these figures came to be addressed as Osorapis. The probability remains that the king established the worship in Alexandria and sought to make Sarapis an imperial deity. There is some evidence to show that the cult, along with that of Isis, was accepted and propagated by Greeks and Macedonians in the royal civil and military services. The cult of Sarapis did not grow rapidly at Alexandria, however. Although Isis and Sarapis were included in the royal oath by the end of the third century, they do not appear in the oath used in Alexandria. The creation of the cult was marked by the introduction of the worship into Alexandria and, according to tradition, was accomplished through the assistance of Demetrius of Phaleron, the Eumolpid Timotheus, and Manetho. In fact, Demetrius seems to have given the earliest testimony concerning the miraculous powers of Sarapis, since, in his *Paeans*, he is supposed to have shown his gratitude to the god for having restored his sight. The Sarapeum at Alexandria, accounted one of the wonders of the world, was said to have been designed by Parmeniscus, while the cult-statue, a great sitting figure adorned with precious metals, was attributed to Bryaxis. The tradition is consistently uniform that those who had a hand in shaping the external features of the cult were men of Greek speech and culture. Manetho, an Egyptian priest who assisted in the formation of the cult, had some familiarity with Hellenic culture, since he wrote in Greek. It is not surprising that this deity combined the attributes of many potent Hellenic gods with some of the characteristics of Osiris. He was represented with the benign and bearded countenance of Zeus, his head crowned with a modius (emblem of fertility). At the right knee of the seated god was the three-headed dog Cerberus, an attribute borrowed from Hades, while the upraised left hand grasped a staff or sceptre, reminiscent of Zeus and Asclepius. Sarapis was a healer of the sick, a worker of miracles, a deity who was superior to fate and who retained from Osiris the character of a god of the underworld. He spoke to his followers in dreams as Asclepius did, yet partook of their festive banquets as a jovial lord of Olympus might have done. He was identified at times not only with the gods already mentioned, but also with Dionysus, Helios, Jupiter, and others. He was associated with Dolichenus and other powerful deities. At Memphis, as well as at Abydos and elsewhere, we know of people called *katochoi* who seem to have considered themselves bound to the temple precincts until the god should set them free. Except when identified with another god, Sarapis seldom receives an epithet. Yet, in one inscription of the Roman period, a man with an Alexandrian deme name calls Sarapis the god of the city and addresses him as Sarapis Polieus. Sarapis was the chief god in the cult of the Egyptian deities. His cult usually went with that of Isis and Harpocrates, Anubis and others being included on occasion. In the Aegean area we find that most of the public cults of the Egyptian deities were called cults of Sarapis, even though other deities were included. In many Greek cities there were cult societies of *Sarapiastai* who held banquets on certain days, passed decrees, voted crowns to officials of the society and to distinguished strangers, and who set up *stelae* recording thereon their official acts. In the period of the Roman Empire, when the mysteries of Isis were quite widespread throughout the Mediterranean world, the worship of Isis tended to eclipse that of Sarapis. Since the worship of both these gods was spread by commercial contacts as well as by zealots, the cults were strong in those cities which had commercial connexions with the East. The acclamation 'There is one Zeus Sarapis', a cry of enthusiasm for the deity, has come down to us in numerous inscriptions.

ANCIENT SOURCES. Th. Hopfner, *Fontes Historiae Religionis Aegyptiacae* (1922–5), contains the literary sources. The inscriptions are scattered through *IG*, *CIL*, *CIG*, and *Sammelbuch griechischer Urkunden aus Ägypten* (Preisigke). The Delian inscriptions are collected in P. Roussel, *Les Cultes égyptiens à Délos* (1916), and in *Inscriptions de Délos*. Papyri documents may be found in U. Wilcken, *Urkunden der Ptolemäerzeit* i (1922–7), and in *PCairo Zen.*, *PTeb.*, *POxy.*, and elsewhere. Other sources are collected in O. Weinreich, *Neue Urkunden zur Sarapis-Religion* (1919). Statuary: H. Haas, *Bilderatlas zur Religionsgeschichte*, 9–11 Lief. (1926).
MODERN LITERATURE. The classic discussion of the origin of Sarapis is found in part 1 of U. Wilcken, *Urkunden der Ptolemäerzeit* (1922–7). Other works are: Cumont, *Rel. or.*; G. Lafaye, *Histoire du culte des divinités d'Alexandrie* (1884); J. Toutain, *Les Cultes paiens dans l'empire romain* (1907– ).
For the Serapeum at Alexandria, founded by Euergetes see I, A. Rowe, *Discovery of the Famous Temple and Enclosure of Sarapis at Alexandria* (*Ann. Serv.*, Supp. cahier 2, 1946); for the dispersion of the cult in the Ptolemaic period, T. A. Brady, *The Reception of the Egyptian cults of the Greeks* (330–30 B.C.) (U.S.A. 1935); P. M. Fraser, *Opusc. Atheniensia* (4°) 3, 1960, 1 ff.            T. A. B.; P. M. F.

**SARCOPHAGI.** A sarcophagus is a coffin for inhumation which in ancient times was often richly decorated, especially if it was to be interred in a chamber-tomb or hypogaeum. In Crete two standard shapes of coffin—the bath-tub and the chest on four legs with a gable roof —were in general use throughout the fourteenth and thirteenth centuries B.C., and some, including the famous Hagia Triada sarcophagus, were richly painted. In the late Archaic period the Clazomenian sarcophagi of painted clay are rectangular or slightly trapezoidal in form. Sculptured sarcophagi appear first in the fifth century B.C. but not in the Greek world itself; a number of anthropoid and casket sarcophagi with sculptured reliefs were made by Greek craftsmen for the kings of Sidon from the fifth century to about 300 B.C. The latest in the series is the famous Alexander Sarcophagus. Some Hellenistic wooden sarcophagi with painted decoration have survived in southern Russia.

The Etruscans used sculptured sarcophagi of clay and stone from the sixth century B.C.; the two commonest types are the casket form with gabled lid and the form with a reclining effigy of the dead. A few sculptured sarcophagi have survived from Republican Rome. The prevailing rite of cremation in Rome gave way to inhumation in the early second century A.D. and the rich series of Roman sculptured marble sarcophagi begins about the time of Trajan. Sculptured sarcophagi were made all over the Roman world; two of the best-known centres were in Athens and Asia Minor. An important series of lead coffins comes from Roman Syria.

*CVA* Brit. Mus. fasc. 8, 45 ff.; Hamdy Bey and Reinach, *Une nécropole royale à Sidon* (1892–6); W. Altmann, *Architectur und Ornamentik der antiken Sarkophage* (1902); C. Robert, *Die antiken Sarkophagreliefs* (1890– ). D. E. S.

**SARDES** (Σάρδεις), the chief city of Lydia, lying under a fortified hill in the Hermus valley, near the junction of the roads from Ephesus, Smyrna, Pergamum, and inner Asia Minor. As the capital of the Lydian kingdom, especially under Croesus, and later as the headquarters of the principal Persian satrapy, it was the political centre of Asia Minor in the pre-Hellenistic period, and it also attained fame for its progress in the arts and crafts— its kings were the first to mint gold and silver coins. It was captured and burnt by the Ionians in 498 B.C., and Xerxes mustered his troops at Sardes before he crossed the Hellespont. In the Macedonian period it belonged in succession to Antigonus, the Seleucids, and the Attalids, and in 133 B.C. it passed to the Romans, who made it the capital of a *conventus* in the province Asia. It was one of the 'Seven Churches' of the Apocalypse. Diocletian made it capital of the province Lydia. Its temple of Artemis has been excavated; and since 1958 large-scale excavations in the city have disclosed substantial remains of different periods over a wide area.

H. C. Butler, *Sardis* (1922 ff.). For the most recent discoveries, G. M. A. Hanfmann, *A Short Guide to the Excavations at Sardis* (1962). W. M. C.; J. M. C.

**SARDINIA** (Σαρδώ), a large island off western Italy containing *nuraghi* and other megalithic monuments of its prehistoric inhabitants (traditionally a mixture of Libyans, Iberians, and Ligurians). It is more fertile, less mountainous, and much more unhealthy than Corsica. The Greeks apparently never colonized Sardinia. Carthage annexed it (*c.* 500 B.C.), but failed to pacify the rugged interior. Rome seized the island from Carthage in 238 B.C. (reject Diod. 15. 27) and organized it, with Corsica, as a province in 227 (Corsica became a separate province in imperial times). The Romans despised the Sardinians ('Sardi uenales: alius alio nequior': Festus, 428 L.) and in republican times allowed them not one free city; Sardinia was treated as conquered land that sent money and grain to Rome (it remained an important granary throughout antiquity). The frequent Sardinian revolts ceased in 114 B.C., but brigandage continued. This was gradually suppressed under the Empire (Tac. *Ann.* 2. 85) and Sardinia achieved a little prosperity: Carales obtained Roman civic rights; Turris Libisonis, Uselis, and Cornus became *coloniae*; and the silver- and iron-mines were worked. But the island never really flourished. Finally it fell successively to Vandals, Goths, Byzantine Emperors, and Saracens.

Ancient writers mention Sardinia infrequently. The important references are: Strabo 5. 223 f.; Pliny, *HN* 3. 83 f.; Paus. 10. 17. 2 f.; Diod. 4. 29 f., 5. 15; Justin, bks. 18 and 19; Cic. *Pro Scauro*; Livy, bks. 21–30.
MODERN LITERATURE. E. S. Bouchier, *Sardinia in Ancient Times* (1917); E. Pais, *Storia della Sardegna e della Corsica* (1923); A. Taramelli, *Bibliografia romano-sarda* (1939); G. Pesce, *Sardegna punica* (1961); id. *Tharros* (1966); P. Cao, *Sardegna romana* (1940); M. Guido, *Sardinia* (1963). E. T. S.

**SARMATAE** (Σαρμάται, Σαυρομάται), a nomad tribe, closely related to the Scythians, and speaking a similar Indo-European language, but showing some points of difference in culture. Their women had a freer position, and, in the days of Herodotus at least, hunted and fought alongside the men (4. 116–17). Their troops were all mounted, but while the rank and file were archers, the chieftains and their retainers wore armour and used heavy lances. Until *c.* 250 B.C. the Sarmatae dwelt east of the river Tanais. During the next 300 years they

moved slowly westwards, displacing the Scythians. Of their two main branches, the Roxolani advanced to the Danube estuary, the Iazyges (q.v.) crossed the Carpathians and occupied the plain between the middle Danube and the Theiss. The Roxolani, checked by the generals of Augustus and Nero (*ILS* 986), became clients of Rome; and the Iazyges entered into similar relations, serving as a buffer between the Dacians and the province of Pannonia. In the second and third centuries the Sarmatae were again set moving by the pressure of German tribes. The Iazyges allied with the Marcomanni against M. Aurelius, and the Roxolani shared the Gothic raids into Moesia. Eventually large numbers of them were settled within Roman territory by Constantine; the rest were partly absorbed by their German neighbours, partly driven back into the Caucasus. M. C.

**SARPEDON,** in mythology, commander of the Lycian contingent of Priam's allies (*Iliad* 2. 876). He takes a prominent part in the fighting, leading an assaulting column of the allies on the Greek wall (12. 101), and making the first breach (290 ff.). He is finally killed by Patroclus (16. 426 ff.), mourned by his father Zeus (459 ff.), and carried off to Lycia for burial by Sleep and Death (666 ff.).

Post-Homeric accounts make him one of the sons of Zeus and Europa, the difference in mythological dating being got over by supposing that he lived for three generations (Apollod. 3. 6). Ancient critics had already noticed that his connexion with Crete was secondary, schol. *Il.* 6. 199, which makes the difference of time six generations. It is possible that some historical relationship between the two countries lies behind it. At all events, there was an historical cult of him in Lycia, with which the Homeric story of his burial is presumably to be connected; his hero-shrine is mentioned, for instance, by schol. *Il.* 16. 673. The rather wide distribution of place-names formed from his (see Immisch in Roscher's *Lexikon* iv. 393 ff.) suggests that his worship is old and famous, which may well have drawn Homer's attention to him.
H. J. R.

**SASERNA,** a cognomen of the gens Hostilia. Two Sasernae, father and son, wrote on husbandry about the beginning of the first century B.C. and were used by Varro, Pliny (*HN*), and Columella.

Schanz–Hosius i⁴. 242.

**SASSANIDS,** kings of the New Persian Empire A.D. 224–636. The dynasty derived its name from Sāsān, grandfather of Artaxerxes I (q.v. 4), who took over the inheritance of the Achaemenids and Arsacids. Their Empire at its greatest extent stretched from Syria to India and from Iberia to the Persian Gulf. The Sassanids constantly sought to drive the Romans from Asia; and the forts of the Euphrates *limes* were fortified against attacks from them. Major campaigns were undertaken against them by various Roman Emperors. Valerian was defeated and captured by Sapor I (q.v.), Constantius defeated Sapor II in 345, Julian died on an invasion of Mesopotamia, Kavadh was defeated by Belisarius; Khosroes II conquered Asia Minor and even threatened Constantinople, but was driven back by Heraclius. On their north-east boundary the Sassanids were menaced by the Hephthalites ('White Huns') and Turks. They were driven from Mesopotamia by the Arabs (A.D. 636), but lingered on as a local dynasty in Iran.

The strongly centralized despotic government of the Sassanid Empire was upheld by the powerful priesthood of the Mazdaean State religion.

SOURCES. (1) Classical: Ammianus Marcellinus; Zosimus; Procopius, *Persica*; Agathias (based on the official records at Ctesiphon). (2) Oriental: various Pehlevi works and numerous traditions are partially preserved in the Avesta and in the works of Firdausi and many other Arab and Persian writers (T. Nöldeke, *Tabari*, 1879). (3) Numismatic: E. Herzfeld, *Kushano-Sasanian Coins*, Mem. Arch. Survey of India, no. 38 (1930); F. D. I. Paruck, *Sāsānian Coins* (Bombay, 1924).

MODERN WORKS. A. Christensen, *L'Empire des Sassanides* (1907), *L'Iran sous les Sassanides*[2] (1944); K. Güterbock, *Byzanz und Persien* (1908); T. Nöldeke, *Geschichte der Perser and Araber zur Zeit der Sassaniden* (1879); *Das national-iranische Epos* (1896–1904); E. Stein, *Histoire du Bas-Empire* i[2] (1959), ii (1949); *PW*, articles on individual kings; *CAH* xii, ch. 4; R. Ghirshman, *Iran, Parthians and Sassanians* (1962). *See also* ARTAXERXES (4) (*Ardashir*) and SAPOR.

M. S. D.; E. W. G.

**SATRAP** (OP *\*khshathrapāvan*), the title held by Persian provincial governors. The satrap was in effect a vassal king, with wide powers within his own province (Xen. *Oec.* 4. 5), but owing allegiance to the Great King. Certain military and civil officials, responsible only to the latter, acted as checks on his autonomy. The political organization of the Persian Empire into satrapies, at first based on the boundaries of the conquered nations, was revised by Darius; his division into twenty satrapies (Hdt. 3. 89–94), though modified by subsequent territorial conquests and losses, remained the basis for later kings; Alexander preserved the satrapal system and it was continued by the Parthians. The Sassanids (q.v.) had local governors who partly corresponded in function to the old satraps, but the title 'satrap' had declined to mean 'mayor of a city and surroundings'.

A. Buchnolz, *Quaestiones de Persarum satrapis* (Leipzig, 1896); O. Leuze, *Die Satrapieeinteilung in Syrien und im Zweistromlande von 520–320* (1935); *PW*, s.v. 'Satrap' (Lehmann-Haupt).

M. S. D.; R. N. F.

**SATRICUM** (1), modern *Conca*, between Antium and Velitrae in Latium (qq.v.). Volsci and Romans fought fiercely for it. Finally, the latter destroyed it (346 B.C.), sparing only the Temple of Mater Matuta. The temple has been excavated and many terracotta revetments found.

A. Andren, *Architectural Terracottas from Etrusco-Italic Temples* (Lund, 1939–40), 153 ff.

(2) Like-named town in the Liris valley (modern *Monte San Giovanni?*), severely punished by Rome for revolting after the Caudine Forks disaster (320 B.C.) (Livy 9. 12–16; Cic. *QFr.* 3. 1. 4.). E. T. S.

**SATURA**, satire, the only literary form created by the Romans, was so free and personal that its character changed with each satirist. Still, it may be loosely defined as a piece of verse, or prose mingled with verse, intended both to entertain, and to improve society by exposing to derision and hatred the follies, vices, and crimes of men. Among its salient characteristics are spontaneity (real or apparent), topicality, ironic wit, coarse humour, colloquial language, frequent intrusions of the author's personality or *persona*, and incessant variations of tone and style.

NAME. *Satura*, from *satur*, 'full', means 'a medley' full of different things. A mixed stuffing was called *satura* too, and the phrase *lex per saturam* meant a legal bill combining several different enactments. Since variety was essential to satire, the Romans accepted this derivation: Juvenal alludes to it when he says every type of human conduct is the *farrago* of his book (1. 85–6). Other suggested derivations—Etruscan *satir*, 'speech'; Etruscan √*sāt*, 'fertility'; *saturi* and *σάτυροι*, 'full-fed'—have found little acceptance.

ORIGINS. *Rome.* (1) Roman sources say Ennius (q.v.) was the first to write satires in verse. They were in four books, using several different metres. Scanty fragments survive, showing that they contained an animal fable, a debate between Life and Death personified, a boastful monologue by a parasite, and at least one utterance by the poet himself. Thus, they had many characteristics of later satire: variety, colloquialism, argument, humour,

moralizing folk-wisdom (cf. Hor. *Serm.* 2. 2, 2. 6. 77 f.), interest in rascals, and the personal touch. But Ennius apparently included no invective and did not use satire to attack anyone personally: for him the title *Satura* or *Saturae* meant *Miscellany*. (The name *Satura* also appears among the writings of Naevius (q.v.), with a citation of a single line in an imposing style: serious or mock-heroic? dramatic or non-dramatic? We cannot tell.)

(2) Livy (7. 2, doubtless copying Varro) describes the evolution of Roman drama. The first complete play with a plot, he says, was put on by Livius Andronicus, but before that Roman actors staged productions combining song, music, and mimic dancing: he calls them *impletas modis saturas*, 'medleys full of (different) rhythms'. Critics disagree about the value of this account; but many think such plotless vaudeville shows did exist. However, no Roman authority suggests they were genetically linked with poetic satire. The most we can say is that poetic and dramatic *saturae* may have grown out of the same impulses and shared some central qualities.

*Greece.* Quintilian, comparing types of literature in Greece and Rome, remarks 'satura . . . tota nostra est' (10. 1. 93). This is sometimes translated 'Satire is a Roman invention', but means 'We are supreme in satire'; and indeed there was no single form of literature in Greek which the Roman satirists copied and emulated (Hor. *Serm.* 1. 10. 66). But several Greek influences helped to build it up.

(1) Horace says Athenian Old Comedy was the chief model for Lucilius (q.v.) (*Serm.* 1. 4. 1–7): he means that Lucilius' language (frank, colloquial, often obscene), his style (irreverent, versatile, humorous), his topics (foibles and failures of prominent men), and above all his role as a social and political critic coincided with the techniques and attitudes of Aristophanes and other comedians of his time.

(2) Another inspiration came from the Hellenistic philosophical discourse (διατριβή), a popular variant of the academic lecture. Touring Cynic and Stoic propagandists discussed ethical problems in virtuoso speeches, partly disguising their serious import by epigrams, jokes, bold colloquialisms, vivid imagery, character-sketches, anecdotes, fables, quotations of poetry, parodies, rhetorical questions, and dialogues with imaginary opponents. Their manner, σπουδογέλοιον, was adopted by Roman satirists: 'ridentem dicere uerum' says Horace (*Serm.* 1. 1. 24). Horace acknowledges his own debt to the witty Bion (q.v.) of Borysthenes (*Epist.* 2. 2. 60), and many passages of Roman satire—such as Pers. 5. 132 f. and Juv. 8—owe both theme and manner to the Greek 'diatribe'. (On it see W. Capelle, *RAC* 3. 990 ff.)

(3) Greek philosophical satire was too limited in range to mean much for the Romans; but from the Cynic Menippus (q.v. 1), Varro (q.v. 2) took the curious technique of interweaving prose with passages of verse. The iambics of Archilochus and Callimachus (3) (qq.vv.) had less influence on Roman satire than on narrower works such as Horace's *Epodes*.

DEVELOPMENT. Horace (*Serm.* 1. 10. 66) calls Ennius the *auctor* of satire, because he originated it, and Lucilius its *inuentor* (1. 10. 48) because he gave it its true nature. Lucilius' innovations were these. He made verse satire a weapon of attack on folly and vice, naming the contemporary fools and knaves he belaboured (Pers. 1. 114–15, Juv. 1. 153–4). He fixed the dactylic hexameter as its medium, applying this ancient and versatile metre to new purposes. He increased the prestige of satire by devoting his whole career to it: for Ennius it was a minor experiment. He emphasized the personal element in it (Hor. *Serm.* 2. 1. 30–4), gave it a wide range of themes, and made its language heavily unliterary, conversational, even coarse. Coarse and careless, thought Horace; but, like his successors Persius and Juvenal, he admired Lucilius greatly. The loss of Lucilius' thirty volumes is a disaster.

Equally original, even more energetic, though apparently less bitter, Varro (q.v. 2) extended the range of the genre still further by introducing the new form of prose with verse-interludes in a remarkable variety of metres. Of 150 books of his Menippean satires, just enough fragments remain to show their brilliant versatility of style and incisive criticism of human folly. Varro also wrote four books of verse satire and a treatise *De compositione saturarum*: all lost.

It is dangerous to write satire about contemporaries: it provokes resentment and retaliation. Horace discovered this, and all his successors felt it strongly. His earliest satires—perhaps some which he later suppressed—provoked severe criticism, against which he rather unconvincingly defended himself (*Serm.* 1. 4, 1. 10, 2. 1). He left two books, containing ten and eight satires respectively. Although he followed Lucilius, he made his poems notably gentler. They contain no invective against really important individuals such as Antony, no exposures of major vice and crime, but attack such peccadilloes as social climbing (1. 9) and *gourmandise* (2. 4). There is some quite charming autobiography in them: in time he turned away from satire, to write poetic letters to his friends.

A later admirer of Lucilius, Persius (q.v.), felt the danger too (1. 107–23). Before publishing his six satires, his executor Cornutus altered a phrase that might have angered Nero. However, the gibes in his poems are mostly too vague to give offence to any particular person; and behind his Stoic armour of rectitude there glows a warm and kindly heart.

The last extant Lucilian satirist, Juvenal (q.v.), who under Trajan and Hadrian published five books containing sixteen satires, expressed his concern even more drastically: 'pone Tigellinum, taeda lucebis in illa | qua stantes ardent' (1. 155–6). He resolved therefore to attack only the dead (1. 170–1), and did indeed pillory Domitian and other evil figures of the past. Still, some of the names of his victims coincide with those of influential living contemporaries: perhaps, insured by his disclaimer, he took the risk. The range of his denunciations is far wider than that of Horace and Persius: it is as wide as Rome itself (*Sat.* 3); it takes in most men and all women (*Sat.* 6). Juvenal looks back over the history of the Roman emperors (e.g. 2. 99–109, 8. 211–30 and 237–44, 10. 56–94 and 329–42) with the sombre pessimism of Tacitus scarcely concealed by a satiric smile. With him satire rises higher than ever before, to rival tragedy (6. 634–7) and command many of the powers of oratory (e.g. 10. 133–87).

In Nero's reign two brilliantly cruel Menippean satires appeared: Seneca's (q.v. 2) *Apocolocyntosis*, a Saturnalian caricature of the deification of Claudius, and Petronius' (q.v. 3) *Satyricon*, an enormous picaresque anti-romance of which only fragments remain. The moral intent of the former comes out in the hopeful prophecy of young Nero's greatness (4) and Augustus' speech to the gods (10–11); that of the latter (apparently one of the least improving books ever written) in its Epicurean contempt for human follies and passions and the exposure of bad taste by the Arbiter of Elegance. Three centuries later the Emperor Julian (q.v.) published a book which, although written in Greek, deserves to rank among Roman satires: his *Caesars*. Perhaps inspired by Seneca's skit, he shows all his predecessors down to Constantine trying to enter heaven and being judged on their characters and records. This is the last of classical Menippean satires, not unworthy of its ancestry. (Martianus (q.v.) Capella's *Marriage of Mercury and Philology* and Boethius' (q.v.) *Consolation of Philosophy* are Menippean in form but not satiric in purpose.)

ANCIENT SOURCES. References collected in F. Marx, *Lucilii Reliquiae* i (Leipzig, 1904), cxx–cxxv.
MODERN STUDIES. P. Lejay, *Les Satires d'Horace* (1911), introduction; J. Geffcken, *Jahrb.* 1919, 393 ff., 469 ff.; A. Kusch, *De saturae Romanae hexametro* (Borna, 1915); A. H. Weston, *Latin satirical writing subsequent to Juvenal* (U.S.A. 1915); R. Heinze, introduction to Horace's *Satires*, ed. by A. Kiessling (Leipzig, 1921⁵) + Nachwort and bibliographischen Nachträge by E. Burck (repr., Berlin, 1957); A. Oltramare, *Origines de la diatribe romaine* (1926); J. W. Duff, *Roman Satire* (U.S.A. 1937); N. Terzaghi, *Per la storia della satira²* (1944); O. Weinreich, *Römische Satiren* (1949); U. Knoche, *Die römische Satire²* (1957); P. Green, *Essays in Antiquity* (1960), ch. 8; G. Highet, *The Anatomy of Satire* (U.S.A. 1962); W. Krenkel (ed.), *Röm. Satire* (1966). See also W. S. Anderson's surveys of work in satire: 1937–55 (*Classical World* 1956) and 1955–62 (ibid. 1964).
                                                                G. H.

**SATURNIA,** hill town in the *Albegna* valley in central Etruria. It received a Citizen Colony in 183 B.C., but is otherwise unrecorded in antiquity. Its surviving polygonal walls and interesting necropolis, however, attest its early importance.

A. Minto, *Mon. Ant.* 1925, 585 ff.                    E. T. S

**SATURNIAN METRE,** a type of early Latin verse used, e.g., by Livius Andronicus (*Odyssia*; e.g. 'uirum mihi Camena ǀ insece uersutum'), by Naevius (*Bellum Punicum*; e.g. 'nouem Iouis concordes | filiae sorores'), in inscriptions (e.g. Scipionic epitaphs). About 160 indubitable examples are extant; few, if any, can be called primitive; the most frequently quoted is: 'dabunt malum Metelli | Naeuio poetae' (*see* NAEVIUS). Ennius (*Ann.* 214 Vahl.) despised the metre; to Horace (*Epist.* 2. 1. 157) it was 'horridus', to Virgil (*G.* 2. 386) 'incomptus'. Roman grammarians (e.g. Caesius Bassus) in bewilderment tried to equate its many metamorphoses with various Greek metres; but Servius (ad Verg. *G.* 2. 385) speaks of it as composed 'ad rhythmum solum'. Modern scholars agree that each line falls into two parts; otherwise controversy reigns. The 'accentual' theory (e.g. O. Keller) which disregards quantity and imposes on Saturnians the rhythm of 'The quéen was iń her párlour | eáting bréad and hóney' involves incredibly artificial accentuations (e.g. 'dedét Tempéstatébus'). W. M. Lindsay's view is that three ordinary word-accents in the first part of the line (normally of 7 syllables) and two in the second part (normally of 6 syllables) function as metrical stresses. Saturnians can, indeed, be so read; but most readers would unconsciously introduce a third (non-accentual) stress into the second part. W. J. W. Koster regards the metre as a double 'tripudium' (cf. 'enos Lases iuuate' in hymn of Fratres Arvales) which later came under the influence of Greek ideas of quantity. The quantitative analysis (the only metrical system found elsewhere in extant classical Latin) relies on prosodic devices demonstrable in Plautus. It starts from the idea that the line is of the type known to Greek metricians as ἀσυνάρτητα—see Hephaestion, ch. 15, who deals with Greek analogues to the Saturnian from Archilochus, Cratinus, Euripides, and Callimachus (e.g. Ἐρασμονίδη Χαρίλαε, χρῆμά τοι γελοῖον); but the most significant example comes from the non-literary cult-hymn to Zeus Dictaeus (Diehl, *Anth. Lyr.* ii. 6, 131): ἰὼ μέγιστε κῶρε, χαῖρέ μοι Κρόνειε (probably early fourth century B.C.). Like certain elements of the *Carmen Arvale* (q.v.) (in which cola of Saturnian type can be identified) and probably like the *versus quadratus* (see METRE, LATIN), the Saturnian would have reached Rome from centres of Greek influence by non-literary routes. The basic system would then be an iambic dimeter catalectic, followed by an ithyphallic (∪ – ∪ – ∪ – ∪̆   – ∪ – ∪ – –). Many variations, however, must be supposed in the basic pattern (not implausible in terms of Plautine *cantica*, but surprising in an epic metre and motivated, presumably, by a desire to avoid monotony), or appeal must be made to the uncertainty of the textual tradition. It is reasonable to assume that Livius Andronicus and Naevius will have introduced substantial changes and refinements into a metrical system which originally owed much to rhythmical devices characteristic of the early *carmen* (q.v.) style (extensive traces of which are easily visible in extant Saturnians).

Schanz–Hosius i, § 6; O. Keller, *Der sat. Vers als rhythmisch erwiesen* (Prague, 1883–6); W. M. Lindsay, *AJPhil.* 1893, 139 ff., 305 ff.; F. Leo, *Der saturnische Vers* (1905); C. Zander, *Versus Saturnii* (1918); W. J. W. Koster, *Mnemos.* 1929, 267 ff.; O. J. Todd, 'Servius on the Saturnian Metre', *CQ* 1940, 133 ff.; W. Beare, *Latin Verse and Europaean Song* (1957); G. Pasquali, *Preistoria della poesia romana* (1936); E. Fraenkel, *JRS* 1937, 262 ff., *Eranos* 1951, 170 f.; G. B. Pighi, *I ritmi e i metri della poesia latina* (1958), 121 ff.; M. Barchiesi, *Nevio Epico* (1962), 294 ff. J. F. M.; G. W. W.

**SATURNINUS** (1), LUCIUS APPULEIUS (*PW*, 'Apuleius' 29), of praetorian family and a good popular orator, as quaestor at Ostia was superseded in his *cura annonae* by Scaurus (q.v. 1) and turned violently against the oligarchy. Co-operating with the consul Marius as tribune in 103 B.C., he assigned land in Africa to Marius' veterans and passed a law establishing a special court for a crime vaguely called *maiestas* (*minuta*), intended for use against unpopular aristocrats, and also—then or more probably in 100—a grain law, against the violent opposition of the Optimates. Turbulent in the next two years, he was almost expelled from the Senate by Metellus (q.v. 6) Numidicus, but held another tribunate in 100 and, again co-operating with the consul Marius, proposed to settle the veterans of the German war in Transalpine Gaul and to give Marius a limited (and perhaps traditional) right of enfranchisement in new colonies. An oath of obedience, to be taken by all senators and magistrates, was attached to the law, which was passed by violence. Marius and Saturninus, after manœuvring their common enemy Metellus into being the only senator to refuse it, forced him to go into exile. With the help of the praetor Glaucia (q.v.), who had the support of the *equites* because of his *repetundae* law, Saturninus also proposed colonies and land distributions for the settlement of veterans (Roman and Italian) of other armies and of *proletarii* (q.v.), and was hoping for another tribunate (in 99) to carry out his plans, while Glaucia stood for the consulate. But Glaucia's competitor Memmius (q.v. 1) was killed in a riot, and Marius, worried by Saturninus independent policy, now intervened and suppressed the agitators under the terms of a '*senatus consultum ultimum*' moved by the *princeps Senatus* Scaurus. They were imprisoned in the *Curia* and murdered there (probably late summer 100). Their surviving adherents, active during the next few years, were embittered against Marius, whose powerful faction now began to disintegrate. Saturninus' colonies were not founded; but there is no reason to doubt that his assignations were carried out. He (or a relative) adopted a son of Decius (q.v. 5); and a relative of his married Lepidus (q.v. 2).

H. H. Scullard, *From the Gracchi to Nero*[2] (1963), 56, 60, with notes (including recent bibliography). E. B.

**SATURNINUS** (2), GAIUS SENTIUS (*PW* 9) (*cos.* 19 B.C.), of a reputable family from Atina, which acquired note with C. Sentius (praetor 94 B.C.). Further, he was related to that Scribonia who married Octavian in 40 (*ILS* 8892). Consul in 19, without colleague for the greater part of the year, he dealt firmly with electoral disorders, refusing to admit the candidature of Egnatius (q.v. 2) Rufus and thwarting his alleged conspiracy. Proconsul of Africa (*c.* 14); legate of Syria (*c.* 9–6), Sentius next appears as legate under Tiberius in Germany (A.D. 4–5); in A.D. 6 he led the army of the Rhine eastwards to participate in the campaign against Maroboduus. Velleius praises warmly this useful public servant and friend of Tiberius—

'uirum multiplicem in uirtutibus, nauum, agilem prouidum', etc. (2. 105. 1).

For the origin and history of the Sentii see R. Syme, *Hist.* 1964, 156 ff. R. S.

**SATURNINUS** (3), LUCIUS ANTONIUS (*PW* 96), governor of Upper Germany, raised revolt at Moguntiacum (probably 1 Jan. A.D. 89). On receipt of the news Domitian left Rome and marched northwards. In the meantime, however, the governor of Lower Germany, Lappius Maximus, who remained loyal, defeated and killed Saturninus in a battle fought beside the Rhine (perhaps near Coblenz). It is stated that German allies of the usurper were unable to cross the Rhine to his assistance because of a sudden thaw (Suet. *Dom.* 6 f.; Dio 67. 11; Mart. 4. 11; 9. 84; *CIL* vi. 2066 (*Acta fratrum arvalium*)). Saturninus was the first senator of his family, and the causes of his action are a mystery. The episode marked a turning-point in the reign of Domitian. R. S.

**SATURNUS, SATURNALIA.** Saturnus is one of the most puzzling gods in Roman cult. His festival (see below) is part of the 'Calendar of Numa', and its position, 17 Dec., midway between Consualia and Opalia, is intelligible if we suppose, as has commonly been done (e.g. by Wissowa, *RK* 204), that his name (Sāturnus, also Saeturnus) is to be connected with *sātus* and taken to be that of a god of sowing, or of seed-corn. It would represent the ritual following on the completion of the autumn sowing, and would come appropriately enough between commemorations of the deities of the store-bin and, apparently (*see* OPS), of plenty. But serious difficulties attend any such explanation. One remarkable fact is that we have clear evidence that he was sacrificed to in Greek fashion, i.e. with the head uncovered (Festus, 432. 1 Lindsay), and none at all that he was ever worshipped in any other manner. The ancients themselves supposed that he was not a native god, but imported from Greece, a story which blends with the flight of Kronos from Zeus, as in Verg. *Aen.* 8. 319 ff. His name seems to find its nearest parallels in Etruria (F. Altheim, *Griechische Götter* (1930), 8, 178), both as to stem (if we reject the connexion with *satus*) and suffix. It is therefore by no means impossible that he is a very old importation from Etruria, and conceivable that the Romans were right in identifying him with Kronos (q.v.).

His temple, the ruins of which are still conspicuous, stands on the clivus Capitolinus, and served as a treasury (*aerarium Saturni*), see Platner–Ashby, 463 ff.; Nash, *Pict. Dict. Rome* ii. 294 ff. His cult-partner is the obscure goddess Lua, whose name seems connected with *lues*, an odd colleague for a god of sowing, but more intelligible if he really had something of the grim character of Kronos. See Gellius 13. 23. 2.

Of the early history of his festival nothing is known; Livy (2. 21) speaks as if it originated in 496 B.C., which is obviously not so (see above). At most, some modification of the ritual, in the direction of hellenization, took place then. In historical times it was the merriest festival of the year, 'optimus dierum', Catullus 14. 15. Slaves were allowed temporary liberty to do as they liked, presents were exchanged, particularly wax candles and little pottery images or dolls, *sigillaria* (q.v.): Macrob. *Sat.* 1. 7. 18 ff., see Wissowa, op. cit. 206, note 2 ff., for more references. There was also a sort of mock king, or Lord of Misrule, *Saturnalicius princeps* (Sen. *Apocol.* 8. 2). By about the fourth century A.D. much of this was transferred to New-year's Day, and so became one of the elements of the traditional celebrations of Christmas (M. P. Nilsson, *ARW* 1921, 52 ff.). The resemblance to the Kronia was noticed by the ancients

(Accius in Macrob. *Sat.* 1. 7. 36–7); it may be pointed out that there is also a resemblance to the Sacaea (q.v.), though the evidence for killing or pretended killing of the mock king is of the weakest (Frazer, *GB* ii. 310 ff.). The connexion between these various festivals is as yet very obscure.　　　　　　　　　　　　　　　　H. J. R.

**SATYRS** and **SILENI** are 'spirits of wild life in woods and hills' (Rose, *Handb. Gk. Myth.* 156), bestial in their desires and behaviour, and having details of animal nature, either of a horse or of a goat. Classical authors constantly confused Satyrs and Sileni, but from the fourth century B.C. on Sileni are usually old and retain horse-ears, while Satyrs are usually young (Paus. 1. 23. 5) and have taken over from Pan the traits of a goat. It seems that Satyrs and Sileni had a different origin, but we are ill informed about the early history of the Satyrs, though it has been argued that they possessed an Illyrian origin (H. Krahe, *Festschr. Havers* (1949), 37). Hesiod (ap. Strabo 471) makes them brothers of the Nymphs (q.v.) and calls them 'good-for-nothing and mischievous'. Apollodorus refers to one Arcadian Satyr who stole cattle and was killed by Argus (2. 1. 2), but clearly identifiable Satyrs first appear in satyr-plays, such as Euripides' *Cyclops* and Sophocles' *Ichneutae*, and on representations of satyr-plays in art (F. Brommer, *Satyrspiele²* (1959); J. Boardman, *BICS* 1958, 6). At that point Satyrs are human beings with some details of a horse (Pollux, *Onom.* 4. 142), although the Ichneutae give one rather the impression of dogs (F. R. Walton, *Harv. Stud.* 1935, 167). The famous wine-pouring Satyr of Praxiteles (H. Gallet de Santerre, *Hommages à A. Grenier* (1962), 721) and the later more idyllic and rustic Satyrs of Hellenistic art and poetry are associated with Dionysus and his circle.

The history of Sileni is much more clear. Attic vases of the early sixth century B.C. (Ch. Blinkenberg, *Lindos* (1931), pl. 126; *Hesperia* 1935, 436) show the shaggy, bearded man with horse-ears, sometimes also a horse-tail and horse-legs, pursuing the Nymphs (*Hymn. Hom. Aphrod.* 262), and an inscription on the François vase dispels all doubt of his identity. He is not at first attached to any god, but seems to resemble folklore men of the forest such as the Russian *leshiy*. He knows important secrets and is captured to make him reveal them. There may have been many stories on this pattern. On the François vase Silenus is captured by two wild men named Oreios and Therytas. The story that became famous is that of King Midas who caught Silenus after having made him drunk (Theopomp. *FHG* i, frs. 74–7). Ovid links this story with the punishment of Midas for his avarice (*Met.* 11. 90). In Virgil (*Ecl.* 6) Silenus is caught by two young shepherds and sings them mythological stories (Z. Stewart, *Harv. Stud.* 1959, 179). About the middle of the sixth century B.C. Silenus (or Sileni, the plural being a matter of small importance in this lower layer of folk mythology) is drawn into the circle of Dionysus. He accompanies Dionysus in the triumphant return of Hephaestus (F. Brommer, *JDAI* 1937, 198), goes along to fight the giants, frolics in the thiasus, rides in the *carrus navalis*, makes music, and helps to make and drink wine. The behaviour of the Sileni is not always the best, and they are apt to attack even Hera or Iris (E. Haspels, *Attic Black-Figured Lekythoi* (1936), 20). When Pratinas introduced the satyr-play, the Sileni provided the distinctive costume but suffered a transformation into comic drunkards and cowards. The Silenus *par excellence* in these plays is the old Papposilenus, who has many weaknesses but also has intellectual talents. He is entrusted with the education of Dionysus, and even voices a proverbial philosophy in Pindar (schol. Ar. *Nub.* 223) and in the story of Midas. The comparison of Socrates with Silenus is based not only on common ugliness (K.

Kerényi, *Dioniso* (1949), 17) but also on common irony and wisdom. Portraits of Socrates and idealized heads of Sileni show great similarity (C. Weickert, *Festschrift J. Loeb* (1930), 103). Silenus is often represented as a good father and the Satyrs as his children. Hellenistic art depicts Silenus either as dignified, inspired, and musical, as the painting of the Villa dei Misteri (P. B. Mudie Cook, *JRS* 1913, 157), or as an old drunkard, as in many sculptural and decorative groups.

Kuhnert in Roscher, *Lex.*, s.v. 'Satyros'; F. Brommer, *Satyroi* (1937); H. Jeanmaire, *Mélanges Picard* (1949), 463; M. Edwards, *JHS* 1960; F. Jesi, *Aegyptus* 1962, 257; E. de Saint-Denis, *Rev. Phil.* 1963, 23.　　　　　G. M. A. H.; J. R. T. P.

**SATYRUS** (1) (fl. 3rd c. B.C.), Peripatetic biographer from Callatis Pontica, wrote mainly at Oxyrhynchus and Alexandria. Works: (1) Βίοι of famous men of all types, including Philip II, Sophocles, Demosthenes, Pythagoras, etc. Fragments in Diog. Laert. and Ath.; also four pages of the Βίος Εὐριπίδου, found at Oxyrhynchus. (2) Περὶ χαρακτήρων (Ath. 4. 168 e). Περὶ δήμων Ἀλεξανδρέων is by another Satyrus (*FGrH* 631).

Satyrus widened the scope of biography to include all celebrities; he takes an uncritical delight in anecdotes and personalities. The Oxyrh. fragment (in dialogue form) reveals a careful and attractive style.

*FHG* iii. 159–66; A. S. Hunt, *POxy.* ix. 1176.　　　F. W. W.

**SATYRUS** (2) (2nd c. B.C.) nicknamed *Zeta*, pupil of Aristarchus, was perhaps the author of a collection of ancient myths (*FGrH* i. 20).

**SATYRUS** (3) (fl. *c.* 150 B.C.), physician, pupil of Quintus (q.v. 1) of Rome, and teacher of Galen at Pergamum. He was a faithful follower of Quintus in the exegesis of Hippocrates and in the teaching of anatomy and pharmacology.

**SAXON SHORE** (*Litus Saxonicum*), name given to the coastline in Gaul and Britain either because exposed to Saxon raids or because settled by Saxon *laeti*.

(1) *Not. Dign.* [*occ.*] (xxxvii, xxxviii) mentions two ports, Grannona and Marcae, under local military *duces*: their sites are uncertain (Grenier, *Manuel* i. 389, 392).

(2) In Britain the *Not. Dign.* [*occ.*] (xxviii) lists nine forts under a *Comes litoris Saxonici*, who appears in Ammianus' narrative of A.D. 367 (27. 8. 1). They seem to be grouped in pairs (? for naval organization). Actually ten forts are known from Brancaster (Norfolk) to Portchester (Hants), nine of which are certainly those of the *Notitia* list. Outliers are found in Lincolnshire and Wales. All but two have external bastions and all but two others have roughly rectangular ground-plans. The areas are 6–10 acres. The original idea may be due to Carausius (not later), but one fort, Anderida (Pevensey, Sussex), seems later (*c.* 330).

D. A. White, *Litus Saxonicum* (U.S.A. 1961), with full bibliography but some rather doubtful inferences; J. N. L. Myres in *Dark Age Britain*, ed. D. B. Harden (1956), 37.　　　　　C. E. S.

**SAXONS,** a German tribe first mentioned by Ptolemy (2. 11. 7) as settled in the Cimbric Chersonese (modern *Holstein*). By *c.* A.D. 200 they seem to have displaced and subdued the Chauci of the lower Elbe; their distinctive pottery is found in Frisia and towards the lower Rhine, where from the fourth century they engaged in warfare with the Franks, while eastward they reached Swabia and Thuringia, and even penetrated into Italy (568). At sea they attracted the attention of ancient authors by their ruthless piracy (cf. Sid. Apoll. 8. 6. 13–15). Their raids were succeeded by permanent settlement. In Gaul documents and place-names show them established around Bayeux, near Boulogne, and in south-west Flanders; while in conjunction with their neighbours the Angli and the mysterious Jutes, they began towards the middle of the fifth century to establish themselves permanently in Britain. Saxon settlements were mainly in the south (Wessex, Essex, Middlesex, Sussex), but their name was applied by themselves and others indiscriminately to all the Teutonic invaders.

Full bibliographies in Collingwood–Myres, *Roman Britain*; R. H. Hodgkin, *History of the Anglo-Saxons*[2] (1939); see also L. Schmidt, *Gesch. der deutschen Stämme*[2] (1937); F. Tischler, *Der Stand der Sachsen-Forschung im liii. Bericht der R.-G. Kommission* (1955). C. E. S.

**SCAEVOLA** (1), Gaius Mucius (*PW* 10), according to some authors originally bore the *cognomen* Cordus, which he subsequently changed for Scaevola, and which may have been borrowed from the story of the Athenian king Codrus. Now *scaevola* was an amulet worn by Roman children, but popular etymology wrongly connected it with *scaeva*, the left hand; thence arose the story of the brave Roman who, having failed to kill Porsenna (q.v.), showed his indifference to physical pain by holding his right hand in fire. The surmise that the legend merely is a misinterpretation of a monument, which represented a young man stretching his right hand over an altar, is improbable. And equally improbable is the surmise that the story is connected with the ritual punishment for perjury.

G. De Sanctis, *Per la scienza dell'antichità* (1909), 321 ff.; Ogilvie, *Coman. Livy 1–5*, 262 ff. P. T.

**SCAEVOLA** (2), Publius Mucius (*PW* 17), brother of Crassus (q.v. 1), whom he succeeded as *pontifex maximus*. As tribune in 141 B.C. he instituted a tribunal to try the corrupt ex-praetor L. Hostilius Tubulus, who went into exile. As consul (133), being an eminent lawyer and enemy of Scipio (q.v. 11) Aemilianus, he was one of the senior advisers of Ti. Gracchus (q.v. 3). Despite the request of some senators, he refused to use violence against the tribune, but later defended the action of Scipio (q.v. 12) Nasica in killing him. He followed in the footsteps of his father (consul 175) as a jurist, firmly establishing his family's pre-eminence in this field, and he seems to have published (and perhaps edited) the series of *annales maximi* (*see* ANNALS).

E. S. Gruen, *Athenaeum* 1965, 321 ff. E. B.

**SCAEVOLA** (3), Quintus Mucius (*PW* 21), called 'Augur' (cf. 4), Stoic, eminent lawyer, son-in-law of Laelius (q.v. 2), but probably, like (2), moderately Gracchan in sympathy (his daughter married Glabrio, q.v. 2). Praetor *c.* 120 B.C., he was accused *repetundarum* after governing Asia, but acquitted. (The trial was satirized by Lucilius, (q.v. 1). He was consul in 117, and in 100 opposed Saturninus (q.v. 1). He taught (among others) his son-in-law L. Crassus (q.v. 3) and, in his old age, Cicero, who venerated his memory and introduced him into several dialogues. Alone among the *principes* present in the city, he opposed Sulla after his march on Rome (88) and aided Marius, who had married his grand-daughter. He died soon after. E. B.

**SCAEVOLA** (4), Quintus Mucius (*PW* 22), called 'Pontifex' (cf. 3), son of (2), whom he surpassed as an orator and even as a lawyer. He published the first systematic treatise on the civil law, providing the foundation for many later commentaries. In his most famous case, the *causa Curiana* (Cic. *De Or.* 1. 180 *et al.*), he defended the strict wording of a will, against the defence of *aequitas* and intention by L. Crassus (q.v. 3). As consuls (95 B.C.), he and Crassus passed the *lex Licinia Mucia* instituting a *quaestio* against aliens who had been illegally enrolled as citizens. Perhaps on the motion of

Scaurus (q.v. 1), he was sent as proconsul to govern Asia and settle its troubles by a complete reorganization, which he achieved with the aid of his legate Rutilius (q.v. 1). His arrangements were made binding on his successors by the Senate, and were a model for other governors. Departing from Asia after nine months, he left Rutilius in charge and later helped in his defence when he was prosecuted *repetundarum*. He himself escaped prosecution, probably through his connexion with Marius. *Pontifex maximus* in 89, he was threatened by Fimbria (q.v.) after Marius' death (86), but protected by the Cinnan government, under which he stayed in Rome. He was killed by Brutus (q.v. 3) in 82, probably when (like many others) he was on the point of joining Sulla.

Badian, *Stud. Gr. Rom. Hist.*, see index. E. B.

**SCAEVOLA** (5), Quintus Cervidius (*PW* 1), a leading Roman jurist of the later second century A.D., *praef. vigilum* 175, legal adviser of Marcus Aurelius, and teacher of Paulus (q.v. 1). The works attributed to him include *Quaestiones* (20 books), *Digesta* (40 books), *Responsa* (6 books), and *Regulae* (4 books). He was evidently in great demand as a consultant jurist: his works are heavily casuistic in character, and the cases are apparently drawn from practice. They often come from the provinces, and he sometimes gives the facts in the original Greek. This, and some Graecisms, has led to the supposition that he was himself a Greek, but the more likely explanation lies in his popularity as a consultant. Moreover, it is likely that both the *Digesta* and the *Responsa* are post-classical compilations of his *responsa*. His style is very terse, and he rarely gives reasons for his opinions. Modestinus (q.v.) speaks of him, with Ulpian (q.v. 1) and Paulus (q.v. 1), as a leader among the jurists. A. B.; B. N.

**SCAMANDER,** a river of the Troad (now called *Menderes su*), rising in Mt. Ida and flowing into the Hellespont after a course of *c.* 60 miles. Despite Pliny's phrase 'amnis navigabilis' (*HN* 5. 124), it can never have been open to shipping. Lechevalier's view that the perennial stream flowing from the springs at Bunarbashi (Kirk Göz) was Homer's Scamander is now abandoned. J. M. C.

**SCANDINAVIA.** The earliest information about Scandinavia is Pytheas' account (*c.* 325 B.C.) of Thule (q.v.), if its identification with Norway is correct. Mela (3. 3) mentions 'islands' in the Sinus Codanus 'north of the Elbe'; Pliny states (*HN* 4. 96) that the largest and most fertile of these is the island of Scatinavia and mentions Sevo Mons, which may be the mountains between south Sweden and Norway. Tacitus (*Germ.* 44, 45) knows of the Suiones (Svear, Swedes), a seafaring nation which evidently came within the ken of the amber traders at the mouth of the Vistula; Ptolemy mentions several tribes in Scandia. Jutland was better known to the Romans, a naval expedition having sailed as far as the Skaw in A.D. 5 (*Mon. Anc.* 26).

The Scandinavian Neolithic Age, fertilized by influences coming with the Megalithic culture from the south-west, was one of considerable achievement, and the subsequent Bronze Age culture in which the trade in Jutland amber (q.v.) with the south played an important part, was of a high order. There was a falling-off in the Early Iron Age, and by the end of the first century B.C. a number of peoples (Langobardi, Vandili, Burgundiones, Gutones) had migrated, in part at any rate, to the German mainland. The home-staying Scandinavians entered on a new period of prosperity in the first century A.D. and enjoyed a lively intercourse with other peoples, as the great quantity of Roman goods in their graves shows. In the third and fourth centuries they came under the influence of the culture stream from the Gothic settlements on the Black Sea and in the Danube lands.

H. Shetelig, H. Falk, and E. V. Gordon, *Scandinavian Archaeology* (1937); O. Klindt-Jensen, *Denmark before the Vikings* (1957); M. Stenberger, *Sweden* (1962); A. Hagen, *Norway* (1967).     O. B.

**SCAURUS** (1), MARCUS AEMILIUS (*PW* 140), of patrician (but recently impoverished and undistinguished) family, had to work his way up like a *novus homo*. He amassed wealth (not always reputably), gained the support of the Metelli, and was consul (with a Metellus) in 115 B.C., defeating Rutilius (q.v. 1). As consul he humiliated Decius (q.v. 5), was made *princeps Senatus* by the censors (one a Metellus) though probably not the senior patrician, and triumphed over Ligurian tribesmen. Henceforth increasingly powerful in the Senate, he married Metella (q.v. 1) and became the head of the Metellan faction, then at the height of its glory. Though himself involved in negotiations with Jugurtha (q.v.), he became one of the chairmen of the tribunal set up by Mamilius (q.v. 3). Censor in 109, he had to be forced to resign on the death of his colleague Drusus (q.v. 1). Some time before 103, he received a *cura annonae*, superseding the quaestor Saturninus (q.v. 1). In 100 he moved the '*senatus consultum ultimum*' against Saturninus and his supporters. In the 90s he was sent to Asia and, on his return, may have brought about the mission to Asia of Scaevola (q.v. 4) Pontifex. After the conviction of Rutilius (q.v. 1) he was one of the chief advisers of Drusus (q.v. 2) and was attacked by Varius (q.v. 1), but crushed him with a haughty reply. He was dead by late 89, when Metella married Sulla. Throughout his life he was involved in numerous trials, not always successful in prosecution, but never convicted. He was the last great *princeps Senatus*, exercising vast power through *factio* and *auctoritas*.

He wrote an autobiography; but it was soon forgotten. Cicero's admiration for him has coloured most of our tradition. Traces of a very different view remain, especially in Sallust. See G. Bloch, *Mélanges d'histoire ancienne* 1909 (inadequate).     E. B.

**SCAURUS** (2), MARCUS AEMILIUS (*PW* 141), son of (1) and Metella (q.v. 1), hence stepson of Sulla. Quaestor under Pompey (*c.* 65 B.C.), he intervened in Judaea and Nabataea, chiefly for his personal profit. As aedile in 58 he issued coins (Sydenham, *CRR* 912–14) commemorating his inglorious campaign against the king of the Nabataeans as a victory. In this office he also gave extravagant games, spending his enormous wealth. As praetor (56), he presided over the trial of Sestius (q.v.), then governed Sardinia (55), where he tried to recoup his fortunes. Prosecuted *repetundarum* in 54 (before Cato, q.v. 5), he briefed Cicero and other eminent men and was acquitted. Standing for the consulship of 53, he was accused (like the other candidates) of *ambitus*, defended by Cicero, but convicted through the hostility of Pompey, whose divorced wife Mucia he had married. He went into exile.

Cicero, especially the fragments of *Pro Scauro* (with Asconius' comments).     E. B.

**SCAURUS** (3), MAMERCUS AEMILIUS (*PW* 139), the last male member of the distinguished republican family of Aemilii Scauri, was a man of unsavoury character, but a distinguished orator and advocate (Sen. *Controv.* 10, praef. 2–3; Tac. *Ann.* 6. 29). Though disliked by Tiberius, he was suffect consul, probably in A.D. 21, but did not govern a province. Twice prosecuted for *maiestas*, in 32 and 34, on the second occasion he committed suicide.     J. P. B.

**SCEPSIS,** a city of the Troad, reputed to be a foundation of Scamandrius and Ascanius, whose descendants ruled there. It seems to have been an Aeolic settlement but reinforced by Milesians. Released by Lysimachus from incorporation in Alexandria Troas (301 B.C.), Scepsis enjoyed a vigorous cultural life into Roman times; Aristotle's library was kept there for two centuries. The site is on Kurşunlu Tepe in the upper Scamander valley; there is little to be seen since the surviving remains were carted off by the Muteselim of Bayramiç about 1800.

W. Leaf, *Strabo on the Troad* (1923), 269–84.     J. M. C.

**SCEPTICS,** philosophers who assert the impossibility of knowledge. On their view, the real nature of things is beyond our grasp; and we must therefore suspend judgement on any issue that presents itself to us. This leads to a rejection of all dogmatic systems of thought.

In antiquity, Scepticism proper began with Pyrrhon (q.v.) and his school, though it had its roots in earlier thought, particularly in the Sophistic movement. Pyrrhon's scepticism, and that of his most prominent pupil, Timon (q.v. 2), was essentially practical in its aims; its object was to produce imperturbability of mind (ἀταραξία), thus far resembling Epicureanism. According to Diogenes Laertius (9. 115), Timon had no immediate successor. (*See* SOPHISTS, EPICURUS.)

Scepticism was introduced into the Academy by Arcesilaus (q.v. 1), and formed the basis of Academic teaching until the headship of Antiochus of Ascalon. It was of a more disinterested and theoretical kind than that of Pyrrhon; the proof of the impossibility of knowledge was regarded as an end in itself, criticism being centred on the Stoic notion of 'conceptual perception' (καταληπτικὴ φαντασία), which provided for direct apprehension of reality. But Academic scepticism too had its more positive side: Carneades (q.v.) put forward a detailed theory of probability, on which action was to be based.

Outside the Academy, Pyrrhonism was revived by Aenesidemus (q.v.), if not earlier. Pyrrhonian and Academic ideas were combined and systematized; Aenesidemus himself reduced the arguments against knowledge to a series of ten formulae (τρόποι τῆς ἐποχῆς), and these were further reduced by Agrippa (5) and Menodotus (3) (qq.v.). The new tradition had important links with the so-called empirical physicians, finally culminating in Sextus (q.v. 2) Empiricus, who gives us in his works an account of the whole system.

Zeller, *Phil. d. Gr.* iii a⁴. 494 f.; iii b. 1 f.; R. Hirzel, *Unters. zu Cicero's philos. Schriften* iii (1883); V. Brochard, *Les Sceptiques grecs* (1887); reprinted 1959); R. Richter, *Der Skeptiz. in Philos.* i (1904); A. Goedeckemeyer, *Die Geschichte d. griech. Skeptiz.* (1905); E. Bevan, *Stoics and Sceptics* (1913); Ueberweg–Praechter, *Grundriss*¹¹, §§ 63, 64, 75; M. M. Patrick, *The Greek S.* (1929); K. Deichgräber, *Die griech. Empirikerschule* (1930). K. Janáček's *Index* to the Teubner *Sextus Empiricus*, vol. iv (2nd ed. 1962), is indispensable.     C. J. R.

**SCERDILAIDAS,** an Illyrian chieftain, probably the son of King Pleuratus and brother of King Agron. When the latter in 230 B.C. was succeeded by his widow Teuta (q.v.) who acted as regent for her stepson Pinnes, Scerdilaidas led her forces against Epirus. But after her defeat by Rome, when Demetrius (q.v. 6) of Pharos became effective ruler and a 'friend' of Rome, Scerdilaidas' position is obscure. He co-operated with Demetrius in a naval attack on Pylos (220), and made an alliance with Philip V of Macedon (220/19). On the defeat of Demetrius by Rome, he presumably seized the guardianship of Pinnes, but he soon appears as king. He broke with Philip. An appeal to Rome brought him ten ships (216), but Philip attacked and seized Lissus and other places (213/12). Scerdilaidas joined with Rome in signing the Aetolian treaty (212/11), but did not live to join in the Peace of Phoenice (205): before then he had been succeeded by his son Pleuratus II (*c.* 207–180).     H. H. S.

**SCHERIA** (Σχερία, epic Σχερίη), the land of the Phaeacians, at which Odysseus (q.v.) arrives after his shipwreck (*Od.* 5. 451 ff., cf. 34). It is a fertile country, apparently an island (6. 204), having an excellent, almost land-locked harbour (263 ff.), by which its city stands, at least one river (5. 451), and a mild climate (cf. 7. 117 ff.; fruits grow all the year round). The population are enterprising and very skilful seafarers, great gossips, boastful and rather impudent, not very warlike or athletic, fond of pleasure, but kindly and willing to escort strangers in their wonderful ships. Various real places have been suggested as the original of Scheria, the most popular in ancient and modern times being Corfú; but as that is within some 80 miles of Ithaca, whereas Scheria is distant a night's voyage for one of the magical Phaeacian ships (*Od.* 13. 81 ff.), the identification is unlikely. See, however, A. Shewan, *Homeric Essays* (1935), 242 ff. That details of real places have been used for the picture is likely. H. J. R.

## SCHOLARSHIP, GREEK, IN ANTIQUITY.
Until the end of the sixth century B.C. Greek literature depended for its survival on oral tradition. Rhapsodes claimed to be exact about the actual words of Homer (Xen. *Mem.* 4. 2. 10). But textual corruption and variation were inevitable. Pisistratus is said to have had an official text of Homer compiled, but the method of recension is unknown, and interpolations were alleged in antiquity. From the sixth to the fourth century Homeric criticism was not so much philological as directed against the morality of his mythology, as in Plato's famous attack (*Resp.* 377 d). Texts were prepared by Antimachus and Aristotle; a treatise was written by Democritus, and a commentary by Ion of Ephesus, but their nature and value are uncertain.

2. Towards the end of the fifth century books became more common, and private collections became possible, though on a small scale (cf. the library of Euripides). But this development did not secure texts from corruption. The absence, in many cases, of an authoritative text, the difficulties presented to the copyist by the form of the fifth-century book, which lacked word-division and punctuation, careless or ignorant transcription, and, in the case of the drama, actors' tampering with the text, were continual sources of danger. Tragedy suffered so badly in the fourth century that in 330 B.C. Lycurgus ordered that a public copy of the text of the three great tragic poets should be deposited in the State archives. This was perhaps merely a copy of the best acting-version. That it was not regarded as presenting the original text of the poets seems clear from Alexandrian criticism. Autograph manuscripts of Plato and Aristotle may have been kept in the Academy and Lyceum. Aristotle made the first important contribution to literary history with his *Didascaliae*, and other Peripatetics devoted themselves to the history and criticism of literature and to grammatical and scientific scholarship, e.g. Theophrastus and Demetrius of Phalerum.

3. The last-named was credited with advising Ptolemy Soter (305–285 B.C.) to found a library at Alexandria. With the establishment of this library in the Brucheum, of the smaller library in the Serapeum, and of the collegiate body in the Museum, the prerequisites for scholarship became available. The libraries contained a huge collection of papyrus rolls, which grew in number from 200,000 c. 285 B.C. to 700,000 in the first century B.C. The successive librarians were learned scholars (e.g. Zenodotus, Aristophanes). Research was facilitated by their careful classification of authors and texts (cf. Callimachus, *Pinakes*), by their determination of genuine and spurious works, and by their introduction of rolls of standard size, which made possible the division of large works, formerly

inconvenient to handle, into groups of rolls. These Alexandrian scholars sought to reconstitute the original text of the classical writers, especially Homer. They adopted the sound practice of comparing manuscripts and studying the usage of each writer; but they also followed too subjective criteria. Caution grew with experience and knowledge, Aristophanes and Aristarchus modifying the arbitrary method of Zenodotus. Their work is best shown in the Venetian scholia to the *Iliad*. In their recensions (διορθώσεις) they used marginal signs, of which the most important were the *obelus* (ὀβελός —), used by Zenodotus and later scholars to mark a spurious line, the asterisk (ἀστερίσκος *), used by Aristophanes to mark incomplete sense and by Aristarchus to mark a verse wrongly repeated elsewhere, the κεραύνιον (T) marking a succession of spurious lines, the ἀντίσιγμα (Ɔ), used by Aristophanes to indicate erroneous repetition and by Aristarchus to mark disturbed word-order, the διπλῆ (>) marking anything noteworthy. The authors thus edited formed the basis of the Alexandrian canon of the best poets, later extended to include prose-writers. Besides such critical editions, the Alexandrians produced exegetical commentaries (ὑπομνήματα), filled with antiquarian and mythological lore, works of literary history and criticism, and lexicographical studies; they also pursued research in metric, grammar, and accentuation. Concurrently with the development of literary studies in Alexandria went the growth of Pergamum as a rival centre of learning with a large library, in which parchment was first used on a considerable scale for books. Here scholarship was exercised rather upon prose than upon poetry, and although editions and commentaries were produced (notably by Crates of Mallos), its best work was probably done in the fields of antiquarian and grammatical research.

4. From the second century B.C. the demand for popular editions and handbooks brought forth variorum commentaries, published separately from the text, but having lemmata (*see* SCHOLIA), and compilations (cf. especially the writings of Didymus), which preserved the best features of Alexandrian scholarship and from which much of the older scholia on classical authors is derived. These commentaries were of great importance in preventing a text's corruption, since the notes would fit only the particular text for which they had been written (cf. the excellent preservation of the nine annotated plays of Euripides, and the seven comedies of Aristophanes in the Venetian MS.).

5. From the time of Hadrian Greek scholarship declined. The systematic study of grammar (e.g. by Apollonius Dyscolus and Herodian), of metric (e.g. by Hephaestion), and the compilation of lexica (e.g. by Harpocration and Hesychius) continued the preservation of the results of Alexandrian research. But the steadily diminishing interest in Greek classical authors and the preference for select editions and anthologies (cf. the works of Proclus and Stobaeus) caused the disappearance of the writings of many earlier authors. The process of disappearance was further helped by the transfer of texts from the decaying papyrus rolls to durable vellum codices in the fourth and fifth centuries, when only such texts as were valued were copied. Although readers might add marginal notes to their text, the medieval combination of text and scholia on the same page is scarcely found in antiquity; the commentary, however abbreviated and compilatory in character, is still a separate book. Although the Roman and early Byzantine ages were a period of loss, texts were not seriously corrupted. The evidence of papyri shows that the quality of texts suffered little between the second and eleventh centuries. Poets were more fortunate than prose-writers in escaping corruption, thanks to the transmission of the Alexandrian

commentaries, but some prose-authors, notably Herodotus, Isocrates, Plato, Demosthenes, have come down to us in a good state.

**6.** After the eighth century, which was the darkest age for Greek literature and scholarship, there came a revival in the ninth century, begun by Photius and Arethas, whose enthusiasm probably helped, along with the industry of lexicographers like the compiler of the *Suda*, q.v. (10th c.), to save many texts, and many of our best manuscripts belong to this time. Rare classical texts were sought out and transcribed from the cumbersome majuscule to the new minuscule hand, an operation which often involved problems of word-division, breathing, accentuation, etc. In the twelfth century Tzetzes annotated the *Iliad* and Eustathius produced his important Homeric commentary and struggled to secure the preservation of the monastic libraries. Under the Palaeologi at Byzantium there was a renaissance of learning which produced editions of classical authors, commentaries, handbooks, and lexica. But scholars like Thomas Magister and Demetrius Triclinius (early 14th c.) were often wilful and drastic in textual criticism, and their unsatisfactory views of metre and language led them into frequent error. Nevertheless, they were trying to do what the great Alexandrians had done 1,500 years earlier, and without them the scholarship of the Renaissance would have been impossible. Their texts became current in Italy, and, but for the fall of Constantinople, their method would have left an indelible mark on Greek literature.

A. Gudeman, *Grundriss der Gesch. der Klass. Philologie²* (1909); F. W. Hall, *A Companion to Classical Texts* (1913); J. W. White, *The Scholia on the 'Aves' of Aristophanes* (1914); A. C. Pearson, *The Fragments of Sophocles* i (1917); J. E. Sandys, *A History of Classical Scholarship* i³ (1921); U. v. Wilamowitz-Moellendorff, *Einleitung in die griechische Tragödie* (1921); Christ–Schmid–Stählin ii⁶, *Die nachklassische Periode* (1920–4); D. L. Page, *Actors' Interpolations in Greek Tragedy* (1934); R. Browning, *Past and Present* 1964, 3 ff.; L. D. Reynolds and N. G. Wilson, *Scribes and Scholars* (1968).

J. F. L.; R. B.

**SCHOLARSHIP, LATIN, IN ANTIQUITY.** Interest in systematic Latin scholarship began in Rome with the visit of Crates (q.v. 3) of Mallos *c.* 168 B.C. His influence may be seen in the orthographical and literary investigations of L. Accius (170–*c.* 85) and in the satires of Lucilius (180–102). But the first Roman 'scholar' was L. Aelius Stilo Praeconinus of Lanuvium (*c.* 154–*c.* 74), whose studies included, besides grammar and literary history (he made a list of the genuine plays of Plautus), etymological, antiquarian, and historical subjects. He inspired M. Terentius Varro (116–27) to his encyclopedic studies: Varro's antiquarian researches (*Antiquitates rerum humanarum et divinarum*), his grammatical writings (*De lingua Latina*), his educational treatises (*Disciplinarum libri novem*) formed a storehouse and model for later critics and scholars. The interest aroused by Varro and his predecessors in grammar and the history of Roman literature is seen in Cicero, Horace, and Caesar amongst others. Varro's scholarship was rivalled by that of P. Nigidius Figulus (98–45), who wrote *Commentarii grammatici* and shares with Varro the credit of inventing the terminology of Latin grammar. Other professed scholars of the same period are L. Ateius Praetextatus and Valerius Cato. A great stimulus to scholarship was given by the founding of the Palatine Library with its collections of Greek and Latin literature in 28 B.C. and the appointment of C. Julius Hyginus (64 B.C.–A.D. 17), who wrote a commentary on Virgil, as librarian. At the close of the Augustan period Fenestella's *Annales* continued the encyclopedic scholarship of Varro; Verrius Flaccus wrote his *De orthographia* and in his *De verborum significatu* produced the first Latin lexicon, a storehouse of information later abridged by Pompeius Festus and drawn upon by all subsequent scholars.

Later, in the first century A.D., Q. Remmius Palaemon, the teacher of Quintilian, wrote an *Ars Grammatica*, the first formal Latin grammar. The tradition of literary criticism was continued by L. Annaeus Seneca, Petronius, and Persius. Q. Asconius Pedianus (A.D. 3–88 or, according to others, 9 B.C.–A.D. 76) wrote a commentary on Cicero's orations and a defence of Virgil, and the Elder Pliny (A.D. 23–79) wrote on *dubius sermo*. M. Valerius Probus (d. A.D. 88) of Berytus not merely studied the *sermo antiquus* (upon which he wrote a *Silva observationum*) but produced careful texts based upon a study of early manuscripts of a number of Latin authors. Fabius Quintilianus (d. 95?), in the *Institutio Oratoria*, summed up the current views upon grammar and literary criticism. In the next century C. Suetonius Tranquillus (d. *c.* 140) wrote, besides lives of orators, poets, and scholars (*De viris illustribus*), a treatise upon critical signs. His younger contemporary Aulus Gellius, in his *Noctes Atticae*, supplies valuable details on the earlier language and literature and on lexicography and grammar. At the end of the century Terentianus Maurus published a manual on prosody and metre; Acron commented on Terence and Horace; and Festus abridged Verrius Flaccus.

In the third century Porphyrion commented on Horace, C. Julius Romanus wrote on grammar, and Solinus wrote an epitome of Pliny, while the learned Censorinus compiled his *De die natali* (A.D. 238). Early in the next century Nonius Marcellus compiled his *De compendiosa doctrina* from the works of earlier scholars; C. Marius Victorinus wrote on metre and commented on Cicero; Aelius Donatus compiled his celebrated grammar, wrote a noted commentary on Terence and another on Virgil; Charisius and Diomedes compiled grammars. At the end of the century Maurus Servius Honoratus wrote his famous commentary on Virgil (extant in a longer and shorter form), omitting nothing but literary criticism. St. Jerome (*c.* 348–420) revised the Latin Bible, wrote *De viris illustribus* (after Suetonius), and translated the chronicle of Eusebius. At the end of the century Macrobius wrote a commentary on Cicero's *Somnium Scipionis*, and in his *Saturnalia* discussed Virgil and ancient Latin literature and language. Martianus Capella, early in the fifth century, summarized ancient learning in his *Nuptiae Philologiae et Mercurii*. The list of Latin scholars closes with the name of Priscian, early in the sixth century, who wrote a grammar in eighteen books, sixteen of which dealt with accidence, in which was summed up all the grammatical learning of previous centuries. *See also* LITERARY CRITICISM, and separate articles on the writers mentioned.

J. E. Sandys, *A History of Classical Scholarship* i (1903); W. Kroll, *Studien z. Verst. d. röm. Lit.* (1924), 87 ff., 308 ff.          R. M. H.

**SCHOLIA.** The word σχόλιον is first found in Cicero (*Att.* 16. 7. 3); its plural is now generally used to describe a body of notes (preserved in the margins of texts) which expound or criticize the language or subject-matter of an author. An individual scholium usually consists of a lemma (i.e. a word or phrase repeated from the text of the author) and an interpretation. In default of a lemma, a reference mark or the mere position of the item in the margin indicates the passage with which the note is concerned. Though the distinctions between scholia, glosses, and commentaries cannot be rigidly drawn, the term 'gloss' is usually applied to sporadic interpretations of the meanings of separate words and the term 'commentary' (*commentum*, *commentarius*) to an exposition which (except for interspersed lemmata) is continuous and is generally transmitted as a separate work (e.g. Porphyrius on Aristotle, Asconius on Cicero). In a collection of scholia, however, while many items do not differ in length or substance from glosses, others have clearly come from a learned source. In general, scholia can be regarded as the *disiecta membra* of lost commentaries; and it is often possible to trace them with some probability to their immediate or ultimate sources. The breaking up of a commentary into marginal scholia met the convenience of readers of a text, but inevitably caused the loss of much that we should have valued. Where space permitted, the successive owners of a manuscript would sometimes add notes of their own or excerpts from commentaries not previously incorporated; and this heterogeneous material was always at the mercy of copyists who sometimes curtailed or recast it. Yet despite many trivialities and much useless lumber, scholia often throw valuable light on points of fact or problems of exegesis (especially when based on the work of one of the great scholars of antiquity), and sometimes their interpretations contain evidence for the author's text. Their lemmata, however, which were frequently adjusted by copyists, need to be used with the utmost caution. Individual manuscripts or groups of manuscripts of a single author often present sets of scholia which bear little immediate relationship to each other; for example, the Homeric scholia in cod. Venetus A are quite distinct from those in cod. Venetus B, and both sets differ from the scholia in cod. Townleianus.

2. GREEK SCHOLIA. The notes found in the Venice codex (A) of Homer afford a good illustration of the origin of scholia. Though they cite the views of Zenodotus of Ephesus, Aristophanes of Byzantium, and Aristarchus, they are not based directly on the continuous commentaries (ὑπομνήματα) and special treatises (συγγράμματα) of the great Alexandrians. Nor are they directly derived from the work of the indefatigable Didymus (q.v. 1) Chalcenterus, who in the first century B.C. summed up the countless Homeric προβλήματα, ζητήματα, and λύσεις of earlier scholars; for they contain references to Aristonicus (the younger contemporary of Didymus) and to Herodian and Nicanor (both of the 1st c. A.D.) who wrote on Homer's prosody and on punctuation. Their chief immediate source is a lost commentary composed not earlier than the middle of the second century A.D.; and on the reliability of its author we depend for our knowledge of the work of his many predecessors. The extant scholia (or, rather, sets of scholia) on Hesiod, Pindar, Aeschylus, Sophocles, Euripides, and Aristophanes are all indebted ultimately to Didymus; but in every instance there are probably several intermediate stages between him and them. Behind the scholia on the Alexandrian poets Apollonius Rhodius, Theocritus, Lycophron, and Nicander lies the work of Theon (q.v. 1), a scholar of the age of Tiberius. Scholia on prose authors, apart from Plato and Demosthenes, are comparatively scanty. Late manuscripts of the poets frequently contain scholia taken from Byzantine scholars such as Tzetzes (12th c.), Eustathius (12th c.), Demetrius Triclinius (early 14th c.), and Thomas Magister (early 14th c.).

3. LATIN SCHOLIA. None of the collections of scholia on Latin authors is earlier than the third century A.D. and many are as late as the sixth or seventh century. Despite attributions made in the Middle Ages, they are all several stages removed from the work of first- and second-century scholars (Cornutus, Probus, Velius Longus, Arruntius Celsus, Aemilius Asper, Terentius Scaurus). Of prose authors, only the speeches of Cicero have scholia. Terence is the only republican poet whose text is thus annotated (the scholia in the cod. Bembinus being particularly important). The various but not extensive sets of scholia on Virgil are overshadowed by the great commentary of Servius, but the scholia Bernensia (closely related to Philargyrius, q.v.) are valuable. For Horace there are collections attributed to Acron and Porphyrion (qq.v.) as well as the less important notes of the 'commentator Cruquianus'. The *Ibis* of Ovid and the *Aratea* of Germanicus both have scholia; and of the poets of the first century A.D., Persius, Lucan, Statius, and Juvenal each has two or more sets of annotations.

A. Gudeman, art. 'Scholien' (Greek only) in *PW*; P. Faider, *Répertoire des éditions de scolies et commentaires d'auteurs latins* (1931); J. E. Sandys, *Hist. of Class. Scholarship* i² (1906); F. W. Hall, *Companion to Classical Texts* (1913). Ample information can be found in the sections devoted to individual authors in Christ–Schmid–Stählin and Schanz–Hosius; to the editions there mentioned add: J. F. Mountford, *Scholia Bembina* (1934); H. J. Botschuyver, *Scholia in Horatium* λφψ *codicum Parisinorum* (1935); P. Wessner, *Scholia in Iuvenalem vetustiora* (1931); J. Irigoin, *Les Scholies métriques de Pindare* (1958); A. La Penna, *Scholia in P. Ovidi Nasonis Ibin* (1959); H. Erbse, *Beiträge zur Überlieferung der Iliasscholien* (1960); L. M. Positano, D. Holwerda, W. J. W. Koster, *Scholia in Aristophanem* (1960–2); L. M. Positano, *Demetrii Triclinii in Aeschyli Persas Scholia* (1963).　　　　　　　　　　　　　　　　　　　J. F. M.

**SCIPIO** (1) **BARBATUS**, LUCIUS CORNELIUS (*PW* 343), consul 298 B.C.; his sarcophagus was the oldest discovered in the Scipios' tomb. The inscription subsequently carved on this sarcophagus records Scipio's exploits in Samnium and Lucania (Dessau, *ILS* 1), and is more trustworthy than Livy (10. 12 f.), who describes his Etruscan successes.　　　　　　　　　　　　E. T. S.

**SCIPIO** (2), LUCIUS CORNELIUS (*PW* 323), son of (1) above, was curule aedile, consul (259 B.C.), and censor (258). In 259 he attempted to use the new Roman fleet to deprive the Carthaginians of a naval base against Italy: he captured Aleria and reduced Corsica, but failed to storm Olbia in Sardinia. Two inscriptions (*ILS* 2, 3; Degrassi, *ILLRP*, no. 310) record his career, but do not mention the triumph which the *Fasti Triumphales* assign to him. Near the Porta Capena he dedicated a temple to the Tempestates which had spared his fleet.　　　H. H. S.

**SCIPIO** (3) **CALVUS**, GNAEUS CORNELIUS (*PW* 345), son of Lucius (2) above, brother of Publius (4), and uncle of Africanus Major (5). As consul in 222 B.C. with his colleague Marcellus (q.v. 1) he defeated the Insubres and captured Mediolanum. In 218 he was sent to Spain, probably as his brother's legate, to prevent reinforcements reaching Hannibal in Italy and to break the Carthaginian power in Spain. His strategy was to advance southwards along the coast, winning adequate bases and command of the sea. In 217 he probably received proconsular *imperium* and won a decisive naval victory off the Ebro. His brother Publius arrived to take supreme command, and together they advanced to Saguntum (traces of their camp survive at Almenara, 5 miles north). In 215 they inflicted a crushing defeat near Ibera on Hasdrubal, who was attempting to break through to Italy. By 212 they had captured Saguntum, from which base they could advance further south. In 211, while Publius was defeated on the upper Baetis, Gnaeus was destroyed with his army at Ilorci in the hinterland of Carthago Nova (on the site see H. H. Scullard, *Scipio Africanus* (1930), 50 ff., 143).

SOURCES. A. Schulten, *Fontes Hispaniae Antiquae* iii (1935), 52 ff.　　　　　　　　　　　　　　　　　　　　　　　　　H. H. S.

**SCIPIO** (4), PUBLIUS CORNELIUS (*PW* 330), was younger brother of Gnaeus (3) above, and father of Africanus Major (5). Consul in 218 B.C., Scipio had to divert his army, destined for Spain, to suppress a Gallic rising in north Italy. With fresh troops he reached the mouth of the Rhône, only to find that Hannibal had slipped past. Scipio hastened back to north Italy, where he hoped to fight delaying actions along the tributaries of the Po. Beaten back and wounded in a cavalry skirmish at Ticinus, he retired to Trebia where he was joined by Sempronius who insisted on engaging Hannibal. The Romans were defeated and lost two-thirds of their army (Dec. 218). In 217 Scipio was sent as proconsul to join his brother in Spain. For his campaign there and his death in 211 see Scipio (3).　　　　　　　　　　　　　　　H. H. S.

**SCIPIO** (5) **AFRICANUS MAJOR,** PUBLIUS CORNE-LIUS (*PW* 336) (236–184/3 B.C.), son of Publius (4) above, and husband of Aemilia, the sister of Paullus (q.v. 2); father of two sons (8 and 9 below) and two daughters, Cornelia, wife of Scipio (10) Nasica, and Cornelia (q.v. 1), mother of the Gracchi. Born in 236 B.C., Scipio is said to have saved his father's life at the battle of Ticinus (218) and as military tribune to have rallied the survivors of Cannae at Canusium (216). After being curule aedile (213), he was appointed by the People to the command in Spain, being the first *privatus* to be invested with proconsular *imperium* (210). In Spain he followed his father's offensive strategy rather than the cautious policy of his own predecessor, Nero (q.v. 2). He seized the enemy's base, Carthago Nova (q.v.), by a brilliant *coup de main* (209). He drilled his army in new tactics, by which the three lines of the Roman army acted with greater mutual independence; he possibly adopted the Spanish sword and improved the *pilum*. In 208 he defeated Hasdrubal Barca at Baecula (*Bailen*) in Baetica: screened by his light troops, his main forces divided and fell on the enemy's flanks, a movement which was a complete break with traditional Roman tactics. He wisely avoided a wild-goose chase after the fleeing Hasdrubal (q.v. 2) and decided to fight on in Spain, where he finally defeated the two other Carthaginian armies at Ilipa (*Alcala del Rio*, near *Seville*): he held the enemy's main forces while the wings outflanked them (206). Thus Roman domination was established in Spain. Before he left Spain Scipio settled some veterans at Italica (q.v.).

As consul for 205, Scipio carried through his determination to invade Africa, despite senatorial opposition led by Fabius (q.v. 5). With an army composed partly of volunteers he crossed to Sicily; he also succeeded in snatching Locri from Hannibal. In 204 as proconsul he landed with perhaps 35,000 men in Africa, where he besieged Utica and wintered on a nearby headland (Castra Cornelia). Early in 203 he successfully attacked and burnt the camps of Syphax and Hasdrubal (q.v. 3) some 6 miles to the south. At Campi Magni (*Souk el Kremis*) on the upper Bagradas, Scipio defeated another enemy army by a double outflanking operation. When he captured Tunis, Carthage sought peace. During an armistice terms were referred to Rome, but after Hannibal's return to Africa the Carthaginians renewed the war in 202. After joining Masinissa, Scipio finally defeated Hannibal in the battle of Zama (q.v.), where neither side could outflank the other and the issue was decided by the Roman and Numidian cavalry, which broke off its pursuit of the Punic horsemen and fell on the rear of Hannibal's army. Scipio was named Africanus after the country he had conquered.

In 199 Scipio was elected censor and became *princeps senatus*. A keen supporter of a philhellenic policy, he prudently but vainly urged in his second consulship (194) that Greece should not be completely evacuated lest Antiochus of Syria should invade it. In 193 he was sent on an embassy to north Africa and perhaps also to the East. When his brother Lucius (7) was given the command against Antiochus (190), Africanus, who could not constitutionally yet be re-elected consul, was 'associated' with the command and served as his brother's legate. After crossing to Asia, where he received back from Antiochus his captured son Lucius (9), Scipio fell ill and took no active part in his brother's victory at Magnesia (189). Meanwhile in Rome political attacks, led by Cato, were launched on the Scipios, culminating in the 'Trials of the Scipios', on which the ancient evidence is conflicting. Africanus intervened when Lucius was accused in 187; whether he himself was formally accused either in 187 or 184 is not beyond doubt. But his influence was undermined and he withdrew embittered and ill to Liternum where he died soon afterwards (184/3).

An outstanding man of action, Scipio may nevertheless on occasion have felt himself to have been divinely inspired and the favourite of Jupiter Capitolinus. This aspect of his character gave rise to the 'Scipionic legend', born during his lifetime but later elaborated (e.g. by parallels with Alexander the Great). Profoundly convinced of his own powers, Scipio personified a new era in which Greek ideas swept over Roman life. By his tactical reforms and strategic ideals he forged a new weapon with which he asserted Rome's supremacy in Spain, Africa, and the Hellenistic East, championing Rome's imperial and protectorate mission in the world. He turned a city-militia into a semi-professional army, which for ten years he commanded at the People's wish; his victory at Zama gave him the most powerful position yet held by a Roman general. But the time had not yet come when the individual challenged the power of the Senate. Scipio offered no threat to the nobility except through the normal channels of political life in which he showed no particular ability. Factional jealousies, the size of his *clientela*, and reaction against his generous foreign policy and his enthusiasm for Greek culture created *invidia* and led to his downfall amid personal and political rivalries, but had demonstrated that Rome's destiny was to be a Mediterranean, not merely an Italian, power.

On the ancient sources (chiefly Polybius and Livy) see Ed. Meyer, *Kl. Schr.* ii (1924), 331 ff., H. H. Scullard, *Scipio Africanus in the Second Punic War* (1930); id. *Sc. A. Soldier and Politician* (1970); W. Schur, *Scipio Africanus und die Begründung der römischen Weltherrschaft* (927); H. H. Scullard, op. cit. and (on Ilipa) *JRS* 1936, 19 ff.; R. M. Haywood, *Studies on Scipio Africanus* (U.S.A. 1933). On Scipio's politics see Scullard, *Rom. Pol.*, see index; A. H. McDonald, *JRS* 1938, 153 ff.; Taylor, *Voting Districts*, 306 ff.; F. Cassola, *I gruppi politici romani nel III sec. a. C.* (1962). On the 'Trials' see P. Fraccaro, *Opusc.* i (1956), 263 ff., and Scullard, op. cit. 290 ff. On Scipio's portrait, M. L. Vollenweider, *MH* 1958, 27 ff. On the legend, F. W. Walbank, *PCPS* 1967, 54 ff. *See further* s.v. PUNIC WARS.        H. H. S.

**SCIPIO** (6) **NĀSĬCA,** PUBLIUS CORNELIUS (*PW* 350) (*cos.* 191 B.C.), son of Scipio (3), received the Magna Mater (204), was curule aedile (197), praetor in Further Spain (194), defeating the Lusitanians at Ilipa, and consul in 191, when he completed the subjugation of Boian territory (191–190). His failure in the censor elections of 189 and 184 marks the Scipionic decline, and apart from the founding of Aquileia (181) and his action as patron in the Spanish inquiry of 171, he played no further part in public life.

Scullard, *Rom. Pol.* 122, 137 ff.        A. H. McD.

**SCIPIO** (7) **ASIATICUS** (ASIAGENUS, ASIAGENES), LUCIUS CORNELIUS (*PW* 337) (*cos.* 190 B.C.), brother of Scipio Africanus, whose legate he was in Spain (207–206), Sicily (205), and Africa (204–202), was curule aedile (195) and praetor in Sicily (193). In 191 he was with M'. Acilius Glabrio at Thermopylae, and in 190 succeeded him as consul. This marked the Scipionic control of policy against Antiochus, and Scipio Africanus accompanied him to the East in effective command. Making a truce with the Aetolians, he crossed to Asia Minor to defeat Antiochus at Magnesia (probably Jan. 189). After preliminary peace negotiations he was succeeded by Manlius Vulso, returning to triumph in 188, with votive games in 186. The senatorial opposition to Africanus' dominance, however, brought on him a demand for accounts and for inquiry into moneys received from Antiochus, and eventually a charge of peculation, on which he would have been imprisoned except, for the intervention of Sempronius Gracchus (cf. PETILLIUS and MINUCIUS 3). Cato degraded him from equestrian status in 184. An undistinguished figure, his career follows that of his great brother.

W. Schur, *Scipio Africanus* (1927); Scullard, *Rom. Pol.* 128 ff., 290 ff.        A. H. McD.

**SCIPIO** (8) PUBLIUS CORNELIUS (*PW* 331), elder son of Africanus Major, adopted the later Africanus Minor before 168 B.C. Augur in 180, he was precluded from a public career by ill health; an outstanding orator, he also wrote an historical work in Greek (Cic. *Brut.* 77). An inscription in Saturnian verse from the Tomb of the Scipios probably refers to him (Dessau, *ILS* 4; Degrassi, *ILLRP* 311).                                    H. H. S.

**SCIPIO** (9), LUCIUS CORNELIUS (*PW* 325), son of Africanus Major, was captured in the war with Antiochus (192 B.C.), but was released unransomed before Magnesia in 190. He gained the praetorship (174) with the help of C. Cicereius, his father's secretary, but incurred the censors' displeasure. Details of his capture and personality are confused.                                              H. H. S.

**SCIPIO** (10) **NASICA CORCULUM,** PUBLIUS CORNELIUS (*PW* 353), curule aedile in 169 B.C., distinguished himself in the Pydna campaign (168); his account of it in an ἐπιστόλιον is preserved by Plutarch (*Aem.* 15–18). On account of irregular election, he resigned the consulship of 162. Censor in 159, he removed unauthorized statues from the Forum. Consul in 155, he ended the Dalmatian War. He checked the building of a theatre on grounds of public morality. Against Cato's policy of destroying Carthage, he urged the moral stimulus of Carthage to Rome, presumably representing the traditional liberal Scipionic policy in Africa. In 152 he forced Masinissa to withdraw from Carthaginian territory. He was envoy to Andriscus (150), *pontifex maximus* (150), and *princeps senatus* (147). Learned in pontifical and civil law, he upheld traditional standards of morality and politics, at home and abroad.

M. Gelzer, *Kl. Schr.* (1963), ii. 39; Scullard, *Rom. Pol.* 226, 240.
                                                    A. H. McD.

**SCIPIO** (11) **AEMILIANUS AFRICANUS NUMANTINUS,** PUBLIUS CORNELIUS (*PW* 335), 185/4–129 B.C., second son of L. Aemilius Paullus (q.v. 2), was adopted by P. Scipio, son of Scipio Africanus. In 168 he fought under Paullus at Pydna. While in Greece he met Polybius (q.v. 1), with whom he afterwards formed an especially close friendship. In 151 he volunteered to serve in Spain under the consul Lucullus when many others were reluctant to do so. Sent by Lucullus to fetch reinforcements from Masinissa (q.v.), he witnessed the great battle between the Carthaginians and the Numidians, subsequently presiding over some abortive negotiations. In 149 and early 148 he achieved great distinction as a military tribune in the Third Punic War (*see* PUNIC WARS). He was a candidate for the aedileship of 147 but was elected consul, although he was under age and had not held the praetorship. This required special legislation, which was carried only after great dissension. As consul, with his closest friend Laelius (q.v. 2) as his chief *legatus*, he restored the discipline of the army in Africa and devoted great energy to making the blockade of Carthage effective. The construction of the famous mole to close the entrance to the harbour was an enormous undertaking. The city fell in the spring of 146, and after supervising its destruction Scipio celebrated a magnificent triumph.

Elected censor in 142, he wished to perform his duties strictly and severely but was thwarted by his colleague, L. Mummius (q.v.). In 140–139 he headed an embassy to the countries of the eastern Mediterranean, taking as a companion the philosopher Panaetius (q.v.), who also stayed with him in Rome for a time. In 137–136 he was much involved in the intrigues surrounding the *foedus Mancinum* (*see* MANCINUS). Constant failures in the Numantine War (*see* NUMANTIA) led to his election to

the consulship of 134. Since second consulships were prohibited this also required special legislation. He again had to restore military discipline, but by the autumn was able to encircle Numantia with an elaborate series of fortifications. When the city fell in the late summer of 133 he destroyed it utterly, returning home in 132 to a second triumph. Finding the political scene transformed by the tribunate and death of Tiberius Gracchus (q.v. 3), he soon took the lead among the anti-Gracchans. Early in 129, championing the discontented Italians, he initiated moves against Tiberius' legislation, provoking a major political storm. By this time he had forfeited much of the mass enthusiasm which he had inspired earlier. His sudden death at the height of the crisis gave rise to rumours, probably false, that he was murdered. Among the suspects was his wife Sempronia, sister of the Gracchi. His marriage to her had been childless and unhappy.

He was a man of strict personal morality, courageous, cultured, and intellectual, with philhellenic leanings (*see* SCIPIONIC CIRCLE), but he could be cruel and ruthless. An able speaker, he had a ready and often caustic wit. He was a competent general, with great powers of organization. Interpretations of his policies, his influence, and his significance have differed widely. He had powerful enemies and never achieved a position of unchallenged leadership, though for nearly twenty years he was a key personality in Roman politics. For this and other reasons it is a mistake to stress his personal responsibility for the policies pursued in the Viriathic and Numantine wars (*see* VIRIATHUS *and* NUMANTIA), although he probably approved of what was done. He may have influenced Roman policy towards the Hellenistic powers, but there is little evidence. Despite his philhellenism he was averse to certain changes in social customs, perhaps in part because he judged them detrimental to military vigour. It is not clear what solutions, if any, he had to offer to the social and demographic problems of the time.

His combination of cultured interests, military success, and political eminence, fortified by his opposition to the Gracchans, roused the admiration of Cicero, who idealized him as the paragon of the wise, beneficent statesman. Cicero used him as the central character of his *De Republica* and also in his *De Senectute*; the *De Amicitia* dwells on the friendship between Scipio and Laelius.

Livy, *Epit.* 48 ff.; Polyb. 31. 23 ff. and bks. 32–9; App. *Pun.* 71 f. and 98 ff.; *Hisp.* 84 ff.; *BCiv.* 1; 'Plut.' *Apophth. Scip. Min.*; Cic. *De Or.*; *Brut.*; Val. Max.
Malcovati, *ORF*² 122; A. Schulten, *Numantia* i (1914), 273, 366; iii (1927), 9; S. Gsell, *Hist. anc. de l'Afrique du Nord* iii (1918), 336; K. Bilz, *Die Politik des P. Cornelius Scipio Aemilianus* (1935); H. H. Scullard, *JRS* 1960, 59; A. E. Astin, *Scipio Aemilianus* (1967).
                                                    A. E. A.

**SCIPIO** (12) **NASICA SERAPIO,** PUBLIUS CORNELIUS (*PW* 354), son of (10), as consul in 138 B.C. (with Brutus, q.v. 2) was involved in trouble with the tribunes about the army levy. In 133 he vigorously opposed his cousin Ti. Gracchus (q.v. 3). When Tiberius sought re-election and was accused of aiming at tyranny, and the consul Scaevola (q.v. 2) refused to use force against him, Scipio led a charge by senators and their clients in which Tiberius was killed. The deed was ever after applauded by Optimates, and execrated by Populares (see, e.g., *Rhet. Her.* 4. 68). Sent to Asia as head of a mission (132)—partly to escape popular fury—he died at Pergamum. He was *pontifex maximus* (it is not clear for how long).   E. B.

**SCIPIONIC CIRCLE.** Scipio Aemilianus (q.v. 11) and certain of his friends, especially Laelius (q.v. 2) and Furius (q.v. 2) Philus, shared a philhellenic outlook and a considerable interest in literature and philosophy. In their earlier years they were the patrons of Terence (q.v.); later they had close contacts with Panaetius (q.v.) and fostered the work of Lucilius (q.v. 1). This group is often referred to as 'the Scipionic Circle', though the term is almost entirely modern, resting on only one rather imprecise ancient reference (Cic. *Amic.* 69). The concept has been abused, by unduly extending its scope, by giving it political significance and by exaggerating the uniqueness of these philhellenic and literary interests, but it is true that the figures patronized by this particular 'Circle' were outstanding and exercised a considerable influence upon the development of Latin literature and thought. The persons chiefly associated with the 'Circle' are usually taken to be those used by Cicero as the *dramatis personae* of his *De Republica*.

K. Büchner, *Römische Literaturgeschichte* (1957), 142; R. M. Brown, *A Study of the Scipionic Circle* (1934), which greatly extends the scope of the concept; H. Strasburger, *Hermes* 1966, 60 ff.; A. E. Astin, *Scipio Aemilianus* (1967), 294.                              A. E. A.

**SCIRAS,** writer of phlyax-plays, like Rhinthon, also of Tarentum, probably in third century B.C. One title, Μελέαγρος, survives, with one fragment of 2 vv. (parody of Eur. *Hipp.* 75).

CGF 190.

**SCIRON** (Σκίρων), a brigand infesting the dangerous Scironian Way (Σκιρωνὶς ὁδός, Hdt. 8. 71. 2) over the Scironian Cliffs (Σκιρωνίδες πέτραι, Strabo 9. 1. 4) near Megara. He made passers-by wash his feet and, as they did so, kicked them over the cliff, where, according to some, they were devoured by a great tortoise (Apollod. *Epit.* 1. 2; Plut. *Thes.* 10; Hyg. *Fab.* 38. 4; and other authors, see O. Waser in Roscher, art. 'Skiron'). Theseus (q.v.), on his way to Athens, threw him into the sea, where, according to Ov. *Met.* 7. 444 ff., his bones turned into the cliffs bearing his name. The Megarian account made him no brigand but a most respectable and highly connected person (Plut. loc. cit.).          H. J. R.

**SCIROPHORIA,** an Athenian festival, also called *Scira*, celebrated the 12th Scirophorion (June/July) and, according to ancient texts, in honour of Demeter and Kore. (The attempt to claim it for Athena alone must be rejected.) The name indicates that something was carried, the σκίρα. The ancient interpretation was that these were parasols, and it is said that the priestess of Athena Polias and the priest of Poseidon-Erechtheus went from the Acropolis to a place called Scira walking under a great white baldacchino. Some modern scholars maintain that they were the sucking-pigs, serpent- and phallus-shaped cakes thrown into underground *megara* and brought up at the Thesmophoria (q.v.).

E. Gjerstad, *ARW* 1929, 189 ff., justly criticized by L. Deubner, *Attische Feste* (1932), 40 ff.                    M. P. N.; J. H. C.

**SCOLIA,** drinking-songs, especially Attic. Athenaeus (15. 693 f.) preserves a collection for the late sixth and early fifth centuries. They were sung in the Prytaneum; a singer held a myrtle-branch and, when he had finished, passed the branch to another and called on him for a song. The process is illustrated in Ar. *Vesp.* 1216 ff., cf. schol. Pl. *Grg.* 451 e, Plut. *Quaest. conv.* 1. 1. 5. There were also choral σκόλια, possibly of a later date, like two pieces in a papyrus at Berlin (*Scol. Anon.* 30).

TEXT. Page, *Poet. Mel. Gr.* 472–8; R. Reitzenstein, *Epigramm und Skolion* (1893), 3 ff.; C. M. Bowra, *Greek Lyric Poetry*[2] (1962), 373 ff.          C. M. B.

**SCOPAS** (4th c. B.C.), sculptor, of Paros; possibly son of Aristander, who was working in 405 B.C., if the Parian sculptor, Aristander, son of Scopas, known from signatures of the first century B.C., is a descendant. Pliny dates him 420 B.C., perhaps by his birth. Selected works, (i) *dated*: 1. Temple of Athena Alea at Tegea; after 395

B.C. Scopas was ἀρχιτέκτων and made marble statues of Asclepius and Hygieia; he must have designed and supervised the pediments (A. Calydonian boar-hunt, B. Achilles and Telephus). The surviving fragments are the basis of all attributions (Winter, *KB* 300. 2–4). A copy of the Asclepius has been recognized. He also made a beardless Asclepius for Gortys (Arcadia). 2. One column in Artemis temple at Ephesus, after 356 B.C. Doubtful, since *una a Scopa* should perhaps read *imo scapo*. 3. East side of Mausoleum, after 351 B.C. Slab 1022 (Winter, *KB* 304. 3) recalls the Tegea sculptures in style.

(ii) *Undated*: 4. Heracles in Sicyon, marble. Copies have been recognized in the Lansdowne Heracles, etc. (Winter, *KB* 300. 8; 301. 1). 5. Bacchant, marble. Callistratus' description justifies recognition of Dresden Maenad (Winter, *KB* 306. 4) as copy. 6. Apollo from Rhamnus, later in Palatine temple. Marble, represented as Citharode. Reproduced on Sorrento base. 7. Poseidon, Thetis, Achilles, Nereids, Tritons, etc. In temple of Neptune at Rome (built by Cn. Domitius Ahenobarbus, 32 B.C.). The base has been recognized (Winter, *KB* 384. 5). The Tritoness of Ostia may derive from the group. 8. Seated Mars and Venus in temple of Mars at Rome (built by D. Junius Brutus Callaicus, 138 B.C.). 9. Apollo Smintheus at Chryse. Represented on coins. 10. Aphrodite Pandemus at Elis, bronze. Represented on coins. 11. Niobid group. Attributed to Scopas or Praxiteles. The style of surviving copies (Winter, *KB* 307) suggests neither.

(iii) *Attributed*: 12. Meleager (Winter, *KB* 300. 7, 301. 2). The Tegea sculptures are remarkable for the expression of violent emotion and movement. His influence is seen in many later works, e.g. the Pergamene gigantomachy (Winter, *KB* 352–5).

Overbeck, 755, 766, 1149–89, 1227, K. A. Neugebauer, *Studien über Skopas* (1913); C. Picard, *Rev. Ét. Gr.* 1934, 385; 1935, 475; Lippold, *Griech. Plastik*, 249; P. E. Arias, *Scopas* (1952).

T. B. L. W.

**SCOPELIANUS,** famous Sophist in Smyrna, in the reigns of Domitian and Hadrian; author of an epic Γιγαντία.

Philostr. *VS* 1. 21.

**SCORDISCI** were a Celtic tribe, later intermingled with Illyrians and Thracians, who invaded Greece in the early third century B.C. and then settled around the confluence of the Savus and the Danube to the east of Sirmium and southward to the upper Margus (Just. 32. 3). In the later second and early first century B.C. many Roman governors of Macedonia undertook campaigns against them. As late as 16 B.C. they were still raiding Macedonia but had been conquered or won over by 12 B.C., when they co-operated with Tiberius in attacks on the Pannonian Breuci (Cass. Dio 54. 30. 3; 31. 2–4). A *civitas Scordiscorum* is attested on inscriptions in the late first century A.D. under the rule of *principes* and *praefecti* (A. Mócsy, *Hist.* 1957, 488 f.).

G. Alföldy, 'Des Territoires occupés par les Scordisques', *Act. Ant. Acad. Scient. Hung.* 1964, 107 ff.          J. J. W.

**SCRIBAE** meant originally all persons who practised writing. Subsequently, when copyists came to be called *librarii*, the term was restricted to secretaries of private individuals, who wanted assistance in correspondence and book-keeping, or of magistrates, especially those concerned with finance and municipal affairs. These public *scribae* were generally freeborn citizens, belonged to the class of the knights, and received a regular salary. They formed several corporations, e.g. the *scribae quaestorii*. Divided into three *decuriae*, they kept the archives of the Senate, transcribed documents, and acted as cashiers and accountants at the *aerarium*. With the growth of bureaucracy in the imperial age, *scribae* were generally appointed to assist any financial, military, or municipal magistracy. *See also* APPARITORES.

Mommsen, *Röm. Staatsr.* i³. 346 ff.; C. Lécrivain,Dar.-Sag. iv. 2. 1123 f.; A. H. M. Jones, *Stud. in Roman Government and Law* (1960), 154 ff. P. T.

**SCRIBONIA** (*PW* 32), sister of L. Scribonius (q.v. 1) Libo, was married at least three times. Her first two husbands, both of whom held the consulship, are hard to identify; by one of them she was the mother of Cornelia, wife of Paullus (4). The third was Octavian, who married her in 40 B.C. in order to conciliate Sextus Pompeius, Libo's son-in-law, but in 39, on the birth of their daughter Julia (q.v. 2), divorced her, 'pertaesus, ut scribit, morum peruersitatem eius' (Suet. *Aug.* 62. 2). She accompanied Julia into exile in 2 B.C., remaining with her till her death in A.D. 14. She herself was still alive in 16.

Syme, *Rom. Rev.* 213, 229; E. F. Leon, *TAPA* 1951, 168 ff. T. J. C.

**SCRIBONIANUS** (1), LUCIUS ARRUNTIUS (*PW* 14) CAMILLUS, was consul in A.D. 32. He was legate of Dalmatia under Gaius and Claudius. In 42, at the instigation of Annius Vinicianus and many Roman senators and *equites*, he persuaded his two legions (VII and XI) to revolt against Claudius. After four days the legions abandoned the revolt, and he was murdered.

*PIR²* 'A', 1140. J. P. B.

**SCRIBONIANUS** (2), L. ARRUNTIUS (*PW* 21) (FURIUS), son of (1) above, claimed descent from Pompeius Magnus (*ILS* 976). He was banished in A.D. 52 for consulting astrologers and died soon afterwards.

*PIR²* 'A', 1147. J. P. B.

**SCRIBONIUS** (1, *PW* 20) **LIBO**, LUCIUS, of senatorial family, father-in-law of Sextus Pompeius, supported Pompey's pretensions to an Egyptian command in 56 B.C. and later commanded a division of his fleet in the Adriatic (49–48). By the end of 46 he had made his peace with Caesar, but must have been proscribed in 43, as in 40 he is one of Sextus' principal adherents sent by him to Antony to arrange an alliance against Octavian. However, he agreed readily to Octavian's marriage with his sister Scribonia (q.v.), and in 39 crossed over from Sicily to prepare the ground for the Pact of Misenum. In 36 he accompanied Sextus to Asia, but abandoned him for Antony in 35. He was consul in 34, and perhaps still alive in 21.

Syme, *Rom. Rev.*, see index. T. J. C.

**SCRIBONIUS** (2, *PW* 23) **LIBO DRUSUS**, MARCUS, great-grandson of Pompeius Magnus. His trial before the Senate in A.D. 16 was the first of the important treason trials of Tiberius' Principate. Tacitus (*Ann.* 2. 27 ff.) considered him an innocent, if half-witted, victim of conspiracy, a judgement which is not impugned by *Fasti Amiternini* (Sept. 13) (Syme, *Tacitus*, 399 f.). He committed suicide during the trial. J. P. B.

**SCRIBONIUS** (3) **LARGUS**, Roman physician *c.* A.D. 1–50, studied at Rome in the time of Tiberius. In 43 he accompanied Claudius on his British campaign, probably on the recommendation of his patron C. Julius Callistus, secretary to Claudius, who also procured the Emperor's patronage for Scribonius' writings. In gratitude Scribonius dedicated to Callistus his only work to come down to us, the *Compositiones* (prescriptions). The contents of this show him to be an empiricist in method, closely akin to Celsus. His work was largely used by (among other writers) Marcellus Empiricus.

Ed. G. Helmreich (1887); K. Deichgräber, *Professio Medici. Zum Vorwort des S. Largus* (1950). W. D. R.

**SCROFA**, GNAEUS TREMELLIUS, quaestor in 71 B.C. and agrarian commissioner in 59, was friendly with Cicero and Atticus, and chief interlocutor in the first two books of Varro's *De re rustica*. Importing elegance into his work on agriculture, he thought little of the matter-of-fact Sasernae (q.v.; Varro, *Rust.* 1. 2. 25). Varro, Pliny, Columella used him. J. W. D.

**SCULPTURE, GREEK.** Archaic period, *c.* 650–480 B.C. During the geometric period of the ninth, the eighth, and the early seventh century statuettes in various materials had been produced, but, as far as is now known, it was not until about 650 B.C. that monumental sculpture was practised in Greece. The inspiration evidently came from Egypt, with which close contact is attested during this very time; also, but to a less extent, from Mesopotamia; and perhaps through a few Mycenaean survivals. From this time on there was an active output of life-size and over life-size statues and reliefs in all parts of Greece —Asia Minor, the Aegean Islands, Greece proper, and southern Italy. The majority of the statues consist of standing and seated male and female figures; but occasionally figures in motion were attempted, especially for the pedimental groups. The chief materials employed were wood, limestone, Island marble, terracotta, and bronze. The sculptures in terracotta and marble were regularly coloured. Those in bronze were first hammered over a core and riveted together, later they were cast solid, and finally cast hollow. The wooden sculptures have practically all disappeared. The standing male figures— the so-called kouroi—are almost all represented in the same general pose: erect, with left leg advanced, and both arms lowered. In contrast to the similar Egyptian statues, they are shown mostly nude and free-standing, with no support at the back. What gives these archaic Greek statues a unique interest is that they show a progressive knowledge of the anatomy of the human body. Step by step, decade by decade, the Greek sculptor learned to represent the complicated structure of the head, the trunk, the arms, the legs and feet, in every detail and in their respective interrelations. By about 480 B.C. an anatomically functioning human figure was achieved—for the first time in the history of the world. Among the earliest and most complete examples of kouroi which have survived are a statue from Delos, two from Sunium, a statue now in New York, and the Cleobis and Biton in Delphi. The series continues with the kouroi from Tenea (in Munich), from Volomandra (in Athens), from Melos (in Athens), and from Attica (in Munich); and it terminates with examples from Ceos (in Athens), Boeotia (in Athens), and the now famous Aristodikos (in Athens). The so-called Omphalos Apollo (a Roman copy of an original of *c.* 460 B.C.) shows the resultant statue of a youth standing in a free, natural pose, with all parts of the body convincingly rendered.

The female standing figures were generally represented clothed, with only the head and limbs showing the same anatomical evolution as do the kouroi. The chief interest here, therefore, centres in the rendering of the drapery, which gradually develops from a foldless, undifferentiated covering to a more lifelike garment. First are observable a few shallow folds cut into the flat surfaces; presently an increase of such folds with a progressive ability to differentiate both those of the thin (linen) and of the heavier (woollen) garments. For this purpose a set of conventions was evolved consisting of ridges and grooves going in various directions and terminating in zigzags. Here too the derivation from Egyptian prototypes is evident. Gradually a more naturalistic treatment was achieved, always, however, within the framework of a decorative scheme. Well-preserved examples of such korai, as they are commonly called, are first the Nikandre, a Naxian dedication found at Delos, now in Athens; a small statue from Auxerre in southern France, in the Louvre; several statues from Samos, now in the Museum there, in the Louvre, and in Berlin; and, above all, the famous series of Maidens which came to light on the Athenian Acropolis, buried there after the sack by the Persians in 480 B.C., and refound, many still resplendent in their original colours, during the eighties of the last century.

The seated male and female figures are best exemplified by the statues from Miletus in the British Museum and in the Louvre, by the Athena perhaps by Endoios in the Acropolis Museum, and by the goddess from Tarentum in Berlin. The pose, at first stiff and motionless, gradually becomes more relaxed and animated, while the drapery, which almost always covers the body, goes through the same changes as in the standing figures.

In a few statues and in the pediments, metopes, and friezes of buildings which have survived from various regions one can catch a glimpse of the development of the other stances that were attempted by the archaic sculptors. Figures reclining and in movement—striding, flying, running, falling—are rendered with progressive ability; and gradually the various parts of a composition become interrelated. One can watch this evolution in a few statues, such as a series of flying Victories, and in the pedimental group of Corcyra in Corfu, the metopes of the Sicyonian Treasury at Delphi, the figures on a limestone relief from Mycenae, and in the superb friezes of the Siphnian Treasury and the metopes of the Athenian Treasury, both at Delphi.

In addition to free-standing statues and architectural sculptures, grave monuments played an important part in archaic Greece. These early gravestones consisted of tall, narrow shafts, generally decorated with a standing male figure in relief and surmounted by a sphinx carved in the round. A few of these monuments are signed by their makers; for instance, the well-known gravestone of Aristion in Athens bears the signature of Aristocles, and one from Boeotia is signed by Alxenor of Naxos.

It is noteworthy that the steady progression from conventional to naturalistic representations was similar throughout the Greek world, uniformly shared by Greek artists all over the Mediterranean. Only occasionally, one can observe the work of progressives and of conservatists among the artists.

2. The classical period of the fifth and fourth centuries, c. 480–330 B.C.

(a) The fifth century. The archaic period was followed first by the so-called early classical epoch—a time of experimentation in various directions, such as in the expression of emotion and in the rendering of complicated stances; then by the classical age proper, characterized by an elevation of spirit combined with a superbly competent rendering of naturalistic form. In both epochs there were great achievements, symbolized for us today by two groups of sculptures: the pediments and metopes of the temple of Zeus at Olympia (c. 465–457 B.C.), and the metopes, friezes, and pediments of the temple of Athena at Athens, known as the Parthenon (447–431 B.C.). In both periods great sculptors arose whose names live to this day. In the first, Pythagoras, who, according to ancient authors, was particularly interested in harmonious composition; Calamis, known for the delicacy and grace of his works, and famous for his representations of horses; and Myron, several of whose statues are preserved in Roman copies. In the second epoch came Phidias (q.v.) of Athens and Polyclitus (q.v. 2) of Argos. In antiquity Phidias' fame rested chiefly on his colossal chryselephantine statues of Athena in the Parthenon and of Zeus at Olympia; today his name is associated with the extant architectural sculptures of the Parthenon, for

which he must have been responsible since, according to Plutarch (*Pericles* 13. 4 and 9), Pericles made him general manager and overseer of all artistic undertakings. Under him Greek sculpture attained the grandeur and sublimity which to us remain the chief characteristics of Greek art. Polyclitus was famous for his quietly standing figures in harmonious poses. Of two of his bronze works—the Doryphorus, 'a youth carrying a lance', and the Diadumenus, 'a youth winding a fillet round his head'—several Roman copies in marble exist, which can give an idea of the harmonious design of the originals. They represent the consummation of the long struggles in the representation of the standing human figure and acted as models for future sculptors.

In addition to these two great sculptors there were a host of other gifted artists, of whom Cresilas, Alcamenes, Agoracritus, Strongylion, Callimachus, and Paeonius (qq.v.) are perhaps the best known today. They and their contemporaries produced the sculptural decoration of the many buildings that arose all over Attica and Greece during this incomparable time—e.g. the Erechtheum, the temple of Athena Nike and its 'balustrade', the temple of Apollo at Phigalea, the temple of Hera at Argos—as well as many a splendid single monument, such as the Nike by Paeonius at Olympia.

(b) The fourth century. The Peloponnesian War (431–404 B.C.) in which most of Greece was engaged, and which finally spread to Sicily, put an end to this artistic activity, especially in Athens. The lull, however, was only temporary. Soon important buildings again arose, not only in Greece but in Asia Minor. Of some of these the sculptural decoration has in part survived; for instance, of the temple of Asclepius at Epidaurus (first quarter of the fourth century); of the temple of Athena Alea at Tegea (c. 370–350 B.C.); of the Mausoleum of Halicarnassus (c. 350–330 B.C.); and of the temple of Artemis at Ephesus (c. 350–330 B.C.). Again great figures arose whose names can be associated with these activities, and who are also known for their single statues. Thus a statue of Eirene by Cephisodotus, which was perhaps erected to celebrate the peace which followed the Athenian victory over Sparta in 375 B.C., has been recognized in several Roman copies. Timotheus and Thrasymedes are associated with the sculptures from Epidaurus; Bryaxis made a statue of which the decorated base with his signature is preserved; Leochares, to whom a number of statues have been tentatively attributed. But the leading sculptors of the time were Praxiteles of Athens, Scopas of Paros, and Lysippus of Sicyon. Of Praxiteles we are in the happy position of possessing an original work in the Hermes found at Olympia in the temple of Hera, at the very spot at which Pausanias saw it during his journeys over Greece. Its superb workmanship and the charm of its composition help us to visualize Praxiteles' much praised masterpiece, the Aphrodite of Cnidus, which survives only in second-rate Roman copies. Other works by Praxiteles which have been more or less securely identified are the Apollo Sauroctonus ('the Lizard-Slayer'), a Satyr, and several Aphrodites. Of Scopas there remain some heads and fragments from the temple of Athena Alea at Tegea, perhaps a slab from the Mausoleum, with which he is known to have been associated, and a Pothos, of which Roman copies have been tentatively identified. Of the third great figure of the fourth century, Lysippus, much is known from the statements of ancient writers, but little of his work has survived to our day. The most convincingly identified statue by him is the Apoxyomenus, 'youth scraping himself', of which a Roman copy has been recognized in a marble statue in the Vatican. Instead of the squarely built statues of Polyclitus, he introduced a slenderer figure with long legs and a small head. In addition there have been recognized a standing statue of Heracles, the so-called Heracles Farnese in Naples, and a seated statue of Heracles, the so-called Heracles Epitrapezius, of which a colossal version has recently been found at Lucus Fucens. A Greek original statue of Agias at Delphi may be an adaptation of a work by him. He was especially famous for his large compositions, some consisting of over twenty figures, and for his portraits. Thus Alexander the Great is said to have preferred him as a portraitist to all others. He was also pre-eminent in representations of animals.

These three artists gave to Greek sculpture a new direction. Instead of the majesty and grandeur of the fifth century they imbued their works with a sober grace. The former spiritual quality has given way to a more human approach, with an increased interest in the individual. These new elements are also observable in the fourth-century Athenian grave monuments with their moving yet restrained rendering of the sorrow of parting, and in the portraits of Thucydides, Plato, and Socrates, which show a gradually heightened sense for a specific individuality.

3. Hellenistic period, c. 330–100 B.C. With the conquests of Alexander the Great the boundaries of the Greek world were greatly enlarged, and Hellenic civilization spread throughout this new eastern, Hellenistic empire. Inevitably the enlargement brought with it fundamental changes also in art. The most important was an increased realism—in movement, in modelling, in expression, and in the range of subjects treated. It is best exemplified by the sculptures from Pergamum, by the Laocoon, by some of the statues recently found at Sperlonga, as well as by many a single work that has survived in a Roman copy. Instead of the quiet stances of former times contortions were favoured, and in relief work strong contrasts between light and shade were produced by a deep carving into the surface. Old age, childhood, deformity, racial differences, strong emotion were now studied with new insight. An increased realism may also be observed in the portraiture of this period, for instance, in the statue of Demosthenes, the blind Homer, the Pseudo-Seneca, and some of the penetrating portraits on Hellenistic coins. Another trend was the so-called *sfumato* style, with delicate modelling and serene expressions—a development from the Praxitelean sculptures.

4. The 'Graeco-Roman' period, c. 100 B.C. and later. The conquest of Greece by Rome initiated still another period in Greek sculpture. The Roman admiration for Greek art brought with it a taste for the works of the past, resulting in an age of copying. Greek sculptors who for almost six centuries had produced masterpieces in ever-changing styles were now engaged all over the Roman Empire in copying the works of a bygone age. To this practice we owe much of our knowledge of Greek sculpture, for many a lost Greek original has survived in such copies. But it spelled the end of an original output, except that it initiated Roman art as such, in which Greek types were borrowed and adapted to form new compositions, and in which the art of portraiture was further developed. *See also* ART, GREEK RELIGIOUS, and the individual sculptors.

J. Overbeck, *Die antiken Schriftquellen* (1868); E. Loewy, *Inschriften griechischer Bildhauer* (1885); A. W. Lawrence, *Later Greek Sculpture* (1927), and *Classical Sculpture* (1929); G. M. A. Richter, *The Sculpture and Sculptors of the Greeks* (1930, 1950), *Three Critical Periods in Greek Sculpture* (1951), *Handbook of Greek Art* (1959, 5th ed. 1967), 45 ff.; J. D. Beazley and B. Ashmole, *Greek Sculpture and Painting*[1] (1966); S. Casson, *The Technique of Early Greek Sculpture* (1933); C. Picard, *Manuel d'archéologie, La Sculpture*, 4 vols. (1935–63); J. Charbonneaux, *La Sculpture grecque archaïque* (1945), and *La Sculpture grecque classique* (1946); Lippold, *Griech. Plastik*; Bieber, *Sculpt. Hellenist. Age*; R. Lullies and M. Hirmer, *Greek Sculpture* (1957); R. Carpenter, *Greek Sculpture, A Critical Review* (1960).
G. M. A. R.

**SCULPTURE, ROMAN.** Etruscan sculptors are recorded to have worked in Rome during the regal period, and some fragments in terracotta, of regal or early republican date, have been discovered. Etruscan sculpture, heavily indebted in its early stages to archaic Greek art, is well known from the seventh to the first century B.C. The Etruscans produced votive sculpture in bronze and clay, and architectural sculpture in the latter material: stone they reserved for tomb sculpture and sarcophagi. Early sculptures of local style have also come to light in other regions of Italy. From the fourth century onward later Greek artistic currents percolated into Rome through Etruria and Campania, and many Greek statues reached the city as war booty. In the second century sculptors from Hellenistic lands began to flock to Rome and Italy, but no sculptures from Rome that can be securely dated before the late second and early first centuries have survived. Under the late Republic marble (usually assisted by colour) came into use for portraiture (q.v.), other statuary, and architectural ornament.

One of the most important products of Roman sculpture is the great series of historical and commemorative reliefs on public buildings of the capital and other cities. The historical relief originated in late republican times, but came into prominence under the Empire. The Ara Pacis (q.v.) illustrates the idealizing Greek style favoured under Augustus. In Flavian times the panels on the Arch of Titus show greater feeling for pictorial effect and the rendering of depth, while the two Domitianic friezes from the Palazzo della Cancelleria reveal a classicizing tendency. The columns of Trajan and Marcus Aurelius exemplify the 'continuous' narrative style in which the stories of Rome's wars with the barbarians are unrolled as in a film in unbroken sequence round the shafts. Between these two columns fall the again more classicized reliefs of Hadrian's reign, followed under the Antonines by a rich, pictorial style of panel carving with experiments in perspective, crowd-representation, and deep-cut contrasts of light and shade. The reliefs on the arches of Septimius Severus in the Roman Forum and at Lepcis Magna in Tripolitania combine Antonine picturesqueness with a new interest in repetitive and frontal poses for the figures. No State reliefs of the third century have come down to us. In the contemporary reliefs on the Arch of Constantine the new Severan tendencies are developed and intensified and they now became the hallmark of the 'late-antique'.

Other types of relief were: decorative, for interior walls (stucco and terracotta were here employed as well as marble); and sepulchral: to the first and early second centuries belong the funerary altars (q.v.) and from the second to the early fourth century there was a large output of sarcophagi (q.v.) with mythological, battle, or genre scenes. Christian sarcophagi of the third, fourth, and fifth centuries are completely Roman in their style. Of Roman pedimental sculpture little remains, although some information is provided by coins and other representations. Sculpture in the round was largely confined to adaptations of Greek types. But there were some original creations; and honorific portrait statues appear in toga, cuirass, or heroic nudity. The sculptors of the eastern provinces, possessing artistic traditions of their own, in some respects led the capital, as is clear from such works as the historical reliefs from Ephesus and the series of Attic and Asiatic sarcophagi. In the western provinces sculpture was mainly funerary and votive. Characteristic are the carved grave *stelai* and such local manifestations as the Jupiter-columns of Roman Germany. The fusion of Celtic with classical traditions in the style and content of the art of these regions is of special interest.

E. Strong, *La scultura romana* (1923, 1926); D. E. Strong, *Roman Imperial Sculpture* (1961); P. G. Hamberg, *Studies in Roman Imperial*

*Sculpture, with special reference to the State Reliefs of the Second Century* (1945); G. Becatti, *La colonna coclide istoriata* (1960); M. F. Squarciapino, *La scuola di Afrodisia* (1943); E. Espérandieu, R. Lantier, *Recueil général des bas-reliefs, statues et bustes de la Gaule romaine* (1907–55), with an additional volume on *La Germanie romaine* (1931); S. Ferri, *Arte romana sul Danubio* (1933); J. M. C. Toynbee, *Art in Britain under the Romans* (1964).

F. N. P.; J. M. C. T.

**SCYLACIUM (or SCYLLETIUM)**, modern *Squillace*, on the 'sole' of the Italian 'boot', overlooking the stormy *Scylleticus Sinus* and dominating the narrowest part of the Bruttian peninsula. Greek in origin, its early history is unknown. Becoming the *colonia* Minervia *c.* 122 B.C., it attained some prosperity. Cassiodorus (q.v.) was born here.

E. T. S.

**SCYLAX** of Caryanda, by order of Darius I, is said to have sailed down the Indus to its mouth, and thence, in a voyage of thirty months, to have reached the isthmus of Suez (Hdt. 4. 44). Though the voyage has been doubted, the book that he wrote is quoted apparently by Hecataeus (q.v. 1) (cf. F 295, 296), as well as by later authors like Aristotle, Strabo, and Avienius (q.v.). No MS. has survived; the *Periplus* that bears his name was written in the fourth century B.C.

*GGM* i. xxxiii–li; 15–96 (text of Periplus); *FGrH* iii C, no. 709. W. A. Heidel, *The Frame of the ancient Gk. Maps* (1937), esp. 47 ff.; Hyde, *Greek Mariners*, 174 ff.

E. H. W.

**SCYLLA** (Σκύλλη, -α), (1) a sea-monster, living in a cave opposite Charybdis (q.v.); she had six heads, each with a triple row of teeth, and twelve feet. She lived on fish of all sorts, but if a ship came near enough, she would seize six men at a time from it and devour them. The only way to restrain her was to implore the intervention of her mother Cratais. She was immortal and irresistible (see Homer, *Od.* 12. 85 ff., 245 ff.). Later authors (e.g. Verg. *Ecl.* 6. 75) say she had a girdle of dogs' heads about her loins. There were also stories, of uncertain date and origin, to the effect that she had once been of human shape but was turned by magic into a monster: e.g. Ovid (*Met.* 13. 730 ff., 14. 1 ff.) says she was loved by Glaucus (q.v. 2) the merman, and changed by Circe (q.v.), who was her rival. Tzetzes on Lycophron, 46 and 650, makes Poseidon the lover and Amphitrite the rival. Rationalizations of her into a rock (cf. Ovid, *Met* 14. 73) or other natural danger of the sea are fairly common; her father is regularly Phorcys, q.v. She is often (as Verg. loc. cit.) confused with (2), daughter of Nisus (q.v. 1) king of Megara.

H. J. R.

**SCYMNUS**, a Greek of Chios, fl. *c.* 185 B.C., alleged author of a lost prose περιήγησις. He is not the author of the extant Περιήγησις, an unpoetical geographical summary in iambics, written *c.* 90 B.C. or earlier: introduction, Europe, especially coasts of Spain, Italy, Sicily, Adriatic, Euxine; then Asia. The rest is lost. The author, usually referred to now as Pseudo-Scymnus, using various sources, is worth little, except on the Euxine, Ligurian, and Spanish coasts, and Greek colonies.

*GGM* i. lxxiv ff., 196 ff.; A. Diller, *The Tradition of the Minor Greek Geographers* (1952), 165 ff., 189; E. H. Bunbury, *Hist. Anc. Geog.* (1879), ii. 69 ff.; Thomson, *Hist. Anc. Geog.* 210.

E. H. W.

**SCYTHIA** was the name given by the Greeks to the country between the Carpathians and the river Don. The term 'Scythian' is frequently used to denote an association of central Asian tribes of Indo-European origin and speech who started penetrating into eastern Europe and the Caucasian area early in the first millennium B.C. By *c.* 650 B.C. they had made themselves the masters of what are now north-western Iran and eastern Turkey as far as the river Halys. After ruling there for some twenty-

eight years they were expelled from Asia by the Medes. Retreating to the north-west, they settled first in the Kuban basin, then moved into what is now southern Russia. There the group to which, strictly speaking, the term Scythian should alone apply, first founded a kingdom—Royal Scythia—on the lower reaches of the Dnieper; when expelled from that area (*c.* 2nd C. B.C.) by the Sarmatians they transferred it to the Crimea. From as early as the fifth century B.C. groups of Scythians also penetrated as far west as Hungary and north as Pomerania.

The Royal Scyths traded with the Greeks living on the Black Sea's northern shore, exchanging wheat, which they levied from the native population, fish, honey, furs, and other foodstuffs for luxuries such as pottery and jewelry, even though they were themselves highly skilled at working metals. They were a pastoral people and adhered to the nomadic way of life till their disappearance from the pages of history in *c.* second century A.D. Warlike and brave, they were among the very first to master the art of horsemanship. They owed much of their military success to the skill of their mounted archers, even defeating a Macedonian army commanded by Alexander's general Zopyrion (*c.* 325 B.C.). However, it was partly owing to the effects of their scorched-earth policy that Darius was obliged to abandon his invasion of their territory (*c.* 512 B.C.).

The Scyths worshipped the elements, the Great Goddess, and—above all—the graves of their ancestors. For their kings and chieftains they built elaborate, richly furnished tombs, all of which took the form of horse burials. Many of the objects and horse trappings recovered from these are of considerable intrinsic value, being of gold or bronze, often enhanced with enamel inlays or jewels. All are profusely decorated, the majority with animal designs which endow them with permanent artistic value. Indeed, the technical skill, linear mastery, intense vitality, and profound sensibility of these renderings is so remarkable that the designs form a distinct school of art. It is one which ensures its Scythian creators of an important place in the history of European culture.

Hdt. 4. 1–144. E. H. Minns, *Scythians and Greeks* (1913); M. Rostovtzeff, *Iranians and Greeks in South Russia* (1922) and *Skythien und der Bosporus* i (1931); G. Borovka, *Scythian Art* (1928); T. Talbot Rice, *The Scythians* (1958); M. I. Artamonov, *Treasures from Scythian Tombs* (1969).

T. T. R.

**SCYTHINUS** of Teos, contemporary of Plato, wrote Ίαμβοι which expressed Heraclitus' doctrine in verse, and also a prose work Περὶ φύσεως and a Ἱστορία which was a novelistic account of Heracles' deeds as benefactor of the human race.

Ed. Diels, *PPF* 169.

W. D. R.

**SEALS** (σφραγίς, *signum*, *sigillum*) played an important part in ancient life, taking the place of the modern signature on documents and, to some extent, of locks and keys. The materials for sealings were lead and wax for documents; in commerce a lump of clay was commonly pressed down over the cordage. In Roman times small seal-cases were frequently employed to protect the impression from damage. The seals themselves were generally of stone or metal, sometimes of ivory, glass, and other materials; some early seals, pierced by string holes, were worn round the neck or wrist but ancient seals were usually worn as signet rings.

The use of seals began in Neolithic times in Greece and they were in common use in EH. Seals of ivory, hard stones, and precious metals were made in Crete where they appear in EM II; the two main types were the stamp and the cylinder-seal. The finest Minoan and Mycenaean seals were cut in hard stone and precious metal. The techniques of cutting stone seals were revived in the later Geometric period, the most notable series being the so-called Island Gems; hard stones—

chalcedony, cornelian, rock crystal, and others—were used again from the middle of the sixth century. The scarab form which had been popular in Egypt from the ninth dynasty was adopted in archaic Greece and the scaraboid was the commonest form in the fifth century. Gold signet rings were also popular.

The principal device on ancient seals was usually pictorial—a favourite deity, a mythical hero, animals, and, later, portraits. The seal devices of several prominent men of Roman times are known; Augustus first used a sphinx and later a portrait of Alexander the Great.

Greek cities possessed civic seals, for public documents or public property; the Romans utilized a magistrate's personal seal.

V. E. G. Kenna, *Cretan Seals* (1960); J. Boardman, *Greek Island Gems* (1963), *Archaic Greek Gems* (1968); V. Chapot, Dar.-Sag., s.v. 'signum'.                    F. N. P.; D. E. S.

**SECESSIO** means the 'withdrawal' of the *plebs* from the rest of the Roman community. It implies detachment from public life and emigration from town. The plebeians *en masse* retired outside the *pomerium*, often to the Aventine, which was turned over to them not later than 450 B.C. We have no means of deciding how many secessions (five are recorded between 494 and 287 B.C.) actually occurred. It would be too radical to accept only the last, for the account of it differs widely from that of the earlier ones, so that a mere anticipation would be incomprehensible. The first secession (traditionally dated to 494), which was stopped by Menenius (q.v.), and the second of 449, which is reputed to have caused the fall of the decemvirs, are perhaps retrojections, though plebeian agitation is in both episodes likely. Nor is the third, with which Canuleius (q.v.) is credited, beyond suspicion, although the *Lex Canuleia* (445) may have been forced through by a secession. The fourth, which is not beyond suspicion either, was merely a military rebellion (342). The fifth secession of 287 is indisputably historical. Social troubles, arising from the pressure of debts, led the *plebs* to withdraw to the Janiculum. A plebeian dictator, Q. Hortensius (q.v. 1), was appointed, and his law terminated the struggle of the Orders.

Ed. Meyer, *Kl. Schr.* i² (1924), 373 ff.; De Sanctis, *Stor. Rom.* ii. 4 ff.; Ogilvie, *Comm. Livy 1–5*, 309 ff.                    P. T.

**SECOND ATHENIAN LEAGUE,** the modern name name for the alliance formed by Athens in 378 B.C. to exploit the widespread resentment caused by Sparta's abuse of her power as champion of the King's Peace (386). The alliance resembled the Delian League (q.v.) but specific guarantees of autonomy ensured that there would be neither tribute nor garrisons, nor interference in the internal affairs of member States; a carefully prescribed procedure accorded the *synedrion* of the Allies a probouleutic function in questions of peace and war and an independent power in certain other matters. Only six States (including Thebes) joined in 378, but, after Athens had by the Decree of Aristotle of spring 377 renounced all claims to allied territory whether as cleruchy (q.v.) or as private possession, numbers steadily increased. The Common Peace of 375 represented the triumph of the new power. With the defeat of Sparta at Leuctra in 371, the *raison d'être* of the League disappeared and, when Athens was unwilling that Sparta should be completely destroyed, Thebes seceded from the League taking with her the States of Euboea and central Greece, and proceeded to the liberation of Peloponnesian States. At the same time Athens began to concentrate all her efforts and the funds of the League on the recovery of two important assets of her former Empire, viz. Amphipolis and the Chersonese. Although Athens formally did not break her promise of 377 not to settle cleruchies in allied States, she

ceased to recruit new members and, when Timotheus (q.v. 2) recaptured Samos in 365, a cleruchy was established there which doubtless encouraged Epaminondas (q.v.) to intervene in the Aegean (364) and so to shake the loyalty of the leading allies, Byzantium, Chios, and Rhodes. Athenian generals, for their part, were severe in exacting war-contributions (*syntaxeis*), and although the *synedrion* continued to function, the plain aim of many Athenians was the recovery of empire. In 357 under the protection of Mausolus (q.v.) Rhodes and Chios joined Byzantium in revolt, and in the ensuing Social War Athens was unable to subject them. After 355 the League lingered on (the *synedrion* playing a part in the peace negotiations of 346), but it had ceased to count for much in Greek affairs and was dissolved after Chaeronea.

F. H. Marshall, *The Second Athenian Confederacy* (1905); S. Accame, *La lega ateniese* (1941); J. A. O. Larsen, *Representative Government in Greek and Roman History* (1955), ch. iii.     G. L. C.

**SECULAR GAMES,** scenic games (*ludi*) and sacrifices performed by the Roman State to commemorate the end of one *saeculum* and the beginning of a new one. The *saeculum*, defined as the longest span of human life, was fixed in the Republic as an era of a hundred years. The celebration was ordered by the Sibylline Books and was under the direction of the *duumviri* (later *decemviri* (q.v.) or *quindecimviri*) *sacris faciundis*. The ceremony took place in the Campus Martius, near the Tiber, at a spot which was known as Tarentum or Terentum. The gods honoured in the republican *ludi* are said to have been Dis and Proserpina, who had an altar near by. The games were associated in origin with the Valerian *gens*, and Valerius Corvus' first consulship, 348 B.C., may have been the date of the first celebration. The secular games of 249 B.C. are much better authenticated. Many scholars believe that the ceremony was actually introduced in that year from Tarentum, though the connexion of the site of the games with the south Italian city is by no means certain. The next celebration took place in 146 B.C. (a date attested by contemporary writers, and therefore more trustworthy than Livy's assignment of the games to 149. Like modern centennials, the *saeculum* was not always celebrated punctually. No games were held a century later, although, if we may trust the indications of coins with symbols of the *saeculum* on them (Alföldi, *Hermes* 1930, 369 ff.), there were plans in 45–42 B.C. to celebrate the *ludi* in the near future. The Fourth Eclogue has been interpreted as a prediction—not fulfilled—of games to be held in 40 B.C.

Augustus' plans to celebrate the beginning of a new age were known to Virgil, who died two years before the games took place, and were referred to in the familiar words 'aurea condet saecula' (*Aen.* 6. 792–3). At Augustus' request the *quindecimviri* made calculations for the celebration and fixed the length of the *saeculum* at 110 years. Augustus' *ludi* in 17 B.C. are well known from Horace's *Carmen Saeculare* and from an inscription, found near the Tiber, which gives details of the complicated ritual. They consisted of three nights and three successive days of sacrifices and archaic scenic games, and of seven supplementary days of more modern entertainment in theatre and circus. Dis and Proserpina do not appear among the gods honoured. Each night Augustus and Agrippa made appropriate offerings and sacrifices beside the Tiber to the Moerae, to the Eilithyiae, and to Terra Mater. On the first two days they made sacrifices on the Capitol to Jupiter and Juno Regina; on the third day they made offerings to Apollo and Diana on the Palatine. The scenic games continued night and day, and 110 matrons held *sellisternia* for Juno and Diana. As we know from the inscription, it was after the offerings on the third day that twenty-seven boys and twenty-seven girls, whose fathers and mothers were living, sang Horace's hymn, first on the Palatine and then on the Capitol. In the hymn Horace brings into great prominence Augustus' patron god Apollo in his new Palatine temple.

The antiquarian Emperor Claudius revived the *saeculum* of a hundred years and held games in A.D. 47 for the eight-hundredth birthday of Rome. Following his example, Philip in 248 celebrated the thousandth anniversary of the city. Domitian in 88 and Septimius Severus in 204 calculated their festivals by use of the Augustan *saeculum* of a hundred and ten years. From Septimius Severus' celebration extensive inscriptional records have been discovered, including a fragmentary secular hymn written in hexameters by an unknown poet.

Hor. *Carmen Saeculare* and the *scholia*; Censorinus, *D.N.* 17; Livy, *Per.* 49; Val. Max. 2. 4. 5; Zosimus 2. 1 ff.; *CIL* vi. 32323–36; *Not. Scav.* 1931, 313 ff.; Latte, *RR* 246 ff. For full collection of sources, including the inscriptions, see G. B. Pighi, *De Ludis Saecularibus Populi Romani Quiritium* (Milan, 1941). On Roman topographical problems, see F. Castagnoli, *Mem. Accad. Lincei* 1947, 97 ff., 152 ff.                     L. R. T.

**SECUNDUS,** JULIUS (*PW* 470), among recent orators specially mentioned by Quintilian (*Inst.* 10. 1. 120; 3. 12). Like M. Aper, another of the *personae* in Tacitus' *Dialogus*, he came from Gaul. A quiet and elegant speaker, he also wrote a biography of Julius Africanus (q.v. 1). He was secretary to Otho.

G. W. Bowersock, *Greek Sophists in the Roman Empire* (1969), Appendix i.                     J. W. D.

**SECURITAS,** commonly associated with the Emperor or the State as a 'virtue' or 'desirable state' (*res expetenda*). Securitas was commonly invoked when some imminent danger had been averted or on an occasion, like 10 Jan., A.D. 69, when the Arval Brethren sacrificed to her on the adoption of Piso. Her characteristic attribute is the column on which she leans.

Wissowa, *RK* 335.                     H. M.

**SECURITY** in Roman law was given to the creditor in the form either of a surety (*see* STIPULATIO) or of rights over the property of the debtor. By the earliest real security, *fiducia*, the creditor acquired ownership of the pledged object by *mancipatio* (q.v.) or *in iure cessio* (*see* DOMINIUM), subject to an agreement or trust for its reconveyance after payment of the debt. The agreement would also usually regulate the creditor's right of sale, etc. By a later form of pledge (*pignus*) the creditor acquired only interdictal possession (*see* POSSESSIO) by a simple delivery. Because of the inconvenience of the debtor's losing possession the Praetor intervened—at first probably in the case of pledges by agricultural tenants to their landlords (of slaves, cattle, agricultural implements)—to enable the creditor to assert his interest without the need for the transfer of possession. This non-possessory 'charge' was later called *hypotheca*. The debtor could hypothecate the same object successively to several creditors, but the earlier mortgage had priority; later mortgagees might enforce their rights only if the preceding one was satisfied. Some mortgages, as for taxes due to the *fiscus* or (by a reform of Justinian's) for the dowry of a woman, were implied by law and privileged (i.e. given overriding priority).                     A. B.; B. N.

**SEDULIUS** (first half of 5th c. A.D.), a Christian Latin poet, author of the *Paschale carmen*, a free adaptation of the Gospel narrative, with a prose version *Paschale opus*, in five books, and two hymns.

TEXT. J. Huemer, *CSEL* x. F. Corsaro, *Sedulio poeta*, with trans. (1956).                     A. H.-W.

**SEGESTA** (Greek Ἔγεστα, the Greeks apparently not appreciating the native initial sibilant), principal city of the Elymi in north-west Sicily, on and below Monte Varvaro a little north-west of modern Calatafimi. By the fifth century B.C. it was considerably hellenized. The Segestans wrote their language in Greek characters and built at least three Doric temples—the largest remaining unfinished. They developed a traditional hostility with Selinus (q.v.), in pursuit of which they allied themselves with Athens (*IG* i². 19—458/7 or 454/3 B.C.) and with Carthage (410 B.C.). There was war between them in 454 (if Diod. Sic. 11. 86 be thus interpreted) and in 416, when Athenian intervention was successfully encouraged with a false display of wealth (Thuc. 6. 6–8 and 46). In 409 Carthage achieved what Athens had not: Selinus was sacked, but Segesta passed into the Carthaginian sphere of domination. Agathocles seized it in 307, treating the population with exceptional barbarity; it also came briefly under Pyrrhus' control (276).

In the First Punic War Segesta immediately surrendered to and was generously treated by the Romans, who like the Segestans claimed Trojan descent. It became a *civitas libera et immunis*, but declined after the Servile War (103–100). Still a significant community in A.D. 25 (Tac. *Ann.* 4. 43), it subsequently disappeared. The site is now, save for tourist facilities, deserted; the remains and their setting are alike magnificent.

Principal temple, A. M. Burford, *CQ* 1961, 87 ff.; recent discoveries, V. Tusa, *Atti del VIImo Congresso internazionale di Archeologia classica* ii (1961), 31 ff.; inscriptions, id. Κώκαλος 1960, 34 ff.                     A. G. W.

**SEIA,** an obscure Roman goddess, said to be the guardian of corn while underground (August. *De civ. D.* 4. 8). Her statue, with that of Segetia (Segesta in Pliny, *HN* 18. 8) and a third who must not be named indoors (Tutulina?), stood in the Circus Maximus (cf. Tert. *De Spect.* 8, Macrob. *Sat.* 1. 16. 8).                     H. J. R.

**SEJANUS** (LUCIUS AELIUS (*PW* 133) SEIANUS; d. A.D. 31), of Volsinii (*Bolsena*). The maternal ancestry of Sejanus was distinguished; his father was an *eques*, L. Seius Strabo. He was made his father's colleague as Prefect of the Praetorian Guard by Tiberius on his accession, and soon, on his father's appointment as Prefect of Egypt, he became sole commander of the Guard, whose strength he increased by quartering the cohorts in a barracks near the Porta Viminalis. Over Tiberius he exercised a steadily increasing influence. After the death of Tiberius' son Drusus in 23 (which Sejanus was suspected of compassing) his influence in the Senate was paramount, and in a succession of treason trials he attacked his enemies (chiefly adherents of Agrippina). He failed to secure Tiberius' consent for a marriage with Livia, the widow of Tiberius' son Drusus, in 25, but his influence increased through Tiberius' retirement (which he encouraged) to Capreae in 27. In 29 he secured the arrest and deportation of Agrippina and her eldest son Nero; her second son Drusus was imprisoned in the Palace in 30. In 31 Sejanus perhaps planned to strike at the principate. He was consul, had been granted *imperium proconsulare*, and had hopes of *tribunicia potestas*. Tiberius, however, warned by Antonia, the widow of his brother Drusus, sent a letter to the Senate. Sejanus was arrested, brought before the Senate, and executed, the command of the Guard having been transferred to Macro (q.v.). The ease with which he was suppressed shows that his conspiracy was still in an early stage.

Syme, *Tacitus*, 401 ff.; A. Boddington, *AJPhil.* 1963, 1 ff.   J. P. B.

**SELENE,** Greek moon-goddess (Roman Luna), was daughter of the Titans Hyperion and Theia, according to Hesiod (*Theog.* 371), sister of Helius and Eos; but different parents are named by other authorities—the Titan Pallas or Helius as father, Euryphaessa as mother. Selene drives the moon chariot, drawn by a pair of horses or oxen, or she rides on a horse or mule or ox.

Selene has few myths. Best known is the story of her love for Endymion which caused Zeus to cast him into an eternal sleep in a cave on Mount Latmus, where Selene visits him. In another story Pan loved Selene and lured her into the woods. We are also told that Zeus and Selene were parents of Herse, the dew (Alcman, fr. 39 Bergk), and that Helius and Selene were parents of the Hours (Quint. Smyrn. 10. 337).

Selene was identified with Artemis, probably before the fifth century B.C., perhaps because both had been identified with Hecate. Selene had little cult in Greece. There was an oracular shrine of Selene Pasiphae near Thalamai in Laconia (Plut. *Agis* 9; Paus. 3. 26. 1). Representations of the moon on ancient Cretan rings and gems do not necessarily indicate a Minoan moon cult, but may do so. In later times, however, the Phrygian moon-god Men (q.v.; Selene was sometimes called Mene) received worship in several Greek cities. It is the luminary itself rather than the goddess Selene that played a role in Greek magic, folklore, and poetry.

W. H. Roscher, *Über Selene und Verwandtes* (1890).    J. E. F.

**SELEUCEIA** (1) **ON TIGRIS** was founded *c.* 312 B.C. by Seleucus I Nicator, as the capital of his empire. It became the great outpost of Greek civilization in the Orient, and replaced Babylon as the entrepôt of trade between east and west. Built beside the ancient Opis, on a natural lake where the Nahrmalka canal from the Euphrates joined the Tigris, Seleuceia was a port for maritime shipping (Strabo 16. 739). The city had a mixed Greek and Babylonian population and a large Jewish colony; Pliny estimated the total population as 600,000 in his day (*HN* 6. 122). Even after the centre of Seleucid power had shifted to Syria, Seleuceia maintained its essentially Greek character. When the Parthians conquered Babylonia, they preserved its free constitution, and kept their troops and administrative officials at Ctesiphon (q.v.) on the opposite river bank. In the Parthian period Seleuceia was still a great commercial centre, in spite of the rivalry of Vologesocerta. But it became the seat of violent factions and dynastic quarrels; after a seven years' revolt (A.D. 35–42, Tac. *Ann.* 11. 9. 6) it was heavily punished. Excavations show that the city thenceforward gradually became orientalized; burnt down by Trajan, it was rebuilt in Parthian style. Its final destruction in A.D. 164 by Avidius Cassius marks the end of Hellenism in Babylonia.

M. Streck, 'Seleukeia und Ktesiphon', *Alte Orient* xvi. 3/4 (1917); O. Reuther, *Antiquity* 1929, 434 ff.; L. Waterman, *First and Second Prelim. Reports upon the Excavations at Tell Umar* (U.S.A. 1931–3); R. H. McDowell, 'Stamped Objects from Seleucia' and 'Coins from Seleucia' (*Univ. of Michigan Studies, Hum. Ser.* xxxvi and xxxvii, 1935); W. W. Tarn, *The Greeks in Bactria and India* (1950).
M. S. D.

**SELEUCEIA** (2) **IN PIERIA** was founded *c.* 300 B.C. by Seleucus I to be his capital, a function that was, however, soon transferred to Antioch, whose seaport it thenceforward remained. Captured by Ptolemy III *c.* 245, it was recovered in 219 by Antiochus III; its adult male citizens then numbered 6,000. It issued municipal coinage from Antiochus IV's reign, coined as one of the Brother Peoples (149–147), and in 108 received its freedom, which was confirmed by Pompey (64 B.C.) in reward for its resistance to Tigranes. It was the station of an imperial fleet; Vespasian improved the harbour, whence St. Paul had sailed on his first mission *c.* A.D. 46.
A. H. M. J.; H. S.

**SELEUCUS** (1) **I** (NICATOR) (*c.* 358–281 B.C.), son of Antiochus (presumably a Macedonian noble). He ac-

companied Alexander to Asia, but was never among his most prominent generals, though probably a close personal associate. After Alexander's death he obtained the satrapy of Babylonia (321), where he supported Antigonus against Eumenes, but nevertheless lost his satrapy and fled to Egypt (316). He regained Babylon by a spectacular exploit, and soon gained Media and Susiana also: from this year the Seleucid Era begins (7 Oct. 312, Macedonian calendar; but 3 Apr. 311, Babylonian).

Seleucus naturally joined the coalition of 'separatist' generals against Antigonus, and the victory of Ipsus (301) gave his kingdom access to the Mediterranean through Syria and (296) Cilicia. Henceforth his policy had a predominantly western bias, as illustrated by the founding of Antioch (300) to balance Seleuceia (q.v. 1), by his marriage to Stratonice daughter of Demetrius (298), and by the avenues for expansion which he sought in Syria and Asia Minor. He saw presumably that it was only by continued Greek immigration that a Graeco-Macedonian empire in Asia could survive. In the East he ceded the Indian provinces to Chandragupta early in his reign (304?). He finally won Asia Minor with the victory of Corupedium over Lysimachus (281), which also gave him hopes of seizing the vacant throne of Macedonia. He invaded Europe, but was murdered by Ptolemy Keraunos, who wanted Macedonia for himself.

The achievement of Seleucus was inferior only to that of Alexander, for he reassembled most of Alexander's empire in Asia. The dual character of his dominion, Mediterranean and continental, was implicit in his two capitals and his two wives (he never repudiated the Bactrian Apama, his wife since 324). He assured the succession by elevating his son Antiochus (q.v. 1) to share his throne (292). In character he seems the most humane, and certainly was one of the ablest, of the Successors.

ANCIENT SOURCES. For the Seleucids in general the sources are too scattered to be indicated briefly. See bibliographies to *CAH* vi, ch. 15 (W. W. Tarn); vii, chs. 3 (Tarn), 5 (M. Rostovtzeff), and 22 (Tarn); viii, chs. 6 and 7 (M. Holleaux) and 16 (E. R. Bevan). MODERN LITERATURE. *CAH* vi–viii; E. R. Bevan, *The House of Seleucus* (1902); E. Bikerman, *Institutions des Séleucides* (1938); R. A. Parker and W. H. Dubberstein, *Babylonian Chronology, 626 B.C.–A.D. 85* (1956); Bengtson, *Strategie* ii. 1 ff.; Rostovtzeff, *Hellenistic World*, esp. i. 422 ff; ii. 695 ff., 841 ff.; C. Edson, *CPhil.* 1958, 153 ff.
G. T. G.

**SELEUCUS** (2) **II** (CALLINICUS) (*c.* 265–225 B.C.) was the eldest son of Antiochus II and Laodice. In this reign (commencing in 246) the Seleucid Empire first suffered severely from the same centrifugal tendencies which had previously beset the Persian Empire. In the Far East, Bactria became definitely independent, and the native kingdom of Parthia also came into existence (248–247): in the West, Seleucid Asia Minor was lost temporarily. Seleucus was hampered throughout by dynastic troubles: first, the pretensions of his stepbrother which produced the invasion of Ptolemy III with its spectacular (though ephemeral) successes ('Third Syrian War', 246–241), and, later, those of his younger brother Antiochus (q.v. 8) Hierax in Asia Minor. Seleucus spent his life on campaign, but it remained for his son Antiochus ('the Great') to restore the kingdom.

W. W. Tarn, *CAH* vii. 716 ff.
G. T. G.

**SELEUCUS** (3) **III** (SOTER) (*c.* 245–223 B.C.), eldest son of Seleucus II, reigned three years only, being murdered (for reasons unknown) on a campaign against Attalus I of Pergamum.

**SELEUCUS** (4) **IV** (PHILOPATOR) (*c.* 218–175 B.C.), second son of Antiochus III, in whose lifetime he already held important commands, till finally he was associated with him in the kingship after the battle of Magnesia (189).

In his sole reign (which commenced in 187) he maintained correct relations with Rome and observed the terms of the peace of Apamea (188), which forbade political adventures in the West, and rendered them impossible by reason of the severe indemnity which it imposed upon him. But he also kept up friendly relations with Macedonia and Egypt, the two Powers of the Near East which remained independent of Rome. He was murdered by his minister Heliodorus for reasons which remain obscure.

E. R. Bevan, *CAH* viii. 495 ff. G. T. G.

**SELEUCUS** (5, *PW* 38) of Seleuceia on the Tigris (? *c.* 150 B.C.), described by Strabo (16. 1. 6) as a Chaldaean, i.e. member of a Babylonian astronomical fraternity, stands alone as a thoroughgoing supporter of Aristarchus (q.v. 1) of Samos' heliocentric hypothesis, which he tried to demonstrate (Plut. *Quaest. Plat.* 8. 1, 1006 c; *Dox. Graec.* 383). He wrote on the tides in opposition to Crates (q.v. 3) of Mallos; he attributed the tides to the moon's resisting the rotation of the earth; Strabo (3. 5. 9) says that he discovered periodical inequalities in the flux and reflux of the Red Sea, which he attributed to the position of the moon in the zodiac. T. H.

**SELEUCUS** (6) **HOMERICUS** of Alexandria was perhaps at the court of the Emperor Tiberius (Suet. *Tib.* 56). He is said to have written commentaries in Greek on practically every Greek poet. Besides works on Greek language and style and on Alexandrian proverbs, he wrote a criticism of the critical signs used by Aristarchus, a biographical work probably on literary figures, a theological treatise, a paradoxographical study, a miscellany, and a commentary on the *axones* of Solon. It is doubtful whether the Περὶ φιλοσοφίας mentioned by Diogenes Laertius is by this Seleucus.

*FHG* iii. 500; *FGrH* iii. 341; M. Müller, *de Seleuco Homerico* (1891); R. Reitzenstein, *Geschichte der griechischen Etymologika* (1897), 157 ff. J. F. L.; R. B.

**SELINUS** (Σελινοῦς, modern *Selinunte*), founded by Megara Hyblaea on the south-west coast of Sicily in 651 B.C. (Diod. Sic. 13. 59. 4) or 628 (Thuc. 6. 4. 2), lies on two low eminences commanding a fertile plain. Prospering quickly, it colonized Heraclea Minoa. As the westernmost Greek city it was in uncomfortable proximity to both Phoenicians and Elymians, and a pro-Punic policy, followed by tyrants in the early period, aligned Selinus with Carthage in 480 (Diod. Sic. 13. 55). Making their peace with Syracuse thereafter, the Selinuntines were wealthy enough to build a series of temples, the shattered remains of which still impress with their magnificence. Long-standing enmity with Segesta (q.v.; cf. Tod i², no. 37) brought Athenian intervention in Sicily (415) and the Carthaginian invasion of 409, when Hannibal sacked Selinus. Refounded soon after by the refugees, the city remained within Carthage's orbit until, for the better defence of Lilybaeum (q.v.), the Carthaginians destroyed it (250 B.C.). Its site became, and still is, deserted (disregard Pliny, *HN* 3. 91).

Bérard, *Bibl. topogr.* 89 ff.; Dunbabin, *Western Greeks*, 301 ff.; G. Vallet and F. Villard, *BCH* 1958, 16 ff.; I. Marconi-Bovio, *Atti del VIImo Congresso internazionale di Archeologia classica* ii (1961), 11 ff. A. G. W.

**SELLA CURULIS** was an ivory folding seat, without back or arms, used by Roman magistrates *cum imperio*. Its Etruscan origin was maintained by the ancient authorities, and their conjecture is supported by archaeological evidence, chiefly from Caere. The name was derived (Gell. 3. 18. 3 ff.) from the chariot (*currus*) in which the chief magistrate was conveyed to the place of judgement, and originally the *sella curulis* served as the seat of justice. Subsequently it became the attribute of all the higher ('curule') magistrates.

Mommsen, *Röm. Staatsr.* i³. 399 ff. P. T.

**SEMELE** (Σεμέλη), otherwise called **Thyone** (Θυώνη), in mythology, a daughter of Cadmus and mother of Dionysus (qq.v.). Whether or not Semele is Zemelo and originally the name of a Thraco-Phrygian earth-goddess (see e.g. Nilsson, *GGR* i². 568), it is certainly not Greek, whereas Thyone is. Such double namings are not uncommon, cf. Alexander–Paris. Her story consists almost wholly of her relations with Zeus and Dionysus. The former's association with her aroused Hera's jealousy, and the goddess, disguising herself (Ov. *Met.* 3. 259 ff.; Hyg. *Fab.* 167, 179, from older sources, cf. e.g. Eur. *Bacch.* 6 ff.), advised her to test the divinity of her lover by bidding him come to her in his true shape. She persuaded him to give whatever she should ask, and he was thus tricked into granting a request which he knew would result in her death. The fire of his thunderbolts killed her, but made her son immortal (cf. Ov. *Fasti* 3. 715 f.; Rose, *CR* 1922, 116). Zeus put the unborn child in his thigh, whence he was born at full time, and, after coming to maturity, he descended into Hades and brought Semele up (Pind. *Ol.* 2. 25 ff.; Paus. 2. 37. 5—Argive legend of the place where he went down to fetch her; and elsewhere); she thus became an Olympian goddess. This, if she was originally a goddess, is evidently secondary. She had a cult in Thebes in historical times (Eur. loc. cit.; Paus. 9. 12. 3–4).

The statement of Hesychius, s.v. Ἐγχώ, that this was another name for her, is pretty obviously due to a misunderstanding of a lost comedian's joke. Someone had said that Dionysus was son of 'Pour-out' or 'Fill-up' and his words had been taken seriously; see Rose, *CQ* 1932, 58. For Actaeon's love of her (in which case he can hardly have been her nephew) see Acusilaus in Apollod. 3. 30, and cf. ACTAEON. H. J. R.

**SEMIRAMIS** (Σεμίραμις), in Greek legend, the daughter of the Syrian goddess Derceto (*see* ATARGATIS). Exposed at birth, she was tended by doves till found by shepherds. Her first husband was Onnes, her second Ninus, king of Assyria, after whose death she ruled many years, renowned in war and as builder of Babylon (this point Berosus, *FHG* ii. 507, denies). At death she was changed into a dove, which was accordingly held sacred (Diod. Sic. 2. 4–20). The historical figure behind this legend is almost certainly Sammuramat, wife of the Assyrian king Shamshi-Adad V, and herself regent 810–805 B.C. in the minority of her son Adad-Nirari III. F. R. W.

**SEMO SANCUS DIUS FIDIUS** (for the full name see Dion. Hal. *Ant. Rom.* 4. 58. 4). A deity of puzzling origin and functions, said to be Sabine (e.g. Prop. 4. 9. 74; he is there identified with Hercules (q.v.), apparently from the interpretation of Dius Fidius as *Iouis filius*, and Sancus is, as often, corrupted, whether by Propertius himself or a copyist, into Sanctus). Semo appears to be his name, and suggests the Semunes of the Arval hymn, usually taken to be deities of sowing; Sancus would seem to be an epithet, perhaps connected with *sancire*, cf. the adj. *sanqualis*, which also shows a *u*-stem. Fidius pretty certainly is to be explained as cognate with *fides*, and Dius is simply 'divine' or 'heavenly'. Wissowa (*RK* 130 ff.) argued against differentiating Semo Sancus from Dius Fidius (cf. Warde Fowler, *Roman Festivals* (1899), 135 ff.), but Latte (*RR* 126 ff.) thinks that originally they were separate deities. In historical times he is connected with oaths and treaties (Wissowa in Roscher's *Lexikon* iv. 318 f., cf. *RK* loc. cit.), hence the common oath *medius fidius*. Hence he has some connexion with thunder. His temple stood on the Quirinal (Platner–Ashby, 469 f.); ascribed to Tarquinius Superbus and dedicated in 466 B.C., it contained a bronze statue of Tanaquil. He had some sort of cult on Tiber island also (Wissowa, locc. cit.). There was a temple of Semo Sancus at Velitrae. Conceivably a deity of sowing had been absorbed by Jupiter (q.v.).                    H. J. R.; H. W. P.

**SEMONIDES,** iambic and elegiac poet, originally of Samos, but connected especially with Amorgos (*Suda* s.v. Σημωνίδης, Strabo 487, Steph. Byz. s.v. Ἀμοργός). The *Suda* makes him a contemporary of Archilochus, Cyril places him in 664–661 (*Adv. Iul.* I. 12), and modern critics have tended to place him later still because of an alleged dependence, not only on Archilochus (fr. I and Archil. fr. 84), but also on Phocylides (fr. 7 and Phoc. fr. 2). A piece of elegiac verse on the shortness of life which some MSS. of Stobaeus (4. 34) attribute to Simonides of Ceos has been ascribed with some reason to Semonides. He is also said to have written a history of Samos in two books of elegiacs (*Suda*). Of his iambic fragments the longest, fr. 7, describes various types of women by comparing them to animals and shows the influence of popular fables; another, fr. I, discourses on the illusions and uncertainties of life and prescribes a mean between desire and despair. Semonides has plenty of humour and some satirical gift; he writes easily. His language is Ionic. *See also* IAMBIC POETRY, GREEK.

TEXT. Diehl, *Anth. Lyr. Graec.* i. 3. 50–64.          C. M. B.

**SEMOS** of Delos (*c*. 200 B.C.), Greek antiquarian, was a careful, scholarly compiler.

WORKS. (1) Geographical and antiquarian: *Delias* or *Deliaca*, on the geography, antiquities, institutions, products, etc., of Delos; *Nesias*, a work on islands; *On Paros*, *On Pergamum*, *Periodoi*.

(2) *On Paeans*, of which a valuable fragment survives describing the masks, dress, and performance of αὐτοκάβδαλοι, ἰθύφαλλοι, φαλλοφόροι.

FGrH iii. 396.                    J. F. L.

**SENATUS. I. REGAL AND REPUBLICAN ROME**

(*a*) *Composition.* The Senate was the council of the kings and survived the monarchy. Tradition attributes to Romulus the institution of a Senate of 100 members, but the oldest certain number is 300, evidently connected with the 3 tribes and 30 curiae. Sulla increased the number to 600, Caesar to 900, and Augustus reverted to 600. The distinction between patrician and plebeian senators, whatever its origin, must have been already definite in the second half of the fifth century B.C. The patrician senators, called *patres*, continued to retain certain prerogatives (cf. below). Plebeian senators were called *adlecti* or *conscripti*. Patricians and plebeians together were called *qui patres qui conscripti* or *patres ⟨et⟩ conscripti*. *Senatores pedarii*, who voted but did not speak, were probably at first those who had not held magistracies, and later magistrates of low rank. The senators were chosen first by the kings, later by the consuls, and at least after the *plebiscitum* of Ovinius (q.v.) by the censors. Late in the third century it was the rule to choose first ex-curule magistrates, who could take part in the sessions before formal appointment. In the time of the Gracchi plebeian aediles and, by the *plebiscitum Atinium*, *tribuni plebis* secured the same privileges. Sulla made admission to the Senate depend mainly on the quaestorship. Thus the Senate was recruited indirectly by popular election. Censors could remove qualified persons only if guilty of misconduct; the exclusion could be revoked by their successors. Certain professions (e.g. petty industry) and certain civic punishments or moral transgressions disqualified from admission. Freedmen or sons of freedmen were not usually admitted. A property qualification (1,000,000 sesterces) was first imposed by Augustus, but the senators usually had at least equestrian census.

Senators wore the *clavus latus* (q.v.) and special shoes. They had reserved seats at religious ceremonies and public entertainments. They were not allowed to leave Italy without the Senate's permission. Being excluded from State contracts and the possession of large ships (*see* CLAUDIUS 7), they were predominantly a landlord class. They had at times an exclusive or privileged position as judges in criminal and civil courts (*see* QUAESTIONES). As office depended mainly on wealth and birth, 'new men' were rare, and the Senate tended to become hereditary (*see* NOVUS HOMO, OPTIMATES). Membership being *de facto* permanent, senators exerted great influence on internal and foreign policy. The transformation of the Senate into a body of ex-magistrates avoided serious clashes between the *imperium* of the magistrates and the *auctoritas* of the Senate and made the Senate responsible in the last centuries B.C. for the direction of the Roman State. The Republic collapsed when military leaders destroyed the authority of the Senate.

(*b*) *Procedure.* The Senate was summoned by the presiding magistrates, either holders of *imperium* or, later, tribunes, according to an order of precedence. Sessions were held between dawn and sunset, but were forbidden by a *Lex Pupia* (2nd or 1st c. B.C.) during the *Comitia*. Only during the Empire were the times of meeting fixed—usually two each month. The meeting had to take place either in Rome (*see* CURIA 2), or within a mile of the city, in a place both public and consecrated. The first sitting of the year was in the temple of Jupiter Capitolinus.

Sittings were held in private, but with opened doors, the tribunes of the *plebs* sitting in the vestibule in the period before their admission to sessions. Each senator spoke from his seat. Freedom of speech was unlimited during the Republic. Augustus imposed a time-limit. First came the report (*relatio*) of the chairman or another magistrate, who submitted it in writing. Each senator was asked (*interrogatio*) his opinion (*sententia*), according to his rank (*censorii, consulares, praetorii, aedilicii*, etc.). Within each category the patricians took precedence, the senior patrician *censorius* of the *gentes maiores* (after 209 B.C. any patrician *censorius*) heading the list as *princeps senatus*. After Sulla the magistrate gave priority to the consuls designate or, in their absence, to any *consularis*; and *princeps senatus* became a merely social title open to plebeians. After the debate the different opinions were put to vote by a division (*discessio*). Sometimes *relatio* was followed by *discessio* without *interrogatio*. Certain resolutions required a quorum. Any resolution, called either *decretum* or, more commonly, *senatus consultum* (q.v.), could be vetoed by the tribunes. The urban quaestors kept the records in the *aerarium*. The publication of official reports in the *acta rerum urbanarum*, ordered by Caesar, was suppressed in part by Augustus. Improvements in shorthand made accurate reports possible.

(*c*) *Functions.* The Senate existed, formally, to advise the magistrates. The patrician senators retained two special functions. The first, which became a pure formality, was to ratify the deliberations of the People (and probably of the *plebs*) and was called *patrum auctoritas* (q.v.). The second was to elect an *interrex* (q.v.) for the arrangement of elections, if no magistrates were available.

The Senate advised the magistrates in matters of domestic and foreign policy, finance and religion, and on their legislative proposals. It could invalidate laws already voted by pointing out technical flaws in procedure. It suggested the nomination of a dictator, assigned the various duties to the magistrates, decided the *prorogatio imperii*, established the equipment (*ornatio*) for each magistrate and pro-magistrate, and marked out the two provinces destined for the consuls. In wartime it influenced the choice and the extension of commissions, fixed the number of the levies, and criticized the conduct of war. In finance it determined the rate of the tribute, supervised revenue and expenditure, and controlled the *aerarium*. It could order the censors to redraft contracts and regulated the coinage (at least of the mint of Rome). The practical decision of war, the conclusion of peace treaties, and the conduct of foreign policy were usually in the hands of the Senate, but the formal declaration of war and ratification of treaties belonged to the *Comitia*. It often received ambassadors and appointed senators to help the magistrates or pro-magistrates in concluding treaties and in settling the organization of conquered territory. The arbitration of the Senate was often asked by Italian communities, by provincials and client States. Religious life was controlled by the Senate, which contained the members of the principal priestly colleges and could order religious ceremonies and introduce new cults. In urgent cases the Senate could order dispensation from the observance of law, subject usually to ratification by the *Comitia*, and after the Gracchan period it could pass the *senatus consultum ultimum* (q.v.).

## II. THE IMPERIAL AGE

(*a*) *The ordo.* In Augustus' view the preservation of the Senate's prestige was vital to his intended restoration of the Republic. The Senate was left to govern Italy and those provinces which required only small garrisons (*see* PROVINCIA). Consequently it retained the *aerarium*. But the Emperor soon acquired control both of the *aerarium* and of the whole senatorial administration. The Senate retained only the supervision of copper coinage. Tacitus' statement (*Ann.* 1. 15) that in A.D. 14 Tiberius transferred to it the actual election of the magistrates must be somewhat qualified after the discovery of the *Tabula Hebana* (q.v.). Even in the Senate the imperial *nominatio* and *commendatio* (q.v.) reduced the importance of elections to a minimum. Thus the self-recruitment of the Senate by the quaestorian elections was influenced by the will of the Emperors, who could also, by *adlectio* (q.v.), directly introduce new members to any senatorial rank.

The Senate became a hereditary order, since, except for new men introduced by the Emperor, only the sons of the senators could become senators. Most of the high offices in the State (governments of provinces, with few exceptions, commands of legions, *praefectus urbi*, *praefecti aerarii*, *legati iuridici*, *correctores*, etc.) were reserved for senators. The senators became a privileged class interested in preserving the Empire. Future senators served at first a year in the army as *tribuni laticlavii*, then held the vigintivirate and entered the Senate at twenty-five through the quaestorship. The senators were called *clarissimi*, a title extended during the second century to wife, sons, and daughters.

(*b*) *Functions and authority.* The Senate developed judicial functions from republican precedents. A legislative power grew out of its advisory capacity. *Senatus consulta* had acquired full recognition as laws at least by A.D. 200. The Emperor had the right of convening, presiding over and laying matters before the Senate, and had the titular position of *princeps senatus*. The *relatio* of the Emperor took precedence. It was usually a written speech (*oratio*), which the later jurists quoted as authoritative rather than the subsequent *senatus consultum*. The number of senators attending meetings continually decreased. Mere *acclamationes* were often substituted for discussion. On the whole, the Senate lost its independence; its freedom was restricted to the choice of a new

Emperor when the throne was vacant, or during a revolution. The Senate, however, was always, in formal connexion with the People, the true repository of the *imperium*: it conferred his powers on the *Princeps*. The acknowledgement of the Senate, therefore, was the condition of the legitimacy of an Emperor (*see* AUGUSTUS, PRINCEPS). Furthermore, the Senate preserved a tradition of discussion, of competence, of respect for the public interest and for republican procedure, and represented a sort of public opinion—of the wealthy classes. Friendly relations between Senate and Emperors were taken to distinguish 'good' Emperors from tyrants. 'Good' Emperors allowed the Senate to try its members. *Damnatio memoriae* (q.v.) depended on the Senate.

(*c*) *From the Principate to the Late Empire.* In the late Republic numbers of municipal Italians and even some provincials entered the Senate, especially under Julius Caesar. Under the Empire, the number of provincial senators increased almost continuously, but until the time of Septimius Severus the majority were Italian. In the first century the provincials came mostly from Spain and Gallia Narbonensis; afterwards Orientals and Africans prevailed. The Danubian provinces never supplied many members.

The distinction between senatorial and imperial provinces was gradually eliminated and the *aerarium* became simply the city-treasury of Rome. Gallienus deprived senators of the command of legions and greatly reduced their share of provincial government. The increasing importance of the *equites* resulted under Constantine and his successors in a virtual fusion of the two orders. This new senatorial order recovered much administrative authority; it drew its recruits chiefly from the palatine *militiae*, the lawyers and other learned professions, and the army. Consequently the number of senators greatly increased. Constantine matched the Senate of Rome with another in Constantinople, which in A.D. 359 was made completely equal to that of Rome. Admission to the Senate was a complex procedure, based on an imperial codicil and subsequent election (normally formal by the Senate). Senators were divided into three groups, with different privileges: *clarissimi*; (*clarissimi et*) *spectabiles*; (*clarissimi et*) *illustres*. By *c.* A.D. 384 each Senate had about 2,000 members. By 450 the two lower classes were excused from attending in the capital. Under Justinian only the *illustres* were entitled to speak, *sententiam dicere*. The *praefectus urbi* usually presided. Senators were (with exceptions) free from curial burdens, but subject to special taxes. As a political body the Senate naturally declined still further; but it remained the representative of the Roman People and continued to legislate. As a body of great landlords, the Senate—or rather the two Senates—remained an essential element of the social structure of the Empire. The Senators of Rome were wealthier and more conservative than those of Constantinople. In the fourth century senators led the defence of Paganism in Italy and in the fifth many assisted the barbarian generals to destroy imperial authority. The Roman Senate is last mentioned in A.D. 603.

1. Mommsen, *Röm. Staatsr.* iii. 2 (1888), is fundamental, but does not entirely supersede earlier works (e.g. G. Bloch, *Les Origines du sénat romain* (1883); P. Willems, *Le Sénat de la république romaine²* (1885)). O'Brien Moore, *PW* Suppl. vi. 660, is very good. A. H. J. Greenidge, *Roman Public Life* (1901), 261 ff., 377 ff. E. Meyer, *Röm. Staat und Staatsgedanke²* (1961); A. Ormanni, *Sul regolamento interno del Senato* (1960). For the origins see also G. Pacchioni, *Att. Acc. Scienze Torino* 1925, 875 ff. A. Magdelain, 'Auspicia ad patres redeunt', *Hommages J. Bayet* (1964), 427 ff. On a special development, E. Gabba, 'Senati in esilio', *Bull. Ist. Dir. Rom.* 1960, 221 ff. Further bibliography in J. Gaudemet, *Institutions de l'antiquité* (1967).

2. *The Senate of the Principate*: Th. A. Abele, *Der Senat unter Augustus* (1907); M. Hammond, *The Augustan Principate²* (1968); H. Volkmann, *Zur Rechtsprechung im Prinzipat des Augustus* (1935), 93 ff.; A. v. Premerstein, *Vom Werden und Wesen des Prinzipats* (1937), 218 ff.; O. T. Schulz, *Das Wesen des römischen Kaisertums der ersten zwei Jahrhunderte* (1916). G. Forni, *Mem. Acc. Lincei* 1953; J. Crook,

Consilium Principis (1955); F. de Marini Avonzo, *La funzione guirisdizionale del senato* (1957); J. Bleicken, *Senatsgericht und Kaisergericht* (1962); H. Bellen *Sav. Zeitschr.* 1962, 143 ff.
3. *The Transformation of the Senatorial Class*: P. Willems, op. cit.; F. Münzer, *Römische Adelsparteien und Adelsfamilien* (1920); Scullard, *Rom. Pol.*; L. R. Taylor, *Party Politics in the Age of Caesar* (1949); H. Hill, 'Sulla's new senators in 81 B.C.', *CQ* 1932, 170 ff.; R. Syme, 'Caesar, the Senate and Italy', *PBSR* 1938, 1 ff.; id. *Rom. Rev.*; S. J. de Laet, *De Samenstelling van den Romeinschen Senaat gedurende de eerste eeuw van het Principaat* (1941); J. Willems, 'Le Sénat romain en l'an 65 après J. Chr.', *Mus. Belge* 1900, 236 ff., 1901, 82 ff., and 1902, 100 ff.; B. Stech, 'Senatores Romani qui fuerint inde a Vespasiano usque ad Traiani exitum', *Klio*, Beih. x (1908); C. S. Walton, 'Oriental senators in the Service of Rome', *JRS* 1929, 38 ff.; P. Lambrechts, *La Composition du sénat romain de l'accession au trône d'Hadrien à la mort de Commode* (1936); id. *La Composition du sénat romain de Septime Sévère à Dioclétien* (1937); G. Barbieri, *L'Albo senatorio di Settimio Severo a Carino* (1952); M. Hammond, *JRS* 1957, 74 ff.; id. *The Antonine Monarchy* (1959); A. Pelletier, *Latomus* 1964, 511 ff.; J. Gagé, *Les Classes sociales dans l'empire romain* (1964).
4. *For the Late Empire*: Ch. Lécrivain, *Le Sénat romain depuis Dioclétien* (1888); J. B. Bury, *History of the Later Roman Empire* i² (1923); J. Sundwall, *Weströmische Studien* (1915); id. *Abhandlungen zur Geschichte des ausgehenden Römertums* (1919). E. Stein, *Bull. Acad. Belgique* 1939, 308 ff.; P. de Francisci, *Rend. Acc. Pont. Arch.* 1946–7, 275 ff.; P. Petit, *Ant. Class.* 1957. 347 ff.; Jones, *Later Rom. Emp.* ii. 523 ff.; A. Chastagnol, *Le Sénat romain sous le règne d'Odoacre* (1966).
A. M.

**SENATUS CONSULTUM** was the advice of the Senate to the magistrates. In republican times it had no legislative force, but *de facto* it was binding. If it was vetoed, it lost its binding force, but conserved the *senatus auctoritas*. During the Empire the *senatus consulta* were at first implemented by a clause in the praetor's edict; after Hadrian certain *senatus consulta* immediately had the force of law. The *senatus consultum* was drafted after the session of the Senate in the presence of the presiding magistrate and some witnesses, usually including the proposer. If necessary, it was translated into Greek. Many *senatus consulta* are preserved in their Greek translation.
A *senatus consultum* usually contained: (1) the name of the presiding magistrate, date, place of assembly, witnesses; (2) the magistrate's report; (3) the introductory formula: 'd(e) e(a) r(e) i(ta) c(ensuerunt)'; (4) the terms of the *consultum*, which often confirmed its own advisory nature in references to the magistrates such as 's(i) e(is) u(idebitur); i(ta) u(tei) e(is) e r(e)p(ublica) f(ideue) s(ua) u(ideatur)'; (5) the letter *C* ( = *censuere*), indicating senatorial approval. In the imperial age was added the number of the senators present.
The texts of *senatus consulta* were deposited in the *aerarium*. Another copy was in ancient times given to the plebeian sanctuary of Ceres. The documents were classified, but not sufficiently to avoid losses and falsifications. The jurists often named them after one of the consuls of the year (*SC Orfitianum*) or more rarely after the Emperor who proposed them (*SC Claudianum*) or after the occasion of the *SC* (*SC Macedonianum*).
Many *senatus consulta* are collected in Bruns, *Fontes*⁷ (1909), and in Riccobono, *FIRA* i. For the Greek texts, P. Viereck, *Sermo graecus quo S P Q R magistratusque populi romani...usi sunt* (1888), is fundamental. P. Willems, *Le Sénat de la république romaine*² i. 248; ii. 204; O'Brien Moore, *PW* Suppl. vi. 800 ff. (with a list of *SC*). A. M.

**SENATUS CONSULTUM ULTIMUM**, a declaration of public emergency by the Senate, usually interpreted as authorizing the magistrates to employ every means of repression against public enemies (not necessarily specified *nominatim*), without being subjected to *provocatio* and *intercessio* (Sall. *Cat.* 29). The formula was: 'senatus decreuit darent operam consules ne quid respublica detrimenti caperet' (Sall. loc. cit., cf. e.g. Caes. *BCiv.* 1. 5). The proper name was *SC de republica defendenda*. The name *SC ultimum*, which is used in modern times, is derived from Caesar, loc. cit.
Its first certain use concerned C. Gracchus. The other assured instances are: the 'tumultus' of Saturninus and Glaucia (100 B.C.), against Sulla (83), Lepidus (77), Catiline (63), in the disturbances of 62 (Metellus Nepos)

and 52 (Clodius), against Caesar (49), M. Caelius Rufus (48), the disturbances of Dolabella (47), against M. Antonius, and against Octavian (43). It was last employed against Salvidienus Rufus in 40.
The exercise of this power by the Senate was hotly contested, e.g. in connexion with C. Rabirius (q.v.). The law of Clodius *de capite civis Romani* in 58 was also a partial condemnation of the *senatus consultum ultimum*.
Mommsen, *Röm. Staatsr.* i. 687 ff.; iii. 1243; *Strafr.* 257 ff.; C. Barbagallo, *Una misura eccezionale dei Romani: il S.C.U.* (1900); J. L. Strachan-Davidson, *Problems of the Roman Criminal Law* i (1912), 225 ff.; E. G. Hardy, *Some Problems in Roman History* (1924), 27 ff., 99 ff.; G. Plaumann, *Klio* 1913, 321 ff.; H. Last, *JRS* 1943, 94 ff.; Ch. Wirszubski, *Libertas as a political idea at Rome* (1950), 55 ff.; S. Mendner, *Philol.* 1966, 258 ff.; A. W. Lintott, *Violence in Rep. Rome* (1968). A. M.

**SENECA** (1), Lucius Annaeus, writer on rhetoric, was born of equestrian family at Corduba in Spain about 55 B.C. Of his life we know little; he was certainly in Rome both as a young man and after his marriage, and his knowledge of the contemporary schools of declamation implies that he spent much time there. He amassed a considerable fortune and may have held an official post in Spain or engaged in trade. By his marriage with Helvia, a fellow countrywoman, he had three sons—Annaeus Novatus, who after adoption by L. Junius Gallio became governor of Achaea, L. Annaeus Seneca (q.v. 2) the philosopher, and M. Annaeus Mela, the father of Lucan. He died between A.D. 37 and 41, after the death of Tiberius and before the exile of his son the philosopher.
His history of his own times, which began with the outbreak of the civil war, is lost. The *Oratorum sententiae divisiones colores*, addressed to his sons, consists of extracts, supplied by his retentive memory, from the declaimers whom he had heard during his long life, interspersed with digressions and comments of his own. The work comprised ten books devoted to *controversiae*, each with a preface, and at least two devoted to *suasoriae*. In our manuscripts only five books (1, 2, 7, 9, and 10) of the *controversiae* and one of the *suasoriae* have survived and these have suffered some mutilation: an abridgement made for school use (probably 4th c.) gives us some knowledge of the contents of the missing books of *controversiae* and, what is more important, supplies two of the missing prefaces.
Shrewd observation, a phenomenal memory, and an experience extending from Cicero's age into the reign of Gaius make Seneca's work a most valuable source for the literary history of the early Empire. The rhetorical schools were his lifelong interest, but he clearly recognized their excesses and their dangers. While the new movement fascinated him, his own sympathies were with the oratorical tradition of Cicero. The specimens of the handling of some forty themes by more than a hundred *rhetores*, great and small, if they are not verbally exact quotations, show remarkable skill in reproducing the styles and mannerisms of others; they are relieved by pithy incidental criticisms and scraps of literary reminiscence which serve to maintain the atmosphere of informality. Seneca's own views, both on individual declaimers and on the general tendencies of his time, are developed at greater length in the prefaces, written in an easy but terse and incisive prose which represents the transition from the periodic to the pointed style. The work bears out the character ascribed to him by his son: he was 'maiorum consuetudini deditus', a man of old-fashioned Roman strictness, fair-minded but suspicious of novelty and of Greek culture, critical of the decadence of contemporary society but combining seriousness with an ironic humour. *See also* DECLAMATIO *and* LITERARY CRITICISM, § 9.
EDITIONS. A. Kiessling (Teubner, 1872), H. J. Müller (Vienna, 1887), H. Bornecque (1902, with Fr. tr. and notes); *Suas.*, W. A.

Edward (1928, with tr. and comm.). H. Bornecque, *Les Déclamations et les déclamateurs d'après Sénèque le Père* (1902); W. Hoffa, *De Seneca patre quaestiones selectae* (Göttingen, 1909); H. Bardon, *Le Vocabulaire de la critique littéraire chez Sénèque le Rhéteur* (1940).

C. J. F.

SENECA (2), LUCIUS ANNAEUS, was born at Corduba, in southern Spain, between 4 B.C. and A.D. 1. He was born into a wealthy equestrian family of Italian stock, being the second son of the Elder Seneca and Helvia; his brothers were Annaeus Novatus, known as Iunius Gallio (q.v.) after his adoption by the orator of that name, and Annaeus Mela (q.v. 2), the father of Lucan. He was happily married to a woman younger than himself, Pompeia Paulina; the evidence for an earlier marriage is tenuous. He had one son, who died in 41.

He was brought to Rome by an aunt on his mother's side, the wife of C. Galerius, prefect of Egypt from 16 to 31. Little is known about his life before A.D. 41. He studied grammar and rhetoric and at some time practised in the courts, but turned at an early age to philosophy. His philosophical training was varied: he attended lectures by Sotion, a Sextian eclectic, Attalus the Stoic, and Papirius Fabianus, also a Sextian; he was later an intimate friend of the Cynic Demetrius. At some time he joined his aunt in Egypt, who nursed him through a period of ill health, returning about 31; through her influence he was shortly afterwards elected quaestor. On the strength of works which have largely been lost he had achieved a considerable reputation as a writer and orator by the time of Gaius' accession, and in 39, according to a story in Dio, his brilliance so offended the Emperor's megalomania that it nearly cost him his life; jealousy may not have been the only motive. In 41 he was banished to Corsica for alleged adultery with Julia Livilla, a sister of Gaius, and remained in exile until 49, when he was recalled through the influence of Agrippina and made praetor. He was also appointed tutor to the young Nero. In 51 Burrus (q.v.), who was to become Seneca's congenial ally and colleague during his years of political influence, was made prefect of the praetorian guard; and with Nero's accession in 54 Seneca exchanged the role of tutor for that of political adviser and minister.

During the next eight years the Empire, virtually under the joint control of Seneca and Burrus, enjoyed a period of good government. As *amicus Principis* and *senator consularis* (he was suffect consul in 56), with influential allies both at court and among the army commanders, unrivalled as an orator and man of letters, Seneca's power was ill-defined but real. His party is difficult to assess and he is reticent about his friends; almost all his addressees are *equites*. His policy, based on compromise and diplomacy rather than innovation or idealism, was modest but successful. But, as Nero fell under the influence of men more willing to condone and even encourage his crimes, Seneca's power declined and his position became intolerable. Nero's murderous acts had tarnished for ever the reputation of his minister, and in 62 the death of Burrus snapped his power. Seneca asked to retire and relinquish his vast wealth to Nero. The retirement was tacitly permitted, the wealth not accepted until later; in practice he withdrew from public life, spent little time in Rome, and devoted his remaining years to philosophy and the company of a circle of congenial friends. In 65 he was forced to commit suicide for alleged participation in the unsuccessful Pisonian conspiracy; the manner of his death, sympathetically described by Tacitus (*Ann.* 15. 64), makes painful reading but reveals an ultimate courage.

Seneca's extant works comprise, first, the ten ethical treatises which are found in the Ambrosian MS. (C. 90 inf.) under the name *dialogi*. They are, with the exception of the *De ira*, comparatively short, and their general content is readily inferred from their traditional titles; the dating is in many cases controversial. They comprise: the *De providentia*, dedicated to Lucilius Iunior, maintaining the theme that no evil can befall the good man, and probably late; *De constantia sapientis*, addressed to Annaeus Serenus and written sometime after 47; *De ira*, divided into three books, dedicated to Seneca's brother Novatus, and probably belonging to the early years of Claudius' reign; *Ad Marciam de consolatione*, a belated and politically inspired attempt to console the daughter of Cremutius Cordus for the death of her sons, perhaps his earliest extant work and probably written in 40; *De vita beata*, incomplete, addressed to Novatus (now called Gallio) and composed during the late 50s, partly as an apologia for his own way of life; *De otio*, of which only eight chapters survive, dated with some probability by its general theme to the period of Seneca's own retirement; *De tranquillitate animi*, which begins with a semi-dialogue with Serenus, of unknown but probably late date; *De brevitate vitae*, addressed to Paulinus, *praefectus annonae* under Nero and (now or later) Seneca's father-in-law, dated with considerable probability to 55; *Ad Polybium de consolatione*, an unattractive piece, written about 43 to win the favour of Claudius' freedman; *Ad Helviam de consolatione*, sent to his mother to console her for her son's exile, an agreeable essay despite the formal nature of the *locus*.

Besides the Ambrosian dialogues, we have four other prose works. The first is the *De clementia*, an eloquent recommendation of mercy to the autocrat, presented to Nero and written Dec. 55/6; of the original three books, only the first and the beginning of the second survive. The codex Nazarianus (Vat. Pal. 1547), the fundamental source for the text of this treatise, also contains the *De beneficiis*, an elaborate and rambling work in seven books, often dry and technical; it is addressed to Aebutius Liberalis and was written sometime after the death of Claudius, with 56 as a *terminus post quem* for book 2. Of much more interest is the *Naturales Quaestiones*, dedicated to Lucilius and written during the period of Seneca's retirement; it deals mainly with natural phenomena, though ethics often impinge on physics, and is of great scientific and some literary interest. The text is corrupt and broken, and the original books, apparently eight in number, have a disturbed sequence. To the same period belongs the longest of the prose works, the *Epistulae Morales*, consisting of 124 letters divided into twenty books; more were extant in antiquity. Their advertised recipient is again Lucilius, but the letters are not real letters and the fiction of a genuine correspondence is only sporadically maintained. Though the form may have been suggested by the publication (perhaps recent) of Cicero's letters, their antecedents are to be found rather in the philosophical letter, the declamation, and the diatribic tradition. The use of the letter-form adds a degree of artificiality absent from the other works, but their variety and informality have made them the most popular of Seneca's works at all times.

In a category of its own is the obscurely entitled *Apocolocyntosis*, a Menippean satire written in a medley of prose and verse. It is a clever, original, and amusing skit on the deification of Claudius, containing some serious political criticism and much bitter personal malice.

Other prose works have been lost, for the titles or fragments of over a dozen survive. These included letters and speeches, a *Vita patris*, some ethical works, geographical treatises on India and Egypt, and books on physics and natural history.

The bulk of Seneca's prose work is philosophical in content and an important source for the history of Stoicism. His own Stoicism, mellowed by eclecticism, human experience, and common sense, has a protreptic and practical purpose and subordinates philosophy to moral exhortation. The moralizing is given all the force which an accomplished rhetorician can provide and is enlivened by anecdote, hyperbole, and vigorous denunciation. The style is brilliant, exploiting to the full the literary fashions of the day while remaining essentially individual, and has an important place in the history of European prose. Non-periodic and highly rhythmical, antithetical, and abrupt, it relies for its effect on rhetorical device, vivid metaphor, striking vocabulary, paradox, and point; the point, a product of the philosophical as much as the rhetorical tradition, is refined to excess by the unflagging ingenuity of the writer. Aimed at immediate impact, the structure is often deliberately loose and need not imply an inability to develop a sustained theme. The brilliance and artifice, rarely letting up and unsupported by any real depth or originality of thought, is apt to cloy.

His most important poetical works are nine tragedies: *Hercules* [*Furens*], based generally on the *Hercules Furens* of Euripides; *Troades*, with a dual source in Euripides' *Troades* and *Hecuba*; *Phoenissae*, reminiscent at first of Sophocles' *OC*, but bringing in Jocasta (an unfinished, or mutilated, text); *Medea*, mainly drawn from Euripides, but other sources may here and there be latent; *Phaedra*, the Euripidean myth, but with a repentant Phaedra; *Oedipus*, with a considerable Sophoclean basis; *Agamemnon*, in which a debt to Aeschylus is rather to be assumed than easily traced; *Thyestes*, a horrific treatment of the gruesome myth, without extant source; *Hercules Oetaeus*, of dubious authenticity, with little in it, apart from subject, to suggest the *Trachiniae*—long, dull, and psychologically incredible.

A tenth tragedy, *Octavia* (q.v.), interesting as the sole surviving *praetexta*, and for its subject, but for little else, is obviously, from internal evidence, not by Seneca.

The tragedies suffer from the same weaknesses as Silver Latin epic, a tendency to exaggeration and a love of rhetoric. Some of the dramatic effects are spoilt by overdone horror, which leads sometimes to the bizarre, sometimes to the grotesque. The characterization, too, is often crude; but the characters of Hecuba, Medea, Phaedra, and Hippolytus are quite convincingly drawn, if not very subtly. In form the plays are modelled closely, like earlier Roman tragedy, on Greek, that is, dramatic episodes, interspersed with odes to be sung by a chorus (though it seems likely that the author thought of the plays as to be read rather than acted). The odes are written in a rather limited number of metres, chiefly the anapaestic, which tends to become monotonous. Some are written in sapphics, glyconics, and asclepiads. The odes are simple and direct in style, but they lack originality, and not much poetry is to be found in them. On the other hand, the episodes, which are written in iambic senarii, are often dramatic; the Latin can be crisp and pointed; and the stichomythia is sometimes even more telling, in style if not in matter, than it is in the Greek tragedians. The *Troades* is free from Seneca's usual vices; and in the *Medea* he has contrived a more dramatic end than Euripides.

Besides the tragedies we have seventy-seven epigrams, a few handed down under Seneca's name, and others attributed to him. Apart from the three epigrams specified as Seneca's in the *Codex Salmasianus*, their authenticity is highly dubious.

Seneca the man has appealed to few; his failings are obvious and out of place in a moral teacher; there were nobler Stoics. But the disconcerting rift between his preaching and his practice has tended to monopolize too much attention and so obscure the complexity of both his character and his achievement. To postulate a close correlation between the formal utterances of stock philosophical or rhetorical *loci* and the realities of biography is out of keeping with the literary convention, and leads to over-simplification. At the same time orator, statesman, diplomat, financier, master of a variety of genres, man of wide learning and experience, there is more to Seneca than his moralizing; he conformed to his principles too late to save his reputation, but this should not obscure the subtlety of the politician, the artistry and psychological insight of the writer, and the humanity of the man.

TEXTS AND EDITIONS. **Dialogues**, M. C. Gertz (1886), E. Hermes (Teubner, 1905), A. Bourgery and R. Waltz (Budé, 4 vols., 1922–42), L. Castiglioni and I. Viansino (Paravia, 3 vols., 1946–63, *dial.* iii–vi, ix–xii only); **De clementia and de beneficiis**, M. C. Gertz (1876), C. Hosius (Teubner, 1914²), F. Préchac (Budé, 1921, 1927); **Natural Questions**, A. Gercke (Teubner, 1907), P. Oltramare (Budé, 1929); **Epistulae**, O. Hense (Teubner, 1914²), A. Beltrami (1931²), F. Préchac (Budé, 5 vols., 1945–64), L. D. Reynolds (O.C.T. 1965); **Apocolocyntosis**, F. Bücheler–G. Heraeus (1922⁶), R. Waltz (Budé, 1961²), C. F. Russo (1965⁴). Various commentaries, including those of J. D. Duff (*dial.* x–xii, 1915), C. Favez (*dial.* vi (1929) and xii (1918)), H. Dahlmann (*dial.* x, 1949), P. Grimal (*dial.* ii (1953) and x (1959)), P. Faider, C. Favez, P. van de Woestijne (*de clem.* I, 1928, II, 1950), W. C. Summers (*Select Letters*, 1910), O. Weinreich (*Apoc.*, 1923).

GENERAL STUDIES. *PIR²* 617; R. Waltz, *Vie de Sénèque* (1909); P. Faider, *Études sur Sénèque* (1921); F. Giancotti, *Cronologia dei 'Dialoghi' di Seneca* (1957); A. Bourgery, *Sénèque prosateur* (1922); E. Albertini, *La Composition dans les ouvrages philosophiques de Sénèque* (1923); B. Axelson, *Senecastudien* (1933) and *Neue Senecastudien* (1939); C. Martha, *Les Moralistes sous l'Empire romain* (1865). There is a critical bibliography of the *Apocolocyntosis* for the years 1922–58 by M. Coffey in *Lustrum* 1961, 239 ff., and a survey of recent scholarship on the prose works, 1940–57, by A. L. Motto, *Classical World* 1960, 13 ff., 37 ff., 70 ff., 111 f.

**Tragedies.** F. Leo, 2 vols. (1878–9: repr. 1963); G. Richter (1902); H. Moricca, 3 vols. (1947); G. Carlsson, *Die Überlieferung d. Sen.-Trag.* (1926): *Zu Senecas Trag.* (1928–9); Translations: F. J. Miller, 2 vols. (Loeb, 1917); Thomann (Zürich, 1961—with notes). Bibliographical survey: M. Coffey, 'Seneca, *Tragedies*, 1922–55', *Lustrum* 1957, 113 ff.

**Epigrams.** *Anth. Lat.* I. H. Bardon, *Rev. Ét. Lat.* 1939, 63 ff.

A. K. and L. D. R.

**SENONES,** the last Gauls to settle in Italy, came from a parent stock which in Caesar's time inhabited the Seine basin (Caes. *BGall.* 2. 2, etc.). In Italy, ousting the Umbrians, they established themselves on the Adriatic coast between Ariminum and Ancona (qq.v.), the Ager Gallicus of historical times. Diodorus and Livy, but not Polybius, say that Senones led the marauding Gallic band that captured Rome in 390 B.C. Thereafter Senones remained a constant menace for 100 years until Rome subjugated them in 283 (Polyb. 2. 17 f.; Diod. 14. 113 f.; Livy 5. 35). They then disappeared from Italy, being either expelled or massacred. Their territory was used partly for colonies (Sena, Ariminum), partly for the allotments which Flaminius assigned to individual Roman citizens in 232.

For bibliography *see* CISALPINE GAUL. [ E. T. S.

**SENTENTIA,** in the language of Roman literary and rhetorical criticism, means the finished expression of a thought. In post-Augustan times the word is used especially to denote the terse, pointed, epigrammatic expression of a striking thought (cf. Quint. 8. 5. 2), which often is of general application (in which case *sententia* is equivalent to 'aphorism', 'wise saw'), but is not necessarily so; any striking thought expressed in this terse, pointed manner can be denoted by the word *sententia*.

Such *sententiae* are found in early Latin literature, e.g. in the Elder Cato (from whom Seneca (*Ep.* 94. 27) quotes 'emas non quod opus est, sed quod necesse est; quod non opus est, asse carum est', as an example of a thought 'packed into a *sententia*'). Quintilian (12. 10. 48) tells us that he finds such *sententiae* in Cicero; they are found also in the fragments of Varro's *Saturae Menippeae* and in the historian Sallust; and the mime of the late Republic afforded ample scope for their use (cf. the surviving *Sententiae* of Publilius (q.v. 3) Syrus; e.g. 'tam deest auaro quod habet quam quod non habet'). It was in the

Silver Age, however, when the influence of the rhetorical schools on literature became much more marked, that the employment of *sententiae* reached its full development. In prose, for instance, the moralizing essays of Seneca are full of them, and Tacitus uses them with masterly effect (e.g. *Agr.* 30. 6 'ubi solitudinem faciunt, pacem appellant'). So too in verse: e.g. the dramas of Seneca, the epic of Lucan (whom Quintilian, with references to this characteristic, calls 'sententiis clarissimus' (10. 1. 90); e.g. 1. 128 'uictrix causa deis placuit sed uicta Catoni'), the satires of Juvenal (e.g. 1.74 'probitas laudatur et alget'), and, of course, the epigrams of Martial.

W. C. Summers, *Select Letters of Seneca*, Introduction A ('The pointed style in Greek and Roman literature'); J. Wight Duff, *Lit. Hist. Rome* (*Silver Age*)², 1964, index and *passim*; K. Barwick, *Martial u. d. zeitgenössische Rhetorik* (1959). *See also* GNOME (γνώμη).
W. S. W.

**SENTINUM,** near modern *Sassoferrato*, on the eastern slopes of the Apennines in Umbria. Here the Romans defeated Samnites, Gauls, and possibly some other peoples in the decisive battle for the supremacy of Italy (295 B.C.). Both the Samnite general, Egnatius (1), Gellius, and the Roman, Decius (3) Mus (qq.v.), fell, the latter allegedly by *devotio*.

P. Sommella, *Antichi campi di battaglia in Italia* (1967), 35 ff.
E. T. S.

**SEPTIMIUS** (1), PUBLIUS, a republican writer on architecture mentioned by Vitruvius (7. *praef.* 14).

**SEPTIMIUS** (2) **SERENUS,** one of the 'neoteric' school in Hadrian's time, wrote rural poems.

Morel, *FPL* 148 ff.

**SEPTIZODIUM** or (**SEPTIZONIUM**), a freestanding ornamental façade, screening the south-east corner of the Palatine Hill at Rome, and dedicated by Severus in A.D. 203 (*CIL* vi. 31229). It closed the vista of the Via Appia like a stage-background, in which the elements were three large niches girt with three stories of colonnading. Earlier examples of *septizodium* occur in Rome (Suet. *Titus* 2, schol. cod. Berolin. fol. 337) and Lambaesis (*CIL* viii. 2657). The adjective ἐπτάζωνος is applied to the seven planets (Dio Cass. 37. 18), and although the word is not itself used metathetically of the days of the week which they govern (see Dombart, *PW*, s.v.), the representation of these gods upon calendars is a commonplace. Perhaps, therefore, these great ornamental façades, filled with statuary, mosaics, and numbers, served as public calendars as well as embellishments.

Ch. Hülsen, *Das Septizonium des Septimius Severus*, Winckelmannsprogramm, n. 46 (1886); Th. Dombart, *Das Septizonium zu Rom* (1922); L. Crema, *L'architettura romana* (1959), 545 ff.; G. Carretoni, *Forma Urbis Romae* (1960), 66 f.
I. A. R.

**SEPTUAGINT** (in abbreviation, LXX), the collection of writings which became the Old Testament of the Greek-speaking Christians. They are mainly translated from the Hebrew (or Aramaic) Scriptures but include, in books later called by Protestants the Apocrypha, some pieces composed in Greek and others translated from lost Semitic originals.

The name is derived from a story told in Greek by a Jewish writer professing under the name Aristeas to be writing a letter to Philocrates before the middle of the third century B.C. It relates that Ptolemy II Philadelphus, the contemporary king of Egypt, in response to a suggestion of his librarian, Demetrius of Phalerum, asked for a translation of the Jewish Law, and was sent from Jerusalem seventy-two (or seventy) learned Jews who on the island of Pharos near Alexandria made a Greek translation of it for the royal library. The story which at first

had some verisimilitude was embellished by later writers with legendary elements and was extended to include beside the Law the other translated books.

The translation was evidently done by different hands at different times. Nearly all of it was finished before the Christian era. Like subsequent translations into vernacular languages, it was intended primarily for those Jews who having migrated into Egypt and other Greek-speaking lands became more at home with the Greek language than with the Hebrew. Since the Christian movement very early became less Jewish than Gentile the Septuagint became its Bible and is quoted in the New Testament and in later Christian writers as well as by the Jews Philo and Josephus. Apart from Jews or Christians few ancient writers show any knowledge of it. Greek and Roman references to things Jewish are not derived directly from it. The citation of Genesis in the anonymous treatise *On the Sublime* 9. 9 is a single exception that 'proves the rule'. The influence of the LXX is probably first manifest in less literary circles, as in the Corpus Hermeticum and in the magical papyri. Translations of the Old Testament into Latin and some other languages were chiefly based upon the Greek, though Jerome in preparing the Latin Vulgate made increasing use of the Hebrew.

The Greek translations of the several books or parts of them vary in style and in degree of literalness. When not influenced by the original Semitic idiom, their Greek, as in the New Testament, and in non-literary documents of the period, represents the vernacular Hellenistic (*Koine*).

Since the Hebrew from which the LXX was translated is older than the major Hebrew MSS. known to us and than the standardized (Massoretic) text of the Old Testament, its apparent differences reflect some variation in the underlying Hebrew. The discovery in 1947 and thereafter of Hebrew scrolls or fragments at Qumran by the Dead Sea show that such differences existed before A.D. 70. These early MSS. sometimes agree with the Septuagint against the Massoretic text, sometimes vice versa, and (in the Law) sometimes with the Samaritan Hebrew. Just what is the history of such variant texts is still under debate.

In like manner the Greek MSS. show variation, suggesting that they were corrupted in copying or were deliberately edited or revised. This variation also is the object of continuing study. Again limited finds near the Dead Sea or elsewhere of fragmentary early Greek MSS. of parts of the Old Testament have provided fresh grounds for conjecture in this field. Each form of text whether Hebrew or Greek had its own associations and history.

Perhaps just because the Christians used the LXX, later Jews, if they wished a Greek translation at all, made new ones or revived earlier ones. Three of these are attached to the names of Theodotion, Aquila, and Symmachus, and were copied in columns parallel to the Hebrew and the Septuagint in the famous *Hexapla* of Origen in the third century of the Christian era. They are no longer extensively preserved.

ARISTEAS. TEXT. Teubner (Wendland, 1900), Swete (Introduction, see below). Translation: Thackeray (1917). Commentary: H. G. Meecham (1935), M. Hadas (1951), A. Pelletier (1962).
HANDY EDITIONS OF THE LXX TEXT WITH MINIMAL APPARATUS. H. B. Swete, 3 vols. (1887–94) and later editions; A. Rahlfs, 2 vols. (Stuttgart, *c.* 1935). Text with critical apparatus: A. E. Brooke, N. McLean *et al.* (1906– ), in progress; A. Rahlfs, J. Ziegler *et al.* (Göttingen, 1931– ), in progress.
INTRODUCTION. H. B. Swete, revised by R. R. Ottley (1914). Handbook: R. R. Ottley (1920). Grammar: R. Helbing (1907); H. St. J. Thackeray (1909); F.-M. Abel (1927). Concordance: E. Hatch and H. A. Redpath, 2 vols. and supplement (1897–1906); Lexicon: J. F. Schleusner (2nd ed., 3 vols., 1822).
INFLUENCE. A. Deissmann, 'Die Hellenisierung des Semitischen Monotheismus', *Neue Jahrb.* 1903; H. St. J. Thackeray, *The Septuagint and Jewish Worship*² (1923); C. H. Dodd, *The Bible and the Greeks* (1934).
SUMMARIES OF RECENT RESEARCH. H. M. Orlinsky, *Journal of American Oriental Society* 1941, 81 ff., and later essays; P. Katz in

*The Background of the New Testament*, ed. by W. D. Davies and D. Daube (1956), 176 ff.; J. W. Wevers, *Theologische Rundschau* 1954, 85 ff., 171 ff., and later essays.

ON THE HEXAPLA. F. Field, *Origenis Hexaplorum quae supersunt*, 2 vols. (1867–74). H. J. C.

**SERAPION** (1) of Alexandria, founder of the empirical school of medicine (*c.* 200–150 B.C.), wrote (1) Πρὸς τὰς διαιρέσεις; (2) Θεραπευτικά. He placed individual observation and experiment first, the statements of recognized authorities second, and argument from analogy third —to be used when the other two are lacking. He is much praised by Galen. W. D. R.

**SERAPION** (2) of Antiocheia, a mathematical geographer (2nd or 1st c. B.C.), held that the sun is eighteen times the size of the earth. He also wrote on astrology. He may probably be dated later than Hipparchus and Panaetius, and earlier than Ptolemy.

Ed. in *CCAG*. W. D. R.

**SERENUS** (1) **SAMMONICUS**, a voluminous writer of the time of Septimius Severus, was murdered by Caracalla's orders in A.D. 212. His only known work is *Res reconditae*. He had a library of 62,000 books.

G. W. Bowersock, *Greek Sophists in the Roman Empire* (1969), ch. 8.

**SERENUS** (2) (or **SERENIUS**), QUINTUS (or QUINCTIUS), author of a medical textbook in verse, *Liber medicinalis*, which may be dated between the end of the second and the fourth century. It depends in the main on the *Medicina Plinii* and on Pliny's *Natural History*. The author *may* have been the poet Serenus Sammonicus (son of the other Serenus Sammonicus, q.v.), who was a friend of Gordian I (b. *c.* A.D. 159) and the teacher of Gordian II (b. *c.* 192), and died before 235.

Ed. F. Vollmer, *CML* ii. 3; R. Pépin (1950). W. D. R.

**SERENUS** (3), mathematician, from Antinoeia in Egypt (formerly thought to be of Antissa in Lesbos), may probably be dated between Pappus and Theon of Alexandria (i.e. *c.* A.D. 300–50). Two of his works are extant: Περὶ κυλίνδρου τομῆς and Περὶ κώνου τομῆς; both edited by J. L. Heiberg (1896). A commentary on the κωνικά of Apollonius of Perga has been lost. Serenus is not of first-rate importance, but preserves much that is of value from earlier writers, notably Apollonius. W. D. R.

**SERES**, the Chinese and Tibetans, first known to Greeks left by Alexander in inner Asia. Aristotle knew vaguely of silk, but not of China. They became famous from Augustus' time as producers of silk sent by land to Asia Minor and by sea to Egypt. As trade developed, the name Seres was applied to Chinese and Tibetans as approached by land, 'Sinae' being their name as approached by sea from India. By Nero's reign further Chinese products were reaching the Roman Empire, the Seres were definitely placed above India, and some geographical details filtered through. In A.D. 97, after Chinese conquests in central Asia, Kan Ying visited Antioch, and *c.* 120 a 'Roman' Maes Titianus sent agents, probably to Kashgar and Daraut Kurghan (where 'Chinese' were met) and beyond. These learnt of cities— Daxata (*Singanfu?*, where Roman coins have been found) and Sera (*Loh Yang?*), seven months from Kashgar (or Daraut Kurghan), and gained rough ideas of Pamir, Tian Shan, and Altai Mountains, and of rivers (Hwang-ho and Yang tsze-Kiang?), but nothing of the sea east of China. They proved that silk was an animal product. Meanwhile one Alexander had sailed from India to Cattigara (q.v.); others reached the Sinae in China itself, naming their capital 'Thinae' (*Nanking?*). Yet Ptolemy made the Chinese coast face west and join Africa. In 166

a mission reached China from Marcus Aurelius, another in 284. About 550, silk-moth eggs were smuggled to Constantinople. By the sixth century A.D. it was known, e.g. by Cosmas Indicopleustes, that east of China lay sea, not land; and that in order to reach China by sea one must end by sailing northwards.

Some of the early glass vessels found in China are thought to be Roman—C. G. Seligman, 'The Roman Orient and the Far East', *Antiquity* 1937, 5 ff. In *Rome and China* (1939) F. Teggart develops a theory that coincidence of ancient barbarian migrations and invasions with war in the Middle East was caused by interruption of commerce by Chinese and (as a less disturbing factor) Roman aggression.

Ptol. *Geog.* 6. 16. 1 ff. (Seres); 7. 3. 1 ff. (Sinae); 1. 11. 7 (Maes); Warmington, *Indian Commerce*, 36–7, 71–2, etc. F. Hirth, *China and the Roman Orient* (1885). Honigmann, *PW*, s.v.; R. E. M. Wheeler, *Rome beyond the Imperial Frontiers* (1955), 183 ff., 201 ff.; Thomson, *Hist. Anc. Geog.* 131 f., 174 f., 300 ff., 366 ff., 411 f.; on Maes, M. Cary, *CQ* 1956, 130 ff. *See also* J. T. Miller, *The Spice Trade of the Roman Empire* (1969), index. E. H. W.

**SERGIUS**, author (date unknown) of *Explanationes in Donatum* (ed. Keil, *Gramm. Lat.* iv. 486–565; cf. also 475–85). In MSS. his name is often confused with that of Servius.

**SERMO** bears a variety of meanings in Latin. Besides being used for conversation, verse in conversational manner and with satiric bent (as in Lucilius and Horace), for style, and for the language of a nation (*in Latino sermone*, Cic. *De Or.* 3. 42), *sermo* is in rhetoric especially applied to the sketch of effective lines of argument well illustrated in the set of shorter pseudo-Quintilianean *declamationes* (q.v.). J. W. D.

**SERPENTS, SACRED.** As the δεισιδαίμων in Theophrastus (*Char.* 16. 4) when he sees a snake in his house takes it for a warning to invoke a god or found a *heroon*, it may be assumed that less pietistic persons had similar feelings regarding some serpents. They are, indeed, the regular accompaniment of heroes and of some, especially chthonian, deities. Sabadius is mentioned in Theophrastus; the god whom Aeschines' mother is alleged to have served, apparently Attis (Dem. 18. 260), had snakes in his ritual, which were handled by some of the officiants; Zeus Meilichius is represented by a huge snake (Harrison, *Prolegomena* (1922), 18 and fig. 1). When, therefore, Alexander of Abonutichus produced his new god in serpent form (Lucian, *Alex.* 7 ff.) he was following time-honoured tradition. In Italy the serpent was connected with the genius (q.v.), cf. Cic. *Div.* 2. 62, where Ti. Sempronius Gracchus, father of the tribunes, sees two snakes, a male and a female, in his bedroom and is told that according as he kills one or the other, he or Cornelia will die, which duly comes to pass. However, they are not found only in this context. Apart from foreign cults (as that of Aesculapius, see especially Ov. *Met.* 15. 669 ff., where the god in serpent form follows the embassy sent to bring him to Rome) and stories of foreign colour (as Tac. *Ann.* 11. 11. 6), in the old Italian worship of Juno Sospita the serpent played a part (Prop. 4. 8. 3 ff.). *See also* ANIMALS, SACRED; ASCLEPIUS, § 5; RELIGION, MINOAN-MYCENAEAN. H. J. R.

**SERRANUS**, an epic poet who died prematurely, mentioned with Saleius Bassus (q.v. 3) by Quintilian (*Inst.* 10. 1. 89–90) and Juvenal (7. 80).

**SERTORIUS** (*PW* 3), QUINTUS, a Sabine *eques* from Nursia, served under Caepio (q.v. 1) and Marius in Gaul and (with distinction) under Didius (q.v. 1) in Spain. Quaestor in 90 B.C., then legate in the Social War, he was offended by Sulla and joined Cinna, taking part in his capture of Rome (87), but opposing Marius' terror. Failing to gain advancement under Cinna, he became praetor (probably) in 83 and was given the whole of Spain (which he knew) as his province. He went there at the end of the year, but was driven out by 81 and, after many adventures, fled to Mauretania. Summoned back by the Lusitanians, he accepted their invitation and soon gained widespread support among the tribes, owing to his bravery, justice, and skill in exploiting their superstition. (His white fawn was regarded as a sign of divine protection.) Successful against many Roman commanders (especially—for several years—Metellus (q.v. 7) Pius), he at one time held most of Roman Spain. Popular with the natives, he tried to romanize their chieftains and acted throughout as a Roman commander, relying heavily on anti-Sullan Romans and Italians in the country, and even creating a 'counter-Senate' from among them and refugees from Italy. Claiming to be the heir of the lawful government ousted by Sulla's rebellion, he had much support and concealed sympathy in Rome, and Lepidus (q.v. 2) tried to co-operate with him against the Sullan order. After the arrival of Pompey (76), he fought (on the whole) successfully against him for three years, but less successfully against Metellus, who now knew his methods; and the two armies gradually wore him down. He tried to establish links with Mithridates—but refused to surrender Asia to him—and with the pirates. Finally, having lost some of his popularity and become embittered by failure, he was murdered (in 73 or 72) by Perperna (q.v. 3), who had joined him after Lepidus' defeat. His memory probably helped Caesar later.

A. Schulten, *Fontes Hispaniae Antiquae* iv (1937); the chief source is Plutarch, *Sertorius* (based in part on Sallust). A. Schulten, *Sertorius* (Leipzig, 1926); E. Gabba, *Athenaeum* 1954, 293 (with bibliography).
E. B.

**SERVASIUS,** SULPICIUS LUPERCUS, JUNIOR ('Serbastus', cod. Leid. Voss. of Ausonius; 'Sebastus', Schryver, Baehrens; 'Servastus', Wernsdorf), a fourth-century A.D. schoolman of uncertain name, has left three Sapphic stanzas *De vetustate*, and forty-two elegiac lines *De cupiditate*.

TEXT WITH TRANSLATION. Duff, *Minor Lat. Poets.*         J. W. D.

**SERVIANUS,** L. IULIUS (*PW* 538) URSUS (b. *c.* A.D. 47), married the young (Aelia) Domitia Paullina, older (?) sister of Hadrian (q.v.). He was *cos. suff.*, probably in 93 (unless he was the Sex. Iulius (?) Servianus given by the *Fasti Potent.* in 90). He succeeded Trajan (q.v.) as legate of Upper Germany (Oct. 97), and, apparently in 98, became legate of Upper Pannonia. Trajan allowed him to become *cos. II ord.* in 102 with Sura (q.v.), and may have regarded him as worthy to be his successor (so Xiphilinus; Zonar. and S.H.A. name Hadrian). His relationship with Hadrian may have been less close; Hadrian showed no special honour to his sister Paullina on her death (130), and allowed Servianus to be *cos. III ord.* only in 134, though Servianus seems to have been the last *privatus* to receive this honour. When Hadrian adopted L. Aelius (q.v. 2) as his successor, Servianus and Cn. Pedianus Fuscus Salinator (either Servianus' son-in-law who had been *cos. ord.* with Hadrian in 118, or this man's son) expressed dissatisfaction. The already ailing Hadrian ordered their deaths, perhaps by suicide, despite the ninety-year-old Servianus' protestation of innocence. Possibly Servianus had hoped that Salinator would be chosen as successor and Hadrian feared lest they create trouble for his successor.

B. Stech, *Klio*, Beiheft x (1912), no. 183; Syme, *Tacitus* ii. 636 and index; *Kl. Pauly* s.v. Iulius 93.         M. H.

**SERVILIA** (*PW* 101) was daughter of Q. Caepio (2) and Livia (sister of M. Drusus (2)), stepsister of M. Cato (5), and mistress of Caesar. By her first husband, M. Brutus (4), she was mother of M. Brutus (5) and by her second, D. Silanus (q.v.), of three daughters who became the wives of M. Lepidus (3), P. Servilius (2), and C. Cassius (6). With these and other connexions, her own high birth, and her strong character, her political influence was undoubtedly far-reaching, though best attested within the circle of the Liberators after Caesar's death (see e.g. Cic. *Att.* 15. 11. 1 f., *ad Brut.* 1. 18. 1 f.).

Münzer, *Römische Adelsparteien* (repr. 1963),336 ff., 426 f.; Syme, *Rom. Rev.*, see index; G. Gianelli, *Donne di Roma antica* iii (1945).
T. J. C.

**SERVILIUS** (1, *PW* 93) **VATIA (ISAURICUS),** PUBLIUS, grandson of Metellus (q.v. 3), praetor and propraetor (perhaps in Sardinia), he was given a triumph in 88 B.C. by Sulla and intended for the consulate of 87, but was defeated by Cinna (q.v. 1) owing to Sulla's unpopularity. Serving with distinction in the *bellum Sullanum* (83–81), he became consul (79) and, as proconsul in Cilicia, fought successfully against pirates and mountain tribes and first properly organized a territorial province there. Triumphing again (74), he became an influential politician, reaching the censorship in 55 (with Valerius Messalla (2)—they regulated the Tiber). He failed to become *pontifex maximus* in 63 (see CAESAR 1). During the 60s and 50s he generally shared Cicero's views. He died in 44, aged 90.

For his campaigns see H. A. Ormerod, *JRS* 1922, 35 ff.; Magie, *Rom. Rule Asia Min.* i. 287 ff. (with notes in vol. ii).         E. B.

**SERVILIUS** (2, *PW* 67) **ISAURICUS,** PUBLIUS, son of (1) above, as praetor in 54 B.C. supported Cato, but became a Caesarian and Caesar's colleague as consul in 48. After suppressing the disturbances of Caelius he governed Asia, whence he corresponded with Cicero in 46. After Caesar's murder Cicero affected to regard him as an ally, but knew him for a man of straw or worse (cf. *ad Brut.* 2. 2. 3, if genuine), and in 43 Servilius betrothed his daughter to Octavian and became reconciled with Antony. Octavian jilted Servilia, but compensated her father with the consulate of 41, in which he showed his usual caution during the Perusine War.         G. E. F. C.

**SERVILIUS** (3) **NONIANUS,** MARCUS (*cos.* A.D. 35), famous for his *recitationes*, the applause on one occasion attracting Claudius Caesar to join his audience (Pliny, *Ep.* 1. 13. 3). For his style in history see Quint. *Inst.* 10. 1. 102; Tac. *Dial.* 23; Peter, *HRRel.* ii. cxxviii, 98.

Syme, *Tacitus*, see index.

**SERVITUTES.** In classical Roman law this term was applied to restrictions on the ownership (*see* DOMINIUM) of land in favour of neighbouring land (e.g. a right of way from one plot over another to the highway, or a right to draw water from one plot for the benefit of another, or a right that nothing shall be built on one plot so as to obstruct the light to a building on the other). The term expresses the idea that one plot serves or is enslaved to the other (hence the modern expressions *praedium dominans, serviens*). A distinction was made between rustic and urban servitudes (*iura praediorum rusticorum, urbanorum*) according as they served a predominantly agricultural purpose or not (e.g. right of way or of water as opposed to right of light). Rustic servitudes were *res mancipi* (*see* MANCIPATIO), and were the older. Unlike a contractual right which could bind and entitle only the parties to the contract, servitudes bound and entitled whoever were the owners for the time being of the land in question.

Justinian included in the category of servitudes another class of restrictions on ownership, comprising usufruct (*ususfructus*)—the right to use and take the fruits of another's property, movable or immovable—*usus*—right simply to use—and *habitatio* and *operae servorum*, which were merely modifications of *usus*, applicable to houses and the services of slaves respectively. These personal servitudes (*servitutes personarum*) are like the others (now distinguished as praedial—*servitutes praediorum*) in that they bind whoever is the owner for the time being of a thing, but are unlike them in that they entitle a particular person, irrespective of his ownership of anything. They are personal to him and inalienable, and can be created only for his life or some shorter period. They serve, moreover, a different purpose. Praedial servitudes effect a permanent enhancement of the content of one ownership at the expense of another, whereas personal servitudes effect (to some extent) a division in time of a single ownership. Thus, usufruct was a method by which a Roman could give a life-interest to one person and a reversionary interest to another (e.g. to a widow and then to a child). *See also* FIDEICOMMISSUM, VINDICATIO.

P. Bonfante, *Corso di diritto romano* iii (1933); W. W. Buckland, *Law Quarterly Review* 1927, 326 ff.; 1928, 426 ff.; 1930, 447 ff. B. Biondi, *La categoria romana delle servitutes* (1938); G. Grosso, *Usufrutto*[1] (1958). See also the textbooks of Roman Law under LAW AND PROCEDURE, ROMAN, I. B. N.

**SERVIUS (1) TULLIUS,** the sixth king of Rome (traditionally 578–535 B.C.), is an indisputably historical figure, whose Roman or Latin origin (despite his later identification with the Etruscan *Mastarna*, q.v.) is attested by his character as an interloper in an age of Etruscan domination of Rome, and by his having built the temple to the Latin goddess Diana on the Aventine. Here the text of a treaty between Rome and the Latin League, traditionally attributed to Servius and known to authors of the Augustan age, was preserved. There is no reason to doubt the authenticity of the treaty, the invention of which would have been wholly purposeless. The tradition that Servius was the son of a maidservant, and that he built the walls of Rome (*see* WALL OF SERVIUS) rather than merely an *agger*, must be rejected. The constitutional reforms attributed to him (as a reputedly liberal ruler) are rejected by some modern scholars as fictitious precedents for laws passed in the fourth century on behalf of the *plebs*, but are accepted by others (*see* CENTURIA, CLASSIS). For his death, *see* TULLIA (1).

For papyrological evidence, see *POxy.* 2088; M. A. Levi, *Riv. Fil.* 1928; A. Piganiol, *Scritti in onore di B. Nogara* (1937), 373 ff. For Dionysius of Halicarnassus on Servius, see E. Gabba, *Athenaeum* 1961, 98 ff. For a conservative view of the Servian reforms see H. Last, *JRS* 1945, 30 ff. A. Alföldi, *Early Rome and the Latins* (1964), 212 ff.; Ogilvie, *Comm. Livy 1–5*, 156 ff. A. Momigliano, *JRS* 1963, 106 ff., confirms (*contra* Alföldi) the tradition that Servius did establish a sanctuary (though an *ara* rather than an *aedes*) of Diana on the Aventine as a federal sanctuary for the Latins; see also op. cit. 119 ff. for his views on the Servian organization. For recent attempts to lower the traditional date of Servius' reign, *see* TARQUINIUS (1). P. T.

**SERVIUS (2)** (4th c. A.D.—a young man about A.D. 384 according to Macrobius, q.v.), grammarian and commentator (called *Marius* or *Maurus Servius Honoratus* in MSS. from the 9th c. onwards). His greatest work was a commentary on Virgil (in the order *Aen.*, *Ecl.*, *G.*), for which he directly or indirectly brought under contribution much of the earlier Virgilian criticism. He relied greatly on Aelius Donatus, though he names him only when he disagrees with him. Since his work was designed for school purposes, he stresses grammatical, rhetorical, and stylistic points, but he does not neglect subject-matter, on which some of his notes show considerable learning. By way of illustration he quotes freely not only from Virgil but also from Terence, Cicero, Sallust, Lucan, Statius, and Juvenal. Often he reports conflicting views, but he retains his own judgement and is always a keen defender of his author. The Servian

commentary is found in a longer and a shorter version in manuscripts; but only the shorter was printed until Pierre Daniel in 1600 published the longer form, which he regarded as the original Servius. G. Thilo, however, in the nineteenth century showed that the so-called Servius Auctus or Servius Danielis consisted of (*a*) Servius and (*b*) the remains of a much more learned commentary (composed in the order *Ecl.*, *G.*, *Aen.*) which he attributed to some Irish monk of the seventh or eighth century (possibly Adamnan). In his edition he printed what he judged to belong to this hypothetical commentary in italics. The current opinion (cf. e.g. E. K. Rand, *CQ* 1916, 158 ff.) is that the 'additions' in Servius Danielis may be parts of the commentary of Aelius Donatus which Servius himself had not incorporated. The other extant works of Servius are: *Explanatio in artem Donati, De finalibus, De centum metris, De metris Horatii.* The *Glossae Servii grammatici* are an apocryphal compilation. *See also* SCHOLARSHIP, LATIN, IN ANTIQUITY.

Ed. G. Thilo (vols. i, ii, iii, pt. 1, 1881–7; vol. iii, pt. 2 = Appendix Serviana, ed. H. Hagen, 1902). Vol. ii (*Aen.* i–ii) of a new edition by a group of Harvard scholars appeared in 1946, vol. iii. (*Aen.* iii–v) in 1965. *Explanatio*, etc., ed. Keil, *Gramm. Lat.* iv. 405–48, 449–55, 456–67, 468–72). *Glossae* ed. G. Goetz, *Corp. Gloss. Lat.* ii. 507–33; E. Fraenkel, *JRS* 1948, 131 ff.; 1949, 145 ff. (= *Kleine Beiträge* (1964), 339 ff.). Schanz–Hosius, § 248. 2 and § 835. J. F. M.

**SESOSTRIS** (Hdt. 2. 102–11) was a mythical Egyptian king to whom were ascribed great conquests in Africa and Asia. In Ptolemaic times he was regarded as a person who had once lived and been heroized. Little of historical value can be gained from the somewhat lengthy discussion of the story by Herodotus.

K. Lange, *Sesostris* (1954). T. A. B.

**SESTIUS** (*PW* 6), PUBLIUS, as quaestor (63 B.C.) and proquaestor served under Antonius (q.v. 3) in Italy (against Catiline) and Macedonia. As tribune designate and tribune (58/7) he worked hard in the interests of Cicero and against Clodius (q.v. 1), suffering injuries in street fighting. Accused *de vi* (56), he was defended by Crassus (q.v. 4), Hortensius (q.v. 2), and Cicero (whose published speech propounds an Optimate programme) and acquitted. Praetor by 54, he was accused (perhaps twice) of *ambitus* and again acquitted with Cicero's help. Proconsul of Cilicia in 49, he joined Caesar after Pharsalus and served under him, remaining in touch with Cicero. He was married to a daughter or grand-daughter of Scipio (7) Asiagenus. He was not prominent after Caesar's death; but his son, a fierce Republican, became consul in 23 (as suffect to Augustus). Cicero (writing confidentially) thought Sestius' temperament morose and his style undistinguished (*Att.* 7. 17).

Cicero, *Pro Sestio*, is the main source. E. B.

**SESTOS,** a city of the Thracian Chersonese, possessing the best harbour in the Dardanelles, and commanding the chief crossing of the straits (to Abydos). Its original Greek population came from Lesbos. Darius returned by way of Sestos from his Scythian Expedition, and Xerxes here set foot on Europe, crossing the Dardanelles by a bridge of boats. Athenian interest in Sestos began with the occupation of the Chersonese by Miltiades; at this time perhaps it received an Athenian settlement. It was the first town to be freed from Persia by the Athenian fleet (479–478), and it was the chief Athenian station during the naval operations against Sparta in the Dardanelles (411–404). After a brief Spartan occupation (404 to 393 or 386) it reverted to Athens in 365. A rebellion against Athens in 357 led to its recapture by Chares, the enslavement of the population, and the establishment of an Athenian cleruchy (352). After a frequent change of overlords in the Hellenistic age it became a free city under Roman rule, but it lost its position as the principal crossing-point between Europe and Asia to Byzantium.

S. Casson, *Macedonia, Thrace and Illyria* (1926), 210 ff.; U. Kahrstedt, 'Beiträge zur Geschichte der Thrakischen Chersones', *Deutsche Beiträge zur Altertumwissenschaft* vi (1954). M. C.

**SET** (called **Typhon** by the Greeks) was a god of Upper Egypt. He appears in the myth of Osiris as the wicked brother who murders the great god of the underworld and wounds his son Horus. The role of Set in this myth was well known to the Greeks, hence he is the wicked Typhon in Plutarch's essay concerning Isis and Osiris (13 ff.). The Greek Typhon (q.v.) was a wicked son of Gaea and Tartarus who was overcome by Zeus, just as Horus finally overcame Set.

A. Erman, *Die Religion der Ägypter* (1934); G. Roeder, art. 'Set' in Roscher's *Lexikon*; J. G. Griffiths, *The Conflict of Horus and Seth* (1960). T. A. B.

**SEVERUS** (1), LUCIUS SEPTIMIUS (*PW* s.v. Severus, 13), Emperor A.D. 193–211. Born A.D. 145 or 146, he came from an equestrian family, with senatorial connexions, from Lepcis Magna in north Africa. He had a distinguished military career, was consul in 190, and subsequently governor of Upper Pannonia. He was hailed as Emperor at Carnuntum on 13 Apr. 193 after the murder of Pertinax and elevation of Didius Julianus, and entered Rome without resistance on 9 June. His first act was to dismiss the Praetorians and constitute a new guard for which all legionaries were eligible. The memory of Pertinax was rehabilitated, and after granting the title of Caesar to Clodius Albinus, governor of Britain, he set out for the East against a rival claimant, Pescennius (q.v.) Niger.

Victories by Septimius' guards at Perinthus, Cyzicus, and Nicaea were followed by a decisive battle at Issus (194), and punitive expeditions in 195 against the Osroeni and other Parthian vassals who had helped Niger. To prevent a recurrence of civil war Syria was divided into two provinces, Coele and Phoenice. Septimius was determined to found a vast dynasty and hastened the inevitable conflict with Albinus; before returning to Europe, he raised his son Caracalla to the rank of Caesar and adopted himself into the family of the Antonines (196). The issue was settled at a battle near Lugdunum (Feb. 197). Britain, like Syria, was divided into two provinces, and a rigorous persecution of the senatorial adherents of Niger and Albinus initiated.

After a short stay in Rome Septimius moved east to retaliate against Parthia for its support of Niger. A successful campaign culminated in the fall of Ctesiphon (Dec. 197). After two abortive attacks on the desert fortress of Hatra the war ended with the annexation of Osroene and Mesopotamia (199). The next two years were spent in Syria and Egypt, where Alexandria was given a municipal council. On 1 Jan. 202 Septimius and Caracalla became joint-consuls at Antioch, and then returned to Rome.

Septimius spent much of the next six years in Rome but visited Africa in 203–4. In 208 he set out with his wife and two sons for Britain. In the hope of intimidating the Caledonians Scotland was invaded, but the Roman losses were severe, and a temporary peace was patched up in the autumn of 210. Worn out by sickness and broken in spirit by Caracalla's unfilial conduct he died at York in 211.

Septimius wanted a more thorough control of all aspects of imperial life, and found the equestrian order the best source of recruits for the administration. The number of equestrian posts was substantially increased at all levels, and occasionally *vicarii*, who were equestrian procurators, replaced regular senatorial governors. The Senate as a body lost authority, though individual senators of Italian, African, and Oriental origin still pursued influential careers. Severus was keenly interested in the administration of justice, and humane and equitable tendencies persisted; the jurist Papinian was praetorian prefect from 205, and Paulus and Ulpian were active at the same time.

A new department of the treasury was set up, the *res privata*; it included all the extensive properties confiscated by Severus, and most of the inherited Antonine properties. Severus was ruthless in his exactions, but his expenditures were large both on campaigns and in the raising of new legions. The pay of the soldiers was increased from 300 to 500 *denarii*. More to be criticized were six *liberalitates* to the people of Rome, the revival of the alimentary system, and a substantial public building programme in Rome which included an arch in the Forum, a palace on the Palatine, and the Septizodium (q.v.). Yet he left a huge surplus at his death.

The chief military reform was the constitution of the new Guard, which henceforth served as a seminary for officers. This change represents not a barbarization but a democratization of the army, just as the stationing of Legio II Parthica at Albanum illustrates Septimius' policy of placing Italy on a level with the provinces. New concessions were made to the soldiers, who were allowed to marry during their service and on their discharge enjoyed special benefits.

In the provinces Hadrian's Wall was repaired and outposts south of the *Limes Tripolitanus* established. New colonies, which frequently received *ius Italicum*, were founded, notably in Africa and Syria, where there was a generally high level of prosperity. Elsewhere, e.g. in Lydia and Egypt, the government seems to have been unable to prevent the exploitation of the peasants by landlords or officials. Severus' alleged 'un-Roman' outlook is highly doubtful; he had a thoroughly realistic appreciation of the military basis of the imperial power; the army was the factor that determined his policy, and to maintain its cost the civil population was subjected to a variety of imperial requisitions. On his death-bed the Emperor is said to have exhorted his sons to live in peace, enrich the soldiers, and despise the rest of the world.

Herodian 2. 11–3. fin.; Dio Cass. bks. 73–6; S.H.A. J. Hasebroek, *Untersuchungen zur Geschichte des Kaisers Septimius Severus* (1921); M. Platnauer, *The Life and Reign of the Emperor L. Septimius Severus* (1918); H. U. Instinsky, *Klio* 1942, 200 ff.; T. D. Barnes, *Hist.* 1967, 87 ff.; A. M. McCann, *The Portraits of S. S.* (1968). H. M. D. P.; B. H. W.

**SEVERUS** (2) **ALEXANDER**, MARCUS AURELIUS (*PW* 221), Emperor A.D. 222–35. This was the title by which Alexianus (b. A.D. 208/9) son of Julia (9) Mamaea was known, when he was adopted by Elagabalus at the age of 13 and made sole Emperor on the murder of the latter in 222. Throughout his reign he was under the influence of his mother.

Alexander's reign is represented in the *Historia Augusta* (q.v.) as a resuscitation of senatorial power, but this is largely illusory. The interests of the Senate were, however, apparently protected by its having some elected members on the Emperor's council. The humane trend in the administration of justice was carried on under jurists like Paulus and Ulpian. The violence of the soldiers was never far away, however; Alexander had to acquiesce in the murder of Ulpian by the praetorians who resented his discipline as prefect, and the historian Dio Cassius narrowly escaped the same fate.

In 231 Alexander and his mother left Rome for Antioch, to repel an invasion of Mesopotamia by the Persian king Artaxerxes (q.v. 4). The campaign, which took place in 232, was not an unqualified success, but Mesopotamia was recovered.

Alexander returned to a triumph in Rome (233),

but his stay was short, as news of unrest in Germany necessitated his presence on the Rhine. The army, part of which was sent direct from Syria, was concentrated at Mainz, but Alexander made the fatal mistake of trying to buy peace. This pacifism was interpreted as cowardice by the legions; looking for a leader of courage and energy, their choice fell on a Thracian peasant called Maximinus (235). Soon afterwards Alexander and his mother, deserted even by the Oriental troops they had favoured, were murdered.

Herodian, bk. 6; Dio Cass. bks. 79–80; N. H. Baynes, *The Historia Augusta* (1926), 57 ff., 118 ff. A. Jardé, *Études critiques sur la vie et le règne de Sévère Alexandre* (1925). H. M. D. P.; B. H. W.

**SEVERUS** (3), SEXTUS JULIUS, shows the preceding names Cn. Minicius (*PW* 11) Faustinus; the *praenomina* are occasionally reversed as *Sex. . . . Cn. . . .* He was a Dalmatian by birth, who rose to senatorial rank and had a brilliant career (*ILS* 1056) under Hadrian (q.v.). Preliminary and urban offices once discharged, he was successively commander of Legio XIV Gemina, governor of Dacia (c. 120–6), *cos. suff.* in 127 (*CIL* xvi. 72; *Fasti Ost.* s.a.), governor of Lower Moesia (128–30), of Britain (c. 130–3), of Judaea (c. 133–5), and then—the first to hold this office—of the newly formed Syria Palaestina (*AE.* 1904, 295, no. 9).

Lambrechts, *Sénat*, no. 93; A. Stein, *Die Legaten von Moesien* (1940), 66 ff. and *Die Reichsbeamten von Dacien* (1944), 19 ff. C. H. V. S.; M. H.

**SEVERUS** (4, *PW* 15), FLAVIUS VALERIUS, an Illyrian soldier of humble origin and boon companion of Galerius, chosen at his wish to succeed as Caesar in the West in A.D. 305. On the death of Constantius Chlorus in 306 Severus succeeded him as Augustus, and Constantine, proclaimed in Britain, was fitted into the system as his Caesar. When Maxentius rose in Rome (Oct. 306), Galerius ordered up Severus from Milan to suppress him. Baffled by the walls of Rome and deserted by his own men, Severus retired to Ravenna and surrendered, on the promise of his life, to the old Maximian. When Galerius invaded Italy in 307, Severus was treacherously put to death by Maxentius at Tres Tabernae. H. M.

**SEVERUS** (5), SULPICIUS—Latin historian who was born in Aquitania c. A.D. 360. A member of a prominent family, he studied law in Bordeaux and became a convert to Christianity c. 389 together with his friend Paulinus (q.v.) of Nola. After the death of his aristocratic wife, he organized under the influence of Bishop Martin of Tours a sort of monastic life on his own estates for himself and his friends. In old age he seems to have passed through a period of Pelagianism. He died c. A.D. 420. Gennadius wrote a brief biography of him (*Vir. ill.* 19), and we have also thirteen letters to him by Paulinus. His extant works are: (1) a life of (Saint) Martin of Tours which is an apology for asceticism and is supplemented by three letters on Martin's miracles and death and by a dialogue which compares Martin's feats with those of the Egyptian hermits; (2) a universal chronicle to A.D. 400 which is an important source for the history of fourth-century events, especially of the Priscillianist heresy (Severus disapproved of the execution of Priscillianus). The whole book is an interesting attempt to present a 'breviarium' of history from the Christian point of view: it uses Christian chronographers, especially St. Jerome, but also Pagan writers. J. Bernays suggested that for the destruction of Jerusalem in A.D. 70 Sulpicius followed the lost account of Tacitus. Sallust and Tacitus are his models in the matter of style.

Best ed. C. Halm (1866); ed. in preparation in *Corpus Christian.* by B. M. Peebles. For the Chronicle also A. Lavertujon (1896–9), with important commentary; for the life of Martin, J. Fontaine's commentary (1968). J. Bernays, *Ges. Abhandl.* ii. 1885, 81 ff.; Schanz–Hosius iv. 2, 472 ff.; H. Delehaye, *Anal. Boll.* 1920, 5 ff.; P. Hylten,

*Studien zu Sulpicius Severus* (1940), on style and text; S. Prete, *I Chronica di S. S.* (1955); H. Montefiore, *Hist.* 1962, 156 ff.; Ch. Saumagne, *Rev. Hist.* 1964, 67 ff.; J. Fontaine, *Mél. Chr. Mohrmann* (1964), 84 ff. A. M.

**SEXI**, a Phoenician settlement at Almuñecar on the coast of southern Spain in Baetica, at least as old as the eighth century B.C. Egyptian alabaster vessels with the seals of the XXII Dynasty (870–847) from Tanais in Egypt have been found; also seventh-century protocorinthian pottery. The later coinage depicts the tunny fish; salt-fish was a chief industry in Roman times.

M. Pellicer, *Excavaciones en el Cerro de S. Cristóbal* (1962), *Madrider Mitteil.* 1963, 9 ff.; A. Vives, *La Moneda hispánica* (1926), iii. 19 ff. H. H. S.

**SEXTIUS** (1, *PW* 13), TITUS, of obscure family, perhaps from Ostia, was a *legatus* of Caesar's in Gaul (53–50 B.C. ?) and perhaps also in the Civil War. In 44 he became governor of Africa Nova (Numidia). After Mutina he was ordered by the Senate to send two of his legions back to Italy for the defence of the State and to transfer the third to Cornificius (q.v. 1), governor of Africa Vetus. Later he attacked Cornificius on behalf of the Triumvirs, defeated him (42), and ruled both provinces till 41, when on request from L. Antonius he handed them over to Octavian's lieutenant C. Fuficius Fango. During the Perusine War he recovered them for Antony, and in 40 surrendered them to Lepidus. His descendants, some of whom assumed the surname Africanus, held several consulships.

Syme, *Rom. Rev.*, see index; T. P. Wiseman, *CQ* 1964, 130 f. G. W. R.; T. J. C.

**SEXTIUS** (2), QUINTUS, philosopher of the time of Augustus, founded a philosophical school which met with great success at first but did not last long. He claimed to be the founder of a native school of philosophy, but was in fact an eclectic, borrowing from Stoicism his ethical views, from Plato the theory that the soul is an incorporeal entity, and from the Pythagoreans a belief in vegetarianism. *See* DIATRIBE. He is probably identical with the botanical and medical writer Sextius Niger, whose work Περὶ ὕλης ἰατρικῆς was used by Pliny and Dioscorides. W. D. R.

**SEXTUS** (1) of Chaeronea, nephew of Plutarch, Platonist, teacher of Marcus Aurelius and Varus.

**SEXTUS** (2) **EMPIRICUS**, doctor of medicine and sceptical philosopher; date very uncertain, but probably between Galen and Diogenes Laertius, c. A.D. 200. He was a Greek (*Math.* 1. 246—use of 1st person plural), not from Athens; he may have spent time in Rome. He was taught by one Herodotus (Diog. Laert. 9. 116), who was well known as a doctor in Rome. The name Empiricus, which is mentioned by Diogenes (9. 117), puts him into the 'empirical' school of doctors.

Three works survive:

(1) Πυρρώνειοι ὑποτυπώσεις (= *Outlines of Pyrrhonism*) in three books, the first an outline of the case for philosophical scepticism, the last two a summary rejection of dogmatic philosophies, divided by subject-matter.

(2) Πρὸς λογικούς A–B, Πρὸς φυσικούς A–B, and Πρὸς ἠθικούς (= *Adversus Mathematicos* VII–XI), a fuller critique of various philosophical systems.

(3) Πρὸς μαθηματικούς (= *Adversus Mathematicos* I–VI = *Against the Professors* I–VI), divided as follows: *Against I the Grammarians*; II *the Rhetoricians*; III *the Geometers*; IV *the Arithmeticians*; V *the Astrologers*; VI *the Musicians*.

Although he used compilations rather than original sources, Sextus is a valuable source of information on earlier philosophy. He has a much better appreciation of an argument than the idiotic and scandalous Diogenes Laertius. In particular, he is one of the best sources for Stoic logic. His original contribution is small.

Greek text, ed. Mutschmann, rev. J. Mau and K. Janáček (Teubner 1954– ); Gk. text and Eng. trans., ed. J. B. Bury (Loeb Classical Library, 1933–49). N. MacColl, *The Greek Sceptics, Pyrrho to Sextus* (1869); M. Patrick, *The Greek Sceptics* (1929); V. Brochard, *Les Sceptiques grecs*[1] (1923); W. Heintz, *Studien zu Sextus Empiricus* (1932); K. Janáček, *Prolegomena to Sextus Empiricus* (Acta Universitatis Palackianae Olomucensis 4, 1948); B. Mates, 'Stoic Logic and the text of S. E.' *AJPhil.* 1949, 295 ff.; P. P. Hallie and G. Etheridge, *Scepticism, Man and God* (1964; sel. Eng. trans. with notes).  D. J. F.

**SEXTUS** (3), originator of a collection of gnomes, Σέξτου γνῶμαι, mentioned by Origen and translated into Latin by Rufinus, who gave it the name of *Anulus*. The Syriac translation bears the title *Dicta selecta sancti Xysti episcopi Romani*, but Jerome argues against the authorship of Xystus (A.D. 256–8) and calls the author Sextus Pythagoreus. The original collection was probably non-Christian and made in the second century A.D., but additions implying a Christian background were gradually made, though definite allusions to Christ or to Christian doctrine were avoided.

Ed. A. Elter (1891–2). H. Chadwick, *The Sentences of Sextus* (1959).  W. D. R.

**SHIPS.** The shipping of the ancient Mediterranean consisted of two main types of vessels—the slim, light-draught war-galley (*see* TRIREME, QUINQUEREME) and the heavy, slow merchant ship. The distinction between these, which accompanied the separation of merchant and pirate in the archaic Greek period, reflects the wide difference in functions: the merchant ship kept the sea night and day with heavy cargoes, in all but the worst weather; for the warship, considerations of seaworthiness were subordinate to efficiency and handiness in battle. Fleets of war, in consequence, often found blockades and long cruises dangerous.

The proportion of length to breadth, in the galley about 7:1, approximated to 4:1 for the transport. Merchant and war-vessels alike were constructed from wood, chiefly larch, cypress, and fir (Theophrastus, *Hist. Pl.* 5. 7). As today, a keel was set upon ways in a dockyard; to this shipwrights attached ribs, upon which the planking of the hull was nailed. Strengthening cables seem to have taken the place of stringers parallel to the keel in some cases. The prow of the merchant vessel was simple, without ram or voluted prow-post; the stern-post, which curved back towards the prow, on cargo ships often resembled a goose's neck. While war-galleys were at most decked only on prow and stern, other craft were usually completely decked by 400 B.C. and had a cabin aft. In the stern were a ladder for use if the ship were beached, usually an anchor in addition to the prow-anchor, and the tutelary image of some god, from which the ship might take its name. This name, or some indicative symbol, was often placed on the prow. The steering-gear consisted of two large rudder-oars, one projecting on either side of the stern.

Merchant craft, having a permanent mast, relied chiefly on sail, though long sweeps could be used. At first they had one mast, which bore a square sail, made from linen or sometimes from hides; later a small forward mast was added, and in the Roman Empire two or three main masts are sometimes found, with triangular sails above the main yard. Such sailing-vessels apparently made three to four knots in normal conditions (*see* NAVIGATION).

With the spread of commerce merchant vessels ncreased in size. The unique *Alexandreia* of Hieron II could carry perhaps 1,600 tons, and the Alexandrian grain-ship *Isis*, of the second century A.D., measured

roughly 180 by 45 feet, with a depth of 44 feet and a carrying capacity of 1,200 tons. These were exceptional; but by the Roman Empire the average *navis oneraria* rated perhaps at 50 tons.

Acts xxvii–xxviii; Lucian, *The Ship*. E. Assmann, 'Seewesen' in A. Baumeister's *Denkmäler des klassischen Altertums* (1888; numerous reproductions); F. Miltner, *PW*, s.v. 'Seewesen'; C. Torr, *Ancient Ships* (1894); J. S. Morison and R. J. Williams, *Greek Oared Ships, 900–322 B.C.* (1968); L. Casson, *The Ancient Mariners* (U.S.A. 1959); id. 'Harbour and River Boats of Ancient Rome', *JRS* 1965, 31 ff.  C. G. S.

**SIBYLLA.** This word, of uncertain etymology, appears first in Heraclitus (ap. Plut. *Pyth. Or.* 6; Clem. Al. *Strom.* 1. 70. 3), and was early used as a proper name (e.g. Ar. *Pax* 1095, 1116). As a single prophetic female the Sibyl was variously localized, and legends of her wanderings account for her presence at different spots, but as early as Heraclides Ponticus (Clem. *Strom.* 1. 108. 3) she became pluralized, and thereafter we find two, three, four, five, six, or ten Sibyls, in different places and some bearing individual names, since the term Sibyl had now become generic. Varro's *Res Divinae* (ap. Lact. *Inst.* 1. 6. 8–12) lists ten: 1. Persian; 2. Libyan; 3. Delphic; 4. Cimmerian (in Italy); 5. Erythraean; 6. Samian; 7. Cumaean (named Amalthea, Herophile, Demophile, or, in Verg. *Aen.* 6. 36, Deiphobe); 8. Hellespontic (at Marpessus near Troy); 9. Phrygian (at Ancyra); 10. Tiburtine (named Albunea). Sibyls at Delos, Clarus, Colophon, Sardis, Dodona, and elsewhere (A. Bouché-Leclercq, *Hist. de la divination* ii (1880), 175, 183. Buchholz in Roscher, *Lexikon* iv. 796–803) are doubtful and perhaps to be identified with some of those in Varro's list. For a legend of the Cumaean Sibyl *see* APOLLO, § 6.

The ecstatic character of Sibylline prophecy (cf. Heraclitus ap. Plut. loc. cit.) is described by Virgil, *Aen.* 6. 77–102. The content of such utterances was early reduced to written form, in Greek hexameter verses, the genuineness of which was often guaranteed by acrostics (Cic. *Div.* 2. 112; Dion. Hal. 4. 62. 6). They were originally, in the case of the Cumaean Sibyl (Varro ap. Serv. *Aen.* 3. 444), inscribed on palm-leaves. Collections of these verses were made for later consultation, and there is a famous story (Dion. Hal. 4. 62. 1–6; Pliny, *HN* 13. 88; Lact. *Inst.* 1. 6. 10–11; Serv. *Aen.* 6. 72, etc.) of the sale to Tarquinius Priscus of one such collection which was put into the charge of a special priestly college (*see* QUINDECIMVIRI SACRIS FACIUNDIS), to be consulted only at the command of the Senate, in contrast to the unrestricted consultation of Sibyls elsewhere. After these Sibylline Books had been destroyed in the burning of the Capitol in 83 B.C. a new collection was made from various sources to replace them. To the Jewish-Hellenistic culture and later to Christian influence are due many blatant forgeries, and fourteen somewhat miscellaneous books of oracles are still extant (ed. by A. Rzach, 1891; J. Geffcken, 1902: annotated collection, with good introduction by A. Kurfess (Tusculum, 1951)). The last known consultation of the books was in 363 (Amm. Marc. 23. 1. 7), and the official collection was burned in the time of Stilicho (Rut. Namat. 2. 52). The influence of Jewish and Christian interpolations, however, combined with the prophecy of the Cumaean Sibyl in Virgil's *Fourth Eclogue* to give to all the Sibyls a position in Christian literature and art somewhat similar to that accorded the Old Testament prophets.  A. S. P.

**SICCA VENERIA**, modern *le Kef*, a Roman town in Tunisia. Originally a Libyan community under Carthaginian rule, it became a *colonia* under Augustus (Colonia Iulia Veneria Cirta Nova Sicca). It was the centre of a cult of Venus, said to have been introduced from Eryx.

The town was the birthplace of Arnobius, and received substantial fortifications in the Byzantine period.

L. Teutsch, *Das Städtewesen in Nordafrika* (1962), 6, 173 ff.
B. H. W.

**SICELS** (*Siculi*). 'Sicel' appears to be a generic term applied by Greeks to the indigenous peoples they encountered when founding their colonies on the east coast of Sicily towards the end of the eighth century B.C.; they were supposed to have arrived comparatively recently from the Italian mainland (Hellanicus, *FGrH* i F 79b; Dion. Hal. *Ant. Rom.* 1. 22; Thuc. 6. 25), where their presence is traditionally attested in the south and perhaps linguistically also in Latium. Archaeology has shown conclusively that the Pantalica-Cassibile-Finocchito culture of the Late Bronze–Early Iron Age in eastern Sicily has affinities with the east Mediterranean and not with the Italian late Apennine Culture, as the sources would lead one to expect: this is in sharp contrast to the contemporary Ausonian culture of the Aeolian Islands (*see* AEOLIAE INSULAE). P. Orsi in 1892 divided Sicilian prehistory into four post-Neolithic 'Siculan' periods, and christened as 'Sicels' all the people of eastern Sicily throughout the Early Bronze Age Castelluccio and Middle Bronze Age Thapsos cultures: these two cultures are, however, considerably earlier than the period suggested by the ancient sources for the Sicel incursion, and their affinities are once more with the east Mediterranean. *See also* SICILY.

Dunbabin, *Western Greeks*; J. Bérard, *La Colonisation grecque*² (1957); L. Bernabò Brea, *Sicily before the Greeks*² (1967).
D. W. R. R.

**SICILY.** PREHISTORY. Ancient writers distinguished three native peoples—Sicani in west-central, Siceli in eastern, and Elymi in western Sicily. Thucydides (6. 2) attributes an Iberian origin to the Sicans, Italic to the Sicels, and Trojan to the Elymi. Archaeologically there is no differentiation of culture between east and west corresponding to the Sicel–Sican distinction, but the Italic origin of immigrants to Sicily in the Late Bronze Age is confirmed by evidence from the Lipari islands and north-eastern Sicily, showing phases of the 'Apennine' culture known as Ausonian. Surviving Sicel linguistic elements argue in the same direction. In south-east Sicily the pre-Greek culture does not show clear Italic affinities (*see* SICELS).

2. THE GREEK SETTLEMENT. Despite Thucydides' account, the Phoenicians did not apparently settle in Sicily before the Greeks, and their colonization was limited to Motya, Panormus, and Soloeis. The Elymi, whose principal centres were Segesta, Eryx, and Entella, became traditional allies of the Carthaginians. From *c.* 735 B.C. (Thucydides' date-indications in 6. 3–5 form the chronological basis) there followed a prolonged period of Greek colonization (*see* COLONIZATION and under the various Greek cities). The natives were ejected from the colonized sites, or (as at Syracuse) reduced to dependent status; occasionally (as at Leontini) there was peaceful coexistence. Once established, the Greeks themselves and their civilization by degrees penetrated and transformed the native area; in some places (e.g. Morgantina) the process was quite rapid. By the Hellenistic period the island was a Siculo-Greek amalgam. The Greeks exploited the island's economic potentialities, and imported Corinthian, Rhodian, and (later) Attic pottery illustrates the considerable trade with Greece. Markets in Africa, south Italy, and (after *c.* 500) Rome were also available. Temple-building and rapid urbanization attest the wealth and culture of the archaic period; the first Sicilian coinage belongs to the second half of the sixth century. The Phoenicians acquiesced in the Greek settlement, but

defended their enclave against Pentathlus (*c.* 580) and Dorieus (*c.* 510).

3. EARLY TYRANNIES. As in Greece, tyranny emerged, but the aristocracies were tenacious, while the threat, potential or actual, of Carthage and the Sicels affected internal politics; this in turn produced greater social instability. Early tyrannies in Acragas and elsewhere foreshadowed the despotism of Hippocrates (q.v. 1) of Gela, who was the first of the great classical tyrants in Sicily. His successor Gelon (q.v.) transferred his capital to Syracuse. A Carthaginian attempt, at the instance of some still independent Greek cities, to check Gelon and his ally Theron (q.v.) of Acragas met disaster at Himera (480). Under Gelon and Hieron (q.v. 1) Siceliot–Greek culture reached its classical zenith. It penetrated the Phoenician colonies, and the Elymi became increasingly Hellenized. After the deaths of Theron and Hieron the tyrannies soon came to an end. The attempt of the Sicel leader Ducetius (q.v.) to organize a national movement proved abortive.

4. THE AGE OF DIONYSIUS. In the latter part of the fifth century the cities maintained their mutual independence and were democratically governed. But democracy did not strike roots in Sicily as in Greece, and external dangers demanded a more authoritarian organization. The Athenians twice intervened in the island (427–424 and 415–413) on the basis of alliances with Leontini and Segesta, with hopes of ultimately controlling it; the first intervention did not succeed and the second (great) expedition ended in utter failure. Carthage now profited by the exhaustion of Syracuse to attempt the complete conquest of Sicily (409). Selinus and Himera fell in 409, Acragas and Gela in 406/5. In the days of crisis Dionysius I succeeded in establishing himself as tyrant of Syracuse; the Carthaginians were repulsed, and Syracuse, which came to control all Sicily outside Carthage's 'area' in the far west, prospered; but the cost was tyranny and the loss of political freedom. Dionysius' death (367) was followed, after a decade, by civil war; petty tyrants established themselves in the various cities, and the Carthaginians again intervened.

5. THE HELLENISTIC PERIOD. At this low ebb in their fortunes the Syracusans sent for Timoleon (q.v.), who defeated the Carthaginians and re-established settled government. His arrangements did not long survive his death (*c.* 336), and oligarchy prevailed. In 317 Agathocles seized the Syracusan tyranny and subjugated most of the island. When he died (289) fresh anarchy ensued; there were more local tyrants, Carthage again threatened, and the tyrant's ex-mercenaries (Mamertini) carved out a dominion for themselves in Messana. City-state Sicily was in fact in dissolution. Pyrrhus (q.v.) of Epirus was called in, but despite quick successes produced no lasting effect. Hieron II (q.v.) of Syracuse to some extent halted the decline, but his defeat of the Mamertini brought on a Carthaginian occupation of Messana and was the occasion for Roman interference and the First Punic War (264–241), after which most of the island became a Roman province. Hieron's kingdom remained autonomous and prosperous until his death in 215, when Syracuse went over to Carthage. After the Roman capture of Syracuse (211) all Sicily was unified under the provincial government.

6. THE ROMAN PROVINCE. The government consisted of a praetor (later proconsul or propraetor) with a quaestor in Syracuse and another in Lilybaeum. A provincial Sicilian council had no real power. Messana and Tauromenium, which had voluntarily accepted Rome's alliance, were distinguished as *civitates foederatae*; a few other communities were *liberae et immunes* (e.g. Segesta, Panormus). Of the remainder some paid a tithe (*civitates decumanae*) on a system established by Hieron II; the

land of others became *ager publicus*, for which they paid rent in addition to the tithe (*civitates censoriae*). All had some local autonomy, infringed by such governors as C. Verres (73–71) but generally respected, and issued small-denomination coinage until the early Empire. Under the Republic wheat-growing, cardinal to Rome's food-supply, was fostered; large *latifundia* grew up as a result of big Roman purchases of real estate. These were worked by slaves whose conditions provoked the serious rebellions of 135–132 and 104–100 B.C. The north-east of the island also suffered in 36 when Octavian expelled Sex. Pompeius, in whose occupation of Sicily he and Antony had acquiesced in 39.

7. THE IMPERIAL PERIOD. The island continued to prosper under the Empire until the barbarian invasions, and Latin and Greek culture long coexisted. Caesar apparently granted the Sicilians Latin rights. Antony claimed he had intended to make them full citizens, but Octavian was less generous. As Augustus he gave Messana and a few other cities Roman citizenship, and he founded veteran-colonies at Catana, Panormus, Syracuse, Tauromenium, Thermae, and Tyndaris. The old administrative system was replaced by one of (*a*) tax-free Roman *coloniae* and *municipia*, (*b*) tax-free Latin *municipia*, (*c*) tax-paying Latin *municipia*. A fixed levy replaced the tithe. *Latifundia*, among them large imperial estates, remained the prevalent agricultural pattern, especially as wheat-growing declined in importance. Yet village life, and therefore smallholdings, evidently flourished also, and in general the population in no way declined, even though some of the old cities (e.g. Morgantina) had by then decayed.

GENERAL. J. Bérard, *Bibl. topogr.* (1941); L. Bernabò Brea, *Musei e monumenti della Sicilia* (1958); L. von Matt and P. Griffo, *Das antike Sizilien* (1959); E. Manni, 'Recenti studi sulla Sicilia antica, Κώκαλος 1961, 216 ff.; M. I. Finley, *Hist. of Sicily* (1968).
PREHISTORY. L. Bernabò Brea, *Sicily before the Greeks* (1957); Lord William Taylour, *Mycenean pottery in Italy and adjacent areas* (1958).
GREEK AND ROMAN PERIODS. General histories of Greece and Rome; E. A. Freeman, *History of Sicily* (4 vols., 1890–4); B. Pace, *Arte e civiltà della Sicilia antica* (4 vols., 1935–49); Dunbabin, *Western Greeks*; A. G. Woodhead, *The Greeks in the West* (1962); A. Schenk, Graf von Stauffenberg, *Trinakria* (1963); J. Boardman, *The Greeks Overseas* (1964); R. van Compernolle, *Étude de chronologie et d'historiographie siciliotes* (1959); H. Wentker, *Sizilien und Athen* (1956); V. Scramuzza in Frank, *Econ. Survey* iii.
INSCRIPTIONS. *IG* xiv, with supplementary material in *SEG*; *CIL* x, pars ii.
COINS. G. F. Hill, *Coins of Ancient Sicily* (1903); G. E. Rizzo, *Monete greche della Sicilia* (1946).                           A. M.; A. G. W.

**SICINIUS** (*PW* 9), GNAEUS, a witty orator, as tribune 76 B.C. tried unsuccessfully to restore the powers of the tribunate.                                                              E. B.

**SICULUS FLACCUS,** *gromaticus* (q.v.), of unknown date; author of a treatise on categories of land-tenure in Italy.

**SICYON,** Corinth's western neighbour, stood in a rich plain 2 miles from the sea. The archaic town lay at the foot of a large triangular plateau which was the acropolis. Demetrius Poliorcetes transplanted it to the acropolis. The remains of this town include the theatre, stadium, agora with fountains and portico, and large Roman buildings.

Sicyon was founded from Argos, and owed Argos religious and originally also political duties. These were set aside by the tyranny which, begun by Orthagoras *c.* 660 B.C., and favouring the non-Dorian elements, lasted over 100 years. Its greatest power was attained under Cleisthenes, who led the forces which destroyed Crisa in the first Sacred War (*c.* 580), and also had relations further west. He celebrated his daughter's wedding with fabulous magnificence (Hdt. 6. 126). Sparta put down the tyranny and Sicyon became her faithful ally. In the third century its chief citizen, Aratus, gave it an important position in the Achaean Confederacy. Sicyon was a famous centre of art. In the archaic period it was a home of painting and pottery (Pliny, *HN* 35. 151–2), but the attribution of the 'Protocorinthian' vases to Sicyon is now discredited (H. Payne, *Necrocorinthia*, 1931, 35 ff.). In the fourth century it possessed the leading school of painters and produced the sculptor Lysippus.

P–K, *GL* iii. 1. 158 ff.; C. H. Skalet, *Ancient Sicyon* (U.S.A. 1928); A. Andrewes, *The Greek Tyrants* (1956), 57 ff.             T. J. D.

**SIDE** (Σίδη), city and harbour on the coast of Pamphylia. Founded, according to Eusebius, in 1405 B.C., it remained a barbarian city till resettled by colonists from Aeolian Cyme, probably in the seventh or sixth century. Arrian says, quoting the Sidetans themselves, that the colonists at once forgot their Greek and began to speak an unknown barbaric tongue. This story is illustrated by the peculiar script and dialect on coins and inscriptions of the city down to about 300 B.C. This has not yet been interpreted. The Sidetans were on bad terms with their neighbours of Aspendus, and were called by Stratonicus the most rascally of mankind. Side submitted quietly to Alexander, and in 190 B.C. was the scene of an indecisive naval battle between Antiochus III and the Rhodians, who were supporting Rome. In the second and first centuries Side was deeply implicated in the Cilician piracy, affording the pirates both a dockyard and a market for their prisoners. Under the early Empire the city was very rich and influential, but in the later third and fourth centuries became impoverished, largely owing to the inroads of the Isaurians. The ruins at Selimiye, or Eski Antalya, are extensive and were excavated from 1947 to 1966 by the Turks. Best preserved are the Hellenistic walls and the Roman theatre.

Arif Müfit Mansel, *Die Ruinen von Side* (1963).          G. E. B.

**SIDICINI,** Oscan-speaking neighbours of the Aurunci (q.v.) immediately north of Campania (q.v.). By threatening their chief town, Teanum, the Samnites precipitated the First Samnite War (343 B.C.) (*see* SAMNIUM). The Sidicini came under Roman domination, probably during the Second Samnite War, but remained technically independent until the Social War. They were rapidly romanized thereafter.                                       E. T. S.

**SIDON,** a city on the coast of Phoenicia, was ruled under Persia by a native dynasty which had close commercial relations with Athens and was already hellenized, as the sarcophagi of the kings show. The dynasty was confirmed by Alexander but suppressed in the early third century (the last known king was the Ptolemaic admiral Philocles), and Sidon became a republic, ruled by Suffetes. From Antiochus IV's reign it issued municipal coinage, still mostly inscribed in Phoenician. In 111 B.C. it gained its freedom, which was recognized by Pompey. It received from Augustus a great accession of territory up to Mount Hermon (*see* ITURAEA). Under Elagabalus it became a Roman colony. Sidon was a great commercial city and also possessed two important industries, purple-dyeing and glass-blowing; the latter art was discovered in the first century B.C. at Sidon, and the names of many Sidonian glass-blowers of the early Principate are known, chiefly from signatures on extant pieces.          A. H. M. J.

**SIDONIUS APOLLINARIS** (GAIUS SOLLIUS APOLLINARIS SIDONIUS), a Gallo-Roman of noble family, was born at Lugdunum (*Lyon*) about A.D. 430. He married Papianilla, daughter of Avitus, and through her acquired the estate of Avitacum in Auvergne. Avitus was proclaimed emperor, July 455. Sidonius accompanied him to Rome, and there recited in his honour, 1 Jan. 456, a panegyric in verse (*Carm.* 7), which was rewarded with a statue in Trajan's Forum. Avitus was soon dethroned. Sidonius then joined an insurrection with headquarters at Lyon, but was finally reconciled to Majorian, the new Emperor, and delivered at Lyon (458) a panegyric on him (ibid. 5). In 459 or 460 he held some government post at Rome. After Majorian's fall (461) he spent some years in his native country. In 467 he led a Gallo-Roman deputation to the Emperor Anthemius at Rome. On 1 Jan. 468 he recited his third and last panegyric (ibid. 2), after which he became *praefectus urbi*. He returned to Gaul in 469 and accepted the bishopric of Auvergne with seat at Clermont-Ferrand. Although ill-equipped for ecclesiastical office, he discharged his sacred duties with earnestness and success; above all, he upheld his people in resisting the Goths. In 475 Rome, to his dismay, ceded Auvergne to Euric. Sidonius was subjected to a mild imprisonment in the fortress of Liviana, near Carcassonne. Released in 476, he was ultimately allowed to resume his bishopric. The usual date for his death, 479, is probably a little too early. He was canonized.

WORKS. (1) *Carmina*: (*a*) 1–8, the three long panegyrics (in reversed chronological order) together with prefaces and dedications; (*b*) 9–24, professedly youthful poems, ranging from 4 to 512 lines, practically all addressed to, or concerned with, friends. (2) *Epistulae*, nine books, addressed to many friends and relations. Books 1–2 belong to the period before his episcopate. Some letters were specially written for the collection, the others were carefully revised. Both poems and letters throw important light on the fifth century. They show Sidonius as a genial and sympathetic man, a loyal friend and ardent patriot, but also as a rather narrow-minded aristocrat and literary pedant. His originality was limited, but he had a keen eye for external details. His language is absurdly stilted and obscure, with all manner of rhetorical tricks exaggerated *ad nauseam*. He had only a superficial knowledge of Greek, and his acquaintance with philosophy did not go beyond the scanty equipment provided in the schools. The Younger Pliny was his model for his letters, Claudian for his panegyrics.

TEXT. Ed. Luetjohann (1887; 'Life' by Mommsen); Mohr (1895); with notes, Savaro (Paris, 1609); Sirmond (Paris, 1652); W. B. Anderson, with transl. and notes (bibliog.), 2 vols. (1936 and 1965); A. Loyen, *Budé ed.* i (1960). O. M. Dalton, free transl. of Letters (2 vols.; 1915); C. E. Stevens, *Sidon. Apoll. and His Age* (bibliog.; 1933); A. Loyen, *Sidoine Apollinaire et l'esprit précieux en Gaule aux derniers jours de l'empire* (1943), and 'Recherches historiques sur les panégyriques de Sidoine Apollinaire', *Bibl. de l'École des hautes Études* (1942), with bibliog. W. B. A.; F. J. E. R.

**SIEGECRAFT, GREEK.** The art of taking fortified citadels or cities may be divided into three periods in Greek military history.

I. BRONZE AGE TO PERSIAN WARS. The scanty evidence (e.g. Hom. *Il.* 12; Paus. 10. 37. 7–8: Crisa *c.* 600) suggests that Greek siegecraft was in a backwater into which ideas occasionally filtered from the main stream of development further east (see Y. Yadin, *The Art of Warfare in Biblical Lands*, 1963). Alyattes took Old Smyrna *c.* 600 (*BSA* 1958/9, 1 ff.), Persian siegecraft overwhelmed several Cypriot and Ionian cities, 497–493, most Athenians abandoned their city in 480 because it could not withstand a Persian siege; but the fortifications in question would probably have sufficed to resist Greek besiegers.

II. TRANSITION, PERSIAN WARS TO PHILIP II. Apart from surprise or treachery, besiegers relied mainly on blockade, normally involving circumvallation. Samos surrendered to Pericles after nine months (440; Thuc. 1. 115 ff.); little Potidaea resisted Athenian siege for three years (432–430). Such blockades were expensive: Samos

cost Athens 1,400 talents, Potidaea 2,000. But some besiegers were beginning to appreciate the value of machines and storming. Pericles possibly used engines at Samos (Diod. 12. 28); Plataea finally fell to blockade, though the Peloponnesians employed mound (χῶμα), battering-ram (κριός), and fire (429–427; Thuc. 2. 75 ff.—a show-piece). Comparatively simple defences could withstand this limited siege-technique, and Pericles based his strategy on the then valid assumption that the Athens-Peiraeus fortress was impregnable. Shortage of archers and slingers, to cover assaults and keep casualties down, partly accounts for Greek weakness. About 400, the invention of artillery (q.v.) gave the Greeks powerful means of providing effective covering 'fire'; later artillery could smash battlements and even help destroy walls. Thus, Dionysius I successfully attacked Motya with a mole, six-story mobile siege-towers, rams, and *gastraphetai* (397; Diod. 14. 49 ff.). Philip II's siege-train profoundly impressed the Greeks, though his eighty-cubit towers and arrow-shooting catapults failed at Perinthus (340; Diod. 16. 74 f.); siegecraft had almost reached maturity.

III. ALEXANDER AND AFTER. Philip II founded the Macedonian engineering school; Alexander reaped the benefit. Confident in the capacity of his engineers (Diades, Charias, Poseidonius) and his more powerful artillery, he displayed fully developed siege-technique in taking Miletus, Halicarnassus, Tyre, Gaza. His siege-train played a vital part in the conquest of Persia. Demetrius' sieges of Salamis (Diod. 20. 48) and Rhodes (Diod. 20. 85–8; 93–7) provide illuminating evidence for Hellenistic siegecraft. Siege-devices included mining, *stoas* (heavily timbered galleries), artillery, *helepoleis* (giant siege-towers carrying catapults and sometimes drawbridges, ἐπιβάθραι), mechanical scaling ladders (σαμβύκαι), various mobile sheds, χελῶναι—χωστρίδες (for ditch-filling), ὀρυκτρίδες (for digging saps), κριοφόροι (ram-carrying). Of course, cities rapidly learned to construct elaborate defences—better walls, numerous chambered towers, ditch-systems, outworks. They deployed defensive artillery, so that sieges often included artillery-duels (e.g. Rhodes). A well-fortified and equipped city could resist a vigorous Hellenistic assault, but few could afford the expense. Hence, after Alexander, besiegers generally had the whip hand, e.g. the interesting attack of Philip V on Echinus (210; Polyb. 9. 41). About 200, Philon Mechanicus, whose poliorcetic manual excellently describes Hellenistic methods of defence and attack, observes significantly: 'Walls are easily taken by stone-throwing artillery and stoas.'

Aeneas Tacticus, *Poliorketika*; Athenaeus and Biton in C. Wescher, *Poliorcétique des Grecs* (1867); Philon Mechanicus v, ed. R. Schoene (1893). E. Schramm in J. Kromayer and G. Veith, *Heerwesen und Kriegführung der Griechen und Römer* (1928), ch. 5; E. W. Marsden, *Greek and Roman Artillery* (1969). E. W. M.

**SIEGECRAFT, ROMAN.** Early Roman besiegers employed blockade (*obsidio*) with methodical circumvallation, exploited surprise, and sometimes, especially after weakening the besieged by *obsidio*, clinched matters by assault (*oppugnatio*), using the shield-tortoise (*testudo*), ladders (*scalae*), and possibly mound (*agger*) and primitive ram (*aries*). Veii, blockaded 405–396 B.C., fell to assault by mine (*cuniculus*), Livy 5. 15 ff.

From the third century B.C., the Romans assimilated the machinery and techniques of Hellenistic siegecraft (*see* SIEGECRAFT, GREEK), but continued to use elaborate field-works, thus effectively combining *obsidio* and *oppugnatio*. The sieges of Syracuse by Marcellus (213–211 B.C. Livy 24. 32 ff.; Polyb. 8. 3 ff.), the Peiraeus by Sulla (87–86 B.C. App. *Mith.* 30 ff.), and of Avaricum, Alesia, and Massilia by Caesar are particularly instructive. Equipment included large and small bolt-shooting artillery (*catapultae, scorpiones*), stone-throwers (*ballistae*) mobile towers (*turres ambulatoriae = helepoleis*), mechanical ladders (*sambucae*), movable siege-sheds (e.g. ram-carrying tortoise, *testudo arietaria* = χελώνη κριοφόρος; for sapping, the *musculus* = χελώνη διορυκτρίς; light mantlets, *vineae* = ἄμπελοι), protective galleries (*porticus* = stoas, sometimes formed by a line of *vineae*), mobile screens (*plutei*), wall-borer (*terebra* = τρύπανον), hooks and crowbars for dislodging masonry (*falces murales, vectes*). The Roman catapult fragments found at Ampurias and Vitruvius' descriptions (10. 10 ff.) show that Roman engines corresponded closely to Greek artillery (q.v.). The same is true of other siege-machinery (Vitr. 10. 13 ff.). Thus the quality of equipment was good, but its quantity, dependent on the initiative of individual commanders (cf. Scipio's efforts to acquire artillery for siege of Utica, 204 B.C., Livy 29. 35. 8), tended to be inadequate.

Every imperial legion had over fifty *catapultae* (one illustrated on C. Vedennius Moderatus' tombstone, *ILS* 2034) and *ballistae*, a workshop (see *JRS* 1961, 158 ff. for *fabrica* at Inchtuthil), and artificers. Thus commanders —and engineers like Trajan's Apollodorus (q.v. 7)— possessed, or could manufacture, any machine of Hellenistic type necessary for a vigorous siege—whether of a hill-fort (see R. E. M. Wheeler, *Maiden Castle* (1943), 61 ff.) or of sophisticated defences like Jotapata (besieged by Vespasian, Joseph. *BJ* 3. 166 ff.), Jerusalem (Titus' siege, id. 5. 263 ff.), and Masada (id. 7. 276 ff.; *JRS* 1962, 142 ff.).

By the fourth century A.D., artillery comprised the one-armed stone-throwing *onager*—mainly defensive— powerful arrow-shooting *ballistae* (first indicated on Trajan's Column), and small non-torsion arrow-shooting *arcuballistae*. Ammianus' accounts (e.g. 24. 4; Maozamalcha) show that Roman siegecraft was still not to be despised.

Vegetius, *De re militari* iv. H. S. Jones, *Companion to Roman History* (1912), 215 ff.; J. Kromayer and G. Veith, *Heerwesen und Kriegführung der Griechen und Römer* (1928), 373 ff., 442 ff., 600 ff.; E. W. Marsden, *Greek and Roman Artillery* (1969).　　E. W. M.

## SIGILLARIA.
The custom of making presents of little pottery figures at the Saturnalia (q.v.) was so firmly fixed at Rome that there was a regular market for them, where apparently other trifling wares were also sold (Auson. *Cent. Nupt.* 206. 7 Peiper). It was usual to give dependants money for this fair (e.g. Suet. *Claud.* 5). The origin of the custom is not known; the date of the fair was, in imperial times, the last of the seven days which the Saturnalia then lasted (Macrob. *Sat.* 1. 10. 24).　H. J. R.

## SIGNA MILITARIA.
The earliest standard of the Roman army was the *signum* of the maniple. Its primitive form was a hand on the top of a pole, which later was replaced by a spearhead decorated with *phalerae, coronae*, and zodiac emblems. When the cohort superseded the maniple as the tactical unit, the *signum* of the leading maniple in each cohort became the chief standard of the cohort. The century had no separate *signum*.

In the pre-Marian army there were also five legionary standards, which were placed for safety in battle between the first two lines. In substitution for these Marius gave each legion an *aquila* of silver or silver gilt with *coronae* as its sole decoration. The *aquila* was the *numen legionis*; its loss sometimes entailed the disbandment of the legion.

Under the Principate the legion retained its *aquila* and *signa*, and to these were added *imagines*, standards containing medallions with the portraits of the reigning and deified Emperors. *Vexilla*, traditionally the standards of the cavalry, were employed in the legions to mark detachments (*vexillationes*), and, in the first century, the corps of veterans serving *sub vexillo*.

In cohorts of *auxilia* the infantry had *signa*, the mounted men *vexilla*: in the *alae* there was a regimental standard carried by the *vexillarius alae*, and the *turmae* had *signa* in addition. Imagines came to be carried by all units, including the *numeri*, except the Praetorian Guard, who had only *signa* and *vexilla*.

In the Late Empire the traditional standards, with the exception of the *imagines*, were retained, and two new ones added, the *draco* and the *labarum*. The former was probably barbarian in origin and adopted from the Dacians, the latter was not so much a military standard as the symbol of triumphant Christianity. *See also* VEXILLUM; STANDARDS, CULT OF.

A. von Domaszewski, *Die Fahnen im römischen Heere* (1885); Parker, *Roman Legions*, 36 ff.; Kromayer–Veith, *Heerwesen und Kriegführung der Griechen und Römer* (1928); M. Marin y Pena, *Instituciones militares romanas* (1956), 375 ff.
　　　　　　　　　　　　　　　　H. M. D. P.; G. R. W.

## SIGNIA,
modern *Segni*, strongly placed at the north-east angle of the Volscian Mountains in Latium (q.v.). A Latin colony here (495 B.C.) helped contain the Volsci. Sulla defeated the Marians near by (Battle of Sacriportus, 82 B.C.). Ancient ruins include spectacular polygonal walls, corbelled gate (*Porta Saracena*), temple in squared masonry, large open-air reservoir.

G. Lugli, *La tecnica edilizia romana* (1957), 121 ff.　E. T. S.

## SILA,
name given to the forests and mountains in the 'toe' of Italy. Rome annexed much of this region after the Pyrrhic War and exploited its pitch and ship's timbers.
　　　　　　　　　　　　　　　　　　E. T. S.

## SILANION
(4th c. B.C.), sculptor, of Athens, dated by Pliny 328 B.C. Selected works: 1. Theseus, in Athens. 2. Dying Iocasta, bronze with admixture of silver in the face. 3. Sappho, in Syracuse, later in Rome. 4. Corinna (M. Bieber, *Sculpt. Hellenist. Age*, figs. 120–2, cf. *Lustrum* 1961, 19). 5. Plato, erected in the Academy by Mithridates the Persian; after 387 (foundation of Academy). The original of surviving Plato busts (Winter, *KB* 317. 2), which differ too much to justify further attribution to Silanion. 6. The sculptor Apollodorus (noted mainly for his irritable temper). 'Nec hominem ex aere fecit sed iracundiam' (Pliny, *HN* 34. 81). 7. The boxer Satyrus, at Olympia, after 327. 8. Signature from Miletus, about 328 B.C. Silanion wrote *Praecepta symmetriarum*. His pupil Zeuxiades made a statue of Hyperides, who died 322.

Overbeck, 1350–63; E. Schmidt, *JDAI* 1932, 239; 1934, 180; R. Boehringer, *Platon, Bildnisse und Nachweise* (1935); Lippold, *Griech. Plastik*, 273.　　　　　　　　　T. B. L. W.

## SILANUS,
(1) DECIMUS JUNIUS (*PW* 163), husband of Servilia (q.v.), as consul designate (63 B.C.) proposed the 'extreme penalty' for the Catilinarians and, after Caesar's speech, explained he had meant imprisonment. As consul, with Murena (q.v.), he passed the *lex Licinia Iunia* on promulgation. Cassius (q.v. 6) and Lepidus (q.v. 3) were his sons-in-law.　　　　　　　　　　　　　E. B.

Many Junii Silani were prominent in the Early Empire, though lacking outstanding individual contribution. Some may be listed:

(2) M. Junius (*PW* 172) Silanus (*cos.* 25 B.C.), of varied political allegiance. In 44 B.C. he supported his brother-in-law Lepidus, went over to Antony at Mutina (43), fell out of favour with the triumvirs, fled to Sextus Pompeius (39), served under Antony in Greece (34–32), but before Actium went over to Octavian, who later raised him to the patriciate (30) and held the consulship with him in 25. (For the suggestion that the consul of 25 should be differentiated from the legate of 43, see Broughton, *MRR, Suppl.* 32.)

(3) M. Junius (*PW* 175) Silanus Torquatus (consul A.D. 19, for the whole year), grandson of no. 2. He was responsible, with his colleague Norbanus, for the *lex Iunia Norbana* (*see* LATINI IUNIANI). He was proconsul of Africa (36–9?). He married Aemilia Lepida, a great-granddaughter of Augustus, and all his five children (nos. 4–7 below) suffered from being descendants of Augustus.

(4) M. Junius (*PW* 176) Silanus (consul A.D. 46, for the whole year), son of no. 3. Born in A.D. 14, a great-great-grandson of Augustus, he was proconsul of Asia in 54. Although he lacked ambition (the Emperor Gaius called him a 'golden sheep', *pecus aurea*), Agrippina thought that his Augustan connexion might jeopardize the succession of her son Nero and that Silanus might be tempted to avenge the death of his brother (no. 6) for which she was responsible. He was put to death.

(5) D. Junius (*PW* 183) Silanus Torquatus (*cos.* A.D. 53), son of no. 3, was forced by Nero to commit suicide (64) because he was alleged to have boasted of his descent from Augustus.

(6) L. Junius (*PW* 180) Silanus Torquatus (praetor A.D. 48), son of no. 3, was betrothed to Octavia, daughter of the Emperor Claudius. He went with Claudius to Britain and received from him the *ornamenta triumphalia*. Through the intrigues of Agrippina he was expelled from the Senate (allegedly for incest with his sister, no. 7 below) and was deprived of his praetorship. He committed suicide on the day that Claudius married Agrippina (49).

(7) Junia (*PW* 198) Calvina, daughter of no. 3, 'festivissima omnium puellarum', married a son of L. Vitellius (q.v. 2) who as censor (A.D. 48) accused her of incest (see no. 6 above) in order to help Agrippina. She was banished (49), but was recalled by Nero after Agrippina's death; she survived till late in Vespasian's reign.

(8) L. Junius (*PW* 183) Silanus Torquatus was a son of the consul of 46 (no. 4) and a nephew of Junia Lepida, the consul's sister. She had married the jurist Cassius (q.v. 8). Silanus was brought up in their home. In 65 Nero accused him of treason and of incest with his aunt Lepida. He was exiled, but was murdered before he could leave Italy (cf. L. Petersen *Hist.* 1966, 328 ff.)

(9) C. Junius (*PW* 158) Silanus represents a collateral branch of the family. His three sons (nos. 10–12) were prominent.

(10) C. Junius (*PW* 159) (*cos.* A.D. 10), son of no. 9, was proconsul of Asia (20/1), and mover of the *senatusconsultum Silanianum*, dealing with the torture of slaves. Accused of *maiestas*, he was exiled (22).

(11) M. Junius (*PW* 174) Silanus (*cos. suff.* A.D. 15), son of no. 9, had considerable influence with Tiberius and the Senate. In 33 his daughter Junia Claudia married Gaius (Caligula), who killed Silanus in 38 (Dio wrongly calls him the 'golden sheep', see no. 4).

(12) D. Junius (*PW* 164) Silanus. When his affair with the Younger Julia (q.v. 3), the granddaughter of Augustus, became known, he voluntarily went into exile (A.D. 8). Thanks to the influence of his brother (no. 11), Tiberius allowed him to return (A.D. 20), but not to hold office.

(13) C. Appius Junius (*PW* 155) Silanus (*cos.* A.D. 28). His parentage is uncertain: he is not likely to have been the son of either no. 9 or 10. He was acquitted on a charge of *maiestas* (32) and was governor of Hispania Tarraconensis (40/1). He enjoyed the friendship of the Emperor Claudius who married him to Domitia Lepida, mother of Claudius' wife Messallina (41). Having refused the advances of Messallina, Silanus was accused by her and Narcissus of treason and executed (42). H. H. S.

**SILENUS,** probably of Kale Acte in Sicily (*FGrH* 175), accompanied Hannibal to Italy and composed a history

of his campaigns for a Greek public; it served as a source for Polybius and for Coelius Antipater, whom Livy used considerably in the third decade. How objective this work was is uncertain; but it contained digressions in the Hellenistic fashion and a romantic element exemplified by the story of Hannibal's dream before he crossed the Ebro (Cic. *Div.* 1. 48–9). Silenus also wrote at least four books of *Sicelica*. F. W. W.

**SILIUS** (1, *PW* 4), GAIUS, grandson of P. Silius Nerva (*cos.* 20 B.C.), consul-designate for A.D. 48 and described as 'iuuentutis Romanae pulcherrimus' (Tac. *Ann.* 11. 12), attracted the guilty passion of Messalina and was involved in a liaison, perhaps in a plot to displace Claudius. The lovers openly celebrated a marriage while the Emperor was absent at Ostia. The imperial freedmen, in alarm, took counsel together and compelled Claudius to act. Silius and his paramour were put to death (48). R. S.

**SILIUS** (2, *PW* 17) **ITALICUS** (an inscription gives his full name, TIBERIUS CATIUS ASCONIUS SILIUS ITALICUS: see *CR* 1935, 216 f.). His birthplace is uncertain, perhaps Patavium (*CR* 1936, 56 ff.), but not Italica in Spain. He died *c.* A.D. 101 aged 75, from voluntary starvation to shorten an incurable ailment (Pliny, *Ep.* 3. 7): this fixes his birth in 26. As a pleader he won fame, and was consul in 68; he supported Vitellius for the succession (Tac. *Hist.* 3. 65), and later, about 77, gained high praise for his administration of Asia. Thereafter, he enjoyed an elegant retirement amongst numerous friends in Rome and Campania; a connoisseur of books, pictures, and statuary, he owned many country-houses, including one of Cicero's, for whom he showed great reverence, as for Virgil, whose tomb in Naples he repaired. From Martial's flattering references to him after 88 it seems that his poetic interest began only late in life. He was acquainted with Epictetus (Arr. *Epict. Diss.* 3. 8. 7) and was as Stoic in his outlook as he was in his death.

WORKS. *Punica*, the longest Latin poem, an historical epic in 12,200 verses on the Second Punic War. The seventeen books begin with Hannibal's oath and, except for digressions on Regulus and Anna, proceed in regular order of events to Scipio's triumph after Zama. The poem was planned by 88, but probably only books 1–6 appeared under Domitian (E. Bickel, *Rh. Mus.* 1911, 505); as 14. 686 dates from the close of Nerva's Principate, hasty workmanship would explain the inferiority of the final books. Since he wrote 'maiore cura quam ingenio' (Pliny, *Ep.* 3. 7. 5), sources should be traceable for his facts; though owing most to Livy's Third Decad, he is not a mere free versifier than Livy. On geography Varro is his chief source, along with Hyginus; his ethnography rests ultimately on Posidonius. His poetry owes most to the *Aeneid*, but adaptations occur from Lucan's and the other epics. Despite his clinging to a mythological scheme and the outworn epic machinery, Silius has some vitality. His learning, displayed in endless epithets and catalogues, is tiresome; he has too many rhetorical speeches; his language is not really poetic, and accounts of battles are confused and gruesome; but the versification is not monotonous; his similes are clear and lifelike; and short passages show good narrative skill or straightforward description. Scipio fails as hero, and Hannibal comes nearer the part.

TEXTS. A. Drakenborch (Utrecht, 1717); G. A. Ruperti (Göttingen, 1795–8); L. Bauer (Teubner, 1890–2).
TRANSLATION. With text, J. D. Duff (Loeb, 1933).
SOURCES. A. Klotz, *Rh. Mus.* 1933, 1 ff.; J. Nicol, *The Historical and Geographical Sources used by Sil. Ital.* (1936); B. Rehm, *Philol.* Suppl. xxiv. 2. 97 ff. D. J. C.

**SILK.** The mulberry silkworm (bombyx mori), the cocoons of which are unwound to produce true silk, was not bred in the Mediterranean world before the sixth century A.D., and the secret of unwinding cocoons also appears to have remained confined to China. But true silk (σῆρες, serica vestis) was imported into western Asia, as cloth (which was sometimes undone and rewoven) or as yarn or raw silk (μέταξα), probably by the fifth century B.C. and perhaps earlier (cf. Hdt. i. 135, Μηδικὴ ἐσθής). From Alexander's time onwards it spread further west, until in the Early Roman Empire it, and its costliness, could become a favourite target of moralists. For some time 'silk' garments were only half silk (subserica, tramoserica), with linen warp or weft, and even so they were by law confined to women. Pure silk material (holoserica vestis), which is said to have been worth its weight in gold, is not mentioned before the early third century A.D., when Elagabalus was the first to wear it. Meanwhile, however, wild or tussore silk, derived from the spinning of material scraped from the cocoons of other species, had been known as Coa vestis (from its manufacture on the island of Cos) or bombycina vestis. (Coa vestis was probably a dark silk derived from saturnia pyri, bombycina a lighter silk from pachypasa otus.) The Coan industry, first mentioned by Aristotle (HA 5. 19. 6; cf. Pliny, HN 11. 76) but probably older, is not referred to after Pliny, and may have succumbed to the competition of imports of true silk.

H. Blümner, Technologie der Gewerbe und Künste i² (1912), 201 ff.; Forbes, Stud. And. Technol. iv³. 50 ff.; J. I. Miller, The Spice Trade of the Roman Empire (1969), see index. L. A. M.

**SILURES,** a tribe in south-east Wales, an offshoot of the Iron Age B culture with C influences. Under Caratacus, they gave trouble to the Roman armies, but were finally subdued by Frontinus (A.D. 74–8), who planted a legionary fortress at Isca (Caerleon). A Roman town in the plain (Venta Silurum, Caerwent) replaced their hill forts.

Collingwood–Myres, Roman Britain, 94 ff., 110 ff.; V. E. Nash-Williams, The Roman Frontier in Wales (1954), 1 ff.; Frere, Britannia, 52 ff., 81 ff. C. E. S.

**SILVA,** like ὕλη, could mean raw material, and, perhaps with a suggestion of its Ciceronian sense of a forest-like abundance, was extended as a literary title to work of varied content (cf. Suetonius' Pratum). Quintilian (Inst. 10. 3. 17) explains it as a rapid draft, and this applies to Statius' Silvae, which are occasional poems hastily composed. Ben Jonson's definition, 'the Ancients call'd that kind of body Sylva, or Ὕλη, in which there were workes of divers nature, and matter congested', indicates why it remained an appropriate title for miscellaneous verses into the Renaissance, e.g. Mantuanus' 'subitaria carmina' (Bologna, 1502) or Politian's 'Sylvae'. J. W. D.

**SILVANUS,** the Roman god of uncultivated land beyond the boundaries of the tillage. He was thus uncanny and dangerous, see PILUMNUS. His personality also seems to have been very vague, for, Siluanus being merely an adjective, he has no name, unless, with Wissowa (RK 213), we suppose that the substantive Faunus (q.v.) is to be supplied. Clearly it would be well to propitiate him when making inroads into his domain, so it is quite understandable that 'every estate has three Silvani' (Gromatici, 302. 14 Lachmann), one for the boundary, one domesticus, possessioni consecratus (watching over the farmhouse itself?), and one for the herdsmen; of course a late and somewhat fossilized form of the worship, which itself dated from times when such land represented the felling of trees and other interferences with the wild country. Silvanus thus bears a kind of resemblance to Greek satyrs and Sileni, and is freely identified with them and with Pan (Wissowa, ibid. 215), also with foreign, especially barbarian, gods somehow connected with untilled land, or supposed to be, regard-

less of their relative importance. Silvanus also occurs as a title of Mars (q.v.; Cato, Agr. 83), unless Marti Siluano is archaic asyndeton for Marti et Siluano.

H. J. R.

**SILVER.** Though known in remote antiquity, silver was for long a rarer and more valuable metal than gold, which could be easily obtained from alluvial deposits by simple washing, whereas silver had to be extracted by regular mining processes. The Phoenicians are said to have been the first to bring silver into general use; several of the silver objects mentioned in Homer have Sidonian associations. The main sources for classical Greece were Bactriana, Colchis, Lydia, Mt. Pangaeus in Thrace, and Laurium, which provided abundant supplies for Athens down to 413 B.C. In the western Mediterranean Spain was the most prolific source of supply, with Sardinia, Gaul, and Britain as minor sources. The conquests of Spain and Asia made silver plentiful at Rome, where it had previously been rare.

Silver was worked with a hammer into plates which were soldered or riveted together and then decorated with repoussé work (ἐμπαιστική), stamping, chasing, and engraving. Vases might be hammered or cast from a mould and were often adorned with reliefs (emblemata), let into the body of the vessel or crustae soldered upon the surface. For coins molten dumps were struck between dies. To provide colour contrast silver objects were often gilded with gold leaf or, in the Roman period, with the help of a mercury amalgam. Niello, a black metallic sulphide used as inlay, was employed in the Bronze Age, and from the Hellenistic period on.

Less popular than gold for jewellery, silver was especially used for valuable and luxurious specimens of objects for which bronze was the common material. It was extensively used for statuettes, but rarely for larger sculpture; for the domestic furniture of wealthy Romans; and, above all, for services of dinner-plate. Many of these services (ministeria) have been preserved, examples being the Treasures of Hildesheim (q.v.) in Berlin, and of Boscoreale in Paris, both of the Early Empire; and the Esquiline and Mildenhall Treasures in London, of the Late Empire. They include flat dishes for eating (lances), flat or hemispherical bowls for drinking (calices, scyphi), jugs (urceoli), saucepans (trulli), buckets for fruit (situlae), spoons (cochlearia), pepper-castors (piperatoria), etc. Cups were the special subjects of artists of whom Pliny gives a list dating from the fourth and third centuries B.C.; he remarks that while no names of goldsmiths have been preserved, the silversmiths (argentarii) are numerous.

Pliny, HN bk. 33. H. B. Walters, Catalogue of Silver Plate in the British Museum (1921); Forbes, Stud. Anc. Technol. viii, ch. 6; R. Higgins, Greek and Roman Jewellery (1961); D. Strong, Greek and Roman Gold and Silver Plate (1966). F. N. P.; J. B.

**SILVIUS,** son of Aeneas (q.v.) and Lavinia, father of Silvius Aeneas and ancestor of the Alban royal house of Silvii (Verg. Aen. 6. 760–7; Livy 1. 3). A legend due to the name, but unknown to Virgil, told that Lavinia, fearing the jealousy of Ascanius, fled to the woods and there gave birth to her son (Dion. Hal. 1. 70). C. B.

**SIMMIAS** (1) (or **Simias**) of Thebes, a member of the inner circle of Socrates' friends, one of those who were prepared to put up money to secure his escape from prison, and who were with him on the day of his death. He had previously associated with the Pythagorean Philolaus, but the theory which he defends in the Phaedo is almost certainly not Pythagorean, involving as it does a denial of the soul's immortality. In the Phaedrus Plato praises highly his philosophical ability. Diogenes Laertius ascribes to him twenty-three dialogues (not extant), but it is doubtful whether this ascription is sound. W. D. R.

**SIMMIAS** (2) of Rhodes, poet and grammarian, lived in Rhodes (Strabo 364, 655) about 300 B.C., wrote three books of γλῶσσαι and four of ποιήματα (*Suda* s.v. Σιμμίας). Of the first Athenaeus gives a few quotations (327 e, 472 e, 479 c, 677 c) about the meanings of words. The poems vary in character. Fragments survive of a hexametric epic on Apollo (fr. 1 Powell), and others called *Gorgo* and *Μῆνες* (frs. 6–8), and of lyrical poems (frs. 13–17). There are also three complete *Technopaegnia* called *Wings* (fr. 24), *Axe* (fr. 25) and *Egg* (fr. 26) and epigrams (frs. 18–22) which are in the epideictic manner of the time. His style shows affinities to the Coan circle of Theocritus, and though he calls himself Δωρία ἀηδών, he does not write in any single dialect.

TEXT. Diehl, *Anth. Lyr. Graec.* ii. 257–75; Powell, *Coll. Alex.* 109–20.
CRITICISM. H. Fränkel, *De Simia Rhodio* (1915).          C. M. B.

**SIMON** of Athens, a shoemaker, was according to a late tradition a friend of Socrates, who used to visit him in his workshop and discuss philosophical questions with him. He plays a considerable part in the (late) *Socraticae epistulae*, and Diogenes Laertius says he was the first to write reminiscences of Socrates in dialogue form. But he is never mentioned by Plato or Xenophon, and his very existence as a real personage is not quite certain.
                                                        W. D. R.

**SIMONIDES** (c. 556–468 B.C.), lyric and elegiac poet, born at Iulis in Ceos (fr. 147 D), the son of Leoprepes. In the last years of the sixth century he wrote Epinician Odes for Glaucus of Carystus (fr. 509 P, Paus. 6. 10. 1) and Eualcidas of Eretria (fr. 518 P). He was the guest of Hipparchus at Athens ([Pl.] *Hipparch.* 228 c), and to this period may have belonged some of his fifty-six victories in dithyrambic competitions (fr. 79 D). A couplet honouring the murderers of Hipparchus, though attributed to him (fr. 76 D), is not necessarily by him, while his epitaph on Hippias' daughter, Archedice, shows his affection for the family (fr. 85 D). About 514 he went to Thessaly, where he was the guest of the Scopads, and celebrated their chariot victories (Theoc. 16. 42–7). He was miraculously preserved when their house fell and destroyed them (Callim. fr. 71, Cic. *De Or.* 2. 86. 353). He lamented them in a Dirge (schol. Theoc. 16. 36). To the same period belong his dirge on Antiochus the son of Echecratidas (ibid. 44), but the only substantial fragment from this time is his lines to Scopas on the nature of virtue (fr. 542 P) in which he seeks to substitute a good conscience as the right test for a good man instead of all-round excellence. He was back in Athens in 490, when his epitaph on the fallen of Marathon was preferred to that of Aeschylus (*Vit. Aesch.* 4). In the wars of 480–479 he rose to great prominence and wrote a commemorative hymn for the Spartans who fell at Thermopylae (fr. 531 P), a hymn of thanksgiving for the victory of Artemisium (frs. 532–5 P), and epitaphs for the fallen, including his own friend Megistias (fr. 83 D) and the Spartans who died with Leonidas (fr. 92 D). At this time he was a friend of Themistocles (Plut. *Them.* 5, Cic. *Fin.* 2. 32. 104), in whose interest he carried on a verbal warfare with Timocreon (frs. 169–70 D, Diog. Laert. 2. 25, 40). About 476 B.C. he went to Syracuse as the guest of Hieron, with whom various stories connect him (Pl. *Ep.* 2. 311 a, Ath. 656 d, Ael. *VH* 9. 1), and made peace between him and Theron (Timaeus ap. schol. Pind. *Ol.* 2. 29). He died in 468 (*Marm. Par.* 73) and was buried at Acragas (Callim. fr. 71). He was said to be ugly (Plut. *Them.* 5), fond of money (Ar. *Pax* 698, Callim. fr. 77), and the inventor of a technique for remembering (Cic. *De Or.* 2. 357). His work falls into the following classes: (1) Hymns, of which very little survives, except frs. 531–5 P. (2) Scolia and Encomia, including his poem to

Scopas (fr. 542 P) and his quatrain on the four best things (*Scol. Att.* 7). (3) Dirges, for which he was extremely renowned (Quint. *Inst.* 10. 1. 64), notably frs. 520–31 P. The famous lines on Danae (fr. 543 P) do not necessarily come from a Dirge. (4) Epinicians, written for many patrons, including Astylus of Croton (fr. 506 P), Crius of Aegina (fr. 507 P), Xenocrates of Acragas (fr. 513 P), Anaxilas of Rhegium (fr. 515 P). In these he seems to have been much more playful than Pindar. (5) Elegies, frs. 62–6, 84, 99, 128, 130 D, including both poems on public events such as the battle of Plataea and short, sympotic poems. (6) Inscriptional epigrams for dedications and epitaphs. The authenticity of these is very doubtful in many cases, as they were probably not collected till the fourth century and would not have the author's name on the stone. The most likely to be genuine are frs. 79, 83, 85, 91 D; *see* EPIGRAM, GREEK, § 2. (7). Since many apophthegms are attributed to him, a collection of such may have existed. He was admired for his choice of words (Dion. Ha . ii. 205. 7, *De Imit.*), his sweetness (Cic. *Nat. D.* 1. 22), his harmonious style (Dion. Hal. *Comp.* 23).

TEXT. Page, *Poet. Mel. Gr.* 238–323; for elegiacs, Diehl, *Anth. Lyr. Graec.* ii. 84–118.
CRITICISM. U. von Wilamowitz-Moellendorff, *Sappho und Simonides* (1913), 137 ff. C. M. Bowra, *Greek Lyric Poetry*[2] (1961), 308 ff.; A. Hauvette, *Les Épigrammes de Simonide*; M. Boas, *De Epigrammatis Simonideis* (1905).                    C. M. B.

**SIMPLICIUS** (Σιμπλίκιος), sixth century A.D., Aristotelian commentator. Born in Cilicia, he studied at Alexandria and Athens and subsequently made his home in the latter city save for a short period of exile in Persia (A.D. 531–3). His learned and sober commentaries on the *De Caelo, Categories, Physics*, and *De Anima* (*Comm. in Arist. Graeca*, vols. 7–11) contain much valuable material, including many fragments of pre-Socratic philosophers. Also extant are a commentary on the *Manual* of Epictetus (ed. J. Schweighäuser, 1800) and a work on Quadratures (ed. F. Rudio, 1907).                    E. R. D.

**SIMYLUS,** (1) Greek didactic iambographer, of whom a few fragments survive, of the third or second, or even of the first, century B.C. Probably not identical with a comic poet of the same name (*CAF* ii. 444).

(2) Greek author of an elegy or epigram on Tarpeia, perhaps slightly earlier than the Augustan age. *Anth. Lyr. Graec.* ii. 248.

Meineke, *FCG*, praef. xiii ff.; J. E. Sandys, *History of Classical Scholarship* (1903), i. 56; J. W. H. Atkins, *Literary Criticism in Antiquity* (1924), i. 179; *PW* iii A. 1, 216 f.        J. D. D.

**SIN.** The various words which may be translated by 'sin' and the ideas which they represent fall into two classes, a lower and a higher. In the former the act is one which brings about undesirable relations between the agent and his supernatural environment; it may be the breach of a taboo, disobedience to the command of a supernatural being, departure from the recognized standard of conduct (ὁσία, *fas*) of his community. It need not be what we should regard as immoral; it does not necessarily connote any evil intention, or any intention at all, on the agent's part; it often is not individual in itself, very often not individual in its consequences. Indeed, the fact that its consequences are supposed to extend far beyond the sinner is the main reason for general objection to it. In the latter the act is itself considered wrong, offending a deity or deities because the god or gods are supposed to be righteous and interested in human morality. The history of Greek thought in this respect is a progress from the lower to the higher conception. Rome seems of herself to have made but small advance in this direction till enlightened by Greek theology.

Of the former stage, in Greece, Hesiod furnishes a good

example (cf. SUPERSTITION). He forbids, with equal earnestness and apparently equal assuredness that divine vengeance will follow transgression, on the one hand a number of acts of which any moral code would disapprove, such as the ill-treatment of orphans and of one's own parents (*Op.* 330 ff.), and on the other purely ritual offences such as omitting to wash the hands before pouring libation (ibid. 724 ff.; full list in R. Pettazzoni, *La confessione dei peccati* iii (1936), 174 ff.). This is in a poem which repeatedly and emphatically insists on the justice of Zeus. In some archaic rites, such as that of the Samothracian gods, confession of offences was a preliminary to initiation; it does not appear that anything more was needed, the confession being simply a process of getting rid of the state of sinfulness and so leaving the candidate ritually pure; Pettazzoni, op. cit. 163 ff., cf. i. 60 ff.; *Harv. Theol. Rev.* 1937, 1 ff., the last giving other examples of confession in ancient ritual, especially oriental cults.

For Rome, a similar state of things can be detected for early times. It is significant that the word *scelus*, perhaps the nearest classical equivalent of 'sin', can also, in Plautus and other Republican authors, mean 'illluck', such as would naturally come mechanically from the violation of some taboo. A legend, the more significant because it is probably pure invention and therefore shows fairly early ideas of what is proper in such matters, represents grave consequences befalling as the result of a wholly accidental *vitium*, or shortcoming, in the celebration of games to Jupiter (Livy 2. 36). The XII Tables show at least the beginnings of a movement towards a more enlightened view, for they make provision for lenient treatment of a merely accidental homicide (Cic. *Top.* 64).

Greece, as early as Homer and more articulately and thoroughly in later authors down to about the end of the fifth century B.C., develops a theory which strongly stresses the moral aspect. Sin is the result of ὕβρις or overweening disregard of the rights of others; Theognis in a famous passage declares this due to κόρος, satiety, in other words too much prosperity, but adds 'when wealth attends a base man' (Theog. 153, cf. Solon, fr. 3. 9 Diehl), while Aeschylus (*Ag.* 751 ff.) emphatically denies that prosperity of itself has any such result (contrast Hdt. 1. 32. 6–9). In any case, this ὕβρις results in ἄτη, a state of blindness to both moral and prudential considerations, in which 'the evil appears good' (Soph. *Ant.* 622, see Jebb ad loc.), and this brings about utter ruin. These sins appear in no case to be mere ritual offences, but serious wrongdoings. It was further held that punishment might not overtake the actual sinner, but either his descendants (as Solon, fr. 1. 29 ff. Diehl) or those somehow associated with him (Hes. op. cit. 240; cf. e.g. Hor. *Carm.* 3. 2. 29 f.), despite their innocence. This problem seems to have exercised Aeschylus greatly, for several of his plays deal with the problem of the hereditary curse, as the surviving trilogy and that of which the *Seven against Thebes* remains. His solution would appear to be that the children of the sinful inherit a certain tendency to sin, but are nevertheless free agents who may return to better ways.

Some of the more mystical religious systems, notably Orphism (q.v.), occupied themselves with the relations between sin and suffering, and seem to have found a solution in the theory that sins committed in one life may be atoned for in another, see especially Pind. *Ol.* 2. 56 ff. (probably Pythagorean). Orphism seems actually to have had a kind of dogma of original sin (Pind. fr. 127 Bowra, see Rose in *Greek Poetry and Life* (1936), 79 ff.).

Further examination of this and kindred problems was mostly left to the philosophic schools (it is worth noting that one of the Christian words for sin, ἁμαρτία,

may derive from a Stoic technicality, see WilamowitzMoellendorff, *Glaube der Hellenen* ii (1932), 120). Many of the later, orientalizing cults elaborately developed the idea of punishment for sin after death, which in Homer hardly exists, save for the penalties inflicted on a few who had directly and personally offended the gods (*Od.* 11. 576 ff.), but expanded under philosophico-religious influences (Orphic-Pythagorean?) into such schemes of Hell, Purgatory, and Paradise as are found in Verg. *Aen.* 6 and became extremely minute and particular in later documents (see A. Dieterich, *Nekyia*², 1913).

LITERATURE. Besides the works mentioned in the text, see a good summary by A. W. Mair in Hastings, *ERE* xi. 545 ff., cf. J. S. Reid, ibid. 569 ff., and on the philosophical aspects A. W. H. Adkins, *Merit and Responsibility* (1960). H. J. R.

**SINGARA,** a city in northern Mesopotamia situated on the southern slope of the range of the same name (modern *Jebel Sinjar*). Captured by Trajan and again in Verus' campaign, it became part of the Roman eastern *limes* defences and was an important military base in the frontier province created by Septimius Severus. Under Severus Alexander it became a *colonia*, but it was captured by the Persian Sapor II in 360 and in 363 was ceded to Persia by Jovian. The Romans made skilful use of the Singara hills in the organization of their Mesopotamian *limes*. Singara's importance in this was due to its position on the central Mesopotamian trade route that came into being in the Parthian period (*see* HATRA).

R. Cagnat, *Syria* 1927, 53 ff.; A. Poidebard, *La Trace de Rome dans le Désert de Syrie* (1934), ch. 6. E. W. G.

**SINIS,** a brigand who lived on the Isthmus of Corinth. He made all comers contend with him at holding down a pine-tree, which, when they could no longer hold it, flung them into the air and so killed them (so Apollod. 3. 218 and others, see for details Wörner in Roscher, s.v.), or, more intelligibly, tied them to two such trees which were then let go and tore them asunder (so Diod. Sic. 4. 59. 3 and others). Hence he was surnamed Pityocamptes (Πιτυοκάμπτης), i.e. pine-bender. Theseus (q.v.), on his way to Athens, killed him in the same manner, Plut. *Thes.* 8, who adds that Perigune (Περιγούνη), Sinis' daughter, became the concubine first of Theseus and later of Deïoneus son of Eurytus of Oechalia. H. J. R.

**SINNIUS CAPITO,** scholar of the Augustan age whose *Epistulae* (containing grammatical discussions), *Liber de syllabis*, and *Libri spectaculorum* are mentioned by later writers.

Schanz–Hosius, § 353; Funaioli, *Gramm. Rom. Frag.* 458–66.

**SINON,** a pretended deserter from the Greek forces at Troy, who told the Trojans a long and false tale of the building of the Trojan Horse (Verg. *Aen.* 2. 57–194) and after it had been taken within the walls released the Greek soldiers inside it and joined in the sack of the city. The story is derived from the epic cycle and is treated by several extant writers.

O. Immisch in Roscher, *Lex.* iv. 935 ff.; A. C. Pearson, *Fragments of Sophocles* ii (1917), 181 ff.; R. G. Austin, Verg. *Aen.* 2 ad loc. A. S. P.

**SINOPE,** a town situated almost at the midpoint of the south shore of the Euxine on an easily defended peninsula with two good harbours about its base, and near the place where the crossing to the Crimea is shortest. The promontory is well watered and fertile (Strabo speaks of market-gardens), the tunny catch was famous, and the mountains noted for their timber and cabinet woods. Founded by Miletus probably in the late seventh century (traditionally founded before 756 B.C., destroyed by the Cimmerians and refounded before 600), it early commanded the maritime trade of much of both coasts of the Pontic region and established many colonies along the coast, some of which were tributary to it in Xenophon's time. In spite of mountain barriers it drew trade from the interior, notably in Sinopic earth (cinnabar). About 437 it was freed from a tyrant by Pericles and received Athenian settlers. It was attacked and occupied briefly by the Persian satrap Datames (c. 375). The town probably maintained its freedom under Alexander and his immediate successors, and with the assistance of Rhodes repulsed Mithridates III of Pontus in 220, but was finally occupied by Pharnaces I in 183 and soon became the Pontic capital. In the Third Mithridatic War it was captured and constituted a free town by Lucullus. It was occupied and suffered severely at the hands of Pharnaces II (q.v.), but Caesar repaired its losses by settling a Roman colony with the title of Colonia Iulia Felix Sinope. In the third century it possessed *Ius Italicum*. An abundant coinage attests its prosperity both in the early and the imperial periods, and the appearance of men of Sinope all about the Euxine, the Aegean, at Athens, and at Rhodes attests the wide commercial connexions of the city. Its vigorous hellenism is shown by the names of Diogenes the Cynic, Diphilus the comic poet and other men of letters. Strabo describes it as a city with fine buildings, market-place, porticoes, gymnasium, and fortifications.

Strabo 12. 545. D. M. Robinson, *Ancient Sinope* (1906); C. Roebuck, *Ionian Trade and Colonization* (1959), 117 ff., and index; Magie, *Rom. Rule Asia Min.* 183 ff., and index. T. R. S. B.

**SIPONTUM** ('Sepontum' *Rav. Cosm.*; 'Sopontum' *Tab. Peut.*) lay at the northern end of the Gulf of Manfredonia in northern Apulia where the coastal dunes meet the limestone outcrops of the Gargano peninsula. Its site is marked by the Norman church of S. Maria di Siponto, a mile south-west of Manfredonia. Its role as the port of Arpi (q.v.) made it important in the republican period and it was a stage on the Adriatic coastal road. The town was quadrilateral in shape and was enclosed by a massive wall of free-standing limestone blocks reminiscent of the wall circuit at Paestum.

*CIL* ix. 65 ff. G. D. B. J.

**SIRENS**, sea-songstresses, whose appearance is not described in Homer. In the *Odyssey* (12. 39, 184) the Sirens live on an island near Scylla and Charybdis. Sailors charmed by their song land and perish; the meadow is full of decaying corpses. But Odysseus following the advice of Circe passes safely. Similarly Orpheus saves the Argonauts by competing with them (Ap. Rhod. 4. 893; Apollod. 1. 9. 25). In other stories the Sirens must die if a mortal can resist their song (Hyg. *Fab.* 141). The escape of Odysseus and of Orpheus and their defeat by the Muses (q.v.) lead to their death. The Sirens are omniscient and have the power to quiet the winds (with their song? Hes. fr. 69 Rzach). They are sometimes called daughters of Earth (J. Pollard, *AJ Arch.* 1949, 357); they sing the strains of Hades (Soph. fr. 861 Pearson), and they live in Hades (Pl. *Cra.* 403 d). Sirens accompany the dead on their voyage to the lower world and crown tombs, from very early times. This leads some authorities to assume that they were originally birds inhabited by souls of the dead. A poetical interpretation makes these funereal Sirens grieve for the dead with mournful songs just as they mourn for Persephone (Dositheus 8 in Hyg. *Fab.* ed. Rose; Eur. *Hel.* 167 f.). When definite geographical locations began to be attached to Homeric geography, it was held that Sirens ranged along the coast of south Italy, where they were worshipped by the seafaring population (Strabo 1. 22) in Naples (C. G. Pugliese, *PP*

1952, 420), Sorrentum, and Sicily. They probably figured in Timaeus (q.v. 2).

In art Sirens are represented as half women and half birds, though male bearded Sirens preponderate among the earlier examples. They are frequently attached to bronze cauldrons (O. Muscarella, *Hesp.* 1962, 317). Not all are associated with music. Some apparently represent omens, familiars of deities, or unworldly powers (E. Kunze, *MDAI(A)* 1932, 135). The rapacious monsters of the archaic period are ennobled in classical art to mournful, beautiful beings; in Hellenistic art and literature they are representative of music almost as much as Muses (E. Buschor, *Die Musen des Jenseits* (1944); J. Pollard, *CR* 1952, 60) and are said to be daughters of a Muse (Ap. Rhod. 4. 896). Occasionally they are given an erotic character (Attic comedy).

For a possible connexion between Σειρήν and Σείριος cf. K. Latte, *Festschrift der Göttinger Akademie* 1951.

Weicker in Roscher's *Lexicon* s.v. 'Sirenen'; H. Payne, *Necrocorinthia* (1931), 139; E. Haspels, *Attic Black-figured Lekythoi* (Paris, 1936), 150; K. Marót, *Die Anfänge der griechischen Literatur* (1960); J. Pollard, *Seers, Shrines and Sirens* (1965); G. Benwell and A. Waugh, *Sea Enchantress* (1965). G. M. A. H.; J. R. T. P.

**SIRIS**, seventh-century Greek colony on the Gulf of Tarentum (q.v.) (modern *Nova Siri*: the R. Siris [*Sinno*] has buried any ancient remains). An allegedly Ionian, but possibly Achaean foundation, Siris occupied the site of earlier Trojan and Chonic settlements and itself disappeared in the sixth century, destroyed by Sybaris and Metapontum (qq.v.). Heraclea (q.v. 1) replaced it (432 B.C.). E. T. S.

**SIRMIUM**, a city on the Savus in Pannonia (Inferior), was probably originally the *oppidum* of the Amantini (Pliny, *HN* 3. 148). It was occupied by the Romans probably during the *Bellum Pannonicum* of 12–9 B.C., and became an important Roman military base in the first century A.D. (Cass. Dio 55. 29). A *colonia* was established there under Vespasian. In the Later Empire it was often the residence of Emperors and high officials, due largely to its importance as a road-junction in the Danube area. It possessed an imperial arms factory (*Not. Dign.* [*occ.*] 9. 18), was a fleet station (loc. cit. 32, 50), and the site of an imperial mint which flourished 336–6, 351–65 (gold, silver, and copper) and 379 and possibly 394–6 (gold only). Large numbers of laws were issued at Sirmium from Diocletian onwards.

A. Mócsy, *Die Bevölkerung von Pannonien bis zu den Markomannenkriegen* (Budapest, 1959), 76 f. On the coinage cf. Mattingly–Sydenham, *RIC* vii. 462; ix. 156 f.; R. A. G. Carson *et al.*, *Late Roman Bronze Coinage, 324–498* (1960), 76. J. J. W.

**SISCIA**, called also *Segesta* (from the island between the rivers Savus and Colapis on which it stood, Pliny, *HN* 3. 148, cf. App. *Ill.* 10. 22 f.), was a city in Pannonia (Superior). Probably taken by Roman commanders in 119 B.C. (App. *Ill.* 10), it was captured by Octavian in 35 B.C. and a garrison established there. During the early first century A.D. it may have been the station of Legio IX Hispana (cf. the possible military building inscription of Tiberius *CIL* iii. 10849). Under Vespasian a *colonia* was settled there, which later acquired the title *Septimia* from Severus. Siscia functioned as an imperial mint (c. A.D. 260–385). Its natural strength was increased by the construction of a canal across the confluence of the rivers under Tiberius (Cass. Dio 49. 37. 3), and it served both as a fleet station (*Not. Dign. occ.* 32. 56) and probably a customs post (*CIL* iii. 10821, 13408).

Coinage. A. Alföldi, *Siscia* (1931), and *Numizmatikai Közlöny* (1927–8). Topography. G. Veith, *Die Feldzüge des C. Iulius Caesar Octavianus in Illyrien* (1914), 51 ff., cf. fig. 7. Colonia. A. Mócsy, *Die Bevölkerung von Pannonien bis zu den Markomannenkriegen* (Budapest, 1959), 25 f. J. J. W.

**SISENNA,** Lucius Cornelius (*PW* 374), the historian, praetor in 78 B.C., defended Verres (70), and was legate to Pompey in 67, dying in Crete. His *Historiae*, in at least twelve books (scarcely the twenty-three of fr. 132), after a reference to Roman origins treated the Social War and Sullan Civil War, certainly from 90 to 82, probably to Sulla's death; it may have continued the work of Sempronius Asellio (q.v.). The composition was literary, not chronological, the style vivid and striking, on the model of Cleitarchus (Cic. *Leg.* 1. 2. 7). This Hellenistic influence appears in his translation of Aristides' *Milesiaca*, associating him with Petronius and Apuleius. His historical authority, however, was recognized by Sallust and Varro. He is not the Plautine commentator of this name.

Peter, *HRRel.* i². cccxxxiv, 276; A. Schneider, *De Sis. hist. reliquiis* (1882); Badian, *Stud. Gr. Rom. Hist.* 212 ff., and *Athenaeum* 1964, 422 ff.; R. Syme, *Sallust* (1964), 48.       A. H. McD.

**SISYPHUS,** in mythology, son of Aeolus (q.v. 2). In *Od.* 11. 593 ff. he is one of those tormented in Hades, having eternally to roll a rock up a hill, from the top of which it always rolls down again. In *Il.* 6. 154–5 he lives in Ephyre in the Argolid and is grandfather of Bellerophon (q.v.), and 'most crafty of men'. The reason for his damnation is not stated in Homer; others, as Eustathius and the schol. on Homer, ll.cc. (cf. Rose, *Handb. Gk. Myth.* 270, 294, and notes), connect it with his offence against Zeus in telling Asopus where the god had taken his daughter Aegina. For the associated folktale of how Sisyphus befooled Death and Hades *see* THANATOS. Being clearly the familiar trickster of popular tales, he is naturally brought into association with Autolycus (q.v. 1); thus, Polyaenus (*Strat.* 6. 52, cf. Hyg. *Fab.* 201) says Autolycus used to steal his cattle, but Sisyphus stopped him by attaching to their hooves lead tablets with the words 'stolen by Autolycus', whereby he tracked them. He is also father of Odysseus in post-Homeric accounts, cf. ANTICLEA. His name is a not infrequent nickname for cunning persons (see Wilisch in Roscher's *Lex.* iv. 964. 22 ff.). A more serious side of his character is reflected in his shrine, the Sisypheion, on the Acrocorinthus (Strabo 8. 6. 21) and his grave on the Isthmus (Paus. 2. 2. 2).       H. J. R.

**SITALCES,** son of Teres, king of the Odrysae of Thrace (q.v.). Sitalces continued the policy of his father, and under him the Odrysian kingdom took shape, until it covered a larger area than the whole of central Greece, extending from the Danube on the north to the Aegean on the south, and the Euxine on the east, a kingdom more powerful and better equipped than the Macedonian. In 431 B.C. through the agency of Nymphodorus (q.v.) of Abdera, Athenian *proxenos* in Thrace, whose sister was married to Sitalces, the Athenians approached Sitalces to obtain his help in controlling Perdiccas (q.v. 2) of Macedon and the towns of Thrace (Thuc. 2. 29). In the following year (430) the Spartans tried in vain (Thuc. 2. 67) to persuade Sitalces to abandon his alliance with Athens and to send an army to relieve Potidaea, which was being besieged by the Athenians. In 429 B.C. Sitalces marched against Perdiccas and the Chalcidians, taking with him Amyntas, son of Philip, brother of Perdiccas, whom he intended to put on the throne of Macedonia. Sitalces overran Chalcidice (q.v.) and Bottiaea, but, after a campaign of thirty days, he returned to his own country having achieved nothing. In taking this action he seems to have acted on the advice of his nephew, Seuthes, who later married Perdiccas' daughter, Stratonice. In 424 B.C. Sitalces organized an expedition against the Triballi, which ended in disaster and his death (Thuc. 4. 101).

Thuc. 2. 29, 95–101. A. Hoeck, 'Das Odrysenreich in Thrakien', *Hermes* 1891, 76 ff.; S. Casson, *Macedonia, Thrace and Illyria* (1926).       J. M. R. C.

**SITOPHYLAKES** (σιτοφύλακες) were Athenian officials appointed annually by lot to supervise the sale of corn and prevent overcharging for barley-meal and bread. There were originally five for the city of Athens and five for Peiraeus, but later the numbers were increased to twenty and fifteen respectively.

Lysias 22; Arist. *Ath. Pol.* 51. 3.       D. M. M.

**SITTIUS** (*PW* 3), Publius, of Nuceria, a wealthy *eques* and friend of Cicero and of Sulla (q.v. 2), with business interests in Spain and Mauretania. Going to Spain in 64 B.C., when in debt and suspected of Catilinarian sympathies, he proceeded to Mauretania to restore his fortunes as a mercenary leader. Attacking Juba (q.v. 1) in support of Caesar (46), he defeated the Pompeian remnants after Thapsus and was rewarded by Caesar with a principality centred on Cirta (q.v.), which he settled chiefly with his mercenaries and perhaps with other (mostly Campanian) families. He was assassinated by a native chieftain in 44, but his *Sittiani* long retained a distinct identity.       E. B.

**SKYTALE,** a secret method of communication used by Spartan magistracies during wartime, especially between ephors and king or general. Each of them had a stick of equal size, so that a message written on a strip of leather wound round the stick of the sender, and then detached, became illegible until the strip was rewound on the stick of the recipient. The skytale is described by Plut. *Lys.* 19, and Gell. 17. 9.       V. E.

**SLAVERY.** The jurist Florentinus defined slavery as 'an institution of the *ius gentium* whereby someone is subject to the *dominium* of another contrary to nature' (*Dig.* 1. 5. 4. 1). In non-juristic contexts the ancients regularly employed the various words we translate 'slave' (as well as words whose root-sense is not servile at all) much more loosely, though not carelessly. The Greeks in particular, whose servile vocabulary was unusually varied, extended the terms to other categories of bondage, such as helots (q.v.), in which the property relationship between master and bondsman was, strictly speaking, not present. Thus in classical Greek δοῦλος (rather than, e.g., ἀνδράποδον) was customary when the contrast with a free man was the point, and in that context it was also appropriate for a helot, as it would not be when contrasting Spartan and Athenian institutions. Nevertheless, the property element remained essential in the end, whether the owner was a private individual, a corporate body, an organ of state, or a god. At the same time, the slave was also a person, and that ambiguity permeated the history of the institution throughout antiquity.

**2.** Origins. Conversion of a person into property is tolerable only for complete outsiders (including the children born to slaves). Within the community itself, a variety of dependent statuses existed, chiefly in the more backward or archaic societies, such as debt-bondsmen, *hektemoroi* (q.v.), or clients (q.v.), involving severe loss of freedom but always stopping short of total, permanent loss. Outright enslavement was also permitted in certain special circumstances, but then physical ejection from the community was required (fictitiously in the case of exposed children) or the step was allowed because it was a commutation of capital punishment (the Roman *servi poenae*). Enslavement of outsiders and their conversion into property meant *ipso facto* deracination: loss of name (Varro, *Ling.* 8. 10, 21), of all the normal ties of kin and 'nation', even of gods, replaced by new focuses of attachment provided by the master and his society.

Casual enslavement of individual outsiders, especially of captive women, went on as far back as our evidence goes. The many references in the Linear B tablets to *doeri*, the Mycenaean form of δοῦλοι, indicate that some sort of bondage was important in the Bronze Age. Subsequently in some areas of Greece—Crete, the Peloponnese, Thessaly—there was subjugation *in situ* of whole populations (helots, *penestai*, etc.), repeated later by Greek migrants elsewhere. When that occurred, chattel slavery was unnecessary and tended to remain insignificant even in the Classical Period. Elsewhere among the archaic Greeks as in early Rome, the labour force seems to have been adequately provided through the dependent relationships already mentioned. At least neither the Homeric poems nor the traditions about early Rome suggest widespread slavery, despite the presence of some slaves. In Athens slavery became important only after the abolition by Solon (q.v.) of the status of *hektemoroi* and of debt-bondage, and in Rome following the abolition of *nexum* (q.v.).

**3.** NUMBERS. Only a few unreliable figures have come down to us. It may be doubted whether precise numbers were known to contemporaries save in those exceptional societies, such as Egypt, in which censuses were carefully taken for fiscal reasons. A reasonable guess would be that even in cities with a high slave density the ratio of slaves to free did not exceed 1:3 (excluding helots from consideration), comparable with other slave societies, such as the American South. More revealing than raw totals is the location of slaves within the economy and among the social classes. Slave ownership was widely distributed among the free, appearing well down in the social and economic scale; as late as the fourth century A.D. Libanius complained (*Or.* 31. 11) that his teachers were too impoverished to afford more than two or three slaves. At the top, the political and intellectual élites in all the great centres of the classical Greek world, except Sparta, and of the Roman Republic and Early Empire depended heavily, though not exclusively, on slave labour for their incomes and for personal services.

Because the level of personal fortunes and of governmental operations was much higher in the Roman world, slave concentrations were proportionately also greater. No Greek could match the 800 slaves Pompey's son recruited from his personal shepherds and attendants (Caes. *BCiv.* 3. 4. 4), as no Greek State could match the 700 slaves who were the regular maintenance staff of imperial Rome's aqueducts (Frontin. *Aq.* 116–17). On the other hand, the number in the Attic silver mines (see LAURIUM) may have reached 30,000 in the fourth century B.C.

**4.** EMPLOYMENT OF SLAVES. Slaves were employed throughout the gamut of human activity, skilled and unskilled, other than political. There were no uniquely slave tasks; the distinction was rather one of status and condition of employment. However, there were two areas in which the preponderance of labour was slave: domestic in the broadest sense (including, e.g., household textile-making) and mining (q.v.). In commerce, banking, and manufacture (see INDUSTRY) there was widespread independent activity by small shopkeepers and craftsmen, but establishments which outgrew the manpower of the family almost invariably expanded by acquiring slaves, sometimes, though rarely, reaching 100 or more men. In the latter these managers and overseers were usually slaves as well. And there were slaves in the professions, both 'liberal' and 'illiberal'.

In agriculture (q.v.) the picture seems more complicated. Peasant farming always coexisted with larger estates and the latter were either worked by slaves (or other kinds of dependent labour) or leased out in smaller units, the tenants being in the same position, with respect to labour, as small proprietors. The extent to which slaves figured in large-scale agriculture in classical Greece is hard to measure. On the one hand, for example, there is Thucydides' remark (1. 141) that in the Peloponnese most men were self-employed (αὐτουργοί). And, on the other hand, there is his evidence of numerous slaves in the countryside in Corcyra (3. 73), or the implication underlying Xenophon's *Oeconomicus* that the gentleman farmer lived in the city and left his estate to a slave bailiff and slave workmen. Size apart, Xenophon's picture is not really different from that of the Roman *latifundia* (q.v.) before tenancy and the colonate (see COLONUS (*b*)) made heavy inroads in the course of the Empire. In the absence of all quantitative evidence, caution is essential in discussing the position in the Empire. Occasional grumbling remarks in the literature are not a sufficient basis for generalization. Columella favoured tenants for holdings too far away to permit the owner to visit (*Rust.* 1. 7. 6–7), but only under those conditions, and he assumed that vine-dressers and other specially skilled workers would continue to be slaves.

Ps.-Aristotle's description of the slave's life as one of 'work, punishment and food' (*Oec.* 1344ᵃ35) is tempered by his recommendation (ᵇ15) that the incentive be held out of freedom at a predetermined date. No statistics are available, but the practice of manumission seems to have been more common in domestic and urban employments than in agriculture or mining (see FREEDMEN). In the cities one procedure was to provide a slave with what the Romans called a *peculium* (q.v.), from the profits of which he eventually purchased his freedom.

Direct ownership and employment of slaves by the State were limited by the practice of contracting out most public enterprises. Hence the Greek δημόσιοι were restricted to the police, a few clerks, and some miscellaneous posts. Imperial Rome, with its extended governmental activity, required more public slaves: in the imperial 'household', for the maintenance of the aqueducts (q.v.), and later in the State factories. Contractors were free to employ whatever labour they wished. In the military sphere the privately owned slave batman was common, but slaves were freed and armed only in moments of crisis, and their use in the navies was infrequent and spasmodic.

It is impossible to discuss the profitability of ancient slavery. Complicated calculations have been attempted but they rest on too few data to be meaningful. The domestic sector stood outside all such considerations anyway. For the rest, the wealth of the owners of large estates and manufactures and the fortunes drawn from mines cannot mean anything other than the profitability of the system. In the peak centuries slaves were cheap: two years' keep would buy a skilled workman. When the sources of supply shrank in the Roman Empire, prices rose and numbers of slaves began to drop: the *pax Romana* had closed off too large a part of the world to slave recruitment.

**5.** SLAVE SUPPLY. Although the statement that war and piracy (q.v.) were the chief sources of slave supply is true in a way, it diverts attention from the indispensable slave-trader. An army which seized a large number of captives either marched them to some near-by market or sold them on the spot to traders who came along for the purpose. 'Piracy' was often a cover-word for an organized slaving system, the most famous being the one based in south-western Asia Minor after 150 B.C., with Delos the transshipment centre (Strabo 14. 5. 2). Neither war nor piracy could have maintained the necessary flow without the complementary efforts of slave-dealers who regularly brought in 'barbarians' obtained from the latter's own territories, where they were made available either through warfare among themselves or by 'peaceful' practices, such as sale of children.

Ancient sources rarely mention the slave-trade, apart from the many figures of captives in particular battles or campaigns and from accounts of particular phases in the persistent, and often equivocal, struggle with piracy. Only by accident, for example, do we know that Ephesus was a major slave-market during a period of at least 400 years (cf. Hdt. 8. 105 and Varro, *Ling.* 8. 21). Nor is a systematic account possible of the distribution of slaves by nationality. Certain nationalities were traditionally believed to be better suited for certain occupations (*Dig.* 21. 1. 31. 21), but the surviving literature shows little interest in accuracy in this matter. As for breeding, we are reduced to guesswork. Evidence in the Delphic manumission inscriptions, papyri, and Roman legal texts on slave-sales perhaps implies more breeding than many modern writers allow.

**6.** REVOLTS. The mixture of nationalities usually found in any large body of slaves was, among other things, a deterrent to revolt (Arist. [*Oec.*] 1344$^b$18). In any event, large-scale slave revolts have always been extremely difficult to organize and, unlike helot revolts, they played no role in Greek history. It was flight which slave-owners feared and to which the law devoted much attention, a danger which was much increased during war or social turmoil (e.g. Thuc. 7. 27. 5). The three great revolts in Roman history occurred during a period of very severe social strain, the first two in Sicily, *c.* 139–132 and 104–100 (Diod. 34–6), the third that led by Spartacus (q.v.) in Italy, 73–71 B.C. (App. *BCiv.* 1. 14). Among the special circumstances were the large concentration of co-nationals —from the hellenized east in Sicily, from the north under Spartacus—and the presence of slaves capable of giving leadership. The numbers participating were said to exceed 100,000, a claim substantiated by the long and considerable military effort which suppression required. The revolts ended in failure, despite the rather mysterious way they were echoed at long distance, in the Attic silver mines and in Pergamum.

The Pergamene revolt of 133–129, led by Aristonicus (q.v. 1), developed utopian features and attracted free men. With that one exception, the slave revolts were not socially revolutionary: they sought to change the position of the slaves actually involved, either by taking possession of the territory or by forcing their way home, but not to change society, and, in particular, not to abolish slavery as an institution. Nor did they obtain significant support from the free poor, who saw in the struggles none of their affair.

**7.** LAW. Because the slave was, in the American phrase, a 'peculiar property', the law had to deal with him more often than with any other single subject. Every act or relationship, civil or criminal, contractual or delictual or familial, required special regulations and modifications if a slave were involved. In a sense there was no law of slavery apart from the rules defining and determining a man's status; there were only special provisions respecting slaves within the law of sales, of contracts, and so forth. And they varied, within rather narrow limits, according to the social structure, as between Gortyn and Athens or between the Rome of the XII Tables (q.v.) and the Rome of Cicero. As society and the economy became more complex, more slaves were employed in managerial and quasi-independent roles, and that required new legal regulations, about the *peculium*, for example. Inevitably there was a tendency to give greater recognition to *de facto* personality, to quasi-marriage rights (*see* CONTUBERNIUM), or to the right of asylum At best, however, amelioration touched only the edges of the institution, leaving the essence unaltered: it is enough

to note that Justinian's lawyers still had to pack the *Corpus Iuris* with classical law about slaves.

**8.** THE HELLENISTIC EAST. In the Greek cities slavery played its traditional role on the whole, and numbers were relatively high because the major cities were so much more populous than those of Greece itself. In the countryside, however, and specifically in the areas not part of the territory of a Greek city, chattel slavery remained essentially insignificant, as it had been before Alexander's conquests. Royal and noble claims to the land included certain rights over the peasantry, whether they were known as λαοί or βασιλικοὶ γεωργοί or by some other name. Hence there was no need for a substantial slave labour force, and indeed important interests against it.

**9.** PSYCHOLOGY. As with the law so with every other aspect of behaviour and thinking: the ubiquity of the slave was an integral factor. That can be seen in the enormously complex variations in rules and practices with respect to slave participation in cult, in the history of prostitution and of sexual habits and attitudes generally, in the writings of philosophers about human nature or about Greeks and barbarians (including the debate about whether or not slavery was a 'natural' institution), in expressed attitudes to labour or in the fragmentary instances of utopian thinking. What one cannot expect is any systematic contemporary discussion of the impact of slavery because no one in antiquity was in a position to analyse the system from outside, and modern scholars are understandably reluctant to attempt the difficult analysis the ancients were unable to make for themselves. Yet somehow one must grasp the psychology of Xenophon when he made the proposal in all seriousness that the Athenian State acquire enough 'publicly owned slaves to work in the mines so that 'every Athenian be maintained at public expense' (*Vect.* 4. 33); or of Horace, a court poet seemingly oblivious of his servile ancestry.

A critical bibliographical essay is appended to M. I. Finley. ed. *Slavery in Classical Antiquity* (1960, with suppl. 1968), and there is a very long list of titles in W. L. Westermann, *The Slave Systems of Greek and Roman Antiquity* (1955). Part i of Ja. A. Lencman, *Die Sklaverei in mykenischen und homerischen Griechenland* (1966), systematically analyses the literature on ancient slavery from the beginning of the nineteenth century. On legal aspects full bibliographies will be found under the appropriate rubrics in A. Berger, *Encyclopedic Dictionary of Roman Law* (1953). In what follows, therefore, emphasis is on important books and monographs and recent articles. (Mainz = *Abhandlungen* of the Akad. d. Wiss. u. d. Lit. in Mainz, Geistes- u. sozialwiss. Klasse.)

GENERAL. S. Lauffer, 'Die Sklaverei in der griechisch-römischen Welt', *Gymnasium* 1961, 370 ff., with discussion by E. Ch. Welskopf, and Lauffer, *Acta Antiqua* 1964, 311 ff.; M. I. Finley, 'Between Slavery and Freedom', *Comp. Studies in Soc. and Hist.* vi (1964), 233 ff.; on debt-bondage, *Rev. Hist. Dr. Fr.* 1965, 159 ff.; on slave-trade, *Klio* 1962, 51 ff.; J. Vogt, *Sklaverei und Humanität* (1965); F. Bömer, *Untersuchungen über die Religion der Sklaven in Griechenland und Rom* (Mainz, 1957, no. 7; 1960, no. 1; 1961, no. 4; 1963, no. 10); H. Wallon, *Histoire de l'esclavage dans l'antiquité*² (3 vols., 1879).

GREECE. F. Gschnitzer, *Studien zur griechischen Terminologie der Sklaverei* i (Mainz, 1963, no. 13); V. Ehrenberg, *The People of Aristophanes*² (1951), ch. 7; S. Lauffer, *Die Bergwerksklaven von Laureion* (Mainz, 1955, no. 12; 1956, no. 11); E. Kazakevich, 'Slave Agents in Athens' (in Russian), *Vestnik Drevnei Istorii* 1961, no. 3, 3 ff.; C. Mossé, *La Fin de la démocratie athénienne* (1962), 179 ff.

HELLENISTIC. Rostovtzeff, *Hellenistic World*; H. Volkmann, *Die Massenversklavungen der Einwohner eroberter Städte in der hellenistisch-römischen Zeit* (Mainz, 1961, no. 3); T. Zawadzki, *The Social and Agrarian Structure of Asia Minor in the Hellenistic Period* (in Polish, 1952); J.-C. Dumont, 'A propos d'Aristonicos', *Eirene* 1966, 189 ff.; I. Bieżuńska-Malowist on Roman Egypt, *Studii Classice* iii (1961), 147 ff.

ROME. C. A. Yeo, 'The Economics of Roman and American Slavery', *Finanzarchiv* 1952, 445 ff.; P. P. Spranger, *Historische Untersuchungen zu den Sklavenfiguren des Plautus und Terenz* (Mainz, 1960, no. 8); M. I. Finley, *Ancient Sicily* (1968), ch. 11; R. H. Barrow, *Slavery in the Roman Empire* (1928); J. Češka, *Differentiation among Slaves in Italy in the First Two Centuries of the Principate* (in Czech, 1959); P. R. C. Weaver on *servi Caesaris*, *PCPS* 1964, 74 ff.; *Past and Present* 1967, 3 ff.

LAW. G. R. Morrow, *Plato's Law of Slavery in Its Relation to Greek Law* (1939); R. Taubenschlag, *The Law of Greco-Roman Egypt*² (1955); W. W. Buckland, *The Roman Law of Slavery* (1908).
M. I. F.

**SMYRNA** (Σμύρνα or Ζμύρνα), a city on the west coast of Asia Minor at the head of the gulf into which flows the Hermus, the natural outlet of the trade of the Hermus valley and within easy reach of the Maeander valley. Old Smyrna lay at the north-eastern corner of the gulf. Occupied by Greeks c. 1000 B.C. and originally Aeolic, it seems soon to have become Ionic; excavation has shown that the old village-like layout was replaced in the seventh century by a handsome fortified city with regular streets. After its capture by Alyattes of Lydia c. 600 Smyrna ceased to exist as a city; it was refounded on its present site around Mount Pagus by Alexander or his successors Antigonus and Lysimachus, and at once became one of the chief cities of Asia. Throughout the Roman period it was famous for its wealth, its fine buildings, and its devotion to science and medicine. It sided with Rome against Mithridates, and in the imperial period owed much to Roman favour. It was made a 'temple-warden' (νεωκόρος) in the imperial cult by Tiberius and was restored after its destruction by earthquakes in A.D. 178 and 180 by Marcus Aurelius. It was one of the 'Seven Churches' of the Apocalypse. Homer was reputed to be a Smyrnaean by birth; other famous poets of Smyrna were Mimnermus, Bion, and Quintus Smyrnaeus.

C. J. Cadoux, *Ancient Smyrna* (1938). For Old Smyrna, J. M. Cook, *BSA* 1958. W. M. C.; J. M. C.

**SOCIAL WAR** is the name given to a war against rebellious allies (*socii*).

(1) ὁ συμμαχικὸς πόλεμος, the revolt of the allies of Athens (357–355 B.C.), led by Rhodes, Cos, and Chios, with the support of Byzantium and Mausolus of Caria, caused by discontent at Athenian supremacy and the exactions imposed by Athenian generals and mercenaries. The defeat of Athens at sea at Embata (356) and the threat of Persian intervention (355) led to negotiations and peace.

(2) The war (220–217) in which the Aetolians and their allies, Sparta and Elis, opposed Philip V of Macedon and his Hellenic League. Philip's campaigns brought it to a successful conclusion in the Peace of Naupactus, the terms of which were very favourable to him.

(3) The Social, Marsic, or Italic War (91–87; the main fighting being in 90–89), waged by Rome's Italian allies (*socii*, among whom the Marsi were prominent) against her predominance. Rome gained the victory largely through the political concession of granting her citizenship to the enemy. Thereafter Italy, south of the Po, was united by the common bond of citizenship. H. H. S.

**SOCII.** The Roman confederation consisted, apart from Latini (q.v.), of the *socii Italici* and allies from beyond Italy. The Italian peoples—Etruscan, Umbrian, Sabellian, and Greek—were allied to Rome by formal treaties (*see* FOEDUS). But frequent revolts led to the final subordination of the federate allies to Rome by the formal requirement that they must 'preserve the greatness (*maiestas*) of the Roman people'. The Italian allies provided Rome with troops *e formula togatorum*—the Greeks giving sailors for the fleet—both in defensive and offensive wars. Otherwise they were sovereign peoples, but tended in the second century B.C. to fall under the general supervision of Rome, until their autonomy became in practice limited. The allies sometimes imitated Roman institutions, notably at Bantia in Bruttium, which romanized its constitution (*see* MEDDIX), while Rome occasionally granted them certain privileges of the Latins, chiefly *commercium*, *conubium*, or *ius exsilii*. But generally the *socii Italici* differed from Rome and the Latins in language, custom, and laws, and being less privileged than the Latins felt more deeply the deterioration in the

Roman attitude, which led to the Social War. This was fought in the defence of local and personal liberty against the abuse of the unrestricted *imperium* by Roman magistrates, claims finally met by the grant of Roman citizenship under the Julian and Plautian laws of 90–89 B.C. (*see* CAESAR 2; PLAUTIUS 1).

From early times Rome had allies outside Italy, notably Carthage and Massilia. After 200 B.C. the number of these *civitates foederatae* rapidly increased. Greek city-states, confederations, and kings became allies, on nominally equal terms. With Rome's rise to world power the position of these *foederati* deteriorated, till they became merely the most highly privileged class of provincial communities, though in theory their rights depended upon a bilateral agreement. They were never included in the *formula togatorum*, although they sometimes provided auxiliary troops, cavalry or light-armed. They did not normally receive the social *iura*, though *exsilium* was valid among them. But they were immune from interference by provincial governors and in internal affairs were in practice freer than the Italian allies, notably in the right of coinage. *Foederati* did not commonly survive in the Western Provinces; for when they rebelled, Rome reduced them to the status either of ordinary provincial communities, *stipendiarii*, or of *civitates liberae*. The latter originally were the Greek States of Sicily and mainland Greece declared free after the defeat of the Hellenistic kings, notably by Flamininus in 196 B.C. Their freedom depended upon a revocable decision of Rome. This 'freedom' later became a substitute for or modification of direct provincialization, as in Macedon (167 B.C.), and Africa (145). Special conditions added to the declaration secured for Rome the substantial advantages—notably the payment of tribute—without the burden of provincial government. Such free States were also known as *socii*, or *socii et amici populi Romani*, terms also applied to the ordinary provincial subjects of Rome. In the Ciceronian age *socius* came to mean any community which had been received *in fidem populi Romani*, though surviving 'free States' continued to exercise diminishing privileges under the Principate.

ANCIENT SOURCES. Livy, Polybius, Cicero (esp. *pro Balbo*) *passim*, and many inscriptions in *CIL*, *SIG*, *OGI*.
MODERN LITERATURE. Inside Italy: Beloch, *Römische Geschichte*; Mommsen Marquardt, *Manuel* vi. 2 (*Röm. Staatsr.* iii. 1); Rosenberg, *Staat der alten Italiker* (1913). E. Badian, *Foreign Clientelae* (1958), Part i. A. J. Toynbee, *Hannibal's Legacy* (1965), i, chs. 3, 5; ii, ch. 4. E. Gabba, *Le origini della Guerra Sociale* (1954), with P. Brunt, *JRS* 1965, 90 ff. A. N. Sherwin-White, *The Roman Citizenship* (1939, esp. Part i); Outside Italy: above, and Abbott and Johnson, *Municipal Administration of the Roman Empire* (documents); Jones, *Cities E. Rom. Prov.*; E. Taubler, *Imperium Romanum* (for the treaty forms, A. Heuss, *Klio* 1934). A. N. S.-W.

**SOCRATES** (1) (469–399 B.C.), son of Sophroniscus and Phaenarete, Athenian of the deme of Alopece. His father is said to have been a sculptor or stonemason and was apparently reasonably well-to-do. At any rate Socrates served in the army as a hoplite, though he was reduced to poverty later. He married late in life Xanthippe, who became notorious in subsequent generations for the stories of her bad temper, though these are very likely to have been exaggerated. There is some evidence that this was his second marriage.

In early life, if we are to judge from Aristophanes' caricature of him in the *Clouds* and the autobiography that Plato puts into his mouth in the *Phaedo*, he was interested in the scientific philosophy of his time. He is said to have associated with Archelaus the physicist, but Aristophanes' picture of him as head of a definite philosophical school is not to be taken seriously and Xenophon seems to have denied any such period in his development. At any rate by the time at which we know most about him he had abandoned these interests and devoted himself to the work of inquiry into the right conduct of life, carried on by the familiar Socratic method of cross-questioning the people with whom he came in contact. If this represents a change of interest, it is probably to be dated some years before the Peloponnesian War and has been plausibly connected with the response made by the Delphic oracle to his friend Chaerephon, to the effect that no one was wiser than Socrates. Of the external events of his life we know comparatively little. He served in the army and we hear of him taking part in the fighting at Potidaea, Amphipolis, and Delium, where he gained a great reputation for courage. He found himself one of the Presidents of the Assembly at the time of the trial of the generals after Arginusae and courageously refused to put the illegal motion to the vote in spite of the fury of the multitude. After the fall of Athens we hear of him defying the orders of the Thirty Tyrants when they tried to implicate him in their misdeeds.

In 399 B.C. he was brought to trial before a popular jury on the charge of introducing strange gods and of corrupting the youth. There has been considerable dispute as to the precise significance of this charge. But the available evidence suggests that the accusation of introducing strange gods was never clearly formulated or pressed very hard. It may well have been put in just to create prejudice, while the real gravamen of the charge lay in the accusation of being a subversive influence on the minds of the young men. This was undoubtedly connected, whether avowedly or not, with his known friendship with some of the men who had been most prominent in attacks on democracy in Athens. After a not very conciliatory speech in his defence he was condemned to death. He refused to take advantage of a plan for his escape, made by some of his friends, and thirty days after the condemnation he drank the hemlock.

His general appearance and manner of life are probably more familiar to us than those of any figure in Greek history. He was a man of strong physique and great powers of endurance, and completely indifferent to comfort and luxury. He was remarkable for his unflinching courage, both moral and physical, and his strong sense of duty. Together with this went an extremely genial and kindly temperament and a keen sense of humour, while he was obviously a man of the greatest intellectual ability. It was the combination of these qualities which secured for him a devoted circle of friends of very varied types, from young men of good family looking forward to a public career to serious thinkers who seem to have come to him for light on the problems which interested them. His circle included both Athenians and men from other cities of Greece. Several of them became known later as founders of philosophical schools of their own representing very diverse views. Such were Plato and Antisthenes at Athens, Eucleides at Megara, and, possibly, Phaedo at Elis.

Socrates' religious views have also been the subject of some debate. He was undoubtedly a man of strong religious sense and scrupulous in religious observances. But he is very likely to have applied the dissolvent influence of his critical method to some of the conventional religious beliefs of the time. On the other hand, there is no real evidence of definite membership of any unorthodox religious body or sect. One of the best-known things about him is the experience, which he had at intervals throughout his life, of a divine sign or warning which determined his action for him from time to time. The exact nature of this has been the subject of much discussion, but still remains a mystery.

The precise significance of Socrates' contribution to thought has been a matter of considerable debate in recent times. There are some who ascribe to him a great part of the positive philosophical doctrines usually associated with the name of Plato. But this does not commend itself to the majority of scholars, who accept as the literal truth the statement frequently ascribed to him by the earliest authorities that he had no set of positive doctrines to teach. None the less his influence on subsequent thought was undoubtedly very great. Later authors in ancient times represented him as being the first thinker to turn men's minds towards questions of morality and the conduct of life. This can hardly be literally true, as an interest in these matters seems to have been developing in Greece in the earliest years of his life. But he does seem to have been the first person to apply serious critical and philosophical thought to these questions, and to examine systematically the fundamental assumptions from which current discussions about conduct started. In the course of this he was the first to lay stress on the importance of systematic definition of the general terms used in discussion. In this way he may be regarded as the inspiration for the development, not only of moral philosophy, but also of logic. To understand his influence fully we have to remember both his own striking personality and the intellectual tendencies of the time. He worked in an age of widespread criticism and discussion which was beginning to produce a sceptical attitude about the foundations of morality and the possibility of knowledge alike. And the example of his strong moral sense and devotion to truth combined with his readiness or even eagerness to face squarely any criticism and discussion was what established his influence most firmly among the men of his age.

PRIMARY ANCIENT SOURCES. Plato; Xenophon, *Mem., Ap., Symp.*; Aeschines Socraticus (fragments, Teubner text); Aristotle, *Metaph., Eth. Nic., Mag. Mor.* (for philosophical contribution).

MODERN AUTHORS. (*a*) General : Zeller ii. 1⁴; J. Burnet, *From Thales to Plato* (1914); H. Maier, *Sokrates* (1913); C. Ritter, *Sokrates* (1931); A. E. Taylor, *Socrates* (1932); W. Jaeger, *Paideia* ii, ch. 2 (Engl. Transl. 1943); O. Gigon, *Sokrates* (1947) and commentaries on Xenophon, *Mem.* (1953, 1956).

(*b*) On the Socratic controversy, particularly relations of Socrates and Plato: A. E. Taylor, *Varia Socratica* (1911); W. D. Ross, *Aristotle's Metaphysics*, introd. ii (1924); A. Diès, *Autour de Platon* i (1927); G. C. Field, *Plato and his Contemporaries* (1930); R. Hackforth, *The Composition of Plato's Apology* (1933). The question of the authenticity of Plato's and Xenophon's portraits of Socrates is bound up with the question how far they were taking part in the battle of pamphleteers which began with Polycrates' Κατηγορία Σωκράτους: see A. Chroust, *Socrates, Man or Myth* (1957), ch. 4, E. R. Dodds, *Plato's Gorgias* (1959), 28 f. On the development in Plato's account of Socrates see G. Rudberg, *Symb. Osl.* 1953.                           G. C. F.

**SOCRATES** (2) (*c.* A.D. 380–*c.* 450), a Constantinopolitan lawyer, continued the *Historia Ecclesiastica* of Eusebius from 305 to 439, trying to give an objective account based on documents and first-hand testimony. Books 1–2, at first dependent on Rufinus, were revised from fuller knowledge of Athanasius' historical writings. Socrates knew little of the West, but for the eastern church assembled many documents, including a collection of conciliar *Acta* made by Sabinus, bishop of Heraclea, in 375 (now lost). Though he made some bad mistakes and did not always understand doctrinal issues, he is generally sensible and straightforward, plain in style, interesting for his lay outlook (e.g. his dislike of episcopal squabbles, sympathy with Novatianist schismatics, ambivalent estimate of Chrysostom). In principle, but insufficiently in practice, he saw the necessity of relating ecclesiastical to secular affairs. His history was the principal source of Sozomen and Theodoret; the three histories were edited to provide the Latin manual, *Historia Tripartita*.

EDITIONS. H. Valesius (Paris, 1686); W. Bright (1893²). S. L. G.

**SODALES**, 'companions' or 'associates', members the minor priesthoods at Rome, which ranked below the *Collegia* (q.v.) and differed from them in that they acted only as a body and not as individuals. The chief of these were the Fetiales (q.v.), who had charge of the *ius* *fetiale* and made treaties (Livy 1. 24) and declared war (Livy 1. 32). Three other *sodalitates* were concerned with annual rites; the Salii (q.v.), priests of Mars, active in March and October, at the opening and closing of the campaigning season; the Luperci, executants of the ritual of the Lupercalia (q.v.) in February; and the Fratres Arvales (q.v.), celebrants of agricultural rites, associated later with the cult of the imperial house. Besides these there were the Sodales Titii or Titienses, of whom nothing is known but their name; Roman tradition (Tac. *Ann.* 1. 54) connected them with the Sabine king Titus Tatius; some recent scholars look to the Etruscan deity Mutinus Titinius and suspect that their ritual was originally phallic. To these ancient *sodalitates* were added after the death of Augustus the Sodales Augustales, who were charged with the cult of the two Divi, Julius and Augustus; later imperial families instituted Sodales Flaviales, Hadrianales, and Antoniniani. C. B.

**SOL.** The name of the Sun is given to two utterly different deities in Rome. The older is Sol Indiges, of whom we know that he had a sacrifice on 9 Aug. (Augustan calendars for that date: *Soli Indigiti in colle Quirinale*), while calendars for 11 Dec., especially the Fasti Antiates, give AG(onium) IND(igetis). Nothing more is known with any certainty; the indication for 11 Dec. is supplemented by Lydus (*Mens* 4. 155, 172. 22 Wuensch), who says that the festival was in honour of Helios. See Koch, *Gestirnverehrung im alten Italien* (1933), 63 ff., against Wissowa, *RK* 317; but some of Koch's combinations are very hazardous, see H. J. Rose, *Harv. Theol. Rev.* 1937, 165 ff. This cult was native, apparently, and is connected by Latte (*RR* 44) with the agricultural calendar.

Much later and certainly foreign (Syrian) was the worship of Sol Invictus, to give him his most characteristic title. Eastern sun-gods had been making their way in the west, helped no doubt by the current identification of Apollo with Helios (e.g. Hor. *Carm. Saec.* 9), for some time; but the first attempt to make the Sun's the chief worship was that of Elagabalus (A.D. 218–22) (S.H.A. *Vit. Ant. Heliogab.* 6. 7 and 17. 8), who introduced the god of Emesa, whose priest and, apparently, incarnation he was, El Gabal. Elagabalus' excesses and consequent unpopularity and assassination checked the cult, but Aurelian (270–5) reintroduced a similar worship, also oriental; he was himself the child of a priestess of the Sun (see S.H.A. *Vit. Aurel.* 5. 5 and 35. 3). This remained the chief imperial and official worship till Christianity displaced it, although the cult of the older gods, especially Jupiter, did not cease, but rather the new one was in some sort parallel to it, the Sun's clergy being called *pontifices Solis*, a significant name which was part of a policy of romanizing the oriental god. Sol had a magnificent temple on the campus Agrippae, see Platner–Ashby, 491 ff. Its dedication day (*natalis*) was 25 Dec.

Wissowa, *RK* 365 ff.; Cumont, *Rel. or.*[4] 106 ff.; Latte, *RR* 231 ff. H. J. R.

**SOLINUS,** GAIUS IULIUS, wrote (probably soon after A.D. 200) *Collectanea Rerum Memorabilium*, a geographical summary of parts of the known world, with remarks on origins, history, customs of nations, and products of countries. Almost the whole is taken from Pliny's *Natural History* and Mela without acknowledgement. There is a meagre addition about the British Isles which gives us Tanatus (*Thanet*); the stone jet, found abundantly in Britain; and the absence of snakes in Ireland. He introduced the name 'mare Mediterraneum'.

Edition. Mommsen, 1895[2], repr. 1958. That of Saumaise, prefixed to his *Plinianae exercitationes* (1689), is still useful. Transl. A. Golding, 1587, reproduced in facsimile 1955. H. Walter *Die Coll. R. M. des C. Iul. Solinus* (1968). E. H. W.

**SOLON,** Athenian statesman and poet, was of noble descent but moderate means; perhaps, as the tradition stated and his travels and economic measures suggest, he was a merchant. He was prominent in Athens' war with Megara for the possession of Salamis, urging his countrymen to renewed effort when they despaired of success (*c.* 600?). In 594/3 he was chief archon, and in later times it was believed that this was the occasion of his reforms; but many difficulties are removed if we date them about twenty years later. It was further believed that he spent the ten years after his reforms in overseas travel, visiting Egypt (where he met Amasis, q.v. 1), Cyprus, and perhaps Lydia (the story of a meeting with Croesus, q.v., was already rejected on chronological grounds in antiquity), and returning to find Athens torn by the 'regional' strife (*see* PISISTRATUS, MEGACLES) which ended only with the establishment of the tyranny. He vainly endeavoured to dissuade the Athenians from supporting Pisistratus, and survived his first usurpation, just how long was not agreed; according to one version, he died in Cyprus and his bones were scattered in the island of Salamis.

It was probably not till the fourth century that written accounts of Solon's work, based on his poems, on surviving fragments of his law-code, and on oral tradition, began to be composed; hence the large speculative element both in the extant sources and in modern reconstructions: the general lines are, however, clear. Attica in the early sixth century laboured under grave economic distress and political conflict. The Eupatridai (q.v.) not only controlled the machinery of government but had reduced many of their poorer countrymen to a condition of serfdom as *Hektemoroi* (q.v.). These, it seems, and any other propertyless Athenians who contracted debts, having no security to offer but their persons, were liable, when they defaulted in the payment of their dues or the restoration of what they had borrowed, to be sold into actual slavery in Attica or overseas. The discontent of the unprivileged classes had risen to a dangerous level, and Solon, who apparently had the confidence of all parties, was appointed to resolve the crisis and legislate for the future.

He first cancelled all debts for which land or liberty was the security (we do not indeed know whether credit was as yet obtainable on any other terms), and so released the peasants from serfdom, restored their farms, and redeemed those who had been sold into slavery; and he forbade all borrowing on the security of the person in future. These measures, known as the *Seisachtheia*, or shaking-off of burdens, though drastic, fell short of the wholesale redistribution of the land which some of his poorer supporters had demanded. Other economic reforms, such as the introduction of a native Attic coinage approximating to the 'Euboic' standard used by Corinth and the western Greeks (*see* COINAGE, GREEK), a corresponding alteration of the system of weights and measures, a prohibition of the export of agricultural produce other than olive-oil, and the granting of citizenship to immigrant craftsmen, were designed to encourage trade and industry and so provide a long-term solution of the country's economic problems.

Solon also reformed the constitution. He divided the citizens into four census-classes (τέλη) called *pentakosiomedimnoi*, *hippeis*, *zeugitai*, and *thetes* (qq.v.), according to their annual production of corn, oil, and wine (it is generally agreed that an equivalent rating in money-income for those who made their living in other ways, if not provided by Solon, must have been introduced sooner or later), and gave each class a proportionate measure of political responsibility. He reserved the chief offices (*see* ARCHONTES) and the Areopagus (q.v.) for the two highest classes; the *zeugitai* were admitted to minor offices and the new *boule*; and the *thetes* to the *ekklesia* and Heliaea (qq.v.). He probably defined the rights and duties of the *ekklesia* for the first time, and strengthened its position in relation to the Areopagus by the institution of a *boule* (q.v.) with probouleutic functions. By granting a right of appeal to the Heliaea he freed the individual from the unfettered power of the magistrates and gave the people some control over them. Lastly, he issued a new and more humane code of justice abolishing all the ordinances of Draco (q.v.) except those concerning homicide.

In attempting to satisfy all parties Solon inevitably satisfied none. Yet his economic reforms not only relieved immediate distress but permanently ended the major evils of serfdom and slavery for debt; and although poverty and discontent were not abolished, they were progressively diminished by the expansion of trade and industry which he encouraged: in this respect his work was carried further by Pisistratus. His constitutional reforms, again, did not prevent further internal strife; but by substituting wealth for birth as the criterion of political privilege and securing the rights of all citizens to some share in the government he broke the monopoly of the Eupatridai and laid the foundations of the future democracy. His laws (i.e. the constitution and the code of justice) were of course added to and in large part superseded; the official copies (*see* AXONES) were lost and the text of some obsolete provisions forgotten; but those which remained in force were incorporated, with appropriate modifications, in the revision begun in 410 (*see* NOMOTHETAI).

Fragments of Solon's poems: Diehl, *Anth. Lyr. Graec.* i³. 20–47; laws: E. Ruschenbusch, Σόλωνος νόμοι, *Hist.* Einzelschriften 9, 1966; Arist. *Ath. Pol.* 1–14; Plut. *Sol.* I. M. Linforth, *Solon the Athenian* (1919); Busolt–Swoboda, *Griech. Staatsk.* ii³. (1926), see index iii; K. Freeman, *Life and Work of Solon* (1926); W. J. Woodhouse, *Solon the Liberator* (1938); R. Hönn, *Solon* (1948); Hignett, *Hist. Athen. Const.*, see index; A. Andrewes, *Greek Tyrants* (1956), 78 f.; A. Masaracchia, *Solone* (1958); G. Ferrara, *La politica di S.* (1964). Date of the reforms: Hignett, op. cit., appendix iii; A. French, *Growth of the Athenian Economy* (1964), 181 ff. Land and Debt. R. J. Hopper in *Ancient Society and Institutions* (1966), 139 ff. *See also under* HEKTEMOROI. The Income-Classes. U. Wilcken, *Hermes* 1928, 236 ff.; K. M. T. Chrimes, *CR* 1932, 2 ff.; J. H. Thiel, *Mnemos.* 1950, 1 ff.; C. M. A. van der Oudenrijn, *Mnemos.* 1952, 19 ff.; K. H. Waters, *JHS* 1960, 181 ff.; French, *Hist.* 1961, 510 ff.; op. cit. 18 ff. Coinage, Weights, and Measures. A. W. Gomme, *JHS* 1926, 171 ff.; J. G. Milne, *JHS* 1930, 179 ff., 1938, 96 f.; J. Johnston, *JHS* 1934, 180 ff.; A. French, op. cit. 22 ff.                              A. W. G.; T. J. C.

**SOPATER** (Σώπατρος) of Paphos, Greek parodist and writer of *phlyakes*, flourished from the time of Alexander to that of Ptolemy II. Fr. 19 mentions Thibron, who put Harpalus to death in 324 B.C. It may be inferred from frs. 1 and 24 that Sopater lived in Alexandria. Fourteen titles of plays survive: three (Βακχίς, Βακχίδος μνηστῆρες, Βακχίδος γάμος) seem to form a triad, unless merely varied descriptions of the same piece; Ἱππόλυτος, Νέκυια, Ὀρέστης are burlesques of mythology or tragedy cf. (MIDDLE COMEDY). From Γαλάται, *The Gauls*, fr. 6 (12 vv.)—the longest extant *phlyax*-fragment—contains raillery of the Stoics; this passage, far removed from the buffoonery of the original *phlyakes*, approaches the spirit and language of Attic Comedy.

*CGF* 192 ff. T. B. L. Webster, *Hellenistic Poetry and Art* (1964), 126 f.                              W. G. W.; W. G. A.

**SOPHAENETUS** of Stymphalus (fl. *c.* 400 B.C.), author of an *Anabasis* of Cyrus and one of the generals who led the Greek army back to the Black Sea. Where Diodorus' account of the expedition differs from Xenophon's, we may suppose that his source, Ephorus, who used Xenophon, drew his divergent information from Sophaenetus.

*FGrH* ii B, 109.                              G. L. B.

**SŌPHILUS**, comic poet, τῆς μέσης κωμῳδίας and 'Sikyonian or Theban' (*Suda*), but he certainly wrote for

the Attic theatre (Ath. 123 d, 228 b). We have nine titles; it is conceivable that his *Androkles* refers to the man mentioned in Menander, *Sam.* 261 ff.

*FCG* iii. 581 ff.; *CAF* ii. 444 ff.; *FAC* ii. 546 ff.                              K. J. D.

**SOPHISTS.** The word σοφιστής does not appear to have been in use before the fifth century B.C. In its earliest use it simply means a wise man or a man skilled at any particular kind of activity. From the first there is, however, perhaps some suggestion of a man who made a special job of being wise, and it gradually came to be specially, though never exclusively, applied to members of a particular profession. This was the profession of itinerant teachers who went from city to city giving instruction for a fee. The subjects of instruction varied somewhat in content, but always had a relation to the art of getting on, or of success in life. Some Sophists, such as Protagoras, claimed to teach 'virtue', which was almost equivalent to efficiency in the conduct of life. Others, like Gorgias and his successors, confined themselves to the teaching of oratory, which in democratic cities was one of the chief roads to success. Instruction in this was, indeed, included in the teaching even of those who made the wider claim. We hear of other aspects of their teaching, such as the system of memory-training ascribed to Hippias, but all have reference to this central practical aim. Their nearest modern parallel is to be found in the numerous institutions at the present day which advertise their ability to train people for success in business, or in life in general. Their activities met a very real demand for higher education, and the leading Sophists enjoyed great success and amassed large fortunes. *See also* EDUCATION, III. 3–4.

It is important to remember that the Sophists were a profession and not a school of thought, though some of them, such as Protagoras, taught definite philosophic views. But the very nature of the profession tended to produce a certain attitude of mind, which placed emphasis on material success and on the ability to argue for any point of view irrespective of its truth. The general influence of the Sophists was therefore necessarily in the direction of scepticism both about the claims of reasoning to arrive at the truth and about the claims of any moral code to determine one's conduct. At the best they taught no more than uncritical acceptance of the conventional moral code of one's particular society. At the worst, in the teaching, for instance, of men like Antiphon and Thrasymachus, they encouraged a cynical disbelief in all moral restraints on the pursuit of selfish, personal ambitions. Some of the early Sophists were men of high character and unblemished reputation. But others were not so, and there were apparently good grounds in their activities for the undesirable associations which the word came to have and which have passed over into its English derivative.

Under the Roman Empire, particularly from the second century A.D. onwards, the word acquired a more specialized meaning and became restricted to teachers and practitioners of rhetoric, which by this time was tending to become a purely literary exercise practised for its own sake. It was, however, a very popular pursuit, and successful practitioners in it enjoyed a high reputation. It became the most valued part of higher education, and teachers of rhetoric were endowed at many of the great centres of population. In later centuries the movement tended to become specially associated with paganism and died out after the final triumph of Christianity.

Testimonia and fragments in Diels, *Vorsokr.*¹¹ ii. 252–416, M. Untersteiner, *I Sofisti* (1949– ). H. Gomperz, *Sophistik und Rhetorik* (1912); J. Burnet, *Greek Philosophy: Thales to Plato* (1914); W. Jaeger, *Paideia* (1939–45); E. R. Dodds, *The Greeks and the Irrational* (1951), ch. 6. Later Sophistic: Philostratus and Eunapius, for lives of the Sophists; Norden, *Ant. Kuntspr.* i; G. W. Bowersock, *Greek Sophists in the Roman Empire* (1969).                              G. C. F.

## SOPHOCLES (1).

### I. LIFE (c. 496–406 B.C.)

Sophocles, son of Sophilus, a wealthy industrialist, was born in or about 496 B.C. at Colonus (*Marm. Par.* 56 and 64), to the praise of which one of his loveliest odes is dedicated (*OC* 668 ff.). His youthful beauty and his skill in dancing and music attracted attention, and he led the paean of victory after Salamis with his lyre. His master in music was Lamprus, one of the great teachers of the old school (*Life*: cf. Plut. *De mus.* 31). His first victory in tragedy was won in 468 B.C. (*Marm. Par.* 56: *IG*² ii. 2325), when he defeated Aeschylus; Plutarch (*Cim.* 8) says that it was his first appearance as a tragic poet—this has been doubted—and that owing to the excitement of popular feeling the archon entrusted the award of the prize to Cimon and his fellow generals. One of his plays on this occasion was probably the *Triptolemus*. In two other early plays he made his mark —as a ball-player in the character of Nausicaa (in the Πλύντριαι ἢ Ναυσικάα) and as a player on the lyre in that of Thamyras (in the play of that name); but the weakness of his voice caused him to give up acting in person (*Life*). His early life coincided with the expansion of the Athenian Empire, and he himself took an honourable share in the duties of citizenship. In 443/2 he was *Hellenotamias* or imperial treasurer (*IG*² i. 202); he was elected general twice at least—in 440, when he was a colleague of Pericles in the suppression of the Samian revolt (*Life*; Plut. *Per.* 8, etc.), and later with Nicias (Plut. *Nic.* 15); and after the Sicilian disaster he was one of the πρόβουλοι appointed to deal with the crisis (Arist. *Rh.* 3. 18, etc.). Whether he owed his appointment in 440 to the success of the *Antigone* may be doubted. There is a pleasant record of his conversations with Ion at Chios in the course of the Samian Expedition (Ath. 13. 603 ff.), and two other friends of Cimon are connected with him in different ways—Polygnotus, who depicted him in the *Stoa Poikile* holding the lyre, and Archelaus the philosopher, to whom he wrote an elegiac poem. He also wrote (c. 441 B.C.) a poem to Herodotus, with whom there are a number of points of contact in his work (Plut. *An seni* 3). He was priest of the healing deity Amynos, Alcon, or Halon (the exact name is doubtful) and made his own house a place of worship for Asclepius until the temple built for him was ready (Plut. *Num.* 3, *Etym. Magn.* s.v. Δεξιών); in recognition of this he was honoured as a hero with the title Δεξιών after his death. He also composed a paean to Asclepius. These and other indications suggest that he accepted the religion of his day without misgivings, just as in other ways he showed himself a healthy minded and normal, as well as a distinguished, Athenian, and he is said to have refused all invitations to leave Athens for the courts of kings (*Life*, cf. fr. 789). His interest in the theory and criticism as well as in the writing of poetry was shown in the composition of a prose work *On the Chorus*, in the story of his discussion of poetical expressions with Ion (Ath. loc. cit.), and in his founding of a literary club (the θίασος of the Muses). He seems to have distinguished his own conscious technique from the inspiration which carried Aeschylus away (εἰ καὶ τὰ δέοντα ποιεῖς ἀλλ' οὐκ εἰδώς γε ποιεῖς). He died late in 406, and Aristophanes in the next year summed up his genial and kindly temperament in the line ὁ δ' εὔκολος μὲν ἐνθάδ', εὔκολος δ' ἐκεῖ (*Ran.* 82). It was characteristic that a few months before his death he appeared with his chorus and actors in mourning for Euripides at the *proagon* (q.v.) before the Great Dionysia. Phrynichus (the Comic poet) spoke of him as εὐδαίμων ἀνὴρ καὶ δεξιός, who died a good death and was taken from the evil to come.

He is said to have composed (probably) 123 plays, and with these he won 24 victories, which means that 96 of his plays were successful; in his other contests he was placed second, but never third.

### II. WORKS

Sophocles, according to Plut. *De prof. virt.* 7, distinguished three periods in his own style: first the 'bombastic' style (ὄγκος) of Aeschylus; secondly, a harsh and artificial style (πικρὸν καὶ κατάτεχνον) of his own, and thirdly, the best type of style and most suited for the expression of character (ἠθικώτατον καὶ βέλτιστον). The extant plays, the earliest of which must fall about twenty-five years after his first appearance, seem all to belong to the third period, though the fragments of some lost early plays recall in matter and vocabulary some of the characteristics of Aeschylus, and some critics have professed to find traces of the second style (whatever Plutarch's words may mean) in the *Ajax* and *Antigone*. The latter was probably produced in 441; the *Ajax* is probably rather earlier; for the *Oedipus Tyrannus* a year soon after 430 seems probable, and the *Trachiniae* may belong to the same period, though the indications are very uncertain. It is disputed whether the *Electra* preceded or followed Euripides' *Electra* (413), and it is variously placed by scholars between 418 and 410. The *Philoctetes* was produced in 409 (arg.), and the *Oedipus Coloneus* posthumously in 401 (arg.). The date of the satyric *Ichneutae* is uncertain (see Powell and Barber, *New Chapters* iii. 93 f.). Of the lost plays, the *Telepheia*, if it was in fact a Trilogy dealing with the story of Telephus (and consisting perhaps of the *Aleadae*, the *Mysi*, and the Ἀχαιῶν σύλλογος), is likely to have been an early group (see ibid. iii. 68 ff.). More than one-third of the known titles are those of plays taken from the Trojan cycle of legend (including that of the house of Atreus); the remainder cover a wide range; about twenty are those of satyric plays. A. W. P.-C.

### III. CHARACTER OF HIS WORK (*See also* TRAGEDY)

1. Sophocles is credited by Aristotle (*Poet.* 4) with three changes in the form of tragedy: he introduced the third actor, introduced 'scene-painting' (σκηνογραφία), and enlarged the chorus from twelve to fifteen. What the scene-painting amounted to is uncertain, and we can only guess at the purpose of enlarging the chorus. The third actor was a fundamental development. It would be interesting to know what actually had happened when 'Sophocles introduced the third actor'. Since it meant altering the rules of the dramatic contest some kind of official consent was presumably necessary, and therefore general agreement among the practising dramatists. Although it is easy to see why Sophocles wanted a third actor, the change would have represented a general rather than a personal desire. Drama must have been moving away from the lyrical towards the histrionic. It is also to be noted that Sophocles did not follow the example of Aeschylus in composing connected trilogies.

2. The third actor enabled the dramatist to increase the number of his *dramatis personae* considerably, since the actors might 'double'. Therefore he could make both plot and situation more complex, and thereby draw character more fully. For example, the heroine of the *Electra* faces in succession at least ten distinct situations: first alone, then with the chorus, then with Chrysothemis, Clytemnestra, the Messenger, and so on. Each situation brings out a different facet of her nature. The new complexity of situation is best illustrated by the triangular scenes in which Aeschylus and Euripides had little interest and Sophocles no rival: three persons are simultaneously involved in the same situation, but with contrasting hopes or fears. Thus, the Messenger in the *Electra* tells his false tale in order to deceive Clytemnestra and further Orestes' vengeance: for Clytemnestra, as she listens, it is

deliverance from terror, but for Electra, the end of everything. The best of such scenes occur in the later plays. An interesting variant is *Philoctetes* 974–1080, where one of the three persons, though he says nothing until the final verses, undergoes a most humiliating experience.

**3.** Sophocles' delicate though powerful delineation of character was well matched by the flexibility of his style. Like Shakespeare, he had at his command the whole range of dramatic speech, from weight and dignity to extreme swiftness and lightness, even casualness: though, unlike Shakespeare, he did not (especially in the later plays) write many 'poetical' passages (lyrics excepted). It is no disparagement of Aeschylus and Euripides to say that Sophocles' style was much more varied than theirs: his conception of drama demanded, as theirs did not, that the speech of his characters should be able to respond instantly to the thought or emotion of the moment. Therefore he will sometimes write four- or five-word verses which have weight without any trace of stiffness, while at the other extreme he once performs the feat, astonishing in an inflected language, of getting twenty-one words into twenty-four syllables (*OT* 370 f.; cf. *Electra* 624 f., 359). Light verse-endings are common, as *Electra* 332 and 426, ending with ὅτι, or a verse may end with an elision, as *Electra* 1017, *OT* 29. Sophocles' rhetoric, when he is rhetorical, is superb; no less moving is the utter simplicity of his simple passages. It has often been suggested that his rhetoric owes something to contemporary sophists who studied the art of rhetoric: perhaps it is an open question if Sophocles learned more from the professors, or the professors from Sophocles.

**4.** His use of the chorus is no less flexible. There are six odes in the *Antigone* (counting the formal parodos), only one in the *Philoctetes*, four in the (later) *Coloneus*. No one formula, such as 'ideal spectator', can properly describe the uses that Sophocles found for the chorus. Usually he gives it a markedly dramatic character, but when it suits him he will allow that character to lapse, and use the chorus as a purely lyrical instrument. The chorus of the *OT* consists of citizens intensely loyal to Oedipus, but in the third ode this character is in abeyance. So it is too in the second and fifth odes of the *Antigone*, although elsewhere in the play it is so much of a dramatic character that it says the right things but about the wrong person—about Antigone, not Creon; at which moments it is certainly no 'ideal spectator'.

Not a few of the odes easily bear comparison with the very best of Greek lyric poetry, though they are essentially dramatic both in structure and function. Changes of rhythm within a stanza are much more frequent and strongly marked than in Euripides, even than in Aeschylus, and often the effect of the change is obvious. (See for example the sudden anapaestic verses at *OT* 469 f. and 479 f.) They suggest that the dance-movements must have been vividly dramatic. Euripides' odes are rhythmically uninteresting by comparison; perhaps he relied more on melody.

The chief actor was usually given a generous share in the lyrical part of the play. At a rough computation Electra's role comprises 640 verses, of which rather more than a quarter were sung or chanted; Antigone sings 75 out of about 220 verses. The lyrical element, taken as a whole, is markedly smaller than is usual in Aeschylus, though it is proportionately as big in the *Ajax*, *Antigone*, and *Philoctetes* as in the *PV* and *Persae*.

**5.** *Structure and Thought.* Sophocles' plots raise an acute problem. By universal consent, the design of some of the plays, notably of the *OT*, is masterly; of others, apparently inept, for the *Ajax* finishes with a new set of characters, and there has been much discussion whether the central character of the *Trachiniae* was meant to be Deianira or Heracles. Sophocles appears even to have forgotten Antigone in the last hundred verses of that play. Since he was a competent dramatist it is likely that he so designed his plots as to help him say what he meant; in which case his plot-structure and his thought should be considered together. There is little profit in making special assumptions to explain one puzzling structure—as for example that Ajax, being an Attic Hero (as Sophocles does not point out), must have his tomb and therefore must be buried—when they do nothing to explain similar puzzles in other plays.

The vividness with which Sophocles portrays his persons and their motives and conflicts reinforces the modern idea that tragic drama first and foremost represents persons. Aristotle thought differently: he is emphatic that 'tragedy is a mimesis not of persons but of an action (πρᾶξις)' (*Poet.* 49ᵇ24, 50ᵃ16, 50ᵇ3), and it is possible that he was right. Inspecting the action of the plays, one finds that it is usually shared, in one way or another, by the human agents and by gods. Therefore the meaning of his religion is of critical importance. If it was no more than a general piety, whether conventional or deeply felt, then a play like the *Trachiniae* is no more than two personal tragedies not very securely joined by piety; further, one is left wondering why Sophocles was not inspired to strengthen the unity of the play (as of the *Antigone* also) by bringing on the heroine's body in the final scenes. But it may have been more than piety. For example, what happens to Creon in the *Antigone* is represented as the outcome, perfectly natural in the circumstances, of what he has done to Polynices' body, to Antigone, to Haemon, to Eurydice (cf. 1301–5); yet Tiresias declares that it is going to be brought about by the angry gods and their Erinyes. In the *Electra*, the act of vengeance and restitution, so ardently desired by Electra, for so many reasons, is undertaken, on no divine prompting (vv. 32–7), by Orestes out of personal and public motives (cf. vv. 67–72), and it is achieved entirely by their own efforts. Guile, δόλος, answers guile (vv. 37, 197, 490, 1392, 1397). Yet there is the constant implication that the gods—Apollo, and Zeus (160–3, 174–6), Dike and Ares, Hermes, and the Erinyes (1384–97)—are acting with them. Such instances suggest that for Sophocles and his audiences the participation of the gods in actions that are already completely explained in human terms implied something like the operation of some universal law; in which case it would be at once intelligible that the action would take precedence over the persons, and that the persons, and what they do, should be displayed as vividly and naturally as possible.

The *praxis* of the *Trachiniae* (to take perhaps the most critical example) involves the following: that Zeus has already punished Heracles for one unjustifiable action, his killing of Iphitus; that his final exploit, which is to end either in his death or in the lasting peace that Deianira so desperately longs for, is the wanton destruction of a whole city for the sake of getting a girl; that the girl is going to supplant the loyal wife; that in such a sudden crisis Deianira does what is entirely natural, for her, in the circumstances; that the poison that she innocently uses is activated by the heat of the fire upon which Heracles is making to Zeus his thank-offering for his destruction of the city. In the first ode the chorus sings of the regular order of nature, in accordance with which Deianira's long anxiety should be followed by peace and joy, especially since Zeus keeps an eye upon his offspring (vv. 139 f.). But instead of joy there is total catastrophe, and the cause of it is plain. The question whether Deianira or Heracles was meant to be the central character seems unimportant, especially if we can believe the last line of the play: 'Nothing is here but Zeus.' Aristotle seems to have been right. The structural difficulties vanish if Sophocles drew his persons for the sake of the action, not vice versa, and if his religion reflected not a mere pious attitude but active thinking about the ways of the universe.

LIFE AND WORKS. A. E. Haigh, *Tragic Drama of the Greeks* (1896); M. Pohlenz, *Die griechische Tragödie* (1954); T. von Wilamowitz, *Die dramatische Technik des Sophokles* (1917); H. Weinstock, *Sophokles* (1931); T. B. L. Webster, *Introduction to Sophocles* (1936); A. von Blumenthal, *Sophokles* (1936); C. M. Bowra, *Sophoclean Tragedy* (1944); A. Lesky, *Die tragische Dichtung der Hellenen* (1956); G. M. Kirkwood, *Sophoclean Drama* (1957); H. D. F. Kitto, *Greek Tragedy* (1961).
TEXT. O.C.T. (A. C. Pearson, 1923); Budé (A. Dain and P. Mazon, 1955–8; with French translation).
COMMENTARIES. R. C. Jebb (each play separately with translation, 1883 onwards); J. C. Kamerbeek, *Ajax, Trachiniae*. See also *Lexicon Sophocleum*, F. Ellendt (2nd ed. by H. Genthe (1872)).
TRANSLATIONS. *Prose*: R. C. Jebb. *Verse*: E. F. Watling (Penguin, 1947 and 1953); *The Complete Greek Tragedies* (U.S.A. 1959); D. Fitts, *Greek Plays in modern translation* (1947); H. D. F. Kitto, *Sophocles, Three Plays* (1962); F. L. Lucas, *Greek Drama for Everyman* (1954). H. D. F. K.

**SOPHOCLES** (2) the Younger, son of Ariston and grandson of the great Sophocles, produced his grandfather's *Oedipus Coloneus* in 401 B.C., and plays of his own from 396 onwards. The numbers of his plays and victories are uncertain (*Suda* s.v., Arg. Soph. *OC*).

**SOPHONISBA** (*Sophoniba* Livy; Σοφωνίβα Appian; the correct name is Saphanba'al), daughter of Hasdrubal (q.v. 3); she married Syphax (q.v.), whom she thus won over to the Carthaginian cause. When Masinissa and Laelius overthrew Syphax (203 B.C.) Sophonisba took poison which according to the romantic story (Livy 30. 12–15) was sent to her by Masinissa, now enamoured of her and unable by any other means to save her from captivity at Rome. Details of her story (e.g. that before her marriage to Syphax she had been betrothed to Masinissa) may be false, but the outline need not be questioned. H. H. S.

**SOPHRON** (Σώφρων) (fifth c. B.C.), Syracusan writer of mimes. His mimes were divided according to subject-matter into ἀνδρεῖοι and γυναικεῖοι. We have one important papyrus fragment and some 170 short citations, mostly preserved to illustrate the Doric dialect. Of the ἀνδρεῖοι may be mentioned Θυννοθήρας ('The Tunny-fisher') and Ἁλιεύς (i.e. ὁ ἁλιεύς) τὸν ἀγρώταν (possibly a dispute between a fisherman and a farmer); of the γυναικεῖοι—Ἀκέστριαι ('The Sempstresses'), Συναριστῶσαι ('Women at breakfast'), Ταὶ γυναῖκες αἳ τὰν θεόν (i.e. Hekate) φαντι ἐξελᾶν (i.e. 'The Sorceresses'). Sophron's mimes were written in some kind of rhythmical prose (schol. Greg. Naz. [in Kaibel, *CGF* 153] ῥυθμοῖς τισι καὶ κώλοις ἐχρήσατο). Their subject-matter was the events of everyday life. Sophron, who was probably the first writer to give literary form to the mime, was greatly admired by Plato (Douris of Samos, *FGrH* 76 F 72). Herodas possibly and Theocritus certainly owed much to him—a schol. on Theoc. 2 says that Theocritus adapted (μεταφέρει) one of Sophron's mimes.
Kaibel, *CGF* 152 ff.; Olivieri, *FCGM* iii. M. P.; K. J. D.

**SOPHRONIUS**, *c.* A.D. 560–638, patriarch of Jerusalem (from 634) at the time of the Arab conquest. He wrote a theological manifesto against the doctrine that though Christ had two natures he had only one will, panegyrics on Egyptian saints (Cyrus and John, John the almsgiver, Maria the penitent prostitute), sermons for Christmas and other feasts, and twenty-three anacreontic odes of esoteric difficulty.
Ed. Migne, *PG* lxxxvii (3), 3147 ff.; *Odes*, ed. M. Gigante (1957). H. G. Beck, *Kirche und theologische Literatur im byzantinischen Reich* (1959), 434 ff. H. C.

**SORA**, 60 miles south-east of Rome at the big bend of the River Liris (q.v.). Rome took Sora from the Volsci in

345 B.C., but Samnites disputed her control until a Latin Colony was established there (303 B.C.). It has always been an important town with a picturesque acropolis but few ancient remains. E. T. S.

**SORACTE**, modern *Soratte*, the isolated 2,420-foot limestone mountain, easily visible from Rome 26 miles to the south, which Horace celebrated (*Odes* 1. 9). Here priests called *Hirpi*, resembling Roman *Luperci*, worshipped Apollo Soranus by walking over hot coals (Pliny, *HN* 7. 19; Serv. *ad Aen.* 11. 787). Sant' Oreste, a village on the lower slopes, preserved the name in corrupted form through medieval times. E. T. S.

**SORANUS** of Ephesus, physician under Trajan and Hadrian (98–138), studied in Alexandria and practised in Rome. He was one of the greatest physicians, a man of erudition, of objective judgement, full of love for his native Greece, critical towards the Romans of the world metropolis.

Of his books, almost twenty in number, dealing with history of medicine, terminological problems, and medicine proper, there are preserved in Greek: 1. Γυναικεῖα I–IV (I. Hygiene of midwife, conception, etc.; II. Childbed, care of the infant; III and IV. Pathology). 2. Π. σημείων καταγμάτων and Π. ἐπιδέσμων, fragments of a surgical treatise.

Soranus restored the Methodical school by moderating its exaggerations in the spirit of the new classical era and by harmonizing it with the tradition. Though believing in general symptoms, he did not neglect individual factors, distinguished the different forms of diseases, and observed accurately the course of an illness. A terse but excellent author, his books in Latin translations or adaptations were widely read in the West. See ANATOMY and PHYSIOLOGY, § 11.

TEXT. J. Ilberg, *CMG* iv (1927); cf. also M. and I. Drabkin, 'Caelius Aurelianus, *Gynaecia*', *Bull. Hist. Medicine*, Suppl. xiii (1951). Transl. of *Gynaeceia*: O. Temkin, *Soranus' Gynecology* (U.S.A. 1956). The βίος Ἱπποκράτους spurious, L. Edelstein, *PW* Suppl. vi. 1293, s.v. 'Hippokrates'. Latin translations, Caelius Aurelianus, *De morbis acutis et chronicis* (cf. Ilberg, *Sitz. Leipz.* 1925), ed. and transl. I. E. Drabkin, *Caelius Aurelianus, On Acute Diseases and On Chronic Disorders* (U.S.A. 1950); Muscio, *Gynaeceia*. Ps.-Soran., see Rose, *Anecdota Graeca* ii.
LITERATURE. Survey, E. Kind, *PW* iii A. 1113; Edelstein, loc. cit. Text-history of *Gynaikeia*, Ilberg, *Abh. Sächs. Akad.* (1910). Doxography, H. Diels, *Dox. Graec.* 207, *Sitz. Berl.* (1893). Influence on Tertullian, H. Karpp, *Zeitschr. f. neutestamentl. Wiss.* (1934). Medicine, T. C. Allbutt, *Greek Medicine in Rome* (1921). L. E.

**SORTITION** (κλήρωσις), election by lot, a method of appointing officials in Greek city-states, especially in democracies. It was based on the idea of equality and reduced outside influence. Little is known of its use except at Athens. It remains uncertain when sortition was introduced there, perhaps as early as Solon. From 487/6 B.C. the archons were appointed by lot out of nominated candidates (πρόκριτοι); later, this became a double sortition. From the time when the archons began to be elected by lot, they lost political leadership. But all ordinary magistrates, a few excepted, were thus appointed; also the Council (a Prytany of fifty from each *phyle*) and the juries (by a very complicated procedure). Lot decided very many questions in political and social life. Politically, sortition, combined with the prohibition or at least severe restriction of re-election, enabled rotation in office, and electoral contests were avoided by its use; moreover, the power of magistrates was reduced, and thus the sovereignty of the popular assembly guaranteed. Sortition was practicable, as almost every citizen had a minimum of political experience, and nobody could be elected without having presented himself. Certain precautions were always taken, and military and some technical (especially financial) officials were appointed by vote.

Except for a few critics like Socrates, the principle of sortition was never discussed. It was, indeed, a necessary and fundamental element of the democratic *polis*.

Arist. *Ath. Pol.* T. W. Headlam, *Election by Lot at Athens* (1891, 2nd ed. 1933); V. Ehrenberg, *PW*, s.v. 'Losung'.　　　　V. E.

**SOSIBIUS** of Lacedaemon. In the reign of Ptolemy I (323–283 B.C.) he went to Egypt and became closely associated with the Alexandrian school. He is probably to be identified with the grammarian Sosibius ὁ λυτικός, so called because of his ability to deal with Homeric problems. He is important for his studies in the history of Sparta (Περὶ τῶν ἐν Λακεδαίμονι θυσιῶν and Χρόνων ἀναγραφή).

*FGrH* iii B, 595.　　　　G. L. B.

**SOSICRATES**, local historian and biographer perhaps from Rhodes, fl. mid second century B.C. Works (*FHG* iv. 500–3): (1) Φιλοσόφων διαδοχή, a biographical study of various philosophers, following the teacher–pupil relation. Sosicrates used Hermippus and perhaps Satyrus. Whether he used Apollodorus is disputed: a common source in Eratosthenes may explain similarities. (2) Κρητικά(*FGrH*461) which Apollodorus used; this may be the earlier work. If he is the Sosicrates mentioned in Timachidas (*Lind. Temp. Chron.* 317, Blinkenberg), he flourished 150–130 B.C.: but the identification is uncertain.

F. W. W.

**SOSIGENES**, astronomer, earlier confused with a Stoic and a Peripatetic of the same name, was Caesar's astronomical expert in his introduction of the Julian calendar in 47 B.C.

**SOSIPATER** (Σωσίπατρος), Greek comic poet: fr. 1, cookery—a sublime science. Apparently among the earlier writers of the New Comedy (v. 11 Chariades is named as living, whereas in Euphron fr. 1. 7 he appears to be dead).

*FCG* iv. 482 ff.; *CAF* iii. 314 ff.

**SOSIPHANES** of Syracuse, tragic poet, flourished about the last third of the fourth century B.C., though some date him later and there may have been two poets of the name. He is credited with seventy-three tragedies (*Suda*, s.v.), and seven victories. He is included in some lists of the *Pleiad* (*see* TRAGEDY § 22). A short but striking fragment on the transitoriness of human happiness survives.

*TGF* 819–20.　　　　A. W. P.-C.

**SOSITHEUS**, of Alexandria Troas, lived in Athens, Syracuse, and Alexandria, was a member of the *Pleiad* (*see* TRAGEDY § 22), and wrote tragedies and satyric plays, including a *Daphnis or Lityerses*, in which a sarcastic reference to the Stoic Cleanthes occurred; twenty lines of this play survive, as well as a laudatory epigram on the poet by Dioscorides (*Anth. Pal.* 7. 707).

*TGF* 821–4.　　　　A. W. P.-C.

**SOSIUS** (1, *PW* 2), GAIUS, probably son of a praetor, served Antony as quaestor *c.* 40 B.C., was 'appointed by him governor of Syria and Cilicia in 38, captured Jerusalem for Herod (q.v. 1) in 37, and triumphed 'ex Iudaea' in Sept. 34. In 32 he and Domitius (5) were consuls. Both supported Antony. Sosius began the year with a diplomatic attack on Octavian; Octavian made a vigorous rejoinder, and the consuls and many senators fled to Antony. Sosius commanded the left wing of Antony's fleet at Actium. He was subsequently pardoned by Octavian at the instance of Arruntius (q.v. 1). He restored the temple of Apollo near the theatre of Marcellus, and

took part in the *Ludi Saeculares* of 17 B.C. as *quindecimvir sacris faciundis*.

Syme, *Rom. Rev.*, see index; M. Grant, *From Imperium to Auctoritas* (1946), 39 ff.; Platner–Ashby, 15 f.; Nash, *Pict. Dict. Rome* i. 28 ff.
　　　　G. W. R.; T. J. C.

**SOSIUS** (2, *PW* 11) **SENECIO**, QUINTUS (*cos. ord.* A.D. 99, II *ord.* 107), is revealed by the convergence of casual evidence as one of the most important members of the governmental oligarchy under Trajan. Of his origin, family, and official career before the consulate nothing is recorded. The link with an influential consular (Sex. Julius Frontinus was his father-in-law) and the friendship of the new Emperor explain his conspicuous advancement: Sosius and Cornelius Palma are the first pair of *consules ordinarii* appointed by Trajan. The date of his second consulate, held with the great Licinius Sura as colleague, and the honour of a public statue (Dio Cass. 68. 12. 2), support the conjecture that he held a high command in the Second Dacian War (A.D. 105–6). Sympathetic, like others of his class and rank (for example, C. Minicius Fundanus, *cos. suff.* 107), to the pursuits of philosophy and letters, Sosius might be claimed for a representative figure in a 'proto-Antonine' period of imperial civilization—Plutarch of Chaeronea enjoyed his friendship and commemorated it by the dedication of several works. He was also a friend of Pliny.

Sosius did not leave a son to perpetuate the family, but his daughter married Q. Pompeius Falco (*cos. suff.* 108), and that line is prominent in the Antonine aristocracy, with manifold connexions and a much-advertised pedigree, as witness the polyonymous consul of A.D. 169 (Dessau, *ILS* 1104), who has thirty-four names, apart from *praenomina*.　　　　R. S.

**SOSTRATUS**, surgeon and zoologist, probably practised in Alexandria after 30 B.C. His medical works dealt chiefly with gynaecology. In zoology he perhaps ranks next after Aristotle among the Greeks.

WORKS: Περὶ ζῴων or Περὶ φύσεως ζῴων; Περὶ βλητῶν καὶ δακέτων. Aelian and the scholia to Nicander preserve much information about his zoological works.

W. D. R.

**SOSYLUS** of Lacedaemon (fl. 218 B.C.), who accompanied Hannibal on his campaigns and wrote a methodical and impartial history of the latter (Περὶ Ἀννίβου πράξεων) in seven books towards the end of the third century B.C. One of the more important sources of Polybius, whose harsh verdict on him (Polyb. 3. 20. 5) must be toned down in the light of a papyrus fragment from his fourth book.

*FGrH* ii B, 176.　　　　G. L. B.

**SOTADES**(1), Athenian comic poet, τῆς μέσης κωμῳδίας according to the *Suda*, and (fr. 3, cf. Harp. s.v. κρωβύλος) a contemporary of Demosthenes. We have three titles and three fragments; fr. 1 is a long description of the cooking of fish.

*FCG* iii. 585 ff.; *CAF* ii. 447 ff.; *FAC* ii. 552 ff.　　　　K. J. D.

**SOTADES** (2), Iambic poet, of Maronea, lived in the time of Ptolemy Philadelphus, of whose marriage with Arsinoë he disapproved strongly (Ath. 621 a, fr. 1 Powell). He invented the *versus sotadeus*, a minor ionic metre which allowed great variations. Some fragments of his work survive, notably from his transcription of the *Iliad* into sotadeans (frs. 4 a–c), and lines to the flute-player Theodorus (fr. 2). The sotadeans preserved by Stobaeus (frs. 6–14) are commonly thought not to be his, and may be moralizing verses composed for the education of Greek children in Egypt. *See* IAMBIC POETRY, GREEK.

TEXT. Diehl, *Anth. Lyr. Graec.* ii. 286–94; Powell, *Coll. Alex.* 238–45.
C. M. B.

**SOTER** (Σωτήρ), fem. **SOTEIRA** (Σώτειρα), a title of several deities, expressing their power to save their worshippers from dangers. It has no Latin equivalent (Cic. *Verr.* 2. 2. 154), unless it be Juno's epithet Sispes or Sospita. It is used, for example, of Zeus (as Xenophon, *An.* 1. 8. 16, and often) and of Kore (Ar. *Ran.* 379, cf. Farnell, *Cults* iii. 198). In Hellenistic times it comes to be used of men, especially kings, often implying some measure of deification; Antigonus Doson was called Euergetes in life, Soter after his death (Polyb. 5. 9. 10). The most famous holder of the title was perhaps Ptolemy I. Like all such titles, it was later cheapened, being given, for instance, to the notorious Verres (Cic. loc. cit. See Nilsson, *GGR* ii. 174 ff., 371 ff.). Its transcendental use is Christian, cf. A. D. Nock in *Essays on the Trinity and the Incarnation* (ed. A. E. J. Rawlinson, 1928), 87 ff.
H. J. R.

**SOTERIA.** The term σωτήρια was appropriate for any sacrifice(s), with or without attendant *agones*, etc., performed either once or several times in commemoration, or in hope, of the deliverance of one man or a group from oppression, sickness, or danger. Commonly Σωτήρια designated certain more or less elaborate city or national festivals celebrated at regular intervals to commemorate major events. (Compare the (older) Ἐλευθέρια, at Plataea, Syracuse, Samos; a third usage consisted in naming festivals in honour of the deliverer himself, e.g. the Diogeneia at Athens after 230/29 B.C.). The known Soteria, some sixteen in all (*PW*, s.v.) are Hellenistic (or later), part of the efflorescence of festivals at that time. The Soteria at Delphi, to commemorate the defeat of Brennus and his Celts in winter 279/8 B.C., are best known: inscriptions furnish a considerable body of detail (as yet not synthesized) about the performances, and data important for third-century chronology. Soon after the departure of the Gauls, the Amphictiones founded annual Soteria. It was not until 243/2 that the Aetolians refounded the same festival: the positive dating in that year of the Athenian archon Polyeuctus has settled a controversy (*Hesp.* 1938, 121, no. 24; for the whole problem, R. Flacelière, *Les Aitoliens à Delphes*, 1937).

**SOTERICHUS** (*c.* A.D. 300), epic poet, author of Greek poems on Dionysus, Alexander, and other subjects (*Suda*).

**SOTION** (1) of Alexandria, Peripatetic, wrote (? between 200 and 170 B.C.) (1) a Διαδοχὴ τῶν φιλοσόφων in thirteen books, in which each philosopher is treated as the definite successor of another; (2) a book on Timon's Σίλλοι. The former work is a main though not a direct source of Diogenes Laertius' information, as well as of the doxographic summaries in such patristic writers as Eusebius and Theodoretus. Sotion seems to have introduced the ultra-simple division of the philosophical successions into Ionian and Italian.

Diels, *Dox. Graec.* 147–9.
W. D. R.

**SOTION** (2), Peripatetic, not earlier than the reign of Tiberius (A.D. 14–37).
WORKS: Κέρας Ἀμαλθείας; *Strange Stories* (ed. A. Westermann, in Παραδοξογράφοι, 1839, 183), about rivers, springs, and pools; Dioclean Disputations (against Epicurus); a commentary on the *Topics*.
W. D. R.

**SOUL.** Apart from philosophic doctrines concerning the soul, there are traces in vocabulary and usage of comparatively primitive ideas surviving in both Greece and Italy. Savages not infrequently believe that a man has several souls (e.g. Frazer, *GB* iii. 27, 80); now in Greek, notably in Homer, there are several words which mean something like 'soul' and seem to refer to parts of a man having different functions. Ψυχή, to judge by its etymology, means the breath-soul, which corresponds to the unsubstantial nature of departed ψυχαί as phantoms, εἴδωλα (*Od.* 11. 51, cf. 83; *Il.* 23. 104). Such phantoms have no φρένες, midriff and the parts adjacent, vitals; to give them more than a faint semblance of life they need to drink blood. It seems not improbable that the θυμός, the 'hot' or 'reeking' part, is the blood-soul; to kill is to take away the θυμός, to save the θυμός is to save life (*Il.* 22. 68 and often; *Od.* 11. 105). In Latin the evidence is less strong, partly no doubt because early documents are lacking; *anima* and *animus* correspond rather to later, philosophical uses respectively of ψυχή and θυμός than to the above meanings. But we may note the existence of *umbra* in the sense of ghost, suggesting belief in a shadow-soul; cf. Lucretius' insistence (4. 364 ff.) on the true nature of shadows. *See, further,* AFTER-LIFE, GENIUS, PSYCHE.

Rose in *Actes du congrès international d'histoire des religions tenu à Paris en octobre 1923* (1925), ii. 138 ff.; and for some criticism of these views as too rigid, Nilsson, *GGR* i². 192 ff.; B. Snell, *The Discovery of the Mind* (E.T. 1953), ch. 1; W. Jaeger, *Theology of the Early Greek Philosophers* (1947), ch. 5; R. B. Onions, *The Origins of European Thought* (1955), 93 ff.
H. J. R.

**SOZOMEN** (d. *c.* A.D. 450), a lawyer in Constantinople, wrote a history of the Church from 324 to 439, of which the conclusion has perhaps been lost. It depends heavily upon Socrates (whom it never mentions), is similar in outlook and content, less critical but more stylish. Sozomen had some additional information, particularly for monasticism; book 9, which uses Olympiodorus, is almost independent of Socrates (q.v. 2).

Ed. J. Bidez and G. C. Hansen (Berlin, 1960).
S. L. R.

**SPAIN.** 1. PREHISTORY. The Spanish peninsula, split by mountains and diverse in climate, has never known ethnical unity. Related to southern France in some of its cave-paintings (e.g. the late palaeolithic Altamira), it also produced the indigenous 'Capsian' culture of the south, and the Bell-beaker people who spread to central Europe. Iberians from Africa began exploiting its metals in early Neolithic times, and later expanded from Almeria over most of the south and east; Celts, invading from the north in the Late Bronze and Iron Ages, eventually mixed with Iberians in some parts of the centre and west (*see* CELTIBERIANS, LUSITANIA), but remained typically Celtic in the north-west, where scattered hill-forts contrast with the thickly urbanized Mediterranean regions. Everywhere the tribal units were much smaller than the general ethnic terms imply.

2. PHOENICIANS, GREEKS, CARTHAGINIANS. Traditionally, Phoenicians of Tyre discovered Tartessus (q.v.) and colonized Gades (q.v.) *c.* 1100 B.C. Some accept the date, others lower it to the eighth or seventh century. In the later seventh century Samian and Phocaean metal-traders reached Tartessus. The Phocaeans planted colonies at Mainake, near Malaca (q.v.) and Ebusus (*Ibiza*); their colony Massilia founded others on the east Spanish coast, notably Emporion (q.v.), Rhodae (*Rosas*), and Artemision (Dianium, now *Denia*). All the Greek centres south of Emporion disappeared when Carthage, during the third century, asserted itself in Spain. Hamilcar Barca and Hannibal conquered large territories, founded Carthago Nova (q.v.), and mobilized Spanish manpower and mineral wealth for the attack on Rome. The Second Punic War, starting from Hannibal's siege of Rome's

ally Saguntum (q.v.) and his approach to the Ebro, continued on the Spanish front until Carthage was driven out by Scipio Africanus in 206.

3. THE ROMAN PROVINCES. In 205 Rome held a narrow east coastal strip (Hispania Citerior) carrying the main road south to Carthago Nova, and beyond it a territory (Hispania Ulterior) including the south-east coast and the Baetis (*Guadalquivir*) valley. Two commands were necessary. In 197 two new praetors (q.v.) were created for Spain. Both provinces were gradually extended inland in punitive campaigns against rebels, guerrillas, and finally the big coalitions of Viriathus (q.v.) and the Celtiberians (q.v.). On the fall of Numantia (q.v.) in 133, Scipio Aemilianus with a senatorial commission drew up *leges* for both provinces, which covered at most two-thirds of the peninsula. The process of conquest halted, except for minor additions by Pompey in the war against Sertorius (q.v.). Further operations—sorties by triumph-hunting generals, and Caesar's civil war against the Pompeians (49-45)—were not attempts at expansion. That the Republic tried and failed to subdue the whole peninsula was a thesis of propaganda to enhance Augustus' conquests north of the Tagus and up to the Biscay coast. They resulted in a largely new province of Lusitania (q.v.) and a great new extension of Citerior (renamed Tarraconensis) to the north and west Ocean. These provinces were assigned to the Emperor; most of Ulterior (renamed Baetica, q.v.) was returned to the Senate in 27 B.C.

The Republic had imposed a tribute of one-twentieth in corn and a fixed sum in silver, for which local mints were introduced (not only at Osca, though the coinage was commonly called *argentum Oscense*). The further duty of military service was illustrated by the mounted lancer on many of the coins; cavalry and Balearic slingers were Spain's chief auxiliary troops. Mines (those of Carthago Nova yielded 25,000 drachmae a day) were public property at first, later mostly sold to private owners. They drew swarms of Italian businessmen to the south and east, which were also rich in crops and herds. Here, besides the mercantile groups, were Roman veterans settled at Italica and half-Spanish *libertini* at Carteia (qq.v.). Elsewhere Rome disarmed resistance and fostered agriculture by moving peoples from the hill-forts, distributing land, and planting native towns (e.g. Gracuris, founded in 179 by Ti. Gracchus, q.v. 2). Cases of misgovernment led in 171 to the institution of trials *de repetundis*, but the picture of oppression was exaggerated by unreliable sources.

Two Roman colonies may have existed before Caesar and Augustus added 21, with many Roman and Latin *municipia*. Augustus formed juridical *conventus*, which in Tarraconensis developed their own emperor-cults (here the provincial cult began in A.D. 15; in Baetica not till Flavian times). The new Augustan conquest required three legions in north-west Tarraconensis; Vespasian reduced them to one, VII Gemina. Discoveries of gold, iron, and tin repaid the annexation. The older Roman territories reached a peak of economic development in the first and second centuries A.D.; Pliny (*HN* 37. 203) reckoned that Spain as a whole was even richer than Gaul, counting manpower among the assets of its barren parts. But standards of civilized life varied widely. It was not as a reward for 'romanization' that Vespasian gave Latin rights to all the Spanish communities, from the Latin-speaking towns of Baetica to Celts still in round huts; the north-west was not suddenly urbanized, as some have inferred. Existing towns, however, prospered under their new charters (for which *see* MALACA); municipal decline scarcely began before the fourth century. The colonies were sending more senators to Rome than any provincial land except Narbonese Gaul. In literature they

had produced the Senecas and Lucan; Columella, Quintilian, and Martial were of native stock.

In the third century northern Spain was hard hit by the Frankish invasions. The peninsula, with the Balearics and Tingitana, was divided into six provinces by Diocletian. Early in the fourth century a powerful church emerged at the Council of Illiberis (Elvira, near modern *Granada*). Hosius (Ossius), bishop of Corduba (q.v.), confirmed its influence; it inspired the works of Prudentius (q.v.) and Orosius (q.v.), survived the barbarian invasions of the fifth century, converted the Visigothic kings to the Athanasian faith, and transmitted a residual legacy of Roman culture through the bishop of Seville, Isidorus (q.v. 2).

CLASSICAL SOURCES. *Fontes Hispaniae Antiquae* i–viii (1922–59), ed. A. Schulten, P. Bosch-Gimpera, L. Pericot; Strabo bk. 3; Pliny, *HN* bks. 3 and 4. 20–3; Ptolemy bk. 2. 3–5. Inscriptions: *CIL* ii and Suppl. Coins: A. Vives, *La Moneda Hispánica* (1928); G. F. Hill, *Ancient Coinage of Hispania Citerior* (1931); G. K. Jenkins, *Jahrbuch für Numismatik* 1961, 75 ff. Monuments: *Catálogo monumental de España* (by districts; various dates and authors).
MODERN WORKS. (*a*) *General*: A. Schulten, *PW*, s.v. 'Hispania', and *Iberische Landeskunde* i (1955); J. R. Mélida, *Arqueología española* (1929); *Historia de España* (ed. R. Menéndez Pidal), vols. i (1947), ii (1935), iii (1940); Jones, *Later Rom. Emp.*; F. Vittinghoff, *Römische Kolonisation* (1951).
(*b*) *Early Spain*: P. Bosch-Gimpera, *Etnología de la península ibérica* (1932), *La Formación de los pueblos de España* (1944); L. Pericot, *L'Espagne avant la conquête romaine* (1952); R. Carpenter, *The Greeks in Spain* (1925); A. Arribas, *The Iberians* (1964); A. García Bellido, *Hispania Greca* (Barcelona, 1948); Dunbabin, *Western Greeks*.
(*c*) *Roman Spain*: A. Schulten, *Numantia* (1914–31); *Geschichte von Numantia* (1933); C. H. V. Sutherland, *The Romans in Spain 217 B.C.–A.D. 117* (1939); E. Albertini, *Les Divisions administratives de l'Espagne romaine* (1923); R. Syme, 'The Spanish war of Augustus', *AJPhil.* 1934; R. K. McElderry, 'Vespasian's reconstruction of Spain', *JRS* 1918 and 1919; M. I. Henderson, 'Julius Caesar and Latium in Spain', *JRS* 1942; G. Alföldy, *Fasti Hispanienses* (1969).

M. I. H.

**SPARTA. 1.** NAME AND SITUATION. Σπάρτη, more probably from σπάρτος ('Spanish broom') than from σπαρτή, 'the sown land' or 'the place of scattered settlements', is used indifferently in Homer with Λακεδαίμων for the dwelling-place of Menelaus. The latter is the official name in historic times, Σπάρτη having poetic or patriotic associations and never being used to describe the territory as contrasted with the city. Sparta is situated on low hills and level ground *c*. 650–700 feet above sea-level on the west bank of the Eurotas, between two tributaries which flow from the slopes of Taÿgetus, and covered a roughly elliptical area measuring *c*. 2 miles (north to south) by 1¼, with the acropolis slightly north of the centre. It was partially walled before the end of the fourth century, completely not before 184 (Livy 34. 38; 38. 34; Paus. 7. 8. 5) when the circuit measured 48 stades (Polybius 9. 21. 2; confirmed by excavation in 1906). Several other landmarks of Spartan topography have also been identified, including the sanctuary of Athena Chalkioikos on the Acropolis overlooking the vast theatre of early imperial date which replaced a smaller Hellenistic structure; the sanctuary of Artemis Orthia, where the Spartan boys were flogged, in the 'Contest of the Whips', on the bank of the Eurotas, which fixes the position of the quarter 'Limnai'; the quarter of 'Pitane' to the north-west of the Acropolis; and, most probably, the Agora south-east of the theatre. The position of the other two quarters Kynosura and Mesoa remains uncertain, but with the data obtained, Pausanias' account of the topography of the city becomes much more intelligible.

**2.** HISTORY. (*a*) Sparta itself, unlike neighbouring Therapne and Amyclae (qq.v.), has produced few pre-Dorian traces, suggesting at most minor occupation in the LH III period, nor did the catastrophe of *c*. 1200 B.C. (*see* DORIANS *and* LACONIA) lead to immediate settlement. But, during the tenth century, at least four Dorian villages grew up around the acropolis and despite early political union (this is the most likely explanation of the dual kingship of Agiads and Eurypontids (qq.v.)) Sparta long retained the appearance and traditions of its village origin (Thuc. 1. 10). The course of her expansion in Laconia cannot be plotted, but by 700 at the latest all but the eastern coastal strip had been reduced and the population, pre-Dorian and Dorian, reduced to the status either of *Perioikoi* (q.v.), who retained partial independence subject to the obligation to serve in Sparta in war, or of helots (q.v.), who were serfs bound to the soil which they cultivated for their Spartan masters.

(*b*) In a great war between about 735 and 715 B.C. much of neighbouring Messenia (q.v.) was annexed and its population helotized. Thus Sparta committed herself to an agricultural future and saddled herself with the lasting problem of holding her gains during the seventh century against outside attack (she was heavily defeated by Argos (q.v.) at Hysiae in 669) and internal discontent (there was a serious Messenian revolt *c*. 660—the exact date is disputed: *see* ARISTOMENES 1 *and* MESSENIA). During the sixth century the external problem was solved by the annexation of Cynuria and Cythera (q.v.), by a long war against Arcadian Tegea to reverse a serious defeat, a defeat of Argos, and the institution of a new policy (*c*. 550; perhaps due to the ephor Chilon, q.v.), by which the Arcadian cities were admitted to alliance. Thus she formed the nucleus of what was to be formally organized *c*. 510–500 into the Peloponnesian League (q.v.). To the period 556–510 belong a series of campaigns which was to earn her later reputation as an enemy of tyranny (*see* SICYON, POLYCRATES 1, LYGDAMIS, HIPPIAS 1). But at home the Messenian problem remained and there was a further revolt *c*. 490 (*see* ANAXILAS 1, ZANCLE).

(*c*) Modern scholars place Sparta's acquisition of the constitution and socio-military institutions which tradition ascribed to Lycurgus (q.v.) anywhere between *c*. 800 and 600 B.C. with a majority for some point in the seventh century. Whatever the date they gave her a defined constitution earlier and therefore more primitive than that of any other significant city and, thanks to the stability of the Spartan economy and of Spartan problems, its essential provisions remained unchanged for centuries. Thus the young Spartan was devoted from the age of 7 to a deadening regime of military training and militaristic obedience which produced the finest army in Greece (*see* ARMIES, GREEK, § 3) but, much more gradually, a notorious austerity of life and an absolutely rigid oligarchic government (*see* APELLAI 1, EPHORS, GEROUSIA).

(*d*) Sparta's leadership in Greek affairs, which she maintained with increased credit in the invasion of Xerxes, began to decline soon after 479, partly as a result of the disgrace of Pausanias (q.v. 1) and Leotychides (q.v.), the anti-Spartan activities of Themistocles, and, above all, the growth of the Delian League under Athens; and it was more seriously impaired by the loss of life in the earthquake of 465 B.C. and the strain of another Messenian War (*c*. 465–460). But she survived the first Peloponnesian War with Athens (460–446) without disgrace and, in 431, her jealousy and fear of Athenian expansion, exacerbated by her allies, prompted her to begin another war (*see* PELOPONNESIAN WAR). The pre-eminence which she regained by the overthrow of Athens in 404 was nevertheless precariously based on a dwindling citizen-population, on the individualist ambitions of Lysander and Agesilaus (qq.v.), and on an increasing disregard for the traditional equality of possessions and for the prohibition of monied wealth and of the alienation of land-lots; and it is not surprising that she never recovered her strength after the disaster of Leuctra (371) and the restoration of Messenian independence by Epaminondas (q.v.).

(*e*) During the next hundred years or more the number of her citizens and her political importance were steadily declining. The deadening effects of her conservative regime were realized, far too late, in 242 B.C. by Agis IV, whose proposals to revive the strictness of the Lycurgan training and to admit *Perioikoi* and foreigners to the citizen-body were obstructed by the ephors and the few remaining *Spartiatai*; and, after his violent death, by Cleomenes III, who by revolutionary methods abolished the ephorate and raised the number of citizens to 4,000, but, ruling as a tyrant, was opposed and overthrown by the Achaean Confederacy and Antigonus (q.v. 3) Doson at Sellasia (222 or 221). Of the various tyrants who followed him, Nabis, who styled himself king, was the most successful, but was defeated by Flamininus (q.v. 1) in 195, and Sparta was compelled to join the Achaean Confederacy and finally incorporated as a *civitas foederata* in the province of Achaea. A remarkable revival of prosperity under the Roman Empire, especially in the second century, is attested by inscriptions and architectural remains, and a revival of the Lycurgan regime is a picturesque, if unpleasant, feature of the age of Septimius Severus. Surviving the destructive raid of the Heruli in A.D. 267, Sparta finally succumbed in ruins at the hands of the Goths under Alaric in 395.

KING-LIST. Before *c*. 800 B.C. the list is very hypothetical. Until 491/90, the Spartans claimed, son had succeeded father; though it is difficult to believe, there is no evidence to refute the claim. Thereafter relationship is indicated in brackets, the reference being to the preceding king.

| AGIADS | EURYPONTIDS |
|---|---|
| Agis, 930–900. | Eurypon, 890–860. |
| Echestratus, 900–870. | Prytanis, 860–830. |
| Leobotes, 870–840. | Polydectes, 830–800. |
| Dorussus, 840–820. | Eunomus, 800–780. |
| Agasilas, 820–790. | Charillus, *c*. 780–750. |
| Archelaus, *c*. 790–760. | Nicandrus, *c*. 750–720. |
| Teleclus, *c*. 760–740. | Theopompus (q.v. 1), *c*. 720–675. |
| Alcamenes, *c*. 740–700. | |
| Polydorus, *c*. 700–665. | Anaxandridas, *c*. 675–665. |
| Eurycrates, *c*. 665–640. | Archidamus I, *c*. 665–645. |
| Anaxandrus, *c*. 640–615. | Anaxilas, *c*. 645–625. |
| Eurycratidas, *c*. 615–590. | Leotychidas I, *c*. 625–600. |
| Leon, *c*. 590–560. | Hippocratides, *c*. 600–575. |
| Anaxandridas, *c*. 560–520. | Agasicles, *c*. 575–550. |
| Cleomenes I, *c*. 520–490. | Ariston, *c*. 550–515. |
| Leonidas I (q.v.) (brother), 490–480. | Demaratus (q.v.), *c*. 515–491. |
| Pleistarchus (son), 480–459. | Leotychidas II (q.v.) (cousin—great-grandson of Hippocratidas), 491–469. |
| Pleistoanax (son), 459–409. | |
| Pausanias (q.v. 2) (son), 409–395. | Archidamus II (q.v.) (grandson), 469–427. |
| Agesipolis I (son), 395–380. | Agis II (q.v.) (son), 427–399. |
| Cleombrotus I (brother), 380–371. | Agasilaus II (q.v.) (brother), 399–360. |
| Agesipolis II (son), 371–370. | Archidamus III (q.v.) (son), 360–338. |
| Cleomenes II (brother), 370–309. | Agis III (q.v.) (son), 338–331. |
| Areus I (q.v.) (grandson), 309–265. | Eudamidas I (brother), 331–*c*. 305. |
| Acrotatus (son), 265–262. | Archidamus IV (son), *c*. 305–275. |
| Areus II (son), 262–254. | Eudamidas II (son), *c*. 275–245. |
| Leonidas II (grandson of Cleomenes II), 254–235. | Agis IV (son), *c*. 244–241. |
| Cleomenes III (q.v. 2) (son), 235–221. | Eudamidas III (son), 241–*c*. 228. |

| AGIADS (cont.) | EURYPONTIDS (cont.) |
|---|---|
| Agesipolis III (grandson of Cleombrotus II), 219–215. | Archidamus V (uncle), 228–227. |
| | Eucleidas (Agiad—brother of Cleomenes III), 227–221. |

ANCIENT SOURCES. (a) Documents: IG v. 1 (1913); BSA xxvi–xxx (1923–30). Public documents prior to Hellenistic times are extremely scarce, and the great majority of surviving inscriptions are statue-bases and lists of magistrates of the imperial age.

(b) Authors. Poets: see Alcman and Tyrtaeus; Homer, esp. Od. iv. Prose: Hdt. 1. 65 ff.; bks. 5–6 passim (Cleomenes), bks. 7–9 (Persian Wars). Thuc. 1. 10, 18, 89 ff., 101–3, 128 ff. (Pausanias); bks. 2–8 passim (Peloponnesian War). Xen. Hell. (passim), Lac. Pol.; Arist. Pol. 2. 9; 5. 7 and passim. Plut. Lycurgus, Lysander, Agesilaus, Agis (IV), Cleomenes (III), Apophthegmata Laconica. For topography, Strabo 8. 4–6 (Laconia); Pausanias 3. 11–20 (Sparta).

MODERN WORKS. The article 'Sparta' in PW gives full accounts of topography (E. Bölte), Constitution and History (V. Ehrenberg), Religion and Art (L. Ziehen), and a bibliography to 1924. More recent works are: F. Ollier, Le Mirage spartiate i (1933), ii (1943); P. Roussel, Sparte² (1960); K. M. T. Chrimes, Ancient Sparta (1949); H. Michell, Sparta (1952); W. den Boer, Laconian Studies (1954); F. Kiechle, Lakonien und Sparta (1962); G. L. Huxley, Early Sparta (1962); A. H. M. Jones, Sparta (1967); A. J. Toynbee, Some Problems of Greek History (1969), 152 ff. Most of these have detailed bibliographies.

EXCAVATIONS AND ANTIQUITIES. BSA xii–xvi (1905–10), xxvi–xxx (1923–30), 1949; R. M. Dawkins and others, The Sanctuary of Artemis Orthia at Sparta (1929); E. A. Lane, BSA xxxiv (1933–4); J. Boardman, BSA lviii (1963); G. Lippold, Frühgriechische Bildhauerschulen (1950), with references.

MAPS. Graecia Antiqua (Frazer and van Buren, 1930), pl. xxxv.
A. M. W.; W. G. F.

**SPARTA, CULTS AND MYTHS.** The former are well discussed in general by Ziehen in PW, s.v. 'Sparta'. Prominent among them were those of Apollo at Amyclae (Hyacinthia, see HYACINTHUS; his throne and archaic statue there were famous, Paus. 3. 19. 1 ff.); of Artemis, who became identified with a Dorian goddess, Ortheia (the name has various forms, see 'Artemis Orthia', JHS Suppl. v, 1929, esp. 399 ff.); Athena, whose principal temple was the Bronze House, hence her epithet Chalkioikos; Aphrodite, here worshipped as an armed goddess, Areia or ὡπλισμένη; Enyalios, apparently regarded as separate from Ares, with some interesting ritual, including sacrifice of puppies and a sham-fight; Zeus, who in Hellenistic times had (inter alia) the title of Agamemnon, a curious blend of the cults of a god and a hero, if the somewhat doubtful evidence is correct. Of heroes and heroines, the Dioscuri (q.v.) were prominent, often in connexion with Helen (q.v.); see F. Chapouthier, Les Dioscures au service d'une déesse (1935), especially 143 ff. Helen herself was worshipped in a way indicating that she is more goddess than heroine. The Leucippides also (see DIOSCURI) had a cult. Of festivals, one of the most prominent was the Carnea (q.v.).

Really Spartan myths are quite uncommon, most of the fabulous history of the place representing attempts to attach pre-Dorian mythology to the Dorians. The Pelopidae, including Agamemnon, who is killed at Amyclae as early as Pindar, Pyth. 11. 31, the hint being taken from Od. 4. 514 ff., are claimed as a kind of Spartans, and Heracles has a series of adventures there and is made out to be an ancestor, though he had little cult.

See bibliography s.v. SPARTA (Excavations). H. J. R.

**SPARTACUS,** Thracian gladiator who led a revolt at Capua in 73 B.C. Numerous Thracian, Celtic, and German renegades quickly joined him. Spartacus defeated two Roman armies, then devastated southern Italy, continually attracting additional fugitives; ultimately his army numbered 90,000. In 72, after losing his Celtic associate Crixus, he defeated three Roman armies and reached Cisalpine Gaul whence, he hoped, his followers would disperse to their homes. They, however, preferred to plunder Italy. Spartacus accordingly marched south again, conquered two more Roman armies, desolated

Lucania, and would have invaded Sicily, had not piratical transports failed him. In 71 Crassus, after unsuccessfully attempting to corner Spartacus in the 'toe' of Italy, finally caught and destroyed him in Lucania, subsequently crucifying any rebels he captured. Pompey, returning from Spain, annihilated the few who escaped. Spartacus quickly became a legend; he was competent, brave, physically powerful, and apparently humane.

The primary source was apparently Sallust's Histories. Plutarch (Crass. 8 f.; Pomp. 21) and Appian (BCiv. 1. 116 f.) give continuous, but not wholly trustworthy, accounts, the writers who follow Livy (Epit. 95 f.; Florus 2. 8; Eutrop. 6. 7; Oros. 5. 24) sketchier versions. See T. Rice Holmes, Roman Republic (1923), i. 156 f.; L. Pareti, Storia di Roma iii (1953), 687 ff. E. T. S.

**SPARTOCIDS,** a dynasty which established itself at Panticapaeum (q.v.) in 438 B.C., and ruled most of the Crimea and the Taman peninsula until c. 110 B.C.: see BOSPORUS (2), CIMMERIAN. It was called after its founder, Spartocus I. The Spartocids were probably of Thracian origin, but soon became hellenized. The earlier members of the dynasty avoided regal style and were known simply as ἄρχοντες Βοσπόρου; but they kept a mercenary force and probably owned most of the Crimean land. From the time of Spartocus III (304–284) they bore the title of kings. They so developed the cultivation of wheat in their dominions as to become the greatest exporters of grain to Greece. In the fifth century they probably conceded a right of pre-emption to Athens; in the next two centuries they still cultivated the Athenian market, but dealt freely with other Aegean cities. Their wealth is attested by their magnificently furnished rock-tombs near Panticapaeum. In the second and first centuries the Spartocids suffered from Scythian and Sarmatian invasions of the Crimea, and c. 110 they were displaced by Mithridates VI of Pontus, whose help was sought by Paerisades V. This last Spartocid ruler was killed in an uprising led by the Scythian Saumacus whom he had probably been forced to adopt. The Bosporan kingdom thus became part of Mithridates' empire.

The dynasty comprised (cf. R. Werner, op. cit.): Spartocus I (438/7–433/2), Seleucus (with Satyrus I, 433/2–393/2), Satyrus I (433/2–389/8, alone 393/2–389/8), Leucon I (389/8–349/8), Spartocus II (with Paerisades I 349/8–344/3), Paerisades I (349/8–311/10, alone 344/3–311/10), Satyrus II (311/10–310/09), Prytanis (310/09), Eumelus (310/09–304/3) Spartocus III (304/3–284/3), Paerisades II (284/3–c. 245). Hereafter less is known of the dynasty: Spartocus IV (c. 245–c. 215), Comasarye (c. 215–c. 175), Paerisades III (between 215 and 190?), Paerisades IV Philometor (c. 190?–after 160), Spartocus V (between 160 and 150), Leucon II (between 160 and 150), Hygiaenon (c. 150), Paerisades V (after 150–108/7).

M. Rostovtzeff, CAH viii, ch. 18; R. Werner, Hist. 1955, 412 f.
M. C.; H. H. S.

**SPARTOI,** see CADMUS. Their descendants had a birthmark in the shape of a spearhead, Arist. Poet. 1454^b22 (from Euripides' Antigone?), by which they could be known.

**SPELUNCA,** natural grotto on the Tyrrhenian coast of Italy immediately east of Tarracina (q.v.), where the Emperor Tiberius had a villa. Sejanus (q.v.) rescued him from death in a cave-in there. Modern Sperlonga preserves the name. Recently the grotto has yielded thousands of fragments of Hellenistic-type sculptures, mostly of marine monsters, and a Greek inscription naming three Rhodian sculptors.

P. MacKendrick, The Mute Stones Speak (1962), 173 ff.; G. Jacobi, L'antro di Tiberio a Sperlonga (1963); G. Saeflund, Fynden: Tiberiusgrottan (1966). E. T. S.

**SPES,** a *res expetenda* rather than an actual 'virtue'. A temple was built to her by A. Atilius Calatinus in the First Punic War. Burnt down in 31 B.C., it was restored by Germanicus in A.D. 17. 'Spes P.R.' is the rising generation, the hope of the race, 'Spes Augusta' imperial promise centred in the princes (cf. *supplicatio Spei et Iuuentuti*, 18 Oct., for the *toga uirilis* of Augustus). She bears an opening flower and catches up her skirt as if in haste. Her temple in the Forum Holitorium is identified with one of the three temples under S. Nicola in Carcere (Platner–Ashby, 493; Nash, *Pict. Dict. Rome* i. 418 ff.).

G. Wissowa, *RK* 263, 329 f.                                    H. M.

**SPEUSIPPUS** (*c.* 407–339 B.C.), Athenian philosopher, son of Eurymedon and of Plato's sister Potone. He accompanied Plato on his last visit to Sicily (361) and succeeded him as head of the Academy from 347 to 339. Of his voluminous writings (Diog. Laert. 4. 4) only fragments and later reports remain, but Aristotle treats him with respect and it is clear that he continued and helped to shape some major philosophical interests which the Academy had acquired under Plato.

(*a*) DEFINITION. Speusippus argued that, since a definition is designed to identify its subject and differentiate it from everything else, it can only be established by knowing everything there is. This can hardly have been intended, as some ancient critics thought, to refute all attempts at defining. More probably it was this view of definition which prompted Speusippus in his ten books of Ὅμοια to set about collecting the observable resemblances between different sorts of plant and animal, for he may have thought (as Aristotle sometimes did, *An. Post. B* 13) that a species can be defined by discovering a set of characteristics which it shares with various other species, taken collectively, but not with any one other species.

The Academy's interest in definition had led to the recognition that some expressions have more than one meaning. Speusippus marked this by drawing distinctions comparable to, but fuller than, those familiar from Aristotle's logic. Where a single word is in question, it may have one sense or more than one (συνώνυμα, ὁμώνυμα); where more than one word is in question, they may stand for one thing or for quite different things, or one may derive its sense from the other (πολυώνυμα, ἑτερώνυμα, παρώνυμα). This in itself would give Speusippus his place at the birth of logic in the Academy.

(*b*) PHILOSOPHY AND EXACT SCIENCE. Speusippus wrote on Pythagorean mathematics, endorsing the search for the elements of numbers which Plato had taken over from the Pythagoreans (see the newly discovered fragment of Speusippus, *Plato Latinus* iii. 40 1–5). But he refused to equate numbers with Platonic Ideas, which like others in the Academy he rejected; and he further denied the claim, which Aristotle ascribes to the Pythagoreans and Plato, that the elements of number are the elements of everything else. Other sorts and levels of reality, he argued, need other sorts of element. Hence Aristotle accuses him of making the universe 'episodic', disconnected; but it is Speusippus' theory that underlies Aristotle's attempt in *Metaph. A* to show that it is not strictly true, but only true 'by analogy', that all things have the same elements.

(*c*) ETHICS. In the Academic debate which can be heard behind Plato's *Philebus* and the ethical writings of Aristotle Speusippus makes two appearances. He holds, first, that pleasure is neither good nor evil in itself, and second, that goodness is to be found only in the final stages of development and not in the origins.

Under all these heads it is likely that the best of his work has been digested in that of Aristotle and his successors,

and in particular that his biological observations in the Ὅμοια were largely absorbed in the treatises of the Lyceum.

Testimonia and fragments in P. Lang, *De Speusippi Academici Scriptis* (1911). Zeller ii. 1⁴. 982–1010; E. Hambruch, *Logische Regeln der plat. Schule in der aristotel. Topik* (1904); J. Stenzel in *PW* iii A. 1636 ff.; H. Cherniss, *Aristotle's Crit. of Plato and the Acad.* i (1944), esp. ch. 1; P. Merlan, *From Platonism to Neoplatonism²* (1961).                                           G. E. L. O.

**SPHAERUS** of Borysthenes (b. *c.* 285 or 265, lived at least to 221 B.C.), a pupil first of Zeno, then of Cleanthes; friend and adviser of the Spartan reformer Cleomenes. His numerous writings dealt with all branches of philosophy (especially with morals and politics) and with certain of the older philosophers. His definitions were highly esteemed in the Stoic school.

Testimonia in von Arnim, *SVF* i. 139–42.                       W. D. R.

**SPHINX,** a mythological monster, with human head and the body of a lion. Originating in Egypt, probably as a type of the king, the Sphinx became known early to Syrians, Phoenicians, and Mycenaean Greeks. Already in the Near East it was transformed into a female being and remained female in Greek literature, although in art bearded male Sphinxes are known in the archaic period (H. Payne, *Necrocorinthia*, 1931, 89). Sphinxes were at first adopted by the Greek artists as a type of ghost-like monsters who carry off boys or youths and are present at fatal combats. Like many other monsters, the Sphinx acquired an apotropaic significance and was placed on tombs (Diog. Laert. 1. 89) and depicted on shields (Aesch. *Sept.* 522). In Boeotia, the native land of Hesiod's great mythological system, the Sphinx became a central figure of the native cycle concerned with the mythical dynasty of the Labdacidae. In an early version the Sphinx, sent by Hera to Thebes, asked the Thebans the riddle about the three ages of men (Apollod. 3. 5. 7 f.; a piece of folklore). They failed to solve it, and after each effort the Sphinx carried away and devoured one of them, including Haemon, son of Creon (E. Haspels, *Attic Black-Fig. Lekythoi*, 1938, 131), until Oedipus (q.v.) solved the riddle. The Sphinx committed suicide, or was killed by Oedipus (Corinna in schol. Eur. *Phoen.* 26). Later accounts, attesting the growth of Delphic religion, make Apollo send the Sphinx. These versions were used by Sophocles (*OT*) and Euripides (*Phoen.*).

In art sphinxes appear in great abundance in the 'animal friezes' of the orientalizing period; marble statues of Sphinxes, such as the Sphinx of the Naxians in Delphi, are given as votives to Apollo (Ch. Picard, *Manuel d'archéol.* i. 570, fig. 197), or guard the tombs of Attica (G. M. A. Richter, *Mélanges Picard*, 1949, 863). In Classical art the Sphinx is humanized. The Sphinx from Aegina and those of later Attic vases have beautiful serious faces, sometimes female breasts. Instead of the Hesiodic monster, the child of Echidna and Orthros (*Theog.* 326), the Sphinx becomes the wise, enigmatic, and musical messenger of divine justice; the tragic poets call her 'the wise virgin' and say that she sang her riddle (Eur. *Phoen.* 48, 1507).

J. Ilberg in Roscher, *Lex.*, s.v.; H. J. Rose, *Handb. Gk. Myth.* 188 and 297; P. Wolters, *Gnomon* 1925, 46; M. Renard, *Latomus* 1950, 303; F. Matz, *JDAI* 1950–1, 91; G. M. A. Hanfmann, *Archaeology* 1953, 229; A. Dessenne, *Le Sphinx, étude iconographique* (1957); H. Walter, *Art and Archaeology*, 1960, 63.
                                               G. M. A. H.; J. R. T. P.

**SPINA,** an Etruscan port situated on what was the mouth of the southern branch of the Po. It was established towards the end of the sixth century (by Greeks or Etruscans?). The site was identified by air-photography in 1956; this city of the marshes had an elaborate canal system. Together with Adria (q.v.), it supplied the earlier foundation of Felsina (q.v.), Etruria Padana, and ultimately Europe with the products of the rich fifth-century Greek commerce. A great quantity of Attic red-figure and other Greek pottery has been recovered from the Valle Trebba and Valle Pega cemeteries; it is now in the museum at Ferrara. Spina exercised considerable naval influence in the Adriatic and maintained a 'Treasury' at Delphi.

P. E. Arias, *Il museo archeologico di Ferrara* (1955); id. *CVA Feriara Museo Nazionale I* (Italy fasc. xxvii, 1963); *Atti I Conv. Stud. Etr.* 1957. *Suppl. Stud. Etr.* xxv (1959); *Mostra dell'Etruria Padana e della città di Spina*, 2 vols. (Bologna, 1960); Scullard, *Etr. Cities*, 209 ff., S. Aurigemma, *Scavi di Spina, la necropoli di Valle Trebba*, i (1960), i. 2 (1965). D. W. R. R.

**SPINNING.** In an ancient household a large amount of a woman's time was spent in wool-work; and on the tomb of a virtuous Roman matron the crowning words of praise were 'Lanam fecit'. The fleeces were brought into the house in their rough state and had first to be washed. The wool was then teased and pulled into fluff before being treated by an instrument called *epinetron* which separated the fibres and arranged them lengthways, making them ready for spinning. The spindle—κλωστήρ, *fusus*—was a straight piece of reed, wood, or metal about 12 inches long; the whorl was a disk of clay, wood, or ivory attached to the end of the spindle; and the operation of spinning was as follows. The wool was placed on the distaff (ἠλακάτη, *colus*), and from it a little was drawn, twisted, and fixed to a hook at the top of the spindle. With the help of the whorl the spindle was spun round, and as it spun more wool was paid out from the distaff and twisted into yarn.

Forbes, *Stud. Anc. Technol.* iv. 149 f. F. A. W.

**SPOLETIUM,** mountain town in Umbria: modern *Spoleto*, with spectacular ancient remains. Becoming a Latin colony (241 B.C.), Spoletium rendered yeoman service against Hannibal (q.v.). After suffering severely in Social and Civil Wars, it became a flourishing *municipium*, the Via Flaminia (q.v.) being diverted to serve it. Later it was a Lombard duchy and is still an important city. *See* UMBRIANS.

C. Pietrangeli, *Spoletium* (Rome, 1939). E. T. S.

**SPOLIA OPIMA** were spoils offered by a Roman general who had slain an enemy leader in single combat. Three kinds are distinguished, *prima*, *secunda*, and *tertia* according to the rank of the winner and the deity to which the spoils were dedicated. *Prima spolia* (or *opima*) were consecrated in the temple of Jupiter Feretrius (*secunda* and *tertia* to Mars and Quirinus respectively). *Spolia opima* were traditionally won on three occasions. Romulus' victory was obviously invented to credit him with the building of the temple of Jupiter Feretrius and the institution of the custom. But the historicity of the victories of A. Cornelius Cossus (q.v.) over Tolumnius (*c*. 428) and of M. Claudius Marcellus (q.v. 1) over Viridomarus (222 B.C.) is attested by epigraphical and literary evidence. Interest in *spolia opima* revived in 29 B.C. owing to the victory of Licinius Crassus (q.v. 6) over Deldo, the chief of the Bastarnae, and Octavian's rejection of Crassus' claim.

J. Marquardt, *Röm. Staatsverw.* ii. 560 f.; Ogilvie, *Comm. Livy 1–5*, 71 ff., 563 f. P. T.

**SPRINGS, SACRED.** The worship of springs (or wells), a phenomenon of the highest antiquity and widespread all over the world, is in essential points similar to that of rivers (*see* RIVER-GODS). Flowing water, especially when bubbling up from the interior of the earth, was to the primitive mind animate and divine, and the plastic creative imagination of the Greeks personified such spirits of fountains as nymphs (*see* NYMPHS). Fountains with

extraordinary qualities gained special significance and acquired corresponding myths—warm healing fountains were attached to the cults of Hephaestus, Heracles, and Artemis. Mantic springs were attached to several famous oracles, as those of Apollo at Didyma (q.v.) near Miletus and at Delphi (Cassotis); cf. the spring at Claros, that of Daphne near Antioch, and that in the Troad near the grave of the Sibyl. Poseidon was said to have caused fountains to spring up (e.g. the salty fountain on the Athenian Acropolis, in the Erechtheum); so also Dionysus (thus a fountain near Haliartus reminded men of the wine-god and his nurses because of the ruddy colour of its waters: Plut. *Lys.* 28. 7). The fountain on the summit of the Boeotian Helicon, Hippocrene, was brought forth by a blow of the hoof of Pegasus, said to have been the horse of Poseidon. Fountains were also named after heroes, as Achilles and Agamemnon; those that disappear into the earth were considered to be entrances to Hades (as Styx in Arcadia, Asterion in Argos). A number of myths (cf. Dirce, s.v. AMPHION, *and* AMYMONE) and cults (cf. the nymphs of the spring) clearly show the strong fascination which springs exercised on Greek minds. The Roman festival Fontinalia (13 Oct.), when flowers were thrown into the fountains, was important. The Romans also threw coins into wells (Pliny, *Ep.* 8. 8. 2). Horace sacrifices a kid to the Bandusian spring (*Carm.* 3. 13. 3).

M. Ninck, *Philol.* Suppl. xiv. 2 (1921); J. H. Croon, *The Herdsman of the Dead* (1952); A. Carnoy, *Muséon* 1956, 187 ff.; J. Fontenrose, *Python* (1959), App. 6. S. E.; J. E. F.

**SPURINNA,** TITUS VESTRICIUS (*PW* s.v.), born in Transpadane Italy *c.* A.D. 25, commanded part of Otho's (q.v.) advanced guard in A.D. 69, and successfully defended Placentia after quelling a mutiny. *Cos. suff.* under Vespasian, he is almost certainly one of two men (Pliny, *Pan.* 60–1) who received a second consulate from Nerva and a third from Trajan: his second consulate is definitely attested by the *Fasti Ostienses*. Nerva honoured him with a statue for a campaign against the Bructeri, but it is uncertain when that operation took place. In his old age Spurinna lived an active life in the country and wrote Greek and Latin lyrics; he was still alive *c.* 105, a friend of the Younger Pliny, and possibly an oral source for Tacitus' *Histories*.

Syme, *Tacitus*, App. 6. G. E. F. C.

**STABERIUS EROS,** a scholar, originally a slave, who taught the children of the Sullan *proscripti* free. Brutus and Cassius were his pupils (Pliny, *HN* 35. 199; Suet. *Gram.* 13).

**STABIAE,** modern *Castellamare* in Campania just south of Pompeii (q.v.). It was taken by the insurgents and destroyed by Sulla in the Social War (90/89 B.C.). In the Early Empire it was a fashionable resort until the Vesuvius eruption buried it (A.D. 79). The Elder Pliny perished here. Excavations have uncovered exceptionally fine frescoes.

L. d'Orsi, *Gli scavi di Stabia* (1954); O. Elia, *Pitture di Stabia* (1957). E. T. S.

**STADIUM.** The Greek στάδιον, the running-track, was a long parallelogram, about 200 yards long and 30 yards wide. In the sprint race (also known as στάδιον) the competitors ran the length of the track; in the longer events they went up and down the straight, turning sharply round pillars at the end. When possible the stadium lay between two hills with an embankment at the two ends which were either left square or rounded in a half-circle, for the convenience of the spectators. The four best-known extant stadia are those at Delphi, Olympia, Epidaurus, and Athens. At Delphi the present structure, dating from the second century A.D., is largely due to

Herodes Atticus, who also rebuilt the stadium at Athens with forty-six rows of marble seats holding some 50,000 people. In all four stadia the start and finish are marked with pillars and stone slabs divided into sections, one for each runner. At Epidaurus there are also small pillars every hundred feet on each side of the track, and a stone channel with basins at intervals to provide the spectators with water.

E. N. Gardiner, *Athletics of the Ancient World* (1930), 128 ff.
F. A. W.

**STANDARDS, CULT OF.** Every permanent station of a Roman military unit, especially a legion, and every camp regularly constructed contained a chapel, which, at least in imperial times (Vegetius, *De re mil.* 2. 6), was under the charge of the first cohort, or headquarters company. In this were kept, besides the statues of gods worshipped by the troops and of the emperors, the standards of the unit and its component parts. These, from an unknown date (Pliny, *HN* 13. 23; our information does not go back to republican times), received divine or quasi-divine honours. They were anointed and otherwise tended on feast-days (Pliny, ibid., cf. ROSALIA). A suppliant might take refuge at them (Tac. *Ann.* 1. 39. 7); an altar was on occasion dedicated at least partly to them, or at all events to the most important, the eagle of the legion (*CIL* iii. 7591; no. 14 v. Domaszewski); the *natalis* of the eagle, presumably the anniversary of the day when the unit was first commissioned, was celebrated (*CIL* ii. 6183; no. 3 v. Domaszewski); sacrifice was made to them particularly on the occasion of a victory (Joseph. *BJ* 6. 316, where the troops who took Jerusalem make offerings to their ensigns in the Temple, not in their camp). Tertullian even says with rhetorical exaggeration that the soldiers venerated them beyond all gods (*Apol.* 16). They are not precisely gods, but are associated with *genius* and *uirtus* (*CIL* iii. 7591, above), and are 'propria legionum numina' (Tac. *Ann.* 2. 17. 2). This perhaps goes to the heart of the matter; they are the embodiment of the luck or power of their unit and hence worthy of respect and to be kept sacredly. *See* SIGNA MILITARIA.

A. von Domaszewski, *Die Religion des römischen Heeres* (*Westdeutsche Zeitschrift* 1895), 9 ff.
H. J. R.

**STAPHYLUS** (1), personification of the grape-cluster, σταφυλή. He is vaguely attached to Dionysus, as his son by Ariadne (q.v.; Plut. *Thes.* 20); his favourite (schol. Ar. *Plut.* 1021); an Assyrian king who welcomes him during his Indian campaign (Nonnus, *Dion.* 18. 5 ff.). Or he discovered the vine and informed Oeneus (q.v.; 'Probus' on Verg. *G.* 1. 9).
H. J. R.

**STAPHYLUS** (2) of Naucratis, an Alexandrian to whom are assigned histories of Athens and Thessaly (Περὶ Ἀθηνῶν and Θεσσαλικά). Perhaps c. 300 B.C.

*FGrH* iii. 269.

**STASEAS** of Naples, the first Peripatetic philosopher known to have settled in Rome. M. Calpurnius Piso became his pupil c. 92 B.C. He is frequently mentioned by Cicero. He seems to have occupied himself particularly with the problem of the normal length of human life.
W. D. R.

**STASINUS** of Cyprus (? 8th c. B.C.), epic poet, possibly author of the *Cypria* (Ath. 15. 682 d), *See* EPIC CYCLE, § 5.

*EGF* 15-32.

**STATILIUS** (*PW* 34) **TAURUS**, TITUS (*cos. suff.* 37 B.C., *cos.* II 26 B.C.), the greatest Augustan marshal after Agrippa. Of uncertain origin (perhaps Lucanian), by military talent and steadfast loyalty he rose to wealth and honours; he was thrice acclaimed *imperator* by the legions and held several priesthoods (*ILS* 893; 893 a). His earliest recorded service for Octavian was as an admiral in the *Bellum Siculum* (36). After the conquest of Sicily he crossed to Africa and secured that province, holding a triumph in 34 (the amphitheatre erected in commemoration on the Campus Martius was completed in 30). He also fought in Illyricum (34-33), commanded the land army in the campaign of Actium (31), and conducted operations in Spain (29). After his second consulate (26) the only record of him is that he was put in charge of Rome as *praefectus urbi* in 16 when Augustus departed to the provinces of the West (Dio Cass. 54. 19. 6; Tac. *Ann.* 6. 11). He probably died not long after. Of his descendants the last and brightest was Statilia Messallina (q.v. 2), the third wife of Nero.

Syme, *Rom. Rev.*, see index.
R. S.

**STATIUS**, PUBLIUS PAPINIUS (c. A.D. 45-96), was born at Naples, where his father, himself a poet, was a schoolmaster. From his father, whom he eulogizes in *Silvae* 5. 3, he learned much of the poetic technique he was afterwards to develop. Settling in Rome, he established there his fame and popularity as a poet. From his *Silvae* we learn that he recited his works to fashionable audiences (cf. Juv. 7. 82-6), that he became intimately acquainted with several of the leading men of his day, and that he was admitted to the court of Domitian, to whose good graces he owed the running water in an estate he acquired at Alba (3. 1. 61 ff.), where his father was buried (5. 3. 35-40). He won the prize, probably in 89, at the annual festival instituted by Domitian at Alba, but was, much to his chagrin, unsuccessful at the quinquennial Capitoline contest, probably in 94. To his wife Claudia he pays graceful compliments (3. 5). They had no children, though Claudia had a daughter by a previous marriage and Statius adopted a son who died young (5. 5). Statius' health was not robust, and we hear of one serious illness through which he was nursed by his wife. Towards the end of his life he retired to his native city, where he died, seemingly before the murder of Domitian (Sept. 96). He appears to have been of an amiable disposition, deeply attached to his relations and capable of warm friendship. Though not of great wealth, he was probably in easy circumstances, at any rate during his later years. Real hardship does not seem ever to have fallen to his lot and, generally speaking, it is only of the pleasant sides of life that we have glimpses in his poems. The least pleasing aspect of his nature is to be seen in the extravagant flattery lavished on Domitian (e.g. *Silv.* 4. 1-3), which may be partially extenuated by the conditions of the age.

WORKS. A poem on Domitian's German wars and the *Agave*, a libretto for a pantomimus mentioned by Juvenal 7. 87, have perished. The epic *Thebais*, published about 91, took twelve years to complete and tells in twelve books the story of the quarrel between Eteocles (q.v. 2) and Polynices. The *Achilleis*, brought to a conclusion in the second book by the poet's death, deals with the education of Achilles under the Centaur Chiron, his disguise as a girl during his sojourn at the court of Lycomedes in Scyros, his amour with Deidameia, his detection by Ulysses and Diomedes, and his departure for Troy. The *Silvae* in five books published at different times from 92 onwards, the fifth being posthumous, consist of thirty-two occasional poems addressed to the poet's friends celebrating their marriages, villas, baths, *objets d'art*, or public benefactions, offering congratulations on recovery from illness, the birth of an heir, or attainment of high office, or consolations on the loss of relatives, and sometimes dealing with lighter subjects. The most famous is the short address to Sleep (5. 4). These poems are mostly in hexameters, though four are in hendecasyllabics, one in sapphics, and one in alcaics. They were lost in medieval times till Poggio discovered a manuscript containing them at Constance in 1417.

Statius' verse is fluent and highly polished, even in the hastily composed *Silvae*. The *Thebais* requires episodic treatment and lacks a real hero. There are frequent imitations of Virgil in word and thought, and the gods take part in the action. Excessive use of hyperbole is perhaps the chief fault in taste. But the various episodes, highly coloured and rhetorical though they be, are generally successful regarded as separate wholes, the descriptive passages striking, and the narrative lively. The sentiment rarely reaches sublimity, but telling effects are achieved in 'pathetic' passages. The epics were much admired throughout medieval times, and Statius, regarded by Dante as a Christian, is an important character in the *Purgatorio*. He was a favourite also of Chaucer's.

LIFE. F. Vollmer's edition of *Silvae* (Teubner, 1898).
MSS. OF EPICS. A. Klotz, *Hermes*, 1905. See too, Garrod's edition of *Thebais* (1906), for theory (arising from nature of MS. variants) of a second edition of *Thebais* by Statius himself.
MSS. OF SILVAE. All MSS. of *Silvae* derive from M, i.e. Codex Matritensis Biblioth. Nation. 3678. For different views on problems connected with the tradition, e.g. whether M is the MS. discovered by Poggio or only a copy of it, a question not yet decided, see Teubner editions by Klotz (1911) and Marastoni (1961).
R. Sweeney, *Prolegomena to an edition of the Scholia of S.* (1969).
Source and Models. R. Helm, *De P. Papinii Statii Thebaide* (1892); Essenfeldt, *Philol.* 1904. Literary Appreciation. L. Legras, *Étude sur la Thébaïde de Stace* (1905); G. Krumbholz, 'Der Erzählungsstil in der Thebais des Statius', *Glotta* 1955, 93 ff., 231 ff.; W. Schetter, *Untersuchungen zur epischen Kunst des Statius* (1960). *Achilleis*: O. A. W. Dilke (1954), with extensive bibliography.
E. J. W.

**STELE.** Stone slabs as grave markers are found occasionally in Bronze Age Greece, the most notable being those with relief decoration above the Shaft Graves at Mycenae. In Geometric and early Archaic Greece such *stelai* are rare, but in Athens about 600 begins a distinguished series with relief decoration on the shaft, topped first by a sphinx, then by a palmette finial. The latter type originated in east Greece, and it persisted after 500 in the islands, after the Athenian series had already ended. A new type of stele in Athens appears after the mid fifth century. It is broader, with pilasters at the side and a pediment above, and carries relief representations of the dead or scenes of parting. The series was stopped by decree of Demetrius of Phalerum at the end of the fourth century and later grave markers are simple short cylindrical blocks. The word is also applied to the upright rectangular slabs on which decrees and similar public documents were inscribed, and to *horoi* marking the limits of property.

G. M. A. Richter, *The Archaic Gravestones of Attica* (1961); K. F. Johansen, *The Attic Grave-Reliefs* (1951); L. H. Jeffery, *BSA* 1962, 115 ff.
J. B.

**STENTOR,** a man who could shout as loudly as fifty ordinary people (*Iliad* 5. 785–6). He is evidently known to Homer, but no later author has anything worth quoting to say of him.

**STEPHANUS of Byzantium** was a Greek grammarian, probably a contemporary of Justinian, and apparently a teacher in the imperial university in Constantinople. Nothing is known in detail of his life. He is the author of 'Εθνικά, in sixty books, an alphabetical list of place-names together with the adjectives derived from them. The original work, which contained information on foundation-legends, etymologies, changes of name, oracles, historical anecdotes, proverbs, etc., is lost. The surviving epitome, consisting mainly of jejune entries, was compiled some time between the sixth and tenth centuries A.D. It may be the work of one Hermolaus, mentioned in the *Suda*, but some scholars believe that it is actually a

conflation of at least two epitomes, made on slightly different principles. There are fragments of the original extensive text embedded in the *De Administrando Imperio* and *De Thematibus* of Constantine Porphyrogenitus.

Stephanus was neither a geographer—he makes no direct use of Ptolemy—nor a historian—he puts down side by side information dating from different epochs—but a grammarian. His prime interest is the correct formation of ethnic adjectives, for which he has two criteria, morphological regularity and regional usage. His direct sources, which he sometimes mentions, include Herodian, Oros of Miletus, Philo of Byblos Περὶ πόλεων, Dionysius Periegetes, Strabo, historians from Hecataeus to Polybius, and lost grammarians and antiquarians. He is not entirely uncritical in his handling of his sources, but his main value is as a compilation of material from writers whose works are lost. The surviving epitome was used by the *Etymologicum Magnum*, Eustathius, and probably the *Suda*. The last writer to use the original version was Constantine Porphyrogenitus. The 'Εθνικά are preserved in a large number of MSS., mainly dating from the Renaissance. There is no satisfactory critical edition.

Ed. A. Meineke, Berlin (1849, repr. 1958).　　R. B.

**STEROPE** or **ASTEROPE,** (1) one of the Pleiads, wife of Oenomaus (q.v.; Paus. 5. 10. 6); (2) daughter of Cepheus king of Tegea (Apollod. 2. 144). Heracles gave her (in Paus. 8. 47. 5, Athena gave Cepheus) some of the hair of Medusa, bidding her lift it thrice above the city wall, to put attackers to flight.　　H. J. R.

**STERTINIUS,** in the Augustan Age, turned Stoic tenets into Latin verse and, according to Acro (ad Hor. *Epist.* 1. 12. 20), wrote 220 books.

**STESICHORUS,** lyric poet, said to have been born at Mataurus (Steph. Byz. s.v. Μάταυρος) and to have lived at Himera (Pl. *Phdr.* 244 a, Arist. *Rh.* 1393ᵇ). His real name was said to be Teisias (*Suda* s.v. Στησίχορος), and it is quite possible that Στησίχορος was a title. His dates are confused by *Marm. Par.* 50, which places his arrival in Greece in 485 B.C. This seems a mistake, and there can be little doubt that he was alive in the first half of the sixth century, since he is connected with Phalaris (Arist. *Rh.* 1393ᵇ) and the *Suda* places his birth at 632–629 B.C. and his death 556–553 B.C. His works were collected in twenty-six books, and seem to have been lyrical poems composed on a big scale, in which the narrative element was strong. Titles of several poems survive and indicate that he told stories gathered from widely different epic sources. It is not known what type of poems he composed, though it is possible that some were Dithyrambs, since narrative predominated in this type, and Stesichorus may have been influenced by the voyage of Arion in the West. Though the fragments are scanty, something may be learned of his work. In his *Funeral-games of Pelias* he drew on the Argonautic saga and described the games in some detail (frs. 178–80). His *Geryoneis* told of Heracles' quest of the cattle of Geryon, and was remarkable for its knowledge of the silver-mines of Tartessus (fr. 184), its conception of Heracles as a great drinker (fr. 181), its account of the Sun's magic cup which Heracles borrowed for his voyage (fr. 185), and for the notion that Geryon was winged (schol. Hes. *Th.* 287), which was soon popularized by painters. His *Boar-hunters* (frs. 221–2) seems to have been about the Calydonian boar-hunt, and his *Eriphyle* (fr. 194) dealt with a famous Theban legend. His *Iliupersis* drew on the epic, and was interesting for its account of Epeus who made the Wooden Horse (fr. 200), though attempts to connect it with the legend of Aeneas remain unproved. In his *Helen* he seems to have told the conventional story in a first version, which contained an account of her marriage to Menelaus (fr. 187). But legend (Pl. *Phdr.* 243 a) told that he was blinded for this and did not recover until he recanted in a second poem, his famous *Palinode*, in which he denied that Helen ever went to Troy (fr. 192) and put the blame on Homer for the story (fr. 193). In a second Palinode (ibid.) he put the blame on Hesiod. Perhaps the truth behind this is that Stesichorus outraged opinion which regarded Helen as a goddess, as it did in Sparta. His *Oresteia* in two books seems also to have been sung at Sparta at a spring festival (frs. 211–12), and differed from Homer in placing the death of Agamemnon in Lacedaemon. It contained an account of Clytemnestra's dream (fr. 219), and gave some part to the nurse of Orestes (fr. 218). The *Rhadine*, attributed to him, seems more likely to be a later, romantic work by another poet, perhaps of the same name (cf. *Marm. Par.* 73). The fragments show that he wrote in the traditional language of choral lyric, used a kind of 'dactylo-epitrite' metre, and was an ingenious inventor of episodes later very popular, such as the birth of Athene in full armour from the head of Zeus (*Etym. Magn.* 772. 49). He was admired for his dignity (Quint. *Inst.* 10. 1. 62) and grandeur in plot and character (Dion. Hal. *Vett. Cens.* 2. 27). *See also* PASTORAL POETRY, GREEK.

TEXT. Page, *Poet. Mel. Gr.* 97–141.
CRITICISM. J. Vürtheim, *Stesichoros' Fragmente und Biographie* (1919): C. M. Bowra, *Greek Lyric Poetry*[2] (1962). C. M. B.

**STESIMBROTUS** (fl. late 5th c. B.C.), biographer from Thasos, who taught at Athens.

WORKS (*FGrH* ii B. 107): (1) Homeric studies; (2) Περὶ τελετῶν, on the Samothracian mysteries; (3) Περὶ Θεμιστοκλέους καὶ Θουκυδίδου καὶ Περικλέους (frs. in Plut.). Stesimbrotus gives full biographical details, but criticizes Themistocles and Pericles and lauds Cimon; no preserved fragments concern Thucydides (son of Melesias). F. W. W.

**STHENELUS,** a tragic poet of the fifth century B.C., chosen by Aristotle (*Poet.* 22) as the example of a poet who avoided all use of poetic vocabulary and was in consequence commonplace in style. His insipidity is ridiculed by Aristophanes (*Vesp.* 1313 and schol.), and Plato Com. (fr. 70) says that he appropriated other poets' verses.

*TGF* 762. A. W. P.-C.

**STHENIDAS** of Locri, the nominal author of a Pythagorean treatise on kingship, of which Stobaeus quotes a fragment; it has been variously dated between the early third century B.C. and the second century A.D.

Stobaeus 4. 270–1 W-H. *See* ECPHANTUS. G. T. G.

**STICHOMETRY.** (1) GREEK. Στίχος means primarily a line of verse, and metrical texts were naturally measured by the number of their verses; but for bibliographical purposes the equivalent of a hexameter line was taken as a unit of measurement for prose works also. For this purpose the hexameter line was reckoned as approximately 16 syllables or 36 letters (Galen, *De placitis Hippocratis et Platonis* 8. 1. 655). This does not mean that prose works were habitually written in lines of this length. On the contrary, the evidence of papyri found in Egypt shows that the lines in prose manuscripts were usually not much more than half of this. The στίχος was simply a unit of measurement indicating the extent of the book, or of portions of a work, and serving to fix the remuneration of the copyist. Thus Josephus (*AJ* 20. 11. 3) states that his work consists of twenty books and 60,000 στίχοι, and according to Diogenes Laertius the works of Aristotle comprised 445,270 στίχοι; while the Edict of Diocletian

fixes a scribe's wage at 25 to 20 *denarii* per 100 στίχοι. Callimachus, in his catalogue (πίνακες) of the Alexandrian Library, recorded the number of στίχοι in each work. Many extant manuscripts contain notes of the number of στίχοι, e.g. several of the Herculaneum rolls, the Chester Beatty papyrus and the Codex Claromontanus of the Pauline Epistles, the Laurentian manuscripts of Herodotus and Sophocles, etc.

(2) LATIN. In Latin manuscripts the same system was in force, the unit being the Virgilian line of 16 syllables. This is stated explicitly in Phillipps MS. 12266, where the writer, in order to check the dishonesty of copyists, states that he had calculated on this basis the number of lines in the books of the Bible and the writings of Cyprian. Stichometrical notes are, however, not common in Latin manuscripts.

Stichometry, a purely mechanical device, is distinct from colometry, the method of dividing texts according to sense-lines. This, according to Jerome (pref. to Isaiah) was common in manuscripts of Demosthenes and Cicero, and was adopted in his Vulgate version of the Prophets. There is no trace of it in extant Greek papyri, but it is found in bilingual manuscripts (where its utility is obvious), and in some later Vulgate manuscripts.

C. Graux, *Rev. Phil.* 1878, 97; F. Ritschl, *Opusc.* (1866), i. 74; V. Gardthausen, *Griechische Paläographie*[2] (1913), ii. 70 ff.; E. M. Thompson, *Introd. to Gr. and Lat. Palaeography* (1912), 67 ff.; R. Devreesse, *Introduction à l'étude des manuscrits grecs* (1954), 60, 163. F. G. K.

**STICHOMYTHIA** (στιχομυθία, Poll. 4. 113, τὸ παρ' ἓν ἰαμβεῖον ἀντιλέγειν) is a form of dramatic dialogue in which two characters speak a single line each for a considerable stretch (cf. *Henry VI*, III. iii. 2). Sometimes they speak two lines each with similar regularity (Eur. *Bacch.* 935 ff.). As Gross shows, Aeschylus was less strict in his use of stichomythia in later plays than in earlier, whereas Euripides grew more strict. Sophocles, avoiding in this as in other respects stiffness in the structure of his iambic verse, is far freer than either; and in comedy, with its naturalistic technique of dialogue and ready tolerance of *antilabe* (breaking of a line between speakers), there is hardly a trace of stichomythia (Ar. *Ach.* 1097 ff., a special case; 305 ff., pairs; *Plut.* 163 ff.). Stichomythia can be highly effective, as in the tensely concentrated dialogue between Orestes and his mother (Aesch. *Cho.* 908 ff.), and that between Oedipus and the Herdsman (Soph. *OT* 1147 ff.); but it tends to involve the introduction of padding (e.g. Soph. *OT* 559, Eur. *Ion* 1002). Even in a long and otherwise regular series stichomythia is sometimes broken, particularly towards the end. Editors occasionally emend needlessly through a mistaken desire for symmetry.

A. Gross, *Die Stichomythie in d. griech. Trag. u. Kom.* (1905); W. Jens, *Die Stichomythie in der frühen griechischen Tragödie* (1955). J. D. D.

**STILICHO,** FLAVIUS, Roman general, was the effective ruler of the Western Empire from A.D. 395 until 408. On the accession of Arcadius (q.v. 2) to the Eastern throne in 395 Stilicho brought about the downfall and death of the new Emperor's chief adviser, Rufinus (q.v. 1). About this time the poet Claudian began to publish his poems in praise of Stilicho. In 395 and 397 he ineffectively invaded Greece in order to defeat the Visigoths of Alaric; but in 402 and 403 he defeated Alaric at Pollentia (*Pollenza*) and Verona respectively, withdrawing troops from Britain and other provinces to make up his army. In 405 he annihilated at Fiesole a horde of Ostrogoths and other barbarians, led by Radagaisus, who had invaded Italy. He was beheaded on the orders of Honorius (q.v.) in 408. Little is known of his character.

S. Mazzarino, *Stilicone* (1942). E. A. T.

**STILO PRAECONINUS**, Lucius Aelius (Suet. *Gram.* 3; Pliny, *HN* 33. 29), the first great Roman scholar, born at Lanuvium about 150 B.C., of equestrian rank, and a Stoic by training. He interested himself in literary criticism, antiquities, grammar, and etymologies; though not an orator, he composed speeches for others. Amongst his pupils he numbered Varro and Cicero (*Brutus* 205–7), and his aims and methods profoundly influenced his own and succeeding generations. His work on literature included interpretations of the *carmina Saliorum*, comments on the language of the XII Tables, critical editions of Ennius and Lucilius, and the establishing of a canon of twenty-five plays of Plautus, whose language he rated highly (Quint. 10. 1. 99). It is difficult to estimate his debt to Greek grammarians, but his treatise on sentences (*De proloquiis*; Gell. 16. 8. 1) was probably inspired by the Περὶ ἀξιωμάτων of Chrysippus.

Cf. G. Funaioli, *Gramm. Rom. Frag.* 57–76. Schanz–Hosius, § 76 a.
J. F. M.

**STILPON** (c. 380–300 B.C.), third head of the Megarian school, may have studied under Diogenes the Cynic, as well as under Eucleides the founder of the Megarian school. During his headship the school was the most popular in Greece; *inter alios* the originally Socratic school of Eretria came under its influence, and Zeno, the founder of Stoicism, acquired from Stilpon his skill in dialectic. Stilpon is said to have written at least twenty dialogues, and the names of some are preserved. In metaphysics he maintained the monism characteristic of the Megarian school, denied the Platonic distinction between universals and individuals, and asserted the wrongness of all assertion that was not tautologous; in ethics, under Cynic influence, he extolled the virtue of ἀπάθεια, but did not press the doctrine to such extremes as the Cynics. His influence on Stoic logic was probably considerable. W. D. R.

**STIMULA**, Roman goddess of unknown functions. She had a grove (Livy 39. 12. 4, cf. Ov. *Fasti* 6. 503), where the Bacchanals met in 186 B.C.; hence identified with Semele (q.v.). Ovid (ibid.; August. *De civ. D.* 4. 11) derives her name 'de stimulis quibus . . . homo impellitur'. H. J. R.

**STIPENDIUM** means a payment in money. As applied to the Roman provinces it meant a direct tax (*see* TRIBU-TUM). It was also applied to soldiers' pay. Since this was originally issued at the end of the campaigning season, *stipendium* came to mean also, first a campaign, and ultimately a year of service. In the latter sense we regularly find in the auxiliary diplomata (q.v.) the phrase 'quinis et vicenis pluribusve stipendiis emeritis'. The other meaning, however, persisted, and from Caesar to Domitian, and from Severus onwards, was applied to the four-monthly payments made to the troops in January, May, and September: hence Suetonius (*Dom.* 7) could describe the Domitianic increase of pay by the words 'addidit et quartum stipendium militi, aureos ternos.'

(a) YEARS OF SERVICE. Polybius states that every Roman citizen with the requisite property-qualification was liable to serve for 16 years between his 17th and 46th years, or for 20 years in an emergency. These terms were observed by Augustus when in 13 B.C. he drew up the regulations for his permanent standing army: 16 years of service +4 as a veteran became the period for a legionary, while the praetorian was favoured with the shorter period of 12 years. He was soon obliged to lengthen the prescribed terms, and in A.D. 5 these became for the legionary 20 years+5 as a veteran; for the praetorian, 16 years; for the auxiliary, 25 years. Many men were willing to serve beyond their time, and there are instances of

service as long as 40 years. Under the Flavians service with the veterans was absorbed into the regular service, and legionaries then served for the same number of years as the auxiliaries. Service in the fleet was for 26 years.

(b) PAY. Pay was issued as early as the siege of Veii (c. 400 B.C.), but it is not until the second century B.C. that we have much evidence as to its amount.

From c. 170 to c. 122 B.C. the basic legionary rate was 5 *asses* a day, with substantial deductions for food, clothing, and arms: at the then prevailing tariffing of 10 *asses* to the *denarius* this meant an annual rate of 180 *denarii*. From the retariffing of the *as* at 16 to the *denarius* until the time of Caesar the rate remained at 5 *asses* a day: this meant a reduction to 112½ *denarii* in the annual rate, but stoppages were now made for food and arms only. Caesar doubled the pay to 225 *denarii* and brought back the deductions for clothing. The rate remained unchanged until the time of Domitian, who increased it to 300 *denarii*. It was increased further to 500 *denarii* by Septimius Severus, and to 750 *denarii* by Caracalla.

Praetorian pay was probably 375 *denarii* a year for the greater part of the reign of Augustus, and was increased to 750 *denarii* in his later years. The urban cohorts then received 375 *denarii*, half the scale of the praetorians. The pay of the *vigiles* and the fleet is uncertain.

Auxiliary pay varied according to arm, members of *alae* receiving more than members of cohorts, and the mounted men in the cohorts more than the *pedites*, whose basic rate was as low as 75 *denarii* a year before the increase under Domitian.

The *principales* (non-commissioned officers) were paid more than the private soldiers, and for pay purposes were graded as *duplicarii* (double-pay men) and *sesquiplicarii* (pay-and-a-half men) according to rank.

In the third century inflation made nonsense of the previous scales and the monetary content of the pay became of little value. Real pay became increasingly made in kind.

*Comparison of Basic Pay from Domitian to Severus (in denarii)*

| | | | |
|---|---|---|---|
| Praetorians | 1,000 | Alae | 200 |
| Urban Cohorts | 500 | Cohorts—equites | 150 |
| Legions | 300 | pedites | 100 |

R. E. Smith, *Service in the Post-Marian Roman Army* (1958); A. von Domaszewski, *Neue Heidelberger Jahrbücher* 1900, 218 ff.; P. A. Brunt, *PBSR* 1950, 54 ff.; R. Marichal, *Annuaire de l'Institut de Philologie et d'Histoire orientales et slaves* 1953, *Mélanges Isidore Lévy*, 399 ff.; G. R. Watson, *Hist.* 1956, 332 ff.; 1958, 113 ff.; 1959, 372 ff.; id. *The Roman Soldier* (1969). G. R. W.

**STIPULATIO**, a formal contract concluded orally in the form of question (made by the future creditor, *stipulator*: 'centum dari spondes?'), and answer (by the future debtor: 'spondeo'). From the use of *spondeo* was derived the more restricted term *sponsio*. Stipulatio was one of the oldest institutions of Roman private law (for its existence in the time of the XII Tables see Gai. *Inst.* 4. 17 a), and it gradually developed into a 'fulcrum' of the whole Roman system of obligations. Any agreement could be given legal effect by being incorporated in this simple oral form (*see* CONTRACT, ROMAN LAW OF). Other verbs (*promittere, dare, facere*, and Greek equivalents) were permissible in the classical law and (unlike *spondere*) were open to foreigners.

*Stipulatio* was also used for some special purposes. Romans commonly required security for a debt in the form of a surety (*see also* SECURITY). The earliest forms (called *sponsio* and *fidepromissio*, from the verbs used) were available only when the principal debt had been created by *stipulatio*. The surety promised to discharge the same obligation as the principal debtor. The later (but still Republican) *fideiussio* was available whether the principal debt arose from a *stipulatio* or in any other way.

There were other technical differences. Another use was *novatio*: one or more obligations concluded in another form could be confirmed and transferred into a stipulation.

*Stipulatio* was also extensively used in civil proceedings, e.g. to oblige a defendant or his representative to fulfil a judgement (*iudicatum solvi*). In many cases a *stipulatio* could be ordered by a magistrate, especially by the praetor (*stipulationes praetoriae*), either to reinforce an already existing obligation, or to create a new obligation for the protection of an interest otherwise not protected (e.g. at the beginning of a usufruct (*see* SERVITUTES), or in case of damage threatened to a neighbour's property by the dangerous condition of a building, etc.).

*Stipulatio* underwent a 'degeneration' the character of which is disputed. On the one hand, its oral form was relaxed. It is usually thought that by the time of Gaius (*Inst.* 3. 92) the use of any particular verb was unnecessary, the formality residing only in an oral question and answer (provided that the same verb was used in both, and that the parties were present together). Many think that by the time of Justinian even this was made unnecessary by an obscure constitution of Leo (*Cod. Iust.* 8. 37. 10; *Inst. Iust.* 3. 15. 1) of A.D. 472 which removed the need for 'sollemnia verba'. On the other hand, the emphasis shifted from the oral form to the written evidence of it. For since witnesses were unnecessary, it became usual to draw up a written memorandum (*instrumentum, cautio*), and already in the time of Cicero (*Top.* 26. 96) *stipulatio* could be classed as a written act. It is probable that well before Justinian the document had in practice replaced the oral form, and Justinian ruled that even a document made *inter absentes* should be valid unless the parties could be proved to have been in different places for the whole day in question.

S. Riccobono, *Sav. Zeitschr.* 1914, 214 ff., 1922, 262 ff (E.T. with supplements and notes by B. Beinart, *Stipulation and the Theory of Contract*, 1957); B. Nicholas, *Law Quart. Rev.* lxix (1953), 63 ff., 233 ff.; J. C. van Oven, *Tijdschr. voor Rechtsgesch.* xxvi (1958), 409 ff. *And see* textbooks s.v. LAW AND PROCEDURE, ROMAN, I. B. N.

**STOA** (1), philosophical school or sect, founded by Zeno of Citium in about 300 B.C., named after the Stoa Poikile, a public hall in Athens, in which Zeno and his successors used to teach. Though the school was probably less strictly organized than the Academy and the Peripatos, it had a continuous succession of official heads (προστάται) from Zeno to at least A.D. 260 (the latest date known) and probably some time later. But it had faded out long before Justinian closed the last philosophical schools at Athens in A.D. 529.

The history of the school is usually divided into three periods: (I) the Early Stoa (from Zeno to the first half of the second century B.C.); (II) the Middle Stoa (second and first centuries B.C.); (III) the Late Stoa (time of the Roman Empire).

I. The *Early Stoa* is represented by: (1) Zeno (until 263); (2) disciples of Zeno: Cleanthes (προστάτης from 263 to 232), Ariston of Chios, Herillus of Carthage, Dionysius "ὁ Μεταθέμενος", Persaeus, Aratus of Soli; (3) disciples of Cleanthes: Chrysippus (προστάτης from 232 to 207) and Sphaerus; (4) disciples of Chrysippus: Zeno of Tarsus and Diogenes the Babylonian, who followed Zeno of Tarsus as προστάτης (exact date unknown); (5) disciples of Diogenes: Antipater of Tarsus (προστάτης from *c.* 150 to 129 B.C.), Archedemus of Tarsus, and Boethus of Sidon.

Zeno was the author of all the fundamental doctrines of the Early Stoa. His system was taken over in its entirety by Cleanthes—while Ariston and Herillus developed doctrines of their own and were later considered heretics—and it was elaborated and corrected by Chrysippus. The philosophy of Chrysippus became later so much identified with Stoic orthodoxy that it super-seded the Zenonian system in the mind of posterity. This makes it difficult to determine exactly in what respects Chrysippus differed from his predecessors, since neither his nor their works have survived.

The system of the Early Stoics was divided into three parts: (*a*) τὸ λογικόν (comprising theory of knowledge, logic, rhetoric); (*b*) τὸ φυσικόν (ontology, physics, theology); (*c*) τὸ ἠθικόν (ethics). Their main doctrines were the following:

(1) Virtue is based on knowledge. Only the wise man who not only knows the truth but also knows with certainty that he knows it can be really virtuous. Since knowledge is the agreement of one's mental conceptions with reality, the wisdom of the wise man consists in his having such mental conceptions as are caused by real things, correspond exactly to (or are accurate images of) these things, and could not have been produced by other causes. Conceptions of this kind are called καταληπτικαὶ φαντασίαι. In the first part of their system (τὸ λογικόν) the Stoics tried to prove that such conceptions are possible and discussed how they are acquired, how they differ from other conceptions, and how they can be expressed in language.

(2) It is the aim of the philosopher to live in harmony (Zeno), or, as Chrysippus added, in harmony with nature (ὁμολογουμένως φύσει ζῆν). The formative and guiding principle in nature is the λόγος (reason), which is identified with God and manifests itself as εἱμαρμένη (fate, necessity) and πρόνοια (divine providence). In a special way it manifests itself in human reason. Among the elements fire is most closely related to the λόγος. The universe is periodically consumed by fire, from which in due course a new world arises.

(3) To be virtuous, that is to live in harmony with reason, is the only good, not to be virtuous the only evil. Everything else is indifferent (ἀδιάφορον). But the orthodox Stoics—in contrast to heretics like Ariston—admitted that there were also προηγμένα (for instance: self-preservation, health) which the wise man chooses and ἀποπροηγμένα (death, illness, pain, etc.) which he avoids if he can do so without acting unvirtuously. Yet their presence or absence does not affect his happiness. For since he always acts in harmony with reason he is always possessed of the only real good and therefore completely independent of the vicissitudes of fortune. He is also absolutely brave, since he knows that pain and death are no evils; absolutely continent, since he knows that pleasure is not a good; and absolutely just, since he is not influenced by prejudice or favour.

II. The *Middle Stoa* is chiefly represented by Panaetius, Diogenes the Babylonian's successor as προστάτης, and by his disciples Posidonius and Hecaton.

Zeno of Tarsus and his disciples had begun to doubt some special doctrines of their predecessors, for instance the doctrine of a periodical world conflagration (ἐκπύρωσις). Panaetius was the first to reject this doctrine altogether and to undertake a thorough revision of the whole Stoic system of philosophy, partly under the influence of Platonic and Aristotelian ideas. In ethics he rejected the belief that only the absolutely wise man can be virtuous. He considered it the duty of the philosopher to help those who without aspiring to absolute wisdom are making progress in wisdom and virtue (προκόπτοντες). He tried to adapt Stoic ethics to the needs of active statesmen and soldiers. It was through him that Stoicism became so important an element in the life of the best representatives of Roman nobility. His ethical views had great influence on P. Scipio Aemilianus, in whose company he spent some years of his life, and on Scipio's friends P. Rutilius Rufus, C. Laelius, Q. Aelius Tubero, Q. Mucius Scaevola the augur, Q. Mucius Scaevola the pontifex and famous jurist, etc. Through his writings he influenced the younger Cato, Brutus, and Cicero, though the latter professed himself an Academic. His disciple Hecaton created a system of moral casuistry, discussing in detail how the virtuous man would act under certain circumstances, especially when there is a seeming conflict of duties. Posidonius subjected the system of the Early Stoics to an even more thorough revision than Panaetius. He was the author of a new natural philosophy comprising all sciences. Mainly through him Stoicism influenced many scientists, such as the astronomers Geminus and Cleomedes and the geographer Strabo.

III. During the latest period in the history of the Stoa purely theoretical questions, though still discussed (cf. Seneca's *Quaestiones Naturales*, and, in the second century, the dispute between Academics, Peripatetics, and Stoics over the categories), receded into the background, giving way to a philosophy which was almost exclusively concerned with ethical questions.

Most important among the Stoic philosophers of the first century after Christ were L. Annaeus Seneca, L. Annaeus Cornutus, C. Musonius Rufus, and, towards the end of the century, Epictetus. At the same time Stoicism gave a philosophical foundation for the aristocratic opposition to those of the Emperors who tried to rule without or against the Senate. Helvidius Priscus, Paetus Thrasea, Rubellius Plautus, the famous opponents of Nero, and Junius Rusticus, who was condemned to death under Domitian, professed Stoicism.

The most important representative of Stoicism in the second century was the Emperor M. Aurelius. The names of a great many Stoic philosophers of minor importance who lived at that time have come down to us. None of the important representatives of the school taught in Athens during that period.

From the third century onward the school gradually faded out. But Stoic doctrine had an important influence on later Neoplatonism and on the philosophy of some of the Fathers of the Christian Church. While the Stoic school ceased to exist, Stoicism spread far beyond the ranks of professional philosophers, and continued to exercise an important influence on the life and thought of many.

*See also* ALLEGORY, GREEK, § 3; ASTROLOGY; ARCESILAUS (1) (for the sceptical criticism of the Stoic doctrine of knowledge).

*Stoicorum veterum fragmenta*, coll. von Arnim, 4 vols. (1921-4). A. Schmekel, *Die Philosophie der mittleren Stoa* (1892); W. L. Davidson, *The Stoic Creed* (1907); E. Bevan, *Stoics and Sceptics* (1913); O. Reith, *Grundbegriffe der stoischen Ethik* (1933); M. Pohlenz, *Die Stoa* (1949-55); B. Mates, *Stoic Logic* (1951); S. Sambursky, *The Physics of the Stoics* (1959); R. MacMullen, *Enemies of the Roman Order* (1967), ch. 2; J. Rist, *Stoic Philosophy* (1969). K. VON F.

**STOA** (2). The name stoa is applied to various types of building with a roof supported by columns, but principally to a long open colonnade. This, besides being an appendage of various structures, was developed by the Greeks as a building in its own right. The stoa may be considered a sophisticated version of the simple lean-to shed, or alternatively, in some forms, as a long hall or *megaron* (*see* TEMPLE) with one side thrown open.

It was employed especially in shrines and in the agora. Archaic examples are found at Delos and in the Heraeum at Samos (see *Ath. Mitt.* 1957, 52 ff.). Greater depth was given to the colonnade by inserting an inner row of columns, which were commonly Ionic (the outer being Doric) and twice as widely spaced.

At Athens the Poikile or Painted Stoa, decorated with pictures by Polygnotus (q.v.) and other famous artists, was built about 460 B.C. Later in the century the Stoa of Zeus Eleutherios, which may also be the Basileios or Stoa of the archon called Basileus, was built in the

Athenian agora. Its remains (*Hesp.* 1937, 6 ff.) show that it was embellished with short projecting wings at either end, a form copied in several later examples.

In the fourth century and the Hellenistic Age stoas of enormous length became fashionable. The South Stoa at Corinth is a splendid example (*Corinth*, vol. i. 4, U.S.A. 1954). Like many stoas, it had a series of rooms opening behind the colonnade. In the same period, magnificent two-storied colonnades were built, notably at Pergamum (q.v.). The Stoa of Attalus II at Athens, now rebuilt to serve as a Museum, shows vividly what this type of building looked like.

Colonnades were also combined in various rectangular schemes (*see* TOWNS); and the peristyle, or enclosed court with colonnades on all sides, was used in shrines, gymnasia (q.v.), and on a modest scale in houses (q.v.).

The stoa was the general-purpose building of the Greeks. It offered shelter from sun, wind, and rain. It could be used as council-chamber or court-house, market-hall or class-room; and also for informal conversation as in several Socratic dialogues.

R. Martin, *Recherches sur l'Agora grecque* (1951), 449 ff.; R. E. Wycherley, *How the Greeks Built Cities*² (1962), 110 ff. R. E. W.

**STOBAEUS** (Ἰωάννης Στοβεύς), author of an anthology of excerpts from poets and prose-writers, intended in the first instance for the instruction of his son Septimius. The work was probably composed in the early fifth century A.D.; it consisted originally of four books, which came to be grouped later under the titles Ἐκλογαί and Ἀνθολόγιον, though subject-matter and treatment are essentially homogeneous. It deals with a variety of topics, from metaphysics to household economy; from book 2 onwards it is concerned chiefly with ethical questions. The illustrative extracts, which Stobaeus probably owed in large measure to earlier collectors, are arranged under successive headings, being grouped generally in the same order, beginning with the poets. Stobaeus cites a multitude of authors, from Homer to Themistius; the writers of the Second Sophistic are scarcely represented, but there are many excerpts from the Neoplatonists; Christian authors are not excerpted. Photius (9th c.) commends the work for its usefulness, especially to writers and speakers. Its value for us consists in the large number of citations from earlier literature, which not only supplement our knowledge of classical authors, but often throw light upon difficulties in the regular manuscript tradition.

*Suda* (s.v. Ἰωάννης); Photius, *Bibl.*, cod. 167. EDITION. C. Wachsmuth and O. Hense (1884-1923). CRITICISM. A. Elter, *De Ioh. St. cod. Phot.* (1880); id. *De gnom. graec. hist. et orig.* (1893-6); O. Hense, *PW* xx. 2549 ff. W. M. E.; R. B.

**STOLO**, GAIUS LICINIUS (*PW* 161), and L. Sextius Lateranus, traditionally tribunes of the *plebs* from 376 to 367 B.C., were celebrated as the authors of the law that opened the consulship to the *plebs*, by enacting that one consul might be a plebeian. L. Sextius was in all likelihood the first plebeian consul and he may have been appointed in 366: but the details of the long struggle, which preceded the passing of the Licinian-Sextian laws, and most of the laws themselves, must be rejected either as anticipating events of the Gracchan Age, or as inventions of Licinius Macer designed to glorify his family. By the enactment which increased from two to ten the number of the officials who superintended various religious ceremonies, the plebeians secured an equal representation. The existence of a law on debts and usury, providing that interest should be deducted from the principal and the balance paid in three equal annual instalments, is sometimes denied. By far the most disputed measure is that which limited tenancies of public land; even if Stolo took some such step to meet the economic crisis of his time, the details are obviously borrowed from the agrarian policy of the Gracchan Age.

B. Niese, *Hermes* 1888; G. Niccolini, *Fasti d. tribuni d. plebe* (1934), 56 ff.; H. H. Scullard, *Hist. Roman World*³ (1962), 94 f.; K. v. Fritz, *Hist.* 1951, 1 ff. P. T.

**STONES, SACRED.** The Greeks and Romans preserved many survivals of religious primitivism, some of which may be due to the pre-Greek and pre-Roman cultures (especially where there was no clear explanation or legend). Good specimens are the many stones (and rocks) that because of their remarkable appearance or mysterious efficacy were regarded as holy, possessing unusual power (or *mana*), in fact fetishes (cf. the Greek *baitylos*). Unhewn stones were the Eros of Thespiai, the Charites of Orchomenus, the healing 'Heracles' at Hyettus (characteristically all Boeotian cults), the 'Zeus Descender' (Καππώτας) at Gythium (probably a meteorite); at Delphi was shown the very stone which Kronos swallowed in place of the newborn Zeus, and oil was daily poured on it. Here they also possessed the much-revered omphalos (q.v.). Thirty squared stones were reverenced at Pharae and had individual divine names; an obelisk at Megara was named Apollon Karinos, and the small stone columns which commonly stood before the doors of Athenian houses were called by the name of Apollo Agyieus. At Pheneus in Arcadia solemn oaths were taken by the *petroma* of Demeter, which was 'two great stones joined to one another' (Paus. 8. 15. 1). We know of representations of Zeus as a pillar (Tarentum) (pillar-cult was well known to the Cretans of pre-Greek times), as a pyramid (Sicyon), and as an omphalos (on Mount Casius). Herms were extremely popular—square columns with human heads and a *membrum virile*. From the Near East we may adduce the black stone (a meteorite) belonging to the Mother of the Gods at Pessinus, the white conical stone of Aphrodite at Paphos, and the cones and pyramids which often occur on coins from Asia Minor.

At Rome an ancient boundary-stone on the Capitol passed as Jupiter Terminus, who here followed on the old god Terminus. The Romans also swore on 'Jupiter the stone' (cf. E. Harrison, *Essays Ridgeway*, 92 ff.); and the *lapis manalis*, which was carried from the Porta Capena by the pontifices and over which water was probably poured, was important as a rain charm.

M. W. de Visser, *Die nichtmenschengestaltigen Götter der Griechen* (1903); Chr. Blinkenberg, *The Thunderweapon in Religion and Folklore* (1911), esp. 13 ff. S. E.; J. E. F.

**STRABO** (64/3 B.C.–A.D. 21 at least), historian and geographer, a Greek (partly Asiatic in descent) of Amaseia, Pontus. He studied grammar under Aristodemus, and, later, geography under Tyrannion, philosophy under Xenarchus, and knew Posidonius. He was in Rome in 44–35, *c.* 31, and 7 B.C.; in Egypt 25–*c.* 19 B.C. (collecting geographical material); and in Amaseia *c.* 7 B.C. to his death. A Peripatetic, Strabo became a Stoic, with some contempt for religion, and admired the Romans and their Empire; independent but no great traveller, he knew various parts of Asia Minor and Egypt, but little of Greece or Italy, and probably wrote for persons in political positions (he emphasizes the use of geography in public affairs—1. 1. 16–18), but whether at Rome for Romans or at Amaseia or Alexandria for Greeks is disputed. Apparent ignorance and omissions do point to some special purpose.

His *Historical Sketches* ('Ιστορικὰ ὑπομνήματα), forty-seven books excluding the era covered by Polybius, are lost; his *Geography* (Γεωγραφία), seventeen books, has survived. Books 1–2: introductory. 1. Homer; Eratosthenes criticized. 2. Mathematical geography; criticism of Eratosthenes and Polybius, examination of Posidonius (especially zones); Eudoxus' voyages. Strabo's opinions on the earth; cartography on sphere and plane. 3. Spain, Isles of Scilly. 4. Gaul, Britain, etc. 5–6. Italy, Sicily; the Roman Empire. 7. North and east Europe, north Balkans (some is lost). 8–10. Greece (very antiquarian and mythological). 11. Euxine-Caspian, etc., Taurus, Armenia. 12–14. Asia Minor (some mythology and history). 15. India, Persia. 16. Mesopotamia, Palestine, Ethiopian coasts, Arabia. 17. Egypt, Ethiopia, north Africa.

Strabo brings Eratosthenes more up to date. On a geocentric sphere, the one land-mass is ocean-girt. He knows Mediterranean lands, Egypt, Asia Minor; little of British Isles; nothing of northernmost Europe and Asia; Caspian by Alexander's writers and Megasthenes; Africa is a triangle north of the equator. Strabo gives geographical and historical information readably, without details except where interesting or important. Having moderate (and not up-to-date) mathematical and astronomical knowledge, he underestimates both; latitudes, longitudes, and 'climata' he treats lightly, and is inadequate in physical geography and phenomena, being predisposed towards his own ideas of what is important. He reveres Homer, undervalues Herodotus, scorns Pytheas. He adds Roman to Greek authorities, despising (rightly?) Roman geographers. But his work is a storehouse of information, an historical geography, and a philosophy of geography.

Text, translation, and full bibliographies in H. L. Jones, *The Geog. of S.* (Loeb, 1917–33). W. Aly, 'Strabon von Amaseia', *Antiquity* i. 5 (1957), and *PP* 1950, 228 ff.; F. Sbordone, *Strab. Geogr.* i (1963). Strabo on Spain: A. García y Bellido, *España y los Españoles* (1945); A. Schulten, *Estrabon. Geografía de Iberia, Fontes Hisp. Antiquae* (1952); on Gaul: W. Hering in *Wiss. Zeitschr. d. Univ. Rostock* iv (1954–5), 289 ff. Cf. also Thomson. *Hist. Anc. Geog.* 224 f., 321 ff.; on Europe: 122, 188, 192 ff., 198 (cf. D. R. Dicks, *Geog. Fragments of Hipparchus* (1960), 189 ff.); Asia: 171, 286 ff., 301, 304; Africa: 182 ff., 259; W. Aly, *PW* s.v. Strabo (3). E. H. W.

**STRATEGOI** (στρατηγοί) was the ordinary term for military commanders in Greece, but in Athens in the fifth century B.C. *strategoi* had political as well as military importance. Nothing is known of Athenian *strategoi* in the sixth century, when the army was commanded by the *polemarchos* (q.v.), but in 501/500 a new arrangement was introduced by which the people annually elected ten *strategoi*, one from each of the ten *phylai* (q.v.) (Arist. *Ath. Pol.* 22. 2). Each *strategos* commanded the regiment of his own *phyle*, while the *polemarchos* retained the supreme command. From 487/6 onwards the *polemarchos*, like the other *archontes*, was appointed by lot. Good leaders, whether military or political, obviously could not be regularly selected by lot; and so the *polemarchos* ceased to command the army, and the *strategoi*, who continued to be elected, not only became the chief military commanders, but in some cases became political leaders too.

Themistocles and Cimon were early examples of *strategoi* who were politicians as well as generals. Pericles was a *strategos* very often throughout his career; from 443 he held the office almost continuously until his death in 429. Cleon, Nicias, and Alcibiades were all *strategoi*. But at the end of the fifth century, with the collapse of the military and naval power of Athens, and later because of an increasing tendency to specialization, military office ceased to be a means of acquiring political influence.

The annual election of *strategoi* was held in the spring, and their term of office coincided with the ordinary Athenian year, from midsummer to midsummer. If a *strategos* died or was dismissed from office, a by-election might be held to replace him for the remainder of the year. The original rule that one *strategos* was elected from each *phyle* underwent some modification: in several years (the earliest is 441/40; cf. *FGrH* 324 F 38) one *phyle* is known to have supplied two *strategoi* simultaneously, leaving another *phyle* unrepresented. The reason for this relaxation of the rule may have been that Pericles' long tenure of the office would otherwise have excluded other members of his *phyle* for many years. (But the view of some modern scholars that in such cases one *strategos* had powers superior to the others seems to be without foundation.) By Aristotle's time the rule had been entirely abandoned, and *strategoi* were elected without regard to *phylai*.

After the *strategoi* took over the supreme command from the *polemarchos*, they ceased to command the regiments of the *phylai* individually. (This function was taken over by the *taxiarchoi*.) A particular military or naval expedition might have one or several *strategoi* in command; only occasionally did all ten go together. A *strategos* might be given special powers to take decisions in the field without reference back to Athens (στρατηγὸς αὐτοκράτωρ). At home, the *strategoi* were responsible for recruitment and the calling up of citizens for military or naval service, and for organizing the maintenance and command of ships by the system of trierarchies (q.v.). When a legal case arose from any of these matters, such as a prosecution for desertion or evasion of military service, or a dispute over the duty to perform a trierarchy (*see* ANTIDOSIS), the *strategoi* were the magistrates responsible for bringing the case to a lawcourt and presiding over the trial (*see* DIKASTERION). In the fourth century a systematic division of duties was made: one *strategos* commanded the infantry, one was in charge of the defence of Attica, two were in charge of the defence of Peiraeus, and one supervised the trierarchies, leaving five available for other duties (Arist. *Ath. Pol.* 61. 1).

The Athenian people kept a close watch on their *strategoi*. At the end of their term of office they were subject to *euthyna* (q.v.) like other magistrates. But in addition every prytany (*see* PRYTANEIS) each *strategos* was subject to a vote, by show of hands, on the question whether his conduct in office was satisfactory. If the vote went against him, he was tried in a lawcourt; but if he was acquitted by the court, he resumed his office (Arist. *Ath. Pol.* 61. 2). These arrangements illustrate one of the most striking features of the Athenian democracy: reluctance to give power to able men and fear that it might be abused.

In the Hellenistic age *strategos* was the title of officials with wide powers, political as well as military, in the Aetolian Confederacy (q.v.) and in the Achaean Confederacy (q.v.). It was also used for the governor of a district in Ptolemaic Egypt (*see* NOMOS) and elsewhere in the Hellenistic empires, and it became the regular Greek word for the Roman *praetor* (q.v.).

ATHENS. Hignett, *Hist. Athen. Const.* 169 ff., 244 ff., 347 ff.; A. H. M. Jones, *Athenian Democracy* (1957), 124 ff.; K. J. Dover, *JHS* 1960, 61 ff.
HELLENISTIC AGE. Bengtson, *Strategie*.                                    D. M. M.

**STRATOCLES** (b. *c.* 350 B.C.) was one of Demosthenes' accusers in the Harpalus trial (324–323). He became the agent of Demetrius Poliorcetes in Athens from 307 and directed the immoderate adulation shown to him. In 303 his authority was upheld by Demetrius against an attempted revolt by the party of Cassander, but was shattered after Demetrius' defeat at Ipsus (301). In 294 he was reinstated by Demetrius, but had to share his power with more moderate politicians. The date of his death is unknown. His main characteristic was unscrupulous demagogy.

W. B. Dinsmoor, *Archons of Athens* (1931).               F. W. W.

**STRATON** (1) of Lampsacus, Aristotelian philosopher, head of the Peripatetic School after Theophrastus until

his death (*c.* 287–269 B.C.). The preserved list of his books (Diog. Laer. 5. 59–60) includes ethics, cosmology, zoology, psychology, physics, and logic; his work on physic sand cosmology earned him the name of ὁ Φυσικός. Fragments of several books survive; a substantial portion of his doctrine about void may be preserved in the Introduction to Hero's *Pneumatica* (*see* GOTTSCHALK).

He contradicted Aristotle in asserting the existence of void in the cosmos. This has been taken for a concession to the Atomists, but it seems unlikely; Strato argued only for 'disseminate void'—i.e. void interstices of small dimensions separating particles of matter. His reasoning was drawn chiefly from the penetration of apparently solid objects by 'physical powers' like heat and sound, and perhaps also from compression (but this is doubtful). The origin of this theory is Theophrastus' theory of 'pores', rather than anything in the Atomists.

Strato argued that the processes of nature were to be explained by natural causes, not by the action of any god. This is mainly an attack on the Stoics, but it also dispenses, apparently, with the very limited part played by Aristotle's divine unmoved movers. Strato rejected the universal teleology of the Stoics; the evidence is not sufficient to decide to what extent he denied that kind of teleology which is the characteristic feature of Aristotelian biology.

Strato was an orthodox Aristotelian in his view of the cosmos as unique, uncreated, and geocentric. He modified the Aristotelian theory of the natural motions of the primary bodies (as the Stoics also did) to give fire and air not absolute lightness but simply less weight than the other two elements; and he dispensed with the fifth body (aether) with its natural circular motion.

He was the last Head of the Peripatetic School to do important original work. His theory about the void, his most famous contribution, was important in the history of physiology through its adoption by Erasistratus, and in technology through its adoption by Hero.

FRR. and COMM. F. Wehrli, *Die Schule des Aristoteles* v (1950); H. B. Gottschalk, *Strato of Lampsacus: Some Texts* (*Proceedings of the Leeds Philosophical and Literary Society* Lit. and Hist. Section, XI, vi (1965), 95 ff.).
GENERAL. H. Diels, 'Über das physikalische System des Strato', *S.-Ber. Akad. Berlin*, 1893, 101 ff.; G. Rodier, *La Physique de Straton de Lamsaque* (1890); W. Capelle, 'Straton der Physiker', *PW* iv A (1931), 278 ff.; A. Schmekel, *Die positive Philosophie* (1938), i. 106 ff..                                                 D. J. F.

**STRATON** (2), New Comedy poet. The only extant fragment is a skit upon the glossomania of the time, in which a bombastic cook describes common things in obsolete poetical words and phrases, and causes his patron to call him 'ex-slave of some kind of rhapsode' (ῥαψῳδοτοιούτου τινὸς | δοῦλος γεγονώς), and therefore filled with Homeric vocables. The play *Phoenicides* (*Phoenix*, according to the *Suda*) is dated *c.* 300 B.C. by the reference (v. 43) to the work of Philetas of Cos.

The author: *FCG* i. 426 ff. Traditional version of the text (from Ath. 9. 382 b): *FCG* iv. 545 f.; *CAF* iii. 361 f. Papyrus version (with additional vv.) and free from actors' (?) interpolations: Guéraud and Jouguet, *Un Livre d'écolier* (1938), 34 ff.; Page, *GLP*, no. 57. See also Webster, *Later Greek Comedy* (1953), 145; H. Dohn, *Mageiros* (1964), 198 ff.                                        W. G. W.; W. G. A.

**STRATON** (3) of Sardis, who lived in Hadrian's time, made a collection of poetic epigrams about homosexual love and lust, the remains of which survive (mainly in book 12) in the Greek Anthology (q.v.). Among them are about 100 of his own poems, which are usually either coarse or mawkish.                                        G. H.

**STRATONICEIA** (Στρατονίκεια, now *Eskihisar*, an important Seleucid foundation in the interior of Caria, called after Stratonice, wife of Antiochus I, and probably founded by him; it was peopled with Macedonians. The city was presented to Rhodes by 'Antiochus and Seleucus' (Polyb. 30. 31. 6), i.e. Antiochus I and his son Seleucus (?), who had previously endowed it lavishly. Lost by Rhodes, probably to Philip V, it was recovered in 197 B.C. (Livy 30. 18. 22). Rhodian possession was confirmed by the Romans at Apamea in 188, but revoked in 167. Like Mylasa (q.v.), Stratoniceia gained favour by resisting Q. Labienus in 40 B.C., and was a free city under the Empire. According to Steph. Byz. (s.v.) it was refounded by Hadrian as Hadrianopolis, but this name never came into general use. Stratoniceia possessed two important sanctuaries: the famous temple of Hecate at Lagina, and that of Zeus Chrysaoreus near the city. The latter served as the religious and political centre of a Chrysaoric League common to all Carians, of which the village was the basis; at its meetings the cities possessed votes in proportion to the number of villages on their territory. The Stratoniceans were admitted, though not Carian by race, by virtue of their possession of Carian villages (Strabo 660). Under the early Empire Stratoniceia, surprisingly in view of her origin, claimed the title of 'authochthonous' (*SEG* iv. 263); the explanation is perhaps that the city was founded on the site of an earlier Carian town (Steph. Byz. mentions a Carian city of Idrias, 'formerly called Chrysaoris', which is not otherwise known). The ruins at Eskihisar are not extensive, but include a theatre and a large building known as the Serapeum.

P. M. Fraser–G. E. Bean, *The Rhodian Peraea* (1954), Chs. iii and iv.                                                                G. E. B.

**STRATONICUS** (fl. *c.* 410–360 B.C.), of Athens, musician and wit, contemporary of Timotheus and Polyeidus (Ath. 8. 352 a–b) and of the actor Simycas (ibid. 348 a). His witticisms, Εὐτράπελοι λόγοι, were well known soon after his death and excerpts made of them (Ath. 350 d). Characteristic examples are: 'Who is more barbarous—the Boeotians or the Thessalians?' The Eleans' (ibid. 350 b); and on a small city: αὕτη οὐ πόλις ἐστίν, ἀλλὰ μόλις (ibid. 352 a).                        C. M. B.

**STRATTIS**, Athenian comic poet, produced Ἄνθρωπ-ορέστης after Eur. *Or.* (408) and *Atalanta* 'long after' (Schol. Ar. *Ran.* 146) Ar. *Ran.* (405). We have nineteen titles and seventy fragments; many titles suggest tragic parody (rather than mythological burlesque, so far as the distinction can be drawn), e.g. *Medea, Philoctetes, Phoenissae*. A traditional figure, the gluttonous Heracles, was a character (fr. 11) in *Callippides*.

FCG ii. 763 ff.; CAF i. 711 ff.; FAC i. 812 ff.           K. J. D.

**STRENAE.** This name was given by the Romans to the luck-bringing twigs which at the New Year were brought from the grove of the goddess Strenia and were exchanged by way of gift as bearers of luck and blessing. This oldest form of *strenae* was preserved in cult, since on the old New Year's Day (1 Mar.) the old laurel branches before the doors of the *rex sacrorum*, the great *flamines*, the *Curiae*, and the temple of Vesta were replaced by new branches. The *strena* is a Spring ceremony and is related to the German May tree. Later it came to be a gift, usually money, but twigs retained an aspect of luck in popular usage. The fact that the use involved an omen led to the word *strena* receiving the meaning 'omen' as early as Plautus.

L. Deubner, *Glotta* 1912, 34 ff.; U. Wilcken, *Arch. Pap.* xi. 297.                                                                L. D.

**STYX**, a river of Arcadia, which plunges from a snow-fed spring on the north-east side of Mt. Chelmos, down a black rock to a depth of 600 feet, and flows through a wild gorge to join the Crathis. Its water was thought poisonous. It was one of the rivers of the underworld; the gods in Homer, and the Arcadians in fact, took oath by it (Hdt. 6. 74).

Hes. *Theog.* 775 ff.; Paus. 8. 17–18, and Frazer ad loc. P–K, *GL* III. 1. 1. 219 ff.; J. Pollard, *Journey to the Styx* (1955).        T. J. D.

**SUBSCRIPTIONES.** (1) GREEK. In rolls of the Classical Period (so far as our evidence goes) information as to the contents of a manuscript is appended at the end. It gave principally the name of the author and title of the work. In extant papyri the subscriptions are of this simplest type. In one of the earliest Biblical papyrus codices (Chester Beatty Pap. II, of the Pauline Epistles), the number of στίχοι (*see* STICHOMETRY) in each epistle has been added, but in a different hand.

Medieval codices often add more information, such as the name of the scribe, the fact that the text has been corrected, or the date of writing. Thus the *Codex Sinaiticus* has notes at the end of Esdras and Esther recording the correction of the text from a manuscript by Pamphilus. In later times prayers for faithfulness in transcription, or curses against inaccuracy or theft, are sometimes added. We should note that later manuscripts may recopy earlier subscriptions (sometimes inaccurately, e.g. as regards date).

(2) LATIN. Early Latin classical manuscripts not infrequently have subscriptions recording the name of a corrector, often a man of considerable standing; e.g. the Medicean codex of Virgil, "Turcius Rufius Apronianus Asterius . . . legi et distinxi codicem fratris Macharii"; Asterius, who was consul in 494, also revised Sedulius. Other subscriptions are: (Martial) 'Ego Torquatus Gennadius emendaui feliciter'; (Apuleius) 'Ego Crispus Sallustius emendaui Romae felix' (with dates = 395 and 397); (Persius) 'Flauius Julius temptaui emendare sine antigrapho' (A.D. 402). These men represent not only the copying but the late Roman scholarship of the fourth century. Their work may have affected the textual tradition; e.g. many manuscripts of Terence contain the text as revised by Calliopius. Most manuscripts of the first decade of Livy bear the subscriptions of Nicomachus Flavianus, his son Nicomachus Dexter, and of Victorianus, all men associated with Symmachus (q.v. 2) in the senatorial literary circle that about A.D. 400 upheld the pagan traditions of Rome.

V. Gardthausen, *Gr. Palaeographie* ii (1913), 425; R. Devreesse, *Introduction à l'étude des manuscrits grecs* (1954); O. Jahn, *Sitz. Sächs. Gesellsch. Wiss.* 1851, 327; L. Traube, *Vorles. u. Abhandl.* ii (1911), 123; E. Bickel, *Gesch. röm. Literatur* (1937), 10; *The Conflict between Paganism and Christianity in the Fourth Century* (ed. A. Momigliano, 1963), 214.                              F. G. K.; A. H. McD.

**SUBURA,** the valley between the Viminal and Esquiline Hills of Rome, opening out of the Argiletum and Forum Transitorium. The district was notorious for its bustle, noise, dirt, and shady morality. Its reputable traders sold provisions and delicacies, and manufacturing trades are also known (*CIL* vi (1953), 9824, 9399, 9491, 33862). Here lay a Jewish synagogue (*CIG* 6447). Distinguished residents included Julius Caesar.

Juv. 11. 51, 141; Mart. 2. 17; 5. 22. 5–9; 7. 31; 10. 94. 56; 12. 18. 2; Pers. 5. 32.                                                    I. A. R.

**SUDA** (ἡ Σοῦδα) or **SUIDAS** is the name of a lexicon, not an author: the word is borrowed from Latin and means *Fortress* or *Stronghold*: see F. Dölger, *Der Titel d. S.* (1936), who instances other fanciful names of such collections, e.g. Pamphilus' Λειμών. The lexicon, which is a historical and literary encyclopedia rather than a mere word-list, was compiled about the end of the tenth century A.D. Texts (with scholia) of Homer, Sophocles, Aristophanes, and the *Anth. Pal.* were directly consulted; otherwise, the work is mainly based not on copies of the writings of authors or commentators but on abridgements and selections from these made by late hands, e.g. the Συναγωγή (*see* LEXICA SEGUERIANA), Harpocration, and Diogenianus (qq.v.). The historians are quoted from the *Excerpts* of Constantine Porphyrogenitus; biography comes mainly from Hesychius of Miletus. The work is marred by contradictions and other ineptitudes. Many of its sources were already corrupt, and like most works of its kind it has suffered from interpolation. Nevertheless, it is of the highest importance, since it preserves (however imperfectly) much that is ultimately derived from the earliest or best authorities in ancient scholarship, and includes topics from many departments of Greek learning and civilization.

EDITIONS. Gaisford, 1834; Bekker, 1854; Bernhardy, 1853; Adler (Teubner's *Lexicog. Gr.* I, i–v), 1929–38.
SOURCES, ETC. A. Adler, *PW* 7 A. 675 ff.　P. B. R. F.; R. B.

**SUEBI**, a term applied by Tacitus in his *Germania* to an extensive group of Germanic peoples living east of the Elbe and including the Hermunduri, Marcomanni, Quadi, Semnones, and others. Roman writers other than Tacitus do not give so wide an extension to Suebia, and Tacitus himself in his later works limits the name to the Marcomanni and Quadi. The central tribe of the Suebi was the Semnones living in Brandenburg who controlled a shrine which was respected by all other Suebi and was the scene of human sacrifices. We do not know what was the relationship between the Suebi of whom Tacitus speaks and the Suebi who crossed the Rhine in A.D. 406, entered Spain in 409, and founded a kingdom in Gallaecia which lasted until destroyed by the Visigoths in 585. The Spanish Suebi were converted to Catholicism by St. Martin of Braga *c.* 560.

Tac. *Germ.*, ed. Anderson (1938), 178 ff.　E. A. T.

**SUEIUS**, a pedantic writer of rural idylls. Ribbeck identifies him with Seius, a friend of Cicero and of Varro.

Baehr, *FPR* 285; Morel, *FPL* 53. H. Bardon, *La Littérature latine inconuue* i (1952), 186 ff.

**SUESSULA**, inland town of Campania, midway between Capua and Nola (qq.v.): modern *Cancello*. It came under Roman control along with Capua in 338 B.C. Later it was the headquarters for Claudius Marcellus' successful operations against Hannibal (q.v.). Although unmentioned thereafter, it evidently remained a fair-sized town throughout antiquity.　E. T. S.

**SUETONIUS** (1) **PAULINUS**, GAIUS, as ex-praetor in A.D. 41, commanded against the Mauretanians and was the first Roman to cross the Atlas mountains, of which he wrote a description (Pliny, *HN* 5. 14). He was probably *consul suffectus c.* 42. In 58 he was appointed governor of Britain and at once began a forward movement reaching the Irish Sea and subduing Mona (Anglesey), a stronghold of Druidism. During the campaign he learnt of Boudicca's revolt (60) and swiftly returned with his advance-guard, but unable to concentrate an adequate force was compelled to abandon Londinium and Verulamium to sack. Retreating (along Watling Street) to his main force, he routed Boudicca's attack. His severity towards the rebels led to discords with the *procurator* Classicianus and his own recall (60). In 69 he supported Otho, and took a leading part in the campaign of Bedriacum, after which he came to terms with Vitellius.

Collingwood–Myres, *Roman Britain*, 98 ff.; Syme, *Tacitus*, 762 ff.
C. E. S.

**SUETONIUS** (2, *PW* 4) **TRANQUILLUS**, GAIUS (b. *c.* A.D. 69), son of the equestrian Suetonius Laetus, tribune of Legio XIII at Bedriacum in 69 (*Otho* 10), and originating perhaps from Pisaurum, perhaps from Hippo Regius in Numidia; while his grandfather seems

to have been associated with Caligula's court (*Cal.* 19). Suetonius is mentioned or addressed several times in the Younger Pliny's letters, as a quiet and scholarly man, who, after some experience at the bar, settled down as a writer. Presumably to qualify him for a career in the imperial service, he obtained through Pliny's agency a military tribunate, but did not take it up (*Ep.* 3.8. 1). He may well have accompanied Pliny to Bithynia about A.D. 111; for from this province Pliny wrote to Trajan and obtained for the childless Suetonius the *ius trium liberorum* (*Tra.* 10. 94–5). Shortly after this must begin the series of appointments to the palace, culminating in the three secretarial posts of *a studiis, a bibliothecis,* and *ab epistulis,* which figure in a fragmentary inscription found at Bône in Algeria in 1952. The last post he held under Hadrian, by whom he was dismissed in 121/2, together with the praetorian prefect Septicius Clarus (S.H.A. *Hadr.* 11. 3), to whom Suetonius had not long before dedicated the first books of his *Caesars* (Joh. Lyd. *de Mag.* 2. 6). We hear nothing more of his career; but he probably continued writing for some years, and his work *On Public Offices* may have been connected with Hadrian's reorganization of the civil service. Altogether Suetonius represents the new type of professional scholars who come to prominence in the second century.

WORKS

1. *De viris illustribus*, composed during the reign of Trajan, biographies of Roman literary men arranged by classes. Of these, *De grammaticis et rhetoribus* is partly preserved in a MS.; and a few lives, variously abbreviated or corrupted, have come down in MSS. of the authors' works. *Terence, Horace, Lucan,* and the Donatus *Virgil* are generally regarded as coming from *De poetis*: the claims of *Tibullus* and *Persius* have been argued. Jerome, in his chronological table, gives brief items from Suetonius' work, including thirty-three poets, down to Lucan; fifteen orators, including Passienus Crispus, part of whose life is preserved in the Schol. to Juvenal, 4. 81; and six historians, including the Elder Pliny, a brief fragment on whom has come down with his own *Natural Histories*. The remains of this work are to be found in Reifferscheid, 80 ff., and in Roth, 257–72, 287–301.

2. *De vita Caesarum*, twelve biographies from Julius Caesar to Domitian. The first few chapters of Julius were lost between the sixth and ninth centuries.

3. Lost works, in Greek as well as Latin, some known only from the list in the *Suda*, s.v. Τράγκυλλος, others from isolated citations in later writers. These included *Ludicra Historia*, on Roman games and festivals; and works on Greek games, on famous courtesans, on kings, on public offices, on Rome and its customs, on the Roman year, on Cicero's *Republic*, on terms of abuse (in Greek), on the correct names for clothes, etc., on critical marks in texts, on bodily faults. Several of these may have been included in the *Pratum* or *Prata*, a miscellany probably also referred to as *De variis rebus*. The evidence for these works is found most conveniently in Schanz–Hosius iii. 58 ff., Roth, 275 ff.

Since nearly all earlier Greek and Roman biography has been lost, the originality of Suetonius is hard to assess. Some contribution must have been made by Alexandrian biography, political and literary, some by Roman *tituli* and *laudationes*. However this may be, the *Caesars* differs from earlier works, as from the nearly contemporary *Lives* of Plutarch, in being arranged *per species* rather than chronologically: after a section on the subject's ancestors, a chronological passage outlines his life from birth to accession; then his activities and characteristics are treated as if under a series of rubrics, varied according to the individual and illustrated with a number of relevant anecdotes; and the chronological sequence is resumed for an account of his death, sometimes followed by a description of his physical and other personal peculiarities. For the historian, this scheme is irritating, since many of the anecdotes can barely be understood thus removed from their proper contexts; nor is this drawback compensated by any real biographical gift on Suetonius' part, which might enable the separate details to add up to a whole. The grammarian's touch is seen in the frequent employment of *divisio*, a statement of the main heads to be dealt with in the following sections, as most clearly in *Jul.* 44. 4: 'ea quae ad formam et habitum et cultum et mores, nec minus quae ad ciuilia et bellica eius studia pertineant, non alienum erit summatim exponere.' Unfortunately the plan of the subsequent material is often not easy to recognize, and is sometimes even obscured by this method of introduction.

Suetonius has few stylistic pretensions, beyond that of simplicity. Indeed he marks a departure in Latin historiography in that he is prepared to quote verbatim from earlier writers and from documents of various sorts, in prose and in verse, in Greek as well as Latin—a practice which was to be continued by such other scholars as Gellius and Macrobius. In particular, he quotes extensively from the letters of Augustus, which he presumably studied while working in the palace. The fact that, while Augustus' letters are drawn upon for the lives of Tiberius, Caligula and Claudius, there is no direct quotation from the correspondence of any later Emperor, suggests that Suetonius had completed only the first two lives when he was dismissed from office. The rare occasions when he seriously analyses a problem (e.g. *Tib.* 21. 2, *Cal.* 8) show that he possessed real critical ability; but all too often he is content simply to set down statements from one source or another, without choosing either to reconcile them or even to indicate the discrepancy. The great number of scurrilous anecdotes in most of the lives may be due to the nature of his sources; but he evidently found it harder to pass over a good scandal, however improbable, than Tacitus did. Moreover, his encyclopedist's mind was more attracted by curiosities of every sort than by major historical events or characters, which tend to be ignored unless they throw direct light on the Emperor's own personality. There is some justification in the judgement of the author of S.H.A. *Probus*, 2. 7, that Sallust, Livy, and Tacitus wrote *diserte*, Suetonius *vere*. Certainly he appears to reproduce his sources closely, without rhetorical perversion or deliberate ambiguity.

Suetonius was followed, in his series of imperial lives, by Marius Maximus and a number of other lost biographers, referred to only by the *Augustan History*, itself modelled on Suetonius, although displaying less skill and considerably less honesty. The sheer interest of the subject and the simplicity of the style have made Suetonius popular almost uninterruptedly since his death. He served as a model for Einhard's *Life of Charlemagne*, and lost his position as the classic biographer only when Plutarch was translated into the modern European languages.

LIFE AND WORKS. Schanz–Hosius iii. 48–67; Mommsen, *Hermes* 1869, 43 ff.; A. Macé, *Essai sur Suétone* (1900); F. della Corte, *Suetonio eques Romanus* (1958); Syme, *Tacitus*, 778 ff.; F. Grosso, *Rend. Linc.* 1959, 265 ff.; G. B. Townend, *Hist.* 1961, 99 ff. and *CQ* 1959, 285 ff.; D. R. Stuart, *Epochs of Gr. and Rom. Biography* (1928); W. Steidle, *Sueton und die antike Biographie* (1951).

TEXTS. C. Roth (Teubner, 1862). *Caesares*: M. Ihm (Teubner, 1907–8). *Gram. et Rhet.*: R. P. Robinson (1925); F. della Corte² (1954); E. Brugnoli (Teubner, 1960). *Suet. praeter Caesarum libros Reliquiae*, A. Reifferscheid (1860).

COMMENTARIES. Baumgarten–Crusius (1816–18). **Julius**, H. E. Butler–M. Cary (1927); **Jul.–Aug.**, H. T. Peck² (1893), Westcott–Rankin (1918); **Aug.**, E. S. Shuckburgh (1896), M. Adams (1939), M. A. Levi (1951); **Tib.** 1–23, M. J. du Four (1941), 24–40, J. H. Rietra (1927); **Cal.** 1–21, J. A. Maurer (1949); **Claud.**, H. Smilda (1896); **Galba–Vit.**, C. Hofstee (1898); **Galba–Dom.**, G. W. Mooney (1930, with translation); **Vesp.**, A. W. Braithwaite (1927); **Titus**, H. Price (1919); **Dom.**, J. Janssen (1919); *De Poetis*, A. Rostagni (1944).

TRANSLATIONS. Philemon Holland (1606); J. C. Rolfe (Loeb, 1914); H. Ailloud (Budé, 1931–3); R. Graves (Penguin, 1957).
STYLE AND DICTION. L. Damasso, *La gram. di C.S.T.* (1906); G. d'Anna, *Le idee letterarie di S.* (1954). *Index to S.*, A. A. Howard and C. N. Jackson (repr. 1963).
SPECIAL STUDIES. C. Brutscher (*Julius*, 1958); H. R. Grap (*Vesp.*, 1937); E. Paratore (*de Poetis*, 1946).                    G. B. T.

**SUFFECTIO** was the procedure by which a substitute (*suffectus*) was appointed, whenever a Roman magistrate resigned or died during his term of office. It was employed to fill vacancies even of very short duration: there are examples of *suffecti* who exercised their power only for a few hours. Under the Empire, when the consulship ceased to be held for a full year, the consuls appointed after the original pair were also called *suffecti*. No *suffectus* ever gave his name to the year, although he kept the rank and title of an ex-magistrate (e.g. *vir consularis, praetorius, quaestorius*).

Mommsen, *Röm. Staatsr.* i³. 592.                    P. T.

**SUILLIUS** (*PW* 4) **RUFUS**, PUBLIUS, married first Vistilia (mother by other husbands of Corbulo and of Gaius Caligula's wife Caesonia), then Ovid's stepdaughter. Banished by Tiberius, recalled by Gaius, under Claudius he was consul, proconsul of Asia, and in Rome a notorious prosecutor. Seneca secured his banishment in A.D. 58.                    J. P. B.

**SULLA** (1) **FELIX**, LUCIUS CORNELIUS (*PW* 392), born *c.* 138 B.C. of an old (but not recently prominent) patrician family (going back to the Rufini); after a dissolute—but financially successful—youth, he first distinguished himself as quaestor under Marius, finally securing the surrender of Jugurtha by Bocchus, by which he later—rightly, but tactlessly—claimed to have won the war. He served against the Germans under Marius, then under Catulus (q.v. 2). *Praetor urbanus* (after a failure) in 97, he was assigned Cilicia *pro consule* (96) and then instructed to instal Ariobarzanes in Cappadocia, which he successfully accomplished, displaying Roman power to eastern kingdoms (including, for the first time, Parthia). His future greatness and his death at the height of good fortune were there foretold to him by a Chaldaean. Prosecuted on his return, he was unable to advance to the consulship. In 91, seeking and obtaining support from the Optimates, he brought to a head a feud against Marius, who had incurred their disfavour by his action against Rutilius (q.v. 1). The Social War supervened, and Sulla fought successfully in the southern theatre. In 89, with the help of the Metelli, he gained the consulship of 88 (with Pompeius (q.v. 2), whose son married his daughter) and married Metella (q.v. 1), whose husband Scaurus (q.v. 1) had recently died. He was now an acknowledged power in the State.

Given the command against Mithridates by the Senate, he was deprived of it by the tribune Sulpicius (q.v. 1), who transferred it to Marius in order to gain his alliance. Sulla pretended to acquiesce, but finding support among his troops (though not among his officers, except for one quaestor, probably his *adfinis* Lucullus, q.v. 2), he boldly marched on Rome and took the city by force. Even his friends were shocked by his methods: he had Sulpicius killed in office and his laws repealed, while Marius and other opponents escaped with difficulty. After passing several laws by threat of force, he had to send his army away and allow the election of Cinna (q.v. 1) as consul for 87, against his own candidate Servilius (q.v. 1); and he failed to gain control of the army of Pompeius (q.v. 3) Strabo through his colleague and *adfinis* Pompeius (q.v. 2), who was killed in the attempt. Despite these reverses, and ignoring a summons to stand trial, he embarked for Greece, where Q. Bruttius Sura, legate of the governor of Macedonia, had already driven the enemy back to the sea: his hope of safety lay in winning the eastern war.

Outlawed, but not molested, under Cinna, he agreed (it seems) to refrain from attacking Valerius Flaccus (q.v. 6) when he marched against Mithridates. Forcing Sura to abandon his campaign, he himself twice defeated Archelaus (q.v. 3) and sacked the Piraeus and (in part) Athens. Having saved Mithridates from Fimbria (see LUCULLUS, 2), he made peace with the king at Dardanus, granting him recognition as an ally of Rome and impunity for his adherents in return for his surrendering his conquests and supporting Sulla with money and supplies. He then dealt with Fimbria, reconciled his own army (disgruntled at the peace with the enemy of Rome) by quartering it on the cities of Asia (which he bled of their wealth), and on hearing of Cinna's death, abandoned negotiations with Rome and openly rebelled (84). Invading Italy, he was soon joined by most eminent men—especially Metellus (q.v. 7) Pius, M. Crassus (q.v. 4) and Pompey—and within a year defeated all the loyalist forces in Italy (see CARBO 2, CARRINAS, MARIUS 2, NORBANUS 1). Finding the Italians hostile, he undertook not to diminish their rights of citizenship, but he massacred those who continued resistance (especially the Samnites: see PAPIUS) and imposed severe penalties and confiscations on their communities. In Rome, under a law of Flaccus (q.v. 5)—who became his *magister equitum*—he was elected Dictator and granted complete immunity. He continued and legalized his massacres by publishing 'proscription' lists (sometimes fraudulently added to by subordinates: see CHRYSOGONUS).

During 81 he enacted a legislative programme designed to put power firmly in the hands of the Senate, whose numbers (traditionally 300) he raised to 600 by adlecting *equites* supporting him. In addition to various minor reforms, he (1) curbed the tribunate by requiring the Senate's approval for tribunician bills, limiting the veto, and barring senior magistracies to ex-tribunes (which made the office unattractive to ambitious men); (2) restored the *quaestiones*—the number of which he raised to at least seven—to the enlarged Senate; (3) raised the number of praetors to eight and that of quaestors to twenty, chiefly to cope with the number of provinces without (in general) prolonging tenure beyond a year; (4) laid down a strict *cursus honorum*, with the quaestorship and praetorship compulsory before the consulship could be reached at a minimum age of 42, and made quaestors automatically members of the Senate; (5) subjected holders of *imperium* outside Rome to stricter control by the Senate. At the same time he settled his veterans on confiscated land (especially in Campania and Etruria) as guarantors of his order. Then, convinced by the old prophecy (in which he fully believed) that he had not long to live, he gradually divested himself of power and restored constitutional government, becoming consul in 80 (with Metellus Pius) and returning to private status in 79. He retired to Campania, where he died in 78 of a long-standing disease. His funeral was impressively arranged to display the power of his veterans, especially in view of the agitation of the consul Lepidus (q.v. 2). But his constitutional reforms, weakened by a series of concessions, were largely overthrown in 70 by his old adherents Pompey and Crassus.

Despite his mystical belief in his luck (hence his *agnomen* and the *praenomina* of his twin children: see SULLA 3), despite his arrogance and ruthlessness, Sulla never aimed at permanent tyranny: he did not even put his portrait on his coins. He undoubtedly wished his settlement to succeed, and he thought it out carefully (no doubt with the help of his associates, who were basically the faction that had supported M. Drusus, q.v. 2), to eliminate the 'two-headedness' (in Varro's phrase) that

had been the bane of Roman politics since C. Gracchus. His arrangements were consistent, practical, and neither visionary nor romantically reactionary. Yet he had no appreciation of deep-seated problems (including the ones he had created). The quick disintegration of his constitution was due both to his own example and to the decline in the morale, public spirit, and authority of the oligarchy that he made supreme—a decline that he had done much to foster. He set the precedent for the use of military force against the State—and for its success; he spared the only powerful enemy of Rome for his personal advantage and prepared the ground for that enemy's future success by ruining the cities of Asia; he weeded out, both in Rome and in Italy, those most loyal to the State and prepared to defend it, while rewarding those who were not; he threw Italy into turmoil by giving much confiscated land to veterans unfitted to work it and accustomed to violence in pursuit of their aims; worst of all, he exposed both the hollowness of Republican forms in the new conditions of power and the moral weakness of most of the ruling élite, which rushed to welcome the political and economic profits of successful rebellion. It was soon evident that honour and public service were not to be expected of these men. A generation later, Italy, which had flocked to defend the Republic against Sulla, showed no eagerness to defend his beneficiaries against one who imitated his methods; and for much of the ruling class itself, *clementia* now made a rebel seem unobjectionable. Sulla's positive achievement was to instil men with a horror of civil war that delayed it for a generation; but it is largely due to him that, when the memory faded, the coming of that war, and the end of the Republic that he had tried to re-establish, were made all but inevitable.

Sulla's *Commentarii* (probably an account not unlike Caesar's, though more egotistical), were edited by Lucullus (q.v. 2) and are an important ultimate source, recognizable in Plutarch, Appian, and Livy. Another major strand, especially of the Livian tradition, goes back to Sisenna. Cicero has many personal memories of the period. Of modern works, Mommsen's *History of Rome* is still highly profitable. For recent work, see E. Badian, *Hist.* 1962, 222, 228 (with bibliography); add Badian, *Stud. Gr. Rom. Hist.*, see index; E. Gabba, *Annali della Scuola Normale Superiore di Pisa* 1964, 1 ff.; U. Laffi, *Athenaeum* 1967, 177 f., 255 f.                                    E. B.

**SULLA** (2), PUBLIUS CORNELIUS (*PW* 386), relative of (1), in whose proscriptions he amassed wealth and under whom he helped to found a veteran colony at Pompeii. With Autronius (q.v.), he was elected consul for 65 B.C., then convicted of *ambitus* (thus struck with *infamia*) and said to be involved in the 'first conspiracy' of Catiline. Prosecuted as a Catilinarian in 62, he secured the support of Hortensius (q.v. 2) and Cicero—whom he rewarded well—and was acquitted. In the Civil War he joined Caesar and secured his rehabilitation, increasing his wealth in the sales of Pompeian properties. He died *c.* 45.

Cicero, *Pro Sulla*.                                    E. B.

**SULLA** (3) (**FELIX**), FAUSTUS CORNELIUS (*PW* 377), son of (1) and of Metella (1): his *praenomen* and that of his twin sister Fausta were intended to symbolize Sulla's luck. He inherited most of his father's wealth, but soon spent it (especially on lavish memorial games in 60 B.C.). Marrying Pompey's daughter, he served under him in the East and was the first to mount the walls of the Temple at Jerusalem. He was quaestor in 54 (see his coins, Sydenham, *CRR* 882 f.) and assisted Milo (Fausta's husband) in 52; and he restored the *Curia* burnt after the death of Clodius (q.v. 1). Taking Pompey's side in the Civil War, he was killed by Sittius' men after Thapsus (46).                                    E. B.

**SULMO**, modern *Sulmona*, town of the Paeligni at the centre of Italy. It resisted Hannibal (211 B.C.) and supported Julius Caesar (49 B.C.), but is famed chiefly as

Ovid's birthplace (43 B.C.). A late republican terraced sanctuary has been recently excavated in its vicinity. The Sulmo Sulla sacked was probably elsewhere (modern *Sermoneta?*), in Latium.

E. T. Salmon, *Ovidiana* (ed. N. I. Herescu, 1958), 3 ff.; F. Castagnoli (ed.), *Studi di urbanistica antica* (1966), 107 ff.        E. T. S.

**SULPICIA** (1, *PW* s.v. Sulpicius 114), daughter of Servius Sulpicius Rufus, and ward of Valerius Messalla (q.v. 3) Corvinus, is not to be confused with her namesake celebrated by Martial (10. 35 and 38). She composed six short elegies incorporated in the Tibullus collection (4. 7–12), in which with unique frankness and rare warmth she passionately avows her love for Cerinthus, a young gentleman of her own sphere, not a freedman or the Cornutus mentioned by Tibullus (2. 2 and 3). Though Sulpicia's literary remains amount to only forty lines and show traces of amateurishness, they nevertheless completely lack conventionality and affectation and constitute a splendid human document. Here is the first poetry we have written by a *docta puella*, and it throws light on certain social tendencies of the Augustan Age. *See also* ELEGIAC POETRY, LATIN.

Text in editions of Tibullus; commentaries in editions of K. F. Smith and Postgate (*see* TIBULLUS). G. Némethy, *Tibulli Carmina, Acc. Sulpiciae Elegidia* (1905). Schanz–Hosius.        J. H.

**SULPICIA** (2, *PW* s.v. Sulpicius 115), wife of Calenus, in Martial's time, and by him praised as authoress of poetry of honourable love (10. 35 and 38). A 'satira' of seventy lines is questionably ascribed to her.

Text in O. Jahn's ed. of Persius and Juvenal; *PLM* v 91; I. Lana (1949), with Ital. transl.). See G. Thiele, 'Die Poesie unter Domitian', *Hermes* 1916, 233 ff.; J. W. Duff, *Roman Satire* (1937); Schanz–Hosius, § 416.

**SULPICIUS** (1, *PW* 92) **RUFUS,** PUBLIUS, was a member (with Drusus, q.v. 2, and Cotta, q.v. 1) of a circle of brilliant and ambitious young nobles taught by L. Crassus (q.v. 3). In 95 B.C. he prosecuted Norbanus (q.v.), and as tribune in 88 tried to carry on Drusus' ideas by securing the fair distribution of the enfranchised Italians in the tribes. Opposed by the Optimates (including his friend, the consul Pompeius, q.v. 2), he began to stress the *Popularis* aspects of his programme and turned for support to Marius, with whom he had found himself accidentally collaborating in opposition to the consular candidature of Caesar (q.v. 3). In return for transferring the command against Mithridates from Sulla to Marius, he was able to pass his laws (with some violence), but, when Sulla reacted by marching on Rome, had to flee. He was captured and executed and his laws were annulled.

E. Badian, *Foreign Clientelae* (1958), 230; id. *Hist.* 1969, 481 ff. E. B.

**SULPICIUS** (2, *PW* 95) **RUFUS,** SERVIUS (*cos.* 51 B.C.), prosecuted Murena (q.v.) when defeated by him in the consular elections for 62 B.C. He waited eleven years for his consulate, and in 51 seems to have resisted the extreme policies of his colleague M. Marcellus (q.v. 4—Cic. *Fam.* 4. 3. 1): in 49 he attended Caesar's Senate; he governed Achaea for Caesar in 46. He died on an embassy to Antony in Jan. 43, and was honoured with a public funeral and a statue on the Rostra. The *Ninth Philippic* is Cicero's eulogy on him, a man of peace and great sanctity of character, chiefly famous as a jurisconsult. He wrote to Cicero two celebrated letters—a description of the murder of M. Marcellus (*Fam.* 4. 12) and a consolation for Tullia's death (ibid. 4. 5).        G. E. F. C.

**SULPICIUS** (3) **BLITHO** (1st c. B.C.), one of Nepos' sources (*Hannibal* 13. 1). For confusion with Sulpicius Galba, grandfather of the Emperor Galba, see Schanz–Hosius i, § 112. 6; Peter, *HRRel.* ccclxxix.

**SULPICIUS** (4), SERVIUS, author of love-poems, mentioned by Horace (*Sat.* 1. 10. 86) and Ovid (*Tr.* 2. 441).

**SULPICIUS** (5) **CAMERINUS,** QUINTUS, epic poet (Ovid, *Pont.* 4. 16. 19) and possibly same as consul of A.D. 9.

**SULPICIUS** (6) **APOLLINARIS** (2nd c. A.D.), scholar, the teacher of Aulus Gellius and the Emperor Pertinax. He wrote learned letters (*epistolicae quaestiones*, now lost), verse summaries of the *Aeneid* (6 hexameters for each book; see Baehrens, *PLM* iv. 169), and metrical summaries of the plays of Terence (cf. e.g. W. M. Lindsay's ed. of Ter.).

Schanz–Hosius, § 597.        J. F. M.

**SUMMANUS,** perhaps originally an epithet of Jupiter (q.v.), as 'dweller in the most high places'; but distinguished from him (Festus, 254. 3) as the god who sends nocturnal thunderbolts. Latte (*RR* 208) derives the cult from an omen during the war with Pyrrhus when a temple was founded; this may, however, have replaced an altar ascribed to Titus Tatius (Platner–Ashby, 502). Wheel-shaped cakes called *summanalia* were offered to him (Festus, 474. 17). His identification with Pluto (Martianus Capella, 2. 161) is fanciful.

Wissowa, *RK* 135.        H. J. R.

**SUNIUM,** a bold promontory at the south apex of Attica, was crowned by a marble temple of Poseidon built *c.* 440 B.C. on the foundations of a temple destroyed by the Persians. There was also a slightly older Ionic temple of Athena of unusual design (Vitr. *De Arch.* 4. 8. 4), later removed to Athens. The early importance of the sanctuary is attested by a mass of Egyptian objects, evidence of overseas trade, and by several archaic marble statues. Sunium was fortified in 413 for the security of the Athenian corn-ships; the circuit of the walls and the boat-houses are well preserved. The fort was also involved in the wars of the third century and the revolt of the slaves from Laurium (q.v.).

Thuc. 8. 4; Paus. 1. 1; 'Α.Ν. Οἰκονομίδης, Σούνιον, ἀρχαιολογικὸς ὁδηγός (1957).        C. W. J. E.

**SUPERSTITION.** The word 'superstition' is relative, for it may be taken to mean indulgence in beliefs or practices which have been abandoned by general, or at least by educated, opinion of the time. For instance, the Emperor Tiberius cannot be called superstitious for believing in astrology, but a modern could be, since its falsity is now well known. It is doubtful whether a Greek or Latin word exists for superstition, since δεισιδαιμονία (cf. RELIGION), when derogatory, as it most often is, means rather excessive pietism or religiosity, whereas *superstitio* itself is implied by Virgil to be unenlightened and meaningless worship ('uana superstitio ueterumque ignara deorum', *Aen.* 8. 187, see W. Warde Fowler, *Aeneas at the Site of Rome*, 1918, 57), perhaps with reference especially to oriental cults of the poet's day. It is hardly possible here to do more than give examples of the existence of magico-religious rites or beliefs known to have been condemned by the more enlightened people of the time.

Whereas Homer evidently writes for a remarkably free-thinking public, he has traces of a state nearer the primitive. For example, although his Achaean characters regard fish merely as very poor food, he speaks of one as ἱερός, holy or taboo (*Il.* 16. 407). This plainly refers to some belief like that of the Syrians with regard to the holy fish of their goddess (Hyg. *Fab.* 197). Hesiod, writing some time later but from a peasant environment, is full of scruples which a Homeric hero would laugh at, e.g. *Op.* 750, against a boy of twelve years or twelve months sitting on a tomb; 753, against a man using a woman's bath, besides the elaborate observation of certain days of the month, 765 ff., if that is really Hesiodic.

The prevalent use of amulets (q.v.) was evidently regarded as superstitious by the more enlightened minds of the fifth and fourth centuries B.C.; hence the point of the story in Theophrastus, ap. Plut. *Pericles* 38, that that statesman during his last illness apologized to a friend for having one about his neck, put there by the women of his household, saying that he must be very low to submit to such folly. A similar contempt is expressed by Plato, *Resp.* 2. 364 b ff., for practitioners of magic (q.v.), and some of the lower forms of purificatory rites which clung to the fringes of Orphism (q.v.). The former of these gained ground with the degeneracy of natural science, as may be seen by comparing the earlier works on medicine, e.g. the Hippocratic corpus, above all *De morbo sacro*, which protests against the unscientific ascription of diseases to supernatural agencies, with some of the later productions, especially the extraordinary mixture of traditional remedies and conjuring which has come down to us from Marcellus of Bordeaux.

In Rome one of the most frequently denounced forms of superstition is the adoption of fragments of foreign ritual, especially the more spectacular kinds. Thus Juvenal's women consult all manner of foreign diviners, indulge in extraordinary orgiastic rites, and perform more or less Egyptian penances (*Sat.* 6. 314 ff., 511 ff.). A fairly common form of this seems to have been the observance of some Jewish rites, especially the Sabbath, by those who were neither Jews nor proselytes (Juv. 14. 96, cf. Hor. *Sat.* 1. 9. 69).

With the coming of Christianity, many who were superstitiously inclined developed two new forms of their aberration. One was the retention, despite all the Doctors of the Church could say, of purely pagan beliefs; e.g. St. Augustine complains, *Expos. epist. ad Galat.* 35, of Christians who tell him 'to his face' that they will not start on a journey the day after the Kalends, which in pagan Roman belief was *religiosus* (cf. Plut. *Quaest. Rom.* 25). The other was the employment of Christian names, holy books, etc., for magic, as the Christian charms, Preisendanz ii. 189 ff., and cf. the strictures of St. Augustine (*in Iohan. evang. tract.* vii. 12) against those who use a Gospel as a remedy for headache. Similar uses had long been made of Jewish formulae, etc., see, e.g., M. Rist in *Journ. Bib. Lit.* 1938, 289 ff. *See* MAGIC.

There is no comprehensive and authoritative work, but material will be found in all large treatises on ancient religion, e.g. Nilsson, *GGR* i². 795 ff., ii. 207 ff., 392 ff.; cf. E. R. Dodds, *The Greeks and the Irrational* (1951). H. J. R.

**SUPPLICATIONES.** On the occasion of a great national calamity (as after the battle of Lake Trasimene, Livy 22. 10. 8) or success (as after the crushing of Vercingetorix' revolt, Caesar, *BGall.* 7. 90. 8) it was the custom at Rome and elsewhere (cf. *ILS* 108: Cumae) to give opportunity for general adoration of the gods, or certain of them, by providing access to their statues or other emblems, often at least placed on *pulvinaria* (q.v.). This was known as a *supplicatio*, from the kneeling or prostrations of the worshippers (commoner in Italy than Greece, C. Sittl, *Gebärden*, 177 f., but cf. H. Bolkestein, *Theophrastos' Charakter der Deisidaimonia* (1929), 23 ff.). It was at least on occasion associated with a *lectisternium* (q.v.), as in Livy, loc. cit., but is to be distinguished from it, as Livy there does. It is apparently a genuinely Roman procedure, older than the foreign use of statues to represent the gods. That it is often said to have taken place *ad* (*circa*) *omnia pulvinaria* is held by Wissowa (*RK* 424) to indicate, along with the fact that it generally followed a consultation of the Sibylline Books, that in the

form familiar from our authorities it was fully hellenized; but see A. K. Lake, *Quantulacumque* (1937), 243 ff., and Latte, *RR* 245 ff. H. J. R.

**SURA,** LUCIUS LICINIUS (*PW* 167), was born in Hispania Tarraconensis. A *novus homo*, he rose in the senatorial career as a *candidatus Caesaris*, probably of Domitian, and eventually commanded Legio I Minervia at Bonn c. A.D. 93–7, became governor of Gallia Belgica 97, and *cos. I suff.* in 97 or 98. A fellow-countryman of Trajan and, like him, versed in frontier-defence, he became his intimate, and possibly influenced Nerva to adopt Trajan. Governor of Lower Germany, then *cos. II ord.* in 102, he served with distinction on Trajan's staff in both Dacian Wars. He received *ornamenta triumphalia* with a statue at public expense. He became *cos. III ord.* in 107 (a rare honour) and died soon after 110. Rich and cultured, he wielded immense influence. Pliny in one letter (*Ep.* 4. 30) submits a physical problem to him, and in another (*Ep.* 7. 27) a psychic one. Sura was a patron of Martial (6. 64. 12–13), who admired the old-fashioned style of his oratory (7. 47. 1–2). It is recorded that he composed speeches for Trajan (S.H.A. *Hadr.* 3. 11).

Dio Cass. 68. 15. 3 ff.; *ILS* 1022, though the name is lost, undoubtedly gives his career; for dedications from near Tarraco, *ILS* 1952, 6956; see also B. Stech, *Klio* Beiheft x (1912), no. 811; Syme, *Tacitus*, see index. C. H. V. S.; M. H.

**SURENAS,** i.e. the Suren. The Surens, one of the seven great Parthian families, ruled Seistan as vassals of the Arsacids, with their capital at Alexandria-Prophthasia The best-known Surenas formed a highly trained professional army of 10,000 horse-archers, with 1,000 swift Arabian camels carrying a huge reserve of arrows. With this force he overthrew Mithridates III and restored Orodes II to his throne, and then defeated Crassus' invasion (*see* CARRHAE). For a moment his genius had made the horse-archer, the common man who had won Carrhae, potential master of the world; but the Parthian nobles were jealous, and Orodes put to death his too brilliant vassal. Another 'Surena' in A.D. 36 crowned the pretender Tiridates king of Parthia, 'patrio more' (Tac. *Ann.* 6. 42). The Surens played an important role in later wars between their Sassanid overlords and Rome and Byzantium.

E. Herzfeld, *Sakastan* (1932), 70 ff. W. W. T.; E. W. G.

**SURGERY.** I. BEFORE 300 B.C.

1. In the Homeric poems references to surgery are mainly in the *Iliad* and concerned with the treatment of the wounds there recorded. The wound is cleaned; blood squeezed or sucked out; edges united by bandaging; and an analgesic of dried herbs rubbed in and applied as an air-tight pad. The only wound-spell is in the *Odyssey* (19. 457–8 ἐπαοιδή, cf. Pindar, *Pyth.* 3. 45 ff.). Homeric treatment resembles the best Egyptian practice. Moreover, instruments early in Greek use, notably the trephine, closely resemble Mesopotamian finds. Thus there is presumption that Greek surgery drew on the traditions of both these civilizations. The first historic Greek practitioner after Asclepius and his sons (*Il.* 2. 731–2; 4. 194; 11. 518 and 614, etc.) was Democedes of Croton. He treated King Darius surgically and had certainly Persian contacts (Hdt. 3. 125, 129, 137).

2. The surgical part of the Hippocratic Collection is in confusion. *Fractures*, *Dislocations* (i.e. ἀρθρῶν, of joints), and *Wounds of the head* are of about 400 B.C., the two former being parts of a larger work. *The nature of bones* is of about 350 B.C. *On surgery* and *Mochlicon* (= *Instruments of reduction*) are later abbreviations of earlier works, but the introductory chapter of *Mochlicon* is the displaced first part of *The nature of bones*. Treatises covering the whole medical field were, Galen indicates,

commonly called 'Concerning the things of surgery'. Some idea of such a work is gained by reading the above works in the following order: *On Surgery*, being a greatly abbreviated introduction to the whole; introductory chapter of *Mochlicon*, being descriptions of the bones; *The nature of bones*, a sketch of theoretical anatomy for the surgeon, omitting bones (despite title); *Fractures*; *Dislocations*; remaining chapters of *Mochlicon*; *Wounds of the head*. It must be remembered that the parts differ greatly in age and state and that there is repetition and overlapping.

**3.** Startlingly modern are the minute directions for preparation of the operating room, and such points as the management of light—both artificial and natural—scrupulous cleanliness of hands, care and use of instruments with special precautions for those of iron, decencies of the operating chamber, modes of dressing wounds, use of splints, and need for tidiness, cleanliness, after-care, and nursing. The directions for bandaging and for diagnosis and treatment of dislocations and fractures, especially of depressed fractures of the skull, are very impressive. In *Fractures* and *Dislocations* certain procedures for reduction are identical with those now in use, but other passages are incompatible with the facts of anatomy. *Wounds of the head* has a special place in the history of surgery. It is a practical work by a highly skilled craftsman, and every sentence suggests experience. Although its treatment of depressed fractures has been criticized from an early date, the book was in current use until the middle of the eighteenth century. It introduces technical terms, two of which, *bregma* and *diploe*, survive in modern usage.

**4.** Among instruments described is the 'bench of Hippocrates', a bed for reducing dislocations, especially of the hip. The form is so ancient as to antedate the screw as a mechanical power. Lever, crank, windlass, and pulley are employed. With minor changes it was in continuous use for at least 2,000 years. There is no reason to associate it with Hippocrates; it may well be more ancient than he, but the name is late.

## II. ALEXANDRIA AND THE EMPIRE

**5.** After 300 B.C. anatomical knowledge enters surgery from the Alexandrian school. Thus *Dislocations* has an obvious interpolation (on the anatomy of the shoulder-joint) of at least a century later than the main text. Similarly the surgeon Hegetor can be approximately dated from a fragment of his work (preserved by Apollonius of Citium) describing the anatomy of the hip-joint in a way discoverable only by dissection. We have no complete surgical work of Alexandrian origin.

**6.** Passing by the stories of Pliny, the first professed surgeon at Rome of whom we have news is Meges of Sidon early in the first century A.D. Heliodorus soon after gave the first account of ligation and torsion of blood-vessels, treated stricture by internal section, performed radical cures for hernias, and was especially skilled in skull operations. Amputations were fully described by Archigenes of Apamea. Antyllus treated cataracts surgically and removed aneurysms by applying two ligatures and cutting down between them—an operation still known by his name alternatively with that of John Hunter (1728–93). These surgeons of the first and second centuries A.D. acted with resource and confidence. The fragments of their works have the authentic tang of experience.

**7.** The standard account of Roman surgery of the first century A.D. is the seventh book of *De medicina* of Aulus Cornelius Celsus. The professional standing of Celsus—whether lay or professional, bond or free—and the character of his book—whether translated from a Greek text, or

product of personal experience, or a compilation—are disputed, but it is certain from the articulation of the book that its author or compiler had practical surgical experience. He gives details of the very dangerous operations for extirpating a goitre and for cutting for stone, and describes well what might be thought to be the modern operation for removing tonsils and for other procedures on the face and mouth and for the removal of polypus from the nose. He gives the first account of dental practice, which includes wiring of loose teeth and use of a dental mirror. His attitude and line of treatment are sensible and humane.

**8.** Galen was no surgeon but his works include accounts of his surgical predecessors. Useful details are also preserved in the works of later Greek writers, notably Oribasius and Paul of Aegina. (For organization of the surgical service in the imperial army *see* MEDICINE.)

**9.** Graphic representations have a place in the history of surgery. The most important are: (*a*) A kylix of about 490 B.C., painted by Sosias, of Achilles bandaging Patroclus. The drawing is excellent, but the bandaging execrable. (*b*) A vase-painting of about 400 B.C. of a surgeon treating patients in his surgery. (*c*) A few votives, murals, memorial slabs, etc., showing instruments for operations. The best is a tablet of instruments from the Asclepieum at Athens. (Details of (*a*), (*b*), and (*c*) are discussed by Charles Singer, *Greek Medicine and Greek Biology*, 1922.) (*d*) Surgical instruments. The best collection is from Pompeii, where over 200 have been found. (*e*) Trajan's column shows an advanced dressing-station of a legion. (*f*) A Laurentian manuscript of about 900, copied from a very early MS. contains illustrations of Soranus of Ephesus *On bandaging* and *On the uterus* and of Apollonius of Citium *On reduction of dislocations*.

**10.** There was interest in veterinary surgery, especially under the Empire. The army had hospitals for animals (Hyginus, *Liber de munitionibus castrorum* 21. 22). Much can be gleaned from agricultural writings, but there was also a considerable veterinary literature. The *Mulomedicina Chironis* of about A.D. 100 survives in a philologically curious Latin version of about A.D. 300. It formed the basis for the larger *Digesta artis mulomedicinae* of Publius Vegetius Renatus (383–450), unexpectedly scientific and well arranged, which long remained in use. Abstracts of a collection of ancient works called *Hippiatrica*, said to have been made for Constantine Porphyrogenitus (905–59), have been in use ever since his time.

The surgical works of 'Hippocrates' are mostly in vol. iii of the Loeb *Hippocrates* by E. T. Withington (1927). Two older works of permanent importance are: J. E. Petrequin, *Chirurgie d'Hippocrate* (2 vols., 1877–8), product of 30 years' study by an accomplished surgeon, and Francis Adams, *The Genuine Works of Hippocrates* (2 vols., 1849), by the last great Greek scholar who practised under almost the circumstances of an ancient surgeon. For Celsus the Loeb edition of W. G. Spencer (3 vols., 1936–8) covers most needs. M. Wellmann, *Celsus, eine Quellenuntersuchung* (1913), is important. For texts, H. Kühlewein, *Hippocratis Opera Omnia* (2 vols., 1894–1902); F. Marx, *Celsi opera quae supersunt* (1915); U. C. Bussemaker and C. Daremberg, *Œuvres d'Oribase* (6 vols., 1851–76). The notes and comments of Francis Adams, *The Seven Books of Paulus Aegineta* (3 vols., 1844–7), are without rival. Werner R. Lewek, 'Die Bank des Hippokrates', *Janus* 1936, is exhaustive. See also PW Suppl. vi, Nachträge (Hippokrates) cols. 1290 ff.; J. S. Milne, *Surgical Instruments in Greek and Roman times* (1907); J. Scarborough, *Roman Medicine* (1969). Veterinary surgery. Sir Frederic Smith, *Early History of Veterinary Literature* (1919); E. Lommatzsch, *P. Vegeti Renati Mulomedicina* (1903); H. Ahlquist, *Studien zur Mulomedicina Chironis* (1909).  C. S.

**SURRENTUM,** modern *Sorrento*, on the southern headland of the Bay of Naples, celebrated for its charming surroundings, delightful climate, and salubrious wine. Surrentum spoke Oscan in republican times and was a *municipium* under the Empire, but is rarely mentioned in history. Ancient remains include the villa of Pollius Felix, elaborately described by Statius (*Silv.* 2. 2).  E. T. S.

**SUSA,** the 'city of lilies', was the capital of Elam, and afterwards of the Achaemenids, where Darius I built his palace (Apadāna). Under Seleucids and Parthians its name was Seleuceia-on-the-Eulaeus; the excavations have furnished numerous Greek inscriptions. In A.D. 1 there were still Greek cleruchs in charge of the citadel, i.e. some early Seleucid had planted a military colony there; probably it became a *polis* under Antiochus III. In A.D. 21 it was still a full-Greek city, with a Council, Assembly, and elected magistrates whose qualifications were scrutinized; it could send embassies, and was therefore a State; though subject to Parthia, it had more than local autonomy. Beside Greeks, other peoples can be traced—Persians, Syrians, Jews, Anatolians, Babylonians, Elymaeans; its city-goddess was the Elamite Nanaia, renamed Artemis, in whose temple Greeks manumitted their slaves. Four Greek poems are known, one a lyric ode (1st c. B.C.) addressed to Apollo by a Syrian title, Mara (Lord); it belongs to a known class of acrostic poems, and that and the forms of decrees and manumissions show that Susa was well within the Greek culture-sphere.

*SEG* vii. 1–33; Fr. Cumont, *CRAcad. Inscr.* 1930–3; W. W. Tarn, *The Greeks in Bactria and India* (1938), 27, 39, 68; G. le Rider, *Suse sous les Séleucids et les Parthes* (1965). W. W. T.

**SUSARION** is first mentioned in the Parian Marble, under some year between 581 and 560, as having originated Comedy in the Attic deme Icaria. A later tradition makes him a Megarian, and he calls himself υἱὸς Φιλίνου Μεγαρόθεν Τριποδίσκιος in the only putative citation from his work. This citation is in normal Attic, and its authenticity is highly improbable; Susarion may indeed be a fictitious person.

*FCG* ii. 3 f.; *CGF* 77 f.; Pickard-Cambridge–Webster, *Dithyramb²*, 183 ff. K. J. D.

**SUTRIUM,** the modern *Sutri*, a small but strategically important Etruscan town, 28 miles north-west of Rome and 6 miles west of Nepete (q.v.). Founded perhaps as late as the fifth century B.C. to control the important road (later the Via Cassia) through the Ciminian forest, it played an important part in the fighting that followed the destruction of Veii in 396 B.C. (Livy 6. 9. 3), very soon after which date it became a Latin colony. Its subsequent history was mainly uneventful until the early Middle Ages, when its position made it once more an important defensive outpost of Rome. It became a *municipium* after the Social War and received a fresh group of colonists soon after the death of Caesar, under the name of Colonia Coniuncta Iulia Sutrina.

*CIL* xi. 489. G. Duncan, *PBSR* 1958, 63 ff. J. B. W.-P.

**SYBARIS** (Σύβαρις), an Achaean-Troezenian foundation (*c.* 720 B.C.) near a similarly named river on the Gulf of Tarentum: the site has been identified near modern *Sibari* in the *Piana del Crati*. By expanding its territory, dispatching colonies (Laus, Scidrus, Posidonia-Paestum), and monopolizing Etruscan trade Sybaris became powerful; her wealthy luxuriousness was proverbial. But in 510 internal dissensions enabled Croton (q.v.) to obliterate Sybaris; the neighbouring river Crathis was diverted from its course to flow over the sacked city. Sybarite exiles, after twice unsuccessfully attempting to refound Sybaris, joined the Athenian foundation at Thurii (q.v.) (443). Thurii quickly expelled them, whereupon they established a new Sybaris on the river Traeis, never an important place.

Strabo 6. 263; Hdt. 5. 44 f.; Diod. 12. 9 f.; Ath. 12. 518 c f. J. S. Calaway, *Sybaris* (U.S.A. 1950); F. Rainey, *AJArch.* 1969, 261 ff. See, too, bibliography s.v. MAGNA GRAECIA. E. T. S.

**SYENE** (*Assuan*), on the southern frontier of ancient Egypt, on the right bank of the Nile, just below the First

Cataract. It was a trading town, and from its quarries came the valuable 'syenite' stone. Under the Ptolemies it replaced Elephantine as the frontier outpost; in 25 B.C. it was freed from Ethiopian invaders by the Romans, who established a garrison there. The fact that the sun's rays fell vertically in Syene at midsummer was utilized by Eratosthenes (q.v.) to make a remarkable calculation of the earth's circumference. E. H. W.

**SYKOPHANTAI** (συκοφάνται). In Athens there were, for most offences, no public prosecutors, but any citizen who wished was allowed to prosecute in a public case (*see* DIKE 2. § 2). Some individuals made a habit of bringing prosecutions, either to gain the financial rewards given to successful prosecutors in certain types of case (notably *phasis* and *apographe*; *see* DIKE 2, § 3 (*f*) and (*g*)), or to gain money by blackmailing a man who was willing to pay to avoid prosecution, or to earn payment from someone who had personal reasons for wanting a man to be prosecuted, or to make a political or oratorical reputation. Such persons came to be called *sykophantai* (literally 'fig-denouncers'; the origin of the usage is obscure). The word is often used as a term of disparagement or abuse in Aristophanes and the Attic orators.

The Athenians wished to check *sykophantai*, especially blackmailers, but not to discourage public-spirited volunteer prosecutors. Therefore the rewards for successful prosecution were not abolished, but penalties were introduced, in most kinds of public case, for a prosecutor who dropped a case after starting it, or whose case was so weak that he failed to obtain one-fifth of the jury's votes (*see* DIKE 2, § 2 (*d*)). In addition, being a *sykophantes* was an offence for which a man could be prosecuted. *Graphe*, *eisangelia*, *probole*, *apagoge*, and *endeixis* (*see* DIKE 2. § 3) are all said to have been possible methods of accusing *sykophantai*, but it is not known how the offence was legally defined.

R. J. Bonner and G. Smith, *The Administration of Justice from Homer to Aristotle* ii (1938), 39 ff. D. M. M.

**SYLE** (ἡ σύλη, τὸ σῦλον) was (1) robbery, cattle-reiving in general; (2) an act of reprisal by an injured person or his kinsmen for a deed of violence or a default on a debt. In early Greece this was often the only means of obtaining satisfaction from members of another tribe or city, and was therefore sanctioned by custom. In time of war *syle* was permitted against all enemy traders. From the sixth century it was gradually circumscribed by commercial treaties and by grants of *asylia* (q.v.) to certain individuals, cities, or sanctuaries. But even in Hellenistic times belligerent States still licensed privateering, and *syle* did not disappear until the Roman era.

H. A. Ormerod, *Piracy in the Ancient World* (1924), ch. 2. M. C.

**SYMBOLON** (σύμβολον, συμβολή), originally a 'mark', 'sign', or 'tally' as a material indication of identification or agreement. Such were used for identification in inter-State relations, as in *IG*² ii. 141. 19 between Athens and a king of Sidon; or between an individual and a ruler, as in Lysias 19. 25: a gold *phiale* given by the Great King of Persia for this purpose. Agreed *symbola* between Athens and her tribute-paying allies are mentioned in the Decree of Kleinias (*IG*² i. 66) to be used for sealing purposes to prevent fraud in the conveyance of the tribute. A distinction must be made between the related word συμβόλαιον (adj. συμβόλαιος or συμβολιμαῖος) which came to mean a contractual relation or obligation (in writing a συγγραφή) and the plural term σύμβολα (συμβολαί) meaning an inter-State agreement dealing with contractual and other legal relations between individuals of different States, and between a State and an individual. The need for these arose when, for trading and other reasons, individuals travelled abroad and needed the protection from personal injury and distraint (ἀσφάλεια and ἀσυλία) which traditional guest-friendship and προξενία could not give. The position is well demonstrated in the treaty between the Ozolian Locrian States of Oiantheia and Chaleion (Tod, *GHI²* 34). If in earlier times treaties secured only basic protection from σῦλαι exercised by private persons or a State, the need developed in the fifth century B.C. for a regulation of disputes arising from contracts of all sorts, and especially trading. Particularly desired were the expediting of decisions and the protection of the interests of the States concerned. The possible confusion of interpretation should be noted between συμβόλαιαι δίκαι (relating to συμβόλαια) and δίκαι ἀπὸ συμβόλων (based on σύμβολα), as in Thucydides 1. 77. 1 and the treaty between Athens and Phaselis (Tod, *GHI²* 32).

It would appear from [Demosthenes] 7. 12-13 that the normal practice was for σύμβολα to provide for cases to be settled in the courts of the State of the respondent, and for the plaintiff to present himself to these. It might also be implied here that such settlements were based on a code of law agreed in the σύμβολα. Σύμβολα existed in the Delian League, and it is clear that they were subject to revision, and might be modified in spirit and practice, if not in theory, according to the relationship existing between Athens and the State in question. They were not necessarily uniform and could be felt to be oppressive, if they contained, e.g., compulsory appeal to the Athenian courts (ἔφεσις) or removed the right of appeal to a third State.

In the fourth century, when Athens had no dominant position, and was, indeed, forced to placate merchants in particular, the ἐμπορικαὶ δίκαι (described in [Demosthenes] 7. 12-13 as ἀκριβεῖς and κατὰ μῆνα) in part replaced σύμβολα as far as mercantile cases were concerned, and had the additional advantage that they were dealt with where the contract was made, which benefited Athens as a banking centre. The same speech, however, seems to show that σύμβολα were still used. The Thesmothetai, who administered the ἐμπορικαὶ δίκαι, also had the duty of supervising the conclusion of σύμβολα (which were confirmed by a special court according to a special *nomos*) and of introducing cases under them. It is clear from the evidence that σύμβολα might cover a wide range of property and other legal relations. They functioned as a check on primitive 'self-help', and as a stage on the road to legal equality of foreigners, later secured by *isopoliteia*.

H. G. Robertson, *Administration of Justice in the Athenian Empire* (1924); R. J. Bonner and G. Smith, *Administration of Justice from Homer to Aristotle* i (1930), 310 ff.; J. W. Jones, *The Law and Legal Theory of the Greeks* (1956), 55 ff.; A. R. W. Harrison, *CQ* 1960, 248 ff.; G. E. M. de Ste Croix, *CQ* 1961, 94 ff.; full details and discussion in A. W. Gomme, *Commentary on Thucydides* i (1945), on 1. 77. 1. R. J. H.

**SYMMACHIA** (συμμαχία, 'fellowship in fighting') was used with several meanings: informal co-operation in war, a treaty of alliance, and a confederacy of allies. Treaties of alliance, of which the earliest Greek example preserved dates from the sixth century, could be of two kinds: defensive (*epimachia*) or offensive and defensive. The latter generally included a clause pledging the signatories to have the same friends and enemies. In such treaties the contracting States frequently had equal rights, but the clause could be so expanded as to subordinate one partner to the other. Thus in 404 B.C. Athens promised to have the same friends and enemies as the Lacedaemonians and follow their leadership. *Symmachia* has been used in a special sense as the name for a confederacy of allies under the *hegemonia* (leadership) of one State. The *hegemonia* included command in war and generally also the presidency of the assembly of the allies. Such leagues were not federal States but recognized the freedom of their members and could

continue to exist even under the King's Peace. The Peloponnesian and Delian Leagues are described in separate articles. More advanced was the Second Athenian League organized *c.* 378 B.C., when a congress or constitutional convention of allies of Athens met and adopted by decrees (δόγματα) the principles or constitution of the League, which was ratified by treaties between Athens and the members. Athens next in the spring of 377 issued a decree inviting States to join on the terms of freedom, self-government, and exemption from garrisons and the payment of tribute. Other documents show that the entire war-policy of members was controlled by the League. Athens held the *hegemonia*, and the members of the assembly (*synedrion*) of the allies, in which each State cast one vote, remained permanently in Athens so that meetings could be called on short notice. The policy of 'the Athenians and their Allies' was determined by agreement between the *synedrion* and the Athenian *ekklesia*. The *synedrion* also exercised some judicial authority. The reference in a decree to a Theban serving as chairman makes it likely that the *synedrion* had a presiding committee similar to the *proëdroi* of the later Hellenic League. The guarantee against tribute (φόρος) did not prevent the collection of contributions (συντάξεις) from members. The League finally was dissolved in 338 B.C. A special variety of *symmachia* is constituted by the Hellenic Leagues of Philip II, Antigonus Monophthalmus, and Antigonus Doson, in which the *hegemonia* was held by kings, while a committee of five *proëdroi* presided over the assembly.

ANCIENT SOURCES. Collected by R. von Scala, *Die Staatsverträge des Altertums* (1898). Add *IG²* iv. 1. 68; Accame (*infra*) 230.
MODERN LITERATURE. *General*: W. S. Ferguson, *Greek Imperialism* (U.S.A. 1913), chs. 1-3 and 7; G. Busolt, *Griechische Staatskunde* ii (1926), 1250 ff. and 1320 ff.; V. Martin, *La Vie internationale dans la Grèce des cités* (1940), 121 ff.; I. Calabi, *Ricerche sui rapporti tra le poleis* (1953), chs. 2 and 3; Larsen, *Representative Govt. in Greek and Roman History* (U.S.A., 1955), ch. 3; V. Ehrenberg, *The Greek State* (1960), ch. 3.
*Special*: F. H. Marshall, *The Second Athenian Confederacy* (1905); F. Hampl, *Die griechischen Staatsverträge des 4. Jahrhunderts* (1938). S. Accame, *La Lega Ateniese del sec. IV a. C.* (1941). J. A. O. L.

**SYMMACHUS** (1) (fl. *c.* A.D. 100) wrote a commentary with ὑποθέσεις on Aristophanes which owed much to Didymus and was one of the main sources of the oldest scholia to Aristophanes. He probably produced the first edition of the latter's select plays.

**SYMMACHUS** (2), QUINTUS AURELIUS (*c.* A.D. 340-*c.* 402), belonged to a distinguished family. Trained by a Gallic *rhetor*, he became the greatest orator of his day, and thus attained the highest positions in the State. He had a knowledge of Greek, but his culture was almost purely literary. His acquaintance with philosophy was superficial. In 369 he was sent on deputation to Gaul and there won the close friendship of Ausonius (q.v.). In 373 he was appointed proconsul of Africa. Holding fast to the pagan religion, he proved the most prominent opponent of Christianity in his time. The influence of Julian had in part re-established paganism, and a storm arose over the removal of the altar of Victory in the senate-house at Rome, when Gratian in 382 by imperial edict disestablished and disendowed the pagan religion. The pagan party struggled for the restoration of the altar and the repeal of the edict, especially when Symmachus was *praefectus urbi* (384, 385), but was defeated largely through the efforts of Ambrosius (q.v.). Symmachus nevertheless attained the consulship in 391 and lived till about 402.

During this last period he wrote the greater part of the numerous letters that have come down to us. Fragments of his carefully composed speeches are also preserved. The letters, in ten books, are addressed to leading persons of the day; their arrangement imitates that of the Younger

Pliny, nine books private, one official correspondence. His literary circle was conspicuous in the pagan scholarship of the period, e.g. in editing Livy (*see* SUBSCRIPTIONES, LATIN).

Ed. O. Seeck (1883). S. Dill, *Roman Society in the last century of the Western Empire* (1905); T. R. Glover, *Life and Letters in the fourth century* (1901); F. Homes Dudden, *Life and Times of St. Ambrose* (1935); *The Conflict between Paganism and Christianity in the fourth century* (ed. A. Momigliano, 1963), ch. 8 (H. Bloch); bibliography relating to Symmachus' prose style, in K. Polheim, *Die lat. Reimprosa* (1963), 235. A. S.; F. J. E. R.

**SYMMORIA.** An official group of taxpayers in Athens in the fourth century B.C., which performed certain public services as a corporate body. The law of Periander (357/6 B.C.) introduced a reform of the *trierarchy*, which was later improved by Demosthenes. It divided the twelve hundred wealthiest citizens into twenty equal *symmoriai*. The upkeep of a number of ships was allotted to them on a proportional basis. Their *epimeletai*, who were, perhaps, identical with the *symmoriarchai*, the wealthiest members of a *symmoria*, divided the *symmoria* into *synteleiai* of members according to their wealth, so that each *synteleia* found one ship.

Earlier in date than Periander's law were the *symmoriai* created in 378/7 in connexion with the reform of the *eisphora* (q.v.). These included practically all Athenian taxpayers and special *symmoriai* of *metoikoi*. They seem to have been organized in the same way as the trierarchic *symmoriai*. Outside Athens, in Teos and possibly Nysa, the term meant bodies analogous to the Attic γένη, and in later antiquity private clubs. *See* DEMOSTHENES (2); EISPHORA; LITURGY; TRIERARCHY.

A. M. Andreades, *A History of Greek Public Finance* (U.S.A. 1933), index; G. Busolt-H. Swoboda, *Griechische Staatskunde* i, ii (1920–6), index; Michell, *Econom. Anc. Gr.*, index. F. Poland, in *PW*, s.v. 'Symmoria', 'Symmoriarches'. F. M. H.

**SYMPHOSIUS** (perhaps 4th–5th c. A.D.), the reputed author of a series of a hundred riddles, each consisting of three hexameters, claimed in the preface to have been composed *ex tempore* during the *Saturnalia*. The work was regarded as a model for the poetic riddle and had an important influence on medieval books of riddles, e.g. Aldhelm's. *See also* RIDDLES.

TEXTS. *PLM* iv; Riese, *Anth. Lat.* i²; with trans. and comm. R. T. Ohl (1928). A. H.-W.

**SYMPLEGADES** (Συμπληγάδες, sc. πέτραι), the Clashing Rocks through which the Argonauts (q.v.) had to pass into the Hellespont. The story is essentially the same as that of the Planctae (Πλαγκταί, *Odyssey* 12. 59 ff.), i.e. the Wandering Rocks, which not even the doves which carry ambrosia to Zeus can get through without losing one of their number; these, however, are not definitely located. The Argo is said there to have passed them, whence it seems that Planctae is the older name, though later authors (as Ap. Rhod. 4. 860 ff.) suppose two sets of clashing or moving rocks, one to the east and the other to the west of the Mediterranean. There is no need to seek a rationalizing explanation of either, see J. Bacon, *Voyage of the Argonauts* (1925), 79. H. J. R.

**SYMPOLITEIA** (the sharing of citizenship or political life) is employed—as it was by Polybius—as a descriptive name for a federal State. The earliest-known use of the word in this sense is in a Lycian inscription of about 180 B.C. The word commonly used in documents as a part of the name of a federal State is *koinon*, which can also be used about a *symmachia* (q.v.) or almost any association or corporation. In English federal States are best called confederacies rather than leagues. Characteristic is a division of power between the central and local govern-

ments and a double citizenship and allegiance, local and federal, symbolized at times by such identifications as 'an Aetolian from Naupactus'. To the federal government belonged foreign affairs, the army, and jurisdiction in cases of treason; in local government and institutions there was a tendency to uniformity. While a citizen normally could exercise political rights only in one community, he apparently possessed civil rights, including the right to acquire real property (*enctesis*), in all communities within the confederacy. Exceptions were the Thessalian Confederacy organized by Flamininus and other confederacies founded under Roman influence. (For accounts of the chief *sympoliteiai*, *see* ACHAEAN CONFEDERACY, AETOLIAN CONFEDERACY, *and* FEDERAL STATES.) *Sympoliteia* is applicable also to any merging of citizenship, and the related verb is used in a Phocian inscription of the second century B.C. referring to the absorption of the city of Medeon by Stiris. Similar expressions are common in connexion with the union of cities in Asia Minor.

ANCIENT SOURCES. *Koinon* in names of confederacies: *SIG* 653. 'Aetolian from Naupactus': ibid. 380 and 500; Stiris–Medeon: ibid. 647 (cf. 546 B). *Sympoliteia*: *SEG* xviii. 570, line 62.
MODERN LITERATURE. E. Szanto, *Das griechische Bürgerrecht* (1892), ch. 3; G. Busolt, *Griechische Staatskunde* i (1920), 156 ff.; V. Ehrenberg, *The Greek State²* (1969); J. A. O. Larsen, *Greek Federal States* (1968). The nature of federal citizenship is discussed by W. Kolbe in *Sav. Zeitschr.* 1929 and Larsen in *Symb. Oslo.* 1957. Anatolian *sympoliteiai*, by L. Robert, *Villes d'Asie mineure²* (1962), 54 ff. J. A. O. L.

**SYMPOSIUM** (συμπόσιον). A symposium was a Greek drinking-party that followed the evening meal. After libations had been poured and a hymn sung there was drinking according to an agreed procedure; the wine was diluted with water in various proportions. The participants were garlanded and many used perfume. Some did not drink; others displayed riotous intemperance. In addition to conversation the guests told riddles and fables, and sang capped drinking-songs (*see* SCOLIA), and pieces of verse from traditional classics or recent drama. Games were played, particularly κότταβος (*see* GAMES). There was usually a woman pipe-player, and displays of dancing, acrobatics, and miming were often given by hired performers.

Ar. *Vesp.* 1208–64; Xen. *Symp.*; Athenaeus, esp. 15; P. Jacobsthal, *Göttinger Vasen* (1912), 33 ff. M. Co.

**SYMPOSIUM LITERATURE.** Descriptions of the conversations at symposia made up a loosely defined literary genre. Precedents were sought in Homeric descriptions of banquets, but the masterpiece of the genre was the *Symposium* of Plato, in which a drinking-party is the setting for a series of contrasting speeches on a single philosophical topic diversified by exchanges of dialogue and the arrival of an uninvited guest. The other important 'Socratic symposium' (cf. Hermog. *Rhet.* 2. 455 f. Spengel) is that of Xenophon, possibly later than Plato's; here more than one topic is discussed, and there are long descriptions of the entertainments provided. Aristotle's *Symposium* is generally identified with his Περὶ μέθης.

Dialogues with the same name were used particularly by Academics and Peripatetics as a framework for philosophical discussions and also by Epicurus, whose *Symposium* was criticized by Ath. (186 e) for lack of artistry. The genre was used, often in the form of unconnected symposiac questions, as a vehicle for miscellaneous learning and lore, e.g. in the σύμμικτα συμποτικά of Aristoxenus on musical problems (Ath. 632 a). The *Symposium* of Heraclides of Tarentum dealt with the medical effects of food and drink (Ath. 64 a).

Maecenas wrote a *Symposium*, in which Virgil, Horace, and other contemporaries appeared (Serv. on *Aen.* 8. 310). Plutarch's *Symposiaca* are miscellaneous topics discussed on various occasions; his *Conv. sept. sap.* describes a single gathering of the Seven Sages and their discursive and sometimes gnomic discussions. Later examples of the symposium framework for literary and antiquarian exposition are the *Deipnosophists* of Athenaeus and the *Saturnalia* of Macrobius (qq.v.).

The serious philosophical symposium was parodied by Menippus (q.v. 1) and also by Lucian in his *Symposium*.

A closely allied form is the δεῖπνον, or description, with or without mockery of the feast itself. Philoxenus, Hegemon of Thasos (Ath. 5 b), and Matron of Pitane (Ath. 134 d) wrote about banquets in verse which parodied high poetry. The early Hellenistic δειπνητικαὶ ἐπιστολαί by Hippolochus and Lynceus described sumptuous banquets (Ath. 128 c). Censorious descriptions of vulgar banquets are found in Roman satire, notably Hor. *Sat.* 2. 8 and the *Cena Trimalchionis* of Petronius.

R. Hirzel, *Der Dialog* (1895); J. Martin, *Symposion* (1931), (analysis of τόποι). M. Co.

**SYNCRETISM,** a word with a curious history, for which see J. Moffatt in Hastings, *ERE*, s.v. It is now used to denote a phenomenon very common in the later stages of ancient religion. While in the earlier periods the theory of the identity of the gods of different nations (cf. INTERPRETATIO ROMANA) was prevalent, in practice each community normally continued to worship its own deities, or if it imported those of another, regarded them as foreign and often gave them a more or less foreign cult. But from about the generation after Alexander it became more and more usual to identify gods of various nations in practice, thus producing cults of a mixed nature, and also to blend together deities of the same racial or national origin but different functions. Perhaps the earliest example of the former process is the Alexandrian cult of Sarapis (q.v.). Here we have an Egyptian god, Usar-Api, i.e. Osiris-Apis, himself no doubt the result of a certain amount of blending of native worships. But his cult-legend represents him as coming from the Black Sea, the foundation of his Alexandrian ritual was partly due to the Eumolpid Timotheus, the initiative in the matter was taken by Ptolemy I, the god was variously identified with Asclepius, Zeus, and Pluto (Tac. *Hist.* 4. 83 f.), and the statue was a Greek work, a Hades with some attributes foreign to him on Greek soil. All this was a State cult, intended perhaps to reconcile Greek and Egyptian elements in the mixed Ptolemaic kingdom. It does not appear to have excited any opposition or nationalistic feeling, at all events among Greeks, if only because earlier movements had tended somewhat in the same direction (see Kern, *Relig. d. Griech.* iii. 145 ff.). Certainly the spread of similar mixed cults was rapid, and current theological speculation at least kept pace with the facts of actual worship. At once an example of these movements and an instance of syncretism involving comparatively little but the blending of native elements is the very common Hellenistic identification of Apollo (q.v.) with Helios, and hence with various non-Greek sun-gods.

Naturally, syncretism is most conspicuous in those worships which never had been national within the classical area, for instance that of Isis. The *locus classicus* for this is Apuleius, *Met.* 11. 5, where a long speech put into the goddess's mouth identifies her with ten different figures of Mediterranean or Anatolian cult. Mithraism (q.v.) manifestly had syncretistic elements; indeed, solar religions seem to have lent themselves especially to it, see, e.g., the long and fantastic list of identifications of the 'Heracles' of Tyre, Nonnus, *Dion.* 40. 369 ff., while theoretically the tendency in late times to identify all gods with the sun (Macrob. *Sat.* 1. 17. 2) worked in the same direction. Two incidental results were the occasional formation of compound names for deities, as Κουραφροδίτη (Proclus, *Hymn* 5. 1), and the not uncommon occurrence of late statues showing one god with the attributes of one or several others. Syncretism is perhaps especially characteristic of magic (q.v.): see S. Eitrem in *Symb. Oslo.* 19 (1939), 57 ff.

LITERATURE. No one important work is devoted to the subject, but all treatises on Hellenistic and imperial cults have chapters or sections dealing with it. The latest is Nilsson, *GGR* i². 602 and ii. 555 ff., who tends to regard all identification of Greek and foreign deities whether in early or late periods as a form of syncretism. Cf. also F. C. Grant *et al.*, *Hellenistic Religions, The Age of Syncretism* (U.S.A. 1953). H. J. R.; H. W. P.

**SYNESIUS** of Cyrene, *c.* A.D. 370–413, Christian Neoplatonist. He was a pupil of Hypatia at Alexandria, but more an orator and poet than a thinker and scholar. He is at his best in his 9 hymns, 156 letters, and rhetorical discourses on Kingship and Dion, the latter being a powerful attack on the contemporary decline of humane culture, whether in the exaggerated asceticism of Christian monks or in the superstitious theurgy of pagans. He shared Neoplatonic interest in the occult (e.g. the Chaldaean oracles, q.v.) and wrote on divination by dreams. His wife and brother were Christians; he was probably a catechumen as early as 399 when he visited Constantinople to win tax remission for Libya. Partly because of his ability to deal with government authorities he was elected bishop of Ptolemais (Libya) in 410. He accepted the charge after six months of hesitation, since the decision required surrendering the cultivated life of a sporting gentleman and accepting doctrines like the resurrection which to him were symbol rather than plain prose.

Opuscula and hymns, ed. N. Terzaghi (1939–44); Letters, ed. R. Hercher, *Epist. Gr.* (1873). H.-I. Marrou in A. Momigliano (ed.), *The Conflict between Paganism and Christianity in the fourth century* (1963). H. C.

**SYNOECISMUS** (συνοικισμός), the joining of several communities into one city-state (*see* POLIS). According to the common Greek opinion it was a single act, performed by a single person, as in the case of the most famous synoecismus, that of Athens by Theseus. In fact, the unification of Attica into one State was produced by a long-continued development, and so it may have been in many other instances. There were different kinds of synoecismus. (1) Several towns of a district effected a political union, the government being centred in one of them, or in a newly founded city. (2) In districts containing only one town the rural population was gathered into this as the only fortified place. (3) Two cities were amalgamated into one, perhaps by the will of some superior authority, e.g. a Hellenistic king. (4) In a tribal State a city was founded as a political centre for the districts occupied by villages and farms. In the second and third type of synoecismus the population was actually transplanted; in most cases the synoecismus was a merely political act (cf. Thuc. 2. 15). It was the most important means by which a tribal State could turn into a *polis*, and it always meant the common recognition of one or more city gods.

V. Ehrenberg, *The Greek State*² (1969). V. E.

**SYPHAX** (Σόφαξ), chief of a Numidian tribe, the Masaesyles, in north Africa, with capitals at Siga and Cirta. He wore a diadem like a Hellenistic monarch, while Phoenician, not Berber, was his official court language. In a war against Carthage (ending in 212 B.C.), he received some support from the Scipios in Spain. He overran part of the territory of his neighbour Masinissa (q.v.) and tried to retain the friendship of both Rome and Carthage, but was won over to the latter by Sophonisba (q.v.). He fought against the Roman expeditionary force led by Scipio, who burnt his camp. Defeated at Campi

Magni, he fled to his kingdom where he was beaten in battle and captured by Laelius and Masinissa (203). He died in imprisonment in Italy.

For coinage see J. Mazard, *Corpus Nummorum Numidiae Maure-taniaeque* (1955), 17 ff. H. H. S.

**SYRACUSE** (*Συράκουσαι*, modern *Siracusa*), on the east coast of Sicily, was founded by the Corinthians, led by the *oikistes* Archias, *c.* 734 B.C. Its early government was aristocratic, the *gamoroi* forming an élite whose lands were worked by underprivileged natives (*killyrioi*). Seventh- and sixth-century prosperity is attested by colonies at Acrae and Camarina (qq.v.) and at Casmenae (*Monte Casale*), as well as by surviving architectural remains. Defeated by Hippocrates (q.v. 1), the *gamoroi* were expelled in a democratic revolution. Gelon (q.v.) espoused their cause, making himself tyrant of the city of whose empire he thus became the founder. His brother Hieron (q.v. 1) confirmed Syracusan primacy and added a cultural splendour.

Soon after Hieron's death Syracuse regained demo-cratic freedom but lost her empire. The democracy operated through an assembly and council (*βουλή*); annual *στρατηγοί*, whose number varied, formed the chief execu-tive. For a short time a device resembling ostracism (q.v.), called *πεταλισμός*, sought to check abuse of power. In 412, after Athens' defeat, the democracy became more com-plete by the reforms of Diocles (q.v. 1), but Dionysius I (q.v.) soon established his tyranny, preserving neverthe-less the accepted organs of the constitution.

The new democracy after 466 had difficulties with the tyrants' ex-soldiers and new citizens, and faced wars with Acragas and with the Sicels under Ducetius (q.v.). But these were surmounted, as later were the wars with Athens (427–424 and 415–413), in which the statesman-ship of Hermocrates (q.v.) was influential. After 406 Carthage was the chief enemy. Dionysius I fought three Carthaginian wars, and more than once the Syracusans were reduced to great straits. But the early fourth century was a period of great prosperity. Rigorously but astutely guided by her tyrant, Syracuse controlled the greater part of Sicily and much of south Italy. Dionysius II enjoyed ten peaceful years before Dion (q.v.) challenged his rule (356); thereafter Syracusan affairs became in-creasingly anarchic, and the city's power and population declined. Timoleon (q.v.) restored the situation, intro-ducing a moderately oligarchic government on the Corin-thian model, but after twenty years this was overthrown by Agathocles (q.v.), who made himself first tyrant (317) and later king (305/4).

At Agathocles' death (289) a further period of insta-bility ensued. A new tyrant Hicetas (288–278) was de-feated by Carthage; Pyrrhus (q.v.) remedied the situation but was unable to revive the empire of Dionysius and Agathocles. After his withdrawal, conflict with the Mamertini in Messana produced a new leader who as King Hieron II (q.v.) led Syracuse into a prosperous Indian summer. By now, however, Syracusan indepen-dence existed by courtesy of the Romans, and when in 215 Hieronymus, Hieron's successor, preferred Carthage to Rome its end was at hand. After a long siege (213–211), in which Archimedes (q.v.) played a substantial part, M. Claudius Marcellus sacked the city.

Under Rome Syracuse became a *civitas decumana* and the governmental centre, retaining both its beauty and a comparative importance. It suffered at Verres' hands, and in 21 B.C. received an Augustan colony, but its prosperity continued beyond the Frankish spoliation of A.D. 280 to its capture by the Arabs in A.D. 878. Exten-sive catacombs attest its importance in the early Christian period.

The original foundation lay on the island of Ortygia

but soon spread to the mainland (Achradina), the two sections being linked by a causeway and bridge. Further expansion took in the districts of Tyche and Temenites, also referred to as Neapolis, where the theatre and other monuments survive. Dionysius I's great fortifications in-cluded the plateau of Epipolae within the defended area.

K. Fabricius, 'Das antike Syrakus', *Klio*, Beiheft 28 (1932); Bérard, *Bibl. topogr.* 96 ff.; Dunbabin, *Western Greeks*; A. G. Woodhead, *The Greeks in the West* (1962); M. P. Loicq-Berger, *Syracuse* (Brussels, 1967); H. P. Drögemüller, *Syrakus* (1969). Constitution. W. Hüttl, *Verfassungsgeschichte von Syrakus* (1929). Coinage. E. Boehringer, *Die Münzen von Syrakus* (1929). A.. G. W.

**SYRIA.** This country (often called by the Greeks Coele Syria, to distinguish it from 'Syria between the rivers' or Mesopotamia) was a satrapy ('Beyond the River') of the Persian Empire till in 332 B.C. it was conquered by Alexander. On his death (323) it was assigned to Lao-medon, who was in 319–318 ejected by Ptolemy I. There-after it was disputed between Ptolemy and Antigonus, till on the latter's death in 301 it was partitioned between Seleucus I, who occupied the north (Syria Seleucis), and Ptolemy I, who retained the south, to which the name Coele Syria was now restricted; the boundary was the river Eleutherus. Despite the three Syrian wars this arrangement remained substantially unchanged till in 201 Antiochus III conquered Coele Syria. During this period the four Phoenician dynasties which had ruled most of the coast were suppressed, and the maritime towns became republics, governed by *suffetes*. The Seleucids, especially Seleucus I, colonized their area intensively, founding at least eight cities and six military colonies of Macedonians. Aradus (q.v.) became a vassal State within the Seleucid empire as early as 259 B.C. Antiochus IV (175–163) encouraged the hellenization of the upper classes, which had already made some progress, and its corollary, civic autonomy. He allowed both the principal Greek colonies and the chief Phoenician towns to issue their own coins, and granted civic charters to many native towns in the interior. The Ptolemies seem to have founded no colonies and governed the interior on a bureaucratic system like the Egyptian.

After Antiochus IV's death the Seleucid power grad-ually declined owing to constant wars between rival claimants to the throne, complicated by Ptolemaic inter-ventions. Taking advantage of the weakness of the central Government, many of the cities obtained their freedom (Tyre, 126 B.C.), and scores of local chiefs carved out principalities for themselves, while four native dynas-ties, those of Commagene, the Ituraeans, the Jews, and the Nabataeans (qq.v.), built up considerable kingdoms. The two branches of the Seleucid house were gradually pushed back to Antioch and to Damascus and its neigh-bourhood, to which the term Coele Syria was now re-stricted. Finally, in 83, Tigranes of Armenia occupied the country, and on his defeat Pompey made Syria a Roman province (64–63). Pompey re-established a num-ber of cities which had been subdued or destroyed by dynasts, notably those subject to the Jewish kingdom, but in general confirmed the existing situation. The pro-vince of Syria thus comprised besides the cities, a few of which were free, the client kingdoms of Commagene and Arabia, the ethnarchy of the Jews, the tetrarchy of the Ituraeans, and many minor tetrarchies in the north. The Parthians invaded Syria in 40 and were ejected by Ven-tidius in 39. Antony gave to Cleopatra the Ituraean tetrarchy, the coast up to the Eleutherus (except Tyre and Sidon), Damascus and Coele Syria, and parts of the Jewish and Nabataean kingdoms.

Syria (which probably included Cilicia Pedias from *c.* 44 B.C. to A.D. 72) was under the Principate an im-portant military command; its legate, a consular, had down to A.D. 70 normally four legions at his disposal.

The client kingdoms were gradually annexed. Commagene (q.v.) was finally incorporated in the province in A.D. 72, Ituraea partly in 24 B.C., partly (Agrippa II's kingdom) c. A.D. 93. Judaea, at first governed by procurators, became in A.D. 70 a regular province ruled by a praetorian legate, who commanded a legion withdrawn from Syria; under Hadrian the province, henceforth usually known as Syria Palaestina, became consular, a second legion being added. The Nabataean kingdom became in A.D. 105 the province of Arabia, ruled by a praetorian legate with one legion. Septimius Severus divided Syria into a northern province with two legions (Syria Coele) and a southern with one legion (Syria Phoenice). Urbanization made little progress under the Empire. Commagene and Arabia were on annexation partitioned into cities, but much of Ituraea was added to the territories of Berytus, Sidon, and Damascus, and in the rest the villages became the units of government. In Judaea the centralized bureaucracy established by the Ptolemies and maintained by the Seleucids, Maccabees, and Herodians survived in some areas throughout the Principate; in others cities were founded by Vespasian, Hadrian, and the Severan Emperors. Of the minor principalities some, such as Chalcis ad Belum, Emesa, and Arca, became cities, but most seem to have been incorporated in the territories of existing towns. Cities being so scarce, Syria remained a predominantly rural country—hence its importance as a recruiting-ground both for the local legions and for many auxiliary units—and only superficially hellenized: not only the peasants of the wide city territories but even the proletariat of the towns always continued to speak Aramaic.

Wine was grown for export in many parts, chiefly along the coast. Other agricultural products of commercial importance were nuts, various fruits, such as the plums of Damascus or the dates of Jericho, and vegetables, e.g. Ascalonite onions. The principal industries were linen-weaving (at Laodicea and in several Phoenician and north Palestinian towns), wool-weaving (at Damascus), purple-dyeing (on the Phoenician and Palestinian coast), and glass-blowing (at Sidon). The country was greatly enriched by the transit trade from Babylonia, Arabia Felix, and the Far East, much of which passed by caravan over the Arabian desert to such emporia as Palmyra, Damascus, Bostra, and Petra, and thence to the coastal ports.

**Seleucid Rulers:**

Seleucus I Nicator 305–281; Antiochus I 281–261; Antiochus II 261–246; Seleucus II 246–226; Ant. Hierax, usurper 241–227; Seleucus III 226–223; Antiochus III the Great 223–187; Achaeus, usurper 220–213; Seleucus IV 187–175; Antiochus IV Epiphanes 175–164; Antiochus V Eupator 164–162; Demetrius I Soter 162–150; Alexander I Balas 150–145; Demetrius II Nicator first reign 145–140; Antiochus VI Dionysus 145–141; Tryphon, usurper, 141–138; Antiochus VII Sidetes 138–129; Demetrius II Nicator, second reign 129–125; Alexander II Zabinas 128–123; Seleucus, son of Demetrius II and Cleopatra was promptly killed by his mother when he declared himself king as Seleucus V; Cleopatra Thea 126; Cleopatra and Antiochus VIII Grypus 125–121; Antiochus VIII Grypus 121–96; Antiochus IX Cyzicenus 114–95; Seleucus VI Epiphanes Nicator 96–95; Demetrius III Philopator 96–88; Antiochus X, Eusebes 95–92; Antiochus IX Philadelphus 93; Philippus I Philadelphus 93–84; Demetrius III Philopator 96–88; Antiochus XII Dionysus 87–84; Tigranes 83–69; Antiochus XIII Asiaticus 69; Philippus II 67–66.

Seleucus I to Antiochus IV: A. J. Sachs and D. I. Wiseman, *Iraq* 1954, 202 ff. From Demetrius I to the end: A. R. Bellinger, *Transactions of the Connecticut Academy of Arts* 1949, 51 ff.

Mommsen, *The Provinces of the Roman Empire* ii (1886), 1–231; E. S. Bouchier, *Syria as a Roman Province* (1916); U. Kahrstedt, 'Syrische Territorien in hellenistische Zeit', *Abh. Ges. Gött., phil.-hist. Kl.*, N.F. xix (1926); R. Dussaud, *Topographie historique de la Syrie antique et médiévale* (1927); id. *La Pénétration des Arabes en Syrie avant l'Islam²* (1955); F. Cumont, *CAH* xi, ch. 15; Jones, *Cities E. Rom. Prov.* 227 ff.; F. M. Heichelheim, *An Economic Survey of Ancient Rome* iv (1938), 120 ff.; A. Poidebard, *La Trace de Rome dans le désert de Syrie* (1934). A. H. M. J.; H. S.

**SYRIAN DEITIES.** Almost all the deities worshipped in Greek and Roman Syria were Semitic. In spite of regional differences, a few main types of cult can be distinguished. One group comprises the cults of high places, of waters and springs, of trees and of stones, especially meteorites. Secondly, the close associations between some animals and certain anthropomorphic deities—particularly the bull, lion, horse, camel, snake, dove, and fish—may imply earlier identifications. The largest group comprises the deities of human form. These are often divinities of agriculture and fertility, of the sky and thunder; they may be protectors, or bringers of military or commercial success; they may represent the sun, moon, or stars. Annual death and resurrection occur in some cults. Most characteristic of Syrian religion were the 'Lord' and 'Lady', the Baal and his consort the Baalat (or El and Elat), pairs of deities who could take many of the above-mentioned forms. Each pair originally protected a Semitic tribe; when the tribe settled, the pair owned the territory, and sometimes their influence spread beyond it.

Certain religious developments reveal the continuing influence of the Babylonian astrologers, the Chaldaei. Deities may be grouped into triads (god, goddess, son; Bel, sun, moon, etc.). Furthermore, when the eternity of astral revolutions was recognized, deities of the skies and stars (e.g. Baalshamin) became omnipotent masters of the universe and eternity, and so of the whole of human life and after-life. Finally, in the Roman period, the Chaldaean syncretistic doctrines tended to weld the Syrian deities into one eternal and omnipotent power, manifest in the Sun.

Worship included ritual banquets, processions in which symbols or statues of the deity were carried, dancing, libations, and sacrifices, divination, sacred prostitution, and mysteries. Imposing temples still stand at Palmyra and Baalbek; others stood at Hierapolis-Bambyce, etc.

The deities of human form are usually depicted in Hellenistic or Roman guise, although many symbols and occasional items of costume survive from earlier periods. Armour and military equipment often aid deities in protection.

Many Semitic deities received approximate Greek or Roman identifications: Bel-Zeus, Allat-Athena, Nergal-Heracles, etc. The Baal was often romanized as Jupiter (Dolichenus, Heliopolitanus, Damascenus; Baalshamin as J. Caelestis). Syrian cults were carried west mostly during the Roman and especially the Severan period, usually by soldiers, slaves, and merchants. Elagabalus and Aurelian (qq.vv.) attempted to establish Syrian solar cults as supreme in Rome. *See also*: ADONIS; ASTARTE; ASTROLOGY; ATARGATIS; BABYLONIA; BELUS; ELAGABALUS; EUROPUS, DURA; FISH, SACRED; JUPITER DOLICHENUS; METRAGYRTES; PROSTITUTION, SACRED; SOL.

ANCIENT SOURCES. Lucian, *De dea Syria*; Philo of Byblos (*FGrH* 790); Apuleius; *Corpus Inscriptionum Semiticarum*.
ARCHAEOLOGICAL EVIDENCE AND DISCUSSION. Useful synthesis in Cumont, *Rel. or.*, ch. 5. See also: W. W. Baudissin, *Adonis und Eshmun* (1911); J. Février, *La Religion des Palmyréniens* (1932); Du Mesnil du Buisson, *Les Tessères et les monnaies de Palmyre* (1962); Dura Europos, Preliminary and Final Excavation Reports; articles in *Syria* and *Mélanges de l'Université St.-Joseph*. M. A. R. C.

**SYRINX** (Σύριγξ), a nymph loved by Pan (q.v.). She ran away from him and begged the earth, or the river nymphs, to help her; she became a reed-bed, from which Pan made his pipe (σύριγξ).

Ov. *Met.* 1. 689 ff.; Servius on Verg. *Ecl.* 2. 31.

**SYRTES,** the shallow waters lying between Tunisia, Tripolitania, and Cyrenaica. The Greater Syrtis (*Gulf of Sidra*) formed the south-east corner of this ill-reputed Mediterranean bay, the Lesser Syrtis (*Gulf of Gabès*) the south-west. Legends, possibly propagated to protect Phoenician trade-monopoly, exaggerated the dangers of the Syrtic Sea, which failed to hamper the commerce of the Phoenician Tripolis to the south or the Greek Pentapolis to the west; to the west Meninx (*Djerba*), the mythical island of the Lotus-eaters, did a prosperous trade in purple dye, and Tacape (*Gabès*) and Taparura (*Sfax*) were flourishing ports. W. N. W.

**SYSSITIA** (συσσίτια; technically ἀνδρεῖα or φιδίτια) were mess-companies, among which the citizen body was apportioned at Sparta and in the cities of Crete. At Sparta membership (obtained by co-optation) was a necessary qualification for full citizenship, and each mess-mate was bound to provide from his allotted estate a fixed ration of food on pain of disfranchisement. On their size ancient opinion varied between about fifteen and about 300. How they were related to other social institutions (*see* SPARTA) is unknown. The Cretan *syssitia* were formed by voluntary grouping round a leader of good family; their upkeep was at State cost.

According to Aristotle (*Pol.* 1272<sup>b</sup>33) *syssitia* also existed at Carthage. These probably were confined to the aristocracy.

Plut. *Lyc.* 12; Strabo 10. 480, 483. M. C.; W. G. F.

# T

**TABELLARII,** freedmen or slaves employed as couriers by the State and by companies and private citizens of importance. To reduce costs, friends might share their services; and under the Republic the couriers of the State and of the *publicani* would carry private mail for important men. An eminent Roman, when abroad, would put someone in Rome in charge of forwarding (as Caesar did when in Gaul). But for reasons of security—especially in times of trouble—it was essential to have one's own trusted letter-carriers for confidential messages. A good messenger, in the best conditions, could apparently cover 60 Roman miles or more in a day. In the Principate, the *cursus publicus* (*see* POSTAL SERVICE) used highly organized imperial *tabellarii*, but did not carry private mail. These *tabellarii* disappear by the third century A.D. Their functions were in the main taken over by *frumentarii* and later *agentes in rebus* (q.v.).

The word is also used (cf. *ILS* 23) for stones showing subdivisions of a mile on Roman roads (q.v.). E. B.

**TABULA BANTINA** is a bronze tablet found in the eighteenth century near Bantia (q.v.). On one side is inscribed the Oscan text of a local law which is of great importance for the study of Oscan; on the other the fragmentary Latin text of a Roman law. The only extant clauses of the Roman measure concern the prescription of penalties for failure to obey and the imposition of an oath of obedience upon magistrates and senators. The demand for a senatorial oath strongly suggests that the measure was the work of a Popularis (q.v.) in the post-Gracchan years. Precise identification is more difficult, but the law is almost certain provision for the appointment of non-senatorial *iudices* and its apparently extensive publication lend weight to the view that it was one of a series of measures regulating the operations and composition of the extortion court (*see* REPETUNDAE). The *lex Servilia* of Glaucia (101 or 100 B.C.) is a possibility; so is the *lex Acilia* (perhaps of *c.* 111 B.C.).

Mommsen, *CIL* i². 440 f.; E. Vetter, *Handbuch der italischen Dialekte* (1953), i. 13 ff.; A. Passerini, *Athenaeum* 1934, 122 ff.; G. Tibiletti, *Athenaeum* 1953, 57 ff.; E. Yarnold, *AJPhil.* 1957, 163 ff. E. S. S.

**TABULA HEBANA** is a bronze tablet found in 1947 at Magliano in the Tiber valley near the site of the ancient township of Heba. It is probably the second tablet of at least three on which was inscribed the text of a *rogatio* of A.D. 19 conferring honours upon the dead Germanicus

(cf. Tac. *Ann.* 2. 83). The *rogatio* is worded in the form of a senatorial decree, and its publication in this form on permanent tablets suggests that its projected presentation to the people for conversion into a *lex* was viewed as purely ceremonial. The inscription is important chiefly for the light which it throws on the conduct of consular and praetorian elections in the early Principate and for the details which it provides of the procedure known as *destinatio* (q.v.). Other major issues upon which it has with less justification been claimed to have some bearing include the procedure of voting in the reformed centuriate assembly of the Republic, and the nature and structure of the newly reorganized *ordo equester* (*see* EQUITES).

TEXT. *Not. Scav.* 1947, 49 ff.; *AJPhil.* 1954, 225 ff.; Ehrenberg and Jones, *Documents* (1954), 76 ff.
COMMENT. *PP* 1950, *passim*; G. Tibiletti, *Principe e magistrati repubblicani* (1953), *passim*, with accompanying bibliography. *See also under* DESTINATIO. E. S. S.

**TABULA PONTIFICUM,** a whitened board set up yearly by the Pontifex Maximus in the Regia, with the magistrates' names, recorded by the day events in which the pontifical college took ceremonial action, e.g. dedications, festivals, triumphs, eclipses, famines, prodigies; political events entered solely in their sacral connexion. The use of the *tabula* may date from the fifth century B.C., but—to judge from Livy's records of prodigies and the state of the *fasti* (q.v.)—its material was not given systematic archival form until *c.* 300 B.C., presumably on the Ogulnian reform of the pontifical college. In due course it formed the basis for the composition of the *annales maximi* (*c.* 123 B.C.).

Cic. *De Or.* 2. 12. 52; Servius ad Verg. *Aen.* 1. 373; Cato, *Orig.* bk. 4, fr. 77 (Peter). O. Seeck, *Die Kalendartafel der Pontifices* (1885); De Sanctis, *Stor. Rom.* i. 16; Beloch, *Röm. Geschichte*, 86; J. E. A. Crake, *CPhil.* 1940, 375 ff.; P. Fraccaro, *JRS* 1957, 59 ff. A. H. McD.

**TABULAE IGUVINAE.** At Gubbio (Iguvium, q.v.), there were discovered in 1444 nine bronze tablets of varying sizes (the largest now surviving measures 33 by 22 in., the smallest 16 by 12), engraved on one or both sides partly in the native, partly in the Latin alphabet. Two of them were taken to Venice in 1540 and lost; the remaining seven are still at Gubbio. These are the famous Iguvine Tables. The oldest was written *c.* 200 B.C. and the latest probably after the conclusion of the Social War in 89 B.C. The text contains the proceedings and liturgy of a brotherhood of priests, the *frater atiieřiur* ('Fratres

Atiedii', apparently in origin a *nomen gentilicium*), not unlike the Roman Arval brethren. This religious corporation was connected with one of the original ten divisions of the Iguvine people (cf. the Roman *curiae*) and in it certain *gentes* (Petronii, Vucii) were prominent.

The ceremonies include the purification of the Fisian Mount (the city of Iguvium), in which sacrifice is offered to the triad Jupiter Grabovius, Mars Grabovius, and Vofionus Grabovius (cf. the Roman triad Jupiter, Mars, Quirinus) before the three gates of the city and to Treba Jovia, Fisus Sancius (cf. Dius Fidius, Sancus), and Tefer Jovius (god of the hearth) behind the three gates of the city; the lustration of the people of Iguvium in which sacrifice is offered to the triad Çerfus Martius (a male equivalent of Ceres), Prestota Çerfia daughter of Çerfus Martius (cf. Persephone-Hecate), and Torsa Çerfia daughter of Çerfius Martius (cf. Core) and a threefold circuit of the assembled people is made (cf. the Roman *lustratio* in which sacrifice was offered to Mars); sacrifices in the event of unfavourable auspices offered to Dicamnus Jovius, Ahtus Jupiter, and Ahtus Mars (Jupiter and Mars as oracles; cf. Latin *Aius*); a private sacrifice of a dog on behalf of the *gens* Petronia (? part of an ancestor cult) to Hondus (cf. Χθόνιος) Jovius; sacrifices at the festival of Semo on behalf of the ten 'decuries' of the Iguvine people offered to Jupiter Sancius; the procession through the fields to the grove (of Jupiter) where sacrifice is made to Pomonus Popdicus (cf. Etr. *Fufluns* = Bacchus-Dionysus) and Vesona Pomoni Popdici (a spring-time vegetation ritual for which cf. the Roman *floralia* and the Oscan bronze table from Agnone). In scope, content, and antiquity the Iguvine Tables surpass all other documents for the study of Italic religion. In many details they show resemblance to Roman ritual and cult but such analogies must be used with extreme caution, particularly since the Tables record a relatively developed stage of Iguvine religion. *See* LUSTRATION. They are also the main source of our knowledge of Umbrian.

F. Buecheler, *Umbrica* (1883), is still important. C. D. Buck, *A Grammar of Oscan and Umbrian²* (1928), texts and glossary; A. von Blumenthal, *Die iguvinischen Tafeln* (1931), discusses numerous details, but is prone to dubious conjecture; G. Devoto, *Tabulae Iguvinae³* (1962), gives much attention to matters of religion; I. Rosenzweig, *Ritual and Cults of Pre-Roman Iguvium* (1937), is a usable compilation; J. W. Poultney, *The Bronze Tables of Iguvium* (1959); A. J. Pfiffig, *Religio Iguvina* (1964). *See also* the bibliography to the article RELIGION, ITALIC. J. W.; R. M. O.

**TABULARIUM.** (1) The record-office at Rome, probably serving chiefly the adjacent *aerarium Saturni*, built by Q. Lutatius Catulus (q.v. 3) in 78 B.C. (*CIL* vi. 1314–15). The building is trapezoidal in plan and lies between the two summits of the Capitol; its main front was towards the Campus Martius. On the opposite side, closing the west end of the Forum, the elevation consisted of a massive substructure of ashlar masonry with an arcade of eleven arches flanked by Doric half columns above it. A second story of Corinthian columns, now disappeared, was probably added in Flavian times. A stairway from the *Forum* climbed through the ground-floor of the substructure to the front hall of the building. The first floor contained a service corridor, leading from the top of the *Porticus Deorum Consentium* to two floors of eastern strong-rooms. The arcade with shops or offices masks two inaccessible vaulted undercrofts suggestive of two large asymmetrical halls, now vanished, at the level of the upper story. *See* ARCHITECTURE II. I.

R. Delbrueck, *Hellenistische Bauten in Latium* (1907), i. 23 ff.; Nash, *Pict. Dict. Rome* ii. 402 ff.

(2) Other *tabularia* in Rome were the Aventine *Templum Cereris*, for plebiscites and *senatus consulta*; *Atrium Libertatis*, the censors' registry of punishments and citizen-rolls; *Aedes Nympharum*, the censors' tax-registry; *Tabularium Caesaris*, for cadastral records; *Tabularium castrense*, for the imperial household.

(3) Taxation sub-offices (*CIL* vi. 8431).

(4) *Tabularium Caesaris* in provinces for imperial rescripts, etc. (*CIL* x. 7852).

(5) *Tabularium Caesaris* in provincial capitals for tax-returns, census, imperial domain-land, birth-registration (S.H.A. *Vit. Marc.* 6).

(6) Military *tabularia* in legionary fortresses and frontier forts (*CIL* viii. 2852).

(7) *Tabularia civitatum* for municipal or cantonal records and local taxation.

See for (2–7), O. Hirschfeld, *Die kaiserlichen Verwaltungsbeamten³* (1963); J. Marquardt, *Römische Staatsverwaltung²* i, ii (1881–5); Mommsen, *Ges. Schr.* (1905–13), v. 329. I. A. R.; D. E. S.

**TACFARINAS,** a Numidian, formerly an auxiliary trooper, took to brigandage and stirred up a serious insurrection in Africa (A.D. 17). Despite victories won by three proconsuls in succession, Furius Camillus, L. Apronius, and Q. Junius Blaesus (the last of whom was acclaimed *imperator* by the troops), the elusive enemy prosecuted his depredations until trapped and killed at Auzia by P. Cornelius Dolabella (24). The dedication of Dolabella to *Victoria Augusta* has been found at Lepcis (*AE* 1961, 107).

R. Syme, *Studies in Rom. Econ. and Soc. Hist. in Honour of A. C. Johnson* (1951), 113 ff. R. S.

**TACHYGRAPHY.** (1) GREEK. Diogenes Laertius (*Vit. Xen.* 2. 48) says that Xenophon was the first to use signs to represent spoken words (πρῶτος ὑποσημειωσάμενος τὰ λεγόμενα); but whether this represents anything like systematic tachygraphy is quite uncertain. The same may be said of the word ὀξυγράφος in the LXX version of Ps. xlv. 2. Nothing is really known of Greek shorthand except from papyri and wax-tablets found in Egypt, which give specimens of tachygraphy from the second century A.D. onwards, and portions of manuals from the end of the third century. These show a fully organized system, composed of a syllabary and a (so-called) Commentary, consisting of groups of words, arranged in fours or occasionally eights, with a sign attached to each, which had to be memorized. The tetrads include some element of association (e.g. one sign represents Γανυμήδης, οἰνοχοεῖ, νέκταρ, μιξοβάρβαρος), but oftener it is not discernible. Such a system is referred to in Basil. *De Virg.* 31 (Migne, *PG* xxx. 733). The British Museum has a portion of two manuals (Papp. 2561, 2562), and a wax-tablet book with exercises; and this material is supplemented by papyri from Antinoë and elsewhere.

(2) LATIN. According to Plutarch (*Cato Mi.* 23), Cicero introduced shorthand at Rome, and as he refers to it by a Greek name (διὰ σημείων, *Att.* 13. 32) he probably derived it from Greece. The Latin system, which shows affinity with the Greek, is associated with the name of Cicero's freedman, Tiro, and the lists of symbols which have come down to us are known as *notae Tironianae*, but the medieval representations of them have been elaborated to an extent that would make them useless for actual reporting. They are sometimes used for scholia.

In the ancient systems of shorthand, as in the modern, one sign may have several interpretations, and in order to interpret shorthand records it is necessary to have a clue to the subject, and (often) to remember something of what was said. Thus stock phrases such as ὦ ἄνδρες Ἀθηναῖοι or τί δεῖ μακρολογεῖν were represented by single signs.

H. J. M. Milne, *Greek Shorthand Manuals* (1934); C. Wessely, *Ein System altgriechischer Tachygraphie* (1895); A. Mentz, *Arch. Pap.* viii. 34; F. W. G. Foat, *JHS* xxi. 238; V. Gardthausen, *Griechische*

*Palaeographie*² (1913), ii. 270 ff.; E. M. Thompson. *Introd. to Gr. and Lat. Palaeography* (1912), 71 ff.; H. Foerster, *Abriss Lat. Paläographie* (1949), 191. F. G. K.

**TACITUS** (1), CORNELIUS (*PW* 395). We do not know Tacitus' parentage, year of birth or death, or even *praenomen*. He was born *c.* A.D. 56, probably of Gallic or north Italian stock, and began his official career under Vespasian. He married Agricola's daughter in 77, became *praetor* and *XVvir* in 88 (*Agr.* 9. 6, *Hist.* 1. 1, *Ann.* 11. 11). Away from Rome when Agricola died in 93, he returned to witness the last years of Domitian's savagery (*Agr.* 3. 2 and 44). *Consul suffectus* in 97, he pronounced the funeral oration over Verginius Rufus (q.v.), and in 100 led Pliny in prosecuting Marius Priscus for extortion. His reputation for eloquence was high, but he had already turned to historical writing, and the *Histories* appear to have been completed during the following decade. He may have governed a military province; he was proconsul of Asia, probably in 112/13. A sentence in *Ann.* 2. 61 has been taken as written after 115; but this may well be a false inference. It is not even known whether he lived to finish the *Annals*.

The *Dialogus* is no longer regarded as Tacitus' first work from about 80, but dated at least twenty years later. A few scholars still deny its Tacitean authorship; most accept it as exemplifying the difference of style required by a non-historical work. The author, discussing the decline of Roman oratory, reveals mastery of argument and characterization, and a rare sense of historical perspective. The *De vita Iulii Agricolae*, published in 98, describes the life of his father-in-law, the larger part being devoted to the scene of Agricola's greatest achievements, Britain. Basically a *laudatio* of the dead man, the work is at the same time an apology for the loyal administrator under the tyranny of Domitian—not least Tacitus himself, and the Emperor Trajan. The full narrative of affairs in Britain was to be given in the *Histories*.

To 98, too, belongs the *De origine et situ Germanorum*, a description of the various tribes north of Rhine and Danube. Again Tacitus employs a familiar genre, though as an ethnological treatise it is singularly incoherent and based on out-of-date material. Subsidiary themes are that of the noble savage, contrasted with the corruption of Rome, and of the constant threat to the Empire: 'tam diu Germania vincitur'.

These are short monographs. Two longer works narrate imperial history from A.D. 14 to 96. The first has no manuscript title, but is usually called the *Histories*: beginning in 69, it presumably ended with Domitian's assassination. Four books and twenty-six chapters of the fifth alone survive, but they give a comprehensive picture of Civil War, containing an extraordinary gallery of ambitious intriguers and incompetent rulers, with one Emperor who 'changed for the better', Vespasian. What Tacitus related of Domitian may be gauged from the *Agricola*, and from the portrait of him in 70—'nondum ad curas intentus, sed stupris et adulteriis filium principis agebat' (*Hist.* 4. 2).

The second is the *Annals*, a conventional title (cf. *Ann.* 4. 32, 13. 31), for in the MS. the heading is 'ab excessu diui Augusti'. We know of sixteen books, though parts of 5 and 6 and the whole of 7–10 are missing, and 16 breaks off in A.D. 66, before Nero's death. The number of books in *Histories* and *Annals* is uncertain: St. Jerome appears to know of thirty altogether (*Comm. in Zach.* 3. 14), but scholars do not agree whether the *Annals* contained eighteen books and the *Histories* twelve, or sixteen and fourteen respectively. The hexadic structure visible in the *Annals* supports the former division. The arrangement is basically annalistic, each year containing sections on home and provincial affairs; but often the doings of the Emperor take up virtually the whole year (e.g. *Ann.*

14. 1–19), while elsewhere a single provincial episode takes precedence (*Ann.* 6. 31–7), even running over the year's limit, with the characteristic reason, 'quo requiesceret animus a domesticis malis' (ibid. 38).

In composing these works, Tacitus drew partly on historical works now lost (of Aufidius Bassus, the Elder Pliny, Cluvius Rufus, Fabius Rusticus, Vipstanus Messalla), partly on public records and his own experience. Very rarely does he refer explicitly to conflicts between his sources (*Hist.* 3. 28; *Ann.* 13. 20, 14. 2); normally he appears to select and combine their evidence without acknowledgement, as if regarding controversy as unfitting to a serious work of history. His technique for the later books of the *Histories*, for which few written sources would be available, we must judge from the uncertain evidence of Pliny (*Ep.* 6. 16, 7. 33).

But his view is also coloured by his own experience. Reacting against the Principate, Tacitus looks back longingly on the 'free' institutions of the Republic ('libertatem et consulatum', *Ann.* 1. 1; cf. 4. 63); the Principate may have benefited the provinces and secured peace (*Ann.* 1. 2; *Hist.* 1. 1), but the overwhelming power thus centred in one man blunted the moral sense of even experienced rulers (*Ann.* 6. 48), and rapidly reduced the ruled to servility and flattery. Thus the Principate tended towards *regnum*, where Tacitus found 'fugas ciuium, urbium euersiones, fratrum coniugum parentum neces aliaque solita regibus' (*Hist.* 5. 8; cf. *Ann.* 6. 1, and 12. 66) and even Augustus is damned with faint praise, or belauded only for contrast with his worse successors (e.g. *Ann.* 1. 46; 3. 5; 13. 3). Roman *virtus* had stagnated into an inactive and inglorious temper; Augustus had lured citizens into the Principate 'dulcedine otii' (*Ann.* 1. 2); *pax* merely cloaked *ignavia*. The Emperors had neglected military glory: Tiberius preferred diplomacy to arms (*Ann.* 2. 64 and 4. 32); Caligula's campaigns were a farce (*Germ.* 37 and *Hist.* 4. 15); Claudius had merely reconquered Britain (*Agr.* 13); and Nero's crimes had alienated the soldiery (*Ann.* 15. 67). Domitian had been warlike, but in the wrong way, and Tacitus shrinks from enumerating the Roman lives he lost (Orosius 7. 10. 4).

Nor was the vaunted *pax Augusta* fruitful or prosperous, at least in Rome (*Hist.* 1. 1; *Ann.* 1. 10); what galls Tacitus is the lack of independence and courage among those who should most have shown it. While lower ranks provided shining examples of loyalty and heroism (*Ann.* 13. 44 and 15. 57), most nobles and senators could only cringe to a despot, 'homines ad seruitutem paratos' (*Ann.* 3. 65; cf. 14. 13), and though L. Silanus *did* put up a fight (*Ann.* 16. 9), the 'patientia seruilis' of Nero's victims rouses Tacitus' scornful pity (*Ann.* 16. 16). Yet he disapproves of the Stoic-minded and their theatrical gestures: his ideal was the prudence of Agricola (*Agr.* 42) or of L. Piso (*Ann.* 6. 10).

Throughout these eighty odd years, Tacitus discerns the wrath of the gods working, gods more eager to punish than to save (*Hist.* 1. 3; *Ann.* 4. 1; 16. 16). His task is gloomy, to record the suspicions of Tiberius, played upon by informers; Claudius the helpless tool of freedmen or wives; the vanity and vice of Nero—all resulting in baseless accusations and judicial murders. 'Primum facinus noui principatus' (*Ann.* 1. 6) is echoed by 'prima nouo principatu mors' (*Ann.* 13. 1) for the reign of Nero. Given the opportunity of recounting victories won by Germanicus or Corbulo, Tacitus can expand indeed (*Ann.* 2. 18; 13. 39); otherwise he feels a painful contrast with republican historians—'nobis in arto et inglorius labor' (*Ann.* 4. 32). Better times undeniably had come with Nerva (*Agr.* 3; *Hist.* 1. 1), but he fears that the past century, in his account, will seem a sombre period (*Ann.* 4. 33).

To dissipate this feeling of monotony and rivet the

reader's attention Tacitus marshals all his resources, forming a style unique and perfectly adapted to purpose. He keeps us continually on the alert. His vocabulary is large and varied: note the different phrases for dying or committing suicide or for 'evening was approaching'. To the classical word Tacitus prefers an older, a simple verb to the usual compound, new forms to hackneyed. Echoes of poetry, subtle reminiscences of Virgil, Graecisms, all make their appeal. Words are left uncoupled, grouped in strange and striking order ('tamen' pushed to the end; *Ann.* 2. 57), or thrust into violent prominence.

Though Tacitus can elaborate sentences of length and complexity, he prefers (like Sallust) rapidity and shortness; periodic structure is deliberately abandoned. Gone are the temporal clauses of Livy, gone the superlatives of Cicero. Instead we have intensity and brevity, gained by skilful use of Historic Infinitives, or adjectives that become practically Active Past Participles ('gnarus', 'certus', 'dubius'), by omission of verbs, by compression, the eventual effect being often to question the validity of the original assertion or to lead the reader unawares into accepting the least creditable of several alternative explanations of a character's action. So intensely personal is his style that he rarely quotes verbatim, save for damning effect—a phrase revealing Tiberius' tortured soul, a brutal joke of Nero's, a tribune's bluntness (*Ann.* 6. 6, 14. 59, 15. 67). His normal method of adaptation may be seen most clearly (and perhaps typically) in his version of a speech of Claudius in *Ann.* 11. 24, compared with the extant original (*ILS* 212).

Throughout shines the quality Pliny noted in Tacitus' speeches, elevation. Tacitus believes in the dignity and moral effect of history (*Ann.* 3. 65). He will not chronicle petty events (*Ann.* 13. 31): his unwillingness to mention spades and shovels (*Ann.* 1. 65), or a garden-cart (*Ann.* 11. 32) leads to circumlocutions recalling French tragedy, but he never drops into mere pomposity; he knows history is a great theme, to be adorned by *fides* and *eloquentia* worthy of it (*Ann.* 4. 34). This consciousness informs his whole manner, whether in comment on nobles who competed at Nero's bidding, 'quos fato perfunctos ne nominatim tradam, maioribus eorum tribuendum puto' (*Ann.* 14. 14), or sad reflection on the 'ludibria rerum mortalium cunctis in negotiis' (*Ann.* 3. 18).

The style, indeed, is inescapable, making its effect sometimes by long passages, sometimes by sentences, sometimes by one phrase of psychological insight. We may instance Agrippina's murder by her son (*Ann.* 14. 1–9), or the rise and collapse of the Pisonian conspiracy (*Ann.* 15. 48–71); Vitellians and Vespasianists fighting ferociously in the heart of Rome, with onlookers applaud (*Hist.* 3. 82–3), or Germanicus' visit to the Varian camp (*Ann.* 1. 61–2), or the terrible picture of Tiberius' end (*Ann.* 6. 50–1). Great and fatal characters stalk across the stage—Tiberius, Sejanus, the Younger Agrippina, Nero—and these are drawn at length, but Tacitus can in a phrase sum up person or situation: Galba, 'omnium consensu capax imperii nisi imperasset' (*Hist.* 1. 49); Vitellius, 'principatum ei detulere qui ipsum non nouerant' (*Hist.* 3. 86); Claudius Sanctus, pusillanimous leader of disgraced troops, 'effosso oculo dirus ore, ingenio debilior' (*Hist.* 4. 62).

Always the irony remains keen—'proprium humani ingenii est odisse quem laeseris' (*Agr.* 42), 'acerrima proximorum odia' (*Hist.* 4. 70), 'obliuione magis quam clementia' (*Ann.* 6. 14)—or we have Nero's admiral advising him to destroy Agrippina; and after?—'additurum principem defunctae templum et aras et cetera ostentandae pietati' (*Ann.* 14. 3).

His bias against the dynastic system is plain; yet his accuracy, though severely probed by modern criticism, can rarely be impugned. Though sometimes an unfavour-

able interpreter of his facts, he will not blacken even Tiberius or Nero by crediting stupid rumours about them (*Ann.* 4. 11; 16. 6). His picture of capital and court is terrible, but its general truth is incontestable. His gaze is focused upon Rome; when he looks further he approves the sturdy simplicity of north Italy and the provinces (*Ann.* 16. 5), and can pen a moving appeal for the preservation of the Empire (*Hist.* 4. 74). Though mistrustful of 'civilization' and of its debilitating effects, he never despairs of human nature: even the Civil War produced examples of heroism, loyalty, and friendship (*Hist.* 1. 3), and virtue is not confined to past ages (*Ann.* 3. 55). Napoleon called Tacitus a 'traducer of humanity': from one who spent his powers in annihilating humanity this verdict is interesting, but simply untrue. In independent selection and judgement, in essential truth, in the dramatic power and nobility of an enthralling style, Tacitus claims his place among the greatest historians.

Yet his survival hangs upon a slender thread. He was little read in succeeding centuries; later, Orosius (q.v.) and Sidonius (q.v.) appear to know him, and Iordanes paraphrases a passage from the *Agricola*. Then darkness falls, though in the ninth century monks at Fulda apparently possessed the early *Annals*, and the *Germania*. Even now we are dependent upon one manuscript (discovered about 1510) for *Annals* 1–6, and upon one manuscript (the Second Medicean, discovered about 1430) for *Annals* 11–16 and *Histories* 1–5; though the independence of Leidensis B.P.L. 16B has been argued by Mendell and exploited, with questionable success, in Koestermann's recent Teubner texts. *See also* LITERARY CRITICISM, LATIN, § 5.

LIFE AND WORKS. G. Boissier, *Tacite*[6] (1926); C. Marchesi, *Tacito* (1924); P. Wuilleumier, *Tacite, l'homme et l'œuvre* (1949); C. W. Mendell, *Tacitus, the man and his work* (1957: particularly on the MSS.); Syme, *Tacitus*; E. Paratore, *Tacito*[2] (1962); Wight Duff, *Literary History of Rome in the Silver Age*[2] (1964), 447 ff.; *PW* Suppl. xi, 373 ff.

TEXTS. O.C.T. (C. D. Fisher; H. Furneaux); Teubner (Halm–Andresen–Koestermann).

COMMENTARIES. **Annals,** Furneaux–Pelham–Fisher (1896–1907); Draeger–Heraeus–Becher; Nipperdey–Andresen; E. Koestermann (1963– ). **Hist.,** W. A. Spooner (1891); Wolff–Andresen (1914–26); Goelzer (1920); Heraeus[6] (1929); Heubner (1963– ). **Agr. and Germ.,** J. H. Sleeman (1914); **Agr.,** Ogilvie–Richmond (1967); **Germ.,** W. Reeb (1930); Robinson (1935); J. G. C. Anderson (1938); Much–Kienast (1959). **Dial.,** W. Peterson (1893); A. Gudemann[2] (1914).

TRANSLATIONS. **Ann.,** G. C. Ramsay (1904); Goelzer (Budé, 1923–5); J. Jackson (Loeb, 1931); M. Grant (Penguin, 1956). **Hist.**, W. H. Fyfe (1912); Ramsay (1915); C. H. Moore (Loeb, 1925–31); Goelzer (Budé, 1921); K. Wellesley (Penguin, 1964). **Minor Works,** W. H. Fyfe (1908); W. Peterson–M. Hutton (Loeb, 1914). **Agr. and Germ.,** H. Mattingly (Penguin, 1948); A, E. de St. Denis (Budé, 1942); **Germ.,** J. Perret (Budé, 1949). **Dial.,** Goelzer–Bornecque (Budé, 1947).

STYLE, DICTION, AND THOUGHT. Besides works listed above, see: E. Courbaud, *Les Procédés d'art de T. dans les 'Histoires'* (1918); N. Eriksson, *Studien zu den Annalen des T.* (1934); A. Draeger, *Über Syntax und Stil des T.* (1882); E. Löfstedt, *Syntactica* (1933); E. Fraenkel, *Neue Jahrb.* 1932, 218 ff.; B. Walker, *Annals of Tacitus*[2] (1960); C. Questa, *Studi sulle fonti degli Annales*[2] (1963).

LEXICON. A. Gerber and A. Greef, *Lexicon Taciteum* (1903).

M. P. C.; G. B. T.

**TACITUS** (2), MARCUS CLAUDIUS (*PW* 361), was chosen by the Senate to succeed Aurelian in Nov. A.D. 275, being then an elderly senator. He marched east and gained a victory over the Goths who had broken into Pontus, but succumbed to murder, or the threat of it, from his own troops at Tyana (*c*. June 276).

Tacitus certainly favoured the Senate, but he did not effectively restore its authority or give back to it the commands in the army. It was only the hopeful fancy of later historians that painted his reign as a late summer of constitutional government under the Senate.

H. M.; B. H. W.

**TAENARUM** (*Ταίναρον*, more rarely *Ταίναρος*). (1) The central peninsula of south Peloponnesus and its terminal cape, near which stood a Temple of Poseidon of which scanty traces remain. Through a cave near by Heracles traditionally dragged up Cerberus from Hades. The sanctuary enjoyed a right of asylum (cf. Thuc. 1. 133), and private slaves were manumitted there, before an ephor (*IG* v. 1. 1228 ff.). In the later fourth century the district was an important headquarters for mercenaries. Iron was mined near the cape.

(2) A city on the west coast of the above peninsula, later a member of the Eleutherolaconian League (*see* LACONIA), alternatively known as Caenepolis.

A. M. W.; W. G. F.

**TAGES,** an important figure of Etruscan mythology, childlike in appearance but of divine wisdom. Tages was unearthed by a peasant in the fields near Tarquinii and revealed the Etruscan discipline (*libri Tagetici*) to the twelve *lucumones* of Etruria. *See also* TARCHON.

Cf. A. S. Pease on Cic. *Div.* 2. 50; S. Weinstock, *PBSR* 1950, 44; A. Piganiol, *Bull. Soc. Antiqu. de France* 1950, i, 32; R. Herbig, *Charites E. Langlotz* (1957); J. Préaux, *Latomus* 1962, 379.
G. M. A. H.

**TAGOS** (ταγός), the official title borne by the chief magistrate of Thessaly. When a *tagos* was in office, he was the military and civil leader of the Thessalians and their *perioikoi;* but it was not unusual for the *tageia* to be left vacant for some years, and during these periods there was no central organization for the whole country. Although a *tagos* was most commonly appointed to deal with some emergency involving all Thessaly, the office was not a temporary one; once elected, a *tagos* retained his powers indefinitely. The term *tagos* is not used by historians except Xenophon, but the principal leaders, such as Thorax the Aleuad who negotiated the submission to Xerxes, certainly held the *tageia*. Jason (q.v. 2) revived the office in 374 B.C. to legalize his control of Thessaly, but Alexander (5), who claimed the *tageia*, cannot have been legitimately elected. When a new Thessalian Confederacy was formed under Theban influence (*c.* 369), the federal *tageia* ceased to exist, and the principal magistrate was an ἄρχων. A municipal *tageia*, as is attested by inscriptions, survived until Roman times.

E. Meyer, *Theopomps Hellenika* (1909), 218 ff.; F. Gschnitzer, *Anzeiger für die Altertumswissenschaft* 1954, 191; J. A. O. Larsen, *CPhil* 1960, 238 ff.
H. D. W.

**TALOS** (Τάλως, Τάλος), perhaps originally a god (ταλῶς is the Sun and Talaios a Cretan title of Zeus, Hesych. s.vv.), but in mythology the guardian of Crete (originally of Europa, Ap. Rhod., *infra*). He is generally said to have been made of bronze by Hephaestus, but animated; for other accounts see Roscher's *Lexikon*, s.v. He kept strangers off by throwing stones (Ap. Rhod.), or burned them (Simonides in schol. Pl. *Resp.* 337 a), or heated himself red-hot and then clasped them in his arms (Eustathius on Homer, 1893. 6). His vital fluid was kept in by a membrane in his foot; Medea (q.v.) cast him into a magic sleep and cut the membrane, thus killing him.

See Ap. Rhod. *Argon.* 4. 1638 ff., the most circumstantial account, and Cook, *Zeus* i. 719 ff.
H. J. R.

**TALTHYBIUS,** Agamemnon's herald (*Iliad* 1. 320). For some reason his name remains familiar in later writings, while his comrade Eurybates (ibid.) is forgotten. He was the eponym of a herald-clan at Sparta, the Talthybiadae (see Hdt. 7. 134. 1).

**TAMIAI** (ταμίαι) means 'treasurers'. In Athens the most important officials with this title were the *tamiai* of Athena. They were ten in number, appointed annually by lot, one from each of the ten *phylai* (q.v.). According to a law attributed to Solon (q.v.) only *pentakosiomedimnoi* (q.v.) were eligible, but by the fourth century B.C. this

rule was no longer enforced. Their year of office began and ended at the time of the Panathenaea (q.v.). They had charge of the money and treasures of Athena Polias, Athena Nike, and Hermes, on the acropolis. They kept the money in a building called the *opisthodomos* (the location of which is doubtful), and they received and made payments in accordance with the decisions of the people. They paid out money not only for religious purposes, but also for military use (especially during the Peloponnesian War) and to defray other secular expenses. Many of their records are preserved on stone, and are an important source of information about Athenian finance.

In 434 B.C. a similar board of ten *tamiai* of 'the other gods' was instituted to take charge of money and treasures belonging to other Attic shrines, which were now brought together into a single fund. It also was kept in the *opisthodomos*, but separately from the money of Athena. In 406/5 the two boards were replaced by a single board of ten *tamiai* of 'Athena and the other gods'. The two separate boards were re-established by 385, but by 341 they were again replaced by a single board.

After the abolition of the *kolakretai* (q.v.) and the *hellenotamiai* (q.v.) other *tamiai* were instituted to take charge of various funds: the *tamias* of the assembly (ταμίας τοῦ δήμου), the *tamias* of the board for the construction of triremes, the *tamias* of the military fund, and so on.

Inscriptions; Arist. *Ath. Pol.* 47. 1. W. S. Ferguson, *The Treasurers of Athena* (1932).
D. M. M.

**TANAGRA,** the chief town of east Boeotia, with a territory extending to the sea, was more closely bound with Attica, with which it had easy connexions, than was the rest of Boeotia (cf. Hdt. 5. 57). It was an early rival to Thebes; after the Persian Wars it probably stood at the head of the Boeotian Confederacy (Head, *Historia Numorum²*, 348). In 457 the Athenians were defeated here by the Spartans and their allies, and the battles of Oenophyta and Delium were also fought in this district. In the fourth century Tanagra declined in importance, contributing only one boeotarch to the Confederacy, but it flourished in Hellenistic and Roman times (Strabo 403). It is now best known for the lively little Hellenistic terracotta figures, women and groups from daily life, found in its graves. It was the birthplace of the poetess Corinna. The walls are preserved, but little else. *See also* FEDERAL STATES, § 3.

Paus. 9. 20, and Frazer, ad loc.; P-K, *GL* I. ii. 514 f.   T. J. D.

**TANAÏS,** the river Don, and a city at its estuary. The river was usually regarded as the boundary between Europe and Asia. A trade route to Central Asia, by which Ural gold came to the Black Sea, and Greek textiles were carried as far as Mongolia, probably followed the Tanaïs valley. But the Greeks knew little of the river: it was at first confused with the Phasis, and Aristotle and Alexander mistook it for a branch of the Jaxartes (q.v.).

Greek goods were passing up the Don by *c.* 600 B.C. but the city of Tanaïs was probably founded by Panticapaeum *c.* 500 B.C. (to judge by the fairly rich finds beginning at that date). In the first century A.D. it was rebuilt higher up the river, near modern Rostov, but it lost its former prosperity.

E. H. Minns, *Scythians and Greeks* (1913), 566 ff.   M. C.; J. B.

**TANAQUIL,** a woman of noble family of Tarquinii, may well be a historical character (cf. Etruscan θανχvil, etc.). According to the Roman story she married Tarquinius Priscus, son of the Corinthian Demaratus who had settled in Tarquinii and married an Etruscan wife. Spurred on by her forceful character, Tarquinius migrated to Rome where he gained the throne. After his murder by the sons of Ancus Marcius, her bold action secured the succession for her son-in-law Servius Tullius. Another tradition named Tarquin's wife Gaia Caecilia: Pliny (*HN* 8. 194) took this to be an alternative (Roman) name of Tanaquil. He adds that her distaff was preserved in the temple of Sancus, and the robe she made for Tullius in that of Fortuna. In his classic *Die Sage von Tanaquil* (1870) J. Bachofen argued, unacceptably, for matriarchy (*Mutterrecht*) in Etruscan society. H. H. S.

**TANTALUS** (*Τάνταλος*), in mythology, king of Sipylos and the neighbourhood in Lydia, son of Zeus and Pluto (*Πλουτώ*), Hyg. *Fab.* 82. 1; the name is variously corrupted in sundry authors (see Scheuer in Roscher's *Lexikon* v. 75. 25 ff. If Pluto was a minor being of the same kind as Plutus (q.v.), this would seem one of the numerous variants of a union of the sky-father with the earth-mother. It is natural, therefore, that their child should be proverbially wealthy (*Ταντάλου τάλαντα*, Anacreon in Photius, s.v., is an older equivalent of 'the riches of Croesus') and king of a fertile district. He is the ancestor of the Pelopidae (*see* PELOPS), the line being

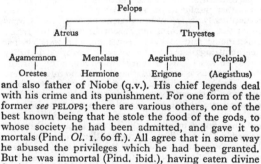

Tantalus
|
Pelops

Atreus — Thyestes

Agamemnon — Menelaus — Aegisthus — (Pelopia)

Orestes — Hermione — Erigone — (Aegisthus)

and also father of Niobe (q.v.). His chief legends deal with his crime and its punishment. For one form of the former *see* PELOPS; there are various others, one of the best known being that he stole the food of the gods, to whose society he had been admitted, and gave it to mortals (Pind. *Ol.* 1. 60 ff.). All agree that in some way he abused the privileges which he had been granted. But he was immortal (Pind. ibid.), having eaten divine food, and so his penalty must be everlasting, for he could not be killed. In Homer (*Od.* 11. 583 ff.) and in most authors (it became almost proverbial for 'tantalizing' in our sense, see Plato, *Prt.* 315 c) he is hungry and thirsty; he stands in water up to his chin, with fruit-laden trees over his head, but when he tries to drink, the water disappears, and if he reaches for the fruit, the wind blows it away. Pindar (ibid. 57 ff.) says a great stone is hung over his head, always threatening to fall, so that the penalty is everlasting fear. Euripides (*Or.* 4 ff.) follows this version, putting Tantalus in the air, not, as usual, in Tartarus. H. J. R.

**TANUSIUS** (*PW* 2) **GEMINUS,** historian of the Late Republic, used by Plutarch (*Caes.* 22. 3) and by Suetonius (*Iul.* 9. 2). Seneca speaks of his Annals as 'ponderosi' (*Ep.* 93. 11), where 'quid vocentur' probably means that Catullus' description of Volusius' histories (36. 1) was applied in jest to Tanusius.

R. Syme, *Sallust* (1964), 96. C. J. F.

**TAPROBANE** (also **Palaesimundu**; later **Salice** and **Sielediba**), Ceylon. First described by Onesicritus and Megasthenes (*c.* 325–300 B.C.) as an island south of India, it was believed by many to be a large land-mass projecting towards Africa (Strabo 15. 690–1; *Peripl. M. Rubr.* 61). It was rediscovered by accident, probably late in the reign of Augustus who died in A.D. 14 (Pliny, *HN* 6. 81 ff.; D. Meredith in *JRS* 1953, 38; R. E. M. Wheeler, *Rome beyond the Imperial Frontiers* (1955), 150, 155 f., 162, 165, 168, 172, 175); Ceylonese envoys visited Rome, and Greek traders henceforth frequented the island.

Yet Ptolemy (*Geog.* 7. 4. 1 ff.), while giving considerable detail and the correct shape, made it fourteen times too large. Many Roman coins, dating from the third century, have been found in Ceylon, though western trade was now conducted intermediately through the Axumites.

Warmington, *Indian Commerce*, esp. 117 ff.; H. Codrington, *Ceylon Coins* (1924); Still, *Journ. R. Asiatic Soc.*, Ceylon Branch xix. E. H. W.

**TARCHON,** founder of Tarquinii and, according to some authorities, of the Etruscan dodecapolis. Tarchon is the son (or brother) of Tyrrhenus, the legendary leader of the Etruscans on their migration from Lydia (Strabo 5. 219), and an ally of Evander (Verg. *Aen.* 8. 506). He is shown on an Etruscan mirror in Florence, watching Tarchies (Tages?) examining a liver for omens (M. Pallottino, *Etruscologia⁵* (1963), pl. xxvii). G. M. A. H.

**TARENTUM** (*Τάρας*, modern *Taranto*), in the 'instep' of the boot-shaped coastline of south Italy, lies on a promontory (now artificially made an island) between a tidal lagoon and a larger bay sheltered by protecting islets, and has a fertile agricultural hinterland. It was founded (traditional date 706 B.C.) by the Partheniae, Spartans supposedly the product of liaisons between Spartan women and Helots; the *oikistes* was Phalanthus. Pottery from Mycenaean date onwards suggests that the site had long been in continuous native occupation before the Greeks established themselves. Tarentine cults and archaic art emphasize the city's Spartan affinities.

Aristocratically governed in the archaic period, Tarentum became a democracy *c.* 475 B.C., perhaps as a repercussion of a heavy defeat at the hands of the Messapii, who had long been hostile neighbours. The decline of Croton after *c.* 450 left it as the leading Greek city in south Italy. In 433/2 it founded a colony at Heraclea (q.v. 1), which became the headquarters of a league of Italiot Greeks. Under the administration of the philosopher Archytas (q.v.) Tarentum reached its zenith in the fourth century. It had a great tradition of artistic and industrial activity, evidenced especially by the sixth-century krater of Vix, by the jewellery and coinage of the fourth and third centuries, and terracotta products throughout the period. Coinage distribution bears witness to considerable trade in the north Adriatic area.

However, the Tarentines had difficulty in maintaining themselves against pressure from the Italian tribes of the interior, and came to depend on the support of foreign mercenary leaders. King Archidamus II of Sparta was defeated by the Lucanians (338); Alexander I of Epirus defeated the Lucanians but quarrelled with his employers (334); Cleonymus of Sparta both quarrelled and was defeated (303). Finally, Pyrrhus (q.v.) of Epirus, at first successful, ultimately abandoned Tarentum to the Romans. The Tarentines, concerned at the Romans' southward advance, had pledged them by treaty (334 B.C.?) not to send warships into the Tarentine gulf. In 282 the Romans assumed a protectorate over Thurii and emphasized the fact by the dispatch of a fleet; the Tarentines forced on a war, relying on Pyrrhus' help. But despite early victories over Rome Pyrrhus went campaigning in Sicily and, on his return, was defeated by the Romans. He withdrew from Italy in 275 and his garrison left Tarentum three years later. Roman terms of surrender and alliance were generous, and Tarentum like the other Greek cities enjoyed greater security henceforward. Livius (q.v. 1) Andronicus, a Tarentine war captive, was a major figure of early Roman literature.

In 213 Hannibal took the city by treachery. Recaptured in 209, it was thoroughly plundered by the Romans. This disaster, and the foundation of a Latin colony at Brundisium (q.v.), led to its decline. Attempts by C. Gracchus and Nero to revive it with Italian settlers largely transformed it into a purely Italian town. In 37 B.C. Antony and Octavian renewed the Second Triumvirate at Tarentum; but thereafter little is heard of it. Horace mentions it (*Carm.* 3. 5. 53–6) as a quiet country retreat suitable for a tired business man.

Bérard, *Bibl. topogr.* 104 ff.; P. Wuilleumier, *Tarente, des origines à la conquête romaine* (1939); Dunbabin, *Western Greeks*; H. Klumbach, *Tarentiner Grabkunst* (1938).  M. C.; A. G. W.

**TARIUS** (*PW* 3) **RUFUS**, LUCIUS, of very humble origin, perhaps from Picenum, served as an officer in Octavian's fleet at Actium, as proconsul of Cyprus, and (*c.* 27 B.C.) as a commander in the Balkans. Augustus rewarded him with the suffect consulship (16) and with gifts totalling ten million sesterces which he invested in land in Picenum. He was *curator aquarum* from A.D. 23 to 24, when he probably died. His clemency to his only son, who tried to murder him, is noted by Seneca (*Clem.* 1. 15).

Syme, *Rom. Rev.*, see index.  T. J. C.

**TARPEIA**, a legendary figure of early Rome. Daughter of the commander of the Capitol when it was attacked by the Sabines, she betrayed the citadel in return for a promise of what the Sabines had on their arms, but in place of their golden armlets (*armillae*) they rewarded her by hurling their shields on her. The legend took various forms (e.g. love for the enemy general replaced love of gold as her motive). It explained the name of the Tarpeian Rock (q.v.), the name being Etruscan (cf. Tarquinius, etc.).

Ogilvie, *Comm. Livy 1–5*, 74 f.  H. H. S.

**TARPEIAN ROCK.** The site of this famous cliff (*rupes*), whence murderers and traitors were thrown, is located by Dionysius (7. 35. 4; 8. 78. 5) as overhanging the Roman forum, while Varro (*Ling.* 5. 41) and others, equating *saxum Tarpeium* with *rupes*, place it close to the temple of Jupiter Capitolinus. Lucan (3. 154) connects it with the temple of Saturn. This leads to the conclusion that the cliff was at the south-west corner of the Capitol.

H. Jordan, *Topographie der Stadt Rom* (1871), i. 2. 127 ff.; Nash, *Pict. Dict. Rome* ii. 409 ff.  I. A. R.

**TARQUINII** (Etr. *Tarχ(u)na*-; modern *Tarquinia*, formerly *Corneto*), the chief of the twelve cities of Etruria and the reputed home of two of the kings of early Rome, Tarquinius Priscus and Superbus (qq.v.; *and see* TARCHON), stood on a high plateau about 60 miles from Rome and 5 miles from the sea. The greatest glory of Tarquinii is the series of painted chamber tombs which starts in the mid-sixth century B.C. The wealth of material found in the extensive necropoleis has made them basic to the study of the Villanovan and successive periods in southern Etruria. Tarquinii has produced the earliest orientalizing tomb in Etruria, containing a vase with the cartouche of the Egyptian Pharaoh Bocchoris (reigned *c.* 718–712 B.C.) associated with local imitations of Protocorinthian (*see* ISCHIA, VILLANOVANS). As at Veii and probably Capena (qq.v.), the city walls, about 5 miles in circuit, may well reflect the mid-fourth-century hostility between Tarquinii and Rome. The chief surviving monument in the city is a fourth-century temple, the so-called Ara della Regina. In 1948 fragments of some late (Latin) inscriptions were published. These Elogia Tarquiniensia commemorate the careers and exploits of earlier famous citizens and thus reflect local Etruscan history.

M. Pallottino, *Mon. Ant.* 1937; id. *La Peinture étrusque* (1952); P. Romanelli, *Tarquinia* (Rome, 1951); id. *Not. Scav.* 1948, 193 ff.; C. M. Lerici, *Nuove testimonianze dell'arte e della civiltà etrusca* (1960), 64 ff.; M. Moretti, *Nuovi monumenti della pittura etrusca* (Milan, 1966); G. A. Mansuelli, *Rév. Arch.* 1967, 41 ff.; Scullard, *Etr. Cities*, 84 ff.; H. Hencken, *Tarquinia, Villanovans and Early*

*Etruscans* I, II (Amer. Soc. Prehistoric Research, 1968), *Tarquinia and Etruscan Origins* (1968). For the *elogia* see P. Romanelli, *Not. Scav.* 1948, 260 ff., J. Heurgon, *Mél. École fr. Rome* 1951, 119 ff., M. Pallottino, *Stud. Etr.* xxi (1950–1), 147 ff.  D. W. R. R.

**TARQUINIUS** (1) **PRISCUS** according to tradition was the fifth king of Rome (616–579 B.C.) and the son of Demaratus of Corinth, who is said to have migrated to Tarquinii in Etruria. Archaeological discoveries confirm both that in the era of the Tarquins Rome was under Etruscan sway and that cultural and trade relations between Etruria and Greece (chiefly Corinth) were then very active. The Tarquins, however, appear to have closer connexions with Caere than with Tarquinii (the latter link being due perhaps to homophony). The Tarquins are indisputably historical figures, though no clear differentiation and distribution of exploits between the two Tarquin kings Priscus and Superbus (q.v.) may have existed before the later annalistic tradition and manipulation developed, and though some stories of Priscus, e.g. about Tanaquil (q.v.), are probably late inventions. His Etruscan origins, apart from archaeology, are also indirectly proved by the story of Mastarna (q.v.) and confirmed by the Roman belief that Tarquin brought to Rome Etruscan customs, cults, and craftsmen. The foundation of the temple of the Capitoline Triad and other public works are attributed to Tarquin, and undoubtedly this building activity (e.g. the Circus Maximus, and draining the Forum) belongs to the period when he is said to have been king. His wars against neighbouring States also are probably historical, but they betray so much similarity with those fought by Tarquinius Superbus as to suggest that Priscus and Superbus are merely names attributed indiscriminately to members of the same Etruscan dynasty. Priscus is also said to have enlarged the Senate. He is said to have been murdered at the instigation of the sons of Ancus Marcius (q.v. 1), but they failed to secure the throne because Tanaquil helped Servius Tullius to power. Tarquin's two sons, Lucius and Aruns, are said later to have married daughters of Servius Tullius (*see* TULLIA 1), while of his daughters one married Servius Tullius, the other M. Brutus and thus became the mother of L. Brutus (q.v. 1).

A. Blakeway, 'Demaratus', *JRS* 1935, 129 ff.; G. Pasquali, *Terze pagine stravaganti* (1942), 1 ff. (against him A. Alföldi, *Early Rome and the Latins*, 1964, 318 ff.); Ogilvie, *Comm. Livy 1–5*, 145 ff. For a summary of Gjerstad's controversial views on the lower dating of the Tarquins (*c.* 530/525–*c.* 500 for Priscus) see E. Gjerstad, *Legends and Facts of Early Roman History* (Lund, 1962), esp. 50 ff. They are rejected by A. Momigliano, *JRS* 1963, 102 ff., M. Pallottino, *Stud. Etr.* 1963, esp. 19 ff.  P. T.

**TARQUINIUS** (2) **SUPERBUS.** The historicity of the last king of Rome (traditionally 534–510 B.C.) is probably proved by the tradition of his capture of Latin towns, of his dedication of the temple of Capitoline Jupiter, and of the treaty between Rome and Gabii ascribed to him, which survived in the temple of Semo Sancus till the time of Augustus (the forgery of such a document would be unintelligible). But, as the name 'Superbus' would not appear in its text (nor for that matter in *any* text), tradition proves only that *a* king Tarquinius existed, thereby supporting the surmise that the two Tarquins are merely names of members of the same dynasty. The records of the Tarquinian sovereignty were later embellished by borrowings from Greek history, both to find similarities between Greece and Rome, and in order to justify the surname of Superbus and to explain the fall of the monarchy. Popular legends or folktales or epic poems were combined with tales of probable or indisputable Greek origin, such as Tarquinius' conspiracy against Servius Tullius and the decapitation of the tallest poppies at Gabii.

For the story of his accession *see* TULLIA 1, for that of his fall *see* LUCRETIA, BRUTUS 1. After his expulsion from

Rome Tarquin is said to have fled to Caere, and to have persuaded Veii and Tarquinii to attack Rome. After their defeat at Silva Arsia, he appealed to Porsenna (q.v.) of Clusium to attack Rome. Next he took refuge with his son-in-law Mamilius Octavius of Tusculum who led the Latins against Rome at the battle of Lake Regillus. Finally, Tarquin escaped to Aristodemus (q.v. 2) of Cumae, where he died. The general pattern of these events may well be historical, but the part in them that legend assigns to Tarquin is much more doubtful.

Ogilvie, *Comm. Livy 1–5*, 194 ff. *See also* TARQUINIUS (1) on Gjerstad's improbable lower dating (he would put Superbus' fall *c.* 450). P. T.

**TARQUINIUS** (3) **COLLATINUS,** LUCIUS, was traditionally the husband of Lucretia (q.v.). When her story was connected with the fall of the monarchy, Collatinus was regarded as a founder of the Republic, and one of the first consuls (509 B.C.). The legend of his consulship also served to harmonize the double tradition about the dedication of the temple of the Capitoline Triad, which was associated both with a Tarquin and with the beginning of the Republic: a consul Tarquinius replaced his royal namesake. It equally served in the post-Sullan age to supply evidence for and against the right of the people to abrogate a consul's *imperium*, while the story of Collatinus' self-imposed exile as a relative of the Tarquins is probably a borrowing from the story of Athenian ostracism.

Ogilvie, *Comm. Livy 1–5*, 232, 238 ff. P. T.

**TARQUITIUS** (*PW* 7) **PRISCUS** is known to us only from a few scattered references. He is mentioned by Pliny (*HN* 1 in his lists of authorities for books 2 and 11,) as one of his sources for 'Etruscan lore', *Etrusca disciplina* (*see* RELIGION, ETRUSCAN), though it is not certain that Pliny had direct access to his writings. Macrobius (*Sat.* 3. 7. 2) quotes from a book of his, *Ostentarium*, a translation of an Etruscan work on prognostication, and from his *Prognostication from Trees*. The literary evidence, supported by *ILS* 2924, seems to indicate that he was an important intermediary for the transmission of Etruscan prognostic learning and ritual to the Romans. Probably he lived about a century earlier than the Tarquitius Priscus of Tac. *Ann.* 12. 59 and 14. 46, who may have been the dedicator of *ILS* 2924.

J. Heurgon, *Latomus* 1953, 402 ff. A. L. P.; A. M. D.

**TARRACINA,** (modern *Terracina*), formerly Volscian Anxur, on the west coast of Italy 65 miles south of Rome. Rome made it a Citizen Colony (329 B.C.). Tarracina was the southern terminus of the Pomptine Marshes canal and an important station on the *Via Appia* (q.v.). Its spectacular ancient remains include the temple of Jupiter on the acropolis.

G. Lugli, *Forma Italiae, Regio I* i. 1 (Rome, 1926); O. A. W. and M. S. Dilke, *Greece and Rome* 1961, 172 ff.; G. Lugli, *La tecnica edilizia romana* (1957), 144 ff. E. T. S.

**TARRACO** (modern *Tarragona*), on the north-east coast of Spain, was placed on or near the Iberian Cese (*Κίσσα*, Cissis), city of the tribe Cessetani. In 218 B.C. it was the base of P. and Cn. Scipio, who fortified it (Pliny, *HN* 3. 21). The earliest stronghold and the largest mint of republican Spain, it became Colonia Iulia (? Victrix) Triumphalis under Caesar. Within the Scipionic walls it was virtually rebuilt by Augustus, to whom it dedicated an altar and, on his death, a temple—the first provincial institution of the emperor-cult. Under him it had superseded Carthago Nova as the chief city of the province, now called Hispania Tarraconensis; it was the governor's winter residence and the centre of the provincial *concilium*. It was sacked by the Franks in A.D. 264; although

Ausonius poetically praised its citadel, excavations show it still in ruins in the fifth century, and the primacy had passed to Barcino (q.v.). Its Roman remains include a large stretch of the walls and of the great 'Devil's Bridge' aqueduct, the so-called 'tomb of the Scipios' (cf. *Madr. Mitteil.* 1966, 162 ff.), and a big cemetery (partly Christian); the plan of the Augustan citadel, reminiscent of central Rome, can still be traced.

S. M. de Navascuéz, *Tarragona* (1929); A. Fick, *Arch. Anz.* 1933; J. S. Vilaro, *Rivista di archeologia cristiana* 1937; on walls, J. S. Vilaro, *Archivo Espanol di Arqueologia* 1949, 221 ff. M. I. H.

**TARSUS.** Though Tarsus later claimed Triptolemus, Perseus, or Heracles as its founder, it was probably a native Cilician town. It was the capital of the Cilician kings and of the Persian satraps, but the Greek coins which it issued during the fifth and fourth centuries B.C. show that it was early hellenized and autonomous. It was renamed 'Antioch on the Cydnus' by Seleucus I or Antiochus I and issued municipal coins under this name from Antiochus IV's reign; on its later autonomous coins it used its old name. Annexed by Pompey in 66, it was granted freedom and immunity by Antony; it was the capital of the province of Cilicia from *c.* A.D. 72. Its constitution was timocratic, a fee of 500 drachmas being charged for admission to citizen rights. This disfranchised the mass of the population, the workers in the linen industry, on which the city's prosperity was based. During the first century B.C. Tarsus was the seat of a celebrated philosophical school and the birthplace of St. Paul. It retains its ancient name unchanged. A. H. M. J.

**TARTESSUS,** a region of south Spain, round the middle and lower Baetis (*Guadalquivir*). The name was also given to the river and to a town at its mouth. Probably visited by the Minoans, it was temporarily occupied by the Phoenicians. About 650 B.C. the Samian Colaeus was driven there; *c.* 600 Phocaeans came, making friends with the Tartessian ruler. The trade of Tartessus with Phoenicians and Carthaginians and (in tin) with Brittany and south-west Britain made it proverbially wealthy. About 500 the town was probably destroyed by the Carthaginians. Geographic writers confused it with Gades. Later poets used Tartessus of all Spain or all west Europe. Tartessus was probably the biblical Tarshish.

Hdt. 1. 163, 4. 152, 196; Strabo 3. 148–51; Mela 1. 2. 6; Avienius, *Ora Maritima* 224 ff. A. Schulten, *Tartessos* (1922), and in *PW*, s.v.; Thomson, *Hist. Anc. Geog.* 29, 53 ff.; J. M. Blazquez, *Tartessos* (Salamanca, 1968). E. H. W.

**TASCIOVANUS,** king of the British Catuvellauni (*c.* 20 B.C.–A.D. 5) and father of Cunobelinus, was perhaps the grandson of Cassivellaunus (qq.v.). His mint was at Verulam, where the Prae Wood site was no doubt his capital. Some of his coins were among the earliest in Britain to imitate classical designs, though his policy was not philo-Roman.

D. F. Allen, *Archaeologia* 1944; C. E. Stevens in W. F. Grimes (ed.), *Aspects of Archaeology in Britain* (1951), 332 ff.; Frere, *Britannia*, ch. iv. S. S. F.

**TATIUS,** TITUS, traditionally a Sabine king, who after the Romans had carried off the Sabine women is said to have captured the Capitol through the treason of Tarpeia (q.v.); after the women had effected a reconciliation, Tatius and Romulus ruled jointly over the two peoples. Tatius may have been a king of Rome, as there is evidence that he enlarged the city and established several cults (Varro, *Ling.* 5. 74). The suggestions that he was merely the eponym of the Roman tribe Tities, or that his connexion with Romulus was invented as a precedent for collegiate magistracy are equally uncertain.

Ogilvie, *Comm. Livy 1–5*, 72, 81. P. T.

**TAURISCUS** (1), an anomalist grammarian, pupil of Crates (q.v. 3) of Mallos, first used τρόπος (trope) as contrasted with κυριολεξία: cf. Sext. Emp. *Math.* 1. 248 f.

**TAURISCUS** (2) (1st c. B.C.), sculptor, son of Artemidorus, of Tralles. Works (owned by Asinius Pollio): 1. Hermerotes, probably a pair of herms (q.v.) with bodies and heads of Erotes. 2 (with his brother, Apollonius). Marble group from Rhodes of Zethus, Amphion, Dirce, and the bull, inspired by a painting and by earlier sculpture. The Farnese bull from the baths of Caracalla (Winter, *KB* 357. 1) is a copy with the added figure of Antiope, etc.

Bieber, *Sculpt. Hellenist. Age,* 133 ff. T. B. L. W.

**TAUROMENIUM** (*Ταυρομένιον,* modern *Taormina*), in eastern Sicily above Naxos (q.v.), was established in 396 B.C. by the Carthaginian Himilco (q.v. 2), who planted there on the site of a small existing settlement the Sicels to whom Dionysius I (q.v.) had given the site of Naxos. Dionysius captured it and refounded it as a Greek city (392). In 358 Andromachus, father of the historian Timaeus (q.v. 2), gathered the Naxian refugees there and became tyrant. The Tauromenites gave prompt support to Timoleon (q.v.) and Pyrrhus (q.v.) in 344 and 278; *c.* 316 Tauromenium passed under the control of Agathocles (q.v.) and under that of a local tyrant Tyndarion *c.* 285. Under Hieron II (q.v.) it again formed part of the Syracusan dominions, but at his death it submitted to Rome, becoming a *civitas foederata.* Seized by the rebels in the first Servile War it was recaptured with difficulty by Rutilius Lupus (132). In 36 Sex. Pompeius (q.v. 6) inflicted a near-fatal reverse on Octavian there. Becoming an Augustan *colonia* Tauromenium flourished in the imperial period.

Bérard, *Bibl. topogr.* 111 f.; G. Manganaro, *Arch. Class.* 1963, 13 ff. A. G. W.

**TAURUS MONS,** properly the mostly well-wooded heights (average 7,000 feet) beginning in south-west Asia Minor, and continuing along the Lycian coast and through Pisidia and Isauria to the borders of Cilicia and Lycaonia. It then divides into: (1) Antitaurus, apparently the heights going north-east through Cappadocia (Mons Argaeus) and Armenia (Mons Capotes) towards the Caucasus; (ii) Abus or Macis (Massis), through Armenia towards the Caspian, keeping the name Taurus and sending southwards Mons Amanus (q.v.) and (beyond the Euphrates) Mons Masius. There were subsidiary ranges south of the Euphrates, and Mt. Zagrus separating Media from Assyria and Babylonia. The name Taurus was extended to include not only the heights of north Iran, but also the Paropamisus (*Hindu Kush*) and Emodus or Imaus (*Himalayas*); and was continued by hearsay to the Eastern Ocean at 'Tamus Headland'. The whole range was regarded as the backbone of Asia, and along it Dicaearchus (*c.* 300 B.C.) fixed for geographers a parallel or median in cartography, dividing the land mass into the cool and warm regions. E. H. W.

**TAXILES,** i.e. 'king Taxila', his personal name being Omphis (Āmbhi), king of the country between the Indus and the Jhelum with his capital at Taxila. From fear of his neighbour Porus he welcomed Alexander; Taxila became Alexander's advanced base, and Taxiles fought for him against Porus. At first Taxiles was subjected to the Macedonian satrap Philippus; after Philippus' murder he ruled nominally as Alexander's governor but soon in complete independence. By 312 B.C. at latest the Taxila kingdom had become part of Chandragupta's empire. W. W. T.

**TEANUM APULUM,** a town in northern Apulia. Its site, known as *Civitate,* overlooks the Fortore valley

9 miles north-west of San Severo and lay on the main Adriatic coastal route between Larinum and Sipontum. As at Arpi and Canusium (q.v.), the course of its earthen rampart circuit shows that it supported a large population in the Daunian period but prosperity had apparently declined by late Republican times. A group of concrete tomb cores survives outside the town.

*CIL* ix. 67 ff. G. D. B. J.

**TECHNOPAIGNIA,** poems intended to show the author's skill, especially by the shape which they make on the page. This art was popular at the beginning of the third century B.C., which produced Simmias' *Axe, Wings,* and *Egg,* Theocritus' *Pipe,* and Dosiadas' *Altar.*

C. M. B.

**TEGEA** lay in the south-east Arcadian plain, across the roads from Sparta to the Argolid and the Isthmus. In this exposed position it developed politically before the other Arcadian towns. About 550 B.C. Sparta came to terms with Tegea after a long war; and for two centuries it followed the Spartan lead, though at times unwillingly, for the Tegeans were tough fighters (cf. Hdt. 9. 26). It was a favourite place of residence for Spartan and other exiles (Leotychidas; Micythus of Rhegium; King Pausanias). About 471 Tegea revolted and joined Argos, but submitted after a defeat (*Anth. Pal.* 7. 512; Hdt. 9. 35). Later, out of hostility to Mantinea (q.v.), Tegea was pro-Spartan. She looked unfavourably on the foundation of Megalopolis.

The temple of Athena Alea, burnt down in 395, was rebuilt with great magnificence, with Scopas as architect and sculptor (Paus. 8. 45. 5). On the borders of Tegean territory and Kynouria, on the Hill of the Analipsis (near Vourvoura) the remains have been discovered of a classical town (? Iasos), and also important Mycenaean finds.

*IG* v. 2. 1 ff. V. Bérard, 'Tegée et la Tegéatide', *BCH* 1892, 529 ff.; 1893, 1 ff.; Hiller von Gaertringen, *PW,* s.v. 'Tegea'; C. Dugas and others, *Sanctuaire d' Aléa Athéna a Tegée* (1924); *BCH* 1921, 335 ff. (older temple). T. J. D.

**TELAMON** (1), in mythology, brother of Peleus (q.v.). On his banishment he settled in Salamis, and as a reward for helping Heracles against Troy received Hesione (q.v.) as his slave-concubine. He was a stern father to her son Teucer (q.v. 2), and on the latter returning from Troy without Aias (q.v. 1), Telamon banished him (Eur. *Hel.* 91 ff.). For his hero-cult see e.g. Hdt. 8. 64. 2. His name ('shield-strap') seems derived from the original notion of his son, Aias, as the bearer of a huge man-covering shield. H. J. R.; H. W. P.

**TELAMON** (2), modern *Talamone* on the coast of Etruria, mid-way between Rome and Pisa. Here the Romans annihilated the Celts of Cisalpine Gaul in 225 B.C. (Polyb. 2. 27–31). Here too Marius landed in 87 B.C. (Plut. *Mar.* 41. 2). Otherwise the village played little part in recorded history.

M. Santangelo, *L' Antiquarium di Orbetello* (1954), 92 ff.; P. Sommella, *Antichi campi di battaglia in Italia* (1967), 11 ff. E. T. S.

**TELCHINES** (Τελχῖνες), semi-divine beings living in Rhodes who were skilled in all manner of metal-work, and so also in magic. Consequently they were dangerous, mischievous, and had the 'evil eye'. Our accounts of them are late and contradictory, but agree more or less in the above points, and also that they were finally destroyed by one of the greater gods, Zeus, Poseidon, or Apollo, or at least driven from Rhodes. They have a certain resemblance to the dwarfs or gnomes of northern European mythology.

See especially Strabo 14. 2. 7, 653–4; Eustathius ad *Iliad.* 771. 55 ff. (from Strabo and Suetonius); *Suda,* s.v.; more in Friedländer in Roscher, s.v., with literature; Herter in *PW,* s.v. *See also* MAGIC, § 4. H. J. R.

**TELECLIDES,** Athenian comic poet, won three victories at the City Dionysia, the first *c.* 445 B.C. (*IG* ii². 2325. 54), and five at the Lenaea, the first *c.* 440 (ibid. 119). We have eight titles (including *Eumenides* and 'Ησίοδοι [cf. CRATINUS]) and seventy fragments. The largest fragment, fr. 1 (*Amphictyons*), describes the Golden Age in extravagant terms; frs. 39 and 40 associate Socrates with Euripides, and frs. 42 and 44 attack Pericles.

FCG ii. 361 ff.; CAF i. 209 ff.; FAC i. 180 ff.　　K. J. D.

**TELEMACHUS** (Τηλέμαχος), son of Odysseus and Penelope (qq.v.). He is prominent in the *Odyssey*, where his character develops throughout those parts of the poem in which he appears. At first he is an untried youth, a good and dutiful son but timid and unenterprising. At the behest of Athena he bids his mother's suitors depart, and when they will not, still with her help he takes ship, goes to the mainland, and then inquires after his father, first from Nestor and then from Menelaus (*Od.* 1–4). Athena warns him to return home and sail by a different route, since the one by which he came is beset by the suitors, who plan to kill him. He does so, and on the way takes the fugitive prophet Theoclymenus aboard. He shows from now on more energy and resource, even before meeting his father (*Od.* 15–16. 153); and, having met him, acts as an intelligent and even enterprising helper, astonishing his mother by taking command of the house (21. 343 ff.) and fighting valiantly against the suitors (22. 91 ff.).

Outside Homer he appears in a few episodes. Palamedes, to detect Odysseus' feigned madness, put Telemachus, then a baby, in the road of his father's plough (Hyg. *Fab.* 95. 2). After his father's death he married Circe according to the *Telegonia* (*see* EPIC CYCLE).

**TELEMUS** (Τήλεμος), in mythology, a prophet who foretold to Polyphemus the Cyclops that Odysseus (q.v.) would one day blind him; *Od.* 9. 507 ff.

**TELEPHUS** (1) (Τήλεφος), in mythology, son of Heracles (q.v.) and Auge, daughter of King Aleos, the eponym of Alea in Arcadia. She bore him in a shrine of Athena; a pestilence ensued, and Aleos when he discovered the matter had the child exposed and gave Auge to be sold overseas. She came into the possession of Teuthras, king and eponym of Teuthrania in Mysia, who married her; the child was suckled by a hind and picked up by shepherds, who called him Telephus (as if from "θηλᾶν", to suckle, and ἔλαφος, a deer or hind; Apollod. 2. 146). In the version preserved by Hyginus (*Fab.* 99. 3) Auge was adopted by Teuthras, who was childless. For some reason (accounts vary in different authors) Telephus when he grew up went to Mysia; here, according to Hyginus' story (very doubtfully traced to Sophocles), Auge was given him in marriage, and they discovered their relationship at the last moment. At all events he became king of Mysia, and here joins with the Epic tradition (post-Homeric), the first part of his story being apparently Tragic. In the *Cypria* the Greeks on their way to Troy mistook Teuthrania for it; Telephus resisted them and was wounded by Achilles. The wound would not heal, and he (at least according to Euripides, *Telephus*) made his way to the Greek camp at Aulis and in accordance with an oracle asked Achilles to cure him; this was done by applying the rust of the spear, for the oracle had said that the wounder should be the healer. He then guided the Greeks to Troy. His legend was adopted by the Attalids as a kind of foundation-myth for their own kingdom. See further Schmidt in Roscher, s.v.
　　H. J. R.

**TELEPHUS** (2) of Pergamum (2nd c. A.D.), a Stoic grammarian, teacher of the Emperor Lucius Verus, wrote on Homer, on the history of literature and of scholarship, on bibliography and antiquities, and on *Attic Syntax* (five books); he compiled an alphabetical lexicon of things in common use, and an 'Ωκυτόκιον (in ten books) of adjectives for the aid of writers and orators. His works are lost.

C. Wendel, PW 9 A. 369 ff.　　P. B. R. F.

**TELES** (Τέλης) (fl. *c.* 235 B.C.), Cynic philosopher, probably of Megara, is the oldest of the many authors of Cynic or Stoic διατριβαί (short ethical discussions), fragments of whose works have been preserved (in his case, in the pages of Stobaeus). His διατριβαί have no claim to philosophical distinction; they simply commend the Cynic way of life in popular language; but he is interesting because of his references to earlier writers like Bion of Borysthenes, Stilpon, and Crates the Cynic.

Ed. O. Hense² (1909).　　W. D. R.

**TELESILLA** (Τελέσιλλα), Argive poetess of the fifth century B.C., famous for arming the women of Argos after its defeat by Cleomenes (Hdt. 6. 76 ff., Polyaenus 8. 33). Nine fragments of her work survive, and seem to come from Hymns, especially to Apollo and Artemis, with whom six are concerned. The Telesilleion (*see* METRE, GREEK, III 9) or acephalous glyconic is called after her. She seems to have written mainly for women (Paus. 2. 20. 8). An Epidaurian Hymn to the Mother of the Gods sometimes ascribed to her seems to be a later imitation.

FRAGMENTS. Page, *Poet. Mel. Gr.* 372–4; J. M. Edmonds, *Lyra Graeca* (1952), ii. 236–45.
CRITICISM. U. von Wilamowitz-Moellendorff, *Textg. d. gr. Lyr.* (1900), 76; P. Maas, *Epidaurische Hymnen* (1933), 134 ff.　C. M. B.

**TELESPHORUS** (Τελεσφόρος), a child-god associated with Asclepius (q.v.). He is commonly shown in art, but seldom mentioned in literature; his name occurs on several inscriptions in his honour, however.

See Schmidt in Roscher, s.v.; Schwen in PW, s.v.　　H. J. R.

**TELESTES,** dithyrambic poet of Selinus (Ath. 616 f, Diod. Sic. 46. 6), won victory at Athens 402/1 B.C. (*Marm. Par.* 79). Titles of his Dithyrambs are *Argo*, *Asclepius*, and *Hymenaeus*, of which in all four fragments survive. The comedian Theopompus referred to him (Ath. 501 f). In style and music he resembled Timotheus and Philoxenus (Dion. Hal. *Comp.* 132). Alexander read him (Plut. *Alex.* 8), and the tyrant Aristratus of Sicyon put up a statue to him (Pliny, *HN* 35. 109).

Page, *Poet. Mel. Gr.* 419–22.　　C. M. B.

**TELETE** (τελετή). Being related to τελεῖν as, for instance, ταφή to θάπτειν, this word properly means no more than 'accomplishment', 'performance', which suits its very rare non-sacral use (perhaps only *Batrachom.* 303, where it is equivalent to the usual Epic τέλος). But from a comparatively early date it was specialized (it does not occur in any sense earlier than Pindar) to mean the accomplishment of a religious or quasi-religious ceremony. So Pindar, *Ol.* 10. 52, uses it of the first celebration of the Olympic Games by Heracles; *Pyth.* 9. 97 and *Nem.* 10. 34, of Athenian festivals including athletic contests; *Ol.* 3. 40, of the celebration of *theoxenia* (q.v.). Only in the last case is the rite purely religious. In Euripides (Aeschylus and Sophocles use only τέλος) it repeatedly means a rite, and perhaps especially one somewhat out of the ordinary, as those of Dionysus, *Bacch.* 22, or any orgiastic ceremonies, ibid. 73. Aristophanes uses it for rites of any kind, as *Pax* 418–20. But there seems to have been a growing tendency about this time to use it especially of mystic ceremonials; thus, Herodotus employs it in speaking of those of Demeter and Dionysus, Andocides (1. 111) of the Eleusinian Mysteries, while it is a favourite word of Plato to signify an initiation. After Alexander this tendency is accentuated, the word very frequently meaning a rite supposed to contain some hidden philosophic or gnostic meaning. It can also signify a magical or supernatural action or even force. This finally develops, especially in Philon of Alexandria, into the sense of 'inner meaning', even 'allegorical interpretation'.

C. Zijderveld, Τελετή; *Bijdragen tot de kennis der religieuse terminologie in het Grieksch* (1934).                    H. J. R.

**TELLUS,** the Roman earth-goddess, probably very old, though her temple on the Esquiline dates only from 268 B.C. (Platner–Ashby, 511). For the question of Greek influence on her ritual see F. Altheim, *Terra Mater* (1931); S. Weinstock in *PW*, s.v. 'Terra Mater'. She is associated in cult with Tellumo (Varro in August. *De civ. D.* 7. 23); with Altor ('Feeder') and Rusor ('Ploughman'?), ibid.; perhaps with the doubtful Tellurus (Mart. Capella 1. 49). No festival is named after her and she has no flamen; but she is the deity concerned in the *feriae sementivae* (Ovid, *Fasti* 1. 657 ff., whereon see Frazer); the Fordicidia of 15 Apr. (ibid. 4. 629 ff., whereon see Frazer; the offering, a cow in calf, is typical for powers of fertility); and the sacrifice of the *porca praecidanea* (Varro in Nonius, 163 M., Gellius 4. 6. 8, who adds Ceres), a sin-offering for neglect of rites, especially those of the dead.

See further Weinstock, loc. cit.                    H. J. R.

**TEMENOS** (τέμενος), in Homeric usage, signifies either a king's or a god's domain, a space marked off and assigned to his use. In later times it is nearly always used of a god's domain.

In the narrower sense it is the sanctuary (ἱερόν) or precinct (περίβολος), the consecrated and enclosed area surrounding the god's altar, which was the centre of worship and the only indispensable cult structure. It usually included a temple also, whose primary purpose was to house the image and votive offerings. Larger precincts, like Apollo's at Delphi, or the Altis at Olympia, also enclosed the treasuries built to house the offerings of a single city, sacred groves, statues, theatres, and the temples of associated deities. The rules governing the sanctity of precincts varied from cult to cult; entrance was sometimes forbidden except to certain persons at certain times. In most cults whoever entered the precinct had to be purified first. The Roman *fanum* or *templum* (in the original sense) corresponds to *temenos* in this narrower meaning.

In the broader sense the *temenos* is all the land that belongs to a god's cult. Some cults owned large tracts of forest, pasture, cultivable land, and even factories and fisheries, from which they received revenues. Though sometimes cultivation of the god's domain was forbidden, it was usually worked either by the god's slaves or by contractors.

See *SIG* 977–94, and many of the inscriptions in von Prott–Ziehen, *Leges Graecorum sacrae et titulis collectae* (1896–1906), for cult-laws relating to this subject. P. Stengel, *Griechische Kultusaltertümer* (1920), 17 ff.; A. Fairbanks, *Handbook of Greek Religion* (1910), 65 ff. For Roman religion see Wissowa, *RK* 467 ff.                    J. E. F.

**TEMENUS** (Τήμενος), (1) king of Stymphalus, founder of the cult of Hera as Maid, Wife, and Widow, *see* HERA, ARCADIA; Paus. 8. 22. 2. (2) Son of Phegeus king of Psophis; he and his brother Axion murdered Alcmaeon (q.v.), Paus. 8. 24. 10. (3) One of the Heraclidae (q.v.; exact genealogy uncertain). After taking a prominent part in the Return of the Heraclidae, he got Argos for his portion of the conquered land. He had a daughter Hyrnetho, and favoured her husband Deïphontes (q.v.) above his own sons, who therefore murdered their father. The people then decided that Deïphontes and Hyrnetho should be king and queen (see Apollod. 2. 172 ff.). One of Temenus' sons (Perdiccas, according to Hdt. 8. 137; Archelaus, Hyg. *Fab.* 219; the latter account is somehow connected with Euripides, *Archelaus*) founded the royal house of Macedonia.

See further O. Waser in Roscher's *Lex.*, art. 'Temenos'. H. J. R.

**TEMPE,** a narrow valley, nearly 5 miles in length, in northern Thessaly, through which the Peneus flows between the massifs of Olympus and Ossa. The gorge was caused by erosion and not, as Greek tradition maintained, by an earthquake. Because it lay on the easiest route between Thessaly and Macedonia and was so narrow that it could be closed by a very small force, its strategic importance was considerable. There were, however, practicable routes over the mountains further inland, and armies not controlling both ends of Tempe normally chose to follow one of these. In 480 B.C. the Greeks sent troops to hold Tempe against Xerxes, but they evacuated it owing to distrust of the Thessalians. It was the scene of operations in 336, when Alexander overcame Thessalian opposition, and also in the Third Macedonian War.

P–K, *GL* i. 1. 111 ff.                    H. D. W.

**TEMPLE.** The Greek temple was the house of the god. It was not an assembly place for a congregation of worshippers. The altar (q.v.) was normally outside to the east, opposite the front of the building (the commonest orientation was east-to-west). The basic element of the temple was a simple room, the *naos* or *cella*. This had various shapes, especially in the earlier period. It could be hairpin-shaped, or occasionally round or squarish; but the usual form, which may be akin to the Mycenean *megaron*, was a rectangle, with the entrance at one end, and the side walls commonly continued to form a porch. On this the more elaborate forms of temple were based. Columns were placed between the projecting walls, or in a row in front. Small temples were commonly 'distyle in antis', i.e. with two columns between the antae or ends of the side walls. The 'treasuries', small temples dedicated by cities at shrines such as Delphi and Olympia (qq.v.), to display their wealth and piety, were mostly of this form. Other small temples were 'tetrastyle prostyle', i.e. with four columns in front. For symmetry a dummy porch, without an entrance door, could be placed at the back of the temple too, making it 'amphiprostyle' (for example, Athena Nike at Athens). The addition of a colonnade (*pteron*, see ARCHITECTURE) all round the nuclear building was not due merely to an extension of the porches; the *pteron* was a new and dominant element. It is seen, already fully developed, in the Heraeum at Olympia (c. 600 B.C.; *see* OLYMPIA). From the sixth century onwards most large temples are peripteral, usually with six columns at each end and twelve to fourteen on the sides. Some large temples were dipteral, with two rows of columns, or pseudo-dipteral (*see* HERMOGENES 1), i.e. with a single row in the same position as the outer row in a dipteral building. A few temples attained enormous size—the curious temple of Zeus at Acragas was over 173 by 361 feet (*see* also OLYMPIEUM)—but such colossi were very rare in comparison with more modest shrines. Besides the regular types, many temples had odd or complicated forms due to the peculiar requirements of the cult (*see* ERECHTHEUM, for example).

The larger temples might have interior columns too,

both for decoration and support for the roof (on the subject of roofing, which presents many difficult problems, see A. T. Hodge, *Woodwork of Greek Roofs*, 1960). Sometimes, in the archaic period, there was a single central row, as in the so-called 'Basilica' at Paestum, but more often there were two rows, creating side aisles. The interior columns were commonly in two tiers as seen in the temple of Aphaea at Aegina or Poseidon at Paestum, and were occasionally carried round the back of the cult-statue at the far end. Some temples had an inner sanctum or *adyton*, or, as in the Parthenon (q.v.), a back chamber opening not into the main *cella* but the back porch. Several large temples were hypaethral, i.e. the *cella* or the greater part of it was open to the sky. In this case a small temple (*naiskos*) might be placed within, as in the temple of Apollo at Didyma near Miletus; the interior then became something between a *cella* and a courtyard.

(For the orders and for sculptural and painted decoration *see* ARCHITECTURE.)

The cult-statue stood on a pedestal at the end of the cella opposite the door. More statues and other offerings might be placed between the side columns or in the porches.

The temple stood in a *temenos* or precinct, often with a wall entered through a *propylon* (columnar gateway; *see* PROPYLAEA). Many small shrines of course consisted of a mere enclosure with an altar and no temple. Offerings were placed about the *temenos*, and there might be a *stoa* (q.v.) on one or more sides. Before the Hellenistic period the relation of the temple to its surrounding structures was variable and usually informal and unsymmetrical.

Roman temples closely resembled Greek ones in external form and treatment, but the Corinthian Order, with steeper pediments and richly carved friezes, was generally used. The temple floor was on a raised platform enclosed by a wall-base (plinth) and this was thrust forward beyond the porch—which was given great importance—to enclose the entrance stepway. These ideas were probably borrowed from non-peripteral Etruscan temples, and Roman temples were often nonperipteral, or pseudo-peripteral (i.e. with engaged columns on the flanks). Internally, the architectural treatment sometimes given to the west end of the *cella* (e.g. in the Temple of Bacchus, Baalbek) is significant in its resemblance to the sanctuary element of the Christian church.

For bibliography *see* ARCHITECTURE; also H. Berve and G. Gruben, *Greek Temples* (Munich, 1961, London, 1963). T. F.; R. E. W.

**TEMPLE OFFICIALS.** A priest (q.v.) presided over every temple and sanctuary in the Greek and Italian States. No other official was needed in the numerous small cults. But at the larger shrines the priest received the assistance of minor officials.

In the administration of the cult and the performance of ritual he was assisted by *hieropoioi* (ἱεροποιοί), who likewise received, as their due, portions of the sacrifices and other honours and perquisites. In Athens two boards of *hieropoioi* of ten each were chosen by lot: one (οἱ ἐπὶ τὰ ἐκθύματα) to perform all sacrifices appointed by oracle, the other (οἱ κατ' ἐνιαυτόν) to administer the four-yearly festivals except the Panathenaea (Arist. *Ath. Pol.* 54). Directly charged with the offering of sacrifices were θύται, among whom a higher rank was sometimes distinguished, the ἱεροθύται or ἀρχιεροθύται. The larger and more important the cult, the more attendants were necessary at the sacrifices. We find mention of sacred heralds (ἱεροκήρυκες), libation-pourers (οἰνοχόοι), overseers (ἐπιμεληταί).

In the care and management of the temple and precinct the priest was assisted by ναοφύλακες, νεωποιοί, or νεωκόροι. They guarded the sanctuary, kept it clean, and purified entrants.

In the administration of cult-finances, sacred treasures, votive offerings, and the revenue-producing parts of the god's domain, the priest was assisted by treasurers or stewards (ἱεροταμίαι). In some cities, as Miletus, a board of ἱεροταμίαι was appointed that looked after the properties of all State-cults.

Since there was no fixed hierarchy in Greek religion, and each State, even each cult, was a law to itself, the evidence shows great variety of practice and much overlapping of the functions of the three principal types of subordinate cult-official. There were also such minor functionaries as cantors (ἀοιδοί), musicians, and *agonothetai*, who supervised the sacred games. *See also* AEDITUUS.

For inscriptions concerning Greek temple officials see *SIG*[1] 1002–54; C. Michel *Recueil d'inscriptions grecques* (1897–1927), 669–735, 810–39, 857–78; many inscriptions in von Prott-Ziehen, *Leges Graecorum sacrae e titulis collectae* (1896–1906). A. Fairbanks, *Handbook of Greek Religion* (1910), 76 ff.; P. Stengel, *Griechische Kultusaltertümer*[3] (1920), 31 ff. J. E. F.

**TENES** (Τένης), the eponym of Tenedos, for whose story, probably not very early, see Plutarch, *Quaest. Graec.* 28 (*Mor.* 350 d–f), with Halliday there and in *CQ* 1927, 37 ff. He was son of Apollo, but nominally of Cycnus king of Coloni; his stepmother accused him as Potiphar's wife did Joseph, and Cycnus set him and his sister Hemithea adrift in a chest which landed at Tenedos. Later, Cycnus discovered the truth and tried to be reconciled, but Tenes with an axe cut the moorings of his boat when Cycnus visited Tenedos, hence the proverb 'Tenedian axe' for a rash deed. Tenes was finally killed by Achilles in defending Hemithea; hence at his hero-shrine Achilles may not be named nor a flute-player enter, because a flute-player bore false witness against him to Cycnus. For the 'Tenedian axe', see further Nilsson, *Minoan-Mycenaean Religion*[2] (1950), 193 ff. H. J. R.

**TEOS** (Τέως), one of the twelve cities of the Ionian League, on the coast north of Ephesus. Tradition said that it was founded first by Minyans from Orchomenus, then by Ionians and Athenians under the sons of Codrus. After the Persian occupation of Ionia the Teians sailed in a body to Thrace, where they founded Abdera; many soon returned and took part in the battle of Lade in 494 B.C. In the Delian League Teos was assessed at six talents, on a par with Ephesus. Antigonus proposed to synoecize Teos and Lebedus, but this was never carried out. About 200 B.C. Teos was chosen as the seat of the Artists of Dionysus, but these soon made themselves unpopular and were moved elsewhere. The ruins at Sığacık are only moderately well preserved; they include a theatre, an odeum, and the famous temple of Dionysus by Hermogenes. The city's two harbours, mentioned by Livy 37. 27–8, are identifiable on the north and south sides of the isthmus.

G. E. Bean, *Aegean Turkey* (1966), 136 ff. G. E. B.

**TERENCE**: PUBLIUS TERENTIUS AFER. A *Vita* has been preserved by Donatus (deriving from Suetonius *De poetis*). Born perhaps c. 190 B.C. in N. Africa, he came as a slave to Rome to the household of a senator, Terentius Lucanus (of whom nothing is known), and adopted his name when manumitted. Date of death is unknown: the last performance of a play was 160 B.C., and he is said to have died on a journey to Greece in 159 B.C. There was much speculation after his death about his relationship with certain Roman *nobiles*: it all derived from *Ad.* 15 ff., which is simply evidence of interest taken in him by important people.

CHRONOLOGY OF HIS PLAYS: this can be established

with certainty because the *didascaliae*, giving full details, have been preserved with all his plays:

| | | |
|---|---|---|
| 166 B.C. | *Andria* | *ludi Megalenses* |
| 165 B.C. | *Hecyra* (1st attempt—a failure) | ,, ,, |
| 163 B.C. | *Heauton-timorumenos* | ,, ,, |
| 161 B.C. | *Eunuchus* | |
| 161 B.C. | *Phormio* | *ludi Romani* |
| 160 B.C. | *Adelphi* | *ludi funebres* for L. Aemilius |
| | *Hecyra* (2nd attempt—a failure) | Paullus (*cos.* 182, 168 B.C.) |
| 160 B.C. | *Hecyra* (3rd attempt) | ? *ludi Romani* |

All of the plays were produced by Ambivius Turpio (who had produced for Caecilius (q.v. 1) also), and the music was written by a man called Flaccus, slave of Claudius.

Of these plays, *Hecyra* and *Phormio* were 'translated' from originals of Apollodorus of Carystus ('Ἐπιδικαζόμενος and 'Εκύρα), an admirer and imitator of Menander. The other four were 'translated' from plays of Menander, but in his adaptation of the *Andria* he added material from Menander's *Perinthia*; for his *Eunuchus* he took the characters of the parasite and the soldier from Menander's *Kolax*; and for his *Adelphi* (Menander wrote two plays of this name: the other supplied the original of Plautus' *Stichus*) he took a scene from Diphilus' *Synapothnescontes*. His critics condemned this procedure as *contaminare* (*see* CONTAMINATIO). The *Hecyra* lost its audience at the beginning of the first two performances (to a rope-dancer and boxer, and to a gladiatorial combat) and succeeded only at the third attempt.

The technique and style of Terence differ widely from those of Plautus: (i) Most noticeable is a total absence of polymetric *cantica* and of opera-type scenes (such as lengthy meeting-scenes between slaves). In this respect Terence is close to Menander: a half of his lines are *senarii*, the rest are trochaic *septenarii* or iambic *octonarii* (only a very few lines in any play are lyric). (ii) Terence invented a new type of prologue, completely unrelated to the play and dealing with questions of literary criticism. He dispensed entirely with the type of prologue, invariable (so it seems) in New Comedy, that informs the spectators about the action. Instead Terence inserts essential information into the action of the play (e.g. *An.* 215 ff., *Hecyra* 572 ff.). With this goes an avoidance of any address by the actors to the audience such as breaks the dramatic illusion (such addresses are quite common in Greek New Comedy and in Plautus), and a restrained use of asides and comments by a hidden actor. He has also a distinct aversion to monologue, and has converted some scenes (e.g. the opening scene of *Andria* or *Eun.* 540 ff.) into a dialogue by adding a πρόσωπον προτακτικόν. (iii) Terence has a careful eye for the coherence of the plot as a whole, and his additions from other plays (often most complicated, as in *Eun.*) are integrated so well that agreement among scholars on the details is not yet attained. (iv) Terence preserves the Greek atmosphere both positively (e.g. in *Eun.* 540 ff. he invents a young man and a party—but it is a Greek-type party, ἔρανος) and negatively (in the sense that, unlike Plautus, he does not introduce Roman customs and objects). But he also avoids excessively abstruse Greek details (contrast *An.* 726 with, e.g., Plautus, *Aul.* 394 ff.; both refer to the rude statue of Ἀπόλλων Ἀγυιεύς outside a house, but the passage of Plautus must puzzle an audience), and, e.g. in *Phorm.* 125 ff., he steers through the thorny Greek law of inheritance with great tact. (v) Terence's style is much closer to real everyday conversation than Plautus':

exclamations, interjections, interruptions, aposiopesis, ellipse—all the characteristic constructions of colloquial speech are freely used. For more solemn effects, in the long metres, coupled synonyms, anaphora, alliteration, asyndeton are all used, but on the whole without the boisterous, fantastic extravagance of Plautus. Clearly distinct in style from the actual dramas are the prologues, in which a deliberate use of all the artifices of rhetoric is obvious—a fact which harmonizes with the status of the prologues as addresses to the audience, completely outside the action of the drama. The general impression given by the drama of Terence is a deliberate step in the direction of realism on stage, not only as compared with Plautus but even with Menander (his two strongest criticisms of Luscius Lanuvinus concern the reproduction of stereotyped situations of Greek comedy: the running slave, *Heaut.* 30 ff., and the visions of the young man in love, *Phorm.* 6 ff.). On the problem of act-division, *see* PLAUTUS, § 5.

The importance and influence of Terence in later times was great: it can be seen in quotations in Cicero, imitations in Horace and Persius, in the grammatical activities of the first century A.D., in the Church Fathers, in the commentaries collected under the name Donatus (q.v. 2), in the early MSS. with scholia and miniature illustrations, in the dramatic rhyming dramas of Hrothswitha of Gandersheim, in the interest taken by the humanists, especially Petrarch, and in the way in which his text has attracted the attention of great scholars like Bentley.

TEXT. Kauer and Lindsay (O.C.T. 1926); *Andria*, A. Thierfelder (1951).
COMMENTARIES. *Andria*, G. P. Shipp (1960²); *Hecyra*, T. F. Carney (1963); *Phormio*, Dziatzko–Hauler (1913⁴); *Adelphoe*, Dziatzko–Kauer (1903²).
TEXT AND TRANSLATION. J. Sargeaunt, 2 vols. (Loeb, 1918); J. Marouzeau, 3 vols. (Budé, 1947–9). Syntax: J. T. Allardice, *The Syntax of Terence* (1929). Metre: W. A. Laidlaw, *The Prosody of Terence* (1938), and P. W. Harsh, 'Early Latin Meter and Prosody, 1904–55', *Lustrum* 1958, 215 ff.
GENERAL. F. Leo, *Gesch. d. röm. Lit.* (1913), 232 ff.; H. Haffter, 'Terenz und seine künstlerische Eigenart', *MH* 1953, 1 ff. and 73 ff. (with very useful bibliography 101 f.). O. Rieth, *Die Kunst Menanders in den 'Adelphen' des Terenz* (1964). General survey of bibliography: J. Marti, 'Terenz 1909–59', *Lustrum* 1961, 114 ff. For the history of the text and illustrations: G. Jachmann, *Die Gesch. des Terenztextes im Altertum* (1924), and *Terentius, Codex Vaticanus Latinus 3868* (1929); L. W. Jones and C. R. Morey, *The Miniatures of the MSS. of Terence prior to the Thirteenth Century* (1930–1). E. B. Jenkins, *Index Verborum Terentianus* (1932); P. McGlynn, *Lexicon Terentianum* (1963–7).                                        G. W. W.

**TERENTIA** (*PW*, 'Terentius' 95), first wife of Cicero (q.v. 1), wealthy and noble (related to the Fabii), frequently addressed and mentioned in his *Letters*, bore him Tullia (q.v. 2) and Cicero (q.v. 4) and is said to have had great influence over him, e.g. to have incited him against Clodius (q.v. 1) through dislike of Clodia (q.v.). During his exile she worked in his interest and was still on good terms with him on his return from Cilicia and early in the Civil War. During 48 B.C. he began to suspect her of financial dishonesty and soon divorced her, though he had great difficulty in repaying her dowry. She later married Sallust, then Valerius Messalla (q.v. 3), and lived to be 103.

G. Boissier, *Cicero and his Friends* (1897).                    E. B.

**TERENTIANUS MAURUS** (late 2nd c. A.D.), grammarian and metrist. His *De litteris syllabis et metris Horatii* (ed. Keil, *Gramm. Lat.* vi. 325–413) is written entirely in verse (2,981 lines). *See also* SCHOLARSHIP, LATIN.

Schanz–Hosius, § 514.                                        J. F. M.

**TERENTIUS SCAURUS**, QUINTUS (early 2nd c. A.D.), grammarian. His *Ars grammatica* and his commentary (in at least ten books) on Horace are lost. The *Liber de orthographia* (ed. Keil, *Gramm. Lat.* vii. 11–33) attributed to him is probably genuine.

Schanz–Hosius, §§ 594–5.                                    J. F. M.

**TERGESTE,** modern *Trieste*, at the head of the Adriatic, is first mentioned in 104 B.C.; it was strengthened by Augustus and flourished in the Flavian-Trajanic period. Remains of a gateway (Augustan?), Capitolium (Claudian), *forum* with Trajanic basilica, and a theatre survive. It was an important point in the road system of north-east Italy.

V. Scrinari, *Tergeste* (Rome, 1951). H. H. S.

**TERMINUS,** a boundary-mark; in Roman religion, especially the *numen* of such marks, which were set up with ceremony, sacrifice being made and blood and other offerings, with the ashes of the fire, put into the hole which was to contain the *terminus* (Siculus Flaccus in *Gromat. Lat.* 141. 4 ff. Lachmann). This filling of the mark with power was reinforced by a yearly sacrifice and feast (Ov. *Fasti* 2. 638 ff.) by the neighbours, on 23 Feb. (Terminalia). It is therefore not remarkable that there was a god Terminus, a kind of concentration of the *numen* of all the boundary-marks. Traditionally, the Terminus on the Capitol had been there before the temple of Jupiter Optimus Maximus was built, and refused to move; he therefore was left inside the temple, with an opening in the roof above, as he must be under the open sky (Ov. ibid. 669 ff.), but this legendary explanation has been denied (see Latte, *RR* 80, n. 3).

Wissowa, *RK* 136 ff.; Frazer on Ovid, loc. cit. H. J. R.

**TERPANDER** (*Τέρπανδρος*) (fl. 647 B.C. Hieron.–Eus., 645 B.C. *Marm. Par.* 34), musician and poet, of Antissa in Lesbos (Timoth. *Pers.* 240), but worked in Sparta (Ath. 635 d) in the middle of the seventh century. He is said to have written: (1) Nomes, in which he set his own or Homer's lines to lyre-music (Plut. *De mus.* 3); (2) *Προοίμια* or Preludes, which may have been of the same genre as the Homeric Hymns (ibid.); (3) scolia (ibid. 28). It is doubtful whether any of the fragments ascribed to him are genuine. Fr. 1 is a libation-song, but indicates a later date in its use of pure spondees, its theology, and its play on the word *ἀρχά*. Fr. 4 seems to be an adaptation of Pind. *Ol.* 13. 22–3. Fr. 2 and fr. 3 have been less disputed. But it may be doubted whether his works were known at Alexandria. *See also* MUSIC, § 10.

Page, *Poet. Mel. Gr.* 362–3, cf. frs. 941 and 1027 (c); Wilamowitz, *Timotheos* (1903), 92 f. C. M. B.

**TERRA SIGILLATA,** pottery of the Roman period, including moulded vessels with reliefs and plain wheel-made forms, is characterized by a red gloss-coat, often glaze-like. Handleless cups, bowls, and plates predominate. Both the forms and the decoration were often copies of metal-work. The general term includes pottery of widely different date and origin. (1) Arretine ware, and related Italian products, made from *c.* 30 B.C. to the mid first century A.D. were widely used in the Mediterranean and also popular in Gaul. Potters' stamps demonstrate frequent use of slave artisans. (2) Later Italian derivatives, mainly plain wares, such as *terra sigillata chiara*. (3) Eastern *sigillata*, although apparently with local Hellenistic precursors, belongs mainly to the first century A.D., when imitations of Arretine plain forms were made in Asia Minor (Tschandarli) and possibly Samos (Pliny, *HN* 35. 160). (4) Gaulish *sigillata*, known in Britain as samian ware (q.v.). (5) Spanish ware of local distribution inspired by the Gaulish tradition. (6) Fourth-century A.D. stamped pottery from the Argonne (Marne ware). (7) North African and Eastern red wares, sometimes with stamped decoration, of the late Roman and Byzantine periods are now usually described as Late Roman A and B Wares.

GENERAL. H. Comfort, *PW* Suppl. vii, s.v.
WESTERN. *General*: F. Oswald and T. D. Pryce, *Terra Sigillata* (1920).

ARRETINE. A. Stenico, *La ceramica arretina* i (1960); A. Oxé, *Arretinische Reliefgefässe vom Rhein* (1933); H. Dragendorff and C. Watzinger, *Die Arretinische Reliefkeramik* (1948).
GAULISH. J. Déchelette, *Les Vases céramiques ornés de la Gaule romaine* (1904); F. Hermet, *La Graufesenque* (1934); J. A. Stanfield and G. Simpson, *Central Gaulish Potters* (1958).
SFANISH. M. A. Mesquiriz de Catalan, *Terra sigillata hispánica* (1961).
LATE ROMAN. G. Chenet, *La Céramique gallo-romaine d' Argonne* (1941).
EASTERN. S. Loeschcke, 'Sigillatatöpfereien in Tschandarli', *Ath. Mitt.* 1912, 344 ff.; J. H. Iliffe, 'Sigilata Wares in the Near East', *Quart. Depart. Antiquities in Palestine* 1938, 4 ff.; K. Kubler, 'Spätantike Stempelkeramik', *Ath. Mitt.* 1931, 75 ff. B. R. H.

**TERRACOTTAS.** The term properly includes all objects made of fired clay; commonly, vases and household vessels are treated separately. Fabricants (*κοροπλάθοι*, *κοροπλάσται*) were originally potters; later they were specialists who occasionally inscribed shop or personal names. Earlier terracottas were modelled freehand; after the sixth century B.C. they were usually made in moulds. Decoration was at first in vase technique; from the mid sixth century onward figurative work was covered with a white slip and painted in earth colours and in copper frit green-blue.

ARCHITECTURAL. Terracotta was used for: sarcophagi (Crete, Clazomenae, Etruria), ash-urns (Etruria), altars (*arulae*), incense-burners (*thymiateria*) and roofing. Revetment adorned all buildings in archaic times; it was somewhat superseded by stone in Greece, but survived in Italy and Sicily. Roof tiles (*κεραμίδες, tegulae*) were commonly of terracotta, constructed on two systems: Laconian (curvilinear), Corinthian (rectilinear). Western colonies copied the system of mother cities. Ornamental elements, simas, metopes, antefixes, acroteria, etc., were gaily decorated with geometric and floral designs in vase technique. Modelled figures were added in pediments, water-spouts, and acroteria. These were especially popular in Italy and Sicily. Large tiles were employed in Roman heating systems: to support the flooring and to permit hot air to circulate through walls (*t. mammatae*). Large moulded relief plaques (Campanian) were set on the walls of Roman houses and bust modillions under their cornices.

FIGURATIVE. Representational terracottas of large size were sometimes made in Greece as votives (Olympia); in Etruria they were common. Corinth led Greek production, exporting widely and teaching the technique to Etruria, where a flourishing school developed (Veii). Etruscan repertory was largely religious, but also included sarcophagi with life-size figures reclining on the lid. Sicily favoured large busts of the Eleusinian deities. Representational terracottas of small scale, masks, reliefs, and figurines, were made as votives for sanctuaries, graves, and house-shrines. Crude human figures appear in Greece in Neolithic times, steatopygous females, a few males, and animals. Rare in the earlier Bronze Age, female figures and animals recur in LH III. Primitive humans and bell figures, numerous horses and riders characterize the terracottas of the Late Iron Age. In the seventh century orientalizing types (first with moulded heads), masks and horses move from Cyprus and Rhodes via Crete all over the classical world. Archaic local schools developed, particularly in Asia Minor, Boeotia, Corinth, Laconia, Argos, Magna Graecia, and Etruria. Relatively few and chiefly hieratic types were made in the fifth century B.C. Votive plaques (Locrian, Melian) were popular. In the fourth century the craft flowered, especially in Athens and Boeotia (Tanagra). The repertory contained few religious types (Aphrodite and Eros), and many of theatrical genre (actors and comic figures). Cemeteries near Tanagra supplied so many charming figures in the 1870s that Greek figurines became the craze in Europe under the name 'Tanagras'. During the third century these types spread everywhere. Fine local shops developed in Alexandria, Sicily, south Italy (Tarentum). Later Hellenistic types were varied, including new religious themes, imaginative genre, and echoes of sculpture. The most active shops were in Asia Minor: Amisus, Troy, Pergamum, Priene, Myrina, Smyrna, Tarsus. Roman shops continued the Hellenistic repertory with local additions. Prolific centres were established in the Rhône and Rhine valleys during the first two Christian centuries. Figurines were also produced in the rest of the Empire, often adapting Mediterranean types to local cults, until *c.* A.D. 200. Thereafter they died out in the north, continuing in the south for another two centuries, particularly in Athens, Corinth, the Fayum, Jordan, Mesopotamia. With the establishment of Christianity, the craft ended completely in the fifth century A.D.

MISCELLANEOUS. Many minor objects were made in terracotta, often as substitutes for more expensive materials. These include ornaments applied to wooden furniture and sarcophagi. Relief decoration was used for vases imitating metal-work. It consisted of moulded figures affixed to the body or modelled vases in the form of animals or figures (plaquette ware, plastic vases). Cheap votives include miniatures of all sorts; jewellery, wreaths and flowers, furniture, implements, armour, vehicles, theatrical masks. Toys are numerous, particularly rattles and dolls. Categories that have been well classified are: lamps, loom-weights, spindle-whorls, stamps, sealings, tokens, metal-impressions, moulds. Excavators find these useful for dating stratification.

ARCHITECTURAL. *PW*, s.v. *Tegula* (Ebert); Å. Åkerström, *Die Architektonischen Terrakotten Kleinasiens* (Skrifter utgivna av Svenska institutet i Athen, series in 4°, vol. xi; Lund, 1966).
FIGURATIVE. Technical: R. V. Nicholls, *BSA* 1952; B. Neutsch, *Jahrb. Ergänzungsheft* 1952.
GENERAL. F. Winter, *Die Typen der figürlichen Terrakotten* (1903); S. Mollard-Besques, *Les Terres cuites grecques* (1963); R. A. Higgins, *Greek Terracottas* (1968). Recent Catalogues: id., *Cat. of the Terracottas . . . British Museum* (1954 on); S. Mollard-Besques, *Cat. raisonné des figurines . . . Mus. du Louvre* (1954 on); D. B. Thompson, *Troy*, Suppl. Monograph 3 (1963); C. Grandjouan, *Agora* vii (1961) (Roman).
MISCELLANEOUS. Consult excavation publications, especially of Delos, Corinth, Olynthus, Perachora, Priene, Pergamum, Alexandria, etc. D. B. T.

**TERRAMARA** derives from the Emilian dialect expression ('terra marna') for the rich black soil whose exploitation as a fertilizer first brought a distinctive type of settlement site to the notice of nineteenth-century archaeologists. It has given its name to an important culture of the Italian Middle and Late Bronze Age, concentrated west of the river Panaro in the modern provinces of Modena, Reggio Emilia, Parma, and Piacenza.

The *terramara* settlements consisted of open, or more usually protected, villages of huts rounded or occasionally rectangular in shape. In low-lying areas the villages had eventually to be built on piles after a deterioration in climate at the beginning of the first millennium B.C. brought about periodic inundations, of which the practical results were not fully overcome until Roman times.

The economy of the *terremare* seems to have been based on hunting (bear, boar, deer), cattle-raising (cows, goats, pigs, sheep), and agriculture. A highly developed bronze industry, no doubt controlled by specialist smiths, suggests trans-Alpine and trans-Adriatic contacts, with supplies of metal presumably being drawn from the Austrian Alps. The stylistic affinities of *terramara* pottery and bronzes must in fact be sought in the repertoire of the Hungarian Early and Middle Bronze Age, notable for its population movements and the consequent spread of cremation as a burial rite: an off-shoot could very well have been dispatched to northern Italy, where the presence of the horse in the Terramara Culture may be inferred from the presence of a Hungarian type of horn cheek-piece. These affinities, and the fact that the best

*terramara* pottery is also the earliest, confirm one aspect of the 'Pigorini theory': the *terramaricoli* were invaders, and appeared with their culture already fully formed. The extension of this theory—i.e. that the *terramaricoli* were the prehistoric ancestors of the Romans, and went south in the twelfth century B.C.—is now quite unacceptable.

Contact between the Terramara Culture and the peninsular Apennine Culture (q.v., known until 1931 as the *cultura extraterramaricola*) heralded the opening of the Italian Late Bronze Age and led ultimately to a complete fusion between the two cultures that was far-reaching in its shaping of the Italian Iron Age. The *terramara* impact on the south was made possible above all by metal, in which Apennine Italy was notoriously poor. *Terramara* products could now travel south as objects of trade: the many parallels between the finds from the *terremare* and from Scoglio del Tonno underline the role of the Tarentino in particular as an area specializing by then in East Mediterranean trade, well illustrated by the find in a LH IIIB house at Mycenae of a mould for casting a *terramara* type of winged axe.

G. Saflund, *Le Terremare . . .* (Lund, 1939), discussed by C. F. C. Hawkes and E. Stiassny, *JRS* 1940, 89 ff.; D. H. Trump, *Proc. Prehist. Soc.* 1958, 165 ff.; V. G. Childe in *Civiltà del Ferro* (Bologna, 1960); S. M. Puglisi, *La civiltà appenninica* (1959); G. A. Mansuelli and R. Scarani, *L'Emilia prima dei Romani* (1961); *Preistoria dell'Emilia e Romagna*, 2 vols. (Bologna, 1962-3). D. W. R. R.

**TERTULLIAN** (QUINTUS SEPTIMIUS FLORENS TERTULLIANUS) (*c.* A.D. 160–*c.* 240), born in or near Carthage, the son of a centurion, was trained in law, and early attracted to Stoicism. Disgust at pagan moral excesses, combined with admiration for the spirit of martyrs, brought him to Christianity (*c.* 195). From then on, he used his brilliant gifts of advocacy, rhetoric, and irony in favour of the rigorist party among the Carthaginian Christians. From the first he was steeped in the spirit of the martyrs. His *Ad Martyras*, *Ad Nationes*, and *Apologeticus* (all written *c.* 197) combined embattled defence of Christianity against popular charges of atheism and black magic with the view that in martyrdom alone the Christian assured himself salvation. Next (198–205) he devoted himself largely to Christian moral and ethical problems. His *De Spectaculis*, *De Oratione*, *De Testimonio Animae*, *Ad Uxorem*, *De Paenitentia*, *De Baptismo*, and *De Praescriptione haereticorum* all show a zeal for a puritan interpretation of the Christian ideal. The *De Praescriptione* was also a brilliant attack both on those who hoped to absorb pagan philosophy into Christianity and on the Gnostic heretics, and contains much of the Western view of tradition and authority. It was followed by works directed against the Valentinians and (between 207 and 211) five books against Marcion, in which Tertullian expounds the unity of God and identity of Jesus Christ with the Jewish messiah.

Meantime Tertullian, probably by now a presbyter in the Carthaginian Church, dissatisfied with his colleagues, and perhaps after a dispute with the clergy in Rome, joined the Montanist movement. This step involved only the hardening of attitudes previously held and fitted his constant conviction that the Last Days were rapidly approaching. The New Prophecy 'dispelled all previous ambiguities', and summoned the Christian to final battle against the world and its representatives. The transition seems to have taken place by 207. He now became more fanatical against 'idolatry' in every form, against those who counselled caution in face of the authorities, and against the traditions of the Roman Empire. His works of this period (*De Fuga in Persecutione*, *Ad Scapulam*, *De Corona Militis*, *De Jejunio*, *De Monogamia*) read like political journalism at its most virulent, characterized by topicality, debating power, and a superb sense of irony. Even his longer and more serious *De Carne Christi*, *De*

*Resurrectione Carnis, De Anima,* and *Adversus Praxean* bear the stamp of the brilliant pleader. His open letter to the proconsul, Scapula, in 212, is a finely documented and biting protest against the official policy of repressing Christianity and a plea for religious liberty. His last surviving work, *De Pudicitia,* was most probably directed against measures by Callistus, Bishop of Rome (217–22), to relax the traditional Christian penitential system. In this Tertullian gives classic expression to the theology of the gathered Church and it is fundamental for the study of the Western doctrine of the Holy Spirit.

Tertullian seems to have lived to a ripe old age, and finally to have broken with the Montanists to found his own sect of Tertullianists more rigorous even than they. Despite his excesses and exaggerations, he remains the first Latin churchman. He turned Christian thought in the West into channels in which it has never ceased to flow. His *Adversus Praxean* answered Patripassianism decisively and contributed towards the formulation of the doctrine of the Trinity. He may also be called the father of Donatism and of all Puritan nonconformity, of radical individualism and of political protest based on Biblical concepts. He is one of the founders of political and religious thought in the West. Thirty-one of his works survive. *See also* DONATISTS.

Ed. *Apologeticus* and *De Spectaculis,* T. R. Glover (Loeb series); *De Anima,* J. H. Waszink (Amsterdam, 1947); *De Baptismo, Adv. Praxean, De Oratione, De Carne Christi,* and *De Resurrectione Carnis,* E. Evans (1957–64). Other works ed. A. Reifferscheid, E. Kroymann, and V. Buhlart, *CSEL* xx, lxx, and lxxvi. *Bibl.,* P. Monceaux, *Histoire littéraire de l' Afrique chrétienne* i (1901); A. d'Alès, *La Théologie de Tertullien* (1905); K. Adam, *Der Kirchenbegriff Tertullians* (1907); J. Berton, *Tertullien le Schismatique* (1928); T. R. Glover, *Conflict of Religions in the Early Roman Empire* (1909), 305 ff.; E. Allo Isichei, *Political Thinking and Social Experience: Some Christian Interpretations of the Roman Empire from Tertullian to Salvian* (1964). W. H. C. F.

**TESSERA,** a ticket or token, used in Rome, as in all ages, for a great variety of purposes, and represented by small pieces, often circular, of lead, bronze, terracotta, bone, etc.

The *tesserae nummulariae,* formerly known erroneously as *tesserae gladiatoriae,* were tabs attached to bags of silver *denarii,* to show that they had been tested for genuineness (*specto*). The surviving examples belong to the last century of the Republic.

Under the Empire there were *tesserae frumentariae,* for the recipients of free corn, *tesserae* for games and public shows, and *tesserae* given in largess by the Emperor and exchangeable for various presents. Many of these *tesserae* bear types, similar to those of coins, but less often legends, and are often of lead. One series of bronze *tesserae* shows imperial heads on the obverse and numbers on the reverse. The attribution of *tesserae* to their particular uses is largely conjectural, but the principles of classification have been determined by Rostovtzeff.

*Tesserae* were, of course, used in private as well as in public life. Among private *tesserae* may be mentioned the *tesserae hospitales,* which established the claim of the bearer to hospitality on his travels abroad, and *tesserae lusoriae,* used for games.

M. Rostovtzeff, 'Römische Bleitesserae', *Klio,* Beiheft 3, 1905. H. M.

**TESTAMENTUM PORCELLI,** a satiric parody (3rd or 4th c. A.D.) of a will imagined to be by a pig, Grunnius Corocotta, just before being killed. It is mentioned by Jerome (praef. *Comment. in Isaiam*) as causing amusement in boys' schools.

Text at end of Bücheler's ed. of Petronius. A. d'Ors, *Rev. internationale des Droits d'Antiquité* 1955, 219 ff. J. W. D.

**TESTIMONIUM** signifies in its widest sense all types of evidence (Gai. 3. 131; Cic. *Top.* 19. 73); the term *instrumentum* was later used in the same sense (*Dig.* 22. 4. 1). In a narrower sense the term signifies the testimony of a witness (*testis*), which was in ancient times the only evidence in legal proceedings. It maintained its importance also in the classical period, though documentary proof gained more and more ground. In the oldest law we already find another activity of witnesses: some solemn legal transactions and acts required for their validity the presence of witnesses, e.g. *mancipatio* and other transactions *per aes et libram* (five witnesses), *confarreatio* (ten), also some important acts in civil procedure (as *in ius vocatio, litis contestatio*) and such legal acts as the opening of a will. When a crime (e.g. of *furtum*) was being investigated, some processes open to the parties to the case required the participation of witnesses. But the widest field of their activity was in testamentary law, because in all forms of will their presence was necessary for the validity of the act (*see* INHERITANCE, LAW OF). The two functions were closely connected, for presence at a legal transaction entailed an obligation on the witness to give evidence if there was litigation. Refusal of testimony made a man *intestabilis,* i.e. incapable of being a witness or calling a witness, and hence also of making a will.

In course of time various forms of written evidence (*instrumenta, documenta*) were developed. On the one hand, a transaction may itself be made in writing and attested by witnesses; on the other, some event or act may be recorded in writing and the truth of the record attested by persons who have been present at the occurrence; or again, a person may make some statement and other persons simply attest the identity of the deponent and the fact that he made the statement. The object of this last process is to make the evidence available in subsequent court proceedings, when it can be read aloud in the absence of the witness himself.

Some persons were generally excluded from testimony: slaves, *impuberes,* women (only from transactions), *intestabiles,* persons convicted of crimes, and those who followed an infamous profession. In particular cases all persons connected by a bond of kinship or moral obligation with a party interested in the lawsuit or in the transaction (*testimonium domesticum*) were excluded. Capacity to witness a will was regulated by special rules.

The deposition of a witness was made personally and usually under oath. Recitation of a written *testatio,* which became the later practice, carried less conviction. Apart from witnesses to legal transactions, persons could not be forced to give evidence except in criminal proceedings. Citation of a witness was called *denuntiatio.* In post-classical law, under the influence of the Hellenistic East, documents acquired greater evidentiary value than the evidence of witnesses, which became more and more distrusted. The testimony of one witness had no value at all.

False witness was severely punished (*Lex Cornelia testamentaria*); according to some laws even with death (XII Tables: 'deicere e saxo Tarpeio'; *Lex Cornelia de sicariis*).

S. Riccobono, *Sav. Zeitschr.* 1913, 231 ff.; L. Wenger, *Institutes of the Roman Law of Civil Procedure* (1940), 195 ff., 293 ff.; W. Hellebrand, *Das Prozesszeugnis im Rechte der Papyri* (1934). A. B.

**TETHYS** (Τηθύς), in mythology, daughter of Earth and Heaven, sister of Ocean (Hes. *Theog.* 136); becomes the consort of Ocean and bears the Rivers, also the three thousand Oceanids, whose work it is to aid the rivers and Apollo to bring young men to their prime, and Styx, chief of them all (ibid. 337 ff.). H. J. R.

**TETRARCHY** (τετραρχία, i.e. the fourth part of an ἀρχή) was first used to denote one of the four political divisions of Thessaly ('tetrad' being a purely geographical term). The tetrarchies were Thessaliotis, Hestiaeotis, Pelasgiotis, and Phthiotis. Their origin is obscure. Some scholars maintain that they were originally separate and independent tribal States which united to form the Thessalian κοινόν. It is much more likely that the κοινόν existed before the tetrarchies and that the latter were artificial divisions of Thessaly created to serve as the basis of its political and military organization. The rapid development of cities towards the end of the fifth century, together with the decay of the κοινόν, caused the tetrarchies to lose much of their importance. In 342 B.C. Philip of Macedon, now Archon of Thessaly, revived them in order to overcome the resistance of the cities through tetrarchs who were his partisans. How long this system lasted is unknown.

The term found its way to the Hellenistic East and was applied to the four divisions into which each of the three tribes of the Galatians was subdivided. In Roman times many hellenized princes in Syria and Palestine were styled 'tetrarch', but the number of tetrarchies in any political organization ceased to be necessarily four, the term denoting merely the realm of a subordinate dynast.

F. Gschnitzer, *Hermes* 1954, 451 ff.; M. Sordi, *La lega tessala* (1958), 316 ff.                                                          H. D. W.

**TETRICUS,** GAIUS PIUS ESUVIUS (*PW* 1), governor of Aquitania, was made Emperor in Gaul on the death of his relative Victorinus. Ruling from A.D. 270 to 274, he was less successful than the preceding 'Gallic' emperors. He finally appealed to Aurelian and, when Aurelian invaded Gaul, deserted his army at the battle of Châlons. Led in triumph, he was afterwards appointed 'corrector Lucaniae'. His son, Tetricus II, shared his fortunes as Caesar and again as a senator of Rome. H. M.; B. H. W.

**TEUCER** (Τεῦκρος), (1) ancestor of the Trojan kings, the genealogy being

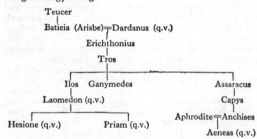

Teucer
|
Batieia (Arisbe)⸗Dardanus (q.v.)
|
Erichthonius
|
Tros
|
Ilos   Ganymedes                    Assaracus
|                                    |
Laomedon (q.v.)                      Capys
|                        Aphrodite⸗Anchises
Hesione (q.v.)   Priam (q.v.)         |
                                    Aeneas (q.v.)

For authorities, see Schmidt in Roscher, v. 406. Ramsay, *Asianic Elements*, 225, identifies him with the Hittite god Tarku. (2) Son of Telamon (q.v. 1) by Hesione. Throughout the *Iliad* he is a valiant archer, and faithful comrade of his half-brother, the greater Ajax. This character is maintained in later works, e.g. the *Ajax* of Sophocles. He was absent at the time of Ajax's suicide (*Ajax* 342–3), but returned (974) in time to take a leading part in the struggle to secure him honourable burial. After his banishment (*see* TELAMON 1) he founded Salamis in Cyprus (Hor. *Carm.* 1. 7. 27 ff., and often). There is no consistent tradition of the manner or place of his death.
H. J. R.

**TEUCER** (3) of Cyzicus (1st c. B.C.) wrote on the Mithridatic Wars, Tyre, the Arabs, Jewish history, Byzantium, and Cyzicus, his work covering Pompey's settlement of the East, and reflecting the part played by Cyzicus at this time. His Περὶ χρυσοφόρου γῆς does not necessarily identify him with Teucer (q.v. 4) of Babylon.

*FGrH* iii A, 126; a, 314.                                   A. H. McD.

**TEUCER** (4) of Babylon (probably the Babylon in Egypt), astrologer, is conjectured to belong to the first century A.D. He expounded the traditional astrology of Egypt and united with it oriental and Greek elements. He had a great influence on Arabian and medieval astrology, through his description of the constellations. Fragments of his works have been preserved.

Ed. F. Boll, *Sphaera* (1903), 16, 31; *CCAG* vii. 194 ff., viii. 196 ff. ix. 2. 180 ff.                                                    W. D. R.

**TEUTA,** Illyrian queen and regent after Agron's death in 231 B.C. for his young son Pinnes by an earlier wife (*see* ILLYRICUM). She followed up Agron's victory over the Aetolians at Medeon by aggression against Epirus, and directed Illyrian piracy against Italian commerce with Greece. She refused Rome satisfaction for the murder of Italian merchants in 230 and even for an attack on the Roman envoys. In 229 she took Corcyra, defeating the Achaeans, and was besieging Issa and Dyrrhachium when Rome intervened, in the First Illyrian War, and forced her to withdraw and submit (Polyb. 2. 2–12).

Badian, *Stud. Gr. Rom. Hist.* 1 ff.; N. G. L. Hammond, *JRS* 1968, 4.                                                                A. H. McD.

**TEUTOBURGIENSIS,** SALTUS, the district where, in A.D. 9, the army of Varus (q.v. 2) was destroyed on the march from summer to winter quarters, by the Cheruscian prince Arminius (q.v.). Despite much discussion, the *Saltus Teutoburgiensis* has not been located, neither is it certain whether *saltus* here means a forest or a mountain pass. The Teutoburger Wald of modern maps is an archaizing name given in the seventeenth century. The site of the disaster must lie somewhere between the middle Weser and the upper Ems, between the Lippe and the Dümmer See. W. John has argued that by the phrase 'medio campi' Tacitus (*Ann.* 1. 61) places the last stand within the camp, on the parade ground where the survivors had dug themselves in; thus the site may one day be discovered by aerial photography.

W. John, *Die Ortlichkeit der Varusschlacht bei Tacitus* (1950).; id. *PW* xxiv, 922 ff.                                          O. B.; J J. W.

**TEUTONES,** a Germanic tribe, chiefly known from their migration in company with the Cimbri (q.v.), whose neighbours they had been in Jutland, to southern France, where Marius annihilated them in the battle of Aquae Sextiae in 102 B.C. The Aduatuci whom Caesar (*BGall.* 2. 29) defeated in Gaul claimed to be descended from the Cimbri and Teutones. From *ILS* 9377 *inter Toutonos*, etc., it has been inferred, perhaps hazardously, that a remnant of them survived at Miltenberg on the Main. Curiously, Tacitus does not mention them or the Ambrones, who marched with them and the Cimbri. The name Teuton became a synonym for German and was used by Latin poets long after the Teutones became extinct.                                                       E. A. T.

**TEXTUAL CRITICISM,** the technique and art of restoring a text to its original state, as far as possible, in the editing of Greek and Latin authors (for papyrus documents *see* PAPYROLOGY, for stone inscriptions *see* EPIGRAPHY). We know ancient texts only from a process of successive copying by hand (*see* PALAEOGRAPHY), which was subject to corruption by faulty transcription and emendation, before the resulting vulgate (*textus receptus*) was committed to print. The modern editor has to review this fallible process in the light of the surviving evidence, which is all too often inadequate. His task is usually defined as (i) *recensio*: to study the manuscript tradition; (ii) *examinatio*: to determine critically what may be taken as authentic; (iii) *divinatio*: to attempt the remedy of error by conjecture. In practice, however, the complexity of evidence may often involve all three phases at once in establishing a text.

The manuscripts representing an original text have a genealogy (*stemma*), but we may not be able to construct it. Copying causes the loss of earlier versions, scribal emendation obscures the line of tradition, inter-borrowing (*contaminatio*) mixes the relations of manuscripts, and the surviving evidence may defy analysis. Learned copying dates for Greek authors from Alexandrian times (3rd c. B.C.), for Latin authors from the fourth century A.D., and it continued for popular authors during the Middle Ages, in Byzantium and the West, to the scholarship of the Renaissance. The effect on transmission may vary according to time, place, and author, but it must be borne in mind; here the history of scholarship is relevant.

An editor should begin by looking for a *stemma*. The evidence is strictly limited to such significant errors as may indicate specific lines of descent; for authentic readings could survive in any line. P. Maas established a formula of analysis. Significant errors are *separative* or *conjunctive*. (i) *Separative*: if one manuscript shows an error where another preserves the authentic reading, the latter has descended independently of the former—but how does one distinguish an authentic reading from a plausible emendation? (ii) *Conjunctive*: two or more manuscripts may share an idiosyncratic error, that is, one which need not be attributed to coincidence in misreading, and it will associate them in a specific line of descent—but what if emendation has removed the evidence of association? Maas would not apply his formula where the manuscript tradition was subject to emendation or 'contamination', and this limits its use—rightly so, for it is unfair to a text to edit it on an uncertain 'stemmatic' basis. Further, the *stemma* must cover a 'closed tradition': otherwise any individual manuscript may contain variants—in text or margin—that come from an external source, not least in the Renaissance (as Pasquali argued) when scholars were searching for fresh manuscripts.

How far may one apply Maas's formula more freely in order to gain a general impression? There must be some evidence for the earlier stages of transmission ('vertically') and a large enough number of manuscripts to allow the possibility of grouping (to reduce the individual vagaries of 'contamination') and of reasonable argument in terms of probability: then it is worth the attempt, providing one heeds the warnings of Maas and Pasquali. There is little excuse these days for neglecting to examine a 'quorum' of the available manuscripts, even initially on a basis of selective collation.

For an increasing number of authors, however, as scholars study more of their manuscripts by stricter methods, the 'stemmatic' procedure shows its dangers: emendation and 'contamination' demand analysis of mutual interrelations ('horizontally'). Let us illustrate the problem by a diagram:

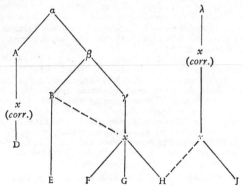

(The Roman capitals show extant manuscripts, the Greek letters their lost ancestors; italic $x$ indicates lost intermediaries, some emended (*corr.*); the dotted lines mark 'contamination'.) We have a main group descended from $a$, which could only too easily be taken as the 'archetype' of a *stemma*, reconstructed from A and the descendants of $\beta$ (though distorted by $x$'s borrowing from B); D and E could be eliminated as derived from A and B respectively, D more doubtfully in view of $x$ (*corr.*). But there is a second line from $\lambda$, which appears late in J and by 'contamination' in H. In practice one might prove the relations of the $a$ group but miss the $\lambda$ evidence. But suppose—and this is no idle assumption—that the earlier manuscripts were lost and we had only D–J of varying dates? The 'stemmatic' analysis would not work: we should have to classify the manuscripts in groups, on evidence already distorted by emendation and 'contamination'. FGH might fit together, but H with some doubt, at a lower level; if $a$ had significant errors we might also associate D and E, but loosely; and only a bold man would argue back from H's borrowings and J to a $\lambda$ line, already corrected.

This is the kind of problem which editors, more often than not, have to face: no clear-cut 'stemmatic' procedure but the difficult examination of emended and 'contaminated' manuscripts. Such manuscripts may vary in date (especially among popular authors), from medieval Western and Byzantine to Renaissance times, and it is always important to know the conditions of scholarship. Too few manuscripts limit the evidence, too many complicate the method of analysis; and late manuscripts may preserve a newly discovered tradition: *recentiores non deteriores* (in Pasquali's words). It is hazardous, though often necessary, to argue from assumption about what could or could not have been soundly corrected: intelligent men, whether scholarly or not, if they thought in the language, might well complete a context by conjecture. We should not underestimate Byzantine learning, the effect of medieval annotation, or the skill of Renaissance emendation. In any event the editor should control the escalation of hypotheses: it is better to plot the evidence and survey its indications. Modern bibliography and photographic copying give him no excuse for not studying the general field of his manuscript tradition. Seven manuscripts of Aeschylus suggested a *stemma*, seventeen have destroyed it, and there are more manuscripts of Aeschylus! The moral is that one should not draw definite conclusions without examining the balance of the evidence. An editor of Polybius or Livy may show a *stemma* and a 'closed tradition' of the main line of descent, but only after collating *all* the known manuscripts; Polybius and Livy, however, were too voluminous to be continually popular. At the same time, as life is short and 'the best may be enemy of the good', there is a place for preliminary investigation, working up from the earlier manuscripts: an 'elenchus' of, say, 1,000 readings allows rapid collation and a choice of the manuscripts that merit closer study. It is no hardship to apply this method to 100 manuscripts, which would cover most lines of tradition.

The recension of manuscripts, even allowing for adequate evidence, may involve argument from probability, as a 'working hypothesis', and emendation and 'contamination' can baffle analysis. We must consider the technical expedients. A 'distribution chart' may assist—the variants plotted in relation to the manuscripts—so that one may discern their relationship. Or there may be recourse to statistical examination, a 'calculus of variants', which does not make any assumption about the authenticity of readings or their successive corruption. This method belongs to that of mathematical symbolism, recording the patterns of variants, and the 'calculus' indicates the possible choice of classes under which the manuscripts may be studied. It is scientific in the sense that an editor should know the *possibly valid* classes rather than argue from a cumulative series of assumptions. Statistical work may now be handed to a computer, once the data are suitably prepared. The benefit here is not only to save time but to overcome human fallibility in judging the evidence: 'punch-cards' will produce their patterns. There is no short-cut in collation; for minor palaeographical differences, depending on the scribe and the script he is copying, could distort the statistical correlation and one must define the significant data: only then can the machine provide the reasonable answers. The result will be not a mechanical result but a context of judgement, as individual readings come up for consideration. The editor has then to use his scholarship and understanding of his author and the subject-matter and style.

L. Havet, *Manuel de critique verbale appliquée aux textes latins* (1911), for the logical problems; F. W. Hall, *Companion to Classical Texts* (1913); W. W. Greg, *The Calculus of Variants* (1927); A. Dain, *Les Manuscrits* (1949); A. A. Hill, 'Postulates for Distributional Studies of Texts', *Papers Bibliograph. Soc. Univ. Virginia* iii (1950–1), 63; G. Pasquali, *Storia della tradizione e critica del testo*² (1952); P. Maas, *Textual Criticism* (rev. ed., 1958), with 'Retrospect'; V. A. Dearing, *Manual of Textual Analysis* (1959); M. Bodmer *et al.*, *Geschichte der Textüberlieferung* i (1961); S. Timpanaro, *La genesi del metodo del Lachmann* (1963); B. M. Metzger, *The Text of the New Testament* (1964); (Dom) Jacques Froger, 'La collation des manuscrits à la machine électronique', *Institut de Recherche et d'Histoire des Textes, Bulletin* xiii (1964–5), 135 ff.
'STEMMATICS'. A. H. McDonald, *T. Livi Libri* xxxi–xxxv (O.C.T. 1965); J. M. Moore, *The Manuscript Tradition of Polybius* (1965).
CONTAMINATED TRANSMISSION. Homer, *Iliad*, ed. T. W. Allen (1931); Greek New Testament, ed. H. von Soden (1913).
NOTE R. D. Dawe, *Manuscripts of Aeschylus* (1964).
ON JUDGEMENT IN TEXTUAL CRITICISM. J. N. Madvig, *Adversaria Critica* i (1871); W. M. Lindsay, *Introduction to Latin Textual Emendation* (1896); A. E. Housman in his editions of *Lucan* (1927), *Manilius* (1937), and *Juvenal* (1938).
TECHNIQUE OF CRITICAL EDITIONS. O. Stählin, *Editionstechnik*² (1914); J. Bidez et A. B. Drachmann, *Emploi des signes critiques*² (1938).
*See* SCHOLARSHIP IN ANTIQUITY *and* PALAEOGRAPHY (with bibliography). A. H. McD.

**THALES,** son of Examyes of Miletus, perhaps of Semitic stock (Hdt. 1. 170), was universally accounted one of the Seven Sages and by Aristotle (*Metaph. A* 3, 983ᵇ20) the founder of physical science. Stories were told of his versatility in many spheres, political (his advice to the Ionians to found a federal capital at Teos, Hdt. loc. cit.), economic, engineering, geographical, astronomical, and mathematical. The tradition that he foretold to within a year the solar eclipse which occurred during the battle of the Halys (28 May 585 B.C.) appears to be as old as Xenophanes (fr. 19 Diels, cf. Hdt. 1. 74, Eudem. fr. 144 Wehrli) but its basis is doubtful (Neugebauer, *Exact Sciences in Antiquity*² (U.S.A. 1957), 142). More plausible is the belief that he founded geometry by studying and generalizing Egyptian 'land-measurement'. He probably wrote nothing, but we must accept Aristotle's attribution to him of the view that the world not only originates from but returns to water, which is thus both eternal (and so divine) and the stuff of which everything consists. With this is connected his saying that 'all things are full of gods'. His cosmology has Egyptian and Semitic affinities.

Diels, *Vorsokr.*¹¹ i. 67–81; Burnet, *EGP.* 40 ff.; Kirk–Raven, *Presocratic Philosophers*, 74 ff.; Zeller–Mondolfo, *La filosofia dei Greci* I. ii (1938), 100 ff.; Guthrie, *Hist. Gk. Phil.* i. 45 ff., A. H. C.

**THALETAS,** of Gortyn in Crete (Paus. 1. 14. 4), worked at Sparta in the seventh century B.C. ('Plut.' *De mus.* 9). He wrote songs which exhorted to law-abidingness (Plut. *Lyc.* 4) and paeans ('Plut.' *De mus.* 10, but cf. 42). Nothing of his work survives. He used paeonic and cretic rhythms ('Plut.' *De mus.* 10). C. M. B.

**THALLUS** published a chronological work in three books, from the Trojan War to Ol. 167 (112–109 B.C.) according to Eusebius; but on the evidence of the fragments, from Belus to at least the death of Christ. If Eusebius is right, Thallus' work must have been later extended. Euhemeristic in character, it was used by the Christian apologists. He may, perhaps, be the Samaritan Thallus, Augustus' secretary or Tiberius' freedman.

*FGrH* ii B, 1156; BD, 835. A. H. McD.

**THAMUGADI** (modern *Timgad*), a settlement in Numidia 20 miles east of Lambaesis (q.v.). Founded in A.D. 100 by Trajan as a veteran colony (*ILS* 6841), the original town was designed on camp lines; *cardo* and *decumanus* intersected at right angles, *curia*, basilica, and forum were placed at this intersection, and smaller streets ran parallel to the two main roads. Thamugadi had many public baths and a theatre, and public-spirited citizens gave it a library and a market-place. When it outgrew its original rectangle, an enormous Capitoline temple was built outside the walls.

The fertile countryside brought great prosperity under the Septimian dynasty; in the fourth century it was still growing, and was a centre of the Donatist Schism in the African church. In the Vandal period, Saharan raiders sacked it; the Byzantines built a protecting fortress, but it fell to the first Arab invasion. Excepting Lepcis, Timgad has the most complete Roman remains in Africa, and has been completely excavated.

A. Ballu, *Les Ruines de Timgad*² (1904); R. Cagnat, *Carthage, Timgad, etc.*¹ (1909); C. Courtois, *Timgad, antique Thamugadi* (1951). W. N. W.

**THAMYRIS** (Θάμυρις) or **THAMYRAS** (Θαμύρας), a Thracian bard, who boasted that he would win a contest even if the Muses opposed him, whereat they blinded him and made him forget his skill (*Il.* 2. 594 ff.). Later authors attribute a multitude of musical inventions to him and add some unimportant tales.

Höfer in Roscher's *Lexikon*, s.v. H. J. R.

**THANATOS.** Death, as a person, hardly rises to the level of a mythological figure, belonging rather to folk-lore or poetical fancy. Thus he is a healer (Eur. *Hipp.* 1373, i.e. only death will ease Hippolytus' pain); he keeps Polybus in the grave (Soph. *OT* 942); he begat the poison which kills Heracles (Soph. *Trach.* 833); he is the only god who loves not gifts (Aesch. in Ar. *Ran.* 1392, i.e. death is inexorable, and, incidentally, is not worshipped as a god). In Epic he is a little more concrete; he is the brother of Sleep, and the two carry away the body of Sarpedon (*Iliad* 14. 231; 16. 671 ff.). Cf. Hesiod, *Theog.* 212 (Death, son of Night), 764 (he is iron-hearted, hated even by gods).

In Euripides' *Alcestis* he is a clearly defined figure, the 'dark-robed lord of the dead' (843), armed with a sword (76), and Euripides borrows him from Phrynichus (Serv. Dan. on *Aen.* 4. 694), who very likely had him from popular belief. Heracles rescues Alcestis (q.v.) by literal physical wrestling with Thanatos. Except for its successful issue, this is not unlike the modern Greek stories of a hero contending with Charos.

A merry tale of Sisyphus (q.v.) is preserved from Phrynichus (fr. 119 Jacoby) by schol. *Iliad* 6. 153. Sisyphus told Asopus what had become of Aegina (q.v.), and Zeus therefore sent Thanatos against him; but Sisyphus bound Thanatos, so no one died until Ares rescued him and gave Sisyphus to him. Before dying, Sisyphus bade his wife Merope give him no funeral dues; she obeyed, and he got permission from Hades to re-ascend to earth and remonstrate. He neglected to return till he died of old age, and Hades set him to roll the rock to keep him from running away again.

For Thanatos in art see O. Waser in Roscher's *Lexikon*, s.v. H. J. R.

**THARGELIA,** an Ionian festival attributed to Apollo and celebrated the 7th Thargelion (May–June), also known from Asia Minor (Hipponax), Abdera, Massilia. The most discussed rite took place the day before. A man (the φαρμακός) was fed, led around in the town, flogged with green plants, driven out, and sometimes stoned or killed. He is certainly a scapegoat, absorbing all evil and then removed. On the other hand, certain rites point to the conception of a spirit of vegetation whose power is to be reinforced. The festival is named after the θάργηλα which were brought on the chief day, first fruits (q.v.) of the still-unripe crops cooked in a pot; the word signifies also the first bread baked of the new crop. The mixing of the two mentioned motifs is explained by the fact that the Thargelia were celebrated a little before the harvest, partly to protect and partly to promote the crops. The θάργηλα rite has been interpreted as the breaking of the taboo on the unripe crops.

L. Deubner, *Attische Feste* (repr. 1959), 179 ff.; Nilsson, *Feste*, 105 ff.; J. E. Harrison, *Proleg. to the Study of Greek Religion³* (1922), 77 ff.: the *pharmakos* is much discussed, e.g. Frazer, *GB⁹* ix; Nilsson, *GGR* i². 107 ff. M. P. N.

**THASOS,** an island of the north Aegean, colonized from Paros, probably *c.* 680 B.C. From the gold-mines in its soil (the first exploitation of which Herodotus (2. 44. 4) ascribed, probably without good reason, to the Phoenicians), and from others on the mainland under Mt. Pangaeus, it derived a revenue rising to 200–300 talents. A dispute with Athens about the mainland mines led to its secession from the Delian League (465), followed by its reduction (463). If we may judge by the fluctuations in the tribute of Thasos (3 talents in 454, and 30 in 446), it was deprived of the mainland mines in 463, but recovered them soon after. Despite a massacre of its Athenian partisans by Lysander (404), it again allied with Athens in 389 and was a permanent member of Athens' Second League. In 340 it was subdued by Philip, and it remained a Macedonian dependency until freed by the Romans in 196. After 300 its waning revenues from the mines were supplemented by the profits of a carefully regulated export of wine. The volume of this trade is attested by widely distributed finds of wine-jars (identified by an official stamp; *see* AMPHORA STAMPS) in the Balkan lands, where Thasian coinage also circulated freely.

Thasos had a flourishing school of sculpture from the seventh to the sixth century, and it was the home of the painter Polygnotus. It preserves impressive remains of its sixth- and fifth-century walls and several buildings of its Agora and a theatre have been excavated.

P-K, *GL* iv. D i; *IG* xii. 8; S. Casson, *Macedonia, Thrace and Illyria* (1926), *passim*; *Études thasiennes* i– (1944– ); *Guide de Thasos* (École française, 1967). M. C.; J. B.

**THEAETETUS** (*c.* 414–369 B.C.) of Athens, mathematician, friend and pupil of Plato in philosophy and of Theodorus of Cyrene in mathematics, contributed much to the foundations (*a*) of Euclid book 10, by investigating the various species of irrationals (cf. Pl. *Tht.* 147 d–148 b), and (*b*) of Euclid book 13, by constructing theoretically the five regular solids and discovering the methods of inscribing them in spheres.

E. Sachs, *De Theaeteto* (1914); A. Wasserstein, *CQ* 1958. W. D. R.

**THEAGENES** (1) of Megara slaughtered the flocks and herds of the wealthy, secured a bodyguard, and made himself tyrant; constructed a tunnelled conduit and pillared fountain; married his daughter to Cylon of Athens, and supported Cylon's unsuccessful attempt to make himself tyrant. He was himself subsequently banished from Megara. The date of Theagenes' tyranny depends on that of Cylon (victor Olymp. XXXV, coup

before Draco), and in spite of recent questionings is probably to be put between 640 and 620 B.C.

Arist. *Pol.* 1305ᵃ, *Rh.* 1. 2; Paus. 1. 28, 40, 41; Thuc. 1. 126; Plut. *Quaest. Graec.* 18. B. Dunkley, *BSA* 1935–6, 145 f. P. N. U.

**THEAGENES** (2) of Rhegium (fl. *c.* 525 B.C.), contemporary of Cambyses and author of a work Περὶ Ὁμήρου, was the first scholar to attempt an allegorical interpretation of Homer by suggesting that the names of the gods represented natural elements (*see* ALLEGORY).

Diels, *Vorsokr.⁵* i. 51 f.; F. Wehrli, *Zur Geschichte der allegorischen Deutung Homers im Altertum* (1928). J. F. L.

**THEAGES,** pupil of Socrates. Plato refers in the *Republic* (496 b) to 'the bridle of Theages', the bad health which kept him out of politics and saved him for philosophy. On the basis of this reference an imitator of Plato wrote a *Theages* dealing with the relation between philosophy and politics, and this is included in the corpus of Plato's works. W. D. R.

**THEANO** is said to have been the wife of Pythagoras, but another tradition describes her as being among his pupils, and the wife of his disciple Brotinus or Brontinus. Several apocryphal books were ascribed to her in antiquity. Seven apocryphal letters are to be seen in Hercher, *Epistolographi*, 603–7. W. D. R.

**THEATRES, STRUCTURE.** The Greek theatre consisted essentially of the orchestra, the flat dancing place used for the choral song and dance out of which grew tragedy (q.v.) and comedy (q.v.); and the auditorium (the *theatron* proper, Latin *cavea*), normally a convenient slope on which spectators could sit or stand. It may possibly have a forerunner in the theatral areas of Minoan palaces (*see* MINOAN CIVILIZATION). In some primitive theatres wooden stands were used for seating. Seats were sometimes cut in the rock; normally they consisted of stone benches of simple form, rising in tiers. The orchestra was normally, but not always, circular, and consisted of hard earth—paving was not introduced till Roman times. The *skene* (tent or hut) was in origin a simple structure for the convenience of the performers, which could also form a background for the plays. In the course of the fifth century it became a more solid building, ultimately acquiring a handsome architectural form with projecting wings. The fully developed auditorium was rather more than a semicircle in plan, opening out a little at the outer ends, where the line of seats was drawn on a slightly greater radius. The outer sectors required embankments and solid retaining walls, while the inner was hollowed out of the hill-side; there were no elaborate substructures as in Roman theatres. The auditorium did not link up with the *skene*, except perhaps by means of light gateways, and the intervening passages on either side were called *parodoi*. Stairways radiated from the orchestra, dividing the seating into 'wedges', and in large theatres there were horizontal passages too. The front tiers were sometimes provided with more elaborate and comfortable seating for priests and officials.

In the fifth century the action took place at orchestra level, with at most a low wooden platform, easily accessible by steps, in front of the *skene* (*see* TRAGEDY, COMEDY). In the late fourth century the *proskenion* was introduced, a row of columns in front of the *skene* supporting a high platform (seen to good advantage at Oropus, where it has been recently reconstructed). This came to be used as a raised stage, a feature appropriate to New Comedy, which would have been out of place in the theatre of Sophocles or Aristophanes. *Proskenia* were usual in Hellenistic theatres, and were added to old theatres at Athens and elsewhere.

Certain small theatres in the Attic demes (Icaria, Thoricus) give a good idea of the primitive form. At Athens itself tradition speaks of an early theatre in the agora. The theatre attached to the shrine of Dionysus Eleuthereus on the south slope of the Acropolis developed from crude beginnings in the latter part of the sixth century B.C.; its peculiar and complicated history is the subject of much dispute. Architecturally it was still simple and undeveloped in the time of the great fifth-century dramatists. The theatre at the shrine of Asclepius near Epidaurus shows the perfection of design achieved in the fourth century. Even then the theatre was by no means standardized and there are many local variations.

Roman theatres conformed to a type which made a complete building, though, in larger examples, the auditorium—a semicircle—was probably only partly roofed. The stage, certainly roofed and close to the semi-circular 'orchestra', was a wide and fairly deep raised platform, backed by a wall (*scenae frons*) as high as the top of the *cavea*, treated as an elaborate front towards the stage, with columns, niches, etc. Substructures of *cavea* and stage consisted of vaulted passages, etc., with staircases, and the outer walls enclosing the back of the *cavea*, sometimes squared, were of arched construction in tiers, with order treatments. Good examples are at Pompeii (small theatre), Orange, Aspendus, Miletus, Taormina, and Dougga (N. Africa). This type of theatre was favoured in Greece too in the Roman imperial period, though in some cases a natural slope was still used, avoiding the need for substructures (*see* ODEUM).

A. W. Pickard-Cambridge, *The Theatre of Dionysus in Athens* (1946); M. Bieber, *History of the Greek and Roman Theatre²* (U.S.A. 1961) (bibliography, 325 ff.); A. von Gerkan and W. Müller-Wiener, *Das Theater von Epidauros* (1961); *see also* ARCHITECTURE (all the books mentioned have sections on the theatre). T. F.; R. E. W.

**THEBES** (1) on the south edge of the east plain of Boeotia replaced, according to tradition, Orchomenus (q.v.) as leading city of Boeotia. It plays an important part in Greek saga in the generations before the Trojan War. The particular connexion with the Near East implied by the story of Cadmus has hitherto been discounted, though a portion of a Mycenaean palace in the centre of the modern town was excavated in 1909 and assumed to be the 'House of Cadmus', mentioned by Pausanias (9. 16. 5) as associated in tradition with the classical temple of Demeter Thesmophorus: τὸ δὲ τῆς Δήμητρος ἱερὸν τῆς Θεσμο-φόρου Κάδμου καὶ τῶν ἀπογόνων οἰκίαν ποτὲ εἶναι λέγουσι. Recent excavations at Thebes (*BCH* 1964, 775 ff., *ILN* 1964, 859 ff.) have revealed a classical structure over-lying a Mycenaean building to the south of the earlier discovery. Among the finds is a 'treasure' including Mesopotamian (?) cylinder-seals, one of them of the period of or at any rate referring to a Kassite king of 1381–1354. The associated objects are of diverse dates; the pottery is LH IIIB (13th c.). Not far away another find has revealed Middle Helladic cist graves and a Mycenaean building above them, with arms, ivories, and Linear B tablets associated with LH IIIB pottery. The find is of little aid in the vexed problem of Linear B dating; the same is true of the cylinder-seals, but some as yet unevaluated confirmation is given to the idea of an oriental connexion and so to saga-tradition, in which the gruesome fates of Theban princes were, next to the tale of Troy, the favoured material of Greek epic and tragedy. Thebes was destroyed by the Epigoni and laid waste. The Catalogue of the Ships (*Il.* 2. 505) names only Ὑποθῆβαι, though, according to Thucydides (1. 12), the forerunners of invasion were already in the 'Cadmean land' whence they went to Troy.

When the 'Boeotian' invasion was completed Thebes outstripped the other Boeotian towns, but was never strong enough to combine them into a unitary State.

It was friendly with the Pisistratids (Hipparchus made a dedication to Apollo Ptoos, *BCH* 1920, 237 ff.); its hostility to Athens dates from the Athenian reception of the Plataeans in *c.* 519 B.C. (*see* PLATAEA). As a punish-ment for the support which it gave to the Persians in 480–479, Thebes lost its predominant position in the Boeotian Confederacy, and recovered it only in 446. During the Peloponnesian War it grew at the expense of its small neighbours. Its territory, with subject towns, was nearly half Boeotia, and it elected four of eleven boeotarchs (*Hell. Oxy.* xii. 3). Dissatisfied with the Spartan peace in 404, Thebes joined Athens and Argos in the Corinthian War. The peace of 387 enabled the Spartans to detach the other Boeotian towns from Thebes, and in 382 they garrisoned the citadel. The Thebans retook it in 378, and at Leuctra in 371 drove the Spartans out of central Greece. For a brief period Thebes, led by Epaminondas (q.v.), was the chief power of Greece, but its hegemony did not survive him. Thebes joined Athens in resisting Philip; it was punished by destruction for a revolt against Alexander, and though refounded was never again a great city. Thebes was a pleasant place, with trees and fresh water ([Dicaearchus] 1. 12 ff. in *FHG* ii. 258). The temple of Apollo Ismenios, where Herodotus (5. 59) saw the ancient tripods bearing Καδμήια (? Mycenaean) γράμματα (and other inscriptions in Greek?), has been excavated. *See also* FEDERAL STATES, § 3.

P-K, *GL* I. ii. 501 ff. *passim.* L. Ziehen, *PW*, s.v. 'Thebai'; A. W. Gomme, *BSA* 1910–11, 29 ff. (topography). T. J. D.; R. J. H.

**THEBES** (2), formerly capital of Egypt, was still an important city at the Greek conquest, but suffered considerably during revolts in 206 and 88 B.C. of which it was the centre. It was sacked by Cornelius Gallus in 30 or 29 B.C.; Strabo found it a group of villages. The temples prospered under the Ptolemies: building was done on the east bank, and the temple of Deir-el-Medineh on the west was begun under Philopator. Occasional records of works occur till *c.* A.D. 150. Thebes had then become a tourist centre, the great attractions, as shown by graffiti, being the statue of 'Memnon' and the Pharaonic tombs. Papyri and numerous ostraca have been found there, almost all dealing with finance or taxation.

The fullest account of the buildings is in A. E. P. Weigall, *Guide to Antiquities of Upper Egypt²* (1913), 60 ff.; cf. also Baedeker, *Egypt³* (1929), 287 ff. For details see Porter and Moss, *Topographical Survey of Ancient Egyptian Hieroglyphic Texts, Reliefs and Paintings* i² (1–11), Theban Necropolis (1964); ii, Theban Temples. For the Graeco-Roman period see A. Bataille, *Les Memnonia* (1952), and (for the colossus of 'Memnon') A. and E. Bernard, *Les Inscriptions grecques et latines du Colosse de Memnon* (1960). J. G. M.

**THEMIS,** a goddess originally akin to or even identical with Gaea (Aesch. *Eum.* 2; *PV* 209–10). In the former passage the oracle at Delphi was once hers; in the latter, she is still a prophetess, and warns her son Prometheus of the future. The same powers are shown in Pindar, *Isthm.* 8. 34 ff., cf. THETIS. In all probability, her name means 'steadfast' (root θε). In Hesiod, *Theog.* 135, she is a daughter of Earth; ibid. 901 ff. she is Zeus' second consort, mother of the Horae and Moerae. But, as her name is used also to mean 'firmly established custom or law, justice', she tends to become an abstraction, Justice or Righteousness. For example, Medea, when betrayed, invokes her as guardian of oaths (Eur. *Med.* 160 ff.); Plato, *Leg.* 936 e, suggests an oath by Zeus, Apollo, and Themis. Her several cults may be supposed to have originated with her earlier nature for the most part.

Weniger in Roscher, s.v.; V. Ehrenberg, *Die Rechtsidee im frühen Griechentum* (1921). H. J. R.

**THEMISON** of Laodicea, pupil of Asclepiades and pre-cursor of Thessalus of Tralles, lived in Rome under

Augustus (31 B.C.–A.D. 14). His views being most inconsistent, his system is no unity. He agreed with Asclepiades in the theory of corpuscles. On the other hand, he introduced into medicine the conception of the *communia* ('status strictus, fluens, et mixtus'), referring to excretion which is either too much or too little, or too much from one part, too little from another. This defect, which he probably thought of as hindering the free movement of the atoms, he tried to remedy by an alteration of the state of the body as the physician finds it. Moreover, he was the first to study methodically the problem of chronic diseases and to encourage their treatment by physicians.

TEXT. Fragments, not collected. Περὶ τῶν ὀξέων καὶ χρονίων νοσημάτων (R. Fuchs, *Rh. Mus.* 1903) not Themison but Herodotus, M. Wellman, *Hermes* 1905, 1913.
LITERATURE. General survey, K. Deichgräber, *PW* v A. 1632. Th. Meyer-Steineg, 'Das medizinische System d. Methodiker', *Jenaer med.-hist. Beiträge* 1916. Themison the 'Vorbereiter der methodischen Lehre', Deichgräber, op. cit. 1632. 40; not the founder of the Methodical school, L. Edelstein, *PW*, Suppl. vi. 358, s.v. 'Methodiker'. L. E.

**THEMISTIUS,** Greek philosopher and rhetorician, was born in Paphlagonia *c*. A.D. 317 of a cultured family of pagan landowners, and studied in the eastern provinces and in Constantinople, where he opened a school (*c*. 345). Attracting the attention of the imperial government, he was soon appointed to an official chair and became a member of the Constantinopolitan Senate. His eloquent and often constructive exposition of the ideology of monarchy in a succession of panegyrics and other speeches won and retained for him the favour of every Emperor from Constantius II to Theodosius I, who appointed him prefect of the city (383–4) and entrusted him with the education of his son, the future Emperor Arcadius. He travelled widely in the Empire, in attendance on the imperial court and on official missions, such as that to the Roman Senate in 357. He died in Constantinople about 388.

In spite of his professed admiration for Plato, Themistius found the pragmatic and realistic approach of Aristotle more congenial, and he was little influenced by contemporary Neoplatonism, with its other-worldly overtones. In his early years as a teacher he wrote explanatory paraphrases of many of Aristotle's works, setting a pattern of exegesis which continued to be followed throughout the Middle Ages. A convinced pagan, he yet refrained from overt attacks on Christianity except in an address to Julian, now lost, which evoked from the Emperor the celebrated letter (253–67 Spanheim) setting out the principles of his proposed restoration of paganism.

Of his numerous works there survive: thirty-four speeches, mainly official addresses to Emperors, but including an interesting funeral oration on his father (*Or.* 20); and paraphrases of Aristotle's *Posterior Analytics*, *Physics*, *De Anima* (in the Greek original), *De Caelo* and *Metaphysics XII* (in a medieval Hebrew translation made from an Arabic version). Themistius was neither a great philosopher nor a great statesman, yet his speeches are valuable as sources for the history of his time and as specimens of pagan political ideology in the Christian empire, and his Aristotelian paraphrases embody material from lost commentaries.

*Orationes*, ed. W. Dindorf (1828); ed. G. Downey, vol. i (1965); *Paraphrases*, ed. M. Wallies, H. Schenkl, R. Heintze, and S. Landauer, in *Commentaria in Aristotelem Graeca* v (1899–1900). R. B.

**THEMISTO,** name of several heroines, the only one of importance being the daughter of Hypseus (Nonnus, *Dionys.* 9. 305 f.), wife of Athamas (q.v.). Herodorus, in schol. Ap. Rhod. 2. 1144, makes her his first wife and mother of several children, including Phrixus and Helle.
See Höfer in Roscher, s.v. H. J. R.

**THEMISTOCLES** (*c*. 528–462), Athenian democratic statesman, was a member of the ancient Lycomid family but, it is said, base-born, perhaps of a non-Greek mother. If so, he owed his unquestioned citizenship to the reform of Cleisthenes (q.v. 1). The tradition about him is predominantly anti-democratic and hostile; Thucydides almost alone gives a more favourable picture of him. Herodotus' informants accused him of corruption, and said that in 480 he had 'newly come to the front'; yet he had been elected eponymous archon in 493 (Dion. Hal. 6. 34) and general of his tribe in 490. As archon he began the development of Piraeus as a port.

The fall of Miltiades (q.v.) in 489 was followed by repeated resorts to ostracism (q.v.). Of nearly 1,500 known ostraka, mostly of these years, no less than 542 bear Themistocles' name. It looks as if rival leaders tried to get rid of him as dangerous; but Themistocles was able to direct enough votes to get rid successively of Hipparchus the friend of Hippias, Megacles the Alcmeonid, Xanthippus, and the middle-class leader Aristides (qq.v.). He was then (483) able to secure the application of a large surplus revenue from the silver mines of Laurium (q.v.) to building up the navy from 70 to 200 triremes, just in time to save Greece from Xerxes' invasion. During his rise to supremacy (487; though no source connects his name with it), a very important reform took place: the opening of the archonships to 'knights' in good standing, *by lot*; which at once transferred the leadership in war to the *strategoi* (who could be re-elected, thus gaining experience), and was bound in time to reduce the prestige of the conservative Aeropagus, recruited from ex-archons.

As *strategos*, then, Themistocles commanded Athens' fleet in 480. He secured the Spartan high command's support for his strategy of fighting as far forward as possible, at Artemisium (q.v.). But for this, the Persians could have avoided disastrous storm-damage on the Thessalian coast by passing it in squadrons able to use the small beaches. He was also responsible for the decisive battle of Salamis (*see* PERSIAN WARS) being fought 'in the Narrows, which most obviously saved our cause' (Thuc. 1. 74). For this he received unprecedented honours at Sparta.

In 479, the chief Athenian commands went to his rivals, recalled from exile in 481 (*see* ARISTIDES, XANTHIPPUS); but Themistocles was still important in the next winter, when he 'spun out the time' at Sparta while the Athenians refortified their city, against Sparta's wishes. Piraeus was also powerfully fortified, on his motion. But in the following years he lost influence to a coalition of the more conservative leaders. About 471 he was ostracized and went to live at Argos, 'also visiting other places in the Peloponnese', where several States were moving towards democracy. Sparta grew alarmed, and (*c*. 468?) claimed to have evidence that he was involved with Pausanias (q.v. 1) in intrigues with Persia. Themistocles escaped to Asia after an adventurous flight by way of Corcyra, Epirus, and Macedonia; he was condemned to death at Athens in absence. King Artaxerxes I made him governor of Magnesia-ad-Maeandrum, where he died, of sickness, Thucydides believed, though he knew also a report of his suicide.

Hdt. 7–8; Thuc. 1. 74, 93, 135–8; Plut. *Them.* (of which A. Bauer's ed., 1881, has a good study of sources). H. T. Wade-Gery, 'Themistocles' Archonship', in his *Essays* (from *BSA* 1940); Beloch, *Gr. Gesch.* ii². 2. 134 ff.; W. G. Forrest, *CQ* 1960; D. M. Lewis, *CQ* 1961; A. R. Burn, *Persia and the Greeks* (1962); A. Andrewes, *Phoenix* 1964. On the Ostia bust of Th., see G. M. A. Richter, *Latomus* 1955. On 'Themistocles' Decree' in an inscription from Troezen (believed by a majority of scholars to be a later Athenian composition), see M. H. Jameson, *Hesp.* 1960; *SEG* 18 (text) and 19 (bibliography). A. R. B.

**THEMISTOGENES** of Syracuse, quoted by Xenophon (*Hell.* 3. 1. 2) as the author of an *Anabasis* of Cyrus.

The *Suda*'s vague notice accepts this statement, but it is unlikely that there was a third account of the expedition in addition to those of Xenophon and Sophaenetus. Themistogenes was probably the pseudonym under which Xenophon published his *Anabasis*.

*FGrH* ii B, 108.                                                    G. L. B.

**THEOCRITUS** (*c.* 300–*c.* 260 B.C.?) was a native of Syracuse, but seems to have lived mostly outside Sicily, first perhaps in southern Italy and later in Cos and at Alexandria. He made several unsuccessful attempts to find a patron. These are mentioned in 16, addressed to Hieron of Syracuse probably in 275/4. However, recognition soon came from Ptolemy Philadelphus, for whom before 270 he composed a panegyric (17). 270 is also the latest possible date for 15 (*Adoniazusai*), which is set in Alexandria.

A few autobiographical details can be gathered from 7 (*Thalusia*) if we may identify the Simichidas of that poem with Theocritus himself. The setting is Cos, and the incident described seems to occur at a moment (perhaps 274/3) when Ptolemy knows of Theocritus' compositions, but has not yet issued an invitation (91–3). From this poem it is clear that Theocritus in Cos has close friends and well-connected acquaintances. He has also won a reputation as a composer of bucolic poems. It is these that have attracted Ptolemy's notice, and it was these presumably that had accompanied his appeals to Hieron and others.

Although the theme of 6 and 11 is Sicilian, and the setting of 4 and 5 ostensibly that of southern Italy, there is little reason to think that any of the bucolic poems were written before Theocritus left the West. Most of them contain details, often botanical, that connect them with Cos and other parts of the East, and most, if not all, may have been composed in Cos.

Subsequently Theocritus was occupied with other forms of composition. 15 was composed for an Alexandrian clientele and may have been closely followed by the other non-bucolic mimes, 14 (which pays a compliment to Ptolemy) and 2. Several pieces are hymns or short epics (13, 22, 24, 26: the distinction is not always easy to draw). Another, written like the mimes in Doric, is an epithalamium addressed to Helen (18). None can be securely dated. A problem of priority arises in connexion with 13 (*Hylas*) and part of 22 (Polydeuces and Amycus), where Theocritus handles episodes from the Argonaut legend. These have been thought to be his contribution to a controversy in which he sided with Callimachus against Apollonius in the latter's attempt to revive the long epic. But there are doubts about Theocritus' position in the controversy, and it is by no means certain if the *Argonautica* preceded his compositions, or even if the quarrel was of this nature at all.

Three poems, 28–31, the last of which is a fragment, are written in Aeolic dialect and metres. In 30 Theocritus is no longer young, and the whole group is probably late. Epigrams, such as 17 and 22, which presuppose a wide reputation, may likewise be late. Whether Theocritus ever left Alexandria for Cos or elsewhere is unknown, and so too is the date of his death.

Theocritus shares with other poets of his age a preference for the short, highly finished poem, for fresh and sometimes exotic themes, and for new forms or old forms used in new ways. Nevertheless, he transcends his age in his ability to select and concentrate his material, in the freshness of his observation of people and scenes, in the vivacity of his narratives and descriptions, in his imagery and lyricism, and above all in his dramatic power. Displays of erudition are normally avoided by him. Two instances, however, are instructive, and possibly were

meant to be. In 7 topographical knowledge is used effectively for cajoling and threatening Pan (107–14), while in 12 two glosses and an *aition* are used, perhaps less naturally, to imply that the love affair is of a kind long sanctioned by custom.

Most of Theocritus' outstanding qualities, dramatic, descriptive, and lyric, are displayed in his bucolic poems. In 1 (*Thyrsis*) the courteous opening dictates the tone while it sets the scene, the description of the cup is dramatized, and the song is concentrated upon Daphnis' predicament and shows no concern for its cause. In 4 a series of changes in the emotional temperature is skilfully conveyed, the offensive-defensive opening leading eventually to a friendly close. In 5 mutual antipathy is gradually intensified until it explodes in the triumph of Comatas. 10 in its dialogue and in its songs vividly contrasts the dreamy lover Bucaeus with the hard-working, hard-headed, bluff but not unkindly Milon. The theme of 6 and 11 is the love of Polyphemus for Galatea. In 11 Theocritus no doubt enjoyed the difficult feat of presenting the physically repulsive Polyphemus as an acceptable lover. 7 is baffling. Its beginning and end are splendidly conceived with a wealth of evocative detail, but the songs, the kernel of the poem, have little immediate appeal. Their full significance no doubt escapes us. Theocritus may have meant to imply that Simichidas, who is presumably the writer himself, is not a rustic turned poet, like Lycidas, but a townsman writing about the countryside, and not exclusively about that. Simichidas' song could have formed the plot of a non-bucolic mime.

The non-bucolic mimes share many of the features of the bucolic. 2, like 3, is a lyrical monologue; 14, like 4, is entirely a dialogue; 15, like 1, consists of a dialogue followed by a song. 2 and 14, like 3 and 10, and the Aeolic poems 29 and 30, pursue the theme of unhappy love. 2 (*Pharmakeutria*) is notable for a contrast of moods—feverish tension and then calm recollection—and for the sympathy which Simaetha wins against all the odds. When we have heard her story, we know that, although she has no one to blame but herself, her lover is vain, selfish, and plausible, while she is credulous and unprotected. In 15 the characterization in a comic situation is no less skilful: Praxinoa is nervous, voluble, and scatterbrained; Gorgo enterprising, phlegmatic, and observant. Theocritus' use of the hexameter for his mimes was a bold stroke, perhaps facilitated by its long association with popular modes of thought in the shape of *gnomai*.

Of the epic narratives, the most strongly characteristic are, first, 13, where Heracles and Hylas occupy the scene almost in isolation, stress is laid on Heracles' affection for Hylas, and Hylas' fall is described in a powerful but non-heroic simile; and secondly, the fight between Polydeuces and Amycus in 22, where again the two chief characters monopolize the drama, and where the setting is pastoral and the fight preceded by a passage of stichomythia, a unique feature. Here the technique of drama is transplanted into epic.

In 16, an appeal to Hieron, the manner and the matter of the choral lyric are transposed into hexameters. The poem reproduces some of Pindar's resonance, and the imagery is moving. Theocritus' poems are depicted as crouching, dejected and reproachful, at the bottom of their chest after a fruitless search for patronage. Appropriately they are personified as Graces.

*See also* PASTORAL POETRY, CALLIMACHUS (3).

TEXTS. J. M. Edmonds, *The Greek Bucolic Poets* (Loeb, 1912); R. J. Cholmeley, *The Idylls of Theocritus*[2] (1919); P. Legrand, *Bucoliques grecs* (1925–7); A. S. F. Gow, *Theocritus*[2] (1952).
GENERAL LITERATURE. P. Legrand, *Étude sur Théocrite* (1898); U. von Wilamowitz-Moellendorff, *Die Textgeschichte der griechischen Bukoliker* (1906); *PW*, v A 2, 'Theokritos (1)' (von Blumenthal); G. Lawall, *Theocritus' Coan Pastorals* (1967).                     D. E. E.

**THEODECTES** (*c.* 375–334 B.C.), born at Phaselis (in Lycia), probably lived mainly at Athens, where he studied under Plato, Isocrates, and Aristotle and won fame as an orator (Cicero, *Orat.* 172, praises his polished style), a writer on rhetorical subjects, and a composer of popular riddles in verse. As a tragic poet he composed 50 plays and in 13 competitions won 8 victories (*Suda,* s.v.), of which 7 were at the Great Dionysia (*IG*² ii. 2325). He died at the age of 41 and was buried on the way to Eleusis ([Plut.] *X orat.* 837 d, Steph. Byz. s.v. Φασηλίς); his monument at Phaselis was honoured by Alexander the Great, his fellow student under Aristotle (Plut. *Alex.* 17). His plays included a *Lynceus* (the crisis of which is praised by Aristotle, *Poet.* 11), a *Mausolus* (in honour of the late king of Caria, but the treatment is unknown), and a *Philoctetes* (Aristotle, *Eth. Nic.* 7. 7, refers to the hero's brave resistance to pain; his hand, not, as in Sophocles, his foot, had been bitten by the serpent). The fragments consist mainly of rather commonplace but well-expressed reflections, and suggest that the poet was in the Euripidean tradition (*TGF* 801–7). Aristotle's *Theodectea,* was a, work on rhetoric so named in his honour. A. W. P.-C.; D. W. L.

**THEODORET,** *c.* A.D. 393–466. After a good education he became a monk and from 423 bishop of Cyrrhus, Syria. From 428 he was involved in the Christological controversy between his friend Nestorius and Cyril (q.v. 1) of Alexandria. He became Cyril's leading critic. Deposed by the monophysite Council of Ephesus (449) he was rehabilitated at Chalcedon in spite of strenuous protests (451), but his attacks on Cyril received posthumous condemnation under Justinian at the council of Constantinople (553). His well-composed letters, written in elegant prose, are informative about both secular and ecclesiastical matters. His *Graecarum Affectionum Curatio* is painstaking and thorough in contrasting Christianity and paganism. His *Church History* from Constantine to 428 contains many invaluable documents. The *Religious History* contains biographies of ascetics. The rest of his work is biblical exegesis and theological controversy, both of which he conducted well.

Ed. Migne, *PG* lxxx–lxxxiv. *Graec. Aff. Cur.,* ed. J. Raeder (Teubner, 1904). *Hist. Eccl.,* ed. L. Parmentier (1911). Letters, ed. Y. Azéma (1955–65, 3 vols.). J. Quasten, *Patrology* iii (1960), 536 ff. H. C.

**THEODORIC** 'the Great', Ostrogothic king of Italy (A.D. 493–526), served when young as a hostage in Constantinople, where he received a Roman upbringing, though it is said that he never learned to write. On the death of his father Theodemer (471) he became king of the Ostrogoths, who were then living in Pannonia. From 471 to 489 he and his followers were involved in the confused and complex politics of the Eastern Empire. In 484 he was consul, and in 489 the Emperor Zeno sent him and his people to Italy to supersede Odoacer (q.v.), whom he defeated and treacherously killed at Ravenna (493). Although in many ways an independent ruler thereafter, he recognized the overlordship of the Eastern Emperors. He retained the Roman civil administration in Italy, though the army there was now Gothic. Intermarriage between Romans and Goths was still forbidden by Roman law. Himself an Arian, his religious policy was tolerant. He was on friendly terms with the barbarian kingdoms of the West, and confirmed his peaceful policies by a series of matrimonial alliances with the various barbarian royal houses. His declining years were darkened by tension with Constantinople, and by the execution of Boethius. He died in 526. His tomb at Ravenna still survives. E. A. T.

**THEODORIDAS** (second half of 3rd c. B.C.), Syracusan poet, wrote poems against his contemporaries in the form of sepulchral epigrams, against Mnasalces (*Anth. Pal.* 13. 21), and Euphorion (ibid. 7. 406). Also genuine epitaphs (ibid. 7. 282, 439, 527, 528) and dedications (ibid. 6. 155, 156). Also poem to Eros (Ath. 475 f), dithyramb *The Centaur* (id. 699 e), iambic and hexameter poems (id. 229 b, 302 c), cinaedic songs (*Suda,* s.v. 'Sotades').

Cf. Susemihl, *Gesch. gr. Litt. Alex.* i. 246. 24, ii. 541 ff. C. M. B.

**THEODORUS** (1), of Samos, a Greek artist of *c.* 550 B.C. He made a silver bowl for Croesus, and an emerald seal for Polycrates. He was said to have invented the line, rule, lathe, and lever, and to have been associated with Rhoecus in inventing, or introducing into Samos, the arts of modelling in clay and of casting images in bronze and iron. Pliny describes a bronze self-portrait by him, and includes him in his list of notable painters. Athenagoras (*Legatio,* ch. 17) says that he and Telecles made the Pythian Apollo at Samos; and Diodorus (1. 98) that they brought back the canon of proportion for the human figure from Egypt. Pausanias mentions a building called 'Scias' at Sparta, apparently an assembly hall, which was attributed to him; and Vitruvius cites a book by him on the Heraeum at Samos which (according to Herodotus) was built for Croesus by Rhoecus, and which is probably identical with the 'Labyrinth' which Pliny attributes to Theodorus himself. Diogenes Laertius (2. 103) says that he advised the inclusion of a layer of charcoal in the foundations of the Artemisium at Ephesus.

Hdt. 1. 51, 3. 41, 60; Pl. *Ion* 533 b; Vitr. 7, *praef.*; Pliny, *HN* 7. 198; 34. 83; 35. 146, 152; 36. 95; Paus. 3. 12. 10; 9. 41. 1. H. W. R.

**THEODORUS** (2) of Cyrene (b. *c.* 460 B.C.), mathematician, teacher of Plato and Theaetetus (Pl. *Tht.* 147 d–148 b), was originally a pupil of Protagoras but turned early to mathematics. Plato represents him as proving separately that $\sqrt{3}$, $\sqrt{5}$, and the roots of the other non-square numbers up to 17 are irrational (the irrationality of $\sqrt{2}$ being known already). W. D. R.

**THEODORUS** (3) of Gadara (fl. 33 B.C.), rhetor. He taught Tiberius at Rhodes (Suet. *Tib.* 57, Sen. *Suas.* 3. 7), and was an important teacher, the principal rival of Apollodorus (q.v. 5), from whom he differed in allowing more freedom in the arrangement and composition of speeches. It has been held that the differences between the two are symptomatic of a real difference of outlook on literature, but this is an exaggeration.

Some evidence in Anonymus Seguerianus (q.v.), but see esp. Quintilian: discussion by G. M. A. Grube, *AJPhil.* 1959, 337 ff. D. A. R.

**THEODOSIUS** (1) Count, a wealthy landowner of Cauca in Spain, was a general of Valentinian I. In A.D. 367 he recovered Britain which had been overrun by Saxons, Picts, and Scots; the invaders had reached the vicinity of London. From 373 to 375 he was active in Africa and suppressed the revolt of the local chieftain Firmus. He was put to death for unknown reasons in Carthage in 376. E. A. T.

**THEODOSIUS** (2) I, 'the Great', the son of Count Theodosius (q.v. 1), was born *c.* A.D. 346. He was promoted early, serving as *dux* of Moesia Superior in 374. On his father's sudden disgrace and execution in 376 he retired to Cauca, but in 378, after the defeat and death of Valens (q.v. 2), Gratian (q.v.) appointed him *magister militum* to fight the Goths, and shortly afterwards (19 Jan. 379) proclaimed him Augustus of the Eastern parts including the dioceses of Dacia and Macedonia. For the next few years Theodosius conducted campaigns against the Visigoths, basing himself at first at Thessalonica

(379–80), then at Constantinople. He failed to eject them from the Empire, and on 3 Oct. 382 signed a treaty with them, recognizing them as federates and assigning them lands in Thrace. In about 386 he signed a treaty with Persia, whereby the long-disputed kingdom of Armenia was partitioned between the two empires. When the usurper Magnus (q.v. 2) Maximus killed Gratian in 383 and occupied the Gauls, Theodosius recognized him, but when in 387 Maximus expelled Valentinian II from Italy, he marched west, defeated Maximus at Siscia and Poetovio, and put him to death at Aquileia. He stayed in Italy for three years. Valentinian II was established in Gaul. Theodosius' elder son Arcadius, whom he had proclaimed Augustus in 383, was left in nominal charge of the East. Theodosius returned to Constantinople in 391, but again had to move west in 394 to subdue the usurper Eugenius, who had succeeded Valentinian II in 392. He again left Arcadius in charge of the East, and took with him to the West his younger son Honorius, proclaimed Augustus in 393. He defeated Eugenius at the Frigidus on 6 Sept. 394, but died at Milan 17 Jan. 395.

Theodosius was a pious Christian and a bigoted adherent of the Nicene creed. He was baptized very early in his reign, during a serious illness. On 27 Feb. 380 he issued a constitution declaring that the faith professed by Pope Damasus and Peter, bishop of Alexandria, was the Catholic faith. He deposed Demophilus, the Arian bishop of Constantinople and recognized the Nicene protagonist, Gregory Nazianzen. On 10 Jan. 381 he ordered that all churches be surrendered to the Catholic bishops as defined by himself. This done he called a council of about 150 bishops at Constantinople, and this council duly ratified Theodosius' action, but refused to accept Gregory Nazianzen. Theodosius asked them to produce a short list and himself chose Nectarius as bishop of Constantinople.

Theodosius was very severe against heretics, issuing eighteen constitutions against them; he even ordained the death penalty for some extremist sects. Towards the pagans his policy was at first ambivalent. He did not forbid sacrifice, but was so severe against divination as to prevent it. He did not close the temples, but he allowed fanatical Christians to destroy them or granted them to petitioners. In 391 he abruptly closed all temples and banned all forms of pagan cult. This step was probably taken under the influence of Ambrose, bishop of Milan, who had obtained a great ascendancy over him since 387. In 388 Ambrose forced him to leave unpunished the bishop of Callinicum, who had burnt down a synagogue. In 390, when Theodosius had ordered a massacre at Thessalonica to avenge the killing of the general Butheric, he refused him communion until he had done penance.

E. Stein, *Histoire du bas-empire* i (1959), 191 ff.; Jones, *Later Rom. Emp.* 156 ff. A. H. M. J.

**THEODOSIUS** (3) **II**, son of Arcadius, born in A.D. 401, was proclaimed Augustus in 402. He succeeded his father in 408 and reigned rather than ruled the Empire until his death in 450. He was very piously educated by his elder sister, Pulcheria, who exercised a strong influence over him until the early 440s. He was also much influenced by his wife Eudoxia, whom he married in 421, until the two of them fell from favour in the early 440s. During the earlier part of his reign the Empire was in fact governed by Anthemius, praetorian prefect of the East from 405 to 414, and then probably by Helio, master of the offices from 414 to 427. From the early 440s the Emperor was controlled by Chrysaphius, an imperial eunuch, and Nomus, master of the offices.

The chief military events of the reign were two successful Persian wars (421–2 and 441), the defeat of the usurper John in the West, and the installation of Valen-

tinian III at Rome (425), an unsuccessful naval expedition against the Vandals (441), and a series of wars and negotiations with Rua and Attila, kings of the Huns. The Roman armies proved helpless against the Huns, and peace was obtained only by paying ever increasing subsidies (350 lb. gold per annum from 422, 700 lb. from 434, 2,100 lb. from 443).

The chief ecclesiastical events were the condemnation of Nestorius, bishop of Constantinople, by the Council of Ephesus in 431, and of Flavian, bishop of Constantinople, by the second Council of Ephesus in 449; Cyril and Dioscurus, bishops of Alexandria, were moving spirits in these two councils.

In 429 a commission was appointed under Antiochus, praetorian prefect and former quaestor, to codify all laws issued since 312. This attempt to reform the law failed, but in 435 a second commission under the same Antiochus carried out the task and in 438 the Theodosian Code was promulgated in both parts of the Empire (*see* CODEX, legal).

J. B. Bury, *A History of the Later Roman Empire* (1923); E. Stein, *Histoire du bas-empire* i (1959). A. H. M. J.

**THEODOSIUS** (4) of Bithynia (probably between 150 and 70 B.C.), mathematician and astronomer, mentioned by Strabo, is probably to be identified with Theodosius the inventor of a sun-dial for use in any locality, mentioned by Vitruvius, and with an author Theodosius mentioned by the *Suda*.

WORKS: extant (1) Σφαιρικά, the oldest extant Greek work on sections of the sphere, a compilation of earlier discoveries, (2) Περὶ οἰκήσεων (astronomical tables for different parts of the earth), (3) Περὶ ἡμερῶν καὶ νυκτῶν; lost (1) Ὑπόμνημα εἰς τὸ Ἀρχιμήδους ἐφόδιον; (2) Ἀστρολογικά; (3) Διαγραφαὶ οἰκιῶν.

*Sphaerica*, ed. J. L. Heiberg, 1927. W. D. R.

**THEOGNETUS**, one of the later poets of the New Comedy. Fr. 1 ridicules excessive preoccupation with philosophy, fr. 2 mentions Pantaleon, whom Chrysippus describes as ὁ πλάνος.

*FCG* iv. 549 f.; *CAF* iii. 364 f.

**THEOGNIS** (1) (fl. 544–541 B.C.; *Suda*, s.v. Θέογνις), elegiac poet, of Megara. Some 1,389 lines survive in good MSS. under his name, and there is much dispute about their authenticity. The chief difficulties are: (1) among these lines are passages written by other poets, or only slightly altered from them, notably Mimnermus (795–6, 1020–2), Tyrtaeus (935–8, 1003–6), Solon (227–32, 315–18, 585–90, 1253–4), Euenus (465–96 and possibly 667–82, 1345–50). These are not cases of the practice of 'paradiorthosis', by which a line was taken and slightly altered in a different sense, as in most cases they are either unaltered or altered in some quite trivial way. (2) In the text of Theognis there are repetitions, which look like variations of the same theme, and it is hard to believe that both sets were written by the same man. (3) There are chronological difficulties. 894 refers to the Cypselids, who disappear from history *c.* 580 B.C., while 773–82 is a prayer to Apollo to keep the Medes away from Megara and cannot be much earlier than 490 B.C. (4) The existing text does not agree with either of the two books mentioned by the *Suda*, the *Maxims* in 2,800 verses and the *Gnomology to Cyrnus*. It seems therefore probable that the original work of Theognis has been supplemented, especially as we find many variations on a given theme, which suggest that the book is a collection of σκόλια intended for the use of singers who had to cap one song with another on a similar subject. A clue for detecting the authentic Theognis ought to lie in 19–23, where the poet speaks of a 'seal' on his work which cannot be stolen or replaced by a substitute, but there is no agreement on what this seal is. It has been thought to be the excellence of the work, the name 'Theognis' in 22, the name Cyrnus, which appears in many poems. If the last is right we may perhaps have a means for restoring at least the *Gnomology to Cyrnus* which the *Suda* mentions. Otherwise the problem seems insoluble. The poems to Cyrnus show marked individuality. Their poet has a strong aristocratic bias, is very frank about his emotions, uses bold and vivid metaphors, went into exile (1197–2000), believed in traditional tenets of Greek morality, and was not without some worldly wisdom. The whole collection agrees with this section in its political temper, and we may conjecture that it was popular, if not composed, in aristocratic circles in Athens in the fifth century. The separate poems are sympotic elegies, and the book may have been a songbook used by those who did not wish to improvise when called on for a song over the wine. Book II, which consists of love-poems, seems to be Athenian, and the whole collection begins with four introductory pieces whose themes recall those of Attic σκόλια. But otherwise it is hard to mark breaks in the collection, though some regard the promise of immortality to Cyrnus, 237–54, as the end of one section and 753–6 as the end of another. The section 1–254 is much more quoted by fourth-century writers than the rest of the book, and may perhaps have had a separate circulation. The whole collection is interesting as being the poetry of a small class with clear ideas about morals and politics and a strong interest in personal relations. Reference in it to Simonides (469, 667, 1349) and to Onomacritus (503) may be to the familiar bearers of these names.

TEXT. D. Young, *Theognis* (1961).
COMMENTARY. T. Hudson-Williams, *The Elegies of Theognis* (1910).
CRITICISM. E. Harrison, *Studies in Theognis* (1902); T. W. Allen, *Theognis* (1934); F. Jacoby, *Theognis* (*Sitz. d. Preußischen Akademie d. Wissenschaften* 1931); J. Kroll, *Theognis-Interpretationen* (1936); C. M. Bowra, *Early Greek Elegists* (1938), ch. 5. C. M. B.

**THEOGNIS** (2), a tragic poet spoken of contemptuously by Aristophanes (*Ach.* 11, 140; *Thesm.* 170) as one who ψυχρὸς ὢν ψυχρῶς ποιεῖ. He is identified by some with the Theognis who was one of the Thirty Tyrants (q.v. 1). If so, he resembled Critias in combining 'tyranny' with poetry.
*TGF* 769. A. W. P.-C.

**THEOI PATROOI, PATRIOI: DI PATRII** (θεοὶ πατρῷοι, πάτριοι). Of the two adjectives, the former means *connected with a father*, or *fathers*, as οὐσία πατρῴα, an estate inherited from one's father; the latter, in dialects (such as Attic) which use both, is vaguer, meaning *ancestral, time-honoured, traditional*. Applied to gods, the former has therefore the more intimate meaning; a θεὸς πατρῷος is at least the god whom the speaker's father, or his ancestors generally, worshipped, while a πάτριος θεός may be merely one whom it is customary to worship in his community, or in the Greek world generally.

The narrowest and most exact meaning of πατρῷος θεός is a god from whom descent is claimed. Aesch. fr. 162 Nauck may serve as an example:

οἱ θεῶν ἀγχίσποροι
οἱ Ζηνὸς ἐγγύς, ὧν κατ' Ἰδαῖον πάγον
Διὸς πατρῴου βωμός ἐστ' ἐν αἰθέρι,
κοὔπω σφιν ἐξίτηλον αἷμα δαιμόνων.

'Those near akin to the gods, close to Zeus, whose altar of Zeus Patroos lies on Ida's heaven-kissing slope, in whose veins the blood of the deities is yet fresh.' The exact context is unknown, but clearly the poet is speaking of heroes who are but a generation or two from their ancestor Zeus. It is in this sense that Athenians worshipped Apollo Patroos. Every candidate for the archon-

ship was tested, and one of the questions put was whether he had a cult of Zeus Herkeios and Apollo Patroos. The former question was meant to ensure that he belonged to a respectable family, having its own proper domestic cult; the latter, to make it clear that he was, what all Athenians claimed to be, a good Ionian, since Ion (q.v. 1) is son of Apollo and ancestor of the Ionian stock. See Arist. *Ath. Pol.* 55. 3. Another not uncommon use of πατρῷος is in such a context as Ar. *Nub.* 1468 (paratragic), καταιδέσθητι π. Δία. Here Zeus is named by a father appealing to his son's sense of duty. He is evidently the god who cares for fathers and their rights. When Orestes (Eur. *El.* 671) says ὦ Ζεῦ πατρῷε καὶ τροπαῖ' ἐχθρῶν ἐμῶν, he may very well be combining the two senses, for Zeus is his ancestor (*see* TANTALUS) and he wants his help to revenge the murder of Agamemnon.

But that πατρῷος cannot always have this sense is clear from the fact that it is used as a title of Artemis at Sicyon (Paus. 2. 9. 6), where her rude and archaic image attested the antiquity of her cult, but clearly, being virgin, she was not an ancestress. Again, the epithet is applied to Hestia, *IG* xiv. 980 (from Rome), and certainly Hestia is a virgin in all our sources; the dedicator perhaps meant to differentiate her from the Roman Vesta (q.v.). In much the same manner, other inscriptions in the same collection (nos. 971, 962, 972) apply the title to the Palmyrene gods and the (Thracian?) Ares. This is in contrast, on the one hand with πατρῷος applied to the obscure Eumelos as ancestor-god of the Eumelidae (ibid. 715), on the other hand with the use, not of πατρῷος but of πάτριος of Aeneas in an inscription from Ilium, *CIG* 3606, where the dedicators might certainly claim him as an ancestor. A long list of examples will be found in Roscher's *Lexikon* iii. 1688–9, of gods of all sorts, from (probably) actual ancestors thought of as deified to ordinary gods traditionally worshipped by the persons in question, who seem to be called quite indifferently πατρῷοι or πάτριοι, with one or two instances of θεοὶ μητρῷοι, whether deified maternal ancestors or gods worshipped in the household of the dedicator's mother.

In Rome, *di patrii* manifestly cannot have the narrower sense of θεοὶ πατρῷοι, at least in official cult, since no Roman god was officially an ancestor; the theories, e.g., about the identity of Romulus and Quirinus (qq.v.) had no effect on the State cult of the latter. A good example of its use is in Verg. *G.* 1. 498, 'di patrii Indigetes et Romule Vestaque mater'. The expression is ambiguous, but either he calls the Indigetes, Quirinus and Vesta, all *patrii*, or he uses that epithet of the first of these only; the former is the more likely. Since no one, even mythologically, seems to have claimed the Indigetes (q.v.) for ancestors, and certainly no one laid such a claim to Vesta, the sense 'worshipped by our fathers, ancestral' is perfectly clear. Nor does it mean only those gods to whom the epithet *pater* (or *mater*) is applied, for while such titles are known for Quirinus and Vesta, no such collocation as *Indigetes patres* is to be found. There is, however, a somewhat specialized sense in which the word is used; it applies above all to the Penates. In this sense *paternus* is once or twice employed; the evicted tenant in Hor. *Carm.* 2. 18. 26 goes his way 'paternos (πατρῴους) in sinu ferens deos'. These would be his *di penates*, represented by images or other symbols, which he piously takes away as Anchises did his in leaving Troy (Verg. *Aen.* 2. 717), though here they are called *patrii*, appropriately, for they are not merely the gods of the individual house but the future objects of national Roman worship, the *Penates publici*, which are not venerated because they formed part of anyone's *sacra domestica*, but because they had been adored by Rome and the States supposedly her ancestors from time immemorial, cf. PENATES. Examples of this use are: Cic. *Har.* 37, 'patrii penatesque di';

*Dom.* 144; cf. Dion. Hal. *Ant. Rom.* 1. 67. 3, some say *di penates* means Πατρῷοι (θεοί).

Roscher's *Lexikon*, arts. 'Patrii di' (J. Ilberg), 'Patrioi theoi', 'Patroa' (Höfer), 'Patrooi theoi' (Ilberg).     H. J. R.

**THEOLOGUMENA ARITHMETICAE.** This work has been thought to be by Iamblichus (q.v. 2), because he apparently wrote about the properties of the Monad. But it does not bear the name of Iamblichus in the MSS., and is merely a compilation from Anatolius and Nicomachus (q.v. 3).

Ed. V. de Falco (1922).     W. D. R.

**THEON**(1) of Alexandria (1st c. B.C.), son of Artemidorus of Tarsus, and successor of Apion (q.v.) at Alexandria. He wrote, *inter alia*, alphabetical lexica of Tragedy and Comedy, probably based (mainly) on the unalphabetical collections of Didymus. His main claim to fame, however, lies in his exhaustive commentaries on the chief Alexandrian poets, which dominated all subsequent scholarship in this field and which form the basis of the surviving scholia. He also wrote one of the first treatises on Greek syntax.

C. Giese, *De Theone eiusque reliquiis* (1867); C. Wendel, *PW* 10 A. 2054 ff.     P. B. R. F.; R. B.

**THEON** (2) of Smyrna (fl. *c.* A.D. 115–40), Platonist, author of an extant work Τὰ κατὰ τὸ μαθηματικὸν χρήσιμα εἰς τὴν Πλάτωνος ἀνάγνωσιν, and of a lost commentary on the *Republic* and a lost work on the order of Plato's writings. The extant book is an elementary work on arithmetic (especially on the types of numbers), the theory of musical harmony, and astronomy.

Ed. E. Hiller (1878).     W. D. R.

**THEON** (3, *PW* 5), AELIUS, of Alexandria (2nd c. A.D.), rhetor, wrote ὑπομνήματα on Xenophon, Isocrates, and Demosthenes, as well as a Τέχνη and other rhetorical works, of which the sole survivor is the *Progymnasmata* (q.v.), a teacher's manual which proved very popular.

TEXT. Spengel, *Rhet.* ii. 59 ff.     D. A. R.

**THEON** (4, *PW* 15) of Alexandria, mathematician and astronomer (fl. A.D. 364). Extant works are (1) a commentary on Ptolemy's *Almagest* (the sections on book 11 and parts of other books are lost); (2) large commentary on the *Handy Tables* of Ptolemy; (3) small introduction to the *Handy Tables*. He is also important for his 'editions' (i.e. reworkings) of (*a*) Euclid (*Elements, Data,* and *Optics*); (*b*) Ptolemy's *Handy Tables*. The latter are extant only in Theon's version. Theon was a competent but completely unoriginal mathematician. His importance lies in the historical data he preserves. It was in his version and under his name that Ptolemy's astronomical tables were known to Islamic science, whence they passed to medieval Europe.

EDITIONS. *Comm. on Almagest*: books 1–4 ed. A. Rome, *Studi e Testi* 72 and 106 (1936, 1943). For the remainder it is still necessary to consult the 1538 Basel edition of the *Almagest* ('apud Ioannem Vualderum'). The *Handy Tables* in the Theonic version were published by Halma in 3 vols. (Paris, 1822, 1823, 1825, with French trans.), the 'small introduction', 27 ff. of the first volume. The 'large commentary' has never been published.
COMMENT. On Theon's 'edition' of Euclid: Heiberg, *Litterargesch. Studien über Euklid* 1882). General: Heath, *Hist. of Greek Maths.* i. 58 ff., ii. 526 ff. See also the introductions of Rome, op. cit., and to his edition of Pappus' commentary, *Studi e Testi* 54 (1931).     G. J. T.

**THEOPHANES** of Mytilene, the historian of Pompey, after a pro-Roman part in home politics, accompanied him in the Third Mithridatic War, and, receiving Roman citizenship, fought in the Civil War. His work appears to have treated only Pompey's campaigns, which he com-

pared to those of Alexander, and was written probably in 63/2 B.C. to further Pompey's cause in Rome.

*FGrH* ii B, 919; BD, 614.     A. H. McD.

**THEOPHILUS** (1), Athenian comic poet; he won a victory in 329 B.C. Eight titles and twelve fragments survive (frs. 6 and 12 are gnomic).

*FCG* iii. 626 ff.; *CAF* ii. 473 ff.; *FAC* ii. 566 ff.     K. J. D.

**THEOPHILUS** (2) of Alexandria, patriarch A.D. 385–412, was no thinker but a zealous pastor who vigorously suppressed Egyptian paganism and advanced the power of Alexandria against Constantinople by opposing John Chrysostom. He appears in a kind light in Synesius' letters.

Migne, *PG* lxv. 33 ff.; M. Richard, *DTC.* xv/1 (1946), 523 ff.     H. C.

**THEOPHRASTUS** (*c.* 370–288/5 B.C.) of Eresos in Lesbos, pupil, collaborator, and successor of Aristotle. In spite of a tradition that he had been a pupil of Plato, it is more probable that he first joined Aristotle while the latter was at Assos (*see* W. W. Jaeger, *Aristotle* (E.T. 1948), 115). From Asia Minor he accompanied Aristotle to Macedonia and thence to Athens (335). From the beginning of this association came the researches, especially in botany (and perhaps also in political science; Philod. *Rhet.* ii, p. 57 Sudhaus), which were later to form the basis of his lectures and published work. Upon Aristotle's retirement to Chalcis (322), he succeeded him as scholarch of the Peripatos.

He is said to have lectured to 2,000 students. His lectures were continually revised (Diog. Laert. 5. 37) and chronological indications in the extant works show that they received their present form in the period of his scholarchate. His most famous pupil was Demetrius of Phaleron, through whose influence he, though a metic, was allowed to own property, the disposition of which he treats in his Will. After the end of Demetrius' regime, he left Athens for a period when a law moved by Sophocles was passed forbidding the operation of philosophical schools without the permission of the Athenian demos. The law was soon repealed. He was also on friendly terms with Cassander and Ptolemy I. He was succeeded as a scholarch by Straton.

WORKS

Four catalogues of his writings (with some duplication and pseudigrapha) are preserved in D. L. 5. 42–50. It is certain that at least the first two and longest of these originated in the Alexandrian library but the traditional (since Usener's *Analecta Theophrastea* (1859) 23) ascription of them to Hermippus (q.v. 2) is based on weak evidence (see *Hermes*, forthcoming). Some of the writings were later edited by Andronicus of Rhodes. The text of all the extant works is notoriously defective, and they are not all yet well represented in modern editions.

Only a minuscule amount of Theophrastus' total output has been preserved. *Plant-researches* (Περὶ φυτῶν ἱστορίας: 9 books) followed by *Plant-Aetiology* (Περὶ φυτῶν αἰτιῶν: 6 books), the first a description and classification, the second a physiology of plant-life. They are a counterpart of and methodologically influenced by Aristotle's biological works. *Characters* (Χαρακτῆρες), a collection of thirty descriptive sketches of types exhibiting deviations from proper norms of behaviour; the preface and some of the contents are Byzantine interpolations. In modern times, they are Theophrastus' most famous and most imitated work. Although they were formerly interpreted as moral essays, influenced by Aristotle's classification of virtuous qualities in *Ethics*, recent scholarship stresses their utility for rhetorical handbooks or comic poetics. *Metaphysics* (τῶν μετὰ τὰ φυσικά), a brief discussion of some problems of first philosophy. Theophrastus shows himself capable of criticizing weaker points in Aristotle's *Metaphysics*, but otherwise marks no advance on Aristotle. A number of short essays on scientific subjects, the first three perhaps extracts from the *Physics*: *On fire*, *On winds*, *On stones*, *On weather-signs*, *On odours*, *On weariness*, *On swooning*, *On sweat*, *On paralysis*. Tne treatise *On sense-perception* is part of the *Phys. Dox.*

His two most valuable and influential works are preserved only in fragments: the *Doctrines of natural philosophers* (Φυσικῶν δόξαι) and the *Laws* (Νόμοι), each in eighteen books. The first was the standard history of opinions about the major problems of science and philosophy, in which he systematized the material used by Aristotle for his own criticism of his predecessors. The *Laws* was a comparative collection of laws and customs of Greek States, and was based on the material used by Aristotle in his *Constitutions* and *Politics* 4–6.

Theophrastus' place in the history of philosophy can be summed up in Cicero's (*Fin.* i. 6) remark that he *tractat locos ab Aristotele ante tractatos*. A scientific researcher and scholar rather than a speculative philosopher, he pursued his researches on topical and methodological lines already laid down by Aristotle. His occasional disagreement on points of doctrine (e.g. a more 'naturalist' ethics; a reaction against excessive teleology in natural processes) or fact are due to his emphasis on science and empirical observation. After Aristotle, he was the most prolific and most famous member of the Peripatetic school, and his works continued to be influential until the first centuries of the Christian era (Cicero, Seneca, Plutarch, Porphyry, commentators to Aristotle).

LIFE AND WORKS. Diogenes Laertius 5. 36–57; Zeller, *Phil. d. Gr.* ii. 2. 806; Ueberweg–Praechter, *Grundriss* 401; O. Regenbogen, s.v. 'Theophrastos' *PW* Suppl. vii. 1354; O. Gigon, *Lex. d. Alten Welt* 3057.
TEXTS (selection). J. G. Schneider, 5 vols. (1818–21); F. Wimmer, with fragments (very incomplete) and Latin transl. (1866); *de igne*, A. Gercke (1896).
WITH COMMENTARY OR TRANSLATION (a selection, generally restricted to recent works). *Hist. Plant.* (with *de odor, de sign. temp.*): A. F. Hort, 2 vols. (Loeb, 1916); *Caus. Plant.*: R. E. Dengler, book I (Diss. Penn., 1927), B. Einarson–G. Link (Loeb, in preparation); *Char.*: R. G. Ussher (1960), P. Steinmetz, 2 vols. (1960–2); *Met.*: W. D. Ross–F. H. Fobes (1929); *de sens.*: G. M. Stratton (1927), J. B. McDiarmid (in pr.); *de lap.*: D. Eicholz (1965). FRAGMENTS. *Major Fragments*, D. Eicholz (Loeb, in pr.); Περὶ εὐσεβείας, W. Pötscher (1964); Φυσ. δοξ., H. Diels, *Doxographi Graeci* (1879); *Nomoi*: H. Hager, *JournPhil* 6 (1927) 1.
STUDIES. The following list includes only studies appearing since the full survey article of Regenbogen in *PW*. Botany: G. Senn, *Die Pflanzenkunde des T. von Eresos* (1956); *Ethics*: C. O. Brink, *Phronesis* 1 (1956) 123; *Physics*: P. Steinmetz, *Die Physik des T. von Eresos* (1964). H. B. Gottschalk finds the teaching of Theophrastus in *Meteor.* 4 (*CQ* 1961, 67) and in *de coloribus* (*Hermes* 1964, 59), both ascribed to Aristotle. *Met.*: G. Reale, *Teofrasto e la sua aporetica metafisica* (1964); *Logic*: I. M. Bocheński, *La Logique de Theophraste* (1947); *Epistem.*: E. Barbotin, *La Théorie aristotelicienne de l'intellect d'après Théophraste* (1957); Φυσ. δοξ.: J. B. McDiarmid, *Harv. Stud.*, 1953, 85; *Laws*: H. Bloch, *Harv. Stud.* 1940, 357, A. E. Raubitschek, *Classica et Mediaevalia* 1958, 78 (on ostracism). Important but neglected fragments of a political work were discovered in a Vatican palimpsest and published by W. Aly, *Fragmentum Vaticanum de eligendis magistratibus* (Studi e testi, 104 [1943]): another discussion by F. Sbordone, *PP* 1948, 269. J. J. K.

**THEOPOMPUS** (1), Eurypontid king of Sparta from c. 720–? c. 670 B.C. and leader in the First Messenian War (Tyrtaeus fr. 4; *see* MESSENIA). He was credited by fourth-century writers with two constitutional reforms—a stricter control of the assembly by the kings and Gerousia (*see* APELLAI 1), and the institution of the ephorate. It is possible that the ephorate was of earlier origin (*see* EPHORS), but that it obtained wider powers under Theopompus. W. G. F.

**THEOPOMPUS** (2), Athenian comic poet, was active from c. 410 B.C. (probably not earlier) to c. 370. Twenty-four plays were ascribed to him; we have twenty titles (including *Odysseus, Penelope*, and *Sirens*) and 100 fragments (many of them only glosses).

*FCG* ii. 792 ff.; *CAF* i. 733 ff.; *FAC* i. 848 ff. K. J. D.

**THEOPOMPUS** (3) of Chios (b. c. 378 B.C.), historian, banished with his father Damasistratus c. 334 for Spartan sympathies and restored by Alexander as a supporter against the pro-Persian oligarchy. On the latter's death he fled to Egypt.

Theopompus, a contemporary of Ephorus, was a pupil of Isocrates and adopted his view of history as the handmaid of politics. Little remains of numerous writings except fragments from the two works on which his fame rests, the *Hellenica* ('Ελληνικαὶ ἱστορίαι) and *Philippica* (Φιλιππικά). The former, a continuation of Thucydides from 411, reached the battle of Cnidos, 394, in twelve books, and took the supremacy of Sparta as its main theme. Our knowledge of the *Hellenica* is meagre unless we accept R. Laqueur's arguments (*PW*, s.v. 'Theopompos') for the identification of the author of the Oxyrhynchus *Hellenica* (*see* OXYRHYNCHUS, THE HISTORIAN FROM) with Theopompus. These arguments rest on style, methods, and the evidence of personal views and research embodied in the papyrus agreeing with characteristics of Theopompus.

Theopompus was able to view events in Greece from a detached standpoint, as is shown by his choice of Philip of Macedon as the connecting theme of the fifty-eight books of *Philippica*. Beginning with Philip's accession, this prolific work was a world history depicted in a series of extensive digressions. Certain of these acquired separate titles (Τὰ θαυμάσια, Περὶ δημαγωγῶν, etc.). Theopompus was remarkable for wide and critical research and for the harshness of his verdicts. *See also* HISTORIOGRAPHY, GREEK, § 4.

*FGrH* ii B, 115; E. Meyer, *Theopomps Hellenika* (1909); F. Jacoby, *Nachrichten Gesellsch. d. Wissensch. zu Göttingen* 1942, i; A. Momigliano, *Terzo contributo alla storia degli studi classici* (1966), 367 ff.; W. R. Connor, *Theopompus and Fifth-century Athens* (1968). G. L. B.

**THEORIKA**, State allowances made to the poorer citizens of Athens to enable them to visit the theatres, introduced, it is said, by Pericles. Two obols were paid per head at each performance to all persons registered for the purpose on the roll of citizens. Later, allowances were paid on other occasions also. In the fourth century B.C. a regulation was made that all surpluses of the State should be used for *theorika* (except during wartime, as an enactment of Demosthenes provided). Another law of the same period punished with death anyone suggesting the use of these funds for army purposes during times of peace. The administrators of the *theorika*, οἱ ἐπὶ τὸ θεωρικόν, were elective magistrates who had considerable, and during the time of Eubulus (q.v. 1) even a controlling, power over financial administration.

The term occurs in Roman Egypt, too, where it seems to mean funds for religious local festivals, which had to be supplied by taxation.

A. M. Andreades, *A History of Greek Public Finance* (1933), index; J. J. Buchanan, *Theorika* (1962); G. Busolt–H. Swoboda, *Griechische Staatskunde* i, ii (1920–6), index; Michell, *Econom. Anc. Gr.* 369 ff.; W. Schwahn, *PW*, s.v.; S. L. Wallace, *Taxation in Egypt from Augustus to Diocletian* (1938), 454. F. M. H.

**THEOROI** (θεωροί), 'observers', a word originally applied to sight-seeing travellers and to the attendants at festivals of distant cities. It became an official title given to a city's representatives at another city's festival. The great panhellenic festivals were attended by theoric delegations (θεωρίαι) from every Greek State. Cities to which *theoroi* regularly came assigned the duty of receiving them to official *theorodokoi* (θεωροδόκοι). At the festivals the *theoroi* offered sacrifices in the name of their cities, and so the title was likewise given to the envoys that a city sent to a distant shrine to offer sacrifice in its name and to the envoys that it sent to consult a distant oracle. The envoys that were sent round to announce the coming celebration of a festival and, after the creation of new panhellenic agonistic festivals in the third century B.C. and later, to announce the new games to all the Greek States were also called *theoroi*. It thus became the accepted title of all sacred envoys. The religious functions of *theoroi* eventually obscured the original purpose of their office, and as early as Thucydides several cities gave the title to annually elected religious magistrates. At Thasos the *theoroi* were eponymous magistrates.

F. Poland, *De legationibus Graecorum publicis* (Leipzig, 1885); C. P. Bill, *TAPA* 1901, 196 ff.; P. Boesch, Θεωρός (1908); A. Boethius, *Die Pythais* (Uppsala, 1918). J. E. F.

**THEOS** (θεός) denotes a god, especially one of the great gods, from his anthropomorphic aspect; from the aspect of power he is also called δαίμων (*see* DAIMON). When there is no room for doubt, θεός often takes the place of the proper noun: thus ἡ θεός is at Athens Athena. There is no reason for assuming anonymous gods. At Eleusis τὼ θεώ are Demeter and Kore, ὁ θεός and ἡ θεά Pluto and Persephone. Noteworthy is the predicative use of θεός in phrases like: 'Recognition of your own kin is *theos*.' The indefinite expressions θεός τις, θεοί alternate in Homer with δαίμων to denote some unknown divine power; in later authors τὸ θεῖον is an equivalent. This abstraction becomes finally an expression for the irrational in human life, that which cannot be explained by natural causes. No plausible etymology exists.

H. J. Rose *et al.*, *La Notion du divin* (Entretiens sur l'ant. class. I 1952). M. P. N.; J. H. C.

**THEOXENIA** (Θεοξένια), or **THEODAISIA** (Θεοδαίσια), a Greek rite 'held on certain fixed days on the supposition that the gods in person were visiting the cities' (schol. Pind. *Ol.* 3, 105, 14 ff. Drachmann). The statement of Hesych., s.v., that it was 'a festival in common for all the gods', may go back to a gloss relating to a particular (unknown) example. The characteristic feature was that a god or gods were considered to be present as guests at a banquet given by their worshippers. This might apparently be a public or private ceremony; if the former, it was often an important one, hence the fairly common occurrence of a month called Theoxenios or Theodaisios. The best known was at Delphi, in Theoxenios (Mar.–Apr.); for this the sixth Paean of Pindar (q.v.) was written. Here Apollo (q.v.) appears to have acted as host to the other gods: θεῶν ξενίᾳ (Pind., op. cit. 60); for an indication that Leto was present cf. Ath. 372 a. The meal was shared by human beings, witness the setting aside, as late as Plutarch's time (*De sera* 557 f), of a portion for Pindar's descendants. Another was that in honour of the Dioscuri and Helen (qq.v.) at Acragas, Pind. *Ol.* 3; this seems to have been rather a domestic feast of the Eumenidae on a magnificent scale than a public festival proper. Several other instances are recorded; see F. Pfister in *PW*, s.v. 'Theodaisia', 'Theoxenia'.

Nilsson, *GGR* i². 135, 409. H. J. R.

**THERA**, one of the Sporades, a treeless semicircular island, forming part of the cone of an ancient volcano, and famous for its wine. It had been colonized from Minoan Crete before the disastrous eruption in *c.* 1500 B.C. which reduced it to its present state. Later came colonists from Laconia, who built the temple to the Carnean Apollo. Its importance in the Archaic period is shown by its rich cemeteries and early sculpture, but in the 630s it had to dispatch part of its population to colonize Cyrene. The islanders took no part in the Persian wars, but, though Dorians, appear as allies of Athens in the Peloponnesian war. The island was a Ptolemaic naval base during the third and part of the second century B.C.

German archaeological excavations (1895–1902) have revealed a fine capital city, with a theatre, of Hellenistic and Roman times. A Minoan colony of pre-eruption days is being excavated.

P-K, *GL* iv. C VII (c); *IG* xii. 3; *Thera*, ed. H. von Gaertringen (1899–1904). Pfuhl, *Ath. Mitt.* 1903, 1 ff. (tombs, etc.). Dörpfeld, *Ath. Mitt.* 1904, 57 ff. (theatre); Kontoleon, *Arch. Eph.* 1939–41, 1 f.; *AM* 1958, 117 f. W. A. L.; J. B.

**THERAMENES** (d. 404/3 B.C.), Athenian statesman. He was one of the principals in establishing the Four Hundred (q.v.). Four months later he was active in overthrowing them and establishing the Five Thousand. When full democracy was restored in 410 he was in the Hellespont, assisting in the recovery of Athens' naval supremacy (*see* PELOPONNESIAN WAR). At Arginusae (406) he commanded only a single ship. The abandonment of survivors from ships wrecked in the battle was probably due only to bad weather, but later at Athens the blame was disputed between Theramenes and the generals, and after a largely illegal trial six generals were put to death. Xenophon blames him for this appalling miscarriage of justice; but Aristophanes in the *Frogs* next spring treated him lightly, merely as an adroit politician. In 404 he was sent to negotiate with Lysander (q.v.), and Xenophon (*Hell.* 2. 2. 16) said that he deliberately wasted three months while the hunger at Athens grew; but he was then sent to Sparta and brought back the final terms of peace. He was appointed one of the 'Thirty Tyrants' (q.v. 1), but soon quarrelled with the extremists, especially Critias (q.v.), who had him condemned and executed.

His frequent changes of side were censured both by democrats like Lysias and by oligarchs like Critias, but for Aristotle and for others in the fourth century he was a moderate seeking a genuine political mean. If he was sincere, he must nevertheless bear much of the blame for the internal troubles which lamed Athens in the last phase of the war. A. A.

**THERAPNE,** the site of a sanctuary (the Menelaeum) Polyb. 5. 18. 3; the temple of Menelaus, Paus. 3. 19. 9, on a steep cliff on the left bank of the Eurotas, to the south-east of Sparta. Some scanty remains of an extensive Late Helladic settlement, destroyed in LH IIIB–C, were excavated in 1910. Votive offerings attest a cult from the late Geometric period to the fourth century B.C. The massive remains of a fifth-century building (excavated in 1909) represent the altar (and temple?) of Helen, who was worshipped here together with the Dioscuri and Menelaus. The cult of the Twins was later transferred to Sparta itself.

*BSA* 1908–9, 108 ff., 1909–10, 4 ff.; J. M. Cook, Γέρας 'Αντωνίου Κεραμοπούλλου (1953), 112 ff.; H. Waterhouse and R. Hope-Simpson, *BSA* 1960, 72. A. M. W.; W. G. F.

**THERMOPYLAE** ('Hot Gates', from its hot sulphur springs) was probably the original meeting-place of the famous Amphictiony (q.v.), whence the delegates were called Pyl-agorai. As a defence position, where the road defiled between fierce cliffs and the sea, then hard by, its weakness was that there is easy ground above, 'along the spine of the mountain' (Hdt. 7. 216), could an invader but find his way to it; and thus the pass was outflanked repeatedly, by sixth-century Thessalians, by the Persians, by the Gauls in 279 (Paus. 10. 22), and by Cato in 191 (Plut. *Cato Maior* 13).

W. K. Pritchett, *AJArch.* 1958; Burn, *Persia and the Greeks* (1962), 407 ff. (G. B. Grundy, *The Great Persian War* (1901), 298 ff., is misleading.) A. R. B.

**THERMUM,** religious centre of Aetolia. Situated north-east of L. Trichonis on a natural rock-castle, it commanded the central plains of Aetolia and formed the meeting-place for the Aetolian Confederacy. Extensive excavation has revealed its occupation from the Bronze Age and its importance as a cult centre for the worship of Apollo Thermios, Apollo Lyseios, and Artemis; oval houses, early type of *megaron*, three temples of *c.* 600 B.C., and terracotta metopes and antefix heads revealing Corinthian influence are the most important discoveries. Its historical importance coincides with the Aetolian Confederacy, until its sack in 218 B.C. by Philip V of Macedon.

'Αρχ. 'Εφ. 1900, 167 f.; 'Αρχ. Δελτ. 1915 and 1916; W. J. Woodhouse, *Aetolia* (1897), 252 f.; P–K, *GL* 2. 2. 342. N. G. L. H.

**THERON,** tyrant of Acragas (488–472 B.C.), married his daughter Demarete to Gelon (q.v.), whose firm ally he became. In 483 he seized Himera from its tyrant Terillus, whose appeal to Carthage resulted in the expedition of 480, when Theron and Gelon won a crushing victory. On Gelon's death Theron supported Polyzelus, younger brother of Hieron I (q.v.), but conflict with Syracuse was avoided and Hieron warned Theron of a plot against his regime. Theron's building programme and patronage of the arts made Acragas one of the most beautiful and renowned of Greek cities.

Dunbabin, *Western Greeks*, ch. 14: A. Schenk, Graf von Stauffenberg, *Trinakria* (1963), 176 ff.; H. Berve, *Die Tyrannis bei den Griechen* i (1967), 132 ff., ii. 595 ff. A. G. W.

**THERSANDER** (Θέρσανδρος), name of five mythological persons, for whom see Höfer in Roscher, s.v.; the one of most genealogical importance is son of Polynices and Argeia (*see* ADRASTUS), from whom Theron of Acragas claimed descent (Pind. *Ol.* 2. 43 ff.); he was one of the Epigoni (q.v.). H. J. R.

**THERSITES,** in mythology, an ugly, foul-tongued fellow, who rails at Agamemnon (*Iliad* 2. 212 ff.), until beaten into silence by Odysseus. Evidently, from his description, he is of low birth; but in post-Homeric tradition (schol. *Il.* ibid.) he is of good family, son of Agrios brother of Oeneus (q.v.), therefore akin to Diomedes (q.v. 2). Hence, when Achilles slays him for railing at him when he mourns for Penthesilea (*Aethiopis*), a quarrel arises and Achilles goes to Lesbos to be purified.

H. J. R.

**THESEUS** (Θησεύς), son of Aegeus (q.v.) or Poseidon, i.e. of a sea-god, and national hero of Athens. This explains his prominence in ancient, especially Attic, literature; the chief surviving continuous accounts of him, however, are Plutarch, *Theseus*, and Apollod. 3. 216 ff., continued by *Epit.* 1. His legend had manifestly been influenced by that of Heracles (q.v.; encounters with brigands and monsters; campaign against the Amazons), and it is not surprising that he is made Heracles' friend and contemporary. There is no proof that any real person lies behind the legend, but that is not impossible.

*Childhood and youth.* When Aegeus departed from Troezen, he left instructions with Aethra that when her son was able, he should lift a certain rock, under which Aegeus had hidden a sword and sandals. Meanwhile, the boy was educated by Pittheus, his tutor being a certain Connidas, a hero honoured in Attica the day before the Theseia (Plut. op. cit. 4). On reaching young manhood (sixteen years old, Paus. 1. 27. 8) he lifted the rock easily (Plut. 6) and determined not to sail to Athens to find his father but go the more dangerous way by land. He thus encountered Periphetes, or Corynetes, Sinis, Sciron, Procrustes, Phaea the sow of Crommyon (qq.v.), and other dangerous men and beasts; the exact numbers and names vary in different accounts. Plutarch (9) says that Theseus was eager to emulate Heracles, and in fact this is one of the most obvious places in which the latter's legend has influenced his. The difference (emphasized by Nilsson, *Cults, myths, oracles and politics in Ancient Greece* (1951), 51 ff.) is that Heracles conquers folktale monsters, Theseus mostly human enemies of travellers.

*Attic and Cretan adventures.* Arrived in Attica, he was in danger from Medea (q.v.), who persuaded Aegeus to send him against the Marathonian bull, which in some accounts was Pasiphae's bull brought from Crete by Heracles (q.v.). On the way there, an old woman named Hecale hospitably entertained him; having killed the bull, he found her dead on his return, and ordered that her memory should be honoured (Callim., frs. of *Hecale*, 230–377 Pf.; Plut. 14). Coming back to Athens, he narrowly escaped an attempt of Medea to poison him (Apollod. *Epit.* 1, 5), thanks to Aegeus' recognizing him in time. He now heard of the tribute yearly sent to the Minotaur, and volunteered, or was specially chosen by Minos (q.v.), to be one of the youths included in it (Plut. 17). On the voyage to Crete he proved his divine ancestry by leaping overboard and coming back safely from the palace of Amphitrite with a gold ornament which Minos had thrown in (Bacchyl. 16). In Crete he killed the Minotaur by the help of Ariadne (q.v.), who gave him a clue of thread to find his way out of the Labyrinth and afterwards fled with him. He left her at Dia (Naxos); in the original story this was probably due to some magical forgetfulness (cf. Theoc. 2. 45–6), but, this detail having fallen out, various reasons were given for his ingratitude (Plut. 20). Thence he sailed to Delos, where he and his comrades danced a complicated figure, in commemoration of the Labyrinth, said to be preserved in the traditional Delian dance known as the 'crane' (Plut. 21). This may serve as an example of the numerous ceremonies, Attic and other, said in later times to commemorate some part of his adventures. For his return *see* AEGEUS.

*Kingship.* Theseus succeeded his father and is supposed to have brought about the συνοικισμός or union of the various communities of Attica into one State with Athens for the capital (Plut. 24). The event is itself historical, but its age and author unknown. He took part with Heracles in the expedition against the Amazons, or went against them on his own account, and won Antiope, or Hippolyte (cf. HIPPOLYTUS 1) for himself; the Amazons in their turn, invaded Attica, held the Areopagus against Theseus, and were finally defeated in a desperate battle. Pirithous the Lapith raided Marathon, was met by Theseus, and became his friend and ally; Theseus came to his wedding-feast and took part in the resultant fight with the Centaurs (q.v.), and later helped Pirithous to invade the lower world in an attempt to carry off Persephone (q.v.). According to the most familiar of the many versions of this story, Theseus was ultimately rescued by Heracles from imprisonment, but Pirithous remained below. Theseus also carried off Helen (q.v.) while she was very young, and consequently Attica was invaded by the Dioscuri (q.v.).

*Death and posthumous honours.* Apart from the variant of his permanent detention by Hades (Verg. *Aen,* 6. 617–18, perhaps already in *Od.* 11. 631) his reign is generally said to have been ended by a rebellion (headed by Menestheus, a descendant of Erechtheus, q.v., Plut.

32), which led to his banishment; he went to Scyros and was there murdered by King Lycomedes (Plut. 35). Long after, some bones alleged to be his were brought from Scyros by Cimon (Plut. 36), and a hero-shrine built for them (not the temple now popularly called the Theseum).

*Contact with other legends.* Besides Heracles, Theseus is said to have been one of the helpers of Meleager (q.v. 1) in the boar-hunt (Plut. 29), and an Argonaut (q.v., ibid.); he brought about the burial of the bodies of the Seven against Thebes (Eur. *Suppl.*), and kindly received Oedipus (q.v., Soph. *OC*).

The Minotaur adventure appears widely in Greek art from the seventh century. Other deeds, individually or as a cycle, became very popular in Athenian sculpture and vase-painting from the later sixth century. He is generally shown as a youth, but the elder statesman of Attic tragedy is anticipated on a vase by Execias of the third quarter of the sixth century (see J. D. Beazley, *Development of Attic Black-figure* (1951), 68 and pl. 27. 3).

Steuding in Roscher's *Lexikon*, s.v. (abundant references to ancient literature and art); H. Herter in *Rh. Mus.* 1936 and 1938–9; C. Dugas and R. Flacelière, *Thésée, images et récits* (1958); Brommer. *Vasenlisten²*, 151 ff.           H. J. R.; H. W. P.; C. M. R.

**THESMOPHORIA,** a women's festival in honour of Demeter (q.v.) common to all Greeks, regularly celebrated in the autumn. In Athens it took place on the 11th–13th Pyanopsion (Oct./Nov.). The women (men being strictly excluded) erected bowers with couches of plants and sat on the ground. The second day was a fast. The name of the third day, Καλλιγένεια, hints at the fecundity of mankind also, but the chief purpose of the festival was to promote the fertility of the corn which was about to be sown. Pigs had been thrown down into subterranean caves (μέγαρα), probably at the Scirophoria (q.v.); the putrefied remains were brought up, laid on an altar, and mixed with the seed-corn. The myth of Eubuleus, the swineherd swallowed up by the earth when Pluto carried off Kore, is an *aition* to account for this custom.

Nilsson, *Feste*, 313 ff.; L. Deubner, *Attische Feste* (1932), 50 ff.
                                                        M. P. N.

**THESMOTHETAI** (θεσμοθέται) in Athens were the six junior of the nine *archontes* (q.v.), appointed annually. They were instituted not later than the seventh century B.C., but nothing is known for certain about their functions at that time. Later their duties were mainly legal. Acting together, as a college, they were the magistrates responsible for many types of case, including most sorts of *graphe* (q.v.), cases arising from *eisangelia* (q.v.), *probole*, or *dokimasia* (q.v.), some other public cases, and some private cases (*see* DIKE). Their court was the *heliaia* (q.v.). They also presided over juries which ratified, on behalf of Athens, legal regulations concerning trade between Athens and other States, and tried cases which arose from them (*see* SYMBOLON). Sometimes they could impose penalties without reference to a jury: in particular, they could authorize the execution without trial of persons exiled for homicide who were afterwards found in Attica. In the fourth century they had to examine the laws for anomalies and inconsistencies, and, if necessary, ask for the appointment of *nomothetai* (q.v.); and, after magistrates ceased to sit regularly in the same courts, it was the *thesmothetai* who allotted courts to magistrates and fixed the days of trials (*see* DIKASTERION). Finally, they drew the lots for the appointment of *archontes* and other officials for the next year.

The Attic orators; Arist. *Ath. Pol.* 59.           D. M. M.

**THESPIAE,** near the east foot of Mt. Helicon, was the chief town of south Boeotia. The Thespians, alone of

Boeotians, fought in full strength at Thermopylae and Plataea. They took a prominent part in the restored Boeotian Confederacy after 446 B.C., providing two boeotarchs. The Spartans used Thespiae as a base for their anti-Theban policy after 382, and it remained important after their expulsion. It was in Roman times still one of the chief Boeotian cities (Strabo, 403, 410). Visitors came to see the Eros of Praxiteles (Cic. *Verr.* 2. 4. 135), and the sanctuary and games of the Muses (*see* HELICON).

Fiehn in *PW*, s.v. 'Thespeia'; P–K, *GL* I. ii. 452 f., 507; G. Roux, 'Le Val des Muses et les musées chez les auteurs anciens', *BCH* 1954, 22 ff.           T. J. D.

**THESPIS** won the prize when tragedy was performed for the first time at the Dionysia at Athens in one of the years 535–533 B.C. (*Marm. Par.* 43, T. J. Cadoux, *JHS* 1948, 109). His invention of the speaking actor must have been made some time before this, and the story which brings him into contact with Solon (Plut. *Sol.* 29, Diog. Laert. 1. 59), though suspect, is not impossible. His invention of the actor who delivered prologues and conversed with the chorus-leader was vouched for by Aristotle (ap. Themistium 26. 316 d) and probably in the previous century by (?) Charon of Lampsacus (*FGrH* 262 F 15). He may have introduced improvements in the mask, but that he invented it (*Suda*, s.v.) is incredible. The same source gives a few titles of plays including a *Pentheus*, but those which circulated under his name in the fourth century B.C. were forgeries (Diog. Laert. 5. 92). Horace's description of him (*Ars P.* 275 ff.) as taking his plays about on wagons, with a chorus whose faces were stained with wine-lees, probably rests on a confusion of early tragedy with early comedy. *See also* TRAGEDY.

*TGF* 832–3; Pickard-Cambridge–Webster, *Dithyramb²*, 69 ff.
                                                A. W. P. C.; D. W. L.

**THESPROTI,** a people mentioned in the *Odyssey* with a king at Ephyra in the Acheron valley (in this region a tholos-tomb and Mycenaean weapons have been found) and probably extending over Epirus in the Late Bronze Age. Later confined to south-west Epirus, their territory included for a time Dodona (q.v.) and always the Nekyomanteion or Oracle of the Dead. The Thesproti formed a tribal State (*koinon*), which entered the Epirote Alliance and the Epirote Confederacy, sided with Rome in 170 B.C., and survived under the Roman settlement.

S. I. Dakaris, *Antike Kunst*, Beiheft i (1963); Hammond, *Epirus*.
                                                        N. G. L. H.

**THESSALONICA,** a city of Macedonia, founded by Cassander, who synoecized the small towns at the head of the Thermaic Gulf; perhaps on the site of Therme (Strabo, fr. 24). It was named after Cassander's wife. It stood at the junction of the Morava–Vardar route from Europe with the route from the Adriatic to Byzantium (the later Via Egnatia). An open roadstead sheltered by Chalcidice, Thessalonica became the chief Macedonian port, displacing Pella when its harbour was silted up. Strongly fortified, it withstood the Roman siege, surrendered after the battle of Pydna, and became the capital of the Roman province (146 B.C.); in the Civil War it served as Pompey's base. A free State and the main station on the Via Egnatia, it enjoyed great prosperity, shown by its prolific coinage, and was made a Roman colony by Decius *c.* A.D. 250. The population included a large Roman element and a Jewish colony, visited by St. Paul, one of whose disciples, Aristarchus, became the first bishop of Thessalonica. Second city to Constantinople in the Byzantine Empire, Thessalonica reached a height of prosperity to which the extant walls and early Byzantine churches bear witness, until it was sacked by Saracens in 904.                                    N. G. L. H.

**THESSALUS** (1) of Cos (fl. *c.* 421–411 B.C.), the more famous of Hippocrates' two sons. Galen considered him to be the author of books 5 and 7, and the part-author of books 2 and 6, of the Hippocratic work on epidemics, and thinks he may have been the author of the *Κατ' ἰητρεῖον.*
W. D. R.

**THESSALUS** (2) of Tralles, the *Iatronikes* as he styled himself, lived in Rome and died before A.D. 79. Pliny the Elder quotes his epitaph. The new medical school to which he laid claim in a letter to Nero was that of the 'Methodists'.

Thessalus accepted Themison's doctrine of the *communia* but did not understand them as a dogmatic conception. He rather took them to mean the morbid change visible in the patient, indicating what, of necessity, the physician should do: change the existing state into its opposite. In short, he interpreted the *communia* as a true sceptic would (Sext. Emp. *Pyr.* I. 236). The degree of the necessary change he determined by considering the size of the *communia*, the locality affected, and the seasons, so that his treatment did not much differ from the usual one. Medical theory, however, was greatly simplified in this way. Thessalus' school was the only new sect seriously to compete with the older Hellenistic schools. Galen's attacks are such as one would expect from a convinced dogmatist without understanding of the modernist attitude of Nero's time.

TEXT. Fragments not collected. The treatise on remedies (F. Cumont, *Rev. Phil.* 1918) probably not by Thessalus.
LITERATURE. H. Diller, *PW* vi A. 168 (but he did not merely reconstitute the Methodical School, but is its founder); cf. L. Edelstein, *PW*, Suppl. vi. 358, s.v. 'Methodiker'. The dependence of the Methodical doctrine on those of Themison (q.v.) had been acknowledged by the 'Methodists' from the beginning (e.g. Celsus, *Prooemium*). The fact that later surveys trace the origin of the school to Asclepiades and Themison (e.g. Galen 14. 684) expresses this dependence in the usual historical categories of beginning and perfecting. Medical doctrine, Th. Meyer-Steineg, *Das medizinische System d. Methodiker*, Jenaer med.-hist. Beiträge (1916); T. C. Allbutt, *Greek Medicine in Rome* (1921).
L. E.

**THESSALY**, a district of northern Greece. Thessaly proper, comprising the four tetrads, Thessaliotis, Hestiaeotis, Pelasgiotis, and Phthiotis (q.v. for the distinction between Thessaly and its Perioecis), consists of two large and level plains separated by hilly country. Mountain barriers impede communication by land with neighbouring areas, and the only outlet to good harbours is a low pass leading to the Bay of Volo. Because of the extent of its plains Thessaly was richer in grain, horses, and cattle than other parts of Greece, but extremes of temperature discouraged the cultivation of olives and vines.

Although the archaeological picture of early Thessaly is incomplete, it is evident that in the Late Helladic period Mycenaean influences spread from Iolcus (q.v.) over most of the country. During the twelfth century invaders from the north and north-west infiltrated into Thessaly. Most of these pressed on southwards, but the Thessali, who migrated from Thesprotia, remained and dominated the plains, reducing the conquered to serfdom or driving them into the mountains. A few baronial families gradually became supreme, and their enterprise in organizing a loosely-knit national State headed by a *tagos* (q.v.) made Thessaly a formidable power in the sixth century. At this time the Thessalians dominated northern Greece, partly by controlling the Amphictionic League (see AMPHICTIONIES) through the votes of small tribes on their borders owing allegiance to them. The rivalries of aristocratic houses and the medism of the Aleuadae (q.v.) soon caused a decline, which was intensified during the fifth century by social unrest, as the urbanization of this backward district gradually broke down baronial domination. In the wars between Athens

and Sparta the Thessalians favoured the former but rendered little assistance, and the foundation of a Spartan colony at Heraclea (q.v. 4) Trachinia illustrates their impotence.

Late in the fifth century Lycophron (q.v. 1) established a tyranny at Pherae, and a protracted struggle began between the Pheraean tyrants and the bulk of the Thessalians led by Larissa, where the Aleuadae had become a city aristocracy. This conflict was disastrous, because both sides enlisted external support from powers whose chief aim was to secure advantages for themselves by exploiting Thessalian disunity. It was only during the tyranny of Jason (q.v. 2), who revived the national State and had himself elected *tagos*, that Thessaly was united and formidable to the rest of Greece. Anarchy returned under Alexander (q.v. 5) of Pherae and his successors, and Thessaly fell an easy prey to Philip of Macedon, who adroitly turned local quarrels to his own advantage. In theory the Thessalians retained their independence, but the kings of Macedon held the archonship of the Thessalian League for life, and Thessaly remained virtually a Macedonian province. Its contingent of cavalry was invaluable to Alexander in Asia. An unsuccessful attempt was made in the Lamian War to throw off Macedonian suzerainty, and in the Hellenistic period Thessaly was often overrun by rival powers, some parts falling under Aetolian control.

In 196 Rome liberated Thessaly from Macedonian rule and established a new Thessalian Confederacy, which was maintained even after 148, when Thessaly was absorbed in the Roman province of Macedonia.

GEOGRAPHY AND TOPOGRAPHY. F. Stählin, *Das hellenische Thessalien* (1924); P-K, *GL.* i. 1.
HISTORY. H. D. Westlake, *Thessaly in the Fourth Century B.C.* (1935); M. Sordi, *La lega tessala* (1958).
POLITICAL AND SOCIAL DEVELOPMENT. U. Kahrstedt, *Gött. Nachr.* 1924, 128 ff.; G. Busolt, *Griechische Staatskunde* ii (1926), 1478 ff.; J. A. O. Larsen, *Greek Federal States* (1968), 12 ff., 281 ff.  H. D. W.

**THESTIUS**, in mythology, king of Pleuron, father of Lynceus and Idas (Argonauts and hunters of the Calydonian boar) and of Althaea, wife of Oeneus (q.v.; Ov. *Met.* 8. 304, 446 and elsewhere).

**THESTOR** (Θέστωρ). Of the five persons so called (Höfer in Roscher, s.v.), the least obscure is the father of Calchas (q.v.; *Iliad* 1. 69). He has no legend, the tale in Hyginus, *Fab.* 190, being manifestly late romance.

**THETES** (θῆτες), hired labourers, the humblest class of free men in a Greek city. At Athens, after Solon (q.v.), the lowest of the four census-classes, men with an estimated annual income of less than 200 *medimnoi* of corn or the equivalent in other produce or money. Solon admitted them to the *ekklesia* and Heliaea (qq.v.), but not to magistracies nor, presumably, to his *boule* (q.v.). This limitation was never formally abrogated, but towards the end of the fifth century it came to be ignored in practice. Because they could not afford a suit of armour, Thetes did not serve in the hoplite ranks; but when Athens became mainly a naval power they had even more important duties as rowers, sailors, marines, and naval officers, the State providing any equipment necessary. On land they probably furnished bowmen and 'light-armed' men (ψιλοί), including peltasts and unarmed pioneers. For their numbers see POPULATION (GREEK).
A. W. G.; T. J. C.

**THETIS** (Θέτις), a Nereid, who was fated to bear a son mightier than his father. This being revealed by Themis to the gods, Pind. *Isthm.* 8. 34 ff. (in Aesch. *Prom. Bound* and *Prom. Unbound* she reveals it to her son Prometheus, who discloses it as the price of his liberation; cf. PROMETHEUS), Zeus and Poseidon gave up all thoughts of possessing her, and instead gave her to Peleus (q.v.), as the most deserving of mankind. Their wedding was attended by all the gods, who brought various gifts (Pind. *Pyth.* 3. 92 ff.; Catullus 64. 31 ff., etc.). She bore one child, Achilles (q.v., *Iliad* 18. 55 ff.; Pind. ibid. 100); Lycophron, 178, says there were seven, of whom the rest perished in the fire when she tried to make them immortal, cf. PELEUS.

The capture by Peleus and her wedding to him are exceedingly popular in art from the sixth century. She is also shown getting the arms from Hephaestus for Achilles; and very often bringing them to him, helped by her sister Nereids, from the mid fifth century riding dolphins and other sea creatures. She balances Eos in pictures of the *psychostasia* and combat with Memnon.

Roscher's *Lexikon*, s.vv. 'Peleus', 'Thetis'. In art, Brommer, *Vasenlisten*², 241 ff., 270 ff. H. J. R.; C. M. R.

**THEVESTE** (modern *Tebessa*), an old Berber town, at the east end of the High Plateaux, commanding the upper Ampsaga. Hanno conquered it for Carthage in the third century B.C. Early in the first century A.D. the Legio III Augusta was stationed near Theveste, which became a *colonia*, probably under Trajan, when the legion moved to Lambaesis. Connected with Carthage by one of the main roads in N. Africa, it became the economic centre of a wide area covering part of southern Algeria and Tunisia. Substantial and impressive ruins, mainly from the Late Empire, include an arch of Caracalla, temple of Jupiter, a large basilica of the fourth and later centuries, and a complete set of Byzantine fortifications.

R. Cagnat, *Carthage, Timgad, Tebessa*² (1909); S. de Roch, *Tebessa, antique Theveste* (1952). B. H. W.

**THIASOS** (θίασος), a group of persons (θιασῖται, -ῶται) associated in the worship of a particular deity or deities, Greek or foreign. Such groups already existed at Athens in the time of Solon, who guaranteed their rights of association; and the epigraphic evidence, mainly of Hellenistic date, reveals them as a common feature of the private life of both Greeks and aliens in the Greek cities of the Aegean and Pontic areas. Their organization resembled that of Greek private societies in general (*see* CLUBS, GREEK). The term *thiasoi* was also used for the small groups into which some, and perhaps all, of the Attic phratries (q.v.) were divided by the early fourth century B.C., and possibly for analogous subdivisions of the citizen-body in other cities.

F. Poland, *Geschichte der griechischen Vereinswesens* (1913), see indexes; Busolt–Swoboda, *Griech. Staatsk.*³ i (1920), ii (1926), see indexes; W. S. Ferguson, *Harv. Theol. Rev.* 1944, 61 ff., A. Andrewes, *JHS* 1961, 1 ff. T. J. C.

**THIBRON,** a Spartan sent to Ionia in the autumn of 400 B.C. with a force of 5,000 Peloponnesians and Helots, in response to an appeal for aid from the Greek cities in the area, who were threatened by the Persian satrap Tissaphernes. He captured Magnesia and was unsuccessful at Trales, but eventually augmented his forces by enlisting most of the surviving Greeks who had served with the Younger Cyrus. In the following year he received the adherence of Pergamus and some minor cities of Aeolis, took several more by storm, but his siege of Egyptian Larisssa was a failure, and the ephors ordered him to attack Caria instead. At Ephesus, however, in the midst of his preparations, he was superseded in command by Dercyllidas (q.v.). On his return to Sparta, he was prosecuted on a charge of allowing his men to plunder friendly Greek cities, condemned, and sent into exile. Subsequently he procured his recall, and in 391 was again sent to Asia Minor with a force of 8,000 men, this time to operate against Struthas the new Persian officer appointed to administer Ionia and the Aegean seaboard. Basing himself on Ephesus and the cities of the Maeander valley, Thibron did little more than conduct plundering expeditions in an incompetent and reckless manner. Struthas, observing this, surprised him one morning with a body of cavalry as he headed a disorderly raiding party, and in the ensuing fight Thibron and a large number of his men were killed. Such was the fate of the last ever Spartan campaign in Asia. Remiss, inefficient, and a poor disciplinarian, Thibron differed from the average Spartan commander and during his stay in Asia achieved virtually nothing.

Xen. *Anab.* 7. 6. 1, 7. 8. 24; id. *Hell.* 3. 1. 4–8, 4. 8. 17–19; Diod. 14. 36, 37. 4, 38. 2, 99. 1–3. E. I. McQ.

**THIRTY TYRANTS** (1). At the end of the Peloponnesian War (Apr. 404 B.C.) the oligarchs at Athens already had the upper hand, Critias leading the extremists, Theramenes the moderates. Both sections joined in asking Lysander for help against the democrats; under pressure from him the *ekklesia* was compelled to appoint thirty ξυγγραφεῖς to draw up a new constitution κατὰ τὰ πάτρια. The Thirty at once seized full power, constituted a new *boule* under their control, and a board of Ten to rule Piraeus, abolished the dicasteries, and began the removal of obnoxious democrats and *sykophantai* (June). This developed into a reign of terror, many respectable citizens and metics being executed and their property confiscated; a Spartan garrison was stationed on the Acropolis; no new constitution was promulgated. To meet the protests of Theramenes, Critias agreed to draw up a list of 3,000 to constitute the citizen body; he never published it, and he stifled further opposition from Theramenes by executing him. 1,500 men in all are said to have been executed; many were exiled or fled. But the Thirty failed to prevent the capture of Piraeus by a band of exiles under Thrasybulus (q.v.), and Critias was killed in a battle (Dec.–Jan. 404/3). They were now deposed by the moderate oligarchs, who constituted themselves as the 3,000 and appointed a board of Ten, who eventually became reconciled with Thrasybulus' party by the good offices of the Spartan king Pausanias (q.v. 2). The full democracy was now restored (late summer 403), and the remnant of the Thirty, who had retired to Eleusis, were exterminated there two or three years later.

Xen. *Hell.* 2. 3. 4; Arist. *Ath. Pol.* 34. 3–41. 1 (less trustworthy than Xenophon, especially in chronology); Diod. 14. 3–6 (from Ephorus). Details in Lysias (esp. *Or.* 12 and 13), Andocides, and Isocrates. Hignett, *Hist. Athen. Const.*, ch. 11 and app. xiii–xiv. A. W. G.

**THIRTY TYRANTS** (2), the name given in the *Historia Augusta* (Pollio) to the pretenders who arose in the provinces in the mid third century A.D. The author's original plan was to write on twenty, but the number was raised to that of the 'thirty tyrants' of Athens by admitted padding; thirty-two names appear in the collection, including two women. The object was to denigrate Gallienus, in whose reign most of the pretenders are said to have lived; in fact only nine are authenticated for his reign. Of the others, some were children of pretenders, some certainly never wore the purple, others are almost certainly fictions, and a few occurred in other reigns. The whole collection is worthless as a historical source. In the list which follows (not in the order of the *Historia*) italicized names are known from coins or other sources.

In Gaul: *Postumus* (q.v.) = M. Cassianius Latinius Postumus Aug., 259–68; Postumus Junior, said to be Caesar, and son of Postumus; *Lollianus* = C. Ulpius Cornelius Laelianus Aug., 268, rebelled against Postumus; *Marius* = M. Aurelius Marius Aug., 268; *Victorinus* = M. Piavonius Victorinus Aug., 268–70; Victorinus Junior, said to be son of Victorinus, existence doubtful; *Tetricus* (q.v.) = C. Pius Esuvius Tetricus Aug., 270–4; *Tetricus Junior*, Caesar, son of Tetricus.

In Illyricum: *Ingenuus*, full name unknown, *c.* 259; *Regalianus* = P. C.... Regalianus Aug., *c.* 260; *Aureolus*, full name unknown, 268.

In Greece: Piso, 261, an invention; *Valens*, 261.

In Isauria: Trebellianus: highly dubious.

In Syria: *Cyriades* = Mareades, *c.* 258, never emperor; *Macrianus* = (Fulvius) Macrianus, 260, never emperor; *Macrianus* (q.v.) *Junior* = T. Fulvius Macrianus Aug., 260–1; *Ballista* (q.v.), 260–1, never emperor; *Quietus* = T. Fulvius Junius Quietus Aug., 260–1; *Odaenathus* (q.v.) = Septimius Odaenathus, 260–7, never emperor; Herodes, Herennianus and Timolaus, *c.* 268 ff., said to be sons of Odaenathus, never emperors; *Maeonius, c.* 268, a relative of Odaenathus, never emperor.

In Egypt: *Aemilianus* = L. Mussius Aemilianus, *c.* 261.

Others: Celsus and Saturninus, both fictions; *Victoria*, mother of Victorinus; *Zenobia* (q.v.), wife of Odaenathus; *Valens Superior*, at Rome in 250; *Titus*, probably = Quartinus, 238; Censorinus, a fiction.

R. Syme, *Ammianus and the Historia Augusta* (1968).

B. H. W.

**THOMAS MAGISTER** (*Theodulos* in religion) of Thessalonica was the Secretary of Andronicus II (A.D. 1282–1328), but withdrew to a monastery, where he devoted himself to scholarship.

WORKS. (1) *Ecloga Vocum Atticarum* ('Εκλογὴ ὀνομάτων καὶ ῥημάτων Ἀττικῶν), based especially on Phrynichus, Ammonius, Herodian, and Moeris, but with much added material that is less valuable, drawn from his own reading, e.g. in Herodotus, Thucydides, Aelius Aristides, and Synesius.

(2) Texts, with scholia, of Aeschylus, Sophocles *Aj., El., OT*, Euripides *Hec., Or., Phoen.*, Aristophanes *Plut., Nub., Ran.*, and Pindar. These give an insight into the oral instruction provided by a late Byzantine teacher. Thomas is well informed on *realien*, tolerably knowledgeable on rare words, and totally ignorant of metre. Lives of these poets appear under his name in some MSS.

(3) Declamations on set themes in the manner of the ancient orators, e.g. *De Regis Officiis* (Π. βασιλείας); panegyrics on famous personalities of earlier date, e.g. Gregory Naz.; eulogistic addresses to contemporaries; deliberative discourses on questions of the moment.

(4) Letters.

*Ecloga*, F. Ritschl (1832); J. P. Migne, *PG* cxlv; F. W. Lenz, *Fünf Reden Th. M.'s* (1963); T. Hopfner, *Sitz. Wien. Akad.* 1912; A. Turyn, *The Manuscript Tradition of the Tragedies of Aeschylus* (1943), 67 ff.; id. *Studies in the Manuscript Tradition of the Tragedies of Sophocles* (1952), 31 ff.; J. Irigoin, *Histoire du texte de Pindare* (1952), 180 ff.; A. Turyn, *The Byzantine Manuscript Tradition of the Tragedies of Euripides* (1957), 165 ff.
J. F. L.; R. B.

**THRACE.** The boundaries of Thrace varied at different times; in the fifth century B.C. the kingdom of the Odrysae, the leading tribe of Thrace, extended over present-day Bulgaria, Turkish Thrace (east of the Hebrus), and Greece between the Hebrus and the Strymon, except for the coastal strip with its Greek cities, i.e. from the Danube on the north to the Hellespont and the Greek fringe on the south, and from Constantinople to the sources of the Strymon in south-west Bulgaria, whereas the Roman province of Thrace was bounded on the north by Haemus, on the east by the Euxine, on the south by the Propontis, Hellespont, and Aegean, and on the west by the Nestus.

By ancient writers the Thracians (who were of Indo-European stock) were considered as a primitive people, consisting of the warlike and ferocious tribes dwelling in the mountains of Haemus and Rhodope, and the peaceable dwellers in the plain, who came into contact with the Greek colonies on the Aegean and Propontis. Until classical times the Thracians lived in open villages; only in Roman times was urban civilization developed. Herodotus remarks (5. 3) that, if they could have been united under a single king, they would have been invincible, a view corroborated by Thucydides (2. 95–101); in fact, unlike the Macedonians, the Thracians never achieved a national history. From the eighth century B.C. the coast of Thrace was colonized by Greeks at Abdera (q.v.), Maroneia, Aenus, Perinthus, Byzantium (qq.v.), Apollonia, and Mesambria, but the Thracians resisted Greek influence.

We have very little historical information about the Thracians, except when they were brought into contact with the Greeks. (For the prehistoric period, as revealed by excavation, see S. Casson, op. cit. *infra*, 102 ff.) The Thracians were subdued by the Persians *c.* 516 B.C., and some of them fought against the Greeks under Xerxes (q.v.) in 480 B.C. Shortly afterwards the first king of the Odrysae, Teres, attempted to carve an empire out of the territory occupied by the Thracian tribes (Thuc. 2. 29), and his sovereignty extended as far as the Euxine and the Hellespont. His son Sitalces (q.v.) enlarged his kingdom, subjugating the tribes of Rhodope as far as the Strymon, and the Getae, north of Haemus. Thenceforward the king of the Odrysae called himself king of the Thracians. Sitalces allied himself with the Athenians against the Macedonians, but his invasion of Macedonia in 429 B.C. achieved nothing. Sitalces was succeeded by Seuthes, his nephew, who married Stratonice, sister of Perdiccas (q.v.). In 382 B.C. Cotys succeeded to the monarchy and made war on Athens, assisted by his son-in-law Iphicrates (q.v.), the Athenian. After Cotys' death in 358 B.C. three princes claimed the succession, Cersobleptes (q.v.), his son, Berisades, and Amadocus.

On the collapse of the Odrysian power in mid fourth century, Philip II (q.v.) of Macedon invaded Thrace and made its princes tributary; he founded Philippopolis (q.v.) in his own honour. After the death of Alexander (q.v. 3) the Great, who had left Thrace under his generals, Thrace fell to Lysimachus (q.v.), who founded Lysimacheia in 308 B.C., and thereafter it was a protectorate of the successive rulers of Macedonia. After the Roman victory at Pydna in 168 B.C., Thrace west of the Hebrus was incorporated in Macedonia, and in 129 B.C. the coastal cities were included.

For the religion of the Thracians, *see* RELIGION, THRACIAN; RIDER-GODS AND HEROES; MACEDONIAN CULTS.

S. Casson, *Macedonia, Thrace, and Illyria* (1926); W. Wiesner, *Der Thraker* (1963); D. P. Dimitrov, *Bulgaria, Land of Ancient Civilizations* (Sofia, 1961; bibl.); V. Beševliev and J. Irmscher, *Antike und Mittelalter in Bulgarien* (1960; esp. V. Velkov, 70 ff.); Head, *Hist. Num.*² 246 ff.; G. Mihailov, 'La Thrace aux IVᵉ et IIIᵉ siècles avant notre ère', *Athenaeum* 1961, 33 ff.; id. *Inscriptiones Graecae in Bulgaria Repertae* (Sofia, i– , 1956– ); A. Hoeck, 'Das Odrysenreich in Thrakien', *Hermes* 1891, 76 ff.; G. Kazarow, *Beiträge zur Kulturgeschichte der Thraker* (Sarajevo, 1916); P. Perdrizet, 'Cultes et mythes du Pangée', *Annales de l'Est* 1910.
J. M. R. C.

THRACE AND ROME. The Romans were slow to realize that the destruction of the Macedonian monarchy would involve them with the Thracians, but when Andriscus (q.v.) revolted (149 B.C.) he drew most of his support from Thrace (Florus i. 30), and the subsequent annexation of Macedon made Rome responsible for the eastern border of Macedon with Thrace. Later raids by Thracian tribes into Macedonia and punitive campaigns by Roman proconsuls of Macedonia are regularly attested. Some peoples in Thrace, however, made alliances with Rome. The Dentheletae had long been faithful allies when wantonly attacked by Piso (q.v. 5), and Cicero calls Rabocentus, chief of the Bessi, a faithful ally, although hitherto they had been troublesome (Cic. *Pis.* 84). Later

Thrace was consolidated into a kingdom ruled by a dynasty from the Sapaei, who lived in the south close to Macedonia. The first-known ruler was Rhascuporis (or Rhescuporis), son of Cotys, who helped Pompey against Caesar and later Brutus and Cassius against Antony and Octavian, while his brother Rhascus supported the latter. He was succeeded as king by his son Cotys (*IG* iii. 552, 553), who strengthened the dynasty by a marriage alliance with the Astae, whose capital was at Bizye in eastern Thrace. A Cotys of this family had sent his son Sadalas to help Pompey; later Sadalas' widow Polemocratia entrusted his infant son Cotys to Brutus, who seized the royal treasure and sent the boy to Cyzicus. This Cotys, who was restored to his kingdom apparently while still a boy, married the daughter of Cotys the Sapaean. The latter acted as regent for his son-in-law and he was followed by his son Rhoemetalces, who acted as regent for his nephews, the sons of Cotys, when the latter died. When the Bessi, already subdued by M. Lollius (19–18 B.C.), broke away from the Astae (*c.* 11 B.C.) and killed Rhascuporis, the only surviving son of Cotys, the Romans awarded the kingdom to Rhoemetalces, Rhascuporis' uncle and guardian, who later ruled the whole of Thrace. When Rhoemetalces died (A.D. 12) Augustus partitioned the kingdom between his son Cotys, who received the civilized coastal area, and his brother Rhascuporis, who received the barbarous interior with only the title of dynast (Tac. *Ann.* 2. 64). In A.D. 19 Rhascuporis killed Cotys and Tiberius deposed him, dividing the kingdom between Rhoemetalces, son of Rhascuporis, as dynast, and the sons of Cotys under a Roman guardian, Trebellenus Rufus. One of these sons, Rhoemetalces, was made king of his father's portion by Gaius in A.D. 38. Later the kingdom was reunited, since in A.D. 46 a certain Rhoemetalces was murdered by his wife and his kingdom became the Roman province of Thrace.

The province was governed by procurators until the reign of Trajan when they were superseded by praetorian legates, assisted by procurators, both of whom were based at Perinthus. Although defence was in the hands of the legate in Moesia, some troops were maintained; late in Nero's reign there were 2,000 (Joseph. *BJ* ii. 16. 4). With very few cities Thrace was administered on a centralized system, the province being divided into *strategiai*, each under a *strategos* appointed by the governor. Colonies were founded at Aprus (*colonia Claudia Aprensis*) by Claudius or Nero, and at Deultum (*colonia Flavia Pacensis Deultum*) under Vespasian. Reorganization under Trajan produced at least seven new cities, based mostly on older settlements, although the mass of the population continued to live in villages. Under Diocletian Thrace was split into a number of small provinces, and more cities were founded. From the third century A.D. onwards Thrace was periodically ravaged by barbarian invaders. After the reconstruction of the defences under Justinian there were 100 forts in the Thracian provinces (Procop. *Aed.* 4. 11).

See bibliography above and, on the client kings, R. M. Dawkins and F. W. Hasluck, *BSA* 1905/6, 175–7; H. Dessau, *Eph. Epigr.* 1913, 696 ff. A. Stein, *Römische Reichsbeamte der Provinz Thracia* (Sarajevo, 1920); Jones, *Cities E. Rom. Prov.* 1 ff. J. J. W.

**THRASEA PAETUS, PUBLIUS CLODIUS** (*cos. suff.* A.D. 56), Stoic, renowned for his uprightness and republican sympathies. He modelled himself on Cato Uticensis, of whom, utilizing Munatius Rufus, he composed a *Life* which Plutarch consulted (*Cato Min.* 25, 37). Condemned under Nero (A.D. 66), he ended his life in noble fashion. *See also* ARRIA (2) MINOR.

Tac. *Ann.* 13. 49; 14. 12, 48–9; 15. 20–1; 16. 21–35. Syme, *Tacitus*, 556 ff. G. C. W.

**THRASYBULUS** (d. 388 B.C.), son of Lycus, Athenian general and statesman. In 411 he was a leader of the democratic State formed by the navy at Samos in opposition to the Four Hundred. He was responsible for the recall of Alcibiades and contributed largely to the naval success of the following years.

He was banished by the Thirty and fled to Thebes where he organized a band of seventy exiles and occupied Phyle (late autumn, 404). When his followers had increased to a thousand, he seized the Piraeus and defeated the troops of the Thirty. Thanks to an amnesty proclaimed at the instance of Sparta, he led his men to Athens, and the democracy was restored. In the Corinthian War he played a prominent part, and in 389/8 he commanded a fleet which gained many allies but suffered from lack of financial support. At Aspendus his troops plundered the natives, who murdered him in his tent.

Thrasybulus showed ability and gallantry as a military leader. He was a staunch champion of democracy but was wise enough to make concessions in order to restore Athenian unity. In his last years he failed to appreciate that the imperialistic policy to which he gave his support was far beyond the material resources of Athens at that time.

Thuc. bk. 8; Xen. *Hell.* bks. 1–4; Diod. bks. 13–14. H. D. W.

**THRASYLLUS** of Alexandria (d. A.D. 36), astrologer. Tiberius made his acquaintance during his stay in Rhodes (6 B.C.–A.D. 2) and came to believe in him implicitly; Thrasyllus remained till his death in close contact with the Emperor, who granted him Roman citizenship. He was a man of good education and a serious student of astrology.

WORKS: (1) a work or works on astrology, epitomized later in a Συγκεφαλαίωσις τοῦ Ἱεροκλέα Θρασύλλου πίνακος; (2) Περὶ τῶν ἕπτα τόνων. In addition he was, with Dercyllides, responsible for the division of Plato's works into tetralogies.

F. Cumont, *CCAG* viii, 3, 99 ff. F. H. Cramer, *Astrology in Roman Law and Politics* (U.S.A. 1954), 92 ff. W. D. R.

**THRASYMACHUS** of Chalcedon (fl. *c.* 430–400 B.C.), sophist and rhetorician, is best known from his defence, in the *Republic*, of the thesis that justice is the interest of the stronger. He played an important part in the development of Greek oratory, by his elaboration of the appeal to the emotions by means of elocution and 'action', and in the development of prose style by his attention to rhythm and to the building up of periods.

Testimonia and fragments in Diels, *Vorsokr.*[11] 2. 319–26. W. D. R.

**THRASYMEDES** (Θρασυμήδης), a son of Nestor who takes a minor part in the *Iliad*: 10. 255; 16. 321 ff., and elsewhere. In the Wooden Horse, Quint. Smyrn. 12. 319.

**THUBURSICU(M) NUMIDARUM** (modern *Khamissa*), a market-town on the road from Hippo Regius (q.v.) to Theveste. Lying in the richly phosphated Bagradas valley, it became a prosperous centre of the agricultural life which Masinissa introduced into his territory. Under Roman rule it was the centre of one of the tribes called Numidae, which continued a separate existence after the town obtained higher status. After being administered jointly by native chieftains and military prefects, it was made a *municipium* by Trajan, and became a colony before A.D. 270. Its extensive ruins have yielded many excellent specimens of Greek and Roman art.

S. Gsell and C. A. Joly, *Khamissa, Mdaourouch, Announa* (Paris, 1922). W. N. W.; B. H. W.

**THUCYDIDES** (1), son of Melesias, Athenian politician. He was of good family, connected by marriage with Cimon (q.v.), and according to Plato active both in war and peace and influential in Athens and Greece generally. A formidable speaker, he replaced Cimon as 'leader of the rich' and political rival of Pericles, whose building-programme he attacked. The issues between them were resolved by his ostracism (443 B.C.?). He seems to have returned after the statutory ten years, but further activity on his part is not well attested; though he was prosecuted in his old age by one Cephisodemus (c. 426). He had two sons Melesias and Stephanus and a grandson Thucydides, son of the former, a young man about 420; by which time he himself was dead. He may have been the historian's maternal grandfather.

Hill-Meiggs-Andrewes, *Sources of Greek History* (1951), see index vi; H. T. Wade-Gery, *JHS* 1932, 205 ff. (*Essays in Greek History* (1958), 239 ff.); D. Kienast, *Gymnasium* 1953, 210 ff.; A. E. Raubitschek, *Phoenix* 1960, 81 ff.; F. J. Frost, *Hist.* 1964, 385 ff.; H. D. Meyer, *Hist.* 1967, 141 ff.  A. W. G.; T. J. C.

**THUCYDIDES** (2), author of the (incomplete) History of the War between Athens and Sparta, 431–404 B.C., in eight books.

LIFE. He was born probably between 460 and 455 B.C.: he was general in 424 (4. 104) and must then have been at least 30 years old; while his claim in 5. 26. 5 that he was of years of discretion from beginning to end of the war perhaps suggests that he was not much more than grown up in 431. He probably died about 400. He shows no knowledge of fourth-century events. The revival of Athenian sea power under Conon and Thrasybulus, from 394 on, made the decision of Aegospotami less decisive than it seemed to Thucydides (compare e.g. 5. 26. 1 with Xen. *Hell.* 5. 1. 35). Of the three writers who undertook to complete his History, only Xenophon took his view that the story ended in 404 (or 401). Theopompus took it down to 394, and so probably did Cratippus (Plut. *Mor.* 345 d). If, as seems likely, the very respectable author of the *Hellenica Oxyrhynchia* is Cratippus, q.v., then both his work and Theopompus' are on a very much larger scale than Xenophon's, a scale like Thucydides' own. This fact, as well as considerations of language and outlook, makes it likely that Xenophon, q.v., wrote his continuation (*Hell.* books 1–2) earlier than the others, and indeed, before the battle of Coronea in 394. But if this be so, then Thucydides cannot have lived more than a year or so into the fourth century. Marcellinus, in his *Life*, c. 34, says that Thucydides was 'over 50' when he died. If he was born about 455 and died about 400, this will be true. The figure may be from Cratippus, who evidently gave some biographical data: Marcellinus quotes him just before (33) for the view that Thucydides died in Thrace.

Thucydides, then, was part of that ardent youth whose abundance on both sides seemed to him to distinguish the war he wrote of. Something of his ardour may be felt in 2. 31: his pride in the soldier's profession and his devotion to the great commander, Pericles.

He caught the Plague, some time between 430 and 427, but recovered, and in 424 failed in the task of saving Amphipolis from Brasidas. Not to have been a match for Brasidas does not prove him a bad soldier: from his history one receives the impression of a first-rate regimental officer, ashore or afloat, who saw war as a matter of style; perhaps his defence of the generals before Megara in 4. 73. 4 (cf. 108. 5) says worse of his judgement of problems of high command than his failure against Brasidas. He was exiled for this (424 winter) and returned twenty years later, after the war was over, and died within a few years.

He had property and influence in the mining district of Thrace (4. 105. 1). His father's name was Olorus

(4. 104. 4), the name of Cimon's Thracian grandfather; his tomb was in Cimon's family vault. It is almost certain he was related by blood to Cimon, and probably to Thucydides the statesman (*JHS* 1932, 210); born in the anti-Pericles opposition, he followed Pericles with a convert's zeal.

PARTS OF THE HISTORY. The incomplete history falls into five parts: A, an introduction (book 1). B, the 10 years war (2. 1–5. 24) C, the precarious peace (5. 25–end). D, The Sicilian war (6 and 7). E, fragment of the Decelean war (8). It is convenient to take first B and D, the two complete wars.

B is enclosed between two statements that 'the continuous war has herein been described'. It was therefore provisionally finished (if these are Thucydides' words). It contains one allusion to the fall of Athens (2. 65. 12) and several allusions to events late in the 27 years: these are no doubt additions made to an already existing narrative, since one passage certainly (2. 23. 3) was not written as late as the last decade of the century. The narrative gets rather more summary after Thucydides' exile (424): e.g. after the futile embassy to Artaxerxes I (4. 50) nothing is said of the important negotiations with Darius II.

D is the most finished portion. As it stands it is adapted to a history of the whole war (6. 7. 4, 6. 93. 4, 7. 18. 4, cf. 7. 9 etc., also 7. 44. 1, 7. 87. 5), and twice at least refers to events of 404 or later (7. 57. 2, 6. 15. 3–4). But these may be revisions and it has been suggested that Thucydides published it separately; and this opinion, though little held now, is not disproved. B and D are connected by C, sequel to B and introduction to D, and provided accordingly with a second preface. For symptoms of incompleteness, see below. C covers 5½ years, very unequally. Its two outstanding features are the description of the Mantinea campaign, and the Melian Dialogue. The former should perhaps be regarded, with B and D, as a third completed episode. The latter foreshadows the dramatic style of D; but if we read 5. 111 with 8. 27 we shall draw no facile moral (see 8. 27. 5).

E has the same symptoms of incompleteness as C and, moreover, stops abruptly in the middle of a narrative. It is very full, covering barely two years in its 109 chapters.

A consists of (i) 1. 1–23, a long preface, illustrating the importance of Thucydides' subject by comparison with earlier history (the so-called 'archaeology') and stating his historical principles: (ii) the causes of the war— that is, for the most part, an account of the political manœuvres of 433–432; he adds important digressions, especially 1. 89–117, a history of the years 479/8–440/39, partly to illustrate his view that the war was an inevitable result of Athens' power, partly to make his history follow without interval on that of Herodotus (1. 97. 2). The second motive perhaps explains the length of another digression (1. 128–38) on the fate of Pausanias and Themistocles.

INCOMPLETENESS. E stops in mid narrative, in winter 411: Thucydides intended to go down to 404 (5. 26. 1). It shares with (roughly) C two peculiarities, absence of speeches and presence of documents, which are thought to show incompleteness; for these see below. The plan to make of BCDE a continuous history of the 27 years is only superficially achieved, even to 411: e.g. there is nothing of Atheno–Persian relations between 424 and 412, vital though these were (2. 65. 12). We shall see below that Thucydides kept his work by him and revised continually; so he left double treatments of the same theme, one of which he meant no doubt to suppress— e.g. the tyrannicides (1. 20, 6. 54–59); possibly 1. 23. 1–3 is a short early variant of 1. 1–19; 3. 84 of part of 82–3 (Schwartz 286 f.). It may be even suspected that 8. 82. 2 is a less accurately informed version of 86. 4–5 and the two have been merely harmonized by 85. 4. If this last suspicion were just, it would be good evidence that Thucydides' remains were put into shape by an editor, whose hand may be further suspected in the misplacement of 3. 17, in 1. 56–7 (whose author—as it stands—surely misconceived the course of events), perhaps even in 1. 118. 2 (where the last sentence seems to leap from the 50s to 432); an editorial hand has, indeed, been suspected wholesale. Though no single case is quite decisive, it is unlikely Thucydides left his unfinished work in need of no editing. If we look for an editor, one thinks naturally of Xenophon, who wrote the continuation (it seems) immediately after Thucydides' death; the suggestion was made in antiquity (Diog. Laert. 2. 57). His soldierly (if not his intellectual) qualities might commend him to Thucydides, but if it was indeed he, he worked with extreme piety, and his hand is very little apparent. Xenophon's limits and virtues alike disqualify him for the authorship of 1. 56–7.

SPEECHES AND DOCUMENTS. Ancient craftsmen, and Thucydides notably, aimed at exactness; but in his speeches, Thucydides admits (1. 22. 1) that exactness was beyond his powers of memory. Here, then, as in reconstructing the far past (1. 20–1), he had to trust to his historical imagination, whose use generally he planned to avoid (ὡς ἂν ἐδόκουν ἐμοὶ εἰπεῖν: this meant applying to the speeches the sort of rationalizing schematism that, e.g., Hecataeus applied to geography); and even here, he promises he will control its use as rigorously as he can by the tenor of the actual words. It is much debated whether he made this profession early; and it has been much explained away. But it is unreasonable to doubt that from the start Thucydides took notes himself, or sought for hearers' notes, of the speeches he considered important. But since he used speeches dramatically, to reveal the workings of men's minds and the impact of circumstance, it is clear that verbatim reports would not have served even if he could have managed to get them, and he was bound to compromise (unconsciously) between dramatic and literal truth. It is likely that, as his technique developed, dramatic truth would tend to prevail; it is tempting to put his profession of method early, a young man's intention. Even so, while we cannot suppose that, at a moment when morale was vital, Pericles used the words in 2. 64. 3; while it is unlikely that the Athenian debater at Melos developed exactly the same vein of thought as Phrynichus before Miletus (5. 111–8. 27); while Pericles' first speech (1. 140 ff.) is perhaps composite, and hard to assign to a single occasion; it is yet dangerous to treat the speeches as free fiction: their dramatic truth was combined with the greatest degree of literal truth of which Thucydides was capable. He tried to recreate real occasions.

There are no speeches in E, and (except the Melian Dialogue) none in C: Cratippus (a younger contemporary) says Thucydides had decided to drop their use. Modern critics treat their absence as a symptom of incompleteness; they would have been added had he lived. But it is possible that these parts without speeches are experiments in new techniques. Thucydides may have felt, as many readers do, that the narrative of the 10 years is a compromise between the methods of tragedy and of a laboratory notebook, so that between the profoundest issues and the particular detail, the middle ranges (e.g. an intelligible account of strategy) are neglected. In the later narrative the methods are more separated. The Sicilian war was capable of almost purely dramatic treatment; C and E evidently not. And in consequence in E at least a new technique is developed, less like either drama or chronicle, more of an organized narrative, with more of the writer's own judgements of values and interpretations of events. It is questionable if E would be improved by speeches, that is, could be profitably (or at all?) trans-

formed into the style of B or D: was Cratippus perhaps right about Thucydides' intention?

This would not prevent some of the speeches in books 1–4 being composed (or revised) very late. The new experiment would not entail eliminating the dramatic from those books; Thucydides experimented to the end and never solved his problem. It is commonly thought that the Funeral Speech was written or rewritten after Athens' fall; and 2. 64. 3 surely was. The Corcyra debate (1. 31–44), on the contrary, has good chances of being an actual report, written up soon after delivery. Though some speeches aim at dramatic characterization (Gorgiastic, 4. 61. 7: Laconic, 1. 86), all are in Thucydides' idiom. But the personalness of this idiom is often overestimated (Finley, op. cit. infra).

It is noteworthy that those portions which lack speeches have (instead?) transcriptions of documents: that is, E and (roughly speaking) C.* If, then, we take C and E as experiments in a new method, the experiment begins in the latter part of B. These documents are usually thought (like the absence of speeches) a sign of incompleteness, since they offend against a 'law of style' which forbids the verbatim use of foreign matter in serious prose. We need not debate the general validity of this law: with so inventive a writer as Thucydides, his laws of style are to be deduced from his practice, and 5. 24. 2 (cf. 2. 1) suggests that the end of B is provisionally finished. Are they part of the experiment? One may be surprised (though grateful) that Thucydides thought the full text of the Armistice (4. 118–19) worth its room. One of the documents (5. 47) is extant in fragments (IG i². 86) and confirms the substantial accuracy of the copies. One conflicts gravely with the narrative (5. 23, 5. 39. 3): it would seem the narrative was written in ignorance of the exact terms, and has not been revised.

'EARLY' AND 'LATE'. Thucydides says (1. 1. 1) he began to write his history as soon as war started; and it is at least arguable that much of the existing narrative, in all five parts of the work, was written, substantially as we have it, very soon after the events. But he worked slowly, and, as he says at 1. 22. 3, laboriously; correcting in the light of better information (we only detect this process where it is incomplete; e.g. 5. 39. 3 was due for correction in the light of 5. 23) or of later events (1. 97. 2; 4. 48. 5, where the qualification ὅσα γε may have been put merely ex abundanti cautela, but more likely when the troubles started again in 410). If his point of view, or his method, changed materially during this process, it becomes of importance to know from which point of view this or that portion is written. More than a century ago, Ullrich called attention to this, believing that an important change of approach came with his discovery (announced in the second preface, 5. 26) that the war had not ended in 421.

Two criteria have been used to determine earliness or lateness: (a) reference to, or ignorance of, datable events or conditions; (b) the stage in Thucydides' own development which a passage reveals.

(a) References to late events cannot be written early, but they may be inserted in early contexts: e.g. those who think D early regard 6. 15. 3–4 and 7. 57. 2 as additions. Ignorance of late events is very much harder to establish: those same who think D early may suspect in 6. 41. 3 ignorance of Dionysius' tyranny, or even (a very slippery question) in 6. 54. 1 ignorance of Herodotus' history—but cannot prove their suspicions; yet where such ignorance is certain (see below), we may be sure that the narrative (or line of thought) which warrants them was conceived early. The results of this method are modest:

*Not exactly C: C ends with the Melian Dialogue (which in colour belongs to D?) and B has documents instead of speeches in its latter part, i.e. after the occasion of Thucydides' exile.

e.g. (i) 1. 10. 2 was not written after the catastrophe of 404: therefore the war against which earlier wars are being measured is not the completed 27 years, and the 'end of war' mentioned in 1. 13. 3–4, 1. 18. 1, is presumably 421; (ii) 2. 23. 3 was not written after the loss of Oropus in 411: therefore some of the narrative of B was written much as we have it before 411; (iii) 2. 65. 12 refers to the fall of Athens: therefore B received additions down to 404 at least.

(b) More has been hoped from the second method. Thucydides worked from his twenties to his fifties, his material growing under his eyes: there must surely be some intellectual or spiritual growth, some change of outlook. The best exponent of this method is Schwartz, who gives (op. cit. *infra* 217–42) an eloquent account of Thucydides' growth. The danger of this method is evident: in the ablest hands it yields quite different results (Meyer, Schwartz), and its first postulate may be doubted, namely, that Thucydides' opinion on the 'true cause' of the war (1. 23. 6) was not formed till after the fall of Athens. No doubt that was his view after 404; no doubt 1. 23. 6 and 1. 88 were written (inserted?) pretty late. But much the same view is expressed by the Corcyran envoy in 1. 33. 3 (cf. 42. 2); and whether the envoy said it or not it was surely Pericles' view. Pericles believed that if Athens used her opportunity in 433 she was bound to provoke in Sparta an enmity that must be faced; all his career, against Cimon and his successors, he had fought for his conviction that Athens and Sparta were natural enemies and Greece not large enough for both. His admirers held that this clear principle (1. 140. 1) was obscured in debate by the irrelevant particulars (1. 140. 4–141. 1). We have not to consider whether Pericles was right: rather, the effect on Thucydides. The devout disciple saw the story unfold in the terms his master had foreseen (2. 65). How far such a 'Pericles-fixation' may have warped Thucydides' judgement, see below.

If this first postulate go, the second will follow it, viz. that only after 404 was Pericles given the importance he now has in books 1–2, since after 404 Thucydides started to rewrite his history as a 'defence of Pericles' (Schwartz 239). It hardly needs to be said that many hold to these postulates and the present writer's disbelief is as subjective as their belief. If these are untrue, truer postulates may be found: the attempt to recreate Thucydides' experience should (and will) never be dropped.

TRUTHFULNESS. Perhaps no good historian is impartial; Thucydides certainly not, though singularly candid. His tastes are clear: he liked Pericles and disliked Cleon. He had for Pericles a regard comparable to Plato's for Socrates and an equal regard for Pericles' Athens. These things were personal: but in principle, concentrations of energy (like Athens or Alcibiades) were to his taste. Their impact on a less dynamic world was likely to be disastrous—but whose fault was that? The world's, he says, consistently (1. 99; 1. 23. 6 etc.; 6. 15; 6. 28; cf. 2. 64. 3–5): and though this consistency may surprise us, we need not quarrel with it. Such judgements are rare, since Thucydides conceives his task as like medical research (see below, and cf. 3. 82. 2) where blame is irrelevant; the disconcerting simplicity of 2. 64. 3 (power and energy are absolute goods) is the more striking.

We need not here investigate Thucydides' possible mistakes. The present writer believes that Pericles (having planned an offensive war) lost his striking power, first because Potidaea revolted, next because of the Plague. Forced to the defensive, he left that as his testament. Thucydides was reluctant to face the fact of this failure, and accepted the testament, siding with the defeatist officer class against the revived offensive of Cleon (4. 27. 5, 28. 5, 65. 4, 73. 4: cf. 5. 7. 2). This is why Pericles' huge effort against Epidaurus (6. 31. 2; motive, cf. 5. 53)

is recorded as a minor futility (2. 56. 4); why Phormion's first campaign in Acarnania (2. 68. 7–9; of 432?) is left timeless; why we hear nothing of the purpose of the Megara decree; why, when that nearly bore fruit at last, Thucydides suggests that the capture of Megara was of no great moment (4. 73. 4; but cf. 72. 1).

Such criticisms hardly detract much from his singular truthfulness. Readers of all opinions will probably agree that he saw more truly, inquired more responsibly, and reported more faithfully than any other ancient historian. That is a symptom of his greatness, but not its core. Another symptom is his style: it is innocent of those clichés of which Isocrates hoped to make the norm of Attic style; in its 'old-fashioned wilful beauty' (Dionysius) every word tells. Like English prose before Dryden and Addison, it uses a language largely moulded by poets: its precision is a poet's precision, a union of passion and candour. After Thucydides history mostly practised the corrupting art of persuasion (cf. Isocr. 4. 8): his scientific tradition survived in the antiquarians, of whom he is the pioneer (1. 8. 1, 2. 15. 2, 3. 104. 4–6, 6. 55. 1), but the instinctive exactness of early Greek observation was lost. To combine his predecessors' candour of vision with his successors' apparatus of scholarship was a necessity laid on him by his sense of the greatness of his subject: he could no more distort or compromise with what he wished to convey than Shakespeare or Michelangelo could.

Thucydides would no doubt prefer to substitute, for these great names, the practice of any honest doctor. He was not modest, but in his statement of his principles he is singularly unaware of his unique equipment, and claims rather that he has spared no pains. The proper context for this statement (1. 20–2) is, first, his very similar statement about his own account of the Plague (2. 48. 3), and then the physician Hippocrates' maxim, 'ars longa vita brevis'. The 'art' which outlasts individual lives is the scientific study of man: the physician studied his clinical, Thucydides his political, behaviour. To know either so well that you can control it (and civilization is largely made up of such controls) is a task for many generations: a piece of that task well done is something gained for ever (1. 22. 4). H. T. W.-G.

STYLE. In a famous sentence (*Thuc.* 24) Dionysius gives as the four 'tools' in Thucydides' workshop τὸ ποιητικὸν τῶν ὀνομάτων, τὸ πολυειδὲς τῶν σχημάτων, τὸ τραχὺ τῆς ἁρμονίας, τὸ τάχος τῶν σημασιῶν. The first, third, and fourth of these criticisms are undoubtedly true. Thucydides' style has a poetical and archaistic flavour (it is often difficult to distinguish clearly between the two), as a reader sees at once when he turns from Thucydides to Andocides and Lysias. His consistent use of αἰεί for ἀεί, ξύν for σύν, and σσ for ττ is one of the signs of this tendency. 'Roughness' is to be seen in his bold changes of construction and his violent hyperbata, in which he wrests an emphatic word from its natural place in the sentence to give it more prominence (1. 19 κατ' ὀλιγαρχίαν, 1. 93. 4 τῆς θαλάσσης). 'Speed' is perhaps the most striking of all his characteristics. He achieves an extreme concision, hardly to be paralleled in Greek prose except in the gnomic utterances of Democritus. A sentence like δοκεῖ . . . καταστροφή (2. 42. 2) is gone in a flash, and no orator, composing for the ear, could have risked such brevity. At 2. 37. 1 (μέτεστι . . . προτιμᾶται) two antitheses are telescoped into one. τὸ πολυειδὲς τῶν σχημάτων is much more open to question, especially as Dionysius has just before credited Thucydides with the use of the θεατρικὰ σχήματα (parisosis, paronomasia, and antithesis) affected by Gorgias and other writers of the sophistic school. Thucydides' thought is, it is true, markedly antithetical in cast (e.g. 1. 70. 6), and antithesis is sometimes strained (e.g. 2. 43. 3). But, unlike the Gorgianists, he has no affection for merely external antithesis, and he often deliberately avoids formal balance (e.g. 4. 59. 2). He eschews almost entirely certain other common adornments of style. He is too austere to use metaphor at all freely, or asyndeton (more suited to the spoken word). He does employ certain devices of assonance, neither, like Gorgias, as ἡδύσματα, nor, like Demosthenes, for emphasis pure and simple, but for the emphasizing of a contrast (3. 82. 8 εὐσεβεία . . . εὐπρεπεία, 6. 76. 2 κατοικίσαι . . . ἐξοικίσαι, 76. 4 ἀξυνετωτέρου . . . κακοξυνετωτέρου). He has a strong leaning, as Dionysius observed (*Amm.* 2. 5), towards abstract expression (e.g. 3. 82–3), sometimes carried to the length of personification (πόλεμος 1. 122. 1, ἐλπίς 5. 103. 1). He probably coined abstracts (especially in -σις) freely, as Euripides did, according to the fashion of the late fifth century, and sometimes used them out of season (7. 70. 6 ἀποστέρησιν, and the odd-looking negatived abstracts, 1. 137. 4 οὐ διάλυσιν, etc.). Like Antiphon, he experimented freely with the use of neuter adjective, or even participle (1. 142. 8 ἐν τῷ μὴ μελετῶντι), to convey an abstract idea. His periods are usually loosely constructed (e.g. 3. 38. 4–7), of clauses longer in actual words, and far richer in content, than those of other Greek prose-writers (e.g. 2. 43. 2–6). J. D. D.

TEXTS. H. Stuart-Jones (O.C.T. 1898–1902, reprinted 1942 with *apparatus criticus* revised by J. E. Powell); C. Hude (Teubner, ed. maior 1913–25, ed. minor 1920–8 with scholia; new ed. by O. Luschnat, bks. 1–2, 1954).

TRANSLATIONS. R. Crawley (*Everyman*, 1910); Jowett's translation, abridged, is used by P. A. Brunt, *Thucydides* (in Trevor-Roper's series, *The Great Histories*, U.S.A. 1963).

COMMENTARIES. A. W. Gomme, *Historical Commentary on T.* (bk. 1, 1945; bks. 2–5. 24, 1956; the remaining books in preparation by A. Andrewes and K. J. Dover); in German, J. Classen (revised by J. Steup, 1892–1922); in Latin, E. F. Poppo (revised by J. M. Stahl, 1886).

CRITICISM. Ancient: Cratippus, *FGrH* 64: Dion. Hal. *Thuc.* [cf. *ad Amm. de T. idiom., ad Pomp.*] (=*opuscula*, ed. Usener–Radermacher, i. 325 ff. [421 ff., ii. 221 ff.]); Marcellinus, *Life of T.*, prefixed to most texts of Thucydides. Modern. F. E. Adcock, *T. and his History* (1963); C. N. Cochrane, *T. and the Science of History* (1929; relation to Hippocratics); J. H. Finley, *Thucydides²* (1947); A. W. Gomme, *Essays in Gk. Hist. and Lit.* (1937, nos. vi–ix); G. B. Grundy, *T. and the History of his Age²* (1948); W. Jaeger, *Paideia* (Engl. Transl. 1938, 379 ff.); O. Luschnat, *Die Feldherrnreden im Gesch. des T.* (1942, *Philologus* Suppl. xxxiv. 2); E. Meyer, *Forschungen* ii (1899, no. v); H. Patzer, *Das Problem der Geschichtsschreibung des T.* (1937); J. de Romilly, *Histoire et Raison chez T.* (1956); *T. and Athenian Imperialism* (Engl. Transl. 1963); W. Schadewaldt, *Die Geschichtsschreibung des T.* 1929; esp. bks. 6–7); E. Schwartz, *Das Geschichtswerk des T.* (1919; *Stilgesetz*, 28 ff.); F. W. Ullrich, *Beiträge zur Erklärung des T.* (1846–52); K. Weidauer, *T. und die Hippokratischen Schriften* (1954); R. Zahn, *Die erste Periklesrede* (1934; diss. with notes by Jacoby); H. D. Westlake, *Individuals in T.* (1968), id. *Essays on Greek Historians* (1969); A. G. Woodhead, *T. on the Nature of Power* (1970).

INDEX. M. H. N. von Essen, *Index Thucydideus*, 1887.

**THUGGA** (modern *Dougga*), a hill-town of Africa proconsularis west of the military road from Carthage to Theveste. The site was occupied in neolithic times. Under Masinissa and his successors it was the seat of a native chieftain and much influenced by Carthaginian civilization; a mausoleum, the most notable pre-Roman building in North Africa, survives. Marian colonists were settled in the vicinity, and in the first century members of the *colonia* of Carthage had lands near by. A curious double community of native *civitas* and Roman *pagus* existed till they were united by Septimius Severus, and became Colonia Licinia Septimia Aurelia Alexandriana Thugga. The Roman remains are among the finest in North Africa, and include a beautiful Capitoline temple, temples of Caelestis and Saturn, a theatre, and Byzantine fortifications.

C. Poinssot, *Les Ruines de Dougga* (1958); A. Golfetto, *Dougga* (Basle, 1961). B. H. W.

**THULE** (Θούλη), a northern land first heard of and described by Pytheas (q.v.). It lay six days' sail to north of Britain. At midsummer the sun's and the Bear's

paths, as seen at Thule, coincided, and neither set. The inhabitants ate berries, 'millet' (oats?) threshed in barns because of the dampness and lack of sun, herbs, fruits, roots, and honey. Round Thule everything was held in an impalpable mass (perhaps thick freezing fog?) which Pytheas himself saw. (On this consult Hyde, 131; Nansen, *In Northern Mists* (1911), i. 66 f.; Thomson, 149; Deman, *Latomus* 1958, 364.) It is uncertain whether Thule was Iceland or Norway. Beyond Thule was the frozen sea; and in fact the sea does freeze now round the north-east of Iceland. Nothing further was discovered about it, but it was henceforth regarded as the northernmost part of the inhabited world. Eratosthenes drew a parallel through Thule at 66° (Arctic circle) which remained for long on maps. Ptolemy gave Thule a north–south extension of 55 miles and located it at Mainland (Shetland), though he retained the belief in its midsummer midnight sun. The land of Thule which Agricola's fleet claimed to have seen (Tac. *Agr.* 10) was no doubt a Shetland island, but not necessarily Foula, the name of which is Norse 'Fowl-island', not derived from Thule.

It may be that Procopius of the sixth century A.D. was right in a wrong way when he called the Scandinavian 'island', old home of the Goths, 'Thule', ten times as large as Britain and far to the north of it, most being desolate, but the rest containing the Gauti and twelve other large tribes. Other writers also seem to mean Scandinavia by 'Thule'. For earlier knowledge of Scandinavia, see Mela 3. 3. 31–2; Pliny 4. 96; Tac. *Germ.* 44; Ptol. 7. 5. 2.

Strabo 63–4, etc.; Pliny, *HN* 2. 187, 4. 104; Diod. 5. 26; Cleomedes, *Cycl. Theor.* i. 7. 37–8, etc.; Geminus, *Elem. Astron.* 6; Ptol. *Geog.* 2. 3. 14, 2. 6. 22, 8. 3. 3. Procop. *Goth.* 2. 15. 4 ff. Cary–Warmington, *Explorers*, 36 ff.; (Pelican) 50 ff.; G. E. Broche, *Pythéas le Massaliote* (1936), 145 ff., to be used with caution. See also Thomson, *Hist. Anc. Geog.* 145 ff., 235 ff., 323, 326, 339, 355, 358, 373 ff.; Hyde, *Greek Mariners*, 128 ff.; D. R. Dicks, *The Geographical Fragments of Hipparchus* (1960), 179 ff., 190 ff.; V. Stefansson, *Ultima Thule* (1942); *Greenland* (1943; use with caution!); H. Shetelik, *Antiquity* 1949, 161 ff.; F. M. Heichelheim, *Antiquity* 1952; M. Cary, *CR* 1949, 112; M. Ninck, *Die Entdeckung von Europa durch die Griechen* (1945), 222, 275. E. H. W.

**THURII** (Θούριοι), Pericles' panhellenic foundation (443 B.C.), which Herodotus and Lysias reputedly joined. It replaced, and occupied a site close to, Sybaris (q.v.): see H. Philipp, *PW* vi A. 646 f. It was originally inhabited by Messapii (q.v.) (J. Whatmough, *Foundations of Roman Italy* (1937), 336). Despite *stasis*, quarrels with other Greeks, and Lucanian wars, Thurii flourished for a time, but finally became voluntarily a Roman dependency, and as such opposed Pyrrhus (q.v.). To revive Thurii after its spoliation by Hannibal Rome founded the Latin colony of Copia here, 193 B.C. (App. *Hann.* 57; Livy 34. 53; 35. 9). But, although remaining strategically important, Thurii gradually declined and ultimately was abandoned (App. *BCiv.* 1. 117; 5. 56. 58; Diod. 12. 9 f.; Strabo 6. 263).

V. Ehrenberg, *AJPhil.* 1948, 149 ff. (= *Polis und Imperium* (1965), 298 ff.); K. Freeman, *Greek City States* (1950), 21 ff. And see bibliography s.v. MAGNA GRAECIA. E. T. S.

**THYIA** (Θυία), apparently the same word as θυιάς, a Bacchante. There being a spot so named at Delphi (Hdt. 7. 178. 2), she is occasionally heard of (as ibid.) as the nymph of the place.

**THYMOETES** (Θυμοίτης) (1), a brother of Priam, Hom. *Il.* 3. 146; Verg. *Aen.* 2. 32, whereon see Servius for his quarrel with Priam; Diod. Sic. 3. 67. 5. (2) Son of the above, Diod. Sic. ibid.

**THYSDRUS** (modern *El Djem*), a Tunisian market-town, lying inland south of Hadrumetum. A not very significant *oppidum liberum* in the first centuries B.C. and A.D., it subsequently obtained the rank of *colonia* and became the centre of a prosperous agricultural district; its amphitheatre, of which striking ruins survive, was built for 60,000 spectators and is the largest Roman building in North Africa. The elder Gordian (q.v.) was proclaimed Emperor at Thysdrus in A.D. 238. W. N. W.

**TIBER** rises as a creek in the Apennines near Arretium, develops into central Italy's greatest river, meanders south to Narnia (confluence with the Nar), then southwest past Rome (where it divides about the *Insula Tiberina*), and enters the Tyrrhenian Sea at Ostia (q.v.). The silt it carries down with it on its 250-mile journey accounts for its tawny colour ('flauus Tiberis'); it accumulates at its mouth to choke the harbour works (*portus*) built by Trajan and others (Claudius even excavated a separate, artificial mouth), and constantly advances the coastline at Ostia. Tributaries: Tinia-Clitumnus, Clanis, Nar, Anio, Allia (qq.v.) and numerous brooks (Pliny's 42 is actually an underestimate). Navigation, although possible as far as Narnia (q.v.), was hazardous owing to the swift current. Inundations are first recorded in 241 B.C. (Oros. 4. 11), but were frequent in all periods, even after Augustus instituted 'curatores riparum et alvei Tiberis', (Suet. *Aug.* 37). The salt deposits at its mouth were worked in very early times, although the settlement at Ostia which traditionally dates from Ancus Marcius' period is not demonstrably older than the fourth century B.C. The Tiber formed the eastern border of Etruria (and hence is frequently called *Tyrrhenus* or *Lydius*) and the northern boundary of Latium. In imperial times opulent villas studded the banks of its lower course.

Strabo 5. 218; 232 f.; Pliny, *HN* 3. 53 f.; Dion. Hal. 3. 44. S. A. Smith, *Tiber and its Tributaries* (1877); J. le Gall, *Le Tibre* (1953). E. T. S.

**TIBERIANUS,** a poet of the fourth century A.D. whose best-known piece is the *Amnis ibat*, 20 trochaic tetrameters. Its feeling for nature prompted Baehrens's suggestion that Tiberianus also composed the *Pervigilium Veneris* (q.v.). For his other brief poems and fragments (text and tr.) see Duff, *Minor Lat. Poets*. J. W. D.

**TIBERIAS,** on L. Galilee, was founded by Herod (q.v. 2) Antipas. Despite its Greek constitution, it was a completely Jewish city. It was the capital of a toparchy, and also of Galilee, till Nero gave Galilee to Agrippa II. In the Jewish war the proletariat was anti-Roman, but the aristocracy on the whole loyal to the king and to Rome; it surrendered to Vespasian and was spared. After the Second Jewish War Tiberias was paganized by Hadrian, but it later became once more a thoroughly Jewish city, the seat of a rabbinical school and of the Jewish patriarch. A. H. M. J.

**TIBERIUS** (1), the Emperor (TIBERIUS JULIUS (*PW* 154) CAESAR AUGUSTUS), was the son of Ti. Claudius Nero and Livia, born in 42 B.C. His mother was divorced, in order to marry Octavian, early in 38 shortly before the birth of her second son Drusus. From 20 B.C., when, accompanying Augustus to the East, he received back the standards lost to the Parthians at Carrhae, until A.D. 12, when he returned to Rome after retrieving the situation on the Rhine after the disaster of Varus, Tiberius had a brilliant military career (interrupted only from 6 B.C. to A.D. 4). Between 12 and 9 B.C. he reduced Pannonia. From 9 B.C. (after the death of his brother) to 7 B.C. and again from A.D. 4 to 6 he campaigned in Germany. From A.D. 6 to 9 he was engaged in suppressing the great revolts of Pannonia and Illyricum. (See, for details of these campaigns, R. Syme, *CAH* x, ch. 12.)

After Agrippa's death Tiberius was forced in 12 B.C. to divorce Vipsania Agrippina, mother of his son Drusus, in order to marry Augustus' daughter, Agrippa's widow,

Julia. A son born of this—most unhappy—marriage died in infancy. In 6 B.C. Tiberius was granted *tribunicia potestas* for five years and invited to carry out a diplomatic mission in the East. Augustus hoped, however, to be succeeded by one of his young grandsons, Gaius or Lucius, and, perhaps through pique on that account, Tiberius retired to Rhodes in 6 B.C. He returned to Rome, though not to Augustus' favour, in A.D. 2. In A.D. 4, both his grandsons having died, Augustus was forced to recognize Tiberius as his likely successor. He adopted him, together with Agrippa Postumus, forcing Tiberius to adopt his nephew Germanicus. Tiberius was given *tribunicia potestas* for ten years, and this was renewed in A.D. 13 for a further ten years. He was also, at the time of his adoption and again in A.D. 13, given *imperium proconsulare*, like that held by Augustus.

Augustus died on 19 Aug. A.D. 14 and Tiberius, in virtue of the *imperium* which he already possessed, was able to discharge urgent administrative duties in the interval before Sept. 17, when (*Fast. Amitern.*, CIL 1. i². 244), after an embarrassing and unprecedented debate (Tac. *Ann.* 1. 10–13) he was, on the proposal of the consuls, proclaimed Emperor. He reigned until his death on 16 Mar. A.D. 37.

Loyalty to Augustus was the keystone of Tiberius' policy. While Augustus was consecrated and a *templum divi Augusti* was built at Rome, Tiberius refused to accept any extravagant honours for himself (Tac. *Ann.* 4. 37 f.; cf. the inscriptions from Gythium, *SEG* xi. 922–3). In foreign policy he followed the 'consilium coercendi intra terminos imperii' bequeathed to him by Augustus (Tac. *Ann.* 1. 11) and, when Germanicus was recalled from the Rhine at the end of 16, the project of conquering Germany was at last abandoned. Cappadocia was made a province on the death of its king Archelaus in 17. The revolt of Florus and Sacrovir in Gallia Lugdunensis in 21 was suppressed with little difficulty by the Upper German army. Trouble with Parthia threatened on two occasions, but was settled by diplomatic negotiation, by Germanicus in 18 and by L. Vitellius at the very end of Tiberius' principate. Tiberius' only innovation in provincial administration lay in lengthening the tenure of office of imperial *legati* in the provinces, whether from slackness or of set purpose (see Marsh, op. cit. *infra*, 157 ff.). In finance Tiberius exercised rigid economy, built little, gave donations sparingly and games hardly at all; he therefore bequeathed great wealth (more than 2,000 millions of sesterces; Suet. *Calig.* 37, Dio Cass. 59. 2).

Tiberius' difficulties in administration were many. His accession coincided with legionary revolts in Pannonia and in Lower Germany, the German legions being ready to proclaim their commander, Germanicus, Emperor. In the Senate he was persistently irritated and insulted by such men as L. Arruntius and Asinius Gallus (q.v.). Within his own family there was jealousy concerning the selection of his prospective successor. After the death of Germanicus in 19 and of Tiberius' son Drusus in 23, the way lay open to the sons of Agrippina and Germanicus: Nero, Drusus, and Gaius. Nero and Drusus fell through the schemes of Sejanus, and Gaius, while his life was saved, received little preparation for government from Tiberius.

The reign of Tiberius was disfigured (cf. Tac. *Ann.* 1. 72 f.; 4. 6, 'legesque, si maiestatis quaestio eximeretur, bono in usu') by the heavy incidence, especially after 23, of trials, chiefly before the Senate, for *maiestas* (q.v.). There is record of more than 100 such prosecutions, of which those of M. Scribonius (q.v. 2) Libo Drusus in 16 and of Cn. Calpurnius Piso (q.v. 7) in 20 were outstanding. Tiberius' own responsibility is hard to assess. Though he showed no vindictiveness or cruelty (cf. Tac. *Ann.* 3. 51), a stronger man might have checked the abuse. There is no evidence that he was ever in serious danger of assassination; yet he had a morbid fear of it, and was encouraged in this fear by L. Aelius Sejanus (q.v.), prefect of the Praetorian Guard and, after 23, Tiberius' chief adviser. Tiberius was encouraged by him to leave Rome for Capreae in 26; he did not return to Rome again, but corresponded by letter with the Senate. Agrippina and Nero were arrested in 29, Drusus in 30, and were all subsequently put to death or committed suicide. Sejanus himself was arrested and executed in Rome on the charge of conspiracy, in 31. His death was followed by that of many of his supporters.

While stories of Tiberius' vice on Capreae may be discounted, his mind was almost unhinged in the last six years of his life (cf. Tac. *Ann.* 6. 6). Lacking the affability ('ciuile ingenium') of his brother Drusus and nephew Germanicus, apt to speak in language of obscure and, it was thought, sinister ambiguity (cf. especially Dio Cass. 57. 1), austere, not even possessing, like his son Drusus, the pardonable and popular weakness of fondness for games, he neither sought popularity nor won it; in Rome itself the news of his death was welcomed.

ANCIENT SOURCES. We have a contemporary account of Tiberius' campaigns under Augustus and of the first sixteen years of his reign in Velleius Paterculus 2. 94–131. This account (published in A.D. 30) is favourable to Tiberius (and also to Sejanus). It is in sharp contrast to the other Roman accounts of the reign, viz. Tacitus, *Annals* 1–6 (most of book 5, with its account of the arrest and trial of Sejanus, is lost), Suetonius, *Tiberius*, and Dio Cassius, bks. 57 f. Tacitus' bias against Tiberius, displayed often in strikingly inept comment and innuendo, has been variously explained. Possibly he saw in Tiberius the prototype of Domitian; though, for a different explanation, see T. S. Jerome, *Aspects of the Study of Roman History* (U.S.A. 1923), chs. 15–17. Without doubt Tacitus' chief sources, the historians who wrote at the end of the Julio-Claudian period, whose works have perished (e.g. Servilius Nonianus, Aufidius Bassus, and, in her memoirs, to which Tacitus once refers, *Ann.* 4. 53, the Younger Agrippina), gave an extremely unfavourable account of Tiberius. See, on Tacitus' sources and his treatment of them, P. Fabia, *Les Sources de Tacite* (1893), F. B. Marsh, *The Reign of Tiberius* (1931), appendix 1, and Syme, *Tacitus*. The Jewish writers, Philo—a contemporary—and Josephus, are friendly to Tiberius and unfriendly to Sejanus.

MODERN LITERATURE. F. B. Marsh, *The Reign of Tiberius* (1931), with full bibliographies; C. E. Smith, *Tiberius and the Roman Empire* (U.S.A. 1942); E. Ciaceri, *Tiberio*[2] (1944); D. M. Pipidi, *Autour de Tibère* (1944); G. Marañón, *Tiberius, a Study in Resentment* (1956: the reconstruction of a psychologist); E. Kornemann, *Tiberius* (1960); on the Gythium inscriptions, M. Rostovtzeff, *Rev. hist.* 1930; *see also* bibliography s.v. MAIESTAS.          J. P. B.

**TIBERIUS** (2) **JULIUS** (*PW* 156) **CAESAR GEMELLUS**, one of twin sons born in A.D. 19 to Drusus, son of Tiberius, and Livia. Tiberius made him joint heir with Gaius to his personal property. Though the Senate annulled the will, Gaius adopted Tiberius Gemellus and allowed him to be hailed as *princeps iuuentutis*. He was put to death, however, during the first year of Gaius' principate.          J. P. B.

**TIBERIUS** (3) **JULIUS** (*PW* 59) **ALEXANDER**, of an opulent Jewish family of Alexandria, nephew of Philon (q.v. 4), but a renegade from the ancestral faith, rose high in the service of Rome. He was procurator governing Judaea (c. A.D. 46–8), when he executed the sons of Judas the Galilean; general staff officer under Corbulo in Armenia (63) and soon after Prefect of Egypt. His long edict, published soon after Galba's accession, has been preserved (*OGI* 669). Tiberius Alexander made his troops take the oath in the name of Vespasian on 1 July 69, which date was adopted as the 'dies imperii'. Enjoying high favour with the new dynasty, he was present with Titus at the siege of Jerusalem in the same function as he had held under Corbulo, but he now held the title of *praefectus praetorio* as appears from *PHib.* ii. 215. He vainly tried to have the Temple preserved.

E. G. Turner, *JRS* 1954, 54 ff.; V. Burr, *Tiberius Julius Alexander* (1955); G. Chalon, *L'Édit de Tiberius Julius Alexander* (1964). R. S.

**TIBULLUS**, ALBIUS (*PW* 1), born between 55 and 48 B.C. Little is known of him except what can be gathered from his poetry and from references in Horace and Ovid. An anonymous and corrupt *Vita*, possibly derived from Suetonius, tells us also that he was of equestrian rank, won *dona militaria*, and was something of a dandy. It is preceded by an epigram of Domitius Marsus, which fixes the date of Tibullus' death in 19 B.C.

Tibullus implies that his patrimony was diminished, presumably by confiscation (1. 1. 41 f.), but his complaints of *paupertas* belong to the conventional picture of the poetic lover. He is contradicted by Horace, who suggests that he was well-off and had a villa at Pedum, between Tibur and Praeneste (*Epist.* 1. 4). He refused or did not attract the patronage of the *princeps* and Maecenas, and celebrated instead the exploits of M. Valerius Messalla (q.v. 3) Corvinus. He set out to the East in Messalla's entourage, but fell ill at Corcyra and returned to Italy (1. 3); it is uncertain whether he served under him in Gaul (1. 7. 9 and *Vita*).

Tibullus' MSS. contain three books, of which the third was divided into two by Italian scholars of the fifteenth century; these are commonly called the *Corpus Tibullianum* and only the first two belong to Tibullus himself. The dates of publication are uncertain: book 1 refers to Messalla's triumph (25 Sept. 27 B.C.), book 2 to the installation of his son as one of the *quindecimviri sacris faciundis* (perhaps not long before Tibullus' death).

The first book deals impartially with his love for a mistress, Delia (1, 2, 3, 5, 6), and for a boy, Marathus (4, 8, 9). Apuleius tells us that Delia existed and that her name was Plania (*Apol.* 10); we need not doubt this, though her attributes (and those of Marathus, for that matter) are largely conventional. Book 2 celebrates a different mistress, whom the poet calls Nemesis (3, 4, 6). Apart from the love poems, the books contain poems in honour of Messalla (1. 7, 2. 5), an elegy on the blessings of peace (1. 10), and a charming representation of a rustic festival and the poet's song at it (2. 1). Book 2 is only just over 400 lines long, and may be either defective or posthumous.

The third book is a collection of poems from the circle of Messalla. It begins with six elegies by Lygdamus (q.v.), and also contains the *Panegyricus Messallae* (q.v.), five poems on the love of Sulpicia for Cerinthus (known as the Garland of Sulpicia), and six short poems by Sulpicia herself (q.v. 1). The poems on Sulpicia are conceivably by Tibullus himself. The elegy and epigram which conclude the book are certainly by somebody else, and have nothing to do with the fictitious Glycera mentioned by Horace (*Carm.* 1. 33).

In Quintilian's view, Tibullus was the most *tersus atque elegans* of the Roman elegists (10. 1. 93). The judgement is justified by the smooth finish of his poems and by the choice, though limited, vocabulary that makes his style a model of the *genus tenue*; no other Roman poet writes with such refined plainness. Yet his simplicity is sometimes deceptive: the transitions by which he glides from one scene or subject to another often baffle analysis. The total loss of his predecessor, Cornelius Gallus (q.v.), makes it difficult to estimate his originality, but it was probably considerable. He rejects myth, both ornamental and structural, and replaces it by pictures of an idealized, but actual, countryside. This owes something to Virgil's *Eclogues*; yet there is novelty in the fusion of an Italian landscape with the Hellenistic and urban themes of elegy.

Appreciation of Tibullus is not constant, and many critics of Latin poetry write him down; he deserves more attention than he currently gets. *See also* ELEGIAC POETRY, LATIN.

BIBLIOGRAPHY. Schanz–Hosius.

EDITIONS. J. P. Postgate (1914); M. Ponchont (1924); F. Calonghi (1927); F. W. Lenz (1937); with comm.: K. F. Smith (1913); E.

Cesareo (1938). Selections: Postgate (1928); K. Harrington (1914). Translations (verse): T. C. Williams (1905); A. S. Way (1936); (prose) J. P. Postgate (1912).

STUDIES. A. Cartault, *A propos du Corpus Tibullianum* (1906); *Le Distique élégiaque chez Tib. Sulp. Lygd.* (1911); M. Ponchont, *Étude sur le texte de T.* (1923); K. Witte, *Die Geschichte der röm. Elegie* i: *Tibullus* (1924); J. Hammer, *Prolegomena* (see MESSALLA 3); N. Salanitro, *Tibullo* (1938); M. Schuster, *Tibull-Studien* (1968). M. E. H.

**TIBUR,** modern *Tivoli* with numerous monuments. Famed for fruits, building-stone (travertine), and cults (e.g. Hercules, Vesta, Albunea), it lies 18 miles east-north-east of Rome, where the Anio (q.v.) leaves the Sabine mountains (Strabo 5. 238). Founded before Rome, possibly by Siculi, Tibur was a powerful member of the Latin League with several dependent towns (Pliny, *HN* 16. 237; Dion. Hal. 1. 16; Cato fr. 58 P.). In the fourth century B.C., aided occasionally by Gauls or Praenestines, it frequently fought Rome until deprived of territory in 338 (Livy 7–8. 14). Tibur, however, remained independent and could harbour Roman exiles (Dessau, *ILS* 19; Livy 9. 30). Acquiring Roman citizenship *c.* 90 B.C. (App. *BCiv.* 1. 65), it became a fashionable resort: Catullus, Horace (possibly), Augustus, and Hadrian had Tiburtine villas. Propertius' Cynthia and captive potentates like Syphax (201 B.C.) and Zenobia (A.D. 273) also sojourned here.

Catullus 44; Prop. 3. 16; Livy 30. 45; S.H.A. *Tyr. Trig.* 30. 27; J. Mancini, *Inscriptiones Italiae* (1936), i. 1. E. Bourne, *A Study of Tibur* (U.S.A. 1916); G. Cascioli, *Bibliografia di Tivoli* (1923); C. Carducci, *Tibur* (Rome, 1940); S. Aurigemma, *The Villa Adriana near Tivoli* (Rome, 1955). E. T. S.

**TICIDAS,** one of the *neoterici* (see ALEXANDRIANISM, LATIN), wrote erotic poems to 'Perilla', i.e. Metella (Ov. *Tr.* 2. 433; Apul. *Apol.* 10). See Baehr. *FPR* 325; Morel, *FPL* 90.

**TICINUM,** in northern Italy near the confluence of the Ticinus and Padus (q.v.). Hannibal defeated the Romans here (218 B.C.), but Ticinum itself is unrecorded until imperial times. In the Late Empire it was an important fortress which Attila sacked, Theodoric strengthened, and the Lombards made their capital, calling it Papia (modern *Pavia*). E. T. S.

**TIFATA,** mountain overlooking Capua (q.v.) in Campania: the name allegedly means oak-grove (Festus 503 L.). The basilica of *Sant'Angelo in Formis* has occupied the site of its famous sanctuary to Diana (*ILS* 6306; Vell. 2. 25. 4) since the tenth century.

A. Maiuri, *Passeggiate Campane* (1957), 159 ff.; D. Mustilli, *Enc. Ital.* 1950, s.v. 'Tifata'; J. Heurgon, *Capoue préromaine* (1942), 299 ff. E. T. S.

**TIGELLINUS,** GAIUS (?) OFONIUS (see *PW*), a low-born Sicilian, was brought up in the households of the Emperor Gaius' sisters, and in A.D. 39 was exiled for adultery with them. Under Claudius he lived in obscurity, but Nero (q.v. 1) made him first *praefectus vigilum* and then in 62 *praefectus praetorio*. He recommended the numerous executions of the following years; and for his part in unmasking the Pisonian conspiracy of 65 he was given triumphal ornaments and other distinctions. He deserted Nero at the last, but after Nero's death he was removed from his prefecture by his colleague Nymphidius (q.v.) Sabinus. Through the influence of Vinius (q.v.) he lived unharmed through Galba's reign, but under Otho he was forced to suicide (Tac. *Hist.* 1. 72). G. E. F. C.

**TIGRANES** (1) **I** 'the Great', son of Artavasdes; king of Armenia. Shortly after 100 B.C. he was set on the throne of Armenia by the Parthians (with whom he had been a hostage for some years) in return for the cession of 'seventy valleys' in Armenia (Strabo 11. 14. 15). He rapidly consolidated his power, forming an alliance with Mithridates of Pontus, whose daughter, Cleopatra, he married. The interference of the two kings in Cappadocia led to Roman intervention and a *démarche* by Sulla. Tigranes turned his attention to expansion at the expense of Parthia, temporarily weakened by invasions on its eastern frontier. He ravaged Media as far as Ecbatana and Assyria as far as Arbela, deprived the Parthians of northern Mesopotamia and made vassals of the kings of Gordyene, Atropatene, and Osroene. In 83 he occupied Syria, Phoenicia, and Cilicia, ejecting warring Seleucid rivals. Greek cities that sided with him were given autonomy and coinage rights, but others, e.g. Soli in Cilicia and Cappadocian Mazaca, were destroyed and their inhabitants transferred to his new southern metropolis, Tigranocerta (q.v.). The empire of Tigranes the Great, 'King of Kings', proved to be an ephemeral affair. In 69 his alliance with Mithridates of Pontus involved him in war with Rome. Lucullus captured Tigranocerta, but the issue remained undecided until Pompey in 66 succeeded in separating the Armenian and Pontic kings. Tigranes' son rebelled and fled to Pompey; together they marched on Artaxata and Tigranes finally surrendered. He lost all his territories except Armenia proper. Henceforward, though engaging in frontier disputes with Parthia, he remained a peaceful vassal of Rome until his death in *c.* 56.

H. Seyrig, *Syria* (1950); *B.M. Cat. Seleucid Kings of Syria,* 103 ff. (coin portraits); see also ARMENIA, LUCULLUS 2, POMPEY. E. W. G.

**TIGRANES** (2) **II** (*PW* 3) (20 B.C.–*c.* 6 B.C.) son of King Artavasdes of Armenia. Captured and sent to Egypt by Antony, he lived for many years in Rome. After the murder of his brother Artaxes, the Armenians sent a request to Augustus that he be sent to reign instead (Tac. *Ann.* 2. 3; *Res Gestae* 27). Tiberius accompanied him with an army, and Tigranes was crowned without opposition. Armenia was thus restored to the ostensible control of Rome, although Tigranes' coins bear Parthian titles.

E. T. Newell, *Numism. Notes and Monogr.* n. 30. 13 ff. M. S. D.; E. W. G.

**TIGRANES** (3) **III** (*PW* 4) (*c.* 6–2 B.C.), son of Tigranes II. On his father's death he was crowned by the pro-Parthian party in Armenia, to reign jointly with his sister-consort Erato. He was expelled by the Romans, but returned after the murder of the Roman nominee a few years later. Attacked by Augustus' adoptive son C. Caesar, he made overtures for peace, but died fighting on his eastern frontier.

*PW*, s.v. 'Erato'. M. S. D.

**TIGRANES** (4) **V** (*PW* 6), great-grandson of Archelaus of Cappadocia (Tac. *Ann.* 14. 26). In A.D. 60 he was sent from Rome to replace Tiridates (q.v. 4) on the throne of Armenia. When he proceeded to lay Adiabene waste, Vologeses of Parthia sent his general Monaeses to invade Armenia, and Tigranes was shut up in Tigranocerta; but the siege was raised after negotiations. He was withdrawn by the Romans in 62 and disappeared from history.

M. S. D.

**TIGRANOCERTA** (modern *Silvan*), city in Armenia, in Arzanene; later rechristened Martyropolis. It was founded by Tigranes I (App. *Mith.* 67) as a southern metropolis to balance the northern capital Artaxata (q.v.). He swelled its citizen body by netting the cities of conquered Cappadocia, Adiabene, and Gordyene (Plut. *Luc.* 25 f.; Strabo 12. 2. 27). Its fortifications were incomplete when Lucullus (q.v. 2) defeated Tigranes nearby in 69 B.C. and easily secured its capitulation. The captured exiles were sent home, but Tigranocerta was still an important fortified city, e.g., in A.D. 59 when Corbulo (q.v.) occupied it. In the wars of Sapor II against Rome and Armenia in the fourth century A.D. it was destroyed by the Sassanians, but it emerges again in the fifth century as Martyropolis, site of a famous Church of the Martyrs.

The site of Tigranocerta has been much disputed: T. Rice Holmes, *Roman Republic* (1923), i. 409 ff., but see C. F. Lehmann-Haupt, *Armenien einst und jetzt* (1910–31), and *PW*, s.v.                    E. W. G.

**TIGRIS,** the more easterly of the Two Rivers of Mesopotamia. Rising in Armenia, it flows south-east through Assyria and Babylonia to the Persian Gulf. On its left bank it receives three main tributaries, the Greater and Lesser Zâb and the Diyâla. At Seleuceia it is only *c.* 18 miles from the Euphrates (q.v.) and the rivers were joined in antiquity by a network of canals. At the double mouth of the Tigris was the kingdom of Mesene of Characene. Both rivers frequently change their course. The Tigris is the faster; the journey downstream could be made on rafts, Seleucia being the limit for shipping.                    M. S. D.

**TIMACHIDAS** of Lindus in Rhodes composed the list of dedications to Athena (the *Anagraphe* of Lindus) which was commissioned in 99 B.C., and subsequently discovered in the excavations there. He also wrote commentaries on several Greek authors, a Δεῖπνα (in eleven books or more—Ath. 1. 5a) and a miscellaneous glossary.

*FGrH* iii. 532.

**TIMAEUS** (1) of Locri in Italy, Pythagorean, the chief speaker in Plato's *Timaeus*. We have no knowledge of him independent of this, and he may have been a fictitious character. The work in ps.-Doric dialect Περὶ ψυχᾶς κόσμω καὶ φύσιος, which passes under the name of Timaeus Locrus, is a late (probably 1st c. A.D.) paraphrase of the *Timaeus*: ed. (with Plato's *Timaeus*) C. F. Herman (Leipzig, 1852).

Testimonia in Diels, *Vorsokr.*¹¹ 1. 441. *PW* vi A. 1203. W. D. R.

**TIMAEUS** (2) of Tauromenium (*c.* 356–260 B.C.). His father Andromachus was ruler of Tauromenium where the Naxians expelled by Dionysius II were settled (358), and by his moderate rule and friendship with Timoleon succeeded in retaining his position after the latter's liberation of Sicily (343). However, Timaeus fled to Athens perhaps as late as 317, when Agathocles drove his enemies from Syracuse to Acragas, or when he seized Tauromenium (312). There remained for fifty years, studied rhetoric under Philiscus, pupil of Isocrates, came into contact with the Peripatetic School, and probably returned to Sicily under Hieron II.

The *History* (Ἱστορίαι) in thirty-eight books was primarily concerned with Sicily, and its importance was great in standardizing previous accounts of Sicilian history and origins. Timaeus aimed to focus attention on the importance of the Greeks in Sicily and their contribution to Hellenism. The *History* dealt mainly with events in Sicily, Italy, and Libya, but included references to events in Greece and reached its conclusion either with Pyrrhus' death (272) or before the Romans attacked Carthage in Sicily (264). The books on Agathocles and Pyrrhus (34–8) seem to have been added to the original plan, perhaps after Timaeus' return. He is also credited with a treatise on the Olympic victors.

Timaeus is praised by Polybius (12. 10. 4) for his accuracy in chronology and research, qualities to which Cicero's description, *longe eruditissimus*, may also refer (*De Or.* 2. 58). His work remained popular at least until the first century A.D. and played an important part as a

basis for Roman historical writing. Timaeus' failings as an historian largely resulted from his rhetorical training and were common to most of his contemporaries. He showed little critical ability in his fondness for rationalizing myths and reliance on etymologies. But charges of wilful ignorance or falsification (Diod. Sic. 13. 90; Polyb. 12. 25) cannot be substantiated; and we must recognize in him the cultivation of wide interests characteristic of the Peripatetics, diligence in collecting information, and a reasonable impartiality, except in the case of Agathocles.

*FGrH* iii B, 566; T. S. Brown, *Timaeus of Tauromenium* (1958); A. Momigliano, *Terzo contributo alla storia dei studi classici* (1966), 23 ff.                    G. L. B.

**TIMAEUS** (3) (probably 4th c. A.D.), under the influence of Neoplatonism, compiled an extant lexicon of Plato.

EDITIONS. Ruhnken (1789); Koch (1833); Dübner (in Baiter's *Plato*, 1839).

**TIMAGENES** of Alexandria, captured and brought to Rome in 55 B.C., where he taught rhetoric and knew Augustus, but subsequently fell out of favour with him. He was a friend of Asinius Pollio, at whose villas he lived. The reference to him in Hor. *Epist.* 1. 19. 15 is obscure. He wrote a *History of Kings* (Βασιλεῖς), which was used by Pompeius Trogus.

*FHG* iii. 317–23; *FGrH* ii. 88; *PW*, s.v. (2).                    J. D. D.

**TIMANTHES** (late 5th c. B.C.), painter, of Cythnus, later of Sicyon, contemporary of Zeuxis; famed for his *ingenium*. In his 'sacrifice of Iphigenia' he showed degrees of grief culminating in the veiled Agamemnon (reflections on late reliefs, Pfuhl, figs. 638–9). He also painted an ideal Hero, and a sleeping Cyclops with a tiny Satyr beside him.

Overbeck, 1734–44; Rumpf, *Malerei u. Zeichn.* 120.  T. B. L. W.

**TIMBER** had an important place in the economies of Greece and Rome. Sea power depended on access to forests; ambitious architecture required strong wood, often in long lengths. Less selective but more continuous was the need for timber for house-building, furniture, tools, and charcoal for cooking. The more rainy western side of Greece still carries a fair supply, though not of the best quality, but rainfall in eastern Greece is inadequate to sustain forests, except on the higher hills and mountains. By the Classical Period the more accessible stands had been overcut and the States near the isthmus were probably the worst sufferers, Athens, Megara, and Corinth. Corinth could draw supplies from the mountains of Achaea and from the north-west through her colonies; and Megara could probably rely on the same sources, except when she was at war with Corinth. Athens looked primarily to the north-east.

Theophrastus (q.v.), who wrote knowledgeably about trees, knew that the finest timber for ship-building came from Macedonia and Thrace. Mount Ida, the south coast of the Euxine, south Italy, and Sicily were alternative sources but the silver firs and pine of Macedonia were nearer to Athens and relations with the Macedonian kings, who exercised a royal monopoly, became important. In an alliance with Athens in the fifth century Perdiccas pledged himself by oath to allow the export of oars only to Athens. Alcibiades had the western forests in Sicily and south Italy in mind when he pressed for action against Syracuse; when her fleet was destroyed Athens depended for survival on the friendship of Archelaus the Macedonian king. Most of the timber used in temple construction at Athens also had to be imported; a decree survives praising the people of the island of Carpathos for sending a specially fine cypress for the restoration of a temple on the Acropolis. In the Hellenistic Period forests continued to be important objectives of policy, military and diplomatic; Macedonia, Syria, Cyprus, and Cilicia held the main reserves. Cleopatra's fleet was built from forests in Cilicia, presented to her by Antony.

In Rome the timber shortage was never so acute as in Greece. The hills of Latium were well stocked with firs, pine, chestnut, and beech, and local supplies could be supplemented by timber floated down the Tiber from the forests of Etruria. When the need for ship timber arose in the third century, there were ample resources near the western coast. Timber was recognized as a useful farm crop and some towns owned woods to ensure the supply of timber for the construction and maintenance of public buildings and for the furnaces that heated water in public baths. In the Empire, as wealth increased, the Roman timber trade became more ambitious and went further afield to satisfy more sophisticated demands. Larch, whose special qualities were first discovered by Caesar, became a favourite timber for building, though it did not grow in central Italy. Under the Emperor Tiberius a large parcel of larch was shipped to Rome from the Rhaetian Alps (in the neighbourhood of the Brenner Pass). It was specially ordered by the Emperor for the restoration of the deck on the lake where mock naval battles were fought, and the tallest of the trees produced a beam more than 100 feet in length. Among exotic timbers the most valuable was the Numidian tree known to the Romans as *citrus* and to the modern trade as African Thuya. It was valued for its distinctive grain and tables made from it fetched record prices. In the Republic Rome had been mainly satisfied with native timber; under the Empire she drew on all the finest timbers from the eastern and western Mediterranean including pine from Paphlagonia, cedars from Syria and Cyprus, and even teak from India.

Theophr. *Enquiry into Plants*; Pliny, *Natural History*, book xvi. A. C. Johnson, 'Ancient Forests and Navies', *TAPA* 1927; E. C. Semple, *Geography of the Mediterranean Region* (1932), 261 ff.
R. M.

**TIME-RECKONING.** The ancients, like all civilized peoples, were faced with a grave difficulty in the reckoning of time, apart from the incidental ones which must have confronted their earliest attempts to observe its passage accurately. For reasons of 'ancestral custom', quite as much religious as scientific or practical, they tried 'to conduct their years in accordance with the sun, their days and months in accordance with the moon' (Geminus of Rhodes, 8. 7). Now the three natural divisions of time, day, lunar month, and solar year, are incommensurables. Taking the day as 1, the lengths of the other two are approximately 29½ and 365¼ respectively, but these last two figures are far from accurate, and the inaccuracy is bound to show itself in any calendar, however carefully reckoned, which tries to combine them.

**2.** TIME (χρόνος). In the Homeric Epics, the word for 'time' (χρόνος) had a very definite and limited meaning (H. Fränkel, 'Die Zeitauffassung in der frühgriechischen Literatur', *Wege und Formen frühgriechisches Denkens* (1955), 1 ff.). It is never a point of time or in time, but always a 'duration', and indeed a lengthy duration—'much time'. If a short duration is to be indicated, it has to be expressed by 'not much time'.

**3.** THE DAY (ἦμαρ, ἡμέρα, *dies*). Although the Babylonians divided day and night (24 hours, νυχθήμερον in Greek) into twelve periods (double hours, cf. Hdt. 2. 109. 3, but see J. Enoch Powell, *CR* 1940, 69 f.), the Greeks made little use of this measurement for any but purely scientific calculations till Hellenistic times (cf. CLOCKS).

Ordinarily, in classical times, they did not speak of hours but of 'cock-crow', 'time of full market' (i.e. mid-morning), 'noon', 'lamp-lighting', 'time of first sleep', and the like. When hours were used, they were not of fixed length, but each 1/12 of the day (or night), consequently varying with the season. Our hour is the ὥρα ἰσημερινή, *hora aequinoctialis*, 1/12 of the day or night at the equinox. Besides the natural reckoning of the day from dawn, it was common in Greece to reckon it officially, for calendar purposes, from sunset to sunset; the Romans reckoned from midnight.

**4.** THE WEEK was little used, save, in Hellenistic times, by believers in astrology (*see* ASTROLOGY). It is a grouping of days in accordance with the supposed governing of the first hour of each by the planet whose name it bears; for details see F. H. Colson, *The Week* (1926; not always quite accurate, but the fullest and best account in English). Strictly speaking, neither Jews nor Christians observe a week, since both officially reject astrology, but a festival (Sabbath and Sunday respectively) which occurs at intervals of seven days. The planetary week becomes important about the third century A.D., and is called ἑβδομάς, *septimana*. In Italy it was customary to have market-days (*nundinae*) at intervals of eight days (a *nundinum*). This might loosely be called a week, but was of very small importance for reckoning time. On calendars it was marked by a continuous series of letters, A–H, the first being the day of the *nundinae*.

**5.** MONTHS (*see further* CALENDARS) were (except as noted below) lunar, more or less accurately reckoned. They always consisted of an integral number of days, which varied slightly so that the average length approximated to 29½ days in any given calendar. It was early noticed that while 12 of these months were about equal to a (solar) year (354 or 355 days as against 365¼) the difference was great enough for such a calendar to be about three months too short in eight years. Hence the practice of inserting extra months (μῆνες ἐμβόλιμοι). Astronomers, beginning with Meton and Eudoxus (1) (qq.v.), constructed elaborate and accurate cycles (see, e.g., Geminus 8. 50), but the influence of these on the civic calendars was apparently slow and slight.

**6.** THE YEAR (ἔτος, ἐνιαυτός, *annus*) consequently was unsatisfactory, since it never exactly coincided with the solar year. As the chief industry of antiquity was agriculture, a demand existed, and was met by the above-named astronomers and others after them, for a perpetual calendar which should show the astronomical facts* and the supposed meteorological events (prevailing winds, etc.) connected with them. Examples of these are the calendar at the end of Geminus (see bibliography, *infra*), the fragments of a calendar found at Miletus in 1899 (W. Kubitschek, *Grundriss der antiken Zeitrechnung* (1928), 173), and the so-called Italian rustic calendars (ibid. 120). They are founded upon the signs of the zodiac, not on civic months. Since a movable pin often enabled the owner to note the day of the local calendar alongside the day given on the perpetual one, the name παράπηγμα was commonly given to such a device. But in Egypt, from very early times, there had been in use a calendar beginning with the rising of Sirius (considered as the sign of the coming rise of the Nile) which consisted of 365 days divided into 12 months having nothing to do with the moon but consisting of 30 days each, with 5 extra days (ἐπαγόμεναι in Greek) at the end of the year. This, of course, meant that in four years the calendar was a day wrong, and in 1,460 years (a Sothis-period, so called from the Egyptian name of Sirius) it righted itself. This

*The Greek peasant was a tolerable practical astronomer from the days of Hesiod and earlier, see, e.g., *Op.* 383; so must the Italian farmers have been.

difference was well known and its reform proposed (Decree of Canopus, 238 B.C.; see Kubitschek, 89) by the insertion of a day every fourth year. On this basis Caesar's reform was founded (*see* CALENDARS), and adopted by Romans and to some extent by others.

7. SEASONS. A method of dating by the natural seasons of the solar year was widespread among Greek authors: G. Busolt, *Griechische Geschichte* (1893–1904), iii. 675 ff. A. W. Gomme (*Commentary on Thucydides* iii (1956), 699 ff.) believes that Thucydides had in mind fixed dates for the beginning of his spring and winter, and W. K. Pritchett and van der Waerden (*BCH* 1961, 17 ff.) have suggested that these dates were those of Euctemon's *parapegma*: vespertinal rising of Arcturus (Mar. 6) and the setting of the Pleiades (Nov. 8). Efforts to date events in Thucydides later than these termini have proved inconclusive, but since the historian nowhere explains his system, the theory of astronomical exactitude must rely primarily on the interpretation of the passage in Thuc. 5. 20. 1–3.

8. GENEALOGIES. The most ancient sort of chronology was by genealogies. The three stages of the development have been traced by W. den Boer, *Laconian Studies* (1954). The first is linked with the name of Simonides (c. 556–468 B.C.). Its time-reckoning connects with undated lists of kings. The second phase is linked with the name of Herodotus, who, however, does not use the genealogical system to the exclusion of all others. His normal method is to reckon with three generations in the century. But he also uses a 'generation' of forty years which probably derived from a Spartan list of kings. The third phase is linked with the names of Eratosthenes (c. 275–194 B.C.) and Apollodorus (b. c. 180 B.C.). It introduces dated lists of kings, a dating made possible by the development of time-reckoning by means of the Olympiads.

9. ERAS. Ancient years, however calculated, were not numbered on any generally understood system, as with us, but merely named ('in the archonship of so-and-so', 'in the consulate of X and Y', 'in the tenth year of the reign of A', etc.), which was next to useless for chronology. This defect was felt, especially by historians, and several eras were proposed. The most familiar were the Olympiads (first celebration of Olympian games, traditionally 776 B.C., thereafter every four years), used quite commonly by chronologists from the fourth century B.C. on; the years from the foundation of Rome, A(nno) V(rbis) C(onditae) or A(b) V(rbe) C(ondita), an event reckoned by Varro (q.v. 2) at 753 B.C. in our dating; and some important local eras, as that of the Seleucidae, from 312 B.C.; several Roman provinces had eras of their own, see Kubitschek, 76 ff. Chronographers from Eratosthenes (q.v.) to the great Christian historian Eusebius of Caesarea and his Latin adapter St. Jerome (see Rose, *Handbook of Lat. Lit.* 492) also used, for earlier dates, such events as the fall of Troy (1183 B.C., Eratosthenes) or the birth of Abraham (2016 B.C., Eusebius). Our era was introduced by the abbot Dionysius Exiguus (d. c. A.D. 540); the practice of reckoning early dates backwards from it is quite recent and a little complicated by the fact that astronomers do and historians generally do not insert a year 0 between 1 B.C. and A.D. 1.

LITERATURE: mostly cited in text. The most convenient summary of relevant facts, with good account of earlier works, is E. Bickerman, *Chronology of the Ancient World* (1968). See also Nillson, *GGR* i². 561 ff., 644 ff. who overstresses the influence of Apollo and Delphi. Latte, *RR* 1 ff. and 36. The most important ancient author, Geminus of Rhodes, is best edited by Manitius (1898; critical text and German version). *See also* CALENDARS. H. J. R.

**TIMESITHEUS,** GAIUS FURIUS (*PW* 89) SABINUS AQUILA, rose from the ranks and entered the equestrian service by way of the centurionate. His career is remarkable for its accumulation of vicarial procuratorships held under Severus Alexander, Maximinus, and Gordian III. In A.D. 241 he was appointed Praetorian Prefect by Gordian and till his death at Nisibis in the winter of 243/4 exercised virtual control over the young Emperor.

*ILS* 1330, *and see under* GORDIAN III. H. M. D. P.

**TIMOCLES,** Middle Comedy poet, late in the period, but he practised with wit and, originality the ἰαμβική ἰδέα of the Old Comedy, attacking, among many others, Demosthenes and Hyperides. Almost one-half of the fragments are personal references. He won the first prize once at the Lenaea between 330 and 320 (*IG* ii². 2325. 158): the latest datable reference (fr. 32. 3) in his work is mention of the γυναικονόμοι instituted (317–307 B.C.) by Demetrius of Phaleron. Of twenty-seven known titles four denote mythological burlesques (Ἥρωες, Κένταυρος), two refer to characters (Ἐπιχαιρέκακος, Πολυπράγμων). An original formation is Ὀρεσταυτοκλείδης, i.e. Autocleides suffering the fate of Orestes—obsessed, however, not by Furies, but by old women. Fr. 1, the strange gods of Egypt; fr. 6, consolation from Tragedy, which outdoes human woes; fr. 8, defence of the parasite's life; fr. 12, Demosthenes 'never uttered an antithesis'.

*FCG* iii. 590 ff.: *CAF* ii. 451 ff.: *FAC* ii. 600 ff. W. G. W.; K. J. D.

**TIMOCREON** (first half of 5th c. B.C.), lyric and elegiac poet of Ialysus in Rhodes (frs. 1–3 P. = Plut. *Them.* 21). He probably took the Persian side when they occupied Rhodes, went to Susa as the guest of the Great King (Ath. 10. 415 f), engaged in controversy with Themistocles after 479 for failing to take him home, and mocked him for his failure to win favour at the Isthmus, and, apparently, for not being made general c. 477 B.C. He also had interchanges with Simonides, who criticized his style (fr. 162 D.) and character (fr. 99 D.). He was a pentathlic victor and a great glutton (Ath. loc. cit.). He wrote σκόλια (fr. 5 P.; with a possible reference to his taking money from the Persians) and epigrams (fr. 6 D.; with a possible reference to Themistocles) in a mixture of colloquial and literary language.

TEXT. Page, *Poet. Mel. Gr.* 375–8.
CRITICISM. C. M. Bowra, *Greek Lyric Poetry*² (1961), 349 ff. C. M. B.

**TIMOLEON** (d. c. 334 B.C.), a Corinthian who liberated Greek Sicily from the domination of military dictators and Carthaginian invaders. After overthrowing the tyranny of his brother, he lived in retirement for many years until in 345 the Corinthians sent him to Sicily with a small mercenary force in response to an appeal by Syracusan aristocrats for help against Dionysius II, who had become tyrant of Syracuse once more. Timoleon had also to contend with Hicetas, an ambitious adventurer who planned to supplant Dionysius and was supported by a strong force of Carthaginians. By a mixture of bold strategy and somewhat unscrupulous diplomacy Timoleon got the better of his opponents and liberated Syracuse. He initiated a programme of political and social reconstruction at Syracuse, where dictatorial powers were conferred on him, and he also began a crusade against the tyrants ruling other cities. When in 341 the Carthaginians sent a large army to Sicily, he took the offensive and, seizing the opportunity to attack them while they were crossing the river Crimisus, gained a decisive victory. Losing the initiative when the tyrants and the Carthaginians allied against him, he was for a time in great difficulties. Eventually he made peace with Carthage and was able to crush the tyrants separately and to extend his programme of reconstruction throughout Greek Sicily. Retiring from public life when his eyesight began to fail, he passed his last years at Syracuse as its most honoured citizen.

The extravagant eulogies of Timoleon by the Sicilian

Timaeus, and perhaps the success of his own propaganda, render suspect the extant records of his career. He must, however, have been an inspiring leader and an astute negotiator. He succeeded, where Dion failed, in bringing peace to Greek Sicily and providing a basis for the revival of its prosperity.

Plut. *Tim.*; Diod. bk. 16; Nepos, '*Timoleon*. H. D. Westlake, *Timoleon and his Relations with Tyrants* (1952); M. Sordi, *Timoleonte* (1961). H. D. W.

**TIMON** (*Τίμων*) (1) of Athens, the famous misanthrope, a semi-legendary character. He seems to have lived in the time of Pericles. Aristophanes is the first to allude to him. He became known to Shakespeare through Plutarch (*Ant.* 70) and Lucian's dialogue.

*Prosop. Att.* 13845. V. E.

**TIMON** (2) of Phlius (*c.* 320–230 B.C.), sceptical philosopher, follower of Pyrrho. After a period of poverty in youth, when he earned a living as a dancer, he studied in Megara with Stilpo and then in Elis with Pyrrho, and later worked as a sophist in Chalcedon. When he had enough money he went to Athens where he lived until his death.

Only fragments of his numerous writings survive. He wrote (1) *Silloi* (lampoons) in hexameters, against the dogmatic philosophers, including a dialogue between himself and Xenophanes; (2) *Ἰνδαλμοί* (Images? Fantasies?) in elegiacs; (3) tragedies, satyr-plays, *kinaidoi*; (4) prose works—*The Funeral Feast of Arcesilaus, On Sensations, Against the Physicists*; (5) Python—a dialogue between Pyrrho, on his way to Delphi, and somone called Python.

Frr. in H. Diels, *Poetarum Philosophorum Fragmenta* (1901), 173 ff. V. Brochard, *Les Sceptiques grecs*[2] (1923). D. J. F.

**TIMOSTRATUS,** one of the latest comic poets of Athens whose fragments survive. A man of good Athenian family, Timostratus obtained in 188 B.C. fifth place with *Λυτ[ρούμενος*, in 183 third place with *Φιλοίκειος* (*IG* ii². 2323, lines 141, 155). His son Ariston and grandson Poses seem also to have been comic poets (E. Preuner, *Rh. Mus.* 1894, 362 ff.).

*FCG* iv. 595 f.; *CAF* iii. 355 ff. W. G. W.; W. G. A.

**TIMOTHEUS** (1) (*c.* 450–*c.* 360 B.C.; *Marm. Par.* 76), dithyrambic poet, of Miletus. After failures in Athens he succeeded with the *Persae*, a lyric nome, for which Euripides wrote the prologue (Satyr. *Vit. Eur.* fr. 39, col. 22) *c.* 419–416 B.C. Large portions of this are preserved in a papyrus of the fourth century B.C. It is an account of Salamis, in which a crude realism is combined with a grotesque imitation of the high style. It closes with the poet's claim to have revolutionized music. Though written out as prose, the *Persians* is constructed on easily distinguishable metrical principles. It is astrophic and composed of various *metra*. His works were collected in eighteen books, but few other fragments are of interest except fr. 20, in which he proclaims the newness of his art. He is said to have influenced Euripides, and parallels have been noted between the speech of the Phrygian in *Persians* 152 with that of the Phrygian in Eur. *Or.* 1365 ff. *See* MUSIC, § 10.

TEXT. Page, *Poet. Mel. Gr.* 399–18. COMMENTARY. U. von Wilamowitz-Moellendorff, *Timotheos: Die Perser* (1903). C. M. B.

**TIMOTHEUS** (2), son of Conon and pupil of Isocrates. Elected *strategos* in 378 B.C., when the Second Athenian League was founded, he won many members for the League by his tour of north-west Greece in 375. Recalled in 374, he broke the peace just concluded with Sparta by restoring democratic exiles in Zacynthus, and

was given the command against Sparta in 373. Paralysed by lack of funds, he was impeached but acquitted; to restore his fortunes he served for Persia against Egypt. Upon the fall of Callistratus in 366 he returned to power with an imperialist policy, which alienated Persia and the League; in spite of Epaminondas' naval campaign he achieved considerable success, but failed repeatedly to capture Amphipolis. Discontent among the allies, which his policy evoked, resulted in the Social War; in 356 Timotheus, Iphicrates, and Chares, sharing the command at Embata, failed to co-operate, and, impeached by Chares, he was sentenced to a fine of 100 talents, left Athens, and died in 354. A wealthy aristocrat with little sympathy for the *demos*, he pursued an individualist and short-sighted policy with outstanding ability.

P. Cloché, *La Politique étrangère d'Athènes 404–338 av. J.-C.* (1934). N. G. L. H.

**TIMOTHEUS** (3), Greek sculptor, active during the first half and middle of the fourth century B.C. He took part in two important monuments of which sculptural remains survive—the temple of Asclepius at Epidaurus and the Mausoleum at Halicarnassus. His share in the sculptures at Epidaurus is attested by the building inscription in which his name appears as having contracted to furnish *typoi* (reliefs?) and acroteria. The style of some of these extant sculptures, with their transparent draperies and massive folds, resembles that current in the late fifth century B.C. Pliny (36. 80) mentions Timotheus along with Scopas (q.v.), Bryaxis, and Leochares (q.v.) as having produced the friezes of the Mausoleum. It has not been possible, however, to attribute to him any specific slabs of these friezes with any confidence, though attempts have been made. Nor have any convincing identifications been made of the single statues—athletes, an Artemis, an Asclepius, etc.—which Pliny and Pausanias ascribed to him. G. M. A. R.

**TIN,** as a component of bronze, occurs very early in Mesopotamia, apparently derived from a distant source, probably Drangiana. Bronze is found sporadically in the later Early Minoan period, and regularly from Middle Minoan times; it probably reached the rest of Europe at a rather later date. Tin was smelted in Nigeria by the second century A.D., but seems not to have been used for bronze. The principal sources available to the classical world were the Erzgebirge (cf. Scymnus 493) and western Europe. Small quantities were mined in Etruria in pre-Roman times, and tin was worked near Delphi. The Phoenicians tried at times to monopolize the western sources, but by the third century Massilia established an overland route. The main Punic source was probably Galicia. Breton tin was worked at an early date, but not much in Roman times; the mines of central Gaul closed soon after the Roman conquest. Cornish tin was hardly known before the Late Bronze Age; it was worked all through the Roman period under native supervision. In Cornwall must be located the Cassiterides. They were known to Massiliots from the fifth century, but the searoute thither from Spain was discovered by P. Crassus (q.v. 2) probably about 95 B.C. *See also* CASSITERIDES.

Metallic tin must have been known to alloy in exact proportions with copper; little has survived, mainly owing to oxidization, but also because it was not of great use unalloyed. Classical writers confuse tin and lead, because they had no clear idea of the atomic difference of metals. Mining was largely in placers; in Cornwall vein-mining was not started before late medieval times.

See especially Strabo 3. 175–6, Polyb. 34. 10. H. Hencken, *Archaeology of Cornwall and Scilly* (1932); W. C. Borlase, *Tin-mining in Spain Past and Present* (1897); O. Davies, *Roman Mines in Europe* (1935); *Proc. Belfast Natural History Society* 1931/2, 41; Forbes, *Stud. Anc. Technol.*, vol. ix. O. D.

**TINCOMMIUS,** son of Commius (q.v.), and king of the British Atrebates, c. 25 B.C.–A.D. 1. His coinage suggests that he came under Roman influence, and he may have been supported by Augustus to counterbalance growing Catuvellaunian power north of the Thames. Before A.D. 7 he had been driven into exile by his brother Eppillus and his name appears on the Monumentum Ancyranum (ch. 32).

D. F. Allen, *Archaeologia* 1944, 1 ff.; C. E. Stevens in W. F. Grimes (ed.), *Aspects of Archaeology in Britain* (1951), 332 ff.; Frere, *Britannia*, ch. iv.                                S. S. F.

**TINGI(S)** (modern *Tangier*), a seaport nearly facing Gibraltar across the Straits. It was a Phoenician settlement in the fifth century B.C. or before. It received Roman citizenship from Octavian, being detached from the client kings of Mauretania. On the provincialization of the latter under Claudius, it became the capital of the procurator of Mauretania Tingitana. It was cut off from Rusaddir (*Melilla*) by the Riff mountains, but was connected with Volubilis (q.v.) and Sala by military roads. Its importance as a naval base lasted till the Arab conquest.

L. Teutsch, *Das Städtewesen von Nordafrika* (1962), 191 ff., 205 ff.                                W. N. W.; B. H. W.

**TIPASA,** a Roman town on the Algerian coast. A Carthaginian settlement, it was given Latin rights by Claudius and was a *colonia* before A.D. 200. Substantial defences survive from the fourth century when it was important in the control of dissident tribes in the Kabylie mountains. There are also numerous remains of Christian character, in particular the chapel of St. Salsa.

P. Cintas, *Fouilles puniques à Tipasa* (1949); J. Baradez, *Tipasa* (Algiers, 1956).                                B. H. W.

**TIRESIAS** (Τειρεσίας), a legendary blind Theban seer, so wise that even his ghost still has its wits (φρένες, cf. SOUL) and is not a mere phantom (*Odyssey* 10. 493–5). Later legends account for his wisdom and blindness chiefly thus: (*a*) He saw Athena bathing; since his mother was her friend, she did not cause his death, but blinded him and gave him the power of prophecy by way of compensation (Callim. *Lav. Pall.* 57 ff.). (*b*) He one day saw snakes coupling and struck them with his stick, whereat he became a woman; later the same thing happened again and he turned into a man. Being asked by Zeus and Hera to settle a dispute as to which sex had more pleasure of love, he decided for the female; Hera was angry and blinded him, but Zeus recompensed him by giving him long life and power of prophecy. So Hyginus, *Fab.* 75, see Rose, ad loc. His advice was sought throughout the times of the Labdacidae, and he finally died after the evacuation of Thebes when besieged by the Epigoni, from drinking of the spring Tilphussa (Apollod. 3. 84, cf. Athenaeus 41 e).                                H. J. R.

**TIRIDATES** (1) **I,** the supposed brother, partner in revolt and successor in rule of Arsaces I, founder of the Parthian Empire, is apocryphal.

Wolski, *Hist.* 1959, 222 ff.                                E. W. G.

**TIRIDATES** (2) **II,** a pretender to the Parthian throne in revolt against Phraates IV (q.v.) shortly before 31 B.C. and temporarily successful in dislodging him. On Phraates' recovery both contestants sought the support of Octavian. In 30/29 B.C. Octavian let Tiridates stay as a refugee in Syria, retaining for himself as a hostage a son of Phraates kidnapped by Tiridates, but making no open offer to assist the latter. In 26 and 25 B.C. Tiridates carried out spring offensives as far as Babylonia with at least the connivance of Augustus; but Augustus had no further use for Tiridates after his final ejection by Phraates (by May 25 B.C.), when he made an appeal for help to

Augustus in Spain. Augustus' failure to eject Phraates through the instrumentality of Tiridates is ignored in his *Res Gestae*.

N. C. Debevoise, *A Political History of Parthia* (1938), 135 ff.                                E. W. G.

**TIRIDATES** (3) **III,** grandson of Phraates IV, was sent by Tiberius to contest the Parthian throne, with the military support of L. Vitellius, governor of Syria (Tac. *Ann.* 4. 32). Expelling Artabanus II, he was welcomed by the pro-Roman faction in the cities of Mesopotamia, and was crowned at Ctesiphon (A.D. 35); he was subsequently again driven out by Artabanus.                                M. S. D.

**TIRIDATES** (4), brother of Vologeses I (q.v.) of Parthia, who set him on the throne of Armenia (A.D. 54). He fled before the Romans and was temporarily displaced by Tigranes V (q.v.), but was reinstated by Vologeses. By a compromise with Corbulo (q.v.) Tiridates agreed to journey to Rome and receive the crown of Armenia ceremonially from Nero (A.D. 66). In c. A.D. 72 nomad Alani overran his kingdom. Tac. *Ann.* 12 ff.; Joseph. *BJ* 7. 244–51.                                M. S. D.

**TIRO,** MARCUS TULLIUS (*PW* 52), confidential slave, secretary, and literary adviser of Cicero (q.v. 1), who freed him in 53 B.C., perhaps on his fiftieth birthday. Ailing after 51, he survived Cicero, published some of his speeches and letters and wrote a biography of him. He also wrote works on grammar (*De usu atque ratione linguae Latinae*) and miscellaneous questions (Gell. *NA* 13. 9. 1). For his system of shorthand (usually called *notae Tironianae*) see TACHYGRAPHY.

See especially Cic. *Fam.* 16.                                E. B.

**TIRYNS** occupies a rocky hill in the Argive plain, 2½ miles north of Nauplia and 1 mile from the sea. A few neolithic fragments show that the site was early inhabited, and with the Early Bronze Age (c. 2800–2100 B.C.) it became important. A round house, perhaps that of the chief, stood on the summit with huts clustered round, and the main settlement spread in the plain below. In the Middle Bronze Age a settlement on the hill with the pottery, houses, and tombs characteristic of the age seems to have been fortified. Its inhabitants belonged to what was probably the first wave of Greek-speaking people in Greece. To this succeeded (1600–1400) in the Late Bronze Age a prince's house of which only a few fresco fragments remain. About 1400 Tiryns began to assume its present form. In the first stage a great wall was built round the south of the hill with a gate on the east. In the second stage the fortress was enlarged at a higher level created by terracing. The wall was extended to the north to include the middle part of the hill, and on the east a great gate, like the Lion Gate at Mycenae, was built. In the third stage the vaulted galleries with store chambers on the south and east were added. A bastion with a side gate was thrown out on the west and a massive wall was built round the north of the hill to protect flocks and herds and refugees. Within the south citadel arose a complex of buildings comprising an earlier and a later royal residence. The earlier palace on the east is well built though small, and is approached through a court. The west or great megaron was a noble hall entered through two courts with propylons, and the inner court contained an altar and a colonnade. It was richly decorated with frescoes, like its predecessors, and by the hearth was a place for a throne. At the side were a bathroom and chambers with upper stories. The lower town on the plain developed similarly, and Tiryns at this time was a rich and powerful State. Attempts to reconcile the plans of the palace and the two megara with the Homeric house divided into men's and women's apartments are based on the false assumption that the two megara were contemporaneous and parts of one homogeneous structure. Like other Mycenaean centres (Mycenae, Athens) Tiryns had cause to fear attack and siege at the end of the thirteenth century, and the same preparation as at Mycenae and Athens, a fortified spring approached from within the walls, has been found at Tiryns (*BCH* 1963, 751 ff.). The palace perished by fire at the end of the Late Helladic IIIB, but Tiryns continued to be inhabited through the geometric and archaic periods, and a temple seems to have arisen on the ruins of the palace. Late Helladic IIIC sherds show continued or renewed occupation after the disaster. Tombs from sub-Mycenaean to geometric have been found south of the acropolis, one of which has produced a unique sub-Mycenaean bronze helmet (*BCH* 1958, 707). Tiryns survived into the classical period as an independent town and sent a contingent to Plataea, but was destroyed by Argos *c.* 470 B.C. The refugees went to Halieis (*Porto Cheli*) where remains have recently been found from the second quarter of the fifth century on into the fourth.

H. Schliemann, *Tiryns* (1886); A. Frickenhaus, G. Rodenwaldt, K. Müller, *Tiryns* i–iv (1912–39); G. Karo, *Führer durch Tiryns*² (1934). A. J. B. W.; R. J. H.

**TISIAS** of Syracuse (5th c. B.C.), an early teacher of rhetoric (q.v.), pupil of Corax (q.v.). Plato (*Phaedrus* 267 a ff.) provides evidence for his having discussed probability (εἰκός) and the power of speech to revalue things.

L. Radermacher, *Artium Scriptores* (1951), 28 ff.; G. A. Kennedy, *The Art of Persuasion in Greece* (1963), 58 ff. D. A. R.

**TISSAPHERNES,** satrap of the Anatolian coastal provinces from 413 B.C., after he had suppressed the revolt by Pissuthnes of Lydia. In 412, prompted by Alcibiades, he began the policy of intervention in the Peloponnesian War, though his support for Sparta was intermittent and half-hearted, his real objective being the exhaustion of both sides. The conspiracy of his brother Teriuchmes against Darius II may have been a contributory factor in Tissaphernes' relegation to Caria in 408, when Cyrus initiated a vigorous pro-Spartan policy. In 401 Cyrus began to mobilize his army, and Tissaphernes, who had previously denounced him on Artaxerxes' accession, rode post-haste to warn the Great King. At Cunaxa his cavalry charge decided the day. He was restored to his command of the coastal provinces, and had to bear the brunt of the Spartan offensive which followed. Though he diplomatically diverted most of the attacks against Pharnabazus, he was crushingly defeated by Agesilaus near Sardis in 395. The hatred of Parysatis (Artaxerxes' daughter) had long made his position insecure, and after this disaster Artaxerxes decided to remove him. He was lured by Tithraustes to Colossae and assassinated.

W. Judeich, *Kleinasiatische Studien* (1892), ch. 2. For coin portraits, C. M. Kraay, *Greek Coins* (1966), nos. 621, 622. D. E. W. W.

**TITAN** (Τιτάν, -ῆν), one of the older gods who were before the Olympians, children of Heaven and Earth. Hesiod (*Theog.* 132 ff.) lists Oceanus, Coeus, Crius, Hyperion, Iapetos, Theia, Rhea, Themis, Mnemosyne, Phoebe, Tethys, and Kronos (q.v.). These names are an odd mixture of Greek and non-Greek, personal names and abstractions. For the battle between them and Zeus *see* KRONOS. The etymology of Τιτῆνες is highly uncertain; Hesiod (ibid. 209) fancifully derives it from τιταίνειν, to strain, and τίσις, vengeance, in allusion to their relations with their father. Later poetry often uses Titan and Titanis for Hyperion and Phoebe, Sun and Moon.

On the problem of their origin, Nilsson, *GGR* i². 510 ff. *See also* ORPHISM. H. J. R.

**TITHE,** δεκάτη, the tenth part of a revenue offered as thank-offering to a god; the sense is often the same as that of votive offering, ἀπαρχή (q.v.). For example, a certain Aeschines offered a statue to Athena as δεκάτη (*IG* i². 543). Best known are the tithes which the Athenians brought to the Eleusinian goddesses and in a decree exhorted all Greeks to bring (*IG* i². 76; *SIG* 83). M. P. N.

**TITIANUS,** JULIUS (*PW* 512) (2nd c. A.D.), writer of fictitious letters of famous women (Ciceronian in style), miscellanist, and grammarian. His studies of Virgil are mentioned by Servius ad *Aen.* 10. 18. His son wrote prose fables. The elder Titianus was nicknamed 'ape of the orators' (*oratorum simia*, Sid. Apoll. *Ep.* 1. 1. 2) by his fellow *Frontoniani* (q.v.) in disapproval of his copying Cicero's epistolary style. In *Historia Augusta* (*Maximini Duo* 27. 5) he is referred to as one *qui dictus est simia temporis sui quod cuncta esset imitatus.*

Schanz–Hosius, § 136. J. W. D.; G. B. A. F.

**TITINIUS** (1), Latin poet; earliest known composer of *fabulae togatae* of the type called *tabernariae*, in lively popular Plautine style. He survived Terence, with whom he was classed in character-drawing, especially feminine.

FRAGMENTS. O. Ribbeck, *CRF*² 133 (3rd ed. Teubner, 1897). E. H. W.

**TITINIUS** (2) **CAPITO,** GNAEUS OCTAVIUS (*PW* 89), a Roman knight who after a successful army career held the post of *ab epistulis* continuously under Domitian, Nerva, and Trajan, and later became *praefectus vigilum* (*ILS* 1448). He was a friend of the Younger Pliny, whom he advised to write history and received a notable reply (*Ep.* 5. 8). A painstaking patron of literature (ibid. 8. 12), he himself wrote the deaths of famous men: he also commemorated the traditional Republican 'martyrs' by keeping statues of Brutus, Cassius, and Cato in his house. G. E. F. C.

**TITIUS** (1, *PW* 7), GAIUS (2nd c. B.C.), orator and tragic writer. The abundance of *argutiae* in his speeches is mentioned by Cicero, *Brut.* 167.

**TITIUS** (2, *PW* 18), MARCUS, was apparently proscribed with his father Lucius in 43 B.C. The father made his way to Sextus Pompeius; the son raised a private fleet. In 40 he was captured by Menodorus (q.v.), but spared by Sextus for his father's sake; in 39 he was restored under the terms of the Pact of Misenum. He served as a quaestor under Antony in the Parthian expedition; in 35, sent by him to Asia to apprehend Sextus, he put him to death at Miletus, perhaps on Antony's instructions; subsequently he became proconsul of Asia (35/4?). In 32 he and his maternal uncle Plancus (q.v. 1) deserted Antony for Octavian. In 31 he was *consul suffectus*, and fought in the campaign of Actium. Later he was governor of Syria (13–9 B.C.?). He has been identified with the subject of the *elogium ILS* 918 (*see* QUIRINIUS). His wife Paullina was a daughter of Q. Fabius Maximus (*cos. suff.* 45 B.C.); the origin of his own family is not known.

T. Corbishley, *JRS* 1934, 43 ff.; L. R. Taylor, *JRS* 1936, 161 ff.; Syme, *Rom. Rev.*, see index; K. M. T. Atkinson, *Hist.* 1958, 315. G. W. R.; T. J. C.

**TITIUS** (3, *PW* 27a) **ARISTO** (*c.* A.D. 100), a Roman jurist, friend of the Younger Pliny, who warmly praises him (*Ep.* 1. 22; cf. 5. 3, 8. 14). He was active both as a respondent jurist and as an advocate, and he was perhaps a member of Trajan's *consilium*, but he is not known to have held any public office (possibly because he was a freedman or descended from a freedman). His writings are known only through citations by other jurists in Justinian's *Digesta* (q.v.). B. N.

**TITUS** (T. FLAVIUS (*PW* 207) VESPASIANUS), Emperor A.D. 79–81, was born 30 Sept. 39, the elder son of Vespasian (q.v.), and was educated along with the Emperor Claudius' son Britannicus (q.v.). After serving in Germany and Britain as military tribune he became quaestor (? 65), but had held no other office in the *cursus* when in 67 he accompanied his father to Judaea and was made legate of Legio XV Apollinaris. Late in 68 he was sent to bear Vespasian's congratulations to Galba (q.v. 1), but at Corinth he turned back on hearing of Galba's death; he consulted the priest at Paphos on his return journey, and brought encouraging advice to his father and Mucianus (q.v.); in all the subsequent negotiations which led to Vespasian's coup on 1 July he played a most active part. After the Flavian victory he was made consul (in absence) for 70 and given supreme command over the Jewish war. In Aug. 70 he captured Jerusalem.

His troops saluted him 'imperator', and on his way home he was crowned at Memphis during the celebrations of a new Apis. The legions at Alexandria begged him to take them with him, and at this point it is not surprising that he was accused of aiming at more power than Vespasian was prepared to concede him. But he returned alone; and though the independent triumph which the Senate had voted him was converted into a joint triumph with his father, he was quickly made a partner in Vespasian's rule. Like his brother he became *princeps iuventutis*; but unlike him he received a *tribunicia potestas* (dated from 1 July 71), became his father's colleague in all the consulates the latter subsequently held, and accumulated imperatorial salutations with his father.

He also became praetorian prefect, in succession to his brother-in-law Arrecinus Clemens. This made him the military arm of Vespasian's regime, and by his ruthlessness in suppressing disaffection he incurred unpopularity. This was enhanced by his liaison with Berenice (q.v. 4), which had begun while he was in Judaea. She came to Rome *c.* 75, and perhaps remained for three or four years, but before his father's death he was compelled to dismiss her. About the same time he had Eprius (q.v.) Marcellus and Caecina (q.v. 3) Alienus executed for alleged conspiracy.

At Vespasian's death on 23 June 79 he succeeded without challenge; and when Berenice returned to Rome he promptly, though reluctantly, sent her away once more. All fears which Roman society had entertained of him were soon dispersed. Affable, and possessed of remarkable good looks, he also won a reputation for generosity, some of which represented personal largess but much of it lavish expenditure from public funds. He repaired the two great disasters of his short reign, the destruction caused by Vesuvius in 79, and the plague and fire in Rome in 80; but he also completed the Colosseum and built the Baths which carry his name. It was a further source of popularity that these months saw no executions or trials for *maiestas*, and that certain informers were scourged or exiled. With his brother Domitian (q.v.), who was eventually suspected of poisoning him, relations were uneasy. But Titus' death, which occurred outside Rome on 13 Sept. 81, was almost certainly due to natural causes. He was immediately deified: a generation later he was described as 'amor ac deliciae generis humani' (Suet. *Tit.* 1).

His first wife was Arrecina Tertulla, daughter of the Emperor Gaius' praetorian prefect. On her death he married Marcia Furnilla, whose father was almost certainly a senator, and who bore his only child Julia (q.v. 5); but he divorced her *c.* 64.

Suet. *Tit.* (ed. G. Mooney, 1930); Dio (in Epitome) 66. J. Crook, *AJPhil.* 1951, 162 ff.; G. Townend, *JRS* 1961, 54 ff.; M. Fortina, *L'Imperatore Tito* (1955). G. E. F. C.

**TITYUS,** a son of Earth, whom Odysseus saw in Hades, covering nine acres of ground, while two vultures tore at his liver, as a punishment for assaulting Leto (*Od.* 11. 576–81). The seat of desire is appropriately punished. He was killed by Zeus (Hyg. *Fab.* 55), Apollo (Ap. Rhod. 1. 759 ff.), Artemis (Pind. *Pyth.* 4. 90; in Euphorion, fr. 105 Powell, she was defending herself, not her mother), or Apollo and Artemis (Apollod. 1. 23). For variants in his story, which are numerous, see Waser in Roscher, s.v. H. J. R.

**TMOLUS** (*Τμῶλος*), the deity of the Lydian mountain so named. He appears, with Midas, as judge of the contest between Apollo and Pan (Ov. *Met.* 11. 156 ff.), and as a coin-figure.

**TOGA.** The toga was the formal and official civilian dress of the Roman citizen, and also his shroud. The *toga praetexta* with a purple hem was worn by curule magistrates and also by boys until they received the plain *toga uirilis* on reaching manhood. Mourners wore a *toga pulla* of dark grey wool. In early times the toga had been worn also by women, but later it was reserved for prostitutes and other *infames*.

The toga was a heavy, expensive garment of fine white wool which needed frequent cleaning. The shape of the material before it was draped is uncertain. Most probably it was semicircular (Dion. Hal. 3. 61), or more precisely a segment of a circle slightly less than a semicircle. The area no doubt varied according to the size, taste, importance, or self-importance of the wearer. Normal dimensions may have been a straight edge of *c.* 18 feet with a maximum depth of *c.* 7 feet.

The straight edge was folded lengthwise and placed on the left shoulder, with a third of its length falling in front of the wearer: the curved outer edge rested on the lower left arm. The rest of the straight edge was drawn across the back, under the right arm, and again over the left shoulder so as to hang behind. Correspondingly, the curved outer edge passed down the back to the right leg, and up again to the left arm and shoulder before falling down the back.

Sculptures show that towards the end of the Republic styles, at least for a time, became more elaborate. The straight edge was often passed over the right shoulder, and not under the right arm, which was thus enclosed as if in a sling. A curving, projecting pocket (*sinus*) could be formed in front. To facilitate this, the straight edge may have been replaced by a slightly curved one.

The toga was dignified, but difficult to drape and keep in place, certainly stuffy, and probably draughty. Several Emperors had to issue decrees so as to enforce its use on public occasions.

Quint. 11. 3. 137–42: Tert. *De Pallio* 5. L. Wilson, *The Roman Toga* (1924). D. E. E.

**TOGATA** (sc. *fabula*). Terence seems to have so fully exploited the resources of Greek New Comedy that new impetus was given to attempts to found a native comic drama, based on Italian resources (as Naevius had tried to do for tragedy with the *praetexta*). Hence the *togata* and the literary *Atellana* (q.v.). Three writers of this genre are known: Titinius, L. Afranius, and T. Quinctius Atta (died in Rome, 77 B.C.). The scenes of the plays seem to have been Italian towns (as with the *Atellana*): a title of Afranius is *Brundisinae*, of Titinius, *Ferentinatis*, *Setina*, and *Veliterna*. Roman names, both *gentilicia* and *cognomina*, occur in the fragments, and some interesting differences from *palliata* are reported: Donatus on Ter. *Eun.* 57 *concessum est in palliata poetis comicis servos dominis sapientiores fingere, quod idem in togata non fere licet*, and Quintilian (10. 1. 100) remarks on the pederastic themes in the plays of Afranius (they are more or less excluded from plays of New Comedy and *palliata*). But, like those of *Atellana*, the dramatic motifs seem often to have been derived still from Greek New Comedy (Afranius declares his debt to Menander in prol. to *Compitalia*, quoted by Macrob. *Sat.* 6. 1. 4: here he followed the prologue-technique invented by Terence), and some details can still be traced in the fragments (see Leo, op. cit. *infra*), including the use by Afranius of Menander's method of introducing a play by means of a divine creature or an abstract concept, so, e.g. Remeligo (= Goddess of Delay) or *Sapientia*. The fragments suggest that these poets made use of polymetric *cantica* and in this respect disregarded Terence and went back to the practice of Naevius, Plautus, and Caecilius.

FRAGMENTS. O. Ribbeck. F. Leo, *Gesch. d. röm. Lit.* (1913), 374 ff.; W. Beare, *The Roman Stage*³ (1964), 128 ff.                          G. W. W.

**TOILET.** Most of the aids to beauty known today were to be found in ancient times on a lady's toilet table; and both in Greece and Rome men gave much more attention to their bodies than is usual with us. The Greeks were constantly rubbing themselves with olive-oil, and the Romans under the Empire devoted much time to massage and bathing: dandies went further and would remove the hair from every part of their body with tweezers, pitch-plaster, and depilatories.

Many specimens have been found of ancient toilet implements, such as mirrors, combs, razors, scissors, curling-tongs, hair-pins, safety-pins, nail-files, and ear-picks. Mirrors were usually made of burnished metal, for though glass was known it was seldom used. Combs were of the tooth-comb pattern, with one coarse and one fine row of teeth. Razors, made of bronze, were of various shapes, the handle often beautifully engraved. Safety-pins (*fibulae*) and brooches had many forms elaborately inlaid with enamel and metal. Ear-picks—*auriscalpia*—were in general use at Rome.

Cosmetics and perfumes were freely used. Athenian wives attached importance to white cheeks, as distinguishing them from sunburned working women; they applied white lead, and also used a rouge made from orchid. Roman ladies also had a great variety of salves, unguents, and hair-dyes, kept in a toilet box with separate compartments for powders, paints, and toothpastes. Several recipes for these commodities are given by Ovid in his mock-didactic poem *De medicamine faciei*, the strangest being one for a lotion 'halcyon cream', made apparently from birds' nests and guaranteed to cure spots on the face.

Greek women usually wore their hair arranged simply in braids, with a parting in the middle, drawn into a knot behind; and the same style was frequently adopted in Rome. But under the Empire a fashion arose of raising a structure of hair on the top of the head, painfully arranged by a lady's maid. Blondes were fashionable in Rome, and brunettes could either dye their hair or use the false hair which was freely imported from Germany.

Men in early Greece and Rome wore beards and allowed the hair of the skull to grow long. From the fifth century the Greeks cut the hair of their skulls short, and from the time of Alexander they shaved their chins. The Romans followed suit in the third century B.C., but from the time of Hadrian they again wore beards.

Ov. *De medicamine faciei*. Forbes, *Stud. Anc. Technol.* iii. 24 f.                          F. A. W.

**TOLOSA,** town in Gallia Narbonensis, modern *Toulouse*, a typical river-plain site (of pre-Roman origin), which under Augustus completely superseded the important Halstatt-La Tène *oppidum* of Vieille-Toulouse. In 106 B.C. Tolosa was wantonly sacked by the consul Caepio (q.v. 1), who carried off a huge spoil. Under the Empire Tolosa possessed *ius Latii* and perhaps the title of colony (Ptolemy 2. 10: 6). Famous for literary culture, its most famous son was, however, the warrior Antonius Primus (q.v.). From 418 it was the capital of the Visigothic kingdom (*regnum Tolosanum*). Its ancient remains are scanty.

M. Labrousse, *Toulouse antique* (1970).                          C. E. S.

**TOMIS** (Τόμις, Τόμαι; Tomi; modern *Constanţa*) was a Milesian colony, perhaps as early as the sixth century. It had a trade route to the Danube across the Dobrudja, but until the third century it played a subordinate part to its neighbour Istria (q.v.). It was brought under Roman rule by M. Lucullus (72 B.C.), but continued to suffer from raids by the hinterland peoples until it was incorporated in the province of Moesia. Under Roman rule, if not before, it was the head of a league of neighbouring Greek cities. The poet Ovid, who was relegated to Tomis by Augustus, held rank there as ἀγωνοθέτης.

C. M. Danoff, *PW* Suppl. ix. 1397 ff.                          M. C.

**TORCH-RACE,** a relay race in which sacred fire was carried by competing teams from one altar to another. At Athens it formed part of the Prometheia, Hephaesteia, and Panathenaea, and was extended to other cults, as that of Pan (Hdt. 6. 105). In the festival of Bendis at Piraeus it was a horse-race (Pl. *Resp.* 328 a) but for Athenians of the fifth century this was apparently a Thracian novelty. The contest probably originated in the belief that fire through use loses its purity, and that fresh fire must be periodically fetched from the altar of a fire-god. The ritual was common to many cults in all Greece and maintained its sacral character throughout antiquity.

See articles 'Lampadedromia' in *PW* and Dar.-Sag.
F. R. W.; R. L. H.

**TORQUATUS** (1), TITUS MANLIUS (*PW* 57). Popular tradition and annalistic speculation made Manlius a striking embodiment of Roman virtue. He reputedly killed a gigantic Celt in a duel and despoiled him of his collar (*torques*), thereby winning the *cognomen* Torquatus (361 B.C.); the story is probably an aetiological myth invented to explain the surname Torquatus borne by a branch of the Manlii. His piety was displayed in saving his father from prosecution, and his stern justice in sentencing his son to death, while he was consul for the third time (340), as the son engaged the enemy against his father's orders. We may believe the accounts of Manlius' successful campaign as dictator against Caere (353), and against the Latins, whose subjugation, the main object of his policy, he secured by the battle of Trifanum (340).

P. T.

**TORQUATUS** (2), TITUS MANLIUS (*PW* 82), as consul (235 B.C.) campaigned in Sardinia and celebrated a triumph. He closed the Temple of Janus, a symbol of restored peace, on the only occasion between Numa and Augustus. Censor 231, but abdicated because *vitio creatus*. Consul II (224), he defeated the Boii, crossed the Po, and attacked the Insubres. He deprecated ransoming Roman prisoners after Cannae. Granted *imperium* in 215 he defeated a Carthaginian expeditionary force in Sardinia, celebrated games as dictator (208), and died in 203.                          H. H. S.

**TORTURE** was applied in the Roman criminal procedure at an early time, but only to slaves to make them confess when accused or to force the truth out of them as witnesses. The procedure was called *quaestio*; a slave's evidence was never *testimonium*. In Republican times the use of torture was fairly common, but the Emperors of the first two centuries A.D. tried to restrict it by admitting it only in cases of grave crime and when the delinquent was so near conviction, 'ut sola confessio seruorum deesse . . . uideatur'. (See the discussion in *Dig.* 48. 18.) From the time of Tiberius the application of torture extended to free persons (to witnesses in the second century), except the *honestiores* (q.v.). Stricter provisions were introduced with regard to some special crimes such as adultery and *crimen maiestatis*, where slaves could be examined under torture against their *domini*, though normally they were not allowed to give evidence against them. In post-classical times torture was extended to civil proceedings (*Cod. Theod.* 2. 27. 1. 2 a), and even Justinian with his distrust of witnesses maintained it, though with restriction to low-born and suspected individuals. A. B.

**TOWNS.** I. GREEK AND HELLENISTIC. Greek towns grew on a great variety of sites. Many spread around an acropolis or citadel, or on one side of it. Some occupied the top of a hill or a plateau. Maritime towns were built on peninsulas, or fanned out from a good harbour. Some important cities were the successors of Mycenaean settlements; many grew on new sites. Defensibility, commerce, and water-supply were amongst the factors which decided which of the villages of early archaic times were to grow into cities. Interesting examples of simple early towns have recently been investigated at Chios (*JHS* 1954, 163; 1955, *Arch. Rep.* 20 f.; 1956, *Arch. Rep.* 35) and Smyrna (*BSA* 1958–9, 1 ff.).

The old acropolis tended in time to become a religious centre, though still used on occasion as a fortress or refuge. Temples (q.v.) frequently occupied other dominant sites too. Small modest shrines were ubiquitous. The form of the city followed no fixed pattern. Its centre was the agora, an open space devoted to religious, political, social, and commercial life, and surrounded by shrines and public buildings. Here the assembly (see EKKLESIA) originally met; later it found a special meeting-place (see PNYX) or used the theatre. Amongst the public buildings was the Bouleuterion (see BOULE, PRYTANIS) or Council-House, which might take the form of a covered hall of moderate size, or a simple stoa. The stoa (q.v. 2) or open colonnade was a constant feature of the agora and other public places. The extensive commercial sections of the agora had a bazaar-like character.

The streets in most old towns were narrow and tortuous, with little systematic paving or drainage. Water supply depended mainly on wells and cisterns in the courtyards of the houses, and on fountain-houses in the agora and elsewhere. The houses (q.v.) had severely plain outer walls and gave little monumental character to the streets.

Increasingly from early archaic times a powerful outer wall was built, following an irregular course in search of defensible terrain. Fortified gates were placed in the line of the most important streets, and well-constructed towers were strategically inserted (see ARCHITECTURE).

The theatre (q.v.) was usually placed on a convenient slope, often at the foot of the acropolis. The gymnasia (q.v.) and the stadium (q.v.), needing plenty of space, were commonly out in the suburbs. The streets leading from the main gates were lined by cemeteries (see DEAD, DISPOSAL OF).

The foundation of numerous colonies and other new cities, often on virgin sites, gave the Greeks ample opportunity to develop more regular and systematic methods of town-planning. They adopted the rectangular or 'gridiron' system; in its Greek context this is called 'Hippodamian', after the famous fifth-century architect (*see* HIPPODAMUS), but it is increasingly clear that the use of a simple rectangular layout goes well back into archaic times (cf. *Arch. Anz.* 1964, ii. 214 ff.). Its development can be particularly associated with Ionia and especially Miletus (q.v.), but recent evidence tends to show that the method was used quite early in the West too. It was ingeniously applied, with little concession to the terrain, even on hill-slopes and ridges.

In these planned towns the streets tended to be given somewhat greater width, especially certain selected main thoroughfares, but they were still architecturally plain. Long colonnaded streets were not built till late Hellenistic times. Shrines, gymnasia, and other buildings were ingeniously incorporated, and in the process more compact and standardized forms were evolved. The stoas of the agora developed into a rectangular complex; most typically, three continuous stoas were built along three sides of the square, while an important street, with a detached stoa beyond it, occupied the fourth side. The city wall still went its own way independent of the grid.

Miletus itself, replanned with extraordinary foresight after its destruction by the Persians early in the fifth century, offers an outstanding example of the method. The excavations of Olynthus (q.v.; *see also* HOUSES) have provided a good example of the late fifth and fourth century. Priene (q.v.), replanned in the latter part of the fourth century, is a model Greek city. In the West, Agrigentum, Selinus, and Metapontum (*Rend. Linc.* 1959, 49 ff.) are noteworthy.

In the Hellenistic period the pattern was extensively and somewhat mechanically reproduced throughout the hellenized east. Dura-Europus (q.v.) is a good example. But at the same time more spectacular modes of planning were developed, notably at Pergamum (q.v.) where a series of monuments rose in terraces along a crescent-shaped ridge. Meanwhile, Athens and most of the ancient cities of Greece proper remained for the most part obstinately old-fashioned in architectural character.

R. E. W.

II. ROMAN. Roman town-planning was of mixed parentage. The dominant strain was the established Graeco-Hellenistic tradition, based on an orthogonal grid of streets and *insulae*, as already widely represented in south Italy. A secondary but powerful influence was that of military architecture, particularly in north Italy and the provinces, where so many of the new urban foundations were military colonies. Good examples of this are Aosta (2 B.C.) and Timgad (A.D. 100). If there was also an Etruscan strain, this did not come from a native Etruscan tradition (the old Etruscan cities were as formless as Rome itself) but at second-hand from Greece, through such Etruscan colonial foundations as Marzabotto (q.v.) and, presumably, Capua. Yet another formative influence was that of the land-surveyors (*agrimensores*), whence the terms *cardo* and *decumanus* for the north–south and east–west streets respectively. Compared with the earlier, Greek foundations, those of the Roman period are marked by a tendency towards more compact, centralized planning, focused upon the forum at the intersection of the two main streets; by a closer integration of street-plan and defences; and by a greater flexibility in adapting the plan to the terrain (contrast Cosa, in Etruria (273 B.C.), with Hellenistic Priene or Dura). But these are developments within a single tradition rather than major innovations. The differences between the Greek cities and those of the Roman world lay rather in the introduction of new constructional techniques, new types of building, and new amenities, such as improved water-supply and drainage, than in new principles of planning.

In Italy Pompeii, a busy market-town, and Herculaneum, a seaside residential resort, present a vivid picture of town-life still developed horizontally in the Hellenistic manner, whereas Ostia, later in date, reflects the very different conditions of Rome itself, where high land values and a developed technology (*see* ARCHITECTURE) led to streets with continuous blocks of houses three stories high. A notable Roman innovation in the cities of the eastern provinces was the use of streets flanked by monumental colonnaded streets (e.g. Antioch, Ephesus, Palmyra).

III. GENERAL. The fundamental distinction, in classical as at all other times, is not between Greek and Roman but between those cities which grew up spontaneously and unplanned, as did Athens and Rome, and those created *ex novo* on some specific historical occasion.

A. von Gerkan, *Griechische Städteanlagen* (1924); R. Martin, *L'Urbanisme dans la Grèce antique* (1956); R. E. Wycherley, *How the Greeks Built Cities*[2] (1962); F. Castagnoli, *Ippodamo di Mileto e l'urbanistica a pianta ortogonale* (1956); J. B. Ward-Perkins, *Town Planning Review* 1955; *see also* ARCHITECTURE (most of the books mentioned have chapters on town-planning). J. B. W.-P.

**TOXARIS,** a Scythian visitor to Athens, given heroic honours there after his death in gratitude for good medical advice sent by him in a dream in time of plague, Lucian, *Scythes* 1.

**TOYS** (παίγνια, *ioculi*). Specimens from children's tombs, and representations on Greek painted vases (in particular on small Attic red-figure jugs, which are surmised to have been presents to children on the feast of Choes) provide our knowledge of ancient toys, which did not differ essentially from modern ones. For the infant there were clappers and rattles (πλαταγή, *crepitaculum*), hinged surfaces of wood or revolving circles with bells or rings of metal, or in animal form with loose pebbles inside. *Crepundia* (γνωρίσματα) were miniature objects and charms hung around the infant's neck; in literature these often served to identify abandoned or kidnapped children. Bells (κώδων, *tintinnabulum*) served the double purpose of amusement and of averting the evil eye. For a more advanced age the doll of rag, bone, wood, or clay was the customary plaything; the limbs were often movable (νευρόσπαστα). Doll's house furniture, chairs, couches, toilet and kitchen utensils, were used as toys as well as for votive offerings; it was customary for girls on marriage and for boys on arrival at puberty to dedicate their playthings to deities. Animals, chariots and horses in wood or clay, go-carts, and whip-tops are represented in museums, while the use of the ball (σφαῖρα, *pila*) and hoop (τροχός, *trochus*) is illustrated on vase-paintings, as are the swing and see-saw. Regular games were played with knucklebones (ἀστράγαλος, *talus*), dice (κύβος, *tessara*), and other pieces.

Anita E. Klein, *Child Life in Greek Art* (U.S.A. 1932); *British Museum Guide to the Exhibition illustrating Greek and Roman Life*, s.v. 'Toys'; L. Becq de Fouquières, *Les Jeux des anciens* (1873). F. N. P.

**TRABEA,** QUINTUS, Latin writer of *comoediae palliatae*, contemporary with Caecilius; could stir the emotions, says Varro. Two fragments in O. Ribbeck, *CRF*[2] 31 (3rd ed. Teubner, 1897).

**TRAGEDY,** GREEK (Introductory). At the beginning of the fifth century B.C. tragedy at Athens formed part of the Great Dionysia, the spring festival of Dionysus Eleuthereus, probably organized some decades earlier by Pisistratus and reorganized towards the turn of the century by Cleisthenes. Three poets competed, each presenting three tragedies and one satyric play. In the former, the actors—originally one only, but Aeschylus introduced

a second very early in the century—and the chorus all presented human beings or divine beings in human form; in the latter the chorus were disguised as satyrs, mainly human in form but with characteristics of horses and goats and wearing the phallus, and the play presented parts of ancient legend which were grotesque in themselves or could easily be made so. Contests of dithyrambs, danced by fifty singers in circular formation (whereas the tragic chorus was arranged in a rectangle), were performed at the festival before the end of the century; the addition of the satyric plays to the tragedies probably took place about 500 B.C.

**2.** The scenes of a tragedy consisted of set speeches or dialogue as might be required; in Aeschylus dialogue is mostly between an actor and the chorus leader and, even in some of his later plays, there is little conversation between two actors. The scenes are separated by choral odes of considerable length and of high excellence as lyric poetry. This suggests that tragedy sprang from a performance which was entirely lyric, and in fact the introduction of a single actor, delivering a prologue and set speeches, is attributed, on what seems to be good authority, to Thespis (q.v.), who gave a performance at Athens about 534 B.C. and probably began the use of the iambic trimeter metre for such speeches, though the trochaic tetrameter was never entirely abandoned for dialogue. The actors and chorus in tragedy wore masks (the actor's mask is credited to Thespis, but it is generally believed that masks were a part of Dionysiac ritual from early times), and must have had some kind of σκηνή or tent to change in. The number of the chorus employed by Thespis and by Aeschylus in his early days is disputed; some scholars think that it was fifty, as in the dithyramb (Poll. 4. 110), but now that the *Supplices* with its chorus representing Danaus' fifty daughters is no longer believed to be an early play, it becomes harder to accept that the chorus numbered fifty, and the argument is weakened; others, who doubt the derivation of tragedy from dithyramb, point to the fact that the chorus in other plays consisted of twelve, or later, fifteen singers.

**3.** The attempt to trace back the development of tragedy before the fifth century is beset with uncertainties at every point. Phrynichus, indeed, a slightly senior contemporary of Aeschylus, seems to have written plays predominantly lyric and not unlike the early plays of Aeschylus himself. But of Thespis nothing more is certainly known than what has been stated above, though one account brings him to Athens from Icaria (in Attica), where his performances may have been connected with the autumn festival of the vintage; and some scholars, relying upon late and doubtful notices, think that these or some similar performances may have been a grotesque affair, which, developing in different directions, gave rise to both tragedy and comedy. No ancient authority attributes satyric plays or satyr-choruses to Thespis. We hear (Poll. 4. 123) of a time 'before Thespis' when 'someone' got up on a table and answered the chorus, and Thespis may have turned this 'someone' into a regular actor, impersonating a character. A late notice (*Suda*, s.v. Ἀρίων) ascribes to Arion of Corinth (about 600 B.C.) the invention of the τραγικὸς τρόπος, i.e. probably the style or mode in music which afterwards belonged to tragedy, and a statement (Joannes Diaconus *in Hermogenem*) attributed to Solon's elegies says that Arion composed the first δρᾶμα τῆς τραγῳδίας, though these cannot be Solon's actual words. Further, Herodotus (5. 67) records that at Sicyon the τραγικοὶ χοροί commemorating the sufferings of the hero Adrastus were transferred by the tyrant Cleisthenes to the worship of Dionysus, and very late sources (*Suda*, s.v. Ἀρίων and οὐδὲν πρὸς τὸν Διόνυσον) mention a 'tragic poet' Epigenes of Sicyon, who was upbraided for introducing into the worship of Dionysus themes which had nothing to do with the god. It may have been some such originally Dorian performance into which Thespis imported an actor. Some scholars believe that the story of Thespis' performances in Icaria was a late invention, intended to deprive the Dorians of the credit for an Athenian institution. The connexion of early tragic lyrics with Dorian people is supported by language. The language of tragedy is, in its main substance, Attic, but not only is there a considerable infusion of Epic and Ionic forms (due to a tradition from days when 'Homer' in a broad sense was the only literature), but in the lyric portions the use of ᾱ for η is probably Doric in origin. A considerable number of Doric words and forms is also to be found in the iambic, as well as in the lyric, portions of tragedy. The explanations which treat these forms as old Attic are less probable (see Pickard-Cambridge–Webster, *Dithyramb²*, 111, and refs. there given). Such forms (as well as the Ionic) doubtless came naturally to a poet who was moved to express himself in language possessing greater distinction than ordinary speech. The theory of the origin of tragedy which is probably still most popular is based mainly on the literal acceptance of statements made by Aristotle (*Poet.* 3–5). According to this theory, the original lyric performance was identical with dithyramb, and its chorus was composed of satyrs, exhibiting some of the physical characteristics of goats (τράγοι). The actor was developed out of the leader (ἐξάρχων) of the dithyramb (cf. Archil. fr. 77 D.); the abandonment of the grotesque language and dancing of the satyrs coincided with the introduction of the iambic trimeter, a more serious metre than the trochaic tetrameter, and the plots, originally short, became longer. The *Suda*'s statement that Pratinas of Phlius (about 500 B.C.) was the first to compose satyric plays is explained away by supposing that the original satyr-plays of tragedies (there being at first *ex hypothesi* no difference) had been drifting too far from Dionysus and subjects connected with him, and that what Pratinas really did was to reintroduce from Phlius the old type of satyric play, which now or shortly afterwards became a pendant to three non-satyric tragedies. (The date at which tragedy on this view discarded the satyric dress for its chorus is not specified.)

**4.** In support of this theory are usually adduced the names τραγῳδία and τραγῳδοί (goat-singers), explained as referring to the goat-like satyrs, and transferred, it is supposed, to the horse-tailed satyrs of Attica; and the fact that the *Suda* ascribes to Arion the composition of literary dithyrambs and the production of satyrs speaking verse, as well as the invention of the τραγικὸς τρόπος, it being assumed that in all three points one and the same type of composition is referred to—an assumption for which there seems to be no ground. It is also the fact that in the fifth century satyric plays were always the work of the same composers as tragedies, and were generally like tragedies in structure.

**5.** But this theory presents great difficulties. There is no clear evidence that a dithyramb was ever danced in satyr-costume (see Webster in Pickard-Cambridge, op. cit. 34, 96), nor is there any trace of dramatic elements in dithyramb before Bacchylides (well on into the fifth century); the dithyrambic chorus was circular, the tragic rectangular. The *Suda*'s notice about Pratinas is more naturally interpreted to mean that he introduced satyric plays for the first time into a festival of non-satyric tragedies; the names 'dithyramb' and 'tragedy' or 'tragic chorus' are never interchangeable in the Classical Period, and Arion's 'tragic' song and the tragic choruses of Sicyon were probably quite distinct from dithyramb; the word τραγῳδοί, 'goat-singers', may mean, not singers in goat-costume (a meaning inappropriate to the mainly equine satyrs of Attica), but singers competing for the

goat as a prize (such as Thespis received), or at the sacrifice of a goat (as perhaps at Icaria, though the evidence is not very satisfactory). Possibly, therefore, Aristotle was theorizing, inferring that the more crude and primitive satyr-drama must have preceded the finer tragedy, and that both might have sprung from the dithyramb, which had come by its own day to include dramatic elements, and which was also known once to have had more riotous forms than later, so that it would not be absurd to connect it with satyr-play. It is difficult to imagine that the noble seriousness of tragedy can have grown so quickly, if at all, out of the ribald play of satyrs. It is far from certain that Aristotle possessed reliable evidence from any period before the late sixth century. On the other hand, it is strange if he invented a development of tragedy which fits so ill with the definition of tragedy in ch. 6 of the *Poetics* as fundamentally serious.

**6.** If it is assumed that Aristotle was guessing and that his account has no authority, then we seem to be left with the following probabilities: (1) The conditions of performance in the precinct of Dionysus at Athens and the intimate association of tragedy with the unquestionably Dionysiac satyr-play confirm the connexion between tragedy and the cult of Dionysus. It may well be relevant that Dionysus was peculiar among Greek gods in taking possession of his worshippers and that the masked actor surrenders his own personality. (2) Since the lyrical element is increasingly dominant as we trace the development of tragedy back towards its source, there is no reason to doubt that it arose, at least in part, from a purely lyric performance and that Thespis introduced the speaking actor. The τραγικὸς τρόπος may have been connected with the dithyramb, and Arion may have been concerned in the development of both. (3) The Dionysiac element is conspicuously lacking in the subject-matter of tragedy, which, like the τραγικὸς χορός at Sicyon, was about mythical heroes. So it would make sense if a non-choral mummery in honour of the Attic Dionysus of Eleutherae were combined with 'tragic' choruses of Peloponnesian origin, which, in part at least, were or had been non-Dionysiac, to form tragedy. But the traces of any Attic cult of the required nature are faint indeed. (For a full presentation and discussion of the evidence and of the main theories see Pickard-Cambridge–Webster, *Dithyramb²*.)

**7.** The history of tragedy in the fifth century will mainly be found in the articles on Aeschylus, Sophocles, and Euripides (*see also* AGATHON, ION, IOPHON). The present article deals mainly with some general aspects of tragedy, its subjects, form, production, etc.

**8.** Tragedy in Greece was a religious ceremony in the sense that it formed part of the festivals of Dionysus, and that it dealt with the myths which were the medium of early religious thought; but it was not an act of worship in the same way as was dithyramb, in which the chorus represented the Athenian people itself paying honour to the god, and its members remained in their own persons. The tragic chorus was always dramatic and 'in character', and from the first the action and the lyrics had most commonly no reference to Dionysus, but presented in dramatic form themes chosen freely from the whole range of epic story and floating legend, gradually settling down, as Aristotle says (*Poet.* 14) to a narrower range (largely non-Dionysiac) as it was found that the legends of certain houses furnished better material than others for dramatic treatment. If the chorus sings an ode to Dionysus, it is because the dramatic situation suggests it (as in Sophocles, *Ant.* 1115), not as an Athenian act of worship. But the tragedy of the three great poets and their contemporaries was always religious, until the closing years of the fifth century, in the sense that the interest was not simply in the action as an exciting series of events, nor simply in the study of striking characters (though both these interests were strong), but in the meaning of the action as exemplifying the relation of man to the powers controlling the universe, and the relation of these powers to his destiny. In the choral odes, and implicitly in the action, the character of these ultimate powers is set forth, and even if (as often with Euripides) the conclusion drawn or to be inferred is a sceptical one, the spectator or reader is usually in contact with the ultimate problems of human life and world-order. (The articles on the three great tragedians will illustrate this.) At the same time, tragedy shows a growing interest in the character of human beings as such. The personages of Aeschylus, though they include some very striking individuals, tend to be types or embodiments of a principle; Sophocles devotes himself mostly to displaying the effect upon certain noble and well-marked, but not abnormal, characters, of some terrible crisis or strain; the characters of Euripides are less raised above ordinary human life; his plays are often studies in distracted or abnormal mentality; he specializes and analyses with a minuteness entirely foreign to Aeschylus and almost absent from the plays of Sophocles.

**9.** With the growing interest in individual character went an increasing attention to art. Aeschylus is never entirely free from the crudities of primitive drama; in Sophocles we find the perfectly balanced and controlled use of all the resources of tragedy; in Euripides an indulgence, highly skilful, but in the judgement of many critics excessive, in more sensational effects both in action and in language. The importance of the actor's art grew correspondingly, until in the fourth century Aristotle (*Rhet.* 3. 1 (1403$^b$33)) could say that the actors now counted for more than the poets. Where attention is concentrated on the performer there is less attention to the message; and whereas Aeschylus was a teacher and a prophet, and Sophocles always maintained the highest religious and moral earnestness, and Euripides was taken so seriously as to provoke strong antagonism, there is no reason to suppose that tragedy was so taken in the fourth century. It was simply a form of art, and perhaps not a particularly successful one; and the chorus, which had embodied the essence of the poet's teaching a century before, came to be, very often, only a singer of interludes. Aristotle does not allude to the religious interest of tragedy at all.

**10.** The poets were free to vary the legends which they found current, for the sake either of their moral or of dramatic art. Aeschylus made some modifications for the sake of religious truth; Euripides, for whom the legends had little religious value and were merely human inventions, himself invents freely; but it was Agathon who first composed a tragedy in which both characters and plot were entirely invented (Arist. *Poet.* 9). Very rarely a subject might be taken from contemporary or recent history: Phrynichus' *Phoenissae* and *Taking of Miletus*, Aeschylus' *Persae*, Theodectes' *Mausolus*, and Moschion's *Men of Pherae* are instances.

**11.** The poets might also indicate political views, though only to a subordinate extent. In Sophocles, indeed, there is little discernible allusion to contemporary issues, and he keeps wholly within the limits of his heroic plot. But in Aeschylus the contemporary reference and the moral are often unmistakable, while Euripides sometimes offers political discourses out of all proportion to their dramatic appropriateness, and alludes frequently to events and questions of his own day. Indeed, hatred of Sparta sometimes leads him to insert passages suggested as much by the contemporary as by the dramatic situation. That in all three poets there should be passages in praise of Athens is natural enough, and both Aeschylus and Euripides like to trace back to a legendary source the beginnings of some honoured institution, religious or political. The poets tend also to modify in the direction

of constitutional monarchy or democracy the legendary traditions of absolute power.

**12.** The presentation of tragedies at the Great Dionysia in groups of three, followed by a satyric play, was regular throughout the fifth century, though the satyric play might be replaced by a play which, if not a tragedy, was at least of a serious kind, like the *Alcestis* of Euripides, few of whose satyric plays survived till the Alexandrian age. From about the middle of the fourth century the satyric play dropped out, except for the performance of a single one at the beginning of each festival. (This is first recorded for 341 B.C. (*IG* ii². 2320).) Aeschylus often presented groups of plays, trilogies or tetralogies, connected in subject; the practice was probably his invention and was little followed by other poets, but Polyphradmon composed a Λυκούργεια, dramatizing the story of Lycurgus, Sophocles (possibly, but not certainly) a Τηλέφεια, Philocles a Πανδιονίς, and Meletus an Οἰδιπόδεια; and now and then there seems to have been a looser connexion of subject between a group of plays exhibited by Euripides, as, for instance, between the *Alexander*, *Palamedes*, and *Troades* in 415, and between the *Chrysippus*, *Oenomaus*, and *Phoenissae* about 409. It was only occasionally that the satyric play presented a lighter version of part of the same story as the preceding trilogy, as did the *Sphinx*, *Lycurgus*, and *Amymone* of Aeschylus.

**13.** The addition of an actor to the original chorus was attributed to Thespis (see above), and Aristotle in his brief summary (*Poet.* 4) says that Aeschylus increased the number of actors to two, diminished the part taken by the chorus, and made the dialogue predominant; Sophocles introduced a third actor and scene-painting. (Both these innovations were adopted by Aeschylus in his latest plays.) In the *Oedipus Coloneus*, written in his last years, Sophocles probably required four actors. As the importance of the actor's part increased, tragedy passed from oratorio into drama, but not completely; for the lyric element long remained an essential part, and there was never a complete presentation of the action. The critical or fatal act took place, with the rarest exceptions, off the scene or even outside the play; the dialogue and the speeches of the actors lead up to it or develop its consequences, but on the scene itself there is very little action. Exceptions will be found at the end of Aesch. *Agam.*, and in the *Supplices* and *Eumenides*; in Soph. *OC*, and Eur. *Andr.* and *Heraclidae*. Obviously the interplay of characters and motives was impossible until there were more actors than one, and on this side of dramatic art Aeschylus himself only gradually acquired the consummate skill which he shows in the *Oresteia*. The single actor could do little more than narrate or ask and answer questions. (The name ὑποκριτής by which he was called probably means interpreter (of the situation to the chorus), though some prefer 'answerer', which hardly fits the speaker of the prologue.)

**14.** In Aeschylus the chorus never loses its importance as the vehicle of his most profound reflection and the lessons which he draws from the action; when not itself the leading personage (as in the *Supplices* and *Eumenides*) it is always closely connected with the hero and his fortunes, and may take a not unimportant share in the development of the action. In Sophocles, though it takes no part in the action, it is intimately interested in it and usually attached closely to one of the leading personages, though the choral odes may lack some of the religious intensity of those of Aeschylus, and their reflections may be rather those of a wise and right-minded spectator, not deficient in relevance or appropriateness. In some plays of Euripides, on the other hand, the chorus seem to be on the spot accidentally and may even be in the way; they may be detached from the hero and the action, and their chants may at times seem to be almost callously irrelevant; but in the *Ion* the chorus intervenes decisively. Neither in Sophocles nor in Euripides have the choral odes the magnitude which they regularly display (except in the *Prometheus*) in Aeschylus. With Agathon (according to Arist. *Poet.* 18) the chorus is said to have been reduced to the singing of interludes unconnected with the play, and this may often have happened in the fourth century. The entry of the chorus is very commonly made to the accompaniment of marching anapaests, and these with the lyric ode which follows when the chorus is in position for dancing (or the lyric or semi-lyric passage substituted for it) form the *parodos* or entrance-song. The succeeding choral odes are termed *stasima*; but there is a form of lyric dialogue between the chorus and a principal actor, the κομμός, which often takes the place of a *stasimon* and probably reproduces a traditional form of lamentation such as is recorded in Homer (e.g. *Il.* 18. 49 ff., 24. 720 ff.), though it is not, in tragedy, confined to lamentations. The parodos is regularly preceded (except in two plays of Aeschylus) by a speech or a scene forming a prologue, and after the parodos the normal structure may be said to be a regular alternation of *epeisodia* or Acts (in which the actors take the main part, though the chorus-leader may join in dialogue or make brief comments on the speeches) and *stasima*. The number of *epeisodia* and *stasima* may be as small as three of each or as many as five or six, according to the view taken of the composition of the particular play. But the limits of variation in this typical structure are very wide. In Aeschylus in particular there are frequently scenes which are mainly lyric, with brief speeches by an actor or snatches of dialogue between the lyrics, the whole sometimes forming a more or less (though not completely) symmetrical structure of the type known as epirrhematic (lyrics and *epirrhemata* of speech or dialogue), and in most plays of Sophocles and several of Euripides there are similar reminiscences of what may have been an original epirrhematic form. This form is also not rare in the κομμός. Again, an *epeisodion* (particularly if long) may be broken up by the insertion of lyrics or anapaests, or (more rarely) the strophe and antistrophe of a choral ode may be separated and interlaced with the parts of an *epeisodion*. The structure of some plays of Euripides (e.g. the *Hippolytus*, *Hercules Furens*, and *Troades*) is in parts very free, though the normal alternation of *epeisodia* and *stasima* is always observed in considerable parts of the play. Rarely in Aeschylus or Sophocles, much more commonly in Euripides, an anapaestic or lyric monody by one of the actors may be introduced, and in such monodies (and more rarely in choral lyrics), the regular antistrophic form of composition (in strophe and antistrophe, with or without epode) may be abandoned for free lyrics (μέλος ἀπολελυμένον) in which the music as well as the words was highly emotional (*see* EURIPIDES). Scholars differ as to the extent to which the choral lyrics written continuously in our manuscripts were divided up, particularly at moments of excitement or uncertainty, between several members of the chorus; but there was certainly the possibility of expressing conflicting views through the two halves of the chorus. In some plays there was a secondary chorus (for instance in the *Supplices* and *Eumenides* of Aeschylus, the *Hippolytus* of Euripides and some lost plays), which might play a not unimportant part (see Lammers, *Die Doppel- und Halb-Chöre in der antiken Tragödie*, 1931). The beginning and end of an *epeisodion*, or the entrance of a character, were often marked, particularly in Aeschylus, by a passage in anapaestic dimeters. The play concluded with a final scene (*exodos*) very variable in structure; but there was never a great choral finale, like that of a modern oratorio; the chorus at most utter a few quiet words.

**15.** It is certain that the several metres used by the poets possessed different emotional values, though they can no longer be fully appreciated. In dialogue the trochaic tetrameter usually implies greater excitement than the iambic trimeter in which dialogue and set speeches are mainly composed. The anapaestic dimeter is used either in marching (and in similar movements at the beginning and end of a scene), or, with less strict metrical rules, in lamentation; in the latter case, and possibly in the former, the words were sung. Hexameter passages are very rare; there is a remarkable lament in elegiacs in Euripides' *Andromache*. Of purely lyric metres, the dochmiac expresses the greatest emotional excitement or distress.

**16.** The plot of an ancient tragedy, partly because it was shorter, displays far less variety than a play of Shakespeare, and Aristotle regards as the ideal plot one in which each step arises out of what precedes it as its necessary or probable consequence, and everything irrelevant to the main causal sequence is excluded, though the poet's skill is shown in so arranging the sequence that pity, fear, and amazement are aroused in the highest degree. So he prefers plots in which the crisis is a περιπέτεια, in which the action brings about just the reverse of what the agent expects, or an ἀναγνωρισμός, the revelation at the critical moment of a close relationship, unsuspected until some dreadful deed was done or about to be done, or events had reached an impasse. (Many forms of recognition are classified in *Poetics* 16.) Best of all is a plot in which περιπέτεια and ἀναγνωρισμός are combined. It is noteworthy that Aeschylus, whom Aristotle almost leaves out of account, seems to have made little use of either.

**17.** The fact that the chorus was normally present throughout the action imposed certain conditions upon tragedy from which the modern dramatist is free. The action must take place out of doors, and change of place is very rare, though it occurs, e.g., in Aeschylus' *Eumenides* and Sophocles' *Ajax*, the chorus having been sent away for sufficient reasons; interiors of houses, otherwise invisible, may be displayed by means of the ἐκκύκλημα or the throwing open of doors. It might be expected that the constant presence of the chorus would also require that the action should be continuous in time; but in fact this so-called 'Unity of Time' was not strictly observed. Aristotle (*Poet.* 5) notes that it was the usual practice to represent (in a play lasting up to 3 hours) events which could fall within about 24 hours, so that considerable intervals of time might be supposed to elapse during a choral ode, and if usually the intervals were not long enough to cause any trouble with audiences accustomed to the convention, they might if required be much longer, as in Aeschylus' *Agamemnon* and *Eumenides*; there is great compression of the events happening off the stage in Sophocles' *Trachiniae*, Euripides' *Andromache* and *Supplices*, and in some other plays; the choral ode separated the scenes as effectively as a modern curtain, and less abruptly. In a number of plays, all, of course, acted in broad daylight, the action is supposed to take place at early dawn or even at night. There is no reason to suppose that a Greek audience was more troubled by this than an Elizabethan.

**18.** Tragedy in Athens was probably performed at first in a circular orchestra in the precinct of Dionysus with no fixed background, except possibly the tent or shelter in which the actors dressed. In the earliest plays of Aeschylus all the scenery that is needed is a raised structure on the far side of the orchestra from the audience, to serve in the *Persae* as the Tomb of Darius; in the *Septem* as an altar, with statues of gods; in the *Supplices* as a stepped altar, with the statues of a number of gods grouped round behind it; and in all three plays the plain background (probably the side of the actors' σκηνή) could represent whatever the play required—the Persian council chamber (*Pers.* 140–1), possibly the palace of Eteocles (or any building on the Theban acropolis) in the *Septem*, the wall of Artemis' sacred precinct (*Supp.* 144–6). There can have been no raised stage, as is shown by the movements of the chorus, and the orchestra must have been large enough to accommodate considerable crowds. It is probable, but not certain, that a few stones still remain to mark the position of this early orchestra. By the date of the *Oresteia* Aeschylus had evidently adopted the background representing a palace or temple-front with a practicable roof, and this remained the normal setting of tragedy to the end of the classical period. In the *Ajax* of Sophocles the background represents the tent of Ajax, though there are difficult scenic problems connected with the play; special scenery must have been arranged for the *Philoctetes* and *Oedipus Coloneus*, Sophocles' two last plays, and stagecraft had doubtless developed considerably by the end of the century. In the satyric *Ichneutae* a very simply decorated background may have represented the χλωρὸς ὑλώδης πάγος, with the entrance to Cyllene's Cave, and the *Cyclops* of Euripides, with the cave of Polyphemus, may have been somewhat similarly staged. Possibly there was a satyr-play set which was used also for tragedies of which the scene was the country. The normal façade suffices for most plays of Euripides, with additions or modifications when required, e.g. in the *Electra*, in which the front is that of a peasant's cottage, and in the *Andromache*, in which the shrine of Thetis as well as the palace of Neoptolemus was required. In four plays the scene was laid before a temple (*Heraclidae, Supplices, Ion, Iphigenia in Tauris*), in front of which in the *Heraclidae* must have been a large stepped altar, while the *Iphigenia* and probably the *Ion* need a portico. In other plays the background consists of one or more tents.

It is generally agreed that there was no high stage until after the great period of Greek Tragedy was ended. The action frequently requires that there shall be easy contact between players and chorus, and none of the remains suggest foundations for a stone platform at this date. On the other hand, a low wooden stage would present no obstacle to movement and would leave no visible remains. The stage building could hardly have risen d'rect from the level of the orchestra, and we may suppose one or more steps of which the top level must have been large enough to take the ἐκκύκλημα, and it may have been extended to cover an appreciable area in front of the back-scene. In the fourth century and subsequently theatres were constructed in many parts of Greece and Asia Minor, and the loftier stage may have been introduced in different places at different times, but probably not before the second century B.C.

**19.** The Athenian poets made use of various somewhat crude mechanical devices, the μηχανή to display actors (usually gods) in the air, the ἐκκύκλημα to reveal the interior of a house or temple, and others; it is often impossible to tell whether a deity was hoisted in on the μηχανή or stood on the θεολογεῖον, a high platform on or near the roof. Probably Aeschylus experimented freely; Sophocles used the μηχανή little if at all; Euripides certainly used the μηχανή or θεολογεῖον in many plays, though perhaps he employed the ἐκκύκλημα less often than is sometimes supposed.

**20.** *Tragedy at the City Dionysia.* Immediately after his election soon after midsummer the Archon (Eponymus) appointed the three *choregoi* for the tragic poets (*see* CHOREGIA); it is not known when he 'gave a chorus' to the three poets whom he selected. It is inferred from Plato (*Leg.* 817 d) that the aspiring poets read their plays to the Archon, who on one occasion refused a chorus to

Sophocles (Cratinus, fr. 15). The actor was originally the poet himself; when a second actor was introduced the poet supplied him and, if he did not perform himself, the protagonist as well. The next development was that the State supplied a protagonist to each poet, and the protagonist supplied the subordinate actors. This may have coincided with the introduction of prizes for actors in 449 B.C. Finally, in the mid fourth century the acting talent was shared equally and each protagonist performed in one tragedy of each poet.

The festival took the form of a contest with prizes, and great pains were taken to ensure a fair verdict. Names of judges from each of the ten tribes were sealed in an urn and one name drawn for each tribe on the day of the contest. At the end the judges each produced an order of merit, but only five of the lists were used to determine the verdict (Isoc. 17. 33–34, Lys. 4. 3). According to Plato the decisions of the judges were determined mainly by the applause (*Leg.* 659 a, 700 c). The victorious poet was crowned with a wreath of ivy, but there were probably money prizes as well. At a dithyrambic contest at the Piraeus established in the fourth century the prizes were 10, 8, and 6 minae.

**21.** *Tragedy at the Lenaea and Rural Dionysia.* The arrangements at the Lenaea were similar except that the (Archon) Basileus was in charge, and metics could take part in the performance. Tragedy was introduced *c.* 432; in 419 and 418 two poets competed, each with two tragedies (no satyric play) (*IG* ii². 2319); an Agathon won the victory in 416 (Ath. 5. 217 a). There are many records of Lenaean tragedy for the fourth century (*IG* ii². 2325; Diod. Sic. 15. 74; Plut. *X Orat.* 839 d) and among the victors named are Dionysius of Syracuse, Aphareus, Theodectes, and Astydamas. At the Rural Dionysia there were frequent performances of tragedy, which may have helped to familiarize the inhabitants of Attica with the great masterpieces. The festivals at the Piraeus and at Salamis seem to have been of special importance. We hear also of festivals at Collytus, Eleusis, and Icaria, and an inscription from Aixone records the exhibition of tragedies (including Sophocles' Τηλέφεια) and comedies there (see A. W. Pickard-Cambridge, *Dramatic Festivals of Athens²*, 45 ff., and Powell and Barber, *New Chapters* iii. 69 ff.).

**22.** *Later Tragedy.* In the century after his death the influence of Euripides on the drama was probably stronger than it was in his lifetime, and a certain inferiority of contemporary writers to the great three of the fifth century seems to have been acknowledged: old plays were sometimes performed (*IG* ii². 2318, Wilhelm, 23), and from about 341 B.C. one such play was regularly exhibited at the beginning of the festival after the single satyric play (*IG* ii². 2320). Dramatic festivals now came to be held all over the Greek world and theatres sprang up everywhere, though we have little evidence as to the plays presented. Aeschines acted in the *Oenomaus* and *Antigone* of Sophocles, which Demosthenes (18. 180, 19. 246) speaks of as often exhibited. The extant *Rhesus*, ascribed to Euripides, is possibly a fourth-century play, in which some of the characteristic idioms of all three of the great tragedians are imitated; but if not strong in character-drawing, it is a good acting play with an impressive final scene. The century was more famous for great actors than great poets (see above); but the reputation of Theodectes, Astydamas, and others must have had some foundation. Apart from the historical plays mentioned above, mythological subjects unknown to the fifth century were sometimes chosen, such as the stories of Adonis and of Leda. There may have been experiments in form, such as the *Centaur* of Chaeremon (q.v.), and Chaeremon and others either wrote to be read, not acted, or at least are regarded by Aristotle as better fitted for reading (ἀναγνωστικοί), being characterized by a vivid descriptive style (γραφικὴ λέξις, as opposed to ἀγωνιστική) (Arist. *Rh.* 3. 12 (1413ᵇ13)). The fact that several of the poets of the century were rhetoricians as well as (or more than) poets may be connected with this. In the third century, when Alexandria was the chief literary centre of the world, we hear of the *Pleiad* of seven tragic poets at the court of Ptolemy Philadelphus (285–247 B.C.); five of these were Homerus, Lycophron (2), Philicus, Sositheus, and Alexander (8) Aetolus (qq.v.); for the remaining two places various names are given. Over 60 names of tragic poets of the Hellenistic period are preserved; the titles of their plays suggest that they often took subjects seldom, if at all, treated in the classical period.

**23.** In the fourth and third centuries satyric plays were sometimes composed which were more like comedies in their topical and personal allusions. (*See* PYTHON, LYCOPHRON 2, SOSITHEUS.) There seems to have been some revival of this form of composition under the influence of Sositheus, and it did not die out entirely, at least outside Athens, before the Christian era.

**24.** It appears that new tragedies were occasionally composed down to the second century A.D., but not later (see Haigh, *Tragic Drama*, 444).

GENERAL. A. E. Haigh, *Tragic Drama of the Greeks* (1896); G. Norwood, *Greek Tragedy⁴* (1948); M. Pohlenz, *Die griechische Tragödie* (1954); A. Lesky, *Die griechische Tragödie²* (1958; Eng. transl. 1965); U. von Wilamowitz-Moellendorff, *Einleitung in die griechische Tragödie* (1907); Pickard-Cambridge–Webster, *Dithyramb²*; H. D. F. Kitto, *Greek Tragedy* (1961); D. W. Lucas, *The Greek Tragic Poets²* (1959); C. del Grande, *ΤΡΑΓΩΔΙΑ²* (1962).

ESSAYS, SPECIAL ASPECTS, ETC. E. Petersen, *Die attische Tragödie als Bild- und Bühnen-Kunst* (1915); W. Schadewaldt, *Monolog und Selbstgespräch* (1926); W. Kranz, *Stasimon* (1933); J. Jones, *On Aristotle and Greek Tragedy* (1962).

GREEK TRAGEDY AND GREEK ART. J. H. Huddilston, *Greek Tragedy in the Light of Vase-paintings* (1898) and *The Attitude of the Greek Tragedians towards Art* (1898); L. Séchan, *Études sur la Tragédie grecque* (1926); T. B. L. Webster, *Greek Art and Literature* (1939); F. Brommer, *Satyrspiele* (1959).

THEATRE, PERFORMANCE, ETC. Wilhelm, *Urkunden*; R. C. Flickinger, *The Greek Theater and its Drama²* (U.S.A. 1936); M. Bieber, *Die Denkmäler zum Theaterwesen im Altertum* (1920) and *The History of the Greek and Roman Theater* (1939); H. Bulle, *Untersuchungen an griechischen Theatern* (1928); E. R. Fiechter, *Das Dionysios-Theater in Athen* (1935–6); A. W. Pickard-Cambridge, *The Theatre of Dionysius in Athens* (1946); *The Dramatic Festivals of Athens²* (1968); T. B. L. Webster, *Greek Theatre Production* (1956).

BIBLIOGRAPHY. T. B. L. Webster in *Fifty Years of Classical Scholarship²* (ed. Platnauer, 1968); A. Lesky, *Die tragische Dichtung der Hellenen* (1964). A. W. P.-C.; D. W. L.

**TRAGICOCOMOEDIA** (τραγικοκωμῳδία), a play blending tragic and comic elements (Plaut. *Amph.* 50–63).

**TRAJAN** (MARCUS ULPIUS TRAIANUS), Roman Emperor A.D. 98–117, was son of M. Ulpius (q.v.) Traianus and a Spanish mother. Born at Italica in Baetica in 53 (less probably 56), he served his vigintivirate *c.* 70, and spent the next ten years as military tribune, accompanying his father to Syria *c.* 75; he was subsequently quaestor and (before 86) praetor. During a legionary command in Spain, he was called to counter the revolt of Saturninus (q.v. 3) in Upper Germany *c.* 88; he was *cos. I ord.* in 91. Governor of Upper Germany in 97, he there learned of his adoption by Nerva (q.v. 1). The choice reflected Nerva's need to placate the Praetorians and legions. Trajan was Spanish born, his family was 'new'; he had seen little of Rome; and Nerva had collateral kinsmen. But Trajan was an experienced soldier, respected but popular as a general, and probably possessing influence at Rome (*see* SURA).

After Nerva's death on 27 or 28 Jan. 98, Trajan, *cos. II ord.* with him since 1 Jan., was unwilling to hasten to Rome or to stress his Nervan connexion, which he honoured but never emphasized. He preferred to inspect and organize the Rhine and Danube frontiers. This, with his discharge or execution of the mutinous Praetorians (Dio. 68. 5. 4; *see* NERVA 1), and his halving of the normal donative, showed his capacity to deal firmly with the troops. Senatorial privileges were at once confirmed. Early in 99 he returned to Rome, amid general welcome, and in 100 held his third consulship (refused in 99; others in 101, 103, 112). Pliny's (q.v. 2) *Panegyric*, delivered in that year, elaborated on his excellent character. Popular with the army, affable to senators, protector of the people, he was *princeps*, not *dominus*; a natural leader, he did not abuse his powers. Personally modest and simple like his wife Plotina (q.v.), he nevertheless insisted on traditional forms.

His social and financial policy, however, was the reverse of reactionary. *Congiaria* (presumably of 75 *denarii* a head) were given in 99 and 102. Free distributions of corn continued, with more recipients, and the corn supply received special attention. The system of *alimenta* (q.v.) was probably initiated by him rather than by Nerva (q.v. 1); accession-gifts were remitted; the scope of the inheritance tax was narrowed; provincial burdens were lightened. There was an ever-increasing programme of public works; at first mainly repairs, supervision, and sundry road-building, but after 107 new building increased; this (with the vast *congiarium* paid in 107 of 500 *denarii* a head) was doubtless financed by the treasure won in the Second Dacian War (5 million pounds of gold and twice as much of silver; the figures are not easily disproved). New baths, the Aqua Traiana, the Naumachia, the magnificent Forum Traiani (q.v.), and new roads and bridges, at home and abroad, were constructed after 107, when there were also sumptuous games celebrating the Dacian conquest.

For Trajan's Dacian and Parthian wars there was justification. Domitian's arrangement with Decebalus (q.v.) rendered the Danube and Moesia unsafe. Trajan left Rome in 101, crossed the Danube at Lederata and marched by way of Bersovia and Aizis (Prisc. *Inst.* 6. 13) to Tibiscum, to be joined perhaps by a parallel column proceeding via Tsierna (cf. *ILS* 5863) and the Teregova Keys pass. At Tapae he fought an apparently indecisive battle, and retired to winter on the Danube. In 102 he advanced up the Aluta valley to the Red Tower pass, and, helped by Lusius (q.v.) Quietus, finally forced the surrender of Decebalus and of his capital Sarmizegethusa. Trajan returned to Rome to claim his triumph and the title *Dacicus*. The peace was short; by 105 Decebalus had attacked the Iazyges and besieged the Roman garrisons left in Dacia. Trajan, proceeding through Illyricum to Drobetae, relieved the garrisons. In 106 he crossed Apollodorus' (q.v. 7) great new bridge at Drobetae, recaptured Sarmizegethusa, and drove Decebalus to suicide. Dacia was annexed as a province, with its capital at Sarmizegethusa, now a colony. The gold- and salt-mines were quickly opened; one legion, XIII Gemina, soon sufficed as a garrison, with *auxilia*. Dacia thus became a bastion protecting the lower Danube. Monuments and a town called Tropaeum Traiani at Adamklissi (q.v.) commemorated Trajan's triumph.

In Numidia Roman occupation was quietly strengthened by the founding of Thamugadi and Lambaesis (qq.v.). In the East, too, Trajan began modestly in 105–6 with the annexation of Arabia Petraea or Nabataea (q.v.) by Palma (q.v.); thus the Flavian eastern frontier was rounded off. But Parthia was still a menace, and when, after 110, its king Osroes dethroned Axidares, Rome's Parthian vassal in Armenia, Trajan set out in Oct. 113, probably intending to annex Armenia. He advanced to Elegeia; Armenia fell easily into his hands in 114 and was incorporated with Cappadocia and Lesser Armenia. Trajan (now officially *Optimus*), perhaps elated by effortless conquest, moved south into Upper Mesopotamia to take Nisibis and (through Lusius Quietus) Singara. Coins proclaimed *Armenia et Mesopotamia in potestatem p. R. redactae*. In 115 he crossed and descended the Tigris, and captured Ctesiphon, the Parthian capital, while a parallel force descended the Euphrates. Winter found him (now *Parthicus*) at the Tigris mouth. With Mesopotamia and its valuable trade-routes captured, consolidation and organization became essential. But in 116 southern Mesopotamia revolted, while Parthian forces successfully attacked Trajan's base-lines in Armenia, Adiabene, and northern Mesopotamia. Trajan suppressed the revolt, making Parthamaspates client-king at Ctesiphon (cf. on coins, *Rex Parthis datus*). Lusius Quietus repelled attacks in the north. But the Empire was restless; since 115 Jews had been in savage revolt in Cyrene, Egypt, Cyprus, and the Levant; Trajan himself was infirm. Leaving his new and precarious conquests, he turned homeward in 117, but died at Selinus in Cilicia *c.* 8 Aug. (*see* HADRIAN). While the Dacian wars had brought solid gain, the expense of the Parthian campaigns was out of all proportion to their material advantages; so much so that his judgement may have been warped by delusive megalomania.

Trajan's administration was economical and strict, but humane and progressive. Provincial governors, lax under Nerva, were now well chosen; provincial and local finances, often unsound, were entrusted to special administrators, such as Pliny (q.v. 2) in Bithynia and Maximus (q.v. 1) in Achaea, and to local *curatores* (q.v.). *Equites* continued to replace freedmen in the Civil Service; more provincials—eastern as well as western—were made senators. But, as Pliny's correspondence shows, Trajan personally directed the administration and discouraged local initiative on the part of governors or provincials. His rulings on problems presented to him by Pliny, notably that on the Christians (*Ep.* 10. 97), illustrate the combination of firmness and humanity which also characterizes such of his general legislation as is preserved. Trajan was fully conscious of his imperial mission to secure *Felicitas, Securitas, Aequitas, Iustitia*—in short, *Salus Generis Humani*. The Principate was a burden laid by heaven upon an earthly vicegerent (cf. Pliny, *Pan.* 80. 3), the servant of mankind, a public exemplar. The title *Optimus*, used unofficially as early as 100, emphasized by the great *Optimo Principi* coin-series of 103 onwards, and official from 114, rehabilitated the Principate in the mystical aura (second only to that of Jupiter *Optimus Maximus*) originally enjoyed by Augustus but since dissipated.

Trajan's ashes were deposited in the base of the column in his Forum. His consecration was no mere compliment; in the Late Empire it is reported by Eutropius (8. 5. 3) that the Senate acclaimed Emperors as *felicior Augusto, melior Traiano*.

ANCIENT SOURCES. *Literary*: Dio Cass. bk. 68; Pliny, *Pan.* (ed. M. Durry, 1938) and *Epp.* esp. bk. 10. One sentence of Trajan's *Dacian Commentaries* is preserved in Priscian, *Inst. Gramm.* 6. 13. Critique of sources, A. Passerini, *Il regno di T.* (1950).
*Inscriptions*: sel. in E. M. Smallwood, *Documents illustrating the Principates of Nerva, Trajan and Hadrian* (1966).
*Coins*: B.M. *Coins, Rom. Emp.* iii (1936); Strack, *Reichsprägung* ii; M. Durry, *Rev. Hist.* 1932. 316 ff.; H. Mattingly, *Num. Chron.* 1926, 232 ff.
MODERN LITERATURE. *General*: R. Paribeni, *Optimus Princeps* (2 vols., 1926–7); C. de la Berge, *Essai sur le règne de Trajan* (1877); B. W. Henderson, *Five Roman Emperors* (1927), chs. 8–12; R. Hanslik, *PW* Suppl. x. 1035 ff. *General bibliography*: A. Garzetti, *L'impero da Tiberio agli Antonini* (1960), 660 ff.; A. Piganiol, *Hist. de Rome*[2] (1962), 303 f., 580; W. H. Gross, *Die Bildnisse T.* (Röm. Herrscherbild II, 1940); Bengtson, *Röm. Gesch.* 326, 329 ff.
*Special*: (*a*) *Finance, and the Dacian treasure*: J. Carcopino, *Dacia* i (1924), 28 ff., revised in *Les Étapes de l'impérialisme romain* (1961), 106 ff.; F. Heichelheim, *Klio* 1932, 124 ff.; R. Syme, *JRS* 1930, 55 ff.; C. H. V. Sutherland, *JRS* 1935, 150 ff.; G. Biraghi, *PP* 1951, 271 ff.; for the *alimenta*, R. Duncan-Jones, *PBSR* 1964, 124 ff.; for the commemoration on the *plutei* (*anaglypha*) *Traiani* in the Roman Forum, Nash, *Pict. Dict. Rome* ii. 176, with bibl.; M. Hammond,

*Mem. Am. Acad. Rome* 1953, 147 ff., with refs. in 169 nn. 120–1 for Trajan's Arch at Beneventum; F. J. Hassel, *Der Trajansbogen in Benevent* (1966); F. A. Lepper, *JRS* 1969, 250 ff. (*b*) *Public works*: R. Paribeni, op. cit. ii. chs. 14–16; for Trajan's column and Forum: E. Nash, *Pict. Dict. Rome* i. 283, 450, with bibl.; L. Rossi, *T.'s Column and the Dacian Wars* (1970). (*c*) *Wars*: (i) *Dacia*: G. A. T. Davies, *JRS* 1917, 74 ff., 1920, 1 ff.; E. Petersen, *Trajans dakische Kriege* (2 vols., 1899–1903); I. A. Richmond, *PBSR* 1935, 1 ff.; H. Stuart Jones, ibid. 1910, 435 ff.; E. T. Salmon, *TAPA* 1936; C. Patsch, *Der Kampf um den Donauraum unter Domitian und Trajan* (1937). (ii) *Parthia, etc.*: R. P. Longden, *JRS* 1931, 1 ff.; J. Guey, *Essai sur la guerre parthique de Trajan* (1937); F. A. Lepper, *Trajan's Parthian War* (1948). See also under ALIMENTA, EQUES, SENATUS.
C. H. V. S.; M. H.

**TRALLES** (Τράλλεις), a city sometimes attributed to Lydia, sometimes to Caria, on a strong position on the north side of the richest section of the Maeander valley; its wealth and commercial advantages are inherited by the modern Aydin. First mentioned by Xenophon (*Hell.* 3. 2. 19), it belonged to the Hecatomnids in the mid fourth century and was an important city in the Hellenistic period (being called Seleucia while under the kings of Syria before 188 B.C.); it was restored by Augustus after an earthquake and given the name Caesarea. Its organization and cult are relatively well known from numerous coins and inscriptions, Zeus Larasios being the principal deity. Its Church received a Letter from Ignatius.
W. M. C.; J. M. C.

**TRANSMIGRATION.** Although the belief that the soul after the death of the body passes into some other corporeal substance is widespread, cogent evidence is lacking that it existed in Greece otherwise than as a philosophical tenet or theological doctrine of non-popular origin. There is even less trace of it in Italy. Pherecydes of Syros is the earliest to whom the theory is attributed (Cic. *Tusc. Disp.* 1. 38). It was certainly taught by the Pythagoreans and regarded as one of their most characteristic dogmas, e.g. Hor. *Carm.* 1. 28. 10, where see commentators; cf. Empedocles, 375, Pind. *Ol.* 2. 56 ff. It is also Orphic, as Pindar, fr. 127 Bowra. Hence opinions as to its ultimate origin must vary with the theories held as to the sources of these systems. From one or both of them it passes into Platonism (e.g. Pl. *Resp.* 10. 614 d ff.), and so, e.g., to the mixed eschatology of Verg. *Aen.* 6. 713 ff. Its existence outside the then civilized world was remarked, e.g., among the Druids (Caes. *BGall.* 6. 14. 5; Luc. 1. 454 ff.).

Nilsson, *GGR* i[2]. 691 ff.                H. J. R.; H. W. P.

**TRAPEZUS,** a colony of Sinope (q.v.), traditionally founded in 756 B.C. as a trading-post on the south-east coast of the Euxine. Its mediocre harbour and inhospitable neighbours retarded its development, so that in 399 it was still a small town tributary to Sinope. It formed part of the kingdoms of Mithridates VI, Deiotarus I (qq.v.), and the line of Polemon, and grew steadily in importance in the early Empire, since it was the nearest port to the Armenian frontier. It became a free city in A.D. 64, when Eastern Pontus was annexed, and received harbour works from Hadrian. Its prosperity was destroyed when it was sacked by the Goths in 259, although it remained a garrison town of some importance.

F. Cumont, *Studia Pontica* ii (1906), 362 ff.; Jones, *Cities E. Rom. Prov.*; Magie, *Rom. Rule Asia Min.*, see index.        T. R. S. B.

**TRASIMENUS LACUS,** the largest lake in Etruria, where Hannibal ambushed and destroyed the consul Flaminius (q.v.) and his army (217 B.C.). It is not a water-filled volcanic crater, but a shallow depression amid olive-covered hills with artificial *emissaria*. The Roman disaster probably occurred at its northern end.    E. T. S.

**TRAVEL.** From the very earliest times the Greeks were great travellers by sea. But travel was not undertaken for pleasure. Indeed, it was strenuous and dangerous, in view of the nature of ancient ships and the constant risk of meeting with pirates (*see* SHIPS, PIRACY). Most sailors were either pirates themselves, or merchants and their crews, running the risk for the sake of large profits. Others were emigrants travelling to new homes. In all cases, sailing was a means of making a living or searching for a place where a living could be made (*see* COMMERCE, COLONIZATION). These men, though they often reached distant countries, never ventured far inland. Travel by land was, in fact, considerably more difficult and dangerous, with means of conveyance, supplies, and safety posing major problems. In most parts of the world, travel by land was possible only in large and well-protected caravans, and was confined to long-established routes (often following river valleys), where traders were known to be welcome. Widely travelled men, like Thales and Solon, generally had a commercial background.

The Persian Empire, establishing a system of policed roads with staging-posts, opened up the possibility of land travel even to distant parts, and men like Hecataeus and Herodotus took advantage of the opportunity, travelling partly from curiosity and partly for pleasure: they are perhaps the first tourists. In fifth- and fourth-century Greece, travel began to be taken for granted. There was much coming and going—even as far as the Persian court —of diplomatic missions; mercenaries travelled freely; and ordinary citizens (e.g. of Athens) saw much service in distant parts. The great festivals attracted large crowds from wherever Greeks lived. After Alexander, in the far-flung and fairly closely-knit Hellenistic world, travel, even over long distances, became still more common. Artists and athletes were now added to those who regarded it as a normal part of their lives, and educated men were expected to travel widely, both to see famous men and places and to study at recognized centres of learning, or to work, at least for a while, at Alexandria or Athens. Even the poor could travel more widely than ever as mercenaries, and an occasional trip to a famous sanctuary or festival must have been within the reach of most Greeks, to judge by the large-scale preparations made at such places for their reception and entertainment. Travel had become much safer and a little more comfortable. Important families had far-flung networks of guest-friends, and for ordinary people inns (of varying quality) could easily be found (*see* CARRIAGES, INNS).

Roman customs easily fitted into those developed in the Hellenistic world, and Hellenistic developments were simply taken much further under Roman rule. From the third century B.C. Italian businessmen had begun to appear all over the Mediterranean; and Roman aristocrats soon began to visit famous centres of art, learning, and religion, when they went out to fight Rome's wars or govern her provinces. They rarely returned without substantial souvenirs, acquired by purchase or less legitimate means. Gradually—and especially after the coming of the Empire—both the need and the opportunities for travel multiplied further. Commerce and administration now embraced the known civilized world: many men had frequent business at provincial capitals and in Rome itself. When an Emperor appeared in a province, immense crowds would flock to see him. For travel on official business the *cursus publicus* (*see* POSTAL SERVICE) provided efficient transport. But for everyone there was a network of good roads, with troops stationed on them to keep them safe, and the safety of the seas was guaranteed by the imperial fleets. A regular tourist industry on quite a modern scale seems to have developed in times of peace and prosperity. Inns, mules, and carriages, under legal regulation, were available in all civilized places: means of conveyance could be hired in one city and left at the gate of the next. While travel for serious study, as well as

exploration and trade even beyond the frontiers, continued and flourished, travel for pleasure became part of the well-to-do pattern of life. At the more famous sites guides and guide-books specially written for the tourist could be obtained, and the souvenir and art-reproduction trade became an important industry. Hadrian's villa at Tivoli is only an extreme example of the influence of travel on upper-class life. Travel—especially to famous spas and places with special climatic features—was also prescribed for health, as medical works attest. Even at lower social levels, the army made men travel widely, and the names of Roman soldiers are engraved on the pyramids.

Even in Roman times, though, safety and comfort never reached modern standards, and such standards were probably not even thought attainable. The ancients never knew sprung carriages, and useless luxury seems to have taken the place of comfort (*see* CARRIAGES). Travel was always very slow. Except in the Postal Service (q.v.) and by private couriers (*see* TABELLARII), 40 Roman miles seems to have been a very good day's journey at the best.

The troubles of the third century brought this fully developed tourism to an end, as prosperity declined and the roads became unsafe again. But as long as the Empire lasted, the upper class, at least, remained ready and accustomed to travel.

*See also* NAVIGATION, ROADS.

L. Friedländer, *Roman Life and Manners* (E.T. 1908–13), i, chs. 6–7; Cary–Warmington, *Explorers*; Dar.-Sag., s.v. 'Viator' (with cross-references).                                                                  E. B.

**TREBATIUS** (*PW* 7) **TESTA**, GAIUS, a Roman jurist, younger contemporary and protégé of Cicero, who dedicated his *Topica* to him. Recommended by Cicero to Caesar as legal adviser, he enjoyed his favour, and later that of Augustus (cf. also Hor. *Serm.* 2. 1. 74 ff.). His writings are known to have included works *de religionibus* and *de iure civili*. No excerpts survive, but his opinions are frequently cited by subsequent jurists. He was the teacher of Labeo (q.v. 1), who regarded him highly, and his reputation rested partly on this fact, but he was evidently an independent and constructive jurist.

A. B.; B. N.

**TREBIUS NIGER** (date doubtful: perhaps 1st c. A.D., see Cichorius, *Röm. Stud.*) is several times quoted on points in natural history by Pliny (e.g. 9. 80; 89; 93; 10. 40; 32. 15).

**TREBONIANUS GALLUS**, GAIUS VIBIUS (*PW* 58), of Perusia (Emperor A.D. 251-3), was proclaimed Emperor by the army in Moesia, of which he was *legatus*, after Decius' death in battle against the Goths near Abrittus. An uneasy peace was arranged with the invaders. In 253 the Persians launched an attack on Syria, while the Goths again raided Thrace. The latter attack was successfully resisted by the legate of Moesia, Aemilianus (q.v.), who was then hailed as Augustus by his army. Trebonianus, who had hoped for peaceful conditions and had lost influence with the troops, was murdered with his son and colleague Volusianus at Interamna. The Empire was ravaged by a severe plague at this time.

A. T. Olmstead, *CPhil.* 1942, 398 ff.                                B. H. W.

**TREBONIUS** (*PW* 6), GAIUS, quaestor *c.* 60 B.C., *tribunus plebis* in 55, when he carried the *Lex Trebonia* conferring five-year commands on Pompey and Crassus. As *legatus* he did good service in Gaul (55–50) and in 49 conducted the siege of Massilia. Praetor in 48, he was sent next year to Spain, but failed against the Pompeians.

Though appointed *consul suffectus* by Caesar in 45, he is said to have plotted against him in that year, and he took part in the actual assassination in 44, detaining Antony outside. Proconsul of Asia in 43, he was treacherously murdered by Dolabella at Smyrna. He published a collection of Cicero's witticisms. C. E. S.

**TREES,** SACRED. Tree worship, characteristic of primitive religion, took a prominent place in Minoan religion. Not only growing trees, often seen inside the doors of shrines or behind walls, but also boughs were the objects of adoration and sacrifice (orgiastic dancing apparently belonged to the ritual). Prehistoric Crete knew trees as deities (epiphanies of goddesses are recognizable in some tree-cults); the connexion of Helena and Ariadne with trees is a survival; to the Greeks, however, trees (and groves) were simply sacred objects. The tree 'having its own soul' (Sil. Ital., cf. δρυάς and art. NYMPHS), was only the abode or the property of a deity (just as springs, mountains, etc. were): so in the story of the Thessalian king, Erysichthon (q.v.), who cut down the holy oak (or attacked the holy grove of poplars) and was correspondingly punished by Demeter. In general it seems to have been a common custom, when clearing a virgin forest, to leave a tree or a clump of trees unhewn, as 'holy' (often dedicated to Artemis). The oak (cf. the mantic oak of Dodona) was mostly associated with Zeus (an inheritance from Indo-European times), the olive-tree with Athena, the laurel with Apollo (cf. the metamorphosis of Daphne), the plane sometimes with Dionysius (cf. his epithet δενδρίτης), the cedar and the nut-tree with Artemis (cf. the metamorphosis of the Caryatids), the myrtle with Aphrodite, the *agnus castus* (important for medicine) with Asclepius. But trees and plants were often sacred to a deity simply because they grew near to the temple or altar (cf. the wild olive used for crowns at Olympia. Cypress, elms, white poplar may have adorned burial places and were accordingly characteristic of the infernal regions. Sacrifices and all sorts of gifts to sacred trees are known from Homeric times. Greek mythology knows the Tree of Life (the Gardens of the Hesperides), but not the originally Oriental World-tree.

In the Forum of Rome the sacred *ficus Ruminalis* or fig-tree of Romulus was one of the most holy emblems of the Eternal City (cf. the cornel-tree on the Palatine, Plut. *Rom.* 20).

C. Boetticher, *Der Baumkultus der Hellenen* (1856); W. Mannhardt *Wald- und Feldkulte²* (1904); J. G. Frazer, *GB* ii. 9 ff.; O. Gruppe, *Gr. Mythologie* ii. 779 ff., 'Pflanzenfetische'. S. E.; J. H. C.

**TREVERI,** a Gallic tribe in the Moselle basin. Strong Germanic admixture is attested by ancient authors, who are supported by archaeological evidence of German penetration *c.* 200 B.C. They furnished cavalry to Caesar, but gave him much trouble to subdue; and were active in rebellion under the early Empire (29 B.C., A.D. 21, A.D. 70), so that they lost their privilege of 'libertas'. Nevertheless, the presence of the Rhine army as a market tempted them to loyalty; and the second century shows an era of great prosperity based on large-scale agricultural organization (cf. the Igel-Säule of the Secundinii). The invasions of the third century destroyed this culture, but the land recovered somewhat with the establishment of the Emperor's and prefect's court at Trier (Augusta Treverorum, q.v.). Trier fell finally to the barbarians *c.* 430.

J. Steinhausen, *Siedelungskunde des Triererlandes* (1936). C. E. S.

**TRIARIUS,** GAIUS VALERIUS (*PW* 363), defeated Lepidus (q.v. 2) in Sardinia (77 B.C.). He successfully served as legate of Lucullus (q.v. 2) against Mithridates, taking several cities and winning a naval victory at Tenedos, but in 67 suffered a disastrous defeat at Zela (q.v.). E. B.

**TRIBONIANUS** (*PW* 1) (d. A.D. 542–5), a confidant and the most intimate collaborator of the Emperor Justinian (q.v.) in the composition and publication of his legislative works. His birth-place was (probably) Side in Pamphylia. He began as an advocate, but soon he rose to the high offices of the *magister officiorum* and *quaestor sacri palatii*. As a lawyer of great learning, especially in the legal literature of the past centuries (Justinian mentions this in particular praise of him) he was invited by the Emperor to assist in the work of codification, first in the composition of the first *Codex* (q.v.) as an ordinary member of the Commission and subsequently, when he had given proof of his quality in this task, as the director (*gubernator*) of the work on the compilation of the *Digesta* (q.v.). For this mighty undertaking he was allowed to choose his collaborators himself. He was likewise given the direction of the work on the *Institutiones* and the second *Codex* (qq.v.).

Tribonian was evidently a man of the greatest ability and versatility (though he is said to have been irreligious and avaricious: he was temporarily removed from the office of *quaestor sacri palatii* in 532 as a concession to popular hostility in the 'Nike' riots (*see* JUSTINIAN)). It is impossible to determine what part he played in the inspiration and conception of Justinian's compilation, but in its execution he was obviously pre-eminent. It is with some reason therefore that the interpolations (*see* DIGESTA) in the work have been in modern times called *emblemata Triboniani*.

There are notices of Tribonian in Procopius (*Pers.* 1. 24–5), Hesychius, and the *Suda*. The last named has articles on two distinct Tribonians. If the identity of these two persons is assumed (as B. Kübler tried to demonstrate), Tribonianus might be the author of some philosophical writings and of dissertations about planets, prosody, and various other topics.

B. Kübler, *Acta cong. iurid. internat.* (Rome, 1935), i; E. Stein, *Bull. Acad. Royale de Belgique, Classe des Lettres,* 1936. A. B.; B. N.

**TRIBUNI AERARII** were the magistrates or officials who collected the war-tax and distributed pay to the soldiers of the several tribes (although they were soon superseded in this office by the *quaestores*). Whether they originally were the heads of the tribes is doubtful, as these officials later were named *curatores*. In the first century B.C. the tribunes appear as a class somewhat similar to, but less wealthy than, the knights, and from them the third *decuria* of judges was taken (70 B.C.). A *Lex Iulia* (46) exempted them from this task.

Mommsen, *Staatsr.* iii³. 18 ff., 532 f.; T. Rice-Holmes, *The Roman Republic,* (1923) i. 391 ff. P. T.

**TRIBUNI MILITUM** in the Republican army were the senior officers of the legions. Elected by the people they ranked as magistrates, and six were assigned to each legion. They were attached directly to the legion and not to its subdivisions, hence they never functioned as mere tactical sub-commanders with fixed duties to attend to. When the number of legions was increased, only the tribunes of the four *legiones urbanae* were elected by the people (*tribuni militum a populo*); the remainder were nominated by the commanders-in-chief.

In the Caesarian period the tribunes were mainly of equestrian origin and their importance declined with the rise of the *legati*. Under the Principate the tribunate was divided into two groups according to birth, the *laticlavii* of senatorial, the *angusticlavii* of equestrian descent. The *tribunus laticlavius* was a young man embarking on a senatorial career, the *angusticlavius* was usually somewhat older and had already shown administrative ability in municipal life. From the time of Nero onwards the regular equestrian career was that of the *tres militiae—praefectus cohortis, tribunus militum, praefectus alae*.

*Tribuni* also commanded cohorts in the Household Troops and *cohortes milliariae* in the *auxilia*. In the Constantinian army the title is borne by officers of the imperial guard and the *vexillationes, auxilia*, and legions of the field army, and also of the cohorts of the *limitanei*.

J. Suolahti, *The Junior Officers of the Roman Army in the Republican Period* (1955), 35 ff.; Eric Birley, *Roman Britain and the Roman Army* (1953), 133 ff.; G. L. Cheesman, *The Auxilia of the Roman Imperial Army* (1914), 36, 94; Jones, *Later Rom. Emp.* 640 ff.

H. M. D. P.; G. R. W.

**TRIBUNI PLEBIS (or PLEBI,** δήμαρχοι**)** were officers of the *plebs* first created in 500–450 B.C. The name is evidently connected with *tribus*, but it is uncertain whether the tribunes were at first chiefs of the tribes, who later became officers of the *plebs*, or whether the name simply imitated that of the *tribuni militum* already existing. The original number of the tribunes is variously given as two, four, or five; but the only certain fact is that before 449 B.C. it had risen to ten. The tribunes were charged with the defence of the lives and property of the plebeians. Their power was not derived from any statute, but from an oath of the plebeians to uphold their *sacrosanctitas* or inviolability—an oath which the patricians never effectually challenged. The tribunes asserted a right of veto (*intercessio*) against any act performed by the magistrates, against elections, laws, *senatus consulta*. The only magistrates exempted were (until *c.* 300 B.C.) the dictator, and perhaps the *interrex*. The tribunes further summoned the *plebs* to assemblies (*concilia plebis*, more usually called *comitia plebis tributa*), elicited resolutions (*plebiscita*), and asserted a right of enforcing the decrees of the *plebs* and their own rights (*coercitio*). *Coercitio* probably could go as far as the infliction of death. Connected with the *coercitio* was a certain amount of jurisdiction. Tribunes were elected by the *concilium plebis*. Each tribune could stop the action of his colleagues by veto. Thus the office was better equipped for obstruction than for getting things done.

This revolutionary power was gradually recognized by the State. The tribunes became indistinguishable from magistrates of the State, although without *imperium* and insignia. The full acknowledgement of their power coincided with the recognition of *plebiscita* as laws with binding force (*c.* 287 B.C.). The tribunes were first admitted to listen to the debates of the Senate; at least from the third century B.C. they obtained the right of convening the Senate; in the second century the tribunate became a sufficient qualification for entry to the Senate. From the fourth and third centuries B.C. the tribunate became partially an instrument by which the Senate could control the magistrates through the veto. In certain trials of public interest the tribunes conducted the prosecution in the *comitia centuriata*. They normally confined their activities to the city of Rome and to the first mile outside it. But the tribunate never forgot its revolutionary traditions. In this period a custom sprang up which rendered re-election to the tribunate unconstitutional; but this custom was broken by C. Gracchus. From the time of Gracchus the tribunician veto was curtailed by special clauses of laws and *senatus consulta*. Sulla excluded the tribunes from the magistracies of the Roman People and abolished or curtailed their power of moving legislation and their judicial powers. In 75 B.C. they were re-admitted to the magistracies, and in 70 the tribunician power was restored to its full extent. The builders of the Principate appreciated the value of the tribunician power in the construction of their personal power. Caesar assumed at least the tribunician *sacrosanctitas*. Augustus, probably in three steps (36, 30, 23 B.C.), obtained a per-

manent *tribunicia potestas*. The Republican tribunate remained, but lost all its independence and nearly every practical function. Until the third century A.D. the tribunate remained a step in the senatorial career for plebeians alternatively with the aedileship. There is still evidence for the tribunate in the fifth century A.D.

Mommsen, *Staatsr.* ii. 1 (1887), 272 ff.; A. H. J. Greenidge, *Roman Public Life* (1901), 93 ff.; E. Meyer, *Kleine Schriften* i² (1924), 333 ff.; De Sanctis, *Stor. Rom.* ii. 26 ff., iv. 1. 534 ff.; Beloch, *Röm. Gesch.* 264 ff.; G. Niccolini, *Il tribunato della plebe* (1932); id. *I fasti dei tribuni della plebe* (1934); J. L. Myres, *Essays presented to C. G. Seligman* (1934), 227 ff.; H. Siber, *Die plebejischen Magistraturen bis zur Lex Hortensia* (1936); C. H. Brecht, 'Zum römischen Komitialverfahren', *Sav. Zeitschr., Rom. Abt.* lix (1939), 261 ff.; F. Altheim, *Lex Sacrata. Die Anfänge der plebeischen Organisation* (1940); H. Siber, *PW* xxi. 1 (1951), 170; J. Bleicken, *Das Volkstribunat* (1955); E. Meyer, *Röm. Staat und Staatsgedanke³* (1964) with bibl.; W. Kunkel, *Sav. Zeitschr., Rom. Abt.* lxxvii (1960), 375 ff. Cf. PLEBS.     A. M.

**TRIBUS.** In Rome the tribe was a division of the State. An analogous division existed in Etruscan Mantua (Serv. ad *Aen.* 10. 202). The *trifu* of the *Tabulae Iguvinae* is on the contrary the whole community. The connexion of *tribus* with *tres* is uncertain. The three original Roman tribes were Titienses (Tities), Ramnenses (Ramnes), and Luceres. It is nearly certain that these tribes were originally ethnic and not local; they probably included the *plebs* from the first.

The ethnic tribes were virtually eliminated by the creation of new local tribes, which consisted of four urban tribes and an increasing number of 'rustic' tribes. The urban tribes were traditionally ascribed to Servius Tullius; but this tradition is not universally accepted by modern scholars. The sixteen oldest rustic tribes bore the names of patrician families, who evidently owned a large part of their territory. The location of most of the oldest tribes is uncertain. The newer tribes included territories in which settlements of Roman citizens were founded, or citizenship was conferred on the native inhabitants. The number of thirty-five, which was attained in 241 B.C. by the progressive addition of rustic tribes, was never exceeded. Later enrolments of citizens into tribes were made without necessary reference to geographic contiguity.

All citizens were probably registered at all times in the local tribes, but with the censorship of Appius Claudius (312 B.C.) the registration of the lower social orders, and especially of the freedmen, in the rustic tribes became a serious political issue. The punishment of 'expulsion from a tribe' (*tribu movere*), which the censors possessed, had by the second century come to mean relegation to an urban tribe.

The extension of the Roman franchise to a great part of Italy after the Social War introduced the question of the balance between new and old citizens. The attempt to confine new citizens to a few tribes in order to check their importance in the *comitia* ultimately failed. But in general freedmen were admitted only to the urban tribes. From the Ciceronian age the name of the tribe in abbreviated form had a regular place in the citizen's full name (the first instance of a regulation of the matter is *CIL* i². 583). Provincials, both individuals and *civitates*, who in imperial times received the Roman citizenship, had to be enrolled in some specified tribe. No absolute rule was followed, but, for instance, people or *civitates* of Gallia Narbonensis were enrolled by preference in tribus Voltinia, the Orientals in the Collina and Quirina.

The territorial tribes were the units for census, taxation, and the military levy. Officials called *tribuni aerarii* (q.v.) long had charge of the financial obligations of the tribe. The relation between the *tribuni aerarii* and other officers called *curatores tribuum* is uncertain. The assemblies of the *plebs* and special less important assemblies of the whole people were arranged by territorial tribes (*see*

COMITIA). If a tribe was small the value of the individual's vote increased. It has been maintained (L. R. Taylor) that the ruling nobility of the Republic derived advantage from controlling the expansion of certain tribes.

There is evidence also for the tribes as a voting section of the citizens in some *municipia* (Lilybaeum) and *coloniae* (Genetiva Urso, Iconium).

Mommsen, *Röm. Staatsr.* iii (1887), 161 ff.; W. Kubitschek, *De Romanorum tribuum origine ac propagatione* (1882); id. *Imperium Romanum tributim descriptum* (1889); E. Meyer, *Kl. Schr.* i². 333 ff.; A. Rosenberg, *Der Staat der alten Italiker* (1913), 118 ff.; De Sanctis, *Stor. Rom.* i. 247 ff.; ii. 16 ff., 230 ff.; Beloch, *Röm. Gesch.* 264; G. Niccolini, 'Le tribù locali romane', *Studi in onore Bonfante* ii (1930), 235 ff.; E. Täubler, 'Die umbrisch-sabellischen und die römischen Tribus', *Sitz. Heidelb. Akad.* 1929–30; P. Fraccaro, 'Tribules ed aerarii', *Athenaeum* 1933, 142 ff. (= *Opuscula* ii (1957), 149 ff.); H. Last, *AJPhil.* 1937, 467 ff.; id. *JRS* 1945, 30 ff.; G. Forni, *Carnuntina* 1956), 40 ff.; id. *Omagiu lui C. Daicoviciu* (1960), 233 ff.; Taylor, *Voting Districts*, cf. E. Badian, *JRS* 1962, 200 ff.; A. Alföldi, *Early Rome and the Latins* (1965), 304 ff.    A. M.

## TRIBUTE LISTS

**TRIBUTE LISTS** at Athens are the records of the firstfruits (ἀπαρχαί: one sixtieth, a mina on the talent) presented to the goddess Athena from the annual contributions (φόροι) of the members of the Athenian League (or Empire). These audited accounts of the *hellenotamiai* (q.v.) began in 454/3 B.C., when the treasury of the Delian League (q.v.) was moved to Athens, and were inscribed annually until 406/5. No tribute was collected in 449/8, after the signing of the Peace of Callias with Persia, or in the years 414/13 to 411/10, when a five per cent tax (εἰκοστή) on allied shipping was substituted (Thuc. 7. 28. 3–4). The payments of the first fifteen years (454/3–440/39) were published on the four sides of a block (*lapis primus*) of Pentelic marble 3·583 m (minimum) in height, 1·109 m in width, 0·385 m in thickness; 180 fragments are known. For the next eight years another block (*lapis secundus*), 2·192 m. (minimum)× 1·471 m× 0·34 m, was used, of which 73 fragments are known. Henceforth each year had its own *stele*. The two large monuments, reconstructed, stand in the Epigraphical Museum at Athens. A prescript numbers each list (except 7) serially by the ἀρχή of the *hellenotamiai* from 454/3; the archon Aristion in List 34 (421/20) establishes the dating. The names (usually ethnics) of the tributaries, preceded by the amounts of quota (in List 1 the order is reversed), are arranged in columns of 30 to 35 lines, normally one entry to a line, cut in the pattern called *stoichedon*. The tribute-records, collectively, include 341 States but no more than 170 paid in any one year. List 1 is unique in that a summation of the quotas, representing a tribute of 396–406 talents from about 140 States, is added on the right lateral surface; in 444/3 some 163 States paid a tribute of over 376 talents. From 443/2 the tributaries are recorded in geographic panels under the headings Ionic, Hellespontine, Thracian, Caric, Nesiotic; in 438/7 Ionic and Caric panels were merged when Athens abandoned about forty inland Caric states. No list can be restored in its entirety, although a few (7, 12, 13) fall little short; but some complete geographic panels (e.g. Thrace in List 23, 432/1 B.C.) allow identification of defaulters. Assessments (from 300 drachmai to the 30 talents of Aegina and Thasos), changing little in scale before the Peloponnesian War, were revised, on average, every four years. Payments normally remained constant within an assessment-period. Regularity of payment, the *stoichedon* pattern, and the geographic order make possible extensive restoration, which assists in the reconstruction of Athenian finances during the Empire. We know 44 fragments of the great assessment ('Cleon's') of 425 with its accompanying decrees (the *stele* has been rebuilt in the Epigraphic Museum); we have three fragments of the assessment of 421 and five from 410/9. Craterus apparently quoted from the first and last assessments; five excerpts have been allocated to 454 and seven to 410/9.

The standard work on the tribute-records is B. D. Merritt, H. T. Wade-Gery, and M. F. McGregor, *The Athenian Tribute Lists*. Volume i (1939) includes bibliography, commentary, photographs, and drawings, fragment by fragment, of lists, assessments, and certain pertinent decrees, along with Testimonia, a Register of payment and non-payment, and a Gazetteer. Volume ii (1949) is primarily a revision of the texts and an expanded collection of decrees. Epigraphic and historical problems are studied in volume iii (1950), which is devoted chiefly to the naval Confederacy and Empire. Volume iv (1953), in addition to indexes, contains an exhaustive bibliography, printed chronologically, from 1752 to 1953. Since 1953 questions have been raised about the missing list and the original appearance of the *lapis primus*. Description of the controversies and pertinent bibliography may be found in M. F. McGregor, *Phoenix* 1962, 267 ff.; *GRBS* 1967, 103 ff.    M. F. M.

**TRIBUTUM** was a direct tax paid by individuals to the Roman State. Until 167 B.C. the citizens of Rome were liable to pay a *tributum*, which was raised only in exceptional circumstances and might be repaid. Thereafter the word applied only to direct taxes raised in the provinces, either in the form of a land-tax (*tributum soli*) or poll-tax (*tributum capitis*). These were paid by all inhabitants of the provinces, whether Roman citizens or not, except by citizens of *coloniae* (*see* COLONIZATION, ROMAN) which normally possessed the *ius Italicum* (q.v.) and were consequently exempt, usually from both taxes (*Dig.* 50. 15. 1 and 8), by citizens of *civitates immunes* or *foederatae* (*see* IMMUNITAS) or by persons specifically exempted by a *lex, senatus consultum,* or imperial decree (*SEG* ix. 8. 3). Under the Republic the *tributum soli* was normally either a fixed sum (*stipendium*), as in Spain and Africa, or a tithe (*decumae*, q.v.) paid in kind and leased by the censors (q.v.) in Rome to *publicani* (q.v.), as in Asia after the *lex Sempronia* (App. *BCiv.* 5. 4. 17–20); Sicily retained the system established by the *lex Hieronica*, and the *decumae* there were contracted for locally (Cic. 2 *Verr.* 3. 6. 12–15). The system of *decumae* contracted for by *publicani* was already disappearing in the late Republic (it seems never to have been introduced in the Tres Galliae), and under the Empire we find almost universally a fixed *tributum* based on the *census* (q.v.) and collected by local magistrates (e.g. Joseph. *BJ* 2. 405) who were responsible for paying it to the provincial officials.

The *tributum capitis* seems first to have been imposed, along with *tributum soli*, in Africa in 146 (App. *Lib.* 135). Thereafter it is most fully attested in inscriptions from the Greek provinces; it is probable, but not quite certain, that it was levied in all provinces. Nothing is known of the rate at which it was levied beyond the statement of Ulpian (*Dig.* 50. 15. 3; cf. App. *Syr.* 50) that the inhabitants of Syria and Cilicia paid 1 per cent of their census valuation annually, from age 14 for men and 12 for women to 65.

In Egypt the Romans raised a complex pattern of taxes in cash and kind (especially in grain) on the land and its produce, and also imposed a poll-tax (*laographia*) paid by native Egyptian males from 14 to 60 or 62, by the inhabitants of the *metropoleis* at reduced rates, but not by the citizens of the Greek cities.

J. Marquardt, *Organisation financière* (1888); S. L. Wallace, *Taxation in Egypt* (1937).    F. G. B. M.

**TRICLINIUM.** Civilized Greeks dined reclining on a couch (κλίνη, *lectus*) and the Romans, who had originally dined seated round the hearth, imitated them. In Greece there were usually two (sometimes more) places to a couch; that on the left was the place of honour. In Rome an arrangement of couches with three places each round three sides of a square table became usual. This was the *triclinium*, and the name was also transferred to a room built to accommodate the arrangement. The diner would lean on his left elbow (supported by a cushion), his feet sloping away from the table and perhaps supported by a footstool. Each couch and seat had its significance: the left couch was the lowest in rank, where the family would dine, the host at the top (i.e. on the left); the guests would recline on the other two, the middle one (next to the host) being more honourable: the place on the right was the position of chief honour (*locus consularis*—see Plut. *Mor.* 619 a f.). The first couch had a head-rest, the third a foot-rest. Couches with backs appear from the first century B.C. By the late Republic, the *sigma* (a single horseshoe-shaped couch, going with a round table) was gaining popularity in place of the three traditional couches: it admitted of greater comfort and informality and was favoured for open-air meals.

A wealthy family would have several *triclinia*, including some with folding doors opening on the garden, both for large-scale hospitality and for use in different seasons. Vitruvius gives precise specifications. Cushions, blankets, bedspreads, and precious ornaments were lavishly used on dining-couches in rich households: luxurious dining-couches were a sign of elegant living. Slaves and the poor dined on pallets or sitting upright, and the class of inns (q.v., e.g. at Pompeii) can be gathered from the sort of dining accommodation provided.

Dar.-Sag., s.v. (also 'lectus'); C. L. Ransom, *Studies in Ancient Furniture* (1905); G. Richter, *Ancient Furniture* (1926), 130 f.   E. B.

**TRICLINIUS**, DEMETRIUS (early 14th c.), one of the most important scholars of his day, lived probably at Salonica. He prepared editions of numerous classical poets, using his knowledge of metre to improve the text, and in some cases he also revised the accompanying corpus of scholia. A number of his emendations are generally accepted; but though he was a better metrician than his contemporaries many of his alterations to the text are violent and unnecessary. He is known to have worked on Aeschylus, Sophocles, Euripides, Aristophanes, Pindar, Hesiod, Theocritus, and Babrius. Several autograph MSS. survive. His scientific interests are demonstrated by a recently published treatise on lunar theory.

A. Turyn, *The Byzantine Manuscript Tradition of the Tragedies of Euripides* (Urbana, 1957), esp. 23 ff., 32 ff.; N. G. Wilson, *CQ* 1962, 32 ff.; G. Zuntz, *An Inquiry into the Transmission of the Plays of Euripides* (1965), *passim*; A. Wasserstein, *Jahrb. d. oesterreichischen byzantinischen Gesellschaft* 1967, 153 ff.; L. D. Reynolds–N. G. Wilson, *Scribes and Scholars* (1968), 65 ff., 157 ff.   N. G. W.

**TRIERARCHY.** A liturgy (q.v.), for naval purposes, the trierarchy was of special importance at Athens, from which a few other States copied the institution. From the early fifth century the Athenian *strategoi* chose for one year from the wealthy adult citizens a number of trierarchs corresponding to the number of triremes to be manned. Furnished with the hull and tackling of a trireme, along with the pay and food of the crew, the trierarch, who acted also as captain, bore all expense of maintenance and repair, totalling some forty to sixty *minae* (Lysias 21. 2, 32. 26–7). After 411 B.C. two citizens usually shared each trierarchy; revisions in 357 and again, at the urging of Demosthenes (*De Corona* 102 ff.), in 340 spread the burden more equitably. Demetrius of Phalerum abolished the liturgy in 317–307 B.C. Elsewhere in Greece the term 'trierarch' denoted merely captain of a trireme; in the Hellenistic and Roman periods, a trierarch might command any warship.

꜠ Orations of Demosthenes, especially 14 (*On the Symmories*) and 51 (*On the Crown of the Trierarchy*). M. Brillant, Dar.-Sag., s.v. 'Trierarchia' (1918).   C. G. S.

**TRINOVANTES**, a British tribe in Essex, probably of Belgic origin. Mandubracius, their prince, fled to Caesar from Cassivellaunus' aggression; the tribe later surrendered (54 B.C.) and brought over other tribes, making a turning-point in Caesar's British war. The Trinovantes were protected in Caesar's peace-terms; they maintained an independent monarchy under Addedomarus and Dubnovellaunus down to Cunobelin's accession, c. A.D. 5. In 43 they were freed from Catuvellaunian rule, but in 49 suffered deprivation of territory on the foundation of the *colonia* at Camulodunum (q.v.). Aggravated by the subsequent behaviour of the colonists, in 60 they joined Boudicca's rebellion, and the colony was destroyed. After its refoundation, the primacy of Camulodunum as an emporium and provincial capital became eclipsed by London, but the provincial centre of the imperial cult remained there. The *caput* of the Trinovantes possibly lay at Caesaromagus (*Chelmsford*). The *civitas* was mainly agricultural with important timber and pottery industries, and salt-boiling and oyster-fisheries along the coast, which from the late third century was defended by the Saxon Shore fort of Othona (*Bradwell*).

C. E. Stevens, *Engl. Hist. Rev.* lii (1937); A. L. F. Rivet, *Town and Country in Roman Britain* (1958), 162 f.; C. F. C. Hawkes and M. R. Hull, *Camulodunum* (1947), 1 ff.; I. A. Richmond, *VCH, Essex* iii. 1 ff.   S. S. F.

**TRINUNDINUM** (or **TRINUM NUNDINUM**) was the interval between three *nundinae*, i.e. the space of twenty-four days (by inclusive reckoning), required between moving and voting a resolution, or between the nomination of candidates and the polling, or between the promulgation and execution of a sentence, etc. The legal force of this measure of publicity, which also guaranteed the legislative power against any abuse on the part of the executive, was confirmed by the *Lex Caecilia Didia* (98 B.C.).

Mommsen, *Röm. Staatsr.* iii³. 1229 ff.; Ogilvie, *Comm. Livy 1–5*, 459 f.; A. Lintott, *CQ* 1965, 281 ff.; A. K. Michels, *Calendar of the Roman Republic* (1967), 191 ff.   P.T.

**TRIOPAS** (Τριόπας), in mythology, father (Callim. *Cer.* 79) of Erysichthon (q.v.); the latter's sin and punishment are sometimes ascribed to him, as Hyg. *Poet. Astr.* 2. 14. Triopas (occasionally called Triops, Τρίοψ) is usually Thessalian, but appears in bewildering and mutually contradictory genealogies (see Mayer in Roscher's *Lexikon*, s.v.). There seems to be no doubt that he is somehow connected with the place Triopion in Caria (Steph. Byz. s.v.). It is also possible that his name ('Three-eye') covers an old sky-god, cf. the three-eyed Zeus in Paus. 2. 24. 3.   H. J. R.

**TRIPOLIS** (1). The three cities of Sabratha, Oea, and Lepcis (qq.v.) on the north African coast. Founded as Phoenician or Punic *emporia*, they were havens on an inhospitable shore but owed their importance largely to the trans-Saharan trade. For long dependencies of Carthage, they were annexed by Masinissa and remained loosely subject to the Numidian kings until the Jugurthine War. Under Augustus they became part of Africa Proconsularis, which extended eastward as far as the Arae Philaenorum on the Greater Syrtis. Their southern frontier zone was given to the Legate of Numidia by Caligula. The Tripolis had bishops by the mid third century. Diocletian constituted the whole area into the new province of Tripolitana, governed from Lepcis. It fell to the Vandals in 455 and was recovered by the Byzantines in 533. Under Justinian Lepcis was the seat of the *Dux limitis Tripolitanae provinciae*. Fierce Berber revolts occurred during the mid sixth century and were suppressed by John Troglita. After the Arab invasion (643–4) Sabratha and Lepcis disappear as towns; Oea, now called *Tripoli* (Trablus al-Gharb), and Tacapae (Gabes) on the western border of the province, survived.

J. M. Reynolds and J. B. Ward-Perkins, *Inscriptions of Roman Tripolitania* (1952); D. E. L. Haynes, *The Antiquities of Tripolitania* (1956); R. W. Hill, *A Bibliography of Libya* (1959).   O. B.

**TRIPOLIS** (2) (in Phoenicia) is said to have been a joint foundation of Tyre, Sidon, and Aradus. Between 104 and 95 B.C. it obtained its freedom from Antiochus IX, but it later fell under a tyrant, who was executed by Pompey; its autonomy was then restored. Its territory produced a noted wine.                                    A. H. M. J.; H. S.

**TRIREME.** The earliest type of Greek warship, the simple *pentekontor* with twenty-five oarsmen on a side, was supplanted in the sixth century B.C. by the more complex trireme, which remained the standard war-galley throughout the ancient period, except in Hellenistic times (*see* QUINQUEREME). Light in structure, undecked, and slim in comparison with merchant craft, the Athenian trireme of the fourth century B.C., probably standard, measured about 120 ft. by 20 ft. The prow of the galley, rising into a lofty prow-post which was given a hooked shape by the Greeks and was voluted by the Romans, bore a ram of wood and bronze. On each side of this was painted a large apotropaic eye. A cross-beam, introduced in the Peloponnesian War, strengthened the prow and projected from the sides sufficiently to protect the 'oar-box', an outrigger construction which compensated for the curving sides of the galley.

The trireme in part sacrificed seaworthiness for efficiency in battle. During storms and at night it was often beached, for its crew (about 200 men) had but cramped quarters. It made an average speed of some four to five knots, aided by a square sail. In battle the mast was lowered or put on shore, and the trireme, formidable chiefly for its ram (*see* DIEKPLUS), was propelled by the easily directed force of oarsmen.

The arrangement of these rowers, which marks the great advance of the trireme over the *pentekontor*, has been much debated, for the ancient evidence is obscure. The long-accepted view that the rowers sat in three superimposed banks is now generally rejected; it seems probable that, the rowing-benches being slanted forward, the rowers sat three on a bench, each rower pulling an individual oar.

E. Assmann, *Seewesen* in A. Baumeister's *Denkmäler des klassischen Altertums* (1888; full reproduction of ancient representations); W. W. Tarn, 'The Greek Warship', *JHS* 1905, and *Hellenistic Military and Naval Developments* (1930); C. G. Starr, 'The Ancient Warship', *CPhil.* 1940; J. S. Morrison and R. T. Williams, *Greek Oared Ships* (1968).                                    C. G. S.

**TRITON** (Τρίτων), the merman of Greek, or rather pre-Greek mythology. The meaning of the name is unknown, but since the syllable *trit*- recurs in the name of the sea-goddess Amphitrite, also non-Greek, it is permissible to suppose that it is a pre-Hellenic vocable meaning something like 'water'. The Tritons remain quite vague figures, mostly appearing as a decoration of sea-pieces and other works of art, but they sometimes play a subordinate part in a legend. For example, a Triton in human form appears to the Argonauts (q.v.) at Lake Tritonis and gives them the clod of earth which was the pledge of future possession of Cyrene; Virgil (*Aen.* 6. 171 ff.) has a story of a Triton who, furious at the presumption of the human trumpeter Misenus in daring to challenge him to a contest (Tritons are commonly represented as playing on conches), drowns him. Pausanias (9. 20. 4; 21. 1) had seen what were represented as bodies of Tritons, possibly sea-beasts of some kind.                                    H. J. R.

**TRITOPATORES** (Τριτοπάτορες), **TRITOPATREIS** (Τριτοπάτρεις), obscure figures of Attic cult, worshipped at Marathon on the eve of the Skira (Deubner, *Att. Feste* (1932), 44). Their name seems to mean 'great-grand-fathers', and they are said to be wind-gods, also the first ancestors of mankind, and to be prayed to for children

before a marriage (Photius, s.v.), perhaps an Orphic practice, cf. Cook, *Zeus* iii. 112 ff.                    H. J. R.

**TRITTYES** (τριττύες), 'thirds', divisions both of the old and of the new *phylai* (q.v.) at Athens. Of the twelve old *trittyes* little is known: alternative guesses in antiquity were that they were identical with the *phratriai* (q.v.) and that they were territorial divisions each containing four of the *naukrariai* (q.v.). They still existed in the late fifth century. The thirty new *trittyes* were territorial divisions made by Cleisthenes (q.v. 1); each of his ten new *phylai* contained three, one from each of his three regions of Attica. We know the approximate locations of all of them and the names of more than half. Each was subdivided into a number of *demoi* (q.v.). They did not become active corporations to the same extent as the *demoi* and *phylai*, but served as mustering-units for the navy, apparently under officers called trittyarchs, and helped to spread the choice of Councillors (*see* BOULE) and of some minor officials over the whole of Attica.

Busolt–Swoboda, *Griech. Staatsk.*³ i (1920); ii (1926), see indexes; W. S. Ferguson, *Studies . . . E. Capps* (1936), 144 ff.; H. Hommel, *Klio* 1940, 181 ff.; Hignett, *Hist. Athen. Const.*, see index; D. W. Bradeen, *TAPA* 1955, 22 ff.; F. R. Wüst, *Hist.* 1957, 176 ff.; D. M. Lewis, *Hist.* 1963, 22 ff.; W. E. Thompson, *Hist.* 1966, 1 ff.
                                    A. W. G.; T. J. C.

**TRIUMPH,** the procession of a victorious Roman general to the temple of Jupiter Capitolinus. Originally Etruscan, later affected by Hellenistic influences, it remained subject to strict rules and retained its ritual character. The route, in classical times, passed from the Campus Martius through the *Porta triumphalis*, the Circus Flaminius and Circus Maximus, round the Palatine, along the Via Sacra and to the Capitol. The procession comprised, basically, the magistrates and 'Senate, the spoils (including eminent captives) and sacrificial animals, the *triumphator* and his army. Increasingly costly and elaborate details were added at suitable points, including banners, paintings and allegorical groups, musicians, and torch-bearers. The *triumphator*, preceded by his lictors, stood on a four-horse chariot, with a slave (murmuring apotropaic words) holding a crown over him; his family usually accompanied him. He was dressed in *tunica palmata* and *toga picta* (chiefly gold and purple) and adorned as a god-king. The army shouted 'Io triumphe!' and sang apotropaic verses (*see* FESCENNINI).

The prerequisites were victory over a foreign enemy, with at least 5,000 of them killed, by a magistrate with *imperium* and his own *auspicia* (q.v.); and the presence of the army, to show the war was won. These rules were gradually relaxed, to admit pro-magistrates (by the first century even *privati* with special *imperia*, like Pompey, and after 45 B.C. *legati*), and to allow a mere token presence of the army. But there was always room for intrigue and favour in their interpretation. Where they disallowed a triumph, an *ovatio* (q.v.) would usually be granted. But—we cannot tell precisely in what conditions —an unofficial triumph *in monte Albano* (*see* ALBANUS MONS), at the *triumphator*'s expense, was possible. These would be officially recorded together with proper triumphs.

Under the Empire, triumphs soon became a monopoly of the Emperor or—with his permission—his family. The victorious general was granted 'triumphal ornaments'; but these were deliberately cheapened and even in the first century A.D. lost all connexion with military exploits.

Mommsen, *Röm. Staatsr.* i³. 412; Dar.-Sag., s.v. 'Triumphus'. *Fasti triumphales* in *Inscriptiones Italiae* 13. 1.                    E. B.

**TRIUMPHAL ARCH,** the term generally used to denote the honorific arch (*fornix, arcus*; ἁψίς πύλη) which was one of the most characteristically Roman of classical buildings. Though regularly erected to commemorate military victories, such arches often had religious or topographical associations that reflect the complex origins of the type, e.g. the posthumous Arch of Titus on the Via Sacra, with its representations both of his Jewish triumph and of his apotheosis; or the frequent use of such arches on bridges or to mark provincial or city boundaries. The earliest recorded examples were built in the first years of the second century B.C. in Rome itself, and the principal subsequent development took place in Rome and Italy (over 100 known arches, many of early imperial date), Gaul (36) and Africa (118); but examples are recorded from every province of the Empire. The earliest surviving arches, of Augustan date, are simple rectangular masses of masonry, with a single archway framed between a pair of half-columns or pilasters and a trabeated entablature (Rimini, 27 B.C.; Susa, 8 B.C.) and surmounted by an attic, which served as the basis for the statuary (frequently a chariot group) which was an integral and essential feature of the monument. The subsequent architectural development was towards a steadily greater elaboration of the decorative framework and in certain cases (e.g. the arches of Severus, A.D. 203, and of Constantine, A.D. 312, in Rome) the addition of two smaller lateral arches. A specialized form, the tetrapylon, with two carriageways intersecting at right-angles, though represented in Rome (arch in the Forum Boarium), was especially common in Africa (e.g. Lepcis Magna, Trajan, Septimius Severus; Tripoli, M. Aurelius; Tebessa, Caracalla).

Systematic lists of all known arches in *PW*, s.v. 'Triumphbogen', and in *Enciclopedia dell'arte antica*, s.v. 'Arco Onorario'.

J. B. W.-P.

**TRIUMVIRI** (properly **TRESVIRI**), in Roman public life, a board of three, usually appointed by the People. For the annual *tresviri monetales* and *capitales* see VIGINTISEXVIRI. Land-commissioners were normally, and if founding a colony always, boards of three (*tresviri agris dandis adsignandis, coloniae deducendae*), appointed as required (*see* AGER PUBLICUS *and* COLONIZATION, ROMAN). Some *tresviri* appear once only, e.g. the *mensarii* of 216 B.C. (Livy 23. 21. 6, cf. 7. 21. 5) and the *tresviri legendi senatus* of A.D. 4 (Suet. *Aug.* 37, Cass. Dio 55. 13. 3). The office of *tresviri recognoscendi turmas equitum*, also instituted under Augustus (Suet. ibid.), lasted at least into the next reign. The *epulones* (q.v.) were originally *tresviri*. *Tresviri* also appear as officials of Italian and other Western towns.

The triumvirate of Antony, Lepidus (qq.v.), and Octavian (*see* AUGUSTUS), though unique, resembled the single dictatorship of Sulla in that they were *tresviri 'rei publicae constituendae'* and had practically absolute powers (probably *imperium maius*), including, at least implicitly, inappellable criminal jurisdiction (*see* PROSCRIPTIO). They were appointed to this office by the *lex Titia* of 27 Nov. 43 for five years, retained it after its legal termination (31 Dec. 38), and after the Pact of Tarentum (q.v.) renewed it for a second quinquennium, probably reckoned from 1 Jan. 37. Lepidus was deposed in Sept. 36. Antony continued to use the title after 33; Octavian appears to have dropped it.

The coalition formed between Caesar, Pompey, and Crassus in 60 B.C. was wholly unofficial, and it is misleading to call them triumvirs and to speak of the 'First' and 'Second' Triumvirates.

Mommsen, *Röm. Staatsr.* ii³. 594 ff., 624 ff., 702 ff. (*Droit publ. rom.* iv. 301 ff., 336 ff., 426 ff.); T. Rice Holmes, *Architect of the Roman Empire* i (1928), 72 ff., 231 ff.; Syme, *Rom. Rev.*, see index; F. de Visscher, *Nouvelles études de droit romain public et privé* (1949), 1 ff.

T. J. C.

**TRIVIA**, Latin translation of Τριοδῖτις, title of Hecate (q.v.) as goddess of cross-roads. Since the identification of Hecate with Artemis and Selene was popular in

Hellenistic times and Diana (q.v.) was identified with Artemis, the epithet is often used of Diana, as Lucretius 1. 84; Catullus 34. 15; cf. Verg. *Aen.* 6. 35 (Hecate and Diana).

H. J. R.

**TROAS**, the mountainous north-west corner of Asia Minor forming a geographical unit dominated by the Ida massif and washed on three sides by the sea. Its name derives from the belief that all this area was once under Trojan rule. The interior is inaccessible, and the more important cities were situated on the coast. The historical significance of the Troad derives from its strategic position flanking the Hellespont (a factor which may already have weighed with the Achaeans in their attack on Troy). From the sixth century Athens became increasingly interested in holding the straits, but after Aegospotami Persia nominally controlled the Troad. It became the battlefield in the struggle between east and west when Alexander routed the Persian first line of resistance at the Granicus. Later the Troad was ruled by Antigonus, who founded Antigoneia—afterwards Alexandria Troas—and from him the country passed successively under the power of Lysimachus, the Seleucids, and Attalus I of Pergamum. The Attalids bequeathed it to Rome, and the Troad suffered severely in the wars of the Republic; but under the Empire it enjoyed a long period of tranquillity until the Arab incursions of the eighth century.

W. Leaf, *Strabo on the Troad* (1923); J. M. Cook, *Greek Archaeology in Western Asia Minor* (*Arch. Rep.* 1959-60), 29 ff.

D. E. W. W.

**TROGODYTAE** (Τρωγοδύται) were a primitive people of 'Ethiopia', in particular northern Sudan. In MSS. of classical authors we frequently find a reading which, by inclusion of the letter *l*, gives or implies the name Troglodytae, 'cave-enterers', 'cave-dwellers'. This latter name may be applied rightly to people with that name placed by classical writers on the northern side of the Caucasus, where 'Troglodytes' lived in caves because of the cold; to a people in north-western Africa; to a people in the interior of northern Africa; and possibly to peoples on the eastern coast of the Red Sea. But when the people concerned are located in Egypt and to the south of it, the name Troglodytae must be taken as false, reflecting no doubt a common confusion, the true name, as various MSS. and papyri show, being Trogodytae with no reference to caves. Trogodytica included the whole coastline from Suez to the Straits of Bab-el-Mandeb; and the Trogodytes ranged southwards to the Abyssinian escarpment. There were and are no natural caves in the eastern deserts of Africa; and it is probable that the Trogodytes lived in huts of wickerwork as the Bega do now. Their lands on the Red Sea coast were explored by agents of Ptolemy II and III. They mostly went naked, ate the bones and hides as well as the flesh of their cattle, and drank a mixture of milk and blood. They squeaked like bats, talked gibberish, and buried their dead by pelting them with stones. They kept women in common, and were governed by 'tyrants'.

Hdt. 4. 183; Diod. 3. 32–3 (from Agatharchides); Strabo 16. 775–6.

E. H. W.

**TROGUS**, POMPEIUS (*PW* 142), the Augustan historian, a Vocontian from Gallia Narbonensis, whose grandfather was enfranchised by Pompey and whose father served under Caesar, wrote zoological, and perhaps botanical, works, used by the Elder Pliny, and a Universal History in forty-four books, entitled *Historiae Philippicae*. Beginning with the Ancient Orient and Greece (books 1–6), he treated Macedon (books 7–12) and the Hellenistic kingdoms to their fall before Rome (books 13–40). Books 41–2 contained Parthian history to 20 B.C., books 43–4 the kingly period of Rome, and Gallic and Spanish history to Augustus' Spanish victory. His main source, which is independent of the patriotic Roman tradition, was probably Timagenes of Alexandria. The narrative was elaborate, in the Hellenistic fashion, with dramatic presentation and a moralizing tendency; speeches were as a rule reported indirectly (Just. 38. 3. 11; but note Mithridates' speech, 38. 4). This character is reflected in the epitome of Justinus (q.v.) by which, in addition to the *prologi* (tables of contents), the work is preserved.

L. E. Hallberg, *De Trogo Pompeio* (1869); F. Seck, *De Pomp. Trog. sermone* (1881); E. Schneider, *De Pomp. Trog. hist. Philipp. consilio et arte* (1913); A. Momigliano, *Athenaeum* 1934, 56 ff.; O. Seel, *Pompei Trogi Fragmenta* (1956). A. H. McD.

**TROILUS** (Τρωΐλος), son of Priam (q.v.), mentioned *Iliad* 24. 257 as dead. Later accounts, as the *Cypria* (Proclus), specify that he was slain by Achilles (q.v.; cf. Verg. *Aen.* 1. 474 and Servius thereon; more in Mayer in Roscher, s.v.). 'Troilus and Cressida' (i.e. Chryseis) is a purely medieval fiction, having no connexion with antiquity.

Achilles' ambush of Troilus (accompanied by Polyxena) at the fountain, the pursuit, the slaughter of the boy on the altar of Apollo, and the battle over the mutilated body, are among the most popular themes in archaic art from the early sixth century and found occasionally later (Brommer, *Vasenlisten²*, 264 ff.). H. J. R.; C. M. R.

**TROPHIES** (τρόπαια, trophaea, from τροπή). The act of dedicating on the field of battle a suit of enemy armour set up on a stake is a specifically Greek practice. Originally intended as a miraculous image of the *theos tropaios* who had brought about the defeat of the enemy, a trophy marked the spot where the enemy had been routed. Trophies were also dedicated in the sanctuary of the deity to whom victory was ascribed. They appear in art at the end of the sixth century B.C. and were certainly in use during the Persian Wars.

The trophies of the fourth century became permanent monuments. The Battle of Leuctra (371 B.C.) was commemorated by a tower surmounted by a trophy of arms, and from this period onwards the name was applied to various kinds of towers and buildings commemorating military and naval victories. Trophies became a common motif of art; sculptured trophies accompanied by statues of captives and victors decorated the buildings of Hellenistic kings and took an important place in Roman triumphal art from the first century B.C. The word trophy is also applied, though not with strict accuracy, to the masses of arms on sculptured monuments which appear first at Pergamum and later on ·a number of Roman commemorative monuments. The best-known Roman trophy monuments are those of Augustus at La Turbie and of Trajan at Adamklissi (q.v.).

G. C. Picard, *Les Trophées romains* (1957). D. E. S.

**TROPHONIUS** (Τροφώνιος), apparently 'the Feeder', a Boeotian oracular god (description of his shrine at Lebadea, P. Philippson, *Symb. Osl.*, fasc. suppl. ix. 11 ff.). Of him and his brother Agamedes practically the same story is told as that of the architect of Rhampsinitus (q.v.; Paus. 9. 37. 4 ff.). His oracle was held in great reverence. Pausanias (who had himself made an inquiry there) describes the elaborate preliminary ritual, after which the inquirer was supposed to be snatched away underground and given direct revelations (ibid. 39. 5 ff.); for its legend see ibid. 40. 1 f. As Nilsson suggests (*GGR* ii. 450), the ceremonies may have been modified to suit later developments. H. J. R.; H. W. P.

**TROY** (modern *Hissarlık*). In north-western Asia Minor, some 4 miles from the Aegean Sea and slightly nearer the Hellespont on the north, are the ruins of the ancient stronghold, called by the Turks Hissarlik, which was identified as the site of Troy by H. Schliemann. Between 1870 and 1890 he excavated much of the mound which had grown to a height of 50 feet and more through gradual accumulation of debris from human habitation. After his death renewed digging by W. Dörpfeld in 1893 and 1894 and by the University of Cincinnati from 1932 to 1938 contributed much to supplement what had previously been learned. The earth cover was not a single uniform deposit; it was composed of forty-six recognizable strata which could be grouped in ten major layers, each obviously representing a period of occupation.

Layers I to V, counting from the bottom, belong to the Early Bronze Age; Layer VI to the Middle and much of the Late Bronze Age; Layers VIIa and VIIb to the remainder of the Late Bronze Age.

From the outset Troy I, seat of a ruler, was a fortified stronghold which lasted through ten phases. Three successive stone walls supported battlements of crude brick; an entrance gate was flanked by projecting towers. Within were free-standing rectangular houses built of crude brick set on a stone socle; one house comprised a portico and doorway and a long room containing a hearth, an early example of the 'megaron' type. Copper was known; stone and bone were used for tools and weapons. A stele of limestone bearing a human face carved in relief displays progress in art beyond the primitive. Abundant pottery was made without use of the wheel. Close connexions with Lesbos and Lemnos and some with the Aegean existed.

Troy II, showing a marked advance in grandeur, survived through seven phases. Three successive fortification walls were erected, each surpassing its predecessor; imposing gates and towers built of stone·and crude brick evince engineering skill. Inside the citadel, facing a court, stood a palatial hall or 'megaron' and many other similar buildings. Wealth and luxury are demonstrated by the gold jewellery and vessels of gold, copper, and bronze and the bronze and stone weapons recovered in the celebrated 'treasures' found by Schliemann. The potter's wheel appears in Phase IIb. Vessels of distinctive shapes were exported; and relations with the Aegean were maintained. Troy II ended in a devastating fire which laid the whole town in ruins.

Three towns of less importance, III, IV, and V, followed. Each, expanding over an enlarged area, had a defensive wall, though little is left of them. From Troy I to V there was evidently a continuity of people and culture with no unmistakable signs of new elements in the population. The Early Bronze Age at Troy, extending over the greater part of the third Millennium, terminated shortly after 2000 B.C.

Troy VI ushers in the Middle Bronze Age. People of a new stock, who brought the horse, took over the citadel. They were great builders: remains of three successive fortification walls of increasing strength and magnificence survive. The third with smoothly sloping outer face was constructed of large neatly squared blocks of hard limestone. There were at least four gateways, two protected by massive towers. Inside the citadel the ground rose in concentric terraces: the royal palace no doubt stood at the summit, but no remains are left, since the whole top of the hill was sliced away in Hellenistic times to make room for the temple of Athena. Spacious free-standing houses occupied the lower terraces, many equipped with stone bases for interior wooden columns. Outside the acropolis to the south was a cremation cemetery containing remnants of some 200 cinerary urns. In its eighth phase, about 1300 B.C., Troy VI was utterly demolished by a violent earthquake—far beyond the destructive power of man in the Bronze Age.

Survivors maintaining the same culture patched the defensive walls and built modest new houses inside the fortress. This was Troy VIIa which lasted a generation or two only to be razed again probably about the middle of the thirteenth century. This time it was a great fire which reduced the town to ruins. Remnants of human bones found in houses and streets suggest that violence accompanied the disaster.

Some of the inhabitants escaped, and once more the town was rebuilt and reoccupied for a time in a phase called Troy VIIb 1. In a still later stage, Troy VIIb 2, a primitive people, evidently coming from Thrace, seized and held dominion over the region to the end of the twelfth century. Thenceforth the site seems to have been virtually deserted for four centuries until early Greek colonists settled on the old ground. The ensuing period, Troy VIII, maintained itself in a small way and was ultimately succeeded by Troy IX which endured through the Hellenistic and Roman eras.

The situation of Hissarlik fits reasonably well with the account of Troy in Homer, Greek tradition, and folk memory. Searching exploration has discovered no rival capital site in north-west Troad. The destruction of Troy VIIa in the mid thirteenth century coincides with the flourishing period of the great royal palaces in Mycenaean Greece. Leadership, manpower, and wealth were there abundantly sufficient to organize a coalition. If there ever was a Troy of Priam with some basis of reality it must have stood in this place and at this time. Archaeological and linguistic discoveries during the past twenty years have convinced many scholars that there is a residue of historical truth in many Greek traditions and legends, and Schliemann's identification of Troy has surely been confirmed.

H. Schliemann, *Troy and its Remains* (1875), *Ilios* (1880), *Troja* (1884), *Bericht ... 1890* (1891); W. Dörpfeld, *Troja und Ilion* (1902), W. Leaf, *Troy* (1912); Blegen, Boulter, Caskey, Rawson, Sperling, *Troy* i–iv (1950–58); D. L. Page, *History and the Homeric Iliad* (1959); C. W. Blegen, *Troy and the Trojans* (1963). C. W. B.

**TRYPHIODORUS, correctly TRIPHIODORUS** (3rd or 4th c. A.D.), epic poet, native of Egypt. He wrote *Marathoniaca, The Story of Hippodamea* (cf. PIRITHOUS), an Ὀδυσσεία λειπογράμματος (cf. NESTOR 2), a paraphrase of Homer's similes, and *The Capture of Troy*. Only the last, in 691 verses, survives, showing a style midway between that described under NONNUS and the more Homeric manner adopted by Quintus Smyrnaeus.

TEXT. Weinberger, 1896 (Teubner, with Colluthus). With translation and brief notes: A. W. Mair, 1928 (Loeb, with Oppian and Colluthus).
GENERAL. L. Ferrari, *Sulla Presa di Ilio di Trifiodoro* (1962). M. L. W.

**TRYPHON** (1, *PW* 7) was the name adopted by a slave called Salvius, who led a slave revolt in central Sicily in 104 B.C. Collecting a large army and gaining the help of another slave leader, Athenion, he took a fortress and defeated a Roman army. He died in 102 and Athenion succeeded to his power. E. B.

**TRYPHON** (2, *PW* 25), son of Ammonius, an important Greek grammarian at Rome under Augustus. His works, which were used by his contemporary Didymus, by Apollonius Dyscolus, and very freely by Herodian, included musical, botanical, zoological, and important dialect glossaries; as Atticist and analogist (*see* GLOSSA (Greek) *and* CRATES (3) OF MALLOS) he wrote Περὶ Ἑλληνισμοῦ, Περὶ ὀρθογραφίας, on disputed breathings, and on etymological pathology, which 'science' (including, for him, dialectal variation) he founded. His works are lost. Our Tryphon Περὶ παθῶν is a late abridgement.

A. von Velsen, *Tryphonis grammatici Alexandrini fragmenta* (1859). P. B. R. F.

**TUBERO** (1), LUCIUS AELIUS (*PW* 150), friend of M. Cicero and *legatus* to Q. Cicero in Asia, engaged in writing history; but of publication we have no proof. It possibly descended as material to his son, Q. Aelius Tubero (q.v. 2), who shared his father's interest both in history and in the Pompeian cause. J. W. D.

**TUBERO** (2), QUINTUS AELIUS (*PW* 156), jurist and annalist, who fought on Pompey's side but became reconciled with Caesar, left politics after an unsuccessful prosecution of the Republican Q. Ligarius in 46 B.C., and wrote on jurisprudence and history (Pompon. *Dig.* 1. 2. 2. 46). He was reputed to be an expert in public and private law; he published several legal works which, however, did not enjoy a great popularity because of his *sermo antiquus*. In at least fourteen books, he treated Roman history from the origins to his own times; these fragments, however, may be from a monograph addressed to Oppius (Gell. 6. 9. 11). Livy cites him with Macer (4. 23. 1; 10. 9. 10). Pliny cites a Q. Tubero for astronomical data (*HN* 18. 235).

Peter, *HRRel.* i². ccclxvi and 308; Beloch, *Röm. Gesch.* 106; Ogilvie, *Comm. Livy 1–5*, 16 ff. A. H. McD.

**TUDER,** modern *Todi* with well-preserved pre-Roman and Roman walls, 62 miles due north of Rome in Umbria. First mentioned *c.* 100 B.C., when already under Roman domination (Plut. *Mar.* 17. 4), it became a *colonia c.* 30 B.C. (Pliny, *HN* 3. 113). Tuder has bequeathed a large bronze statue inscribed in Umbrian of Mars, the god it especially worshipped (Sil. 4. 222; 8. 462). E. T. S.

**TUDITANUS** (1), PUBLIUS SEMPRONIUS (*PW* 96) (*cos.* 204 B.C.), military tribune at Cannae (216), curule aedile in 214, praetor in 213, commanding at Ariminum until 211, became censor in 209. A leading diplomat, he closed the First Macedonian War by the Peace of Phoenice (205). Consul in 204, he won a success over Hannibal near Croton, dedicating a temple to *Fortuna Primigenia* (194). His Greek experience placed him on the embassy to Greece, Syria, and Egypt in 200, which opened the new Roman policy in the East, with the Second Macedonian War.

F. W. Walbank, *Philip V of Macedon* (1940), 102 ff., 305, 313. A. H. McD.

**TUDITANUS** (2), GAIUS SEMPRONIUS (*PW* 92), consul in 129 B.C. when he triumphed over the Iapydes, wrote *Libri magistratuum* in at least thirteen books, treating intercalation, the *maius* and *minus imperium*, the origin of the tribunate, and the *nundinae*. Fragments about the Aborigines, the books of Numa, the death of Regulus, and (probably) Flamininus' triumph, indicate an historical work.

Peter, *HRRel.* i². cci; 143. Cf. C. Cichorius, *Wien. Stud.* 1902, 588 ff. A. H. McD.

**TULLIA** (1), the younger daughter of Servius (q.v. 1) Tullius, was said to have impelled her brother-in-law, the future Tarquinius Superbus, to murder her husband, Aruns Tarquinius, and subsequently her father, in order that she might marry him and become his queen. Tullia then drove her chariot over her dead father's body, in a street thereafter named Vicus Sceleratus. The story, for which a Greek origin has been claimed, merely because it was cast by Roman authors into the mould and technique of Greek tragedy, is probably best explained as an aetiological myth invented to explain the street name and the gesture of a statue, which was popularly believed to represent Servius Tullius.

Ogilvie, *Comm. Livy 1–5*, 185 ff.; A. Alföldi, *Early Rome and the Latins* (1964), 152 f. P. T.

**TULLIA** (2, *PW* 'Tullius' 60), Cicero's daughter, born *c.* 79 B.C.; first (by 63) married to a C. Piso (quaestor 58), who died in 57; then (56) to a Furius Crassipes (quaestor 51), who divorced her *c.* 51; finally, to Dolabella (q.v. 3) (50, in Cicero's absence). This marriage—never a success —ended late in 46. In Feb. 45 Tullia died, shortly after bearing a son who did not long survive her. Her death was a heavy blow to Cicero, who (though he loved her) had taken little account of her happiness during her life, but now proposed to build a shrine to her. He had to abandon the project and turned to philosophy for consolation.

                                                                E. B.

**TULLIANUM**, the underground execution-cell of the prison at Rome, flanking the *comitium*, and connected with Servius Tullius (Varro, *Ling.* 5. 151; Festus 356). The derivation from *\*tullus*, a spring, is more attractive, for the existing work is a well-chamber, once circular, built in coursed peperino (Tenney Frank, *Buildings of the Roman Republic* (1924), 39 ff.) of the third century B.C. The room above it has a travertine front repaired in A.D. 22 or 45 (*CIL* vi. 31674; cf. *ILS* iii, 342). The frontal orientation, as of the *comitium*, is by the cardinal points. A spring still rises in the present floor, higher than the original. Here were executed most State prisoners, including Jugurtha, the Catilinarian conspirators, and Vercingetorix.

Nash, *Pict. Dict. Rome* i. 206 ff.                         I. A. R.

**TULLUS HOSTILIUS**, traditionally the third king of Rome (673–642 B.C.), is probably an historical figure, and the suggestion that he is a duplication of Romulus can be dismissed. His capture and destruction of Alba Longa, which ceased to be an independent city during the regal period, and his founding of the *Curia Hostilia*, may be accepted as facts. The Curia was indisputably built by an eponymous king, because no Hostilius is mentioned as consul in the early Fasti, nor does the gens Hostilia seem to have come to the forefront till the end of the second century B.C. But most of his wars were related, or imagined, merely to explain his name and as examples of his *ferocitas*; and his story was almost lost in folklore tales such as the battle of the Champions (*see* HORATII), and the punishment of Mettius Fufetius.

Ogilvie, *Comm. Livy 1–5*, 105 ff.                         P. T.

**TUMULTUS** was the state of fear (*timor*) and confusion resulting from a war fought on the frontiers of Italy (or, originally, near the walls of Rome). Cicero (*Phil.* 8. 1. 3) attests that there were only two examples of *tumultus*, namely *tumultus Italicus* (i.e. war in Italy and, later, civil war) 'quod erat domesticus' and *tumultus Gallicus* (as Gaul was the only province that had a common frontier with Italy), 'quod erat Italiae finitimus'. The term probably came into use after the Gallic capture of Rome (387 B.C.). When the *tumultus* was announced, business and the administration of justice stopped (*iustitium*), army leave was cancelled, and all the citizens, wearing the military dress called *sagum*, were levied, even if previously exempted from service, to form a supplementary corps named *tumultuarii milites*.

E. Pottier, Dar.–Sag., s.v.; Kromayer–Veith, *Heerwesen u. Kriegführung* (1928), 285, 305.                         P. T.

**TUNIS** (or **TUNES**), a Libyan town on the site of modern Tunis. It is frequently mentioned in connexion with fighting in the vicinity of Carthage in the campaigns of Agathocles, Regulus, and Scipio Africanus. Although overshadowed by Carthage, situated only a few miles away, it remained a separate community to the end of the Roman period.                         B. H. W.

**TURBO**, QUINTUS MARCIUS (*PW* 107), bears on inscriptions also the succeeding names *Gallonicus* (?) *Fronto Publicius Severus Iulius* (?) *Priscus*, though the full series does not occur in any one inscription. He was born in Dalmatia and possibly began his career as a centurion (*CIL* iii. 14349. 2). In A.D. 114, he was prefect of the fleet at Misenum (*CIL* xvi. 60). Trajan (q.v.) sent him, probably in 116 or 117, to quiet Jewish disturbances in Egypt and Cyrene (Euseb. *Hist. Eccl.* 4. 2. 4). Hadrian (q.v.), whose confidence he enjoyed (S.H.A. *Hadr.* 4. 2), sent him in 117, probably to succeed the consular Lusius (q.v.) Quietus, as a procuratorial governor to quiet one or both the Mauretanias (*Hadr.* 5. 8). In 118, Hadrian put him in charge of Pannonia and Dacia with a rank which the S.H.A. equates with the prefecture of Egypt (*Hadr.* 6. 7, 7. 3), and, probably in 119, made him *praefectus praetorio* with Septicius Clarus in succession to Attianus (q.v.) (*Hadr.* 9. 3–5). Though as prefect Turbo was loyal and vigorous (Dio 69. 18), Hadrian in his later years became suspicious of him (as of others; *Hadr.* 15. 7) and dismissed him from office, probably not as early as he did Clarus (*c.* 122) but perhaps before the date (136) at which Dio gives a retrospective estimate of Turbo, although S.H.A. *Ael.* 6. 4–5 may refer to Turbo as the prefect whom Hadrian discharged (after 136) for publicizing his regret over the adoption of the ailing Aelius. Whether Turbo survived Hadrian is not known.

S.H.A. *Hadr.*; for his origin and early career, Dio bk. 69. 18; *AE* 1955, 230, no. 225; R. H. Lacey, *The Equestrian Officials of Trajan and Hadrian* etc. (Diss. Princeton, 1917), 17, no. 39; A. Stein, *Die Reichsbeamten von Dazien* (1944), 14 ff. and *Die Präfekten von Ägypten* (1950), 59 ff.; R. Syme, *JRS* 1962, 87 ff., who assigns the inscription from Caesarea (*Ann. Épigr.* 1946, 198, no. 113) to another Turbo, active under Antoninus; H. G. Pflaum, *Les Carrières procuratoriennes* etc. (1960), i. 199 ff.                         M. H.

**TURIA**, wife of Q. Lucretius Vespillo (*cos.* 19 B.C.), concealed her husband during the proscriptions of 43–42 until his pardon was obtained. She has been identified with the subject of the so-called *Laudatio Turiae* (*ILS* 8393).

W. Warde Fowler, *CR* 1905, 261 ff.; E. Weiss, *PW* xii. 995 ff.; M. Durry, *Une Éloge funèbre d'une matrone romaine* (1950) (text, trans., and comm.); A. E. Gordon, *AJArch.* 1950, 223 ff.; F. della Corte, *Giornale italiano di filologia* 1950, 146 ff.                         G. W. R.

**TURNUS** (1), Italian hero, son of Daunus and the nymph Venilia, and brother of the nymph Juturna; king of the Rutulians, whose capital was Ardea. He was the accepted suitor of Lavinia, daughter of Latinus (q.v.), but Latinus subsequently betrothed her to Aeneas against the will of his wife Amata. The Latins, roused by Juno, join with the Rutulians to make war on the Trojans. Turnus fights bravely, leads the attack on the Trojan camp and defends Lavinium. He slays Pallas, son of Evander, and is twice saved by Juno from Aeneas, who finally pursues and kills him (*Aen.* 7–12).                         C. B.

**TURNUS** (2), satirist under Domitian, brother of the tragic poet Scaeva Memor (q.v.), and credited with 'ingentia pectora' by Martial (7. 97. 7; 11. 10; Probus (Vallae) *ad Iuven.* 1. 20; Rut. Namat. 1. 603–4; Lydus, *Mag.* 1. 41).

**TURPILIUS**, SEXTUS (died old, 103 B.C.), Latin composer of *comoediae palliatae*, livelier and more popular than Terence's. Of thirteen surviving titles six come from Menander.

Fragments: O. Ribbeck, *CRF*² 85 (3rd. ed. Teubner, 1897).
                                                                E. H. W.

**TURRANIUS GRACILIS** (of uncertain date), an authority on Spain, used by the elder Pliny (*HN*, books 3, 9, and 18, *index auctorum*).

**TURRĪNUS,** CLODIUS, name of two rhetoricians, father and son, discussed by the Elder Seneca (*Controv.* 10, *pr.* 14–16). The senior lost force in speaking by too strict adherence to Apollodorean rules: he held a distinguished position in Spain. The son, in whom Seneca saw high promise, was treated as one of his own sons.

J. W. D.

**TUSCULUM,** a city near *Frascati* 15 miles south-east of Rome. Its extensive remains occupy a strong, bracing site 2,198 feet above sea-level. Myths shroud its origin, but Tusculum was certainly powerful in early Latium. Its dictator Octavius Mamilius allegedly supported his son-in-law Tarquinius Superbus (508 B.C.); but traditions associating Tusculum with Etruscans may be mere aetiological fictions to explain its name. More credibly, Tusculum reputedly led the Latins at Lake Regillus (q.v.) *c.* 496, when Mamilius himself fell. Thereafter, however, being exposed to Aequian attacks via Algidus, it became Rome's ally and staunchly resisted Aequi, Volsci, and Gauls. Tusculum, the first Latin city to obtain Roman citizenship (381), supplied Rome with several illustrious families (Mamilii, Fulvii, Fonteii, Juventii, Porcii). Some Tusculans joined the Latin revolt in 340 B.C. but usually Tusculum remained loyal (e.g. against Hannibal). A *municipium* under late Republic and early Empire, Tusculum was a fashionable resort where wealthy Romans sojourned: Lucullus, Maecenas, and especially Cicero, who composed several philosophical treatises in his Tusculan villa (at *Poggio Tulliano*?). Subsequently Tusculum is seldom mentioned, but was still an important stronghold when destroyed in medieval times. Cato the Censor was born here.

Strabo 5. 239; Livy 1. 49; 2. 15 f.; 3. 7 f.; 4. 33 f.; 6. 21; 8. 7 f.; 26. 9; Dion. Hal. bk. 10 *passim*. G. McCracken, *A Short History of Ancient Tusculum* (U.S.A. 1939).     E. T. S.

**TŪTĬCĀNUS,** friend of Ovid from youth, whose name could not appear in elegiac verse without the playful scansions of *Pont.* 4. 12. 10–11: cf. 4. 14. He retold Homeric themes in Latin.

**TWELVE TABLES,** the earliest Roman code of laws, and the starting-point in the development of Roman law. The circumstances under which it was drawn up are not clear, and the authenticity of the XII Tables has therefore been called in question by some scholars. But it may be regarded as certain that the XII Tables were actually drawn up by a special commission of *decemviri legibus scribundis* in 451–450 B.C. (*see* DECEMVIRI). Enacted by the *Comitia Centuriata* as a statute (*lex duodecim tabularum* appears often in the sources), the XII Tables were published in the Forum on tablets of bronze (or wood). The original Tables perished when Rome was burnt by the Gauls. The object of the code was to collect the most important rules of the existing customary law, the knowledge of which had been till then confined to the patrician *pontifices*, and to reduce patrician privilege. It is unlikely, however, that the *decemviri* departed much from the customary law, though certainty is impossible, in default of authentic sources about the law in pre-decemviral times and for lack of a complete text of the Code, which is known only through quotations and references in legal and lay literature. The surviving text (a collection of very brief and abrupt imperatives) is mostly in a later and modernized Latin, but it contains a few passages in archaic language, whose meaning is not always clear. Some few similarities to Greek institutions may possibly be attributable to the embassy to Athens which, according to tradition, preceded the decemviral work. The XII Tables contained rules from all spheres of law: private and criminal, sacral and public, but procedure seems to

have been dealt with in more detail than substantive law. The statement of Livy (3. 34. 6) that they were 'fons omnis publici priuatique iuris' is an exaggeration. We cannot tell what proportion the surviving fragments bear to the whole, but their scale suggests that only the more salient rules were expressed. The XII Tables were never abolished (even in Cicero's youth schoolboys learnt them by heart); but the later development of Roman law made much of them obsolete. Some fundamental rules nevertheless remained operative until Justinian. *See also* LAW AND PROCEDURE, ROMAN, I.

Reconstructions of the decemviral code have been attempted since the sixteenth century; the one now generally accepted (for convenience) is that of R. Schoell, *Legis duodecim tabularum reliquiae* (1866). Modern editions are to be found in the collections of *Fontes iuris Romani* by Bruns–Mommsen–Gradenwitz, and Riccobono (second edition i, 1941).

H. F. Jolowicz, *Hist. Intro. to the Study of Roman Law*[2] (1952), and other works on History and Sources cited s.v. LAW AND PROCEDURE, ROMAN, I. F. Wieacker, *Entretiens Hardt* xiii (1966), 293 ff.     A. B.; B. N.

**TYCHE,** formed from the verb τυγχάνειν, and reflecting its varied use, can mean either 'success' or 'fortune', 'happenstance': what a person 'attains' on his own, or whatever 'befalls' him of good or bad. The two ideas are not necessarily distinct: to 'Saviour Tyche, child of Zeus the Deliverer', Pindar ascribes not only good fortune divinely bestowed, as in the liberation of Himera, but also success won by skill, in matters such as navigation, warfare, and government (*Ol.* 12. 1–5); Alcman calls Tyche 'sister of Order and Persuasion, and daughter of Forethought' (Plutarch, *De fort. Rom.* 4. 318 a). Most often, however, *tyche* is merely 'luck', divorced from human effort, and like the English word it may be either neutral or favourable: '*tyche* and *moira* give everything to man', says Archilocus (Stob. 1. 6. 3), meaning one's 'luck' and one's 'lot'; Eudore and Tyche, 'Bounty' and 'Luck', are named together as Oceanids (Hes. *Theog.* 360; Tyche appears beside 'Flockgrazing', a special form of Bounty, at *Hom. Hymn to Demeter* 420).

*Tyche* works obscurely, lifting up one man and pushing down another (Soph. *Ant.* 1158 f.), and is finally heard as 'chance', a principle ruling all of human life (Demetrius of Phaleron *apud* Polybium 29. 21; cf. Plato, *Leg.* 709 b); such *tyche* is 'a blind and wretched thing' (Menander *apud* Stobaeum 1. 7. 3), and—wearing the aspect of the old gods whom it supersedes—even jealous (Polyb. 39. 8. 2) or punitive (id. 23. 10. 2). In stricter usage of the fourth century pure chance was *automaton*, distinguished from *tyche*, good or bad 'fortune' (Arist. *Ph.* 2, 4–6). Conceived absolutely, *tyche* excludes belief in the gods (*fr. trag. adesp.* 169; cf. Eur. *Cycl.* 606 f.). No use praying for riches or distinction, because all that man gets is *tyche* (Theognis 129 f.). In pious language, to be sure, the gods are 'masters' of *tyche* (Eur. *El.* 890 f.); we hear that *tyche* depends on 'the goodwill of the gods' (Demosthenes 2. 22), or that 'god has awarded to each' his own *tyche* (id. 18. 208). Tyche herself is invoked in a lyric hymn of early Hellenistic times (Stobaeus 1. 6. 13), and praised as 'noblest of the gods', all-powerful, wise, and gracious. Menander sees in Tyche 'a divine breath or understanding that guides and preserves all things' (Stobaeus 1. 6. 1). But the plain meaning of the word defies such moral glozing.

Feeling for *tyche* is strongest in risky situations: in athletic contests (Pind. *Isth.* 8. 66), in the drawing of lots (*Eur.* fr. 989), in love (on vases Tyche is named among the attendants of Aphrodite), and above all in seafaring (Aesch. *Ag.* 664), whence Tyche's commonest attribute in art, the rudder (cf. Pindar *apud* Plutarch, *loc. cit.*). But a man may see his whole life governed by *tyche*:

Oedipus calls himself 'the child of Tyche', for mere luck, not royal parentage, has made him eminent (Soph. *OT.* 1080–5). *Tyche* was used to form personal names of good omen, like Eutyches; such names, always current (Tychius at *Il.* 7. 220), are immensely common from the first century B.C. onwards. In popular belief each person has a separate *tyche*, which is born with him, and appears in all the particulars of his life (Demosthenes 18. 252–66, weighing his own *tyche* against Aeschines'; Philemon *apud* Stobaeum 1. 6. 11). So *tyche* is much like *daimon*, and sometimes both are invoked together as personal deities (Soph. *Ichn.* 73; Eur. *IA.* 1136; cf. Plato, *Leg.* 877 a). In a household cult of the third century B.C. offerings are prescribed for the *agathos daimon* of a married couple, and for the *agathe tyche* of the man's parents. The *tyche* of a Hellenistic king or Roman Emperor was a power to be adjured and even worshipped —often, no doubt, out of flattery more than faith; but it is clear that the *fortuna* of magnates like Sulla and Caesar could be the object of popular superstition.

Cities too were subject to *tyche*. Melos relies on 'the saving luck conferred by heaven' (Thuc. 5. 112); from the early fourth century onward the formula 'with good luck' was usually prefaced to records of Athenian decrees, and above a decree from Tegea Tyche is represented with her rudder, adorning a trophy. The Thebans, in the years of their supremacy, founded a cult of Tyche, the earliest known; the statue showed her holding, like Eirene, the child Plutus, and was thus an allegorical creation, no less than all later types of the goddess. In the same century Agathe Tyche received sacrifice at Athens, on one occasion together with Eirene; her statue, by Praxiteles, stood near the Prytaneion. A city, like a man, might have its special *tyche* (the oracle at Dodona affirmed that the *tyche* of Athens was 'good', while the *tyche* of mankind, in the same period, was 'hard and terrible', Demosthenes 18. 253), and in the third century this idea too issued in cult, first evident at Antioch and Alexandria: at the outset it seems that only the *tyche* of a great city, as of a great man, was honoured, but during imperial times many towns large and small, especially in Asia Minor and the East, worshipped their own Luck, that is Tyche designated by the place-name in the genitive.

G. Herzog-Hauser, *PW* s.v. Tyche; H. Herter, *Glück und Verhängnis. Über die altgriechische Tyche*, Hellas 1963, 1 ff.    N. R.

**TYDEUS** (Τυδεύς), in mythology, father, by Deipyle daughter of Adrastus (q.v.), of Diomedes (q.v. 2), and son of Oeneus (q.v.) (Apollod. 1. 75). He was a small but powerful and valiant man (*Iliad* 5. 801). Being sent on an embassy to Thebes by the Seven, he took part in sports there and defeated all the rest; the Thebans laid an ambush for him, but he killed all but one of the fifty who composed it (4. 384 ff.). Later poems, drawing more or less on the Cyclic Thebaid, and still later ones which use the *Thebais* of Antimachus, tell of his part in the attack on Thebes, his furious battle-rage (as Aesch. *Sept.* 377 ff.), and the manner of his death (*see* MELANIPPUS). A sixth-century vase shows Tydeus killing Ismene, as in the story told by Mimnermus (Brommer, *Vasenlisten*², 345).    H. J. R.

**TYNDAREOS** (Τυνδάρεως or -ος), in mythology, husband of Leda and father, real or putative, of Helen, Clytemnestra, and the Dioscuri (qq.v.). He was king of Lacedaemon (Apollod. 2. 145, and often), brother of Leucippus (q.v. 1), and of Aphareus and Icarius (Apollod. 1. 87); for his varying genealogy, see Roscher's *Lexikon* v. 1406 f. He has not much legend of his own; Hesiod (fr. 93 Rzach) says that when sacrificing to the gods he forgot Aphrodite, who therefore made his daughters light

and unfaithful. He is also associated with Heracles (q h.s the hero had a serious quarrel with Hippocoön and (iv sons, wherefore he invaded Lacedaemon, their kingdom, overcame and killed them in a desperate battle in which he lost his brother Iphicles (q.v.), and gave Lacedaemon to Tyndareos (Alcman, fr. 1. 5 Diehl; Apollod. 2. 143 ff.).    H. J. R.

**TYNNICHUS,** poet of Chalcis, whose reputation rested on a single poem, a paean to Apollo, of which nothing survives, but which was admired by Aeschylus (Porph. *Abst.* 2. 18) and mentioned with high praise by Plato.

Page, *Poet. Mel. Gr.* 707.

**TYPHON, TYPHOEUS** (Τυφών, Τυφωεύς), a monster, often confused with the Giants (q.v.), as Horace, *Carm.* 3. 4. 53, but originally and properly distinct from them. He was born by Earth to Tartarus after the defeat of the Titans (Hes. *Theog.* 820 ff.). He had a hundred heads of dragon-shape, which uttered the sounds of all manner of beasts, also mighty hands and feet (presumably a hundred, or a hundred pairs, of each, though Hesiod does not say so) and would have done enormous harm if Zeus had not at once attacked him with his thunderbolts, overthrown him, and cast him into Tartarus, setting Aetna on fire by the way (in Homer, *Il.* 2. 783, he lies in the land of the Arimi; cf. Verg. *Aen.* 9. 715–16, and commentators on both passages). His shape suggests oriental rather than Greek myth, and this is confirmed by his regular connexion with Cilicia. The story, therefore, in Apollod. 1. 41–4 Nonnus, *Dion.* 1. 154 ff., may be eastern and ancient. Typhon strove with Zeus, stole his thunderbolts, and cut out his sinews with his own sword; but Hermes and Aegipan stole all back (or Cadmus, q.v., disguised as a shepherd, beguiled Typhon with his music), so Zeus was finally victorious, and buried Typhon under Aetna.

H. J. R.

**TYRANNIO** (1) the Elder (early 1st c. B.C.). Theophrastus, son of Epicratides, of Amisus (where his teacher nicknamed him Tyrannio), afterwards a pupil of Dionysius Thrax, was brought by Lucullus as prisoner to Rome, where he was freed and enjoyed the patronage of Pompey, being the first Aristarchan to teach in the city. He was a friend of Cicero, Caesar, and Atticus, and interested in the Latin language, which he regarded as derived from an Aeolic Greek dialect. He was among those who examined the MSS. brought by Sulla from Athens, 86 B.C. His works, on metre (a comparatively rare topic), on Homeric and other criticism and exegesis, and on grammar (which, under Atticist influence, he defined as θεωρία μιμήσεως), have perished.

C. Wendel, *PW* 7 A. 1811 ff.    P. B. R. F.; R. B.

**TYRANNIO** (2) the Younger, son of Artemidorus, a Phoenician, was brought as a prisoner to Rome and freed by Terentia, the widow of Cicero. He was a pupil of Tyrannio the Elder, and became an eminent grammarian at Rome, Strabo being among his pupils. He wrote on accents and other grammatical topics, but his works have been confused with those of the elder Tyrannio, the fate of which they have shared.

C. Wendel, *PW* 7 A. 1819 f.    P. B. R. F.

**TYRANNY** (τυραννίς, perhaps a Lydian word) was the illegal monarchy which was usurped by individuals in many oligarchic city-states of the seventh and the sixth centuries B.C., the 'age of tyrants'. The earliest occurrence of the word is in Archilochus (fr. 22 D.). It was not a special form of constitution or a reign of terror; that bad sense was attached to it later, especially by the democratic *polis* of the fifth century which glorified the tyrannicide, and by the political philosophers, e.g. Plato, to whom tyranny meant the worst constitution possible. Tyranny hardly ever lasted more than two generations. The best known of the tyrants were Pheidon, Polycrates, Cypselus and Periander, Cleisthenes of Sicyon, Pisistratus (qq.v.). The last representatives of the early period of tyranny were the Sicilian tyrants Theron, Gelon, and Hieron, who rose to power mainly as military leaders. A second epoch of tyranny was introduced by Dionysius I (q.v.). Tyranny of the older type mostly arose from political and economic leadership of the lower classes, and often prepared the rise of democracy. The outlines of the constitution did not change, but the tyrants used laws and institutions as instruments of their own policy. They fostered popular cults, and generally contributed greatly to the enrichment and civilization of their States; without being 'business men' they actively participated in the great economic changes of their time. Later tyrants, though military dictators, inaugurated a new age of monarchy (q.v.).

P. N. Ure, *The Origin of Tyranny* (1922); A. Andrewes, *The Greek Tyrants* (1956); H. Berve, *Die Tyrannis beiden Griechen* (1967).
V. E.

**TYRE** (*Τύρος*, *Tyrus*), HELLENISTIC AND ROMAN, an important city on the Phoenician coast, some 20 miles south of Sidon. In 332 B.C. it offered an obstinate resistance to Alexander and was captured only after a famous siege. Though destroyed, it made a rapid recovery and became a Ptolemaic possession, at first under a native dynasty till 274, then as a republic, ruled by *Suffetes*. Conquered by the Seleucids in 200 B.C., it became free in 126. It early struck a *foedus* with Rome. It was made a colony by Septimius Severus, who granted it the *ius Italicum*, and also made it the capital of Syria Phoenice. It revolted under Elagabalus. It was a great commercial city, maintaining a *statio* at Puteoli and at Rome during the Principate, and was the seat of a famous purple-dyeing industry. It ruled a large territory, stretching to the upper waters of the Jordan.          A. H. M. J.; H. S.

**TYRRHENUS** (*Τυρρηνός*), eponym of the Tyrrhenians (Etruscans, q.v.), Dion. Hal. *Ant. Rom.* 1. 27. 1, where he is son of King Atys and comes from Maeonia (Lydia); in schol. Pl. *Ti.* 25 b, he is Atys' grandson; son of Heracles, Dion. Hal. 1. 28. 1, or of Telephus (q.v. 1), ibid.; apparently god of the Tyrrhenian Sea (Valerius Flaccus 4. 715). He invented trumpets (Hyg. *Fab.* 274. 20).
H. J. R.

**TYRTAEUS,** elegiac poet of the seventh century B.C., said by some to be an Athenian schoolmaster, who was sent to Sparta as the result of an oracle (Pl. *Leg.* 629 a, Paus. 4. 15. 6). It seems more likely that he was really a Spartan, since he was a general (Ath. 14. 630 f, Diod. Sic. 8. 36), and his fragments show him giving orders (frs. 1 and 8), which would hardly be tolerated by Spartans in a foreigner. He led the Spartans in the second Messenian War and helped to take Messene (*Suda* s.v. *Τυρταῖος*). His poems were collected at Alexandria in five books and contained: (1) war-songs, of which two specimens have been recognized in pieces of undoubted Spartan origin but not necessarily his (frs. 15–16 Bergk = *Carm. Pop.* 18–19); (2) exhortations in elegiac verse; and (3) a poem called *Πολιτεία* for the Lacedaemonians. Most of the existing fragments seem to belong to the second class.

Fr. 1 seems to be concerned with some definite occasion in war, since it gives orders for tactical arrangements and is concerned with a siege. Fr. 6–7 is a single poem which begins by praising the virtue of dying for one's country and ends by urging the young men to valour. Fr. 8 begins with a general praise of courage at a time that seems to be after a defeat and ends with specific advice on conduct in battle. Fr. 9 is more elaborate; it is concerned with the nature of *ἀρετή* and of the *ἀνὴρ ἀγαθός*, whom Tyrtaeus finds in the brave fighter. There is no good reason to suspect the authenticity of these pieces, since the type of warfare which they describe belongs to the seventh century, and all show a similar use of language, even of repeated phrases. Other fragments may belong to the third class, notably fr. 2 on the origin of the Spartans, fr. 3 on the alleged Delphian origin of their constitution, frs. 4 and 5 on the First Messenian War. Tyrtaeus was certainly connected with the political reforms of his time, though he was not necessarily a prophet of the so-called Lycurgan constitution. He writes in an epic language, with many echoes of Homer, and at times he is unskilful in his adaptation of a Homeric motive to new uses (fr. 6–7. 21–6 and *Il.* 22. 71–6, fr. 8. 29–34 and *Il.* 16. 215–17). His importance is more political than literary, though he seems to have influenced Solon. The Spartans are said to have sung his songs on the march (Ath. 630 e).

TEXT. Diehl, *Anth. Lyr. Graec.* i. 1. 6–22.
COMMENTARY. T. Hudson-Williams, *Early Greek Elegy* (1926), 106–15.
CRITICISM. U. von Wilamowitz-Moellendorff, *Textgeschichte der gr. Lyriker* (1900), 97 ff.; W. Jaeger, 'Tyrtaios über die wahre *ἀρετή*', *Sitz. Preuß. Ak.* 1932; C. M. Bowra, *Early Greek Elegists* (1938), 39 ff.          C. M. B

**TZETZES,** JOHANNES (12th C. A.D.), a copious, careless, quarrelsome, Byzantine polymath. In his youth he wrote (A.D. 1143) a commentary on the *Iliad* of which the greater part is still unpublished, followed by *Allegories* on *Iliad* and *Odyssey* (in 10,000 verses), and other verse works on *Antehomerica*, *Homerica*, and *Posthomerica*. His other writings include scholia on Hesiod, Aristophanes, Lycophron, and others, and a poem on prosody. His chief work, *Βίβλος Ἱστορική*, by its first editor named *Χιλιάδες*, is a review (in 12,674 verses) of Greek literature and learning, with quotations from over 400 authors. In regard to his poverty and slighted merits Tzetzes displays an engaging lack of reticence. He was not always without taste or discretion; e.g., once, when reduced to selling the rest of his library he retained his Plutarch; nor is felicity of expression lacking in (for example) his objurgation of Thucydides' cross-word style (*λοξοσυστρόφοις λόγοις*). Generally, however, his manner is dull, and he is extremely inaccurate (perhaps owing to his frequent separation from his books). His uncorroborated evidence is accordingly viewed with much suspicion. Nevertheless, he preserves much valuable information from ancient scholarship, and offers an engaging glimpse of the life of a Byzantine scholar in a period of intense interest in ancient Greek literature.

EDITIONS. *Letters*: Pressel, 1851; *Chiliades*: Kiessling, 1826; (scholia) Cramer, *Anecd. Ox.* 3 (1836); *Allegories*: *Iliad*: Boissonade (1851); *Odyssey*: H. Hunger, *Byz. Zeitschr.*, 1955; (scholia) Cramer, *Anecd. Ox.* 3. On *Iliad*: Hermann, 1812–14; Bachmann (in schol. *Iliad*) 1835–8; *Homerica*, *AnteH.*, *PostH.*: Jacobs, 1793; Bekker, 1816; (reprinted, Lehrs, 1868); *On Theogony*: Bekker (1842), Matranga, *Anecd. Gr.* 2 (1850); *Schol. on W.D. and Shield*: Gaisford, *Poet. Gr. Min.* 3. *Schol. on Aristophanes*: Koster and others (1960–4); *Schol. on Lycophron*: Scheer (1908). *Allegories ἐκ τῆς χρονικῆς*, etc.: Morellus, 1616; Studemund, *Anecd. Gr. varia*, 1886; *Schol. on Oppian*: Bussemaker (Didot), 1849; *Περὶ διαφορᾶς ποιητῶν*, etc.: Kaibel, *CGF* i. *On Death of Emperor Manuel* (1180): Matranga, *Anecd. Gr.* 2 (1850); C. Wendel, *PW* 7 A. 1959 ff.
P. B. R. F.; R. B.

# U

**UBII,** a German tribe on the east of the Rhine, between the Main and the Westerwald, which besought Caesar's help against the Suebi (q.v.) in 55 B.C. Under renewed Suebic pressure in 38 B.C. Agrippa brought them across the river at their own request, and settled them on land formerly belonging to the Eburones, in which Cologne was later to rise (*see* COLONIA AGRIPPINENSIS). The Ubii furnished recruits to the Roman army; they only joined Civilis in A.D. 70 under duress and returned to their allegiance to Rome at the earliest possible moment.    O. B.

**ULPIANUS** (1), DOMITIUS (*PW* 88), one of the last great Roman jurists, born of a family long established at Tyre. He was, with Paulus (q.v. 1), assessor to Papinian q.v.) as *praefectus praetorio*, and at some time held the office *a libellis*. He is said to have been banished, like Paul, by Elagabalus, but already in A.D. 222 he is *praefectus annonae*, and in the same year *praefectus praetorio*. He had great influence as adviser of the young Emperor, but was killed (223) by the mutinous Praetorians, ostensibly for his severity and some plans of reform unfavourable to this privileged corps. Like Paul, Ulpian was pre-eminent as an encyclopedic compiler and synthesizer. (It is possible to see a rivalry between them: both cite other jurists freely, but never cite each other, and their major literary works are parallel.) Ulpian was perhaps less original and acute than Paul, but he had greater clarity and ease of exposition. His aim seems to have been to sum up the learning of his predecessors so well that direct reference to previous authorities would be unnecessary, and his citations of earlier literature are accordingly numerous and thorough. Justinian's compilers paid him the compliment of using him far more than any other writer: nearly a third of the *Digesta* (q.v.) is taken from his works (more than twice as much as from Paul, his nearest competitor). The original extent of his writings was very great—we know of nearly 280 books— and is the more remarkable because his literary activity seems to have been almost entirely confined to the reign of Caracalla (212–17). His principal works: *Ad edictum libri 81*, a long commentary on the Praetor's Edict, with an annexe in two books on the Edict of the *aediles curules*; a comprehensive work *Ad Sabinum* in fifty-one books (perhaps unfinished, and certainly subsequently re-edited) with several supplementary monographs on various *Leges* or on special branches of the private law (*sponsalia, fideicommissa*); general works for practitioners (*disputationes, Responsa*); short textbooks: *Institutiones, Regulae* (seven books); monographs on various magistracies. The work known as *Tituli ex corpore Ulpiani* (or *Epitome Ulpiani*), which is preserved independently of the *Digest*, is probably a fourth-century epitome of a *Liber singularis regularum*, itself also attributed to Ulpian but more probably compiled by an unknown writer from edited texts of Gaius, Ulpian, and other jurists. The *Opiniones*, known only from the *Digest*, are probably also spurious.

*See* bibliography s.v. JURISPRUDENCE. For date of his death, *POxy* xxxi. 2665. F. Schulz, *Sabinus-Fragmente in Ulpians Sabinus-Kommentar* (1906). On the *Epitome* and *Liber singularis*: F. Schulz, *Die Epitome Ulpiani* (1926) and *Roman Legal Science* (1946); W. W. Buckland, *Law Quart. Rev.* xl (1924), 184 ff., liii (1937), 508 ff.; and literature on transmission of texts s.v. LAW AND PROCEDURE, ROMAN, I.
                                                              A. B.; B. N.

**ULPIANUS** (2) of Ascalon taught rhetoric at Emesa and Antioch in the reign of Constantine (A.D. 324–37) and wrote a number of declamations and rhetorical works.

He is the reputed author of scholia to eighteen speeches of Demosthenes; they are of little independent value. He was a teacher of Libanius and Prohaeresius.

**ULPIUS TRAIANUS,** MARCUS, father of the Emperor Trajan (q.v.), was a native of Italica in Baetica, of which province he later became governor. He commanded Legio X Fretensis in the Jewish War *c.* A.D. 67–8, and became consul (the first of his family to reach this rank) soon afterwards. In 73–4 he was created a patrician. Governor of Syria *c.* 73–6 (cf. *AE* 1933, no. 205), he won *ornamenta triumphalia* (*ILS* 8970), doubtless due to his wise handling of Parthian threats, and became proconsul of Asia *c.* 79–80. He died before 100 (cf. Pliny, *Pan.* 89); consecrated *c.* 112, he was honoured on his son's coinage as *Divus Pater Traianus*.

R. Paribeni, *Optimus Princeps* i (1926), 45 ff.; B. Stech, *Klio*, Beiheft x (1912), no. 34; Strack, *Reichsprägung* i. 199 ff.; *B.M. Coins, Rom. Emp.* iii (1936); R. Hanslik, *PW* Suppl. x. 1032 ff.; Syme, *Tacitus*, 1. 30 f. and index.                    C. H. V. S.; M. H.

**UMBRIANS.** The word 'Umbrian' has been used by ancient and modern authors to denote a variety of ethnic, linguistic, cultural, and geographical entities. Pliny (*HN* 3. 14. 112) refers to the Umbrians as the *gens antiquissima Italiae*, and derives their Greek name of Ombrikoi from their having survived the flood. Attempts to equate the Umbrians of the ancient sources with a range of archaeological terms extending from the Villanovans (q.v.) to the Germanic Ambrones have brought little save confusion or a clarity that is at best illusory. Evidence for the Indo-European Italic dialect known as Umbrian is found in that part of central Italy where the urnfield and inhumation rite overlapped; it is closely related to Oscan, from southern Italy (outside the urnfield area), and is written in a script derived via Etruscan from the western Greek alphabet. The longest documents are the ritual texts known as the Tabulae Iguvinae (q.v.).

Umbria, together with Ager Gallicus, formed the Sixth Regio of Italy (q.v.) under Augustus. As such, it included territory bounded by the Adriatic, the Crustumium, and the Aesis on the east, and by Sabine territory and the Tiber to south and west. Important towns included Iguvium, Camerinum, Asisium, Tuder, Sentinum, Spoletium, Carsulae, Ameria, Interamna Nahars, Narnia, Ocriculum (qq.v.), and Hispellum, and in Ager Gallicus Pisaurum and Sena Gallica.

G. Devoto, *Tabulae Iguvinae* (Rome, 1937); id. *Origini Indoeuropee* (1962); M. Pallottino, *X Cong. int. scienze storiche* ii (1955), 3 ff.; *Atti del I° Convegno di Studi Umbri* (Perugia, 1964); *PW* Suppl. ix. 1745 ff.                                    D. W. R. R.

**URBANUS,** a Virgilian scholar repeatedly cited by Servius in his commentary on Virgil. He is certainly later than Cornutus (q.v. 1) whom he criticizes; and Thilo, *Serv. praef.* 16, puts him as late as the fourth century.

**URSO** (modern *Osuna*), a native settlement in Spain about 60 miles east of Seville. A centre of Pompeian resistance in 45 B.C., it was stormed by Caesar, who later replaced the inhabitants with colonists. Bronze tablets containing part of the colonial charter (*Lex Coloniae Genetivae Iuliae*) survive. It is an administrative regulation (*lex data*) based on a legislative act (*lex rogata*) issued by M. Antonius on behalf of Julius Caesar. From Pliny (*HN* 3. 12) it seems that this was one of Caesar's colonies for the *plebs urbana* of Rome. It included freedmen on equal terms.

Dessau, *ILS* 6087; Bruns, *Font.* 28; translation and commentary in E. G. Hardy, *Roman Laws and Charters* (1913).
J. J. van N.; M. I. H.

**USURY.** Loans at interest were not customary in Greece and Italy during the Early Iron Age, except perhaps for cattle and seed. Our earliest records come from Megara, and from Athens, where Solon removed all restrictions of interest, and made provisions for all types of loans. Usury with or without security became a profitable business during the Classical Period, both for private individuals and for temples and State institutions. Athens, from Solon's time, most Hellenic States, and Rome forbade lending on the security of the debtor's person, a practice prevalent in the East until the Hellenistic age, which was a period of large borrowing transactions throughout the civilized world. Usury was absolutely forbidden at Rome in, perhaps, 342 B.C., but the law became inoperative from the second century. The pitiless treatment of debtors by the upper classes at Rome during the later Republic is only too well known. After 51 B.C. interest might not exceed 12 per cent, except for seed loans; but usury by legal subterfuge is attested by authors and papyri. These evasions were gradually made more difficult, under the impact of Aristotle and the Judaeo-Christian tradition, until in the Late Roman period a limit was fixed (50 per cent!), extending to seed loans. Unlimited usury was henceforth illegal.

*See* BOTTOMRY LOANS; INTEREST, RATE OF. Michell, *Econom. Anc. Gr.* 29 f.; M. Schnebel, *Aegyptus* 1933, 35 f. F. M. H.

**UTICA** (modern *Utique*), traditionally the oldest Phoenician settlement on the north African coast, some 30 miles north-west of Carthage; its earliest remains appear to be of the eighth century B.C. Though now lying 5 miles inland, in antiquity it was a port on the mouth of the Bagradas river. Within the Carthaginian Empire it always retained a special position. Utica was besieged by Scipio (204) and supported Masinissa (q.v.) against Carthage in 149. Rome rewarded Utica with lands of the fallen city and made her the capital of the Roman province of Africa; Italian financiers and merchants settled in the Free City. Pompey made the port his base for the swift campaign which won Africa from the Marians (81). Later Utica remained loyal to the Pompeian cause against the forces of Curio and Caesar, and was the scene of Cato's suicide. Heavily fined for its senatorial sympathies, Utica lost ground as Roman Carthage became important, but received municipal rights under Augustus and colonial under Hadrian. A substantial part of the residential section of the Roman town has recently been uncovered.

Excavation reports in *Karthago* 1951, 1954, 1958, etc. L. Teutsch, *Das Städtwesen in Nordafrika* (1962), see index; A. Lézine, *Carthage. Utique* (1968). W. N. W.; B. H. W.

**UXELLODUNUM**, an *oppidum* of the Cadurci. In 51 B.C. it was the scene of the last Gallic resistance to Caesar who, after Drappes and Lucterius had been defeated while out foraging, finally took it by diverting the spring which supplied it. The place is generally identified with *Puy d'Issolu* (near *Vayrac*), where in 1862 Cessac discovered diversionary works at a spring on the west side of the hill-fort, but other details do not fully agree and *l'Impernal* (*Luzech*) and *Murcens* (north-east of *Cahors*) still claim some adherents.

Hirtius, *BGall.* 8. 30-4. C. Jullian, *Hist. de la Gaule* iii (1909), 553 ff. Puy d'Issolu: Grenier, *Manuel* i. 201 ff. L'Impernal: M. A. Cotton in Wheeler and Richardson, *Hill-Forts of Northern France* (1957), 186 ff. Murcens: Cotton, op. cit. 183 ff. A. L. F. R.

# V

**VABALLATHUS**, SEPTIMIUS, or in Greek ATHENO-DORUS, the son of Odaenathus (q.v.) by his second wife Zenobia (q.v.), was an infant when his father was killed but was his titular successor, under the guardianship of his mother. He at first assumed the title of king of kings and *corrector totius orientis*. In A.D. 270 Aurelian recognized him as *vir consularis, rex, imperator, dux Romanorum*. In 271 he was proclaimed *Imperator Caesar Vaballathus Athenodorus Augustus*. In 274 he was apparently not carried in Aurelian's triumph, and may have died before.
A. H. M. J.; H. S.

**VACUNA**, a Sabine goddess, Horace, *Epist.* 1. 10. 49. He probably puns on her name, as if she were 'uacationis dea' (so Cruquius' commentator ad loc.), but her real functions were already forgotten. Varro identified her with Victoria (q.v.; 'Acron' ad loc.), others with Bellona, Diana, Minerva, and Venus (qq.v.; ibid. and Porphyrio ad loc.). She had groves at Reate and by the Lacus Velinus (Pliny, *HN* 3. 109).

E. C. Evans, *Cults of the Sabine Territory* (1939), index s.v.
H. J. R.

**VAGELLIUS**, Neronian poet and friend of Seneca (*QNat.* 6. 2. 9). Morel, *FPL* 124. The same name is accepted by Ribbeck and others, but queried by Schanz, for the doubtful 'Vallegius' mentioned by Donatus (auctarium, Suet. *Vit. Ter.*) as a witness to the Younger Scipio's share in Terence's plays. J. W. D.

**VALENS** (1), FABIUS (*PW* 151) (*cos. suff.* A.D. 69), born at Anagnia of equestrian family, 'procax moribus neque absurdus ingenio' (Tac. *Hist.* 3. 62). Commander of Legio I in Germania Inferior, he supported Galba, suppressed the governor Fonteius Capito, and incited Vitellius to proclaim himself Emperor. An army-commander in the invasion of Italy and at Bedriacum, and honoured by Vitellius, he was impeded by ill health from reaching northern Italy in time to oppose the troops of Antonius Primus. Learning of the fall of Cremona, he made his way to Gallia Narbonensis, but was captured there and subsequently put to death. R. S.

**VALENS** (2), Eastern Emperor (A.D. 364-78), was elevated by his brother Valentinian I (q.v.) to rule the East. The chief event of his reign was the crossing of the Danube by the Visigoths, who completely defeated Valens in the battle of Adrianople (9 Aug. 378); his body was never recovered. He was an ardent Arian and was considerably less tolerant in religious matters than his brother. E. A. T.

**VALENTIA** (modern *Valencia*), on the south-east coast of Hispania Citerior. Decimus Brutus settled the former soldiers of Viriathus (138 B.C.) either here or at another Valentia (?*Valença do Minho* in Portugal). Its inhabitants supported Sertorius' cause even after his death. Its Roman name was known to Sallust in connexion with the Sertorian war. It became a full Roman colony at some time in the first century B.C. The prosperity of the city is proved by Iberian ceramics, Ibero-Roman coins, numerous inscriptions, and the fact of Byzantine occupation.                                     J. J. van N.; M. I. H.

**VALENTINIAN** (1) **I**, Roman Emperor (A.D. 364–75), a Pannonian, was an army officer who was elevated by the troops at Nicaea in Feb. 364 after the death of Jovian. At Constantinople in March he elevated his brother Valens (q.v. 2) to rule in the East, while he himself took over the government of the West. Most of his reign was spent in the defence of the northern frontiers. In this work he showed great skill and energy. In 367 he proclaimed his son Gratian (q.v.) as Emperor. Although cruel and irritable he showed consistent toleration in religious matters. He died at Brigetio (375).                          E. A. T.

**VALENTINIAN** (2) **II**, Roman Emperor (A.D. 375–92), was the son of Valentinian I. He was elevated by the troops at Aquincum (375) without the consent of Valens or Gratian (qq.v.), but they gave him Italy, Africa, and Illyricum to rule. Expelled from Italy by Magnus Maximus (q.v. 2) he was restored by Theodosius I. He was found dead, perhaps murdered, at Vienne in 392.

**VALENTINIAN** (3) **III**, Western Roman Emperor (A.D. 425–55), was the son of Constantius III and Placidia (qq.v.) and was born in 419. First Placidia and then Aetius were the effective rulers of his part of the Empire, for he never took much interest in public affairs; but in 444 he issued his famous Novel 17 which gave the bishop of Rome supremacy over provincial churches. He murdered Aetius with his own hands in 454; but two barbarian retainers of Aetius avenged their master by murdering Valentinian in 455.                          E. A. T.

**VALĔRIANUS**, Publius Licinius (PW 173) (Emperor A.D. 253–60). A senator of distinguished origin, he held an important military command in Raetia under Trebonianus Gallus. The troops he collected to help Gallus against Aemilianus hailed him as Emperor on the death of Gallus. When Aemilianus was killed by his own troops, Valerian and his son Gallienus were universally recognized as Augusti. During their reigns, the Empire nearly collapsed under external attacks and internal revolts, but the chronology is exceptionally obscure.

Probably about the beginning of his reign, the Borani ravaged the coast of Pontus; a few years later, perhaps c. 256, the Goths, who were also settled on the Sea of Azov, raided south by land and sea, sacking Nicomedia, Nicaea, and other Bithynian cities. A few years later again another Gothic raid plundered the Ionian cities, destroying the Artemision at Ephesus.

The success of these raids was due to lack of city walls, an unarmed populace, and the concentration of troops on the frontiers, especially the Euphrates. Here Sapor (q.v.) was increasingly aggressive, launching attacks into Syria. The important frontier fort of Dura fell in 256, and even Antioch was captured, or its territory ravaged, perhaps twice. Valerian, who was probably in the East from 256, was able to do little, and the final catastrophe came in 260 when he was captured by the Persians at Edessa. His subsequent fate is unknown. Christian writers perhaps exaggerate his defects because he issued edicts of persecution, but Valerian seems to have been quite overwhelmed by the series of disasters in the East.

G. Walser and Th. Pekáry, Die Krise des römischen Reiches (1962), 28 ff.; A. T. Olmstead, CPhil. 1942, 241 ff., 398 ff.; Magie, Rom. Rule Asia Min. 705 ff.                          B. H. W.

**VALĔRIUS** (1, PW 302) **POPLICOLA**, Publius, traditionally one of the first consuls in 509 B.C., is a figure of doubtful historicity, despite the objectively attested connexion of the Valerii with the Velia. His story rests mainly on the account of Valerius Antias, who claimed descent from him, and was the main source of Plutarch's biography. His alleged victories over Rome's neighbours, his work as a popular lawgiver (e.g. a Lex Valeria, establishing the right of provocatio), his consequent cognomen Poplicola (populum colere), his raising of the number of senators, and his institution of the quaestorship are all suspect.

Ogilvie, Comm. Livy 1–5, 250 ff.                          P. T.

**VALERIUS** (2, PW 304) **POTITUS**, Lucius, and M. Horatius Barbatus, the consuls who are said in 449 B.C. to have replaced the Decemvirs, were traditionally patrician benefactors of the plebs who reconciled the Orders. In all likelihood they acted as peacemakers, although their programme of appeasement probably consisted (apart from the restoration of the consulship) in the de facto recognition of the measures taken by the plebeians for their government (tribal assemblies) and their defence (the appointment of plebeian magistrates). The laws ascribed to Valerius and Horatius (Livy 3. 55) were: (1) the recognition that plebiscita were binding on the whole community; (2) the restoration of the right of appeal (prouocatio); (3) the sacrosanctity of plebeian magistrates. Their historicity should be seriously doubted or rejected outright because plebiscita were given force of law only by the Lex Hortensia (c. 287 B.C.); the right of appeal had already been secured by the XII Tables; and the recognized sacrosanctity of plebeian magistrates, however welcome, juridically meant nothing except that they were now magistrates of the Roman community. They were attributed to the consuls of 449 because the fall of the Decemvirs seemed a landmark in the plebeian advance, or rather because the annalists liked to connect the basic elements of the Roman constitution with either the beginnings of the Republic (laws attributed to Valerius Poplicola) or the restoration of the consulship.

De Sanctis, Stor. Rom. ii. 51 ff.; G. W. Botsford, The Roman Assemblies (1909), 274 ff.; H. H. Scullard, Hist. Roman World³ (1961), 432 ff.; E. S. Staveley, Athenaeum 1955, 12 ff.; K. v. Fritz, The Theory of the Mixed Constitution in Antiquity (1954); Ogilvie, Comm. Livy 1–5, 497 ff.                          P. T.

**VALERIUS** (3, PW 137) **CORVUS**, Marcus. Roman hero of the fourth century B.C., traditionally a simple farmer who lived to be a hundred. He was consul in 348 (when only 22 years old), 346, 343, 335, 300, 299 (suffectus), dictator in 342, 301; altogether he occupied the curule chair twenty-one times. When military tribune (349) he engaged a giant Gaul in single combat: a raven (corvus), by flapping in the Gaul's eyes, presented Valerius with victory and a cognomen. Valerius is also said to have defeated Volsci (346), Samnites (343), the inhabitants of Cales (335), Aequi (300), Etrusci (299), and to have quelled a mutiny (342) and promulgated a law of appeal (300). Even Livy (cf. 7. 42; 10. 3) hesitated to ascribe all these exploits to him. Some of the exaggerations in surviving accounts probably derive from Valerius Antias. Modern writers are more critical.

Livy, bks. 7–10; Val. Max. 8. 13. 1; 8. 15. 5; App. Gall. 10; BCiv. 3. 88; Aul. Gell. 9. 11; Zonar. 7. 25; [Aur. Vict.] De vir. ill. 29. F. Münzer, De gente Valeria (Diss. Berlin, 1891).          E. T. S.

**VALERIUS** (4, PW 95) **AEDITUUS** (fl. c. 100 B.C.), like Lutatius Catulus and Porcius Licinus, wrote epigrams, often erotic, after Greek models. Gellius (19. 9. 10) praises the verses of all three as unequalled for neatness and charm.

Morel, FPL.                          J. W. D.

VALERIUS (5, *PW* 98) ANTIAS, the Roman annalist of the immediate post-Sullan period, wrote a history of Rome in at least seventy-five books, from the origins to his own times. Book 2 included Numa, book 22 Mancinus at Numantia, book 45 (probably) the year 110 B.C.; the latest date preserved is 91 B.C., the latest book 75. This shows an increase in scale for contemporary events, but even for early times he wrote more fully than the records justified (Livy 3. 5. 12). He represents the rhetorical fashion in historiography, elaborating battle-scenes, inventing casualty figures, and composing reports of debates and speeches. To information often false he added confusion and misrepresentation, under the political and family influences of his time, e.g. on early Valerian tradition. He glorified Scipio Africanus (Livy 38. 50–60) and admired Sulla. Livy criticizes his numbers (26. 49. 3; 33. 10. 8; 36. 38. 6), but followed him throughout his work. His style was vigorous and rhetorical, if without grace, bringing annalistic history to its highest literary point before Livy.

Peter, *HRRel.* i². cccv; 238; K. W. Nitzsch, *Die röm. Annalistik* (1873), 349; F. Münzer, *De gente Valeria* (1891); Ogilvie, *Comm. Livy 1–5*, 12 ff.                                    A. H. McD.

VALERIUS (6, *PW* 345) SORANUS (i.e. of Sora), QUINTUS, *trib. pleb.* 82 B.C., was a linguistic and antiquarian scholar often quoted by Varro, *Ling.*: cf. Gell. 2. 10. 3; Cic. *De Or.* 3. 43; *Brut.* 169. Two hexameters of his on the fatherhood of Jupiter are quoted from Varro by St. Augustine, *De civ. D.* 7. 9.

Morel, *FPL.* Schmekel (*Die Philosophie der mittleren Stoa* (1892), 446) placed him in the Scipionic Circle, and Büttner (*Porcius Licinus u. der litter. Kreis des Lutatius Catulus*, 123) sought to identify him with Valerius (q.v. 4) Aedituus.                                    J. W. D.

VALERIUS (7, *PW* 117) CATO, PUBLIUS, scholar and poet, born in Cisalpine Gaul probably *c.* 100–90 B.C. Almost all our knowledge of him comes from Suetonius (*Gram.* 11) and nothing has survived from his writings. They included, besides works of scholarship (in which a special interest in Lucilius may have appeared), an *Indignatio*, in which he repudiated aspersions on his birth and complained of the loss of his patrimony in the time of Sulla, and two poems, *Lydia*, probably amatory, and *Diana* or *Dictynna*, a narrative poem on the story of Britomartis. He was an outstanding teacher of whom it was said 'solus legit ac facit poetas'. Cinna, Ticida, and Furius Bibaculus were among his pupils: their complimentary references to his poetry and his teaching show that he embraced the ideals and standards of the Alexandrian school and suggest that its development owed something to his inspiration.                                    C. J. F.

VALERIUS (8, *PW* 239) MAXIMUS, a Roman historian in Tiberius' reign with strong rhetorical and philosophical bias. A poor man, he was befriended by Sextus Pompeius (*cos.* A.D. 14), and accompanied him to his governorship in Asia about A.D. 27. After his return Valerius composed a handbook of illustrative examples for rhetoricians, *Factorum ac dictorum memorabilium libri IX.* This is dedicated to Tiberius, to whom constant flattery is addressed; and the violent denunciation of Sejanus (9. 11 Ext. 4) suggests that it was published soon after his downfall in 31. The subject-matter of the nine books has no clearly defined plan, but is divided under headings mostly moral or philosophical in character (e.g. Omens, Moderation, Gratitude, Chastity, Cruelty), which are usually illustrated by Roman (*domestica*) and foreign (*externa*) examples. The latter, chiefly Greek, are admittedly less important, and in keeping with the strongly national spirit of the compilation are outnumbered by the *domestica* by two to one. The work is shallow, sententious, and bombastic, full of the boldest

metaphor and rhetorical artifices of the Silver Age, especially forced antitheses and far-fetched epigrams, only occasionally relieved by touches of poetic fancy or neat passages of narrative or dialogue. His chief sources seem to have been Livy and Cicero, but there are indications of many others, such as Varro, Coelius Antipater, Pompeius Trogus, and several Greek writers. His use of this material is almost entirely non-critical, and varies greatly in extent and accuracy. Yet the variety and convenience of the compilation ensured some measure of success in antiquity, and considerably more in the Middle Ages. It is referred to by Pliny the Elder, Plutarch, and others. Most significant, however, is the existence of two later epitomes. The first is by Julius Paris (4th c. ?) and has attached to it a summary on Roman names, *De praenominibus*, ascribed to a certain C. Titius Probus and elsewhere erroneously included in MSS. as book 10 of Valerius' own work. The second, by Januarius Nepotianus (5th c. ?), breaks off early in book 3.

EDITIONS. A. Torrenius (1726; notes and index); C. Kempf (Berlin, 1854: Teubner, 1888); P. Constant (1935: Fr. trans.).
STUDIES. C. Bosch, *Die Quellen des Val. Max.* (1929); A. Klotz, 'Studien', *Sitz. Wien* 1942, 5; D. M. Schullian, 'A Prelim. List of MSS.', in *Studies in Honor of Ullman* (1960).                                    G. C. W.

VALERIUS (9, *PW* 106) ASIATICUS, DECIMUS (?), born at Vienna (q.v.), and *consul suffectus* in A.D. 35, was rich, proud, and athletic. Used by Gaius with contemptuous familiarity, he publicly approved his murder and was thought to have been in the plot. Under Claudius he served in Britain and held a second consulship (46). In 47, through the contrivance of Messallina, he was condemned by Claudius on charges of treason and adultery and committed suicide. Claudius attacked his memory in a famous speech (*ILS* 212. 2. 14–17).

P. Fabia, *La Table claudienne de Lyon* (1929), 104 ff.        T. J. C.

VALERIUS (10) FESTUS, C. CALPETANUS (*PW* 2) RANTIUS QUIRINALIS, *cos. suff.* A.D. 71, was legate of the African legion in 69. He arranged the murder of the proconsul L. Piso (q.v. 10): it was alleged that, as a relative of the defeated Vitellius, he wanted to demonstrate his loyalty to the new Emperor Vespasian. He then campaigned against the Garamantes, and was given consular decorations. After his consulship he became curator of the Tiber, legate of Pannonia (73), and of Tarraconensis (79–80). He died, still an *amicus* of the Emperor, early in Domitian's reign (Mart. 1. 78).                                    G. E. F. C.

VALERIUS (11, *PW* 170) FLACCUS, GAIUS, a poet. Nothing is known of his life save that he was a *quindecimvir sacris faciundis* (1. 5, 8. 239–41), that he probably began his poem in A.D. 80 (see references to Titus and his *Templum Divi Vespasiani*, 1. 13–16, and to the eruption of Vesuvius, 3. 208–9, 4. 507–9), and that premature death overtook him before he completed the eighth book of his *Argonautica* in 92 or 93; for the only certain reference to him in Roman literature is Quintilian's brief expression of regret at his demise (*Inst.* 10. 1. 90).

His only known work is the *Argonautica*, which is indebted to but not a close imitation of the similar work of Apollonius (q.v. 1) Rhodius. The poem takes the reader in the company of the Argonauts from Iolcos to Colchis, where Jason secures the Golden Fleece and escapes with Medea. Nearly all the well-known incidents of the myth are described in detail—the story of Hypsipyle and the Lemnian women, the tragic battle at Cyzicus, Hercules' loss of Hylas to the Nymphs, the boxing-match between Pollux and Amycus, the passage of the Argo between the Clashing Rocks, the meeting with Medea, who helps him to sow the dragons' teeth. But the poem breaks off abruptly with the pursuit of the Argo by her brother Absyrtus. Valerius' Jason is a much more successful character, as a leader of heroes, but his Medea is a less subtle psychological study, than Apollonius'.

Valerius is strongly influenced by Virgil, like the other epic writers of the early Empire, but is a better poet than they, in so far as he is less excessively rhetorical than Lucan and a more original genius than Statius. Unlike them, however, he was unknown in the Middle Ages until the Florentine humanist Poggio Bracciolini discovered at St. Gall in 1416 a MS. (now lost).

TEXTS. G. Thilo (1863; best critical apparatus); J. B. Bury, Postgate's *Corp. Poet. Lat.* (1905); C. Giarratano (1904; highly conservative); O. Kramer (Teubner, 1913).
COMMENTARIES. P. Burman (1724; useful variorum edition); P. Langen (1897).
TRANSLATION. J. H. Mozley (Loeb, 1934).
STUDIES. K. Schenkl, *Stud. z. d. Argonautica* (1871); W. C. Summers, *A Study of the Argonautica* (1894); F. Mehmel, *Valerius Flaccus* (1934). R. J. G.; A. K.

**VALERIUS** (12) **LICINIANUS**, LUCIUS, from Bilbilis (Mart. 1. 61. 11; 4. 55. 1), an advocate whom Martial considered a Spanish Cicero, was exiled by Domitian, but permitted by Nerva to settle in Sicily, where he professed oratory (Pliny, *Ep.* 4. 11).

**VALGIUS** (*PW* 7) **RUFUS** (*cos. suff.* 12 B.C.), one of the poetic circle patronized by Maecenas (Hor. *Sat.* 1. 10. 82), was consoled by Horace (*Carm.* 2. 9) on the death of a favourite slave, Mystes, whom he had himself commemorated in elegiac laments. Besides elegies he composed epigrams, translated Apollodorus' rhetorical precepts (Quint. *Inst.* 3. 1. 18), wrote on grammatical questions and on herbs.

Schanz–Hosius; Baehrens, *FPR*; Morel, *FPL*. J. W. D.

**VALLIUS SYRIACUS**, a distinguished rhetorician in the Elder Seneca's *Controversiae* (1. 1. 11 and 21; 2. 1. 34 ff.; 7. 6. 11; 9. 4. 18). He proclaimed himself a pupil of Theodorus (q.v. 3), and therefore not a slavish employer of *narratio* (q.v.) in his speeches.

**VANDALS**, a Germanic people, who left their original homes in southern Scandinavia before the beginning of the Christian era, and settled on the south coast of the Baltic Sea. Pliny speaks of the *Vandilii*, as he and Tacitus call them, as including various other peoples, e.g. the Goths and Burgundians, who at any rate in later times would by no means have considered themselves to be Vandals. At least as early as the second century A.D. they were divided into two sections, the Asdings and the Silings. Before the year 200 they had moved southwards into the lands lying east of the Tisza, where they became the western neighbours of the Visigoths (*see* GOTHS) when the latter occupied Transdanubian Dacia (*c.* 270). The Vandals frequently raided, and were raided by, the Visigoths and also attacked the Roman provinces in the third and fourth centuries. But they did not seriously affect the Romans until on 31 Dec. 406, having probably been driven westwards by the advancing Huns, they crossed the Rhine near Mainz in company with the Alans (q.v.) and Suebi. For three years they severely devastated wide areas of Gaul and in 409 crossed into Spain. Here, too, they ravaged extensively, but then settled down apparently with the intention of living there permanently. The Silings occupied Baetica, the Alans Lusitania, and the Asdings and Suebi Gallaecia. The Silings were all but exterminated by the Visigoths, who were acting under Roman instructions. Those Alans who escaped the Visigoths joined the Asdings, whose kings henceforth were known as the 'kings of the Vandals and Alans'. Under King Gunderic they moved into southern Spain, leaving the Suebi in Gallaecia (where their kingdom lasted until 585). Gunderic died in 428, and in the following year the Asding Vandals and the Alans,

numbering in all 80,000 persons, crossed into Africa. For their subsequent history *see* s.vv. GAISERIC, GELIMER.

L. Schmidt, *Geschichte der Wandalen*[2] (1942); C. Courtois, *Les Vandales et l'Afrique* (1955). Article in *PW* is concluded in Suppl. x. 957 ff. E. A. T.

**VARGUNTEIUS**, QUINTUS (2nd c. B.C.), junior to Lampadio (q.v.) among early lecturers on old Latin poets, expounded Ennius in public lectures, attracting large audiences (Suet. *Gram.* 2).

**VARIUS** (1, *PW* 7) **'HYBRIDA'**, QUINTUS, of Sucro in Spain, as tribune in 90 B.C. unsuccessfully attacked Scaurus (q.v. 1) and irregularly passed a law setting up a special court with equestrian jurors, which tried and convicted several of the supporters of Drusus (q.v. 2) for having incited the Italians to revolt. Trials continued even after the other *quaestiones* had been suspended owing to the war. In 89, in circumstances not clear (but perhaps connected with the jury reform of Plautius, q.v. 1), he was convicted under his own law and went into exile (Cic. *Brut.* 305).

E. S. Gruen, *JRS* 1965, 122 ff.; E. Badian, *Hist.* 1969, 447 ff. E. B.

**VARIUS** (2, *PW* 21) **RUFUS**, a distinguished elegiac, epic, and tragic Augustan poet, friend of Virgil (*Catal.* 7; *Ecl.* 9. 35), Maecenas, and Horace (*Sat.* 1. 5. 40; 6. 55), who praises his epic highly (*Carm.* 1. 6; *Sat.* 1. 10. 43). His epics included a *De morte* based on Epicurean principles, with special reference to Julius Caesar's death) and perhaps a *Panegyric* on Augustus. His tragedy *Thyestes*, performed at the games after Actium (29 B.C.), won deep admiration and comparison with the Greek masterpieces (Quint. 3. 8. 45, 10. 1. 98; Tac. *Dial.* 12). Assisted by Plotius Tucca (q.v.), he edited the *Aeneid* by Augustus' orders after Virgil's death.

Morel, *FPL* 100–1; Ribbeck, *TRF*[2] 229. G. C. W.

**VARRO** (1), GAIUS TERENTIUS (*PW* 83) (*cos.* 216 B.C.), was represented in the hostile aristocratic tradition (deriving probably from Fabius Pictor) as of humble origin (a butcher's son) and as a radical demagogue opposed to the Senate (cf. C. Flaminius), whereas his career shows that he enjoyed the Senate's confidence, while his father may have been a rich merchant. He was praetor in 218 B.C. As consul he commanded at Cannae (q.v.); he was probably no more responsible than his colleague, L. Aemilius Paullus, for the subsequent disaster, after which he was thanked by the Senate for not despairing of the State. He served as proconsul in Picenum (215–213), and with *imperium pro praetore* held Etruria against Hasdrubal's advance (208–207), and went as an ambassador to Africa in 200.

Scullard, *Rom. Pol.* 49 ff., *BICS* 1955, 19 f. H. H. S.

**VARRO** (2), MARCUS TERENTIUS (*PW* 84, Suppl. vi) (116–27 B.C.), was born probably at Reate in Sabine country (Symmachus, *Ep.* 1. 2. 21; according to Augustine, *De civ. D.* 4. 1, 'Romae natus et educatus'). He was a pupil of the first Roman philologist L. Aelius Stilo, who made himself known by his researches into the genuineness of the comedies bearing Plautus' name. At Athens his teacher of philosophy was the Academic Antiochus of Ascalon. In public life Varro rose to be a praetor. He fought as a partisan of Pompey in Spain in 49, but without success. Caesar restored him to favour and appointed him keeper of the future public library in 47. After Caesar's death he was outlawed by Antony in 43, but escaped death. His libraries, however, were plundered. When the Civil War was over he was allowed to devote himself entirely to peaceful study. According to Gellius (3. 10. 17) he had already edited 490 books at the beginning of his 78th year. We know the titles of fifty-five works, a catalogue of Varro's writings (but not of all) having been preserved in a fragment of Jerome (Ritschl, *Opusc.* iii. 522 ff.). We possess only two of his works substantially: *De lingua latina* (in part) and *Rerum rusticarum libri III.*

WORKS

1. *De lingua latina libri XXV*, of which books 5–10 are partly extant (only 5 and 6 entirely). Book 1 contained an introduction, probably a general view of the subject, books 2–7 explained how words had originated and were applied to things and ideas, 8–13 treated declension and conjugation, 14–25 dealt with syntax. Books 2–4 were dedicated by Varro to his quaestor Septumius, but starting from book 5 the remaining books are dedicated to Cicero. The work was published before Cicero's death, probably in 43 B.C. The derivations are often fanciful, but the work has preserved many quotations, especially from the old Latin poets.

2. *Rerum rusticarum libri III* (37 B.C.); book 1 treats of agriculture in general; 2 of cattle- and sheep-breeding; 3 of the smaller livestock kept on a farm, such as birds, bees, fishes, etc. Varro's aim was to rouse the diminished interest in country-life. The author has a tiresome tendency to group subject-matter under various headings and divide these again into subdivisions, but his prefaces are enjoyable and his book is not without wit.

Of Varro's lost works we may mention:

1. *Saturarum Menippearum libri CL*, probably between 81 and 67 B.C., humorous essays seasoned with verses, in which Varro followed, but in his own original way, the dialogues of the Cynic philosopher Menippus of Gadara (first half of 3rd c. B.C.). Varro proves himself here an enemy to the luxury and other foibles of his time. Ninety titles and 600 fragments have come down to us.

2. *Antiquitatum rerum humanarum et divinarum libri XLI* (47 B.C.). The first twenty-five books dealt with *res humanae*, and the last sixteen books with *res divinae* (Augustine, *De civ. D.* 6. 3). To arrange his subject-matter he put the questions: Who? Where? When? What? After an introductory book, 2–25 were divided into four parts: 2–7 treated of persons (e.g. inhabitants of Italy), 8–13 of places (e.g. Rome, Italy), 14–19 of the times, 20–5 of the actions of men.

The sixteen books that contained the *res divinae* began with an introductory book; the rest were divided into five parts: 27–9, priests; 30–2, temples, etc.; 33–5, festal days, games, etc.; 36–8, *sacra*; 39–41, the gods.

3. *Logistoricon libri LXXVI* (44 B.C.– ?), a collection of dialogues on various subjects—education of children, madness, chastity, etc. Every book took its name from a celebrated character, e.g. *Marius de fortuna, Tubero de origine humana.*

4. *Hebdomades vel de imaginibus* (libri xv; 39 B.C.). This work treated of famous Romans and Greeks, and contained 700 portraits illustrating the text (Pliny, *HN* 35. 11). It was called *Hebdomades* (Gell. 3. 10. 1), because the number 7 played an important part throughout.

5. *Disciplinarum libri IX*, an encyclopaedia of the *artes liberales*, i.e. of the branches of learning essential for a freeborn man (cf. ENCYCLOPEDIC LEARNING).

Varro's writings cover nearly every domain of science—history (*De vita populi Romani*, 'a social history of the Roman people'; *De gente populi Romani*, on primitive Rome and chronology), geography, rhetoric, jurisprudence (*De iure civili lib. XV*), philosophy, music, medicine, architecture, literary history (*De scaenicis originibus lib. III*; *De comoediis Plautinis*). He was the greatest scholar among the Romans; as to his method, he was a pupil of the Greeks, but he collected his matter

largely himself. His works were a mine of information for pagan and Christian authors, and even for medieval compilers. *See also* GRAMMAR; SCHOLARSHIP, LATIN.

LIFE AND WORKS. G. Boissier, *La Vie et les ouvrages de M. T. Varron* (1861); H. Dahlmann, *PW* Suppl. vi (1935), 1172.

TEXTS. **Ling. Lat.**: Weidmann (Spengel), Teubner (Schoell and Goetz); **Rer. rust.**: Teubner (Goetz); **Fragm. Gramm. and Lit.**: Funaioli, *Gramm. Rom. frag.* i. 183 (Teubner); **Sat. Men.**: Weidmann (Bücheler–Heraeus, Petron. *Sat.* 1922, 181); **Antiq.**: R. Merkel, *Ovidi Fasti* (1841), cvi; P. Mirsch, *Leipz. Stud.* v. 1 (1882); **Logist., Imag.**: Ch. Chappuis, *Fragm. des ouvr. de Varron* (1868); **Disc.**: F. Ritschl, *Opusc.* iii. 372; **Hist. fr.**: H. Peter, *HRRel.* ii (1906), 9.

COMMENTARIES. **Ling. Lat.** bk. 8, H. Dahlmann (1940). **Rer. Rust.**: J. G. Schneider, *Script. rei rust.* i (1794); H. Keil, *Comment. in Varronis rer. rust. libros tres* (critical, 1891).

TRANSLATIONS. **Ling. Lat.**: R. G. Kent (with text, Loeb); **Rer. Rust.** 1: L. Storr-Best (1912); W. D. Hooper and H. B. Ash (with text, Loeb).

STYLE AND DICTION. G. Heidrich, *Der Stil des Varro* (1892); R. Krumbiegel, *De Varroniano scribendi genere quaestiones* (1892); E. Norden, *Ant. Kunstpr.* i (1909), 194.

SPECIAL STUDIES. **Ling. Lat.**: H. Dahlmann, *V. und die hellenistische Sprachtheorie* (1932); **Sat. Men.**: L. Riccomagno, *Studio sulle Sat. Men. di Varrone* (1931); J. W. Duff, *Roman Satire* (U.S.A. 1936); F. della Corte, *La Poesia di V. ricostituita* (1938); **Antiq.**: R. Agahd, *Fleck. J. Suppl.* 1898; **Logist.**: R. Müller, *Klass. Phil. Stud.* 1938; **De gente Pop. Rom.**: P. Fraccaro, *Studi Varroniani* (1907); **De vita Pop. Rom.**: B. Riposati (1939).

*Varron (Entretiens Hardt* ix) includes bibliography of Varro 1950–62.

                                                 P. J. E.

**VARRO** (3) **ATACINUS**, PUBLIUS TERENTIUS (*PW* 88), was born in the Atax valley in Gallia Narbonensis in 82 B.C. Nothing is known of his life, and his work is represented only by fragments. His *Bellum Sequanicum* was a historical poem, presumably in the Ennian tradition, on Caesar's campaign of 58 B.C.: later he seems to have come under the new Greek influence (*see* ALEXANDRIANISM) in his *Argonautae*, a translation or adaptation of Apollonius Rhodius (Ov. *Am.* 1. 15. 21, Quint. 10. 1. 87), in amatory verse (probably elegiac) addressed to one 'Leucadia' (Prop. 3. 34. 85, Ov. *Tr.* 2. 439), and in two didactic works, *Chorographia*, a geographical poem, and *Epimenis* (?: the title is uncertain), in which he used Aratus' *Phaenomena* and on which Virgil drew in the *Georgics*. (The passage *Georgics* 1. 374–89 closely follows some lines of Varro quoted by Servius.) That he wrote satires we know from a passing reference in Horace (*Sat.* 1. 10. 46).

Fragments in Morel, *FPL.*                          C. J. F.

**VARRO** (4) **MURENA**, AULUS TERENTIUS (*PW* 92), probably a Licinius Murena adopted by an A. Terentius Varro, was brother-in-law of Maecenas (q.v.) and known to Horace (*Sat.* 1. 5. 38; cf. *Carm.* 3. 19). In 25 B.C. he ruthlessly subdued the Salassi of the Val d'Aosta (*see* AUGUSTA PRAETORIA). While consul with Augustus in 23 he defended M. Primus, ex-governor of Macedonia on a charge of *maiestas* and then joined Fannius Caepio (q.v. 3) and others in a conspiracy and was condemned and executed.

Syme, *Rom. Rev.*, see index; W. C. McDermott, *TAPA* 1941, 255 ff.; K. M. T. Atkinson, *Hist.* 1960, 440 ff.; F. Millar, *A Study of Cassius Dio* (1964), 88 ff.; D. Stockton, *Hist.* 1965, 18 ff.; S. Jameson, *Hist.* 1969, 204 ff.                  T. J. C.

**VARUS** (1), PUBLIUS ATTIUS (*PW* 32), of undistinguished family, praetor and then governor of Africa before 51 B.C., took Pompey's side in the Civil War. In 49, after failing to hold Caesar in Picenum, he established himself in his old province of Africa (*see* LIGARIUS). Assaulted by Curio (q.v. 2) at Utica, he was relieved by Juba (q.v. 1). After Pharsalus he had to yield the supreme command to Metellus (q.v. 11) Scipio, and served under him in the Thapsus campaign, from which he escaped to Spain. He fell at Munda.              T. J. C.

**VARUS** (2), PUBLIUS QUINCTILIUS (*PW* 20) (*cos.* 13 B.C.), of a patrician family that had been of no importance for centuries. He owed his career to the favour of Augustus, being the husband of Claudia Pulchra, the grandniece of the Princeps, and was able to acquire some political influence (his two sisters made good marriages, cf. the table in *PW* xvii. 870). Varus became proconsul of Africa (? 7–6 B.C.), and then legate of Syria. When Judaea revolted after the death of Herod the Great he marched rapidly southwards and dealt firmly with the insurgents (Joseph. *BJ* 2. 39 ff., etc.). Varus is next heard of as legate of the Rhine army in A.D. 9. When marching back with three legions from the summer-camp near the Weser, he was treacherously attacked in difficult country by Arminius (q.v.) whose professions he had trusted. The Roman army was destroyed in the Saltus Teutoburgiensis (q.v.; there has been much debate on the site) and Varus took his own life (Dio 56. 18–22; Vell. Pat. 2. 117–20; Florus 2. 30). Varus was made the scapegoat for the signal failure of Augustus' whole German policy. He is alleged to have been grossly extortionate in Syria, torpid and incompetent in his German command—'ut corpore ita animo immobilior, otio magis castrorum quam bellicae adsuetus militiae' (Vell. Pat. 2. 117. 2).

*CAH* x. 943 (bibliography). R. S.

**VARUS** (3), QUINCTILIUS, son of (2) above, was as a speaker trained under the pre-Tiberian rhetor Cestius Pius from Smyrna.

**VARUS** (4), ARRIUS (*PW* 36), a Roman knight, served with distinction as *praefectus cohortis* under Corbulo, but later is said to have defamed his old commander to Nero. In A.D. 69, when a *primus pilus* in one of the Danubian legions, he lent vigorous help to Antonius Primus on the Flavian side in the invasion of Italy, being rewarded after the final victory with the office of *praefectus praetorio*. Mucianus, however, soon arrived at Rome, put a check upon his ambitions (cf. the treatment of Antonius Primus), and reduced him to the post of *praefectus annonae*. He is not heard of afterwards. R. S.

**VASE-PAINTING.** Vase-painting not only records the development of Greek Painting (q.v.), but is also a prime source for the Greek conception of gods and heroes through their history and for the external appearance of everyday life.

MYCENAEAN. In the early period Mycenaean vases are strongly influenced by naturalistic Minoan vase-painting. After the fine fifteenth-century Palace Style vase-painting gradually becomes increasingly formal and abstract, although many interesting pictures survive till the end of the period.

ELEVENTH TO TENTH CENTURY B.C. The new Protogeometric style with precise shapes and simple geometric ornaments including compass-drawn concentric circles starts in Attica and spreads rapidly to other areas.

NINTH TO EIGHTH CENTURY B.C. The ornament gradually becomes more complicated and spreads over more of the surface of the vase. By the mid eighth century in Attica (and rather later and more sparingly elsewhere) the pattern bands are interspersed with bands of animals and human figures in silhouette—battles, dances, funerals, including some scenes which are certainly mythical and suggest a similar interpretation for all.

SEVENTH CENTURY. *Orientalizing.* From *c.* 725 B.C. patterns become more naturalistic and the decoration less orderly, with larger figures in partial outline; later the black-figure style (silhouette with incised inner markings) comes in. Athenian vases are divided into Early Proto-Attic (reminiscent of geometric), 'black and white', Late Proto-Attic (predominantly black-figure). In

Corinth Middle and Late Proto-Corinthian, 700–625 (neat and orderly; some small polychrome vases of superlative merit), is followed by Early Corinthian, 625–600 (black-figure; animal friezes and heroic scenes). Melian vases have large, untidy, heroic scenes. East Greek vases have processions of animals on white ground; figure-scenes are rare.

SIXTH CENTURY. *Black-figure.* In Athens two lines can be traced: 1. *Vigorous style.* Massive figures and often violent scenes. Originates in seventh century with Nessus painter. Continued by Sophilus, *c.* 570, the C painter, 575–550, Execias (q.v.), Andocides (q.v. 2) painter, 560–530) and Leagrus group, *c.* 515. 2. *Delicate style.* Drawing, neat and fine, sometimes formal. Begins with Clitias, 560. and painters of Little Master cups, *c.* 550, then Amasis (q.v. 2) painter and Menon painter (*see* ANDOCIDES 2).

Corinthian vase-painting continues till about 550, with some excellent pictures, e.g. 'Departure of Amphiaraus'. Chalcis carries on the best Corinthian tradition until 520, but the later Phineus group shows Ionian influence. The finest Laconian vases, e.g. Arcesilas cup, are produced 590–550. The chief East Greek styles are Fikellura, 570–500 (derives from Rhodian; drawing often witty), Clazomenian, 560–530, including Northampton group (formal and decorative), Caeretan, 540–525 (lively scenes of 'Heracles and Busiris', etc.; possibly made in Italy, but, unlike Pontic and allied groups, shows no Etruscan influence).

*530–400. Red-figure.* Figures reserved against black background, inner markings in black or brown. In Athens starts with Andocides (q.v.) painter and Menon painter. The vigorous style is continued by Euphronius Euthymides (qq.v.), Cleophrades painter (*see* EPICTETUS I), Panaetius painter (*see* EUPHRONIUS), Brygus (q.v.) painter; and the delicate style by Epictetus (q.v. I), Phintias (formal and elaborate), Berlin painter (rhythmical line and quiet beauty), Pan painter (mannerist), Duris (q.v.). After 480 Niobid painter and Penthesilea painter (*see* EUPHRONIUS) reflect composition of Micon and Polygnotus (q.v.); Chicago painter and the Phiale painter are quieter. White-ground vases, particularly *lecythi*, are now common; Achilles painter, 460–440, develops tradition of Berlin painter; Reed painter (430–410) is more passionate. In red-figure Eretria painter (440–420) begins a rich style which Meidias painter elaborates (*see* MEIDIAS); Dinos painter is realistic and vigorous. Red-figure painting starts in south Italy about 440 and at first is strongly influenced by Athens.

FOURTH CENTURY. In Athens the rich style continues in the work of Meidias painter's successors. The vigorous style can be traced through successive groups of Kertch vases. In south Italy local groups, Lucanian, Apulian (including Gnathia), Paestan, Campanian, Sicilian, Etruscan, develop on their own lines; their subjects are often interesting. Gnathia ware has echoes of Sicyonian painting. Vase-painting ends in the third century with the magnificent polychrome ware of Centuripe.

GENERAL. *Corpus Vasorum Antiquorum*; E. Pfuhl, *Malerei und Zeichnung der Griechen* (1923, 1940); Rumpf, *Malerei und Zeichnung der Griechen* (1953); R. M. Cook, *Greek Painted Pottery* (1960); P. Arias, M. Hirmer, and B. Shefton, *History of Greek Vase-Painting* (1962). (*See also under* GREEK PAINTING.)

SPECIAL. Mycenaean: A. Furumark, *Mycenaean Pottery* (1941). Protogeometric: V. Desborough, *Protogeometric Pottery* (1952). Geometric: J. N. Coldstream, *Greek Geometric Pottery* (1968); J. M. Davison, *Attic Geometric Workshops* (1961). Corinthian: H. G. G, Payne, *Necrocorinthia* (1931); *Protokorinthische Vasenmalerei* (1933). Chalcidian: A. Rumpf, *Chalkidische Vasen* (1927). Black-figure (Attic): J. D. Beazley, *Development of Attic Black-figure* (1951); *Attic Black-figure Vase-painters* (1956). Red-figure (Attic): J. D. Beazley, *Attic Red-figure Vase-painters* (1963). South Italian: A. D. Trendall, *Paestan Pottery* (1936); *Frühitalistische Vasen* (1938); (with A. Cambitoglou) *Apulian red-figured vase-painters of the plain style* (1961); *Red-figure vases of Lucania, Campania, and Sicily* (1967). Etruscan: J. D. Beazley, *Etruscan Vase-painting* (1947). T. B. L. W.

**VATICAN,** originally the district on the west bank of the Tiber extending from the territory of Veii to the reaches below Rome, but later forming the northern sector of the last of the fourteen regions into which Augustus divided the city of Rome. Its most distinctive feature was the *Mons Vaticanus,* descending sharply to a valley on the south and, on its east side, adjoining the Tiber, to the *Campus Vaticanus.* The region was noted for its clay (Juv. *Sat.* 6. 344), for the poor quality of the wine from its vineyards (Mart. *Epigr.* 6. 92. 3, etc.), and for its unhealthy air (Tac. *Hist.* 2. 93). Here lay the *Naumachiae* and the *Circus Gai et Neronis* (the traditional scene of St. Peter's martyrdom), the latter, in the *Vallis Vaticana,* probably being situated within the bounds of an imperial park, the *Horti Agrippinae* (Pliny, *HN* 16. 201; 36. 74; Tac. *Ann.* 14. 14; 15. 39, 44; Suet. *Claud.* 21). *Vaticanus* is also associated with a shrine of the Magna Mater (*CIL* xiii. 1. 1751; xiii. 2, 1, 7281), whose altars (*CIL* vi. 497–504) have been found on the site of St. Peter's façade. The two Roman highways that crossed this suburban area, the *Via Cornelia,* running from east to west, and the *Via Triumphalis,* running from south-east to north-west, were lined with tombs. Just to the north of where the former road must have lain there came to light under St. Peter's, during World War II, two rows of richly decorated mausolea all facing south and dating from the second century: predominantly pagan, they contain a few Christian burials and are aligned with some first-century graves and with the shrine that, from *c.* 160 onwards, marked the reputed site of the Apostle's resting-place. Of the tombs, found since the War on the Vatican City car-park site, which bordered the Via Triumphalis, a number date from the first century.

For books that deal in part with Vatican topography and cemeteries, see J. M. C. Toynbee and J. B. Ward-Perkins, *The Shrine of St. Peter and the Vatican Excavations* (1956); E. Kirschbaum, *The Tombs of St. Peter and St. Paul* (1959). I. A. R.; J. M. C. T.

**VATINIUS** (*PW* 3), PUBLIUS, tribune 59 B.C., sponsored the bills granting Caesar (q.v. 1) Cisalpine Gaul and Illyricum, and confirming Pompey's Eastern settlement; he also figures prominently in attacks on Bibulus and in the affair of Vettius (q.v. 3). In 56 Cicero, defending Sestius (q.v.), delivered the invective *In P. Vatinium testem interrogatio,* but in 54, obedient to the triumvirs, successfully defended Vatinius (who had been praetor in 55) on a bribery charge. After serving with Caesar in Gaul, Vatinius won a victory in the Adriatic in 47, and in December received the consulate, an office he had always boasted he would hold. His proconsulate, in Illyricum, was recognized by a *supplicatio* in 45; and though he surrendered to Brutus (q.v. 5) in 43 he triumphed in 42. Vatinius was made an easy butt by his personal disabilities, weak legs, and scrofulous swellings; but he took raillery well, and in later life was genuinely reconciled with Cicero, to whom in 45 he wrote *Fam.* 5. 10. (Cf. Catull. 14. 3 and 52–3.)

L. G. Pocock, *A Commentary on Cicero In Vatinium* (1926).
G. E. F. C.

**VECTIGAL** meant primarily revenue derived from public land, mines, saltworks, etc., and in general rents derived from State property. Such sources provided the basic revenues of the early Republic, and remained the most important forms of income for the *municipia* and *civitates* of the Empire. The term was also extended to cover indirect taxes, of which the only ones in the Republican period were the *portoria* (q.v.) and the *vicesima libertatis,* a tax of 5 per cent on the value of manumitted slaves. In the Principate the number of the *vectigalia* was increased, and they provided a considerable part of the State revenue. Only *vectigalia* were paid by the inhabitants of Italy, who

were exempt from *tributum* (q.v.). The most important of the *vectigalia* were the *portoria.* In order to raise revenue for the provision of discharge-donatives for veterans Augustus founded the *aerarium militare,* into which was paid the yield of two new taxes. The *centesima rerum venalium,* a tax of 1 per cent on sales by auction, was reduced to ½ per cent by Tiberius and abolished, in Italy, by Gaius. The *vicesima hereditatum* was a charge of 5 per cent on significant sums bequeathed to persons other than near relatives (see Pliny, *Pan.* 37–40). The death-duties were paid by citizens only, and their introduction was resented by Italians, who objected to any form of taxation. The extension of the citizenship had the effect of increasing their yield. The *quinta et vicesima venalium mancipiorum,* a 4 per cent tax on sales of slaves, was established by Augustus in A.D. 7 to provide the pay of the *vigiles* (q.v.). A number of minor *vectigalia* were established by Gaius (Suet. *Cal.* 40); one of them, on prostitutes, is attested in the second and third centuries. The collection of *vectigalia* was in the early Principate let out to companies of *publicani* (q.v.). In the second, and occasionally in the first, we find imperial *procuratores* (q.v.) of the *vicesima hereditatum* and *vicesima libertatis;* their precise function is unknown. *Portoria* came in the second century to be collected by individual *conductores* (q.v.) and then *procuratores.* G. H. S.; G. F. B. M.

**VEDIOVIS, VEIOVIS, VEDIVS,** an ancient deity, worshipped at Rome on the Capitol and on Tiber island (Platner–Ashby, 548 f.) and at Bovillae. His offering was a she-goat, sacrificed *ritu humano* (Gell. 5. 12. 12), whether that means on behalf of the dead (cf. Festus, 91. 24 Lindsay) or as a surrogate for a human victim (Preller–Jordan, *Röm. Mythol.*³ i. 265). This suggests a chthonian god, but his name is puzzling. The ancients, deriving *Iuppiter* from *iuuare,* took Vediouis as 'the non-helper' (Gell. ibid. 8), i.e. harmful, or as 'little Iuppiter', on the analogy of *uegrandis* (Ov. *Fasti* 3. 445–8, cf. Festus, 519. 22 Lindsay, both from Verrius Flaccus); Wissowa, *RK* 237, as a sort of anti-Iuppiter, a god of the dead; C. Koch, *Der römische Juppiter* (1937), 68, as meaning an abnormal form of Iuppiter, Latte (*RR* 81) as a Iuppiter who disappoints. His festival was on 21 May. The temple, which stood behind the Tabularium between the two summits of the Capitol, was discovered in 1939. The excavated temple is a restoration of 78 B.C.; below it are traces of the first temple, dedicated in 192 B.C., and of a temple of the mid second century. See Nash, *Pict. Dict. Rome* ii. 490 ff. The marble cult-statue of Apolline type (probably 2nd c. A.D.), found at the same time, replaced an earlier one of cypress wood. H. J. R.

**VEDIUS** (*PW* 8) **POLLIO,** PUBLIUS, a freedman's son and friend of Augustus, attained equestrian rank. Rich and cruel, he used to punish slaves by throwing them alive to his lampreys. He was one of Augustus' influential private assistants and appears to have been active in Asia both in an official capacity and as a private benefactor. He died in 15 B.C., leaving to Augustus much of his property, including his villa Pausilypon (*see* PAUSILYPUS MONS) and his immense town house on the Esquiline, on the site of which Augustus built the Porticus Liviae.

K. Scott, *AJPhil.* 1939, 459 f.; R. Syme, *JRS* 1961, 23 ff.; K. M. T. Atkinson, *Revue internationale des Droits del'Antiquité* 1962, 261 ff.; Platner–Ashby, 197, 423. A. M.; T. J. C.

**VEGETIUS RENATUS,** FLAVIUS, is the author of an *Epitoma rei militaris* in four books, which is the only ancient manual of Roman military institutions to have survived intact. Written between A.D. 383—Gratian is called *divus* (1. 20)—and 450, when a critical revision was produced by Eutropius at Constantinople, it is addressed to a single Emperor. If, as seems probable, Theodosius the Great is meant, the work may be dated to the years 383–95, and perhaps even more closely to Theodosius' stay in Italy from Aug. 388 to June 391.

The plan of the treatise is simple: book 1 deals with the recruit, book 2 with organization, book 3 with tactics and strategy, and book 4 with fortifications and naval warfare. Not quite so simple, however, is its composition. Vegetius himself was neither a historian nor a soldier: he was a bureaucrat by profession—he may have been *comes sacrarum largitionum*—and in temperament he was an antiquary. The result is a compilation carelessly constructed from material of all ages, a congeries of inconsistencies. To impress the reader with the weight of his authority he names some of his sources—Cato the Elder, Frontinus, and Paternus, and the *constitutiones* of Augustus, Trajan, and Hadrian. It is naïve to assume that these were the only sources he used, or even that he used these always at first hand. Schenk's view was that Paternus was his most recent source: it followed that all later additions must be from Vegetius' own day and experience. This led him to refer the *antiqua legio* of book 2, which is clearly not from Vegetius' own time, but from something which he has read, right back to the age of Hadrian: the majority of scholars have concurred in placing it in the third century, though details differ.

The real importance of Vegetius' work lies perhaps not so much in the mass of information which he gives us about the Roman army, for much of this is unfortunately unstratified, as in the very considerable influence which he had upon the military thinking of the Middle Ages and Renaissance.

TEXT. C. Lang² (1885). TRANSLATION. John Clarke (1767).
STUDIES. Dankfrid Schenk, 'Flavius Vegetius Renatus: die Quellen der Epitoma rei militaris', *Klio*, Beiheft 22 (1930); A. Anderson, *Studia Vegetiana* (1938); V. A. Sirago, *Galla Placidia* (1961), app. 2. A. R. Neumann, *PW* Suppl. x. 992 ff. Cf. G. R. Watson, *The Roman Soldier* (1969). G. R. W.

**VEIENTO,** AULUS DIDIUS GALLUS FABRICIUS (*PW* 15), was consul three times under the Flavian Emperors (his second tenure, in A.D. 80 under Titus, is the only one securely dated), and was evidently one of the most powerful senators of the period. Under Nero he had been exiled for circulating libels on eminent persons and for selling honours (Tac. *Ann.* 14. 50). But to Juvenal (4. 113; see also Schol. to line 94) he is 'prudens Veiento', prominent in Domitian's council; and he retained imperial favour under Nerva (Pliny, *Ep.* 4. 22), though his influence was then challenged (ibid. 9. 13. 13 ff.). He is not heard of after 97.

*ILS* 1010; Syme, *Tacitus*, app. 5. G. E. F. C.

**VEII,** founded by Villanovan settlers from the coast in the ninth–eighth century B.C., was Rome's nearest neighbour among the Etruscan cities, only 9 miles to the north. Relations with Rome were at first close and friendly, but the expansion of Roman power in Latium led to rivalry; after a long siege the city was destroyed in 396 B.C. (Livy 5. 1–22; Plut. *Cam.* 2–6) and its territory annexed, the population being grouped into four new rustic tribes. A small urban nucleus survived and shortly before 2 B.C. became the *municipium Augustum Veiens*; but the Roman town was of little importance and was progressively deserted in later antiquity. The site, about 480 acres in extent, was enclosed in the late fifth century B.C. by a powerful wall and rampart; but although the cemeteries have been extensively explored, little is known of the city itself. Etruscan Veii was famous for its statuary. Pliny (*HN* 35. 157) records the name of Vulca, commissioned to furnish statues for Jupiter's temple on the Roman Capitol. His school was responsible for the terracotta statues of Apollo and other divinities from one of the temples of Veii, now in the Museo di Villa Giulia at Rome.

*CIL* xi. 1. 556–7. J. B. Ward-Perkins, 'Veii : Historical Topography', *PBSR* 1965; 'The Ager Veientanus', *PBSR* 1968; *Not. Scav.* 1963, 77 ff.; 1967, 87 ff.; Scullard, *Etr. Cities*, 104 ff. J. B. W.-P.

**VELABRUM** was the low ground between the Capitol and Palatine in Rome, originally a swamp open to Tiber floods. The Cloaca Maxima (q.v.) passed riverwards through it, and by draining made of it one of the busiest centres in the city (Macrob. 1. 10. 15), contained between the Vicus Tuscus and Vicus Iugarius and carrying all traffic between the Forum and the river. Here lay Acca Larentia's shrine. I. A. R.

**VELIA,** now a narrow ridge or spur connecting the Palatine and Oppian hills of Rome at the head of the Via Sacra (q.v.). The summit was probably modified by levelling for the vestibule of Nero's *Domus Aurea* (q.v.) in A.D. 64, where later stood the temple of Venus and Roma, built under Hadrian. The saddle was crowned by the Arch of Titus. I. A. R.

**VELITES.** In the early Republican army the light-armed troops were recruited from citizens unable to provide themselves with hoplite armour and were called *rorarii*. By the Second Punic War their title had been changed to *velites*. The number in each legion was the same as that of *hastati* or *principes*. In battle they were employed probably as *iaculatores* (γροσφομάχοι) in conjunction with cavalry to open the attack. The chief period of their use was in the second half of the Second Punic War. During the succeeding century their importance declined with the increasing use of foreign contingents (e.g. Balearic slingers), and they were perhaps finally abolished by Lucullus.

J. Kromayer and G. Vieth, *Heerwesen und Kriegführung der Griechen und Römer* (1928); Parker, *Roman Legions²*; M. J. V. Bell, *Hist.* 1965, 419 ff. H. D. M. P.; G. R. W.

**VELITRAE** (modern *Velletri*): Volscian town on the southern rim of the Alban hills in Latium. It frequently fought early Rome, until annexed by the latter (338 B.C.). It still spoke Volscian then, but was soon completely latinized. Augustus originated from Velitrae. Claudius made it a *colonia*. E. T. S.

**VELIUS LONGUS** (early 2nd c. A.D.), scholar, who interested himself in the language of Republican authors, and wrote a commentary on the Aeneid. Only his *De orthographia* (ed. Keil, *Gramm. Lat.* vii. 46–81) is extant.

Schanz–Hosius, § 596; Conington–Nettleship, *The Works of Virgil* (1898) I. lxxxvii ff.

**VELLEIUS** (*PW* 5) **PATERCULUS** (*c.* 19 B.C.–after A.D. 30), was of Campanian descent. All our information concerning his life and writing is derived from his own works, in which he inserts references to the loyalty to Rome of his maternal ancestors, the Magii, and to the distinction of his grandfather and father as adherents of the Elder and Younger Tiberius Nero respectively. The historian, after several military campaigns, served under the latter for eight years in Germany and Pannonia, was quaestor in A.D. 7 and praetor, together with his brother, in A.D. 15. We learn nothing of his career during the following fifteen years, but he probably failed to reach the consulate. His adulation of Sejanus (2. 127–8) suggests that he may have been involved in the prefect's fall in the following year. However, two Velleii Paterculi appear as suffect consuls in 60 and 61, probably sons of the historian. The *praenomen* of the senior, Gaius, confirms the uncertain evidence of the text concerning his father's names.

The *Historiae Romanae* is a compendium of Roman history addressed to Velleius' friend M. Vinicius (who married Julia, daughter of Germanicus) on attaining the consulship, A.D. 30. Book 1, of which the opening and the part dealing with the period from Romulus to the battle of Pydna are missing, begins with the history of the Orient and Greece and ends with the fall of Carthage and Corinth (146 B.C.); book 2, covering the period 146 B.C. to A.D. 30, becomes more detailed as it approaches the author's own day, doubtless because, as he tells us, he projected a fuller history from the Civil War onwards. He inserted two historical excursuses, on Roman colonization (1. 14–15) and on the Roman provinces (2. 38–9), and three on literary topics, one on early Latin literature (2. 9), and another on the Ciceronian and Augustan period (2. 36), in which he couples Virgil with the minor poet Rabirius, while a third (1. 16–17) points out that the flourishing periods in Greek and Latin literature were confined within very brief limits. He shows some knowledge of Greek literature, mentioning Homer, Hesiod, tragic and comic writers, Isocrates, Plato, Aristotle. He cites only Cato and Hortensius among his sources (1. 7. 3; 2. 16. 3). A considerable controversial literature discusses authors possibly used by him and his general reliability (see Dihle in *PW* and Schanz); but most recent work on Velleius has been concerned only with the elucidation of particular historical problems.

Velleius as a historian is enthusiastic rather than critical and has all the pretentiousness of the novice who has fallen under the spell of contemporary rhetoric. Though his work is one of the earliest extant specimens of post-Augustan prose, his style has all the characteristics of the Silver Age. His attempts at pointed phraseology, though occasionally effective, are often puerile. He indulges in lengthy sentences which are not periods but mere strings of clauses interspersed with parentheses, and he has an irritating fondness for exclamations and interrogations. He admits that he wrote hurriedly, and the stream of his narrative, if it sometimes carries the reader along with it, certainly lacks profundity. His interest is chiefly in individuals, and he portrays, often with some skill, the lesser lights as well as the protagonists of history. His admiration for his old chief Tiberius and for the whole imperial house is unbounded; even Tiberius' ministers, such as Sejanus, can do no wrong. His work is a valuable source for the reigns of Augustus and Tiberius; but generally represents the adulatory type of history condemned by Tacitus (*Hist.* 1. 1), who ignores Velleius, as do all ancient authorities.

The text, derived from a single lost MS. from Murbach, is thoroughly corrupt.
LIFE AND WORKS. Schanz–Hosius, §422; Teuffel, *Gesch. d. römisch. Lit.* (1913–20), §278; J. Wight Duff, *Lit. Hist. Rome, Silver Age²* (1960), 68 ff.; W. C. Summers, *Silver Age of Lat. Lit.* (1920), 139 ff.; H. Sauppe, *Schweiz. Museum* (1837), i. 133 (= *Ausgew. Schr.* 39 ff.); F. Münzer, *Zur Komposition des Vell.* in *Festschrift zur 49. Philol. Vers.* (1907), 247 ff.; Dziech, *Eos* 1919, 18 ff.; I. Lana, *Vell. Pat. o della propaganda* (1952); A. Dihle, *PW* viii. A. 1 (1955), 637 ff.; J. Hellegouar'ch, *Latomus* 1964, 669 ff.
TEXTS. O.C.T. (R. Ellis, 1898); Teubner (Haase, 1840; Halm, 1863; Stegman de Pritzwald, 1933); E. Bolaffi (1930).
COMMENTARIES. Ruhnken–Frotscher (1830–9); Lemaire (1822); Orelli (1835); Kritz (1840); Rockwood (Civil War and reigns of Augustus and Tiberius) (1893).
TRANSLATIONS. F. W. Shipley, with text (Loeb, 1924); Hainsselin–Watelet (French, 1932).
STYLE AND DICTION. N. Oestling, *De elocutione Vell.* (1874); C. de Oppen, *De Vell.* (1875); H. Georges, *De elocutione Vell.* (1877); O. Lange, *Zum Sprachgebr. des Vell.* (1878); F. Milkau, *De Vell. genere dicendi* (1888); C. von Morawski, *Philol.* 1875, 715; E. Bolaffi, *De Velleiano sermone* (1925); Norden, *Ant. Kunstpr.* 302.
LEXICON. G. A. Koch (1857). E. S. F.; G. B. T.

**VENAFRUM**, modern *Venafro*, on the Latium–Campania border. It spoke Oscan in the third century B.C. and was probably a Samnite town brought under Roman domination *c.* 290 B.C. The Social War insurgents captured it and slaughtered its Roman garrison (90 B.C.). Famous for its olives, it became a flourishing *colonia* in imperial times.

E. Vetter, *Handbuch der italischen Dialekte* (1953), i. 135. E. T. S.

**VENANTIUS HONORIUS CLEMENTIANUS FORTUNATUS** (*c.* A.D. 540–*c.* 600), born near Treviso in northern Italy and educated at Ravenna, left Italy in 565 and subsequently lived in Poitiers, where he ultimately became bishop. A versatile poet, he wrote numerous poems on both secular and religious themes (including the great Passion hymns *Pange lingua* and *Vexilla regis*); he also wrote in prose. Fortunatus has been termed both the last of the Roman poets and the first of the medieval.

TEXT. F. Leo (poems) and B. Krusch (prose), *MGH, AA* iv. A. H.-W.

**VENATIONES.** Fights of man against beast or beast against beast were introduced into Rome in the second century B.C. They grew more elaborate, until under the Empire the whole world was ransacked for animals, which were transported (as illustrated in mosaics of Piazza Armerina in Sicily) to Rome and to amphitheatres all over the Empire. Lions, panthers, bears, bulls, hippopotami, crocodiles were matched against each other or against *bestiarii*. Five thousand wild and four thousand tame animals were slaughtered when the Flavian amphitheatre was opened; eleven thousand when Trajan celebrated his triumph over the Dacians.

Friedländer *Rom. Life* ii. 62–74; J. P. Balsdon, *Life and Leisure in Anc. Rome* (1969), 302 ff. F. A. W.; J. P. B.

**VENETI** (1), Gallic tribe occupying modern *Morbihan*. Their strongly 'Atlantic' culture was but slightly touched by Celticism in the La Tène period, but they themselves strongly influenced south-west British cultures by their trade, which stimulated their resistance to Caesar. They were defeated by D. Brutus in a naval battle (56 B.C.). Under the Empire their commerce declined, but a prosperous agricultural life is indicated by villa-finds. The region was occupied by emigrant Britons in the fifth century.

Caes. *BGall.* 3. 8–16. C. Jullian, *Hist. de la Gaule* (1907–26), ii. 486 ff.; vi. 437 ff. C. E. S.

**VENETI** (2) inhabited fertile country about the head of the Adriatic. Chief cities: Ateste in prehistoric times, Patavium in historic (*see* ANTENOR 1). They may be of Illyrian extraction (cf. Hdt. 1. 196), although their surviving inscriptions (5th–1st c. B.C.) are not demonstrably in an Illyrian language. Archaeological evidence reveals that they immigrated into north Italy *c.* 950; here they preceded and later successfully resisted Etruscans and Gauls. They were highly civilized, preferred horse-breeding and commerce to war, and early organized the Baltic amber (q.v.) trade. They particularly worshipped a goddess of healing, Rehtia. Always friendly to Rome, the Veneti aided her against Gauls (390 B.C.) and Hannibal. Later from allies they became subjects, though retaining local autonomy. Presumably they obtained Latin rights in 89, full citizenship in 49 B.C. Their romanization ensued.

Strabo 5. 212; Polyb. 2. 17 f.; Livy 1. 1; 5. 33; 10. 2. R. S. Conway, *Prae-Italic Dialects* i (1933), 230; J. Whatmough, *Foundations of Roman Italy* (1937), 171 (with bibliography); M. S. Beeler, *The Venetic Language* (U.S.A. 1949). For their alleged Paphlagonian origin see Serv. ad *Aen.* 1. 242; Hom. *Il.* 2. 852; Strabo 12. 543. E. T. S.

**VENILIA**, a goddess of forgotten nature and functions. It is implied by Varro (*Ling.* 5. 72) that she is associated with Neptunus (q.v., cf. August. *De civ. D.* 7. 22). Some insignificant stories, patently late inventions, are told of her by poets.

**VENNONIUS,** an early Roman author, now lost, whose history Cicero greatly regrets not to have at hand (*Att.* 12. 3. 1; cf. *Leg.* 1. 6). He is cited by Dionysius of Halicarnassus, 4. 15.

Peter, *HRRel.* i. 142.

**VENTA SILURUM,** a town of Roman Britain in South Wales (modern *Caerwent*), the *caput* of the *civitas* of the Silures (*It. Ant.* 485. 9: *Rav. Cosm.* 48). A dedication to Ti. Claudius Paulinus, former commander of Legio II Augusta (. . . *ex decreto ordinis respubl(ica) civit(atis) Silurum*; Collingwood–Wright, *RIB* 311) forms important evidence for the character of local government in Britain. Founded in the late first century A.D., the town was defended by earthworks in the late second and a town wall was added in the late third century; this was supplemented with external towers probably by Count Theodosius (369). These defences enclosed only 44 acres. The town survived into the fifth century, but much of it was finally destroyed by fire, possibly by Irish raiders.

*Archaeologia* lviii–lxii (early excavations 1892–1910); V. E. Nash-Williams, ibid. 1930, 229 ff. (defences); *Bull. Board of Celtic Studies* 1953, 159 ff.; *A Hundred Years of Welsh Archaeology* (1946), 80 ff.
S. S. F.

**VENTIDIUS** (*PW* 5), PUBLIUS (*cos. suff.* 43 B.C.), the proverbial upstart of the Roman revolutionary wars: probably of quite reputable municipal origin. Captured in infancy at Asculum and led in the triumph of Pompeius Strabo (89 B.C.), he made his livelihood with difficulty. Abusively designated as a *mulio*, he was probably an army-contractor (cf. Gell. 15. 4, the best account of his early life). Like other representatives of the defeated and impoverished Italians, he became an adherent of Caesar, through whose patronage he entered the Senate. Praetor in 43, Ventidius, who had been raising three legions in his native Picenum, reinforced Antony, after his defeat at Mutina. As a reward, he became consul later in the year. In 41–40 B.C. he intervened indecisively in the *Bellum Perusinum*. After the Pact of Brundisium he was sent to drive the Parthians out of Asia and Syria, in which task he won brilliant victories at the Cilician Gates and at Mt. Amanus (39), and at Gindarus (38). Superseded by Antony (there were allegations of taking bribes from the king of Commagene), he returned to Rome to celebrate his Parthian triumph (38), and died soon after, being honoured with a public funeral. His Parthian triumph was long remembered (cf. Tac. *Germ.* 37. 4: 'infra Ventidium deiectus Oriens'). No official or contemporary evidence gives P. Ventidius the *cognomen* 'Bassus'; nor can he quite be proved identical with Sabinus, the *mulio* of Virgil, *Catal.* 10.

Syme, *Rom. Rev.*, see index.
R. S.

**VENUS,** an Italian goddess, not originally Roman (Varro, *Ling.* 6. 33: 'cuius nomen ego antiquis litteris . . . nusquam inueni'). Her cult was later widespread in Italy (see Latte, *RR* 183 ff.). She is so obscure that the only clues to her functions are her name, a few passing remarks of antiquaries, and her identification. The name should by all analogies be neuter and apparently is feminine merely because it denotes a female; as a common noun it means 'charm, beauty', and so may be compared to Charis (cf. CHARITES). Varro (op. cit. 6. 20) says that on the Vinalia Rustica (a day mistakenly supposed to be her festival) gardeners keep holiday. Cf. *Rust.* 1. 1. 6, Venus has *procuratio hortorum*; Festus, 322. 19; 366. 35 Lindsay; Pliny, *HN* 19. 50. Naevius, *fr. com.* 122 Ribbeck, speaks of eating 'Venus that has felt Vulcan's power', i.e. boiled vegetables. We may therefore suppose that she was the *numen* whose power made herb-gardens look 'charmingly' prosperous and fertile. There is no evidence that she had anything to do with animal fertility, including that of

mankind. However, perhaps through the association of Aphrodite (q.v.) with Charis, or the Charites, she somehow became identified with her at an unknown date. It would seem that the cult of Aphrodite of Eryx (Venus Erucina) was the first point of contact (temple on the Capitol in 217 B.C.). To classical Rome Venus was Aphrodite; so much so that the Greek metonymies (Aphrodite = love-making, highest throw at dice, luck, etc.) were taken over by her. As Venus Genetrix (= mother of the *gens Iulia*) she was prominent in imperial cult.

Wissowa, *RK* 288 ff.; Keune in Roscher's *Lexikon*, s.v. For the temples of Venus in Rome see Platner–Ashby, 551 ff. See also Nash, *Pict. Dict. Rome* i. 491 (Venus Erucina, dedicated in 181 B.C., outside the Porta Collina; later called Venus Hortorum Sallustianorum); i. 424 ff. (Venus Genetrix, dedicated in 46 B.C. by Caesar, in the Forum Iulium); ii. 496 ff. (Venus et Roma, on the site of the vestibule of Nero's Golden House, built by Hadrian and consecrated in A.D. 136 or 137; rebuilt by Maxentius after a fire in 307; apart from the podium, all the surviving remains belong to the rebuilding); ii. 423 ff. (Venus Victrix, built by Pompey in his theatre and dedicated in 55 B.C.).
H. J. R.

**VENUSIA,** a town, probably of Peucetian origin, in Apulia near the Lucanian border, famed as Horace's birthplace (*Sat.* 2. 1. 34); modern *Venosa*. When Rome took Venusia it was probably Samnite and certainly populous, 292 B.C.; it received a Latin colony one year later (Dion. Hal. 17–18. 5 incredibly numbers the colonists at 20,000). Venusia immediately became a military stronghold and important station on the Via Appia (Strabo 5. 250). Resisting Hannibal, it harboured the fugitives from Cannae, thereby repeating the role it had probably played in 280 after Heraclea (Polyb. 3. 116 f.; Zonar. 8. 3). In 200 Rome reinforced Venusia (Livy 31. 49). Roman arrogance presumably provoked its defection in the Social War (Malcovati, *ORF²* 192; App. *BCiv.* 1. 39). In 43 the Triumvirs settled veterans here and Venusia remained a *colonia* in imperial times (App. *BCiv.* 4. 3).

N. Jacobone, *Venusia* (1909). E. T. S.

**VER SACRUM,** literally, consecrated (produce of the) spring. In times of distress, or merely when the population was superabundant, Italian communities and others, including Greek also (Dionysius, Strabo), used to consecrate to a god, often Jupiter, all that should be born in the spring. The beasts were apparently sacrificed; but the human beings (*sacrani*), when twenty years old (Festus, 150. 21), were veiled and sent out of the country. They might go where they would and found a new settlement. The ceremony (without human participation) was revived in 217 B.C.

Festus, 150, 424, 519 Lindsay; Dion. Hal. *Ant. Rom.* 1. 16; Strabo 5. 4. 12, 250; Livy 22. 10; 33. 44; 34. 44. J. Heurgon, *Trois Études sur le Ver Sacrum* (1957). H. J. R.

**VERCELLAE,** modern *Vercelli*, town of the Libici near the gold-mines of north-western Cisalpine Gaul (q.v.), which attained consequence in imperial times. The *Campi Raudii*, where Marius and Catulus annihilated the Cimbri (101 B.C.), although usually sought near here, possibly lay much further east: J. Zennari, *I Vercelli dei Celti e l'invasione celtica* (1956). E. T. S.

**VERCINGETORIX,** son of Celtillus, formerly king of the Arverni, raised the revolt against Caesar in 52 B.C., and was acclaimed king of the tribe and general of the confederates. Defeated by Caesar's cavalry at Noviodunum Biturigum, he adopted 'Fabian' tactics, hampering Caesar's supply by systematic destruction. With this was combined the strategy of tempting Caesar to attack or ingloriously decline the attack on impregnable ground. The policy succeeded admirably near Avaricum, where Caesar did not attack, and at Gergovia, where he did. Vercingetorix was led to risk another attack on Caesar in the field, which was badly defeated, so that he retreated to another prepared fortress, Alesia (q.v.). Caesar had an unexpected weapon, the circumvallation, with which he beat off not only Vercingetorix but the Gallic army summoned from outside to break it. Vercingetorix surrendered and was put to death after Caesar's triumph (46).

Caes. *BGall.* bk. 7. C. Jullian, *Vercingétorix* (1921).          C. E. S.

**VERGILIOMASTIX,** 'the scourge of Virgil', is a bombastic name given to critics of Virgil.

Servius ad *Ecl.* 2. 23; *Aen.* 5. 521; Ribbeck, *Proleg. ad Verg.*, ch. 8 (1866); Donatus 16. 61–2 (E. D:ehl, *Die Vitae Vergilianae u. ihre antike Quellen*, 1911); Conington–Nettleship, *Works of Virgil* (1898), I⁵. xxix–liii; C. G. Hardie, *praef.* to *Vitae Vergilianae Antiquae* (1954).          R. M.

**VERGINIA** was traditionally killed by her own father to save her from the lust of the decemvir Appius Claudius. This murder is said to have precipitated the revolution leading to the overthrow of the decemvirs (449 B.C.). The poetical details of the legend show that the story, although probably based on that of Lucretia, was not invented by jurists as a precedent for the protection of individual liberty, or by annalists desirous of explaining the fall of the decemvirs. The lateness of the connexion of the legend with the story of Appius Claudius' lust and tyranny is proved by the fact that the so-called plebeian heroes Verginius and Verginia in fact belonged to a family that was indisputably patrician. However 'devoid of historical foundation', the story of Verginia is a landmark in the development of historical consciousness and historical writing at Rome.

A. Alföldi, *Early Rome and the Latins* (1964), 153 ff.; Ogilvie, *Comm. Livy 1–5*, 476 ff. (with bibliography).          P. T.

**VERGINIUS** (1, *PW* 29) **FLAVUS,** a famous Neronian teacher who had Persius for a pupil. His renown brought exile on him (Tac. *Ann.* 15. 71). Quintilian held his authoritiy in great respect, mentioning him in several passages.

**VERGINIUS** (2, *PW* 27) **RUFUS,** LUCIUS, from Mediolanum, consul A.D. 63, became legate of Upper Germany in 67. In 68 he was prepared to make a deal with Vindex (q.v.), but, being compelled by his own soldiers to fight, he crushed the rebel. He refused to be hailed as Emperor and recognized Galba, who, still suspicious, replaced him in Germany. Consul II under Otho, he again refused the sovereignty after Otho's death. He became an example of loyalty to the State, and Nerva chose him as his colleague in the consulate (97). He died that year or a little later. His panegyric was pronounced by Tacitus, and his memory was celebrated by Pliny the Younger, whose *tutor* he had been (*Ep.* 2. 1). His epitaph is preserved (Pliny, *Ep.* 9. 19):

Hic situs est Rufus, pulso qui Vindice quondam
Imperium adseruit non sibi sed patriae.

C. M. Kraay, *Num. Chron.* 1949, 129 ff.; P. A. Brunt, *Latomus* 1959, 531 ff.; D. C. A. Shotter, *CQ* 1967, 370 ff.          A. M.

**VERONA,** a town on the river Athesis in Cisalpine Gaul (q.v.), astride the routes to the Brenner Pass in fertile wine-producing country (Verg. *G.* 2. 94). Although probably founded by Raeti, it is first mentioned in history as a town of the Cenomani (Pliny, *HN* 3. 130; Livy 5. 35). Prior to imperial times little is known of Verona except that it was Catullus' birthplace. A large, flourishing city, Verona had the title of *colonia* in A.D. 69 (Strabo 5. 212; Tac. *Hist.* 3. 8). Numerous Roman remains (including magnificent first-century amphitheatre, third-century walls, etc.) and the fact that Constantine (312), Theodoric (499), and the Lombards

(568) thought it worth while to occupy it, demonstrate its importance.

P. Marconi, *Verona romana* (1938); I. A. Richmond–W. G. Holford, 'Roman Verona', *PBSR* 1935, 69 f.; G. Radke, *PW* 8 A, 2. Nachtrag 2426 ff. For, its Raetic origin see J. Whatmough, *Harv. Stud.* 1937, 181.          E. T. S.

**VERRES** (*PW* 1), GAIUS, perhaps the son of one of Sulla's new senators who, as an ex-*divisor* (*see* CANDIDATUS), had considerable influence. As quaestor in 84 B.C., he deserted from Carbo (q.v. 2) to Sulla, appropriating his *fiscus*; as legate (eventually *pro quaestore*) of Dolabella (q.v. 2) in Cilicia, he plundered Cilicia and Asia with him, but on their return helped to secure his conviction. As *praetor urbanus* (74) he flagrantly sold justice; as proconsul (73–71) in Sicily, he exploited and oppressed the province (except for his ally Messana), and even some Romans living there, by force and chicanery. Unwisely offending several senators and ill-treating clients of Pompey, he yet evaded the effect of Senate disapproval (*see* GELLIUS 1) through his father's influence. On his return, he used his great wealth and his connexions, as well as the hostility of powerful nobles (especially the leading Metelli) to Pompey, to win strong support. Hortensius (q.v. 2), consul designate with the friendly Metellus (q.v. 8), defended him against the prosecution launched by Cicero as a patron of the Sicilians (70), and tried to drag the case on into his consulate. Outwitted by Cicero's speed and forensic tactics, and seeing Pompey's full influence used against him, amid Popular agitation for jury reform (*see* COTTA 3), Hortensius advised his client to anticipate conviction by fleeing to Massilia. Cicero nevertheless published the second *actio* (for *comperendinatio see* REPETUNDAE), to drive home the extent of Verres' guilt and advertise his own skill; and the evidence, though presented *ex parte*, seems overwhelming. Having won, Cicero conciliated Verres' powerful friends by agreeing to a low *litis aestimatio*. His *Ver ines* give us our best insight into provincial administration and its abuses in the late Republic. Verres later died at Massilia, proscribed (for his art treasures, we are told) by Antonius (q.v. 4).

Cic. *Verr.*          E. B.

**VERTUMNUS (VORTUMNUS),** an Etruscan god (Varro, *Ling.* 5. 46; Prop. 4. 2. 4, who says he came from Volsinii). A statue of him stood in the Vicus Tuscus in Rome, and Propertius (ibid. 13 ff.) indicates that the tradespeople there made frequent offerings to him. Nothing is known of his functions; his name may be connected with the Etruscan family *ultimni*, latinized Veldumnius. The Romans etymologized it from *uertere*, e.g. Prop. ibid. 21 ff. Dedications, of imperial times, have been found at Tuder, Ancona, Canusium, etc.

See Wissowa in Roscher, s.v.; Latte, *RR* 191 f.          H. J. R.

**VERULAMIUM,** a town in Britain near modern St. Albans (Herts.). After a short military occupation the town grew up in the valley below the site of Tasciovanus' capital (*Verlamio*) and was probably accorded the status of *municipium* by Claudius (Tac. *Ann.* 14. 33). The earliest shops were half-timbered multiple buildings in quasi-military style, suggesting the employment of army architects. After the sack by Boudicca (A.D. 60) rebuilding was delayed some fifteen to twenty years; but by 79 a new masonry forum of Gallic design was dedicated, under Julius Agricola, as the inscription (*JRS* 1956, 147) shows, and the half-timbered shops were rebuilt. The earliest defensive earthwork (perhaps pre-Flavian) enclosed 119 acres; it became obsolete early in the second century and the town expanded over it. Stone public buildings of the late first and early second centuries include two temples of non-classical type and a market hall; but domestic building was still in half-timber. About 155 much of the town, including the forum, was burnt down; in the restoration a theatre and palatial town houses in masonry were built. Late in the second century a new earthwork defence was begun, but was replaced before 250 by a town wall on a different line enclosing 200 acres. Two monumental arches in the main street now marked the vanished original boundary, and a third was added near the theatre *c.* 300. There was much building activity early in the fourth century, continuing here and there to its end and beyond. At least one large house was built after *c.* 370 and structural activity on its site can be traced to perhaps *c.* 450. Here Alban was martyred (perhaps under Severus); in 429 Germanus visited his shrine (*Script. rer. Meroving.* 7. 262). The site became deserted in the late fifth or sixth century and the ruins were much pillaged for the monastic buildings of St. Albans in the early Middle Ages.

Summary of earlier information *VCH, Herts.* i. 125 ff.; R. E. M. and T. V. Wheeler, *Verulamium* (1936); K. M. Kenyon, *Archaeologia* 1935, 213 ff. (theatre); *Ant. Journ.* 1937, 28 ff.; *Trans. St. Albans Architect. Archaeolog. Soc.* 1953, 13 ff.; S. S. Frere, *Ant. Journ.* 1956-62 (interim reports 1955–61); *Bulletin Institute of Archaeology* (*London*) 1964, 61 ff.; *Antiquity* 1964, 103 ff. (general summaries).
S. S. F.

**VERUS, LUCIUS,** Roman co-Emperor A.D. 161–9, was born in 130 and named L. Ceionius (*PW* 8) Commodus. He was son of L. Aelius (q.v. 2). On the death of Aelius, Hadrian (q.v.) in 138 required Antoninus (q.v. 1) to adopt his son along with the ten years older Marcus Aurelius (q.v. 1). Antoninus as Emperor did not, however, advance him equally with Marcus. The youth assumed the *toga virilis* in 145, became quaestor in 153, and consul in 154, with a second consulship in 161. On Pius' death in 161, Verus lacked the special standing of his adoptive 'twin', Marcus Aurelius. Marcus, however, at once created him (as 'L. Aurelius Verus') *Augustus* and colleague with tribunician power. Thus for the first time the imperial powers, except for the position of *pontifex maximus*, were fully shared. In 164 Marcus married Verus to his daughter Lucilla (q.v.), some eighteen years younger. Verus was weak and indulgent, and a poor administrator. Nevertheless, he commanded in the East in 163–6 and celebrated a triumph, though Avidius (q.v. 2) Cassius probably did the real work. Verus joined Marcus on the Danube in 168. His death on their return to Rome early in 169 was probably a benefit for the Empire and perhaps a relief to Marcus.

S.H.A. *Verus*; Dio Cass. bks. 71–2; P. Lambrechts, *Ant. Class.* 1934, 173; C. H. Dodd, *Num. Chron.* 1911, 209 ff.; Wegner, *Herrscherbild* ii. 4 (1939), 56 ff., 226 ff.; *B.M. Coins, Rom. Emp.* iv (1940); Bengtson, *Rom. Gesch.* 349 f. See also under AURELIUS (1), MARCUS.
C. H. V. S.; M. H.

**VESONTIO** (modern *Besançon*), capital of the Sequani, a Celtic tribe of Gallia Comata, was occupied by Caesar in 58 B.C. and in A.D. 68 was the scene of a decisive battle between the forces of Vindex (q.v.) and Verginius (q.v. 2) Rufus. Included in Gallia Belgica by Augustus, the Sequani were transferred under the Flavians to Germania Superior, and in the Late Empire Vesontio became the provincial capital of Maxima Sequanorum. The site is accurately described by Caesar, in a bend of the river Dubis (modern *Doubs*). The most important surviving monument is the Porte Noire, but the forum and amphitheatre are also known.

Caes. *BGall.* 1. 38–9; Plut. *Galba* 6; Dio Cass. 63. 24; Grenier, *Manuel* i. 560 ff. (Porte Noire), iii. 353 ff. (forum), ibid. 692 ff. (amphitheatre).
A. L. F. R.

**VESPAE IUDICIUM COCI ET PISTORIS IUDICE VULCANO,** contest between baker and cook in ninety-nine hexameters by a travelling rhetorician Vespa. Witty and full of puns, the poem is familiar with mythology and Roman folklore, and shows no trace of Christianity but cannot be older (and may well be later) than the third century A.D. because of its prosody (*in caccabō, Meleāger*). Metre pleasing, although final syllable is admitted in the fifth rise, and hiatus and *syllaba anceps* at the main caesura.

Baehrens, *PLM* iv. 326; F. Pini, Rome, 1958 (text, transl., comm.). See V. Tandoi, *Atene e Roma* 1960, 198 ff.
O. S.

**VESPASIAN** (TITUS FLAVIUS (*PW* 206) VESPASIANUS), Emperor A.D. 69–79, was born in A.D. 9 at Sabine Reate. His father Flavius Sabinus (for his elder brother of the same name *see* SABINUS 3) was a tax-gatherer; his mother also was of equestrian family, but her brother had entered the Senate. After his praetorship in 40 his career was advanced by the freedman Narcissus (q.v. 2). Legate of II Augusta in the Claudian invasion of Britain, he commanded the left wing in the subsequent advance (43–4), and for his distinguished services was awarded triumphal ornaments and two priesthoods. He became suffect consul in 51, and was later proconsul of Africa (*c.* 63): his lack of employment in the interval was perhaps due to Narcissus' death. In 66 he accompanied Nero to Greece, and fell into disfavour for sleeping during the Emperor's singing; but in Feb. 67 he was appointed as special commander to suppress the Jewish rebellion. By Nero's death he had largely subdued Judaea apart from Jerusalem itself, but he then stopped campaigning.

He decided to accept Galba (q.v.—*see also* TITUS), but he reconciled himself with the governor of Syria, Mucianus (q.v.), and on the news of Galba's murder these two Eastern legates considered action. They ostensibly supported Otho against Vitellius (q.v. 1), but after Otho's suicide they began collecting force. On 1 July 69 the two Egyptian legions, under their prefect Tiberius (q.v. 3) Alexander, acclaimed Vespasian Emperor, and the legions in Judaea and Syria quickly followed. Mucianus set out with an expeditionary force to threaten Italy while Vespasian held up the corn ships at Alexandria. But in August the Danubian armies joined the Flavian cause, and Antonius Primus (q.v.) entered Italy. It was alleged that he had done so against orders, and that Vespasian's victory could have been bloodless. However this may be, Antonius after winning a crushing battle at Cremona pressed on to Rome, and entered the city on 21 Dec., the day after Vitellius' death. Vespasian was immediately adopted by the Senate, though he continued to date his rule from 1 July.

His recognition was accompanied by the formal grant of miscellaneous powers, for some of which the Julio-Claudian Emperors had not sought explicit sanction. Whether similar grants had been made to Galba, Otho, and Vitellius—or were to be made to Vespasian's successors—is not clear; but it so happens that in Vespasian's case a fragment of the enabling law has survived (*ILS* 244). More important, however, than any legal enactment was the acquisition of *auctoritas* by the members of an upstart house, and Vespasian was careful to publicize a number of divine omens which portended his accession. Later measures to achieve the same end included frequent tenure of the consulate, for brief periods of the year, by himself and his sons, and the accumulation of numerous imperatorial salutations. Throughout his reign Vespasian insisted that the succession would devolve on his sons (*see* TITUS *and* DOMITIAN). Controversy over the dynastic principle may have caused his quarrel with doctrinaire senators like Helvidius (q.v.) Priscus, who was executed *c.* 76.

Vespasian returned to Italy *c.* Oct. 70. While at Alexandria he had been concerned with raising money, and his sales of imperial estates caused discontent in Egypt. He announced that 40,000 million sesterces were needed to put the State to rights, and both before and after his return he promoted his financial programme. He increased, and sometimes doubled, provincial taxation, and revoked imperial immunities. Some such measures were essential after the deficit incurred by Nero and the devastation of the civil wars, but contemporaries inevitably charged Vespasian with 'avarice'. How much he collected for public funds is unknown, but he was able to restore the Capitol, to build his Forum and Temple of Peace, and to begin work on the Colosseum. He probably also left a considerable surplus to his successors.

It was probably in part for financial reasons that in 73 he assumed the censorship with Titus. But in this office he also recruited many new members, both Italian and provincial, to the Senate, and conferred Roman and Latin rights on communities abroad. Chief among these grants was that of Latin rights to all native communities in Spain.

He effectively restored discipline to the armies after the events of 68–9. Before his return Mucianus had reduced the praetorian guard, greatly enlarged by Vitellius, to approximately its old size; and the legions were soon regrouped to ensure that Vitellian troops would not occupy dangerous positions. In the East Vespasian substituted three armies, with a total of six legions, in Syria, Cappadocia, and Judaea, for the single army (until Nero's time only four legions) in Syria. After the Jewish and Rhineland rebellions (see TITUS, CIVILIS) had been suppressed, Vespasian was able to undertake some rectification of the frontiers: most significantly in Britain, with the annexation of northern England and the pacification of Wales, and an advance into Scotland (see AGRICOLA 1); but to some extent also in southern Germany.

On his death on 23 June 79 (his last words are reported as 'Vae, puto deus fio') he was immediately accorded deification. By his unassuming behaviour he had largely conciliated the aristocracy (but see EPRIUS MARCELLUS), and Tacitus (Hist. 1. 50) says he was the first Emperor who changed for the better. He was industrious, and the simplicty of his life was taken as a model by contemporary senators. Matching his rugged and uncompromising features he cultivated a bluff manner, characteristic of the humble origins he liked to recall. His initial appointments (see e.g. PAETUS CAESENNIUS, PETILLIUS CERIALIS) reflect his astuteness in building a powerful party, of which the core was his own family. The policies of his reign do not reveal any great break with tradition. But to have ended the civil wars was no mean achievement, and PAX, with some reason, was a principal motif on his coinage.

He had married one Flavia Domitilla, who was believed to be of only Latin status until her father Flavius Liberalis successfully proved her Roman citizenship. She bore his two sons, and a daughter also named Flavia Domitilla (later deified); but both wife and daughter died before he became Emperor. He then lived with an earlier mistress named Caenis, who had been a freedwoman of Tiberius' sister-in-law Antonia.

SOURCES. Vespasian's rise to power is excellently documented by Suetonius, as well as by Tac. *Hist.* 2–4. But after this point Suetonius' 'Life' (ed. A. W. Braithwaite, 1927) tends to degenerate into a series of interesting anecdotes designed to illustrate Vespasian's character; and the absence of a chronological framework is little remedied by the Epitomators of Dio Cassius, 65–6. Epigraphical and numismatic evidence is of prime importance: see M. McCrum and A. G. Woodhead, *Documents of the Principates of the Flavian Emperors 68–96* (1961). See also Syme, *Tacitus*, index; A. Briessmann, 'Tacitus und das flavische Geschichtsbild', *Hermes, Einzelschr.* 10 (1955).

G. E. F. C.

**VESTA, VESTALS.** Vesta is the Roman hearthgoddess, the etymological equivalent of Hestia (q.v.), as she is in cult. She was prominent in family worship (see WORSHIP, HOUSEHOLD; PENATES), and is sometimes depicted in *lararia* (as G. K. Boyce, *Amer. Acad. Rome* 1937, plate 24) with her favourite beast, the ass ([Verg.] *Copa* 26). Not much is known of her domestic ritual, but see Cato, *Agr.* 143. 2.

For her as for Hestia it is evident that the royal hearthcult must have been supremely important in early times. Hence it is very natural that her State worship (*Vesta publica populi Romani Quiritium*) should not be in a temple but in a round building near the Regia, doubtless an imitation in stone of the ancient round hut (the modern *capanna*). This contained no image (Ov. *Fast.* 6. 295–6), but a fire which never was let out ('ignis inextinctus', ibid. 297; 'ignem illum sempiternum', Cic. *Dom.* 144). Curtained off from the rest of the building was the *penus* (Festus, 296. 12 Lindsay), which was opened for some days at the Vestalia, 9 June, a time of ill-omen, for the building was cleaned then and the days were *religiosi* and *nefasti* till the dirt had been disposed of on 15 June, *Q(uando) ST(ercus) D(elatum) F(as)*. The *penus* contained various sacred objects, but as none but the Vestals might enter it, their nature was never known but widely guessed at (e.g. Livy 26. 27. 14; cf. Dion. Hal. *Ant. Rom.* 2. 66. 3). This cult, though old (founded by Numa, Dion. Hal. ibid. 1 and other authors), was not primitive, for the Forum is not part of the oldest Rome. Preceding it was the cult of Caca, on the Palatine (Servius on *Aen.* 8. 190), of like character.

Vesta was served by the Vestal Virgins, representing the daughters of the royal house (see H. J. Rose, *Mnemos.* 1926, 2 ff.). They are said to have been originally two, then four, but in historical times normally six (Plut. *Num.* 10). They served originally for five years (Dion. Hal. 1. 76. 3), in historical times for thirty, during which time they must remain virgin, but after which they might marry, though few did, as it was supposedly unlucky (Plut. ibid.). Candidates must be between the ages of six and ten, and were chosen by the *pontifex maximus*, with the formula *te, Amata, capio*, from a total of twenty (if so many offered). They were not necessarily patricians. They received numerous honours, including emancipation from their fathers' tutelage, but were under the control of the *pontifex*, who could scourge any who let the sacred fire out or committed other offences short of unchastity; for that the culprit was entombed alive (obviously a judicial ordeal; Vesta might set her free if she was innocent). See Plut. loc. cit.; Gell. 1. 12.

Not much is known of the ritual, save that it was oldfashioned, not using water from mains and relighting the fire, if ever it went out, by friction of wood (Wissowa, 254). The Vestals wore the old sacral dress otherwise used by brides only. *See* MIRACLES, ATRIUM VESTAE.

Wissowa in Roscher's *Lexikon*, s.v.; Latte, *RR* 108 ff.; A. Brelich, *Vesta* (Zürich, 1949), gives an 'unconvincing picture of Vesta' (S. Weinstock, *JRS* 1950, 150). For her temples near the Regia and on the Palatine, see Platner–Ashby, 557 f.; Nash, *Pict. Dict. Rome* ii. 505 ff., 511 ff.

H. J. R.

**VESTINI,** a central Italian tribe living near the *Gran Sasso*, highest peak of the Apennines (q.v.). They spoke an Oscan-type dialect. Chief towns: Pinna, Aternum. Their became allies of Rome before 300 B.C. but joined their close associates, the Marsi, Marrucini, and Paeligni (qq.v.) in the Social War rebellion against her. Their romanization quickly ensued.

A. la Regina, *Mem. dei Lincei* 1968, 360 ff.

E. T. S.

**VESUVIUS,** the famous volcano on the Bay of Naples, rises isolated out of the surrounding plain of Campania (q.v.). Its base is some 30 miles in circumference, its central cone over 4,000 feet high, and its general appearance picturesque since the mountain-sides have been largely blown away. Vesuvius is mentioned only twice during the Roman Republic: in the Latin War of 340, where the allusion (Livy 8. 8. 19) seems erroneous, and in the revolt of Spartacus (q.v.) who used its crater as a stronghold in 73. It appeared extinct (Diod. 4. 21. 5), and its fertile slopes were extensively cultivated, with vineyards mostly (Strabo 5. 4. 8, 247). On 5 Feb. A.D. 63 a damaging earthquake presaged the first recorded eruption, the severe one of 24 Aug. 79 that buried Pompeii (q.v.) in sand, stones, and mud, Herculaneum (q.v.) in liquid tufa, and Stabiae (q.v.) in ashes, asphyxiated Pliny the Elder (q.v.), and is described by Pliny the Younger (q.v.), an eyewitness, in letters to Tacitus (*Ep.* 6. 16, 20). Antiquity witnessed three subsequent eruptions (in 202, 472, and 512), and violent activity still periodically recurs. E. T. S.

**VETERA**, near Birten, on the Rhine, was a major base for the Augustan invasions of Germany and became the station of two legions. The fortress had been completely rebuilt before it was destroyed by Civilis (q.v.) in A.D. 70. A new fortress for one legion was subsequently erected on a new site, was occupied till *c.* 260, and may have been refortified by Julian. A colony (*colonia Ulpia Traiana*), fortified from the beginning, was founded (between 98 and 107) near by at Xanten on a site which continued to be occupied apparently into the fifth century.

H. v. Petrikovits, *Bonner Jahrb.* 1952; *Das römische Rheinland* (1960); and *PW* s.v.; H. Hinz, in (*Gymnasium*) *Germania Romana: I, Römerstädte in Deutschland* (1960). P. S.

**VETTIUS** (1, *PW* 13) **PHILOCOMUS**, a friend of Lucilius, on whose satires, like Laelius Archelaus, he lectured and commented (Suet. *Gram.* 2).

**VETTIUS** (2, *PW* 16) **SCATO**, PUBLIUS, as Marsic 'praetor' in the Social War in the summer of 90 B.C. won several victories, finally killing the consul P. Rutilius Lupus; when driven back by Rutilius' legate Marius (q.v. 1), he marched on Aesernia, which he captured after defeating the other consul Caesar (q.v. 2). In 89 he tried to negotiate with the consul Pompeius (q.v. 3) Strabo through his guest-friend Sextus Pompeius, the consul's brother. (Cicero, q.v. 1, serving under Pompeius, was present.) Later, defeated by Pompeius, he was surrendered by his army and asked a slave to kill him. E. B.

**VETTIUS** (3, *PW* 6), LUCIUS, an *eques* from Picenum, served under Pompeius (q.v. 3) and Sulla and became a friend of Catiline. Involved in his conspiracy (63 B.C.), he turned informer and gave Cicero useful help, but came to grief trying to denounce Caesar. In 59—apparently now Caesar's agent—he denounced an Optimate 'plot' against Pompey, involving many prominent men, including the Curiones (*see* CURIO 1 and 2) and Lucullus (q.v. 2). Disbelieved, he was gaoled and mysteriously killed. The facts remain obscure.

C. Meier, *Hist.* 1961, 88 (with bibliography). E. B.

**VETTIUS** (4, *PW* 67) **VALENS,** astrological writer of the second century A.D.

Ed. W. Kroll, 1908.

**VETULONIA** (Etr. *Vetluna*), in the hills to the west of the bay that is now the Grosseto plain, was one of the twelve cities of Etruria. Excavation has been mainly confined to the extensive necropoleis. The earliest material comes from Villanovan *pozzo*-graves, the most notable from a series of wealthy orientalizing 'circle tombs', consisting of trenches surrounded by stones and covered by a tumulus. The *Circolo dei Lebeti* contained bronze cauldrons with siren heads and griffin protomes that have Greek and oriental parallels respectively. The

Pietrera tumulus contained a single chamber with a corbelled dome supported by a central pillar: it has produced the earliest stone statuary in Etruria. According to Silius Italicus (8. 484–8) the Romans assumed the Etruscan royal insignia of *fasces, sella curulis*, etc., from Vetulonia: an axe bound with iron rods was found in an early tomb there.

I. Falchi, *Vetulonia e la sua necropoli antichissima* (1891); *Stud. Etr.* 1931, *passim*; G. Renzetti, ibid. 1950–1, 291 ff.; A. Talocchini, ibid. 1963, 437 ff.; G. Camporeale, ibid. 1964, 3 ff.; id. *La tomba del Duce* (1967); id. *I commerci di Vetulonia in età orientalizzante* (1968); Scullard, *Etr. Cities*, 134 ff. D. W. R. R.

**VEXILLUM.** In the Republican army *vexilla* were the standards of the legionary cavalry. Hence, *vexilla* were carried by cavalry units, such as *alae*, at all periods. The *vexillum* was used also as the standard of a detachment (*vexillatio*), or, in the first century A.D., of a corps of veterans after their period of service under the *aquila* had been completed. Hence, *vexillum* itself was often used for a detachment. The flag of a general or an admiral was a scarlet *vexillum*. *See also* SIGNA MILITARIA.

M. Rostovtzeff, *JRS* 1942, 92 ff. G. R. W.

**VIA AEMILIA**, named after its builder M. Aemilius Lepidus, *cos.* 187 B.C. (Livy 39. 2), and subsequently repaired by Augustus and Trajan, ran from Ariminum 176 miles north-west to Placentia (with later extensions to Augusta Praetoria, to Segusio, to Aquileia, all somewhat inaccurately called Via Aemilia). The Aemilia helped to romanize Cisalpine Gaul rapidly: with its extensions it touched every important city of the district (still called Emilia) except Ravenna.

It is to be distinguished from the Via Aemilia Scauri (q.v.).

⊦ Strabo 5. 217. N. Lamboglia, *Athenaeum* 1937. E. T. S.

**VIA AEMILIA SCAURI,** highway built by M. Aemilius Scaurus, censor 109 B.C., linking the Viae Aurelia and Postumia (qq.v.). It ran from Vada Volaterrana through Pisae, Genua, and Vada Sabatia and thence inland to Dertona. From Vada Sabatia the Via Iulia Augusta (built by Augustus) continued along the coast to beyond Albintimilium (*Ventimiglia*). E. T. S.

**VIA ANNIA** (1), highway built in northern Italy, perhaps by T. Annius Luscus, *cos.* 153 B.C. It probably linked Bononia with Aquileia via Patavium, Altinum, and Concordia.

(2) The extension of the Via Appia (q.v.), which ran from Capua through Nola, Nuceria, Consentia, and Vibo to Rhegium, may also have been a Via Annia (not Via Popillia, q.v., as usually stated), built perhaps by T. Annius Rufus, propraetor 131 B.C.

(3) Road near Falerii in Etruria.

T. P. Wiseman, *PBSR* 1964, 21 ff.; F. T. Hinrichs, *Hist.* 1967, 167 ff. E. T. S.

**VIA APPIA**, the Romans' principal route to south Italy and beyond (Strabo 6. 283). Appius Claudius Caecus, censor 312 B.C., built and named the 132-mile section from Rome to Capua (Livy 9. 29). It had probably been extended by 244 through Beneventum, Venusia, and Tarentum to Brundisium (234 miles). Paving of the Appia commenced in 295 and apparently was complete by Gracchan times (Livy 10. 23; Plut. *C. Gracch.* 7; reject Diod. 20. 36). In imperial times a praetorian *curator* kept the road in order. Its exact line can be traced most of the way to Beneventum, but not beyond, since the shorter route to Brundisium via Canusium and Barium, which the Via Traiana (q.v.) later used, led to neglect of the Appia. Between Rome and Beneventum, however, one can still see roadside tombs (e.g. the

Scipios', Caecilia Metella's), the ancient pavement (*c.* 20 ft. wide at *Itri*), a rock-cutting (at Tarracina), embankments (e.g. at Aricia and *Itri*), bridges (three between Caudium and Beneventum), and milestones. One of these proves that, even though travellers preferred the 19-mile-long ship canal, the Appia from its earliest days crossed the Pomptine marshes (q.v.) (C. Hülsen, *Röm. Mitt.* 1889, 83 ff.). Various branches, e.g. the one to Rhegium [*see* VIA ANNIA (2)], were also somewhat inaccurately called Via Appia.

T. Ashby, *Roman Campagna* (1927), 174 ff.; A. Maiuri, *Passeggiate Campane* (1957), 347 ff. E. T. S.

**VIA AURELIA,** important highway (Cic. *Phil.* 12. 9) of unknown date, but presumably built before its extension, the Via Aemilia Scauri (q.v.) of 109 B.C. It was 175 miles long, running from Rome north-west to Alsium, thence along the Etruscan coast to Vada Volaterrana. Later prolongations to Dertona and to Arelate are also called Via Aurelia in the Itineraries. *See also* VIA POSTUMIA.

D. Anziani, *Mélanges d'arch.* 1913; F. Castagnoli (ed.), *La Via Aurelia* (1968). E. T. S.

**VIA CASSIA,** highway running north from Rome through Sutrium, Volsinii, and Clusium in central Etruria to Arretium, whence the Via Flaminia Minor (187 B.C.) led across the Apennines to Bononia. It was apparently built in the late third or early second century B.C. Between Veii and Sutrium it diverged from the older Via Amerina which continued to Nepete, Falerii Novi, and the North. The Via Cassia was ultimately prolonged from Arretium to Florentia and Mutina with an extension to Pistoria, Luca, and Luna.

Cic. *Phil.* 12. 22. F. Martinori, *Via Cassia e sue deviazioni* (1930); *and see* s.v. VIA CLODIA. E. T. S.

**VIA CLODIA,** highway running north from Rome through western Etruria, of uncertain, but evidently republican date (3rd c.?), though in part following older Etruscan roads. Its course is often confused with that of the Via Cassia (q.v.), which probably followed the same line to near Veii; thence Via Clodia turned north-west and certainly touched Blera, Tuscania, and Saturnia (q.v.).

J. B. Ward-Perkins, *JRS* 1957, 139 ff.; id. *PBSR* 1955, 44 ff.; 1957, 67 ff. E. T. S.

**VIA DOMITIA,** a very ancient route from the Rhône to Spain, improved by the Romans apparently before the death of Polybius (124 B.C.; cf. 3. 39. 8), but owing its name to the conqueror of Narbonensis, Cn. Domitius (q.v. 2) Ahenobarbus (121); a milestone of Domitius survives (Degrassi, *ILLRP* n. 460a). It was repaired by M. Fonteius (*c.* 75), and under the Empire by Tiberius (A.D. 31–2), Claudius (41), Antoninus Pius (145), Maximinus (235–8), and Diocletian (284–305).

Grenier, *Manuel* ii. 26 ff. C. E. S.

**VIA DOMITIANA,** highway built by Domitian (A.D. 95), running from Sinuessa on the Via Appia (q.v.) through Volturnum, Liternum, and Cumae to Puteoli, where it joined a road to Neapolis (q.v.).

Stat. *Silv.* 4. 3. E. T. S.

**VIA EGNATIA,** Roman road built *c.* 130 B.C. from the Adriatic coast to Byzantium; named after Egnatia on the Apulian coast, where the corresponding road from Rome to Brundisium touched the sea, the Via Egnatia was the main route from Rome to the East. Two branches of the road, starting respectively from Dyrrhachium and Apollonia, united in the Skumbi valley, crossed the Balkan range by Lake Lychnidus (*Ochrida*), and descended to Thessalonica via Heraclea, Eordaea, Aegae,

and Pella, whence it followed the Thracian coast to Byzantium. It followed the line of a trade-route through the Balkan range which Corinth had exploited.

N. G. L. H.

**VIA FLAMINIA,** the great northern highway of Italy, built 220 B.C. by C. Flaminius, when censor (Livy, *Epit.* 20; reject Strabo 5. 217). It was 209 miles long from Rome via Narnia, Mevania, Nuceria, and Helvillum to Fanum Fortunae (q.v.), where it turned north-west and followed the Adriatic coastline via Pisaurum to Ariminum (q.v.). After A.D. 69 the section between Narnia and Nuceria was provided with an alternative, 6-mile longer route via Interamna (q.v.), Spoletium, and Fulginium. From its earliest days the Flaminia was much frequented; its importance was, if anything, enhanced in late imperial times when the imperial court was at Milan or Ravenna. Large towns grew up along its tomb-lined course. The road was often repaired: by C. Gracchus, Augustus (parts of whose bridge at Narnia (q.v.) and whose honorific arch at Ariminum survive), Vespasian (whose tunnel through Intercisa Pass still exists near Calles), Trajan, Hadrian. Various branches, e.g. from Nuceria to Ancona, were also inaccurately called Via Flaminia.

T. Ashby–R. A. L. Fell, *JRS* 1921. E. T. S.

**VIA LABICANA,** highway running south-east from Rome to Labici and the country of the Hernici (q.v.). Avoiding the Alban Hills, it joined the Via Latina (q.v.) near Anagnia. E. T. S.

**VIA LATINA,** one of the arterial highways radiating from Rome, is not named after its builder—a fact suggesting high antiquity. It ran south-east and, after surmounting the outer rim of the Alban Hills at Algidus, followed the Trerus valley through the Hernici country where the Via Labicana (q.v.) joined it near Anagnia. It crossed the Liris at Fregellae, then proceeded via Aquinum, Casinum, Venafrum, Teanum, and Cales across the Volturnus to Casilinum where it merged with the Appia. (A later short cut via Rufrae avoided Venafrum.) The 135-mile Latina was much frequented (Strabo 5. 237); important branches ran from it into Samnium. Pyrrhus and Hannibal both used it, presumably because it followed an easier line than the Appia. Its exact line can still be traced without much difficulty.

T. Ashby, *Roman Campagna* (1927), 153 f. E. T. S.

**VIA POPILLIA,** highway in northern Italy, linking Ariminum, Atria, and Altinum with Aquileia, built by P. Popillius (q.v. 2), *cos.* 132 B.C. (Dessau, *ILS* 5807). The road from Capua to Rhegium in southern Italy is also often attributed to him, but probably incorrectly: *see* VIA ANNIA (2). E. T. S.

**VIA POSTUMIA,** north Italian highway centring on Cremona, whence it ran in one direction through Placentia and Dertona to Genua, and in the other through Bedriacum, Verona, Vicetia, and Opitergium to Aquileia. Built by Sp. Postumius Albinus (*cos.* 148 B.C.), it consolidated the conquest of the Transpadane region (*see* CISALPINE GAUL). The Itineraries regard its western section as part of the Via Aurelia. Ancient authors virtually ignore it.

Dessau, *ILS* 5806, 5946; Tac. *Hist.* 3. 21. E. T. S.

**VIA SACRA,** the street connecting the *Forum Romanum* with the Velia, affording access to the Palatine. The name probably comes from the hallowed buildings which the street passed, connected with the shrines of Vesta and the Regia. The earliest-known monument at its end is the *fornix Fabianus* (*JRS* 1922, 27 f.) of 121 B.C., whence the road straggled towards the Velia, passing many private houses and shops, its pavement being still visible. In A.D. 64 Nero planned the street anew as a noble colonnaded avenue flanked by large bazaars for jewellers, florists, and luxury-traders. The northern bazaar was smaller and was obliterated by the basilica of Maxentius; the southern, though curtailed by Hadrian's extensions of the Atrium Vestae (q.v.), occupied the considerable space between that house and the Arch of Titus.

Nash, *Pict. Dict. Rome* ii. 284 ff. I. A. R.

**VIA SALARIA,** highway built in prehistoric times to facilitate the salt trade from the Tiber mouth. It ran north-east from Rome to Reate (q.v.) in the Sabine country. Later extensions, (1) through Amiternum and (2) through Asculum, carried it to the Adriatic. E. T. S.

**VIA TRAIANA,** highway built (A.D. 109) by Trajan, which replaced the Via Appia (q.v.) as the usual route between Beneventum and Brundisium. It touched Aequum Tuticum, Aecae, Herdoniae, Canusium, Barium, and Gnathia. Its identification with the Republican Via Minucia mentioned by Cicero (*Att.* 9. 6. 1) and others is very dubious.

T. Ashby–R. Gardner, *PBSR* 1914, 104 f. E. T. S.

**VIA VALERIA,** important highway running eastwards from Rome to Aternum on the Adriatic. Its first 18 miles comprised the very ancient Via Tiburtina. This was prolonged, possibly *c.* 300 B.C., to Carsioli, Alba Fucens, and apparently Cerfennia (Livy 10. 1. 3; Diod. 20. 90, emending Σερεννία. Livy 9. 43 records a road-building Valerius, censor 306 B.C.). This extension later became a paved highway, perhaps in the censorship of M. Valerius Messalla (154 B.C.), and was the Via Valeria proper (cf. Strabo 5. 238). Finally, the Emperor Claudius continued the road as the Via Claudia Valeria from Cerfennia to the Adriatic. Pliny's estimate of 136 miles as the breadth of Italy is based on the Valeria (*HN* 3. 44).

T. Ashby, *PBSR* 1906, 84 ff. (Via Tiburtina); C. C. van Essen, ibid. 1957, 22 ff. (centre); R. Gardner, ibid. 1920, 75 ff. (Via Claudia Valeria). E. T. S.

**VIATORES** were public bailiffs, mostly freedmen or of low birth, whose chief business was to run errands for the magistrates and summon senators to meetings. They also seized confiscated goods, made arrests, and executed the commands and sentences issued by their respective magistrates. They formed a corporation divided into several *decuriae* according to the rank of the magistracies (the first was therefore the *decuria consularis*). Municipal magistrates also employed *viatores* chiefly to collect taxes.

Mommsen, *Röm. Staatsr.* i³. 360 ff.; A. H. M. Jones, *Stud. in Rom. Government and Law* (1960), 154 ff. P. T.

**VIBENNA,** CAELIUS, an Etruscan who, according to Roman tradition, came to help Tarquinius Priscus (Tac. *Ann.* 4. 65; Romulus, according to Varro, *Ling.* 5. 46) and, as a reward, settled on the hill later known as the Caelius Mons (q.v.). He is also known from Etruscan tradition: the François tomb-painting at Vulci depicts him being rescued by his brother Aulus Vibenna and Mastarna (q.v.) from Cn. Tarquinius. According to the Emperor Claudius (*ILS* 212, representing a romanized version of the Etruscan tradition?), Mastarna, Caelius' friend and fellow adventurer, driven from Etruria, settled with the remains of Caelius' army on the Caelian hill and changed his name to Servius Tullius. The name of A. Vibenna appears on a mid-sixth-century *bucchero*

vase, dedicated at Veii (M. Pallottino, *Stud. Etr.* 1939, 456 ff.).

A. Momigliano, *Claudius*² (1961), 10 ff., 84 ff. H. H. S.

**VIBIUS** (1, *PW* 39) **MARSUS,** GAIUS, of unknown descent, *consul suffectus* in A.D. 17, was a *legatus* of Germanicus in the East and after his death conducted Agrippina back to Rome (19). From 27 to 30 he was proconsul of Africa. In 37 he was accused of treason and adultery but saved by the death of Tiberius. As *legatus* of Syria (42–45) he was hostile to Agrippa (q.v. 1), and checked the designs on Armenia of Vardanes, king of Parthia. T. J. C.

**VIBIUS** (2, *PW* 48) **RUFUS,** GAIUS (*cos. suff.* A.D. 16), a declaimer of Tiberius' reign. His arguments are often cited in the Elder Seneca's *Controversiae* (e.g. 2. 1. 2 and 28; 2. 3. 8; 2. 6. 10; 7. 3. 4; 9. 2. 2).

**VIBIUS** (3, *PW* 28) **CRISPUS,** QUINTUS, born at Vercellae in Transpadane Italy, was *cos. suff.* under Nero, and twice more before A.D. 83. He was *curator aquarum* 68–71, probably proconsul of Africa in 71, and legate of Tarraconensis in 73. His wit and oratory are praised by Quintilian (see also Suet. *Dom.* 3, Dio 65. 2. 3), and were probably the source of his great influence with Vespasian (Tac. *Dial.* 8, 13): his tact (Juvenal 4. 81 ff.) enabled him to survive where others, like Epirus (q.v.) Marcellus, came to grief. Yet Tacitus (*Hist.* 2. 10, 4. 41–2) regarded him as a sinister character.

R. Syme, *Rev. Ét. Anc.* 1956, 256 ff. G. E. F. C.

**VIBIUS** (4, *PW* 40) **MAXIMUS,** GAIUS, *praefectus coh. III Alpinorum* in Dalmatia A.D. 94 (*CIL* iii. 859), prefect of Egypt from Apr. 103 to Mar. 107, was a friend of both Martial (11. 106) and Statius, whose *Silv.* 4. 7 was written in his honour. Its close suggests that Vibius produced some kind of handbook of world-history with an epitome of Sallust and Livy.

W. Keil, *B. phil. Woch.* 1919, 1075; H. A. Musurillo, *The Acts of the Pagan Martyrs* (1954), 150 ff.; R. Syme, *Hist.* 1957, 480 ff. J. W. D.; G. B. A. F.

**VICA POTA,** a goddess, whose shrine lay on the Velia in Rome (Livy 2. 7. 12). Though it existed in his time, her functions were unknown, some explaining her as Victoria (q.v.; *uincere, potiri*; Cic. *Leg.* 2. 28), some as goddess of food and drink (*uictus, potus*; Arn. *Adv. Nat.* 3. 25). H. J. R.

**VICARIUS.** During the first two centuries A.D. *vicarius* meant a substitute for an absent or deceased provincial governor. In the third century *vicarii* were equestrian procurators who were specially appointed by the Emperor to administer provinces in place of the regular senatorial governors. When Diocletian divided the Empire into dioceses, each was entrusted to a *vicarius*, officially a deputy of the praetorian prefects (*vices agentes praefectorum praetorio*). They acted as judges of appeal from the courts of the provincial governors of their dioceses and had a general supervision over their administration. As the powers of the prefects continued to increase, the position of *vicarii* tended to decline in importance. (*See* DIOECESIS.)

H. M. D. P.; B. H. W.

**VICOMAGISTRI** were presidents of sub-districts (*vici*) in town or city wards (*regiones*) charged with the upkeep of local cults, particularly the cult of the *lares compitales* and the organization of the *ludi compitales* (Wissowa, *RK* 171 ff.). They are attested by republican inscriptions (Degrassi, *ILLRP* 701–4), and in the political strife of the late Republic their organization attained notoriety, being abolished by *senatus consultum* in the middle 60s and revived by Clodius in 58 (Asc., p. 7 C; Cic. *Pis.* 4. 9; cf. *Red. Sen.* 13. 33; *Sest.* 15. 34, 25. 55). The institution was probably not abolished again (cf. J. V. A. Fine, *CPhil.* 1932, 268) though Augustus transformed it in 7 B.C. (Dio Cass. 55. 8: *CIL* vi. 343, 2222) or perhaps earlier (*ILS* 3617, 3620), apparently in connexion with his creation of the fourteen regions (*see* REGIO); each *vicus* now elected four *magistri* and their cults included those of the *lares Augusti* and the *genius* of the Emperor (*ILS* 3613–21); they also had some responsibility for fire-fighting (cf. Dio loc. cit.) until A.D. 6. Whereas earlier the *magistri* had been freeborn, though of low social standing, by Hadrian's time they were all freedmen (*ILS* 6073, of A.D. 136). Pliny (*HN* 3. 5. 66) gives the number of *vici* as 265; there were therefore 1,060 *magistri* in his day, but by the fourth century the number had been reduced to 48 to a *regio*.

I. A. R.; J. N.

**VICTIMARIUS.** At a Roman sacrifice, the officiant did not, at least normally and in the classical epoch, kill the victim himself; this was done by a *victimarius* or sacred slaughterman. These formed a *collegium* in imperial times, attendant (*CIL* vi. 971) on the Emperor, priests, and magistrates.

H. J. R.

**VICTORIA,** the Roman equivalent of Nike (q.v.). There is no evidence that she is anything more, mentions of an early cult of Victory being referable to Vacuna or Vica Pota (qq.v.; Dion. Hal. *Ant. Rom.* 1. 15. 1; Asc. *Pis.*, p. 13. 15 Clark). She is associated in cult with Jupiter (Victor), as in the *acta Arualium* (p. cxcviii Henzen), oftener with Mars (as ibid., p. clxv), also with other deities. She was worshipped by the army, as was natural (Domaszewski, *Rel. des röm. Heeres* (*Westd. Zeit.* 1895), 4 ff.), and hence is given surnames associating her with particular legions and more commonly still with Emperors (list in Roscher, vi. 299; cf. J. Gagé, *Rev. Arch.* 1930, 1 ff., *Rev. Hist.* 1933, 1 ff.). Her temple on the Clivus Victoriae leading up to the Palatine dates from 294 B.C. (see Platner–Ashby, 570; Nash, *Pict. Dict. Rome* i. 257). Her most famous monument was perhaps her altar in the senate-house, put there by Augustus in 29 B.C., removed under Constantius, replaced by the pagan party in Rome, removed again by Gratian in 382, replaced for a short time by Eugenius and perhaps once more by Stilicho, and finally vanishing with the other vestiges of pagan cult (Ambrosius, *Epp.* 17; 18; 57. 6, cf. Paulinus, *Vit. Ambros.* 26; Symmachus, *Relat.* 3 Claudian; 28. 597).

Latte in Roscher, s.v. and *RR*, see index; S. Weinstock, *Harv. Theol. Rev.* 1957, 211 ff.

H. J. R.

**VICTORINUS** (1), GAIUS MARIUS (4th c. A.D.), was the author of philosophical (Neoplatonic), rhetorical, and grammatical works. His reputation was such that a statue in his honour was set up in the forum Traianum. After becoming a Christian, he wrote theological treatises. Most of his *Ars grammatica* (ed. Keil, *Gramm. Lat.* vi. 3–184) has been ousted in our MSS. by the *De metris* of Aphthonius (q.v.). His translations of Plato, Aristotle, and Porphyrius are lost, as is his commentary on Cicero's *Topica*; but his *explanationes* of the *De inventione* of Cicero are preserved (ed. Halm, *Rhet. Lat. Min.* 155–304). His Christian writings (in Migne, *PL* viii) included commentaries on some Pauline epistles, *De trinitate contra Arium, De ὁμοουσίῳ recipiendo,* and possibly a work against the Manichaeans.

Schanz–Hosius, §§ 828–31 a.

J. F. M.

**VICTORINUS** (2), MAXIMUS, grammarian of unknown date, author of a *De ratione metrorum* (ed. Keil, *Gramm. Lat.* vi. 216–28). Certain other treatises: *Ars Victorini, De metris, De finalibus metrorum* (ed. Keil, *Gramm. Lat.* 6. 187–205; 206–15; 229–242) are attributed in MSS. to an unspecified 'Victorinus'.

Schanz–Hosius, § 829.

J. F. M.

**VI(C)TORIUS MARCELLUS,** the man to whom Quintilian dedicated his *Institutio Oratoria* as a manual for Marcellus' son and for his own boy, of whom, however, he was bereaved before his work was half completed (*Inst.* 1, *prooem.* 6; 6, *prooem.* 1–16). Statius addresses *Silvae,* book 4, to him (*prooem.* 1). He was *consul suffectus* in A.D. 105.

R. Hanslik, *PW* Suppl. ix. 1744.

J. W. D.

**VICUS** was the smallest agglomeration of buildings forming a recognized unit, either a country village or a ward of a town. The former were subordinate to a *pagus* of the *civitas* in which they lay, the latter directly to the municipal authority. *Vici* could also exist on private or imperial estates withdrawn from the municipal system, where they depended upon the local landlord or imperial procurator. They were administered by *magistri* or *aediles* elected by the villagers. Priestly officials, *dicatores,* are also known. *Vici* in towns, too, had their *vicomagistri* (q.v.). Those of Rome, revived by Augustus, had charge of the street shrines, and for a while of the fire-brigade. A *vicus* could be a *praefectura* (q.v.) but was normally subordinate to an intermediate authority.

For bibliography *see under* MUNICIPIUM (REPUBLIC). A. N. S.-W.

**VIENNA,** town in Gallia Narbonensis, modern *Vienne*; capital of the Allobroges. Perhaps created *colonia Latina* by M. Antonius (43 B.C.); given probably by Gaius the title of *colonia civium Romanorum.* In the third century A.D. it possessed *ius Italicum.* In 69 it narrowly escaped destruction from Vitellius' army, encouraged by its jealous neighbour Lugdunum. A large straggling town with Augustan *enceinte* is partially preserved. Its most notable surviving building is the temple of Rome and Augustus, enlarged and rededicated by Tiberius. Like Lugdunum, it was an important seat of early Christianity.

*CIL* xii. 217; Grenier, *Manuel* i. 323 ff.; J. Formigé, *Le Théâtre romain de Vienne* (1950).

C. E. S.

**VIGILES** (νυκτοφύλακες). Except for the existence of *triumviri nocturni,* about whose function little is known, the city of Rome under the late Republic possessed neither fire-brigade nor police force. After the fire of 23 B.C. Augustus established a fire-brigade of 600 slaves commanded at first by the aediles but after 7 B.C. (when Rome was divided into 14 *regiones* and 265 *vici,* each with four *vicomagistri*) by the *vicomagistri* (q.v.). After another serious fire (A.D. 6) Augustus effected a lasting reorganization. He created a corps of 7,000 *Vigiles,* all freedmen, who were organized in seven cohorts, each consisting of seven centuries, and each commanded by a tribune. Over the whole body was set a *Praefectus Vigilum,* who was appointed directly by the Emperor; he was an *eques* and ranked below the *Praefectus Annonae* and *Praefectus Praetorio* (Dio Cass. 55. 26; Suet. *Aug.* 30). From Trajan's time he was assisted by a Sub-Prefect. To his original duties were added later those of a judge, and he presided over trials for incendiarism and petty larceny (*Dig.* 1. 15. 3); in the third century A.D. the office, like that of *Praefectus Praetorio,* was held by eminent jurists.

Each cohort of *Vigiles* was responsible for two *regiones* of the city. The troops were quartered at first in private houses (Dio Cass. 57. 19. 6; cf. Suet. *Tib.* 37), but later had sub-stations, *excubitoria*, one in each *regio*. They were occasionally called on in emergencies to perform military duties, e.g. in A.D. 31, at the time of the arrest of Sejanus (q.v.), when Macro (q.v.), their commander, was promoted to the praetorian Prefecture, and in A.D. 69. In such emergencies they normally came, with their prefect, under the command of the *Praefectus Urbi*.

P. K. Baillie Reynolds, *The Vigiles of Imperial Rome* (1926).
J. P. B.

**VIGINTISEXVIRI.** This collective denomination embraces twenty-six Roman civil *magistratus minores* who had no special official titles, being indicated only by their functions and number (*duoviri, tresviri, quattuorviri*). Some of them were endowed with particular juridical competence, notably the *decemviri stlitibus iudicandis* (q.v.). Another group were the four *praefecti (iure dicundo) Capuam Cumas*, exercising the delegated jurisdiction of the *praetor urbanus* in these and eight other Campanian towns. The remainder had administrative functions: the *tresviri (triumviri) monetales* (more precise title: *tresviri aere argento auro flando feriundo*), the masters of the mint; the *quattuorviri viis in urbe purgandis*, and the *duoviri viis extra urbem purgandis*, who provided for the maintenance of the streets in Rome and in the environs respectively; and finally the *tresviri capitales* responsible for prisons (*carceris custodia*) and executions. In their capacity as guardians of nocturnal peace they were also called *tresviri nocturni*. Under Augustus the number of these magistrates was reduced to twenty, six of them (four *praefecti Capuam Cumas* and *duoviri viis extra urbem purgandis*) having been abolished. Hence their new collective name: *vigintiviri*. One of these magistracies was, as it seems, a necessary preliminary to the quaestorship.

On the *tresviri capitales* see W. Kunkel, *Untersuchungen zur Entwicklung des röm. Kriminalverfahrens* (1962), 71 ff.; G. Pugliese, *Processo civile romano* i (1962), 211 ff. A. B.; B. N.

**VILLA** was the Latin name for a rural dwelling associated with agriculture. The traditional Italian farm of this kind is described in detail by Varro (*Rust.* 1. 11–13) and Vitruvius (6. 6. 1) as a courtyard edifice comprising house, stables, and workshops, run by slave labour for the benefit of an urban proprietor. Such farms, however, were always matched by those of smallholders and yeomanry, and Campanian examples of both kinds have been studied (R. Carrington, *JRS* 1931, 110 f.) and may be compared with Istrian farms of the same type (Gnirs, *JÖAI* 1915, Beiblatt 101). *See* AGRICULTURE. The residential villa, or country seat of the well-to-do, is a later development of the second century B.C., wherein are seen the first relations of architectural design to landscape or vistas and the development of large courtyard houses or seaside palaces.

In the provinces the development of country houses is primarily of the imperial age, our knowledge of republican examples being negligible. Local types of house undoubtedly existed, though understanding of their development is very uneven as between provinces. In Syria the age-old eastern type of courtyard house (*liwan*) existed side by side with smaller flat-roofed dwellings, while in Africa mosaics attest a two-story house based upon a corridor, with larger tower-like rooms at either end. This type of house occurs very widely throughout the north-west provinces on estates of medium size, while larger houses there follow the more Roman courtyard type or the open-fronted style associated with landscape architecture. In Britain and Belgica there were hybrids between large courtyard houses and the openfronted corridor-house, while the so-called 'basilican' house, a barn-like building of nave and aisles, also appears.

Socially, most of the provincial villas known to us are the dwellings of large landowners or smallholders, and there is little trace of the Italian *latifundia*.

C. Swoboda, *Römische und romanische Paläste* (1919); A. Gnirs, *JÖAI* 1907, Beiblatt; ibid. 1915; P. Gauckler, *Mon. Piot* 1897, 185 ff.; id. *Inventaire des mosaïques* ii. 1 (Tunisie), no. 940; E. Littman, *Ruinenstätten und Schriftdenkmäler Syriens* (1917), 31; H. C. Butler, *Publ. of an Amer. Arch. Exped. to Syria, 1899–1900* i–iv (1904–5), *Publ. of Princeton Univ. Exp. to Syria, 1904–5* i–iii (1907–16); B. Thomas, *Römische Villen in Pannonien* (1964); Grenier, *Manuel* ii. 782 ff.; F. Cumont, *Comment la Belgique fut romanisée²* (1918); R. de Maeyer, *De Romeinsche Villa's in Belgie* (1937); P. Steiner, *Römische Landhäuser im Trierer Bezirk* (1923); F. Oelmann, 'Ein gallorömischen Bauernhof bei Mayen', *Bonner Jahrb.* 1928, 51 ff.; R. G. Collingwood and I. A. Richmond, *Archaeology of Roman Britain³* (1969); P. Corder (ed.), *Romano-British Villas: Some Current Problems* (1955); A. L. F. Rivet, *Town and Country in Roman Britain* (1964), 99 ff.; id. (ed.), *The Roman Villa in Britain* (1969); J. T. Smith, 'Romano-British Aisled Houses', *Arch. Journ.* 1963, i ff. I. A. R.; A. L. F. R.

**VILLANOVANS.** The word 'Villanovan' derives from the small town near Bologna where in 1853 Gozzadini found the first of many Iron Age cemeteries in the modern provinces of Bologna, Faenza, Forli, and Ravenna. The name is now used to denote the period and people represented not only in these cemeteries but also in those of Etruria, where they precede the cemeteries of the great Etruscan cities; it may also be applied to the cemeteries of Pontecagnano and Sala Consilina near Salerno, and to the isolated cemetery of Fermo in the Marche. It is convenient to retain the distinction between 'Northern' and 'Southern' Villanovans. Both are characterized above all by biconical ossuaries with incised decoration. Although many archaeologists have argued that the Villanovans came to Italy from north of the Alps, they do not seem to have been immigrants: their material culture, like that of the other cultures of the Italian Iron Age, derives ultimately from a combination of the Terramara and Apennine cultures (qq.v.) of the Bronze Age, via an independent ('proto-Villanovan') Italian version of the European Urnfield culture typified in central Italy at Tolfa and Allumiere.

An alternative to the old chronology of the Northern Villanovans (i.e. San Vitale, Benacci I and II, and Arnoaldi periods, or more simply Villanovan I–IV: see Chevalier, *Latomus* 1962, 120 ff.) has recently been suggested by Müller-Karpe. His Bologna I invites comparison with certain typological aspects of contemporary central and southern Italy and is datable in general to the ninth century B.C., starting perhaps in the tenth. There are even more secure central Italian parallels for his eighth-century Bologna II, especially at Tarquinii (q.v.), the starting-point for any discussion of the Iron Age in Etruria. Unlike their Northern counterparts, the Southern Villanovans, situated between the Tiber and the Tyrrhenian seaboard, were open to influences from outside. These began to arrive in the first half of the eighth century with the Greek prospectors who landed on Ischia (q.v.) and at Cumae presumably on their way to the metal-rich regions of north-west Etruria: their effect on the Southern Villanovans is clearly seen in the infiltration into southern Etruria of painted pottery imitating Greek Geometric which accompanies an increased awareness of the industrial possibilities of iron. These early Greeks heralded the great colonizing movements from the east Mediterranean of which we see an early sign in the form of the Bocchoris vase at Tarquinii (q.v.), matched now by a Bocchoris scarab from a late-eighth-century context on Ischia. In southern Etruria, at least, the transition from Villanovan to orientalizing, and so eventually to Etruscan, was complete. The fact that from the mid eighth century onwards there is a considerable amount of material in the north (including some orientalizing) that would be equally at home in the south indicates a northward transmission of artistic—and doubtless other—influences. At the same time, it should not be forgotten that at least some complementary influences were crossing the Apennines in the opposite direction to certain sites in southern Etruria, notably Vetulonia (q.v.).

Unfortunately, our knowledge of the Villanovans is based almost exclusively on the evidence of their cemeteries: a Villanovan habitation has, however, recently been excavated at San Giovenale (q.v.). It seems safe to conclude that Villanovan economy was based on agriculture, stock-raising, and hunting; an extensive use of the horse is indicated by the numerous horse-bits found in both Northern and Southern tombs. By at least the middle of the eighth century the fine quality both of pottery and of cast and sheet bronze indicates that their production had passed into the hands of professional craftsmen. The density of the Villanovan concentration around Bologna must surely mean that it was playing an important part in commercial expansion to the north long before it passed into the Etruscan orbit with the foundation of Felsina (q.v.) in the sixth century.

D. Randall-MacIver, *Villanovans and Early Etruscans* (1924); M. Pallottino, *Mon. Ant.* 1937; id. *Stud. Etr.* 1939, 85 ff.; id. *Rend. Pont.* xxii (1946–7), 31 ff.; A. Akerström, *Der Geometrische Stil in Italien* (Lund, 1943) x, discussed by T. J. Dunbabin and C. F. C. Hawkes, *JRS* 1949, 137 ff.; H. Müller-Karpe, *Beiträge zur Chronologie der Urnenfelderzeit nördlich und südlich der Alpen* (1959), discussed by Pallottino, *Stud. Etr.* 1960, 11 ff.; *Mostra dell'Etruria Padana e della città di Spina* (Bologna, 1960); *Civiltà del Ferro* (Bologna, 1960); G. A. Mansuelli and R. Scarani, *L'Emilia prima dei Romani* (1961); R. Pittioni, *PW* Suppl. ix, s.v. *Italien Urgeschichte*, esp. 262 ff.; *Preistoria dell'Emilia e Romagna*, 2 vols. (Bologna, 1962, 1963; B. d'Agostino, *Enc. Arte. Ant.* vii (1966), s.v. 'Villanovia civiltà'; J. Close-Brooks and D. Ridgway, *Stud. Etr.* 1967, 311 ff.; H. Hencken, *Tarquinia, Villanovans and Early Etruscans* i, ii (Amer. Soc. Prehistoric Research, 1968).                    D. W. R. R.

**VILLIUS** (*PW* 5), LUCIUS, tribune of the *plebs* in 180 B.C., carried the first *lex annalis*, which established minimum age-limits for tenure of the curule magistracies (42 for the consulship). It was possibly this same law which required an interval of two years between curule magistracies. These provisions remained largely unchanged until the Principate, when the minimum ages were lowered. *See also* CURSUS HONORUM.

Livy 40. 44. 1. A. Astin, *The Lex Annalis before Sulla* (1958) and refs. there to other interpretations; Mommsen, *Röm. Staatsr.* i³. 529.
                                                                            A. E. A.

**VIMINACIUM**, modern *Kostolac* on the Danube east of Belgrade, was a Celtic settlement which became a legionary fortress and city in Moesia Superior. Its permanent garrison (probably from A.D. 56/7) was Legio VII Claudia; for a period under Trajan it was also occupied by Legio IV Flavia. The civil settlement became a *municipium* (*Aelium*) under Hadrian and a *colonia* under Gordian III.                    J. J. W.

**VINDELICI**, a people of mainly Celtic origin but including Illyrian and other elements, inhabited the Schwabian–Bavarian plateau and reached from the northern slopes of the Alps up to the Danube. They were conquered by Tiberius and Drusus (15 B.C.). Later they occupied the eastern part of the province of Raetia (Vindelicia) and their name was commemorated in the city of Augusta Vindelicorum (q.v.) which became a *municipium* under Hadrian.                    J. J. W.

**VINDEX**, GAIUS JULIUS (*PW* 534), of regal Aquitanian family, son of a Roman senator (who had presumably been adlected by Claudius), rebelled against Nero (early spring, A.D. 68) when legate of Gallia Lugdunensis, for unknown reasons. He sought to inveigle other provincial governors, vainly, except Sulpicius Galba (q.v. 1), whose claims to the throne he promised to support. Masses of native Gauls, the notables, and their clients joined

Vindex. The city of Vienna in Narbonensis declared for him, but the Roman veteran colony of Lugdunum refused to admit him. In the meantime, Verginius (q.v. 2) Rufus mustered the army of Germania Superior and marched to crush the rising. Vindex was defeated and killed in a great battle at Vesontio. Much remains uncertain about this important episode.

P. A. Brunt, *Latomus* 1959, 531 ff.; J. B. Hainsworth, *Hist.* 1962, 86 ff.                                                                  R. S.

**VINDICATIO** was the action by which the owner of a thing (including, in early law, persons in *patria potestas* (q.v.)) could assert his title against anyone having *possessio* (q.v.) of the thing (*rei vindicatio*), or, more widely, the actions by which title was asserted to *servitutes* (q.v.) (*vindicatio servitutis, ususfructus*), or by which the freedom of a supposed slave was asserted by an *adsertor libertatis* (*vindicatio in libertatem, causa liberalis*). The term signified in the early Roman process the formal assertions of the right of ownership made by both the parties (Gai. *Inst.* 4. 16; *see* SACRAMENTUM). When the plaintiff was not quiritary owner, a *rei vindicatio* would not lie, but if he were *in via usucapiendi* (*see* DOMINIUM) the Praetor would allow a variant (*utilis*) form of the action with the fiction that the time necessary for *usucapio* had elapsed (*actio Publiciana*: Gai. *Inst.* 4. 36). In the formulary procedure the successful plaintiff in a *rei vindicatio* could not compel the defendant to return the thing (*see* LITIS AESTIMATIO), but the plaintiff was allowed to swear to its value by *iusiurandum* (q.v.) *in litem* and thus by judicious over-valuation to encourage its return.                    B. N.

**VINDOBONA**, modern *Vienna* on the Danube, lay in the territory of the Boii, a Celtic people included within Pannonia (Superior). In the first century A.D. it was garrisoned by the *Ala Flavia Domitiana Augusta Britannica milliaria civium Romanorum* (under Domitian CIL iii. 15197). At the beginning of Trajan's reign, probably on the occasion of his visit in 98, Legio XIII Gemina was moved there from Poetovio (q.v.) and began the construction of a legionary fortress before it departed for the Dacian Wars. In its place came Legio XIV Gemina Martia Victrix which remained until the end of Trajan's reign when it moved to Carnuntum (q.v.), while Legio X Gemina was moved from Aquincum (q.v.) to become the permanent garrison at Vindobona.

At some date in the third century the civil settlement became a *municipium* (CIL iii. 4557) while Vindobona was also a *statio* of the *classis Histrica* (*Not. Dign.* [occ.] xxxiv. 28). Though not in administrative terms the equal of Carnuntum, Vindobona was an important fortress, especially in the Marcomannic Wars, during which it was apparently destroyed, though rebuilt almost immediately. M. Aurelius died there. In 395 part of the fortress was burnt down, and later (perhaps *c.* 406) Vindobona was abandoned by the Romans.

A. Neumann, 'Die Fortschritte der Vindobonaforschung 1948 bis 1954', *Carinthia* i. 146 (1956), 453 ff.; id. *Forschungen in Vindobona* 1948–67 (1968).                    F. A. W. S.; J. J. W.

**VINDONISSA**, modern *Windisch*, Switzerland, a prehistoric site on the lower Aar, occupied *c.* A.D. 12 by Legio XIII, which was replaced in 45–6 by Legio XXI Rapax, whose violent behaviour to the Helvetii in 69 induced Vespasian to send it elsewhere. Its place was taken by Legio XI Claudia Pia Fidelis, until *c.* 100 when it was realized that Vindonissa was too far from any theatre of war. A considerable civil population remained for whom the military fortress was reconstructed *c.* 260 under pressure of Alamannic attacks. The fortress and the *forum* of the *canabae* have been partially excavated. It was an important centre of lamp manufacture.

R. Laur-Belart, *Vindonissa, Lager und Vicus* (1935).    C. E. S.

**VINICIANUS**, ANNIUS (*PW* 98), son of Vinicianus who conspired in A.D. 42, and son-in-law of Corbulo (q.v.), was legate of Legio V Macedonica in 63 when he was not yet quaestor. In 65 he escorted Tiridates to Rome. He gave his name to a plot against Nero at Beneventum (66). A. M.

**VINICIUS** (1, *PW* 6), MARCUS (*cos. suff.* 19 B.C.), a *novus homo* from Cales in Campania, is first mentioned as legate of Augustus in Gaul (25 B.C.). In Illyricum (13, perhaps as proconsul) he and Agrippa began the *Bellum Pannonicum* terminated by Tiberius (12–9). Vinicius is next (and last) heard of in A.D. 1 or 2 as commander of the Rhine army. The acephalous elogium from Tusculum, recording operations against Transdanubian peoples (*ILS* 8965) is now generally attributed to Vinicius, but the details and dating of that campaign are uncertain (14–13, 10, and *c*. 1 B.C. have been suggested). The historian Velleius Paterculus enjoyed the patronage of the Vinicii, dedicating his work to the grandson, M. Vinicius.

R. Syme, *CQ* 1933, 142 ff.; *Hist.* 1962, 148; A. v. Premerstein, *JÖAI* 1934, 60 ff. R. S.

**VINICIUS** (2), PUBLIUS (*cos.* A.D. 2), Augustan orator and declaimer; an admirer of Ovid, he combined originality with good taste (Sen. *Controv.* 7. 5. 11, 10. 4. 25). He was son of (1) above and father of M. Vinicius (*cos.* A.D. 30 and 45 and husband of Julia, q.v. 4, who fell a victim to Messalina in 46).

**VINICIUS** (3), LUCIUS (*cos. suff.* 5 B.C.), Augustan orator and declaimer; famous for his quick wit (Sen. *Controv.* 2. 5. 20).

**VINIUS** (*PW* 5) TITUS, close adviser of Galba (q.v. 1) and his colleague as consul in A.D. 69, had been imprisoned after a scandal when military tribune in Germany in 39. Released by Claudius he became praetor and legionary legate, but he again met disgrace when the emperor accused him of stealing some gold plate. Emerging from a retarded career as proconsul of Narbonensis, he was in Spain at the time of Galba's rising, though it is uncertain what post he held. Later he urged Galba to adopt Otho (q.v.), but he was murdered along with Galba by Otho's troops in Jan. 69. Tacitus (*Hist.* 1. 48) says he was then aged 57, but this is hard to reconcile with the date of his military tribunate. G. E. F. C.

**VIRGIL** (PUBLIUS VERGILIUS MĀRO; 70–19 B.C.), poet. The spelling with an 'i' is traditional; contemporary inscriptions give the name Vergilius. It was corrupted by the fourth or fifth centuries, and so passed into all vernaculars. A 'Life' of Virgil was included in Suetonius' *de Poetis*. This survives in various forms: expanded by Donatus (q.v. 1), abbreviated by Servius, Phocas, and others, and expanded again into 'Donatus auctus' (early 15th c.). Though these *Lives* may attribute poems of the *Appendix Vergiliana* (q.v.) to Virgil, they make no use of them for biographical purposes. Varius (q.v. 2), who edited the *Aeneid* after Virgil's death, wrote something about Virgil (Quint. 10. 3. 8). A reference in Gellius (*NA* 17. 10. 2) to *amici familiaresque* who wrote on Virgil may mean no more than Varius. Legend soon grew about Virgil, and anecdotes are attributed to recollections long after his death (e.g. of Eros, his amanuensis, in extreme old age: Donat. 34). As information was lacking, allegorization was applied to the *Eclogues* to supply it.

Virgil was born on 15 Oct. 70 B.C. (in view of the dislocation of the pre-Julius calendar, Dante by the words 'nacqui sub Julio' (*Inf.* 1. 70) may mean that Virgil was really born in July), at Andes, a *pagus* near Mantua. Tradition has identified this much-disputed site with Pietole, south-south-east of Mantua (see B. Nardi, *Mantuanitas Vergiliana* (1963), 69 ff.). The gentile *nomen* Vergilius is widely distributed, mostly in Etruscan regions; the *cognomen* Maro may be Etruscan rather than Greek (*Od.* 9. 197): see M. L. Gordon, *JRS* 1934, 188. Virgil himself stresses the Etruscan element in Mantua (*Aen.* 10. 198 ff.). There is no reason to think that he was in any way Celtic. His father, though described as of humble origin (Macrob. *Sat.* 5. 2. 1), as a potter or courier who married his master's daughter, was probably an *eques*, a landowner rich enough to give his son an excellent education and to prepare him for a senatorial career. He had married a Magia, whose family, like the Vergilii, achieved several magistracies in Rome, though not the consulship.

**2.** Virgil was presumably brought up in Mantua and at his father's suburban villa and farm, but for his higher education he went to Cremona. He assumed the *toga virilis* on his fifteenth birthday (Donatus 6 wrongly says seventeenth). Tradition had it that Lucretius (q.v. 2) died on the same day. From Cremona Virgil proceeded to Milan, and soon after to Rome, where he studied rhetoric under prominent teachers. He seems to have entered what survived of the circle of Catullus (q.v. 1), as his friendship with Pollio (q.v.) and the admiring reference (*Ecl.* 9. 35) to Cinna (q.v. 3) show. He was deeply influenced by Catullus and by Alexandrian ideals of poetry (*see* ALEXANDRIANISM, LATIN). Some of the poems in the *Catalepton*, if they are his, belong to this period. He made one appearance as an advocate in the courts, but abandoned all thought of a political career, perhaps when the civil war broke out (49 B.C.) and retired to Naples to study philosophy under the Epicurean Siro (*Catal.* 5, variously dated), whose small villa and holding of land he seems to have inherited before 41 B.C. (*Catal.* 8).

**3.** When land in Italy was distributed to war veterans in 41 B.C. (*see* AUGUSTUS), Virgil's father was expropriated and took refuge with his son near Naples (*Catal.* 8). The *Lives* and Commentators assert that *Ecl.* 1 celebrates the subsequent restoration of the estate to Virgil by Octavian owing to the intercession of his friends, but *G.* 1. 198–9 surely implies that the loss was permanent. (In *Ecl.* 1 the situation of Meliboeus, a free citizen who loses his ancestral estate, fits Virgil much more closely than that of Tityrus, an old slave who is granted his liberty and his *peculium*: Virgil is Tityrus in *Ecl.* 1 only in the sense that both are pastoral poets, as *Ecl.* 6. 4 shows.) Appian's account shows that the alleged *triumviri agris dividundis*, (by a happy coincidence all Virgil's friends, Pollio, Alfenus Varus, and Cornelius Gallus) could not have existed, since Antony's friends complained that Octavian kept the whole distribution in his own hands (App. *BCiv.* 5. 14. But cf. Broughton, *MRR* ii. 377).

The *Lives* and Commentators also assert that Virgil began the *Eclogues* when he was 28 (i.e. 42 B.C.) and finished them in three years. This is based on the certain dating of four *Eclogues*: 1 and 9 to 41 B.C.; 4 to 40; and 8 to 39. But 2, 3, and 5 (and probably 7) are earlier than 9 (itself earlier than 1, as a comparison of 9. 50 with 1. 73 shows) and can scarcely be crowded into 42. 10 may belong to 38 or 37. Pollio's encouragement of Virgil to transpose the Theocritean pastoral into Latin (*Ecl.* 8. 11–12) was more probably due to a renewal of personal contact, interrupted since 49, than to correspondence. But Pollio was not in Italy from 49 until late 45, when he was probably praetor. Later he was in Spain (44), returned to Italy (July 43), and was made governor of Cisalpine Gaul by Antony. If then 45 is the most likely year for him to reassemble his literary circle, the *Eclogues* are to be spread over eight years (45–37). Their probable order is 2, 7, 3, 5, 9, 1, 4, 6, 8, 10 (but 7 is put later by some). Their present order is due to artistic reasons of symmetry and alternation. They were appreciated more widely than by the circles which admired Alexandrianism, and, adapted as mimes to the stage (Donat. 27; Servius on *Ecl.* 6. 11), made Virgil a popular, though elusive (Donat. 39), figure. The salutations of the crowd in the theatre (Tac. *Dial.* 13) must have been due to the *Eclogues*.

4. Virgil came into contact with Horace (q.v.) and gained his friendship (*Carm.* 1. 3, 8), probably in 41 (if *Ecl.* 1. 70–1 seems to heighten, and therefore to quote, the bitter words of *Epode* 16. 9–14; the *Epode* and *Ecl.* 4 have common elements). Despite social and temperamental differences, the two poets had much in common, in their poetic ideals, in the loss of their patrimony, and in their (later) admiration of Augustus. When the *Eclogues* were collected and published under Virgil's name, Maecenas (q.v.) seems to have captured Virgil for Octavian from the Antonian Pollio. But earlier, as Servius says (on *Ecl.* 1. 12 and 70), *Ecl.* 1 had not been unqualified praise of Octavian (and it is too lightly assumed that the *iuvenis* of 1. 42 must be Octavian, see J. Liegle, *Hermes* 1943, 209 ff., and the context of 'Caesar's star' in *Ecl.* 9 shows that the hopes it aroused were delusory). Virgil recommended Horace to Maecenas, who nine months later admitted him to the circle which included Varius and Plotius Tucca. In this company the famous journey to Brundisium (*Sat.* 1. 5) was made in 37.

Virgil is said to have spent seven years on the *Georgics*. The possibility of a free poetic handling of this topic may have been suggested by the publication of Varro's *Res Rustica* in 37. The reference (*G.* 2. 161–4) to the Portus Iulius near Avernus, completed in 37, provides the earliest date, the reference (*G.* 4. 560–2) to Octavian in the East after Actium (31) gives the latest. After Octavian's return in 29, Virgil read the poem to him in his villa at Atella (Donat. 27). Virgil was then living at Naples (*G.* 4. 563–4). If the Vergilius of Horace *Carm.* 1. 3 is the poet, a journey to Greece may be reflected in the references to Greece in the proem of *G.* 3. The poem honoured Maecenas, to whom each book is addressed (1. 2; 2. 41; 3. 41; 4. 2: a symmetrical arrangement).

5. The *Aeneid* does not seem to be the epic that is projected in *Georgics* 3. 8–48. Ancient tradition asserts that it took eleven years to write, viz. 29 to 19, but Donatus himself (31) supplies the evidence to disprove this: when Augustus wrote to Virgil from Spain in 26, he had not seen either the first outline (ὑπογραφή) or any episode (κῶλον) of the poem, though he had been in Italy in 27. Virgil (quoted by Macrob. 1. 24. 11) refused to send any specimen to Augustus, saying that he needed 'much profounder studies' (i.e. than those of the years 29–27) and that he must have embarked on his epic task 'in a moment of aberration' (*paene vitio mentis*). The *Life* by Probus confirms this dating: *Aeneida ingressus bello Cantabrico*, and Propertius (2. 34 B, 63–6, 91–2), writing after Gallus' death in 26, salutes the birth of the *Aeneid*, a poem greater than the *Iliad*.

Later, however, Virgil read books 2, 4, and 6 (the last after the death of Marcellus in 23, since lines 860–6 caused his mother, Octavia, to faint) to Augustus and his circle. In 19 he left Italy to travel in Greece and Asia for three years, during which he would complete and polish the *Aeneid*, and afterwards devote himself to philosophy. At Athens, however, he met Augustus and was persuaded to return home with him. He fell ill at Megara, and was brought back as far as Brundisium, where he died on 20 Sept. His body was brought to Naples and buried within 2 miles on the road to Puteoli (the tomb now shown as Virgil's is *more* than 2 miles from the ancient

city). No doubt he had built the tomb for himself, and is said to have dictated the inscription for it on his deathbed:

> Mantua me genuit, Calabri rapuere, tenet nunc
> Parthenope; cecini pascua rura duces.

Before leaving Italy, Virgil—for whatever reason—had made Varius, his literary executor, promise to burn the *Aeneid*, if anything should happen to him. Augustus ordered that this wish should be disregarded and the poem published in its unfinished state.

6. Virgil is described as tall and broad, with a dark complexion; cf. the mosaic from Hadrumetum (q.v.). An attempt has been made to establish a Virgilian type among portrait busts of Augustan date (V. Poulsen, *Vergil*, Bremen, 1959). He suffered from ill health (Donat. 25). He never married, and homosexual tendencies were inferred from this and from the appearance in the *Eclogues* of that traditional Greek theme. Gifts from his friends (presumably Augustus and Maecenas) made him a rich man, with houses in Rome and near Naples, and a villa in Nola (Servius on *G.* 2. 224).

7. WORKS

(1) *Early Poems.* Fourteen short poems (**Catalepton**) and five longer, **Culex, Ciris, Copa, Moretum,** and, more doubtfully, **Aetna,** were attributed to the youth of Virgil. But in modern times the attribution of almost all has been disputed and generally rejected. *See* APPENDIX VERGILIANA.

(2) **Eclogues** ('Εκλογή, a single 'selected' occasional poem, including odes and epistles of Horace, not a collection of such); in the Middle Ages and up to Spenser the word was taken to mean 'goat-song' (αἰγλογ); more properly *Bucolics* (βουκολικά, songs of cowherds), a title taken from Theocritus: all Virgil's poems have Greek titles.

With the exceptions of 4 and 6, the *Eclogues* are modelled on the *Idylls* of Theocritus and Pseudo-Theocritus. Sometimes an *Eclogue* is a transposition of a single *Idyll*, as *Ecl.* 9 is of *Id.* 7; the two halves of *Ecl.* 8 are based on *Id.* 1 and 2. *Ecl.* 5 and 10 grow out of the situation of *Id.* 1. The 'amoebaean' competitions of 3 and 7 reflect *Id.* 4 and 5. *Ecl.* 1 has no Greek model, as the situation is new and Roman. *Ecl.* 2 (Corydon to Alexis) uses *Id.* 11 (Cyclops to Galatea), but the name of Corydon comes from *Id.* 4 and of Alexis from epigrams of Plato and Meleager, and the homosexual theme from *Id.* 7, 8, 12, 23, etc. *Id.* 20 provides the contrast of country and city. As *Id.* 11 provides the moral 'poetry is the medicine of love' (cf. Callim. *Epigr.* 46 Pf.), so it provides most of the verbal echoes, but in company with several other *Idylls* and other Hellenistic poems, especially epigrams. *Ecl.* 2. 24 seems pure Greek, but is not Theocritean; its hiatus and line-ending are also Greek. Sometimes the translation is close; sometimes Virgil is very free, or may adopt an idea to work it out independently. Already in *Ecl.* 2 Virgil enters seriously into the sentiments of Corydon, even identifies himself with him, without the ironical and patronizing distance of Theocritus. In general the names, the setting, and scenery are all Greek, Sicilian, or Arcadian. But Virgil infuses a realistic Italian element. Arcadian shepherds appear on the banks of the Mincius (*Ecl.* 7); in *Ecl.* 3 two Greek astronomers figure, and then suddenly Pollio, in person in contrast to the rival poets, Bavius and Maevius; and the riddle in 104–5 may have a Roman reference. *Ecl.* 5 *may* perhaps allude to the death and deification of Julius Caesar. His 'star' (the comet of July 44) and his name appear in *Ecl.* 9. 47, but the comet was interpreted also as pointing to the young Caesar (Pliny, *HN* 2. 22–3, 89–94). Mantua and Cremona, Varius and Cinna, are named also, and in *Ecl.* 1. 19 the name of Rome sounds for the first time. Gallus forms the climax of *Ecl.* 6, and is the protagonist of 10. The dedications of 4 and 8 to Pollio and of 6 to (Alfenus) Varus are one thing: quite another is the occurrence of Roman persons and places within Greek settings, and is in itself enough to refute all identifications of the Greek names as masks for contemporary Romans. Menalcas in 9 and Tityrus in 1 are not simply Virgil, but personifications of some aspect of him, as Meliboeus is also in 1 or Lycidas in 9. They are not Virgil, but his creations and projections, carrying some of his personal experience of the evictions.

*Ecl.* 4 and 6 stand apart as 'paulo maiora', embodying an element of prophecy or revelation. The identity of the child in *Ecl.* 4, under whose rule peace and the Golden Age will be restored, has provoked age-long debate. If the boy is real and Roman, as he surely is, and not a god or a personification, he is more probably the expected child of Antony and Octavia, whose marriage was to seal the Peace of Brundisium, not the expected child of Octavian and Scribonia, who proved to be a girl, the unfortunate Julia. The Christian interpretation of the poem was launched, in a naïve form, by Constantine at Nicaea in 325 (Euseb. *Oratio ad Sanctos*). Lactantius and St. Augustine adopt a carefully qualified attitude to it: St. Jerome is hostile. *Ecl.* 6 has in this century excited great interest. Silenus, like Proteus in *G.* 4, utters a prophecy to his captors. The cosmology with which he begins is Lucretian in language, but it is not Epicurean since the four elements compose a living and sentient universe. The enigmatic series of myths culminates in Gallus, and then lines 11, 75–7, and 81 are, with two small changes, quoted in the *Ciris* 59–61, 51.

The *Eclogues*, thus blending Greek with Italian elements, and an idealized Arcadia with contemporary history, created a new and enchanting art, exquisite in its sentiment and in its music, endlessly imitated (*see* PASTORAL POETRY, LATIN): 'all the charm of all the Muses flowering in a lonely word'. In them Virgil develops from an Alexandrian into a Roman.

(3) **Georgics** (Γεωργικά, 'husbandry'; on the model of Nicander's Γεωργικά, Θηριακά, etc.), a poem of 2,188 lines, in four books. According to Donatus 22, Virgil dictated in the morning a large number of lines that he had rehearsed, and spent the day reducing them to a very few, 'licking them into shape'. If the poem took seven years (36–29), the rate of composition was less than one line a day. Book 1 deals with the cultivation of crops; book 2 with that of fruit-trees, especially the vine; 3 with the rearing of animals, and 4 with bees. The share of bees is out of all proportion to that of farmers' manuals: thus the *villaticae pastiones* (poultry and fish) of Varro's third book vanish.

Virgil describes his poem as 'Hesiodic' (2. 176, *Ascraeum*), but it is not so in the sense that the *Eclogues* are Theocritean. He invokes Hesiod in the spirit of Callimachus, as the patron of didactic poetry, and in book 1 twice follows him directly in the description of the plough (169–75) and of the 'days' (276–86), and in an occasional phrase or precept. The loose and desultory, almost conversational, development of book 1 seems deliberately Hesiodic. In detail Virgil owes more to Alexandrian didactic poets; to the *Diosemeia* of Aratus (q.v. 1) for weather signs (1. 204 ff.), sometimes (esp. 375–87) adapting the Latin version of Varro Atacinus (not of Cicero), and to his *Phaenomena* for constellations (244–6); to Eratosthenes (q.v.) for the zones of sky and earth (233–51); and to Nicander, though the debt cannot be traced. The story of Aristaeus (4. 315–558), the αἴτιον of the βουγονία, is Callimachean, especially in the linking of myths together. It is an exquisite example of the Alexandrian 'epyllion', where the two stories of Aristaeus, and of Orpheus and Eurydice, are causally linked,

not merely juxtaposed as in Catullus' sixty-fourth poem. But it is also Homeric, in the direct borrowing of Proteus from the *Odyssey*, and it follows on the miniature epic of the first half of the book, like the *Batrachomyomachia* (pseudo-Homeric, but perhaps, to Virgil, Homeric), of the small animals treated heroically with affectionate humour. There are also imitations of Homer already in book 1: e.g. 104–10 cf. *Il.* 21. 257–62 (irrigation); 281–3 cf. *Od.* 11. 596 (Pelion on Ossa). What Virgil owes to prose writers on agriculture, whether Greek or Latin, cannot be determined. He ignores the basis of Cato's economy, the large estate run with slaves, and dwells on the smallholder. Varro made a systematic handling unnecessary, but perhaps his Ciceronian dialogue form suggested something of the tone, especially of book 1, and the culmination in a myth, as in Cicero's *de Republica* (*Somnium Scipionis*) and several dialogues of his model, Plato. The twelve gods of Virgil's invocation are a variant on the twelve *Di Consentes* of Varro's proem. A tragic incident of civil disorder at the end of Varro's first book may have pointed to Virgil's set piece on the civil war at the end of book 1. But Virgil's greatest debt is to the Latin didactic epic of Lucretius (q.v. 2), not only in the phrases of didactic argument and transition, in countless epithets and turns of style, in reminiscences of themes, which show how Virgil's mind was saturated with Lucretius, and in the all but naming of Lucretius in 2. 490–2, but also in the set pieces of higher tone which elevate and diversify the *Georgics* as they do the *de rerum natura*, notably the meditation on the power of love and the description of the plague in 3 (after Lucretius 4 and 6), and the fact that the *Georgics* are basically an answer to Lucretius, often in his own phrases. The naturalistic explanation in 1. 415–23 (from dense and rare, not *divinitus*) seems a concession to Lucretius, but 4. 219–27 offers a Stoic reply (as already in *Ecl.* 6). Virgil reasserts divine providence, and a religious attitude expressed even in the mystery of sacrifice, and the importance of death (contrast: *nil igitur ad nos mors est*) and of the underworld. It is this implicit depth, and Virgil's sympathy with nature, animals, and men, that has led critics, like Dryden, to feel that the *Georgics* are 'the best poem of the best poet', whereas the *Aeneid* may seem too explicit and too Augustan. The more the poem is treated as a practical guide to husbandry, and Virgil's technical accuracy stressed, the less relevant must appear the 'set pieces' (and much less relevant than they are in Lucretius), some eleven of them of various lengths, making up a third of the whole poem, culminating in the longest, the 'episode' of Aristaeus. Already Seneca (*Ep.* 86. 15–17) detects an inaccuracy and suggests that Virgil's aim was to give pleasure, not instruction.

In style and metre, and in command of all resources of artistic expression, in control over long periods (1. 5–42) or brief (4. 445–56), in every device of 'rhetoric', in range of emotional tone, from solemn to playful, from lyrical to conversational, the *Georgics* are fully mature and show the freedom of a master.

(4) **Aeneid**, 'the story of Aeneas' (the title Αἰνηΐς is modelled on Ἡρακληΐς), begun in 26 and left almost finished in 19, an epic in twelve books, of 12,847 lines according to the anonymous verses *Summa Vergilii* (Baehrens, *PLM* iv, n. 182, p. 178), but our texts have 12,913 owing to the inclusion of the Helen-episode in 2. 567–88 and 1. 1 a–d, and to interpolations. If the *Aeneid* were the poem on Augustus explicitly projected in the *Georgics* (3. 8–48), Virgil might have begun it in 29, but Aeneas is not mentioned in this passage which glorifies Augustus, while in the *Aeneid* Augustus is hardly *in medio*. Why then the three-year delay (see above § 5)? And what attracted Virgil to his Aeneas (*Aeneas meus*)? Virgil must have come to see that a contemporary

epic of Ennian type (Ennius' epitaph is quoted in *G*. 3. 8–9) on Augustus could not give him adequate scope; only later did the imperial house accidentally provide in Marcellus an example of Virgil's type of tragedy, the young man who dies before his parents and before their eyes (*Ecl*. 5. 22–3; *G*. 3. 258–63; 4. 477; in *Aen*., Euryalus, Lausus, Pallas). The matrimonial complexities of the *domus Augusta*, disastrous enough, were hardly the tragic theme of love that Virgil, in the spirit of *Ecl*. 10. 69, felt bound to graft on to Aeneas in defiance of history and chronology, even of the legend of the chaste Dido, who killed herself to avoid a second marriage. For us the connexion of Trojan Aeneas with Rome first appears in Naevius (q.v.). Ennius developed the theme of Aeneas in Italy, and Cato (q.v. 1) too in his *Origines*. At first Virgil might well dismiss Aeneas as an exhausted theme, until he saw how to expand Fabius Pictor's prophetic dream (Cic. *Div*. 1. 21. 43) as an Odyssean and Orphic κατάβασις into book 6, to draw in Dido and place the Kingdom of Saturn in Latium and Arcadia on the Palatine and also to include the whole of Roman 'history' down to Augustus by means of various 'prophetic' devices (the unborn heroes of 6. 756 ff.; the scenes on the shield, 8. 626 ff. and utterances of Jupiter, 1. 257; 10. 6–15; even Dido's curse, 4. 625–9, and the boat-race, 5). Aeneas had been known and located in the West, 'Hesperia', not much, if at all, later than Heracles (*Aen*. 8. 185 ff.) or Odysseus (father of Latinus already in Hesiod, *Theog*. 1011–13), and he appealed more to the Romans. Numa was said to have imposed on Roman magistrates the obligation to sacrifice to Aeneas' *Penates* at Lavinium (Luc. 7. 394–6: cf. Serv. on *Aen*. 2. 296), and his other act of 'piety', in carrying Anchises from Troy, is depicted on vases and seals from Veii before 500 B.C. (cf. K. Schauenburg, *Gymnasion* 1960, 176 ff.). But he excited a new interest when a family, transferred to Rome from Alba Longa on its fall, the gens Iulia of Bovillae (Tac. *Ann*. 2. 41), which for centuries had claimed descent from him, provided the first two Caesars.

Aeneas had always been unique in the *Iliad* (20. 307–8: cf. *Hymn. Hom. Ven*., 196–7, and *Aen*. 3. 97–8) in that he has a future as well as a past, and a kingdom is prophesied for his descendants. Strabo (608) records without approval the Roman interpretation and reading in *Iliad* 20. 307 of πάντεσσιν for Τρώεσσιν: Αἰνείαο γένος πάντεσσιν ἀνάξει.

The *Aeneid* was thus much more than the revival of a Greek myth; it was an epic of Rome, and, like that of Ennius, brought its action down to the present. It was not, however, annalistic, but Homeric and Aristotelian in its unity of action. It was a commonplace among ancient critics (Donat. 21; Macrob. *Sat*. 5. 2. 6) that the first half of the *Aeneid* was an *Odyssey*, the second half an *Iliad*, with Turnus as the new Achilles (6. 89; 9. 742; 11. 438), and correspondences between the two halves have been worked out, perhaps to excess. It seems true of both halves that the even-numbered books are more exciting and dramatic, the odd lower in tone but more cheerful (Conway). A tripartite division into the calling, the preparation, and the execution of the task, has some plausibility, as also has the contrast of luxurious, Epicurean (4. 34, 379) Carthage with the pastoral simplicity of Pallanteum (8. 362–5). 6 is usually seen as the turning-point in Aeneas' 'development', but 6, 7, and 8 form a series of arrivals, in Italy, in Latium, and in Rome. Virgil himself marks 7. 45 (*maius opus moveo*) as the ascent to a higher theme.

Virgil's debt to Homer ranges from over-all structure, the compositional device of retrospective narrative (in 2 and 3, where, however, it serves to impress on both Aeneas and Dido the impossibility of his permanence in Carthage, and so increases the tragic error of both, cf.

Tib. Donatus on *Aen*. 4. 172), the adaptation of whole episodes, games, νέκυια, shield, catalogues, Doloneia (Nisus and Euryalus), to the transformation of incidents (Elpenor and Palinurus, Ajax and Dido, cf. Macrob. 5. 2. 14–15), the imitation of similes in particular, and of turns of thought or phrase.

Virgil drew on other Greek poets also (more than any Greek, according to Macrob. 5. 2. 2), Pisander for book 2 (Macrob. 5. 2. 4), and Apollonius Rhodius, especially for book 4 (Serv. on *Aen*. 4. 1: 'inde totus hic liber translatus est'), where Greek tragedy, whether directly or in Latin versions by Ennius, Pacuvius, and Accius, contribute also. Of Latin works, the *Annales* of Ennius contribute largely, also Lucretius and Catullus. The *Aeneid* commemorates the literature as well as the history of Rome, and preserved what was otherwise lost (cf. Macrob. 6. 5–6).

Virgil left the *Aeneid* uncompleted, but how seriously? Enough to require three years' work? It was known that Virgil, having drawn up a plan of the *Aeneid* in prose, composed it piecemeal (Donat. 23: *particulatim*) leaving transitions 'propped up by scaffolding' in the form of provisional lines or half-lines. Inconsistencies were observed, especially between book 3 and the rest (3. 256–7 and 7. 122–3; 3. 389–93 and 8. 47–8); its chronology can scarcely be extended beyond three years, yet elsewhere Aeneas' Odyssey takes seven years (1. 755–6; 5. 626). But Servius, who points out (on 5. 626) that these two passages are inconsistent (if in 1 seven years have passed, in 5 it should be the eighth year), concludes that this is one of the 'insoluble' passages (twelve in all, according to him on 9. 361). But too much can easily be made of such points, and a large change of plan, making 3 part of Aeneas' narrative instead of the poet's (curiously third person for first is found at 3. 686) and the games of 5 to occur on the anniversary of Anchises' death instead of at his funeral, seems unlikely. Speculation about the order of composition of separate books or parts of books is hazardous. The half-lines were always taken as proof of incompleteness, and attempts were made to complete them. Virgil may well have been at work on his various drafts for the Helen passage, when he died. 1. 1 a–d were probably added by an ingenious editor to introduce the poet's portrait in an *édition de luxe* (E. Brandt, *Philol*. 1927/8, 331 ff.).

Virgil's greatness was recognized by some of his contemporaries, and he was fairly soon established as 'the poet' *par excellence*, like Homer in Greek. The *Aeneid* became a school textbook, and the standard of Latin grammar and syntax and poetic propriety. But the poem was also the target of much criticism. At first, the extent of Virgil's adaptations of other poets, 'plagiarisms', filled critics with an almost dismayed amazement (even Macrobius speaks of Virgil's *studii circa Homerum nimietas*); one compiled eight books of what he called neutrally 'likenesses', but another called them '*furta*'. A third collected the '*vitia*': Gellius (*NA* 9. 9. 12), comparing 1. 494 unfavourably with *Od*. 6. 102, probably quotes one of them. A Carvilius Pictor wrote an *Aeneidomastix*, and is referred to by Servius as 'Vergiliomastix'. Vipsanius Agrippa accused Virgil of a new kind of 'affectation' (κακοζηλία; F. Marx, *Rh. Mus*. 1925, 174 ff.), consisting in the misuse of ordinary words. Horace (*Ars P*. 46–7) praises this, and Macrobius (6. 6. 1–9) compiles the debris of the controversy, treating all his examples as merits. Modern, but not ancient critics, have attacked the character of Aeneas. His desertion of Dido has been blamed from the point of view of courtly or romantic love, but the ancient world blamed Antony for his infatuation with Cleopatra (Virgil associates her with Dido, 4. 644 and 8. 709) and commended Titus for leaving Berenice. No ancient critic had any doubt, such as many moderns have, but that Aeneas was in love with Dido. The excuse urged on Aeneas' behalf, that obedience to the gods must override his personal preference, is turned into derision of his automatic 'piety'. Such critics have ignored Aeneas' repeated flouting of divine command in 2 (not to mention his doubts as late as 5. 700–3) and determination to fulfil the heroic ideal of a glorious death when the cause is lost. Virgil sympathizes indeed with Dido and Turnus, but also implicitly criticizes the old ideal. But it is very doubtful if any 'development' should be found in Aeneas' character. 'Piety', a warm devotion to his gods, his city, and his family (the English word has misleading associations), is his mark throughout, despite his forgetfulness and ferocity (10. 517–20).

It has been said that the poem fails as a story, 'partly perhaps through its length and the magnitude of the conception'. But it is shorter than the *Iliad* and the *Odyssey*, and if denser, also more tightly organized. Whereas Homer is concerned with only a personal fate, Virgil introduces into epic a theme of national, even world-shaking, importance, and it was just this religious view of Aeneas' mysterious vocation and Rome's function in the world that made the *Aeneid* an 'actual' and contemporary work. It has not the simplicity of primary oral epic, but the philosophical reflectiveness of a later age and an Alexandrian *labor limae* in every line and word. 'With Virgil European poetry grows up' (C. S. Lewis), and Aeneas is a man, an adult, whereas 'Achilles had been little more than a passionate boy'. For us perhaps the great books and climaxes come too early, in 2, 4, and 6, but for Virgil and the Romans the second half, as Iliadic, was '*maius opus*', and the abrupt, un-Greek, ending with Turnus' death is designed to preclude a thirteenth book such as Maffeo Veggio supplied. One of Virgil's own reasons for discontent with the poem was perhaps that he could not support his 'myth' with an adequate philosophy. The one great explicitly philosophical discourse, of Anchises (6. 724–51), expresses a Neopythagorean pessimism and other-worldly dualistic hostility to the body. But Virgil's view of the providential function of 'Roma aeterna' *within* the world, and of Augustus as a god in the flesh restoring the Golden Age in Italy, implies a philosophy of embodiment (not to say 'incarnation'). Furthermore, what is the λόγος of the Descent into the Underworld, if the Gates of Hell remain dualistically impregnable to the Gods of Heaven (6. 552–4)? Dante expanded Virgil's *Descent* into the whole *Comedy*, giving it a Christian meaning by linking it with the celebration of Christ's Death, Harrowing of Hell, and Resurrection at Easter, but he puts his finger on two errors of Virgil, as excluding him from heaven: namely, his belief in the impregnability of Hell and his hostility to the body.

There are Stoic elements in Virgil: *G*. 4. 217–27; *exercite*, 3. 182 and 5. 725 (cf. Sen. *Dial*. 1. iv. 7 and 13); *praecipere*, 6. 103–5 (cf. Cic. *Off*. 1. 81); Sen. *Ep*. 76. 33, but the boast of 6. 103–5 is quickly refuted by events. The two rhyming stanzas *Ad Maronis Mausoleum* (by an anonymous poet at Paris in the twelfth–thirteenth century (?) —see B. Nardi, *Mantuanitas Vergiliana* (1963), 149 ff.) express what many have felt before and since: at Virgil's tomb St. Paul laments that the poet died a pagan:

> 'Quem te', inquit, 'reddidissem
> Si te vivum invenissem
> Poetarum maxime.'

## 8. THE PROGRESS OF CRITICISM

If the populace saluted Virgil as the writer of its most exquisite mimes, and Propertius (2. 34. 65) before the event, and Horace after (*Sat*. 1. 10. 44), saluted the *Aeneid*, the controversy about his plagiaristic and asso-

ciative method (like that of T. S. Eliot in our times) tended to obscure his originality and greatness, until 'purloining Hercules' club' and 'picking pearls out of dung-hills' was recognized as difficult, bold, and meritorious. In *c*. 28 B.C. Nepos (*Att*. 12. 4) mentions a L. Julius Calidus, not Virgil, as the successor to Lucretius and Catullus; and as late as A.D. 27 Velleius Paterculus (2. 36. 3) cites Rabirius with and before Virgil as 'principes carminum nostri aevi'. Augustus' librarian, Hyginus, wrote much about Virgil, but Gellius preserves chiefly unfavourable judgements. After Maecenas (Sen. *Suas*. 1. 12), the first defender in public was Asconius (Donat. 46), and under Nero Valerius Probus set himself to determine Virgil's text. When Virgil was established in the schools of the *grammatici* and *rhetores*, the learning of the Greek scholiasts on Homer, the tragedians, and Alexandrians was transferred, not always aptly, to Virgil. Our surviving commentaries of the late fourth century, when the pagan opposition in Rome to the Church was using Virgil as its bible, draw on the first century of Virgilian criticism; ineptitudes may be suspected of lateness. Neoplatonic exegesis displaces the earlier Stoic. This deification of Virgil begins in the first century A.D. with Calpurnius (*Ecl*. 4. 70), Seneca (*Ep*. 108. 26: *tanquam missum oraculo*), and the cult by Silius Italicus of Virgil's work and tomb (Pliny, *Ep*. 3. 7. 8), Quintilian's veneration (1. 8. 5, etc.) and Statius' adoration of the 'divine' *Aeneid* from afar (*Theb*. 12. 816–17, cf. *Silv*. 4. 4. 54). Lucan alone refuses to take Virgil as a model for epic. Rhetoricians like Arellius Fuscus (Sen. *Suas*. 3. 5) and historians like Tacitus, especially in the *Germania*, show his influence. The archaizing fashion of the second century may have caused a slight recession, but the first consultations of the *Sortes Vergilianae* are attributed (possibly anachronistically) to Hadrian (S.H.A. *Hadr*. 2. 8, despite 16. 6!). Copies of the *Aeneid* were enshrined in temples for consultation (*Clod. Alb*. 4. 5. 4). Virgil was treated as the supreme poet, orator, philosopher, prophet, and theologian. Christian writers composed Virgilian centos to tell Bible stories, and pagans (Ausonius) for other purposes. St. Jerome (*Ep*. 53. 7) ridicules this 'christianizing' of Virgil, in words that Alcuin later uses to deprecate the epic lays of Anglo-Saxon paganism. But not much later the ideas as well as the words of Virgil were rendered innocuous by allegory in the work of Fulgentius (q.v.). This tradition of turning the *Aeneid* into an allegory of the stages of human life (*Aen*. 2 represents the trauma of birth; 6 the acquisition of philosophical enlightenment) persisted in Bernardus Silvestris (fl. *c*. A.D. 1150), John of Salisbury (1115–80), Dante (*Convivio* 4. 26 and *de Vulg. Eloq*. 2. 4, but not in the *Comedy*), and Petrarch. But Petrarch's unfinished Latin epic, the *Africa* on Scipio Africanus, shows a new appreciation of Virgil's art, especially in point of structure and unity of plot.

Domenico Comparetti's *Virgilio nel Medio Evo* (1872; Engl. Transl. 1895) remains a classic, but his view of the popular origin of the legends of Virgil the magician at his tomb in Naples needs to be corrected. The legends are the work of scholars such as Gervase of Tilbury, Alexander Neckam, Conrad of Querfurt, developing hints from Donatus and attributing alien stories to Virgil (see G. Pasquali, Preface in the 1943 reprint of Comparetti). Comparetti's work has been amplified by C. G. Leland, *The Unpublished Legends of Virgil* (1899), and J. W. Spargo, *Vergil the Necromancer* (1934), and continued by V. Zabughin, *Virgilio nel Rinascimento italiano* (1921–3).

As for Virgilian scholarship since the Renaissance, a word can perhaps be spared for the period since the date (1903–8) of Sandys's *History of Classical Scholarship*. R. Heinze's *Virgils Epische Technik* (1903) inaugurated a new era of Virgilian studies and kindled a new interest for Virgil in Germany, which had been under the 'tyranny' of Greece (1903 is also the year of Norden's edition of book 6). Much of what is new in this century, especially on the *Eclogues*, has come from Germany. The continuity and unity of Virgil's work from *Eclogues* to *Aeneid* has been brought out (Klingner), and his art of cumulative imagery or symbolism (Pöschl) studied (see e.g. B. M. W. Knox, *AJPhil.* 1950). Virgil's metre and language have been analysed, with a more precise discrimination of archaic and poetic language from that of ordinary life (Cordier, Axelson, Wilkinson).

BIBLIOGRAPHIES. F. Peeters, *A Bibliography of Vergil* (U.S.A. 1933); G. Mambelli, *Gli studi virgiliani nel secolo xx.* 2 vols. (1940); J. van Ooteghem, *Bibliotheca Graeca et Latina²*, *LEC* 1947, 267 ff., and (supplement) ibid. 1961, 76 ff.; G. E. Duckworth, *Recent Work on Vergil 1940–56* (the Vergilian Society, New Hampshire, 1958), 1957–63 (ibid. 1964) = *Classical World* 1957 and 1964; R. G. Austin, *Joint Assoc. of Classical Teachers* 1963, 78 ff.
TEXTS. O. Ribbeck (1894–5); A. Hirtzel (1900); G. Janell (1920); R. Sabbadini (1930); R. A. B. Mynors (O.C.T. 1969); Appendix Vergiliana, Clausen *et al.* (1965).
ANCIENT LIVES. Ed. H. Nettleship (1879); E. Diehl (1911); J. Brummer (1912); C. Hardie (O.C.T. 1954); K. Bayer (1958).
COMMENTARIES. Servius, ed. G. Thilo and H. Hagen (1881–7) (repr. 1961), *Aen.* 1–2, ed. Rand, etc. (U.S.A. 1946); *Aen.* 3–4, ed. Stocker and Travis (1965); J. Conington, revised by H. Nettleship and F. Haverfield (latest ed. 1883–96). *Aeneid*: J. Henry, *Aeneidea* (1873–89). Separate books: 1, R. S. Conway (1935); 2, R. G. Austin (1964); 3, R. D. Williams (1962); 4, A. S. Pease (U.S.A. 1935), R. G. Austin (1955); 5, R. D. Williams (1960); 6, E. Norden (1903, 3rd ed. 1926), H. E. Butler (1920). *Georgics*: W. Richter (Munich, 1957); J. Martyn (1746).
INDEXES AND LEXICONS. H. Merguet (1912); M. N. Wetmore (U.S.A. 2nd ed. 1930); index to Servius, J. F. Mountford and J. T. Schultz (U.S.A. 1930).
TRANSLATIONS (English). Verse: J. Dryden (1697); J. Conington (1866); Henry Howard, Earl of Surrey, *Aen.* 2 and 4 (1557); C. Day Lewis, *Ecl.* (1963); *G.* (1940); *Aen.* (1952). Prose: J. W. Mackail (1889, 1905), J. Jackson (1908), W. F. J. Knight (1956); *Eclogues*: E. V. Rieu (1949).

CRITICAL WORKS:
GENERAL. W. Y. Sellar (3rd ed. 1897); R. Heinze, *Virgils Epische Technik³* (1928); H. W. Prescott, *The Development of Virgil's Art* (1927); V. Pöschl, *Die Dichtkunst Virgils* (1950; Engl. Transl. 1962); J. Perret, *Virgile, l'homme et l'œuvre* (1952); F. Klingner, *Römische Geisteswelt* (1956), 221 ff.; Brooks Otis, *Virgil, A Study in Civilized Poetry* (1963); ed. Oppermann, *Wege zu Vergil* (1963); E. Nitchie, *Vergil and the English Poets* (1919).
SPECIAL. Ed. A. Cartault, *Étude sur les B. de V.* (1897); F. Skutsch, *Aus Vergils Frühzeit* (1901); *Gallus und Vergil* (1906); H. J. Rose, *The Eclogues of V.* (1942).
*Georgics*: F. Klingner, *V.'s Georgica* (1963); L. P. Wilkinson, *The G. of V.* (1969).
*Aen.* M. M. Crump, *The Growth of the Aeneid* (1920); J. Sparrow, *Half-lines and Repetitions in Virgil* (1931); F. Bömer, *Rom und Troia* (1951); P. Boyancé, *La Religion de Virgile* (1963); H. Georgii, *Die antike Aeneiskritik* (1893); G. N. Knauer, *Die Aeneis und Homer* (1964). C. G. H.

**VIRIATHUS,** a Lusitanian shepherd, escaped from the massacre of Galba (q.v. 3), rallied his people, and became their commander-in-chief (*c.* 147 B.C.). Exploiting Roman commitments in Africa and Greece (until 145) and his superior knowledge of the terrain, he defeated a series of Roman commanders in both provinces, and won the co-operation of other tribes. He finally defeated Q. Fabius Maximus Servilianus, from whom he secured a favourable peace and recognition as an ally of the Roman people (140). But Fabius' brother Q. Caepio, succeeding him, persuaded the Senate to denounce the peace and, in the course of fresh negotiations, secured Viriathus' assassination. Viriathus received a splendid funeral, but the Lusitanians soon surrendered. He remains a national hero in Portugal.

A. Schulten, *Fontes Hispaniae Antiquae* iv (1937); H. Simon, *Roms Kriege in Spanien* (1962), *passim.* E. B.

**VIROCONIUM** (*Uriconium*), a town in Roman Britain, modern *Wroxeter* (Shropshire). The site was first occupied, perhaps in A.D. 48–9, by *Cohors I* (?) *Thracum equitata*; later, perhaps 52–8, the fortress of Legio XIV was established close by. The Twentieth replaced the Fourteenth on the latter's withdrawal from Britain (66), and the site remained in military occupation until 87 or 90. After the loss of Scotland Legio XX moved to Deva (*Chester*), and Wroxeter was developed as the *caput* of the Cornovii. Late-first-century baths, perhaps intended for the legion, were left incomplete, to be swept away by Hadrian, in whose reign a normal forum-with-basilica replaced them: the forum is dated by a dedication to Hadrian of 129–30 by the *civitas Cornoviorum* (*RIB* 288). Big new public baths, architecturally combined with a shopping precinct and large public latrine, were built shortly after 150; they were provided with a great open-air swimming bath and a covered exercise hall. About 165 the centre of the town was damaged by fire, but was soon rebuilt. Air photographs have revealed numerous large private houses and an aqueduct. An earth rampart was provided towards the end of the second century, enclosing *c.* 200 acres, and a town wall was inserted in its front perhaps early in the third. Before 300 the forum was destroyed by fire and not rebuilt, but the town apparently prospered until late in the fourth century, when the withdrawal of Legio XX from Chester must have left the region exposed to Irish raiders. Two coins of Carausius with mint mark BRI have been claimed for a temporary mint at Viroconium (= Briconium) (*Num. Chron.⁵ v. 336; Sutherland, *Coinage and Currency in Roman Britain* (1937), 63).

Summary of old excavations: *VCH, Shropshire* i. 220 ff.; later Bushe-Fox 1st, 2nd, and 3rd *Reports* (1912–14); K. M. Kenyon, *Archaeologia* 1940, 175 ff.; D. Atkinson, *Report on Excavations at Wrox. 1923–27* (1942); G. Webster and B. Stanley, *Trans. Shropshire Arch. Soc.* lvii (ii) (1962–3); I. A. Richmond in Foster and Alcock, *Culture and Environment* (1963), 251 ff. S. S. F.

**VIRUNUM,** a city in southern Noricum near the river Glan at modern *Zollfeld*. It lay in the territory of the Celtic Norici, whose centre was on the Magdalensberg 1,058 metres south-east of Klagenfurt. At first the site of a Celtic *oppidum*, terraces on the hillside were occupied by more than three square kilometres of buildings, including a forum, a temple, and a centre for the imperial cult constructed by the Norican peoples under Augustus. Most of the buildings are in the classical style and date from the late first century B.C. to the reign of Claudius. From here the Norici were administered by a Roman *conventus* (q.v.) organization and the place was also the centre of the *concilium provinciae.* Under Claudius a *municipium* was established at Virunum (*CIL* iii. 11555: *municipium Claudium Virunum*) enrolled in the voting-tribe Claudia. Until the establishment of the legionary fortress at Lauriacum (q.v.) under Marcus Aurelius, Virunum was the provincial capital and the residence of the governing procurator. Gradually the buildings on the Magdalensberg fell out of use as the centre of administration was transferred to Virunum. The forum, *capitolium*, baths, amphitheatre, and private dwellings of Virunum have been discovered while its street-grid occupied over one kilometre square. Destroyed by fire during the Marcomannic invasions (169–75), the city was later rebuilt. In the provincial reorganization of Diocletian it was the capital of Noricum Mediterranea.

R. Egger, *Die Stadt auf dem Magdalensberg* (1961). J. J. W.

**VIS** (*Violence*). (*a*) POLITICAL VIOLENCE. In the early history of the Roman Republic violence, where recorded, seems to have stemmed mainly from the self-help of the *plebs* in defence of their tribunes and the resistance of the patricians and their clients. From 133 B.C. until Caesar's dictatorship it dominated city politics. Here it was no mass revolutionary movement, but a political weapon employed for limited ends. The lack of a police force weakened executive measures against it, and often the only counter was a state of emergency (*see* 'SENATUS CONSULTUM ULTIMUM'). From 78 B.C. violence against the State was an offence under the *leges Lutatia* and *Plautia*. Laws passed *per vim* were sometimes annulled by the Senate. Comprehensive legislation against all armed violence was provided by a *lex Iulia de vi publica* (probably of Augustus): practical security was afforded by Augustus' creation of the urban cohorts and the *vigiles*.

(*b*) PRIVATE VIOLENCE. 'Self-help' was generally regarded as a proper means of securing justice, when legal redress was unobtainable or slow. Certain forms were even incorporated into the XII Tables, e.g. for dealing with thieves and debtors. Violence was often employed in property disputes, but was limited by the interdicts concerning possession and *vis* (by 161 B.C. and 111 B.C. respectively). After Sulla interdicts were directed against the use of armed gangs, and the action for the recovery of property extorted by force was instituted. In addition to these measures providing restitution and compensation, a *lex Iulia de vi privata* (possibly the same bill as that *de vi publica*) established penalties, and the field of this law was extended during the Principate so that gradually violence was superseded by official action.

A. W. Lintott, *Violence in Republican Rome* (1968).    A. W. L.

**VITELLIUS** (1), AULUS (A.D. 15–69), Emperor in A.D. 69, was a friend of Gaius and Claudius, being the son of their powerful *amicus* L. Vitellius (q.v. 2). He was consul in 48, proconsul in Africa and legate there under his brother. In 68 he was sent by Galba to command the legions of Lower Germany. On 2 Jan. 69 he was hailed as Emperor by his troops, at the instigation of his legates Caecina Alienus and Fabius Valens, and was immediately recognized by the Upper German army, which had already revolted; he also obtained the adherence of Gaul, Raetia, Britain, and Spain. His expeditionary force to Italy had started before news arrived of Galba's death. Caecina (4) and Valens (1) (qq.v.) converged on north Italy and easily overcame Otho (q.v.). Vitellius was still in Germany when he heard of the victory. His march to Rome (Apr.–July) was like that of a conqueror. He posed as the successor of Nero and later adopted the title of *consul perpetuus*. He humiliated the defeated soldiers, and doubled his mistake by not dismissing them: he disbanded only the Praetorians and *cohortes urbanae* whom he replaced with a much larger force from among his own legionaries. He was allegedly incompetent and became notorious for his gluttony. The Eastern legions swore allegiance to him, yet immediately afterwards they hailed Vespasian (q.v.) as their Emperor. The Danubian troops, many of whom had fought for Otho, went over to Vespasian and invaded Italy under Antonius Primus. Valens was ill, and Vitellius had to rely on Caecina, who was plotting with the commander of the fleet at Ravenna. Vitellius, with four legions and detachments from four others, decided to hold the line of the Po at Cremona and Hostilia. The troops at Hostilia refused to support Caecina's treachery, and retired to Cremona after having arrested their commander. A battle before Cremona, with a demoralized army, was a defeat for the absent Vitellius (Oct. 69). Valens, who had recovered, failed to organize a second army in Gaul. In Germany Civilis (q.v.) rose in arms. The fleet at Misenum abandoned Vitellius. In Rome, Vespasian's brother, Flavius Sabinus (q.v. 3), had nearly persuaded Vitellius to abdicate, but the mob compelled him to remain. Vitellius had to attack Sabinus in the Capitol, where the temple of Jupiter was burned. Primus arrived and defeated the Vitellians after a desperate resistance. Vitellius was

discovered hiding, led through the Forum, and cruelly killed (20 Dec. 69).

Suetonius, *Vitellius*, etc. *See further under* GALBA, VESPASIAN.
                                                                          A. M.

**VITELLIUS** (2, *PW* Suppl. ix, s.v. 7a), LUCIUS (*cos.* A.D. 34, *cos.* II 43, *cos.* III 47), son of P. Vitellius (a Roman knight from Nuceria, procurator of Augustus), was an intimate friend of the Emperor Claudius and the most successful politician of the age: when he died he was honoured with a public funeral and a statue in the Forum bearing the inscription 'pietatis immobilis erga principem' (Suet. *Vit.* 3). In fact, he links the political history of three reigns; and a close nexus can be discovered between Vitellii, Plautii, and Petronii. Legate of Syria from A.D. 35 to 37, he displayed great vigour, dealing firmly with Parthian affairs, inducing Artabanus to pay homage to Rome, and conciliating the Jews: 'regendis prouinciis prisca uirtute egit' (Tac. *Ann.* 6. 32). At Rome, however, he earned a different reputation —'exemplar apud posteros adulatorii dedecoris habetur' (ibid.). But Claudius left him in charge of Rome when going away for the invasion of Britain in 43. He also chose him for colleague in the censorship (47). Vitellius had a large share in devising the ruin of Valerius Asiaticus; and, cleverly adopting the cause of Agrippina, he acted as the mouthpiece of a loyal Senate in advocating her marriage to Claudius. He probably died soon after (last mentioned in 51).
                                                                          R. S.

**VITICULTURE.** The vine and its cultivation were known in Eastern Mediterranean countries as far back as the neolithic period. Minoan Crete had vines in plenty, as had the larger landowners of the periods of Homer and Hesiod. In many parts of Greece, and in Italy after 150 B.C. grapes were a more important crop than grain. Sour wine and vinegar were essential for improving the drinking water. Famous wines came from Cos, Cnidos, Thasos, Chios, Lesbos, Rhodes, Ephesus, and Aminea, Berytus and Laodicea, Tarraco in Spain, several districts of Sicily, the *Falernus mons* in Campania, etc. Plantations in which vines grew side by side with fruit-trees and vegetables were often preferred to those confined to the vine alone, though these became more usual after the Hellenistic age. The plantations were enclosed by walls or fences. The methods of Graeco-Roman culture are familiar to us from the recorded practice of Hellenistic Egypt and Roman Italy, which later spread to the Roman provinces.

Many species of vines were known, some being imported. In laying out a vineyard the land was first ploughed and dug over, and provision was made for irrigation. Then the vines were planted in long trenches and bound with bast to reeds or stakes or (as often in Greece and Italy) to trees, and subsequently pruned. The whole vineyard was next dug over and manured, and the soil was loosened (*ablaqueatio*) so as to lead more water to the roots. There followed a second digging, a picking off of young sterile shoots, a third digging, a second picking of shoots. The vines were tied up and a thorough irrigation undertaken before the crop was harvested. The vineyards had to be well guarded against thieves, a precaution as necessary then as it is today. In course of time new vines had to be planted to replace those that had died. An Italian model vineyard of *c*. 66 acres described by Cato needed 2 oxen, 3 asses, and many implements, with a slave overseer, his wife, and 16 slaves to work it.

States took a great interest in viticulture. A law of Thasos dating from the fourth century B.C. protected native growers by forbidding the import of foreign, and regulating dealings in home-produced wines. Rome seems to have put restrictions on viticulture in certain areas outside Italy with a similar view. Ptolemaic Egypt introduced heavy duties on wine imports, together with State control of the culture of vines in the Nile country by imposing a special tax, the *apomoira*.

See AGRICULTURE, CATO (I), COLUMELLA. For the Thasian wine law see *BCH* 1921, 46 ff.; R. Dion, *Histoire de la vigne et du vin en France des origines au XIXᵉ siècle* (1959); Frank, *Econ. Survey* i–v, index s.v. 'vineyard'; J. Hasebroek, *Griechische Wirtschafts- und Gesellschaftsgeschichte bis zur Perserzeit* (1931), index s.v. 'Weinbau'; S. Loeschke, *Denkmäler vom Weinbau aus der Zeit der Römerherrschaft an Mosel, Saar und Ruwer* (1934); Michell, *Econom. Anc. Gr.*, index s.v. 'viticulture', 'vineyards'; F. Orth, *Weinbau und Weinbereitung der Römer* (1902); Cl. Préaux, *L'Économie royale des Lagides* (1939), 165 ff.; P. Remark, *Der Weinbau im Römerreich* (1927); Rostovtzeff, *Hellenistic World*. *Roman Empire²* (indexes s.v. 'vineyards', 'viticulture'); S. L. Wallace, *Taxation in Egypt from Augustus to Diocletian* (1938), 53 ff.; P. Weise, *Über den Weinbau der Römer* i (1897).                    F. M. H.

**VITRUVIUS POL(L)IO** (or **MAMURRA** q.v.), a Roman architect and military engineer under the second triumvirate and early in Augustus' reign. He built a basilica at Fanum; but his fame rests chiefly on a treatise, *De architectura*, on architecture and engineering, compiled partly from his own experience, and partly from similar works by Hermogenes (q.v. 1) and other noted architects, mostly Greeks. His outlook is essentially Hellenistic, and there is a marked absence of reference to important buildings of Augustus' reign. *De architectura*, the only work of its kind which has survived, is divided into ten books. Book i treats of town-planning, architecture in general, and of the qualifications proper in an architect; ii of building-materials; iii and iv of temples and of the 'Orders'; v of other civic buildings; vi of domestic buildings; vii of pavements and decorative plaster-work; viii of water-supplies; ix of geometry, mensuration, astronomy, etc.; x of machines, civil and military. The information on materials and methods of construction in ii and vii, and on rules of proportion in iii and iv is of great value.

P. Thielscher (*PW* ix A. 427 ff.) identifies Vitruvius with Mamurra (q.v.), Caesar's *praefectus fabrum*. Following Choisy he rejects the cognomen Pollio by inserting a comma between *Vitruvius* and *Polio* in the passage *Vitruvius Polio aliique auctores* which appears in Cetius Faventinus' epitome *ad init*. This identification is contested by P. Ruffel and J. Sonbiran, *Pallas* 1962, 123 ff.

TEXT. F. Krohn (Teubner, 1912); with Fr. Transl. and comm. A. Choisy (1909); with Engl. Transl. F. Granger (Loeb, 1931–4); with Germ. Transl. and notes C. Fensterbusch (1964); Transl. only: M. H. Morgan (U.S.A. 1914, new ed. 1960). See also H. Koch, *Vom Nachleben Vitruvs* (1951); F. Pellati, *Vitruvio* (1938); W. Sackur, *Vitruv u.d. Poliorketiker, V.u.d. christliche Antike. Bautechnisches aus d. Literatur d. Altertums* (1925); Schanz–Hosius, § 355.
H. W. R.; A. M. D.

**VOCONIUS ROMANUS**, an able orator in Pliny's circle who wrote letters which read as if the Muses were speaking in Latin (*Ep.* 2. 13. 7)—a hint at the propriety of a poetic ingredient in letter-writing. A former president of the council of Hispania Tarraconensis, he was recommended by Pliny for equestrian and then senatorial status.

**VOCONTII**, a Celtic tribe of Gallia Narbonensis who, from at least the third century B.C. (Livy 21. 31) occupied the western foot-hills of the Alps south of the Allobroges (q.v.). Under Roman control they remained a *civitas foederata* with the unusual arrangement of two *capita* (Pliny, *HN* 3. 37), each enjoying *ius Latii*. These were Vasio (*Vaison-la-Romaine*) and Lucus Augusti (*Luc-en-Diois*), while Die became *Colonia Dea Augusta Vocontiorum* (*CIL* xii. 690). Vaison, extensively excavated, appears to have originated in a hill-fort south of the Ouvèze, but the Roman town lay mainly north of the river (crossed by a Roman bridge) and the structures

uncovered include a theatre (Tiberian), the so-called portico of Pompey, and two groups of houses. Prominent citizens of Vasio were Burrus, Trogus, and perhaps Tacitus himself (Syme, *Tacitus*, 613–24). Vocontian cavalry fought for Pompey in Spain and later contributed *alae* to the imperial *auxilia*.

Vaison: J. Sautel, *Vaison dans l'Antiquité²* (1942); *FOR* vii (1939), 50 ff.; A. Grenier, *Manuel* iii. 194 ff. Luc: Sautel, *FOR* xi (1957), 39 ff. Die: ibid. 44 ff.                    A. L. F. R.

**VOCULA**, C. DILLIUS (*PW* 2), from Corduba in Spain, was legate of Legio XXII Primigenia in Upper Germany in A.D. 69. Placed in charge of the operations against Civilis (q.v.) he succeeded in relieving Vetera in the Lower province, but was forced back and had difficulty in holding his own camp Mogontiacum (*Mainz*). In spring 70 he was murdered at Novaesium by a Roman deserter on the orders of Classicus (q.v.). His earlier career, a normal senatorial *cursus*, is recorded on a dedication at Rome by his wife Helvia Procula (*ILS* 953).                    G. E. F. C.

**VOLATERRAE** (Etr. *Velaθri*; modern *Volterra*), one of the most powerful of the twelve cities of Etruria, and the capital of the metal-rich zone between the river Cecina, whose valley it dominates, and Massa Marittima, was established in Villanovan times on a hill 20 miles from the sea. Volaterrae is notable for its carved funerary stelae, and for its production of alabaster funerary caskets, carved with mythological scenes, dating from the third–second centuries. Tomb types include 'tholoi' with round chambers, domes, and central pillars. One tomb contained 109 cremations, the associated material ranging in time from local fourth-century red-figure craters to Arretine. Volaterrae withstood a two-year (82–80 B.C.) siege by Sulla's army, and subsequently became a colony for his veterans; Cicero defended a native of the town against the loss of his rights of citizenship (Cic. *Caecin.*).

L. Consortini, *Volterra nell'antichità* (1940); E. Fiumi, *Stud. Etr.* 1957, 367 ff., 463 ff.; Scullard, *Etr. Cities* 146 ff.                    D. W. R. R.

**VOLCACIUS** (1) **SEDIGITUS** (fl. *c.* 100 B.C.) is the author of thirteen senarii, in which ten writers of the *comoedia palliata* are enumerated and characterized by him with great self-confidence. Gellius (15. 24) quotes the verses from Volcacius' lost work *De poetis*. In his list Caecilius Statius is first, Plautus second, Naevius third, Licinius fourth, Atilius fifth, Terence sixth, Turpilius seventh, Trabea eighth, Luscius ninth, and Ennius tenth 'causa antiquitatis' (cf. Suet. *Vit. Ter.* 7).

Baehrens, *FPR* (Teubner, 1886); W. Morel, *FPL* (Teubner, 1927).
A. S.

**VOLCACIUS** (2) **MOSCHUS**, rhetor, a Greek from Pergamum (Porph. ad Hor. *Epist.* 1. 5. 9), who may have owed his name and citizenship to Volcacius Tullus, consul of 33 B.C. (Kiessling, *Hermes* 1891, 634 f.). Exiled after a trial for poisoning, he opened a school at Massilia, where he died about A.D. 25. A distinguished speaker, according to Seneca, but too much given to tricks of style (*Controv.* 10 *pr.* 10, 2. 5. 13); Tac. *Ann.* 4. 43).                    C. J. F.

**VOLCANUS (VOLKANUS, VULCANUS)**, an ancient Italian fire-god, apparently of volcanic fire (this would explain why he is worshipped at Puteoli, near the *zolfatare*, Strabo 5. 246; perhaps also his association with Maia, Gellius 13. 23. 2, 'Maiam Volcani', if her name is to be derived from the root *mag* and explained as the power which makes something, perhaps crops, increase; cf. also Pliny, *HN* 2. 240, fire comes out of the ground near Mutina 'statis Volcano diebus'), certainly of destructive fire, which explains why his temple should always stand outside a city (Vitr. 1. 7. 1), on the authority of the Etruscan haruspices. He was worshipped at Rome from the earliest-known times, having a flamen (q.v.) and a festival, the Volcanalia, on 23 Aug. (calendars). His shrine, the Volcanal, stood in the Area Volcani in the Roman Forum at the foot of the Capitol; it may therefore go back to a time when the Forum was still outside the city (see Platner–Ashby, 583 f.; Nash, *Pict. Dict. Rome* ii. 517 ff.). A newer temple (before 214 B.C.) stood in the Campus Martius. His name is certainly not Latin, the nearest to it in sound being the Cretan Ϝελχανός (for whom see Cook, *Zeus* ii. 946 ff.), who, however, seems to have no resemblance to him in functions. For Etruscan names suggesting Volcanus see F. Altheim, *Griechische Götter* (1930), 172. It is thus possible, but unproved, that he came in from the eastern Mediterranean, through Etruria. He seems to have been worshipped principally to avert fires, hence his by-name Mulciber ('qui ignem mulcet'), his title Quietus, and his association with Stata Mater (Dessau, *ILS* 3295, 3306), apparently the goddess who makes fires stand still. On the Volcanalia, when sacrifice was also made to Juturna, the Nymphs, Ops Opifera, and Quirinus, he was given a curious and (at least for Rome) unexampled sacrifice, live fish from the Tiber being flung into a fire (see calendars and Varro, *Ling.* 6. 20, Festus, 274. 35 ff. Lindsay). This also can be readily explained as an offering of creatures usually safe from him to induce him to spare those things which at so hot a time of year are particularly liable to be burned. He had a considerable cult at Ostia, where he seems to have been the chief god (R. Meiggs, *Roman Ostia* (1960), 337 ff.). In classical times he is fully identified with Hephaestus, q.v.

Wissowa in Roscher's *Lexikon*, s.v.; H. J. Rose, *JRS* 1933, 46 ff.; Latte, *RR* 129 ff. H. J. R.

**VOLOGESES I,** King of Parthia, A.D. 51/52–79/80. His family belonged to Media Atropatene. Much of his reign was spent in wars with Rome and on his eastern frontier. In 54 Vologeses set his brother Tiridates (q.v. 3) on the throne of Armenia (Tac. *Ann.* 12. 50). Cn. Corbulo (q.v.), sent to re-establish Roman influence, was at first successful, Vologeses being occupied on his eastern frontier with a rebellion. Tiridates fled, and a Roman nominee Tigranes (q.v. 4) was crowned as king of Armenia. But Vologeses returned to continue the war, and at one time gained an advantageous treaty from Paetus (q.v.), after the latter's capitulation at Rhandeia. Finally, peace was made and Tiridates agreed (63) to go to Rome and pay homage to Nero for his throne: this he did in 66. Vologeses' later relations with Rome were friendlier; he sought Vespasian's help against the invading Alani (Suet. *Dom.* 2. 2). In his reign Zoroastrianism made great advances, and the books of the Avesta were collected. He founded Vologesia near Seleucia, as a commercial rival to Seleucia. In his reign began a strong reaction against Hellenic influences. Pehlevi first appears along with Greek on his coins.

For Vologeses II–V, *see* ARSACIDS.

On the wars with Corbulo see M. Hammond, *Harv. Stud.* 1934; A. Momigliano, *Atti del II° congresso naz. di studi romani* i (1931), 368 ff.; W. Schur, *Klio* 1925, 75 ff., and 1926, 215 ff.; N. C. Debevoise, *Political History of Parthia* (1938), 174 ff. M. S. D.; E. W. G.

**VOLSCI** descended from central Italy in the sixth century B.C. and by 500 had established themselves in the middle Liris valley and regions south-east of the Alban Hills. Chief towns: Sora, Arpinum, Atina, Privernum, Ecetra, Antium, Circeii, Anxur (= Tarracina), Velitrae, and possibly Pometia (qq.vv.). Casual mention of Volsci in regal times is untrustworthy,

but thereafter they became, and for 200 years remained, a threat which Rome met by signing an alliance with Latins and Hernici c. 493 (*see* CASSIUS 1). The Aequi (q.v.) aided the Volsci. Fifth-century Volscian operations are known only from garbled Roman accounts; but Coriolanus' exploits and defensive Latin colonies at Signia (495), Norba (492), and Ardea (442) imply Volscian successes. In 431, however, the Latin allies defeated the Aequi, then repulsed the Volsci; Latin colonies at Circeii (393), Satricum (385), Setia (382) mark their advance. Volsci opposed Rome in the Latin War, but were defeated by C. Maenius (q.v.). By 304 all Volsci were subject to Rome and so rapid and complete was their romanization that their original civilization can scarcely be discovered. Their language resembles Umbrian (cf. Festus, 204 L.). Although often represented as a unitary nation, they were not cohesive. Some Volscian cities faced Rome singly (Pometia, Ecetra in the fifth century; Antium, Privernum in the fourth), and those in the Liris valley obviously acted independently of those near the Tyrrhenian coast.

Diodors *Römische Annalen*, ed. Drachmann xi. 37–xiv. 102; Livy, bks. 2–8; Dion. Hal., bks. 6–11, 14. L. Pareti, *Storia di Roma* i (1952); E. Vetter, *Handbuch der italischen Dialekte* (1953), i. 156. For their alleged Illyrian origin see Serv. ad *Aen.* 12. 842; J. Whatmough, *Foundations of Roman Italy* (1937), 300. E. T. S.

**VOLSINII** (Etr. *Velzna-*). The original Volsinii has been identified variously with modern Orvieto by K. O. Müller since 1898 and with Bolsena by R. Bloch. The former is perhaps more probable, in view of the rich sixth–fifth-century Crocefisso del Tufo cemetery at Orvieto; little that is earlier than the fourth century has been found at Bolsena, or nearer to it than the Villanovan and Etruscan cemetery and habitation sites in the Civita and Gran Carro localities about 6 miles to the south. This could agree with the statement by Zonaras (8. 7. 8) that the survivors of the Volsinian rebellion of 294 B.C. were resettled elsewhere. Not far from the Etruscan city was Fanum Voltumnae, which was from the end of the fifth century the religious and political headquarters of the twelve cities of Etruria: it has yet to be identified archaeologically.

P. Perali, *Orvieto etrusca* (1928); S. Puglisi, *Studi e ricerche su Orvieto etrusca* (1934); R. Bloch, *Mélanges d'arch.* 1947, 9 ff., 1950, 53 ff., 1958, 7 ff.; M. Bizzari, *Stud. Etr.* 1962, 1 ff., ibid. 1966, 2 ff.; W. V. Harris, *PBSR* 1965, 282 ff.; G. Colonna, *Stud. Etr.* 1967, 3 ff.; Scullard, *Etr. Cities*, 126 ff.; on Bolsena, Castagnoli, *Stud. urb.* 71 ff. D. W. R. R.

**VOLTACILIUS PITHOLAUS** (? *Plotus*, Reifferscheid), LUCIUS, according to Nepos the first freedman to write history, opened a school of rhetoric, 81 B.C. He had as a pupil Pompeius Magnus, whose biography, as well as his father's, he wrote (Suet. *Rhet.* 3).

**VOLTUMNA,** an Etruscan goddess, at whose shrine the Etruscan federal council met (Livy 4. 23. 5; 25. 7; 61. 2; 5. 17. 6; 6. 2. 2). Nothing more is known of her and the site of the shrine is uncertain (*see* VOLSINII). Some connexion with Vertumnus (q.v.) etymologically is likely.

L. R. Taylor, *Local Cults of Etruria* (1923), 230 ff.

**VOLTURNUS,** the principal river of Campania (q.v.), a considerable stream often mentioned in ancient accounts of Samnite and Hannibalic Wars. It rises in Samnium and flows southward past Aesernia, Venafrum, and Allifae (qq.v.) until joined by its tributary, the Calor, whereupon it turns abruptly westward to enter the Tyrrhenian about 20 miles below Casilinum (q.v.). E. T. S.

**VOLUBILIS** (modern *Oubili*), town in the Djebel Zerhoun plain in Morocco. It was already important in the second century B.C. and under Juba II it became a flourishing town. The influence of Carthaginian civilization was pronounced and its magistrates were called *suffetes*. It was rewarded by Claudius *c.* A.D. 44 with the rank of *municipium* for its support of Rome against Aedemon's rebellion. Substantial remains survive, especially of Severan date. The town was near the frontier and sometimes threatened by the tribe of the Baquates; it was apparently evacuated when Diocletian reorganized the frontier.

J. Carcopino, *Le Maroc antique* (1949), i; L. Chatelain, *Le Maroc des Romains* (1944), 139 ff.; R. Thouvenot, *Volubilis* (Paris, 1949); R. Étienne, *Le Quartier nord-est de Volubilis* (1960); A. Momigliano, *Claudius²* (1961), 66 ff., 114, 139 f.                    B. H. W.

**VOLUMNIUS,** PUBLIUS, a philosopher who accompanied M. Brutus (q.v. 5) in his campaign against the triumvirs. He recorded, perhaps in a biography, prodigies which preceded Brutus' last battle (Plut. *Brut.* 48).

**VOTIENUS MONTANUS,** orator, from Narbo; prosecuted for treason in A.D. 25 and died in exile a few years later. He condemned the showiness of declamations (Sen. *Controv.* 9. *praef.* 1). His passion for repetitions which did not leave well alone led to his being called 'the Ovid of speakers'.                    J. W. D.

**VOTING.** (1) IN GREEK CITY STATES most resolutions of the Assembly, as well as elections of magistracies, were decided by show of hands (χειροτονία), in some rare cases by acclamation, e.g. in the election of the Spartan ephors. For questions concerning individuals (ἐπ' ἀνδρί), voting was accomplished by secret ballot (ψήφισμα from ψῆφος = voting-stone); but already in early times *all* decrees of people were so called. The same method was used for passing sentences by juries, and voting by sherds was similar (*see* OSTRACISM).                    V. E.

(2) AT ROME voting took place in the assemblies of the *curiae*, centuries, and tribes. In the curiate assemblies it very early became a mere formality, the voting units being represented by thirty lictors. The procedure in the centuriate and tribal assemblies followed a broadly similar pattern. Voting was generally preceded by a *contio* (q.v.). When the presiding magistrate dissolved this and ordered the voting to begin (*discedere*), non-citizens were summoned to withdraw (*populus summouetur*), and ropes were stretched across the Assembly to divide it into as many enclosures as there were centuries or tribes. These enclosures, called at first *licium*, then *ovile*, and finally *saepta* (q.v.), were connected with the platform of the magistrate by galleries (*pontes*). Before 139 B.C. voters intimated their decision orally and singly to officials named *rogatores* who stood at the exit of the enclosures and recorded the votes by means of dots on special tablets (*ferre punctum*). From 139 to 107, however, a series of *leges tabellariae* were enacted instituting a secret ballot. The formulas used in the voting did not change: in legislation, *Uti rogas* (V) and *antiquo* (A), this negative answer properly meaning 'I confirm the old state of things'; in jurisdiction *libero* (L) and *damno* or *condemno* (hence the abbreviated form C); in elections *dico* or *facio*. But now these were written on official tablets (*tabellae*) which were thrown into an urn (*cista*) at the exit of each *pons* under the surveillance of guardians (*custodes*), and then conveyed to the tellers (*diribitores*) for counting. When the counting was over, the result of the voting in each tribe or century was communicated to the presiding magistrate who then made an announcement of all the results (*renuntiatio*) either at random or, sometimes in the case of multiple elections, in an order determined by lot.

Group voting was universal in Roman assemblies.

Thus a majority of votes within a century determined the vote of that century, and a majority of centuries determined the will of the assembly. Furthermore, in elections designed to fill two or more places on a board or college, the counting of votes within a unit and the final *renuntiatio* of results came to a stop as soon as the required number of candidates had secured an absolute majority.

Voting was allowed only between sunrise and sunset, on days especially appointed in the Calendar. Throughout the Republic it was essential for a citizen to attend the assembly in Rome, if he was to vote at all, although Augustus did experiment with a postal vote in the last days of comitial activity.

Mommsen, *Röm. Staatsr.*'iii³. 397 ff.; G. W. Botsford, *The Roman Assemblies* (1909), 446 ff.; Taylor, *Voting Districts*; id. *Roman Voting Assemblies* (1966); U. Hall, *Hist.* 1964, 267 ff. *See also* TABULA HEBANA.
P. T.; E. S. S.

**VOTIVE OFFERINGS** are gifts of a permanent character to supernatural beings (ἀναθήματα, later ἀναθέματα, as distinct from δῶρα, gifts to human beings), thus differing from sacrifices and taxes (tithes and first-fruits are here not included). They have their source in religious feeling and in the worship of divine powers to whom the dedicant ascribes the occasion (see under 2) of the gift. This dedication is a voluntary act, but it may have been recommended by religious tradition or sometimes ordered by an oracle (e.g. for unbelief, breach of religious custom, blood-guilt; cf. the two statues of the Spartan regent Pausanias dedicated in the Brazen House of Athena). For the gods they may mean an increase of their authority: the gift and its publicity 'magnify' the gods, at the same time intensifying the feeling of connexion and sympathy on both sides. For the main difference from a sacrifice is that the object dedicated is not destroyed; it remains as a perpetual glory to the dedicant, and more specifically to his community: conduct which was too self-complacent was severely censured, cf. the case of Pausanias (Thuc. 1. 132).

The motives generally are: thanksgiving (e.g. for deliverance from sickness, perils on the sea, and all sorts of calamity), intercession (sometimes accompanied by sacrifice, or taking its place, or reminding the deity of it), or propitiation (each Athenian archon swore to dedicate a golden statue, probably not a portrait of himself, if he broke his oath; cf. corresponding sacrifices from similar motives). The occasions are manifold. States (or monarchs) returned thanks for victory in war and thus commemorated other forms of divine aid (so tripods of gold were sent to Delphi after the battles of Plataea, Himera, Cumae, Diod. 11. 21). Statues of Victory were common as war-dedications (cf. the Athenian temple inventories, the most famous examples being the Nike of Paeonius at Olympia, and the Nike of Samothrace now in the Louvre). The statue of Nemesis at Rhamnus was a memorial of the Persian War, the temple of Athena at Pergamum of the defeat of the Gauls. A crown of honour was dedicated to the Athenian people by 'the Euboeans saved and set free' (Dem. xxiv. 180). The people (alone, or with the *boule*) dedicated statues of officials in sacred precincts; later such compliments to the Roman Emperors became quite commonplace.

We must not forget the many feasts and ceremonials, often annually repeated, which served the State or private individuals as occasions for showing their loyalty or gratitude to the State divinities or national heroes. Many finds of innumerable standardized figures in the earliest strata of ancient shrines may have their origin in such festivals, e.g. miniature reproductions of the cult-image of the temple or other forms of the deity in question (as the votive offerings to (Artemis) Orthia at Sparta), objects of use, robes (cf. Hecuba's gift to Athena in the *Iliad*), mirrors, weapons, etc., finally the ἀνδριάντες and κόραι of all sizes and different materials (falling into disuse in the 5th c. B.C.). We may especially mention the *peplos* offered at the Panathenaea at Athens. Sacred missions (θεωρίαι, *see* THEOROI) regularly brought with them offerings for dedication, thus supplementing their sacrifices.

Private people dedicated on similar principles, for help in disease (cf. the sanctuaries of Asclepius), in danger and every sort of calamity, for good luck and further aid, often accompanying the offering with a prayer and sacrifice for further success. Victories in games and contests of other kinds (cf. the legendary competition between Homer and Hesiod) were eagerly glorified, the offering of the prize becoming traditional and often compulsory (cf. the many statues of athletes, and the Charioteer at Delphi). We may add as appropriate occasions of offering: every great moment or crisis of human life, birth, puberty (e.g. the offering of one's hair), marriage, election to an office, acquittal in court, etc. Book 6 of the *Anthology* and the treasure-lists of Athens (the treasures of Athena, Artemis Brauronia, or Asclepius), Delos, Delphi give an impression of the endless varieties of motive; dedication of slaves, chiefly as a form of emancipation, is also to be noted. The holy precincts thus in course of time were filled with gifts; they became real museums. Treasure-houses were built, and in the inner chambers of the temples (the *opisthodomoi*) their always increasing treasures were kept, but still these overflowed. The clearing-up did not mean destroying, since the ex-votos were commonly tabu and accordingly much can still be found by archaeologists within the sacred enclosures.

As for the meaning of these ex-votos, and the objects dedicated, they might be of direct use to the god. In myth or history many temples are recorded as being due to the gratitude of heroes, monarchs, cities (Danaus, Heracles, Theseus; the temple of Apollo at Bassae commemorates deliverance from pestilence). We may add altars (often with inscriptions), colonnades, idols, garments for the idols, etc. The throne of Xerxes, the manger of Mardonius, and other trophies were offered to the gods; cf. also the many statues of the Apollo or Kouros type. But pious people dedicated also what had been useful to themselves, thanks to the benevolence of a god or the gods; artisans their tools, etc. (also specimens of their skill and their gains), a shipowner an image of his ship (cf. Catullus 4; Agamemnon dedicated his rudder to Hera at Samos), a courtesan her mirror—in general things well used or now useless, or but once used (so a cauldron used for the bride's bath before marriage) and for ever to be remembered. Acts, blessed by the gods (birth, victory, etc.) were also thus immortalized. An impulse was in this way given to art (e.g. sculpture) and even to poetry. The historians drew facts from the inscriptions employed, and the makers of legend a fresh start for their imagination (cf. the Lindian temple-chronicle). The homage thus paid to the gods is also a reliable barometer as to the curve of religious feeling in antiquity (as today in the Catholic Church).

E. Reisch, *Griechische Weihgeschenke* (1890). The chief work is W. H. D. Rouse, *Greek Votive Offerings* (1902). The religious background: J. Rudhardt, *Notions fondamentales de la pensée religieuse* (1958), 214 ff.        S. E.; J. H. C.

**VOTUM.** Greeks and Romans alike made promises to gods that, if this or that favour was granted, they would do this or that act in return, and felt under an obligation to do as they had promised. Nevertheless, the practical and juridical character of Roman religion, as distinct from Greek, is seen in the Roman public use of vows, *uota*, public or private, which oblige either of the two parties engaged in the act to keep the bargain if the god

(or gods) is willing, and even in the formulae of many private vows: *u(otum) s(oluit) l(ibens) m(erito)* and in the phrases *uoti reus, uoti damnatus*. The reciprocity involves the State (or the private individual) taking the initiative. In the name of the State the magistrate undertakes to offer to the god or the gods sacrifices, games, the building of a temple, the dedication of an altar, a share of the booty, or some other thing if the god on his side will give his assistance in winning the war, averting the famine or pestilence, achieving some success, etc. The publicity of such vows was compulsory. The vows made by the State were in most cases extraordinary, but vows were also made regularly for a definite period, e.g. the annually renewed *uota* of the higher magistrates for the welfare of the State (on 3 Jan., before the first regular sitting of the Senate) and the *uota* at the termination of the *lustrum*. The periodicity of public *uota* may originate in the terms defined for the magistrates. Such vows found their direct continuation under the Empire in the *uota pro salute imperatoris* (for the Emperor and his family, since 30 B.C., the periodicity becoming regular *uota quinquennalia, decennalia*, etc.). Vows for the safe return of the Emperor (from expeditions or war), for his health, his reign, for the delivery of the empress, etc. were customary. The text of the *uotum* was regularly fixed in the presence of the pontifices, and the document went into the archives. As modalities of the *uotum* we have to consider the devotion of the enemy's army (*see* DEVOTIO) and the evocation of the gods of a besieged city *see* EVOCATIO). Good examples of private vows are Verg. *Aen.* 5. 235 ff. (Cloanthus vows a bull if he wins the boat-race) and Hor. *Carm.* 1. 5.

Wissowa, *RK* 380 ff. J. Toutain, art. 'Votum' in Dar.–Sag. Warde Fowler, *Rel. Exper.* 200 ff. Latte, *RR* 46 f. The periodical vows for the welfare of the Emperor were regularly commemorated by coin-issues, for which see Mattingly, *Proc. Brit. Acad.* 1950, 155 ff.; ibid. 1951, 219 ff.        S. E.; R. M. O.

**VULCI** (Etr. *Velχ-*), 13 miles north-west of Tarquinii, situated on a plateau overlooking the river Fiora and with a commanding view of Monte Argentario and Cosa (q.v.), was one of the twelve cities of Etruria. It was an important centre by the late eighth century, rich in painted pottery and bronze; its orientalizing period has much in common with that of Vetulonia (q.v.). From the late seventh century onwards, Vulci was the centre of a school of stone carving, and of the manufacture of bronze utensils that were widely exported. Attention has been mainly concentrated on the tombs, dating from the Villanovan period onwards, several thousands of which had been opened by the mid nineteenth century.

S. Gsell, *Fouilles dans la nécropole de Vulci* (1891); F. Messerschmidt, A. von Gerkan, *JDAI Ergänzungsheft* xii (1930); R. Bartoccini, *Atti VII Cong. int. arch. class.* ii (1961), 257 ff.; W. L. Brown, *The Etruscan Lion* (1960), ch. 4; Scullard, *Etr. Cities*, 119 ff.; G. Colonna, *Stud. Etr.* 1961, 47 ff.; *Arch. Class.* 1961, 9 ff.; A. Giuliano, *JDAI* 1963, 183 ff. with *Arch. Anz.* 1967, 7 ff.; M. Torelli, *Enc. Arte Ant.* vii (1966), s.v. 'Vulci'.        D. W. R. R.

**VULGATE** (*versio vulgata*), Latin version of the Bible. The ever-increasing divergences, the defective textual tradition, and the lack of literary elegance in the Old Latin versions of the Bible (i.e. those used in the Church before the Vulgate) led Pope Damasus to urge (c. A.D. 382) Hieronymus (*see* JEROME) to undertake a revision which might, so it was hoped, become the common biblical text of the Western Church. In the New Testament Jerome made, as he declares in his Preface *Novum opus*, comparison with ancient Greek MSS. and altered the Old Latin text only when it seemed absolutely necessary, retaining in all other cases what had become familiar phraseology. This procedure accounts for the presence of quite diverse renderings of identical expressions in Greek (e.g. 'high priest' is usually translated in Matthew and Luke by *princeps sacerdotum*, in Mark by *summus sacerdos*, and in John by *pontifex*).

In the Old Testament Jerome began with the Psalms, making two revisions, both based on the (Greek) Septuagint. The first, produced hastily (*cursim*), has been commonly identified with the 'Roman Psalter' (still used in St. Peter's Basilica in Rome); the second, known as the 'Gallican Psalter', was based on Origen's Hexaplaric text, and is the text which is used for the Psalms in the official Roman Catholic Bible (the Clementine text of 1592). A growing interest in Hebrew led Jerome in 387 to take up residence in Bethlehem, where, in the course of some fifteen years, he translated the Old Testament directly from the Hebrew (including a fresh translation of the Psalms).

Scribal corruption of Jerome's revision prompted several medieval scholars to purify the Vulgate text; notable among these were the successive efforts of Alcuin, Theodulf, Lanfranc, and Stephen Harding. Unfortunately, however, each of these attempts resulted eventually in still further textual corruption through mixture of the several types of Vulgate text that developed at various European centres of scholarship. As a result, the more than 8,000 Vulgate MSS. extant today exhibit the greatest amount of cross-contamination of textual types.

CRITICAL EDITIONS. *Biblia Sacra iuxta Latinam Vulgatam Versionem* [Benedictine ed.], *Genesis–* (1926–  ); J. Wordsworth and H. J. White, *Nouum Testamentum Latine* (1889–1954); ed. minor (1911), corrected edition (1920).
GRAMMAR. W. E. Plater and H. J. White, *A Grammar of the Vulgate* (1926).
LEXICOGRAPHY. F. [P.] Kaulen, *Sprachliches Handbuch zur biblischen Vulgata*[2] (1904); G. C. Richards, *A Concise Dictionary to the Vulgate New Testament* (1934).

CONCORDANCES. F. P. Dutripan[8] (1880); E. Peultier–L. Étienne–L. Gantois[2] (1939).
STUDIES. S. Berger, *Histoire de la Vulgate pendant les premiers siècles du moyen-âge* (1893); H. Quentin, *Mémoire sur l'établissement du texte de la Vulgate* (1922); H. J. Vogels, *Vulgatastudien* (1928); F. Stummer, *Einführung in die lateinischen Bibel* (1928); H. Glunz, *History of the Vulgate in England from Alcuin to Roger Bacon* (1933); P. McGurk, *Latin Gospel Books from A.D. 400 to A.D. 800* (1961).
B. M. M.

**VULSO** (1) **LONGUS**, LUCIUS MANLIUS (*PW* 101), as consul (256 B.C.) with Regulus (q.v. 1) won the naval battle of Ecnomus and led the expeditionary force to Africa. He returned to Rome to receive a triumph, leaving Regulus in sole command in Africa. As consul II (250) he blockaded Lilybaeum without success. H. H. S.

**VULSO** (2), GNAEUS MANLIUS (*PW* 91), curule aedile in 197 B.C., praetor in Sicily in 195, succeeded L. Scipio as consul in 189 in the East, concluding the peace with Antiochus and subduing the Galatians in defence of law and order in Asia Minor; the campaign was also profitable in booty. In 188 he settled Asia and returned through Thrace, suffering losses. His triumph in 187 was opposed by L. Furius Purpurio and Aemilius Paullus, probably as part of Scipionic criticism of his policy. Tradition made him introduce luxury to Rome, and certainly the effects of Eastern spoil became apparent with the close of the Syrian War.

Magie, *Rom. Rule Asia Min.* 279, 1156; Scullard, *Rom. Pol.* 135 ff.
A. H. McD.

# W

**WALL OF ANTONINUS**, a Roman frontier-wall, 37 miles long, running from Bridgeness on the Forth to Old Kilpatrick on the Clyde, built for Antoninus Pius (S.H.A. *Pius* 5. 4) in A.D. 142 by Q. Lollius (q.v. 4) Urbicus. The wall was of turf, standing upon a cobbled foundation 14 feet wide and systematically built (*JRS* 1921, 1 f.) in long sectors by Legions II, VI, and XX, who marked their work by inscribed slabs (Collingwood and Wright, *RIB* 2139, 2173, 2184–6, 2193–4, 2196–2200, 2203–6, 2208). Twenty feet or more in front of the wall lay a ditch, approaching 40 feet wide and not less than 12 feet deep. Forts occur at Carriden, Kinneil, Inveravon, Mumrills (7·1 acres), Falkirk, Rough Castle (1·5 acres), Seabegs, *Castlecary* (3·9 acres), Westerwood (2·3 acres), Croy Hill (2·4 acres), Bar Hill (3·6 acres), Auchendavy, Kirkintilloch, Cadder (3·2 acres), *Balmuildy* (4·3 acres), New Kilpatrick, Castlehill (3·4 acres), Duntocher, Old Kilpatrick (4·7 acres), those italicized having stone walls. Minor structures are signalling-platforms, occurring in pairs at high points, and fortlets (0·2 acres), one of them at the passage of the northward road at Watling Lodge, near Falkirk. Thus, the Antonine Wall is structurally an advance upon Hadrian's Turf Wall (*see* WALL OF HADRIAN) in its economy of material and rubble foundation, allowing better drainage, while its garrison was distributed in small close-spaced forts instead of large forts and milecastles. Beyond the wall outpost-forts of the north road were held as far as Strathearn on the east, while on the west a road led towards Dumbarton, to a fortified port as yet unknown. Posts on the flanks are also known.

*History.* Excavation of the forts reveals two principal periods of occupation, a suspected third being probably no more than traces of levelling and tidying-up at evacua-

tion. Period I (*c.* 142–54) is thought to end with demolition when the troops were withdrawn to quell a rebellion of the Brigantes and Selgovae. The reoccupation of period II was begun before the death of Antoninus Pius, perhaps under Julius Verus *c.* 158, and ended in the first year of Commodus (180) when Dio (71. 16) records the overthrow of a frontier-wall and the dispatch of Ulpius Marcellus to Britain (for the date see *RIB* 1329). After inflicting heavy punishment on the Caledonians, Marcellus withdrew the frontier to Hadrian's Wall *c.* 184–5.

Sir G. Macdonald, *The Roman Wall in Scotland*[2] (1934); A. S. Robertson, *The Antonine Wall* (1960); K. A. Steer, *Arch. Ael*[4] 1964, 1 ff.; Frere, *Britannia*, ch. 8. Map 2½ in. (Ordnance Survey, 1969). I. A. R.; S. S. F.

**WALL OF AURELIAN**, the City Wall of Rome, constructed by Aurelian in A.D. 271–5 in anticipation of a sudden barbarian inroad (S.H.A. *Aurel.* 21. 9; 39. 2; Aurel. Vict. *Caes.* 35; Ioh. Malalas, *Chron.* xii, 299), was completed by Probus (Zosim. 1. 49). The original wall was some 20 feet high excluding the wide-set battlements. It extended for 12 miles, with 381 rectangular towers, at an interval of *c.* 100 feet, except on the long river-walls. The wall was usually solid but occasionally galleried and sometimes treated as a revetment-wall. It frequently embodied earlier structures, such as the retaining-wall of the Horti Aciliani (*muro torto*), the *castra praetoria*, private houses and tenements, the so-called *amphitheatrum castrense*, the *domus Lateranorum*, and the pyramid-tomb of Cestius. It surrounded the Fourteen Regions, enclosing, however, a relatively small part of *Transtiberim*. The gates, mostly named from the principal roads, were Portae *Flaminia*, Pinciana, Salaria, Nomentana, 'Chiusa', Tiburtina, Praenestina–

Labicana, Asinaria, Metrobia, Latina, *Appia, Ostiensis, Portuensis,* Aurelia-Pancraziana, Septimiana, Aurelia-Sancti Petri. All were flanked by simple semicircular towers, those italicized having twin portals originally. There were also at least six postern gates. The wall was thus designed to repel a raid rather than stand siege. The wall was doubled in height by adding a gallery, while gates were remodelled and fitted with vantage-courts, by Maxentius (A.D. 306–12), who also began a ditch. Wall, and especially gates, were repaired by Stilicho in 401–3 (*CIL* vi. 1188–90; Claud. *VI cons. Hon.* 529). Later repairs occurred under Valentinian III, probably after the earthquake of 442, and under Theoderic in 507–11. Belisarius, in preparation for the siege of 536, refurbished the wall and dug a large ditch in front of it.

    I. A. Richmond, *The City Wall of Imperial Rome* (1930); Nash, *Pict. Dict. Rome* ii. 86 ff.      I. A. R.

**WALL OF HADRIAN,** a frontier-wall of Roman Britain, running for 80 Roman miles from Wallsend-on-Tyne to Bowness-on-Solway. Erected in A.D. 122–6, it was first designed to start at *Pons Aelius,* Newcastle-upon-Tyne, the eastern 45 miles being in stone (10 feet thick and some 15 feet high, excluding battlements), and the western 31 miles in turf (20 feet thick at the base and some 12 feet high). Twenty feet in front of the wall ran a V-shaped ditch (27 feet wide and 15 feet deep). Patrols lay in attached fortlets or milecastles, with towered gates to north, at every 1,620 yards, and in intermediate turrets (20 feet square) at every 540 yards. As work progressed, changes came. The Stone Wall was changed to $7\frac{1}{2}$ feet in width, and extended 4 miles eastwards, to Wallsend, and 4 miles westward (replacing the Turf Wall) to Banks. Garrison forts were also built, at Wallsend, Newcastle, *Benwell, Rudchester, Halton, Chesters, Housesteads,* Carvoran, *Birdoswald,* Castlesteads, Stanwix, *Burgh-by-Sands,* and *Bowness* (those italicized being of standard pattern for a *cohors milliaria* or an *ala quingenaria*). At Stanwix the milliary *ala Petriana* was posted; the rest probably held *cohortes quingenariae* and were soon augmented by Carrawburgh, Drumburgh, and Greatchesters. Forts and turrets continued down the Cumberland coast to Moresby; outpost-forts·existed at Birrens, Netherby, and Bewcastle.

    Behind the wall, enclosing all forts but Carvoran on the Stanegate (see below), ran a boundary-ditch (20 feet wide, 10 feet deep, and 8 feet across the flat bottom) with upcast disposed in two equidistant turf-kerbed mounds, 100 feet apart from crest to crest. A patrol-track ran along the south side of the ditch, reached by causeways at the milecastles. Public passages pierced both mounds at the forts and crossed the ditch on a causeway faced in stone and barred by a non-defensive gate. Lateral communication was first supplied by branches from the Stanegate, the pre-Hadrianic road from Corbridge to Carlisle. Later, the Military Way, between the boundary-ditch and wall, connected forts and milecastles.

    *History.* Soon after the accession of Antoninus Pius the frontier was advanced to the Forth–Clyde line, and Hadrian's Wall was opened by slighting the boundary-ditch and removing the gates from milecastles. Apparently *c.* 158 (Collingwood and Wright, *RIB* 1389) and with the intention of separating the Selgovae and Brigantes under supervision, the wall was reoccupied simultaneously with the Antonine Wall in its second period, and remained the frontier when the latter was abandoned *c.* 180. The garrison was depleted by Albinus in 196–7, and on his defeat was savagely overthrown, to be restored by Severus in 205–7. In place of the Antonine Wall a forward zone was now held by outpost-forts

at Risingham, High Rochester, Bewcastle, and Netherby, a system which with its pacific supervision of the Lowland tribes kept the peace until the defeat of Allectus in 296 invited another Pictish inroad, followed by the restoration by Constantius I. Under Constans in 343 and Julian in 360 the forward zone suffered, and was abandoned after attacks by Picts, Scots, and Attacotti in 367–8, which again overwhelmed the wall. The restoration by Count Theodosius in 369 introduced changes of garrison; thereafter occupation outlasted the expedition of Magnus Maximus (383) to come to an end finally *c.* 400, after which the frontier became the sole responsibility of the allied principalities in the Lowlands, which had been established by Valentinian I.

    J. C. Bruce, *The Handbook to the Roman Wall*[12] (ed. I. A. Richmond, 1966); R. G. Collingwood, *JRS* 1921, 37 ff.; 1931, 36 ff.; F. G. Simpson and I. A. Richmond, *JRS* 1935, 1 ff.; I. A. Richmond, *JRS* 1950, 43 ff. and *Northumberland County History* xv for outpost-forts; E. Birley, *Research on Hadrian's Wall* (1961); Frere, *Britannia,* ch. 7 and *passim*; C. E. Stevens, 'The building of Hadrian's Wall', *Cumberland Westm. Antiqu. and Archaeol. Soc.* 1966.
     I. A. R.; S. S. F.

**WALL OF SERVIUS,** the city-wall of Republican Rome, traditionally assigned to King Servius Tullius, actually belongs to 378 B.C. It is of Grotta Oscura tufa, built in headers and stretchers, 4·50 m thick and at least 8·50 m high, retaining an earth bank or terrace, and is comparable with the contemporary wall of Pompeii II (*see* FORTIFICATIONS). The masons' marks, with Hellenistic affinities, suggest Greek contractors. The wall enclosed an irregular area dictated by contours, embracing the Quirinal, Viminal, Oppian, Caelian, Aventine, and fortified Capitoline hills. There is, however, room for difference of opinion (cf. von Gerkan, *Röm. Mitt.* 1931, 153 ff.) as to the course between the last two points, while the time-space relation of the Palatine fortification to the wall is another crux. Gates are well known by name, hardly by structure. In the second century B.C. the wall was heightened to some 50 feet (cf. Pompeii III), and was also supplied with casemates for *ballistae,* covering approaches to the gates. During the first century B.C. neglect and encroachment made the course hard to find by the time of Augustus.

    The original work of Servius is represented by the *agger,* which, revetted by the Republican Wall just described, crosses the neck of land between Quirinal and Oppian (cf. E. Gjerstad, *Acta Instit. Rom. Regin. Sueciae* xvii. 3, 1960, 32 ff.). It is a typical promontory defence, as at Ardea, and covered tombs of the sixth century B.C. in Villa Spithoever. It is later than such works as the *murus terreus Carinarum,* which, if defensive, would mark an independent Oppian circuit. The rest of the fortification, as at Ardea, would depend upon scarped cliffs, 'ex omni parte arduis praeruptisque montibus', as Cicero observed (*Rep.* 2. 6. 11).

    G. Saeflund, *Le mura di Roma repubblicana* (1932); Nash, *Pict. Dict. Rome* ii. 104 ff.      I. A. R.

**WAR, ART OF** (GREEK). Homer was commonly credited by ancient readers with having intended to provide instruction in the art of war. But the attempt to deduce some kind of theory from military practice does not seem properly to have begun till the latter half of the fifth century, when the Sophists applied their abstract methods to this subject among others. Of the textbooks derived from this movement there are preserved only the small treatise of Xenophon on the duties of a cavalry officer and an extract dealing with siege-warfare from a comprehensive textbook by Aeneas Tacticus. The other technical writers on the subject date from the Roman period. Of contemporary historians Thucydides, Xenophon, and Polybius in their different ways show appreciation of the art of war as a factor in history.

The Homeric battles cannot be reduced to technical terms. Sometimes they consist of duels between chieftains, taking place in front of masses of imperfectly armed retainers; at others the Greeks and Trojans meet in ranks of infantry, called phalanxes, and ranged closely shoulder to shoulder. Chariots are normally used to convey chieftains into or out of the fighting-line.

In Tyrtaeus the references to warfare are too full of Homeric echoes to give independent evidence on archaic warfare. The chief source of information before the Peloponnesian War is Herodotus. From him it appears that Greek warfare till his day was based on the hoplite (q.v.). Campaigning was mostly confined to the period of the year from March to October, the only season when (in the absence of military roads) it was easy to move bodies of heavy troops. Wars were usually limited to the border struggles of neighbouring States; the invader's objective was to destroy the corn and fruit-trees of the enemy and so compel them to offer battle or capitulate. There was no science of manœuvring before or during action, the only tactical device being the ambush. When hoplites met on level ground the deciding factor was usually weight of numbers. The troops were massed in ranks reckoned as the depth of so many shields. The side which first broke under pressure was defeated. The victors set up a trophy: the vanquished asked for a truce to bury their dead. Light-armed troops were quite unorganized; cavalry also were few, and were not used with any special effect.

The Peloponnesian War revealed the absurdity of annual raids on the enemy's corn lands. The Athenians by retiring into their fortified area and importing their food supplies were able to ignore the Spartan invasions. Hence the Spartans were forced at last to adopt the method of creating a permanent fortified base at Decelea. Also the constant fighting in various kinds of terrain showed up the lack of adaptability of the hoplites and the advantages of the occasional use of light-armed troops. The development of the peltast (q.v.) in the early fourth century provided a more mobile unit, which did not cost so much to maintain all the year round.

The hoplite battle was first revolutionized by Epaminondas. It had been a convention to put the best troops on the right of the line, But Epaminondas placed a massed body on the left to crush the enemy's right in a slanting advance, and by this element of surprise he broke the Spartan front at Leuctra. This manœuvre was only a more intelligent use of an old Boeotian device, but out of it Philip and Alexander, by means of the Macedonian phalanxe (q.v.), developed the method of attacking with part of their front, while the rest held back. For the purpose of delivering the main thrust Alexander used the excellent cavalry which Thessaly and Macedon provided, and exploited the charge from the flank. The further step of holding part of one's forces in reserve to use at a later point in the action is not found before the battle of Arbela. The other special innovation in Alexander's warfare is the pressing of pursuit, by which the enemy was prevented from re-forming.

After Alexander there were no drastic changes. The main evolution consists in the further modification of the phalanx. Also a few special varieties of warfare added to the complexity of fighting: heavy-armed cavalry and elephants (q.v.) were first known from oriental sources, but were soon used throughout the Hellenistic world. Generally war became more and more an activity for professionals and was too complex for the ordinary citizen; but as it became more specialized, it also became more stereotyped. Alexander's attack in its fresh vigour was never twice the same, but the Hellenistic generals'

methods were quite fixed when the Romans met them on Greek soil.

ANCIENT TEXTBOOKS. Xen. *Hipparchicus*; Aeneas Tacticus. Later technical writers are not of great value.

MODERN DISCUSSIONS. J. Kromayer and G. Veith, *Heerwesen und Kriegführung der Griechen und Römer* (1928); F. E. Adcock, *The Greek and Macedonian Art of War* (1957).

HOPLITE WAR. G. B. Grundy, *Thucydides and His Age* (1911); A. M. Snodgrass, *Arms and Armour of the Greeks* (1967).

HELLENISTIC WARFARE. W. W. Tarn, *Hellenistic Military and Naval Developments* (1930).         H. W. P.

**WAR, ART OF** (ROMAN). The earliest Roman battle-order was probably the phalanx (*see* preceding article). In the fourth century B.C. (after the Gallic invasions or during the Samnite Wars) this was replaced by the manipular system, a type of warfare of which an essential feature was open-order fighting. This innovation was accompanied by the adoption of *pilum* and *gladius* as the national weapons, the effective use of which required space for free movement. In this system the legion was drawn up in three lines of maniples with intervals equal to the frontage of each unit between the maniples, the units in the rear lines covering off the intervals in the lines in front of them. The plan of battle was at first schematic. After preliminary skirmishing by light-armed troops and cavalry stationed on the flanks of the legions, the front line (*hastati*) on coming into range hurled their *pila* and, if successful, advanced and decided the issue by hand-to-hand fighting with the *gladius*; if unsuccessful, they retired through the gaps in the second line, and their place was taken by the *principes*. Finally, a stand might be made with closed ranks at the third line (*triarii*), which at first retained the *hasta*. (*See* ARMS AND ARMOUR, ROMAN.)

During the Punic Wars much practical experience was acquired. Each line of maniples became more independent of the others, and experiments were made with a larger unit, the cohort, which after Marius permanently superseded the maniple. The fullest development was reached under Caesar. The *triplex acies* was no longer rigidly adhered to (e.g. *BGall.* 3. 24. 1), but dispositions varied with topographical conditions. The possibilities of flank attacks or of holding troops in reserve for the decisive onslaught were frequently exploited, while archers and slingers were increasingly employed in country unsuited to heavy infantry. Roman warfare was thus emancipated from stereotyped theories. Its success depended partly on the general's ability but mainly on the discipline of the soldiers. (*See* MANIPULUS, COHORS.)

During the first two centuries A.D. tactics for the most part followed the Caesarian model. But with the increasing efficiency of the auxiliary cavalry and light infantry a greater variety of manœuvres resulted. The legions still normally sustained the brunt of attack and defence, but the auxiliaries not infrequently played a decisive part (e.g. Tac. *Hist.* 2. 25; 2. 41; 5. 18; *Agr.* 35). Even during the anarchy of the third century the Roman army retained a high fighting spirit. Its defects were by then twofold, one the consequence of its very professionalism, which tended to separate the soldier in sentiment from the civilian population, the other a growth of regionalism, which divided the main army groups, of Britain, the Rhine, the Danube, and the East, from one another in spirit.

A marked feature of Roman warfare was the emphasis placed on camp construction. Even on short campaigns a camp with ditch and rampart was laid out as a base for attack and a safe retreat in the event of defeat (*see* CAMPS). During the Republic these camps were usually temporary, but in the scheme of frontier defence gradually perfected in the Principate permanent garrisons for legions and *auxilia* were established (*see* LIMES). The defensive attitude which this system inevitably inculcated finally proved to be a weakness, and it was necessary in the fourth century to divide the army permanently into a frontier force and a field army of higher status (*see* ARMIES, ROMAN).

Two methods of advance were commonly adopted. If attack was not expected, the army moved in one long column with a vanguard of scouts and cavalry, which also protected the flanks and rear (Joseph. *BJ* 3. 6. 2). If danger was anticipated, a formation easily convertible into an *acies* was adopted (*agmen quadratum*, Tac. *Ann.* 1. 51).

Despite the technical difficulties and the lack of maps more detailed than itineraries (q.v.), converging movements involving long marches and careful synchronization were increasingly attempted and sometimes succeeded. On the whole Roman strategy aimed at the destruction of the enemy in pitched battle rather than at a war of attrition.

J. Kromayer and G. Veith, *Heerwesen und Kriegführung der Griechen und Römer* (1928); H. Delbrück, *Geschichte der Kriegskunst*[3] (1920); F. Lammert, *PW* Suppl. iv. 1060 ff., s.v. 'Kriegskunst (römische)'; Parker, *Roman Legions*[2]; F. E. Adcock, *The Roman Art of War under the Republic* (1940). H. M. D. P.; G. R. W.

**WAR, RULES OF.** These, like much other international law, depended on custom and showed a constant conflict between the higher standard of the best public opinion and harsher measures permitted by usage, while passion and expediency frequently caused the most fundamental rules to be violated. Thus, the temptation to profit from a surprise at times led to the opening of hostilities without a declaration of war. Probably the law most generally observed was that of the sanctity of heralds, for heralds were essential to communications between belligerents. Nor did Greeks frequently refuse a defeated army a truce for burying its dead, for the request of such a truce meant an admission of defeat and usually was followed by retreat. Beyond this there were few restraints except humanitarian considerations and the universal condemnation of excessive harshness. Plundering and the destruction of crops and property were legitimate, and were carried on both by regular armies and fleets, and by informal raiding-parties and privateers, and even were the sanctity of temples was not always respected. Prisoners, if not protected by special terms of surrender, were at the mercy of their captors, who could execute them or sell them into slavery. The warfare of the Hellenistic Age was somewhat more humane, though with the actions of the Achaean general Aratus against 'tyrants' and still more with the wars of Rome and Philip V deterioration began once more. Roman warfare at its worst was extremely cruel and sometimes went to the length of killing all living things, even animals, in cities taken by storm, but it was often tempered by mercy. Though surrender (*deditio*) gave full power to the captors, it was unusual to use extreme measures against a city that surrendered and appealed to the *fides* of Rome. The protection of the rules of war was not extended to pirates and not always to barbarians.

The sources are ancient accounts of wars, especially those of Thucydides, Polybius, and Livy.

MODERN WORKS. C. Phillipson, *The International Law and Custom of Ancient Greece and Rome* (1911), chs. xxii–xxviii; Rostovtzeff, *Hellenistic World*, 140 ff., 192 ff., 603 ff., 1258 f.

SPECIAL. Piganiol, 'Venire in fidem', *Revue internationale des droits de l'antiquité* 1950; Aymard, 'Le Partage des profits de la guerre dans les traités d'alliance antiques', *Rev. Hist.* 1957.
J. A. O. L.

**WATER** had several functions in the ancient world. First, although hygienic standards were not comparable to ours, cleanliness was very highly valued. The Greeks inherited bathing practices from Minoan-Mycenaean civilization, and developed them, both in domestic life and in public baths (esp. also in the *gymnasia*). The Romans transformed these into a regular social institution (*see* BATHS). Secondly, water was a primal element in cosmogonic thought. This applies equally to philosophy (*see* THALES) and to the early mythical cosmogonies (on which cf. Kirk–Raven, *Presocratic Philosophers*, ch. 1, esp. 41 ff. and for Oceanus as the source of all 11 ff.). Thirdly, it was (together with fire) very important in purificatory and other religious rites. The new-born child, the bride (cf. the use of *loutrophoroi*) and bridegroom, the bodies of the dead and the mourners, the initiates (*see* MYSTERIES), and the consultants of oracles were purified by water; the prophet received inspiration by drinking from the holy source. Sea water and water from natural springs were considered particularly efficacious. As regards spring water (*see* SPRINGS), this has two aspects, both connected with the nether world. First, it is, apart from its purificatory function, a giver of fertility to all nature. Second, it has the purely chthonic function of serving the dead, who are 'thirsty' (cf. the di-pi-si-jo-i on Pylos tablets). Water, therefore, was a usual gift to the dead, together with other liquids. In the texts on gold plates, usually labelled 'Orphic', the soul is 'parched with thirst' and wants to drink the water of Memory. In the eschatological myths of Plato and Virgil, *Aeneid* 6. 714, 749, the souls drink the water of Oblivion.

S. Eitrem, *Opferritus und Voropfer der Griechen und Römer* (1915), ch. 2; M. Ninck, 'Die Bedeutung des Wassers im Kult und Leben der Alten', *Philol.* Suppl. xiv. 2 (1921); R. Ginouvès, *Balaneutikè. Recherches sur le bain dans l'ant. grecque* (1962). J. H. C.

**WEAVING.** The weaving of cloth for ordinary household use in Greece and Rome was usually done at home. The more elaborate forms of weaving were left to professional craftsmen, and the best specimens of their work, often imported from Persia, Egypt, and Phoenicia, seem by the descriptions in literature to have been equal to the finest modern tapestry. These were all made by hand on an upright loom (ἱστός, *tela*) differing very little in principle from that used by Penelope in the *Odyssey*. Its operation was as follows.

The framework was simple: two upright posts joined at the top by a transverse beam (ζυγόν, *jugum*). To this beam were fastened the threads of the warp (πηνίον, *stamina*) with weights attached at the bottom to make them hang straight. These threads were then divided into two groups by means of two horizontal rods (κανόνες, *arundines*) so that the shuttle (κερκίς, *radius*) might pass alternately over and under them. The warp was much stouter than the weft thread, which was placed on a bobbin (πήνη, *panus*) revolving on a cane and delivering the thread through a hole in the front of the shuttle. After the shuttle had passed to and fro several times the weft was driven upwards by a comb (κτείς, *pecten*) the teeth of which were inserted between the warp threads. For weaving in its simplest form this was all that was necessary; when a pattern was required a system of leashes and heddles, such as we have now, was used and worked by hand. In early times the web began at the top and the weaver worked standing; but at some time in the last century B.C. the Egyptian fashion of sitting and starting at the bottom was introduced in Rome.

In the process of weaving, rich robes for women or for goddesses were often decorated with θρόνα or δαίδαλα—elaborate patterns of flowers, animals, or human figures. Vase-paintings, particularly of the geometric and archaic periods, show goddesses or other female beings wearing garments with deep bands of such figures. It is probable that the epithets in -θρονος (ποικιλόθρονος, χρυσόθρονος, ἀργυρόθρονος, εὔθρονος, etc.), applied in the epics and elsewhere in Greek literature to female beings, may show the root word θρόνα, not θρόνος, and may denote 'wearing garments with bright (or golden, or silver, or fair, etc.) figures'.

Forbes, *Stud. Anc. Technol.* iv²; A. J. B. Wace, 'Weaving or Embroidery?', *AJArch.* 1948, 51 ff.; Lillian B. Lawler, 'On Certain Homeric Epithets', *Philological Quarterly* xxvii (1948), 80 ff.; G. M. Bolling, '*Poikilos* and *Throna*', *AJPhil.* 1958, 275 ff.

F. A. W.; L. B. L.

**WEIGHING-INSTRUMENTS.** The balance (σταθμός, *libra*, *bilanx*) of two pans at equal distances from the point of suspension is an invention of primitive times; in Mycenaean tablets it is the symbol for the largest unit of weight, and Homer is familiar with its use, which persisted through antiquity. The steelyard, in which the rod is unequally divided, the object to be weighed being suspended from the short arm against a sliding weight on the longer, does not appear before Roman times (*statera*: originally *statera campana*, from an alleged Campanian origin); but from its greater convenience it became the most popular form of balance. Examples in museums show great variety; several scales and as many suspension-points may be combined; the pans may be replaced by hooks or by receptacles for liquids. *Trutina* is a pan-balance for large masses; *momentana* and *moneta* are for small objects, or coins.

E. Michon, Dar.–Sag., s.v. 'Libra'; M. della Corte, *Mon. Ant.* xxi (1912), 1 ff.　　　　　　　　　　　　　　　F. N. P.; M. L.

**WEIGHTS.** Weights of the Greek Bronze Age are usually flattened cylinders of stone or metal, incised circles on the upper surface indicating the denomination. Other forms are the duck and bull's head, the slingstone of haematite, and from Cnossus comes a flattened stone pyramid, the weight of a light talent (29 kg) or of a standard copper ingot. Several standards appear to have been current, extant Minoan weights having been related to the Egyptian, Babylonian, and Phoenician systems.

Mycenaean texts from Cnossus, Pylus, and Mycenae present a system of weights in which the largest unit is equal to 30 of the next, which is made up of four smaller units, etc. The absolute value of the largest unit may be somewhat under 30 kg.

The typical weight of historic Greece is a square plaque of lead with a badge, and sometimes the denomination, the name of the issuing city, or other official guarantees on the top in relief. The principal types on the most widespread series of Attic weights are the astragalos (stater), dolphin (mna), amphora (one-third stater with half-amphora as one-sixth), tortoise (one-fourth stater with half-tortoise as one-eighth). There were many other forms, as caprice or local custom dictated. Roman weights show less variety, the common form being a spheroid of stone or metal, with flattened top and bottom; the denomination is generally expressed in punctured characters on the top.

Several weight standards were used in Greece; the principal ones were the Aeginetic, traditionally associated with Pheidon of Argos, and the Euboic, introduced by Solon into Attica. The Attic-Euboic in later times tended to oust the Aeginetic. The historical origin of these standards is disputed; the Greeks held that they were based on natural units, e.g. in the Attic-Euboic system on the barley-corn, of which twelve went to the obol. Extant weights often show considerable variations from the norm. A theoretical Greek table is:

|  | Attic-Euboic standard | Aeginetic standard |
|---|---|---|
| The *obol*, or metal spit | 0·72 gm | 1·05 gm |
| The *drachma*, bundle of six spits | 4·31 „ | 6·30 „ |
| The *mina*, 100 *drachmae* | 431·00 „ | 630·00 „ |
| The *talent*, 60 *minae* | 25·86 kg | 37·80 kg |

The talent represented a man's load. The Attic-Euboic mina weighed almost a pound avoirdupois.

The Roman system was based upon the pound, *libra*, of 327·45 grammes = 0·721 of the pound avoirdupois, which was divided into 12 ounces, *unciae*. The names and symbols of the subdivisions are:

| *libra* or *as* | 1 pound | I |
|---|---|---|
| *deunx* | 11 oz. | S = = = |
| *dextans* | 10 „ | S = = |
| *dodrans* | 9 „ | S = |
| *bes* | 8 „ | S = |
| *septunx* | 7 „ | S– |
| *semis* | 6 „ | S |
| *quincunx* | 5 „ | = = – |
| *triens* | 4 „ | = = |
| *quadrans* | 3 „ | = – |
| *sextans* | 2 „ | = |
| *sescuncia* | 1½ „ | ⎨– |
| *uncia* | 1 „ | – |
| *semuncia* | ½ „ | ⎨ |
| *sicilicus* | ¼ „ | ⎬ |
| *sextula* | ⅙ „ | ⎬ |
| *semisextula* | 1/12 „ | ⎬δ |
| *scriptulum* | 1/24 „ | ⋆ |

A. J. Evans, 'Minoan Weights', in *Corolla Numismatica* (1906), 336 ff.; *British Museum Guide to the Exhibition illustrating Greek and Roman Life* (1929), s.v. 'Weights'; E. Michon, Dar.–Sag., s.v. 'Libra', 'Pondus'; O. Viedebandt, *Antike Gewichtsnormen* (1923); W. Ridgeway, *Origin of Metallic Currency and Weight Standards* (1892); M. Ventris and J. Chadwick, *Documents in Mycenaean Greek* (1956); M. Lang and M. Crosby, *Weights, Measures and Tokens, Athenian Agora* x (1964); F. Hultsch, *Reliquiae Scriptorum Metrologicorum* (1882).　　　　　　　　　F. N. P.; M. L.

**WIND-GODS** were worshipped both by the Greeks and the Romans. Their ruler, Aeolus, might shut them up in a sack (Homer), but they were also regarded as well-defined personalities (so especially Boreas and Zephyrus). Originally they were represented as horses (the swift-footed horses of Achilles are the offspring of Zephyrus and one of the Harpies), later as anthropomorphic, often winged (under oriental influence). Homer speaks of four winds (later also the traditional number), Hesiod names three as children of Astraeus (the Starry Man) and Eos (the Dawn); the 'Tower of the Winds' at Athens has eight. The winds were regarded as fertilizing or impregnating, and astrologers assigned them to the planet Jupiter; they were also regarded as destructive, and their cult had a corresponding character (a black lamb is sacrificed to the 'typhos' according to Aristophanes, *Ran.* 847–8). The Athenians were especially interested in Boreas, for whom they organized a state-cult because he destroyed a large part of the Persian fleet. (Dedication to the winds at Pergamum, *Ath. Mitt.* 1910, 547.) Even magic practices were employed in order to conciliate the winds (cf. the 'windlullers' at Corinth, Hesych, s.v.).

In Italy the name of the north wind (*aquilo*) still reminds us of the idea of the wind as a mighty bird. Here the west wind, Favonius (Zephyrus), was the favourite. The Romans had a temple of the *Tempestates* (near to the Porta Capena) from the third century B.C. In imperial times the winds were often represented on sarcophagi.

J. Stengel, *Hermes* 1900, 627 ff.; F. Cumont, *Rev. Arch.* 1929, 26 ff.; Nilsson, *GGR* i². 116 f.　　　　　　　　　　S. E.; J. H. C.

**WINE** (cf. VITICULTURE). Both in Greece and in Italy wine, which (except in ritual and as medicine) was almost always diluted with water, formed part of the staple diet, and even slaves were allowed their ration. In both countries the grapes were gathered, trodden, and then pressed in wedge, beam, or screw presses (all of them classical inventions). The juice that flowed before (πρότροπος) or during treading was separated from that produced by pressing, which was always considered second rate. A third-rate wine (στεμφυλίτης), produced from a further pressing of the lees mixed with water, was drunk only by the very poor. Some of the juice (γλεῦκος, *mustum*) was used at once; but the greater part was stored in cellars in large pottery fermenting vats ($\pi i \theta o \iota$, *dolia*), often smeared with resin or pitch, in which it was left to ferment for about six months with frequent skimming during this period. In Rome, where by the first century B.C. Italian wines had largely replaced the earlier Greek imports, fermentation sometimes took place in the open air or, in jars (*amphorae*), in the upstairs storeroom (*apotheca*), which was normally reserved for wine that had been filtered after fermentation through cloth or metal sieves, transferred to jars, and sealed and labelled. (For trading purposes, however, large skins [$\dot{a}\sigma\kappa o i$, *cullei*] and, in Roman times, wooden casks were also used.) During fermentation the Romans sometimes added inspissated must (*defrutum*) to increase the alcoholic content. The Greeks found it difficult to arrest fermentation completely, with the result that their wines normally had to be drunk within 3–4 years. The Romans took elaborate steps (including sometimes heat treatment in the *fumarium*) to stop fermentation; but they too normally drank their wines within 3–4 years, though some Italian wines took 10–15 years to ripen, and there are occasional references to much older vintages. Wines were classified either by colour (black, red, white, yellow) or by taste (dry, harsh, light, sweet), and artificial additions to improve lustre, bouquet, or taste were not unknown. Very many different varieties, usually based on locality, are enumerated by ancient authors (especially Pliny, *HN*, bk. 14, Athenaeus, bks. 1–10), with Chian, Thasian, Lemnian, and Coan among the Greek, and Setine, Caecuban, Falernian, and Alban among the Italian most highly thought of. In general, wine was so central a feature of Graeco-Roman life that the boundaries of wine-drinking largely coincided with those of classical civilization.

Forbes, *Stud. Anc. Technol.* iii. 106 ff.; C. Seltman, *Wine in the Ancient World* (1957); A. D. Fitton Brown, *CR* 1962, 192 ff. L. A. M.

## WOMEN, POSITION OF. GREECE. (a) Upper-class women as pictured by Homer and the tragedians enjoyed a moderately free social life within their own circle. Similar conditions are discernible in Sparta among Spartiate women, in Lesbos (Sappho's circle, q.v.) in tyrants' families, and in Athens before the radical democracy (Plut. *Cim.* 4). Except at Sparta, however, women did not certainly have the right to dispose of property, and all women, even of the highest class, spun, wove, and made clothes.

(b) Middle- and lower-middle-class women are known mainly from democratic Athens. Their lives were much more restricted, since they were married very early in life (too early in Xenophon's opinion (*Lac. Pol.* 1, 3–6) and in Plato's (*Resp.* 460 d–e)), and stayed almost entirely in their homes, being regarded as responsible for the three duties of raising children, producing clothes, with their maidservants' help, protecting the house (Xen. *Oec.* 7. 17–37). Some women received elementary education, knew something of civic affairs, and had a considerable influence on their husbands; all took part in the family's religious life, and shared in that of the State. They suffered from the middle-cass snobbery which ordains that gentlewomen should not work (Xen. *Mem.* 2. 7, 2–12). Women had no political rights and could not act in law except to divorce their husbands (by $\dot{a}\pi o\lambda\epsilon\iota\psi\iota s$) and give evidence under oath; they could not own property, but the State took elaborate precautions to protect them from being left destitute, and to secure the marriage of orphans and $\dot{\epsilon}\pi i\kappa\lambda\eta\rho o\iota$ (girls without brothers), and to ensure that the elderly were protected (Arist. *Ath. Pol.* 56, 6–7). The requirement (after 451 B.C.) that citizens must have both parents citizens, and formally married, ensured that almost all citizen-girls would marry; public opinion regarded failure to secure

marriages for womenfolk as discreditable. However, the above regulation also created a preoccupation with chastity, which caused young women to be excessively guarded. Older women, especially widows, had more freedom and independence.

(c) Poor women, especially widows, went out to work; known occupations include spinning for pay (Hom. *Il.* 12. 433–5), wet-nurse (Dem. 57. 31–35), selling ribbons (ibid.), festival garlands (a soldier's widow), bread, potherbs in the market, etc. (Ar. *Thesm.* 446–52, etc.). Foundlings, non-citizens, and slaves often became kept women, either concubines (a class recognized at law, Dem. 23. 53–6), or courtesans ($\dot{\epsilon}\tau\alpha\hat{\iota}\rho\alpha\iota$), who were often highly educated and talented, and acted as the female company at men's social gatherings. Hetaereae (q.v.) also included flute-girls and other musicians who entertained at rowdier parties. The lowest class were common prostitutes ($\pi\dot{o}\rho\nu\alpha\iota$), who frequented the lodging-houses of Peiraeus. The trade of keeper of girls ($\pi o\rho\nu o\beta o\sigma\kappa\dot{o}s$) was followed by retired hetaerae; hetaerae sometimes married young citizens, but such marriages did not usually last long (Isae. 3. 28–9); the marriage of Pericles and Aspasia (q.v.) was exceptional, as was their son's receipt of citizenship.

PHILOSOPHERS' VIEWS. Plato (in *Laws*) abandoned his attempt (in *Republic*) to oust the family from its central position in Greek society: Aristotle accepted it as basic (*Pol.* 1. 1, *Nic. Eth.* 8, 12). Both believed that men and women should have the same education and training; Plato approved of women as 'Guardians'. Both advocated controlling the size of their city's population, and regulating the family as the focus of man's acquisitive instincts. Cynics (e.g. Crates 2 q.v.) rejected family life; Stoics (e.g. Musonius q.v. Rufus) supported ideas of equality for women.

HELLENISTIC AGE. Royal women ejoyed great influence and took a large part in dynastic intrigues; many of the Ptolemies (qq.v.) married their sisters. Upper-class women in Alexandria enjoyed considerable freedom (Theoc. *Id.* 15), and papyri (private letters etc.) show widespread literacy among the Greeks of Egypt. The society of New Comedy (q.v.) has some social contacts between the sexes, but the situations portrayed do not suggest a socially mature society.

ROME. In early Rome *paterfamilias* (see PATRIA POTESTAS) was all-powerful; his wife (like his children) owned no property: she was *in manu*, and was protected financially only by her position *filiae loco* and by the difficulty of divorce, but marriage without *manus* (q.v.) antedated the XII Tables. Thereafter women had to have a guardian through whom alone they could conduct important business; until Augustus only Vestal Virgins (q.v.) were excepted; thereafter women with three children became independent, freedwomen with four.

Upper-class Roman women were influential; the republican senatorial class was very small and extensively intermarried; senators' houses were used for much public business and for administering *clientelae*. Many women were educated and witty (*sermone lepido*, *ILS* 8430, and Sulpicia's poems, q.v. 1); some craved power (Fulvia, q.v.); many remained domesticated (Cornelia—Prop. 4, 11, 'Turia' q.v.). Divorce and adultery were frequent (e.g. Clodia q.v.), and were attacked by Augustus' legislation (q.v.), although its success was limited (Juvenal 6 etc.).

Middle- and lower-class women are little known; peasant life probably changed little; women managed the clothing trade (evidence at Pompeii, q.v.); literature (Plautus, Horace, elegiac poets, satire, q.v.) mentions courtesans, etc.; after Augustus, prostitutes, procuresses, and actresses suffered from legal disabilities.

The breakdown of the patriarchal system liberated

women of the citizen class, but deprived them of their importance for marriage. Augustus allowed any non-senatorial Roman to marry a freedwoman, and the *de facto* marriages of soldiers were legalized and their children were enfranchised.

GREECE. *See under* MARRIAGE, LAW OF; V. Ehrenberg, *The People of Aristophanes* (1943), ch. 8; H. D. F. Kitto, *The Greeks* (1951), ch. 12; R. Flacelière, *Daily Life in Greece at the Time of Pericles* (1965; 1959 in French), ch. 3; Joseph Vogt, *Von der Gleichwertigkeit der Geschlechter in der bürgerlichen Gesellschaft der Griechen* (1960); W. K. Lacey, *The Family in Classical Greece* (1968).
ROME. *See under* MARRIAGE, LAW OF; PATRIA POTESTAS; J. P. V. D. Balsdon, *Roman Women* (1962).
For older views see *Companion Gr. Stud.* 610 ff.; *Comp. Lat. Stud.* 185 ff.          W. K. L.

**WORSHIP, HOUSEHOLD.** A Greek householder might have a particularly close association with some god or hero (as Ariston king of Sparta with Astrabacus, Hdt. 6. 69. 3; Pindar with Alcmeon, *Pyth.* 8. 56 ff., and with the Mother of the Gods, *Pyth.* 3. 77 ff.: for private *sacra* cf. Theopomp. ap. Porph. *Abst.* 2. 16), but this was exceptional, and no part of domestic cult proper. The centre of the latter seems to have been the hearth, respectful treatment of which is recommended as early as Hesiod, *Op.* 733–4. At the ordinary family meals it was customary to begin by offering a little of the food, probably to Hestia (q.v.; Theophrastus in Porph. *Abst.* 2. 20). Before drinking wine, which formed a regular part of the meal, a little was poured on the floor to the Good Daimon, i.e. the luck of the house, and a little drunk neat, thus establishing a communion with him (cf. W. W. Tarn, *JHS* 1928, 210 ff.; Athenaeus, 692 ff.; Ar. *Eq.* 85 (with schol.), 106). After a more formal dinner, when the tables were cleared and the drinking-bout (*symposium*) began, it was customary, at all events in Athens, to offer three libations, to Zeus, the heroes, and Zeus Soter (Aeschylus, fr. 55 Nauck; see further Cook, *Zeus* ii. 1123, note 7). Of these, Zeus Soter is not the great Zeus, but rather a domestic deity, see H. Sjövall, *Zeus im altgr. Hauskult* (Diss. Lund, 1931), 85 ff.; see the whole dissertation for various domestic deities called Zeus, including Zeus Ktesios (53 ff.), who is hardly more than a deified store-jar in origin; cf. Cook, 1092 ff. Nilsson, *GGR* i². 402 ff. A householder also made private celebrations of recognized public festivals (Nock, *Harv. Theol. Rev.* 1936, 85, n. 105; cf. *SIG* 695, 86 ff.).

For Rome cf. CHILDREN, LARES, PENATES, VESTA. The cult was essentially the same as the Greek, though there were marked differences in detail; the objects of worship were the hearth (Vesta), the *numina* of the store-cupboard (Penates), and the Lar Familiaris; but there might be added to the *lararium*, or domestic chapel, at all events in classical times, almost any deity the householder fancied, as is shown by the figures represented in the Pompeian *lararia* (see Boyce in *Am. Ac. Rome* xiv, and add S.H.A. *Alex. Sev.* 29. 2). Cf. Hor. *Sat.* 2. 2. 123 ff. for a domestic cult of Ceres. *See also* RELIGION, MINOAN-MYCENAEAN; MEALS, SACRED; VESTA.

There is no treatise on the subject as a whole. The handbooks of private antiquities are inadequate here. Some useful works are cited above; add M. P. Nilsson in *Symb. Philol. Danielsson* (Uppsala, 1932), 218 ff.; id. *Opuscula Selecta* iii (1960), 271 ff.; H. J. Rose, 'The religion of the Greek household', *Euphrosyne* 1957, 95 ff.    H. J. R.

**WRESTLING.** This was a popular exercise among the Greeks. They used a wide variety of holds and throws, many of which are illustrated in vase-paintings. The object was to throw an opponent to the ground, and generally three throws were required for victory. In the major festivals wrestling was the last of the events in the pentathlon (q.v.) and, though weight was an advantage in this event, general athletic ability was required in order to qualify for it. Wrestling was also practised extensively to acquire general physical fitness and was considered particularly valuable, together with boxing, as a part of military training.      R. L. H.

# X

**XANTHIPPUS** (1), husband of Cleisthenes' niece Agariste and father of Pericles. As a political ally of the Alcmaeonids (q.v.), he probably brought Miltiades (q.v.) to trial in 493 B.C., and he secured his condemnation in 490–489. He was ostracized in 484, but was recalled in the general amnesty before Xerxes' invasion. Elected general for 479 he commanded the Athenian contingent at Mycale and had a large share in this victory. In 478, after a winter siege, he captured Sestos and had the Persian governor and his children massacred.

J. Kirchner, *Prosopographia Attica* ii. 152 f., no. 11169; J. Carcopino, *L'Ostracisme athénien*² (1935), 148 f., and *passim*; H. Willrich, *Perikles* (1936), 62 ff.      P. T.

**XANTHIPPUS** (2), a Spartan mercenary captain, helped Carthage against Regulus (q.v.). He reorganized the Carthaginian army and annihilated the Roman expeditionary force, making brilliant use of the Carthaginian elephants and cavalry to outflank and mow down the Romans (255 B.C.). After this victory he left Carthage. The story that he was treacherously killed by the Carthaginians on his homeward journey may be rejected. That he is the same Xanthippus who later served Ptolemy Euergetes is conjectural.      H. H. S.

**XANTHUS** (1), poet of Magna Graecia or Sicily in seventh century B.C., mentioned by Stesichorus (Ath. 12. 513 a), who is said to have drawn on his *Oresteia* for his own (ibid.). He said that Electra was originally called Laodice, but had her name changed by the Argives because she remained unmarried (Ael. *VH* 4. 26).

J. M. Edmonds, *Lyra Graeca* (Loeb repr. 1952), ii. 12–13. C. M. B.

**XANTHUS** (2) of Lydia, author of Λυδιακά in four books, was a contemporary of Herodotus, coupled with Hellanicus and Damastes (qq.v.) as 'extending down to the time of Thucydides' (Dion. Hal. *De Thuc.* 5). Ephorus (Ath. 12. 515 d) says that Herodotus used him, but the evidence of the fragments is inconclusive. Surviving fragments illustrate his taste for romance and folktales (often of non-Greek origin) and speculation about geological changes in the countryside, in the Herodotean manner. Nicolaus (q.v.) of Damascus records many details of Lydian history and legend not mentioned by Herodotus; the language he uses in these passages retains Ionic forms and traces of a style reminiscent of Herodotus, and he is probably using Xanthus or a later adaptation of his *Lydiaca*. *See also* LOGOGRAPHERS.

*FHG* i. 36–44; iv. 628–9; *FGrH* ii. A, 90 (Nic. Dam.), iii C, 765. L. Pearson, *Early Ionian Historians* (1939), ch. 3; H. Diller in *Navicula Chiloniensis, Stud. in hon. F. Jacoby* (1956), 66 ff.    L. P.

**XENAGORAS** (fl. *c.* 90 B.C.), a Greek, wrote Χρόνοι (Chronologies) of Greek (and Italian?) towns, and Περὶ νήσων.

FGrH ii. 240.

**XENARCHUS** (1), Sicilian mime-writer (*see* MIMUS) of the late fifth century B.C., son of Sophron (q.v.).

Arist. *Poet.* 1447ᵇ3; Kaibel, *CGF*, p. 182.

**XENARCHUS** (2), Middle Comedy poet, of considerable frankness and liveliness; 8 titles survive, mainly from daily life. Fr. 1, parody of tragic style: fr. 7, illegal watering of fish; fr. 14, happy cicalas, their wives have no voice.

FCG iii. 614 ff.; CAF ii. 467 ff.

**XENOCLES** (1), son of the Elder Carcinus (q.v. 1), is said (Ael. *VH* 2. 8) to have defeated Euripides in 415 B.C. with a group of plays consisting of *Oedipus*, *Lycaon*, *Bacchae*, and *Athamas* (satyric). His *Licymnius* was parodied by Aristophanes (*Nub.* 1264–5), and there are contemptuous references to him in Ar. *Thesm.* 169, *Ran.* 86. Epithets applied to him (μηχανοδίφης, δωδεκαμήχανος) may refer to a fondness for strange mechanical devices (*TGF*, p. 770).

(2) Son of the Younger Carcinus (q.v. 2), wrote tragedies in the fourth century B.C. (schol. Ar. *Ran.* 86).

A. W. P.-C.

**XENOCRATES** (1) of Chalcedon, son of Agathenor, disciple of Plato and head of the Academy from 339 to 314 B.C. He is presented to us as a man of impressive personality, with a combination of austere dignity and kindliness which exercised a great influence on all who came in contact with him. He was generally respected in Athens and was employed by the citizens as ambassador to Antipater in 322 B.C.

His philosophical contributions, so far as we can reconstruct them from the scanty evidence, were less impressive. He seems, in general, to have attempted to reproduce Plato's thought in a stereotyped and formalized system, though on one or two points he probably preserved the correct tradition of interpretation as against Aristotle. He also interested himself in giving a systematic account of the nature of the gods and daemons and their relations to the heavenly bodies, in a way which foreshadowed the fantasies of later Neoplatonism. From the titles of his works we may conjecture that his chief interest lay in moral questions, but rather in the direction of teaching a practical morality than of ethical analysis, a line which his immediate successors in the Academy appear to have followed. His only known excursion into mathematics issued in a defence of 'indivisible lines', which Aristotle thereupon proved indefensible.

R. Heinze, *Xenocrates* (1892); S. Pines, 'A New Fragment of Xenocrates', *TAPA* 1961. G. C. F.

**XENOCRATES** (2) of Aphrodisias, physician of the time of Nero and the Flavians (54–96).

WORKS. Περὶ τῆς ἀπὸ τοῦ ἀνθρώπου καὶ τῶν ζῴων ὠφελείας, full of superstitious means of treatment, borrowed largely from previous works such as Ps.-Democritus' Λιθογνώμων, a lexicon of gems (frs. ed. M. Wellmann in *Quellen u. Studien zur Geschichte der Naturwissenschaften u. der Medizin*, 1935); Περὶ τῆς τῶν ἐνύδρων τροφῆς; *On the healing properties of plants*; *On the names of plants*; *On the meaning of the flight of birds*.

Frs. ed. J. L. Ideler in *Physici et Medici Graeci Minores* (1841), i. 121. W. D. R.

**XENOPHANES** of Colophon left home at the age of 25 (probably on the Persian conquest of Ionia in 545

B.C.) and lived an exile's life for at least sixty-seven years (fr. 8 Diels), at some time in Zancle and Catana, and latterly perhaps at the court of Hieron of Syracuse. He is said to have written epic verses on the Foundation of Colophon and the Colonization of Elea, but extant fragments are either from his *Satires* (Σίλλοι) in hexameters and iambics (including those traditionally attributed to a philosophic poem) or from elegiac occasional pieces.

An accomplished and original writer in the tradition of Tyrtaeus and Solon, Xenophanes became the poet in Magna Graecia of the Ionian intellectual enlightenment. In ruthless criticism of Homer and Hesiod he denies that the gods resemble men in conduct, shape, or understanding; there is a single eternal self-sufficient Consciousness, which, without stirring, sways the universe (with which it is itself identical) through thought. His physical theories are based on keen observation but are clearly dependent on Milesian science, as his theology may be on ideas of Pythagoras. In his elegies he turns his criticism to society, denouncing the accepted canons of ἀρετή (athletic and military prowess) as of less social value than his own intellectual achievement. Throughout he claims for his views not truth but probability and propriety. Neither sceptic nor mystic, he is more a searching and constructive critic of convention than a systematic thinker. But he is named by Heraclitus in the same breath with Hesiod, Pythagoras, and Hecataeus, and Plato treats him, perhaps seriously, as a founder of the Eleatic school. As the first writer to consider the impact of natural theology on conduct he exercised a lasting influence on religious thought.

Diels, *Vorsokr.*¹¹ i. 113–39; Diehl, *Anth. Lyr. Graec.* i³. 63–74; J. Burnet, *EGP* 112 ff.; C. M. Bowra, *Early Greek Elegists* (1938), 106–35; W. Jaeger, *The Theology of the Early Greek Philosophers* (1947) 38 ff.; Guthrie, *Hist. Gk. Phil.* i. 360 ff. A. H. C.

**XENOPHON** (1). LIFE. Xenophon, the son of Gryllus of the Athenian deme Erchia, lived from *c.* 428/7 B.C. to *c.* 354 B.C. By his wife Philesia Xenophon had two sons, Gryllus and Diodorus, of whom the former died in the battle of Mantinea in 362 B.C. Xenophon was born of a comparatively wealthy family, but his life was not easy and undisturbed, and his various experiences had a corresponding effect on the sympathies and interests which he reveals in his writings. Xenophon approached maturity at a time of oligarchic revolution at Athens and perhaps participated in the battle of Arginusae, which was the occasion of unhappy political events. As a young aristocrat, a member of the cavalry, and an associate of Socratic circles he probably found life politically difficult during the oligarchic revolution and even precarious after the democratic restoration, and left Athens in 401. In that year, at the invitation of Proxenus and in spite of Socrates' advice, he joined the army in Asia Minor which turned out to be in the service of Cyrus who aspired to the Persian throne. After the failure of the expedition, the Anabasis, Xenophon was elected a general and extricated the army which came to Trapezus in 400. After service with Seuthes of Thrace he offered the troops under his command to the Spartan general Thibron and campaigned in Asia Minor with him and his successor Dercylidas in 399/7. It was probably in 399, the year of Socrates' death and a time of difficulty for Socratic associates, that Xenophon was formally exiled. His sons were born in the following years. In 396/4 he served under the Spartan king Agesilaus, to whom he became strongly attached. When Agesilaus was recalled at the start of the Corinthian War, Xenophon accompanied him and was present at the battle of Coronea in 394, when Spartan forces were ranged against his native Athens. Unable to return home Xenophon was allowed to stay at first with his family in Sparta, and was then presented by the Spartans with an estate near Olympia, at Scillus. It was while he was at Scillus that Xenophon was elected Spartan *proxenos* for the entertainment of Spartans visiting Olympia. In 371, in defiance of Sparta, Elis claimed Scillus and Xenophon was obliged to leave his estate there, whence he and his family went to Corinth and stayed in the region of the Isthmus. As relations between Athens and Sparta improved, the decree of exile was rescinded c. 368. In 366/5 when the Athenians were expelled from Corinth he returned to Athens, where he lived until c. 354, when he died, possibly on a visit to Corinth (D.L. 2. 56).

2. WORKS. (1) **Hellenica** ('Ελληνικά). As it stands the work is a history of Greek affairs, in seven books, from 411 to 362. The work, however, was neither conceived as a unity, nor moulded into one. It consists of three major sections. Books 1–2, covering the years 411 to 403, are a continuation of Thucydides. He probably used Thucydides' notes to 2. 3, 10, and continued his annalistic method; as Xenophon was then in Athens, books 1–2 were centred on Athens. Books 3. 1 to 5. 3, covering the years 399–379, were written at Scillus c. 379/8. He left a gap for the years 402 and 401; and the part of the Anabasis which had already been written covered what he wanted to say for 401–399. Book 3 was very much based on Xenophon's experiences with Thibron, Dercylidas, and Agesilaus; for book 4, covering 395–389, Xenophon relied on his memory and to a great extent on Peloponnesian sources. He displays little knowledge of Athenian politics or sources and possibly wrote for a limited Spartan circle. When he wrote these books Xenophon was disillusioned by Sparta's conduct over the King's Peace and his attitude was more anti-Theban than pro-Spartan. The remainder of book 5, covering 379 to 375, was written at Corinth, c. 369. Books 6–7, which draw on a wider variety of sources, were written at Athens after 362, at which point he ended his narrative. It was then that the various sections were probably published together without revision and 2. 4, 43 was added as a link to cover the gap in Athenian history from 403 to 401. Significantly Xenophon did not mention the Common Peace (κοινὴ εἰρήνη) or the Second Athenian Confederacy.

(2) **Anabasis** (Κύρου ἀνάβασις), an account, now in seven books, of the expedition of the Greek mercenaries under Cyrus and of their return to safety (401–399). The first part to 5. 3, 6, dealing with the expedition proper, was written soon after 386 at Scillus when peace had been restored between Persia and Sparta. Since Xenophon had participated in the Anabasis and then supported Agesilaus' campaigns in Asia Minor he published the first part under the pseudonym of Themistogenes of Syracuse (Xen., *Hell.* 3. 1, 2). Whereas the first part is calm and amusing, that from 5. 3, 6, written about 377, is tense and aggressive and Xenophon casts aside the pseudonym and magnifies the importance of his role in order to answer his critics both among those who served and among official circles at Sparta.

(3) **Cynegeticus** (Κυνηγετικός), a treatise on hunting the hare especially, but also wild boar and deer, written early in Xenophon's literary career, perhaps at Scillus. Xenophon is concerned with the educational value of hunting in developing character and in training for war, and violently attacks the morally subversive effects of the sophists.

(4) **Spartan Constitution** (Λακεδαιμονίων πολιτεία), written c. 388 in a mood of gratitude to the Spartans who had settled him at Scillus. It is a laudatory and uncritical account of the Spartan system, which attracted the attention of the philosophers for its apparent stability. Ch. 14 is a partial palinode possibly written after 371, when Xenophon had become disillusioned with Spartan foreign policy and designed to excite notice at Athens.

(5) **Apology** (Άπολογία Σωκράτους). During his exile Xenophon probably kept in touch with philosophical developments through the schools at Elis and Phlius, and perhaps also through Callias and Hermogenes. Professing to record the words of the latter, Xenophon sets out to give a better interpretation of Socrates, some fifteen years after Socrates died, showing that Socrates was not incompetent and preferred to die.

(6) **Memorabilia** (Άπομνημονεύματα), recollections of Socrates in four books, of which 1–2 were written c. 381, and 3–4 c. 355/4. Books 1–2 consist of a defence absolving Socrates from the charges of 399 and deal with matters of education and the dangers of youth, which were perhaps of interest to his youthful sons. Books 3–4 deal with problems of wealth and management of household and State, which probably never concerned Socrates but which were of interest to Xenophon and of current concern in Athens.

(7) **Oeconomicus** (Οἰκονομικός), dialogues on estate management between Socrates and Critobulus (1–5) and Socrates and Ischomachus (7–21), perhaps published c. 362/1, but the dialogue with Critobulus may be contemporary with *Memorabilia* 1–2 as it is concerned with the good family-life and moral codes upheld by the countryman—a matter of importance when Xenophon's sons were maturing on the estate at Scillus.

(8) **On Horsemanship** (Περὶ ἱππικῆς), the oldest extant complete work on the subject. It is an authoritative work written by an expert; possibly compiled c. 380 for the instruction of Xenophon's sons.

(9) **Symposium** (Συμπόσιον) consists of pleasant recollections of an imaginary party held at Callias' house c. 422 with Socrates as one of the guests. Xenophon possibly aimed to pay homage to Socrates after returning from exile, but the work may have been part of Xenophon's attempt to re-establish himself politically with Callias, who helped in the *rapprochement* of Athens and Sparta.

(10) **Cyropaedia** (Κύρου παιδεία). Plato and others wrote on the problem of finding and educating statesmen and leaders. This work, which is Xenophon's counterblast, is a historical novel, now in eight books, with Cyrus the Elder as the model hero. There is a lengthy treatment of Xenophon's notions on the maintenance of authority and empire, political and military organization, moral reform and the value of family-life. The impressions made by Cyrus the Younger on Xenophon diminished and in the 360s it was apparent that the Persian system was not conducive to efficiency or progress, and so 8. 8, showing the confusion resulting from the death of Cyrus, was written as a palinode. Xenophon's ideas on the family prompted Plato to reply in the 'Laws'.

(11) **Hieron** ('Ιέρων), a dialogue between the Elder Hieron of Syracuse and Simonides of Ceos, who visited Syracuse in 476. Xenophon took up the popular theme of the position of tyrants, perhaps as a postscript to the *Cyropaedia*, and discussed whether the position of a tyrant could be a happy one and how a tyrant could secure the goodwill of his subjects.

(12) **Hipparchicus** ('Ιππαρχικός), a work on the duties of a cavalry commander, dealing with problems of manœuvre, organization, supply, and discipline in the State cavalry as matters of urgency. It was perhaps written with an eye to the position of Athens c. 357, when a final chapter on the armour of a horse and knight may have been added to (8) 'On Horsemanship'.

(13) **Agesilaus** (Άγησίλαος), written in praise of Agesilaus, who died in 360. It includes borrowings from *Hell.* 3–4, but they are given a twist and display Agesilaus as a hero in the Panhellenic cause.

(14) **Ways and Means** (Περὶ πόρων), offers a policy of

'peace through strength' for Athens consonant with that of Eubulus c. 355/4. It suggests many practical ways of increasing public resources by stimulating commercial and industrial enterprises.

**The Constitution of Athens** (Ἀθηναίων Πολιτεία), an oligarchic pamphlet written c. 431 by an unknown critic ot the policy and system of the Athenian democracy, but conceding that, as democracies go, the Athenian system is efficient. Style and subject-matter preclude the possibility of Xenophon's authorship.

**3.** Xenophon was one of the most prolific writers of antiquity and the variety of his work surpasses that of most others. His language and style are simple and fluent, containing no highly individualistic or eccentric features, and he has traditionally been considered to represent classical Attic prose at its best. Xenophon also achieved a considerable originality of form; in the *Anabasis*, by relating at length events in which he had participated; in the *Memorabilia*, by relating versions of conversations and personal recollections of Socrates; in the *Cyropaedia*, by employing the form of an historical romance.

In antiquity, if we follow the biography of Xenophon written by Diogenes Laertius, Xenophon was regarded primarily as a philosopher (cf. Cic. *Tusc.* 2. 26) and in more recent times as an historian. But neither approach is sufficient for an appreciation of Xenophon, for neither the historian who turns from Thucydides nor the philosopher who turns from Plato will discover an identical approach in Xenophon. The attitude of Xenophon was less that of the dedicated and inspired scholar than that of the practical Athenian gentleman of cultural and social attainments, who drew upon his own experiences and environment to set down and record for others practical information according to his own interests and from his own point of view. To the extent that his interests were 'utilitarian' perhaps Xenophon could rightly look upon himself as a follower of Socrates. Physical and metaphysical speculations were matters which Xenophon was content to leave to others.

Xenophon's favourite personal interests seem to have lain in hunting and horsemanship, in both of which he displays a scientific and detailed knowledge. He regarded them, however, as pursuits likely to develop a sound physique and virtuous habits which were conducive to good leadership and efficiency, especially in war (*Cyn.* 1. 18; *Cyr.* 1. 1, 16). Xenophon placed great emphasis on the development of such qualities, for in the *Hipparchicus* he gives less prominence to advice on battle tactics than to the moral qualities of a leader, and in the *Oeconomicus* he lays less emphasis on scientific aspects of agricultural and estate management than on the need for efficient management of men, family, slaves, and workers.

In Xenophon's writings we find his attitude to the conventions of family life and religious observances. In the *Oeconomicus* he gives the conventional picture of a man of means and maturity obtaining a youthful wife, who is sufficiently young and malleable to be trained and instructed in her habits and duties according to her husband's notions on the maintenance of the household (3. 10 f.; 7. 32 f. cf., *Mem.* 1. 1, 8; 3, 14). Xenophon reveals his attitude to the treatment of slaves, who respond to kindness and favours, and whose instincts can be trained in the same manner as those of animals by the provident owner (*Oec.* 13. 9; 14. 8–10). Xenophon conformed to the orthodox religious observances of his age. He consulted the Delphic Oracle before joining Proxenus and the Ten Thousand, even if he did so frame his question as to receive the answer which he desired (*An.* 3, 1. 5–6). At the end of the march, although he had made frequent offerings to Zeus, he made a further sacrifice to Zeus the Gracious at the behest of a sooth-sayer (id. 5. 6, 29). Then, when he was installed at Scillus, he dedicated gifts to Artemis (id. 5, 3. 7–8), for it was to her as well as to Apollo that the huntsman devoted a share of his captures (*Cyn.*, 6. 13). Above all, the gods were to be respected, for they were present everywhere (*Mem.* 1. 1, 19), they had the power to grant or deny good fortune (*Oec.* 11. 8) and were inclined to help those who helped themselves (*Cyr.* 1. 6, 5).

Xenophon was an idealist, but one who was prepared to work within the limits of circumstances. At Scillus and Corinth, for example, he was content to record history in so far as he knew of events without searching far afield for news. In the *Hieron* he considered how efficient the rule of one man in a State could be, but instead of devising entire programmes of education based on idealistic and epistemological preconceptions he sought to explain how the ruler ought to present himself to the people and conciliate their opinion. In the *De Vectigalibus* he did not speculate on the relevance and morality of material wealth, but set forward practical and inventive suggestions to increase the revenue of State by such means as investment in hotels and accommodations for rent to visitors and investment in slaves to lease to operators (3. 12; 4. 4; 23).

Xenophon was preoccupied with his interests in education, which he considered to be a most important matter (*Ap.* 21), and was of the opinion that a man ought to pursue education to the limits that his material resources permitted (*Cyn.* 2. 1), in order that he might be fitted for the noblest occupation, namely, governing and leading men (*Mem.* 3. 6, 2). It is in the *Cyropaedia* that Xenophon sets out most fully ideas on formal education (e.g. 1. 2, 2), but although discussions are introduced on ethics and concepts such as justice and there is a recognition of the need for development of powers of oral communication and of reasoning, the formal programme has a distinct bias toward physical activities, such as patrol duties and hunting. A leader had to be ready to give active leadership (*Hipp.* 1. 24; *Oec.* 12. 19–20) and not follow the opinion of the masses (cf. *Mem.* 3. 1, 4), who could be misled by demagogues and sophists (cf. *Mem.* 1. 7, 5; *Cyn.*, 13. 11).

Just as Xenophon's historical work was affected by his material limitations and circumstances and just as his social ideals reflected his status as a man of means (cf. *Cyn.*, 2. 1), so too were his political views affected by his experience. For he was brought up in the Peloponnesian War, in years of demoralizing political and military crisis for the Athenian democracy. In the post-war period he had little experience of normal political conditions until his return, late in life, to Athens. The men whose leadership he had directly experienced were Clearchus, Proxenus, and Menon on the March of the Ten Thousand, and subsequently Agesilaus the Spartan king and military leader. Xenophon consequently developed a sympathy for autocratic and tightly disciplined procedures, but eventually his earlier approval of the Spartan system of organization gave way to disapproval (*Lac.* 14) and he showed signs of recognizing the merits of the Athenian democratic system of the fourth century B.C.

Xenophon probably achieved his greatest popularity among the Romans for his sense of the practical, his support of the aristocratic ideals, and virtues in politics, war, and country life, and for his pursuit of the ideal of 'mens sana in corpore sano'.

LIFE AND WORKS. Diog. Laert. 2. 48–59. G. Grote, *History of Greece* viii (1888), *Plato* iii (1875); K. Münscher, 'Xenophon in Greek and Latin Literature', *Philol. Suppl.* xiii (1920); L. V. Jacks, *Xenophon Soldier of Fortune* (1930); J. Luccioni, *Les idées politiques et sociales de Xénophon* (1947); E. Delebecque, *Essai sur la vie de Xénophon* (1957). TEXTS. O.C.T. (Marchant); Teubner (Gemoll, Hude, etc.). *Opuscula*, G. Pierleoni (1937).

COMMENTARIES. *Hell.*: G. E. Underhill (1906). *An.*: W. Vollbrecht (1907–12). *Lac.*: F. Ollier (1934). *Mem.*: O. Gigon, I (1953), 2 (1956). *Cyr., Oec.*: H. A. Holden (1883–9). *Hieron*: J. Luccioni (1948). *Horsemanship*: E. Delebecque (1950). *Symp.*: G. J. Woldinga (1938/9). *Vect.*: J. H. Thiel (1922). *Ath.*: L. Stecchini (1950). Le opere socratiche (*Mem. Symp. Ap. Oec.*): R. Laurenti (1961).
TRANSLATIONS. H. G. Dakyns (Everyman, 1890). R. Warner, *Anabasis* (1949), *Hellenica* (1966). With text: Loeb Series and Budé Series (French).
STYLE AND LANGUAGE. L. Gautier, *La Langue de X.* (1911); J. Bigalke, *Einfluss der Rhetorik auf X. Stil* (1933); A. W. Persson, *Zur Textgeschichte X.* (1914); F. W. Sturz, *Lexicon X.* (1801–4, repr. 1964).
STUDIES OF PARTICULAR WORKS. *Hell.*: W. P. Henry, *Greek Historical Writing* (1966); G. Colin, *X. Historien* (1933). *An.*: E. Delebecque, *Rev. Ét. Gr.* 1946–7. *Cyn.*: W. Baehrens, *Mnemos.* 1926; O. Manns, *Über die Jagd bei den Griechen* (1889–90). *Lac.*: K. M. T. Chrimes 1948. *Ap.*: O. Gigon, *M.H.* 1946. *Mem.*: J. Luccioni 1953. *Oec.*: E. Delebecque, *Rev. Ét. Gr.* 1951. *Horsemanship*: K. Widdra 1965; M. H. Morgan 1894, repr. 1962. *Cyr.*: A. Champdor 1952. *Hieron*: L. Strauss 1963. *Hipp.*: E. Ekman 1933. *Ages.*: W. Seyffert 1909. *Vect.*: K. von der Lieck 1933. *Ath.*: H. Frisch 1942.                    D. J. M.

**XENOPHON** (2) **EPHESIUS**, Greek romancer, author of a novel entitled the *Ephesiaca* or *Anthia and Habrocomes* (Τὰ κατὰ Ἀνθίαν καὶ Ἀβροκόμην Ἐφεσιακά). Practically nothing is known about him, and both parts of his name have been suspected by scholars of being spurious. The critics have assigned him to every century A.D. from the second to the fifth: his mention (2. 13. 3) of the Eirenarch of Cilicia, a magistrature which is not attested before Trajan, is an unquestionable *terminus post quem*, and the destruction of the Artemision (A.D. 263)— a temple whose description occurs in the *Ephesiaca*—is regarded as a probable *terminus ante quem*.

His work narrates how a couple of young lovers from Ephesus, soon after being married, became separated whilst on a voyage, and were subjected to all sorts of trials and tribulations (shipwrecks, attacks by pirates and robbers, enslavement, advances by powerful suitors, etc.) which they managed to overcome without ever forgetting, or being unfaithful to, each other, until they met again and returned to Ephesus, where they lived happily ever after.

The traditional plot-ingredients of the genre are all present: the plot itself is so disjointed and unclear that most critics believe the novel (which is in five books) to be the clumsy and lacunose abridgement of a longer original (the *Suda*, in fact, says that Xenophon's novel was in ten books). Xenophon's characterization is extremely poor (his figures have been called 'bloße Marionetten' by Rohde), and his language, although he often draws from the vocabulary of the Attic Xenophon, is far removed from Atticistic purity and full of vulgarisms.

EDITIO PRINCEPS. A. Cocchia (London, 1726).
STANDARD EDITION. G. Dalmeyda (Paris, 1926, with French translation and excellent Introduction on the dating problem, language, and style, etc.).
COMMENTARY. A. E. Locella (Wien, 1796) (still useful).
CRITICISM. Rohde, *Gr. Roman*, 409 ff.; Christ–Schmid–Stählin ii. 2⁶, 810 ff.; M. Schnepf: cf. ad HELIODORUS; E. Mann, *Über den Sprachgebrauch des Xen. Ephes.* (Programm Kaiserslautern, 1896); O. Schissel von Fleschenberg, *Die Rahmenerzählung in den Ephesischen Geschichten des Xen. Ephes.* (1909); B. Lavagnini, *Studi sul romanzo greco* (1950), 145 ff.                    G. G.

**XERXES I** O.P. *Khshayārshan*, son of Darius and Atossa, king of Persia 486–465 B.C. He inherited from his father the task of punishing the Greeks for their participation in the Ionian revolt. Securing the co-operation of Carthage, and promises of support from several Greek States, he prepared a great fleet and army, bridged the Hellespont, and dug a canal through the Athos peninsula. In the spring of 480 his forces set out. At first they met with success; the fleet was victorious at Artemisium, the army forced Thermopylae, Attica was laid waste, and the Greeks forced back to their last line of defence, the Isthmus of Corinth. But at Salamis Themistocles with the Greek fleet won a victory which decided the future of Greece. His supplies from Asia cut off, Xerxes was forced to retreat; Mardonius, whom he left in command, was defeated at Plataea, and a final Persian failure at Mycale encouraged the defection of the Greeks of Asia Minor.

Of Xerxes' subsequent career little is known. In his reign the circumnavigation of Africa was attempted. After his defeats in Greece, Xerxes retired to his harem. He built extensively at Persepolis, Ecbatana, etc. But the Empire, though still vast in extent and resources, was weakened by court intrigues, in one of which he was murdered.

Beloch, *Gr. Gesch.* ii; G. B. Grundy, *The Great Persian War* (1901); A. T. Olmstead, *History of the Persian Empire* (U.S.A. 1948); A. R. Burn, *Persia and the Greeks* (1962). *See also* PERSIA, PERSIAN WARS.                    M. S. D.; R. N. F.

# Z

**ZALEUCUS**, the lawgiver of Italian Locri. As his laws are said to have been the first Greek codification, he probably lived *c.* 650 B.C. His legislation was notorious for its severity. The older tradition (4th c.) seems to have preserved some good material, e.g. his use of the *lex talionis* ('eye for eye') and prescription of exact penalties for each crime. Like other Greek lawgivers, he also issued sumptuary laws. Zaleucus was famous, too, as a conciliator of social factions; the constitution of Locri, however, remained extremely aristocratic. His laws were accepted by many cities of Italy and Sicily. The later tradition about him is mostly legendary (cf. *FGrH* 566, F 130 with Jacoby's comment).

Arist. *Pol.* 1274ᵃʼᵇ; Diod. 12, 19ᵇ. F. E. Adcock, *CHJ* 1927; M. Mühl, *Klio*, Beiheft xxii (1929).                    V. E.

**ZALMOXIS (Salmoxis)** (Ζάλμοξις, Σάλμοξις), the deity of the Getae (Hdt. 4. 94–6). He seems to have been a god of the dead, for the Getae are said to 'make immortal' a man every four years, by throwing him upon spear-points, after charging him with messages for the other world. Plato (*Chrm.* 156 d) speaks of certain 'physicians of Zalmoxis' and their doctrines; this seems his own invention. Other authors (*see* commentators *ad locc.*) add nothing but a conjecture of Mnaseas (in Photius, s.v. Ζάμολξις [*sic*] that he was the same as Kronos (q.v.).

Cf. A. D. Nock, *CR* 1926, 184 ff.                    H. J. R.

**ZAMA** was the name of one or more towns in North Africa. The view that a Zama lay at Sidi Abd el Djedidi, 31 miles north-west of Kairoʼuan, should probably be rejected (cf. L. Poinssot, *Rev. Africaine* 1928, 165 ff.). Further west lay Zama Maior and Zama Regia, unless these should be identified as one town. Modern Jama and Seba Biar are the most probable sites for one or both. Ksar Toual Zouameul or Zammel, 4½ miles east of Seba Biar, is now identified with Vicus Maracitanus, 'attributed' to Zama Regia, and not with Zama Regia itself (Déroche, *op. cit. infra*). The question must remain open until new epigraphic evidence is found. Zama Regia lay in the Numidian kingdom. It was besieged unsuccessfully by Metellus during the Jugurthine War (109 B.C.); later it was Juba's capital, and after capture by T. Sextius (41 B.C.) it was temporarily destroyed. It may have become a *municipium c.* 29 B.C.; it was a colony under Hadrian (Col. Ael. Hadr. Augusta Zama Regia). Zama is best known as the traditional site of Hannibal's defeat by Scipio Africanus in 202, an identification which rests on no better authority than Nepos. The battle was almost certainly not fought there, although Hannibal camped at Zama before advancing still further west to the actual battlefield which Polybius calls Margaron (otherwise unknown) and Livy Naraggara (Sidi Youssef); it probably lay between Naraggara and western Zama in a plain Draa-el-Metnan, south-west of Sicca Veneria (El Kef).

T. Rice Holmes, *The Roman Republic* iii (1923), 536 ff.; H. H. Scullard, *Scipio Africanus in the Second Punic War* (1930), 310; id. *Scipio Africanus: Soldier and Politician* (1970);;L. Déroche, *Mélanges d'arch.* 1948, 55 ff. For the *municipium*, M. Grant. *From Imperium to Auctoritas* (1946), 182; L. Teutsch, *Das röm, Städtewesen in Nordafrika* (1962), 187 ff. H. H. S.

**ZELA,** an ancient temple State of Pontus with a large and fertile territory, and a considerable population of hierodules attached to the land and service of Anaïtis and the 'Persian Deities'. Here Mithridates VI (q.v.) defeated Triarius in 67, and Caesar Pharnaces II (q.v.) in 47. Originally under priestly rule, it was one of Pompey's Pontic cities. Under Antony it became a temple State again, in the kingdom of Polemo I (q.v.), but when this was annexed in A.D. 64 it appears as a city again.

Strabo 11. 512; 12. 559. F. Cumont, *Studia Pontica* ii (1906), 188 ff; iii (1910), 233 ff; Jones, *Cities E. Rom. Prov.*, see index; Magie, *Rom. Rule Asia Min.* 183 and index. T. R. S. B.

**ZENO** (*Ζήνων*) (1) of Elea, pupil and friend of Parmenides (q.v.), was probably born *c.* 490 B.C. (Pl. *Prm.* 127 b). His most famous and perhaps only book was written in his youth and supported Parmenides' monism by drawing pairs of contradictory conclusions from the premisses of its opponents (Pl. *Prm.* 128 c), whence Aristotle (fr. 65) calls him the inventor of dialectic. Thus he argued that, if many things exist, they must each be (*a*) self-identical and one and therefore so small as to have no magnitude, yet nevertheless (*b*) infinitely large, since each, if it is not to be nothing, must have some magnitude and every magnitude is divisible into an infinite number of magnitudes (Simpl. *in Phys.* 139–41). Further arguments showed that any group of many things must be both limited and unlimited in number (fr. 3) and both like and unlike, one and many, at rest and in motion (Pl. *Phdr.* 261 d). To the last antinomy probably belong the four arguments for the impossibility of motion paraphrased by Aristotle, *Phys.* 6. 9 (the *Dichotomy*, the *Achilles*, the *Arrow*, and the *Stadium*).

Plato asserts that the 'many things' which Zeno's arguments aimed to prove unreal were physical objects (*ὁρώμενα Prm.* 130 a, 135 e). And in fact the exhaustiveness of the arguments shows that they were not designed to refute a special physical or metaphysical theory; they appear rather to be a systematic development of Parmenides' views about the foundations of the 'beliefs of mortals' and to seek to show that the units of which any plurality must consist cannot be so defined that they can be considered as genuine units.

Though polemical in intention, Zeno's arguments were influential in education (Pl. *Alc.* 1. 119 a, Plut. *Per.* 4) and probably also in the development of mathematical and physical views connected with the notions of unity, continuity, and infinity.

Diels, *Vorsokr.*¹¹ i. 247–58; Burnet, *EGP* 310ff.; W. D. Ross, *Aristotle's Physics* (1936), xi–xii, 71 ff., 479 f., 655 f.; H. D. P. Lee, *Zeno of Elea* (1936); H. Fränkel, 'Zeno of Elea's attacks on plurality', *AJPhil.* 1942, 1 ff., 193 ff. (revised in German in *Wege und Formen frühgriechischen Denkens* (1960)); G. E. L. Owen, 'Zeno and the Mathematicians', *Proc. Ar. Soc.* 1958, 199 ff. A. H. C.

**ZENO** (2) (335–263 B.C.), son of Mnaseas of Citium (Cyprus), probably of Phoenician race, founder of the Stoic school. He came to Athens in 313 and attended the lectures of Polemon, head of the Academy, and of the Megarian philosopher Diodorus *ὁ Κρόνος*, but was converted to Cynicism by Crates of Thebes. His earlier writings, especially his *πολιτεία*, are said to have been entirely Cynic in outlook. Later he turned to Socratic philosophy through study of the works of Antisthenes, and finally developed his own system. He taught in the Stoa Poikile, a public hall in Athens, from which the name of his school is derived, and soon acquired a large audience, though he tried to keep out the general public and wanted to teach real philosophers only. He became a friend of King Antigonus Gonatas and was invited to stay with him at his court at Pella, but declined and sent his disciple Persaeus instead.

Unlike most of the Socratics he created a complete philosophical system, consisting of logic and theory of knowledge (*λογικόν*), physics (*φυσικόν* and *θεολογικόν*), and ethics (*ἠθικόν*). In physics he admittedly followed Heraclitus, but was also strongly influenced by Aristotelian philosophy. In logic and theory of knowledge he was influenced by Antisthenes and Diodorus, the Megarian. His ethical doctrine gave great comfort to many during the troubled times of the successors of Alexander. According to this doctrine the only real good is virtue, the only real evil moral weakness. Everything else, including poverty, death, pain, is indifferent. Since nobody can deprive the wise man of his virtue he is always in possession of the only real good and therefore happy.

A. C. Pearson, *Fragments of Zeno and Cleanthes* (1891); von Arnim, *SVF* i. 3–72; Diog. Laert. 7. 1–160; M. Pohlenz, 'Zenon und Chrysipp', *Nachricht. Götting. Gesellsch.*, Fachgruppe i, N.F. id, no. 9; id. *Die Stoa*² (1948–55). K. VON F.

**ZENO** (3) of Tarsus, Stoic, successor of Chrysippus as head of the school in 204 B.C. He left behind him few books but many disciples.

Testimonia in von Arnim, *SVF* iii. 209. See Zeller, *Phil. d. Griechen* iii. 1⁴. 45 f.

**ZENO** (4) of Rhodes (early 2nd c. B.C.), wrote a history of Rhodes from the beginnings to his own times, which Polybius used (with Antisthenes), although he criticized his patriotic exaggeration (Polyb. 16. 14); his tradition may also appear in Diodorus.

*FGrH* iii. 523.

**ZENO** (5) of Sidon (b. *c.* 150 B.C.), Epicurean, pupil of Apollodorus and probably head of the school between him and Phaedrus. Cicero heard him lecture in Athens in 79–78. Philodemus' *Περὶ παρρησίας* was a selection from Zeno, and his *Περὶ σημείων* borrows lectures by him. He is probably the source of part of Cic. *Nat. D.* 1.

Zeller, *Phil. d. Griechen* iii. 1⁴. 384–6. W. D. R.

**ZENO** (6) of Sidon, Stoic, pupil of Diodorus Cronus (Diog. Laert. 38. 16).

Zeller, *Phil. d. Griechen* iii. 1⁴. 40.

**ZENOBIA (Septimia),** or in Aramaic *Bat Zabbai*, the second wife of Odaenathus (q.v.). She was perhaps responsible for the murder of her husband and his son by a previous marriage; at any rate she thereupon secured the power for herself in the name of her infant son Vaballathus (q.v.). Gallienus sent Heraclianus against her, but he was defeated, and Zenobia, having secured Syria and devastated Bostra (q.v.), in A.D. 269 conquered Egypt, and next year overran Asia Minor except Bithynia. Aurelian at first acquiesced, granting to Vaballathus the same position as his father, but when in 271 Zenobia, not content with this partial recognition, proclaimed her son Augustus, he marched against her. His general Probus was killed while attempting to conquer Egypt, but he himself reoccupied Asia Minor with little resistance, defeated Zabdas, Zenobia's general, at Antioch and again at Emesa, and finally captured Palmyra and the queen herself and her sons. Having been exhibited in Aurelian's triumph she was granted a pension and a villa at Tibur. Zenobia is highly praised for her beauty, intelligence, and virtue, but was evidently a ruthless woman. She sacrificed to her personal ambition the fortune of her native city, which Odaenathus had by his loyalty to the Empire preserved. *See also* AURELIANUS.

J. G. Février, *Histoire de Palmyre* (1931), 103 ff.    A. H. M. J.

**ZENODORUS,** author, between 200 B.C. and A.D. 90, of a treatise Περὶ ἰσομέτρων σχημάτων. Several propositions from it are preserved in the commentary of Theon of Alexandria on book 1 of Ptolemy's *Syntaxis*. He was followed closely in his treatment of the subject by Pappus, whose treatment is, however, more complete. His style is not unlike that of Euclid and Archimedes.    W. D. R.

**ZENODOTUS** of Ephesus (b. *c.* 325 B.C.), pupil of Philetas, became the first head of the Library at Alexandria (*c.* 284) and undertook the classification of the Greek epic and lyric poets, some of whom he edited.

WORKS

(1) Lexicography: *Homeric Glossary* (Γλῶσσαι), which often relied on guesswork to give the meaning of difficult words, but opened the way for the scholarly study of language; Λέξεις ἐθνικαί, a compilation of foreign expressions occurring in literary texts. (2) Editions (διορθώσεις). His recension of the *Iliad* and *Odyssey*, in which for the first time the poems were divided into twenty-four books, represented the first scientific attempt to get back to the original Homeric text by the collation of several MSS. He marked lines of the genuineness of which he felt doubt with an *obelus* (*see* SCHOLARSHIP, GREEK, § 3), and altered the text by the transposition or telescoping of verses, by the introduction of new readings, and sometimes even by the insertion of new lines. But the extremely subjective nature of his criteria—he laid great emphasis on τὸ πρέπον—made him sometimes rash in emendation. He produced also recensions of Hesiod, *Theog.*, Anacreon, Pindar (*POxy.* v. 841).

H. Düntzer, *De Zenodoti studiis Homericis* (1848); K. Lehrs, *De Aristarchi studiis Homericis*[3] (1882); A. Römer, *Über die Homerrezension des Zenodot* (1886); D. B. Monro, *Homer's Odyssey*, Appendix (1901); G. M. Bolling, *External Evidence for Interpolation in Homer* (1925); M. van der Valk, *Researches on the Text and Scholia of the Iliad* ii (1964), 1 ff.    J. F. L.; R. B.

**ZEPHYRUS,** god of the West Wind, sometimes said to be husband of Iris (rainy wind and rainbow), as Alcaeus, fr. 8 Diehl; a subordinate figure in a few legends, as that of Hyacinthus (q.v.). His parents are Eos and Astraeus (Hes. *Theog.* 379). Cf. WIND-GODS.

**ZEUGITAI** (ζευγῖται), at Athens, before Solon a name for the citizens of moderate substance, roughly corresponding with the 'farmers' (*see* EUPATRIDAI) and Demiourgoi (q.v.) and so called either from the yoke of oxen (ζεῦγος) normally possessed by the former, or as serving in the army in close ranks (cf. Plut. *Pel.* 23), i.e. as hoplites (q.v.). Solon used the name for his third census-class, of men with an estimated annual income of between 300 and 200 *medimnoi* of corn, or the equivalent in other produce or money. In effect, the majority of the farmers and craftsmen of Attica fell into this class and it provided the bulk of the city's force of hoplites, each man furnishing his own arms. Under Solon's constitution the *zeugitai* enjoyed full citizen rights, except that

they were admitted to the minor magistracies only. From the time of Cleisthenes they could be elected as *strategoi* (q.v.), and from 457/6 were eligible for appointment as *archontes* (q.v.).    A. W. G.; T. J. C.

**ZEUGITANA.** The name, of unknown origin, sometimes applied to the northern part of the province of Africa, centred on Carthage. It is used by Pliny (*HN* 5. 23), but then seems to have gone out of use, to reappear in the fourth century when it was occasionally used of Africa (Proconsularis), now much smaller in area after the division of the old province of Africa by Diocletian.    B. H. W.

**ZEUGMA** (modern *Bâlkîs*, opposite *Birecik*), in Syria on the right bank of the Euphrates at its chief crossing, about 70 miles below Samosata. Twin colonies Seleuceia (right bank) and Apamea (left bank) were founded by Seleucus I at this point (Pliny, *HN* 5. 86), which came to be known by the generic name Zeugma ('junction'); it superseded an earlier Zeugma near Thapsacus. As a frontier post and a meeting-place of trade-routes from East and West across the Parthian Empire, it became extremely prosperous. Justinian fortified it against the Sassanids, but in 639 it fell to the Arabs.

M. S. D.; E. W. G.

**ZEUS** is the only Greek god whose Indo-European origin can be proved with certainty. He is found as 'Father', which attribute is very common in Greek too, among the Romans, Indians, and Illyrians (Jupiter, Dyaus pita, Deipatyros); the name of the German god Ziu (cf. Tuesday) is akin. The word signifies 'sky', and according to a general opinion the bright sky; yet this is of no importance to primitive man, and the cults prove that Zeus is the weather-god, i.e. the sky as the sphere of atmospheric phenomena, thunder, rain, etc. Mountain peaks give weather signs, and Zeus is enthroned on them; Olympus is a pre-Greek word signifying 'mountain'; and among other peoples also the thunder-god became the supreme god. The epithet 'Father' is generally understood according to the Homeric phrase 'Father of gods and men'. But Zeus created neither gods nor men and it is unbelievable that in Indo-European times a nobility traced its descent from Zeus—this is probably due to the heroic Mycenaean age; again, the divine children of Zeus, Athena, Artemis, Apollo, Ares, Dionysus, include pre-Greek and immigrant gods. Consequently 'Father' is to be taken in the sense of *pater familias*, protector and ruler of the family. This implies a moral notion, the maintenance of customary laws; and these, e.g. the respect for suppliants and guest-friends (Zeus Hikesios, Xenios), were always bound up with Zeus. This explains why Zeus was the god of the courtyard and the household (Zeus Herkeios, Ktesios). The Greek State being founded on the family, Zeus was, as Homer shows, the protector of the king and his rights. The Mycenaean age formed the supreme god and the State of the gods after the model of its mighty kings and knights. Zeus is surrounded by recalcitrant vassals who sometimes show him respect, sometimes mock him. He rules according to power rather than according to righteousness, and has innumerable loves and children.

Homer impressed this Zeus upon the Greek mind. In the historical age, although kingship was abolished, Zeus was not dethroned. Zeus became the highest civic god, often with the epithet Polieus and together with Athena Polias, the old Minoan-Mycenaean palace goddess and protectress of the king. As protector of political freedom he was called Soter, Eleutherios, and festivals were instituted in his honour. He had little to do with other concerns of the people—agriculture, war, crafts, etc. It was never forgotten that Zeus was the protector of law and morals. Hesiod invokes him as such in his cry for justice and places Dike at his side. The loftiest conception of Zeus is found in Aeschylus, who enhances his righteousness and overwhelming power. In the Hellenistic age his name was very freely given to the chief deity of any non-Greek tribe or region (the most famous precursor in classical times being Zeus Ammon in Libya). Cosmological ideas were not in any large measure attached to Zeus; Stoic philosophy, however, identified him with its highest principle, fire, which at the same time is the reason which pervades and animates the universe. This idea is expressed very beautifully in the hymn by Cleanthes (q.v.).

Certain myths are important, among them the most peculiar Cretan myth of the birth of Zeus, according to which the child was hidden in a cave in order that Kronos might not swallow it up, and nourished by animals, and the Curetes danced around it. The Cretans told also that Zeus was dead and buried. This is certainly a Minoan conception, the spirit of vegetation, as born and dying annually. This Cretan deity, the *kouros*, who may be the consort of the great vegetation-goddess, was identified with the Greek supreme god. Zeus dethroned Kronos and together with the Olympian gods fought against the Titans and imprisoned them. The Titans are believed to be pre-Greek gods but the evidence is slight. The myth is perhaps modelled on the cosmological myth according to which Kronos dethroned his father Uranus. These myths are mixed up with the folktale motives.

Zeus in art is a kingly, bearded figure, in the archaic period robed, later sometimes naked. Pheidias' gold and ivory enthroned colossus at Olympia was perhaps the most celebrated of all statues in antiquity and set the type for future generations. Pausanias (1. 17. 1) saw in the Heraeum at Olympia an early image of Zeus standing, wearing a helmet; and it is likely that the numerous small bronzes of helmeted warriors from the eighth and seventh centuries found at Olympia represent the god (see E. Kunze, *Olympia Bericht* iv (1950), 123 ff.).

Cook, *Zeus*; M. P. Nilsson, *ARW* 1938, 156 ff.; *GGR* i². 383 ff. and 510 ff. (the Titans). M. P. N.; J. H. C.; C. M. R.

**ZEUXIS,** painter, of Heraclea in Lucania, pupil of Neseus of Thasos or Damophilus of Himera. Pliny dates him 397 B.C., and rejects 424. Quintilian dates both him and Parrhasius in the time of the Peloponnesian War. In Plato's *Protagoras* (dramatic date about 430) he is young and a newcomer in Athens. His rose-wreathed Eros is mentioned in Ar. *Ach.* 991–2 (425). He painted Alcmena for Acragas before 406, and Archelaus' palace between 413 and 399. He 'entered the door opened by Apollodorus and stole his art'; he added the use of highlights to shading, and Lucian praises in the Centaur family (an instance of the unusual subjects which Zeuxis preferred) the subtle gradation of colour from the human to the animal body of the female Centaur; his grapes (possibly on the scenery for satyr-plays) were said to have deceived the birds. His figures lacked the ἦθος of Polygnotus, although his Penelope was morality itself, and his Helen, for Croton, an ideal picture compiled from several models; πάθος rather than ἦθος distinguished the Autoboreas with Titan look and wild hair, and the Menelaus drenched in tears. He also painted monochromes on white, and *figlina opera* (clay plaques).

Overbeck, 1077, 1121, 1647–91; Pfuhl, 739; O. Brendel, *JDAI* 1932, 191; Rumpf, *Malerei u. Zeichn.* 126. T. B. L. W.

**ZOÏLUS** (Ζωΐλος) of Amphipolis (4th c. B.C.), the cynic philosopher, pupil of Polycrates and teacher of Anaximenes of Lampsacus; is described by the *Suda* as ῥήτωρ καὶ φιλόσοφος, by Aelian, *VH* 11. 10, as κύων ῥητορικός and ψογερός. He was notorious for the bitterness of his

attacks on Isocrates, Plato, and especially Homer. He probably visited Alexandria when the Library and Museum were being established.

WORKS

(1) *Against Isocrates.* (2) *Against Plato*, favourably mentioned by Dion. Hal. *Pomp.* 1. (3) *Against Homer* (Καθ' Ὁμήρου or Κατὰ τῆς Ὁμήρου ποιήσεως or perhaps Ὁμηρομάστιξ, which became the author's nickname). This work was chiefly devoted to severe, though often captious, criticism of the poet's invention, of the credibility of incidents (e.g. *Il.* 23. 100), and of the characters (e.g. *Il.* 1. 50). Aristotle's lost Ἀπορήματα Ὁμηρικά was a reply to Zoïlus and his followers. (4) *Censure of Homer* (Ψόγος Ὁμήρου), probably a declamation. (5) *Panegyric on the People of Tenedos.* (6) *On Figures*, a technical rhetorical treatise; his definition σχῆμά ἐστιν ἕτερον μὲν προσποιεῖσθαι ἕτερον δὲ λέγειν is criticized by Quintilian (9. 1. 14). He was the first to use σχῆμα in this technical sense. (7) *On Amphipolis.* (8) A history of Greece from the Theogony to the death of Philip of Macedon.

*FGrH* ii. A, 71; U. Friedländer, *De Zoilo aliisque Homeri obtrectatoribus* (1895). J. F. L.; R. B.

**ZONARAS,** JOHANNES, Byzantine historian and canonist of the twelfth century. A commander of the body-guard and imperial secretary, he retired to monastic life at Hagia Glykeria (isle of Niandro) where he devoted himself to writing. He composed an authoritative commentary to Byzantine Canon Law, commentaries on the poems of Gregory of Nazianzus and on the terminology of religious poetry—and probably the various other exegetic books and lives of saints which go under his name; he is also the author of at least one religious poem. As a historian he wrote an *epitome of histories* which in modern editions is divided into eighteen books: it is a universal history to A.D. 1118 and was composed before 1143 under John II Comnenus. Zonaras never claimed to be more than a compiler and complained gracefully about the lack of books in his little island. For Greek history he mainly used Herodotus, Xenophon, Plutarch, and Arrian. For Roman history to the destruction of Carthage he excerpted Plutarch and the first twenty-one books of Dio Cassius, for which he is our only important source. He was compelled to omit the history of the late Roman Republic because he did not have the relevant books of Dio (he only gives some excerpts from Plutarch's *Pompey* and *Caesar*), but was able to use Dio's books 44–68 and is, together with Xiphilinus our main source for the reconstruction of Dio's books 61–8. For the period after Domitian he followed Xiphilinus instead of the original Dio. He added information from other sources (e.g. Eusebius). Petrus Patricius was his chief source for the period between Severus Alexander and Constantine. The rest derives from various chronicles, not all of which have been identified. Zonaras is especially important as a source for the period A.D. 450–550. His excerpts are faithful in content, but stylistically independent. See DIO (2) CASSIUS.

His works collected in Migne, *PG* xxxviii, cxxxiv–cxxxvii. CRITICAL EDITIONS OF THE HISTORIES. M. Pinder-Th. Büttner-Wobst (1841–97); L. Dindorf (1868–75). ON SOURCES. Th. Büttner-Wobst, *Commentationes Fleckeisenianae* (1890), 123 ff.; V. Ph. Boissevain, *Hermes* 1891, 440 ff.; F. Millar, *A Study of Cassius Dio* (1964), 2 ff., 195 ff. IN GENERAL. K. Krumbacher, *Gesch. Byz. Lit.²* (1897), 370 ff.; Ph. Meyer, *Reallex. Protest. Theol. Kirche* 21 (1908), 715; E. Amann, *Dict. Théol. Cath.* 15 (1950), 3705; G. Moravcsik, *Byzantinoturcica* i² (1958), 344 ff. A. M.

**ZONAS** of Sardis (fl. 80 B.C.) was a distinguished orator, and left a few poetic epigrams in the Greek Anthology. The finest is a poignant epitaph asking Charon to help the little dead boy who cannot walk very well in his first sandals (*Anth. Pal.* 7. 365); his pastoral pieces in the manner of Anyte (q.v.) are charming too, e.g. *Anth. Pal.* 9. 226 and 312. His family name was Diodorus, and some epigrams appearing in the Anthology under that name may be his.                    G. H.

**ZOOLOGY.** Excellent early vase-paintings of animals are scattered over the Greek world with special schools in Cyprus, Boeotia, Chalcis, etc. Marine creatures are particularly well rendered. The name for a painter, *zōgraphos*, suggests attention to animal forms. Much accurate observation is displayed on coins and mosaics, both Greek and Imperial, and on some of them the actual species of small marine invertebrates can be easily recognized.

2. With some effort a classificatory system may be read into the arrangements of animals by habit in *On diet* of the Hippocratic Collection. More scientific are various fragments of the Sicilian school on the structure of animals (*see* ANATOMY AND PHYSIOLOGY, §2). In the true scientific tradition is a work of the Hippocratic Collection (artificially divided under titles *On Generation, On the Nature of the Embryo*, and *On Diseases*, book 4) of about 380 B.C. It sets forth in some detail a doctrine of pangenesis astonishingly like that of Darwin (*Animals and Plants under Domestication*, 1868). To explain heredity it supposes that vessels reach the seed carrying samples from all parts of the body. It contains the first account of a controlled biological experiment. 'Take 20 eggs and let them be incubated by hens. Each day, from the second to that of hatching, remove an egg, break it, and examine it. You will find that the nature of the bird can be likened to that of man. The membranes proceed from the umbilical cord, and all that I have said on the subject of the infant you will find in the bird's egg, in which you will be surprised to find an umbilical cord.'

3. With almost the sole exception of this able work, ancient zoology begins and ends with Aristotle. Among his positive contributions are:

(a) Records of the life, breeding, habits, and structure of about 540 species of animals.

(b) Investigations of the developing chick, which has ever since been the classical embryological subject.

(c) Accounts of the habits and development of octopuses and squids, in some cases surpassed only in quite modern times.

(d) Anatomical accounts of the four-chambered stomach of ruminants, of the complex relations of the ducts, vessels, and organs in the mammalian generative system, and of the mammalian character of porpoises, dolphins, and whales, all unsurpassed until the seventeenth century.

(e) Accounts of exceptional modes of development of fish, among them of a dog-fish (*Mustelus laevis*) the young of which is linked to the womb by a navel cord and placenta much as in a mammal. Nothing has contributed more to Aristotle's modern scientific reputation than the rediscovery of this phenomenon a century ago.

(f) Observations on paternal care in fish, verified only in the last century by Louis Agassiz, who named the fish concerned *Parasilurus Aristotelis*; and on the hectocotylization of one of the tentacles in the octopus.

(g) Stress on the heart and vascular system on embryological grounds. He is often quoted as calling the heart 'the first to live and last to die'. The idea is in his works but the phrase is not.

(h) A permanent addition to the technique of scientific instruction was his introduction of diagrams to explain anatomical relations. Some of his diagrams can be restored from his descriptions.

4. Aristotle seems not to have been interested in taxonomy, and there is no attempt in his work to produce a taxonomic scheme. His main concern is to ascertain the causes of the observed differences between animals: the *Historia animalium* is a collection of materials for this purpose, and his own title for the treatise known as the *Parts of Animals* is 'the Causes of the Parts of Animals'. (It should be noted that although he attaches great importance to morphological differences, drawing attention to differences which are merely of degree—of 'the more and less'—and wider differences 'by analogy', these are not the only differences which he records, and his survey includes differences in methods of reproduction, of locomotion, diet, disposition, habitat, and manner of life generally.) He does, however, for practical purposes of exposition, make use of the general division into blooded (i.e. red-blooded) and bloodless animals; and under these two headings we find the following 'main groups': (1) under blooded animals, Viviparous quadrupeds, Oviparous quadrupeds, Cetacea, Birds, and Fishes; (2) under bloodless animals, the four groups Crustacea, Cephalopods, Insects, and Testacea. These groupings are, however, used for convenience of treatment, and the fundamental principle of degrees of heat (see §7 below) cuts across them. It is also obvious that some animals, such as man and the serpents, are not catered for by these groupings. Aristotle also draws attention to the continuous gradation of things in nature, from lifeless objects upwards: they can be arranged in a sort of ladder, the *scala naturae* discussed by naturalists until the mid nineteenth century. In the eighth book of the *Historia animalium* he writes as follows: 'Nature gradually advances from things that are without soul (life) to the animals (living things) in such a way that the continuity prevents us from seeing where the boundary comes and from determining to which side of it an intermediate example belongs. First after the lifeless things stands the tribe of plants; and of these one kind of plant differs from another in that it appears to possess a greater share of life: the whole tribe of plants, when compared with other objects, seems almost to be endued with soul (life), yet when compared with the tribe of animals it appears to be without soul (life). The advance from plants to animals is continuous, as I have said. Thus, in the sea there are creatures of which one would be at a loss to say whether they are animals or plants . . .' (*HA* 588ᵇ4 ff.).

5. It is sometimes said that Aristotle's view of reproduction is that the material part of the embryo is contributed by the female parent, and the 'form' (which in a living creature is the 'soul', the principle of life) by the male parent. There are times when Aristotle does in fact express himself in these terms, but a more precise statement of his view is that the male contributes the *sentient faculty* of 'soul': the possession of this faculty is the distinctive feature of an animal as contrasted with a plant. The material contributed by the female is also endowed with 'soul', but only with the lower faculties of it. It is thus true to say that the male contributes no material part to the embryo; but some material must pass from the male to the female, and this material is the 'connate pneuma' (σύμφυτον πνεῦμα) contained in the semen. The function of the connate pneuma is to act as the vehicle of the 'movements' proper to the species or 'form' concerned (in Greek εἶδος can mean both species and 'form'); and this function of transmitting the 'form' (by means of the appropriate 'movements') to the new embryo is really only an extension of its normal function of maintaining the 'form' in the already existing fully grown animal. Aristotle describes the connate pneuma as the chief of the 'instruments' used by Nature, comparing it with the instruments of the smith, which similarly

convey to the material on which he is working the 'movements' proper to the 'form' of the article into which he intends to fashion the material. In the body, the connate pneuma is carried in the blood, which is charged with it by the heart, the seat of 'soul' or the vital principle, and this pneumatization of the blood is effected by the heat resident in the heart. The semen, being blood which has undergone a further stage of 'concoction' by heat, is thus, like the blood, capable of acting as the vehicle of the 'movements' proper to 'soul', and of reproducing them in the embryonic material supplied by the female parent. The difference between semen and catamenia (which Aristotle identified with the embryonic material) is due to the fact that the female, being less 'hot' than the male, is unable to carry the concoction of this portion of the blood to the stage when it acquires the movements proper to sentient soul.

According to Aristotle, semen is one of the 'useful residues'; others include milk, catamenia, and marrow: Nature employs for useful purposes the blood which is surplus to the maintenance requirements of the body.

**6.** In view of what has been said it is not surprising that Aristotle explicitly rejected any theory of pangenesis such as had been propounded by some of his predecessors. None of the parts of the body is present as such in the embryo when it is first constituted: they are fashioned by the 'movements' supplied by the male parent. (But see § 7 below.) These 'movements' are complex, and include those proper not only to 'animal' and to the species concerned, but also to the sex and to the individual, and even to grandparents and more remote ancestors. The final determination of the sex of the embryo and of its resemblance or lack of resemblance to parents or ancestors is the result of a contest between the 'movements' and the material upon which they are operating: if the movement of the male 'departs from type' it changes over to the female; if the immediate movements 'relapse' they fall back into those of grandparents or more remote ancestors. This principle Aristotle applies not only to general resemblance of the body as a whole, but also to resemblance of individual parts of it. When the 'movements' become unduly confused, no family resemblance can be traced in the offspring; when the 'movement' cannot master the embryonic material, the result is a monstrosity—merely 'an animal'.

These matters are discussed by Aristotle at considerable length and in great detail; his discussion on this subject is one of the most remarkable in the whole of his zoological works. With his notion of the *scala naturae* and his theory of the 'relapsing' of the 'movements,' it might perhaps have been expected that the stage was set for Aristotle to go on to propound a theory of evolution. He does not, however, go back to what has been stated above. Perhaps one reason which prevented him from doing so was his view of the place of animals in the whole scheme of the universe. The perpetual succession of generations was for him a process in which the sublunary or lower part of the cosmos approached as closely as was possible for it to the unchanging individual eternity of the things in the upper cosmos; in the lower cosmos it is the 'forms' (species) only, not the individuals, which are eternal, and it would no doubt have seemed a contradiction of the whole scheme of the universe to suggest that these 'forms' were liable to change.

**7.** The importance of heat (or, more precisely, hot substance) in Aristotle's theory of living things cannot be overestimated. Hot substance is in fact one of the four fundamental constituents of the physical universe recognized by him, and the connate pneuma itself, the essential intermediary between 'form' and 'matter', is a special kind of hot substance. If it were necessary to

say that there is any typically Aristotelian classification of animals, it would have to be that which he himself indicates, based on the principle of degrees of heat. For him, the 'most perfect' animals are those which are the hottest: they produce 'perfect' offspring because they are able to carry the 'concoction' of the embryo to the point when it is identical in form (though not of course in size) with the parent. Colder animals can produce only eggs; even colder ones only larvae. The coldest animals reproduce in a manner comparable to that of plants. It has already been noted that the difference between the sexes is accounted for by a difference of heat. Heat, however, is not merely an enabling or concomitant factor: it is an active one, and in this regard cold is associated with it. It is true that the 'movements' proper to 'form', which are conveyed to the embryonic material, are responsible for fashioning the embryo into an animal of the required species; but the lower stages of the work can be left to the 'movements' of the hot and the cold, which are able of themselves to fashion the uniform parts of the body, such as flesh, bone, hair, and sinew, though they cannot deal with the next stage, the formation of the non-uniform parts such as head, hand, and foot. The doctrine of spontaneous generation has a somewhat similar basis. Animals and plants are formed in earth and fluid because there is water in the earth, and there is pneuma in water, and there is 'soul-heat' (θερμότης ψυχική) in all pneuma; indeed, Aristotle can go so far as to say that in the case of spontaneous generation of natural things the matter can be set in movement *by itself*: it can supply itself with the same movement as that which the semen normally would supply.

The passive ingredients upon which the active ones, especially the hot, operate are the solid (dry) and the fluid (moist), particularly the latter, which is the best suited for supporting life (ζωτικόν). It is the relationship between these four factors, especially between the hot and the fluid, which determines much of the behaviour and the observable features of animals, and of which these are symptoms. In this connexion Aristotle pays special attention to the habitat, and the places of feeding and breeding of animals: e.g. some spend all their time in the water, others on land, while others are amphibious. Again, some animals are cooled by taking in air, others by taking in water, others are cooled sufficiently by their environment, and so forth. These phenomena, which exhibit many different combinations, are to be explained by the 'blend' (κρᾶσις) of the animals' physical composition, and especially by the balance between the hot and the fluid. The notion of 'blend' is an important one in Greek thought, and it is in fact a special case of συμμετρία, right proportion, proper balance of ingredients of all kinds; a notion applied elsewhere by Aristotle and found also in other writers. Like one of the Hippocratic authors (in *Regimen*), Aristotle holds that an animal's physical 'blend' determines not only its physical health but also its disposition (whence our 'temperament') and its sensitivity and intelligence. The excellence of man's physical 'blend' is shown by the fact that he is the most intelligent of the animals. After Aristotle there is no scientific observation of a zoological character. (However, *see* ANATOMY AND PHYSIOLOGY, §§ 12, 18.)

**8.** The largest collections of animal stories are those of Pliny and Aelian. Much accurate nature-knowledge can be gleaned from general literature, especially Latin. Roman country gentlemen had their game preserves and aviaries, of which Varro gives details (*Rust.* 3. 49. 13). A mural in the Villa Livia shows a bird-sanctuary. Under the Empire many strange beasts were brought to Rome for the circus. Lions, tigers, elephants both African and Indian, rhinoceroses, bears, bisons, boars, leopards, panthers, hyenas, and crocodiles were in the imperial menageries. These sometimes contained prodigious numbers; Trajan owned 11,000 beasts, Augustus 420 tigers, Nero 400 bears, and Gordian I 300 ostriches. Curiosity accounted for the presence of serpents, camels, hippopotamuses, antelopes, zebras, and giraffes. The first giraffe came to Europe for Commodus about 190, and Gordian I (237) is said to have had 100 of them.

The Hippocratic work *On Generation* is given in the edition of E. Littré, vol. iii (1851). Practically all the zoological work of Aristotle is in his three works *Historia animalium, De partibus animalium, De generatione animalium* (*see* ARISTOTLE). Discussion with bibliography in Charles Singer, *Studies in the History and Method of Science* ii (1921), and *Greek Biology and Greek Medicine* (1922). See also the introductions and appendixes in the Loeb editions of *De gen. an.* and *Hist. an.*; and D. M. Balme, 'γένος and εἶδος in Aristotle's biology', *CQ* 1962, 81 ff., and id. 'Aristotle's Use of Differentiae in Zoology' in *Aristote et les problèmes de méthode* (Symposium Aristotelicum, 1962). O. Keller, *Die antike Tierwelt* (1909). Representation of animals in ancient art: Imhof-Blumer and O. Keller, *Tier -und pflanzenbilder auf Münzen und Gemmes des klassischen Altertums* (1889); J. Morin, *Dessins des animaux en Grèce* (1911). Menageries in great detail by G. Loisel, *Histoire des ménageries* (3 vols., 1912); G. Jennison, *Animals for Show and Pleasure in Ancient Rome* (1937).

C. S.; A. L. P.

**ZOPYRUS,** writer on physiognomy, known from his judgement on Socrates' appearance.

See Förster, *Scriptores Physiognomonici* i, prol. vii ff.

**ZOROASTER** (Ζωροάστρης), the best-known form of the name of Zarathuštra; for others see Bidez–Cumont i. 36 ff. The Greeks had heard of him as early as the fifth century B.C. (Xanthus of Lydia in Diog. Laert. proem, 2), and mentions of him are common in the Hellenistic period. Apart from an aberrant tradition, due perhaps to Ctesias (q.v.), which made him a king of Bactria conquered by Ninus and Semiramis (Bidez–Cumont ii. 41 ff.), a fairly correct idea of his teachings was current in philosophic circles from about the time of Plato, the intermediary being probably Eudoxus of Cnidos. Legendary details of all sorts accumulated about him, some doubtless of oriental origin, and he was credited with the authorship of an immense number of works (2,000,000 lines or some 10,000,000 words, Hermippus in Pliny, *HN* 30. 4, were ascribed to him), dealing with theology, natural science, astrology, magic, etc., much of their contents being not only spurious but also quite foreign to his real interests and teachings.

J. Bidez and F. Cumont, *Les Mages hellénisés* (1938); J. Duchesne-Guillemin, *The Western Response to Zoroaster* (1958).

H. J. R.; J. D.-G.

**ZOSIMUS,** a Greek historian. Little is known of his life except that he had been *advocatus fisci* and obtained the dignity of *comes.* His identification either with the sophist Zosimus of Ascalon or with the sophist Zosimus of Gaza is doubtful. He wrote a history (*Historia nova*) of the Roman Empire from Augustus to A.D. 410. He must have completed it after A.D. 498, as he mentions the abolition of the *auri lustralis collatio* (2. 38), but before the composition of the chronicle of Eustathius of Epiphania in which he is quoted (first decades of the 6th c.). Book 1 summarizes the history of the first three centuries of the Empire (the section on Diocletian is lost), in books 2–4 Zosimus gives a more precise account of the fourth century and particularly of the years 395–410, for which he is our most important source. He uses Eunapius and Olympiodorus (qq.v.) extensively and his excursus on secular games (2. 1–6) derives from Phlegon (q.v.). He imitates Polybius. His interpretation of events is determined by his paganism. He sees the decadence of the Empire as a consequence of the rejection of paganism. He is naturally hostile to Constantine and Theodosius I and favourable to Julian. His attitude towards Stilicho is ambivalent.

Best edition by L. Mendelssohn (1887) with important introd. on sources. Cf. Christ–Schmid–Stählin, ii. 2. 1037; E. Stein, *Hist. Bas-Empire* ii (1949), 707 ff.; S. Mazzarino, *La fine del mondo antico* (1959), 61 ff.; G. Moravcsik, *Byzantinoturcica* i² (1958), 577 ff. A. Cameron, *Philologus*, 1969, 106 ff.

A. M.

# APPENDIX
# GENERAL BIBLIOGRAPHY

(*Note*. The works here listed are those currently in use in 1969. For special bibliographies see the article concerned.)

A. General bibliographies covering a period.

1. W. Engelmann, *Bibliotheca scriptorum classicorum*, 8th ed. by E. Preuss, 2 vols. (Leipzig, 1880–2), publications between 1700 and 1878.

2. R. Klussmann, *Bibliotheca scriptorum classicorum*, 2 vols. (Leipzig, 1900–13), publications between 1878 and 1896.

3. S. Lambrino, *Bibliographie de l'antiquité classique 1898–1914*, Tome I, Auteurs et textes (1951). Tome II in preparation.

4. J. Marouzeau, *Dix années de bibliographie classique. Bibliographie critique et analytique de l'antiquité gréco-latine*, 2 vols. (1927–8), publications between 1914 and 1924.

5. D. Rounds, *Articles on antiquity in 'Festschriften': an index* (Cambridge, Mass., 1962).

B. General bibliographies, annual.

1. *Bibliotheca philologica classica*, 65 vols., 1873–1941 (listing publications until 1938). This was published as an appendix to *Bursians Jahresberichte* (see C. 1 below) and gives titles of books and articles only.

2. *L'Année philologique. Bibliographie critique et analytique de l'antiquité gréco-latine* (1927– . In progress). This gives titles of books and titles and abstracts of articles, from 1924 on.

C. Critical surveys of work in the main fields in systematic order.

1. *Jahresberichte über die Fortschritte der klassischen Altertumswissenschaft*, begründet von Conrad Bursian (usually referred to as *Bursians Jahresberichte*, or merely *Bursian*), 285 vols., Berlin, 1873–98, Leipzig, 1898–1945 (published 1956). Successive general editors were C. Bursian, Iwan Müller, W. Kroll, K. Münscher, and A. Thierfelder. This gave at regular intervals critical, and in principle exhaustive, surveys of recent work in all the main fields of classical study. There is a 'Generalregister' to volumes i–lxxxvii, published in 1897 without volume number. Subsequently indexes to reports appeared in vol. cxxxviii (1908), vol. clxvi (1914), and vol. cci (1925). From 1938 to 1945 an annual index to reports was published. Two annual appendices were published with Bursian:
   (*a*) *Bibliotheca philologica classica* (B. 1 above)
   (*b*) *Biographisches Jahrbuch*, containing obituaries of classical scholars, which ceased publication in 1943.

2. *Lustrum. Internationale Forschungsberichte aus dem Bereich des klassischen Altertums*, herausgegeben von H. J. Mette und A. Thierfelder (Göttingen, 1956– . In progress). This publishes periodical reports similar to those of *Bursian*, written by scholars from different countries; the languages used are German, French, and English.

3. *Year's Work in Classical Studies*, 34 vols. (1906–47). This gave selective annual surveys arranged by subject-matter.

4. *Fifty Years of Classical Scholarship*, edited by M. Platnauer (2nd edition, 1968). Critical and selective surveys by subject-matter of work done in the first half of the present century.

D. General bibliographies of works in particular languages, or published in particular countries.

1. I. Borzsák, *A magyar klasszika-filológiai irodalom bibliográfiája 1926–50* (*Bibliographia philologiae classicae in Hungaria*) (Budapest, 1952).

2. G. Pianko, *Filologia klasyczna w Polsce. Bibliografia za lata 1945–1949* (Warsaw, 1952); *Bibliografia za lata 1950–1954* (Warsaw, 1958).

3. K. Svoboda, *Bibliografie českých a slovenských prací o antice za léta 1901–50* (Prague, 1961); L. Vidman, Bibliografie řeckých a latinských studií v Československu za léta 1951–1960 (Prague, 1966).

4. A. Voronkov, *Drevnjaja Gretsija i drevnij Rim. Bibliograficheskij ukazatel' izdanij, vyshedshikh v SSSR (1895–1959 gg)* (Moscow, 1961).

5. L. S. Thompson, *A Bibliography of American Doctoral Dissertations in Classical Studies and Related Fields* (1968).

## E. Special bibliographies of particular fields.

1. N. I. Herescu, *Bibliographie de la littérature latine* (1943). Useful, but rather uneven.

2. J. Cousin, *Bibliographie de la langue latine* (1951).

3. Linguistic Bibliography, Utrecht–Antwerp, 1939– (annual; in progress). Indo-European Languages, Sections VIII and IX deal with Greek and Latin respectively.

4. H. Bengtson, *Einführung in die alte Geschichte*[4] (1962).

5. *Archäologische Bibliographie*, published since 1913 as an appendix to the *Jahrbuch des Deutschen Archäologischen Instituts*.

6. *Fasti archaeologici: Annual Bulletin of Classical Archaeology* (Florence, 1948– . In progress).

7. W. Bonser, *A Romano-British Bibliography* (1964).

## F. Collections of comprehensive presentations of main subjects.

1. Iwan von Muller's *Handbuch* (in progress), ten sections with many subdivisions (1885– ). The full title was originally *Handbuch der klassichen Altertumwissenschaft*; in 1920 its scope was extended to cover pre-history and the ancient Near East, and its title changed to *Handbuch der Altertumwissenschaft*. The first edition (1885–91) has now been almost completely superseded by later editions, usually very much enlarged. The latest volumes of the *Handbuch* are authoritative and detailed surveys of their field, and are referred to above in the bibliographies to individual articles, including those on Greek and Latin grammar and literature.

2. A. Gercke and E. Norden (Ed.), *Einleitung in die Altertumswissenschaft*, 3rd and 4th ed. (Leipzig, 1931–5). Published in three volumes, with ten, six, and five sections respectively. The sections have separate pagination, were on sale separately, and in some cases have been published separately in new and enlarged editions since 1935. Gercke–Norden provides compact and reliable outlines of the main fields; but some of these are now somewhat out of date.

3. L. Whibley, *A Companion to Greek Studies*[4] (1931).

4. J. E. Sandys, *A Companion to Latin Studies*[3] (1929).

5. L. Laurand, *Manuel des études grecques et latines*, new ed. by P. d'Hérouville, 4 vols. (1946).

6. *Enciclopedia classica* (1959– . In progress). There are three sections, devoted respectively to History and Antiquities, Language and Literature, and Archaeology and History of Art. Each will comprise several volumes. Those published by 1968 were:

    I. ii. 2, *L'imperio romano*, by M. A. Levi;

    I. iii. 1–6, *Antichità greche*, edited by C. Del Grande;

    II. v. 1, *Storia della lingua greca*, by V. Pisani;

    II. v. 2, *Le metrica greca*, by C. Del Grande;

    II. v. 3, *Grammatica storica della lingua greca*, by L. Heilmann;

    III. x. 1, *L'Archeologia*, by P. E. Arias;

    III. x. 2, *Il Mediterraneo, l'Europa, l'Italia durante la preistoria*, by P. Laviosa-Zambotti;

    III. x. 3, *Topografia di Roma antica*, by F. Castagnoli;

    III. x. 4, *Geografia e topografia storica*, by G. A. Mansuelli, N. Alfieri, and F. Castagnoli;

    III. xi. 5, *Storia della ceramica di età arcaica, classica, ed ellenistica e della pittura di età arcaica e classica*, by P. E. Arias;

    III. xii. 1, *L'architettura romana*, by L. Crema.

7. V. Ussani and F. Arnaldi, *Guida allo studio della civiltà romana antica*, 2 vols. (1952–4).

## G. Collections of articles in alphabetical order.

1. Pauly–Wissowa, *Realenzyklopädie der klassischen Altertumswissenschaft* (Stuttgart, 1893– . In progress). The work is now (1969) complete from *A* to *Zenius*. There are so far thirty-three volumes, plus ten volumes of supplements, containing in all more than 95,000 columns. The earlier articles are often now out of date, and the later articles are sometimes too long and detailed for easy reference. An index to Suppl. vols. i–iv appears after the article *molaris lapis* (1932).

2. *Der kleine Pauly. Lexikon der Antike* (1964– ). Aachen–Nasidienus had appeared by 1969. Brief articles, with select bibliographies.

3. *Lexikon der alten Welt*, ed. C. Andresen and others (Zürich–Stuttgart, 1965). Similar in arrangement to the present dictionary and slightly larger in scale.

4. *Reallexikon für Antike und Christentum* (1950– . In progress). By 1969 vols. i–vi and part of vol. vii, dealing in all with *A und O* to *Fortschritt*, had appeared. Valuable for late antiquity.

5. *Enciclopedia dell'arte antica*, 7 vols., 1958–66. Up-to-date and authoritative articles, copiously illustrated.

## H. General catalogues of printed books.

1. British Museum. *General Catalogue of Printed Books* (in progress), 263 vols. plus five additional vols. (1931–66); Additions 1963, 5 vols. (1964); Ten-Year Supplement 1956–65. In progress (1968– ).

2. Library of Congress, *Catalogue of Printed Cards*, 167 vols. (1958–60); *First Supplement*, 42 vols. (1960); *Author Catalogue 1948–52*, 24 vols. (1960); *National Union Catalog 1952–5*, 30 vols. (1961); ibid. *1953–7*, 28 vols. (1958); ibid. *1958–62*, 54 vols. (1963) *Cumulative Author List 1963*, 5 vols. (1964); 1964, 5 vols. (1965); 1965, 7 vols. (1966); 1966, 7 vols. (1967).

3. Bibliothèque Nationale, *Catalogue général des livres imprimés*, 197 vols. (1924–67), *Aach–Vacquant*. *Catalogue général des livres imprimés 1960–4*, 12 vols. (1965–7).

## I. Miscellaneous.

1. *Nairn's Classical Handlist*[3] (1953) is an excellent selective bibliography though rapidly becoming out of date.

2. M. R. P. McGuire, *Introduction to Classical Scholarship: a Syllabus and Bibliographical Guide* (U.S.A. 1961).

3. Many classical periodicals publish index volumes. Worthy of mention among these are:
   (*a*) *Revue des études grecques*. Tables générales for vols. xxxi–l, 1918–37 (1937); for vols. li–lxxiii, 1938–60 (1962).
   (*b*) *Revue des études latines*. Tables—Index at five-yearly intervals, the last in vol. xliii, 1965.
   (*c*) *Classical Review*. Index to vols. i–lxiv, 1887–1950 (1962).
   (*d*) *Journal of Roman Studies*. Consolidated Index to vols. i–xx, 1911–30 (1930); to vols. xxi–xl, 1931–50 (1955).
   (*e*) *Journal of Hellenic Studies*. Index to vols. ix–xvi (1898), and to vols. xliii–lx (1941).

4. Some 27,400 dissertations on classical subjects are listed in *Catalogus Dissertationum Philologicarum classicarum*, ed. II *et* III (Leipzig, 1910 and 1935).

R. B.

# INDEX OF NAMES, ETC.
## WHICH ARE NOT TITLES OF ENTRIES IN THE DICTIONARY

# INDEX TO INITIALS OF CONTRIBUTORS

# INDEX TO INITIALS OF CONTRIBUTORS